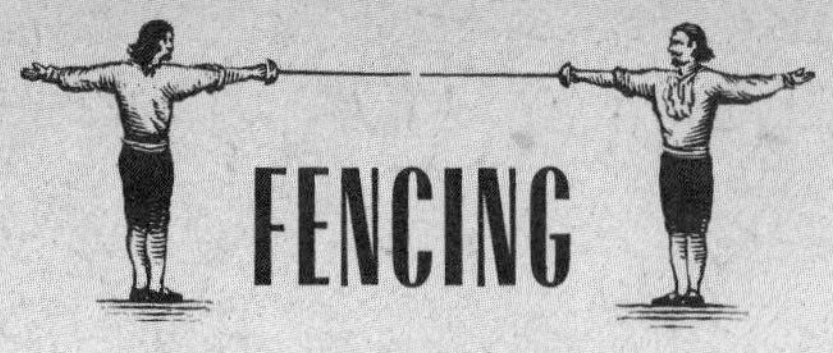

Participants:

Principals-The duelists.

Seconds-Each principal selects a close friend to be his second. The seconds are to watch over the details, ensure fair play and guard a principal's honor at all turns.

Surgeons-Two doctors of competent skill.

Weapons:

Epées will measure 43 inches long, weigh no more than 27 ounces and employ a three-sided blade.

Grip:

The hilt should rest in the palm of one's hand with the thumb placed flat along the top.

Footwork:

Steps should be kept small and fast. The man who lifts his feet too far off the ground is sure to be buried in it.

Starting Position:

Principals stand facing one another with sword in hand.

"En garde!":

After taking a moment to steady the nerves, one of the principals shall say, "En garde!" Both men will adopt the on-guard stance, tap swords once and the fighting will commence.

On-Guard Position:

Feet should be at right angles, falling under the shoulders. Knees should be bent, also at right angles. The right arm should be three-quarters extended.

The left hand should be raised. The elbow should be at shoulder height so that the arm, forearm and hand form a curve.

To Attack:

WORTH FIGHTING OVER.

From the vine, to the press, to the barrel, to the bottle, all in the same location.

THE SINGLE VINEYARD, ESTATE MERLOT.

CHATEAU STE. MICHELLE

Wine Spectator's

Ultimate Guide To Buying Wine

5TH EDITION

WINE SPECTATOR PRESS

New York

Contents

Wine Spectator's
Ultimate Guide to Buying Wine
Fifth Edition

ISBN 1-881659-34-8
ISSN 1058-5729

A Publication of:
M. Shanken Communications, Inc.
387 Park Avenue South
New York, NY 10016
Telephone: 212-684-4224
Fax: 212-684-5424

San Francisco office:
601 Van Ness Ave., Suite 2032
San Francisco, CA 94102
Telephone: 415-673-2040
Fax: 415-673-0103

Distributed by:
Running Press
125 South 22nd Street
Philadelphia, PA 19103
Telephone: 215-567-5080
Fax: 215-568-2919

Manufactured in the United States of America

Cover photograph by Jeff Harris

Introduction

Get acquainted with *Wine Spectator*'s tasting system, and learn several ways to get the most for your wine-buying dollar.

Great Vintages, Great Wines

Geared especially to the collector, this section rates wines from the recent outstanding vintages of six of the world's most prestigious wine types.

Top-Rated Current Releases

Discover the best currently available wines in your favorite categories, and use this "shopping list" when you visit your local wine store.

The Main Listings: Wines by Country and Producer

Following a general introduction to the wines of each country—complete with maps of the major wine regions—you'll find *Wine Spectator*'s ratings and current retail prices for nearly 40,000 wines, and the many tasting notes that describe a wine's special character.

Winery Index

Find the exact page number in the main listings on which each winery's ratings begin.

Top right, Tom Rochioli, co-owner/winemaker of J. Rochioli Vineyards; top left, Warren Winiarski, owner Stag's Leap Wine Cellars; bottom, Bo Barrett, winemaker, and his father Jim Barrett, owner, of Chateau Montelena.

Editor and Publisher Marvin R. Shanken

Executive Editor Michael Moaba
Managing Editor, *Wine Spectator*, Jim Gordon

Editorial Director, Book Division Ann Berkhausen
Assistant Editors Tara Collins, Amy Lyons
Assistant Copy Editor James Rothschild
Editorial Assistant Alan Richtmyer

Writer Ben Giliberti

Tasting Director Bruce Sanderson
Tasting Coordinators Wayne Young (New York), Thomas Garrett (San Francisco)
Assistant Tasting Coordinators Molly Ferrell (New York), Wells Guthrie (San Francisco)

Vice President, Creative Services Martin Leeds
Art Director Jeffrey Felmus
Cover Art Director Ken Newbaker
Cover Designer Diane Miljat
Production Manager Connie McGilvray
Production Services Noble Desktop Publishers

President and Group Publishing Director Robert Beleson
Senior Vice President, Marketing Jay Morris
Vice President, Director of Advertising Miriam Morgenstern
Vice President, Western Advertising Manager Cynthia A. McGregor
Vice President, Advertising Services Director Elizabeth Ferrero
Advertising Services Manager Virginia Juliano
Vice President, Retail Sales Christine Carroll
Vice President, Circulation Laura Zandi

Foreword

Wine lovers have been asking us for an update of *Wine Spectator's Ultimate Guide to Buying Wine* ever since the great success of our last edition. And here it is. But we thought it wasn't enough merely to publish an update. For the Fifth Edition we redesigned the *Ultimate Guide,* made it easier to read and more authoritative than ever.

We want you to be able to use this book at home to plan your wine purchases and take it with you to wine shops when you buy. It's like having at your fingertips all 240 issues of Wine Spectator magazine that we have published since 1985, when we began our wine-tasting program in its current form.

The scope of the wines reviewed here is as broad as the charter of *Wine Spectator*, the world's most widely read consumer wine publication, founded in 1976. In exclusive "blind" tastings we rate the best—and the best-selling—wines from California, Bordeaux, Burgundy, Italy, Washington, Germany and Spain, to mention just a few regions. From Chardonnay and Cabernet Sauvignon, to Champagne and vintage Port, our editors give you their independent views on which are the best wines in each category.

Our guide enables you to quickly look up our editors' ratings of nearly 40,000 wines we have reviewed—including 14,000 wines newly evaluated since the last edition. We tell you how good (or bad) the wines are, and what the fair prices are. In addition, you'll find many thousands of notes that describe what a wine actually tastes like, and advise you whether to drink it now or hold on to it for a while.

This year we've added 240 pages. We've created new features to give you more information for your money, including *Wine Spectator*'s Top 100 Values and a general introduction to the wines of each major country. And we've added hot new vintages to the Great Vintages, Great Wines section for people buying 1994 California Chardonnay, 1995 Bordeaux futures and 1992 California Cabernet, just to name a few.

The efforts of the entire *Wine Spectator* staff have made this book possible. But special thanks go to Book Division editorial director Ann Berkhausen and her team, for compiling such a massive guide; to researcher and proofreader James Rothschild, for guarding the accuracy of the information; and to tasting director Bruce Sanderson, for making all the timely ratings possible.

The Ultimate Guide to Buying Wine, Fifth Edition, is the largest and most up to date collection of wine ratings and price data available. It is an incomparable reference for wine consumers and wine-trade members to use throughout the year. To further improve the guide, we need your help. Please write us with any criticisms or suggestions.

Marvin R. Shanken
Editor and Publisher

Wine-Buying Strategies

By James Laube

If you're new to wine, you're in for an adventure. Devising a buying strategy can be as simple as choosing a few brands you like and sticking with them, or it can be as complex as collecting verticals of the world's greatest wines or buying wine futures.

For many wine drinkers, maintaining brand loyalty is a tried-and-true way to keep your cellar stocked with reliable wines that suit your taste and budget. More daring collectors expand their hobby of wine collecting into a more sophisticated enterprise. They keep tabs on new wines and vintages from old-guard producers in Bordeaux, Burgundy, Italy, Spain or Germany, and a watchful eye on up-and-coming producers from the New World, such as California, Oregon, Washington, Australia, New Zealand and Chile.

Regardless of your level of interest in wine, you're in for some fun and challenges. Wine is a living thing and is constantly changing. Every year you'll be presented with a seemingly endless stream of new wines, producers, appellations and vintages. Even when you find a winery or style of wine that appeals to you, your taste will likely change over time, and you'll discover new things that appeal to you. The combination of possibilities is endless.

Rule No. 1 of buying wine is to trust your own taste. No one knows your taste preferences better than you, so it's important to be comfortable deciding which wines appeal to you and which don't. The best advice is to taste a wine by buying a single bottle before you commit to several bottles or a case. The importance of this rule is further magnified for expensive wines. It makes no sense to pay $20, $30 or $40 for a wine you've never tried and might not like. You'll be far happier with your buying decisions if you taste a wine and decide you like it before committing to more bottles. There's a big wine world to choose from, with literally thousands of different wines. Even if your friends or wine critics rave about a wine, there's no guarantee that you'll like it.

Gaining experience with the world's fine wines takes time, but it is a fascinating journey. You're likely to learn as much from your buying mistakes as you will from your triumphs. Part of the fun of wine is learning where and how it's grown and vinified, which food types match well with different wines, and which wine types and vintages improve with cellaring and bottle age.

Before you start buying wine, it's a good idea to assess your needs. How much wine do you drink and on what occasions? Do you want to cellar young wines for drinking in a few years? You may also decide to budget money for your wine hobby so you can determine how much you can realistically afford to spend on wine. For some people it's easy to identify their wine needs. For others it's wiser to plan a strategy before heading to the wine shop. Remember, it's easier to buy a case of wine than it is to drink it.

It's also easy to buy more wine than you realistically need. Buying wine on a whim can be fun, particularly when you spot a special bottle you've been looking for. But fanciful buying also increases the odds that you'll end up with a wine you may not need for which you may have paid too much. Planning ahead allows you to set aside a specific amount of money for buying wine by the case. Many retailers and wineries offer a 10 percent discount for case purchases. Discount stores, however, usually pass along the 10 percent discount on all purchases.

Once you've outlined your needs, you'll need a place to shop. Years ago, about the only source to buy fine wine was the traditional fine-wine merchant. Today your options abound. You see fine wine in scores of discount chain stores and upscale supermarkets, some of which present a dazzling selection. Retailers have also become more aggressive with sales promotions, selling wine through ads in newspapers and magazines via telephone and toll-free "800" numbers. A growing list of retailers publish catalogs, especially during the holiday season, offering hundreds of wines and special gift packages. There are even wine-of-the-month clubs. Once you join, the club selects wines for you and ships them to your home for you to sample. Most

10 Tips to Better Wine Buying

1. Always taste before you buy. Don't get trapped buying what your friends or critics call the best. Trust your own palate. Taste a bottle before you buy six bottles or a case.

2. Diversify your collection. You may have passions for one kind of wine or another, but variety is the spice of life with wine, so shop around for different styles of wine.

3. Shop for values. Go out of your way to look for best buys to get the most mileage out of your wine dollar.

4. Drink your wines before they get too old. Even the most age-worthy reds from Bordeaux or California reach drinkability in 10 years. You've paid good money for your wines; don't let them slide over the hill.

5. Keep costs in perspective. A few fine wines are expensive, but far too many well-made, reasonably priced wines are ignored because they lack the image and prestige of higher-priced wines.

6. Buy wine by the case. Most retailers give you a 10 percent discount or one bottle free.

7. Beware of last year's superstar. Last year's hero could be this year's goat.

8. Stockpile wine you like so that you don't run out or hesitate to open the last bottle.

9. Investing in futures can be risky business.

10. Assemble your wines with rhyme and reason. Think about your needs before parting with your cash.

of the time, though, you'll be purchasing wine at a retail store, so it helps to get to know your local wine stores and merchants, including what kinds of wines they stock and their pricing strategies.

A well-informed retailer is an excellent source of sound buying advice and tips about what's new and interesting in his store. Retailers can also help find special wines that may be hard to find. Some retail stores even do the shopping for their customers. When a special wine comes in, they set aside a few bottles or a case and bill the customer, holding the wine until it's picked up.

While you're visiting wine shops, take special notice of how the wines are stored and if the temperature is cool. Light and heat are enemies of wine. Wine shops that are warm or hot in summer months may not be the best place to buy your wines. It's also wise to examine wine bottles to make sure the fill level is good-up to the neck of the bottle-and that wine hasn't leaked through the cork. If wine leaks out, that means air is getting into the bottle and oxidizing the wine. Avoid bottles with low fills or leaks.

As wine gets costlier, it makes greater sense to develop a buying strategy. One fun way to defray costs and taste a broad selection of wines is to join a club or group that tastes wines regularly. This way you can spread out some of the costs and taste expensive wines such as Château Lafite-Rothschild, Romanée-Conti, Gaja or Château d'Yquem. Each member brings a bottle of wine to the tasting and shares it among six, eight or 12 people. Some wine syndicates even order cases of wines together, which is another way to cut costs (with a 10 percent discount) and broaden your exposure to the world of fine wines.

For those who like to take risks, buying wine futures, where you pay a discounted price in advance of a wine's delivery, is one way to obtain hard-to-get wines, presumably at reduced prices. Buying futures works like this: Young, unbottled wines are sold at discounted prices through retailers or wineries. Once the wine is bottled and ready for sale, it is delivered to the consumer. Most of the time, consumers pay less for futures, and futures can be a good way to obtain hard-to-get wines.

Others buy wine futures for speculation purposes. They hope that the price they pay for futures is sufficiently lower than the price will be when the wine is released. If that's true, they can resell the wine at a profit. But there are risks in buying futures. The major danger is that you're buying a wine you haven't tried. Unless you're intimately familiar with the producer, vintage or style of wine, you're gambling. You could also pay more for a wine than is necessary. If the economy sours, the price on release may be far less than anticipated, reducing the savings you hoped to achieve. Finally, in buying futures you may tie up your money with one or two producers and miss out on some of the other bargains once that vintage is released. There's also the possibility that your retailer may go out of business before the wine is released, making your wine and your money difficult to recover.

When you're on the road touring wine country, you'll also discover that many wineries have specialty wines or older vintages no longer on the market that they sell only at the winery. Be on the lookout for some of those rarities, but don't necessarily expect to find great bargains. Most wineries give a 10 percent discount on sales, but they mark their wines up to full retail price. You can often find them less expensive at your local retail outlet.

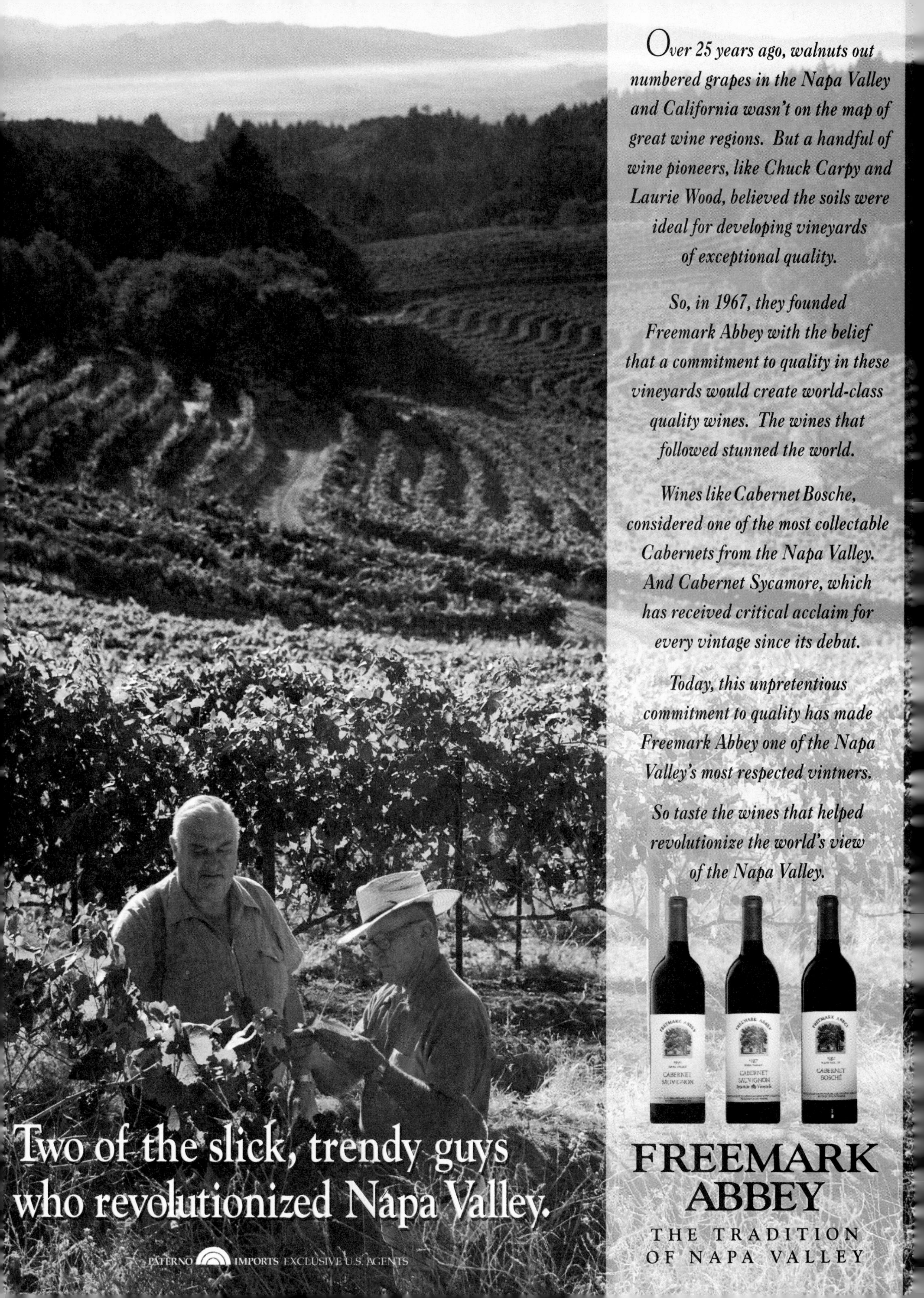
Over 25 years ago, walnuts out numbered grapes in the Napa Valley and California wasn't on the map of great wine regions. But a handful of wine pioneers, like Chuck Carpy and Laurie Wood, believed the soils were ideal for developing vineyards of exceptional quality.
So, in 1967, they founded Freemark Abbey with the belief that a commitment to quality in these vineyards would create world-class quality wines. The wines that followed stunned the world.
Wines like Cabernet Bosche, considered one of the most collectable Cabernets from the Napa Valley. And Cabernet Sycamore, which has received critical acclaim for every vintage since its debut.
Today, this unpretentious commitment to quality has made Freemark Abbey one of the Napa Valley's most respected vintners.
So taste the wines that helped revolutionize the world's view of the Napa Valley.
Two of the slick, trendy guys who revolutionized Napa Valley.
FREEMARK ABBEY
THE TRADITION OF NAPA VALLEY
PATERNO IMPORTS EXCLUSIVE U.S. AGENTS

How We Taste Wine

The wine ratings and tasting notes contained in this book are the result of thousands of tastings by the senior editors of *Wine Spectator*. Two types of tastings are used to review wines for the magazine and for this book. First are the weekly blind tastings of newly released wines by our tasting panels in San Francisco and New York. Second are special blind tastings, conducted by our senior editors, of a particular type or vintage of wine, frequently conducted on location around the world. (A small percentage of the scores in this book, notably those of very old vintages, were not conducted under blind conditions.)

The weekly blind tastings are arranged by our tasting coordinators, who bag and code the wine bottles. They do not participate in the tastings. All capsules and corks are removed from the bottles prior to tasting, and when necessary other efforts are made to conceal the wines' identity from the tasters. Tasters are told only the general type of wine (varietal or region) and the vintage. Price is not taken into account in scoring, although the notes are often edited after the scores are determined to include comments about price and value.

Wines are chosen for tasting from those sent to our offices for review and from wines we purchase at retail. Wines scoring below 70 are automatically retasted under blind conditions from a different bottle. We also retaste many other wines to confirm our impressions.

Tasters for *Wine Spectator* score wines using our 100-point scale. Ratings reflect how highly our tasting panel regards each wine relative to other wines. Ratings are based on immediate quality, as well as on how good a wine will be when it's at its peak, regardless of how soon that will be.

A range of scores (for example, 85-89) indicates a preliminary evaluation, and is used mainly in conjunction with barrel tastings, which are conducted before wines are released.

THE TASTERS

MARVIN R. SHANKEN
EDITOR AND PUBLISHER

Marvin Shanken, 52, was a partner in a Wall Street investment firm in the early 1970s when he bought *Impact*, then a little-known beverage-industry newsletter. In 1975, he left Wall Street to run *Impact* full-time. His interest in wine led him to purchase, in 1979, the *Wine Spectator*—today, the largest and most influential wine publication in the world. Shanken is chairman of M. Shanken Communications Inc., publisher of *Cigar Aficionado, Impact, Impact International, Market Watch* and *Food Arts,* and event chairman of the New York and California Wine Experiences.

JIM GORDON
MANAGING EDITOR

Jim Gordon, 44, supervises the editorial staff and wine tasting operations in New York, San Francisco and Europe. His experience covering the wine industry goes back to 1979 when he began working as a journalist in Napa Valley. He joined *Wine Spectator* in San Francisco in 1984, and was promoted to managing editor in 1987. He moved to the magazine's New York headquarters in 1993. Gordon participates in weekly blind tastings and has traveled and reported extensively on U.S. and European wine regions.

HARVEY STEIMAN
EDITOR AT LARGE

Harvey Steiman, 49, tastes and reports on a wide variety of wine regions, including Australia, California and the Pacific Northwest. Steiman joined *Wine Spectator* in 1984, after serving as food and wine editor of the San Francisco Examiner. Among his accomplishments as a critic, Steiman sounded the alarm on the poor quality of the 1983 vintage in Burgundy and introduced readers to the era of modern winegrowing in Italy's Piedmont. Steiman is also a master at explaining the wonderful affinity between wine and good cooking. He creates the monthly *Wine Spectator* menus and has authored three cookbooks.

JAMES LAUBE
SENIOR EDITOR

James Laube, 45, is *Wine Spectator*'s senior expert on the major wine types of California, most notably Cabernet Sauvignon and Chardonnay. He has been writing for the magazine since 1980, and joined the staff full-time in 1983. Laube's third book, *California Wine,* was recently published. As the leading authority on California wine, Laube cautioned consumers about the troubled 1989 Chardonnay vintage while most other critics were defending the wineries, and he was the first major writer to recognize the excellence of the 1990 through 1992 Cabernet vintages. His reviewing and reporting have helped bring numerous wineries to the forefront of recognition.

JAMES SUCKLING
SENIOR EDITOR/EUROPEAN BUREAU CHIEF

James Suckling, 37, joined *Wine Spectator* in 1981 and in 1985 he was assigned to Europe. His specialties as a critic are Bordeaux, vintage Port and Tuscany. Suckling cut his teeth on the heralded 1982 vintage in Bordeaux and now blind tastes every vintage three times before the wines are released. Suckling was the first major critic to tip off Americans to the great quality of the 1989 and 1990 vintages in Bordeaux. His 1990 book, *Vintage Port,* is the Port aficionados' bible, and his writing was instrumental in bringing international acclaim to the modern era-wines of Tuscany.

PER-HENRIK MANSSON
SENIOR EDITOR

Per-Henrik Mansson, 45, is *Wine Spectator*'s leading expert on Burgundy, and also does regular tasting and reporting on Piedmont, Bordeaux, Tuscany and other regions. Mansson joined *Wine Spectator* in 1987 and has been based in Europe since 1989. His reviews of red Burgundy helped bring the excellent 1989 and classic 1990 vintage to the forefront of attention. But he also warned consumers off the much weaker 1991 and 1992 vintages and endured severe criticism from other critics and the wine trade for his tough stance. Mansson's reporting skills were developed in earlier jobs with daily newspapers.

THOMAS MATTHEWS
SENIOR EDITOR/NEW YORK BUREAU CHIEF

Thomas Matthews, 43, began writing for *Wine Spectator* in 1987, while living in Bordeaux. In 1988, he joined the magazine's staff as a reporter in the London bureau, moving back to the United States in 1989 to become *Wine Spectator*'s New York bureau chief. His first book, *A Village in the Vineyards,* was published in 1993.

Matthews got his start in the wine business in 1979, picking grapes in Bordeaux and Cognac. From 1982 to 1986, he worked in New York City as the wine buyer for Odeon Restaurant and Café Luxembourg. He has a bachelor's degree in literature and philosophy from Bennington College in Vermont and a master's degree in political science from Yale University in Connecticut.

KIM MARCUS
ASSISTANT MANAGING EDITOR

Kim Marcus, 37, joined the *Wine Spectator* staff in 1988 and has been a regular taster since 1990. Marcus is in charge of the magazine's Upfront section, and edits the annual vintage reports, which give readers a sneak preview of each vintage's potential quality in all the world's major wine regions. Marcus filed *Wine Spectator*'s first staff-written report from Chile in 1992. He also has been a key behind-the-scenes reporter on the California wine industry. He wrote the 1992 cover story, "California's Billion Dollar Nightmare," which related the denial and damage that accompanied the phylloxera epidemic in the vineyards.

BRUCE SANDERSON
TASTING DIRECTOR

Bruce Sanderson, 40, joined *Wine Spectator* in 1993 after working for the previous five years as a wine steward and in retail wine sales. He manages the tasting operations in New York, San Francisco and Europe, and is a regular taster in the New York office, where a wide variety of wines from Europe, South America, the eastern United States and other regions are reviewed. He writes the "Spectator Picks" column in the Buying Guide. Sanderson has been studying toward a Master of Wine degree, and has taught wine appreciation classes.

JEFF MORGAN
WEST COAST EDITOR

Jeff Morgan, 42, joined *Wine Spectator* full time in 1995 after writing for the magazine on a freelance basis since 1992. Morgan is now the magazine's principal West Coast news reporter, a feature writer and a wine taster. His in-depth story on the wines of California's South Central Coast brought overdue recognition to the Chardonnays, Pinot Noirs and other wines of this up-and-coming area. Morgan once worked as a winery manager and has written on wine for other national magazines and *The New York Times*.

Vintage Charts

The best guarantee of satisfaction in evaluating a wine for purchase is the quality behind the producer's name. Once you've picked a producer with a track record for quality, often the next question is, "Which vintage should I buy?" Knowing the relative merits of each vintage can help you make more informed buying decisions.

This section presents our qualitative ratings—using *Wine Spectator*'s 100-point scale—of vintages in the world's major wine regions for the past 10-20 years. The vintage ratings have been updated according to ongoing wine evaluations by our senior editors. For each vintage year you will find the score, our rating, a comment on the characteristics of that vintage or the wines from the vintage, and our drinkability recommendation.

Wine Spectator's 100-Point Scale

95-100—Classic, a great wine

90-94—Outstanding, a wine of superior character and style

80-89—Good to Very Good, a wine with special qualities

70-79—Average, a drinkable wine that may have minor flaws

60-69—Below Average, drinkable but not recommended

50-59—Poor, undrinkable, not recommended

Vintage charts are, by necessity, general in nature. Vintage ratings listed here are averages for year and region. Many good wines are produced in "bad" years, just as bad wines are produced in "good" years. Use our vintage charts as a general guide to overall quality.

FRANCE | ALSACE

Vintage	Score	Rating	Comment	Drinkability
1993	87	Very Good	Rainy year, but ripe grapes; intense, steely wines	Drink
1992	84	Good	A huge crop; producers who limited yields made solid wines	Drink
1991	77	Average	Harvest rains hurt quality; some late-harvest success	Drink
1990	93	Outstanding	Exceptionally ripe year; stunning Rieslings, some fine late-harvest wines	Drink or Hold
1989	96	Classic	A ripe year; rich, round wines and superb late-harvest wines	Drink or Hold
1988	95	Classic	Excellent balance; firm and opulent	Drink or Hold
1987	85	Very Good	Steely, lean and fresh	Drink
1986	84	Good	Light, elegant and delicious	Drink
1985	90	Outstanding	Concentrated and intensely fruity, with good backbone	Drink or Hold
1984	74	Average	Slightly unripe, thin and simple	Drink
1983	93	Outstanding	Very rich and superbly structured; many dessert wines	Drink

FRANCE | RED BORDEAUX

Vintage	Score	Rating	Comment	Drinkability
1995	88-92	Very Good–Outstanding	Solid, aromatic wines with racy tannins and fruit to balance; stick to top estates	Not Released
1994	80-84	Good	Firm tannins, with above-average fruit flavor but some dilution and dryness	Not Released
1993	82	Good	Good color, perfumey, fruity and balanced; Pomerol and St.-Emilion best	Drink
1992	72	Average	Light, simple, early-maturing and often diluted; many unripe wines	Drink
1991	72	Average	Lean, tough and light; top names only	Drink
1990	97	Classic	Opulent, well structured and harmonious; Right Bank great	Hold
1989	98	Classic	Bold, dramatic fruit character; tannic and long-aging	Hold
1988	93	Outstanding	Marvelous structure; ripe, concentrated fruit, firm tannins	Hold
1987	76	Average	Delicate and ripe, yet diluted	Drink
1986	95	Classic	Powerful, intense and tannic; best in Médoc	Hold
1985	93	Outstanding	Balanced, supple and fruity; defines finesse	Drink or Hold
1984	70	Average	Unripe, astringent and dry; most fading	Drink
1983	86	Very Good	Rich and ripe in fruit and tannins; some overly tannic	Drink
1982	94	Outstanding	Intensely ripe fruit, plenty of ripe tannins; best in Médoc	Drink or Hold
1981	82	Good	Elegant, balanced and charming; some starting to fade	Drink
1980	78	Average	Light, pleasant wines for early drinking	Drink
1979	83	Good	Supple, fruity and delicate; perfect now	Drink
1978	86	Very Good	Structured, fleshy and complex; best are improving	Drink or Hold
1977	60	Below Average	Poor, unripe and acidic; well past their prime	Drink
1976	80	Good	Early promise unfulfilled; fully matured now	Drink
1975	85	Very Good	Hard, tannic, slowly evolving; time will tell	Drink or Hold
1974	58	Poor	Unripe and diluted; not worth much	Drink

BUSINESS REPLY MAIL

FIRST-CLASS MAIL PERMIT NO. 1302 BOULDER, CO

POSTAGE WILL BE PAID BY ADDRESSEE

Wine Spectator

PO BOX 50463
BOULDER CO 80323-0463

NO POSTAGE
NECESSARY
IF MAILED
IN THE
UNITED STATES

BUSINESS REPLY MAIL

FIRST-CLASS MAIL PERMIT NO. 1302 BOULDER, CO

POSTAGE WILL BE PAID BY ADDRESSEE

Wine Spectator

PO BOX 50463
BOULDER CO 80323-0463

BEST BUY

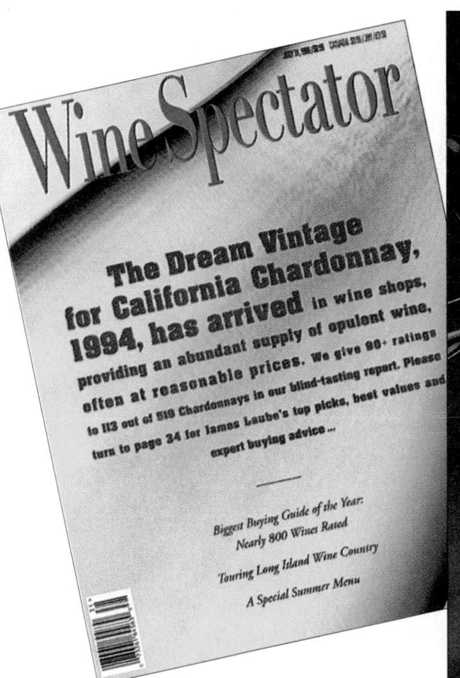

Now you can save 29% off the newsstand price of *Wine Spectator* magazine. The one magazine with a real nose for what's happening in wine. The magazine that talks about wine in a way that's entertaining, accessible and easy to swallow.

Best of all, every issue comes with the famous **Wine Spectator Buying Guide,** full of lively reviews and ratings of over 200 wine releases. With its convenient pull-out shopping guide, *Wine Spectator* maximizes your enjoyment of buying and drinking wine.

Plus, you'll get expanded coverage of outstanding restaurants around the globe, exciting travel destinations, and world class cuisine.

Call or write today to enjoy 19 issues of *Wine Spectator* for just $40. It's a Best Buy you can't afford to be without.

Call 1-800-752-7799

Introductory Offer

❑ YES! Please send me 1 year (19 issues) of Wine Spectator for $40. That's a 29% savings off the cover price. **Mail to: Wine Spectator, P.O. Box 50462, Boulder, CO 80322-0462.**

Name____________________

Company____________________

Address____________________

City/State/Zip____________________

Charge to: ❑ Visa ❑ Mastercard ❑ American Express
❑ Check enclosed ❑ Bill me

Card #____________________ Exp.__________

Signature____________________

Please Check: ❑ Consumer (06) ❑ Food & Beverage Director (07)
❑ Retailer (05) ❑ Importer (02) ❑ Winery (03) ❑ Distributor (04)
❑ Other (99) ____________________

Please allow 6 - 8 weeks for delivery of first issue. Send foreign orders prepaid in U.S. dollars. Canada $53.50 (including GST); all others $125. 56HZ5

1973	68	Below Average	Early-maturing luncheon wines; most faded	Drink
1972	60	Below Average	Acidic, light wines; not very interesting	Drink
1971	80	Good	Uneven quality; Pomerol and St.-Emilion still good, but Médoc and Graves fading quickly	Drink
1970	91	Outstanding	Excellent all-around vintage; structured, with lots of fruit	Drink or Hold
1966	89	Very Good	Typical but hard wines; most at their peaks	Drink
1964	80	Good	Uneven quality; outstanding Pomerol and St.-Emilion, diluted in Médoc	Drink
1961	99	Classic	Best vintage since 1945; great concentration, structure and longevity, best are still youthful	Drink or Hold

FRANCE | RED BURGUNDY

Vintage	Score	Rating	Comment	Drinkability
1993	91	Outstanding	Top domaines made exuberant, racy, balanced wines	Hold
1992	79	Average	Pleasant at best, diluted and light at worst	Drink
1991	86	Very Good	Uneven quality, but some wines improving as tannins soften and they flesh out	Drink or hold
1990	98	Classic	Classic balance, formidable fruit and refined tannins	Hold
1989	93	Outstanding	Seductive and harmonious; delicious now	Drink or Hold
1988	90	Outstanding	Muscular and firm; some losing fruit, others improving	Drink or Hold
1987	85	Very Good	Lovely and supple; at its peak now	Drink
1986	79	Average	Lean and drying; some past their peak	Drink
1985	95	Classic	Ripe, supple, soft, very appealing; many peaking now	Drink
1984	74	Average	Many thin, watery wines	Drink
1983	79	Average	Most are drying and over the hill, but a few gems escaped widespread rot	Drink
1982	78	Average	Huge crop; some good, but many disappointing	Drink
1981	74	Average	Light and thin	Drink
1980	79	Average	Drinkable, but past its peak	Drink
1979	80	Good	The best are still good, with others past their peak	Drink
1978	92	Outstanding	Best wines have extraordinary richness and finesse	Drink or Hold
1977	65	Below Average	Past its peak	Drink
1976	87	Very Good	Tough wines; some coming around	Drink or Hold
1975	65	Below Average	Past its peak	Drink
1974	65	Below Average	Past its peak	Drink
1973	69	Below Average	Lighter style, but charming	Drink
1972	81	Good	Lean wines with style	Drink
1971	89	Very Good	Fully mature vintage	Drink
1970	81	Good	Forgotten vintage; holding up	Drink
1969	93	Outstanding	Authentic structure; flavorful	Drink

■ ■ ■ ■

FRANCE | WHITE BURGUNDY

Vintage	Score	Rating	Comment	Drinkability
1995	89-93	Very Good–Outstanding	Rich, thick and generous, with good acidity and aging potential	Not Released
1994	87	Very Good	Charming, soft, honeyed, fruity; many delicious on release	Drink or Hold
1993	82	Good	Austere, lean; best are elegant	Drink or Hold
1992	89	Very Good	Balanced; great finesse and lovely fruit	Drink or Hold
1991	85	Very Good	Fruity, charming, delicious already	Drink
1990	92	Outstanding	Racy, graceful, round; will improve with age	Drink or Hold
1989	92	Outstanding	Rich, opulent; the best will age well	Drink or Hold
1988	88	Very Good	Firm; good concentration and balance	Drink or Hold
1987	84	Good	Fresh, simple; enjoy while fruit flavor lasts	Drink
1986	92	Outstanding	Seductive, opulent, honeyed; peaking now	Drink
1985	94	Outstanding	Bold, powerful; some remain tough	Drink or Hold
1984	78	Average	Light, tart, very simple	Drink
1983	85	Very Good	Uneven; some are rich and heavy	Drink
1982	83	Good	Some surprises, but generally light	Drink
1981	82	Good	Difficult, uneven vintage; high acidity	Drink
1980	73	Average	Mostly unripe and diluted	Drink

FRANCE | CHAMPAGNE

Vintage	Score	Rating	Comment	Drinkability
1989	88-92	Very Good–Outstanding	Potentially outstanding; ripe and rich	Drink or Hold
1988	90	Outstanding	Outstanding quality; great balance	Drink or Hold
1987	81	Good	Acceptable, but few vintage cuvées	Drink
1986	86	Very Good	Good quality; lean and firm	Drink
1985	96	Classic	Superb balance, with great structure and ripe fruit	Drink
1984	79	Average	Large harvest; unexceptional quality	Drink
1983	83	Good	Large harvest; pleasant	Drink
1982	94	Outstanding	Rich and complex, with abundant fruit	Drink
1981	84	Good	Angular and hard, with clean fruit; some surprises	Drink
1980	82	Good	Generous and very fruity with average structure	Drink
1979	91	Outstanding	Classy, elegant and firm; aging well	Drink

FRANCE | NORTHERN RHÔNE RED

Vintage	Score	Rating	Comment	Drinkability
1993	75	Average	Wet harvest left many wines diluted	Drink
1992	78	Average	Light year for early drinking	Drink
1991	87	Very Good	Elegant, with fine tannins and silky fruit; early maturing	Drink or Hold
1990	97	Classic	Massive and rich, with loads of tannin and fruit	Hold
1989	92	Outstanding	Round and opulent, with great texture and backbone	Hold

1988	90	Outstanding	Solid and tough; excellent aging potential	Hold
1987	85	Very Good	Soft and short, but drinking well	Drink
1986	87	Very Good	Tannic and medium-bodied, very firm; starting to come around	Drink
1985	90	Outstanding	Rich, round, loads of fruit	Drink
1984	76	Average	Late, wet harvest; light on fruit and sometimes green	Drink
1983	90	Outstanding	Big and tannic, very solid; best appellations need more time	Drink or Hold
1982	86	Very Good	Ripe and fruity; lacking in backbone but drinking well	Drink

FRANCE | SOUTHERN RHÔNE RED

Vintage	Score	Rating	Comment	Drinkability
1993	78	Average	Inconsistent; best are balanced	Drink
1992	74	Average	Diluted, lean; few successful wines	Drink
1991	73	Average	Most wines hard and green	Drink
1990	95	Classic	Massive wines with great concentration	Hold
1989	96	Classic	Hot year with average crop; powerful, concentrated reds built for aging	Hold
1988	90	Outstanding	Dry and temperate year; balanced wines with focused fruit and firm backbones	Hold
1987	75	Average	Wet weather with rot prevalent; light, fruity wines, some lacking character	Drink
1986	88	Very Good	Racy wines with plenty of steely tannins and clean fruit; underrated	Hold
1985	86	Very Good	Ripe and exuberant, with loads of fruit that's evolving quickly	Drink or Hold
1984	78	Average	A difficult growing season; many unripe wines, but a few surprises	Drink
1983	89	Very Good	Small crop of Grenache; tannic, powerful wines coming into their own	Drink or Hold
1982	84	Good	Variable year, but many wines still fresh; balanced, with an abundance of fruit	Drink

FRANCE | SAUTERNES

Vintage	Score	Rating	Comment	Drinkability
1992	72	Average	Light, straightforward, diluted and medium-sweet	Drink
1991	77	Average	Moderately sweet, attractive apéritif wines	Drink
1990	99	Classic	Fabulous balance; rich and racy, with power and elegance	Hold
1989	98	Classic	Incredibly rich, with lots of botrytis; built for aging	Hold
1988	93	Outstanding	Extremely fine and firm, well balanced and concentrated	Hold
1987	79	Average	Clean and appealing, with little botrytis	Drink
1986	90	Outstanding	Harmonious, charming, focused and honeyed; lively acidity	Hold
1985	85	Very Good	Little botrytis character; clean and sweet	Drink
1984	68	Below Average	A few good wines; a wet, difficult harvest	Drink
1983	95	Classic	Intense, complex and stylish; abundant botrytis character	Drink or Hold

1982	77	Average	Mostly fat, alcoholic and sweet	Drink
1981	83	Good	Medium richness; finely balanced wines	Drink
1980	82	Good	Good year; balanced, lightly botrytized wines	Drink

GERMANY | RIESLING

Vintage	Score	Rating	Comment	Drinkability
1994	86	Very Good	Solid quality, high acidity, medium extract; focus on top estates	Drink or Hold
1993	89	Very Good	Great surprise: plenty of fruit, acidity and character; stick to top estates	Drink or Hold
1992	88	Very Good	Uneven quality; some late-harvest, botrytized classics, but many soft, diluted wines	Drink or Hold
1991	85	Very Good	Crisp, racy acidity, but uneven quality	Drink or Hold
1990	97	Classic	Powerful, great acidity and extract, harmonious	Hold
1989	92	Outstanding	High rating for botrytized, late-harvest wines, but others tough and unexceptional	Drink or Hold
1988	93	Outstanding	Balanced, firm; best from middle Mosel	Drink or Hold
1987	83	Good	Fresh, light, high acidity; surprisingly good	Drink or Hold
1986	86	Very Good	Aromatic, elegant; best from Pfalz	Drink
1985	87	Very Good	Racy, well structured; some problems in Rheingau, Pfalz	Drink or Hold
1984	74	Average	Unripe, aggressive acidity; only top producers drinkable	Drink
1983	93	Outstanding	Very fruity, ripe, round; little botrytis	Drink or Hold
1982	78	Average	Overproduction, diluted, soft; very good ausleses	Drink
1981	81	Good	Clean, lean, light	Drink
1980	65	Below Average	Very green, unripe, thin	Drink
1979	88	Very Good	Small crop; fresh, well structured	Drink
1978	68	Below Average	Green, thin, not recommended	Drink
1977	78	Average	Light, crisp, elegant; most already consumed	Drink
1976	96	Classic	Huge, ripe, powerful; plenty of botrytis	Drink
1975	93	Outstanding	Superb, great balance, firm structure	Drink
1974	66	Below Average	Mean, no harmony, little fruit	Drink
1973	84	Good	Better than expected; ripe acidity, good fruit	Drink
1972	69	Below Average	High acidity, lean; most past their prime	Drink
1971	97	Classic	Powerful, elegant, superb structure; long-lived	Drink

ITALY | PIEDMONT | BAROLO & BARBARESCO

Vintage	Score	Rating	Comment	Drinkability
1993	83-87	Good-Very Good	Some are delicious and fruity; medium body	Drink
1992	72	Average	Diluted; many estates didn't bottle	Drink
1991	80	Good	Mostly light, some pleasant; a few very good wines	Drink
1990	97	Classic	Firm, ripe and long-aging	Hold
1989	97	Classic	Ripe, opulent and supple	Hold
1988	90	Outstanding	Firm, focused and generous	Drink or Hold

1987	83	Good	Light, but with pretty fruit	Drink or Hold
1986	86	Very Good	Soft and generous	Drink or Hold
1985	94	Outstanding	Rich, ripe, concentrated and elegant	Hold
1984	80	Good	Light style; spicy and fruity	Drink
1983	75	Average	Very light, sometimes thin	Drink
1982	90	Outstanding	Powerful, tannic and long-lived	Hold
1981	73	Average	Light; mature now	Drink
1980	70	Average	Very light; some are thin	Drink
1979	86	Very Good	Supple and flavorful	Drink or Hold
1978	90	Outstanding	Firm and authentically built	Drink or Hold

ITALY | TUSCANY | BRUNELLO DI MONTALCINO

Vintage	Score	Rating	Comment	Drinkability
1990	98	Classic	Super structure; powerful and ripe, yet balanced	Drink or Hold
1989	80	Good	Light, aromatic and fresh	Drink
1988	94	Outstanding	Rich and harmonious, with outstanding structure	Drink or Hold
1987	81	Good	Lean and aromatic, with delicate fruit	Drink
1986	85	Very Good	Medium weight; better than expected, with firm tannins	Drink or Hold
1985	94	Outstanding	Superripe, concentrated and powerful; some wines overdone	Drink or Hold
1984	72	Average	Light, diluted and weak	Drink
1983	88	Very Good	Well rounded, with luscious fruit and good tannins	Drink
1982	87	Very Good	Hot year; ripe, firm and delicious	Drink
1981	82	Good	Fine and fruity, with medium structure; fading	Drink
1980	79	Average	Better than expected, with elegant fruit and firm tannins	Drink
1979	89	Very Good	Very balanced, with beautiful aromas, lovely fruit and ripe tannins	Drink

ITALY | TUSCANY | CHIANTI AND SUPER TUSCANS

Vintage	Score	Rating	Comment	Drinkability
1993	79	Average	Light, aromatic and fruity wines; less diluted than '92	Drink
1992	77	Average	Very light, very diluted; buy only the best names	Drink
1991	81	Good	Delicate, aromatic, fresh wines for early drinking	Drink
1990	98	Classic	Concentrated, highly extracted, with firm tannins and fresh acidity	Drink or Hold
1989	79	Average	Some light, pleasant wines; others very diluted	Drink
1988	96	Classic	Balanced, with excellent concentration, firm acidity and fine tannins	Drink or Hold
1987	82	Good	Variable quality, but some good surprises	Drink
1986	86	Very Good	Slightly lean but solid wines, with good fruit	Drink
1985	95	Classic	Hot, superripe year; big and rich wines, with tons of fruit	Drink
1984	75	Average	Light, difficult vintage; most wines insipid	Drink
1983	88	Very Good	Pretty wines, with good intensity and backbone	Drink
1982	90	Outstanding	Very ripe fruit, with plenty of tannins; rich, round wines	Drink

1981	85	Very Good	Focused fruit, firm tannins; some exceptional wines	Drink
1980	77	Average	Tricky weather for most of vintage; uneven quality, with some unripe wines	Drink

PORTUGAL | VINTAGE PORT

Vintage	Score	Rating	Comment	Drinkability
1994	95-100	Classic	Classic, muscular tannins; layers of fruit and character	Not Released
1992	94	Outstanding	Concentrated, tannic and fruity; best are classics	Hold
1991	93	Outstanding	Racy, harmonious, rich	Hold
1987	88	Very Good	Balanced and elegant, with good finesse	Hold
1986	80	Good	Firm, gutsy and a little simple	Hold
1985	96	Classic	Opulent and intense, with a solid backbone	Hold
1984	81	Good	Lean, linear, one-dimensional	Drink or Hold
1983	92	Outstanding	Powerful, tannic and age-worthy	Hold
1982	84	Good	Sweet and raisiny; unbalanced	Drink or Hold
1980	87	Very Good	Solid and well structured, with focused fruit	Drink or Hold
1979	74	Average	Light, sweet and insipid	Drink
1978	84	Good	Fruity, soft and ready	Drink
1977	97	Classic	Tough, tannic and complex; ageless	Hold
1976	76	Average	Simple, variable and short	Drink
1975	80	Good	Light and one-dimensional, but fruity	Drink
1974	74	Average	Aromatic and angular; small production	Drink
1972	79	Average	Light, fragrant and easy to drink	Drink
1970	95	Classic	Harmonious and well structured, with intense fruit	Drink or Hold
1969	72	Average	Light and simple; tiny production	Drink
1968	77	Average	One-dimensional and fruity; small crop	Drink
1967	88	Very Good	Focused fruit; angular and elegant	Drink
1966	93	Outstanding	Iron backbone; fresh, with good concentration	Drink or Hold
1965	80	Good	Rich and focused fruit; tiny production	Drink
1964	81	Good	Appealing fruit; stylish, soft and round	Drink
1963	98	Classic	Copious fruit; forceful and extremely age-worthy	Drink or Hold
1962	82	Good	Pleasant, fruity and soft	Drink
1961	80	Good	Very ripe, roasted flavors; sweet	Drink
1960	87	Very Good	Balanced, sweet and elegant; at its peak	Drink
1958	84	Good	Fragrant, fragile and fruity	Drink
1957	85	Very Good	Angular, tannic and lively; tiny production	Drink
1955	94	Outstanding	Harmonious, refined, fruity and solid	Drink
1954	85	Very Good	Fragrant, balanced, fresh and fruity	Drink
1952	80	Good	Fruity, simple and sweet; tiny production	Drink
1950	86	Very Good	Subtle, sweet and soft	Drink
1948	99	Classic	Massive, superripe and powerful	Drink or Hold
1947	93	Outstanding	Balanced, integrated and attractive	Drink

1945	98	Classic	Youthful and concentrated; superlative quality	Drink or Hold
1942	86	Very Good	Pleasant, elegant and fruity	Drink
1938	80	Good	Useful; light but pleasant	Drink
1935	95	Classic	Aromatic, refined and firmly structured	Drink
1934	93	Outstanding	Ripe, powerful and concentrated	Drink
1931	95	Classic	Luscious, rich and complete	Drink
1927	100	Classic	Superb concentration with balance and breeding; large production	Drink
1920	85	Very Good	Elegant, balanced and fruity	Drink
1917	88	Very Good	Ripe, rich, flavorful	Drink
1912	98	Classic	Concentrated, powerful and superbly structured	Drink
1911	80	Good	Attractive; fruity and ripe	Drink
1908	94	Outstanding	Fine, balanced and flavorful	Drink
1904	90	Outstanding	Delicate, balanced and fruity	Drink
1900	90	Outstanding	Classy, balanced and delicate	Drink

UNITED STATES | CALIFORNIA | CABERNET SAUVIGNON

Vintage	Score	Rating	Comment	Drinkability
1995	90-94	Outstanding	Rich, complex and flavorful out of barrel	Not Released
1994	89-93	Very Good-Outstanding	Ripe, dark and concentrated	Not Released
1993	83-87	Good-Very Good	Simple, fruity and uncomplicated	Not Released
1992	93	Outstanding	Supple, rich and fruity, with soft tannins	Hold
1991	94	Outstanding	Intense, tannic, age-worthy; best in Napa	Hold
1990	95	Classic	Ripe, supple, complex; best in Napa	Hold
1989	84	Good	Austere, tannic; uneven quality	Drink
1988	82	Good	Lean, crisp and simple	Drink
1987	94	Outstanding	Deep, rich, complex, tannic; best in Napa	Drink or Hold
1986	95	Classic	Classic structure, tight, age-worthy	Drink
1985	97	Classic	California's finest: elegant, rich, stylish	Drink
1984	94	Outstanding	Rich, fruity, opulent	Drink
1983	81	Good	Lean, tannic; uneven quality	Drink
1982	78	Average	Austere, lean; uneven quality	Drink
1981	85	Very Good	Supple, charming, balanced	Drink
1980	84	Good	Ripe, firm; fading now	Drink
1979	88	Very Good	Austere but age-worthy; the best are long-lived	Drink
1978	93	Outstanding	Ripe, flavorful, complex	Drink
1977	82	Good	Elegant and charming	Drink
1976	75	Average	Ripe but awkward	Drink
1975	86	Very Good	Charming, supple, elegant, balanced	Drink
1974	91	Outstanding	Bold, rich, opulent, dramatic	Drink
1973	87	Very Good	Elegant, charming, subtle, balanced	Drink

1972	67	Below Average	Rainy harvest; simple, watery, uninspired	Drink
1971	68	Below Average	Rainy harvest; mediocre quality	Drink
1970	95	Classic	Deep, complex, elegant, age-worthy	Drink
1969	92	Outstanding	Elegant, supple, balanced, charming	Drink
1968	96	Classic	Rich, concentrated, powerful, tannic	Drink
1967	82	Good	Elegant, supple and balanced, with early charm	Drink
1966	91	Outstanding	Rich, complex, balanced, delightful	Drink
1965	83	Good	Ripe, balanced and charming; serviceable	Drink
1964	91	Outstanding	Ripe, complex and balanced; enduring	Drink
1963	69	Below Average	Frost damage, short crop with uneven quality, not memorable	Drink
1962	69	Below Average	Frost damage, mediocre vintage, uninspiring	Drink
1961	71	Average	Severe frosts; decent quality but past their prime	Drink
1960	84	Good	Fruity, elegant and balanced; commendable	Drink
1959	87	Very Good	Elegant, balanced and complex; enduring	Drink
1958	95	Classic	Amazingly youthful; complex, elegant, age-worthy	Drink
1957	78	Average	Elegant, balanced and fruity; uneven quality	Drink
1956	86	Very Good	Supple, balanced, complex, age-worthy	Drink
1955	89	Very Good	Great depth, balance, finesse and ageability	Drink
1954	85	Very Good	Elegant, balanced, charming	Drink
1953	67	Below Average	Decent and drinkable, but not notable	Drink
1952	85	Very Good	Severe frosts; low expectations but sound wines	Drink
1951	94	Outstanding	Great depth, character and balance; age-worthy	Drink
1950	90	Outstanding	Fine depth, character and ageability	Drink
1949	86	Very Good	Heavy frosts; firm-structured and age-worthy	Drink
1948	69	Below Average	Wet spring, cool harvest with low sugars; uneven quality	Drink
1947	85	Very Good	Warm year; elegant, balanced, age-worthy	Drink
1946	91	Outstanding	Heavy frosts, early harvest; deeply flavored and early-maturing	Drink
1945	84	Good	Elegant, gentle, delicate	Drink
1944	78	Average	Heavy frosts, good season, decent wines	Drink
1943	79	Average	Wet winter, spring frosts; good crop, average quality	Drink
1942	88	Very Good	Ripe and balanced, aging well	Drink
1941	89	Very Good	Rich, deep, concentrated, age-worthy	Drink
1939	87	Very Good	Ripe, balanced, age-worthy	Drink

UNITED STATES | CALIFORNIA | CHARDONNAY

Vintage	Score	Rating	Comment	Drinkability
1994	95	Classic	Uniformly ripe, rich, complex; greatest year in memory	Drink or Hold
1993	88	Very Good	Forward, fruity and balanced, but many lean and simple; variable	Drink
1992	93	Outstanding	Elegant and flavorful, with fine depth	Drink or Hold
1991	92	Outstanding	Intense, ripe, complex and balanced	Drink
1990	92	Outstanding	Ripe, rich and concentrated, with fine depth	Drink
1989	85	Very Good	Uneven quality, but some are fine	Drink

1988	89	Very Good	Ripe, balanced, delicate, forward	Drink
1987	85	Very Good	Hard, austere, uneven quality, but some are fine	Drink
1986	91	Outstanding	Deep, rich, concentrated, complex	Drink
1985	92	Outstanding	Ripe, elegant, concentrated, harmonious	Drink
1984	87	Very Good	Very ripe, fleshy, early-maturing	Drink
1983	81	Good	Austere, uneven quality; most have faded	Drink
1982	79	Average	Huge crop; very ripe but unbalanced	Drink
1981	87	Very Good	Ripe, forward, charming	Drink
1980	86	Very Good	Very rich, ripe, full-bodied	Drink

UNITED STATES | CALIFORNIA | MERLOT

Vintage	Score	Rating	Comment	Drinkability
1994	88-92	Very Good–Outstanding	Ripe, complex, promising; could be great	Drink or Hold
1993	83	Good	Variable quality, with few stars	Drink or Hold
1992	89	Very Good	Complex wines; best are well balanced	Drink or Hold
1991	88	Very Good	Ripe, large crop; well balanced	Drink or Hold
1990	90	Outstanding	Ripe and complex; best since '87	Drink or Hold
1989	84	Good	Large crop, but uneven quality	Drink or Hold
1988	86	Very Good	Small crop; fruity and balanced	Drink or Hold
1987	91	Outstanding	Rich and complex; best of decade	Drink or Hold
1986	87	Very Good	Huge crop; ripe and powerful	Drink or Hold
1985	88	Very Good	Ripe and balanced, but variable	Drink or Hold
1984	86	Very Good	Fleshy, ripe and forward	Drink
1983	86	Very Good	Intense and tannic; better than Cabernet	Drink
1982	86	Very Good	Uneven quality; diluted wines	Drink
1981	84	Good	Ripe and fruity, but only good	Drink
1980	83	Good	Large crop; early-drinking wines	Drink

UNITED STATES | CALIFORNIA | PINOT NOIR

Vintage	Score	Rating	Comment	Drinkability
1994	91-94	Outstanding	Should be excellent; rich and dark	Not Released
1993	86	Very Good	Light in color and body, but appealing	Drink
1992	90	Outstanding	Ripe and fruity; best in Russian River	Drink or Hold
1991	90	Outstanding	Complex and concentrated; best in Russian River	Hold
1990	92	Outstanding	Rich, complex and concentrated	Drink or Hold
1989	84	Good	Huge crop; uneven quality, light style	Drink
1988	87	Very Good	Forward, balanced, pleasant wines	Drink
1987	85	Very Good	Light, simple, pleasant	Drink
1986	89	Very Good	Firm, deep and intense; has aged well	Drink
1985	88	Very Good	Elegant, balanced, complex	Drink
1984	86	Very Good	Ripe, opulent and complex	Drink

1983	79	Average	Uneven quality; tannic, average wines	Drink
1982	81	Good	Tight and firm, but uneven quality	Drink
1981	87	Very Good	Ripe and fruity; early drinkers	Drink
1980	83	Good	Hot harvest, uneven quality	Drink

UNITED STATES | CALIFORNIA | ZINFANDEL

Vintage	Score	Rating	Comment	Drinkability
1994	95	Classic	Dark, rich, intense and complex; classy vintage	Drink or Hold
1993	88	Very Good	Fruity, complex; fine balance	Drink or Hold
1992	93	Outstanding	Very ripe, opulent and complex	Drink or Hold
1991	92	Outstanding	Ripe, elegant, complex	Drink or Hold
1990	93	Outstanding	Rich, complex and concentrated	Drink or Hold
1989	82	Good	Huge crop; uneven quality, tannic	Drink
1988	84	Good	Uneven crop; forward-balanced wines	Drink
1987	92	Outstanding	Bright, rich and complex	Drink
1986	91	Outstanding	Firm, intense, tannic yet age-worthy	Drink
1985	93	Outstanding	Wonderful balance and harmony	Drink
1984	88	Very Good	Ripe, opulent and complex	Drink
1983	79	Average	Uneven quality, tannic, average	Drink
1982	82	Good	Tight and firm, but uneven quality	Drink
1981	85	Very Good	Ripe, fruity, early-drinking	Drink
1980	82	Good	Hot harvest; uneven quality	Drink

UNITED STATES | OREGON | PINOT NOIR

Vintage	Score	Rating	Comment	Drinkability
1993	85	Very Good	Uneven, but the best wines are elegant	Drink or Hold
1992	90	Outstanding	Very ripe; some opulent wines	Drink or Hold
1991	88	Very Good	Ripe wines; most are clean	Drink
1990	86	Very Good	Drinkable, with ripe flavors	Drink
1989	85	Very Good	Drinkable; some starting to fade	Drink
1988	85	Very Good	Ripe flavors; starting to fade	Drink
1987	75	Average	Thin, light and simple	Drink
1986	82	Good	Lean, hard and tannic	Drink
1985	88	Very Good	Very ripe early, but most are faded	Drink
1984	75	Average	Thin, hard wines	Drink
1983	87	Very Good	Early excitement, but most are gone	Drink

The Top 100

Each year the editors of *Wine Spectator* choose 100 of the most exciting wines from the thousands reviewed to present our Top 100 wines of the year in the December 31 issue. All of the wines considered for our Top 100 were evaluated in blind tastings in our offices or on location in Europe. The result each year is 100 wine choices that would make splendid drinking for even the toughest wine critic.

We could have simply given you a list of the highest-scoring wines, but that would only be part of the story. A wine's score simply reflects how good it is, regardless of price or where it comes from. Many of the most exciting wines we review are worth special attention because they represent a unique style or make a real contribution to the great diversity that makes wine so much fun. Absolute quality is only one component of this "excitement factor." We also consider:

Overall Value
We expect more of higher-priced wines. A $100 Bordeaux has to carry an extremely high rating to make the Top 100. Conversely, a $10 Cabernet Sauvignon could make the Top 100 with a lower score.

Relative Value within Type
The Top 100 favors highly rated wines that are priced below average for their type. In other words, a $25 Chassagne-Montrachet is a good relative value. A $25 Chilean Chardonnay is not.

Availability
The Top 100 favors wines that are not in extremely short supply. Some wines made in tiny quantities, however, such as cru Burgundies, were so highly rated and reasonably priced in their categories that we decided they are well worth searching for. We made exceptions to the rule for wines such as these.

Rarity of Excellence within Type
We like to find outstanding wines in categories that don't usually produce outstanding quality. For example, the best Sauvignon Blanc may make the list while a Chardonnay with the same score and price may not, because we find fewer outstanding Sauvignon Blancs.

In the following pages are the Top 100 rankings for 1995, 1994 and 1993.

Top 100: Best Wines Released in 1995

RANK	SCORE	PRICE*	WINE
1	97	$100	**PENFOLDS** Shiraz South Australia Grange **1990**
2	99	$100	**CAYMUS** Cabernet Sauvignon Napa Valley Special Selection **1991**
3	94	$18	**THE HESS COLLECTION** Cabernet Sauvignon Napa Valley **1992**
4	96	$45	**FONSECA** Vintage Port **1992**
5	96	$140	**COMTE GEORGES DE VOGÜÉ** Musigny Cuvée Vieilles Vignes **1993**
6	94	$13	**ZACA MESA** Syrah Santa Barbara County Zaca Vineyards **1993**
7	95	$43	**CAMPOGIOVANNI** Brunello di Montalcino **1990**
8	94	$40	**KISTLER** Chardonnay Sonoma Valley Kistler Vineyard **1992**
9	95	$45	**BERINGER** Cabernet Sauvignon Napa Valley Private Reserve **1992**
10	96	$27	**TRIMBACH** Riesling Alsace Cuvée Frédéric Emile **1990**
11	95	$22	**TURLEY** Zinfandel Napa Valley Hayne Vineyard **1993**
12	98	$60	**ALTESINO** Brunello di Montalcino Montosoli **1990**
13	97	$150	**E. GUIGAL** Côte-Rôtie La Landonne **1991**
14	96	$40	**ARAUJO** California Cabernet Sauvignon Eisele Vineyard **1992**
15	97	$90	**DANIEL RION** Clos Vougeot **1993**
16	96	$28	**ARROWOOD** California White Riesling Late Harvest Russian River Valley Oak Meadow Vineyard Special Select **1993** (375ml)
17	96	$40	**FLORA SPRINGS** Cabernet Sauvignon Napa Valley Rutherford Reserve **1992**
18	95	$37	**TAYLOR FLADGATE** Vintage Port **1992**
19	94	$30	**LEWIS** Cabernet Sauvignon Napa Valley Oakville Ranch **1992**
20	93	$30	**ANDERSON'S** Conn Valley Cabernet Sauvignon Napa Valley Estate Reserve **1992**
21	93	$45	**FAR NIENTE** Cabernet Sauvignon Napa Valley **1992**
22	95	$72	**CAPARZO** Brunello di Montalcino Vigna la Casa **1990**
23	96	$185	**LEROY** Volnay-Santenots **1993**
24	93	$9	**CHATEAU STE. MICHELLE** Washington White Riesling Late Harvest Columbia Valley Chateau Reserve **1991** (375ml)
25	93	$30	**JEAN-MARC BOILLOT** Volnay **1993**
26	94	$15	**BONNY DOON** California Muscat Canelli Vin de Glacière **1994** (375ml)
27	94	$26	**MONTICELLO** Chardonnay Napa Valley Corley Estate Reserve **1992**
28	93	$44	**MONTHELIE-DOUHAIRET** Volnay En Champans **1993**
29	92	$16	**PENFOLDS** South Australia Cabernet-Shiraz Bin 389 **1992**
30	93	$18	**RABBIT RIDGE** Zinfandel Sonoma Country San Lorenzo Reserve **1993**
31	92	$17	**A. RAFANELLI** Cabernet Sauvignon Dry Creek Valley **1992**
32	92	$18	**ROMBAUER** Chardonnay Carneros **1993**
33	92	$20	**BERINGER** Chardonnay Napa Valley Private Reserve **1993**
34	94	$27	**MASTROJANNI** Brunello di Montalcino **1990**
35	94	$49	**QUINTA DO VESÚVIO** Vintage Port **1992**
36	93	$28	**WHITEHALL LANE** Cabernet Sauvignon Napa Valley Morisoli Vineyard **1992**
37	91	$20	**GROTH** Cabernet Sauvignon Napa Valley **1992**
38	93	$60	**MÉO-CAMUZET** Nuits-St.-Georges Aux Murgers **1993**
39	93	$30	**FORMAN** Cabernet Sauvignon Napa Valley **1992**
40	93	$45	**SHAFER** Cabernet Sauvignon Stags Leap District Hillside Select **1991**
41	93	$55	**DOMINUS** Napa Valley Napanook Vineyard **1991**
42	93	$30	**ETUDE** Cabernet Sauvignon Napa Valley **1992**
43	92	$29	**BERINGER** Merlot Howell Mountain Bancroft Ranch **1992**
44	92	$30	**CHATEAU MONTELENA** Cabernet Sauvignon Napa Valley The Montelena Estate **1991**
45	92	$40	**PENFOLDS** Cabernet Sauvignon South Australia Bin 707 **1992**
46	93	$59	**ORNELLAIA** Masseto **1992**
47	92	$20	**ALION** Ribera del Duero Reserva **1991**
48	91	$17	**MARKHAM** Chardonnay Napa Valley Barrel Fermented **1993**
49	93	$30	**CASTELLO BANFI** Brunello di Montalcino **1990**

*PRICE ON RELEASE

Top 100: Best Wines Released in 1995

RANK	SCORE	PRICE*	WINE
50	93	$42	**OLIVIER LEFLAIVE FRÈRES** Volnay Frémiets **1993**
51	91	$23	**MATANZAS CREEK** Chardonnay Sonoma Valley **1993**
52	92	$25	**ARROWOOD** Cabernet Sauvignon Sonoma County **1992**
53	93	$54	**CONTI COSTANTI** Brunello di Montalcino **1990**
54	91	$16	**BODEGAS ESMERALDA** Cabernet Sauvignon Mendoza Agrelo Vineyard Catena **1992**
55	92	$180	**BODEGAS VEGA SICILIA** Ribera del Duero Unico Reserva **1970**
56	92	$65	**DOMAINE LEFLAIVE** Puligny-Montrachet Clavaillon **1992**
57	92	$35	**DOMAINE ZIND-HUMBRECHT** Gewürztraminer Grand Cru Goldert **1993**
58	92	$35	**HENSCHKE** Cabernet Sauvignon Eden Valley Cyril Henschke **1991**
59	92	$20	**RIDGE** California Chardonnay Santa Cruz Mountains **1992**
60	91	$15	**GLORIA FERRER** Chardonnay Carneros **1993**
61	92	$27	**KUMEU RIVER** Chardonnay Kumeu **1993**
62	91	$17	**CAYMUS** California Conundrum **1994**
63	91	$12	**MARIENBERG** Shiraz McLaren Vale **1992**
64	92	$35	**SIMI** Cabernet Sauvignon Alexander Valley Reserve **1991**
65	91	$19	**CHALK HILL** Chardonnay Chalk Hill **1993**
66	91	$20	**FERRARI-CARANO** Chardonnay Alexander Valley **1993**
67	91	$30	**EL MOLINO** Pinot Noir Napa Valley **1992**
68	92	$68	**MONGEARD-MUGNERET** Echezeaux Vieilles Vignes **1993**
69	92	$21	**STONESTREET** Chardonnay Sonoma County **1993**
70	92	$45	**NOZZOLE** Il Pareto **1993**
71	92	$28	**ROSEMOUNT** Chardonnay Hunter Valley Roxburgh **1991**
72	91	$12	**KIONA** Merlot Columbia Valley **1992**
73	90	$11	**MARQUÉS DE RISCAL** Rioja Riserva **1989**
74	90	$10	**ROSEMOUNT** Shiraz South Australia **1994**

*PRICE ON RELEASE

RANK	SCORE	PRICE	WINE
75	91	$29	**LEONETTI WASHINGTON** Merlot **1992**
76	91	$32	**SILVER OAK** Cabernet Sauvignon Alexander Valley **1991**
77	91	$30	**MATANZAS CREEK** Merlot Alexander Valley **1993**
78	91	$55	**ROBERT MONDAVI** Cabernet Sauvignon, Napa Valley Reserve **1992**
79	91	$20	**RIDGE** Zinfandel Blend Sonoma County Geyserville **1993**
80	90	$12	**FRANCISCAN** Chardonnay Napa Valley Oakville Estate Barrel Fermented **1993**
81	91	$37	**RUINART** Champagne R de Ruinart **NV**
82	91	$25	**TALBOTT** Chardonnay Monterey **1992**
83	91	$30	**HENSCHKE** Shiraz Keyneton Mount Edelstone **1992**
84	91	$18	**ST. FRANCIS** Zinfandel Sonoma Valley Old Vines **1993**
85	91	$20	**MARIMAR TORRES** Chardonnay Sonoma County Green Valley Don Miguel **1992**
86	90	$25	**CHATEAU STE. MICHELLE** Chardonnay Columbia Valley Cold Creek Vineyard **1993**
87	90	$15	**FERRARI-CARANO** Fumé Blanc Sonoma County Reserve **1994**
88	90	$18	**FONTODI** Chianti Classico Riserva **1991**
89	90	$14	**E. & J. GALLO** Zinfandel Dry Creek Valley Frei Ranch Vineyard Gallo **1990**
90	90	$20	**GLEN CARLOU** Chardonnay Paarl **1994**
91	90	$15	**GREEN & RED** Zinfandel Napa Valley Chiles Mill Vineyard **1993**
92	90	$18	**HEITZ** Cabernet Sauvignon Napa Valley **1990**
93	90	$32	**LAURENT PERRIER** Champagne Brut L.P. **NV**
94	90	$18	**SIRO PANCENTI** Rosso di Montalcino **1993**
95	90	$18	**SANFORD** Chardonnay Santa Barbara County **1993**
96	90	$18	**STEELE** Pinot Noir Carneros **1993**
97	90	$20	**THELEMA** Cabernet Sauvignon-Merlot Stellenbosch **1992**
98	90	$16	**ROEDERER ESTATE** Anderson Valley Brut **NV**
99	90	$65	**ANTINORI** Solaia **1991**
100	91	$89	**MOËT & CHANDON** Cuvée Dom Pérignon **1988**

Top 100: Best Wines Released in 1994

RANK	SCORE	PRICE*	WINE
1	98	$75	**CAYMUS** Cabernet Sauvignon Napa Valley Special Selection **1990**
2	98	$135	**E. GUIGAL** Côte-Rôtie La Mouline **1990**
3	97	$33	**FLORA SPRINGS** Cabernet Sauvignon Napa Valley Reserve **1991**
4	96	$25	**LEONETTI** Merlot Washington **1992**
5	93	$20	**FERRARI-CARANO** Chardonnay Alexander Valley **1992**
6	96	$45	**DOMAINE ZIND-HUMBRECHT** Gewürztraminer Alsace Grand Cru Goldert Vendange Tardive **1990**
7	96	$46	**SANDRONE** Barolo Cannubi Boschis **1990**
8	96	$63	**J. L. CHAVE** Hermitage **1990**
9	94	$32	**CROFT** Vintage Port **1991**
10	93	$16	**RIDGE** Zinfandel Sonoma Valley Pagani Ranch Late Picked **1992**
11	96	$40	**CONTERNO FANTINO** Barolo Sorô Ginestra **1990**
12	95	$25	**ST. CLEMENT** Oroppas Napa Valley **1992**
13	95	$29	**LEONETTI** Cabernet Sauvignon Washington **1991**
14	93	$17	**SILVERADO** Cabernet Sauvignon Stags Leap District **1991**
15	93	$20	**CAYMUS** Cabernet Sauvignon Napa Valley **1991**
16	95	$41	**PIO CESARE** Barolo Ornato **1990**
17	94	$35	**GUENOC** Cabernet Sauvignon Napa Valley Beckstoffer Vineyard Reserve **1991**
18	94	$37	**TAYLOR FLADGATE** Vintage Port Quinta de Vargellas **1991**
19	94	$40	**BENI DI BATASIOLO** Barolo La Corda della Briccolina **1990**
20	94	$45	**GROTH** Cabernet Sauvignon Napa Valley Reserve **1990**
21	93	$26	**KISTLER** Chardonnay Sonoma County **1992**
22	93	$29	**WOODWARD CANYON** Cabernet Sauvignon Columbia Valley **1991**
23	93	$30	**PIPER-HEIDSIECK** Brut Rosé Champagne **NV**
24	93	$35	**FONSECA** Vintage Port Guimaraens **1991**
25	93	$35	**E. GUIGAL** Hermitage **1990**

RANK	SCORE	PRICE	WINE
26	93	$38	**VERGET** Puligny-Montrachet Sous le Puits **1992**
27	93	$41	**NOZZOLE** Il Pareto **1990**
28	93	$45	**PAOLO SCAVINO** Barolo Bric dël Fiasc **1990**
29	93	$45	**GRAHAM** Vintage Port **1991**
30	92	$10	**GUNDLACH BUNDSCHU** Zinfandel Sonoma Valley **1992**
31	98	$12	**YALUMBA MUSCAT RUTHERGLEN** Museum Show Reserve **NV** (375 ml)
32	92	$12	**CHATEAU REYNELLA** Fine Old Tawny Port Old Cave **NV**
33	92	$14	**DOMAINE DU CLOSEL** Savennières Cuvée Spéciale **1992**
34	92	$14	**ROBERT MONDAVI** Zinfandel Napa Valley **1992**
35	92	$18	**THE HESS COLLECTION** Cabernet Sauvignon Napa Valley **1991**
36	92	$22	**CHATEAU STE. MICHELLE** Chardonnay Columbia Valley Chateau Reserve **1992**
37	92	$22	**WYNNS** Cabernet Sauvignon Coonawarra John Riddoch Limited Release **1990**
38	92	$23	**BYRON** Chardonnay Santa Barbara County Reserve **1992**
39	94	$60	**CAPARZO** Brunello di Montalcino Vigna la Casa **1988**
40	94	$81	**BOUCHARD PÈRE & FILS** Chevalier-Montrachet Domaines du Château de Beaune **1992**
41	91	$10	**CAYMUS** Sauvignon Blanc Napa Valley Barrel Fermented **1992**
42	91	$10	**HOGUE** Chardonnay Columbia Valley **1992**
43	91	$11	**GEORGES DUBOEUF** Moulin-à-Vent Aged in Oak **1991**
44	91	$12	**WYNNS** Chardonnay Coonawarra **1992**
45	91	$12	**RAVENSWOOD** Zinfandel Sonoma County **1992**
46	92	$25	**DOMAINES SCHLUMBERGER** Gewürztraminer Alsace Grand Cru Kessler **1989**
47	92	$25	**TRIMBACH** Riesling Alsace Cuvée Frédéric Emile **1989**
48	92	$25	**DR. LOOSEN** Riesling Spätlese Mosel Urziger Würzgarten **1993**
49	92	$25	**DALLA VALLE** Cabernet Sauvignon Napa Valley **1991**

*PRICE ON RELEASE

Top 100: Best Wines Released in 1994

RANK	SCORE	PRICE*	WINE
50	92	$25	**AU BON CLIMAT** Chardonnay Santa Barbara County Bien Nacido Vineyard Le Bouge d'à Côté **1992**
51	92	$26	**CASTELLO DI VOLPAIA** Coltassala **1990**
52	92	$28	**ROBERT MONDAVI** Chardonnay Napa Valley Reserve **1992**
53	92	$28	**KUMEU RIVER** Chardonnay Kumeu **1992**
54	92	$30	**KISTLER** Chardonnay Russian River Valley Dutton Ranch **1992**
55	92	$30	**PONZI** Pinot Noir Oregon Reserve **1992**
56	92	$35	**GOULD CAMPBELL** Vintage Port **1991**
57	91	$15	**GLORIA FERRER** Chardonnay Carneros **1992**
58	91	$15	**ST. FRANCIS** Chardonnay Sonoma Valley Estate Reserve **1992**
59	91	$16	**TRUCHARD** Chardonnay Napa Valley Carneros **1992**
60	91	$17	**BERINGER** Chardonnay Napa Valley Private Reserve **1992**
61	91	$18	**PESQUERA** Ribera del Duero Crianza **1991**
62	91	$18	**CUNE RIOJA** Viña Real Gran Reserva **1985**
63	91	$19	**CLOUDY BAY** Chardonnay Marlborough **1992**
64	90	$10	**MCWILLIAMS** Chardonnay South Eastern Australia Mount Pleasant **1992**
65	90	$10	**PAUL THOMAS** Chardonnay Columbia Valley **1993**
66	90	$10	**FOREST GLEN** Chardonnay Sonoma County **1992**
67	91	$20	**ROBERT PECOTA** Cabernet Sauvignon Napa Valley Kara's Vineyard **1991**
68	91	$23	**DEHLINGER** Pinot Noir Russian River Valley Reserve **1991**
69	91	$25	**MUMM** Cuvée Napa DVX Napa Valley **1990**
70	91	$25	**AU BON CLIMAT** Pinot Noir Santa Barbara County Bien Nacido Vineyard La Bauge Au-dessus **1991**
71	91	$30	**DOMAINE DROUHIN** Pinot Noir Oregon Laurène **1992**
72	91	$26	**MARCARINI** Barolo Brunate **1990**
73	90	$12	**JACKY JANODET** Morgon **1991**
74	90	$14	**RIDGE** Zinfandel Paso Robles Dusi Ranch **1992**
75	90	$14	**E. & J. GALLO** Zinfandel Dry Creek Valley Frei Ranch Vineyard Gallo Sonoma **1990**
76	90	$14	**BODEGAS ISMAEL ARROYO** Ribera del Duero Mesoneros de Castilla Crianza **1990**
77	91	$28	**ALTESINO** Brunello di Montalcino **1988**
78	91	$29	**ARGIANO** Brunello di Montalcino **1988**
79	91	$30	**DAVID BRUCE** Pinot Noir Santa Cruz Mountains Estate Reserve **1990**
80	91	$34	**BEAUX FRÈRES** Pinot Noir Willamette Valley Unfined and Unfiltered **1992**
81	90	$15	**LUCIEN CROCHET** Sancerre **1992**
82	90	$15	**GREENWOOD RIDGE** Pinot Noir Anderson Valley Roederer Estate Vineyards **1992**
83	90	$15	**MARKHAM** Chardonnay Napa Valley Barrel Fermented **1992**
84	90	$15	**A. RAFANELLI** Cabernet Sauvignon Dry Creek Valley Unfiltered **1991**
85	90	$15	**CHATEAU MONTELENA** Cabernet Napa Valley Calistoga Cuvée **1992**
86	90	$16	**DOMAINE DENIS GAUDRY** Pouilly-Fumé Coteaux du Petit Boisgibault **1992**
87	90	$18	**SWANSON** Sangiovese Napa Valley **1992**
88	91	$35	**POGGIO ANTICO** Brunello di Montalcino **1988**
89	90	$16	**ROEDERER ESTATE** Brut Anderson Valley **NV**
90	90	$16	**STEFANO FARINA** Barolo **1989**
91	90	$16	**SEQUOIA GROVE** Cabernet Sauvignon Napa Valley **1990**
92	90	$16	**ST. CLEMENT** Chardonnay Napa Valley Carneros **1992**
93	90	$17	**PUNSET** Barbaresco **1989**
94	91	$39	**ROBERT CHEVILLON** Nuits-St.-Georges Les Vaucrains **1991**
95	90	$18	**GROTH** Cabernet Sauvignon Napa Valley **1991**
96	90	$18	**BELVEDERE** Chardonnay Sonoma County Preferred Stock **1992**
97	90	$18	**ROBERT MONDAVI** Cabernet Sauvignon Napa Valley Unfiltered **1991**
98	90	$19	**ANDREW WILL** Merlot Washington **1992**
99	90	$19	**ROCHIOLI** Pinot Noir Russian River Valley **1991**
100	91	$45	**G. ROUMIER** Bonnes Mares **1991**

*PRICE ON RELEASE

Top 100: Best Wines Released in 1993

RANK	SCORE	PRICE*	WINE
1	100	$80	**CHÂTEAU LATOUR** Pauillac **1990**
2	96	$60	**GAJA** Barolo Sperss **1989**
3	97	$40	**SILVERADO** Cabernet Sauvignon Napa Valley Limited Reserve **1990**
4	94	$14	**CHÂTEAU LA LOUVIÈRE** Pessac-Léognan **1990**
5	95	$83	**LOUIS LATOUR** Corton-Charlemagne **1990**
6	97	$40	**CHÂTEAU PICHON-LONGUEVILLE** Comtesse de Lalande Pauillac **1990**
7	94	$15	**MOUNT VEEDER** Cabernet Sauvignon Napa Valley **1990**
8	96	$42	**ORNELLAIA** Tuscany Vino da Tavola **1990**
9	95	$26	**CHÂTEAU LAGRANGE** St.-Julien **1990**
10	97	$85	**CHÂTEAU LAFITE-ROTHSCHILD** Pauillac **1990**
11	98	$139	**GAJA** Barbaresco Sorô San Lorenzo **1989**
12	96	$32	**CHÂTEAU LE GAY** Pomerol **1990**
13	96	$26	**LEONETTI** Cabernet Sauvignon Washington **1990**
14	97	$150	**E. GUIGAL** Côte-Rôtie La Turque **1989**
15	98	$400	**CHÂTEAU PÉTRUS** Pomerol **1990**
16	96	$63	**CHÂTEAU TROTANOY** Pomerol **1990**
17	96	$65	**CA' DEI GANCIA** Barolo Cannubi **1989**
18	95	$25	**CHÂTEAU ST. JEAN** Johannisberg Riesling Late Harvest Alexander Valley Special Selection **1989** (375ml)
19	95	$29	**CHÂTEAU GRAND-PUY-LACOSTE** Pauillac **1990**
20	95	$30	**CHÂTEAU CANON-LA-GAFFELIÈRE** St.-Emilion **1990**
21	95	$30	**CHÂTEAU LAGRANGE** Pomerol **1990**
22	95	$33	**CHÂTEAU CORDEILLAN-BAGES** Pauillac **1990**
23	95	$45	**PAOLO SCAVINO** Barolo Bric dël Fiasc **1989**
24	95	$50	**LUCIANO SANDRONE** Barolo Cannubi Boschis **1989**
25	94	$24	**CHÂTEAU LARMANDE** St.-Emilion **1990**
26	94	$25	**CHÂTEAU COS-LABORY** St.-Estèphe **1990**
27	94	$28	**CHÂTEAU BOURGENEUF** Pomerol **1990**
28	94	$28	**CHÂTEAU LA CROIX DE GAY** Pomerol **1990**
29	94	$30	**BADIA A COLTIBUONO** Sangioveto **1988**
30	94	$30	**CHÂTEAU CLERC-MILON** Pauillac **1990**
31	94	$32	**G. MASCARELLO** Barbaresco Marcarini **1988**
32	94	$38	**BENI DI BATASIOLO** Barolo La Corda della Briccolina **1989**
33	95	$45	**CHÂTEAU BEAUSÉJOUR-DUFFAU-LA-GARROSSE** St.-Emilion **1990**
34	96	$195	**LOUIS LATOUR** Montrachet **1990**
35	94	$71	**DOMAINE DES COMTES LAFON** Meursault Désirée **1990**
36	95	$150	**DOMAINE LEFLAIVE** Bâtard-Montrachet **1990**
37	93	$20	**CHÂTEAU DE PEZ** St.-Estèphe **1990**
38	93	$20	**DUCKHORN** Cabernet Sauvignon Napa Valley **1990**
39	93	$22	**CHÂTEAU LES ORMES DE PEZ** St.-Estèphe **1990**
40	93	$22	**CHÂTEAU SMITH HAUT-LAFITTE** Pessac-Léognan **1990**
41	93	$22	**CHÂTEAU PAVIE-DECESSE** St.-Emilion **1990**
42	93	$23	**PRUNOTTO** Barolo **1988**
43	93	$23	**WILLIAMS-SELYEM** Pinot Noir Russian River Valley **1991**
44	94	$24	**PAHLMEYER** Chardonnay Napa Valley **1991**
45	93	$24	**TALBOTT** Chardonnay Monterey **1990**
46	93	$23	**DR. LOOSEN** Riesling Auslese Mosel Wehlener Sonnenuhr **1992**
47	93	$25	**DALLA VALLE** Cabernet Sauvignon Napa Valley **1990**
48	93	$31	**CHÂTEAU LÉOVILLE-BARTON** St.-Julien **1990**
49	93	$31	**CHÂTEAU TALBOT** St.-Julien **1990**
50	94	$80	**VEUVE CLICQUOT** La Grande Dame **1985**
51	94	$80	**DOMAINE DE CHEVALIER** Pessac-Léognan **1989**
52	94	$110	**DOMAINE DE LA ROMANÉE-CONTI** Echézeaux **1990**

*PRICE ON RELEASE

Top 100: Best Wines Released in 1993

RANK	SCORE	PRICE*	WINE
53	92	$14	**BYRON** Chardonnay Santa Barbara County **1991**
54	92	$15	**BONNY DOON** Muscat Canelli Vin de Glacière **1992** (375ml)
55	92	$16	**ROSEMOUNT** Syrah Show McLaren Vale Reserve **1990**
56	92	$17	**GUNDERLOCH** Riesling Spätlese Rheinhessen Nackenheimer Rothenberg **1992**
57	92	$18	**CAYMUS** Conundrum **1991**
58	93	$36	**CHÂTEAU LE BON PASTEUR** Pomerol **1990**
59	93	$37	**RUINART** Brut Champagne R de Ruinart **NV**
60	92	$34	**DOMAINE GUY ROULOT** Meursault Les Tessons Clos de Mon Plaisir **1990**
61	91	$9	**MICHELE CHIARLO** Barbera d'Asti **1990**
62	91	$12	**COLUMBIA** Chardonnay Columbia Valley Woodburne Cuvée **1991**
63	91	$13	**GREENWOOD RIDGE** Zinfandel Sonoma County Scherrer Vineyards **1991**
64	91	$13	**WILLIAM WHEELER** Chardonnay Sonoma County **1991**
65	91	$15	**GUENOC** Meritage Lake County **1990**
66	91	$15	**NAVARRO** Chardonnay Anderson Valley Premiere Reserve **1991**
67	91	$15	**SHAFER** Chardonnay Napa Valley Barrel Select **1991**
68	91	$15	**ROMBAUER** Chardonnay Carneros **1991**
69	91	$15	**MARKHAM** Merlot Napa Valley **1990**
70	91	$16	**ALPHONSE MELLOT** Sancerre Domaine La Moussière **1991**
71	91	$16	**COVEY RUN** Chardonnay Yakima Valley Reserve **1990**
72	91	$18	**RIDGE** Zinfandel Dry Creek Valley Lytton Springs **1991**
73	91	$17	**CHÂTEAU FONTENIL** Fronsac **1990**
74	91	$17	**DOMAINE DE LA VIELLE JULIENNE** Châteauneuf-du-Pape **1990**
75	91	$17	**CLOS PEGASE** Cabernet Sauvignon Napa Valley **1990**
76	91	$18	**STAG'S LEAP WINE CELLARS** Cabernet Sauvignon Napa Valley **1990**

*PRICE ON RELEASE

RANK	SCORE	PRICE	WINE
77	90	$9	**MARKHAM** Sauvignon Blanc Napa Valley **1991**
78	90	$9	**BYRON** Sauvignon Blanc Santa Barbara County **1992**
79	90	$10	**ESTATE WILLIAM BACCALA** Merlot Napa Valley **1990**
80	90	$10	**MEEKER** Zinfandel Dry Creek Valley Gold Leaf Cuvée **1990**
81	90	$11	**CHÂTEAU SOUVERAIN** Cabernet Sauvignon Alexander Valley **1990**
82	90	$11	**SELBACH-OSTER** Riesling Spätlese Mosel Zeltinger Sonnenuhr **1992**
83	91	$21	**DOMAINE RENÉ MANUEL** Meursault Clos de la Baronne **1991**
84	91	$25	**LOUIS JADOT** Meursault **1990**
85	92	$23	**MICHELE CHIARLO** Barolo **1988**
86	91	$25	**MARCARINI** Barolo Brunate **1989**
87	90	$13	**FIRESTONE** Chardonnay Santa Ynez Barrel Fermented **1991**
88	90	$13	**BERINGER** Cabernet Sauvignon Knights Valley **1990**
89	90	$14	**ESTANCIA** Meritage Alexander Valley **1990**
90	91	$31	**LOUIS LATOUR** Puligny-Montrachet **1990**
91	91	$33	**E. GUIGAL** Hermitage **1989**
92	91	$35	**PONZI** Pinot Noir Willamette Valley 20th Anniversary Edition **1990**
93	92	$22	**LEONETTI** Merlot Washington **1991**
94	92	$30	**E.&J. GALLO** Chardonnay Northern Sonoma Estate **1991**
95	92	$35	**DRAPPIER** Champagne Carte d'Or **1989**
96	92	$35	**ROEDERER ESTATE** Brut Anderson Valley L'Ermitage **1989**
97	92	$40	**CHÂTEAU DE BEAUCASTEL** Châteauneuf-du-Pape **1990**
98	90	$16	**PODERE IL PALAZZINO** Chianti Classico **1990**
99	90	$20	**FERRARI-CARANO** Siena Sonoma County **1991**
100	90	$30	**DOMAINE DROUHIN** Pinot Noir **1990**

Best Wine Values

To help you find many of the outstanding values in wine that this book covers, we have narrowed the choices down to 100 great values that are easy to find at wine shops, and a supplementary list of 90 other good wines at very affordable prices.

The Top 100 Great Values were the focus of a *Wine Spectator* cover story (May 31, 1996) and constitute what our editors found to be really exciting, high quality wines at $12 and under.

In the section entitled Other Best Buys, we have collected the additional recently released wines that rated 83 or higher and cost $10 a bottle or less. You'll find a broad selection of varietal and regional wines under this lower price ceiling.

The wines in both categories are organized by general wine type—red and white—to make it easy to use this list to plan your purchases before shopping, or to refer to while in the wine shop. For complete tasting notes on these wines, look in the main listings under the country of origin and the winery's name.

50 Great Red Wine Values at a Glance

WINE	SCORE	PRICE
CABERNET SAUVIGNON		
MONTES Chile Cabernet Sauvignon Curicó 1991	88	$8
SANTA AMELIA Chile Cabernet Sauvignon Colchagua 1994	88	$6
CAMELOT California Cabernet Sauvignon North Coast 1993	87	$12
EXPRESSIONS California Cabernet Sauvignon Napa Valley 1993	87	$10
GALLO SONOMA California Cabernet Sauvignon Sonoma County 1992	87	$12
J. LOHR California Cabernet Sauvignon Paso Robles Seven Oaks 1993	87	$12
NAPA RIDGE California Cabernet Sauvignon North Coast Coastal Oak Barrel 1993	87	$7
SEBASTIANI California Cabernet Sauvignon Sonoma County 1992	87	$10
ALAMEDA Chile Cabernet Sauvignon Maipo Valley Vintner's Selection 1993	85	$5
BANDIERA California Cabernet Sauvignon Napa Valley 1993	85	$8
CANYON ROAD California Cabernet Sauvignon California 1993	85	$6
HESS SELECT California Cabernet Sauvignon California 1993	85	$9
LINDEMANS Australia Cabernet Sauvignon South Australia Bin 45 1994	85	$6
MCDOWELL California Cabernet Sauvignon Mendocino 1992	85	$6
MILBURN PARK Australia Cabernet Sauvignon Victoria 1994	85	$6
OXFORD LANDING Australia Cabernet Sauvignon-Shiraz South Eastern Australia 1993	85	$6
M.G. VALLEJO California Cabernet Sauvignon California 1992	85	$6
WENTE BROS. California Cabernet Sauvignon Livermore Valley Wente Family Estate Selection 1993	85	$8
MERLOT		
COLUMBIA CREST Washington Merlot Columbia Valley 1993	85	$8
PARDUCCI California Merlot California 1994	85	$8
SEBASTIANI California Merlot Sonoma County 1993	85	$8
ALAMEDA Chile Merlot Maipo Valley Santa Maria Vineyard 1993	85	$8
J. LOHR California Merlot California Cypress 1993	85	$8
SANTA AMELIA Chile Merlot Colchagua 1994	85	$8

WINE	SCORE	PRICE
MONTES Chile Merlot Curicó Special Cuvée 1994	85	$8
MONTES Chile Merlot Curicó Villa Montes 1994	85	$8
PINOT NOIR		
PARDUCCI California Pinot Noir Mendocino County 1994	85	$8
FIRESTEED Oregon Pinot Noir Oregon 1994	85	$8
NAPA RIDGE California Pinot Noir North Coast Coastal 1994	85	$8
CARNEROS CREEK California Pinot Noir Carneros Fleur de Carneros 1994	85	$8
SHIRAZ		
ROSEMOUNT Australia Shiraz South Australia 1994	85	$8
MCGUIGAN BROTHERS Australia Black Shiraz South Eastern Australia 1994	85	$8
PENFOLDS Australia Shiraz-Cabernet Sauvignon Australia Koonunga Hill 1994	85	$8
ROTHBURY Australia Shiraz South Eastern Australia 1994	85	$8
ZINFANDEL		
VILLA MT. EDEN California Zinfandel California Cellar Select 1994	85	$8
BERINGER California Zinfandel Napa Valley 1994	85	$8
CHATEAU SOUVERAIN California Zinfandel Dry Creek Valley 1994	85	$8
SEGHESIO California Zinfandel Sonoma County 1994	85	$8
EUROPEAN REDS		
GEORGES DUBOEUF France Fleurie Flower Label 1994	85	$8
MONTE ANTICO Italy 1994	85	$8
BODEGAS BERBERANA Spain Rioja Reserva 1994	85	$8
GEORGES DUBOEUF France Beaujolais-Villages Flower Label 1994	85	$8
GEORGES DUBOEUF France Morgon Flower Label 1994	85	$8
GEORGES DUBOEUF France Moulin-à-Vent Flower Label 1994	85	$8
SOGRAPE Portugal Dão Duque de Viseu 1992	85	$8
GEORGES DUBOEUF France Brouilly Flower Label 1994	85	$8
FARNESE Italy Montepulciano d'Abruzzo 1994	85	$8
MASCIARELLI Italy Montepulciano d'Abruzzo 1994	85	$8
COOPERATIVA REGUENGOS DE MONSARAZ Portugal Reguengos 1994	85	$8
LUIGI RIGHETTI Italy Valpolicella Classico Superiore Campolieti 1993	85	$10

50 Great White Wine Values at a Glance

WINE	SCORE	PRICE
CHARDONNAY		
CHATEAU SOUVERAIN California Chardonnay Sonoma County 1994	91	$12
BERINGER California Chardonnay Napa Valley 1994	90	$11
CHATEAU ST. JEAN California Chardonnay Sonoma County 1994	90	$11
J. LOHR California Chardonnay Monterey Riverstone 1994	90	$12
WYNNS Australia Chardonnay Coonawarra 1994	90	$12
MERIDIAN California Chardonnay Santa Barbara County 1994	89	$10
ROSEMOUNT Australia Chardonnay Hunter Valley 1995	89	$10
BELVEDERE California Chardonnay Sonoma County 1994	88	$9
EXPRESSIONS California Chardonnay Sonoma County 1994	88	$10
HOGUE Washington Chardonnay Columbia Valley 1994	88	$9
MILBURN PARK Australia Chardonnay Victoria 1994	88	$9
PENFOLDS Australia Chardonnay Australia Koonunga Hill 1995	88	$9
PENFOLDS Australia Chardonnay South Australia Barrel Fermented Reserve Bin 1994	88	$12
WOLF BLASS Australia Chardonnay South Australia 1995	87	$11
PARDUCCI California Chardonnay Mendocino County 1994	87	$8
R.H. PHILLIPS California Chardonnay Dunnigan Hills Barrel Cuvée 1994	87	$8
RAYMOND California Chardonnay Monterey Estates 1994	87	$12
RODNEY STRONG California Chardonnay Sonoma County 1994	87	$11
WATERBROOK Washington Chardonnay Columbia Valley 1994	87	$10
BANDIERA California Chardonnay Napa Valley 1994	86	$8
JOLIESSE California Chardonnay California Reserve 1994	86	$7
BEL ARBOR California Chardonnay California Vintner's Selection 1994	85	$5
BRIDGEVIEW Oregon Chardonnay Oregon 1994	85	$6
CHATEAU POTELLE California Chardonnay Napa Valley-Central Coast 1994	85	$9
FOREST GLEN California Chardonnay California Barrel Fermented 1994	85	$10
HAYWOOD California Chardonnay California Vintner's Select 1994	85	$8

WINE	SCORE	PRICE
J. LOHR California Chardonnay California Cypress 1993	85	$9
LOUIS M. MARTINI California Chardonnay Napa Valley 1994	85	$9
ROTHBURY Australia Chardonnay Hunter Valley 1995	85	$8
PAUL THOMAS Washington Chardonnay Washington 1994	85	$9
TYRRELL'S Australia Chardonnay South Eastern Australia Old Winery Premier Selection 1994	85	$8
SAUVIGNON BLANC		
DUCKHORN California Sauvignon Blanc Napa Valley 1994	89	$12
GEYSER PEAK California Sauvignon Blanc Sonoma County 1995	89	$8
FERRARI-CARANO California Fumé Blanc Sonoma County 1994	88	$11
BUENA VISTA California Sauvignon Blanc Lake County 1994	87	$7
CHATEAU ST. JEAN California Fumé Blanc Sonoma County 1994	87	$8
KENWOOD California Sauvignon Blanc Sonoma County 1994	87	$9
MARKHAM California Sauvignon Blanc Napa Valley 1994	87	$8
MATUA New Zealand Sauvignon Blanc Hawke's Bay 1994	87	$10
HOGUE Washington Fumé Blanc Columbia Valley 1994	86	$7
NAPA RIDGE California Sauvignon Blanc North Coast Coastal 1994	86	$5
SILVERADO California Sauvignon Blanc Napa Valley 1994	86	$9
CHATEAU SOUVERAIN California Sauvignon Blanc Alexander Valley Barrel Fermented 1994	85	$8
OTHER WHITES AND BLENDS		
PENFOLDS Australia Sémillon-Chardonnay South Australia Koonunga Hill 1995	87	$8
COLUMBIA CREST Washington Johannisberg Riesling Columbia Valley 1994	86	$6
SAUVION & FILS France Muscadet de Sèvre et Maine Sur Lie Sauvion du Cléray 1995	86	$7
COLUMBIA CREST Washington Sémillon Columbia Valley 1994	85	$6
GEYSER PEAK California Johannisberg Riesling North Coast Soft 1994	85	$6
MCGUIGAN BROTHERS Australia Sémillon-Chardonnay South Eastern Australia 1994	85	$7
WYNDHAM Australia Sémillon-Chardonnay South Eastern Australia Bin 777 1995	85	$6

Other Best Buys

RED, $7 AND UNDER

87 LAUREL GLEN Reds Rouge Rosso Tinto California 1993 • $7.00 • (11/30/95)
86 BOGLE Petite Sirah California 1993 • $7.00 • (11/15/95)
86 PARDUCCI Petite Sirah Mendocino County 1992 • $6.50 • (09/30/95)
85 BOGLE Cabernet Sauvignon California 1993 • $6.50 • (11/30/95)
85 JEAN CLAUDE BOISSET Cabernet Sauvignon Vin de Pays d'Oc 1994 • $6.00 • (10/31/95)
85 CEDAR BROOK Pinot Noir California 1993 • $7.00 • (11/15/95)
85 MCGUIGAN BROTHERS Black Shiraz South Eastern Australia 1994 • $7.00 • (11/15/95)
85 OXFORD LANDING Merlot South Eastern Australia 1993 • $7.00
84 BEL ARBOR Merlot California Vintner's Selection 1994 • $6.00 • (06/30/96)
84 LA BOUVERIE Merlot Vin de Pays d'Oc Cuvée Spéciale 1993 • $7.00 • (10/31/95)
84 CHEVALIER DE RODILAN Cabernet Vin de Pays d'Oc 1994 • $6.00 • (12/31/95)
84 FETZER Cabernet Sauvignon California Bel Arbors 1993 • $7.00 • (12/15/95)
84 HASKOVO ESTATES Merlot Haskovo 1993 • $5.50 • (12/31/95)
84 NICOLAS Merlot Vin de Pays d'Oc Maison Nicolas Réserve 1993 • $6.00 • (10/31/95)
83 LA MARCA Cabernet Sauvignon Piave 1993 • $6.00 • (05/31/96)

WHITE, $7 AND UNDER

88 STEPHEN ZELLERBACH Sauvignon Blanc Sonoma County 1993 • $7.00 • (08/31/95)
87 FETZER Bonterra Organically Grown Grapes Mendocino County 1993 • $7.00 • (07/31/95)
87 FORIS Gewürztraminer Rogue Valley 1993 • $7.00 • (03/31/96)
87 SNOQUALMIE Johannisberg Riesling Columbia Valley 1993 • $6.00 • (09/15/95)
86 BOGLE Fumé Blanc California 1994 • $5.00 • (05/15/96)
86 CHATEAU STE. MICHELLE Sémillon Columbia Valley Barrel Fermented 1994 • $7.00 • (07/31/95)
86 GEYSER PEAK Gewürztraminer California 1995 • $7.00 • (06/15/96)
86 HANWOOD Sémillon Chardonnay Australia 1993 • $6.00 • (10/15/95)
85 COLUMBIA Sémillon Columbia Valley 1994 • $6.50 • (08/31/95)
85 GLEN ELLEN Chardonnay California Proprietor's Reserve 1993 • $5.00 • (07/31/95)
85 KNUDSEN ERATH Riesling Willamette Valley 1994 • $7.00 • (01/31/96)
85 MCGUIGAN BROTHERS Sémillon Chardonnay South Eastern Australia 1994 • $7.00 • (10/31/95)
84 ASHLAND Riesling Oregon Dry 1994 • $5.00 • (01/31/96)
84 COLUMBIA CREST Johannisberg Riesling Columbia Valley 1995 • $6.00 • (06/15/96)
84 FORESTVILLE Chardonnay California 1994 • $6.00 • (06/30/96)

■ ■ ■ ■

84 **HARDY'S** Chardonnay South Eastern Australia Nottage Hill 1995 • $7.00 • (03/31/96)

84 **TYRRELL'S** Long Flat White South Eastern Australia 1995 • $6.00 • (03/31/96)

83 **BARRIER REEF** Sauvignon Blanc South Eastern Australia 1993 • $7.00

83 **BRIDGEVIEW** Riesling Oregon Blue Moon Limited Edition NV • $6.00 • (01/31/96)

RED, $7.25 TO $10

89 **BLACKSTONE** Merlot Napa County Reserve 1993 • $10.00 • (04/30/96)

89 **STONEHEDGE** Cabernet Sauvignon Napa Valley Winemaker's Reserve 1992 • $10.00 • (11/30/95)

88 **MARQUES DE GRINON** Rioja 1994 • $10.00 • (06/30/96)

88 **HOUGHTON** Cabernet Sauvignon Western Australia Wildflower Ridge 1992 • $8.00 • (10/31/95)

88 **PARDUCCI** Cabernet Sauvignon Mendocino County 1992 • $8.00 • (11/15/95)

88 **R.H. PHILLIPS** Syrah California EXP 1993 • $10.00 • (12/31/95)

88 **SANTA ALICIA** Merlot Maipo Valley Reserve 1992 • $8.00 • (12/31/95)

88 **SAUSAL** Zinfandel Alexander Valley 1993 • $9.00 • (07/31/95)

87 **BERTANI** Valpolicella Valpantena Secco-Bertani 1992 • $10.00 • (06/15/96)

87 **BONNY DOON** Grenache California Clos de Gilroy 1994 • $8.00 • (11/15/95)

87 **CHATEAU REYNELLA** Cabernet Merlot Basket Pressed McLaren Vale 1992 • $10.00 • (12/15/95)

87 **KARLY** Zinfandel Amador County Pokerville 1993 • $8.00 • (10/15/95)

87 **CASA LAPOSTOLLE** Cabernet Sauvignon Colchagua 1994 • $9.00 • (06/30/96)

87 **MCDOWELL** Syrah Mendocino 1993 • $10.00 • (10/15/95)

87 **NAPA RIDGE** Cabernet Sauvignon Central Coast 1992 • $8.00 • (10/15/95)

87 **STE. CHAPELLE** Cabernet Sauvignon Washington 1993 • $10.00 • (11/15/95)

87 **TRAPICHE** Malbec Mendoza Oak Cask Vintner's Selection Lujan de Coyo County 1991 • $8.00 • (08/31/95)

87 **TUALATIN** Pinot Noir Willamette Valley Barrel Aged 1994 • $10.00 • (01/31/96)

86 **ARIES** Pinot Noir Los Carneros 1994 • $10.00 • (01/31/96)

86 **BODEGAS BERBERANA** Rioja Tempranillo Dragon Label 1994 • $10.00 • (06/30/96)

86 **BUENA VISTA** Pinot Noir Carneros 1993 • $10.00 • (10/15/95)

86 **CA' DEL SOLO** Big House White California 1994 • $7.50 • (10/15/95)

86 **J. LOHR** Cabernet Sauvignon California Cypress 1992 • $9.00 • (11/30/95)

86 **ROSEMOUNT** Shiraz Cabernet Australia 1995 • $10.00 • (06/15/96)

86 **SEAVIEW** Shiraz McLaren Vale 1992 • $7.50

86 **TESSERA** Merlot California 1994 • $9.00 • (06/30/96)

86 **TRAPICHE** Malbec Mendoza Oak Cask Vintner's Selection Lujan de Cuyo County 1990 • $8.00 • (07/31/95)

85 **COLUMBIA CREST** Cabernet Sauvignon Columbia Valley 1992 • $9.00 • (07/31/95)

85 **FETZER** Merlot California Eagle Peak 1994 • $8.00 • (06/15/96)

85 **LOUIS M. MARTINI** Pinot Noir Los Carneros 1993 • $8.00 • (01/31/96)
85 **NAPA RIDGE** Merlot North Coast Coastal 1993 • $10.00 • (06/30/96)
84 **STONE CREEK** Merlot Washington Special Selection 1993 • $8.00 • (05/15/96)

WHITE, $7.25 TO $10

90 **BERNARDUS** Sauvignon Blanc Monterey County 1994 • $10.00 • (12/31/95)
88 **J.B. ADAM** Riesling Alsace Réserve 1993 • $9.00 • (09/15/95)
88 **BONNY DOON** Riesling California Pacific Rim 1994 • $8.00 • (09/15/95)
88 **HARDY'S** Chardonnay Padthaway 1994 • $11.00 • (03/31/96)
88 **LOCKWOOD** Sauvignon Blanc Monterey 1994 • $9.00 • (05/31/96)
88 **NEIRANO** Gavi 1994 • $10.00 • (02/29/96)
88 **HERMANN J. WIEMER** Johannisberg Riesling Finger Lakes Semi-Dry 1994 • $10.00 • (01/31/96)
87 **BERINGER** Sauvignon Blanc-Sémillon Meritage Knights Valley 1993 • $9.00 • (08/31/95)
87 **CARNEROS CREEK** Chardonnay California Fleur de Carneros 1993 • $9.00 • (09/30/95)
87 **FRANZ HAAS** Pinot Grigio Kris Alto Adige 1994 • $10.00 • (10/31/95)
87 **HESS SELECT** Chardonnay California 1994 • $9.50 • (06/30/96)
87 **DOMAINES SCHLUMBERGER** Pinot Blanc Alsace 1993 • $10.00 • (07/31/95)
87 **VAN DUZER** Riesling Dry Oregon Reserve 1994 • $8.00 • (01/31/96)
87 **PETER ZEMMER** Pinot Grigio Alto Adige 1995 • $10.00 • (06/15/96)
86 **ARCIERO** Chardonnay Paso Robles 1994 • $9.00 • (06/15/96)
86 **CHAPPELLET** Chenin Blanc Napa Valley Dry 1993 • $7.50 • (10/15/95)
86 **COTES DE SONOMA** Chardonnay Sonoma County 1994 • $8.00 • (10/15/95)
86 **DUCK POND** Chardonnay Willamette Valley Barrel Fermented 1994 • $8.00 • (11/15/95)
86 **HOGUE** Fumé Blanc Columbia Valley 1994 • $7.50 • (09/15/95)
86 **TAFT STREET** Chardonnay Sonoma County 1994 • $10.00 • (06/15/96)
85 **MILBURN PARK** Sauvignon Blanc Victoria 1994 • $8.00 • (03/31/96)
84 **AURORA** Chardonnay Willamette Valley 1994 • $8.00 • (03/31/96)

Great Vintages, Great Wines

In the following pages you will find *Wine Spectator*'s ratings for the recent outstanding vintages of six of the world's most prestigious—and therefore collectible—wine types: red Bordeaux, red Burgundy, white Burgundy, vintage Port, California Cabernet and blends, and California Chardonnay. Also listed are current retail or auction prices.

The wines are organized in descending order of score, to make it easy to identify the best wines of each vintage. If you know the name of a wine already and you want to look up its score and tasting note, turn to the main listings section and look under the country name and then under the producer's name.

Château Margaux
in Bordeaux.

Red Bordeaux

Here are *Wine Spectator*'s ratings and prices for the major château wines from the six best recent vintages—1995 (based on barrel samples), 1990, 1989, 1988, 1986 and 1982. The wines are organized by vintage, and in descending order of score, to make it easy to identify the best wines of each vintage. For ratings from years omitted from this section, turn to the main listings section, where you will find complete ratings under the château names.

We bring you the newest vintage, 1995, even though it was not released at press time, because many consumers are buying these wines as "futures." 1995 Bordeaux is superior to 1994—also still in barrel— and is clearly the best vintage since 1990. The 1993 vintage, currently on sale, is the best of three week years beginning in 1991. We recommend you skip most wines from 1991-1993 if you are looking for high-quality Bordeaux that will improve significantly with age.

The date of the issue of *Wine Spectator* in which the rating was first published is in parentheses. In general, wines for which no issue date appears were tasted between April 15, 1994 and June 15, 1996.

1995 Red Bordeaux | Vintage Rating: 88-92

95-100 CHÂTEAU AUSONE St.-Emilion 1995 • $NA • (05/15/96)
95-100 CHÂTEAU CERTAN DE MAY Pomerol 1995 • $NA • (05/15/96)
95-100 CHÂTEAU DUCRU-BEAUCAILLOU St.-Julien 1995 • $NA • (05/15/96)
95-100 CHÂTEAU L'EVANGILE Pomerol 1995 • $NA • (05/15/96)
95-100 CHÂTEAU LAFITE ROTHSCHILD Pauillac 1995 • $NA • (05/15/96)
95-100 CHÂTEAU MARGAUX Margaux 1995 • $NA • (05/15/96)
95-100 CHÂTEAU MOUTON-ROTHSCHILD Pauillac 1995 • $NA • (05/15/96)
95-100 CHÂTEAU PICHON-LONGUEVILLE-LALANDE Pauillac 1995 • $NA • (05/15/96)
90-94 CHÂTEAU BOURGNEUF Pomerol 1995 • $NA • (05/15/96)
90-94 CHÂTEAU CALON-SÉGUR St.-Estèphe 1995 • $NA • (05/15/96)
90-94 CHÂTEAU CANON(ST.-EMILION) St.-Emilion 1995 • $NA • (05/15/96)
90-94 CHÂTEAU CANON-LA GAFFELIÈRE St.-Emilion 1995 • $NA • (05/15/96)
90-94 CHÂTEAU CHEVAL-BLANC St.-Emilion 1995 • $NA • (05/15/96)
90-94 CHÂTEAU CLERC MILON Pauillac 1995 • $NA • (05/15/96)
90-94 CHÂTEAU CLINET Pomerol 1995 • $NA • (05/15/96)
90-94 CHÂTEAU CORDEILLAN-BAGES Pauillac 1995 • $NA • (05/15/96)
90-94 CHÂTEAU COS-D'ESTOURNEL St.-Estèphe 1995 • $NA • (05/15/96)
90-94 CHÂTEAU FERRIÈRE Margaux 1995 • $NA • (05/15/96)
90-94 CHÂTEAU FIGEAC St.-Emilion 1995 • $NA • (05/15/96)
90-94 CHÂTEAU GLORIA St.-Julien 1995 • $NA • (05/15/96)
90-94 CHÂTEAU GRAND-MAYNE St.-Emilion 1995 • $NA • (05/15/96)
90-94 CHÂTEAU GRAND-PUY-LACOSTE Pauillac 1995 • $NA • (05/15/96)
90-94 CHÂTEAU HAUT-BRION Pessac-Léognan 1995 • $NA • (05/15/96)
90-94 CHÂTEAU KIRWAN Margaux 1995 • $NA • (05/15/96)
90-94 CHÂTEAU L'ANGÉLUS St.-Emilion 1995 • $NA • (05/15/96)
90-94 CHÂTEAU LA LOUVIÈRE Pessac-Léognan 1995 • $NA • (05/15/96)
90-94 CHÂTEAU LA MISSION-HAUT-BRION Pessac-Léognan 1995 • $NA • (05/15/96)
90-94 CHÂTEAU LA POINTE Pomerol 1995 • $NA • (05/15/96)
90-94 CHÂTEAU LA VRAYE-CROIX-DE-GAY Pomerol 1995 • $NA • (05/15/96)
90-94 CHÂTEAU LAFON-ROCHET St.-Estèphe 1995 • $NA • (05/15/96)
90-94 CHÂTEAU LAGRANGE(ST.-JULIEN) St.-Julien 1995 • $NA • (05/15/96)
90-94 CHÂTEAU LARMANDE St.-Emilion 1995 • $NA • (05/15/96)
90-94 CHÂTEAU LATOUR Pauillac 1995 • $NA • (05/15/96)
90-94 CHÂTEAU LE BON-PASTEUR Pomerol 1995 • $NA • (05/15/96)
90-94 CHÂTEAU LE GAY Pomerol 1995 • $NA • (05/15/96)
90-94 CHÂTEAU LE PIN Pomerol 1995 • $NA • (05/15/96)

90-94 **CHÂTEAU LYNCH-BAGES** Pauillac 1995 • $NA • (05/15/96)
90-94 **CHÂTEAU LÉOVILLE BARTON** St.-Julien 1995 • $NA • (05/15/96)
90-94 **CHÂTEAU LÉOVILLE POYFERRÉ** St.-Julien 1995 • $NA • (05/15/96)
90-94 **CHÂTEAU MONBOUSQUET** St.-Emilion 1995 • $NA • (05/15/96)
90-94 **CHÂTEAU PALMER** Margaux 1995 • $NA • (05/15/96)
90-94 **CHÂTEAU PAPE CLÉMENT** Pessac-Léognan 1995 • $NA • (05/15/96)
90-94 **CHÂTEAU PAVIE-MACQUIN** St.-Emilion 1995 • $NA • (05/15/96)
90-94 **CHÂTEAU PETIT-VILLAGE** Pomerol 1995 • $NA • (05/15/96)
90-94 **CHÂTEAU PICHON-LONGUEVILLE-BARON** Pauillac 1995 • $NA • (05/15/96)
90-94 **CHÂTEAU PRIEURÉ-LICHINE** Margaux 1995 • $NA • (05/15/96)
90-94 **CHÂTEAU PÉTRUS** Pomerol 1995 • $NA • (05/15/96)
90-94 **CHÂTEAU SIRAN** Margaux 1995 • $NA • (05/15/96)
90-94 **CHÂTEAU SMITH-HAUT-LAFITTE** Pessac-Léognan 1995 • $NA • (05/15/96)
90-94 **CHÂTEAU ST.-PIERRE** St.-Julien 1995 • $NA • (05/15/96)
90-94 **CHÂTEAU TROPLONG-MONDOT** St.-Emilion 1995 • $NA • (05/15/96)
90-94 **CHÂTEAU TROTANOY** Pomerol 1995 • $NA • (05/15/96)
90-94 **CHÂTEAU D'ISSAN** Margaux 1995 • $NA • (05/15/96)
90-94 **CHÂTEAU DE VALANDRAUD** St.-Emilion 1995 • $NA • (05/15/96)
90-94 **CLOS DE L'ORATOIRE** St.-Emilion 1995 • $NA • (05/15/96)
90-94 **CHATEAU RAUZAN-SEGLA** Margaux 1995 • $NA • (05/15/96)
90-94 **VIEUX-CHÂTEAU-CERTAN** Pomerol 1995 • $NA • (05/15/96)
85-89 **ABEILLE DE FIEUZAL** Pessac-Léognan 1995 • $NA • (05/15/96)
85-89 **CARRUADES DE LAFITE ROTHSCHILD** Pauillac 1995 • $NA • (05/15/96)
85-89 **CHÂTEAU BAHANS HAUT-BRION** Pessac-Léognan 1995 • $NA • (05/15/96)
85-89 **CHÂTEAU BEAU-SÉJOUR BÉCOT** St.-Emilion 1995 • $NA • (05/15/96)
85-89 **CHÂTEAU BEAUREGARD** Pomerol 1995 • $NA • (05/15/96)
85-89 **CHÂTEAU BEAUSÉJOUR** St.-Emilion 1995 • $NA • (05/15/96)
85-89 **CHÂTEAU BEL-ORME-TRONQUOY-DE-LALANDE** Haut-Médoc 1995 • $NA • (05/15/96)
85-89 **CHÂTEAU BELGRAVE** Haut-Médoc 1995 • $NA • (05/15/96)
85-89 **CHÂTEAU BEYCHEVELLE** St.-Julien 1995 • $NA • (05/15/96)
85-89 **CHÂTEAU BISTON-BRILLETTE** Moulis 1995 • $NA • (05/15/96)
85-89 **CHÂTEAU BRANAIRE-DUCRU** St.-Julien 1995 • $NA • (05/15/96)
85-89 **CHÂTEAU BÉLAIR** St.-Emilion 1995 • $NA • (05/15/96)
85-89 **CHÂTEAU CANON(CANON-FRONSAC)** Canon-Fronsac 1995 • $NA • (05/15/96)
85-89 **CHÂTEAU CANON-MOUEIX** Canon-Fronsac 1995 • $NA • (05/15/96)
85-89 **CHÂTEAU CANTENAC-BROWN** Margaux 1995 • $NA • (05/15/96)
85-89 **CHÂTEAU CANUET** Margaux 1995 • $NA • (05/15/96)
85-89 **CHÂTEAU CARONNE-STE.-GEMME** Haut-Médoc 1995 • $NA • (05/15/96)
85-89 **CHÂTEAU CHAMBERT-MARBUZET** St.-Estèphe 1995 • $NA • (05/15/96)
85-89 **CHÂTEAU CHARLEMAGNE** Canon-Fronsac 1995 • $NA • (05/15/96)
85-89 **CHÂTEAU CHASSE-SPLEEN** Moulis 1995 • $NA • (05/15/96)
85-89 **CHÂTEAU CISSAC** Haut-Médoc 1995 • $NA • (05/15/96)
85-89 **CHÂTEAU CITRAN** Haut-Médoc 1995 • $NA • (05/15/96)
85-89 **CHÂTEAU CORBIN-MICHOTTE** St.-Emilion 1995 • $NA • (05/15/96)
85-89 **CHÂTEAU COS-LABORY** St.-Estèphe 1995 • $NA • (05/15/96)
85-89 **CHÂTEAU COUFRAN** Haut-Médoc 1995 • $NA • (05/15/96)
85-89 **CHÂTEAU CROIZET-BAGES** Pauillac 1995 • $NA • (05/15/96)
85-89 **CHÂTEAU DAUZAC** Margaux 1995 • $NA • (05/15/96)
85-89 **CHÂTEAU DEYREM-VALENTIN** Margaux 1995 • $NA • (05/15/96)
85-89 **CHÂTEAU DUHART-MILON ROTHSCHILD** Pauillac 1995 • $NA • (05/15/96)
85-89 **CHÂTEAU FAIZEAU** Montagne-St.-Emilion Sélection Vieilles Vignes 1995 • $NA • (05/15/96)
85-89 **CHÂTEAU FLEUR-CARDINALE** St.-Emilion 1995 • $NA • (05/15/96)
85-89 **CHÂTEAU FONROQUE** St.-Emilion 1995 • $NA • (05/15/96)
85-89 **CHÂTEAU FONTENIL** Fronsac 1995 • $NA • (05/15/96)
85-89 **CHÂTEAU FOURCAS-HOSTEN** Listrac 1995 • $NA • (05/15/96)
85-89 **CHÂTEAU GAZIN** Pomerol 1995 • $NA • (05/15/96) • RT
85-89 **CHÂTEAU GISCOURS** Margaux 1995 • $NA • (05/15/96)
85-89 **CHÂTEAU GRAND-PONTET** St.-Emilion 1995 • $NA • (05/15/96)
85-89 **CHÂTEAU GREYSAC** Médoc 1995 • $NA • (05/15/96)
85-89 **CHÂTEAU HAUT-BAGES-AVÉROUS** Pauillac 1995 • $NA • (05/15/96)
85-89 **CHÂTEAU HAUT-BAGES-LIBÉRAL** Pauillac 1995 • $NA • (05/15/96)
85-89 **CHÂTEAU HAUT-BAILLY** Pessac-Léognan 1995 • $NA • (05/15/96)
85-89 **CHÂTEAU HAUT-BEAUSÉJOUR** St.-Estèphe 1995 • $15 • (05/15/96)
85-89 **CHÂTEAU HAUT-CORBIN** St.-Emilion 1995 • $NA • (05/15/96)
85-89 **CHÂTEAU HAUT-LAGRANGE** Pessac-Léognan 1995 • $NA • (05/15/96)
85-89 **CHÂTEAU HAUT-MARBUZET** St.-Estèphe 1995 • $NA • (05/15/96)
85-89 **CHÂTEAU JONQUEYRES** Bordeaux Supérieur 1995 • $NA • (05/15/96)
85-89 **CHÂTEAU LA COMMANDERIE** Pomerol 1995 • $NA • (05/15/96)
85-89 **CHÂTEAU LA CONSEILLANTE** Pomerol 1995 • $NA • (05/15/96)
85-89 **CHÂTEAU LA CROIX DU CASSE** Pomerol 1995 • $NA • (05/15/96)
85-89 **CHÂTEAU LA CROIX-DE-GAY** Pomerol 1995 • $NA • (05/15/96)
85-89 **CHÂTEAU LA DOMINIQUE** St.-Emilion 1995 • $NA • (05/15/96)
85-89 **CHÂTEAU LA FLEUR** St.-Emilion 1995 • $NA • (05/15/96)
85-89 **CHÂTEAU LA FLEUR DE GAY** Pomerol 1995 • $NA • (05/15/96)
85-89 **CHÂTEAU LA FLEUR-POURRET** St.-Emilion 1995 • $NA • (05/15/96)
85-89 **CHÂTEAU LA FLEUR-PÉTRUS** Pomerol 1995 • $NA • (05/15/96)
85-89 **CHÂTEAU LA GARDE** Pessac-Léognan 1995 • $NA • (05/15/96)
85-89 **CHÂTEAU LA GRAVE TRIGANT DE BOISSET** Pomerol 1995 • $NA • (05/15/96)
85-89 **CHÂTEAU LA GURGUE** Margaux 1995 • $NA • (05/15/96)

85-89 CHÂTEAU LA SERRE St.-Emilion 1995 • $NA • (05/15/96)
85-89 CHÂTEAU LA TOUR CARNET Haut-Médoc 1995 • $NA • (05/15/96)
85-89 CHÂTEAU LA TOUR-HAUT-BRION Pessac-Léognan 1995 • $NA • (05/15/96)
85-89 CHÂTEAU LA TOUR-DE-BY Médoc 1995 • $NA • (05/15/96)
85-89 CHÂTEAU LA VIEILLE CURE Fronsac 1995 • $NA • (05/15/96)
85-89 CHÂTEAU LABÉGORCE Margaux 1995 • $NA • (05/15/96)
85-89 CHÂTEAU LABÉGORCE-ZÉDÉ Margaux 1995 • $NA • (05/15/96)
85-89 CHÂTEAU LAFLEUR Pomerol 1995 • $NA • (05/15/96)
85-89 CHÂTEAU LAFLEUR-GAZIN Pomerol 1995 • $NA • (05/15/96)
85-89 CHÂTEAU LANGOA BARTON St.-Julien 1995 • $NA • (05/15/96)
85-89 CHÂTEAU LARCIS-DUCASSE St.-Emilion 1995 • $NA • (05/15/96)
85-89 CHÂTEAU LARRIVET-HAUT-BRION Pessac-Léognan 1995 • $NA • (05/15/96)
85-89 CHÂTEAU LASCOMBES Margaux 1995 • $NA • (05/15/96)
85-89 CHÂTEAU LATOUR À POMEROL Pomerol 1995 • $NA • (05/15/96)
85-89 CHÂTEAU LE BOSCQ St.-Estèphe 1995 • $NA • (05/15/96)
85-89 CHÂTEAU LE PRIEURÉ St.-Emilion 1995 • $NA • (05/15/96)
85-89 CHÂTEAU LES GRANDS CHÊNES Médoc Cuvée Préstige 1995 • $NA • (05/15/96)
85-89 CHÂTEAU LES ORMES-DE-PEZ St.-Estèphe 1995 • $NA • (05/15/96)
85-89 CHÂTEAU LILIAN LADOUYS St.-Estèphe 1995 • $NA • (05/15/96)
85-89 CHÂTEAU MAGDELAINE St.-Emilion 1995 • $NA • (05/15/96)
85-89 CHÂTEAU MARSAU Côtes de Francs 1995 • $NA • (05/15/96)
85-89 CHÂTEAU MAZERIS Canon-Fronsac 1995 • $NA • (05/15/96)
85-89 CHÂTEAU MEYNEY St.-Estèphe 1995 • $NA • (05/15/96)
85-89 CHÂTEAU MONBRISON Margaux 1995 • $NA • (05/15/96)
85-89 CHÂTEAU MONTROSE St.-Estèphe 1995 • $NA • (05/15/96)
85-89 CHÂTEAU MONTVIEL Pomerol 1995 • $NA • (05/15/96)
85-89 CHÂTEAU MOULIN DU CADET St.-Emilion 1995 • $NA • (05/15/96)
85-89 CHÂTEAU MOULIN-ST.-GEORGES St.-Emilion 1995 • $NA • (05/15/96)
85-89 CHÂTEAU PATACHE D'AUX Médoc 1995 • $NA • (05/15/96)
85-89 CHÂTEAU PAVIE St.-Emilion 1995 • $NA • (05/15/96)
85-89 CHÂTEAU PAVIE-DECESSE St.-Emilion 1995 • $NA • (05/15/96)
85-89 CHÂTEAU PHÉLAN-SÉGUR St.-Estèphe 1995 • $NA • (05/15/96)
85-89 CHÂTEAU PLINCE Pomerol 1995 • $NA • (05/15/96)
85-89 CHÂTEAU PONTET-CANET Pauillac 1995 • $NA • (05/15/96)
85-89 CHÂTEAU POUJEAUX Moulis 1995 • $NA • (05/15/96)
85-89 CHÂTEAU PUYGUERAUD Côtes de Francs 1995 • $NA • (05/15/96)
85-89 CHÂTEAU ROCHER BELLEVUE FIGEAC St.-Emilion 1995 • $NA • (05/15/96)
85-89 CHÂTEAU SOCIANDO-MALLET Haut-Médoc 1995 • $NA • (05/15/96)
85-89 CHÂTEAU TALBOT St.-Julien 1995 • $NA • (05/15/96)
85-89 CHÂTEAU TOUR-BALADOZ St.-Emilion 1995 • $NA • (05/15/96)
85-89 CHÂTEAU TRONQUOY-LALANDE St.-Estèphe 1995 • $NA • (05/15/96)
85-89 CHÂTEAU VERDIGNAN Haut-Médoc 1995 • $NA • (05/15/96)
85-89 CHÂTEAU VIEUX-ROBIN Médoc 1995 • $NA • (05/15/96)
85-89 CHÂTEAU D'ANGLUDET Margaux 1995 • $NA • (05/15/96)
85-89 CHÂTEAU D'ARMAILHAC Pauillac 1995 • $NA • (05/15/96)
85-89 CHÂTEAU DE CAMENSAC Haut-Médoc 1995 • $NA • (05/15/96)
85-89 CHÂTEAU DE CARLES Fronsac 1995 • $NA • (05/15/96)
85-89 CHÂTEAU DE CRUZEAU Pessac-Léognan 1995 • $NA • (05/15/96)
85-89 CHÂTEAU DE FIEUZAL Pessac-Léognan 1995 • $NA • (05/15/96)
85-89 CHÂTEAU DE LA DAUPHINE Fronsac 1995 • $NA • (05/15/96)
85-89 CHÂTEAU DE LA TOUR Bordeaux Supérieur 1995 • $NA • (05/15/96)
85-89 CHÂTEAU DE PEZ St.-Estèphe 1995 • $NA • (05/15/96)
85-89 CHÂTEAU DE SALES Pomerol 1995 • $NA • (05/15/96)
85-89 CLOS FOURTET St.-Emilion 1995 • $NA • (05/15/96)
85-89 CLOS MARSALETTE Pessac-Léognan 1995 • $NA • (05/15/96)
85-89 CLOS L'EGLISE Pomerol 1995 • $NA • (05/15/96)
85-89 DOMAINE DE CHEVALIER Pessac-Léognan 1995 • $NA • (05/15/96)
85-89 LA CHAPELLE DE LA MISSION-HAUT-BRION Pessac-Léognan 1995 • $NA • (05/15/96)
85-89 LES FORTS DE LATOUR Pauillac 1995 • $NA • (05/15/96)
85-89 PENSÉES DE LAFLEUR Pomerol 1995 • $NA • (05/15/96)
85-89 TOURELLES DE LONGUEVILLE Pauillac 1995 • $NA • (05/15/96)
80-84 CHÂTEAU CANON-LA-GAFFELIERE Canon-Fronsac 1995 • $NA • (05/15/96)
80-84 CHÂTEAU ANDRON-BLANQUET St.-Estèphe 1995 • $NA • (05/15/96)
80-84 CHÂTEAU ARNAULD Haut-Médoc 1995 • $NA • (05/15/96)
80-84 CHÂTEAU BEAUMONT Haut-Médoc 1995 • $NA • (05/15/96)
80-84 CHÂTEAU BRANE-CANTENAC Margaux 1995 • $NA • (05/15/96)
80-84 CHÂTEAU CANTEMERLE Haut-Médoc 1995 • $NA • (05/15/96)
80-84 CHÂTEAU CARBONNIEUX Pessac-Léognan 1995 • $NA • (05/15/96)
80-84 CHÂTEAU CLÉMENT PICHON Haut-Médoc 1995 • $NA • (05/15/96)
80-84 CHÂTEAU CÔTE ROL St.-Emilion 1995 • $NA • (05/15/96)
80-84 CHÂTEAU DILLON Haut-Médoc 1995 • $NA • (05/15/96)
80-84 CHÂTEAU FERRAND Pomerol 1995 • $NA • (05/15/96)
80-84 CHÂTEAU FEYTIT-CLINET Pomerol 1995 • $NA • (05/15/96)
80-84 CHÂTEAU FONBADET Pauillac 1995 • $NA • (05/15/96)
80-84 CHÂTEAU FOURCAS-DUPRÉ Listrac 1995 • $NA • (05/15/96)
80-84 CHÂTEAU FRANC-MAYNE St.-Emilion 1995 • $NA • (05/15/96)
80-84 CHÂTEAU GRAND-PUY-DUCASSE Pauillac 1995 • $NA • (05/15/96)
80-84 CHÂTEAU GRUAUD-LAROSE St.-Julien 1995 • $NA • (05/15/96)
80-84 CHÂTEAU HAUT-GARDÈRE Pessac-Léognan 1995 • $NA • (05/15/96)
80-84 CHÂTEAU LA GOMERIE St.-Emilion 1995 • $NA • (05/15/96)
80-84 CHÂTEAU LA TOUR MARTILLAC Pessac-Léognan 1995 • $NA • (05/15/96)

80-84 **CHÂTEAU LA TOUR-ST.-BONNET** Médoc 1995• $NA • (05/15/96)
80-84 **CHÂTEAU LA VIOLETTE** Pomerol 1995• $NA• (05/15/96)
80-84 **CHÂTEAU LAGRANGE(POMEROL)** Pomerol 1995• $NA • (05/15/96)
80-84 **CHÂTEAU LE BONNAT** Graves 1995• $NA• (05/15/96)
80-84 **CHÂTEAU LE CROCK** St.-Estèphe 1995• $NA • (05/15/96)
80-84 **CHÂTEAU LES CHARMES-GODARD** Côtes de Francs 1995 • $NA• (05/15/96)
80-84 **CHÂTEAU MALARTIC-LAGRAVIÈRE** Pessac-Léognan 1995 • $NA• (05/15/96)
80-84 **CHÂTEAU MALESCASSE** Haut-Médoc 1995• $NA • (05/15/96)
80-84 **CHÂTEAU MOULIN-RICHE** St.-Julien 1995• $NA • (05/15/96)
80-84 **CHÂTEAU PAVILLON LA CROIX FIGEAC** St.-Emilion 1995 • $NA• (05/15/96)
80-84 **CHÂTEAU PETIT-FIGEAC** St.-Emilion 1995• $NA • (05/15/96)
80-84 **CHÂTEAU PIBRAN** Pauillac 1995• $NA• (05/15/96)
80-84 **CHÂTEAU POUGET** Margaux 1995• $NA• (05/15/96)
80-84 **CHÂTEAU POUMEY** Pessac-Léognan 1995• $NA • (05/15/96)
80-84 **CHÂTEAU PUY-BLANQUET** St.-Emilion 1995• $NA • (05/15/96)
80-84 **CHÂTEAU ROLLAND-MAILLET** St.-Emilion 1995• $NA • (05/15/96)
80-84 **CHÂTEAU SOUDARS** Haut-Médoc 1995• $NA• (05/15/96)
80-84 **CHÂTEAU ST.-ANDRÉ-CORBIN** St.-Georges-St.-Emilion 1995• $NA• (05/15/96)
80-84 **CHÂTEAU TEYSSIER** Montagne-St.-Emilion 1995• $NA • (05/15/96)
80-84 **CHÂTEAU D'OLIVIER** Pessac-Léognan 1995• $NA • (05/15/96)
80-84 **CHÂTEAU DE MARBUZET** St.-Estèphe 1995• $NA • (05/15/96)
80-84 **CHÂTEAU DE SOURS** Bordeaux 1995• $NA• (05/15/96)
80-84 **CHÂTEAU DU CARTILLON** Haut-Médoc 1995• $NA • (05/15/96)
80-84 **CHÂTEAU DU GLANA** St.-Julien Vieilles Vignes 1995 • $NA• (05/15/96)
80-84 **CLOS LARCIS** St.-Emilion 1995• $NA• (05/15/96)
80-84 **L DE LA LOUVIÈRE** Pessac-Léognan 1995• $NA • (05/15/96)
80-84 **LES FIEFS DE LAGRANGE** St.-Julien 1995• $NA • (05/15/96)
80-84 **PAUILLAC DE CHÂTEAU LATOUR** Pauillac 1995• $NA • (05/15/96)
80-84 **CHATEAU RAUZAN-GASSIES** Margaux 1995• $NA • (05/15/96)
80-84 **SEGLA** Margaux 1995• $NA• (05/15/96)
75-79 **CHÂTEAU BONNET** Bordeaux Reserve 1995• $NA • (05/15/96)
75-79 **CHÂTEAU CLOS DES JACOBINS** St.-Emilion 1995• $NA • (05/15/96)
75-79 **CHÂTEAU LE JURAT** St.-Emilion 1995• $NA• (05/15/96)
75-79 **CHÂTEAU LE SARTRE** Pessac-Léognan 1995• $NA • (05/15/96)
75-79 **CHÂTEAU LIVERSAN** Haut-Médoc 1995• $NA• (05/15/96)
75-79 **CHÂTEAU PLAGNAC** Médoc 1995• $NA• (05/15/96)
75-79 **CHÂTEAU VILLEMAURINE** St.-Emilion 1995• $NA • (05/15/96)
75-79 **CHÂTEAU DE ROCHEMORIN** Pessac-Léognan 1995• $NA • (05/15/96)
75-79 **VILLA BEL-AIR** Graves 1995• $NA• (05/15/96)
70-74 **CHÂTEAU MARJOSSE** Bordeaux 1995• $NA• (05/15/96)
70-74 **CHÂTEAU PRIEURS DE LA COMMANDERIE** Pomerol 1995 • $NA• (05/15/96)

1990 Red Bordeaux
Vintage Rating: 97

100 **CHÂTEAU LATOUR** Pauillac 1990• $80
98 **CHÂTEAU PETRUS** Pomerol 1990• $594• (03/31/93)
97 **CHÂTEAU LAFITE-ROTHSCHILD** Pauillac 1990• $153 • (03/31/93)• CS
97 **CHÂTEAU LE PIN** Pomerol 1990• $275• (03/31/93)
97 **CHÂTEAU PICHON-LONGUEVILLE-LALANDE** Pauillac 1990 • $55• (03/15/93)• SS
96 **CHÂTEAU HAUT-BRION** Pessac-Léognan 1990• $76 • (04/30/93)• CS
96 **CHÂTEAU LE GAY** Pomerol 1990• $49• (03/31/93)
96 **CHÂTEAU MARGAUX** Margaux 1990• $400• (03/31/93)
96 **CHÂTEAU TROTANOY** Pomerol 1990• $46• (03/31/93)
95 **CHÂTEAU BEAUSEJOUR-DUFFAU-LAGARROSSE** St.-Emilion 1990• $50• (03/31/93)
95 **CHÂTEAU CANON-LA-GAFFELIERE** St.-Emilion 1990• $30 • (03/15/93)
95 **CHÂTEAU CORDEILLAN-BAGES** Pauillac 1990• $33 • (03/31/93)
95 **CHÂTEAU GRAND-PUY-LACOSTE** Pauillac 1990• $26 • (03/31/93)
95 **CHÂTEAU LA FLEUR DE GAY** Pomerol 1990• $75 • (03/31/93)
95 **CHÂTEAU LA LAGUNE** Haut-Médoc 1990• $24 • (10/15/94)
95 **CHÂTEAU LA MISSION-HAUT-BRION** Pessac-Léognan 1990 • $65• (03/31/93)
95 **CHÂTEAU LAFLEUR** Pomerol 1990• $200• (05/15/94)
95 **CHÂTEAU LAGRANGE** Pomerol 1990• $30• (03/31/93)
95 **CHÂTEAU LAGRANGE** St.-Julien 1990• $30• (03/31/93) • SS
95 **CHÂTEAU MOUTON-ROTHSCHILD** Pauillac 1990• $104 • (05/15/93)• CS
94 **CHÂTEAU AUSONE** St.-Emilion 1990• $95• (03/31/93)
94 **CHÂTEAU BOURGNEUF** Pomerol 1990• $23• (03/31/93)
94 **CHÂTEAU CLERC-MILON** Pauillac 1990• $30• (03/31/93)
94 **CHÂTEAU COS-LABORY** St.-Estèphe 1990• $25 • (03/31/93)
94 **CHÂTEAU FONROQUE** St.-Emilion 1990• $28• (03/31/93)
94 **CHÂTEAU LA CONSEILLANTE** Pomerol 1990• $110 • (03/31/93)
94 **CHÂTEAU LA CROIX DE GAY** Pomerol 1990• $28 • (03/31/93)
94 **CHÂTEAU LA LOUVIERE** Pessac-Léognan 1990• $21 • (03/31/93)
94 **CHÂTEAU LAFITE-ROTHSCHILD** Pauillac 1990• $NA • (11/30/91)
94 **CHÂTEAU LARMANDE** St.-Emilion 1990• $24• (03/31/93)
94 **CHÂTEAU LE PIN** Pomerol 1990• $275• (05/15/94)
94 **CHÂTEAU LYNCH-BAGES** Pauillac 1990• $58 • (03/31/93)
94 **CHÂTEAU MONTROSE** St.-Estèphe 1990• $154 • (03/31/93)
94 **CHÂTEAU PAVIE** St.-Emilion 1990• $38• (03/31/93)
94 **CHÂTEAU PICHON-LONGUEVILLE-BARON** Pauillac 1990 • $38• (03/31/93)
94 **CLOS DE L'ORATOIRE** St.-Emilion 1990• $28• (03/31/93)
94 **LES FORTS DE LATOUR** Pauillac 1990• $34• (03/31/93)
93 **CHÂTEAU BELAIR** St.-Emilion 1er Grand Cru Classé 1990• $45

93 **CHÂTEAU DE PEZ** St.-Estèphe 1990 • $20 • (03/31/93)
93 **CHÂTEAU L'ANGELUS** St.-Emilion 1990 • $67 • (03/31/93)
93 **CHÂTEAU LA TOUR-HAUT-BRION** Pessac-Léognan 1990 • $35 • (03/31/93)
93 **CHÂTEAU LAFLEUR** Pomerol 1990 • $200 • (03/31/93)
93 **CHÂTEAU LE BON-PASTEUR** Pomerol 1990 • $33 • (03/31/93)
93 **CHÂTEAU LEOVILLE-BARTON** St.-Julien 1990 • $48 • (03/31/93)
93 **CHÂTEAU LES ORMES DE PEZ** St.-Estèphe 1990 • $22 • (03/31/93)
93 **CHÂTEAU PAVIE-DECESSE** St.-Emilion 1990 • $22 • (03/31/93)
93 **CHÂTEAU PIBRAN** Pauillac 1990 • $25 • (03/31/93)
93 **CHÂTEAU SMITH-HAUT-LAFITTE** Pessac-Léognan 1990 • $24 • (03/31/93)
93 **CHÂTEAU TALBOT** St.-Julien 1990 • $24 • (03/31/93)
92 **CHÂTEAU CANTENAC-BROWN** Margaux 1990 • $24 • (03/31/93)
92 **CHÂTEAU DE FIEUZAL** Pessac-Léognan 1990 • $29 • (03/31/93)
92 **CHÂTEAU DUHART-MILON** Pauillac 1990 • $25 • (10/15/94)
92 **CHÂTEAU FIGEAC** St.-Emilion 1990 • $45 • (03/31/93)
92 **CHÂTEAU GISCOURS** Margaux 1990 • $35 • (03/31/93)
92 **CHÂTEAU HAUT-MARBUZET** St.-Estèphe 1990 • $32 • (03/31/93)
92 **CHÂTEAU L'EVANGILE** Pomerol 1990 • $83 • (03/31/93)
92 **CHÂTEAU LA GRAVE TRIGANT DE BOISSET** Pomerol 1990 • $28 • (03/31/93)
92 **CHÂTEAU LEOVILLE-POYFERRE** St.-Julien 1990 • $31 • (03/31/93)
92 **CHÂTEAU PAPE-CLEMENT** Pessac-Léognan 1990 • $47 • (03/31/93)
92 **CHÂTEAU PETIT-VILLAGE** Pomerol 1990 • $47 • (03/31/93)
92 **CHÂTEAU ST.-PIERRE** St.-Julien 1990 • $26 • (03/31/93)
92 **CHÂTEAU TROTANOY** Pomerol 1990 • $65 • (05/15/94)
92 **CHÂTEAU VILLEMAURINE** St.-Emilion 1990 • $28 • (03/31/93)
92 **DOMAINE DE CHEVALIER** Pessac-Léognan 1990 • $42 • (03/31/93)
91 **CHÂTEAU BRANE-CANTENAC** Margaux 1990 • $28 • (03/31/93)
91 **CHÂTEAU CANON** St.-Emilion 1990 • $41 • (03/31/93)
91 **CHÂTEAU CERTAN DE MAY** Pomerol 1990 • $85 • (10/15/94)
91 **CHÂTEAU CHEVAL BLANC** St.-Emilion 1990 • $182 • (03/31/93)
91 **CHÂTEAU DE CRUZEAU** Pessac-Léognan 1990 • $16 • (03/31/93)
91 **CHÂTEAU DESMIRAIL** Margaux 1990 • $27 • (03/31/93)
91 **CHÂTEAU FONTENIL** Fronsac 1990 • $17 • (03/31/93)
91 **CHÂTEAU FRANC-MAYNE** St.-Emilion 1990 • $23 • (03/31/93)
91 **CHÂTEAU HAUT-BAGES-AVEROUS** Pauillac 1990 • $22 • (03/31/93)
91 **CHÂTEAU HAUT-CORBIN** St.-Emilion 1990 • $18 • (03/31/93)
91 **CHÂTEAU LA TOUR-MARTILLAC** Pessac-Léognan 1990 • $25 • (03/31/93)
91 **CHÂTEAU LANGOA BARTON** St.-Julien 1990 • $27 • (03/31/93)
91 **CHÂTEAU MONBRISON** Margaux 1990 • $22 • (03/31/93)
91 **CHÂTEAU MOULIN DU CADET** St.-Emilion 1990 • $NA • (03/31/93)
91 **CHÂTEAU PALMER** Margaux 1990 • $42 • (03/31/93)
91 **CHÂTEAU PHELAN-SEGUR** St.-Estèphe 1990 • $20 • (03/31/93)
91 **CHÂTEAU POUGET** Margaux 1990 • $22 • (03/31/93)
91 **CHÂTEAU SOCIANDO-MALLET** Haut-Médoc 1990 • $29 • (03/31/93)
91 **CHÂTEAU TROPLONG-MONDOT** St.-Emilion 1990 • $32 • (03/31/93)
91 **CHÂTEAU TROTTE VIEILLE** St.-Emilion 1990 • $29 • (03/31/93)
90 **CHÂTEAU BEAU-SITE** St.-Estèphe 1990 • $23 • (03/31/93)
90 **CHÂTEAU BELAIR** St.-Emilion 1990 • $35 • (03/31/93)
90 **CHÂTEAU BRANAIRE-DUCRU** St.-Julien 1990 • $25 • (03/31/93)
90 **CHÂTEAU CHASSE-SPLEEN** Moulis 1990 • $27 • (03/31/93)
90 **CHÂTEAU COS D'ESTOURNEL** St.-Estèphe 1990 • $72 • (03/31/93)
90 **CHÂTEAU FONPLEGADE** St.-Emilion 1990 • $25 • (03/31/93)
90 **CHÂTEAU GRUAUD LAROSE** St.-Julien 1990 • $35 • (03/31/93)
90 **CHÂTEAU KIRWAN** Margaux 1990 • $28 • (03/31/93)
90 **CHÂTEAU LA FLEUR-PETRUS** Pomerol 1990 • $70 • (03/31/93)
90 **CHÂTEAU LAFLEUR-GAZIN** Pomerol 1990 • $30 • (03/31/93)
90 **CHÂTEAU LALANDE-BORIE** St.-Julien 1990 • $19 • (03/31/93)
90 **CHÂTEAU LARCIS-DUCASSE** St.-Emilion 1990 • $25 • (03/31/93)
90 **CHÂTEAU LATOUR A POMEROL** Pomerol 1990 • $60 • (10/15/94)
90 **CHÂTEAU MAGDELAINE** St.-Emilion 1990 • $36 • (03/31/93)
90 **CHÂTEAU MEYNEY** St.-Estèphe 1990 • $15 • (03/31/93)
90 **CHÂTEAU OLIVIER** Pessac-Léognan 1990 • $20 • (12/31/92)
90 **CHÂTEAU PETIT-FIGEAC** St.-Emilion 1990 • $24 • (03/31/93)
90 **CHÂTEAU SIRAN** Margaux 1990 • $22 • (03/31/93)
90 **CLOS FOURTET** St.-Emilion 1990 • $30 • (03/31/93)
90 **LES TOURELLS DE LONGUEVILLE** Pauillac 1990 • $24 • (03/31/93)
89 **CHÂTEAU CANON-DE-BREM** Canon-Fronsac 1990 • $17 • (03/31/93)
89 **CHÂTEAU CANUET** Margaux 1990 • $18 • (03/31/93)
89 **CHÂTEAU D'ARMAILHAC** Pauillac 1990 • $22 • (03/31/93)
89 **CHÂTEAU DE ROCHEMORIN** Pessac-Léognan 1990 • $12 • (03/31/93)
89 **CHÂTEAU DUCRU-BEAUCAILLOU** St.-Julien 1990 • $40 • (03/31/93)
89 **CHÂTEAU FAIZEAU** Montagne-St.-Emilion Vieilles Vignes 1990 • $15 • (03/31/93)
89 **CHÂTEAU GLORIA** St.-Julien 1990 • $20 • (03/31/93)
89 **CHÂTEAU LA FLEUR** St.-Emilion 1990 • $22 • (03/31/93)
89 **CHÂTEAU LA TOUR-DE-MONS** Margaux 1990 • $20 • (03/31/93)
89 **CHÂTEAU LABEGORCE-ZEDE** Margaux 1990 • $22 • (03/31/93)
89 **CHÂTEAU LAFON-ROCHET** St.-Estèphe 1990 • $21 • (03/31/93)
89 **CHÂTEAU LIVERSAN** Haut-Médoc 1990 • $19 • (03/31/93)
89 **CHÂTEAU MALMAISON** Moulis 1990 • $14 • (03/31/93)
89 **CHÂTEAU MOULIN HAUT-LAROQUE** Fronsac 1990 • $14 • (03/31/93)

■ ■ ■ ■

Red Bordeaux

89 **CHÂTEAU TOUR-HAUT-CAUSSAN** Médoc 1990 • $18 • (03/31/93)
89 **PAUILLAC DE CHÂTEAU LATOUR** Pauillac 1990 • $29 • (03/31/93)
89 **VIEUX CHÂTEAU CERTAN** Pomerol 1990 • $61 • (03/31/93)
88 **CHÂTEAU ANDRON BLANQUET** St.-Estèphe 1990 • $18 • (03/31/93)
88 **CHÂTEAU BOUSCAUT** Pessac-Léognan 1990 • $18 • (03/31/93)
88 **CHÂTEAU CISSAC** Haut-Médoc 1990 • $18 • (03/31/93)
88 **CHÂTEAU COUFRAN** Haut-Médoc 1990 • $17 • (03/31/93)
88 **CHÂTEAU DE CHANTEGRIVE** Graves Cuvée Edouard 1990 • $16 • (03/31/93)
88 **CHÂTEAU DU GLANA** St.-Julien 1990 • $20 • (03/31/93)
88 **CHÂTEAU DURFORT-VIVENS** Margaux 1990 • $22 • (03/31/93)
88 **CHÂTEAU GAZIN** Pomerol 1990 • $32 • (03/31/93)
88 **CHÂTEAU HAUT-BAILLY** Pessac-Léognan 1990 • $28 • (03/31/93)
88 **CHÂTEAU HAUT-MAILLET** Pomerol 1990 • $25 • (03/31/93)
88 **CHÂTEAU LA DOMINIQUE** St.-Emilion 1990 • $35 • (03/31/93)
88 **CHÂTEAU LA FLEUR-ST.-GEORGES** Lalande-de-Pomerol 1990 • $NA • (03/31/93)
88 **CHÂTEAU LA SERRE** St.-Emilion 1990 • $22 • (03/31/93)
88 **CHÂTEAU LA VIEILLE CURE** Fronsac 1990 • $19 • (03/31/93)
88 **CHÂTEAU LACHESNAYE** Haut-Médoc 1990 • $17 • (03/31/93)
88 **CHÂTEAU LESTAGE** Listrac 1990 • $18 • (03/31/93)
88 **CHÂTEAU MAZERIS-BELLEVUE** Canon-Fronsac 1990 • $15 • (03/31/93)
88 **CHÂTEAU MOULIN-PEY LABRIE** Canon-Fronsac 1990 • $16 • (03/31/93)
88 **CHÂTEAU NENIN** Pomerol 1990 • $25 • (03/31/93)
88 **CHÂTEAU POUJEAUX** Moulis 1990 • $20 • (03/31/93)
88 **CHÂTEAU ROUGET** Pomerol 1990 • $29
88 **CHÂTEAU ST.-ANDRE-CORBIN** St.-Georges-St.-Emilion 1990 • $15 • (03/31/93)
88 **LES FIEFS DE LAGRANGE** St.-Julien 1990 • $18 • (03/31/93)
88 **PIERRE DOURTHE** Bordeaux Numero 1 1990 • $9 • (05/15/94) • BB
87 **CHÂTEAU BEYCHEVELLE** St.-Julien 1990 • $34 • (03/31/93)
87 **CHÂTEAU BRILLETTE** Moulis 1990 • $18 • (03/31/93)
87 **CHÂTEAU CARBONNIEUX** Pessac-Léognan 1990 • $19 • (03/31/93)
87 **CHÂTEAU DE CHANTEGRIVE** Graves 1990 • $14 • (03/31/93)
87 **CHÂTEAU HAUT-MAZIERES** Bordeaux 1990 • $10 • (11/15/94) • BB
87 **CHÂTEAU LA CABANNE** Pomerol 1990 • $27 • (03/31/93)
87 **CHÂTEAU LA GURGUE** Margaux 1990 • $27 • (03/31/93)
87 **CHÂTEAU LA MAZEROLLE** Bordeaux 1990 • $9 • (03/15/93) • BB
87 **CHÂTEAU LA TOUR-LEOGNAN** Pessac-Léognan 1990 • $21 • (03/31/93)
87 **CHÂTEAU LACOSTE-BORIE** Pauillac 1990 • $18 • (03/31/93)
87 **CHÂTEAU LE SARTRE** Pessac-Léognan 1990 • $19 • (03/31/93)
87 **CHÂTEAU LOUDENNE** Médoc 1990 • $17 • (03/31/93)
87 **CHÂTEAU LYNCH-MOUSSAS** Pauillac 1990 • $18 • (03/31/93)
87 **CHÂTEAU MALESCOT-ST.-EXUPERY** Margaux 1990 • $24 • (02/28/94)
87 **CHÂTEAU PUY-BLANQUET** St.-Emilion 1990 • $13 • (03/31/93)
87 **CHÂTEAU RAUSAN-SEGLA** Margaux 1990 • $38 • (03/31/93)
87 **DOMAINE DE L'EGLISE** Pomerol 1990 • $37 • (03/31/93)
86 **CHÂTEAU ARNAULD** Haut-Médoc 1990 • $19 • (03/31/93)
86 **CHÂTEAU BERGAT** St.-Emilion 1990 • $19 • (03/31/93)
86 **CHÂTEAU CHAMBERT-MARBUZET** St.-Estèphe 1990 • $25 • (03/31/93)
86 **CHÂTEAU CITRAN** Haut-Médoc 1990 • $20 • (03/31/93)
86 **CHÂTEAU D'ANGLUDET** Margaux 1990 • $22 • (03/31/93)
86 **CHÂTEAU D'ISSAN** Margaux 1990 • $25 • (03/31/93)
86 **CHÂTEAU DALEM** Fronsac 1990 • $20 • (03/31/93)
86 **CHÂTEAU DE LAMARQUE** Haut-Médoc 1990 • $18 • (03/31/93)
86 **CHÂTEAU DE MARBUZET** St.-Estèphe 1990 • $19 • (09/15/93)
86 **CHÂTEAU L'EGLISE-CLINET** Pomerol 1990 • $45 • (06/15/93)
86 **CHÂTEAU LA POINTE** Pomerol 1990 • $27 • (03/31/93)
86 **CHÂTEAU LAFLEUR-POURRET** St.-Emilion 1990 • $23 • (03/31/93)
86 **CHÂTEAU LANESSAN** Haut-Médoc 1990 • $16 • (03/31/93)
86 **CHÂTEAU LASCOMBES** Margaux 1990 • $22 • (03/31/93)
86 **CHÂTEAU LE BOUSCAT** Bordeaux Grand Réserve 1990 • $9 • (11/15/94)
86 **CHÂTEAU PRIEURE-LICHINE** Margaux 1990 • $20 • (03/31/93)
86 **CHÂTEAU ST.-GEORGES** St.-Georges-St.-Emilion 1990 • $23 • (08/31/95)
86 **CHÂTEAU TRIMOULET** St.-Emilion 1990 • $20 • (09/15/93)
86 **CHÂTEAU YON-FIGEAC** St.-Emilion 1990 • $24 • (03/31/93)
85 **CHÂTEAU BALAC** Haut-Médoc 1990 • $12 • (09/15/93)
85 **CHÂTEAU CANON-FRONSAC** Canon-Fronsac 1990 • $18 • (03/31/93)
85 **CHÂTEAU DAUZAC** Margaux 1990 • $23 • (03/31/93)
85 **CHÂTEAU DE FRANCE** Pessac-Léognan 1990 • $20 • (03/31/93)
85 **CHÂTEAU FOURCAS-HOSTEN** Listrac 1990 • $20 • (03/31/93)
85 **CHÂTEAU VERDIGNAN** Haut-Médoc 1990 • $17 • (03/31/93)
85 **CLOS LARCIS** St.-Emilion 1990 • $25 • (03/31/93)
84 **CHÂTEAU CANON MOUEIX** Canon-Fronsac 1990 • $15 • (03/31/93)
84 **CHÂTEAU DE BELCIER** Côtes de Castillon 1990 • $NA • (03/31/93)
84 **CHÂTEAU GREYSAC** Médoc 1990 • $12 • (03/31/93)
84 **CHÂTEAU HAUT-BATAILLEY** Pauillac 1990 • $23 • (03/31/93)
84 **CHÂTEAU RAMAGE LA BATISSE** Haut-Médoc 1990 • $18 • (03/31/93)
84 **CHÂTEAU ROMEFORT** Médoc 1990 • $10 • (02/28/94)
84 **CHÂTEAU SIAURAC** Lalande-de-Pomerol 1990 • $19 • (05/15/94)
84 **CHÂTEAU SIAURAC** Lalande-de-Pomerol 1990 • $19
84 **CHÂTEAU SOUDARS** Haut-Médoc 1990 • $18 • (03/31/93)
84 **MOUTON-CADET** Bordeaux 1990 • $10
83 **CHÂTEAU CLARKE** Listrac 1990 • $15 • (11/15/94)

83 **CHÂTEAU DU BEAU-VALLON** St.-Emilion 1990 • $14 • (08/31/95)
83 **CHÂTEAU FONREAUD** Listrac 1990 • $16 • (03/31/93)
83 **CHÂTEAU HAUT-BAGES-LIBERAL** Pauillac 1990 • $22 • (06/15/93)
83 **CHÂTEAU LE PAPE** Pessac-Léognan 1990 • $16 • (08/31/95)
83 **CHÂTEAU LES GRANGES** Haut-Médoc 1990 • $NA • (03/31/93)
83 **CHÂTEAU ROUSSELLE** Fronsac 1990 • $NA • (03/31/93)
83 **CHÂTEAU TERTRE-ROTEBOEUF** St.-Emilion 1990 • $76 • (06/15/93)
83 **CHÂTEAU VILLARS** Fronsac 1990 • $17 • (03/31/93)
83 **VERDILLAC** Bordeaux 1990 • $7 • (09/15/93) • BB
82 **BARTON & GUESTIER** Merlot Bordeaux 1990 • $6 • (11/30/92) • BB
82 **BARTON & GUESTIER** Bordeaux Fondation 1725 1990 • $9 • (03/15/93)
82 **CHÂTEAU BONNET** Bordeaux Réserve 1990 • $NA • (03/31/93)
82 **CHÂTEAU DE BIROT** Premières Côtes de Bordeaux 1990 • $10 • (05/15/94)
82 **CHÂTEAU FOURCAS-DUPRE** Listrac 1990 • $17 • (03/31/93)
82 **CHÂTEAU LA TOUR DE BY** Médoc 1990 • $12 • (03/31/93)
82 **CHÂTEAU LABEGORCE** Margaux 1990 • $20 • (03/31/93)
82 **CHÂTEAU PLINCE** Pomerol 1990 • $25
82 **CHÂTEAU PONTET-CANET** Pauillac 1990 • $29 • (03/31/93)
82 **CHÂTEAU TOUR CALON** Montagne-St.-Emilion 1990 • $13 • (08/31/95)
82 **JEAN-PIERRE MOUEIX** Merlot Bordeaux 1990 • $10 • (11/15/94)
82 **MARQUIS DE CHASSE** Bordeaux 1990 • $7 • (03/15/93) • BB
81 **CHÂTEAU CANTEMERLE** Haut-Médoc 1990 • $25 • (03/31/93)
81 **CHÂTEAU DE LA DAUPHINE** Fronsac 1990 • $17 • (03/31/93)
81 **CHÂTEAU HANTEILLAN** Haut-Médoc 1990 • $17 • (03/31/93)
81 **CHÂTEAU LA TONNELLE** Premières Côtes de Blaye 1990 • $8 • (03/15/93)
81 **CHÂTEAU PUYGUERAUD** Côtes de Francs 1990 • $18 • (03/31/93)
81 **MAITRE D'ESTOURNEL** Bordeaux 1990 • $9 • (11/30/92)
80 **CHÂTEAU BEAUMONT** Haut-Médoc 1990 • $13 • (03/31/93)
80 **CHÂTEAU LA CLAVERIE** Côtes de Francs 1990 • $19 • (03/31/93)
80 **CHÂTEAU MAZERIS** Canon-Fronsac 1990 • $18 • (05/15/94)
80 **CHÂTEAU PITRAY** Côtes de Castillon 1990 • $9 • (03/15/93)
80 **LUCIEN DESCHAUX** Médoc 1990 • $8 • (01/31/92) • BB
79 **CHÂTEAU LAMARTINE** Bordeaux Supérieur 1990 • $NA • (03/31/93)
79 **CHÂTEAU LAPELLETRIE** St.-Emilion 1990 • $19 • (02/28/94)
79 **CHÂTEAU ROCHER-BELLEVUE-FIGEAC** St.-Emilion 1990 • $15 • (03/31/93)
78 **BARTON & GUESTIER** Cabernet Sauvignon Bordeaux 1990 • $6 • (11/30/92)
78 **CHAI DE BORDES-QUANCARD** Bordeaux Vieilli dans nos Chais 1990 • $10 • (03/15/93)
78 **CHÂTEAU TAYAC** Côtes de Bourg 1990 • $12 • (06/15/93)
77 **CHÂTEAU CLOS DES JACOBINS** St.-Emilion 1990 • $35 • (03/31/93)
76 **CHÂTEAU DE PAILLET QUANCARD** Premières Côtes de Bordeaux 1990 • $14 • (06/15/93)
76 **CHÂTEAU LA FLEUR CRAVIGNAC** St.-Emilion 1990 • $18 • (08/31/95)
75 **CHÂTEAU LAROSE-TRINTAUDON** Haut-Médoc 1990 • $12 • (03/31/93)
75 **LUCIEN DESCHAUX** Bordeaux 1990 • $6 • (01/31/92)
75 **MOULIN DE DUHART** Pauillac 1990 • $14 • (02/28/94)
74 **CHÂTEAU FOMBRAUGE** St.-Emilion 1990 • $20 • (02/28/94)
74 **CHÂTEAU TOUMALIN** Canon-Fronsac 1990 • $14 • (03/31/93)
68 **CHÂTEAU ROC DE CAMBES** Côtes de Bourg 1990 • $16 • (06/15/93)

1989 RED BORDEAUX
VINTAGE RATING: 98

99 **CHÂTEAU MARGAUX** Margaux 1989 • $106 • (03/15/92) • CS
99 **CHÂTEAU MOUTON-ROTHSCHILD** Pauillac 1989 • $130 • (03/15/92)
98 **CHÂTEAU LA FLEUR DE GAY** Pomerol 1989 • $117 • (03/15/92)
98 **CHÂTEAU LYNCH-BAGES** Pauillac 1989 • $71 • (03/15/92)
98 **CHÂTEAU PICHON-LONGUEVILLE-BARON** Pauillac 1989 • $60 • (03/15/92)
97 **CHÂTEAU HAUT-BRION** Pessac-Léognan 1989 • $135 • (03/15/92)
97 **CHÂTEAU LATOUR** Pauillac 1989 • $97 • (03/15/92)
96 **CHÂTEAU CLERC-MILON** Pauillac 1989 • $33 • (03/15/92)
96 **CHÂTEAU CORDEILLAN-BAGES** Pauillac 1989 • $26 • (03/15/92)
96 **CHÂTEAU L'EGLISE-CLINET** Pomerol 1989 • $45 • (08/31/92)
96 **CHÂTEAU LA MISSION-HAUT-BRION** Pessac-Léognan 1989 • $100 • (03/15/92)
96 **CHÂTEAU LAFLEUR** Pomerol 1989 • $190 • (03/15/92)
96 **DOMAINE DE CHEVALIER** Pessac-Léognan 1989 • $59 • (03/15/92)
95 **CHÂTEAU BEYCHEVELLE** St.-Julien 1989 • $47 • (03/15/92)
95 **CHÂTEAU CALON-SEGUR** St.-Estèphe 1989 • $27 • (03/15/92)
95 **CHÂTEAU CHASSE-SPLEEN** Moulis 1989 • $30 • (03/15/92)
95 **CHÂTEAU COS D'ESTOURNEL** St.-Estèphe 1989 • $46 • (03/15/92)
95 **CHÂTEAU DE FIEUZAL** Pessac-Léognan 1989 • $32 • (03/15/92)
95 **CHÂTEAU LA POINTE** Pomerol 1989 • $17 • (03/15/92)
95 **CHÂTEAU LA TOUR-HAUT-BRION** Pessac-Léognan 1989 • $44 • (03/15/92)
95 **CHÂTEAU LAFITE-ROTHSCHILD** Pauillac 1989 • $113 • (03/15/92)
95 **CHÂTEAU LAGRANGE** St.-Julien 1989 • $29 • (03/15/92)
95 **CHÂTEAU LARMANDE** St.-Emilion 1989 • $18 • (03/15/92)
95 **CHÂTEAU MONTROSE** St.-Estèphe 1989 • $55 • (03/15/92)
95 **CHÂTEAU OLIVIER** Pessac-Léognan 1989 • $23 • (03/15/92) • SS
95 **CHÂTEAU PALMER** Margaux 1989 • $91 • (03/15/92)
95 **CHÂTEAU PIBRAN** Pauillac 1989 • $25 • (03/15/92)

■ ■ ■ ■

Red Bordeaux

94 **CHÂTEAU BRANE-CANTENAC** Margaux 1989 • $31 • (03/15/92)

94 **CHÂTEAU D'ARMAILHAC** Pauillac 1989 • $22 • (03/15/92)

94 **CHÂTEAU FRANC-MAYNE** St.-Emilion 1989 • $28 • (03/15/92)

94 **CHÂTEAU L'ANGELUS** St.-Emilion 1989 • $67 • (03/15/92)

94 **CHÂTEAU LANGOA BARTON** St.-Julien 1989 • $25 • (03/15/92)

94 **CHÂTEAU LE PIN** Pomerol 1989 • $250 • (03/31/94)

94 **CHÂTEAU LEOVILLE-BARTON** St.-Julien 1989 • $33 • (03/15/92)

94 **CHÂTEAU ST.-PIERRE** St.-Julien 1989 • $39 • (03/15/92)

94 **LES TOURELLS DE LONGUEVILLE** Pauillac 1989 • $27 • (03/15/92)

93 **CHÂTEAU AUSONE** St.-Emilion 1989 • $94 • (03/15/92)

93 **CHÂTEAU BARET** Pessac-Léognan 1989 • $18 • (03/15/92)

93 **CHÂTEAU BOUSCAUT** Pessac-Léognan 1989 • $22 • (03/15/92)

93 **CHÂTEAU CITRAN** Haut-Médoc 1989 • $20 • (03/15/92)

93 **CHÂTEAU COS-LABORY** St.-Estèphe 1989 • $22 • (03/15/92)

93 **CHÂTEAU FIGEAC** St.-Emilion 1989 • $48 • (03/15/92)

93 **CHÂTEAU GRAND-MAYNE** St.-Emilion 1989 • $22 • (03/15/92)

93 **CHÂTEAU GRUAUD LAROSE** St.-Julien 1989 • $36 • (03/15/92)

93 **CHÂTEAU L'ARROSEE** St.-Emilion 1989 • $40 • (04/30/92)

93 **CHÂTEAU LAFLEUR** Pomerol 1989 • $246 • (03/31/94)

93 **CHÂTEAU MEYNEY** St.-Estèphe 1989 • $30 • (03/15/92)

93 **CHÂTEAU MONBRISON** Margaux 1989 • $28 • (03/15/92)

93 **CHÂTEAU TERTRE-ROTEBOEUF** St.-Emilion 1989 • $79 • (03/15/92)

93 **CHÂTEAU VILLEMAURINE** St.-Emilion 1989 • $30 • (03/15/92)

93 **DOMAINE DE L'EGLISE** Pomerol 1989 • $33 • (03/15/92)

92 **CHÂTEAU DURFORT-VIVENS** Margaux 1989 • $28 • (03/15/92)

92 **CHÂTEAU GISCOURS** Margaux 1989 • $27 • (03/15/92)

92 **CHÂTEAU GLORIA** St.-Julien 1989 • $29 • (03/15/92)

92 **CHÂTEAU HAUT-BAILLY** Pessac-Léognan 1989 • $28 • (03/15/92)

92 **CHÂTEAU L'EVANGILE** Pomerol 1989 • $60 • (03/15/92)

92 **CHÂTEAU LA CABANNE** Pomerol 1989 • $20 • (03/15/92)

92 **CHÂTEAU LA COMMANDERIE** St.-Emilion 1989 • $19 • (03/15/92)

92 **CHÂTEAU LA CONSEILLANTE** Pomerol 1989 • $96 • (03/15/92)

92 **CHÂTEAU LA GURGUE** Margaux 1989 • $30 • (03/15/92)

92 **CHÂTEAU LA TOUR CARNET** Haut-Médoc 1989 • $24 • (03/15/92)

92 **CHÂTEAU LAFON-ROCHET** St.-Estèphe 1989 • $31 • (03/15/92)

92 **CHÂTEAU PICHON-LONGUEVILLE-LALANDE** Pauillac 1989 • $58 • (03/15/92)

92 **CLOS LARCIS** St.-Emilion 1989 • $28 • (03/15/92)

91 **CHÂTEAU BEAUSEJOUR-DUFFAU-LAGARROSSE** St.-Emilion 1989 • $44 • (03/15/92)

91 **CHÂTEAU CANTEMERLE** Haut-Médoc 1989 • $35 • (03/15/92)

91 **CHÂTEAU DUCRU-BEAUCAILLOU** St.-Julien 1989 • $53 • (10/15/92)

91 **CHÂTEAU GAZIN** Pomerol 1989 • $27 • (03/15/92)

91 **CHÂTEAU GRAND-PUY-LACOSTE** Pauillac 1989 • $22 • (03/15/92)

91 **CHÂTEAU LA DOMINIQUE** St.-Emilion 1989 • $33 • (03/15/92)

91 **CHÂTEAU LA LOUVIERE** Pessac-Léognan 1989 • $22 • (03/15/92)

91 **CHÂTEAU LARCIS-DUCASSE** St.-Emilion 1989 • $28 • (03/15/92)

91 **CHÂTEAU LE GAY** Pomerol 1989 • $43 • (03/15/92)

91 **CHÂTEAU SMITH-HAUT-LAFITTE** Pessac-Léognan 1989 • $19 • (03/15/92)

91 **CHÂTEAU ST.-ANDRE-CORBIN** St.-Georges-St.-Emilion 1989 • $15 • (04/30/92)

91 **CHÂTEAU ST.-PIERRE** St.-Julien 1989 • $21 • (10/15/92)

91 **LES FORTS DE LATOUR** Pauillac 1989 • $NA • (03/15/92)

91 **VIEUX CHÂTEAU CERTAN** Pomerol 1989 • $46 • (03/15/92)

90 **CHÂTEAU BAHANS-HAUT-BRION** Pessac-Léognan 1989 • $36 • (03/15/92)

90 **CHÂTEAU BEAU-SITE** St.-Estèphe 1989 • $20 • (03/15/92)

90 **CHÂTEAU BOURGNEUF** Pomerol 1989 • $32 • (03/15/92)

90 **CHÂTEAU BRANAIRE-DUCRU** St.-Julien 1989 • $35 • (03/15/92)

90 **CHÂTEAU CANON** St.-Emilion 1989 • $44 • (03/15/92)

90 **CHÂTEAU CHEVAL BLANC** St.-Emilion 1989 • $114 • (03/15/92)

90 **CHÂTEAU DAUZAC** Margaux 1989 • $26 • (03/15/92)

90 **CHÂTEAU DE MALLERET** Haut-Médoc 1989 • $NA • (03/15/92)

90 **CHÂTEAU DU TERTRE** Margaux 1989 • $29 • (03/15/92)

90 **CHÂTEAU DUHART-MILON** Pauillac 1989 • $25 • (03/15/92)

90 **CHÂTEAU HAUT-BAGES-AVEROUS** Pauillac 1989 • $26 • (03/15/92)

90 **CHÂTEAU HAUT-MARBUZET** St.-Estèphe 1989 • $35 • (03/15/92)

90 **CHÂTEAU LATOUR A POMEROL** Pomerol 1989 • $55 • (03/15/92)

90 **CHÂTEAU LEOVILLE-POYFERRE** St.-Julien 1989 • $42 • (03/15/92)

90 **CHÂTEAU LYNCH-MOUSSAS** Pauillac 1989 • $18 • (03/15/92)

90 **CHÂTEAU PAVIE** St.-Emilion 1989 • $36 • (03/15/92)

90 **CHÂTEAU PAVIE-DECESSE** St.-Emilion 1989 • $29 • (03/15/92)

90 **CHÂTEAU PETIT-FIGEAC** St.-Emilion 1989 • $21 • (03/15/92)

90 **CHÂTEAU POUJEAUX** Moulis 1989 • $21 • (03/15/92)

90 **CHÂTEAU PUY-BLANQUET** St.-Emilion 1989 • $14 • (03/15/92)

90 **CHÂTEAU SOCIANDO-MALLET** Haut-Médoc 1989 • $28 • (03/15/92)

90 **CHÂTEAU TALBOT** St.-Julien 1989 • $32 • (03/15/92)

90 **CHÂTEAU TROTANOY** Pomerol 1989 • $87 • (03/15/92)

90 **CHÂTEAU TROTTE VIEILLE** St.-Emilion 1989 • $44 • (03/15/92)

90 **CHÂTEAU VERDIGNAN** Haut-Médoc 1989 • $17 • (03/15/92)

89 **BARON PHILIPPE DE ROTHSCHILD** Médoc 1989 • $11 • (11/15/94)

89 **CARRUADES DE LAFITE** Pauillac 1989 • $34 • (03/15/92)

89 **CHÂTEAU BARON DE BRANE** Margaux 1989 • $NA • (03/15/92)

89 **CHÂTEAU BELAIR** St.-Emilion 1989 • $37 • (03/15/92)

89 **CHÂTEAU CANTENAC-BROWN** Margaux 1989 • $32 • (03/15/92)

89 **CHÂTEAU CERTAN DE MAY** Pomerol 1989 • $65 • (10/15/94)

89 **CHÂTEAU COUFRAN** Haut-Médoc 1989 • $14 • (03/15/92)

89 **CHÂTEAU DE FRANCE** Pessac-Léognan 1989 • $22 • (03/15/92)

89 **CHÂTEAU DE LAMARQUE** Haut-Médoc 1989 • $26 • (03/15/92)

89 **CHÂTEAU DE MARBUZET** St.-Estèphe 1989 • $21 • (03/15/92)

89 **CHÂTEAU DE PEZ** St.-Estèphe 1989 • $21 • (03/15/92)

89 **CHÂTEAU GLORIA** St.-Julien 1989 • $22 • (10/15/92)

89 **CHÂTEAU HAUT-BAGES-LIBERAL** Pauillac 1989 • $17 • (03/15/92)

89 **CHÂTEAU HAUT-CORBIN** St.-Emilion 1989 • $26 • (03/15/92)

89 **CHÂTEAU LACOSTE-BORIE** Pauillac 1989 • $15 • (03/15/92)

89 **CHÂTEAU LARRIVET-HAUT-BRION** Pessac-Léognan 1989 • $33 • (03/15/92)

89 **CHÂTEAU PONTET-CANET** Pauillac 1989 • $17 • (03/15/92)

89 **CHÂTEAU TROPLONG-MONDOT** St.-Emilion 1989 • $26 • (03/15/92)

89 **CLOS FOURTET** St.-Emilion 1989 • $28 • (03/15/92)

89 **COUVENT DES JACOBINS** St.-Emilion 1989 • $28 • (04/30/92)

88 **CHÂTEAU ARNAULD** Haut-Médoc 1989 • $14 • (03/15/92)

88 **CHÂTEAU CANON-LA-GAFFELIERE** St.-Emilion 1989 • $36 • (03/15/92)

88 **CHÂTEAU D'AGASSAC** Haut-Médoc 1989 • $20 • (03/15/92)

88 **CHÂTEAU DE CHANTEGRIVE** Graves 1989 • $20 • (03/15/92)

88 **CHÂTEAU DE ROCHEMORIN** Pessac-Léognan 1989 • $16 • (03/15/92)

88 **CHÂTEAU DUPLESSIS-FABRE** Moulis 1989 • $9 • (03/15/92)

88 **CHÂTEAU FONROQUE** St.-Emilion 1989 • $24 • (03/15/92)

88 **CHÂTEAU GRANDES-MURAILLES** St.-Emilion 1989 • $NA • (03/15/92)

88 **CHÂTEAU LA CLAVERIE** Côtes de Francs 1989 • $21 • (03/15/92)

88 **CHÂTEAU LA CROIX DE GAY** Pomerol 1989 • $27 • (03/15/92)

88 **CHÂTEAU LA FLEUR-PETRUS** Pomerol 1989 • $57 • (03/15/92)

88 **CHÂTEAU LA GRAVE TRIGANT DE BOISSET** Pomerol 1989 • $35 • (03/15/92)

88 **CHÂTEAU LA TOUR-DE-MONS** Margaux 1989 • $25 • (03/15/92)

88 **CHÂTEAU LA VIEILLE CURE** Fronsac 1989 • $16 • (03/15/92)

88 **CHÂTEAU LALANDE-BORIE** St.-Julien 1989 • $17 • (03/15/92)

88 **CHÂTEAU LE BON-PASTEUR** Pomerol 1989 • $38 • (04/30/92)

88 **CHÂTEAU MAGDELAINE** St.-Emilion 1989 • $38 • (03/15/92)

88 **CHÂTEAU PAPE-CLEMENT** Pessac-Léognan 1989 • $43 • (03/15/92)

88 **CHÂTEAU PETIT-VILLAGE** Pomerol 1989 • $47 • (03/15/92)

88 **CHÂTEAU PLAGNAC** Médoc 1989 • $12 • (03/15/92)

88 **CHÂTEAU RAMAGE LA BATISSE** Haut-Médoc 1989 • $15 • (03/15/92)

88 **CHÂTEAU RAUSAN-SEGLA** Margaux 1989 • $44 • (03/15/92)

88 **CHÂTEAU SIRAN** Margaux 1989 • $25 • (03/15/92)

87 **CHÂTEAU CAP DE MOURLIN** St.-Emilion 1989 • $23 • (03/15/92)

87 **CHÂTEAU D'ANGLUDET** Margaux 1989 • $20 • (03/15/92)

87 **CHÂTEAU DU GLANA** St.-Julien 1989 • $NA • (03/15/92)

87 **CHÂTEAU FOURCAS-HOSTEN** Listrac 1989 • $19 • (03/15/92)

87 **CHÂTEAU HAUT-BATAILLEY** Pauillac 1989 • $26 • (03/15/92)

87 **CHÂTEAU KIRWAN** Margaux 1989 • $32 • (03/15/92)

87 **CHÂTEAU LA LAGUNE** Haut-Médoc 1989 • $29

87 **CHÂTEAU LA TOUR-DE-BESSAN** Margaux 1989 • $NA • (03/15/92)

87 **CHÂTEAU LAFLEUR-GAZIN** Pomerol 1989 • $NA • (03/15/92)

87 **CHÂTEAU LAGRANGE** Pomerol 1989 • $29 • (03/15/92)

87 **CHÂTEAU LAROSE-TRINTAUDON** Haut-Médoc 1989 • $12 • (03/15/92)

87 **CHÂTEAU LIVERSAN** Haut-Médoc 1989 • $18 • (03/15/92)

87 **CHÂTEAU MALESCOT-ST.-EXUPERY** Margaux 1989 • $27 • (03/15/92)

87 **CHÂTEAU SOUTARD** St.-Emilion 1989 • $27 • (09/15/93)

87 **CHÂTEAU TOUR-HAUT-CAUSSAN** Médoc 1989 • $20 • (03/15/92)

87 **PAVILLON ROUGE DU CHÂTEAU MARGAUX** Margaux 1989 • $40 • (04/30/92)

86 **CHÂTEAU BRILLETTE** Moulis 1989 • $17 • (03/15/92)

86 **CHÂTEAU CAMENSAC** Haut-Médoc 1989 • $16 • (03/15/92)

86 **CHÂTEAU CANON MOUEIX** Canon-Fronsac 1989 • $22 • (03/15/92)

86 **CHÂTEAU DE CRUZEAU** Pessac-Léognan 1989 • $14 • (03/15/92)

86 **CHÂTEAU DESMIRAIL** Margaux 1989 • $27 • (03/15/92)

86 **CHÂTEAU FOURCAS-DUPRE** Listrac 1989 • $25 • (03/15/92)

86 **CHÂTEAU GRAND-PUY-DUCASSE** Pauillac 1989 • $23 • (04/30/92)

86 **CHÂTEAU LA LAGUNE** Haut-Médoc 1989 • $27 • (03/15/92)

86 **CHÂTEAU LABEGORCE-ZEDE** Margaux 1989 • $20 • (03/15/92)

86 **CHÂTEAU LES CHARMES-GODARD** Côtes de Francs 1989 • $NA • (03/15/92)

86 **CHÂTEAU LES ORMES DE PEZ** St.-Estèphe 1989 • $24 • (03/15/92)

86 **CHÂTEAU MOULIN DU CADET** St.-Emilion 1989 • $NA • (03/15/92)

86 **CHÂTEAU PLAISANCE** Premières Côtes de Bordeaux Cuvée Spéciale Red 1989 • $13 • (01/31/92)

86 **CHÂTEAU PRIEURE-LICHINE** Margaux 1989 • $25 • (03/15/92)

85 **CHÂTEAU BALESTARD LA TONNELLE** St.-Emilion 1989 • $28 • (03/15/92)

85 **CHÂTEAU BELLEGRAVE-VAN DER VOORT** Pauillac 1989 • $20 • (09/15/93)

85 **CHÂTEAU BONNET** Bordeaux en Fûts de Chêne Reserve 1989 • $11 • (07/15/92)

85 **CHÂTEAU CARBONNIEUX** Pessac-Léognan 1989 • $26 • (03/15/92)

85 **CHÂTEAU CISSAC** Haut-Médoc 1989 • $19 • (03/15/92)

85 **CHÂTEAU CLARKE** Listrac 1989 • $16 • (03/15/92)

85 **CHÂTEAU CLOS DES JACOBINS** St.-Emilion 1989 • $45 • (03/15/92)

85 **CHÂTEAU DE CHANTEGRIVE** Graves Cuvée Edouard 1989 • $22 • (03/15/92)

85 **CHÂTEAU LA SALLE DE POUJEAUX** Moulis 1989 • $15 • (03/15/92)

85 **CHÂTEAU LA TOUR DE BY** Médoc 1989 • $19 • (03/15/92)
85 **CHÂTEAU LANESSAN** Haut-Médoc 1989 • $20 • (03/15/92)
85 **CHÂTEAU MALARTIC-LAGRAVIERE** Pessac-Léognan 1989 • $24 • (03/15/92)
85 **CHÂTEAU MALMAISON** Moulis 1989 • $16 • (03/15/92)
85 **CHÂTEAU PHELAN-SEGUR** St.-Estèphe 1989 • $23 • (03/15/92)
85 **CHÂTEAU PLAISANCE** Premières Côtes de Blaye Cuvée Spéciale Red 1989 • $9 • (02/28/91) • BB
85 **CHÂTEAU SOUDARS** Haut-Médoc 1989 • $15 • (03/15/92)
84 **CHÂTEAU CANON-DE-BREM** Canon-Fronsac 1989 • $23 • (03/15/92)
84 **CHÂTEAU CAPBERN-GASQUETON** St.-Estèphe 1989 • $27 • (03/15/92)
84 **CHÂTEAU D'ISSAN** Margaux 1989 • $4 • (03/15/92)
84 **CHÂTEAU DULUC** St.-Julien 1989 • $NA • (03/15/92)
84 **CHÂTEAU GOFFRETEAU** Bordeaux Rouge 1989 • $8 • (05/15/91) • BB
84 **CHÂTEAU LA FLEUR** St.-Emilion 1989 • $18 • (03/15/92)
84 **CHÂTEAU MALESCASSE** Haut-Médoc 1989 • $13 • (03/15/92)
84 **DEMOISELLE DE SOCIANDO-MALLET** Haut-Médoc 1989 • $21 • (03/15/92)
84 **MOULIN DE DUHART** Pauillac 1989 • $20 • (12/31/92)
84 **MOUTON-CADET** Bordeaux 1989 • $8 • (07/15/92) • BB
83 **CHÂTEAU LA TOUR-DU-PIN-FIGEAC-BELIEVIER** St.-Emilion 1989 • $24 • (04/30/92)
83 **CHÂTEAU PUYGUERAUD** Côtes de Francs 1989 • $18 • (03/15/92)
83 **CHÂTEAU TERTRE-DAUGAY** St.-Emilion 1989 • $29 • (04/30/92)
83 **JEAN-PIERRE MOUEIX** Merlot Bordeaux Christian Moueix 1989 • $9 • (11/30/92)
82 **CHÂTEAU BEAUMONT** Haut-Médoc 1989 • $14 • (03/15/92)
82 **CHÂTEAU CANON-FRONSAC** Canon-Fronsac 1989 • $24 • (03/15/92)
82 **CHÂTEAU CANUET** Margaux 1989 • $18 • (03/15/92)
82 **CHÂTEAU D'ARSAC** Haut-Médoc 1989 • $9 • (03/15/92)
82 **CHÂTEAU L'ENCLOS** Pomerol 1989 • $30 • (04/30/92)
82 **CHÂTEAU LA FLEUR-POURRET** St.-Emilion 1989 • $NA • (03/15/92)
82 **CHÂTEAU LA GROLET** Côtes de Bourg 1989 • $9 • (08/31/91) • BB
82 **CHÂTEAU LAPELLETRIE** St.-Emilion 1989 • $19 • (07/15/92)
82 **CHÂTEAU ROC MIGNON D'ADRIEN** Bordeaux Supérieur 1989 • $6 • (02/28/91) • BB
82 **LA CAVE TROISGROS** Bordeaux 1989 • $9 • (05/15/91)
81 **BEAUCLAIRE** Bordeaux 1989 • $7 • (06/15/93) • BB
81 **CHÂTEAU BATAILLEY** Pauillac 1989 • $19 • (03/15/92)
81 **CHÂTEAU DE TERREFORT-QUANCARD** Bordeaux 1989 • $14 • (12/31/92)
81 **CHÂTEAU LE BONNAT** Graves 1989 • $18 • (04/30/92)
81 **CHÂTEAU LOUDENNE** Médoc 1989 • $13 • (03/15/92)
81 **CHÂTEAU MONT BELAIR** St.-Emilion 1989 • $12 • (11/15/91)
81 **FONT VILLAC** St.-Emilion 1989 • $14 • (11/30/92)
80 **CHÂTEAU DE LA DAUPHINE** Fronsac 1989 • $15 • (03/15/92)
80 **CHÂTEAU MOULIN DE CITRAN** Haut-Médoc 1989 • $14 • (03/15/92)
80 **CHÂTEAU PEYRAUD** Premières Côtes de Blaye 1989 • $8 • (03/31/91)
79 **CHÂTEAU BONNET** Bordeaux 1989 • $9 • (07/15/92)
79 **CHÂTEAU GRAND CHEMIN** Côtes de Bourg 1989 • $9 • (11/30/92)
79 **CHÂTEAU GREYSAC** Médoc 1989 • $12 • (03/15/92)
79 **CHÂTEAU LA TERRASSE** Bordeaux Supérieur 1989 • $8 • (03/31/91)
79 **CHÂTEAU LAGRAVE PARAN** Bordeaux 1989 • $8 • (02/28/91)
79 **CHÂTEAU VILLEGEORGE** Haut-Médoc 1989 • $14 • (03/15/92)
79 **PIERRE JEAN** Bordeaux Supérieur 1989 • $9 • (07/15/92)
78 **AUGEY** Bordeaux 1989 • $7 • (11/30/92)
78 **CHÂTEAU LES DONATS** Premières Côtes de Blaye Red 1989 • $9 • (11/30/92)
78 **CHÂTEAU PERENNE** Premières Côtes de Blaye 1989 • $9 • (03/31/91)
78 **CHÂTEAU PLANTEY** Pauillac 1989 • $NA • (03/15/92)
78 **CHÂTEAU TOUR CALON** Montagne-St.-Emilion 1989 • $13 • (11/30/92)
78 **CHÂTEAU VILLARS** Fronsac 1989 • $16 • (06/15/93)
77 **CHÂTEAU GUIRAUD-CHEVAL-BLANC** Côtes de Bourg 1989 • $6 • (11/30/92)
77 **CHÂTEAU HANTEILLAN** Haut-Médoc 1989 • $14 • (03/15/92)
77 **CHÂTEAU MERIC** Graves 1989 • $16 • (07/15/92)
77 **CHÂTEAU MOULIN DE BEL-AIR** Médoc 1989 • $NA • (03/15/92)
77 **VERDILLAC** Bordeaux 1989 • $8 • (11/30/92)
76 **CHÂTEAU DU MOULIN DE PEYRONIN** Bordeaux 1989 • $10 • (07/15/92)
76 **MAITRE D'ESTOURNEL** Bordeaux 1989 • $9 • (11/30/92)
75 **BARTON & GUESTIER** Bordeaux Fondation 1725 1989 • $9 • (07/31/91)
75 **CHÂTEAU BARRYES** Haut-Médoc 1989 • $10 • (07/15/92)
75 **CHÂTEAU GUIBON** Bordeaux 1989 • $8 • (07/15/92)
75 **CHÂTEAU TOUR PRIGNAC** Médoc 1989 • $9 • (07/15/92)
75 **COLLECTION FOLLE EPOQUE** Bordeaux Supérieur 1989 • $9 • (11/30/92)
74 **CHÂTEAU TALMONT** Bordeaux 1989 • $8 • (02/28/91)
74 **JEAN-PIERRE MOUEIX** St.-Emilion 1989 • $13 • (06/15/93)
71 **ARMAND ROUX** Bordeaux Verdillac 1989 • $7 • (01/31/92)
71 **CHÂTEAU TOUR-DU-ROC** Haut-Médoc 1989 • $13 • (06/15/93)

1988 Red Bordeaux
Vintage Rating: 93

100 **CHÂTEAU MOUTON-ROTHSCHILD** Pauillac 1988 • $89
97 **CHÂTEAU LYNCH-BAGES** Pauillac 1988 • $58 • (10/15/94)
97 **CHÂTEAU MARGAUX** Margaux 1988 • $61 • (03/31/91) • CS
96 **CHÂTEAU PALMER** Margaux 1988 • $39 • (02/28/91) • CS
95 **CHÂTEAU COS D'ESTOURNEL** St.-Estèphe 1988 • $36 • (07/15/91) • CS
95 **CHÂTEAU LE PIN** Pomerol 1988 • $230 • (06/30/91) • CS
95 **CHÂTEAU LEOVILLE-LAS CASES** St.-Julien 1988 • $46 • (02/15/92)
95 **CHÂTEAU PICHON-LONGUEVILLE-BARON** Pauillac 1988 • $39 • (03/31/91) • SS
94 **CHÂTEAU CLERC-MILON** Pauillac 1988 • $26 • (04/30/91) • SS
94 **CHÂTEAU HAUT-BAILLY** Pessac-Léognan 1988 • $35 • (04/30/91)
94 **CHÂTEAU L'ARROSEE** St.-Emilion 1988 • $21 • (03/15/91)

94 **CHÂTEAU LA FLEUR DE GAY** Pomerol 1988 • $67 • (06/30/91)
94 **CHÂTEAU LAFITE-ROTHSCHILD** Pauillac 1988 • $104 • (11/30/91)
94 **CHÂTEAU LARRIVET-HAUT-BRION** Pessac-Léognan 1988 • $25 • (04/30/91)
94 **CHÂTEAU PAVIE-DECESSE** St.-Emilion 1988 • $16 • (03/31/91)
94 **CHÂTEAU PETRUS** Pomerol 1988 • $379 • (08/31/91)
93 **CHÂTEAU BEYCHEVELLE** St.-Julien 1988 • $26 • (04/30/91)
93 **CHÂTEAU CHEVAL BLANC** St.-Emilion 1988 • $63 • (12/31/90) • CS
93 **CHÂTEAU FIGEAC** St.-Emilion 1988 • $45 • (06/30/91)
93 **CHÂTEAU HAUT-BAGES-AVEROUS** Pauillac 1988 • $20 • (04/30/91)
93 **CHÂTEAU L'ANGELUS** St.-Emilion 1988 • $43 • (03/31/91)
93 **CHÂTEAU LATOUR** Pauillac 1988 • $67 • (04/30/91)
93 **CHÂTEAU PAPE-CLEMENT** Pessac-Léognan 1988 • $40 • (12/31/90)
92 **CHÂTEAU CLINET** Pomerol 1988 • $56 • (02/28/91)
92 **CHÂTEAU DE FRANCE** Pessac-Léognan 1988 • $18 • (02/28/91) • SS
92 **CHÂTEAU DE MARBUZET** St.-Estèphe 1988 • $17 • (07/15/91) • SS
92 **CHÂTEAU DUCRU-BEAUCAILLOU** St.-Julien 1988 • $30 • (10/15/92)
92 **CHÂTEAU LA LOUVIERE** Pessac-Léognan 1988 • $24 • (08/31/91) • SS
92 **CHÂTEAU MARQUIS DE TERME** Margaux 1988 • $23 • (04/30/91)
92 **CHÂTEAU MONBRISON** Margaux 1988 • $16 • (02/28/91)
92 **CHÂTEAU RAUSAN-SEGLA** Margaux 1988 • $35 • (03/15/91)
92 **LES FIEFS DE LAGRANGE** St.-Julien 1988 • $17 • (04/30/91)
91 **CHÂTEAU BALESTARD LA TONNELLE** St.-Emilion 1988 • $25 • (04/30/91)
91 **CHÂTEAU CITRAN** Haut-Médoc 1988 • $20 • (04/30/91)
91 **CHÂTEAU DE FIEUZAL** Pessac-Léognan 1988 • $33 • (04/30/91)
91 **CHÂTEAU FRANC BIGAROUX** St.-Emilion 1988 • $24 • (07/31/91)
91 **CHÂTEAU HAUT-MARBUZET** St.-Estèphe 1988 • $32 • (12/31/90) • SS
91 **CHÂTEAU L'EGLISE-CLINET** Pomerol 1988 • $47 • (12/31/90)
91 **CHÂTEAU LA LAGUNE** Haut-Médoc 1988 • $17 • (04/30/91)
91 **CHÂTEAU LA TOUR-HAUT-BRION** Pessac-Léognan 1988 • $30 • (06/15/91) • CS
91 **CHÂTEAU LEOVILLE-BARTON** St.-Julien 1988 • $29 • (03/31/91)
91 **CHÂTEAU OLIVIER** Pessac-Léognan 1988 • $25 • (02/15/91)
91 **CHÂTEAU PICHON-LONGUEVILLE-LALANDE** Pauillac 1988 • $45 • (04/30/91)
91 **CHÂTEAU TAILHAS** Pomerol 1988 • $20 • (04/30/91)
91 **CHÂTEAU TRIMOULET** St.-Emilion 1988 • $16 • (06/15/91)
91 **DOMAINE DE CHEVALIER** Pessac-Léognan 1988 • $40 • (07/15/91)
91 **VIEUX CHÂTEAU CERTAN** Pomerol 1988 • $39 • (03/31/91)
90 **CHÂTEAU BATAILLEY** Pauillac 1988 • $30 • (04/30/91)
90 **CHÂTEAU BEAUREGARD** Pomerol 1988 • $36 • (07/31/91)
90 **CHÂTEAU BOURGNEUF** Pomerol 1988 • $21 • (06/30/91)
90 **CHÂTEAU CANON** St.-Emilion 1988 • $30 • (06/30/91)
90 **CHÂTEAU CERTAN DE MAY** Pomerol 1988 • $67 • (06/30/91)
90 **CHÂTEAU CLOS DES JACOBINS** St.-Emilion 1988 • $26 • (04/15/91)
90 **CHÂTEAU DAUZAC** Margaux 1988 • $20 • (06/30/91)
90 **CHÂTEAU GLORIA** St.-Julien 1988 • $20 • (03/31/91)
90 **CHÂTEAU GRAND-PUY-LACOSTE** Pauillac 1988 • $28 • (04/30/91)
90 **CHÂTEAU LA CONSEILLANTE** Pomerol 1988 • $48 • (03/31/91)
90 **CHÂTEAU LA GURGUE** Margaux 1988 • $34 • (04/30/91)
90 **CHÂTEAU LA MISSION-HAUT-BRION** Pessac-Léognan 1988 • $90 • (11/15/91)
90 **CHÂTEAU LAFLEUR** Pomerol 1988 • $130 • (10/31/91)
90 **CHÂTEAU LATOUR A POMEROL** Pomerol 1988 • $29 • (10/15/94)
90 **CHÂTEAU MOUTON-BARONNE-PHILIPPE** Pauillac 1988 • $25 • (04/30/91)
90 **CHÂTEAU PRIEURE-LICHINE** Margaux 1988 • $18 • (04/30/91)
90 **CHÂTEAU TALBOT** St.-Julien 1988 • $21 • (03/15/91)
90 **CHÂTEAU TERTRE-ROTEBOEUF** St.-Emilion 1988 • $56 • (06/15/91)
89 **CHÂTEAU CADET-PIOLA** St.-Emilion 1988 • $20 • (07/15/91)
89 **CHÂTEAU CANTENAC-BROWN** Margaux 1988 • $25 • (04/30/91)
89 **CHÂTEAU CERTAN-GIRAUD** Pomerol 1988 • $23 • (02/28/91)
89 **CHÂTEAU CHASSE-SPLEEN** Moulis 1988 • $32 • (03/31/91)
89 **CHÂTEAU FONBADET** Pauillac 1988 • $16 • (08/31/91)
89 **CHÂTEAU GISCOURS** Margaux 1988 • $23 • (04/30/91)
89 **CHÂTEAU GRAND-MAYNE** St.-Emilion 1988 • $20 • (04/30/91)
89 **CHÂTEAU GRAND-PUY-DUCASSE** Pauillac 1988 • $21 • (04/30/91)
89 **CHÂTEAU GRUAUD LAROSE** St.-Julien 1988 • $31 • (02/28/91)
89 **CHÂTEAU LA CROIX DE GAY** Pomerol 1988 • $30 • (06/30/91)
89 **CHÂTEAU LACOSTE-BORIE** Pauillac 1988 • $19 • (04/30/91)
89 **CHÂTEAU LEOVILLE-LAS CASES** St.-Julien 1988 • $45 • (10/31/91)
89 **CHÂTEAU MALESCOT-ST.-EXUPERY** Margaux 1988 • $23 • (04/30/91)
89 **CHÂTEAU PAVIE** St.-Emilion 1988 • $34 • (03/31/91)
89 **CHÂTEAU TROTANOY** Pomerol 1988 • $65 • (08/31/91)
89 **LE PETIT CHEVAL** St.-Emilion 1988 • $35 • (03/31/91)
88 **CHÂTEAU CANON** St.-Emilion 1988 • $42
88 **CHÂTEAU D'ISSAN** Margaux 1988 • $22 • (04/30/91)
88 **CHÂTEAU DUHART-MILON** Pauillac 1988 • $24 • (08/31/91)
88 **CHÂTEAU GLORIA** St.-Julien 1988 • $18 • (10/15/92)
88 **CHÂTEAU HAUT-BAGES-LIBERAL** Pauillac 1988 • $19 • (03/15/91)
88 **CHÂTEAU LA TOUR-MARTILLAC** Pessac-Léognan 1988 • $24 • (02/28/91)
88 **CHÂTEAU LES ORMES DE PEZ** St.-Estèphe 1988 • $21 • (04/30/91)
88 **CHÂTEAU MOULINET** Pomerol 1988 • $17 • (07/31/91)
88 **CHÂTEAU POUJEAUX** Moulis 1988 • $16 • (02/28/91)
88 **CHÂTEAU SIRAN** Margaux 1988 • $26 • (06/30/91)
88 **CHÂTEAU SOUDARS** Haut-Médoc 1988 • $15 • (04/30/91)

■ ■ ■ ■

88 **CHÂTEAU ST.-PIERRE** St.-Julien 1988 • $27 • (10/15/92)
88 **CHÂTEAU TOUR DU HAUT-MOULIN** Haut-Médoc 1988 • $20 • (04/30/91)
88 **CLOS RENE** Pomerol 1988 • $24 • (04/30/91)
88 **PAVILLON ROUGE DU CHÂTEAU MARGAUX** Margaux 1988 • $30 • (04/30/91)
88 **RESERVE DE LA COMTESSE** Pauillac 1988 • $26 • (03/15/91)
87 **CHÂTEAU BEAU-SEJOUR BECOT** St.-Emilion 1988 • $21 • (06/30/91)
87 **CHÂTEAU BEAUSEJOUR-DUFFAU-LAGARROSSE** St.-Emilion 1988 • $28 • (04/30/91)
87 **CHÂTEAU BOUSCAUT** Pessac-Léognan 1988 • $25 • (04/30/91)
87 **CHÂTEAU DE CRUZEAU** Pessac-Léognan 1988 • $14 • (02/28/91)
87 **CHÂTEAU GAZIN** Pomerol 1988 • $27 • (06/30/91)
87 **CHÂTEAU GRAND-MAYNE** St.-Emilion 1988 • $15 • (07/15/91)
87 **CHÂTEAU GREYSAC** Médoc 1988 • $15 • (04/30/91)
87 **CHÂTEAU HAUT-BATAILLEY** Pauillac 1988 • $19 • (08/31/91)
87 **CHÂTEAU KIRWAN** Margaux 1988 • $28 • (04/30/91)
87 **CHÂTEAU L'EVANGILE** Pomerol 1988 • $48 • (06/30/91)
87 **CHÂTEAU LA MISSION-HAUT-BRION** Pessac-Léognan 1988 • $90 • (04/30/91)
87 **CHÂTEAU LALANDE-BORIE** St.-Julien 1988 • $17 • (04/30/91)
87 **CHÂTEAU LATOUR A POMEROL** Pomerol 1988 • $55 • (05/15/94)
87 **CHÂTEAU LE BONNAT** Graves 1988 • $18 • (12/31/90)
87 **CHÂTEAU LIVERSAN** Haut-Médoc 1988 • $15 • (07/31/91)
87 **CHÂTEAU MONTROSE** St.-Estèphe 1988 • $27 • (03/31/91)
87 **CHÂTEAU PHELAN-SEGUR** St.-Estèphe 1988 • $20 • (07/15/91)
87 **CHÂTEAU ROCHER-BELLEVUE-FIGEAC** St.-Emilion 1988 • $18 • (04/30/91)
87 **CHÂTEAU SOCIANDO-MALLET** Haut-Médoc 1988 • $26 • (03/31/91)
87 **CHÂTEAU TAILLEFER** Pomerol 1988 • $22 • (06/30/91)
86 **CHÂTEAU AUSONE** St.-Emilion 1988 • $105 • (10/15/94)
86 **CHÂTEAU CANON-LA-GAFFELIERE** St.-Emilion 1988 • $30 • (06/30/91)
86 **CHÂTEAU CARBONNIEUX** Pessac-Léognan 1988 • $20 • (02/28/91)
86 **CHÂTEAU DE LA DAME** Margaux 1988 • $15 • (02/15/91)
86 **CHÂTEAU DE LAMARQUE** Haut-Médoc 1988 • $20 • (04/30/91)
86 **CHÂTEAU DU TERTRE** Margaux 1988 • $30 • (06/30/91)
86 **CHÂTEAU GRAND PONTET** St.-Emilion 1988 • $21 • (07/15/91)
86 **CHÂTEAU LA DOMINIQUE** St.-Emilion 1988 • $25 • (06/30/91)
86 **CHÂTEAU LA TOUR DE BY** Médoc 1988 • $13 • (06/15/91)
86 **CHÂTEAU LANGOA BARTON** St.-Julien 1988 • $20 • (07/15/91)
86 **CHÂTEAU LARMANDE** St.-Emilion 1988 • $23 • (04/30/91)
86 **CHÂTEAU VERDIGNAN** Haut-Médoc 1988 • $15 • (04/30/91)
86 **CLOS FOURTET** St.-Emilion 1988 • $27 • (10/31/91)
85 **CHÂTEAU BEL AIR** Haut-Médoc 1988 • $15 • (04/30/91)
85 **CHÂTEAU BERTINERIE** Premières Côtes de Blaye Red 1988 • $10 • (07/15/90)
85 **CHÂTEAU CALON-SEGUR** St.-Estèphe 1988 • $25 • (07/15/91)
85 **CHÂTEAU CANTEMERLE** Haut-Médoc 1988 • $19 • (03/15/91)
85 **CHÂTEAU CORMEIL-FIGEAC** St.-Emilion 1988 • $20 • (04/30/91)
85 **CHÂTEAU COS-LABORY** St.-Estèphe 1988 • $20 • (04/30/91)
85 **CHÂTEAU D'ANGLUDET** Margaux 1988 • $20 • (02/28/91)
85 **CHÂTEAU FOMBRAUGE** St.-Emilion 1988 • $14 • (11/30/92)
85 **CHÂTEAU FONPLEGADE** St.-Emilion 1988 • $18 • (06/30/91)
85 **CHÂTEAU L'ENCLOS** Pomerol 1988 • $17 • (03/15/91)
85 **CHÂTEAU LE BON-PASTEUR** Pomerol 1988 • $25 • (02/28/91)
85 **CHÂTEAU LYNCH-MOUSSAS** Pauillac 1988 • $25 • (08/31/91)
85 **CHÂTEAU RAUZAN-GASSIES** Margaux 1988 • $35 • (08/31/91)
85 **CHÂTEAU ST.-PIERRE** St.-Julien 1988 • $32 • (04/30/91)
85 **CHÂTEAU TERTRE-DAUGAY** St.-Emilion 1988 • $20 • (04/30/91)
85 **CHÂTEAU TROPLONG-MONDOT** St.-Emilion 1988 • $31 • (07/15/91)
85 **CHÂTEAU TROTTE VIEILLE** St.-Emilion 1988 • $51 • (04/30/91)
85 **PIERRE JEAN** St.-Emilion 1988 • $10 • (06/30/91) • BB
84 **BARTON & GUESTIER** Merlot Bordeaux 1988 • $6 • (02/15/90) • BB
84 **CHÂTEAU ARNAULD** Haut-Médoc 1988 • $15 • (04/30/91)
84 **CHÂTEAU CAP DE MOURLIN** St.-Emilion 1988 • $20 • (04/30/91)
84 **CHÂTEAU CHAUVIN** St.-Emilion 1988 • $20 • (06/30/91)
84 **CHÂTEAU COUFRAN** Haut-Médoc 1988 • $15 • (04/30/91)
84 **CHÂTEAU GRUAUD LAROSE** St.-Julien 1988 • $27 • (03/31/91)
84 **CHÂTEAU HAUT-FAUGERES** St.-Emilion 1988 • $17 • (04/30/92)
84 **CHÂTEAU LA GAFFELIERE** St.-Emilion 1988 • $38 • (04/30/91)
84 **CHÂTEAU LAROSE-TRINTAUDON** Haut-Médoc 1988 • $9 • (04/30/91)
84 **CHÂTEAU LE BONNAT** Graves White 1988 • $17 • (03/31/90)
84 **CHÂTEAU LE BOSCQ** Médoc 1988 • $20 • (04/30/91)
84 **CHÂTEAU LES ORMES-SORBET** Médoc 1988 • $20 • (04/30/91)
84 **CHÂTEAU MALARTIC-LAGRAVIERE** Pessac-Léognan 1988 • $32 • (07/15/91)
84 **CHÂTEAU TRONQUOY-LALANDE** St.-Estèphe 1988 • $14 • (07/15/91)
84 **CHÂTEAU VIEUX GABRIAN** Bordeaux Supérieur 1988 • $11 • (04/30/91)
83 **CHÂTEAU BELLEGRAVE-VAN DER VOORT** Pauillac 1988 • $20 • (08/31/91)
83 **CHÂTEAU DASSAULT** St.-Emilion 1988 • $17 • (07/15/91)
83 **CHÂTEAU DE PEZ** St.-Estèphe 1988 • $19 • (06/15/91)
83 **CHÂTEAU DUCLA** Bordeaux Cuvée Extrème 1988 • $11 • (07/15/92)
83 **CHÂTEAU FOURCAS-DUPRE** Listrac 1988 • $22 • (04/30/91)
83 **CHÂTEAU FOURCAS-LOUBANEY** Listrac 1988 • $17 • (02/28/91)
83 **CHÂTEAU FRANC-MAYNE** St.-Emilion 1988 • $21 • (07/15/91)
83 **CHÂTEAU HAUT-SARPE** St.-Emilion 1988 • $19 • (06/30/91)
83 **CHÂTEAU LA POINTE** Pomerol 1988 • $13 • (07/31/91)

83 **CHÂTEAU LABEGORCE-ZEDE** Margaux 1988 • $20 • (04/30/91)
83 **CHÂTEAU LE GAY** Pomerol 1988 • $23 • (04/30/91)
83 **CHÂTEAU PITRAY** Côtes de Castillon 1988 • $7 • (02/28/91) • BB
83 **CHÂTEAU TROCARD** Bordeaux Supérieur 1988 • $8 • (01/31/92) • BB
83 **CLOS L'EGLISE** Pomerol 1988 • $26 • (06/30/91)
82 **CHÂTEAU BEAUMONT** Haut-Médoc 1988 • $15 • (07/15/91)
82 **CHÂTEAU DE LA GRAVE** Bordeaux Supérieur 1988 • $8 • (07/15/90) • BB
82 **CHÂTEAU DEMERAULMONT** St.-Estèphe 1988 • $10 • (08/31/91) • BB
82 **CHÂTEAU FONREAUD** Listrac 1988 • $15 • (04/30/91)
82 **CHÂTEAU FOURCAS-HOSTEN** Listrac 1988 • $14 • (07/15/91)
82 **CHÂTEAU LA CROIX** Pomerol 1988 • $24 • (07/31/91)
82 **CHÂTEAU LA TOUR CARNET** Haut-Médoc 1988 • $15 • (08/31/91)
82 **CHÂTEAU LAGARENNE** Bordeaux Supérieur 1988 • $8 • (07/31/90) • BB
82 **CHÂTEAU LAGRAVE PARAN** Bordeaux 1988 • $6 • (07/15/90) • BB
82 **CHÂTEAU LARCIS-DUCASSE** St.-Emilion 1988 • $20 • (04/30/91)
82 **CHÂTEAU LASCOMBES** Margaux 1988 • $33 • (08/31/91)
82 **CHÂTEAU LESTAGE** Listrac 1988 • $20 • (08/31/91)
82 **CHÂTEAU LOUDENNE** Médoc 1988 • $10 • (08/31/91)
82 **CHÂTEAU MAUCAILLOU** Moulis 1988 • $14 • (07/31/91)
82 **CHÂTEAU PETIT-FAURIE-DE-SOUTARD** St.-Emilion 1988 • $20 • (04/30/91)
82 **CHÂTEAU SEGUR** Haut-Médoc 1988 • $15 • (12/31/90)
82 **JEAN-PIERRE MOUEIX** St.-Emilion 1988 • $13 • (04/30/92)
81 **CHÂTEAU BRILLETTE** Moulis 1988 • $15 • (08/31/91)
81 **CHÂTEAU CLARKE** Listrac 1988 • $18 • (04/30/91)
81 **CHÂTEAU DESTIEUX** St.-Emilion 1988 • $19 • (06/30/91)
81 **CHÂTEAU GOFFRETEAU** Bordeaux Supérieur 1988 • $6 • (02/28/91) • BB
81 **CHÂTEAU HAUT RIAN** Premières Côtes de Bordeaux 1988 • $7 • (05/15/90) • BB
81 **CHÂTEAU LA MOULINE** Moulis 1988 • $20 • (02/15/91)
81 **CHÂTEAU LA VIEILLE CURE** Fronsac 1988 • $19 • (10/31/91)
81 **CHÂTEAU LEOVILLE-POYFERRE** St.-Julien 1988 • $21 • (07/15/91)
81 **CHÂTEAU MAGDELAINE** St.-Emilion 1988 • $27 • (10/31/91)
81 **CHÂTEAU ST.-SULPICE** Bordeaux 1988 • $7 • (08/31/91) • BB
81 **COUVENT DES JACOBINS** St.-Emilion 1988 • $28 • (03/31/91)
81 **MAISON MOUEIX** Bordeaux 1988 • $6 • (01/31/92) • BB
81 **MAITRE D'ESTOURNEL** Bordeaux 1988 • $9 • (11/30/92)
81 **MOUTON-CADET** Bordeaux 1988 • $9 • (04/30/91) • BB
80 **CHÂTEAU LA SERRE** St.-Emilion 1988 • $18 • (06/15/91)
80 **CHÂTEAU LANESSAN** Haut-Médoc 1988 • $20 • (07/31/91)
80 **CHÂTEAU LE GRAND VERDUS** Bordeaux Supérieur 1988 • $7 • (10/31/91) • BB
80 **CHÂTEAU PATACHE D'AUX** Médoc 1988 • $17 • (04/30/91)
80 **CHÂTEAU POTENSAC** Médoc 1988 • $12 • (10/31/91)
80 **CHÂTEAU RAHOUL** Graves 1988 • $18 • (08/31/91)
80 **CLOS DU MARQUIS** St.-Julien 1988 • $16 • (10/31/91)
80 **ST.-JOVIAN** Bordeaux Supérieur 1988 • $5 • (07/31/91) • BB
79 **ARMAND ROUX** Bordeaux Verdillac 1988 • $6.25 • (07/15/90) • BB
79 **BEAUCLAIRE** Bordeaux Supérieur 1988 • $6 • (12/31/90)
79 **CHÂTEAU BELGRAVE** Haut-Médoc 1988 • $28 • (07/31/91)
79 **CHÂTEAU LA COMMANDERIE** St.-Emilion 1988 • $15 • (10/31/91)
79 **CHÂTEAU PLAGNAC** Médoc 1988 • $8 • (04/30/91)
79 **CHÂTEAU TERTRE-ROTEBOEUF** St.-Emilion 1988 • $40 • (03/31/91)
79 **CHÂTEAU TOUR-HAUT-CAUSSAN** Médoc 1988 • $13 • (07/15/91)
78 **BARTON & GUESTIER** Bordeaux 1988 • $6 • (03/31/90)
78 **CHÂTEAU BONNET** Bordeaux Reserve 1988 • $11 • (07/15/91)
78 **CHÂTEAU CLEMENT-PICHON** Haut-Médoc 1988 • $15 • (08/31/91)
78 **CHÂTEAU GRAND CLARET** Premières Côtes de Bordeaux 1988 • $7 • (07/31/91)
78 **CHÂTEAU JACQUES-BLANC** St.-Emilion Cuvée du Maitre 1988 • $23 • (04/30/91)
78 **CHÂTEAU SENEJAC** Haut-Médoc 1988 • $14 • (04/30/91)
78 **CHÂTEAU TAYAC** Côtes de Bourg 1988 • $10 • (01/31/92)
78 **CHÂTEAU TRINITE VALROSE** Bordeaux Supérieur Ile de Patiras 1988 • $7 • (08/31/91)
78 **MARQUIS DES TOURS** Bordeaux 1988 • $5 • (02/28/91)
77 **CHÂTEAU BONNET** Bordeaux 1988 • $7 • (04/30/91)
77 **CHÂTEAU LA TOUR-DU-PIN-FIGEAC** St.-Emilion 1988 • $24 • (07/15/91)
77 **SIRIUS** Bordeaux 1988 • $15 • (08/31/91)
77 **YVON MAU** Bordeaux Officiel du Bicentenaire de la Revolution 1988 • $4 • (07/31/89)
76 **CHÂTEAU BRANE-CANTENAC** Margaux 1988 • $42 • (08/31/91)
76 **CHÂTEAU DE LA MEULIERE** Premières Côtes de Bordeaux 1988 • $9 • (02/28/91)
76 **CHÂTEAU FOURNAS BERNADOTTE** Haut-Médoc 1988 • $18 • (06/15/91)
76 **CHÂTEAU MERIC** Graves 1988 • $17 • (04/30/91)
76 **JEAN-PIERRE MOUEIX** Merlot Bordeaux Christian Moueix 1988 • $9 • (11/30/92)
76 **MICHEL LYNCH** Bordeaux 1988 • $8 • (10/31/91)
75 **CHÂTEAU COLOMBIER-MONPELOU** Pauillac 1988 • $15 • (10/31/91)
75 **CHÂTEAU DU PINTEY** Bordeaux Supérieur 1988 • $11 • (08/31/91)
75 **PIERRE JEAN** Bordeaux Supérieur 1988 • $8 • (07/31/91)
74 **CHÂTEAU DUCLA** Bordeaux 1988 • $7 • (08/31/91)
73 **BARTON & GUESTIER** Cabernet Sauvignon Bordeaux 1988 • $6 • (02/15/90)
73 **CHÂTEAU CROIZET-BAGES** Pauillac 1988 • $28 • (08/31/91)
73 **CHÂTEAU DURFORT-VIVENS** Margaux 1988 • $40 • (08/31/91)
73 **CHÂTEAU ST.-GEORGES** St.-Georges-St.-Emilion 1988 • $18 • (04/30/92)
72 **CHÂTEAU CORBIN-MICHOTTE** St.-Emilion 1988 • $15 • (07/15/91)
71 **CHÂTEAU BALLUE-MONDON** Bordeaux 1988 • $8 • (03/31/90)
69 **CHÂTEAU BAULOS** Bordeaux Prince Albert Poniatowski 1988 • $8 • (08/31/91)
65 **CHÂTEAU JONQUEYRES** Bordeaux Supérieur Cuvée Vieilles Vignes 1988 • $12 • (03/31/91)

55 **CHÂTEAU CAMENSAC** Haut-Médoc 1988 • $16 • (07/15/91)

1986 Red Bordeaux
Vintage Rating: 95

98 **CHÂTEAU CHEVAL BLANC** St.-Emilion 1986 • $83 • (06/30/89) • CS
98 **CHÂTEAU MARGAUX** Margaux 1986 • $105 • (06/15/89) • CS
98 **CHÂTEAU MARGAUX** Margaux 1986 • $154 • (12/15/89)
98 **CHÂTEAU MOUTON-ROTHSCHILD** Pauillac 1986 • $114 • (05/31/89) • CS
97 **CHÂTEAU CLERC-MILON** Pauillac 1986 • $38 • (05/31/89)
97 **CHÂTEAU LA MISSION-HAUT-BRION** Pessac-Léognan 1986 • $60 • (11/15/91)
97 **CHÂTEAU MOUTON-ROTHSCHILD** Pauillac 1986 • $245 • (05/15/91)
97 **CHÂTEAU PICHON-LONGUEVILLE-BARON** Pauillac 1986 • $58 • (05/31/89)
97 **CHÂTEAU PICHON-LONGUEVILLE-LALANDE** Pauillac 1986 • $65 • (05/31/89)
96 **CHÂTEAU DE SALES** Pomerol 1986 • $23
96 **CHÂTEAU LAFITE-ROTHSCHILD** Pauillac 1986 • $141 • (11/30/91)
96 **CHÂTEAU MONTROSE** St.-Estèphe 1986 • $53 • (05/15/89) • SS
96 **CHÂTEAU PETRUS** Pomerol 1986 • $299 • (02/15/91)
95 **CHÂTEAU CANON** St.-Emilion 1986 • $45 • (05/15/89)
95 **CHÂTEAU LA DOMINIQUE** St.-Emilion 1986 • $40 • (06/30/89)
95 **CHÂTEAU LA FLEUR DE GAY** Pomerol 1986 • $53 • (10/31/89) • CS
95 **CHÂTEAU LE PIN** Pomerol 1986 • $200 • (06/15/89)
95 **CHÂTEAU LEOVILLE-LAS CASES** St.-Julien 1986 • $86 • (02/15/92)
95 **CHÂTEAU PETRUS** Pomerol 1986 • $320 • (11/15/89)
94 **CHÂTEAU CLOS DES JACOBINS** St.-Emilion 1986 • $34 • (06/30/89)
94 **CHÂTEAU L'ANGELUS** St.-Emilion 1986 • $27 • (06/30/89)
94 **CHÂTEAU LA MISSION-HAUT-BRION** Pessac-Léognan 1986 • $60 • (06/15/89)
94 **CHÂTEAU LAFLEUR** Pomerol 1986 • $145 • (05/15/94)
94 **CHÂTEAU LE GAY** Pomerol 1986 • $33
94 **CHÂTEAU LYNCH-BAGES** Pauillac 1986 • $50 • (10/31/89)
94 **CHÂTEAU MAGDELAINE** St.-Emilion 1986 • $48 • (02/15/90)
94 **CHÂTEAU PALMER** Margaux 1986 • $41 • (06/15/89)
94 **CHÂTEAU SOCIANDO-MALLET** Haut-Médoc 1986 • $29 • (11/30/89)
94 **CLOS RENE** Pomerol 1986 • $22 • (06/15/89) • SS
93 **CHÂTEAU BEYCHEVELLE** St.-Julien 1986 • $41 • (05/31/89)
93 **CHÂTEAU CANON** St.-Emilion 1986 • $41 • (06/30/89)
93 **CHÂTEAU CERTAN DE MAY** Pomerol 1986 • $63 • (09/15/89)
93 **CHÂTEAU CHEVAL BLANC** St.-Emilion 1986 • $122 • (02/15/91)
93 **CHÂTEAU COS D'ESTOURNEL** St.-Estèphe 1986 • $51 • (05/31/89)
93 **CHÂTEAU GRUAUD LAROSE** St.-Julien 1986 • $35 • (05/31/89)
93 **CHÂTEAU HAUT-MARBUZET** St.-Estèphe 1986 • $30 • (05/31/89)
93 **CHÂTEAU LA CONSEILLANTE** Pomerol 1986 • $59 • (06/15/89)
93 **CHÂTEAU LA FLEUR-PETRUS** Pomerol 1986 • $52 • (02/15/90) • CS
93 **CHÂTEAU LATOUR** Pauillac 1986 • $85 • (03/31/90)
93 **CHÂTEAU LE PIN** Pomerol 1986 • $383 • (05/15/94)
93 **CHÂTEAU LYNCH-BAGES** Pauillac 1986 • $37 • (05/31/89)
93 **CHÂTEAU MOUTON-BARONNE-PHILIPPE** Pauillac 1986 • $23 • (05/31/89)
93 **CHÂTEAU PAVIE** St.-Emilion 1986 • $35 • (06/30/89)
93 **CHÂTEAU PAVIE-DECESSE** St.-Emilion 1986 • $21 • (06/30/89)
93 **VIEUX CHÂTEAU CERTAN** Pomerol 1986 • $65 • (06/15/89)
92 **CHÂTEAU BERNADOTTE** Pauillac 1986 • $22 • (11/30/89)
92 **CHÂTEAU COS D'ESTOURNEL** St.-Estèphe 1986 • $62 • (05/15/90)
92 **CHÂTEAU DE MARBUZET** St.-Estèphe 1986 • $16 • (06/30/89)
92 **CHÂTEAU HAUT-BRION** Pessac-Léognan 1986 • $88 • (06/30/89)
92 **CHÂTEAU HAUT-MARBUZET** St.-Estèphe 1986 • $31 • (11/30/89)
92 **CHÂTEAU L'ENCLOS** Pomerol 1986 • $20 • (06/15/89)
92 **CHÂTEAU LE BON-PASTEUR** Pomerol 1986 • $46 • (06/15/89)
92 **CHÂTEAU LE CROCK** St.-Estèphe 1986 • $21 • (11/30/89)
92 **CHÂTEAU MONBRISON** Margaux 1986 • $23 • (11/30/89)
92 **CHÂTEAU PAPE-CLEMENT** Pessac-Léognan 1986 • $36 • (06/30/89)
92 **CHÂTEAU PRIEURE-LICHINE** Margaux 1986 • $32 • (06/15/89)
92 **CHÂTEAU ST.-PIERRE** St.-Julien 1986 • $24 • (09/15/89) • SS
92 **CHÂTEAU TRONQUOY-LALANDE** St.-Estèphe 1986 • $16 • (11/30/89)
91 **CHÂTEAU BEAUSEJOUR-DUFFAU-LAGARROSSE** St.-Emilion 1986 • $34 • (06/30/89)
91 **CHÂTEAU CANON-LA-GAFFELIERE** St.-Emilion 1986 • $21 • (06/30/89)
91 **CHÂTEAU D'ANGLUDET** Margaux 1986 • $28 • (06/15/89)
91 **CHÂTEAU DUCRU-BEAUCAILLOU** St.-Julien 1986 • $51 • (06/30/89)
91 **CHÂTEAU HAUT-BAGES-LIBERAL** Pauillac 1986 • $38 • (05/31/89)
91 **CHÂTEAU HAUT-BAILLY** Pessac-Léognan 1986 • $28 • (06/15/89)
91 **CHÂTEAU L'EGLISE-CLINET** Pomerol 1986 • $55 • (06/15/89)
91 **CHÂTEAU LA LOUVIERE** Pessac-Léognan 1986 • $30 • (06/15/89)
91 **CHÂTEAU LABEGORCE-ZEDE** Margaux 1986 • $22 • (11/30/89)
91 **CHÂTEAU LALANDE-BORIE** St.-Julien 1986 • $17 • (11/30/89)
91 **CHÂTEAU LARMANDE** St.-Emilion 1986 • $26 • (06/30/89)
91 **CHÂTEAU TALBOT** St.-Julien 1986 • $51 • (05/31/89)
91 **CLOS J. KANON** St.-Emilion 1986 • $17 • (11/15/89)
90 **CHÂTEAU CANON** St.-Emilion 1986 • $45
90 **CHÂTEAU CHASSE-SPLEEN** Moulis 1986 • $28 • (11/30/89)
90 **CHÂTEAU CLARKE** Listrac 1986 • $18 • (11/15/89)
90 **CHÂTEAU D'ANGLUDET** Margaux 1986 • $29 • (11/30/89)
90 **CHÂTEAU DE FIEUZAL** Pessac-Léognan 1986 • $23 • (06/30/89)

90 **CHÂTEAU DE PEZ** St.-Estèphe 1986 • $21 • (06/30/89)
90 **CHÂTEAU DESMIRAIL** Margaux 1986 • $22 • (06/30/89)
90 **CHÂTEAU DUHART-MILON** Pauillac 1986 • $30 • (05/31/89)
90 **CHÂTEAU DURFORT-VIVENS** Margaux 1986 • $25 • (06/15/89)
90 **CHÂTEAU HAUT-BAGES-AVEROUS** Pauillac 1986 • $21 • (11/30/89)
90 **CHÂTEAU LA POINTE** Pomerol 1986 • $21 • (06/15/89)
90 **CHÂTEAU LA TOUR-DE-MONS** Margaux 1986 • $17 • (06/15/89)
90 **CHÂTEAU LA TOUR-DE-MONS** Margaux 1986 • $19 • (11/30/89)
90 **CHÂTEAU LA TOUR-MARTILLAC** Pessac-Léognan 1986 • $15 • (02/15/90)
90 **CHÂTEAU LAFLEUR** Pomerol 1986 • $145 • (10/31/89)
90 **CHÂTEAU LEOVILLE-BARTON** St.-Julien 1986 • $36 • (05/31/89)
90 **CHÂTEAU LES ORMES DE PEZ** St.-Estèphe 1986 • $21 • (05/31/89)
90 **CHÂTEAU MALARTIC-LAGRAVIERE** Pessac-Léognan 1986 • $23 • (06/15/89)
90 **CHÂTEAU MEYNEY** St.-Estèphe 1986 • $19 • (06/30/89)
90 **CHÂTEAU ST.-PIERRE** St.-Julien 1986 • $24 • (10/15/92)
90 **CHÂTEAU TERTRE-ROTEBOEUF** St.-Emilion 1986 • $39 • (06/30/89)
90 **CHÂTEAU TOUR DU HAUT-MOULIN** Haut-Médoc 1986 • $16 • (11/30/89)
90 **RESERVE DE LA COMTESSE** Pauillac 1986 • $30 • (05/31/89)
89 **CHÂTEAU AUSONE** St.-Emilion 1986 • $65 • (10/15/94)
89 **CHÂTEAU CANTEMERLE** Haut-Médoc 1986 • $30 • (06/30/89)
89 **CHÂTEAU CHAMBERT-MARBUZET** St.-Estèphe 1986 • $29 • (11/30/89)
89 **CHÂTEAU DU TERTRE** Margaux 1986 • $22 • (06/15/89)
89 **CHÂTEAU FIGEAC** St.-Emilion 1986 • $51 • (06/30/89)
89 **CHÂTEAU GLORIA** St.-Julien 1986 • $23 • (10/15/92)
89 **CHÂTEAU GRUAUD LAROSE** St.-Julien 1986 • $59 • (02/28/91)
89 **CHÂTEAU LA GRAVE TRIGANT DE BOISSET** Pomerol 1986 • $36 • (03/31/90)
89 **CHÂTEAU LA LAGUNE** Haut-Médoc 1986 • $34 • (06/30/89)
89 **CHÂTEAU PONTET-CANET** Pauillac 1986 • $31 • (05/31/89)
89 **DOMAINE DE CHEVALIER** Pessac-Léognan 1986 • $36 • (06/15/89)
88 **CHÂTEAU BEL-AIR** Haut-Médoc 1986 • $9 • (11/15/89) • BB
88 **CHÂTEAU CANUET** Margaux 1986 • $15 • (11/30/89)
88 **CHÂTEAU CORBIN** St.-Emilion 1986 • $15 • (06/30/89)
88 **CHÂTEAU GRAND-PUY-LACOSTE** Pauillac 1986 • $31 • (05/31/89)
88 **CHÂTEAU L'EVANGILE** Pomerol 1986 • $44 • (09/15/89)
88 **CHÂTEAU LE CROCK** St.-Estèphe 1986 • $21 • (06/30/89)
88 **CHÂTEAU MALESCASSE** Haut-Médoc 1986 • $9 • (11/30/89)
88 **CHÂTEAU MALESCOT-ST.-EXUPERY** Margaux 1986 • $29 • (06/15/89)
88 **CHÂTEAU MEYNEY** St.-Estèphe 1986 • $31 • (11/30/89)
88 **CHÂTEAU MOULIN RICHE** St.-Julien 1986 • $20 • (11/30/89)
88 **CHÂTEAU PIBRAN** Pauillac 1986 • $18 • (11/30/89)
88 **CHÂTEAU POUJEAUX** Moulis 1986 • $19 • (11/30/89)
88 **CHÂTEAU RAUZAN-GASSIES** Margaux 1986 • $25 • (06/30/89)
88 **CHÂTEAU TOUR-HAUT-CAUSSAN** Médoc 1986 • $14 • (11/30/89)
88 **CHÂTEAU TROPLONG-MONDOT** St.-Emilion 1986 • $23 • (06/30/89)
87 **CHÂTEAU BEAUREGARD** Pomerol 1986 • $24 • (06/15/89)
87 **CHÂTEAU BRANE-CANTENAC** Margaux 1986 • $27 • (06/15/89)
87 **CHÂTEAU CAP DE MOURLIN** St.-Emilion 1986 • $18 • (06/30/89)
87 **CHÂTEAU CARBONNIEUX** Pessac-Léognan 1986 • $18 • (09/15/89)
87 **CHÂTEAU DE CRUZEAU** Pessac-Léognan 1986 • $10 • (06/30/89)
87 **CHÂTEAU FIGEAC** St.-Emilion 1986 • $38 • (10/31/91)
87 **CHÂTEAU GRAND-MAYNE** St.-Emilion 1986 • $16 • (06/30/89)
87 **CHÂTEAU L'ARROSEE** St.-Emilion 1986 • $36 • (02/15/89)
87 **CHÂTEAU LABEGORCE-ZEDE** Margaux 1986 • $22 • (06/15/89)
87 **CHÂTEAU LES ORMES DE PEZ** St.-Estèphe 1986 • $22 • (11/30/89)
87 **CHÂTEAU MOULIN ROUGE** Haut-Médoc 1986 • $14 • (11/30/89)
87 **CHÂTEAU RAUSAN-SEGLA** Margaux 1986 • $82 • (09/15/89)
87 **CHÂTEAU ST.-GEORGES** St.-Georges-St.-Emilion 1986 • $14 • (07/15/90)
87 **CHÂTEAU TERREY-GROS-CAILLOUX** St.-Julien 1986 • $20 • (11/30/89)
86 **CHÂTEAU BAHANS-HAUT-BRION** Pessac-Léognan 1986 • $27 • (09/15/89)
86 **CHÂTEAU BEAU-SITE** St.-Estèphe 1986 • $18 • (11/30/89)
86 **CHÂTEAU CALON-SEGUR** St.-Estèphe 1986 • $34 • (05/31/89)
86 **CHÂTEAU CANON-DE-BREM** Canon-Fronsac 1986 • $15 • (03/31/90)
86 **CHÂTEAU CERTAN-GIRAUD** Pomerol 1986 • $22 • (06/30/89)
86 **CHÂTEAU DE MARBUZET** St.-Estèphe 1986 • $16 • (11/30/89)
86 **CHÂTEAU DE SALES** Pomerol 1986 • $23 • (06/30/89)
86 **CHÂTEAU FOMBRAUGE** St.-Emilion 1986 • $19 • (06/30/89)
86 **CHÂTEAU LA GURGUE** Margaux 1986 • $23 • (06/15/89)
86 **CHÂTEAU LABEGORCE** Margaux 1986 • $15 • (02/15/90)
86 **CHÂTEAU LAGRANGE** St.-Julien 1986 • $33 • (02/15/90)
86 **CHÂTEAU LATOUR A POMEROL** Pomerol 1986 • $50 • (10/15/94)
86 **CHÂTEAU LEOVILLE-POYFERRE** St.-Julien 1986 • $27 • (05/31/89)
86 **CHÂTEAU LYNCH-MOUSSAS** Pauillac 1986 • $18 • (06/30/89)
86 **CHÂTEAU PHELAN-SEGUR** St.-Estèphe 1986 • $20 • (11/30/89)
86 **CHÂTEAU POTENSAC** Médoc 1986 • $16 • (11/30/89)
86 **CLOS L'EGLISE** Pomerol 1986 • $33 • (02/15/90)
85 **CHÂTEAU AUSONE** St.-Emilion 1986 • $120 • (06/30/89)
85 **CHÂTEAU CHASSE-SPLEEN** Moulis 1986 • $28 • (06/30/89)
85 **CHÂTEAU CLEMENT-PICHON** Haut-Médoc 1986 • $11 • (11/30/89)

85 **CHÂTEAU COUFRAN** Haut-Médoc 1986 • $15 • (06/30/89)

85 **CHÂTEAU GRAND-PUY-DUCASSE** Pauillac 1986 • $21 • (06/30/89)

85 **CHÂTEAU GREYSAC** Médoc 1986 • $10 • (11/30/89)

85 **CHÂTEAU HAUT-BAGES-AVEROUS** Pauillac 1986 • $19 • (05/31/89)

85 **CHÂTEAU HAUT-BATAILLEY** Pauillac 1986 • $23 • (05/31/89)

85 **CHÂTEAU LA GURGUE** Margaux 1986 • $23 • (11/30/89)

85 **CHÂTEAU LA TOUR-LEOGNAN** Pessac-Léognan 1986 • $11 • (02/15/89)

85 **CHÂTEAU LAROSE-TRINTAUDON** Haut-Médoc 1986 • $10 • (11/15/89)

85 **CHÂTEAU LESTAGE-SIMON** Haut-Médoc 1986 • $13 • (11/30/89)

85 **CHÂTEAU MALESCASSE** Haut-Médoc 1986 • $9 • (06/30/89)

84 **CHÂTEAU BEAUMONT** Haut-Médoc 1986 • $12 • (06/30/89)

84 **CHÂTEAU DE ROCHEMORIN** Pessac-Léognan 1986 • $15 • (06/15/89)

84 **CHÂTEAU DU BEAU-VALLON** St.-Emilion 1986 • $10 • (09/30/89)

84 **CHÂTEAU DU CAUZE** St.-Emilion 1986 • $15 • (06/30/89)

84 **CHÂTEAU DU GLANA** St.-Julien 1986 • $17 • (11/30/89)

84 **CHÂTEAU FIGEAC** St.-Emilion 1986 • $51 • (10/15/94)

84 **CHÂTEAU LA CARDONNE** Médoc 1986 • $10 • (02/15/90)

84 **CHÂTEAU LA TOUR DE BY** Médoc 1986 • $12 • (02/15/89)

84 **CHÂTEAU LACOSTE-BORIE** Pauillac 1986 • $15 • (06/30/89)

84 **CHÂTEAU LALANDE-BORIE** St.-Julien 1986 • $17 • (11/15/89)

84 **CHÂTEAU NENIN** Pomerol 1986 • $22 • (06/30/89)

84 **CHÂTEAU PUYGUERAUD** Côtes de Francs 1986 • $12 • (06/15/89)

84 **CHÂTEAU SOCIANDO-MALLET** Haut-Médoc 1986 • $25 • (06/30/89)

84 **CHÂTEAU TOUR DU HAUT-MOULIN** Haut-Médoc 1986 • $16 • (06/30/89)

84 **CLOS DU MARQUIS** St.-Julien 1986 • $19 • (09/15/89)

84 **PAVILLON ROUGE DU CHÂTEAU MARGAUX** Margaux 1986 • $22 • (06/30/89)

83 **CHÂTEAU CAMENSAC** Haut-Médoc 1986 • $14 • (06/30/89)

83 **CHÂTEAU D'ISSAN** Margaux 1986 • $25 • (06/15/89)

83 **CHÂTEAU DUCLUZEAU** Listrac 1986 • $11 • (11/30/89)

83 **CHÂTEAU GISCOURS** Margaux 1986 • $24 • (06/15/89)

83 **CHÂTEAU POUJEAUX** Moulis 1986 • $22 • (06/30/89)

83 **CHÂTEAU RAHOUL** Graves 1986 • $18 • (12/31/90)

83 **CHÂTEAU TROTANOY** Pomerol 1986 • $70 • (10/31/89)

83 **CHÂTEAU VERDIGNAN** Haut-Médoc 1986 • $15 • (06/30/89)

82 **CHÂTEAU ARNAULD** Haut-Médoc 1986 • $18 • (11/30/89)

82 **CHÂTEAU BELAIR** St.-Emilion 1986 • $26 • (03/31/90)

82 **CHÂTEAU COUFRAN** Haut-Médoc 1986 • $15 • (11/30/89)

82 **CHÂTEAU GOFFRETEAU** Bordeaux Supérieur 1986 • $6 • (06/15/89) • BB

82 **CHÂTEAU KIRWAN** Margaux 1986 • $25 • (06/30/89)

82 **CHÂTEAU LA FLEUR** St.-Emilion 1986 • $14 • (02/15/90)

82 **CHÂTEAU LARRIVET-HAUT-BRION** Pessac-Léognan 1986 • $17 • (06/15/89)

82 **CHÂTEAU LES HAUTS DE BRAME** St.-Estèphe 1986 • $19 • (10/31/89)

82 **CHÂTEAU PERENNE** Premières Côtes de Blaye 1986 • $7 • (06/30/89)

82 **CHÂTEAU PLAGNAC** Médoc 1986 • $9 • (11/30/89)

82 **CHÂTEAU RAMAGE LA BATISSE** Haut-Médoc 1986 • $14 • (11/30/89)

82 **CLOS LABARDE** St.-Emilion 1986 • $15 • (06/30/89)

81 **CHÂTEAU BELGRAVE** Haut-Médoc 1986 • $16 • (03/31/90)

81 **CHÂTEAU CHAMBERT-MARBUZET** St.-Estèphe 1986 • $29 • (05/31/89)

81 **CHÂTEAU DE PARENCHERE** Bordeaux Supérieur 1986 • $9 • (06/30/89)

81 **CHÂTEAU HANTEILLAN** Haut-Médoc 1986 • $15 • (11/30/89)

81 **CHÂTEAU HAUT-GARDERE** Pessac-Léognan 1986 • $11 • (09/30/89)

81 **CHÂTEAU LA CROIX ST.-JEAN** Bordeaux Supérieur 1986 • $6 • (11/30/88) • BB

81 **CHÂTEAU LA VALADE** Fronsac 1986 • $5.25 • (05/15/89) • BB

81 **CHÂTEAU LA VIEILLE CURE** Fronsac 1986 • $15 • (05/15/91)

81 **CHÂTEAU LESCALLE** Bordeaux Supérieur 1986 • $8 • (06/30/89)

81 **CHÂTEAU PITRAY** Côtes de Castillon 1986 • $6 • (09/30/89) • BB

81 **CHÂTEAU SAUVAGE** Premières Côtes de Bordeaux Red 1986 • $9 • (04/15/90)

81 **CHÂTEAU TOUR CALON** Montagne-St.-Emilion 1986 • $10 • (09/30/89)

81 **MOUTON-CADET** Bordeaux 1986 • $7.25 • (02/15/89) • BB

80 **CHÂTEAU BEAUSEJOUR** Côtes de Castillon 1986 • $5 • (06/15/89) • BB

80 **CHÂTEAU BELLEGRAVE-VAN DER VOORT** Pauillac 1986 • $19 • (10/31/91)

80 **CHÂTEAU BRASSAC** Bordeaux Supérieur 1986 • $5 • (08/31/88) • BB

80 **CHÂTEAU LA TOUR DE BY** Médoc 1986 • $12 • (11/30/89)

80 **CHÂTEAU LES HAUTS DE BRAME** St.-Estèphe 1986 • $22 • (03/31/91)

80 **CHÂTEAU PETIT-FAURIE-DE-SOUTARD** St.-Emilion 1986 • $15 • (06/30/89)

80 **CHEVALIER DUCLA** Bordeaux 1986 • $5 • (05/15/89) • BB

80 **CLOS FOURTET** St.-Emilion 1986 • $41 • (06/30/89)

80 **DOMAINE DE GRAND MAISON** Pessac-Léognan 1986 • $8 • (04/15/90)

79 **CHÂTEAU BEAU-SEJOUR BECOT** St.-Emilion 1986 • $22 • (07/31/89)

79 **CHÂTEAU BELLERIVE** Médoc 1986 • $4 • (02/15/89)

79 **CHÂTEAU CISSAC** Haut-Médoc 1986 • $12 • (11/30/89)

79 **CHÂTEAU FAURIE-PASCAUD** Bordeaux 1986 • $5 • (06/30/88)

79 **CHÂTEAU FOURCAS-HOSTEN** Listrac 1986 • $14 • (11/15/89)

79 **CHÂTEAU LA CROIX DE MILLORIT** Côtes de Bourg 1986 • $9 • (05/15/91)

79 **CHÂTEAU LAURETAN** Bordeaux 1986 • $5 • (05/15/89)

79 **CHÂTEAU MARQUIS DE TERME** Margaux 1986 • $25 • (06/30/89)

79 **CHÂTEAU PEDESCLAUX** Pauillac 1986 • $18 • (02/15/90)
79 **CHÂTEAU PLAGNAC** Médoc 1986 • $9 • (06/30/89)
79 **CHÂTEAU ROLAND** St.-Emilion 1986 • $12 • (06/30/89)
79 **CHÂTEAU SEGONZAC** Premières Côtes de Blaye 1986 • $9 • (06/30/89)
79 **CHÂTEAU SOUDARS** Haut-Médoc 1986 • $13 • (11/30/89)
79 **CHÂTEAU TOUR-DU-MIRAIL** Haut-Médoc 1986 • $12 • (11/30/89)
78 **CHÂTEAU BARREYRES** Haut-Médoc 1986 • $8.25 • (06/30/89)
78 **CHÂTEAU BOUSCAUT** Pessac-Léognan 1986 • $14 • (02/15/89)
78 **CHÂTEAU BRILLETTE** Moulis 1986 • $14 • (11/30/89)
78 **CHÂTEAU CANDELAY** Bordeaux Supérieur 1986 • $5 • (06/15/89)
78 **CHÂTEAU CANTELAUDE** Haut-Médoc 1986 • $17 • (06/30/89)
78 **CHÂTEAU CLINET** Pomerol 1986 • $29 • (09/15/89)
78 **CHÂTEAU CROIZET-BAGES** Pauillac 1986 • $15 • (06/30/89)
78 **CHÂTEAU DE SOURS** Bordeaux Supérieur 1986 • $7 • (09/30/89)
78 **CHÂTEAU LAROSE-TRINTAUDON** Haut-Médoc 1986 • $10 • (11/30/89)
78 **CHÂTEAU MOULIN HAUT-LAROQUE** Fronsac 1986 • $11 • (11/15/89)
78 **CHÂTEAU RICHETERRE** Margaux 1986 • $13 • (02/15/89)
78 **LA PETITE EGLISE** Pomerol 1986 • $15 • (09/15/89)
78 **ST.-JOVIAN** Cabernet Sauvignon Bordeaux 1986 • $4 • (07/31/88)
77 **CHÂTEAU L'ESPERANCE** Bordeaux 1986 • $7 • (09/30/89)
77 **CHÂTEAU LA PIERRIERE** Côtes de Castillon 1986 • $6 • (12/31/88)
77 **CHÂTEAU LES GRANDS JAYS** Bordeaux Supérieur 1986 • $6 • (05/15/89)
77 **CHÂTEAU PHELAN-SEGUR** St.-Estèphe 1986 • $20 • (06/30/89)
77 **CHÂTEAU ST.-ANDRE-CORBIN** St.-Georges-St.-Emilion 1986 • $22 • (03/31/90)
77 **CHÂTEAU TOUR DE BELLEGARDE** Bordeaux Supérieur 1986 • $4 • (05/15/89)
77 **LA COUR PAVILLON** Bordeaux 1986 • $7.25 • (02/28/91)
76 **BARONS EDMOND & BENJAMIN ROTHSCHILD** Haut-Médoc 1986 • $48 • (03/31/91)
76 **CHÂTEAU CAPBERN-GASQUETON** St.-Estèphe 1986 • $20 • (11/30/89)
76 **CHÂTEAU CLEMENT-PICHON** Haut-Médoc 1986 • $11 • (09/30/89)
76 **CHÂTEAU FONTENIL** Fronsac 1986 • $15 • (02/15/90)
76 **CHÂTEAU LA CROIX DE GIRON** Bordeaux Supérieur 1986 • $5.25 • (05/15/89)
76 **CHÂTEAU LA TERRASSE** Bordeaux Supérieur 1986 • $8 • (06/30/89)
76 **CHÂTEAU TOUR-DU-ROC** Haut-Médoc 1986 • $11 • (11/30/89)
76 **CHÂTEAU VERDIGNAN** Haut-Médoc 1986 • $15 • (11/30/89)
76 **ST.-JOVIAN** Merlot Bordeaux 1986 • $5 • (05/15/89)
75 **CHÂTEAU CHAUVIN** St.-Emilion 1986 • $15 • (06/30/89)
75 **CHÂTEAU CORMEIL-FIGEAC** St.-Emilion 1986 • $12 • (06/30/89)
75 **CHÂTEAU DE LAMARQUE** Haut-Médoc 1986 • $18 • (11/30/89)
75 **CHÂTEAU LE BOSCQ** Médoc 1986 • $10 • (06/30/89)
74 **CHARTRON LA FLEUR** Bordeaux 1986 • $4 • (05/15/89)
74 **CHÂTEAU DUPLESSIS-FABRE** Moulis 1986 • $7 • (11/30/89)
74 **CHÂTEAU LOUDENNE** Médoc 1986 • $12 • (11/30/89)
73 **CHÂTEAU BONNET** Bordeaux 1986 • $6 • (05/15/89)
73 **CHÂTEAU DU MOULIN DE PEYRONIN** Bordeaux 1986 • $10 • (03/31/90)
73 **LAURIOL** Côtes de Francs 1986 • $8 • (06/15/89)
72 **CHÂTEAU GRAND-BARRAIL-LAMARZELLE-FIGEAC** St.-Emilion 1986 • $15 • (06/30/89)
72 **CHÂTEAU LOUDENNE** Bordeaux 1986 • $12 • (03/31/89)
72 **YVON MAU** Bordeaux Officiel du Bicentenaire de la Revolution Francaise 1986 • $4 • (06/30/89)
71 **CHÂTEAU DU CHEVALIER** Montagne-St.-Emilion 1986 • $19 • (03/31/91)
70 **ALEXIS LICHINE** Bordeaux 1986 • $4 • (03/31/89)
70 **CHÂTEAU DU PINTEY** Bordeaux Supérieur 1986 • $8 • (12/10/90)
70 **CHÂTEAU LA TONNELLE** Haut-Médoc 1986 • $11 • (11/30/89)
70 **CHÂTEAU LES ALOUETTES** Bordeaux Kosher 1986 • $10 • (03/31/90)
70 **CHÂTEAU MAROTTE** Bordeaux 1986 • $3 • (04/30/88)
69 **CHÂTEAU LAMOTHE-CISSAC** Haut-Médoc 1986 • $12 • (11/30/89)
67 **CHÂTEAU TOUR-DU-ROC** Haut-Médoc 1986 • $11 • (09/30/89)
62 **CHÂTEAU DU MOULIN-MEYNEY** Bordeaux 1986 • $6
50 **CHÂTEAU LA TOUR-HAUT-BRION** Pessac-Léognan 1986 • $NA

1982 Red Bordeaux
Vintage Rating: 94

99 **CHÂTEAU HAUT-BRION** Graves 1982 • $120 • (08/31/92)
99 **CHÂTEAU LATOUR** Pauillac 1982 • $150 • (03/31/90)
98 **CHÂTEAU LEOVILLE-LAS CASES** St.-Julien 1982 • $93 • (02/15/90)
98 **CHÂTEAU MARGAUX** Margaux 1982 • $138 • (12/15/89)
97 **CHÂTEAU CHEVAL BLANC** St.-Emilion 1982 • $175 • (02/15/91)
97 **CHÂTEAU LA LAGUNE** Haut-Médoc 1982 • $43 • (05/01/89)
97 **CHÂTEAU LA MISSION-HAUT-BRION** Graves 1982 • $152 • (08/31/92)
97 **CHÂTEAU LAFITE-ROTHSCHILD** Pauillac 1982 • $243 • (08/31/92)
97 **CHÂTEAU LATOUR** Pauillac 1982 • $150 • (05/01/89)
97 **CHÂTEAU LATOUR A POMEROL** Pomerol 1982 • $77 • (08/31/92)
97 **CHÂTEAU PICHON-LONGUEVILLE-LALANDE** Pauillac 1982 • $163 • (08/31/92)
96 **CHÂTEAU CHEVAL BLANC** St.-Emilion 1982 • $175 • (05/15/89)
96 **CHÂTEAU LA CONSEILLANTE** Pomerol 1982 • $75 • (05/15/89)
96 **CHÂTEAU LA MISSION-HAUT-BRION** Graves 1982 • $85 • (05/01/85)
96 **CHÂTEAU PETRUS** Pomerol 1982 • $675 • (02/15/91)
96 **CHÂTEAU TROTANOY** Pomerol 1982 • $170 • (08/31/92)
95 **CHÂTEAU CHEVAL BLANC** St.-Emilion 1982 • $373 • (08/31/92)

95 **CHÂTEAU D'ANGLUDET** Margaux 1982 • $25 • (12/01/85) • CS
95 **CHÂTEAU GRAND-PUY-LACOSTE** Pauillac 1982 • $72 • (08/31/92)
95 **CHÂTEAU LE PIN** Pomerol 1982 • $320 • (05/15/89)
95 **CHÂTEAU LEOVILLE-LAS CASES** St.-Julien 1982 • $100 • (02/15/92)
95 **CHÂTEAU MAGDELAINE** St.-Emilion 1982 • $53 • (05/15/89)
95 **CHÂTEAU MARGAUX** Margaux 1982 • $305 • (08/31/92)
95 **CHÂTEAU MOUTON-ROTHSCHILD** Pauillac 1982 • $344 • (08/31/92)
95 **CHÂTEAU TROTANOY** Pomerol 1982 • $170 • (10/15/88)
94 **CHÂTEAU CANON** St.-Emilion 1982 • $78 • (08/31/92)
94 **CHÂTEAU GRUAUD LAROSE** St.-Julien 1982 • $83 • (08/31/92)
94 **CHÂTEAU LA LAGUNE** Haut-Médoc 1982 • $62 • (08/31/92)
94 **CHÂTEAU LA LOUVIERE** Graves 1982 • $25 • (10/16/85) • SS
94 **CHÂTEAU LATOUR** Pauillac 1982 • $280 • (08/31/92)
94 **CHÂTEAU LE BON-PASTEUR** Pomerol 1982 • $130 • (08/31/92)
94 **CHÂTEAU LEOVILLE-LAS CASES** St.-Julien 1982 • $168 • (08/31/92)
94 **CHÂTEAU LYNCH-BAGES** Pauillac 1982 • $54 • (03/01/85) • CS
94 **CHÂTEAU PAVIE** St.-Emilion 1982 • $54 • (08/31/92)
94 **CHÂTEAU PETRUS** Pomerol 1982 • $878 • (08/31/92)
93 **CHÂTEAU AUSONE** St.-Emilion 1982 • $160 • (05/15/89)
93 **CHÂTEAU COS D'ESTOURNEL** St.-Estèphe 1982 • $112 • (08/31/92)
93 **CHÂTEAU DE PEZ** St.-Estèphe 1982 • $22 • (08/31/92)
93 **CHÂTEAU DUCRU-BEAUCAILLOU** St.-Julien 1982 • $99 • (08/31/92)
93 **CHÂTEAU FIGEAC** St.-Emilion 1982 • $67 • (10/31/91)
93 **CHÂTEAU GAZIN** Pomerol 1982 • $31 • (08/31/92)
93 **CHÂTEAU HAUT-BATAILLEY** Pauillac 1982 • $45 • (08/31/92)
93 **CHÂTEAU L'EVANGILE** Pomerol 1982 • $169 • (05/15/89)
93 **CHÂTEAU LA CONSEILLANTE** Pomerol 1982 • $75 • (02/16/85)
93 **CHÂTEAU LA GAFFELIERE** St.-Emilion 1982 • $29 • (08/31/92)
93 **CHÂTEAU LA MISSION-HAUT-BRION** Graves 1982 • $85 • (11/15/91)
93 **CHÂTEAU LAFLEUR** Pomerol 1982 • $275 • (05/15/94)
93 **CHÂTEAU LEOVILLE-LAS CASES** St.-Julien 1982 • $93 • (05/01/89)
93 **CHÂTEAU LEOVILLE-POYFERRE** St.-Julien 1982 • $NA
93 **CHÂTEAU ST.-PIERRE** St.-Julien 1982 • $28 • (12/16/85) • CS
93 **CHÂTEAU VILLEMAURINE** St.-Emilion 1982 • $40 • (08/31/92)
93 **DOMAINE DE CHEVALIER** Graves 1982 • $42 • (08/31/92)
93 **LES FORTS DE LATOUR** Pauillac 1982 • $58 • (08/31/92)
92 **CHÂTEAU BELAIR** St.-Emilion 1982 • $39 • (08/31/92)
92 **CHÂTEAU CANTEMERLE** Haut-Médoc 1982 • $30 • (05/01/89)
92 **CHÂTEAU CERTAN DE MAY** Pomerol 1982 • $204 • (05/15/89)
92 **CHÂTEAU DUCRU-BEAUCAILLOU** St.-Julien 1982 • $76 • (05/01/85)
92 **CHÂTEAU HAUT-MARBUZET** St.-Estèphe 1982 • $57 • (11/30/89)
92 **CHÂTEAU LALANDE-BORIE** St.-Julien 1982 • $17 • (11/30/89)
92 **CHÂTEAU MALARTIC-LAGRAVIERE** Graves 1982 • $34 • (08/31/92)
92 **CHÂTEAU MONTROSE** St.-Estèphe 1982 • $56 • (08/31/92)
92 **CHÂTEAU PALMER** Margaux 1982 • $68 • (08/31/92)
92 **CHÂTEAU PETIT-VILLAGE** Pomerol 1982 • $60 • (05/15/89)
92 **CHÂTEAU PICHON-LONGUEVILLE-BARON** Pauillac 1982 • $39 • (08/31/92)
92 **CHÂTEAU PLINCE** Pomerol 1982 • $15 • (05/15/89)
92 **CHÂTEAU SOCIANDO-MALLET** Haut-Médoc 1982 • $40 • (08/31/92)
92 **MOULIN DES CARRUADES** Pauillac 1982 • $34 • (08/31/92)
91 **CHÂTEAU BOYD-CANTENAC** Margaux 1982 • $29 • (05/01/85)
91 **CHÂTEAU CANON** St.-Emilion 1982 • $60 • (05/15/89)
91 **CHÂTEAU CANON-DE-BREM** Canon-Fronsac 1982 • $16 • (08/31/92)
91 **CHÂTEAU CANTENAC-BROWN** Margaux 1982 • $22 • (05/01/85)
91 **CHÂTEAU CAPBERN-GASQUETON** St.-Estèphe 1982 • $22 • (09/16/85)
91 **CHÂTEAU D'ANGLUDET** Margaux 1982 • $23 • (08/31/92)
91 **CHÂTEAU DAUZAC** Margaux 1982 • $28 • (08/31/92)
91 **CHÂTEAU DE CRUZEAU** Graves 1982 • $20 • (08/31/92)
91 **CHÂTEAU DUHART-MILON** Pauillac 1982 • $49 • (08/31/92)
91 **CHÂTEAU FEYTIT-CLINET** Pomerol 1982 • $37 • (05/15/89)
91 **CHÂTEAU L'ARROSEE** St.-Emilion 1982 • $46 • (05/15/89)
91 **CHÂTEAU LA CROIX DE GAY** Pomerol 1982 • $27 • (05/15/89)
91 **CHÂTEAU LA GRAVE TRIGANT DE BOISSET** Pomerol 1982 • $40 • (05/15/89)
91 **CHÂTEAU LA LOUVIERE** Graves 1982 • $25 • (08/31/92)
91 **CHÂTEAU LALANDE-BORIE** St.-Julien 1982 • $17 • (08/31/92)
91 **CHÂTEAU LANESSAN** Haut-Médoc 1982 • $23 • (08/31/92)
91 **CHÂTEAU LANGOA BARTON** St.-Julien 1982 • $32 • (08/31/92)
91 **CHÂTEAU LARMANDE** St.-Emilion 1982 • $13 • (05/15/89)
91 **CHÂTEAU LE BON-PASTEUR** Pomerol 1982 • $51 • (05/15/89)
91 **CHÂTEAU LYNCH-BAGES** Pauillac 1982 • $106 • (08/31/92)
91 **CHÂTEAU MAGDELAINE** St.-Emilion 1982 • $68 • (08/31/92)
91 **CHÂTEAU MEYNEY** St.-Estèphe 1982 • $25 • (08/31/92)
91 **CHÂTEAU PETIT-VILLAGE** Pomerol 1982 • $86 • (08/31/92)
91 **CHÂTEAU PHELAN-SEGUR** St.-Estèphe 1982 • $34 • (08/31/92)
90 **CHÂTEAU BEAUSEJOUR-DUFFAU-LAGARROSSE** St.-Emilion 1982 • $30 • (05/15/89)
90 **CHÂTEAU BELAIR** St.-Emilion 1982 • $41 • (05/15/89)
90 **CHÂTEAU BOYD-CANTENAC** Margaux 1982 • $29 • (08/31/92)

90 **CHÂTEAU BRANAIRE-DUCRU** St.-Julien 1982 • $41 • (08/31/92)
90 **CHÂTEAU CANTEMERLE** Haut-Médoc 1982 • $38 • (08/31/92)
90 **CHÂTEAU CAP DE MOURLIN** St.-Emilion 1982 • $18 • (08/31/92)
90 **CHÂTEAU CERTAN-GIRAUD** Pomerol 1982 • $41 • (05/15/89)
90 **CHÂTEAU CHASSE-SPLEEN** Moulis 1982 • $41 • (11/30/89)
90 **CHÂTEAU CLERC-MILON** Pauillac 1982 • $41 • (08/31/92)
90 **CHÂTEAU D'ANGLUDET** Margaux 1982 • $25 • (11/30/89)
90 **CHÂTEAU DASSAULT** St.-Emilion 1982 • $20 • (05/15/89)
90 **CHÂTEAU DE PEZ** St.-Estèphe 1982 • $22 • (04/01/86)
90 **CHÂTEAU DE ROCHEMORIN** Graves 1982 • $22 • (08/31/92)
90 **CHÂTEAU DURFORT-VIVENS** Margaux 1982 • $25 • (08/31/92)
90 **CHÂTEAU FIGEAC** St.-Emilion 1982 • $110 • (08/31/92)
90 **CHÂTEAU FOURCAS-HOSTEN** Listrac 1982 • $18 • (08/31/92)
90 **CHÂTEAU GRUAUD LAROSE** St.-Julien 1982 • $51 • (05/01/89)
90 **CHÂTEAU HAUT-MARBUZET** St.-Estèphe 1982 • $59 • (08/31/92)
90 **CHÂTEAU L'EVANGILE** Pomerol 1982 • $85 • (05/01/89)
90 **CHÂTEAU LA FLEUR-PETRUS** Pomerol 1982 • $103 • (08/31/92)
90 **CHÂTEAU LA TOUR-DE-MONS** Margaux 1982 • $16 • (11/30/89)
90 **CHÂTEAU LAFON-ROCHET** St.-Estèphe 1982 • $86 • (08/31/92)
90 **CHÂTEAU LEOVILLE-BARTON** St.-Julien 1982 • $58 • (08/31/92)
90 **CHÂTEAU LYNCH-BAGES** Pauillac 1982 • $54 • (10/31/89)
90 **CHÂTEAU MAUCAILLOU** Moulis 1982 • $25 • (11/30/89)
90 **CHÂTEAU MONBRISON** Margaux 1982 • $22 • (11/30/89)
90 **CHÂTEAU MOULIN RICHE** St.-Julien 1982 • $22 • (11/30/89)
90 **CHÂTEAU OLIVIER** Graves 1982 • $21 • (08/31/92)
90 **CHÂTEAU PAVIE** St.-Emilion 1982 • $57 • (03/16/85)
90 **CHÂTEAU PIBRAN** Pauillac 1982 • $18 • (11/30/89)
90 **CHÂTEAU PONTET-CANET** Pauillac 1982 • $25 • (08/31/92)
90 **CHÂTEAU TOUR-HAUT-CAUSSAN** Médoc 1982 • $16 • (08/31/92)
89 **CHÂTEAU BEAUREGARD** Pomerol 1982 • $20 • (05/15/89)
89 **CHÂTEAU BEYCHEVELLE** St.-Julien 1982 • $62 • (08/31/92)
89 **CHÂTEAU FONROQUE** St.-Emilion 1982 • $21 • (08/31/92)
89 **CHÂTEAU GRUAUD LAROSE** St.-Julien 1982 • $51 • (02/28/91)
89 **CHÂTEAU HAUT-BAGES-AVEROUS** Pauillac 1982 • $25 • (11/30/89)
89 **CHÂTEAU LA CROIX** Pomerol 1982 • $30 • (05/15/89)
89 **CHÂTEAU LA TOUR DE BY** Médoc Cuvée Prestige 1982 • $20 • (08/31/92)
89 **CHÂTEAU LA TOUR-FIGEAC** St.-Emilion 1982 • $22 • (05/15/89)
89 **CHÂTEAU LAGRANGE** St.-Julien 1982 • $36 • (08/31/92)
89 **CHÂTEAU LE GAY** Pomerol 1982 • $38 • (05/15/89)
89 **CHÂTEAU LEOVILLE-POYFERRE** St.-Julien 1982 • $53 • (06/01/85)
89 **CHÂTEAU NENIN** Pomerol 1982 • $31 • (05/15/89)
89 **CHÂTEAU OLIVIER** Graves 1982 • $21 • (03/15/87)
89 **CHÂTEAU PAVIE** St.-Emilion 1982 • $57 • (05/15/89)
89 **CHÂTEAU PAVIE MACQUIN** St.-Emilion 1982 • $28 • (05/15/89)
89 **CHÂTEAU PAVIE-DECESSE** St.-Emilion 1982 • $30 • (08/31/92)
89 **CHÂTEAU PRIEURE-LICHINE** Margaux 1982 • $30 • (05/01/85)
89 **CHÂTEAU SIRAN** Margaux 1982 • $30 • (08/31/92)
89 **CHÂTEAU ST.-PIERRE** St.-Julien 1982 • $28 • (08/31/92)
89 **CHÂTEAU TROTTE VIEILLE** St.-Emilion 1982 • $24 • (08/31/92)
89 **VIEUX CHÂTEAU CERTAN** Pomerol 1982 • $60 • (05/15/89)
88 **CHÂTEAU BEAUSEJOUR-DUFFAU-LAGARROSSE** St.-Emilion 1982 • $30 • (08/31/92)
88 **CHÂTEAU BRANE-CANTENAC** Margaux 1982 • $29 • (08/31/92)
88 **CHÂTEAU CADET-PIOLA** St.-Emilion 1982 • $23 • (05/15/89)
88 **CHÂTEAU CHAMBERT-MARBUZET** St.-Estèphe 1982 • $30 • (11/30/89)
88 **CHÂTEAU D'ISSAN** Margaux 1982 • $27 • (08/31/92)
88 **CHÂTEAU DE CHANTEGRIVE** Graves 1982 • $70 • (08/31/92)
88 **CHÂTEAU DE SALES** Pomerol 1982 • $32 • (05/15/89)
88 **CHÂTEAU GAZIN** Pomerol 1982 • $30 • (05/15/89)
88 **CHÂTEAU GISCOURS** Margaux 1982 • $34 • (08/31/92)
88 **CHÂTEAU GREYSAC** Médoc 1982 • $18 • (08/31/92)
88 **CHÂTEAU L'ANGELUS** St.-Emilion 1982 • $37 • (05/15/89)
88 **CHÂTEAU LA CLUSIERE** St.-Emilion 1982 • $20 • (05/15/89)
88 **CHÂTEAU LA FLEUR DE GAY** Pomerol 1982 • $75 • (05/15/89)
88 **CHÂTEAU LA GAFFELIERE** St.-Emilion 1982 • $25 • (05/15/89)
88 **CHÂTEAU LA LOUBIERE** Pomerol 1982 • $13 • (05/15/89)
88 **CHÂTEAU LA TOUR-DE-MONS** Margaux 1982 • $18 • (08/31/92)
88 **CHÂTEAU LA TOUR-DU-PIN-FIGEAC** St.-Emilion 1982 • $21 • (05/15/89)
88 **CHÂTEAU LA VIOLETTE** Pomerol 1982 • $25 • (05/15/89)
88 **CHÂTEAU LABEGORCE** Margaux 1982 • $20 • (08/31/92)
88 **CHÂTEAU LOUDENNE** Médoc 1982 • $17 • (08/31/92)
88 **CHÂTEAU MOUTON-BARONNE-PHILIPPE** Pauillac 1982 • $37 • (08/31/92)
88 **CHÂTEAU PHELAN-SEGUR** St.-Estèphe 1982 • $29 • (11/30/89)
88 **CHÂTEAU POUJEAUX** Moulis 1982 • $22 • (11/30/89)
88 **CHÂTEAU RAUSAN-SEGLA** Margaux 1982 • $30 • (08/31/92)
88 **CHÂTEAU RIPEAU** St.-Emilion 1982 • $18 • (05/15/89)
88 **CHÂTEAU TALBOT** St.-Julien 1982 • $92 • (05/01/89)
88 **CLOS FOURTET** St.-Emilion 1982 • $35 • (06/01/85)
88 **CLOS L'EGLISE** Pomerol 1982 • $29 • (05/15/89)
87 **CHÂTEAU BEAUMONT** Haut-Médoc 1982 • $18 • (08/31/92)

87 **CHÂTEAU BEAUREGARD** Pomerol 1982 • $23 • (08/31/92)
87 **CHÂTEAU CALON-SEGUR** St.-Estèphe 1982 • $61 • (08/31/92)
87 **CHÂTEAU FEYTIT-CLINET** Pomerol 1982 • $20 • (03/16/85)
87 **CHÂTEAU GLORIA** St.-Julien 1982 • $48 • (10/15/92)
87 **CHÂTEAU HAUT-SARPE** St.-Emilion 1982 • $20 • (05/15/89)
87 **CHÂTEAU L'EGLISE-CLINET** Pomerol 1982 • $53 • (05/15/89)
87 **CHÂTEAU LA CONSEILLANTE** Pomerol 1982 • $120 • (08/31/92)
87 **CHÂTEAU LABEGORCE-ZEDE** Margaux 1982 • $21 • (11/30/89)
87 **CHÂTEAU LES ORMES DE PEZ** St.-Estèphe 1982 • $25 • (11/30/89)
87 **CHÂTEAU MOULINET** Pomerol 1982 • $10 • (05/15/89)
87 **CHÂTEAU TROTTE VIEILLE** St.-Emilion 1982 • $35 • (05/15/89)
87 **CHÂTEAU YON-FIGEAC** St.-Emilion 1982 • $25 • (05/15/89)
87 **CLOS FOURTET** St.-Emilion 1982 • $35 • (05/15/89)
87 **CLOS RENE** Pomerol 1982 • $32 • (05/15/89)
86 **CHÂTEAU BATAILLEY** Pauillac 1982 • $32 • (08/31/92)
86 **CHÂTEAU BEAU-SITE** St.-Estèphe 1982 • $18 • (08/31/92)
86 **CHÂTEAU CAP DE MOURLIN (JACQUES)** St.-Emilion 1982 • $NA • (05/15/89)
86 **CHÂTEAU CLERC-MILON** Pauillac 1982 • $34 • (04/01/85)
86 **CHÂTEAU COS-LABORY** St.-Estèphe 1982 • $24 • (08/31/92)
86 **CHÂTEAU DE MARBUZET** St.-Estèphe 1982 • $22 • (11/30/89)
86 **CHÂTEAU FONBADET** Pauillac 1982 • $16 • (08/01/85)
86 **CHÂTEAU HANTEILLAN** Haut-Médoc 1982 • $18 • (08/31/92)
86 **CHÂTEAU L'ENCLOS** Pomerol 1982 • $43 • (05/15/89)
86 **CHÂTEAU LA CARDONNE** Médoc 1982 • $20 • (08/31/92)
86 **CHÂTEAU LA CROIX** Pomerol 1982 • $27 • (05/01/89)
86 **CHÂTEAU LA GRAVE TRIGANT DE BOISSET** Pomerol 1982 • $43 • (08/31/92)
86 **CHÂTEAU LA TOUR DE BY** Médoc 1982 • $20 • (02/01/85) • BB
86 **CHÂTEAU MEYNEY** St.-Estèphe 1982 • $22 • (11/30/89)
86 **CHÂTEAU MOULINET** Pomerol 1982 • $10 • (04/01/85)
86 **CHÂTEAU ROUGET** Pomerol 1982 • $28 • (05/15/89)
86 **CHÂTEAU TRONQUOY-LALANDE** St.-Estèphe 1982 • $20 • (11/30/89)
86 **LES FORTS DE LATOUR** Pauillac 1982 • $55 • (10/15/90)
85 **CHÂTEAU BEAU-SEJOUR BECOT** St.-Emilion 1982 • $25 • (05/15/89)
85 **CHÂTEAU BRILLETTE** Moulis 1982 • $19 • (11/30/89)
85 **CHÂTEAU COUFRAN** Haut-Médoc 1982 • $24 • (08/31/92)
85 **CHÂTEAU DU GLANA** St.-Julien 1982 • $12 • (11/30/89)
85 **CHÂTEAU GRAND-BARRAIL-LAMARZELLE-FIGEAC** St.-Emilion 1982 • $25 • (05/15/89)
85 **CHÂTEAU JEAN FAURE** St.-Emilion 1982 • $14 • (11/16/85)
85 **CHÂTEAU LA GURGUE** Margaux 1982 • $24 • (11/30/89)
85 **CHÂTEAU LA POINTE** Pomerol 1982 • $36 • (05/15/89)
85 **CHÂTEAU LA ROSE FIGEAC** Pomerol 1982 • $25 • (05/15/89)
85 **CHÂTEAU LA TOUR DE BY** Médoc 1982 • $20 • (08/31/92)
85 **CHÂTEAU LARCIS-DUCASSE** St.-Emilion 1982 • $27 • (08/31/92)
85 **CHÂTEAU LIVERSAN** Haut-Médoc 1982 • $24 • (08/31/92)
85 **CHÂTEAU POUJEAUX** Moulis 1982 • $22 • (08/31/92)
85 **CHÂTEAU TAILLEFER** Pomerol 1982 • $23 • (05/15/89)
85 **CHÂTEAU TERTRE-ROTEBOEUF** St.-Emilion 1982 • $30 • (09/16/85)
85 **PAVILLON ROUGE DU CHÂTEAU MARGAUX** Margaux 1982 • $69 • (07/15/87)
85 **VIEUX CHÂTEAU CERTAN** Pomerol 1982 • $62 • (08/31/92)
84 **CHÂTEAU BOUSCAUT** Graves 1982 • $18 • (08/31/92)
84 **CHÂTEAU CURE-BON-LA-MADELAINE** St.-Emilion 1982 • $30 • (05/15/89)
84 **CHÂTEAU DE CRUZEAU** Graves 1982 • $7 • (12/16/85)
84 **CHÂTEAU HAUT-BAILLY** Pessac-Léognan 1982 • $42
84 **CHÂTEAU LA CABANNE** Pomerol 1982 • $23 • (08/31/92)
84 **CHÂTEAU LA POINTE** Pomerol 1982 • $31 • (08/31/92)
84 **CHÂTEAU LA VIEILLE CURE** Fronsac 1982 • $15 • (08/31/92)
84 **CHÂTEAU LAGRANGE** Pomerol 1982 • $30 • (05/15/89)
84 **CHÂTEAU LES ORMES DE PEZ** St.-Estèphe 1982 • $43 • (08/31/92)
84 **CHÂTEAU LESTAGE-SIMON** Haut-Médoc 1982 • $15 • (11/30/89)
84 **CHÂTEAU PAPE-CLEMENT** Graves 1982 • $33 • (02/01/85)
84 **CHÂTEAU RAUZAN-GASSIES** Margaux 1982 • $32 • (08/31/92)
84 **CHÂTEAU SOUTARD** St.-Emilion 1982 • $31 • (05/15/89)
84 **CHÂTEAU TOUR DU HAUT-MOULIN** Haut-Médoc 1982 • $16 • (11/30/89)
84 **CHÂTEAU TOUR-DU-ROC** Haut-Médoc 1982 • $12 • (11/30/89)
84 **CHÂTEAU VILLEGEORGE** Haut-Médoc 1982 • $18 • (08/31/92)
83 **CHÂTEAU BALESTARD LA TONNELLE** St.-Emilion 1982 • $25 • (05/15/89)
83 **CHÂTEAU BOURGNEUF** Pomerol 1982 • $25 • (05/15/89)
83 **CHÂTEAU CAPBERN-GASQUETON** St.-Estèphe 1982 • $22 • (11/30/89)
83 **CHÂTEAU CARBONNIEUX** Graves 1982 • $26 • (08/31/92)
83 **CHÂTEAU CLOS DES JACOBINS** St.-Emilion 1982 • $35 • (05/15/89)
83 **CHÂTEAU COUFRAN** Haut-Médoc 1982 • $24 • (11/30/89)
83 **CHÂTEAU CROQUE-MICHOTTE** St.-Emilion 1982 • $25 • (05/15/89)
83 **CHÂTEAU GOMBAUDE-GUILLOT** Pomerol 1982 • $28 • (05/15/89)
83 **CHÂTEAU HERMITAGE** Pomerol 1982 • $NA • (05/15/89)
83 **CHÂTEAU LAFLEUR DU ROY** Pomerol 1982 • $28 • (05/15/89)
83 **CHÂTEAU PATACHE D'AUX** Médoc 1982 • $20 • (05/01/85)
83 **CHÂTEAU PRIEURE-LICHINE** Margaux 1982 • $38 • (08/31/92)
83 **CHÂTEAU ST.-PIERRE** St.-Julien 1982 • $28 • (10/15/92)
83 **CHÂTEAU TOUR-HAUT-CAUSSAN** Médoc 1982 • $10 • (11/30/89)

83 **CHÂTEAU VERDIGNAN** Haut-Médoc 1982 • $16 • (02/16/85) • BB
83 **CHÂTEAU VIEUX SARPE** St.-Emilion 1982 • $NA • (05/15/89)
83 **CHÂTEAU VILLEMAURINE** St.-Emilion 1982 • $40 • (05/15/89)
83 **CLOS DU CLOCHER** Pomerol 1982 • $33 • (05/15/89)
83 **CLOS FOURTET** St.-Emilion 1982 • $20 • (08/31/92)
82 **CHÂTEAU BALESTARD LA TONNELLE** St.-Emilion 1982 • $24 • (08/31/92)
82 **CHÂTEAU CLOS DES JACOBINS** St.-Emilion 1982 • $35 • (08/31/92)
82 **CHÂTEAU CROIZET-BAGES** Pauillac 1982 • $26 • (08/31/92)
82 **CHÂTEAU DE FIEUZAL** Graves 1982 • $22 • (08/31/92)
82 **CHÂTEAU DE LAMARQUE** Haut-Médoc 1982 • $18 • (08/31/92)
82 **CHÂTEAU LA TOUR-DU-PIN-FIGEAC-BELIEVIER** St.-Emilion 1982 • $22 • (05/15/89)
82 **CHÂTEAU LARMANDE** St.-Emilion 1982 • $29 • (08/31/92)
82 **CHÂTEAU MALESCASSE** Haut-Médoc 1982 • $18 • (11/30/89)
82 **CHÂTEAU TAILHAS** Pomerol 1982 • $15 • (05/15/89)
82 **CHÂTEAU VIEUX-FERRAND** Pomerol 1982 • $NA • (05/15/89)
81 **CHÂTEAU CAP DE MOURLIN (JEAN)** St.-Emilion 1982 • $NA • (05/15/89)
81 **CHÂTEAU CISSAC** Haut-Médoc 1982 • $21 • (11/30/89)
81 **CHÂTEAU DE FIEUZAL** Graves 1982 • $22 • (05/01/85)
81 **CHÂTEAU DUCLUZEAU** Listrac 1982 • $16 • (08/31/92)
81 **CHÂTEAU GRANDES-MURAILLES** St.-Emilion 1982 • $NA • (05/15/89)
81 **CHÂTEAU HANTEILLAN** Haut-Médoc 1982 • $12 • (11/30/89)
81 **CHÂTEAU HAUT-BAGES-AVEROUS** Pauillac 1982 • $25 • (08/31/92)
81 **CHÂTEAU HAUT-COUTELIN** St.-Estèphe 1982 • $13 • (02/15/88)
81 **CHÂTEAU LA TOUR DU PIN** St.-Èmilion 1982 • $12 • (05/01/85)
81 **CHÂTEAU LAROSE-TRINTAUDON** Haut-Médoc 1982 • $11 • (02/16/86) • BB
81 **CHÂTEAU LASCOMBES** Margaux 1982 • $34 • (08/31/92)
81 **CHÂTEAU LYNCH-MOUSSAS** Pauillac 1982 • $22 • (08/31/92)
81 **CHÂTEAU SMITH-HAUT-LAFITTE** Graves 1982 • $18 • (08/31/92)
81 **CHÂTEAU TRIMOULET** St.-Emilion 1982 • $15 • (05/15/89)
80 **CHÂTEAU DU TERTRE** Margaux 1982 • $29 • (08/31/92)
80 **CHÂTEAU DUCLUZEAU** Listrac 1982 • $12 • (11/30/89)
80 **CHÂTEAU LA TOUR DE BY** Médoc 1982 • $20 • (11/30/89)
80 **CHÂTEAU LE CROCK** St.-Estèphe 1982 • $20 • (11/30/89)
80 **CHÂTEAU MOULIN ROUGE** Haut-Médoc 1982 • $13 • (11/30/89)
80 **CHÂTEAU VERDIGNAN** Haut-Médoc 1982 • $16 • (08/31/92)
80 **VIEUX CHÂTEAU GUIBEAU** St.-Emilion 1982 • $8 • (09/16/85)
79 **CHÂTEAU CARTEYRON** St.-Emilion 1982 • $7.25 • (09/01/85)
79 **CHÂTEAU DE FRANCE** Graves 1982 • $17 • (08/31/92)
79 **CHÂTEAU DE LAMARQUE** Haut-Médoc 1982 • $14 • (11/30/89)
79 **CHÂTEAU DUPLESSIS-FABRE** Moulis 1982 • $10 • (11/30/89)
79 **CHÂTEAU DURAND-LAPLAGNE** St.-Emilion 1982 • $7 • (09/16/85)
79 **CHÂTEAU FOURCAS-DUPRE** Listrac 1982 • $27 • (08/31/92)
79 **CHÂTEAU LA DOMINIQUE** St.-Emilion 1982 • $45 • (08/31/92)
79 **CHÂTEAU LAROSE-TRINTAUDON** Haut-Médoc 1982 • $16 • (11/30/89)
79 **CHÂTEAU PERENNE** Premières Côtes de Blaye 1982 • $5 • (11/16/85) • BB
79 **CHÂTEAU TOUR-DU-MIRAIL** Haut-Médoc 1982 • $9 • (11/30/89)
79 **DOMAINE DE CHEVALIER** Graves 1982 • $42 • (10/15/94)
79 **LES DOUELLES** Bordeaux 1982 • $3 • (10/01/85) • BB
78 **CHÂTEAU CHANGROLLE** Lalande-de-Pomerol 1982 • $6 • (12/16/84)
78 **CHÂTEAU CITRAN** Haut-Médoc 1982 • $12 • (04/01/85)
78 **CHÂTEAU CLINET** Pomerol 1982 • $38 • (05/15/89)
78 **CHÂTEAU FONROQUE** St.-Emilion 1982 • $6 • (05/15/89)
78 **CHÂTEAU LE COUVENT** St.-Emilion 1982 • $13 • (06/16/86)
78 **CHÂTEAU PIQUE-CAILLOU** Graves 1982 • $20 • (08/31/92)
78 **CLOS DE L'ORATOIRE** St.-Emilion 1982 • $NA • (05/15/89)
77 **CHÂTEAU FONPLEGADE** St.-Emilion 1982 • $25 • (05/15/89)
77 **CHÂTEAU LANDAY** Haut-Médoc 1982 • $6 • (02/16/85)
77 **PONTALLIER JOHNSON** Merlot Bordeaux 1982 • $8 • (10/15/87)
76 **CHÂTEAU LALANDE-BORIE** St.-Julien 1982 • $17 • (10/15/86)
76 **CHÂTEAU LE BOSCQ** Médoc 1982 • $6 • (10/01/85) • BB
76 **CHÂTEAU VERDIGNAN** Haut-Médoc 1982 • $16 • (11/30/89)
75 **CHÂTEAU SEGUR** Haut-Médoc 1982 • $6 • (04/16/85)
75 **CHÂTEAU VILLADIERE** St.-Emilion 1982 • $8 • (09/01/85)
74 **CHÂTEAU LA TERRASSE** Bordeaux Supérieur 1982 • $4 • (11/16/85)
74 **CHÂTEAU LOUDENNE** Médoc 1982 • $12 • (11/30/89)
74 **G. MICHELOT** Bordeaux Supérieur 1982 • $5 • (01/01/86) • BB
73 **CHÂTEAU BONNET** Bordeaux 1982 • $4 • (04/16/85)
73 **CHÂTEAU DE LUSSAC** Lussac-St.-Emilion 1982 • $6 • (05/01/84)
73 **CHÂTEAU ST.-SULPICE** Bordeaux 1982 • $6 • (05/15/87)
72 **CHÂTEAU BELLERIVE** Bordeaux Supérieur 1982 • $8 • (12/16/85)
71 **CHÂTEAU ARNAULD** Haut-Médoc 1982 • $17 • (11/30/89)
71 **CHÂTEAU DE LUCAT** Bordeaux Supérieur 1982 • $4 • (10/01/85)
70 **CHÂTEAU DE LA GRAVE** Côtes de Bourg 1982 • $5.25 • (02/16/85)
68 **CHÂTEAU CLARKE** Listrac 1982 • $13 • (10/15/86)
68 **CHÂTEAU RAMAGE LA BATISSE** Haut-Médoc 1982 • $11 • (11/30/89)
64 **CHÂTEAU LE MAYNE** Puisseguin-St.-Emilion 1982 • $7 • (12/01/85)

Domaine Leroy in Auxey-Duresses.

Red Burgundy

The five most recent outstanding vintages of red Burgundy—1993, 1990, 1989, 1988 and 1985—are listed in this section, with ratings and prices. The wines are organized by vintage and then in descending order of score, to make it easy to identify the best wines of each year. For ratings of wines from other vintages, see the main listings.

The 1993 vintage came to market beginning in late 1995, and it's of exceptional quality, especially if you look for the most reputable domaines. Some of the big negociant firms didn't fare as well. 1993 contrasts with 1990, another outstanding year and a vintage in which you can hardly go wrong when buying. We skipped over 1991 and 1992 in this section; neither year was a washout, and 1991 in particular produced some very good wines, but both are significantly weaker overall than the years covered here.

Red Burgundy is generally made in small quantities, and many of the best wines are bought up quickly on release. But diligent shoppers can find them on sale at retail, at auction and on restaurant wine lists.

The date of the issue of *Wine Spectator* in which the rating was first published is in parentheses. In general, wines for which no issue date appears were tasted between April 15, 1994 and June 15, 1996.

1993 RED BURGUNDY | VINTAGE RATING: 91

98 **DOMINIQUE LAURENT** Mazis-Chambertin 1993 • $117 • (05/15/96)
97 **BERTRAND AMBROISE** Corton Le Rognet 1993 • $75 • (11/15/95)
97 **DOMAINE DANIEL RION** Clos Vougeot 1993 • $90
97 **LEROY** Musigny 1993 • $500
96 **BERTRAND AMBROISE** Clos Vougeot 1993 • $90 • (11/15/95)
96 **COMTE DE VOGUE** Musigny Cuvée Vieilles Vignes 1993 • $140
96 **DOMINIQUE LAURENT** Ruchottes-Chambertin 1993 • $117 • (05/15/96)
96 **JEAN GRIVOT** Richebourg 1993 • $128 • (05/15/96)
96 **LEROY** Volnay Santenots 1993 • $185
96 **LEROY** Clos de Vougeot 1993 • $250
96 **LEROY** Richebourg 1993 • $500
96 **SERAFIN PERE & FILS** Charmes-Chambertin 1993 • $90
95 **DOMAINE ANNE & FRANCOIS GROS** Clos Vougeot Le Grand Maupertuis 1993 • $55
95 **DOMINIQUE LAURENT** Gevrey-Chambertin Vieilles Vignes 1993 • $NA • (05/15/96)
95 **EMMANUEL ROUGET** Echézeaux 1993 • $80 • (05/15/96)
95 **EMMANUEL ROUGET** Vosne-Romanée Cros Parantoux 1993 • $72 • (05/15/96)
95 **JAYER-GILLES** Echézeaux Du Dessus 1993 • $135
95 **LEROY** Chambertin 1993 • $500
95 **LEROY** Romanée-St.-Vivant 1993 • $500
95 **LEROY** Nuits-St.-Georges Les Vigne Rondes 1993 • $185
94 **COMTE DE VOGUE** Bonnes Mares 1993 • $115
94 **COMTE DE VOGUE** Chambolle-Musigny Amoureuses 1993 • $125
94 **DENIS MORTET** Chambertin 1993 • $115
94 **DENIS MORTET** Clos Vougeot 1993 • $80
94 **DOMAINE DANIEL RION** Nuits-St.-Georges Aux Vignerondes 1993 • $50
94 **DOMAINE GROS FRERE & SOEUR** Richebourg 1993 • $110
94 **DOMAINE JACQUES PRIEUR** Musigny EP 1993 • $63
94 **DOMAINE JEAN-JACQUES CONFURON** Chambolle-Musigny Premier Cru EP 1993 • $60
94 **DOMAINE JEAN-JACQUES CONFURON** Vosne-Romanée Les Beaux Monts 1993 • $63
94 **DOMAINE MEO-CAMUZET** Richebourg 1993 • $175
94 **DOMAINE DE LA ROMANÉE-CONTI** La Tâche 1993 • $270 • (05/15/96)
94 **DOMAINE DE LA ROMANÉE-CONTI** Romanée-Conti 1993 • $850 • (05/15/96)
94 **DOMINIQUE LAURENT** Clos Vougeot 1993 • $NA • (05/15/96)
94 **J. CONFURON-COTETIDOT** Gevrey-Chambertin 1993 • $NA • (05/15/96)
94 **JEAN GRIVOT** Vosne-Romanée Les Beaux Monts 1993 • $32 • (05/15/96)
94 **JEAN GROS** Richebourg 1993 • $160
94 **LEROY** Clos de la Roche 1993 • $325
94 **LEROY** Vosne-Romanée Les Beaux Monts 1993 • $185
94 **PHILIPPE CHARLOPIN-PARIZOT** Charmes-Chambertin 1993 • $94 • (05/15/96)

■ ■ ■ ■

Red Burgundy

93 **DOMAINE DANIEL RION** Vosne-Romanée Les Chaumes 1993 • $50
93 **DOMAINE DANIEL RION** Nuits-St.-Georges Les Grandes Vignes 1993 • $32
93 **DOMAINE GROS FRERE & SOEUR** Grands Echézeaux 1993 • $69
93 **DOMAINE MEO-CAMUZET** Nuits-St.-Georges Aux Murgers 1993 • $60
93 **DOMAINE MEO-CAMUZET** Vosne-Romanée Les Chaumes 1993 • $70
93 **DOMAINE MEO-CAMUZET** Vosne-Romanée Aux Brûlées 1993 • $75
93 **DOMAINE MICHEL LAFARGE** Volnay Clos du Château des Ducs 1993 • $65
93 **DOMAINE MONTHELIE-DOUHAIRET** Volnay Champans 1993 • $44
93 **DOMAINE DES COMTES LAFON** Volnay-Santenots Les Santenots du Milieu 1993 • $NA • (05/15/96)
93 **DOMINIQUE LAURENT** Pommard Les Epenots 1993 • $85 • (05/15/96)
93 **DOMINIQUE LAURENT** Pommard Vieilles Vignes 1993 • $48 • (05/15/96)
93 **JAYER-GILLES** Nuits-St.-Georges Les Haut Poirets 1993 • $70
93 **JEAN-MARC BOILLOT** Volnay 1993 • $30 • (11/15/95)
93 **JOSEPH DROUHIN** Corton Bressandes 1993 • $70
93 **LECHENEAUT** Chambolle-Musigny Premier Cru 1993 • $68
93 **LECHENEAUT** Nuits-St.-Georges Les Damodes # 1993 • $68
93 **LEROY** Vosne-Romanée Les Brûlées 1993 • $185
93 **MONGEARD-MUGNERET** Clos de Vougeot 1993 • $71
93 **MONGEARD-MUGNERET** Clos de Vougeot Red 1993 • $71
93 **MAURICE ECARD** Savigny-lès-Beaune Aux Serpentières 1993 • $94 • (05/15/96)
93 **OLIVIER LEFLAIVE** Volnay Frémiets 1993 • $42
93 **ROBERT ARNOUX** Romanée-St.-Vivant 1993 • $NA • (11/15/95)
92 **CLAUDE DUGAT** Gevrey-Chambertin Lavaux St.-Jacques EP 1993 • $65
92 **DOMAINE DANIEL RION** Chambolle-Musigny Les Charmes 1993 • $63
92 **DOMAINE DANIEL RION** Vosne-Romanée Les Beaux Monts 1993 • $50
92 **DOMAINE FOREY** Vosne-Romanée Les Gaudichots LD 1993 • $45
92 **DOMAINE JACQUES PRIEUR** Clos Vougeot EP Red 1993 • $54
92 **DOMAINE ROSSIGNOL-TRAPET** Latricières-Chambertin 1993 • $64
92 **DOMAINE DE L'ARLOT** Nuits-St.-Georges Clos des Forêts St.-Georges 1993 • $40 • (05/15/96)
92 **DOMAINE DE LA ROMANÉE-CONTI** Romanée St.-Vivant 1993 • $135 • (05/15/96)
92 **JAYER-GILLES** Nuits-St.-Georges Les Damodes 1993 • $85
92 **JEAN GRIVOT** Clos de Vougeot 1993 • $45 • (05/15/96) • CS
92 **JEAN GRIVOT** Echézeaux 1993 • $45 • (05/15/96)
92 **JEAN-MARC BOILLOT** Volnay Pitures 1993 • $42 • (11/15/95)
92 **JACQUES-FREDERIC MUGNIER** Bonnes Mares 1993 • $90 • (05/15/96)
92 **JEAN & JEAN-LOUIS TRAPET** Chambertin 1993 • $NA • (05/15/96)
92 **LEROY** Pommard Les Vignots 1993 • $94
92 **LEROY** Corton Renardes 1993 • $185
92 **LOUIS JADOT** Clos de Vougeot 1993 • $NA
92 **LOUIS JADOT** Corton Pougets 1993 • $46
92 **MARQUIS D'ANGERVILLE** Volnay Premier Cru 1993 • $20 • (05/15/96)
92 **MONGEARD-MUGNERET** Echézeaux Vieille Vigne 1993 • $60
91 **ARMAND GIRARDIN** Pommard Charmots 1993 • $60
91 **CLAUDE DUGAT** Gevrey-Chambertin Premier Cru 1993 • $50
91 **DAMOY** Chambertin Red 1993 • $69
91 **DAMOY** Chambertin Clos de Bèze Red 1993 • $55
91 **DAMOY** Chapelle-Chambertin 1993 • $57
91 **DENIS MORTET** Chambolle-Musigny Les Beaux Bruns 1993 • $43
91 **DOMAINE ANNE & FRANCOIS GROS** Richebourg 1993 • $100
91 **DOMAINE DUJAC** Clos St.-Denis 1993 • $79 • (05/15/96)
91 **DOMAINE FOREY** Echézeaux 1993 • $45
91 **DOMAINE GROS FRERE & SOEUR** Vosne-Romanée 1993 • $35
91 **DOMAINE JACQUES PRIEUR** Volnay-Santenots 1993 • $34
91 **DOMAINE LALEURE-PIOT** Corton Bressandes 1993 • $51
91 **DOMAINE LUCIEN BOILLOT** Volnay Les Caillerets 1993 • $38 • (11/15/95)
91 **DOMAINE LUCIEN BOILLOT** Pommard Les Fremiers 1993 • $38 • (11/15/95)
91 **EMMANUEL ROUGET** Vosne-Romanée Les Beaux Monts 1993 • $55 • (05/15/96)
91 **FAIVELEY** Echézeaux 1993 • $56 • (05/15/96)
91 **FAIVELEY** Chambertin Clos de Bèze 1993 • $113 • (05/15/96)
91 **JEAN GROS** Vosne-Romanée Clos des Réas 1993 • $60
91 **JOSEPH DROUHIN** Chambertin 1993 • $119
91 **LECHENEAUT** Clos de la Roche 1993 • $90
91 **LEROY** Latricières-Chambertin 1993 • $325
91 **LEROY** Nuits-St.-Georges Aux Boudots 1993 • $185
91 **MICHEL GROS** Chambolle-Musigny 1993 • $35
91 **MONGEARD-MUGNERET** Echézeaux 1993 • $50
91 **ROBERT ARNOUX** Clos de Vougeot 1993 • $80 • (11/15/95)
91 **SERAFIN PERE & FILS** Gevrey-Chambertin Les Cazetiers 1993 • $70
91 **SERAFIN PERE & FILS** Gevrey-Chambertin Le Fonteny 1993 • $65
91 **TOLLOT-BEAUT** Corton 1993 • $57
90 **ARMAND GIRARDIN** Pommard Epenots 1993 • $60
90 **BERTRAND AMBROISE** Nuits-St.-Georges Les Vaucrains 1993 • $65 • (11/15/95)
90 **BOUCHARD PERE & FILS** La Romanée Château de Vosne-Romanée 1993 • $120 • (11/15/95)
90 **BERTAGNA** Clos St.-Denis 1993 • $71 • (05/15/96)
90 **CLAUDE DUGAT** Charmes-Chambertin EP 1993 • $90
90 **CLAUDE DUGAT** Gevrey-Chambertin EP 1993 • $40
90 **DENIS MORTET** Gevrey-Chambertin 1993 • $42
90 **DENIS MORTET** Gevrey-Chambertin En Champs Vieille Vigne 1993 • $50
90 **DENIS MORTET** Gevrey-Chambertin En Motrot 1993 • $46
90 **DENIS MORTET** Gevrey-Chambertin Lavaux-St.-Jacques 1993 • $58
90 **DENIS MORTET** Gevrey-Chambertin Les Champeaux 1993 • $58
90 **DOMAINE ALETH GIRARDIN** Beaune Clos des Mouches 1993 • $48
90 **DOMAINE COSTE-CAUMARTIN** Pommard Clos des Boucherottes 1993 • $42
90 **DOMAINE DANIEL RION** Vosne-Romanée 1993 • $32
90 **DOMAINE DE COURCEL** Pommard Les Rugiens 1993 • $42
90 **DOMAINE JACQUES PRIEUR** Volnay-Santenots Clos des Santenots 1993 • $37

90 **DOMAINE JEAN-JACQUES CONFURON** Clos Vougeot EP 1993 • $85
90 **DOMAINE JEAN-JACQUES CONFURON** Nuits-St.-Georges Les Fleurières LD 1993 • $45
90 **DOMAINE MEO-CAMUZET** Nuits-St.-Georges Aux Boudots 1993 • $60
90 **DOMAINE PARENT** Corton Les Renardes 1993 • $62
90 **DOMAINE ROSSIGNOL-TRAPET** Beaune Les Teurons 1993 • $33
90 **DOMAINE ROSSIGNOL-TRAPET** Chambertin 1993 • $77
90 **DOMAINE DE LA ROMANÉE-CONTI** Echézeaux 1993 • $95 • (05/15/96)
90 **DOMAINE DE LA ROMANÉE-CONTI** Richebourg 1993 • $190 • (05/15/96)
90 **EMMANUEL ROUGET** Nuits-St.-Georges 1993 • $NA • (05/15/96)
90 **FAIVELEY** Nuits-St.-Georges Porrets St.-Georges 1993 • $43 • (05/15/96)
90 **FONTAINE-GAGNARD** Volnay Clos des Chânes 1993 • $43
90 **FREDERIC ESMONIN** Ruchottes-Chambertin 1993 • $65
90 **GEANTET-PANSIOT** Charmes-Chambertin 1993 • $60 • (05/15/96)
90 **GEANTET-PANSIOT** Gevrey-Chambertin Poissenot 1993 • $45 • (05/15/96)
90 **JAYER-GILLES** Bourgogne Hautes Côtes de Beaune 1993 • $22
90 **JAYER-GILLES** Côte de Nuits-Villages 1993 • $36
90 **JEAN GRIVOT** Nuits-St.-Georges Les Boudots 1993 • $32 • (05/15/96)
90 **JEAN-MARC BOILLOT** Pommard Les Jarollières 1993 • $50 • (11/15/95)
90 **JEAN-MARC PAVELOT** Savigny-lès-Beaune Aux Guettes 1993 • $28
90 **JEAN-MARC PAVELOT** Savigny-lès-Beaune La Dominode 1993 • $28
90 **JACQUES-FREDERIC MUGNIER** Chambolle-Musigny Les Fuées 1993 • $69 • (05/15/96)
90 **LECHENEAUT** Nuits-St.-Georges Premier Cru 1993 • $60
90 **LEROY** Chambolle-Musigny Les Charmes 1993 • $200
90 **LOUIS JADOT** Chambertin Clos de Bèze 1993 • $87
90 **MARQUIS D'ANGERVILLE** Volnay En Champans 1993 • $29 • (05/15/96)
90 **MICHELE & PATRICE RION** Chambolle-Musigny Les Cras 1993 • $38
90 **MAUME** Gevrey-Chambertin 1993 • $NA • (05/15/96)
90 **PRINCE FLORENT DE MERODE** Ladoix Les Chaillots 1993 • $17
90 **PHILIPPE CHARLOPIN-PARIZOT** Clos St.-Denis 1993 • $94 • (05/15/96)
90 **PHILIPPE ROSSIGNOL** Gevrey-Chambertin Les Corbeaux Cuvée Vieilles Vignes 1993 • $NA • (05/15/96)
90 **TOLLOT-BEAUT** Savigny-lès-Beaune Lavières 1993 • $25
90 **TOLLOT-BEAUT** Corton Bressandes 1993 • $57
89 **DAMOY** Gevrey-Chambertin Clos Tamisot LD 1993 • $30
89 **DENIS MORTET** Marsannay Les Longeroies Red 1993 • $30
89 **DOMAINE JEAN-JACQUES CONFURON** Romanée-St.-Vivant 1993 • $150
89 **DOMAINE JEAN-JACQUES CONFURON** Nuits-St.-Georges Les Chaboeufs 1er 1993 • $60
89 **DOMAINE LALEURE-PIOT** Corton Le Rognet 1993 • $47
89 **DOMAINE MICHEL ESMONIN** Gevrey-Chambertin Clos St.-Jacques 1993 • $64
89 **DROUHIN-LAROZE** Clos de Vougeot 1993 • $62
89 **DOMAINE DE L'ARLOT** Nuits-St.-Georges Clos de L'Arlot 1993 • $34 • (05/15/96)
89 **DOMAINE DES LAMBRAYS** Clos des Lambrays 1993 • $NA
89 **DOMINIQUE LAURENT** Nuits-St.-Georges Les Vaucrains 1993 • $NA
89 **EDMOND CORNU** Ladoix Les Carrières 1993 • $27
89 **EMMANUEL ROUGET** Savigny-lès-Beaune 1993 • $NA
89 **FONTAINE-GAGNARD** Chassagne-Montrachet Morgeot 1993 • $27
89 **HAEGELEN-JAYER** Clos de Vougeot 1993 • $NA
89 **J. CONFURON-COTETIDOT** Clos de Vougeot 1993 • $NA
89 **J. CONFURON-COTETIDOT** Nuits-St.-Georges Premier Cru 1993 • $NA
89 **J. CONFURON-COTETIDOT** Nuits-St.-Georges 1993 • $NA
89 **JEAN GROS** Vosne-Romanée 1993 • $35
89 **JEAN-MARC BOILLOT** Volnay Carelle Sous La Chapelle 1993 • $42 • (11/15/95)
89 **JEAN-MARC PAVELOT** Savigny-lès-Beaune Aux Gravains 1993 • $30
89 **JACQUES PRIEUR** Chambertin 1993 • $NA
89 **LA POUSSE D'OR** Volnay Caillerets-Clos des 60 Ouvrées 1993 • $60
89 **LABOURE-ROI** Echézeaux 1993 • $54
89 **LEONARD DE SAINT-AUBIN** Volnay 1993 • $26 • (05/15/96)
89 **LEROY** Savigny-lès-Beaune Les Narbantons 1993 • $70
89 **LEROY** Gevrey-Chambertin Les Combottes 1993 • $220
89 **LEROY** Nuits-St.-Georges 1993 • $110
89 **LOUIS JADOT** Corton Pougets 1993 • $NA
89 **LOUIS JADOT** Gevrey-Chambertin Estournelles St.-Jacques 1993 • $48
89 **LOUIS LATOUR** Romanée St.-Vivant Les Quatre Journaux 1993 • $NA
89 **MOMMESSIN** Beaune Les Cent Vignes 1993 • $30
89 **MOMMESSIN** Bonnes Mares 1993 • $80
89 **PHILIPPE ROSSIGNOL** Gevrey-Chambertin Les Corbeaux 1993 • $NA
89 **ROBERT ARNOUX** Echézeaux 1993 • $80 • (11/15/95)
89 **TOLLOT-BEAUT** Aloxe-Corton Les Vercots 1993 • $37
88 Frantin Grands Echézeaux 1993 • $60 • (11/15/95)
88 **ANTONIN RODET** Nuits-St.-Georges Roncières 1993 • $45
88 **BERTRAND AMBROISE** Vosne-Romanée Aux Damaudes 1993 • $45 • (11/15/95)
88 **BICHOT** Grands Echézeaux Domaine du Clos Frantin 1993 • $NA
88 **BONNEAU DU MARTRAY** Corton 1993 • $45 • (11/15/95)
88 **BOUCHARD PERE & FILS** Chambolle-Musigny Domaines du Château de Beaune 1993 • $36 • (11/15/95)
88 **BOUCHARD PERE & FILS** Vosne-Romanée Aux Reignots 1993 • $51
88 **BERTAGNA** Clos de Vougeot 1993 • $90 • (05/15/96)
88 **CHATEAU DE POMMARD** Pommard 1993 • $36
88 **CHOPIN-GROFFIER** Clos Vougeot 1993 • $85
88 **COMTE DE VOGUE** Chambolle-Musigny 1993 • $60
88 **COSTE-CAUMARTIN** Pommard Les Fremiers 1993 • $NA • (05/15/96)
88 **DENIS MORTET** Gevrey-Chambertin Au Vellé 1993 • $46
88 **DENIS MORTET** Bourgogne Les Charmes au Chatelain 1993 • $15
88 **DOMAINE ANNE & FRANCOIS GROS** Chambolle-Musigny La Combe d'Orveau 1993 • $29
88 **DOMAINE ANNE & FRANCOIS GROS** Vosne-Romanée 1993 • $40
88 **DOMAINE DANIEL RION** Nuits-St.-Georges Les Hauts Pruliers 1993 • $50
88 **DOMAINE DANIEL RION** Nuits-St.-Georges Clos des Argillières 1993 • $50
88 **DOMAINE DE COURCEL** Pommard Grand Clos des Epenots 1993 • $33

88 **DOMAINE DUJAC** Morey-St.-Denis 1993 • $37 • (05/15/96)
88 **DOMAINE DUJAC** Gevrey-Chambertin Aux Combottes 1993 • $65 • (05/15/96)
88 **DOMAINE FOREY** Vosne-Romanée 1993 • $26
88 **DOMAINE JACQUES PRIEUR** Volnay En Champans 1993 • $36
88 **DOMAINE JACQUES PRIEUR** Beaune Clos de la Feguine EP 1993 • $30
88 **DOMAINE JACQUES PRIEUR** Corton Bressandes EP 1993 • $70
88 **DOMAINE LEJEUNE** Pommard Les Argillières 1993 • $36
88 **DOMAINE LUCIEN BOILLOT** Gevrey-Chambertin Les Cherbaudes 1er 1993 • $40 • (11/15/95)
88 **DOMAINE MEO-CAMUZET** Clos de Vougeot 1993 • $55
88 **DOMAINE ROSSIGNOL-TRAPET** Gevrey-Chambertin Petite Chapelle 1993 • $43
88 **DOMAINE DE L'ARLOT** Nuits-St.-Georges 1993 • $22 • (05/15/96)
88 **DOMAINE DE LA ROMANÉE-CONTI** Grands Echézeaux 1993 • $135
88 **DOMAINE DES COMTES LAFON** Volnay Clos des Chànes 1993 • $NA
88 **FONTAINE-GAGNARD** Bourgogne 1993 • $14
88 **GEORGES MUGNERET** Nuits-St.-Georges Les Chaignots 1993 • $NA
88 **J. CONFURON-COTETIDOT** Chambolle-Musigny 1993 • $NA
88 **JEAN GRIVOT** Vosne-Romanée 1993 • $22 • (05/15/96)
88 **JOSEPH DROUHIN** Volnay Chevret 1993 • $38
88 **JOSEPH DROUHIN** Bonnes Mares 1993 • $100
88 **JOSEPH DROUHIN** Musigny 1993 • $130
88 **JACQUES-FREDERIC MUGNIER** Chambolle-Musigny 1993 • $39 • (05/15/96)
88 **LA POUSSE D'OR** Volnay Clos de la Bousse d'Or 1993 • $70
88 **LECHENEAUT** Chambolle-Musigny 1993 • $48
88 **LEROY** Chambolle-Musigny Les Fremières 1993 • $125
88 **LOUIS JADOT** Gevrey-Chambertin Estournelles St.-Jacques 1993 • $NA
88 **LOUIS JADOT** Romanée-St.-Vivant 1993 • $135
88 **LOUIS JADOT** Vosne-Romanée Les Suchots 1993 • $46
88 **LOUIS JADOT** Beaune Clos des Ursules 1993 • $35 • (11/15/95)
88 **LOUIS LATOUR** Corton Corton Grancey 1993 • $43
88 **MICHELE & PATRICE RION** Bourgogne Les Bons Bâtons 1993 • $15
88 **MOMMESSIN** Chambolle-Musigny Premier Cru 1993 • $45
88 **MONGEARD-MUGNERET** Richebourg 1993 • $110
88 **MICHEL LAFARGE** Volnay Clos des Chênes 1993 • $94
88 **P. DUBREUIL-FONTAINE PÈRE & FILS** Corton Les Perrières 1993 • $NA
88 **P. DUBREUIL-FONTAINE PÈRE & FILS** Corton Bressandes 1993 • $NA • (05/15/96)
88 **PRINCE FLORENT DE MERODE** Pommard Clos de la Platière 1993 • $31
88 **PRINCE FLORENT DE MERODE** Corton Clos du Roi 1993 • $44
88 **PHILIPPE CHARLOPIN-PARIZOT** Gevrey-Chambertin Cuvée Vieilles Vignes 1993 • $NA
88 **ROBERT ARNOUX** Vosne-Romanée Les Chaumes 1993 • $55 • (11/15/95)
88 **ROBERT JAYER-GILLES** Bourgogne Hautes-Côtes de Nuits 1993 • $22
88 **TOLLOT-BEAUT** Beaune Clos du Roi 1993 • $35
88 **THIERRY MORTET** Gevrey-Chambertin Clos Prieur 1993 • $NA • (05/15/96)
87 **BICHOT** Vosne-Romanée Les Malconsorts Domaine du Clos Frantin 1993 • $NA • (11/15/95)
87 **BOUCHARD PERE & FILS** Chassagne-Montrachet Red 1993 • $25 • (11/15/95)
87 **DOMAINE A.-F. GROS** Vosne-Romanée Maizières 1993 • $50
87 **DOMAINE A.-F. GROS** Vosne-Romanée Aux Réas 1993 • $44
87 **DOMAINE DANIEL RION** Côte de Nuits-Villages 1993 • $17
87 **DOMAINE LALEURE-PIOT** Chorey-lès-Beaune Les Champs Longs 1993 • $17
87 **DOMAINE LUCIEN BOILLOT** Volnay Les Brouillards 1993 • $37 • (11/15/95)
87 **DOMAINE LUCIEN BOILLOT** Gevrey-Chambertin Les Corbeaux 1993 • $40 • (11/15/95)
87 **DOMAINE PARENT** Pommard Les Epenots 1993 • $57
87 **DOMAINE PIERRE LABET** Beaune Clos des Monsnières 1993 • $20
87 **DOMAINE ROSSIGNOL-TRAPET** Chapelle-Chambertin 1993 • $77
87 **DOMAINE ROSSIGNOL-TRAPET** Gevrey-Chambertin 1993 • $28
87 **DOMAINE THIERRY MORTET** Chambolle-Musigny Les Beaux Bruns 1993 • $58 • (05/15/96)
87 **EDMOND CORNU** Corton Bressandes 1993 • $57
87 **FONTAINE-GAGNARD** Chassagne-Montrachet 1993 • $23
87 **JEAN-MARC PAVELOT** Savigny-lès-Beaune Les Narbantons 1993 • $29
87 **JOSEPH DROUHIN** Chambolle-Musigny Premier Cru 1993 • $45
87 **JOSEPH DROUHIN** Morey-St.-Denis Clos Sorbè 1993 • $43
87 **JEAN & JEAN-LOUIS TRAPET** Chapelle-Chambertin 1993 • $NA
87 **LA POUSSE D'OR** Santenay Clos de Tavannes 1993 • $40
87 **LABOURE-ROI** Gevrey-Chambertin 1993 • $22
87 **LOUIS JADOT** Beaune Clos de Couchereaux 1993 • $25
87 **LOUIS JADOT** Fixin 1993 • $18
87 **LEJEUNE** Pommard Les Poutures 1993 • $NA
87 **MOMMESSIN** Savigny-lès-Beaune 1993 • $21
87 **MOMMESSIN** Nuits-St.-Georges Aux Chaignots 1993 • $57
87 **MOMMESSIN** Vosne-Romanée Premier Cru 1993 • $46
87 **MONGEARD-MUGNERET** Grands Echézeaux 1993 • $100
87 **MONGEARD-MUGNERET** Savigny-lès-Beaune 1993 • $22 • (11/15/95)
87 **MICHEL GROS** Vosne-Romanée Clos de la Fontaine 1993 • $NA
87 **P. DUBREUIL-FONTAINE PÈRE & FILS** Corton Clos du Roi 1993 • $NA
87 **PRINCE FLORENT DE MERODE** Corton Maréchaudes 1993 • $32
87 **ROBERT ARNOUX** Vosne-Romanée Les Suchots 1993 • $80 • (11/15/95)
87 **TOLLOT-BEAUT** Chorey-Côte-de-Beaune 1993 • $18
87 **TOLLOT-BEAUT** Beaune Grèves 1993 • $35
86 **ALAIN GRAS** Auxey-Duresses Rouge 1993 • $20
86 **ANTONIN RODET** Vosne-Romanée 1993 • $30
86 **BERTRAND AMBROISE** Nuits-St.-Georges 1993 • $40 • (11/15/95)
86 **BOUCHARD PERE & FILS** Beaune Teurons Domaines du Château de Beaune 1993 • $28 • (11/15/95)
86 **BOUCHARD PERE & FILS** Gevrey-Chambertin 1993 • $29 • (11/15/95)
86 **BERTAGNA** Vougeot Clos de la Perrière 1993 • $58 • (05/15/96)
86 **DOMAINE BRUNO CLAIR** Marsannay Les Grasses Têtes 1993 • $25 • (05/15/96)
86 **DOMAINE BRUNO CLAIR** Gevrey-Chambertin 1993 • $47 • (05/15/96)

86 **DOMAINE DUJAC** Chambolle-Musigny 1993 • $37 • (05/15/96)
86 **DOMAINE LALEURE-PIOT** Savigny-lès-Beaune Les Vergelesses 1993 • $25
86 **DOMAINE MICHEL VOARICK** Corton Renardes 1993 • $60
86 **DOMAINE PARENT** Pommard Les Chaponnières 1993 • $50
86 **DOMAINE CHOFFLET-VALDENAIRE** Givry 1993 • $20 • (05/15/96)
86 **DOMINIQUE LAURENT** Vosne-Romanée 1993 • $NA
86 **DOMINIQUE LAURENT** Beaune Premier Cru Vieilles Vignes 1993 • $NA
86 **DOMINIQUE LAURENT** Volnay 1993 • $NA
86 **F. CHAUVENET** Charmes-Chambertin 1993 • $78
86 **FREDERIC ESMONIN** Gevrey-Chambertin Clos Prieur 1993 • $30
86 **JAFFELIN** Volnay 1993 • $24
86 **JEAN-MARC BOILLOT** Bourgogne 1993 • $17 • (11/15/95)
86 **JOSEPH DROUHIN** Beaune Clos des Mouches 1993 • $50
86 **JEAN & JEAN-LOUIS TRAPET** Latricières-Chambertin 1993 • $NA
86 **JEAN-MARC MILLOT** Echézeaux 1993 • $NA
86 **L'HERITIER-GUYOT** Corton Les Renardes 1993 • $60
86 **LABOURE-ROI** Pommard Les Bertins 1993 • $29
86 **LABOURE-ROI** Charmes-Chambertin 1993 • $59
86 **LOUIS JADOT** Beaune Clos des Ursules 1993 • $NA
86 **LEJEUNE** Pommard Les Rugiens 1993 • $NA
86 **MAUME** Gevrey-Chambertin Lavaut St.-Jacques 1993 • $NA
86 **OLIVIER LEFLAIVE** Pommard Rugiens 1993 • $48
86 **PRINCE FLORENT DE MERODE** Corton Bressandes 1993 • $37
86 **SIMON BIZE & FILS** Savigny-lès-Beaune Les Marconnets 1993 • $25 • (05/15/96)
86 **TOLLOT-BEAUT** Aloxe-Corton 1993 • $29
85 **BICHOT** Echézeaux 1993 • $NA • (11/15/95)
85 **BOUCHARD PERE & FILS** Beaune Clos de la Mousse Domaines du Château de Beaune 1993 • $28 • (11/15/95)
85 **COMTE ARMAND** Pommard Clos des Epeneaux 1993 • $52
85 **DOMAINE BRUNO CLAIR** Marsannay Les Vaudenelles 1993 • $22 • (05/15/96)
85 **DOMAINE FOREY** Nuits-St.-Georges Les Perrières 1993 • $33
85 **DOMAINE LALEURE-PIOT** Pernand-Vergelesses Ile des Vergelesses 1993 • $33
85 **DOMAINE LEJEUNE** Pommard Les Poutures 1993 • $31
85 **DOMAINE LUCIEN BOILLOT** Nuits-St.-Georges Les Pruliers 1993 • $40 • (11/15/95)
85 **DOMAINE MICHEL VOARICK** Pernand-Vergelesses 1993 • $20
85 **DOMAINE MICHEL VOARICK** Corton Clos du Roi 1993 • $60
85 **DOMAINE PARENT** Beaune Les Epenotes 1993 • $57
85 **DOMAINE DES COMTES LAFON** Volnay En Champans 1993 • $NA
85 **EDMOND CORNU** Savigny-lès-Beaune 1993 • $22
85 **JEAN-MARC BOILLOT** Beaune Les Montrevenots 1993 • $30 • (11/15/95)
85 **JEAN-MARC PAVELOT** Savigny-lès-Beaune 1993 • $22
85 **JOSEPH DROUHIN** Pommard Epenots 1993 • $35
85 **JOSEPH DROUHIN** Charmes-Chambertin 1993 • $84
85 **JACQUES-FRÉDÉRIC MUGNIER** Chambolle-Musigny Les Amoureuses 1993 • $100
85 **JEAN & JEAN-LOUIS TRAPET** Gevrey-Chambertin 1993 • $NA
85 **JEAN GRIVOT** Vosne-Romanée Les Suchots 1993 • $NA
85 **LA POUSSE D'OR** Pommard Les Jarolières 1993 • $65
85 **LA POUSSE D'OR** Volnay Les Caillerets 1993 • $53
85 **LEONARD DE SAINT-AUBIN** Pommard 1993 • $27 • (05/15/96)
85 **LOUIS JADOT** Santenay Clos de Malte 1993 • $16
85 **MOMMESSIN** Beaune 1993 • $23
85 **MOMMESSIN** Charmes-Chambertin 1993 • $68
85 **MONGEARD-MUGNERET** Bourgogne Hautes Côtes de Nuits 1993 • $17
85 **P. DUBREUIL-FONTAINE PÈRE & FILS** Pernand-Vergelesses 1993 • $NA • (05/15/96)
85 **PRINCE FLORENT DE MERODE** Corton Renardes 1993 • $37
85 **ROBERT ARNOUX** Pinot Noir Bourgogne 1993 • $18 • (05/15/96)
85 **ROPITEAU FRERES** Santenay 1993 • $16
85 **SERAFIN PERE & FILS** Gevrey-Chambertin Vieilles Vignes 1993 • $55
84 **ALAIN GRAS** St.-Romain 1993 • $18
84 **ANTONIN RODET** Volnay-Santenots 1993 • $35
84 **ANTONIN RODET** Chambolle-Musigny 1993 • $30
84 **ANTONIN RODET** Gevrey-Chambertin Les Cazetiers 1993 • $45
84 **BICHOT** Monthelie 1993 • $NA • (11/15/95)
84 **BOUCHARD PERE & FILS** Volnay Fremiets Clos de la Rougeotte 1993 • $35
84 **CHATEAU DE LA TOUR** Clos Vougeot 1993 • $53
84 **DOMAINE LALEURE-PIOT** Pernand-Vergelesses Les Vergelesses 1993 • $24
84 **DOMAINE LALEURE-PIOT** Pernand-Vergelesses Premier Cru 1993 • $22
84 **DOMAINE LALEURE-PIOT** Bourgogne Passetoutgrain 1993 • $15
84 **DOMAINE MUSSY** Beaune Montremenots 1993 • $26
84 **DOMAINE PIERRE LABET** Bourgogne Pinot Noir 1993 • $14
84 **DOMAINE THIERRY MORTET** Bourgogne 1993 • $NA • (05/15/96)
84 **FAIVELEY** Mercurey Clos du Roy 1993 • $25 • (05/15/96)
84 **FREDERIC ESMONIN** Gevrey-Chambertin Estournelles-St.-Jacques 1993 • $40
84 **J. CONFURON-COTETIDOT** Vosne-Romanée Les Suchots 1993 • $NA
84 **JAFFELIN** Santenay Clos Rousseau 1993 • $17
84 **JOSEPH DROUHIN** Maranges Premier Cru 1993 • $20
84 **L'HERITIER-GUYOT** Clos de Vougeot 1993 • $35
84 **L'HERITIER-GUYOT** Gevrey-Chambertin Les Cazetiers 1993 • $45
84 **LABOURE-ROI** Pommard 1993 • $24
84 **LEONARD DE SAINT-AUBIN** Gevrey-Chambertin 1993 • $26 • (05/15/96)
84 **LEONARD DE SAINT-AUBIN** Chambolle-Musigny 1993 • $30 • (05/15/96)
84 **LOUIS JADOT** Santenay Clos de Malte 1993 • $NA
84 **LOUIS JADOT** Pernand-Vergelesses Clos de la Croix de Pierre 1993 • $19
84 **LOUIS JADOT** Chambolle-Musigny 1993 • $28
84 **LOUIS LATOUR** Chambertin Red 1993 • $102
84 **LEJEUNE** Pommard 1993 • $NA
84 **MOMMESSIN** Santenay Clos Rousseau 1993 • $26
84 **MOMMESSIN** Pommard 1993 • $35
84 **MOMMESSIN** Clos de Tart 1993 • $86
84 **OLIVIER LEFLAIVE** Pommard 1993 • $32
84 **PIERRE ANDRE** Corton Pougets 1993 • $48 • (11/15/95)
84 **PIERRE BITOUZET** Pommard Platières 1993 • $40 • (11/15/95)

84 **SIMON BIZE & FILS** Savigny-lès-Beaune Aux Grands Liards 1993 • $19 • (05/15/96)
83 **BICHOT** Volnay Premier Cru 1993 • $25 • (11/15/95)
83 **BOUCHARD PERE & FILS** Volnay Caillerets Ancienne Cuvée Carnot 1993 • $37
83 **BOUCHARD PERE & FILS** Volnay Caillerets 1993 • $NA
83 **CHOPIN-GROFFIER** Côte de Nuits-Villages 1993 • $22
83 **DOMAINE A.-F. GROS** Echézeaux 1993 • $84
83 **DOMAINE COSTE-CAUMARTIN** Bourgogne 1993 • $18
83 **DOMAINE LEJEUNE** Pommard Rugiens 1993 • $65
83 **DOMAINE MICHEL ESMONIN** Gevrey-Chambertin 1993 • $29
83 **DOMAINE SIRUGUE** Gevrey-Chambertin 1993 • $25 • (11/15/95)
83 **DOMAINE SIRUGUE** Côte de Nuits-Villages Clos de la Belle Marguerite 1993 • $15
83 **EMMANUEL ROUGET** Vosne-Romanée 1993 • $NA
83 **JOSEPH DROUHIN** Chorey-lès-Beaune 1993 • $20
83 **L'HERITIER-GUYOT** Côte de Nuits-Villages 1993 • $15
83 **LABOURE-ROI** Meursault 1993 • $22
83 **MOMMESSIN** Gevrey-Chambertin Premier Cru 1993 • $45
83 **MONGEARD-MUGNERET** Savigny-lès-Beaune Les Narbantons 1993 • $26
83 **MONGEARD-MUGNERET** Bourgogne 1993 • $16
83 **MUGNERET-GIBOURG** Vosne-Romanée 1993 • $NA
83 **PIERRE BITOUZET** Savigny-lès-Beaune 1993 • $25 • (11/15/95)
83 **REINE PEDAUQUE** Corton Les Renardes 1993 • $50
82 **BICHOT** Bourgogne Pinot Noir 1993 • $12 • (11/15/95)
82 **BOUCHARD PERE & FILS** Beaune Grèves Vigne de l'Enfant Jésus 1993 • $50 • (11/15/95)
82 **BOUCHARD PERE & FILS** Nuits-St.-Georges Clos-St.-Marc 1er EP 1993 • $47
82 **CHOPIN-GROFFIER** Nuits-St.-Georges Les Chaignots 1993 • $60
82 **DOMAINE FOREY** Nuits-St.-Georges 1993 • $24
82 **DOMAINE JACQUES PRIEUR** Meursault Clos de Mazeray 1993 • $30
82 **DOMAINE MICHEL VOARICK** Aloxe-Corton 1993 • $30
82 **DOMAINE MUSSY** Pommard 1993 • $34
82 **EDMOND CORNU** Ladoix 1993 • $22
82 **JAFFELIN** Pernand-Vergelesses 1993 • $14
82 **JEAN CLAUDE BOISSET** Chassagne-Montrachet Red 1993 • $18 • (11/15/95)
82 **JEAN CLAUDE BOISSET** Savigny-lès-Beaune 1993 • $12 • (11/15/95)
82 **JOSEPH DROUHIN** Vosne-Romanée 1993 • $38
82 **JACQUES-FRÉDÉRIC MUGNIER** Chambolle-Musigny Les Fuées 1993 • $NA
82 **LOUIS JADOT** Clos St.-Denis 1993 • $62
82 **LOUIS LATOUR** Pommard 1993 • $28
82 **LOUIS LATOUR** Aloxe-Corton Domaine Latour 1993 • $21
82 **LUPE-CHOLET** Nuits-St.-Georges Chateau Gris 1er 1993 • $35
82 **MICHEL GROS** Bourgogne Hautes Côtes de Nuits 1993 • $16
82 **MONGEARD-MUGNERET** Vosne-Romanée Les Orveaux 1993 • $40
82 **OLIVIER LEFLAIVE** Pommard Epenots 1993 • $46
82 **PIERRE ANDRE** Savigny-lès-Beaune Clos des Guettes 1993 • $25 • (11/15/95)
82 **PIERRE ANDRE** Gevrey-Chambertin Champlain 1993 • $21 • (11/15/95)
82 **PIERRE PONNELLE** Beaune Les Grèves 1993 • $21
82 **PIERRE PONNELLE** Corton le Clos du Roi 1993 • $43
82 **SIMON BIZE & FILS** Savigny-lès-Beaune Aux Fournaux 1993 • $25 • (05/15/96)
81 **BICHOT** Gevrey-Chambertin 1993 • $30 • (11/15/95)
81 **DOMAINE ANNE & FRANCOIS GROS** Bourgogne Pinot Noir 1993 • $13
81 **DROUHIN-LAROZE** Chambertin Clos de Bèze 1993 • $68
81 **EDMOND CORNU** Chorey-lès-Beaune Les Bons Ores 1993 • $20
81 **J. CONFRUON-COTETIDOT** Echézeaux 1993 • $NA
81 **JOSEPH DROUHIN** Ladoix 1993 • $20
81 **JOSEPH DROUHIN** Morey-St.-Denis 1993 • $NA
81 **LEJEUNE** Pommard Les Argillières 1993 • $NA • (05/15/96)
81 **MOMMESSIN** Morey-St.-Denis La Forge 1993 • $57
81 **MOMMESSIN** Vosne-Romanée 1993 • $40
81 **P. DUBREUIL-FONTAINE PÈRE & FILS** Savigny-lès-Beaune Aux Vergelesses 1993 • $NA
81 **ROBERT ARNOUX** Nuits-St.-Georges Les Poisets 1993 • $50 • (11/15/95)
81 **ROBERT ARNOUX** Nuits-St.-Georges Les Corvées Pagets 1993 • $55 • (11/15/95)
80 **DOMAINE COSTE-CAUMARTIN** Pommard 1993 • $37
80 **DOMAINE GROS FRERE & SOEUR** Bourgogne Hautes Côtes de Nuits 1993 • $15
80 **DOMAINE LEJEUNE** Bourgogne Passetoutgrain 1993 • $13
80 **DOUDET-NAUDIN** Savigny-lès-Beaune Domaine Doudet 1993 • $18
80 **DROUHIN-LAROZE** Latricières-Chambertin 1993 • $52
80 **F. CHAUVENET** Beaune Les Grèves 1993 • $29
80 **F. CHAUVENET** Bourgogne Pinot Noir Château Marguerite de Bourgogne 1993 • $14
80 **J. CONFURON-COTETIDOT** Vosne-Romanée 1993 • $NA
80 **JOSEPH DROUHIN** Savigny-lès-Beaune 1993 • $25
80 **LABOURE-ROI** Clos de Vougeot 1993 • $57
80 **LABOURE-ROI** Bourgogne Pinot Noir 1993 • $9
80 **LOUIS LATOUR** Beaune Domaine Latour 1993 • $22
80 **LOUIS LATOUR** Beaune Vignes Franches 1993 • $26
80 **MOMMESSIN** Volnay Taillepieds 1993 • $40
80 **PIERRE ANDRE** Pommard Premier Cru 1993 • $38 • (11/15/95)
80 **REINE PEDAUQUE** Pommard 1993 • $30
80 **ROPITEAU FRERES** Chassagne-Montrachet Red 1993 • $17
80 **ROPITEAU FRERES** Pommard 1993 • $25
79 Ladoix 1993 • $NA
79 **CAVE DES VIGNERONS DE MANCEY** Bourgogne Cuvée Spéciale Vieille en Fûts de Chêne 1993 • $9 • (05/15/96)
79 **CHOPIN-GROFFIER** Nuits-St.-Georges 1993 • $45
79 **DOMAINE FOREY** Bourgogne 1993 • $12
79 **DOMAINE MUSSY** Pommard Premier Cru 1993 • $38
79 **DOMAINE MUSSY** Pommard Epenots 1993 • $45
79 **DOMAINE MUSSY** Volnay 1993 • $NA
79 **EDOUARD DELAUNAY** Côte de Beaune-Villages 1993 • $18
79 **JAFFELIN** Bourgogne Hautes Côtes de Beaune 1993 • $12
79 **JEAN CLAUDE BOISSET** Clos de Vougeot Red 1993 • $46 • (11/15/95)
79 **JEAN GROS** Nuits-St.-Georges 1993 • $32
79 **OLIVIER LEFLAIVE** Chassagne-Montrachet Morgeot Red 1993 • $34
79 **OLIVIER LEFLAIVE** Santenay 1993 • $20
79 **PIERRE ANDRE** Santenay 1993 • $NA • (11/15/95)
79 **PIERRE ANDRE** Santenay Domaine du Prieuré Sainte Agathe 1993 • $18 • (11/15/95)
79 **PIERRE ANDRE** Ladoix Clos des Chagnots 1993 • $20 • (11/15/95)

79 **REINE PEDAUQUE** Gevrey-Chambertin 1993 • $25
79 **ROBERT ARNOUX** Bourgogne Pinot Noir 1993 • $18 • (11/15/95)
79 **ROPITEAU FRERES** Gevrey-Chambertin 1993 • $23
79 **ROPITEAU FRERES** Pinot Noir Bourgogne 1993 • $9
78 **BICHOT** Pommard Le Clos du Pavillon 1993 • $26 • (11/15/95)
78 **DOMAINE MUSSY** Beaune Epenottes 1993 • $26
78 **DOMAINE PARENT** Pommard Les Chanlins 1993 • $47
78 **DROUHIN-LAROZE** Bonnes Mares 1993 • $62
78 **EDOUARD DELAUNAY** Bourgogne Pinot Noir En Fleur 1993 • $15
78 **F. CHAUVENET** Corton 1993 • $54
78 **F. CHAUVENET** Chambolle-Musigny 1993 • $37
78 **F. CHAUVENET** Nuits-St.-Georges 1993 • $40
78 **JAFFELIN** Chambolle-Musigny 1993 • $24
78 **JAFFELIN** Bourgogne Bourgogne du Chapitre 1993 • $10
78 **LEONARD DE SAINT-AUBIN** Nuits-St.-Georges 1993 • $26 • (05/15/96)
78 **LOUIS LATOUR** Nuits-St.-Georges 1993 • $31
78 **ROBERT ARNOUX** Vosne-Romanée Les Hautes Maizières 1993 • $50 • (11/15/95)
78 **ROPITEAU FRERES** Meursault Red 1993 • $16
77 **BICHOT** Côte de Nuits-Villages 1993 • $15 • (11/15/95)
77 **DROUHIN-LAROZE** Gevrey-Chambertin Lavaux St.-Jacques 1993 • $38
77 **JEAN CLAUDE BOISSET** Charmes-Chambertin 1993 • $56 • (11/15/95)
77 **L'HERITIER-GUYOT** Vougeot Les Cras 1er 1993 • $35
77 **P. DUBREUIL-FONTAINE PÈRE & FILS** Pernand-Vergelesses Ile des Vergelesses 1993 • $NA
77 **PIERRE ANDRE** Clos Vougeot 1993 • $70 • (11/15/95)
77 **PIERRE PONNELLE** Clos de Vougeot 1993 • $57
77 **ROPITEAU FRERES** Côte de Nuits-Villages 1993 • $14
76 **DOMAINE LEJEUNE** Bourgogne 1993 • $14
76 **DOUDET-NAUDIN** Vosne-Romanée Les Suchots 1993 • $36
76 **JAFFELIN** Fixin 1993 • $17
76 **JEAN CLAUDE BOISSET** Gevrey-Chambertin 1993 • $16 • (11/15/95)
76 **MOMMESSIN** Pommard Premier Cru 1993 • $40
76 **PIERRE ANDRE** Nuits-St.-Georges 1993 • $30 • (11/15/95)
76 **PIERRE BITOUZET** Savigny-lès-Beaune Les Lavières 1993 • $30 • (11/15/95)
76 **PIERRE PONNELLE** Bonnes Mares 1993 • $66
75 **DOMAINE A.-F. GROS** Bourgogne Hautes Côtes de Nuits 1993 • $20
75 **JEAN CLAUDE BOISSET** Bourgogne Pinot Noir Charles de France 1993 • $NA • (11/15/95)
75 **LABOURE-ROI** Nuits-St.-Georges 1993 • $27
75 **REINE PEDAUQUE** Nuits-St.-Georges 1993 • $25
75 **ROPITEAU FRERES** Volnay Clos des Chênes 1993 • $30
75 **ROPITEAU FRERES** Côte de Beaune-Villages 1993 • $13
74 **BICHOT** Côte de Beaune-Villages 1993 • $15 • (11/15/95)
74 **JAFFELIN** Auxey-Duresses 1993 • $12
74 **JAFFELIN** Aloxe-Corton 1993 • $20
74 **JAFFELIN** Nuits-St.-Georges 1993 • $25
74 **JEAN CLAUDE BOISSET** Bourgogne Pinot Noir 1993 • $NA • (11/15/95)
74 **L'HERITIER-GUYOT** Chambolle-Musigny 1993 • $30
74 **ROPITEAU FRERES** Vosne-Romanée 1993 • $26
73 **DOMAINE PIERRE LABET** Beaune Coucherias 1993 • $26
73 **EDOUARD DELAUNAY** Clos de Vougeot Red 1993 • $85
73 **JAFFELIN** Beaune Champs-Pimont (1er) 1993 • $19
73 **LUPE-CHOLET** Bourgogne Clos de Lupé 1993 • $12
73 **PIERRE ANDRE** Chassagne-Montrachet Chanvennes 1993 • $25 • (11/15/95)
72 **PIERRE ANDRE** Aloxe-Corton 1993 • $35 • (11/15/95)
72 **ROPITEAU FRERES** Bourgogne Hautes- Côtes de Nuits 1993 • $12
71 **CHARLES VIENOT** Côte de Nuits-Villages Cuvée Roi de Saxe 1993 • $15
70 **F. CHAUVENET** Beaune 1993 • $24

1990 Red Burgundy
Vintage Rating: 98

100 **COMTE DE VOGUE** Musigny Cuvée Vieilles Vignes 1990 • $140
99 **COMTE DE VOGUE** Bonnes Mares 1990 • $110 • (12/15/92)
99 **DOMAINE MEO-CAMUZET** Vosne-Romanée Cros Parantoux 1990 • $81 • (06/15/93)
98 **DOMAINE LEROY** Richebourg 1990 • $299 • (12/15/92)
97 **CHRISTOPHE ROUMIER** Ruchottes-Chambertin 1990 • $80 • (12/15/92)
97 **DOMAINE ANNE & FRANCOIS GROS** Richebourg 1990 • $130 • (12/15/92)
97 **DOMAINE DANIEL RION** Clos Vougeot 1990 • $100 • (12/15/92)
97 **DOMAINE LEROY** Pommard Les Vignots 1990 • $74 • (12/15/92)
97 **DOMAINE LEROY** Clos de la Roche 1990 • $289 • (12/15/92)
97 **DOMAINE LEROY** Vosne-Romanée Aux Réas 1990 • $58 • (12/15/92)
97 **DOMAINE LEROY** Romanée-St.-Vivant 1990 • $299 • (12/15/92)
97 **DOMAINE LEROY** Clos de Vougeot 1990 • $155 • (12/15/92)
97 **DOMAINE MEO-CAMUZET** Richebourg 1990 • $242 • (06/15/93)
97 **DOMAINE ROSSIGNOL-TRAPET** Latricières-Chambertin 1990 • $83 • (12/15/92)
97 **JAYER-GILLES** Echézeaux du Dessus 1990 • $100 • (12/15/92)
97 **JAYER-GILLES** Nuits-St.-Georges Les Hauts Poirets 1990 • $48 • (12/15/92)
96 **ARMAND ROUSSEAU** Ruchottes-Chambertin Clos des Ruchottes 1990 • $80 • (12/15/92)
96 **DOMAINE G. ROUMIER** Bonnes Mares 1990 • $100 • (12/15/92)
96 **DOMAINE GROS FRERE & SOEUR** Richebourg 1990 • $51 • (12/15/92)
96 **DOMAINE LEROY** Chambertin 1990 • $456 • (12/15/92)
96 **DOMAINE LEROY** Latricières-Chambertin 1990 • $204 • (12/15/92)
96 **JOSEPH DROUHIN** Charmes-Chambertin 1990 • $81 • (12/15/92)
96 **MOMMESSIN** Charmes-Chambertin 1990 • $45 • (12/15/92)
96 **TOLLOT-BEAUT** Corton Bressandes 1990 • $40
95 **ARMAND ROUSSEAU** Chambertin-Clos de Bèze 1990 • $135 • (12/15/92)
95 **DOMAINE ANNE & FRANCOIS GROS** Clos Vougeot Le Grand Maupertuis 1990 • $75 • (12/15/92)
95 **DOMAINE COSTE-CAUMARTIN** Pommard Clos des Boucherottes 1990 • $37 • (12/15/92)
95 **DOMAINE DANIEL RION** Vosne-Romanée Les Chaumes 1990 • $70 • (12/15/92)
95 **DOMAINE LEROY** Vosne-Romanée Les Beaux Monts 1990 • $200 • (12/15/92)

95 **DOMAINE LEROY** Pommard Trois Follots 1990 • $69 • (12/15/92)

95 **DOMAINE LEROY** Nuits-St.-Georges Aux Allots 1990 • $67 • (12/15/92)

95 **DOMAINE LEROY** Nuits-St.-Georges Aux Vigne Rondes 1990 • $100 • (12/15/92)

95 **DOMAINE LEROY** Vosne-Romanée Les Genaivrières 1990 • $61 • (12/15/92)

95 **DOMAINE MICHEL LAFARGE** Volnay 1990 • $75 • (12/15/92)

95 **DOMAINE ROSSIGNOL-TRAPET** Chambertin 1990 • $106 • (12/15/92)

95 **DOMAINE ROSSIGNOL-TRAPET** Chapelle-Chambertin 1990 • $83 • (12/15/92)

95 **F. CHAUVENET** Clos St.-Denis 1990 • $65 • (12/15/92)

95 **JOSEPH DROUHIN** Musigny 1990 • $129 • (12/15/92)

95 **MOMMESSIN** Clos de Tart 1990 • $96 • (12/15/92)

94 **BERTRAND AMBROISE** Corton Le Rognet 1990 • $60 • (12/15/92)

94 **BOUCHARD PERE & FILS** Pommard Premier Cru Domaines du Château de Beaunè 1990 • $39 • (12/15/92)

94 **CHOPIN-GROFFIER** Clos Vougeot 1990 • $70 • (12/15/92)

94 **COMTE DE VOGUE** Chambolle-Musigny Les Amoureuses 1990 • $66 • (12/15/92)

94 **DOMAINE A.-F. GROS** Richebourg 1990 • $180 • (12/15/92)

94 **DOMAINE BACHELET** Charmes-Chambertin 1990 • $53 • (12/15/92)

94 **DOMAINE COSTE-CAUMARTIN** Pommard 1990 • $28 • (12/15/92)

94 **DOMAINE COSTE-CAUMARTIN** Pommard Les Fremiers 1990 • $32 • (12/15/92)

94 **DOMAINE DE LA ROMANEE-CONTI** Echézeaux 1990 • $182 • (12/31/93) • CS

94 **DOMAINE DE LA ROMANEE-CONTI** Grands Echézeaux 1990 • $160 • (12/31/93) • CS

94 **DOMAINE LEROY** Chambolle-Musigny Les Fremières 1990 • $79 • (12/15/92)

94 **DOMAINE LEROY** Nuits-St.-Georges Aux Lavières 1990 • $59 • (12/15/92)

94 **DOMAINE LEROY** Nuits-St.-Georges Aux Boudots 1990 • $108 • (12/15/92)

94 **DOMAINE MEO-CAMUZET** Vosne-Romanée Les Chaumes 1990 • $55 • (02/15/93)

94 **DOMAINE MICHEL LAFARGE** Volnay Clos des Chênes 1990 • $75

94 **DOMAINE MORTET FILS** Clos de Vougeot 1990 • $NA • (12/15/92)

94 **F. CHAUVENET** Corton 1990 • $60 • (12/15/92)

94 **GUY CASTAGNIER** Mazis-Chambertin Mazy-Chambertin 1990 • $NA • (12/15/92)

94 **GUY CASTAGNIER** Bonnes Mares 1990 • $NA • (12/15/92)

94 **J. LABET & N. DECHELETTE** Clos Vougeot Château de la Tour 1990 • $NA • (12/15/92)

94 **JEAN GROS** Richebourg 1990 • $150 • (12/15/92)

94 **JEAN-MARC BOILLOT** Pommard Les Jarolières 1990 • $67 • (12/15/92)

94 **JEAN-MARC BOILLOT** Volnay Pitures 1990 • $55 • (12/15/92)

94 **JOSEPH DROUHIN** Griotte-Chambertin 1990 • $84 • (12/15/92)

94 **PHILLIPE CHARLOPIN** Chambertin 1990 • $90 • (08/31/92)

94 **PRINCE FLORENT DE MERODE** Corton Renardes 1990 • $54 • (12/15/92)

94 **TOLLOT-BEAUT** Corton 1990 • $56 • (12/15/92)

93 **ARMAND ROUSSEAU** Mazis-Chambertin Mazy-Chambertin 1990 • $75 • (12/15/92)

93 **BOUCHARD PERE & FILS** Beaune Les Marconnets Domaines du Château de Beaune 1990 • $28 • (12/15/92)

93 **CHOPIN-GROFFIER** Vougeot 1990 • $44 • (12/15/92)

93 **CHRISTOPHE ROUMIER** Charmes-Chambertin 1990 • $105 • (12/15/92)

93 **COMTE ARMAND** Pommard Clos des Epeneaux 1990 • $57 • (12/15/92)

93 **COMTE SENARD** Corton En Charlemagne 1990 • $NA • (12/15/92)

93 **COMTE SENARD** Corton Le Clos du Roi 1990 • $55 • (12/15/92)

93 **COMTE SENARD** Corton Clos des Meix 1990 • $NA • (12/15/92)

93 **DOMAINE BRUNO CLAIR** Chambertin-Clos de Bèze 1990 • $70 • (12/15/92)

93 **DOMAINE DANIEL RION** Nuits-St.-Georges Clos des Argillières 1990 • $52 • (12/15/92)

93 **DOMAINE DANIEL RION** Vosne-Romanée Les Chaumes 1990 • $70

93 **DOMAINE DE LA ROMANEE-CONTI** Romanée-Conti 1990 • $750 • (12/31/93) • CS

93 **DOMAINE GROS FRERE & SOEUR** Clos Vougeot Musigni 1990 • $68 • (12/15/92)

93 **DOMAINE MEO-CAMUZET** Vosne-Romanée 1990 • $36 • (02/15/93)

93 **DOMAINE MEO-CAMUZET** Vosne-Romanée Aux Brûlées 1990 • $81 • (06/15/93)

93 **DOMAINE MORTET FILS** Gevrey-Chambertin Clos Prieur 1990 • $38 • (12/15/92)

93 **DUBREUIL-FONTAINE** Corton Clos du Roi 1990 • $61 • (12/15/92)

93 **FAIVELEY** Chambertin Clos de Bèze 1990 • $130 • (12/15/92)

93 **GEORGES MUGNERET** Ruchottes-Chambertin 1990 • $78 • (12/15/92)

93 **GHISLAINE BARTHOD** Chambolle-Musigny Aux Beaux-Bruns 1990 • $50 • (12/15/92)

93 **GUY CASTAGNIER** Clos St.-Denis Red 1990 • $NA • (12/15/92)

93 **JAFFELIN** Romanée St.-Vivant 1990 • $75 • (12/15/92)

93 **JEAN GROS** Vosne-Romanée Clos des Réas 1990 • $48 • (12/15/92)

93 **JOSEPH DROUHIN** Beaune Clos des Mouches 1990 • $52 • (12/15/92)

93 **JOSEPH DROUHIN** Volnay Clos des Chênes 1990 • $42 • (12/15/92)

93 **JOSEPH DROUHIN** Chambolle-Musigny Les Amoureuses 1990 • $80 • (12/15/92)

93 **JOSEPH DROUHIN** Bonnes Mares 1990 • $91 • (12/15/92)

93 **LA POUSSE D'OR** Volnay Clos de la Bousse d'Or 1990 • $75 • (11/30/92) • CS

93 **MUGNERET-GIBOURG** Echézeaux 1990 • $66 • (12/15/92)

93 **PHILIPPE BATACCHI** Morey-St.-Denis Premier Cru 1990 • $44 • (12/15/92)

93 **PHILIPPE BATACCHI** Clos de la Roche 1990 • $59 • (12/15/92)

93 **TOLLOT-BEAUT** Aloxe-Corton 1990 • $38 • (12/15/92)

92 **ARMAND ROUSSEAU** Chambertin 1990 • $150 • (12/15/92)

92 **ARMAND ROUSSEAU** Clos de la Roche 1990 • $78 • (12/15/92)

92 **BOUCHARD PERE & FILS** Volnay Taillepieds Domaines du Château de Beaune 1990 • $34 • (12/15/92)

92 **CHARLOPIN-PARIZOT** Charmes-Chambertin 1990 • $70 • (08/31/92)

92 **DOMAINE BRUNO CLAIR** Savigny-lès-Beaune La Dominode 1990 • $32 • (12/15/92)

92 **DOMAINE BRUNO CLAIR** Gevrey-Chambertin Clos du Fonteny 1990 • $45 • (12/15/92)

92 **DOMAINE DANIEL RION** Nuits-St.-Georges Les Grandes Vignes 1990 • $42 • (12/15/92)

92 **DOMAINE DANIEL RION** Nuits-St.-Georges Aux Vignerondes 1990 • $70 • (12/15/92)

92 **DOMAINE DANIEL RION** Vosne-Romanée Les Beaux Monts 1990 • $70 • (12/15/92)

92 **DOMAINE DUJAC** Charmes-Chambertin 1990 • $75 • (12/15/92)

92 **DOMAINE DUJAC** Gevrey-Chambertin Aux Combottes 1990 • $67 • (12/15/92)

92 **DOMAINE DUJAC** Clos de la Roche 1990 • $83 • (12/15/92)

92 **DOMAINE FOREY** Echézeaux 1990 • $65 • (12/15/92)

92 **DOMAINE G. ROUMIER** Chambolle-Musigny Les Amoureuses 1990 • $55 • (12/15/92)

92 **DOMAINE G. ROUMIER** Clos Vougeot 1990 • $65 • (12/15/92)

92 **DOMAINE HENRI GOUGES** Nuits-St.-Georges Clos des Porrets St.-Georges 1990 • $58 • (12/15/92)

92 **DOMAINE HENRI GOUGES** Nuits-St.-Georges Les St.-Georges 1990 • $60 • (12/15/92)

92 **DOMAINE LEJEUNE** Pommard Les Rugiens 1990 • $49 • (12/15/92)

92 **DOMAINE LEROY** Corton Renardes 1990 • $111 • (12/15/92)

92 **DOMAINE LEROY** Savigny-lès-Beaune Les Narbantons 1990 • $138 • (12/15/92)

92 **DOMAINE LEROY** Gevrey-Chambertin Les Combottes 1990 • $111 • (12/15/92)

92 **DOMAINE PONSOT** Clos de la Roche Cuvée Vieilles Vignes 1990 • $150 • (03/15/93)

92 **F. CHAUVENET** Clos de Vougeot 1990 • $69 • (12/15/92)

92 **FAIVELEY** Morey-St.-Denis Clos des Ormes 1990 • $12 • (12/15/92)

92 **FAIVELEY** Clos de Vougeot 1990 • $50 • (12/15/92)

92 **FAIVELEY** Gevrey-Chambertin Les Marchais 1990 • $45 • (12/15/92)

92 **HUBERT LIGNIER** Clos de la Roche 1990 • $90 • (12/15/92)

92 **JAFFELIN** Charmes-Chambertin 1990 • $55 • (12/15/92)

92 **JEAN-MARC BOILLOT** Beaune Les Montrevenots 1990 • $39 • (12/15/92)

92 **JEAN-MARC BOILLOT** Pommard Les Saussilles 1990 • $48 • (12/15/92)

92 **JEAN-MARC BOILLOT** Volnay 1990 • $40 • (12/15/92)

92 **JEAN-MARC PAVELOT** Savigny-lès-Beaune Aux Guettes 1990 • $33 • (12/15/92)

92 **LOUIS JADOT** Vosne-Romanée 1990 • $30 • (12/15/92)

92 **LOUIS JADOT** Chambertin Clos de Bèze 1990 • $105

92 **MOMMESSIN** Volnay Taillepieds 1990 • $23 • (12/15/92)

92 **OLIVIER LEFLAIVE** Pommard 1990 • $30 • (12/15/92)

92 **OLIVIER LEFLAIVE** Volnay 1990 • $36 • (12/15/92)

92 **PHILIPPE LECLERC** Gevrey-Chambertin Combes aux Moines 1990 • $70 • (12/15/92)

92 **ROBERT CHEVILLON** Nuits-St.-Georges Les St.-Georges 1990 • $63

92 **TOLLOT-BEAUT** Beaune Les Grèves 1990 • $40 • (12/15/92)

91 **BOUCHARD PERE & FILS** Le Corton Domaines du Château de Beaune 1990 • $50 • (12/15/92)

91 **CHOPIN-GROFFIER** Nuits-St.-Georges Aux Chaignots 1990 • $40 • (12/15/92)

91 **DOMAINE B. SERVEAU** Chambolle-Musigny Les Amoureuses 1990 • $68 • (12/15/92)

91 **DOMAINE B. SERVEAU** Nuits-St.-Georges Chaînes Carteaux 1990 • $46 • (12/15/92)

91 **DOMAINE BACHELET** Gevrey-Chambertin Vieilles Vignes 1990 • $43 • (12/15/92)

91 **DOMAINE DANIEL RION** Vosne-Romanée 1990 • $42 • (12/15/92)

91 **DOMAINE DE LA ROMANEE-CONTI** La Tâche 1990 • $428 • (12/31/93)

91 **DOMAINE DE LA ROMANEE-CONTI** Richebourg 1990 • $310 • (12/31/93)

91 **DOMAINE DUJAC** Echézeaux 1990 • $88 • (12/15/92)

91 **DOMAINE GROS FRERE & SOEUR** Grands Echézeaux 1990 • $85 • (12/15/92)

91 **DOMAINE HENRI GOUGES** Nuits-St.-Georges Les Vaucrains 1990 • $60 • (12/15/92)

91 **DOMAINE MEO-CAMUZET** Nuits-St.-Georges Aux Boudots 1990 • $68 • (02/15/93)

91 **DOMAINE MICHEL LAFARGE** Volnay 1990 • $75 • (12/15/92)

91 **DOMAINE MORTET FILS** Gevrey-Chambertin Champeaux 1990 • $45 • (12/15/92)

91 **DOMAINE PONSOT** Morey-St.-Denis 1990 • $68 • (03/15/93)

91 **DOMAINE ROSSIGNOL-TRAPET** Beaune Les Teurons 1990 • $46 • (12/15/92)

91 **DOMAINE TAUPENOT-MERME** Charmes-Chambertin 1990 • $58 • (11/30/94)

91 **DUBREUIL-FONTAINE** Pommard Les Epenots 1990 • $59 • (12/15/92)

91 **F. CHAUVENET** Echézeaux 1990 • $62 • (12/15/92)

91 **FAIVELEY** Mazis-Chambertin 1990 • $52 • (12/15/92)

91 **FAIVELEY** Echézeaux 1990 • $71 • (12/15/92)

91 **FAIVELEY** Nuits-St.-Georges Les Damodes 1990 • $45 • (12/15/92)

91 **GEORGES MUGNERET** Clos Vougeot 1990 • $89 • (12/15/92)

91 **J. CONFURON-COTETIDOT** Echézeaux 1990 • $65 • (12/15/92)

91 **J. CONFURON-COTETIDOT** Nuits-St.-Georges Premier Cru 1990 • $28 • (12/15/92)

91 **JACQUES GERMAIN** Beaune Les Teurons 1990 • $48 • (12/15/92)

91 **JACQUES GERMAIN** Beaune Cents-Vignes 1990 • $46 • (12/15/92)

91 **JACQUES GERMAIN** Beaune Les Vignes Franches 1990 • $46 • (12/15/92)

91 **JAFFELIN** Gevrey-Chambertin Lavaut St.-Jacques 1990 • $42 • (12/15/92)

91 **JEAN GARAUDET** Pommard Les Charmots 1990 • $48 • (08/31/92)

91 **JOSEPH DROUHIN** Pommard Epenots 1990 • $48 • (12/15/92)

91 **JOSEPH DROUHIN** Chambertin 1990 • $113 • (12/15/92)

91 **JOSEPH DROUHIN** Gevrey-Chambertin Champeaux 1990 • $70 • (12/15/92)

91 **JOSEPH DROUHIN** Echézeaux 1990 • $69 • (12/15/92)

91 **JOSEPH DROUHIN** Clos de Vougeot 1990 • $71 • (12/15/92)

91 **JOSEPH DROUHIN** Grands Echézeaux 1990 • $100

91 **LA POUSSE D'OR** Volnay Les Caillerets-Clos des 60 Ouvrées 1990 • $62 • (12/15/92)

91 **LOUIS JADOT** Beaune Clos des Ursules 1990 • $44 • (12/15/92)

■ ■ ■ ■

Red Burgundy

91 **LOUIS JADOT** Griotte-Chambertin 1990 • $70 • (12/15/92)
91 **LOUIS JADOT** Chambolle-Musigny 1990 • $30 • (12/15/92)
91 **LOUIS JADOT** Bonnes Mares 1990 • $75 • (12/15/92)
91 **LOUIS JADOT** Clos Vougeot 1990 • $55 • (12/15/92)
91 **MOILLARD** Beaune Grèves Domaine Thomas-Moillard 1990 • $40 • (12/15/92)
91 **MOMMESSIN** Aloxe-Corton 1990 • $20 • (12/15/92)
91 **MOMMESSIN** Vosne-Romanée Les Suchots 1990 • $35 • (12/15/92)
91 **OLIVIER LEFLAIVE** Pommard Rugiens 1990 • $35 • (12/15/92)
91 **PHILIPPE BATACCHI** Gevrey-Chambertin Les Evocelles 1990 • $32 • (12/15/92)
91 **PHILIPPE LECLERC** Gevrey-Chambertin Champeaux 1990 • $50 • (12/15/92)
91 **SERAFIN PERE & FILS** Gevrey-Chambertin Les Cazetiers 1990 • $56 • (12/15/92)
91 **TOLLOT-BEAUT** Corton Les Bressandes 1990 • $40 • (12/15/92)
90 **ALAIN BURGUET** Gevrey-Chambertin Vieilles Vignes 1990 • $43 • (12/15/92)
90 **ARMAND ROUSSEAU** Gevrey-Chambertin Le Clos St.-Jacques 1990 • $85 • (12/15/92)
90 **BERTRAND AMBROISE** Nuits-St.-Georges En Rue de Chaux 1990 • $48 • (12/15/92)
90 **BERTRAND AMBROISE** Nuits-St.-Georges Les Vaucrains 1990 • $44 • (12/15/92)
90 **BOUCHARD PERE & FILS** Volnay Caillerets Ancienne Cuvée Carnot Domaines du Château de Beaune 1990 • $37 • (12/15/92)
90 **CHARLOPIN-PARIZOT** Gevrey-Chambertin Cuvée Vieilles Vignes 1990 • $40 • (04/30/92)
90 **COMTE DE VOGUE** Chambolle-Musigny 1990 • $45 • (12/15/92)
90 **DOMAINE A.-F. GROS** Echézeaux 1990 • $90 • (12/15/92)
90 **DOMAINE BRUNO CLAIR** Morey-St.-Denis En La Rue de Vergy 1990 • $37 • (12/15/92)
90 **DOMAINE DANIEL RION** Nuits-St.-Georges Les Hauts Pruliers 1990 • $70 • (12/15/92)
90 **DOMAINE DE LA ROMANEE-CONTI** Romanée St.-Vivant 1990 • $175 • (12/31/93)
90 **DOMAINE DUJAC** Clos St.-Denis 1990 • $83 • (12/15/92)
90 **DOMAINE HENRI GOUGES** Nuits-St.-Georges Les Pruliers 1990 • $58 • (12/15/92)
90 **DOMAINE LALEURE-PIOT** Corton Bressandes 1990 • $NA • (12/15/92)
90 **DOMAINE LALEURE-PIOT** Pernand-Vergelesses Ile des Vergelesses 1990 • $NA • (12/15/92)
90 **DOMAINE LUCIEN BOILLOT** Volnay Les Brouillards 1990 • $32 • (12/15/92)
90 **DOMAINE MEO-CAMUZET** Nuits-St.-Georges Aux Murgers 1990 • $68 • (02/15/93)
90 **DOMAINE MICHEL LAFARGE** Volnay 1990 • $43 • (12/15/92)
90 **DOMAINE MORTET FILS** Gevrey-Chambertin 1990 • $NA • (12/15/92)
90 **DOMAINE MORTET FILS** Chambolle-Musigny Les Beaux Bruns 1990 • $45 • (12/15/92)
90 **DOMAINE ROSSIGNOL-TRAPET** Gevrey-Chambertin Petite Chapelle 1990 • $21 • (12/15/92)
90 **DOMAINE TAUPENOT-MERME** Chambolle-Musigny 1990 • $22 • (11/30/94)
90 **F. CHAUVENET** Gevrey-Chambertin Lavaut St.-Jacques 1990 • $56 • (12/15/92)
90 **F. CHAUVENET** Nuits-St.-Georges Les Pruliers 1990 • $52 • (12/15/92)
90 **FAIVELEY** Corton Clos des Cortons 1990 • $86 • (12/15/92)
90 **FAIVELEY** Pommard Les Chaponnières 1990 • $65 • (12/15/92)
90 **FAIVELEY** Nuits-St.-Georges Clos de la Maréchale 1990 • $36 • (11/30/92)
90 **FAIVELEY** Nuits-St.-Georges Porrets St.-Georges 1990 • $45 • (12/15/92)
90 **FAIVELEY** Nuits-St.-Georges Aux Chaignots 1990 • $48 • (12/15/92)
90 **GHISLAINE BARTHOD** Chambolle-Musigny Les Charmes 1990 • $50 • (12/15/92)
90 **GHISLAINE BARTHOD** Chambolle-Musigny Les Véroilles 1990 • $50 • (12/15/92)
90 **GUY CASTAGNIER** Clos de la Roche 1990 • $NA • (12/15/92)
90 **J.-M. GAUNOUX** Volnay Le Clos des Chênes 1990 • $NA • (12/15/92)
90 **JAFFELIN** Beaune Champs Pimont 1990 • $25 • (12/15/92)
90 **JAYER-GILLES** Côte de Nuits-Villages 1990 • $34 • (12/15/92)
90 **JOSEPH DROUHIN** Volnay 1990 • $33 • (12/15/92)
90 **JOSEPH DROUHIN** Grands Echézeaux 1990 • $102 • (12/15/92)
90 **JOSEPH DROUHIN** Vosne-Romanée Les Petits-Monts 1990 • $NA • (12/15/92)
90 **LOUIS JADOT** Corton Pougets 1990 • $50 • (12/15/92)
90 **LOUIS JADOT** Pommard Les Arvelets 1990 • $42 • (12/15/92)
90 **LOUIS JADOT** Mazis-Chambertin 1990 • $70 • (12/15/92)
90 **LOUIS JADOT** Gevrey-Chambertin Clos St.-Jacques 1990 • $48 • (12/15/92)
90 **MOILLARD** Morey-St.-Denis Monts Luisants 1990 • $33 • (12/15/92)
90 **MOMMESSIN** Beaune Les Cents Vignes 1990 • $20 • (12/15/92)
90 **MOMMESSIN** Savigny-lès-Beaune 1990 • $14 • (12/15/92)
90 **MOMMESSIN** Gevrey-Chambertin Lavaux St.-Jacques 1990 • $45 • (12/15/92)
90 **MOMMESSIN** Nuits-St.-Georges Aux Chaignots 1990 • $29 • (12/15/92)
90 **OLIVIER LEFLAIVE** Pommard Epenots 1990 • $35 • (12/15/92)
90 **PAUL PERNOT** Beaune Les Teurons 1990 • $33 • (04/30/92)
90 **PHILIPPE BATACCHI** Gevrey-Chambertin Les Jeunes Rois 1990 • $38 • (12/15/92)
90 **PHILIPPE LECLERC** Gevrey-Chambertin Les Platières 1990 • $35 • (12/15/92)
90 **PIERRE BOUREE FILS** Gevrey-Chambertin Le Clos St.-Jacques 1990 • $60 • (12/15/92)
90 **PIERRE BOUREE FILS** Clos de la Roche 1990 • $70 • (12/15/92)
90 **PRINCE FLORENT DE MERODE** Corton Clos du Roi 1990 • $64 • (12/15/92)
90 **PRINCE FLORENT DE MERODE** Pommard Clos de la Platière 1990 • $48 • (12/15/92)
90 **SIMON BIZE & FILS** Savigny-lès-Beaune Aux Vergelesses 1990 • $29 • (12/15/92)
90 **SIMON BIZE & FILS** Savigny-lès-Beaune Les Marconnets 1990 • $33 • (12/15/92)
90 **TOLLOT-BEAUT** Beaune Clos du Roi 1990 • $48 • (12/15/92)
90 **TOLLOT-BEAUT** Savigny-lès-Beaune Lavières 1990 • $35 • (12/15/92)

89 **ALAIN BURGUET** Gevrey-Chambertin 1990 • $NA • (12/15/92)
89 **BERTRAND AMBROISE** Nuits-St.-Georges 1990 • $38 • (12/15/92)
89 **BOUCHARD PERE & FILS** Echézeaux 1990 • $42 • (10/31/92)
89 **CHARLOPIN-PARIZOT** Clos St.-Denis 1990 • $76 • (08/31/92)
89 **CHATEAU DES HERBEAUX** Chambertin 1990 • $75 • (02/15/93)
89 **CHOPIN-GROFFIER** Nuits-St.-Georges 1990 • $43 • (12/15/92)
89 **DOMAINE BERTAGNA** Nuits-St.-Georges Aux Murgers 1990 • $NA • (12/15/92)
89 **DOMAINE BRUNO CLAIR** Gevrey-Chambertin Les Cazetiers 1990 • $55 • (12/15/92)
89 **DOMAINE G. ROUMIER** Morey-St.-Denis Clos de La Bussière 1990 • $53 • (12/15/92)
89 **DOMAINE LALEURE-PIOT** Pernand-Vergelesses Les Vergelesses 1990 • $NA • (12/15/92)
89 **DOMAINE MEO-CAMUZET** Corton Clos Rognet 1990 • $68 • (06/15/93)
89 **DOMAINE PARENT** Pommard Les Epenots 1990 • $NA • (12/15/92)
89 **DOMAINE PIERRE GUILLEMOT** Savigny-lès-Beaune Serpentières 1990 • $24 • (12/15/92)
89 **DOMAINE PIERRE LABET** Beaune Clos des Monsnières 1990 • $30 • (12/15/92)
89 **DUBREUIL-FONTAINE** Corton Bressandes 1990 • $59 • (12/15/92)
89 **EDMOND CORNU** Corton Bressandes 1990 • $60 • (12/15/92)
89 **F. CHAUVENET** Beaune Les Grèves 1990 • $35 • (12/15/92)
89 **F. CHAUVENET** Gevrey-Chambertin Estournelles St.-Jacques 1990 • $56 • (12/15/92)
89 **FAIVELEY** Gevrey-Chambertin Les Cazetiers 1990 • $49 • (12/15/92)
89 **FAIVELEY** Chambolle-Musigny Les Fuées 1990 • $36 • (12/15/92)
89 **GUY CASTAGNIER** Charmes-Chambertin 1990 • $NA • (12/15/92)
89 **GUY CASTAGNIER** Latricières-Chambertin 1990 • $NA • (12/15/92)
89 **JACQUES GERMAIN** Beaune Les Boucherottes 1990 • $42 • (12/15/92)
89 **JACQUES GERMAIN** Beaune Aux Cras 1990 • $46 • (12/15/92)
89 **JAFFELIN** Pommard 1990 • $30 • (12/15/92)
89 **JEAN-MARC PAVELOT** Savigny-lès-Beaune 1990 • $22 • (12/15/92)
89 **JOSEPH DROUHIN** Clos de la Roche 1990 • $69 • (12/15/92)
89 **LOUIS LATOUR** Corton Château Corton Grancey 1990 • $43 • (12/15/92)
89 **LOUIS LATOUR** Romanée St.-Vivant Les Quatre Journaux 1990 • $139 • (12/15/92)
89 **MACHARD DE GRAMONT** Nuits-St.-Georges Les Damodes 1990 • $48 • (05/31/95)
89 **MOILLARD** Corton Clos des Vergennes 1990 • $53 • (12/15/92)
89 **SERAFIN PERE & FILS** Gevrey-Chambertin 1990 • $45 • (12/15/92)
89 **SIMON BIZE & FILS** Savigny-lès-Beaune Aux Fournaux 1990 • $28 • (12/15/92)
88 **BOUCHARD PERE & FILS** Nuits-St.-Georges Clos des Argillières 1990 • $31 • (10/31/92)
88 **BOUCHARD PERE & FILS** Aloxe-Corton Domaines du Château de Beaune 1990 • $30 • (12/15/92)
88 **BOUCHARD PERE & FILS** Chambertin Domaines du Château de Beaune Red 1990 • $NA • (12/15/92)
88 **BOUCHARD PERE & FILS** Beaune Grèves Vigne de l'Enfant Jésus 1990 • $53
88 **CHATEAU DE POMMARD** Pommard 1990 • $60 • (12/15/92)
88 **COMTE SENARD** Corton Bressandes 1990 • $NA • (12/15/92)
88 **DOMAINE B. SERVEAU** Chambolle-Musigny Les Sentiers 1990 • $35 • (12/15/92)
88 **DOMAINE COSTE-CAUMARTIN** Bourgogne 1990 • $16 • (12/15/92)
88 **DOMAINE DU CLOS FRANTIN** Echézeaux 1990 • $42 • (11/30/92)
88 **DOMAINE FRANCOIS LEGROS** Chambolle-Musigny Les Noirots 1990 • $40 • (03/15/93)
88 **DOMAINE FRANCOIS LEGROS** Nuits-St.-Georges Les Perrières 1990 • $39 • (03/15/93)
88 **DOMAINE G. ROUMIER** Chambolle-Musigny 1990 • $28 • (12/15/92)
88 **DOMAINE HENRI GOUGES** Nuits-St.-Georges 1990 • $40 • (12/15/92)
88 **DOMAINE HENRI GOUGES** Nuits-St.-Georges Les Vaucrains Premier Cru 1990 • $60
88 **DOMAINE LEJEUNE** Pommard Les Argillières 1990 • $40 • (12/15/92)
88 **DOMAINE LEROY** Nuits-St.-Georges Au Bas de Combe 1990 • $58 • (12/15/92)
88 **DOMAINE LUCIEN BOILLOT** Gevrey-Chambertin Les Corbeaux 1990 • $33 • (12/15/92)
88 **DOMAINE MEO-CAMUZET** Nuits-St.-Georges 1990 • $38 • (02/15/93)
88 **DOMAINE PIERRE LABET** Beaune Aux Coucherias 1990 • $35 • (12/15/92)
88 **DOMAINE TAUPENOT-MERME** Morey-St.-Denis 1990 • $22 • (11/30/94)
88 **DUBREUIL-FONTAINE** Pernand-Vergelesses Ile des Vergelesses 1990 • $37 • (12/15/92)
88 **GEORGES MUGNERET** Nuits-St.-Georges Les Chaignots 1990 • $45 • (12/15/92)
88 **HUBERT LIGNIER** Morey-St.-Denis Premier Cru 1990 • $36 • (12/15/92)
88 **JAFFELIN** Monthelie 1990 • $17 • (12/15/92)
88 **JEAN GARAUDET** Pommard Les Noizons 1990 • $40 • (08/31/92)
88 **JEAN-MARC BOILLOT** Bourgogne 1990 • $19 • (12/15/92)
88 **JOSEPH DROUHIN** Aloxe-Corton 1990 • $33 • (12/15/92)
88 **JOSEPH DROUHIN** Corton 1990 • $58 • (12/15/92)
88 **JOSEPH DROUHIN** Beaune Hospices de Beaune Cuvée Maurice Drouhin 1990 • $NA • (12/15/92)
88 **JOSEPH DROUHIN** Gevrey-Chambertin 1990 • $36 • (12/15/92)
88 **JOSEPH DROUHIN** Chambolle-Musigny Les Hauts Doix 1990 • $53 • (12/15/92)
88 **JOSEPH DROUHIN** Morey-St.-Denis 1990 • $33 • (12/15/92)
88 **JOSEPH DROUHIN** Nuits-St.-Georges Les Boudots 1990 • $57 • (12/15/92)
88 **LOUIS JADOT** Pernand-Vergelesses Clos de la Croix de Pierre 1990 • $18 • (12/15/92)
88 **LOUIS JADOT** Savigny-lès-Beaune La Dominode 1990 • $23 • (12/15/92)
88 **LOUIS JADOT** Vosne-Romanée Les Suchots 1990 • $49 • (12/15/92)
88 **LOUIS LATOUR** Pommard Epenots 1990 • $37

■ ■ ■ ■

88 **MOILLARD** Savigny-lès-Beaune Domaine Thomas-Moillard 1990 • $20 • (12/15/92)

88 **PHILIPPE BATACCHI** Côte de Nuits-Villages 1990 • $20 • (12/15/92)

88 **PIERRE BITOUZET** Aloxe-Corton Valozières 1990 • $NA • (12/15/92)

88 **PIERRE BITOUZET** Savigny-lès-Beaune Les Lavières 1990 • $NA • (12/15/92)

88 **PRINCE FLORENT DE MERODE** Ladoix Les Chaillots 1990 • $23 • (12/15/92)

87 **A. & P. DE VILLAINE** Côte Chalonnaise Bouzeron La Digoine 1990 • $16 • (11/30/92)

87 **BOUCHARD PERE & FILS** Vosne-Romanée Aux Raignots Château de Vosne-Romanée 1990 • $40 • (10/31/92)

87 **DOMAINE DE L'ARLOT** Nuits-St.-Georges Clos des Forêts St.-Georges 1990 • $49 • (12/15/92)

87 **DOMAINE DUJAC** Morey-St.-Denis 1990 • $41 • (12/15/92)

87 **DOMAINE FRANCOIS LEGROS** Vougeot Les Crâs 1990 • $45 • (03/15/93)

87 **DOMAINE FRANCOIS LEGROS** Nuits-St.-Georges Aux Bousselots 1990 • $39 • (03/15/93)

87 **DOMAINE HENRI PERROT-MINOT** Morey-St.-Denis En la Rue de Vergy 1990 • $25 • (03/15/94)

87 **DOMAINE LUCIEN BOILLOT** Volnay Les Angles 1990 • $32 • (12/15/92)

87 **DOMAINE MORTET FILS** Bourgogne Les Charmes au Châtelain 1990 • $NA • (12/15/92)

87 **DOMAINE MUSSY** Beaune Montrevenots 1990 • $45 • (12/15/92)

87 **DOMAINE Y. CLERGET** Volnay Premier Cru 1990 • $37 • (12/15/92)

87 **F. CHAUVENET** Monthelie Les Champs-Fulliot 1990 • $NA • (12/15/92)

87 **F. CHAUVENET** Pommard Les Chanlins 1990 • $59 • (12/15/92)

87 **F. CHAUVENET** Clos de la Roche 1990 • $76 • (12/15/92)

87 **GHISLAINE BARTHOD** Chambolle-Musigny 1990 • $25 • (12/15/92)

87 **GHISLAINE BARTHOD** Chambolle-Musigny Les Crâs 1990 • $50 • (12/15/92)

87 **GUY CASTAGNIER** Gevrey-Chambertin 1990 • $NA • (12/15/92)

87 **GUY CASTAGNIER** Chambolle-Musigny 1990 • $NA • (12/15/92)

87 **GUY CASTAGNIER** Clos de Vougeot Red 1990 • $NA • (12/15/92)

87 **JAFFELIN** Beaune Les Bressandes 1990 • $27 • (12/15/92)

87 **JEAN GARAUDET** Beaune Red Le Clos des Mouches 1990 • $35 • (08/31/92)

87 **JEAN-LUC DUBOIS** Chorey-lès-Beaune 1990 • $30 • (06/15/93)

87 **JOSEPH DROUHIN** Pernand-Vergelesses 1990 • $21 • (12/15/92)

87 **JOSEPH DROUHIN** Chambolle-Musigny 1990 • $36 • (12/15/92)

87 **LOUIS JADOT** Beaune Les Avaux 1990 • $28 • (12/15/92)

87 **LOUIS JADOT** Côte de Beaune-Villages 1990 • $15 • (12/15/92)

87 **LOUIS JADOT** Santenay Clos de Malte 1990 • $18 • (12/15/92)

87 **LOUIS JADOT** Volnay 1990 • $28 • (12/15/92)

87 **LOUIS LATOUR** Beaune Domaine Latour 1990 • $21 • (12/15/92)

87 **MARIUS DELARCHE PERE & FILS** Corton Les Renardes 1990 • $49 • (06/15/93)

87 **MARIUS DELARCHE PERE & FILS** Pernand-Vergelesses Ile des Vergelesses 1990 • $28 • (06/15/93)

87 **MOILLARD** Beaune 1990 • $26 • (12/15/92)

87 **PHILIPPE BATACCHI** Fixin 1990 • $23 • (12/15/92)

87 **SERAFIN PERE & FILS** Gevrey-Chambertin Le Fonteny 1990 • $63 • (12/15/92)

87 **SERAFIN PERE & FILS** Gevrey-Chambertin Vieilles Vignes 1990 • $50 • (12/15/92)

87 **SIMON BIZE & FILS** Savigny-lès-Beaune Aux Grands Liards 1990 • $22 • (12/15/92)

87 **SIMON BIZE & FILS** Bourgogne Les Perrières 1990 • $17 • (12/15/92)

86 **ALAIN GRAS** St.-Romain 1990 • $24 • (12/15/92)

86 **ALBERT MOROT** Les Bressandes 1990 • $38 • (12/15/92)

86 **BOUCHARD PERE & FILS** Volnay Frémiets Clos de la Rougeotte Domaines du Château de Beaune 1990 • $NA • (12/15/92)

86 **BOUCHARD PERE & FILS** Chambolle-Musigny Domaines du Château de Beaune 1990 • $NA • (12/15/92)

86 **BOUCHARD PERE & FILS** Nuits-St.-Georges Clos des Argillières 1990 • $31 • (12/15/92)

86 **DOMAINE DU CLOS FRANTIN** Vosne-Romanée Les Malconsorts 1990 • $37 • (11/30/92)

86 **DOMAINE GROS FRERE & SOEUR** Côte de Nuits-Villages 1990 • $18 • (12/15/92)

86 **DOMAINE HENRI PERROT-MINOT** Morey-St.-Denis La Riotte 1990 • $40 • (12/31/93)

86 **DOMAINE LUCIEN BOILLOT** Bourgogne 1990 • $14 • (12/15/92)

86 **DOMAINE MEO-CAMUZET** Bourgogne Passe-tout-grains 1990 • $17 • (03/31/92)

86 **DOMAINE MORTET FILS** Chambertin 1990 • $92 • (12/15/92)

86 **DOMAINE MUSSY** Pommard Les Epenots 1990 • $50 • (12/15/92)

86 **DOMAINE PRIEUR-BRUNET** Beaune Clos du Roi 1990 • $32 • (02/15/93)

86 **DOMAINE Y. CLERGET** Volnay Les Cailleres 1990 • $45 • (12/15/92)

86 **F. CHAUVENET** Pommard 1990 • $45 • (12/15/92)

86 **F. CHAUVENET** Volnay Clos de Chênes 1990 • $58 • (12/15/92)

86 **FREDERIC ESMONIN** Ruchottes-Chambertin 1990 • $71 • (10/31/92)

86 **GEISWELLER & FILS** Bourgogne 1990 • $NA • (12/15/92)

86 **HUBERT LIGNIER** Morey-St.-Denis 1990 • $36 • (12/15/92)

86 **JAFFELIN** Clos de Vougeot 1990 • $55 • (12/15/92)

86 **JEAN-NOEL GAGNARD** Chassagne-Montrachet Morgeot Red 1990 • $25 • (02/15/93)

86 **JOSEPH DROUHIN** Vosne-Romanée Les Suchots 1990 • $58 • (12/15/92)

86 **LABOURE-ROI** Nuits-St.-Georges 1990 • $20 • (06/15/93)

86 **LEROY** Bourgogne Leroy 1990 • $18 • (12/15/92)

86 **LOUIS JADOT** Monthelie 1990 • $18 • (12/15/92)

86 **LOUIS LATOUR** Bourgogne Cuvée Latour 1990 • $11 • (12/15/92)

86 **MOILLARD** Pommard Rugiens 1990 • $50 • (12/15/92)

86 **MOMMESSIN** Santenay Clos Rousseau 1990 • $14 • (12/15/92)

86 **MOMMESSIN** Chambolle-Musigny 1990 • $22 • (12/15/92)

86 **MUGNERET-GIBOURG** Bourgogne 1990 • $18 • (12/15/92)

86 **PIERRE PONNELLE** Bonnes Mares 1990 • $56

86 **PIERRE PONNELLE** Clos de Vougeot 1990 • $48

86 **PRINCE FLORENT DE MERODE** Aloxe-Corton Premier Cru 1990 • $37 • (12/15/92)

86 **PRINCE FLORENT DE MERODE** Corton Maréchaudes 1990 • $49 • (12/15/92)
86 **SIMON BIZE & FILS** Savigny-lès-Beaune Aux Guettes 1990 • $33 • (12/15/92)
86 **TOLLOT-BEAUT** Chorey-Côte-de-Beaune 1990 • $26 • (12/15/92)
85 **ALAIN GRAS** Auxey-Duresses Rouge 1990 • $29 • (12/15/92)
85 **ALBERT MOROT** Beaune Les Teurons 1990 • $39 • (12/15/92)
85 **BERNARD MOREY** Chassagne-Montrachet Red 1990 • $28 • (06/15/93)
85 **BOUCHARD PERE & FILS** Vosne-Romanée Aux Reignots Château de Vosne-Romanée 1990 • $53 • (12/15/92)
85 **DOMAINE B. SERVEAU** Chambolle-Musigny Les Chabiots 1990 • $35 • (12/15/92)
85 **DOMAINE BERTAGNA** Vougeot Clos de la Perrière 1990 • $NA • (12/15/92)
85 **DOMAINE DANIEL RION** Côte de Nuits-Villages 1990 • $25 • (12/15/92)
85 **DOMAINE FOREY** Vosne-Romanée 1990 • $30 • (12/15/92)
85 **DOMAINE JEAN CHARTRON** Bourgogne Clos de la Combe 1990 • $11 • (03/31/92)
85 **DOMAINE LEJEUNE** Bourgogne 1990 • $18 • (12/15/92)
85 **DOMAINE LUCIEN BOILLOT** Gevrey-Chambertin Les Cherbaudes 1990 • $35 • (12/15/92)
85 **DOMAINE MEO-CAMUZET** Bourgogne 1990 • $20 • (06/15/93)
85 **DOMAINE PARENT** Beaune Les Epenotes 1990 • $NA • (12/15/92)
85 **DOMAINE PRIEUR-BRUNET** Pommard La Platière 1990 • $40 • (02/15/93)
85 **DOMAINE PRIEUR-BRUNET** Volnay-Santenots 1990 • $35 • (02/15/93)
85 **DOMAINE PRIEURE ROCH** Vosne-Romanée Les Clous 1990 • $30 • (06/15/93)
85 **EDMOND CORNU** Bourgogne 1990 • $15 • (12/15/92)
85 **F. CHAUVENET** Chambolle-Musigny 1990 • $45 • (12/15/92)
85 **FAIVELEY** Nuits-St.-Georges 1990 • $36 • (12/15/92)
85 **FAIVELEY** Bourgogne Joseph Faiveley 1990 • $11 • (12/15/92)
85 **GUY CASTAGNIER** Morey-St.-Denis 1990 • $NA • (12/15/92)
85 **JACQUES GERMAIN** Chorey-Côte-de-Beaune Château de Chorey-lès-Beaune 1990 • $24 • (12/15/92)
85 **JAFFELIN** Chassagne-Montrachet 1990 • $16 • (12/15/92)
85 **JAFFELIN** Pernand-Vergelesses 1990 • $16 • (12/15/92)
85 **JAFFELIN** Santenay 1990 • $16 • (12/15/92)
85 **JAFFELIN** Volnay 1990 • $24 • (12/15/92)
85 **JEAN GARAUDET** Monthelie 1990 • $25 • (08/31/92)
85 **JEAN GROS** Nuits-St.-Georges 1990 • $30 • (12/15/92)
85 **LABOURE-ROI** Pommard 1990 • $20 • (06/15/93)
85 **LABOURE-ROI** Charmes-Chambertin 1990 • $45 • (06/15/93)
85 **LOUIS JADOT** Fixin 1990 • $15 • (12/15/92)
85 **LOUIS JADOT** Nuits-St.-Georges Clos des Corvées 1990 • $36 • (12/15/92)
85 **LOUIS LATOUR** Pommard Epenots 1990 • $37 • (12/15/92)
85 **MICHEL GROS** Côte de Nuits-Villages 1990 • $NA • (12/15/92)
85 **MOILLARD** Gevrey-Chambertin 1990 • $33 • (12/15/92)
85 **MOILLARD** Fixin Clos de la Perrière 1990 • $30 • (12/15/92)
85 **OLIVIER LEFLAIVE** Chassagne-Montrachet 1990 • $17 • (12/15/92)
85 **OLIVIER LEFLAIVE** Santenay Les Gravières 1990 • $17 • (12/15/92)
85 **PHILIPPE LECLERC** Gevrey-Chambertin Les Cazetiers 1990 • $65 • (12/15/92)
85 **PRINCE FLORENT DE MERODE** Corton Bressandes 1990 • $54 • (12/15/92)
85 **SIMON BIZE & FILS** Savigny-lès-Beaune 1990 • $20 • (12/15/92)
84 **ALAIN BURGUET** Bourgogne 1990 • $18 • (12/15/92)
84 **ALBERT MOROT** Beaune Les Marconnets 1990 • $38 • (12/15/92)
84 **ALBERT MOROT** Beaune Toussaints 1990 • $38 • (12/15/92)
84 **BOUCHARD PERE & FILS** Beaune Les Teurons Domaines du Château de Beaune 1990 • $30 • (12/15/92)
84 **CHARLOPIN-PARIZOT** Marsannay en Montchenovoy 1990 • $19 • (04/30/92)
84 **CHATEAU DE PULIGNY-MONTRACHET** Monthelie 1990 • $21 • (08/31/92)
84 **DOMAINE ANNE & FRANCOIS GROS** Bourgogne 1990 • $17 • (12/15/92)
84 **DOMAINE BACHELET** Côte de Nuits-Villages 1990 • $18 • (12/15/92)
84 **DOMAINE DU CLOS FRANTIN** Gevrey-Chambertin 1990 • $28 • (11/30/92)
84 **DOMAINE MARCHAND-GRILLOT** Gevrey-Chambertin 1990 • $20 • (06/15/93)
84 **DOMAINE MEO-CAMUZET** Clos de Vougeot 1990 • $77 • (09/30/93)
84 **DOMAINE Y. CLERGET** Volnay 1990 • $34 • (12/15/92)
84 **DOMAINE Y. CLERGET** Volnay Clos du Verseuilles 1990 • $42 • (12/15/92)
84 **F. CHAUVENET** Monthelie 1990 • $21 • (12/15/92)
84 **FREDERIC ESMONIN** Gevrey-Chambertin Estournelles St.-Jacques 1990 • $39 • (10/31/92)
84 **J. CONFURON-COTETIDOT** Vosne-Romanée 1990 • $30 • (12/15/92)
84 **JAFFELIN** Auxey-Duresses 1990 • $16 • (12/15/92)
84 **JAFFELIN** Santenay La Maladière 1990 • $19 • (12/15/92)
84 **JEAN GARAUDET** Bourgogne Passe tout grains 1990 • $10 • (06/15/92)
84 **JEAN GRIVOT** Richebourg 1990 • $NA • (12/15/92)
84 **JEAN-LUC DUBOIS** Ladoix La Combe 1990 • $19 • (06/15/93)
84 **JEAN-NOEL GAGNARD** Chassagne-Montrachet 1990 • $50 • (11/30/92)
84 **JOSEPH DROUHIN** Chassagne-Montrachet Red 1990 • $22 • (12/15/92)
84 **JOSEPH DROUHIN** Savigny-lès-Beaune 1990 • $22 • (12/15/92)
84 **LABOURE-ROI** Chambolle-Musigny 1990 • $20 • (06/15/93)
84 **LABOURE-ROI** Richebourg 1990 • $71 • (06/15/93)
84 **LOUIS LATOUR** Aloxe-Corton Domaine Latour 1990 • $22 • (12/15/92)
84 **MARIUS DELARCHE PERE & FILS** Pernand-Vergelesses Les Vergelesses 1990 • $25 • (06/15/93)
84 **MOILLARD** Beaune Grèves Domaine Thomas-Moillard 1990 • $29 • (08/31/92)
84 **MOILLARD** Charmes-Chambertin 1990 • $35 • (12/31/93)
84 **PIERRE BOUREE FILS** Chambertin 1990 • $85 • (12/15/92)
84 **PIERRE PONNELLE** Corton le Clos du Roi 1990 • $36
83 **DOMAINE BRUNO CLAIR** Marsannay Les Longeroies 1990 • $18 • (12/15/92)
83 **DOMAINE COTTIN** Chambolle-Musigny 1990 • $22 • (06/15/93)

■ ■ ■ ■

Red Burgundy

83 **DOMAINE PARENT** Corton Les Renardes 1990• $NA • (12/15/92)
83 **DOMAINE PIERRE GUILLEMOT** Savigny-lès-Beaune Jarrons 1990• $24• (12/15/92)
83 **DOMAINE PRIEURE ROCH** Clos de Vougeot 1990• $65 • (06/15/93)
83 **F. CHAUVENET** Nuits-St.-Georges Aux Chaignots 1990 • $53• (12/15/92)
83 **FRANCOISE & DENIS CLAIR** Santenay Clos de Tavannes 1990• $29• (02/15/93)
83 **FREDERIC ESMONIN** Mazis-Chambertin Mazy-Chambertin 1990• $71• (10/31/92)
83 **FREDERIC ESMONIN** Gevrey-Chambertin Lavaut St.-Jacques 1990• $39• (10/31/92)
83 **GHISLAINE BARTHOD** Bourgogne 1990• $23• (12/15/92)
83 **J. CONFURON-COTETIDOT** Vosne-Romanée Les Suchots 1990• $44• (12/15/92)
83 **JOSEPH DROUHIN** Maranges Premier Cru 1990• $19 • (12/15/92)
83 **JOSEPH DROUHIN** Santenay 1990• $22• (12/15/92)
83 **LABOURE-ROI** Clos de Vougeot 1990• $44• (06/15/93)
83 **LABOURE-ROI** Gevrey-Chambertin 1990• $20 • (06/15/93)
82 **BOUCHARD PERE & FILS** Savigny-lès-Beaune Les Lavières Domaines du Château de Beau 1990• $NA • (12/15/92)
82 **DOMAINE HENRI PERROT-MINOT** Chambolle-Musigny 1990 • $32• (03/15/94)
82 **DOMAINE MICHEL LAFARGE** Bourgogne Pinot Noir 1990 • $18• (12/15/92)
82 **DOMAINE PRIEURE ROCH** Vosne-Romanée Hautes Maizières 1990• $50• (06/15/93)
82 **DOMAINE SIRUGUE** Côte de Nuits-Villages Clos de la Belle Marguerite 1990• $10• (06/15/93)
82 **DOMAINE Y. CLERGET** Bourgogne 1990• $15 • (12/15/92)
82 **FREDERIC ESMONIN** Gevrey-Chambertin Les Corbeaux 1990• $39• (10/31/92)
82 **GUFFENS-HEYNEN** Mâcon-Pierreclos En Chavigne Cuvée Bois Neuf 1990• $18• (08/31/92)
82 **JAFFELIN** Bourgogne du Châpitre 1990• $11 • (12/15/92)
82 **JEAN CLAUDE BOISSET** Gevrey-Chambertin 1990• $17
82 **JOSEPH DROUHIN** Pommard 1990• $36• (12/15/92)
82 **JOSEPH DROUHIN** Côte de Nuits-Villages 1990• $20 • (12/15/92)
82 **OLIVIER LEFLAIVE** Monthelie Premier Cru 1990• $19 • (12/15/92)
82 **PIERRE PONNELLE** Corton Clos du Roi 1990• $NA • (12/31/93)
82 **PIERRE PONNELLE** Clos de Vougeot 1990• $45 • (12/31/93)
81 **DOMAINE CHANTAL LESCURE** Vosne-Romanée Les Suchots 1990• $26• (06/15/93)
81 **DOMAINE DU CLOS FRANTIN** Nuits-St.-Georges 1990• $29 • (11/30/92)
81 **DOMAINE DU CLOS FRANTIN** Corton 1990• $53 • (11/30/92)
81 **DOMAINE PARENT** Pommard Les Chaponnières 1990 • $NA• (12/15/92)
81 **DOMAINE TAUPENOT-MERME** Gevrey-Chambertin Bel Air 1990• $30• (01/31/95)
81 **DUBREUIL-FONTAINE** Savigny-lès-Beaune Aux Vergelesses 1990• $25• (12/15/92)
81 **FRANCOISE & DENIS CLAIR** Santenay Clos de la Comme 1990• $26• (02/15/93)
81 **JEAN GROS** Bourgogne 1990• $16• (12/15/92)
81 **MOILLARD** Echézeaux 1990• $45• (12/31/93)
80 **BOUCHARD PERE & FILS** Chassagne-Montrachet 1990 • $21• (12/15/92)
80 **DOMAINE B. SERVEAU** Morey-St.-Denis Les Sorbets 1990 • $35• (12/15/92)
80 **DOMAINE BRUNO CLAIR** Marsannay Les Grasses Têtes 1990• $28• (12/15/92)
80 **DOMAINE CHANTAL LESCURE** Nuits-St.-Georges Les Damodes 1990• $25• (06/15/93)
80 **DOMAINE F. & L. SAIER** Clos des Lambrays 1990• $73 • (03/15/93)
80 **F. CHAUVENET** Bourgogne 1990• $NA• (12/15/92)
80 **JAYER-GILLES** Bourgogne Hautes-Côtes de Beaune 1990 • $24• (12/15/92)
80 **JEAN-NOEL GAGNARD** Santenay Clos de Tavannes 1990 • $16• (11/30/92)
80 **LABOURE-ROI** Echézeaux 1990• $36• (06/15/93)
80 **MICHEL JUILLOT** Côte Chalonnaise 1990• $13 • (10/31/92)
80 **MONGEARD-MUGNERET** Savigny-lès-Beaune Les Narbantons 1990• $33• (06/15/93)
80 **OLIVIER LEFLAIVE** Rully 1990• $20• (11/30/92)
79 **CHATEAU DE PULIGNY-MONTRACHET** St.-Aubin En Remilly 1990• $25• (08/31/92)
79 **CHATEAU DE PULIGNY-MONTRACHET** Pommard 1990• $40 • (08/31/92)
79 **DOMAINE A.-F. GROS** Vosne-Romanée Aux Réas 1990 • $40• (12/15/92)
79 **DOMAINE DE L'ARLOT** Nuits-St.-Georges 1990• $33 • (12/15/92)
79 **DOMAINE FOREY** Nuits-St.-Georges Les Perrières 1990 • $40• (12/15/92)
79 **DOMAINE MICHEL VOARICK** Aloxe-Corton 1990• $26 • (12/15/92)
79 **DOMAINE Y. CLERGET** Pommard Les Rugiens 1990• $48 • (12/15/92)
79 **JEAN GRIVOT** Nuits-St.-Georges Les Boudots 1990• $NA • (12/15/92)
79 **LABOURE-ROI** Mazis-Chambertin 1990• $29• (06/15/93)
79 **LOUIS LATOUR** Bourgogne Pinot Noir 1990• $10 • (12/15/92)
79 **MOILLARD** Bourgogne Hautes Côtes de Beaune Les Alouettes 1990• $16• (12/15/92)
79 **MOILLARD** Nuits-St.-Georges Clos de Thorey Domaine Thomas-Moillard 1990• $50• (12/15/92)
79 **PAUL PERNOT** Meursault-Blagny La Pièce sous le Bois 1990• $33• (04/30/92)
78 **BOUCHARD PERE & FILS** Côte de Nuits-Villages 1990 • $NA• (12/15/92)
78 **CHATEAU DE PULIGNY-MONTRACHET** Côte de Nuits-Villages 1990• $21• (08/31/92)
78 **DOMAINE DE L'ARLOT** Nuits-St.-Georges Clos de L'Arlot 1990• $45• (12/15/92)
78 **DOMAINE DU CLOS FRANTIN** Vosne-Romanée 1990• $28 • (11/30/92)
78 **LABOURE-ROI** Bonnes Mares 1990• $56• (06/15/93)
78 **LOUIS LATOUR** Côte de Beaune-Villages 1990• $16 • (12/15/92)
78 **LOUIS LATOUR** Gevrey-Chambertin 1990• $32 • (12/15/92)
77 **DOMAINE PRIEUR-BRUNET** Santenay La Maladière 1990 • $23• (02/15/93)
77 **DOMAINE VINCENT PRUNIER** Chassagne-Montrachet Red 1990• $16• (06/15/93)
77 **LOUIS JADOT** Bourgogne 1990• $NA• (12/15/92)
77 **MOMMESSIN** St.-Aubin 1990• $NA• (12/15/92)
77 **MONGEARD-MUGNERET** Fixin 1990• $26• (03/15/93)

76 **DOMAINE CHANTAL LESCURE** Pommard Les Bertins 1990 • $22 • (06/15/93)
76 **DOMAINE CHANTAL LESCURE** Clos de Vougeot 1990 • $44 • (06/15/93)
76 **JEAN GRIVOT** Vosne-Romanée Les Beaux Monts 1990 • $NA • (12/15/92)
75 **DOMAINE MICHEL VOARICK** Corton Clos du Roi 1990 • $36 • (12/15/92)
75 **MOILLARD** Bourgogne Passe-tout-grains Notre Dame des Ceps 1990 • $9 • (08/31/91)
74 **DOMAINE MAURICE PROTHEAU** Rully Red La Chatalienne 1990 • $14 • (06/15/93)
74 **J.-M. GAUNOUX** Corton Les Renardes 1990 • $60 • (12/15/92)
73 **DOMAINE MICHEL VOARICK** Corton Les Bressandes 1990 • $36 • (12/15/92)
72 **DOMAINE ANNE & FRANCOIS GROS** Chambolle-Musigny La Combe d'Orveau 1990 • $40 • (12/15/92)
72 **DOMAINE RENE JACQUESON** Gevrey-Chambertin Le Fonteny 1990 • $24 • (06/15/93)
71 **PIERRE PONNELLE** Musigny 1990 • $125 • (12/31/93)
70 **LOUIS LATOUR** Corton Domaine Latour 1990 • $35 • (12/15/92)
69 **DOMAINE MICHEL VOARICK** Romanée St.-Vivant 1990 • $76 • (12/15/92)
69 **JEAN GRIVOT** Vosne-Romanée 1990 • $NA • (12/15/92)
69 **PROSPER MAUFOUX** Mâcon-Viré Château de Viré Red 1990 • $12 • (03/31/93)
65 **DOMAINE LALEURE-PIOT** Côte de Nuits-Villages 1990 • $NA • (12/15/92)

1989 Red Burgundy
Vintage Rating: 93

98 **JEAN GROS** Richebourg 1989 • $180 • (01/31/92)
97 **DOMAINE A.-F. GROS** Richebourg 1989 • $130 • (01/31/92)
97 **DOMAINE DE LA ROMANEE-CONTI** Romanée-Conti 1989 • $850 • (10/31/92)
97 **DOMAINE MEO-CAMUZET** Richebourg 1989 • $270 • (11/15/91)
96 **COMTE DE VOGUE** Musigny Cuvée Vieilles Vignes 1989 • $134 • (01/31/92)
96 **DOMAINE G. ROUMIER** Musigny 1989 • $95 • (01/31/92)
96 **DOMAINE LEROY** Pommard Les Vignots 1989 • $70 • (01/31/92)
96 **DOMAINE LEROY** Richebourg 1989 • $206 • (01/31/92)
95 **DOMAINE DU CLOS FRANTIN** Richebourg 1989 • $117 • (01/31/92)
95 **DOMAINE GROS FRERE & SOEUR** Richebourg 1989 • $81 • (01/31/92)
95 **DOMAINE LEROY** Corton Renardes 1989 • $117 • (01/31/92)
95 **DOMAINE LEROY** Nuits-St.-Georges Aux Boudots 1989 • $117 • (01/31/92)
95 **DOMAINE LEROY** Romanée-St.-Vivant 1989 • $197 • (01/31/92)
95 **DOMAINE LEROY** Clos de Vougeot 1989 • $88 • (01/31/92)
95 **DOMAINE MEO-CAMUZET** Vosne-Romanée Au Cros-Parantoux 1989 • $91 • (11/15/91)
95 **DOMAINE MICHEL LAFARGE** Volnay 1989 • $67 • (01/31/92)
95 **FAIVELEY** Mazis-Chambertin 1989 • $46 • (01/31/92)
94 **BERTRAND AMBROISE** Nuits-St.-Georges Les Vaucrains 1989 • $38 • (01/31/92)
94 **BOUCHARD PERE & FILS** Caillerets Ancienne Cuvée Carnot Château Red 1989 • $52 • (02/29/92) • CS
94 **CHARLES MORTET** Chambertin 1989 • $68 • (01/31/92)
94 **CHOPIN-GROFFIER** Clos Vougeot 1989 • $72 • (01/31/92)
94 **CHRISTOPHE ROUMIER** Ruchottes-Chambertin 1989 • $70 • (01/31/92)
94 **COMTE DE VOGUE** Bonnes Mares 1989 • $93 • (01/31/92)
94 **DOMAINE LEROY** Chambolle-Musigny Les Fremières 1989 • $80 • (01/31/92)
94 **DOMAINE LEROY** Clos de la Roche 1989 • $148 • (01/31/92)
94 **DOMAINE LEROY** Vosne-Romanée Les Brûlées 1989 • $111 • (01/31/92)
94 **DOMAINE MEO-CAMUZET** Nuits-St.-Georges Aux Murgers 1989 • $81 • (11/15/91)
94 **DOMAINE MEO-CAMUZET** Vosne-Romanée Aux Brûlées 1989 • $91 • (11/15/91)
94 **DOMAINE MEO-CAMUZET** Clos de Vougeot 1989 • $91 • (11/15/91) • CS
94 **DOMAINE MICHEL LAFARGE** Volnay 1989 • $67 • (01/31/92)
94 **EMMANUEL ROUGET** Vosne-Romanée Cros Parantoux 1989 • $83 • (11/15/91)
94 **F. CHAUVENET** Pommard Epenots 1989 • $45 • (01/31/92)
94 **JAFFELIN** Clos St.-Denis 1989 • $53 • (01/31/92)
94 **JAYER-GILLES** Red 1989 • $101 • (01/31/92)
94 **MONGEARD-MUGNERET** Vosne-Romanée Les Orveaux 1989 • $43 • (01/31/92)
94 **PIERRE BOUREE FILS** Clos de la Roche 1989 • $65 • (01/31/92)
94 **TOLLOT-BEAUT** Corton Bressandes 1989 • $58
93 **ARMAND ROUSSEAU** Chambertin- Clos de Bèze 1989 • $135 • (01/31/92)
93 **BERTRAND AMBROISE** Corton Le Rognet 1989 • $45 • (01/31/92)
93 **BOUCHARD PERE & FILS** Vosne-Romanée Aux Reignots Château de Vosne-Romanée 1989 • $55 • (01/31/92)
93 **CHOPIN-GROFFIER** Nuits-St.-Georges Les Chaignots 1989 • $40 • (01/31/92)
93 **COMTE DE VOGUE** Chambolle-Musigny Les Amoureuses 1989 • $93 • (01/31/92)
93 **COMTE DE VOGUE** Musigny Cuvée Vieilles Vignes 1989 • $134
93 **DOMAINE B. SERVEAU** Chambolle-Musigny Les Sentiers 1989 • $30 • (01/31/92)
93 **DOMAINE DANIEL RION** Nuits-St.-Georges Aux Vignerondes 1989 • $63 • (01/31/92)
93 **DOMAINE DE LA ROMANEE-CONTI** Grands Echézeaux 1989 • $111 • (10/31/92)
93 **DOMAINE DU CLOS FRANTIN** Echézeaux 1989 • $45 • (01/31/92)
93 **DOMAINE G. ROUMIER** Bonnes Mares 1989 • $46 • (01/31/92)
93 **DOMAINE LEROY** Chambertin 1989 • $212 • (01/31/92)
93 **DOMAINE LEROY** Gevrey-Chambertin Les Combottes 1989 • $68 • (01/31/92)
93 **DOMAINE LEROY** Latricières-Chambertin 1989 • $151 • (01/31/92)
93 **DOMAINE MEO-CAMUZET** Corton 1989 • $76 • (11/15/91)
93 **DOMAINE MICHEL LAFARGE** Volnay 1989 • $67
93 **F. CHAUVENET** Corton 1989 • $50 • (01/31/92)
93 **GUY CASTAGNIER** Latricières-Chambertin 1989 • $62 • (01/31/92)
93 **GUY CASTAGNIER** Mazis-Chambertin Mazy-Chambertin 1989 • $62 • (01/31/92)

■ ■ ■ ■

Red Burgundy

93 **JEAN GRIVOT** Richebourg 1989 • $NA • (01/31/92)

93 **JOSEPH DROUHIN** Bonnes Mares 1989 • $99 • (01/31/92)

93 **LOUIS JADOT** Corton Pougets 1989 • $64 • (01/31/92)

93 **LOUIS JADOT** Chambertin Clos de Bèze Red 1989 • $105 • (01/31/92)

93 **LOUIS LATOUR** Bonnes Mares 1989 • $60 • (01/31/92)

93 **LOUIS LATOUR** Romanée-St.-Vivant Les Quatre Journaux 1989 • $140 • (01/31/92)

93 **MOILLARD** Vosne-Romanée Malconsorts Domaine Thomas-Moillard 1989 • $60 • (01/31/92)

93 **MONGEARD-MUGNERET** Echézeaux Vieille Vigne 1989 • $59 • (01/31/92)

93 **MONGEARD-MUGNERET** Grands Echézeaux 1989 • $95 • (01/31/92)

93 **MONGEARD-MUGNERET** Vougeot Les Cras 1989 • $NA • (01/31/92)

93 **OLIVIER LEFLAIVE** Clos St.-Denis 1989 • $56 • (01/31/92)

92 **BOUCHARD PERE & FILS** Corton Le Corton Domaines du Château de Beaune 1989 • $79 • (01/31/92)

92 **BOUCHARD PERE & FILS** Pommard Clos du Pavillon 1989 • $NA • (01/31/92)

92 **BOUCHARD PERE & FILS** Chambertin Clos de Bèze Red 1989 • $92 • (01/31/92)

92 **DOMAINE COSTE-CAUMARTIN** Pommard Les Fremiers 1989 • $35 • (01/31/92)

92 **DOMAINE COSTE-CAUMARTIN** Pommard Clos des Boucherottes 1989 • $38 • (01/31/92)

92 **DOMAINE DANIEL RION** Nuits-St.-Georges Les Hauts Pruliers 1989 • $63 • (01/31/92)

92 **DOMAINE DANIEL RION** Vosne-Romanée Les Chaumes 1989 • $63 • (01/31/92)

92 **DOMAINE DANIEL RION** Clos Vougeot 1989 • $94 • (01/31/92)

92 **DOMAINE FRANCOIS LEGROS** Chambolle-Musigny Les Noirots 1989 • $30 • (11/15/91)

92 **DOMAINE GROS FRERE & SOEUR** Grands Echézeaux 1989 • $80 • (01/31/92)

92 **DOMAINE LEROY** Nuits-St.-Georges Aux Allots 1989 • $45 • (01/31/92)

92 **DOMAINE LEROY** Nuits-St.-Georges Les Vignes Rondes 1989 • $53 • (01/31/92)

92 **DOMAINE LEROY** Vosne-Romanée Les Beaux Monts 1989 • $83 • (01/31/92)

92 **DOMAINE MEO-CAMUZET** Nuits-St.-Georges 1989 • $52 • (11/15/91)

92 **DUBREUIL-FONTAINE** Corton Clos du Roi 1989 • $63 • (01/31/92)

92 **F. CHAUVENET** Echézeaux 1989 • $56 • (01/31/92)

92 **FAIVELEY** Nuits-St.-Georges Les St.-Georges 1989 • $28 • (01/31/92)

92 **FREDERIC ESMONIN** Griotte-Chambertin 1989 • $80 • (03/31/92)

92 **GEORGES MUGNERET** Ruchottes-Chambertin 1989 • $NA • (01/31/92)

92 **JACQUES GERMAIN** Beaune Les Teurons 1989 • $50 • (01/31/92)

92 **JEAN GROS** Vosne-Romanée Clos des Réas 1989 • $70 • (01/31/92)

92 **JOSEPH DROUHIN** Beaune Clos des Mouches 1989 • $47 • (02/29/92)

92 **JOSEPH DROUHIN** Chambolle-Musigny Les Sentiers 1989 • $55 • (01/31/92)

92 **JOSEPH DROUHIN** Chambolle-Musigny Les Feusselottes 1989 • $55 • (01/31/92)

92 **JOSEPH DROUHIN** Charmes-Chambertin 1989 • $80 • (01/31/92)

92 **JOSEPH DROUHIN** Mazis-Chambertin 1989 • $86 • (01/31/92)

92 **JOSEPH DROUHIN** Romanée-St.-Vivant 1989 • $94 • (01/31/92)

92 **LA POUSSE D'OR** Volnay Clos de l'Audignac 1989 • $45 • (01/31/92)

92 **LABOURE-ROI** Bonnes Mares 1989 • $55 • (08/31/92)

92 **MOMMESSIN** Clos de Tart 1989 • $52 • (01/31/92)

92 **MONGEARD-MUGNERET** Richebourg 1989 • $95 • (01/31/92)

92 **OLIVIER LEFLAIVE** Volnay 1989 • $38 • (01/31/92)

92 **SERAFIN PERE & FILS** Charmes-Chambertin 1989 • $43 • (01/31/92)

92 **SERAFIN PERE & FILS** Gevrey-Chambertin Vieilles Vignes 1989 • $45 • (01/31/92)

92 **TOLLOT-BEAUT** Corton Bressandes 1989 • $67 • (01/31/92)

91 **BERTRAND AMBROISE** Nuits-St.-Georges En Rue de Chaux 1989 • $38 • (01/31/92)

91 **BOUCHARD PERE & FILS** Beaune Grèves Vigne de l'Enfant Jésus 1989 • $59

91 **CHOPIN-GROFFIER** Nuits-St.-Georges 1989 • $32 • (01/31/92)

91 **DOMAINE BRUNO CLAIR** Vosne-Romanée Les Champs Pedrix 1989 • $30 • (01/31/92)

91 **DOMAINE DANIEL RION** Nuits-St.-Georges Clos des Argillières 1989 • $63 • (01/31/92)

91 **DOMAINE DE LA ROMANEE-CONTI** La Tâche 1989 • $368 • (10/31/92)

91 **DOMAINE DE LA ROMANEE-CONTI** Romanée St.-Vivant 1989 • $118 • (10/31/92)

91 **DOMAINE DU CLOS FRANTIN** Nuits-St.-Georges 1989 • $29 • (02/29/92)

91 **DOMAINE DU CLOS FRANTIN** Clos de Vougeot 1989 • $56 • (01/31/92)

91 **DOMAINE DUJAC** Clos St.-Denis 1989 • $80 • (01/31/92)

91 **DOMAINE GROS FRERE & SOEUR** Vosne-Romanée 1989 • $39 • (01/31/92)

91 **DOMAINE GROS FRERE & SOEUR** Clos Vougeot Musigni 1989 • $80 • (01/31/92)

91 **DOMAINE LEROY** Savigny-lès-Beaune Les Narbantons 1989 • $65 • (01/31/92)

91 **DOMAINE LEROY** Vosne-Romanée Les Genevrières 1989 • $75 • (01/31/92)

91 **DOMAINE MEO-CAMUZET** Vosne-Romanée 1989 • $47 • (11/15/91)

91 **DOMAINE MEO-CAMUZET** Vosne-Romanée Les Chaumes 1989 • $62 • (01/31/92)

91 **EMMANUEL ROUGET** Vosne-Romanée 1989 • $48 • (11/15/91)

91 **F. CHAUVENET** Beaune Grèves 1989 • $30 • (01/31/92)

91 **F. CHAUVENET** Gevrey-Chambertin Estournelles St.-Jacques 1989 • $40 • (01/31/92)

91 **F. CHAUVENET** Nuits-St.-Georges Les Chaignots 1989 • $45 • (01/31/92)

91 **FAIVELEY** Corton Clos des Cortons 1989 • $100 • (01/31/92)

91 **FREDERIC ESMONIN** Ruchottes-Chambertin 1989 • $80 • (03/31/92)

91 **GEORGES MUGNERET** Ruchottes-Chambertin 1989 • $66 • (04/30/92)

91 **GUY CASTAGNIER** Bonnes Mares 1989 • $67 • (01/31/92)

91 **GUY CASTAGNIER** Clos St.-Denis Red 1989 • $62 • (01/31/92)

91 **J. CONFURON-COTETIDOT** Clos de Vougeot 1989 • $60 • (09/15/92)

91 **JACQUES GERMAIN** Beaune Vignes-Franches 1989 • $45 • (01/31/92)

91 **JACQUES-FREDERIC MUGNIER** Chambolle-Musigny 1989 • $41 • (01/31/92)

91 **JAFFELIN** Corton 1989 • $54 • (01/31/92)

91 **JAFFELIN** Echézeaux 1989 • $60 • (01/31/92)

91 **JAFFELIN** Romanée-St.-Vivant 1989 • $80 • (01/31/92)

91 **JEAN GARAUDET** Beaune Clos des Mouches 1989 • $32 • (11/15/91)

91 **JEAN GARAUDET** Pommard Noizons 1989 • $34 • (11/15/91)

91 **JOSEPH DROUHIN** Volnay Clos des Chênes 1989 • $50 • (01/31/92)

91 **JOSEPH DROUHIN** Chambolle-Musigny 1989 • $41 • (01/31/92)

91 **JOSEPH DROUHIN** Grands Echézeaux 1989 • $114 • (01/31/92)

91 **JOSEPH DROUHIN** Gevrey-Chambertin Les Cazetiers 1989 • $70 • (01/31/92)

91 **JOSEPH DROUHIN** Griotte-Chambertin 1989 • $90 • (01/31/92)

91 **JOSEPH DROUHIN** Clos St.-Denis 1989 • $76 • (01/31/92)

91 **JOSEPH DROUHIN** Vosne-Romanée Les Beaumonts 1989 • $70 • (01/31/92)

91 **LA POUSSE D'OR** Santenay Clos de Tavannes 1989 • $29 • (01/31/92)

91 **LOUIS JADOT** Beaune Clos des Ursules 1989 • $73 • (02/29/92)

91 **LOUIS LATOUR** Beaune Domaine Latour 1989 • $22 • (01/31/92)

91 **MOMMESSIN** Corton Les Grèves 1989 • $45 • (01/31/92)

91 **PHILLIPE CHARLOPIN** Chambertin 1989 • $35 • (11/15/91)

91 **PIERRE BOUREE FILS** Beaune Les Epenottes 1989 • $30 • (01/31/92)

91 **TOLLOT-BEAUT** Beaune Clos du Roi Premier Cru 1989 • $52 • (01/31/92)

90 **ARMAND ROUSSEAU** Gevrey-Chambertin Le Clos St.-Jacques 1989 • $95 • (01/31/92)

90 **ARMAND ROUSSEAU** Mazis-Chambertin Mazy-Chambertin 1989 • $80 • (01/31/92)

90 **ARMAND ROUSSEAU** Ruchottes-Chambertin Clos des Ruchottes 1989 • $85 • (01/31/92)

90 **BERTRAND AMBROISE** Nuits-St.-Georges 1989 • $30 • (01/31/92)

90 **BOUCHARD PERE & FILS** Beaune Marconnets Domaines du Château de Beaune 1989 • $39 • (01/31/92)

90 **CHARLES MORTET** Gevrey-Chambertin Les Champeaux 1989 • $34 • (01/31/92)

90 **CHOPIN-GROFFIER** Chambolle-Musigny 1989 • $32 • (01/31/92)

90 **DOMAINE A.-F. GROS** Clos Vougeot Le Grand Maupertuis 1989 • $NA • (01/31/92)

90 **DOMAINE BRUNO CLAIR** Morey-St.-Denis en La Rue de Vergy 1989 • $36 • (01/31/92)

90 **DOMAINE DANIEL RION** Vosne-Romanée Les Beaux Monts 1989 • $63 • (01/31/92)

90 **DOMAINE DE L'ARLOT** Nuits-St.-Georges Clos des Forets St.-Georges 1989 • $55 • (01/31/92)

90 **DOMAINE DE LA ROMANEE-CONTI** Echézeaux 1989 • $114 • (10/31/92)

90 **DOMAINE DE LA ROMANEE-CONTI** Richebourg 1989 • $214 • (10/31/92)

90 **DOMAINE DU CLOS FRANTIN** Grands Echézeaux 1989 • $56 • (01/31/92)

90 **DOMAINE DUJAC** Charmes-Chambertin 1989 • $72 • (01/31/92)

90 **DOMAINE FOREY** Echézeaux 1989 • $NA • (01/31/92)

90 **DOMAINE G. ROUMIER** Chambolle-Musigny 1989 • $38 • (01/31/92)

90 **DOMAINE HENRI GOUGES** Nuits-St.-Georges Les Vaucrains 1989 • $49 • (01/31/92)

90 **DOMAINE JEAN-JACQUES CONFURON** Romanée-St.-Vivant 1989 • $113 • (10/31/92)

90 **DOMAINE JOBLOT** Givry Clos du Cellier aux Moines 1989 • $25 • (01/31/92)

90 **DOMAINE MEO-CAMUZET** Nuits-St.-Georges Aux Boudots 1989 • $81 • (11/15/91)

90 **F. CHAUVENET** Volnay Clos de Chênes 1989 • $40 • (01/31/92)

90 **F. CHAUVENET** Clos de Vougeot Red 1989 • $60 • (01/31/92)

90 **FAIVELEY** Beaune Champs-Pimont 1989 • $34 • (01/31/92)

90 **FAIVELEY** Pommard Les Chaponnières 1989 • $50 • (01/31/92)

90 **FAIVELEY** Chambertin Clos de Bèze 1989 • $63 • (01/31/92)

90 **FAIVELEY** Nuits-St.-Georges Les Damodes 1989 • $45 • (01/31/92)

90 **GEORGES MUGNERET** Nuits-St.-Georges Les Chaignots 1989 • $43 • (01/31/92)

90 **GUY CASTAGNIER** Charmes-Chambertin 1989 • $62 • (01/31/92)

90 **GUY CASTAGNIER** Clos de la Roche 1989 • $62 • (01/31/92)

90 **JACQUES GERMAIN** Beaune Les Crâs 1989 • $48 • (01/31/92)

90 **JACQUES-FREDERIC MUGNIER** Chambolle-Musigny Les Amoureuses 1989 • $62 • (01/31/92)

90 **JAFFELIN** Nuits-St.-Georges Les Damodes 1989 • $36 • (01/31/92)

90 **JEAN GROS** Vosne-Romanée 1989 • $39 • (01/31/92)

90 **JOSEPH DROUHIN** Volnay Chevret 1989 • $50 • (01/31/92)

90 **JOSEPH DROUHIN** Chambertin 1989 • $114 • (01/31/92)

90 **JOSEPH DROUHIN** Grands Echézeaux 1989 • $114

90 **LA POUSSE D'OR** Volnay Clos de la Bousse d'Or 1989 • $60 • (01/31/92)

90 **LOUIS JADOT** Beaune Boucherottes 1989 • $38 • (01/31/92)

90 **LOUIS JADOT** Gevrey-Chambertin Clos St.-Jacques 1989 • $22 • (01/31/92)

90 **MOMMESSIN** Beaune 1989 • $18 • (01/31/92)

90 **MOMMESSIN** Nuits-St.-Georges Les Vaucrains 1989 • $45 • (01/31/92)

90 **RENE ENGEL** Grands Echézeaux 1989 • $75 • (11/15/91)

90 **TOLLOT-BEAUT** Aloxe-Corton 1989 • $60 • (01/31/92)

90 **TOLLOT-BEAUT** Beaune Grèves 1989 • $44 • (01/31/92)

90 **TOLLOT-BEAUT** Corton 1989 • $67 • (01/31/92)

90 **TOLLOT-BEAUT** Savigny-lès-Beaune Lavières 1989 • $38 • (01/31/92)

89 **BOUCHARD PERE & FILS** Clos de la Roche 1989 • $NA • (01/31/92)

89 **BOUCHARD PERE & FILS** Nuits-St.-Georges Clos-St.-Marc 1989 • $59 • (01/31/92)

89 **BOUCHARD PERE & FILS** Nuits-St.-Georges La Richemone 1989 • $NA • (01/31/92)

89 **CHARLES MORTET** Chambolle-Musigny Les Beaux Bruns 1989 • $34 • (01/31/92)

89 **COMTE DE VOGUE** Chambolle-Musigny 1989 • $44 • (01/31/92)

89 **DOMAINE BRUNO CLAIR** Savigny-lès-Beaune La Dominode 1989 • $24 • (01/31/92)

89 **DOMAINE BRUNO CLAIR** Gevrey-Chambertin Les Cazetiers 1989 • $61 • (01/31/92)

89 **DOMAINE CHANTAL LESCURE** Vosne-Romanée Les Suchots 1989 • $25 • (08/31/92)

89 **DOMAINE DANIEL RION** Chambolle-Musigny Aux Beaux Bruns 1989 • $45 • (01/31/92)

89 **DOMAINE DANIEL RION** Vosne-Romanée 1989 • $37 • (01/31/92)

89 **DOMAINE DU CLOS FRANTIN** Vosne-Romanée 1989 • $30 • (01/31/92)

89 **DOMAINE DUJAC** Clos de la Roche 1989 • $80 • (01/31/92)

89 **DOMAINE FOREY** Nuits-St.-Georges Les Perrières 1989 • $NA • (01/31/92)

89 **DOMAINE HENRI GOUGES** Nuits-St.-Georges Les St.-Georges 1989 • $49 • (01/31/92)

89 **DOMAINE HENRI GOUGES** Nuits-St.-Georges Les Vaucrains Premier Cru 1989 • $49

89 **DOMAINE LEROY** Nuits-St.-Georges Aux Lavières 1989 • $75 • (01/31/92)

89 **F. CHAUVENET** Gevrey-Chambertin Clos St.-Jacques 1989 • $45 • (01/31/92)

89 **FAIVELEY** Echézeaux 1989 • $53 • (01/31/92)

89 **FAIVELEY** Gevrey-Chambertin Les Cazetiers 1989 • $47 • (01/31/92)

89 **FAIVELEY** Latricieres-Chambertin 1989 • $53 • (01/31/92)

89 **FREDERIC ESMONIN** Mazis-Chambertin Mazy-Chambertin 1989 • $80 • (03/31/92)

89 **J. CONFURON-COTETIDOT** Vosne-Romanée 1989 • $27 • (10/31/92)

89 **J. CONFURON-COTETIDOT** Chambolle-Musigny 1989 • $32 • (11/30/92)

89 **JAFFELIN** Aloxe-Corton 1989 • $27 • (01/31/92)

89 **JAFFELIN** Beaune Les Champimonts 1989 • $27 • (01/31/92)

89 **JAFFELIN** Volnay 1989 • $29 • (01/31/92)

89 **JAFFELIN** Chambolle-Musigny 1989 • $28 • (01/31/92)

89 **JAFFELIN** Clos de Vougeot 1989 • $60 • (01/31/92)

89 **JOSEPH DROUHIN** Aloxe-Corton 1989 • $27 • (01/31/92)

89 **JOSEPH DROUHIN** Pommard Epenots 1989 • $56 • (01/31/92)

89 **JOSEPH DROUHIN** Chambolle-Musigny Les Baudes 1989 • $52 • (01/31/92)

89 **JOSEPH DROUHIN** Chambolle-Musigny Premier Cru 1989 • $50 • (01/31/92)

89 **JOSEPH DROUHIN** Vosne-Romanée Les Suchots 1989 • $70 • (01/31/92)

89 **LOUIS JADOT** Vosne-Romanée 1989 • $40 • (01/31/92)

89 **LOUIS LATOUR** Corton Château Corton Grancey 1989 • $48 • (01/31/92)

89 **MOILLARD** Beaune Grèves Domaine Thomas-Moillard 1989 • $28 • (01/31/92)

89 **MOILLARD** Corton Clos des Vergennes 1989 • $40 • (01/31/92)

89 **MOILLARD** Morey-St.-Denis Monts Luisants 1989 • $28 • (01/31/92)

89 **MOILLARD** Nuits-St.-Georges Clos de Thorey Domaine Thomas-Moillard 1989 • $35 • (01/31/92)

89 **MOMMESSIN** Vosne-Romanée Aux Brûlées 1989 • $38 • (01/31/92)

89 **MUGNERET-GIBOURG** Echézeaux 1989 • $62 • (01/31/92)

89 **MUGNERET-GIBOURG** Vosne-Romanée 1989 • $34 • (01/31/92)

89 **RENE ENGEL** Echézeaux 1989 • $47 • (11/15/91)

89 **ROBERT CHEVILLON** Nuits-St.-Georges 1989 • $36 • (01/31/92)

89 **ROBERT CHEVILLON** Nuits-St.-Georges Les Vaucrains 1989 • $65 • (01/31/92)

89 **ROBERT DROUHIN** Clos de Vougeot Red 1989 • $88 • (01/31/92)

89 **SERAFIN PERE & FILS** Gevrey-Chambertin Les Cazetiers 1989 • $54 • (01/31/92)

88 **ARMAND ROUSSEAU** Gevrey-Chambertin 1989 • $NA • (01/31/92)

88 **BICHOT** Corton Hospices de Beaune Cuvée Docteur-Peste 1989 • $100 • (01/31/92)

88 **BOUCHARD AINE** Chambertin Clos de Bèze Domaine Marion 1989 • $NA • (01/31/92)

88 **BOUCHARD PERE & FILS** Volnay Taillepieds Domaines de Château de Beaune 1989 • $48 • (01/31/92)

88 **BOUCHARD PERE & FILS** Echézeaux 1989 • $62 • (01/31/92)

88 **CHARLES MORTET** Gevrey-Chambertin Clos Prieur 1989 • $30 • (01/31/92)

88 **CHARLES MORTET** Gevrey-Chambertin 1989 • $25 • (01/31/92)

88 **CHARLOPIN-PARIZOT** Gevrey-Chambertin Cuvée Vieilles Vignes 1989 • $75 • (11/15/91)

88 **DOMAINE CHANTAL LESCURE** Beaune Les Chouacheux 1989 • $19 • (08/31/92)

88 **DOMAINE D'AUVENAY** Auxey-Duresses Red 1989 • $42 • (01/31/92)

88 **DOMAINE DANIEL RION** Nuits-St.-Georges Les Grandes Vignes 1989 • $38 • (01/31/92)

88 **DOMAINE DU CLOS FRANTIN** Chambertin 1989 • $73 • (01/31/92)

88 **DOMAINE G. ROUMIER** Chambolle-Musigny Les Amoureuses 1989 • $62 • (01/31/92)

88 **DOMAINE JOBLOT** Givry Clos de la Servoisine 1989 • $25 • (01/31/92)

88 **DOMAINE MICHEL LAFARGE** Volnay 1989 • $41 • (01/31/92)

88 **F. CHAUVENET** Volnay Premier Cru 1989 • $36 • (01/31/92)

88 **F. CHAUVENET** Gevrey-Chambertin Lavaux St.-Jacques 1989 • $45 • (01/31/92)

88 **F. CHAUVENET** Nuits-St.-Georges Les Pruliers 1989 • $45 • (01/31/92)

88 **FAIVELEY** Morey-St.-Denis Clos des Ormes 1989 • $44 • (01/31/92)

88 **FAIVELEY** Vosne-Romanée 1989 • $35 • (01/31/92)

88 **FREDERIC ESMONIN** Gevrey-Chambertin Les Corbeaux 1989 • $42 • (03/31/92)

88 **FREDERIC ESMONIN** Gevrey-Chambertin Lavaux St.-Jacques 1989 • $42 • (03/31/92)

88 **GUY CASTAGNIER** Chambolle-Musigny 1989 • $39 • (01/31/92)

88 **JACQUES-FREDERIC MUGNIER** Musigny 1989 • $125 • (01/31/92)

88 **JAFFELIN** Gevrey-Chambertin 1989 • $30 • (01/31/92)

88 **JOSEPH DROUHIN** Beaune Grèves 1989 • $47 • (01/31/92)

88 **JOSEPH DROUHIN** Clos de la Roche 1989 • $77 • (01/31/92)

88 **LABOURE-ROI** Chambertin 1989 • $55 • (08/31/92)

88 **LOUIS JADOT** Pommard Grands Epenots 1989 • $50 • (01/31/92)
88 **LOUIS JADOT** Fixin 1989 • $21 • (01/31/92)
88 **LOUIS JADOT** Chambertin Clos de Bèze Red 1989 • $100
88 **MARIE-PIERRE GERMAIN** Aloxe-Corton Les Vercots Red 1989 • $NA • (01/31/92)
88 **MAURICE ECARD** Savigny-lès-Beaune Les Serpentières 1989 • $25 • (11/15/91)
88 **MOILLARD** Fixin 1989 • $NA • (01/31/92)
88 **MOMMESSIN** Aloxe-Corton Les Valozières 1989 • $28 • (01/31/92)
88 **MOMMESSIN** Pommard 1989 • $28 • (01/31/92)
88 **MUGNERET-GIBOURG** Echézeaux 1989 • $62 • (04/30/92)
88 **MUGNERET-GIBOURG** Bourgogne 1989 • $17 • (01/31/92)
88 **OLIVIER LEFLAIVE** Pommard Epenots 1989 • $40 • (01/31/92)
88 **OLIVIER LEFLAIVE** Charmes-Chambertin 1989 • $60 • (01/31/92)
88 **POTHIER-RIEUSSET** Beaune Les Boucherottes 1989 • $28 • (11/30/92)
87 **BOUCHARD PERE & FILS** Aloxe-Corton Red 1989 • $36 • (01/31/92)
87 **CHARLES MORTET** Bourgogne 1989 • $14 • (01/31/92)
87 **DOMAINE BRUNO CLAIR** Marsannay Les Longeroies 1989 • $18 • (01/31/92)
87 **DOMAINE CHANTAL LESCURE** Pommard Les Bertins 1989 • $25 • (08/31/92)
87 **DOMAINE COSTE-CAUMARTIN** Bourgogne 1989 • $15 • (01/31/92)
87 **DOMAINE FRANCOIS LEGROS** Nuits-St.-Georges Les Perrières 1989 • $29 • (11/15/91)
87 **DOMAINE G. ROUMIER** Clos Vougeot Red 1989 • $62 • (01/31/92)
87 **DOMAINE HENRI GOUGES** Nuits-St.-Georges Clos des Porrets-St.-Georges 1989 • $45 • (01/31/92)
87 **F. CHAUVENET** Clos St.-Denis Red 1989 • $60 • (01/31/92)
87 **FAIVELEY** Gevrey-Chambertin 1989 • $34 • (01/31/92)
87 **FAIVELEY** Gevrey-Chambertin La Combe Aux Moines 1989 • $47 • (01/31/92)
87 **GEORGES MUGNERET** Chambolle-Musigny Les Feusselottes 1989 • $47 • (04/30/92)
87 **JAFFELIN** Monthelie 1989 • $19 • (01/31/92)
87 **JAFFELIN** Charmes-Chambertin 1989 • $66 • (01/31/92)
87 **JAYER-GILLES** Red 1989 • $32 • (01/31/92)
87 **JEAN GROS** Nuits-St.-Georges 1989 • $39 • (01/31/92)
87 **JEAN-NOEL GAGNARD** Chassagne-Montrachet Morgeot Red 1989 • $25 • (11/15/91)
87 **JOSEPH DROUHIN** Chassagne-Montrachet 1989 • $23 • (01/31/92)
87 **JOSEPH DROUHIN** Pommard Rugiens 1989 • $56 • (01/31/92)
87 **JOSEPH DROUHIN** Santenay 1989 • $44 • (01/31/92)
87 **JOSEPH DROUHIN** Savigny-lès-Beaune 1989 • $23 • (01/31/92)
87 **LOUIS JADOT** Monthelie 1989 • $21 • (01/31/92)
87 **LOUIS JADOT** Clos Vougeot 1989 • $74 • (01/31/92)
87 **LOUIS LATOUR** Gevrey-Chambertin 1989 • $35 • (01/31/92)
87 **MAURICE ECARD** Savigny-lès-Beaune Les Peuillets 1989 • $25 • (11/15/91)
87 **MOMMESSIN** Maranges 1989 • $13 • (01/31/92)
87 **MOMMESSIN** Fixin 1989 • $15 • (01/31/92)
87 **MONGEARD-MUGNERET** Clos de Vougeot 1989 • $77 • (01/31/92)
87 **OLIVIER LEFLAIVE** Morey-St.-Denis 1989 • $30 • (01/31/92)
87 **RENE ENGEL** Vosne-Romanée Les Brûlées 1989 • $35 • (11/15/91)
87 **SIMON BIZE & FILS** Savigny-lès-Beaune Aux Vergelesses 1989 • $27 • (01/31/92)
87 **TOLLOT-BEAUT** Chorey-Côte-de-Beaune 1989 • $28 • (01/31/92)
86 **BERTRAND AMBROISE** Red 1989 • $20 • (01/31/92)
86 **BICHOT** Pommard Hospices de Beaune Cuvée Cyrot-Chaudron 1989 • $70 • (01/31/92)
86 **CHARLES MORTET** Clos de Vougeot 1989 • $47 • (01/31/92)
86 **CHATEAU DE POMMARD** Pommard 1989 • $65 • (01/31/92)
86 **DOMAINE B. SERVEAU** Morey-St.-Denis Les Sorbets 1989 • $30 • (01/31/92)
86 **DOMAINE DU CLOS FRANTIN** Corton 1989 • $58 • (01/31/92)
86 **DOMAINE DUJAC** Gevrey-Chambertin Aux Combottes 1989 • $65 • (01/31/92)
86 **DOMAINE HENRI GOUGES** Nuits-St.-Georges Les Pruliers 1989 • $45 • (01/31/92)
86 **EMMANUEL ROUGET** Nuits-St.-Georges 1989 • $48 • (11/15/91)
86 **F. CHAUVENET** Pommard Les Chanlins 1989 • $45 • (01/31/92)
86 **FREDERIC ESMONIN** Gevrey-Chambertin Estournelles St.-Jacques 1989 • $42 • (03/31/92)
86 **GEORGES MUGNERET** Nuits-St.-Georges Les Chaignots 1989 • $43 • (04/30/92)
86 **GUY CASTAGNIER** Morey-St.-Denis 1989 • $NA • (01/31/92)
86 **JAFFELIN** Chassagne-Montrachet 1989 • $18 • (01/31/92)
86 **JAFFELIN** Pernand-Vergelesses 1989 • $19 • (01/31/92)
86 **JAFFELIN** Morey-St.-Denis Les Ruchots 1989 • $30 • (01/31/92)
86 **JAFFELIN** Vosne-Romanée 1989 • $29 • (01/31/92)
86 **JAYER-GILLES** Bourgogne Hautes Côtes de Nuits 1989 • $24 • (01/31/92)
86 **JEAN GARAUDET** Monthelie 1989 • $22 • (11/15/91)
86 **JOSEPH DROUHIN** Gevrey-Chambertin Lavaux St.-Jacques 1989 • $70 • (01/31/92)
86 **JOSEPH DROUHIN** Morey-St.-Denis Clos Sorbè 1989 • $45 • (01/31/92)
86 **LOUIS JADOT** Pernand-Vergelesses Clos de la Croix de Pierre 1989 • $21 • (01/31/92)
86 **LUPE-CHOLET** Bourgogne Pinot Noir Comte de Lupé 1989 • $7 • (01/31/92)
86 **MOILLARD** Fixin Clos d'Entre Deux Velles 1989 • $28 • (01/31/92)
86 **MOMMESSIN** Beaune Les Cent Vignes 1989 • $23 • (01/31/92)
86 **PRINCE FLORENT DE MERODE** Pommard Clos de la Platière 1989 • $48 • (11/30/92)
86 **ROBERT CHEVILLON** Nuits-St.-Georges Les St.-Georges 1989 • $53
86 **SERAFIN PERE & FILS** Gevrey-Chambertin Le Fonteny 1989 • $50 • (01/31/92)
85 **BICHOT** Château de Montpatey Pinot Noir Red 1989 • $10 • (06/15/92) • BB
85 **DOMAINE B. SERVEAU** Chambolle-Musigny Les Amoureuses 1989 • $50 • (01/31/92)

85 **DOMAINE DANIEL RION** Vosne-Romanée Les Chaumes 1989 • $63
85 **DOMAINE F. & L. SAIER** Clos des Lambrays 1989 • $68 • (11/15/91)
85 **DOMAINE FOREY** Vosne-Romanée 1989 • $NA • (01/31/92)
85 **DOMAINE G. ROUMIER** Morey-St.-Denis Clos de La Bussière 1989 • $38 • (01/31/92)
85 **DOMAINE MICHEL LAFARGE** Bourgogne 1989 • $19 • (01/31/92)
85 **F ROBLET-MONNOT** Volnay Les Caillerets 1989 • $37 • (11/15/93)
85 **FAIVELEY** Chambolle-Musigny 1989 • $34 • (01/31/92)
85 **FAIVELEY** Fixin 1989 • $21 • (01/31/92)
85 **FAIVELEY** Nuits-St.-Georges Clos de la Maréchale 1989 • $25 • (01/31/92)
85 **FAIVELEY** Clos de Vougeot 1989 • $41 • (01/31/92)
85 **GUY CASTAGNIER** Clos de Vougeot Red 1989 • $64 • (01/31/92)
85 **JAFFELIN** Auxey-Duresses 1989 • $16 • (01/31/92)
85 **JAFFELIN** Beaune Les Bressandes 1989 • $28 • (01/31/92)
85 **JAFFELIN** Ladoix Côte de Beaune 1989 • $13 • (01/31/92)
85 **JAFFELIN** Pommard 1989 • $33 • (01/31/92)
85 **JAFFELIN** Santenay 1989 • $17 • (01/31/92)
85 **JAFFELIN** Savigny-lès-Beaune 1989 • $18 • (01/31/92)
85 **JAFFELIN** Fixin 1989 • $18 • (01/31/92)
85 **JEAN-NOEL GAGNARD** Santenay Clos de Tavannes 1989 • $25 • (11/15/91)
85 **JOSEPH DROUHIN** Bourgogne Pinot Noir Laforàt 1989 • $9 • (04/30/91) • BB
85 **JOSEPH DROUHIN** Maranges Première Cru 1989 • $20 • (01/31/92)
85 **JOSEPH DROUHIN** Pommard 1989 • $43 • (01/31/92)
85 **LEROY** Bourgogne Leroy 1989 • $18 • (01/31/92)
85 **LOUIS JADOT** Nuits-St.-Georges Clos des Corvées 1989 • $56 • (01/31/92)
85 **LOUIS LATOUR** Pommard Epenots 1989 • $38
85 **MICHEL JUILLOT** Mercurey Clos Tonnerre Red 1989 • $24 • (08/31/92)
85 **MOILLARD** Corton Clos du Roi Domaine Thomas-Moillard 1989 • $41 • (01/31/92)
85 **MOILLARD** Ladoix Côte de Beaune 1989 • $NA • (01/31/92)
85 **MOMMESSIN** Gevrey-Chambertin Lavaux St.-Jacques 1989 • $45 • (01/31/92)
85 **MONGEARD-MUGNERET** Bourgogne 1989 • $9 • (01/31/92)
85 **MONGEARD-MUGNERET** Vosne-Romanée 1989 • $34 • (01/31/92)
85 **MUGNERET-GIBOURG** Vosne-Romanée 1989 • $34 • (11/15/91)
85 **PIERRE BOUREE FILS** Gevrey-Chambertin 1989 • $35 • (01/31/92)
85 **RENE ENGEL** Clos Vougeot 1989 • $66 • (11/15/91)
85 **RENE ENGEL** Vosne-Romanée 1989 • $34 • (11/15/91)
85 **SIMON BIZE & FILS** Savigny-lès-Beaune Les Bourgeots 1989 • $19 • (01/31/92)
84 **A. & P. DE VILLAINE** Bourgogne La Digoine Bouzeron 1989 • $17 • (11/15/91)
84 **DOMAINE DU CLOS FRANTIN** Gevrey-Chambertin 1989 • $29 • (01/31/92)
84 **DOMAINE DUJAC** Morey-St.-Denis 1989 • $40 • (01/31/92)
84 **DOMAINE JEAN-JACQUES CONFURON** Côte de Nuits-Villages Les Vignottes 1989 • $16 • (11/30/92)
84 **DOMAINE MEO-CAMUZET** Bourgogne Passe-tout-grains 1989 • $17 • (07/15/91)
84 **DUBREUIL-FONTAINE** Pernand-Vergelesses Ile des Vergelesses 1989 • $40 • (01/31/92)
84 **FAIVELEY** Bourgogne Joseph Faiveley 1989 • $12 • (01/31/92)
84 **FAIVELEY** Nuits-St.-Georges Les Porêts St.-Georges 1989 • $42 • (01/31/92)
84 **JACQUES GERMAIN** Chorey-Côte-de-Beaune Château de Chorey-lès-Beaune 1989 • $24 • (01/31/92)
84 **JAFFELIN** St.-Aubin 1989 • $14 • (01/31/92)
84 **JAFFELIN** Cote de Nuits-Villages 1989 • $15 • (01/31/92)
84 **JAYER-GILLES** Bourgogne Hautes Côtes de Beaune 1989 • $24 • (01/31/92)
84 **LABOURE-ROI** Chambertin Clos de Bèze 1989 • $60 • (08/31/92)
84 **LOUIS JADOT** Côte de Beaune-Villages 1989 • $18 • (01/31/92)
84 **LOUIS JADOT** Côte de Beaune-Villages 1989 • $19 • (08/31/92)
84 **LOUIS LATOUR** Aloxe-Corton Domaine Latour 1989 • $24 • (01/31/92)
84 **LOUIS LATOUR** Savigny-lès-Beaune 1989 • $NA • (01/31/92)
84 **MICHEL JUILLOT** Mercurey Les Champs Martins Red 1989 • $24 • (08/31/92)
84 **MOILLARD** Bourgogne Hautes Côtes de Nuits Les Vignes Hautes 1989 • $NA • (01/31/92)
84 **MONGEARD-MUGNERET** Nuits-St.-Georges Les Boudots 1989 • $49 • (01/31/92)
84 **OLIVIER LEFLAIVE** Pommard 1989 • $32 • (01/31/92)
84 **POTHIER-RIEUSSET** Pommard Les Rugiens 1989 • $49 • (11/30/92)
84 **PRINCE FLORENT DE MERODE** Corton Bressandes 1989 • $56 • (11/30/92)
83 **BICHOT** Beaune Hospices de Beaune Cuvée Guigone-de-Salins 1989 • $68 • (01/31/92)
83 **BICHOT** Crox St.-Louis Pinot Noir Red 1989 • $9 • (06/15/92) • BB
83 **DOMAINE B. SERVEAU** Bourgogne 1989 • $10 • (01/31/92)
83 **DOMAINE B. SERVEAU** Chambolle-Musigny 1989 • $27 • (01/31/92)
83 **DOMAINE DE L'ARLOT** Clos du Châpeau 1989 • $24 • (01/31/92)
83 **DOMAINE JEAN-JACQUES CONFURON** Nuits-St.-Georges Les Chaboeufs 1989 • $32 • (11/30/92)
83 **DOMAINE MEO-CAMUZET** Bourgogne 1989 • $23 • (11/15/91)
83 **FAIVELEY** Nuits-St.-Georges 1989 • $33 • (01/31/92)
83 **J. CONFURON-COTETIDOT** Echézeaux 1989 • $1 • (10/31/92)
83 **JAFFELIN** Bourgogne Pinot Noir 1989 • $10 • (01/31/92)
83 **JAFFELIN** Nuits-St.-Georges 1989 • $27 • (01/31/92)
83 **LABOURE-ROI** Bourgogne Pinot Noir 1989 • $8 • (08/31/92)
83 **LOUIS JADOT** Bourgogne Pinot Noir 1989 • $NA • (01/31/92)
83 **MOILLARD** Aloxe-Corton Les Affouages Red 1989 • $NA • (01/31/92)
83 **MOILLARD** Bourgogne Hautes Côtes de Beaune Les Alouettes 1989 • $17 • (01/31/92)
83 **MONGEARD-MUGNERET** Fixin 1989 • $25 • (01/31/92)
83 **POTHIER-RIEUSSET** Pommard Clos de Verger 1989 • $44 • (11/30/92)

82 **BICHOT** Château de Dracy Pinot Noir Red 1989 • $9 • (06/15/92)

82 **BOUCHARD PERE & FILS** Savigny-lès-Beaune 1989 • $29 • (01/31/92)

82 **COMTE ARMAND** Pommard Clos des Epeneaux 1989 • $50 • (11/30/92)

82 **DOMAINE CHANTAL LESCURE** Clos de Vougeot 1989 • $45 • (08/31/92)

82 **DOMAINE GROS FRERE & SOEUR** Bourgogne Hautes Côtes de Nuits 1989 • $NA • (01/31/92)

82 **JAFFELIN** Côte de Beaune-Villages 1989 • $14 • (01/31/92)

82 **JAFFELIN** Santenay La Maladière 1989 • $20 • (01/31/92)

82 **MARIUS DELARCHE PERE & FILS** Pernand-Vergelesses 1989 • $15 • (04/30/91)

82 **MICHEL GROS** Bourgogne Hautes Côtes de Nuits 1989 • $NA • (01/31/92)

82 **MOILLARD** Rully 1989 • $14 • (08/31/91)

82 **MOMMESSIN** Auxey-Duresses Red 1989 • $13 • (01/31/92)

82 **MUGNERET-GIBOURG** Bourgogne 1989 • $17 • (06/15/92)

82 **OLIVIER LEFLAIVE** Clos de la Roche 1989 • $63 • (03/15/93)

82 **PIERRE BITOUZET** Aloxe-Corton Valozières 1989 • $28 • (11/30/92)

82 **POTHIER-RIEUSSET** Pommard 1989 • $32 • (11/30/92)

82 **POTHIER-RIEUSSET** Pommard Les Epenots 1989 • $49 • (11/30/92)

81 **BERNARD MOREY** Chassagne-Montrachet Red 1989 • $23 • (11/30/92)

81 **DOMAINE BRUNO CLAIR** Marsannay Les Vaudenelles 1989 • $18 • (01/31/92)

81 **DOMAINE JEAN-JACQUES CONFURON** Nuits-St.-Georges Aux Boudots 1989 • $32 • (11/30/92)

81 **DOMAINE JEAN-JACQUES CONFURON** Chambolle-Musigny 1989 • $35 • (11/30/92)

81 **DOMAINE ROBERT GROFFIER** Bonnes Mares 1989 • $79 • (01/31/92)

81 **F. CHAUVENET** Monthelie Les Champs-Fulliot 1989 • $20 • (01/31/92)

81 **JAFFELIN** Gevrey-Chambertin Lavaux St.-Jacques 1989 • $40 • (01/31/92)

81 **MUGNERET-GIBOURG** Vosne-Romanée 1989 • $34 • (04/30/92)

81 **PATRIARCHE** Bourgogne-Hautes-Côtes de Nuits Cuvée Varache 1989 • $11 • (01/31/92)

81 **PHILIPPE LECLERC** Gevrey-Chambertin Les Platières 1989 • $44 • (10/31/92)

80 **DOMAINE SIRUGUE** Gevrey-Chambertin 1989 • $20 • (08/31/92)

80 **JOSEPH DROUHIN** Nuits-St.-Georges Les Boudots 1989 • $70 • (01/31/92)

80 **LOUIS LATOUR** Bourgogne Cuvée Latour 1989 • $NA • (01/31/92)

80 **LOUIS LATOUR** Santenay 1989 • $NA • (01/31/92)

79 **DOMAINE B. SERVEAU** Chambolle-Musigny Les Chabiots 1989 • $30 • (01/31/92)

79 **F. CHAUVENET** Auxey-Duresses Red Le Val 1989 • $NA • (01/31/92)

78 **DOMAINE A.-F. GROS** Bourgogne Hautes Côtes de Nuits 1989 • $19 • (06/15/92)

78 **DOMAINE DE L'ARLOT** Nuits-St.-Georges Clos de L'Arlot 1989 • $48 • (01/31/92)

78 **DOMAINE ROBERT GROFFIER** Bourgogne 1989 • $14 • (01/31/92)

78 **HENRI DE VILLAMONT** Bourgogne Pinot Noir 1989 • $11 • (03/31/91)

78 **LOUIS LATOUR** Chambertin Cuvée Hèritiers Latour Red 1989 • $90 • (01/31/92)

78 **MONGEARD-MUGNERET** Savigny-lès-Beaune Les Narbantons 1989 • $28 • (01/31/92)

77 **JEAN GRIVOT** Nuits-St.-Georges Les Boudots 1989 • $NA • (01/31/92)

77 **MICHEL GOUBARD** Bourgogne Côte Chalonnaise Mont-Avril Pinot Noir 1989 • $10 • (03/15/93)

77 **MONGEARD-MUGNERET** Bourgogne Hautes Côtes de Nuits 1989 • $16 • (01/31/92)

77 **ROBERT CHEVILLON** Bourgogne 1989 • $16 • (01/31/92)

76 **JEAN CLAUDE BOISSET** Bourgogre Conférie des Chevaliers du Tastevin Red 1989 • $7 • (06/15/92)

76 **LABOURE-ROI** Chambolle-Musigny Domaine Cottin 1989 • $30 • (03/31/92)

76 **LOUIS JADOT** Bourgogne Pinot Noir Jadot 1989 • $12 • (06/15/93)

76 **MUGNERET-GIBOURG** Bourgogne 1989 • $17 • (11/15/91)

75 **BICHOT** Bourgogne Château de Dracy Pinot Noir 1989 • $10 • (03/31/92)

75 **JAFFELIN** Chorey-Côte-de-Beaune 1989 • $13 • (01/31/92)

75 **JEAN GRIVOT** Vosne-Romanée Les Beaumonts 1989 • $NA • (01/31/92)

75 **MICHEL JUILLOT** Mercurey Red 1989 • $21 • (08/31/92)

69 **DOMAINE JEAN-JACQUES CONFURON** Nuits-St.-Georges Les Fleurières 1989 • $26 • (11/30/92)

1988 Red Burgundy
Vintage Rating: 90

98 **JEAN GROS** Richebourg 1988 • $190 • (02/28/91)

97 **DOMAINE A.-F. GROS** Richebourg 1988 • $190 • (02/15/91)

96 **DOMAINE MEO-CAMUZET** Richebourg 1988 • $253 • (11/30/90)

96 **EMMANUEL ROUGET** Echézeaux 1988 • $81 • (11/15/90)

96 **LOUIS JADOT** Chambertin Clos de Bèze Red 1988 • $97 • (03/15/91)

95 **ARMAND ROUSSEAU** Chambertin- Clos de Bèze 1988 • $188 • (05/15/91)

95 **DOMAINE LEROY** Romanée-St.-Vivant 1988 • $431 • (04/30/91)

94 **DOMAINE DE LA ROMANEE-CONTI** Richebourg 1988 • $216 • (04/30/91)

94 **DOMAINE MEO-CAMUZET** Vosne-Romanée Au Cros-Parantoux 1988 • $84 • (11/30/90)

94 **HENRI JAYER** Echézeaux 1988 • $59 • (05/15/91)

94 **JEAN GROS** Vosne-Romanée Clos des Réas 1988 • $50 • (02/28/91)

94 **JOSEPH DROUHIN** Chambertin 1988 • $83 • (02/15/91)

94 **LOUIS JADOT** Griotte-Chambertin 1988 • $75 • (03/15/91)

93 **ARMAND ROUSSEAU** Chambertin 1988 • $201 • (05/15/91)

93 **BERTRAND AMBROISE** Nuits-St.-Georges En Rue de Chaux 1988 • $40 • (05/15/91)

93 **COMTE DE VOGUE** Musigny Cuvée Vieilles Vignes 1988 • $134 • (12/31/90)

93 **DOMAINE CECI** Clos de Vougeot Red 1988 • $48 • (07/15/91)

93 **DOMAINE DANIEL RION** Nuits-St.-Georges Aux Lavières 1988 • $33 • (02/15/91)

■ ■ ■ ■

Red Burgundy

93 DOMAINE DANIEL RION Vosne-Romanée Les Chaumes 1988 • $54 • (01/31/91)

93 DOMAINE LEROY Nuits-St.-Georges Aux Boudots 1988 • $230 • (04/30/91)

93 DOMAINE LEROY Vosne-Romanée Les Beaux Monts 1988 • $74 • (04/30/91)

93 DOMAINE ROBERT GROFFIER Chambolle-Musigny Amoureuses 1988 • $66 • (11/15/90)

93 DROUHIN-LAROZE Bonnes Mares 1988 • $81 • (12/31/90)

93 GUY CASTAGNIER Latricières-Chambertin 1988 • $63 • (07/15/91)

93 HENRI JAYER Vosne-Romanée Cros Parantoux 1988 • $180 • (05/15/91)

93 JOSEPH DROUHIN Echézeaux 1988 • $60 • (11/15/90)

93 JOSEPH DROUHIN Charmes-Chambertin 1988 • $65 • (11/15/90)

93 JOSEPH DROUHIN Clos de la Roche 1988 • $73 • (02/15/91)

93 LOUIS JADOT Corton Pougets 1988 • $61 • (03/31/91)

93 LOUIS JADOT Chapelle-Chambertin 1988 • $75 • (03/15/91)

92 BERTRAND AMBROISE Corton Le Rognet 1988 • $43 • (11/30/90)

92 CHOPIN-GROFFIER Vougeot 1988 • $32 • (05/15/91)

92 DOMAINE DANIEL RION Vosne-Romanée Les Beaux Monts 1988 • $48 • (02/15/91)

92 DOMAINE DANIEL RION Clos Vougeot 1988 • $53 • (01/31/91)

92 DOMAINE DANIEL RION Nuits-St.-Georges Aux Vignerondes 1988 • $54 • (01/31/91)

92 DOMAINE DE LA ROMANEE-CONTI Echézeaux 1988 • $158 • (04/30/91)

92 DOMAINE DE LA ROMANEE-CONTI Grands Echézeaux 1988 • $153 • (04/30/91)

92 DOMAINE GROS FRERE & SOEUR Clos Vougeot Musigni 1988 • $95 • (03/31/91)

92 DOMAINE MEO-CAMUZET Nuits-St.-Georges Aux Boudots 1988 • $80 • (11/30/90)

92 DOMAINE MEO-CAMUZET Clos de Vougeot 1988 • $95 • (11/30/90)

92 DOMAINE PONSOT Chambolle-Musigny Les Charmes 1988 • $58 • (04/30/91)

92 DROUHIN-LAROZE Chambertin Clos de Bèze 1988 • $88 • (12/31/90)

92 GEORGES MUGNERET Ruchottes-Chambertin 1988 • $69 • (11/15/90)

92 JOSEPH DROUHIN Corton Bressandes 1988 • $60 • (11/15/90)

92 JOSEPH DROUHIN Morey-St.-Denis Monts-Luisants 1988 • $38 • (02/28/91)

92 LOUIS JADOT Beaune Boucherottes 1988 • $33 • (03/31/91)

92 LOUIS TRAPET Chambertin 1988 • $111 • (07/15/91)

92 RENE ENGEL Echézeaux 1988 • $41 • (03/31/91)

92 ROSSIGNOL-FEVRIER Volnay 1988 • $32 • (03/31/91)

92 SERAFIN PERE & FILS Gevrey-Chambertin 1988 • $35 • (03/31/91)

92 SERAFIN PERE & FILS Gevrey-Chambertin Le Fonteny 1988 • $50 • (05/15/91)

92 TOLLOT-BEAUT Corton Bressandes 1988 • $59

91 A. CHOPIN Nuits-St.-Georges Aux Murgers 1988 • $28 • (07/15/90)

91 ALAIN MICHELOT Nuits-St.-Georges 1988 • $39 • (07/15/91)

91 ALBERT MOROT Beaune Cent Vignes 1988 • $30 • (04/30/91)

91 ARMAND ROUSSEAU Clos de la Roche 1988 • $75 • (05/15/91)

91 BOUCHARD PERE & FILS Corton Le Corton Domaines du Château de Beaune 1988 • $77 • (03/31/91)

91 BOUCHARD PERE & FILS Beaune Grèves Vigne de l'Enfant Jésus 1988 • $19 • (04/30/91)

91 CHARLES MORTET Gevrey-Chambertin Clos Prieur 1988 • $41 • (02/15/91)

91 DOMAINE A.-F. GROS Echézeaux 1988 • $84 • (02/15/91)

91 DOMAINE CECI Chambolle-Musigny Aux Echanges 1988 • $33 • (07/15/91)

91 DOMAINE DANIEL RION Nuits-St.-Georges Les Hauts Pruliers 1988 • $54 • (01/31/91)

91 DOMAINE DANIEL RION Nuits-St.-Georges Clos des Argillières 1988 • $48 • (01/31/91)

91 DOMAINE DANIEL RION Vosne-Romanée Les Chaumes 1988 • $54

91 DOMAINE F. & L. SAIER Clos des Lambrays 1988 • $75 • (03/31/91)

91 DOMAINE GROS FRERE & SOEUR Richebourg 1988 • $192 • (02/28/91)

91 DOMAINE MEO-CAMUZET Nuits-St.-Georges Aux Murgers 1988 • $80 • (11/30/90)

91 DOMAINE MEO-CAMUZET Nuits-St.-Georges 1988 • $50 • (11/30/90)

91 DOMAINE PONSOT Latricières-Chambertin 1988 • $150 • (05/15/91)

91 DROUHIN-LAROZE Latricières-Chambertin 1988 • $68 • (12/31/90)

91 GUY CASTAGNIER Mazis-Chambertin Mazy-Chambertin 1988 • $63 • (07/15/91)

91 GUY CASTAGNIER Clos de la Roche 1988 • $63 • (07/15/91)

91 J. JAYER Echézeaux 1988 • $100 • (03/15/91)

91 J. LABET & N. DECHELETTE Clos Vougeot Château de la Tour 1988 • $56 • (11/30/90)

91 JOSEPH DROUHIN Griotte-Chambertin 1988 • $81 • (11/15/90)

91 LOUIS JADOT Gevrey-Chambertin Estournelles St.-Jacques 1988 • $50 • (03/15/91)

91 LOUIS JADOT Ruchottes-Chambertin 1988 • $75 • (03/15/91)

91 LOUIS JADOT Beaune Clos des Ursules 1988 • $56 • (03/31/91)

91 MOILLARD Morey-St.-Denis Monts Luisants 1988 • $30 • (12/15/90)

91 PIERRE BOUREE FILS Clos de la Roche 1988 • $85 • (03/31/91)

91 RENE ENGEL Clos Vougeot 1988 • $37 • (03/15/91)

91 ROBERT ARNOUX Romanée-St.-Vivant 1988 • $250 • (11/15/90)

91 SERAFIN PERE & FILS Gevrey-Chambertin Les Cazetiers 1988 • $53 • (05/15/91)

90 ALAIN MICHELOT Nuits-St.-Georges Les Chaignots 1988 • $56 • (05/15/91)

90 BERNARD HERESZTYN Gevrey-Chambertin Les Goulots 1988 • $44 • (07/15/91)

90 BOUCHARD PERE & FILS Pommard 1988 • $37 • (04/30/91)

90 COMTE ARMAND Pommard Clos des Epeneaux 1988 • $46 • (02/28/91)

90 COMTE DE VOGUE Musigny Cuvée Vieilles Vignes 1988 • $108

90 DOMAINE DES CHEZEAUX Griotte-Chambertin 1988 • $110 • (05/15/91)

90 DOMAINE DUJAC Clos de la Roche 1988 • $75 • (03/31/91)

90 **DOMAINE DUJAC** Echézeaux 1988 • $75 • (03/31/91)
90 **DOMAINE MICHEL LAFARGE** Volnay 1988 • $65 • (07/15/91)
90 **DOMAINE MICHEL LAFARGE** Volnay 1988 • $65 • (07/15/91)
90 **DOMAINE ROBERT GROFFIER** Bonnes Mares 1988 • $80 • (11/15/90)
90 **FAIVELEY** Corton Clos des Cortons 1988 • $120 • (03/31/91)
90 **JACQUES GERMAIN** Beaune Les Teurons 1988 • $42 • (02/15/91)
90 **JEAN GARAUDET** Pommard Les Charmots 1988 • $46 • (11/15/90)
90 **JEAN GROS** Vosne-Romanée 1988 • $38 • (02/28/91)
90 **JEANNE-MARIE DE CHAMPS** Nuits-St.-Georges Les Terres Blanches 1988 • $39 • (07/15/91)
90 **JOSEPH DROUHIN** Clos de Vougeot Red 1988 • $85 • (02/15/91)
90 **JOSEPH DROUHIN** Vosne-Romanée Les Suchots 1988 • $57 • (02/28/91)
90 **LOUIS JADOT** Beaune Clos des Couchereaux 1988 • $35 • (03/31/91)
90 **REMOISSENET** Beaune Les Grèves 1988 • $38 • (11/30/90)
90 **ROBERT CHEVILLON** Nuits-St.-Georges Les St.-Georges 1988 • $59
89 **ALAIN MICHELOT** Nuits-St.-Georges Les Richemone 1988 • $54 • (05/15/91)
89 **BERTRAND MACHARD DE GRAMONT** Vosne-Romanée Les Réas 1988 • $32 • (07/15/91)
89 **BOUCHARD PERE & FILS** Pommard Premier Cru Domaines du Château de Beaunè 1988 • $53 • (03/31/91)
89 **BOUCHARD PERE & FILS** Chambertin Clos de Bèze Red 1988 • $82 • (04/30/91)
89 **CHARLES MORTET** Gevrey-Chambertin 1988 • $35 • (02/15/91)
89 **COMTE DE VOGUE** Chambolle-Musigny Les Amoureuses 1988 • $93 • (02/28/91)
89 **COMTE DE VOGUE** Bonnes Mares 1988 • $65 • (03/31/91)
89 **DOMAINE CHANDON DE BRIAILLES** Corton Bressandes 1988 • $75 • (02/28/91)
89 **DOMAINE G. ROUMIER** Chambolle-Musigny 1988 • $30 • (07/15/91)
89 **DOMAINE GROS FRERE & SOEUR** Vosne-Romanée 1988 • $46 • (03/31/91)
89 **DOMAINE LEROY** Nuits-St.-Georges Aux Allots 1988 • $49 • (04/30/91)
89 **DOMAINE LEROY** Clos de Vougeot 1988 • $89 • (04/30/91)
89 **DOMAINE MEO-CAMUZET** Vosne-Romanée Aux Brûlées 1988 • $84 • (11/30/90)
89 **DOMAINE MICHEL LAFARGE** Volnay 1988 • $72
89 **DOMAINE PIERRE AMIOT** Gevrey-Chambertin Les Combottes 1988 • $64 • (03/15/91)
89 **DOMAINE PONSOT** Griotte-Chambertin 1988 • $150 • (05/15/91)
89 **DOMAINE PONSOT** Clos de la Roche Cuvée William 1988 • $150 • (05/15/91)
89 **DOMAINE ROBERT GROFFIER** Chambolle-Musigny Les Sentiers 1988 • $45 • (11/15/90)
89 **DROUHIN-LAROZE** Clos de Vougeot 1988 • $81 • (12/31/90)
89 **FAIVELEY** Gevrey-Chambertin Les Cazetiers 1988 • $57 • (03/31/91)
89 **GUY CASTAGNIER** Clos St.-Denis Red 1988 • $63 • (07/15/91)
89 **HAEGELEN-JAYER** Nuits-St.-Georges Les Damodes 1988 • $39 • (05/15/91)
89 **HENRI JAYER** Vosne-Romanée Les Beaumonts 1988 • $160 • (05/15/91)
89 **JACQUES THEVENOT-MACHAL** Volnay-Santenots 1988 • $36 • (11/15/90)
89 **JACQUES-FREDERIC MUGNIER** Chambolle-Musigny Les Fuées 1988 • $60 • (05/15/91)
89 **JEAN GRIVOT** Nuits-St.-Georges Les Pruliers 1988 • $53 • (04/30/91)
89 **JEANNE-MARIE DE CHAMPS** Nuits-St.-Georges Les Didiers Hospices de Nuits Cuvée Jacques 1988 • $49 • (09/30/90)
89 **LOUIS JADOT** Nuits-St.-Georges Clos des Corvées 1988 • $49 • (02/28/91)
89 **LOUIS TRAPET** Chambertin Cuvée Vieilles Vignes 1988 • $119 • (07/15/91)
89 **LOUIS TRAPET** Chapelle-Chambertin 1988 • $84 • (07/15/91)
89 **MOILLARD** Nuits-St.-Georges Hospices de Nuits Cuvée Jacques Duret 1988 • $68 • (08/31/91)
89 **MOILLARD** Nuits-St.-Georges Clos de Thorey Domaine Thomas-Moillard 1988 • $50 • (12/31/90)
89 **MUGNERET-GIBOURG** Echézeaux 1988 • $70 • (11/15/90)
89 **PIERRE BOUREE FILS** Charmes-Chambertin 1988 • $75 • (03/31/91)
89 **RENE ENGEL** Vosne-Romanée Les Brûlées 1988 • $45 • (02/28/91)
88 **ALAIN BURGUET** Gevrey-Chambertin Vieilles Vignes 1988 • $45 • (12/31/90)
88 **BERTRAND MACHARD DE GRAMONT** Nuits-St.-Georges Les Hauts Pruliers 1988 • $37 • (07/15/91)
88 **BOUCHARD PERE & FILS** Volnay Taillepieds Domaines de Château de Beaune 1988 • $50 • (03/31/91)
88 **CHATEAU DES HERBEAUX** Volnay Santenots 1988 • $36 • (11/30/90)
88 **DOMAINE B. SERVEAU** Morey-St.-Denis Les Sorbets 1988 • $35 • (02/28/91)
88 **DOMAINE CHANTAL LESCURE** Pommard Les Bertins 1988 • $22 • (11/30/90)
88 **DOMAINE JEAN CHARTRON** Beaune Hospices de Beaune Cuvée Cyrot-Chaudron 1988 • $40 • (02/15/91)
88 **DOMAINE LEROY** Pommard Les Vignots 1988 • $84 • (04/30/91)
88 **DOMAINE PONSOT** Clos de la Roche Cuvée Vieilles Vignes 1988 • $185 • (05/15/91)
88 **DROUHIN-LAROZE** Chapelle-Chambertin 1988 • $68 • (12/31/90)
88 **DROUHIN-LAROZE** Gevrey-Chambertin Clos Prieur 1988 • $44 • (12/31/90)
88 **GHISLAINE BARTHOD** Chambolle-Musigny 1988 • $50 • (03/15/91)
88 **JAFFELIN** Gevrey-Chambertin 1988 • $25 • (08/31/91)
88 **JAFFELIN** Volnay 1988 • $30 • (08/31/91)
88 **JAFFELIN** Chambolle-Musigny 1988 • $32 • (12/31/90)
88 **JAYER-GILLES** Bourgogne Hautes-Côtes de Beaune 1988 • $26 • (05/15/91)
88 **JEAN GARAUDET** Pommard 1988 • $37 • (11/15/90)
88 **JEAN GARAUDET** Monthelie 1988 • $23 • (11/15/90)
88 **JEAN-MARC BOILLOT** Beaune Les Montrevenots 1988 • $37 • (05/15/91)
88 **JOSEPH DROUHIN** Beaune Clos des Mouches 1988 • $50 • (02/15/91)
88 **JOSEPH DROUHIN** Grands Echézeaux 1988 • $85
88 **LA POUSSE D'OR** Pommard Les Jarolières 1988 • $27 • (08/31/91)

88 **LOUIS JADOT** Nuits-St.-Georges Les Boudots 1988 • $49 • (02/28/91)

88 **LOUIS JADOT** Gevrey-Chambertin Clos St.-Jacques 1988 • $52 • (03/15/91)

88 **LOUIS JADOT** Bonnes Mares 1988 • $65 • (03/15/91)

88 **LOUIS JADOT** Chambertin Clos de Bèze Red 1988 • $90

88 **MARQUIS D'ANGERVILLE** Volnay Clos des Ducs 1988 • $47 • (10/31/93)

88 **MOILLARD** Beaune Hospices de Beaune Cuvée Clos des Avaux 1988 • $80 • (08/31/91)

88 **MOILLARD** Vosne-Romanée Malconsorts Domaine Thomas-Moillard 1988 • $50 • (03/31/91)

88 **MONGEARD-MUGNERET** Echézeaux Vieille Vigne 1988 • $61 • (02/15/91)

88 **POTHIER-RIEUSSET** Beaune Les Les Boucherottes 1988 • $35 • (11/30/90)

88 **TOLLOT-BEAUT** Chorey-lès-Beaune 1988 • $25 • (12/31/90)

87 **ALAIN MICHELOT** Nuits-St.-Georges Les Vaucrains 1988 • $56 • (05/15/91)

87 **ALBERT MOROT** Beaune Bressandes 1988 • $30 • (03/31/91)

87 **BICHOT** Vosne-Romanée Les Beaux Monts 1988 • $34 • (07/15/90)

87 **BICHOT** Pommard 1988 • $25 • (08/31/90)

87 **BICHOT** Hospices de Beaune Cuvée Blondeau Red 1988 • $60 • (06/15/92)

87 **BOUCHARD PERE & FILS** Volnay Taillepieds Domaines de Château de Beaune 1988 • $47 • (03/31/91)

87 **CHANSON PERE & FILS** Vosne-Romanée Suchots 1988 • $55 • (09/30/90)

87 **CHARLES MORTET** Gevrey-Chambertin Les Champeaux 1988 • $46 • (03/15/91)

87 **CHARTRON & TREBUCHET** Pommard Les Epenots 1988 • $45 • (02/28/91)

87 **CHATEAU DE MEURSAULT** Volnay Clos des Chênes 1988 • $47 • (07/15/91)

87 **CHATEAU DE POMMARD** Pommard 1988 • $53 • (09/15/92)

87 **CHATEAU DES HERBEAUX** Chambertin 1988 • $75 • (12/31/90)

87 **CHOPIN-GROFFIER** Clos Vougeot 1988 • $70 • (05/15/91)

87 **DOMAINE ALETH GIRARDIN** Pommard Charmots 1988 • $44 • (07/15/91)

87 **DOMAINE DANIEL RION** Chambolle-Musigny Aux Beaux Bruns 1988 • $37 • (01/31/91)

87 **DOMAINE DE L'ARLOT** Nuits-St.-Georges Clos de L'Arlot 1988 • $43 • (03/31/91)

87 **DOMAINE DU CLOS FRANTIN** Gevrey-Chambertin 1988 • $37 • (07/15/90)

87 **DOMAINE MEO-CAMUZET** Vosne-Romanée 1988 • $50 • (12/31/90)

87 **DOMAINE MICHEL LAFARGE** Volnay 1988 • $44 • (07/15/91)

87 **GHISLAINE BARTHOD** Chambolle-Musigny Les Crâs 1988 • $45 • (02/28/91)

87 **GUY CASTAGNIER** Bonnes Mares 1988 • $67 • (07/15/91)

87 **JEAN GRIVOT** Nuits-St.-Georges Les Boudots 1988 • $54 • (04/30/91)

87 **JOSEPH DROUHIN** Chambolle-Musigny Les Amoureuses 1988 • $76 • (12/31/90)

87 **JOSEPH DROUHIN** Latricières-Chambertin 1988 • $72 • (02/15/91)

87 **LAROCHE** Nuits-St.-Georges 1988 • $28 • (11/15/90)

87 **LEROY** Bourgogne d'Auvenay 1988 • $15 • (04/30/91)

86 **ALBERT MOROT** Savigny-lès-Beaune Vergelesses La Bataillère 1988 • $26 • (03/31/91)

86 **ALBERT MOROT** Beaune Grèves 1988 • $32 • (07/15/91)

86 **CHATEAU DES HERBEAUX** Clos Vougeot 1988 • $65 • (11/30/90)

86 **DOMAINE B. SERVEAU** Chambolle-Musigny Les Chabiots 1988 • $39 • (02/28/91)

86 **DOMAINE CHANDON DE BRIAILLES** Savigny-lès-Beaune Les Lavières 1988 • $31 • (02/28/91)

86 **DOMAINE DUJAC** Gevrey-Chambertin Aux Combottes 1988 • $54 • (03/31/91)

86 **DOMAINE MAUME** Charmes-Chambertin 1988 • $60 • (07/15/91)

86 **DOMAINE PIERRE AMIOT** Clos de la Roche 1988 • $75 • (03/15/91)

86 **DOMAINE ROUX PERE & FILS** Volnay En Champans 1988 • $35 • (03/31/90)

86 **GEORGES MUGNERET** Chambolle-Musigny Les Feusselottes 1988 • $54 • (11/15/90)

86 **GERARD MUGNERET** Vosne-Romanée 1988 • $37 • (02/28/91)

86 **GUY CASTAGNIER** Clos de Vougeot Red 1988 • $65 • (08/31/91)

86 **JACQUES-FREDERIC MUGNIER** Chambolle-Musigny Les Amoureuses 1988 • $80 • (05/15/91)

86 **JACQUES-FREDERIC MUGNIER** Chambolle-Musigny 1988 • $96 • (05/15/91)

86 **JEAN GARAUDET** Beaune Clos des Mouches 1988 • $40 • (11/15/90)

86 **JEAN-NOEL GAGNARD** Chassagne-Montrachet Morgeot Red 1988 • $20 • (12/31/90)

86 **JESSIAUME PERE & FILS** Santenay Gravières 1988 • $21 • (03/31/91)

86 **LABOURE-ROI** Chambolle-Musigny 1988 • $35 • (02/28/91)

86 **LOUIS JADOT** Pernand-Vergelesses Clos de la Croix de Pierre 1988 • $17 • (03/31/91)

86 **LOUIS JADOT** Pommard Grands Epenots 1988 • $38 • (03/31/91)

86 **PAUL PERNOT** Beaune Les Teurons 1988 • $33 • (03/31/91)

86 **ROBERT ARNOUX** Vosne-Romanée Les Suchots 1988 • $60 • (02/28/91)

86 **TOLLOT-BEAUT** Beaune Clos du Roi 1988 • $53 • (02/28/91)

85 **BOUCHARD PERE & FILS** Chassagne-Montrachet Red 1988 • $22 • (04/30/91)

85 **BOUCHARD PERE & FILS** Beaune Grèves Vigne de l'Enfant Jésus 1988 • $59

85 **CHANSON PERE & FILS** Pernand-Vergelesses Les Vergelesses 1988 • $24 • (08/31/90)

85 **DOMAINE DE L'ARLOT** Nuits-St.-Georges Clos des Forets St.-Georges 1988 • $53 • (03/31/91)

85 **DOMAINE DUJAC** Charmes-Chambertin 1988 • $60 • (03/31/91)

85 **DOMAINE LEROY** Auxey-Duresses Les Clous 1988 • $52 • (05/15/91)

85 **DOMAINE MARC MOREY** Beaune Les Paules 1988 • $24 • (08/31/90)

85 **DOMAINE PONSOT** Morey-St.-Denis Monts Luisants 1988 • $40 • (04/30/91)

85 **DOMAINE PONSOT** Clos St.-Denis Cuvée Vieilles Vignes 1988 • $165 • (07/15/91)

85 **DOMAINE PRIEUR-BRUNET** Volnay-Santenots 1988 • $35 • (11/30/90)

85 **FAIVELEY** Nuits-St.-Georges Les Damodes 1988 • $52 • (03/31/91)

85 **FRANCOISE & DENIS CLAIR** Santenay Clos de la Comme 1988 • $25 • (06/15/92)

85 **G. VACHET-ROUSSEAU** Gevrey-Chambertin 1988 • $30 • (12/31/90)

85 **JEAN GRIVOT** Clos de Vougeot 1988 • $70 • (04/30/91)

85 **JOSEPH DROUHIN** Volnay Clos des Chênes 1988 • $45 • (02/15/91)

85 **LA POUSSE D'OR** Volnay Les Caillerets 1988 • $49 • (08/31/91)

85 **LOUIS JADOT** Chassagne-Montrachet Morgeot Clos de la Chapelle Domaine du Duc de Magenta 1988 • $20 • (03/31/91)

85 **PIERRE BOILLOT** Volnay Santenots 1988 • $37 • (08/31/90)

84 **BICHOT** Volnay 1988 • $25 • (08/31/90)

84 **CHANSON PERE & FILS** Beaune Clos des Fèves 1988 • $35 • (08/31/90)

84 **DOMAINE B. SERVEAU** Chambolle-Musigny Les Amoureuses 1988 • $66 • (02/28/91)

84 **DOMAINE B. SERVEAU** Nuits-St.-Georges Chaînes Carteaux 1988 • $39 • (03/31/91)

84 **DOMAINE JOBLOT** Givry Clos du Cellier aux Moines 1988 • $26 • (12/31/90)

84 **DOMAINE MICHEL ESMONIN** Gevrey-Chambertin Estournelles St.-Jacques 1988 • $40 • (03/31/91)

84 **FAIVELEY** Mercurey Clos du Roy 1988 • $22 • (03/31/91)

84 **GEORGES MUGNERET** Clos Vougeot 1988 • $90 • (11/15/90)

84 **GERARD MUGNERET** Vosne-Romanée Les Suchots 1988 • $57 • (02/28/91)

84 **JAFFELIN** Santenay La Maladière 1988 • $21 • (08/31/91)

84 **JEAN-NOEL GAGNARD** Santenay Clos de Tavannes 1988 • $25 • (11/15/90)

84 **JOSEPH DROUHIN** Bourgogne Pinot Noir Laforàt 1988 • $10 • (03/31/91) • BB

84 **LOUIS TRAPET** Latricières-Chambertin 1988 • $84 • (07/15/91)

84 **MOILLARD** Fixin Confrérie des Chevaliers du Tastevin 1988 • $19 • (08/31/91)

84 **REMOISSENET** Bonnes Mares 1988 • $80 • (12/31/90)

83 **ALAIN MICHELOT** Nuits-St.-Georges Les Porets-St.-Georges 1988 • $56 • (05/15/91)

83 **ALAIN MICHELOT** Nuits-St.-Georges Les Cailles 1988 • $54 • (05/15/91)

83 **BOUCHARD PERE & FILS** Savigny-lès-Beaune Les Lavières Domaines du Château de Beau 1988 • $29 • (04/30/91)

83 **CHATEAU DE PULIGNY-MONTRACHET** Pommard 1988 • $34 • (08/31/90)

83 **CHATEAU DES HERBEAUX** Musigny 1988 • $75 • (12/31/90)

83 **DOMAINE CHANDON DE BRIAILLES** Pernand-Vergelesses Ile des Vergelesses 1988 • $35 • (02/28/91)

83 **DOMAINE G. ROUMIER** Morey-St.-Denis Clos de La Bussière 1988 • $30 • (07/15/91)

83 **DOMAINE PRIEUR-BRUNET** Chassagne-Montrachet Red Morgeot 1988 • $17 • (11/15/90)

83 **DOMAINE SIRUGUE** Côte de Nuits-Villages Clos de la Belle Marguerite 1988 • $16 • (03/31/91)

83 **GHISLAINE BARTHOD** Chambolle-Musigny Les Beaux-Bruns 1988 • $45 • (02/28/91)

83 **HENRI DE VILLAMONT** Chambolle-Musigny 1988 • $39 • (02/15/91)

83 **JEANNE-MARIE DE CHAMPS** Nuits-St.-Georges Les Didiers Hospices de Nuits Cuvée Cabet 1988 • $26 • (09/30/90)

83 **LA POUSSE D'OR** Santenay Clos de Tavannes 1988 • $28 • (08/31/91)

83 **LABOURE-ROI** Bourgogne 1988 • $12 • (03/31/91)

83 **LOUIS JADOT** Pommard 1988 • $36 • (03/31/91)

83 **LOUIS JADOT** Beaune Premier Cru 1988 • $26 • (06/15/93)

83 **LUPE-CHOLET** Bourgogne Pinot Noir Comte de Lupé 1988 • $9 • (02/28/90) • BB

83 **MOILLARD** Bourgogne Hautes Côtes de Beaune Les Alouettes 1988 • $15 • (07/15/91)

83 **P. MISSEREY** Nuits-St.-Georges Les Vaucrains 1988 • $35 • (08/31/92)

83 **REMOISSENET** Mercurey Clos Fortoul 1988 • $17 • (03/31/91)

83 **VALENTIN BOUCHOTTE** Savigny-lès-Beaune Hauts-Jarrons 1988 • $31 • (02/28/91)

82 **BICHOT** Beaune 1988 • $15 • (08/31/90)

82 **CHATEAU DE MEURSAULT** Pinot Noir du Château Bourgogne 1988 • $16 • (01/31/92)

82 **CHATEAU DE PULIGNY-MONTRACHET** Côte de Nuits-Villages 1988 • $17 • (03/31/91)

82 **DOMAINE LEROY** Nuits-St.-Georges Aux Lavières 1988 • $84 • (04/30/91)

82 **DOMAINE PRIEUR-BRUNET** Beaune Clos du Roi 1988 • $30 • (12/31/90)

82 **DUVERNAY** Rully Les Cloux 1988 • $18 • (12/31/90)

82 **GHISLAINE BARTHOD** Bourgogne 1988 • $20 • (03/31/91)

82 **PHILIPPE LECLERC** Gevrey-Chambertin Les Cazetiers 1988 • $66 • (07/15/91)

82 **PHILIPPE LECLERC** Gevrey-Chambertin La Combe aux Moines 1988 • $72 • (07/15/91)

82 **STANISLAS HERESZTYN** Gevrey-Chambertin Les Champonnets 1988 • $37 • (12/31/90)

81 **FAIVELEY** Mercurey Domaine de la Croix Jacquelet Red 1988 • $18 • (03/31/91)

81 **GHISLAINE BARTHOD** Chambolle-Musigny Les Véroilles 1988 • $45 • (02/28/91)

81 **JEAN GROS** Nuits-St.-Georges 1988 • $42 • (02/28/91)

81 **LABOURE-ROI** Gevrey-Chambertin 1988 • $35 • (12/31/90)

81 **LOUIS LATOUR** Pommard Epenots 1988 • $38

81 **LOUIS TRAPET** Gevrey-Chambertin 1988 • $40 • (07/15/91)

81 **RENE ENGEL** Vosne-Romanée 1988 • $30 • (07/15/90)

80 **ALBERT MOROT** Beaune Les Teurons 1988 • $20 • (07/15/91)

80 **DOMAINE A.-F. GROS** Bourgogne Hautes Côtes de Nuits 1988 • $22 • (03/31/91)

80 **DOMAINE BRUNO CLAIR** Marsannay 1988 • $16 • (11/15/91)

80 **DOMAINE DE L'ARLOT** Côte de Nuits-Villages Clos du Châpeau 1988 • $21 • (03/31/91)

80 **DOMAINE F. & L. SAIER** Mercurey Les Champs Martins 1988 • $17 • (08/31/91)

80 **DOMAINE PIERRE AMIOT** Morey-St.-Denis Les Ruchots 1988 • $57 • (02/28/91)

80 **DOMAINE PRIEUR-BRUNET** Santenay Maladière 1988 • $20 • (11/15/90)

80 **DOMAINE RAPET** Bourgogne en Bully 1988 • $19 • (03/31/91)

80 **DROUHIN-LAROZE** Gevrey-Chambertin Lavaux-St.-Jacques 1988 • $44 • (12/31/90)

80 **GEORGES MUGNERET** Nuits-St.-Georges Les Chaignots 1988 • $47 • (11/15/90)

80 **HENRI DE VILLAMONT** Savigny-lès-Beaune Le Village 1988 • $18 • (03/31/91)

80 **JOSEPH DROUHIN** Vosne-Romanée Les Beaumonts 1988 • $46 • (03/31/91)

80 **PHILIPPE NADDEF** Gevrey-Chambertin 1988 • $25 • (07/15/91)

80 **ROBERT ARNOUX** Vosne-Romanée Les Chaumes 1988 • $45 • (02/28/91)

79 **CHARLOPIN-PARIZOT** Gevrey-Chambertin Cuvée Vieilles Vignes 1988 • $31 • (12/31/90)

79 **CHARTRON & TREBUCHET** Côte de Beaune-Villages 1988 • $16 • (02/28/91)

79 **DOMAINE B. SERVEAU** Chambolle-Musigny Les Sentiers 1988 • $39 • (02/28/91)

79 **DOMAINE RAPET** Pernand-Vergelesses 1988 • $31 • (02/28/91)

79 **DOMAINE RENE MANUEL** Meursault Red Clos de la Baronne 1988 • $18 • (03/31/91)

78 **BICHOT** Savigny-lès-Beaune Hospices de Beaune Cuvée Fouquerand 1988 • $39 • (01/31/92)

78 **CHANSON PERE & FILS** Givry Red 1988 • $13 • (12/31/90)

78 **PIERRE BOUREE FILS** Gevrey-Chambertin Clos de la Justice 1988 • $54 • (03/31/92)

78 **ROBERT ARNOUX** Clos Vougeot 1988 • $70 • (03/15/91)

78 **VOLPATO-COSTAILLE** Chambolle-Musigny 1988 • $34 • (02/28/91)

77 **CHATEAU DE PULIGNY-MONTRACHET** Monthelie 1988 • $16 • (11/15/90)

77 **JEAN-MARC BOILLOT** Pommard Les Saucilles 1988 • $47 • (05/15/91)

77 **PIERRETTE & JEAN-CLAUDE RATEAU** Beaune Clos Des Mariages 1988 • $25 • (01/31/92)

76 **FAIVELEY** Nuits-St.-Georges Clos de la Maréchale 1988 • $25 • (03/15/91)

76 **GERARD MUGNERET** Nuits-St.-Georges Les Boudots 1988 • $48 • (02/28/91)

76 **L'HERITIER-GUYOT** Clos de Vougeot 1988 • $51 • (03/15/93)

76 **OLIVIER LEFLAIVE** Givry Red 1988 • $16 • (10/31/92)

75 **MICHEL JUILLOT** Corton Perrieres 1988 • $54 • (08/31/92)

74 **PHILIPPE LECLERC** Gevrey-Chambertin Les Platières 1988 • $40 • (07/15/91)

73 **HAEGELEN-JAYER** Chambolle-Musigny 1988 • $39 • (05/15/91)

73 **HAEGELEN-JAYER** Clos de Vougeot 1988 • $69 • (05/15/91)

73 **JEAN-CLAUDE VOLPATO** Bourgogne Passe-tout-grains 1988 • $13 • (03/31/91)

73 **LOUIS JADOT** Clos Vougeot 1988 • $68 • (11/15/91)

73 **PIERRE BOUREE FILS** Bourgogne 1988 • $15 • (03/31/92)

72 **DOMAINE ROY PERE & FILS** Gevrey-Chambertin Vieilles Vignes 1988 • $30 • (12/31/90)

72 **JEAN CLAUDE BOISSET** Bourgogne Tastevinage 1988 • $11 • (08/31/91)

71 **DOMAINE A.-F. GROS** Vosne-Romanée Aux Réas 1988 • $41 • (02/28/91)

71 **DOMAINE ALETH GIRARDIN** Beaune Clos des Mouches 1988 • $36 • (07/15/91)

69 **PHILIPPE NADDEF** Mazis-Chambertin 1988 • $60 • (07/15/91)

68 **BICHOT** Bourgogne Château de Dracy Pinot Noir 1988 • $8 • (02/28/90)

68 **DOMAINE ROY PERE & FILS** Gevrey-Chambertin Clos Prieur 1988 • $35 • (12/31/90)

68 **REMOISSENET** Givry du Domaine Thénard 1988 • $19 • (03/31/91)

67 **DOMAINE F. & L. SAIER** Mercurey Les Chenelots 1988 • $17 • (04/30/91)

67 **HAEGELEN-JAYER** Echézeaux 1988 • $61 • (08/31/91)

64 **MUGNERET-GIBOURG** Vosne-Romanée 1988 • $34 • (12/31/90)

64 **PHILIPPE LECLERC** Bourgogne Les Bons Bâtons 1988 • $22 • (08/31/91)

60 **ROBERT ARNOUX** Vosne-Romanée Les Suchots 1988 • $76 • (12/31/90)

1985 Red Burgundy

Vintage Rating: 95

99 **DOMAINE DE LA ROMANEE-CONTI** Romanée-Conti 1985 • $1080 • (01/31/90)

99 **HENRI JAYER** Richebourg 1985 • $625 • (05/15/91)

98 **DOMAINE DE LA ROMANEE-CONTI** La Tâche 1985 • $605 • (02/29/88)

98 **LOUIS LATOUR** Romanée-St.-Vivant Les Quatre Journaux 1985 • $110 • (03/15/88)

97 **ARMAND ROUSSEAU** Chambertin 1985 • $49 • (03/15/88)

97 **DOMAINE MEO-CAMUZET** Richebourg 1985 • $235 • (03/31/88)

97 **F. CHAUVENET** Corton Hospices de Beaune Docteur-Peste 1985 • $155 • (07/15/88)

97 **F. CHAUVENET** Charmes-Chambertin 1985 • $72 • (07/31/87)

97 **JOSEPH DROUHIN** Clos de la Roche 1985 • $60 • (11/15/87)

97 **TOLLOT-BEAUT** Corton 1985 • $75 • (03/15/88)

96 **DOMAINE DE LA ROMANEE-CONTI** Echézeaux 1985 • $176 • (02/29/88)

96 **DOMAINE DE LA ROMANEE-CONTI** Romanée-Conti 1985 • $375 • (02/29/88)

96 **DOMAINE DU CLOS FRANTIN** Echézeaux 1985 • $37 • (09/15/87)

96 **F. CHAUVENET** Corton 1985 • $53 • (07/31/87)

96 **FAIVELEY** Chambertin Clos de Bèze 1985 • $105 • (03/15/88)

96 **HENRI JAYER** Echézeaux 1985 • $264 • (05/15/91)

96 **JAFFELIN** Clos de Vougeot 1985 • $49 • (06/15/88)

96 **JEANNE-MARIE DE CHAMPS** Nuits-St.-Georges Les Didiers Hospices de Nuits Cuvée Cabet 1985 • $53 • (03/15/88)

96 **LOUIS JADOT** Nuits-St.-Georges Clos des Corvées 1985 • $46 • (03/15/88)

95 **DOMAINE DANIEL RION** Vosne-Romanée Les Beaux Monts 1985 • $55 • (02/29/88)

95 **DOMAINE DU CLOS FRANTIN** Vosne-Romanée Les Malconsorts 1985 • $55 • (09/30/87)

95 **DOMAINE DUJAC** Charmes-Chambertin 1985 • $100 • (03/15/88)

95 **DOMAINE DUJAC** Clos de la Roche 1985 • $85 • (03/15/88)

95 **F. CHAUVENET** Pommard Epenots 1985 • $48 • (07/31/87)

95 **HENRI JAYER** Vosne-Romanée Cros Parantoux 1985 • $230 • (05/15/91)

95 **JOSEPH DROUHIN** Pommard Epenots 1985 • $41 • (11/15/87)

95 **JOSEPH DROUHIN** Chambertin 1985 • $107 • (11/15/87)

95 **JOSEPH DROUHIN** Griotte-Chambertin 1985 • $68 • (11/15/87)

95 **LOUIS JADOT** Beaune Clos des Ursules 1985 • $55 • (03/15/88) • SS

95 **LOUIS JADOT** Bonnes Mares 1985 • $78 • (03/15/88)

95 **LOUIS LATOUR** Chambertin Cuvée Hèritiers Latour Red 1985 • $87 • (03/15/88)
95 **MOILLARD** Vosne-Romanée Malconsorts Domaine Thomas-Moillard 1985 • $47 • (07/31/88)
94 **DOMAINE DANIEL RION** Nuits-St.-Georges Clos des Argillières 1985 • $75 • (03/15/88)
94 **DOMAINE DE LA ROMANEE-CONTI** Grands Echézeaux 1985 • $323 • (02/29/88)
94 **DOMAINE PONSOT** Chambolle-Musigny Les Charmes 1985 • $75 • (06/15/88)
94 **DOMAINE TORTOCHOT** Chambertin 1985 • $90 • (12/31/88)
94 **F. CHAUVENET** Clos St.-Denis Red 1985 • $67 • (07/31/87)
94 **JOSEPH DROUHIN** Clos de Vougeot Red 1985 • $38 • (11/15/87)
94 **JOSEPH DROUHIN** Vosne-Romanée Les Suchots 1985 • $42 • (11/15/87)
94 **LOUIS JADOT** Gevrey-Chambertin Clos St.-Jacques 1985 • $75 • (03/31/88)
94 **MOILLARD** Charmes-Chambertin 1985 • $55 • (05/31/88)
94 **MOILLARD** Echézeaux 1985 • $47 • (04/15/88)
94 **PHILIPPE NADDEF** Gevrey-Chambertin 1985 • $25 • (04/15/88)
94 **PRINCE FLORENT DE MERODE** Pommard Clos de la Platière 1985 • $45 • (03/15/88)
93 **DOMAINE MEO-CAMUZET** Clos de Vougeot 1985 • $105 • (03/31/88)
93 **HENRI JAYER** Vosne-Romanée Les Brûlées 1985 • $300 • (05/15/91)
93 **JOSEPH DROUHIN** Pommard 1985 • $33 • (11/15/87)
93 **JOSEPH DROUHIN** Chambolle-Musigny 1985 • $33 • (11/15/87)
93 **JOSEPH DROUHIN** Grands Echézeaux 1985 • $75 • (11/15/87)
93 **JOSEPH DROUHIN** Nuits-St.-Georges Les Roncières 1985 • $38 • (11/15/87)
93 **JOSEPH DROUHIN** Vosne-Romanée Les Beaumonts 1985 • $31 • (11/15/87)
93 **MUGNERET-GIBOURG** Echézeaux 1985 • $57 • (02/29/88)
93 **PARIGOT PERE & FILS** Pommard Les Charmots 1985 • $34 • (06/15/87) • CS
93 **PIERRE BOUREE FILS** Nuits-St.-Georges Les Vaucrains 1985 • $68 • (05/31/88)
93 **PIERRE GELIN** Gevrey-Chambertin 1985 • $25 • (04/15/88)
93 **POTHIER-RIEUSSET** Volnay 1985 • $34 • (02/15/88)
93 **PRINCE FLORENT DE MERODE** Corton Bressandes 1985 • $52 • (02/15/88)
92 **ARMAND ROUSSEAU** Gevrey-Chambertin Le Clos St.-Jacques 1985 • $85 • (10/15/88)
92 **CAPTAIN-GAGNEROT** Corton Les Renardes 1985 • $70 • (12/31/88)
92 **CHANSON PERE & FILS** Beaune Clos des Fèves 1985 • $33 • (01/31/89)
92 **CHARLES MORTET** Gevrey-Chambertin Clos Prieur 1985 • $29 • (07/31/88)
92 **COMTE DE VOGUE** Musigny Cuvée Vieilles Vignes 1985 • $103 • (03/31/88)
92 **DOMAINE DE COURCEL** Pommard Rugiens 1985 • $32 • (04/30/88)
92 **DOMAINE G. ROUMIER** Morey-St.-Denis Clos de La Bussière 1985 • $27 • (04/30/88)
92 **DOMAINE HENRI GOUGES** Nuits-St.-Georges Clos des Porrets Premier Cru 1985 • $NA
92 **DOMAINE JEAN-MARC BOULEY** Pommard Les Rugiens 1985 • $30 • (10/31/88)
92 **DOMAINE MEO-CAMUZET** Vosne-Romanée Les Chaumes 1985 • $80 • (03/31/88)
92 **DOMAINE ROUX PERE & FILS** Volnay En Champans 1985 • $25 • (03/15/87)
92 **DROUHIN-LAROZE** Chambertin Clos de Bèze 1985 • $110 • (10/15/88)
92 **F. CHAUVENET** Vosne-Romanée Les Suchots 1985 • $46 • (07/31/87)
92 **FAIVELEY** Gevrey-Chambertin Les Cazetiers 1985 • $53 • (03/31/88)
92 **FAIVELEY** Mazis-Chambertin 1985 • $91 • (03/15/88)
92 **GASTON & PIERRE RAVAUT** Corton Hautes-Mourottes 1985 • $46 • (07/31/88)
92 **GEORGES MUGNERET** Ruchottes-Chambertin 1985 • $150 • (02/15/88)
92 **JOSEPH DROUHIN** Corton 1985 • $48 • (11/15/87)
92 **JOSEPH DROUHIN** Nuits-St.-Georges 1985 • $29 • (11/15/87)
92 **LOUIS JADOT** Beaune Hospices de Beaune Cuvée Nicolas-Rolin 1985 • $85 • (03/15/88)
92 **MOILLARD** Corton Clos des Vergennes 1985 • $36 • (05/31/87)
92 **MOILLARD** Pommard Clos des Epeneaux 1985 • $45 • (06/30/88) • CS
92 **MONGEARD-MUGNERET** Richebourg 1985 • $123 • (03/15/88)
92 **PHILIPPE LECLERC** Gevrey-Chambertin Combes aux Moines 1985 • $70 • (10/15/88)
92 **PIERRE BOUREE FILS** Chambertin 1985 • $81 • (05/31/88)
91 **B. MUGNERET-GOUACHON** Echézeaux 1985 • $29 • (12/31/88)
91 **BICHOT** Pommard Hospices de Beaune Cuvée Cyrot-Chaudron 1985 • $60 • (10/31/88)
91 **BITOUZET-PRIEUR** Volnay Pitures 1985 • $36 • (07/31/88)
91 **BONNEAU DU MARTRAY** Corton 1985 • $62 • (10/15/88)
91 **BOUCHARD PERE & FILS** Beaune Grèves Vigne de l'Enfant Jésus 1985 • $32 • (01/31/89)
91 **COMTE ARMAND** Pommard Clos des Epeneaux 1985 • $44 • (03/15/88)
91 **DOMAINE B. SERVEAU** Chambolle-Musigny Les Amoureuses 1985 • $75 • (06/15/88)
91 **DOMAINE DANIEL RION** Nuits-St.-Georges Aux Vignerondes 1985 • $40 • (03/15/88)
91 **DOMAINE DANIEL RION** Vosne-Romanée Les Chaumes 1985 • $60
91 **DOMAINE DES CHEZEAUX** Chambolle-Musigny Les Charmes 1985 • $75 • (06/15/88)
91 **DOMAINE DES CHEZEAUX** Griotte-Chambertin 1985 • $150 • (06/15/88)
91 **DOMAINE DU CLOS FRANTIN** Vosne-Romanée 1985 • $29 • (10/15/87)
91 **DOMAINE DUJAC** Clos St.-Denis 1985 • $89 • (03/15/88)
91 **DOMAINE F. BUFFET** Volnay 1985 • $35 • (10/15/88)
91 **DOMAINE FRANCOIS LAMARCHE** Vosne-Romanée Suchots 1985 • $36 • (10/15/88)
91 **GEORGES LIGNIER** Clos St.-Denis 1985 • $54 • (03/15/88)
91 **JOSEPH DROUHIN** Savigny-lès-Beaune 1985 • $25 • (11/15/87) • SS
91 **JOSEPH DROUHIN** Gevrey-Chambertin 1985 • $33 • (11/15/87)
91 **JOSEPH DROUHIN** Pernand-Vergelesses 1985 • $17 • (11/15/87)

■ ■ ■ ■

Red Burgundy

91 **LOUIS JADOT** Beaune Boucherottes 1985 • $35 • (03/15/88)
91 **LOUIS JADOT** Beaune Clos des Couchereaux 1985 • $34 • (03/15/88)
91 **LOUIS JADOT** Beaune Les Chouacheux 1985 • $30 • (03/15/88)
91 **LOUIS JADOT** Pommard Chaponnières 1985 • $39 • (03/15/88)
91 **LOUIS JADOT** Chambolle-Musigny 1985 • $27 • (05/15/88)
91 **LOUIS JADOT** Nuits-St.-Georges 1985 • $30 • (04/15/88)
91 **LOUIS JADOT** Beaune Clos des Ursules 1985 • $44 • (03/15/89)
91 **MOMMESSIN** Corton 1985 • $28 • (02/15/88)
91 **MOMMESSIN** Volnay 1985 • $80 • (03/15/88)
91 **MOMMESSIN** Clos de Tart 1985 • $77 • (02/15/88)
91 **PIERRE BOUREE FILS** Bonnes Mares 1985 • $85 • (05/31/88)
91 **PIERRE BOUREE FILS** Gevrey-Chambertin Les Cazetiers 1985 • $67 • (05/31/88)
91 **REMOISSENET** Chambertin 1985 • $100 • (03/15/88)
91 **REMOISSENET** Clos de la Roche 1985 • $72 • (03/15/88)
91 **REMOISSENET** Vosne-Romanée Les Suchots 1985 • $75 • (03/15/88)
91 **REMOISSENET** Richebourg 1985 • $138 • (03/15/88)
90 **A.R. CHOPPIN** Beaune Bressandes 1985 • $32 • (09/30/87)
90 **BOUCHARD PERE & FILS** Vosne-Romanée Aux Reignots Château de Vosne-Romanée 1985 • $51 • (02/28/89)
90 **CHARLES MORTET** Chambertin 1985 • $64 • (06/15/88)
90 **DOMAINE B. SERVEAU** Chambolle-Musigny Les Chabiots 1985 • $39 • (06/15/88)
90 **DOMAINE FRANCOIS LAMARCHE** Clos de Vougeot 1985 • $48 • (10/15/88)
90 **DOMAINE JEAN-MARC BOULEY** Volnay Caillerets 1985 • $27 • (10/15/88)
90 **DOMAINE MEO-CAMUZET** Nuits-St.-Georges Aux Murgers 1985 • $73 • (04/15/88)
90 **DOMAINE PONSOT** Clos de la Roche Cuvée Vieilles Vignes 1985 • $200 • (06/15/88)
90 **DROUHIN-LAROZE** Mazis-Chambertin 1985 • $47 • (10/15/88)
90 **DUBREUIL-FONTAINE** Corton Clos du Roi 1985 • $65 • (07/15/88)
90 **FAIVELEY** Gevrey-Chambertin 1985 • $38 • (04/15/88)
90 **FAIVELEY** Nuits-St.-Georges 1985 • $40 • (03/15/88)
90 **HAEGELEN-JAYER** Clos de Vougeot 1985 • $64 • (04/15/88)
90 **J. LABET & N. DECHELETTE** Clos Vougeot Château de la Tour 1985 • $60 • (06/15/88)
90 **JEHAN JOLIET** Fixin Clos de la Perrière 1985 • $25 • (07/31/88)
90 **JOSEPH DROUHIN** Aloxe-Corton 1985 • $23 • (11/15/87)
90 **LA POUSSE D'OR** Volnay Les Caillerets 1985 • $35 • (03/15/88)
90 **LOUIS JADOT** Beaune Hospices de Beaune Cuvée Dames-Hospitalier 1985 • $85 • (03/15/88)
90 **LOUIS JADOT** Chapelle-Chambertin 1985 • $54 • (03/15/88)
90 **LOUIS LATOUR** Beaune Vignes Franches 1985 • $51 • (03/15/88)
90 **LOUIS LATOUR** Corton Domaine Latour 1985 • $38 • (03/15/88)
90 **MACHARD DE GRAMONT** Nuits-St.-Georges Les Hauts Pruliers 1985 • $36 • (02/15/88)
90 **MOILLARD** Vosne-Romanée Malconsorts Domaine Thomas-Moillard 1985 • $21 • (12/15/86)
90 **MOMMESSIN** Gevrey-Chambertin 1985 • $25 • (02/15/88)
90 **PHILIPPE LECLERC** Gevrey-Chambertin Les Platières 1985 • $56 • (10/15/88)
90 **PIERRE ANDRE** Corton Pougets 1985 • $45 • (07/15/88)
90 **PIERRE GELIN** Mazis-Chambertin 1985 • $25 • (03/15/88)
90 **RENE ENGEL** Echézeaux 1985 • $32 • (10/15/87)
90 **RENE MUGNERET** Vosne-Romanée 1985 • $27 • (04/30/88)
90 **ROBERT ARNOUX** Vosne-Romanée Les Suchots 1985 • $52 • (07/31/88)
89 **BARTON & GUESTIER** Gevrey-Chambertin 1985 • $21 • (04/30/88)
89 **BOUCHARD PERE & FILS** Beaune Marconnets Domaines du Château de Beaune 1985 • $35 • (01/31/89)
89 **BOUCHARD PERE & FILS** Beaune Grèves Vigne de l'Enfant Jésus 1985 • $61 • (02/28/95)
89 **CHATEAU DE LA MALTROYE** Chassagne-Montrachet Clos St.-Jean Red 1985 • $19 • (10/15/88)
89 **DOMAINE DE COURCEL** Pommard Clos des Epeneaux 1985 • $37 • (04/30/88)
89 **DOMAINE FRANCOIS LAMARCHE** Vosne-Romanée La Grande Rue 1985 • $60 • (10/15/88)
89 **DOMAINE MICHEL LAFARGE** Volnay 1985 • $75
89 **DOMAINE RENE MONNIER** Beaune Cent Vignes 1985 • $25 • (10/31/87)
89 **DOMAINE RENE MONNIER** Pommard Les Vignots 1985 • $30 • (11/15/88)
89 **F. CHAUVENET** Echézeaux 1985 • $47 • (07/31/87)
89 **FAIVELEY** Chambolle-Musigny 1985 • $45 • (05/15/88)
89 **FAIVELEY** Echézeaux 1985 • $74 • (03/31/88)
89 **HERVE ROUMIER** Chambolle-Musigny Les Amoureuses 1985 • $65 • (03/31/88)
89 **JAFFELIN** Pommard 1985 • $38 • (03/15/88)
89 **JEAN-MARC PAVELOT** Savigny-lès-Beaune Aux Guettes 1985 • $20 • (02/15/88)
89 **JOSEPH DROUHIN** Charmes-Chambertin 1985 • $60 • (11/15/87)
89 **LOUIS JADOT** Corton Pougets 1985 • $52 • (03/15/88)
89 **LOUIS JADOT** Chambertin Clos de Bèze Red 1985 • $80 • (03/15/88)
89 **LOUIS LATOUR** Corton Château Corton Grancey 1985 • $61 • (03/15/88)
89 **LOUIS LATOUR** Corton Clos de la Vigne au Saint 1985 • $43 • (03/15/88)
89 **LOUIS LATOUR** Pommard Epenots 1985 • $46 • (03/15/88)
89 **MACHARD DE GRAMONT** Beaune Les Chouacheux 1985 • $34 • (05/31/88)
89 **MACHARD DE GRAMONT** Savigny-lès-Beaune Les Guettes 1985 • $25 • (07/31/88)
89 **MACHARD DE GRAMONT** Nuits-St.-Georges En la Perrière Noblot 1985 • $41 • (05/31/88)
89 **MARIUS DELARCHE PERE & FILS** Pernand-Vergelesses Ile des Vergelesses 1985 • $23 • (10/15/88)
89 **MOILLARD** Beaune Grèves Domaine Thomas-Moillard 1985 • $25 • (03/15/87)
89 **MOILLARD** Volnay Clos des Chênes 1985 • $32 • (07/15/88)
89 **MOILLARD** Nuits-St.-Georges Clos de Thorey Domaine Thomas-Moillard 1985 • $38 • (05/31/87)
89 **PHILIPPE LECLERC** Gevrey-Chambertin Les Cazetiers 1985 • $70 • (10/15/88)

89 **PHILIPPE ROSSIGNOL** Côte de Nuits-Villages 1985 • $10 • (07/31/88)

89 **ROBERT CHEVILLON** Nuits-St.-Georges Les St.-Georges 1985 • $75

89 **TOLLOT-BEAUT** Aloxe-Corton 1985 • $29 • (03/15/88)

88 **BICHOT** Volnay 1985 • $53 • (04/30/89)

88 **BOUCHARD PERE & FILS** Volnay 1985 • $35 • (01/31/89)

88 **DOMAINE B. SERVEAU** Morey-St.-Denis Les Sorbets 1985 • $39 • (06/15/88)

88 **DOMAINE DANIEL RION** Chambolle-Musigny Aux Beaux Bruns 1985 • $33 • (03/31/88)

88 **DOMAINE DANIEL RION** Nuits-St.-Georges Les Hauts Pruliers 1985 • $43 • (03/15/88)

88 **DOMAINE DE LA ROMANEE-CONTI** Romanée St.-Vivant 1985 • $201 • (02/29/88)

88 **DOMAINE F. BUFFET** Pommard Rugiens 1985 • $40 • (10/15/88)

88 **DROUHIN-LAROZE** Clos de Vougeot 1985 • $60 • (10/15/88)

88 **DUBREUIL-FONTAINE** Savigny-lès-Beaune Les Vergelesses 1985 • $24 • (01/31/89)

88 **F. CHAUVENET** Beaune Theurons 1985 • $23 • (07/31/87)

88 **F. CHAUVENET** Gevrey-Chambertin Charreux 1985 • $33 • (10/15/87)

88 **FAIVELEY** Latricières-Chambertin 1985 • $77 • (03/15/88)

88 **G. BARTHOD-NOELLAT** Chambolle-Musigny Les Cras 1985 • $37 • (07/31/88)

88 **GASTON & PIERRE RAVAUT** Aloxe-Corton 1985 • $35 • (07/31/88)

88 **GASTON & PIERRE RAVAUT** Ladoix La Corvée 1985 • $26 • (07/31/88)

88 **HENRI MAGNIEN** Gevrey-Chambertin Les Cazetiers 1985 • $35 • (10/15/87)

88 **HENRI MEURGEY** Chassagne-Montrachet Clos de la Boudriotte Red 1985 • $40 • (10/31/88)

88 **J. JAYER** Nuits-St.-Georges Les Lavières 1985 • $38 • (03/15/88)

88 **JAFFELIN** Volnay 1985 • $30 • (03/15/88)

88 **JEAN CHAUVENET** Nuits-St.-Georges Les Bousselots 1985 • $49 • (05/31/88)

88 **JOSEPH DROUHIN** Santenay 1985 • $17 • (11/15/87)

88 **JOSEPH DROUHIN** Volnay 1985 • $29 • (11/15/87)

88 **LOUIS CLAIR** Santenay Gravières Domaine de L'Abbay 1985 • $17 • (10/15/87)

88 **LOUIS JADOT** Musigny Le Musigny 1985 • $74 • (03/31/88)

88 **LOUIS JADOT** Chambertin Clos de Bèze 1985 • $113

88 **LOUIS LATOUR** Pommard Epenots 1985 • $46

88 **LOUIS TRAPET** Chambertin 1985 • $101 • (03/15/88)

88 **LUPE-CHOLET** Nuits-St.-Georges Château Gris 1985 • $39 • (02/15/88)

88 **PIERRE ANDRE** Corton Clos du Roi 1985 • $45 • (07/15/88)

88 **PIERRE BOUREE FILS** Santenay Gravières 1985 • $30 • (05/31/88)

88 **PIERRE BOUREE FILS** Charmes-Chambertin 1985 • $68 • (05/31/88)

88 **TOLLOT-BEAUT** Corton Bressandes 1985 • $75

87 **A.R. CHOPPIN** Beaune Teurons 1985 • $32 • (10/31/87)

87 **A.R. CHOPPIN** Savigny-lès-Beaune Vergelesses 1985 • $25 • (10/31/87)

87 **BOUCHARD PERE & FILS** Volnay Frémiets Clos de le Rougeotte Domaines de Château de Beaune 1985 • $44 • (01/31/89)

87 **BOUCHARD PERE & FILS** Nuits-St.-Georges Clos-St.-Marc 1985 • $53 • (02/28/89)

87 **CHARLES VIENOT** Gevrey-Chambertin 1985 • $32 • (04/30/88)

87 **CHATEAU DE MEURSAULT** Beaune Cent-Vignes 1985 • $31 • (02/28/90)

87 **COMTE DE VOGUE** Musigny Cuvée Veilles Vignes 1985 • $206

87 **DOMAINE BERTAGNA** Vougeot Clos de la Perrière 1985 • $40 • (04/15/89)

87 **DOMAINE CLAUDINE DESCHAMPS** Gevrey-Chambertin Bel-Air 1985 • $28 • (03/31/88)

87 **DOMAINE G. ROUMIER** Chambolle-Musigny 1985 • $26 • (02/15/88)

87 **DOMAINE JEAN-MARC BOULEY** Volnay Clos des Chênes 1985 • $27 • (10/15/88)

87 **DOMAINE MONTHELIE-DOUHAIRET** Volnay Champans 1985 • $25 • (07/15/88)

87 **JEAN GRIVOT** Vosne-Romanée 1985 • $31 • (04/30/88)

87 **JEAN GROS** Vosne-Romanée Clos des Réas 1985 • $58 • (07/31/88)

87 **JEAN MICHELOT** Pommard 1985 • $29 • (04/30/88)

87 **JEANNE-MARIE DE CHAMPS** Corton Hospices de Beaune Cuvée Charlotte-Dumay 1985 • $76 • (10/15/88)

87 **LA POUSSE D'OR** Pommard Les Jarolières 1985 • $39 • (03/15/88)

87 **LOUIS JADOT** Beaune Bressandes 1985 • $35 • (03/15/88)

87 **LOUIS LATOUR** Echézeaux 1985 • $49 • (03/15/88)

87 **MOILLARD** Morey-St.-Denis Monts Luisants 1985 • $21 • (05/31/87)

87 **PROSPER MAUFOUX** Santenay Les Gravières 1985 • $18 • (10/15/88)

87 **REMOISSENET** Nuits-St.-Georges Aux Argillats 1985 • $34 • (10/15/88)

87 **REMY GAUTHIER** Volnay Santenots 1985 • $27 • (03/15/88)

86 **ARMAND ROUSSEAU** Charmes-Chambertin 1985 • $63 • (10/15/88)

86 **BICHOT** Monthelie Hospices de Beaune Cuvée Lebelin 1985 • $52 • (10/15/87)

86 **CAPTAIN-GAGNEROT** Clos Vougeot Red 1985 • $67 • (12/31/88)

86 **CHATEAU DE LA MALTROYE** Chassagne-Montrachet Boudriottes Red 1985 • $17 • (10/15/88)

86 **DOMAINE B. SERVEAU** Nuits-St.-Georges Chaînes Carteaux 1985 • $39 • (06/15/88)

86 **DOMAINE LEQUIN-ROUSSOT** Chassagne-Montrachet Morgeot 1985 • $24 • (05/31/88)

86 **DOMAINE LEQUIN-ROUSSOT** Corton Les Languettes 1985 • $39 • (07/15/88)

86 **DOMAINE LUCIEN BOILLOT** Volnay Les Angles 1985 • $33 • (07/15/88)

86 **DOMAINE MUSSY** Pommard 1985 • $35 • (10/15/88)

86 **DUBREUIL-FONTAINE** Corton Bressandes 1985 • $50 • (01/31/89)

86 **FAIVELEY** Beaune Champs-Pimont 1985 • $36 • (03/15/88)

86 **GEORGES LIGNIER** Morey-St.-Denis Clos des Ormes 1985 • $28 • (03/15/88)

86 **JEAN CLAUDE BOISSET** Volnay Clos des Chênes 1985 • $28 • (04/15/88)

86 **JEAN-CHARLES FORNEROT** Chassagne-Montrachet La Maltroie 1985 • $19 • (07/31/89)

86 **JOSEPH DROUHIN** Côte de Nuits-Villages 1985 • $19 • (11/15/87)

86 **JOSEPH DROUHIN** Grands Echézeaux 1985 • $75

Red Burgundy

86 **LA POUSSE D'OR** Volnay Les Caillerets-Clos des 60 Ouvrées 1985 • $55 • (03/15/88)
86 **LOUIS JADOT** Gevrey-Chambertin Estournelles St.-Jacques 1985 • $41 • (03/31/88)
86 **LOUIS JADOT** Vosne-Romanée 1985 • $33 • (03/31/88)
86 **LOUIS LATOUR** Vosne-Romanée Beaumonts 1985 • $36 • (03/15/88)
86 **MACHARD DE GRAMONT** Nuits-St.-Georges Les Allots 1985 • $35 • (05/31/88)
86 **PAUL PILLOT** Chassagne-Montrachet Red Clos St.-Jean 1985 • $24 • (11/15/88)
86 **RENE ENGEL** Grands Echézeaux 1985 • $43 • (10/15/87)
85 **ARMAND ROUSSEAU** Mazis-Chambertin Mazy-Chambertin 1985 • $63 • (10/15/88)
85 **BOUCHARD PERE & FILS** Beaune Teurons Domaines du Château de Beaune 1985 • $35 • (01/31/89)
85 **CHARLES VIENOT** Mercurey 1985 • $12 • (04/30/88)
85 **DOMAINE BERTAGNA** Vougeot Les Crâs 1985 • $30 • (03/31/88)
85 **DOMAINE BERTAGNA** Nuits-St.-Georges Aux Murgers 1985 • $41 • (02/28/89)
85 **DOMAINE DANIEL RION** Nuits-St.-Georges 1985 • $28 • (03/15/88)
85 **DOMAINE DUCHET** Beaune Cent-Vignes 1985 • $27 • (03/15/88)
85 **DOMAINE LEQUIN-ROUSSOT** Santenay La Comme 1985 • $24 • (05/31/88)
85 **FAIVELEY** Nuits-St.-Georges Clos de la Maréchale 1985 • $51 • (03/15/88)
85 **FONTAINE-GAGNARD** Chassagne-Montrachet 1985 • $16 • (12/31/88)
85 **GEORGES LIGNIER** Clos de la Roche 1985 • $63 • (03/15/88)
85 **JEAN GROS** Nuits-St.-Georges 1985 • $36 • (07/31/88)
85 **JOSEPH DROUHIN** Côte de Beaune-Villages 1985 • $14 • (11/15/87)
85 **LOUIS JADOT** Pernand-Vergelesses 1985 • $18 • (04/15/88)
85 **LOUIS LATOUR** Charmes-Chambertin 1985 • $50 • (03/15/88)
85 **MOILLARD** Pommard Rugiens 1985 • $40 • (06/30/88)
85 **MOMMESSIN** Côte de Nuits-Villages 1985 • $17 • (07/31/88)
85 **MOMMESSIN** Côte de Beaune-Villages 1985 • $13 • (02/15/88)
85 **MUGNERET-GIBOURG** Vosne-Romanée 1985 • $33 • (02/29/88)
85 **PIERRE ANDRE** Savigny-lès-Beaune Clos des Guettes 1985 • $20 • (07/31/88)
85 **PIERRE BOUREE FILS** Gevrey-Chambertin Clos de la Justice 1985 • $51 • (05/31/88)
85 **PROSPER MAUFOUX** Santenay Les Gravières 1985 • $17 • (10/15/89)
85 **RENE ENGEL** Vosne-Romanée Les Brûlées 1985 • $28 • (10/15/87)
85 **RENE ENGEL** Clos Vougeot 1985 • $75 • (10/15/87)
85 **ROBERT CHEVILLON** Nuits-St.-Georges 1985 • $40 • (04/30/88)
84 **CHARLES VIENOT** Corton Maréchaudes 1985 • $57 • (07/15/88)
84 **CHEVALIER DE BEAUBASSIN** Nuits-St.-Georges 1985 • $31 • (04/30/88)
84 **DOMAINE FRANCOIS LAMARCHE** Vosne-Romanée Malconsorts Red 1985 • $44 • (10/15/88)
84 **DOMAINE MARC MOREY** Beaune Les Paules 1985 • $15 • (12/31/88)
84 **F. CHAUVENET** Santenay 1985 • $18 • (07/31/87)
84 **F. CHAUVENET** Nuits-St.-Georges Les Plâteaux 1985 • $34 • (07/31/87)
84 **F. CHAUVENET** Côte de Beaune-Villages 1985 • $16 • (07/31/87)
84 **JAFFELIN** Santenay La Maladière 1985 • $22 • (03/15/88)
84 **JEAN-LUC JOILLOT** Bourgogne Tastevinage 1985 • $15 • (06/30/88)
84 **LOUIS TRAPET** Chapelle-Chambertin 1985 • $64 • (03/15/88)
84 **LUPE-CHOLET** Aloxe-Corton 1985 • $18 • (03/15/88)
84 **MACHARD DE GRAMONT** Chorey-lès-Beaune Les Beaumonts 1985 • $22 • (07/31/88)
84 **MACHARD DE GRAMONT** Nuits-St.-Georges Les Hauts Poirets 1985 • $41 • (06/15/88)
84 **MOILLARD** Chassagne-Montrachet Morgeot Red 1985 • $15 • (05/31/87)
84 **PIERRE GELIN** Chambertin Clos de Bèze 1985 • $77 • (03/15/88)
83 **A. CHOPIN** Côte de Nuits-Villages 1985 • $9 • (10/31/87) • BB
83 **DOMAINE F. & L. SAIER** Mercurey Les Champs Martins 1985 • $20 • (03/31/88)
83 **DOMAINE ROUX PERE & FILS** Santenay 1985 • $21 • (10/31/87)
83 **JEAN-CHARLES FORNEROT** Chassagne-Montrachet Les Champs Gain 1985 • $19 • (07/31/89)
83 **JOSEPH DROUHIN** Mercurey 1985 • $17 • (11/15/87)
83 **LOUIS JADOT** Chassagne-Montrachet Morgeot Clos de la Chapelle Domaine du Duc de Magenta 1985 • $19 • (04/15/88)
83 **LOUIS JADOT** Pernand-Vergelesses Clos de la Croix de Pierre 1985 • $18 • (04/15/88)
83 **LUPE-CHOLET** Savigny-lès-Beaune Les Serpentières 1985 • $17 • (03/15/88)
83 **MICHEL CLERGET** Chambolle-Musigny Les Charmes 1985 • $41 • (05/15/88)
83 **MOMMESSIN** Charmes-Chambertin 1985 • $45 • (02/15/88)
83 **OLIVIER LEFLAIVE** Chassagne-Montrachet 1985 • $32 • (10/31/88)
83 **POTHIER-RIEUSSET** Bourgogne 1985 • $7 • (06/30/88) • BB
83 **TOLLOT-BEAUT** Chorey-Côte-de-Beaune 1985 • $18 • (04/15/88)
82 **DOMAINE BERTAGNA** Vosne-Romanée Les Beaux Monts Bas 1985 • $35 • (10/15/88)
82 **DOMAINE RENE LECLERC** Gevrey-Chambertin Combes aux Moines 1985 • $41 • (10/31/88)
82 **GELIN & MOLIN** Fixin Clos du Châpitre Domaine Marion 1985 • $25 • (04/30/88)
82 **GEORGES LIGNIER** Morey-St.-Denis 1985 • $23 • (03/15/88)
82 **JEAN-CHARLES FORNEROT** St.-Aubin Les Perrières 1985 • $15 • (07/31/89)
82 **LOUIS JADOT** Clos Vougeot 1985 • $85 • (03/31/88)
82 **MICHEL CLERGET** Echézeaux 1985 • $51 • (07/31/88)
82 **MONGEARD-MUGNERET** Vosne-Romanée Les Orveaux 1985 • $32 • (03/15/88)
82 **REMOISSENET** Bonnes Mares 1985 • $88 • (03/15/88)
81 **A.R. CHOPPIN** Beaune Cent Vignes 1985 • $32 • (10/31/87)
81 **BARTON & GUESTIER** Pommard 1985 • $21 • (11/30/87)
81 **BICHOT** Bourgogne Le Bourgogne Bichot Pinot Noir 1985 • $8 • (11/15/87)
81 **CHARLES VIENOT** Pommard 1985 • $33 • (04/30/88)

81 **DOMAINE HENRI CLERC & FILS** Beaune Chaume Gaufriot 1985 • $29 • (11/15/88)
81 **DOMAINE MONTHELIE-DOUHAIRET** Monthelie 1985 • $16 • (06/30/88)
81 **F. CHAUVENET** Puligny-Montrachet Red 1985 • $16 • (06/15/87)
81 **FAIVELEY** Mercurey Clos du Roy 1985 • $23 • (04/30/88)
81 **HENRI & GILLES REMORIQUET** Nuits-St.-Georges Rue de Chaux 1985 • $22 • (07/31/88)
81 **HENRI MAGNIEN** Gevrey-Chambertin 1985 • $25 • (10/15/87)
81 **JEAN GRIVOT** Clos de Vougeot 1985 • $62 • (04/30/88)
81 **MACHARD DE GRAMONT** Bourgogne Pinot Noir Domaine de la Vierge Romaine 1985 • $13 • (06/30/88)
81 **MOILLARD** Volnay Clos des Chênes 1985 • $32 • (05/31/87)
81 **PRINCE FLORENT DE MERODE** Corton Maréchaudes 1985 • $49 • (03/15/88)
80 **DOMAINE BRUNO CLAIR** Savigny-lès-Beaune La Dominode 1985 • $24 • (03/15/88)
80 **F. CHAUVENET** Nuits-St.-Georges Les Perrières 1985 • $48 • (07/31/87)
80 **F. CHAUVENET** Bourgogne Pinot Noir Château Marguerite de Bourgog 1985 • $10 • (06/30/88)
80 **HENRI MAGNIEN** Gevrey-Chambertin Premier Cru 1985 • $29 • (10/15/87)
80 **J. JAYER** Vosne-Romanée Les Rouges 1985 • $44 • (03/15/88)
80 **MACHARD DE GRAMONT** Aloxe-Corton Les Morais 1985 • $34 • (07/15/88)
80 **MARQUIS D'ANGERVILLE** Volnay Clos des Ducs 1985 • $49 • (03/15/88)
80 **MOMMESSIN** Savigny-lès-Beaune 1985 • $17 • (07/31/88)
80 **PHILIPPE NADDEF** Gevrey-Chambertin Champeaux 1985 • $29 • (03/31/88)
79 **A.R. CHOPPIN** Beaune Grèves 1985 • $32 • (09/30/87)
79 **FAIVELEY** Corton Clos des Cortons 1985 • $100 • (03/15/88)
79 **JEAN CLAUDE BOISSET** Nuits-St.-Georges 1985 • $25 • (04/30/88)
79 **JEAN-NOEL GAGNARD** Chassagne-Montrachet Morgeot Red 1985 • $18 • (11/30/87)
79 **LABOURE-ROI** Pommard Les Bertins 1985 • $29 • (03/15/88)
79 **LOUIS JADOT** Côte de Beaune-Villages 1985 • $17 • (04/15/88)
79 **LOUIS TRAPET** Gevrey-Chambertin 1985 • $40 • (05/31/88)
79 **LUPE-CHOLET** Bourgogne Clos de Lupé 1985 • $15 • (03/31/88)
79 **MOILLARD** Fixin Clos d'Entre Deux Velles 1985 • $16 • (05/31/87)
79 **PHILIPPE LECLERC** Gevrey-Chambertin Les Champeaux 1985 • $55 • (10/31/88)
78 **CHARLES VIENOT** Bourgogne 1985 • $9 • (06/15/89)
78 **DOMAINE DANIEL RION** Vosne-Romanée 1985 • $28 • (02/29/88)
78 **DOMAINE F. & L. SAIER** Clos des Lambrays Domaine des Lambrays 1985 • $55 • (02/15/88)
78 **DOMAINE LEQUIN-ROUSSOT** Santenay 1985 • $18 • (05/31/88)
78 **FAIVELEY** Clos de la Roche 1985 • $105 • (03/15/88)
78 **JEAN CLAUDE BOISSET** Pommard 1985 • $28 • (04/30/88)
78 **JOSEPH DROUHIN** Bourgogne Pinot Noir Laforàt 1985 • $8 • (11/15/87)
78 **LOUIS JADOT** Bourgogne Pinot Noir 1985 • $11 • (04/30/88)
78 **MACHARD DE GRAMONT** Nuits-St.-Georges Les Vallerots 1985 • $47 • (05/31/88)
78 **MOILLARD** Bourgogne Pinot Noir 1985 • $7 • (03/31/88)
77 **DOMAINE JEAN MORETEAUX** Bourgogne Pinot Noir Les Clous 1985 • $9 • (11/15/87)
77 **LOUIS LATOUR** Gevrey-Chambertin 1985 $36 • 10/15/88)
77 **REMOISSENET** Givry du Domaine Thénard 1985 • $18 • (04/30/88)
77 **RENE ENGEL** Vosne-Romanée 1985 • $24 • (10/15/87)
76 **DOMAINE B. SERVEAU** Bourgogne 1985 • $13 • (11/15/87)
76 **FAIVELEY** Nuits-St.-Georges Les Porêts St.-Georges 1985 • $47 • (03/15/88)
76 **HENRI BOILLOT** Bourgogne 1985 • $13 • (12/31/88)
76 **JEAN CLAUDE BOISSET** Pommard Rugiens 1985 • $33 • (03/15/88)
76 **LOUIS LATOUR** Aloxe-Corton Les Chaillots 1985 • $37 • (04/15/88)
76 **PIERRE GELIN** Fixin Clos Napolèon 1985 • $25 • (04/30/88)
75 **CAVE DES VIGNERONS DE BUXY** Bourgogne Pinot Noir Grande Réserve 1985 • $7 • (06/30/88)
75 **DOMAINE GROS FRERE & SOEUR** Clos Vougeot Musigni 1985 • $102 • (03/31/88)
75 **DOMAINE LEQUIN-ROUSSOT** Nuits-St.-Georges 1985 • $39 • (04/15/88)
75 **FAIVELEY** Mercurey Clos des Myglands Red 1985 • $20 • (04/30/88)
75 **LOUIS JADOT** Nuits-St.-Georges Les Boudots 1985 • $42 • (03/15/88)
75 **REMOISSENET** Echézeaux 1985 • $73 • (03/15/88)
74 **DOMAINE DUJAC** Chambolle-Musigny Les Gruenchers 1985 • $43 • (03/31/88)
73 **DOMAINE BRUNO CLAIR** Morey-St.-Denis 1985 • $20 • (05/15/88)
73 **LEROY** Bourgogne d'Auvenay 1985 • $12 • (03/31/88)
73 **MICHEL CLERGET** Chambolle-Musigny 1985 • $38 • (05/15/88)
71 **CLEMANCEY FRERES** Fixin Les-Hervelets 1985 • $21 • (04/30/88)
71 **DOMAINE GROS FRERE & SOEUR** Grands Echézeaux 1985 • $75 • (03/31/88)
71 **LEONARD DE ST.-AUBIN** Nuits-St.-Georges 1985 • $25 • (11/30/87)
70 **DOMAINE GROS FRERE & SOEUR** Vosne-Romanée 1985 • $35 • (04/15/88)
70 **JEAN CHOFFLET** Givry Red 1985 • $12 • (11/15/87)
68 **DOMAINE HENRI GOUGES** Nuits-St.-Georges Les St.-Georges 1985 • $45 • (02/15/88)
67 **LA POUSSE D'OR** Santenay Clos de Tavannes 1985 • $22 • (03/15/88)
67 **PIERRE BITOUZET** Savigny-lès-Beaune Les Lavières 1985 • $19 • (03/15/88)
66 **BICHOT** Santenay Les Gravières 1985 • $15 • (03/15/88)
66 **LEONARD DE ST.-AUBIN** Gevrey-Chambertin 1985 • $25 • (11/30/87)
64 **CHARLOPIN-PARIZOT** Gevrey-Chambertin 1985 • $22 • (11/30/87)

The vineyards of Louis Latour.

White Burgundy

Here are *Wine Spectator*'s ratings and prices for the four best recent vintages of white Burgundy—1994, 1992, 1990 and 1989. These Burgundian Chardonnays are organized by vintage and then in descending order of score, to make it easy to identify the best wines of each vintage.

If you can find the increasingly rare 1990s and 1989s for sale at reliable wine shops where you believe they have been properly stored, they are worth buying. Both vintages are rated Outstanding (92) by *Wine Spectator*. The 1992 and 1994 vintages are very good, but perhaps not quite as remarkable. 1991 and 1993 weren't as good overall, and make for riskier shopping. White Burgundy looks potentially outstanding in 1995, probably the best year since 1990, but too few of the wines had been released at press time to include them here. Ratings for past years not covered here can be found in the main listings.

The date of the issue of *Wine Spectator* in which the rating was first published is in parentheses. In general, wines for which no issue date appears were tasted between April 15, 1994 and June 15, 1996.

1994 WHITE BURGUNDY | VINTAGE RATING: 87

96 **MARC COLIN** Montrachet 1994 • $200 • (05/31/96)

96 **VERGET** Montrachet 1994 • $160 • (05/31/96)

95 **MICHEL BOUZEREAU** Meursault Les Genevrières 1994 • $45 • (05/31/96)

94 **BOUCHARD PÈRE & FILS** Montrachet 1994 • $185 • (05/31/96)

94 **MICHEL BOUZEREAU** Puligny-Montrachet Champs Gains 1994 • $45 • (05/31/96)

94 **PIERRE COLIN** Bâtard-Montrachet 1994 • $NA • (05/31/96)

93 **CHARLES & RÉMI JOBARD** Meursault Les Genevrières 1994 • $45 • (05/31/96)

93 **GUFFENS-HEYNEN** Pouilly-Fuissé La Roche 1994 • $40 • (05/31/96)

93 **J. A. FERRET** Pouilly-Fuissé Tournant de Pouilly 1994 • $45 • (05/31/96)

93 **JACQUES PRIEUR** Chevalier-Montrachet 1994 • $150 • (05/31/96)

93 **JEAN PILLOT** Chassagne-Montrachet Les Vergers 1994 • $32 • (05/31/96)

93 **JEAN-MARC BOILLOT** Puligny-Montrachet Les Combettes 1994 • $62 • (05/31/96)

93 **MICHEL COLIN-DELÉGER** Chassagne-Montrachet En Remilly 1994 • $40 • (05/31/96)

93 **ROBERT & RAYMOND JACOB** Corton-Charlemagne 1994 • $NA • (05/31/96)

92 **ANTONIN GUYON** Meursault Les Charmes-Dessus 1994 • $32 • (05/31/96)

92 **DOMAINE ROULOT** Meursault Les Charmes 1994 • $63 • (05/31/96)

92 **GUFFENS-HEYNEN** Pouilly-Fuissé Clos des Petits-Croux 1994 • $34 • (05/31/96)

92 **MICHEL NIELLON** Chevalier-Montrachet 1994 • $135 • (05/31/96)

92 **VERGET** Chassagne-Montrachet La Romanée 1994 • $50 • (05/31/96)

92 **VERGET** Corton-Charlemagne Cuvée Vieilles Vignes 1994 • $57 • (05/31/96)

92 **VERGET** Meursault Les Porusot 1994 • $44 • (05/31/96)

91 **BOUCHARD PÈRE & FILS** Corton-Charlemagne 1994 • $60 • (05/31/96)

91 **DOMAINE ROULOT** Meursault Le Tesson Clos de Mon Plaisir 1994 • $13 • (05/31/96)

91 **JOSEPH DROUHIN** Puligny-Montrachet Les Folatières 1994 • $54 • (05/31/96)

91 **LOUIS JADOT** Puligny-Montrachet Les Perrières 1994 • $38 • (05/31/96)

91 **OLIVIER LEFLAIVE FRÈRES** Rully Premier Cru 1994 • $19 • (05/31/96)

91 **VERGET** Meursault Les Charmes Cuvée Vieilles Vignes 1994 • $52 • (05/31/96)

90 **ALBERT GRIVAULT** Meursault Les Perrières 1994 • $39 • (05/31/96)

90 **BLAIN-GAGNARD** Chassagne-Montrachet Morgeot 1994 • $45 • (05/31/96) • 90

90 **CHARTRON & TRÉBUCHET** Puligny-Montrachet 1994 • $26 • (05/31/96)

90 **CHÂTEAU FUISSÉ** Pouilly-Fuissé Vieilles Vignes 1994 • $44 • (05/31/96)

90 **FERNAND PILLOT** Chassagne-Montrachet Les Vergers 1994 • $NA • (05/31/96) • 89

90 **FERNAND PILLOT** Chassagne-Montrachet Vide Bourse 1994 • $NA • (05/31/96) • 90

90 **FRANÇOISE & DENIS CLAIR** St.-Aubin Les Murgers des Dents de Chien 1994 • $27 • (05/31/96)

90 **G. MICHELOT** Meursault 1994 • $NA • (05/31/96)

90 **JACQUES PRIEUR** Meursault Clos de Mazeray 1994 • $35 • (05/31/96)

90 **JACQUES PRIEUR** Puligny-Montrachet Les Combettes 1994 • $50 • (05/31/96)

90 **JEAN BOILLOT** Puligny-Montrachet Les Pucelles 1994 • $45 • (05/31/96)

90 **JEAN-MARC BOILLOT** Puligny-Montrachet Les Folatières 1994 • $51 • (05/31/96)

90 **JEAN-MARC BOILLOT** Puligny-Montrachet Les Pucelles 1994 • $58 • (05/31/96)

90 **JOSEPH DROUHIN** St.-Aubin 1994 • $22 • (05/31/96)

90 **LOUIS LATOUR** Corton-Charlemagne 1994 • $78 • (05/31/96) • 91

90 **MARC COLIN** Chassagne-Montrachet Vide Bourse 1994 • $38 • (05/31/96) • 90

90 **MARC MOREY** Chassagne-Montrachet Les Vergers 1994 • $40 • (05/31/96) • 90

90 **MICHEL BOUZEREAU** Meursault Les Charmes 1994 • $45 • (05/31/96)

90 **MICHEL NIELLON** Chassagne-Montrachet Clos de la Maltroie 1994 • $NA • (05/31/96)

90 **MOILLARD** Bâtard-Montrachet 1994 • $85 • (05/31/96)

90 **PATRICK JAVILLIER** Puligny-Montrachet Les Levrons 1994 • $NA • (05/31/96)

90 **VERGET** Meursault Les Genevrières Hospices de Beaune 1994 • $35 • (05/31/96)

89 **CHARTRON & TRÉBUCHET** Chassagne-Montrachet Les Morgeot 1994 • $25 • (05/31/96) • 88

89 **CHARTRON & TRÉBUCHET** Santenay 1994 • $15 • (05/31/96)

89 **CHÂTEAU FUISSÉ** Pouilly-Fuissé Les Combettes 1994 • $34 • (05/31/96)

89 **CHÂTEAU FUISSÉ** Pouilly-Fuissé Le Clos 1994 • $34 • (05/31/96)

89 **FRANÇOISE & DENIS CLAIR** Puligny-Montrachet La Garenne 1994 • $44 • (05/31/96)

89 **GEORGES DUBOEUF** Mâcon-Villages Glen Carlou Chard Reserve 1994 • $NA

89 **GUY AMIOT** Chassagne-Montrachet Les Champs Gain 1994 • $44 • (05/31/96) • 90

89 **JEAN PILLOT** Chassagne-Montrachet Morgeot 1994 • $NA • (05/31/96) • 89

89 **JEAN-JACQUES & SYLVAINE MARTIN** Pouilly-Fuissé Les Chevrières 1994 • $NA • (05/31/96)

89 **L'HÉRITIER-GUYOT** Vougeot Clos Blanc de Vougeot 1994 • $40 • (05/31/96)

89 **LOUIS JADOT** Meursault Perrières 1994 • $38 • (05/31/96)

89 **MICHEL COLIN-DELÉGER** Chassagne-Montrachet Les Chenevottes 1994 • $45 • (05/31/96) • 90

89 **MICHEL NIELLON** Chassagne-Montrachet Clos St.-Jean 1994 • $NA • (05/31/96) • 90

89 **MOILLARD** Meursault Charmes 1994 • $37 • (04/30/96)

89 **PAUL GARAUDET** Meursault Vieille Vigne 1994 • $26 • (05/31/96)

89 **VERGET** Pouilly-Fuissé Tête de Cuvée 1994 • $25 • (05/31/96)

89 **VERGET** Puligny-Montrachet Les Enseignères 1994 • $33 • (05/31/96)

88 **ALBERT GRIVAULT** Meursault 1994 • $25 • (05/31/96)

88 **CORDIER PÈRE & FILS** Pouilly-Fuissé Lot No.1 1994 • $21 • (05/31/96)

88 **DOMAINE THOMAS** St.-Véran Vieille Vigne Cuvée Préstige 1994 • $16 • (08/31/95)

88 **DOMAINE ROULOT** Meursault Les Luchets 1994 • $36 • (05/31/96)

88 **FERNAND PILLOT** Chassagne-Montrachet Les Grandes Ruchottes 1994 • $NA • (05/31/96) • 88

88 **FERNAND PILLOT** Puligny-Montrachet 1994 • $NA • (05/31/96)

88 **FONTAINE-GAGNARD** Criots-Bâtard-Montrachet 1994 • $90 • (05/31/96) • 88

88 **GOISOT** Bourgogne Aligoté 1994 • $NA • (05/31/96)

88 **HENRI NAUDIN-FERRAND** Bourgogne Hautes-Côtes de Beaune 1994 • $NA • (05/31/96) • 88

88 **JEAN CHARTRON** Puligny-Montrachet Clos de la Pucelle 1994 • $NA • (05/31/96)

88 **JEAN PILLOT** Chassagne-Montrachet Les Macherelles 1994 • $NA • (05/31/96)

88 **LALEURE-PIOT** Pernand-Vergelesses Premier Cru 1994 • $34 • (05/31/96)

88 **MICHEL COLIN-DELÉGER** Chassagne-Montrachet Morgeot 1994 • $40 • (05/31/96) • 88

88 **MICHEL MOREY-COFFINET** Chassagne-Montrachet La Romanée 1994 • $37 • (05/31/96) • 89

88 **MICHEL MOREY-COFFINET** Chassagne-Montrachet Caillerets 1994 • $34 • (05/31/96) • 88

88 **MICHEL NIELLON** Bâtard-Montrachet 1994 • $135 • (05/31/96)

88 **MICHEL NIELLON** Chassagne-Montrachet 1994 • $45 • (05/31/96)

88 **MOMMESSIN** Pouilly-Fuissé 1994 • $25 • (05/31/96)

88 **THIBERT PÈRE & FILS** Pouilly-Fuissé 1994 • $15 • (05/31/96)

88 **THOMAS** Pouilly-Fuissé Vieilles Vignes 1994 • $25 • (05/31/96)

87 **BACHELET-RAMONET** Chassagne-Montrachet Caillerets 1994 • $NA • (05/31/96)

87 **BLAIN-GAGNARD** Chassagne-Montrachet Caillerets 1994 • $45 • (05/31/96)

87 **BOUCHARD PÈRE & FILS** Bâtard-Montrachet 1994 • $96 • (05/31/96) • 85

87 **BOUCHARD PÈRE & FILS** Beaune Clos St.-Landry 1994 • $32 • (05/31/96) • 87

87 **BOUCHARD PÈRE & FILS** Beaune Premier Cru 1994 • $28 • (05/31/96) • 87

87 **BOUCHARD PÈRE & FILS** Puligny-Montrachet Les Pucelles 1994 • $46 • (05/31/96)

87 **CHARTRON & TRÉBUCHET** Bourgogne Chardonnay 1994 • $10 • (05/31/96)

87 **CORDIER PÈRE & FILS** Pouilly-Fuissé Les Vignes Blanches 1994 • $34 • (05/31/96)

87 **DOMAINE CORSIN** St.-Véran 1994 • $15

87 **DANIEL BARRAUD** Pouilly-Fuissé La Verchère 1994 • $21 • (05/31/96)

87 **DOMAINE MICHELOT** Meursault Les Narvaux 1994 • $40 • (05/31/96)

87 **DOMAINE THOMAS-MOILLARD** Corton-Charlemagne 1994 • $60 • (05/31/96)

87 **GEORGES DUBOEUF** Pouilly-Fuissé Oak-Aged 1994 • $17 • (05/31/96)

87 **GUY AMIOT** Chassagne-Montrachet Clos St.-Jean 1994 • $44 • (05/31/96) • 86

87 **GUY AMIOT** Chassagne-Montrachet Les Vergers 1994 • $44 • (05/31/96)

87 **JEAN-CLAUDE THEVENET** St.-Véran Clos de l'Ermitage; Cuvée Vieilles Vignes White 1994 • $16

87 **JACQUES SAUMAIZE** Pouilly-Fuissé La Roche 1994 • $17 • (05/31/96)

87 **JEAN PILLOT** Chassagne-Montrachet Les Chenevottes 1994 • $30 • (05/31/96)

87 **JEAN-MARC BOILLOT** Puligny-Montrachet Les Referts 1994 • $47 • (05/31/96)

87 **JOSEPH DROUHIN** Puligny-Montrachet 1994 • $39 • (05/31/96)

87 **LOUIS CARILLON** Puligny-Montrachet 1994 • $35 • (05/31/96)

87 **MARC MOREY** Chassagne-Montrachet Morgeot 1994 • $48 • (05/31/96)

87 **MOILLARD** Puligny-Montrachet Les Perrières 1994 • $39 • (05/31/96)

87 **OLIVIER LEFLAIVE FRÈRES** St.-Aubin En Remilly 1994 • $22 • (05/31/96)

87 **PHILIPPE CHAVY** Puligny-Montrachet Corvée des Vignes 1994 • $30 • (05/31/96)

87 **ROUX PÈRE & FILS** Chardonnay Bourgogne 1994 • $NA • (05/31/96)

87 **VERGET** Chassagne-Montrachet Premier Cru 1994 • $27 • (05/31/96)

87 **VINCENT PRUNIER** Puligny-Montrachet La Garenne 1994 • $NA • (05/31/96)

86 **ANTONIN RODET** Meursault Les Perrières 1994 • $53 • (05/31/96)

86 **BLAIN-GAGNARD** Criots-Bâtard-Montrachet 1994 • $95 • (05/31/96) • 86

86 **CHÂTEAU DE PULIGNY-MONTRACHET** Puligny-Montrachet 1994 • $16 • (05/31/96)

86 **DOMAINE CORSIN** Mâcon-Villages 1994 • $12

86 **FONTAINE-GAGNARD** Bâtard-Montrachet 1994 • $90 • (05/31/96) • 85

86 **FONTAINE-GAGNARD** Chassagne-Montrachet La Boudriotte 1994 • $46 • (05/31/96)

86 **GEORGES DUBOEUF** Pouilly-Fuissé Flower Label 1994 • $16 • (06/30/95)

86 **GEORGES DUBOEUF** St.-Véran 1994 • $9 • (06/30/95)

86 **GEORGES DUBOEUF** Mâcon-Lugny Chardonnay Fête des Fleurs 1994 • $8 • (06/30/95) • BB

86 **GEORGES BURRIER** Pouilly-Fuissé 1994 • $18 • (05/31/96)

86 **GUY AMIOT** Chassagne-Montrachet Les Macherelles 1994 • $39 • (05/31/96)

86 **JEAN-MARC BOILLOT** Puligny-Montrachet 1994 • $37 • (05/31/96)

86 **JEAN-MARC BROCARD** Bourgogne Domaine Ste.-Claire 1994 • $11 • (05/31/96)

86 **L'HÉRITIER-GUYOT** St.-Romain 1994 • $16 • (05/31/96)

86 **LEONARD DE SAINT-AUBIN** Puligny-Montrachet 1994 • $27 • (05/31/96)

86 **LOUIS LATOUR** Montrachet 1994 • $230 • (05/31/96)

86 **MARC MOREY** Chassagne-Montrachet Les Chenevottes 1994 • $40 • (05/31/96)

86 **MARC MOREY** Puligny-Montrachet Les Pucelles 1994 • $60 • (05/31/96)

86 **MICHEL JUILLOT** Mercurey 1994 • $23 • (05/31/96)

86 **MME. R. GUÉRIN** Pouilly-Fuissé La Roche Sélection Vieilles Vignes Cuvée No. 1 1994 • $NA • (05/31/96)

86 **MOILLARD** Puligny-Montrachet 1994 • $30 • (05/31/96)

86 **PIERRE BITOUZET** Corton-Charlemagne 1994 • $50 • (05/31/96) • 86

86 **RAPET PÈRE & FILS** Corton-Charlemagne 1994 • $70 • (05/31/96) • 85

86 **RENÉ GUERIN** Pouilly-Fuissé La Roche Sélection Vieilles Vignes No. 2 1994 • $21 • (05/31/96)

86 **ROGER BELLAND** Chassagne-Montrachet Morgeot-Clos Pitois 1994 • $NA • (05/31/96)

86 **THIBERT PÈRE & FILS** Pouilly-Fuissé Vieilles Vignes 1994 • $16 • (05/31/96)

86 **VERGET** Meursault Les Rougeots 1994 • $31 • (05/31/96)

86 **VERGET** Puligny-Montrachet Sous Le Puits 1994 • $38 • (05/31/96)

85 **ANDRÉ AUVIGUE** Pouilly-Fuissé Solutré 1994 • $18 • (05/31/96)

85 **BLAIN-GAGNARD** Chassagne-Montrachet Clos St.-Jean 1994 • $45 • (05/31/96)

85 **BLAIN-GAGNARD** Chassagne-Montrachet La Boudriotte 1994 • $45 • (05/31/96)

85 **BOUCHARD PÈRE & FILS** Meursault Les Genevrières 1994 • $46 • (05/31/96)

85 **CAVE DE VIRE** Mâcon-Viré Cuvée Spéciale 1994 • $NA

85 **CATHERINE & PASCAL ROLLET** Pouilly-Fuissé Domaine de la Chapelle 1994 • $16 • (05/31/96)

85 **CHARLES & RÉMI JOBARD** Bourgogne Chardonnay 1994 • $20 • (05/31/96)

85 **CHARTRON & TRÉBUCHET** Auxey-Duresses 1994 • $14 • (05/31/96) • 85

85 **CHARTRON & TRÉBUCHET** Meursault 1994 • $22 • (05/31/96)

85 **CHARTRON & TRÉBUCHET** Pernand-Vergelesses 1994 • $15 • (05/31/96)

85 **CHARTRON & TRÉBUCHET** St.-Aubin La Chatenière 1994 • $17 • (05/31/96)

85 **CHÂTEAU POUILLY** Pouilly-Fuissé 1994 • $27 • (05/31/96)

85 **CHÂTEAU DE PULIGNY-MONTRACHET** St.-Aubin En Remilly 1994 • $11 • (05/31/96)

85 **DOMAINE DES DEUX ROCHES** Mâcon-Villages 1994 • $13

85 **DOMAINE DES DEUX ROCHES** St.-Véran 1994 • $NA

85 **DOMAINE THOMAS** St.-Véran 1994 • $12 • (08/31/95)

85 **DOMAINE MICHELOT** Meursault Les Charmes 1994 • $50 • (05/31/96)

85 **DOMAINE MICHELOT** Meursault Clos du Cromin 1994 • $38 • (05/31/96)

85 **DOMAINE MICHELOT** Meursault Les Perrières 1994 • $60 • (05/31/96)

85 **DOMAINE MICHELOT** Meursault Sous la Velle 1994 • $30 • (05/31/96)

85 **FERNAND PILLOT** Chassagne-Montrachet Morgeot 1994 • $NA • (05/31/96)

85 **FONTAINE-GAGNARD** Chassagne-Montrachet La Maltroie 1994 • $46 • (05/31/96)

85 **GUY AMIOT** Chassagne-Montrachet Caillerets 1994 • $50 • (05/31/96)

85 **HENRI PLUMET HÉRITIERS** Pouilly-Fuissé Clos du Chalet Pouilly 1994 • $NA • (05/31/96)

85 **J. A. FERRET** Pouilly-Fuissé Tête de Cru 1994 • $40 • (05/31/96) • 84

85 **JACQUES PRIEUR** Meursault Les Perrières 1994 • $70 • (05/31/96)

85 **JEAN BOILLOT** Puligny-Montrachet Clos de la Mouchère 1994 • $44 • (05/31/96)

85 **JEAN CHARTRON** Puligny-Montrachet Clos du Cailleret 1994 • $42 • (05/31/96)

85 **JEAN PILLOT** Chassagne-Montrachet Caillerets 1994 • $42 • (05/31/96)

85 **JEAN PILLOT** Chassagne-Montrachet Champs Gain 1994 • $32 • (05/31/96)

85 **JEAN PILLOT** Puligny-Montrachet 1994 • $NA • (05/31/96)

85 **LATOUR-GIRAUD** Puligny-Montrachet Champ Canet 1994 • $NA • (05/31/96)

85 **LOUIS LATOUR** Chevalier-Montrachet Les Demoiselles 1994 • $148 • (05/31/96)

85 **LOUIS LATOUR** Chassagne-Montrachet Les Chenevottes 1994 • $37 • (05/31/96)

85 **LUPÉ-CHOLET** Chassagne-Montrachet 1994 • $NA • (05/31/96) • 85

85 **MARC COLIN** Chassagne-Montrachet Les Caillerets 1994 • $45 • (05/31/96)

85 **MARC COLIN** Chassagne-Montrachet Les Champs-Gains 1994 • $40 • (05/31/96)

85 **MARC COLIN** Puligny-Montrachet Le Trézin 1994 • $40 • (05/31/96)

85 **MARC COLIN** St.-Aubin Le Charmois 1994 • $24 • (05/31/96)

85 **MARC COLIN** St.-Aubin Les Cortons 1994 • $24 • (05/31/96)

85 **MARC MOREY** Chassagne-Montrachet 1994 • $33 • (05/31/96)

85 **MARC MOREY** Chassagne-Montrachet En Virondot 1994 • $40 • (05/31/96)

85 **MICHEL BOUZEREAU** Meursault Les Grands Charrons 1994 • $30 • (05/31/96)

85 **MICHEL BOUZEREAU** Meursault Le Tesson 1994 • $35 • (05/31/96)

85 **MICHEL NIELLON** Chassagne-Montrachet Les Champs Gains 1994 • $55 • (05/31/96)

85 **MOILLARD** Meursault 1994 • $29 • (04/30/96)

85 **RAPET PÈRE & FILS** Pernand-Vergelesses 1994 • $21 • (05/31/96)

85 **ROGER BELLAND** Puligny-Montrachet Champ Gain 1994 • $NA • (05/31/96)

85 **ROGER LUQUET** Pouilly-Fuissé Clos du Bourg 1994 • $19 • (05/31/96)

85 **ROGER SAUMAIZE** Pouilly-Fuissé Vigne Blanche 1994 • $NA • (05/31/96)

85 **ROGER SAUMAIZE-MICHELIN** Pouilly-Fuissé Les Ronchevats 1994 • $NA • (05/31/96)

85 **ROUX PÈRE & FILS** Chassagne-Montrachet 1994 • $NA • (05/31/96) • 85

85 **THIERRY GUÉRIN** Pouilly-Fuissé La Roche Vieilles Vignes 1994 • $22 • (05/31/96)

84 **ANTONIN RODET** Chassagne-Montrachet La Grande Montagne 1994 • $48 • (05/31/96)

84 **ANTONIN RODET** Puligny-Montrachet Le Cailleret 1994 • $53 • (05/31/96)

84 **BÉATRICE & JEAN-MICHEL DROUIN** Pouilly-Fuissé Domaine des Gerbeaux Cuvée Préstige 1994 • $16 • (05/31/96)

84 **BOUCHARD PÈRE & FILS** Puligny-Montrachet Les Folatières 1994 • $38 • (05/31/96)

84 **BRUNO CLAIR** Morey-St.-Denis En La Rue de Vergy 1994 • $40 • (05/31/96)

84 **CAVE DE LUGNY** Mâcon-Lugny Les Charmes 1994 • $9

84 **CAVE DE VIRE** Mâcon-Viré Grande Réserve 1994 • $NA

84 **CAVE DE VIRE** Mâcon-Viré 1994 • $NA

84 **CHANSON PÈRE & FILS** Montagny Premier Cru 1994 • $13 • (05/31/96)

84 **CHANSON PÈRE & FILS** Pouilly-Fuissé St.-Vincent 1994 • $19 • (05/31/96)

84 **CHARLES & RÉMI JOBARD** Meursault Les Chevalières 1994 • $32 • (05/31/96)

84 **CHARTRON & TRÉBUCHET** Puligny-Montrachet Les Referts 1994 • $29 • (05/31/96) • 84

84 **CHÂTEAU DE PULIGNY-MONTRACHET** Meursault Les Perrières 1994 • $16 • (05/31/96)

84 **COLLIN & BOURISSET** Pouilly-Fuissé Domaine Tranchand 1994 • $16 • (05/31/96)

84 **CORDIER PÈRE & FILS** Pouilly-Fuissé Vieilles Vignes 1994 • $30 • (05/31/96)

84 **FONTAINE-GAGNARD** Chassagne-Montrachet La Grande Montagne 1994 • $46 • (05/31/96)

84 **FONTAINE-GAGNARD** Chassagne-Montrachet Les Chenevottes 1994 • $46 • (05/31/96)

84 **FRANÇOIS GAGNEROT & FILS** Corton-Charlemagne 1994 • $36 • (05/31/96) • 85

84 **GEORGES DUBOEUF** Pouilly-Fuissé Clos Reissier 1994 • $17 • (06/30/95)

84 **GEORGES BURRIER** Chardonnay Mâcon-Villages 1994 • $10 • (05/31/96)

84 **GUY AMIOT** Puligny-Montrachet Les Demoiselles 1994 • $60 • (05/31/96)

84 **J.J. VINCENT** Pouilly-Fuissé Cuvée Première 1994 • $NA • (05/31/96) • 84

84 **JEAN-CLAUDE THEVENET** Mâcon-Villages 1994 • $10

84 **JACQUES SAUMAIZE** Pouilly-Fuissé Vieilles Vignes 1994 • $16 • (05/31/96)

84 **JEAN-MARC BOILLOT** Puligny-Montrachet Champ-Canet 1994 • $47 • (05/31/96)

84 **JOSEPH DROUHIN** Beaune Clos des Mouches 1994 • $60 • (05/31/96) • 84

84 **JOSEPH DROUHIN** Meursault Perrières 1994 • $52 • (05/31/96)

84 **LEONARD DE SAINT-AUBIN** Chassagne-Montrachet 1994 • $26 • (05/31/96)

84 **LES VIGNERONS D'IGE** Mâcon-Igé 1994 • $NA

84 **LATOUR-GIRAUD** Meursault Les Genevrières 1994 • $NA • (05/31/96)

84 **LOUIS JADOT** Savigny-lès-Beaune 1994 • $20 • (05/31/96)

84 **LOUIS LATOUR** Montagny La Grande Roche 1994 • $13 • (05/31/96)

84 **LUPÉ-CHOLET** Puligny-Montrachet 1994 • $NA • (05/31/96)

84 **MANCIAT-PONCET** Pouilly-Fuissé Les Crays 1994 • $18 • (05/31/96)

84 **MARC COLIN** Chassagne-Montrachet 1994 • $35 • (05/31/96) • 84

84 **MICHEL COLIN-DELÉGER** Chassagne-Montrachet Les Vergers 1994 • $40 • (05/31/96)

84 **MOILLARD** Pouilly-Fuissé Domaine Greffet 1994 • $22 • (05/31/96)

84 **MONTHÉLIE-DOUHAIRET** Meursault 1994 • $34 • (05/31/96)

84 **PIERRE FERRAUD & FILS** St.-Véran 1994 • $10

84 **PHILIPPE CHAVY** Puligny-Montrachet Les Nosroyes 1994 • $30 • (05/31/96)

84 **PIERRE LABET** Savigny-lès-Beaune Aux Vergelesses 1994 • $34 • (05/31/96)

84 **ROGER SAUMAIZE-MICHELIN** Pouilly-Fuissé Clos de la Roche 1994 • $NA • (05/31/96)

84 **ROUX PÈRE & FILS** Meursault Clos des Poruzots 1994 • $NA • (05/31/96)

84 **THOMAS** Pouilly-Fuissé 1994 • $17 • (05/31/96)

83 **ANDRÉ GUÉRIN** Pouilly-Fuissé La Roche No #1 1994 • $NA • (05/31/96)

83 **CELLIER DES TOURNONS** Pouilly-Fuissé Rocqenvert 1994 • $19 • (05/31/96)

83 **CHARTRON & TRÉBUCHET** Rully White La Chaume 1994 • $14 • (05/31/96)

83 **DEMESSEY** Mâcon-Villages 1994 • $12

83 **DOMAINE LEFLAIVE** Bâtard-Montrachet 1994 • $140 • (05/31/96)

83 **DOMAINE MICHELOT** Meursault Clos St.-Félix 1994 • $35 • (05/31/96)

83 **DOMAINE MICHELOT** Meursault Poruzot 1994 • $40 • (05/31/96)

83 **F. CHAUVENET** Mâcon-Blanc-Villages Les Jumelles 1994 • $8

83 **FONTAINE-GAGNARD** Chassagne-Montrachet Les Vergers 1994 • $46 • (05/31/96)

83 **GEORGES DUBOEUF** Mâcon-Villages Domaine les Chenevières 1994 • $NA

83 **GEORGES DUBOEUF** Mâcon-Villages 1994 • $NA

83 **JEANNE ROUSSEAU** Pouilly-Fuissé 1994 • $13 • (06/30/95)

83 **JEAN BOILLOT** Puligny-Montrachet 1994 • $49 • (05/31/96)

83 **JOSEPH DROUHIN** Pernand-Vergelesses 1994 • $24 • (05/31/96)

83 **LOUIS LATOUR** St.-Véran 1994 • $11

83 **LOUIS JADOT** St.-Aubin 1994 • $19 • (05/31/96)

83 **MARC COLIN** Puligny-Montrachet La Garenne 1994 • $45 • (05/31/96)

83 **MICHEL COLIN-DELÉGER** Chassagne-Montrachet Les Chaumées 1994 • $40 • (05/31/96)

83 **PATRICK JAVILLIER** Meursault Les Casses-Têtes 1994 • $39 • (05/31/96)

83 **PAUL BEAUDET** Pouilly-Fuissé Domaine des Trois Tilleuls Vieilles Vignes 1994 • $NA • (05/31/96)

83 **ROUX PÈRE & FILS** St.-Aubin White Les Cortons 1994 • $NA • (05/31/96)

82 **ANTONIN GUYON** Pernand-Vergelesses 1994 • $20 • (05/31/96)

82 **BOUCHARD PERE & FILS** Mâcon-Villages Mâcon-Villages; Le Chamville 1994 • $11

82 **CAVE DE CHAINTRE** St.-Véran 1994 • $NA

82 **CHÂTEAU DE PULIGNY-MONTRACHET** Puligny-Montrachet Les Folatières 1994 • $20 • (05/31/96)

82 **CORDIER PÈRE & FILS** Pouilly-Fuissé Lot No. 2 1994 • $21 • (05/31/96)

82 **DOMAINE DES DEUX ROCHES** St.-Véran Les Terres Noires 1994 • $17

82 **FONTAINE-GAGNARD** Chassagne-Montrachet Morgeot 1994 • $46 • (05/31/96)

82 **JOSEPH DROUHIN** Meursault 1994 • $37 • (05/31/96)

82 **LOUIS LATOUR** Chassagne-Montrachet 1994 • $34 • (05/31/96) • 82

82 **MOILLARD** Meursault Clos du Cromin 1994 • $28 • (05/31/96)

82 **MOILLARD** Chardonnay Bourgogne Hautes-Côtes de Beaune Les Alouettes 1994 • $15 • (05/31/96)

82 **MOILLARD** St.-Véran Domaine de la Verchère 1994 • $12 • (05/31/96)

82 **MONTHÉLIE-DOUHAIRET** Meursault Les Santenots 1994 • $34 • (05/31/96)

82 **THIERRY GUÉRIN** Pouilly-Fuissé Clos de France 1994 • $22 • (05/31/96)

82 **VERGET** St.-Aubin Premier Cru 1994 • $18 • (05/31/96)

81 **BÉATRICE & JEAN-MICHEL DROUIN** Pouilly-Fuissé Domaine des Gerbeaux 1994 • $NA • (05/31/96)

81 **CHARTRON & TREBUCHET** Mâcon-Villages 1994 • $12

81 **CHÂTEAU DE RULLY** Rully 1994 • $20 • (05/31/96)

81 **DUVERGEY-TABOUREAU** Mâcon-Villages 1994 • $14

81 **DOMAINE MICHELOT** Meursault Les Grands Charrons 1994 • $38 • (05/31/96)

81 **DOMAINE THOMAS-MOILLARD** Chardonnay Bourgogne Hautes-Côtes de Nuits 1994 • $14 • (05/31/96)

81 **GEORGES DUBOEUF** Mâcon-Villages Domaine les Chenevières 1994 • $8 • (06/30/95)

81 **JEAN CHARTRON** Puligny-Montrachet Les Folatières 1994 • $42 • (05/31/96)

81 **JOSEPH DROUHIN** Chassagne-Montrachet Marquis de Laguiche White 1994 • $54 • (05/31/96) • 81

81 **LATOUR-GIRAUD** Meursault Les Narvaux 1994 • $NA • (05/31/96)

81 **LOUIS LATOUR** Pouilly-Fuissé 1994 • $21 • (05/31/96)

81 **MAILLARD PÈRE & FILS** Corton 1994 • $NA • (05/31/96) • 80

81 **PAUL GARAUDET** Puligny-Montrachet 1994 • $27 • (05/31/96)

81 **PIERRE MATROT** Bourgogne Chardonnay 1994 • $17 • (05/31/96)

81 **ROGER LASSARAT** Pouilly-Fuissé Cuvée Prestige 1994 • $NA • (05/31/96)

81 **ROGER LUQUET** Pouilly-Fuissé 1994 • $16 • (05/31/96)

80 **ALBERT BICHOT** St.-Véran 1994 • $NA • (05/31/96)

80 **BACHELET-RAMONET** Chassagne-Montrachet La Grande Montagne 1994 • $NA • (05/31/96)

80 **CHARTRON & TRÉBUCHET** St.-Véran Château du Chasselas White 1994 • $15

80 **CHARTRON & TRÉBUCHET** Mercurey 1994 • $15 • (05/31/96)

80 **CHÂTEAU DE BEAUREGARD** Pouilly-Fuissé 1994 • $23 • (05/31/96)

80 **CHÂTEAU DE CHAMIREY** Mercurey 1994 • $20 • (05/31/96)

80 **DOMAINE DE LA CROIX SENAILLET** St.-Véran 1994 • $NA

80 **DANIEL BARRAUD** Pouilly-Fuissé La Roche 1994 • $24 • (05/31/96)

80 **DANIEL BARRAUD** Pouilly-Fuissé Cuvée Vieilles Vignes 1994 • $28 • (05/31/96)

80 **DOMAINE ROULOT** Chardonnay Bourgogne 1994 • $19 • (05/31/96)

80 **FRANÇOIS GAGNEROT & FILS** Ladoix Les Gréchons 1994 • $NA • (05/31/96)

80 **JEAN CLAUDE BOISSET** Mâcon-Blanc-Villages 1994 • $8 • (08/31/95)

80 **JEAN-MARC AUJOUX** St.-Véran 1994 • $11 • (08/31/95)

80 **JEAN PILLOT** Chassagne-Montrachet 1994 • $25 • (05/31/96)

80 **L'HÉRITIER-GUYOT** Auxey-Duresses 1994 • $18 • (05/31/96) • 80

80 **L'HÉRITIER-GUYOT** Chassagne-Montrachet 1994 • $28 • (05/31/96) • 79

80 **LOUIS LATOUR** Meursault Les Gouttes d'Or 1994 • $40 • (05/31/96)

80 **MONTHÉLIE-DOUHAIRET** Bourgogne Aligoté 1994 • $14 • (05/31/96)

80 **P. DUBREUIL-FONTAINE PÈRE & FILS** Pernand-Vergelesses 1994 • $56 • (05/31/96)

80 **PATRICK JAVILLIER** Bourgogne Cuvée Oligocène 1994 • $23 • (05/31/96)

80 **PAUL GARAUDET** Bourgogne 1994 • $NA • (05/31/96)

80 **ROGER LUQUET** St.-Véran 1994 • $10

80 **ROLAND BOUCHACOURT** Mâcon-Villages Château de Péronne 1994 • $7

80 **ROPITEAU FRERES** St.-Véran 1994 • $11

80 **ROBERT-DENOGENT** Pouilly-Fuissé Les Reisses Vieilles Vignes 1994 • $24 • (05/31/96)

80 **ROBERT-DENOGENT** Pouilly-Fuissé Les Carrons 1994 • $34 • (05/31/96)
80 **ROBERT-DENOGENT** Pouilly-Fuissé Cuvée Claude Denogent 1994 • $28 • (05/31/96)
80 **VERGET** St.-Romain 1994 • $17 • (05/31/96)
80 **VINCENT PRUNIER** Auxey-Duresses 1994 • $NA • (05/31/96) • 81
79 **ANTONIN RODET** Chassagne-Montrachet Morgeot 1994 • $43 • (05/31/96)
79 **BACHELET-RAMONET** Bâtard-Montrachet 1994 • $NA • (05/31/96) • 79
79 **CAVE DE CHAINTRE** Mâcon-Fuissé 1994 • $NA
79 **CHANSON PÈRE & FILS** Bourgogne Cuvée Alexis Chanson 1994 • $10 • (05/31/96)
79 **CHARTRON & TRÉBUCHET** St.-Romain 1994 • $14 • (05/31/96)
79 **FRANÇOIS PAQUET** Mâcon Blanc-Villages Cépage Chardonnay 1994 • $9 • (08/31/95)
79 **FONTAINE-GAGNARD** Chassagne-Montrachet Caillerets 1994 • $46 • (05/31/96)
79 **GEORGES DUBOEUF** Mâcon-Villages Flower Label 1994 • $8 • (06/30/95)
79 **GEORGES DUBOEUF** St.-Véran Domaine St.-Martin 1994 • $9
79 **HENRI DE VILLAMONT** St.-Véran Clos de l'Ermitage White 1994 • $NA
79 **L'HÉRITIER-GUYOT** Hautes Côtes de Nuits 1994 • $13 • (05/31/96)
79 **LABOURE-ROI** Mâcon-Blanc-Villages 1994 • $10
79 **LOUIS LATOUR** Meursault 1994 • $30 • (05/31/96)
79 **LOUIS LATOUR** Puligny-Montrachet Les Folatières 1994 • $45 • (05/31/96)
79 **LUPÉ-CHOLET** Meursault 1994 • $NA • (05/31/96)
79 **MOMMESSIN** St.-Véran Domaine de l'Evèque 1994 • $14 • (05/31/96)
79 **OLIVIER LEFLAIVE FRÈRES** St.-Romain 1994 • $18 • (05/31/96)
79 **PIERRE FERRAUD & FILS** Mâcon-Villages 1994 • $9
79 **ROGER LUQUET** Mâcon Clos de Condemine 1994 • $9
79 **ROPITEAU FRERES** Mâcon-Villages Les Chanterelles 1994 • $9
79 **RAPET PÈRE & FILS** Pernand-Vergelesses Premier Cru 1994 • $30 • (05/31/96)
79 **ROGER LASSARAT** Pouilly-Fuissé Clos de France 1994 • $NA • (05/31/96)
79 **THIBERT PÈRE & FILS** Pouilly-Fuissé Vignes Blanches 1994 • $14 • (05/31/96)
79 **THIERRY GUÉRIN** St.-Véran Clos des Pierres Brûlées 1994 • $13 • (05/31/96)
78 **ALBERT BICHOT** Chassagne-Montrachet 1994 • $NA • (05/31/96) • 78
78 **ALBERT BICHOT** Meursault 1994 • $25 • (05/31/96)
78 **ANTONIN RODET** Puligny-Montrachet Hameau de Blagny 1994 • $45 • (05/31/96)
78 **CHÂTEAU FUISSÉ** Pouilly-Fuissé 1994 • $NA • (05/31/96)
78 **CLAUDE NOUVEAU** Santenay 1994 • $NA • (05/31/96)
78 **DEMESSEY** Pouilly-Fuissé 1994 • $20 • (05/31/96)
78 **DOMAINE MICHELOT** 1994 • $55 • (05/31/96) • 77
78 **FRANÇOISE & NICOLAS MELIN** Pouilly-Fuissé Domaine La Soufrandise Vieilles Vignes 1994 • $25 • (05/31/96) • 78
78 **JEAN-PAUL PAQUET** Pouilly-Fuissé Domaine Les Vieux Murs 1994 • $NA • (05/31/96)
78 **JOSEPH DROUHIN** Chassagne-Montrachet 1994 • $38 • (05/31/96) • 78
78 **LALEURE-PIOT** Pernand-Vergelesses 1994 • $28 • (05/31/96)
78 **LOUIS JADOT** Santenay Clos de Malte 1994 • $17 • (05/31/96)
78 **LOUIS LATOUR** Pernand-Vergelesses 1994 • $20 • (05/31/96)
78 **MOILLARD** Chardonnay Bourgogne Tradition 1994 • $12 • (05/31/96)
78 **THIERRY GUÉRIN** Pouilly-Fuissé La Roche 1994 • $19 • (05/31/96)
78 **VINCENT PRUNIER** St.-Aubin White Premier Cru 1994 • $NA • (05/31/96)
77 **AUVIGUE & REVEL** Pouilly-Fuissé Vieilles Vignes 1994 • $24 • (05/31/96)
77 **JEAN-MARC AUJOUX** Mâcon-Villages 1994 • $9 • (06/30/95)
77 **JEAN BOILLOT** Puligny-Montrachet Les Perrières 1994 • $45 • (05/31/96)
77 **L'HÉRITIER-GUYOT** Bourgogne 1994 • $12 • (05/31/96)
77 **LABOURE-ROI** St.-Véran 1994 • $8
77 **LAROCHE** Mâcon-Villages 1994 • $9
77 **LES VIGNERONS D'IGE** Mâcon-Igé Château London 1994 • $10
77 **LUPÉ-CHOLET** Mâcon-Villages 1994 • $NA • (05/31/96) • 76
77 **ROLAND BOUCHACOURT** Mâcon-Villages 1994 • $7
77 **VINCENT PRUNIER** Meursault 1994 • $NA • (05/31/96) • 75
76 **CAVE DES VIGNERONS DE MANCEY** Mâcon-Villages Vieilles Vignes 1994 • $9 • (08/31/94)
76 **HENRI NAUDIN-FERRAND** Bourgogne Aligoté 1994 • $NA • (05/31/96)
76 **JAFFELIN** St.-Véran 1994 • $10
76 **MARC COLIN** St.-Aubin La Chatenière White 1994 • $24 • (05/31/96)
76 **MICHEL JUILLOT** Corton-Charlemagne 1994 • $94 • (05/31/96)
76 **MICHEL MOREY-COFFINET** Chassagne-Montrachet 1994 • $24 • (05/31/96)
76 **ROUX PÈRE & FILS** Puligny-Montrachet Les Enseignères 1994 • $NA • (05/31/96)
75 **ALAIN GRAS** St.-Romain 1994 • $22 • (05/31/96)
75 **ALBERT BICHOT** Mâcon-Villages 1994 • $10 • (05/31/96)
75 **CAVE DES VIGNERONS DE MANCEY** Mâcon-Villages 1994 • $7
75 **GEORGES DUBOEUF** Pouilly-Fuissé 1994 • $15 • (05/31/96)
75 **JAFFELIN** Mâcon-Villages 1994 • $9
75 **JEAN CLAUDE BOISSET** Pouilly-Fuissé 1994 • $NA • (06/30/95)
75 **JEAN CLAUDE BOISSET** Pouilly-Fuissé 1994 • $14 • (06/30/95)
75 **LAROCHE** Mâcon-Lugny 1994 • $10
75 **LALEURE-PIOT** Corton-Charlemagne 1994 • $70 • (05/31/96) • 75
75 **LATOUR-GIRAUD** Meursault Clos du Cromin 1994 • $NA • (05/31/96) • 75
75 **RENÉ GUERIN** Pouilly-Fuissé La Roche Oak-aged Cuvée No. 2 1994 • $19 • (05/31/96)
75 **ROBERT-DENOGENT** Pouilly-Fuissé La Croix 1994 • $23 • (05/31/96)
74 **FONTAINE-GAGNARD** Chassagne-Montrachet 1994 • $40 • (05/31/96) • 74
74 **MICHEL JUILLOT** Bourgogne 1994 • $14 • (05/31/96) • 74
74 **OLIVIER LEFLAIVE FRÈRES** 1994 • $20 • (05/31/96)

73 **LUPÉ-CHOLET** Bourgogne Chardonnay Comtesse de Lupé White 1994 • $NA • (05/31/96)

73 **MARC COLIN** St.-Aubin En Remilly White 1994 • $24 • (05/31/96) • 73

73 **PIERRE ANDRE** St.-Véran 1994 • $9 • (08/31/95)

73 **ROUX PÈRE & FILS** St.-Aubin White Les Pucelles 1994 • $NA • (05/31/96)

72 **ALBERT BICHOT** Mâcon-Lugny 1994 • $NA • (05/31/96) • 74

72 **JEAN-PAUL PAQUET** Pouilly-Fuissé Domaine de Fuissiacus Vieilles Vignes 1994 • $15 • (05/31/96)

72 **LOUIS JADOT** Puligny-Montrachet 1994 • $34 • (05/31/96)

72 **LOUIS LATOUR** Puligny-Montrachet 1994 • $35 • (05/31/96)

71 **CHANSON PÈRE & FILS** Pernand-Vergelesses White 1994 • $16 • (05/31/96) • 71

70 **ALBERT BICHOT** Puligny-Montrachet 1994 • $26 • (05/31/96)

70 **CHÂTEAU DE MONTPATEY** Bourgogne Chardonnay White 1994 • $10 • (05/31/96)

70 **HENRI DE VILLAMONT** Mâcon-Villages 1994 • $NA

70 **OLIVIER LEFLAIVE FRÈRES 1994** • $14 • (05/31/96) • 70

70 **PIERRE LABET** Beaune Clos des Monsnières 1994 • $26 • (05/31/96)

70 **REINE PEDAUQUE** Mâcon-Villages Coupées 1994 • $9

67 **PIERRE ANDRE** Mâcon-Villages Mâcon André 1994 • $9 • (08/31/95)

62 **LES VIGNERONS D'IGE** St.-Véran 1994 • $NA

1992 White Burgundy
Vintage Rating: 89

97 **DOMAINE JACQUES PRIEUR** Montrachet 1992 • $200 • (08/31/94)

96 **DOMAINE JEAN CHARTRON** Chevalier-Montrachet Clos des Chevaliers 1992 • $95 • (08/31/94)

95 **DOMAINE RAMONET** Montrachet 1992 • $268

95 **LOUIS LATOUR** Montrachet 1992 • $170 • (08/31/94) • CS

95 **PIERRE COLIN** Bâtard-Montrachet 1992 • $50 • (08/31/94)

94 **BOUCHARD PERE & FILS** Chevalier-Montrachet Domaines du Château de Beaune 1992 • $81 • (08/31/94)

94 **DOMAINE ETIENNE SAUZET** Bienvenues-Bâtard-Montrachet 1992 • $127 • (08/31/94)

94 **DOMAINE RAMONET** Bâtard-Montrachet 1992 • $NA

94 **DOMAINE RAMONET** Montrachet Harvey Steiman White 1992 • $550

94 **DOMAINE DES COMTES LAFON** Meursault Les Genevrières 1992 • $75

94 **JEAN-NOEL GAGNARD** Bâtard-Montrachet 1992 • $100 • (08/31/94)

94 **JOSEPH DROUHIN** Montrachet Marquis de Laguiche 1992 • $162 • (08/31/94)

93 **DOMAINE ETIENNE SAUZET** Puligny-Montrachet Champ Canet 1992 • $68 • (08/31/94)

93 **DOMAINE LEFLAIVE** Chevalier-Montrachet Grand Cru 1992 • $155 • (05/15/95)

93 **DOMAINE MARC MOREY** Bâtard-Montrachet 1992 • $92 • (08/31/94)

93 **DOMAINE DES COMTES LAFON** Meursault Les Charmes 1992 • $75 • (08/31/94)

93 **GUFFENS-HEYNEN** Pouilly-Fuissé Clos des Petits-Croux 1992 • $NA

93 **J.-F. COCHE-DURY** Corton-Charlemagne 1992 • $170 • (08/31/94)

93 **J.-F. COCHE-DURY** Meursault Les Rougeots 1992 • $NA

93 **J.-F. COCHE-DURY** Meursault Les Perrières 1992 • $83

93 **LOUIS JADOT** Corton-Charlemagne 1992 • $56 • (08/31/94)

93 **VERGET** Bâtard-Montrachet 1992 • $125 • (08/31/94)

93 **VERGET** Puligny-Montrachet Sous Le Puits 1992 • $38 • (08/31/94)

92 **CHARTRON & TREBUCHET** Bâtard-Montrachet 1992 • $82 • (07/31/94)

92 **CHATEAU DE PULIGNY-MONTRACHET** Meursault Les Porusot 1992 • $30 • (08/31/94)

92 **DOMAINE ETIENNE SAUZET** Chevalier-Montrachet 1992 • $114 • (08/31/94)

92 **DOMAINE JACQUES PRIEUR** Meursault Perriéres 1992 • $45 • (08/31/94)

92 **DOMAINE JACQUES PRIEUR** Puligny-Montrachet Les Combettes 1992 • $NA • (08/31/94)

92 **DOMAINE LEFLAIVE** Puligny-Montrachet Clavoillon 1992 • $65 • (05/15/95)

92 **JOSEPH DROUHIN** Bâtard-Montrachet 1992 • $120 • (08/31/94)

92 **JOSEPH DROUHIN** Puligny-Montrachet Clos de la Garenne 1992 • $43 • (08/31/94)

92 **LOUIS JADOT** Puligny-Montrachet Clos de la Garenne Duc de Magenta Monopo 1992 • $33 • (08/31/94)

92 **OLIVIER LEFLAIVE** Bâtard-Montrachet 1992 • $100

92 **OLIVIER LEFLAIVE** Bienvenues-Bâtard-Montrachet White 1992 • $85

92 **PATRICK JAVILLIER** Meursault Les Narvaux 1992 • $35 • (08/31/94)

92 **TOLLOT-BEAUT** Corton-Charlemagne 1992 • $70 • (08/31/94)

91 **AMIOT-BONFILS** Puligny-Montrachet Les Demoiselles 1992 • $65 • (08/31/94)

91 **DOMAINE ETIENNE SAUZET** Bâtard-Montrachet 1992 • $127 • (08/31/94)

91 **DOMAINE ETIENNE SAUZET** Puligny-Montrachet Les Folatières 1992 • $68 • (08/31/94)

91 **DOMAINE GUY ROULOT** Meursault Les Perrières 1992 • $58 • (08/31/94)

91 **DOMAINE LEFLAIVE** Puligny-Montrachet Les Combettes 1992 • $83 • (05/15/95)

91 **DOMAINE RAMONET** Chassagne-Montrachet Caillerets 1992 • $52

91 **DOMAINE RAMONET** Chassagne-Montrachet Les Vergers 1992 • $NA

91 **DOMAINE RENE MANUEL** Meursault Clos des Bouches Chères 1992 • $NA • (08/31/94)

91 **FAIVELEY** Corton-Charlemagne 1992 • $62 • (08/31/94)

91 **G. MICHELOT** Meursault Clos du Cromin 1992 • $38 • (08/31/94)

91 **JEAN-MARC BOILLOT** Puligny-Montrachet Les Referts 1992 • $NA • (08/31/94)

91 **LOUIS JADOT** Chevalier-Montrachet Les Demoiselles 1992 • $93 • (08/31/94)

91 **MICHELOT-BUISSON** Meursault Charmes 1992 • $57 • (08/31/94)

91 **VAUCHER** Corton-Charlemagne 1992 • $NA • (08/31/94)

90 **BONNEAU DU MARTRAY** Corton-Charlemagne 1992 • $44 • (08/31/94)

90 **C. MICHELOT** Meursault Grands Charrons 1992 • $NA • (08/31/94)

90 **CHARTRON & TREBUCHET** Puligny-Montrachet Les Referts 1992 • $28 • (08/31/94)

90 **CHARTRON & TREBUCHET** Puligny-Montrachet 1992 • $25 • (07/31/94)

90 **DOMAINE D'AUVENAY** Puligny-Montrachet Les Folatières 1992 • $96 • (08/31/94)

90 **DOMAINE D'AUVENAY** Meursault Les Narvaux 1992 • $NA • (08/31/94)

90 **DOMAINE GUY ROULOT** Meursault Les Luchets 1992 • $32 • (08/31/94)

90 **DOMAINE JEAN CHARTRON** Puligny-Montrachet Clos du Cailleret 1992 • $34 • (08/31/94)

90 **DOMAINE MARC MOREY** Chassagne-Montrachet Virondot 1992 • $35 • (08/31/94)

90 **DOMAINE MARC MOREY** Puligny-Montrachet Les Pucelles 1992 • $53 • (08/31/94)

90 **DOMAINE DES COMTES LAFON** Meursault Clos de la Barre 1992 • $55 • 90

90 **DOMAINE DES COMTES LAFON** Meursault Perrières 1992 • $80 • 85

90 **HENRI GERMAIN** Meursault Le Limozin 1992 • $33 • (08/31/94)

90 **J.-F. COCHE-DURY** Meursault 1992 • $NA • (08/31/94)

90 **JEAN CLAUDE BOISSET** Chassagne-Montrachet Talley RINGER 1992 White 1992 • $NA

90 **JEAN PILLOT** Chassagne-Montrachet Les Champs Gain 1992 • $32 • (08/31/94)

90 **LEGER-PLUMET** Pouilly-Fuissé Domaine des Gerbaux Fût de Chêne 1992 • $NA

90 **LOUIS CARILLON** Puligny-Montrachet 1992 • $33 • (08/31/94)

90 **LOUIS CARILLON** Puligny-Montrachet Les Perrières 1992 • $41 • (08/31/94)

90 **LOUIS CARILLON** Puligny-Montrachet 1992 • $33 • (08/31/94)

90 **LOUIS CARILLON** Puligny-Montrachet Les Champs Canet 1992 • $43 • (08/31/94)

90 **LOUIS CARILLON** Puligny-Montrachet Les Perrières 1992 • $41 • (08/31/94)

90 **LOUIS LATOUR** Corton-Charlemagne 1992 • $60 • (08/31/94)

90 **OLIVIER LEFLAIVE** Puligny-Montrachet Les Folatières 1992 • $52 • (08/31/94)

90 **VERGET** Pouilly-Fuissé 1992 • $17

89 **BERNARD MOREY** Chassagne-Montrachet Morgeot 1992 • $33 • (02/28/94)

89 **BLAIN-GAGNARD** Bâtard-Montrachet 1992 • $90 • (08/31/94)

89 **BOUCHARD PERE & FILS** Corton-Charlemagne Domaines du Château de Beaune 1992 • $50 • (08/31/94)

89 **CHATEAU DE PULIGNY-MONTRACHET** Puligny-Montrachet Les Folatières 1992 • $34 • (08/31/94)

89 **DOMAINE JEAN CHARTRON** Puligny-Montrachet Clos des Pucelles 1992 • $36 • (08/31/94)

89 **DOMAINE JOSEPH MATROT** Meursault Charmes 1992 • $33 • (08/31/94)

89 **DOMAINE LEFLAIVE** Puligny-Montrachet Les Pucelles 1992 • $86 • (05/15/95)

89 **DOMAINE RENE MONNIER** Meursault Charmes 1992 • $40 • (08/31/94)

89 **FRANCOIS JOBARD** Meursault Poruzots 1992 • $50

89 **JEAN PILLOT** Chassagne-Montrachet Les Chenevottes 1992 • $30 • (08/31/94)

89 **LOUIS JADOT** Meursault-Charmes 1992 • $35 • (08/31/94)

89 **LOUIS LATOUR** Meursault Goutte d'Or 1992 • $31 • (08/31/94)

89 **LOUIS LATOUR** Puligny-Montrachet Les Folatières 1992 • $34 • (08/31/94)

89 **MESTRE-MICHELOT** Meursault Le Limozin 1992 • $38 • (08/31/94)

89 **MESTRE-MICHELOT** Meursault Poruzot 1992 • $NA • (08/31/94)

89 **MICHEL BOUZEREAU** Les Grands Charrons 1992 • $NA • (08/31/94)

89 **MOMMESSIN** Corton-Charlemagne 1992 • $70 • (08/31/94)

89 **PATRICK JAVILLIER** Meursault Les Tillets 1992 • $33 • (08/31/94)

89 **PIERRE BITOUZET** Corton-Charlemagne 1992 • $52 • (08/31/94)

88 **ALBERT GRIVAULT** Meursault 1992 • $28 • (08/31/94)

88 **ANTONIN RODET** Corton-Charlemagne 1992 • $NA • (08/31/94)

88 **BOUCHARD PERE & FILS** Puligny-Montrachet Les Pucelles 1992 • $30 • (08/31/94)

88 **CHARTRON & TREBUCHET** Corton-Charlemagne 1992 • $56 • (07/31/94)

88 **DOMAINE DES COMTES LAFON** Meursault 1992 • $48 • (05/15/95)

88 **DOMAINE ETIENNE SAUZET** Puligny-Montrachet Les Combettes 1992 • $79 • (08/31/94)

88 **DOMAINE ETIENNE SAUZET** Puligny-Montrachet La Garenne 1992 • $62 • (08/31/94)

88 **DOMAINE ETIENNE SAUZET** Puligny-Montrachet Les Combettes 1992 • $79 • (08/31/94)

88 **JAFFELIN** Meursault Les Cras 1992 • $34 • (08/31/94)

88 **JOSEPH DROUHIN** Meursault Perriéres 1992 • $40 • (08/31/94)

88 **MICHEL BOUZEREAU** Meursault Genevriéres 1992 • $NA • (08/31/94)

88 **MICHEL COLIN-DELEGER** Chassagne-Montrachet Les Chenevottes 1992 • $36 • (08/31/94)

88 **MICHEL NIELLON** Chassagne-Montrachet Clos St.-Jean 1992 • $NA • (08/31/94)

88 **MOMMESSIN** Meursault 1992 • $25 • (08/31/94)

88 **PIERRE MATROT** Meursault 1992 • $20 • (08/31/94)

88 **VAUCHER** Puligny-Montrachet 1992 • $NA • (08/31/94)

87 **ALBERT GRIVAULT** Meursault Clos des Perrières 1992 • $80 • (08/31/94)

87 **BERNARD MOREY** Chassagne-Montrachet Baudines 1992 • $33 • (02/28/94)

87 **CHARTRON & TREBUCHET** Chassagne-Montrachet Les Morgeots 1992 • $22 • (08/31/94)

87 **CHATEAU DE PULIGNY-MONTRACHET** Puligny-Montrachet 1992 • $26 • (08/31/94)

87 **DOMAINE GUY ROULOT** Meursault Le Tesson Clos de Mon Plaisir 1992 • $40 • (08/31/94)

87 **DOMAINE JOSEPH MATROT** Meursault Les Chevalières 1992 • $25 • (05/15/95)

87 **DOMAINE LEFLAIVE** Puligny-Montrachet 1992 • $49 • (05/15/95)

87 **DOMAINE RAMONET** Chassagne-Montrachet Les Ruchottes 1992 • $68

87 **DOMAINE VALETTE** Pouilly-Fuissé Clos Reyssié 1992 • $NA

87 **FRANCOIS JOBARD** Meursault Genevrières 1992 • $50 • (08/31/94)

87 **JEAN CLAUDE BOISSET** Meursault 1992 • $15 • (05/31/94)

87 **JEAN PILLOT** Puligny-Montrachet 1992 • $26 • (08/31/94)

87 **JEAN-MARC BOILLOT** Puligny-Montrachet 1992 • $NA • (08/31/94)

87 **JEAN-NOEL GAGNARD** Chassagne-Montrachet Les Caillerets White 1992 • $47 • (08/31/94)

87 **LABOURE-ROI** Meursault 1992 • $NA • (08/31/94)
87 **LEONARD DE SAINT-AUBIN** Puligny-Montrachet 1992 • $24 • (11/15/94)
87 **LOUIS LATOUR** Puligny-Montrachet 1992 • $27 • (08/31/94)
87 **MICHEL COLIN-DELEGER** Chassagne-Montrachet Les Chaumées 1992 • $45 • (08/31/94)
87 **MICHEL MOREY-COFFINET** Chassagne-Montrachet La Romanée White 1992 • $39 • (07/31/94)
87 **MICHEL NIELLON** Chassagne-Montrachet Clos de la Maltroie 1992 • $NA • (08/31/94)
87 **MOMMESSIN** Meursault Les Charmes 1992 • $34 • (08/31/94)
87 **OLIVIER LEFLAIVE** Meursault Les Perrières 1992 • $45 • (08/31/94)
87 **OLIVIER LEFLAIVE** Montrachet 1992 • $175
87 **VERGET** Meursault Genevriéres 1992 • $50 • (08/31/94)
87 **VERGET** Chassagne-Montrachet Morgeot 1992 • $44 • (08/31/94)
86 **DOMAINE JEAN CHARTRON** Puligny-Montrachet Les Folatières 1992 • $35 • (07/31/94)
86 **DOMAINE RAMONET** Chassagne-Montrachet Morgeot 1992 • $50
86 **DOMAINE RENE MONNIER** Meursault Les Chevalières 1992 • $25 • (08/31/94)
86 **GUY BOCARD** Meursault-Charmes Cru 1992 • $36 • (05/15/95)
86 **JEAN CLAUDE BOISSET** Rully 1992 • $9 • (02/28/95) • BB
86 **LOUIS JADOT** Chassagne-Montrachet 1992 • $23 • (08/31/94)
86 **M. VINCENT** Pouilly-Fuissé Château Fuissé 1992 • $37 • (11/15/94)
86 **M. VINCENT** Pouilly-Fuissé Château Fuissé Vieilles Vignes 1992 • $50 • (11/15/94)
86 **M. VINCENT** Pouilly-Fuissé Château Fuissé Vieilles Vignes 1992 • $50 • (11/15/94)
86 **MARC COLIN** Chassagne-Montrachet Les Caillerets 1992 • $32 • (08/31/94)
86 **MICHEL BOUZEREAU** Meursault Les Tessons 1992 • $29 • (08/31/94)
86 **MICHEL COLIN-DELEGER** Chassagne-Montrachet Les Vergers 1992 • $40 • (08/31/94)
86 **MICHEL NIELLON** Chassagne-Montrachet 1992 • $32 • (08/31/94)
86 **OLIVIER LEFLAIVE** Puligny-Montrachet Les Champs-Canet 1992 • $50 • (08/31/94)
86 **VERGET** Chassagne-Montrachet La Romanée 1992 • $50 • (08/31/94)
85 **ALBERT MOREY** Bâtard-Montrachet 1992 • $114 • (02/28/94)
85 **AMIOT-BONFILS** Chassagne-Montrachet 1992 • $NA • (08/31/94)
85 **ANTONIN RODET** Meursault Rodet 1992 • $NA • (08/31/94)
85 **CHARTRON & TREBUCHET** Chassagne-Montrachet Clos St.-Marc 1992 • $30 • (07/31/94)
85 **CHARTRON & TREBUCHET** Auxey-Duresses 1992 • $18 • (07/31/94)
85 **DOMAINE ETIENNE SAUZET** Puligny-Montrachet Les Referts 1992 • $62 • (08/31/94)
85 **DOMAINE MARC MOREY** Chassagne-Montrachet Morgeot 1992 • $36 • (08/31/94)
85 **FAIVELEY** Bourgogne Georges Faiveley 1992 • $16 • (08/31/94)
85 **HENRI GERMAIN** Chassagne-Montrachet Morgeot White 1992 • $39 • (08/31/94)
85 **J.J. VINCENT** St.-Véran 1992 • $9 • BB
85 **JEAN-NOEL GAGNARD** Chassagne-Montrachet Les Chenevottes White 1992 • $36 • (08/31/94)
85 **JOSEPH DROUHIN** Chassagne-Montrachet Marquis de Laguiche White 1992 • $42 • (08/31/94)
85 **MOMMESSIN** Puligny-Montrachet 1992 • $27 • (08/31/94)
85 **OLIVIER LEFLAIVE** Chassagne-Montrachet Morgeot White 1992 • $45 • (08/31/94)
85 **OLIVIER LEFLAIVE** Corton-Charlemagne 1992 • $65
85 **PATRICK JAVILLIER** Meursault Les Casses-Têtes 1992 • $30 • (08/31/94)
85 **PIERRE ANDRE** Puligny-Montrachet Les Folatières 1992 • $28 • (08/31/94)
85 **PIERRE MATROT** Puligny-Montrachet Les Chalumeaux 1992 • $30 • (08/31/94)
85 **REINE PEDAUQUE** Meursault Les Charmes 1992 • $29 • (08/31/94)
85 **SYLVAIN LANGOUREAU** Meursault La Pièce Sous Le Bois 1992 • $32 • (08/31/94)
85 **TOLLOT-BEAUT** Bourgogne 1992 • $15 • (08/31/94)
84 **ANTONIN RODET** Meursault Les Perriéres 1992 • $NA • (08/31/94)
84 **BERNARD MOREY** Chassagne-Montrachet Les Embazées 1992 • $33 • (02/28/94)
84 **CHARTRON & TREBUCHET** Rully White La Chaume 1992 • $15
84 **CHARTRON & TREBUCHET** Mercurey 1992 • $15
84 **COMTE SENARD** Corton En Charlemagne 1992 • $52
84 **CUVEE NICOLE** Puligny-Montrachet 1992 • $40 • (05/15/95)
84 **DOMAINE ETIENNE SAUZET** Puligny-Montrachet 1992 • $46 • (08/31/94)
84 **DOMAINE MARC MOREY** Chassagne-Montrachet Les Chenevottes 1992 • $35 • (08/31/94)
84 **DOMAINE MAURICE PROTHEAU** Rully White 1992 • $8 • (02/28/95)
84 **DOMAINE ROUX PERE & FILS** St.-Aubin White La Chatenière 1992 • $NA • (08/31/94)
84 **DUBREUIL-FONTAINE** Corton-Charlemagne 1992 • $61 • (08/31/94)
84 **GEORGES DUBOEUF** Pouilly-Fuissé 1992 • $11 • (09/15/93)
84 **JAFFELIN** Chassagne-Montrachet Les Vergers White 1992 • $30 • (08/31/94)
84 **M. VINCENT** Pouilly-Fuissé 1992 • $18
84 **MARC COLIN** Chassagne-Montrachet 1992 • $20 • (08/31/94)
84 **MOMMESSIN** Chassagne-Montrachet 1992 • $26 • (08/31/94)
84 **OLIVIER LEFLAIVE** Puligny-Montrachet 1992 • $38 • (08/31/94)
84 **PROSPER MAUFOUX** Chassagne-Montrachet Les Chenevottes 1992 • $25 • (08/31/94)
84 **PROSPER MAUFOUX** Puligny-Montrachet 1992 • $22 • (08/31/94)
84 **YVES DARVIOT** Beaune Clos des Mouches White 1992 • $43 • (08/31/94)
83 **BERNARD MOREY** St.-Aubin Les Charmois 1992 • $23 • (02/28/94)
83 **BOUCHARD PERE & FILS** Meursault 1992 • $20 • (08/31/94)
83 **CHARTRON & TREBUCHET** St.-Aubin La Chatenière Premier Cru 1992 • $18 • (08/31/94)
83 **CHARTRON & TREBUCHET** St.-Romain 1992 • $16 • (07/31/94)

White Burgundy

83 **CHATEAU DE CHAMIREY** Marsannay White 1992 • $17 • (08/31/94)

83 **DOMAINE MARC MOREY** Chassagne-Montrachet 1992 • $30 • (08/31/94)

83 **JEAN PILLOT** Chassagne-Montrachet Morgeot 1992 • $37 • (08/31/94)

83 **LOUIS JADOT** Marsannay 1992 • $NA • (08/31/94)

83 **M. VINCENT** St.-Véran 1992 • $15

83 **MARQUIS DE MACMAHON** Meursault Les Meix Chavaux 1992 • $NA • (08/31/94)

83 **MOREY-BLANC** Meursault Charmes 1992 • $57 • (08/31/94)

83 **PIERRE ANDRE** Ladoix Le Rognet White 1992 • $17 • (08/31/94)

83 **REINE PEDAUQUE** Corton-Charlemagne 1992 • $52 • (08/31/94)

83 **RENE GUERIN** Pouilly-Fuissé La Roche 1992 • $20 • (11/15/94)

82 **AMIOT-BONFILS** Chassagne-Montrachet Les Vergers 1992 • $56 • (08/31/94)

82 **CAVE DE VIRE** Mâcon-Viré Fûts de Chêne Neufs 1992 • $NA

82 **CHARLES VIENOT** Bourgogne Clos Le Village 1992 • $9

82 **CHARTRON & TREBUCHET** Pernand-Vergelesses White 1992 • $18 • (07/31/94)

82 **DOMAINE RENE MONNIER** Puligny-Montrachet Les Folatières 1992 • $40 • (08/31/94)

82 **DOMAINE ROUX PERE & FILS** St.-Aubin White Les Cortons 1992 • $NA • (08/31/94)

82 **DUBREUIL-FONTAINE** Pernand-Vergelesses White 1992 • $NA • (11/15/94)

82 **J.J. VINCENT** Mâcon-Villages Pièce d'Or 1992 • $7

82 **JAFFELIN** Auxey-Duresses 1992 • $13 • (08/31/94)

82 **JEAN CLAUDE BOISSET** Chassagne-Montrachet 1992 • $16 • (08/31/94)

82 **JEAN CLAUDE BOISSET** Meursault 1992 • $16 • (02/28/94)

82 **JEAN-NOEL GAGNARD** Chassagne-Montrachet Les Masures White 1992 • $30 • (08/31/94)

82 **LOUIS LATOUR** Chassagne-Montrachet 1992 • $26 • (08/31/94)

82 **OLIVIER LEFLAIVE** Meursault 1992 • $32 • (08/31/94)

82 **REINE PEDAUQUE** Chassagne-Montrachet 1992 • $22 • (08/31/94)

81 **BERNARD MOREY** Chassagne-Montrachet Les Caillerets 1992 • $33 • (02/28/94)

81 **BLAIN-GAGNARD** Chassagne-Montrachet Les Caillerets 1992 • $35 • (08/31/94)

81 **DOMAINE PONSOT** Morey-St.-Denis White Monts Luisant Vieilles Vignes 1992 • $59 • (08/31/94)

81 **JAFFELIN** St.-Aubin Premier Cru White 1992 • $13 • (08/31/94)

81 **JAFFELIN** Rully 1992 • $14 • (08/31/94)

81 **JEAN CLAUDE BOISSET** Meursault 1992 • $15 • (08/31/94)

81 **JEAN CLAUDE BOISSET** Bourgogne White Charles de France Chardonnay de Bourgogne 1992 • $8

81 **LABOURE-ROI** Chassagne-Montrachet 1992 • $NA • (08/31/94)

81 **LOUIS JADOT** Puligny-Montrachet 1992 • $29 • (05/15/95)

80 **BERNARD MOREY** Chassagne-Montrachet Vieilles Vignes 1992 • $29 • (02/28/94)

80 **JAFFELIN** Montagny 1992 • $12 • (08/31/94)

80 **JEAN PILLOT** Chassagne-Montrachet 1992 • $NA • (08/31/94)

80 **LEROY** Bourgogne Leroy White 1992 • $19 • (08/31/94)

80 **MARC COLIN** St.-Aubin En Remilly White 1992 • $14 • (08/31/94)

80 **OLIVIER LEFLAIVE FRÈRES** Chevalier-Montrachet 1992 • $NA • (05/31/96) • 79

79 **BARTON & GUESTIER** Pouilly-Fuissé 1992 • $16 • (03/31/95)

79 **BOUCHARD PERE & FILS** Beaune Clos Saint Landry Domaines du Château de White 1992 • $24 • (08/31/94)

79 **DUBREUIL-FONTAINE** Pernand-Vergelesses Clos Berthet Monopole White 1992 • $30 • (08/31/94)

79 **MARQUIS DE MACMAHON** Puligny-Montrachet La Garenne 1992 • $NA • (08/31/94)

79 **MOREY-BLANC** Meursault Les Narvaux 1992 • $40 • (08/31/94)

79 **PIERRE ANDRE** Corton-Charlemagne 1992 • $52 • (08/31/94)

79 **R. BALLOT-MILLOT & FILS** Meursault Charmes 1992 • $NA • (08/31/94)

79 **ROPITEAU-MIGNON** Meursault 1992 • $NA • (08/31/94)

78 **DOMAINE MICHEL LAFARGE** Meursault 1992 • $NA • (08/31/94)

78 **JEAN CLAUDE BOISSET** Puligny-Montrachet 1992 • $25 • (08/31/94)

78 **JEAN CLAUDE BOISSET** Bourgogne White Chardonnay Charles de France 1992 • $8 • (02/28/94)

78 **LEONARD DE SAINT-AUBIN** Meursault 1992 • $NA • (11/15/94)

78 **MICHEL MOREY-COFFINET** Chassagne-Montrachet Les Caillerets White 1992 • $36 • (07/31/94)

78 **MICHEL MOREY-COFFINET** Chassagne-Montrachet 1992 • $25 • (07/31/94)

78 **PIERRE MOREY** Bourgogne White 1992 • $19 • (08/31/94)

77 **ANTONIN RODET** Rully White Château de Rully 1992 • $16 • (08/31/94)

77 **HENRI GERMAIN** Meursault Charmes 1992 • $40 • (08/31/94)

77 **J.J. VINCENT** Pouilly-Fuissé 1992 • $11

77 **MARQUIS DE MACMAHON** Chassagne-Montrachet Abbaye de Morgeot 1992 • $NA • (08/31/94)

77 **MOMMESSIN** Puligny-Montrachet La Garenne 1992 • $36 • (08/31/94)

77 **PIERRE BITOUZET** Savigny-lès-Beaune Les Goudelettes White 1992 • $20 • (08/31/94)

77 **SYLVAIN LANGOUREAU** St.-Aubin Les Remilly White 1992 • $17 • (08/31/94)

76 **BLAIN-GAGNARD** Chassagne-Montrachet La Boudriotte 1992 • $35 • (08/31/94)

76 **LABOURE-ROI** Bourgogne White 1992 • $8

76 **OLIVIER LEFLAIVE** Bourgogne Chardonnay White 1992 • $9

75 **DOMAINE JACQUES PRIEUR** Meursault Clos de Mazeray 1992 • $32 • (08/31/94)

74 **DOMAINE MONTHELIE-DOUHAIRET** Meursault Les Cras 1992 • $37 • (11/15/94)

73 **JEAN CLAUDE BOISSET** Chassagne-Montrachet 1992 • $17 • (02/28/94)

73 **JOSEPH ROTY** Bourgogne White Grande Ordinaire Cuvée Philippe Roty 1992 • $NA

73 **R. BALLOT-MILLOT & FILS** Meursault Les Criots 1992 • $38 • (08/31/94)

70 **PROSPER MAUFOUX** Puligny-Montrachet Les Folatières 1992 • $30 • (08/31/94)

69 **DOMAINE BRUNO CLAIR** Bourgogne White 1992 • $19

68 **GEORGES DUBOEUF** Bourgogne Blanc Flower Label 1992 • $9

1990 White Burgundy
Vintage Rating: 92

97 **DOMAINE DES COMTES LAFON** Montrachet 1990 • $413 • (10/15/93) • CS

97 **DOMAINE DE LA ROMANEE-CONTI** Montrachet White 1990 • $500 • (10/15/93)

97 **PAUL PERNOT** Bâtard-Montrachet 1990 • $175 • (02/28/93)

97 **PIERRE MOREY** Montrachet 1990 • $375 • (01/31/93)

96 **DOMAINE DE LA ROMANEE-CONTI** Montrachet 1990 • $650

96 **DOMAINE RAMONET** Montrachet 1990 • $500

96 **LOUIS LATOUR** Montrachet 1990 • $195 • (10/15/93)

95 **DOMAINE ETIENNE SAUZET** Bâtard-Montrachet 1990 • $188 • (11/30/92)

95 **DOMAINE LEFLAIVE** Chevalier-Montrachet 1990 • $165 • (01/31/93)

95 **DOMAINE LEFLAIVE** Bâtard-Montrachet 1990 • $150 • (10/15/93)

95 **DOMAINE RAMONET** Montrachet 1990 • $400 • (11/30/92)

95 **LOUIS LATOUR** Corton-Charlemagne 1990 • $83 • (09/30/93) • CS

94 **DOMAINE DES COMTES LAFON** Meursault Désirée 1990 • $71 • (10/15/93)

94 **DOMAINE DES COMTES LAFON** Meursault Genevrières 1990 • $109 • (10/15/93)

94 **DOMAINE DES COMTES LAFON** Meursault Charmes 1990 • $85 • (10/15/93)

94 **DOMAINE LEFLAIVE** Chevalier-Montrachet 1990 • $165 • (10/15/93)

94 **DOMAINE RAMONET** Chassagne-Montrachet Les Ruchottes White 1990 • $60 • (11/30/92)

94 **DOMAINE RAMONET** Bienvenues-Bâtard-Montrachet White 1990 • $180 • (01/31/93)

94 **DOMAINE RAMONET** Bâtard-Montrachet 1990 • $200 • (02/28/93)

94 **G. MICHELOT** Meursault Les Tillets 1990 • $NA • (10/15/93)

94 **J.-F. COCHE-DURY** Corton-Charlemagne 1990 • $150 • (10/15/93)

94 **LOUIS LATOUR** Chevalier-Montrachet Les Demoiselles 1990 • $133 • (10/15/93)

94 **MESTRE-MICHELOT** Meursault Le Limozin 1990 • $NA • (10/15/93)

93 **AMIOT-BONFILS** Montrachet 1990 • $190 • (10/15/93)

93 **BOUCHARD PERE & FILS** Chevalier-Montrachet 1990 • $124 • (10/15/93)

93 **BOUCHARD PERE & FILS** Montrachet 1990 • $210 • (10/15/93)

93 **DOMAINE D'AUVENAY** Puligny-Montrachet Les Folatières 1990 • $100 • (10/15/93)

93 **DOMAINE DES COMTES LAFON** Meursault Clos de la Barre 1990 • $69 • (10/15/93)

93 **DOMAINE GUY ROULOT** Meursault Perrières 1990 • $48 • (10/15/93)

93 **DOMAINE LEFLAIVE** Bâtard-Montrachet 1990 • $150 • (02/28/93)

93 **J.-F. COCHE-DURY** Meursault 1990 • $36 • (10/15/93)

93 **LABOURE-ROI** Montrachet Le Montrachet White 1990 • $160 • (07/15/92)

93 **LOUIS JADOT** Chevalier-Montrachet Les Demoiselles 1990 • $115 • (07/31/93)

93 **LOUIS JADOT** Puligny-Montrachet Les Pucelles 1990 • $NA • (10/15/93)

93 **LOUIS LATOUR** Meursault Goutte d'Or 1990 • $35 • (10/15/93)

92 **BONNEAU DU MARTRAY** Corton-Charlemagne 1990 • $60 • (10/15/93)

92 **DOMAINE DES COMTES LAFON** Meursault Perrières 1990 • $120 • (10/15/93)

92 **DOMAINE DES COMTES LAFON** Meursault 1990 • $68 • (10/15/93)

92 **DOMAINE ETIENNE SAUZET** Puligny-Montrachet Les Referts 1990 • $83 • (01/31/93)

92 **DOMAINE GUY ROULOT** Meursault Les Tessons Clos de Mon Plaisir 1990 • $34 • (10/15/93)

92 **DOMAINE LEFLAIVE** Puligny-Montrachet Les Pucelles 1990 • $88 • (10/15/93)

92 **FAIVELEY** Corton-Charlemagne 1990 • $125 • (10/15/93)

92 **GUFFENS-HEYNEN** Pouilly-Fuissé Clos des Petits-Croux 1990 • $50 • (07/31/92)

92 **JOSEPH DROUHIN** White 1990 • $75 • (05/15/92)

92 **JOSEPH DROUHIN** Clos des Mouches White 1990 • $64 • (05/15/92) • CS.

92 **LOUIS JADOT** Corton-Charlemagne 1990 • $67 • (10/15/93)

92 **LOUIS LATOUR** Puligny-Montrachet Les Folatières 1990 • $37 • (10/15/93)

92 **OLIVIER LEFLAIVE** Meursault Les Poruzots 1990 • $40 • (10/15/93)

92 **OLIVIER LEFLAIVE** Puligny-Montrachet Les Champs-Canets 1990 • $40 • (10/15/93)

92 **OLIVIER LEFLAIVE** Puligny-Montrachet Les Champs Gains 1990 • $40 • (10/15/93)

92 **PIERRE BITOUZET** White 1990 • $84 • (08/31/92)

91 **BOUCHARD PERE & FILS** Domaines du Château de Beaune White 1990 • $99 • (08/31/92)

91 **CHARTRON & TREBUCHET** Bâtard-Montrachet 1990 • $115 • (03/31/92)

91 **DOMAINE GUY ROULOT** Meursault Charmes 1990 • $48 • (10/15/93)

91 **DOMAINE JEAN CHARTRON** Puligny-Montrachet Clos de la Pucelle 1990 • $55 • (03/31/92)

91 **JEAN-NOEL GAGNARD** Chassagne-Montrachet Morgeot White 1990 • $60 • (08/31/92)

91 **JOSEPH DROUHIN** White 1990 • $32 • (05/15/92)

91 **LOUIS JADOT** Meursault 1990 • $25 • (10/15/93)

91 **LOUIS LATOUR** Puligny-Montrachet 1990 • $31 • (09/30/93)

91 **LOUIS LATOUR** Chassagne-Montrachet Morgeot 1990 • $NA • (10/15/93)

91 **LOUIS LATOUR** Bienvenues-Bâtard-Montrachet 1990 • $107 • (10/15/93)

91 **MICHEL COLIN-DELEGER** Chassagne-Montrachet Les Chaumées 1990 • $45 • (02/28/93)

91 **MICHEL COLIN-DELEGER** Chassagne-Montrachet Morgeot White 1990 • $38 • (10/15/93)

91 **MICHEL COLIN-DELEGER** Chassagne-Montrachet Les Vergers 1990 • $38 • (10/15/93)

91 **MICHELOT-BUISSON** Meursault Genevrières 1990 • $NA • (10/15/93)

91 **OLIVIER LEFLAIVE** Puligny-Montrachet Les Folatières 1990 • $42 • (10/15/93)

91 **PAUL PERNOT** Bâtard-Montrachet 1990 • $130 • (07/15/92)

91 **PAUL PERNOT** Puligny-Montrachet Folatières 1990 • $60 • (04/15/92)

91 **TOLLOT-BEAUT** Corton-Charlemagne 1990 • $95 • (10/15/93)

■ ■ ■ ■

White Burgundy

90 **AMIOT-BONFILS** Chassagne-Montrachet Les Vergers White 1990 • $36 • (10/15/93)

90 **BOUCHARD PERE & FILS** Meursault Genevrières 1990 • $51 • (10/15/93)

90 **CHATEAU DES HERBEAUX** Puligny-Montrachet Les Combettes 1990 • $45 • (12/15/92)

90 **DOMAINE ETIENNE SAUZET** Puligny-Montrachet Champ-Canet 1990 • $83 • (01/31/93)

90 **DOMAINE ETIENNE SAUZET** Chassagne-Montrachet 1990 • $50 • (02/28/93)

90 **DOMAINE GUY ROULOT** Meursault Les Luchets 1990 • $34 • (10/15/93)

90 **DOMAINE JOSEPH MATROT** Meursault 1990 • $37 • (08/31/92)

90 **DOMAINE LEFLAIVE** Bienvenues-Bâtard-Montrachet White 1990 • $109 • (10/15/93)

90 **DOMAINE LEFLAIVE** Puligny-Montrachet Les Combettes 1990 • $86 • (10/15/93)

90 **DOMAINE LEFLAIVE** Puligny-Montrachet 1990 • $53 • (10/15/93)

90 **DOMAINE LEQUIN-ROUSSOT** Chassagne-Montrachet Morgeot White 1990 • $34 • (08/31/92)

90 **DOMAINE VALETTE** Pouilly-Fuissé Clos Reyssié Réserve Particulière 1990 • $NA

90 **FAIVELEY** Meursault 1990 • $39 • (10/15/93)

90 **GUFFENS-HEYNEN** Pouilly-Fuissé La Roche 1990 • $45 • (07/31/92)

90 **J.M. BOILLOT** Meursault 1990 • $50 • (10/15/93)

90 **JOSEPH DROUHIN** Charmes White 1990 • $48 • (05/15/92)

90 **JOSEPH DROUHIN** White 1990 • $128 • (05/15/92)

90 **LABOURE-ROI** Corton-Charlemagne 1990 • $48 • (07/15/92)

90 **LOUIS JADOT** Meursault Genevrières 1990 • $NA • (10/15/93)

90 **LOUIS JADOT** Meursault Perrières 1990 • $39 • (10/15/93)

90 **MARC COLIN** Chassagne-Montrachet Les Caillerets White 1990 • $40 • (10/15/93)

90 **MICHELOT-BUISSON** Meursault Perrières 1990 • $NA • (10/15/93)

89 **ALBERT MOREY** Chassagne-Montrachet Morgeot 1990 • $40 • (08/31/92)

89 **BOUCHARD PERE & FILS** Meursault Genevrières Domaines du Château de Beaun 1990 • $35 • (08/31/92)

89 **DOMAINE ETIENNE SAUZET** Puligny-Montrachet Les Combettes 1990 • $99 • (01/31/93)

89 **DOMAINE ETIENNE SAUZET** Puligny-Montrachet Les Perrières 1990 • $83 • (01/31/93)

89 **DOMAINE JEAN CHARTRON** Puligny-Montrachet Les Folatières 1990 • $48 • (03/31/92)

89 **DOMAINE RAMONET** Chassagne-Montrachet Les Caillerets White 1990 • $56 • (11/30/92)

89 **FERNAND COFFINET** Bâtard-Montrachet 1990 • $112 • (06/15/93)

89 **J.M. BOILLOT** Puligny-Montrachet 1990 • $55 • (10/15/93)

89 **J.M. BOILLOT** Chassagne-Montrachet Morgeots White 1990 • $75 • (10/15/93)

89 **JEAN-MARC BOILLOT** Puligny-Montrachet La Truffière 1990 • $45 • (11/30/92)

89 **JEAN-MARC BOILLOT** Bâtard-Montrachet 1990 • $105 • (10/15/93)

89 **JEAN-NOEL GAGNARD** Chassagne-Montrachet Premier Cru White 1990 • $55 • (08/31/92)

89 **LOUIS JADOT** Pernand-Vergelesses White 1990 • $18 • (10/15/93)

89 **LOUIS LATOUR** Meursault 1990 • $27 • (10/15/93)

89 **MADAME FRANCOIS COLIN** Puligny-Montrachet Les Demoiselles 1990 • $75 • (01/31/93)

89 **MARC COLIN** Chassagne-Montrachet 1990 • $30 • (10/15/93)

89 **PAUL PERNOT** Puligny-Montrachet Les Pucelles 1990 • $75 • (07/15/92)

89 **R. BALLOT-MILLOT & FILS** Meursault Charmes 1990 • $38 • (10/15/93)

88 **BOUCHARD PERE & FILS** Meursault Clos des Corvées de Citeaux 1990 • $50 • (10/15/93)

88 **CHATEAU DE PULIGNY-MONTRACHET** Puligny-Montrachet 1990 • $62 • (08/31/92)

88 **DOMAINE DU CLOS FRANTIN** Corton-Charlemagne 1990 • $50 • (05/15/93)

88 **DOMAINE JEAN CHARTRON** Puligny-Montrachet Clos du Cailleret 1990 • $57 • (03/31/92)

88 **DOMAINE JOSEPH MATROT** Puligny-Montrachet Les Chalumeaux 1990 • $55 • (08/31/92)

88 **DOMAINE LEQUIN-ROUSSOT** Bâtard-Montrachet 1990 • $86 • (08/31/92)

88 **DOMAINE LEQUIN-ROUSSOT** Chassagne-Montrachet Les Caillerets White 1990 • $34 • (08/31/92)

88 **DOMAINE RAMONET** Chassagne-Montrachet Les Vergers White 1990 • $41 • (11/30/92)

88 **JEAN-MARC MOREY** Chassagne-Montrachet Les Caillerets White 1990 • $47 • (02/28/93)

88 **LABOURE-ROI** Chassagne-Montrachet Les Morgeots White 1990 • $25 • (07/15/92)

88 **LEROY** Bourgogne 1990 • $17 • (07/31/93)

88 **LOUIS LATOUR** Meursault Chateau de Blagny 1990 • $32 • (10/15/93)

88 **LOUIS LATOUR** Chassagne-Montrachet 1990 • $30 • (10/15/93)

88 **MICHEL COLIN-DELEGER** Chassagne-Montrachet En Remilly 1990 • $36 • (10/15/93)

88 **MOILLARD** Meursault Charmes 1990 • $45 • (08/31/92)

88 **OLIVIER LEFLAIVE** Bâtard-Montrachet 1990 • $100 • (10/15/93)

88 **OLIVIER LEFLAIVE** Meursault 1990 • $28 • (10/15/93)

88 **PIERRE MOREY** Bâtard-Montrachet 1990 • $122 • (06/15/93)

88 **ROGER SAUMAIZE** Pouilly-Fuissé Les Ronchevats 1990 • $29 • (11/30/92)

88 **TOLLOT-BEAUT** Bourgogne White 1990 • $18 • (10/15/93)

87 **AMIOT-BONFILS** Chassagne-Montrachet Les Champgains White 1990 • $36 • (10/15/93)

87 **BERNARD MOREY** Chassagne-Montrachet Morgeot White 1990 • $34 • (08/31/92)

87 **BERNARD MOREY** Puligny-Montrachet Sous Le Puits 1990 • $40 • (08/31/92)

87 **BERNARD MOREY** Chassagne-Montrachet Les Embazées 1990 • $34 • (08/31/92)

87 **CHARTRON & TREBUCHET** Meursault Les Charmes 1990 • $44 • (03/31/92)

87 **CHATEAU DE PULIGNY-MONTRACHET** Côte de Nuits-Villages White 1990 • $24 • (08/31/92)

87 **DOMAINE ETIENNE SAUZET** Puligny-Montrachet 1990 • $50 • (12/15/92)

87 **FAIVELEY** Puligny-Montrachet Les Champgain 1990 • $47 • (10/15/93)

87 **FAIVELEY** Chassagne-Montrachet 1990 • $42 • (10/15/93)

87 **JAFFELIN** White 1990 • $28 • (05/15/92)

87 **JEAN-NOEL GAGNARD** Chassagne-Montrachet Les Caillerets White 1990 • $62 • (08/31/92)

87 **JOSEPH DROUHIN** Perrières White 1990 • $48 • (05/15/92)

87 **LOUIS JADOT** Savigny-lès-Beaune White 1990 • $18 • (07/31/93)

87 **LOUIS JADOT** Beaune Grèves White 1990 • $38 • (10/15/93)

87 **LOUIS LATOUR** Puligny-Montrachet Truffières 1990 • $38 • (10/15/93)

87 **MICHEL COLIN-DELEGER** Chassagne-Montrachet Les Vergers 1990 • $50 • (02/28/93)

87 **MICHEL COLIN-DELEGER** Chassagne-Montrachet Les Chenevottes 1990 • $36 • (10/15/93)

87 **OLIVIER LEFLAIVE** Puligny-Montrachet 1990 • $35 • (10/15/93)

87 **PIERRE BOUZEREAU-EMONIN** Meursault Charmes 1990 • $36 • (08/31/92)

87 **PIERRE MOREY** Meursault Les Tessons 1990 • $50 • (01/31/93)

86 **BOUCHARD PERE & FILS** Beaune Cru Beaune du Château 1990 • $NA • (10/15/93)

86 **BOUCHARD PERE & FILS** Puligny-Montrachet 1990 • $34 • (10/15/93)

86 **CHARTRON & TREBUCHET** St.-Romain 1990 • $20 • (03/31/92)

86 **CHARTRON & TREBUCHET** Chassagne-Montrachet Les Morgeots White 1990 • $40 • (03/31/92)

86 **DOMAINE D'AUVENAY** Auxey-Duresses White 1990 • $40 • (10/15/93)

86 **DOMAINE JEAN CHARTRON** Chevalier-Montrachet 1990 • $120 • (03/31/92)

86 **DOMAINE LEQUIN-ROUSSOT** Chassagne-Montrachet Les Vergers White 1990 • $34 • (08/31/92)

86 **DOMAINE LEROY** Meursault Les Narvaux 1990 • $75 • (01/31/93)

86 **DOMAINE LEROY** Corton-Charlemagne 1990 • $153 • (05/15/93)

86 **DOMAINE PRIEUR-BRUNET** Meursault Chevalières 1990 • $27 • (12/15/92)

86 **JEAN-MARC MOREY** Chassagne-Montrachet Les Chaumées White 1990 • $48 • (02/28/93)

86 **JOSEPH DROUHIN** Les Pucelles White 1990 • $64 • (05/15/92)

86 **JOSEPH DROUHIN** Chassagne-Montrachet Marquis de Laguiche White 1990 • $48 • (07/15/92)

86 **LOUIS JADOT** Puligny-Montrachet Champ Gain 1990 • $35 • (07/31/94)

86 **LOUIS JADOT** Chassagne-Montrachet 1990 • $28 • (10/15/93)

86 **LOUIS JADOT** Chassagne-Montrachet Morgeot Duc de Magenta White 1990 • $32 • (10/15/93)

86 **MARC COLIN** St.-Aubin Les Combes White 1990 • $30 • (10/15/93)

86 **MARC COLIN** Chassagne-Montrachet Les Champs-Gains White 1990 • $40 • (10/15/93)

86 **MARIUS DELARCHE PERE & FILS** Pernand-Vergelesses White 1990 • $16 • (12/15/92)

86 **MICHEL COLIN-DELEGER** Chassagne-Montrachet Les Chaumées 1990 • $34 • (10/15/93)

86 **MICHELOT-BUISSON** Meursault Charmes 1990 • $NA • (10/15/93)

86 **MOILLARD** Meursault Clos du Cromin 1990 • $27 • (10/15/93)

86 **OLIVIER LEFLAIVE** Meursault Perrières 1990 • $40 • (10/15/93)

86 **OLIVIER LEFLAIVE** Puligny-Montrachet Les Referts 1990 • $40 • (10/15/93)

86 **PAUL PERNOT** Bourgogne Chardonnay Champierrier White 1990 • $17 • (08/31/92)

86 **PIERRE MOREY** Meursault Perrières 1990 • $67 • (12/15/92)

86 **ROGER SAUMAIZE** Pouilly-Fuissé Vigne Blanche 1990 • $25 • (03/31/93)

85 **ALBERT MOREY** Chassagne-Montrachet 1990 • $47 • (08/31/92)

85 **BERNARD MOREY** Chassagne-Montrachet Les Baudines White 1990 • $34 • (11/30/92)

85 **CHATEAU DE MEURSAULT** Meursault 1990 • $40 • (05/15/95)

85 **DOMAINE LEQUIN-ROUSSOT** Santenay Clos Rousseau White 1990 • $24 • (08/31/92)

85 **DOMAINE RENE MANUEL** Meursault Clos de la Baronne 1990 • $22 • (08/31/92)

85 **FAIVELEY** Puligny-Montrachet 1990 • $42 • (10/15/93)

85 **GUFFENS-HEYNEN** Pouilly-Fuissé Les Croux 1990 • $34 • (07/31/92)

85 **JAFFELIN** Chassagne-Montrachet Les Vergers White 1990 • $32 • (04/15/92)

85 **JAFFELIN** Puligny-Montrachet La Garenne 1990 • $34 • (04/15/92)

85 **JAFFELIN** White 1990 • $75 • (04/15/92)

85 **JEAN-MARC MOREY** Chassagne-Montrachet Les Chenevottes White 1990 • $47 • (02/28/93)

85 **JOSEPH DROUHIN** Les Folatières White 1990 • $60 • (05/15/92)

85 **JOSEPH DROUHIN** White 1990 • $36 • (05/15/92)

85 **LABOURE-ROI** Bâtard-Montrachet 1990 • $80 • (07/15/92)

85 **LOUIS JADOT** Pouilly-Fuissé Cuvée Réserve Spéciale 1990 • $22 • (11/30/92)

85 **LOUIS JADOT** Meursault 1990 • $25 • (05/15/93)

85 **MARC COLIN** St.-Aubin La Chatenière White 1990 • $30 • (10/15/93)

85 **MICHEL COLIN-DELEGER** Chassagne-Montrachet 1990 • $39 • (02/28/93)

85 **PIERRE BOUZEREAU-EMONIN** Meursault 1990 • $23 • (08/31/92)

85 **PIERRE PONNELLE** Côte de Beaune Les Pierre Blanches 1990 • $12 • (07/31/94)

84 **CHARTRON & TREBUCHET** St.-Aubin Les Combes White 1990 • $23 • (03/31/92)

84 **DOMAINE JEAN MANCIAT** Mâcon-Villages Vielles Vignes 1990 • $13 • (07/31/92)

84 **DOMAINE JOSEPH MATROT** Meursault Blagny 1990 • $53 • (08/31/92)

84 **EMMANUEL ROUGET** Bourgogne Aligoté 1990 • $13 • (05/15/93)

84 **FRANCOISE & DENIS CLAIR** St.-Aubin Les Murgers des Dents de Chien White 1990 • $27 • (08/31/92)

84 **JAFFELIN** Corton-Charlemagne 1990 • $55 • (04/15/92)

84 **JAFFELIN** White 1990 • $24 • (05/15/92)

84 **JAFFELIN** St.-Aubin 1990 • $17 • (07/15/92)

84 **JAFFELIN** St.-Romain 1990 • $14 • (07/15/92)

84 **JOSEPH DROUHIN** Rully 1990 • $18 • (07/15/92)

84 **LOUIS JADOT** Mâcon-Lugny Jadot Les Petites Pierres 1990 • $8 • (11/30/92)

84 **LOUIS JADOT** Auxey-Duresses Duc de Magenta White 1990 • $17 • (10/15/93)

84 **OLIVIER LEFLAIVE** Bourgogne Chardonnay Les Sétilles White 1990 • $15 • (05/15/93)

84 **OLIVIER LEFLAIVE** St.-Aubin En Remilly White 1990 • $21 • (10/15/93)

83 **DOMAINE LEFLAIVE** Bourgogne 1990 • $28 • (10/15/93)

83 **JAFFELIN** Pouilly-Fuissé 1990 • $18 • (07/31/91)

■ ■ ■ ■

White Burgundy

83 **JEAN-NOEL GAGNARD** Chassagne-Montrachet 1990 • $50 • (08/31/92)

83 **LOUIS JADOT** Puligny-Montrachet 1990 • $29 • (02/28/93)

83 **MICHEL GOUBARD** Bourgogne Aligoté 1990 • $9.25 • (02/28/93) • BB

83 **PIERRE BITOUZET** Savigny-lès-Beaune Les Goudelettes White 1990 • $33 • (08/31/92)

82 **CHARTRON & TREBUCHET** Rully La Chaume White 1990 • $20 • (03/31/92)

82 **CHATEAU DE PULIGNY-MONTRACHET** St.-Aubin en Remilly White 1990 • $28 • (08/31/92)

82 **CHATEAU DE PULIGNY-MONTRACHET** Meursault Les Perrières 1990 • $53 • (08/31/92)

82 **DOMAINE PRIEURE ROCH** Bourgogne Chardonnay Grand Ordinaire White 1990 • $16 • (07/31/93)

82 **DOMAINE RAMONET** Chassagne-Montrachet Morgeot White 1990 • $62 • (02/28/93)

82 **J.J. VINCENT** Pouilly-Fuissé 1990 • $18 • (08/31/91)

82 **JEAN CLAUDE BOISSET** Pouilly-Fuissé 1990 • $12 • (07/31/92)

82 **LABOURE-ROI** Meursault 1990 • $20 • (05/15/93)

82 **LOUIS JADOT** Pouilly-Fuissé 1990 • $19 • (11/30/92)

82 **LOUIS JADOT** Mâcon-Viré 1990 • $9 • (11/30/92)

82 **MICHELOT-BUISSON** Bourgogne 1990 • $NA • (10/15/93)

82 **OLIVIER LEFLAIVE** Bourgogne Les Sétilles White 1990 • $15 • (10/15/93)

82 **PIERRE BOUZEREAU-EMONIN** Meursault Les Narvaux 1990 • $24 • (08/31/92)

82 **POTHIER-RIEUSSET** Meursault Les Caillerets 1990 • $36 • (08/31/92)

81 **DOMAINE RENE MANUEL** Meursault Poruzot 1990 • $30 • (08/31/92)

81 **FAIVELEY** Meursault Les Bouchères 1990 • $52 • (10/15/93)

81 **J.J. VINCENT** Mâcon-Villages Pièce d'Or 1990 • $9 • (08/31/91)

81 **JAFFELIN** Bourgogne Chardonnay du Châpitre White 1990 • $9 • (07/31/91) • BB

81 **JAFFELIN** Chassagne-Montrachet 1990 • $28 • (04/15/92)

81 **JAFFELIN** Rully 1990 • $14 • (07/15/92)

81 **JOSEPH DROUHIN** White 1990 • $36 • (05/15/92)

81 **PAUL PERNOT** Puligny-Montrachet 1990 • $45 • (04/15/92)

80 **CHATEAU DE PULIGNY-MONTRACHET** Meursault Les Porusot 1990 • $51 • (08/31/92)

80 **DOMAINE BRUNO CLAIR** Marsannay White 1990 • $20 • (11/30/92)

80 **DOMAINE MAROSLAVAC** Puligny-Montrachet Clos du Vieux Château 1990 • $25 • (08/31/92)

80 **DOMAINE VINCENT PRUNIER** Auxey-Duresses White 1990 • $18 • (07/31/93)

80 **GUFFENS-HEYNEN** En Chavigne Cuvée Vieilles Vignes White 1990 • $21 • (07/31/92)

80 **J.J. VINCENT** St.-Véran 1990 • $13 • (03/31/93)

80 **LOUIS JADOT** La Fontaine White 1990 • $10 • (07/31/92)

80 **MARIUS DELARCHE PERE & FILS** Corton-Charlemagne 1990 • $50 • (12/15/92)

80 **OLIVIER LEFLAIVE** St.-Romain 1990 • $16 • (10/15/93)

80 **PIERRE BITOUZET** Corton-Charlemagne 1990 • $84 • (05/15/93)

80 **PIERRE MOREY** Meursault Charmes 1990 • $67 • (05/15/93)

79 **BARTON & GUESTIER** Pouilly-Fuissé 1990 • $14 • (03/31/93)

79 **BOUCHARD PERE & FILS** Beaune Clos St.-Landry Domaines du Château de Beaune White 1990 • $28 • (08/31/92)

79 **DOMAINE JOSEPH MATROT** Meursault Les Chevalières 1990 • $39 • (05/15/93)

79 **JOSEPH DROUHIN** White 1990• $18 • (07/31/92)

78 **CHATEAU DE PULIGNY-MONTRACHET** St.-Romain White 1990 • $24 • (08/31/92)

78 **DOMAINE JOSEPH MATROT** Bourgogne Chardonnay White 1990 • $19 • (02/28/93)

78 **DOMAINE PRIEUR-BRUNET** Bourgogne Chardonnay Cuvée Ste.-Jehanne de Chantal White 1990 • $13 • (02/28/93)

78 **OLIVIER LEFLAIVE** Puligny-Montrachet 1990 • $40 • (05/15/93)

78 **VERGET** Mâcon-Villages 1990 • $15 • (11/30/92)

77 **DOMAINE RENE MANUEL** Bourgogne White 1990 • $9 • (08/31/92)

77 **DOMAINE RENE MANUEL** Meursault Clos des Bouches Chères 1990 • $31 • (10/15/93)

77 **MICHEL COLIN-DELEGER** Chassagne-Montrachet 1990 • $30 • (10/15/93)

77 **OLIVIER LEFLAIVE** Rully Premier Cru White 1990 • $20 • (05/15/93)

77 **PRINCE FLORENT DE MERODE** Ladoix Hautes Mourottes White 1990 • $38 • (06/15/93)

77 **PROSPER MAUFOUX** St.-Véran 1990 • $13 • (11/30/92)

76 **CHATEAU DE LA TOUR DE L'ANGE** Chardonnay 1990 • $9 • (07/31/92)

76 **DOMAINE BRUNO CLAIR** Bourgogne White 1990 • $17 • (11/30/92)

76 **MOILLARD** Puligny-Montrachet 1990 • $39 • (08/31/92)

76 **VERGET** St.-Véran 1990 • $17 • (11/30/92)

75 **DOMAINE PONSOT** Morey-St.-Denis Monts Luisants White 1990 • $66 • (05/15/93)

75 **JOSEPH DROUHIN** Bourgogne Chardonnay Laforàt White 1990 • $9 • (08/31/92)

75 **LABOURE-ROI** Puligny-Montrachet 1990 • $24 • (05/15/93)

75 **LEONARD DE ST.-AUBIN** Pouilly-Fuissé 1990 • $15 • (08/31/91)

74 **CHARTRON & TREBUCHET** Bourgogne Chardonnay White 1990 • $11 • (03/31/92)

74 **MICHEL GOUBARD** Bourgogne Chardonnay 1990 • $9 • (02/28/93)

74 **MOILLARD** Bourgogne Aligoté Long du Bois White 1990 • $12 • (08/31/91)

73 **LABOURE-ROI** Chassagne-Montrachet 1990 • $22 • (05/15/93)

72 **BARTON & GUESTIER** Mâcon St.-Louis 1990 • $8 • (03/31/92)

72 **FERNAND COFFINET** Chassagne-Montrachet Blanchot-Dessus 1990 • $43 • (05/15/93)

72 **MOILLARD** Chassagne-Montrachet 1990 • $20 • (08/31/92)

71 **CHATEAU DE MEURSAULT** Bourgogne Clos du Chateau White 1990 • $19

71 **PROSPER MAUFOUX** White 1990 • $20 • (07/31/92)

70 **CAVE DE CHARDONNAY** Mâcon-Chardonnay Chardonnay de Chardonnay 1990 • $10 • (11/30/92)

70 **DOMAINE D'AZENAY** Mâcon-Azé 1990 • $12 • (03/31/92)

68 **JEAN CLAUDE BOISSET** White 1990 • $7 • (07/31/92)

68 **MOREAU** Mâcon-Villages 1990 • $9 • (03/31/92)

64 **LUCIEN DESCHAUX** Pouilly-Fuissé La Cuvée du Maitre 1990 • $14 • (03/31/92)

1989 WHITE BURGUNDY
VINTAGE RATING: 92

98 **DOMAINE DE LA ROMANEE-CONTI** Montrachet 1989 • $800

98 **FAIVELEY** Corton-Charlemagne 1989 • $125 • (08/31/91)

98 **JOSEPH DROUHIN** Montrachet Marquis de Laguiche White 1989 • $222 • (08/31/91)

97 **DOMAINE D'AUVENAY** Puligny-Montrachet Les Folatières 1989 • $95 • (08/31/91)

97 **DOMAINE ETIENNE SAUZET** Bâtard-Montrachet 1989 • $160 • (08/31/91)

97 **JEAN-NOEL GAGNARD** Bâtard-Montrachet 1989 • $140 • (08/31/91)

97 **JOSEPH DROUHIN** Corton-Charlemagne 1989 • $62 • (08/31/91)

96 **DOMAINE D'AUVENAY** Meursault Les Narvaux 1989 • $60 • (08/31/91)

96 **DOMAINE LEFLAIVE** Chevalier-Montrachet 1989 • $180 • (08/31/91)

96 **DOMAINE RAMONET** Montrachet White 1989 • $550

96 **JAFFELIN** Montrachet Le Montrachet White 1989 • $150 • (08/31/91)

95 **BONNEAU DU MARTRAY** Corton-Charlemagne 1989 • $80 • (08/31/91)

95 **JOSEPH DROUHIN** Chevalier-Montrachet 1989 • $120 • (08/31/91)

94 **BOUCHARD PERE & FILS** Montrachet Domaines du Château de Beaune White 1989 • $240 • (08/31/91)

94 **CHARTRON & TREBUCHET** Chassagne-Montrachet Les Morgeots White 1989 • $54 • (02/15/91)

94 **DOMAINE JEAN CHARTRON** Chevalier-Montrachet 1989 • $173 • (02/28/91)

94 **DOMAINE LEFLAIVE** Puligny-Montrachet Clavoillon 1989 • $71 • (08/31/91)

94 **F. CHAUVENET** Meursault Genevrières 1989 • $42 • (08/31/91)

94 **F. CHAUVENET** Meursault Les Poruzots 1989 • $53 • (08/31/91)

94 **F. CHAUVENET** Criots-Bâtard-Montrachet 1989 • $NA • (08/31/91)

94 **JAFFELIN** Corton-Charlemagne 1989 • $75 • (08/31/91)

94 **JOSEPH DROUHIN** Puligny-Montrachet Les Folatières 1989 • $67 • (08/31/91)

94 **PIERRE MOREY** Meursault Perrières 1989 • $64 • (08/31/91)

93 **DOMAINE GUY ROULOT** Meursault Les Tessons Clos de Mon Plaisir 1989 • $50 • (08/31/91)

93 **DOMAINE JOSEPH MATROT** Meursault Blagny 1989 • $63 • (08/31/91)

93 **DOMAINE LEFLAIVE** Bâtard-Montrachet 1989 • $125 • (08/31/91)

93 **HENRI GERMAIN** Meursault Charmes 1989 • $55 • (08/31/91)

93 **JEAN-MARC BOILLOT** Bâtard-Montrachet 1989 • $105 • (08/31/91)

93 **LOUIS JADOT** Puligny-Montrachet Clos de la Garenne Domaine du Duc de Mag 1989 • $61 • (08/31/91)

93 **LOUIS JADOT** Bâtard-Montrachet 1989 • $120 • (08/31/91)

93 **LOUIS LATOUR** Corton-Charlemagne 1989 • $95 • (08/31/91)

93 **MICHEL BOUZEREAU** Meursault Genevrières 1989 • $46 • (05/31/91)

93 **MICHEL COLIN-DELEGER** Chassagne-Montrachet Les Vergers 1989 • $57 • (08/31/91)

93 **PAUL PERNOT** Bâtard-Montrachet 1989 • $160 • (02/28/91)

93 **PIERRE MATROT** Puligny-Montrachet Les Combettes 1989 • $45 • (08/31/91)

92 **ANTONIN RODET** Bâtard-Montrachet 1989 • $NA • (08/31/91)

92 **ANTONIN RODET** Corton-Charlemagne 1989 • $65 • (08/31/91)

92 **BOUCHARD PERE & FILS** Chevalier-Montrachet Domaines du Château de Beaune 1989 • $150 • (08/31/91)

92 **CHARTRON & TREBUCHET** Bâtard-Montrachet 1989 • $120 • (02/28/91)

92 **DOMAINE JACQUES PRIEUR** Montrachet White 1989 • $100 • (08/31/91)

92 **DOMAINE RAMONET** Chassagne-Montrachet Les Caillerets White 1989 • $56 • (09/30/91)

92 **DOMAINE ROUX PERE & FILS** Chassagne-Montrachet Morgeot White 1989 • $55 • (08/31/91)

92 **OLIVIER LEFLAIVE** Corton-Charlemagne 1989 • $88 • (08/31/91)

91 **ANTONIN RODET** Chassagne-Montrachet Morgeot White 1989 • $40 • (08/31/91)

91 **CHARTRON & TREBUCHET** Meursault Les Charmes 1989 • $57 • (02/28/91)

91 **CHATEAU DE PULIGNY-MONTRACHET** Meursault Les Perrières 1989 • $57 • (02/28/91)

91 **DOMAINE ETIENNE SAUZET** Puligny-Montrachet Les Referts 1989 • $81 • (08/31/91)

91 **DOMAINE GUY ROULOT** Meursault Les Luchets 1989 • $39 • (08/31/91)

91 **DOMAINE GUY ROULOT** Meursault Charmes 1989 • $65 • (08/31/91)

91 **F. CHAUVENET** Meursault Les Perrières 1989 • $41 • (08/31/91)

91 **HENRI GERMAIN** Chassagne-Montrachet Morgeot White 1989 • $NA • (08/31/91)

91 **JAFFELIN** Puligny-Montrachet La Garenne 1989 • $30 • (08/31/91)

91 **JAFFELIN** Bienvenues-Bâtard-Montrachet White 1989 • $75 • (08/31/91)

91 **JEAN GERMAIN** Meursault Goutte d'Or 1989 • $NA • (08/31/91)

91 **JEAN GERMAIN** Puligny-Montrachet Les Champs Gains 1989 • $54 • (08/31/91)

91 **JEAN-MARC BOILLOT** Meursault 1989 • $NA • (08/31/91)

91 **JEAN-MARC BOILLOT** Puligny-Montrachet 1989 • $NA • (08/31/91)

91 **JEAN-MARC MOREY** Chassagne-Montrachet Les Chenevottes White 1989 • $54 • (03/31/92)

91 **JEAN-NOEL GAGNARD** Chassagne-Montrachet Les Caillerets White 1989 • $64 • (08/31/91)

91 **JEAN-PHILIPPE FICHET** Meursault Perrières 1989 • $43 • (08/31/91)

91 **JOSEPH DROUHIN** Corton-Charlemagne 1989 • $92 • (02/28/91)

91 **JOSEPH DROUHIN** Meursault Charmes 1989 • $65 • (08/31/91)

91 **LOUIS JADOT** Meursault Perrières 1989 • $NA • (08/31/91)

91 **LOUIS JADOT** Puligny-Montrachet 1989 • $39 • (08/31/91)

91 **MICHEL BOUZEREAU** Puligny-Montrachet Les Champs-Gains 1989 • $42 • (05/31/91)

■ ■ ■ ■

White Burgundy

91 **MICHEL COLIN-DELEGER** Chassagne-Montrachet Les Chaumées 1989• $38• (08/31/91)

91 **MICHEL COLIN-DELEGER** Chassagne-Montrachet Les Remilly 1989• $38• (08/31/91)

91 **OLIVIER LEFLAIVE** Puligny-Montrachet Les Champs Gains 1989• $53• (08/31/91)

91 **OLIVIER LEFLAIVE** Bâtard-Montrachet 1989• $137 • (08/31/91)

91 **PIERRE MATROT** Meursault Perrières 1989• $40 • (08/31/91)

91 **PROSPER MAUFOUX** Bâtard-Montrachet 1989• $88 • (08/31/91)

91 **PROSPER MAUFOUX** Criots-Bâtard-Montrachet 1989 • $87• (08/31/91)

91 **REINE PEDAUQUE** Meursault Genevrières 1989• $48 • (08/31/91)

91 **ROGER SAUMAIZE** Pouilly-Fuissé Clos de la Roche 1989 • $28• (07/31/91)

91 **ROPITEAU FRERES** Meursault Perrières 1989• $32 • (05/15/93)

90 **BICHOT** Meursault Genevrières 1989• $33 • (08/31/91)

90 **BICHOT** Meursault Poruzots 1989• $31• (08/31/91)

90 **BOUCHARD PERE & FILS** Puligny-Montrachet Les Pucelles 1989• $50• (08/31/91)

90 **CHATEAU DE PULIGNY-MONTRACHET** Meursault Les Porusot 1989• $55• (02/28/91)

90 **DOMAINE ETIENNE SAUZET** Chassagne-Montrachet 1989 • $60• (08/31/91)

90 **DOMAINE ETIENNE SAUZET** Puligny-Montrachet 1989 • $63• (08/31/91)

90 **DOMAINE ETIENNE SAUZET** Puligny-Montrachet Les Combettes 1989• $84• (08/31/91)

90 **DOMAINE GUY ROULOT** Meursault Perrières 1989• $65 • (08/31/91)

90 **DOMAINE JACQUES PRIEUR** Puligny-Montrachet Les Combettes 1989• $33• (08/31/91)

90 **DOMAINE PRIEUR-BRUNET** Meursault Chevalières 1989 • $45• (08/31/91)

90 **DOMAINE ROUX PERE & FILS** Puligny-Montrachet La Garenne 1989• $55• (08/31/91)

90 **FAIVELEY** Chassagne-Montrachet Les Vergers White 1989• $83• (08/31/91)

90 **JAFFELIN** Bâtard-Montrachet 1989• $110• (08/31/91)

90 **JEAN-MARC MOREY** Chassagne-Montrachet Champs-Gains 1989• $54• (03/31/92)

90 **JEAN-NOEL GAGNARD** Chassagne-Montrachet Morgeot White 1989• $63• (08/31/91)

90 **JOSEPH DROUHIN** Chassagne-Montrachet Marquis de Laguiche White 1989• $58• (02/15/91)

90 **JOSEPH DROUHIN** Puligny-Montrachet Les Pucelles 1989 • $68• (02/28/91)

90 **JOSEPH DROUHIN** Meursault 1989• $45• (08/31/91)

90 **JOSEPH DROUHIN** Puligny-Montrachet Clos de la Garenne 1989• $67• (08/31/91)

90 **JOSEPH DROUHIN** Bâtard-Montrachet 1989• $155 • (08/31/91)

90 **LAROCHE** Chassagne-Montrachet 1989• $45 • (02/28/91)

90 **LOUIS JADOT** Chassagne-Montrachet Morgeot Clos de la Chapelle Domaine du D White 1989• $50 • (08/31/91)

90 **LOUIS JADOT** Puligny-Montrachet Les Combettes 1989 • $67• (08/31/91)

90 **LOUIS LATOUR** Puligny-Montrachet Les Folatières 1989 • $52• (08/31/91)

90 **LOUIS LATOUR** Chevalier-Montrachet Les Demoiselles 1989• $152• (08/31/91)

90 **MARC COLIN** Chassagne-Montrachet 1989• $NA • (08/31/91)

90 **MARC COLIN** Montrachet 1989• $NA• (08/31/91)

90 **MICHEL BOUZEREAU** Meursault Les Grands Charrons 1989• $33• (05/31/91)

90 **MICHEL POUHIN-SEURRE** Meursault Poruzots 1989• $64 • (11/15/91)

90 **OLIVIER LEFLAIVE** Chassagne-Montrachet Les Chaumées White 1989• $NA• (08/31/91)

90 **OLIVIER LEFLAIVE** Meursault Charmes 1989• $NA • (08/31/91)

90 **OLIVIER LEFLAIVE** Puligny-Montrachet 1989• $43 • (08/31/91)

90 **REINE PEDAUQUE** Puligny-Montrachet Les Folatières 1989• $42• (08/31/91)

89 **ANTONIN RODET** Montrachet 1989• $195• (08/31/91)

89 **DOMAINE HENRI CLERC & FILS** Bienvenues-Bâtard-Montrachet White 1989• $113• (08/31/91)

89 **DOMAINE JACQUES PRIEUR** Perrières White 1989• $30 • (08/31/91)

89 **DOMAINE JEAN CHARTRON** Puligny-Montrachet Clos du Cailleret 1989• $79• (02/28/91)

89 **DOMAINE JOSEPH MATROT** Meursault Charmes 1989 • $65• (08/31/91)

89 **DOMAINE JOSEPH MATROT** Puligny-Montrachet Les Chalumeaux 1989• $66• (08/31/91)

89 **DOMAINE LEROY** Auxey-Duresses White 1989• $37 • (08/31/91)

89 **DOMAINE PRIEUR-BRUNET** Meursault Les Forges Dessus 1989• $NA• (08/31/91)

89 **DOMAINE PRIEUR-BRUNET** Meursault Charmes 1989 • $54• (08/31/91)

89 **DOMAINE RENE MANUEL** Meursault Clos de la Baronne 1989• $29• (01/31/92)

89 **DOMAINE ROUX PERE & FILS** Chassagne-Montrachet 1989• $45• (08/31/91)

89 **DOMAINE ROUX PERE & FILS** Meursault Clos des Poruzots 1989• $45• (08/31/91)

89 **DOMAINE ROUX PERE & FILS** Puligny-Montrachet Les Enseignères 1989• $45• (08/31/91)

89 **JEAN GERMAIN** Mersault Meix-Chavaux 1989• $38 • (08/31/91)

89 **JEAN GERMAIN** Meursault Clos des Meix-Chavaux 1989 • $NA• (08/31/91)

89 **JEAN-NOEL GAGNARD** Chassagne-Montrachet Premier Cru White 1989• $60• (08/31/91)

89 **JEAN-PIERRE DICONNE** Meursault Les Narvaux 1989 • $NA• (08/31/91)

89 **LABOURE-ROI** Pouilly-Fuissé 1989• $15• (07/15/92)

89 **LABOURE-ROI** Meursault 1989• $38• (08/31/91)

89 **LOUIS CARILLON** Puligny-Montrachet Les Perrières 1989 • $50• (08/31/91)

89 **LOUIS JADOT** Chassagne-Montrachet 1989• $39 • (08/31/91)

89 **LOUIS JADOT** Meursault 1989• $35• (08/31/91)

89 **LOUIS JADOT** Corton-Charlemagne 1989• $115 • (08/31/91)

89 **LOUIS LATOUR** Meursault 1989• $38• (08/31/91)

89 **MARIUS DELARCHE PERE & FILS** Corton-Charlemagne 1989• $60• (08/31/91)

89 **MICHEL COLIN-DELEGER** Chassagne-Montrachet Les Chenevottes 1989• $66• (08/31/91)

89 **MICHEL POUHIN-SEURRE** Meursault Le Limosin 1989 • $44• (11/15/91)

89 **PAUL PERNOT** Puligny-Montrachet Folatières 1989• $70 • (02/28/91)

89 **PROSPER MAUFOUX** Montrachet 1989 • $172 • (08/31/91)

89 **ROGER SAUMAIZE** Pouilly-Fuissé Les Ronchevats 1989 • $31 • (07/31/91)

88 **ALBERT GRIVAULT** Meursault 1989 • $48 • (08/31/91)

88 **ANTONIN RODET** Meursault Perrières 1989 • $NA • (08/31/91)

88 **BICHOT** Puligny-Montrachet 1989 • $30 • (08/31/91)

88 **BICHOT** Puligny-Montrachet Les Chalumeaux 1989 • $35 • (08/31/91)

88 **BOUCHARD PERE & FILS** Chassagne-Montrachet 1989 • $17 • (04/30/91)

88 **CHARTRON & TREBUCHET** Chassagne-Montrachet 1989 • $46 • (02/15/91)

88 **CHARTRON & TREBUCHET** Meursault 1989 • $41 • (02/28/91)

88 **DOMAINE ETIENNE SAUZET** Puligny-Montrachet Les Perrières 1989 • $84 • (08/31/91)

88 **DOMAINE JEAN CHARTRON** Puligny-Montrachet Les Folatières 1989 • $62 • (02/28/91)

88 **DOMAINE JEAN CHARTRON** Puligny-Montrachet Clos de la Pucelle 1989 • $69 • (02/28/91)

88 **DOMAINE LEFLAIVE** Puligny-Montrachet Les Pucelles 1989 • $79 • (08/31/91)

88 **DOMAINE PRIEUR-BRUNET** Chassagne-Montrachet Les Embazées 1989 • $54 • (08/31/91)

88 **DOMAINE PRIEUR-BRUNET** Meursault 1989 • $NA • (08/31/91)

88 **DOMAINE ROUX PERE & FILS** Chassagne-Montrachet Morgeot 1989 • $55 • (02/28/91)

88 **FAIVELEY** Meursault Les Bouchères 1989 • $82 • (08/31/91)

88 **FAIVELEY** Puligny-Montrachet 1989 • $72 • (08/31/91)

88 **HENRI GERMAIN** Meursault Clos du Cromin 1989 • $55 • (08/31/91)

88 **HENRI GERMAIN** Meursault Le Limozin 1989 • $50 • (08/31/91)

88 **JAFFELIN** Santenay Les Gravières White 1989 • $25 • (08/31/91)

88 **JEAN CLAUDE BOISSET** Puligny-Montrachet Les Folatières 1989 • $38 • (08/31/91)

88 **JEAN-MARC MOREY** Chassagne-Montrachet Les Caillerets 1989 • $54 • (03/31/92)

88 **JEAN-NOEL GAGNARD** Chassagne-Montrachet 1989 • $55 • (08/31/91)

88 **JEAN-PHILIPPE FICHET** Meursault 1989 • $28 • (08/31/91)

88 **JOSEPH DROUHIN** Chassagne-Montrachet 1989 • $50 • (08/31/91)

88 **JOSEPH DROUHIN** Chassagne-Montrachet Clos St.-Jean 1989 • $NA • (08/31/91)

88 **LABOURE-ROI** Chassagne-Montrachet 1989 • $42 • (08/31/91)

88 **LABOURE-ROI** Corton-Charlemagne 1989 • $59 • (04/15/92)

88 **LOUIS CARILLON** Puligny-Montrachet 1989 • $50 • (08/31/91)

88 **LOUIS JADOT** Auxey-Duresses Domaine du Duc de Magenta White 1989 • $25 • (08/31/91)

88 **LOUIS LATOUR** Chassagne-Montrachet 1989 • $42 • (08/31/91)

88 **OLIVIER LEFLAIVE** Meursault 1989 • $39 • (08/31/91)

88 **PIERRE PONNELLE** Corton-Charlemagne 1989 • $85 • (08/31/91)

88 **PROSPER MAUFOUX** Chassagne-Montrachet Les Chenevottes White 1989 • $37 • (08/31/91)

88 **REINE PEDAUQUE** Chassagne-Montrachet 1989 • $35 • (08/31/91)

88 **SIMON BIZE & FILS** Savigny-lès-Beaune 1989 • $22 • (08/31/91)

87 **ALBERT GRIVAULT** Meursault Clos des Perrières 1989 • $64 • (08/31/91)

87 **BICHOT** Puligny-Montrachet Hameau de Blagny 1989 • $38 • (01/31/92)

87 **BOUCHARD PERE & FILS** Corton-Charlemagne 1989 • $77 • (08/31/91)

87 **CHATEAU DE LA MALTROYE** Chassagne-Montrachet Morgeot Vigne Blanche 1989 • $40 • (02/28/91)

87 **DOMAINE ETIENNE SAUZET** Puligny-Montrachet Champ Canet 1989 • $85 • (08/31/91)

87 **DOMAINE JOSEPH MATROT** Meursault Les Chevalières 1989 • $48 • (08/31/91)

87 **DOMAINE MONTHELIE-DOUHAIRET** Meursault Les Santenots 1989 • $NA • (08/31/91)

87 **DOMAINE RAMONET** Chassagne-Montrachet 1989 • $45 • (09/30/91)

87 **F. CHAUVENET** Chassagne-Montrachet Les Caillerets 1989 • $NA • (08/31/91)

87 **F. CHAUVENET** Puligny-Montrachet Champs-Gain 1989 • $30 • (08/31/91)

87 **FAIVELEY** Meursault 1989 • $68 • (08/31/91)

87 **FAIVELEY** Puligny-Montrachet Les Combettes 1989 • $89 • (08/31/91)

87 **GERARD THOMAS** St.-Aubin La Chatenière White 1989 • $28 • (08/31/91)

87 **JAFFELIN** Chassagne-Montrachet 1989 • $40 • (08/31/91)

87 **JAFFELIN** Chassagne-Montrachet Les Vergers 1989 • $30 • (08/31/91)

87 **JEAN GERMAIN** Meursault Bouchères 1989 • $NA • (08/31/91)

87 **JEAN-PIERRE DICONNE** Meursault Clos des Luchets 1989 • $NA • (08/31/91)

87 **JOSEPH DROUHIN** Auxey-Duresses 1989 • $22 • (02/28/91)

87 **JOSEPH DROUHIN** Chassagne-Montrachet Marquis de Laguiche 1989 • $60 • (08/31/91)

87 **JOSEPH DROUHIN** Meursault Perrières 1989 • $60 • (08/31/91)

87 **LOUIS CARILLON** Puligny-Montrachet Les Champs Gains 1989 • $50 • (08/31/91)

87 **LOUIS JADOT** Pouilly-Fuissé Cuvée Réserve Spéciale 1989 • $21 • (07/31/91)

87 **LOUIS JADOT** Pernand-Vergelesses 1989 • $NA • (08/31/91)

87 **LOUIS LATOUR** Puligny-Montrachet 1989 • $43 • (08/31/91)

87 **MICHEL BOUZEREAU** Meursault Les Tessons 1989 • $35 • (05/31/91)

87 **PIERRE ANDRE** Puligny-Montrachet 1989 • $32 • (08/31/91)

87 **PIERRE MOREY** Meursault Les Tessons 1989 • $43 • (08/31/91)

87 **PROSPER MAUFOUX** Puligny-Montrachet 1989 • $36 • (08/31/91)

87 **TOLLOT-BEAUT** Bourgogne Chardonnay 1989 • $NA • (08/31/91)

86 **CHARTRON & TREBUCHET** St.-Aubin La Chatenière White 1989 • $24 • (02/28/91)

86 **CHATEAU DE LA MALTROYE** Chassagne-Montrachet Grandes Ruchottes 1989 • $40 • (02/28/91)

86 **DOMAINE BRUNO CLAIR** Morey-St.-Denis en La Rue De Vergy White 1989 • $30 • (08/31/91)
86 **DOMAINE ETIENNE SAUZET** Bourgogne Chardonnay White 1989 • $31 • (08/31/91)
86 **DOMAINE HENRI CLERC & FILS** Bourgogne Chardonnay Les Champs Perriers White 1989 • $20 • (08/31/91)
86 **DOMAINE JACQUES PRIEUR** Meursault Clos de Mazeray 1989 • $25 • (08/31/91)
86 **DOMAINE LEFLAIVE** Puligny-Montrachet 1989 • $54 • (08/31/91)
86 **F. CHAUVENET** Meursault Les Gouttes d'Or 1989 • $NA • (08/31/91)
86 **F. CHAUVENET** Puligny-Montrachet La Garenne 1989 • $NA • (08/31/91)
86 **GEORGES DUBOEUF** Pouilly-Fuissé 1989 • $15 • (10/31/90)
86 **JAFFELIN** Chassagne-Montrachet Les Caillerets White 1989 • $30 • (08/31/91)
86 **JAYER-GILLES** Bourgogne Hautes Côtes de Beaune White 1989 • $24 • (08/31/91)
86 **JEAN CLAUDE BOISSET** Chassagne-Montrachet Les Vergers White 1989 • $38 • (08/31/91)
86 **JEAN CLAUDE BOISSET** Corton-Charlemagne Grand Cru 1989 • $NA
86 **JEAN GERMAIN** Meursault 1989 • $40 • (08/31/91)
86 **JEAN GERMAIN** Puligny-Montrachet 1989 • $NA • (08/31/91)
86 **JOSEPH DROUHIN** Rully 1989 • $18 • (02/28/91)
86 **JOSEPH DROUHIN** Pernand-Vergelesses 1989 • $23 • (08/31/91)
86 **JOSEPH DROUHIN** Meursault Genevrières 1989 • $60 • (08/31/91)
86 **LABOURE-ROI** Bourgogne Chardonnay 1989 • $8 • (08/31/92)
86 **LOUIS JADOT** Puligny-Montrachet 1989 • $36 • (01/31/92)
86 **LOUIS LATOUR** Meursault Château de Blagny 1989 • $95 • (08/31/91)
86 **MARC COLIN** Chassagne-Montrachet Les Caillerets White 1989 • $NA • (08/31/91)
86 **MARC COLIN** Chassagne-Montrachet Les Champs-Gains White 1989 • $NA • (08/31/91)
86 **MICHEL COLIN-DELEGER** Chassagne-Montrachet 1989 • $32 • (08/31/91)
86 **MOMMESSIN** Meursault Premier Cru 1989 • $NA • (08/31/91)
86 **OLIVIER LEFLAIVE** Meursault Les Poruzots 1989 • $NA • (08/31/91)
86 **OLIVIER LEFLAIVE** Puligny-Montrachet Les Garennes 1989 • $56 • (08/31/91)
86 **OLIVIER LEFLAIVE** St.-Aubin En Remilly White 1989 • $29 • (06/15/93)
86 **REINE PEDAUQUE** Bâtard-Montrachet 1989 • $100 • (08/31/91)
85 **BICHOT** Montrachet 1989 • $170 • (08/31/91)
85 **BOUCHARD PERE & FILS** Pouilly-Fuissé 1989 • $25 • (04/30/91)
85 **BOUCHARD PERE & FILS** Meursault Genevrières Domaines du Château de Beaun 1989 • $63 • (08/31/91)
85 **BOUCHARD PERE & FILS** Puligny-Montrachet Les Champs Gain 1989 • $NA • (08/31/91)
85 **CHANSON PERE & FILS** Chassagne-Montrachet Les Embazées White 1989 • $37 • (08/31/91)
85 **CHARTRON & TREBUCHET** St.-Romain 1989 • $20 • (02/28/91)
85 **CHARTRON & TREBUCHET** Corton-Charlemagne 1989 • $105 • (02/28/91)
85 **DOMAINE DU CLOS FRANTIN** Corton-Charlemagne 1989 • $NA • (08/31/91)
85 **DOMAINE MONTHELIE-DOUHAIRET** Meursault 1989 • $25 • (08/31/91)
85 **DOMAINE ROUX PERE & FILS** St.-Aubin La Pucelle 1989 • $26 • (02/28/91)
85 **F. CHAUVENET** Meursault Les Casses Têtes 1989 • $26 • (08/31/91)
85 **FAIVELEY** Bourgogne Chardonnay Cuvée Joseph Faiveley White 1989 • $21 • (08/31/91)
85 **FERNAND COFFINET** Chassagne-Montrachet Blanchot-Dessus 1989 • $36 • (03/31/92)
85 **GEORGES DUBOEUF** St.-Véran White 1989 • $10 • (10/31/90)
85 **JAFFELIN** Auxey-Duresses 1989 • $16 • (08/31/91)
85 **JAFFELIN** Meursault 1989 • $25 • (08/31/91)
85 **JAYER-GILLES** Bourgogne Hautes Côtes de Nuits 1989 • $18 • (08/31/91)
85 **JEAN GERMAIN** St.-Romain Clos Sous le Château White 1989 • $24 • (08/31/91)
85 **JEAN GERMAIN** Puligny-Montrachet Les Grands Champs 1989 • $48 • (08/31/91)
85 **JOSEPH DROUHIN** St.-Véran 1989 • $16 • (02/28/91)
85 **LABOURE-ROI** St.-Aubin Le Charmois 1989 • $23 • (07/15/92)
85 **M. VINCENT** Pouilly-Fuissé Château Fuissé 1989 • $24 • (08/31/91)
85 **MARC COLIN** St.-Aubin La Chatenière 1989 • $NA • (08/31/91)
85 **MOMMESSIN** Chassagne-Montrachet Première Cru White 1989 • $NA • (08/31/91)
85 **OLIVIER LEFLAIVE** Chassagne-Montrachet 1989 • $41 • (08/31/91)
85 **PROSPER MAUFOUX** Puligny-Montrachet Folatières 1989 • $43 • (08/31/91)
85 **REINE PEDAUQUE** Corton-Charlemagne 1989 • $78 • (08/31/91)
85 **ROGER LASSARAT** Pouilly-Fuissé Cuve Prestige 1989 • $NA
85 **ROPITEAU FRERES** Meursault Le Meursault de Ropiteau 1989 • $22 • (05/15/93)
84 **ALAIN GRAS** St.-Romain 1989 • $20 • (08/31/91)
84 **BICHOT** Meursault 1989 • $26 • (08/31/91)
84 **BICHOT** Bienvenues-Bâtard-Montrachet 1989 • $84 • (08/31/91)
84 **CHANSON PERE & FILS** Puligny-Montrachet 1989 • $37 • (08/31/91)
84 **CHARLES VIENOT** Meursault 1989 • $35 • (08/31/91)
84 **CHATEAU DE MEURSAULT** Meursault 1989 • $54 • (02/28/94)
84 **DOMAINE CHANTAL LESCURE** Côte de Beaune Les Grandes Chatelaines 1989 • $38 • (08/31/91)
84 **DOMAINE RENE MANUEL** Meursault Clos des Bouches Chères 1989 • $68 • (08/31/91)
84 **DUBREUIL-FONTAINE** Corton-Charlemagne 1989 • $71 • (03/31/92)
84 **GEORGES DUBOEUF** Mâcon-Lugny Fête des Fleurs 1989 • $9 • (10/31/90)
84 **JACQUES GERMAIN** Pernand-Vergelesses 1989 • $NA • (08/31/91)
84 **JAFFELIN** Puligny-Montrachet 1989 • $42 • (05/31/91)
84 **JEAN-PIERRE DICONNE** Auxey-Duresses 1989 • $NA • (08/31/91)
84 **JOSEPH DROUHIN** Meursault Perrières 1989 • $60 • (02/28/91)
84 **JOSEPH DROUHIN** Auxey-Duresses 1989 • $22 • (08/31/91)

84 **JOSEPH DROUHIN** St.-Romain 1989 • $22 • (08/31/91)
84 **JOSEPH DROUHIN** Puligny-Montrachet Les Pucelles 1989 • $68 • (08/31/91)
84 **LAROCHE** Meursault 1989 • $25 • (08/31/92)
84 **MOMMESSIN** Meursault 1989 • $NA • (08/31/91)
84 **MOMMESSIN** Puligny-Montrachet 1989 • $NA • (08/31/91)
84 **OLIVIER LEFLAIVE** St.-Aubin Premier Cru 1989 • $31 • (08/31/91)
84 **P. MISSEREY** Meursault Charmes Hospices de Beaune Cuvee de Bahè 1989 • $87 • (08/31/92)
84 **PIERRE ANDRE** Meursault 1989 • $23 • (08/31/91)
84 **PIERRE MOREY** Meursault Charmes 1989 • $64 • (11/30/91)
84 **PROSPER MAUFOUX** Montagny Première Cru White 1989 • $20 • (08/31/91)
84 **SIMON BIZE & FILS** Bourgogne Chardonnay Les Champlains White 1989 • $NA • (08/31/91)
83 **BICHOT** Mâcon-Villages 1989 • $9 • (07/15/90)
83 **BICHOT** Savigny-lès-Beaune Savigny Blanc White 1989 • $19 • (08/31/91)
83 **BOUCHARD PERE & FILS** Meursault 1989 • $37 • (04/30/91)
83 **CHARLES VIENOT** Puligny-Montrachet Champs Gain 1989 • $42 • (08/31/91)
83 **CHATEAU DE PULIGNY-MONTRACHET** Côte de Nuits-Villages White 1989 • $27 • (02/28/91)
83 **DOMAINE PRIEUR-BRUNET** Bourgogne Chardonnay Prieur White 1989 • $NA • (08/31/91)
83 **DOMAINE ROUX PERE & FILS** Puligny-Montrachet Champs Gains 1989 • $55 • (02/28/91)
83 **FAIVELEY** Chassagne-Montrachet 1989 • $70 • (08/31/91)
83 **GERARD THOMAS** St.-Aubin Murgers des Dents Chien White 1989 • $25 • (08/31/91)
83 **JAFFELIN** St.-Aubin 1989 • $16 • (08/31/91)
83 **JAFFELIN** Puligny-Montrachet 1989 • $42 • (08/31/91)
83 **JOSEPH DROUHIN** Puligny-Montrachet 1989 • $50 • (08/31/91)
83 **MARC COLIN** St.-Aubin Les Combes 1989 • $NA • (08/31/91)
83 **MICHEL JUILLOT** Corton-Charlemagne 1989 • $89 • (08/31/92)
83 **MOMMESSIN** Chassagne-Montrachet 1989 • $NA • (08/31/91)
83 **PAUL PERNOT** Bourgogne Chardonnay Champerrier White 1989 • $16 • (04/30/91)
83 **PRINCE FLORENT DE MERODE** Ladoix Côte de Beaune Hautes Mourottes White 1989 • $37 • (08/31/92)
83 **PROSPER MAUFOUX** Pouilly-Fuissé 1989 • $23 • (08/31/91)
82 **ANTONIN RODET** Puligny-Montrachet Les Clavoillons 1989 • $43 • (08/31/91)
82 **BICHOT** Puligny-Montrachet Les Combettes 1989 • $40 • (07/15/92)
82 **CHARLES VIENOT** Savigny-lès-Beaune 1989 • $24 • (08/31/91)
82 **CHATEAU DE PULIGNY-MONTRACHET** Meursault 1989 • $42 • (02/28/91)
82 **DOMAINE BRUNO CLAIR** Bourgogne 1989 • $13 • (08/31/91)
82 **DOMAINE DU VIEUX ST.-SORLIN** Mâcon-la Roche Vineuse 1989 • $14 • (02/28/91)
82 **DOMAINE JOSEPH MATROT** Meursault 1989 • $42 • (08/31/91)
82 **JAFFELIN** Rully Barrel Fermented White 1989 • $16 • (08/31/91)
82 **JAFFELIN** St.-Romain 1989 • $18 • (08/31/91)
82 **JEANNE-MARIE DE CHAMPS** Meursault Charmes Hospices de Beaune Cuvee Bahèzre 1989 • $75 • (08/31/91)
82 **JOSEPH DROUHIN** Bourgogne Chardonnay Laforàt White 1989 • $9 • (04/30/91) • BB
82 **LABOURE-ROI** Bourgogne Hautes Côtes de Beaune White 1989 • $10 • (08/31/92)
82 **PIERRE MOREY** Meursault Les Tessons 1989 • $44 • (03/31/92)
82 **PIERRE PONNELLE** Vougeot Le Village 1989 • $32 • (08/31/91)
82 **PROSPER MAUFOUX** St.-Véran 1989 • $14 • (08/31/91)
82 **REINE PEDAUQUE** St.-Aubin 1989 • $18 • (08/31/91)
82 **ROPITEAU FRERES** Puligny-Montrachet Champ Gain 1989 • $30 • (05/15/93)
81 **CHANSON PERE & FILS** Bourgogne Chardonnay White 1989 • $10 • (08/31/91)
81 **DOMAINE HENRI CLERC & FILS** Beaune Chaume Gaufriot White 1989 • $30 • (08/31/91)
81 **DOMAINE JOSEPH MATROT** Bourgogne Chardonnay 1989 • $15 • (08/31/91)
81 **DOMAINE ROUX PERE & FILS** St.-Aubin La Chatenière White 1989 • $26 • (08/31/91)
81 **GEORGES DUBOEUF** Mâcon-Villages 1989 • $8 • (10/31/90)
81 **JAFFELIN** Meursault Les Bouchères 1989 • $27 • (08/31/91)
81 **JEAN GERMAIN** Bourgogne Clos de la Fortune White 1989 • $NA • (08/31/91)
81 **OLIVIER LEFLAIVE** Rully Premier Cru White 1989 • $20 • (07/31/91)
81 **OLIVIER LEFLAIVE** Bourgogne Chardonnay Les Sétilles 1989 • $15 • (08/31/91)
81 **PIERRE MOREY** Bourgogne Chardonnay 1989 • $20 • (08/31/91)
81 **PROSPER MAUFOUX** Mâcon-Villages 1989 • $11 • (08/31/91)
81 **PROSPER MAUFOUX** Bourgogne Chardonnay 1989 • $12 • (08/31/91)
81 **PROSPER MAUFOUX** Puligny-Montrachet Hameau de Blagny 1989 • $39 • (08/31/91)
81 **REINE PEDAUQUE** Bourgogne Chardonnay Buchère 1989 • $12 • (08/31/91)
81 **ROBERT SARRAU** Mâcon-Villages 1989 • $8 • (10/31/90)
81 **ROPITEAU FRERES** Chassagne-Montrachet Morgeot White 1989 • $30 • (05/15/93)
80 **CHANSON PERE & FILS** Pernand-Vergelesses 1989 • $18 • (08/31/91)
80 **DOMAINE RENE MANUEL** Bourgogne 1989 • $9 • (08/31/91)
80 **DOMAINE ROUX PERE & FILS** St.-Aubin La Pucelle White 1989 • $26 • (08/31/91)
80 **FERNAND COFFINET** Chassagne-Montrachet 1989 • $34 • (03/31/92)
80 **JAFFELIN** St.-Véran 1989 • $14 • (07/31/91)
80 **JAFFELIN** Bourgogne Chardonnay du Châpitre 1989 • $9 • (08/31/91)
80 **LABOURE-ROI** Mâcon-Villages 1989 • $10 • (04/30/91)
80 **LABOURE-ROI** Puligny-Montrachet 1989 • $45 • (08/31/91)
80 **LAROCHE** Puligny-Montrachet 1989 • $47 • (02/28/91)
80 **MARIUS DELARCHE PERE & FILS** Pernand-Vergelesses Ile des Vergelesses White 1989 • $NA • (08/31/91)
80 **PAUL PERNOT** Puligny-Montrachet 1989 • $52 • (02/28/91)

■ ■ ■ ■

White Burgundy

79 **BOUCHARD PERE & FILS** Beaune Clos St.-Landry Domaines du Château de Beaune White 1989 • $50 • (08/31/91)

79 **CHANSON PERE & FILS** Beaune Clos des Mouches White 1989 • $15 • (08/31/91)

79 **DOMAINE VALETTE** Pouilly-Fuissé Clos Reyssié Réserve Particulière 1989 • $NA

79 **J.J. VINCENT** Pouilly-Fuissé 1989 • $15 • (04/30/91)

79 **MICHEL COLIN-DELEGER** Chassagne-Montrachet Morgeot White 1989 • $40 • (08/31/91)

79 **P. MISSEREY** Pouilly-Loché Domaine du Château de Loché White 1989 • $14 • (08/31/92)

79 **REINE PEDAUQUE** Auxey-Duresses 1989 • $22 • (08/31/91)

79 **THIERRY GUERIN** St.-Véran 1989 • $9 • (03/31/91)

78 **CHANSON PERE & FILS** Meursault 1989 • $30 • (08/31/91)

78 **CHARTRON & TREBUCHET** Bourgogne Chardonnay 1989 • $10 • (02/28/91)

78 **CHARTRON & TREBUCHET** Rully La Chaume White 1989 • $18 • (04/30/91)

78 **DOMAINE CLAUDINE DESCHAMPS** Côte de Beaune 1989 • $NA • (08/31/91)

78 **DOMAINE TALMARD** Mâcon-Chardonnay 1989 • $10 • (10/31/90)

78 **JEAN CLAUDE BOISSET** St.-Aubin Les Charmois White 1989 • $19 • (08/31/91)

78 **LOUIS JADOT** St.-Véran La Chapelle White 1989 • $14 • (08/31/91)

78 **MICHEL POUHIN-SEURRE** Puligny-Montrachet 1989 • $52 • (11/15/91)

78 **MOILLARD** Bourgogne Hautes Côtes de Beaune Les Alouettes White 1989 • $15 • (06/15/91)

78 **PROSPER MAUFOUX** Bourgogne Aligoté 1989 • $12 • (07/31/91)

77 **F. CHAUVENET** St.-Romain 1989 • $NA • (08/31/91)

77 **MOILLARD** Mâcon-Villages Domaine de Montbellet 1989 • $11 • (04/30/91)

77 **PROSPER MAUFOUX** Meursault 1989 • $32 • (04/15/92)

76 **DOMAINE DES ROCHES** Mâcon-Igé 1989 • $9 • (10/31/90)

76 **DOMAINE HENRI CLERC & FILS** Puligny-Montrachet Les Folatières 1989 • $64 • (08/31/91)

76 **JEAN PILLOT** Puligny-Montrachet 1989 • $42 • (04/30/91)

75 **CHANSON PERE & FILS** Bourgogne Hautes Côtes de Beaune White 1989 • $12 • (08/31/91)

75 **LABOURE-ROI** White 1989 • $6 • (07/31/92)

74 **CHATEAU DE PULIGNY-MONTRACHET** Puligny-Montrachet 1989 • $66 • (02/28/91)

74 **DOMAINE ROUX PERE & FILS** Bourgogne Chardonnay White 1989 • $18 • (08/31/91)

74 **PHILIPPE BOUZEREAU** Les Narvaux White 1989 • $37 • (11/30/91)

73 **DOMAINE B. SERVEAU** Bourgogne Chardonnay 1989 • $16 • (04/30/91)

73 **LEONARD DE ST.-AUBIN** Puligny-Montrachet 1989 • $28 • (08/31/91)

72 **CHATEAU DE LA TOUR DE L'ANGE** Mâcon-Villages Chardonnay 1989 • $9 • (08/31/91)

71 **LES ACACIAS** Mâcon-Villages Cave de Viré 1989 • $11 • (02/28/91)

71 **PROSPER MAUFOUX** Château de Viré White 1989 • $12 • (07/31/92)

71 **REINE PEDAUQUE** Savigny-lès-Beaune White 1989 • $22 • (08/31/91)

69 **DUBREUIL-FONTAINE** Bourgogne Aligoté White 1989 • $13 • (08/31/92)

69 **PIERRE PONNELLE** Bourgogne Hautes Côtes de Nuits White 1989 • $15 • (08/31/91)

68 **JEAN CLAUDE BOISSET** St.-Véran 1989 • $12 • (07/31/91)

Domaine Leroy, Burgundy.

Graham's Lodge, Oporto.

Vintage Port

Here are *Wine Spectator's* ratings and prices for the seven most recent "declared" vintages of vintage Port. The Ports are organized by vintage and in descending order of score, to make it easy to identify the best labels in each vintage.

Listed here are scores from the 1992, 1991, 1987, 1985, 1983 and 1977 vintages. 1992 and 1991 are both quite high in quality, but they may be surpassed by 1994, which *Wine Spectator* projects to be of classic quality when it begins to be released in 1997. Scores for 1994 are given as ranges because they are based on barrel samples.

The date of the issue of *Wine Spectator* in which the rating was first published is in parentheses. In general, wines for which no issue date appears were tasted between April 15, 1994 and June 15, 1996.

1994 Vintage Port | Vintage Rating: 95-100

95-100 CROFT Vintage Port 1994 • $NA • (06/15/96)
95-100 DOW Vintage Port 1994 • $38 • (06/15/96)
95-100 FONSECA Vintage Port 1994 • $55 • (06/15/96)
95-100 GRAHAM Vintage Port 1994 • $42 • (06/15/96)
95-100 TAYLOR FLADGATE Vintage Port 1994 • $55 • (06/15/96)
95-100 QUINTA DO VESUVIO Vintage Port 1994 • $42 • (06/15/96)
90-94 CHURCHILL Vintage Port 1994 • $NA • (06/15/96)
90-94 COCKBURN Vintage Port 1994 • $40 • (06/15/96)
90-94 DELAFORCE Vintage Port 1994 • $NA • (06/15/96)
90-94 FERREIRA Vintage Port 1994 • $NA • (06/15/96)
90-94 MARTINEZ Vintage Port 1994 • $40 • (06/15/96)
90-94 MARTINEZ Vintage Port Quinta da Eira Velha 1994 • $40 • (06/15/96)
90-94 NIEPOORT Vintage Port 1994 • $NA • (06/15/96)
90-94 QUINTA DO NOVAL Vintage Port 1994 • $NA • (06/15/96)
90-94 RAMOS-PINTO Vintage Port 1994 • $NA • (06/15/96)
90-94 WARRE Vintage Port 1994 • $38 • (06/15/96)
85-89 CALEM Vintage Port 1994 • $NA • (06/15/96)
85-89 GOULD CAMPBELL Vintage Port 1994 • $NA • (06/15/96)
85-89 KOPKE Vintage Port 1994 • $NA • (06/15/96)
85-89 QUINTA DO PASSADOURO Vintage Port 1994 • $NA • (06/15/96)
85-89 POCAS JUNIOR Vintage Port 1994 • $30 • (06/15/96)
85-89 RAMOS-PINTO Vintage Port Quinta da Ervamoira 1994 • $NA • (06/15/96)
85-89 ROMARIZ Vintage Port 1994 • $NA • (06/15/96)
85-89 QUINTA DE LA ROSA Vintage Port 1994 • $35 • (06/15/96)
85-89 QUINTA DO SAGRADO Vintage Port 1994 • $NA• (06/15/96)
85-89 SANDEMAN Vintage Port Lot A 1994 • $NA • (06/15/96)
85-89 SANDEMAN Vintage Port Lot C 1994 • $NA • (06/15/96)
85-89 SANDEMAN Vintage Port Lot B 1994 • $NA • (06/15/96)
85-89 SKEFFINGTON Vintage Port 1994 • $NA • (06/15/96)
85-89 SMITH WOODHOUSE Vintage Port 1994 • $32 • (06/15/96)
80-84 BARROS Vintage Port 1994 • $NA • (06/15/96)
80-84 BURMESTER Vintage Port 1994 • $NA
80-84 OFFLEY Vintage Port 1994 • $NA • (06/15/96)
80-84 QUARLES HARRIS Vintage Port 1994 • $NA • (06/15/96)
70-74 BURMESTER Vintage Port Quinta do Nova 1994 • $NA

1992 Vintage Port
Vintage Rating: 94

96 FONSECA Vintage Port 1992 • $30 • (06/15/95) • CS
95 TAYLOR FLADGATE Vintage Port 1992 • $37 • (06/15/95)
94 QUINTA DO VESUVIO Vintage Port 1992 • $49 • (06/15/95)
92 DOW Vintage Port Quinta do Bomfim 1992 • $30 • (06/30/95)
91 GRAHAM Vintage Port Malvedos 1992 • $39 • (06/30/95)
91 WARRE Vintage Port Quinta da Cavadinha 1992 • $26 • (06/30/95)
90 DELAFORCE Vintage Port 1992 • $35 • (06/15/95)
90 QUINTA DO INFANTADO Vintage Port 1992 • $35 • (06/15/95)
90 NIEPOORT Vintage Port 1992 • $33 • (06/15/95)
89 CHURCHILL Vintage Port Agua Alta 1992 • $35 • (06/15/95)
89 COCKBURN Vintage Port Quinta da Canias 1992 • $35 • (06/15/95)
89 MARTINEZ Vintage Port Quinta da Eira Velha 1992 • $NA • (06/15/95)
89 ROMANIERA Vintage Port Quinta das Liceiras 1992 • $NA • (06/15/95)
88 OSBORNE Vintage Port 1992 • $28 • (06/15/95)
88 QUINTA DO PASSADOURO Vintage Port 1992 • $NA • (06/15/95)
88 QUINTA DE LA ROSA Vintage Port 1992 • $NA • (06/15/95)
88 SMITH WOODHOUSE Vintage Port 1992 • $33 • (06/15/95)
87 BURMESTER Vintage Port Quinta do Nova 1992 • $NA • (06/15/95)
86 CALEM Vintage Port Quinta do Foz 1992 • $NA • (06/15/95)
85 BURMESTER Vintage Port 1992 • $NA • (06/15/95)
85 GILBERT Vintage Port 1992 • $NA • (06/15/95)

1991 Vintage Port
Vintage Rating: 93

94 **CROFT** Vintage Port 1991 •$32 •(07/31/94)
94 **TAYLOR FLADGATE** Vintage Port Quinta de Vargellas 1991 •$NA •(07/31/94)
93 **FONSECA** Vintage Port Guimaraens 1991 •$35 •(07/31/94)
93 **FONSECA** Vintage Port 1991 •$NA
93 **GRAHAM** Vintage Port 1991 •$45 •(07/31/94)
92 **GOULD CAMPBELL** Vintage Port 1991 •$35 •(07/31/94)
91 **CHURCHILL** Vintage Port 1991 •$35 •(07/31/94)
91 **DOW** Vintage Port 1991 •$42 •(07/31/94)
91 **FERREIRA** Vintage Port 1991 •$19 •(07/31/94)
91 **QUINTA DO VESUVIO** Vintage Port 1991 •$48 •(07/31/94)
91 **WARRE** Vintage Port 1991 •$35 •(07/31/94)
88 **COCKBURN** Vintage Port 1991 •$36 •(07/31/94)
87 **DELAFORCE** Vintage Port 1991 •$29 •(07/31/94)
87 **DELAFORCE** Vintage Port Quinta da Corte 1991 •$29 •(07/31/94)
87 **QUINTA DO NOVAL** Vintage Port 1991 •$25 •(07/31/94)
87 **ROZES** Vintage Port 1991 •$23 •(07/31/94)
87 **SMITH WOODHOUSE** Vintage Port 1991 •$36 •(07/31/94)
86 **BURMESTER** Vintage Port 1991 •$NA •(07/31/94)
86 **RAMOS-PINTO** Vintage Port 1991 •$26 •(07/31/94)
86 **QUINTA DE LA ROSA** Vintage Port 1991 •$NA •(07/31/94)
85 **GILBERT'S** Vintage Port 1991 •$NA •(07/31/94)
85 **QUINTA DO INFANTADO** Vintage Port 1991 •$25 •(07/31/94)
85 **MARTINEZ** Vintage Port 1991 •$NA •(07/31/94)
85 **NIEPOORT** Vintage Port 1991 •$NA •(07/31/94)
84 **PORTO POCAS** Vintage Port 1991 •$NA •(07/31/94)
83 **FEIST** Vintage Port 1991 •$NA •(07/31/94)
82 **KOPKE** Vintage Port 1991 •$NA •(07/31/94)
81 **HUTCHESON** Vintage Port 1991 •$19 •(07/31/94)
80 **CALEM** Vintage Port 1991 •$NA •(07/31/94)
79 **BARROS** Vintage Port 1991 •$NA •(07/31/94)

1987 Vintage Port
Vintage Rating: 88

94 **QUINTA DO NOVAL** Vintage Port Nacional 1987 •$NA •(01/01/90)
93 **TAYLOR FLADGATE** Vintage Port Quinta de Vargellas 1987 •$NA •(02/01/90)
91 **GRAHAM** Vintage Port Malvedos 1987 •$NA •(02/01/90)
91 **NIEPOORT** Vintage Port 1987 •$17 •(11/01/89)
90 **FONSECA** Vintage Port Guimaraens 1987 •$NA •(02/01/90)
89 **QUINTA DO NOVAL** Vintage Port 1987 •$NA •(01/01/90)
88 **FERREIRA** Vintage Port 1987 •$NA •(11/01/89)
88 **OFFLEY** Vintage Port Boa Vista 1987 •$NA •(01/01/90)
87 **DELAFORCE** Vintage Port Quinta da Corte 1987 •$NA •(02/01/90)
86 **DOW** Vintage Port Quinta do Bomfim 1987 •$NA •(02/01/90)
86 **QUINTA DA EIRA VELHA** Vintage Port 1987 •$NA •(05/01/90)
86 **KOPKE** Vintage Port 1987 •$24 •(01/01/90)
86 **ROZES** Vintage Port 1987 •$NA •(06/01/90)
86 **WARRE** Vintage Port Quinta da Cavadinha 1987 •$NA •(02/01/90)
84 **CALEM** Vintage Port Quinta do Foz 1987 •$28 •(06/01/90)
84 **MARTINEZ** Vintage Port 1987 •$NA •(05/01/90)
84 **OFFLEY** Vintage Port 1987 •$NA •(01/01/90)
83 **CHURCHILL** Vintage Port Agua Alta 1987 •$48 •(04/15/91)
83 **QUINTA DE VAL DA FIGUEIRA** Vintage Port 1987 •$NA •(02/01/90)
82 **FONSECA** Vintage Port Quinta do Panascal 1987 •$NA •(02/01/90)
81 **BARROS** Vintage Port 1987 •$28 •(01/01/90)
81 **QUINTA DA ROMANEIRA** Vintage Port 1987 •$NA •(01/01/90)
81 **ROYAL OPORTO** Vintage Port 1987 •$19 •(11/30/91)
80 **QUINTA DO CRASTO** Vintage Port 1987 •$NA •(01/01/90)
80 **C. DA SILVA** Vintage Port Presidential 1987 •$NA •(02/01/90)
79 **CROFT** Vintage Port Quinta da Roeda 1987 •$NA •(02/01/90)

1985 Vintage Port
Vintage Rating: 96

96 **GRAHAM** Vintage Port 1985 •$47 •(06/01/90)
95 **FONSECA** Vintage Port 1985 •$40 •(06/01/90)
95 **QUINTA DO NOVAL** Vintage Port Nacional 1985 •$200 •(11/01/89)
93 **BURMESTER** Vintage Port 1985 •$25 •(01/01/90)
93 **COCKBURN** Vintage Port 1985 •$46 •(10/31/88)
93 **WARRE** Vintage Port 1985 •$38 •(10/31/88)
92 **CROFT** Vintage Port 1985 •$42 •(10/31/88)
92 **FERREIRA** Vintage Port 1985 •$28 •(10/31/88)
92 **GRAHAM** Vintage Port 1985 •$47 •(10/31/88)
92 **NIEPOORT** Vintage Port 1985 •$44 •(06/01/90)
91 **DOW** Vintage Port 1985 •$37 •(09/30/87)
91 **FONSECA** Vintage Port 1985 •$40 •(09/30/87)
91 **GRAHAM** Vintage Port 1985 •$47 •(09/30/87) •CS
91 **QUINTA DO NOVAL** Vintage Port 1985 •$35 •(10/31/88)
91 **TAYLOR FLADGATE** Vintage Port 1985 •$53 •(10/31/88)
91 **WARRE** Vintage Port 1985 •$18 •(06/01/90)
90 **COCKBURN** Vintage Port 1985 •$16 •(06/01/90)
90 **KOPKE** Vintage Port 1985 •$14 •(01/01/90)
90 **TAYLOR FLADGATE** Vintage Port 1985 •$53 •(06/01/90)
89 **DOW** Vintage Port 1985 •$23 •(06/01/90)
89 **MARTINEZ** Vintage Port 1985 •$16 •(06/01/90)
89 **NIEPOORT** Vintage Port 1985 •$33 •(01/31/88)
89 **OFFLEY** Vintage Port Boa Vista 1985 •$31 •(06/01/90)
89 **SMITH WOODHOUSE** Vintage Port 1985 •$34 •(06/01/90)
88 **CALEM** Vintage Port 1985 •$42 •(06/01/90)
88 **ROCHA** Vintage Port 1985 •$32 •(04/15/91)
87 **BURMESTER** Vintage Port 1985 •$30 •(12/31/88)
87 **FERREIRA** Vintage Port 1985 •$28 •(11/01/89)
87 **MARTINEZ** Vintage Port 1985 •$29 •(09/30/87)
87 **QUARLES HARRIS** Vintage Port 1985 •$30 •(09/30/87)
87 **SMITH WOODHOUSE** Vintage Port 1985 •$34 •(09/30/87)
87 **VAN ZELLER** Vintage Port Quinta do Roriz 1985 •$NA •(07/01/90)
86 **QUINTA DO NOVAL** Vintage Port 1985 •$35 •(06/01/90)
85 **GOULD CAMPBELL** Vintage Port 1985 •$33 •(06/01/90)
85 **MORGAN (PORT)** Vintage Port 1985 •$NA •(02/01/90)
85 **OFFLEY** Vintage Port Boa Vista 1985 •$31 •(09/30/87)
85 **POCAS JUNIOR** Vintage Port 1985 •$19 •(02/01/90)
85 **QUARLES HARRIS** Vintage Port 1985 •$30 •(06/01/90)

85 **RAMOS-PINTO** Vintage Port 1985 •$32 •(11/01/89)
84 **CALEM** Vintage Port 1985 •$38 •(09/30/87)
84 **CHURCHILL** Vintage Port 1985 •$39 •(09/30/87)
84 **HOOPER** Vintage Port 1985 •$20 •(09/30/87)
84 **REBELLO-VALENTE** Vintage Port 1985 •$42 •(09/30/87)
83 **SANDEMAN** Vintage Port 1985 •$33 •(06/01/90)
81 **CHURCHILL** Vintage Port 1985 •$39 •(02/01/90)
81 **CROFT** Vintage Port 1985 •$14 •(06/01/90)
81 **DELAFORCE** Vintage Port 1985 •$41 •(06/01/90)
81 **GOULD CAMPBELL** Vintage Port 1985 •$33 •(09/30/87)
81 **REBELLO-VALENTE** Vintage Port 1985 •$42 •(06/01/90)
81 **ROZES** Vintage Port 1985 •$21 •(05/01/90)
81 **WIESE & KROHN** Vintage Port 1985 •$32 •(01/01/90)
80 **BARROS** Vintage Port 1985 •$29 •(01/01/90)
80 **HOOPER** Vintage Port 1985 •$20 •(06/01/90)
80 **SANDEMAN** Vintage Port 1985 •$33 •(09/30/87)
80 **VAN ZELLER** Vintage Port 1985 •$NA •(01/01/90)
78 **C. DA SILVA** Vintage Port Presidential 1985 •$30 •(02/01/90)
78 **FONSECA** Vintage Port Quinta do Panascal 1985 •$NA •(02/01/90)
78 **QUINTA DA ROMANEIRA** Vintage Port 1985 •$29 •(01/01/90)
76 **QUINTA DO INFANTADO** Vintage Port 1985 •$33 •(07/01/90)
76 **MESSIA** Vintage Port 1985 •$19 •(09/30/87)
76 **OSBORNE** Vintage Port 1985 •$26 •(02/01/89)
72 **FEIST** Vintage Port 1985 •$25 •(01/01/90)
72 **FEUERHEERD** Vintage Port 1985 •$NA •(01/01/90)
71 **QUINTA DO CRASTO** Vintage Port 1985 •$24 •(01/01/90)
71 **ROYAL OPORTO** Vintage Port 1985 •$16 •(06/01/90)
70 **BORGES** Vintage Port 1985 •$15 •(05/01/90)
70 **VIEIRA DE SOUSA** Vintage Port 1985 •$NA •(01/01/90)
69 **A. PINTOS DOS SANTOS** Vintage Port 1985 •$NA •(01/01/90)
67 **MESSIA** Vintage Port 1985 •$20 •(02/01/90)

1983 Vintage Port
Vintage Rating: 92

97 **COCKBURN** Vintage Port 1983 •$30 •(06/01/90)
97 **TAYLOR FLADGATE** Vintage Port 1983 •$45 •(03/31/87)
95 **GRAHAM** Vintage Port 1983 •$43 •(10/31/88)
95 **SMITH WOODHOUSE** Vintage Port 1983 •$33 •(03/31/87)
94 **DOW** Vintage Port 1983 •$20 •(06/01/90)
94 **WARRE** Vintage Port 1983 •$43 •(12/31/86) •CS
93 **GRAHAM** Vintage Port 1983 •$43 •(06/01/90)
92 **COCKBURN** Vintage Port 1983 •$45 •(08/31/87) •CS
92 **SMITH WOODHOUSE** Vintage Port 1983 •$12 •(06/01/90)
91 **COCKBURN** Vintage Port 1983 •$45 •(10/31/88)
91 **FERREIRA** Vintage Port Quinta do Seixo 1983 •$26 •(11/01/89)
91 **OFFLEY** Vintage Port Boa Vista 1983 •$35 •(01/01/90)
90 **FONSECA** Vintage Port 1983 •$40 •(06/01/90)
90 **GOULD CAMPBELL** Vintage Port 1983 •$34 •(06/01/90)
90 **QUARLES HARRIS** Vintage Port 1983 •$33 •(03/31/87)
89 **FONSECA** Vintage Port 1983 •$40 •(10/31/88)
89 **QUARLES HARRIS** Vintage Port 1983 •$33 •(02/01/90)
89 **RAMOS-PINTO** Vintage Port 1983 •$35 •(11/01/89)
89 **TAYLOR FLADGATE** Vintage Port 1983 •$45 •(06/01/90)
88 **DOW** Vintage Port 1983 •$36 •(10/31/88)
88 **GOULD CAMPBELL** Vintage Port 1983 •$34 •(03/31/87)
88 **TAYLOR FLADGATE** Vintage Port 1983 •$45 •(10/31/88)
88 **WARRE** Vintage Port 1983 •$16 •(06/01/90)
87 **FERREIRA** Vintage Port Quinta do Seixo 1983 •$26 •(10/31/88)
85 **CROFT** Vintage Port Quinta da Roeda 1983 •$22 •(02/01/90)
85 **KOPKE** Vintage Port 1983 •$23 •(01/01/90)
84 **CALEM** Vintage Port 1983 •$40 •(06/01/90)
84 **NIEPOORT** Vintage Port 1983 •$16 •(06/01/90)
84 **VAN ZELLER** Vintage Port Quinta do Roriz 1983 •$22 •(07/01/90)
84 **VAN ZELLER** Vintage Port 1983 •$36 •(01/01/90)
84 **WARRE** Vintage Port 1983 •$43 •(10/31/88)
79 **FONSECA** Vintage Port Quinta do Panascal 1983 •$NA •(02/01/90)
78 **REBELLO-VALENTE** Vintage Port 1983 •$36 •(06/01/90)
77 **MESSIA** Vintage Port Quinta do Cachâo 1983 •$11 •(02/01/90)
76 **BARROS** Vintage Port 1983 •$33 •(01/01/90)
76 **ROYAL OPORTO** Vintage Port 1983 •$15 •(06/01/90)
70 **BORGES** Vintage Port 1983 •$29 •(05/01/90)
69 **CHURCHILL** Vintage Port Agua Alta 1983 •$41 •(07/01/90)
60 **HOOPER** Vintage Port 1983 •$16 •(03/01/90)

1977 Vintage Port
Vintage Rating: 97

100 **FONSECA** Vintage Port 1977 •$70 •(04/01/90)
98 **TAYLOR FLADGATE** Vintage Port 1977 •$75 •(04/01/90)
94 **DOW** Vintage Port 1977 •$37 •(04/01/90)
94 **GRAHAM** Vintage Port 1977 •$66 •(10/31/88)
93 **CROFT** Vintage Port 1977 •$63 •(10/31/88)
93 **GOULD CAMPBELL** Vintage Port 1977 •$29 •(02/01/90)
92 **DOW** Vintage Port 1977 •$61 •(10/31/88)
92 **TAYLOR FLADGATE** Vintage Port 1977 •$75 •(10/31/88)
92 **WARRE** Vintage Port 1977 •$32 •(04/01/90)
91 **FONSECA** Vintage Port 1977 •$70 •(10/31/88)
91 **GRAHAM** Vintage Port 1977 •$66 •(03/16/84) •CS
90 **FERREIRA** Vintage Port 1977 •$51 •(10/31/88)
90 **GRAHAM** Vintage Port 1977 •$66 •(04/01/90)
89 **NIEPOORT** Vintage Port 1977 •$50 •(04/01/90)
89 **QUARLES HARRIS** Vintage Port 1977 •$43 •(02/01/90)
89 **REBELLO-VALENTE** Vintage Port 1977 •$47 •(02/01/90)
89 **SMITH WOODHOUSE** Vintage Port 1977 •$25 •(02/01/90)
89 **WARRE** Vintage Port 1977 •$61 •(10/31/88)
88 **OFFLEY** Vintage Port Boa Vista 1977 •$18 •(01/01/90)
88 **SANDEMAN** Vintage Port 1977 •$74 •(10/31/88)
86 **FERREIRA** Vintage Port 1977 •$51 •(11/01/89)
85 **CROFT** Vintage Port 1977 •$25 •(04/01/90)
85 **SANDEMAN** Vintage Port 1977 •$28 •(06/01/90)
82 **BURMESTER** Vintage Port 1977 •$37 •(01/01/90)
82 **DIEZ HERMANOS** Vintage Port 1977 •$NA •(04/01/90)
81 **ROCHA** Vintage Port 1977 •$19 •(04/30/91)
80 **DELAFORCE** Vintage Port 1977 •$17 •(02/01/90)
78 **MORGAN (PORT)** Vintage Port 1977 •$NA •(01/01/90)
78 **QUINTA DO NOVAL** Vintage Port 1977 •$50 •(10/31/88)
74 **ROYAL OPORTO** Vintage Port 1977 •$30 •(11/01/89)
72 **C. DA SILVA** Vintage Port Presidential 1977 •$39 •(02/01/90)
69 **CALEM** Vintage Port 1977 •$66 •(11/01/89)
69 **FEUERHEERD** Vintage Port 1977 •$17 •(01/01/90)
68 **KOPKE** Vintage Port 1977 •$23 •(01/01/90)
60 **MESSIA** Vintage Port Quinta do Cachâo 1977 •$20 •(02/01/90)

Clos Pegase in Sonoma Valley.

California Cabernet

Here are *Wine Spectator*'s ratings for the six most recent outstanding vintages of California Cabernet Sauvignon and wines blended from Cabernet and other Bordeaux grapes, including red Meritage wines. Also listed are retail prices. The wines are organized in descending order of score, to make it easy to identify the best wines of each vintage.

The vintages included here are 1992, 1991, 1990, 1987, 1986 and 1985. We omitted the 1993, 1989 and 1988 vintages in this section because they are of lesser quality. Wines from these and other years, however, are to be found in the main listings.

The date of the issue of *Wine Spectator* in which the rating was first published is in parentheses. In general, wines for which no issue date appears were tasted between April 15, 1994 and June 15, 1996.

1992 CALIFORNIA CABERNET | VINTAGE RATING: 93

98 **GROTH** Cabernet Sauvignon Napa Valley Reserve 1992 • $70 • (04/30/96) • CS

96 **ARAUJO** Cabernet Sauvignon Napa Valley Eisele Vineyard 1992 • $40 • (11/15/95) • CS

96 **FLORA SPRINGS** Cabernet Sauvignon Napa Valley Rutherford Reserve 1992 • $40 • (11/15/95)

95 **BERINGER** Cabernet Sauvignon Napa Valley Private Reserve 1992 • $45 • (11/15/95) • CS

95 **ST. CLEMENT** Oroppas Napa Valley 1992 • $25 • (09/30/94) • CS

94 **DALLA VALLE** Maya Napa Valley 1992 • $75 • (12/15/95)

94 **LEWIS CELLARS** Cabernet Sauvignon Napa Valley Oakville Ranch 1992 • $30 • (11/30/95)

94 **STAG'S LEAP WINE CELLARS** S.L.V. Cask 23 Napa Valley 1992 • $80 • (12/15/95) • CS

94 **THE HESS COLLECTION** Cabernet Sauvignon Napa Valley 1992 • $18 • (11/15/95) • SS

93 **ANDERSON'S CONN VALLEY** Cabernet Sauvignon Napa Valley Estate Reserve 1992 • $30 • (11/15/95)

93 **CRONIN** Concerto Stags Leap District Robinson Vineyard 1992 • $17 • (04/30/96)

93 **ETUDE** Cabernet Sauvignon Napa Valley 1992 • $30 • (11/30/95)

93 **FAR NIENTE** Cabernet Sauvignon Napa Valley 1992 • $45 • (11/15/95)

93 **FORMAN** Cabernet Sauvignon Napa Valley 1992 • $30 • (06/15/95) • CS

93 **PAUL HOBBS** Cabernet Sauvignon Carneros Napa Valley Hyde Vineyard 1992 • $30 • (12/15/95)

93 **WHITEHALL LANE** Cabernet Sauvignon Napa Valley Morisoli Vineyard 1992 • $28 • (10/15/95)

92 **A. RAFANELLI** Cabernet Sauvignon Dry Creek Valley Unfiltered 1992 • $17 • (09/30/95) • SS

92 **ALTAMURA** Cabernet Sauvignon Napa Valley 1992 • $28

92 **ARROWOOD** Cabernet Sauvignon Sonoma County 1992 • $25 • (11/15/95)

92 **ARROWOOD** Cabernet Sauvignon Sonoma County Réserve Spéciale 1992 • $35 • (12/15/95)

92 **CAYMUS** Cabernet Sauvignon Napa Valley Special Selection 1992 • $100 • (05/15/96) • CS

92 **CHIMNEY ROCK** Reserve Stags Leap District 1992 • $30 • (12/15/95)

92 **COLGIN** Cabernet Sauvignon Napa Valley Herb Lamb Vineyard 1992 • $29 • (10/15/95)

92 **CORISON** Cabernet Sauvignon Napa Valley 1992 • $28 • (11/30/95) • CS

92 **COSENTINO** Meritage Coz Napa Valley 1992 • $45 • (12/15/95)

92 **DALLA VALLE** Cabernet Sauvignon Napa Valley 1992 • $30 • (12/15/95) • CS

92 **DIAMOND CREEK** Cabernet Sauvignon Napa Valley Gravelly Meadow 1992 • $50 • (11/15/94) • CS

92 **FLORA SPRINGS** Trilogy Napa Valley 1992 • $27 • (11/30/95) • CS

92 **JUSTIN** Isosceles Reserve San Luis Obispo County 1992 • $25 • (12/15/95)

92 **LA JOTA** Cabernet Sauvignon Howell Mountain 11th Anniversary Release 1992 • $38

92 **ST. FRANCIS** Cabernet Sauvignon Sonoma County Reserve 1992 • $24 • (11/30/95)

92 **STONESTREET** Legacy Alexander Valley 1992 • $35 • (09/30/95) • CS

92 **SCREAMING EAGLE** Cabernet Sauvignon Napa Valley 1992 • $50 • (02/29/96)

92 **VILLA MT. EDEN** Cabernet Sauvignon Mendocino Signature Series 1992 • $45 • (03/31/95)

92 **WHITEHALL LANE** Cabernet Sauvignon Napa Valley Reserve 1992 • $23 • (10/15/95)

91 **DIAMOND CREEK** Cabernet Sauvignon Napa Valley Volcanic Hill 1992 • $50 • (11/15/94)

91 **GROTH** Cabernet Sauvignon Napa Valley 1992 • $20 • (09/30/95) • CS

91 **JUDD'S HILL** Cabernet Sauvignon Napa Valley 1992 • $26 • (12/15/95)

91 **KENDALL-JACKSON** Cabernet Sauvignon California Grand Reserve 1992 • $35 • (11/30/95)

91 **OPUS ONE** Napa Valley 1992 • $75 • (12/15/95) • CS

91 **PEJU** Cabernet Sauvignon Napa Valley HB Vineyard 1992 • $35 • (12/15/95)

91 **PHILIP TOGNI** Cabernet Sauvignon Napa Valley 1992 • $32 • (11/15/94) • CS

91 **PINE RIDGE** Cabernet Sauvignon Napa Valley Rutherford Cuvée 1992 • $16 • (11/15/95) • SS

91 **ROBERT MONDAVI** Cabernet Sauvignon 1992 • $28 • (09/30/95)

91 **ROBERT MONDAVI** Cabernet Sauvignon Napa Valley Reserve 1992 • $55 • (07/31/95) • CS

91 **SHAFER** Cabernet Sauvignon Stags Leap District 1992 • $22 • (09/30/95) • CS

91 **STAG'S LEAP WINE CELLARS** Cabernet Sauvignon Napa Valley Fay 1992 • $35 • (12/15/95) • CS

91 **STAGLIN FAMILY** Cabernet Sauvignon Napa Valley 1992 • $28 • (12/15/95)

91 **STONESTREET** Cabernet Sauvignon Alexander Valley 1992 • $25 • (10/31/95)

90 **CHATEAU MONTELENA** Cabernet Sauvignon Napa Valley Calistoga Cuvée 1992 • $15 • (11/15/94) • SS

90 **CONN CREEK** Anthology Napa Valley 1992 • $30 • (12/15/95)

90 **CORNERSTONE** Cabernet Sauvignon Howell Mountain Beatty Ranch 1992 • $33 • (12/15/95)

90 **DIAMOND CREEK** Cabernet Sauvignon Napa Valley Red Rock Terrace 1992 • $50 • (11/15/94)

90 **DUCKHORN** Cabernet Sauvignon Napa Valley 1992 • $24 • (10/31/95) • SS

90 **GUENOC** Cabernet Sauvignon Napa Valley Bella Vista Vineyard Reserve 1992 • $25 • (12/15/95)

90 **GUENOC** Cabernet Sauvignon Napa Valley Beckstoffer IV Vineyard Reserve 1992 • $40 • (12/15/95)

90 **HARRISON** Cabernet Sauvignon Napa Valley 1992 • $33 • (11/15/95)

90 **HARTWELL** Cabernet Sauvignon Stags Leap District 1992 • $50 • (11/15/95)

90 **JARVIS** Cabernet Sauvignon Napa Valley 1992 • $48 • (08/31/95)

90 **JOSEPH PHELPS** Insignia Napa Valley 1992 • $50 • (09/30/95) • CS

90 **MOUNT EDEN** Cabernet Sauvignon Santa Cruz Mountains Old Vine Reserve 1992 • $35 • (06/15/96)

90 **OAKVILLE RANCH** Cabernet Sauvignon Napa Valley 1992 • $24 • (12/15/95)

90 **PETER MICHAEL** Cabernet Sauvignon Knights Valley Les Pavots 1992 • $29 • (12/15/95)

90 **PINE RIDGE** Cabernet Sauvignon Stags Leap District 1992 • $31 • (12/15/95)

90 **SIGNORELLO** Cabernet Sauvignon Napa Valley Founder's Reserve 1992 • $32 • (09/15/95) • CS

90 **SILVERADO** Cabernet Sauvignon Napa Valley 1992 • $19 • (03/31/95) • SS

90 **SPOTTSWOODE** Cabernet Sauvignon Napa Valley 1992 • $39 • (11/30/95) • CS

90 **ST. CLEMENT** Cabernet Sauvignon Napa Valley 1992 • $24 • (10/31/95)

90 **SWANSON** Cabernet Sauvignon Napa Valley 1992 • $22 • (12/15/95)

90 **SEQUOIA GROVE** Cabernet Sauvignon Napa Valley 1992 • $18 • (07/31/95) • SS

90 **THOMAS FOGARTY** Cabernet Sauvignon Napa Valley Vallerga Vineyards 1992 • $25 • (04/30/96)

90 **ZIA CELLARS** Cabernet Sauvignon Napa Valley 1992 • $24 • (04/30/96)

89 **ATLAS PEAK** Cabernet Sauvignon Atlas Peak 1992 • $18 • (12/15/95)

89 **BEAULIEU** Cabernet Sauvignon Napa Valley Georges de Latour Private Reserve 1992 • $40 • (12/15/95)

89 **BRYANT FAMILY VINEYARD** Cabernet Sauvignon Napa Valley 1992 • $32 • (05/31/96)

89 **CAYMUS** Cabernet Sauvignon Napa Valley 1992 • $25 • (09/30/95)

89 **CHATEAU SOUVERAIN** Cabernet Sauvignon Alexander Valley Winemaker's Reserve 1992 • $16 • (12/15/95)

89 **CHATEAU ST. JEAN** Cabernet Sauvignon Sonoma County Cinq Cépages 1992 • $18 • (02/29/96)

89 **CLOS DU BOIS** Marlstone Vineyard Alexander Valley 1992 • $21 • (11/30/95)

89 **CLOS DU BOIS** Cabernet Sauvignon Alexander Valley Briarcrest Vineyard 1992 • $20 • (11/30/95)

89 **DRY CREEK** Cabernet Sauvignon Dry Creek Valley 1992 • $16 • (10/15/95)

89 **E. & J. GALLO** Cabernet Sauvignon Dry Creek Valley Frei Ranch Vineyard Gallo Sonoma 1992 • $16 • (11/15/95)

89 **ELYSE** Cabernet Sauvignon Napa Valley Morisoli Vineyard 1992 • $30 • (04/30/96)

89 **ESTANCIA** Meritage Alexander Valley 1992 • $15 • (09/30/95)

89 **FERRARI-CARANO** Siena Sonoma County 1992 • $20 • (09/30/95)

89 **GREENWOOD RIDGE** Cabernet Sauvignon Anderson Valley 1992 • $18 • (09/15/95)

89 **GUENOC** Meritage Langtry California 1992 • $35 • (12/15/95)

89 **GARY FARRELL** Cabernet Sauvignon Sonoma County Ladi's Vineyard 1992 • $20 • (07/31/95)

89 **JOSEPH PHELPS** Cabernet Sauvignon Napa Valley Backus Vineyard 1992 • $45 • (12/15/95)

89 **LIVINGSTON** Cabernet Sauvignon Napa Valley Moffett Vineyard 1992 • $30 • (12/15/95)

89 **MARTIN RAY** Cabernet Sauvignon California Saratoga Cuvée 1992 • $28 • (10/31/95)

89 **MONTICELLO** Cabernet Sauvignon Napa Valley Jefferson Cuvée 1992 • $18 • (12/15/95)

89 **OPTIMA** Cabernet Sauvignon Alexander Valley 1992 • $25 • (12/15/95)

89 **PAHLMEYER** Napa Valley 1992 • $34 • (12/15/95)

89 **RIDGE** Cabernet Sauvignon Santa Cruz Mountains 1992 • $16 • (11/15/94)

89 **RIDGE** Cabernet Sauvignon Santa Cruz Mountains Monte Bello 1987 • $58 • (11/15/90)

89 **ROSENTHAL** Cabernet Sauvignon California 1992 • $22 • (12/15/95)

89 **S. ANDERSON** Cabernet Sauvignon Stags Leap District Richard Chambers Vineyard 1992 • $46 • (12/15/95)

89 **SEQUOIA GROVE** Cabernet Sauvignon Rutherford Estate Reserve 1992 • $30 • (12/31/95)

89 **SIMI** Cabernet Sauvignon Alexander Valley 1992 • $15 • (10/15/95)

89 **STONEHEDGE** Cabernet Sauvignon Napa Valley Winemaker's Reserve 1992 • $10 • (11/30/95) • BB

88 **BEAULIEU** Tapestry Red Napa Valley Reserve 1992 • $20 • (04/30/96)

88 **CAFARO** Cabernet Sauvignon Napa Valley 1992 • $26 • (12/15/95)

88 **CHIMNEY ROCK** Elevage Stags Leap District 1992 • $30 • (12/15/95)

88 **CINNABAR** Cabernet Sauvignon Santa Cruz Mountains Saratoga Vineyard 1992 • $20 • (12/15/95)

88 **CLOS PEGASE** Cabernet Sauvignon Napa Valley 1992 • $19 • (10/15/95)

88 **CONN CREEK** Cabernet Sauvignon Napa Valley Limited Release 1992 • $18 • (12/15/95)

88 **COSENTINO** Cabernet Sauvignon Napa Valley Punched Cap Fermented Unfined 1992 • $16 • (09/15/95)

88 **CUVAISON** Cabernet Sauvignon Napa Valley 1992 • $26 • (12/15/95)

88 **CLOS LACHANCE** Cabernet Sauvignon Santa Cruz Mountains 1992 • $20 • (07/31/95)

88 **DUNN** Cabernet Sauvignon Napa Valley 1992 • $33 • (12/15/95)

88 **EHLERS GROVE** Cabernet Sauvignon Napa Valley 1992 • $15 • (12/15/95)

88 **GIRARD** Cabernet Sauvignon Napa Valley Reserve 1992 • $40 • (12/15/95)

88 **GUENOC** Meritage Lake County 1992 • $15 • (12/15/95)

88 **JUSTIN** Cabernet Sauvignon San Luis Obispo County 1992 • $18 • (12/15/95)

88 **LA JOTA** Cabernet Sauvignon Howell Mountain Selection 1992 • $18 • (06/15/95)

88 **LAUREL GLEN** Cabernet Sauvignon North Coast Terra Rosa 1992 • $10 • (04/30/95) • SS

88 **LAUREL GLEN** Cabernet Sauvignon Sonoma Mountain Counterpoint 1992 • $16 • (12/15/95)

88 **MARKHAM** Cabernet Sauvignon Napa Valley 1992 • $17 • (11/30/95)

88 **MAZZOCCO** Cabernet Sauvignon Sonoma County 1992 • $18 • (04/30/96)

88 **MERRYVALE** Cabernet Sauvignon Napa Valley 1992 • $24 • (12/15/95)

88 **MOUNT VEEDER** Reserve Napa Valley 1992 • $40

88 **NEWTON** Claret Napa Valley 1992 • $13 • (11/15/94)

88 **PAHLMEYER** Jayson Napa Valley 1992 • $20 • (12/31/94)

88 **PARDUCCI** Cabernet Sauvignon Mendocino County 1992 • $8 • (11/15/95) • BB

88 **PLAM** Cabernet Sauvignon Napa Valley 1992 • $30 • (11/15/94)

88 **RAYMOND** Cabernet Sauvignon Napa Valley 1992 • $17 • (11/30/95)

88 **REMICK RIDGE VINEYARDS** Cabernet Sauvignon Sonoma Valley 1992 • $19 • (05/31/96)

88 **SAUSAL** Cabernet Sauvignon Alexander Valley 1992 • $14 • (10/31/95)

88 **SHENANDOAH** Cabernet Sauvignon Amador County 1992 • $10 • (11/15/94) • BB

88 **SMITH & HOOK** Cabernet Sauvignon Santa Lucia Highlands Masterpiece Edition 1992 • $30 • (12/15/95)

88 **STAG'S LEAP WINE CELLARS** Cabernet Sauvignon Napa Valley S.L.V. 1992 • $35 • (12/15/95)

88 **STERLING** Cabernet Sauvignon Napa Valley Diamond Mountain Ranch Vineyard 1992 • $17 • (10/31/95)

88 **TRUCHARD** Cabernet Sauvignon Napa Valley Carneros 1992 • $20 • (03/31/96)

88 **TOM EDDY** Cabernet Sauvignon Napa Valley 1992 • $36 • (05/15/96)

88 **VILLA MT. EDEN** Cabernet Sauvignon Napa Valley Grand Reserve 1992 • $16 • (04/30/96)

88 **VON STRASSER** Cabernet Sauvignon Napa Valley Diamond Mountain 1992 • $28 • (02/28/95)

88 **VENGE VINEYARDS** Cabernet Sauvignon Napa Valley Family Reserve 1992 • $NA • (06/30/96)

88 **VIADER** Napa Valley 1992 • $28 • (07/31/95)

88 **ZD** Cabernet Sauvignon Napa Valley Reserve 1992 • $34 • (04/30/96)

87 **ARROWOOD** Cabernet Sauvignon Sonoma County Domaine du Grand Archer 1992 • $9 • (11/15/94)

87 **BARNETT** Cabernet Sauvignon Spring Mountain 1992 • $32 • (05/31/95)

87 **BENZIGER** Cabernet Sauvignon Sonoma County 1992 • $13 • (09/15/95)

87 **BERINGER** Meritage Knights Valley 1992 • $13 • (11/15/95)

87 **BERINGER** Cabernet Sauvignon Knights Valley 1992 • $15 • (08/31/95)

87 **BYINGTON** Cabernet Sauvignon Alexander Valley Smith Reichel Vineyard 1992 • $15 • (12/15/95)

87 **CARMENET** Cabernet Sauvignon Sonoma County Moon Mountain Dynamite Cabernet 1992 • $15 • (09/15/95)

87 **COSENTINO** Meritage The Poet Napa Valley 1992 • $24 • (12/15/95)

87 **DOMAIN HILL & MAYES** Cabernet Sauvignon Napa Valley Clos Fontaine du Mont Reserve 1992 • $32 • (12/15/95)

87 **E. & J. GALLO** Cabernet Sauvignon Sonoma County 1992 • $12 • (11/15/95)

87 **FOXEN** Cabernet Sauvignon Santa Barbara County 1992 • $20 • (10/31/94)

87 **FRANCISCAN** Cabernet Sauvignon Napa Valley Oakville Estate 1992 • $15 • (12/15/95)

87 **GUNDLACH BUNDSCHU** Cabernet Sauvignon Sonoma Valley Rhinefarm Vineyards 1992 • $15 • (10/31/95)

87 **HESS SELECT** Cabernet Sauvignon California 1992 • $9 • (11/15/94) • BB

87 **JEKEL** Cabernet Sauvignon Arroyo Seco Sanctuary Estate 1992 • $13 • (12/15/95)

87 **JOSEPH PHELPS** Cabernet Sauvignon Napa Valley 1992 • $20 • (09/30/95)

87 **JUSTIN** Justification San Luis Obispo County 1992 • $20 • (05/15/95)

87 **KENWOOD** Cabernet Sauvignon Sonoma Valley Jack London Vineyard 1992 • $20 • (10/31/95)

87 **LAMBERT BRIDGE** Cabernet Sauvignon Sonoma County 1992 • $15 • (12/15/95)

87 **LIVINGSTON** Cabernet Sauvignon Napa Valley Stanley's Selection 1992 • $18 • (08/31/95)

87 **LYETH** A Red Blend Alexander Valley 1992 • $18 • (08/31/95)

87 **MAZZOCCO** Matrix Dry Creek Valley 1992 • $28

87 **MOUNT VEEDER** Cabernet Sauvignon Napa Valley 1992 • $25 • (12/15/95)

87 **MURPHY-GOODE** Cabernet Sauvignon Alexander Valley Murphy Ranch 1992 • $15 • (05/15/95)

87 **NAPA RIDGE** Cabernet Sauvignon Central Coast 1992 • $8 • (10/15/95) • BB

87 **NORMAN VINEYARD** Cabernet Sauvignon Paso Robles 1992 • $13 • (11/15/94)

87 **PARADIGM** Cabernet Sauvignon Napa Valley 1992 • $28 • (12/15/95)

87 **PEACHY CANYON** Cabernet Sauvignon Central Coast 1992 • $18 • (11/15/94)

87 **PEJU** Meritage Napa Valley 1992 • $24 • (11/15/94)

87 **PINE RIDGE** Cabernet Sauvignon Stags Leap District 1992 • $30 • (11/15/94)

87 **POPE VALLEY CELLARS** Cabernet Sauvignon Napa Valley La Dolce DeVita Vineyard 1992 • $15 • (12/15/95)

87 **PRIDE** Cabernet Sauvignon Napa Valley 1992 • $18 • (12/15/95)

87 **ROBERT CRAIG** Cabernet Sauvignon Napa Valley 1992 • $20 • (10/15/95)

87 **RUTHERFORD VINEYARDS** Cabernet Sauvignon Napa Valley Rutherford Bench 1992 • $8 • (12/15/95)

87 **SADDLEBACK** Cabernet Sauvignon Napa Valley 1992 • $17 • (12/15/95)

87 **SEBASTIANI** Cabernet Sauvignon Sonoma County 1992 • $10 • (11/15/95) • BB

87 **STERLING** Cabernet Sauvignon Reserve Napa Valley 1992 • $40 • (12/15/95)

87 **TREFETHEN** Cabernet Sauvignon Napa Valley 1992 • $21 • (02/29/96)

87 **V. SATTUI** Cabernet Sauvignon Napa Valley Julian Schwinger Reserve Stock 1992 • $50 • (04/30/96)

87 **VICHON** Cabernet Sauvignon California Coastal Selection 1992 • $9 • (01/31/95) • BB

87 **VICHON** Cabernet Sauvignon Napa Valley 1992 • $16 • (12/15/95)

87 **WHITEHALL LANE** Cabernet Sauvignon Napa Valley 1992 • $15 • (10/15/95)

86 **ALEXANDER VALLEY VINEYARDS** Cabernet Sauvignon Alexander Valley Wetzel Family Estate 1992 • $14 • (05/31/95)

86 **BARON HERZOG** Cabernet Sauvignon California 1992 • $9 • (12/31/94) • BB

86 **BEAULIEU** Cabernet Sauvignon Napa Valley Rutherford 1992 • $12 • (11/30/95)

86 **CHAPPELLET** Cabernet Sauvignon Napa Valley Pritchard Hill Estates 1992 • $15 • (09/15/95)

86 **CIRRI** Cabernet Sauvignon Alexander Valley 1992 • $10 • (12/15/95)

86 **CONCANNON** Assemblage Reserve Central Coast 1992 • $15 • (12/15/95)

86 **DE LOACH** Cabernet Sauvignon Russian River Valley 1992 • $15 • (12/15/95)

86 **DEHLINGER** Cabernet Sauvignon Russian River Valley 1992 • $18

86 **DURNEY** Cabernet Sauvignon Carmel Valley Dances On Your Palate Private Reserve 1992 • $31 • (05/31/96)

86 **FATHOM** Cabernet Sauvignon Santa Ynez Valley 1992 • $24 • (11/15/94)

86 **J. LOHR** Cabernet Sauvignon California Cypress 1992 • $9 • (11/30/95) • BB

86 **KENWOOD** Cabernet Sauvignon Sonoma Valley 25th Anniversary Vintage 1992 • $16 • (10/31/95)

86 **LOCKWOOD** Cabernet Sauvignon Monterey 1992 • $14 • (09/30/95)

86 **MARTIN RAY** Cabernet Sauvignon Napa Valley 1992 • $28 • (10/31/95)

86 **RAVENSWOOD** Cabernet Sauvignon Sonoma County 1992 • $15 • (11/15/94)

86 **ROCKING HORSE** Cabernet Sauvignon Stags Leap District Robinson Vineyard 1992 • $24 • (04/15/95)

86 **SANTA BARBARA WINERY** Cabernet Sauvignon Santa Ynez Valley Reserve 1992 • $16 • (12/15/95)

86 **SCHUG** Cabernet Sauvignon Sonoma Valley Heritage Reserve 1992 • $25 • (11/15/94)

85 **CHATEAU MARGARITE** Cabernet Sauvignon Napa Valley 1992 • $15 • (12/15/95)

85 **CHATEAU SOUVERAIN** Cabernet Sauvignon Alexander Valley 1992 • $12 • (03/31/95)

85 **DE LORIMIER** Mosaic Alexander Valley Meritage 1992 • $18 • (03/31/96)

85 **DICKERSON** Ruby Cabernet Napa Valley 1992 • $10 • (05/15/95)

85 **DOMAINE ST. GEORGE** Cabernet Sauvignon California Vintage Reserve 1992 • $6 • (11/15/94) • BB

85 **DUNCAN PEAK** Cabernet Sauvignon Mendocino County 1992 • $16 • (11/15/94)

85 **FETZER** Cabernet Sauvignon North Coast Barrel Select 1992 • $12 • (12/15/95)

85 **GUENOC** Cabernet Sauvignon Lake County 1992 • $15 • (12/15/95)

85 **KONRAD** Mélange à Trois Mendocino 1992 • $13 • (12/15/95)

85 **LAUREL GLEN** Cabernet Sauvignon Sonoma Mountain 1992 • $33 • (12/15/95)

85 **LOS ENCANTOS** Cabernet Sauvignon Napa Valley Covenant Reserve 1992 • $14 • (02/29/96)

85 **M.G. VALLEJO** Cabernet Sauvignon California 1992 • $6 • (11/30/95) • BB

85 **MCDOWELL** Cabernet Sauvignon Mendocino 1992 • $10 • (12/15/95)

85 **MILL CREEK** Cabernet Sauvignon Dry Creek Valley 1992 • $12 • (12/15/95)

85 **ROSENBLUM** Holbrook Mitchell Trio Napa Valley 1992 • $23 • (11/15/94)

85 **ROUND HILL** Cabernet Sauvignon Napa Valley 1992 • $12 • (12/15/95)

85 **ST. FRANCIS** Cabernet Sauvignon Sonoma County 1992 • $10 • (11/15/94)

85 **STERLING** Cabernet Sauvignon Napa Valley 1992 • $14 • (11/30/95)

85 **TAFT STREET** Cabernet Sauvignon California 1992 • $9 • (12/15/95)

85 **TITUS** Cabernet Sauvignon Napa Valley 1992 • $19 • (12/15/95)

85 **WEINSTOCK** Cabernet Sauvignon Sonoma County 1992 • $9 • (05/31/95)

85 **WHITE OAK** Cabernet Sauvignon Alexander Valley 1992 • $14 • (12/15/95)

85 **WILLIAM HILL** Cabernet Sauvignon Napa Valley Reserve 1992 • $24 • (12/15/95)

84 **BUEHLER** Cabernet Sauvignon Napa Valley 1992 • $14 • (12/15/95)

84 **CEDAR BROOK** Cabernet Sauvignon Napa Valley 1992 • $8 • (11/15/94)

84 **CHARLES KRUG** Cabernet Sauvignon Napa Valley 1992 • $12 • (12/15/95)

84 **CHATOM** Cabernet Sauvignon Calaveras County 1992 • $12 • (06/15/95)

84 **CHRISTOPHE** Cabernet Sauvignon Napa County 1992 • $9 • (12/15/95)

84 **CONCANNON** Cabernet Sauvignon Central Coast Selected Vineyard 1992 • $10 • (11/15/94)

84 **DOUGLASS HILL** Cabernet Sauvignon Napa Valley 1992 • $15 • (12/15/95)

84 **GLASS MOUNTAIN QUARRY** Cabernet Sauvignon California 1992 • $10 • (12/15/95)

84 **HANNA** Cabernet Sauvignon Alexander Valley 1992 • $16 • (12/15/95)

84 **J. PEDRONCELLI** Cabernet Sauvignon Alexander Valley Morris Fay Vineyards Single Vineyard Selection 1992 • $13 • (03/31/96)

84 **J. PEDRONCELLI** Cabernet Sauvignon Alexander Valley Fay Vineyard 1992 • $13 • (12/15/95)

84 **LIPARITA** Cabernet Sauvignon Howell Mountain 1992 • $28 • (12/15/95)

84 **MARTIN BROTHERS** Etrusco Paso Robles 1992 • $18 • (11/15/93)

84 **MICHAEL SULLBERG** Cabernet Sauvignon Central Coast 1992 • $6 • (12/15/95)

84 **MOUNT KONOCTI** Cabernet Sauvignon Lake County Kelsey 1992 • $10 • (11/15/94)

84 **PAUL HOBBS** Cabernet Sauvignon Howell Mountain Liparita Vineyard 1992 • $35 • (05/15/96)

84 **PEJU** Cabernet Sauvignon Napa Valley 1992 • $18 • (12/15/95)

84 **RAVENSWOOD** Mountain Claret Sonoma County 1992 • $12 • (09/15/95)

84 **ROBERT MONDAVI** Cabernet Sauvignon Oakville 1992 • $28 • (09/30/95)

84 **SEGHESIO** Cabernet Sauvignon Sonoma County 1992 • $9 • (11/15/94)

84 **STELTZNER** Claret Stags Leap District 1992 • $11 • (03/31/95)

84 **VICHON** Cabernet Sauvignon Stags Leap District 1992 • $31 • (03/31/96)

84 **WELLINGTON** Cabernet Sauvignon Sonoma County Mohrhardt Ridge Vineyard 1992 • $14 • (12/15/95)

84 **WILLIAM HILL** Cabernet Sauvignon Napa Valley 1992 • $14 • (12/15/95)

83 **BANDIERA** Cabernet Sauvignon Napa Valley 1992 • $8 • (09/30/95)

83 **BYINGTON** Cabernet Sauvignon Santa Cruz Mountains Bates Ranch 1992 • $22 • (12/15/95)

83 **CAIN** Cuvée Napa Valley 1992 • $16 • (12/15/95)

83 **CAMELOT** Cabernet Sauvignon Central Coast 1992 • $11 • (11/15/94)

83 **CANYON ROAD** Cabernet Sauvignon California 1992 • $7 • (11/15/94)

83 **CHAPPELLET** Cabernet Sauvignon Napa Valley 1992 • $20 • (03/31/96)

83 **CHIMNEY ROCK** Cabernet Sauvignon Stags Leap District 1992 • $22 • (05/15/96)

83 **CRESTON** Cabernet Sauvignon Paso Robles 1992 • $10 • (12/15/95)

83 **FIRESTONE** Cabernet Sauvignon Santa Ynez Valley 1992 • $12 • (12/15/95)

83 **FOREST GLEN** Cabernet Sauvignon Sonoma County Barrel Select 1992 • $10 • (11/15/94)

83 **HAHN** Cabernet Sauvignon Santa Lucia Highlands 1992 • $10 • (08/31/95)

83 **HUSCH** Cabernet Sauvignon Mendocino La Ribera Red 1992 • $8 • (11/15/94)

83 **JEKEL** Meritage Sanctuary Estate Arroyo Seco 1992 • $13 • (12/15/95)

83 **MONTEVINA** Cabernet Sauvignon California 1992 • $9 • (12/15/95)

83 **MONTICELLO** Cabernet Sauvignon Napa Valley Corley Select Reserve 1992 • $28 • (12/15/95)

83 **MOUNT EDEN** Cabernet Sauvignon Santa Cruz Mountains 1992 • $16 • (05/31/95)

83 **PETERSON** Cabernet Sauvignon Dry Creek Valley 1992 • $16 • (09/15/95)

83 **RODNEY STRONG** Cabernet Sauvignon Sonoma County 1992 • $10 • (06/15/95)

83 **ROUND HILL** Cabernet Sauvignon California 1992 • $7 • (12/15/95)

83 **SMITH & HOOK** Cabernet Sauvignon Santa Lucia Highlands 1992 • $18 • (12/15/95)

83 **STAUB'S; RUSTY*** Cabernet Sauvignon California 1992 • $10 • (12/15/95)

83 **TOPOLOS** Cabernet Sauvignon Sonoma County 1992 • $18 • (11/15/94)

83 **TUDAL** Cabernet Sauvignon Napa Valley 1992 • $18 • (12/15/95)

83 **VINE CLIFF** Cabernet Sauvignon Napa Valley 1992 • $30 • (05/15/96)

83 **WELLINGTON** Cabernet Sauvignon Mount Veeder Random Ridge 1992 • $16 • (12/15/95)

83 **WOODBRIDGE** Cabernet Sauvignon California Barrel Aged 1992 • $6 • (12/15/95)

82 **ARCIERO** Cabernet Sauvignon Paso Robles 1992 • $9 • (12/15/95)

82 **BELVEDERE** Cabernet Sauvignon Sonoma County 1992 • $12 • (03/31/96)

82 **BON MARCHE** Cabernet Sauvignon Napa Valley 1992 • $8 • (03/31/94)

82 **BRUTOCAO** Cabernet Sauvignon Mendocino Albert Vineyard 1992 • $13 • (07/31/95)

82 **COOPER-GARROD** Cabernet Sauvignon Santa Cruz Mountains 1992 • $20 • (03/31/96)

82 **DUNNEWOOD** Cabernet Sauvignon Alexander Valley Seven Arches Vineyard Gold Label Select 1992 • $10 • (02/29/96)

82 **ESTANCIA** Cabernet Sauvignon Alexander Valley 1992 • $10 • (11/15/94)

82 **IRON HORSE** Cabernet Sauvignon Alexander Valley T-T Reserve 1992 • $20 • (04/30/96)

82 **KENDALL-JACKSON** Cabernet Sauvignon California Vintner's Reserve 1992 • $14 • (04/30/95)

82 **LOUIS M. MARTINI** Cabernet Sauvignon North Coast 1992 • $9 • (12/15/95)

82 **MOONDANCE** Cabernet Sauvignon Napa Valley 1992 • $10 • (07/31/95)

82 **NORMAN VINEYARD** Cabernet Sauvignon Paso Robles No Nonsense Red 1992 • $9 • (11/15/94)

82 **PLAM** Cabernet Sauvignon California 1992 • $6 • (12/15/95)

82 **R.H. PHILLIPS** Cabernet Sauvignon California 1992 • $7 • (05/15/96)

82 **RANCHO SISQUOC** Cabernet Sauvignon Santa Maria Valley 1992 • $15 • (12/15/95)

82 **ROBERT MONDAVI** Cabernet Sauvignon California Woodbridge 1992 • $6 • (11/15/94) • BB

82 **STE. CLAIRE** Cabernet Sauvignon California 1992 • $11 • (11/15/94)

82 **STEVENOT** Cabernet Sauvignon Calaveras County Reserve 1992 • $10 • (07/31/95)

81 **BOGLE** Cabernet Sauvignon California 1992 • $6 • (05/15/94)

81 **RICHARDSON** Cabernet Sauvignon Sonoma Valley Horne 1992 • $12 • (11/15/94)

80 **BUENA VISTA** Cabernet Sauvignon Carneros 1992 • $12 • (12/15/95)

80 **IVAN TAMAS** Cabernet Sauvignon Livermore Valley 1992 • $7 • (12/15/95)

79 **GRGICH HILLS** Cabernet Sauvignon Napa Valley 1992 • $26

79 **LONE OAK** Cabernet Sauvignon Monterey 1992 • $6 • (11/15/94)

79 **MARTIN BROTHERS** Etrusco Paso Robles 1992 • $18 • (02/28/95)

79 **MOUNTAIN VIEW** Cabernet Sauvignon North Coast 1992 • $6 • (11/15/94)

79 **NAPA RIDGE** Cabernet Sauvignon North Coast Coastal Oak Barrel 1992 • $8 • (11/15/94)

78 **BEL ARBORS** Cabernet Sauvignon California 1992 • $7 • (01/31/95)

78 **DURNEY** Cabernet Sauvignon Carmel Valley Dances On Your Palate Private Reserve 1992 • $31 • (03/31/96)

78 **FORESTVILLE** Cabernet Sauvignon California 1992 • $6 • (11/15/94)

78 **GICOMA CELLARS** Cabernet Sauvignon Napa Valley Pointer Run Vineyards 1992 • $14 • (03/31/96)

77 **BOEGER** Meritage El Dorado 1992 • $15 • (03/31/96)

77 **MAACAMA CREEK** Cabernet Sauvignon Alexander Valley Reserve 1992 • $12 • (11/15/94)

77 **PHOENIX VINEYARDS** Hillside Rogue Napa Valley 1992 •$16 •(04/30/96)

75 **GROVE STREET** Cabernet Sauvignon California Vineyard Select 1992 •$7 •(11/15/94)

75 **JENNER VINEYARDS** Cabernet Sauvignon Dry Creek Valley 1992 •$6 •(03/31/96)

75 **NOMINEE** Cabernet Sauvignon Napa Valley 1992 •$7 •(11/15/94)

74 **KEENAN** Cabernet Sauvignon Napa Valley 1992 •$20

73 **PAGOR** Cabernet Sauvignon California 1992 •$12 •(03/31/96)

72 **HACIENDA** Cabernet Sauvignon California Clair de Lune 1992 •$7 •(11/15/94)

1991 California Cabernet
Vintage Rating:91

99 **CAYMUS** Cabernet Sauvignon Napa Valley Special Selection 1991 •$100 •(04/15/95) •CS

97 **FLORA SPRINGS** Cabernet Sauvignon Napa Valley Reserve 1991 •$33 •(09/30/94) •CS

95 **GROTH** Cabernet Sauvignon Napa Valley Reserve 1991 •$50 •(04/15/95) •CS

94 **BERINGER** Cabernet Sauvignon Napa Valley Private Reserve 1991 •$40 •(03/31/95) •CS

94 **DIAMOND CREEK** Cabernet Sauvignon Napa Valley Red Rock Terrace Micro-Climate 3 1991 •$50 •(11/15/93) •CS

94 **GUENOC** Cabernet Sauvignon Napa Valley Beckstoffer Vineyard Reserve 1991 •$35 •(09/30/94) •CS

94 **MARTIN RAY** Cabernet Sauvignon Napa Valley 1991 •$28 •(11/15/94)

94 **ST. CLEMENT** Oroppas Napa Valley 1991 •$22 •(10/31/93)

93 **CAYMUS** Cabernet Sauvignon Napa Valley 1991 •$20 •(11/15/94) •SS

93 **CONN CREEK** Anthology Napa Valley 1991 •$30 •(09/30/94) •CS

93 **CORNERSTONE** Cabernet Sauvignon Howell Mountain Beatty Ranch 1991 •$33 •(11/15/94)

93 **DIAMOND CREEK** Cabernet Sauvignon Napa Valley Volcanic Hill Micro-Climate 4 1991 •$50 •(11/15/93) •CS

93 **DOMINUS** Napanook Vineyard Napa Valley 1991 •$55 •(11/15/95) •CS

93 **JUDD'S HILL** Cabernet Sauvignon Napa Valley 1991 •$24 •(09/30/94) •SS

93 **OPUS ONE** Napa Valley 1991 •$65 •(11/15/94) •CS

93 **SHAFER** Cabernet Sauvignon Stags Leap District Hillside Select 1991 •$45 •(11/15/95) •CS

93 **SILVERADO** Cabernet Sauvignon Stags Leap District Limited Reserve 1991 •$40 •(11/15/94) •CS

93 **SILVERADO** Cabernet Sauvignon Stags Leap District 1991 •$17 •(04/30/94) •SS

93 **SPOTTSWOODE** Cabernet Sauvignon Napa Valley 1991 •$40 •(11/15/94) •CS

92 **CHATEAU MONTELENA** Cabernet Sauvignon Napa Valley The Montelena Estate 1991 •$40 •(05/31/95) •SS

92 **CLOS DU BOIS** Cabernet Sauvignon Alexander Valley Winemaker's Reserve 1991 •$30 •(10/15/94) •CS

92 **DALLA VALLE** Cabernet Sauvignon Napa Valley 1991 •$25 •(11/15/94) •SS

92 **DIAMOND CREEK** Cabernet Sauvignon Napa Valley Gravelly Meadow 1991 •$50 •(10/31/93) •CS

92 **HARTWELL** Cabernet Sauvignon Stags Leap District 1991 •$55 •(11/15/94)

92 **OAKVILLE RANCH** Cabernet Sauvignon Napa Valley Reserve 1991 •$32 •(05/15/95)

92 **PRIDE** Cabernet Sauvignon Napa Valley 1991 •$18 •(05/15/94)

92 **SIMI** Cabernet Sauvignon Alexander Valley Reserve 1991 •$35 •(10/15/95)

92 **STAG'S LEAP WINE CELLARS** S.L.V. Cask 23 Napa Valley 1991 •$70 •(12/31/94) •CS

92 **THE HESS COLLECTION** Cabernet Sauvignon Napa Valley 1991 •$18 •(11/15/94) •SS

91 **ARROWOOD** Cabernet Sauvignon Sonoma County 1991 •$25 •(09/30/94) •SS

91 **B.R. COHN** Cabernet Sauvignon Sonoma Valley Olive Hill Vineyard 1991 •$28 •(04/15/95)

91 **BUEHLER** Cabernet Sauvignon Napa Valley Reserve 1991 •$25 •(09/30/95)

91 **CHATEAU SOUVERAIN** Cabernet Sauvignon Alexander Valley Winemaker's Reserve 1991 •$14 •(10/31/94)

91 **CHATEAU ST. JEAN** Cabernet Sauvignon Sonoma County Cinq Cépages 1991 •$18 •(11/15/95)

91 **DIAMOND CREEK** Cabernet Sauvignon Napa Valley Volcanic Hill 1991 •$50 •(11/15/93) •CS

91 **DUNN** Cabernet Sauvignon Howell Mountain 1991 •$39 •(12/15/95) •CS

91 **E. & J. GALLO** Cabernet Sauvignon Northern Sonoma 1991 •$50 •(11/15/94)

91 **GEYSER PEAK** Réserve Alexandre Alexander Valley 1991 •$30 •(07/31/94) •CS

91 **GUENOC** Meritage Langtry California 1991 •$35 •(09/30/94)

91 **HEITZ** Cabernet Sauvignon Napa Valley Martha's Vineyard 1991 •$65 •(04/30/96) •CS

91 **KENDALL-JACKSON** Meritage Cardinale California 1991 •$60 •(12/15/95)

91 **OAKVILLE RANCH** Cabernet Sauvignon Napa Valley Lewis Select 1991 •$28 •(09/30/94)

91 **PAUL HOBBS** Cabernet Sauvignon Carneros Napa Valley Hyde Vineyard 1991 •$30 •(10/31/94)

91 **RIDGE** Monte Bello Santa Cruz Mountains 1991 •$75 •(11/15/95) •CS

91 **ROBERT PECOTA** Cabernet Sauvignon Napa Valley Kara's Vineyard 1991 •$20 •(09/15/94)

91 **ROSENTHAL** Cabernet Sauvignon California 1991 •$20 •(11/15/94)

91 **S. ANDERSON** Cabernet Sauvignon Stags Leap District Richard Chambers Vineyard 1991 •$46 •(12/31/94)

91 **SEQUOIA GROVE** Cabernet Sauvignon Napa Valley Estate Reserve 1991 •$26 •(07/31/94)

91 **SILVER OAK** Cabernet Sauvignon Alexander Valley 1991 •$32 •(11/15/95)

91 **STONESTREET** Legacy Alexander Valley 1991 •$35 •(11/15/94)

91 **THE HESS COLLECTION** Cabernet Sauvignon Napa Valley Reserve 1991 •$39 •(04/30/96)

91 **VIADER** Napa Valley 1991 •$28 •(11/15/94)

90 **A. RAFANELLI** Cabernet Sauvignon Dry Creek Valley Unfiltered 1991 •$15 •(09/15/94) •SS

90 **ARAUJO** Cabernet Sauvignon Napa Valley Eisele Vineyard 1991 •$40 •(10/15/94) •CS

90 **BEAULIEU** Cabernet Sauvignon Napa Valley Georges de Latour Private Reserve 1991 •$40 •(12/15/95)

90 **CHIMNEY ROCK** Elevage Stags Leap District 1991 •$30 •(11/15/94)

90 **COSENTINO** Cabernet Sauvignon Napa Valley Reserve 1991 •$30 •(12/15/95)

90 **DALLA VALLE** Maya Napa Valley 1991 •$50 •(11/15/94)

90 **DIAMOND CREEK** Cabernet Sauvignon Napa Valley Gravelly Meadow Lake Blend 1991 •$50 •(11/15/93)

90 **DIAMOND CREEK** Cabernet Sauvignon Napa Valley Red Rock Terrace 1991 •$50 •(11/15/93)

90 **E. & J. GALLO** Cabernet Sauvignon Sonoma County Gallo Sonoma 1991 •$12 •(03/31/95) •SS

90 **FERRARI-CARANO** Siena Sonoma County 1991 •$20 •(11/15/93)

90 **FOXEN** Cabernet Sauvignon Santa Barbara County 1991 •$20 •(02/28/94)

90 **GEYSER PEAK** Cabernet Sauvignon Alexander Valley Reserve 1991 •$20 •(03/15/94) •SS

90 **GROTH** Cabernet Sauvignon Napa Valley 1991 •$18 •(10/15/94) •SS

90 **HARLAN** Napa Valley 1991 •$65 •(11/30/95)

90 **JOSEPH PHELPS** Insignia Napa Valley 1991 •$50 •(05/31/95) •CS

90 **JOSEPH PHELPS** Cabernet Sauvignon Napa Valley Backus Vineyard 1991 •$35 •(10/15/94) •BB

90 **KISTLER** Cabernet Sauvignon Sonoma Valley Kistler Vineyard 1991 •$30 •(06/15/95)

90 **LA JOTA** Cabernet Sauvignon Howell Mountain 10th Anniversary Release 1991 •$38 •(06/15/94) •CS

90 **LAUREL GLEN** Cabernet Sauvignon Sonoma Mountain Counterpoint 1991 •$15 •(11/30/93) •SS

90 **MERRYVALE** Cabernet Sauvignon Napa Valley Profile 1991 •$36 •(12/15/95)

90 **PARADIGM** Cabernet Sauvignon Napa Valley 1991 •$26 •(11/15/94)

90 **PEACHY CANYON** Cabernet Sauvignon Paso Robles 1991 •$18 •(11/15/93)

90 **PHILIP TOGNI** Cabernet Sauvignon Napa Valley 1991 •$30 •(11/15/93)

90 **ROBERT MONDAVI** Cabernet Sauvignon Napa Valley Unfiltered 1991 •$18 •(11/15/94) •SS

90 **ROBERT MONDAVI** Cabernet Sauvignon Napa Valley Reserve 1991 •$56 •(11/15/94)

90 **ROCKING HORSE** Cabernet Sauvignon Stags Leap District Robinson Vineyard 1991 •$24 •(03/31/94)

90 **ROSENBLUM** Cabernet Sauvignon Napa Valley Holbrook Mitchell Vineyard 1991 •$14 •(10/31/94)

90 **SADDLEBACK** Cabernet Sauvignon Napa Valley 1991 •$17 •(10/31/94)

90 **SHAFER** Cabernet Sauvignon Stags Leap District 1991 •$21 •(08/31/94)

90 **SIGNORELLO** Cabernet Sauvignon Napa Valley Founder's Reserve 1991 •$30 •(09/30/94)

90 **SILVER OAK** Cabernet Sauvignon Napa Valley 1991 •$36 •(11/15/95)

90 **ST. CLEMENT** Cabernet Sauvignon Napa Valley 1991 •$23 •(09/30/94) •SS

90 **TOM EDDY** Cabernet Sauvignon Napa Valley 1991 •$32 •(04/30/95)

90 **V. SATTUI** Cabernet Sauvignon Napa Valley Mario's Stock Reserve 1991 •$35 •(11/15/94)

89 **ABREU** Cabernet Sauvignon Napa Valley Madrona Ranch 1991 •$31

89 **ARROWOOD** Domaine du Grand Archer Sonoma County 1991 •$8.25 •(04/30/94) •SS

89 **CAIN** Five Napa Valley 1991 •$40 •(12/15/95)

89 **CHAPPELLET** Cabernet Sauvignon Napa Valley 1991 •$20 •(11/15/94)

89 **CHARLES KRUG** Cabernet Sauvignon Napa Valley Vintage Selection 1991 •$28 •(12/15/95)

89 **CORISON** Cabernet Sauvignon Napa Valley 1991 •$26 •(10/15/94)

89 **COSENTINO** M. Coz Napa Valley 1991 •$45 •(11/15/94)

89 **CRONIN** Cabernet Sauvignon Santa Cruz Mountains 1991 •$17 •(04/30/96)

89 **DE LOACH** Cabernet Sauvignon Russian River Valley O.F.S. 1991 •$25 •(09/30/95)

89 **DRY CREEK** Cabernet Sauvignon Dry Creek Valley Reserve 1991 •$20 •(10/31/94)

89 **FAR NIENTE** Cabernet Sauvignon Napa Valley 1991 •$40 •(09/15/94)

89 **FIRESTONE** Vintage Reserve Santa Ynez Valley 1991 •$22 •(12/15/95)

89 **FORMAN** Cabernet Sauvignon Napa Valley 1991 •$30 •(03/15/94) •CS

89 **FRANCISCAN** Meritage Magnificat Oakville Estate Napa Valley 1991 •$20 •(12/15/95)

89 **GRGICH HILLS** Cabernet Sauvignon Napa Valley Yountville Selection 1991 •$35 •(12/15/95)

89 **GUENOC** Meritage Lake County 1991 •$15 •(10/31/94) •SS

89 **JOHNSON TURNBULL** Cabernet Sauvignon Napa Valley 1991 •$18 •(10/31/94)

89 **JOSEPH PHELPS** Cabernet Sauvignon Napa Valley Eisele Vineyard 1991 •$45 •(10/15/94)

89 **JOSEPH PHELPS** Cabernet Sauvignon Napa Valley 1991 •$18 •(10/15/94)

89 **KENDALL-JACKSON** Cabernet Sauvignon California Grand Reserve 1991 •$30 •(11/15/94)

89 **KENWOOD** Cabernet Sauvignon Sonoma Valley Artist Series 1991 •$40 •(11/15/94)

89 **LAUREL GLEN** Cabernet Sauvignon Sonoma Mountain 1991 •$30 •(11/15/94)

89 **LIVINGSTON** Cabernet Sauvignon Napa Valley Moffett Vineyard 1991 •$30 •(11/15/94)

89 **LYETH** A Red Blend Alexander Valley 1991 •$14 •(10/15/94) •SS

89 **MARTIN BROTHERS** Etrusco Paso Robles 1991 •$18 •(06/30/93)

89 **NEWLAN** Cabernet Sauvignon Napa Valley 1991 •$16 •(11/30/95)

89 **OAKVILLE RANCH** Cabernet Sauvignon Napa Valley 1991 •$24 •(09/30/94)

89 **RICHARDSON** Cabernet Sauvignon Sonoma Valley Horne 1991 •$14 •(11/15/93)

89 **RIDGE** Cabernet Sauvignon Santa Cruz Mountains 1991 •$16 •(10/15/93)

89 **STAGLIN FAMILY** Cabernet Sauvignon Napa Valley 1991 •$26 •(11/15/94)

89 **SWANSON** Cabernet Sauvignon Napa Valley 1991 •$20 •(11/15/94)

89 **SEAVEY** Cabernet Sauvignon Napa Valley 1991 •$26 •(07/31/95)

89 **WHITEHALL LANE** Cabernet Sauvignon Napa Valley Morisoli Vineyard 1991 •$36 •(05/31/95)

89 **WHITEHALL LANE** Cabernet Sauvignon Napa Valley Reserve 1991 •$26 •(05/31/95)

88 **ALTAMURA** Cabernet Sauvignon Napa Valley 1991 •$25 •(05/31/96)

88 **ANDERSON'S CONN VALLEY** Cabernet Sauvignon Napa Valley Estate Reserve 1991 •$30 •(11/15/94)

88 **BENZIGER** Cabernet Sauvignon Sonoma County 1991 •$12 •(03/15/94)

88 **BERINGER** Meritage Knights Valley 1991 •$13 •(09/15/94)

88 **CAFARO** Cabernet Sauvignon Napa Valley 1991 •$28 •(09/15/95)

88 **CAKEBREAD** Cabernet Sauvignon Napa Valley 1991 •$22 •(11/15/94)

88 **CLOS DU BOIS** Marlstone Vineyard Alexander Valley 1991 •$18 •(01/31/95)

88 **CLOS PEGASE** Cabernet Sauvignon Napa Valley 1991 • $17 • (06/30/94)

88 **CONN CREEK** Cabernet Sauvignon Napa Valley Limited Release 1991 • $18 • (11/15/94)

88 **CUVAISON** Cabernet Sauvignon Napa Valley 1991 • $22 • (11/15/94)

88 **DEHLINGER** Cabernet Sauvignon Russian River Valley 1991 • $15 • (05/15/95)

88 **DUCKHORN** Howell Mountain 1991 • $25 • (11/15/94)

88 **DUNCAN PEAK** Cabernet Sauvignon Mendocino County 1991 • $12 • (10/31/93)

88 **DUNN** Cabernet Sauvignon Napa Valley 1991 • $28 • (11/15/94)

88 **EBERLE** Cabernet Sauvignon Paso Robles 1991 • $16 • (04/15/95)

88 **FISHER** Cabernet Sauvignon Sonoma County Wedding Vineyard 1991 • $28 • (11/15/94)

88 **GRACE FAMILY** Cabernet Sauvignon Napa Valley 1991 • $225 • (11/15/94)

88 **GUILLIAMS** Cabernet Sauvignon Spring Mountain 1991 • $17 • (12/15/95)

88 **GUNDLACH BUNDSCHU** Cabernet Sauvignon Sonoma Valley Rhinefarm Vineyards 1991 • $15 • (10/31/94)

88 **JUSTIN** Cabernet Sauvignon San Luis Obispo Society Reserve 1991 • $19 • (11/15/94)

88 **LOCKWOOD** Cabernet Sauvignon Monterey 1991 • $12 • (10/31/93)

88 **MARKHAM** Cabernet Sauvignon Napa Valley 1991 • $17 • (11/15/94)

88 **MAZZOCCO** Cabernet Sauvignon Sonoma County 1991 • $18 • (11/15/94)

88 **MORGAN** Cabernet Sauvignon Carmel Valley 1991 • $15 • (11/15/94)

88 **MOUNT EDEN** Cabernet Sauvignon Santa Cruz Mountains Old Vine Reserve 1991 • $35 • (04/15/95)

88 **OAKFORD** Cabernet Sauvignon Napa Valley 1991 • $30 • (12/15/95)

88 **OPTIMA** Cabernet Sauvignon Alexander Valley 1991 • $25 • (02/28/95)

88 **PINE RIDGE** Cabernet Sauvignon Stags Leap District 1991 • $30 • (11/15/94)

88 **RAYMOND** Cabernet Sauvignon Napa Valley 1991 • $17 • (11/15/94)

88 **ROBERT SINSKEY** RSV Claret Stags Leap District 1991 • $28 • (11/15/94)

88 **ROSENBLUM** Cabernet Sauvignon Napa Valley George Hendry Vineyard Reserve 1991 • $30 • (11/15/94)

88 **SEBASTIANI** Cabernet Sauvignon Sonoma Valley Cherryblock Old Vines 1991 • $24 • (11/15/94)

88 **SEQUOIA GROVE** Cabernet Sauvignon Napa Valley 1991 • $18 • (11/15/94)

88 **ST. FRANCIS** Cabernet Sauvignon Sonoma County Reserve 1991 • $24 • (11/15/94)

88 **STAG'S LEAP WINE CELLARS** Cabernet Sauvignon Napa Valley Fay 1991 • $30 • (12/31/94)

88 **STERLING** Cabernet Sauvignon Reserve Napa Valley 1991 • $30 • (11/15/94)

88 **STONESTREET** Cabernet Sauvignon Alexander Valley 1991 • $22 • (05/15/95)

88 **TERRACES** Cabernet Sauvignon Napa Valley 1991 • $40 • (10/31/95)

88 **VICHON** Cabernet Sauvignon Stags Leap District SLD 1991 • $28 • (12/15/95)

88 **VINE CLIFF** Cabernet Sauvignon Napa Valley 1991 • $25 • (04/30/95)

88 **VON STRASSER** Cabernet Sauvignon Napa Valley Diamond Mountain 1991 • $25 • (03/31/94)

88 **WHITEHALL LANE** Cabernet Sauvignon Napa Valley 1991 • $14 • (11/15/94)

87 **BEAULIEU** Tapestry Signet Collection Napa Valley 1991 • $20 • (12/15/95)

87 **BEAULIEU** Cabernet Sauvignon Napa Valley Rutherford 1991 • $13 • (10/15/94)

87 **BERINGER** Cabernet Sauvignon Knights Valley 1991 • $13 • (05/31/94)

87 **BERNARD PRADEL** Cabernet Sauvignon Howell Mountain Ranch 1991 • $21 • (09/15/95)

87 **BUENA VISTA** Cabernet Sauvignon Carneros 1991 • $12 • (10/15/94)

87 **CHATEAU MARGARITE** Cabernet Sauvignon Napa Valley 1991 • $15 • (11/15/93)

87 **CLOS DU BOIS** Cabernet Sauvignon Alexander Valley Briarcrest 1991 • $18 • (11/15/94)

87 **CLOS DU VAL** Cabernet Sauvignon Stags Leap District 1991 • $20 • (09/30/95)

87 **CRONIN** Concerto Robinson Vineyard Stags Leap District 1991 • $17 • (02/28/95)

87 **DICKERSON** Cabernet Sauvignon Napa Valley Ruby Cabernet Limited Reserve 1991 • $11 • (11/15/94)

87 **DRY CREEK** Cabernet Sauvignon Sonoma County 1991 • $15 • (11/15/93)

87 **GARY FARRELL** Cabernet Sauvignon Sonoma County Ladi's Vineyard 1991 • $18 • (08/31/94)

87 **GIRARD** Cabernet Sauvignon Napa Valley Reserve 1991 • $35 • (11/15/94)

87 **IRON HORSE** T-T Cabernets Alexander Valley 1991 • $19 • (12/15/95)

87 **J. LOHR** Cabernet Sauvignon Paso Robles VS 1991 • $22 • (11/30/95)

87 **KATHRYN KENNEDY** Cabernet Sauvignon Santa Cruz Mountains 1991 • $54 • (11/15/94)

87 **MAZZOCCO** Matrix Dry Creek Valley 1991 • $28 • (12/15/95)

87 **MERRYVALE** Cabernet Sauvignon Napa Valley 1991 • $23 • (11/15/94)

87 **MIRASSOU** Cabernet Sauvignon Monterey County Fifth Generation Harvest Reserve 1991 • $12 • (12/15/95)

87 **NAPA RIDGE** Cabernet Sauvignon North Coast Coastal Reserve 1991 • $13 • (10/15/95)

87 **NEWTON** Claret Napa Valley 1991 • $12 • (06/15/93)

87 **PETER MICHAEL** Cabernet Sauvignon Knights Valley Les Pavots 1991 • $26 • (05/15/95)

87 **RAYMOND** Meritage Private Reserve Napa Valley 1991 • $40 • (12/15/95)

87 **ROCHIOLI** Cabernet Sauvignon Russian River Valley Neoma's Vineyard Reserve 1991 • $26 • (12/15/95)

87 **RUSTRIDGE** Cabernet Sauvignon Napa Valley 1991 • $20 • (12/15/95)

87 **STAG'S LEAP WINE CELLARS** Cabernet Sauvignon Napa Valley 1991 • $18 • (03/31/94)

87 **TRUCHARD** Cabernet Sauvignon Napa Valley Carneros 1991 • $18 • (11/15/94)

87 **TULOCAY** Cabernet Sauvignon Napa Valley De Celles Vineyard 1991 • $12 • (11/15/94)

87 **V. SATTUI** Cabernet Sauvignon Napa Valley Preston Vineyard Rutherford District 1991 • $22 • (11/15/94)

86 **ATLAS PEAK** Cabernet Sauvignon Atlas Peak 1991 • $18 • (09/15/95)

86 **BOEGER** Meritage El Dorado 1991 • $15 • (12/15/95)

86 **BUEHLER** Cabernet Sauvignon Napa Valley 1991 • $13 • (09/15/94)

86 **CLOS DU BOIS** Cabernet Sauvignon Alexander Valley 1991 • $12 • (02/28/94)

86 **CLOS PEGASE** Hommage Napa Valley 1991 • $25 • (11/15/94)

86 **COSENTINO** Cabernet Sauvignon Napa Valley 1991 • $16 • (10/31/94)

86 **CUVAISON** Meritage Reserve Napa Valley 1991 • $50 • (12/15/95)

86 **DORCICH CELLARS** Cabernet Sauvignon Santa Clara County 1991 • $18 • (07/31/95)

86 **ESTANCIA** Cabernet Sauvignon Alexander Valley 1991 • $9 • (10/31/93) • BB

86 **FERRARI-CARANO** Cabernet Sauvignon Sonoma County 1991 • $16 • (09/15/95)

86 **FLORA SPRINGS** Trilogy Napa Valley 1991 • $25 • (11/15/94)

86 **GIRARD** Cabernet Sauvignon Napa Valley 1991 • $18 • (05/31/94)

86 **KATHRYN KENNEDY** Lateral California 1991 • $18 • (11/15/93)

86 **KONRAD** Mélange à Trois Mendocino 1991 • $12 • (03/15/94)

86 **LIPARITA** Cabernet Sauvignon Howell Mountain 1991 • $28 • (11/15/94)

86 **MARIO PERELLI-MINETTI** Cabernet Sauvignon Napa Valley 1991 • $13 • (05/31/96)

86 **MURRIETA'S WELL** Vendimia Livermore Valley 1991 • $28 • (11/15/94)

86 **PEJU** Cabernet Sauvignon Napa Valley HB Vineyard 1991 • $35 • (09/15/95)

86 **ROBERT PEPI** Cabernet Sauvignon Napa Valley Vine Hill Ranch 1991 • $18 • (12/15/95)

86 **RODNEY STRONG** Cabernet Sauvignon Northern Sonoma Alexander's Crown Vineyard 1991 • $20 • (12/15/95)

86 **RODNEY STRONG** Cabernet Sauvignon Northern Sonoma Reserve 1991 • $30 • (12/15/95)

86 **ROSENBLUM** Holbrook Mitchell Trio Napa Valley 1991 • $22 • (11/15/93)

86 **RUTHERFORD RANCH** Meritage Quintessence Napa Valley 1991 • $20 • (12/15/95)

86 **RUTHERFORD RANCH** Cabernet Sauvignon Napa Valley 1991 • $10 • (11/15/94)

86 **SIERRA VISTA** Cabernet Sauvignon El Dorado Five Star Reserve 1991 • $22 • (11/15/94)

86 **SMITH & HOOK** Cabernet Sauvignon Santa Lucia Highlands 1991 • $18 • (11/15/94)

86 **SONOMA CREEK** Cabernet Sauvignon Sonoma Valley 1991 • $15 • (11/15/93)

86 **SOQUEL** Cabernet Sauvignon Santa Cruz Mountains 1991 • $20 • (04/15/94)

86 **STERLING** Cabernet Sauvignon Napa Valley Diamond Mountain Ranch 1991 • $18 • (11/15/94)

86 **TOBIN JAMES** Cabernet Sauvignon San Luis Obispo County Twilight 1991 • $12 • (11/15/93)

86 **TULOCAY** Cabernet Sauvignon Napa Valley Cliff Vineyard 1991 • $12 • (11/15/94)

86 **V. SATTUI** Cabernet Sauvignon Napa Valley Suzanne's Vineyard 1991 • $16 • (11/15/94)

85 **BANDIERA** Cabernet Sauvignon Napa Valley 1991 • $6 • (09/30/94) • BB

85 **CARMENET** Cabernet Sauvignon Sonoma Valley Dynamite Cabernet 1991 • $15 • (11/15/93)

85 **CHALK HILL** Cabernet Sauvignon Chalk Hill 1991 • $21 • (11/15/94)

85 **CHATEAU SOUVERAIN** Cabernet Sauvignon Alexander Valley 1991 • $11 • (06/30/94)

85 **CONN CREEK** Cabernet Sauvignon Napa Valley Barrel Select 1991 • $18 • (11/15/94)

85 **DE LORIMIER** Meritage Mosaic Alexander Valley 1991 • $18 • (08/31/95)

85 **DOMAINE HILL & MAYES** Cabernet Sauvignon Napa Valley Clos Fontaine du Mont Reserve 1991 • $32 • (12/31/94)

85 **ESTANCIA** Meritage Alexander Valley 1991 • $14 • (09/15/94)

85 **FARELLA-PARK** Cabernet Sauvignon Napa Valley 1991 • $25 • (02/28/95)

85 **FOREST GLEN** Cabernet Sauvignon Sonoma County 1991 • $10 • (04/30/94)

85 **FREEMARK ABBEY** Cabernet Sauvignon Napa Valley 1991 • $17 • (11/15/94)

85 **GUENOC** Cabernet Sauvignon Lake County 1991 • $15 • (11/15/94)

85 **HANNA** Cabernet Sauvignon Alexander Valley 1991 • $14 • (02/28/95)

85 **HEITZ** Cabernet Sauvignon Napa Valley 1991 • $19 • (04/30/96)

85 **KEENAN** Cabernet Sauvignon Napa Valley 1991 • $21 • (12/15/95)

85 **KUNDE** Cabernet Sauvignon Sonoma Valley Reserve 1991 • $23 • (05/31/96)

85 **MONTICELLO** Cabernet Sauvignon Napa Valley Corley Select Reserve 1991 • $25 • (12/15/95)

85 **MOUNT VEEDER** Cabernet Sauvignon Napa Valley 1991 • $18 • (01/31/95)

85 **PEJU** Cabernet Sauvignon Napa Valley 1991 • $18 • (09/15/95)

85 **PINE RIDGE** Cabernet Sauvignon Napa Valley Andrus Reserve 1991 • $60 • (11/15/93)

85 **RIDGE** Cabernet Sauvignon Napa County York Creek 1991 • $16 • (11/15/94)

85 **RITCHIE CREEK** Cabernet Sauvignon Napa Valley 1991 • $18 • (04/15/95)

85 **SEBASTIANI** Cabernet Sauvignon Sonoma County 1991 • $10 • (11/15/94)

85 **SHAFER** Firebreak Stags Leap District 1991 • $20 • (12/15/93)

85 **STAGS' LEAP WINERY** Cabernet Sauvignon Napa Valley 1991 • $20 • (11/15/94)

85 **STELTZNER** Cabernet Sauvignon Stags Leap District Commemorative 1991 • $45 • (03/31/95)

85 **STELTZNER** Cabernet Sauvignon Napa Valley 1991 • $18 • (03/31/95)

85 **SULLIVAN** Cabernet Sauvignon Napa Valley 1991 • $23 • (11/15/94)

85 **V. SATTUI** Cabernet Sauvignon Napa Valley 1991 • $14 • (11/15/94)

85 **WELLINGTON** Cabernet Sauvignon Sonoma County Mohrhardt Ridge Vineyard 1991 • $14 • (11/15/94)

85 **WHITE ROCK** Claret Napa Valley 1991 • $22 • (12/15/95)

85 **WHITEHALL LANE** Meritage Napa Valley 1991 • $15 • (11/15/94)

84 **ALEXANDER VALLEY VINEYARDS** Cabernet Sauvignon Alexander Valley Wetzel Family Estate 1991 • $13 • (11/15/93)

84 **AUSTIN** Cabernet Sauvignon Santa Barbara County Mille Delices 1991 • $20 • (11/15/93)

84 **BENZIGER** Cabernet Blend Sonoma Mountain Estate Tribute 1991 • $20 • (03/31/96)

84 **BENZIGER** Estate Tribute Sonoma Mountain 1991 • $20 • (12/15/95)

84 **BON MARCHE** Cabernet Sauvignon Sonoma County 1991 • $7 • (03/31/93) • BB

84 **DUNNEWOOD** Cabernet Sauvignon North Coast Barrel Select 1991 • $7 • (11/15/94)

84 **FIELD STONE** Cabernet Sauvignon Alexander Valley 1991 • $14 • (11/15/94)

84 **FIRESTONE** Cabernet Sauvignon Santa Ynez Valley 1991 • $12 • (11/15/94)

84 **FISHER** Cabernet Sauvignon Napa Valley Coach Insignia 1991 • $20 • (11/15/94)

84 **GEYSER PEAK** Cabernet Sauvignon Sonoma County 1991 • $10 • (03/15/94)

84 **HUSCH** Cabernet Sauvignon Mendocino La Ribera Vineyard 1991 • $14 • (03/31/95)

84 **J. LOHR** Cabernet Sauvignon Paso Robles Seven Oaks 1991 • $11 • (07/31/94)

84 **JORDAN** Cabernet Sauvignon Alexander Valley 1991 • $25 • (06/15/95)

84 **JUSTIN** Isosceles Reserve San Luis Obispo 1991 • $23 • (11/15/94)

84 **LAMBERT BRIDGE** Cabernet Sauvignon Sonoma County 1991 • $14 • (10/15/94)

84 **LOCKWOOD** Cabernet Sauvignon Monterey Partners Reserve 1991 • $16 • (11/15/94)

84 **MOUNT VEEDER** Reserve Napa Valley 1991 • $40 • (09/15/95)

84 **MURRIETA'S WELL** Vendimia Livermore Valley 1991 • $28 • (05/31/95)

84 **NAPA RIDGE** Cabernet Sauvignon Central Coast Oak Barrel 1991 • $8 • (11/15/94)

84 **PARDUCCI** Cabernet Sauvignon Mendocino County 1991 • $8 • (02/28/95) • BB

84 **PINE RIDGE** Cabernet Sauvignon Napa Valley Rutherford Cuvée 1991 • $17 • (11/15/94)

84 **RANCHO SISQUOC** Cabernet Sauvignon Santa Maria Valley 1991 • $15 • (11/15/94)

84 **RAVENSWOOD** Cabernet Sauvignon Sonoma County 1991 • $14 • (11/15/94)

84 **RAYMOND** Cabernet Sauvignon California Amberhill California Selection 1991 • $8 • (11/15/94)

84 **RAYMOND** Cabernet Sauvignon Napa Valley Private Reserve 1991 • $25 • (12/15/95)

84 **ROCKING HORSE** Cabernet Sauvignon Napa Valley Hillside Cuvée 1991 • $18 • (03/15/94)

84 **ROMBAUER** Cabernet Sauvignon Napa Valley 1991 • $20 • (12/15/95)

84 **RUBISSOW-SARGENT** Cabernet Sauvignon Mount Veeder 1991 • $16 • (12/15/95)

84 **SANTA BARBARA WINERY** Cabernet Sauvignon Santa Ynez Valley Unfiltered Reserve 1991 • $16 • (11/15/94)

84 **SONOMA CREEK** Cabernet Sauvignon Napa Valley Reserve 1991 • $15 • (11/15/94)

84 **ST. FRANCIS** Cabernet Sauvignon Sonoma County 1991 • $10 • (09/15/93)

84 **STELTZNER** Claret Stags Leap District 1991 • $10 • (02/28/94)

84 **STEVENOT** Cabernet Sauvignon Calaveras County Reserve 1991 • $11 • (11/15/94)

84 **TOPAZ** Rouge de Trois Napa Valley 1991 • $17 • (12/15/95)

84 **TREFETHEN** Cabernet Sauvignon Napa Valley 1991 • $19 • (12/15/95)

84 **WELLINGTON** Cabernet Sauvignon Mount Veeder Random Ridge 1991 • $16 • (11/15/94)

84 **WHITE OAK** Cabernet Sauvignon Alexander Valley 1991 • $14 • (11/15/94)

84 **WILLIAM HILL** Cabernet Sauvignon Napa Valley Reserve 1991 • $14 • (10/15/94)

84 **WILLIAM WHEELER** Cabernet Sauvignon Dry Creek Valley Norse Vineyards Reserve 1991 • $12 • (11/15/94)

84 **WINTERBROOK** Cabernet Sauvignon Napa Valley Grand Reserve 1991 • $18 • (01/31/95)

83 **B.R. COHN** Cabernet Sauvignon Sonoma Valley 1991 • $12 • (11/15/94)

83 **BAYVIEW CELLARS** Cabernet Sauvignon Napa Valley 1991 • $12 • (05/31/95)

83 **BELL** Cabernet Sauvignon Baritelle Vineyards 1991 • $40 • (12/15/95)

83 **BONVERRE** Cabernet Sauvignon California Lot Number 9 1991 • $7 • (05/15/94)

83 **BURGESS** Cabernet Sauvignon Napa Valley Vintage Selection 1991 • $20 • (12/15/95)

83 **BRUTOCAO** Cabernet Sauvignon Mendocino Proprietor's Special Reserve 1991 • $35 • (07/31/95)

83 **CAIN** Cuvée Napa Valley 1991 • $15 • (12/31/94)

83 **CASTORO** Cabernet Sauvignon Paso Robles The Wine 1991 • $10 • (11/15/94)

83 **CHATOM** Cabernet Sauvignon Calaveras County 1991 • $12 • (11/15/94)

83 **CLOVERDALE RANCH** Cabernet Sauvignon Alexander Valley Estate Cuvée 1991 • $12 • (11/15/94)

83 **FETZER** Cabernet Sauvignon North Coast Barrel Select 1991 • $12 • (11/15/94)

83 **FOREST LAKE** Cabernet Sauvignon California 1991 • $6 • (05/31/94) • BB

83 **GOLDEN CREEK** Caberlot Reserve Sonoma County 1991 • $15 • (11/15/94)

83 **GRGICH HILLS** Cabernet Sauvignon Napa Valley 1991 • $24 • (12/15/95)

83 **HAMBRECHT** Cabernet Sauvignon Dry Creek Valley Bradford Mountain 1991 • $14 • (11/15/94)

83 **HAYWOOD** Cabernet Sauvignon California 1991 • $8 • (11/15/94)

83 **HOP KILN** Cabernet Sauvignon Russian River Valley 1991 • $14 • (11/15/94)

83 **KENDALL-JACKSON** Cabernet Sauvignon California Vintner's Reserve 1991 • $15 • (07/31/94)

83 **KENWOOD** Cabernet Sauvignon Sonoma Valley Jack London Vineyard 1991 • $20 • (11/15/94)

83 **LIVINGSTON** Cabernet Sauvignon Napa Valley Stanley's Selection 1991 • $20 • (11/15/94)

83 **MILL CREEK** Cabernet Sauvignon Dry Creek Valley 1991 • $12 • (11/15/94)

83 **MURPHY-GOODE** Cabernet Sauvignon Alexander Valley Murphy Ranch 1991 • $15 • (11/15/94)

83 **NOMINEE** Cabernet Sauvignon Napa Valley 1991 • $7 • (07/15/93)

83 **ROBERT MONDAVI** Cabernet Sauvignon North Coast Coastal 1991 • $11 • (09/30/94)

83 **SEGHESIO** Cabernet Sauvignon Sonoma County 1991 • $9 • (03/31/94)

83 **SOQUEL** Cabernet Sauvignon Stags Leap District 1991 • $18 • (05/15/94)

83 **STEVENOT** Cabernet Sauvignon California 1991 • $8 • (04/30/93) • BB

83 **THORNHILL** Cabernet Sauvignon Napa Valley 1991 • $10 • (11/15/94)

83 **TANTALUS** Meritage Sonoma County 1991 • $16 • (07/31/95)

83 **VICHON** Cabernet Sauvignon California Coastal Selection 1991 • $9 • (11/15/93)

83 **VILLA MT. EDEN** Cabernet Sauvignon Napa Valley Grand Reserve 1991 • $14 • (03/31/95)

82 **BEAULIEU** Cabernet Sauvignon Napa Valley Beautour 1991 • $9 • (09/30/94)

82 **BELVEDERE** Cabernet Sauvignon Sonoma County 1991 • $10 • (11/15/94)

82 **BETTINELLI** Cabernet Sauvignon Napa Valley 1991 • $14 • (05/31/95)

82 **CASTORO** Cabernet Sauvignon Paso Robles Reserve 1991 • $12 • (11/15/94)

82 **CHESTNUT HILL** Cabernet Sauvignon California Coastal Cuvée 1991 • $9 • (05/15/94)

82 **CORBETT CANYON** Cabernet Sauvignon Napa Valley Reserve 1991 • $9 • (09/30/94)

82 **FOSS CREEK** Cabernet Sauvignon Sonoma County 1991 • $7 • (11/15/94)

82 **FOXHOLLOW** Cabernet Sauvignon Paso Robles 1991 • $10 • (06/30/94)

82 **FRANCISCAN** Cabernet Sauvignon Napa Valley Oakville Estate 1991 • $13 • (11/15/94)

82 **GODSPEED** Cabernet Sauvignon Mount Veeder 1991 • $15 • (12/15/95)

82 **GREENWOOD RIDGE** Cabernet Sauvignon Anderson Valley 1991 • $14 • (11/15/94)

82 **GUENOC** Cabernet Sauvignon North Coast 1991 • $12 • (11/15/94)

82 **HARRISON** Cabernet Sauvignon Napa Valley 1991 • $30 • (11/15/94)

82 **HESS SELECT** Cabernet Sauvignon California 1991 • $9 • (02/28/94)

82 **INDIAN SPRINGS** Cabernet Sauvignon Nevada County 1991 • $9 • (11/15/94)

82 **J. LOHR** Cabernet Sauvignon California Cypress 1991 • $8 • (11/15/94)

82 **KARLY** Cabernet Sauvignon El Dorado Stromberg Carpenter Vineyard 1991 • $15 • (11/15/94)

82 **KENWOOD** Cabernet Sauvignon Sonoma Valley 1991 • $16 • (11/15/94)

82 **LAWRENCE J. BARGETTO** Cabernet Sauvignon Central Coast Cyrpress 1991 • $9 • (11/15/94)

82 **NAPA CREEK** Cabernet Sauvignon Napa Valley 1991 • $12 • (11/15/94)

82 **OCTOPUS MOUNTAIN** Cabernet Sauvignon Anderson Valley Dennison Vineyard 1991 • $13 • (11/15/94)

82 **ONE WORLD WINERY** Cabernet Sauvignon Russian River Valley 1991 • $15 • (05/15/94)

82 **PAHLMEYER** Napa Valley 1991 • $32 • (11/15/94)

82 **QUIVIRA** Cabernet Cuvée Dry Creek Valley 1991 • $15 • (07/31/95)

82 **R.H. PHILLIPS** Cabernet Sauvignon California 1991 • $8 • (05/15/94)

82 **RODNEY STRONG** Cabernet Sauvignon Sonoma County 1991 • $10 • (11/15/94)

82 **SONOMA CREEK** Cabernet Sauvignon Sonoma Valley 1991 • $15 • (11/15/94)

82 **STERLING** Cabernet Sauvignon Napa Valley 1991 • $14 • (11/15/94)

82 **STONEGATE** Cabernet Sauvignon Napa Valley 1991 • $18 • (12/15/95)

82 **SULLIVAN** Coeur de Vigne Private Reserve Napa Valley 1991 • $30 • (11/15/94)

82 **SUTTER HOME** Cabernet Sauvignon Napa Valley Reserve 1991 • $12 • (11/15/94)

82 **VICHON** Cabernet Sauvignon California Coastal Selection 1991 • $11 • (09/30/94)

82 **VILLA MT. EDEN** Cabernet Sauvignon California Cellar Select 1991 • $10 • (05/15/94)

82 **WENTE BROS.** Cabernet Sauvignon Livermore Valley 1991 • $10 • (11/15/94)

82 **WINDEMERE** Cabernet Sauvignon Napa Valley 1991 • $16 • (03/31/96)

81 **AETNA SPRINGS** Cabernet Sauvignon Napa Valley 1991 • $18 • (05/15/94)

81 **CANYON ROAD** Cabernet Sauvignon California 1991 • $7 • (06/15/93)

81 **CHARLES KRUG** Cabernet Sauvignon Napa Valley 1991 • $12 • (11/15/94)

81 **HOPE FARMS** Claret Paso Robles 1991 • $10 • (11/15/94)

81 **HUSCH** Cabernet Sauvignon Mendocino North Field Select 1991 • $18 • (03/31/95)

81 **LEEWARD** Cabernet Sauvignon Alexander Valley 1991 • $15 • (11/30/93)

81 **MADRONA** Cabernet Sauvignon El Dorado 1991 • $11 • (05/31/95)

81 **MICHEL-SCHLUMBERGER** Cabernet Sauvignon Dry Creek Valley 1991 • $18 • (11/15/94)

81 **MONTERRA** Cabernet Sauvignon Monterey 1991 • $7 • (11/15/94)

81 **RUTHERFORD ESTATE** Cabernet Sauvignon Napa Valley 1991 • $7 • (11/15/94)

81 **RUTHERFORD HILL** Cabernet Sauvignon Napa Valley 1991 • $14 • (11/15/94)

81 **SUTTER HOME** Cabernet Sauvignon California 1991 • $6 • (11/15/94)

81 **TAFT STREET** Cabernet Sauvignon Sonoma County 1991 • $11 • (03/15/94)

81 **VICHON** Cabernet Sauvignon Napa Valley 1991 • $16 • (04/30/94)

81 **WINTERBROOK** Cabernet Sauvignon Napa County 1991 • $8 • (05/15/94)

80 **AUSTIN** Cabernet Sauvignon Santa Barbara County Perry's Reserve 1991 • $15 • (11/15/93)

80 **CONCANNON** Assemblage Livermore Valley 1991 • $15 • (11/15/94)

80 **CORBETT CANYON** Cabernet Sauvignon California Coastal Classic 1991 • $6 • (06/15/93)

80 **HAHN** Cabernet Sauvignon Santa Lucia Highlands 1991 • $10 • (11/15/94)

80 **MASO** Napa Valley 1991 • $8 • (03/31/95)

80 **MONTEREY PENINSULA** Cabernet Sauvignon Monterey County 1991 • $12 • (12/15/95)

80 **ROBERT MONDAVI** Cabernet Sauvignon California Woodbridge 1991 • $7 • (11/15/93)

80 **ROUND HILL** Cabernet Sauvignon California 1991 • $7 • (11/15/94)

79 **BEAUCANON** Cabernet Sauvignon Napa Valley 1991 • $12 • (12/15/95)

79 **CALLAWAY** Cabernet Sauvignon California Hawk Watch 1991 • $10 • (11/15/94)

79 **CASTORO** Dieci Anni Paso Robles 1991 • $16 • (11/15/93)

79 **CIRRI** Cabernet Sauvignon Alexander Valley 1991 • $10 • (11/15/94)

79 **CONCANNON** Cabernet Sauvignon Livermore Valley Concannon Estate Vineyard 1991 • $9 • (11/15/93)

79 **FENESTRA** Cabernet Sauvignon Livermore Valley 1991 • $11 • (06/15/95)

79 **GRAESER** Cabernet Sauvignon Napa Valley 1991 • $14 • (12/15/95)

79 **LA JOTA** Cabernet Sauvignon Howell Mountain Selection 1991 • $NA • (06/15/94)

79 **M.G. VALLEJO** Cabernet Sauvignon California Harvest Select 1991 • $6 • (11/15/94)

79 **MADIGAN** Cabernet Sauvignon Napa Valley 1991 • $10 • (11/15/93)

79 **MICHAEL SULLBERG** Cabernet Sauvignon Napa Valley 1991 • $7 • (11/15/94)

79 **SHENANDOAH** Cabernet Sauvignon Amador County 1991 • $10 • (11/15/94)

79 **TOPOLOS** Riserva Sonoma County 1991 • $18 • (11/15/93)

78 **BOEGER** Cabernet Sauvignon El Dorado 1991 • $12 • (12/15/95)

78 **CASTORO** Cabernet Sauvignon Paso Robles The Wine 1991 • $10 • (11/15/93)

78 **DE LOACH** Cabernet Sauvignon Russian River Valley 1991 • $15 • (11/15/94)

78 **GLEN ELLEN** Cabernet Sauvignon California Proprietor's Reserve 1991 • $6 • (11/15/93)

78 **HAWK CREST** Cabernet Sauvignon California 1991 • $9 • (03/31/94)

78 **LOUIS M. MARTINI** Cabernet Sauvignon Sonoma Valley Monte Rosso Vineyard 1991 • $22 • (12/15/95)

78 **MEEKER** Cabernet Sauvignon Dry Creek Valley Gold Leaf Cuvée 1991 • $14 • (11/15/94)

78 **RENAISSANCE** Cabernet Sauvignon North Yuba 1991 • $12 • (12/15/95)

78 **RIVERSIDE VINEYARDS** Cabernet Sauvignon California 1991 • $7 • (11/15/94)

78 **SONOMA CREEK** Cabernet Sauvignon Sonoma County 1991 • $15 • (11/15/93)

78 **STEPHEN ZELLERBACH** Cabernet Sauvignon California 1991 • $9 • (03/31/94)

77 **IVAN TAMAS** Cabernet Sauvignon Livermore Valley Le Clan des Quatre Vineyards 1991 • $8 • (11/15/93)

77 **LA CROSSE** Cabernet Sauvignon Napa Valley 1991 • $7 • (02/28/95)

77 **NAPA RIDGE** Cabernet Sauvignon North Coast Coastal Oak Barrel 1991 • $8 • (11/15/93)

77 **PEPPERWOOD GROVE** Cabernet Sauvignon California 1991 • $6 • (06/15/93)

77 **ROUDON-SMITH** Cabernet Sauvignon California 1991 • $10 • (11/15/93)

76 **BRINDIAMO** Cabernet Sauvignon California Limited Bottling 1991 • $8 • (11/15/94)

76 **VENDANGE** Cabernet Sauvignon California 1991 • $6 • (11/15/94)

76 **WILDHURST** Cabernet Sauvignon Clear Lake 1991 • $9 • (11/15/93)

75 **CHRISTOPHE** Cabernet Sauvignon Napa County 1991 • $8 • (12/15/95)

75 **J. PEDRONCELLI** Cabernet Sauvignon Dry Creek Valley 1991 • $9 • (11/15/94)

75 **MAACAMA CREEK** Cabernet Sauvignon Alexander Valley Melim Vineyard Reserve 1991 • $9 • (11/15/93)

75 **SANTA BARBARA WINERY** Cabernet Sauvignon Santa Ynez Valley 1991 • $11 • (11/15/94)

74 **J. WILE & SONS** Cabernet Sauvignon Napa Valley 1991 • $7 • (11/15/93)

74 **MIRASSOU** Cabernet Sauvignon Monterey County Fifth Generation Family Selection 1991 • $9 • (12/15/95)

74 **MOUNT PALOMAR** Cabernet Sauvignon Temecula 1991 • $10 • (11/15/94)

73 **DEVLIN** Cabernet Sauvignon Santa Cruz Mountains Beauregard Ranch 1991 • $9 • (02/28/95)

73 **KORBEL** Cabernet Sauvignon Alexander Valley 1991 • $13 • (11/15/94)

72 **ARCIERO** Cabernet Sauvignon Paso Robles 1991 • $9 • (12/15/95)

72 **TWIN HILLS RANCH** Cabernet Sauvignon Paso Robles 1991 • $7 • (11/15/94)

70 **MARIO PERELLI-MINETTI** Cabernet Sauvignon Napa Valley 1991 • $13 • (03/31/96)

68 **RETZLAFF** Cabernet Sauvignon Livermore Valley 1991 • $16 • (11/15/93)

1990 California Cabernet
Vintage Rating: 95

98 **CAYMUS** Cabernet Sauvignon Napa Valley Special Selection 1990 • $192 • (03/31/94) • CS

97 **SILVERADO** Cabernet Sauvignon Napa Valley Limited Reserve 1990 • $40 • (10/31/93) • CS

95 **CHATEAU ST. JEAN** Cabernet Sauvignon Sonoma County Reserve 1990 • $38 • (04/30/96) • CS

94 **GROTH** Cabernet Sauvignon Napa Valley Reserve 1990 • $45 • (11/15/94) • CS

94 **MOUNT VEEDER** Cabernet Sauvignon Napa Valley 1990 • $15 • (10/31/93) • SS

93 **CAIN** Five Napa Valley 1990 • $34 • (09/15/94) • CS

93 **DALLA VALLE** Cabernet Sauvignon Napa Valley 1990 • $25 • (09/30/93)

93 **DUCKHORN** Cabernet Sauvignon Napa Valley 1990 • $20 • (07/31/93) • CS

93 **E. & J. GALLO** Cabernet Sauvignon Northern Sonoma 1990 • $60 • (10/31/93) • CS

93 **OAKVILLE RANCH** Cabernet Sauvignon Napa Valley 1990 • $23 • (10/15/93)

92 **BERINGER** Cabernet Sauvignon Napa Valley Private Reserve 1990 • $40 • (11/15/94) • CS

92 **COSENTINO** M. Coz Napa Valley 1990 • $45 • (11/15/93)

92 **DIAMOND CREEK** Cabernet Sauvignon Napa Valley Volcanic Hill 1990 • $50 • (11/15/92) • CS

92 **DUNN** Cabernet Sauvignon Napa Valley 1990 • $41 • (11/15/93) • CS

92 **GUENOC** Cabernet Sauvignon Napa Valley Beckstoffer Vineyard Reserve 1990 • $35 • (11/15/93)

92 **MOUNT VEEDER** Reserve Napa Valley 1990 • $25 • (09/15/94) • CS

92 **OPUS ONE** Napa Valley 1990 • $65 • (11/30/93) • CS

92 **PHILIP TOGNI** Cabernet Sauvignon Napa Valley 1990 • $34 • (11/15/92)

92 **SIGNORELLO** Cabernet Sauvignon Napa Valley Founder's Reserve 1990 • $30 • (10/15/93)

92 **STAG'S LEAP WINE CELLARS** S.L.V. Cask 23 Napa Valley 1990 • $65 • (10/31/93) • CS

91 **ARROWOOD** Cabernet Sauvignon Sonoma County 1990 • $24 • (10/31/93) • SS

91 **CLOS PEGASE** Cabernet Sauvignon Napa Valley 1990 • $17 • (11/15/93) • SS

91 **CORISON** Cabernet Sauvignon Napa Valley 1990 • $24 • (10/15/93)

91 **DIAMOND CREEK** Cabernet Sauvignon Napa Valley Red Rock Terrace 1990 • $50 • (11/15/92)

91 **DOMINUS** Cabernet Sauvignon Napa Valley 1990 • $64 • (06/30/94) • SS

91 **FERRARI-CARANO** Reserve Sonoma County 1990 • $47 • (11/30/95)

91 **GUENOC** Langtry Lake County Meritage 1990 • $35 • (11/15/93)

91 **GUENOC** Meritage Red Lake County 1990 • $18 • (11/15/93) • SS

91 **HARRISON** Cabernet Sauvignon Napa Valley Reserve 1990 • $40 • (10/15/94)

91 **HEITZ** Cabernet Sauvignon Napa Valley Trailside Vineyard 1990 • $45 • (10/15/95) • CS

91 **KENDALL-JACKSON** Cardinale California 1990 • $50 • (10/15/94)

91 **LIVINGSTON** Cabernet Sauvignon Napa Valley Moffett Vineyard 1990 • $30 • (11/15/93)

91 **ROBERT MONDAVI** Cabernet Sauvignon Napa Valley Reserve 1990 • $55 • (10/31/93)

91 **ROCKING HORSE** Cabernet Sauvignon Stags Leap District Robinson Vineyard 1990 • $22 • (02/15/93)

91 **SILVER OAK** Cabernet Sauvignon Napa Valley 1990 • $32 • (11/15/94) • CS

91 **SPOTTSWOODE** Cabernet Sauvignon Napa Valley 1990 • $56 • (10/31/93) • CS

91 **ST. FRANCIS** Cabernet Sauvignon Sonoma County Reserve 1990 • $24 • (09/30/93)

91 **STAG'S LEAP WINE CELLARS** Cabernet Sauvignon Napa Valley 1990 • $18 • (05/15/93) • SS

91 **VIADER** Napa Valley 1990 • $25 • (07/15/93)

91 **VICHON** Cabernet Sauvignon Stags Leap District SLD 1990 • $24 • (11/15/93)

90 **A. RAFANELLI** Cabernet Sauvignon Dry Creek Valley Unfiltered 1990 • $15 • (09/15/93)

90 **ANDERSON'S CONN VALLEY** Cabernet Sauvignon Napa Valley Estate Reserve 1990 • $25 • (11/15/93)

90 **B.R. COHN** Cabernet Sauvignon Sonoma Valley Olive Hill Vineyard 1990 • $25 • (11/15/93)

90 **BERINGER** Cabernet Sauvignon Knights Valley 1990 • $13 • (11/15/93) • SS

90 **CAYMUS** Cabernet Sauvignon Napa Valley 1990 • $115 • (12/15/93) • SS

90 **CHATEAU MONTELENA** Cabernet Sauvignon Napa Valley The Montelena Estate 1990 • $46 • (11/15/94) • CS

90 **CHATEAU SOUVERAIN** Cabernet Sauvignon Alexander Valley 1990 • $11 • (11/15/93) • SS

90 **DIAMOND CREEK** Cabernet Sauvignon Napa Valley Lake 1990 • $176 • (02/15/93)

90 **ESTANCIA** Meritage Red Alexander Valley 1990 • $14 • (10/15/93) • SS

90 **GARY FARRELL** Cabernet Sauvignon Sonoma County Ladi's Vineyard 1990 • $18 • (11/15/92)

90 **GEYSER PEAK** Réserve Alexandre Alexander Valley 1990 • $30 • (11/15/93)

90 **GEYSER PEAK** Cabernet Sauvignon Alexander Valley Reserve 1990 • $15 • (06/15/93)

90 **GRACE FAMILY** Cabernet Sauvignon Napa Valley 1990 • $225 • (08/31/93)

90 **GROTH** Cabernet Sauvignon Napa Valley 1990 • $17 • (09/30/93) • SS

90 **HEITZ** Cabernet Sauvignon Napa Valley Martha's Vineyard 1990 • $65 • (04/30/95) • CS

90 **HEITZ** Cabernet Sauvignon Napa Valley 1990 • $18 • (04/30/95)

90 **KENDALL-JACKSON** Cabernet Sauvignon California Grand Reserve 1990 • $30 • (11/15/93)

90 **MARKHAM** Cabernet Sauvignon Napa Valley 1990 • $17 • (11/15/93) • SS

90 **NIEBAUM-COPPOLA** Rubicon Napa Valley 1990 • $35 • (12/15/95)

90 **PAHLMEYER** Caldwell Vineyard Napa Valley 1990 • $32 • (10/15/93)

90 **RAYMOND** Meritage Private Reserve Napa Valley 1990 • $40 • (10/31/94)

90 **ROBERT MONDAVI** Cabernet Sauvignon Napa Valley 1990 • $15 • (10/31/93) • SS

90 **S. ANDERSON** Cabernet Sauvignon Stags Leap District Richard Chambers Vineyard 1990 • $42 • (11/15/93)

90 **SEQUOIA GROVE** Cabernet Sauvignon Napa Valley Estate Reserve 1990 • $25 • (12/15/93)

90 **SEQUOIA GROVE** Cabernet Sauvignon Napa Valley 1990 • $16 • (03/31/94) • SS

90 **SHAFER** Cabernet Sauvignon Stags Leap District 1990 • $20 • (11/15/93)

90 **SILVERADO** Cabernet Sauvignon Stags Leap District 1990 • $16 • (06/30/93)

90 **ST. CLEMENT** Cabernet Sauvignon Napa Valley 1990 • $22 • (10/31/93)

90 **THE HESS COLLECTION** Cabernet Sauvignon Napa Valley Reserve 1990 • $38 • (11/15/94)

90 **THE HESS COLLECTION** Cabernet Sauvignon Napa Valley 1990 • $18 • (04/15/94) • CS

89 **BEAULIEU** Cabernet Sauvignon Napa Valley Georges de Latour Private Reserve 1990 • $40 • (11/15/94)

89 **BRAREN PAULI** Cabernet Sauvignon Dry Creek Valley 1990 • $13 • (10/31/93)

89 **CHATEAU SOUVERAIN** Cabernet Sauvignon Alexander Valley Winemaker's Reserve 1990 • $13 • (05/31/94)

89 **CLOS DU BOIS** Cabernet Sauvignon Alexander Valley Briarcrest Vineyard 1990 • $19 • (04/15/94)

89 **CLOS DU VAL** Cabernet Sauvignon Napa Valley Reserve 1990 • $45 • (04/30/95)

89 **DALLA VALLE** Maya Napa Valley 1990 • $50 • (09/30/93)

89 **DIAMOND CREEK** Cabernet Sauvignon Napa Valley Gravelly Meadow 1990 • $50 • (11/15/92)

89 **DRY CREEK** Meritage Dry Creek Valley 1990 • $18 • (11/15/94)

89 **DUNN** Cabernet Sauvignon Howell Mountain 1990 • $50 • (05/15/94)

89 **DURNEY** Cabernet Sauvignon Carmel Valley 1990 • $17 • (11/15/94)

89 **FERRARI-CARANO** Cabernet Sauvignon Sonoma County 1990 • $15 • (09/30/94)

89 **FORMAN** Cabernet Sauvignon Napa Valley 1990 • $30 • (07/15/93)

89 **KATHRYN KENNEDY** Cabernet Sauvignon Santa Cruz Mountains 1990 • $54 • (06/15/94)

89 **LAUREL GLEN** Cabernet Sauvignon Napa Valley Terra Rosa 1990 • $9 • (09/30/93) • BB

89 **LAUREL GLEN** Cabernet Sauvignon Sonoma Mountain 1990 • $30 • (11/15/93)

89 **LIPARITA** Cabernet Sauvignon Howell Mountain 1990 • $28 • (11/15/93)

89 **LONG** Cabernet Sauvignon Napa Valley 1990 • $30 • (08/31/93)

89 **MURRIETA'S WELL** Vendimia Red Livermore Valley 1990 • $28 • (11/15/94)

89 **RIDGE** Monte Bello Santa Cruz Mountains 1990 • $60 • (11/15/93)

89 **SILVER OAK** Cabernet Sauvignon Alexander Valley 1990 • $32 • (11/15/94)

89 **ST. FRANCIS** Cabernet Sauvignon Sonoma County 1990 • $10 • (09/30/93)

89 **STAG'S LEAP WINE CELLARS** Cabernet Sauvignon Napa Valley S.L.V. 1990 • $30 • (03/31/94)

89 **SWANSON** Cabernet Sauvignon Napa Valley 1990 • $23 • (11/15/93)

89 **VICHON** Cabernet Sauvignon Napa Valley 1990 • $16 • (08/31/93)

89 **WILLIAM SEAVEY** Cabernet Sauvignon Napa Valley 1990 • $24 • (08/31/94)

88 **ALEXANDER VALLEY VINEYARDS** Cabernet Sauvignon Alexander Valley Wetzel Family Estate 1990 • $14 • (06/15/93)

88 **ALTAMURA** Cabernet Sauvignon Napa Valley 1990 • $25 • (09/15/95)

88 **BURGESS** Cabernet Sauvignon Napa Valley Vintage Selection 1990 • $18 • (10/15/94)

88 **CHARLES KRUG** Cabernet Sauvignon Napa Valley 1990 • $12 • (10/31/93)

88 **CHIMNEY ROCK** Elevage Stags Leap District 1990 • $30 • (11/15/93)

88 **CLOS DU BOIS** Marlstone Vineyard Alexander Valley 1990 • $20 • (11/15/93)

88 **CUTLER** Cabernet Sauvignon Sonoma Valley 1990 • $19 • (11/15/94)

88 **DEER PARK** Cabernet Sauvignon Howell Mountain Beatty Ranch Reserve 1990 • $24 • (10/31/94)

88 **DIAMOND CREEK** Cabernet Sauvignon Napa Valley Three Vineyard Blend 1990 • $75 • (02/15/93)

88 **FAR NIENTE** Cabernet Sauvignon Napa Valley 1990 • $36 • (09/15/93)

88 **FRANCISCAN** Cabernet Sauvignon Napa Valley Oakville Estate 1990 • $13 • (10/31/93)

88 **FREEMARK ABBEY** Cabernet Sauvignon Napa Valley Sycamore Vineyards 1990 • $23 • (12/15/95)

88 **FROG'S LEAP** Cabernet Sauvignon Napa Valley 1990 • $17 • (09/30/93)

88 **HUSCH** Cabernet Sauvignon Mendocino La Ribera Vineyards 1990 • $14 • (08/31/93)

88 **INNISFREE** Cabernet Sauvignon Napa Valley 1990 • $11 • (04/30/93)

88 **IRON HORSE** Cabernets Alexander Valley 1990 • $19 • (11/15/93)

88 **J. LOHR** Cabernet Sauvignon Paso Robles Seven Oaks 1990 • $11 • (11/15/93)

88 **J. LOHR** Cabernet Sauvignon Paso Robles VS.1 1990 • $22 • (03/31/95)

88 **JOSEPH PHELPS** Cabernet Sauvignon Napa Valley Backus Vineyard 1990 • $30 • (11/15/93)

88 **JUSTIN** Isosceles San Luis Obispo County Reserve 1990 • $23 • (11/15/93)

88 **KATHRYN KENNEDY** Lateral California 1990 • $17 • (10/15/92)

88 **KUNDE** Claret Sonoma Valley Louis Kunde Founder's Reserve 1990 • $17 • (11/15/93)

88 **KUNDE** Cabernet Sauvignon Sonoma Valley 1990 • $15 • (03/15/93)

88 **LAUREL GLEN** Cabernet Sauvignon Sonoma Mountain Reserve 1990 • $75 • (11/15/93)

88 **LIVINGSTON** Cabernet Sauvignon Napa Valley Stanley's Selection 1990 • $20 • (03/15/93)

88 **LOCKWOOD** Cabernet Sauvignon Monterey Partners Reserve 1990 • $18 • (10/31/93)

88 **MARIO PERELLI-MINETTI** Cabernet Sauvignon Napa Valley 1990 • $15 • (11/15/94)

88 **MERRYVALE** Cabernet Sauvignon Napa Valley 1990 • $20 • (06/30/93)

88 **MONTICELLO** Cabernet Sauvignon Napa Valley Corley Reserve 1990 • $25 • (11/15/93)

88 **MOUNT EDEN** Cabernet Sauvignon Santa Cruz Mountains Lathweisen Ridge 1990 • $15 • (06/15/93)

88 **NAVARRO** Cabernet Sauvignon Mendocino 1990 • $17 • (10/15/95)

88 **OAKFORD** Cabernet Sauvignon Napa Valley 1990 • $25 • (11/15/94)

88 **PEJU** Cabernet Sauvignon Napa Valley HB Vineyard 1990 • $35 • (11/15/94)

88 **PRESTON** Cabernet Sauvignon Dry Creek Valley 1990 • $12 • (11/15/94)

88 **QUIVIRA** Cabernet Cuvée Dry Creek Valley 1990 • $15 • (11/15/93)

88 **RANCHO SISQUOC** Red Cellar Select Santa Maria Valley 1990 • $25 • (11/15/93)

88 **RAYMOND** Cabernet Sauvignon Napa Valley Private Reserve 1990 • $25 • (10/31/94)

88 **RAYMOND** Cabernet Sauvignon Napa Valley 1990 • $17 • (11/15/93)

88 **RIDGE** Cabernet Sauvignon Napa County York Creek 1990 • $16 • (11/15/93)

88 **RODNEY STRONG** Cabernet Sauvignon Northern Sonoma Reserve 1990 • $30 • (06/15/94)

88 **SAN SABA** Cabernet Sauvignon Monterey 1990 • $15 • (11/15/94)

88 **SOQUEL** Cabernet Sauvignon Santa Cruz Mountains 1990 • $16 • (03/31/93)

88 **STAG'S LEAP WINE CELLARS** Cabernet Sauvignon Napa Valley Fay 1990 • $30 • (03/31/94)

88 **STELTZNER** Claret Stags Leap District 1990 • $11 • (11/15/92)

88 **TUDAL** Cabernet Sauvignon Napa Valley 1990 • $17 • (02/28/94)

88 **VINCENT ARROYO** Cabernet Sauvignon Napa Valley 1990 • $15 • (11/15/92)

88 **WHITE ROCK** Claret Napa Valley 1990 • $19 • (04/15/94)

88 **WHITEHALL LANE** Cabernet Sauvignon Napa Valley 1990 • $13 • (12/15/93)

88 **WHITEHALL LANE** Cabernet Sauvignon Napa Valley Reserve 1990 • $23 • (02/28/95)

88 **WILLIAM HILL** Cabernet Sauvignon Napa Valley Reserve 1990 • $24 • (11/15/93)

88 **WINDEMERE** Cabernet Sauvignon Napa Valley Diamond Mountain 1990 • $14 • (08/31/93)

87 **ATLAS PEAK** Consenso Atlas Peak 1990 • $22 • (12/15/95)

87 **BANDIERA** Cabernet Sauvignon Napa Valley 1990 • $6 • (04/15/94) • BB

87 **CAKEBREAD** Cabernet Sauvignon Napa Valley Rutherford Reserve 1990 • $42 • (12/15/95)

87 **CHATEAU ST. JEAN** Cabernet Sauvignon Sonoma County Cinq Cépages 1990 • $18 • (09/30/94)

87 **CLOS DU BOIS** Cabernet Sauvignon Alexander Valley 1990 • $13 • (03/31/93)

87 **CLOS PEGASE** Hommage Napa Valley 1990 • $20 • (04/15/94)

87 **COSENTINO** Cabernet Sauvignon Napa Valley Reserve 1990 • $25 • (11/15/94)

87 **FETZER** Cabernet Sauvignon California Barrel Select 1990 • $12 • (11/15/93)

87 **GIRARD** Cabernet Sauvignon Napa Valley Estate Grown 1990 • $16 • (11/15/93)

87 **GRGICH HILLS** Cabernet Sauvignon Napa Valley 1990 • $22 • (04/30/95)

87 **HANNA** Cabernet Sauvignon Alexander Valley 1990 • $18 • (11/15/93)

87 **HARRISON** Cabernet Sauvignon Napa Valley 1990 • $30 • (07/15/93)

87 **HUSCH** Cabernet Sauvignon Mendocino North Field Select 1990 • $18 • (11/15/93)

87 **JOHNSON TURNBULL** Cabernet Sauvignon Napa Valley Vineyard Selection 67 1990 • $34 • (04/30/94)

87 **JORDAN** Cabernet Sauvignon Alexander Valley 1990 • $25 • (06/30/94)

87 **LAKESPRING** Cabernet Sauvignon Napa Valley 1990 • $10 • (05/15/94)

87 **LAUREL GLEN** Cabernet Sauvignon Sonoma Mountain Counterpoint 1990 • $15 • (03/15/93)

87 **LYETH** A Red Blend Alexander Valley 1990 • $13 • (06/30/93)

87 **MERIDIAN** Cabernet Sauvignon Paso Robles 1990 • $14 • (09/30/93)

87 **MURPHY-GOODE** Cabernet Sauvignon Alexander Valley Murphy Ranch 1990 • $15 • (10/15/93)

87 **ROBERT SINSKEY** RSV Claret Carneros 1990 • $28 • (05/15/94)

87 **ROBERT SINSKEY** Cabernet Sauvignon Napa Valley Aries 1990 • $11 • (10/31/93)

87 **ROSENBLUM** Holbrook Mitchell Trio Napa Valley 1990 • $22• (11/15/92)

87 **SMITH & HOOK** Cabernet Sauvignon Santa Lucia Highlands 1990• $18• (03/31/94)

87 **SMOTHERS BROTHERS** Cabernet Sauvignon Sonoma Valley Remick Ridge Ranch 1990• $18• (11/15/94)

87 **SOQUEL** Cabernet Sauvignon Stags Leap District 1990 • $18• (11/15/93)

87 **STERLING** Cabernet Sauvignon Reserve Napa Valley 1990• $30• (11/15/94)

87 **STONESTREET** Cabernet Sauvignon Alexander Valley 1990• $20• (11/15/94)

87 **SUTTER HOME** Cabernet Sauvignon Napa Valley Centennial Selection Reserve 1990• $12 • (10/31/93)

87 **TREFETHEN** Cabernet Sauvignon Napa Valley 1990 • $19• (11/15/95)

87 **TRUCHARD** Cabernet Sauvignon Napa Valley Carneros 1990• $18• (11/15/93)

87 **VON STRASSER** Cabernet Sauvignon Napa Valley Diamond Mountain 1990• $25• (11/15/93)

87 **WHITE OAK** Cabernet Sauvignon Alexander Valley 1990 • $14• (11/15/93)

86 **BEAUCANON** Cabernet Sauvignon Napa Valley 1990 • $11• (02/28/95)

86 **BENZIGER** Cabernet Sauvignon Sonoma County 1990 • $13• (09/30/93)

86 **CHALK HILL** Cabernet Sauvignon Chalk Hill 1990• $17 • (12/15/93)

86 **CHATEAU MARGARITE** Cabernet Sauvignon Napa Valley 1990• $12• (11/15/93)

86 **CHATEAU POTELLE** Cabernet Sauvignon Napa Valley Cuvée 95 1990• $16• (10/15/94)

86 **COSENTINO** Meritage The Poet California 1990• $23 • (05/15/95)

86 **COSENTINO** Cabernet Sauvignon Napa Valley 1990• $15 • (11/15/93)

86 **CRONIN** Joe's Cuvée California 1990• $27 • (03/15/94)

86 **DUCKHORN** Howell Mountain 1990• $25• (11/15/93)

86 **E. & J. GALLO** Cabernet Sauvignon Sonoma County Gallo Sonoma 1990• $10• (11/15/94)• BB

86 **ESTANCIA** Cabernet Sauvignon Alexander Valley 1990 • $9• (06/15/93)• BB

86 **FISHER** Cabernet Sauvignon Napa-Sonoma Counties Coach Insignia 1990• $20• (06/15/93)

86 **GIRARD** Cabernet Sauvignon Napa Valley Reserve 1990 • $25• (04/15/94)

86 **GUILLIAMS** Cabernet Sauvignon Napa Valley Spring Mountain District 1990• $15• (11/15/94)

86 **HALLCREST** Cabernet Sauvignon El Dorado County Covington Vineyard 1990• $19• (11/15/94)

86 **HAMBRECHT** Cabernet Sauvignon Dry Creek Valley Bradford Mountain Vineyard 1990• $13• (11/15/93)

86 **IRON HORSE** Cabernets T-T Vineyards Alexander Valley 1990• $15• (10/31/94)

86 **J. LOHR** Cabernet Sauvignon California Cypress 1990 • $7• (11/15/93)• BB

86 **JOSEPH PHELPS** Insignia Napa Valley 1990• $40 • (11/15/94)

86 **KENWOOD** Cabernet Sauvignon Sonoma Valley Artist Series 1990• $30• (12/15/93)

86 **KISTLER** Cabernet Sauvignon California Kistler Estate Vineyard 1990• $30• (02/28/94)

86 **MURRIETA'S WELL** Vendimia Livermore Valley 1990• $28 • (11/15/93)

86 **NEWLAN** Cabernet Sauvignon Napa Valley 1990• $26 • (02/28/95)

86 **RABBIT RIDGE** Cabernet Sauvignon Sonoma County Rabbit Ridge Ranch Estate Reserve 1990• $20 • (11/15/94)

86 **RAVENSWOOD** Pickberry Vineyards Sonoma Mountain 1990• $26• (11/15/93)

86 **ROBERT PECOTA** Cabernet Sauvignon Napa Valley Kara's Vineyard 1990• $16• (09/15/93)

86 **ROCHIOLI** Cabernet Sauvignon Russian River Valley J. Rochioli Neoma's Vineyard Reserve 1990• $24 • (06/15/93)

86 **RODNEY STRONG** Cabernet Sauvignon Northern Sonoma Alexander's Crown Vineyard 1990• $20• (11/15/93)

86 **ROMBAUER** Cabernet Sauvignon Napa Valley 1990• $18 • (11/15/94)

86 **ST. SUPERY** Cabernet Sauvignon Napa Valley Dollarhide Ranch 1990• $14• (11/15/93)

86 **STEVENOT** Cabernet Sauvignon Calaveras County Reserve 1990• $10• (07/31/93)

86 **TERRACES** Cabernet Sauvignon Napa Valley 1990• $40 • (11/15/94)

86 **VILLA MT. EDEN** Cabernet Sauvignon Napa Valley Grand Reserve 1990• $16• (11/15/93)

86 **WELLINGTON** Cabernet Sauvignon Mount Veeder Random Ridge 1990• $16• (10/15/93)

86 **WENTE BROS.** Cabernet Sauvignon Livermore Valley Charles Wetmore Vineyard Reserve 1990• $16 • (08/31/94)

86 **ZD** Cabernet Sauvignon Napa Valley 1990• $20 • (11/15/92)

85 **BEAULIEU** Meritage Napa Valley 1990• $20 • (11/15/94)

85 **BEAULIEU** Cabernet Sauvignon Napa Valley Rutherford 1990• $11• (10/31/93)

85 **BERNARD PRADEL** Cabernet Sauvignon Napa Valley Limited Barrel Selection 1990• $14• (09/15/95)

85 **BYRON** Cabernet Sauvignon Santa Barbara County 1990 • $16• (08/31/92)

85 **CARMENET** Meritage Sonoma Valley Moon Mountain Estate Vineyard 1990• $25• (11/15/93)

85 **CHIMNEY ROCK** Cabernet Sauvignon Stags Leap District 1990• $20• (04/30/94)

85 **CRONIN** Cabernet Sauvignon Santa Cruz Mountains 1990• $17• (02/28/95)

85 **CUVAISON** Cabernet Sauvignon Napa Valley 1990• $18 • (03/31/94)

85 **DE LOACH** Cabernet Sauvignon Russian River Valley 1990• $16• (03/31/93)

85 **DORCICH CELLARS** Cabernet Sauvignon Santa Clara County 1990• $20• (07/31/95)

85 **DURNEY** Cabernet Sauvignon Carmel Valley 1990• $12 • (11/15/92)

85 **FIRESTONE** Cabernet Sauvignon Santa Ynez Valley Reserve 1990• $20• (11/15/94)

85 **FLORA SPRINGS** Trilogy Napa Valley 1990• $33 • (02/28/94)

85 **FLORA SPRINGS** Cabernet Sauvignon Napa Valley Reserve 1990• $33• (02/28/94)

85 **FRANCISCAN** Meritage Magnificat Napa Valley 1990 • $20• (11/15/94)

85 **HALLCREST** Cabernet Sauvignon El Dorado County De Cascabel Vineyard Proprietors Reserve 1990• $13 • (11/15/94)

85 **HEITZ** Cabernet Sauvignon Napa Valley Bella Oaks Vineyard 1990• $27• (04/30/95)

85 **JOSEPH PHELPS** Cabernet Sauvignon Napa Valley 1990 • $24• (06/15/93)

85 **LA JOTA** Cabernet Sauvignon Howell Mountain 1990 • $28• (11/15/93)

85 **LAWRENCE J. BARGETTO** Cabernet Sauvignon Santa Cruz Mountains Bates Ranch 1990 • $16 • (12/15/95)

85 **LOUIS M. MARTINI** Cabernet Sauvignon Sonoma Valley Monte Rosso 1990 • $23 • (09/30/94)

85 **MARKHAM** Laurent Reserve Napa Valley 1990 • $25 • (12/31/94)

85 **MARTIN BROTHERS** Etrusco Paso Robles 1990 • $18 • (11/15/92)

85 **MAYACAMAS** Cabernet Sauvignon Napa Valley 1990 • $25 • (12/15/95)

85 **MOUNT EDEN** Cabernet Sauvignon Santa Cruz Mountains Old Vine Reserve 1990 • $30 • (11/15/93)

85 **NALLE** Cabernet Sauvignon Dry Creek Valley 1990 • $18 • (11/15/93)

85 **PEACHY CANYON** Cabernet Sauvignon Paso Robles 1990 • $15 • (03/31/93)

85 **QUAIL RIDGE** Cabernet Sauvignon Napa Valley 1990 • $13 • (11/15/94)

85 **QUIVIRA** Cabernet Cuvée Dry Creek Valley 1990 • $15 • (11/15/94)

85 **RUBISSOW-SARGENT** Les Trompettes Mount Veeder 1990 • $18 • (11/15/94)

85 **SANTA CRUZ MOUNTAIN** Cabernet Sauvignon Santa Cruz Mountains Bates Ranch 1990 • $15 • (12/15/95)

85 **STONESTREET** Legacy Alexander Valley 1990 • $35 • (11/15/93)

85 **STONESTREET** Cabernet Sauvignon Alexander Valley 1990 • $24 • (11/15/93)

85 **THE NEGOCIANTS** Cabernet Sauvignon Napa Valley 1990 • $10 • (03/31/94)

85 **VINE CLIFF** Cabernet Sauvignon Napa Valley 1990 • $35 • (11/15/93)

85 **WINTERBROOK** Cabernet Sauvignon Napa Valley Grand Reserve 1990 • $19 • (09/15/93)

85 **YORK MOUNTAIN** Cabernet Sauvignon San Luis Obispo County 1990 • $14 • (12/15/95)

84 **BEAULIEU** Tapestry Signet Collection Napa Valley 1990 • $20

84 **BENZIGER** A Tribute Sonoma Mountain Red 1990 • $27 • (11/15/94)

84 **CAFARO** Cabernet Sauvignon Napa Valley 1990 • $24 • (11/15/93)

84 **CHESTNUT HILL** Cabernet Sauvignon California Coastal Cuvée 1990 • $8 • (05/15/93)

84 **CINNABAR** Cabernet Sauvignon Santa Cruz Mountains 1990 • $20 • (11/15/94)

84 **CLOS DU VAL** Cabernet Sauvignon Napa Valley 1990 • $12 • (06/30/94)

84 **CORBETT CANYON** Cabernet Sauvignon Napa Valley Reserve 1990 • $9 • (09/15/93) • BB

84 **EBERLE** Cabernet Sauvignon Paso Robles 1990 • $15 • (09/15/94)

84 **FIELD STONE** Cabernet Sauvignon Alexander Valley Staten Family Reserve 1990 • $20 • (11/15/94)

84 **FIELD STONE** Cabernet Sauvignon Alexander Valley Vineyard Blend 1990 • $14 • (11/15/93)

84 **FIRESTONE** Cabernet Sauvignon Santa Ynez Valley Vintage Reserve 1990 • $20 • (02/15/93)

84 **FOXEN** Cabernet Sauvignon Santa Barbara County 1990 • $20 • (11/15/92)

84 **GLASS MOUNTAIN QUARRY** Cabernet Sauvignon California 1990 • $9 • (06/15/93)

84 **GUENOC** Cabernet Sauvignon Lake County 1990 • $11 • (04/15/94)

84 **HALLCREST** Cabernet Sauvignon Santa Cruz Mountains Beauregard Ranch Proprietors Reserve 1990 • $23 • (11/15/94)

84 **HOP KILN** Cabernet Sauvignon Russian River Valley 1990 • $14 • (09/15/93)

84 **HOPE FARMS** Cabernet Sauvignon Paso Robles 1990 • $9 • (11/15/94)

84 **JEKEL** Cabernet Sauvignon Arroyo Seco 1990 • $13 • (11/15/94)

84 **JOSEPH SWAN** Cabernet Sauvignon Sonoma Mountain Steiner Vineyard 1990 • $18 • (11/15/93)

84 **KENWOOD** Cabernet Sauvignon Sonoma Valley 1990 • $17 • (11/15/93)

84 **LAUREL GLEN** Cabernet Sauvignon Napa Valley Terra Rosa 1990 • $10 • (11/15/92)

84 **MEEKER** Cabernet Sauvignon Dry Creek Valley Scharf Family Vineyard 1990 • $14 • (11/15/94)

84 **MONTEREY VINEYARD** Cabernet Sauvignon Monterey County Limited Release 1990 • $11 • (11/15/94)

84 **PINE RIDGE** Cabernet Sauvignon Napa Valley Rutherford Cuvée 1990 • $16 • (11/15/93)

84 **POPE VALLEY CELLARS** Cabernet Sauvignon Napa Valley 1990 • $14 • (11/15/94)

84 **RAVENSWOOD** Cabernet Sauvignon Sonoma Valley Gregory Vineyard 1990 • $18 • (04/30/93)

84 **ROSENBLUM** Cabernet Sauvignon Napa Valley George Hendry Vineyard 1990 • $14 • (11/15/93)

84 **ROUND HILL** Cabernet Sauvignon Napa Valley Reserve 1990 • $11 • (11/15/94)

84 **ROUND HILL** Cabernet Sauvignon California 1990 • $7 • (05/31/94) • BB

84 **RUBISSOW-SARGENT** Cabernet Sauvignon Mount Veeder 1990 • $16 • (11/15/94)

84 **SADDLEBACK** Cabernet Sauvignon Napa Valley 1990 • $15 • (11/15/93)

84 **SIMI** Cabernet Sauvignon Sonoma County Centennial Edition 1990 • $14 • (11/15/94)

84 **TOBIN JAMES** Cabernet Sauvignon Paso Robles Private Stash 1990 • $12 • (11/15/92)

83 **ATLAS PEAK** Consenso Napa Valley 1990 • $22 • (11/15/93)

83 **BARNETT** Cabernet Sauvignon Napa Valley 1990 • $25 • (11/15/93)

83 **BOEGER** Cabernet Sauvignon El Dorado 1990 • $12 • (11/15/94)

83 **BOGLE** Cabernet Sauvignon California 1990 • $6 • (11/15/92) • BB

83 **BUEHLER** Cabernet Sauvignon Napa Valley 1990 • $12 • (11/15/93)

83 **BUENA VISTA** Cabernet Sauvignon Carneros Grand Reserve 1990 • $24 • (10/15/94)

83 **CAKEBREAD** Cabernet Sauvignon Napa Valley 1990 • $21 • (09/15/93)

83 **CEDAR MOUNTAIN** Cabernet Sauvignon Livermore Valley Blanches Vineyard 1990 • $20 • (11/15/93)

83 **CLOS DU VAL** Cabernet Sauvignon Stags Leap District 1990 • $18 • (11/15/94)

83 **COTES DE SONOMA** Cabernet Sauvignon Sonoma County 1990 • $6 • (10/31/92) • BB

83 **FETZER** Cabernet Sauvignon California Valley Oaks 1990 • $8 • (03/15/93)

83 **FOREST GLEN** Cabernet Sauvignon Sonoma County 1990 • $12 • (09/15/93)

83 **FREEMARK ABBEY** Cabernet Sauvignon Napa Valley 1990 • $16 • (11/15/94)

83 **GUNDLACH BUNDSCHU** Cabernet Sauvignon Sonoma Valley Rhinefarm Vineyards 1990 • $14 • (11/15/93)

83 **HANZELL** Cabernet Sauvignon Sonoma Valley 1990 • $20 • (11/15/94)

83 **JOULLIAN** Cabernet Sauvignon Carmel Valley 1990 • $14 • (12/15/95)

83 **KENDALL-JACKSON** Cabernet Sauvignon California Vintner's Reserve 1990 • $13 • (11/15/92)

83 **LIBERTY SCHOOL** Cabernet Sauvignon California Vintner Select Series Three 1990 • $7 • (06/15/93)

83 **LONGORIA** Cabernet Sauvignon Santa Ynez Valley 1990 • $15 • (06/15/93)

83 **MILAT** Cabernet Sauvignon Napa Valley 1990 • $14 • (11/15/94)

83 **MONTPELLIER** Cabernet Sauvignon California 1990 • $8 • (11/15/94)

83 **MOUNT PALOMAR** Cabernet Sauvignon Temecula 1990 • $12 • (07/15/93)

83 **NEWTON** Claret Napa Valley 1990 • $12 • (08/31/92)

83 **PINE RIDGE** Cabernet Sauvignon Stags Leap District 1990 • $30 • (11/15/93)

83 **SANTA BARBARA WINERY** Cabernet Sauvignon Santa Ynez Valley 1990 • $11 • (11/15/93)

83 **SANTA BARBARA WINERY** Cabernet Sauvignon Santa Ynez Valley Reserve 1990 • $16 • (11/15/93)

83 **STERLING** Cabernet Sauvignon Napa Valley 1990 • $14 • (11/15/93)

83 **VILLA MT. EDEN** Cabernet Sauvignon California Cellar Select 1990 • $10 • (03/31/93)

83 **WELLINGTON** Cabernet Sauvignon Sonoma County Mohrhardt Ridge Vineyard 1990 • $14 • (09/15/93)

83 **WILDHURST** Cabernet Sauvignon Clear Lake 1990 • $10 • (07/31/92)

82 **BEL ARBORS** Cabernet Sauvignon California 1990 • $6 • (03/15/93) • BB

82 **BRUTOCAO** Cabernet Sauvignon Mendocino Unfiltered Unfined 1990 • $13 • (05/15/94)

82 **BUENA VISTA** Cabernet Sauvignon Carneros 1990 • $11 • (09/15/93)

82 **CASTORO** Cabernet Sauvignon Paso Robles Reserve 1990 • $12 • (11/15/93)

82 **CLONINGER** Cabernet Sauvignon Monterey 1990 • $15 • (07/15/93)

82 **CRONIN** Concerto Stags Leap District Robinson Vineyard 1990 • $17 • (03/15/94)

82 **FENESTRA** Cabernet Sauvignon Livermore Valley 1990 • $12 • (11/15/93)

82 **HAWK CREST** Cabernet Sauvignon California 1990 • $9 • (04/30/93)

82 **HAYWOOD** Cabernet Sauvignon California Vintner's Select 1990 • $8 • (03/15/93)

82 **KONOCTI** Cabernet Sauvignon Lake County 1990 • $10 • (11/15/93)

82 **KUNDE** Cabernet Sauvignon Sonoma Valley Estate Reserve 1990 • $23 • (11/15/93)

82 **LIBERTY SCHOOL** Cabernet Sauvignon California Vintner Select Series Three 1990 • $7 • (08/31/92)

82 **MAZZOCCO** Matrix Sonoma County 1990 • $28 • (11/15/94)

82 **MCDOWELL** Cabernet Sauvignon Mendocino 1990 • $9 • (07/15/93)

82 **MEEKER** Cabernet Sauvignon Dry Creek Valley Gold Leaf Cuvée 1990 • $14 • (09/15/93)

82 **MICHEL-SCHLUMBERGER** Cabernet Sauvignon Dry Creek Valley Reserve 1990 • $35 • (11/15/94)

82 **MISSION VIEW** Cabernet Sauvignon Paso Robles 1990 • $12 • (11/15/94)

82 **NAPA RIDGE** Cabernet Sauvignon North Coast North Coast Reserve 1990 • $13 • (11/15/94)

82 **OAKVILLE BENCH** Cabernet Sauvignon Napa County 1990 • $12 • (05/15/94)

82 **OPTIMA** Cabernet Sauvignon Alexander Valley 1990 • $27 • (06/15/94)

82 **PAHLMEYER** Caldwell Vineyard Napa Valley Minty Cuvée 1990 • $NA

82 **PESENTI** Cabernet Sauvignon Paso Robles Family Reserve 1990 • $12 • (11/15/92)

82 **PHILIPPE-LORRAINE** Cabernet Sauvignon Napa Valley 1990 • $10 • (09/15/93)

82 **RUSTRIDGE** Cabernet Sauvignon Napa Valley 1990 • $30 • (12/15/95)

82 **SILVER HORSE** Cabernet Sauvignon Paso Robles 1990 • $10 • (11/15/94)

82 **STAR HILL** Cabernet Sauvignon Napa Valley Bartolucci Vineyard Doc's Reserve 1990 • $24 • (02/15/93)

82 **TOPAZ** Rouge de Trois Napa Valley 1990 • $16 • (06/30/93)

82 **VICHON** Cabernet Sauvignon California Coastal Selection 1990 • $9 • (11/15/93)

82 **YORK MOUNTAIN** Cabernet Sauvignon San Luis Obispo County Reserve 1990 • $16 • (12/15/95)

81 **ADELAIDA** Cabernet Sauvignon San Luis Obispo County 1990 • $22 • (11/15/93)

81 **CANTERBURY** Cabernet Sauvignon California 1990 • $7 • (11/15/92)

81 **CHAPPELLET** Cabernet Sauvignon Napa Valley 1990 • $25 • (11/15/93)

81 **COSENTINO** Cabernet Sauvignon Napa County 1990 • $15 • (11/15/93)

81 **CRESTON** Cabernet Sauvignon San Luis Obispo 1990 • $10 • (11/15/94)

81 **FIRESTONE** Cabernet Sauvignon Santa Ynez Valley 1990 • $12 • (11/15/93)

81 **GEYSER PEAK** Cabernet Sauvignon Sonoma County 1990 • $10 • (06/15/93)

81 **GREENWOOD RIDGE** Cabernet Sauvignon Anderson Valley Estate Reserve 1990 • $16 • (11/15/92)

81 **GUNDLACH BUNDSCHU** Bearitage Sonoma Valley 1990 • $10 • (05/15/93)

81 **HOPE FARMS** Cabernet Sauvignon Paso Robles 1990 • $9 • (11/15/93)

81 **JOHNSON TURNBULL** Cabernet Sauvignon Napa Valley 1990 • $16 • (03/31/94)

81 **KLEIN** Cabernet Sauvignon Santa Cruz Mountains 1990 • $25 • (11/15/93)

81 **LOCKWOOD** Cabernet Sauvignon Monterey Partners Reserve 1990 • $9 • (11/15/92)

81 **MAACAMA CREEK** Cabernet Sauvignon Alexander Valley Reserve 1990 • $14 • (11/15/92)

81 **MIRASSOU** Cabernet Sauvignon Monterey County Fifth Generation Family Selection 1990 • $9 • (09/15/93)

81 **RENAISSANCE** Cabernet Sauvignon North Yuba 1990 • $14 • (11/15/94)

81 **RETZLAFF** Meritage Livermore Valley 1990 • $18 • (11/15/93)

81 **ROBERT MONDAVI** Cabernet Sauvignon California Woodbridge 1990 • $8 • (10/31/92)

81 **RODNEY STRONG** Cabernet Sauvignon Sonoma County 1990 • $11 • (11/15/93)

81 **STERLING** Cabernet Sauvignon Napa Valley Diamond Mountain Ranch 1990 • $18 • (11/15/93)

81 **STONEGATE** Cabernet Sauvignon Napa Valley 1990 • $14 • (11/15/94)

81 **STRATFORD** Cabernet Sauvignon California 1990 • $12 • (11/15/92)

81 **SUTTER HOME** Cabernet Sauvignon California 1990 • $6 • (09/15/93) • BB

81 **WENTE BROS.** Cabernet Sauvignon Livermore Valley Wente Family Estate Selection 1990 • $8 • (11/15/93)

81 **WINTERBROOK** Cabernet Sauvignon Napa County 1990 • $9 • (08/31/92)

80 **BEAULIEU** Cabernet Sauvignon Napa Valley Beautour 1990 • $8 • (11/15/93)

80 **BEL ARBORS** Cabernet Sauvignon California Founder's Selection 1990 • $6 • (11/15/93)

80 **BLACK MOUNTAIN** Cabernet Sauvignon Alexander Valley Fat Cat 1990 • $18 • (06/15/93)

80 **DEHLINGER** Cabernet Sauvignon Russian River Valley 1990 • $15 • (11/15/94)

80 **FIELD STONE** Cabernet Sauvignon Alexander Valley Hoot Owl Barrel Select 1990 • $16 • (05/15/94)

80 **FOPPIANO** Cabernet Sauvignon Russian River Valley 1990 • $9 • (11/15/94)

80 **GOLDEN CREEK** Cabernet Sauvignon Sonoma County 1990 • $12 • (11/15/94)

80 **HAHN** Cabernet Sauvignon Santa Lucia Highlands 1990 • $10 • (05/15/94)

80 **HESS SELECT** Cabernet Sauvignon California 1990 • $9 • (11/15/92)

80 **INDIAN SPRINGS** Cabernet Sauvignon Nevada County 1990 • $8 • (11/15/93)

80 **JUSTIN** Cabernet Sauvignon San Luis Obispo County 1990 • $19 • (11/15/93)

80 **M.G. VALLEJO** Cabernet Sauvignon California 1990 • $6 • (11/15/92) • BB

80 **MONTEREY VINEYARD** Cabernet Sauvignon Monterey County Classic 1990 • $6 • (03/31/93) • BB

80 **MONTEVINA** Cabernet Sauvignon California 1990 • $9 • (05/15/93)

80 **MORAGA** Cabernet Sauvignon Bel Air 1990 • $50 • (11/15/94)

80 **PAGE MILL** Cabernet Sauvignon Napa Valley V. & L. Eisele Vineyard 1990 • $18 • (03/31/96)

80 **R.H. PHILLIPS** Cabernet Sauvignon California 1990 • $8 • (11/15/92)

80 **SEBASTIANI** Cabernet Sauvignon Sonoma County 1990 • $10 • (11/15/94)

80 **SOQUEL** Cabernet Sauvignon Stags Leap District 1990 • $20 • (02/29/96)

79 **BEAULIEU** Cabernet Sauvignon Napa Valley Claret Special Release 1990 • $7 • (11/15/92)

79 **BRANDER** Bouchet Tête de Cuvée Santa Ynez Valley 1990 • $18 • (11/15/93)

79 **CALLAWAY** Cabernet Sauvignon California 1990 • $8 • (11/15/93)

79 **DOMAINE MICHEL** Cabernet Sauvignon Sonoma County 1990 • $12 • (11/15/94)

79 **LOUIS M. MARTINI** Cabernet Sauvignon North Coast 1990 • $8 • (11/15/94)

79 **MIRASSOU** Cabernet Sauvignon Monterey County Fifth Generation Harvest Reserve Limited 1990 • $12 • (11/15/93)

79 **NEVADA CITY** Claret Sierra Foothills The Directors' Reserve 1990 • $14 • (11/15/93)

79 **PARDUCCI** Cabernet Sauvignon North Coast 1990 • $7 • (11/15/94)

79 **RIVERSIDE FARM** Cabernet Sauvignon California 1990 • $7 • (11/15/92)

79 **SEGHESIO** Cabernet Sauvignon Sonoma County 1990 • $9 • (06/15/93)

79 **STEVENOT** Cabernet Sauvignon California 1990 • $8 • (11/15/92)

79 **TERRA** Cabernet Sauvignon Napa Valley 1990 • $13

78 **ARCIERO** Cabernet Sauvignon Paso Robles 1990 • $7 • (11/15/94)

78 **ARCIERO** Cabernet Sauvignon Paso Robles Reserve 1990 • $14 • (12/15/95)

78 **CHRISTOPHE** Cabernet Sauvignon Napa Valley 1990 • $9 • (07/15/93)

78 **FENESTRA** Livermore Valley 1990 • $35 • (12/15/95)

78 **M.G. VALLEJO** Cabernet Sauvignon California Harvest Select 1990 • $7 • (06/15/93)

78 **MERRYVALE** Profile Napa Valley 1990 • $36 • (12/15/95)

78 **NAPA CELLARS** Cabernet Sauvignon California 1990 • $8 • (11/15/94)

78 **RAYMOND** Cabernet Sauvignon California Amberhill California Selection 1990 • $8 • (11/15/94)

77 **DE LORIMIER** Mosaic Alexander Valley Meritage 1990 • $18 • (06/15/94)

77 **FREMONT CREEK** Cabernet Sauvignon Mendocino Napa Counties Beckstoffer Vineyards 1990 • $9 • (11/15/94)

77 **HAGAFEN** Cabernet Sauvignon Napa Valley 1990 • $20 • (05/15/94)

77 **HARMONY CELLARS** Cabernet Sauvignon Paso Robles 1990 • $12 • (11/15/93)

77 **MORGAN** Cabernet Sauvignon Carmel Valley 1990 • $14 • (11/15/93)

77 **TIJSSELING** Cabernet Sauvignon Mendocino County 1990 • $8 • (11/15/92)

76 **MADDALENA** Cabernet Sauvignon Sonoma County 1990 • $8 • (11/15/94)

76 **MOUNTAIN VIEW** Cabernet Sauvignon North Coast 1990 • $6 • (06/15/93)

76 **RANCHO SISQUOC** Cabernet Sauvignon Santa Maria Valley 1990 • $14 • (11/15/93)

75 **BARON HERZOG** Cabernet Sauvignon California Selection 1990 • $11 • (06/15/93)

75 **GREENWOOD RIDGE** Cabernet Sauvignon Anderson Valley Estate Reserve 1990 • $16 • (06/15/93)

75 **WOODSIDE** Cabernet Sauvignon Santa Cruz Mountains 1990 • $24 • (11/15/93)

74 **MILL CREEK** Cabernet Sauvignon Dry Creek Valley 1990 • $12 • (11/15/93)

74 **PEPPERWOOD GROVE** Cabernet Sauvignon California 1990 • $5 • (11/15/92)

74 **SHENANDOAH** Cabernet Sauvignon Amador County 1990 • $10 • (11/15/92)

74 **TULOCAY** Cabernet Sauvignon Napa Valley Cliff Vineyard 1990 • $12 • (11/15/94)

73 **J. PEDRONCELLI** Cabernet Sauvignon Dry Creek Valley 1990 • $9 • (11/15/93)

73 **RICHARDSON** Cabernet Sauvignon Sonoma Valley Horne 1990 • $12 • (11/15/93)

73 **VENDANGE** Cabernet Sauvignon California 1990 • $6 • (08/31/92)

71 **VILLA HELENA** Cabernet Sauvignon Napa Valley Atlas Peak Baron von Kees Vineyard 1990 • $22 • (11/15/93)

70 **BOCAGE** Cabernet Sauvignon Monterey Proprietor's Cuvée 1990 • $10 • (11/15/94)

70 **BOISSET** Cabernet Sauvignon Sonoma County 1990 • $15 • (11/15/94)

68 **STONE CREEK** Cabernet Sauvignon Napa Valley Chairman's Reserve 1990 • $10 • (11/15/93)

1987 CALIFORNIA CABERNET
VINTAGE RATING: 94

98 **CAYMUS** Cabernet Sauvignon Napa Valley Special Selection 1987 • $115 • (10/31/91) • CS

97 **GRACE FAMILY** Cabernet Sauvignon Napa Valley 1987 • $260 • (06/30/90)

97 **OPUS ONE** Napa Valley 1987 • $96 • (11/15/90) • CS

96 **SPOTTSWOODE** Cabernet Sauvignon Napa Valley 1987 • $62 • (09/15/90) • SS

95 **CHATEAU MONTELENA** Cabernet Sauvignon Napa Valley 1987 • $91 • (10/31/91) • SS

95 **DIAMOND CREEK** Cabernet Sauvignon Napa Valley Volcanic Hill 1987 • $58 • (12/15/89)

95 **DUCKHORN** Cabernet Sauvignon Napa Valley 1987 • $39 • (06/30/90) • CS

95 **DUNN** Cabernet Sauvignon Howell Mountain 1987 • $72 • (11/30/91)

95 **HEITZ** Cabernet Sauvignon Napa Valley Martha's Vineyard 1987 • $86 • (03/31/92) • CS

95 **KENDALL-JACKSON** Cardinale California Meritage 1987 • $44 • (03/31/92)

95 **LA JOTA** Cabernet Sauvignon Howell Mountain 1987 • $31 • (07/31/90) • SS

95 **WILLIAM HILL** Cabernet Sauvignon Napa Valley Reserve 1987 • $39 • (11/15/90) • SS

94 **BERINGER** Cabernet Sauvignon Napa Valley Private Reserve 1987 • $63 • (10/31/91)

94 **DIAMOND CREEK** Cabernet Sauvignon Napa Valley Red Rock Terrace 1987 • $52 • (12/15/89)

94 **DUNN** Cabernet Sauvignon Howell Mountain 1987 • $72 • (04/15/91)

94 **DUNN** Cabernet Sauvignon Napa Valley 1987 • $49 • (11/30/91)

94 **FROG'S LEAP** Cabernet Sauvignon Napa Valley 1987 • $39 • (12/31/89) • SS

94 **LAUREL GLEN** Cabernet Sauvignon Sonoma Mountain Counterpoint 1987 • $13 • (10/31/89)

94 **PHILIP TOGNI** Cabernet Sauvignon Napa Valley 1987 • $33 • (08/31/90)

94 **ROBERT MONDAVI** Cabernet Sauvignon Napa Valley Reserve 1987 • $74 • (11/30/91)

94 **THE HESS COLLECTION** Cabernet Sauvignon Napa Valley 1987 • $17 • (04/15/91) • SS

93 **BENZIGER** Cabernet Sauvignon Sonoma County 1987 • $22 • (09/30/90) • SS

93 **CAYMUS** Cabernet Sauvignon Napa Valley 1987 • $96 • (09/15/90)

93 **DUNN** Cabernet Sauvignon Napa Valley 1987 • $56 • (11/15/90)

93 **FORMAN** Cabernet Sauvignon Napa Valley 1987 • $30 • (09/30/90) • CS

93 **LOUIS M. MARTINI** Cabernet Sauvignon Sonoma Valley Monte Rosso 1987 • $25 • (11/15/90)

93 **MAZZOCCO** Cabernet Sauvignon Alexander Valley Claret Style 1987 • $20 • (08/31/90)

93 **QUAIL RIDGE** Cabernet Sauvignon Napa Valley 1987 • $16 • (09/30/91)

93 **SILVERADO** Cabernet Sauvignon Stags Leap District Limited Reserve 1987 • $45 • (10/31/91)

93 **STERLING** Cabernet Sauvignon Reserve Napa Valley 1987 • $43 • (11/15/90)

92 **B.R. COHN** Cabernet Sauvignon Sonoma Valley Olive Hill Vineyard 1987 • $31 • (06/30/90)

92 **BEAULIEU** Cabernet Sauvignon Napa Valley Georges de Latour Private Reserve 1987 • $38 • (11/15/91)

92 **CAIN** Cabernet Sauvignon Napa Valley Estate 1987 • $25 • (10/15/90)

92 **CHAPPELLET** Cabernet Sauvignon Napa Valley Reserve 1987 • $27 • (02/15/93)

92 **CHATEAU ST. JEAN** Cabernet Sauvignon Alexander Valley 1987 • $17 • (06/30/91) • SS

92 **CHATEAU ST. JEAN** Cabernet Sauvignon Alexander Valley Reserve 1987 • $38 • (07/31/92) • CS

92 **CLOS DU VAL** Reserve Stags Leap District 1987 • $49 • (07/15/92) • CS

92 **CLOS DU VAL** Cabernet Sauvignon Stags Leap District 1987 • $21 • (06/30/91)

92 **CORISON** Cabernet Sauvignon Napa Valley 1987 • $20 • (11/15/90)

92 **CUVAISON** Cabernet Sauvignon Napa Valley 1987 • $25 • (10/31/90)

92 **FOLIE A DEUX** Cabernet Sauvignon Napa Valley 1987 • $18 • (11/15/90)

92 **GUENOC** Cabernet Sauvignon Napa Valley Beckstoffer Vineyard Reserve 1987 • $24 • (06/30/91)

92 **KENWOOD** Cabernet Sauvignon Sonoma Valley Jack London Vineyard 1987 • $19 • (01/31/91)

92 **MORGAN** Cabernet Sauvignon Carmel Valley 1987 • $16 • (09/30/90)

92 **OPTIMA** Cabernet Sauvignon Sonoma County 1987 • $22 • (12/15/90)

92 **RODNEY STRONG** Cabernet Sauvignon Alexander Valley Reserve 1987 • $28 • (09/30/91)

92 **SHAFER** Cabernet Sauvignon Stags Leap District 1987 • $19 • (07/31/90)

92 **SILVERADO** Cabernet Sauvignon Stags Leap District 1987 • $25 • (04/15/90) • SS

92 **SWANSON** Cabernet Sauvignon Napa Valley 1987 • $25 • (10/15/91)

92 **TERRACES** Cabernet Sauvignon 1987 • $38 • (02/29/92)

91 **A. RAFANELLI** Cabernet Sauvignon Dry Creek Valley 1987 • $12 • (08/31/90)

91 **CAIN** Five Napa Valley 1987 • $30 • (04/30/91)

91 **CAKEBREAD** Cabernet Sauvignon Napa Valley Rutherford Reserve 1987 • $23 • (09/15/93)

91 **DIAMOND CREEK** Cabernet Sauvignon Napa Valley Lake 1987 • $220 • (11/15/90)

91 **EDMUNDS ST. JOHN** Les Fleurs du Chaparral Napa Valley 1987 • $15 • (08/31/90)

91 **FLORA SPRINGS** Cabernet Sauvignon Napa Valley Cellar Select 1987 • $25 • (11/15/90)

91 **HACIENDA** Antares Sonoma County 1987 • $28 • (11/15/90)

91 **MAZZOCCO** Matrix Sonoma County 1987 • $28 • (01/31/92)

91 **OAKFORD** Cabernet Sauvignon Napa Valley 1987 • $34 • (11/15/90)

91 **PAHLMEYER** Caldwell Vineyard Napa Valley 1987 • $41 • (11/15/90)

91 **SANTA CRUZ MOUNTAIN** Cabernet Sauvignon Santa Cruz Mountains Bates Ranch 1987 • $16 • (11/15/92)

91 **STERLING** Cabernet Sauvignon Napa Valley 1987 • $14 • (05/15/90)

91 **STERLING** Cabernet Sauvignon Napa Valley Diamond Mountain Ranch 1987 • $16 • (11/15/90)

91 **VINCENT ARROYO** Cabernet Sauvignon Napa Valley 1987 • $12 • (11/15/90)

90 **BENZIGER** Cabernet Sauvignon Sonoma County 1987 • $22 • (08/10/90)

90 **BERINGER** Cabernet Sauvignon Knights Valley 1987 • $20 • (11/15/90)

90 **CAKEBREAD** Cabernet Sauvignon Napa Valley 1987 • $25 • (10/15/90)

90 **CHIMNEY ROCK** Cabernet Sauvignon Stags Leap District 1987 • $29 • (07/31/91) • SS

90 **CLOS DU BOIS** Marlstone Vineyard Alexander Valley 1987 • $27 • (07/31/91)

90 **CLOS PEGASE** Hommage California 1987 • $20 • (08/31/91)

90 **CUTLER** Cabernet Sauvignon Sonoma Valley Batto Ranch 1987 • $17 • (03/31/92)

90 **DIAMOND CREEK** Cabernet Sauvignon Napa Valley Gravelly Meadow 1987 • $50 • (12/15/89)

90 **FLORA SPRINGS** Trilogy Napa Valley 1987 • $33 • (05/15/91)

90 **FREEMARK ABBEY** Cabernet Sauvignon Napa Valley Sycamore Vineyards 1987 • $25 • (11/15/93)

90 **GAN EDEN** Cabernet Sauvignon Alexander Valley 1987 • $18 • (03/31/91)

90 **GEYSER PEAK** Réserve Alexandre Alexander Valley 1987 • $18 • (06/15/91)

90 **HEITZ** Cabernet Sauvignon Napa Valley 1987 • $21 • (04/15/92) • SS

90 **HUSCH** Cabernet Sauvignon Mendocino La Ribera Vineyards 1987 • $12 • (11/15/90)

90 **JORDAN** Cabernet Sauvignon Alexander Valley 1987 • $36 • (11/15/91)

90 **JUSTIN** Reserve Paso Robles 1987 • $20 • (02/15/91)

90 **KENWOOD** Cabernet Sauvignon Sonoma Valley 1987 • $15 • (07/15/91)

90 **LAUREL GLEN** Cabernet Sauvignon Sonoma Mountain 1987 • $34 • (09/15/90)

90 **MONTICELLO** Cabernet Sauvignon Napa Valley Jefferson Cuvée 1987 • $14 • (09/30/90)

90 **MONTICELLO** Cabernet Sauvignon Napa Valley Corley Reserve 1987 • $25 • (11/15/90)

90 **ROBERT MONDAVI** Cabernet Sauvignon Napa Valley Reserve 1987 • $55 • (08/31/90)

90 **ROBERT PECOTA** Cabernet Sauvignon Napa Valley Kara's Vineyard 1987 • $17 • (10/15/90)

90 **ROBERT PEPI** Cabernet Sauvignon Napa Valley Vine Hill Ranch 1987 • $24 • (04/30/91)

90 **ST. CLEMENT** Cabernet Sauvignon Napa Valley 1987 • $23 • (09/30/91) • CS

90 **STRATFORD** Cabernet Sauvignon Napa Valley Partners' Reserve 1987 • $16 • (04/30/91)

90 **WHITEHALL LANE** Cabernet Sauvignon Napa Valley Reserve 1987 • $28 • (11/15/91)

90 **ZD** Cabernet Sauvignon Napa Valley Estate Bottled 1987 • $40 • (01/31/91)

89 **ABREU** Cabernet Sauvignon Napa Valley Madrona Ranch 1987 • $25 • (07/31/91)

89 **ADELAIDA** Cabernet Sauvignon Paso Robles 1987 • $14 • (02/28/91)

89 **BANDIERA** Cabernet Sauvignon Napa Valley 1987 • $7 • (11/15/91) • BB

89 **CARMENET** Red Sonoma Valley 1987 • $24 • (11/15/90)

89 **CONN CREEK** Triomphe Napa Valley 1987 • $26 • (07/15/92)

89 **CRONIN** Cabernet Sauvignon Merlot Stags Leap District Robinson Vineyard 1987 • $17 • (02/28/91)

89 **CUTLER** Satyre Sonoma Valley 1987 • $20 • (07/15/92)

89 **DOMINUS** Napa Valley 1987 • $43 • (11/15/91)

89 **FRANCISCAN** Cabernet Sauvignon Napa Valley Oakville Estate 1987 • $12 • (02/15/91)

89 **GEYSER PEAK** Cabernet Sauvignon Alexander Valley Estate Reserve 1987 • $14 • (06/15/91)

89 **GUENOC** Cabernet Sauvignon Lake County 1987 • $12 • (07/15/91)

89 **GUNDLACH BUNDSCHU** Cabernet Sauvignon Sonoma Valley Rhinefarm Vineyards Vintage Reserve 1987 • $22 • (07/31/92)

89 **GUSTAVE NIEBAUM** Cabernet Sauvignon Napa Valley Mast Vineyard 1987 • $14 • (08/31/92)

89 **INGLENOOK** Cabernet Sauvignon Napa Valley Reserve Cask 1987 • $21 • (11/15/92)

89 **JOHNSON TURNBULL** Cabernet Sauvignon Napa Valley Vineyard Selection 67 1987 • $22 • (06/30/91)

89 **KATHRYN KENNEDY** Cabernet Sauvignon Santa Cruz Mountains 1987 • $46 • (01/31/91)

89 **MURPHY-GOODE** Cabernet Sauvignon Alexander Valley 1987 • $17 • (05/31/90)

89 **NALLE** Cabernet Sauvignon Dry Creek Valley 1987 • $18 • (01/31/91)

89 **ROBERT KEEBLE** Cabernet Sauvignon Napa Valley 1987 • $14 • (10/15/91)

89 **RODNEY STRONG** Cabernet Sauvignon Alexander Valley Alexander's Crown Vineyard 1987 • $17 • (07/15/91)

89 **SILVER OAK** Cabernet Sauvignon Napa Valley 1987 • $44 • (10/15/91)

89 **SILVER OAK** Cabernet Sauvignon Alexander Valley 1987 • $45 • (10/15/91)

89 **SILVER OAK** Cabernet Sauvignon Napa Valley Bonny's Vineyard 1987 • $87 • (10/31/92)

89 **SIMI** Cabernet Sauvignon Sonoma County 1987 • $17 • (05/15/91)

89 **STAGS' LEAP WINERY** Cabernet Sauvignon Stags Leap District 1987 • $18 • (06/30/91)

88 **CLOS DU BOIS** Cabernet Sauvignon Alexander Valley Briarcrest Vineyard 1987 • $30 • (11/15/91)

88 **DEHLINGER** Cabernet Sauvignon Russian River Valley 1987 • $13 • (02/28/91)

88 **ESTANCIA** Meritage Alexander Valley 1987 • $12 • (01/31/91)

88 **FAR NIENTE** Cabernet Sauvignon Napa Valley 1987 • $39 • (11/15/90)

88 **FETZER** Cabernet Sauvignon Sonoma County Reserve 1987 • $22 • (09/30/93)

88 **GEYSER PEAK** Cabernet Sauvignon Sonoma County 1987 • $8 • (11/30/90) • BB

88 **GIRARD** Cabernet Sauvignon Napa Valley Reserve 1987 • $27 • (11/15/91)

88 **GROTH** Cabernet Sauvignon Napa Valley Reserve 1987 • $58 • (03/31/92)

88 **GUENOC** Meritage Langtry Lake-Napa Counties 1987 • $35 • (04/15/91)

88 **HAGAFEN** Cabernet Sauvignon Napa Valley 1987 • $20 • (04/30/90)

88 **JOSEPH PHELPS** Cabernet Sauvignon Napa Valley Backus Vineyard 1987 • $35 • (07/15/91)

88 **KENWOOD** Cabernet Sauvignon Sonoma Valley Artist Series 1987 • $35 • (11/15/90)

88 **LYTTON SPRINGS** Cabernet Sauvignon Mendocino County Private Reserve 1987 • $18 • (09/15/90)

88 **NAVARRO** Cabernet Sauvignon Mendocino 1987 • $16 • (11/15/92)

88 **NEWLAN** Cabernet Sauvignon Napa Valley 1987 • $15 • (11/15/92)

88 **NIEBAUM-COPPOLA** Rubicon Napa Valley 1987 • $30 • (11/15/93)

88 **PRESTON** Cabernet Sauvignon Dry Creek Valley 1987 • $17 • (10/31/90)

88 **RENAISSANCE** Cabernet Sauvignon North Yuba Reserve 1987 • $35 • (12/15/95)

88 **SHAFER** Cabernet Sauvignon Stags Leap District Hillside Select 1987 • $36 • (07/31/92)

88 **SIMI** Cabernet Sauvignon Alexander Valley Reserve 1987 • $37 • (07/15/92)

88 **STAR HILL** Cabernet Sauvignon Napa Valley Doc's Reserve 1987 • $24 • (11/15/91)

88 **V. SATTUI** Cabernet Sauvignon Napa Valley Preston Vineyards Reserve Stock 1987 • $35 • (11/15/92)

88 **VILLA MT. EDEN** Cabernet Sauvignon Napa Valley 1987 • $15 • (02/15/91)

88 **WILD HORSE** Cabernet Sauvignon Paso Robles 1987 • $13 • (04/30/91)

87 **ALEXANDER VALLEY VINEYARDS** Cabernet Sauvignon Alexander Valley 1987 • $17 • (05/31/90)

87 **ARROWOOD** Cabernet Sauvignon Sonoma County 1987 • $26 • (11/15/90)

87 **BEAULIEU** Cabernet Sauvignon Napa Valley Georges de Latour Private Reserve 1987 • $38 • (09/30/91)

87 **CHATEAU SOUVERAIN** Cabernet Sauvignon Alexander Valley 1987 • $9 • (11/15/90)

87 **CONN CREEK** Cabernet Sauvignon Napa Valley Barrel Select 1987 • $18 • (07/15/91)

87 **CONN CREEK** Cabernet Sauvignon Napa Valley Reserve 1987 • $23 • (08/31/92)

87 **DRY CREEK** Meritage Dry Creek Valley 1987 • $24 • (01/31/92)

87 **FRANCISCAN** Meritage Napa Valley 1987 • $24 • (04/30/91)

87 **FREEMARK ABBEY** Cabernet Sauvignon Napa Valley Bosché 1987 • $25 • (11/15/91)

87 **GARY FARRELL** Cabernet Sauvignon Sonoma County 1987 • $16 • (10/31/90)

87 **GEYSER PEAK** Réserve Alexandre Alexander Valley 1987 • $21 • (05/15/93)

87 **GRGICH HILLS** Cabernet Sauvignon Napa Valley 1987 • $29 • (11/15/92)

87 **HUSCH** Cabernet Sauvignon Mendocino North Field Select 1987 • $16 • (11/15/90)

87 **KENDALL-JACKSON** Cabernet Sauvignon California Proprietor's Grand Reserve 1987 • $16 • (03/31/92)

87 **KLEIN** Cabernet Sauvignon Santa Cruz Mountains 1987 • $19 • (10/15/90)

87 **LOUIS M. MARTINI** Cabernet Sauvignon Napa Valley Reserve 1987 • $14 • (10/15/90)

87 **MARIETTA** Cabernet Sauvignon Sonoma County 1987 • $10 • (02/28/91)

87 **MARKHAM** Cabernet Sauvignon Napa Valley 1987 • $17 • (08/31/91)

87 **MEEKER** Cabernet Sauvignon Dry Creek Valley 1987 • $14 • (10/15/91)

87 **NEWTON** Cabernet Sauvignon Napa Valley 1987 • $21 • (11/15/91)

87 **PEJU** Cabernet Sauvignon Napa Valley HB Vineyard 1987 • $20 • (11/15/90)

87 **QUAIL RIDGE** Cabernet Sauvignon Napa Valley Reserve 1987 • $25 • (11/15/92)

87 **QUIVIRA** Cabernet Sauvignon Dry Creek Valley 1987 • $15 • (11/15/90)

87 **ROBERT MONDAVI** Cabernet Sauvignon Napa Valley 1987 • $46 • (05/31/90)

87 **ROMBAUER** Cabernet Sauvignon Napa Valley 1987 • $17 • (11/15/91)

87 **SEQUOIA GROVE** Cabernet Sauvignon Napa Valley Estate 1987 • $31 • (11/15/91)

87 **STAG'S LEAP WINE CELLARS** S.L.V. Cask 23 Stags Leap District 1987 • $60 • (11/15/91)

87 **STERLING** Three Palms Vineyard Napa Valley 1987 • $23 • (11/15/90)

87 **STONEGATE** Meritage Reserve Napa Valley 1987 • $19 • (10/15/92)

87 **VICHON** Cabernet Sauvignon Stags Leap District SLD 1987 • $24 • (07/31/90)

87 **WINDSOR** Cabernet Sauvignon Russian River Valley River West Vineyard 1987 • $20 • (11/15/92)

86 **BERNARD PRADEL** Cabernet Sauvignon Napa Valley 1987 • $20 • (10/15/90)

86 **BYINGTON** Cabernet Sauvignon Napa Valley 1987 • $16 • (11/15/91)

86 **CLOS DU BOIS** Cabernet Sauvignon Alexander Valley 1987 • $11 • (02/15/90)

86 **COSENTINO** Cabernet Sauvignon North Coast Reserve 1987 • $28 • (02/28/91)

86 **EBERLE** Cabernet Sauvignon Paso Robles Reserve 1987 • $26 • (11/15/93)

86 **FREEMARK ABBEY** Cabernet Sauvignon Napa Valley 1987 • $22 • (07/31/91)

86 **GIRARD** Cabernet Sauvignon Napa Valley 1987 • $20 • (11/15/90)

86 **INGLENOOK** Cabernet Sauvignon Napa Valley 1987 • $10 • (11/15/91)

86 **IRON HORSE** Cabernets Alexander Valley 1987 • $20 • (03/15/91)

86 **J. LOHR** Cabernet Sauvignon Paso Robles Seven Oaks 1987 • $12 • (04/30/91)

86 **KEENAN** Cabernet Sauvignon Napa Valley 1987 • $19 • (05/31/90)

86 **LAUREL GLEN** Terra Rosa Napa Valley 1987 • $14 • (07/31/90)

86 **MIRASSOU** Cabernet Sauvignon Monterey County Harvest Reserve 1987 • $13 • (11/15/91)

86 **ROLLING HILLS** Cabernet Sauvignon California 1987 • $7 • (12/15/89) • BB

86 **RUTHERFORD HILL** Cabernet Sauvignon Napa Valley XVS 1987 • $26 • (11/15/92)

86 **SEBASTIANI** Wildwood Sonoma Valley 1987 • $15 • (08/31/91)

86 **STELTZNER** Cabernet Sauvignon Stags Leap District 1987 • $25 • (11/15/91)

86 **STONEGATE** Meritage Reserve Napa Valley 1987 • $17 • (11/15/93)

86 **TREFETHEN** Cabernet Sauvignon Napa Valley 1987 • $16 • (11/15/90)

86 **WENTE BROS.** Cabernet Sauvignon Livermore Valley Charles Wetmore Vineyard Estate Reserve 1987 • $18 • (04/30/91)

85 **BEAULIEU** Cabernet Sauvignon Napa Valley Rutherford 1987 • $11 • (12/15/90)

85 **BENZIGER** A Tribute Sonoma Mountain 1987 • $20 • (12/31/90)

85 **BENZIGER** Cabernet Sauvignon Sonoma Valley Estate Bottled 1987 • $12 • (11/15/90)

85 **BOEGER** Cabernet Sauvignon El Dorado 1987 • $11 • (03/15/91)

85 **BUEHLER** Cabernet Sauvignon Napa Valley 1987 • $21 • (07/31/90)

85 **BURGESS** Cabernet Sauvignon Napa Valley Vintage Selection 1987 • $21 • (10/15/91)

85 **CHAUFFE-EAU** Cabernet Sauvignon Alexander Valley 1987 • $16 • (08/31/92)

85 **COSENTINO** Meritage The Poet California 1987 • $25 • (09/15/90)

85 **DE LOACH** Cabernet Sauvignon Russian River Valley O.F.S. 1987 • $22 • (10/15/90)

85 **ETUDE** Cabernet Sauvignon Napa Valley 1987 • $24 • (11/10/90)

85 **FIELD STONE** Cabernet Sauvignon Alexander Valley 1987 • $14 • (02/28/91)

85 **FISHER** Cabernet Sauvignon Napa-Sonoma Counties Coach Insignia 1987 • $20 • (09/30/90)

85 **GRAND CRU** Cabernet Sauvignon Sonoma County Premium Selection 1987 • $12 • (11/15/91)

85 **GUNDLACH BUNDSCHU** Cabernet Sauvignon Sonoma Valley Rhinefarm Vineyards 1987 • $17 • (05/15/91)

85 **HEITZ** Cabernet Sauvignon Napa Valley Bella Oaks Vineyard 1987 • $33 • (06/30/92)

85 **J. PEDRONCELLI** Cabernet Sauvignon Dry Creek Valley 1987 • $8 • (11/15/90) • BB

85 **KONOCTI** Meritage Red Clear Lake 1987 • $17 • (04/15/91)

85 **MOUNT EDEN** Cabernet Sauvignon Santa Cruz Mountains Young Vine Cuvée 1987 • $12 • (04/15/90)

85 **MOUNT VEEDER** Cabernet Sauvignon Napa Valley 1987 • $22 • (04/30/91)

85 **PINE RIDGE** Cabernet Sauvignon Stags Leap District 1987 • $30 • (01/31/92)

85 **RIDGE** Cabernet Sauvignon Napa County York Creek 1987 • $21 • (11/15/92)

85 **RODNEY STRONG** Cabernet Sauvignon Sonoma County 1987 • $10 • (06/30/91)

85 **RUTHERFORD HILL** Cabernet Sauvignon Napa Valley 1987 • $16 • (11/15/92)

85 **SEGHESIO** Cabernet Sauvignon Sonoma County 1987 • $9 • (04/30/91)

85 **ST. SUPERY** Cabernet Sauvignon Napa Valley Dollarhide Ranch 1987 • $13 • (07/15/90)

85 **STRATFORD** Cabernet Sauvignon Napa Valley 1987 • $12 • (04/30/90)

85 **VIANSA** Obsidian Sonoma-Napa Counties 1987 • $65 • (07/15/91)

85 **WHITE OAK** Cabernet Sauvignon 1987 • $14 • (02/29/92)

85 **WILLIAM HILL** Cabernet Sauvignon Napa Valley Silver Label 1987 • $14 • (11/15/90)

84 **BRAREN PAULI** Cabernet Sauvignon Mendocino 1987 • $8 • (03/31/91) • BB

84 **CAFARO** Cabernet Sauvignon Napa Valley 1987 • $20 • (11/15/90)

84 **CINNABAR** Cabernet Sauvignon Santa Cruz Mountains 1987 • $18 • (03/31/91)

84 **CRONIN** Cabernet Sauvignon Merlot Santa Cruz Mountains 1987 • $17 • (03/31/92)

84 **DOMAINE MICHEL** Cabernet Sauvignon Sonoma County 1987 • $20 • (03/31/91)

84 **DRY CREEK** Meritage Dry Creek Valley 1987 • $24 • (07/31/91)

84 **DRY CREEK** Cabernet Sauvignon Sonoma County 1987 • $13 • (04/15/90)

84 **EVEREST** Cabernet Sauvignon Dry Creek Valley 1987 • $16 • (08/31/92)

84 **FERRARI-CARANO** Cabernet Sauvignon Alexander Valley 1987 • $18 • (07/15/91)

84 **FISHER** Cabernet Sauvignon Napa-Sonoma Counties Coach Insignia 1987 • $20 • (11/15/91)

84 **FLORA SPRINGS** Trilogy Napa Valley 1987 • $35 • (01/31/91)

84 **HANZELL** Cabernet Sauvignon Sonoma Valley 1987 • $29 • (11/15/91)

84 **J. LOHR** Cabernet Sauvignon California 1987 • $7 • (02/15/90) • BB

84 **KONOCTI** Meritage Clear Lake 1987 • $17 • (11/15/92)

84 **LAKESPRING** Cabernet Sauvignon Napa Valley 1987 • $17 • (10/15/91)

84 **LEEWARD** Cabernet Sauvignon Alexander Valley 1987 • $13 • (11/15/90)

84 **PESENTI** Cabernet Sauvignon San Luis Obispo County Family Reserve 1987 • $8 • (12/15/89)

84 **PINE RIDGE** Cabernet Sauvignon Napa Valley Diamond Mountain 1987 • $35 • (11/15/90)

84 **RAVENSWOOD** Cabernet Sauvignon Sonoma Valley 1987 • $13 • (05/31/90)

84 **RUTHERFORD ESTATE** Cabernet Sauvignon Napa Valley 1987 • $6 • (08/31/92) • BB

84 **SEBASTIANI** Cabernet Sauvignon Sonoma Valley Cherryblock 1987 • $14 • (07/15/92)

84 **WEIBEL** Cabernet Sauvignon Mendocino County 1987 • $8 • (02/28/91) • BB

84 **WHITEHALL LANE** Cabernet Sauvignon Napa Valley 1987 • $18 • (09/15/90)

84 **WILLIAM WHEELER** Cabernet Sauvignon Dry Creek Valley 1987 • $14 • (11/15/91)

84 **YORK MOUNTAIN** Cabernet Sauvignon San Luis Obispo County 1987 • $12 • (11/15/92)

83 **BELLEROSE** Cabernet Sauvignon Dry Creek Valley Reserve Cuvée 1987 • $18 • (11/15/91)

83 **BUENA VISTA** Cabernet Sauvignon Carneros 1987 • $11 • (10/15/90)

83 **CHATEAU POTELLE** Cabernet Sauvignon Alexander Valley 1987 • $16 • (08/31/91)

83 **CHATEAU SOUVERAIN** Cabernet Sauvignon Alexander Valley Private Reserve 1987 • $15 • (05/15/91)

83 **CHRISTOPHE** Cabernet Sauvignon Napa Valley Reserve 1987 • $12 • (11/15/91)

83 **CONCANNON** Cabernet Sauvignon Livermore Valley Reserve 1987 • $16 • (07/15/91)

83 **DEUX AMIS** Cabernet Sauvignon Dry Creek Valley 1987 • $14 • (11/15/91)

83 **FERRARI-CARANO** Cabernet Sauvignon Alexander Valley Special Selection 1987 • $24 • (03/31/93)

83 **HALLCREST** Cabernet Sauvignon El Dorado De Cascabel Vineyard 1987 • $13 • (11/15/91)

83 **J.W. MORRIS** Cabernet Sauvignon California Private Reserve 1987 • $8 • (03/31/90)

83 **KISTLER** Cabernet Sauvignon Sonoma Valley Kistler Estate Vineyard 1987 • $33 • (02/28/91)

83 **LAWRENCE J. BARGETTO** Cabernet Sauvignon Santa Cruz Mountains Bates Ranch 1987 • $15 • (11/15/93)

83 **LYETH** Red Alexander Valley 1987 • $15 • (10/15/92)

83 **MARIO PERELLI-MINETTI** Cabernet Sauvignon Napa Valley 1987 • $12 • (04/30/91)

83 **MERRYVALE** Cabernet Sauvignon Napa Valley Profile 1987 • $25 • (11/15/91)

83 **MONTEREY VINEYARD** Cabernet Sauvignon Monterey County Classic 1987 • $6 • (01/31/91) • BB

83 **RAYMOND** Cabernet Sauvignon Napa Valley 1987 • $17 • (02/28/91)

83 **ROMBAUER** Le Meilleur du Chai Napa Valley 1987 • $35 • (11/15/93)

83 **RUTHERFORD RANCH** Cabernet Sauvignon Napa Valley 1987 • $13 • (04/30/91)

83 **SOBON ESTATE** Cabernet Sauvignon Shenandoah Valley 1987 • $15 • (11/30/90)

83 **TOAD HALL** Bodacious Napa Valley 1987 • $20 • (11/15/92)

83 **ZACA MESA** Cabernet Sauvignon Central Coast Reserve 1987 • $25 • (11/15/91)

82 **CLOS PEGASE** Cabernet Sauvignon Napa Valley 1987 • $17 • (08/31/92)

82 **CORBETT CANYON** Cabernet Sauvignon Central Coast Reserve 1987 • $9 • (11/15/91)

82 **CRESTON** Cabernet Sauvignon Paso Robles Winemaker's Selection 1987 • $16 • (11/15/91)

82 **FIRESTONE** Cabernet Sauvignon Santa Ynez Valley 1987 • $11 • (05/31/90)

82 **GAINEY** Cabernet Sauvignon Santa Barbara County 1987 • $13 • (11/15/90)

82 **KENDALL-JACKSON** Cabernet Sauvignon California Vintner's Reserve 1987 • $14 • (11/15/91)

82 **RAYMOND** Cabernet Sauvignon Napa Valley Private Reserve 1987 • $28 • (08/31/92)

82 **STELTZNER** Cabernet Sauvignon Stags Leap District 1987 • $25 • (11/15/90)

82 **STEVENOT** Cabernet Sauvignon Calaveras County Grand Reserve 1987 • $9 • (03/31/92)

82 **STONEGATE** Cabernet Sauvignon Napa Valley 1987 • $14 • (03/31/92)

81 **ARCIERO** Cabernet Sauvignon Paso Robles 1987 • $8 • (11/15/92)

81 **BEAULIEU** Cabernet Sauvignon Napa Valley Beautour 1987 • $8 • (05/31/89) • BB

81 **CAREY** Cabernet Sauvignon Santa Ynez Valley La Cuesta Vineyard Reserve 1987 • $16 • (05/31/91)

81 **DE LORIMIER** Mosaic Alexander Valley 1987 • $18 • (03/31/92)

81 **DOMAINE MICHEL** Cabernet Sauvignon Sonoma County 1987 • $20 • (08/31/92)

81 **GAN EDEN** Cabernet Sauvignon Alexander Valley 1987 • $18 • (11/15/90)

81 **GROTH** Cabernet Sauvignon Napa Valley 1987 • $20 • (10/31/90)

81 **HACIENDA** Cabernet Sauvignon Sonoma County 1987 • $15 • (11/15/92)

81 **JOULLIAN** Cabernet Sauvignon Carmel Valley 1987 • $14 • (07/31/91)

81 **LA VIEILLE MONTAGNE** Cabernet Sauvignon Napa Valley 1987 • $14 • (06/15/91)

81 **MAYACAMAS** Cabernet Sauvignon Napa Valley 1987 • $41 • (11/15/92)

80 **CHESTNUT HILL** Cabernet Sauvignon Sonoma County 1987 • $9 • (03/31/90)

80 **CHRISTOPHE** Cabernet Sauvignon Napa Valley Reserve 1987 • $8 • (08/31/92)

80 **COSENTINO** Cabernet Sauvignon North Coast 1987 • $16 • (06/30/90)

80 **DORE** Cabernet Sauvignon California Limited Release Lot 102 1987 • $8 • (11/15/91)

80 **ESTANCIA** Cabernet Sauvignon Alexander Valley 1987 • $7 • (07/15/90) • BB

80 **HANNA** Cabernet Sauvignon Sonoma County 1987 • $16 • (08/31/90)

80 **JOHNSON TURNBULL** Cabernet Sauvignon Napa Valley 1987 • $16 • (11/15/90)

80 **MONTE VERDE** Cabernet Sauvignon California Proprietor's Reserve 1987 • $6 • (12/15/89)

80 **PARDUCCI** Cabernet Sauvignon North Coast 1987 • $9 • (04/30/91)

80 **PINE RIDGE** Cabernet Sauvignon Napa Valley Rutherford Cuvée 1987 • $18 • (11/15/90)

80 **ROYCE** Cabernet Sauvignon Sonoma County 1987 • $12 • (11/15/92)

80 **SHENANDOAH** Cabernet Sauvignon Amador County Artist Series 1987 • $10 • (02/28/91)

80 **VAN DER HAYDEN** Cabernet Sauvignon Alexander Valley 1987 • $18 • (08/31/92)

79 **CHARLES KRUG** Cabernet Sauvignon Napa Valley 1987 • $11 • (11/15/91)

79 **CHRISTIAN BROTHERS** Cabernet Sauvignon Napa Valley 1987 • $7 • (10/15/91)

79 **CRESTON** Cabernet Sauvignon Paso Robles 1987 • $10 • (11/15/91)

79 **DAVIS BYNUM** Cabernet Sauvignon Sonoma County 1987 • $11 • (11/15/90)

79 **FOX MOUNTAIN** Cabernet Sauvignon Sonoma County Reserve 1987 • $15 • (11/15/94)

79 **GLEN ELLEN** Cabernet Sauvignon California Proprietor's Reserve 1987 • $6 • (01/31/91)

79 **HAWK CREST** Cabernet Sauvignon North Coast 1987 • $8 • (03/31/90)

79 **SAUSAL** Cabernet Sauvignon Alexander Valley 1987 • $14 • (11/15/92)

79 **STREBLOW** Cabernet Sauvignon Napa Valley 1987 • $16 • (10/15/90)

78 **EBERLE** Cabernet Sauvignon Paso Robles Reserve 1987 • $28 • (11/15/94)

78 **J. WILE & SONS** Cabernet Sauvignon Napa Valley 1987 • $10 • (05/31/91)

78 **MCDOWELL** Cabernet Sauvignon California 1987 • $9 • (11/15/90)

78 **POPPY HILL** Cabernet Sauvignon California 1987 • $7 • (05/31/91)

78 **ZD** Cabernet Sauvignon Napa Valley 1987 • $16 • (02/15/91)

77 **JEKEL** Meritage Symmetry The Sanctuary Estate Arroyo Seco 1987 • $25 • (03/31/93)

77 **PINE RIDGE** Cabernet Sauvignon Napa Valley Rutherford Cuvée 1987 • $18 • (03/15/92)

77 **ROUND HILL** Cabernet Sauvignon Napa Valley Reserve 1987 • $11 • (11/15/91)

77 **SANTA BARBARA WINERY** Cabernet Sauvignon Santa Ynez Valley Reserve 1987 • $18 • (11/15/90)

77 **STAG'S LEAP WINE CELLARS** Cabernet Sauvignon Stags Leap District S.L.V. 1987 • $33 • (11/15/90)

77 **SUTTER HOME** Cabernet Sauvignon California 1987 • $5 • (06/30/89)

76 **DE MOOR** Cabernet Sauvignon Napa Valley 1987 • $16 • (11/15/91)

76 **EBERLE** Cabernet Sauvignon Paso Robles 1987 • $22 • (11/15/91)

76 **RENAISSANCE** Cabernet Sauvignon North Yuba 1987 • $15 • (08/31/92)

75 **BELVEDERE** Cabernet Sauvignon Sonoma County Discovery Series 1987 • $6 • (06/15/90)

75 **DOMAINE NAPA** Cabernet Sauvignon Napa Valley 1987 • $13 • (12/15/92)

75 **FENESTRA** Cabernet Sauvignon Monterey Smith & Hook Vineyard 1987 • $14 • (11/15/91)

75 **JOSEPH PHELPS** Cabernet Sauvignon Napa Valley 1987 • $50 • (07/15/91)

75 **STAG'S LEAP WINE CELLARS** Cabernet Sauvignon Napa Valley 1987 • $18 • (08/31/90)

74 **ROBERT MONDAVI** Cabernet Sauvignon California Woodbridge 1987 • $6 • (09/15/89)

74 **TULOCAY** Cabernet Sauvignon Napa Valley Egan Vineyard 1987 • $17 • (02/15/91)

72 **BARON** Cabernet Sauvignon Paso Robles 1987 • $9 • (11/15/92)

72 **FIELD STONE** Cabernet Sauvignon Alexander Valley Staten Family Reserve 1987 • $25 • (11/15/91)

72 **SANTA YNEZ VALLEY** Cabernet Merlot Santa Barbara County 1987 • $13 • (03/31/90)

70 **MONT ST. JOHN** Cabernet Sauvignon Napa Valley 1987 • $14 • (11/15/92)

70 **SEQUOIA GROVE** Cabernet Sauvignon Napa Valley 1987 • $19 • (11/15/91)

65 **MOUNT EDEN** Cabernet Sauvignon Santa Cruz Mountains 1987 • $28 • (04/30/91)

1986 CALIFORNIA CABERNET
VINTAGE RATING: 95

98 **CAYMUS** Cabernet Sauvignon Napa Valley Special Selection 1986 • $135 • (03/01/89)

96 **BERINGER** Cabernet Sauvignon Napa Valley Private Reserve 1986 • $70 • (03/01/89)

96 **DIAMOND CREEK** Cabernet Sauvignon Napa Valley Red Rock Terrace 1986 • $51 • (03/01/89)

96 **DIAMOND CREEK** Cabernet Sauvignon Napa Valley Volcanic Hill 1986 • $43 • (03/01/89)

96 **DUNN** Cabernet Sauvignon Howell Mountain 1986 • $81 • (11/30/91)

96 **JOSEPH PHELPS** Insignia Napa Valley 1986 • $43 • (03/01/89)

96 **TERRACES** Cabernet Sauvignon Napa Valley 1986 • $23 • (01/31/91)

95 **BERINGER** Cabernet Sauvignon Napa Valley Private Reserve 1986 • $69 • (09/15/90) • CS

95 **DUNN** Cabernet Sauvignon Napa Valley 1986 • $70 • (10/15/89) • CS

95 **DUNN** Cabernet Sauvignon Howell Mountain 1986 • $81 • (07/31/90) • CS

95 **HEITZ** Cabernet Sauvignon Napa Valley Martha's Vineyard 1986 • $76 • (04/15/91) • CS

95 **JOHNSON TURNBULL** Cabernet Sauvignon Napa Valley Vineyard Selection 82 1986 • $25 • (08/31/89)

95 **JOSEPH PHELPS** Cabernet Sauvignon Napa Valley Eisele Vineyard 1986 • $40 • (03/01/89)

95 **KENWOOD** Cabernet Sauvignon Sonoma Valley Artist Series 1986 • $25 • (11/30/89) • CS

95 **OPUS ONE** Napa Valley 1986 • $79 • (11/30/89)

95 **ROBERT MONDAVI** Cabernet Sauvignon Napa Valley Reserve 1986 • $44 • (11/30/91)

95 **SPOTTSWOODE** Cabernet Sauvignon Napa Valley 1986 • $82 • (09/15/89)

95 **STERLING** Cabernet Sauvignon Reserve Napa Valley 1986 • $43 • (03/15/90) • CS

95 **WILLIAM HILL** Cabernet Sauvignon Napa Valley Reserve 1986 • $29 • (03/01/89)

94 **B.R. COHN** Cabernet Sauvignon Sonoma Valley Olive Hill Vineyard 1986 • $34 • (05/31/89)

94 **CAYMUS** Cabernet Sauvignon Napa Valley 1986 • $106 • (03/15/90) • SS

94 **CUVAISON** Cabernet Sauvignon Napa Valley 1986 • $30 • (07/15/89)

94 **DIAMOND CREEK** Cabernet Sauvignon Napa Valley Gravelly Meadow 1986 • $53 • (03/01/89)

94 **DUCKHORN** Cabernet Sauvignon Napa Valley 1986 • $39 • (07/31/89) • SS

94 **DUNN** Cabernet Sauvignon Howell Mountain 1986 • $81 • (03/01/89)

94 **FLORA SPRINGS** Trilogy Napa Valley 1986 • $37 • (02/15/90)

94 **FROG'S LEAP** Cabernet Sauvignon Napa Valley 1986 • $42 • (03/01/89)

94 **KEENAN** Cabernet Sauvignon Napa Valley 1986 • $20 • (03/01/89)

94 **KENWOOD** Cabernet Sauvignon Sonoma Valley Artist Series 1986 • $36 • (03/01/89)

94 **ST. FRANCIS** Cabernet Sauvignon Sonoma Valley Reserve (Black Label) 1986 • $20 • (11/30/89)

94 **SILVER OAK** Cabernet Sauvignon Napa Valley 1986 • $55 • (10/31/90) • CS

94 **SILVERADO** Cabernet Sauvignon Stags Leap District 1986 • $25 • (08/31/89) • SS

94 **STERLING** Reserve Napa Valley 1986 • $43 • (03/01/89)

93 **BEAULIEU** Cabernet Sauvignon Napa Valley Georges de Latour Private Reserve 1986 • $38 • (03/31/91)

93 **BERINGER** Cabernet Sauvignon Napa Valley Chabot Vineyard 1986 • $30 • (03/01/89)

93 **BUENA VISTA** Cabernet Sauvignon Carneros Private Reserve 1986 • $25 • (10/15/90)

93 **CAFARO** Cabernet Sauvignon Napa Valley 1986 • $18 • (11/15/89)

93 **CARMENET** Red Sonoma Valley 1986 • $25 • (03/01/89)

93 **CHATEAU MONTELENA** Cabernet Sauvignon Napa Valley 1986 • $53 • (10/15/90)

93 **CINNABAR** Cabernet Sauvignon Santa Cruz Mountains 1986 • $15 • (11/15/89)

93 **CUVAISON** Cabernet Sauvignon Napa Valley 1986 • $30 • (03/01/89)

93 **DIAMOND CREEK** Cabernet Sauvignon Napa Valley Red Rock Terrace 1986 • $51 • (12/31/88)

93 **DOMINUS** Napa Valley 1986 • $50 • (03/01/89)

93 **DUNN** Cabernet Sauvignon Napa Valley 1986 • $53 • (11/30/91)

93 **FORMAN** Cabernet Sauvignon Napa Valley 1986 • $37 • (06/15/89)

93 **GRACE FAMILY** Cabernet Sauvignon Napa Valley 1986 • $250 • (03/01/89)

93 **GROTH** Cabernet Sauvignon Napa Valley Reserve 1986 • $95 • (03/01/89)

93 **GUSTAVE NIEBAUM** Cabernet Sauvignon Napa Valley Tench Vineyard 1986 • $16 • (10/15/89)

93 **JOSEPH PHELPS** Insignia Napa Valley 1986 • $43 • (08/31/90) • CS

93 **JOSEPH PHELPS** Cabernet Sauvignon Napa Valley Backus Vineyard 1986 • $38 • (03/01/89)

93 **KEENAN** Cabernet Sauvignon Napa Valley 1986 • $20 • (08/31/89)

93 **MOUNT VEEDER** Meritage Napa Valley 1986 • $25 • (03/01/89)

93 **PHILIP TOGNI** Cabernet Sauvignon Napa Valley 1986 • $35 • (03/01/89)

93 **ROBERT MONDAVI** Cabernet Sauvignon Napa Valley 1986 • $35 • (07/31/89)

93 **SANTA CRUZ MOUNTAIN** Cabernet Sauvignon Santa Cruz Mountains Bates Ranch 1986 • $15 • (03/01/89)

93 **SHAFER** Cabernet Sauvignon Stags Leap District 1986 • $20 • (09/30/89) • SS

93 **SILVER OAK** Cabernet Sauvignon Alexander Valley 1986 • $48 • (10/31/90) • SS

93 **STAG'S LEAP WINE CELLARS** S.L.V. Cask 23 Stags Leap District 1986 • $70 • (11/15/90)

93 **THE HESS COLLECTION** Cabernet Sauvignon Napa Valley Reserve 1986 • $73 • (09/15/90)

92 **ARROWOOD** Cabernet Sauvignon Sonoma County 1986 • $30 • (10/15/89)

92 **CAYMUS** Cabernet Sauvignon Napa Valley 1986 • $42 • (03/01/89)

92 **CHAPPELLET** Cabernet Sauvignon Napa Valley Reserve 1986 • $20 • (03/01/89)

92 **CHARLES KRUG** Cabernet Sauvignon Napa Valley Vintage Selection 1986 • $28 • (10/31/92)

92 **CLOS DU VAL** Cabernet Sauvignon Stags Leap District 1986 • $23 • (03/01/89)

92 **ETUDE** Cabernet Sauvignon Napa Valley 1986 • $24 • (09/30/89)

92 **GROTH** Cabernet Sauvignon Napa Valley 1986 • $27 • (11/15/89)

92 **HAYWOOD** Cabernet Sauvignon Sonoma Valley 1986 • $19 • (11/15/89)

92 **INGLENOOK** Reunion Napa Valley 1986 • $45 • (03/01/89)

92 **INGLENOOK** Cabernet Sauvignon Napa Valley Reserve Cask 1986 • $25 • (03/01/89)

92 **LA JOTA** Cabernet Sauvignon Howell Mountain 1986 • $44 • (03/01/89)

92 **MONTICELLO** Cabernet Sauvignon Napa Valley Corley Reserve 1986 • $30 • (03/15/90)

92 **NIEBAUM-COPPOLA** Rubicon Napa Valley 1986 • $29 • (03/01/89)

92 **PEJU** Cabernet Sauvignon Napa Valley HB Vineyard 1986 • $20 • (11/15/89)

92 **PINE RIDGE** Cabernet Sauvignon Napa Valley Diamond Mountain 1986 • $30 • (11/30/89)

92 **PINE RIDGE** Cabernet Sauvignon Napa Valley Andrus Reserve 1986 • $47 • (03/01/89)

92 **PLAM** Cabernet Sauvignon Napa Valley 1986 • $24 • (09/15/89)

92 **SHAFER** Cabernet Sauvignon Stags Leap District Hillside Select 1986 • $45 • (03/01/89)

92 **SIMI** Cabernet Sauvignon Alexander Valley Reserve 1986 • $36 • (03/01/89)

92 **STAG'S LEAP WINE CELLARS** SLV Cask 23 Stags Leap District 1986 • $75 • (03/01/89)

91 **A. RAFANELLI** Cabernet Sauvignon Dry Creek Valley 1986 • $9 • (09/30/89)

91 **BUEHLER** Cabernet Sauvignon Napa Valley 1986 • $20 • (03/01/89)

91 **BUENA VISTA** Cabernet Sauvignon Carneros 1986 • $11 • (10/15/89)

91 **BURGESS** Cabernet Sauvignon Napa Valley Vintage Selection 1986 • $20 • (03/01/89)

91 **CAIN** Five Napa Valley 1986 • $30 • (02/15/90)

91 **CARMENET** Red Sonoma Valley 1986 • $25 • (07/31/89)

91 **CLOS DU VAL** Cabernet Sauvignon Stags Leap District 1986 • $23 • (05/31/90)

91 **CLOS DU VAL** Cabernet Sauvignon Napa Valley Joli Val 1986 • $13 • (03/01/89)

91 **CONN CREEK** Cabernet Sauvignon Napa Valley Barrel Select Private Reserve 1986 • $40 • (12/15/90)

91 **DIAMOND CREEK** Cabernet Sauvignon Napa Valley Gravelly Meadow 1986 • $53 • (12/31/88)

91 **DIAMOND CREEK** Cabernet Sauvignon Napa Valley Volcanic Hill 1986 • $53 • (12/31/88)

91 **DOMINUS** Napa Valley 1986 • $45 • (02/28/91)

91 **FAR NIENTE** Cabernet Sauvignon Napa Valley 1986 • $35 • (09/30/89)

91 **FREEMARK ABBEY** Cabernet Sauvignon Napa Valley Sycamore Vineyards 1986 • $25 • (11/15/91)

91 **GIRARD** Cabernet Sauvignon Napa Valley Reserve 1986 • $34 • (03/01/89)

91 **GRGICH HILLS** Cabernet Sauvignon Napa Valley 1986 • $29 • (03/01/89)

91 **GROTH** Cabernet Sauvignon Napa Valley Reserve 1986 • $31 • (04/30/91)

91 **HACIENDA** Antares Sonoma County 1986 • $28 • (07/31/89)

91 **HAYWOOD** Cabernet Sauvignon Sonoma Valley 1986 • $19 • (03/01/89)

91 **INGLENOOK** Cabernet Sauvignon Napa Valley Reserve Cask 1986 • $25 • (10/31/91)

91 **KENDALL-JACKSON** Cabernet Sauvignon California Cardinale 1986 • $65 • (11/15/90)

91 **KISTLER** Cabernet Sauvignon Sonoma Valley Kistler Estate Vineyard 1986 • $30 • (03/01/89)

91 **MARKHAM** Cabernet Sauvignon Napa Valley 1986 • $16 • (03/01/89)

91 **NEWTON** Cabernet Sauvignon Napa Valley 1986 • $21 • (05/31/90)

91 **OPTIMA** Cabernet Sauvignon Sonoma County 1986 • $22 • (02/15/90)

91 **PINE RIDGE** Cabernet Sauvignon Stags Leap District Pine Ridge Stags Leap Vineyard 1986 • $29 • (03/01/89)

91 **PINE RIDGE** Cabernet Sauvignon Napa Valley Diamond Mountain 1986 • $30 • (03/01/89)

91 **SHAFER** Cabernet Sauvignon Stags Leap District Hillside Select 1986 • $45 • (03/15/91)

91 **STAG'S LEAP WINE CELLARS** Cabernet Sauvignon Stags Leap District S.L.V. 1986 • $32 • (11/30/89)

91 **STELTZNER** Cabernet Sauvignon Stags Leap District 1986 • $18 • (12/31/89)

91 **STERLING** Cabernet Sauvignon Napa Valley 1986 • $18 • (03/31/89)

91 **STERLING** Cabernet Sauvignon Napa Valley Diamond Mountain Ranch 1986 • $15 • (03/15/90)

91 **THE HESS COLLECTION** Cabernet Sauvignon Napa Valley 1986 • $18 • (03/01/89)

91 **TUDAL** Cabernet Sauvignon Napa Valley 1986 • $20 • (12/15/89)

91 **VICHON** Cabernet Sauvignon Stags Leap District SLD 1986 • $35 • (10/31/89)

91 **WILLIAM HILL** Cabernet Sauvignon Napa Valley Reserve 1986 • $29 • (11/15/89)

90 **BUENA VISTA** Cabernet Sauvignon Sonoma County 1986 • $11 • (11/15/89)

90 **CAKEBREAD** Cabernet Sauvignon Napa Valley 1986 • $21 • (08/31/89)

90 **CAYMUS** Cabernet Sauvignon Napa Valley Cuvée 1986 • $15 • (08/31/89)

90 **CHATEAU ST. JEAN** Cabernet Sauvignon Alexander Valley 1986 • $19 • (10/15/89)

90 **COSENTINO** Cabernet Sauvignon North Coast Reserve 1986 • $18 • (05/15/90)

90 **DEHLINGER** Cabernet Sauvignon Russian River Valley 1986 • $13 • (03/15/90)

90 **FISHER** Cabernet Sauvignon Sonoma County Coach Insignia 1986 • $20 • (03/01/89)

90 **FREEMARK ABBEY** Cabernet Sauvignon Napa Valley Bosché 1986 • $24 • (03/01/89)

90 **HANZELL** Cabernet Sauvignon Sonoma Valley 1986 • $35 • (10/31/90)

90 **IRON HORSE** Cabernets Alexander Valley 1986 • $22 • (04/15/90)

90 **KENWOOD** Cabernet Sauvignon Sonoma Valley Jack London Vineyard 1986 • $18 • (09/15/89)

90 **LIVINGSTON** Cabernet Sauvignon Napa Valley Moffett Vineyard 1986 • $34 • (03/01/89)

90 **MORGAN** Cabernet Sauvignon Carmel Valley 1986 • $16 • (09/15/89)

90 **MURPHY-GOODE** Cabernet Sauvignon Alexander Valley Premier Vineyard 1986 • $16 • (11/15/89)

90 **PINE RIDGE** Cabernet Sauvignon Napa Valley Rutherford Cuvée 1986 • $19 • (05/31/90)

90 **RAYMOND** Cabernet Sauvignon Napa Valley 1986 • $16 • (05/31/90)

90 **SEQUOIA GROVE** Cabernet Sauvignon Napa Valley Estate 1986 • $28 • (03/01/89)

90 **SPRING MOUNTAIN** Cabernet Sauvignon Napa Valley 1986 • $NA • (03/01/89)

90 **STELTZNER** Cabernet Sauvignon Stags Leap District 1986 • $18 • (03/01/89)

90 **THE HESS COLLECTION** Cabernet Sauvignon Napa Valley 1986 • $18 • (11/15/89)

90 **TREFETHEN** Cabernet Sauvignon Napa Valley Hillside Selection 1986 • $36 • (03/01/89)

90 **VICHON** Cabernet Sauvignon Stags Leap District SLD 1986 • $35 • (03/01/89)

89 **ALEXANDER VALLEY VINEYARDS** Cabernet Sauvignon Alexander Valley 1986 • $18 • (12/31/88)

89 **BEAULIEU** Cabernet Sauvignon Napa Valley Georges de Latour Private Reserve 1986 • $55 • (11/15/90)

89 **BUENA VISTA** Cabernet Sauvignon Carneros Private Reserve 1986• $23• (03/15/91)

89 **CAKEBREAD** Cabernet Sauvignon Napa Valley 1986 • $21• (03/01/89)

89 **CAKEBREAD** Cabernet Sauvignon Napa Valley Rutherford Reserve 1986• $43• (11/15/91)

89 **CHAPPELLET** Cabernet Sauvignon Napa Valley Reserve 1986• $20• (02/15/93)

89 **GAINEY** Cabernet Sauvignon Santa Barbara County Limited Selection 1986• $15• (12/15/89)

89 **GEYSER PEAK** Réserve Alexandre Alexander Valley 1986 • $20• (09/30/90)

89 **GIRARD** Cabernet Sauvignon Napa Valley 1986• $23 • (11/15/89)

89 **GUNDLACH BUNDSCHU** Cabernet Sauvignon Sonoma Valley Rhinefarm Vineyards 1986• $17• (03/01/89)

89 **HEITZ** Cabernet Sauvignon Napa Valley Bella Oaks Vineyard 1986• $26• (04/15/91)

89 **KLEIN** Cabernet Sauvignon Santa Cruz Mountains 1986 • $22• (09/30/89)

89 **LAUREL GLEN** Cabernet Sauvignon Sonoma Mountain 1986• $34• (03/01/89)

89 **MERRYVALE** Red Table Wine Napa Valley 1986• $25 • (03/01/89)

89 **MONTICELLO** Cabernet Sauvignon Napa Valley Jefferson Cuvée 1986• $14• (04/15/89)

89 **NEWLAN** Cabernet Sauvignon Napa Valley 1986• $15 • (04/30/91)

89 **PAHLMEYER** Caldwell Vineyard Napa Valley 1986• $39 • (11/15/89)

89 **PHILIP TOGNI** Cabernet Sauvignon Napa Valley 1986 • $35• (07/31/89)

89 **QUAIL RIDGE** Cabernet Sauvignon Napa Valley 1986 • $15• (11/15/90)

89 **RAVENSWOOD** Pickberry Vineyards Sonoma Mountain 1986• $38• (03/01/89)

89 **ROMBAUER** Le Meilleur du Chai Napa Valley 1986• $45 • (03/01/89)

89 **SANTA CRUZ MOUNTAIN** Cabernet Sauvignon Santa Cruz Mountains Bates Ranch 1986• $15• (11/15/91)

89 **SIMI** Cabernet Sauvignon Alexander Valley Reserve 1986• $36• (07/31/91)

89 **ST. FRANCIS** Cabernet Sauvignon Sonoma County 1986 • $12• (01/31/90)

89 **STAG'S LEAP WINE CELLARS** Cabernet Sauvignon Stags Leap District SLV 1986• $32• (03/01/89)

89 **TUDAL** Cabernet Sauvignon Napa Valley 1986• $20 • (03/01/89)

89 **WHITEHALL LANE** Cabernet Sauvignon Napa Valley 1986 • $16• (08/31/89)

88 **ALEXANDER VALLEY VINEYARDS** Cabernet Sauvignon Alexander Valley 1986• $18• (03/01/89)

88 **BURGESS** Cabernet Sauvignon Napa Valley Vintage Selection 1986• $20• (07/15/90)

88 **CHATEAU CHEVRE** Chevre Reserve Napa Valley 1986 • $25• (07/31/89)

88 **CHRISTIAN BROTHERS** Cabernet Sauvignon Napa Valley 1986• $9• (11/15/90)

88 **CLOS PEGASE** Cabernet Sauvignon Napa Valley 1986 • $17• (09/30/90)

88 **CRONIN** Cabernet Sauvignon Merlot Stags Leap District Robinson Vineyard 1986• $16• (02/15/90)

88 **CRONIN** Cabernet Sauvignon Merlot San Mateo County Shaw & Cronin 1986• $15• (02/28/91)

88 **DRY CREEK** Cabernet Sauvignon Sonoma County 1986 • $11• (03/31/89)

88 **FETZER** Cabernet Sauvignon Sonoma County Reserve 1986• $24• (09/30/91)

88 **GRGICH HILLS** Cabernet Sauvignon Napa Valley 1986 • $29• (11/15/91)

88 **HEITZ** Cabernet Sauvignon Napa Valley 1986• $25 • (04/15/91)

88 **IRON HORSE** Cabernets Alexander Valley 1986• $22 • (03/01/89)

88 **JORDAN** Cabernet Sauvignon Alexander Valley 1986 • $38• (11/15/90)

88 **LAKESPRING** Cabernet Sauvignon Napa Valley 1986 • $17• (03/01/89)

88 **LIVINGSTON** Cabernet Sauvignon Napa Valley Moffett Vineyard 1986• $19• (11/30/89)

88 **LYETH** Red Alexander Valley 1986• $23• (11/15/90)

88 **MONTICELLO** Cabernet Sauvignon Napa Valley Corley Reserve 1986• $30• (03/01/89)

88 **NIEBAUM-COPPOLA** Rubicon Napa Valley 1986• $29 • (11/15/92)

88 **PRESTON** Cabernet Sauvignon Dry Creek Valley 1986 • $13• (03/01/89)

88 **RAVENSWOOD** Cabernet Sauvignon Sonoma County 1986• $17• (12/31/88)

88 **RAYMOND** Cabernet Sauvignon Napa Valley Private Reserve 1986• $28• (11/15/91)

88 **RIDGE** Cabernet Sauvignon Napa County York Creek 1986• $20• (03/01/89)

88 **ROBERT PECOTA** Cabernet Sauvignon Napa Valley Kara's Vineyard 1986• $16• (03/01/89)

88 **ROBERT PEPI** Cabernet Sauvignon Napa Valley Vine Hill Ranch 1986• $19• (10/31/90)

88 **ROMBAUER** Cabernet Sauvignon Napa Valley 1986• $18 • (04/15/90)

88 **RUTHERFORD HILL** Cabernet Sauvignon Napa Valley XVS 1986• $22• (03/01/89)

88 **SEQUOIA GROVE** Cabernet Sauvignon Napa County 1986 • $16• (03/01/89)

88 **SILVER OAK** Cabernet Sauvignon Napa Valley Bonny's Vineyard 1986• $95• (10/15/91)

88 **STERLING** Cabernet Sauvignon Napa Valley Diamond Mountain Ranch 1986• $15• (03/01/89)

88 **V. SATTUI** Cabernet Sauvignon Napa Valley Preston Vineyard 1986• $20• (03/01/89)

87 **BUENA VISTA** L'Année Carneros 1986• $35 • (02/28/91)

87 **CHARLES KRUG** Cabernet Sauvignon Napa Valley Vintage Select 1986• $29• (03/01/89)

87 **CHARLES KRUG** Cabernet Sauvignon Napa Valley 1986 • $11• (02/28/91)

87 **CHIMNEY ROCK** Cabernet Sauvignon Stags Leap District 1986• $19• (09/30/89)

87 **CLOS DU BOIS** Cabernet Sauvignon Alexander Valley Briarcrest Vineyard 1986• $21• (08/31/90)

87 **CLOS DU VAL** Cabernet Sauvignon Napa Valley Joli Val 1986• $13• (12/15/89)

87 **CONN CREEK** Cabernet Sauvignon Napa Valley Barrel Select 1986• $18• (03/01/89)

87 **FISHER** Cabernet Sauvignon Sonoma County Coach Insignia 1986• $20• (01/31/90)

87 **FOX MOUNTAIN** Cabernet Sauvignon Russian River Valley Reserve 1986• $20• (11/15/92)

87 **GIRARD** Cabernet Sauvignon Napa Valley Reserve 1986 • $34• (11/15/90)

87 **GUNDLACH BUNDSCHU** Cabernet Sauvignon Sonoma Valley 1986• $9• (11/15/89)

87 **HACIENDA** Cabernet Sauvignon Sonoma County 1986 • $15• (11/15/91)

87 **HANNA** Cabernet Sauvignon Sonoma County 1986 • $16• (07/31/89)

87 **JOHNSON TURNBULL** Cabernet Sauvignon Napa Valley Vineyard Selection 67 1986 •$20 •(03/01/89)

87 **LAUREL GLEN** Cabernet Sauvignon Sonoma Mountain 1986 •$29 •(05/15/89)

87 **MARKHAM** Cabernet Sauvignon Napa Valley 1986 •$16 •(04/30/91)

87 **MONT ST. JOHN** Cabernet Sauvignon Napa Valley 1986 •$14 •(04/30/91)

87 **MOUNT VEEDER** Cabernet Sauvignon Napa Valley 1986 •$20 •(03/01/89)

87 **NAVARRO** Cabernet Sauvignon Mendocino 1986 •$16 •(10/15/91)

87 **PRESTON** Cabernet Sauvignon Dry Creek Valley 1986 •$13 •(03/15/90)

87 **ST. ANDREW'S WINERY** Cabernet Sauvignon Napa Valley 1986 •$15 •(04/30/90)

87 **ST. CLEMENT** Cabernet Sauvignon Napa Valley 1986 •$25 •(03/01/89)

87 **STREBLOW** Cabernet Sauvignon Napa Valley 1986 •$16 •(07/31/89)

87 **TREFETHEN** Cabernet Sauvignon Napa Valley 1986 •$33 •(03/01/89)

87 **VITA NOVA** Reservatum Santa Barbara County 1986 •$20 •(12/15/89)

86 **BLACK MOUNTAIN** Cabernet Sauvignon Alexander Valley Fat Cat 1986 •$20 •(11/15/91)

86 **CHIMNEY ROCK** Cabernet Sauvignon Stags Leap District 1986 •$19 •(03/01/89)

86 **CLOS DU BOIS** Cabernet Sauvignon Alexander Valley 1986 •$12 •(05/31/89)

86 **COSENTINO** Meritage The Poet California 1986 •$22 •(07/31/89)

86 **CUTLER** Cabernet Sauvignon Sonoma Valley Batto Ranch 1986 •$17 •(11/15/90)

86 **GAN EDEN** Cabernet Sauvignon Alexander Valley 1986 •$15 •(02/15/89)

86 **JOHNSON TURNBULL** Cabernet Sauvignon Napa Valley Vineyard Selection 67 1986 •$20 •(04/15/90)

86 **KENWOOD** Cabernet Sauvignon Sonoma Valley 1986 •$15 •(09/30/89)

86 **LONG** Cabernet Sauvignon Napa Valley 1986 •$45 •(03/01/89)

86 **LOUIS M. MARTINI** Cabernet Sauvignon Sonoma Valley Monte Rosso 1986 •$21 •(03/01/89)

86 **MAYACAMAS** Cabernet Sauvignon Napa Valley 1986 •$45 •(03/01/89)

86 **MERRYVALE** Red Table Wine Napa Valley 1986 •$25 •(10/15/90)

86 **MONTEREY PENINSULA** Cabernet Sauvignon Monterey County Doctors' Reserve 1986 •$18 •(11/15/94)

86 **RAVENSWOOD** Cabernet Sauvignon Sonoma County 1986 •$17 •(03/01/89)

86 **RAYMOND** Cabernet Sauvignon Napa Valley Private Reserve 1986 •$28 •(03/01/89)

86 **ROBERT PECOTA** Cabernet Sauvignon Napa Valley Kara's Vineyard 1986 •$16 •(09/15/89)

86 **ROMBAUER** Cabernet Sauvignon Napa Valley 1986 •$18 •(03/01/89)

86 **SEBASTIANI** Cabernet Sauvignon Sonoma County Reserve 1986 •$13 •(01/31/91)

86 **SHENANDOAH** Cabernet Sauvignon Amador County Artist Series 1986 •$12 •(10/31/88)

86 **STAGS' LEAP WINERY** Cabernet Sauvignon Stags Leap District 1986 •$17 •(03/01/89)

86 **STERLING** Three Palms Vineyard Napa Valley 1986 •$22 •(12/31/89)

86 **STONEGATE** Cabernet Sauvignon Napa Valley 1986 •$17 •(02/28/91)

85 **BANDIERA** Cabernet Sauvignon Napa Valley 1986 •$6 •(10/31/89) •BB

85 **BEAUCANON** Cabernet Sauvignon Napa Valley 1986 •$15 •(12/31/88)

85 **BEAULIEU** Cabernet Sauvignon Napa Valley Rutherford 1986 •$29 •(09/15/89)

85 **BUEHLER** Cabernet Sauvignon Napa Valley 1986 •$20 •(04/30/89)

85 **CAIN** Cabernet Sauvignon Napa Valley 1986 •$16 •(08/31/90)

85 **CHATEAU SOUVERAIN** Cabernet Sauvignon Alexander Valley 1986 •$8 •(11/15/89) •BB

85 **CLOS DU BOIS** Marlstone Vineyard Alexander Valley 1986 •$24 •(08/31/90)

85 **CUTLER** Satyre Sonoma Valley 1986 •$20 •(02/28/91)

85 **DALLA VALLE** Cabernet Sauvignon Napa Valley 1986 •$20 •(06/30/90)

85 **EBERLE** Cabernet Sauvignon Paso Robles 1986 •$15 •(11/15/89)

85 **ESTANCIA** Cabernet Sauvignon Alexander Valley 1986 •$8 •(04/15/89) •BB

85 **FIELD STONE** Cabernet Sauvignon Alexander Valley Hoot Owl Reserve 1986 •$20 •(12/15/90)

85 **FLORA SPRINGS** Trilogy Napa Valley 1986 •$39 •(03/01/89)

85 **FLORA SPRINGS** Cabernet Sauvignon Napa Valley 1986 •$16 •(03/15/90)

85 **FOLIE À DEUX** Cabernet Sauvignon Napa Valley 1986 •$17 •(04/15/90)

85 **FREMONT CREEK** Cabernet Sauvignon Mendocino-Napa Counties 1986 •$8 •(04/30/91) •BB

85 **GEYSER PEAK** Cabernet Sauvignon Alexander Valley Estate Reserve 1986 •$15 •(09/30/90)

85 **GRAND CRU** Cabernet Sauvignon Alexander Valley Collector's Reserve 1986 •$22 •(05/15/90)

85 **INGLENOOK** Cabernet Sauvignon Napa Valley 1986 •$10 •(02/28/91) •BB

85 **KENDALL-JACKSON** Cabernet Sauvignon California Vintner's Reserve 1986 •$11 •(12/31/88)

85 **KENDALL-JACKSON** Cabernet Sauvignon California The Proprietor's 1986 •$24 •(03/15/90)

85 **LA JOTA** Cabernet Sauvignon Howell Mountain 1986 •$38 •(10/15/89)

85 **MOUNT EDEN** Cabernet Sauvignon Santa Cruz Mountains 1986 •$29 •(03/01/89)

85 **RIDGE** Cabernet Sauvignon Santa Cruz Mountains Monte Bello 1986 •$48 •(03/01/89)

85 **STONE CREEK** Cabernet Sauvignon Napa Valley Limited Bottling 1986 •$10 •(06/15/90)

85 **TIJSSELING** Cabernet Sauvignon Mendocino 1986 •$8 •(01/31/90) •BB

84 **CHATEAU POTELLE** Cabernet Sauvignon Alexander Valley 1986 •$15 •(10/31/90)

84 **DAVIS BYNUM** Cabernet Sauvignon Sonoma County 1986 •$10 •(11/15/89)

84 **DE LORIMIER** Mosaic Alexander Valley 1986 •$16 •(10/31/89)

84 **FRANCISCAN** Cabernet Sauvignon Napa Valley Oakville Estate 1986 •$11 •(07/15/90)

84 **HUSCH** Cabernet Sauvignon Mendocino 1986 •$12 •(02/15/90)

84 **J. LOHR** Cabernet Sauvignon California 1986 •$6 •(04/15/89) •BB

84 **KISTLER** Cabernet Sauvignon Sonoma Valley Kistler Estate Vineyard 1986 •$26 •(09/30/89)

84 **LA VIEILLE MONTAGNE** Cabernet Sauvignon Napa Valley 1986 •$14 •(06/30/90)

84 **LAWRENCE J. BARGETTO** Cabernet Sauvignon Santa Cruz Mountains 1986 • $18 • (08/31/92)

84 **MERLION** Cabernet Sauvignon Napa Valley 1986 • $17 • (11/15/90)

84 **MONTEREY PENINSULA** Cabernet Sauvignon Monterey County 1986 • $10 • (11/15/94)

84 **PAUL MASSON** Cabernet Sauvignon California Vintners Selection 1986 • $6 • (06/30/89)

84 **ROMBAUER** Le Meilleur du Chai Napa Valley 1986 • $45 • (05/15/91)

84 **SEQUOIA GROVE** Cabernet Sauvignon Napa Valley Estate 1986 • $28 • (09/30/89)

84 **TREFETHEN** Cabernet Sauvignon Napa Valley 1986 • $33 • (10/31/89)

84 **VILLA MT. EDEN** Cabernet Sauvignon Napa Valley 1986 • $15 • (02/15/91)

84 **YORK MOUNTAIN** Cabernet Sauvignon San Luis Obispo 1986 • $15 • (11/15/90)

84 **YORK MOUNTAIN** Cabernet Sauvignon San Luis Obispo County 1986 • $14 • (11/15/92)

83 **BARON HERZOG** Cabernet Sauvignon Sonoma County Special Reserve 1986 • $14 • (11/15/89)

83 **BEAULIEU** Cabernet Sauvignon Napa Valley Beautour 1986 • $7 • (10/31/88)

83 **BELLEROSE** Cuvée Bellerose Sonoma County 1986 • $11 • (01/31/90)

83 **CECCHETTI SEBASTIANI** Cabernet Sauvignon Alexander Valley 1986 • $8 • (04/15/89)

83 **FENESTRA** Cabernet Sauvignon Monterey Smith & Hook Vineyard 1986 • $14 • (11/15/93)

83 **FREEMARK ABBEY** Cabernet Sauvignon Napa Valley 1986 • $16 • (11/15/90)

83 **GUNDLACH BUNDSCHU** Cabernet Sauvignon Sonoma Valley Rhinefarm Vineyards Reserve 1986 • $25 • (08/31/91)

83 **J. PEDRONCELLI** Cabernet Sauvignon Dry Creek Valley 1986 • $7 • (09/15/89) • BB

83 **JEKEL** Cabernet Sauvignon Arroyo Seco 1986 • $13 • (11/15/90)

83 **JOSEPH PHELPS** Cabernet Sauvignon Napa Valley Backus Vineyard 1986 • $38 • (01/31/90)

83 **LOLONIS** Cabernet Sauvignon Mendocino County Private Reserve 1986 • $15 • (05/15/90)

83 **MIRASSOU** Cabernet Sauvignon California Family Selection 1986 • $9 • (05/31/91)

83 **MONTEREY VINEYARD** Cabernet Sauvignon Monterey County Limited Release 1986 • $10 • (11/15/89)

83 **MOUNT EDEN** Cabernet Sauvignon Santa Cruz Mountains 1986 • $29 • (08/31/90)

83 **MOUNT VEEDER** Cabernet Sauvignon Napa Valley 1986 • $20 • (11/15/90)

83 **RENAISSANCE** Cabernet Sauvignon North Yuba 1986 • $15 • (07/15/91)

83 **WILLIAM WHEELER** Cabernet Sauvignon Dry Creek Valley 1986 • $12 • (08/31/90)

82 **BENZIGER** Cabernet Sauvignon Sonoma County 1986 • $10 • (07/31/89)

82 **BERNARD PRADEL** Cabernet Sauvignon Napa Valley 1986 • $12 • (01/31/90)

82 **BRUTOCAO** Cabernet Sauvignon Mendocino 1986 • $13 • (03/31/92)

82 **CHATEAU DIANA** Cabernet Sauvignon California Limited Edition 1986 • $5 • (10/15/91) • BB

82 **DUNNEWOOD** Cabernet Sauvignon Napa Valley Napa Reserve 1986 • $11 • (06/15/90)

82 **GLEN ELLEN** Cabernet Sauvignon California Proprietor's Reserve 1986 • $4 • (07/15/88) • BB

82 **HAWK CREST** Cabernet Sauvignon North Coast 1986 • $7 • (10/15/88) • BB

82 **M.G. VALLEJO** Cabernet Sauvignon California 1986 • $5 • (06/15/90) • BB

82 **MAYACAMAS** Cabernet Sauvignon Napa Valley 1986 • $45 • (11/15/91)

82 **RIDGE** Cabernet Sauvignon Santa Cruz Mountains Monte Bello 1986 • $31 • (09/15/89)

82 **ROUND HILL** Cabernet Sauvignon Napa Valley 1986 • $8 • (10/15/88)

82 **STAG'S LEAP WINE CELLARS** Cabernet Sauvignon Napa Valley 1986 • $18 • (06/15/89)

82 **SUGARLOAF RIDGE** Cabernet Sauvignon Sonoma Valley 1986 • $13 • (03/31/90)

82 **TREFETHEN** Cabernet Sauvignon Napa Valley Estate Reserve 1986 • $30 • (08/31/92)

82 **WENTE BROS.** Cabernet Sauvignon Livermore Valley Estate Reserve 1986 • $12 • (10/15/90)

82 **WILLOW CREEK** Cabernet Sauvignon Napa-Alexander Valleys 1986 • $9 • (07/31/89)

81 **FIRESTONE** Cabernet Sauvignon Santa Ynez Valley 1986 • $10 • (12/15/89)

81 **KATHRYN KENNEDY** Cabernet Sauvignon Santa Cruz Mountains 1986 • $37 • (03/15/90)

81 **ROUDON-SMITH** Cabernet Sauvignon Santa Cruz Mountains 1986 • $12 • (03/15/91)

80 **ALEXANDER VALLEY VINEYARDS** Cabernet Sauvignon Alexander Valley Library Reserve 1986 • $18 • (06/15/93)

80 **ARCIERO** Cabernet Sauvignon Paso Robles 1986 • $8 • (11/15/90)

80 **CASTORO** Cabernet Sauvignon Paso Robles Hope Farms 1986 • $8 • (12/15/89)

80 **CORBETT CANYON** Cabernet Sauvignon Central Coast Coastal Classic 1986 • $6 • (12/15/89)

80 **DRY CREEK** Meritage Dry Creek Valley 1986 • $22 • (09/15/90)

80 **FERRARI-CARANO** Cabernet Sauvignon Alexander Valley 1986 • $18 • (09/15/90)

80 **KONOCTI** Cabernet Sauvignon Lake County 1986 • $9 • (04/30/90)

80 **LOUIS M. MARTINI** Cabernet Sauvignon North Coast 1986 • $10 • (09/15/89)

80 **PARDUCCI** Cabernet Merlot Cellarmaster Selection Mendocino County 1986 • $15 • (11/15/92)

80 **PINE RIDGE** Cabernet Sauvignon Napa Valley Andrus Reserve 1986 • $47 • (05/15/90)

80 **ROBERT MONDAVI** Cabernet Sauvignon California Cabernet 1986 • $5 • (12/15/88) • BB

80 **ROUND HILL** Cabernet Sauvignon Napa Valley Reserve 1986 • $9 • (06/30/90)

80 **RUTHERFORD ESTATE** Cabernet Sauvignon Napa Valley 1986 • $7 • (11/15/91)

80 **STONE CREEK** Cabernet Sauvignon Napa Valley Special Selection 1986 • $10 • (11/15/91)

80 **WHITE ROCK** Claret Napa Valley 1986 • $18 • (10/31/89)

80 **ZACA MESA** Cabernet Sauvignon Santa Barbara County Reserve 1986 • $15 • (12/15/88)

79 **ARCIERO** Cabernet Sauvignon Paso Robles 1986 • $9 • (12/31/89)

79 **DOMAINE ST. GEORGE** Cabernet Sauvignon Russian River Valley Select Reserve 1986 • $9 • (05/31/90)

79 **FOPPIANO** Cabernet Sauvignon Sonoma County 1986 • $9 • (11/15/90)

79 **FRANCISCAN** Meritage Napa Valley 1986 • $27 • (07/31/90)

79 **GRAND CRU** Cabernet Sauvignon Sonoma County Premium Selection 1986 • $12 • (04/30/90)

79 **LEEWARD** Cabernet Sauvignon Alexander Valley 1986 • $12 • (10/15/89)

79 **MASSON** Cabernet Sauvignon Monterey County Vintage Selection 1986 • $9 • (11/15/89)

79 **MONTEREY VINEYARD** Cabernet Sauvignon Monterey County Limited Release 1986 • $8 • (08/31/92)

79 **MOUNTAIN VIEW** Cabernet Sauvignon Mendocino County 1986 • $6 • (03/31/90)

79 **PARDUCCI** Cabernet Merlot Cellarmaster Selection Mendocino County 1986 • $15 • (04/30/91)

79 **STONEGATE** Cabernet Sauvignon Napa Valley 1986 • $17 • (03/01/89)

79 **SUTTER HOME** Cabernet Sauvignon California 1986 • $5 • (11/30/88)

79 **VENTANA** Meritage Magnus Monterey 1986 • $20 • (10/31/89)

79 **VILLA ZAPU** Cabernet Sauvignon Napa Valley 1986 • $16 • (10/31/89)

78 **BENZIGER** Cabernet Sauvignon Sonoma Valley 1986 • $17 • (04/30/90)

78 **CHARTRONS** Claret California 1986 • $15 • (11/15/91)

78 **CHRISTOPHE** Cabernet Sauvignon Napa Valley Reserve 1986 • $12 • (11/15/90)

78 **DE MOOR** Cabernet Sauvignon Napa Valley Owners Select 1986 • $16 • (02/28/91)

78 **GUENOC** Cabernet Sauvignon Lake County 1986 • $13 • (04/30/91)

78 **J. PEDRONCELLI** Cabernet Sauvignon Dry Creek Valley Reserve 1986 • $14 • (11/15/92)

78 **MAZZOCCO** Cabernet Sauvignon Alexander Valley Claret Style 1986 • $20 • (07/31/89)

78 **RAVENSWOOD** Pickberry Vineyards Sonoma Mountain 1986 • $38 • (02/15/89)

78 **RENAISSANCE** Cabernet Sauvignon North Yuba 1986 • $21 • (11/15/94)

78 **SEQUOIA GROVE** Cabernet Sauvignon Napa County 1986 • $16 • (09/30/89)

78 **ZACA MESA** Cabernet Sauvignon Santa Barbara County 1986 • $9 • (12/15/89)

77 **DOMAINE STE. VINCENT** Cabernet Sauvignon Sonoma County Reserve 1986 • $8 • (11/15/92)

77 **FLORA SPRINGS** Cabernet Sauvignon Napa Valley 1986 • $16 • (03/01/89)

77 **JOSEPH PHELPS** Cabernet Sauvignon Napa Valley Eisele Vineyard 1986 • $40 • (08/31/90)

77 **MADDALENA** Cabernet Sauvignon Alexander Valley Reserve 1986 • $10 • (03/31/90)

77 **MONTEREY PENINSULA** Cabernet Sauvignon Monterey County Monterey Cellars 1986 • $8 • (11/15/92)

77 **VIANSA** Cabernet Sauvignon Sonoma-Napa Counties 1986 • $15 • (07/31/90)

77 **WHITEHALL LANE** Cabernet Sauvignon Napa Valley Reserve 1986 • $30 • (11/15/90)

76 **FREEMARK ABBEY** Cabernet Sauvignon Napa Valley Bosché 1986 • $24 • (07/31/90)

76 **FREMONT CREEK** Cabernet Sauvignon Mendocino-Napa Counties 1986 • $8 • (11/15/89)

76 **MONTEREY VINEYARD** Cabernet Sauvignon Monterey County Classic 1986 • $5 • (10/31/89)

76 **SEGHESIO** Cabernet Sauvignon Northern Sonoma 1986 • $8 • (06/30/90)

75 **DOMAINE MICHEL** Cabernet Sauvignon Sonoma County 1986 • $19 • (06/30/90)

75 **GUGLIELMO** Cabernet Sauvignon Santa Clara County Private Reserve 1986 • $12 • (11/15/93)

75 **J. WILE & SONS** Cabernet Sauvignon Napa Valley 1986 • $7 • (09/15/88)

75 **PARSONS CREEK** Cabernet Sauvignon Sonoma County 1986 • $13 • (11/15/89)

74 **AUSTIN** A Genoux Santa Barbara County 1986 • $15 • (12/15/89)

74 **BARON HERZOG** Cabernet Sauvignon Sonoma County Special Reserve 1986 • $16 • (03/31/91)

74 **INGLENOOK** Niebaum Claret Napa Valley 1986 • $13 • (06/30/91)

74 **KENDALL-JACKSON** Cabernet Sauvignon Lake County 1986 • $7 • (07/31/88)

73 **DUNNEWOOD** Cabernet Sauvignon California 1986 • $7 • (06/15/90)

73 **INNISFREE** Cabernet Sauvignon Napa Valley 1986 • $11 • (06/30/90)

73 **RANCHO SISQUOC** Cabernet Sauvignon Santa Maria Valley 1986 • $10 • (12/15/89)

72 **MEEKER** Cabernet Sauvignon Dry Creek Valley 1986 • $19 • (02/15/90)

72 **MISSION VIEW** Cabernet Sauvignon Paso Robles 1986 • $12 • (12/15/89)

71 **SEBASTIANI ESTATES** Cabernet Sauvignon North Coast Emilia 1986 • $13 • (03/31/92)

70 **GARLAND RANCH** Cabernet Sauvignon Central Coast 1986 • $6 • (10/31/89)

70 **MCDOWELL** Cabernet Sauvignon McDowell Valley 1986 • $8 • (04/30/90)

70 **TULOCAY** Cabernet Sauvignon Napa Valley 1986 • $12 • (06/30/90)

69 **HOP KILN** Cabernet Sauvignon Dry Creek Valley 1986 • $12 • (06/15/89)

68 **RIDGE** Cabernet Sauvignon Santa Cruz Mountains 1986 • $15 • (10/31/89)

68 **RUTHERFORD HILL** Cabernet Sauvignon Napa Valley 1986 • $14 • (02/28/91)

66 **FIRESTONE** Cabernet Sauvignon Santa Ynez Valley 1986 • $10

60 **MIRASSOU** Cabernet Sauvignon Monterey County Harvest Reserve 1986 • $13 • (07/31/91)

55 **CONN CREEK** Cabernet Sauvignon Napa Valley Barrel Select 1986 • $18 • (02/28/91)

1985 California Cabernet
Vintage Rating: 97

99 **CAYMUS** Cabernet Sauvignon Napa Valley Special Selection 1985 • $240 • (04/30/90)

98 **HEITZ** Cabernet Sauvignon Napa Valley Martha's Vineyard 1985 • $163 • (04/30/90)

98 **STAG'S LEAP WINE CELLARS** SLV Cask 23 Stags Leap District 1985 • $180 • (03/01/89)

97 **KENDALL-JACKSON** Cabernet Sauvignon California Cardinale 1985 • $90 • (11/15/89)

96 **BERINGER** Cabernet Sauvignon Napa Valley Private Reserve 1985 • $78 • (03/01/89)

96 **STAG'S LEAP WINE CELLARS** S.L.V. Cask 23 Stags Leap District 1985 • $180 • (11/30/89)

96 **STERLING** Cabernet Sauvignon Reserve Napa Valley 1985 • $42 • (07/15/89) • SS

96 **STERLING** Reserve Napa Valley 1985 • $42 • (03/01/89)

96 **THE HESS COLLECTION** Cabernet Sauvignon Napa Valley 1985 • $69 • (03/01/89)

95 **BEAULIEU** Cabernet Sauvignon Napa Valley Georges de Latour Private Reserve 1985 • $55 • (03/31/91)

95 **BERINGER** Cabernet Sauvignon Napa Valley Private Reserve 1985 • $57 • (12/15/89) • SS

95 **CHATEAU MONTELENA** Cabernet Sauvignon Napa Valley 1985 • $75 • (03/01/89)

95 **DOMINUS** Napa Valley 1985 • $60 • (03/01/89)

95 **GRACE FAMILY** Cabernet Sauvignon Napa Valley 1985 • $260 • (03/01/89)

95 **GROTH** Cabernet Sauvignon Napa Valley Reserve 1985 • $135 • (04/15/90)

95 **INGLENOOK** Cabernet Sauvignon Napa Valley Reserve Cask 1985 • $19 • (03/01/89)

95 **KENDALL-JACKSON** Cabernet Sauvignon California Proprietor's Reserve 1985 • $20 • (12/15/88)

95 **OPUS ONE** Napa Valley 1985 • $95 • (06/15/89)

95 **RIDGE** Cabernet Sauvignon Santa Cruz Mountains Monte Bello 1985 • $65 • (03/01/89)

95 **ROBERT MONDAVI** Cabernet Sauvignon Napa Valley Reserve 1985 • $55 • (11/15/89) • SS

95 **SILVER OAK** Cabernet Sauvignon Alexander Valley 1985 • $60 • (03/01/89)

95 **SPOTTSWOODE** Cabernet Sauvignon Napa Valley 1985 • $105 • (03/01/89)

94 **ARROWOOD** Cabernet Sauvignon Sonoma County 1985 • $36 • (12/15/88)

94 **B.R. COHN** Cabernet Sauvignon Sonoma Valley Olive Hill Vineyard 1985 • $38 • (03/01/89)

94 **BUENA VISTA** Cabernet Sauvignon Carneros Private Reserve 1985 • $23 • (10/15/89) • SS

94 **CLOS DU VAL** Reserve Stags Leap District 1985 • $50 • (11/15/90)

94 **DUNN** Cabernet Sauvignon Napa Valley 1985 • $70 • (03/01/89)

94 **INGLENOOK** Reunion Napa Valley 1985 • $35 • (03/01/89)

94 **JOSEPH PHELPS** Cabernet Sauvignon Napa Valley Eisele Vineyard 1985 • $56 • (03/01/89)

94 **PINE RIDGE** Cabernet Sauvignon Stags Leap District Pine Ridge Stags Leap Vineyard 1985 • $30 • (03/01/89)

94 **ROBERT MONDAVI** Cabernet Sauvignon Napa Valley 1985 • $27 • (12/15/88) • SS

94 **ROBERT MONDAVI** Cabernet Sauvignon Napa Valley Reserve 1985 • $55 • (11/30/91)

94 **SIMI** Cabernet Sauvignon Alexander Valley Reserve 1985 • $30 • (08/31/90) • SS

94 **STAG'S LEAP WINE CELLARS** Cabernet Sauvignon Stags Leap District S.L.V. 1985 • $49 • (03/01/89)

94 **WILLIAM HILL** Cabernet Sauvignon Napa Valley Reserve 1985 • $46 • (03/01/89)

93 **BUEHLER** Cabernet Sauvignon Napa Valley 1985 • $19 • (03/01/89)

93 **BUENA VISTA** Cabernet Sauvignon Carneros Private Reserve 1985 • $23 • (03/01/89)

93 **BURGESS** Cabernet Sauvignon Napa Valley Vintage Selection 1985 • $24 • (03/01/89)

93 **CHAPPELLET** Cabernet Sauvignon Napa Valley Reserve 1985 • $25 • (02/15/93)

93 **CLOS DU VAL** Cabernet Sauvignon Stags Leap District 1985 • $32 • (03/01/89)

93 **DIAMOND CREEK** Cabernet Sauvignon Napa Valley Red Rock Terrace 1985 • $29 • (03/01/89)

93 **DIAMOND CREEK** Cabernet Sauvignon Napa Valley Volcanic Hill 1985 • $32 • (03/01/89)

93 **DUNN** Cabernet Sauvignon Napa Valley 1985 • $64 • (11/30/91)

93 **FORMAN** Cabernet Sauvignon Napa Valley 1985 • $45 • (03/01/89)

93 **FREEMARK ABBEY** Cabernet Sauvignon Napa Valley Bosché 1985 • $39 • (03/01/89)

93 **GRACE FAMILY** Cabernet Sauvignon Napa Valley 1985 • $260 • (12/15/88)

93 **GROTH** Cabernet Sauvignon Napa Valley 1985 • $38 • (11/15/88)

93 **GROTH** Cabernet Sauvignon Napa Valley Reserve 1985 • $119 • (03/01/89)

93 **JOSEPH PHELPS** Insignia Napa Valley 1985 • $52 • (07/31/89) • CS

93 **KATHRYN KENNEDY** Cabernet Sauvignon Santa Cruz Mountains 1985 • $33 • (12/15/88)

93 **KISTLER** Cabernet Sauvignon Sonoma Valley Kistler Estate Vineyard 1985 • $36 • (03/01/89)

93 **LAUREL GLEN** Cabernet Sauvignon Sonoma Mountain 1985 • $85 • (03/01/89)

93 **MARKHAM** Cabernet Sauvignon Napa Valley 1985 • $17 • (03/01/89)

93 **OPTIMA** Cabernet Sauvignon Sonoma County 1985 • $19 • (12/15/88)

93 **PINE RIDGE** Cabernet Sauvignon Napa Valley Rutherford Cuvée 1985 • $20 • (03/01/89)

93 **SHAFER** Cabernet Sauvignon Stags Leap District Hillside Select 1985 • $30 • (03/01/89)

93 **ST. CLEMENT** Cabernet Sauvignon Napa Valley 1985 • $35 • (03/01/89)

93 **STELTZNER** Cabernet Sauvignon Stags Leap District 1985 • $25 • (03/01/89)

93 **STERLING** Three Palms Vineyard Napa Valley 1985 • $22 • (12/31/88)

93 **VICHON** Cabernet Sauvignon Stags Leap District SLD 1985 • $25 • (01/31/89)

93 **WHITEHALL LANE** Cabernet Sauvignon Napa Valley 1985 • $16 • (11/15/88)

92 **ALEXANDER VALLEY VINEYARDS** Cabernet Sauvignon Alexander Valley 1985 • $18 • (11/15/87)

92 **BURGESS** Cabernet Sauvignon Napa Valley Vintage Selection 1985 • $24 • (07/15/89)

92 **CAYMUS** Cabernet Sauvignon Napa Valley Cuvée 1985 • $12 • (07/15/88)

92 **CAYMUS** Cabernet Sauvignon Napa Valley 1985 • $24 • (03/01/89)

92 **CHATEAU MONTELENA** Cabernet Sauvignon Napa Valley 1985 • $59 • (11/15/89) • CS

92 **CLOS DU VAL** Reserve Stags Leap District 1985 • $50 • (11/15/89)

92 **DIAMOND CREEK** Cabernet Sauvignon Napa Valley Gravelly Meadow 1985 • $29 • (03/01/89)

92 **DUCKHORN** Cabernet Sauvignon Napa Valley 1985 • $40 • (03/01/89)

92 **ETUDE** Cabernet Sauvignon California 1985 • $25 • (12/15/88)

92 **FAR NIENTE** Cabernet Sauvignon Napa Valley 1985 • $41 • (03/01/89)

92 **FORMAN** Cabernet Sauvignon Napa Valley 1985 • $67 • (06/15/88)

92 **GRGICH HILLS** Cabernet Sauvignon Napa Valley 1985 • $47 • (03/01/89)

92 **HEITZ** Cabernet Sauvignon Napa Valley Bella Oaks Vineyard 1985 • $36 • (05/15/90) • CS

92 **KISTLER** Cabernet Sauvignon Sonoma Valley Kistler Estate Vineyard 1985 • $20 • (05/31/88)

92 **LAKESPRING** Cabernet Sauvignon Napa Valley 1985 • $19 • (07/15/88)

92 **LONG** Cabernet Sauvignon Napa Valley 1985 • $40 • (03/01/89)

92 **LYETH** Red Alexander Valley 1985 • $23 • (03/01/89)

92 **MAYACAMAS** Cabernet Sauvignon Napa Valley 1985 • $49 • (01/31/90)

92 **MONTICELLO** Cabernet Sauvignon Napa Valley Corley Reserve 1985 • $35 • (07/31/89)

92 **PINE RIDGE** Cabernet Sauvignon Napa Valley Andrus Reserve Cuvée Duet 1985 • $40 • (03/01/89)

92 **RIDGE** Cabernet Sauvignon Napa County York Creek 1985 • $21 • (03/01/89)

92 **RUTHERFORD RANCH** Cabernet Sauvignon Napa Valley 1985 • $11 • (05/15/90) • SS

92 **SANTA CRUZ MOUNTAIN** Cabernet Sauvignon Santa Cruz Mountains Bates Ranch 1985 • $18 • (03/01/89)

92 **SEQUOIA GROVE** Cabernet Sauvignon Napa Valley Estate 1985 • $30 • (03/01/89)

92 **SILVERADO** Cabernet Sauvignon Stags Leap District 1985 • $30 • (03/01/89)

92 **STELTZNER** Cabernet Sauvignon Stags Leap District 1985 • $25 • (11/15/88)

92 **VICHON** Cabernet Sauvignon Stags Leap District SLD 1985 • $25 • (03/01/89)

92 **WILLIAM HILL** Cabernet Sauvignon Napa Valley Reserve 1985 • $46 • (11/15/88)

91 **BEAULIEU** Cabernet Sauvignon Napa Valley Georges de Latour Private Reserve 1985 • $46 • (12/31/89)

91 **BERINGER** Cabernet Sauvignon Napa Valley Chabot Vineyard 1985 • $31 • (03/01/89)

91 **BERNARD PRADEL** Cabernet Sauvignon Napa Valley 1985 • $12 • (04/30/89)

91 **CARMENET** Red Sonoma Valley 1985 • $35 • (03/01/89)

91 **CONN CREEK** Cabernet Sauvignon Napa Valley Barrel Select Private Reserve 1985 • $45 • (09/15/90)

91 **CUTLER** Cabernet Sauvignon Sonoma Valley Batto Ranch 1985 • $20 • (07/31/89)

91 **CUVAISON** Cabernet Sauvignon Napa Valley 1985 • $40 • (03/31/89)

91 **DIAMOND CREEK** Cabernet Sauvignon Napa Valley Red Rock Terrace 1985 • $67 • (11/30/87)

91 **DRY CREEK** Cabernet Sauvignon Sonoma County 1985 • $16 • (05/31/88) • SS

91 **DUCKHORN** Cabernet Sauvignon Napa Valley 1985 • $50 • (06/15/88) • CS

91 **FISHER** Cabernet Sauvignon Sonoma County Coach Insignia 1985 • $22 • (09/15/88)

91 **GROTH** Cabernet Sauvignon Napa Valley 1985 • $38 • (03/01/89)

91 **GUNDLACH BUNDSCHU** Cabernet Sauvignon Sonoma Valley Rhinefarm Vineyards 1985 • $14 • (03/01/89)

91 **HAYWOOD** Cabernet Sauvignon Sonoma Valley 1985 • $20 • (03/15/88)

91 **INGLENOOK** Reunion Napa Valley 1985 • $35 • (07/15/89)

91 **JOSEPH PHELPS** Cabernet Sauvignon Napa Valley Backus Vineyard 1985 • $49 • (12/31/88)

91 **KENWOOD** Cabernet Sauvignon Sonoma Valley 1985 • $15 • (02/15/89)

91 **KENWOOD** Cabernet Sauvignon Sonoma Valley Artist Series 1985 • $39 • (03/01/89)

91 **LA JOTA** Cabernet Sauvignon Howell Mountain 1985 • $43 • (11/15/88)

91 **LAUREL GLEN** Cabernet Sauvignon Sonoma Mountain 1985 • $52 • (04/30/88)

91 **MARKHAM** Cabernet Sauvignon Napa Valley 1985 • $17 • (04/15/90)

91 **MERRYVALE** Red Table Wine Napa Valley 1985 • $26 • (03/01/89)

91 **NIEBAUM-COPPOLA** Rubicon Napa Valley 1985 • $35 • (03/01/89)

91 **PLAM** Cabernet Sauvignon Napa Valley 1985 • $24 • (06/30/88)

91 **RAYMOND** Cabernet Sauvignon Napa Valley Private Reserve 1985 • $30 • (07/15/90) • CS

91 **SHAFER** Cabernet Sauvignon Stags Leap District Hillside Select 1985 • $48 • (05/31/90) • CS

91 **SHAFER** Cabernet Sauvignon Stags Leap District 1985 • $22 • (03/01/89)

91 **SILVERADO** Cabernet Sauvignon Stags Leap District 1985 • $30 • (11/15/88) • SS

91 **SIMI** Cabernet Sauvignon Sonoma County 1985 • $21 • (09/30/89)

91 **THE HESS COLLECTION** Cabernet Sauvignon Napa Valley 1985 • $69 • (11/15/88)

91 **VICHON** Cabernet Sauvignon Napa Valley 1985 • $19 • (11/15/88)

90 **BERINGER** Cabernet Sauvignon Napa Valley Chabot Vineyard 1985 • $31 • (11/15/91)

90 **CAKEBREAD** Cabernet Sauvignon Napa Valley 1985 • $20 • (04/15/88)

90 **CARNEROS CREEK** Cabernet Sauvignon Los Carneros 1985 • $15 • (10/31/89)

90 **CAYMUS** Cabernet Sauvignon Napa Valley 1985 • $55 • (11/15/88)

90 **CHRISTIAN BROTHERS** Cabernet Sauvignon Napa Valley 1985 • $8 • (06/15/88)

90 **CLOS DU VAL** Cabernet Sauvignon Stags Leap District 1985 • $32 • (06/15/89)

90 **CONN CREEK** Cabernet Sauvignon Napa Valley Barrel Select 1985 • $29 • (09/15/90)

90 **CUVAISON** Cabernet Sauvignon Napa Valley 1985 • $40 • (03/01/89)

90 **FAR NIENTE** Cabernet Sauvignon Napa Valley 1985 • $41 • (12/31/88)

90 **FISHER** Cabernet Sauvignon Sonoma County Coach Insignia 1985 • $22 • (03/01/89)

90 **FLORA SPRINGS** Cabernet Sauvignon Napa Valley 1985 • $16 • (07/31/89)

90 **FRANCISCAN** Meritage Napa Valley 1985 • $30 • (03/31/90)

90 **FREEMARK ABBEY** Cabernet Sauvignon Napa Valley Bosché 1985 • $39 • (07/31/89)

90 **GRGICH HILLS** Cabernet Sauvignon Napa Valley 1985 • $35 • (10/31/90)

90 **INGLENOOK** Cabernet Sauvignon Napa Valley Reserve Cask 1985 • $19 • (02/15/91) • CS

90 **JOSEPH PHELPS** Cabernet Sauvignon Napa Valley Backus Vineyard 1985 • $49 • (03/01/89)

90 **ROBERT PEPI** Cabernet Sauvignon Napa Valley Vine Hill Ranch 1985 • $18 • (03/01/89)

90 **ROMBAUER** Le Meilleur du Chai Napa Valley 1985 • $48 • (10/31/89)

90 **SMITH-MADRONE** Cabernet Sauvignon Napa Valley 1985 • $19 • (03/01/89)

90 **STAG'S LEAP WINE CELLARS** Cabernet Sauvignon Stags Leap District SLV 1985 • $49 • (10/31/88)

90 **STAG'S LEAP WINE CELLARS** Cabernet Sauvignon Napa Valley 1985 • $16 • (09/15/88)

90 **STERLING** Cabernet Sauvignon Napa Valley Diamond Mountain Ranch 1985 • $21 • (03/01/89)

90 **TREFETHEN** Cabernet Sauvignon Napa Valley Hillside Selection 1985 • $36 • (03/01/89)

90 **WILLIAM HILL** Cabernet Sauvignon Napa Valley Silver Label 1985 • $12 • (04/30/88)

89 **BUEHLER** Cabernet Sauvignon Napa Valley 1985 • $25 • (04/30/88)

89 **CHARLES KRUG** Cabernet Sauvignon Napa Valley Vintage Select 1985 • $29 • (03/15/92)

89 **DIAMOND CREEK** Cabernet Sauvignon Napa Valley Gravelly Meadow 1985 • $69 • (11/30/87)

89 **DIAMOND CREEK** Cabernet Sauvignon Napa Valley Three Vineyard Blend 1985 • $100 • (03/01/89)

89 **DRY CREEK** Meritage Dry Creek Valley 1985 • $22 • (11/15/89)

89 **DUNN** Cabernet Sauvignon Howell Mountain 1985 • $110 • (03/01/89)

89 **EBERLE** Cabernet Sauvignon Paso Robles 1985 • $17 • (03/01/89)

89 **FRANCISCAN** Meritage Napa Valley 1985 • $30 • (03/01/89)

89 **GIRARD** Cabernet Sauvignon Napa Valley Reserve 1985 • $35 • (03/01/89)

89 **GUSTAVE NIEBAUM** Cabernet Sauvignon Napa Valley Reference 1985 • $14 • (10/31/89)

89 **HAYWOOD** Cabernet Sauvignon Sonoma Valley 1985 • $20 • (03/01/89)

89 **J. LOHR** Cabernet Sauvignon Napa Valley Carol's Vineyard Reserve 1985 • $15 • (12/15/88)

89 **KENWOOD** Cabernet Sauvignon Sonoma Valley Jack London Vineyard 1985 • $27 • (10/15/88)

89 **KONOCTI** Cabernet Sauvignon Lake County 1985 • $7 • (11/15/89) • BB

89 **NEWTON** Cabernet Sauvignon Napa Valley 1985 • $22 • (03/01/89)

89 **PHILIP TOGNI** Cabernet Sauvignon Napa Valley 1985 • $23 • (03/01/89)

89 **PRESTON** Cabernet Sauvignon Dry Creek Valley 1985 • $18 • (03/01/89)

89 **ROBERT PECOTA** Cabernet Sauvignon Napa Valley Kara's Vineyard 1985 • $16 • (12/15/88)

89 **RUTHERFORD HILL** Cabernet Sauvignon Napa Valley XVS 1985 • $29 • (03/01/89)

89 **SEBASTIANI ESTATES** Cabernet Sauvignon Sonoma Valley Cherry Block 1985 • $17 • (03/31/90)

89 **ST. ANDREW'S WINERY** Cabernet Sauvignon Napa Valley 1985 • $11 • (05/15/88)

89 **STERLING** Cabernet Sauvignon Napa Valley 1985 • $17 • (05/15/88)

89 **STREBLOW** Cabernet Sauvignon Napa Valley 1985 • $15 • (06/15/88)

89 **TUDAL** Cabernet Sauvignon Napa Valley 1985 • $25 • (03/01/89)

88 **ALEXANDER VALLEY VINEYARDS** Cabernet Sauvignon Alexander Valley 1985 • $18 • (03/01/89)

88 **CHAPPELLET** Cabernet Sauvignon Napa Valley Reserve 1985 • $25 • (03/01/89)

88 **CHIMNEY ROCK** Cabernet Sauvignon Stags Leap District 1985 • $15 • (10/31/88)

88 **CLOS DU BOIS** Marlstone Vineyard Alexander Valley 1985 • $34 • (03/01/89)

88 **CLOS DU VAL** Cabernet Sauvignon Napa Valley Gran Val 1985 • $8 • (05/31/88)

88 **DIAMOND CREEK** Cabernet Sauvignon Napa Valley Volcanic Hill 1985 • $55 • (11/30/87)

88 **DUNN** Cabernet Sauvignon Howell Mountain 1985 • $110 • (11/30/91)

88 **FLORA SPRINGS** Trilogy Napa Valley 1985 • $33 • (03/01/89)

88 **FLORA SPRINGS** Cabernet Sauvignon Napa Valley 1985 • $16 • (03/01/89)

88 **FRANCISCAN** Cabernet Sauvignon Napa Valley Oakville Estate Reserve 1985 • $20 • (05/31/90)

88 **FRANCISCAN** Cabernet Sauvignon Napa Valley Library Selection 1985 • $18 • (03/01/89)

88 **FREEMARK ABBEY** Cabernet Sauvignon Napa Valley Sycamore Vineyards 1985 • $25 • (10/31/89)

88 **GEYSER PEAK** Réserve Alexandre Alexander Valley 1985 • $19 • (09/30/89)

88 **GIRARD** Cabernet Sauvignon Napa Valley 1985 • $22 • (09/15/88)

88 **IRON HORSE** Cabernets Alexander Valley 1985 • $21 • (12/31/88)

88 **J. LOHR** Cabernet Sauvignon Napa Valley Carol's Vineyard Reserve Lot 2 1985 • $18 • (09/30/90)

88 **JOHNSON TURNBULL** Cabernet Sauvignon Napa Valley 1985 • $18 • (07/15/88)

88 **JORDAN** Cabernet Sauvignon Alexander Valley 1985 • $46 • (09/15/89)

88 **LA JOTA** Cabernet Sauvignon Howell Mountain 1985 • $26 • (03/01/89)

88 **LAKESPRING** Cabernet Sauvignon Napa Valley 1985 • $19 • (03/01/89)

88 **MONTICELLO** Cabernet Sauvignon Napa Valley Corley Reserve 1985 • $35 • (03/01/89)

88 **PINE RIDGE** Cabernet Sauvignon Napa Valley Rutherford Cuvée 1985 • $20 • (02/15/89)

88 **RAYMOND** Cabernet Sauvignon Napa Valley Private Reserve 1985 • $30 • (03/01/89)

88 **RODNEY STRONG** Cabernet Sauvignon Alexander Valley Alexander's Crown Vineyard 1985 • $15 • (09/30/90)

88 **RUTHERFORD HILL** Cabernet Sauvignon Napa Valley XVS 1985 • $29 • (04/30/89)

88 **SHAFER** Cabernet Sauvignon Stags Leap District 1985 • $22 • (11/15/88)

88 **SILVER OAK** Cabernet Sauvignon Napa Valley 1985 • $85 • (10/31/89)

88 **SMITH & HOOK** Cabernet Sauvignon Napa County 1985 • $12 • (09/30/89)

88 **SPRING MOUNTAIN** Cabernet Sauvignon Napa Valley 1985 • $20 • (03/01/89)

88 **ST. FRANCIS** Cabernet Sauvignon California 1985 • $9 • (11/30/87)

88 **STERLING** Cabernet Sauvignon Napa Valley Diamond Mountain Ranch 1985 • $21 • (05/31/89)

88 **VICHON** Cabernet Sauvignon Napa Valley 1985 • $19 • (03/01/89)

88 **WHITEHALL LANE** Cabernet Sauvignon Napa Valley Reserve 1985 • $30 • (11/30/89)

87 **BERINGER** Cabernet Sauvignon Knights Valley 1985 • $20 • (05/31/88)

87 **BLACK MOUNTAIN** Cabernet Sauvignon Alexander Valley Fat Cat 1985 • $18 • (04/30/90)

87 **CAIN** Five Napa Valley 1985 • $43 • (06/15/89)

87 **CHATEAU SOUVERAIN** Cabernet Sauvignon Sonoma County 1985 • $8 • (11/30/88)

87 **CHIMNEY ROCK** Cabernet Sauvignon Stags Leap District 1985 • $15 • (03/01/89)

87 **CLOS DU BOIS** Cabernet Sauvignon Alexander Valley 1985 • $19 • (04/15/88)

87 **CONCANNON** Cabernet Sauvignon Livermore Valley Reserve 1985 • $14 • (02/15/89)

87 **CONN CREEK** Cabernet Sauvignon Napa Valley Barrel Select Private Reserve 1985 • $45 • (03/01/89)

87 **ESTANCIA** Cabernet Sauvignon Alexander Valley 1985 • $6 • (06/15/88) • BB

87 **FETZER** Cabernet Sauvignon California Reserve 1985 • $17 • (11/15/89)

87 **FIELD STONE** Cabernet Sauvignon Alexander Valley Hoot Owl Creek Vineyards 1985 • $20 • (03/31/89)

87 **FLORA SPRINGS** Trilogy Napa Valley 1985 • $33 • (02/15/89)

87 **FRANCISCAN** Cabernet Sauvignon Napa Valley Oakville Estate Reserve 1985 • $20 • (03/01/89)

87 **GUENOC** Cabernet Sauvignon Guenoc Valley Premier Cuvée 1985 • $18 • (12/15/88)

87 **IRON HORSE** Cabernets Alexander Valley 1985 • $21 • (03/01/89)

87 **MERRYVALE** Red Table Wine Napa Valley 1985 • $26 • (11/15/88)

87 **MONTICELLO** Cabernet Sauvignon Napa Valley Jefferson Cuvée 1985 • $12 • (02/29/88)

87 **MOUNT VEEDER** Cabernet Sauvignon Napa Valley 1985 • $20 • (03/01/89)

87 **NAVARRO** Cabernet Sauvignon Mendocino 1985 • $14 • (11/15/90)

87 **NEWLAN** Cabernet Sauvignon Napa Valley 1985 • $15 • (03/31/90)

87 **NIEBAUM-COPPOLA** Rubicon Napa Valley 1985 • $29 • (11/15/90)

87 **RIDGE** Cabernet Sauvignon Santa Cruz Mountains Jimsomare 1985 • $16 • (02/15/89)

87 **RODNEY STRONG** Cabernet Sauvignon Alexander Valley Alexander's Crown Vineyard 1985 • $17 • (05/31/91)

87 **STONEGATE** Cabernet Sauvignon Napa Valley 1985 • $17 • (03/01/89)

87 **V. SATTUI** Cabernet Sauvignon Napa Valley Preston Vineyard 1985 • $20 • (03/01/89)

86 **CHATEAU ST. JEAN** Cabernet Sauvignon Alexander Valley 1985 • $20 • (11/15/88)

86 **CLOS DU BOIS** Cabernet Sauvignon Alexander Valley Briarcrest Vineyard 1985 • $24 • (06/15/89)

86 **CLOS PEGASE** Cabernet Sauvignon Napa Valley 1985 • $17 • (05/31/88)

86 **DURNEY** Cabernet Sauvignon Carmel Valley Private Reserve 1985 • $20 • (11/15/92)

86 **FETZER** Cabernet Sauvignon Sonoma County Reserve 1985 • $24 • (08/31/90)

86 **FRANCISCAN** Cabernet Sauvignon Napa Valley Oakville Estate 1985 • $11 • (05/15/89)

86 **GIRARD** Cabernet Sauvignon Napa Valley Reserve 1985 • $35 • (02/15/90)

86 **GLEN ELLEN** Cabernet Sauvignon Sonoma Valley Imagery Series 1985 • $13 • (02/15/89)

86 **HANNA** Cabernet Sauvignon Sonoma Valley 1985 • $14 • (06/30/88)

86 **INNISFREE** Cabernet Sauvignon Napa Valley 1985 • $9 • (03/15/89)

86 **KEENAN** Cabernet Sauvignon Napa Valley 1985 • $15 • (03/01/89)

86 **LIVINGSTON** Cabernet Sauvignon Napa Valley Moffett Vineyard 1985 • $33 • (03/01/89)

86 **LYETH** Red Alexander Valley 1985 • $19 • (05/31/89)

86 **MOUNT EDEN** Cabernet Sauvignon Santa Cruz Mountains 1985 • $40 • (03/01/89)

86 **PRESTON** Cabernet Sauvignon Dry Creek Valley 1985 • $18 • (09/30/88)

86 **ROBERT PECOTA** Cabernet Sauvignon Napa Valley Kara's Vineyard 1985 • $16 • (03/01/89)

86 **ROUND HILL** Cabernet Sauvignon Napa Valley Reserve 1985 • $11 • (05/31/88)

86 **SEBASTIANI** Cabernet Sauvignon Sonoma County Reserve 1985 • $13 • (11/15/90)

86 **SEQUOIA GROVE** Cabernet Sauvignon Napa County 1985 • $21 • (03/01/89)

86 **SILVER OAK** Cabernet Sauvignon Alexander Valley 1985 • $60 • (10/31/89)

86 **STONEGATE** Cabernet Sauvignon Napa Valley 1985 • $17 • (08/31/90)

85 **BEAULIEU** Cabernet Sauvignon Napa Valley Rutherford 1985 • $17 • (06/15/88)

85 **CAKEBREAD** Cabernet Sauvignon Napa Valley Rutherford Reserve 1985 • $41 • (03/01/89)

85 **CONN CREEK** Cabernet Sauvignon Napa Valley Barrel Select 1985 • $29 • (03/01/89)

85 **CRUVINET** Cabernet Sauvignon Alexander Valley 1985 • $7 • (09/15/88) • BB

85 **FETZER** Cabernet Sauvignon Mendocino Barrel Select 1985 • $10 • (12/15/88)

85 **FROG'S LEAP** Cabernet Sauvignon Napa Valley 1985 • $24 • (03/01/89)

85 **J. PEDRONCELLI** Cabernet Sauvignon Dry Creek Valley Reserve 1985 • $14 • (03/31/90)

85 **JORDAN** Cabernet Sauvignon Alexander Valley 1985 • $36 • (03/01/89)

85 **LIVINGSTON** Cabernet Sauvignon Napa Valley Moffett Vineyard 1985 • $62 • (10/15/88)

85 **MERLION** Cabernet Sauvignon Napa Valley 1985 • $14 • (08/31/88)

85 **RAVENSWOOD** Cabernet Sauvignon Sonoma County 1985 • $20 • (03/01/89)

85 **ROBERT PEPI** Cabernet Sauvignon Napa Valley Vine Hill Ranch 1985 • $18 • (07/31/90)

85 **ROMBAUER** Cabernet Sauvignon Napa Valley 1985 • $20 • (04/30/89)

85 **SILVER OAK** Cabernet Sauvignon Napa Valley Bonny's Vineyard 1985 • $95 • (03/01/89)

85 **SPRING MOUNTAIN** Cabernet Sauvignon Napa Valley 1985 • $20 • (10/15/89)

85 **STAGS' LEAP WINERY** Cabernet Sauvignon Stags Leap District 1985 • $18 • (03/01/89)

85 **WHITE OAK** Cabernet Sauvignon Alexander Valley Myers Limited Reserve 1985 • $18 • (07/31/89)

84 **BUENA VISTA** Cabernet Sauvignon Carneros 1985 • $10 • (11/15/88)

84 **CAKEBREAD** Cabernet Sauvignon Napa Valley 1985 • $18 • (03/01/89)

84 **CHAPPELLET** Cabernet Sauvignon Napa Valley Reserve 1985 • $25 • (02/15/90)

84 **CHARLES KRUG** Cabernet Sauvignon Napa Valley Vintage Select 1985 • $29 • (03/01/89)

84 **COSENTINO** Cabernet Sauvignon North Coast 1985 • $11 • (09/15/88)

84 **DOMINUS** Napa Valley 1985 • $69 • (02/15/90)

84 **FIELD STONE** Cabernet Sauvignon Alexander Valley Turkey Hill Vineyard 1985 • $18 • (02/28/91)

84 **GUENOC** Cabernet Sauvignon Guenoc Valley Premier Cuvée 1985 • $17 • (10/15/90)

84 **HUSCH** Cabernet Sauvignon Mendocino La Ribera Cabernet 1985 • $5 • (11/30/87) • BB

84 **JOSEPH PHELPS** Cabernet Sauvignon Napa Valley 1985 • $61 • (05/15/89)

84 **RAYMOND** Cabernet Sauvignon Napa Valley 1985 • $16 • (12/15/89)

84 **SEGHESIO** Cabernet Sauvignon Northern Sonoma 1985 • $5 • (04/15/89) • BB

84 **SHADOWBROOK** Cabernet Sauvignon Napa Valley 1985 • $9 • (07/15/91)

83 **BEAULIEU** Cabernet Sauvignon Napa Valley Beautour 1985 • $7 • (06/15/88)

83 **BENZIGER** Cabernet Sauvignon Sonoma Valley 1985 • $16 • (12/15/88)

83 **CAREY** Cabernet Sauvignon Santa Ynez Valley 1985 • $10 • (11/15/89)

83 **HACIENDA** Cabernet Sauvignon Sonoma County 1985 • $15 • (09/30/90)

83 **INGLENOOK** Cabernet Sauvignon Napa Valley 1985 • $10 • (03/31/89)

83 **JOHNSON TURNBULL** Cabernet Sauvignon Napa Valley 1985 • $18 • (03/01/89)

83 **KALIN** Cabernet Sauvignon Sonoma County Reserve 1985 • $23 • (04/15/91)

83 **LEEWARD** Cabernet Sauvignon Alexander Valley 1985 • $12 • (10/31/87)

83 **MARIETTA** Cabernet Sauvignon Sonoma County 1985 • $10 • (06/30/90)

83 **NEYERS** Cabernet Sauvignon Napa Valley 1985 • $14 • (07/15/89)

83 **PINE RIDGE** Cabernet Sauvignon Napa Valley Andrus Reserve Cuvée Duet 1985 • $40 • (10/15/88)

83 **RAVENSWOOD** Cabernet Sauvignon Sonoma County 1985 • $20 • (05/31/88)

83 **SILVER OAK** Cabernet Sauvignon Napa Valley Bonny's Vineyard 1985 • $95 • (11/15/90)

83 **STRATFORD** Cabernet Sauvignon California 1985 • $10 • (11/30/88)

83 **WILLIAM WHEELER** Cabernet Sauvignon Dry Creek Valley Norse Vineyard Private Reserve 1985 • $18 • (11/15/90)

83 **YORK MOUNTAIN** Cabernet Sauvignon San Luis Obispo 1985 • $15 • (12/15/89)

82 **BELLEROSE** Cuvée Bellerose Sonoma County 1985 • $19 • (12/15/88)

82 **CLOS DU BOIS** Cabernet Sauvignon Alexander Valley Briarcrest Vineyard 1985 • $24 • (03/01/89)

82 **EBERLE** Cabernet Sauvignon Paso Robles 1985 • $17 • (02/15/89)

82 **FETZER** Cabernet Sauvignon Lake County 1985 • $6 • (08/31/87) • BB

82 **FROG'S LEAP** Cabernet Sauvignon Napa Valley 1985 • $24 • (12/31/87)

82 **INGLENOOK** Niebaum Claret Napa Valley 1985 • $12 • (03/15/89)

82 **MADRONA** Cabernet Sauvignon El Dorado 1985 • $12 • (04/15/92)

82 **MONTEREY PENINSULA** Cabernet Sauvignon Monterey County 1985 • $12 • (11/15/92)

82 **QUAIL RIDGE** Cabernet Sauvignon Napa Valley 1985 • $15 • (07/31/89)

82 **RENAISSANCE** Cabernet Sauvignon North Yuba Reserve 1985 • $45 • (11/15/92)

82 **RUTHERFORD HILL** Cabernet Sauvignon Napa Valley 1985 • $17 • (04/30/90)

82 **VILLA MT. EDEN** Cabernet Sauvignon Napa Valley 1985 • $13 • (03/01/89)

81 **BELVEDERE** Cabernet Sauvignon Alexander Valley Robert Young Vineyard Gifts of the Land 1985 • $16 • (01/31/91)

81 **CAIN** Cabernet Sauvignon Napa Valley 1985 • $16 • (04/15/89)

81 **CLOS DU BOIS** Marlstone Vineyard Alexander Valley 1985 • $34 • (06/15/89)

81 **COSENTINO** Cabernet Sauvignon North Coast Reserve 1985 • $18 • (04/30/89)

81 **DOMAINE NAPA** Cabernet Sauvignon Napa Valley 1985 • $12 • (12/15/88)

81 **GRAND CRU** Cabernet Sauvignon Alexander Valley Collector's Reserve 1985 • $18 • (07/15/89)

81 **JOSEPH PHELPS** Cabernet Sauvignon Napa Valley Eisele Vineyard 1985 • $56 • (05/31/89)

81 **MIRASSOU** Cabernet Sauvignon Napa Valley Harvest Reserve 1985 • $12 • (11/15/89)

81 **MOUNT EDEN** Cabernet Sauvignon Santa Cruz Mountains 1985 • $40 • (11/15/89)

81 **SUNNY ST. HELENA** Cabernet Sauvignon Napa Valley 1985 • $9 • (10/31/87)

81 **ZD** Cabernet Sauvignon Napa Valley 1985 • $14 • (05/15/89)

80 **BELVEDERE** Cabernet Sauvignon Alexander Valley Robert Young Vineyard Gifts of the Land 1985 • $16 • (11/30/89)

80 **E. & J. GALLO** Cabernet Sauvignon Northern Sonoma 1985 • $8 • (08/31/92)

80 **HEITZ** Cabernet Sauvignon Napa Valley 1985 • $34 • (05/15/90)

80 **LA FERRONNIERE** Cabernet Sauvignon Napa Valley 1985 • $14 • (01/31/90)

80 **LOUIS M. MARTINI** Cabernet Sauvignon Sonoma Valley Monte Rosso 1985 • $24 • (03/01/89)

80 **MILANO** Cabernet Sauvignon Mendocino County Sanel Valley Vineyard 1985 • $18 • (09/30/89)

80 **PINE RIDGE** Cabernet Sauvignon Stags Leap District Pine Ridge Stags Leap Vineyard 1985 • $30 • (04/10/89)

80 **R.H. PHILLIPS** Cabernet Sauvignon California 1985 • $6 • (11/30/88)

80 **SEBASTIANI** Cabernet Sauvignon Sonoma County Family Selection 1985 • $8 • (10/15/88)

80 **SOLARI** Cabernet Sauvignon Napa Valley Larkmead Vineyards 1985 • $10 • (03/15/90)

80 **SYLVAN SPRINGS** Cabernet Sauvignon California Vintner's Reserve 1985 • $5 • (09/30/88) • BB

80 **TREFETHEN** Cabernet Sauvignon Napa Valley Hillside Selection 1985 • $36 • (11/15/90)

80 **TREFETHEN** Cabernet Sauvignon Napa Valley 1985 • $19 • (03/01/89)

80 **VANINO** Cabernet Sauvignon Sonoma County 1985 • $11 • (09/30/88)

79 **CORBETT CANYON** Cabernet Sauvignon Santa Barbara-San Luis Obispo Counties Select 1985 • $10 • (05/31/88)

79 **COSENTINO** Meritage The Poet California 1985 • $18 • (08/31/88)

79 **DE MOOR** Cabernet Sauvignon Napa Valley 1985 • $14 • (03/01/89)

79 **FREEMARK ABBEY** Cabernet Sauvignon Napa Valley 1985 • $21 • (10/31/89)

79 **GRAND CRU** Cabernet Sauvignon Sonoma County Premium Selection 1985 • $9 • (06/15/89)

79 **IVAN TAMAS** Cabernet Sauvignon North Coast 1985 • $7 • (12/31/87)

79 **J. PEDRONCELLI** Cabernet Sauvignon Dry Creek Valley 1985 • $7 • (10/15/88)

79 **KEENAN** Cabernet Sauvignon Napa Valley 1985 • $15 • (03/31/89)

79 **LAWRENCE J. BARGETTO** Cabernet Sauvignon Sonoma County Cypress 1985 • $8 • (11/15/89)

79 **ZACA MESA** Cabernet Sauvignon Santa Barbara County Reserve 1985 • $15 • (10/15/88)

78 **A. RAFANELLI** Cabernet Sauvignon Dry Creek Valley 1985 • $8 • (09/15/88)

78 **FREMONT CREEK** Cabernet Sauvignon Mendocino-Napa Counties 1985 • $9 • (03/31/88)

78 **GUNDLACH BUNDSCHU** Cabernet Sauvignon Sonoma Valley Rhinefarm Vineyards 1985 • $14 • (03/31/89)

78 **HACIENDA** Cabernet Sauvignon Sonoma Valley Estate Reserve 1985 • $18 • (11/15/92)

78 **J. WILE & SONS** Cabernet Sauvignon Napa Valley 1985 • $7 • (11/15/87)

78 **M.G. VALLEJO** Cabernet Sauvignon California 1985 • $4 • (02/15/89)

78 **MADDALENA** Cabernet Sauvignon Alexander Valley Reserve 1985 • $11 • (06/30/89)

78 **MASSON** Cabernet Sauvignon Monterey County Vintage Selection 1985 • $8 • (09/15/88)

78 **PAT PAULSEN** Cabernet Sauvignon Sonoma County 1985 • $11 • (12/31/87)

78 **RICHARD MICHAELS** Cabernet Sauvignon California 1985 • $10 • (09/30/88)

78 **RICHARDSON** Cabernet Sauvignon Sonoma Valley 1985 • $12 • (11/30/88)

78 **RIDGE** Cabernet Sauvignon Napa County York Creek 1985 • $21 • (06/10/89)

78 **ROBERT MONDAVI** Cabernet Sauvignon California Cabernet 1985 • $4.25 • (10/31/87) • BB

78 **TAFT STREET** Cabernet Sauvignon California 1985 • $7 • (10/15/88)

78 **WENTE BROS.** Cabernet Sauvignon Central Coast 1985 • $8 • (11/15/89)

77 **ARCIERO** Cabernet Sauvignon Paso Robles 1985 • $6 • (12/31/87)

77 **AUDUBON** Cabernet Sauvignon Napa Valley 1985 • $11 • (06/15/88)

77 **BOEGER** Cabernet Sauvignon El Dorado 1985 • $11 • (02/15/89)

77 **CHARLES KRUG** Cabernet Sauvignon Napa Valley 1985 • $23 • (01/31/90)

77 **CHESTNUT HILL** Cabernet Sauvignon Sonoma County 1985 • $7 • (10/15/88)

77 **GEYSER PEAK** Cabernet Sauvignon Alexander Valley Estate Reserve 1985 • $15 • (05/15/89)

77 **MOUNTAIN VIEW** Cabernet Sauvignon Mendocino County 1985 • $6 • (02/15/89)

77 **PESENTI** Cabernet Sauvignon San Luis Obispo County Family Reserve 1985 • $13 • (12/15/89)

76 **BYRON** Cabernet Sauvignon Central Coast 1985 • $14 • (12/15/89)

76 **LOUIS M. MARTINI** Cabernet Sauvignon North Coast 1985 • $9 • (10/31/88)

76 **MEEKER** Cabernet Sauvignon Dry Creek Valley 1985 • $18 • (04/30/89)

76 **MONTEREY PENINSULA** Cabernet Sauvignon Monterey County Doctors' Reserve 1985 • $25 • (11/15/92)

76 **PACHECO RANCH** Cabernet Sauvignon Marin County 1985 • $10 • (11/15/91)

76 **PARSONS CREEK** Cabernet Sauvignon Sonoma County 1985 • $13 • (06/30/89)

76 **STEVENOT** Cabernet Sauvignon Calaveras County 1985 • $7 • (06/30/89)

76 **WILLIAM WHEELER** Cabernet Sauvignon Dry Creek Valley 1985 • $12 • (07/15/89)

75 **CRESTON** Cabernet Sauvignon Central Coast Winemaker's Selection 1985 • $17 • (12/15/89)

75 **FOX MOUNTAIN** Cabernet Sauvignon Russian River Valley Reserve 1985 • $19 • (09/15/89)

75 **HAWK CREST** Cabernet Sauvignon North Coast 1985 • $6 • (07/31/88)

75 **HOP KILN** Cabernet Sauvignon Dry Creek Valley 1985 • $10 • (10/15/88)

75 **MONTEREY VINEYARD** Cabernet Sauvignon Monterey County Limited Release 1985 • $10 • (08/31/88)

75 **ROMBAUER** Cabernet Sauvignon Napa Valley 1985 • $20 • (02/15/89)

75 **STONEGATE** Cabernet Sauvignon Napa Valley 1985 • $17 • (04/15/90)

74 **CHRISTOPHE** Cabernet Sauvignon Napa Valley Reserve 1985 • $13 • (11/15/89)

74 **DEHLINGER** Cabernet Sauvignon Russian River Valley 1985 • $13 • (05/31/89)

74 **ELLISTON** Cabernet Sauvignon Central Coast Sunol Valley Vineyard 1985 • $16 • (11/15/91)

74 **FITCH MOUNTAIN** Cabernet Sauvignon Napa Valley 1985 • $9 • (04/15/89)

74 **J.W. MORRIS** Cabernet Sauvignon Alexander Valley 1985 • $8 • (02/15/89)

74 **MADDALENA** Cabernet Sauvignon Sonoma County 1985 • $6 • (05/31/88)

74 **SAUSAL** Cabernet Sauvignon Alexander Valley 1985 • $12 • (07/31/89)

74 **SMITH-MADRONE** Cabernet Sauvignon Napa Valley 1985 • $19 • (04/15/90)

73 **MONTEREY VINEYARD** Cabernet Sauvignon Monterey-Sonoma-San Luis Obispo Counties Classic 1985 • $5 • (02/15/89)

72 **DEER VALLEY** Cabernet Sauvignon Monterey 1985 • $5 • (12/31/87)

72 **FIRESTONE** Cabernet Sauvignon Santa Ynez Valley 1985 • $9 • (08/31/88)

72 **RIVERSIDE FARM** Cabernet Sauvignon California 1985 • $4 • (05/31/88)

72 **VIANSA** Cabernet Sauvignon Sonoma-Napa Counties 1985 • $13 • (09/15/89)

71 **FOPPIANO** Cabernet Sauvignon Russian River Valley 1985 • $9 • (06/30/89)

71 **LAURA'S** Cabernet Sauvignon Paso Robles 1985 • $12 • (12/15/89)

70 **AMIZETTA** Cabernet Sauvignon Napa Valley 1985 • $16 • (05/31/88)

70 **CHAPPELLET** Cabernet Sauvignon Napa Valley Reserve 1985 • $25 • (05/31/89)

70 **FIELD STONE** Cabernet Sauvignon Alexander Valley Home Ranch Vineyard 1985 • $14 • (04/15/89)

70 **THOMAS FOGARTY** Cabernet Sauvignon Napa Valley 1985 • $15 • (07/15/91)

70 **VENTANA** Cabernet Sauvignon Monterey Magnus Meritage 1985 • $18

70 **WILD HORSE** Cabernet Sauvignon Paso Robles Wild Horse Vineyards 1985 • $11 • (06/30/88)

69 **BARON HERZOG** Cabernet Sauvignon Sonoma County Special Reserve 1985 • $14

68 **CRESTON** Cabernet Sauvignon San Luis Obispo County 1985 • $12 • (12/15/89)

68 **GUENOC** Cabernet Sauvignon Lake County 1985 • $33

67 **ESTRELLA RIVER** Cabernet Sauvignon Paso Robles 1985 • $9 • (11/15/89)

67 **FIRESTONE** Cabernet Sauvignon Santa Ynez Valley Vintage Reserve 1985 • $25 • (12/15/89)

66 **DELICATO** Cabernet Sauvignon California 1985 • $6 • (06/30/88)

64 **RIDGE** Cabernet Sauvignon Santa Cruz Mountains 1985 • $12 • (06/15/89)

63 **HOUTZ** Cabernet Sauvignon Santa Ynez Valley 1985 • $8 • (12/15/89)

62 **MARION** Cabernet Sauvignon California 1985 • $5 • (12/31/87)

61 **MENDOCINO ESTATE** Cabernet Sauvignon Mendocino 1985 • $5 • (02/15/88)

57 **J. FRITZ** Cabernet Sauvignon Alexander Valley 1985 • $10 • (12/31/88)

The historic Beringer Estate in Napa Valley.

California Chardonnay

Here are *Wine Spectator*'s ratings and prices for the four most recent vintages of California Chardonnay. All are of exceptional quality, and the choice of excellent Chardonnay has never been better. The most recently released year, 1994, is perhaps the easiest vintage in which to find a great bottle of Chardonnay, followed closely by 1993, 1992 and 1991.

The wines are organized in descending order of score, to make it easy to identify the best wines of each vintage. If you know the name of a wine already and you want to look up its score and tasting note, turn to the main listings section of this book, and look under United States and then under the winery name. California Chardonnays from previous years, not listed here, can also be found there.

The date of the issue of *Wine Spectator* in which the rating was first published is in parentheses. In general, wines for which no issue date appears were tasted between April 15, 1994 and June 15, 1996.

1994 CALIFORNIA CHARDONNAY | VINTAGE RATING: 95

95 **BERINGER** Chardonnay Napa Valley Private Reserve 1994 • $20 • (04/30/96) • SS

95 **ROCHIOLI** Chardonnay Russian River Valley Reserve 1994 • $28 • (04/30/96)

95 **SAINTSBURY** Chardonnay Carneros Reserve 1994 • $25 • (05/31/96)

94 **BERINGER** Chardonnay Napa Valley Sbragia Limited Release 1994 • $25 • (05/15/96)

94 **MARCASSIN** Chardonnay Alexander Valley Gauer Vineyard Upper Barn 1994 • $39 • (05/15/96) • CS

94 **PATZ & HALL** Chardonnay Mount Veeder Carr Vineyard 1994 • $38 • (02/29/96)

94 **TRUCHARD** Chardonnay Napa Valley Carneros 1994 • $19 • (03/31/96)

94 **VILLA MT. EDEN** Chardonnay Santa Maria Valley Bien Nacido Vineyard Signature Series 1994 • $30 • (05/31/96)

93 **CHALK HILL** Chardonnay Chalk Hill 1994 • $20 • (06/15/96) • SS

93 **FIDDLEHEAD** Chardonnay Central Coast 1994 • $32 • (05/31/96)

93 **GIRARD** Chardonnay Napa Valley Reserve 1994 • $32 • (05/31/96)

93 **MARCASSIN** Chardonnay Carneros Hudson Vineyard 1994 • $39 • (05/15/96)

93 **MARTIN RAY** Chardonnay California Mariage 1994 • $25 • (05/31/96)

93 **PINE RIDGE** Chardonnay Stags Leap District 1994 • $25 • (05/31/96)

93 **ROMBAUER** Chardonnay Carneros 1994 • $21 • (12/31/95) • SS

93 **SHAFER** Chardonnay Napa Valley Carneros Red Shoulder Ranch 1994 • $23 • (06/15/96)

93 **STEELE** Chardonnay Carneros Sangiacomo Vineyard 1994 • $22 • (05/31/96)

92 **ARROWOOD** Chardonnay Sonoma County Cuvée Michel Berthoud Réserve Spéciale 1994 • $27 • (05/31/96)

92 **CHATEAU ST. JEAN** Chardonnay Alexander Valley Belle Terre Vineyards 1994 • $18 • (04/30/96)

92 **CUVAISON** Chardonnay Napa Valley Carneros Reserve 1994 • $30

92 **E. & J. GALLO** Chardonnay Russian River Valley Laguna Ranch Vineyard 1994 • $16 • (04/30/96)

92 **GARY FARRELL** Chardonnay Russian River Valley Allen Vineyard 1994 • $20 • (04/30/96)

92 **GARY FARRELL** Chardonnay Russian River Valley 1994 • $17 • (05/15/96)

92 **LIPARITA** Chardonnay Howell Mountain 1994 • $18 • (04/30/96)

92 **NICHOLS** Chardonnay Arroyo Grande Valley Talley Vineyards 1994 • $23 • (04/30/96)

92 **PAHLMEYER** Chardonnay Napa Valley 1994 • $34 • (05/31/96)

92 **SIGNORELLO** Chardonnay Napa Valley Founder's Reserve 1994 • $30 • (05/15/96)

92 **STEELE** Chardonnay California 1994 • $18 • (05/15/96) • SS

92 **STEELE** Chardonnay Mendocino Du Pratt Vineyard 1994 • $24 • (05/31/96)

92 **STEELE** Chardonnay Santa Barbara County Goodchild Vineyard 1994 • $24 • (05/31/96)

92 **VILLA MT. EDEN** Chardonnay Napa Valley Grand Reserve 1994 • $16 • (04/30/96)

91 **BEAULIEU** Chardonnay Napa Valley Carneros Reserve 1994 • $18 • (04/30/96)

91 **CHALONE** Chardonnay Chalone 1994 • $27 • (06/15/96) • CS

91 **CHATEAU SOUVERAIN** Chardonnay Sonoma County 1994 • $12 • (04/30/96) • SS

91 **CHATEAU SOUVERAIN** Chardonnay Carneros Winemaker's Reserve 1994 • $16 • (06/15/96)

91 **CLOS DU BOIS** Chardonnay Alexander Valley Calcaire Vineyard 1994 • $18 • (04/30/96) • SS

91 **EL MOLINO** Chardonnay Napa Valley 1994 • $35 • (05/31/96)

91 **FERRARI-CARANO** Chardonnay Alexander Valley Tre Terre 1994 • $24 • (05/15/96)

91 **FORMAN** Chardonnay Napa Valley 1994 • $23

91 **GIRARD** Chardonnay Napa Valley 1994 • $18 • (06/15/96) • SS

91 **LANDMARK** Chardonnay Sonoma County Overlook 1994 • $16 • (03/31/96) • SS

91 **MACROSTIE** Chardonnay Carneros 1994 • $17 • (04/30/96)

91 **NEYERS** Chardonnay Carneros 1994 • $18 • (06/30/96)

91 **PATZ & HALL** Chardonnay Napa Valley 1994 • $28 • (02/29/96)

91 **SOLITUDE** Chardonnay Carneros Sangiacomo Vineyard 1994 • $19 • (01/31/96)

91 **STAG'S LEAP WINE CELLARS** Chardonnay Napa Valley Beckstoffer Ranch 1994 • $24 • (05/31/96)

91 **STEELE** Chardonnay Santa Barbara County Bien Nacido Vineyard 1994 • $24 • (05/31/96)

91 **STONESTREET** Chardonnay Sonoma County 1994 • $25 • (05/31/96) • SS

91 **THOMAS FOGARTY** Chardonnay Santa Cruz Mountains Estate Reserve 1994 • $23 • (06/30/96)

90 **ACACIA** Chardonnay Carneros 1994 • $18 • (04/30/96) • SS

90 **BERINGER** Chardonnay Napa Valley 1994 • $11 • (03/31/96) • SS

90 **BERNARDUS** Chardonnay Monterey County 1994 • $15 • (05/15/96) • SS

90 **BYINGTON** Chardonnay Santa Cruz Mountains Special Reserve Vineyards Spring Ridge Vineyard 1994 • $23 • (06/30/96)

90 **BYRON** Chardonnay Santa Barbara County Reserve 1994 • $23 • (05/31/96)

90 **CALERA** Chardonnay Central Coast 1994 • $15 • (12/31/95) • SS

90 **CHALONE** Chardonnay Chalone Reserve 1994 • $45 • (05/31/96)

90 **CHATEAU ST. JEAN** Chardonnay Sonoma County 1994 • $11 • (04/30/96) • SS

90 **DRY CREEK** Chardonnay Dry Creek Valley Reserve 1994 • $17 • (05/15/96)

90 **ESTANCIA** Chardonnay Monterey Reserve 1994 • $20 • (05/31/96)

90 **FERRARI-CARANO** Chardonnay Alexander Valley 1994 • $22 • (05/15/96) • SS

90 **FRANCISCAN** Chardonnay Napa Valley Oakville Estate Barrel Fermented 1994 • $13 • (04/30/96)

90 **GREENWOOD RIDGE** Chardonnay Anderson Valley Du Pratt Vineyard 1994 • $19 • (04/30/96)

90 **GRGICH HILLS** Chardonnay Napa Valley 1994 • $26 • (05/31/96)

90 **HARRISON** Chardonnay Napa Valley 1994 • $26 • (04/30/96)

90 **J. LOHR** Chardonnay Monterey Riverstone 1994 • $12 • (02/29/96)

90 **KENDALL-JACKSON** Chardonnay California Grand Reserve 1994 • $26 • (03/31/96)

90 **KENDALL-JACKSON** Chardonnay Santa Maria Valley Camelot Vineyard 1994 • $18 • (03/31/96) • SS

90 **LEWIS CELLARS** Chardonnay Napa Valley Oakville Ranch Reserve 1994 • $28 • (05/15/96)

90 **MARKHAM** Chardonnay Napa Valley 1994 • $15 • (06/15/96) • SS

90 **MATANZAS CREEK** Chardonnay Sonoma Valley 1994 • $28 • (05/31/96)

90 **MUELLER** Chardonnay Russian River Valley 1994 • $13 • (05/15/96)

90 **NEWTON** Chardonnay Napa Valley 1994 • $19 • (03/31/96)

90 **RIDGE** Chardonnay Santa Cruz Mountains Monte Bello Ridge Vineyards 1994 • $20 • (05/15/96)

90 **S. ANDERSON** Chardonnay Stags Leap District 1994 • $20 • (04/30/96)

90 **SANFORD** Chardonnay Santa Barbara County 1994 • $17 • (05/31/96) • SS

90 **ST. FRANCIS** Chardonnay Sonoma Valley Reserve Estate 1994 • $20 • (05/15/96)

90 **STEELE** Chardonnay Mendocino Dennison Vineyard 1994 • $22 • (05/31/96)

90 **SELBY** Chardonnay Sonoma County 1994 • $18 • (04/30/96)

90 **THOMAS FOGARTY** Chardonnay Santa Cruz Mountains 1994 • $17 • (02/29/96)

90 **VINE CLIFF** Chardonnay Napa Valley 1994 • $23 • (05/31/96)

89 **BENZIGER** Chardonnay Carneros Reserve 1994 • $13 • (03/31/96)

89 **CAMELOT** Chardonnay Central Coast 1994 • $11 • (06/15/96)

89 **CARMENET** Chardonnay Sonoma Valley Carneros Sangiacomo Vineyard 1994 • $16 • (06/15/96)

89 **CLOS DU BOIS** Chardonnay Dry Creek Valley Flintwood Vineyard 1994 • $17 • (04/30/96)

89 **CLOS LACHANCE** Chardonnay Santa Cruz Mountains 1994 • $18 • (05/31/96)

89 **CLOS PEGASE** Chardonnay Napa Valley Carneros Pegase Circle Reserve 1994 • $23 • (05/15/96)

89 **COOPER-GARROD** Chardonnay Santa Cruz Mountains 1994 • $18 • (02/29/96)

89 **DE LOACH** Chardonnay Russian River Valley O.F.S. 1994 • $25 • (05/15/96)

89 **DRY CREEK** Chardonnay Sonoma County Barrel Fermented 1994 • $14 • (03/31/96)

89 **FLORA SPRINGS** Chardonnay Carneros 1994 • $20 • (06/30/96)

89 **GEYSER PEAK** Chardonnay Alexander Valley Reserve 1994 • $20 • (05/15/96)

89 **J. LOHR** Chardonnay Arroyo Seco VS 1994 • $23 • (06/15/96)

89 **KUNDE** Chardonnay Sonoma Valley Wildwood 1994 • $20 • (05/31/96)

89 **KUNDE** Chardonnay Sonoma Valley Kinneybrook 1994 • $20 • (05/31/96)

89 **LANDMARK** Chardonnay Sonoma County Damaris Reserve 1994 • $23 • (03/31/96)

89 **MERIDIAN** Chardonnay Santa Barbara County 1994 • $10 • (02/29/96) • BB

89 **MUELLER** Chardonnay Alexander Valley Gauer Ranch 1994 • $15 • (05/15/96)

89 **MURPHY-GOODE** Chardonnay Alexander Valley Island Block Reserve 1994 • $24 • (01/31/96)

89 **MURPHY-GOODE** Chardonnay Russian River Valley J & K Murphy Vineyard Reserve 1994 • $24 • (05/31/96)

89 **NAVARRO** Chardonnay Anderson Valley Première Reserve 1994 • $15 • (06/15/96)

89 **OAKVILLE RANCH** Chardonnay Napa Valley ORV 1994 • $28 • (05/15/96)

89 **PAUL HOBBS** Chardonnay Sonoma Mountain Richard Dinner Vineyard 1994 • $28 • (06/30/96)

89 **RAYMOND** Chardonnay Napa Valley Reserve 1994 • $14 • (05/31/96)

89 **RAYMOND** Chardonnay Napa Valley Private Reserve 1994 • $18 • (05/31/96)

89 **ROBERT MONDAVI** Chardonnay Napa Valley 1994 • $17 • (05/31/96)

89 **ROCHIOLI** Chardonnay Russian River Valley 1994 • $17 • (06/15/96)

89 **SIGNORELLO** Chardonnay Napa Valley 1994 • $20 • (03/31/96)

89 **STAG'S LEAP WINE CELLARS** Chardonnay Napa Valley 1994 • $22 • (06/15/96)

89 **VICHON** Chardonnay Napa Valley 1994 • $NA • (02/29/96)

89 **WILD HORSE** Chardonnay Central Coast 1994 • $14 • (06/30/96) • SS

88 **ARROWOOD** Chardonnay Sonoma County 1994 • $21 • (05/31/96)

88 **AU BON CLIMAT** Chardonnay Santa Barbara County 1994 • $15 • (01/31/96)

88 **BABCOCK** Chardonnay Santa Ynez Valley Mt. Carmel Vineyard 1994 • $27 • (01/31/96)

88 **BANNISTER** Chardonnay Russian River Valley Allen Vineyard 1994 • $20 • (05/31/96)

88 **BEAULIEU** Chardonnay Napa Valley Carneros 1994 • $13 • (02/29/96)

88 **BELVEDERE** Chardonnay Russian River Valley 1994 • $13 • (02/29/96)

88 **BELVEDERE** Chardonnay Sonoma County 1994 • $9 • (02/29/96) • BB

88 **BUENA VISTA** Chardonnay Carneros Grand Reserve 1994 • $22 • (06/15/96)

88 **BYRON** Chardonnay Santa Barbara County 1994 • $16 • (05/31/96)

88 **CAMBRIA** Chardonnay Santa Barbara County 1994 • $15 • (02/29/96)

88 **CAMBRIA** Chardonnay Santa Maria Valley Reserve 1994 • $30 • (06/15/96)

88 **CHALONE** Chardonnay Chalone Gavilan 1994 • $16 • (06/15/96)

88 **CINNABAR** Chardonnay Santa Cruz Mountains Saratoga Vineyard 1994 • $23 • (06/15/96)

88 **CLAIBORNE & CHURCHILL** Chardonnay Edna Valley MacGregor Vineyard 1994 • $18 • (05/31/96)

88 **CLOS DU BOIS** Chardonnay Alexander Valley Calcaire Vineyard 1994 • $18

88 **CLOS PEGASE** Chardonnay Napa Valley Carneros Mitsuko's Vineyard 1994 • $17 • (05/15/96)

88 **DE LORIMIER** Chardonnay Alexander Valley Clonal Select 1994 • $20 • (06/30/96)

88 **DEHLINGER** Chardonnay Russian River Valley 1994 • $16 • (05/31/96)

88 **DRY CREEK** Chardonnay Dry Creek Valley Wolcott Vineyard Barrel Fermented Reserve 1994 • $22 • (02/29/96)

88 **EDMEADES** Chardonnay Anderson Valley 1994 • $18 • (05/15/96)

88 **EXPRESSIONS** Chardonnay Sonoma County 1994 • $10 • (04/30/96) • BB

88 **GAINEY** Chardonnay Santa Ynez Valley Limited Selection 1994 • $25 • (06/30/96)

88 **GUENOC** Chardonnay Guenoc Valley Genevieve Magoon Vineyard Estate Reserve 1994 • $23 • (04/30/96)

88 **GUENOC** Chardonnay Guenoc Valley Genevieve Magoon Unfiltered Reserve 1994 • $30 • (05/15/96)

88 **LA CREMA** Chardonnay Sonoma County 1994 • $15 • (03/31/96)

88 **LAKESPRING** Chardonnay Napa Valley 1994 • $12 • (02/29/96)

88 **LONGORIA** Chardonnay Santa Ynez Valley Huber Vineyard 1994 • $21 • (06/30/96)

88 **LOS ENCANTOS** Chardonnay Santa Maria Covenant Reserve 1994 • $14 • (02/29/96)

88 **MERRYVALE** Chardonnay Napa Valley Starmont 1994 • $16 • (05/31/96)

88 **MIRASSOU** Chardonnay Monterey County Fifth Generation Family Selection 1994 • $11 • (06/15/96)

88 **NORMAN VINEYARD** Chardonnay San Luis Obispo County 1994 • $12 • (05/15/96)

88 **OAKVILLE RANCH** Chardonnay Napa Valley Vista Vineyard 1994 • $20 • (05/15/96)

88 **PINE RIDGE** Chardonnay Napa Valley Knollside Cuvée 1994 • $16 • (05/31/96)

88 **QUPE** Chardonnay Santa Barbara County Sierra Madre Reserve 1994 • $25 • (05/31/96)

88 **REMICK RIDGE VINEYARDS** Chardonnay Sonoma Valley 1994 • $16 • (06/15/96)

88 **SCHUG** Chardonnay Carneros Heritage Reserve 1994 • $25 • (06/30/96)

88 **SEAVEY** Chardonnay Napa Valley 1994 • $16 • (05/15/96)

88 **SONOMA-LOEB** Chardonnay Sonoma County Ambassador John L. Loeb Jr.'s 1994 • $18 • (03/31/96)

88 **STEELE** Chardonnay Mendocino Lolonis Vineyard 1994 • $26 • (05/31/96)

88 **STEELE** Chardonnay Sonoma Valley Durell Vineyard 1994 • $24 • (05/31/96)

88 **SONOMA-LOEB** Chardonnay Sonoma County Ambassador John L. Loeb Jr.'s Private Reserve 1994 • $25 • (02/29/96)

88 **WENTE BROS.** Chardonnay Livermore Valley Herman Wente Reserve 1994 • $22 • (06/30/96)

88 **WHITCRAFT** Chardonnay Santa Ynez Valley Sanford & Benedict Vineyard 1994 • $35 • (05/15/96)

88 **WHITCRAFT** Chardonnay Santa Maria Valley Bien Nacido Vineyard 1994 • $17 • (06/15/96)

87 **ABADIA DEL ROBLE** Chardonnay California Barrel Fermented 1994 • $10 • BB

87 **BYINGTON** Chardonnay Santa Cruz Mountains Special Reserve Vineyards 1994 • $18 • (06/30/96)

87 **CAKEBREAD** Chardonnay Napa Valley 1994 • $23 • (01/31/96)

87 **CALE** Chardonnay Carneros Sangiacomo Vineyard 1994 • $20 • (05/15/96)

87 **CAMELOT** Chardonnay Santa Barbara County 1994 • $18 • (06/15/96)

87 **CARPE DIEM** Chardonnay San Luis Obispo County 1994 • $19 • (02/29/96)

87 **CHAPPELLET** Chardonnay Napa Valley Signature 1994 • $24 • (06/15/96)

87 **DREYER SONOMA** Chardonnay Sonoma County 1994 • $9 • (04/30/96)

87 **E. & J. GALLO** Chardonnay Dry Creek Valley Stefani Vineyard 1994 • $16 • (05/15/96)

87 **EDMEADES** Chardonnay Anderson Valley Anderson Crest Vineyard 1994 • $20 • (06/15/96)

87 **FESS PARKER** Chardonnay Santa Barbara County 1994 • $16 • (06/30/96)

87 **FISHER** Chardonnay Sonoma County Whitney's Vineyard 1994 • $26 • (06/15/96)

87 **GUENOC** Chardonnay Guenoc Valley 1994 • $15 • (04/30/96)

87 **HESS SELECT** Chardonnay California 1994 • $9 • (06/30/96) • BB

87 **IRON HORSE** Chardonnay Sonoma County Green Valley 1994 • $18 • (05/15/96)

87 **JOULLIAN** Chardonnay Monterey 1994 • $12 • (06/15/96)

87 **KENWOOD** Chardonnay Sonoma County 25th Anniversary Vintage 1994 • $14 • (12/15/95)

87 **KUNDE** Chardonnay Sonoma Valley Reserve 1994 • $22 • (06/15/96)

87 **LOCKWOOD** Chardonnay Monterey 1994 • $15 • (04/30/96)

87 **LOGAN** Chardonnay Monterey 1994 • $14 • (05/15/96)

87 **LOUIS M. MARTINI** Chardonnay Napa Valley 1994 • $11 • (06/15/96)

87 **LYETH** Chardonnay Sonoma County 1994 • $11 • (02/29/96)

87 **MAZZOCCO** Chardonnay Sonoma County River Lane 1994 • $14 • (06/30/96)

87 **OLIVET LANE** Chardonnay Russian River Valley Pellegrini Family Vineyards 1994 • $12 • (02/29/96)

87 **OPTIMA** Chardonnay Carneros 1994 • $28 • (02/29/96)

87 **PARDUCCI** Chardonnay Mendocino County 1994 • $8 • (09/30/95) • BB

87 **PETER MICHAEL** Chardonnay Napa County Clos du Ciel 1994 • $32 • (06/15/96)

87 **PRIDE** Chardonnay Napa Valley 1994 • $18 • (05/15/96)

87 **R.H. PHILLIPS** Chardonnay Dunnigan Hills Barrel Cuvée 1994 • $8 • (05/31/96) • BB

87 **RABBIT RIDGE** Chardonnay Russian River Valley Rabbit Ridge Ranch Estate Reserve 1994 • $16 • (05/15/96)

87 **RAYMOND** Chardonnay Monterey Estates 1994 • $12 • (03/31/96)

87 **RODNEY STRONG** Chardonnay Sonoma County 1994 • $11 • (06/15/96)

87 **SANTA BARBARA WINERY** Chardonnay Santa Ynez Valley Reserve 1994 • $22 • (06/30/96)

87 **SILVER HORSE** Chardonnay Paso Robles 1994 • $11 • (02/29/96)

87 **STONE CREEK** Chardonnay Napa Valley Chairman's Reserve 1994 • $15 • (11/15/95)

87 **SWANSON** Chardonnay Napa Valley Carneros 1994 • $22 • (05/15/96)

87 **TALLEY** Chardonnay Edna Valley Oliver's Vineyard 1994 • $15 • (06/15/96)

87 **ZACA MESA** Chardonnay Santa Barbara County Zaca Vineyards 1994 • $13 • (05/15/96)

86 **ARCIERO** Chardonnay Paso Robles 1994 • $9 • (06/15/96) • BB

86 **BANDIERA** Chardonnay Napa Valley 1994 • $8 • (09/30/95) • BB

86 **BELVEDERE** Chardonnay Alexander Valley 1994 • $12 • (04/30/96)

86 **CAMBRIA** Chardonnay Santa Maria Valley Katherine's Vineyard 1994 • $18 • (02/29/96)

86 **COTES DE SONOMA** Chardonnay Sonoma County 1994 • $8 • (10/15/95) • BB

86 **FAR NIENTE** Chardonnay Napa Valley 1994 • $32 • (02/29/96)

86 **FERMENTATIONS & MORE** Chardonnay Edna Valley MacGregor Vineyard 1994 • $13 • (04/30/96)

86 **FETZER** Chardonnay North Coast Barrel Select 1994 • $10 • (06/15/96)

86 **FISHER** Chardonnay Sonoma County Coach Insignia 1994 • $18 • (06/15/96)

86 **JOLIESSE VINEYARDS** Chardonnay California Reserve 1994 • $7 • (05/31/96) • BB

86 **KENDALL-JACKSON** Chardonnay California Vintner's Reserve 1994 • $14 • (12/15/95)

86 **KENT RASMUSSEN** Chardonnay Napa Valley 1994 • $21 • (02/29/96)

86 **KUNDE** Chardonnay Sonoma Valley 1994 • $14 • (01/31/96)

86 **MERIDIAN** Chardonnay Santa Barbara County Limited Release 1994 • $17 • (06/30/96)

86 **MICHAEL SULLBERG** Chardonnay Knights Valley Lot 54 Barrel Fermented 1994 • $8 • (02/29/96)

86 **MILL CREEK** Chardonnay Dry Creek Valley 1994 • $12 • (06/30/96)

86 **MURPHY-GOODE** Chardonnay Alexander Valley Barrel Fermented 1994 • $14 • (12/31/95)

86 **NAPA RIDGE** Chardonnay Napa Valley Coastal Reserve 1994 • $12 • (06/30/96)

86 **P & M STAIGER** Chardonnay Santa Cruz Mountains 1994 • $12 • (06/15/96)

86 **PEJU** Chardonnay Napa Valley 1994 • $15 • (06/30/96)

86 **S. ANDERSON** Chardonnay Napa Valley Carneros 1994 • $18 • (05/15/96)

86 **SEBASTIANI** Chardonnay Russian River Valley Dutton Ranch 1994 • $18 • (06/30/96)

86 **SILVER RIDGE** Chardonnay California Barrel Fermented 1994 • $10 • (06/30/96)

86 **TAFT STREET** Chardonnay Sonoma County 1994 • $10 • (06/15/96) • BB

86 **VON STRASSER** Chardonnay Napa Valley 1994 • $30 • (06/15/96)

85 **BEL ARBORS** Chardonnay California Vintner's Selection 1994 • $5 • (05/31/96) • BB

85 **BUEHLER** Chardonnay Russian River Valley 1994 • $13 • (02/29/96)

85 **CAMELOT** Chardonnay Monterey Reserve 1994 • $22 • (06/15/96)

85 **CANEPA** Chardonnay Alexander Valley Gauer Vineyard Adobe 111 1994 • $24 • (04/30/96)

85 **CHATEAU POTELLE** Chardonnay Napa Valley-Central Coast 1994 • $9 • (10/15/95)

85 **COSENTINO** Chardonnay Napa Valley 1994 • $14 • (06/30/96)

85 **COSENTINO** Chardonnay Napa Valley The Sculptor Reserve 1994 • $25 • (06/30/96)

85 **CUVAISON** Chardonnay Napa Valley Carneros Twenty-fifth Anniversary Harvest 1994 • $16 • (06/30/96)

85 **DE LOACH** Chardonnay Russian River Valley 1994 • $15 • (06/30/96)

85 **FOREST GLEN** Chardonnay California Barrel Fermented 1994 • $10 • (05/15/96)

85 **HAYWOOD** Chardonnay California Vintner's Select 1994 • $8 • (11/15/95) • BB

85 **LOUIS M. MARTINI** Chardonnay Napa Valley 1994 • $9 • (05/15/96)

85 **MERIDIAN** Chardonnay Edna Valley Reserve 1994 • $14 • (06/30/96)

85 **MISSION VIEW** Chardonnay Paso Robles 1994 • $10 • (10/31/95)

85 **MONTICELLO** Chardonnay Napa Valley Corley Wild Yeast Estate Reserve 1994 • $33 • (06/15/96)

85 **NAPA RIDGE** Chardonnay Napa Valley Coastal Frisinger Vineyard 1994 • $11 • (06/30/96)

85 **NAPA RIDGE** Chardonnay Central Coast Coastal Vines 1994 • $7 • (10/15/95)

85 **NAVARRO** Chardonnay Mendocino 1994 • $8 • (02/29/96)

85 **RODNEY STRONG** Chardonnay Chalk Hill Chalk Hill Vineyard 1994 • $14 • (04/30/96)

85 **SCHUG** Chardonnay Carneros 1994 • $18 • (06/30/96)

85 **SCHUG** Chardonnay Sonoma Valley 1994 • $14 • (06/30/96)

85 **SILVERADO HILL CELLARS** Chardonnay Napa Valley 1994 • $10 • (06/15/96)

85 **YORK MOUNTAIN** Chardonnay San Luis Obispo County 1994 • $12 • (06/30/96)

84 **BENZIGER** Chardonnay Carneros 1994 • $13 • (05/15/96)

84 **CHIMNEY ROCK** Chardonnay Carneros 1994 • $16 • (06/30/96)

84 **FIRESTONE** Chardonnay Santa Ynez Valley Barrel Fermented 1994 • $13 • (05/15/96)

84 **FORESTVILLE** Chardonnay California 1994 • $6 • (06/30/96) • BB

84 **GREEN & RED** Chardonnay Napa Valley Catacula Vineyard 1994 • $18 • (06/30/96)

84 **GROTH** Chardonnay Napa Valley 1994 • $15 • (06/30/96)

84 **HANNA** Chardonnay Sonoma County 1994 • $14 • (04/30/96)

84 **JAFFURS** Chardonnay Santa Barbara County Bien Nacido Vineyard 1994 • $15 • (03/31/96)

84 **LAWRENCE J. BARGETTO** Chardonnay Central Coast Cypress 1994 • $9 • (05/15/96)

84 **M.G. VALLEJO** Chardonnay California 1994 • $6 • (11/15/95)

84 **MARTIN BROTHERS** Chardonnay Paso Robles in Botti 1994 • $12 • (09/30/95)

84 **MCDOWELL** Chardonnay Mendocino 1994 • $10 • (05/15/96)

84 **MOUNT EDEN** Chardonnay Edna Valley MacGregor Vineyard 1994 • $16 • (06/15/96)

84 **RUTHERFORD ESTATE** Chardonnay California Barrel Select 1994 • $7 • (05/15/96)

84 **SANTA BARBARA WINERY** Chardonnay Santa Barbara County 1994 • $9 • (06/15/96)

84 **SEGHESIO** Chardonnay Russian River Valley Family Home 1994 • $10 • (05/15/96)

84 **SHOOTING STAR** Chardonnay Sonoma County 1994 • $10 • (05/15/96)

84 **ST. CLEMENT** Chardonnay Napa Valley Carneros Abbotts Vineyard 1994 • $21 • (06/30/96)

84 **ST. FRANCIS** Chardonnay Sonoma County 1994 • $10 • (05/15/96)

84 **STEVENOT** Chardonnay Calaveras County Reserve 1994 • $10 • (05/15/96)

84 **TESSERA** Chardonnay California 1994 • $9 • (06/15/96)

84 **TREFETHEN** Chardonnay Napa Valley Eshcol 1994 • $10 • (04/30/96)

84 **VILLA MT. EDEN** Chardonnay California Cellar Select 1994 • $9 • (06/30/96)

84 **WELLINGTON** Chardonnay Sonoma Valley 1994 • $11 • (06/30/96)

84 **WHITE OAK** Chardonnay Russian River Valley Poplar Ranch Private Reserve 1994 • $18 • (06/30/96)

83 **FETZER** Chardonnay Mendocino 1994 • $12 • (03/31/96)

83 **FOREST HILL** Chardonnay Napa Valley Private Reserve 1994 • $32 • (06/30/96)

83 **GRAND CRU** Chardonnay California Premium Selection 1994 • $8 • (06/30/96)

83 **KEENAN** Chardonnay Napa Valley Hillside 1994 • $15 • (06/15/96)

83 **MONTPELLIER** Chardonnay California 1994 • $8 • (06/30/96)

83 **MORRO BAY** Chardonnay Central Coast Special Edition 1994 • $10 • (12/31/95)

83 **NOMINEE** Chardonnay Paso Robles 1994 • $7 • (12/15/95)

83 **PARAISO SPRINGS** Chardonnay Santa Lucia Highlands 1994 • $12 • (06/30/96)

83 **PEJU** Chardonnay Napa Valley HB Vineyard 1994 • $22 • (06/30/96)

83 **SILVERADO HILL CELLARS** Chardonnay Napa Valley Winemaker's Traditional Methode 1994 • $10 • (06/15/96)

83 **STEPHEN ZELLERBACH** Chardonnay California 1994 • $8 • (10/31/95)

83 **STONE CREEK** Chardonnay California Special Selection 1994 • $7 • BB

83 **TREFETHEN** Chardonnay Napa Valley 1994 • $19 • (06/30/96)

83 **TALUS** Chardonnay California 1994 • $8 • (03/31/96)

83 **VICHON** Chardonnay California Coastal Selection 1994 • $10 • (06/15/96)

82 **ALPEN CELLARS** Chardonnay Trinity County 1994 • $7 • (06/15/96)

82 **BAILEYANA** Chardonnay Edna Valley 1994 • $15 • (06/15/96)

82 **BLACKSTONE** Chardonnay Monterey County Grand Reserve 1994 • $10 • (06/15/96)

82 **BOUCHAINE** Chardonnay California Q.C. Fly 1994 • $9 • (06/15/96)

82 **CHRISTOPHE** Chardonnay Napa County 1994 • $9 • (06/15/96)

82 **CLOS DU BOIS** Chardonnay Alexander Valley Barrel Fermented 1994 • $13 • (04/30/96)

82 **GODWIN** Chardonnay Alexander Valley 1994 • $20 • (04/30/96)

82 **HAWK CREST** Chardonnay California 1994 • $9 • (05/15/96)

82 **IVAN TAMAS** Chardonnay Central Coast 1994 • $9 • (06/15/96)

82 **JEPSON** Chardonnay Mendocino County Estate Select 1994 • $14 • (06/15/96)

82 **MONTHAVEN** Chardonnay Napa Valley 1994 • $8 • (03/31/96)

82 **RIDGE** Chardonnay Santa Cruz Mountains 1994 • $16 • (06/15/96)

82 **ROBERT ALISON** Chardonnay California 1994 • $6 • (12/31/95)

82 **ROBERT MONDAVI** Chardonnay Central Coast Coastal 1994 • $10 • (05/15/96)

82 **SEBASTIANI** Chardonnay Sonoma County 1994 • $11 • (06/15/96)

82 **SUMMERFIELD** Chardonnay California Vintner's Reserve 1994 • $8 • (06/15/96)

81 **BOGLE** Chardonnay California Barrel Fermented Cuvee 1994 • $6 • (03/31/96)

81 **CANYON ROAD** Chardonnay California 1994 • $7 • (05/15/96)

81 **CHATEAU DE BAUN** Chardonnay Russian River Valley 1994 • $10 • (05/15/96)

81 **HACIENDA** Chardonnay California Clair de Lune 1994 • $7 • (05/15/96)

81 **HAHN** Chardonnay Monterey 1994 • $10 • (10/31/95)

81 **LA CASA SENA** Chardonnay Santa Clara Valley 1994 • $12 • (04/30/96)

81 **SUTTER RIDGE** Chardonnay Amador County 1994 • $8 • (06/15/96)

81 **WENTE BROS.** Chardonnay Central Coast 1994 • $9 • (06/15/96)

81 **WILDHURST** Chardonnay California 1994 • $11 • (06/15/96)

80 **BEAULIEU** Chardonnay Napa Valley Beautour 1994 • $9 • (06/15/96)

80 **CHAPPELLET** Chardonnay Napa Valley 1994 • $15 • (06/15/96)

80 **CK MONDAVI** Chardonnay California 1994 • $6 • (05/15/96)

80 **CLOS DU BOIS** Chardonnay Alexander Valley Barrel Fermented 1994 • $13 • (04/30/96)

80 **JACKSON VALLEY** Chardonnay Amador County 1994 •$7 •(06/15/96)

80 **MONT ST. JOHN** Chardonnay Carneros 1994 •$13 •(06/15/96)

80 **ROSEWOOD** Chardonnay Monterey 1994 •$10 •(06/15/96)

80 **STEPHEN ZELLERBACH** Chardonnay Sonoma County 1994 •$12 •(05/15/96)

78 **BEAUCANON** Chardonnay Napa Valley 1994 •$12 •(06/15/96)

78 **BORDONI VINEYARDS** Chardonnay Solano County 1994 •$16 •(03/31/96)

76 **RAYMOND** Chardonnay California Amberhill 1994 •$10 •(06/15/96)

1993 California Chardonnay
Vintage Rating: 88

94 **KISTLER** Chardonnay Sonoma Valley Kistler Vineyard 1993 •$40 •(06/30/96) •CS

93 **AU BON CLIMAT** Chardonnay Santa Ynez Valley Sanford & Benedict Reserve 1993 •$34 •(01/31/96)

93 **BYRON** Chardonnay Santa Maria Valley Estate 1993 •$28 •(04/30/96)

93 **FERRARI-CARANO** Chardonnay Alexander Valley Tre Terre 1993 •$22 •(02/29/96)

93 **PETER MICHAEL** Chardonnay Sonoma County Mon Plaisir 1993 •$35 •(01/31/96)

93 **PETER MICHAEL** Chardonnay Sonoma County Cuvée Indigène 1993 •$40 •(01/31/96)

93 **VILLA MT. EDEN** Chardonnay Santa Barbara County Signature Series 1993 •$30 •(07/31/95)

92 **BERINGER** Chardonnay Napa Valley Private Reserve 1993 •$20 •(03/31/95) •SS

92 **CHATEAU DE BAUN** Chardonnay Russian River Valley Creekside Vineyard Reserve 1993 •$18 •(02/29/96)

92 **GARY FARRELL** Chardonnay Russian River Valley Allen Vineyard 1993 •$18 •(04/15/95)

92 **KISTLER** Chardonnay Russian River Valley Vine Hill Vineyard 1993 •$35 •(06/30/96)

92 **MACROSTIE** Chardonnay Carneros Reserve 1993 •$23 •(01/31/96)

92 **MARCASSIN** Chardonnay Alexander Valley Gauer Vineyard Upper Barn 1993 •$36 •(06/30/95)

92 **ROMBAUER** Chardonnay Carneros 1993 •$18 •(03/31/95) •SS

92 **SIMI** Chardonnay Sonoma County Reserve 1993 •$28 •(06/15/96)

92 **STONESTREET** Chardonnay Sonoma County 1993 •$21 •(04/30/95) •SS

91 **ADLER FELS** Chardonnay Sonoma County 1993 •$12 •(03/31/96)

91 **ARROWOOD** Chardonnay Sonoma County Cuvée Michel Berthoud Réserve Spéciale 1993 •$24 •(06/15/95)

91 **BYRON** Chardonnay Santa Barbara County Reserve 1993 •$23 •(07/31/95)

91 **CAMBRIA** Chardonnay Santa Maria Valley Reserve 1993 •$25 •(05/31/95) •SS

91 **CARMENET** Chardonnay Sonoma Valley Carneros Sangiacomo Vineyard 1993 •$16 •(06/30/96) •SS

91 **CHALK HILL** Chardonnay Chalk Hill 1993 •$19 •(05/15/95) •SS

91 **FERRARI-CARANO** Chardonnay Alexander Valley 1993 •$20 •(04/30/95) •SS

91 **FERRARI-CARANO** Chardonnay Napa-Sonoma Counties Reserve 1993 •$30 •(05/15/96)

91 **GLORIA FERRER** Chardonnay Carneros 1993 •$15 •(03/31/95) •SS

91 **GAINEY** Chardonnay Santa Ynez Valley Limited Selection 1993 •$25 •(07/31/95)

91 **KISTLER** Chardonnay Sonoma Valley Durell Vineyard 1993 •$34 •(06/15/95)

91 **KISTLER** Chardonnay Sonoma Mountain McCrea Vineyard 1993 •$35 •(06/30/96)

91 **LITTORAI** Chardonnay Russian River Valley Mays Canyon 1993 •$25 •(12/31/95)

91 **MARCASSIN** Chardonnay Sonoma Coast Lorenzo Vineyard 1993 •$36 •(06/30/95)

91 **MARKHAM** Chardonnay Napa Valley Barrel Fermented 1993 •$17 •(06/15/95) •SS

91 **MATANZAS CREEK** Chardonnay Sonoma Valley 1993 •$23 •(09/30/95) •SS

91 **PATZ & HALL** Chardonnay Napa Valley 1993 •$25 •(06/15/95)

91 **ROBERT MONDAVI** Chardonnay Napa Valley Reserve 1993 •$29 •(07/31/95)

91 **STEELE** Chardonnay Mendocino DuPratt Vineyard 1993 •$24 •(07/31/95)

91 **TALBOTT** Chardonnay Monterey Sleepy Hollow Vineyard 1993 •$26 •(12/31/95) •CS

91 **VILLA MT. EDEN** Chardonnay Carneros Grand Reserve 1993 •$14 •(04/30/95)

91 **WILLIAMS SELYEM** Chardonnay Russian River Valley Allen Vineyard 1993 •$35 •(06/30/95)

90 **ACACIA** Chardonnay Carneros Reserve 1993 •$25 •(04/30/96)

90 **AU BON CLIMAT** Chardonnay Arroyo Grande Valley Talley Vineyard Talley Reserve 1993 •$25 •(07/31/95)

90 **BYRON** Chardonnay Santa Barbara County 1993 •$15 •(07/31/95) •SS

90 **CAMELOT** Chardonnay Santa Barbara County 1993 •$12 •(01/31/95)

90 **DE LOACH** Chardonnay Russian River Valley O.F.S. 1993 •$25 •(09/30/95)

90 **FOXEN** Chardonnay Santa Maria Valley 1993 •$20 •(04/15/95)

90 **FRANCISCAN** Chardonnay Napa Valley Oakville Estate Barrel Fermented 1993 •$12 •(04/15/95) •SS

90 **GEYSER PEAK** Chardonnay Alexander Valley Reserve 1993 •$20 •(04/15/95)

90 **GUENOC** Chardonnay Guenoc Valley Genevieve Magoon Vineyard Reserve 1993 •$25 •(05/31/95)

90 **IRON HORSE** Chardonnay Sonoma County Cuvée Joy 1993 •$19 •(05/15/95)

90 **KENDALL-JACKSON** Chardonnay California Grand Reserve 1993 •$24 •(06/30/95)

90 **KISTLER** Chardonnay Sonoma County Cuvée Cathleen 1993 •$50 •(06/30/96)

90 **KUNDE** Chardonnay Sonoma Valley Kinneybrook Unfiltered 1993 •$17 •(01/31/96)

90 **LANDMARK** Chardonnay Alexander Valley Damaris Reserve 1993 •$19 •(12/31/94)

90 **LEWIS CELLARS** Chardonnay Napa Valley Oakville Ranch Reserve 1993 •$26 •(07/31/95)

90 **LIPARITA** Chardonnay Howell Mountain 1993 •$16 •(10/31/95)

90 **LONG** Chardonnay Napa Valley 1993 •$30 •(01/31/96)

90 **LOS OLIVOS VINTNERS** Chardonnay Santa Barbara County 1993 •$18 •(09/30/95)

90 **MARCASSIN** Chardonnay Carneros Hudson Vineyard 1993 •$36 •(06/30/95)

90 **MOUNT EDEN** Chardonnay Edna Valley MacGregor Vineyard 1993 •$15 •(03/31/95) •SS

90 **MURPHY-GOODE** Chardonnay Russian River Valley J & K Murphy Vineyard Reserve 1993• $24• (07/31/95)

90 **OAKVILLE RANCH** Chardonnay Napa Valley Vista Vineyards 1993• $18

90 **QUPE** Chardonnay Santa Barbara County Sierra Madre Vineyards 1993• $11• (04/30/95)• SS

90 **ROCHIOLI** Chardonnay Russian River Valley Reserve 1993 • $28• (06/15/95)

90 **SANFORD** Chardonnay Santa Barbara County Barrel Select 1993• $30

90 **SANFORD** Chardonnay Santa Barbara County 1993• $18 • (06/30/95)• SS

90 **SANTA BARBARA WINERY** Chardonnay Santa Ynez Valley Lafond Vineyard 1993• $30• (05/15/96)

90 **SOLITUDE** Chardonnay Carneros Sangiacomo Vineyard 1993• $18• (05/31/95)

90 **ST. FRANCIS** Chardonnay Sonoma Valley Reserve 1993 • $19• (04/15/95)

90 **SIGNORELLO** Chardonnay Napa Valley Founder's Reserve 1993• $30• (07/31/95)

90 **STEELE** Chardonnay Mendocino Lolonis Vineyard 1993 • $20• (07/31/95)

90 **TALBOTT** Chardonnay Monterey Diamond T Estate 1993 • $34• (05/31/96)

89 **AU BON CLIMAT** Chardonnay Santa Maria Valley Gold Coast Vineyard 1993• $20• (07/31/95)

89 **BANNISTER** Chardonnay Russian River Valley Allen Vineyard 1993• $18• (06/15/95)

89 **CHATEAU SOUVERAIN** Chardonnay Russian River Valley Rochioli Vineyard Reserve 1993• $16• (04/30/95)

89 **CLOS DU BOIS** Chardonnay Alexander Valley Calcaire Vineyard 1993• $18• (05/15/95)

89 **CLOS LACHANCE** Chardonnay Santa Cruz Mountains 1993 • $18• (07/31/95)

89 **FRANCISCAN** Chardonnay Napa Valley Oakville Estate Cuvée Sauvage 1993• $30• (05/31/95)

89 **GUNDLACH BUNDSCHU** Chardonnay Sonoma Valley Sangiacomo Ranch Special Selection 1993• $15 • (11/15/95)

89 **GARY FARRELL** Chardonnay Russian River Valley Westside Farms 1993• $18• (07/31/95)

89 **HOP KILN** Chardonnay Russian River Valley M. Griffin Vineyards 1993• $15• (02/28/95)

89 **JOSEPH PHELPS** Chardonnay Los Carneros 1993• $17 • (08/31/95)

89 **KISTLER** Chardonnay Sonoma Coast 1993• $26 • (06/15/95)

89 **KISTLER** Chardonnay Russian River Valley Dutton Ranch 1993• $35• (06/30/96)

89 **KUNDE** Chardonnay Sonoma Valley Reserve 1993• $20

89 **KUNDE** Chardonnay Sonoma Valley Wildwood Unfiltered 1993• $17• (01/31/96)

89 **MARK WEST** Chardonnay Russian River Valley 1993• $13 • (05/31/96)• SS

89 **MARTIN RAY** Chardonnay California Mariage 1993• $24 • (08/31/95)

89 **MERRYVALE** Chardonnay Napa Valley Silhouette 1993 • $36• (05/31/96)

89 **MILLBROOK** Chardonnay Central Coast Mistral Vineyard 1993• $8• (02/28/95)

89 **OPTIMA** Chardonnay Carneros Unfiltered 1993• $25 • (10/15/95)

89 **PAHLMEYER** Chardonnay Napa Valley 1993• $30 • (04/30/95)

89 **PINE RIDGE** Chardonnay Stags Leap District 1993• $25 • (06/30/95)

89 **SAINTSBURY** Chardonnay Carneros Reserve 1993• $25 • (05/31/95)

89 **SEBASTIANI** Chardonnay Russian River Valley Dutton Ranch 1993• $18• (05/31/95)

89 **STAG'S LEAP WINE CELLARS** Chardonnay Napa Valley Reserve 1993• $28• (05/31/95)

89 **SANTA BARBARA WINERY** Chardonnay Santa Ynez Valley Reserve 1993• $20• (07/31/95)

89 **SARAH'S VINEYARD** Chardonnay Santa Clara County 1993 • $42• (07/31/95)

89 **SONOMA-LOEB** Chardonnay Sonoma County Ambassador John L. Loeb Jr.'s Private Reserve 1993• $26 • (07/31/95)

89 **V. SATTUI** Chardonnay Napa Valley Carsi Vineyard Barrel Fermented 1993• $18• (02/28/95)

89 **VINE CLIFF** Chardonnay Napa Valley Proprietress Reserve 1993• $35• (05/31/95)

89 **VOSS** Chardonnay Napa Valley 1993• $NA• (02/29/96)

89 **WHITCRAFT** Chardonnay Santa Maria Valley Bien Nacido Vineyard 1993• $22• (05/31/95)

88 **ABADIA DEL ROBLE** Chardonnay Napa Valley Clos Fontaine du Mont Reserve 1993• $20

88 **BEAULIEU** Chardonnay Napa Valley Carneros Reserve 1993• $18• (12/31/95)

88 **BAILEYANA** Chardonnay Edna Valley Paragon Vineyard 1993• $15• (07/31/95)

88 **CALE** Chardonnay Carneros Sangiacomo Vineyard 1993 • $18• (06/15/95)

88 **CALERA** Chardonnay Central Coast 1993• $15 • (02/28/95)

88 **CANEPA** Chardonnay Alexander Valley Canepa Vineyard 1993• $20• (12/15/95)

88 **CAMELOT** Chardonnay Central Coast 1993• $12 • (07/31/95)

88 **CUVAISON** Chardonnay Carneros Napa Valley Reserve 1993• $28• (07/31/95)

88 **DEHLINGER** Chardonnay Russian River Valley 1993• $15 • (05/31/95)

88 **DOMAIN HILL & MAYES** Chardonnay Napa Valley Clos Fontaine du Mont Reserve 1993• $20• (05/31/96)

88 **E. & J. GALLO** Chardonnay Northern Sonoma Estate Bottled 1993• $30• (07/31/95)

88 **EDNA VALLEY** Chardonnay Edna Valley 1993• $15 • (06/30/95)

88 **EL MOLINO** Chardonnay Napa Valley 1993• $30 • (07/31/95)

88 **FESS PARKER** Chardonnay Santa Barbara County American Tradition Reserve 1993• $18• (06/15/95)

88 **FETZER** Chardonnay Mendocino Reserve 1993• $24 • (07/31/95)

88 **GIRARD** Chardonnay Napa Valley Old Vines 1993• $19 • (12/15/95)

88 **GAN EDEN** Chardonnay Sonoma County 1993• $12 • (07/31/95)

88 **KEENAN** Chardonnay Napa Valley 1993• $15• (10/15/95)

88 **KENDALL-JACKSON** Chardonnay Santa Maria Valley Camelot Vineyard 1993• $16• (07/31/95)

88 **LANDMARK** Chardonnay Sonoma County Overlook 1993 • $14• (02/28/95)

88 **LAURIER** Chardonnay Sonoma County 1993• $15 • (03/31/96)

88 **MARIMAR TORRES** Chardonnay Sonoma County Green Valley Don Miguel Vineyard 1993• $20• (05/15/96)

88 **MAYACAMAS** Chardonnay Napa Valley 1993• $18 • (05/15/96)

88 **MORGAN** Chardonnay Monterey Reserve 1993• $23 • (06/15/96)

88 **MUELLER** Chardonnay Sonoma County Gauer Ranch 1993 • $15• (03/31/96)

88 **MERRYVALE** Chardonnay Napa Valley Reserve 1993 • $25 • (07/31/95)

88 **NAPA RIDGE** Chardonnay Napa Valley Frisinger Vineyard 1993 • $11 • (04/15/95)

88 **NAVARRO** Chardonnay Anderson Valley Première Reserve 1993 • $NA • (02/29/96)

88 **PEJU** Chardonnay Napa Valley Barrel Fermented HB Vineyard 1993 • $22 • (12/31/94)

88 **QUPÉ** Chardonnay Santa Barbara County Sierra Madre Reserve 1993 • $25 • (07/31/95)

88 **ROBERT MONDAVI** Chardonnay Carneros 1993 • $23 • (05/15/96)

88 **RABBIT RIDGE** Chardonnay Russian River Valley Rabbit Ridge Ranch Estate Reserve 1993 • $16 • (07/31/95)

88 **SIGNORELLO** Chardonnay Napa Valley 1993 • $20 • (04/15/95)

88 **SCHUG** Chardonnay Carneros Heritage Reserve 1993 • $25 • (07/31/95)

88 **STAG'S LEAP WINE CELLARS** Chardonnay Napa Valley 1993 • $19 • (07/31/95)

88 **STEELE** Chardonnay Santa Barbara County Bien Nacido Vineyard 1993 • $22 • (07/31/95)

88 **SWANSON** Chardonnay Carneros Napa Valley 1993 • $20 • (07/31/95)

88 **TERRA** Chardonnay Carneros Sangiacomo Vineyard 1993 • $19 • (06/30/96)

88 **TALLEY** Chardonnay Arroyo Grande Valley 1993 • $18 • (07/31/95)

88 **WENTE BROS.** Chardonnay Livermore Valley Herman Wente Vineyard Estate Reserve 1993 • $14 • (09/30/95)

88 **WILD HORSE** Chardonnay Central Coast 1993 • $13 • (01/31/95)

88 **ZACA MESA** Chardonnay Santa Barbara County Jim Clendenen Alumni Winemaker Series 1993 • $18 • (02/29/96)

87 **ARROWOOD** Chardonnay Sonoma County 1993 • $20 • (06/15/95)

87 **AU BON CLIMAT** Chardonnay Santa Barbara County 1993 • $16 • (07/31/95)

87 **BEAUCANON** Chardonnay Napa Valley 1993 • $12

87 **BELVEDERE** Chardonnay Russian River Valley 1993 • $12 • (10/15/95)

87 **BERNARDUS** Chardonnay Monterey County 1993 • $15 • (06/30/95)

87 **CAMBRIA** Chardonnay Santa Maria Valley Katherine's Vineyard 1993 • $16 • (02/28/95)

87 **CARNEROS CREEK** Chardonnay California Fleur de Carneros 1993 • $9 • (09/30/95) • BB

87 **CHATEAU DE BAUN** Chardonnay Russian River Valley 1993 • $10 • (04/30/95)

87 **CLOS DANIELLE** Chardonnay Carneros Private Reserve 1993 • $9 • (01/31/95) • BB

87 **CHALONE** Chardonnay Chalone 1993 • $27 • (07/31/95)

87 **CHAUFFE-EAU** Chardonnay Carneros Sans Filtrage Sangiacomo 1993 • $17 • (07/31/95)

87 **CLAIBORNE & CHURCHILL** Chardonnay Edna Valley MacGregor Vineyard 1993 • $17 • (07/31/95)

87 **CLOS PEGASE** Chardonnay Carneros Napa Valley Pegase Circle Reserve 1993 • $20 • (07/31/95)

87 **CONCANNON** Chardonnay Livermore Valley Reserve 1993 • $15 • (07/31/95)

87 **E. & J. GALLO** Chardonnay Sonoma County Gallo Sonoma 1993 • $12 • (06/30/95)

87 **ESTANCIA** Chardonnay Monterey County 1993 • $9 • (04/15/95) • BB

87 **ESTANCIA** Chardonnay Monterey County Reserve 1993 • $20 • (07/31/95)

87 **FESS PARKER** Chardonnay Santa Barbara County 1993 • $13 • (01/31/95)

87 **FETZER** Chardonnay North Coast Barrel Select 1993 • $11 • (06/30/95)

87 **FIRESTONE** Chardonnay Santa Ynez Valley Barrel Fermented 1993 • $12 • (11/30/94)

87 **GIRARD** Chardonnay Napa Valley Viridian Vineyard 1993 • $38 • (12/15/95)

87 **HANDLEY** Chardonnay Dry Creek Valley 1993 • $15 • (06/30/96)

87 **IRON HORSE** Chardonnay Sonoma County Green Valley 1993 • $18 • (05/15/95)

87 **J. LOHR** Chardonnay Monterey Riverstone 1993 • $12 • (12/15/95)

87 **MILL CREEK** Chardonnay Dry Creek Valley 1993 • $12 • (05/15/95)

87 **MIRASSOU** Chardonnay Monterey County Fifth Generation Harvest Reserve 1993 • $12 • (07/31/95)

87 **NAPA RIDGE** Chardonnay Central Coast 1993 • $7 • (06/15/94) • BB

87 **NICHOLS** Chardonnay Arroyo Grande Valley Talley Vineyards 1993 • $20 • (12/31/95)

87 **OJAI** Chardonnay Santa Barbara County Reserve 1993 • $21 • (07/31/95)

87 **PRIDE** Chardonnay Napa Valley 1993 • $18 • (07/31/95)

87 **RAYMOND** Chardonnay Napa Valley 1993 • $14 • (12/15/95)

87 **ROBERT SINSKEY** Chardonnay Carneros 1993 • $20 • (07/31/95)

87 **SEBASTIANI** Chardonnay Sonoma County 1993 • $10 • (06/15/95) • BB

87 **SHAFER** Chardonnay Napa Valley Barrel Select 1993 • $16 • (04/30/95)

87 **SILVERADO** Chardonnay Napa Valley 1993 • $15 • (05/31/95)

87 **TRUCHARD** Chardonnay Carneros Napa Valley 1993 • $17 • (07/31/95)

87 **WHITE OAK** Chardonnay Sonoma County Myers Limited Reserve 1993 • $16 • (10/15/95)

87 **WILSON DANIELS** Chardonnay Napa Valley 1993 • $10 • (05/15/96)

87 **ZACA MESA** Chardonnay Santa Barbara County Zaca Vineyards 1993 • $12 • (01/31/95)

86 **BEAULIEU** Chardonnay Napa Valley Beautour 1993 • $10 • (04/30/95) • BB

86 **BURGESS** Chardonnay Napa Valley Barrel Fermented Debourbage 1993 • $15 • (07/31/95)

86 **CHAPPELLET** Chardonnay Napa Valley 1993 • $15 • (10/31/95)

86 **CHATEAU WOLTNER** Chardonnay Howell Mountain 1993 • $10 • (09/30/94)

86 **CLOS DU VAL** Chardonnay Carneros Special Select 1993 • $20 • (04/30/95)

86 **CLOS PEGASE** Chardonnay Carneros Napa Valley 1993 • $15 • (09/30/95)

86 **COSENTINO** Chardonnay Napa Valley The Sculptor Reserve 1993 • $24 • (02/28/95)

86 **CHATEAU ST. JEAN** Chardonnay Alexander Valley Belle Terre Vineyards 1993 • $18 • (07/31/95)

86 **CHAUFFE-EAU** Chardonnay Russian River Valley Sans Filtrage Dutton 1993 • $18 • (07/31/95)

86 **CLOS DU BOIS** Chardonnay Dry Creek Valley Flintwood Vineyard 1993 • $17 • (07/31/95)

86 **CUVAISON** Chardonnay Carneros Napa Valley 1993 • $15 • (07/31/95)

86 **GRGICH HILLS** Chardonnay Napa Valley 1993 • $24 • (12/15/95)

86 **GUENOC** Chardonnay Guenoc Valley 1993• $15 • (02/28/95)

86 **GAINEY** Chardonnay Santa Barbara County 1993• $14 • (07/31/95)

86 **HESS SELECT** Chardonnay California 1993• $9 • (12/15/94) • BB

86 **HIDDEN CELLARS** Chardonnay Mendocino Organically Grown Grapes 1993• $10• (09/30/95)

86 **HARRISON** Chardonnay Napa Valley 1993• $26 • (07/31/95)

86 **JOULLIAN** Chardonnay Monterey Family Reserve 1993 • $20• (06/15/96)

86 **LAMBERT BRIDGE** Chardonnay Sonoma County Barrel Fermented 1993• $13• (04/15/95)

86 **LEEWARD** Chardonnay Edna Valley Reserve 1993• $15 • (05/31/95)

86 **LOCKWOOD** Chardonnay Monterey Partners Reserve 1993 • $17• (06/30/96)

86 **LOCKWOOD** Chardonnay Monterey 1993• $15 • (12/15/95)

86 **LONGORIA** Chardonnay Santa Ynez Valley Huber Vineyard 1993• $16• (07/31/95)

86 **MURPHY-GOODE** Chardonnay Alexander Valley Barrel Fermented 1993• $13• (07/31/95)

86 **NEYERS** Chardonnay Carneros 1993• $16• (02/28/95)

86 **NAPA RIDGE** Chardonnay Napa Valley Coastal Reserve 1993• $13• (07/31/95)

86 **NEVADA CITY** Chardonnay Nevada County Barrel Fermented 1993• $11• (07/31/95)

86 **OJAI** Chardonnay Arroyo Grande Valley 1993• $18 • (07/31/95)

86 **PARAISO SPRINGS** Chardonnay Santa Lucia Highlands Barrel Fermented 1993• $12• (07/31/95)

86 **PAUL HOBBS** Chardonnay Sonoma Mountain Richard Dinner Vineyard 1993• $28• (07/31/95)

86 **PEJU** Chardonnay Napa Valley 1993• $16• (07/31/95)

86 **ROUND HILL** Chardonnay California 1993• $7 • (04/30/95) • BB

86 **RUTHERFORD VINEYARDS** Chardonnay Napa Valley 1993 • $8• (06/15/95) • BB

86 **S. ANDERSON** Chardonnay Napa Valley Carneros 1993 • $18• (04/30/95)

86 **SALAMANDRE** Chardonnay Santa Cruz Mountains Matteson Vineyard 1993• $16• (07/31/95)

86 **SOQUEL** Chardonnay California Coastal Cellars 1993• $NA

86 **STORRS** Chardonnay Santa Cruz Mountains Vanumanutagi Vineyards 1993• $19• (05/31/95)

86 **SANFORD** Chardonnay Santa Ynez Valley 1993• $24 • (07/31/95)

86 **SONOMA-LOEB** Chardonnay Sonoma County Ambassador John L. Loeb Jr.'s 1993• $16• (07/31/95)

86 **STEELE** Chardonnay California 1993• $18• (07/31/95)

86 **STONY HILL** Chardonnay Napa Valley SHV 1993• $23 • (07/31/95)

86 **TAFT STREET** Chardonnay Sonoma County 1993• $9 • (01/31/95) • BB

85 **ATLAS PEAK** Chardonnay Atlas Peak 1993• $16 • (07/31/95)

85 **BABCOCK** Chardonnay Santa Barbara County 1993• $16 • (01/31/95)

85 **BABCOCK** Chardonnay San Luis Obispo Talley Vineyard 1993• $25• (01/31/95)

85 **BEAULIEU** Chardonnay Napa Valley Carneros 1993• $13 • (09/30/95)

85 **BENZIGER** Chardonnay Carneros 1993• $13• (06/30/95)

85 **BOUCHAINE** Chardonnay Carneros 1993• $15 • (02/29/96)

85 **BOUCHAINE** Chardonnay Napa Valley Carneros Estate Reserve 1993• $22• (06/30/96)

85 **BUEHLER** Chardonnay Russian River Valley 1993• $13 • (01/31/95)

85 **CHATEAU SOUVERAIN** Chardonnay Sonoma County Barrel Fermented 1993• $12• (06/15/95)

85 **CHATEAU ST. JEAN** Chardonnay Sonoma County 1993 • $11• (05/15/96)

85 **CLOS DU VAL** Chardonnay Carneros Napa Valley 1993 • $15• (12/15/95)

85 **CRONIN** Chardonnay Napa Valley 1993• $18• (07/31/95)

85 **CRONIN** Chardonnay Alexander Valley Stuhlmuller Vineyard 1993• $18• (07/31/95)

85 **DE LOACH** Chardonnay Russian River Valley 1993• $15 • (02/29/96)

85 **DE LORIMIER** Chardonnay Alexander Valley 1993• $14 • (02/29/96)

85 **ESTATE WILLIAM BACCALA** Chardonnay Sonoma County 1993• $13• (02/29/96)

85 **EDMEADES** Chardonnay Anderson Valley Dennison Vineyard 1993• $20• (07/31/95)

85 **ELKHORN PEAK** Chardonnay Napa Valley Fagan Creek Vineyards 1993• $15• (07/31/95)

85 **FAR NIENTE** Chardonnay Napa Valley 1993• $32 • (07/31/95)

85 **FISHER** Chardonnay Sonoma County Whitney's Vineyard 1993• $26• (07/31/95)

85 **FOREST HILL** Chardonnay Napa Valley Private Reserve 1993• $28• (07/31/95)

85 **FOXEN** Chardonnay Santa Maria Valley Tinaquaic Vineyard 1993• $28• (07/31/95)

85 **GEYSER PEAK** Chardonnay Sonoma County 1993• $10 • (12/15/94) • BB

85 **GREENWOOD RIDGE** Chardonnay Late Harvest Anderson Valley 1993• $18• (06/15/94)

85 **GLEN ELLEN** Chardonnay California Proprietor's Reserve 1993• $5• (07/31/95) • BB

85 **GODSPEED** Chardonnay Mount Veeder 1993• $15 • (07/31/95)

85 **HAHN** Chardonnay Monterey 1993• $10• (03/31/95)

85 **HANNA** Chardonnay Russian River Valley Reserve 1993 • $18• (06/30/96)

85 **HUSCH** Chardonnay Mendocino 1993• $12• (11/30/94)

85 **J. LOHR** Chardonnay California Cypress 1993• $9 • (12/15/95)

85 **KENDALL-JACKSON** Chardonnay California Vintner's Reserve 1993• $14• (09/15/94)

85 **KORBEL** Chardonnay Russian River Valley 1993• $15 • (06/30/95)

85 **LA CREMA** Chardonnay California Reserve 1993• $12 • (05/31/95)

85 **LA CREMA** Chardonnay California Grand Cuvée 1993• $20 • (05/31/95)

85 **MACKINAW** Chardonnay California 1993• $10• (03/31/95)

85 **MACROSTIE** Chardonnay Carneros 1993• $16• (02/28/95)

85 **MERIDIAN** Chardonnay Edna Valley 1993• $14 • (04/30/95)

85 **MERIDIAN** Chardonnay Santa Barbara County 1993• $10 • (06/15/95)

85 **MADROÑA** Chardonnay El Dorado 1993• $10• (07/31/95)

85 **MONT ST. JOHN** Chardonnay Carneros Organically Grown Grapes 1993• $13• (07/31/95)

85 **MONTEREY VINEYARD** Chardonnay Monterey County Limited Release 1993• $13• (07/31/95)

85 **NAPA RIDGE** Chardonnay Central Coast Coastal Vines 1993• $8• (11/30/94)• BB

85 **PETER MCCOY VINEYARDS** Chardonnay Knights Valley Clos des Pierres 1993 • $20 • (06/15/96)

85 **R.H. PHILLIPS** Chardonnay California Barrel Cuvée 1993 • $7 • (06/30/95) • BB

85 **ROBERT MONDAVI** Chardonnay Napa Valley Unfiltered 1993 • $15 • (07/31/95)

85 **ROCHIOLI** Chardonnay Russian River Valley 1993 • $16 • (07/31/95)

85 **RODNEY STRONG** Chardonnay Chalk Hill Chalk Hill Vineyard 1993 • $14 • (07/31/95)

85 **SCHUG** Chardonnay Sonoma Valley 1993 • $12 • (11/30/94)

85 **STONY HILL** Chardonnay Napa Valley 1993 • $21 • (06/15/96)

85 **SAINTSBURY** Chardonnay Carneros 1993 • $15 • (07/31/95)

85 **SALMON CREEK** Chardonnay Carneros 1993 • $12 • (07/31/95)

85 **STERLING** Chardonnay Napa Valley Sterling Collections Z Lot 1993 • $20 • (07/31/95)

85 **STORRS** Chardonnay Santa Cruz Mountains Christie Vineyard Mountain Vineyard Collection 1993 • $17 • (07/31/95)

85 **TREFETHEN** Chardonnay Napa Valley 1993 • $19 • (07/31/95)

85 **VILLA MT. EDEN** Chardonnay California Cellar Select 1993 • $8 • (04/30/95)

85 **WENTE BROS.** Chardonnay Central Coast Wente Family Estate Selection 1993 • $9 • (04/30/95)

85 **WENTE BROS.** Chardonnay Arroyo Seco Riva Ranch 1993 • $8 • (05/15/96)

85 **WILDHURST** Chardonnay California 1993 • $10 • (07/31/95)

85 **WILDHURST** Chardonnay Sonoma County Reserve 1993 • $12 • (07/31/95)

85 **ZD** Chardonnay California 1993 • $23 • (02/28/95)

84 **ACACIA** Chardonnay Carneros 1993 • $17 • (07/31/95)

84 **ADLER FELS** Chardonnay Sonoma County Coleman Reserve 1993 • $14 • (03/31/96)

84 **B.R. COHN** Chardonnay Carneros 1993 • $28 • (07/31/95)

84 **BELVEDERE** Chardonnay Sonoma County 1993 • $9 • (05/31/95)

84 **BERINGER** Chardonnay Napa Valley 1993 • $11 • (04/30/95)

84 **BOGLE** Chardonnay California Reserve 1993 • $12 • (05/15/96)

84 **BOUCHAINE** Chardonnay California Q.C. Fly 1993 • $8 • (10/15/95)

84 **BANDIERA** Chardonnay Napa Valley 1993 • $8 • (07/31/95)

84 **BRANDER** Chardonnay Santa Ynez Valley Tête de Cuvée 1993 • $15 • (07/31/95)

84 **BYINGTON** Chardonnay Santa Cruz Mountains Redwood Hill Vineyard 1993 • $23 • (07/31/95)

84 **BYINGTON** Chardonnay Santa Cruz Mountains 1993 • $18 • (07/31/95)

84 **CASTLE ROCK** Chardonnay Napa Valley Barrel Fermented 1993 • $10 • (07/31/95)

84 **CLOS DU BOIS** Chardonnay Alexander Valley Barrel Fermented 1993 • $13 • (01/31/95)

84 **COTES DE SONOMA** Chardonnay Sonoma County 1993 • $8 • (04/15/95)

84 **CAKEBREAD** Chardonnay Napa Valley 1993 • $22 • (07/31/95)

84 **CALLAWAY** Chardonnay Temecula Hawk Watch Calla-Lees 1993 • $9 • (07/31/95)

84 **CHALONE** Chardonnay Chalone Gavilan 1993 • $14 • (07/31/95)

84 **CHATEAU MONTELENA** Chardonnay Napa Valley 1993 • $23 • (07/31/95)

84 **CHATEAU WOLTNER** Chardonnay Howell Mountain Estate Reserve 1993 • $17 • (07/31/95)

84 **CHRISTOPHE** Chardonnay North Coast 1993 • $8 • (07/31/95)

84 **CHRISTOPHER CREEK** Chardonnay Russian River Valley 1993 • $14 • (07/31/95)

84 **CONCANNON** Chardonnay Central Coast Selected Vineyard 1993 • $10 • (07/31/95)

84 **CRONIN** Chardonnay Santa Cruz Mountains 1993 • $20 • (07/31/95)

84 **DE LOACH** Chardonnay Sonoma County Sonoma Cuvée 1993 • $10 • (05/15/96)

84 **DOUGLASS HILL** Chardonnay Napa Valley 1993 • $15 • (12/31/95)

84 **DRY CREEK** Chardonnay Sonoma County Barrel Fermented 1993 • $14 • (07/31/95)

84 **FETZER** Chardonnay Mendocino County Bonterra Organically Grown Grapes 1993 • $9 • (06/30/95)

84 **FREEMARK ABBEY** Chardonnay Napa Valley 1993 • $16 • (06/30/96)

84 **FLORA SPRINGS** Chardonnay Napa Valley Barrel Fermented 1993 • $20 • (07/31/95)

84 **GLASS MOUNTAIN QUARRY** Chardonnay California 1993 • $9 • (06/30/95)

84 **GROTH** Chardonnay Napa Valley 1993 • $14 • (04/15/95)

84 **GREEN & RED** Chardonnay Napa Valley Catacula Vineyard 1993 • $16 • (07/31/95)

84 **IVÁN TAMÁS** Chardonnay Livermore Valley Hayes Ranch 1993 • $8 • (07/31/95)

84 **JORDAN** Chardonnay Sonoma County 1993 • $20 • (06/30/96)

84 **KENWOOD** Chardonnay Sonoma Valley Reserve 1993 • $18 • (07/31/95)

84 **KENWOOD** Chardonnay Sonoma Valley 1993 • $14 • (07/31/95)

84 **KENWOOD** Chardonnay Sonoma Valley Beltane Ranch 1993 • $18 • (07/31/95)

84 **LAZY CREEK** Chardonnay Anderson Valley 1993 • $10 • (06/15/96)

84 **LAWRENCE J. BARGETTO** Chardonnay Santa Cruz Mountains 1993 • $16 • (07/31/95)

84 **LOGAN** Chardonnay Monterey 1993 • $14 • (07/31/95)

84 **MAZZOCCO** Chardonnay Sonoma County Winemaker's Select 1993 • $18 • (06/30/96)

84 **MORRO BAY** Chardonnay Central Coast Special Edition 1993 • $10 • (05/15/95)

84 **MERRYVALE** Chardonnay Napa Valley Starmont 1993 • $16 • (07/31/95)

84 **PETERSON** Chardonnay Anderson Valley 1993 • $13 • (07/31/95)

84 **ROBERT MONDAVI** Chardonnay Central Coast Coastal 1993 • $11 • (12/15/94)

84 **RAVENSWOOD** Chardonnay North Coast Vintners Blend 1993 • $9 • (07/31/95)

84 **SONOMA-CUTRER** Chardonnay Sonoma Coast Russian River Ranches 1993 • $14 • (04/30/95)

84 **ST. CLEMENT** Chardonnay Carneros Napa Valley Abbotts Vineyard 1993 • $18 • (07/31/95)

84 **THE HESS COLLECTION** Chardonnay Napa Valley 1993 • $15 • (07/31/95)

84 **WHITEHALL LANE** Chardonnay Napa Valley Barrel Fermented 1993 • $13 • (05/15/95)

84 **WELLINGTON** Chardonnay Sonoma Valley Barrel Fermented 1993 • $12 • (07/31/95)

84 **WHEELER** Chardonnay Sonoma County 1993 • $11 • (07/31/95)

84 **YORK MOUNTAIN** Chardonnay San Luis Obispo 1993 • $12 • (07/31/95)

83 **ALDERBROOK** Chardonnay Dry Creek Valley 1993 • $12 • (07/31/95)

83 **AUDUBON** Chardonnay Sonoma Valley Carneros Sangiacomo Barrel Fermented 1993 • $12 • (07/31/95)

83 **BAYVIEW CELLARS** Chardonnay Napa Valley Carneros 1993 • $12 • (06/30/96)

83 **BABCOCK** Chardonnay Santa Ynez Valley Mt. Carmel Vineyard 1993 • $25 • (07/31/95)

83 **BRUTOCAO** Chardonnay Mendocino Bliss Vineyard 1993 • $10 • (07/31/95)

83 **BYINGTON** Chardonnay Mount Veeder 1993 • $14 • (07/31/95)

83 **CASTLEVIEW** Chardonnay Sonoma County Private Reserve 1993 • $9 • (10/15/95)

83 **COLBY** Chardonnay Napa Valley 1993 • $12 • (05/15/96)

83 **CHATEAU WOLTNER** Chardonnay Howell Mountain St. Thomas Vineyard 1993 • $23 • (07/31/95)

83 **CIRRI** Chardonnay Sonoma County 1993 • $9 • (07/31/95)

83 **CLAUDIA SPRINGS** Chardonnay Anderson Valley 1993 • $10 • (07/31/95)

83 **COSENTINO** Chardonnay Napa Valley 1993 • $15 • (07/31/95)

83 **DUNNEWOOD** Chardonnay Carneros Gold Label Select 1993 • $10 • (07/31/95)

83 **FOREST GLEN** Chardonnay Sonoma County Barrel Fermented 1993 • $10 • (12/31/94)

83 **HACIENDA** Chardonnay California Clair de Lune 1993 • $6 • (02/28/95)

83 **HIDDEN CELLARS** Chardonnay Mendocino County 1993 • $10 • (07/31/95)

83 **KONRAD** Chardonnay Mendocino 1993 • $11 • (06/15/96)

83 **KENWOOD** Chardonnay Sonoma Valley Yulupa 1993 • $14 • (07/31/95)

83 **LA CROSSE** Chardonnay Napa Valley 1993 • $7 • (04/30/95)

83 **LEEWARD** Chardonnay Central Coast 1993 • $11 • (10/15/95)

83 **MAZZOCCO** Chardonnay Sonoma County River Lane 1993 • $15 • (07/31/95)

83 **MOUNT PALOMAR** Chardonnay Temecula Reserve 1993 • $16 • (07/31/95)

83 **NAVARRO** Chardonnay Anderson Valley 1993 • $8 • (07/31/95)

83 **PORTER CREEK** Chardonnay Russian River Valley Unfiltered Reserve 1993 • $23 • (07/31/95)

83 **RAYMOND** Chardonnay California Amberhill California Selection 1993 • $11 • (02/28/95)

83 **RODNEY STRONG** Chardonnay Sonoma County 1993 • $11 • (04/30/95)

83 **RUTZ CELLARS** Chardonnay Russian River Valley 1993 • $18

83 **RODNEY STRONG** Chardonnay Sonoma County 1993 • $11 • (04/30/95)

83 **ROUND HILL** Chardonnay Napa Valley Van Asperen Selection Reserve 1993 • $12 • (07/31/95)

83 **STEPHEN ZELLERBACH** Chardonnay California 1993 • $8 • (01/31/95)

83 **SEQUOIA GROVE** Chardonnay Carneros Napa Valley 1993 • $14 • (07/31/95)

83 **SILVERADO HILL CELLARS** Chardonnay Napa Valley Winemaker's Traditional Methode 1993 • $10 • (07/31/95)

83 **TULOCAY** Chardonnay Napa Valley De Celles Vineyard 1993 • $14 • (07/31/95)

83 **VICHON** Chardonnay Napa Valley 1993 • $14 • (07/31/95)

83 **WHITE OAK** Chardonnay Sonoma County 1993 • $11 • (07/31/95)

83 **ZAYANTE** Chardonnay Santa Cruz Mountains 1993 • $14 • (07/31/95)

82 **B.R. COHN** Chardonnay Carneros Joseph Herman Vineyard Reserve 1993 • $20 • (07/31/95)

82 **BETTINELLI** Chardonnay Napa Valley 1993 • $12 • (05/15/96)

82 **BOGLE** Chardonnay California 1993 • $6.25 • (01/31/95) • BB

82 **CASTLEVIEW** Chardonnay Carneros Private Reserve 1993 • $10 • (10/15/95)

82 **COOPERS' LEGACY** Chardonnay Sonoma County 1993 • $9 • (07/31/95)

82 **CASTORO** Chardonnay San Luis Obispo County 1993 • $10 • (07/31/95)

82 **CHATEAU WOLTNER** Chardonnay Howell Mountain Frederique Vineyard 1993 • $40 • (07/31/95)

82 **CHATEAU WOLTNER** Chardonnay Howell Mountain Titus Vineyard 1993 • $40 • (07/31/95)

82 **CHATOM** Chardonnay Calaveras County 1993 • $10 • (07/31/95)

82 **CHIMNEY ROCK** Chardonnay Carneros 1993 • $16 • (07/31/95)

82 **CHIMÈRE** Chardonnay Santa Barbara County 1993 • $13 • (07/31/95)

82 **EDMEADES** Chardonnay Mendocino 1993 • $12 • (04/15/95)

82 **FENESTRA** Chardonnay Livermore Valley Toy Vineyard 1993 • $12 • (07/31/95)

82 **FIELD STONE** Chardonnay Sonoma County 1993 • $14 • (07/31/95)

82 **HAYWOOD** Chardonnay California Vintner's Select 1993 • $8 • (02/28/95)

82 **J. FRITZ** Chardonnay Sonoma County 1993 • $10 • (07/31/95)

82 **JEKEL** Chardonnay Arroyo Seco Gravelstone Vineyard 1993 • $10 • (07/31/95)

82 **JOULLIAN** Chardonnay Monterey 1993 • $11 • (07/31/95)

82 **LYETH** Chardonnay Sonoma County 1993 • $12 • (12/15/94)

82 **M.G. VALLEJO** Chardonnay California 1993 • $6 • (07/31/95)

82 **MONTICELLO** Chardonnay Napa Valley Corley Estate Reserve 1993 • $26 • (05/15/96)

82 **MONT ST. JOHN** Chardonnay Carneros Napa Valley Madonna Vineyards 1993 • $18 • (07/31/95)

82 **PORTER CREEK** Chardonnay Russian River Valley 1993 • $14 • (07/31/95)

82 **RANCHO SISQUOC** Chardonnay Santa Maria Valley 1993 • $15 • (07/31/95)

82 **ROUND HILL** Chardonnay Napa Valley Reserve 1993 • $11 • (07/31/95)

82 **RUTHERFORD RANCH** Chardonnay Napa Valley 1993 • $9 • (07/31/95)

82 **ST. ANDREW'S VINEYARD** Chardonnay Napa Valley 1993 • $12 • (07/31/95)

82 **ST. FRANCIS** Chardonnay Sonoma County 1993 • $12 • (11/30/94)

82 **SCHUETZ OLES** Chardonnay Napa Valley Chappell Vineyard 1993 • $14 • (07/31/95)

82 **SHOOTING STAR** Chardonnay Mendocino 1993 • $9 • (11/15/94)

82 **STERLING** Chardonnay Napa Valley 1993 • $14 • (04/30/95)

82 **STEVENOT** Chardonnay Sierra Foothills 1993 • $8 • (02/28/95)

■ ■ ■ ■

California Chardonnay

82 **STEVENOT** Chardonnay Calaveras County Reserve 1993 • $11• (02/28/95)

82 **SUMMERFIELD** Chardonnay California Vintner's Reserve 1993• $6• (07/31/95)

82 **SEGHESIO** Chardonnay Sonoma County 1993• $9 • (07/31/95)

82 **SEQUOIA GROVE** Chardonnay Napa Valley Estate Reserve 1993• $18• (07/31/95)

82 **SONOMA MISSION** Chardonnay Sonoma County 1993• $8 • (07/31/95)

82 **VICHON** Chardonnay California Coastal Selection 1993 • $10• (01/31/95)

82 **WHITEHALL LANE** Chardonnay Napa Valley 1993• $11 • (05/15/95)

82 **WHITE OAK** Chardonnay Russian River Valley Poplar Ranch Private Reserve 1993• $18• (07/31/95)

81 **ARCIERO** Chardonnay Paso Robles 1993• $9 • (12/31/95)

81 **CHARLES KRUG** Chardonnay Napa Valley 1993• $11 • (05/15/95)

81 **CORBETT CANYON** Chardonnay Santa Barbara County Reserve 1993• $9• (01/31/95)

81 **DEER VALLEY** Chardonnay Monterey County 1993• $7 • (10/31/95)

81 **FETZER** Chardonnay California Sundial 1993• $8 • (07/31/95)

81 **HANDLEY** Chardonnay Anderson Valley 1993• $11 • (06/15/96)

81 **MARTIN BROTHERS** Chardonnay Paso Robles in Botti 1993 • $12• (07/31/95)

81 **PARDUCCI** Chardonnay Mendocino County 1993• $8 • (02/28/95)

81 **SADDLEBACK** Chardonnay Napa Valley 1993• $13 • (07/31/95)

81 **ST. SUPÉRY** Chardonnay Napa Valley Dollarhide Ranch 1993• $13• (07/31/95)

81 **WOODBRIGE** Chardonnay California Barrel Aged 1993• $6 • (07/31/95)

81 **WELLINGTON** Chardonnay Sonoma County Barrel Fermented Lot 2 1993• $8• (07/31/95)

81 **YORKVILLE CELLARS** Chardonnay Anderson Valley 1993 • $10• (07/31/95)

80 **CEDAR MOUNTAIN** Chardonnay Livermore Valley Blanches Vineyard 1993• $15• (11/15/95)

80 **CHOUINARD** Chardonnay Monterey Ventana Vineyard 1993 • $12• (07/31/95)

80 **CLOS ST. THOMAS** Chardonnay California 1993• $7 • (03/31/95)

80 **CORBETT CANYON** Chardonnay Central Coast Coastal Classic 1993• $5• (01/31/95)

80 **CRESTON** Chardonnay Paso Robles 1993• $10 • (07/31/95)

80 **DOMAINE ST. GEORGE** Chardonnay California Vintage Reserve 1993• $6• (01/31/95)

80 **DUNNEWOOD** Chardonnay North Coast Barrel Select 1993 • $8• (02/28/95)

80 **DEMOOR** Chardonnay Napa Valley 1993• $12• (07/31/95)

80 **EHLERS GROVE** Chardonnay California 1993• $10 • (07/31/95)

80 **J. PEDRONCELLI** Chardonnay Dry Creek Valley 1993• $9 • (07/31/95)

80 **LAWRENCE J. BARGETTO** Chardonnay Central Coast Cypress 1993• $9• (07/31/95)

80 **MOUNTAIN VIEW** Chardonnay Monterey 1993• $6

79 **BLACKSTONE** Chardonnay Monterey County Reserve 1993 • $8• (07/31/95)

79 **BRINDIAMO** Chardonnay California Limited Bottling 1993 • $10• (07/31/95)

79 **CHATEAU JULIEN** Chardonnay Monterey County Grand Reserve 1993• $7• (05/15/96)

79 **CHRISTOPHE** Chardonnay Napa County 1993• $8 • (09/30/94)

79 **MISSION CANYON** Chardonnay Santa Barbara County 1993 • $8• (07/31/95)

79 **MONTEREY VINEYARD** Chardonnay Monterey County Classic 1993• $6• (02/28/95)

79 **MOUNT PALOMAR** Chardonnay Temecula 1993• $10 • (02/28/95)

79 **NOMINEE** Chardonnay Paso Robles 1993• $6 • (06/30/94)

79 **RED HILL** Chardonnay California 1993• $4• (07/31/95)

79 **TWIN HILLS** Chardonnay Paso Robles 1993• $9 • (07/31/95)

79 **VENDANGE** Chardonnay California Autumn Harvest 1993 • $7• (06/30/94)

78 **CANYON ROAD** Chardonnay California 1993• $7 • (01/31/95)

78 **CARTLIDGE & BROWNE** Chardonnay California 1993• $6 • (04/30/95)

78 **CASTORO** Chardonnay Paso Robles Reserve 1993• $12 • (07/31/95)

78 **EBERLE** Chardonnay Paso Robles 1993• $12 • (07/31/95)

78 **GAN EDEN** Chardonnay Sonoma County Reserve 1993 • $14• (07/31/95)

78 **HEITZ** Chardonnay Napa Valley Estate Selection 1993 • $18• (07/31/95)

78 **MASSON** Chardonnay Monterey County 1993• $10

78 **MONTEVIÑA** Chardonnay California 1993• $8 • (07/31/95)

78 **SUNSTONE** Chardonnay Santa Barbara County 1993• $14 • (07/31/95)

78 **SCHUG** Chardonnay Carneros 1993• $16• (07/31/95)

78 **STERLING** Chardonnay Carneros Napa Valley Winery Lake 1993• $18• (07/31/95)

77 **EPOCH** Chardonnay Central Coast 1993• $7 • (10/31/95)

77 **FORESTVILLE** Chardonnay California 1993• $6 • (01/31/95)

77 **GROVE STREET** Chardonnay Sonoma County Healdsburg Vineyard Select 1993• $7• (07/31/95)

77 **MISSION VIEW** Chardonnay San Luis Obispo 1993• $10 • (07/31/95)

77 **SALAMANDRE** Chardonnay Arroyo Seco 1993• $16 • (07/31/95)

76 **CASTLEVIEW** Chardonnay Russian River Valley Private Reserve 1993• $10• (12/15/95)

76 **DURNEY** Chardonnay Carmel Valley Cachagua Dances On Your Palate 1993• $11• (05/15/96)

76 **RENAISSANCE** Chardonnay North Yuba Barrel Select 1993 • $20• (07/31/95)

75 **CHATEAU JULIEN** Chardonnay Monterey County Sur Lie Private Reserve 1993• $17• (12/15/95)

75 **LAZY CREEK** Chardonnay Anderson Valley 1993• $10 • (07/31/95)

74 **CHATEAU JULIEN** Chardonnay Monterey County Grand Reserve 1993• $7

74 **OAK RIDGE VINEYARDS** Chardonnay California Bighorn 1993 • $7• (06/30/94)

74 **SUTTER HOME** Chardonnay California 1993• $6 • (04/30/95)

74 **THE NEGOCIANTS** Chardonnay Central Coast 1993• $7 • (02/28/95)

72 **NAPA CELLARS** Chardonnay Napa Valley 1993• $7 • (07/31/95)

1992 California Chardonnay
Vintage Rating: 93

94 **CHATEAU ST. JEAN** Chardonnay Alexander Valley Robert Young Vineyards Reserve 1992• $50• (04/30/96)

94 **KISTLER** Chardonnay Sonoma Valley Kistler Vineyard 1992 • $40• (03/31/95)• SS

94 **MONTICELLO** Chardonnay Napa Valley Corley Estate Reserve 1992• $26• (04/15/95)

93 **BERINGER** Chardonnay Napa Valley Sbragia Limited Release 1992• $25• (05/31/94)

93 **CHALONE** Chardonnay Chalone Reserve 1992• $35 • (06/30/94)

93 **FERRARI-CARANO** Chardonnay Alexander Valley 1992• $20 • (04/30/94)• SS

93 **KISTLER** Chardonnay Sonoma County 1992• $26 • (05/15/94)• SS

93 **ROCHIOLI** Chardonnay Russian River Valley Reserve 1992 • $26• (05/31/94)

92 **AU BON CLIMAT** Chardonnay Santa Barbara County Le Bouge D'àcôté 1992• $25• (05/31/94)

92 **BYRON** Chardonnay Santa Barbara County Reserve 1992 • $23• (11/30/94)• SS

92 **FOXEN** Chardonnay Santa Maria Valley Tinaquaic Vineyard 1992• $28• (05/15/94)

92 **KISTLER** Chardonnay Russian River Valley Dutton Ranch 1992• $30• (05/15/94)

92 **KISTLER** Chardonnay Sonoma County Cuvée Cathleen 1992• $50• (06/30/95)

92 **MARCASSIN** Chardonnay Alexander Valley Gauer Vineyard Upper Barn 1992• $50• (09/30/94)

92 **MURPHY-GOODE** Chardonnay Alexander Valley Reserve 1992• $22• (06/30/94)

92 **RIDGE** Chardonnay Santa Cruz Mountains 1992• $20 • (03/31/95)• SS

92 **ROBERT MONDAVI** Chardonnay Carneros 1992• $22 • (06/30/94)

92 **ROBERT MONDAVI** Chardonnay Napa Valley Reserve 1992 • $28• (06/15/94)

92 **ROBERT MONDAVI** Chardonnay Carneros 1992• $22 • (06/15/94)

92 **SILVERADO** Chardonnay Napa Valley Limited Reserve 1992 • $33• (12/31/94)• SS

92 **STEELE** Chardonnay Sonoma Valley Durell Vineyard 1992 • $24• (03/31/94)

92 **STEELE** Chardonnay Mendocino Lolonis Vineyard 1992 • $26• (06/15/94)

91 **AU BON CLIMAT** Chardonnay Arroyo Grande Valley Talley Reserve 1992• $25• (05/31/94)

91 **BERINGER** Chardonnay Napa Valley Private Reserve 1992 • $17• (06/30/94)

91 **BERNARDUS** Chardonnay Monterey County 1992• $13 • (11/15/94)• SS

91 **BYRON** Chardonnay Santa Maria Valley Estate 1992• $25 • (07/31/95)

91 **CAMBRIA** Chardonnay Santa Maria Valley Reserve 1992 • $25• (06/30/94)

91 **CHALONE** Chardonnay Chalone 1992• $26• (06/15/94)

91 **CHATEAU POTELLE** Chardonnay Mount Veeder V.G.S. 1992 • $34• (04/30/96)

91 **E. & J. GALLO** Chardonnay Northern Sonoma Estate Bottled 1992• $30• (09/15/94)

91 **FERRARI-CARANO** Chardonnay Napa-Sonoma Counties Reserve 1992• $27• (05/31/95)

91 **GAINEY** Chardonnay Santa Ynez Valley Limited Selection 1992• $25• (06/15/94)

91 **GLORIA FERRER** Chardonnay Carneros Freixenet Vineyards 1992• $15• (04/30/94)

91 **KISTLER** Chardonnay Sonoma Valley Durell Vineyard Sand Hill 1992• $28• (05/15/94)

91 **KISTLER** Chardonnay Russian River Valley Vine Hill Vineyard 1992• $32• (03/31/95)

91 **MACROSTIE** Chardonnay Carneros Reserve 1992• $20 • (02/28/95)

91 **MARIMAR TORRES** Chardonnay Sonoma County Green Valley Don Miguel Vineyard 1992• $20• (04/30/95) • SS

91 **MARTIN RAY** Chardonnay California Mariage 1992• $24 • (11/30/94)

91 **MATANZAS CREEK** Chardonnay Sonoma Valley Journey 1992• $70• (12/31/95)

91 **MER ET SOLEIL** Chardonnay Central Coast 1992• $25 • (08/31/95)• SS

91 **PATZ & HALL** Chardonnay Napa Valley 1992• $25 • (04/15/94)

91 **PETER MICHAEL** Chardonnay Napa County Clos du Ciel 1992• $26• (06/30/94)

91 **ST. FRANCIS** Chardonnay Sonoma Valley Reserve Estate 1992• $15• (04/30/94)• SS

91 **TALBOTT** Chardonnay Monterey Diamond T Estate 1992 • $34

91 **TALBOTT** Chardonnay Monterey 1992• $25• (06/30/95) • SS

91 **TRUCHARD** Chardonnay Napa Valley Carneros 1992• $16 • (06/30/94)

90 **BELVEDERE** Chardonnay Sonoma County Preferred Stock 1992• $18• (11/30/94)

90 **CALE** Chardonnay Carneros Sangiacomo Vineyard 1992 • $18• (03/31/94)

90 **CHATEAU ST. JEAN** Chardonnay Alexander Valley Belle Terre Vineyards 1992• $18• (05/15/94)

90 **CHATEAU WOLTNER** Chardonnay Howell Mountain Estate Reserve 1992• $17• (06/30/94)

90 **CHATEAU WOLTNER** Chardonnay Howell Mountain Frederique Vineyard 1992• $40• (06/30/94)

90 **COOPER-GARROD** Chardonnay Santa Cruz Mountains Premier Release 1992• $16• (12/15/94)

90 **DEHLINGER** Chardonnay Russian River Valley The Montrachet Cuvee 1992• $20• (11/15/94)

90 **FOREST GLEN** Chardonnay Sonoma County 1992• $10 • (06/30/94)• SS

90 **FOREST HILL** Chardonnay Napa Valley Private Reserve 1992• $26• (06/30/94)

90 **FRANCISCAN** Chardonnay Napa Valley Oakville Estate Cuvée Sauvage 1992• $24• (06/30/94)

90 **GREENWOOD RIDGE** Chardonnay Anderson Valley Du Pratt Vineyard 1992• $19• (05/31/94)

90 **JARVIS** Chardonnay Napa Valley 1992• $34• (08/31/95)

90 **KENDALL-JACKSON** Chardonnay Santa Maria Valley Camelot Vineyard 1992• $15• (06/30/94)

90 **KISTLER** Chardonnay Sonoma Mountain McCrea Vineyard 1992• $35• (04/30/95)

90 **LANDMARK** Chardonnay Sonoma Valley Two Williams Vineyards 1992• $14• (06/30/94)

90 **MARKHAM** Chardonnay Napa Valley 1992• $15 • (03/15/94)• SS

90 **MUELLER** Chardonnay Russian River Valley LB Reserve 1992• $30• (07/31/95)

90 **ROCHIOLI** Chardonnay Russian River Valley 1992• $15 • (05/31/94)• SS

90 **SANFORD** Chardonnay Santa Barbara County Barrel Select 1992• $30• (06/30/95)

90 **ST. CLEMENT** Chardonnay Napa Valley Carneros 1992 • $16• (03/31/94)• SS

90 **STAG'S LEAP WINE CELLARS** Chardonnay Napa Valley Reserve 1992 • $28 • (12/31/94)

90 **STAG'S LEAP WINE CELLARS** Chardonnay Napa Valley 1992 • $18 • (06/30/94) • SS

90 **STEELE** Chardonnay Santa Barbara County Bien Nacido Vineyard 1992 • $22 • (03/31/94)

90 **STEELE** Chardonnay Carneros Sangiacomo Vineyard 1992 • $22 • (03/31/94)

90 **STEELE** Chardonnay California 1992 • $18 • (06/15/94)

90 **STONESTREET** Chardonnay Sonoma County 1992 • $20 • (01/31/95) • SS

90 **THOMAS FOGARTY** Chardonnay Santa Cruz Mountains Estate Reserve 1992 • $18 • (02/29/96)

90 **ZACA MESA** Chardonnay Santa Barbara County Alumni Winemaker Series James A. Clenden 1992 • $18 • (01/31/95)

89 **ACACIA** Chardonnay Carneros Reserve 1992 • $22 • (05/15/95)

89 **ARROWOOD** Chardonnay Sonoma County 1992 • $20 • (04/30/94)

89 **CALERA** Chardonnay Central Coast 1992 • $15 • (02/28/94) • SS

89 **CALERA** Chardonnay Mount Harlan 1992 • $33 • (05/31/94)

89 **CHARLES KRUG** Chardonnay Napa Valley Carneros Reserve 1992 • $17 • (06/15/94)

89 **CHAUFFE-EAU** Chardonnay Carneros Sangiacomo Sans Filtrage 1992 • $17 • (04/30/94)

89 **CLOS DU BOIS** Chardonnay Alexander Valley Calcaire Vineyard 1992 • $18 • (05/15/94)

89 **CUVAISON** Chardonnay Napa Valley Carneros 1992 • $15 • (09/15/94)

89 **GIRARD** Chardonnay Napa Valley Reserve 1992 • $28 • (06/30/94)

89 **GRGICH HILLS** Chardonnay Napa Valley Carneros Selection 1992 • $35 • (04/30/95)

89 **GUENOC** Chardonnay Guenoc Valley Genevieve Magoon Vineyard 1992 • $25 • (05/15/94)

89 **HAHN** Chardonnay Monterey 1992 • $10 • (05/31/94) • SS

89 **HIDDEN CELLARS** Chardonnay Mendocino County Reserve 1992 • $17 • (11/30/94)

89 **JOULLIAN** Chardonnay Monterey Family Reserve 1992 • $18 • (07/31/95)

89 **KUNDE** Chardonnay Sonoma Valley Estate Reserve 1992 • $20 • (06/30/94)

89 **LONG** Chardonnay Napa Valley 1992 • $29 • (04/15/95)

89 **MONTICELLO** Chardonnay Napa Valley Corley Family Vineyards 1992 • $15 • (09/30/95)

89 **MOUNT EDEN** Chardonnay Edna Valley MacGregor Vineyard 1992 • $15 • (06/15/94)

89 **PENARD** Chardonnay Carneros 1992 • $16 • (12/15/94)

89 **PINE RIDGE** Chardonnay Stags Leap District Vieille Vigne 1992 • $35 • (11/15/94)

89 **PINNACLES** Chardonnay Monterey 1992 • $15 • (06/15/94)

89 **SANTA BARBARA WINERY** Chardonnay Santa Ynez Valley Reserve 1992 • $20 • (04/30/94)

89 **SONOMA-LOEB** Chardonnay Sonoma County Ambassador John L. Loeb Jr's Private Reserve 1992 • $26 • (09/30/94)

89 **SONOMA-LOEB** Chardonnay Sonoma County Ambassador John L. Loeb Jr.'s 1992 • $25

89 **STEELE** Chardonnay Mendocino Dennison Vineyard 1992 • $20 • (06/15/94)

89 **SWANSON** Chardonnay Napa Valley Carneros 1992 • $18 • (01/31/95)

89 **SANTA BARBARA WINERY** Chardonnay Santa Ynez Valley Lafond Vineyard Unfiltered 1992 • $30 • (07/31/95)

89 **SARAH'S VINEYARD** Chardonnay Santa Clara County 1992 • $42 • (07/31/95)

89 **THE HESS COLLECTION** Chardonnay Napa Valley 1992 • $15 • (12/15/94)

89 **V. SATTUI** Chardonnay Napa Valley Carsi Vineyard Barrel Fermented 1992 • $18 • (06/30/94)

88 **BABCOCK** Chardonnay Santa Ynez Valley Grand Cuvée 1992 • $25 • (09/30/95)

88 **BAILEYANA** Chardonnay Edna Valley Paragon Vineyard 1992 • $14 • (05/31/94)

88 **BAYVIEW CELLARS** Chardonnay Napa Valley Carneros 1992 • $12 • (12/15/94)

88 **BEAULIEU** Chardonnay Napa Valley Carneros Reserve 1992 • $16 • (04/30/95)

88 **BENZIGER** Chardonnay Carneros Premiere Vineyard 1992 • $16 • (06/15/94)

88 **BYRON** Chardonnay Santa Barbara County 1992 • $15 • (04/30/94)

88 **CHATEAU MONTELENA** Chardonnay Napa Valley 1972-1992 Anniversary 1992 • $23 • (06/15/95)

88 **CHATEAU ST. JEAN** Chardonnay Alexander Valley Robert Young Vineyards 1992 • $22 • (05/15/94)

88 **CHATEAU WOLTNER** Chardonnay Howell Mountain St. Thomas Vineyard 1992 • $23 • (06/30/94)

88 **CHATEAU WOLTNER** Chardonnay Howell Mountain Titus Vineyard 1992 • $40 • (06/30/94)

88 **CRONIN** Chardonnay Napa Valley 1992 • $18 • (11/15/94)

88 **CRONIN** Chardonnay Alexander Valley Stuhlmuller Vineyard 1992 • $18 • (11/15/94)

88 **CRONIN** Chardonnay Santa Cruz Mountains 1992 • $22 • (11/15/94)

88 **CUVAISON** Chardonnay Carneros Napa Valley Reserve 1992 • $25 • (05/15/95)

88 **DUNNEWOOD** Chardonnay Carneros Gold Label Select 1992 • $9 • (06/30/94) • BB

88 **ESTANCIA** Chardonnay Monterey County 1992 • $8 • (02/28/94) • SS

88 **FESS PARKER** Chardonnay Santa Barbara County Reserve 1992 • $16 • (04/30/94)

88 **FLORA SPRINGS** Chardonnay Napa Valley Barrel Fermented 1992 • $23 • (06/30/94)

88 **GARY FARRELL** Chardonnay Russian River Valley Allen Vineyard 1992 • $18 • (06/15/94)

88 **GIRARD** Chardonnay Napa Valley Estate 1992 • $18 • (06/30/94)

88 **GRGICH HILLS** Chardonnay Napa Valley 1992 • $24 • (12/15/94)

88 **HIDDEN CELLARS** Chardonnay Mendocino County 1992 • $12 • (02/28/94)

88 **JOSEPH PHELPS** Chardonnay Los Carneros 1992 • $17 • (05/15/94)

88 **KENT RASMUSSEN** Chardonnay Napa Valley 1992 • $19 • (12/31/94)

88 **KUNDE** Chardonnay Sonoma Valley 1992 • $14 • (06/30/94)

88 **LA CREMA** Chardonnay California Reserve 1992 • $20 • (06/30/94)

88 **LAURIER** Chardonnay Sonoma County 1992 • $15 • (06/30/94)

88 **LIPARITA** Chardonnay Howell Mountain 1992 • $16 • (06/15/94)

88 **LYETH** Chardonnay Sonoma County 1992 • $12 • (06/30/94)

88 **MATANZAS CREEK** Chardonnay Sonoma Valley 1992 • $22 • (11/15/94)

88 **MAYACAMAS** Chardonnay Napa Valley 1992 • $16 • (08/31/95)

88 **MAZZOCCO** Chardonnay Sonoma County Winemaker's Select 1992 • $18 • (10/15/95)

88 **MERRYVALE** Chardonnay Napa Valley Starmont 1992 • $16 • (06/30/94)

88 **MORGAN** Chardonnay Monterey Reserve 1992 • $25 • (04/30/95)

88 **MOUNT VEEDER** Chardonnay Napa Valley 1992 • $14 • (06/30/94)

88 **MUELLER** Chardonnay Russian River Valley LB Barrel Fermented 1992 • $13 • (12/15/94)

88 **OAKVILLE RANCH** Chardonnay Napa Valley ORV 1992 • $24 • (09/30/94)

88 **OJAI** Chardonnay Santa Barbara County 1992 • $15 • (12/31/93)

88 **OJAI** Chardonnay Arroyo Grande Valley Reserve 1992 • $21 • (01/31/95)

88 **PRIDE** Chardonnay Napa Valley 1992 • $18 • (02/28/94)

88 **ROBERT MONDAVI** Chardonnay Napa Valley 1992 • $15 • (06/15/94)

88 **ROMBAUER** Chardonnay Carneros 1992 • $16 • (11/15/94)

88 **SANFORD** Chardonnay Santa Barbara County 1992 • $16 • (06/30/94)

88 **SANFORD** Chardonnay Santa Ynez Valley 1992 • $24 • (05/15/95)

88 **SEQUOIA GROVE** Chardonnay Napa Valley Estate Reserve 1992 • $19 • (03/31/95)

88 **SIGNORELLO** Chardonnay Napa Valley Founder's Reserve 1992 • $28 • (06/30/94)

88 **SARAH'S VINEYARD** Chardonnay Santa Clara County Lot II 1992 • $24 • (07/31/95)

88 **SONOMA-CUTRER** Chardonnay Sonoma Coast Cutrer Vineyard 1992 • $21 • (07/31/95)

88 **VENTANA** Chardonnay Monterey Gold Stripe Selection 1992 • $12 • (06/30/95)

88 **VICHON** Chardonnay Napa Valley 1992 • $14 • (06/15/94)

88 **WILLIAM HILL** Chardonnay Napa Valley 1992 • $13 • (01/31/95)

88 **WILLIAMS SELYEM** Chardonnay Russian River Valley Allen Vineyard 1992 • $30 • (04/30/94)

87 **ACACIA** Chardonnay Carneros 1992 • $16 • (06/30/94)

87 **AU BON CLIMAT** Chardonnay Santa Ynez Valley Sanford & Benedict Reserve 1992 • $35 • (07/31/95)

87 **B.R. COHN** Chardonnay Sonoma Valley Carneros 1992 • $12 • (11/30/93)

87 **BELVEDERE** Chardonnay Alexander Valley 1992 • $9 • (11/15/94) • BB

87 **BERINGER** Chardonnay Napa Valley 1992 • $10 • (05/31/94)

87 **CAKEBREAD** Chardonnay Napa Valley 1992 • $23 • (06/30/94)

87 **CLOS LACHANCE** Chardonnay Santa Cruz Mountains 1992 • $18 • (06/30/94)

87 **CAKEBREAD** Chardonnay Napa Valley Reserve 1992 • $30 • (07/31/95)

87 **DE LORIMIER** Chardonnay Alexander Valley Clonal Select 1992 • $20 • (02/28/95)

87 **DOMAINE HILL & MAYES** Chardonnay Napa Valley Clos Fontaine du Mont 1992 • $20 • (12/31/94)

87 **DURNEY** Chardonnay Carmel Valley Dances On Your Palate 1992 • $18 • (02/29/96)

87 **ELKHORN PEAK** Chardonnay Napa Valley Fagan Creek Vineyards 1992 • $15 • (12/15/94)

87 **FRANCISCAN** Chardonnay Napa Valley Oakville Estate 1992 • $11 • (06/30/94)

87 **FISHER** Chardonnay Sonoma County Whitney's Vineyard 1992 • $26 • (07/31/95)

87 **HANZELL** Chardonnay Sonoma Valley 1992 • $25 • (10/31/95)

87 **HARRISON** Chardonnay Napa Valley 1992 • $24 • (06/30/94)

87 **HOP KILN** Chardonnay Russian River Valley 1992 • $15 • (06/30/94)

87 **HERON LAKE** Chardonnay Wild Horse Valley 1992 • $12 • (07/31/95)

87 **JEPSON** Chardonnay Mendocino 1992 • $14 • (02/28/95)

87 **KEENAN** Chardonnay Napa Valley 1992 • $15 • (12/31/94)

87 **KENDALL-JACKSON** Chardonnay California Grand Reserve 1992 • $22 • (06/30/94)

87 **KENWOOD** Chardonnay Sonoma Valley Reserve 1992 • $18 • (06/30/94)

87 **KONOCTI** Chardonnay California Mount Konocti Reserve 1992 • $15 • (02/28/94)

87 **LA CREMA** Chardonnay California 1992 • $12 • (06/30/94)

87 **LANDMARK** Chardonnay Sonoma County Overlook 1992 • $12 • (03/31/94)

87 **LAZY CREEK** Chardonnay Anderson Valley 1992 • $9 • (04/15/94)

87 **LONGORIA** Chardonnay Santa Barbara County 1992 • $18 • (07/31/95)

87 **MILL CREEK** Chardonnay Dry Creek Valley 1992 • $12 • (02/28/94)

87 **MONT ST. JOHN** Chardonnay Carneros Madonna Vineyards 1992 • $18 • (06/30/94)

87 **MONTICELLO** Chardonnay Napa Valley Corley Reserve 1992 • $18 • (06/30/94)

87 **MIRASSOU** Chardonnay Santa Clara County 140th Anniversary Selection Anniversary Bottling 1992 • $14 • (07/31/95)

87 **MIRASSOU** Chardonnay Monterey County Fifth Generation Harvest Reserve 1992 • $12 • (07/31/95)

87 **NAVARRO** Chardonnay Anderson Valley Première Reserve 1992 • $15 • (11/30/94)

87 **NEWTON** Chardonnay Napa Valley 1992 • $16 • (03/15/94)

87 **OAKVILLE RANCH** Chardonnay Napa Valley Vista Vineyards 1992 • $18 • (06/30/94)

87 **RAYMOND** Chardonnay Napa Valley Private Reserve 1992 • $18 • (04/30/95)

87 **ROBERT MONDAVI** Chardonnay Central Coast Coastal 1992 • $11 • (09/15/94)

87 **ROBERT SINSKEY** Chardonnay Los Carneros 1992 • $20 • (06/30/94)

87 **SEAVEY** Chardonnay Napa Valley 1992 • $16 • (03/31/95)

87 **SEGHESIO** Chardonnay Sonoma County 1992 • $9 • (03/31/94) • BB

87 **SILVERADO** Chardonnay Napa Valley 1992 • $16 • (04/30/94)

87 **SILVERADO HILL CELLARS** Chardonnay Napa Valley 1992 • $10 • (06/30/94) • BB

87 **SONOMA CREEK** Chardonnay Carneros Organically Grown 1992 • $15 • (12/15/94)

87 **THE NEGOCIANTS** Chardonnay Central Coast 1992 • $6 • (11/30/94) • BB

87 **WHITE ROCK** Chardonnay Napa Valley 1992 • $17 • (06/30/94)

87 **WILLIAM WHEELER** Chardonnay Sonoma County 1992 • $11 • (04/30/94)

87 **WINTERBROOK** Chardonnay Napa Valley Grand Reserve 1992 • $15 • (02/28/95)

86 **BANNISTER** Chardonnay Russian River Valley Allen Vineyard 1992 • $17 • (04/30/94)

86 **BEAULIEU** Chardonnay Carneros 1992 • $10 • (06/30/94) • BB

86 **BOUCHAINE** Chardonnay Carneros 1992 • $15 • (02/28/95)

86 **BANCROFT** Chardonnay Howell Mountain 1992 • $16 • (07/31/95)

86 **BOGLE** Chardonnay California Barrel Fermented Reserve 1992 • $10 • (07/31/95)

86 **CHATEAU SOUVERAIN** Chardonnay Russian River Valley Allen Vineyard Reserve 1992 • $14 • (06/30/94)

86 **CINNABAR** Chardonnay Santa Cruz Mountains 1992 • $20 • (03/31/95)

86 **CONCANNON** Chardonnay Central Coast Selected Vineyards 1992 • $11 • (05/15/94)

86 **COSENTINO** Chardonnay Napa County 1992 • $15 • (03/31/94)

86 **COTES DE SONOMA** Chardonnay Sonoma County 1992 • $7 • (07/15/93) • BB

86 **CRONIN** Chardonnay Monterey County Ventana Vineyard 1992 • $18 • (04/15/95)

86 **DRY CREEK** Chardonnay Sonoma County Barrel Fermented Reserve 1992 • $16 • (07/31/95)

86 **EL MOLINO** Chardonnay Napa County 1992 • $30 • (06/30/94)

86 **FAR NIENTE** Chardonnay Napa Valley 1992 • $30 • (06/30/94)

86 **FIRESTONE** Chardonnay Santa Ynez Valley Barrel Fermented 1992 • $12 • (11/30/93)

86 **FISHER** Chardonnay Sonoma County Coach Insignia 1992 • $16 • (06/30/94)

86 **FORMAN** Chardonnay Napa Valley 1992 • $22 • (03/31/94)

86 **FOSS CREEK** Chardonnay Central Coast Barrel Fermented 1992 • $7 • (01/31/95)

86 **GAVILAN** Chardonnay Chalone Gavilan 1992 • $13 • (02/28/94)

86 **IRON HORSE** Chardonnay Sonoma County Green Valley Lot #2 1992 • $17 • (06/30/94)

86 **JORY** Chardonnay Santa Clara County Selected Clone 1992 • $17 • (06/30/94)

86 **JORDAN** Chardonnay Alexander Valley 1992 • $21 • (07/31/95)

86 **LOUIS M. MARTINI** Chardonnay Napa Valley 1992 • $8 • (11/15/94) • BB

86 **MACROSTIE** Chardonnay Carneros 1992 • $16 • (06/30/94)

86 **MCDOWELL** Chardonnay Mendocino 1992 • $9 • (01/31/94)

86 **MERIDIAN** Chardonnay Edna Valley 1992 • $14 • (06/30/94)

86 **MURPHY-GOODE** Chardonnay Alexander Valley Barrel Fermented 1992 • $13 • (03/15/94)

86 **NAPA RIDGE** Chardonnay North Coast Coastal Reserve 1992 • $13 • (05/31/94)

86 **NAVARRO** Chardonnay Anderson Valley Table Wine 1992 • $7 • (04/15/94) • BB

86 **NEWLAN** Chardonnay Napa Valley Napa-Villages 1992 • $10 • (09/30/95)

86 **OJAI** Chardonnay Santa Barbara County Reserve 1992 • $21 • (01/31/95)

86 **PAGE MILL** Chardonnay Santa Clara County Elizabeth Garbett Vineyard 1992 • $17 • (07/15/93)

86 **PAHLMEYER** Chardonnay Napa Valley Not Filtered 1992 • $26 • (11/15/94)

86 **PINE RIDGE** Chardonnay Napa Valley Knollside Cuvée 1992 • $14 • (06/30/95)

86 **RUTHERFORD RANCH** Chardonnay Napa Valley 1992 • $9 • (05/31/95) • BB

86 **SEQUOIA GROVE** Chardonnay Carneros Napa Valley 1992 • $14 • (06/30/94)

86 **SHAFER** Chardonnay Napa Valley Barrel Select 1992 • $16 • (03/31/94)

86 **STEELE** Chardonnay Mendocino DuPratt Vineyard 1992 • $22 • (06/30/94)

86 **TAFT STREET** Chardonnay Sonoma County 1992 • $8 • (04/30/94) • BB

86 **WHITEHALL LANE** Chardonnay Napa Valley 1992 • $11 • (02/28/94)

85 **ARROWOOD** Chardonnay Sonoma County Cuvée Michel Berthoud 1992 • $24 • (06/30/94)

85 **ALDERBROOK** Chardonnay Dry Creek Valley 1992 • $15 • (07/31/95)

85 **BANDIERA** Chardonnay Napa Valley 1992 • $6 • (05/15/94) • BB

85 **BEAUCANON** Chardonnay Napa Valley 1992 • $11 • (02/28/94)

85 **BENZIGER** Chardonnay Sonoma County 1992 • $13 • (05/31/94)

85 **BOISSET** Chardonnay Sonoma County 1992 • $15 • (06/30/94)

85 **CHALONE** Chardonnay Chalone 1992 • $26 • (01/31/94)

85 **CHAPPELLET** Chardonnay Napa Valley 1992 • $14 • (12/31/94)

85 **CHATEAU DE BAUN** Chardonnay Russian River Valley 1992 • $10 • (04/15/94) • BB

85 **CIRRI** Chardonnay Carneros 1992 • $11 • (06/30/94)

85 **CLOS DU BOIS** Chardonnay Alexander Valley Barrel Fermented 1992 • $12 • (03/15/94)

85 **DE LORIMIER** Chardonnay Alexander Valley 1992 • $15 • (02/28/95)

85 **FESS PARKER** Chardonnay Santa Barbara County 1992 • $15 • (02/28/94)

85 **FETZER** Chardonnay Mendocino County Barrel Select 1992 • $11 • (04/15/94)

85 **FETZER** Chardonnay Mendocino County Bonterra Organically Grown Grapes 1992 • $9 • (04/15/94) • BB

85 **FOXEN** Chardonnay Santa Maria Valley 1992 • $20 • (04/15/94)

85 **HAGAFEN** Chardonnay Napa Valley 1992 • $14 • (06/30/94)

85 **HANNA** Chardonnay Russian River Valley Reserve 1992 • $16 • (02/28/95)

85 **HUSCH** Chardonnay Anderson Valley Special Reserve 1992 • $18 • (07/31/95)

85 **J. FRITZ** Chardonnay Russian River Valley Barrel Select 1992 • $18 • (07/31/95)

85 **J. LOHR** Chardonnay Monterey Riverstone 1992 • $12 • (05/15/94)

85 **KENWOOD** Chardonnay Sonoma Valley Yulupa Vineyard 1992 • $14 • (06/30/94)

85 **LEEWARD** Chardonnay Edna Valley Reserve 1992 • $15 • (06/30/94)

85 **MAZZOCCO** Chardonnay Sonoma County River Lane 1992 • $15 • (06/30/94)

85 **MERIDIAN** Chardonnay Santa Barbara County 1992 • $10 • (03/15/94)

85 **MIRASSOU** Chardonnay Monterey County Harvest Reserve 1992 • $12 • (05/31/94)

85 **MONT ST. JOHN** Chardonnay Carneros Organically Grown Grapes 1992 • $13 • (06/30/94)

85 **MORGAN** Chardonnay Monterey 1992 • $15 • (12/31/93)

85 **OPTIMA** Chardonnay Sonoma County 1992 • $25 • (04/30/94)

85 **PEJU** Chardonnay Napa Valley 1992 • $14 • (06/30/94)
85 **PETER MCCOY** Chardonnay Knights Valley Clos des Pierres 1992 • $19 • (07/31/95)
85 **RAYMOND** Chardonnay Napa Valley 1992 • $14 • (04/30/95)
85 **ROCHE** Chardonnay Carneros Barrel Select Reserve 1992 • $20 • (06/30/94)
85 **RODNEY STRONG** Chardonnay Chalk Hill Chalk Hill Vineyard 1992 • $13 • (06/30/94)
85 **ROBERT PEPI** Chardonnay Napa Valley Puncheon Fermented 1992 • $15 • (07/31/95)
85 **S. ANDERSON** Chardonnay Stags Leap District 1992 • $20 • (06/30/94)
85 **SAINT GREGORY** Chardonnay Mendocino 1992 • $12 • (04/15/95)
85 **SAINTSBURY** Chardonnay Carneros 1992 • $15 • (06/30/94)
85 **VOSS** Chardonnay Napa Valley 1992 • $13 • (02/28/95)
85 **WHITCRAFT** Chardonnay Santa Maria Valley Bien Nacido Vineyard 1992 • $20 • (12/31/93)
85 **WILLIAM HILL** Chardonnay Napa Valley Reserve 1992 • $18 • (01/31/95)
85 **WILSON DANIELS** Chardonnay Napa Valley 1992 • $10 • (01/31/95)
85 **WENTE BROS.** Chardonnay Arroyo Seco Riva Ranch 1992 • $12 • (07/31/95)
85 **ZACA MESA** Chardonnay Santa Barbara County Chapel Vineyard 1992 • $16 • (06/30/94)
84 **ALEXANDER VALLEY VINEYARDS** Chardonnay Alexander Valley Wetzel Family Estate 1992 • $11 • (05/15/95)
84 **ADLER FELS** Chardonnay Sonoma County 1992 • $12 • (07/31/95)
84 **BOUCHAINE** Chardonnay California Q.C. Fly 1992 • $8 • (04/15/95)
84 **BRUTOCAO** Chardonnay Mendocino Bliss Vineyards 1992 • $10 • (06/30/94)
84 **CANYON ROAD** Chardonnay California 1992 • $7 • (06/15/93) • BB
84 **CARNEROS CREEK** Chardonnay Los Carneros 1992 • $14 • (06/30/94)
84 **CASTORO** Chardonnay San Luis Obispo County 1992 • $10 • (07/15/93)
84 **CHALK HILL** Chardonnay Chalk Hill 1992 • $18 • (05/15/94)
84 **CHARLES KRUG** Chardonnay Napa Valley 1992 • $12 • (03/31/94)
84 **CHATEAU SOUVERAIN** Chardonnay Sonoma County Barrel Fermented 1992 • $11 • (06/30/94)
84 **CHATEAU ST. JEAN** Chardonnay Sonoma County 1992 • $12 • (11/15/94)
84 **CHATEAU WOLTNER** Chardonnay Howell Mountain 1992 • $10 • (09/15/93)
84 **CLOS DU VAL** Chardonnay Carneros 1992 • $15 • (01/31/95)
84 **CLOS PEGASE** Chardonnay Napa Valley 1992 • $9 • (06/30/94) • BB
84 **COASTAL CELLARS** Chardonnay California 1992 • $5 • (07/31/95)
84 **DAVIS BYNUM** Chardonnay Russian River Valley Allen-Griffen Vineyards 1992 • $17 • (04/30/94)
84 **DEHLINGER** Chardonnay Russian River Valley 1992 • $15 • (06/30/94)
84 **EDNA VALLEY** Chardonnay Edna Valley 1992 • $15 • (06/30/94)
84 **GROVE STREET** Chardonnay Sonoma County Vintage Select 1992 • $7 • (05/15/95)
84 **GUENOC** Chardonnay Guenoc Valley 1992 • $15 • (02/28/94)
84 **HACIENDA** Chardonnay California Clair de Lune 1992 • $7 • (06/30/94)
84 **HANNA** Chardonnay Sonoma County 1992 • $14 • (04/30/95)
84 **HART'S DESIRE** Chardonnay Edna Valley MacGregor Vineyard 1992 • $14 • (03/31/95)
84 **HAYWOOD** Chardonnay California Vintner's Select 1992 • $8 • (06/30/94) • BB
84 **HESS SELECT** Chardonnay California 1992 • $9 • (03/31/94)
84 **HIDDEN CELLARS** Chardonnay Mendocino County Organically Grown Grapes 1992 • $14 • (03/31/94)
84 **HUSCH** Chardonnay Mendocino 1992 • $11 • (03/15/94)
84 **HANDLEY** Chardonnay Dry Creek Valley 1992 • $16 • (07/31/95)
84 **LA CROSSE** Chardonnay Napa Valley 1992 • $6 • (05/31/94) • BB
84 **LOCKWOOD** Chardonnay Monterey 1992 • $10 • (05/31/94)
84 **LOGAN** Chardonnay Monterey 1992 • $14 • (06/30/94)
84 **M.G. VALLEJO** Chardonnay California Harvest Select 1992 • $6 • (03/31/95) • BB
84 **MADRONA** Chardonnay El Dorado 1992 • $12 • (06/30/94)
84 **MERRYVALE** Chardonnay Napa Valley Reserve 1992 • $25 • (06/30/94)
84 **MICHAEL SULLBERG** Chardonnay Sonoma County 1992 • $6 • (06/30/94) • BB
84 **MONTEREY VINEYARD** Chardonnay Monterey County Classic 1992 • $6 • (06/30/93) • BB
84 **MOUNT PALOMAR** Chardonnay Temecula Reserve 1992 • $16 • (06/30/94)
84 **NOMINEE** Chardonnay Paso Robles Central Coast 1992 • $6 • (03/31/93) • BB
84 **OLIVET LANE** Chardonnay Russian River Valley 1992 • $12 • (03/15/94)
84 **ORFILA VINEYARDS** Chardonnay California Barrel Fermented 1992 • $10 • (05/31/95)
84 **RAYMOND** Chardonnay California Amberhill California Selection 1992 • $11 • (05/15/94)
84 **SHOOTING STAR** Chardonnay Mendocino 1992 • $9 • (06/30/94) • BB
84 **SONOMA-LOEB** Chardonnay Sonoma County 1992 • $15 • (03/31/94)
84 **ST. FRANCIS** Chardonnay Sonoma County 1992 • $10 • (05/31/94)
84 **STERLING** Chardonnay Napa Valley Diamond Mountain Ranch Vineyard 1992 • $18 • (04/30/95)
84 **STE. CLAIRE** Chardonnay California Barrel Select 1992 • $11 • (07/31/95)
84 **WENTE BROS.** Chardonnay Central Coast Estate Grown 1992 • $9 • (07/15/93) • BB
84 **WINDEMERE** Chardonnay Edna Valley Mac Gregor Vineyard 1992 • $11 • (03/15/94)
83 **BEAULIEU** Chardonnay Napa Valley Beautour 1992 • $8 • (06/30/94)
83 **BETTINELLI** Chardonnay Napa Valley 1992 • $11 • (07/31/95)
83 **BROTHER & SISTER WINERY** Chardonnay Central Coast Epoch 1992 • $5 • (07/31/95)
83 **BUENA VISTA** Chardonnay Carneros 1992 • $10 • (12/31/94)
83 **BURGESS** Chardonnay Napa Valley Triere Vineyard 1992 • $16 • (06/30/94)
83 **CALLAWAY** Chardonnay Temecula Hawk Watch Classic Sur Lie Style Calla-Lees 1992 • $8 • (04/15/95)
83 **CHATEAU CHEVRE** Chardonnay Napa Valley 1992 • $11 • (06/30/94)

83 **COLBY** Chardonnay Napa Valley 1992 • $12 • (05/15/95)

83 **DE MOOR** Chardonnay Napa Valley 1992 • $12 • (06/30/94)

83 **DUNNEWOOD** Chardonnay North Coast Barrel Select 1992 • $7 • (06/30/94) • BB

83 **EBERLE** Chardonnay Paso Robles 1992 • $12 • (06/30/94)

83 **FARELLA-PARK** Chardonnay Napa Valley Barrel Fermented 1992 • $14 • (02/28/95)

83 **FETZER** Chardonnay California Sundial 1992 • $8 • (06/30/94) • BB

83 **FLORA SPRINGS** Chardonnay Napa Valley Floréal 1992 • $11 • (06/30/94)

83 **FROG'S LEAP** Chardonnay Carneros 1992 • $16 • (06/30/94)

83 **FREEMARK ABBEY** Chardonnay Napa Valley 1992 • $16 • (07/31/95)

83 **GABRIELLI** Chardonnay Mendocino Reserve 1992 • $20 • (06/30/94)

83 **GROTH** Chardonnay Napa Valley 1992 • $14 • (03/31/94)

83 **HANDLEY** Chardonnay Anderson Valley 1992 • $12 • (07/31/95)

83 **J. LOHR** Chardonnay California Cypress 1992 • $8 • (06/30/94) • BB

83 **JORY** Chardonnay California White Zeppelin Blimp de Blanc 1992 • $10 • (06/30/94)

83 **KENWOOD** Chardonnay Sonoma Valley 1992 • $14 • (06/30/94)

83 **LAWRENCE J. BARGETTO** Chardonnay Santa Cruz Mountains 1992 • $16 • (01/31/95)

83 **LIMUR** Chardonnay Napa Valley 1992 • $16 • (06/30/94)

83 **LOCKWOOD** Chardonnay Monterey Partners Reserve 1992 • $18 • (07/31/95)

83 **MICHEL-SCHLUMBERGER** Chardonnay Dry Creek Valley 1992 • $18 • (03/31/95)

83 **MOUNT MADRONA** Chardonnay Napa Valley Certified Kosher 1992 • $14 • (07/31/95)

83 **NEVADA CITY** Chardonnay Nevada County Barrel Fermented 1992 • $10 • (06/30/94)

83 **PEJU** Chardonnay Napa Valley HB Vineyard 1992 • $18 • (06/30/94)

83 **R.H. PHILLIPS** Chardonnay California Barrel Cuvée 1992 • $8 • (06/15/94) • BB

83 **RUTHERFORD HILL** Chardonnay Napa Valley Exceptional Vineyard Selection Reserve 1992 • $20 • (07/31/95)

83 **SEBASTIANI** Chardonnay Sonoma County 1992 • $12 • (06/30/94)

83 **SONOMA-CUTRER** Chardonnay Sonoma Coast Russian River Ranches 1992 • $14 • (06/30/94)

83 **ST. ANDREW'S VINEYARD** Chardonnay Napa Valley 1992 • $10 • (06/30/94)

83 **ST. SUPERY** Chardonnay Napa Valley Dollarhide Ranch 1992 • $12 • (06/30/94)

83 **SODA CANYON** Chardonnay Napa Valley 14th Leaf 1992 • $10 • (07/31/95)

83 **STONY HILL** Chardonnay Napa Valley 1992 • $30 • (07/31/95)

83 **TERRA** Chardonnay Carneros 1992 • $16

83 **TREFETHEN** Chardonnay Napa Valley 1992 • $18 • (06/30/94)

82 **ARMIDA** Chardonnay Russian River Valley 1992 • $10 • (06/30/94)

82 **CALISTOGA VINEYARDS** Chardonnay Napa Valley 1992 • $11 • (07/31/95)

82 **CARMENET** Chardonnay Carneros Sonoma Valley Sangiacomo Vineyard 1992 • $17 • (06/30/94)

82 **CHIMNEY ROCK** Chardonnay Stags Leap District 1992 • $15 • (06/30/94)

82 **CORBETT CANYON** Chardonnay Santa Barbara County Reserve 1992 • $9 • (06/30/94)

82 **ESTATE WILLIAM BACCALA** Chardonnay Sonoma County 1992 • $11 • (06/30/94)

82 **ESTRELLA RIVER** Chardonnay California Proprietor's Reserve 1992 • $6 • (06/30/94) • BB

82 **FLEUR DE CARNEROS** Chardonnay California 1992 • $9 • (06/30/94)

82 **GUGLIELMO** Chardonnay Monterey County 1992 • $8 • (03/31/94)

82 **HARMONY CELLARS** Chardonnay Paso Robles 1992 • $11 • (06/30/94)

82 **IVÁN TAMÁS** Chardonnay Livermore Valley Hayes Ranch 1992 • $8 • (07/31/95)

82 **JORY** Chardonnay Santa Clara County Selected Clone 1992 • $17 • (02/28/94)

82 **KORBEL** Chardonnay Sonoma County 1992 • $10 • (06/30/94)

82 **KUNDE** Chardonnay Sonoma Valley Wildwood Vineyard 1992 • $17 • (06/30/94)

82 **KUNDE** Chardonnay Sonoma Valley Kinneybrook Vineyard 1992 • $17 • (06/30/94)

82 **LA TOURNELLE** Chardonnay Monterey 1992 • $8 • (01/31/94)

82 **LANDMARK** Chardonnay Alexander Valley Damaris Reserve 1992 • $16 • (06/30/94)

82 **LAWRENCE J. BARGETTO** Chardonnay Central Coast Cypress 1992 • $9 • (01/31/95)

82 **LEEWARD** Chardonnay Central Coast 1992 • $11 • (06/30/94)

82 **MARION** Chardonnay Sonoma County 1992 • $8 • (09/15/93)

82 **MONTEREY VINEYARD** Chardonnay Monterey County Classic 1992 • $6 • (06/30/94) • BB

82 **RABBIT RIDGE** Chardonnay Sonoma County 1992 • $12 • (06/30/94)

82 **RODNEY STRONG** Chardonnay Sonoma County 1992 • $10 • (10/15/93)

82 **SCHUG** Chardonnay Sonoma Valley 1992 • $12 • (06/30/94)

82 **STEPHEN ZELLERBACH** Chardonnay California 1992 • $9 • (03/31/94)

82 **THOMAS FOGARTY** Chardonnay Santa Cruz Mountains 1992 • $16 • (07/31/95)

82 **V. SATTUI** Chardonnay Napa Valley 1992 • $14 • (06/30/94)

82 **ZODIAC** Chardonnay California Pisces 1992 • $6 • (04/15/94)

81 **ADLER FELS** Chardonnay Sonoma County Coleman Reserve 1992 • $14 • (07/31/95)

81 **BOGLE** Chardonnay California 1992 • $6 • (06/15/94)

81 **BRINDIAMO** Chardonnay California 1992 • $8 • (06/15/94)

81 **COSENTINO** Chardonnay Napa Valley The Sculptor 1992 • $20 • (06/30/94)

81 **FIELDBROOK** Chardonnay Mendocino County Redwood Valley Vineyard 1992 • $12 • (02/28/95)

81 **FOSS CREEK** Chardonnay Sonoma County 85% Barrel Fermented 1992 • $6 • (01/31/95)

81 **GLEN ELLEN** Chardonnay California Proprietor's Reserve 1992 • $6 • (07/15/93) • BB

81 **JOULLIAN** Chardonnay Monterey 1992 • $11 • (06/30/94)

81 **KARLY** Chardonnay Edna Valley MacGregor Vineyard 1992 • $14 • (06/30/94)

81 **LA CASA SENA** Chardonnay Monterey 1992 • $20 • (12/31/93)

81 **LAKESPRING** Chardonnay Napa Valley 1992 • $10 • (06/30/94)

81 **LEEWARD** Chardonnay Ventura County 1992 • $12 • (06/30/94)

81 **ROUND HILL** Chardonnay California 1992 • $7 • (01/31/94)

81 **ROUND HILL** Chardonnay Napa Valley Van Asperen Selection Reserve 1992 • $12 • (06/30/94)

81 **STERLING** Chardonnay Napa Valley 1992 • $14 • (06/30/94)

80 **BEL ARBORS** Chardonnay California Founder's Selection 1992 • $6 • (07/15/93)

80 **BONVERRE** Chardonnay California Lot Number 14 1992 • $7 • (02/28/95)

80 **CLONINGER** Chardonnay Monterey 1992 • $11 • (04/30/96)

80 **DRY CREEK** Chardonnay Sonoma County Barrel Fermented 1992 • $14 • (06/30/94)

80 **FETZER** Chardonnay California Sundial 1992 • $8 • (07/15/93)

80 **FIELD STONE** Chardonnay Sonoma County 1992 • $14 • (06/30/94)

80 **FREMONT CREEK** Chardonnay Mendocino Napa Counties Beckstoffer Vineyards 1992 • $9 • (06/30/94)

80 **GABRIELLI** Chardonnay Mendocino 1992 • $14 • (06/30/94)

80 **GEYSER PEAK** Chardonnay Sonoma County 1992 • $10 • (03/15/94)

80 **GREEN & RED** Chardonnay Napa Valley Catacula Vineyard 1992 • $15 • (06/30/94)

80 **JEKEL** Chardonnay Arroyo Seco Gravelstone 1992 • $10 • (06/30/94)

80 **KENDALL-JACKSON** Chardonnay California Vintner's Reserve 1992 • $13 • (07/15/93)

80 **LAMBERT BRIDGE** Chardonnay Sonoma County 1992 • $13 • (06/30/94)

80 **MAACAMA CREEK** Chardonnay Alexander Valley Melim Vineyard Reserve 1992 • $10 • (06/30/94)

80 **MACKINAW** Chardonnay California 1992 • $9 • (01/31/94)

80 **MADDALENA** Chardonnay Central Coast 1992 • $7 • (06/30/94)

80 **MONTERRA** Chardonnay California 1992 • $7 • (06/30/94)

80 **NAPA RIDGE** Chardonnay North Coast Coastal Vines 1992 • $8 • (06/30/94)

80 **P AND M STAIGER** Chardonnay Santa Cruz Mountains 1992 • $12 • (06/30/94)

80 **REVERE** Chardonnay Napa Valley Berlenbach Vineyards 1992 • $20 • (06/30/94)

80 **REVERE** Chardonnay Napa Valley Reserve 1992 • $22 • (06/30/94)

80 **ROBERT MONDAVI** Chardonnay California Woodbridge 1992 • $8 • (01/31/94)

80 **RUTHERFORD ESTATE** Chardonnay Napa Valley 1992 • $7 • (06/30/94)

80 **SCHUG** Chardonnay Carneros Barrel Fermented 1992 • $16 • (06/30/94)

80 **THE NEGOCIANTS** Chardonnay Central Coast Barrel Fermented 1992 • $7 • (12/15/94)

80 **TWIN HILLS RANCH** Chardonnay Paso Robles Reserve 1992 • $9 • (06/30/94)

80 **VICHON** Chardonnay California Coastal Selection 1992 • $10 • (09/30/94)

80 **YORK MOUNTAIN** Chardonnay San Luis Obispo County 1992 • $12 • (06/30/94)

79 **ARCIERO** Chardonnay Paso Robles 1992 • $8 • (06/30/94)

79 **AUDUBON** Chardonnay Sonoma County Carneros Sangiacomo Barrel Fermented 1992 • $12 • (06/30/94)

79 **BON MARCHE** Chardonnay Sonoma County 1992 • $8 • (01/31/94)

79 **CK MONDAVI** Chardonnay California 1992 • $6 • (06/30/94)

79 **CORBETT CANYON** Chardonnay Central Coast Coastal Classic 1992 • $5 • (03/31/94)

79 **J. PEDRONCELLI** Chardonnay Dry Creek Valley 1992 • $10 • (06/30/94)

79 **KINDERWOOD** Chardonnay Monterey County 1992 • $6 • (06/30/94)

79 **MICHAEL SULLBERG** Chardonnay Central Coast Barrel Fermented 1992 • $6 • (06/30/94)

79 **PAGE MILL** Chardonnay California Cuvee Select 1992 • $24 • (07/15/93)

79 **RIVERSIDE FARM** Chardonnay California 1992 • $6 • (06/30/94)

79 **RIVERSIDE VINEYARDS** Chardonnay California 1992 • $7 • (06/30/94)

79 **STEVENOT** Chardonnay California 1992 • $8 • (09/15/93)

79 **SUTTER HOME** Chardonnay California 1992 • $6 • (01/31/94)

79 **TOPOLOS** Chardonnay Sonoma County Dry Farmed Sonoma Mountain Old Vines Bar 1992 • $12 • (06/30/94)

78 **BARON HERZOG** Chardonnay California 1992 • $11

78 **BRANDER** Chardonnay Santa Ynez Valley Tête de Cuvée 1992 • $15 • (06/30/94)

78 **CASTORO** Chardonnay San Luis Obispo County The Wine 1992 • $10 • (02/28/95)

78 **CHATEAU DE LEU** Chardonnay Solano County Green Valley 1992 • $10 • (06/30/94)

78 **GRAESER** Chardonnay Napa Valley Silverado Summers Vineyard 1992 • $13 • (07/31/95)

78 **SONOMA MISSION** Chardonnay Sonoma County 1992 • $8 • (06/30/94)

78 **TRENTADUE** Chardonnay Alexander Valley 1992 • $10 • (06/30/94)

78 **WOODSIDE** Chardonnay Santa Cruz Mountains 1992 • $18 • (06/30/94)

77 **CRESTON** Chardonnay Paso Robles 1992 • $10 • (06/30/94)

77 **CHRISTINE WOODS** Chardonnay Anderson Valley Estate Reserve 1992 • $14 • (07/31/95)

77 **KONRAD** Chardonnay Mendocino 1992 • $11 • (02/28/95)

77 **ORGANIC WINE WORKS** Chardonnay Mendocino County Redwood Valley Vineyards 1992 • $12 • (04/15/93)

77 **THE NEGOCIANTS** Chardonnay Napa Valley Barrel Select 1992 • $6 • (01/31/94)

76 **FOREST LAKE** Chardonnay California 1992 • $6 • (06/30/94)

76 **HAWK CREST** Chardonnay California 1992 • $9 • (07/15/93)

76 **KONOCTI** Chardonnay California Mount Konocti Kelsey 1992 • $10 • (07/15/93)

76 **MEEKER** Chardonnay Dry Creek Valley White Table Wine Second Rack 1992 • $8 • (02/28/95)

76 **PEPPERWOOD GROVE** Chardonnay California 1992 • $6 • (07/15/93)

75 **FENESTRA** Chardonnay Livermore Valley Toy Vineyard 1992 • $12 • (06/30/94)

75 **GROVE STREET** Chardonnay Sonoma County 1992 • $6 • (06/30/94)

75 **MOUNTAIN VIEW** Chardonnay Monterey 1992 • $6 • (06/30/94)

74 **STEVENOT** Chardonnay Calaveras County Barrell Fermented 1992 • $11 • (06/30/94)

73 **BOGLE** Chardonnay California 1992 • $6 • (01/31/94)

73 **FOXHOLLOW** Chardonnay Monterey 1992 • $10 • (06/30/94)

73 **JOSEPH FILIPPI** Chardonnay Monterey Limited Release Winemaker's Reserve 1992 • $7 • (06/30/94)

73 **SADDLEBACK** Chardonnay Napa Valley Nils Venge 1992 • $13 • (06/30/94)

73 **TWIN HILLS RANCH** Chardonnay Paso Robles A Natural Wine 1992 • $6 • (06/30/94)

72 **MOUNT PALOMAR** Chardonnay Temecula 1992 • $10 • (06/30/94)

72 **MONTEREY PENINSULA** Chardonnay California 1992 • $10 • (07/31/95)

70 **MONTPELLIER** Chardonnay California 1992 • $8 • (06/30/94)

70 **SONOMA CREEK** Chardonnay Carneros Barrel Fermented 1992 • $10 • (09/30/94)

70 **WELLINGTON** Chardonnay Sonoma Valley Barrel Fermented 1992 • $11 • (06/30/94)

67 **STERLING** Chardonnay Carneros Napa Valley Winery Lake 1992 • $18 • (06/30/94)

65 **CILURZO** Chardonnay Temecula Barrel Fermented 1992 • $8 • (06/30/94)

62 **JANKRIS** Chardonnay Paso Robles 1992 • $10 • (06/30/94)

1991 California Chardonnay
Vintage Rating: 92

94 **PAHLMEYER** Chardonnay Napa Valley 1991 • $24 • (06/30/93)

92 **BERINGER** Chardonnay Napa Valley Sbragia Limited Release 1991 • $19 • (07/15/93)

92 **BYRON** Chardonnay Santa Barbara County 1991 • $14 • (05/31/93) • SS

92 **E. & J. GALLO** Chardonnay Northern Sonoma Estate 1991 • $30 • (06/30/93)

92 **KISTLER** Chardonnay Russian River Valley Vine Hill Vineyard 1991 • $32 • (05/31/93)

92 **PAUL HOBBS** Chardonnay Sonoma Mountain Dinner Vineyard 1991 • $27 • (12/31/93)

92 **SAINTSBURY** Chardonnay Carneros Reserve 1991 • $22 • (05/31/94)

92 **STEELE** Chardonnay Mendocino DuPratt Vineyard 1991 • $24 • (03/15/93)

91 **BYRON** Chardonnay Santa Maria Valley Estate 1991 • $23 • (04/30/94)

91 **CHALONE** Chardonnay Chalone 1991 • $29 • (12/31/92) • SS

91 **CHALONE** Chardonnay Chalone Reserve 1991 • $35 • (06/30/94)

91 **CHATEAU POTELLE** Chardonnay Mount Veeder V.G.S. 1991 • $32 • (06/15/95)

91 **CHATEAU ST. JEAN** Chardonnay Alexander Valley Robert Young Vineyards Reserve 1991 • $50 • (04/30/95)

91 **CRONIN** Chardonnay Santa Cruz Mountains 1991 • $20 • (08/31/93)

91 **DE LOACH** Chardonnay Russian River Valley O.F.S. 1991 • $25 • (07/15/93)

91 **FERRARI-CARANO** Chardonnay Alexander Valley 1991 • $20 • (06/30/93)

91 **FLORA SPRINGS** Chardonnay Napa Valley Barrel Fermented 1991 • $23 • (06/15/93) • SS

91 **FRANCISCAN** Chardonnay Napa Valley Oakville Estate Cuvée Sauvage 1991 • $25 • (07/15/93) • SS

91 **IRON HORSE** Chardonnay Sonoma County Green Valley 1991 • $18 • (04/30/93)

91 **KENWOOD** Chardonnay Sonoma Valley Reserve 1991 • $18 • (06/15/93)

91 **LANDMARK** Chardonnay Alexander Valley Damaris Reserve 1991 • $17 • (06/15/93)

91 **LONG** Chardonnay Napa Valley 1991 • $29 • (07/15/93)

91 **MERRYVALE** Chardonnay Napa Valley Reserve 1991 • $25 • (05/31/93)

91 **MUELLER** Chardonnay Russian River Valley Barrel Fermented 1991 • $13 • (10/15/93)

91 **NAVARRO** Chardonnay Anderson Valley Première Reserve 1991 • $15 • (10/31/93) • SS

91 **PATZ & HALL** Chardonnay Napa Valley 1991 • $24 • (12/15/92)

91 **ROCHIOLI** Chardonnay Russian River Valley J. Rochioli Reserve 1991 • $24 • (07/15/93)

91 **ROMBAUER** Chardonnay Carneros 1991 • $15 • (09/15/93) • SS

91 **SANFORD** Chardonnay Santa Barbara County 1991 • $18 • (03/15/93)

91 **SANFORD** Chardonnay Santa Barbara County Barrel Select 1991 • $30 • (06/30/93)

91 **SHAFER** Chardonnay Napa Valley Barrel Select 1991 • $15 • (03/15/93)

91 **SONOMA-LOEB** Chardonnay Sonoma County 1991 • $15 • (01/31/93)

91 **STAG'S LEAP WINE CELLARS** Chardonnay Napa Valley Reserve 1991 • $28 • (03/15/94)

91 **WENTE BROS.** Chardonnay Central Coast Estate Grown 1991 • $8 • (07/15/92) • SS

91 **WILLIAM WHEELER** Chardonnay Sonoma County 1991 • $13 • (04/15/93)

90 **BELVEDERE** Chardonnay Sonoma County Preferred Stock 1991 • $18 • (04/15/94)

90 **CARMENET** Chardonnay Carneros Sonoma Valley Sangiacomo Vineyard Private Selection 1991 • $17 • (06/30/93) • SS

90 **CHATEAU SOUVERAIN** Chardonnay Russian River Valley Allen Vineyard Reserve 1991 • $14 • (07/15/93)

90 **CHATEAU ST. JEAN** Chardonnay Alexander Valley Robert Young Vineyards 1991 • $22 • (05/15/94)

90 **CHATEAU WOLTNER** Chardonnay Howell Mountain Titus Vineyard 1991 • $40 • (09/15/93)

90 **CINNABAR** Chardonnay Santa Cruz Mountains 1991 • $20 • (02/28/94) • SS

90 **DOMAINE DE CLARCK** Chardonnay Carneros Première Réserve 1991 • $20 • (03/15/93)

90 **FERRARI-CARANO** Chardonnay Sonoma-Napa Counties Reserve 1991 • $28 • (04/30/94)

90 **FIRESTONE** Chardonnay Santa Ynez Valley Barrel Fermented 1991 • $13 • (02/15/93)

90 **FOREST HILL** Chardonnay Napa Valley Private Reserve 1991 • $26 • (07/15/93)

90 **GIRARD** Chardonnay Napa Valley Estate 1991 • $18 • (07/15/93)

90 **GLORIA FERRER** Chardonnay Carneros 1991 • $15 • (07/15/93)

90 **KENT RASMUSSEN** Chardonnay Napa Valley 1991 • $18 • (07/15/93)

90 **KISTLER** Chardonnay Russian River Valley Dutton Ranch 1991 • $33 • (02/15/93)

90 **KISTLER** Chardonnay Sonoma Mountain McCrea Vineyard 1991 • $33 • (05/31/93)

90 **KISTLER** Chardonnay Sonoma Valley Kistler Vineyard 1991 • $32 • (02/28/94)

90 **MATANZAS CREEK** Chardonnay Sonoma Valley 1991 • $20 • (11/30/93)

90 **MERRYVALE** Chardonnay Napa Valley Starmont 1991 • $16 • (05/31/93)

90 **ROBERT MONDAVI** Chardonnay Napa Valley Reserve 1991 • $28 • (04/30/93)

90 **ROBERT MONDAVI** Chardonnay Napa Valley 1991 • $15 • (04/30/93) • SS

90 **ROBERT MONDAVI** Chardonnay Carneros 1991 • $20 • (05/15/93)

90 **ROBERT SINSKEY** Chardonnay Los Carneros 1991 • $16 • (07/15/93)

90 **ROCHIOLI** Chardonnay Russian River Valley 1991 • $15 • (07/15/93)

90 **SOLITUDE** Chardonnay Carneros Sangiacomo Vineyard 1991 • $18 • (07/15/93)

90 **ST. CLEMENT** Chardonnay Napa Valley Carneros Abbotts Vineyard 1991 • $18 • (12/31/93)

90 **STEELE** Chardonnay Mendocino Lolonis Vineyard 1991 • $26 • (03/15/93)

90 **TALBOTT** Chardonnay Monterey Diamond Estate 1991 • $30 • (09/15/94)

90 **TRUCHARD** Chardonnay Carneros Napa Valley 1991 • $16 • (07/15/93)

90 **VICHON** Chardonnay Napa Valley 1991 • $14 • (06/15/93)

89 **ACACIA** Chardonnay Napa Valley Carneros Marina Vineyard 1991 • $20 • (08/31/93)

89 **ARROWOOD** Chardonnay Sonoma County Réserve Spéciale 1991 • $50 • (11/30/93)

89 **BERINGER** Chardonnay Napa Valley Private Reserve 1991 • $19 • (07/15/93)

89 **BERNARDUS** Chardonnay California 1991 • $12 • (07/15/93)

89 **BYINGTON** Chardonnay Santa Cruz Mountains Redwood Hill Vineyard 1991 • $18 • (03/31/93)

89 **CALERA** Chardonnay Central Coast 1991 • $14 • (04/15/93)

89 **DEHLINGER** Chardonnay Russian River Valley 1991 • $13 • (05/15/93)

89 **E. & J. GALLO** Chardonnay Sonoma County Gallo Sonoma 1991 • $9 • (06/30/94)

89 **EL MOLINO** Chardonnay Napa County 1991 • $30 • (07/15/93)

89 **FIELD STONE** Chardonnay Sonoma County 1991 • $14 • (07/15/93)

89 **FRANCISCAN** Chardonnay Napa Valley Oakville Estate 1991 • $12 • (07/15/93)

89 **FROG'S LEAP** Chardonnay Carneros 1991 • $16 • (07/15/93)

89 **HUSCH** Chardonnay Mendocino 1991 • $11 • (04/15/93)

89 **J. LOHR** Chardonnay Monterey Riverstone 1991 • $12 • (07/15/93)

89 **KENDALL-JACKSON** Chardonnay Santa Maria Valley Camelot Vineyard 1991 • $16 • (01/31/93)

89 **KUNDE** Chardonnay Sonoma Valley 1991 • $14 • (04/15/93)

89 **LOCKWOOD** Chardonnay Monterey Partners Reserve 1991 • $15 • (07/15/93)

89 **LOUIS M. MARTINI** Chardonnay Napa Valley Reserve 1991 • $14 • (02/28/94)

89 **MIRASSOU** Chardonnay Monterey County Harvest Reserve 1991 • $12 • (06/15/93)

89 **NEWTON** Chardonnay Napa Valley 1991 • $15 • (07/15/93)

89 **OAKVILLE RANCH** Chardonnay Napa Valley 1991 • $18 • (07/15/93)

89 **OJAI** Chardonnay Arroyo Grande Valley Reserve 1991 • $21 • (12/31/93)

89 **RABBIT RIDGE** Chardonnay Russian River Valley Rabbit Ridge Ranch 1991 • $16 • (04/30/93)

89 **RAYMOND** Chardonnay Napa Valley Private Reserve 1991 • $18 • (07/15/93)

89 **S. ANDERSON** Chardonnay Stags Leap District Proprietor's Reserve 1991 • $25 • (07/15/93)

89 **SILVERADO** Chardonnay Napa Valley 1991 • $16 • (07/15/93)

89 **SONOMA-LOEB** Chardonnay Sonoma County Private Reserve 1991 • $28 • (03/15/93)

89 **STEELE** Chardonnay Carneros Sangiacomo Vineyard 1991 • $22 • (03/15/93)

89 **WILDHURST** Chardonnay Sonoma County Reserve 1991 • $16 • (03/31/93)

88 **ADELAIDA** Chardonnay San Luis Obispo County 1991 • $18 • (07/15/93)

88 **ALEXANDER VALLEY VINEYARDS** Chardonnay Alexander Valley Wetzel Family Estate 1991 • $10 • (06/30/93)

88 **ARROWOOD** Chardonnay Sonoma County 1991 • $19 • (07/15/93)

88 **B.R. COHN** Chardonnay Napa Valley Silver Label 1991 • $12 • (03/31/93)

88 **BEAULIEU** Chardonnay Napa Valley Carneros Barrel Fermented Reserve 1991 • $16 • (06/30/94)

88 **BENZIGER** Chardonnay Carneros Premiere Vineyard 1991 • $16 • (07/15/93)

88 **BENZIGER** Chardonnay Sonoma County 1991 • $12 • (07/15/93)

88 **BOUCHAINE** Chardonnay Carneros Napa Valley Reserve 1991 • $20 • (02/28/95)

88 **BRUTOCAO** Chardonnay Mendocino 1991 • $10 • (07/15/93)

88 **BYRON** Chardonnay Santa Barbara County Reserve 1991 • $20 • (07/15/93)

88 **CALE** Chardonnay Carneros Sangiacomo Vineyard 1991 • $18 • (10/31/93)

88 **CANEPA CELLARS** Chardonnay Alexander Valley 1991 • $19 • (07/15/93)

88 **CHATEAU POTELLE** Chardonnay Napa Valley 1991 • $9 • (03/15/94) • BB

88 **CHATEAU SOUVERAIN** Chardonnay Sonoma Valley Durell Vineyard Reserve 1991 • $13 • (07/15/93)

88 **CHATEAU ST. JEAN** Chardonnay Alexander Valley Belle Terre Vineyards Reserve 1991 • $40 • (04/30/95)

88 **DE LOACH** Chardonnay Russian River Valley 1991 • $18 • (03/31/93)

88 **EDNA VALLEY** Chardonnay Edna Valley 1991 • $15 • (12/31/92)

88 **FETZER** Chardonnay Mendocino County Organically Grown Grapes 1991 • $9 • (04/30/93) • BB

88 **FREEMARK ABBEY** Chardonnay Napa Valley Carpy Ranch 1991 • $22 • (06/30/94)

88 **GREEN & RED** Chardonnay Napa Valley Catacula Vineyard 1991 • $16 • (07/15/93)

88 **GUENOC** Chardonnay Guenoc Valley Genevieve Magoon Vineyard Reserve 1991 • $25 • (10/15/93)

88 **HARRISON** Chardonnay Napa Valley 1991 • $24 • (07/15/93)

88 **KISTLER** Chardonnay Sonoma Valley Durell Vineyard Sand Hill 1991 • $32 • (05/31/93)

88 **KONRAD** Chardonnay Mendocino County 1991 • $11 • (04/15/94)

88 **LANDMARK** Chardonnay Sonoma County Overlook 1991 • $12 • (04/15/93)

88 **LAURENT CELLARS** Chardonnay Napa Valley 1991 • $25 • (07/15/93)

88 **MACROSTIE** Chardonnay Carneros 1991 • $16 • (12/15/92)

88 **MARKHAM** Chardonnay Napa Valley 1991 • $15 • (04/30/93)

88 **MERIDIAN** Chardonnay Edna Valley 1991 • $14 • (03/31/93)

88 **OAKVILLE RANCH** Chardonnay Napa Valley Vista Vineyards 1991 • $18 • (07/15/93)

88 **PETER MICHAEL** Chardonnay Napa County Clos du Ciel 1991 • $25 • (07/15/93)

88 **RANCHO SISQUOC** Chardonnay Santa Maria Valley 1991 • $14 • (07/15/93)

88 **ROBERT PEPI** Chardonnay Napa Valley Puncheon Fermented 1991 • $16 • (12/31/93)

88 **SANTA BARBARA WINERY** Chardonnay Santa Ynez Valley Lafond Vineyard 1991 • $30 • (04/30/94)

88 **SONOMA-CUTRER** Chardonnay Sonoma Coast Cutrer Vineyard 1991 • $18 • (07/15/93)

88 **SONOMA-CUTRER** Chardonnay Sonoma Coast Les Pierres 1991 • $19 • (03/31/95)

88 **ST. CLEMENT** Chardonnay Carneros Abbotts Vineyard 1991 • $18 • (07/15/93)

88 **STONY HILL** Chardonnay Napa Valley 1991 • $42 • (06/30/94)

88 **TALBOTT** Chardonnay Monterey 1991 • $24 • (06/30/94)

88 **VENTANA** Chardonnay Monterey Gold Stripe Selection 1991 • $10 • (02/28/94) • BB

88 **WELLINGTON** Chardonnay Sonoma Valley Barrel Fermented 1991 • $11 • (06/15/93)

88 **WENTE BROS.** Chardonnay Livermore Valley Herman Wente Vineyard Reserve 1991 • $15 • (07/15/93)

88 **WHITE OAK** Chardonnay Sonoma County Myers Limited Reserve 1991 • $20 • (06/30/94)

88 **WHITE ROCK** Chardonnay Napa Valley 1991 • $16 • (10/15/93)

88 **ZACA MESA** Chardonnay Santa Barbara County 1991 • $11 • (06/30/93)

87 **ADELAIDA** Chardonnay San Luis Obispo Reserve 1991 • $28 • (06/30/94)

87 **BELVEDERE** Chardonnay Russian River Valley 1991 • $12 • (04/15/94)

87 **BLACK MOUNTAIN** Chardonnay Alexander Valley Douglass Hill 1991 • $11 • (05/15/93)

87 **BOEGER** Chardonnay El Dorado 1991 • $12 • (09/15/93)

87 **BOUCHAINE** Chardonnay Carneros 1991 • $15 • (06/30/94)

87 **CHARLES KRUG** Chardonnay Napa Valley Carneros Reserve 1991 • $16 • (06/15/94)

87 **CHATEAU WOLTNER** Chardonnay Howell Mountain Estate Reserve 1991 • $17 • (09/15/93)

87 **CLOS DU BOIS** Chardonnay Dry Creek Valley Flintwood Vineyard 1991 • $17 • (06/30/94)

87 **CLOS DU VAL** Chardonnay Carneros 1991 • $15 • (07/15/93)

87 **CLOS PEGASE** Chardonnay Napa Valley 1991 • $13 • (07/15/93)

87 **COSENTINO** Chardonnay Napa Valley 1991 • $14 • (01/31/93)

87 **CRONIN** Chardonnay Napa Valley 1991 • $18 • (08/31/93)

87 **CUVAISON** Chardonnay Carneros Napa Valley 1991 • $14 • (07/15/93)

87 **DOMAINE DE CLARCK** Chardonnay Monterey County 1991 • $14 • (03/15/93)

87 **DRY CREEK** Chardonnay Sonoma County 20th Vintage Anniversary Reserve 1991 • $15 • (11/15/94)

87 **FAR NIENTE** Chardonnay Napa Valley 1991 • $30 • (07/15/93)

87 **FISHER** Chardonnay Sonoma County Coach Insignia 1991 • $16 • (07/15/93)

87 **GABRIELLI** Chardonnay Mendocino 1991 • $14 • (07/15/93)

87 **GRGICH HILLS** Chardonnay Napa Valley 1991 • $24 • (03/15/94)

87 **HANZELL** Chardonnay Sonoma Valley 1991 • $25 • (06/30/94)

87 **KENWOOD** Chardonnay Sonoma Valley Yulupa Vineyard 1991 • $14 • (06/15/93)

87 **MARIO PERELLI-MINETTI** Chardonnay Napa Valley 1991 • $13 • (09/30/95)

87 **SAINTSBURY** Chardonnay Carneros 1991 • $15 • (12/15/92)

87 **SONOMA-CUTRER** Chardonnay Sonoma Coast Cutrer Vineyard 1991 • $20 • (06/30/94)

87 **STEELE** Chardonnay California 1991 • $18 • (02/15/93)

87 **SWANSON** Chardonnay Carneros Napa Valley 1991 • $18 • (06/30/94)

87 **THE HESS COLLECTION** Chardonnay Napa Valley 1991 • $14 • (07/15/93)

87 **THOMAS-HSI** Chardonnay Napa Valley 1991 • $18 • (06/30/94)

87 **TULOCAY** Chardonnay Napa Valley DeCelles Vineyard 1991 • $13 • (07/15/93)

87 **VILLA MT. EDEN** Chardonnay Carneros Grand Reserve 1991 • $15 • (03/31/93)

87 **WENTE BROS.** Chardonnay Arroyo Seco Riva Ranch 1991 • $12 • (07/15/93)

86 **ADLER FELS** Chardonnay Sonoma County Coleman Reserve 1991 • $12 • (03/31/94)

86 **ARCIERO** Chardonnay Paso Robles 1991 • $8 • (05/31/93)

86 **BELVEDERE** Chardonnay Alexander Valley 1991 • $8 • (06/30/93) • BB

86 **BOUCHAINE** Chardonnay Carneros Unfiltered Limited Release 1991 • $20 • (06/30/94)

86 **BUENA VISTA** Chardonnay Carneros Grand Reserve 1991 • $20 • (12/31/94)

86 **BURGESS** Chardonnay Napa Valley Triere Vineyard 1991 • $16 • (08/31/93)

86 **CHAMISAL** Chardonnay Edna Valley 1991 • $14 • (03/31/93)

86 **CHATEAU DE BAUN** Chardonnay Russian River Valley 1991 • $10 • (06/30/93)

86 **CHRISTOPHE** Chardonnay Napa Valley Reserve 1991 • $11 • (01/31/93)

86 **CLOS DU BOIS** Chardonnay Alexander Valley Calcaire Vineyard 1991 • $18 • (07/15/93)

86 **ESTANCIA** Chardonnay Monterey 1991 • $8 • (05/31/93) • BB

86 **ESTATE WILLIAM BACCALA** Chardonnay Sonoma County 1991 • $9 • (02/28/94) • BB

86 **FORMAN** Chardonnay Napa Valley 1991 • $25 • (04/15/93)

86 **GARY FARRELL** Chardonnay Russian River Valley 1991 • $16 • (04/15/93)

86 **GARY FARRELL** Chardonnay Russian River Valley Allen Vineyard 1991 • $18 • (07/15/93)

86 **GRGICH HILLS** Chardonnay Napa Valley 1991 • $NA • (07/15/93)

86 **GROTH** Chardonnay Napa Valley 1991 • $14 • (04/30/93)

86 **HAGAFEN** Chardonnay Napa Valley 1991 • $13 • (07/15/93)

86 **HANNA** Chardonnay Sonoma County 1991 • $14 • (04/15/94)

86 **JEKEL** Chardonnay Arroyo Seco Gravelstone 1991 • $10 • (05/31/94) • BB

86 **JOSEPH PHELPS** Chardonnay Napa Valley 1991 • $16 • (07/15/93)

86 **LAZY CREEK** Chardonnay Anderson Valley 1991 • $10 • (07/15/93)

86 **MARK WEST** Chardonnay Russian River Valley 1991 • $12 • (02/15/93)

86 **MAZZOCCO** Chardonnay Sonoma County River Lane 1991 • $15 • (03/31/93)

86 **MONTICELLO** Chardonnay Napa Valley Corley Reserve 1991 • $17.25 • (07/15/93)

86 **MORGAN** Chardonnay Monterey Reserve 1991 • $23 • (12/31/93)

86 **NEWLAN** Chardonnay Napa Valley 1991 • $19 • (06/30/94)

86 **SAINT GREGORY** Chardonnay Mendocino 1991 • $14 • (04/15/94)

86 **SANTA BARBARA WINERY** Chardonnay Santa Ynez Valley 1991 • $12 • (07/15/93)

86 **SANTA BARBARA WINERY** Chardonnay Santa Ynez Valley Reserve 1991 • $20 • (07/15/93)

86 **SEBASTIANI** Chardonnay Sonoma County Reserve 1991 • $13 • (07/15/93)

86 **ST. ANDREW'S WINERY** Chardonnay Napa Valley 1991 • $10 • (07/15/93)

86 **ST. CLEMENT** Chardonnay Napa Valley 1991 • $16 • (04/15/93)

86 **ST. SUPERY** Chardonnay Napa Valley Dollarhide Ranch 1991 • $13 • (03/31/93)

86 **STEVENOT** Chardonnay Calaveras County Reserve 1991 • $10 • (06/30/93)

86 **V. SATTUI** Chardonnay Napa Valley Carsi Vineyard Barrel Fermented 1991 • $23 • (06/30/94)

85 **ACACIA** Chardonnay Napa Valley 1991 • $11 • (03/15/93)

85 **BANDIERA** Chardonnay Napa Valley 1991 • $6 • (01/31/94) • BB

85 **BOUCHAINE** Chardonnay California Q.C. Fly 1991 • $8 • (09/30/92) • BB

85 **CAMBRIA** Chardonnay Santa Maria Valley Katherine's Vineyard 1991 • $16 • (07/15/93)

85 **CAMBRIA** Chardonnay Santa Maria Valley Reserve 1991 • $25 • (06/30/94)

85 **CHARLES KRUG** Chardonnay Napa Valley 1991 • $12 • (12/31/92)

85 **CHATEAU JULIEN** Chardonnay Monterey County Sur Lie Private Reserve 1991 • $13 • (07/15/93)

85 **CHATEAU SOUVERAIN** Chardonnay Sonoma County Barrel Fermented 1991 • $9 • (03/15/93)

85 **CHATEAU ST. JEAN** Chardonnay Sonoma County 1991 • $10 • (07/15/93)

85 **CHATEAU ST. JEAN** Chardonnay Alexander Valley Belle Terre Vineyards 1991 • $17 • (05/15/94)

85 **CHATEAU WOLTNER** Chardonnay Howell Mountain Frederique Vineyard 1991 • $40 • (09/15/93)

85 **COSENTINO** Chardonnay Napa Valley The Sculptor 1991 • $20 • (07/15/93)

85 **DRY CREEK** Chardonnay Sonoma County Barrel Fermented 1991 • $13 • (03/15/93)

85 **EDNA VALLEY** Chardonnay Edna Valley Paragon Vineyard Reserve Bottling 1991 • $20 • (06/30/94)

85 **ELLISTON** Chardonnay Central Coast Sunol Valley Vineyard 1991 • $12 • (11/30/92)

85 **GUENOC** Chardonnay Guenoc Valley 1991 • $14 • (04/30/93)

85 **GUNDLACH BUNDSCHU** Chardonnay Sonoma Valley Sangiacomo Ranch Special Selection 1991 • $16 • (07/15/93)

85 **HOP KILN** Chardonnay Russian River Valley M. Griffin Vineyards 1991 • $15 • (07/15/93)

85 **KENDALL-JACKSON** Chardonnay California Proprietor's Grand Reserve 1991 • $23 • (03/31/93)

85 **KENWOOD** Chardonnay Sonoma Valley 1991 • $10 • (02/15/93)

85 **LA CROSSE** Chardonnay Napa Valley 1991 • $6 • (12/31/92) • BB

85 **LAWRENCE J. BARGETTO** Chardonnay Central Coast Cypress 1991 • $9 • (10/15/93) • BB

85 **LEEWARD** Chardonnay Central Coast 1991 • $11 • (11/30/92)

85 **M.G. VALLEJO** Chardonnay California 1991 • $5 • (11/30/92) • BB

85 **MARIMAR TORRES** Chardonnay Sonoma County Green Valley Don Miguel Vineyard 1991 • $25 • (07/15/93)

85 **MERIDIAN** Chardonnay Santa Barbara County 1991 • $10 • (07/15/93)

85 **MOUNT EDEN** Chardonnay Edna Valley MacGregor Vineyard 1991 • $15 • (07/15/93)

85 **OBESTER** Chardonnay Mendocino County 1991 • $15 • (06/30/94)

85 **PRIDE** Chardonnay Napa Valley 1991 • $18 • (04/30/94)

85 **RAYMOND** Chardonnay Napa Valley 1991 • $15 • (02/28/94)

85 **RIDGE** Chardonnay Santa Cruz Mountains 1991 • $20 • (07/15/93)

85 **ROCHE** Chardonnay Carneros 1991 • $15 • (07/15/93)

85 **S. ANDERSON** Chardonnay Stags Leap District 1991 • $18 • (07/15/93)

85 **SIGNORELLO** Chardonnay Napa Valley 1991 • $20 • (07/15/93)

85 **SIMI** Chardonnay Mendocino-Sonoma-Napa Counties 1991 • $12 • (07/15/93)

85 **SODA CANYON** Chardonnay Napa Valley 13th Leaf 1991 • $10 • (06/30/94)

85 **SOLIS** Chardonnay Santa Clara County Barrel Fermented 1991 • $10 • (11/30/92)

85 **ST. FRANCIS** Chardonnay Sonoma Valley Reserve Estate 1991 • $15 • (07/15/93)

85 **TAFT STREET** Chardonnay Sonoma County 1991 • $8 • (05/15/93) • BB

85 **VOSS** Chardonnay Napa Valley 1991 • $16 • (01/31/93)

85 **WINTERBROOK** Chardonnay Napa Valley Grand Reserve 1991 • $17 • (07/15/93)

84 **BANNISTER** Chardonnay Russian River Valley 1991 • $NA • (07/15/93)

84 **BERINGER** Chardonnay Napa Valley 1991 • $11 • (03/31/93)

84 **BON MARCHE** Chardonnay Sonoma County 1991 • $8 • (03/15/93) • BB

84 **BUENA VISTA** Chardonnay Carneros 1991 • $11 • (07/15/93)

84 **CARNEROS CREEK** Chardonnay Los Carneros 1991 • $13 • (02/15/93)

84 **CASTORO** Chardonnay San Luis Obispo County 1991 • $9 • (06/30/93)

84 **CHARLES KRUG** Chardonnay Napa Valley Carneros Reserve 1991 • $16 • (07/15/93)

84 **CHATEAU WOLTNER** Chardonnay Howell Mountain 1991 • $12 • (07/15/92)

84 **DANIEL GEHRS** Chardonnay Monterey County 1991 • $11 • (07/15/93)

84 **DE LORIMIER** Chardonnay Alexander Valley Prism 1991 • $15 • (03/31/94)

84 **DUNNEWOOD** Chardonnay North Coast Barrel Select 1991 • $6 • (11/30/92) • BB

84 **FARELLA-PARK** Chardonnay Napa Valley 1991 • $15 • (10/15/93)

84 **FETZER** Chardonnay Mendocino County Barrel Select 1991 • $11 • (07/15/93)

84 **GAINEY** Chardonnay Santa Barbara County 1991 • $13 • (07/15/93)

84 **GAUER ESTATE** Chardonnay Alexander Valley 1991 • $16 • (06/15/93)

84 **GAVILAN** Chardonnay Chalone Gavilan 1991 • $13 • (03/31/93)

84 **GLEN ELLEN** Chardonnay California Proprietor's Reserve 1991 • $6 • (01/31/93) • BB

84 **JORDAN** Chardonnay Alexander Valley 1991 • $20 • (06/30/94)

84 **JORY** Chardonnay Monterey Reserve 1991 • $23 • (03/31/93)

84 **JOULLIAN** Chardonnay Monterey 1991 • $10 • (06/15/93)

84 **JOULLIAN** Chardonnay Carmel Valley Family Reserve 1991 • $18 • (06/30/94)

84 **KARLY** Chardonnay Edna Valley MacGregor Vineyard 1991 • $14 • (07/15/93)

84 **KENDALL-JACKSON** Chardonnay California Vintner's Reserve 1991 • $13 • (07/15/92)

84 **LEEWARD** Chardonnay Monterey County 1991 • $14 • (06/30/94)

84 **LOCKWOOD** Chardonnay Monterey 1991 • $9 • (07/15/93)

84 **LOGAN** Chardonnay Monterey 1991 • $14 • (07/15/93)

84 **MIRASSOU** Chardonnay Monterey County Family Selection 1991 • $10 • (02/15/93)

84 **OPTIMA** Chardonnay Sonoma County 1991 • $25 • (07/15/93)

84 **PARAISO SPRINGS** Chardonnay Monterey County Barrel Fermented 1991 • $10 • (06/30/94)

84 **PINNACLES** Chardonnay Monterey 1991 • $16 • (07/15/93)

84 **RABBIT RIDGE** Chardonnay Sonoma County 1991 • $12 • (10/15/93)

84 **REVERE** Chardonnay Napa Valley Reserve 1991 • $22 • (06/30/94)

84 **RODNEY STRONG** Chardonnay Sonoma County 1991 • $9 • (11/15/92) • BB

84 **ROUND HILL** Chardonnay Napa Valley Van Asperen Reserve 1991 • $11 • (07/15/93)

84 **SEBASTIANI** Chardonnay Sonoma County 1991 • $9 • (05/15/93)

84 **SILVER MOUNTAIN** Chardonnay Monterey 1991 • $14 • (06/30/94)

84 **SONOMA-CUTRER** Chardonnay Russian River Valley 1991 • $13 • (07/15/93)

84 **ST. ANDREW'S VINEYARD** Chardonnay Napa Valley Limited Reserve 1991 • $18 • (06/30/94)

84 **ST. FRANCIS** Chardonnay Sonoma County 1991 • $9 • (08/31/92)

84 **STERLING** Chardonnay Carneros Napa Valley Winery Lake 1991 • $18 • (09/30/94)

84 **STERLING** Chardonnay Napa Valley Diamond Mountain Ranch Vineyard 1991 • $18 • (06/30/94)

84 **STONESTREET** Chardonnay Sonoma County 1991 • $24 • (06/30/94)

84 **THE HESS COLLECTION** Chardonnay Mount Veeder 1991 • $22 • (06/30/94)

84 **VILLA MT. EDEN** Chardonnay California Cellar Select 1991 • $10 • (03/15/93)

83 **ACACIA** Chardonnay Napa Valley Carneros 1991 • $17 • (03/15/93)

83 **BEAUCANON** Chardonnay Napa Valley 1991 • $10 • (12/15/92)

83 **CECCHETTI SEBASTIANI** Chardonnay Napa Valley 1991 • $10 • (07/15/93)

83 **CHALK HILL** Chardonnay Chalk Hill 1991 • $10 • (03/15/93)

83 **CHATEAU JULIEN** Chardonnay Monterey County Sur Lie Private Reserve 1991 • $11 • (06/30/94)

83 **CHATEAU MONTELENA** Chardonnay Napa Valley 1991 • $23 • (06/30/94)

83 **CHATOM** Chardonnay Calaveras County 1991 • $NA • (07/15/93)

83 **CLOS DU BOIS** Chardonnay Alexander Valley Barrel Fermented 1991 • $13 • (03/31/93)

83 **COLBY** Chardonnay Napa Valley 1991 • $14 • (03/31/95)

83 **CRESTON** Chardonnay Paso Robles 1991 • $10 • (07/15/93)

83 **CRONIN** Chardonnay Monterey County Ventana Vineyard 1991 • $18 • (08/31/93)

83 **FETZER** Chardonnay Mendocino Reserve 1991 • $18 • (07/15/93)

83 **GREENWOOD RIDGE** Chardonnay Mendocino 1991 • $16 • (03/31/93)

83 **GUNDLACH BUNDSCHU** Chardonnay Sonoma Valley 1991 • $12 • (10/31/93)

83 **HAHN** Chardonnay Monterey 1991 • $10 • (06/15/93)

83 **HIDDEN CELLARS** Chardonnay Mendocino County Organically Grown Grapes 1991 • $14 • (12/15/92)

83 **INGLENOOK** Chardonnay Napa Valley 1991 • $9 • (06/30/94)

83 **KEENAN** Chardonnay Napa Valley 1991 • $15 • (04/15/93)

83 **LA CASA SENA** Chardonnay Monterey La Reina Vineyard 1991 • $19 • (03/31/93)

83 **LAUREL ESTATE** Chardonnay North Coast 1991 • $8 • (11/30/92)

83 **LIMUR** Chardonnay Napa Valley 1991 • $16 • (07/15/93)

83 **LOLONIS** Chardonnay Mendocino County Estate Reserve 1991 • $12 • (07/15/93)

83 **LYETH** Chardonnay Sonoma County 1991 • $12 • (07/15/93)

83 **MCDOWELL** Chardonnay Mendocino 1991 • $9 • (06/30/93)

83 **MIRASSOU** Chardonnay Monterey County Harvest Reserve 1991 • $12 • (05/31/94)

83 **MONTICELLO** Chardonnay Napa Valley 1991 • $9 • (01/31/94)

83 **MOUNT PALOMAR** Chardonnay Temecula 1991 • $10 • (08/31/92)

83 **NEWLAN** Chardonnay Napa Valley Reserve 1991 • $20 • (07/15/93)

83 **NEWLAN** Chardonnay Napa Valley 1991 • $14 • (07/15/93)

83 **PEJU** Chardonnay Napa Valley HB Vineyard 1991 • $18 • (07/15/93)

83 **PENARD** Chardonnay Carneros 1991 • $19 • (03/31/93)

83 **RAYMOND** Chardonnay California Selection 1991 • $8 • (07/15/93) • BB

83 **REVERE** Chardonnay Napa Valley Berlenbach Vineyards 1991 • $20 • (06/30/94)

83 **ROUND HILL** Chardonnay California 1991 • $6 • (02/15/93) • BB

83 **RUTHERFORD HILL** Chardonnay Napa Valley Exceptional Vineyard Selection Reserve 1991 • $19 • (06/30/94)

83 **SEGHESIO** Chardonnay Sonoma County 1991 • $9 • (06/30/93)

83 **SILVER RIDGE** Chardonnay California Barrel Fermented 1991 • $10 • (06/15/93)

83 **STONEGATE** Chardonnay Sonoma County Bella Vista Vineyard 1991 • $14 • (11/30/93)

82 **BEAULIEU** Chardonnay Napa Valley Beaufort 1991 • $8 • (07/15/93)

82 **CONCANNON** Chardonnay Central Coast Selected Vineyards 1991 • $10 • (07/15/93)

82 **CRONIN** Chardonnay California Nancy's Cuvée 1991 • $27 • (06/30/94)

82 **DOMAINE NAPA** Chardonnay Napa Valley 1991 • $13 • (07/15/93)

82 **EBERLE** Chardonnay Paso Robles 1991 • $12 • (07/15/93)

82 **GLASS MOUNTAIN QUARRY** Chardonnay California 1991 • $9 • (06/15/93)

82 **HAGAFEN** Chardonnay Napa Valley Reserve 1991 • $17 • (06/30/94)

82 **HESS SELECT** Chardonnay California 1991 • $10 • (12/15/92)

82 **LIPARITA** Chardonnay Howell Mountain 1991 • $16 • (03/15/94)

82 **LOLONIS** Chardonnay Mendocino County Private Reserve 1991 • $19 • (07/15/93)

82 **LOUIS M. MARTINI** Chardonnay Napa Valley 1991 • $8 • (06/30/93)

82 **MADDALENA** Chardonnay Central Coast San Simeon Collection 1991 • $10 • (06/30/94)

82 **MADRONA** Chardonnay El Dorado 1991 • $10 • (06/30/94)

82 **MARK WEST** Chardonnay Russian River Valley Barrel Fermented 1991 • $11 • (07/15/93)

82 **MICHAEL SULLBERG** Chardonnay Atlas Peak Lot 55 Barrel Fermented 1991 • $6 • (05/15/96)

82 **NAPA CELLARS** Chardonnay Napa Valley 1991 • $7 • (07/15/93)

82 **RIVERSIDE FARM** Chardonnay California 1991 • $7 • (07/15/92) • BB

82 **SEQUOIA GROVE** Chardonnay Carneros 1991 • $14 • (07/15/93)

82 **SEQUOIA GROVE** Chardonnay Napa Valley Estate Reserve 1991 • $21 • (06/30/94)

82 **STAG'S LEAP WINE CELLARS** Chardonnay Napa Valley 1991 • $18 • (07/15/93)

82 **STRATFORD** Chardonnay California 1991 • $9 • (07/15/93)

82 **VICHON** Chardonnay California Coastal Selection 1991 • $10 • (01/31/93)

82 **ZD** Chardonnay California 1991 • $21 • (07/15/93)

81 **BEAULIEU** Chardonnay Napa Valley Carneros Reserve 1991 • $16 • (06/30/94)

81 **BUTTERFLY CREEK** Chardonnay California 1991 • $18 • (07/15/93)

81 **CAKEBREAD** Chardonnay Napa Valley 1991 • $23 • (03/31/93)

81 **DAVIS BYNUM** Chardonnay Russian River Valley Allen-Griffin Vineyards Limited Release 1991 • $17 • (07/15/93)

81 **FENESTRA** Chardonnay Livermore Valley Toy Vineyard 1991 • $12 • (07/15/93)

81 **FLORA SPRINGS** Chardonnay Napa Valley Floréal 1991 • $12 • (07/15/93)

81 **FREEMARK ABBEY** Chardonnay Napa Valley 1991 • $16 • (06/30/94)

81 **GEYSER PEAK** Chardonnay Alexander Valley Reserve 1991 • $17 • (07/15/93)

81 **GUSTAVE NIEBAUM** Chardonnay Napa Valley Reference 1991 • $11 • (03/31/93)

81 **HAYWOOD** Chardonnay California Vintner's Select 1991 • $8 • (03/31/93)

81 **IRONSTONE** Chardonnay California Gold Canyon 1991 • $10 • (04/15/93)

81 **J. KERR** Chardonnay Santa Barbara County 1991 • $30 • (06/30/94)

81 **J.W. MORRIS** Chardonnay California Private Reserve 1991 • $7 • (07/15/93) • BB

81 **MARK WEST** Chardonnay Russian River Valley Estate Reserve 1991 • $14 • (07/15/93)

81 **PARDUCCI** Chardonnay Mendocino County 1991 • $8 • (07/15/93)

81 **R.H. PHILLIPS** Chardonnay California Barrel Cuvée 1991 • $8 • (08/31/92) • BB

81 **ROUND HILL** Chardonnay Napa Valley Reserve 1991 • $11 • (07/15/93)

81 **STONY RIDGE** Chardonnay California 1991 • $6 • (11/30/92)

81 **TALLEY** Chardonnay Arroyo Grande Valley 1991 • $16 • (07/15/93)

80 **CALERA** Chardonnay Mount Harlan 1991 • $33 • (07/15/93)

80 **CLAIBORNE & CHURCHILL** Chardonnay Edna Valley MacGregor Vineyard 1991 • $16 • (07/15/93)

80 **CHÂTEAU JULIEN** Chardonnay Monterey County Private Reserve 1991 • $15 • (07/31/95)

80 **DE MOOR** Chardonnay Napa Valley 1991 • $13 • (07/15/93)

80 **FOREST GLEN** Chardonnay California Barrel Fermented 1991 • $12 • (07/15/93)

80 **GEYSER PEAK** Chardonnay Sonoma County 1991 • $10 • (07/15/93)

80 **HANDLEY** Chardonnay Dry Creek Valley 1991 • $16 • (06/30/94)

80 **HANDLEY** Chardonnay Anderson Valley 1991 • $12 • (06/30/94)

80 **J. PEDRONCELLI** Chardonnay Dry Creek Valley 1991 • $9 • (03/31/94)

80 **KENDALL-JACKSON** Chardonnay Sonoma Valley Durell Vineyard 1991 • $16 • (11/30/92)

80 **MARION** Chardonnay Sonoma County 1991 • $8 • (07/15/93)

80 **MURPHY-GOODE** Chardonnay Alexander Valley Estate Vineyard 1991 • $16 • (12/15/92)

80 **NAPA RIDGE** Chardonnay Central Coast Coastal 1991 • $7 • (07/15/93)

80 **NAPA RIDGE** Chardonnay North Coast Coastal Reserve 1991 • $12 • (07/15/93)

80 **OAK FALLS** Chardonnay Napa Valley Private Reserve 1991 • $7 • (02/15/93)

80 **PURPLE MOUNTAIN** Chardonnay Monterey Barrel Fermented 1991 • $10 • (03/31/93)

80 **ROBERT MONDAVI** Chardonnay California Woodbridge 1991 • $8 • (12/31/92)

80 **SCHUG** Chardonnay Carneros Barrel Fermented 1991 • $15 • (07/15/93)

80 **SEQUOIA GROVE** Chardonnay Napa Valley Carneros 1991 • $14 • (06/30/94)

80 **WHITE OAK** Chardonnay Sonoma County 1991 • $13 • (09/15/92)

80 **WILDHURST** Chardonnay Sonoma County 1991 • $8 • (01/31/94)

79 **AHLGREN** Chardonnay Santa Cruz Mountains Buerge Vineyard 1991 • $15 • (06/30/94)

79 **CEDAR MOUNTAIN** Chardonnay Livermore Valley Blanches Vineyard 1991 • $15 • (07/15/93)

79 **CHATEAU JULIEN** Chardonnay Monterey County Barrel Fermented 1991 • $8 • (07/15/93)

79 **CHIMNEY ROCK** Chardonnay Stags Leap District 1991 • $15 • (03/31/94)

79 **CLONINGER** Chardonnay Monterey 1991 • $15 • (07/15/93)

79 **DOMAINE MICHEL** Chardonnay Dry Creek Valley 1991 • $13 • (02/28/94)

79 **MIRASSOU** Chardonnay Monterey County Family Selection 1991 • $9 • (06/30/94)

79 **MOUNT PALOMAR** Chardonnay Temecula Reserve 1991 • $16 • (08/31/92)

■ ■ ■ ■

California Chardonnay

78 **BABCOCK** Chardonnay Santa Ynez Valley 1991 • $18 • (07/15/93)

78 **BEL ARBORS** Chardonnay California 1991 • $7 • (11/30/92)

78 **BRANDER** Chardonnay Santa Ynez Valley Tête de Cuvée 1991 • $16 • (07/15/93)

78 **BUENA VISTA** Chardonnay Carneros 1991 • $11 • (06/30/94)

78 **CALLAWAY** Chardonnay Temecula Calla-Lees 1991 • $8 • (07/15/93)

78 **CHRISTINE WOODS** Chardonnay Anderson Valley 1991 • $12 • (06/30/94)

78 **GABRIELLI** Chardonnay Mendocino Reserve 1991 • $20 • (07/15/93)

78 **HIDDEN CELLARS** Chardonnay Mendocino County Reserve 1991 • $16 • (07/15/93)

78 **HIDDEN CELLARS** Chardonnay Mendocino County 1991 • $14 • (07/15/93)

78 **M.G. VALLEJO** Chardonnay California Harvest Select 1991 • $7 • (07/15/93)

78 **MOUNTAIN VIEW** Chardonnay Monterey County 1991 • $6 • (03/31/93)

78 **ROUDON-SMITH** Chardonnay Central Coast 1991 • $10 • (06/30/94)

78 **ROYCE** Chardonnay California 1991 • $10 • (02/15/93)

78 **SADDLEBACK** Chardonnay Napa Valley Nils Venge 1991 • $12 • (06/30/94)

78 **STERLING** Chardonnay Napa Valley 1991 • $14 • (07/15/93)

78 **STONE CREEK** Chardonnay California 1991 • $7 • (09/30/92)

78 **WILLIAM HILL** Chardonnay Napa Valley Silver Label 1991 • $12 • (06/30/94)

78 **YORK MOUNTAIN** Chardonnay San Luis Obispo County 1991 • $9 • (07/15/93)

77 **CONCANNON** Chardonnay Livermore Valley Limited Bottling Reserve 1991 • $15 • (06/30/94)

77 **CORBETT CANYON** Chardonnay Central Coast Coastal Classic 1991 • $6 • (11/30/92)

77 **FALLENLEAF** Chardonnay Carneros Sonoma Valley 1991 • $12 • (06/30/94)

77 **GUENOC** Chardonnay North Coast 1991 • $12 • (09/15/92)

77 **HALLCREST** Chardonnay Santa Cruz Mountains Meyley Vineyard 1991 • $17 • (03/31/95)

77 **MAURICE CARRIE** Chardonnay Temecula 1991 • $7 • (06/30/94)

77 **MAURICE CARRIE** Chardonnay Temecula Private Reserve 1991 • $10 • (06/30/94)

77 **MORGAN** Chardonnay Monterey 1991 • $16 • (07/15/93)

77 **STEVENOT** Chardonnay California 1991 • $8 • (04/15/93)

77 **WINDEMERE** Chardonnay Edna Valley MacGregor Vineyard 1991 • $12 • (07/15/93)

76 **BAILEYANA** Chardonnay Edna Valley 1991 • $14 • (07/15/93)

76 **BEAUCANON** Chardonnay Late Harvest Envie 1991 • $11 • (04/15/93)

76 **CONCANNON** Chardonnay Livermore Valley Limited Bottling Reserve 1991 • $15 • (07/15/93)

76 **FETZER** Chardonnay California Sundial 1991 • $8 • (08/31/92)

76 **J. LOHR** Chardonnay California Cypress 1991 • $7 • (07/15/93)

76 **MOUNT VEEDER** Chardonnay Napa Valley 1991 • $16 • (07/15/93)

76 **SUTTER HOME** Chardonnay California 1991 • $6 • (03/31/93)

75 **CALLAWAY** Chardonnay Temecula Calla-Lees Hawk Watch Classic Sur Lie St 1991 • $10 • (06/30/94)

75 **CORBETT CANYON** Chardonnay Santa Barbara County Reserve 1991 • $9 • (07/15/93)

75 **FREMONT CREEK** Chardonnay Mendocino Napa Counties Beckstoffer Vineyards 1991 • $9 • (07/15/93)

75 **INDIAN SPRINGS** Chardonnay Nevada County Sierra Foothills Reserve 1991 • $17 • (03/31/93)

75 **PEJU** Chardonnay Napa Valley 1991 • $15 • (07/15/93)

75 **PHILIPPE-LORRAINE** Chardonnay Napa Valley 1991 • $9 • (03/31/93)

75 **SOQUEL** Chardonnay Santa Cruz Mountains 1991 • $16 • (03/31/93)

75 **VAN DER HAYDEN** Chardonnay Napa Valley 1991 • $9.25 • (01/31/95)

74 **CHESTNUT HILL** Chardonnay California 1991 • $8 • (03/31/93)

74 **DAVID BRUCE** Chardonnay San Ysidro 1991 • $15 • (09/15/93)

74 **LEEWARD** Chardonnay Edna Valley Paragon Vineyard Reserve 1991 • $15 • (07/15/93)

74 **MAGNOLIA** Chardonnay Napa Valley 1991 • $16 • (07/15/93)

74 **RODNEY STRONG** Chardonnay Chalk Hill Chalk Hill Vineyard 1991 • $13 • (07/15/93)

74 **STONY HILL** Chardonnay Napa Valley SHV 1991 • $14 • (03/31/93)

73 **AHLGREN** Chardonnay Santa Cruz Mountains Mayers Vineyard 1991 • $15 • (06/30/94)

73 **DAVID BRUCE** Chardonnay Santa Cruz Mountains Split Rail Vineyard 1991 • $18 • (09/15/93)

73 **HOUTZ** Chardonnay Santa Ynez Valley 1991 • $12 • (07/15/93)

73 **SADDLEGROVE** Chardonnay California 1991 • $7 • (07/15/93)

72 **CALE** Chardonnay Carneros Sangiacomo Vineyard 1991 • $18 • (07/15/93)

72 **GARLAND RANCH** Chardonnay California 1991 • $6 • (07/15/92)

72 **HALLCREST** Chardonnay California Fortuyn Cuvée 1991 • $9 • (03/31/95)

72 **ORGANIC WINE WORKS** Chardonnay Sonoma County Freiberg Vinyard 1991 • $9 • (07/15/92)

72 **ZODIAC** Chardonnay California Gemini 1991 • $6 • (09/15/93)

71 **CHATOM** Chardonnay Calaveras County 1991 • $12 • (06/30/94)

71 **RAVENSWOOD** Chardonnay Sonoma Valley Estate 1991 • $11 • (04/30/93)

70 **COTTONWOOD CANYON** Chardonnay Santa Barbara County 1991 • $20 • (07/31/95)

70 **DAVID BRUCE** Chardonnay Santa Cruz Mountains Meyley Vineyard 1991 • $18 • (09/15/93)

70 **KORBEL** Chardonnay Sonoma County 1991 • $10 • (06/30/94)

69 **DAVIS BYNUM** Chardonnay Sonoma County 1991 • $10 • (07/15/93)

68 **JEPSON** Chardonnay Mendocino 1991 • $14 • (06/30/94)

60 **CILURZO** Chardonnay Temecula Barrel Fermented Reserve 1991 • $12 • (06/30/94)

60 **SYLVESTER** Chardonnay Paso Robles Kiara Reserve 1991 • $9 • (07/15/93)

Top-Rated Current Releases

By Wine Type

This section of the book is where you look if you are interested in a particular wine type and want a "shopping list" of the best currently available wines of that type. (The main listings section, which follows, is where you look if you have a specific wine in mind and want to know *Wine Spectator*'s rating and price.)

Seventeen popular wine types are covered here, with the top-rated wines of the type listed in descending order by score. These cover the most recent vintages reviewed, those that you will find in most wine shops.

RED BORDEAUX

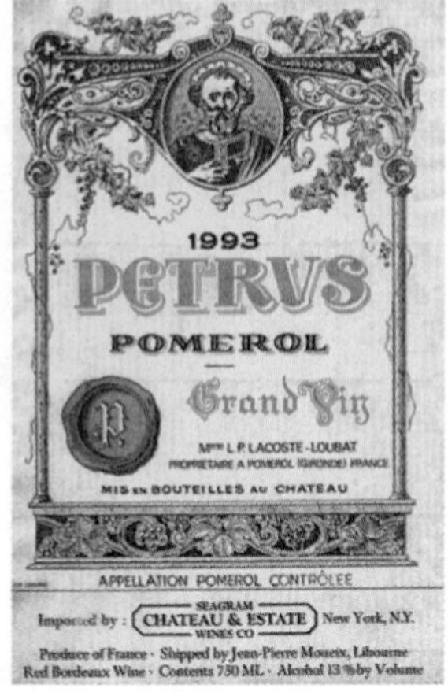

95 **CHATEAU PETRUS** Pomerol 1993 • $225 • (01/31/96) • CS
94 **CHATEAU LA FLEUR DE GAY** Pomerol 1993 • $50 • (01/31/96) • CS
92 **CHATEAU CANON-LA GAFFELIERE** St.-Emilion 1993 • $30 • (01/31/96)
91 **CHATEAU HAUT-BRION** Pessac-Léognan 1993 • $72 • (01/31/96)
91 **CHATEAU LATOUR** Pauillac 1993 • $70 • (01/31/96)
91 **CHATEAU TROTANOY** Pomerol 1993 • $50 • (01/31/96) • CS
90 **CHATEAU L'ANGELUS** St.-Emilion 1993 • $50 • (01/31/96)
90 **CHATEAU CHEVAL-BLANC** St.-Emilion 1993 • $75 • (01/31/96) • CS
90 **CHATEAU CLINET** Pomerol 1993 • $40 • (01/31/96)
90 **CHATEAU MARGAUX** Margaux 1993 • $72 • (01/31/96)
90 **CHATEAU MONTROSE** St.-Estèphe 1993 • $38 • (01/31/96)
90 **CHATEAU MOUTON-ROTHSCHILD** Pauillac 1993 • $72 • (01/31/96)
90 **CHATEAU LE PIN** Pomerol 1993 • $300 • (01/31/96)
89 **CHATEAU D'ARMAILHAC** Pauillac 1993 • $25 • (01/31/96)
89 **CHATEAU CLERC MILON** Pauillac 1993 • $24 • (01/31/96)
89 **CHATEAU LAGRANGE** St.-Julien 1993 • $25 • (01/31/96)
89 **CHATEAU LEOVILLE-LAS CASES** St.-Julien 1991 • $38 • (02/29/96)
89 **CHATEAU LA MISSION-HAUT-BRION** Pessac-Léognan 1993 • $60 • (01/31/96)
89 **CHATEAU PONTET-CANET** Pauillac 1993 • $23 • (01/31/96)
89 **CHATEAU VALANDRAUD** St.-Emilion 1993 • $95 • (01/31/96)
88 **CHATEAU AUSONE** St.-Emilion 1993 • $90 • (01/31/96)
88 **CHATEAU CHASSE-SPLEEN** Moulis 1993 • $22 • (01/31/96)
88 **CLOS DE L'ORATOIRE** St.-Emilion 1993 • $25 • (01/31/96)
88 **CHATEAU COS D'ESTOURNEL** St.-Estèphe 1993 • $33 • (01/31/96)
88 **CHATEAU GRUAUD LAROSE** St.-Julien 1993 • $30 • (01/31/96)
88 **CHATEAU GUILLOT CLAUZEL** Pomerol 1993 • $NA • (01/31/96)
88 **CHATEAU LAFLEUR** Pomerol 1993 • $180 • (01/31/96)
88 **CHATEAU LAFON-ROCHET** St.-Estèphe 1993 • $23 • (01/31/96)
88 **CHATEAU LEOVILLE-BARTON** St.-Julien 1993 • $30 • (01/31/96)
88 **CHATEAU MONBOUSQUET** St.-Emilion 1993 • $23 • (01/31/96)
88 **CHATEAU PALMER** Margaux 1993 • $40 • (01/31/96)
88 **CHATEAU PAVIE** St.-Emilion 1993 • $45 • (01/31/96)
88 **CHATEAU PICHON-LONGUEVILLE-LALANDE** Pauillac 1993 • $33 • (01/31/96)
88 **CHATEAU SOCIANDO-MALLET** Haut-Médoc 1993 • $25 • (01/31/96)
88 **CHATEAU TROPLONG-MONDOT** St.-Emilion 1993 • $35 • (01/31/96)
87 **CHATEAU BEAUREGARD** Pomerol 1993 • $26 • (01/31/96)
87 **CHATEAU BEAUSEJOUR** St.-Emilion 1993 • $30 • (01/31/96)
87 **CHATEAU LE BON-PASTEUR** Pomerol 1993 • $32 • (01/31/96)
87 **CHATEAU LA DOMINIQUE** St.-Emilion 1993 • $30 • (01/31/96)
87 **CHATEAU L'EVANGILE** Pomerol 1993 • $65 • (01/31/96)
87 **CHATEAU FERRIERE** Margaux 1993 • $NA • (01/31/96)
87 **CHATEAU DE FIEUZAL** Pessac-Léognan 1993 • $25 • (01/31/96)
87 **CHATEAU FIGEAC** St.-Emilion 1993 • $33 • (01/31/96)
87 **CHATEAU GAZIN** Pomerol 1993 • $30 • (01/31/96)
87 **LA GRAVE A POMEROL** Pomerol 1993 • $28 • (01/31/96)
87 **CHATEAU LARMANDE** St.-Emilion 1993 • $24 • (01/31/96)
87 **CHATEAU LYNCH-BAGES** Pauillac 1993 • $33 • (01/31/96)
87 **CHATEAU LES ORMES DE PEZ** St.-Estèphe 1993 • $19 • (01/31/96)
87 **CHATEAU RAUSAN-SEGLA** Margaux 1993 • $33 • (01/31/96)

86 **CHATEAU BEAU-SEJOUR BECOT** St.-Emilion 1993 • $25 • (01/31/96)
86 **CHATEAU BONALGUE** Pomerol 1993 • $27 • (12/15/95)
86 **CLOS DU CLOCHER** Pomerol 1993 • $28 • (12/15/95)
86 **CHATEAU DAUZAC** Margaux 1993 • $24 • (01/31/96)
86 **YANNICK FAVREAU** Pomerol 1993 • $NA • (02/29/96)
86 **CHATEAU LA FLEUR-PETRUS** Pomerol 1993 • $39 • (01/31/96)
86 **CHATEAU GISCOURS** Margaux 1993 • $24 • (01/31/96)
86 **CHATEAU GRAND-PONTET** St.-Emilion 1993 • $22 • (01/31/96)
86 **CHATEAU HAUT-BAILLY** Pessac-Léognan 1993 • $30 • (01/31/96)
86 **CHATEAU KIRWAN** Margaux 1993 • $20 • (01/31/96)
86 **CHATEAU LAFITE-ROTHSCHILD** Pauillac 1993 • $72 • (01/31/96)
86 **CHATEAU LANGOA BARTON** St.-Julien 1993 • $25 • (01/31/96)
86 **CHATEAU LARRIVET-HAUT-BRION** Pessac-Léognan 1993 • $19 • (01/31/96)
86 **CHATEAU MEYNEY** St.-Estèphe 1993 • $17 • (01/31/96)
86 **CHATEAU PAVIE MACQUIN** St.-Emilion 1993 • $18 • (01/31/96)
86 **CHATEAU PETIT-VILLAGE** Pomerol 1993 • $35 • (01/31/96)
86 **CHATEAU SMITH-HAUT-LAFITTE** Pessac-Léognan 1993 • $25 • (01/31/96)
86 **CHATEAU ST.-GEORGES** St.-Georges-St.-Emilion 1990 • $23 • (08/31/95)
86 **CHATEAU TALBOT** St.-Julien 1993 • $25 • (01/31/96)

85 **CHATEAU BRANAIRE-DUCRU** St.-Julien 1993 • $25 • (01/31/96)
85 **CHATEAU BRANE-CANTENAC** Margaux 1993 • $25 • (01/31/96)
85 **CHATEAU CANON** St.-Emilion 1993 • $36 • (01/31/96)
85 **CHATEAU CANTENAC-BROWN** Margaux 1993 • $23 • (01/31/96)
85 **CHATEAU CLOS DES JACOBINS** St.-Emilion 1993 • $25 • (01/31/96)
85 **CLOS L'EGLISE** Pomerol 1993 • $25 • (01/31/96)

85 **CHATEAU LA CROIX-DE-GAY** Pomerol 1993 • $20 • (01/31/96)
85 **LES FIEFS DE LAGRANGE** St.-Julien 1993 • $16 • (01/31/96)
85 **CHATEAU LA FLEUR** St.-Emilion 1993 • $17 • (01/31/96)
85 **CHATEAU LA FONTAINE** Fronsac 1993 • $9 • (08/31/95)
85 **CHÂTEAU GRAND-PUY-LACOSTE** Pauillac 1993 • $25 • (01/31/96)
85 **CHATEAU GRESSIER GRAND POUJEAUX** Moulis 1993 • $16 • (01/31/96)
85 **CHATEAU LA GURGUE** Margaux 1993 • $21 • (01/31/96)
85 **CHATEAU HAUT-MARBUZET** St.-Estèphe 1993 • $33 • (01/31/96)
85 **CHATEAU LAFLEUR-GAZIN** Pomerol 1993 • $24 • (01/31/96)
85 **CHATEAU LALANDE-BORIE** St.-Julien 1993 • $18 • (01/31/96)
85 **CHATEAU LIVERSAN** Haut-Médoc 1993 • $15 • (01/31/96)
85 **CHATEAU LA LOUVIERE** Pessac-Léognan 1993 • $23 • (01/31/96)
85 **CHATEAU MAGDELAINE** St.-Emilion 1993 • $36 • (01/31/96)
85 **CHATEAU OLIVIER** Pessac-Léognan 1993 • $23 • (01/31/96)
85 **CHATEAU PAVIE-DECESSE** St.-Emilion 1993 • $24 • (01/31/96)
85 **CHATEAU PICHON-LONGUEVILLE-BARON** Pauillac 1993 • $33 • (01/31/96)
85 **CHATEAU SIRAN** Margaux 1993 • $22 • (01/31/96)
85 **CHATEAU ST.-PIERRE** St.-Julien 1993 • $22 • (01/31/96)
85 **LA TERRASSE** Bordeaux Supérieur La Terrasse sur la Rivière 1993 • $9 • (08/31/95)

RED BURGUNDY

86 **DOMAINE CHOFFLET-VALDENAIRE** Givry 1993 • $20 • (05/15/96)
97 **BERTRAND AMBROISE** Corton Le Rognet 1993 • $75 • (11/15/95)
93 **JEAN-MARC BOILLOT** Volnay 1993 • $30 • (11/15/95)

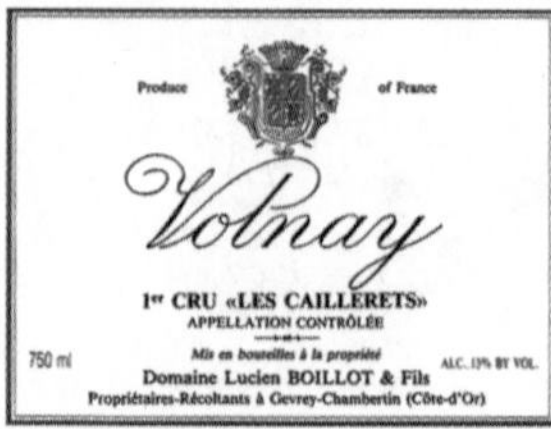

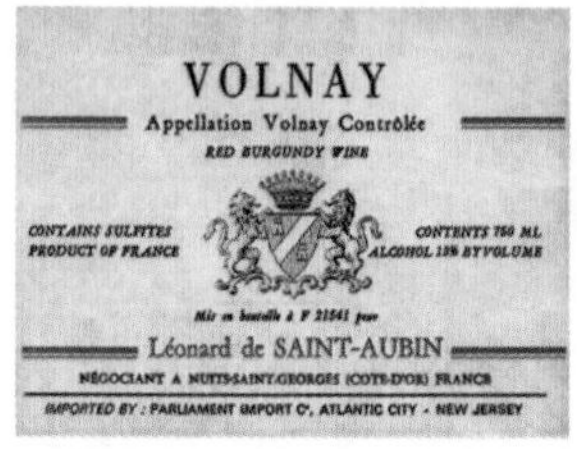

93 **MAURICE ECARD** Savigny-lès-Beaune Aux Serpentières 1993 • $94 • (05/15/96)

93 **DOMAINE DES COMTES LAFON** Volnay-Santenots Les Santenots du Milieu 1993 • $NA • (05/15/96)

93 **DOMINIQUE LAURENT** Pommard Les Epenots 1993 • $85 • (05/15/96)

93 **DOMINIQUE LAURENT** Pommard Vieilles Vignes 1993 • $48 • (05/15/96)

92 **MARQUIS D'ANGERVILLE** Volnay Premier Cru 1993 • $20 • (05/15/96)

92 **JEAN-MARC BOILLOT** Volnay Pitures 1993 • $42 • (11/15/95)

91 **DOMAINE LUCIEN BOILLOT** Volnay Les Caillerets 1993 • $38 • (11/15/95)

91 **DOMAINE LUCIEN BOILLOT** Pommard Les Fremiers 1993 • $38 • (11/15/95)

90 **MARQUIS D'ANGERVILLE** Volnay En Champans 1993 • $29 • (05/15/96)

90 **SIMON BIZE & FILS** Aloxe-Corton Le Suchot 1993. • $24 • (05/15/96)

90 **JEAN-MARC BOILLOT** Pommard Les Jarollières 1993 • $50 • (11/15/95)

89 **JEAN-MARC BOILLOT** Volnay Carelle Sous La Chapelle 1993 • $42 • (11/15/95)

89 **LEONARD DE SAINT-AUBIN** Volnay 1993 • $26 • (05/15/96)

88 **BONNEAU DU MARTRAY** Corton 1993 • $45 • (11/15/95)

88 **COSTE-CAUMARTIN** Pommard Les Fremiers 1993 • $NA • (05/15/96)

88 **P. DUBREUIL-FONTAINE PÈRE & FILS** Corton Bressandes 1993 • $NA • (05/15/96)

88 **LOUIS JADOT** Beaune Clos des Ursules 1993 • $35 • (11/15/95)

87 **DOMAINE LUCIEN BOILLOT** Volnay Les Brouillards 1993 • $37 • (11/15/95)

87 **BOUCHARD PERE & FILS** Chassagne-Montrachet Red 1993 • $25 • (11/15/95)

87 **MONGEARD-MUGNERET** Savigny-lès-Beaune 1993 • $22 • (11/15/95)

86 **SIMON BIZE & FILS** Savigny-lès-Beaune Les Marconnets 1993 • $25 • (05/15/96)

86 **BOUCHARD PERE & FILS** Beaune Teurons Domaines du Château de Beaune 1993 • $28 • (11/15/95)

85 **JEAN-MARC BOILLOT** Beaune Les Montrevenots 1993 • $30 • (11/15/95)

85 **BOUCHARD PERE & FILS** Beaune Clos de la Mousse Domaines du Château de Beaune 1993 • $28 • (11/15/95)

85 **P. DUBREUIL-FONTAINE PÈRE & FILS** Pernand-Vergelesses 1993 • $NA • (05/15/96)

85 **LEONARD DE SAINT-AUBIN** Pommard 1993 • $27 • (05/15/96)

98 **DOMINIQUE LAURENT** Mazis-Chambertin 1993 • $117 • (05/15/96)

96 **BERTRAND AMBROISE** Clos Vougeot 1993 • $90 • (11/15/95)

96 **JEAN GRIVOT** Richebourg 1993 • $128 • (05/15/96)

96 **DOMINIQUE LAURENT** Ruchottes-Chambertin 1993 • $117 • (05/15/96)

95 **DOMINIQUE LAURENT** Gevrey-Chambertin Vieilles Vignes 1993 • $NA • (05/15/96)

95 **EMMANUEL ROUGET** Echézeaux 1993 • $80 • (05/15/96)

95 **EMMANUEL ROUGET** Vosne-Romanée Cros Parantoux 1993 • $72 • (05/15/96)

94 **PHILIPPE CHARLOPIN-PARIZOT** Charmes-Chambertin 1993 • $94 • (05/15/96)

94 **J. CONFURON-COTETIDOT** Gevrey-Chambertin 1993 • $NA • (05/15/96)

94 **JEAN GRIVOT** Vosne-Romanée Les Beaux Monts 1993 • $32 • (05/15/96)

94 **DOMINIQUE LAURENT** Clos Vougeot 1993 • $NA • (05/15/96)

94 **DOMAINE DE LA ROMANÉE-CONTI** La Tâche 1993 • $270 • (05/15/96)

94 **DOMAINE DE LA ROMANÉE-CONTI** Romanée-Conti 1993 • $850 • (05/15/96)

93 **ROBERT ARNOUX** Romanée-St.-Vivant 1993 • $NA • (11/15/95)

93 **J. A. FERRET** Pouilly-Fuissé Tournant de Pouilly 1994 • $45 • (05/31/96)

93 **GUFFENS-HEYNEN** Pouilly-Fuissé La Roche 1994 • $40 • (05/31/96)

92 **DOMAINE DE L'ARLOT** Nuits-St.-Georges Clos des Forêts St.-Georges 1993 • $40 • (05/15/96)

92 **JEAN GRIVOT** Clos de Vougeot 1993 • $45 • (05/15/96) • CS
92 **JEAN GRIVOT** Echézeaux 1993 • $45 • (05/15/96)
92 **JACQUES-FREDERIC MUGNIER** Bonnes Mares 1993 • $90 • (05/15/96)
92 **DOMAINE DE LA ROMANÉE-CONTI** Romanée St.-Vivant 1993 • $135 • (05/15/96)
92 **JEAN & JEAN-LOUIS TRAPET** Chambertin 1993 • $NA • (05/15/96)
91 **ROBERT ARNOUX** Clos de Vougeot 1993 • $80 • (11/15/95)
91 **DOMAINE DUJAC** Clos St.-Denis 1993 • $79 • (05/15/96)
91 **FAIVELEY** Echézeaux 1993 • $56 • (05/15/96)
91 **FAIVELEY** Chambertin Clos de Bèze 1993 • $113 • (05/15/96)
91 **EMMANUEL ROUGET** Vosne-Romanée Les Beaux Monts 1993 • $55 • (05/15/96)
90 **BERTRAND AMBROISE** Nuits-St.-Georges Les Vaucrains 1993 • $65 • (11/15/95)
90 **BERTAGNA** Clos St.-Denis 1993 • $71 • (05/15/96)
90 **BOUCHARD PERE & FILS** La Romanée Château de Vosne-Romanée 1993 • $120 • (11/15/95)
90 **PHILIPPE CHARLOPIN-PARIZOT** Clos St.-Denis 1993 • $94 • (05/15/96)
90 **FAIVELEY** Nuits-St.-Georges Porrets St.-Georges 1993 • $43 • (05/15/96)
90 **GEANTET-PANSIOT** Charmes-Chambertin 1993 • $60 • (05/15/96)
90 **GEANTET-PANSIOT** Gevrey-Chambertin Poissenot 1993 • $45 • (05/15/96)
90 **JEAN GRIVOT** Nuits-St.-Georges Les Boudots 1993 • $32 • (05/15/96)
90 **MAUME** Gevrey-Chambertin 1993 • $NA • (05/15/96)
90 **JACQUES-FREDERIC MUGNIER** Chambolle-Musigny Les Fuées 1993 • $69 • (05/15/96)
90 **DOMAINE DE LA ROMANÉE-CONTI** Echézeaux 1993 • $95 • (05/15/96)
90 **DOMAINE DE LA ROMANÉE-CONTI** Richebourg 1993 • $190 • (05/15/96)
90 **PHILIPPE ROSSIGNOL** Gevrey-Chambertin Les Corbeaux Cuvée Vieilles Vignes 1993 • $NA • (05/15/96)
90 **EMMANUEL ROUGET** Nuits-St.-Georges 1993 • $NA • (05/15/96)
89 **DOMAINE DE L'ARLOT** Nuits-St.-Georges Clos de L'Arlot 1993 • $34 • (05/15/96)
89 **ROBERT ARNOUX** Echézeaux 1993 • $80 • (11/15/95)
88 **BERTRAND AMBROISE** Vosne-Romanée Aux Damaudes 1993 • $45 • (11/15/95)
88 **DOMAINE DE L'ARLOT** Nuits-St.-Georges 1993 • $22 • (05/15/96)
88 **ROBERT ARNOUX** Vosne-Romanée Les Chaumes 1993 • $55 • (11/15/95)
88 **BERTAGNA** Clos de Vougeot 1993 • $90 • (05/15/96)
88 **DOMAINE LUCIEN BOILLOT** Gevrey-Chambertin Les Cherbaudes 1er 1993 • $40 • (11/15/95)
88 **BOUCHARD PERE & FILS** Chambolle-Musigny Domaines du Château de Beaune EP 1993 • $36 • (11/15/95)
88 **DOMAINE DUJAC** Morey-St.-Denis 1993 • $37 • (05/15/96)
88 **DOMAINE DUJAC** Gevrey-Chambertin Aux Combottes 1993 • $65 • (05/15/96)
88 **JEAN GRIVOT** Vosne-Romanée 1993 • $22 • (05/15/96)
88 **THIERRY MORTET** Gevrey-Chambertin Clos Prieur 1993 • $NA • (05/15/96)
88 **JACQUES-FREDERIC MUGNIER** Chambolle-Musigny 1993 • $39 • (05/15/96)
87 **ROBERT ARNOUX** Vosne-Romanée Les Suchots 1993 • $80 • (11/15/95)
87 **BICHOT** Vosne-Romanée Les Malconsorts Domaine du Clos Frantin 1993 • $NA • (11/15/95)
87 **DOMAINE LUCIEN BOILLOT** Gevrey-Chambertin Les Corbeaux 1993 • $40 • (11/15/95)

87 **DOMAINE THIERRY MORTET** Chambolle-Musigny Les Beaux Bruns 1993 • $58 • (05/15/96)
86 **BERTRAND AMBROISE** Nuits-St.-Georges 1993 • $40 • (11/15/95)
86 **BERTAGNA** Vougeot Clos de la Perrière 1993 • $58 • (05/15/96)
86 **JEAN-MARC BOILLOT** Bourgogne 1993 • $17 • (11/15/95)
86 **BOUCHARD PERE & FILS** Gevrey-Chambertin 1993 • $29 • (11/15/95)
86 **DOMAINE BRUNO CLAIR** Marsannay Les Grasses Têtes 1993 • $25 • (05/15/96)
86 **DOMAINE BRUNO CLAIR** Gevrey-Chambertin 1993 • $47 • (05/15/96)
86 **DOMAINE DUJAC** Chambolle-Musigny 1993 • $37 • (05/15/96)
85 **BICHOT** Echézeaux 1993 • $NA • (11/15/95)
85 **DOMAINE LUCIEN BOILLOT** Nuits-St.-Georges Les Pruliers 1993 • $40 • (11/15/95)
85 **DOMAINE BRUNO CLAIR** Marsannay Les Vaudenelles 1993 • $22 • (05/15/96)
85 **ROBERT ARNOUX** Pinot Noir Bourgogne 1993 • $18 • (05/15/96)

WHITE BURGUNDY

91 **OLIVIER LEFLAIVE FRÈRES** Rully Premier Cru 1994 • $19 • (05/31/96)
99 **J.-F. COCHE-DURY** Corton-Charlemagne 1993 • $170 • (05/31/96) • CS
98 **DOMAINE DES COMTES LAFON** Montrachet 1993 • $350 • (05/31/96)
96 **MARC COLIN** Montrachet 1994 • $200 • (05/31/96)
96 **VERGET** Montrachet 1994 • $160 • (05/31/96)
95 **MICHEL BOUZEREAU** Meursault Les Genevrières 1994 • $45 • (05/31/96)
95 **J.-F. COCHE-DURY** Meursault Les Perrières 1993 • $80 • (05/31/96)
95 **DOMAINE LEFLAIVE** Chevalier-Montrachet 1993 • $165 • (05/31/96)
94 **BOUCHARD PÈRE & FILS** Montrachet 1994 • $185 • (05/31/96)
94 **MICHEL BOUZEREAU** Puligny-Montrachet Champ Gain 1994 • $45 • (05/31/96)
94 **PIERRE COLIN** Bâtard-Montrachet 1994 • $NA • (05/31/96)
94 **RAMONET** Bâtard-Montrachet 1993 • $140 • (05/31/96)
93 **JEAN-MARC BOILLOT** Puligny-Montrachet Les Combettes 1994 • $62 • (05/31/96)
93 **J.-F. COCHE-DURY** Meursault 1993 • $45 • (05/31/96)
93 **MICHEL COLIN-DELÉGER** Chassagne-Montrachet En Remilly 1994 • $40 • (05/31/96)
93 **GOISOT** Bourgogne Côtes d'Auxerre Domaine du Corps de Garde 1994 • $NA • (05/31/96)
93 **ROBERT & RAYMOND JACOB** Corton-Charlemagne 1994 • $NA • (05/31/96)
93 **CHARLES & RÉMI JOBARD** Meursault Les Genevrières 1994 • $45 • (05/31/96)
93 **DOMAINE DES COMTES LAFON** Meursault Les Perrières 1993 • $80 • (05/31/96)
93 **JEAN PILLOT** Chassagne-Montrachet Les Vergers 1994 • $32 • (05/31/96)
93 **JACQUES PRIEUR** Chevalier-Montrachet 1994 • $150 • (05/31/96)
92 **J.-F. COCHE-DURY** Meursault Les Rougeots 1993 • $60 • (05/31/96)
92 **GOISOT** Bourgogne Côtes d'Auxerre Chardonnay Domaine du Corps de Garde 1994 • $NA • (05/31/96)
92 **ANTONIN GUYON** Meursault Les Charmes-Dessus 1994 • $32 • (05/31/96)
92 **GUFFENS-HEYNEN** Pouilly-Fuissé Clos des Petits-Croux 1994 • $34 • (05/31/96)
92 **JEAN THÉVENET** Mâcon Clessé Domaine de la Bongran Cuvée Tradition 1993 • $NA • (05/31/96)
92 **DOMAINE LEFLAIVE** Puligny-Montrachet Clavoillon 1993 • $70 • (05/31/96)
92 **DOMAINE LEFLAIVE** Puligny-Montrachet Les Pucelles 1993 • $100 • (05/31/96)

92 **MICHEL NIELLON** Chevalier-Montrachet 1994 • $135 • (05/31/96)
92 **DOMAINE ROULOT** Meursault Les Charmes 1994 • $63 • (05/31/96)
92 **VERGET** Chassagne-Montrachet La Romanée 1994 • $50 • (05/31/96)
92 **VERGET** Corton-Charlemagne Cuvée Vieilles Vignes 1994 • $57 • (05/31/96)
92 **VERGET** Meursault Les Porusot 1994 • $44 • (05/31/96)
91 **BOUCHARD PÈRE & FILS** Corton-Charlemagne 1994 • $60 • (05/31/96)
91 **JOSEPH DROUHIN** Puligny-Montrachet Les Folatières 1994 • $54 • (05/31/96)
91 **LOUIS JADOT** Puligny-Montrachet Les Perrières 1994 • $38 • (05/31/96)
91 **DOMAINE LEFLAIVE** Puligny-Montrachet Les Folatières 1993 • $95 • (05/31/96)
91 **DOMAINE ROULOT** Meursault Le Tesson Clos de Mon Plaisir 1994 • $13 • (05/31/96)
91 **VALETTE** Mâcon-Chaintré Vieilles Vignes 1994 • $NA • (05/31/96)
91 **VERGET** Meursault Les Charmes Cuvée Vieilles Vignes 1994 • $52 • (05/31/96)
90 **BLAIN-GAGNARD** Chassagne-Montrachet Morgeot 1994 • $45 • (05/31/96) • 90
90 **JEAN BOILLOT** Puligny-Montrachet Les Pucelles 1994 • $45 • (05/31/96)
90 **JEAN-MARC BOILLOT** Puligny-Montrachet Les Folatières 1994 • $51 • (05/31/96)
90 **JEAN-MARC BOILLOT** Puligny-Montrachet Les Pucelles 1994 • $58 • (05/31/96)
90 **MICHEL BOUZEREAU** Meursault Les Charmes 1994 • $45 • (05/31/96)
90 **CHARTRON & TRÉBUCHET** Puligny-Montrachet 1994 • $26 • (05/31/96)
90 **FRANÇOISE & DENIS CLAIR** St.-Aubin Les Murgers des Dents de Chien 1994 • $27 • (05/31/96)
90 **MARC COLIN** Chassagne-Montrachet Vide Bourse 1994 • $38 • (05/31/96) • 90
90 **JOSEPH DROUHIN** St.-Aubin 1994 • $22 • (05/31/96)
90 **J. A. FERRET** Pouilly-Fuissé Les Ménétrières 1993 • $45 • (05/31/96)
90 **CHÂTEAU FUISSÉ** Pouilly-Fuissé Vieilles Vignes 1994 • $44 • (05/31/96)
90 **ALBERT GRIVAULT** Meursault Les Perrières 1994 • $39 • (05/31/96)
90 **PATRICK JAVILLIER** Puligny-Montrachet Les Levrons 1994 • $NA • (05/31/96)
90 **LOUIS LATOUR** Corton-Charlemagne 1994 • $78 • (05/31/96) • 91
90 **G. MICHELOT** Meursault 1994 • $NA • (05/31/96)
90 **MOILLARD** Bâtard-Montrachet 1994 • $85 • (05/31/96)
90 **MARC MOREY** Chassagne-Montrachet Les Vergers 1994 • $40 • (05/31/96) • 90
90 **FERNAND PILLOT** Chassagne-Montrachet Les Vergers 1994 • $NA • (05/31/96) • 89
90 **FERNAND PILLOT** Chassagne-Montrachet Vide Bourse 1994 • $NA • (05/31/96) • 90
90 **JACQUES PRIEUR** Meursault Clos de Mazeray 1994 • $35 • (05/31/96)
90 **JACQUES PRIEUR** Puligny-Montrachet Les Combettes 1994 • $50 • (05/31/96)
90 **RAMONET** Chassagne-Montrachet Les Ruchottes 1993 • $75 • (05/31/96)
90 **RAMONET** Puligny-Montrachet Champ Canet 1993 • $75 • (05/31/96)
90 **JEAN THÉVENET** Mâcon Viré Domaine Emilian Gillet Quintaine 1992 • $20 • (05/31/96)
90 **VERGET** Meursault Les Genevrières Hospices de Beaune 1994 • $35 • (05/31/96)
89 **GUY AMIOT** Chassagne-Montrachet Les Champs Gain 1994 • $44 • (05/31/96) • 90
89 **CHARTRON & TRÉBUCHET** Chassagne-Montrachet Les Morgeot 1994 • $25 • (05/31/96) • 88
89 **CHARTRON & TRÉBUCHET** Santenay 1994 • $15 • (05/31/96)
89 **FRANÇOISE & DENIS CLAIR** Puligny-Montrachet La Garenne 1994 • $44 • (05/31/96)

89 **MICHEL COLIN-DELÉGER** Chassagne-Montrachet Les Chenevottes 1994 • $45 • (05/31/96) • 90

89 **CHÂTEAU FUISSÉ** Pouilly-Fuissé Les Combettes 1994 • $34 • (05/31/96)

89 **CHÂTEAU FUISSÉ** Pouilly-Fuissé Le Clos 1994 • $34 • (05/31/96)

89 **PAUL GARAUDET** Meursault Vieille Vigne 1994 • $26 • (05/31/96)

89 **HENRI GERMAIN** Meursault Les Charmes 1993 • $43 • (08/31/95)

89 **L'HÉRITIER-GUYOT** Vougeot Clos Blanc de Vougeot 1994 • $40 • (05/31/96)

89 **LOUIS JADOT** Meursault Perrières 1994 • $38 • (05/31/96)

89 **PATRICK JAVILLIER** Meursault Les Tillets 1993 • $38 • (08/31/95)

89 **FRANÇOIS JOBARD** Meursault Poruzots 1993 • $NA • (05/31/96)

89 **DOMAINE LEFLAIVE** Bienvenues-Bâtard-Montrachet 1994 • $125 • (05/31/96)

89 **JEAN-JACQUES & SYLVAINE MARTIN** Pouilly-Fuissé Les Chevrières 1994 • $NA • (05/31/96)

89 **MOILLARD** Meursault Charmes 1994 • $37 • (04/30/96)

89 **MICHEL NIELLON** Chassagne-Montrachet Clos St.-Jean 1994 • $NA • (05/31/96) • 90

89 **JEAN PILLOT** Chassagne-Montrachet Morgeot 1994 • $NA • (05/31/96) • 89

89 **JEAN THÉVENET** Mâcon Viré Domaine Emilian Gillet Quintaine 1993 • $20 • (05/31/96)

89 **VERGET** Pouilly-Fuissé Tête de Cuvée 1994 • $25 • (05/31/96)

89 **VERGET** Puligny-Montrachet Les Enseignères 1994 • $33 • (05/31/96)

88 **PIERRE BITOUZET** Corton-Charlemagne 1993 • $NA • (08/31/95)

88 **BONNEAU DU MARTRAY** Corton-Charlemagne 1993 • $60 • (08/31/95)

88 **JEAN CHARTRON** Puligny-Montrachet Clos de la Pucelle 1994 • $NA • (05/31/96)

88 **MICHEL COLIN-DELÉGER** Chassagne-Montrachet Morgeot 1994 • $40 • (05/31/96) • 88

88 **CORDIER PÈRE & FILS** Pouilly-Fuissé Lot No.1 1994 • $21 • (05/31/96)

88 **FONTAINE-GAGNARD** Criots-Bâtard-Montrachet 1994 • $90 • (05/31/96) • 88

88 **GOISOT** Bourgogne Aligoté 1994 • $NA • (05/31/96)

88 **ALBERT GRIVAL'LT** Meursault 1994 • $25 • (05/31/96)

88 **FRANÇOIS JOBARD** Meursault 1993 • $NA • (05/31/96)

88 **LALEURE-PIOT** Pernand-Vergelesses Premier Cru 1994 • $34 • (05/31/96)

88 **OLIVIER LEFLAIVE** Meursault Les Perrières 1993 • $42 • (08/31/95)

88 **MOMMESSIN** Pouilly-Fuissé 1994 • $25 • (05/31/96)

88 **MICHEL MOREY-COFFINET** Chassagne-Montrachet Caillerets 1994 • $34 • (05/31/96) • 88

88 **MICHEL MOREY-COFFINET** Chassagne-Montrachet La Romanée 1994 • $37 • (05/31/96) • 89

88 **HENRI NAUDIN-FERRAND** Bourgogne Hautes-Côtes de Beaune 1994 • $NA • (05/31/96) • 88

88 **MICHEL NIELLON** Bâtard-Montrachet 1994 • $135 • (05/31/96)

88 **MICHEL NIELLON** Chassagne-Montrachet 1994 • $45 • (05/31/96)

88 **FERNAND PILLOT** Chassagne-Montrachet Les Grandes Ruchottes 1994 • $NA • (05/31/96) • 88

88 **FERNAND PILLOT** Puligny-Montrachet 1994 • $NA • (05/31/96)

88 **JEAN PILLOT** Chassagne-Montrachet Les Macherelles 1994 • $NA • (05/31/96)

88 **DOMAINE ROULOT** Meursault Les Luchets 1994 • $36 • (05/31/96)

88 **THIBERT PÈRE & FILS** Pouilly-Fuissé 1994 • $15 • (05/31/96)

88 **THOMAS** Pouilly-Fuissé Vieilles Vignes 1994 • $25 • (05/31/96)

88 **DOMAINE THOMAS** St.-Véran Vieille Vigne Cuvée Préstige 1994 • $16 • (08/31/95)

87 **GUY AMIOT** Chassagne-Montrachet Clos St.-Jean 1994 • $44 • (05/31/96) • 86

87 **GUY AMIOT** Chassagne-Montrachet Les Vergers 1994 • $44 • (05/31/96)
87 **BACHELET-RAMONET** Chassagne-Montrachet Caillerets 1994 • $NA • (05/31/96)
87 **DANIEL BARRAUD** Pouilly-Fuissé La Verchère 1994 • $21 • (05/31/96)
87 **BLAIN-GAGNARD** Chassagne-Montrachet Caillerets 1994 • $45 • (05/31/96)
87 **JEAN-MARC BOILLOT** Puligny-Montrachet Les Referts 1994 • $47 • (05/31/96)
87 **BOUCHARD PÈRE & FILS** Bâtard-Montrachet 1994 • $96 • (05/31/96) • 85
87 **BOUCHARD PÈRE & FILS** Beaune Clos St.-Landry 1994 • $32 • (05/31/96) • 87
87 **BOUCHARD PÈRE & FILS** Beaune Premier Cru 1994 • $28 • (05/31/96) • 87
87 **BOUCHARD PÈRE & FILS** Puligny-Montrachet Pucelles 1994 • $46 • (05/31/96)
87 **JEAN-MARC BROCARD** Sauvignon de St.-Bris Domaine Ste.-Claire 1994 • $NA • (05/31/96)
87 **LOUIS CARILLON** Puligny-Montrachet 1994 • $35 • (05/31/96)
87 **CHARTRON & TRÉBUCHET** Bourgogne Chardonnay 1994 • $10 • (05/31/96)
87 **PHILIPPE CHAVY** Puligny-Montrachet Corvée des Vignes 1994 • $30 • (05/31/96)
87 **CORDIER PÈRE & FILS** Pouilly-Fuissé Les Vignes Blanches 1994 • $34 • (05/31/96)
87 **JOSEPH DROUHIN** Puligny-Montrachet 1994 • $39 • (05/31/96)
87 **GEORGES DUBOEUF** Pouilly-Fuissé Oak-Aged 1994 • $17 • (05/31/96)
87 **HENRI GERMAIN** Meursault Les Chevalières 1993 • $NA • (08/31/95)
87 **HENRI GERMAIN** Meursault Le Limozin 1993 • $33 • (08/31/95)
87 **GOISOT** Bourgogne Côtes d'Auxerre Chardonnay 1994 • $NA • (05/31/96)
87 **OLIVIER LEFLAIVE FRÈRES** St.-Aubin En Remilly 1994 • $22 • (05/31/96)
87 **DOMAINE MICHELOT** Meursault Les Narvaux 1994 • $40 • (05/31/96)
87 **MOILLARD** Puligny-Montrachet Les Perrières 1994 • $39 • (05/31/96)
87 **MARC MOREY** Chassagne-Montrachet Morgeot 1994 • $48 • (05/31/96)
87 **JEAN PILLOT** Chassagne-Montrachet Les Chenevottes 1994 • $30 • (05/31/96)
87 **VINCENT PRUNIER** Puligny-Montrachet La Garenne 1994 • $NA • (05/31/96)
87 **DOMAINE GUY ROULOT** Meursault Les Meix Chavaux 1993 • $37 • (08/31/95)
87 **ROUX PÈRE & FILS** Chardonnay Bourgogne 1994 • $NA • (05/31/96)
87 **JACQUES SAUMAIZE** Pouilly-Fuissé La Roche 1994 • $17 • (05/31/96)
87 **DOMAINE THOMAS-MOILLARD** Corton-Charlemagne 1994 • $60 • (05/31/96)
87 **VERGET** Chassagne-Montrachet Premier Cru 1994 • $27 • (05/31/96)
86 **GUY AMIOT** Chassagne-Montrachet Les Macherelles 1994 • $39 • (05/31/96)
86 **DOMAINE D'AUVENAY** Puligny-Montrachet Les Folatières 1993 • $NA • (08/31/95)
86 **ROGER BELLAND** Chassagne-Montrachet Morgeot-Clos Pitois 1994 • $NA • (05/31/96)
86 **PIERRE BITOUZET** Corton-Charlemagne 1994 • $50 • (05/31/96) • 86
86 **BLAIN-GAGNARD** Criots-Bâtard-Montrachet 1994 • $95 • (05/31/96) • 86
86 **JEAN-MARC BOILLOT** Puligny-Montrachet 1994 • $37 • (05/31/96)
86 **JEAN-MARC BROCARD** Bourgogne Domaine Ste.-Claire 1994 • $11 • (05/31/96)
86 **GEORGES BURRIER** Pouilly-Fuissé 1994 • $18 • (05/31/96)
86 **FONTAINE-GAGNARD** Bâtard-Montrachet 1994 • $90 • (05/31/96) • 85
86 **FONTAINE-GAGNARD** Chassagne-Montrachet La Boudriotte 1994 • $46 • (05/31/96)
86 **MME. R. GUÉRIN** Pouilly-Fuissé La Roche Sélection Vieilles Vignes Cuvée No. 1 1994 • $NA • (05/31/96)
86 **RENÉ GUERIN** Pouilly-Fuissé La Roche Sélection Vieilles Vignes No. 2 1994 • $21 • (05/31/96)
86 **L'HÉRITIER-GUYOT** St.-Romain 1994 • $16 • (05/31/96)

86 **LOUIS JADOT** Beaune-Grèves Le Clos Blanc 1994 • $38 • (05/31/96) • 86
86 **MICHEL JUILLOT** Mercurey 1994 • $23 • (05/31/96)
86 **LOUIS LATOUR** Montrachet 1994 • $230 • (05/31/96)
86 **LOUIS LATOUR** Puligny-Montrachet Les Folatières 1993 • $39 • (08/31/95)
86 **LOUIS LATOUR** Meursault Les Gouttes d'Or 1993 • $37 • (08/31/95)
86 **LEONARD DE SAINT-AUBIN** Puligny-Montrachet 1994 • $27 • (05/31/96)
86 **MOILLARD** Puligny-Montrachet 1994 • $30 • (05/31/96)
86 **MARC MOREY** Chassagne-Montrachet Les Chenevottes 1994 • $40 • (05/31/96)
86 **MARC MOREY** Puligny-Montrachet Les Pucelles 1994 • $60 • (05/31/96)
86 **DOMAINE JACQUES PRIEUR** Meursault Les Perrières 1993 • $52 • (08/31/95)
86 **CHÂTEAU DE PULIGNY-MONTRACHET** Puligny-Montrachet 1994 • $16 • (05/31/96)
86 **RAPET PÈRE & FILS** Corton-Charlemagne 1994 • $70 • (05/31/96) • 85
86 **ANTONIN RODET** Meursault Les Perrières 1994 • $53 • (05/31/96)
86 **THIBERT PÈRE & FILS** Pouilly-Fuissé Vieilles Vignes 1994 • $16 • (05/31/96)
86 **VERGET** Meursault Les Rougeots 1994 • $31 • (05/31/96)
86 **VERGET** Puligny-Montrachet Sous Le Puits 1994 • $38 • (05/31/96)
86 **VERGET** Bâtard-Montrachet 1993 • $130 • (08/31/95)
85 **GUY AMIOT** Chassagne-Montrachet Caillerets 1994 • $50 • (05/31/96)
85 **ANDRÉ AUVIGUE** Pouilly-Fuissé Solutré 1994 • $18 • (05/31/96)
85 **ROGER BELLAND** Puligny-Montrachet Champ Gain 1994 • $NA • (05/31/96)
85 **BLAIN-GAGNARD** Chassagne-Montrachet Clos St.-Jean 1994 • $45 • (05/31/96)
85 **BLAIN-GAGNARD** Chassagne-Montrachet La Boudriotte 1994 • $45 • (05/31/96)
85 **JEAN BOILLOT** Puligny-Montrachet Clos de la Mouchère 1994 • $44 • (05/31/96)
85 **BOUCHARD PÈRE & FILS** Meursault Les Genevrières 1994 • $46 • (05/31/96)
85 **MICHEL BOUZEREAU** Meursault Les Grands Charrons 1994 • $30 • (05/31/96)
85 **MICHEL BOUZEREAU** Meursault Le Tesson 1994 • $35 • (05/31/96)
85 **CHARTRON & TRÉBUCHET** Auxey-Duresses 1994 • $14 • (05/31/96) • 85
85 **CHARTRON & TRÉBUCHET** Meursault 1994 • $22 • (05/31/96)
85 **CHARTRON & TRÉBUCHET** Pernand-Vergelesses 1994 • $15 • (05/31/96)
85 **CHARTRON & TRÉBUCHET** St.-Aubin La Chatenière 1994 • $17 • (05/31/96)
85 **JEAN CHARTRON** Puligny-Montrachet Clos du Cailleret 1994 • $42 • (05/31/96)
85 **MARC COLIN** Chassagne-Montrachet Les Caillerets 1994 • $45 • (05/31/96)
85 **MARC COLIN** Chassagne-Montrachet Les Champs-Gains 1994 • $40 • (05/31/96)
85 **MARC COLIN** Puligny-Montrachet Le Trézin 1994 • $40 • (05/31/96)
85 **MARC COLIN** St.-Aubin Le Charmois 1994 • $24 • (05/31/96)
85 **MARC COLIN** St.-Aubin Les Cortons White 1994 • $24 • (05/31/96)
85 **J. A. FERRET** Pouilly-Fuissé Tête de Cru 1994 • $40 • (05/31/96) • 84
85 **FONTAINE-GAGNARD** Chassagne-Montrachet La Maltroie 1994 • $46 • (05/31/96)
85 **THIERRY GUÉRIN** Pouilly-Fuissé La Roche Vieilles Vignes 1994 • $22 • (05/31/96)
85 **PATRICK JAVILLIER** Meursault Les Clou 1993 • $40 • (08/31/95)
85 **CHARLES & RÉMI JOBARD** Bourgogne Chardonnay 1994 • $20 • (05/31/96)
85 **FRANÇOIS JOBARD** Meursault Les Genevrières 1993 • $NA • (05/31/96)
85 **LATOUR-GIRAUD** Puligny-Montrachet Champ Canet 1994 • $NA • (05/31/96)
85 **LOUIS LATOUR** Chevalier-Montrachet Les Demoiselles 1994 • $148 • (05/31/96)

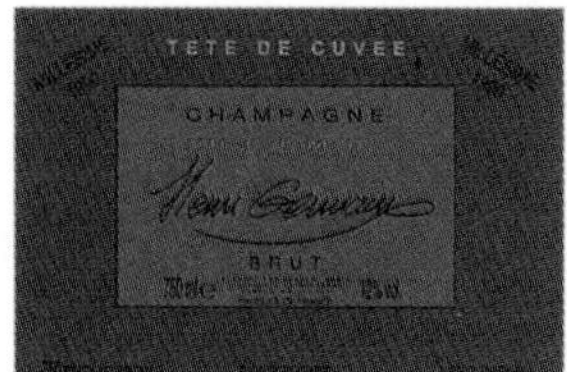

85 **LOUIS LATOUR** Chassagne-Montrachet Les Chenevottes 1994 • $37 • (05/31/96)
85 **LOUIS LATOUR** Puligny-Montrachet La Garenne 1993 • $36 • (08/31/95)
85 **LUPÉ-CHOLET** Chassagne-Montrachet 1994 • $NA • (05/31/96) • 85
85 **ROGER LUQUET** Pouilly-Fuissé Clos du Bourg 1994 • $19 • (05/31/96)
85 **DOMAINE MICHELOT** Meursault Les Charmes 1994 • $50 • (05/31/96)
85 **DOMAINE MICHELOT** Meursault Clos du Cromin 1994 • $38 • (05/31/96)
85 **DOMAINE MICHELOT** Meursault Les Perrières 1994 • $60 • (05/31/96)
85 **DOMAINE MICHELOT** Meursault Sous la Velle 1994 • $30 • (05/31/96)
85 **MOILLARD** Meursault 1994 • $29 • (04/30/96)
85 **MARC MOREY** Chassagne-Montrachet 1994 • $33 • (05/31/96)
85 **MARC MOREY** Chassagne-Montrachet En Virondot 1994 • $40 • (05/31/96)
85 **MICHEL NIELLON** Chassagne-Montrachet Les Champs Gains 1994 • $55 • (05/31/96)
85 **FERNAND PILLOT** Chassagne-Montrachet 1994 • $NA • (05/31/96) • 87
85 **FERNAND PILLOT** Chassagne-Montrachet Morgeot 1994 • $NA • (05/31/96)
85 **JEAN PILLOT** Chassagne-Montrachet Caillerets 1994 • $42 • (05/31/96)
85 **JEAN PILLOT** Chassagne-Montrachet Champs Gain 1994 • $32 • (05/31/96)
85 **JEAN PILLOT** Puligny-Montrachet 1994 • $NA • (05/31/96)
85 **HENRI PLUMET HÉRITIERS** Pouilly-Fuissé Clos du Chalet Pouilly 1994 • $NA • (05/31/96)
85 **CHÂTEAU POUILLY** Pouilly-Fuissé 1994 • $27 • (05/31/96)
85 **JACQUES PRIEUR** Meursault Les Perrières 1994 • $70 • (05/31/96)
85 **DOMAINE JACQUES PRIEUR** Meursault Clos de Mazeray 1993 • $34 • (08/31/95)
85 **CHÂTEAU DE PULIGNY-MONTRACHET** St.-Aubin En Remilly 1994 • $11 • (05/31/96)
85 **RAPET PÈRE & FILS** Pernand-Vergelesses 1994 • $21 • (05/31/96)
85 **CATHERINE & PASCAL ROLLET** Pouilly-Fuissé Domaine de la Chapelle 1994 • $16 • (05/31/96)
85 **CATHERINE & PASCAL ROLLET** Pouilly-Fuissé Domaine de la Chapelle Vieilles Vignes 1994 • $19 • (05/31/96)
85 **ROUX PÈRE & FILS** Chassagne-Montrachet 1994 • $NA • (05/31/96) • 85
85 **ROGER SAUMAIZE-MICHELIN** Pouilly-Fuissé Les Ronchevats 1994 • $NA • (05/31/96)
85 **ROGER SAUMAIZE** Pouilly-Fuissé Vigne Blanche 1994 • $NA • (05/31/96)
85 **DOMAINE THOMAS** St.-Véran 1994 • $12 • (08/31/95)

CHAMPAGNE

92 **CHARLES HEIDSIECK** Brut Champagne Blanc des Millénaires 1983 • $55 • (12/31/95)
92 **KRUG** Brut Blanc de Blancs Champagne Clos du Mesnil 1985 • $229 • (12/31/95)
92 **POL ROGER** Brut Rosé Champagne 1988 • $52 • (12/15/95)
91 **HENRI GERMAIN** Brut Champagne 1990 • $39 • (12/15/95)
91 **CHARLES HEIDSIECK** Brut Champagne Réserve NV • $37 • (12/31/95)
91 **MOET & CHANDON** Brut Champagne Cuvée Dom Pérignon 1988 • $89 • (07/31/95)
90 **PAUL BARA** Brut Champagne 1988 • $45 • (11/30/95)
90 **CATTIER** Brut Rosé Champagne NV • $40 • (12/15/95)
90 **A. CHARBAUT** Brut Rosé Champagne NV • $35 • (12/31/95)

90 **HENRI GERMAIN** Brut Champagne President Germain Grand Cru Chardonnay 1988 • $60 • (12/15/95)

90 **GOSSET** Brut Rosé Champagne Grand Rosé 1988 • $60 • (12/15/95)

90 **LAURENT-PERRIER** Brut Champagne Cuvée Ultra Brut NV • $41 • (11/30/95)

90 **LAURENT-PERRIER** Brut Champagne L.P.NV • $32 • (11/30/95)

90 **G.H. MUMM** Brut Champagne Cordon Rouge NV • $25 • (12/15/95)

90 **BRUNO PAILLARD** Brut Rosé Champagne Première Cuvée NV • $35 • (12/15/95)

90 **PHILIPPONNAT** Rosé Champagne Réserve NV • $32 • (12/15/95)

90 **VRANKEN** Brut Champagne Demoiselle Téte de Cuvée 1989 • $40 • (01/31/96)

89 **HENRI ABELE** Brut Champagne Le Sourire de Reims 1986 • $85 • (11/30/95)

89 **BAUGET-JOUETTE** Brut Rosé Champagne NV • $33 • (12/15/95)

89 **HENRI GERMAIN** Brut Champagne NV • $25 • (12/15/95)

89 **J. LASSALLE** Brut Rosé Champagne Réserve des Grandes Années NV • $40 • (12/15/95)

89 **MOET & CHANDON** Impérial Champagne 1990 • $48 • (11/30/95)

89 **LOUIS ROEDERER** Brut Champagne Brut Premier NV • $25 • (11/30/95)

89 **VEUVE CLICQUOT** Brut Champagne Reserve 1988 • $50 • (07/31/95)

89 **VRANKEN** Champagne Demoiselle Grande Cuvée NV • $27 • (01/31/96)

88 **CHARLES DE CAZANOVE** Brut Champagne Millèsime 1989 • $30 • (07/31/95)

88 **G.H. MUMM** Cordon Rosé Champagne NV • $35 • (12/15/95)

88 **BRUNO PAILLARD** Brut Champagne Première Cuvée NV • $25 • (12/15/95)

88 **POMMERY** Brut Rosé Champagne NV • $29 • (12/15/95)

87 **A. CHARBAUT** Brut Champagne NV • $28 • (12/31/95)

87 **HENRI GERMAIN** Brut Rosé Champagne NV • $30 • (12/15/95)

87 **HENRI GERMAIN** Brut Champagne President Germain NV • $35 • (12/15/95)

87 **PERRIER-JOUET** Brut Rosé Champagne Fleur de Champagne 1988 • $95 • (12/15/95)

87 **RUINART** Brut Blanc de Blancs Champagne Dom Ruinart 1988 • $93 • (12/15/95)

87 **RUINART** Brut Rosé Champagne Dom Ruinart 1986 • $109 • (12/15/95)

87 **TAITTINGER** Brut Rosé Champagne Cuvée Prestige NV • $48 • (12/15/95)

87 **TAITTINGER** Brut Rosé Champagne Comtes de Champagne 1991 • $120 • (12/15/95)

86 **BOLLINGER** Brut Blanc de Noirs Champagne Vieilles Vignes Françaises 1986 • $219 • (12/31/95)

86 **BOLLINGER** Brut Champagne Special Cuvée NV • $38 • (12/31/95)

86 **POL ROGER** Brut Champagne NV • $37 • (12/15/95)

86 **POL ROGER** Brut Champagne NV • $37 • (12/15/95)

86 **VEUVE CLICQUOT** Brut Champagne La Grande Dame 1988 • $100 • (12/15/95)

85 **DEUTZ** Brut Rosé Champagne Cuvée Marie-Damarisse NV • $25 • (12/15/95)

85 **LAURENT-PERRIER** Brut Rosé Champagne Cuvée Rosé Brut NV • $42 • (12/15/95)

85 **PIPER-HEIDSIECK** Brut Champagne Cuvée Brut NV • $30 • (12/31/95)

GERMAN RIESLING

96 **DR. BURKLIN-WOLF** Riesling Trockenbeerenauslese Pfalz Forster Kirchenstück 1994 • $211 • (11/30/95)

96 **H. DONNHOFF** Riesling Trockenbeerenauslese Nahe Niederhäuser Hermannshöhle 1994 • $168 • (11/30/95)

96 **DR. LOOSEN** Riesling Trockenbeerenauslese Mosel-Saar-Ruwer Urziger Würzgarten 1994 • $NA • (11/30/95)

96 **ROBERT WEIL** Riesling Beerenauslese Rheingau Kiedricher Gräfenberg 1994 • $141 • (11/30/95)

95 **GUNDERLOCH** Riesling Trockenbeerenauslese Rheinhessen Nackenheimer Rothenberg 1994 • $NA • (11/30/95)

95 **DR. LOOSEN** Riesling Auslese Long Gold Cap Mosel-Saar-Ruwer Erdener Prälat 1994 • $NA • (11/30/95)

95 **ROBERT WEIL** Riesling Trockenbeerenauslese Rheingau Kiedricher Gräfenberg 1994 • $291 • (11/30/95)

94 **H. DONNHOFF** Riesling Eiswein Nahe Oberhäuser Brücke 1994 • $127 • (11/30/95)

94 **REINHOLD HAART** Riesling Beerenauslese Mosel-Saar-Ruwer Piesporter Goldtröpfchen 1994 • $NA • (11/30/95)

93 **DR. LOOSEN** Riesling Auslese Gold Cap Mosel-Saar-Ruwer Erdener Prälat 1994 • $65 • (11/30/95)

93 **EGON MULLER** Riesling Beerenauslese Mosel-Saar-Ruwer Scharzhofberger 1994 • $NA • (11/30/95)

93 **SELBACH-OSTER** Riesling Beerenauslese Mosel-Saar-Ruwer Zeltinger Sonnenuhr 1994 • $83 • (11/30/95)

92 **DR. BURKLIN-WOLF** Riesling Beerenauslese Pfalz Wachenheimer Goldbächel 1994 • $75 • (11/30/95)

92 **DR. LOOSEN** Riesling Auslese Mosel-Saar-Ruwer Erdener Prälat 1994 • $44 • (11/30/95)

92 **WEGELER-DEINHARD** Riesling Trockenbeerenauslese Pfalz Deidesheimer Herrgottsacker Geheimrat J 1994 • $NA • (11/30/95)

92 **ROBERT WEIL** Riesling Auslese Gold Cap Rheingau Kiedricher Gräfenberg 1994 • $NA • (11/30/95)

91 **LE GALLAIS** Riesling Auslese Gold Cap Mosel-Saar-Ruwer Wiltinger Braune Kupp 1994 • $NA • (11/30/95)

91 **REICHSGRAF VON KESSELSTATT** Riesling Trockenbeerenauslese Mosel-Saar-Ruwer Scharzhofberger 1994 • $NA • (11/30/95)

91 **DR. LOOSEN** Riesling Auslese Mosel-Saar-Ruwer Urziger Würzgarten 1994 • $34 • (11/30/95)

91 **DR. LOOSEN** Riesling Auslese Gold Cap Mosel-Saar-Ruwer Urziger Würzgarten 1994 • $47 • (11/30/95)

91 **WEGELER-DEINHARD** Riesling Auslese Rheingau Winkeler Hasensprung Geheimrat J 1994 • $NA • (11/30/95)

90 **JOSEF BIFFAR** Riesling Spätlese Pfalz Deideshiemer Grainhübel 1994 • (11/30/95)

90 **SCHLOSSGUT DIEL** Riesling Eiswein Nahe 1994 • $142 • (11/30/95)

90 **LE GALLAIS** Riesling Beerenauslese Mosel-Saar-Ruwer Wiltinger Braune Kupp 1994 • $NA • (11/30/95)

90 **GUNDERLOCH** Riesling Spätlese Rheinhessen Nackenheimer Rothenberg 1994 • $21 • (11/30/95)

90 **GUNDERLOCH** Riesling Auslese Gold Cap Rheinhessen Nackenheimer Rothenberg 1994 • $59 • (11/30/95)

90 **GUNDERLOCH** Riesling Beerenauslese Rheinhessen Nackenheimer Rothenberg 1994 • $96 • (11/30/95)

90 **REINHOLD HAART** Riesling Auslese Mosel-Saar-Ruwer Piesporter Goldtröpfchen 1994 • $44 • (11/30/95)

90 **KOEHLER-RUPRECHT** Riesling Trockenbeerenauslese Pfalz Kallstadter Saumagen 1994 • $NA • (11/30/95)

90 **FRANZ KUNSTLER** Riesling Spätlese Rheingau Hochheimer Herrenberg 1994 • $30 • (11/30/95)

90 **FRANZ KUNSTLER** Riesling Trockenbeerenauslese Rheingau Hochheimer Hölle 1994 • $428 • (11/30/95)

90 **DR. LOOSEN** Riesling Spätlese Mosel-Saar-Ruwer Erdener Treppchen 1994 • $27 • (11/30/95)

90 **EGON MULLER** Riesling Auslese Gold Cap Mosel-Saar-Ruwer Scharzhofberger 1994 • $NA • (11/30/95)

90 **DR. PAULY-BERGWEILER** Riesling Beerenauslese Mosel-Saar-Ruwer Bernkasteler Lay 1994 • $33 • (11/30/95)

90 **SELBACH-OSTER** Riesling Auslese Mosel-Saar-Ruwer Wehlener Sonnenuhr 1994 • $34 • (11/30/95)

90 **WEGELER-DEINHARD** Riesling Auslese Mosel-Saar-Ruwer Wehlener Sonnenuhr Geheimrat J 1994 • $NA • (11/30/95)

89 **H. DONNHOFF** Riesling Auslese Nahe Oberhäuser Brücke 1994 • $33 • (11/30/95)

89 **KOEHLER-RUPRECHT** Riesling Beerenauslese Pfalz Kallstadter Saumagen 1994 • $NA • (11/30/95)

89 **FRANZ KUNSTLER** Riesling Beerenauslese Rheingau Hochheimer Hölle 1994 • $104 • (11/30/95)

89 **DR. LOOSEN** Riesling Spätlese Mosel-Saar-Ruwer Urziger Würzgarten 1994 • $29 • (11/30/95)

89 **EGON MULLER** Riesling Auslese Mosel-Saar-Ruwer Scharzhofberger 1994 • $129 • (11/30/95)

89 **SCHLOSS REINHARTSHAUSEN** Riesling Beerenauslese Rheingau Hattenheimer Wisselbrunnen 1994 • $NA • (11/30/95)

89 **PRINZ ZU SALM-DALBERG** Riesling Kabinett Nahe Schloss Wallhausen 1993 • $13 • (12/15/95)

89 **C. VON SCHUBERT** Riesling Spätlese Mosel-Saar-Ruwer Maximin Grünhäuser Abtsberg 1994 • $27 • (11/30/95)

89 **WEGELER-DEINHARD** Riesling Beerenauslese Mosel-Saar-Ruwer Bernkasteler Doctor Geheimrat J 1994 • $NA • (11/30/95)

88 **HANS CRUSIUS & SOHN** Riesling Auslese Trocken Nahe Traiser BasteiAuslese Trocken 1994 • $NA • (11/30/95)

88 **GUNDERLOCH** Riesling Kabinett Rheinhessen Nackenheimer Rothenberg Jean Baptiste 1994 • $15 • (11/30/95)

88 **REINHOLD HAART** Riesling Kabinett Mosel-Saar-Ruwer Piesporter Goldtröpfchen 1994 • $18 • (11/30/95)

88 **REINHOLD HAART** Riesling Spätlese Mosel-Saar-Ruwer Piesporter Domherr 1994 • $24 • (11/30/95)

88 **KOEHLER-RUPRECHT** Riesling Auslese Pfalz Kallstadter Saumagen 1994 • $NA • (11/30/95)

88 **FRANZ KUNSTLER** Riesling Spätlese Trocken Rheingau Hochheimer Hölle 1994 • $30 • (11/30/95)

88 **JOSEF LEITZ** Riesling Auslese Rheingau Rüdesheimer Berg Schlossberg 1994 • $38 • (11/30/95)

88 **MULLER-CATOIR** Riesling Spätlese Pfalz Gimmeldinger Mandelgarten 1994 • $29 • (11/30/95)

88 **C. VON SCHUBERT** Riesling Trockenbeerenauslese Mosel-Saar-Ruwer Maximin Grünhäuser Abtsberg 1994 • $220 • (11/30/95)

88 **SELBACH-OSTER** Riesling Auslese Mosel-Saar-Ruwer Zeltinger Sonnenuhr One Star 1994 • $39 • (11/30/95)

88 **WEGELER-DEINHARD** Riesling Spätlese Mosel-Saar-Ruwer Wehlener Sonnenuhr Geheimrat J 1994 • $NA • (11/30/95)

87 **JOSEF BIFFAR** Riesling Spätlese Trocken Pfalz Wachenheimer Gerümpel 1994 • $NA • (11/30/95)

87 **JOSEF BIFFAR** Riesling Trockenbeerenauslese Pfalz Deidesheimer Kieselberg 1994 • $107 • (11/30/95)

87 DR. BURKLIN-WOLF Riesling Kabinett Pfalz Wachenheimer Rechbächel 1994 • $17 • (11/30/95)

87 DR. BURKLIN-WOLF Riesling Spätlese Trocken Pfalz Wachenheimer Goldbächel 1994 • $22 • (11/30/95)

87 JOH. JOS. CHRISTOFFEL Riesling Auslese Gold Cap Mosel-Saar-Ruwer Urziger Würzgarten Five Stars 1994 • $NA • (11/30/95)

87 HANS CRUSIUS & SOHN Riesling Spätlese Nahe Schlossböckelheimer Felsenberg 1994 • $NA • (11/30/95)

87 HANS CRUSIUS & SOHN Riesling Auslese Nahe Schlossböckelheimer Felsenberg 1994 • $NA • (11/30/95)

87 SCHLOSSGUT DIEL Riesling Beerenauslese Nahe BA Gold Cap 1994 • $NA • (11/30/95)

87 REINHOLD HAART Riesling Spätlese Mosel-Saar-Ruwer Piesporter Goldtröpfchen 1994 • $27 • (11/30/95)

87 HEYL ZU HERRNSHEIM Riesling Spätlese Trocken Rheinhessen Niersteiner Pettenthal 1994 • $22 • (11/30/95)

87 REICHSGRAF VON KESSELSTATT Riesling Spätlese Mosel-Saar-Ruwer Josephshöfer 1994 • $NA • (11/30/95)

87 REICHSGRAF VON KESSELSTATT Riesling Auslese Mosel-Saar-Ruwer Kaseler Nies'chen 1994 • $NA • (11/30/95)

87 KOEHLER-RUPRECHT Riesling Spätlese Pfalz Kallstadter Saumagen 1994 • $NA • (11/30/95)

87 FRANZ KUNSTLER Riesling Spätlese Trocken Rheingau Hochheimer Stielweg 1994 • $30 • (11/30/95)

87 MULLER-CATOIR Riesling Kabinett Pfalz Haardter Bürgergarten 1994 • $21 • (11/30/95)

87 EGON MULLER Riesling Spätlese Mosel-Saar-Ruwer Scharzhofberger 1994 • $NA • (11/30/95)

87 SCHMITT SCHENK Spätlese Mosel-Saar-Ruwer Erdener Treppchen 1994 • $12 • (11/30/95)

87 C. VON SCHUBERT Riesling QbA Mosel-Saar-Ruwer Maximin Grünhäuser Abtsberg 1994 • $16 • (11/30/95)

87 C. VON SCHUBERT Riesling Auslese Mosel-Saar-Ruwer Maximin Grünhäuser Herrenberg Fuder No. 45 1994 • $58 • (11/30/95)

87 SELBACH-OSTER Riesling Auslese Mosel-Saar-Ruwer Zeltinger Schlossberg 1994 • $37 • (11/30/95)

87 WEGELER-DEINHARD Riesling Spätlese Rheingau Rüdesheimer Berg Rottland Geheimrat J 1994 • $NA • (11/30/95)

87 WEGELER-DEINHARD Riesling Spätlese Mosel-Saar-Ruwer Berncasteler Doctor Geheimrat J 1994 • $NA • (11/30/95)

87 ROBERT WEIL Riesling Auslese Rheingau Kiedricher Gräfenberg 1994 • $78 • (11/30/95)

86 JOSEF BIFFAR Riesling Kabinett Pfalz Deideshimer Kieselberg 1994 • $15 • (11/30/95)

86 SCHLOSSGUT DIEL Riesling QbA Nahe 1994 • $12 • (11/30/95)

86 H. DONNHOFF Riesling Auslese Nahe Niederhäuser Hermmanshöhle 1994 • $34 • (11/30/95)

86 GUNDERLOCH Riesling Auslese Rheinhessen Nackenheimer Rothenberg 1994 • $33 • (11/30/95)

86 REICHSGRAF VON KESSELSTATT Riesling Kabinett Mosel-Saar-Ruwer Josephshöfer 1994 • $NA • (11/30/95)

86 REICHSGRAF VON KESSELSTATT Riesling Kabinett Mosel-Saar-Ruwer Scharzhofberger 1994 • $NA • (11/30/95)

86 KOEHLER-RUPRECHT Riesling Spätlese Halbtrocken Pfalz Kallstadter Saumagen 1994 • $NA • (11/30/95)

86 **FRANZ KUNSTLER** Riesling QbA Halbtrocken Rheingau 1994 • $14 • (11/30/95)

86 **PETER NICOLAY** Riesling Auslese Mosel-Saar-Ruwer Erdener Prälat 1994 • $35 • (11/30/95)

86 **DR. PAULY-BERGWEILER** Riesling Spätlese Mosel-Saar-Ruwer Bernkasteler Alte Badstube am Doctorberg 1994 • $27 • (11/30/95)

86 **DR. PAULY-BERGWEILER** Riesling Auslese Mosel-Saar-Ruwer Bernkasteler Lay 1994 • $21 • (11/30/95)

86 **DR. PAULY-BERGWEILER** Riesling Trockenbeerenauslese Mosel-Saar-Ruwer Bernkasteler Badstube am Doctorberg 1994 • $NA • (11/30/95)

86 **SCHLOSS REINHARTSHAUSEN** Riesling Spätlese Rheingau Hattenheimer Wisselbrunnen 1994 • $NA • (11/30/95)

86 **MAX FERD. RICHTER** Riesling Spätlese Mosel-Saar-Ruwer Brauneberger Juffer-Sonnenuhr 1994 • $NA • (11/30/95)

86 **MAX FERD. RICHTER** Riesling Spätlese Mosel-Saar-Ruwer Wehlener Sonnenuhr 1994 • $NA • (11/30/95)

86 **TYRELL** Riesling Auslese Gold Cap Mosel-Saar-Ruwer Eitelsbacher Karthäuserhofberg Füder No. 19 1994 • $52 • (11/30/95)

86 **WEGELER-DEINHARD** Riesling Kabinett Rheingau Oestricher Lenchen Geheimrat J 1994 • $13 • (11/30/95)

86 **ROBERT WEIL** Riesling Spätlese Rheingau Kiedricher Gräfenberg 1994 • $32 • (11/30/95)

85 **DR. BURKLIN-WOLF** Riesling QbA Pfalz Forster 1994 • $14 • (11/30/95)

85 **DR. BURKLIN-WOLF** Riesling Spätlese Pfalz Wachenheimer Altenburg 1994 • $20 • (11/30/95)

85 **JOH. JOS. CHRISTOFFEL** Riesling Spätlese Mosel-Saar-Ruwer Urziger Würzgarten 1994 • $17 • (11/30/95)

85 **JOH. JOS. CHRISTOFFEL** Riesling Auslese Gold Cap Mosel-Saar-Ruwer Urziger Würzgarten Four Stars 1994 • $39 • (11/30/95)

85 **HANS CRUSIUS & SOHN** Riesling Spätlese Nahe Niederhäuser Felsensteyer 1994 • $NA • (11/30/95)

85 **H. DONNHOFF** Riesling Spätlese Nahe Oberhäuser Brücke 1994 • $23 • (11/30/95)

85 **STAATSWEINGUTER KLOSTER EBERBACH** Riesling Rheingau Steinberger 1994 • $14 • (11/30/95)

85 **VON HOVEL** Riesling Kabinett Mosel-Saar-Ruwer Oberemmeler Hütte 1994 • $13 • (11/30/95)

85 **REICHSGRAF VON KESSELSTATT** Riesling Kabinett Mosel-Saar-Ruwer Piesporter Goldtröpfchen 1994 • $NA • (11/30/95)

85 **REICHSGRAF VON KESSELSTATT** Riesling Spätlese Mosel-Saar-Ruwer Scharzhofberger 1994 • $NA • (11/30/95)

85 **KOEHLER-RUPRECHT** Riesling Kabinett Pfalz Kallstadter Steinacker 1994 • $NA • (11/30/95)

85 **DR. LOOSEN** Riesling Kabinett Mosel-Saar-Ruwer Erdener Treppchen 1994 • $17 • (11/30/95)

85 **PETER NICOLAY** Riesling Spätlese Mosel-Saar-Ruwer Urziger Goldwingert 1994 • $NA • (11/30/95)

85 **DR. PAULY-BERGWEILER** Riesling Spätlese Mosel-Saar-Ruwer Bernkasteler Badstube 1994 • $24 • (11/30/95)

85 **DR. PAULY-BERGWEILER** Riesling Spätlese Mosel-Saar-Ruwer Bernkasteler Doctor 1994 • $47 • (11/30/95)

85 **SCHLOSS REINHARTSHAUSEN** Riesling Spätlese Rheingau Erbacher Marcobrunn 1994 • $NA • (11/30/95)

85 **MAX FERD. RICHTER** Riesling Kabinett Mosel-Saar-Ruwer Graacher Himmelreich 1994 • $NA • (11/30/95)

85 **MAX FERD. RICHTER** Riesling Auslese Mosel-Saar-Ruwer Brauneberger Juffer 1994 • $NA • (11/30/95)

85 **PRINZ ZU SALM-DALBERG** Riesling Spätlese Nahe Wallhäuser Johannisberg 1994 • $15 • (12/15/95)

85 **SCHMITT SCHENK** Kabinett Mosel-Saar-Ruwer Urziger Würzgarten 1994 • $9 • (11/30/95)

85 **C. VON SCHUBERT** Riesling Kabinett Mosel-Saar-Ruwer Maximin Grünhäuser Abtsberg 1994 • $21 • (11/30/95)

85 **C. VON SCHUBERT** Riesling Kabinett Mosel-Saar-Ruwer Maximin Grünhäuser Herrenberg 1994 • $21 • (11/30/95)

85 **C. VON SCHUBERT** Riesling Auslese Mosel-Saar-Ruwer Maximin Grünhäuser Abtsberg 1994 • $45 • (11/30/95)

85 **DR. H. THANISCH (MULLER-BURGGRAEFF)** Riesling Kabinett Mosel-Saar-Ruwer Wehlener Sonnenuhr 1994 • $NA • (11/30/95)

85 **DR. H. THANISCH (MULLER-BURGGRAEFF)** Riesling Auslese Mosel-Saar-Ruwer Graacher Himmelreich 1994 • $NA • (11/30/95)

85 **TYRELL** Riesling Kabinett Mosel-Saar-Ruwer Eitelsbacher Karthäuserhofberg 1994 • $17 • (11/30/95)

85 **TYRELL** Riesling Auslese Mosel-Saar-Ruwer Eitelsbacher Karthäuserhofberg 1994 • $35 • (11/30/95)

85 **SCHLOSS VOLLRADS** Riesling Kabinett Rheingau 1994 • $17 • (11/30/95)

85 **SCHLOSS VOLLRADS** Riesling Auslese Rheingau 1994 • $55 • (11/30/95)

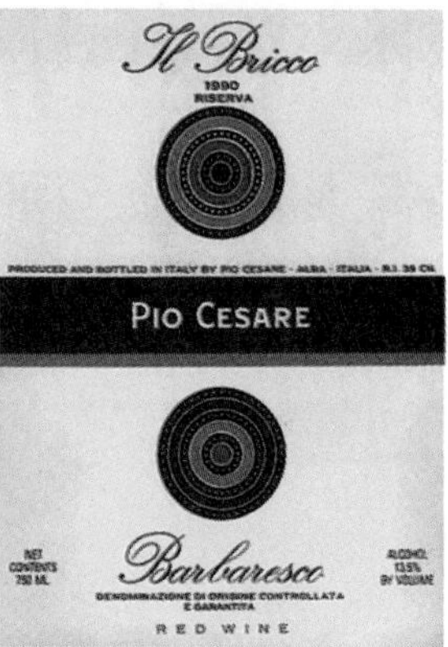

BAROLO & BARBARESCO

96 **LUCIANO SANDRONE** Barolo Cannubi Boschis 1990 • $NA

93 **PAOLO SCAVINO** Barolo Bric dël Fiasc 1990 • $45

91 **CA' DEI GANCIA** Barolo Cannubi 1989 • $65

91 **GIANNI GAGLIARDO** Barolo Preve 1990 • $35

90 **CAPPELLANO** Barolo Gabutti 1990 • $42

90 **ALDO CONTERNO** Barolo Granbussia 1990 • $120

90 **PODERI ROCCHE DEI MANZONI** Barolo Riserva Vigna d'la Roul 1990 • $NA

90 **PAOLO SCAVINO** Barolo Riserva Rocche dell'Annunziata 1990 • $65

89 **PODERI ROCCHE DEI MANZONI** Barolo Riserva 1990 • $35

88 **BREZZA** Barolo Cannubi 1990 • $40

88 **BROVIA** Barolo Monprivato 1990 • $44

88 **CA' DE MONTE** Barolo 1990 • $16 • (02/28/95)

88 **PIO CESARE** Barbaresco Il Bricco Riserva 1990 • $52 • (10/31/95)

88 **MICHELE CHIARLO** Barolo Cerequio 1991 • $60

88 **STEFANO FARINA** Barolo 1990 • $18 • (07/31/95)

87 **BERSANO** Barolo Cascina Badarina 1990 • $30 • (10/31/95)

87 **CAVALOTTO** Barolo Riserva Bricco Boschis 1990 • $39

87 **FONTANAFREDDA** Barolo Vigna Lazzarito 1990 • $39

86 **BREZZA** Barolo Cannubi 1991 • $30

86 **CAPPELLANO** Barolo Gabutti 1991 • $42

86 **MICHELE CHIARLO** Barolo Cannubi 1991 • $60

86 Barolo Dedicato a Claus Riedel 1990 • $NA

86 **FONTANAFREDDA** Barolo di Serralunga d'Alba 1990 • $20

86 **GAJA** Barolo Sperss 1991 • $60

86 **PRODUTTORI DEL BARBARESCO** Barbaresco Rabajà 1990 • $35

86 **VILLADORIA** Barolo 1991 • $NA • (10/31/95)

86 **GIANNI VOERZIO** Barolo La Serra 1991 • $NA

85 **MARZIANO & ENRICO ABBONA** Barolo Vigneto Terlo Ravera 1990 • $25 • (07/31/95)
85 **ELIO ALTARE** Barolo 1991 • $30 • (10/31/95)
85 **MICHELE CHIARLO** Barolo 1991 • $24 • (10/31/95)
85 **CLERICO** Barolo Ciabot Mentin Ginestra 1991 • $30
85 **GIACOMO FENOCCHIO** Barolo Bussia 1990 • $20
85 **FONTANAFREDDA** Barolo Vigna La Villa Paiagallo 1990 • $39
85 **INFERNOTTO** Barolo 1990 • $15 • (02/28/95)
85 **MASSOLINO** Barolo Vigna Rionda 1990 • $40
85 **PAITIN** Barbaresco Sor' Paitin 1991 • $20
85 **PIRA** Barolo 1990 • $40
85 **PAOLO SCAVINO** Barolo Cannubi 1991 • $30
85 **VIETTI** Barolo Rocche 1990 • $60
85 **ROBERTO VOERZIO** Barolo La Serra 1991 • $NA

CHIANTI CLASSICO

93 **CASTELLO DI AMA** Chianti Classico Vigneto Bertinga 1990 • $34 • (02/28/95)
93 **CASTELLO DI AMA** Chianti Classico Vigneto La Casuccia 1990 • $38
93 **FATTORIA DI FELSINA** Chianti Classico Berardenga Rancia Riserva 1990 • $28 • (02/28/95) • ss
93 **FATTORIA VALTELLINA** Chianti Classico Giorgio Regni Riserva 1990 • $25
91 **CASTELLO DI AMA** Chianti Classico Vigneto Bellavista 1990 • $38
91 **FONTODI** Chianti Classico Al Sorbo 1990 • $27
91 **LA MASSA** Chianti Classico Riserva 1990 • $17
91 **POGGERINO** Chianti Classico Riserva 1990 • $NA
90 **CASTELLO DI AMA** Chianti Classico Vigneto San Lorenzo 1990 • $34
90 **FATTORIA DI FELSINA** Chianti Classico Berardenga Riserva 1990 • $18
90 **FONTODI** Chianti Classico Riserva 1991 • $18
90 **RUFFINO** Chianti Classico Ducale Oro (Gold Label) Riserva 1990 • $25
90 **SAN FELICE** Chianti Classico Poggio Rosso Riserva 1990 • $24
89 **ANTINORI** Chianti Classico Riserva 1990 • $NA
89 **ANTINORI** Chianti Classico Badia a Passignano Riserva 1991 • $30
89 **CASTELLO DI CACCHIANO** Chianti Classico Millennio Riserva 1990 • $17
89 **CAROBBIO** Chianti Classico Riserva 1990 • $NA
89 **FONTODI** Chianti Classico Riserva 1990 • $20
88 **LE CINCIOLE** Chianti Classico 1993 • $NA
88 **LA MASSA** Chianti Classico Giorgio Primo 1992 • $57
88 **POGGERINO** Chianti Classico 1993 • $NA
88 **CASTELLO DI QUERCETO** Chianti Classico Riserva Il Picchio 1990 • $27 • (10/31/95)
88 **CASTELLO DEI RAMPOLLA** Chianti Classico Riserva 1990 • $25 • (02/28/95)
88 **RIECINE** Chianti Classico Riserva 1990 • $NA
88 **RIECINE** Chianti Classico Riserva 1991 • $35
88 **VIGNAMAGGIO** Chianti Classico Mona Lisa Riserva 1990 • $17
87 **CASTELLO DI AMA** Chianti Classico Vigneto Bellavista 1991 • $25
87 **ANTINORI** Chianti Classico Tenute Marchese Antinori Riserva 1991 • $22
87 **VILLA CAFAGGIO** Chianti Classico Riserva 1990 • $17
87 **CAROBBIO** Chianti Classico Riserva 1991 • $NA
87 **CARPINETO** Chianti Classico Riserva 1990 • $13
87 **CELLOLE** Chianti Classico Riserva 1990 • $NA

87 **CENNATOIO** Chianti Classico Riserva 1990 • $17
87 **CASA EMMA** Chianti Classico Riserva 1990 • $NA
87 **LILLIANO** Chianti Classico 1993 • $NA
87 **CASTELLO DI QUERCETO** Chianti Classico Riserva 1990 • $14 • (02/28/95)
87 **BARONE RICASOLI** Chianti Classico Brolio Riserva 1990 • $NA
87 **ROCCA DI CASTAGNOLI** Chianti Classico Poggio A'Frati Riserva 1990 • $22
87 **TERRABIANCA** Chianti Classico Vigna della Croce Riserva 1990 • $17
87 **VISTARENNI** Chianti Classico Riserva 1990 • $NA
87 **VITICCIO** Chianti Classico Riserva 1990 • $NA
86 **CASTELLO DI AMA** Chianti Classico Vigneto La Casuccia 1991 • $25
86 **TENUTA BIBBIANO** Chianti Classico Vigna del Capannino 1990 • $NA • (02/28/95)
86 **CASTELLO DI FONTERUTOLI** Chianti Classico Ser Lapo Riserva 1990 • $26
86 **FONTODI** Chianti Classico 1993 • $12
86 **CASTELLO DI GABBIANO** Chianti Classico Riserva 1990 • $15 • (02/28/95)
86 **CASTELLO LA LECCIA** Chianti Classico 1991 • $10
86 **LILLIANO** Chianti Classico Riserva 1990 • $22
86 **CASANUOVA DI NITTARDI** Chianti Classico Nittardi Riserva 1990 • $NA
86 **NOZZOLE** Chianti Classico La Forra Riserva 1990 • $22
86 **PAGLIARESE** Chianti Classico 1993 • $NA
86 **IL PALAGIO** Chianti Classico Riserva 1990 • $NA
86 **IL PALAGIO** Chianti Classico Riserva 1991 • $NA
86 **CASTELLO DELLA PANERETTA** Chianti Classico Riserva 1990 • $NA
86 **POGGIO AL SOLE** Chianti Classico Riserva 1990 • $NA
86 **CASTELLO DEI RAMPOLLA** Chianti Classico Riserva 1991 • $28
86 **ROCCA DI CASTAGNOLI** Chianti Classico 1990 • $14 • (02/28/95)
86 **SAN FELICE** Chianti Classico Riserva Il Grigio 1991 • $16
86 **SAVIGNOLA PAOLINA** Chianti Classico Riserva 1990 • $NA
86 **FATTORIA DI SELVOLE** Chianti Classico Lanfredini Castello di Selvole Riserva 1991 • $13
86 **FATTORIA VALTELLINA** Chianti Classico Giorgio Regni 1992 • $13
86 **CASTELLO DI VERRAZZANO** Chianti Classico 1993 • $9
86 **CASTELLO DI VERRAZZANO** Chianti Classico Riserva 1991 • $9
86 **CASTELLO VICCHIOMAGGIO** Chianti Classico Riserva La Prima 1991 • $NA
86 **CASTELLO DI VOLPAIA** Chianti Classico Riserva 1990 • $14 • (02/28/95)
85 **CASTELLO DI AMA** Chianti Classico 1992 • $15 • (02/28/95)
85 **ANTINORI** Chianti Classico Tenute Marchese Antinori Riserva 1990 • $22 • (02/28/95)
85 **BADIA A COLTIBUONO** Chianti Classico Riserva 1990 • $25 • (02/28/95)
85 **TENUTA BIBBIANO** Chianti Classico Montornello 1993 • $NA • (10/31/95)
85 **FATTORIA LE BOCCE** Chianti Classico Riserva 1990 • $15 • (02/28/95)
85 **CASTELGREVE** Chianti Classico Riserva 1990 • $12
85 **CASTELLARE DI CASTELLINA** Chianti Classico Riserva 1991 • $21
85 **CENNATOIO** Chianti Classico 1993 • $13
85 **CASA EMMA** Chianti Classico 1993 • $NA
85 **CASTELLO DI FONTERUTOLI** Chianti Classico 1992 • $13
85 **FONTODI** Chianti Classico 1992 • $13
85 **FATTORIA LA LOGGIA** Chianti Classico Riserva 1990 • $17
85 **CASANUOVA DI NITTARDI** Chianti Classico 1993 • $12
85 **NOZZOLE** Chianti Classico Riserva 1990 • $12 • (02/28/95)
85 **CASTEL RUGGERO** Chianti Classico 1993 • $NA

85 **LA SALA** Chianti Classico Riserva 1990 • $NA
85 **SAN FELICE** Chianti Classico Il Grigio Riserva 1990 • $16
85 **VECCHIE TERRE DI MONTEFILI** Chianti Classico 1992 • $20
85 **VECCHIE TERRE DI MONTEFILI** Chianti Classico 1993 • $NA
85 **CASTELLO VICCHIOMAGGIO** Chianti Classico Petri Riserva 1990 • $NA
85 **VITICCIO** Chianti Classico Riserva 1991 • $10

SUPER TUSCANS

97 **ANTINORI** Solaia 1990 • $65 • (02/28/95) • CS
96 **COL D'ORCIA** Olmaia Red 1990 • $19 • (02/28/95)
96 **NOZZOLE** Il Pareto 1990 • $41
94 **CASTELLO DI FONTERUTOLI** Siepi 1993 • $30
93 **ORNELLAIA** Masseto 1992 • $59
93 **TENUTA SAN GUIDO** Sassicaia 1990 • $90
92 **CASTELLO DI AMA** Vigna l'Apparita 1991 • $60
92 **ANTINORI** Tignanello 1990 • $39 • (02/28/95) • CS
92 **NOZZOLE** Il Pareto 1993 • $45
91 **AVIGNONESI** Grifi 1990 • $36 • (02/28/95) • cs
91 **COLLE BERETTO** Il Cénno 1990 • $27 • (12/31/95)
91 **FATTORIA DI FELSINA** Fontalloro 1990 • $38
91 **ORNELLAIA** Masseto 1991 • $59
91 **CASTELLO DEI RAMPOLLA** Sammarco 1990 • $55
91 **FATTORIA VALTELLINA** Convivio Giorgio Regni 1991 • $30
90 **ANTINORI** Solaia 1991 • $65 • CS
90 **CASTELLO DI CACCHIANO** RF Red 1990 • $25
90 **CASTELLO DI FONTERUTOLI** Siepi 1992 • $30
90 **FONTODI** Syrah Case Via 1991 • $30
90 **FONTODI** Flaccianello della Pieve 1991 • $32
90 **FRESCOBALDI** Lamaione Castelgiocondo 1991 • $18
90 **FRESCOBALDI** Capitolare di Biturica Mormoreto 1991 • $32
90 **ISOLE E OLENA** Cabernet Sauvignon Collezione de Marchi 1991 • $30
90 **MELINI** Vigneto Coltri Vineyard 2 Red 1990 • $20 • (12/31/95)
90 **RIECINE** La Gioia 1990 • $45
90 **ROCCA DI CASTAGNOLI** Stielle 1990 • $33
90 **VECCHIE TERRE DI MONTEFILI** Chianti Classico Anfiteatro 1991 • $32
90 **VITICCIO** Monile 1991 • $33
89 **CASTELLO BANFI** Mandrielle 1992 • $25 • (02/28/95)
89 **CASTELLO DI BOSSI** Corbaia Red 1990 • $32 • (12/31/95)
89 **CECCHI** Capitolare di Cardisco Spargolo Red 1991 • $29
89 **FRESCOBALDI** Lamaione Castelgiocondo 1992 • $18
89 **RIECINE** La Gioia 1991 • $42
88 **CASTELLO DI AMA** Vigna Il Chiuso 1991 • $25 • (02/28/95)
88 **CASTELLO DI AMA** Vigna l'Apparita 1992 • $60
88 **AVIGNONESI** Merlot 1991 • $36
88 **CASTELLO BANFI** Tavernelle 1992 • $20 • (10/31/95)
88 **CASTELLARE DI CASTELLINA** I Sodi di S. Niccolo Red 1990 • $36
88 **CENNATOIO** Etrusco 1991 • $26
88 **CASTELLO DI FONTERUTOLI** Concerto 1991 • $30
88 **FRESCOBALDI** Capitolare di Biturica Mormoreto 1990 • $32
88 **LILLIANO** Anagallis Red 1990 • $25

88 **CASTELLO DI MONSANTO** Nemo Red 1990 • $29
88 **FATTORIA LE PUPILLE** Saffredi 1990 • $40 • (02/28/95)
88 **ROCCA DI CASTAGNOLI** Stielle Red 1990 • $27 • (07/31/95)
88 **SAN FABIANO CALCINAIA** Cerviolo Rosso 1991 • $15
88 **TENUTA SAN GUIDO** Sassicaia 1989 • $84
87 **CASTELLO BANFI** Colvecchio 1991 • $25 • (02/28/95)
87 **CASTELLO BANFI** Mandrielle 1990 • $25 • (02/28/95)
87 **CAPARZO** Ca' del Pazzo 1992 • $28
87 **CARPINETO** Farnito 1991 • $18
87 **CASTELLARE DI CASTELLINA** I Sodi di S. Niccolo 1991 • $42
87 **CENNATOIO** Rosso Fiorentino 1991 • $26
87 **TENUTA FARNETA** Selezione di Bongoverno 1990 • $25 • (10/31/95)
87 **FONTODI** Pinot Nero Case Via 1993 • $35
87 **CASTELLO DEI RAMPOLLA** Sammarco 1991 • $58
87 **CASTELLO DEI RAMPOLLA** Sammarco 1990 • $55 • (07/31/95)
87 **ROCCA DELLE MACIE** Roccato 1990 • $30
87 **ROCCA DI CASTAGNOLI** Stielle 1991 • $33
87 **FATTORIA DI SELVOLE** Barullo 1991 • $16
86 **ANTINORI** Tignanello 1991 • $38 • (10/31/95)
86 **AVIGNONESI** Aleatico Red 1990 • $28 • (02/28/95)
86 **AVIGNONESI** Merlot 1990 • $55 • (02/28/95)
86 **FATTORIA BAGGIOLINO** Poggio Brandi 1990 • $26
86 **CASTELLO BANFI** Tavernelle 1991 • $22 • (02/28/95)
86 **ISOLE E OLENA** Cepparello Red 1991 • $28
86 **MONTE VERTINE** Le Pergole Torte Red 1992 • $46
86 **ORNELLAIA** Ornellaia Tuscany 1991 • $38
86 **SANT'ANNA** Vigna Il Vallone 1992 • $23
85 **CASTELLO BANFI** Belnero 1992 • $28 • (10/31/95)
85 **MELINI** Vigneto Coltri, Vineyard 1 Red 1990 • $20 • (12/31/95)
85 **MONTE VERTINE** Montevertine Red 1991 • $23
85 **ORNELLAIA** Ornellaia Tuscany 1992 • $44
91 **CASTELLO BANFI** Chardonnay Fontanelle 1993 • $17 • (02/29/96)
88 **COL D'ORCIA** Ghiaie Bianche Chardonnay White 1992 • $19 • (06/30/95)

VINTAGE PORT

96 **FONSECA** Vintage Port 1992 • $30 • (06/15/95) • CS
95 **TAYLOR FLADGATE** Vintage Port 1992 • $37 • (06/15/95)
94 **QUINTA DO VESUVIO** Vintage Port 1992 • $49 • (06/15/95)
93 **FONSECA** Vintage Port 1991 • $NA
92 **DOW** Vintage Port Quinta do Bomfim 1992 • $30 • (06/30/95)
91 **GRAHAM** Vintage Port Malvedos 1992 • $39 • (06/30/95)
91 **WARRE** Vintage Port Quinta da Cavadinha 1992 • $26 • (06/30/95)
90 **DELAFORCE** Vintage Port 1992 • $35 • (06/15/95)
90 **QUINTA DO INFANTADO** Vintage Port 1992 • $35 • (06/15/95)
90 **NIEPOORT** Vintage Port 1992 • $33 • (06/15/95)
89 **CHURCHILL** Vintage Port Agua Alta 1992 • $35 • (06/15/95)
89 **COCKBURN** Vintage Port Quinta da Canias 1992 • $35 • (06/15/95)
89 **MARTINEZ** Vintage Port Quinta da Eira Velha 1992 • $NA • (06/15/95)
89 **ROMANIERA** Vintage Port Quinta das Liceiras 1992 • $NA • (06/15/95)
88 **OSBORNE** Vintage Port 1992 • $28 • (06/15/95)

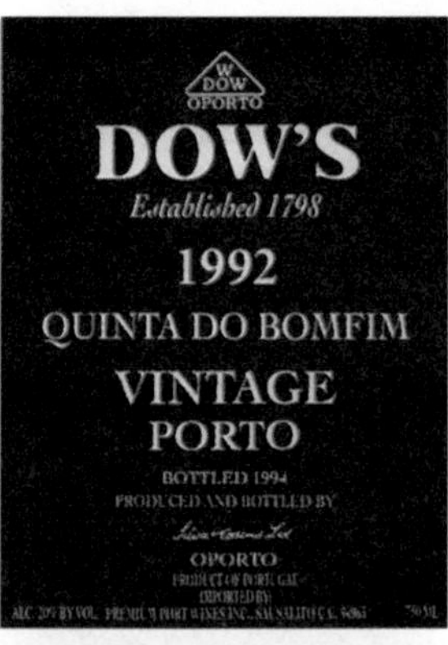

88 **QUINTA DO PASSADOURO** Vintage Port 1992 • $NA • (06/15/95)
88 **QUINTA DE LA ROSA** Vintage Port 1992 • $NA • (06/15/95)
88 **SMITH WOODHOUSE** Vintage Port 1992 • $33 • (06/15/95)
87 **BURMESTER** Vintage Port Quinta do Nova 1992 • $NA • (06/15/95)
86 **CALEM** Vintage Port Quinta do Foz 1992 • $NA • (06/15/95)
85 **BURMESTER** Vintage Port 1992 • $NA • (06/15/95)
85 **GILBERT** Vintage Port 1992 • $NA • (06/15/95)

RIOJA RED

90 **MARQUES DE RISCAL** Rioja Reserva 1989 • $11 • (04/30/95)
89 **BODEGAS MARTINEZ BUJANDA** Rioja Conde de Valdemar Gran Reserva 1989 • $20 • (03/31/96)
89 **BODEGAS MARTINEZ BUJANDA** Rioja Conde de Valdemar Reserva 1990 • $12 • (04/30/95)
88 **MARQUES DE GRINON** Rioja 1994 • $10 • (06/30/96) • BB
88 **BODEGAS MARTINEZ BUJANDA** Rioja Reserva 1989 • $12
88 **REMELLURI** Rioja Reserva 1990 • $14 • (04/30/95)
88 **VIÑA LJALBA** Rioja Ljalba Reserva 1990 • $16 • (06/30/96)
87 **BODEGAS AMEZOLA DE LA MORA** Rioja Reserva Señorio Amezola 1989 • $13 • (04/15/95)
87 **BODEGAS AMEZOLA DE LA MORA** Señorio Amezola Reserva Rioja 1989 • $13 • (04/30/95)
87 **BODEGAS BRETON** Rioja Dominio de Conte Reserva 1991 • $26
87 **MARQUES DE CACERES** Rioja Reserva 1989 • $20 • (03/31/96)
87 **CUNE** Rioja Viña Real Crianza 1989 • $9 • BB
87 **BODEGAS MARTINEZ BUJANDA** Rioja Vendimia Seleccionada Reserva 1990 • $26 • (03/31/96)
87 **BODEGAS MARTINEZ BUJANDA** Rioja Reserva Especial 1989 • $25 • (04/30/95)
87 **BODEGAS MONTECILLO** Rioja Viña Cumbrero Crianza 1990 • $7 • (04/30/95)
86 **BODEGAS BERBERANA** Rioja Tempranillo Dragon Label 1994 • $10 • (06/30/96) • BB
86 **LORINON** Rioja Loriñon Crianza 1990 • $9 • (04/15/95)
86 **BODEGAS CORRAL** Don Jacobo Crianza Rioja 1989 • $7 • (04/30/95)
86 **MARQUES DE GRINON** Rioja 1991 • $10 • (03/31/95)
86 **BODEGAS MARTINEZ BUJANDA** Rioja Reserva Garnacha 1989 • $22 • (04/30/95)
85 **BODEGAS AMEZOLA DE LA MORA** Rioja Crianza Viña Amezola 1990 • $10 • (04/30/95)
85 **BODEGAS BILBAINAS** Rioja Viña Pomal Crianza 1990 • $13 • (03/31/96)
85 **MARQUES DE CACERES** Rioja Gran Reserva 1989 • $NA • (03/31/96)
85 **BODEGAS MARTINEZ BUJANDA** Rioja Conde de Valdemar Crianza 1991 • $8.50 • (03/31/95)
85 **BODEGAS MARTINEZ BUJANDA** Rioja Crianza 1989 • $9 • BB
85 **MARQUES DE RISCAL** Rioja Reserva 1991 • $13 • (03/31/96)
85 **BODEGAS SIERRA CANTABRIA** Rioja Crianza 1989 • $7 • (03/31/95)
85 **VINA SALCEDA** Rioja Crianza 1991 • $11 • (03/31/96)

CALIFORNIA CABERNET SAUVIGNON & BLENDS

98 **GROTH** Cabernet Sauvignon Napa Valley Reserve 1992 • $70 • (04/30/96) • CS
96 **ARAUJO** Cabernet Sauvignon Napa Valley Eisele Vineyard 1992 • $40 • (11/15/95) • CS

96 **FLORA SPRINGS** Cabernet Sauvignon Napa Valley Rutherford Reserve 1992 • $40 • (11/15/95)

95 **BERINGER** Cabernet Sauvignon Napa Valley Private Reserve 1992 • $45 • (11/15/95) • CS

95 **CHATEAU ST. JEAN** Cabernet Sauvignon Sonoma County Reserve 1990 • $38 • (04/30/96) • CS

94 **DALLA VALLE** Maya Napa Valley 1992 • $75 • (12/15/95)

94 **THE HESS COLLECTION** Cabernet Sauvignon Napa Valley 1992 • $18 • (11/15/95) • SS

94 **LEWIS CELLARS** Cabernet Sauvignon Napa Valley Oakville Ranch 1992 • $30 • (11/30/95)

94 **STAG'S LEAP WINE CELLARS** S.L.V. Cask 23 Napa Valley 1992 • $80 • (12/15/95) • CS

93 **ANDERSON'S CONN VALLEY** Cabernet Sauvignon Napa Valley Estate Reserve 1992 • $30 • (11/15/95)

93 **CORNERSTONE** Cabernet Sauvignon Howell Mountain Beatty Ranch 1993 • $33 • (04/30/96)

93 **CRONIN** Concerto Stags Leap District Robinson Vineyard 1992 • $17 • (04/30/96)

93 **DOMINUS** Napanook Vineyard Napa Valley 1991 • $55 • (11/15/95) • CS

93 **ETUDE** Cabernet Sauvignon Napa Valley 1992 • $30 • (11/30/95)

93 **FAR NIENTE** Cabernet Sauvignon Napa Valley 1992 • $45 • (11/15/95)

93 **PAUL HOBBS** Cabernet Sauvignon Carneros Napa Valley Hyde Vineyard 1992 • $30 • (12/15/95)

93 **SHAFER** Cabernet Sauvignon Stags Leap District Hillside Select 1991 • $45 • (11/15/95) • CS

93 **WHITEHALL LANE** Cabernet Sauvignon Napa Valley Morisoli Vineyard 1992 • $28 • (10/15/95)

92 **ARROWOOD** Cabernet Sauvignon Sonoma County 1992 • $25 • (11/15/95)

92 **ARROWOOD** Cabernet Sauvignon Sonoma County Réserve Spéciale 1992 • $35 • (12/15/95)

92 **CAYMUS** Cabernet Sauvignon Napa Valley Special Selection 1992 • $100 • (05/15/96) • CS

92 **CHIMNEY ROCK** Reserve Stags Leap District 1992 • $30 • (12/15/95)

92 **COLGIN** Cabernet Sauvignon Napa Valley Herb Lamb Vineyard 1992 • $29 • (10/15/95)

92 **CORISON** Cabernet Sauvignon Napa Valley 1992 • $28 • (11/30/95) • CS

92 **COSENTINO** Meritage Coz Napa Valley 1992 • $45 • (12/15/95)

92 **DALLA VALLE** Cabernet Sauvignon Napa Valley 1992 • $30 • (12/15/95) • CS

92 **FLORA SPRINGS** Trilogy Napa Valley 1992 • $27 • (11/30/95) • CS

92 **JUSTIN** Isosceles Reserve San Luis Obispo County 1992 • $25 • (12/15/95)

92 **A. RAFANELLI** Cabernet Sauvignon Dry Creek Valley Unfiltered 1992 • $17 • (09/30/95) • SS

92 **SADDLEBACK** Cabernet Sauvignon Napa Valley 1993 • $19 • (05/31/96)

92 **ST. CLEMENT** Oroppas Napa Valley 1993 • $30 • (10/31/95)

92 **ST. FRANCIS** Cabernet Sauvignon Sonoma County Reserve 1992 • $24 • (11/30/95)

92 **SCREAMING EAGLE** Cabernet Sauvignon Napa Valley 1992 • $50 • (02/29/96)

92 **SIMI** Cabernet Sauvignon Alexander Valley Reserve 1991 • $35 • (10/15/95)

92 **STONESTREET** Legacy Alexander Valley 1992 • $35 • (09/30/95) • CS

92 **TAY** Cabernet Sauvignon Napa Valley 1993 • $35 • (04/30/96)

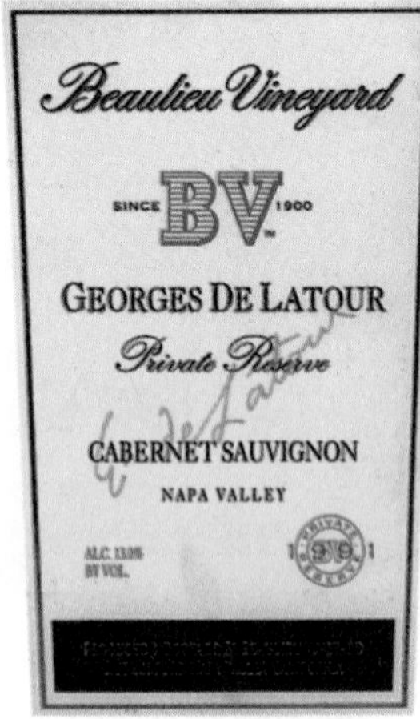

92 **WHITEHALL LANE** Cabernet Sauvignon Napa Valley Reserve 1992 • $23 • (10/15/95)

91 **BUEHLER** Cabernet Sauvignon Napa Valley Reserve 1991 • $25 • (09/30/95)

91 **CHATEAU ST. JEAN** Cabernet Sauvignon Sonoma County Cinq Cépages 1991 • $18 • (11/15/95)

91 **DUNN** Cabernet Sauvignon Howell Mountain 1991 • $39 • (12/15/95) • CS

91 **FERRARI-CARANO** Reserve Sonoma County 1990 • $47 • (11/30/95)

91 **GROTH** Cabernet Sauvignon Napa Valley 1992 • $20 • (09/30/95) • CS

91 **HEITZ** Cabernet Sauvignon Napa Valley Martha's Vineyard 1991 • $65 • (04/30/96) • CS

91 **HEITZ** Cabernet Sauvignon Napa Valley Trailside Vineyard 1990 • $45 • (10/15/95) • CS

91 **THE HESS COLLECTION** Cabernet Sauvignon Napa Valley Reserve 1991 • $39 • (04/30/96)

91 **JUDD'S HILL** Cabernet Sauvignon Napa Valley 1992 • $26 • (12/15/95)

91 **KENDALL-JACKSON** Cabernet Sauvignon California Grand Reserve 1992 • $35 • (11/30/95)

91 **KENDALL-JACKSON** Meritage Cardinale California 1991 • $60 • (12/15/95)

91 **LA JOTA** Cabernet Sauvignon Howell Mountain 12th Anniversary Release 1993 • $42 • (04/30/96)

91 **ROBERT MONDAVI** Cabernet Sauvignon Napa Valley Reserve 1992 • $55 • (07/31/95) • CS

91 **ROBERT MONDAVI** Cabernet Sauvignon 1992 • $28 • (09/30/95)

91 **OPUS ONE** Napa Valley 1992 • $75 • (12/15/95) • CS

91 **PAHLMEYER** Red Napa Valley 1993 • $36 • (05/31/96) • CS

91 **PEJU** Cabernet Sauvignon Napa Valley HB Vineyard 1992 • $35 • (12/15/95)

91 **PINE RIDGE** Cabernet Sauvignon Napa Valley Rutherford Cuvée 1992 • $16 • (11/15/95) • SS

91 **RIDGE** Monte Bello Santa Cruz Mountains 1991 • $75 • (11/15/95) • CS

91 **SHAFER** Cabernet Sauvignon Stags Leap District 1992 • $22 • (09/30/95) • CS

91 **SILVER OAK** Cabernet Sauvignon Alexander Valley 1991 • $32 • (11/15/95)

91 **STAG'S LEAP WINE CELLARS** Cabernet Sauvignon Napa Valley Fay 1992 • $35 • (12/15/95) • CS

91 **STAGLIN FAMILY** Cabernet Sauvignon Napa Valley 1992 • $28 • (12/15/95)

91 **STONESTREET** Cabernet Sauvignon Alexander Valley 1992 • $25 • (10/31/95)

90 **BEAULIEU** Cabernet Sauvignon Napa Valley Georges de Latour Private Reserve 1991 • $40 • (12/15/95)

90 **B.R. COHN** Cabernet Sauvignon Sonoma Valley Olive Hill Vineyard 1993 • $32 • (04/30/96)

90 **CONN CREEK** Anthology Napa Valley 1992 • $30 • (12/15/95)

90 **CORNERSTONE** Cabernet Sauvignon Howell Mountain Beatty Ranch 1992 • $33 • (12/15/95)

90 **COSENTINO** Cabernet Sauvignon Napa Valley Reserve 1991 • $30 • (12/15/95)

90 **ROBERT CRAIG** Cabernet Sauvignon Mount Veeder 1993 • $25 • (10/15/95)

90 **DUCKHORN** Cabernet Sauvignon Napa Valley 1992 • $24 • (10/31/95) • SS

90 **DUCKHORN** Migration Red Napa Valley 1993 • $12 • (02/29/96) • SS

90 **FERRARI-CARANO** Siena Sonoma County 1993 • $24 • (11/30/95)

90 **THOMAS FOGARTY** Cabernet Sauvignon Napa Valley Vallerga Vineyards 1992 • $25 • (04/30/96)

90 **FOXEN** Cabernet Franc Santa Maria Valley Tinaquaic Vineyard 1993 • $24 • (04/30/96)

90 **GUENOC** Cabernet Sauvignon Napa Valley Bella Vista Vineyard Reserve 1992 • $25 • (12/15/95)
90 **GUENOC** Cabernet Sauvignon Napa Valley Beckstoffer IV Vineyard Reserve 1992 • $40 • (12/15/95)
90 **HARLAN** Napa Valley 1991 • $65 • (11/30/95)
90 **HARRISON** Cabernet Sauvignon Napa Valley 1992 • $33 • (11/15/95)
90 **HARTWELL** Cabernet Sauvignon Stags Leap District 1992 • $50 • (11/15/95)
90 **JARVIS** Cabernet Sauvignon Napa Valley 1992 • $48 • (08/31/95)
90 **MARTIN BROTHERS** Cabernet Etrusco Paso Robles 1993 • $16 • (12/15/95)
90 **MERRYVALE** Cabernet Sauvignon Napa Valley Profile 1991 • $36 • (12/15/95)
90 **PETER MICHAEL** Cabernet Sauvignon Knights Valley Les Pavots 1992 • $29 • (12/15/95)
90 **MOUNT EDEN** Cabernet Sauvignon Santa Cruz Mountains Old Vine Reserve 1992 • $35 • (06/15/96)
90 **NIEBAUM-COPPOLA** Rubicon Napa Valley 1990 • $35 • (12/15/95)
90 **OAKVILLE RANCH** Cabernet Sauvignon Napa Valley 1992 • $24 • (12/15/95)
90 **JOSEPH PHELPS** Insignia Napa Valley 1992 • $50 • (09/30/95) • CS
90 **PINE RIDGE** Cabernet Sauvignon Stags Leap District 1992 • $31 • (12/15/95)
90 **RAYMOND** Cabernet Sauvignon Napa Valley Reserve 1993 • $17 • (04/30/96)
90 **SEQUOIA GROVE** Cabernet Sauvignon Napa Valley 1992 • $18 • (07/31/95) • SS
90 **SHAFER** Cabernet Sauvignon Stags Leap District Hillside Select10/11/95 DO NOT USE 1991 1990 • $38 • (12/15/95)
90 **SIGNORELLO** Cabernet Sauvignon Napa Valley Founder's Reserve 1992 • $32 • (09/15/95) • CS
90 **SILVER OAK** Cabernet Sauvignon Napa Valley 1991 • $36 • (11/15/95)
90 **SPOTTSWOODE** Cabernet Sauvignon Napa Valley 1992 • $39 • (11/30/95) • CS
90 **ST. CLEMENT** Cabernet Sauvignon Napa Valley 1992 • $24 • (10/31/95)
90 **STEELE** Cabernet Sauvignon Anderson Valley 1993 • $22 • (04/30/96)
90 **SWANSON** Cabernet Sauvignon Napa Valley 1992 • $22 • (12/15/95)
90 **ZIA CELLARS** Cabernet Sauvignon Napa Valley 1992 • $24 • (04/30/96)
89 **S. ANDERSON** Cabernet Sauvignon Stags Leap District Richard Chambers Vineyard 1992 • $46 • (12/15/95)
89 **ATLAS PEAK** Cabernet Sauvignon Atlas Peak 1992 • $18 • (12/15/95)
89 **BEAULIEU** Cabernet Sauvignon Napa Valley Georges de Latour Private Reserve 1992 • $40 • (12/15/95)
89 **BRYANT FAMILY VINEYARD** Cabernet Sauvignon Napa Valley 1992 • $32 • (05/31/96)
89 **CAIN** Five Napa Valley 1991 • $40 • (12/15/95)
89 **CAYMUS** Cabernet Sauvignon Napa Valley 1992 • $25 • (09/30/95)
89 **CHATEAU SOUVERAIN** Cabernet Sauvignon Alexander Valley Winemaker's Reserve 1992 • $16 • (12/15/95)
89 **CHATEAU ST. JEAN** Cabernet Sauvignon Sonoma County Cinq Cépages 1992 • $18 • (02/29/96)
89 **CLOS DU BOIS** Cabernet Sauvignon Alexander Valley Briarcrest Vineyard 1992 • $20 • (11/30/95)
89 **CLOS DU BOIS** Marlstone Vineyard Alexander Valley 1992 • $21 • (11/30/95)
89 **ROBERT CRAIG** Cabernet Sauvignon Howell Mountain 1993 • $25 • (10/15/95)
89 **CRONIN** Cabernet Sauvignon Santa Cruz Mountains 1991 • $17 • (04/30/96)
89 **DE LOACH** Cabernet Sauvignon Russian River Valley O.F.S. 1991 • $25 • (09/30/95)
89 **DRY CREEK** Cabernet Sauvignon Dry Creek Valley 1992 • $16 • (10/15/95)
89 **DRY CREEK** Meritage Dry Creek Valley 1993 • $20 • (11/30/95)

89 **ELYSE** Cabernet Sauvignon Napa Valley Morisoli Vineyard 1992 • $30 • (04/30/96)

89 **ESTANCIA** Meritage Alexander Valley 1992 • $15 • (09/30/95)

89 **GARY FARRELL** Cabernet Sauvignon Sonoma County Ladi's Vineyard 1992 • $20 • (07/31/95)

89 **FERRARI-CARANO** Siena Sonoma County 1992 • $20 • (09/30/95)

89 **FIRESTONE** Vintage Reserve Santa Ynez Valley 1991 • $22 • (12/15/95)

89 **FRANCISCAN** Meritage Magnificat Oakville Estate Napa Valley 1991 • $20 • (12/15/95)

89 **E. & J. GALLO** Cabernet Sauvignon Dry Creek Valley Frei Ranch Vineyard Gallo Sonoma 1992 • $16 • (11/15/95)

89 **GREENWOOD RIDGE** Cabernet Sauvignon Anderson Valley 1992 • $18 • (09/15/95)

89 **GRGICH HILLS** Cabernet Sauvignon Napa Valley Yountville Selection 1991 • $35 • (12/15/95)

89 **GUENOC** Meritage Langtry California 1992 • $35 • (12/15/95)

89 **CHARLES KRUG** Cabernet Sauvignon Napa Valley Vintage Selection 1991 • $28 • (12/15/95)

89 **LA JOTA** Cabernet Franc Howell Mountain 1992 • $28 • (07/31/95)

89 **LIVINGSTON** Cabernet Sauvignon Napa Valley Moffett Vineyard 1992 • $30 • (12/15/95)

89 **MONTICELLO** Cabernet Sauvignon Napa Valley Jefferson Cuvée 1992 • $18 • (12/15/95)

89 **NEWLAN** Cabernet Sauvignon Napa Valley 1991 • $16 • (11/30/95)

89 **OPTIMA** Cabernet Sauvignon Alexander Valley 1992 • $25 • (12/15/95)

88 **LA JOTA** Cabernet Franc Howell Mountain 1993 • $28 • (04/30/96)

89 **PAHLMEYER** Napa Valley 1992 • $34 • (12/15/95)

89 **JOSEPH PHELPS** Cabernet Sauvignon Napa Valley Backus Vineyard 1992 • $45 • (12/15/95)

89 **RAVENSWOOD** Cabernet Sauvignon Sonoma Valley Gregory 1993 • $20 • (12/15/95)

89 **MARTIN RAY** Cabernet Sauvignon California Saratoga Cuvée 1992 • $28 • (10/31/95)

89 **ROCKLAND ROAD CELLARS** Cabernet Sauvignon Napa Valley 1993 • $30 • (05/15/96)

89 **ROSENTHAL** Cabernet Sauvignon California 1992 • $22 • (12/15/95)

89 **SEAVEY** Cabernet Sauvignon Napa Valley 1991 • $26 • (07/31/95)

89 **SEQUOIA GROVE** Cabernet Sauvignon Estate Reserve 1992 • $30 • (07/31/95)

89 **SEQUOIA GROVE** Cabernet Sauvignon Rutherford Estate Reserve 1992 • $30 • (12/31/95)

89 **SIMI** Cabernet Sauvignon Alexander Valley 1992 • $15 • (10/15/95)

89 **STAGLIN FAMILY** Cabernet Sauvignon Napa Valley 1993 • $30 • (04/30/96)

89 **STONEHEDGE** Cabernet Sauvignon Napa Valley Winemaker's Reserve 1992 • $10 • (11/30/95) • BB

89 **VIADER** Napa Valley 1993 • $29 • (05/15/96)

89 **VON STRASSER** Cabernet Sauvignon Napa Valley Diamond Mountain 1993 • $28 • (04/30/96)

88 **ALTAMURA** Cabernet Sauvignon Napa Valley 1991 • $25 • (05/31/96)

88 **ALTAMURA** Cabernet Sauvignon Napa Valley 1990 • $25 • (09/15/95)

88 **BEAULIEU** Tapestry Red Napa Valley Reserve 1992 • $20 • (04/30/96)

88 **CAFARO** Cabernet Sauvignon Napa Valley 1991 • $28 • (09/15/95)

88 **CAFARO** Cabernet Sauvignon Napa Valley 1992 • $26 • (12/15/95)

88 **CHIMNEY ROCK** Elevage Stags Leap District 1992 • $30 • (12/15/95)

88 **CINNABAR** Cabernet Sauvignon Santa Cruz Mountains Saratoga Vineyard 1992 • $20 • (12/15/95)

88 **CLOS LACHANCE** Cabernet Sauvignon Santa Cruz Mountains 1992 • $20 • (07/31/95)

88 **CLOS PEGASE** Cabernet Sauvignon Napa Valley 1992 • $19 • (10/15/95)

88 **CONN CREEK** Cabernet Sauvignon Napa Valley Limited Release 1992 • $18 • (12/15/95)

88 **COSENTINO** Cabernet Sauvignon Napa Valley Punched Cap Fermented Unfined 1992 • $16 • (09/15/95)

88 **CUVAISON** Cabernet Sauvignon Napa Valley 1992 • $26 • (12/15/95)

88 **DIAMOND CREEK** Cabernet Sauvignon Napa Valley Volcanic Hill 1993 • $50 • (12/15/95)

88 **DICKERSON** Ruby Cabernet Limited Reserve Napa Valley 1993 • $9 • (12/15/95)

88 **DRY CREEK** Cabernet Sauvignon Dry Creek Valley 1993 • $16 • (11/30/95)

88 **DUNN** Cabernet Sauvignon Napa Valley 1992 • $33 • (12/15/95)

88 **TOM EDDY** Cabernet Sauvignon Napa Valley 1992 • $36 • (05/15/96)

88 **EHLERS GROVE** Cabernet Sauvignon Napa Valley 1992 • $15 • (12/15/95)

88 **FORMAN** Cabernet Sauvignon Napa Valley 1993 • $32 • (04/30/96)

88 **FREEMARK ABBEY** Cabernet Sauvignon Napa Valley Sycamore Vineyards 1990 • $23 • (12/15/95)

88 **GEYSER PEAK** Cabernet Sauvignon Alexander Valley Reserve 1993 • $20 • (12/15/95)

88 **GIRARD** Cabernet Sauvignon Napa Valley Reserve 1992 • $40 • (12/15/95)

88 **GUENOC** Meritage Lake County 1992 • $15 • (12/15/95)

88 **GUILLIAMS** Cabernet Sauvignon Spring Mountain 1991 • $17 • (12/15/95)

88 **JARVIS** Cabernet Sauvignon Napa Valley 1993 • $48 • (05/15/96)

88 **JARVIS** Lake William Red Napa Valley 1993 • $45 • (05/15/96)

88 **JUSTIN** Cabernet Sauvignon San Luis Obispo County 1992 • $18 • (12/15/95)

88 **LAUREL GLEN** Cabernet Sauvignon Sonoma Mountain Counterpoint 1992 • $16 • (12/15/95)

88 **LEWIS CELLARS** Cabernet Sauvignon Napa Valley Oakville Ranch 1993 • $32 • (04/30/96)

88 **MARKHAM** Cabernet Sauvignon Napa Valley 1992 • $17 • (11/30/95)

88 **MAZZOCCO** Cabernet Sauvignon Sonoma County 1992 • $18 • (04/30/96)

88 **MERRYVALE** Cabernet Sauvignon Napa Valley 1992 • $24 • (12/15/95)

88 **MURPHY-GOODE** Cabernet Sauvignon Alexander Valley Murphy Ranch 1993 • $16 • (11/15/95)

88 **NAVARRO** Cabernet Sauvignon Mendocino 1990 • $17 • (10/15/95)

88 **OAKFORD** Cabernet Sauvignon Napa Valley 1991 • $30 • (12/15/95)

88 **PARDUCCI** Cabernet Merlot Cellarmaster Selection Mendocino County 1993 • $15 • (11/15/95)

88 **PARDUCCI** Cabernet Sauvignon Mendocino County 1992 • $8 • (11/15/95) • BB

88 **PEACHY CANYON** Cabernet Sauvignon Central Coast 1993 • $20 • (12/15/95)

88 **PINE RIDGE** Cabernet Sauvignon Howell Mountain 1993 • $31 • (12/15/95)

88 **PRIDE** Cabernet Franc Sonoma County 1993 • $20 • (04/30/96)

88 **RAYMOND** Cabernet Sauvignon Napa Valley 1992 • $17 • (11/30/95)

88 **REMICK RIDGE VINEYARDS** Cabernet Sauvignon Sonoma Valley 1992 • $19 • (05/31/96)

88 **SAUSAL** Cabernet Sauvignon Alexander Valley 1992 • $14 • (10/31/95)

88 **SIGNORELLO** Cabernet Sauvignon Napa Valley Founder's Reserve 1993 • $32 • (05/15/96)

88 **SMITH & HOOK** Cabernet Sauvignon Santa Lucia Highlands Masterpiece Edition 1992 • $30 • (12/15/95)

88 **STAG'S LEAP WINE CELLARS** Cabernet Sauvignon Napa Valley S.L.V. 1992 • $35 • (12/15/95)

88 **STERLING** Cabernet Sauvignon Napa Valley Diamond Mountain Ranch Vineyard 1992 • $17 • (10/31/95)

88 **STONEGATE** Reserve Napa Valley 1989 • $24 • (12/15/95)

88 **TERRACES** Cabernet Sauvignon Napa Valley 1991 • $40 • (10/31/95)

88 **TRUCHARD** Cabernet Sauvignon Napa Valley Carneros 1992 • $20 • (03/31/96)

88 **VENEZIA** Cabernet Sauvignon Alexander Valley 1993 • $20 • (04/30/96)

88 **VENGE VINEYARDS** Cabernet Sauvignon Napa Valley Family Reserve 1992 • $NA • (06/30/96)

88 **VIADER** Napa Valley 1992 • $28 • (07/31/95)

88 **VICHON** Cabernet Sauvignon Stags Leap District SLD 1991 • $28 • (12/15/95)

88 **VILLA MT. EDEN** Cabernet Sauvignon Napa Valley Grand Reserve 1992 • $16 • (04/30/96)

88 **VINEYARD 29** Cabernet Sauvignon Napa Valley 1993 • $33 • (03/31/96)

88 **ZD** Cabernet Sauvignon Napa Valley Reserve 1992 • $34 • (04/30/96)

87 **ATLAS PEAK** Consenso Atlas Peak 1990 • $22 • (12/15/95)

87 **BANDIERA** Cabernet Sauvignon Napa Valley Reserve 1993 • $12 • (11/30/95)

87 **BEAULIEU** Tapestry Signet Collection Napa Valley 1991 • $20 • (12/15/95)

87 **BENZIGER** Cabernet Sauvignon Sonoma County 1992 • $13 • (09/15/95)

87 **BERINGER** Cabernet Sauvignon Knights Valley 1992 • $15 • (08/31/95)

87 **BERINGER** Meritage Knights Valley 1992 • $13 • (11/15/95)

87 **BYINGTON** Cabernet Sauvignon Alexander Valley Smith Reichel Vineyard 1992 • $15 • (12/15/95)

87 **CAKEBREAD** Cabernet Sauvignon Napa Valley Rutherford Reserve 1990 • $42 • (12/15/95)

87 **CAMELOT** Cabernet Sauvignon North Coast 1993 • $12 • (12/15/95)

87 **CARMENET** Cabernet Sauvignon Sonoma County Moon Mountain Dynamite Cabernet 1992 • $15 • (09/15/95)

87 **CHATEAU ST. JEAN** Cabernet Sauvignon Sonoma County Reserve 1989 • $38 • (11/15/95)

87 **CLOS DU VAL** Cabernet Sauvignon Stags Leap District 1991 • $20 • (09/30/95)

87 **CLOS PEGASE** Cabernet Sauvignon Napa Valley 1993 • $20 • (03/31/96)

87 **COSENTINO** Meritage The Poet Napa Valley 1992 • $24 • (12/15/95)

87 **ROBERT CRAIG** Cabernet Sauvignon Napa Valley Affinity 1993 • $25 • (10/15/95)

87 **ROBERT CRAIG** Cabernet Sauvignon Napa Valley 1992 • $20 • (10/15/95)

87 **CUTLER** Satyre Sonoma Valley 1989 • $20 • (12/15/95)

87 **DOMAIN HILL & MAYES** Cabernet Sauvignon Napa Valley Clos Fontaine du Mont Reserve 1992 • $32 • (12/15/95)

87 **EXPRESSIONS** Cabernet Sauvignon Napa Valley 1993 • $10 • (04/30/96) • BB

87 **FRANCISCAN** Cabernet Sauvignon Napa Valley Oakville Estate 1992 • $15 • (12/15/95)

87 **E. & J. GALLO** Cabernet Sauvignon Sonoma County 1992 • $12 • (11/15/95)

87 **GUNDLACH BUNDSCHU** Cabernet Sauvignon Sonoma Valley Rhinefarm Vineyards 1992 • $15 • (10/31/95)

87 **IRON HORSE** T-T Cabernets Alexander Valley 1991 • $19 • (12/15/95)

87 **JEKEL** Cabernet Sauvignon Arroyo Seco Sanctuary Estate 1992 • $13 • (12/15/95)

87 **KENWOOD** Cabernet Sauvignon Sonoma Valley Jack London Vineyard 1992 • $20 • (10/31/95)

87 **LA JOTA** Cabernet Sauvignon Howell Mountain Selection 1993 • $24 • (04/30/96)

87 **LAMBERT BRIDGE** Cabernet Sauvignon Sonoma County 1992 • $15 • (12/15/95)

87 **LIVINGSTON** Cabernet Sauvignon Napa Valley Stanley's Selection 1992 • $18 • (08/31/95)

87 **J. LOHR** Cabernet Sauvignon Paso Robles Seven Oaks 1993 • $12 • (11/30/95)

87 **J. LOHR** Cabernet Sauvignon Paso Robles VS 1991 • $22 • (11/30/95)

87 **LYETH** A Red Blend Alexander Valley 1992 • $18 • (08/31/95)

87 **MAZZOCCO** Matrix Dry Creek Valley 1991 • $28 • (12/15/95)

87 **MIRASSOU** Cabernet Sauvignon Monterey County Fifth Generation Harvest Reserve 1991 • $12 • (12/15/95)

87 **MOUNT VEEDER** Cabernet Sauvignon Napa Valley 1992 • $25 • (12/15/95)

87 **NAPA RIDGE** Cabernet Sauvignon Central Coast 1992 • $8 • (10/15/95) • BB

87 **NAPA RIDGE** Cabernet Sauvignon North Coast Coastal Reserve 1991 • $13 • (10/15/95)

87 **NAPA RIDGE** Cabernet Sauvignon North Coast Coastal Oak Barrel 1993 • $7.50 • (11/30/95) • BB

87 **PARADIGM** Cabernet Sauvignon Napa Valley 1992 • $28 • (12/15/95)

87 **PEACHY CANYON** Cabernet Blend Central Coast Para Siempré 1993 • $28 • (03/31/96)

87 **JOSEPH PHELPS** Cabernet Sauvignon Napa Valley 1992 • $20 • (09/30/95)

87 **POPE VALLEY CELLARS** Cabernet Sauvignon Napa Valley La Dolce DeVita Vineyard 1992 • $15 • (12/15/95)

87 **BERNARD PRADEL** Cabernet Sauvignon Howell Mountain Ranch 1991 • $21 • (09/15/95)

87 **PRIDE** Cabernet Sauvignon Napa Valley 1992 • $18 • (12/15/95)

87 **RAVENSWOOD** Cabernet Sauvignon Sonoma County 1993 • $15 • (12/15/95)

87 **RAYMOND** Meritage Private Reserve Napa Valley 1991 • $40 • (12/15/95)

87 **ROCHIOLI** Cabernet Sauvignon Russian River Valley Neoma's Vineyard Reserve 1991 • $26 • (12/15/95)

87 **ROCKING HORSE** Cabernet Sauvignon Napa Valley Garvey Family Vineyard 1993 • $20 • (04/30/96)

87 **RUSTRIDGE** Cabernet Sauvignon Napa Valley 1991 • $20 • (12/15/95)

87 **RUTHERFORD VINEYARDS** Cabernet Sauvignon Napa Valley Rutherford Bench 1992 • $8 • (12/15/95)

87 **SADDLEBACK** Cabernet Sauvignon Napa Valley 1992 • $17 • (12/15/95)

87 **V. SATTUI** Cabernet Sauvignon Napa Valley Julian Schwinger Reserve Stock 1992 • $50 • (04/30/96)

87 **SEBASTIANI** Cabernet Sauvignon Sonoma County 1992 • $10 • (11/15/95) • BB

87 **STERLING** Cabernet Sauvignon Reserve Napa Valley 1992 • $40 • (12/15/95)

87 **PHILIP TOGNI** Cabernet Sauvignon Napa Valley 1993 • $35 • (05/31/96)

87 **TREFETHEN** Cabernet Sauvignon Napa Valley 1992 • $21 • (02/29/96)

87 **TREFETHEN** Cabernet Sauvignon Napa Valley 1990 • $19 • (11/15/95)

87 **TRIA** Claret Dry Creek Valley 1993 • $24 • (05/31/96)

87 **VICHON** Cabernet Sauvignon Napa Valley 1992 • $16 • (12/15/95)

87 **WHITEHALL LANE** Cabernet Sauvignon Napa Valley 1992 • $15 • (10/15/95)

86 **ATLAS PEAK** Cabernet Sauvignon Atlas Peak 1991 • $18 • (09/15/95)

86 **BEAULIEU** Cabernet Sauvignon Napa Valley Rutherford 1992 • $12 • (11/30/95)

86 **BOEGER** Meritage El Dorado 1991 • $15 • (12/15/95)

86 **BRANDER** Bouchet Tête de Cuvée Santa Ynez Valley 1993 • $22 • (12/15/95)

86 **CHAPPELLET** Cabernet Sauvignon Napa Valley Pritchard Hill Estates 1992 • $15 • (09/15/95)

86 **CHATEAU MONTELENA** Cabernet Calistoga Cuvée Napa Valley 1993 • $18 • (12/15/95)

86 **CIRRI** Cabernet Sauvignon Alexander Valley 1992 • $10 • (12/15/95)

86 **CLOS LACHANCE** Cabernet Sauvignon Santa Cruz Mountains 1993 • $23 • (04/30/96)

86 **CONCANNON** Assemblage Reserve Central Coast 1992 • $15 • (12/15/95)

86 **CUVAISON** Meritage Reserve Napa Valley 1991 • $50 • (12/15/95)

86 **DE LOACH** Cabernet Sauvignon Russian River Valley 1992 • $15 • (12/15/95)

86 **DIAMOND CREEK** Cabernet Sauvignon Napa Valley Gravelly Meadow 1993 • $50 • (12/15/95)

86 **DORCICH CELLARS** Cabernet Sauvignon Santa Clara County 1991 • $18 • (07/31/95)

86 **DUNCAN PEAK** Cabernet Sauvignon Mendocino County 1993 • $18 • (04/30/96)

86 **DURNEY** Cabernet Sauvignon Carmel Valley Dances On Your Palate Private Reserve 1992 • $31 • (05/31/96)

86 **FERRARI-CARANO** Cabernet Sauvignon Sonoma County 1991 • $16 • (09/15/95)

86 **FOXEN** Cabernet Sauvignon Santa Barbara County 1993 • $22 • (12/15/95)

86 **GUENOC** Cabernet Sauvignon Guenoc Valley Tephra Ridge Reserve 1993 • $30 • (12/15/95)

86 **JARVIS** Cabernet Franc Napa Valley 1992 • $40 • (08/31/95)

86 **KATHRYN KENNEDY** Lateral California 1993 • $25 • (12/15/95)

86 **KENWOOD** Cabernet Sauvignon Sonoma Valley 25th Anniversary Vintage 1992 • $16 • (10/31/95)

86 **LAMBERT BRIDGE** Cabernet Sauvignon Sonoma County 1993 • $15 • (12/15/95)

86 **LOCKWOOD** Cabernet Sauvignon Monterey 1992 • $14 • (09/30/95)

86 **J. LOHR** Cabernet Sauvignon California Cypress 1992 • $9 • (11/30/95) • BB

86 **LYETH** Meritage California 1993 • $13 • (11/15/95)

86 **ROBERT PECOTA** Cabernet Sauvignon Napa Valley Kara's Vineyard 1993 • $20 • (12/15/95)

86 **PEJU** Cabernet Sauvignon Napa Valley HB Vineyard 1991 • $35 • (09/15/95)

86 **ROBERT PEPI** Cabernet Sauvignon Napa Valley Vine Hill Ranch 1991 • $18 • (12/15/95)

86 **MARIO PERELLI-MINETTI** Cabernet Sauvignon Napa Valley 1991 • $13 • (05/31/96)

86 **MARTIN RAY** Cabernet Sauvignon Napa Valley 1992 • $28 • (10/31/95)

86 **RICHARDSON** Synergy Sonoma Valley 1994 • $15 • (12/15/95)

86 **ROCHIOLI** Cabernet Sauvignon Russian River Valley Neoma's Vineyard Reserve 1993 • $28 • (04/30/96)

86 **RUTHERFORD RANCH** Meritage Quintessence Napa Valley 1991 • $20 • (12/15/95)

86 **SANTA BARBARA WINERY** Cabernet Sauvignon Santa Ynez Valley Reserve 1992 • $16 • (12/15/95)

86 **RODNEY STRONG** Cabernet Sauvignon Northern Sonoma Alexander's Crown Vineyard 1991 • $20 • (12/15/95)

86 **RODNEY STRONG** Cabernet Sauvignon Sonoma County 1993 • $11 • (12/15/95)

86 **RODNEY STRONG** Cabernet Sauvignon Northern Sonoma Reserve 1991 • $30 • (12/15/95)

85 **BANDIERA** Cabernet Sauvignon Napa Valley 1993 • $8 • (11/30/95) • BB

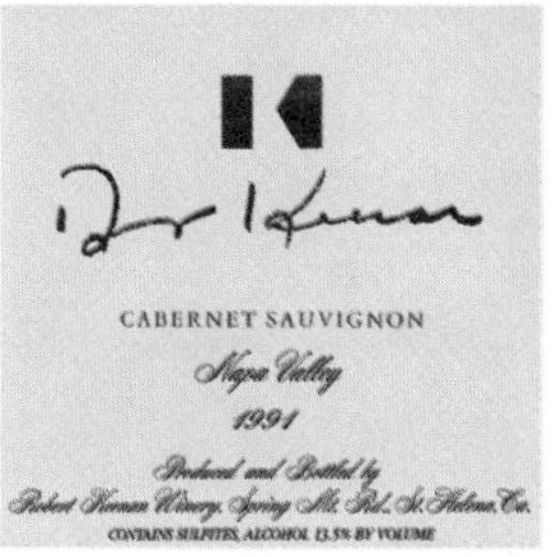

85 **LAWRENCE J. BARGETTO** Cabernet Sauvignon Santa Cruz Mountains Bates Ranch 1990 • $16 • (12/15/95)
85 **BOGLE** Cabernet Sauvignon California 1993 • $6.50 • (11/30/95) • BB
85 **CANYON ROAD** Cabernet Sauvignon California 1993 • $6 • (11/15/95) • BB
85 **CHATEAU MARGARITE** Cabernet Sauvignon Napa Valley 1992 • $15 • (12/15/95)
85 **DE LORIMIER** Meritage Mosaic Alexander Valley 1992 • $18 • (03/31/96)
85 **DE LORIMIER** Meritage Mosaic Alexander Valley 1991 • $18 • (08/31/95)
85 **DIAMOND CREEK** Cabernet Sauvignon Napa Valley Red Rock Terrace 1993 • $50 • (12/15/95)
85 **DORCICH CELLARS** Cabernet Sauvignon Santa Clara County 1990 • $20 • (07/31/95)
85 **FETZER** Cabernet Sauvignon Sonoma County Reserve 1989 • $24 • (12/15/95)
85 **FETZER** Cabernet Sauvignon North Coast Barrel Select 1992 • $12 • (12/15/95)
85 **FOLIE A DEUX** Cabernet Sauvignon Napa Valley 1993 • $14 • (12/15/95)
85 **GRACE FAMILY** Cabernet Sauvignon Napa Valley 1993 • $75 • (05/15/96)
85 **GUENOC** Cabernet Sauvignon Lake County 1992 • $15 • (12/15/95)
85 **HEITZ** Cabernet Sauvignon Napa Valley 1991 • $19 • (04/30/96)
85 **HESS SELECT** Cabernet Sauvignon California 1993 • $9.50 • (11/30/95) • BB
85 **WILLIAM HILL** Cabernet Sauvignon Napa Valley Reserve 1992 • $24 • (12/15/95)
85 **KEENAN** Cabernet Sauvignon Napa Valley 1991 • $21 • (12/15/95)
85 **KENDALL-JACKSON** Cabernet Sauvignon California Vintner's Reserve 1993 • $15 • (03/31/96)
85 **KONRAD** Mélange à Trois Mendocino 1992 • $13 • (12/15/95)
85 **KUNDE** Cabernet Sauvignon Sonoma Valley Reserve 1991 • $23 • (05/31/96)
85 **LAUREL GLEN** Cabernet Sauvignon Sonoma Mountain 1992 • $33 • (12/15/95)
85 **LOS ENCANTOS** Cabernet Sauvignon Napa Valley Covenant Reserve 1992 • $14 • (02/29/96)
85 **MAYACAMAS** Cabernet Sauvignon Napa Valley 1990 • $25 • (12/15/95)
85 **MCDOWELL** Cabernet Sauvignon Mendocino 1992 • $10 • (12/15/95)
85 **MILL CREEK** Cabernet Sauvignon Dry Creek Valley 1992 • $12 • (12/15/95)
85 **ROBERT MONDAVI** Cabernet Sauvignon North Coast Coastal 1993 • $11 • (02/29/96)
85 **MONTICELLO** Cabernet Sauvignon Napa Valley Corley Select Reserve 1991 • $25 • (12/15/95)
85 **PEJU** Cabernet Sauvignon Napa Valley 1991 • $18 • (09/15/95)
85 **BERNARD PRADEL** Cabernet Sauvignon Napa Valley Limited Barrel Selection 1990 • $14 • (09/15/95)
85 **ROUND HILL** Cabernet Sauvignon Napa Valley 1992 • $12 • (12/15/95)
85 **ST. FRANCIS** Cabernet Sauvignon Sonoma County 1993 • $12 • (11/30/95)
85 **SANTA CRUZ MOUNTAIN** Cabernet Sauvignon Santa Cruz Mountains Bates Ranch 1990 • $15 • (12/15/95)
85 **SHENANDOAH** Cab-Shiraz Amador County 1993 • $10 • (12/15/95)
85 **STERLING** Cabernet Sauvignon Napa Valley 1992 • $14 • (11/30/95)
85 **TAFT STREET** Cabernet Sauvignon California 1992 • $9.50 • (12/15/95)
85 **TITUS** Cabernet Sauvignon Napa Valley 1992 • $19 • (12/15/95)
85 **M.G. VALLEJO** Cabernet Sauvignon California 1992 • $6 • (11/30/95) • BB
85 **WENTE BROS.** Cabernet Sauvignon Livermore Valley Wente Family Estate Selection 1993 • $8 • (11/15/95) • BB
85 **WHITE OAK** Cabernet Sauvignon Alexander Valley 1992 • $14 • (12/15/95)
85 **WHITE ROCK** Claret Napa Valley 1991 • $22 • (12/15/95)

85 **YORK MOUNTAIN** Cabernet Sauvignon San Luis Obispo County 1990 • $14 • (12/15/95)

CALIFORNIA CHARDONNAY

95 **BERINGER** Chardonnay Napa Valley Private Reserve 1994 • $20 • (04/30/96) • SS

95 **ROCHIOLI** Chardonnay Russian River Valley Reserve 1994 • $28 • (04/30/96)

95 **SAINTSBURY** Chardonnay Carneros Reserve 1994 • $25 • (05/31/96)

94 **BERINGER** Chardonnay Napa Valley Sbragia Limited Release 1994 • $25 • (05/15/96)

94 **CHATEAU ST. JEAN** Chardonnay Alexander Valley Robert Young Vineyards Reserve 1992 • $50 • (04/30/96)

94 **KISTLER** Chardonnay Sonoma Valley Kistler Vineyard 1993 • $40 • (06/30/96) • CS

94 **MARCASSIN** Chardonnay Alexander Valley Gauer Vineyard Upper Barn 1994 • $39 • (05/15/96) • CS

94 **PATZ & HALL** Chardonnay Mount Veeder Carr Vineyard 1994 • $38 • (02/29/96)

94 **TRUCHARD** Chardonnay Napa Valley Carneros 1994 • $19 • (03/31/96)

94 **VILLA MT. EDEN** Chardonnay Santa Maria Valley Bien Nacido Vineyard Signature Series 1994 • $30 • (05/31/96)

93 **AU BON CLIMAT** Chardonnay Santa Ynez Valley Sanford & Benedict Reserve 1993 • $34 • (01/31/96)

93 **BYRON** Chardonnay Santa Maria Valley Estate 1993 • $28 • (04/30/96)

93 **CHALK HILL** Chardonnay Chalk Hill 1994 • $20 • (06/15/96) • SS

93 **FERRARI-CARANO** Chardonnay Alexander Valley Tre Terre 1993 • $22 • (02/29/96)

93 **GIRARD** Chardonnay Napa Valley Reserve 1994 • $32 • (05/31/96)

93 **MARCASSIN** Chardonnay Carneros Hudson Vineyard 1994 • $39 • (05/15/96)

93 **FIDDLEHEAD** Chardonnay Central Coast 1994 • $32 • (05/31/96)

93 **PETER MICHAEL** Chardonnay Sonoma County Mon Plaisir 1993 • $35 • (01/31/96)

93 **PETER MICHAEL** Chardonnay Sonoma County Cuvée Indigène 1993 • $40 • (01/31/96)

93 **PINE RIDGE** Chardonnay Stags Leap District 1994 • $25 • (05/31/96)

93 **MARTIN RAY** Chardonnay California Mariage 1994 • $25 • (05/31/96)

93 **ROMBAUER** Chardonnay Carneros 1994 • $21 • (12/31/95) • SS

93 **SHAFER** Chardonnay Napa Valley Carneros Red Shoulder Ranch 1994 • $23 • (06/15/96)

93 **STEELE** Chardonnay Carneros Sangiacomo Vineyard 1994 • $22 • (05/31/96)

93 **VILLA MT. EDEN** Chardonnay Santa Barbara County Signature Series 1993 • $30 • (07/31/95)

92 **ARROWOOD** Chardonnay Sonoma County Cuvée Michel Berthoud Réserve Spéciale 1994 • $27 • (05/31/96)

92 **CHATEAU DE BAUN** Chardonnay Russian River Valley Creekside Vineyard Reserve 1993 • $18 • (02/29/96)

92 **CHATEAU ST. JEAN** Chardonnay Alexander Valley Belle Terre Vineyards 1994 • $18 • (04/30/96)

92 **GARY FARRELL** Chardonnay Russian River Valley Allen Vineyard 1994 • $20 • (04/30/96)

92 **GARY FARRELL** Chardonnay Russian River Valley 1994 • $17 • (05/15/96)

92 **E. & J. GALLO** Chardonnay Russian River Valley Laguna Ranch Vineyard 1994 • $16 • (04/30/96)

92 **KISTLER** Chardonnay Russian River Valley Vine Hill Vineyard 1993 • $35 • (06/30/96)

92 **LIPARITA** Chardonnay Howell Mountain 1994 • $18 • (04/30/96)

92 **MACROSTIE** Chardonnay Carneros Reserve 1993 • $23 • (01/31/96)

92 **NICHOLS** Chardonnay Arroyo Grande Valley Talley Vineyards 1994 • $23 • (04/30/96)

92 **PAHLMEYER** Chardonnay Napa Valley 1994 • $34 • (05/31/96)

92 **SIGNORELLO** Chardonnay Napa Valley Founder's Reserve 1994 • $30 • (05/15/96)

92 **SIMI** Chardonnay Sonoma County Reserve 1993 • $28 • (06/15/96)

92 **STEELE** Chardonnay California 1994 • $18 • (05/15/96) • SS

92 **STEELE** Chardonnay Mendocino Du Pratt Vineyard 1994 • $24 • (05/31/96)

92 **STEELE** Chardonnay Santa Barbara County Goodchild Vineyard 1994 • $24 • (05/31/96)

92 **VILLA MT. EDEN** Chardonnay Napa Valley Grand Reserve 1994 • $16 • (04/30/96)

91 **ADLER FELS** Chardonnay Sonoma County 1993 • $12 • (03/31/96)

91 **BEAULIEU** Chardonnay Napa Valley Carneros Reserve 1994 • $18 • (04/30/96)

91 **BYRON** Chardonnay Santa Barbara County Reserve 1993 • $23 • (07/31/95)

91 **BYRON** Chardonnay Santa Maria Valley Estate 1992 • $25 • (07/31/95)

91 **CARMENET** Chardonnay Sonoma Valley Carneros Sangiacomo Vineyard 1993 • $16 • (06/30/96) • SS

91 **CHALONE** Chardonnay Chalone 1994 • $27 • (06/15/96) • CS

91 **CHATEAU POTELLE** Chardonnay Mount Veeder V.G.S. 1992 • $34 • (04/30/96)

91 **CHATEAU SOUVERAIN** Chardonnay Sonoma County 1994 • $12 • (04/30/96) • SS

91 **CHATEAU SOUVERAIN** Chardonnay Carneros Winemaker's Reserve 1994 • $16 • (06/15/96)

91 **CLOS DU BOIS** Chardonnay Alexander Valley Calcaire Vineyard 1994 • $18 • (04/30/96) • SS

91 **EL MOLINO** Chardonnay Napa Valley 1994 • $35 • (05/31/96)

91 **FERRARI-CARANO** Chardonnay Alexander Valley Tre Terre 1994 • $24 • (05/15/96)

91 **FERRARI-CARANO** Chardonnay Napa-Sonoma Counties Reserve 1993 • $30 • (05/15/96)

91 **THOMAS FOGARTY** Chardonnay Santa Cruz Mountains Estate Reserve 1994 • $23 • (06/30/96)

91 **GAINEY** Chardonnay Santa Ynez Valley Limited Selection 1993 • $25 • (07/31/95)

91 **GIRARD** Chardonnay Napa Valley 1994 • $18 • (06/15/96) • SS

91 **KISTLER** Chardonnay Sonoma Mountain McCrea Vineyard 1993 • $35 • (06/30/96)

91 **LANDMARK** Chardonnay Sonoma County Overlook 1994 • $16 • (03/31/96) • SS

91 **LITTORAI** Chardonnay Russian River Valley Mays Canyon 1993 • $25 • (12/31/95)

91 **MACROSTIE** Chardonnay Carneros 1994 • $17 • (04/30/96)

91 **MATANZAS CREEK** Chardonnay Sonoma Valley 1993 • $23 • (09/30/95) • SS

91 **MATANZAS CREEK** Chardonnay Sonoma Valley Journey 1992 • $70 • (12/31/95)

91 **MER ET SOLEIL** Chardonnay Central Coast 1992 • $25 • (08/31/95) • SS

91 **ROBERT MONDAVI** Chardonnay Napa Valley Reserve 1993 • $29 • (07/31/95)

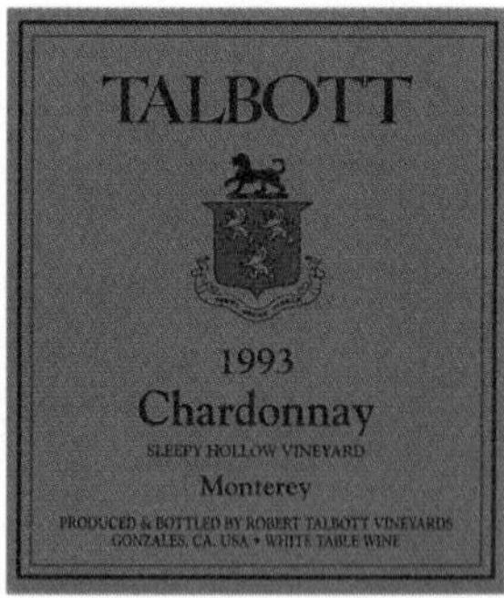

91 **NEYERS** Chardonnay Carneros 1994 • $18 • (06/30/96)

91 **PATZ & HALL** Chardonnay Napa Valley 1994 • $28 • (02/29/96)

91 **SOLITUDE** Chardonnay Carneros Sangiacomo Vineyard 1994 • $19 • (01/31/96)

91 **STAG'S LEAP WINE CELLARS** Chardonnay Napa Valley Beckstoffer Ranch 1994 • $24 • (05/31/96)

91 **STEELE** Chardonnay Santa Barbara County Bien Nacido Vineyard 1994 • $24 • (05/31/96)

91 **STEELE** Chardonnay Mendocino DuPratt Vineyard 1993 • $24 • (07/31/95)

91 **STONESTREET** Chardonnay Sonoma County 1994 • $25 • (05/31/96) • SS

91 **TALBOTT** Chardonnay Monterey Sleepy Hollow Vineyard 1993 • $26 • (12/31/95) • CS

90 **ACACIA** Chardonnay Carneros 1994 • $18 • (04/30/96) • SS

90 **ACACIA** Chardonnay Carneros Reserve 1993 • $25 • (04/30/96)

90 **S. ANDERSON** Chardonnay Stags Leap District 1994 • $20 • (04/30/96)

90 **AU BON CLIMAT** Chardonnay Arroyo Grande Valley Talley Vineyard Talley Reserve 1993 • $25 • (07/31/95)

90 **BERINGER** Chardonnay Napa Valley 1994 • $11 • (03/31/96) • SS

90 **BERNARDUS** Chardonnay Monterey County 1994 • $15 • (05/15/96) • SS

90 **BYINGTON** Chardonnay Santa Cruz Mountains Special Reserve Spring Ridge Vineyard 1994 • $23 • (06/30/96)

90 **BYRON** Chardonnay Santa Barbara County Reserve 1994 • $23 • (05/31/96)

90 **BYRON** Chardonnay Santa Barbara County 1993 • $15 • (07/31/95) • SS

90 **CALERA** Chardonnay Central Coast 1994 • $15 • (12/31/95) • SS

90 **CHALONE** Chardonnay Chalone Reserve 1994 • $45 • (05/31/96)

90 **CHATEAU ST. JEAN** Chardonnay Sonoma County 1994 • $11 • (04/30/96) • SS

90 **DE LOACH** Chardonnay Russian River Valley O.F.S. 1993 • $25 • (09/30/95)

90 **DRY CREEK** Chardonnay Dry Creek Valley Reserve 1994 • $17 • (05/15/96)

90 **ESTANCIA** Chardonnay Monterey Reserve 1994 • $20 • (05/31/96)

90 **FERRARI-CARANO** Chardonnay Alexander Valley 1994 • $22 • (05/15/96) • SS

90 **THOMAS FOGARTY** Chardonnay Santa Cruz Mountains Estate Reserve 1992 • $18.50 • (02/29/96)

90 **THOMAS FOGARTY** Chardonnay Santa Cruz Mountains 1994 • $17 • (02/29/96)

90 **THOMAS FOGARTY** Chardonnay Santa Cruz Mountains Estate Reserve 1992 • $18.50 • (02/29/96)

90 **FRANCISCAN** Chardonnay Napa Valley Oakville Estate Barrel Fermented 1994 • $13 • (04/30/96)

90 **GREENWOOD RIDGE** Chardonnay Anderson Valley Du Pratt Vineyard 1994 • $19 • (04/30/96)

90 **GRGICH HILLS** Chardonnay Napa Valley 1994 • $26 • (05/31/96)

90 **HARRISON** Chardonnay Napa Valley 1994 • $26 • (04/30/96)

90 **JARVIS** Chardonnay Napa Valley 1992 • $34 • (08/31/95)

90 **KENDALL-JACKSON** Chardonnay California Grand Reserve 1994 • $26 • (03/31/96)

90 **KENDALL-JACKSON** Chardonnay Santa Maria Valley Camelot Vineyard 1994 • $18 • (03/31/96) • SS

90 **KISTLER** Chardonnay Sonoma County Cuvée Cathleen 1993 • $50 • (06/30/96)

90 **KUNDE** Chardonnay Sonoma Valley Kinneybrook Unfiltered 1993 • $17 • (01/31/96)

90 **LEWIS CELLARS** Chardonnay Napa Valley Oakville Ranch Reserve 1994 • $28 • (05/15/96)

90 **LEWIS CELLARS** Chardonnay Napa Valley Oakville Ranch Reserve 1993 • $26 • (07/31/95)

90 **LIPARITA** Chardonnay Howell Mountain 1993 • $16 • (10/31/95)

90 **J. LOHR** Chardonnay Monterey Riverstone 1994 • $12 • (02/29/96) • SS

90 **LONG** Chardonnay Napa Valley 1993 • $30 • (01/31/96)

90 **LOS OLIVOS VINTNERS** Chardonnay Santa Barbara County 1993 • $18 • (09/30/95)

90 **MARKHAM** Chardonnay Napa Valley 1994 • $15 • (06/15/96) • SS

90 **MATANZAS CREEK** Chardonnay Sonoma Valley 1994 • $28 • (05/31/96)

90 **MUELLER** Chardonnay Russian River Valley 1994 • $13 • (05/15/96)

90 **MUELLER** Chardonnay Russian River Valley LB Reserve 1992 • $30 • (07/31/95)

90 **MURPHY-GOODE** Chardonnay Russian River Valley J & K Murphy Vineyard Reserve 1993 • $24 • (07/31/95)

90 **NEWTON** Chardonnay Napa Valley 1994 • $19 • (03/31/96)

90 **RIDGE** Chardonnay Santa Cruz Mountains Monte Bello Ridge Vineyards 1994 • $20 • (05/15/96)

90 **SANFORD** Chardonnay Santa Barbara County 1994 • $17 • (05/31/96) • SS

90 **SANTA BARBARA WINERY** Chardonnay Santa Ynez Valley Lafond Vineyard 1993 • $30 • (05/15/96)

90 **SELBY** Chardonnay Sonoma County 1994 • $18 • (04/30/96)

90 **SIGNORELLO** Chardonnay Napa Valley Founder's Reserve 1993 • $30 • (07/31/95)

90 **ST. FRANCIS** Chardonnay Sonoma Valley Reserve Estate 1994 • $20 • (05/15/96)

90 **STEELE** Chardonnay Mendocino Dennison Vineyard 1994 • $22 • (05/31/96)

90 **STEELE** Chardonnay Mendocino Lolonis Vineyard 1993 • $20 • (07/31/95)

90 **TALBOTT** Chardonnay Monterey Diamond T Estate 1993 • $34 • (05/31/96)

90 **VINE CLIFF** Chardonnay Napa Valley 1994 • $23 • (05/31/96)

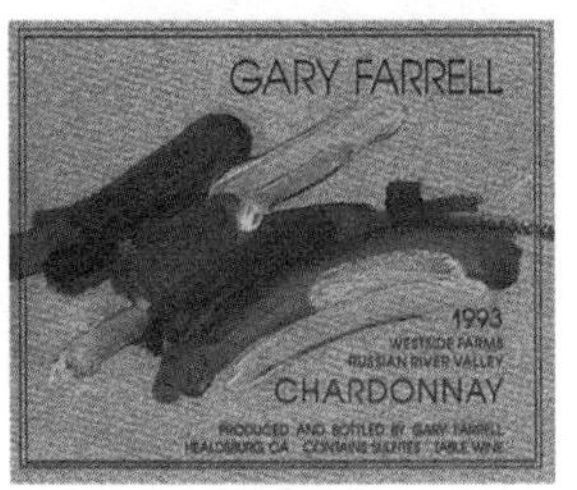

89 **AU BON CLIMAT** Chardonnay Santa Maria Valley Gold Coast Vineyard 1993 • $20 • (07/31/95)

89 **BENZIGER** Chardonnay Carneros Reserve 1994 • $13 • (03/31/96)

89 **CAMELOT** Chardonnay Central Coast 1994 • $11 • (06/15/96)

89 **CARMENET** Chardonnay Sonoma Valley Carneros Sangiacomo Vineyard 1994 • $16 • (06/15/96)

89 **CLOS DU BOIS** Chardonnay Dry Creek Valley Flintwood Vineyard 1994 • $17 • (04/30/96)

89 **CLOS LACHANCE** Chardonnay Santa Cruz Mountains 1994 • $18 • (05/31/96)

89 **CLOS LACHANCE** Chardonnay Santa Cruz Mountains 1993 • $18 • (07/31/95)

89 **CLOS PEGASE** Chardonnay Napa Valley Carneros Pegase Circle Reserve 1994 • $23 • (05/15/96)

89 **COOPER-GARROD** Chardonnay Santa Cruz Mountains 1994 • $18 • (02/29/96)

89 **DE LOACH** Chardonnay Russian River Valley O.F.S. 1994 • $25 • (05/15/96)

89 **DRY CREEK** Chardonnay Sonoma County Barrel Fermented 1994 • $14 • (03/31/96)

89 **GARY FARRELL** Chardonnay Russian River Valley Westside Farms 1993 • $18 • (07/31/95)

89 **FLORA SPRINGS** Chardonnay Carneros 1994 • $20 • (06/30/96)

89 **GEYSER PEAK** Chardonnay Alexander Valley Reserve 1994 • $20 • (05/15/96)

89 **GUNDLACH BUNDSCHU** Chardonnay Sonoma Valley Sangiacomo Ranch Special Selection 1993 • $15 • (11/15/95)

89 **PAUL HOBBS** Chardonnay Sonoma Mountain Richard Dinner Vineyard 1994 • $28 • (06/30/96)

89 **JOULLIAN** Chardonnay Monterey Family Reserve 1992 • $18 • (07/31/95)

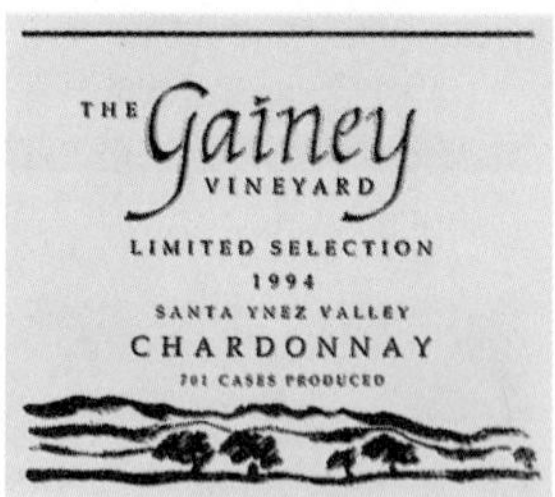

89 **KISTLER** Chardonnay Russian River Valley Dutton Ranch 1993 • $35 • (06/30/96)

89 **KUNDE** Chardonnay Sonoma Valley Wildwood Unfiltered 1993 • $17 • (01/31/96)

89 **KUNDE** Chardonnay Sonoma Valley Wildwood 1994 • $20 • (05/31/96)

89 **KUNDE** Chardonnay Sonoma Valley Kinneybrook 1994 • $20 • (05/31/96)

89 **LANDMARK** Chardonnay Sonoma County Damaris Reserve 1994 • $23 • (03/31/96)

89 **J. LOHR** Chardonnay Arroyo Seco VS 1994 • $23 • (06/15/96)

89 **MARK WEST** Chardonnay Russian River Valley 1993 • $13 • (05/31/96) • SS

89 **MERIDIAN** Chardonnay Santa Barbara County 1994 • $10 • (02/29/96) • BB

89 **MERRYVALE** Chardonnay Napa Valley Silhouette 1993 • $36 • (05/31/96)

89 **ROBERT MONDAVI** Chardonnay Napa Valley 1994 • $17 • (05/31/96)

89 **MONTICELLO** Chardonnay Napa Valley Corley Family Vineyards 1992 • $15 • (09/30/95)

89 **MUELLER** Chardonnay Alexander Valley Gauer Ranch 1994 • $15 • (05/15/96)

89 **MURPHY-GOODE** Chardonnay Alexander Valley Island Block Reserve 1994 • $24 • (01/31/96)

89 **MURPHY-GOODE** Chardonnay Russian River Valley J & K Murphy Vineyard Reserve 1994 • $24 • (05/31/96)

89 **NAVARRO** Chardonnay Anderson Valley Première Reserve 1994 • $15 • (06/15/96)

89 **OAKVILLE RANCH** Chardonnay Napa Valley ORV 1994 • $28 • (05/15/96)

89 **OPTIMA** Chardonnay Carneros Unfiltered 1993 • $25 • (10/15/95)

89 **JOSEPH PHELPS** Chardonnay Los Carneros 1993 • $17 • (08/31/95)

89 **MARTIN RAY** Chardonnay California Mariage 1993 • $24 • (08/31/95)

89 **RAYMOND** Chardonnay Napa Valley Reserve 1994 • $14 • (05/31/96)

89 **RAYMOND** Chardonnay Napa Valley Private Reserve 1994 • $18 • (05/31/96)

89 **ROCHIOLI** Chardonnay Russian River Valley 1994 • $17 • (06/15/96)

89 **SANTA BARBARA WINERY** Chardonnay Santa Ynez Valley Reserve 1993 • $20 • (07/31/95)

89 **SANTA BARBARA WINERY** Chardonnay Santa Ynez Valley Lafond Vineyard Unfiltered 1992 • $30 • (07/31/95)

89 **SARAH'S VINEYARD** Chardonnay Santa Clara County 1992 • $42 • (07/31/95)

89 **SARAH'S VINEYARD** Chardonnay Santa Clara County 1993 • $42 • (07/31/95)

89 **SIGNORELLO** Chardonnay Napa Valley 1994 • $20 • (03/31/96)

89 **SONOMA-LOEB** Chardonnay Sonoma County Ambassador John L. Loeb Jr.'s Private Reserve 1993 • $26 • (07/31/95)

89 **STAG'S LEAP WINE CELLARS** Chardonnay Napa Valley 1994 • $22 • (06/15/96)

89 **VICHON** Chardonnay Napa Valley 1994 • $NA • (02/29/96)

89 **VOSS** Chardonnay Napa Valley 1993 • $NA • (02/29/96)

89 **WILD HORSE** Chardonnay Central Coast 1994 • $14 • (06/30/96) • SS

88 **ARROWOOD** Chardonnay Sonoma County 1994 • $21 • (05/31/96)

88 **AU BON CLIMAT** Chardonnay Santa Barbara County 1994 • $15 • (01/31/96)

88 **BABCOCK** Chardonnay Santa Ynez Valley Mt. Carmel Vineyard 1994 • $27 • (01/31/96)

88 **BABCOCK** Chardonnay Santa Ynez Valley Grand Cuvée 1992 • $25 • (09/30/95)

88 **BAILEYANA** Chardonnay Edna Valley Paragon Vineyard 1993 • $15 • (07/31/95)

88 **BANNISTER** Chardonnay Russian River Valley Allen Vineyard 1994 • $20 • (05/31/96)

88 **BEAULIEU** Chardonnay Napa Valley Carneros 1994 • $13 • (02/29/96)

88 **BEAULIEU** Chardonnay Napa Valley Carneros Reserve 1993 • $18 • (12/31/95)
88 **BELVEDERE** Chardonnay Russian River Valley 1994 • $13 • (02/29/96)
88 **BELVEDERE** Chardonnay Sonoma County 1994 • $9 • (02/29/96) • BB
88 **BUENA VISTA** Chardonnay Carneros Grand Reserve 1994 • $22 • (06/15/96)
88 **BYRON** Chardonnay Santa Barbara County 1994 • $16 • (05/31/96)
88 **CAMBRIA** Chardonnay Santa Barbara County 1994 • $15 • (02/29/96)
88 **CAMBRIA** Chardonnay Santa Maria Valley Reserve 1994 • $30 • (06/15/96)
88 **CAMELOT** Chardonnay Central Coast 1993 • $12 • (07/31/95)
88 **CANEPA** Chardonnay Alexander Valley Canepa Vineyard 1993 • $20 • (12/15/95)
88 **CHALONE** Chardonnay Chalone Gavilan 1994 • $16 • (06/15/96)
88 **CINNABAR** Chardonnay Santa Cruz Mountains Saratoga Vineyard 1994 • $23 • (06/15/96)
88 **CLAIBORNE & CHURCHILL** Chardonnay Edna Valley MacGregor Vineyard 1994 • $18 • (05/31/96)
88 **CLOS PEGASE** Chardonnay Napa Valley Carneros Mitsuko's Vineyard 1994 • $17 • (05/15/96)
88 **CUVAISON** Chardonnay Carneros Napa Valley Reserve 1993 • $28 • (07/31/95)
88 **DEHLINGER** Chardonnay Russian River Valley 1994 • $16 • (05/31/96)
88 **DE LORIMIER** Chardonnay Alexander Valley Clonal Select 1994 • $20 • (06/30/96)
88 **DOMAIN HILL & MAYES** Chardonnay Napa Valley Clos Fontaine du Mont Reserve 1993 • $20 • (05/31/96)
88 **DRY CREEK** Chardonnay Dry Creek Valley Wolcott Vineyard Barrel Fermented Reserve 1994 • $22 • (02/29/96)
88 **EDMEADES** Chardonnay Anderson Valley 1994 • $18 • (05/15/96)
88 **EL MOLINO** Chardonnay Napa Valley 1993 • $30 • (07/31/95)
88 **EXPRESSIONS** Chardonnay Sonoma County 1994 • $10 • (04/30/96) • BB
88 **FETZER** Chardonnay Mendocino Reserve 1993 • $24 • (07/31/95)
88 **GAINEY** Chardonnay Santa Ynez Valley Limited Selection 1994 • $25 • (06/30/96)
88 **E. & J. GALLO** Chardonnay Northern Sonoma Estate Bottled 1993 • $30 • (07/31/95)
88 **GAN EDEN** Chardonnay Sonoma County 1993 • $12 • (07/31/95)
88 **GIRARD** Chardonnay Napa Valley Old Vines 1993 • $19 • (12/15/95)
88 **GUENOC** Chardonnay Guenoc Valley Genevieve Magoon Vineyard Estate Reserve 1994 • $23 • (04/30/96)
88 **GUENOC** Chardonnay Guenoc Valley Genevieve Magoon Unfiltered Reserve 1994 • $30 • (05/15/96)
88 **KEENAN** Chardonnay Napa Valley 1993 • $15 • (10/15/95)
88 **KENDALL-JACKSON** Chardonnay Santa Maria Valley Camelot Vineyard 1993 • $16 • (07/31/95)
88 **LA CREMA** Chardonnay Sonoma County 1994 • $15 • (03/31/96)
88 **LAKESPRING** Chardonnay Napa Valley 1994 • $12 • (02/29/96)
88 **LAURIER** Chardonnay Sonoma County 1993 • $15 • (03/31/96)
88 **LONGORIA** Chardonnay Santa Ynez Valley Huber Vineyard 1994 • $21 • (06/30/96)
88 **LOS ENCANTOS** Chardonnay Santa Maria Covenant Reserve 1994 • $14 • (02/29/96)
88 **MAYACAMAS** Chardonnay Napa Valley 1993 • $18 • (05/15/96)
88 **MAYACAMAS** Chardonnay Napa Valley 1992 • $16 • (08/31/95)
88 **MAZZOCCO** Chardonnay Sonoma County Winemaker's Select 1992 • $18 • (10/15/95)

88 **MERRYVALE** Chardonnay Napa Valley Starmont 1994 • $16 • (05/31/96)

88 **MERRYVALE** Chardonnay Napa Valley Reserve 1993 • $25 • (07/31/95)

88 **MIRASSOU** Chardonnay Monterey County Fifth Generation Family Selection 1994 • $11 • (06/15/96)

88 **ROBERT MONDAVI** Chardonnay Carneros 1993 • $23 • (05/15/96)

88 **MORGAN** Chardonnay Monterey Reserve 1993 • $23 • (06/15/96)

88 **MUELLER** Chardonnay Sonoma County Gauer Ranch 1993 • $15 • (03/31/96)

88 **NAVARRO** Chardonnay Anderson Valley Première Reserve 1993 • $NA • (02/29/96)

88 **NORMAN VINEYARD** Chardonnay San Luis Obispo County 1994 • $12 • (05/15/96)

88 **OAKVILLE RANCH** Chardonnay Napa Valley Vista Vineyard 1994 • $20 • (05/15/96)

88 **PINE RIDGE** Chardonnay Napa Valley Knollside Cuvée 1994 • $16 • (05/31/96)

88 **QUPÉ** Chardonnay Santa Barbara County Sierra Madre Reserve 1994 • $25 • (05/31/96)

88 **QUPÉ** Chardonnay Santa Barbara County Sierra Madre Reserve 1993 • $25 • (07/31/95)

88 **RABBIT RIDGE** Chardonnay Russian River Valley Rabbit Ridge Ranch Estate Reserve 1993 • $16 • (07/31/95)

88 **REMICK RIDGE VINEYARDS** Chardonnay Sonoma Valley 1994 • $16 • (06/15/96)

88 **SARAH'S VINEYARD** Chardonnay Santa Clara County Lot II 1992 • $24 • (07/31/95)

88 **SCHUG** Chardonnay Carneros Heritage Reserve 1994 • $25 • (06/30/96)

88 **SCHUG** Chardonnay Carneros Heritage Reserve 1993 • $25 • (07/31/95)

88 **SEAVEY** Chardonnay Napa Valley 1994 • $16 • (05/15/96)

88 **SONOMA-CUTRER** Chardonnay Sonoma Coast Cutrer Vineyard 1992 • $21 • (07/31/95)

88 **SONOMA-LOEB** Chardonnay Sonoma County Ambassador John L. Loeb Jr.'s Private Reserve 1994 • $25 • (02/29/96)

88 **SONOMA-LOEB** Chardonnay Sonoma County Ambassador John L. Loeb Jr.'s 1994 • $18 • (03/31/96)

88 **STAG'S LEAP WINE CELLARS** Chardonnay Napa Valley 1993 • $19 • (07/31/95)

88 **STEELE** Chardonnay Mendocino Lolonis Vineyard 1994 • $26 • (05/31/96)

88 **STEELE** Chardonnay Sonoma Valley Durell Vineyard 1994 • $24 • (05/31/96)

88 **STEELE** Chardonnay Santa Barbara County Bien Nacido Vineyard 1993 • $22 • (07/31/95)

88 **SWANSON** Chardonnay Carneros Napa Valley 1993 • $20 • (07/31/95)

88 **TALLEY** Chardonnay Arroyo Grande Valley 1993 • $18 • (07/31/95)

88 **TERRA** Chardonnay Carneros Sangiacomo Vineyard 1993 • $19 • (06/30/96)

88 **MARIMAR TORRES** Chardonnay Sonoma County Green Valley Don Miguel Vineyard 1993 • $20 • (05/15/96)

88 **WENTE BROS.** Chardonnay Livermore Valley Herman Wente Reserve 1994 • $22 • (06/30/96)

88 **WENTE BROS.** Chardonnay Livermore Valley Herman Wente Vineyard Estate Reserve 1993 • $14 • (09/30/95)

88 **WHITCRAFT** Chardonnay Santa Ynez Valley Sanford & Benedict Vineyard 1994 • $35 • (05/15/96)

88 **WHITCRAFT** Chardonnay Santa Maria Valley Bien Nacido Vineyard 1994 • $17 • (06/15/96)

88 **ZACA MESA** Chardonnay Santa Barbara County Jim Clendenen Alumni Winemaker Series 1993 • $18 • (02/29/96)

87 **AU BON CLIMAT** Chardonnay Santa Ynez Valley Sanford & Benedict Reserve 1992 • $35 • (07/31/95)

87 **AU BON CLIMAT** Chardonnay Santa Barbara County 1993 • $16 • (07/31/95)

87 **BELVEDERE** Chardonnay Russian River Valley 1993 • $12 • (10/15/95)

87 **BYINGTON** Chardonnay Santa Cruz Mountains Special Reserve Vineyards 1994 • $18 • (06/30/96)

87 **CAKEBREAD** Chardonnay Napa Valley 1994 • $23 • (01/31/96)

87 **CAKEBREAD** Chardonnay Napa Valley Reserve 1992 • $30 • (07/31/95)

87 **CALE** Chardonnay Carneros Sangiacomo Vineyard 1994 • $20 • (05/15/96)

87 **CAMELOT** Chardonnay Santa Barbara County 1994 • $18 • (06/15/96)

87 **CARNEROS CREEK** Chardonnay California Fleur de Carneros 1993 • $9 • (09/30/95) • BB

87 **CARPE DIEM** Chardonnay San Luis Obispo County 1994 • $19 • (02/29/96)

87 **CHALONE** Chardonnay Chalone 1993 • $27 • (07/31/95)

87 **CHAPPELLET** Chardonnay Napa Valley Signature 1994 • $24 • (06/15/96)

87 **CHAUFFE-EAU** Chardonnay Carneros Sans Filtrage Sangiacomo 1993 • $17 • (07/31/95)

87 **CLAIBORNE & CHURCHILL** Chardonnay Edna Valley MacGregor Vineyard 1993 • $17 • (07/31/95)

87 **CLOS PEGASE** Chardonnay Carneros Napa Valley Pegase Circle Reserve 1993 • $20 • (07/31/95)

87 **CONCANNON** Chardonnay Livermore Valley Reserve 1993 • $15 • (07/31/95)

87 **DREYER SONOMA** Chardonnay Sonoma County 1994 • $9 • (04/30/96)

87 **DURNEY** Chardonnay Carmel Valley Dances On Your Palate 1992 • $18 • (02/29/96)

87 **EDMEADES** Chardonnay Anderson Valley Anderson Crest Vineyard 1994 • $20 • (06/15/96)

87 **ESTANCIA** Chardonnay Monterey County Reserve 1993 • $20 • (07/31/95)

87 **FISHER** Chardonnay Sonoma County Whitney's Vineyard 1994 • $26 • (06/15/96)

87 **FISHER** Chardonnay Sonoma County Whitney's Vineyard 1992 • $26 • (07/31/95)

87 **E. & J. GALLO** Chardonnay Dry Creek Valley Stefani Vineyard 1994 • $16 • (05/15/96)

87 **GIRARD** Chardonnay Napa Valley Viridian Vineyard 1993 • $38 • (12/15/95)

87 **GUENOC** Chardonnay Guenoc Valley 1994 • $15 • (04/30/96)

87 **HANDLEY** Chardonnay Dry Creek Valley 1993 • $15 • (06/30/96)

87 **HANZELL** Chardonnay Sonoma Valley 1992 • $25 • (10/31/95)

87 **HERON LAKE** Chardonnay Wild Horse Valley 1992 • $12 • (07/31/95)

87 **HESS SELECT** Chardonnay California 1994 • $9.50 • (06/30/96) • BB

87 **IRON HORSE** Chardonnay Sonoma County Green Valley 1994 • $18 • (05/15/96)

87 **JOULLIAN** Chardonnay Monterey 1994 • $12 • (06/15/96)

87 **KENWOOD** Chardonnay Sonoma County 25th Anniversary Vintage 1994 • $14 • (12/15/95)

87 **KUNDE** Chardonnay Sonoma Valley Reserve 1994 • $22 • (06/15/96)

87 **LOCKWOOD** Chardonnay Monterey 1994 • $15 • (04/30/96)

87 **LOGAN** Chardonnay Monterey 1994 • $14 • (05/15/96)

87 **J. LOHR** Chardonnay Monterey Riverstone 1993 • $12 • (12/15/95)

87 **LONGORIA** Chardonnay Santa Barbara County 1992 • $18 • (07/31/95)

87 **LYETH** Chardonnay Sonoma County 1994 • $11 • (02/29/96)

87 **LOUIS M. MARTINI** Chardonnay Napa Valley 1994 • $11 • (06/15/96)

87 **MAZZOCCO** Chardonnay Sonoma County River Lane 1994 • $14 • (06/30/96)

87 **PETER MICHAEL** Chardonnay Napa County Clos du Ciel 1994 • $32 • (06/15/96)

87 **MIRASSOU** Chardonnay Santa Clara County 140th Anniversary Selection Anniversary Bottling 1992 • $14 • (07/31/95)

87 **MIRASSOU** Chardonnay Monterey County Fifth Generation Harvest Reserve 1992 • $12 • (07/31/95)

87 **MIRASSOU** Chardonnay Monterey County Fifth Generation Harvest Reserve 1993 • $12 • (07/31/95)

87 **NICHOLS** Chardonnay Arroyo Grande Valley Talley Vineyards 1993 • $20 • (12/31/95)

87 **OJAI** Chardonnay Santa Barbara County Reserve 1993 • $21 • (07/31/95)

87 **OLIVET LANE** Chardonnay Russian River Valley Pellegrini Family Vineyards 1994 • $12 • (02/29/96)

87 **OLIVET LANE** Chardonnay Russian River Valley Pellegrini Family Vineyards 1994 • $12 • (02/29/96)

87 **OPTIMA** Chardonnay Carneros 1994 • $28 • (02/29/96)

87 **PARDUCCI** Chardonnay Mendocino County 1994 • $8 • (09/30/95) • BB

87 **FESS PARKER** Chardonnay Santa Barbara County 1994 • $16 • (06/30/96)

87 **MARIO PERELLI-MINETTI** Chardonnay Napa Valley 1991 • $13 • (09/30/95)

87 **R.H. PHILLIPS** Chardonnay Dunnigan Hills Barrel Cuvée 1994 • $8 • (05/31/96) • BB

87 **PRIDE** Chardonnay Napa Valley 1994 • $18 • (05/15/96)

87 **PRIDE** Chardonnay Napa Valley 1993 • $18 • (07/31/95)

87 **RABBIT RIDGE** Chardonnay Russian River Valley Rabbit Ridge Ranch Estate Reserve 1994 • $16 • (05/15/96)

87 **RAYMOND** Chardonnay Monterey Estates 1994 • $12 • (03/31/96)

87 **RAYMOND** Chardonnay Napa Valley 1993 • $14 • (12/15/95)

87 **SANTA BARBARA WINERY** Chardonnay Santa Ynez Valley Reserve 1994 • $22 • (06/30/96)

87 **SILVER HORSE** Chardonnay Paso Robles 1994 • $11 • (02/29/96)

87 **ROBERT SINSKEY** Chardonnay Carneros 1993 • $20 • (07/31/95)

87 **STONE CREEK** Chardonnay Napa Valley Chairman's Reserve 1994 • $15 • (11/15/95)

87 **RODNEY STRONG** Chardonnay Sonoma County 1994 • $11 • (06/15/96)

87 **SWANSON** Chardonnay Napa Valley Carneros 1994 • $22 • (05/15/96)

87 **TALLEY** Chardonnay Edna Valley Oliver's Vineyard 1994 • $15 • (06/15/96)

87 **TRUCHARD** Chardonnay Carneros Napa Valley 1993 • $17 • (07/31/95)

87 **WHITE OAK** Chardonnay Sonoma County Myers Limited Reserve 1993 • $16 • (10/15/95)

87 **WILSON DANIELS** Chardonnay Napa Valley 1993 • $10 • (05/15/96)

87 **ZACA MESA** Chardonnay Santa Barbara County Zaca Vineyards 1994 • $13 • (05/15/96)

86 **S. ANDERSON** Chardonnay Napa Valley Carneros 1994 • $18 • (05/15/96)

86 **ARCIERO** Chardonnay Paso Robles 1994 • $9 • (06/15/96) • BB

86 **BANCROFT** Chardonnay Howell Mountain 1992 • $16 • (07/31/95)

86 **BANDIERA** Chardonnay Napa Valley 1994 • $8 • (09/30/95) • BB

86 **BELVEDERE** Chardonnay Alexander Valley 1994 • $12 • (04/30/96)

86 **BOGLE** Chardonnay California Barrel Fermented Reserve 1992 • $10 • (07/31/95)

86 **BURGESS** Chardonnay Napa Valley Barrel Fermented Debourbage 1993 • $15 • (07/31/95)

86 **CAMBRIA** Chardonnay Santa Maria Valley Katherine's Vineyard 1994 • $18 • (02/29/96)

86 **CHAPPELLET** Chardonnay Napa Valley 1993 • $15 • (10/31/95)

86 **CHATEAU ST. JEAN** Chardonnay Alexander Valley Belle Terre Vineyards 1993 • $18 • (07/31/95)
86 **CHAUFFE-EAU** Chardonnay Russian River Valley Sans Filtrage Dutton 1993 • $18 • (07/31/95)
86 **CLOS DU BOIS** Chardonnay Dry Creek Valley Flintwood Vineyard 1993 • $17 • (07/31/95)
86 **CLOS PEGASE** Chardonnay Carneros Napa Valley 1993 • $15 • (09/30/95)
86 **COTES DE SONOMA** Chardonnay Sonoma County 1994 • $8 • (10/15/95) • BB
86 **CUVAISON** Chardonnay Carneros Napa Valley 1993 • $15 • (07/31/95)
86 **DRY CREEK** Chardonnay Sonoma County Barrel Fermented Reserve 1992 • $16 • (07/31/95)
86 **FAR NIENTE** Chardonnay Napa Valley 1994 • $32 • (02/29/96)
86 **FERMENTATIONS & MORE** Chardonnay Edna Valley MacGregor Vineyard 1994 • $13 • (04/30/96)
86 **FETZER** Chardonnay North Coast Barrel Select 1994 • $10 • (06/15/96)
86 **FISHER** Chardonnay Sonoma County Coach Insignia 1994 • $18 • (06/15/96)
86 **GAINEY** Chardonnay Santa Barbara County 1993 • $14 • (07/31/95)
86 **GRGICH HILLS** Chardonnay Napa Valley 1993 • $24 • (12/15/95)
86 **HARRISON** Chardonnay Napa Valley 1993 • $26 • (07/31/95)
86 **HIDDEN CELLARS** Chardonnay Mendocino Organically Grown Grapes 1993 • $10 • (09/30/95)
86 **PAUL HOBBS** Chardonnay Sonoma Mountain Richard Dinner Vineyard 1993 • $28 • (07/31/95)
86 **JOLIESSE VINEYARDS** Chardonnay California Reserve 1994 • $7 • (05/31/96) • BB
86 **JORDAN** Chardonnay Alexander Valley 1992 • $21 • (07/31/95)
86 **JOULLIAN** Chardonnay Monterey Family Reserve 1993 • $20 • (06/15/96)
86 **KENDALL-JACKSON** Chardonnay California Vintner's Reserve 1994 • $14 • (12/15/95)
86 **KUNDE** Chardonnay Sonoma Valley 1994 • $14 • (01/31/96)
86 **LOCKWOOD** Chardonnay Monterey Partners Reserve 1993 • $17 • (06/30/96)
86 **LOCKWOOD** Chardonnay Monterey 1993 • $15 • (12/15/95)
86 **LONGORIA** Chardonnay Santa Ynez Valley Huber Vineyard 1993 • $16 • (07/31/95)
86 **MERIDIAN** Chardonnay Santa Barbara County Limited Release 1994 • $17 • (06/30/96)
86 **MILL CREEK** Chardonnay Dry Creek Valley 1994 • $12 • (06/30/96)
86 **MURPHY-GOODE** Chardonnay Alexander Valley Barrel Fermented 1993 • $13 • (07/31/95)
86 **MURPHY-GOODE** Chardonnay Alexander Valley Barrel Fermented 1994 • $14 • (12/31/95)
86 **NAPA RIDGE** Chardonnay Napa Valley Coastal Reserve 1994 • $12 • (06/30/96)
86 **NAPA RIDGE** Chardonnay Napa Valley Coastal Reserve 1993 • $13 • (07/31/95)
86 **NEVADA CITY** Chardonnay Nevada County Barrel Fermented 1993 • $11 • (07/31/95)
86 **NEWLAN** Chardonnay Napa Valley Napa-Villages 1992 • $10 • (09/30/95)
86 **OJAI** Chardonnay Arroyo Grande Valley 1993 • $18 • (07/31/95)
86 **PARAISO SPRINGS** Chardonnay Santa Lucia Highlands Barrel Fermented 1993 • $12 • (07/31/95)
86 **PEJU** Chardonnay Napa Valley 1994 • $15 • (06/30/96)
86 **PEJU** Chardonnay Napa Valley 1993 • $16 • (07/31/95)
86 **KENT RASMUSSEN** Chardonnay Napa Valley 1994 • $21 • (02/29/96)
86 **SALAMANDRE** Chardonnay Santa Cruz Mountains Matteson Vineyard 1993 • $16 • (07/31/95)

86 **SANFORD** Chardonnay Santa Ynez Valley 1993 • $24 • (07/31/95)

86 **SEBASTIANI** Chardonnay Russian River Valley Dutton Ranch 1994 • $18 • (06/30/96)

86 **SILVER RIDGE** Chardonnay California Barrel Fermented 1994 • $10 • (06/30/96)

86 **SONOMA-LOEB** Chardonnay Sonoma County Ambassador John L. Loeb Jr.'s 1993 • $16 • (07/31/95)

86 **P & M STAIGER** Chardonnay Santa Cruz Mountains 1994 • $12 • (06/15/96)

86 **STEELE** Chardonnay California 1993 • $18 • (07/31/95)

86 **STONY HILL** Chardonnay Napa Valley SHV 1993 • $23 • (07/31/95)

86 **MICHAEL SULLBERG** Chardonnay Knights Valley Lot 54 Barrel Fermented 1994 • $8 • (02/29/96)

86 **TAFT STREET** Chardonnay Sonoma County 1994 • $10 • (06/15/96) • BB

86 **VON STRASSER** Chardonnay Napa Valley 1994 • $30 • (06/15/96)

85 **ALDERBROOK** Chardonnay Dry Creek Valley 1992 • $15 • (07/31/95)

85 **ATLAS PEAK** Chardonnay Atlas Peak 1993 • $16 • (07/31/95)

85 **BEAULIEU** Chardonnay Napa Valley Carneros 1993 • $13 • (09/30/95)

85 **BEL ARBORS** Chardonnay California Vintner's Selection 1994 • $5 • (05/31/96) • BB

85 **BOUCHAINE** Chardonnay Carneros 1993 • $15 • (02/29/96)

85 **BOUCHAINE** Chardonnay Napa Valley Carneros Estate Reserve 1993 • $22 • (06/30/96)

85 **BUEHLER** Chardonnay Russian River Valley 1994 • $13 • (05/15/96)

85 **CAMELOT** Chardonnay Monterey Reserve 1994 • $22 • (06/15/96)

85 **CANEPA** Chardonnay Alexander Valley Gauer Vineyard Adobe 111 1994 • $24 • (04/30/96)

85 **CHATEAU POTELLE** Chardonnay Napa Valley-Central Coast 1994 • $9.50 • (10/15/95)

85 **CHATEAU ST. JEAN** Chardonnay Sonoma County 1993 • $11 • (05/15/96)

85 **CLOS DU VAL** Chardonnay Carneros Napa Valley 1993 • $15 • (12/15/95)

85 **COSENTINO** Chardonnay Napa Valley 1994 • $14 • (06/30/96)

85 **COSENTINO** Chardonnay Napa Valley The Sculptor Reserve 1994 • $25 • (06/30/96)

85 **CRONIN** Chardonnay Napa Valley 1993 • $18 • (07/31/95)

85 **CRONIN** Chardonnay Alexander Valley Stuhlmuller Vineyard 1993 • $18 • (07/31/95)

85 **CUVAISON** Chardonnay Napa Valley Carneros Twenty-fifth Anniversary Harvest 1994 • $16 • (06/30/96)

85 **DE LOACH** Chardonnay Russian River Valley 1993 • $15 • (02/29/96)

85 **DE LOACH** Chardonnay Russian River Valley 1994 • $15 • (06/30/96)

85 **DE LORIMIER** Chardonnay Alexander Valley 1993 • $14 • (02/29/96)

85 **EDMEADES** Chardonnay Anderson Valley Dennison Vineyard 1993 • $20 • (07/31/95)

85 **ELKHORN PEAK** Chardonnay Napa Valley Fagan Creek Vineyards 1993 • $15 • (07/31/95)

85 **ESTATE WILLIAM BACCALA** Chardonnay Sonoma County 1993 • $13 • (02/29/96)

85 **FAR NIENTE** Chardonnay Napa Valley 1993 • $32 • (07/31/95)

85 **FISHER** Chardonnay Sonoma County Whitney's Vineyard 1993 • $26 • (07/31/95)

85 **FOREST GLEN** Chardonnay California Barrel Fermented 1994 • $10 • (05/15/96)

85 **FOREST HILL** Chardonnay Napa Valley Private Reserve 1993 • $28 • (07/31/95)

85 **FOXEN** Chardonnay Santa Maria Valley Tinaquaic Vineyard 1993 • $28 • (07/31/95)

85 **J. FRITZ** Chardonnay Russian River Valley Barrel Select 1992 • $18 • (07/31/95)

85 **GLEN ELLEN** Chardonnay California Proprietor's Reserve 1993 • $5 • (07/31/95) • BB

85 **GODSPEED** Chardonnay Mount Veeder 1993 • $15 • (07/31/95)

85 **HANNA** Chardonnay Russian River Valley Reserve 1993 • $18 • (06/30/96)

85 **HAYWOOD** Chardonnay California Vintner's Select 1994 • $8 • (11/15/95) • BB

85 **HUSCH** Chardonnay Anderson Valley Special Reserve 1992 • $18 • (07/31/95)

85 **J. LOHR** Chardonnay California Cypress 1993 • $9 • (12/15/95)

85 **MADROÑA** Chardonnay El Dorado 1993 • $10 • (07/31/95)

85 **LOUIS M. MARTINI** Chardonnay Napa Valley 1994 • $9 • (05/15/96)

85 **PETER MCCOY VINEYARDS** Chardonnay Knights Valley Clos des Pierres 1993 • $20 • (06/15/96)

85 **PETER MCCOY** Chardonnay Knights Valley Clos des Pierres 1992 • $19 • (07/31/95)

85 **MERIDIAN** Chardonnay Edna Valley Reserve 1994 • $14 • (06/30/96)

85 **MISSION VIEW** Chardonnay Paso Robles 1994 • $10 • (10/31/95)

85 **ROBERT MONDAVI** Chardonnay Napa Valley Unfiltered 1993 • $15 • (07/31/95)

85 **MONT ST. JOHN** Chardonnay Carneros Organically Grown Grapes 1993 • $13 • (07/31/95)

85 **MONTEREY VINEYARD** Chardonnay Monterey County Limited Release 1993 • $13 • (07/31/95)

85 **MONTICELLO** Chardonnay Napa Valley Corley Wild Yeast Estate Reserve 1994 • $33 • (06/15/96)

85 **NAPA RIDGE** Chardonnay Napa Valley Coastal Frisinger Vineyard 1994 • $11 • (06/30/96)

85 **NAPA RIDGE** Chardonnay Central Coast Coastal Vines 1994 • $7.50 • (10/15/95)

85 **NAVARRO** Chardonnay Mendocino 1994 • $8 • (02/29/96)

85 **ROBERT PEPI** Chardonnay Napa Valley Puncheon Fermented 1992 • $15 • (07/31/95)

85 **ROCHIOLI** Chardonnay Russian River Valley 1993 • $16 • (07/31/95)

85 **SAINTSBURY** Chardonnay Carneros 1993 • $15 • (07/31/95)

85 **SALMON CREEK** Chardonnay Carneros 1993 • $12 • (07/31/95)

85 **SCHUG** Chardonnay Carneros 1994 • $18 • (06/30/96)

85 **SCHUG** Chardonnay Sonoma Valley 1994 • $14 • (06/30/96)

85 **SILVERADO HILL CELLARS** Chardonnay Napa Valley 1994 • $10 • (06/15/96)

85 **STERLING** Chardonnay Napa Valley Sterling Collections Z Lot 1993 • $20 • (07/31/95)

85 **STONY HILL** Chardonnay Napa Valley 1993 • $21 • (06/15/96)

85 **STORRS** Chardonnay Santa Cruz Mountains Christie Vineyard Mountain Vineyard Collection 1993 • $17 • (07/31/95)

85 **RODNEY STRONG** Chardonnay Chalk Hill Chalk Hill Vineyard 1994 • $14 • (04/30/96)

85 **RODNEY STRONG** Chardonnay Chalk Hill Chalk Hill Vineyard 1993 • $14 • (07/31/95)

85 **TREFETHEN** Chardonnay Napa Valley 1993 • $19 • (07/31/95)

85 **WENTE BROS.** Chardonnay Arroyo Seco Riva Ranch 1993 • $8 • (05/15/96)

85 **WENTE BROS.** Chardonnay Arroyo Seco Riva Ranch 1992 • $12 • (07/31/95)

85 **WILDHURST** Chardonnay California 1993 • $10 • (07/31/95)

85 **WILDHURST** Chardonnay Sonoma County Reserve 1993 • $12 • (07/31/95)

85 **YORK MOUNTAIN** Chardonnay San Luis Obispo County 1994 • $12 • (06/30/96)

CALIFORNIA MERLOT

92 **BERINGER** Merlot Howell Mountain Bancroft Ranch 1992 • $29 • (12/15/95) • SS

92 **CHATEAU ST. JEAN** Merlot Sonoma County Reserve 1991 • $32 • (02/29/96) • CS

91 **JUSTIN** Merlot San Luis Obispo County 1992 • $20 • (12/31/95)

91 **PEACHY CANYON** Merlot Paso Robles 1992 • $22 • (07/31/95)

91 **RIDGE** Merlot Santa Cruz 1992 • $16 • (01/31/96)

90 **CLOS PEGASE** Merlot Napa Valley 1992 • $17 • (09/30/95)

90 **DUCKHORN** Merlot Napa Valley 1993 • $24 • (01/31/96)

90 **FOXEN** Merlot Santa Maria Valley Tinaquaic Vineyard 1993 • $24 • (04/30/96)

90 **KENDALL-JACKSON** Merlot California Grand Reserve 1992 • $30 • (09/30/95)

90 **VICHON** Merlot Napa Valley 1992 • $18 • (01/31/96)

89 **ARROWOOD** Merlot Sonoma County 1992 • $28 • (12/15/95)

89 **BERINGER** Merlot Howell Mountain Bancroft Ranch 1993 • $29 • (06/30/96)

89 **BLACKSTONE** Merlot Napa County Reserve 1993 • $10 • (04/30/96) • BB

89 **COSENTINO** Merlot Napa Valley Oakville 1993 • $30 • (12/15/95)

89 **FERRARI-CARANO** Merlot Sonoma County 1992 • $20 • (09/30/95)

89 **FRANCISCAN** Merlot Napa Valley Oakville Estate 1993 • $16 • (12/15/95)

89 **GROTH** Merlot Napa Valley 1992 • $20 • (09/30/95)

89 **MARKHAM** Merlot Napa Valley 1993 • $16 • (12/15/95)

89 **CHARLES KRUG** Merlot Napa Valley 1993 • $20 • (04/30/96)

89 **NIEBAUM-COPPOLA** Merlot Napa Valley 1993 • $18 • (05/15/96)

89 **PRIDE** Merlot Napa Valley 1993 • $20 • (12/15/95)

89 **RAYMOND** Merlot Napa Valley 1992 • $17 • (11/15/95)

89 **TRUCHARD** Merlot Napa Valley Carneros 1993 • $20 • (04/30/96)

88 **AZALEA SPRINGS** Merlot Napa Valley 1992 • $22 • (12/15/95)

88 **BETTINELLI** Merlot Napa Valley 1993 • $25 • (03/31/96)

88 **THE HESS COLLECTION** Merlot Napa Valley 1992 • $18 • (06/30/96)

88 **KENWOOD** Merlot Sonoma County Jack London Vineyard 1992 • $18 • (09/30/95)

88 **KUNDE** Merlot Sonoma Valley 1993 • $17 • (12/31/95)

88 **LIPARITA** Merlot Howell Mountain 1993 • $26 • (04/30/96)

88 **MATANZAS CREEK** Merlot Sonoma Valley 1993 • $38 • (06/30/96)

88 **MONTICELLO** Merlot Napa Valley Corley Family Vineyard 1992 • $18 • (09/30/95)

88 **PARDUCCI** Merlot California 1994 • $8 • (12/31/95) • BB

88 **PEACHY CANYON** Merlot Paso Robles 1993 • $22 • (03/31/96)

88 **REMICK RIDGE VINEYARDS** Merlot Sonoma Valley Marcy's Vineyard 1992 • $30 • (05/31/96)

88 **RIDGE** Merlot Santa Cruz Mountains Monte Bello Ridge 1993 • $24 • (06/15/96)

88 **SHAFER** Merlot Napa Valley 1993 • $24 • (12/15/95)

88 **STAG'S LEAP WINE CELLARS** Merlot Napa Valley 1992 • $24 • (12/15/95)

88 **WHITEHALL LANE** Merlot Napa Valley Leonardini Vineyard Reserve 1993 • $28 • (12/15/95)

87 **CLOS PEGASE** Merlot Napa Valley 1993 • $19 • (02/29/96)

87 **COSENTINO** Merlot Napa Valley Oakville 1994 • $38 • (06/30/96)

87 **DE LOACH** Merlot Russian River Valley 1993 • $14 • (09/30/95)
87 **EXPRESSIONS** Merlot Sonoma County 1994 • $12 • (06/15/96)
87 **GARY FARRELL** Merlot Sonoma County Ladi's Vineyard 1993 • $20 • (04/30/96)
87 **FLORA SPRINGS** Merlot Napa Valley 1994 • $14 • (06/30/96)
87 **FLORA SPRINGS** Merlot Napa Valley 1993 • $12 • (09/30/95)
87 **FROG'S LEAP** Merlot Napa Valley 1993 • $NA • (04/30/96)
87 **E. & J. GALLO** Merlot Northern Sonoma Vineyard Designation Gallo Sonoma 1993 • $15 • (04/30/96)
87 **HANNA** Merlot Alexander Valley 1993 • $16 • (06/15/96)
87 **JADE MOUNTAIN** Merlot Napa Valley 1993 • $25 • (03/31/96)
87 **PINE RIDGE** Merlot Napa Valley Carneros 1994 • $29 • (06/30/96)
87 **SEBASTIANI** Merlot Sonoma County 1993 • $12 • (11/15/95)
87 **ST. CLEMENT** Merlot Napa Valley 1993 • $18 • (04/30/96)
87 **SUMMERS RANCH** Merlot Knights Valley 1992 • $21 • (02/29/96)
87 **TRUCHARD** Merlot Napa Valley Carneros 1992 • $18 • (09/30/95)
86 **ALEXANDER VALLEY VINEYARDS** Merlot Alexander Valley Wetzel Family Estate 1992 • $15 • (07/31/95)
86 **CHATEAU SOUVERAIN** Merlot Alexander Valley 1993 • $13 • (12/15/95)
86 **KEENAN** Merlot Napa Valley 1993 • $25 • (06/30/96)
86 **KENDALL-JACKSON** Merlot California Grand Reserve 1993 • $42 • (06/30/96)
86 **LAMBERT BRIDGE** Merlot Sonoma County 1993 • $15 • (12/15/95)
86 **J. LOHR** Merlot California Cypress 1993 • $10 • (12/31/95)
86 **MACROSTIE** Merlot Carneros 1993 • $19 • (02/29/96)
86 **MONTERRA** Merlot Monterey Sand Hill 1992 • $10 • (02/29/96)
86 **SANTA CRUZ MOUNTAIN** Merlot California 1993 • $15 • (04/30/96)
86 **ST. FRANCIS** Merlot Sonoma Valley RINGER 1992 • $NA • (12/31/95)
86 **STONESTREET** Merlot Alexander Valley 1993 • $30 • (06/30/96)
86 **SWANSON** Merlot Napa Valley 1992 • $16 • (07/31/95)
86 **TESSERA** Merlot California 1994 • $9 • (06/30/96) • BB
86 **VILLA MT. EDEN** Merlot Napa Valley Grand Reserve 1993 • $16 • (12/31/95)
86 **WELLINGTON** Merlot Sonoma County 1992 • $15 • (11/15/95)
86 **WHITEHALL LANE** Merlot Napa Valley 1993 • $18 • (12/15/95)
85 **CHATEAU JULIEN** Merlot Monterey County Grand Reserve 1994 • $9 • (06/30/96)
85 **FETZER** Merlot California Eagle Peak 1994 • $8 • (06/15/96) • BB
85 **FETZER** Merlot North Coast Barrel Select 1994 • $12 • (06/30/96)
85 **KUNDE** Merlot Sonoma Valley 1993 • $17 • (02/29/96)
85 **MERRYVALE** Merlot Napa Valley 1992 • $24 • (09/30/95)
85 **MURPHY-GOODE** Merlot Alexander Valley Murphy Ranches 1993 • $16 • (12/15/95)
85 **NAPA RIDGE** Merlot North Coast Coastal 1993 • $10 • (06/30/96) • BB
85 **ROBERT PECOTA** Merlot Napa Valley Steven André Vineyard Unfiltered 1993 • $20 • (12/15/95)
85 **RUBISSOW-SARGENT** Merlot Mount Veeder 1992 • $16 • (05/15/96)
85 **ROBERT SINSKEY** Merlot Carneros Napa Valley 1992 • $18 • (04/30/96)
85 **SMITH & HOOK** Merlot Santa Lucia Highlands 1992 • $18 • (07/31/95)
85 **VILLA MT. EDEN** Merlot Napa Valley Grand Reserve 1994 • $16 • (06/30/96)

CALIFORNIA ZINFANDEL

96 **TURLEY** Zinfandel Napa Valley Hayne Vineyard 1994 • $27 • (04/30/96)

95 **TURLEY** Zinfandel Napa Valley Hayne Vineyard 1993 • $22 • (09/30/95)
94 **TURLEY** Zinfandel Napa Valley Moore Earthquake Vineyard 1994 • $25 • (04/30/96)
93 **ROBERT BIALE** Zinfandel Napa Valley Aldo's Vineyard Proprietor's Series 1994 • $19 • (05/15/96)
93 **RABBIT RIDGE** Zinfandel Sonoma County San Lorenzo Vineyard Reserve 1993 • $18 • (09/15/95)
93 **TURLEY** Zinfandel Howell Mountain Black-Sears Vineyard 1994 • $24 • (04/30/96)
93 **TURLEY** Zinfandel Napa Valley Aida Vineyard 1993 • $20 • (09/30/95)
92 **EDMEADES** Zinfandel Russian River Valley Hartford Vineyard 1994 • $30 • (04/30/96)
92 **RABBIT RIDGE** Zinfandel Dry Creek Valley Olsen Vineyard 1994 • $16 • (04/30/96)
91 **ROBERT BIALE** Zinfandel Napa Valley Aldo's Vineyard Proprietor's Series 1993 • $18 • (10/15/95)
91 **CRONIN** Zinfandel Sonoma Valley 1992 • $15 • (10/15/95)
91 **ROBERT MONDAVI** Zinfandel Napa Valley 1994 • $16 • (04/30/96)
91 **SAUCELITO CANYON** Zinfandel Arroyo Grande Valley 1993 • $14 • (10/15/95) • SS
91 **ST. FRANCIS** Zinfandel Sonoma Valley Old Vines 1993 • $18 • (10/15/95)
91 **STEELE** Zinfandel Mendocino DuPratt Vineyard 1993 • $18 • (04/30/96)
91 **TURLEY** Zinfandel Napa Valley Whitney Vineyard 1994 • $22 • (04/30/96)
90 **COSENTINO** Zinfandel Napa County Sonoma County The Zin 1994 • $21 • (04/30/96)
90 **D-CUBED CELLARS** Zinfandel Howell Mountain 1994 • $15 • (04/30/96)
90 **GREEN & RED** Zinfandel Napa Valley Chiles Mill Vineyard Unfiltered 1993 • $15 • (09/30/95)
90 **GREENWOOD RIDGE** Zinfandel Sonoma County Scherrer Vineyards 1994 • $15 • (04/30/96)
90 **KENWOOD** Zinfandel Sonoma Valley Nuns Canyon 1993 • $16 • (04/30/96)
90 **NORMAN VINEYARD** Zinfandel Paso Robles 1993 • $13 • (10/15/95)
90 **RAVENSWOOD** Zinfandel Sonoma Valley Old Hill Vineyard 1993 • $22 • (09/15/95)
90 **RIDGE** Zinfandel Sonoma Valley Pagani Ranch 1993 • $20 • (09/15/95) • CS
90 **ROSENBLUM** Zinfandel Napa Valley George Hendry Vineyard Reserve 1993 • $22 • (04/30/96)
90 **STEELE** Zinfandel Clear Lake Catfish Vineyard 1994 • $16 • (04/30/96)
90 **JOSEPH SWAN** Zinfandel Russian River Valley Frati Ranch 1993 • $18 • (10/15/95)
90 **TURLEY** Zinfandel Napa Valley Aida Vineyard 1994 • $20 • (04/30/96)
90 **TURLEY** Zinfandel Napa Valley Moore Earthquake Vineyard 1993 • $20 • (09/30/95)
89 **GARY FARRELL** Zinfandel Russian River Valley Collins Vineyard 1993 • $15 • (07/31/95)
89 **FIFE** Zinfandel Napa Valley Les Vieilles Vignes 1992 • $16 • (09/15/95)
89 **KENWOOD** Zinfandel Sonoma County Geyserville Mazzoni 1993 • $15 • (09/30/95)
89 **MONTEVINA** Zinfandel Amador County Terra d'Oro 1993 • $15 • (04/30/96)
89 **RAVENSWOOD** Zinfandel Sonoma County 1993 • $15 • (09/15/95)
89 **RAVENSWOOD** Zinfandel Napa Valley Dickerson 1993 • $20 • (09/15/95)
89 **RAVENSWOOD** Zinfandel Sonoma Valley Cooke 1993 • $20 • (09/15/95)
89 **RENWOOD** Zinfandel Amador County Old Vine 1993 • $15 • (09/15/95)

89 **ROCKING HORSE** Zinfandel Howell Mountain Lamborn Family Vineyard 1993 • $15 • (04/30/96)
89 **ROSENBLUM** Zinfandel Contra Costa County 1994 • $11 • (04/30/96)
89 **ROSENBLUM** Zinfandel Sonoma Valley Samsel Vineyard Maggie's Reserve 1993 • $22 • (09/30/95)
89 **SHOOTING STAR** Zinfandel Lake County 1994 • $8.50 • (04/30/96)
89 **STEELE** Zinfandel Clear Lake Catfish Vineyard 1993 • $13 • (09/30/95)
89 **STORYBOOK MOUNTAIN** Zinfandel Napa Valley Eastern Exposures 1992 • $17 • (10/15/95)
89 **TRIA** Zinfandel Napa Valley 1994 • $16 • (05/15/96)
89 **VIANO** Zinfandel Contra Costa County Sand Rock Hill Reserve Selection 1992 • $9 • (10/15/95)
89 **WILLIAMS SELYEM** Zinfandel Russian River Valley 1992 • $30 • (04/30/96)
88 **DAVIS BYNUM** Zinfandel Russian River Valley 1992 • $12 • (10/15/95)
88 **CHATEAU POTELLE** Zinfandel Napa Valley V.G.S. 1993 • $28 • (12/31/95)
88 **CLINE** Zinfandel Contra Costa County Reserve 1993 • $16 • (09/15/95)
88 **DE LOACH** Zinfandel Russian River Valley O.F.S. 1994 • $25 • (04/30/96)
88 **DE LOACH** Zinfandel Russian River Valley Pelletti Ranch 1993 • $14 • (10/15/95)
88 **DE LOACH** Zinfandel Russian River Valley Barbieri Ranch 1993 • $14 • (10/15/95)
88 **DICKERSON** Zinfandel Napa Valley Limited Reserve 1993 • $17 • (12/31/95)
88 **DRY CREEK** Zinfandel Sonoma County Old Vines 1993 • $15 • (09/15/95)
88 **EDMEADES** Zinfandel Mendocino 1994 • $16 • (04/30/96)
88 **EDMEADES** Zinfandel Mendocino Zeni Vineyard 1993 • $20 • (08/31/95)
88 **GARY FARRELL** Zinfandel Russian River Valley Collins Vineyard 1994 • $16 • (04/30/96)
88 **FERMENTATIONS & MORE** Zinfandel Paso Robles Benito Dusi Vineyard 1993 • $14 • (04/30/96)
88 **FERRARI-CARANO** Zinfandel Sonoma County 1993 • $14 • (08/31/95)
88 **GREEN & RED** Zinfandel Napa Valley Chiles Mill Vineyard 1994 • $16 • (04/30/96)
88 **GUNDLACH BUNDSCHU** Zinfandel Sonoma Valley Rhinefarm Vineyard 1993 • $14 • (10/15/95)
88 **HENDRY** Zinfandel Napa Valley Hendry Block 7 1992 • $14 • (10/15/95)
88 **LOLONIS** Zinfandel Mendocino County Private Reserve 1992 • $16 • (10/15/95)
88 **LYTTON SPRINGS** Zinfandel Sonoma County 1994 • $18 • (04/30/96)
88 **NORMAN VINEYARD** Zinfandel Paso Robles The Classic 1994 • $13 • (04/30/96)
88 **PEACHY CANYON** Zinfandel Paso Robles Dusi Ranch 1993 • $20 • (10/15/95)
88 **PESENTI** Zinfandel Paso Robles 1993 • $12 • (09/30/95)
88 **QUIVIRA** Zinfandel Dry Creek Valley 1994 • $15 • (04/30/96)
88 **A. RAFANELLI** Zinfandel Dry Creek Valley 1993 • $14 • (12/31/95)
88 **RAVENSWOOD** Zinfandel Sonoma Valley Monte Rosso 1993 • $20 • (09/15/95)
88 **RIDGE** Zinfandel Sonoma County 1993 • $12 • (09/15/95)
88 **ROCHIOLI** Zinfandel Russian River Valley Sodini Vineyard 1993 • $15 • (08/31/95)
88 **ROMBAUER** Zinfandel Napa Valley 1993 • $18 • (07/31/95)
88 **ROSENBLUM** Zinfandel Paso Robles Richard Sauret Vineyard 1993 • $12 • (09/30/95)
88 **ROSENBLUM** Zinfandel Sonoma County Old Vines 1993 • $13 • (09/30/95)
88 **SAUSAL** Zinfandel Alexander Valley 1993 • $9 • (07/31/95) • BB

88 **SCHUETZ OLES** Zinfandel Napa Valley Korte Ranch 1993 • $14 • (10/15/95)
88 **SEBASTIANI** Zinfandel Dry Creek Valley Cuneo-Saini Vineyard 1994 • $12 • (10/15/95)
88 **SPARROW LANE** Zinfandel North Coast 1993 • $12 • (10/15/95)
88 **STEELE** Zinfandel Mendocino Pacini Vineyard 1994 • $15 • (04/30/96)
88 **JOSEPH SWAN** Zinfandel Sonoma Valley Stellwagen Vineyard 1993 • $16 • (10/15/95)
88 **TERRACES** Zinfandel Napa Valley 1992 • $16 • (10/15/95)
88 **TRUCHARD** Zinfandel Napa Valley Carneros 1994 • $15 • (03/31/96)
88 **VILLA MT. EDEN** Zinfandel Sonoma Valley Monte Rosso Vineyard Grand Reserve 1993 • $16 • (09/15/95)
88 **VILLA MT. EDEN** Zinfandel California Cellar Select 1993 • $8 • (09/15/95) • BB
88 **WHITE OAK** Zinfandel Alexander Valley 1993 • $15 • (10/15/95)
87 **ADELAIDA** Zinfandel San Luis Obispo County 1992 • $16 • (04/30/96)
87 **BERINGER** Zinfandel Napa Valley 1992 • $9 • (09/15/95) • BB
87 **BUEHLER** Zinfandel Napa Valley 1994 • $12 • (04/30/96)
87 **CHATEAU MONTELENA** Zinfandel Napa Valley The Montelena Estate 1992 • $12 • (07/31/95)
87 **CHATEAU SOUVERAIN** Zinfandel Dry Creek Valley 1993 • $9.50 • (08/31/95) • BB
87 **CLINE** Zinfandel Contra Costa County 1994 • $12 • (04/30/96)
87 **CLINE** Zinfandel Contra Costa County Bridgehead 1993 • $18 • (09/15/95)
87 **CLINE** Zinfandel Contra Costa County Big Break 1993 • $18 • (09/15/95)
87 **COSENTINO** Zinfandel Sonoma County The Zin Unfined and Unfiltered 1993 • $18 • (09/15/95)
87 **DE LOACH** Zinfandel Russian River Valley Gambogi Ranch 1994 • $15 • (04/30/96)
87 **DE LOACH** Zinfandel Russian River Valley Papera Ranch 1994 • $15 • (04/30/96)
87 **EBERLE** Zinfandel Paso Robles Sauret Vineyard 1994 • $16 • (04/30/96)
87 **ELYSE** Zinfandel Howell Mountain 1994 • $16 • (04/30/96)
87 **ELYSE** Zinfandel Napa Valley Coeur du Val 1994 • $14 • (04/30/96)
87 **E. & J. GALLO** Zinfandel Dry Creek Valley Frei Ranch Vineyard Gallo Sonoma 1993 • $14 • (04/30/96)
87 **THE HESS COLLECTION** Zinfandel Napa Valley 1992 • $15 • (10/15/95)
87 **JANKRIS** Zinfandel Paso Robles 1993 • $9 • (10/15/95)
87 **KARLY** Zinfandel Amador County Pokerville 1993 • $8 • (10/15/95) • BB
87 **LANG** Zinfandel El Dorado Twin Rivers Vineyards 1992 • $6 • (09/15/95)
87 **NALLE** Zinfandel Dry Creek Valley 1993 • $16 • (08/31/95)
87 **NICHELINI** Zinfandel Napa Valley 1991 • $12 • (03/31/96)
87 **NIEBAUM-COPPOLA** Zinfandel Napa Valley Edizione Pennino 1993 • $16 • (10/15/95)
87 **PEACHY CANYON** Zinfandel Paso Robles Eastside 1993 • $12 • (10/15/95)
87 **PEIRANO ESTATE** Zinfandel Lodi 1993 • $10 • (08/31/95)
87 **QUIVIRA** Zinfandel Dry Creek Valley 1993 • $14 • (04/30/96)
87 **RAVENSWOOD** Zinfandel Russian River Valley Wood Road Belloni 1993 • $20 • (09/15/95)
87 **RENWOOD** Zinfandel Fiddletown Old Vine 1993 • $22 • (04/30/96)
87 **RENWOOD** Zinfandel Shenandoah Valley Grandpére 1993 • $21 • (10/15/95)
87 **ROSENBLUM** Zinfandel Paso Robles Richard Sauret Vineyard 1994 • $12 • (04/30/96)
87 **ROSENBLUM** Zinfandel Napa Valley 1993 • $14 • (04/30/96)

87 **ROSENBLUM** Zinfandel Mount Veeder Brandlin Ranch 1993 • $19 • (10/15/95)

87 **SCHERRER** Zinfandel Alexander Valley Old & Mature Vines 1993 • $15 • (10/15/95)

87 **SHENANDOAH** Zinfandel Amador County Special Reserve 1994 • $8.50 • (04/30/96)

87 **SHENANDOAH** Zinfandel Amador County Special Reserve 1993 • $8.50 • (10/15/95)

87 **STEELE** Zinfandel Mendocino Pacini Vineyard 1993 • $14 • (09/30/95)

87 **SUMMIT LAKE** Zinfandel Howell Mountain 1991 • $12 • (10/15/95)

87 **WELLINGTON** Zinfandel Sonoma Valley 100 Year Old Vines 1993 • $15 • (10/15/95)

87 **WILLIAM WHEELER** Zinfandel Dry Creek Valley 1992 • $11 • (08/31/95)

87 **WHITE OAK** Zinfandel Sonoma Valley 1993 • $9 • (10/15/95)

86 **BANNISTER** Zinfandel Dry Creek Valley Bradford Mountain Vineyard 1993 • $15 • (10/15/95)

86 **BYINGTON** Zinfandel Howell Mountain 1992 • $10 • (03/31/96)

86 **DE LOACH** Zinfandel Russian River Valley 1994 • $14 • (04/30/96)

86 **DE LOACH** Zinfandel Russian River Valley Pelletti Ranch 1994 • $15 • (04/30/96)

86 **DE LOACH** Zinfandel Russian River Valley Gambogi Ranch 1993 • $14 • (10/15/95)

86 **DE LOACH** Zinfandel Russian River Valley Papera Ranch 1993 • $14 • (10/15/95)

86 **DEUX AMIS** Zinfandel Sonoma County 1993 • $12 • (10/15/95)

86 **EDMEADES** Zinfandel Mendocino Ciapusci Vineyard 1993 • $20 • (10/15/95)

86 **EDMUNDS ST. JOHN** Zinfandel Amador County 1993 • $16 • (10/15/95)

86 **GABRIELLI** Zinfandel Mendocino 1993 • $12 • (07/31/95)

86 **HENDRY** Zinfandel Mount Veeder Brandlin Vineyard 1992 • $15 • (10/15/95)

86 **HOP KILN** Zinfandel Sonoma County Primitivo 1993 • $18 • (10/15/95)

86 **MAZZOCCO** Zinfandel Sonoma County 1993 • $14 • (08/31/95)

86 **ROBERT MONDAVI** Zinfandel Napa Valley 1993 • $16 • (07/31/95)

86 **PEACHY CANYON** Zinfandel Paso Robles Westside 1993 • $15 • (10/15/95)

86 **RIDGE** Zinfandel Paso Robles Dusi Ranch 1993 • $14 • (09/30/95)

86 **ROSENBLUM** Zinfandel Contra Costa County 1993 • $11 • (09/30/95)

86 **SIGNORELLO** Zinfandel Napa Valley Unfined Unfiltered 1993 • $18 • (09/15/95)

86 **STORYBOOK MOUNTAIN** Zinfandel Napa Valley Reserve 1991 • $25 • (10/15/95)

86 **STORYBOOK MOUNTAIN** Zinfandel Napa Valley 1992 • $14 • (10/15/95)

86 **RODNEY STRONG** Zinfandel Russian River Valley River West Vineyard Old Vines 1992 • $14 • (07/31/95)

86 **TOPOLOS** Zinfandel Sonoma County Ultimo Old Vines Unfined 1993 • $20 • (10/15/95)

86 **WELLINGTON** Zinfandel Sonoma Valley Casa Santinamaria 1993 • $12 • (10/15/95)

86 **WINDEMERE** Zinfandel Paso Robles Benito Dusi Vineyard 1993 • $15 • (03/31/96)

85 **ACACIA** Zinfandel Napa Valley Old Vines 1993 • $10 • (10/15/95)

85 **ALDERBROOK** Zinfandel Dry Creek Valley 1993 • $14 • (10/15/95)

85 **BALLENTINE** Zinfandel Napa Valley 1992 • $14 • (10/15/95)

85 **BENZIGER** Zinfandel Sonoma County 1993 • $14 • (10/15/95)

85 **BERINGER** Zinfandel North Coast 1992 • $10 • (12/31/95)

85 **BLOCKHEADIA RINGNOSII** Zinfandel Rutherford 1993 • $15 • (10/15/95)

85 **BOEGER** Zinfandel El Dorado Walker Vineyard 1993 • $12 • (10/15/95)

85 **CANARD** Zinfandel Napa Valley 1990 • $12 • (04/30/96)

85 **CLAUDIA SPRINGS** Zinfandel Mendocino Pacini Vineyard 1993 • $14 • (10/15/95)

85 **CLINE** Zinfandel Contra Costa County 1993 • $12 • (09/15/95)

85 **CRONIN** Zinfandel Santa Clara County 1992 • $12 • (10/15/95)

85 **DE LOACH** Zinfandel Russian River Valley Barbieri Ranch 1994 • $15 • (04/30/96)

85 **DE LOACH** Zinfandel Russian River Valley 1993 • $13 • (10/15/95)

85 **EDMEADES** Zinfandel Mendocino Ciapusci Vineyard 1994 • $29 • (04/30/96)

85 **ELYSE** Zinfandel Howell Mountain 1993 • $16 • (10/15/95)

85 **EXPRESSIONS** Zinfandel Sonoma County 1993 • $12 • (04/30/96)

85 **FRANUS** Zinfandel Napa Valley Hendry Vineyard 1993 • $14 • (10/15/95)

85 **E. & J. GALLO** Zinfandel Dry Creek Valley Frei Ranch Vineyard Gallo Sonoma 1992 • $15 • (09/15/95)

85 **HART'S DESIRE** Zinfandel Russian River Valley Ponzo Vineyard 1994 • $14 • (05/15/96)

85 **JADE MOUNTAIN** Zinfandel California 1991 • $13 • (10/15/95)

85 **KUNDE** Zinfandel Sonoma Valley The Shaw Vineyard Century Vines 1993 • $14 • (03/31/96)

85 **LIMERICK LANE** Zinfandel Russian River Valley Collins Vineyard 1993 • $14 • (10/15/95)

85 **MARIETTA** Zinfandel Sonoma County 1992 • $11 • (09/15/95)

85 **MILANO** Zinfandel Mendocino County Sanel Valley Vineyard 1993 • $10 • (10/15/95)

85 **J. PEDRONCELLI** Zinfandel Dry Creek Valley Mother Clone Special Vineyard Selection 1993 • $11 • (10/15/95)

85 **RANDON RIDGE** Zinfandel Sonoma Valley Old Wave 1993 • $14 • (10/15/95)

85 **ROUND HILL** Zinfandel Napa Valley 1992 • $8 • (10/15/95)

85 **RUTHERFORD RANCH** Zinfandel Napa Valley 1992 • $8 • (08/31/95)

85 **SEGHESIO** Zinfandel Dry Creek Valley 1993 • $12 • (10/15/95)

85 **SEGHESIO** Zinfandel Sonoma County 1993 • $9 • (10/15/95)

85 **SOBON ESTATE** Zinfandel Shenandoah Valley Rocky Top 1993 • $13.50 • (03/31/96)

85 **JOSEPH SWAN** Zinfandel Russian River Valley V.H.S.R. Bohn Vineyard 1993 • $15 • (10/15/95)

85 **THORNTON** Zinfandel South Coast Limited Bottling 1994 • $12 • (03/31/96)

85 **WHITE OAK** Zinfandel Sonoma County Limited Reserve 1993 • $13 • (10/15/95)

92 **VIANSA** Zinfandel Prindelo Sonoma Valley 1993 • $20 • (10/15/95)

91 **RIDGE** Zinfandel Lytton Springs Dry Creek Valley 1993 • $19 • (07/31/95) • SS

91 **RIDGE** Zinfandel Geyserville Sonoma County 1993 • $20 • (09/15/95) • SS

CALIFORNIA PINOT NOIR

93 **WHITCRAFT** Pinot Noir Santa Maria Valley Bien Nacido Vineyard 1994 • $30 • (12/31/95)

92 **SARAH'S** Pinot Noir Santa Clara County 1993 • $50 • (10/15/95)

92 **WHITCRAFT** Pinot Noir Sonoma Coast Hirsch Vineyard 1994 • $40 • (05/15/96)

91 **AU BON CLIMAT** Pinot Noir Arroyo Grande Valley Rosemary's Talley Vineyard 1993 • $40 • (12/31/95)

91 **MUELLER** Pinot Noir Russian River Valley Emily's Cuvée 1994 • $20 • (04/30/96)

91 **NICHOLS** Pinot Noir Santa Barbara County Sierra Madre Vineyard 1993 • $24 • (12/31/95)

91 **W.H. SMITH WINES** Pinot Noir Sonoma Coast Hellenthal Vineyard Young Vines 1994 • $22 • (04/30/96)

90 **BEAULIEU** Pinot Noir Napa Valley Carneros Reserve 1994 • $19 • (03/31/96)

90 **FOXEN** Pinot Noir Santa Maria Valley Bien Nacido Vineyard 1993 • $26 • (11/15/95)

90 **FOXEN** Pinot Noir Santa Ynez Valley Sanford & Benedict Vineyard 1993 • $30 • (11/15/95)

90 **GREENWOOD RIDGE** Pinot Noir Anderson Valley 1994 • $16 • (01/31/96)

90 **STEELE** Pinot Noir Santa Barbara County Bien Nacido Vineyard 1994 • $20 • (04/30/96)

90 **STEELE** Pinot Noir Carneros 1993 • $18 • (09/15/95)

90 **WILLIAMS SELYEM** Pinot Noir Sonoma Coast 1994 • $30 • (06/30/96)

89 **ACACIA** Pinot Noir Carneros 1994 • $18 • (04/30/96)

89 **AU BON CLIMAT** Pinot Noir Santa Ynez Valley Sanford & Benedict Vineyard 1993 • $35 • (12/31/95)

89 **CAMBRIA** Pinot Noir Santa Maria Valley Julia's Vineyard 1994 • $22 • (02/29/96)

89 **CRONIN** Pinot Noir Santa Cruz Mountains Peter Martin Ray Vineyard 1992 • $22 • (04/30/96)

89 **DELOACH** Pinot Noir Russian River Valley O.F.S. 1994 • $25 • (02/29/96)

89 **HARTFORD COURT** Pinot Noir Russian River Valley Arrendell Vineyard 1994 • $42 • (02/29/96)

89 **ROBERT MONDAVI** Pinot Noir Napa Valley Reserve 1993 • $30 • (05/31/96)

89 **ROBERT MONDAVI** Pinot Noir Carneros Napa Valley Unfiltered 1993 • $26 • (11/30/95)

89 **MONTICELLO** Pinot Noir Napa Valley Monticello Vineyards Estate Reserve 1993 • $30 • (11/30/95)

89 **NICHOLS** Pinot Noir Santa Barbara County Sierra Madre Vineyard 1994 • $24 • (04/30/96)

89 **ROCHIOLI** Pinot Noir Russian River Valley West Block Reserve 1993 • $38 • (10/15/95)

89 **SANTA CRUZ MOUNTAIN** Pinot Noir Santa Cruz Mountains Matteson Vineyard 1992 • $16 • (04/30/96)

89 **SIDURI** Pinot Noir Anderson Valley Rose Vineyard 1994 • $30 • (01/31/96) • RT

89 **WHITCRAFT** Pinot Noir Santa Maria Valley Bien Nacido Vineyard N 1994 • $40 • (05/15/96)

88 **AU BON CLIMAT** Pinot Noir Santa Maria Valley 1994 • $18 • (02/29/96)

88 **BENZIGER** Pinot Noir California 1993 • $14 • (06/15/96)

88 **BYINGTON** Pinot Noir Santa Cruz Mountains Special Reserve Vineyards 1994 • $25 • (02/29/96)

88 **BYINGTON** Santa Cruz Mountains Special Reserve Vineyards 1994 • $25 • (02/29/96)

88 **CARNEROS CREEK** Pinot Noir Los Carneros 1993 • $13 • (09/15/95)

88 **CARNEROS CREEK** Pinot Noir Carneros Signature Reserve 1993 • $28 • (11/15/95)

88 **DEHLINGER** Pinot Noir Russian River Valley 1993 • $20 • (11/30/95)

88 **GARY FARRELL** Pinot Noir Russian River Valley Olivet Lane Vineyard 1994 • $30 • (06/30/96)

88 **FIDDLEHEAD** Pinot Noir Santa Maria Valley 1993 • $25 • (05/31/96)

88 **FOXEN** Pinot Noir Santa Maria Valley 1993 • $20 • (11/15/95)

88 **HITCHING POST** Pinot Noir Santa Maria Valley Bien Nacido Vineyard 1993 • $25 • (10/15/95)

88 **HITCHING POST** Pinot Noir Santa Ynez Valley Sanford & Benedict Vineyard 1993 • $25 • (10/15/95)

88 **KENDALL-JACKSON** Pinot Noir California Vintner's Reserve 1994 • $14 • (11/15/95)

88 **LA CREMA** Pinot Noir Sonoma County 1994 • $17 • (03/31/96)

88 **LAURIER** Pinot Noir Sonoma County 1994 • $15 • (03/31/96)

88 **MONTICELLO** Pinot Noir Napa Valley Corley Family Vineyards 1992 • $18 • (09/15/95)

88 **FESS PARKER** Pinot Noir Santa Barbara County American Tradition Reserve 1994 • $25 • (02/29/96)

88 **RAMSPECK** Pinot Noir Napa Valley 1994 • $16 • (01/31/96)

88 **SAINTSBURY** Pinot Noir Carneros 1994 • $18 • (02/29/96)

88 **SANTA CRUZ MOUNTAIN** Pinot Noir Santa Cruz Mountains Matteson Vineyard 1991 • $15 • (04/30/96)

88 **STEELE** Pinot Noir Carneros Durell Vineyard 1993 • $19 • (09/15/95)

88 **STEELE** Pinot Noir Carneros Sangiacomo Vineyard 1993 • $22 • (09/15/95)

88 **LANE TANNER** Pinot Noir Santa Maria Valley Sierra Madre Plateau 1994 • $20 • (02/29/96)

88 **TRUCHARD** Pinot Noir Carneros 1993 • $18 • (11/30/95)

88 **WILLIAMS-SELYEM** Pinot Noir Russian River Valley Rochioli Vineyard 1993 • $NA • (02/29/96)

88 **WILLIAMS SELYEM** Pinot Noir Anderson Valley Ferrington Vineyard 1993 • $NA • (02/29/96)

87 **ALDERBROOK** Pinot Noir Russian River Valley 1994 • $15 • (01/31/96)

87 **ANCIEN WINES** Pinot Noir Carneros 1993 • $18 • (04/30/96)

87 **AU BON CLIMAT** Pinot Noir Arroyo Grande Valley Talley and Paragon Vineyards 1993 • $20 • (09/15/95)

87 **BYRON** Pinot Noir Santa Barbara County 1994 • $16.50 • (02/29/96)

87 **CARNEROS CREEK** Pinot Noir Carneros 1994 • $16 • (02/29/96)

87 **COSENTINO** Pinot Noir Napa Valley LZ 1994 • $20 • (02/29/96)

87 **DOMAINE CARNEROS** Pinot Noir Carneros 1994 • $20 • (02/29/96)

87 **DOMAINE CARNEROS** Pinot Noir Carneros The Famous Gate 1993 • $30 • (12/31/95)

87 **EL MOLINO** Pinot Noir Napa Valley 1993 • $35 • (05/31/96)

87 **FOXEN** Pinot Noir Santa Maria Valley 1994 • $20 • (01/31/96)

87 **HERON LAKE** Pinot Noir Wild Horse Valley 1994 • $24 • (02/29/96)

87 **HITCHING POST** Pinot Noir Santa Maria Valley 1993 • $16 • (10/15/95)

87 **KENWOOD** Pinot Noir Russian River Valley Olivet Lane 1993 • $22 • (10/15/95)

87 **LA CREMA** Pinot Noir Sonoma County Reserve 1994 • $14 • (02/29/96)

87 **MACROSTIE** Pinot Noir Carneros 1993 • $17 • (01/31/96)

87 **MERIDIAN** Pinot Noir Santa Barbara County San Luis Obispo County Reserve 1993 • $16 • (11/30/95)

87 **NEWLAN** Pinot Noir Napa Valley 1993 • $18 • (05/15/96)

87 **OPTIMA** Pinot Noir Russian River Valley 1994 • $40 • (04/30/96)

87 **PARDUCCI** Pinot Noir Mendocino County 1994 • $8 • (01/31/96) • BB

87 **RUTZ CELLARS** Pinot Noir Russian River Valley Quail Hill Vineyard 1993 • $24 • (01/31/96)

87 **SCHUG** Pinot Noir Carneros 1994 • $16 • (02/29/96)

87 **STONESTREET** Pinot Noir Russian River Valley 1994 • $30 • (02/29/96)

87 **RODNEY STRONG** Pinot Noir Russian River Valley River East Vineyard 1993 • $16 • (12/31/95)
87 **MARIMAR TORRES** Pinot Noir Sonoma County Green Valley Don Miguel Vineyard 1992 • $35 • (04/30/96)
87 **TULOCAY** Pinot Noir Napa Valley Haynes Vineyard 1992 • $15 • (11/30/95)
86 **ACACIA** Pinot Noir Carneros Reserve 1993 • $25 • (04/30/96)
86 **ANDERSON'S CONN VALLEY** Pinot Noir Napa Valley Valhalla Vineyards 1993 • $40 • (04/30/96)
86 **ARIES** Pinot Noir Los Carneros 1994 • $10 • (01/31/96) • BB
86 **BEAULIEU** Pinot Noir Napa Valley Carneros 1993 • $13 • (10/15/95)
86 **BERNARDUS** Pinot Noir Santa Barbara County Bien Nacido Vineyard 1993 • $25 • (01/31/96)
86 **BUENA VISTA** Pinot Noir Carneros 1993 • $10 • (10/15/95) • BB
86 **CARNEROS CREEK** Pinot Noir Carneros Las Lomas 1994 • $18 • (02/29/96)
86 **CRICHTON HALL** Pinot Noir Napa Valley 1993 • $22 • (04/30/96)
86 **EDMEADES** Pinot Noir Anderson Valley Dennison Vineyard 1993 • $20 • (09/15/95)
86 **HARTFORD COURT** Pinot Noir Russian River Valley Dutton Ranch-Sanchietti Vineyard 1994 • $35 • (02/29/96)
86 **HITCHING POST** Pinot Noir Santa Barbara County Sierra Madre and Gold Coast Vineyards 1993 • $14 • (12/31/95)
86 **LEEWARD** Pinot Noir Santa Barbara County 1993 • $14 • (09/15/95)
86 **LONGORIA** Pinot Noir Santa Maria Valley Bien Nacido Vineyard 1994 • $23 • (04/30/96)
86 **LONGORIA** Pinot Noir Santa Maria Valley Bien Nacido Vineyard 1993 • $20 • (09/15/95)
86 **MERIDIAN** Pinot Noir Santa Barbara County 1994 • $14 • (03/31/96)
86 **MIRASSOU** Pinot Noir Monterey County Fifth Generation Harvest Reserve 1992 • $12 • (10/15/95)
86 **ROBERT MONDAVI** Pinot Noir Napa Valley Unfiltered 1993 • $16 • (09/15/95)
86 **NAPA RIDGE** Pinot Noir North Coast Coastal 1994 • $7.50 • (01/31/96) • BB
86 **OLIVET LANE** Pinot Noir Russian River Valley Pellegrini Family Vineyards 1994 • $15 • (01/31/96)
86 **FESS PARKER** Pinot Noir Santa Barbara County 1994 • $16 • (02/29/96)
86 **FESS PARKER** Pinot Noir Santa Barbara County American Tradition Reserve 1993 • $22 • (02/29/96)
86 **PAVONA WINES** Pinot Noir Monterey County Paraiso Springs Vineyard 1994 • $15 • (04/30/96)
86 **SEGHESIO** Pinot Noir Sonoma County 1993 • $12 • (11/15/95)
86 **STEELE** Pinot Noir Santa Barbara County Bien Nacido Vineyard 1993 • $22 • (09/15/95)
86 **JOSEPH SWAN** Pinot Noir Sonoma Mountain Steiner Vineyard 1994 • $17 • (04/30/96)
86 **LANE TANNER** Pinot Noir Santa Maria Valley Bien Nacido 1994 • $20 • (02/29/96)
86 **VILLA MT. EDEN** Pinot Noir Santa Maria Valley Bien Nacido Vineyard Grand Reserve 1994 • $12 • (01/31/96)
86 **WILLIAMS SELYEM** Pinot Noir Russian River Valley 1994 • $28 • (06/30/96)
86 **WILLIAMS SELYEM** Pinot Noir Sonoma County 1994 • $23 • (06/30/96)
85 **AU BON CLIMAT** Pinot Noir Santa Barbara County La Bauge Au-dessus Bien Nacido Vineyard 1993 • $25 • (09/15/95)
85 **BANNISTER** Pinot Noir Russian River Valley 1994 • $18 • (05/31/96)
85 **BYINGTON** Pinot Noir Santa Cruz Mountains St. Charles Vineyard Special Reserve 1993 • $30 • (02/29/96)

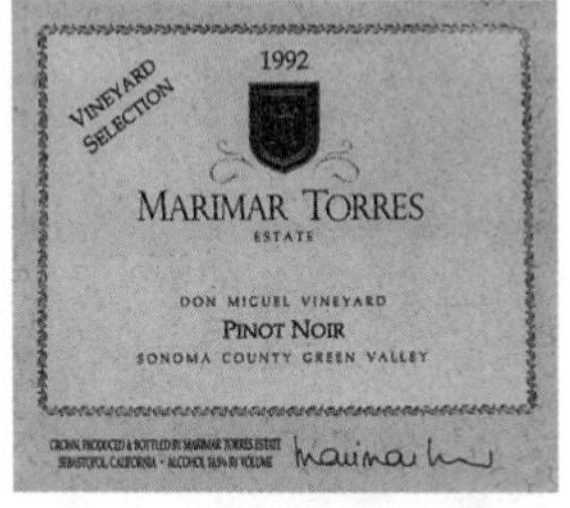

85 **CALERA** Pinot Noir Central Coast 1994 • $16 • (02/29/96)
85 **CARNEROS CREEK** Pinot Noir Carneros Fleur de Carneros 1994 • $10 • (11/30/95) • BB
85 **CEDAR BROOK** Pinot Noir California 1993 • $7 • (11/15/95) • BB
85 **CLOS LACHANCE** Pinot Noir Santa Cruz Mountains 1993 • $19 • (12/31/95)
85 **EDMEADES** Pinot Noir Anderson Valley Anderson Crest Vineyard 1994 • $23 • (03/31/96)
85 **LOUIS M. MARTINI** Pinot Noir Los Carneros 1993 • $8 • (01/31/96) • BB
85 **MORGAN** Pinot Noir California 1994 • $18 • (02/29/96)
85 **NAVARRO** Pinot Noir Anderson Valley Méthode à l'Ancienne 1992 • $15 • (03/31/96)
85 **RUTZ CELLARS** Pinot Noir Russian River Valley Dutton Ranch 1993 • $24 • (01/31/96)
85 **SAINTSBURY** Pinot Noir Carneros Garnet 1994 • $11 • (11/15/95)
85 **SCOTLAND CRAIG** Pinot Noir Russian River Valley Rochioli Vineyard 1993 • $35 • (12/31/95)
85 **SELBY** Pinot Noir Russian River Valley 1994 • $16 • (05/15/96)
85 **SOQUEL** Pinot Noir Santa Cruz Mountains Longridge Vineyard 1994 • $25 • (02/29/96)
85 **WILLIAMS-SELYEM** Pinot Noir Sonoma Coast Summa & Coastlands Vineyards 1993 • $40 • (02/29/96)
85 **WILLIAMS SELYEM** Pinot Noir Russian River Valley Olivet Lane Vineyard 1993 • $28 • (09/15/95)
85 **WILLIAMS SELYEM** Pinot Noir Sonoma Coast 1993 • $26 • (09/15/95)

CALIFORNIA SAUVIGNON BLANC & BLENDS

90 **BERNARDUS** Sauvignon Blanc Monterey County 1994 • $10 • (12/31/95) • BB
90 **BRANDER** Sauvignon Blanc Santa Ynez Valley Cuvée Nicolas 1994 • $21 • (04/30/96)
90 **FERRARI-CARANO** Fumé Blanc Sonoma County Reserve 1994 • $15 • (12/15/95)
90 **NAVARRO** Sauvignon Blanc Mendocino Cuvée 128 1994 • $11 • (02/29/96)
89 **DUCKHORN** Sauvignon Blanc Napa Valley 1994 • $12 • (12/31/95)
89 **GEYSER PEAK** Sauvignon Blanc Sonoma County 1995 • $8 • (05/15/96) • BB
89 **ROBERT PEPI** Sauvignon Blanc Napa Valley Reserve Selection 1994 • $20 • (03/31/96)
89 **SHENANDOAH** Sauvignon Blanc Amador County 1995 • $8 • (05/31/96)
88 **CHALK HILL** Sauvignon Blanc Chalk Hill 1993 • $16 • (08/31/95)
88 **CHATEAU ST. JEAN** Fumé Blanc Russian River Valley La Petite Etoile 1994 • $12 • (04/30/96)
88 **DRY CREEK** Fumé Blanc Dry Creek Valley Barrel Fermented Reserve 1994 • $15 • (02/29/96)
88 **FERRARI-CARANO** Fumé Blanc Sonoma County 1994 • $11 • (12/15/95)
88 **IRON HORSE** Fumé Blanc Alexander Valley T-T Vineyards 1995 • $13 • (06/30/96)
88 **LOCKWOOD** Sauvignon Blanc Monterey 1994 • $9 • (05/31/96) • BB
88 **MAYACAMAS** Sauvignon Blanc Napa Valley 1993 • $10 • (08/31/95)
88 **ROBERT MONDAVI** Sauvignon Blanc Stags Leap District 1993 • $18 • (09/15/95)
88 **SELENE** Sauvignon Blanc Carneros Hyde Vineyards 1994 • $18 • (02/29/96)
88 **STEPHEN ZELLERBACH** Sauvignon Blanc Sonoma County 1993 • $7 • (08/31/95) • BB
87 **ARCIERO** Sauvignon Blanc Paso Robles 1994 • $6 • (05/31/96)

87 **BUENA VISTA** Sauvignon Blanc Lake County 1994 • $7.50 • (09/15/95) • BB
87 **CAKEBREAD** Sauvignon Blanc Napa Valley 1994 • $13 • (08/31/95)
87 **CHATEAU POTELLE** Sauvignon Blanc Napa Valley 1994 • $9.50 • (08/31/95)
87 **CHATEAU ST. JEAN** Fumé Blanc Sonoma County 1994 • $8 • (04/30/96)
87 **FETZER** Bonterra Organically Grown Grapes Mendocino County 1993 • $7 • (07/31/95) • BB
87 **FIRESTONE** Sauvignon Blanc Santa Ynez Valley 1994 • $8 • (02/29/96)
87 **GREENWOOD RIDGE** Sauvignon Blanc Anderson Valley 1994 • $9 • (02/29/96)
87 **GUENOC** Sauvignon Blanc Guenoc Valley 1994 • $11 • (07/31/95)
87 **HANDLEY** Sauvignon Blanc Dry Creek Valley 1993 • $9 • (08/31/95)
87 **HANNA** Sauvignon Blanc Sonoma County 1994 • $10 • (08/31/95)
87 **HUSCH** Sauvignon Blanc Mendocino 1994 • $9 • (08/31/95)
87 **IRON HORSE** Fumé Blanc Alexander Valley T-T Vineyards 1994 • $12 • (08/31/95)
87 **JEPSON** Sauvignon Blanc Mendocino County Estate Select 1994 • $8.50 • (05/31/96)
87 **KENDALL-JACKSON** Sauvignon Blanc California Grand Reserve 1994 • $20 • (06/30/96)

87 **KENWOOD** Sauvignon Blanc Sonoma County 1994 • $9.50 • (12/15/95) • BB
87 **LAKEWOOD** Sauvignon Blanc Clear Lake 1994 • $10 • (12/31/95)
87 **LONG** Sauvignon Blanc Napa Valley 1994 • $14 • (05/15/96)
87 **MARKHAM** Sauvignon Blanc Napa Valley 1994 • $8 • (08/31/95) • BB
87 **MATANZAS CREEK** Sauvignon Blanc Sonoma County 1994 • $15 • (02/29/96)
87 **MURPHY-GOODE** Alexander Valley 1994 • $10 • (07/31/95)
87 **RANCHO SISQUOC** Sauvignon Blanc Santa Maria Valley 1993 • $10 • (08/31/95)
87 **RUTHERFORD VINEYARDS** Fumé Blanc Napa Valley 1993 • $8 • (08/31/95)
87 **ST. CLEMENT** Sauvignon Blanc Napa Valley 1994 • $12 • (08/31/95)
87 **TURLEY** Sauvignon Blanc Napa Valley Turley Vineyard 1994 • $16 • (10/31/95)

87 **VOSS SAUVIGNON BLANC** Napa Valley 1994 • $9 • (07/31/95)
86 **BOGLE** Fumé Blanc California 1994 • $5 • (05/15/96) • BB
86 **COTES DE SONOMA** Sauvignon Blanc Sonoma County 1995 • $9 • (06/15/96)
86 **LOCKWOOD** Sauvignon Blanc Monterey 1993 • $9 • (08/31/95)
86 **MAYACAMAS** Sauvignon Blanc Napa Valley 1994 • $12 • (05/15/96) • BB
86 **MILL CREEK** Sauvignon Blanc Dry Creek Valley 1994 • $8 • (10/31/95)
86 **NAPA RIDGE** Sauvignon Blanc North Coast Coastal 1994 • $5 • (12/15/95) • BB
86 **QUIVIRA** Sauvignon Blanc Dry Creek Valley 1994 • $10 • (06/15/96)
86 **SELENE** Sauvignon Blanc Carneros Napa Valley Hyde Vineyards 1993 • $18 • (08/31/95)
86 **SILVERADO** Sauvignon Blanc Napa Valley 1994 • $9.50 • (02/29/96)
86 **RODNEY STRONG** Sauvignon Blanc Northern Sonoma Charlotte's Home Vineyard 1995 • $10 • (06/15/96)
85 **ALDERBROOK** Sauvignon Blanc Dry Creek Valley 1994 • $8.50 • (08/31/95)
85 **BUTTONWOOD FARM** Sauvignon Blanc Santa Ynez Valley 1993 • $12 • (08/31/95)
85 **CHATEAU SOUVERAIN** Sauvignon Blanc Alexander Valley Barrel Fermented 1994 • $8 • (08/31/95)
85 **FLORA SPRINGS** Sauvignon Blanc Napa Valley 1993 • $8 • (08/31/95)
85 **FOPPIANO** Sauvignon Blanc Dry Creek Valley 1993 • $8.50 • (08/31/95)
85 **GEYSER PEAK** Sauvignon Blanc Sonoma County 1994 • $7.50 • (08/31/95)
85 **HAWK CREST** Sauvignon Blanc California 1994 • $8 • (02/29/96)

85 **HIDDEN CELLARS** Sauvignon Blanc Mendocino 1994 • $9 • (12/15/95)

85 **KENWOOD** Sauvignon Blanc Sonoma Valley Reserve 1994 • $15 • (12/15/95)

85 **LIPARITA** Sauvignon Blanc Howell Mountain 1994 • $14 • (10/31/95)

85 **MIRASSOU** Sauvignon Blanc California 1993 • $6 • (08/31/95)

85 **ROBERT MONDAVI** Fumé Blanc Napa Valley 1994 • $11 • (05/15/96)

85 **MOUNT KONOCTI** Fumé Blanc Lake County 1994 • $8 • (08/31/95)

85 **MURPHY-GOODE** Sauvignon Blanc Alexander Valley Reserve Fumé 1994 • $16 • (02/29/96)

85 **ROBERT PECOTA** Sauvignon Blanc Napa Valley 1994 • $7.50 • (08/31/95)

85 **QUIVIRA** Sauvignon Blanc Dry Creek Valley 1993 • $10 • (08/31/95)

85 **ROUND HILL** Fumé Blanc Napa Valley 1993 • $7 • (08/31/95)

85 **SEGHESIO** Sauvignon Blanc Sonoma County 1994 • $9 • (08/31/95)

85 **STERLING** Sauvignon Blanc Napa Valley 1994 • $9 • (03/31/96)

85 **VENTANA** Sauvignon Blanc Monterey 1994 • $9 • (05/31/96)

89 **KENDALL-JACKSON** Meritage Royale California 1994 • $15 • (07/31/95)

89 **VENEZIA** Bianco Nuovo Mondo Alexander Valley Meritage 1994 • $18 • (03/31/96)

88 **COSENTINO** The Novelist Napa Valley Meritage 1994 • $15 • (12/31/95)

88 **MURRIETA'S WELL** Vendimia Livermore Valley 1992 • $23 • (07/31/95)

87 **ALDERBROOK** Duet Dry Creek Valley 1992 • $11 • (08/31/95)

87 **BERINGER** Sauvignon Blanc-Sémillon Meritage Knights Valley 1993 • $9 • (08/31/95) • BB

87 **VICHON** Chevrignon Napa Valley 1994 • $NA • (02/29/96)

86 **BENZIGER** A Tribute Sonoma Mountain White 1992 • $16 • (08/31/95)

86 **CRESTON** Chevrier Blanc Paso Robles 1994 • $9 • (08/31/95)

86 **LAKEWOOD** Chevriot Clear Lake 1993 • $12 • (08/31/95)

86 **LYETH** Meritage White Sonoma County 1994 • $7.50 • (06/15/96)

CALIFORNIA SPARKLING WINE

91 **JORDAN** Sonoma County J 1990 • $23 • (11/30/95) • SS

91 **KRISTONE** Blanc de Noirs California 1991 • $60 • (11/30/95)

90 **DOMAINE CARNEROS** Brut Carneros Blanc de Blancs 1989 • $25 • (05/15/96)

90 **KRISTONE** Brut Rosé California 1991 • $60 • (11/30/95)

90 **ROEDERER ESTATE** Brut Anderson Valley L'Ermitage 1990 • $35 • (12/31/95)

89 **DOMAINE CARNEROS** Brut Carneros 1991 • $20 • (12/31/95)

89 **MUMM CUVEE NAPA** Brut Carneros Winery Lake 1990 • $18 • (11/30/95)

88 **S. ANDERSON** Brut Napa Valley 1990 • $23 • (11/30/95)

88 **S. ANDERSON** Blanc de Noirs Napa Valley 1991 • $23 • (12/31/95)

88 **HANDLEY** Blanc de Blancs Anderson Valley 1990 • $18 • (12/15/95)

88 **IRON HORSE** Brut Sonoma County Green Valley Late Disgorged 1989 • $45 • (12/31/95)

87 **HANDLEY** Brut Anderson Valley 1990 • $15 • (12/31/95)

87 **IRON HORSE** Wedding Cuvée Sonoma County Green Valley 1993 • $19 • (04/30/96)

87 **KRISTONE** Blanc de Blancs California 1991 • $60 • (11/30/95)

86 **S. ANDERSON** Rosé Napa Valley 1991 • $25 • (12/31/95)

85 **ROBERT HUNTER** Blanc de Noirs Sonoma Valley Brut de Noirs 1991 • $25 • (09/15/95)

The Main Listings

Wines by Country and Producer

This is the *Ultimate Guide*'s main listings section. Here you will find "nuts-and-bolts" information—producer, appellation, vintage, price, date of rating, and score—on nearly 40,000 wines reviewed by *Wine Spectator* during the last 12 years. Listings of the most recently tasted wines also contain descriptive notes that will help you get a sense of what the wine actually tastes like.

Turn the page for detailed information that will help you to understand and make use of our listings.

How to Use These Listings

The wine ratings contained in this guide are taken from the tasting results that have been published in *Wine Spectator* over the past decade. While the majority of the ratings in this book are quite recent, some ratings are not as current.

While we feel that these older ratings can be very useful in presenting a nearly complete vertical representation of a particular wine, we also feel the need to caution you to pay particular attention to the date on each of the ratings. This will tell you how current the rating is. Wines for which no issue date appears were tasted between April 15, 1994 and June 15, 1996.

In general, ratings and tasting notes included here are from *Wine Spectator*'s tasting panel. Other sources for the ratings are individual tasting reports by our senior editors, and tastings conducted by a senior editor as part of the research for one of our Wine Spectator Press books.

There is one other type of rating you will see in this book, primarily in the listings for red Bordeaux and California Cabernet. These are ratings based on barrel tastings. which are tastings conducted on wines before they have been bottled and released for sale. These are, by definition, very preliminary ratings and should be treated as such. Many things can happen to a wine between the time it is tasted in barrel and the time that you purchase it at your local store; wines can improve or decline during that time, and can show signs of poor shipping or storage conditions. Barrel-tasting ratings are indicated by the code (BT) and by a range of scores (e.g. 85-89).

Wine Spectator's 100-Point Scale

95-100—Classic; a great wine
90-94—Outstanding; superior character and style
80-89—Good to very good; wine with special qualities
70-79—Average; drinkable wine that may have minor flaws
60-69—Below average; drinkable but not recommended
50-59—Poor; undrinkable, not recommended

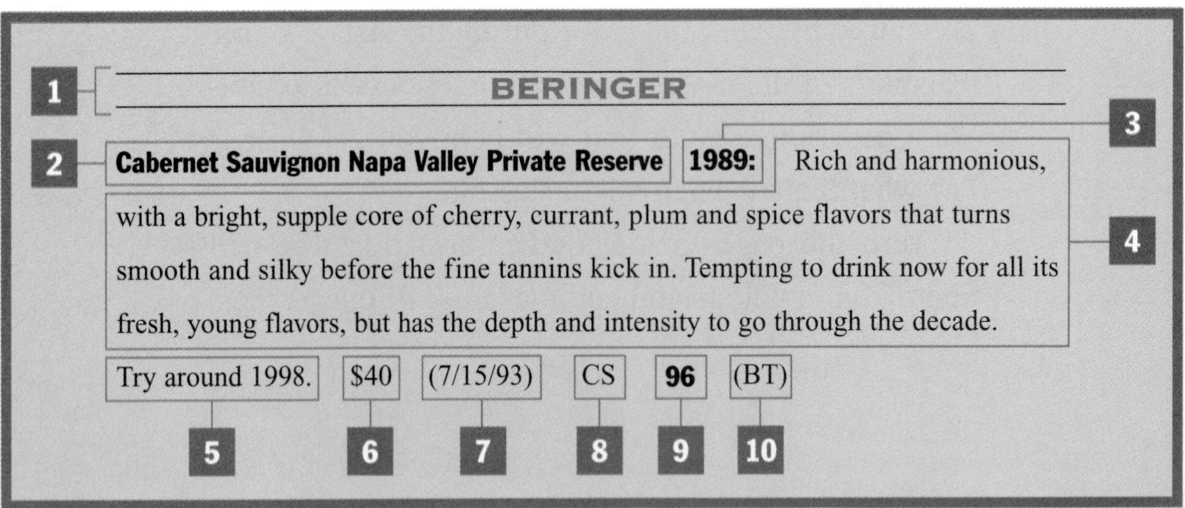

The Ratings: Piece by Piece

Because of the very large number of ratings presented here, each wine listing must be as brief as possible. Therefore, we have used abbreviations and shortcuts throughout this book. A key to these symbols can be found in the lower left-hand corner of every left-hand page in the main listings. At left is a typical wine listing and an explanation for each of the elements.

1. Producer's Name—The name of the winery or producer, set in capital letters to easily distinguish it from the rest of the wine's information.

Producers whose names are preceded by "Château," "Domaine," "Bodegas" and the like are listed by the name following these designations. For example, Château Woltner will be listed under "W" as "Woltner, Château."

Producers' names that include given names are listed alphabetically under the surname. For example, Robert Mondavi will be found under "M" as "Mondavi, Robert."

Producers' names that begin with English and foreign articles such as a, the, de, di, le, la, los, etc., are listed under the main word following the article. Thus, La Vieille Ferme is listed as "Vieille Ferme, La."

Producers' names that begin with "St." or "Ste." are alphabetized as though this word were spelled out. For example, "Saint Laurent, Château" follows "St.-Jovian."

2. Wine Type/Description—Contains the wine type and any varietal name, appellation, or other vineyard or special designation, such as Sonoma Valley or Cask 23.

3. Vintage—The year the wine was harvested and vinified.

4. Tasting Note—The tasting note for the wine, as published in *Wine Spectator*. These notes give the tasters' impressions of the wine, and thus present a more complete picture than the score alone.

5. Drinkability—Tasting notes may also include our estimate as to when a wine will be at its best.

6. Price Data—The wine's price information can come in three distinct forms:

—A single price, such as $37, signifies the estimated current retail price. These are drawn from many sources, including auctions, retailer advertisements and catalogs and wholesale price books, and as such are our "best educated guess." Prices may—and will—vary.

—$NA means that no price data was available; it occurs typically with older wines and very new ones.

—A price followed by the symbol Ⓐ is a recent average auction price.

7. Issue Date—The date of the issue of *Wine Spectator* in which the rating was first published. In general, the wines were tasted within two months prior to this date. Wines for which no issue date appears were tasted between April 15, 1994 and June 15, 1996.

8. Special Ratings—The special designations used here are:

SS (Spectator Selection) — *Wine Spectator*'s highest recommendations in a given issue. Not necessarily the highest-scoring wines, they are the wines we think represent the most outstanding values when quality is balanced against price.

CS (Cellar Selection) — The wines we believe are the best candidates for addition to your cellar. We believe these wines will improve most with bottle age, and show the greatest potential as collectibles.

BB (Best Buy) — Wines that the editors feel show outstanding quality at modest prices; because of their attractive prices, they tend to disappear from retail shelves quickly.

9. Score—This is the number, from the *Wine Spectator*'s 100-point scale, that represents the taster's evaluation of the wine's quality relative to other wines.

Ratings are based on immediate quality, as well as on how good a wine will be when it's at its peak, regardless of how soon that will be.

A range of scores (90-94, for example) indicates a preliminary rating. It is generally used in conjunction with a barrel tasting.

10. Barrel Tasting—The code (BT) appearing after and range of scores indicates a barrel tasting as described above.

Australia

With more than 750 wineries in production, Australia has become a formidable source of quality wine. Almost every major grape variety is cultivated here, and Australia's best wines compete with the elite of Bordeaux, Burgundy and California in price as well as quality.

Australian wines are stylistically similar to California's. Their flavors tend to be full and hearty, and new oak (often the vanilla-tasting American oak) is frequently employed in their production. Also as in California, there is an increasing concentration here on a few major red and white varietals. Cabernet Sauvignon and Chardonnay are extremely successful and are widely planted. The more traditional Shiraz (known as Syrah elsewhere) also thrives here, producing a rich wine that takes oak aging quite well. Sémillon, often blended with Chardonnay, shows unusual viscosity and freshness.

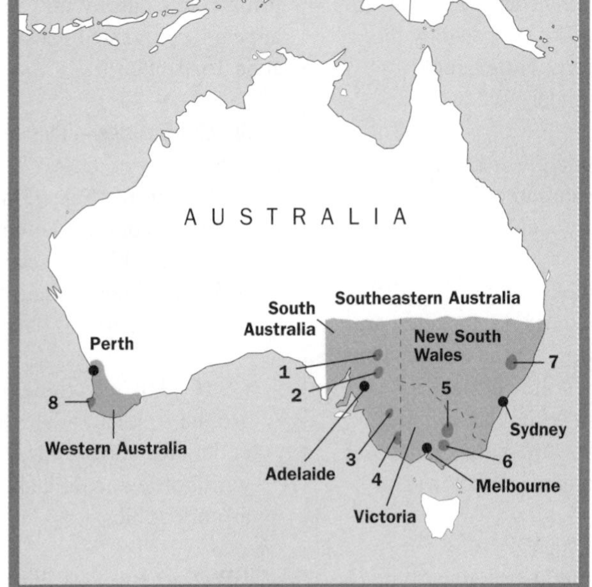

1. Clare
2. Barossa Valley
3. Padthaway
4. Coonawarra
5. Goulburn Valley
6. Yarra Valley
7. Hunter Valley
8. Margaret River

HISTORY OF AUSTRALIAN WINE PRODUCTION

The first vines arrived in Australia with the British Expeditionary Fleet in 1778. However, serious commercial wine production did not begin until the 1890s, in Southeastern Australia, where the vast majority of wine production still takes place. Most wineries were established as family enterprises. Many of these family names—for example, Tyrell's, Smith & Son and Campbells—remain important in the present-day Australian wine industry.

Before 1950, Australian wine production focused on fortified wines. A red wine boom in the 1960s was followed by a white wine boom in the 1980s. There was a rather sudden upswing in prices in the late 1980s that temporarily put a damper on the Australian wine boom, but prices have since stabilized and are now extremely fair.

AUSTRALIAN WINE REGIONS

Australia's chief wine regions are South Australia, New South Wales, and Victoria. Often wines from all three regions are blended and sold under the catch-all Southeastern Australia denomination. The only other significant wine region is Western Australia, located near Perth on the West Coast.

South Australia

More than 60 percent of the country's wine production come from the South Australia region, which includes the well-known Barossa Valley, located about 60 kilometers from Adelaide. Barossa is also the headquarters of many of the country's most famous wineries, including Penfolds, Seppelt, Peter Lehmann and Wolf Blass. South Australia is also the source of Penfolds Grange (formerly Grange Hermitage), generally regarded as Australia's greatest red wine. Made from almost 100 percent Shiraz and always aged in new American oak, it was created by the late Max Schubert, the legendary former head of Penfolds winemaking operations.

The chief grape varieties in South Australia are Shiraz and Grenache for reds, and Sémillon and Riesling for whites. However, Cabernet Sauvignon and Chardonnay are becoming increasingly important, particularly for export markets.

South Australia's finest Cabernet-based reds come from the Coonawarra district, which, like the Médoc of France and the Napa Valley, excels in producing an age-worthy, well-structured Cabernet Sauvignon. Although Coonawarra's climate is among the coolest in Australia, the key feature of its terroir is its unique soil, called terra rossa, which consists of a rich layer of rust-colored earth laid over a thick layer of limestone and clay. The cigar-shaped Coonawarra district, only a mile wide and seven miles long, is virtually the only place in Australia that contains significant acreage of this prized soil. Wynns and Bowen Estate are perhaps the most famous wineries located in Coonawarra, but many other wineries, such as Lindemans, Penfolds, Parker, Seppelt, and Rosemount, obtain considerable production from the region.

South Australia also boasts what many consider Australia's finest white wine district: Padthaway, which is located about 65 miles north of Coonawarra. Padthaway's Chardonnays are particularly distinguished, seeming to combine a California-like generosity with a European-style minerally austerity. The Clare region, north of Adelaide, has developed an excellent reputation for its Riesling and other German varietals.

Rosemount in the Upper Hunter Valley—known for its rich Chardonnays and Shiraz.

New South Wales

Although South Australia now outranks it in production, New South Wales was Australia's first important wine region; some of its vineyards date back to the 1820s. While Cabernet Sauvignon and Chardonnay have been extensively planted in New South Wales in recent decades, the traditional Shiraz and Sémillon remain the most distinctive wines of the region.

The Hunter Valley, about 100 miles north of Sydney, is the most important wine region of New South Wales. Major Hunter Valley wineries include Tyrell's, McWilliams, Wyndham Estate and Rothbury Estate, all of which have achieved international reputations.

Though not widely planted until the 1970s, a subregion called the Upper Hunter Valley—home of Rosemount winery—seems to have a special facility for producing Chardonnays and Shiraz with vigorous fruit and alcoholic richness.

Victoria

Victoria is not as well-known as the other major Australian wine regions, but its wines have great potential. Foremost among these regions is the cool Yarra Valley, which excels at Burgundian-style Pinot Noirs and Chardonnays. Yarra Valley wines often sell at top prices, reflecting the low yields and painstaking production methods typically maintained by the wineries there.

Victoria also excels in the production of sparkling wines, owing to a cool climate that allows the grapes to obtain excellent acidity along with concentrated fruit. Although some of the traditional Champagne grapes, such as Pinot Noir and Chardonnay, are cultivated here, the Sémillon is the dominant sparkling wine grape in Victoria. This variety lends Victoria's sparkling wines a unique herbal dimension that is quite appealing. Well-known sparkling wine producers in Victoria include Yellowglen and Seppelt.

Western Australia

Lying on the western coast near Perth, the Western Australia region is far removed geographically from the rest of Australian winemaking and it accounts for a relatively small percentage of total production. Located at its southwestern extreme is the Margaret River area, Western Australia's most prestigious wine producing area. With high natural acidity and firm tannins, Margaret River products are considered by many the most European-style wines of Australia. Leading Margaret River producers, which tend to be "boutique" wineries (meaning that their wines can be hard to find and expensive), include Leeuwin Estate and Vasse Felix.

AUSTRALIAN DESSERT WINES

Sweet dessert wines are an Australian specialty. Among the best known is the hazelnut-scented Yalumba Galway Pipe Port, which is similar to a Portuguese tawny, with a bit more almondy sweetness. Also well regarded is the pineapple- and butterscotch-scented Peter Lehmann Sémillon Sauternes, which has proven itself a genuine value through the years. Finally, the island of Tasmania, off the coast of Melbourne, specializes in late-harvest Riesling and Gewürztraminer, both of which combine excellent acidity with well-balanced sweetness.

ABADIA DEL ROBLE

Cabernet Sauvignon King Valley High Country 1992: Soft and gentle, with supple texture and spicy raspberry and plum flavors that have plenty of character and richness on the finish. Best from 1997-1998. • $NA • **88**

ADAMS, TIM

Riesling Clare Valley 1994: Crisp and bright, with nicely articulated apple and citrus flavors. Lively finish with a fruity, floral touch. Drinkable now. 2,000 cases made. • $15 • (06/30/95) • **86**

Sémillon Clare Valley 1994: Ripe and generous, flavors centered on pineapple, with a citrusy zing on the finish. Drinkable now. 4,000 cases made. • $17 • (06/30/95) • **87**

Sémillon Clare Valley 1993: Soft and broad, offering delicious pear and slightly lanolin-scented spice flavors. Drinkable now. 3,500 cases made. • $15 • (06/30/95) • **84**

Shiraz Clare Valley 1992: Strong menthol aromas and flavors run through this medium-weight, tasty red. Has a lot of personality, but not for everyone. 3,000 cases made. • $16 • (11/15/95) • **83**

ALTA

Sauvignon Blanc Victoria 1994: Bright and refreshing, with straightforward orange, apple, and lime flavors mingling on the finish. Drinkable now. 2,000 cases made. • $14 • (06/30/95) • **85**

ANGAS

Brut Australia NV • $8 • (12/31/87) • **76**

Brut Rosé Australia NV • $8 • (12/31/87) • **78**

ARROWFIELD

Cabernet Merlot Australia 1990 • $10 • (03/31/93) • **84**

Cabernet Merlot South Eastern Australia 1993: Lean, herbal and smooth-textured, with eucalyptus overtones. Drinkable now. 10,295 cases made. • $11 • (06/30/95) • **81**

Cabernet Merlot South Eastern Australia 1991: Lean and spicy, a little tannic, but lively enough to suggest that the currant and berry flavors will emerge with time. Drinkable now. 4,500 cases made. • $10 • (08/31/94) • **83**

Cabernet Sauvignon Australia Show Reserve 1990 • $15 • (11/30/92) • **84**

Cabernet Sauvignon Hunter Valley Show Reserve 1991: A little tough and rough in texture, but the aromas spread out their minty currant and raspberry flavors nicely and the fruit lingers on the finish. Try now. 2,500 cases made. • $18 • (07/31/94) • **86**

Cabernet Sauvignon McLaren Vale Show Reserve 1992: Crisp, focused, solid, basic berry and currant flavors and a touch of cedar. Tannic enough to want until 1999 to 2001. 2,500 cases made. • $22 • (04/30/96) • **87**

Chardonnay Australia 1991 • $10 • (03/31/93) • **80**

Chardonnay Australia Show Reserve 1991 • $15 • (03/15/93) • **84**

Chardonnay Hunter Valley Show Reserve 1992: Spicy, toasty, buttery flavors are beautifully focused and elegant, although they tend to overshadow the fruit. A tasting wine, good now. 2,500 cases made. • $18 • (07/31/94) • **86**

Chardonnay South Eastern Australia 1994: Simple, straightforward and engagingly fruity, echoing apple and spice. Drinkable now. 10,650 cases made. • $11 • (06/30/95) • **81**

Chardonnay South Eastern Australia 1992: Crisp and spicy, a floral wine with narrowly focused pear and caramel flavors. 5,000 cases made. • $10 • (07/31/94) • **85**

Chardonnay South Eastern Australia 1991 • $10 • (03/31/93) • **75**

Key: SS—Spectator Selection. CS—Cellar Selection. BB—Best Buy. $NA—Price not available. (BT)—Barrel tasting. Ⓐ—Auction Price.
Dates in parentheses represent the issues in which the ratings were published.

Chardonnay South Eastern Australia Show Reserve 1994: Smooth and spicy, a nice mouthful of racy citrus and clove flavors, finishing fresh. 3,000 cases made. • $22 • (04/30/96) • **88**

Chardonnay South Eastern Australia Show Reserve 1993: Supple, round and open-textured, a smooth, polished wine that glows with peach and pear flavors, hinting at vanilla on the finish. Drink now. 2,500 cases made. • $20 • (05/15/95) • **90**

Gewürztraminer South Eastern Australia Late Harvest 1993: Very ripe, unctuously sweet, sporting generous apricot, vanilla and honey flavors. Has some astringency on the finish that actually helps makes it feel more balanced. Drinkable now. 550 cases made. • $11 • (05/15/95) • **88**

Rhine Riesling Late Harvest Cowra Show Reserve 1993: Bright gold in color, deeply spicy and resiny on the nose, rich with nectarine flavor and nicely honeyed right through the finish. Delicious now. 1,000 cases made. • $22 • (05/15/96) • **90**

Sémillon Chardonnay Hunter Valley 1993: Bright and fruity, best while it's fresh-tasting, showing off its simple pear and grapefruit flavors. • $8 • (09/30/94) • **81**

Sémillon South Eastern Australia Show Reserve 1993: Light and pleasantly spicy, a decadent earthy, figgy note runs through the soft finish that shows tobacco and tea. Drinkable now. 1,925 cases made. • $20 • (06/30/95) • **86**

Shiraz Australia Show Reserve 1990 • $15 • (11/30/92) • **85**

Shiraz Cabernet Australia 1990 • $10 • (11/30/92) • **87**

Shiraz Hunter Valley Show Reserve 1991: Ripe and generous, solidly built, with layers of plum, blackberry and spice flavors that hint at coffee on the zippy finish. Drinkable now, fine through 1998. 2,500 cases made. • $18 • (09/30/94) • **89**

Shiraz South Eastern Australia 1993: Smooth and inviting, polished and well mannered, revealing a leathery edge to the plum and spice flavors. Drinkable now. 600 cases made. • $11 • (05/15/95) • **84**

Shiraz South Eastern Australia 1991: Firm in texture, with a buttery edge to the modest spice and plum flavors. Drinkable now. 3,000 cases made. • $10 • (09/30/94) • **82**

Shiraz South Eastern Australia Show Reserve 1992: Smooth and ripe, loaded with smoky blackberry and spice flavors that keep echoing on the bright finish. Drinkable now. 1,120 cases made. • $20 • (05/15/95) • **88**

ARUNDA

Cabernet Shiraz South Eastern Australia 1990 • $6 • (05/31/93) • **81**

ASHWOOD

Cabernet Sauvignon Riverina 1991 • $10 • (07/15/93) • **84**

Cabernet Sauvignon Riverland 1992: Light and supple, a tinge of beet flavor sneaking in with the modest plum and berry. Drinkable now. 2,000 cases made. • $9 • (06/30/95) • **83**

Chardonnay Riverina 1992 • $7 • (07/15/93) • **81**

Chardonnay South Australia Riverland 1992: Round and generous, a spicy Chardonnay with mouth-filling pineapple and pear flavors lurking underneath. Drinkable now. 3,000 cases made. • $10 • (09/30/94) • **84**

River Willow Australia 1992 • $7 • (04/30/94) • **79**

River Willow Red Australia 1991 • $7 • (05/31/93) • **85**

River Willow White Riverland 1993: Soft, vague and undefined, finishing sweet and earthy. 1,500 cases made. • $7 • (06/30/95) • **73**

Sémillon Goulburn Valley 1992 • $9 • (12/31/93) • **74**

Sémillon-Sauvignon Blanc Riverland 1994: Soft and floral, a little sweet, offering some nice pineapple notes on the finish. 1,000 cases made. • $8 • (06/30/95) • **80**

Shiraz Riverland 1993: Firm and somewhat chewy, offering a nice core of red cherry and berry flavor. Finishes slightly tannic. Best in 1998. 2,000 cases made. • $9 • (03/31/96) • **83**

Shiraz Riverland 1992: Smooth, elegant and almost refined, unusual for a Shiraz, showing somewhat gamy prune and spice flavors. Drinkable now. 2,000 cases made. • $9 • (06/30/95) • **83**

BALDIVIS ESTATE

Cabernet Sauvignon Merlot Western Australia 1991 • $9 • (12/15/93) • **84**
Cabernet Sauvignon Merlot Western Australia 1990 • $9 • (06/30/93) • **80**
Chardonnay Australia 1991 • $10 • (03/31/93) • **73**
Chardonnay Western Australia 1992 • $10 • (10/31/93) • **78**

BANNOCKBURN

Pinot Noir Geelong 1990 • $NA • (06/30/93) • **87**
Pinot Noir Geelong 1986 • $26 • (01/31/90) • **73**
Pinot Noir Geelong 1985 • $17 • (03/15/88) • **74**
Shiraz Geelong 1984 • $13 • (10/31/89) • **81**

BAROSSA VALLEY

Cabernet Sauvignon South Australia 1987 • $11 • (01/31/90) • **83**
Shiraz Cabernet Sauvignon Barossa Valley 1985 • $8 • (09/30/89) BB • **86**

BARRAMUNDI

Australia NV • $7 • (05/31/93) • **81**

BARRIER REEF

Cabernet Sauvignon South Eastern Australia 1992: Light and supple, offering straightforward blackberry and vanilla flavors that maintain spiciness on the finish. Drinkable now. 8,000 cases made. • $8 • (11/30/95) • **85**
Cabernet Shiraz South Eastern Australia 1991 • $7 • (06/30/93) • **76**
Chardonnay South Eastern Australia 1993: Ripe, broad and generous with its pear and pineapple notes, finishing supple and a little spicy. 8,000 cases made. • $8 • (12/31/95) • **85**
Chardonnay South Eastern Australia 1991 • $7 • (08/31/92) • **82**
Sauvignon Blanc South Eastern Australia 1993: Ripe and spicy, vanilla-oak flavors weaving through the green apple and spice. 5,000 cases made. • $7 BB • **83**

BARWANG

Cabernet Sauvignon Australia 1992: Solid, chunky Cabernet fruit bounces through this chewy, full-bodied wine, centered around plum and toast aromas and flavors that keep reverberating on the finish. A little on the alcoholic side, but drinkable now. • $18 • (09/30/94) • **89**
Cabernet Sauvignon New South Wales 1994: Ripe in flavor, focused black currant, blackberry, anise and vanilla notes playing generously across the palate and finishing with a touch of tannin that should resolve by around 1998. 4,200 cases made. • $16 • (04/30/96) • **88**
Cabernet Sauvignon New South Wales 1993: Firm and chewy, packing in some ripe currant and blackberry flavors between the layers of minty, spicy tannins. Best in 1998. 2,500 cases made. • $18 • (10/15/95) • **85**
Chardonnay Australia 1993: Bright and flavorful, a sappy white with a nice shot of melon and grapefruit on the palate. Drinkable now. • $18 • (09/30/94) • **83**
Chardonnay New South Wales 1995: Crisp, lively, very distinctive lime and lemon flavors that never smooth out. May be better in 1997. 4,000 cases made. • $16 • (04/30/96) • **81**
Chardonnay New South Wales 1994: Soft and somewhat grassy, a definite green edge running through the modest fruit in this distinctive Chardonnay. Drinkable now. 2,500 cases made. • $18 • (09/30/95) • **86**
Shiraz Australia 1991: Ripe enough to cut through a layer of tannins, showing some nice plum and pepper flavors on the finish. Drinkable now. • $18 • (09/30/94) • **84**
Shiraz New South Wales 1994: Ripe and round, generous with its plum and leather flavors, hinting at spice on the smooth finish. 3,500 cases made. • $16 • (04/30/96) • **86**
Shiraz New South Wales 1992: Lean and crisp, edging into tartness, but with ripe plum and dried cherry flavors that linger on the finish. Best from 1997. 2,500 cases made. • $18 • (11/15/95) • **85**

BERRI

Cabernet Sauvignon Barossa Valley 1985 • $7 • (04/30/88) • **76**
Cabernet Shiraz Australia 1985 • $10 • (07/01/87) • **89**
Shiraz Barossa Valley 1985 • $9 • (02/15/88) • **85**
Shiraz Cabernet South Australia Vintage Selection 1986 • $9 • (03/15/88) • **80**

BLACK MARLIN

South Eastern Australia 1992: Smooth and refreshing, with a nice grapefruit edge to the pear and vanilla flavors that gain some zip on the finish. • $8 • (07/31/94) • **83**
South Eastern Australia 1991 • $7 • (04/30/94) • **81**

BLACK OPAL

Cabernet Merlot South Australia Reserve 1994: Strives for elegance, packing some attractive berry flavors on a lean frame and finishing austere. May be better in 1999. • $14 • (04/30/96) • **80**
Cabernet Merlot South Eastern Australia 1994: Earthy forest-floor, pickle-barrel notes pop up first, offering just enough blackberry to strike a balance on the finish. Seems too tough and acidic for the flavor profile. Try in 2000 or 2001. • $9 • (04/30/96) • **83**
Cabernet Merlot South Eastern Australia 1992 • $10 • (04/30/94) • **81**
Cabernet Merlot South Eastern Australia 1990 • $9 • (04/15/93) BB • **87**
Cabernet Merlot South Eastern Australia 1989 • $9 • (11/30/92) • **82**
Cabernet Sauvignon Hunter Valley 1985 • $8 • (07/15/88) BB • **81**
Cabernet Sauvignon South Eastern Australia 1994: Crisp and fruity, nicely balanced to show off its strawberry and currant flavors without a load of tannins. Drinkable now, but better in 1997. • $9 • (04/30/96) • **85**
Cabernet Sauvignon South Eastern Australia 1992 • $10 • (04/30/94) • **83**
Cabernet Sauvignon South Eastern Australia 1989 • $9 • (11/30/92) • **78**
Cabernet Sauvignon South Eastern Australia 1987 • $8 • (02/28/90) BB • **85**
Chardonnay South Australia Reserve 1995: Smooth and beautifully integrated, cascading its pear, hazelnut, vanilla and peach flavors through a silky texture to a long finish. Drinkable now. • $14 • (04/30/96) • **88**
Chardonnay South Eastern Australia 1995: Smooth and creamy, soft, offering pleasant peach flavors. Drinkable now. • $9 • (04/30/96) • **83**
Chardonnay South Eastern Australia 1993: Soft, almost watery, leaving the spicy fruit high and dry. Drinkable now. Tasted twice with consistent results. • $10 • (09/30/94) • **75**
Chardonnay South Eastern Australia 1992 • $9 • (07/15/93) • **82**
Chardonnay South Eastern Australia 1991 • $9 • (11/15/92) BB • **86**
Shiraz South Eastern Australia 1994: Firm and a little chewy, somewhat shy on the nose but showing pretty plum and floral flavors as aftertaste. Best in 1998. • $9 • (04/30/96) • **82**
Shiraz South Eastern Australia 1991 • $10 • (03/31/94) • **83**
Shiraz South Eastern Australia 1990 • $8 • (11/30/92) • **80**

BLACK SILK

South Australia 1993: Soft, a little watery, but showing some nice fig and herbal flavors. Drinkable now. • $7 • (04/30/94) • **78**

BLASS, WOLF

Cabernet Blend South Australia Black Label 1986 • $26 • (04/30/94) • **87**
Cabernet Merlot South Australia Black Label 1983 • $25 • (04/30/89) • **77**
Cabernet Sauvignon Shiraz Merlot South Australia Black Label 1986 • $25 • (05/31/93) • **90**
Cabernet Sauvignon Shiraz South Australia Black Label 1987: Showing the mature flavors you'd expect at this age. The minty chocolate and currant notes are appealing, but it's also still quite tannic. Best from now to 2002. • $26 • (08/31/94) • **87**
Cabernet Sauvignon South Australia President's Selection 1993: Bright and pretty and nicely focused with its berry, vanilla and spice flavors, finishing smooth and generous. 5,000 cases made. • $16 • (06/15/96) • **87**

Cabernet Sauvignon South Australia President's Selection 1989: Lean and minty, with firm, drying tannins. This is best served alongside food to take away the austere edges. • $15 • (08/31/94) • **83**

Cabernet Sauvignon South Australia President's Selection 1987 • $15 • (05/31/93) • **85**

Cabernet Sauvignon South Australia President's Selection 1986 • $18 • (03/15/92) • **78**

Cabernet Sauvignon South Australia President's Selection 1983 • $14 • (04/30/88) • **76**

Cabernet Sauvignon South Australia Yellow Label 1994: Youthful, flavorful, dripping with blackberry, tar and vanilla flavors that linger on the solid finish. Try in 1998. 15,000 cases made. • $11 • (06/15/96) • **86**

Cabernet Sauvignon South Australia Yellow Label 1992: Earthy and tarry at first, but the ripe blackberry and black cherry flavors come through on the finish in this broad, generous red. Drinkable now. • $10 • (08/31/94) • **85**

Cabernet Sauvignon South Australia Yellow Label 1990 • $10 • (05/31/93) • **86**

Cabernet Sauvignon South Australia Yellow Label 1989 • $10 • (06/30/93) • **81**

Cabernet Sauvignon South Australia Yellow Label 1988 • $10 • (03/15/92) • **88**

Cabernet Sauvignon South Australia Yellow Label 1984 • $10 • (04/30/89) • **78**

Cabernet Sauvignon South Australia Yellow Label 1983 • $9 • (12/15/87) • **86**

Cabernet Shiraz Australia Black Label 1980 • $18 • (07/01/87) • **89**

Cabernet Shiraz Australia Yellow Label 1983 • $8 • (07/01/87) • **87**

Cabernet Shiraz Clare Barossa Valleys Black Label 1982 • $25 • (04/15/88) • **88**

Cabernet Shiraz Langhorne Creek 1981 • $18 • (07/01/87) • **90**

Chardonnay South Australia 1995: Bright with fruit and supple in texture, this harmonious white has a generous dose of peach and pear flavors and a hint of honey on the finish. 15,000 cases made. • $11 • (05/31/96) • **87**

Chardonnay South Australia Barrel Fermented 1993: Soft, even a little sweet, with a nice range of buttery apple and spice flavors. • $10 • (09/30/94) • **82**

Chardonnay South Australia Barrel Fermented 1992 • $10 • (04/30/93) • **86**

Chardonnay South Australia Bilyara Cellars President's Selection 1994: Ripe, supple and complex, with caramel and spice overtones to the pear, pineapple and citrus flavors. It extends into a beautifully balanced, polished finish. Drinkable now, but it should improve through 1997. 1,000 cases made. • $13 • (03/31/95) • **91**

Chardonnay South Australia President's Selection 1995: A bright and fresh mouthful of green apple and spice flavors linger right on through the finish. Delicious now. 7,000 cases made. • $14 • (05/31/96) • **85**

Shiraz South Australia President's Selection 1990: Warm, round and spicy, plummy, with nice overlays of nutmeg, cedar and tar, finishing with generosity and polish. Drinkable now. • $13 • (09/30/94) • **86**

Shiraz South Australia President's Selection 1988 • $15 • (05/31/93) • **85**

BLEASDALE

Cabernet Sauvignon Australia Longhorne Creek 1990: Herbal, slightly gamy flavors add an extra dimension to the soft prune and black cherry flavors. Drinkable now, but may be even better in 1997. 3,100 cases made. • $8 • (06/30/95) BB • **86**

Longhorne Creek White Burgundy Australia 1994: Broad in texture, with a floral, leafy strand of flavor that opens up on the citrusy finish. Lively and drinkable now. 2,700 cases made. • $7 • (04/15/95) • **84**

Malbec Langhorne Creek 1992: Ripe and gamy flavors compete for attention in this light-textured, full flavored wine. 1,600 cases made. • $8 • (03/31/96) • **80**

Shiraz Australia Longhorne Creek 1992: Broad and supple. It wraps gamy plum and blackberry flavors into a chewy package that promises fullest pleasure in 1997 or 1998. 2,100 cases made. • $7 • (05/15/95) BB • **87**

Shiraz-Cabernet Sauvignon Langhorne Creek 1992: Tight and spicy, a lively mouthful of peppery, slightly minty berry flavor. Drinkable now. 1,000 cases made. • $8 • (03/31/96) • **87**

Shiraz Cabernet Sauvignon Langhorne Creek 1989 • $7 • (05/31/93) • **78**

Shiraz Langhorne Creek 1993: Firm, focused and lively with peppery plum flavors that linger nicely through the modestly tannic finish. Give it until 1998. 2,700 cases made. • $8 • (03/31/96) • **87**

Shiraz Langhorne Creek 1987 • $7 • (05/31/93) • **71**

White Burgundy Langhorne Creek 1995: Simple, bright, broad and fruity, a nice mouthful of peach, pear and spice flavors that persist on the sturdy finish. 3,000 cases made. • $8 • (03/31/96) • **85**

BLUE PYRENEES

Cabernet Sauvignon Australia 1982 • $20 • (05/31/87) • **89**

BOWEN ESTATE

Cabernet Sauvignon Coonawarra 1992: Smooth and focused, lively acidity picking up currant, berry and bay leaf flavors, hinting at chocolate on the aftertaste. Has style and power to age through at least 2000. 2,500 cases made. • $22 • (10/31/95) • **89**

Red Coonawarra 1992: Firm in texture, sporting an herbal edge and packed with currant, raspberry and sweet vanilla flavors that persist through a solid finish. Best in 1998. 2,500 cases made. • $22 • (10/31/95) • **89**

BRAND'S LAIRA

Cabernet Sauvignon Coonawarra 1991: Smooth and spicy, a lean red with plum, vanilla and nutmeg flavors. Drinkable now. 5,000 cases made. • $13 • (09/30/94) • **84**

Cabernet Sauvignon Coonawarra Laira 1993: Soft, ripe and generous, brimming with berry and plum flavors that extend into a warm and welcoming finish. Good now. 3,000 cases made. • $15 • (06/30/95) • **87**

Chardonnay Coonawarra 1994: Smooth, spicy and elegant, boasting tiers of hazelnut, pear and toast flavors that linger enticingly on the silky finish. Drinkable now, best in 1997. 3,000 cases made. • $15 • (04/30/96) • **91**

Chardonnay Coonawarra 1991 • $13 • (10/31/93) • **84**

Chardonnay Coonawarra Laira 1993: Geared to the fruity side, with pear and citrus notes ringing on the generous finish. Drinkable now. 3,000 cases made. • $15 • (04/15/95) • **83**

Shiraz Coonawarra 1994: Beautifully proportioned, harmonious, shining its brilliant berry and red cherry flavors in a clear beam through the long, elegant finish. Not a powerhouse but a rich, gentle red that has remarkable length. Approachable now, best from 1998 to 2000. 5,000 cases made. • $15 • (04/30/96) • **90**

Shiraz Coonawarra 1992: Crisp and flavorful, with smoky black cherry flavors up front and modest tannins. Drinkable now. 3,000 cases made. • $15 • (06/30/95) • **84**

Shiraz Coonawarra 1990 • $13 • (10/31/93) • **86**

BRIDGEWATER MILL

Shiraz McLaren Vale Millstone 1993: Fresh, rich and chocolaty, with highly focused berry flavor at the core and spicy accents right through the finish. A bright and round wine of good complexity. 4,000 cases made. • $15 • (05/31/96) • **88**

BROKE ESTATE

Cabernet Sauvignon-Franc Hunter Valley 1993: Earthy, vegetal flavors permeate this soft, slightly chewy Cabernet blend. 5,000 cases made. • $20 • (06/30/95) • **78**

Chardonnay Hunter Valley 1993: Ripe and golden, a toasty tasting, smooth-textured white that finally settles into an oaky finish. Drinkable now. • $20 • (04/30/95) • **86**

Key: SS—Spectator Selection. CS—Cellar Selection. BB—Best Buy. $NA—Price not available. (BT)—Barrel tasting. Ⓐ—Auction Price.
Dates in parentheses represent the issues in which the ratings were published.

BROKENWOOD

Cabernet Sauvignon South Eastern Australia 1990 • $15 • (05/15/94) • **82**
Shiraz South Eastern Australia 1990 • $15 • (10/31/93) • **86**

BROWN BROTHERS

Cabernet Sauvignon King Valley Family Selection 1991: Soft and fruity, offering plenty of ripe cherry and currant flavor on a slightly watery structure. Tasty to drink soon. • $10 • (06/30/94) • **80**
Cabernet Sauvignon Victoria 1987 • $9 • (07/15/90) • **82**
Cabernet Sauvignon Victoria 1985 • $7 • (05/15/89) • **76**
Cabernet Sauvignon Victoria Family Selection Reserve 1988: Displays aromas and flavors of mature Cabernet-meaty plum, currant, prune and spice-wrapped in an extra layer of astringency. Substantial tannins; try in 1998 or 2000. • $17 • **88**
Cabernet Sauvignon Victoria Reserve 1987 • $12 • (09/15/90) • **83**
Cabernet Sauvignon Victoria St.-George Vineyard 1984 • $8 • (05/31/87) • **86**
Chardonnay King Valley Family Selection 1992: Appealing, soft and supple, with generous peach and pear flavor that dances through the finish. • $12 • (07/31/94) • **85**
Chardonnay King Valley Limited Production Family Selection 1992: Lean and harmonious, gently flavorful, ringing with pear, apple and spice, all converging nicely on the finish. Drinkable now. • $12 • (12/15/94) • **87**
Everton Family Selection King Valley 1992: Ripe and generous in flavor, firm and almost aristocratic in structure. This has balanced dark cherry and meaty flavors, should develop well past 2000. • $9 • (06/30/95) • **85**
Everton Family Selection Victoria 1990: Lean and supple, strongly herbal in flavor, with a strong smoky edge to the modest Cabernet flavors. Drink now. • $7 • (03/31/95) • **81**
Muscat of Alexandria Victoria Lexia 1987 • $8 • (07/31/90) • **73**
Muscat of Alexandria Victoria Lexia 1986 • $8 • (05/15/89) • **77**
Muscat Victoria Lexia Family Selection 1993: Soft, sweet and appealing, offering honey, litchi and pineapple flavors that spread out nicely on the finish. Drink now. • $9 • (05/15/95) • **87**
Pinot Noir Victoria 1983 • $9 • (07/01/87) • **83**
Port Victoria 1987 • $13 • (07/31/90) • **84**
Port Victoria Family Selection Wood Matured Reserve NV: Smooth and spicy like a tawny. Opens up to a remarkable range of spice, toast and raisin flavors that linger on the balanced finish. • $8 • (03/31/95) BB • **86**
Sauvignon Blanc King Valley Family Selection 1993: A zinger. Strong herbal flavors pervade this crisp, lemony white. Definitely a Sauvignon character. • $10 • (01/31/95) • **83**
Shiraz Australia 1983 • $9 • (07/15/87) • **92**
Shiraz Cabernet Sauvignon Victoria 1988 • $9 • (05/31/93) • **83**
Shiraz King Valley Family Selection 1991: Light and fruity, generous with its plummy flavors, shaded nicely with cedar and spice overtones. Drinkable now. • $9 • (09/30/94) • **85**
Shiraz Mondeuse Cabernet Sauvignon Australia 1983 • $10 • (07/01/87) • **87**
Shiraz Victoria 1990 • $9 • (05/31/93) • **82**
Shiraz Victoria 1986 • $8 • (07/15/90) • **85**
Shiraz Victoria 1985 • $7 • (05/15/89) BB • **83**
Tarrango Victoria 1993: Bright and fruity, a light, simple, Beaujolais-like red with appealing grapey flavors. Serve cool. Drinkable now. • $8 • (01/31/95) • **83**

CAMPBELLS

Muscat Rutherglen Old NV • $15 • (07/01/87) • **92**
Tokay Rutherglen Old NV • $15 • (07/01/87) • **91**

CAPE MENTELLE

Cabernet Sauvignon 1987 • $18 • (03/15/92) • **69**
Cabernet Sauvignon Margaret River 1992: Earthy, heavily floral flavors characterize this sturdy wine. Not too tannic, but dense enough to want until 1999 or 2000. • $20 • (06/15/96) • **83**
Cabernet Sauvignon Margaret River 1991: Earthy, mildewy flavors rob this red of its charm, killing the fruit. Could be corky. • $19 • (10/31/95) • **77**
Cabernet Sauvignon Margaret River 1988 • $19 • (06/30/92) • **79**
Cabernet Sauvignon Western Australia 1987 • $19 • (03/31/91) • **84**
Chardonnay Margaret River 1993: Ripe and focused, a note of honey shading the pear and fresh-cut apple flavors. Long and lively. Drinkable now. • $19 • (06/30/95) • **87**
Shiraz Margaret River 1992: Distinctive flavors are reminiscent of berries and beets in this lively, generous, youthful and raw red. Give it until 1997 or 1998. • $15 • (10/31/95) • **85**
Shiraz Margeret River 1989 • $15 • (05/31/92) • **84**
Shiraz Margaret River 1988 • $15 • (02/28/91) • **88**

CAPEL VALE

Chardonnay Western Australia 1995: Bright and focused, generous with its citrusy pear and passion fruit flavors, with just a touch of oak to add some spice. Tasty now but better in 1997. 500 cases imported. • $14 • (03/31/96) • **87**
Chardonnay Western Australia 1992: An earthy style with a juniper edge to the pear and spice flavors. Misses the mark for Chardonnay. • $13 • (09/30/94) • **74**
Shiraz Western Australia 1994: Beautifully proportioned plum, berry and toast flavors linger nicely on a lean frame, bordering on austere. May be best from 1997. 500 cases made. • $14 • (03/31/96) • **84**
Shiraz Western Australia 1990 • $11 • (05/31/93) • **70**

CASSEGRAIN

Cabernet Sauvignon Hunter Valley Vintage Selection 1990: Smooth and polished, a spicy, toasty overlay adding an extra dimension to the tarry plum and blackberry flavors. Drinkable now, might improve through 1997. 2,000 cases made. • $16 • (06/30/94) • **87**
Cabernet Sauvignon Merlot South Eastern Australia 1988 • $15 • (08/31/92) • **86**
Cabernet Sauvignon Pokolbin 1986 • $18 • (03/31/91) • **83**
Cabernet Sauvignon Shiraz Merlot South Eastern Australia 1991 • $8 • (11/30/93) • **77**
Cabernet Shiraz Merlot South Eastern Australia 1988 • $8 • (09/30/91) • **69**
Chambourcin New South Wales 1992 • $12 • (04/30/94) • **83**
Chambourcin South Eastern Australia 1990 • $12 • (02/15/92) • **77**
Chardonnay Hastings Valley 1994: Light and lively, with an apple and grapefruit character that keeps bouncing through the finish. Drinkable now. 2,000 cases made. • $16 • (04/15/95) • **86**
Chardonnay Hastings Valley 1993: A ripe and generous Australian Chardonnay, with distinctive fruit character. Balances nectarine, pear and apricot flavors, with a touch of smoke and spice on the round finish. Delicious now, should be fine through 1997. 1,500 cases made. • $16 • (01/31/95) SS • **91**
Chardonnay Hunter River Valley Black Label 1991 • $16 • (04/15/94) • **85**
Chardonnay South Eastern Australia 1991 • $11 • (03/31/93) • **84**
Pinot Noir New South Wales Morrillon Vineyard 1988 • $20 • (02/29/92) • **80**
Sémillon New South Wales Black Label 1993: Ripe and generous, with a mineral edge to the pineapple and fig that keep glowing on the finish. Drinkable now. 1,500 cases made. • $16 • (06/30/95) • **85**
Shiraz Hastings Valley 1993: Firm and a little chewy in texture, with plenty of plum and berry flavors to keep it fresh and lively. Drinkable now. 2,000 cases made. • $16 • (03/31/95) • **88**
Shiraz Hunter Valley Foundation 1989 • $11 • (05/31/93) • **75**
Shiraz Hunter Valley Vintage Selection 1983 • $18 • (05/31/93) • **72**
Shiraz New South Wales Black Label 1993: Ripe and definitely gamy, a pleasant combination of black cherry, berry and wild flavors persist on the finish. Drinkable now. 1,500 cases made. • $16 • (03/31/95) • **86**
Shiraz Pokolbin Leonard Select Vineyard 1987 • $20 • (03/15/91) • **87**
Shiraz South Eastern Australia Black Label 1989 • $16 • (03/31/94) • **82**
Shiraz South Eastern Australia 1988 • $13 • (02/15/92) • **77**

CEDAR CREEK

Cabernet Sauvignon South Eastern Australia Bin 99 1994: Herbal, earthy, floral flavors predominate in this lean, hard-edged red. 10,000 cases made. • $11 • (04/30/96) • **72**

Cabernet Sauvignon South Eastern Australia Bin 99 1992: Light and earthy, a lean Cabernet with simple flavors. 30,000 cases made. • $6 • (09/30/94) • **78**

Cabernet Sauvignon South Eastern Australia Bin 99 1990 • $6 • (03/31/93) BB • **82**

Chardonnay South Eastern Australia Bin 33 1995: Light and appealing, with simple citrusy flavors. Ready now. 20,000 cases made. • $7 • (03/31/96) • **80**

Chardonnay South Eastern Australia Bin 33 1993: Simple and fruity, a soft white with modest flavors. Drinkable now, while it's fresh. 60,000 cases made. • $6 • (09/30/94) • **77**

Chardonnay South Eastern Australia Bin 33 1990 • $6 •(05/31/92) BB • **85**

Sémillon Blend South Eastern Australia Bin 11 1994: Simple and bright, tasty for its citrusy apple flavors. 70,000 cases made. • $6 • (03/31/96) • **81**

Shiraz Cabernet South Eastern Australia Bin 21 1995: This is an odd duck, considering its earthy, floral flavors. Finishes a little sour, too. 20,000 cases made. • $10 • (04/30/96) • **75**

Shiraz Cabernet South Eastern Australia Bin 21 1991: Lean and spicy, with earthy flavors and a chewy texture. Drinkable now. 20,000 cases made. • $5 • (09/30/94) • **79**

CHITTERING

Cabernet Sauvignon Merlot Western Australia 1988 • $18 • (09/30/91) • **79**

CLANCY'S GOLD PREFERENCE

Red Barossa Valley Gold Preference 1992: Firm and chewy at first, it softens on the finish as the plummy, spicy flavors emerge. Nicely done. Approachable now, best in 1998. 3,000 cases made. • $16 • (04/30/96) • **86**

CLYDE PARK

Cabernet Sauvignon Geelong 1984 • $15 • (03/15/88) • **79**

COCKATOO RIDGE

Cabernet Blend South Eastern Australia 1994: Light and silky, offering a nice range of currant, herb and spice flavors that echo gently on the finish. 10,000 cases made. • $9 • (03/31/96) • **82**

Cabernet Merlot South Eastern Australia 1993: Soft and generous, showing straightforward blackberry and plum flavor that lingers gently on the finish. Drink now. • $7 • (10/15/95) • **84**

Cabernet Merlot South Eastern Australia 1990 • $7 • (06/30/92) BB • **82**

Cabernet Sauvignon Merlot South Eastern Australia 1992 • $6 • (05/15/94) BB • **84**

Chardonnay South Eastern Australia 1994: Light and lively, with lots of bright fruit and spice flavors. 10,000 cases made. • $9 • (03/31/96) • **82**

Chardonnay South Eastern Australia 1993 • $6 • (03/15/94) • **80**

Chardonnay South Eastern Australia 1991 • $7 • (08/31/92) • **79**

COLDRIDGE

Sémillon Chardonnay South Eastern Australia 1993: Light and simple, with pear and spice notes. Ready now. 50,000 cases made. • $6 • (09/30/94) • **78**

Sémillon South Eastern Australia 1992 • $6 • (11/30/92) • **77**

Key: SS—Spectator Selection. CS—Cellar Selection. BB—Best Buy. $NA—Price not available. (BT)—Barrel tasting. Ⓐ—Auction Price.
Dates in parentheses represent the issues in which the ratings were published.

Shiraz Cabernet Sauvignon South Eastern Australia 1992 • $6 • (10/31/93) BB • **82**

Shiraz Cabernet South Eastern Australia 1993 • $6 • (06/15/94) • **80**

Shiraz Cabernet South Eastern Australia 1992 • $6 • (05/31/93) BB • **81**

Shiraz Cabernet Victoria 1989 • $6 • (08/31/92) BB • **81**

South Eastern Australia 1994: Youthful, fruity and appealing, light and soft in texture, showing pretty raspberry accents on the finish. 30,000 cases made. • $7 • (06/30/95) • **82**

COLDSTREAM HILLS

Cabernet Sauvignon Lilydale 1987 • $20 • (01/31/90) • **84**

Chardonnay Yarra Valley 1992 • $15 • (03/15/94) • **75**

Pinot Noir Lilydale Miller Vineyard 1987 • $20 • **71**

Pinot Noir Yarra Valley 1992 • $15 • (04/30/94) • **88**

CORIOLE

Cabernet Sauvignon McLaren Vale 1993: Ripe and generous on the nose, offering a strong, minty streak running through the plum and currant flavors, finishing leaner than it starts. Needs until 2000 to 2004 to soften the tannins. 1,000 cases made. • $20 • (04/30/96) • **89**

Sangiovese McLaren Vale 1994: Crisp and flavorful, featuring a floral edge reminiscent of Chianti and finishing with bright, berry notes. Drinkable now. 2,000 cases made. • $16 • (04/30/96) • **86**

Sémillon Sauvignon Blanc McLaren Vale 1994: Lively, snappy green apple and herb notes show a resiny edge to the fruit flavors. More concentration than most. Approachable now. 1,500 cases made. • $14 • (04/30/96) • **87**

Shiraz Cabernet McLaren Vale Redstone 1993: Firm and focused, a solid red of mineral-scented plum and spice flavors. Supple enough to drink now, but wants until 1998 to 2000. 3,000 cases made. • $15 • (04/30/96) • **87**

Shiraz McLaren Vale 1993: Ripe black cherry, licorice and gamy flavors wrap around rich texture, echoing some lovely peppery-floral notes on the velvety finish. Firm tannins should meld nicely upon cellaring until 1998 to 2000. 2,500 cases made. • $20 • (04/30/96) • **87**

COWRA ESTATE

Cabernet Sauvignon New South Wales 1988 • $10 • (03/31/93) • **62**

Chardonnay Australia 1992: Bright, lively and appealing for its lingering green apple, vanilla and spice flavors. 2,000 cases made. • $10 • (12/15/95) • **87**

CRANSWICK ESTATE

Cabernet Sauvignon Riverina 1991 • $8 • (06/15/94) • **82**

Sémillon Colombard Riverina 1992: Soft and flavorful, if a little stale at the edge. • $8 • (09/30/94) • **76**

Shiraz Cabernet South Eastern Australia 1990 • $7 • (05/31/93) • **82**

Shiraz Merlot South Eastern Australia 1990 • $7 • (04/15/93) • **80**

CULLENS

Cabernet Merlot Margaret River 1985 • $15 • (11/15/87) • **87**

D'ARENBERG

Cabernet Sauvignon McLaren Vale High Trellis 1989 • $8 • (07/15/93) • **82**

Chardonnay Australia Barrel Fermented 1992: Supple and flavorful, with a crisp core of green apple and melon flavors that remain lively through the finish. Drinkable now. 1,950 cases made. • $11 • (12/15/94) • **88**

Chardonnay McLaren Vale Barrel Fermented 1991 • $8 • (07/15/93) • **79**

Ironstone Pressings Australia 1991: Dense and aromatic, rich in ripe fruit and cedar notes. Tough tannins, but focused. Aging until 1998 is a good idea. 400 cases made. • $15 • (01/31/95) • **87**

Ironstone Pressings McLaren Vale 1989 • $11 • (05/31/93) • **86**

Port Australia Nostalgia Very Old Tawny Port NV: Rich and aromatic, with plenty of spicy, earthy, raisiny notes lingering on the finish. 400 cases made. • $16 • (03/31/95) • **83**

Port Australia Vintage 1987: Flavorful, smooth, featuring a range of black cherry, prune and toast notes that finish soft. Lacks grip, but makes up for it with charm. Drinkable now. 400 cases made. • $16 • (03/31/95) • **85**

Riesling McLaren Vale Noble Riesling 1992 • $10 • (04/30/94) • **87**

Shiraz Australia Old Vine 1990: Hard, earthy and somewhat dirty around the edges. A jolt of ripe fruit comes through on the finish. 1,200 cases made. • $11 • (03/31/95) • **75**

Shiraz McLaren Vale Old Vine 1989 • $8 • (05/31/93) BB • **85**

DALFARRAS

Cabernet Sauvignon Australia 1989 • $8 • (09/30/93) • **77**

Marsanne Australia 1992 • $9 • (07/15/93) • **83**

DE BORTOLI

Sémillon Australia Noble One 1993: Deep gold color, deep aromas and deep flavors, centering around fig, honey, almond and orange zest. Spicy vanilla notes swirl through the elegant finish. A remarkable wine with a character all its own. 8,000 cases made. • $28 • (06/15/96) • **93**

DENMAN

Cabernet Sauvignon Hunter Valley 1983 • $5 • (11/15/87) • **76**

DEVIL'S LAIR

Cabernet Sauvignon Margaret River 1992: Somewhat tart, but berry and herbal flavors are lively and persist on the crisp finish. Best in 1997. 3,000 cases made. • $20 • (10/15/95) • **82**

Chardonnay Margaret River 1994: Bright and flavorful, laying out its spicy pear and apple flavors with a touch of lime on the lively finish. Drinkable now. 3,500 cases made. • $19 • (06/30/95) • **87**

Chardonnay Margaret River 1993: Ripe, round and spicy, with dark-toned flavors of nutmeg and tobacco. Pineapple and pear come through on the finish. A full-bodied Chardonnay. Drinkable now. 2,300 cases made. • $17 • (06/30/95) • **88**

DRAYTON'S

Cabernet Merlot Hunter Valley 1991: Earthy, dirty flavors take this one out of the running, turns sour on the finish. 5,000 cases made. • $10 • (09/30/94) • **64**

Cabernet Sauvignon Hunter Valley 1993: Firm and focused, weaving a nice strand of spice and smoke through the straightforward currant and plum flavors. Drink now. 10,000 cases made. • $10 • (10/31/95) • **84**

Cabernet Sauvignon Hunter Valley 1991: Soft and spicy, plummy and herb-scented with a plush texture, but the flavors fall off on the finish. Drinkable now. 5,000 cases made. • $10 • (09/30/94) • **79**

Chardonnay Hunter Valley 1995: Bright and grapey, with a resiny edge to the exuberant fruit flavors that form up into a nicely focused line on the finish. Ready now. 12,000 cases made. • $9 • **85**

Chardonnay Hunter Valley 1994: Bright, flavorful and generous, with a nice hint of citrusy apple that keeps spinning on the finish. Drink soon. 15,000 cases made. • $8 • (12/15/94) • **85**

Chardonnay Hunter Valley 1993 • $8 • (04/15/94) BB • **88**

Chardonnay Hunter Valley 1991 • $9 • (10/31/93) • **85**

Chardonnay Hunter Valley C-6 1994: Light, lively and smooth-textured, with snappy green apple and spice flavors that linger on the finish. 15,000 cases made. • $7 • (12/15/94) BB • **85**

Chardonnay Hunter Valley C-6 1993 • $7 • (04/15/94) BB • **85**

Chardonnay South Eastern Australia 1995: Ripe and generous, appealing for its spicy pear and nectarine flavors. 12,000 cases made. • $9 • (04/30/96) • **85**

Chardonnay South Eastern Australia C-6 1995: Soft and maybe a bit sweet, showing some nice apricot, pear and honey flavors that remain zesty on the finish. 12,000 cases made. • $8 • (04/30/96) • **81**

Port Australia Fine Old Pioneer NV: Coffee, tea and spice notes mingle with a touch of plum and vanilla in this solid, forthright tawny. Nicely balanced. 2,400 cases made. • $10 • (03/31/95) • **82**

Port Hunter Valley Old Tawny Port Log Press NV: Smooth and spicy, a lovely mouthful of rich almond, berry and vanilla flavors that linger nicely. Not too sweet, either. 1,800 cases made. • $18 • (03/31/95) • **88**

Sémillon Chardonnay Hunter Valley Oakey Creek 1994: Fruity, supple and charming. Appealing for its green apple and spice flavors. 12,500 cases made. • $7 • (10/15/95) • **85**

Sémillon Hunter Valley 1993: Broad and distinctive, featuring lanolin overtones to the pear and tobacco flavors. Ready now, but should improve through 1997. 12,500 cases made. • $8 • (10/31/95) • **85**

Shiraz Cabernet Sauvignon Hunter Valley Oakey Creek 1993 • $7 • (06/15/94) • **82**

Shiraz Hunter Valley Bin 5555 1994: Indulges in plenty of earthy, barnyardy flavors to accompany the modest fruit. A distinctive style, not for everyone. 10,000 cases made. • $9 • (12/15/95) • **73**

Shiraz Hunter Valley Bin 5555 1990 • $10 • (04/15/94) • **82**

Shiraz Hunter Valley S-5 1994: Smooth, gamy, generous tar, animal and berry flavors. Drink now. 15,000 cases made. • $7 • (10/31/95) • **82**

Shiraz Hunter Valley William 1991: Ripe, somewhat raisiny, chewy with mild tannins, a sturdy red that should be best in 1997. 750 cases made. • $23 • (10/31/95) • **83**

Shiraz Hunter Valley William 1989: Smooth and supple, with ripe cherry, plum and raspberry flavors, but it picks up an earthy, leathery edge on the finish. Ready now. Tasted twice. 2,500 cases made. • $30 • (09/30/94) • **85**

Shiraz South Eastern Australia S-5 1995: Bright and ripe, delivering pretty plum and spice flavors on a thin layer of fine tannins, narrowing somewhat on the finish. Best in 1997. 12,000 cases made. • $7 • (04/30/96) • **84**

Verdelho Hunter Valley 1995: Broad and fruity, a mouthful of green apple and citrusy flavors that linger nicely as the finish turns crisp. Ready now. 2,500 cases made. • $10 • (03/31/96) • **86**

Verdelho Hunter Valley 1994: Broad and spicy, pleasantly fruity, showing pear and hints of tropical flavors. 1,500 cases made. • $10 • (10/31/95) • **83**

ELDERTON

Cabernet Sauvignon Merlot Barossa Valley 1984 • $11 • (04/30/88) • **86**

EVANS & TATE

Cabernet Sauvignon Margaret River 1991 • $14 • (11/15/93) • **82**

Cabernet Merlot Australia Barrique 61 1994: Earthy, cedary, spicy flavors tend to overwhelm the soft currant and berry notes in this high-toned, distinctly herbal red. Shows complexity but seems slightly tough at this stage. Should improve through 2001 to 2003. 5,000 cases made. • $14 • (04/30/96) • **88**

Chardonnay Australia Two Vineyards 1995: A bracing mouthful of apple, peach and orange peel flavors, remaining lively through the finish. Best in 1997. 5,000 cases made. • $14 • (04/30/96) • **86**

Chardonnay Australia Two Vineyards 1994: Light in texture, brash in flavor, a metallic edge to the sweet pear flavor. Drinkable now. 5,000 cases made. • $14 • (06/30/95) • **80**

Chardonnay Margaret River 1991 • $18 • (10/31/93) • **88**

Chardonnay Western Australia Two Vineyards 1993 • $14 • (03/15/94) • **81**

Chardonnay Western Australia Two Vineyards 1992 • $13 • (10/31/93) • **79**

Merlot Australia Margaret River 1992: Fresh and lively, chewy, firm blackberry and currant flavors linger on the finish. Drinkable now. 8,000 cases made. • $15 • (05/31/95) • **85**

Merlot Margaret River 1994: Minty, herbal, earthy flavors dominate the fruit in this simple, modest wine. • $16 • **79**

Merlot Margaret River 1992: Crisp in texture, a bit jammy in flavor, with a minty edge to the soft black cherry notes that give it some distinction. Drinkable now. • $15 • (09/30/94) • **82**

Merlot Margaret River 1991 • $16 • (04/30/94) • **70**

Merlot Margaret River 1990 • $15 • (12/15/93) • **82**

Sauvignon Blanc Western Australia 1995: Light, with a smooth frame. Citrusy herb flavors have a hint of mint. • $14 • **82**

Sémillon Margaret River 1992 • $13 • (11/15/93) • **82**

Sémillon Sauvignon Blanc Margaret River Classic 1993 • $12 • (12/31/93) • **84**

Shiraz Australia Gnangara 1993: Light, fruity and simple, with appealing cherry and spice flavors. A little richer on the finish. Drinkable now. 18,000 cases made. • $10 • (06/30/95) • **85**

Shiraz Cabernet Western Australia Gnangara 1992 • $12 • (03/31/94) • **82**

Shiraz Cabernet Western Australia Gnangara 1991 • $10 • (11/30/93) • **80**

Shiraz Margaret River Hermitage 1991 • $14 • (10/31/93) • **87**

FIVE MILE HOLLOW

Chardonnay Sémillon Sauvignon Blanc Australia 1993: Citrusy, spicy and focused, a round, polished white with an appealing range of grapefruit, pear and spicy oak flavors. Drinkable now. 10,000 cases made. • $10 • (07/31/94) • **84**

Hastings River 1995: Light and silky, offering a resiny edge to the modest apple flavors. Drinkable now. 3,000 cases made. • $12 • (04/30/96) • **82**

Hastings River 1994: Earthy, barnyardy flavors dominate this red mélange, a distinctive mouthful if not bound to please everyone exactly. Drinkable now. 3,000 cases made. • $12 • (04/30/96) • **80**

Red Table Wine Hastings Valley 1993: Earthy, gamy, black cherry and plum character that tapers gradually into the finish. Drinkable now. A blend of Merlot, Shiraz, Chambourcin and Pinot Noir. 3,000 cases made. • $12 • (05/31/95) • **85**

Shiraz Cabernet Merlot Australia 1992: Has a little more polish than most, a smooth, well manicured red that offers appealing plum and leather flavors. Drinkable now. 10,000 cases made. • $10 • (09/30/94) • **85**

White Table Wine Hastings Valley 1994: Ripe and round peach, citrus and pear flavors, with an almond note on the finish. Drinkable now. A blend including Sémillon, Sauvignon Blanc and Chardonnay. 3,000 cases made. • $12 • (05/31/95) • **85**

GARRETT, ANDREW

Blanc de Blanc Australia Chardonnay Cuvée NV • $10 • (03/15/93) • **84**

Brut Pinot Noir Australia Cuvée NV • $10 • (02/15/93) • **81**

Cabernet Blend Australia McLarens Red 1991 • $7 • (11/30/92) • **81**

Cabernet Merlot Australia French Oak Matured 1990 • $10 • (11/30/92) • **83**

Cabernet Sauvignon Merlot South Eastern Australia 1991 • $11 • (04/30/94) • **85**

Chardonnay Australia Barrel Fermented 1991 • $10 • (11/15/92) • **84**

Chardonnay South Eastern Australia 1992 • $11 • (03/15/94) • **79**

McLarens White Australia 1991 • $7 • (11/30/92) BB • **84**

Sémillon Australia Wood Matured 1991 • $9 • (11/30/92) • **80**

Sémillon McLaren Vale 1992 • $12 • (04/30/94) • **76**

Shiraz Australia Bold Style 1991 • $9 • (11/30/92) • **87**

Shiraz South Australia Clarendon Estate 1982 • $8 • (11/15/87) • **80**

Shiraz South Eastern Australia Black Shiraz 1992 • $10 • (03/31/94) • **81**

GOVERNOR PHILLIP

Cabernet Sauvignon Shiraz Barossa Valley 1986 • $6 • (07/31/89) BB • **83**

Classic Australian Red Australia NV • $5 • (07/31/89) BB • **82**

GRANT SMITH LTD.

Chardonnay Riverina Valley Bin 98 Vintner's Reserve 1991 • $6 • (11/30/93) • **80**

Shiraz Cabernet Riverina Valley Bin 95 Vintner's Reserve 1990 • $6 • (12/15/93) BB • **83**

Shiraz Merlot Riverina Bin 101 Vintner's Reserve 1990 • $6 • (04/15/94) BB • **85**

GRANTS

Cabernet Sauvignon Barossa Valley 1984 • $8 • (11/15/87) • **73**

Key: SS—Spectator Selection. CS—Cellar Selection. BB—Best Buy. $NA—Price not available. (BT)—Barrel tasting. Ⓐ—Auction Price.
Dates in parentheses represent the issues in which the ratings were published.

HANWOOD

Cabernet Sauvignon Australia 1993: Soft and a little chewy, with modest blackberry and currant flavors, finishing earthy. Drinkable now. 25,000 cases made. • $8 • (06/30/95) • **81**

Cabernet Sauvignon South Eastern Australia 1994: Light in texture, as appealingly spicy strawberry and vanilla flavors linger gently on the finish. Drinkable now. 35,000 cases made. • $7 • (04/30/96) • **83**

Chardonnay Australia 1993: Bright and fruity, youthful and straightforward, with appealing apple and slightly resiny flavors. Drinkable now. 25,000 cases made. • $8 • (06/30/95) • **84**

Chardonnay South Eastern Australia 1995: Light, fruity and refreshing, showing pleasant nectarine and citrus flavors. Drinkable now. 39,000 cases made. • $7 • (04/30/96) • **84**

Sémillon Chardonnay Australia 1993: Nicely focused pear, fig and tobacco flavors give this soft, appealing wine a classic feel. Attractive both for its character and its price. 12,000 cases made. • $6 • (10/15/95) BB • **86**

Shiraz South Eastern Australia 1994: Light and lean, offering basic berry flavor and a touch of pepper. 14,500 cases made. • $7 • (04/30/96) • **81**

HAPPS

Shiraz Margaret River 1990 • $11 • (03/31/94) • **83**

HARDYS

Brut Australia Grand Reserve Australian Champagne NV: Tasty, straightforward sparkler, with creamy berry flavors lurking in the background. 4,000 cases made. • $8 • (09/15/94) • **81**

Brut Australia Grand Reserve NV • $8 • (02/29/92) BB • **83**

Cabernet Malbec Reynella McLaren Vale Collection No. 9 1984 • $6 • (07/15/88) • **76**

Cabernet Sauvignon Coonawarra 1993: Firm in texture, with light but focused raspberry and plum flavors that turn spicy on the finish. Drinkable now. 10,500 cases made. • $11 • (03/31/96) • **86**

Cabernet Sauvignon Coonawarra 1992: Lean and focused, with hints of bay leaves and tobacco on plum and black cherry. Packed with flavor. It needs until 1997 or 1998 to settle down. 3,500 cases made. • $10 • (06/30/95) BB • **87**

Cabernet Sauvignon Coonawarra 1987 • $11 • (07/15/90) • **81**

Cabernet Sauvignon Coonawarra Collection 1990: Ripe and generous, a smooth-textured wine with plenty of currant, berry, chocolate flavor arcing across the palate, making this stylish and appealing to drink now. Should be fine through 1997 to 2000. Tasted twice. 5,000 cases made. • $10 • (06/30/94) BB • **88**

Cabernet Sauvignon Coonawarra Regional Collection 1992: Silky and generous, offering layers of plum, spice, vanilla and brown sugar aromas and flavors that echo on the solid finish. Drinkable now, but has the stuff to develop through 1997 or 1998 at least. 5,000 cases made. • $10 • (08/31/94) BB • **89**

Cabernet Sauvignon Coonawarra Regional Collection 1991: Firm in texture, with a solid core of plum and spice flavor, chewy enough to want until 1999 to soften. 5,000 cases made. • $10 • (06/30/94) • **84**

Cabernet Sauvignon Coonawarra Thomas Hardy 1991: Ripe, rich and sweet with vanilla and spicy oak overtones to the generous currant, plum and prune flavors that expand on the finish. Harmonious and balanced, aiming for 1998 to 2000 for best drinking. 1,000 cases made. • $20 • (03/31/96) • **89**

Cabernet Sauvignon Coonawarra Thomas Hardy 1989: Ripe, rich and generous. Mature accents of tobacco, cedar and spice grace the blackberry, prune and currant flavors. Nicely balanced and distinctive, drinkable now, but worth cellaring until 1997. 800 cases made. • $27 • (03/31/95) • **88**

Cabernet Sauvignon Keppoch 1986 • $7 • (07/15/90) • **79**

Cabernet Sauvignon Keppoch 1985 • $7 • (10/31/88) • **80**

Cabernet Sauvignon Keppoch Bird Series 1985 • $6 • (09/30/88) BB • **81**

Cabernet Sauvignon McLaren Vale Captain's Selection 1985 • $4 • (07/15/88) • **75**

Cabernet Sauvignon McLaren Vale Collection No. 8 1986 • $11 • (01/31/89) • **76**

Cabernet Sauvignon Shiraz South Eastern Australia Bird Series 1990 • $7 • (05/15/94) • **82**

Cabernet Sauvignon South Australia Bird Series 1988 • $8 • (03/15/92) BB • **83**

Cabernet Sauvignon South Australia Collection 1989 • $12 • (05/31/93) • **83**

Cabernet Sauvignon South Australia Collection 1988 • $10 • (02/15/91) • **83**

Cabernet Sauvignon South Australia Nottage Hill 1989 • $8 • (11/30/92) • **80**

Cabernet Sauvignon South Eastern Australia 1994: Focused and flavorful, fruit balanced on berry and currant. Generous and appealing already. Drink soon. 2,000 cases made. • $8 • (06/30/95) • **81**

Cabernet Sauvignon South Eastern Australia Nottage Hill 1992: Smooth and polished, simple, with a silky texture and ripe currant flavors shaded by a touch of spice. 22,000 cases made. • $7 • (07/31/94) • **82**

Cabernet Sauvignon South Eastern Australia Nottage Hill 1990 • $8 • (03/31/93) • **77**

Cabernet-Shiraz South Eastern Australia Nottage Hill 1994: Crisp and lively, the zingy, herbal currant and cedar flavors jumping through the finish. Approachable now, best in 1998. • $7 • (04/30/96) • **86**

Cabernet-Shiraz South Eastern Australia Nottage Hill 1993: Bright and sharply focused, chewy in texture, displaying plum and berry flavors that remain vibrant through the finish. Drinkable now. 9,000 cases made. • $7 • (04/30/95) • **85**

Chardonnay Australia NV • $10 • (05/31/87) • **86**

Chardonnay Padthaway 1994: Ripe and silky, a generous mouthful of spicy pear and citrus flavors lingering on the smooth finish. A ready-to-drink bargain from Down Under. 14,000 cases made. • $11 • (03/31/96) BB • **88**

Chardonnay Padthaway Eileen Hardy 1993: Broad, generous and spicy, with honey and pear flavors up front followed by floral and buttery notes on the long, elegant finish. Drinkable now. 1,000 cases made. • $19 • (05/15/95) • **89**

Chardonnay Padthaway Eileen Hardy Yarra Glen 1994: Ripe, soft and generous with its pear, spice and honey flavors. Lightens up on the finish. Ready now. 2,500 cases made. • $18 • (06/30/96) • **85**

Chardonnay Padthaway Regional Collection 1992: Earthy and soft-textured with caramel and pineapple flavors echoing on the finish. • $10 • (09/30/94) • **83**

Chardonnay South Australia Eileen Hardy 1992: Lean and spicy, but unfocused and lacking in concentration, showing only modest fruit flavor. Drinkable now. 2,000 cases made. • $20 • (09/30/94) • **79**

Chardonnay South Australia Eileen Hardy 1991 • $20 • (05/15/94) • **85**

Chardonnay South Eastern Australia 1994: Light, simple, pleasantly fruity, with pear and apple flavors that remain bright through the finish. 2,000 cases made. • $8 • (06/30/95) • **82**

Chardonnay South Eastern Australia Bird Series 1993: Light and floral, almost like a Riesling, finishing fresh and lively. Drinkable now. • $9 • (09/30/94) • **83**

Chardonnay South Eastern Australia Bird Series 1992: A Chardonnay with rich but cloying pear and apple flavors. Simple fruity style. 40,000 cases made. • $7 • (09/30/94) • **78**

Chardonnay South Eastern Australian Bird Series 1991 • $7 • (06/30/92) BB • **85**

Chardonnay South Eastern Australia Nottage Hill 1995: Simple, fresh and lively, appealing for its citrusy peach character. Enjoy soon. 20,000 cases made. • $7 • (03/31/96) BB • **84**

Chardonnay South Eastern Australia Nottage Hill 1994: Bright and fruity, a youthful, straightforward wine with appealing apple and slightly resiny flavors. Ready now. 10,000 cases made. • $7 • (06/30/95) BB • **84**

Chardonnay South Eastern Australia Nottage Hill 1993: Soft, supple and pleasantly fruity, brimming with pear, honey and spice flavors that echo on the finish. Drinkable now. 28,000 cases made. • $7 • (03/31/95) BB • **83**

Chardonnay South Eastern Australia Nottage Hill 1992: Ripe and generous, sturdy, seems a little clumsy on the finish. • $7 • (09/30/94) • **82**

Chardonnay South Eastern Australia Nottage Hill 1991 • $8 • (05/31/92) BB • **87**

Merlot South Eastern Australia Nottage Hill 1994: Lean, dark and chewy-showing more tannin than fruit right now, but plummy, spicy flavors emerge on the finish. Try in 1998. 12,000 cases made. • $8 • (03/31/96) • **85**

Merlot South Eastern Australia Nottage Hill 1993: Light and airy, showing nicely focused currant and blackberry flavors that expand and become supple on the finish. Appealing and drinkable now. 7,000 cases made. • $7 • (05/31/95) BB • **86**

Port Australia 1982 • $15 • (07/31/90) • **72**

Port Australia Tall Ships Tawny Port NV: Smooth and rich, offering coffee, raisin, spice and slightly tarry flavors that meld together on the finish. 1,500 cases made. • $10 • (03/31/95) • **86**

Port Australia Vintage Port 1983: Mature, a little earthy, with unfocused prune and tobacco flavors that become chewy and tough on the finish. Tasted twice, with consistent notes. 1,500 cases made. • $15 • (06/30/95) • **73**

Port Australia Vintage Port 1982: Smooth and mature, showing a nice balance of black cherry flavor and tarry, smoky overtones. Drinkable now. 1,500 cases made. • $15 • (03/31/95) • **85**

Premium Classic Dry Red McLaren Vale 1986 • $6 • (05/15/89) • **75**

Premium Classic Dry Red South Australia 1988 • $5 • (07/31/90) BB • **78**

Sémillon Chardonnay South Eastern Australia Captain's Selection 1993: A little on the watery side, soft and pleasant but not very lively. • $7 • (09/30/94) • **74**

Sémillon Chardonnay South Eastern Australia Captain's Selection 1992 • $6 • (03/15/93) • **80**

Sémillon Chardonnay South Eastern Australia Captain's Selection 1991 • $6 • (06/30/92) BB • **83**

Sémillon Chardonnay South Eastern Australia Stamps of Australia 1993: Simple and fruity, sweet up front, but a little citrusy and tart on the finish. 18,000 cases made. • $6 • (09/30/94) • **78**

Shiraz Eileen Hardy 1989 • $7 • (05/31/92) BB • **85**

Shiraz Eileen Hardy 1988 • $19 • (02/15/92) • **91**

Shiraz Cabernet Sauvignon South Eastern Australia Bird Series 1991: Firm and chewy, a solid red with berry and red cherry flavors at the core and some spicy, cedary notes sneaking in on the finish. Drinkable now. 10,000 cases made. • $10 • (09/30/94) • **83**

Shiraz Cabernet Sauvignon South Eastern Australia Captain's Selection 1993: Soft, warm and fruity, smooth-textured, with nice berry, plum and cedar aromas and flavors. Drinkable now. 22,000 cases made. • $6 • (09/30/94) • **83**

Shiraz Cabernet Sauvignon South Eastern Australia Captain's Selection 1992: Lean, thin and weak in flavor, finishing with a light touch of currant and cedar. • $7 • (09/30/94) • **76**

Shiraz Cabernet Sauvignon South Eastern Australia Stamps of Australia 1993: Rough in texture, modest in flavor, this one needs time for its currant and berry flavors to gain some polish. Try in 1997. • $7 • (09/30/94) • **81**

Shiraz Cabernet Sauvignon South Eastern Australia Stamps of Australia 1992: Firm and focused, lively with serious plum, cedar and tar aromas and flavors, a little hot on the finish. 17,600 cases made. • $6 • (09/30/94) • **82**

Shiraz Cabernet South Eastern Australia Captain's Selection 1991 • $6 • (05/31/93) BB • **84**

Shiraz Cabernet South Eastern Australia Captain's Selection 1990 • $6 • (06/30/92) BB • **82**

Shiraz McLaren Vale 1987 • $7 • (07/15/90) BB • **87**

Shiraz McLaren Vale 1986 • $7 • (12/31/88) BB • **89**

Shiraz McLaren Vale Bird Series 1991 • $7 • (04/15/94) BB • **84**

Shiraz McLaren Vale Bird Series 1990 • $7 • (05/31/93) • **80**

Shiraz McLaren Vale Bird Series 1988 • $7 • (09/30/91) BB • **84**

Shiraz McLaren Vale Padthaway Bird Series 1984 • $5 • (07/15/88) • **79**

Shiraz Padthaway McLaren Vale Clare Valley Eileen Hardy 1993: Dark, almost black in color, densely packed with blackberry, black cherry, pepper and licorice flavors that just don't quit, ending in a smoky note. Tight enough to want until 2000 to 2005. Has great depth and a long, fat finish. 2,000 cases made. • $20 • (04/30/96) • **94**

Shiraz South Australia Eileen Hardy 1992: A tightly structured, firmly focused red that packs in lots of chewy blackberry and stewed plum flavors. Needs time to develop, best from 1997. 2,000 cases made. • $20 • (05/15/95) • **87**

Shiraz South Australia Eileen Hardy 1990 • $20 • (03/31/94) • **86**

Shiraz South Australia Eileen Hardy 1989 • $20 • (05/31/93) • **84**

Shiraz South Eastern Australia Nottage Hill 1993: Smooth and minty, marked by oak, but sneaking some ripe berry and chocolate notes into the finish. Best from 1997. 9,000 cases made. • $7 • (11/15/95) • **82**
Tawny Port Australia Tall Ships NV • $11 • (07/31/90) • **83**

HARVARD

Sémillon Chardonnay South Eastern Australia 1991 • $6 • (06/30/93) BB • **83**
Shiraz Cabernet South Eastern Australia 1990 • $6 • (05/31/93) • **78**

HAWTHORN HILL

Merlot South Eastern Australia Bin 8000 1990 • $7 • (11/30/92) • **78**
Shiraz South Eastern Australia Bin 5000 1990 • $7 • (11/30/92) BB • **85**

HEGGIES

Cabernet Blend Cabernets 1985 • $15 • (03/31/93) • **84**
Chardonnay Eden Valley 1994: Ripe, round and focused, offering plenty of spicy pear and honey flavors that linger on the smooth finish. Ready now. 1,000 cases made. • $15 • (05/15/96) • **90**
Merlot Eden Valley 1992: Chunky, almost clumsy, but with some pretty berry flavors under the layer of scratchy tannins. 1,000 cases made. • $16 • (06/30/96) • **80**
Rhine Riesling Late Harvest Barossa Valley Botrytis Affected 1986 • $8 • (02/15/88) • **92**
Viognier Eden Valley 1994: Not fat like most Viogniers, but has plenty of floral, spicy fruit flavors, finishing in a riot of citrus and pear notes. Ready now. 275 cases made. • $15 • (09/30/95) • **86**

HENSCHKE

Cabernet Blend Keyneton Estate 1988 • $14 • (06/30/92) • **82**
Cabernet Blend Keyneton Estate 1985 • $12 • (03/31/89) • **79**
Cabernet Blend Keyneton Estate 1984 • $12 • (02/15/88) • **85**
Cabernet Sauvignon Eden Valley Cyril Henschke 1992: Richly tannic, but warm and supple underneath. Its currant, plum and beefy flavors emerge as it unfolds on the palate. Tannins resolve nicely on the long finish, making this approachable by 2001 to 2003. Tasted twice, with consistent notes. 1,000 cases made. • $36 • (04/30/96) • **92**
Cabernet Sauvignon Eden Valley Cyril Henschke 1990: Has a combination of earthy, leathery flavors and ripe plum and coffee notes. Continues earthy on the finish, where the tannins are drying. 10,000 cases made. • $28 • (08/31/94) • **84**
Cabernet Sauvignon Eden Valley Cyril Henschke 1989 • $23 • (05/31/93) • **86**
Cabernet Sauvignon Keyneton Cyril Henschke 1991: A smooth and harmonious Cab that shows off a pretty core of black cherry, currant, cedar and spice. Mild, elegant tannins and a lingering aftertaste round it off. Drinkable now, but age-worthy, too. 10,000 cases made. • $35 • (06/15/95) CS • **92**
Cabernet Sauvignon Keyneton Cyril Henschke 1988 • $23 • (06/30/92) • **85**
Cabernet Sauvignon Keyneton Cyril Henschke 1986 • $23 • (09/15/89) • **91**
Cabernet Sauvignon Keyneton Cyril Henschke 1985 • $21 • (01/31/89) • **90**
Cabernet Sauvignon Keyneton Cyril Henschke 1984 • $19 • (12/15/87) • **94**
Sémillon Eden Valley 1992: Ripe, smoky and deftly balanced between its fig and pear flavors and the toasty, earthy overtones. 10,000 cases made. • $12 • (07/31/94) • **85**
Sémillon Eden Valley Louis 1995: Ripe, bright and smooth, a nice mouthful of pear, apple and spice flavors, finishing focused enough to suggest it be best from 1997. 1,000 cases made. • $17 • (03/31/96) • **87**
Sémillon Eden Valley Matured in French Oak 1994: Soft, perfumy and generous, a strong woody edge marring its charm. 2,000 cases made. • $11 • (10/31/95) • **77**
Shiraz Hill of Grace 1988 • $27 • (05/31/92) • **88**
Shiraz Hill of Grace 1987 • $27 • (05/31/92) CS • **91**

Key: SS—Spectator Selection. CS—Cellar Selection. BB—Best Buy. $NA—Price not available. (BT)—Barrel tasting. Ⓐ—Auction Price.
Dates in parentheses represent the issues in which the ratings were published.

Shiraz Mount Edelstone 1989 • $17 • (05/31/92) • **88**
Shiraz Mount Edelstone 1988 • $17 • (05/31/92) • **90**
Shiraz Cabernet Malbec Australia Keyneton Estate 1992: Elegant, pretty cherry, blackberry and dusty pepper notes, firm tannins on the finish. • $19 • (06/15/95) • **86**
Shiraz Cabernet Malbec Australia Keyneton Estate 1991: Firm, rich and intense, with a solid core of black cherry, wild berry and spice notes. Turns tannic on the finish, but it keeps pumping out the flavor. Drink now to 1999. 12,000 cases made. • $12 • (08/31/94) • **85**
Shiraz Cabernet Malbec Eden Valley/Barossa Valley Keyneton Estate 1993: Smooth and spicy, with a nice undercurrent of ripe plum and anise flavors, plus a touch of prune. A harmonious and amazingly elegant Australian red that's appealing now. 5,000 cases made. • $22 • (03/31/96) • **93**
Shiraz Keyneton Estate 1989 • $14 • (05/31/93) • **83**
Shiraz Keyneton Hill of Grace 1991: Marked by minty currant aromas with flavors to match. A bit rustic and still tannic, but it unfolds some complex flavors and holds together. Should be even better by 1997. 1,000 cases made. • $65 • (06/30/95) • **91**
Shiraz Keyneton Hill of Grace 1989 • $31 • (05/31/93) • **91**
Shiraz Keyneton Hill of Grace 1986 • $26 • (09/30/89) • **87**
Shiraz Keyneton Mount Edelstone 1993: Luxuriant, opulent, heady, showing spicy plum, blackberry, cherry and gently peppery aromas and flavors that swirl harmoniously and echo long and sweet on the supple finish. Still youthful, this Australian red is already expertly balanced and poised to improve through 2005. 1,500 cases made. • $34 • (03/31/96) CS • **96**
Shiraz Keyneton Mount Edelstone 1992: A full-bodied, concentrated Shiraz that delivers lots of flavor, with ripe cherry, plum and currant, lively spice and cedary oak. Finishes with a complex aftertaste and firm but not overpowering tannins. Drinkable now, but may be better by 1997. 10,000 cases made. • $30 • (06/15/95) SS • **91**
Shiraz Keyneton Mount Edelstone 1991: Intense, with a spicy, minty edge and a core of currant and cherry. Turns thick, chewy and tannic on the finish, approachable now or worth cellaring short-term. 10,000 cases made. • $18 • (09/30/94) • **87**
Shiraz Keyneton Mount Edelstone 1990 • $17 • (05/31/93) • **84**
Shiraz Keyneton Mount Edelstone 1987 • $17 • (05/31/91) • **86**
Shiraz Keyneton Mount Edelstone 1986 • $17 • (10/31/89) • **90**
Shiraz Keyneton Mount Edelstone 1985 • $15 • (03/31/89) • **81**
Shiraz Keyneton Mount Edelstone 1984 • $14 • (02/15/88) • **90**

HILL-SMITH

Cabernet Sauvignon Barossa Valley 1984 • $9 • (08/31/87) • **75**
Cabernet Sauvignon Barossa Valley 1981 • $9 • (07/16/86) • **82**
Cabernet Sauvignon Shiraz Terra Rossa Block 1988 • $11 • (11/30/92) • **81**
Cabernet Sauvignon Shiraz Eden Valley Terra Rossa Block 1992: Rich, broad and generous, a mouthful of plum, prune and black cherry flavor, shaded by tar. Soft and ready now. • $12 • (05/15/96) • **87**
Chardonnay Adelaide Hills Air-Strip Block 1990 • $11 • (03/31/93) • **73**
Chardonnay Eden Valley Air-Strip Block 1994: Bright and brilliantly focused, as lively, citrusy apple and pear flavor and spicy oak weave through it. Delicious now. • $12 • (05/15/96) • **89**
Sémillon Chenin Blanc Varietal White Barossa Valley 1984 • $4 • (11/15/86) BB • **78**
Sémillon Late Harvest Barossa Valley Autumn Harvest Botrytis 1986 • $10 • (03/15/89) • **84**
Sémillon Late Harvest Barossa Valley Autumn Harvest Botrytis 1985 • $8 • (02/15/88) • **88**
Sémillon Late Harvest Barossa Valley Autumn Harvest Botrytis 1983 • $8 • (08/31/86) • **84**
Shiraz Barossa Valley 1986 • $9 • (02/28/91) BB • **86**
Shiraz Barossa Valley 1984 • $6 • (05/15/87) • **82**
Varietal Red Barossa Valley 1985 • $4 • (01/31/88) • **75**

HILLSTOWE

Chardonnay Adelaide Hills Udy's Mill 1994: Crisp, focused and on the lean side. Delicately floral, with a resiny peach flavor that lingers. Give until late 1997 to reach full maturity. • $22 • **87**

Chardonnay Adelaide Hills Udy's Mill 1992: Dark and ripe, spicy and elegant, offering plenty of polished pear, honey and nutmeg aromas and flavors that linger on the finish. 700 cases made. • $21 • (09/30/94) • **90**

Chardonnay McLaren Vale 1992: Supple and fruity, with appealing apple and spice flavors that remain lively on the finish. Drinkable now. 2,000 cases made. • $15 • (09/30/94) • **85**

Chardonnay McLaren Vale 1991 • $15 • (04/30/93) • **87**

Pinot Noir Yarra Valley 1992: Elegant, greets you with mint and cedar notes, picking up light cherry and spice on the finish. Could use a little more richness and depth. Ready now. 700 cases made. • $21 • (07/31/94) • **83**

HOLLICK

Cabernet Merlot Coonawarra 1985 • $16 • (05/31/88) • **72**

Cabernet Sauvignon Coonawalla 1988 • $14 • (03/15/92) • **74**

HOUGHTON

Cabernet Sauvignon Frankland River Wildflower Ridge 1988 • $9 • (07/15/91) • **78**

Cabernet Sauvignon Western Australia Wildflower Ridge 1992: Ripe and generous, offering a lively mouthful of plum, blackberry and a touch of herb and chocolate—all that for a good price. Approachable now, but better from 1997 through 1998. 9,000 cases made. • $8 • (10/31/95) BB • **88**

Cabernet Sauvignon Western Australia Wildflower Ridge 1991: Lean and chewy, a rough-hewn Cabernet with modest flavors, but it holds together on the finish. May be best from 1997. • $7 • (09/30/94) • **82**

Cabernet Sauvignon Western Australia Wildflower Ridge 1990: Lean, chewy and minty, herb-centered, finishes austere and shows a tight beam of berry flavor. Drinkable now. • $7 • (09/30/94) • **82**

Cabernet Shiraz McLaren Vale Wildflower Ridge 1985 • $9 • (12/31/88) • **88**

Chardonnay Western Australia Wildflower Ridge 1993: Petroleum jelly aromas and flavors are a little off-putting in this simple, otherwise fruity everyday white. • $7 • (09/30/94) • **74**

Chardonnay Western Australia Wildflower Ridge 1992: Light and spicy, if a little green around the edges. • $7 • (09/30/94) • **79**

Chardonnay Western Australia Wildflower Ridge 1991 • $9 • (11/15/92) • **84**

Chardonnay Western Australia Wildflower Ridge 1990 • $9 • (11/30/91) BB • **88**

Shiraz McLaren Vale Wildflower Ridge 1985 • $9 • (12/31/88) • **88**

Shiraz Western Australia Wildflower Ridge 1994: An enjoyable wine whose basic berry flavors have distinct herbal and anise overtones. Drinkable now. 3,000 cases made. • $8 • (06/30/96) • **85**

Shiraz Western Australia Wildflower Ridge 1993: Ripe, round and generous, satiny in texture, spicy and plummy in flavor. 5,000 cases made. • $8 • (10/31/95) • **84**

Shiraz Western Australia Wildflower Ridge 1991 • $7 • (06/15/94) BB • **84**

Shiraz Western Australia Wildflower Ridge 1990 • $9 • (05/31/93) • **84**

Shiraz Western Australia Wildflower Ridge 1989 • $9 • (11/30/92) • **83**

White Burgundy Western Australia 1993: Simple and fruity, with a greenish edge. • $6 • (09/30/94) • **77**

White Burgundy Western Australia 1992: Soft and fruity, echoing pear and melon on the pleasant finish. • $6 • (09/30/94) • **81**

HUNGERFORD HILL

Cabernet Merlot Hunter Valley 1985 • $10 • (02/28/90) • **80**

Cabernet Sauvignon Coonawarra 1984 • $11 • (03/15/88) • **79**

Pinot Noir Hunter Valley 1986 • $12 • (02/28/90) • **74**

Pinot Noir Hunter Valley 1984 • $11 • (03/15/88) • **70**

Shiraz Hunter Valley 1988 • $10 • (02/28/90) • **80**

HUNTER PARK

Chardonnay Hunter Valley 1994: Smooth and generous with its pineapple flavor, but it has a woolly character that takes some of the gleam away. 10,000 cases made. • $11 • (06/15/96) • **83**

Chardonnay Hunter Valley Kenmarie Vineyard 1994: Ripe and rich without being heavy, smartly focused to show the pineapple, spice and coconut flavors. Best from 1997. 4,000 cases made. • $15 • (06/15/96) • **88**

Chardonnay Hunter Valley Kenmarie Vineyard 1993: Ripe, soft and rich, pouring out its honeyed pear and almond flavors, long and supple on the finish. Drinkable now. 4,000 cases made. • $20 • (01/31/95) • **89**

HUNTER RIDGE

Chardonnay South Eastern Australia Vanessa's Vale 1995: Bright, youthful, focused and appealing for its nectarine, pear and citrus flavor that remains lively through the long finish. Delicious now. 8,000 cases made. • $9 • (03/31/96) • **88**

Merlot South Eastern Australia Vanessa's Vale 1995: Has a nice floral quality in its spicy blueberry and plum flavors. This is light, but it builds up intensity on the modestly tannic finish. Better in 1997. 6,000 cases made. • $9 • (03/31/96) • **87**

Shiraz South Eastern Australia Vanessa's Vale 1995: Youthful, smooth, polished and effusively fruity, showing lots of nice raspberry and red plum flavors that linger on the simple finish. Ready now. 3,000 cases made. • $9 • (03/31/96) • **85**

HUNTERS

Chardonnay Hunter River Valley 747 1994: Dark color and earthy, somewhat tired flavors make this an unusually mature wine for a 1994. Not for all tastes. 5,000 cases made. • $7 • (03/31/96) • **79**

Merlot Hunter River Valley 565 1993: Earthy, gamy flavors compete with the modest fruit in this one. 3,000 cases made. • $7 • (03/31/96) • **77**

JABIRU

Cabernet Sauvignon Australia 1993: An oddball range of flavors—spicy, toasty and a little like candied orange peel on the finish—but it has style and remains nicely in balance. Drinkable now. 4,000 cases made. • $8 • (03/31/95) BB • **85**

Chardonnay South Eastern Australia 1994: Light and piney, a zippy white that comes off more like a snappy Riesling than a Chardonnay. Pleasant. Drink soon. 4,000 cases made. • $8 • (01/31/95) BB • **84**

Sauvignon Blanc South Eastern Australia 1993: Broad and floral, sharp-flavored, with more herbal tones than fruit. Drinkable now. 3,000 cases made. • $8 • (01/31/95) • **79**

JAMIESONS RUN

Chardonnay Coonawarra 1993: Fruity and fresh, sturdy in style, with solid pear and citrus flavors. Drinkable now. • $10 • (09/30/94) • **83**

Chardonnay Coonawarra 1992 • $10 • (11/15/92) • **85**

Shiraz Cabernet Coonawarra 1991: Strongly herbal, almost minty, a lean blend with a thread of prune and spice at the core. Drinkable now. • $10 • (09/30/94) • **81**

Shiraz Cabernet Coonawarra 1990: Earthy flavors shoulder past the fruit in this otherwise solid red. • $10 • (09/30/94) • **77**

JOHNSTONE

Cabernet Shiraz Hunter Valley 1988 • $6 • (07/15/91) • **75**

JUD'S HILL

Cabernet Sauvignon Merlot Australia 1985 • $13 • (04/30/88) • **80**

KINGSTON ESTATE

Cabernet Sauvignon 1991: Ripe and generous but soft-textured, with lots of appealing berry and currant flavors and a slightly smoky edge. Best to drink soon. 10,000 cases made. • $10 • (07/31/94) • **85**

Cabernet Sauvignon Riverland 1992: Light and polished, a simple wine with appealing but modest red plum, cedar and cherry flavors. 5,000 cases made. • $10 • (03/31/96) • **82**

Chardonnay 1992: Lean and simple, with a mineral edge to the modest pear flavors. Drinkable now. 10,000 cases made. • $10 • (07/31/94) • **82**

KOALA RIDGE

Chardonnay Reserve 1991: Ripe and spicy, with a grapefruit edge to the pineapple and caramel flavors, finishing focused and a little sharp. Drinkable now. 1,000 cases made. • $15 • (07/31/94) • **87**
Merlot Reserve 1989: Fruity, spicy and cedary, a smooth-textured wine with ripe berry flavors balancing the finish. 1,000 cases made. • $15 • (09/30/94) • **83**
Merlot Riverland 1993: Sturdy wine with simple blackberry and toast flavors, finishing with a nice polish. Ready now. 2,000 cases made. • $10 • (03/31/96) • **84**
Mourvèdre Riverland 1993: A little chunky at first, but it turns smooth as the blackberry flavor comes through. Ready now. 1,000 cases made. • $10 • (03/31/96) • **83**
Sémillon 1993: Round and fruity, well-mannered, with a polished texture and nice fig and pineapple notes that carry through the finish. 5,000 cases made. • $9 • (07/31/94) • **81**
Shiraz 1991: Light, smooth and spicy, appealing for its cedary tobacco overtones and plummy flavor at the core. Drinkable now. 5,000 cases made. • $9 • (09/30/94) • **84**
Shiraz Reserve 1991: Ripe, smooth and generous, with lots of plum, prune and spice flavors that remain rich on the finish. Tasty now. 1,000 cases made. • $15 • (01/31/95) • **85**
Shiraz Riverland 1993: Ripe and smooth, a youthful wine with appealing berry and spice flavors. Ready now. 5,000 cases made. • $10 • (03/31/96) • **86**

KOALA RIDGE

Cabernet Sauvignon Barossa Valley 1990 • $9 • (03/31/93) BB • **84**
Cabernet Sauvignon Barossa Valley 1988 • $10 • (03/15/92) • **83**
Cabernet Sauvignon Barossa Valley 1985 • $9 • (01/31/89) • **84**
Chardonnay Barossa Valley 1992 • $9 • (07/15/93) • **79**
Chardonnay Eden Valley 1993: Ripe and sweet, a soft white with spicy pear and nutmeg flavors. 6,000 cases made. • $10 • (09/30/94) • **81**
Hermitage Barossa Valley 1985 • $9 • (01/31/90) • **80**
Hermitage Barossa Valley 1984 • $8 • (08/31/87) • **71**

KOOKABURRA

Cabernet Sauvignon South Eastern Australia 1992: Earthy and somewhat musty notes cut through the modest plum flavor. Finishes herbal. Tasted twice, with consistent notes. 8,500 cases made. • $8 • (06/30/95) • **74**
Chardonnay South Eastern Australia 1993: Sharp-edged and a little coarse, but the bright pineapple and pear flavors come through on the finish. 8,500 cases made. • $6 • (04/15/95) • **80**
Shiraz South Eastern Australia 1992: On the lighter side, with pleasantly earthy plum and vanilla flavors that carry through the crisp finish. Drinkable now. 10,800 cases made. • $6 • (03/31/95) • **81**

KRONDORF

Cabernet Sauvignon Franc McLaren Vale 1984 • $9 • (04/15/87) BB • **89**

LAKE'S FOLLY

Cabernet Hunter Valley 1985 • $16 • (03/31/89) • **80**

LASSETER

Brut Australia 1985 • $17 • (10/31/89) • **87**
Brut Australia NV • $10 • (12/31/88) • **84**

LEASINGHAM

Cabernet Malbec Australia Bin 56 Winemakers Selection 1984 • $7 • (11/15/87) • **84**
Cabernet Malbec Clare Valley Domaine 1992: Soft and generous, supple, with gorgeous vanilla-scented plum, berry and black cherry aromas and flavors. Finishes smooth and elegant. Delicious to drink now through 1998. 7,500 cases made. • $8 • (06/30/94) • **89**
Cabernet Malbec Clare Valley Domaine 1989 • $8 • (08/31/92) • **82**
Cabernet Sauvignon Australia Bin 49 Winemakers Selection 1982 • $7 • (11/15/87) • **83**
Cabernet Sauvignon Clare Valley Classic 1992: Ripe and generous, mouth-filling, chewy and rich in texture, almost opulent. Plum, blackberry and delicate spice flavors broaden and become more polished as the finish persists. Tempting now, best from 1997. 800 cases made. • $16 • (06/15/95) • **90**
Cabernet Sauvignon Malbec Domaine Clare Valley 1993: Light and a little tannic for its modest level of berry flavors. Best in 1997. 1,000 cases made. • $12 • (03/31/96) • **80**
Cabernet Shiraz Australia Bin 68 1983 • $5 • (11/15/87) • **79**
Chardonnay Clare Valley 1993: Ripe and focused, showing resiny nuances on the spicy pear and apple. A little oaky. Drinkable now. 2,500 cases made. • $9 • (06/30/95) • **84**
Chardonnay Clare Valley Domaine 1992: Fresh and direct, brightly fruity, with spicy overtones and firm on the finish. Drinkable now. 7,500 cases made. • $8 • (09/30/94) • **84**
Chardonnay South Australia Hutt Creek 1993: Soft and simple, pleasantly fruity, echoing apple and vanilla on the finish. 8,000 cases made. • $6 • (09/30/94) • **81**
Sauvignon Blanc South Australia Hutt Creek 1993: Fruity and direct, a little astringent, but tasty enough to finish balanced. 7,500 cases made. • $6 • (09/30/94) • **80**
Sauvignon Blanc South Australia Hutt Creek 1992: Dry and austere, earthy, with extremely minor charms. 7,500 cases made. • $6 • (09/30/94) • **77**
Shiraz Australia Bin 61 1982 • $4 • (12/15/87) • **79**
Shiraz Cabernet Malbec Australia Hutt Creek Claret 1984 • $4 • (09/30/87) BB • **81**
Shiraz Cabernet Sauvignon South Australia Hutt Creek 1991: Offers a pretty core of grapey Shiraz-tinged fruit. Well balanced, drinkable now. 2,000 cases made. • $6 • (09/30/94) • **82**
Shiraz Cabernet Sauvignon South Australia Hutt Creek 1989 • $5 • (08/31/92) BB • **87**
Shiraz Clare Valley 1992: Light and chewy, with bright plum and spice aromas and flavors, a bit tannic but smooth enough to be drinkable. 9,000 cases made. • $8 • (09/30/94) • **83**
Shiraz Clare Valley Classic 1992: Smooth and polished, offering a range of plum, black cherry, vanilla and spice flavors, plus a touch of earth on the finish. Try now. 1,000 cases made. • $16 • (06/30/95) • **86**
Shiraz Clare Valley Domaine 1993: Ripe and supple, featuring focused red cherry, berry and spice flavors. Mildly chewy tannins can use until around 1998. 3,000 cases made. • $9 • (02/29/96) • **86**
Shiraz Clare Valley Domaine 1992: Bright, open-textured and disarmingly fruity, juicy with blackberry and black cherry flavors. Only a little tannic on the finish, but drinkable now. 1,000 cases made. • $9 • (06/30/95) BB • **85**

LEEUWIN

Cabernet Sauvignon Margaret River 1988: Crisp, chewy and flavorful, an herbal red that kicks in enough fruit to stay in balance. Drinkable now. 4,000 cases made. • $18 • (07/31/94) • **84**
Cabernet Sauvignon Margaret River 1983 • $18 • (05/31/88) • **86**
Cabernet Sauvignon Margaret River 1979 • $20 • (09/15/89) • **79**
Cabernet Sauvignon Margaret River Art Series 1987 • $20 • (11/30/92) • **70**
Cabernet Sauvignon Margaret River Redgum Ridge 1990 • $15 • (11/15/93) • **83**
Pinot Noir Margaret River Art Series 1988 • $20 • (11/30/92) • **81**
Sauvignon Blanc Margaret River 1992: Crisp and lively, a zinger of a wine with citrus and slightly herbal flavors, echoing nicely on the finish. 2,500 cases made. • $18 • (09/30/94) • **85**
Sauvignon Blanc Margaret River 1991: Distinctive and flavorful, a mouthful of herbal, leafy and anise aromas and flavors, with just enough fruit sneaking in on the finish to keep it in balance. 2,500 cases made. • $19 • (09/30/94) • **85**

Key: SS—Spectator Selection. CS—Cellar Selection. BB—Best Buy. $NA—Price not available. (BT)—Barrel tasting. Ⓐ—Auction Price.
Dates in parentheses represent the issues in which the ratings were published.

LEHMANN, PETER

Cabernet Blend Barossa Valley 1986 • $8 • (02/28/91) • **78**
Cabernet Sauvignon Barossa Valley 1993: Ripe and generous, boasting a subtle, spicy edge to the blackberry and currant flavors packed between its layers of tannin. Shows enough promise to make it worth waiting until 2002 to 2005. 10,000 cases made. • $14 • (04/30/96) • **90**
Cabernet Sauvignon Barossa Valley 1992: Sturdy, simple and easy to drink, showing ripe berry and plum flavors that follow through to the finish. 8,000 cases made. • $13 • (06/30/95) • **80**
Cabernet Sauvignon Barossa Valley 1987 • $8 • (03/31/91) • **80**
Cabernet Sauvignon Barossa Valley 1986 • $9 • (01/31/90) • **85**
Cabernet Sauvignon Barossa Valley 1983 • $9 • (07/01/87) • **81**
Clancy's Gold Preference Barossa Valley 1991: A little thick and chewy, but soft, with muddy, tarry flavors that overshadow the fruit. 6,000 cases made. • $15 • (06/30/95) • **77**
Port Barossa Valley Bin AD 2010 1989: Earthy, toasty, a little charred-tasting, but the blackberry and wild raspberry flavors come through on the finish. Best from 1999. 500 cases made. • $15 • (04/15/95) • **85**
Sémillon Barossa Valley 1994: Bright and spicy, a refreshing wine with citrusy pineapple flavors that echo on the light finish. Ready now. 14,000 cases made. • $10 • (01/31/95) • **85**
Sémillon Late Harvest Barossa Valley Botrytis Sauternes 1992: Sweet and rich, but not opulent, with fig and cigar notes. Drinkable now. 4,000 cases made. • $12 • (06/30/95) • **83**
Sémillon Late Harvest Barossa Valley Botrytis Sauternes 1988 • $6 • (04/15/91) BB • **83**
Sémillon Late Harvest Barossa Valley Botrytis Sauternes 1987 • $8 • (10/31/89) • **89**
Sémillon Late Harvest Barossa Valley Botrytis Sauternes 1984 • $15 • (07/01/87) • **89**
Shiraz Barossa Valley 1993: Brilliantly fruity, as impressive black cherry and pepper flavors keep spilling over on the zippy finish. Approachable now, but best in 1998. 12,000 cases made. • $10 • (04/30/96) • **88**
Shiraz Barossa Valley 1992: Relatively light and smooth, modestly fruity, with a touch of prune to the spicy flavors. Drinkable now. 15,000 cases made. • $10 • (01/31/95) • **81**
Shiraz Barossa Valley 1987 • $8 • (04/15/91) BB • **84**
Shiraz Barossa Valley 1983 • $7 • (07/01/87) • **81**
Shiraz Barossa Valley Dry Red 1985 • $7 • (07/31/89) BB • **84**
Shiraz Barossa Valley Dry Red 1983 • $5 • (04/30/87) • **79**
Shiraz Cabernet Sauvignon Barossa Valley 1985 • $7 • (01/31/90) • **83**

LILLYDALE

Cabernet Merlot Yarra Valley 1990: Dominant aromas suggest fresh sawdust, but the flavors enrich and expand to show some pretty black cherry and plum. Try in 1997. 1,500 cases made. • $14 • (06/30/95) • **82**
Chardonnay Yarra Valley 1993: Light and citrusy, a pineapple note chiming in on the slightly metallic finish. Drinkable now. 1,500 cases made. • $14 • (06/30/95) • **81**
Pinot Noir Yarra Valley 1990: Mature, almost Sherry-like overtones in this soft, comfortable red. Not much Pinot character, but interesting. 1,500 cases made. • $14 • (06/30/95) • **77**

LINDEMANS

Cabernet Blend Pyrus 1986 • $25 • (06/30/92) • **77**
Cabernet Blend Coonawarra Pyrus 1991: Warm and richly flavorful up front, balancing its raspberry, currant and cedar notes against a strong hit of tannin on the finish. Needs until 2001 to 2005 to soften. • $22 • (04/30/96) • **87**
Cabernet Blend Coonawarra Pyrus 1987 • $25 • (05/31/93) • **84**
Cabernet Blend Coonawarra Pyrus 1986 • $24 • (07/31/90) • **78**
Cabernet Blend Coonawarra Pyrus 1985 • $20 • (05/31/88) • **87**
Cabernet Merlot South Australia Padthaway 1990 • $13 • (04/15/93) • **83**
Cabernet Sauvignon Coonawarra 1986 • $14 • (10/31/90) • **83**
Cabernet Sauvignon Coonawarra 1985 • $14 • (04/30/89) • **86**
Cabernet Sauvignon Coonawarra 1984 • $12 • (02/15/88) • **84**
Cabernet Sauvignon Coonawarra 1982 • $8 • (09/30/86) • **79**
Cabernet Sauvignon Coonawarra 150 Years Sequicentenary 1990: Lean, chewy and austere, showing modest black cherry and earthy flavors. Drinkable now. 2,000 cases made. • $13 • (03/31/95) • **80**
Cabernet Sauvignon Coonawarra St. George Vineyard 1991: Ripe, smooth and opulent; a silky-textured Cabernet delivering rich black cherry, tar, spice and mint flavors bubbling around on the gorgeous finish. Approachable now, but youthful enough to want until 2001 or 2002. • $22 • (04/30/96) • **92**
Cabernet Sauvignon Coonawarra St.-George Vineyard 1990: Firm-textured and generous in flavor, unfolding its bright currant and blackberry notes smoothly and gracefully. Tempting now, best from 1997. • $22 • (03/31/95) • **85**
Cabernet Sauvignon Coonawarra St.-George Vineyard 1986 • $25 • (06/30/92) • **82**
Cabernet Sauvignon Coonawarra St.-George Vineyard 1985 • $21 • (04/30/89) • **80**
Cabernet Sauvignon Coonawarra St.-George Vineyard 1984 • $15 • (01/31/88) • **88**
Cabernet Sauvignon Coonawarra St.-George Vineyard Lindemans Classic 1980 • $NA • **64**
Cabernet Sauvignon Coonawarra St.-George Vineyard NV • $15 • (05/31/87) • **88**
Cabernet Sauvignon Coonawarra Special Selection 1993: Tight and tannic, a little astringent for the level of flavor, showing more cedar and spice than berry notes. Give it until 2002 or 2003. • $15 • (04/30/96) • **85**
Cabernet Sauvignon Coonawarra Special Selection 1991: Ripe and generous, smooth-textured, showing a modicum of plum and spicy, peppery berry flavor amidst chewy tannins that emerge on the finish. Best in 1998. • $13 • (11/30/95) • **85**
Cabernet Sauvignon South Australia Bin 45 1994: Smooth and generous on a modest scale, appealing for its ripe currant, mint and spice flavors. Approachable now, best in 1998. 155,000 cases made. • $7 • (04/30/96) • **85**
Cabernet Sauvignon South Australia Bin 45 1993: Smooth and distinctively minty, a supple Cabernet that weaves its plum and currant flavors smoothly with the herbal overtones. Soft tannins make it drinkable now. • $7 • (11/30/95) • **83**
Cabernet Sauvignon South Australia Bin 45 1985 • $6 • (01/31/88) • **79**
Cabernet Sauvignon South Eastern Australia Bin 45 1992: Firm and chewy, packed with minty, spicy black cherry and currant flavors that fan out on the finish. Best from 1997 through 1998. 25,000 cases made. • $7 • (03/31/95) BB • **86**
Cabernet Sauvignon South Eastern Australia Bin 45 1991 • $7 • (04/30/94) BB • **82**
Cabernet Sauvignon South Eastern Australia Bin 45 1990 • $7 • (04/15/93) • **80**
Cabernet Sauvignon South Eastern Australia Bin 45 1989 • $6 • (08/31/92) BB • **81**
Cabernet Shiraz Coonawarra Limestone Ridge 1984 • $15 • (07/01/87) • **87**
Chardonnay Bin 65 1991 • $7 • (05/31/92) BB • **87**
Chardonnay Coonawarra 1994: Youthful, fruity and floral, showing lots of spice and vanilla in the smooth-textured pear and caramel flavors that linger on the finish. Tasty now. 900 cases made. • $15 • (04/30/95) • **87**
Chardonnay Padthaway 1994: Tightly wound, a brilliantly flavorful white that unfolds slowly, displaying Burgundian hazelnut, honey and pear notes which linger on the finish. Delicious now, best in 1997. • $13 • (04/30/96) • **92**
Chardonnay Padthaway 1991 • $13 • (03/15/93) • **80**
Chardonnay Padthaway Vineyard 1993: Youthful, flavorful and delicately spicy. Supple enough to show off its appealing vanilla, pear and toast notes. Drinkable now. 4,000 cases made. • $13 • (03/31/95) • **87**
Chardonnay Padthaway Vineyard 1992 • $13 • (05/15/94) • **89**
Chardonnay South Eastern Australia Bin 65 1995: A light, crisp, simple wine, but with pleasant pineapple and spice flavors that linger nicely on the finish. 208,444 cases made. • $7 • (03/31/96) • **83**
Chardonnay South Eastern Australia Bin 65 1994: Light and fruity, with a green, citrusy tinge to the apple flavor that echoes on the finish. Drinkable now. 195,000 cases made. • $7 • (03/31/95) BB • **85**
Chardonnay South Eastern Australia Bin 65 1993 • $7 • (04/15/94) BB • **83**

Chardonnay South Eastern Australia Bin 65 1992 • $7 • (04/30/93) BB • **83**

Limestone Ridge Vineyard Coonawarra 1990: Very ripe, earthy and big-boned, with herb and pickle aromas and rough-hewn berry and black cherry flavors. Best from 1997. • $22 • (01/31/95) • **87**

Merlot South Australia Bin 40 1994: Broad but still unfocused, a mouthful of tar and berry flavors are just starting to come together. Try in 1997. 50,300 cases made. • $7 • (03/31/96) • **82**

Merlot South Australia Bin 40 1993: Light and nicely focused, with spicy black cherry and currant flavors that ride smoothly to a polished finish. Drinkable now. 30,000 cases made. • $8 • (04/15/95) BB • **87**

Merlot South Australia Reserve 1993: Chewy at first, becoming softer and more elegant, almost velvety on the finish, showing modest tar and blackberry flavors that linger. Best now. • $13 • (12/15/95) • **86**

Merlot South Eastern Australia Bin 40 1992: Earthy, gamy flavors dominate the ripe fruit in this broad-textured, different sort of Merlot. Ends up being appealing. • $7 • (09/30/94) • **80**

Pinot Noir Padthaway 1986 • $12 • (09/15/89) • **73**

Pinot Noir Padthaway 1984 • $12 • (02/15/88) • **82**

Sauvignon Blanc South Eastern Australia Bin 95 1992 • $7 • (04/30/94) • **82**

Sémillon Chardonnay South Eastern Australia Bin 77 1994: Distinctive for its nectarine and pear flavors that remain exuberant right through the finish. Drinkable now. 15,000 cases made. • $7 • (06/15/95) BB • **85**

Sémillon Chardonnay South Eastern Australia Bin 77 1992: This usually does better. Lightly fruity, it loses intensity and depth on the finish. 8,000 cases made. • $7 • (09/30/94) • **80**

Sémillon Chardonnay South Eastern Australia Bin 77 1991 • $7 • (03/15/93) BB • **83**

Sémillon Chardonnay South Eastern Australia Henry Lindeman 1992 • $6 • (06/30/93) • **80**

Sémillon Late Harvest Padthaway Botrytis Griffith 1988 • $12 • (07/31/90) • **83**

Sémillon Late Harvest Padthaway Botrytis Griffith 1987 • $12 • (10/31/89) • **91**

Shiraz Barossa Valley 1986 • $12 • (05/15/89) • **83**

Shiraz Cabernet Coonawarra Limestone Ridge Vineyard 1991: Rich and elegant, an opulent red on a sleek frame, swirling with sweet, tarry plum, currant and black pepper flavors that remain vibrant through the finish. Delicious now, it should keep growing through 2000 to 2002. 9,200 cases made. • $22 • (04/30/96) • **91**

Shiraz Cabernet Coonawarra Limestone Ridge Lindemans Classic 1982 • $38 • (07/31/90) • **70**

Shiraz Cabernet Coonawarra Limestone Ridge Vineyard 1986 • $24 • (07/31/90) • **84**

Shiraz Cabernet Coonawarra Limestone Ridge Vineyard 1985 • $21 • (07/31/89) • **68**

Shiraz Cabernet Limestone Ridge Vineyard 1986 • $25 • (06/30/92) • **86**

Shiraz Cabernet Sauvignon South Eastern Australia Henry Lindeman 1991 • $6 • (05/31/93) • **79**

Shiraz Hunter Valley 1987 • $10 • (02/15/91) • **81**

Shiraz Hunter Valley Bin 3110 Lindemans Classic 1965 • $95 • (09/15/89) • **96**

Shiraz Hunter Valley Bin 4110 Lindemans Classic 1970 • $60 • (09/15/89) • **89**

Shiraz Hunter Valley Bin 5910 Lindemans Classic 1980 • $30 • (07/31/90) • **73**

Shiraz South Australia Bin 50 1994: Smooth-textured, with ripe raspberry and cherry flavors and peppery, earthy grace notes on the finish. Drinkable now. 110,000 cases made. • $8 • (06/30/96) • **86**

Shiraz South Australia Bin 50 1993: Smooth and ripe, medium in weight, featuring appealing plum, spice and tar flavors that soften on the finish. Drink now. • $7 • (12/15/95) • **84**

Shiraz South Australia Bin 50 1986 • $5 • (05/15/89) • **78**

Shiraz South Eastern Australia Bin 50 1992: Earthy flavors against a coarse texture add up to a wine struggling to find its balance. May be best from 1997. • $7 • (01/31/95) • **82**

Key: SS—Spectator Selection. CS—Cellar Selection. BB—Best Buy. $NA—Price not available. (BT)—Barrel tasting. Ⓐ—Auction Price.
Dates in parentheses represent the issues in which the ratings were published.

Shiraz South Eastern Australia Bin 50 1991: Tart and lean, with a signature peppery edge to the Shiraz fruit. Despite firm tannins, it's ready now. 7,800 cases made. • $7 • (09/30/94) • **79**

Shiraz South Eastern Australia Bin 50 1989 • $6 • (05/31/92) • **80**

Shiraz South Eastern Australia Bin 50 1987 • $5 • (07/15/90) BB • **84**

Tawny Port Australia Macquarie Very Special Wood Matured NV • $11 • (07/31/90) • **84**

LONGLEAT

Cabernet Sauvignon Goulburn Valley Revi Resco 1986 • $9 • (09/30/89) • **73**

MACKENZIE ESTATES

Sémillon Chardonnay Hunter Valley 1994: Earthy, toasty flavors come off austere and drying. 4,000 cases made. • $8 • (04/30/96) • **77**

Shiraz Hunter Valley 1994: Tight, tough and tannic, difficult to warm up to, shy of fruit and other flavors. May be better in 2000. 4,000 cases made. • $8 • (04/30/96) • **77**

MARIENBERG

Cabernet Sauvignon McLaren Vale 1992: Earthy, gamy and spicy, showing more smoky oak than plummy flavors, lean and focused. Drink now. 6,000 cases made. • $12 • (10/15/95) • **84**

Chardonnay McLaren Vale 1994: Smooth and supple, with elegantly polished, clove-scented pear and toast flavors that glide through the finish. Drinkable now. 6,000 cases made. • $12 • (06/30/95) • **86**

Chardonnay South Eastern Australia 1993: Firm in texture, with distinctively smoky, almost bitter flavors that shoulder past the fruit. May be better in 1997. 5,000 cases made. • $11 • (03/31/96) • **78**

Lavinia Classic Dry White McLaren Vale 1994: Lean and tight, with focused pineapple and tobacco flavors. Drink now. 3,000 cases made. • $10 • (06/30/95) • **81**

Riesling McLaren Vale Cottage Classic 1994: Unusual tropical fruit and floral flavors combine in this reticent style of Riesling. Drinkable now. 2,000 cases made. • $10 • (06/30/95) • **84**

Sémillon Chardonnay McLaren Vale 1994: Bright and fruity, with lively pear, pineapple and a touch of cedar in the swirl of flavors. Drinkable now. 5,000 cases made. • $11 • (06/15/95) • **86**

Shiraz McLaren Vale 1993: Earthy, herbal, gamy and peppery flavors dominate this one, making it distinctive but out there on the edge. May be best in 1998. 4,500 cases made. • $12 • (04/30/96) • **85**

Shiraz McLaren Vale 1992: Massively flavorful but not heavy, expanding on its tar, prune, black cherry, coffee and cola flavors, then ringing out echoes of berries and spice on the long finish. A distinctive, complex and powerful Australian red. Tempting now, but best from 1999 on. 5,000 cases made. • $12 • (10/31/95) • **91**

MASSONI

Chardonnay Main Creek Vineyard 1992: Crisp and focused, lively, with finely tuned green apple and spice flavors that linger on the finish. Drinkable now. 900 cases made. • $20 • (07/31/94) • **88**

MCGUIGAN BROTHERS

Cabernet Merlot Hunter Valley Shareholders Reserve 1991 • $11 • (02/28/93) • **86**

Cabernet Sauvignon Australia Bin 4000 NV • $9 • (03/31/93) • **81**

Cabernet Sauvignon Australia Personal Reserve 1993: Packs a lot of beautiful currant and blackberry between the layers of anise and vanilla, wrapped in velvety tannins, harmonious and elegantly proportioned. Tempting now, best from 2000 to 2002. 1,000 cases made. • $15 • (04/30/96) • **91**

Cabernet Sauvignon South Eastern Australia Bin 4000 1991 • $8 • (06/15/94) • **80**

Chardonnay Australia Bin 7000 1992 • $8 • (03/15/93) • **83**

Chardonnay Australia Shareholders Reserve 1992 • $11 • (09/30/93) • **76**

Chardonnay Hunter Valley Shareholders Reserve 1991 • $11 • (03/15/93) • **84**

Chardonnay South Eastern Australia Bin 7000 1992: Bright and fruity, pear and apple flavors riding along the polished surface to a lively finish. Drinkable now. 10,000 cases made. • $8 • (06/30/94) BB • **85**

Merlot South Eastern Australia Bin 3000 1995: Light and refreshing, sporting a tropical fruit punch character that lingers appealingly on the bright finish. Drinkable now. 10,000 cases made. • $8 • (04/30/96) • **85**

Merlot South Eastern Australia Bin 3000 1993: Smooth and sweet, sporting a honeylike edge to the cherry flavors. Very unusual, rather like a cough drop. Tasty finish. Drink now. 12,000 cases made. • $8 • (04/15/95) • **85**

Merlot South Eastern Australia Bin 3000 Soft Mellow Dry Red 1994: Soft, almost sweet, showing berry and plum flavors and a touch of spice on the finish. 9,000 cases made. • $9 • **81**

Sémillon Chardonnay South Eastern Australia 1994: A light and fragrant value of a wine. A note of tobacco accents the zingy citrus and pineapple flavors that echo nicely on the finish. 30,000 cases made. • $7 • (10/31/95) BB • **85**

Sémillon Chardonnay South Eastern Australia 1992 • $7 • (11/15/93) • **80**

Shiraz Hunter Valley Hermitage Personal Reserve 1993: Firm, tight and flavorful, chewy in texture but focused with its spicy, almost cinnamon-scented blackberry and plum notes. Stylish, harmonious fruit and spiced oak tones should be at their best in 2001 to 2003. 1,000 cases made. • $15 • (04/30/96) • **91**

Shiraz South Eastern Australia Black 1994: Soft and appealing for its straightforward fruit flavors, swirling with blackberry, currant and cranberry flavors, almost sweet on the finish. 30,000 cases made. • $7 • (11/15/95) BB • **85**

Shiraz South Eastern Australia Black 1992 • $7 • (10/31/93) BB • **83**

Shiraz South Eastern Australia Black 1991 • $7 • (05/31/93) BB • **82**

MCLARENS

Chardonnay South Eastern Australia 1993: Smooth and graceful, its green apple and spice flavors folding nicely into a lingering finish. 5,000 cases made. • $9 • (12/15/94) BB • **86**

Classic Dry White South Eastern Australia 1993: Subdued in aromas, but the flavors have the distinctive floral, piney, green apple notes of a clean, dry Riesling. 2,500 cases made. • $7 • (01/31/95) • **82**

Sémillon Chardonnay South Eastern Australia 1992: Soft, appealing, simple and spicy, with modest fig and pear flavors. 2,500 cases made. • $9 • (01/31/95) • **83**

Shiraz Cabernet Sauvignon South Eastern Australia 1992: Soft and generous, showing a bright, spicy edge to the plum and blackberry flavors, finishes with a hint of tea. Drinkable now. 5,000 cases made. • $9 • (01/31/95) • **82**

Shiraz South Eastern Australia 1991 • $8 • (11/30/93) BB • **87**

MCWILLIAMS

Cabernet Sauvignon Australia Hanwood Estate 1991 • $7 • (12/15/93) • **82**

Cabernet Sauvignon South Eastern Australia Mount Pleasant 1992: Solid Cabernet with appealing currant and anise aromas and flavors that weave through a chunky finish. Drinkable now. 18,000 cases made. • $10 • (09/30/94) • **85**

Cabernet Sauvignon South Eastern Australia Mount Pleasant 1991 • $10 • (12/15/93) • **80**

Chardonnay Australia Hanwood Estate 1992 • $7 • (10/31/93) • **77**

Chardonnay South Eastern Australia Mount Pleasant 1992: Ripe and generous, broad, with some depth and distinction, layering its spicy pear, melon and grapefruit notes nicely. Flavors echo on the long finish. Drinkable now. 18,000 cases made. • $10 • (09/30/94) • **90**

Chardonnay South Eastern Australia Mount Pleasant 1991 • $10 • (10/31/93) • **82**

Shiraz Australia Hanwood 1993: Light in texture, simple, with modest berry flavors. • $7 • (09/30/94) • **77**

MILBURN PARK

Cabernet Sauvignon Victoria 1994: Ripe and focused on currant and berry flavors draped over a supple frame that lets the fruit echo on the finish. Approachable now. 15,000 cases made. • $9 • (03/31/96) • **85**

Chardonnay Victoria 1994: An exuberant mouthful of citrusy pineapple, remaining broad and flavorful through the generous finish. 20,000 cases made. • $9 • (03/31/96) BB • **88**

Sauvignon Blanc Victoria 1994: Light and satiny, with pleasant orange peel and grapefruit notes to keep it lively. 10,000 cases made. • $8 • (03/31/96) BB • **85**

MILDARA

Cabernet Merlot Murray River Valley 1986 • $7 • (03/31/89) • **80**

Cabernet Sauvignon Coonawarra 1986 • $10 • (01/31/89) • **90**

Cabernet Sauvignon Coonawarra 1985 • $8 • (04/15/88) BB • **89**

Cabernet Sauvignon Coonawarra 1984 • $6 • (04/30/87) • **77**

Cabernet Sauvignon McLaren Vale Private Reserve 1985 • $13 • (01/31/89) • **85**

Cabernet Sauvignon Merlot Coonawarra 1985 • $5 • (01/31/88) BB • **80**

Cabernet Sauvignon Merlot Coonawarra 1984 • $5 • (06/15/87) BB • **82**

Cabernet Sauvignon Murray River Valley 1986 • $8 • (01/31/89) • **80**

Shiraz Coonawarra 1986 • $9 • (12/31/88) • **89**

MITCHELL

Shiraz Clare Valley Peppertree Vineyard 1989 • $11 • (02/15/92) • **76**

MITCHELTON

Cabernet Blend South Eastern Australia 1993: Lean and distinctly herbal, with a minty eucalyptus hint to the basic black cherry flavor. Smooth and drinkable now. 15,000 cases made. • $10 • (06/30/95) • **82**

Cabernet Blend South Eastern Australia Cabernet Shiraz Malbec 1992 • $9 • (05/15/94) • **84**

Cabernet Sauvignon Goulburn Valley 1988 • $13 • (04/15/91) • **86**

Cabernet Sauvignon Goulburn Valley 1986 • $13 • (01/31/90) • **73**

Cabernet Sauvignon Goulburn Valley Reserve 1990 • $18 • (03/31/93) • **82**

Cabernet Sauvignon Merlot Australia Print Label 1985 • $17 • (01/31/90) • **78**

Cabernet Sauvignon Shiraz Cabernet Franc South Eastern Australia Thomas Mitchell 1994: Light and crisp, showing sour candy overtones to the light, citrusy berry flavors. Ready now. • $10 • (04/30/96) • **80**

Cabernet Sauvignon Shiraz Merlot South Eastern Australia 1991 • $10 • (11/30/93) • **82**

Cabernet Sauvignon South Eastern Australia Reserve 1992: Rough in texture, youthful and angular. Needs time to soften, may be best from 1998. 5,000 cases made. • $16 • (01/31/95) • **80**

Cabernet Sauvignon South Eastern Australia Reserve 1991 • $14 • (11/15/93) • **81**

Cabernet Sauvignon Victoria Reserve 1993: Generous, supple and velvety, rounding out its chocolaty plum and berry flavors in a note of spicy oak. Close to drinkable; try now. 5,000 cases made. • $16 • (11/30/95) • **90**

Cabernet Shiraz Merlot Victoria 1990 • $10 • (08/31/92) • **87**

Cabernet Shiraz Merlot Victoria 1987 • $9 • (01/31/90) • **86**

Chardonnay Victoria 1994: Bright, fruity and fresh, with a simple pear flavor that has leafy overtones. 15,000 cases made. • $10 • (06/30/95) • **82**

Chardonnay Victoria 1993: A bright and fruity Australian white, with generous nectarine and spice aromas and flavors that linger on the finish. 40,000 cases made. • $9 • (07/31/94) BB • **85**

Chardonnay Victoria 1992 • $9 • (03/15/93) • **87**

Chardonnay Victoria 1991 • $8 • (02/29/92) • **77**

Chardonnay Victoria Reserve 1993: Ripe and supple, a harmonious wine that balances its ripe pear and fig flavors against a welcome touch of spicy vanilla. Ready now. Significantly better than the first tasting. 5,000 cases made. • $16 • (06/30/96) • **89**

Marsanne Goulburn Valley 1991 • $9 • (08/31/92) • **86**

Marsanne Goulburn Valley Reserve 1992: Bright and fruity, with flavors centering around citrus and pineapple that last into a solid finish. Drinkable now. 5,000 cases made. • $16 • (01/31/95) • **85**

Marsanne Goulburn Valley Reserve 1991 • $15 • (04/30/94) • **84**

Marsanne South Eastern Australia 1995: Lean and crisp, adding a citrusy edge to the peach flavors. Drinkable now. 8,000 cases made. • $10 • (04/30/96) • **83**

Marsanne South Eastern Australia 1993: Crisp and floral, with a citrusy edge that's especially pleasant. 12,000 cases made. • $9 • (07/31/94) • **81**
Marsanne Victoria Reserve 1993: Broad and fruity, showing nicely focused peach and apple flavors. Drinkable now. 4,000 cases made. • $16 • (04/30/96) • **81**
MCM Cab Mac Victoria 1992 • $9 • (03/31/93) • **85**
Sémillon Chardonnay Victoria 1991 • $8 • (03/15/93) • **81**
Shiraz Goulburn Valley 1989 • $8 • (02/15/92) • **80**
Shiraz Goulburn Valley 1988 • $8 • (03/15/91) BB • **86**
Shiraz South Eastern Australia 1993: A light, fruity style that echoes with pleasant berry and currant flavors. Drinkable now. 15,000 cases made. • $10 • (06/30/95) • **85**
Shiraz South Eastern Australia Thomas Mitchell 1994: Simple and bright, a little coarse in texture but pleasant for its berry and anise flavors. 9,000 cases made. • $10 • (04/30/96) • **83**
Shiraz Victoria 1991 • $9 • (05/31/93) • **84**
Shiraz Victoria 1990 • $8 • (11/30/92) BB • **84**
Shiraz Victoria Print Label 1991: Ripe, generous and mouth-filling. Packs in plenty of berry, plum, tar and spice flavors, finishing with a bite of tannin. Drinkable now. 1,500 cases made. • $18 • (09/30/94) • **87**
Shiraz Victoria Print Label 1990 • $17 • (05/31/93) • **88**
Shiraz Victoria Reserve 1993: Beautifully rich and aromatically expansive, smooth, elegant and spicy in flavor, weaving a strong bead of blackberry and plum flavor throughout. Drink now. 5,000 cases made. • $16 • **91**

MONTROSE

Cabernet Sauvignon Mudgee 1987 • $10 • (02/28/91) • **81**
Cabernet Sauvignon Mudgee 1986 • $8 • (07/31/89) • **86**
Cabernet Sauvignon Mudgee 1984 • $10 • (04/30/88) • **88**
Cabernet Sauvignon Mudgee Special Reserve 1985 • $16 • (01/31/90) • **80**
Poet's Corner South Eastern Australia 1991 • $6 • (03/31/93) BB • **82**
Shiraz Mudgee 1988 • $9 • (03/15/91) • **78**
Shiraz Mudgee 1984 • $10 • (07/01/87) • **87**
Shiraz Mudgee 1983 • $7 • (03/15/88) • **86**

MORRIS

Tokay Australia Show Reserve NV • $15 • (07/01/87) • **92**

MOUNT LANGI GHIRAN

Shiraz Victoria 1994: Ripe, rich, elegant and a distinctly peppery character make this a highly seasoned mouthful of fruit and tar. It maintains the richness right through the spicy finish. The slightly scratchy tannins will smooth out by late 1997. 1,800 cases made. • $24 • (06/15/96) • **92**

MOUNT PLEASANT

Chardonnay Hunter Valley 1995: Light and crisp, a well-crafted Chardonnay that folds its peach, melon and vanilla flavors around a silky frame. Drinkable now. 8,500 cases made. • $13 • (04/30/96) • **87**
Chardonnay Hunter Valley 1993: Very ripe and generous, offering a mouthful of spicy pear, fig and tobacco flavors that linger on the supple finish. Delicious now, and should be fine at least through 1998. 2,500 cases made. • $12 • (06/30/95) • **88**
Sémillon Hunter Valley Elizabeth 1991: Bright lemon and pineapple flavors characterize this lively, harmonious white, finishing in an earthy, herbal note. Drinkable now. 40,000 cases made. • $13 • (04/30/96) • **87**
Shiraz Hunter Valley 1993: Light in color, as modest peppery, berry flavors swing smoothly through the finish. Approachable now. • $11 • (04/30/96) • **82**
Shiraz Hunter Valley 1992: Distinctly earthy, gamy, animal flavors, smooth-textured. Not for every palate, although it balances elegantly on the finish. Ready now, but should age through 2000. 1,900 cases made. • $12 • (11/30/95) • **83**

MOUNTADAM

Chardonnay Australia 1993: A Chardonnay that's spicy and a little buttery, but the pear and toast flavors come sailing through and linger on the finish. Drinkable now. 8,000 cases made. • $25 • (09/30/95) • **90**
Chardonnay Eden Valley 1994: Very pretty spicy, floral notes swirl around a nice core of pear and nectarine flavors, remaining crisp and elegant through the long finish. Delicious now. 6,000 cases made. • $26 • (04/30/96) • **90**
Chardonnay Eden Valley 1992: Crisp in texture, some subtle herb and citrus notes appear on the earthy finish. Seems to tone down its fruit in favor of longevity. Drink now 5,000 cases made. • $23 • (05/15/95) • **88**
Chardonnay Eden Valley 1991 • $20 • (10/31/93) • **84**
Pinot Noir Eden Valley 1993: Light on the palate, showing pruny, almost chocolaty flavors and a smoky note on the finish. Not especially bright, but it has character. 2,000 cases made. • $26 • (04/30/96) • **81**
Pinot Noir Eden Valley 1992: A fresh, appealing style of Pinot Noir, bright and generous, popping with beautifully focused currant and blackberry flavor, then softening to a light burr of tannin on the finish. Drinkable now through 1998. 1,500 cases made. • $20 • (07/31/94) • **88**
Pinot Noir Eden Valley 1988 • $25 • (03/31/91) • **86**

NORMANS

Cabernet Sauvignon South Australia Chais Clarendon 1991: Lean and chewy, with earthy, ashy notes to the modest black cherry and raisin flavors. 1,000 cases made. • $20 • (06/30/95) • **78**
Cabernet Sauvignon South Australia Chais Clarendon 1989: Soft and herbal, with a minty-cedary edge to the modest cherry flavors. 1,000 cases made. • $19 • (09/30/94) • **78**
Cabernet Sauvignon South Australia Family Reserve 1993: Smooth and flavorful, a nice mouthful of berry and currant notes, approachable now. 7,000 cases made. • $10 • (04/30/95) • **84**
Cabernet Sauvignon South Australia Family Reserve 1992: Dense and bright in color, but a little short on flavor intensity, sneaking in a touch of currant on the chewy finish. Drinkable now. 7,000 cases made. • $10 • (09/30/94) • **79**
Chardonnay Chandlers Hill 1991 • $7 • (02/29/92) BB • **86**
Chardonnay South Australia Chais Clarendon 1991: Lean and lively, showing its pear, apricot, spice, and toast flavors delicately. Stylish, harmonious, and appealing. Drinkable now. 750 cases made. • $19 • (11/30/94) • **88**
Chardonnay South Australia Chandlers Hill 1994: Light and fruity, with a sappy edge to the basic nectarine flavors. Drinkable now. 10,000 cases made. • $8 • (01/31/95) • **81**
Chardonnay South Australia Chandlers Hill 1993: Ripe and spicy, a flavorful white, with generous nutmeg, vanilla and pear flavors that echo on the finish. 10,000 cases made. • $8 • (09/30/94) • **84**
Chardonnay South Australia Family Reserve 1994: Round, generous and fruity, adding spice and mineral nuances to the pear and vanilla flavors at the core. Drinkable now. 10,000 cases made. • $10 • (04/15/95) • **87**
Chardonnay South Australia Family Reserve 1993: Soft, spicy and broad, a mouth-filling white that leans more toward caramel and nutmeg than fruit. Very tasty. 10,000 cases made. • $10 • (09/30/94) • **83**
Shiraz South Australia Chais Clarendon 1992: Smooth and fruity, brimming with plum and spice flavors that persist on the silky finish. Fine through 1997. 750 cases made. • $20 • (04/15/95) • **87**
Shiraz South Australia Chais Clarendon 1990 • $19 • (06/15/94) • **86**
Shiraz South Australia Chandlers Hill 1993: Earthy, chocolaty, raisiny flavors tend to dominate this lean, chewy red. Drink now. 10,000 cases made. • $8 • (04/15/95) • **79**
Shiraz South Australia Chandlers Hill 1992 • $8 • (06/15/94) • **82**

O'SHEA, MAURICE

Chardonnay Australia 1994: Crisp and appealing, offering some nice vanilla and apple flavors. Doesn't show much depth for the price. May be better in 1997. • $25 • (04/30/96) • **82**

Key: SS—Spectator Selection. CS—Cellar Selection. BB—Best Buy. $NA—Price not available. (BT)—Barrel tasting. Ⓐ—Auction Price.
Dates in parentheses represent the issues in which the ratings were published.

Shiraz Hunter Valley 1993: Broad and textured, showing crisp black cherry and spice flavors that linger a bit on the finish. Drinkable now. 500 cases made. • $25 • (04/30/96) • **86**

ORLANDO

Brut Australia Extra Brut Carrington NV: Soft in texture, with a smoky, almost burnt edge to the simple flavors. • $8 • (09/30/94) • **76**

Cabernet Sauvignon Coonawarra Jacaranda Ridge 1989: Very ripe, almost raisiny, offering dark purple plum and tar flavors that turn smoky on the finish. Mature and ready now. • $35 • (10/31/95) • **83**

Cabernet Sauvignon Coonawarra St.-Hugo 1989 • $15 • (12/15/93) • **86**

Cabernet Sauvignon Coonawarra St.-Hugo 1987 • $15 • (05/31/91) • **78**

Cabernet Sauvignon Coonawarra St.-Hugo 1986 • $8 • (02/28/91) • **81**

Cabernet Sauvignon Coonawarra St.-Hugo 1985 • $15 • (04/30/89) • **90**

Cabernet Sauvignon South Eastern Australia Jacob's Creek 1990 • $8 • (12/15/93) • **78**

Cabernet Sauvignon South Eastern Australia Jacob's Creek 1989 • $7 • (06/30/92) • **77**

Cabernet Sauvignon South Eastern Australia Jacob's Creek 1988 • $7 • (07/15/91) BB • **83**

Cabernet Sauvignon South Eastern Australia Jacob's Creek 1987 • $7 • (07/31/90) BB • **85**

Cabernet Sauvignon South Eastern Australia Jacob's Creek 1986 • $7 • (05/15/89) BB • **87**

Chardonnay South Eastern Australia Jacob's Creek 1995: The bright yellow color is odd, but the fresh apple and pineapple flavors are appealing. Drinkable now. 40,000 cases made. • $7 • (03/31/96) • **81**

Chardonnay South Eastern Australia Jacob's Creek 1993: Lean, lithe and spicy, the pear and honey flavors converging into a solid finish. Drinkable now. 200,000 cases made. • $7 • (06/30/94) BB • **82**

Chardonnay South Eastern Australia Jacob's Creek 1992 • $8 • (09/30/93) • **80**

Chardonnay South Eastern Australia Jacob's Creek 1991 • $7 • (05/31/92) BB • **86**

Chardonnay South Eastern Australia St.-Hugo 1992: Simple, generous and spicy, a toasty Chardonnay with definite peach and apple flavors. Drinkable now. 4,000 cases made. • $16 • (06/30/94) • **86**

Merlot South Eastern Australia Jacob's Creek 1994: Crisp and modestly flavorful, fresh with black cherry and spice flavors. • $7 • (03/31/96) • **80**

Merlot South Eastern Australia Jacob's Creek 1992: Simple, fruity and spicy, a modest Merlot with tannins chewier than the flavors can support. Drinkable now. 15,000 cases made. • $8 • (09/30/94) • **77**

Merlot South Eastern Australia Jacob's Creek 1991 • $8 • (12/15/93) • **81**

Merlot South Eastern Australia Jacob's Creek 1990 • $7 • (06/30/92) • **79**

Merlot South Eastern Australia Jacob's Creek 1989 • $7 • (09/30/91) • **82**

Sauvignon Blanc South Eastern Australia Jacob's Creek 1992: Earthy, herbal flavors dominate this austere Sauvignon Blanc, only a wisp of citrus livening it up on the finish. 8,000 cases made. • $7 • (09/30/94) • **79**

Sauvignon Blanc South Eastern Australia Jacob's Creek 1991 • $8 • (09/15/93) • **72**

Sémillon Chardonnay South Eastern Australia Jacob's Creek 1995: Crisp, straightforward and appealing for its soft pear and citrus flavors. 20,000 cases made. • $7 • (03/31/96) • **80**

Shiraz Cabernet South Eastern Australia Jacob's Creek 1994: Smooth and lively, harmonious despite its youth, finishing a little narrow but spicy and fresh. Drinkable now. • $7 • (03/31/96) • **82**

Shiraz Cabernet South Eastern Australia Jacob's Creek 1991 • $8 • (10/31/93) • **80**

Shiraz Padthaway Lawson's 1991: Balances its ripe fruit and earthy components into a fascinating whirl of black cherry, dark plum and meat overtones, extending into a solid finish. Best in 1997. 200 cases made. • $22 • (02/29/96) • **89**

OXFORD LANDING

Cabernet Sauvignon Shiraz Oxford Landing 1989 • $7 • (02/29/92) BB • **82**

Cabernet Sauvignon Shiraz South Australia 1988 • $7 • (09/15/90) • **73**

Cabernet Sauvignon Shiraz South Eastern Australia 1993: Light, lean, silky and spicy, with an herbal, tobacco-like character pushing through the chocolaty black cherry flavors; a lot of depth for the money. Try now. 30,000 cases made. • $7 • (11/30/95) BB • **85**

Cabernet Sauvignon Shiraz South Eastern Australia 1992: Lean in structure but supple in texture, showing spicy, lightly leathery tones in its plum and prune flavors. Drinkable now. 20,000 cases made. • $7 • (06/30/95) • **84**

Cabernet Sauvignon Shiraz South Eastern Australia 1991 • $7 • (04/30/94) • **81**

Chardonnay South Eastern Australia 1995: Crisp at first, with a nice layer of creaminess on the light finish. Ready now. 20,000 cases made. • $8 • (03/31/96) • **84**

Chardonnay South Eastern Australia 1994: Fresh, floral and smooth, a broad-textured white that never gets heavy. Tasty to drink while it's fresh. 20,000 cases made. • $10 • (05/15/95) • **86**

Chardonnay South Eastern Australia 1993 • $7 • (03/15/94) • **83**

Chardonnay South Eastern Australia 1992 • $7 • (04/30/93) BB • **83**

Chardonnay South Eastern Australia 1991 • $7 • (02/29/92) BB • **83**

Merlot South Eastern Australia 1994: Thin and simple, with only modest berry flavors. 10,000 cases made. • $7 • (06/30/96) • **78**

Merlot South Eastern Australia 1993: Supple, generous and spicy, showing a chocolaty edge to the black cherry flavors. At a good price and drinkable now. 10,000 cases made. • $7 BB • **85**

Sauvignon Blanc South Eastern Australia 1994: Soft and spicy, layering some butterscotch over the modest pear and spice flavors. Ready now. 10,000 cases made. • $7 • (03/31/96) • **80**

Sauvignon Blanc South Eastern Australia 1993 • $7 • (04/30/94) • **80**

Sauvignon Blanc South Eastern Australia 1992 • $7 • (04/15/93) BB • **87**

PARKER ESTATE

Cabernet Blend Coonawarra Terra Rossa First Growth 1990: Lean and tannic, with a broad range of decadent plum and cherry-laced fruit that turns earthy on the finish. It has its appeal despite its rough edges. 900 cases made. • $38 • (09/30/94) • **80**

Cabernet Blend Coonawarra Terra Rossa First Growth 1989 • $35 • (05/31/93) • **89**

Cabernet Sauvignon Coonawarra Terra Rossa 1992: Lean and herbal, a volatile, sour edge robbing this of its charm. 1,000 cases made. • $20 • (03/31/95) • **74**

Cabernet Sauvignon Coonawarra Terra Rossa 1991: Lean and austere, with a narrow band of plum and leathery flavors that turn tannic on the finish. Drinkable now. 2,000 cases made. • $22 • (09/30/94) • **82**

Terra Rossa First Growth Coonawarra 1991: Firm and intense, with a tight, rich, chewy core of ripe, meaty currant and black cherry flavors. Gritty tannins, best after 1998 or 2000. 1,000 cases made. • $39 • (03/31/95) • **87**

PENFOLDS

Cabernet Sauvignon Shiraz Bin 389 South Australia 1992: Rich, smooth and plush, with complex currant, black cherry, anise and spice flavors that are bold and intense. Finishes with firm tannins, but the fruit still manages to gush through on the finish. 25,000 cases made. • $16 • (11/30/95) SS • **92**

Cabernet Sauvignon Shiraz Bin 389 South Australia 1991: Ripe and spicy, sporting minty, herbal overtones to the plum and black cherry flavors. Chunky if somewhat rustic with firm, drying tannins. This is a big, intense mouthful that will require cellaring into 1997 or 1998. 25,000 cases made. • $16 • (11/30/95) • **90**

Cabernet Sauvignon Shiraz Bin 389 South Australia 1990: Chunky and tasty, with ripe plum and berry flavors, but it needs time to smooth out. Drinkable now. • $16 • (01/31/95) • **86**

Cabernet Sauvignon Shiraz South Australia 1989 • $16 • (04/15/94) • **87**

Cabernet Sauvignon Shiraz Bin 389 South Australia Koonunga Hill 1987 • $7 • (02/28/91) BB • **86**

Cabernet Sauvignon Shiraz South Australia Koonunga Hill 1986 • $7 • (05/15/89) • **78**

Cabernet Sauvignon South Australia Bin 407 1993: Rich and focused, supple in texture and layered with cedary blackberry and currant flavors, finishing firm and a bit chunky. Worth waiting until 2001 to 2003. • $16 • (04/30/96) • **88**

Cabernet Sauvignon South Australia Bin 407 1992: Bright and flavorful, giving you a zesty mouthful of berry and pickle barrel character that lingers through the finish. The tannins should soften until 1997 or 1998. 35,000 cases made. • $16 • (03/31/96) • **85**

Cabernet Sauvignon South Australia Bin 407 1991: Ripe, a little gamy and dense, with concentrated red cherry, tobacco and herb flavors that finish solidly. Drinkable now. • $16 • (11/30/94) • **86**

Cabernet Sauvignon South Australia Bin 407 1990 • $16 • (03/31/93) • **78**

Cabernet Sauvignon South Australia Bin 707 1992: Ripe and generous, elegantly balanced and velvety. The focused currant and plum flavors are shaded by a touch of smoke and spice, the fruit persisting beautifully on the finish. Best in 1997. 10,000 cases made. • $40 • (10/15/95) CS • **92**

Cabernet Sauvignon South Australia Bin 707 1990: Dark and inviting, with a supple core of wild berry, mint and currant flavors that are rich and elegant, finishing with a long, smooth aftertaste. Retasted because of significant bottle variation; two of four bottles were clearly superior in separate tastings. 10,675 cases made. • $40 • (03/31/95) CS • **92**

Cabernet Sauvignon South Australia Bin 707 1989 • $40 • (05/31/93) • **85**

Cabernet Sauvignon South Australia Bin 707 1987 • $38 • (05/31/91) • **83**

Cabernet Sauvignon South Australia Bin 707 1986 • $28 • (09/30/89) • **90**

Cabernet Sauvignon South Australia Bin 707 1981 • $18 • (07/01/87) • **90**

Cabernet Shiraz Coonawarra Bin 920 1990: Earthy, firmly tannic, with a minty edge to the leathery currant and cherry fruit. A touch rustic and finishing with dry tannins, but doesn't shortchange on flavor. • $110 • (05/15/96) • **86**

Cabernet Shiraz South Australia Bin 389 1993: Dense in color, texture and flavor, a solid mouthful of red plum and currant notes, turning cedary and spicy on the finish. Give it until 2000 to 2002. • $18 • (04/30/96) • **87**

Cabernet Shiraz South Australia Bin 389 1989 • $16 • (06/30/93) • **83**

Cabernet Shiraz South Australia Bin 389 1988 • $16 • (03/31/93) • **81**

Cabernet Shiraz South Australia Bin 389 1987 • $14 • (02/28/91) • **88**

Cabernet Shiraz South Australia Bin 389 1986 • $15 • (01/31/90) • **83**

Cabernet Shiraz South Australia Bin 389 1985 • $14 • (12/31/88) • **86**

Cabernet Shiraz South Australia Bin 389 1983 • $15 • (07/01/87) • **91**

Cabernet Shiraz South Australia Koonunga Hill 1984 • $7 • (07/01/87) • **89**

Chardonnay Australia Koonunga Hill 1995: Light and refreshing, shading its bright nectarine and passion fruit flavors with a touch of citrus. Tangy, bracing to drink now. 130,000 cases made. • $9 • (04/30/96) • **88**

Chardonnay South Australia 1994: Broad and flavorful, a bit medicinal but rich and spicy on the finish. Ready now. • $9 • (05/15/96) • **84**

Chardonnay South Australia 1993: Bright and tightly structured, a lighter style of Chardonnay that shows off its pear and spice flavors as they linger on the finish. Ready now. 154,000 cases made. • $9 • (04/30/95) • **87**

Chardonnay South Australia 1992 • $9 • (05/15/94) • **81**

Chardonnay South Australia 1991 • $9 • (04/30/93) • **84**

Chardonnay South Australia Barrel Fermented Reserve 1992: Very ripe, spicy and complex, with layers of honey, spice, pineapple and pear flavors that cascade into a lavish finish. A lot of wine for the price. Drinkable now. • $12 • (11/30/94) • **89**

Chardonnay South Australia Barrel Fermented Reserve 1994: Crisp, focused and bright with lemony pear and vanilla flavors, a touch of passion fruit sneaking around the edges. Best from 1997. • $12 • (03/31/96) • **88**

Chardonnay South Australia Matured in French Oak Casks 1991 • $16 • (04/30/93) • **89**

Chardonnay Sauvignon Blanc Organically Grown Grapes Clare Valley 1993: Smooth, spicy, light-textured and round, with melon, apple and vanilla flavors and a lingering finish. 1,000 cases made. • $10 • (01/31/95) • **85**

Shiraz South Australia Grange 1990: Amazingly ripe, rich and opulent, with layers of earthy currant, black cherry and anise flavors that are smooth and supple. The silky texture leads into a long, lingering aftertaste that offers echoes of fruit. The tannins are fine but substantial enough to age. Try from 1997 to 2005. 8,000 cases made. • $100 • (11/30/95) CS • **97**

Key: SS—Spectator Selection. CS—Cellar Selection. BB—Best Buy. $NA—Price not available. (BT)—Barrel tasting. Ⓐ—Auction Price.
Dates in parentheses represent the issues in which the ratings were published.

South Australia Grange Hermitage Bin 95 1989: Deep color, with complex, concentrated flavors to match. Has an array of jam, raspberry, anise, black cherry, vanilla and spice flavors that fold together nicely. Finishes with a long, full aftertaste. Has the tannic structure to age, but is delicious now. Try between 1997 and 2005. 8,000 cases made. • $85 • (01/31/95) CS • **96**

South Australia Grange Hermitage Bin 95 1988: Ripe and spicy, with a pretty anise edge to the rich cherry and currant flavors. Well balanced, finishing with firm tannins. Appealing already, but this has a history of improving with age. Best after 1998. 1,000 cases made. • $85 • (03/31/94) • **88**

South Australia Grange Hermitage Bin 95 1987: Ripe, rich, generous, powerful and amazingly complex, offering vanilla, cedar and toast-scented plum, black cherry and spice flavors that extend into a gorgeous finish. A beautifully sculpted wine, with all the elements to grow into a great one with cellaring through 1999 to 2005. 5,500 cases made. • $80 • (05/31/93) CS • **93**

South Australia Grange Hermitage Bin 95 1986: Ripe, round and generous, with smooth, polished smoke- and coffee-scented plum and prune aromas and flavors. Finishes with muscle and the sort of balance to keep it improving through 1996 to 2000. A very good wine, but seems to be missing the breadth and complexity you usually expect from the Grange. 5,790 cases made. • $80 • (05/31/93) • **88**

Grange Hermitage Bin 95 1985 • $80 • (02/29/92) • **88**

Grange Hermitage Bin 95 1984 • $80 • (04/15/91) • **89**

Grange Hermitage Bin 95 1982 • $60 • (04/15/91) • **94**

Grange Hermitage Bin 95 1981 • $49 • (04/15/91) • **89**

Grange Hermitage Bin 95 1980 • $NA • (04/15/91) • **88**

Grange Hermitage Bin 95 1979 • $NA • (04/15/91) • **89**

Grange Hermitage Bin 95 1978 • $NA • (04/15/91) • **85**

Grange Hermitage Bin 95 1977 • $NA • (04/15/91) • **82**

Grange Hermitage Bin 95 1976 • $NA • (04/15/91) • **86**

Grange Hermitage Bin 95 1974 • $NA • (04/15/91) • **79**

Grange Hermitage Bin 95 1971 • $NA • (04/15/91) • **95**

Grange Hermitage Bin 95 1970 • $NA • (04/15/91) • **85**

Grange Hermitage Bin 95 1968 • $NA • (04/15/91) • **87**

Grange Hermitage Bin 95 1967 • $NA • (04/15/91) • **91**

Koonunga Hill South Australia 1993: Broad in texture, adding fig and toast flavors that ride nicely on the finish. Drinkable now. • $9 • (05/31/95) • **83**

Koonunga Hill South Australia 1992: Light and smoothly integrated, showing flavorful plum and spice that linger on the finish. Drinkable now. • $NA • (06/30/95) • **84**

Koonunga Hill South Australia 1991: Lean and somewhat chunky, but ripe currant and plum flavors carry through on the finish. Drinkable now. • $9 • (03/31/95) BB • **85**

Port Australia Club NV: Very spicy, sporting caramel, cinnamon and tarry flavors, sweet and silky on the long finish. • $9 • (05/15/96) • **89**

Rhine Riesling Late Harvest South Australia 1987 • $5 • (03/15/89) BB • **88**

Riesling South Australia Bin 202 1993 • $7 • (04/30/94) • **82**

Sémillon Chardonnay South Australia Koonunga Hill 1995: Bright, fruity, lively peach and pear flavors linger on the finish, echoing toast and fruit. Drinkable now. • $8 • (04/30/96) • **87**

Sémillon Chardonnay South Australia Koonunga Hill 1994: Bright, lively and generous with its spicy, herbal pear and vanilla flavors. Drinkable now. 15,000 cases made. • $9 • (03/31/96) • **85**

Sémillon Chardonnay South Australia Koonunga Hill 1992 • $7 • (07/15/93) • **78**

Sémillon Chardonnay South Australia Koonunga Hill 1991 • $7 • (06/30/93) BB • **83**

Sémillon Late Harvest South Australia 1987 • $6 • (03/15/89) • **84**

Shiraz Cabernet Sauvignon Australia Koonunga Hill 1994: A little shy on the nose but blackberry flavors come through against the chewy, firm-textured background. Best in 1998. • $9 • (04/30/96) • **85**

Shiraz Cabernet Sauvignon Koonunga Hill South Australia 1993: More tannic than you might expect, a tightly austere wine with dark cherry and spice flavors poking though. Tannins need until 1998, but this is made to drink sooner. 210,000 cases made. • $9 • (03/31/96) • **78**

Shiraz Cabernet South Australia Koonunga Hill 1990 • $9 • (02/28/93) BB • **86**

Shiraz Coonawarra Bin 128 1993: Lean and toasty, featuring a strong, peppery oak character running through the narrowly focused blackberry flavors. Give it until 2000 to 2002. • $14 • (04/30/96) • **86**
Shiraz Coonawarra Bin 128 1992: Elegant, almost austere style, flavorful without being gooey, dealing out its black cherry, berry and plum notes and adding a mineral edge. Approachable now, best now to 1999. • $13 • (11/30/95) • **88**
Shiraz Coonawarra Bin 128 1990 • $15 • (03/31/94) • **83**
Shiraz South Australia Grange Hermitage Bin 95 1955 • $NA • (04/15/91) • **93**
Shiraz South Australia Kalimna Bin 28 1993: Smooth and harmonious but tightly wrapped in fine layers of tannin, focusing its blackberry, anise and toasty-peppery flavors in a solid beam that keeps shining through the finish. Best in 2003 to 2005. 35,000 cases made. • $18 • (04/30/96) • **91**
Shiraz South Australia Kalimna Bin 28 1992: Lean in texture, but beautifully aromatic and focused in flavor, showing black cherry and black pepper character that lingers on the tight finish. Best from 1997-1998. 2,000 cases made. • $16 • (11/15/95) • **85**
Shiraz South Australia Magill Estate Vineyard 1988 • $44 • (05/31/93) • **85**
Shiraz South Australia Magill Estate Vineyard 1985 • $45 • (07/31/89) • **87**
South Australia Grange Hermitage Bin 95 1983 • $80 • (03/15/91) • **92**
South Australia Grange Hermitage Bin 95 1966 • $NA • (04/15/91) • **96**
South Australia Grange Hermitage Bin 95 1965 • $NA • (04/15/91) • **84**

PETALUMA

Cabernet Merlot Coonawarra 1984 • $18 • (05/31/87) • **92**
Cabernet Sauvignon Coonawarra 1991: Firm and remarkably flavorful, boasting ripe currant, berry and a touch of red pepper, smooth and generous on the finish. Ready now, but should improve through 1998. 5,000 cases made. • $20 • (04/30/95) • **88**
Cabernet Sauvignon Coonawarra 1984 • $18 • (05/31/87) • **91**
Cabernet Sauvignon Merlot Coonawarra 1988 • $21 • (12/15/93) • **85**
Cabernet Sauvignon Merlot Coonawarra 1986 • $25 • (05/31/91) • **87**
Cabernet Shiraz Coonawarra 1982 • $16 • (07/01/87) • **89**
Chardonnay Australia 1994: Has density but the spicy apple flavors seem unfocused until the finish, when they linger unexpectedly. Could improve by 1997. 4,800 cases made. • $22 • (06/15/96) • **86**
Chardonnay Australia 1986 • $8 • (05/31/87) • **86**
Chardonnay South Australia 1992: Ripe, generous and spicy; a real mouthful of flavor with a smooth, supple texture. Its pear and citrus flavors expand on the finish, picking up some nice honey notes. Delicious already. 5,000 cases made. • $20 • (04/15/95) • **90**
Riesling Clare Valley 1995: Deliciously dry, floral and bursting with nectarine and green apple flavors that are couched in citrus and slightly resiny overtones. Distinctive, invigorating and amazingly tasty. 2,500 cases made. • $16 • (05/31/96) • **90**

PEWSEY VALE

Cabernet Sauvignon Australia Individual Vineyard Selection 1989 • $11 • (04/15/93) • **78**
Rhine Riesling Barossa Valley Individual Vineyard Selection 1987 • $5 • (03/15/89) • **79**
Rhine Riesling Individual Vineyard Selection 1990 • $9 • (07/15/91) • **76**
Rhine Riesling Late Harvest Barossa Valley Botrytis 1986 • $8 • (02/15/88) • **90**
Rhine Riesling Late Harvest Barossa Valley Botrytis Individual Vineyard Selection 1987 • $9 • (10/31/89) • **71**

PIERRO

Chardonnay Australia 1994: Tight and terrifically focused, a closed bud of a wine that shows concentrated apple, pear and spice flavors and need until 1997 to '98 to unfold. A cult favorite in Australia. 1,500 cases made. • $32 • (03/31/96) • **92**

PIPERS BROOK

Chardonnay Tasmania 1990 • $25 • (02/15/92) • **92**
Pinot Noir Tasmania 1990 • $25 • (02/29/92) • **81**

PREECE

Cabernet Sauvignon Goulburn Valley 1990 • $14 • (11/30/92) • **85**
Cabernet Sauvignon Goulburn Valley 1989 • $13 • (03/15/92) • **84**
Cabernet Sauvignon South Eastern Australia 1993: Soft and generous, with an earthy streak in the modest prune and chocolate flavors. Try in 1997. 10,000 cases made. • $12 • (06/30/95) • **82**
Cabernet Sauvignon South Eastern Australia 1992 • $12 • (04/30/94) • **86**
Chardonnay Goulburn Valley 1992 • $12 • (10/31/93) • **77**
Chardonnay Goulburn Valley 1991 • $14 • (11/15/92) • **84**
Chardonnay South Eastern Australia 1994: Smooth and a little spicy, simple, pleasant and lively on the apple-scented finish. 10,000 cases made. • $12 • (06/30/95) • **83**
Chardonnay South Eastern Australia 1993: Bright and fruity, a lively white with generous green apple and melon aromas and flavors that echo convincingly on the finish. Drinkable now. 30,000 cases made. • $11 • (09/30/94) • **86**

REDBANK

Brut Australia Emily NV: Smooth and creamy, delivering simple floral and pear flavors. Ready now. 2,000 cases made. • $12 • (05/15/96) • **85**
Cabernet Blend South Eastern Australia Sally's Paddock 1986 • $32 • (01/31/90) • **86**
Cabernet Sauvignon South Eastern Australia Long Paddock 1986 • $13 • (01/31/90) • **74**
Cabernet Sauvignon South Eastern Australia Long Paddock 1985 • $7 • (07/15/91) • **74**
Cabernet Sauvignon South Eastern Australia Redbank Cabernet 1986 • $54 • (01/31/90) • **89**
Cabernet Sauvignon Victoria Redbank Cabernet 1991: Firm in texture, offering mouth-filling currant, spice and mint flavors that lean toward elegance on the finish but come up a little short. May be best from 1998. • $37 • (10/15/95) • **87**
Chardonnay South Eastern Australia Long Paddock 1994: Soft, ripe and generous with its nectarine and spice flavors. Drinkable now. 5,000 cases made. • $10 • (03/31/96) • **84**
Chardonnay South Eastern Australia Long Paddock 1993: Lean but fragrant, a spicy wine with a touch of earthy pear flavor that finishes solid and simple. Ready now. 5,000 cases made. • $10 • **84**
Chardonnay South Eastern Australia Long Paddock 1992 • $9 • (03/15/94) • **82**
Sally's Paddock Red Victoria 1993: Has complexity, but the plummy, cedary flavors don't quite stand up to oaky notes on aftertaste. May be better in 2000. • $57 • (04/30/96) • **85**
Sémillon South Eastern Australia Long Paddock 1994: Broad and distinctive, boasting fig, hay and citrus peel flavors that build up richness on the palate. 2,000 cases made. • $10 • (03/31/96) • **84**
Shiraz South Eastern Australia Long Paddock 1991 • $9 • (11/30/93) • **82**
Shiraz Victoria Mountain Creek 1985 • $9 • (09/30/91) • **84**

REYNELLA, CHATEAU

Brut Australia NV: Dark, toasty, spicy style, a little sweet on the finish, appealing for its floral notes. 10,000 cases made. • $9 • (04/30/96) • **83**
Brut South Australia NV • $9 • (11/15/91) • **79**
Cabernet Merlot Basket Pressed McLaren Vale 1993: Chewy but supple and flavorful, with nice berry and spice notes. Better in 1997. 2,500 cases made. • $10 • (03/31/96) • **86**
Cabernet Merlot Basket Pressed McLaren Vale 1992: Nicely articulated currant and berry flavors course through this smooth-textured, elegant Australian red. In a supple style that's approachable now, and at a bargain. Try now. 5,000 cases made. • $10 • (12/15/95) BB • **87**
Cabernet Merlot McLaren Vale 1990: Soft and chewy with fine-textured tannins, but only modest flavors of black cherry and a touch of tar. Drinkable now. 2,500 cases made. • $8 • (09/30/94) • **79**
Cabernet Sauvignon Coonawarra 1988 • $8 • (04/30/91) • **86**
Cabernet Sauvignon Coonawarra 1984 • $7 • (04/30/88) • **80**
Cabernet Sauvignon Coonawarra 1980 • $15 • (05/31/87) • **84**
Cabernet Sauvignon McLaren Vale 1994: Ripe, rich and chewy, offering plenty of sweet plum, blackberry and currant flavors that have spicy,

toasty overlays weaving through the finish. Try in 1998. 5,000 cases made. • $12 • (06/30/96) • **88**

Cabernet Sauvignon McLaren Vale Basket Pressed 1993: Lean, lithe and nicely balanced between its blackberry and currant flavors and the smack of spicy oak that shows up on the finish. The tannins need until 1997 or 1998 to quiet down. 3,500 cases made. • $12 • (03/31/96) • **85**

Cabernet Sauvignon McLaren Vale Basket Pressed 1992: Bright and focused, packed with herb and tobacco-scented black cherry flavors. Earthy and has style and distinction. Best from 1997 to 1998. • $10 • (06/30/95) • **86**

Cabernet Sauvignon McLaren Vale Basket Pressed 1991: Smooth, ripe and polished. It's a generous Australian Cab, with lots of plum and currant flavors up front, narrowing a bit on the finish. Drinkable now. 6,000 cases made. • $8 • (07/31/94) BB • **84**

Cabernet Sauvignon McLaren Vale Basket Pressed 1990 • $9 • (05/15/94) • **82**

Chardonnay McLaren Vale 1994: Smooth and spicy, lean at first, but the citrusy, honeyed pear flavors open out on the finish. 3,000 cases made. • $10 • (03/31/96) • **88**

Chardonnay McLaren Vale 1993: Broad, ripe and spicy, a mouthful of flavor, echoing nutmeg, pear and vanilla and a touch of (welcome) maturity. 1,000 cases made. • $8 • (09/30/94) • **84**

Chardonnay McLaren Vale 1992: A good if simple young Chardonnay with straightforward pear and apple flavors. Delivers a nice core of fruit without the oak extras. Ready now. 8,000 cases made. • $10 • (07/31/94) • **83**

Chardonnay McLaren Vale 1990 • $11 • (11/30/91) • **84**

Port McLaren Vale Vintage Port 1992: A strong eucalyptus and medicinal note cuts through unfocused plum and cherry flavors. Seems awfully woody, but might be better by 2000 to 2003. 500 cases made. • $13 • (06/30/95) • **79**

Port South Australia 1981 • $12 • (11/15/91) • **85**

Shiraz McLaren Vale Basket Pressed 1994: A generous mouthful of brilliant berry, black pepper, sweet spice, coffee and chocolate flavors that swirl through the velvety finish. Delicious now, best in 1997. 4,000 cases made. • $12 • (06/30/96) • **92**

Shiraz McLaren Vale Basket Pressed 1993: Firm and chewy, a fountain of generous plum, berry and spice flavors erupting behind a curtain of tannin. Needs until 1998 to soften the tannins, but the fruit is already appealing. 3,000 cases made. • $10 • (03/31/96) • **86**

Shiraz McLaren Vale Basket Pressed 1991: Tough and tannic, chewy, with just a little berry and plum flavor peeking out from behind the screen of tannins. May be best from 1997. 2,500 cases made. • $8 • (09/30/94) • **81**

Tawny Port McLaren Vale Old Cave NV: Focused, flavorful and juicy, setting licorice, cinnamon and green tobacco-cedary notes around a core of spicy black cherry. Long and complex. 8,000 cases made. • $15 • (05/15/96) • **90**

Tawny Port South Australia Old Cave Fine Old NV • $12 • (11/15/91) • **77**

REYNOLDS

Sémillon Hunter Valley Benchmark 1992 • $10 • (07/15/93) • **78**

ROO'S LEAP

Cabernet Sauvignon McLaren Vale 1990 • $10 • (03/31/93) • **81**

Cabernet Sauvignon McLaren Vale 1985 • $10 • (11/30/88) • **89**

Cabernet Sauvignon McLaren Vale Limited Edition 1986 • $9 • (01/31/90) • **85**

Chardonnay Coonawarra Barrel Fermented 1993: Brilliant aromas, although the flavors are more modest, picking up steam on the finish which echoes the spicy pear and toast from the nose. Drinkable now. • $12 • (06/30/94) • **85**

Chardonnay Coonawarra Barrel Fermented 1992 • $10 • (04/30/93) • **80**

Chardonnay Coonawarra Barrel Fermented 1991 • $10 • (06/30/92) • **83**

Fumé Blanc Barossa Valley 1992 • $7 • (04/15/93) • **75**

Key: SS—Spectator Selection. CS—Cellar Selection. BB—Best Buy. $NA—Price not available. (BT)—Barrel tasting. Ⓐ—Auction Price.
Dates in parentheses represent the issues in which the ratings were published.

Fumé Blanc Barossa Valley 1991 • $8 • (06/30/92) • **83**

Pinot Noir McLaren Vale 1988 • $8 • (02/28/91) • **86**

ROSEMOUNT

Brut South Eastern Australia 1994: Bright and fruity, centering its flavors around pear and fig, then opening up to a spicy finish. A good value that's drinkable now. 40,000 cases made. • $8 • (05/31/95) BB • **85**

Brut South Eastern Australia 1989 • $15 • (08/31/92) • **88**

Cabernet Sauvignon Coonawarra Kirri Billi Vineyard 1986 • $20 • (10/31/90) • **88**

Cabernet Sauvignon Coonawarra Show Reserve 1993: Firm and a little chewy, a solid wine with ripe, anise-scented, smoky blackberry flavors, a little gamy at the end. Not quite the depth of the 1992. Best from 1999. 1,200 cases made. • $17 • (03/31/96) • **88**

Cabernet Sauvignon Coonawarra Show Reserve 1992: Rich, smooth and polished, with dense and well focused currant, black cherry and chocolate flavors that are supported by toasty oak nuances in the background. Supple and has a wonderful sense of harmony given its weight. Best Cabernet yet from this Australian winery. 1,800 cases made. • $17 • (11/30/95) • **93**

Cabernet Sauvignon Coonawarra Show Reserve 1991 • $17 • (04/30/94) • **80**

Cabernet Sauvignon Coonawarra Show Reserve 1989 • $17 • (11/30/92) • **85**

Cabernet Sauvignon Coonawarra Show Reserve 1988 • $16 • (05/31/91) • **89**

Cabernet Sauvignon Coonawarra Show Reserve 1987 • $15 • (02/28/91) • **88**

Cabernet Sauvignon Coonawarra Show Reserve 1985 • $14 • (01/31/89) • **82**

Cabernet Sauvignon Coonawarra Show Reserve 1984 • $14 • (02/28/87) • **86**

Cabernet Sauvignon Hunter Valley 1989 • $10 • (09/30/91) • **82**

Cabernet Sauvignon Hunter Valley 1988 • $10 • (01/31/90) • **76**

Cabernet Sauvignon Hunter Valley 1987 • $10 • (07/31/89) • **83**

Cabernet Sauvignon Hunter Valley 1986 • $11 • (01/31/89) SS • **93**

Cabernet Sauvignon Hunter Valley 1985 • $9 • (01/31/88) • **85**

Cabernet Sauvignon Hunter Valley 1984 • $9 • (04/30/87) • **78**

Cabernet Sauvignon South Australia 1994: Wild, herbal flavors run through the exuberant berry notes in this smooth-textured red. Drinkable now. • $10 • (10/15/95) • **84**

Cabernet Sauvignon South Australia 1993: Soft and simple, generous with its black cherry and raspberry flavors, finishing supple and appealing. Drinkable now. 60,000 cases made. • $10 • (04/30/95) • **85**

Cabernet Sauvignon South Eastern Australia 1992: A little chewy, with anise and plum flavors that fade a bit on the finish. Drinkable now. • $10 • (07/31/94) • **83**

Cabernet Sauvignon South Eastern Australia 1991 • $9 • (03/31/93) • **86**

Cabernet Shiraz South Eastern Australia 1989 • $6 • (07/31/90) BB • **81**

Chardonnay Hunter Valley 1995: Ripe, spicy and vibrant apple, pear and citrus flavors whirl and eddy on the zingy finish. A fruit-centered Australian white that has class and depth. 56,000 cases made. • $10 • (04/30/96) SS • **89**

Chardonnay Hunter Valley 1994: Youthful and exuberant. A little coarse but lively, with pear and pineapple flavors. Drinkable now. 80,000 cases made. • $10 • (06/30/95) • **82**

Chardonnay Hunter Valley 1993: Ripe, round and generous, polished enough to show off the fig, pear and pineapple flavors and picking up some toast and spice shadings on the finish. Drinkable now. 40,000 cases made. • $10 • (06/30/94) • **87**

Chardonnay Hunter Valley Matured in Oak Casks 1991 • $9 • (11/15/92) • **81**

Chardonnay Hunter Valley Roxburgh 1993: Ripe, round and spicy, with an earthy undercurrent to the spicy, resiny apple and nectarine flavors, hinting at honey on the long finish. A graceful, distinctive Australian white that's delicious now and has a long future. 2,200 cases made. • $30 • (03/31/96) CS • **92**

Chardonnay Hunter Valley Roxburgh 1991: Deep, rich, complex and mouth-filling. This oozes butter, spice, toast and vanilla flavors around a core of pear and apricot that remains elegant. Delicious now. 1,700 cases made. • $28 • (03/31/95) • **92**

Chardonnay Hunter Valley Show Reserve 1994: Nicely articulated Chardonnay fruit shines through chewy, straight-ahead texture, echoing its pear, spice and vanilla flavors on a solid finish. Tasty now through 1997. • $17 • (12/15/95) • **89**

Chardonnay Hunter Valley Show Reserve 1993: Smooth in texture and graceful on the palate, with spicy pineapple and nectarine flavors that linger enticingly. A joy to drink now. 10,000 cases made. • $16 • (04/30/95) SS • **89**

Chardonnay Hunter Valley Show Reserve 1992: Smooth, polished and generous with its apple, nectarine and vanilla flavors, echoing a touch of honey on the finish. Drinkable now. Tasted twice. • $17 • (06/30/94) • **87**

Chardonnay South Eastern Australia 1992 • $9 • (12/31/93) • **77**

Chardonnay South Eastern Australia Matured in Oak Casks 1991 • $9 • (03/31/93) • **86**

Dry Red Diamond Reserve Hunter Valley 1988 • $6 • (02/28/90) BB • **83**

Dry Red Diamond Reserve Hunter Valley 1986 • $6 • (09/15/87) BB • **86**

Fumé Blanc Hunter Valley 1994: Soft and supple, featuring a green apple-herbal streak cutting through the spicy freshness. Lingering finish. 1,000 cases made. • $10 • **84**

Fumé Blanc South Eastern Australia 1992 • $9 • (09/15/93) • **83**

Merlot South Eastern Australia 1992 • $11 • (12/15/93) • **82**

Pinot Noir Hunter Valley 1989 • $10 • (09/30/91) • **81**

Pinot Noir Hunter Valley 1985 • $9 • (04/30/87) • **84**

Pinot Noir Hunter Valley NV • $9 • (07/01/87) • **80**

Pinot Noir Hunter Valley Giants Creek Vineyard 1987 • $20 • (02/28/90) • **84**

Riesling South Eastern Australia Traminer Riesling 1994: Soft and appealingly fruity, the flavors centered around peach and delicate spices. Fresh and inviting, but drink soon. 40,000 cases made. • $8 • (04/15/95) • **85**

Riesling South Eastern Australia Traminer Riesling 1993: Very pretty stuff, soft and floral, with a vanilla edge to the creamy, flowery flavors. Not sweet, but not sharp either. • $8 • (09/30/94) • **84**

Riesling South Eastern Australia Traminer Riesling 1992 • $8 • (04/30/94) • **84**

Sémillon Chardonnay South Eastern Australia 1995: Round and smooth, with pleasant pineapple flavors and an agreeable touch of wool sneaking in on the finish. Maybe better in 1997. 35,000 cases made. • $8 • (06/15/96) • **83**

Sémillon Chardonnay South Eastern Australia 1993: Smooth and polished, spicy, with appealing fig and vanilla flavors that echo nicely on the finish. 32,000 cases made. • $8 • (09/30/94) • **84**

Sémillon Chardonnay South Eastern Australia 1991 • $7 • (11/30/92) • **77**

Sémillon South Eastern Australia Wood Matured 1991 • $9 • (08/31/92) BB • **83**

Shiraz Cabernet Australia 1995: A light, bright and fruity red with fresh blackberry flavors. It's appealing to drink now, and priced right. 45,000 cases made. • $10 • (06/15/96) BB • **86**

Shiraz Cabernet Sauvignon South Eastern Australia 1993: Smooth and fruity, showing off its plum and spice flavors with an appealing, polished style. 26,000 cases made. • $8 • (06/30/94) • **85**

Shiraz Cabernet Sauvignon South Eastern Australia 1992 • $7 • (10/31/93) BB • **86**

Shiraz Cabernet Sauvignon South Eastern Australia 1991 • $7 • (11/30/92) • **67**

Shiraz Cabernet Sauvignon South Eastern Australia 1990 • $7 • (07/15/91) BB • **84**

Shiraz Hunter Valley 1989 • $8 • (02/15/91) SS • **91**

Shiraz Hunter Valley 1988 • $8 • (01/31/90) SS • **90**

Shiraz Hunter Valley 1987 • $9 • (07/31/89) • **87**

Shiraz Hunter Valley 1986 • $9 • (04/15/89) • **92**

Shiraz Hunter Valley 1985 • $8 • (02/15/88) • **80**

Shiraz Hunter Valley 1984 • $7 • (04/30/87) • **83**

Shiraz Show Reserve 1990 • $8 • (02/15/92) SS • **92**

Shiraz Show Reserve 1989 • $15 • (02/29/92) • **89**

Shiraz South Australia 1994: A ripe, supple and silky Shiraz that is generous with its berry, spice and tar flavors, which also linger enticingly on the finish. Drinkable now. 60,000 cases made. • $10 • (10/31/95) SS • **90**

Shiraz South Australia 1993: Not as good as recent vintages, but it's smooth, almost silky, with modest tannins to balance the sweet plum and spice flavors. Drink now. • $10 • (01/31/95) • **83**

Shiraz South Eastern Australia 1992 • $10 • (01/31/94) SS • **89**

Shiraz South Eastern Australia 1991 • $9 • (04/15/93) • **89**

Syrah McLaren Vale Balmoral 1993: Ripe, rich and velvety, a little more compact than previous vintages, weaving its spicy, peppery flavors around a core of blackberry and plum, echoing nicely on the finish. Best after 1997. 1,100 cases made. • $28 • (03/31/96) • **90**

Syrah McLaren Vale Balmoral 1992: A remarkable balance of powerful flavors and gentle structure. Very ripe and rich in texture, keeps pouring out its blueberry, black cherry, plum and smoke flavors. Fine tannins wrap gently around the finish. Tempting now, but best from 1997. 2,600 cases made. • $25 • (03/31/95) CS • **93**

Syrah McLaren Vale Show Reserve 1991 • $17 • (01/31/94) SS • **90**

Syrah McLaren Vale Show Reserve 1990 • $16 • (04/15/93) • **92**

Traminer Riesling 1991 • $7 • (02/29/92) BB • **83**

Traminer Riesling South Eastern Australia 1995: Spicy, fruity and refreshing, a zingy mouthful of peach, green apple, litchi and spice flavors that remain lively through the finish. Great as an apéritif. 11,500 cases made. • $8 • (05/15/96) • **87**

ROSEWOOD

Muscat Australia Liqueur NV • $50 • (07/01/87) • **91**

Muscat Rutherglen Old Liqueur NV • $40 • (07/01/87) • **90**

Muscat Rutherglen Special Liqueur NV • $30 • (07/01/87) • **91**

ROTHBURY

Cabernet Sauvignon South Eastern Australia 1994: Crisp in texture, with a minty edge to the light currant flavor, though finishing with a bit more tannin than the wine deserves. Best in 1998. 15,000 cases made. • $9 • (06/15/96) • **84**

Chardonnay Hunter Valley 1995: Bright and steely, with a nice bead of fresh apple and pear flavors zinging through it. 40,000 cases made. • $8 • (05/31/96) • **85**

Chardonnay Hunter Valley 1993: Straightforward, showing bright pear and vanilla flavors that finish fresh. Drinkable now. 20,000 cases made. • $9 • (12/15/94) BB • **86**

Chardonnay Hunter Valley 1992: Fleshy, fruity and flavorful, offering apple and honey character, softening a bit on the finish. Drinkable now. 40,000 cases made. • $9 • (07/31/94) • **84**

Chardonnay Hunter Valley 1991 • $9 • (02/29/92) • **83**

Chardonnay Hunter Valley Barrel Fermented 1993: Crisp, showing plenty of apple, pear and tropical fruit character, finishes spicy and lively. Drinkable now. 12,000 cases made. • $11 • (03/31/95) • **85**

Chardonnay Hunter Valley Reserve 1991: Deep gold in color, with rich, opulent and mature honey, pear and butterscotch notes. A bold, high-extract mouthful of Chardonnay that's best consumed now considering the maturity of the colors, but the flavors linger long on the finish. 3,000 cases made. • $13 • (06/30/94) • **89**

Chardonnay Hunter Valley Reserve Bottling 1994: This one weaves plenty of spicy complexity around a thread of lovely apple and pear flavor. Aims for restraint, with impressive length, echoing sweet oak. Best in 1997. 2,000 cases made. • $14 • (06/15/96) • **89**

Chardonnay Hunter Valley Reserve Bottling 1993: Brazen yellow color, tropical fruit and fig aromas and flavors add up to a dramatic Chardonnay with resiny notes on the finish. Drinkable now. 2,500 cases made. • $13 • (03/31/95) • **86**

Shiraz Hunter Valley Herlstone Vineyard 1987 • $9 • (05/31/91) • **85**

Shiraz Hunter Valley Herlstone Vineyard 1986 • $11 • (07/31/89) • **76**

Shiraz Hunter Valley Herlstone Vineyard 1985 • $11 • (03/31/89) • **78**

Shiraz Hunter Valley Herlstone Vineyard 1984 • $9 • (05/15/87) • **90**

Shiraz Hunter Valley Reserve Bottling 1993: Rich in texture and flavor, though the character is offbeat, with powerful minty, earthy, meaty notes offsetting the ripe cherry lurking in the background. Best in 1988. 5,000 cases made. • $20 • (06/30/96) • **88**

Shiraz South Eastern Australia 1993: A sturdy style, with gamy overtones to the delicate black cherry and spice flavors. A value-priced red that's drinkable now. 70,000 cases made. • $8 • (05/31/96) BB • **85**

Shiraz South Eastern Australia 1992: Bright, spicy and lively. Smooth-textured with berry and black cherry flavors weaving through the spice. Ready now. 12,000 cases made. • $9 • (11/30/94) BB • **85**

Syrah Hunter Valley 1989 • $11 • (05/31/93) • **78**

ROUGE HOMME

Cabernet Sauvignon Coonawarra 1984 • $12 • (02/15/88) • **84**

ROVALLEY RIDGE

Cabernet-Barossa Valley 1992: Smooth and generous, but it mixes ripe cherry flavors with green, unripe edge, finishing lean and minty but focused. Best from 1997. • $NA • **85**

Cabernet Shiraz Barossa Valley Limited Release 1991: Smooth and velvety, folding in some nice blackberry and spice flavors that linger gently on the finish. Drinkable now, better in 1997. • $NA • **85**

Cabernet Shiraz Eden Valley Show Reserve 1992: Ripe and plush, a mouthful of currant, wild blackberry and plum fruit that picks up nuances of spice and mint on the rich finish. Has length and style, and the stuffings to age through 2000 at least. • $NA • **92**

Chardonnay Eden Valley Show Reserve 1993: Focused, concentrated and elegantly balanced on a lean frame, packed with crisp pear, passion fruit and honey flavors that linger on the finish. Drinkable now. • $NA • **89**

Chardonnay Eden Valley Show Reserve 1992: Ripe and broad, dark in color and rich in texture. Mature aromas and flavors combine with a touch of honey and pear on the finish. 6,000 cases made. • $18 • (06/30/95) • **84**

Chardonnay New South Wales 1993: Light and floral, with a sappy edge to the simple apple flavors. 4,000 cases made. • $8 • (09/30/94) • **78**

Red New South Wales 1992: Light and simple, with an earthy cherry edge. Solid value for everyday drinking. Ready now. 4,000 cases made. • $6 • (09/30/94) • **81**

Shiraz Barossa Valley Old Vine Show Reserve 1992: Ripe and distinctively peppery, a little rough around its dense core of black cherry and tar flavors. Drinkable now. • $NA • **85**

Shiraz Barossa Valley Old Vine Show Reserve 1991: Spicy, rich and exotic, lightly chewy and substantial from first spicy whiff to finishing echo of the plum, berry and black pepper. Stretches the flavors. Delicious now, but best from 1997. 4,000 cases made. • $18 • (05/15/95) • **92**

Show Reserve Eden Valley 1991: Lean and definitely earthy, but some currant flavor sneaks through on the finish. Might be better in 1997. 5,000 cases made. • $18 • (06/30/95) • **82**

RYECROFT

Chardonnay McLaren Vale Flame Tree 1992 • $8 • (07/15/93) • **82**

Shiraz McLaren Vale Flame Tree 1992 • $8 • (04/30/93) BB • **88**

ST. HALLETT

Gamekeeper's Reserve Barossa 1994: Smooth and silky, a generous mouthful of minty raspberry, red cherry and plum flavors, finishing polished and lively. Drinkable now. 3,000 cases made. • $10 • (03/31/96) • **86**

Poacher's Blend Barossa 1995: Tastes remarkably like fruit cocktail, fresh and generous with its pear, grape and melon flavors from beginning to end. 3,000 cases made. • $10 • (04/30/96) • **84**

Shiraz Barossa Old Block 1992: A rich, ripe and generous red from Australia that shows its depth with layers of black cherry, blackberry, plum and spice flavors that echo long on the finish. A distinguished wine that's delicious now but should improve through 2002. 1,500 cases made. • $23 • (03/31/96) CS • **92**

Key: SS—Spectator Selection. CS—Cellar Selection. BB—Best Buy. $NA—Price not available. (BT)—Barrel tasting. Ⓐ—Auction Price.
Dates in parentheses represent the issues in which the ratings were published.

ST. HUBERTS

Cabernet Sauvignon Yarra Valley 1984 • $13 • (11/15/87) • **84**

Pinot Noir Yarra Valley 1985 • $12 • (11/15/87) • **80**

SALTRAM

Cabernet Sauvignon Coonawarra Pinnacle Selection 1988 • $12 • (06/30/93) • **82**

Cabernet Sauvignon Coonawarra Pinnacle Selection 1984 • $13 • (11/30/92) • **76**

Cabernet Sauvignon Hazelwood 1985 • $8 • (07/31/89) • **79**

Cabernet Sauvignon Shiraz Barossa Valley 1984 • $12 • (01/31/90) • **89**

Cabernet Sauvignon South Australia Classic 1987 • $7 • (06/30/93) • **79**

Chardonnay South Eastern Australia Classic 1992 • $8 • (10/31/93) • **79**

Chardonnay South Eastern Australia Classic 1991 • $7 • (04/30/93) BB • **84**

Shiraz Cabernet South Eastern Australia 1988 • $6 • (05/31/93) • **76**

Shiraz Hazelwood 1984 • $8 • (07/31/89) • **81**

SCARBOROUGH

Chardonnay Hunter Valley 1995: Bright and spicy, showing lots of green apple and vanilla flavors on a crisp frame. Not quite harmonious, but tasty. 2,000 cases made. • $15 • (04/30/96) • **85**

SCOTCHMANS HILL

Chardonnay Geelong 1994: Ripe, rich, supple, delicate butterscotch notes harmonize beautifully with pear, pineapple and caramel flavors that linger appealingly. 4,000 cases made. • $20 • (12/15/95) • **88**

Pinot Noir Geelong 1994: Delicate, supple and refined, folding its currant, spice and smoke flavors into generous swirls as it glides into a silky finish. Tempting through 1997. 4,000 cases made. • $20 • (12/15/95) • **87**

SEAVIEW

Brut South Australia 1990 • $9 • (07/15/93) • **80**

Brut South Australia 1988 • $9 • (11/15/91) BB • **83**

Cabernet Sauvignon McLaren Vale 1993: Crisp and focused, a tight, lighter style of Cabernet that shows some ripe black cherry flavors. • $8 • (03/31/96) • **85**

Cabernet Sauvignon South Australia 1992: Surprisingly tough, tannic and somewhat wild, adding a dusky, wild herb edge to the red currant and beetroot flavors. Needs until 1998. • $7 • (10/31/95) • **83**

Cabernet Sauvignon South Australia 1989 • $6 • (05/15/94) BB • **82**

Cabernet Sauvignon South Australia 1986 • $10 • (07/31/90) • **88**

Cabernet Shiraz South Australia 1987 • $8 • (09/30/91) BB • **82**

Chardonnay McLaren Vale 1995: Bright and citrusy, flavors centered around orange and vanilla. Ready now. • $8 • (03/31/96) • **83**

Chardonnay McLaren Vale 1994: A ripe, resonant, vibrant wine that pours out its beautiful pear, spice and honey flavors and lets them linger on the polished finish. Impressive and drinkable now. 23,000 cases made. • $7 • (04/30/95) SS • **90**

Chardonnay McLaren Vale Edwards & Chaffey 1994: Ripe, spicy and complex, a fascinating mouthful of nutmeg-scented pear, orange and honey flavors that linger nicely on the long finish. Delicious now, better after 1997. 2,972 cases made. • $25 • **89**

Chardonnay South Australia 1992 • $6 • (04/15/94) BB • **86**

Port Australia Flagship NV • $9 • (11/15/91) • **79**

Sauvignon Blanc McLaren Vale 1994: Lean and spicy, with a snappy shot of pure fruit and an interesting overlay of sweet pea character. 17,650 cases made. • $9 • (05/31/96) • **84**

Sauvignon Blanc McLaren Vale 1993: Crisp and distinctively herbal, but silky. A touch of onion skin turns up in the melony fruit flavors. Drinkable now. • $8 • (06/30/95) • **82**

Sémillon Sauvignon Blanc McLaren Vale 1994: Bright, fresh and flavorful. A floral- and tobacco-scented white that follows through with a lovely mouthful of pear and spice flavors. 36,450 cases made. • $9 • (05/31/96) • **85**

Shiraz Cabernet South Australia 1991 • $6 • (05/15/94) BB • **84**

Shiraz McLaren Vale 1993: Lean and a little sharp at the edges, packaging its gamy black cherry flavors in a polished texture. Best from 1998. • $8 • (03/31/96) • **85**
Shiraz McLaren Vale 1992: Ripe, almost sweet with its plum, spice and blackberry flavors that swirl gently through the lean finish. Drinkable now. 2,000 cases made. • $7 BB • **86**
Shiraz South Australia 1987 • $10 • (09/30/91) • **86**
Shiraz South Eastern Australia 1989: This has an earthy, musty edge that cleans up a bit, but it never moves beyond a plain, ordinary red. Drinkable now. 5,000 cases made. • $6 • (09/30/94) • **71**

SEPPELT

Brut Australia Fleur de Lys 1985 • $18 • (12/31/88) • **85**
Brut South Eastern Australia Imperial NV • $10 • (01/31/90) • **82**
Cabernet Sauvignon Australia Dorrien 1989: Round in structure, velvety in texture, with mature flavors that lean more toward cigar and leather than fruit or spice. Chewy and needs until 1997 or 1998. 1,372 cases made. • $26 • (06/30/95) • **83**
Cabernet Sauvignon Barossa Valley Dorrien 1990: With its rich, complex and deep set of aromas, this promises much that the tough, tannic flavors don't quite deliver. Has spice, berry and meaty character that might well outlive the tannins. Best from 2000 to 2002. 200 cases made. • $26 • (03/31/96) • **89**
Cabernet Sauvignon Barossa Valley Dorrien 1987 • $22 • (03/31/93) • **85**
Cabernet Sauvignon Padthaway Black Label 1988 • $12 • (03/31/91) • **81**
Cabernet Sauvignon Shiraz South Eastern Australia Classic 1990 • $6 • (11/30/93) • **76**
Cabernet Sauvignon South Australia Black Label 1994: Ripe, tarry flavors dominate. Soft-textured and straightforward, it's approachable now but probably best after 1998. 2,600 cases made. • $11 • **85**
Cabernet Sauvignon South Australia Black Label 1993: Lean and tough, chewy for the level of fruit which barely peeks through. 3,000 cases made. • $10 • (04/30/96) • **80**
Cabernet Sauvignon South Australia Black Label 1992: Rich, ripe and plush, generous with its plum, red berry and spice flavors that extend into a smooth finish. Tempting now, but can age until 1998. 1,950 cases made. • $10 • (10/31/95) • **90**
Cabernet Sauvignon South Australia Black Label 1991: Sturdy, smooth and flavorful, a generous mouthful of plum and black cherry flavors shaded with cedar and toast. Nicely done. • $10 • (07/31/94) • **86**
Cabernet Sauvignon South Australia Black Label 1990 • $10 • (11/15/93) • **82**
Cabernet Sauvignon South Australia Reserve Bin 1993: Light and lean but it shows attractive red berry and vanilla flavors and a crisp finish. Ready now. 5,400 cases made. • $8 • (10/31/95) • **82**
Cabernet Sauvignon South Eastern Australia Black Label 1985 • $11 • (04/30/88) • **64**
Cabernet Sauvignon South Eastern Australia Black Label 1982 • $13 • (04/01/86) • **78**
Cabernet Sauvignon South Eastern Australia Murray River 1987 • $5 • (04/15/88) • **77**
Cabernet Sauvignon South Eastern Australia Reserve Bin 1991 • $8 • (06/15/94) • **82**
Cabernet Sauvignon South Eastern Australia Reserve Bin 1990 • $8 • (11/15/93) • **84**
Cabernet Sauvignon South Eastern Australia Reserve Bin 1988 • $9 • (07/15/91) • **82**
Cabernet Sauvignon Victoria Drumborg 1989: Funky, strongly earthy and barnyardy. Murky and leathery on the finish. Tasted twice, with consistent notes. 3,000 cases made. • $30 • (06/30/95) • **72**
Cabernet Sauvignon Victoria Harpers Range 1992: Lively, with supple texture. Bursting with fruit, bright currant, berry and slightly tarry flavors. Approachable now, but worth cellaring until 1999-2000 to round it out. 1,000 cases made. • $16 • **89**
Cabernet Shiraz South Australia Classic 1994: Lean and green, even a little sour on the aggressive finish, showing more herb and pickle barrel flavors than fruit or spice. Try in 1999. 5,500 cases made. • $6 • (04/30/96) • **79**
Cabernet Shiraz South Eastern Australia 1986 • $8 • (01/31/90) • **82**
Cabernet Shiraz South Eastern Australia Moyston 1989 • $8 • (11/30/92) • **79**
Chardonnay South Australia Black Label 1995: Lean and spicy, with a citrusy green apple flavor that lingers and gains focus on the finish. 3,800 cases made. • $11 • **85**
Chardonnay South Australia Black Label 1994: Ripe and spicy, broad enough to support a range of resiny pear and citrusy flavors. Drinkable now. 2,000 cases made. • $10 • (12/15/95) • **87**
Chardonnay South Eastern Australia Black Label 1991 • $10 • (10/31/93) • **83**
Chardonnay South Eastern Australia Reserve Bin 1994: Lean and lively, showing more crisp texture than flavor for now. Try now. 24,000 cases made. • $8 • (03/31/96) • **81**
Chardonnay South Eastern Australia Reserve Bin 1993: Light and airy, spicy, with fresh apple flavor. 20,000 cases made. • $8 • (09/30/94) • **80**
Chardonnay South Eastern Australia Reserve Bin 1992 • $8 • (11/30/93) • **76**
Chardonnay South Eastern Australia Reserve Bin 1991 • $8 • (11/15/92) BB • **83**
Chardonnay Victoria Great Western Vineyards 1991: A spicy, barrel-fermented style in spades. Layers in more toasty, smoky flavors than fruit, but echoes apricot on the spicy finish. 3,000 cases made. • $15 • (06/30/95) • **87**
Classic South Australia 1992: Stylish, ripe, smooth and generous, with spicy plum and berry flavors on a polished, supple frame. A lighter style with plenty of flavor. Appealing now. 4,000 cases made. • $6 • (04/15/95) BB • **87**
Port Australia Para No. 113 NV • $25 • (11/15/91) • **83**
Port Barossa Valley Para Port Bin 109 NV • $25 • (02/15/88) • **92**
Port Barossa Valley Para Port No. 110 NV • $25 • (03/15/89) • **79**
Port McLaren Flat Barossa 1978 • $15 • (02/15/88) • **70**
Sémillon Chardonnay Moyston 1991 • $7 • (06/30/92) • **81**
Sémillon Chardonnay South Eastern Australia 1994: Has a definite earthy, haylike character that rolls over the other flavors, although it finishes with a nice touch of citrusy acidity. 1,950 cases made. • $6 • (03/31/96) • **82**
Sémillon Chardonnay South Eastern Australia Classic 1993: Lean and vaguely herbal around a bright core of pear and fig flavors, an appealing white with nicely defined flavors. • $6 • (09/30/94) • **81**
Sémillon Chardonnay South Eastern Australia Classic 1992 • $6 • (11/30/93) BB • **83**
Shiraz Australia Great Western Vineyards Hermitage 1988: Smells rich and spicy, tarry notes adding depth to the dark cherry flavors. Some sour cherry on the finish. Distinctive, but not for everyone. Drinkable now. 2,028 cases made. • $25 • (04/15/95) • **82**
Shiraz South Australia Black Label 1993: Crisp, focused and flavorful, as bright boysenberry and plum notes remain lively through the finish. Appealing now, better when it softens, about 1998. 500 cases made. • $10 • (04/30/96) • **87**
Shiraz South Australia Black Label 1990 • $10 • (10/31/93) • **82**
Shiraz South Australia Black Label 1989 • $10 • (05/31/93) • **85**
Shiraz South Australia Reserve Bin 1992: A little chewy in texture, with plenty of plum and blackberry coming through. Fresh and inviting through the finish. Drinkable now. 22,000 cases made. • $7 • (04/15/95) BB • **87**
Shiraz South Eastern Australia Black Label 1994: Soft, spicy and appealing. Modest berry and tobacco flavors that pick up some scratchy tannins on the finish. Needs until 1998-1999 for tannins to ease. 2,000 cases made. • $11 • **84**
Shiraz South Eastern Australia Black Label 1984 • $12 • (12/31/88) • **87**
Shiraz South Eastern Australia Black Label 1983 • $10 • (02/15/88) • **74**
Shiraz South Eastern Australia Reserve Bin 1993: Light, smooth and plummy, lean, adding spicy overtones. Best in 1997. 2,000 cases made. • $8 • (10/31/95) • **83**
Shiraz South Eastern Australia Reserve Bin 1991: Lean and chewy, with modest berry flavors and a gamy edge. Drinkable now. • $8 • (09/30/94) • **78**
Shiraz South Eastern Australia Reserve Bin 1990 • $8 • (10/31/93) • **82**
Shiraz South Eastern Australia Reserve Bin 1989 • $9 • (08/31/92) • **84**
Shiraz Victoria Black Label 1992: Ripe and expansive, playing out its spicy plum and black cherry flavors against a touch of tar and tobacco. Delicious now, best in 1997. 500 cases made. • $10 • (10/31/95) • **87**
Shiraz Victoria Black Label 1988 • $12 • (08/31/92) • **86**

Shiraz Victoria Chalambar 1992: Ripe, and silky-smooth. Generous flavors—berry, black cherry, plum, anise and vanilla—that linger enticingly on the long finish. Delicious now, but could keep gaining depth through 2002. 900 cases made. • $14 • **92**

Shiraz Victoria Great Western Vineyards Hermitage 1988: Smooth and spicy, a silky mouthful of berry and slightly gamy flavors. Ready now. 3,000 cases made. • $25 • (10/31/95) • **85**

Tawny Port Australia Old Trafford NV • $15 • (03/15/89) • **95**

Tawny Port Barossa Valley Mt. Rufus NV • $12 • (02/15/88) • **78**

Tokay Rutherglen Show D.P. 57 NV: An amazing mouthful of rich, sweet, spicy, toasty nuances swirl around a core of honey, cherry and pear flavors laced with touches of cinnamon and nutmeg. Rich, complex and elegant, heady and delicious. 2,000 cases made. • $39 • (05/31/96) • **95**

SEVENHILL

Riesling Clare Valley 1994: Delicate, dry and glowing with pure Riesling fruitiness. Echoes of apple, peach and pine on the finish. 2,500 cases made. • $14 • (06/30/95) • **86**

STANLEY

Shiraz Cabernet Sauvignon Coonawarra Private Reserve 1985 • $4 • (12/15/87) • **78**

STONIER'S

Cabernet Sauvignon Mornington Peninsula 1992: Firm, focused and straightforward, featuring basic Cabernet fruit and a touch of earthy, herbal character at the edge. Best in 1997. 3,000 cases made. • $20 • (10/15/95) • **84**

Chardonnay Mornington Peninsula Reserve 1994: Smooth and more mature than the vintage would indicate, but very spicy and crisp on the lively finish. Best in 1997. 1,000 cases made. • $24 • (04/30/96) • **87**

SUNNYCLIFF

Cabernet Sauvignon Coonawarra 1991: Firm and toasty, a spicy red that gets a little coarse on the finish. 20,000 cases made. • $7 • (09/30/94) • **79**

Cabernet Sauvignon Coonawarra 1990 • $7 • (04/15/93) BB • **84**

Chardonnay Victoria 1993: Soft and mature for a '93, with spicy, woody flavors that linger on the finish. 25,000 cases made. • $7 • (09/30/94) • **79**

Chardonnay Victoria 1992 • $7 • (04/30/93) • **80**

SWANN, MARK

Cabernet Sauvignon Coonawarra 1987 • $7 • (02/28/91) BB • **84**

Cabernet Sauvignon Coonawarra 1985 • $7 • (10/31/88) BB • **88**

Cabernet Sauvignon Coonawarra 1984 • $8 • (08/31/87) • **77**

Cabernet Sauvignon Coonawarra 1982 • $7 • (03/16/84) • **78**

Cabernet Sauvignon South Australia 1990 • $7 • (03/31/93) • **75**

Cabernet Sauvignon South Australia 1989 • $8 • (03/15/92) • **81**

Cabernet Sauvignon South Australia Proprietor's Reserve 1988 • $5 • (02/28/91) BB • **86**

Cabernet Sauvignon South Australia Proprietor's Reserve 1987 • $5 • (07/31/89) BB • **81**

Cabernet Sauvignon South Australia Proprietor's Reserve 1986 • $5 • (10/31/88) • **78**

Chardonnay Victoria 1992 • $7 • (04/30/93) • **78**

Chardonnay Victoria 1991 • $7 • (08/31/92) • **77**

Dessert Rutherglen Gold Vintner's Select NV • $10 • (12/31/88) • **92**

Port Australia Vintage 1980 • $10 • (04/16/84) • **78**

Shiraz Eden Valley 1980 • $6 • (03/16/84) • **80**

Key: SS—Spectator Selection. CS—Cellar Selection. BB—Best Buy. $NA—Price not available. (BT)—Barrel tasting. Ⓐ—Auction Price.
Dates in parentheses represent the issues in which the ratings were published.

TAHBILK, CHATEAU

Cabernet Sauvignon Goulburn Valley 1992: A solid red, though not much about it that says Cabernet. A bit chewy, but shows enough tarry berry flavors to make it worth cellaring until 2002-2005. • $14 • **85**

Cabernet Sauvignon Goulburn Valley 1990 • $11 • (06/15/94) • **83**

Cabernet Sauvignon Goulburn Valley 1989 • $12 • (11/30/92) • **83**

Cabernet Sauvignon Goulburn Valley 1988 • $12 • (03/31/91) • **87**

Cabernet Sauvignon Goulburn Valley 1987 • $11 • (07/31/90) • **89**

Cabernet Sauvignon Goulburn Valley 1986 • $10 • (03/31/89) • **88**

Cabernet Sauvignon Goulburn Valley 1984 • $7 • (11/15/87) • **81**

Cabernet Sauvignon Victoria 1990 • $11 • (06/30/93) • **78**

Chardonnay Goulburn Valley 1994: Spicy, toasty, nutty flavors dominate this medium-weight, slightly resiny white. Better in 1997 and beyond. • $14 • **83**

Chardonnay Goulburn Valley 1992: Very ripe, with a tinny, canned grapefruit and pineapple edge that gives it a vinegary flavor. Good, but unexceptional. 10,000 cases made. • $10 • (09/30/94) • **80**

Marsanne Goulburn Valley 1995: Fresh and tangy, with lively citrus and pear flavors. A hint of rose petal on the silky finish. • $11 • **84**

Marsanne Goulburn Valley 1993: A soft, ripe and generous white from a Rhône grape variety. It offers a fruit bowl of flavors that keep glowing on the finish. Drink soon. 40,000 cases made. • $10 • (04/15/95) BB • **87**

Marsanne Goulburn Valley 1992 • $9 • (04/30/94) • **82**

Shiraz 1988 • $10 • (02/15/92) • **82**

Shiraz Goulburn Valley 1992: Earthy and chewy. Packing enough berry, anise and spice flavor to warrant cellaring until the modest but hard tannins subside—see what develops around 2000-2005. • $14 • **86**

Shiraz Goulburn Valley 1991 • $10 • (06/15/94) • **84**

Shiraz Goulburn Valley 1989 • $11 • (11/30/92) • **73**

Shiraz Goulburn Valley 1987 • $11 • (03/15/91) • **87**

Shiraz Goulburn Valley 1984 • $6 • (11/15/87) • **77**

Shiraz Victoria 1990 • $10 • (05/31/93) • **84**

Shiraz Victoria 1986 • $10 • (03/31/89) • **88**

TALTARNI

Brut Australia Cuvée Brut NV • $16 • (08/31/92) • **85**

Brut Australia Taché NV • $16 • (06/30/92) • **83**

Cabernet Sauvignon Victoria 1990: Supple, velvety and generous with its spicy black cherry and tobacco flavors that blend harmoniously on the finish. Has enough to want until 2002 to 2005. • $15 • (04/30/96) • **89**

Cabernet Sauvignon Victoria 1989: Smoothly mature, with tobacco-scented prune and currant flavors. Finishes spicy and vaguely earthy. Drinkable now. 5,500 cases made. • $15 • (06/30/95) • **87**

Cabernet Sauvignon Victoria 1988: Mature, herbal, ripe and curranty, this has style and grace and a spicy finish. Drinkable now. • $12 • (06/30/94) • **86**

Cabernet Sauvignon Victoria 1987 • $12 • (08/31/92) • **80**

Cabernet Sauvignon Victoria 1986 • $10 • (09/30/91) • **81**

Cabernet Sauvignon Victoria 1984 • $9 • (11/15/87) • **85**

Cabernet Sauvignon Victoria 1982 • $9 • (04/30/87) • **84**

Cabernet Sauvignon Victoria 1981 • $7 • (05/16/85) • **80**

Cabernet Sauvignon Victoria 1980 • $6 • (03/01/84) • **81**

Merlot Cabernet Franc Victoria 1990: Earthy, gamy flavors give this one a distinctive character that not everyone will like, but it has personality. Ripe cherry notes sneak in on the finish. Drinkable now. • $12 • (07/31/94) • **85**

Merlot Victoria 1992: Minty, cedary notes add depth and style to this cherry-scented, firm-textured, nicely focused, harmonious Merlot. Has a velvety feel and fine balance. • $15 • (04/30/96) • **89**

Merlot Victoria 1991: Lean and a little scratchy, but has ripe black cherry and smoke flavors on the finish. Drinkable now. 1,200 cases made. • $15 • (04/15/95) • **83**

Sauvignon Blanc Victoria 1995: Very fresh and spicy, packed with nectarine and vanilla flavors that linger enticingly on the finish. Big and refreshing at the same time. Drinkable now. • $10 • (04/30/96) • **90**

Sauvignon Blanc Victoria 1993: Crisp and beautifully focused, nicely balanced between citrusy pear and bright herbal overtones, a delicious touch of sweet oak on the finish. Delicious through 1997. 2,000 cases made. • $12 • (05/31/95) • **89**

Sauvignon Blanc Victoria Frenchmans Vineyard 1992: Light and spicy, an attractive white with crisp texture and vanilla-grapefruit flavors. Lingers, too. Drink soon while it's fresh. • $10 • (09/30/94) • **87**

Sauvignon Blanc Victoria Frenchmans Vineyard 1991 • $12 • (06/30/92) • **84**

Shiraz Victoria 1993: Smooth and generous, sprinkling some wonderful pepper and spice notes over the rich black plum, anise and black cherry flavors. Best in 1997. • $15 • (04/30/96) • **90**

Shiraz Victoria 1992: Ripe and round, remarkably generous with its smoky blackberry and spice flavors that turn supple and elegant on the long finish. Delicious now through 1998. • $15 • (03/31/95) • **89**

Shiraz Victoria 1991: Ripe and chewy, complex, layers its spicy, cedary plum, berry and gamy flavors in a tight package, finishing a little austere. Approachable now, but best from 1997. • $13 • (09/30/94) • **88**

Shiraz Victoria 1990 • $13 • (04/30/93) • **92**

Shiraz Victoria 1989 • $14 • (08/31/92) • **88**

Shiraz Victoria 1988 • $14 • (05/31/92) • **89**

Shiraz Victoria 1987 • $10 • (09/30/91) • **82**

Shiraz Victoria 1986 • $10 • (10/31/90) • **84**

Shiraz Victoria 1985 • $10 • (11/30/88) SS • **91**

Shiraz Victoria 1984 • $9 • (02/15/88) • **75**

Shiraz Victoria 1982 • $9 • (04/30/87) • **86**

Shiraz Victoria 1980 • $6 • (03/16/84) • **77**

TARRA WARRA

Pinot Noir Yarra Glen 1989 • $28 • (04/15/92) • **80**

Pinot Noir Yarra Glen 1988 • $25 • (12/31/90) • **86**

Pinot Noir Yarra Valley 1991: Elegant and easy drinking, with spicy cherry, cola and light herbal notes. Light tannins on the finish make it appealing now. 600 cases made. • $26 • (07/31/94) • **85**

Pinot Noir Yarra Valley 1990 • $27 • (08/31/92) • **87**

Pinot Noir Yarra Valley Tunnel Hill 1991 • $15 • (06/30/93) • **81**

TEMPLE BRUER

Cabernet Sauvignon Merlot Cabernet Franc South Australia 1989: Aims for elegance and achieves a supple frame for its smoky, earthy flavors, a centered note of black cherry keeps it in balance. Drinkable now. 1,500 cases made. • $11 • (03/31/95) • **84**

Shiraz Malbec South Australia 1990: Thick and spicy, with a minty edge to the tarry plum flavors. Drinkable now. 1,500 cases made. • $11 • (01/31/95) • **80**

TERRACE VALE

Pinot Noir Hunter Valley 1986 • $9 • (03/15/88) • **81**

Shiraz Hunter Valley Bin 6 1986 • $9 • (03/15/88) • **73**

THISTLE HILL

Cabernet Sauvignon Mudgee 1988 • $18 • (04/30/94) • **79**

Chardonnay Mudgee 1991 • $16 • (04/15/94) • **84**

TOLLEY'S

Pinot Noir Barossa Valley Selected Harvest 1983 • $5 • (11/15/87) • **76**

TUNNEL HILL

Pinot Noir Yarra Valley 1990 • $16 • (02/29/92) • **84**

TYRRELL'S

Brut Pinot Noir Hunter Valley 1983 • $19 • (09/30/88) • **82**

Cabernet Merlot Australia Old Winery 1988 • $7 • (03/31/91) BB • **84**

Cabernet Merlot Hunter Valley 1985 • $9 • (07/31/89) • **84**

Cabernet Merlot New South Wales Victoria 1983 • $8 • (03/15/88) • **84**

Cabernet Merlot South Eastern Australia Old Winery 1994: A nice mouthful of plum and black cherry flavors accompanied by a streak of spicy oak to jazz it up. 20,000 cases made. • $8 • (03/31/96) • **84**

Cabernet Merlot South Eastern Australia Old Winery 1990 • $9 • (03/31/93) • **78**

Cabernet Sauvignon Hunter Valley Classic 1984 • $7 • (09/15/90) BB • **88**

Cabernet Sauvignon Hunter Valley Premier Selection 1983 • $8 • (04/30/88) BB • **87**

Cabernet Sauvignon Merlot Hunter Valley 1987 • $7 • (09/15/90) • **79**

Cabernet Sauvignon Merlot Hunter Valley 1986 • $8 • (01/31/90) BB • **88**

Cabernet Sauvignon Merlot Hunter Valley 1984 • $9 • (07/15/88) • **82**

Cabernet Sauvignon Merlot South Eastern Australia Old Winery 1991 • $8 • (12/15/93) • **81**

Cabernet Sauvignon South Eastern Australia Old Winery 1992: Firm in texture, with clear berry and currant flavors lingering on the smooth finish. Drink now. 4,000 cases made. • $8 • (06/30/95) BB • **83**

Cabernet Sauvignon South Eastern Australia Old Winery 1991 • $8 • (11/15/93) • **80**

Cabernet Sauvignon South Eastern Australia Old Winery 1986 • $9 • (03/15/92) • **84**

Chardonnay Hunter Valley Shee-Oak Individual Vineyard Non-Wooded 1995: Very spicy, nutty tones in a silky, lightly citrusy white. Harmonious and ultimately elegant. Has plenty of flavor and character. Drinkable now. • $10 • (04/30/96) • **88**

Chardonnay Hunter Valley Shee-Oak Individual Vineyard Non Wooded 1994: Ripe and generous at first, offering citrusy pear and nutmeg flavors, lingering nicely on the finish. Ready now. 5,000 cases made. • $10 • (03/31/96) • **88**

Chardonnay Hunter Valley Vat 47 Pinot Chardonnay 1995: Crisp and tart, flavors leaning more toward candied fruit than fresh, nicely framed by spicy oak. May be better in 1997. Tasted twice, with consistent notes. • $15 • (04/30/96) • **83**

Chardonnay Hunter Valley Vat 47 Pinot Chardonnay 1994: A distinctive white from Australia that's crisply focused, packing in its spicy, honeyed, buttery pear and apricot flavors that swirl around beautifully on the long, elegant finish. Drinkable now, but should improve through 1998. 8,000 cases made. • $16 • (04/30/96) • **92**

Chardonnay Hunter Valley Vat 47 Pinot Chardonnay 1993: Very ripe and broad, a resiny flavor snaking through the bright apple and spicy vanilla character that lingers on the finish. Has plenty of personality. Drinkable now. 7,000 cases made. • $15 • (06/30/95) • **86**

Chardonnay Sémillon Long Flat South Eastern Australia 1991 • $7 • (02/15/93) • **82**

Chardonnay South Eastern Australia 1994: Fresh and light, showing pleasant appley and grassy flavors. 7,600 cases made. • $6 • (12/15/95) • **81**

Chardonnay South Eastern Australia 1993: Fresh and fruity, flavors similar to fruit cocktail, light and refreshing. Ready now. 150,000 cases made. • $6 • (06/30/95) • **81**

Chardonnay South Eastern Australia Old Winery 1993: Ripe and generous. Supple enough to show off the peach and spice flavors to best advantage. Drinkable now. 10,000 cases made. • $8 • (06/30/95) BB • **85**

Chardonnay South Eastern Australia Old Winery 1992 • $8 • (10/31/93) • **82**

Chardonnay South Eastern Australia Old Winery 1991 • $9 • (03/31/93) • **78**

Chardonnay South Eastern Australia Old Winery Premier Selection 1995: Fresh and fruity, featuring soft nectarine and vanilla flavors that spread out gently on the finish. Drinkable now. • $7 • (04/30/96) • **87**

Chardonnay South Eastern Australia Old Winery Premier Selection 1994: The pleasant pear and lime flavors remain tart and lively through the finish. 50,000 cases made. • $8 • (03/31/96) BB • **85**

Dry Red Vat 9 Hunter Valley 1987 • $15 • (04/15/93) • **81**

Dry Red Winemaker's Selection Vat 9 1984 • $15 • (02/15/92) • **83**

Hermitage 1982 • $8 • (07/01/87) • **84**

Long Flat Chardonnay Sémillon South Eastern Australia 1992 • $5 • (11/30/93) • **74**

Long Flat Red 1988 • $7 • (02/15/92) BB • **84**

Long Flat Red Hunter Valley 1986 • $6 • (01/31/90) • **79**

Long Flat Red Hunter Valley 1985 • $5 • (07/31/89) BB • **81**

Long Flat Red Hunter Valley 1984 • $6 • (09/30/88) BB • **83**

Long Flat Red Hunter Valley 1983 • $6 • (04/15/88) • **79**

Long Flat Red South Eastern Australia 1992: A smooth, easy-drinking red that offers spice, raspberry and plum flavors through the finish.

Shiraz, Cabernet Sauvignon and Malbec. 125,000 cases made. • $6 • (05/31/95) • **83**

Long Flat Red South Eastern Australia 1991 • $7 • (05/31/93) • **82**

Long Flat Red South Eastern Australia 1990 • $6 • (08/31/92) BB • **84**

Long Flat South Eastern Australia 1994: Light, fruity and simple, showing some nice apple and resin flavors that fade slightly on the finish. 25,000 cases made. • $6 • (06/30/95) • **79**

Long Flat White South Eastern Australia 1995: Soft and fruity, with clean, pleasant grapefruit and tropical fruit flavors that finish light. Drink soon to enjoy its freshness. 100,000 cases made. • $6 • (03/31/96) BB • **84**

Long Flat White South Eastern Australia 1992 • $5 • (11/30/93) BB • **84**

Long Flat White South Eastern Australia 1991 • $7 • (04/15/93) BB • **82**

Old Winery South Eastern Australia 1992: A lighter style of Cabernet, almost transparent in texture, with light currant and blackberry fruit playing against an herbal, slightly tarry edge. Drinkable now. 10,000 cases made. • $8 • (06/30/95) • **84**

Pinot Noir Hunter River 1988 • $14 • (01/31/90) • **68**

Pinot Noir Hunter River 1985 • $10 • (07/01/87) • **87**

Pinot Noir Hunter Valley Old Winery 1995: Crisp and lively, sporting juicy, berry flavors on a lean frame. Best in 1997. • $7 • (04/30/96) • **84**

Pinot Noir South Eastern Australia Old Winery 1993: Delicate and distinctive, with pure plum and berry flavors, supported by fine tannins and textbook balance. A beautifully made Pinot that's easily worth its price. Drinkable now. 7,000 cases made. • $8 • (06/15/95) BB • **88**

Port Australia 8-Year-Old Fine Aged Tawny NV: Smooth and sweet, a lighter style of tawny with modest tea and spice flavors. 4,000 cases made. • $9 • (06/30/95) • **81**

Sémillon Chardonnay South Eastern Australia Long Flat 1995: Bright and fresh, with lively citrus and pear flavors and a touch of herb on the finish. 60,000 cases made. • $6 • (03/31/96) • **82**

Sémillon Hunter Valley Vat 1 1991: Richly flavored, supple in texture, featuring spicy honey and pear notes that linger nicely on the fat finish. Harmonious and drinkable now. • $15 • (04/30/96) • **88**

Shiraz Cabernet South Eastern Australia 1993: Light, fruity and easy to drink, adding a streak of gamy Shiraz character to increase the depth. Ready now. 3,800 cases made. • $6 • (10/15/95) • **83**

Shiraz Cabernet South Eastern Australia 1992: Ripe in flavor, crisp in texture, a tightly wound wine that should be at its best from 1997. 60,000 cases made. • $6 • (06/30/95) BB • **82**

Shiraz Cabernet South Eastern Australia 1991 • $6 • (10/31/93) • **80**

Shiraz Hunter Valley 1982 • $7 • (07/15/88) • **75**

Shiraz Hunter Valley Classic 1986 • $8 • (01/31/90) BB • **84**

Shiraz Hunter Valley Classic 1985 • $9 • **65**

Shiraz Hunter Valley Dry Red Vat 9 1987 • $10 • (06/15/94) • **82**

Shiraz Hunter Valley Hunter River Vat 9 1989: Lean and chewy. Acidity seems out of balance and the fruit is not fresh. May be better in 1997. 10,000 cases made. • $12 • (06/30/95) • **77**

Shiraz Hunter Valley Old Winery 1990: Lean, spicy and chewy, with modest fruit and tobacco overtones. Drinkable now. 7,000 cases made. • $8 • (06/30/95) • **83**

Shiraz Hunter Valley Old Winery 1988 • $10 • (05/31/93) • **77**

Shiraz Hunter Valley Old Winery Premier Selection 1993: Lean and lively bright berry and black cherry flavors, zingy, citrusy acidity and a crisp finish. Approachable now, best in 1997. • $8 • (02/29/96) • **86**

Shiraz Hunter Valley Stevens 1994: Bright and fruity, packed with plum and blueberry flavors on a tightly focused frame. Juicy finish. Drinkable now. 5,000 cases made. • $10 • (02/29/96) • **87**

Shiraz Hunter Valley Vat 9 1991: Rich and distinctively gamy, full-bodied, adding an earthy edge to the crisp plum and berry flavors. Approachable now, best from 1998 to 2000. • $11 • (04/30/96) • **88**

Shiraz Hunter Valley Vat 9 Aged Release 1990: Ripe and sweet, offering raisiny, dried cherry flavors that balance nicely against a grace note of toasty, spicy character. Not fat, but focused and generous. Best in 1997. 8,000 cases made. • $12 • (02/29/96) • **87**

South Eastern Australia Long Flat White 1994: A simple, fruity and tremendously tempting blend of Sémillon, Gewürztraminer and Trebbiano that is generous with its pear, tropical fruit and spicy flavors. Drinkable now. 125,000 cases made. • $6 • (05/31/95) BB • **84**

Tawny Port Australia 8 Barrels NV: Spicy and glowing with litchi fruit flavors like Muscat, sweet and touched by caramel notes on the open finish. • $9 • (05/15/96) • **87**

VASSE FELIX

Cabernet Merlot Margaret River Classic Dry Red 1991 • $12 • (04/30/94) • **82**

Cabernet Sauvignon Margaret River 1990 • $14 • (04/30/94) • **85**

VIRGIN HILLS

Cabernet Sauvignon Bendigo 1984 • $17 • (04/30/88) • **68**

WILKINSON, AUDREY

Cabernet Sauvignon Hunter Valley 1986 • $14 • (09/30/91) • **87**

Shiraz Hunter Valley Hermitage 1985 • $13 • (09/30/91) • **79**

WILLESPIE

Cabernet Sauvignon Margaret River 1990 • $13 • (11/15/93) • **79**

Cabernet Sauvignon Margaret River 1989 • $13 • (06/30/93) • **82**

WIRRA WIRRA

Cabernet Sauvignon McLaren Vale 1984 • $14 • (01/31/88) • **84**

Cabernet Shiraz Merlot McLaren Vale Church Block 1985 • $11 • (03/15/88) • **89**

WOODLEY

Chardonnay South Eastern Australia 1994: Fresh and light, showing pleasant appley and grassy flavors. 7,600 cases made. • $6 • (12/15/95) • **81**

Chardonnay South Eastern Australia 1993: Fresh and fruity, flavors similar to fruit cocktail, light and refreshing. Ready now. 150,000 cases made. • $6 • (06/30/95) • **81**

Chardonnay South Eastern Australia Queen Adelaide 1991 • $6 • (03/31/93) • **78**

Port South Australia Queen Adelaide Tawny NV: Lean in structure, with rich spice and cigar flavors that cut through the sweetness. Has a sense of elegance and impressive length. 20,000 cases made. • $7 • (04/15/95) BB • **87**

Shiraz Cabernet Queen Adelaide 1988 • $7 • (02/29/92) BB • **82**

Shiraz Cabernet South Eastern Australia 1993: Light, fruity and easy to drink, adding a streak of gamy Shiraz character to increase the depth. Ready now. 3,800 cases made. • $6 • (10/15/95) • **83**

Shiraz Cabernet South Eastern Australia 1992: Ripe in flavor, crisp in texture, a tightly wound wine that should be at its best from 1997. 60,000 cases made. • $6 • (06/30/95) BB • **82**

Shiraz Cabernet South Eastern Australia 1991 • $6 • (10/31/93) • **80**

Shiraz Cabernet South Eastern Australia Queen Adelaide 1992: Ripe in flavor, crisp in texture and tightly wound, should be at its best in 1997. 60,000 cases made. • $6 • (06/30/95) • **82**

Shiraz Cabernet South Eastern Australia Queen Adelaide 1989 • $7 • (05/31/93) • **74**

WYNDHAM

Brut Australia Cuvée NV: Smooth, round and toasty, the spicy notes radiating through this deftly balanced sparkling wine. Drinkable now. Excellent value. 10,000 cases made. • $8 • (05/15/95) BB • **86**

Cabernet Merlot Hunter Valley Bin 888 1990: At first whiff it smells like bleach, but after that passes it just seems herbal and light. • $8 • (09/30/94) • **77**

Cabernet Sauvignon Hunter Valley Bin 444 1988 • $7 • (06/30/92) • **80**

Cabernet Sauvignon Hunter Valley Bin 444 1986 • $7 • **60**

Cabernet Sauvignon Hunter Valley Bin 444 1983 • $6 • (07/15/88) BB • **82**

Key: SS—Spectator Selection. CS—Cellar Selection. BB—Best Buy. $NA—Price not available. (BT)—Barrel tasting. Ⓐ—Auction Price.
Dates in parentheses represent the issues in which the ratings were published.

Cabernet Sauvignon South Eastern Australia Bin 444 1993: Smooth and supple, avoiding any apparent tannins to show off only modest cherryish flavor. Ready now. 22,000 cases made. • $7 • (05/15/96) • **79**

Cabernet Sauvignon South Eastern Australia Bin 444 1992: Firm and chewy, but the ripe currant and spice flavors come through on the lively finish. Drinkable now. • $9 • (11/30/94) • **84**

Cabernet Sauvignon South Eastern Australia Bin 444 1991: Lean and velvety, a modest level of black cherry and smoke flavors persisting into the finish. Drinkable now. 25,000 cases made. • $7 • (01/31/95) • **83**

Cabernet Shiraz Hunter Valley 1987 • $7 • (01/31/90) BB • **91**

Cabernet Shiraz Hunter Valley 1986 • $6 • (12/31/88) BB • **87**

Cabernet Shiraz Hunter Valley 1985 • $6 • (03/15/88) BB • **87**

Cabernet Shiraz South Eastern Australia 1989 • $7 • (06/30/92) • **76**

Chardonnay South Eastern Australia Bin 222 1993: Clean, sharply focused and lively, with apple and apricot flavors that linger on the finish. Drinkable now. 35,000 cases made. • $7 • (06/30/95) • **83**

Chardonnay South Eastern Australia Bin 222 1992: Ripe and smooth, balancing the green apple and leesy flavors with a touch of spice and vanilla that lurks behind the scenes on the finish. Drinkable now. 30,000 cases made. • $7 • (11/30/94) BB • **87**

Chardonnay South Eastern Australia Bin 222 1991 • $7 • (03/31/93) • **78**

Chardonnay South Eastern Australia Oak Cask 1993: Smooth and buttery, rich with pear, caramel and vanilla flavors that are balanced beautifully on the finish. Drinkable now. 15,000 cases made. • $9 • (04/30/95) BB • **88**

Chardonnay South Eastern Australia Oak Cask 1992 • $8 • (03/15/94) BB • **87**

Merlot Hunter Valley 1986 • $8 • (01/31/90) BB • **85**

Pinot Noir South Eastern Australia Bin 333 1994: Starts off with lovely plum and berry fruit, picking up a bass note of earthy, barnyardy flavor on the smooth finish. A distinctive style through 1997. 15,000 cases made. • $7 • (05/15/96) • **85**

Pinot Noir South Eastern Australia Bin 333 1987 • $7 • (08/31/92) • **78**

Reserve Bin TR2 Medium Dry White South Eastern Australia 1993: Has the floral and spicy flavors and broad, generous structure of Viognier, round and polished with lots of personality. • $4 • (09/30/94) • **87**

Sémillon-Chardonnay South Eastern Australia Bin 777 1995: A rich, spicy and fragrant Australian blend that keeps its floral, citrus and green apple flavors bouncing brightly on the finish. A lot of character for only a few bucks. 25,000 cases made. • $6 • (05/15/96) BB • **85**

Shiraz Hunter Valley Bin 555 1986 • $7 • (01/31/90) BB • **85**

Shiraz Hunter Valley Bin 555 1985 • $7 • **64**

Shiraz South Eastern Australia Bin 555 1993: Light, smooth and appealing for its smoky strawberry flavors. Not a classically styled Shiraz, but makes a pretty red for immediate enjoyment. 75,000 cases made. • $8 • (06/15/96) • **82**

Shiraz South Eastern Australia Bin 555 1991: Light in texture and flavor, with a slightly gamy edge to the soft raspberry flavors. Drinkable now. • $9 • (09/30/94) • **81**

Shiraz South Eastern Australia Bin 555 1990 • $7 • (02/15/93) BB • **85**

Shiraz South Eastern Australia Bin 555 1988 • $7 • (06/30/92) • **83**

WYNN, DAVID

Chardonnay South Eastern Australia 1994: Light and spicy, offering enough fruit to keep it charming, persisting on the finish. 8,000 cases made. • $10 • (12/15/95) • **84**

Sémillon Chardonnay South Eastern Australia 1993: Soft and floral, generous with its gooseberry and apple flavors. 5,000 cases made. • $9 • (10/15/95) • **83**

Shiraz South Eastern Australia Patriarch 1993: Firm, focused and remarkably silky, concentrating its blueberry, pepper and spice flavors. Tannins need until 1997 to soften. 4,000 cases made. • $15 • (10/31/95) • **86**

WYNNS

Cabernet Hermitage Coonawarra 1984 • $10 • (12/31/88) • **79**

Cabernet Sauvignon Coonawarra 1991: Earthy, barnyardy notes run through the plum and berry flavors in this round, generous red, distinctive, but not for everyone. Drinkable now. 20,000 cases made. • $12 • (04/30/95) • **85**

Cabernet Sauvignon Coonawarra 1989 • $12 • (04/30/94) • **82**

Cabernet Sauvignon Coonawarra 1982 • $15 • (11/30/88) • **90**

Cabernet Sauvignon Coonawarra Estate 1989 • $12 • (04/15/93) • **86**

Cabernet Sauvignon Coonawarra John Riddoch 1992: Richly tannic, a wine of consummate depth and distinction, adding fresh floral-herbal tones to the powerful currant, plum and vanilla flavors. Has plenty of personality and depth. Best to wait until 2003 to 2005. • $40 • (04/30/96) • **91**

Cabernet Sauvignon Coonawarra John Riddoch Limited Release 1990: Chewy, focused and impressively deep in flavor. It's plush and pours out blackberry, currant and spicy-herbal flavors. Finishes with an echo of the minty notes that also sneak in on the aromas, this has style and great potential. Tempting now, but best from 1998. 3,900 cases made. • $22 • (11/30/94) SS • **92**

Cabernet Sauvignon Coonawarra John Riddoch Limited Release 1988 • $22 • (03/31/93) • **84**

Cabernet Sauvignon Shiraz Coonawarra 1990 • $11 • (04/30/94) • **83**

Chardonnay Coonawarra 1994: Smooth, silky and spicy, an elegant mouthful of toasty pear and caramel notes on the finish. Has character and style and should be at its best in 1997. • $12 • (04/30/96) • **90**

Chardonnay Coonawarra 1993: Ripe and rich—a little sweet perhaps—but it rolls out the toasty vanilla, raisin and pear flavors. Polished and flavorful. • $12 • (06/30/95) • **88**

Chardonnay Coonawarra 1992: Ripe and distinctive, expanding and accelerating to the finish. It elevates its spicy, smoky pear and apricot flavors onto another plane on the long finish. Terrific to drink now, should be fine through 1997. • $12 • (11/30/94) • **91**

Chardonnay Coonawarra 1991 • $12 • (04/15/94) • **86**

Chardonnay Coonawarra Estate 1991 • $12 • (03/15/93) • **84**

Shiraz Coonawarra 1992: Bright, fruity and sturdy, appealing berry and spice flavors last on the finish. Drinkable now. 48,000 cases made. • $11 • (03/31/95) • **84**

Shiraz Coonawarra 1991 • $11 • (03/31/94) • **84**

Shiraz Coonawarra Michael 1993: Crisp in texture, with spicy berry and prune flavors that expand and gain a touch of anise on the finish. Has impressive length, needs until 1999-2000 to soften. 4,693 cases made. • $40 • **90**

YALUMBA

Brut Australia Angas NV: A sparkling wine style that favors creamy, buttery, lightly honeyed flavors, finishing with a touch of pear and spice. Balanced and rich in flavor. 20,000 cases made. • $10 • (03/31/96) BB • **86**

Brut Rosé Australia Angas NV: Coral color and earthy Pinot Noir flavors characterize this broad-structured sparkler. 50,000 cases made. • $9 • (09/30/94) • **81**

Brut Rosé South Australia Angas NV • $9 • (12/31/90) • **84**

Brut South Australia Angas NV • $9 • (12/31/90) • **78**

Brut de Brut Australia 1984 • $8 • (03/15/88) • **84**

Cabernet Sauvignon Coonawarra Family Reserve 1989 • $9 • (02/28/93) BB • **84**

Cabernet Sauvignon Coonawarra Octavius 1988 • $30 • (05/15/94) • **90**

Cabernet Sauvignon Shiraz Coonawarra 1984 • $6 • (01/31/88) • **78**

Cabernet Sauvignon Sparkling Australia Cuvée Two Prestige NV: Dense maroon color, rich flavor and spicy flavors add up to a unique sparkling wine that has marvelous cassis and berry fruit at the core. 2,000 cases made. • $15 • (03/31/96) • **88**

Cabernet Shiraz Coonawarra 1985 • $6 • (09/30/89) • **67**

Chardonnay Australia Show Reserve 1993: Smooth and supple, weaving together lovely spice, orange, pear and honey flavors on the polished frame, finishing with plenty of fruit and oak flavors. Appealing now. • $NA • (06/30/96) • **88**

Chardonnay Barossa Valley Family Reserve 1994: Fine textured, flavorful and focused, balancing its citrusy flavors with a touch of spice. Ready now. 1,000 cases made. • $12 • (03/31/96) • **84**

Chardonnay South Australia Family Reserve 1992: Crisp in texture, a sturdy white with appealing if modest pear and spice flavors. Drinkable now. 5,000 cases made. • $10 • (06/30/94) • **82**

Chardonnay South Eastern Australia Oxford Landing 1994: Fresh, floral and smooth, a broad-textured wine that never gets heavy. Tasty to drink while it's fresh. 20,000 cases made. • $7 • (05/15/95) • **86**

Chardonnay Yarra Valley Eden Valley Show Reserve 1993: Strives for elegance, with its understated but focused nectarine, pear, spice and toast flavors that fan out beautifully on the finish. Best from 1997. 1,000 cases made. • $12 • (03/31/96) • **90**

Grenache Barossa Bush Vine 1994: Has a distinctive, nutty flavor that runs through the modest berry notes. Simple but easy to drink. 1,000 cases made. • $12 • (04/30/96) • **80**

Late Harvest Eden Valley Botrytis Sémillon Family Reserve 1991: Smooth and deeply honeyed, rich, with fig, spice and vanilla notes as well. Pretty good ringer for a Sauternes. Drinkable now. 5,000 cases made. • $10 • (09/15/94) • **86**

Merlot South Eastern Australia Oxford Landing 1992: A strong minty-herbal streak characterizes this light-colored, light-bodied wine. Finish is short. 5,000 cases made. • $8 • (09/30/94) • **78**

Muscat Rutherglen Museum Show Reserve NV: Amazingly rich, ripe and powerful, gorgeous and unctuous, with layers and layers of spice, tar, coffee and molasses around a core of prune and apricot flavors. A great dessert wine. 1,000 cases made. • $12 • (09/15/94) • **98**

Oxford Landing South Eastern Australia 1992: Lean in structure but supple in texture, showing a spicy, slightly leathery edge to the plum and prune fruit. Drinkable now. 20,000 cases made. • $7 • (06/30/95) • **84**

Port Australia Galway Pipe NV: Manages to be elegant while it pours out intense and complex spice, coffee, date and caramel flavors that linger elegantly on the sweet finish. 5,000 cases made. • $19 • (05/31/96) • **92**

Port South Australia Clocktower Tawny Port NV: Smooth and spicy, gentle and sweet, with flavors that fade a little on the finish but echo some lovely plum and leather notes. 40,000 cases made. • $9 • (07/31/94) • **86**

Sémillon Late Harvest Barossa Valley Botrytis Affected 1984 • $5 • (03/15/89) • **83**

Sémillon Late Harvest Barossa Valley Botrytis Family Reserve 1994: This Australian dessert wine is sweet and smooth, layering its pear, apricot, honey, caramel and tobacco flavors in a swirl of beautifully balanced sweetness. Long and vibrant on the finish, it should be best starting in 1999. 1,000 cases made. • $12 • (12/31/95) • **94**

Sémillon Late Harvest Barossa Valley Botrytis Sémillon Family Reserve 1993: Deep golden color and luscious, intense ripe pineapple, apricot, honey and vanilla, hinting at toasted marshmallow on the finish. Sensational now, should continue to improve through 2000 to 2003. • $11 • (09/30/95) • **93**

Shiraz Barossa Valley Family Reserve 1993: Focused and flavorful, although it veers off toward an earthy/gamy style, picking up a nice touch of plum on the finish. Best from 1998. 5,000 cases made. • $10 • (03/31/96) • **86**

Shiraz Barossa Valley Family Reserve 1991: Firm, intense and peppery, spewing out lots of spicy currant and wild berry flavors. Finishes with firm tannins, drink now or cellar it short term. 5,000 cases made. • $10 • (09/30/94) • **88**

Shiraz Barossa Valley Family Reserve 1989 • $9 • (11/30/92) • **86**

Sparkling Australia Angas Brut Rosé NV: Fresh and inviting, a lovely mouthful of berry and floral-scented spice and citrus flavors that linger delicately on the finish. 10,000 cases made. • $10 • (03/31/96) • **86**

Sparkling Australia Pinot Noir-Chardonnay Cuvée One Prestige NV: Nice, crisp backbone has some flesh on it with spicy pear, vanilla and toasty flavors that linger on the smooth finish. 5,000 cases made. • $15 • (03/31/96) • **88**

Tawny Port South Australia Clocktower NV: Goes for lightness and elegance and achieves a spicy complexity that's rare in a wine of this price range. Hints of licorice, cinnamon and tar emerge on the smooth finish. 10,000 cases made. • $10 • (05/15/96) BB • **89**

YARRA RIDGE

Pinot Noir Victoria 1993: Light and a little bitter, with soft and modest flavors. Unimpressive. 2,000 cases made. • $12 • (06/30/95) • **74**

Sauvignon Blanc South Eastern Australia 1994: Broad and floral, herbal at the core, with a touch of sweet pear on the finish. 2,000 cases made. • $12 • (06/30/95) • **82**

YARRA YERING

Cabernet Sauvignon Coldstream Dry Red Wine No. 1 1984 • $14 • (05/31/88) • **73**

Key: SS—Spectator Selection. CS—Cellar Selection. BB—Best Buy. $NA—Price not available. (BT)—Barrel tasting. Ⓐ—Auction Price.
Dates in parentheses represent the issues in which the ratings were published.

Chile

Chile has been called a paradise for the production of fine wine. Stretching more than 2500 miles from its northern border in the Atacama Desert to Tierra del Fuego in the south, Chile is squeezed between the cool Pacific in the west and the high Andes Mountains in the east. Because Chile has never been touched by phylloxera, it is one of the few places where vinifera vines can be planted on their own roots, without the necessity of being grafted onto phylloxera-resistant American rootstock. Clean, abundant water from the Andes makes irrigation reliable, and grape vines thrive in Chile's naturally fertile, light soil. Prices for Chilean wines are often quite modest, with many good bottlings in the $5 to $10 range.

HISTORY OF CHILEAN WINEMAKING

Chilean viticulture dates back to the 1850s, when a wave of French immigrants settled in the Santiago region, bringing with them native French grape types such as Cabernet Sauvignon, Malbec, Merlot, Sémillon and Sauvignon Blanc. The French winemaking tradition remains strong here. Chilean wines still tend more toward the elegant, European style than they do toward the heavier, more concentrated style found in much of the rest of the New World (though this is partly attributable to the light Chilean soil).

For many years Chile was held back by a lack of capital and foreign investment. As recently as the early 1980s, for example, Chilean wines were still being fermented and aged in wood barrels made from the local rauli (beech) tree. Much of this wood was musty and old, leading to oxidized whites and tired reds that lacked fruit.

The situation changed dramatically in the mid-1980s, when Chile began to aggressively develop its wine industry as a source of export income. Chilean, American and European interests, including Domaine Rothschild (of Lafite), owners of the Los Vascos estate in Peralillo, the Torres family of Spain and Kendall-Jackson of California have invested in the Chilean wine industry, bringing with them the latest winemaking technology. In addition, leading enologists such as Bordeaux's Michel Rolland and California's Greg Upton have been retained as consultants at leading estates.

1. Aconcagua
2. Casablanca
3. Maipo
4. Rapel
5. Colchagua
6. Maule

CHILEAN WINE REGIONS

Located in the northern part of Chile's central valley, a narrow, 300-mile long valley set between the Andes and a coastal range of mountains to the west, is the Maipo Valley. Starting just below Santiago and extending 25 miles south to the town of Buin, the Maipo is the heart of the Chilean wine industry. The wines from vineyards closer to Santiago, such as Cousiño-Macul and the Bruno Paul estate (a joint venture between Bruno Prats of Château Cos-d'Estournel and Paul Pontallier of Château Margaux), have a distinctly earthy taste that is reminiscent of a red Graves. Further south in the Central Valley, a number of newer sub-regions are being quickly developed. These include Lontue, Colchagua, Curicó and Rancagua. Many producers blend wines from a number of these regions, with the object of producing well balanced reds and whites that combine the flavors of several regions.

The vineyards of Viña Santa Rita in the Maipo Valley south of Santiago—the original home of Chilean viticulture.

MAJOR CHILEAN GRAPE VARIETIES

Much like California wines, Chilean wines are marketed primarily by varietal labeling (for instance, "Chardonnay") rather than by regional appellations such as "Maipo Valley". The most important grape types remain the traditional red and white Bordeaux varieties, with Chardonnay receiving more and more attention.

Cabernet Sauvignon is widely planted. Many Cabernets display the cedary nuances and gentle herbal notes of a red Bordeaux. In place of the old rauli barrels of the past, many winemakers are using combinations of French and American oak to season the wine, adding an appealing vanilla note to the Cabernet varietal character. Concha y Toro, the largest producer, makes wines ranging from light, everyday clarets to impressive oak-aged reservas such as the Don Melchor line, a regular strong performer in *Wine Spectator* tastings. Errazuriz and Santa Rita have also established themselves as fine Cabernet producers.

Because Chilean Cabernet is soft and round, it has rarely needed the softening effect of Merlot to achieve balance. As a result, until recently, Chile had not produced much Merlot, which was thought of primarily as a blending grape. However, with Merlot's rise as a popular varietal in its own right throughout the world, production has increased.

Chilean Merlots are of a high quality, displaying soft, luscious fruit and a nice Graves-like *goût de terroir*. Particularly exciting is Casa Lapostolle, whose first vintage of Merlot scored very well, and promises even better things to come.

Most Chilean wineries also produce decent, sometimes delicious, white wines. Sauvignon Blanc remains the most consistent of the white varieties. Most is now cold-fermented in stainless steel vats, yielding wines that are fresh and ready to be drunk upon release. A more serious style, made in the manner of a white Graves (using barrel fermentation), is also beginning to appear at a somewhat higher price.

Chardonnay is also becoming important, largely because of the almost insatiable international demand for this popular varietal. Generally warm conditions in many regions have meant that Chilean Chardonnays often lack crispness and definition. Several producers, including Los Vascos, Concha y Toro, Santa Rita and Vina Calina are experimenting with barrel fermentation, lees stirring and more careful selection of grapes in an effort to produce Chardonnays with more character.

ALAMEDA

Cabernet Sauvignon Maipo Valley 1988 • $5 • (06/15/92) BB • **84**

Cabernet Sauvignon Maipo Valley Santa Maria Vineyard 1993: This firm red shows herbal, earthy and gamy flavors. Its rich but could use more fruit. 25,000 cases made. • $6 • (02/29/96) • **81**

Cabernet Sauvignon Maipo Valley Vintner's Selection 1993: Fresh, vivid black cherry and chocolate flavors are backed by crisp acidity and firm tannins. Balanced and respectably intense, and shows what Chile does best. 100,000 cases made. • $5 • (02/29/96) BB • **85**

Cabernet Sauvignon Maipo Valley Vintner's Selection 1992: Ripe, jammy berry fruit, accented by peppery and earthy notes give this rich wine liveliness, firm tannins give it structure. A straightforward wine, it makes pleasant drinking now. 70,000 cases made. • $5 • (04/30/95) BB • **85**

Chardonnay Maipo Valley Santa Maria Vineyard 1994: This ripe, oaky white shows good intensity, crisp acidity and fresh pineapple and butter flavors. The oak is a bit heavy, but the wine has verve and style. 16,000 cases made. • $6 • (04/30/95) • **84**

Merlot Maipo Valley Santa Maria Vineyard 1993: This polished Chilean red offers well-balanced flavors of currant, game, black pepper and toast. Drinkable now, but enough structure to improve in the short term. 50,000 cases made. • $6 • (02/29/96) BB • **86**

Merlot Maipo Valley Santa Maria Vineyard 1992: Fresh and clean, good varietal character. Licorice and plum aromas, plum, herb and black olive flavors. Though not very concentrated, it's balanced and ready to drink. 14,000 cases made. • $6 • (06/15/95) • **84**

Merlot Maipo Valley Santa Maria Vineyard 1987 • $5 • (06/15/92) BB • **82**

Sauvignon Blanc Maipo Valley 1993: Round and soft, with lots of vanilla character, this shows melon and fig flavors in a ripe style. Could use more crispness, but an appealing wine. 22,000 cases made. • $5 • (06/15/95) • **83**

Sauvignon Blanc Maipo Valley Vintner's Selection 1994: Ripe and soft flavors of vanilla, butter and melon indicate Chardonnay more than Sauvignon Blanc. Intriguing, but not for everyone. 40,000 cases made. • $5 • (06/30/96) • **81**

ALLISON, ROBERT

Merlot Maipo Valley 1987 • $5 • (06/30/90) • **77**

BRUNO, DOMAINE PAUL

Cabernet Sauvignon Maipo Valley 1994: Good structure and concentration, but despite some black cherry flavor, the dominant feature is bitterness. Notes of burnt coffee, rubber, tar and smoke. • $15 • (06/30/96) • **74**

CALITERRA

Cabernet Sauvignon Maipo 1992 • $7 • (05/31/94) • **82**

Cabernet Sauvignon Maipo 1991 • $6 • (04/30/93) • **83**

Cabernet Sauvignon Maipo 1990 • $5 • (03/15/93) BB • **84**

Cabernet Sauvignon Maipo 1989 • $6 • (06/15/92) BB • **87**

Cabernet Sauvignon Maipo 1988 • $6 • (10/15/91) • **79**

Cabernet Sauvignon Maipo 1987 • $6 • (09/15/90) BB • **86**

Cabernet Sauvignon Maipo 1986 • $6 • (07/31/89) BB • **85**

Cabernet Sauvignon Maipo Reserva 1988 • $9 • (12/15/92) • **86**

Cabernet Sauvignon Maipo Valley 1992: Lean and simple, this Cab tends towards the vegetal end of the varietal spectrum, with tea and light cherry flavors. Drink now. • $NA • (04/30/95) • **78**

Chardonnay Casablanca 1993 • $6 • (05/31/94) BB • **84**

Chardonnay Curicó 1992 • $7 • (04/30/93) • **80**

Chardonnay Curicó 1991 • $6 • (06/15/92) BB • **86**

Sauvignon Blanc Curicó 1992 • $5 • (04/30/93) • **78**

Sauvignon Blanc Curicó 1991 • $5 • (06/15/92) • **79**

CANEPA

Cabernet Sauvignon Curicó Magnificum 1990: Velvety and sweet, this luscious Cabernet gives all its fruit and vanilla flavors up front, leading to a gentle finish. Drink now and enjoy. 400 cases made. • $19 • (05/31/95) • **86**

Cabernet Sauvignon Maipo Valley 1994: Berry and tar flavors emerge from this smooth yet firm wine that's harmonious but not complex. Drink now. • $7 • (06/30/95) • **82**

Cabernet Sauvignon Maipo Valley 1993: Bright cherry and currant flavors are compromised by a smoky, slightly rubbery aroma which carries through to the finish. Drink now. • $6 • (04/30/95) • **79**

Cabernet Sauvignon Maipo Valley 1991 • $6 • (04/30/93) • **82**

Cabernet Sauvignon Maipo Valley 1990 • $6 • (06/15/92) BB • **81**

Cabernet Sauvignon Maipo Valley 1989: Pleasant and simple, at full maturity. The flavors run from dried cherry through tobacco and cedar and linger on the soft, slightly drying finish. Drink now. • $9 BB • **81**

Cabernet Sauvignon Maipo Valley 1986 • $6 • (06/15/90) • **75**

Cabernet Sauvignon Maipo Valley 1985 • $4 • (11/15/87) • **75**

Cabernet Sauvignon Maipo Valley Finisimo Estate Reserve 1990: Dark-colored and still firm, this youthful wine offers tar, bell pepper and black cherry flavors over muscular tannins. It's ripe and concentrated, but lacks finesse. Drink now through 1997. • $NA • (06/30/96) • **83**

Cabernet Sauvignon Maipo Valley Finisimo 1983 • $9 • (06/30/90) • **76**

Cabernet Sauvignon Maipo Valley Private Reserve 1992: There's plenty of ripe fruit here, with jammy black cherry and currant flavors, and lots of tannin, too. This Chilean value-wine needs some time to come together, but it's an ambitious effort that should be ready now. 5,000 cases made. • $8 • (04/30/95) BB • **88**

Cabernet Sauvignon Maipo Valley Reserva 1988 • $6 • (06/15/90) BB • **84**

Cabernet Sauvignon-Malbec Curicó 1994: Round and fruity, this shows good Cabernet character, adding cassis, herbal and smoky flavors and just enough tannin to stand up to food. Balanced and frank. • $5 • (10/31/95) • **85**

Cabernet Sauvignon-Malbec Maipo Valley 1984 • $4 • (03/15/88) • **74**

Cabernet Sauvignon-Malbec Sagrada Familia 1993: Fresh and fruity, this soft red offers bright cherry and blackberry flavors and hints of spice and herb. There's just enough tannin to keep it refreshing. Drink now. • $5 • (05/31/95) • **84**

Chardonnay Rancagua 1994: Clean, subtle and charming, peach, floral and light citrus flavors are fresh and crisp, not weighed down by oak influence. • $6 • (04/30/95) • **84**

Chardonnay Rancagua Private Reserve 1993: Bright and flavorful, if a bit overoaked, this bold Chardonnay marries tingly acidity, crisp fruit and plenty of vanilla and butter tones. • $8 • (04/30/95) • **84**

Merlot Curicó 1994: Merlot character comes through in the fleshy texture and soft cherry and light herbal flavors in this lush red. It's soft enough for drinking now. • $6 • **81**

Merlot Maipo Valley 1990 • $6 • (06/15/92) BB • **84**

Merlot Maipo Valley 1988 • $6 • (06/30/90) BB • **79**

Sauvignon Blanc Curicó 1994: Big, lush body, crisp acidity and ripe flavors of pineapple, vanilla and melon. A bit clumsy at first, but this white has lots going for it, needs food to show its best. • $5 • (05/15/95) • **85**

Sauvignon Blanc Maipo Valley 1992 • $5 • (04/30/93) BB • **83**

Sauvignon Blanc Maipo Valley 1991 • $5 • (05/15/92) BB • **88**

CARMEN

Cabernet Sauvignon Maipo Valley 1993: Decent quality, but on the earthy, smoky side of the flavor spectrum. Could use more fruit. • $6 • (06/30/96) • **78**

Cabernet Sauvignon Maipo Valley 1990 • $6 • (05/31/94) • **70**

Cabernet Sauvignon Maipo Valley Alto Jahuel 1990 • $6 • (07/15/93) BB • **82**

Cabernet Sauvignon Maipo Valley Alto Jahuel Reserve 1989 • $8 • (07/15/93) • **81**

Cabernet Sauvignon Maipo Valley Barrel Select Gold Reserve 1993: Cedary, minty overtones give this deeply flavorful and firmly tannic wine a distinctive profile. It's packed with rich black cherry and plum flavors, backed by smoky oak nuances. Drink now. 2,000 cases made. • $18 • (01/31/95) • **86**

Cabernet Sauvignon Maipo Valley Reserve 1992: An herbal style of Cabernet with accents of mint and raisins. It's sweet, fleshy and a bit cloying. • $10 • (06/30/96) • **78**

Cabernet Sauvignon Maipo Valley Reserve 1991: Ripe-smelling but lean-tasting Cabernet that has more tannin than fruit. Its mineral and herb flavors turn tight and astringent on the finish. 15,000 cases made. • $9 • (01/31/95) • **80**

Cabernet Sauvignon Maipo Valley Reserve 1990 • $8 • (05/31/94) • **72**

Cabernet Sauvignon Rapel 1992: This well-made, sophisticated Chilean red offers polished texture and firm structure for an amazingly low price, and throws in enough cherry and raspberry flavors to fill it out. Minty and light toasty notes add interest, and keep you coming back for more. Drinkable now. 40,000 cases made. • $6 • (04/30/95) BB • **87**

Chardonnay Central Valley 1995: A smooth, polished wine with a nice balance of oak and fruit. Discreet flavors of apples and pears lead to a slightly herbal finish. Good with food. • $6 • (06/30/96) • **83**

Chardonnay Maipo Valley 1993 • $6 • (05/31/94) • **79**

Chardonnay Maipo Valley Reserve 1994: Complete, balanced and harmonious, this wine shows deft use of oak and has ripe, crisp fruit, full body and a long finish. This Chilean has more sophistication than most South American Chardonnays. Drink now. 8,800 cases made. • $9 • (04/30/95) BB • **87**

Chardonnay Maipo Valley Reserve 1992 • $8 • (05/31/94) • **83**

Chardonnay Rapel 1994: A clean, fresh-tasting Chardonnay with pleasant fruit flavors and a touch of buttery complexity. Smooth, soft and almost sweet on the palate. 40,000 cases made. • $6 • (02/28/95) BB • **84**

Merlot Maipo Valley Alto Jahuel 1990 • $6 • (01/31/94) • **80**

Merlot Maipo Valley Reserve 1993: A densely flavored and lavishly oaked Merlot that's deep in color, almost chewy in texture, with firm tannins and a long finish. Drink now. • $9 • (01/31/95) • **85**

Merlot Maule Valley 1994: Light and fruity, fresh in flavor and easy to drink. Reminds us of strawberries. Charming. • $6 • (05/31/96) • **82**

Merlot Maule Valley 1993: Round, fruity and lush, balanced, sporting black cherry, plum and light herbal flavors. Soft tannins, will complement food. Drinkable now. Tasted twice, with consistent notes. 35,000 cases made. • $6 • (06/15/95) • **83**

Merlot Maule Valley Reserve 1994: A tough-textured red of modest fruit flavor that is good and drinkable, but not as filled out as it ought to be. • $10 • (05/31/96) • **80**

Merlot Rapel 1992 • $6 • (05/31/94) • **82**

Merlot Rapel Reserve 1993: Vibrant blackberry and plum aromas follow through on the velvety palate in this ripe wine. It's lush and fruity and shows toasty oak character, the flavors carry through on the finish. Appealing now. 2,080 cases made. • $9 • (05/15/95) BB • **88**

Sauvignon Blanc Maipo Valley 1992 • $6 • (09/15/93) • **77**

Sauvignon Blanc Maipo Valley Reserve 1992 • $8 • (09/15/93) • **82**

Sauvignon Blanc Maule Valley Reserve 1993: Soft and rather delicate for a Sauvignon Blanc, revealing light peach and pine flavors. Tasted twice, with consistent notes. • $9 • (05/31/95) • **79**

Sauvignon Blanc Rapel 1994: Bold, with plenty of Sauvignon Blanc character. This Chilean value shows lemon, light herb, melon and fig flavors in a taut package with good acidity for backbone. The finish is rich and long. 4,400 cases made. • $6 • (05/15/95) • **87**

Sauvignon Blanc Rapel Valley 1995: This round, soft wine offers pear and herbal flavors, an innocuous white that goes down and disappears. • $6 • (06/30/96) • **78**

CARTA VIEJA

Cabernet Sauvignon Maule 1993: Bright and vivid, this shows lively tart cherry and raspberry flavors with crisp acidity and soft tannins. It's fresh and clean on the palate, but finishes a bit short. Drink now. • $4 • (04/30/95) • **82**

Cabernet Sauvignon Maule Valley 1991 • $4 • (05/31/94) • **76**

Cabernet Sauvignon Maule Valley 1990 • $4 • (02/28/93) BB • **81**

Cabernet Sauvignon Maule Valley 1987 • $6 • (06/15/91) • **78**

Cabernet Sauvignon Maule Valley 1986 • $4 • (06/15/90) • **75**

Cabernet Sauvignon Maule Valley 1985 • $3 • (07/31/89) • **68**

Cabernet Sauvignon Maule Valley Antiqua Selection 1988 • $8 • (04/30/93) • **76**

Key: SS—Spectator Selection. CS—Cellar Selection. BB—Best Buy. $NA—Price not available. (BT)—Barrel tasting. Ⓐ—Auction Price.
Dates in parentheses represent the issues in which the ratings were published.

Cabernet Sauvignon Maule Valley Antiqua Selection 1986 • $8 • (06/15/91) • **75**

Chardonnay Maule 1994: Light and crisp, this wine offers green apple and light earthy flavors. It's a bit thin and lacks depth, but would make an acceptable apéritif. • $4 • (04/30/95) • **78**

Chardonnay Maule Proprietor's Reserve 1993: Packs a healthy punch of oak and rich fruit. The flavors range from smoke and nuts to melon and pear, with firm acidity for structure. Shows balance and intensity. 6,000 cases made. • $8 • (04/30/95) BB • **86**

Chardonnay Maule Valley 1993 • $4 • (05/31/94) • **72**

Chardonnay Maule Valley 1992 • $4 • (04/30/93) • **77**

Chardonnay Maule Valley Proprietors Reserve 1992 • $8 • (04/30/93) • **78**

Merlot Maule Valley 1993: Berry and cherry flavors are light but appealing in this simple wine. It's soft and drinkable now. • $4 • **80**

Merlot Maule Valley 1991 • $4 • (02/28/93) BB • **81**

Sauvignon Blanc Maule Valley 1993 • $4 • (05/31/94) BB • **81**

Sauvignon Blanc Maule Valley 1992 • $4 • (04/30/93) BB • **82**

CASABLANCA

Chardonnay Casablanca Valley Santa Isabel Estate 1993: This is full-bodied for a Chilean Chardonnay, with strong toasty oak flavors and ripe fruit, but it shows a marked vegetal streak that detracts from the pleasure. A disappointment from a talented winemaker. Tasted twice with consistent results. 4,000 cases made. • $9 • **72**

Gewürztraminer Santa Isabel Estate Casablanca Valley 1993: This bright, lively wine offers vivid grapefruit and lichi flavors with tangy acidity and a smoky finish, with more the structure than the flavors of Gewurztraminer. It's a vibrant, well-made wine that would show well with shellfish dishes. 400 cases made. • $8 • (04/15/95) • **84**

Sauvignon Blanc Casablanca Valley Santa Isabel Estate 1993: This bold, rich white shows a hint of Sauternes character-honeyed and spicy-but then acidity kicks in and it finishes with clean Sauvignon crispness. 6,000 cases made. • $8 • (05/15/95) • **87**

CASAS DEL TOQUI, LAS

Cabernet Sauvignon Cachapoal 1995: Lively, fresh and chunky, with moderate tannins and soft acidity. Leaning toward the herbal, gamy side of Cabernet. Drinkable now. 8,000 cases made. • $10 • (06/30/96) • **84**

Chardonnay Cachapoal Grande Réserve 1995: Plenty of oak gives this wine rich, toasty, buttery flavors, and there's just enough melon and apple to keep it in balance. 8,000 cases made. • $10 • (06/30/96) • **83**

Sémillon Cachapoal 1995: A firm wine that has little fruit character and a slight musty note on the finish. It's basically neutral. 8,000 cases made. • $8 • (06/30/96) • **78**

CATADORES, LOS

Cabernet Sauvignon Lontue Selección Especial 1986 • $5 • (06/15/92) BB • **84**

Sauvignon Blanc Lontue Selección Especial 1990 • $5 • (06/15/92) • **79**

CAVAS DEL RACO

Cabernet Sauvignon Alto Maipo 1990: An oddball wine with overripe, pruny aromas, murky flavors and an earthy finish. 3,500 cases made. • $10 • **71**

CHATEAU ANDREW

Cabernet Sauvignon Colchagua 1983 • $6 • (12/01/85) • **60**

CONCHA Y TORO

Cabernet Sauvignon Concha Puente Alto Vineyard Marqués de Casa 1987 • $9 • (06/15/92) • **67**

Cabernet Sauvignon Pirque Vineyard Casillero del Diablo 1984 • $9 • (06/15/92) • **74**

Cabernet Sauvignon Puente Alto Vineyard Private Reserve Don Melchor 1988 • $14 • (05/15/92) SS • **91**

Cabernet Sauvignon Maipo 1989 • $5 • (04/30/93) • **81**

Cabernet Sauvignon Maipo 1985 • $5 • (09/15/90) • **69**
Cabernet Sauvignon Maipo 1984 • $5 • (04/30/88) BB • **89**
Cabernet Sauvignon Maipo Casillero del Diablo Reserva Special 1984 • $7 • (11/15/87) • **85**
Cabernet Sauvignon Maipo Casillero del Diablo Special Reserve Pirque Valley 1991 • $9 • (05/31/94) • **81**
Cabernet Sauvignon Maipo Don Melchor Private Reserve 1991: This shows both concentration and elegance. Ripe fruit is clean and true, with just enough new oak to frame it and firm ripe tannins. It's not flashy, but each sip finds new nuances. Drink now. • $13 • (04/30/95) • **87**
Cabernet Sauvignon Maipo Don Melchor Private Reserve 1990 • $13 • (04/15/94) • **84**
Cabernet Sauvignon Maipo Marqués de Casa Concha Puente Alto Vineyard 1991: Ripe and round, with roasted fruit and earthy flavors, this is a big wine that has depth but lacks focus. It has a nice herbal Cabernet character, and will stand up to rich meat dishes. Drink now. Tasted twice with consistent results. • $10 • **82**
Cabernet Sauvignon Maipo Pirque Vineyard Casillero del Diablo Special Reserve 1988 • $9 • (12/15/92) • **81**
Cabernet Sauvignon Maipo Puente Alto Vineyard Don Melchor Private 1989 • $14 • (07/15/93) • **78**
Cabernet Sauvignon Maipo Puente Alto Vineyard Don Melchor Private Reserve 1993: Powerful concentration and balance. Deep color and full body show firm structure, yet the tannins are well-integrated and the plum and cassis flavors marry nicely with toasty oak. A well-made red that's approachable now but will be better in 1997. 10,000 cases made. • $16 • (06/30/96) CS • **91**
Cabernet Sauvignon Maipo Puente Alto Vineyard Marqués de Casa Concha 1991 • $10 • (05/31/94) • **81**
Cabernet Sauvignon Maipo Puente Alto Vineyard Marqués de Casa Concha 1989: • $11 • (06/30/96) • **76**
Cabernet Sauvignon Maipo Puente Alto Vineyard Marqués de Casa Concha 1988 • $11 • (04/30/93) • **73**
Cabernet Sauvignon Maipo Puente Alto Vineyard Private Reserve Don Melchor 1988 • $15 • (04/30/93) • **74**
Cabernet Sauvignon Maipo Puente Alto Vineyard Private Reserve Don Melchor 1987 • $13 • (06/30/90) • **85**
Cabernet Sauvignon Maipo Puente Alto Vineyard Special Reserve 1983 • $8 • (09/15/90) • **75**
Cabernet Sauvignon Maipo Special Reserve 1981 • $6 • (04/30/88) • **80**
Cabernet Sauvignon Maipo Valley Casillero del Diablo 1992: Pleasant mint and black cherry aromas and flavors thin out on the palate, dominated by oak tannins. The Cabernet character winds up somewhat simple. Drink now. • $8 • (04/30/95) • **82**
Cabernet Sauvignon Maipo Valley Trio 1994: Appealing chocolate and mint aromas give way to ripe, fleshy flavors of plum, mint and toast. The tannins are supple but add some backbone to the lush palate. Drinkable now. • $8 • (06/30/96) • **84**
Cabernet Sauvignon Merlot 1988 • $5 • (07/31/92) • **79**
Cabernet Sauvignon Merlot Rapel 1990 • $5 • (04/30/93) • **78**
Cabernet Sauvignon Merlot Rapel 1986 • $4 • (09/15/90) BB • **80**
Chardonnay Casablanca Valley Amelia Private Reserve 1993: Broad-beamed, presenting plenty of oak for structure. Pineapple and mango notes accent toast and hazelnut flavors, good concentration and length. • $13 • (04/30/95) • **85**
Chardonnay Casablanca Valley Casillero del Diablo 1994: Smoky, oaky aromas give way to a tight palate that features crisp acidity and fresh melon flavors. Ambitious and full-blown, if a bit awkward. • $9 • (06/30/96) • **84**
Chardonnay Casablanca Valley Trio 1995: This lively white has a good balance of crisp acidity and sweet oak, with buttery aromas and tropical fruit flavors. It's fresh and clean, if a bit short. • $8 • (06/30/96) • **84**
Chardonnay Maipo 1991 • $5 • (04/30/93) • **81**
Chardonnay Maipo Marqués de Casa Concha Santa Isabel Vineyard 1994: Balanced and clean, fresh and fruity, mingling pear, melon and vanilla flavors with good acidity and firm texture. Brings you back for another sip. • $10 • (04/30/95) • **85**
Chardonnay Maipo Santa Isabel Vineyard Casillero del Diablo Special Reserve 1991 • $9 • (04/30/93) • **71**
Chardonnay Maipo Santa Isabel Vineyard Marqués de Casa Concha 1993 • $10 • (05/31/94) • **85**
Merlot Peumo Valley Trio 1995: Lush, fleshy, characteristic blackberry and tomato flavors, supple tannins and a sweet hint of oak. Plenty of fruit for early drinking. • $8 • (06/30/96) • **85**
Merlot Rapel 1990 • $5 • (04/30/93) BB • **83**
Merlot Rapel 1986 • $4 • (03/15/90) • **76**
Merlot Rapel Marqués de Casa Concha Peumo Vineyard 1993: A beauty. Striking aromas of chocolate, coffee and ripe black plum give way to richly concentrated flavors of plum, toast, licorice and chocolate. It's ripe, balanced and lingers on the finish. A good-value Merlot from Chile. Drink now. 2,000 cases made. • $10 • (05/15/95) BB • **89**
Merlot Rapel Peumo Vineyard Casillero del Diablo 1994: Very good intensity for Chilean Merlot, from bold cherry, toast and spice aromas to firm flavors of fruit, oak and smoke. Drinkable now, could use more time in bottle. • $8 • (05/15/95) • **85**
Merlot Rapel Peumo Vineyard Marqués de Casa Concha 1992 • $10 • (05/31/94) • **85**
Merlot Rapel Peumo Vineyard Marqués de Casa Concha 1990 • $11 • (04/30/93) • **76**
Merlot Rapel Peumo Vineyard Marqués de Casa Concha 1989 • $9 • (05/15/92) • **85**
Sauvignon Blanc Maipo Casillero del Diablo Santa Isabel Vineyard 1991 • $8 • (04/30/93) • **73**
Sauvignon Blanc Maipo Valley Casillero del Diablo 1994: Appealing aromas of melon and vanilla lead to roundness and softness and a touch of oak. It's still crisp, though, and fruit lingers on the finish. • $8 • (05/15/95) • **86**
Sauvignon Blanc Sémillon Rapel 1991 • $5 • (04/15/93) • **66**

CONO SUR

Cabernet Sauvignon 1993: A straightforward wine with good varietal character, this shows ripe plum and cherry flavors with a slight herbaceous note and soft tannins. It's balanced and makes easy-drinking now. 9,500 cases made. • $6 • (04/30/95) • **82**
Cabernet Sauvignon Selection Reserve 1992: Oaky, sweet vanilla and spice notes feature this round, fruity, generous, lively red, plum and black cherry flavors linger on the finish. Drinkable now. 5,500 cases made. • $10 • (04/30/95) • **85**
Pinot Noir 1994: Here's a soft, supple wine for immediate drinking. The flavors run through cherry, tomato and herbal notes, then finish a bit short. Shows a bit of Pinot character, and it's quaffable. 10,000 cases made. • $6 • (04/15/95) • **80**
Pinot Noir Selection Reserve 1994: Smoke and toast notes get the upper hand over the soft plum fruit in this round, fleshy wine. It's clean and the fruit is ripe, but lacks well-defined Pinot character. Drink now. 3,000 cases made. • $10 • (04/15/95) • **81**

COUSINO-MACUL

Cabernet Sauvignon Maipo 1991 • $7 • (05/31/94) • **79**
Cabernet Sauvignon Maipo 1990 • $8 • (04/30/93) • **75**
Cabernet Sauvignon Maipo 1988 • $8 • (05/15/92) • **81**
Cabernet Sauvignon Maipo 1987 • $6 • (09/15/90) • **71**
Cabernet Sauvignon Maipo 1986 • $8 • (09/15/90) • **72**
Cabernet Sauvignon Maipo 1984 • $5 • (02/15/89) BB • **86**
Cabernet Sauvignon Maipo 1983 • $6 • (05/15/88) BB • **85**
Cabernet Sauvignon Maipo Antiguas Reservas 1990: Distinctive, appealing aromas of smoke and eucalyptus give way to soft, polished flavors of black currant and licorice. It's well-focused and varietally correct, but a slight rubbery note on the finish detracts. Drink now. 20,000 cases made. • $9 • **82**
Cabernet Sauvignon Maipo Antiguas Reservas 1989 • $12 • (05/31/94) • **80**
Cabernet Sauvignon Maipo Antiguas Reservas 1988 • $10 • (04/30/93) • **74**
Cabernet Sauvignon Maipo Antiguas Reservas 1987 • $10 • (06/15/92) • **82**
Cabernet Sauvignon Maipo Antiguas Reservas 1986 • $10 • (05/31/92) • **83**
Cabernet Sauvignon Maipo Antiguas Reservas 1985 • $11 • (10/15/91) • **81**
Cabernet Sauvignon Maipo Antiguas Reservas 1984 • $9 • (09/15/90) • **77**
Cabernet Sauvignon Maipo Antiguas Reservas 1981 • $9 • (02/15/89) • **80**
Cabernet Sauvignon Maipo Antiguas Reservas 1980 • $8 • (05/15/88) • **80**
Chardonnay Maipo 1992 • $9 • (05/31/94) • **78**

Chardonnay Maipo 1991 • $8 • (04/30/93) • **80**

Finis Terrae Maipo Valley 1992: Round and ripe, with chocolate, plum and prune aromas, and plum and licorice flavors in a thick, tannic texture. Quite extracted and heavily oaked, it may not age well, but shows attractive, mature character now. Drink while the fruit is still fresh. • $25 • (06/30/96) • **83**

Merlot Maipo 1991: Ripe and lush, this wine shows velvety fruit, with plum, toast and black olive flavors. There's a smoky, charred note that may put off some drinkers. Tasted twice with consistant notes. Drink now. 4,000 cases made. • $10 • **78**

Merlot Maipo Limited Release 1990 • $13 • (05/31/94) • **83**

Merlot Maipo Limited Release 1989 • $11 • (05/31/92) • **85**

Merlot Maipo Limited Release 1988 • $11 • (05/31/92) • **84**

Sauvignon Blanc Maipo 1992 • $6 • (04/30/93) BB • **82**

Sauvignon Blanc Maipo 1991 • $7 • (06/15/92) • **70**

CRANE LAKE

Cabernet Sauvignon Colchagua Valley 1992: Lush ripe fruit gives this wine immediate appeal. Layers of plum, black cherry and raspberry flavors are underpinned by chocolate notes and bright acidity. There's enough tannin to give it grip. Drink now. • $5 • (04/30/95) BB • **86**

Merlot Colchagua Valley 1992: Still tight and unyielding, this wine shows firm structure, and a slight weedy note doesn't detract from the ripe plum and black olive flavors. Drink now. • $5 • **84**

Sauvignon Blanc Colchagua Valley 1994: Light-bodied, this is soft and even a bit sweet on the finish, with light floral and apple notes. An easy quaff, but little true character. • $5 • **79**

DE MARTINO

Cabernet Sauvignon Maipo Valley 1991: Soft, well-knit red for drinking now. Pleasant cherry and mature tobacco flavors, integrated tannins and a lingering finish. 5,500 cases made. • $8 BB • **82**

Cabernet Sauvignon Maipo Valley De Martino Vineyard 1994: Bright cherry, herbaceous and bell pepper notes say Cabernet, offering fresh acidity and just enough backbone for balance. A good food wine for early drinking. 12,000 cases made. • $5 • (02/29/96) • **84**

Cabernet Sauvignon Maipo Valley Prima De Martino Vineyard 1993: Good concentration here. Rich, velvety texture is supported by firm, ripe tannins, giving it intensity, but the coffee and cassis flavors are a bit muted now. Try now. 2,500 cases made. • $8 • (02/29/96) • **87**

Cabernet Sauvignon Maipo Valley Santa Ines Vineyard 1991: Solid structure and some cherry and light herbal notes, short and dry finish. Drinkable now. 30,000 cases made. • $6 • (04/30/95) • **77**

Cabernet Sauvignon Maipo Valley Santa Ines Vineyard 1990 • $5 • (03/15/93) BB • **85**

Cabernet Sauvignon Maipo Valley Santa Ines Vineyard 1989 • $5 • (12/15/92) • **69**

Chardonnay Maipo Valley De Martino Vineyard 1995: Fresh and crisp, featuring enough pear and peach flavors to balance the soft vanilla notes. It's simple but appealing. 5,000 cases made. • $6 • (02/29/96) • **81**

Chardonnay Maipo Valley De Martino Vineyard Reserve 1995: Aggressive toasty vanilla flavors dominate this thick-textured Chardonnay, and light melon notes aren't enough for balance. 3,500 cases made. • $7 • (02/29/96) • **77**

Chardonnay Maipo Valley Santa Ines Vineyard Oak Barrel Fermented 1993: The candy, floral aromas smell like cheap perfume, and the flavors are simple and short. Very little Chardonnay character. 4,800 cases made. • $7 • (04/30/95) • **73**

Merlot Maipo Valley De Martino Vineyard 1994: Smoky and herbal flavors are prominent in this lean, supple Merlot. It's showing more tannin than fruit. 7,000 cases made. • $6 • (02/29/96) • **82**

Merlot Maipo Valley Santa Ines Vineyard 1993: Floral and smoke aromas are appealing, and the wine is round and soft, but it's so diluted that the flavors are gone almost before you swallow it. Too bad, because there's good fruit here. 9,800 cases made. • $6 • **80**

Key: SS—Spectator Selection. CS—Cellar Selection. BB—Best Buy. $NA—Price not available. (BT)—Barrel tasting. Ⓐ—Auction Price.
Dates in parentheses represent the issues in which the ratings were published.

Sauvignon Blanc Maipo Valley De Martino Vineyard 1995: Vivid herbaceous and grassy aromas give way to light-bodied, soft flavors of apples and herbs and a rather cloying finish. 8,000 cases made. • $5 • (02/29/96) • **79**

Sauvignon Blanc Maipo Valley Fumé De Martino Vineyard 1995: Ripe flavors of pineapple and pear are enriched by light vanilla notes in this round white. Though lacking in classic varietal character, it's fresh and clean. 1,000 cases made. • $7 • (02/29/96) • **83**

Sauvignon Blanc Maipo Valley Santa Ines Vineyard 1994: Austere and quite tart, this mingles light green apple and earthy notes in a wine that's crisp without lively freshness. Best for spritzers. 28,000 cases made. • $6 • **78**

DOÑA SOL

Cabernet Sauvignon Colchagua Valley 1992: Alluring aromas of black cherry, licorice and smoke give way to bright fruit on the palate, offering varietal character and a bit of personality. Drink now. • $6 • (04/30/95) • **85**

Chardonnay Colchagua Valley 1994: Crisp and fruity, this lean wine offers green apple and citrus flavors, the lack of oak will please those who like their fruit fresh and pure. 4,100 cases made. • $6 • (04/30/95) • **81**

Chardonnay Colchagua Valley 1993: Aggressive use of oak gives this wine appealing toast, hazelnut and vanilla flavors, along with underlying ripe apple and pear flavors that seem a bit overwhelmed at the moment. There's enough acidity for grip. For fans of oak. 4,100 cases made. • $6 • (04/30/95) • **84**

Merlot Colchagua Valley 1992: A muddled wine with some plum notes but more vegetal and candied fruit flavors, this is round and a bit dull, and the finish is dry. 8,500 cases made. • $6 • **77**

Sauvignon Blanc Colchagua Valley 1994: Very crisp green apple flavors dominate this light-bodied, fresh wine. It's clean, tart and simple. Good for apéritifs or spritzers. 3,800 cases made. • $6 • **80**

ERRAZURIZ

Cabernet Sauvignon Aconcagua Valley 1987 • $9 • (09/15/90) • **82**

Cabernet Sauvignon Aconcagua Valley 1985 • $5 • (09/15/88) • **82**

Cabernet Sauvignon Aconcagua Valley Antigua Reserva Don Maximiano 1984 • $7 • (09/15/88) BB • **87**

Cabernet Sauvignon Aconcagua Valley Antigua Reserva Don Maximiano 1980 • $6 • (11/15/87) • **68**

Cabernet Sauvignon Aconcagua Valley Don Maximiano Estate Reserva 1993: Call this the Martha's Vineyard of Chile, for its strong eucalyptus and cassis flavors and muscular tannins. More power than elegance, but its distinctive character should improve through 1997. • $12 • (10/31/95) • **87**

Cabernet Sauvignon Aconcagua Valley Don Maximiano Estate Reserva 1991 • $9 • (04/15/94) • **82**

Cabernet Sauvignon Aconcagua Valley Don Maximiano Estate Reserva Special Reserve 1993: Rich, harmonious and concentrated, boasting luscious plum, blueberry and mint flavors backed by round, full tannins and a vanilla finish. Drink now through 1998. • $25 • (10/31/95) • **89**

Cabernet Sauvignon Aconcagua Valley Estate Reserva Don Maximiano 1990 • $9 • (04/30/93) • **88**

Cabernet Sauvignon Aconcagua Valley Estate Reserva Don Maximiano 1989 • $10 • (06/15/92) • **87**

Cabernet Sauvignon Aconcagua Valley Estate Reserva Don Maximiano 1988 • $9 • (06/15/92) • **85**

Cabernet Sauvignon Aconcagua Valley Estate Reserva Don Maximiano Special Reserve 1989 • $9 • (04/30/93) • **83**

Chardonnay Maule Valley 1995: Soft and round, this has a pleasant mouth-feel but not much flavor, only light pear and melon with an herbal accent. Easy drinking. • $NA • (10/31/95) • **78**

Chardonnay Maule Valley 1991 • $11 • (06/15/92) • **84**

Chardonnay Maule Valley Reserva 1994: Oak dominates this muscular white, from vanilla aromas to toasty flavors, but there's plenty of acidity for backbone and nice apple and melon notes emerge on the finish. • $12 • (10/31/95) • **84**

Chardonnay Maule Valley Reserva 1993: A tight, understated wine with good balance. The modest apple flavors are fresh and crisp, and finish clean. A good apéritif wine. • $NA • (04/30/95) • **81**
Chardonnay Maule Valley Reserva 1992 • $9 • (04/30/93) • **84**
Chardonnay Maule Valley Reserva 1991 • $9 • (12/15/92) • **82**
Merlot Maule Valley 1994: Acrid, burnt aromas give way to black cherry flavors in this soft, round wine, then re-emerge in the bitter finish. The texture is appealing and there is ripe, clean fruit underneath, but bitterness overwhelms its virtues. 50,000 cases made. • $8 • (06/30/96) • **75**
Merlot Maule Valley 1993 • $9 • (05/31/94) • **83**
Merlot Maule Valley 1992 • $8 • (03/31/93) BB • **85**
Merlot Maule Valley 1991 • $8 • (12/15/92) • **83**
Sauvignon Blanc Maule 1995: Assertive lime and green apple flavors provide a crisp, clean profile. Not rich, but quite refreshing. 30,000 cases made. • $8 • (02/29/96) • **80**
Sauvignon Blanc Maule Valley Reserva 1993 • $9 • (05/31/94) • **84**
Sauvignon Blanc Maule Valley Reserva 1991 • $7 • (06/15/92) BB • **87**

GARZAS, LAS

Cabernet Sauvignon Colchagua Valley 1990 • $7 • (04/30/93) • **80**
Cabernet Sauvignon Colchagua Valley Proprietor Reserve 1990 • $7 • (05/31/94) • **77**

LAPOSTOLLE, CASA

Cabernet Sauvignon Colchagua 1994: Attractive tar and smoke aromas give way to plum and smoky flavors and ample tannins. Good sense of polish and varietal flavor. Should improve through 1997. 20,000 cases imported. • $9 • (06/30/96) BB • **87**
Merlot Colchagua Selection 1994: Ripe, balanced and concentrated, clean, fresh flavors of plum and licorice are supported by firm tannins. Fine now. Made by Pomerol star Michel Rolland. • $9 • (05/15/95) • **87**
Merlot Rapel Valley Cuvée Alexandre 1994: Rich and well-defined. Powerful aromas of plum and toast give way to round, lush tannins and ripe fruit, as chocolate and sweet fruit flavors linger on the finish. Drinkable now, it should improve through 1997. 3,000 cases made. • $15 • (06/30/96) • **90**
Sauvignon Blanc Colchagua 1995: The buttery, bitter almond flavors are atypical of the varietal, and the wine finishes a bit flat. Lacks fruit and verve. 10,000 cases made. • $8 • (06/30/96) • **76**
Sauvignon Blanc Colchagua 1994: Rich texture, good intensity, ripe melon flavor and plenty of vanilla oak character. Full-bodied, and though the acidity is a bit low, it still makes luscious drinking. • $7 • (05/15/95) • **85**

LARA, CASA DE

Cabernet Sauvignon Maule Valley 1991 • $5 • (05/31/94) • **73**
Sauvignon Blanc Maule Valley 1993 • $5 • (05/31/94) • **85**

LIBERTY SCHOOL

Cabernet Sauvignon Lontue NV • $6 • (09/15/88) BB • **80**

LOS BOLDOS, CHATEAU

Cabernet Sauvignon Requinoa 1991: Maturing now, this firm Cab offers licorice and tobacco aromas and flavors and plum and raisin character. The tannins are a bit coarse. • $8 • **75**

MAISON DU LAC

Cabernet Sauvignon Maipo Valley 1989 • $5 • (07/15/93) BB • **82**
Merlot Maipo Valley 1990 • $7 • (01/31/94) • **81**
Sauvignon Blanc Maipo Valley 1992 • $6 • (05/31/94) • **71**

MONTES

Cabernet Sauvignon Curicó 1992: Solid, sturdy, oak-influenced Cabernet with a good core of black cherry flavor and very firm tannins. It's good now, but should hold on through 1998. 20,000 cases made. • $8 • (06/30/96) • **84**
Cabernet Sauvignon Curicó 1991: Appealing blackberry and vanilla aromas follow through on the firm, concentrated palate. This Chilean Cab is still fresh, but with some depth and length. A fruit-driven wine that features balance and verve. Tasted twice, with consistent notes. 20,000 cases made. • $8 • (02/29/96) BB • **88**
Cabernet Sauvignon Curicó 1990: Round, deep, ripe fruit and soft tannins, a strong smoky, rubbery note permeates and seriously detracts from the pleasure. Drinkable now. 10,000 cases made. • $8 • (04/30/95) • **78**
Cabernet Sauvignon Curicó 1989 • $8 • (05/31/94) • **80**
Cabernet Sauvignon Curicó Montes Alpha 1992: Heavy-handed and oaky in flavor, without enough fruit to stand up to the heavily charred, woody character. Some will find it impressive, but it's too tannic and awkward for us. 15,000 cases made. • $14 • (06/30/96) • **78**
Cabernet Sauvignon Curicó Montes Alpha 1991: Delicious in the style. An oaky tasting, but elegant Cabernet with lots of clove and cinnamon notes that come out in the aroma and last through the finish. It is well-balanced, well-integrated, and fruity enough to drink now. 600 cases made. • $14 • (06/15/95) • **87**
Cabernet Sauvignon Curicó Montes Alpha 1990: Sturdy, still fresh, showing ripe black cherry and plum flavors and a smoky note. The tannins are firm, the finish clean and long. 600 cases made. • $14 • (04/30/95) • **84**
Cabernet Sauvignon Curicó Montes Alpha 1989 • $12 • (02/28/94) • **78**
Cabernet Sauvignon Curicó Montes Alpha Private Selection 1988 • $14 • (05/15/92) • **87**
Cabernet Sauvignon Curicó Villa Montes 1993: Light, vivid raspberry flavors that burst, then fade. Simple but pleasant. 20,000 cases made. • $7 • (02/29/96) • **82**
Cabernet Sauvignon Curicó Villa Montes 1992: Bright, perfumed rasberry and cherry aromas are attractive and carry through on the palate, which is rather soft and light but still balanced and fresh. Drink now. 25,000 cases made. • $6 • (04/30/95) • **83**
Cabernet Sauvignon Curicó Villa Montes 1991 • $6 • (02/28/94) • **79**
Cabernet Sauvignon Curicó Villa Montes 1990 • $6 • (02/28/93) BB • **84**
Cabernet Sauvignon Curicó Villa Montes 1989 • $6 • (06/15/92) BB • **84**
Cabernet Sauvignon Curicó Villa Montes 1988 • $4 • (02/15/90) • **73**
Cabernet Sauvignon Curicó Villa Montes 1987 • $7 • (02/15/90) BB • **84**
Cabernet Sauvignon Curicó Villa Montes Special Selection 1987 • $12 • (09/15/90) • **84**
Chardonnay Curicó Montes Alpha Special Cuvée 1995: A jolt of new oak in a light-bodied white that doesn't have enough fruit for balance. 1,500 cases made. • $NA • (06/30/96) • **79**
Chardonnay Curicó Montes Alpha Special Cuvée 1994: Bold, oaky, rich, lots of butter, toast and nutmeg aromas and similarly extreme flavors that are accented with banana and pineapple. Lingering finish, could use a bit more fruit. • $10 • (06/15/95) • **85**
Chardonnay Curicó Oak Barrel Fermented 1995: Full-bodied but basically neutral, this has light apple and vanilla notes but comes across mainly as a round white wine. 5,000 cases made. • $8 • (02/29/96) • **79**
Chardonnay Curicó Oak Barrel Fermented 1994: Vanilla notes add interest to this round yet crisp white, joining pear, apple and citrus flavors. It holds together well. 5,000 cases made. • $8 • (04/30/95) • **84**
Chardonnay Curicó Oak Barrel Fermented 1993 • $9 • (05/31/94) • **80**
Chardonnay Curicó Oak Barrel Fermented 1992 • $9 • (04/30/93) • **83**
Chardonnay Curicó Oak Barrel Fermented 1991 • $9 • (06/15/92) • **78**
Malbec Colchagua 1995: A wine with good varietal character delivering smoky, gamy and pruny flavors, some toasty oak, and enough acidity to maintain liveliness. It's fresh, rich and ready to drink now. 10,000 cases made. • $8 • (06/30/96) • **86**
Merlot Curicó 1991 • $8 • (01/31/94) • **82**
Merlot Curicó 1990 • $8 • (04/30/93) BB • **83**
Merlot Curicó Montes Alpha Special Reserve Aged in French Oak 1994: A fine example of delicacy coexisting with intensity. Bright aromas of plum and cassis give way to ripe fruit flavors enhanced by a touch of oak. Light tannins give just enough grip. Not an ager, but very pleasant now. 2,500 cases made. • $14 • (06/30/95) • **86**
Merlot Curicó Special Cuvée 1994: A stylish, fresh Merlot with deep color, spicy aromas, plum and berry flavors and ample oak accents.

Moderately tannic, but smooth enough to drink now through 1997. 20,000 cases made. • $8 • (05/31/96) • **85**

Merlot Curicó Special Cuvée 1993: A smooth operator. Ripe, plenty of jammy flavors and round texture. The plum and blueberry pie flavors are vibrant and matched by lovely clove and cinnamon notes. 20,000 cases made. • $8 • (12/31/95) • **86**

Merlot Curicó Valley Special Cuvée 1992 • $8 • (05/31/94) • **83**

Merlot Curicó Valley Villa Montes 1989 • $7 • (09/15/90) • **79**

Merlot Curicó Villa Montes 1995: Fresh and very flavorful, like blackberry jam without the sweetness. Deep purple in color, peppery in aroma, smooth and lush in texture. Not tannic, so it's ready to drink. Good value and enjoyment-what the Chileans do best. 15,000 cases made. • $7 • (05/31/96) BB • **85**

Merlot Curicó Villa Montes 1994: Jammy blackberry and licorice flavors have just enough tannin for balance, then fade cleanly and quickly. Pleasant fruit in an up-front style. 10,000 cases made. • $8 • (02/29/96) • **83**

Merlot Curicó Villa Montes 1993: Ripe black cherry flavor and a touch of vanilla from oak, light tannins. More concentration would add depth to what is a clean quaffing wine. 28,000 cases made. • $7 • (06/30/95) • **83**

Merlot Curicó Villa Montes 1991 • $7 • (01/31/94) • **80**

Sauvignon Blanc Curicó Villa Montes 1994: This round, soft wine shows rather dull fruit and finishes heavy and a bit cloying. It lacks acidity for balance, and true Sauvignon Blanc character. 25,000 cases made. • $6 • **77**

Sauvignon Blanc Curicó Villa Montes 1993 • $6 • (05/31/94) • **81**

Sauvignon Blanc Curicó Villa Montes 1992 • $6 • (04/30/93) • **76**

Sauvignon Blanc Curicó Villa Montes 1991 • $6 • (06/15/92) BB • **80**

MUÑOZ, ALEJANDRO HERNANDEZ

Pinot Noir Maipo Viña Portal Del Alto Gran Vino 1984 • $3 • (03/15/90) • **74**

OAK BLUFFS

Cabernet Sauvignon 1990 • $6 • (06/15/92) BB • **85**

ORIENTAL, DOMAINE

Cabernet Sauvignon Maule Valley Clos Centenaire 1991 • $7 • (04/30/93) • **76**

Cabernet-Merlot Maule Valley 1991 • $6 • (04/30/93) • **80**

PEREZ-LLANO

Cabernet Sauvignon Rancagua Gran Vino 1988 • $5 • (06/15/92) • **76**

PLAYA, LA

Cabernet Sauvignon Maipo Valley 1992: Bizarre flavors of milk and paste in a flat, dull structure. Unpleasant, though better than another bottle tasted. 25,000 cases made. • $6 • (06/30/96) • **61**

Cabernet Sauvignon Maipo Valley 1989 • $6 • (05/31/94) • **77**

Cabernet Sauvignon Maipo Valley 1988 • $5 • (04/30/93) BB • **81**

Cabernet Sauvignon Maipo Valley 1986 • $4 • (03/15/90) • **74**

Cabernet Sauvignon Maipo Valley Estate Reserve 1990: An odd marriage of dill pickle and brandied cherries gives this wine distinctive character but not much appeal. 12,000 cases made. • $8 • (06/15/95) • **72**

Cabernet Sauvignon Maipo Valley Estate Reserve 1988 • $8 • (05/31/94) • **81**

Chardonnay Maipo Valley 1995: Melon and candied apple flavors mingle with vanilla and honey notes in this heavy-handed Chardonnay. However, it packs enough acidity to maintain liveliness. 20,000 cases made. • $6 • (02/29/96) • **78**

Chardonnay Maipo Valley 1992 • $8 • (05/31/94) • **78**

Chardonnay Maipo Valley 1991 • $5 • (04/30/93) • **72**

Key: SS—Spectator Selection. CS—Cellar Selection. BB—Best Buy. $NA—Price not available. (BT)—Barrel tasting. Ⓐ—Auction Price.
Dates in parentheses represent the issues in which the ratings were published.

Merlot Maipo Valley 1990 • $6 • (05/31/94) BB • **86**

Merlot Maipo Valley 1988 • $5 • (04/30/93) BB • **81**

Merlot Maipo Valley 1987 • $4 • (03/15/90) • **75**

Sauvignon Blanc Maipo Valley 1992 • $5 • (03/31/93) BB • **85**

PORTAL DEL ALTO

Cabernet Sauvignon Maipo Gran Reserva 1983 • $4 • (09/15/90) BB • **82**

Cabernet Sauvignon Maipo Valley 1992 • $4 • (05/31/94) • **77**

Cabernet Sauvignon Maipo Valley 1990 • $4 • (03/15/93) BB • **84**

Cabernet Sauvignon Maipo Valley 1987 • $3 • (06/15/92) BB • **83**

Cabernet Sauvignon Maipo Valley Gran Reserva 1986 • $3 • (06/15/92) BB • **79**

Cabernet Sauvignon Maipo Valley 1984 • $3 • (03/15/90) • **77**

Cabernet Sauvignon Maipo Valley Gran Reserva 1989 • $4 • (04/30/93) • **72**

Merlot Maipo Valley 1992 • $4 • (05/31/94) • **78**

Merlot Maipo Valley 1990 • $4 • (04/30/93) • **77**

Sauvignon Blanc Maipo Valley 1992 • $4 • (05/31/94) • **73**

Sauvignon Blanc Maipo Valley 1991 • $3 • (06/16/92) • **76**

Sauvignon Blanc Sémillon Maipo Valley 1991 • $4 • (05/31/94) • **66**

PUMAS, LOS

Cabernet Sauvignon Curicó Valley 1988 • $4 • (09/15/90) • **69**

RABAT, DOMAINE

Cabernet Sauvignon Colchagua Valley Apalta Vineyard Reserva 1990: Attractive tobacco and cedar aromas give way to soft, fresh fruit flavors of cherry and berry and a touch of oak still toasty and sweet on the finish. It's well-integrated and drinking nicely now. 6,000 cases made. • $7 • (04/30/95) • **85**

Cabernet Sauvignon Maipo Valley 1991: Ultraripe cassis, roasted plum and tobacco flavors clash with rubbery notes and a slight, unpleasant spritz. 60,000 cases made. • $5 • (04/30/95) • **72**

Chardonnay Colchagua Valley Apalta Vineyard 1993: Lush-textured and slightly sweet, this has simple oak character and some ripe apple and melon flavors, but a sawdust note intrudes. A soft, easy-drinking wine. 5,000 cases made. • $7 • (04/30/95) • **78**

Merlot Colchagua Valley Apalta Vineyard Reserva 1992: Deep-colored and richly-textured, this ripe, concentrated wine shows attractive plum, licorice, coffee and cigar box flavors. This is a big Merlot for Chile. 4,000 cases made. • $7 • **86**

Sauvignon Blanc Maipo Valley 1993: This round, fleshy wines shows tropical fruit and vanilla flavors, but lacks acidity and finishes a bit sweet and dull. A round, easy-drinking style. 50,000 cases made. • $5 • **79**

Sauvignon Blanc Maipo Valley 1992 • $5 • (02/28/93) BB • **83**

RIVER FALLS

Merlot Colchagua 1994: Hearty, definitely on the herbal and tannic side, but fairly rich overall. Some ripe plum and cherry flavors with a touch of bittersweet chocolate on the finish. Needs to smooth out a little. 50,000 cases made. • $6 • (12/31/95) • **83**

SAGE ESTATE

Cabernet Sauvignon Maipo Valley 1990 • $6 • (04/30/93) BB • **84**

Chardonnay Maipo Valley 1992 • $7 • (04/30/93) • **75**

Sauvignon Blanc Maipo Valley 1992 • $6 • (04/30/93) BB • **84**

ST. MORILLON

Cabernet Sauvignon Lontue 1992: A soft, candy-like wine with flavors reminiscent of hard candy and vanilla, this lacks structure and varietal character. It's drinkable, but doesn't stay with you. 50,000 cases made. • $5 • (04/30/95) • **76**

Cabernet Sauvignon Lontue 1986 • $5 • (10/15/91) BB • **83**

Cabernet Sauvignon Lontue 1985 • $4 • (09/15/90) • **75**

Cabernet Sauvignon Maipo 1990 • $6 • (05/31/94) BB • **85**

Cabernet Sauvignon Maipo 1987 • $6 • (03/15/93) BB • **81**

Cabernet Sauvignon Maipo 1986 • $5 • (07/31/92) • **76**

Chardonnay Lontue Reserve Barrel Fermented 1993: Smoky, toasty oak flavors are appealing, but don't leave much room for fruit in this rich but somewhat one-dimensional wine. Will appeal to fans of oak. 2,000 cases made. • $11 • **81**

Sauvignon Blanc Lontue 1994: The crisp structure is appealing, but the flavors are somewhat neutral, except for a hint of herbal and onion notes. It's simple and inoffensive. 30,000 cases made. • $5 • **79**

Sauvignon Blanc Lontue 1992 • $6 • (04/30/93) • **74**

Sauvignon Blanc Lontue 1991 • $5 • (06/15/92) • **79**

SAN CARLOS

Cabernet Sauvignon Colchagua Valley 1991: Light and herbal, with some cherry flavors, this lacks concentration and verve. Straightforward red. • $7 • (10/31/95) • **77**

Chardonnay Colchagua 1995: This snappy white offers light, crisp apple and citrus flavors, fresh and lean. A delightful apéritif. • $6 • (10/31/95) • **82**

Malbec Colchagua Valley Oak Aged 1994: Smoky bacon and licorice flavors are typical of Malbec, while the supple fruitiness is characteristic of Chile. An appealing red for drinking now. • $6 • (02/29/96) • **86**

Merlot Colchagua Valley 1994: A rich, chocolaty Merlot that is fairly soft and round. Generous and well proportioned, with ripe plum, cherry and cassis flavors. Finishes with coffee notes. • $6 • (12/31/95) • **85**

Sauvignon Blanc Colchagua Valley 1994: Round and fleshy for a Sauvignon Blanc, this has ripe pear and herbal flavors and buttery accents. It's soft and full, showing just enough acidity for balance. • $6 • (02/29/96) • **82**

SAN CLEMENTE

Cabernet Sauvignon Maule Valley 1990 • $5 • (04/30/93) • **71**

Sauvignon Sémillon Maule Valley 1991 • $5 • (04/15/93) • **78**

SAN JOSE DE SANTIAGO

Cabernet Sauvignon Colchagua Valley 1990 • $5 • (05/15/92) BB • **85**

Cabernet Sauvignon Maule 1993: An earthy, vegetal quality shades this cranberry flavored red that is rather tart and lean. 15,000 cases made. • $7 • (06/30/96) • **79**

SAN MARTIN

Cabernet Sauvignon Maipo Valley International Series 1987 • $4 • (06/15/90) BB • **78**

SAN PEDRO

Cabernet Sauvignon Las Encinas Vino Tinto Seco 1987 • $NA • (06/15/92) • **80**

Cabernet Sauvignon Lontue Castillo de Molina 1982 • $7 • (02/15/89) • **78**

Cabernet Sauvignon Lontue Castillo de Molina 1981 • $7 • (11/15/87) BB • **83**

Cabernet Sauvignon Lontue Castillo de Molina 1979 • $7 • (03/15/87) • **81**

Cabernet Sauvignon Lontue Gato de Oro 1986 • $4 • (02/15/90) BB • **85**

Cabernet Sauvignon Lontue Gato Negro 1989 • $4 • (06/15/92) • **75**

Cabernet Sauvignon Lontue Gato Negro 1985 • $4 • (11/15/88) BB • **80**

Cabernet Sauvignon Lontue Gato Negro 1984 • $4 • (05/15/88) BB • **83**

Cabernet Sauvignon Lontue Gato Negro 1983 • $4 • (03/15/87) • **76**

Merlot Lontue 1989 • $7 • (05/31/92) BB • **89**

Merlot Lontue 1988 • $5 • (12/31/90) BB • **84**

Merlot Lontue Gato de Oro 1987 • $6 • (02/15/89) BB • **81**

Sauvignon Blanc Lontue 1991 • $7 • (06/15/92) • **79**

Sauvignon Blanc Lontue Gato Blanco 1991 • $4 • (06/15/92) • **75**

SANTA ALICIA

Cabernet Sauvignon Maipo Valley 1990: Cassis and herbal aromas are appealing. The palate is a bit flat but offers plum and licorice flavors backed by modest tannins. Still fresh, best to drink now. • $6 • (10/31/95) • **82**

Cabernet Sauvignon Maipo Valley Reserve 1990: Though light-bodied and somewhat tannic, this Cabernet Sauvignon delivers interesting cassis, black pepper and herbal notes that linger on the finish. A good food wine. • $8 • (10/31/95) • **83**

Chardonnay Maipo Valley 1993: Simple and straightforward, offering more herbal and vegetal character than fruit. • $6 • (10/31/95) • **75**

Chardonnay Maipo Valley Reserve 1993: Vivid and still fresh. Aromas of honey and flowers give way to delicate but lively flavors of tangerine, melon and vanilla. It's harmonious and lingers on the finish. • $8 • (10/31/95) • **86**

Chardonnay-Sémillon Vintage Select Curicó Valley 1993: Simple, slightly musty note, lacking depth and character. • $5 • (02/29/96) • **73**

Merlot Maipo Valley 1992: Ripe and dense, with herbal and green olive flavors and a hint of chocolate and spice. Past its peak, drink now. • $6 • (12/31/95) • **79**

Merlot Maipo Valley Reserve 1992: Effusively young and fresh for a '92, with a dollop of blueberry flavors and aromas. Concentrated, ripe and balanced, with a good backbone of tannins. Easy to like and delicious, this bargain from Chile finishes with a hint of mint. 5,000 cases made. • $8 • (12/31/95) BB • **88**

Sauvignon Blanc Maipo Valley Fumé Blanc 1993: Heavy flavors of vanilla and honey dominate this broad, soft white. Made in the traditional style favored by the Chilean domestic market, it may appeal to American oak lovers. • $6 • (02/29/96) • **79**

Vintage Select Merlot/Cabernet Sauvignon Curicó Valley 1992: Soft and diluted with little fruit, this shows herbal and mushroom flavors, then turns dry on the finish. • $5 • (10/31/95) • **76**

SANTA AMELIA

Cabernet Sauvignon Colchagua 1994: Richer and more structured than most Chilean Cabs, which makes this an especially good value. It offers smoky oak aromas, concentrated plum and black cherry flavors and a lively tobacco note. The tannins are firm, and it's lush and generous. Drinkable now, but may improve through 1997. 50,000 cases made. • $6 • (10/31/95) BB • **88**

Chardonnay Colchagua 1994: Light and refreshing, this features pleasant apple and beeswax aromas, then turns crisp on the palate, though without much fruit. Clean and likable. 25,000 cases made. • $6 • (10/31/95) • **82**

Merlot Colchagua 1994: An easy going Chilean wine that's a good value. Plenty of plum and chocolate flavors, ripe, bold and well balanced, with a touch of herbal character. It finishes with some clovelike flavors. 25,000 cases made. • $6 • (12/31/95) BB • **86**

SANTA CAROLINA

Cabernet Sauvignon Maipo Valley Estrella de Oro 1982 • $8 • (03/15/90) • **76**

Cabernet Sauvignon Maipo Valley Los Toros Vineyard Reserva 1985 • $8 • (04/30/93) BB • **84**

Cabernet Sauvignon Maipo Valley Los Toros Vineyard Special Reserve 1988 • $8 • (04/30/93) • **83**

Cabernet Sauvignon Maipo Valley Reserva Santa Rosa Vineyard 1990: Ripe and blowsy, this still has enough underlying tannin to give it shape, the flavors are roasted red fruits and earth. There's a hint of herbal Cabernet character, too. Drink now. 39,300 cases made. • $8 • (05/31/95) • **84**

Cabernet Sauvignon Maipo Valley Santa Rosa Vineyard 1986 • $4 • (04/30/88) • **78**

Cabernet Sauvignon Maipo Valley Santa Rosa Vineyard Gran Reserva Cinco Estrellas 1987 • $14 • (02/28/94) • **84**

Chardonnay Lontue Valley 1994: A fully fruity, uncomplicated white wine with lots of pear flavor, a tinge of smokiness and a slightly sweet finish. Easy going and soft on the palate. • $6 • (06/15/95) • **80**

Chardonnay Maipo Valley Santa Rosa Vineyard Gran Reserva Cinco Estrellas 1991 • $14 • (01/31/94) • **83**

Chardonnay Maipo Valley Santa Rosa Vineyard Special Reserve 1991 • $8 • (04/30/93) • **83**

Merlot Maipo Valley Santa Rosa Vineyard 1993: Pretty plum, smoke and toast flavors run through this lush, appealingly priced Merlot from

CHILE

Chile. The tannins are soft, and it finishes with plenty of sweet fruit. Easy to like, drink now. 49,000 cases made. • $6 • (05/15/95) BB • **86**

Merlot Maipo Valley Santa Rosa Vineyard 1989 • $6 • (03/31/93) BB • **82**

Merlot Maipo Valley Santa Rosa Vineyard Reserva 1991 • $8 • (04/15/94) • **84**

Merlot Maipo Valley Santa Rosa Vineyard Reserva 1990 • $8 • (04/30/93) • **82**

Merlot Maipo Valley Santa Rosa Vineyard Reserva 1989 • $8 • (04/30/93) BB • **82**

Merlot San Fernando Valley Gran Reserva Cinco Estrellas 1993: Round yet well defined, showing black cherry, light herb and smoke flavors. It's balanced, with enough tannin for grip. Drinkable now. 8,600 cases made. • $10 • (05/15/95) • **86**

Merlot San Fernando Valley Reserva 1993: A light, easy-drinking wine with clean flavors of cherry and light herbs. It's pleasant without showing much Merlot character. 25,700 cases made. • $8 • **81**

Merlot Santa Rosa Vineyard Reserva Especial 1989 • $8 • (06/15/92) BB • **83**

Merlot/Cabernet Sauvignon San Fernando Valley 1993: Ripe fruit flavors of currants, raspberries and cherries give this wine appeal. It's fresh and lush, and if it lacks the structure for aging, it gives plenty of pleasure now. • $6 • (05/15/95) • **85**

Pinot Noir Maipo Valley Reserva Santa Rosa Vineyard 1994: The pleasant cherry and berry fruit flavors are light and overmatched by a green, weedy note in this light, simple wine. There isn't much structure, drink up. 3,000 cases made. • $8 • **77**

Sauvignon Blanc Maipo Valley Santa Rosa Vineyard 1993 • $8 • (04/15/94) BB • **85**

Sauvignon Blanc Maipo Valley Santa Rosa Vineyard Special Reserve 1991 • $8 • (04/30/93) • **75**

SANTA MONICA

Cabernet Sauvignon Rancagua 1993: Acceptable stuff in a pinch, but too vegetal and herbal tasting for our palates. Moderately tannic, ready to drink. • $6 • **77**

Cabernet Sauvignon Rancagua 1992: Average quality, with some structure but dull and vegetal flavors. • $6 • **77**

Cabernet Sauvignon Rancagua 1991: Already mature, light and simple, offering dried-cherry, tea and smoke flavors that quickly disappear. Drink now. • $5 • (04/30/95) • **77**

Cabernet Sauvignon Rancagua 1989 • $5 • (10/15/91) BB • **85**

Cabernet Sauvignon Rancagua 1988 • $6 • (03/15/90) BB • **86**

Cabernet Sauvignon Rancagua Tierra de Sol 1985 • $NA • (06/15/92) • **74**

Cabernet Sauvignon Rancagua Tierra de Sol Reserva 1990: A rich wine with ripe fruit and firm tannins, it shows raisin, tobacco and cedar notes in a thick, rather coarse structure. Still hard, it's maturing rapidly, and may dry out before it softens. Try now. 1,000 cases made. • $12 • (04/30/95) • **81**

Chardonnay Rancagua 1995: Full-bodied, if a bit lean in flavor, for a Chilean Chardonnay. Nice apple notes with hints of herb and smoke. • $6 • (06/30/96) • **83**

Chardonnay Rancagua 1993: A delicate, silky wine with light lemon, pear and vanilla flavors and a nice balance of creaminess and crispness on the palate. It's clean and shows some elegance. • $5 • (04/30/95) • **82**

Chardonnay Rancagua 1992 • $6 • (01/31/94) • **78**

Chardonnay Rancagua Tierra de Sol 1991 • $NA • (06/15/92) • **85**

Chardonnay Rancagua Tierra de Sol Reserva 1993: Rich but neutral, straightforward, lacking fruit and Chardonnay character. 1,000 cases made. • $12 • (04/30/95) • **76**

Merlot Rancagua 1994: Not much fun. It has vegetal, swampy aromas and flavors and very little fruit. • $6 • **73**

Merlot Rancagua 1993: Light and soft, without much fruit or Merlot character, this is a straightforward red with berry fruit flavors and light tannins. Drink now. • $5 • **79**

Merlot Rancagua 1992 • $6 • (01/31/94) • **79**

Key: SS—Spectator Selection. CS—Cellar Selection. BB—Best Buy. $NA—Price not available. (BT)—Barrel tasting. Ⓐ—Auction Price.
Dates in parentheses represent the issues in which the ratings were published.

Sauvignon Blanc Rancagua 1994: Simple, sweet oak flavors dominate this light, dull Sauvignon Blanc. There are some apple tones but the wine is clumsy and somewhat cloying. • $6 • (06/30/96) • **77**

Sauvignon Blanc Rancagua 1993: Delicate floral aromas are appealing but get lost in the soft, dull flavors, which finish a bit sweet and cloying. Drinkable, but lacks Sauvignon Blanc character. • $4 • **78**

Sauvignon Blanc Rancagua 1992 • $6 • (05/31/94) • **76**

Sauvignon Blanc Rancagua 1991 • $6 • (05/15/92) BB • **85**

Sémillon Rancagua 1994: Fresh, lively spice and peach flavors produce enough vivacity for this white to stand on its own, and enough weight to stand up to food. • $5 • (06/30/96) • **83**

Sémillon Rancagua 1993: A crisp, straightforward wine with forward pear and citrus flavors, accented with a pleasant herbal note. It's round and easy to drink. • $4 • (04/15/95) • **82**

Sémillon Rancagua Seaborne 1992 • $5 • (05/31/94) • **79**

Sémillon Rancagua Seaborne 1991 • $5 • (07/31/92) • **78**

SANTA RITA

Cabernet Sauvignon Maipo Valley 120 1990 • $6 • (05/31/94) • **83**

Cabernet Sauvignon Maipo Valley 120 1989 • $7 • (02/15/93) BB • **85**

Cabernet Sauvignon Maipo Valley 120 1988 • $6 • (05/31/92) BB • **86**

Cabernet Sauvignon Maipo Valley 120 1986 • $5 • (05/15/89) BB • **83**

Cabernet Sauvignon Maipo Valley 120 Medalla Real 1987 • $11 • (06/15/90) • **78**

Cabernet Sauvignon Maipo Valley 120 Medalla Real 1984 • $9 • (11/15/87) • **85**

Cabernet Sauvignon Maipo Valley Casa Real 1993: Rich and mouthcoating, offering chewy cherry and cassis flavors, vanilla notes and herbal accents. There's plenty of extract and tannin here. Should improve through 1997. 1,827 cases made. • $25 • (06/30/96) • **88**

Cabernet Sauvignon Maipo Valley Casa Real 1989 • $NA • (06/15/92) • **81**

Cabernet Sauvignon Maipo Valley Medalla Real 1993: A light-bodied wine with pretty cherry flavors, spicy, toasty oak notes and firm tannins on the finish. Not a blockbuster, but has appealing personality, good with food. • $13 • (06/30/96) • **85**

Cabernet Sauvignon Maipo Valley Medalla Real 1992: Vivid fruit and firm structure are augmented by currant and slight herbal flavors. Ripe and balanced. Drinkable now. • $12 • (04/30/95) • **87**

Cabernet Sauvignon Maipo Valley Medalla Real 1990 • $11 • (04/15/94) • **87**

Cabernet Sauvignon Maipo Valley Medalla Real 1989 • $12 • (02/15/93) • **89**

Cabernet Sauvignon Maipo Valley Medalla Real 1988 • $11 • (05/15/92) • **88**

Cabernet Sauvignon Maipo Valley Medalla Real 1987 • $12 • (06/15/91) • **82**

Cabernet Sauvignon Maipo Valley Medalla Real 1986 • $5 • (03/15/90) • **78**

Cabernet Sauvignon Maipo Valley Medalla Real 1985 • $8 • (03/31/88) • **75**

Cabernet Sauvignon Maipo Valley Reserva 1993: Dense and muscular for a Chilean red, with a nice balance of ripe plum and toasty oak. It's still firm and closed, but would match well with hearty food. • $10 • (06/30/96) • **85**

Cabernet Sauvignon Maipo Valley Reserva 1992: Light and crisp flavors mingle light cherry and berry with a marked herbal, green-bean note, the tannins are light but dry. Drink now. • $9 • (04/30/95) • **81**

Cabernet Sauvignon Maipo Valley Reserva 1990 • $9 • (04/15/94) • **85**

Cabernet Sauvignon Maipo Valley Reserva 1989 • $10 • (04/30/93) • **83**

Cabernet Sauvignon Maipo Valley Reserva 1988 • $8 • (06/15/92) • **86**

Cabernet Sauvignon Maipo Valley Reserva 1987 • $12 • (09/15/90) • **85**

Cabernet Sauvignon Maipo Valley Reserva 1986 • $6 • (05/15/89) BB • **87**

Cabernet Sauvignon Rapel 120 1994: Thin, perhaps already fading, the cherry notes are pleasant, but turn slightly sweet and raisiny, and the finish is dry. Might perk up with food, but don't wait. • $6 • (06/30/96) • **79**

Cabernet Sauvignon Rapel 120 1992: A focused wine with ripe berry, cherry flavors accented with light cinnamon and chocolate flavors. The tannins are light but present, and the balance is good. This is fresh and clean, drink now. 65,000 cases made. • $7 • (04/30/95) • **85**

Chardonnay Casablanca Valley Medalla Real 1994: Clean, fresh, simple apple and floral flavors and a hint of sweetness on the palate. Not

much Chardonnay character, but it's a pleasant quaff. • $13 • (04/30/95) • **82**
Chardonnay Maipo Valley 120 1991 • $7 • (05/15/92) BB • **89**
Chardonnay Maipo Valley Casa Blanca 1991 • $NA • (06/15/92) • **78**
Chardonnay Maipo Valley Medalla Real 1993 • $11 • (05/31/94) • **84**
Chardonnay Maipo Valley Medalla Real 1991 • $11 • (05/15/92) • **83**
Chardonnay Maipo Valley Reserva 1995: Vivid and energetic, this light-bodied white is crisp and clean, and offers a nice balance of smoky oak, lime and apple. Good intensity. • $10 • (06/30/96) • **84**
Chardonnay Maipo Valley Reserva 1994: A tight wine in a subdued style, this shows crisp acidity, a hint of smoky oak and straightforward apple fruit. It seems simple at first, but grows on you, a good food wine. • $9 • (04/30/95) • **82**
Chardonnay Maipo Valley Reserva 1992 • $11 • (04/30/93) • **78**
Chardonnay Maipo Valley Reserva 1991 • $10 • (06/15/92) • **90**
Chardonnay Maule Valley 120 1995: A crisp, straightforward wine. The smoky and green apple flavors are lean, but the overall impression is fresh and clean. • $6 • (06/30/96) • **82**
Chardonnay Maule Valley 120 1994: Appealing floral and appley aromas fade on the rather diluted palate, it's straightforward and clean, but doesn't hold your interest. • $7 • (04/30/95) • **80**
Chardonnay Rapel 120 1993 • $6 • (05/31/94) • **82**
Merlot Maipo Valley 120 1990 • $7 • (04/30/93) • **78**
Merlot Maipo Valley 120 1989 • $6 • (06/15/92) BB • **85**
Merlot Maule Valley 120 1994: Soft and simple, showing cherry and light tomato flavors, and pleasant on the palate if slightly dry on the finish. • $6 • (06/30/96) • **79**
Merlot Maule Valley 120 1992: This vivid wine is fresh, if a bit lean, with appealing aromas of toast and plum and tart cranberry and herbal flavors with a firm tannic underpinning. It's a bit green, but shows good concentration. • $7 • **82**
Merlot Rapel 120 1991 • $6 • (05/31/94) • **81**
Sauvignon Blanc Maipo Valley 120 1992 • $7 • (04/30/93) • **78**
Sauvignon Blanc Maipo Valley 120 1991 • $6 • (06/15/92) BB • **84**
Sauvignon Blanc Maipo Valley Medalla Real 1991 • $NA • (06/15/92) • **84**
Sauvignon Blanc Maipo Valley Reserva 1992 • $9 • (04/30/93) • **83**
Sauvignon Blanc Maipo Valley Reserva 1991 • $7 • (06/15/92) BB • **88**
Sauvignon Blanc Maule Valley 120 1995: A snappy wine, with crisp gooseberry flavors, light herbal notes and good acidity. It's fresh and light. • $6 • (06/30/96) • **83**
Sauvignon Blanc Maule Valley 120 1994: Firm and fresh, with a nice mix of acidity and ripe apple and melon flavors, this wine delivers Sauvignon Blanc character in a smooth, easy-drinking package. • $7 • **83**
Sauvignon Blanc Maule Valley 120 1993 • $6 • (05/31/94) • **81**
Sauvignon Blanc Maule Valley Reserva 1995: The oak dominates the apple flavors in this wine and turns a bit bitter on the finish. Fine for a glass or two, might not stand up to food. • $10 • (06/30/96) • **80**
Sauvignon Blanc Maule Valley Reserva 1994: Smooth and fleshy, delivering clean grassy and herbal character and a bit of spice on the finish. It's richer than many Chilean Sauvignons, but still clean and fresh. • $8 • (05/15/95) • **85**
Sauvignon Blanc Maule Valley Reserva 1993 • $8 • (05/31/94) • **82**

SOUTH VALLEY

Cabernet Sauvignon Rancagua 1989 • $9 • (02/28/94) • **83**
Sémillon Rancagua 1991 • $9 • (05/31/94) • **73**

STONELAKE

Cabernet Sauvignon Lontue 1993: Really fruity, fresh and appealing, with definite oak shadings and enough cherry and berry flavors to flesh it out. Moderately tannic, but ready to drink now. • $13 • (06/30/96) • **85**
Chardonnay Lontue La Primavera Vineyard 1994: A satisfying quaff offering good intensity and balance. Thick and fairly rich with ripe, buttery flavors, as well as apple and pear notes. • $13 • (06/30/96) • **84**
Merlot Lontue 1994: A smooth-textured, stylish Merlot that has the appealing flavors of new oak and a modest amount of fruit to back it up. Drink now. • $13 • (05/31/96) • **84**
Pinot Noir Lontue La Primavera Vineyard 1994: Well-made red, featuring supple, crisp tannins, juicy, berry flavors and a judicious touch of smoky oak. It's balanced and fresh and a nice match with food. • $14 • (06/30/96) • **85**

STONY HOLLOW

Cabernet Sauvignon 1988 • $6 • (06/15/92) BB • **84**

TERRANOBLE

Merlot Maule 1994: This light-bodied red sticks to the herbal end of the Merlot flavor spectrum, with smoky notes and light, firm tannins. It's clean but simple. • $8 • **77**
Sauvignon Blanc Maule 1994: Light toast and grassy aromas are appealing, the flavors are delicate, soft and balanced, with lemon and light butter notes. Light and pleasant, Henri Marrionet, the winemaker, is from the Loire Valley. • $8 • **81**

TOLVA, DOMAINE

Cabernet Sauvignon Maule Valley 1991 • $5 • (05/31/94) BB • **82**
Cabernet Sauvignon Maule Valley 1989 • $5 • (12/15/92) • **74**
Chardonnay Maule Valley 1993 • $5 • (05/31/94) BB • **81**
Merlot Maule Valley 1992 • $5 • (05/31/94) BB • **83**
Sauvignon Blanc Maule Valley 1992 • $5 • (05/31/94) • **79**
Sauvignon Blanc Maule Valley 1991 • $5 • (05/31/94) • **79**

TORRES, MIGUEL

Cabernet Sauvignon Curicó 1992: Light cherry, tea and slightly weedy flavors mingle in this rather diluted red. Ready now. 38,000 cases made. • $7 • (06/15/95) • **78**
Cabernet Sauvignon Curicó 1991 • $7 • (05/31/94) • **78**
Cabernet Sauvignon Curicó 1990 • $7 • (06/15/92) BB • **85**
Cabernet Sauvignon Curicó 1989 • $7 • (06/15/91) BB • **82**
Cabernet Sauvignon Curicó 1988 • $4 • (09/15/90) BB • **87**
Cabernet Sauvignon Curicó 1985 • $5 • (03/31/88) • **73**
Cabernet Sauvignon Curicó 1984 • $4 • (01/31/87) • **79**
Cabernet Sauvignon Curicó Manso de Velasco Reserve 1993: Straightforward, rather lean, offering a mix of ripe plum and barnyard flavors and some sweet oak accents. Firm tannins and lingering finish promise further improvement. • $16 • (10/31/95) • **84**
Cabernet Sauvignon Curicó Manso de Velasco Reserve 1990: Lively, young and firm. Appealing ripe blackberry, smoke, spice and sweet vanilla flavors and a slight varnish note. Drinkable now. 3,050 cases made. • $15 • (05/31/95) • **84**
Cabernet Sauvignon Curicó Manso de Velasco Reserve 1989: There are attractive dried cherry, spice and brown sugar flavors in this maturing wine, and its texture is soft and delicate. It's Cab made in a style reminiscent of Rioja. Drink now. 3,500 cases made. • $15 • **83**
Chardonnay Curicó 1992 • $9 • (12/15/92) • **85**
Chardonnay Curicó 1991 • $8 • (06/15/92) • **74**
Chardonnay Curicó Chardonnay de la Cordillera 1994: Straightforward balance of acidity and alcohol, showing little fruit flavor and less Chardonnay character. Use it as a mixer. 5,000 cases made. • $8 • (02/29/96) • **77**
Chardonnay Curicó District Chardonnay de la Cordillera 1993 • $7 • (05/31/94) • **80**
Sauvignon Blanc Curicó 1995: Sour earthy aromas and flavors mar this tart wine, and an unpleasant chalky texture dominates the palate. • $NA • **68**
Sauvignon Blanc Curicó 1994: Light and very crisp, well-defined grassy, herbal flavors are balanced, true and not aggressive. It's not complex, but appealingly fresh and lively. 30,000 cases made. • $7 • (05/15/95) • **84**
Sauvignon Blanc Curicó 1993 • $7 • (05/31/94) • **79**
Sauvignon Blanc Curicó 1992 • $6 • (04/30/93) BB • **84**
Sauvignon Blanc Curicó 1991 • $7 • (04/15/92) BB • **84**

CHILE

TRAVERSO, SERGIO

Cabernet Sauvignon Colchagua 1992: Tart and tight, vegetal aromas are a turnoff, although the green flavors become fairly civilized on the palate. Not likely to improve with age. • $7 • (06/15/95) • **76**

Cabernet Sauvignon Colchagua 1990 • $6 • (12/15/92) • **79**

Merlot Colchagua 1992: Not bad, but might have been better two years ago. It seems slightly vinegary and tired despite modest fruit flavors. 10,000 cases made. • $7 • **77**

Merlot Colchagua 1990 • $6 • (12/15/92) BB • **83**

UNDURRAGA

Cabernet Sauvignon Maipo Valley 1992: This ripe, fleshy wine is thick with cassis, plum and chocolate flavors, full-bodied for Chile, with just enough tannin for grip. Can stand up to a steak. Drink now. • $6 • (04/30/95) • **84**

Cabernet Sauvignon Maipo Valley 1991 • $5 • (05/31/94) • **77**

Cabernet Sauvignon Maipo Valley 1990 • $6 • (07/15/93) • **79**

Cabernet Sauvignon Maipo Valley 1989 • $6 • (06/15/92) • **74**

Cabernet Sauvignon Maipo Valley 1988 • $5 • (09/15/90) BB • **83**

Cabernet Sauvignon Maipo Valley 1987 • $5 • (02/15/90) BB • **87**

Cabernet Sauvignon Maipo Valley Reserve 1991: Rich toast and coffee tones of new oak and ripe, concentrated plum and currant flavors provide depth. Good structure, lingering fruit finish. Approachable now, but will improve through 1997. • $9 • (05/31/95) • **88**

Cabernet Sauvignon Maipo Valley Reserve 1989 • $8 • (05/31/94) • **82**

Cabernet Sauvignon Maipo Valley Reserve Selection 1988 • $9 • (04/30/93) • **81**

Cabernet Sauvignon Maipo Valley Reserve Selection 1987 • $8 • (06/15/92) BB • **87**

Cabernet Sauvignon Maipo Valley Reserve Selection 1986 • $8 • (06/15/91) BB • **83**

Cabernet Sauvignon Maipo Valley Reserve Selection 1985 • $7 • (03/15/90) BB • **85**

Cabernet Sauvignon Maipo Valley Santa Ana 1985 • $5 • (11/15/87) • **78**

Chardonnay Maipo Valley 1995: A light vegetal note detracts from this soft, thin white. It lacks fruit flavor and concentration. • $6 • (06/30/96) • **77**

Chardonnay Maipo Valley 1994: Vivid pineapple and citrus aromas give way to liveliness and tart acidity. It has a different profile than most South American Chards we've tasted, fresh and zingy. • $6 • (04/30/95) • **83**

Chardonnay Maipo Valley 1993 • $6 • (01/31/94) • **82**

Chardonnay Maipo Valley 1992 • $7 • (04/30/93) • **75**

Chardonnay Maipo Valley 1991 • $7 • (06/15/92) • **78**

Merlot Maipo Valley 1993: Flavors of herbs and cherries mingle in this fresh, clean wine, kept brisk by firm tannins. It's a bit austere, but has good Merlot character. • $6 • **82**

Merlot Maipo Valley 1992 • $6 • (04/30/93) • **76**

Pinot Noir Maipo Valley 1992: A generic red, this is soft and light, with some sweet cherry and light herbal flavors, an easy quaff that won't go the distance with a meal. Drink now, try slightly chilled. • $7 • (04/15/95) • **78**

Sauvignon Blanc Maipo Valley 1995: Lively and straightforward, this simple white offers light citrus and pineapple flavors and a clean finish. • $6 • (06/30/96) • **80**

Sauvignon Blanc Maipo Valley 1994: The honey and floral aromas and soft, peachy flavors taste more like Riesling than Sauvignon Blanc, but the wine is delicate and lively. • $6 • **81**

Sauvignon Blanc Maipo Valley 1993 • $5 • (04/15/94) BB • **85**

Sauvignon Blanc Maipo Valley 1992 • $6 • (09/15/93) • **81**

Sauvignon Blanc Maipo Valley 1991 • $6 • (05/15/92) • **79**

Key: SS—Spectator Selection. CS—Cellar Selection. BB—Best Buy. $NA—Price not available. (BT)—Barrel tasting. Ⓐ—Auction Price.
Dates in parentheses represent the issues in which the ratings were published.

VALDIVIESO

Cabernet Sauvignon Maipo Valley 1986 • $7 • (04/30/93) • **83**

Cabernet Sauvignon Maipo Valley 1984 • $8 • (06/15/92) • **71**

Chardonnay Lontue 1992 • $7 • (04/30/93) • **82**

Merlot Maipo Valley 1989 • $8 • (06/15/92) • **79**

VALLE DE SAN FERNANDO

Cabernet Sauvignon San Fernando 1988 • $5 • (06/15/92) BB • **83**

Cabernet Sauvignon San Fernando 1985 • $7 • (07/31/89) • **79**

Cabernet Sauvignon San Fernando 1983 • $4 • (11/15/88) • **77**

Cabernet Sauvignon San Fernando Gran Reserva 1986 • $6 • (04/30/93) • **79**

Cabernet Sauvignon San Fernando Gran Reserva 1984 • $6 • (09/15/90) BB • **81**

Cabernet Sauvignon San Fernando Gran Reserva 1982 • $6 • (11/15/88) BB • **81**

Merlot San Fernando 1990 • $5 • (06/15/92) • **75**

VASCOS, LOS

Cabernet Sauvignon Colchagua 1993: Good presence here. The cassis and plum flavors are concentrated, and firm tannins give the wine structure. It has clean, ripe varietal character, good balance and though drinkable now it should hold. 125,000 cases made. • $7 • (04/30/95) BB • **85**

Cabernet Sauvignon Colchagua 1992 • $7 • (05/31/94) BB • **83**

Cabernet Sauvignon Colchagua 1991 • $9 • (04/15/94) • **82**

Cabernet Sauvignon Colchagua 1990 • $7 • (05/31/92) BB • **88**

Cabernet Sauvignon Colchagua 1989 • $7 • (06/15/92) BB • **83**

Cabernet Sauvignon Colchagua 1988 • $7 • (06/15/91) BB • **82**

Cabernet Sauvignon Colchagua 1987 • $5 • (09/15/90) BB • **86**

Cabernet Sauvignon Colchagua 1985 • $5 • (11/15/87) • **84**

Cabernet Sauvignon Colchagua 1984 • $4 • (04/30/88) BB • **88**

Cabernet Sauvignon Colchagua Grande Reserve 1991 • $12 • (05/31/94) • **83**

Cabernet Sauvignon Colchagua Reserve 1992: There's plenty of lively fresh fruit here, with flavors from cherry to raspberry to strawberry that fill the mouth and linger on the finish. The moderate tannins make it drinkable now. 10,000 cases made. • $12 • (04/30/95) • **84**

Cabernet Sauvignon Colchagua Reserve 1990 • $12 • (05/31/94) • **81**

Cabernet Sauvignon Colchagua Reserve 1989 • $11 • (06/15/92) • **84**

Chardonnay Colchagua 1994: Crisp and lean, light-bodied, almost neutral in character. Could come from any grape, any vineyard. 25,000 cases made. • $7 • (04/30/95) • **75**

Chardonnay Colchagua 1993 • $7 • (05/31/94) • **80**

Chardonnay Colchagua 1992 • $NA • (01/31/94) • **79**

Sauvignon Blanc Colchagua 1994: Heavy, dull, marred by flavors of varnish and earth, lacks freshness and varietal character. Tasted twice, with consistent notes. 35,000 cases made. • $5 • (05/31/95) • **71**

Sauvignon Blanc Colchagua 1993 • $5 • (05/31/94) • **80**

Sauvignon Blanc Colchagua 1991 • $6 • (09/15/93) • **75**

VILLARD

Cabernet Sauvignon Rancagua 1992: A sturdy red, with firm tannins and straightforward cherry and light earthy flavors. It'll stand up to food, but doesn't have much to say on its own. Drink now. 6,500 cases made. • $8 • (04/30/95) • **81**

Cabernet Sauvignon Rancagua 1991 • $8 • (05/31/94) • **76**

Chardonnay Aconcagua Casablanca Vineyard 1993: Fresh and lively, from the alluring peach and toast aromas through the ripe fruit and crisp acidity on the palate. The oak is deftly used, and adds interest to the solid, concentrated fruit. A well-made wine that should improve. Drink now or hold. 5,500 cases made. • $8 • (04/30/95) BB • **88**

Chardonnay Aconcagua Casablanca Vineyard Barrel Fermented Reserve 1993: An unctuous, expressive wine with distinctive character. Rich butter and vanilla flavors show a somewhat heavy hand with the oak, but there's plenty of tropical fruit flavors for balance. Tasted twice with consistent results. 800 cases made. • $10 • **85**

Chardonnay Lontue 1992 • $7 • (05/31/94) • **77**

Merlot Cachapoal 1992: Vibrant yet polished, this wine offers toast, mint, plum and light herbal flavors in a well-focused, varietally-correct package. The lingering finish is clean. Not a blockbuster, but a real pleasure to drink. 2,000 cases made. • $8 • **87**

Sauvignon Blanc Aconcagua 1993 • $5 • (05/31/94) • **77**

Sauvignon Blanc Aconcagua Casablanca Vineyard 1994: An exotic fruit salad with very distinctive style: tart, vibrant citrus, pineapple, hay and herb notes. May be too rambunctious for timid palates, but it makes a statement. 4,800 cases made. • $7 • (05/15/95) • **85**

VIÑA CALINA

Cabernet Franc Chile 1994: Velvety and soft, this ripe red offers black cherry, light herbal and coffee notes. Lots of flavor for current drinking. A joint venture with Kendall-Jackson. • $20 • (02/29/96) • **84**

Cabernet Sauvignon Chile 1993: Jammy raspberry and vanilla flavors are wrapped in a thick, velvety texture, adding mouth-filling tannins and the peppery kick of alcohol. Big, without much subtlety. • $20 • (02/29/96) • **84**

Chardonnay Chile Selección de Las Lomas 1995: This full-flavored wine offers smoky, creamy pineapple and melon notes that linger on the finish, with a slight sweetness. Bright fruit and skillful use of oak give it character. • $16 • (06/30/96) • **86**

Merlot Chile 1994: Vivid cherry and vanilla aromas follow through on the palate in this big, ripe, fleshy red. A joint venture with Kendall-Jackson. • $20 • (02/29/96) • **83**

VIÑA DEL MAR

Cabernet Sauvignon Curicó Selección Especial 35 1988 • $6 • (06/15/91) BB • **81**

Cabernet Sauvignon Curicó Selección Especial 35 1987 • $6 • (09/15/90) BB • **83**

Cabernet Sauvignon Lontue 1988 • $6 • (06/15/92) • **79**

Cabernet Sauvignon Lontue 1985 • $6 • (04/30/88) BB • **86**

Cabernet Sauvignon Lontue Selección Especial 17 1986 • $6 • (02/15/90) BB • **80**

Cabernet Sauvignon Maipo Valley 1992: A soft wine that adds olive and herbal notes to the cherry and plum fruit flavors. It's round and balanced, but lacks depth. Drink now. 24,000 cases made. • $6 • (04/30/95) • **78**

Cabernet Sauvignon Maipo Valley 1990 • $6 • (05/31/94) • **82**

Cabernet Sauvignon Maipo Valley Reserve 1988: Candied cherry and strawberry aromas give way to sweet vanilla and dried fruit flavors in this jammy wine. It's soft and simple. Drink now. 2,000 cases made. • $9 • **77**

Cabernet Sauvignon Maipo Valley Reserve 1987 • $10 • (05/31/94) • **83**

Cabernet Sauvignon Maipo Valley Reserve 1986 • $9 • (06/15/92) • **78**

Chardonnay Lontue 1992 • $6 • (04/30/93) • **72**

Chardonnay Lontue 1991 • $6 • (12/15/92) • **69**

Chardonnay Lontue Reserve 1991 • $9 • (06/15/92) • **83**

Chardonnay Maipo Valley 1994: This light, simple wine would make a good spritzer, except for the flavors of earth and onions that get in the way of the green apple flavors. Tasted twice with consistant results. 9,000 cases made. • $7 • **73**

Chardonnay Maipo Valley 1993 • $6 • (05/31/94) • **78**

Chardonnay Maipo Valley Reserve 1993: Modest lemon and apple cider flavors, soft floral and waxy overtones. Showed better in a previous tasting. 2,000 cases made. • $9 • (04/30/95) • **79**

Fumé Blanc Lontue 1992 • $6 • (04/30/93) • **78**

Fumé Blanc Lontue 1991 • $6 • (06/15/92) BB • **85**

Fumé Blanc Maipo Valley 1994: Floral and sweet herbal aromas give way to candied fruit and an earthy, cloying finish in this disjointed wine. It lacks fresh Sauvignon Blanc character. 18,000 cases made. • $6 • **76**

Fumé Blanc Maipo Valley 1993 • $6 • (05/31/94) • **79**

Merlot Curicó Selección Especial 12 1989 • $6 • (06/15/91) BB • **80**

Merlot Curicó Selección Especial 12 1988 • $6 • (09/15/90) BB • **82**

Merlot Lontue 1990 • $6 • (06/15/92) BB • **83**

Merlot Lontue 1988 • $6 • (07/31/89) BB • **80**

Merlot Maipo Valley 1992: Black cherry and plum flavors are attractive in this soft wine, but there's a creamy lactose flavor that's a bit off-putting. It's ripe and lush, drink now. 25,000 cases made. • $6 • **77**

Merlot Maipo Valley 1991 • $6 • (05/31/94) BB • **82**

Merlot Maipo Valley Reserve 1989 • $9 • (05/15/92) • **78**

VIÑA PORTA

Cabernet Sauvignon Valle del Cachapoal 1994: Really fruity, with lots of straightforward cherry and berry flavors, modest tannins and a crisp bite on the finish. Drinkable now, but should mellow through 1997. 5,000 cases made. • $9 • (06/30/96) • **83**

Cabernet Sauvignon Valle del Cachapoal 1993: Soft and ripe with a tannic finish. Very peppery plum and cherry flavors. Comes off a bit overdone, but still tasty and firm on the finish. 10,000 cases made. • $9 • (12/31/95) • **84**

Cabernet Sauvignon Valle del Cachapoal 1992: Nice complexity for this price. A mix of sweet oak, appealing herbal accents and plenty of bright berry and cherry flavors. The tannins are firm but in balance with the fruit and crisp acidity. From Chile. Drink now. 7,000 cases made. • $9 • (04/30/95) BB • **87**

Cabernet Sauvignon Valle del Cachapoal 1991 • $9 • (05/31/94) • **79**

Cabernet Sauvignon Valle del Cachapoal Reserva 1992: Distinctive, ripe, adding spice, leather and cigar-box aromas and flavors to firm tannins and rich texture. Drinkable now through 1997. 7,000 cases made. • $11 • (04/30/95) • **88**

Chardonnay Maipo Valley Valle del Maipo 1992 • $9 • (04/15/94) BB • **86**

Chardonnay Valle del Cachapoal 1995: Full-bodied for Chile, with attractive spicy oak notes. The flavors lean more towards herbal than fruity. 5,000 cases made. • $9 • (06/30/96) • **82**

Chardonnay Valle del Cachapoal 1994: Nicely balanced, offering pear and apple flavors, light vanilla accents and crisp, lemony acidity. It's clean and has some intensity. 10,000 cases made. • $9 • (02/29/96) • **84**

Chardonnay Valle del Cachapoal 1993: Straightforward and rather neutral, shows some oak and soft acidity. Tasted twice, with consistent notes. 7,000 cases made. • $9 • (04/30/95) • **78**

VIÑA SEGU OLLÉ

Cabernet Sauvignon Maule Valley Doña Consuelo 1994: An average, jug-type wine, with rubbery aromas, lean, smoky flavors and medium body. • $6 • (06/30/96) • **75**

Cabernet Sauvignon Maule Valley Doña Consuelo 1993: Funky and sweet with aromas of sour milk and nail polish remover. Not recommended. Tasted twice, with consistent notes. • $6 • (06/30/96) • **55**

Cabernet Sauvignon Maule Valley Doña Consuelo 1992: Stewed red fruits, tobacco and soft tannins, without varietal character or distinctive personality. Straightforward, drinkable now. 5,000 cases made. • $6 • (04/30/95) • **77**

Cabernet Sauvignon Maule Valley Doña Consuelo Reserve 1993: Fresh and clean, with pleasantly brisk tannins, this is varietally correct, though the flavors fall onto the herbal, green bean side, with light cherry accents. Drink now. 3,000 cases made. • $8 • (06/15/96) • **83**

Cabernet Sauvignon Maule Valley Doña Consuelo Reserve 1992: Tasty but tough Cabernet, from the spicy, oaky aromas to the thick black cherry flavors and dense, rather tannic texture. Drink now through 1997. 2,000 cases made. • $8 • (06/30/96) • **84**

Cabernet Sauvignon Maule Valley Doña Consuelo Reserve 1991: Fading and drying out, this shows raisin, smoke and dead leaf aromas and flavors. Past its prime. 2,000 cases made. • $14 • (06/30/96) • **76**

Chardonnay Maule Valley Doña Consuelo 1995: Crisp, thin and straightforward, this almost neutral white shows little varietal character, its lemony acidity makes it a pleasant apéritif. • $6 • (06/30/96) • **79**

Chardonnay Maule Valley Doña Consuelo 1994: Round and generous, this wine makes a rich impression on the palate, but the flavors are dull, with celery and butter notes and not much fruit. 5,000 cases made. • $6 • (04/30/95) • **78**

Merlot Maule Valley Doña Consuelo 1995: A smoky-tasting Merlot with earthy, herbal flavors and moderate tannins. 7,000 cases made. • $6 • (05/31/96) • **81**

Merlot Maule Valley Doña Consuelo 1994: Pleasant cherry and smoky aromas turn simple on the palate. The wine is round and soft but doesn't show much concentration. Drink now. 5,000 cases made. • $6 • **78**

Moscatel de Alejandria Doña Consuelo Maule Valley 1993: Smooth yet crisp, showing herbal and smoky fig, apple and light honey flavors in a tight, subtle, fresh, well-integrated package. 7,000 cases made. • $6 • (04/15/95) • **84**

Moscatel de Alejandria Maule Valley Doña Consuelo 1994: An exotic wine with a fruit-salad mix of flavors. Orange, pineapple, honey and nutty flavors mingle in this assertive wine that's pleasant and reminiscent of hard candy in its simplicity and slightly sweet finish. 7,000 cases made. • $6 • (06/30/96) • **81**

Sauvignon Blanc Maule Valley Doña Consuelo 1994: Bright pineapple and lime flavors with sweet oak make this a lively white with moderate acidity. Not complex, but vivid enough to pair with food. 7,000 cases made. • $6 • (06/30/96) • **83**

VIÑOS DE CHILE

Blush Lontue Gato Rosado 1994: 10,000 cases made. • $5 • (08/31/95) • **84**

Cabernet Sauvignon Lontue Gato Negro 1993: This brown-tinged wine tastes tired already. There are stewed fruits, weedy notes and earthy flavors in a round, soft frame. It lacks freshness and vibrancy. Drink up. 50,000 cases made. • $5 • (04/30/95) • **75**

Sauvignon Blanc Lontue Gato Blanco 1994: Vibrant and bright with gooseberry and fig flavors and very crisp acidity, this is reminiscent of New Zealand in style. The flavors persist and the finish is clean. A well-made wine. Tasted twice with consistant results. 40,000 cases made. • $5 • (05/31/95) BB • **86**

VIÑOS EXPOSICION

Cabernet Sauvignon Talca Conde del Maule 1988 • $6 • (06/15/92) • **79**

Cabernet Sauvignon Talca Escudo de Talca 1990 • $5 • (06/15/92) BB • **82**

Cabernet Sauvignon Talca Molino Viejo 1990 • $5 • (06/15/92) BB • **82**

Cabernet Sauvignon Talca Reserva de Talca 1989 • $6 • (06/15/92) • **77**

Sauvignon Blanc Talca Conde del Maule 1991 • $6 • (06/15/92) • **75**

VINTERRA

Cabernet Sauvignon Maipo & Napa Valleys NV • $7 • (02/15/90) BB • **86**

VIU MANENT

Cabernet Sauvignon Colchagua Valley Proprietor's Reserve 1991: Initial barnyard aroma is off-putting, but it disappears and ripe, roasted plum and blackberry flavors emerge. Round and velvety, sporting vanilla oak notes on the long finish. • $6 • (10/31/95) • **85**

Chardonnay Colchagua Proprietor's Reserve 1994: On the earthy side, this awkward, disjointed wine shows little fruit or freshness. • $NA • (10/31/95) • **73**

WALNUT CREST

Cabernet Sauvignon Maipo 1987 • $5 • (04/30/93) BB • **82**

Cabernet Sauvignon Maipo 1985 • $4 • (06/30/90) BB • **80**

Merlot Rapel 1993: A rich, ripe, brawny red from Chile. This shows deep color, aromas of plum and smoke, with plum, light herbal and toast flavors in good balance. There's good concentration here for an unbelievable price. Drinkable now. 170,000 cases made. • $5 • (05/15/95) BB • **86**

Merlot Rapel 1992 • $5 • (05/31/94) • **79**

Merlot Rapel 1990 • $5 • (04/30/93) BB • **84**

Merlot Rapel 1989 • $4 • (05/15/92) BB • **83**

Merlot Rapel 1987 • $4 • (06/30/90) BB • **85**

Sauvignon Blanc Maipo Valley 1991 • $5 • (04/30/93) • **78**

Key: SS—Spectator Selection. CS—Cellar Selection. BB—Best Buy. $NA—Price not available. (BT)—Barrel tasting. Ⓐ—Auction Price.
Dates in parentheses represent the issues in which the ratings were published.

France

Although France is not the largest producer of wine, it produces more great wine than any other country. The wines of Bordeaux, Burgundy, the Rhône and Champagne all testify to the centuries-old reputation of quality French wine. Yet, France is not just about tradition. In recent decades, less well-known regions of France such as the Languedoc, Provence, the Ardèche and the Jardin de la France have undergone a viticultural revolution. Where once these vineyards produced simple *vin ordinaire* for everyday domestic consumption, many now turn out quality wines of all types.

1. Loire
2. Champagne
3. Alsace
4. Chablis
5. Côte d'Or
6. Mâcon
7. Beaujolais
8. Bordeaux
9. Languedoc-Roussillion (d'Oc)
10. Rhône
11. Provence

THE FRENCH APPELLATION SYSTEM

Established in the 1930s, the *Appellation (d'Origine) Controllée* laws (AC) are key to understanding French wines. Though widely misperceived as a guarantee of quality, what the AC laws are, in fact, is a guarantee of authenticity—in other words, that the wine in the bottle actually comes from the place stated on its label. This system reflects the basic philosophical underpinning of French winemaking: that soils are unique and that the character and quality of wine flows from the precise interplay of soil, climate, grape variety and the human element contributed by the winemaker.

There are roughly 250 recognized AC wine types, ranging from large regional appellations, such as "AC Bordeaux," which covers tens of thousands of acres, to mini-appellations, such as "Château Grillet," which covers a single estate. As a general rule, the more tightly specified the AC, the better the quality of the soil and the wine that comes from it. Thus, to take Bordeaux as an example, at the top of the AC hierarchy are the specific communes, such as Pauillac, St-Julien, Margaux and Pomerol. At the base of the pyramid are the basic Bordeaux wines, which can come from anywhere in the region. In between are intermediate levels such as Médoc and Haut-Médoc. As one moves up the pyramid, specifications as to yields per acre, alcoholic content, and other factors grow increasingly tighter. Most of the other important regions—including Burgundy, the Rhône, and the Loire—have similar gradations of specificity and quality within their respective appellations.

With the vast improvements in winemaking and viticulture that have taken place in recent decades, the traditional appellation control system has become somewhat inadequate; it does not embrace the dynamic growth and improvement in quality going on outside the original ACs. An intermediate experiment with a category called VDQS (*vins delimités de qualité supérieure*) was initiated in 1949, to recognize regions of special merit that had not quite achieved the quality and consistency expected of a wine in the AC category. This VDQS category has now largely disappeared as many of its original members have been elevated to full AC status.

Many of the most exciting recent developments have taken place in a category created in 1973 called *vin de pays* (VDP). There are now roughly a hundred defined areas that have the right to use this term on their labels. Some of the best known include Vin de Pays d'Oc, Vin de Pays de l'Hérault and Vin de Pays des Côtes du Gascogne. More than 75 percent of the *vins de pays* are from the vast Midi region on France's Mediterranean coast, which in the past had been devoted almost solely to bulk wine production.

The VDP category has become extremely important and now accounts for about one-fifth of total wine production. Development here has been aided by the simple fact that vineyard land in the better-known ACs has become prohibitively expensive. Large, established AC firms such as Louis Latour, Moreau, and Baron de Rothschild (Mouton) have invested heavily in VDP production, believing that with the right production techniques and better vineyard practices, there is significant potential for quality wines.

Many of the VDP wines are sold under their varietal names—as "Chardonnay," for instance—in a frank recognition of the realities of the modern consumer market; consumers appear to understand varietal labels much better than they do the more complex appellation system. This represents a major shift away from the traditional *appellation controllée* philosophy, which has always emphasized geography over grape varieties. It is a safe bet that both systems will continue to coexist and prosper, with the AC wines being marketed to a sophisticated audience of collectors and connoisseurs, while the varietal wines will be sold with increasing success to a mass market which demands good quality at a fair price.

FRENCH WINE REGIONS

Bordeaux

Of all the wines entitled to AC status, Bordeaux accounts for the largest percentage of production by far, about 20 to 25 percent in good years. At more than sixty million cases annually, it also accounts for about 10 percent of total French wine production. Almost 250,000 acres of vineyards are entitled to the Bordeaux appellation, and 80 percent of the total production is devoted to red wines.

The most important Bordeaux grape is the Cabernet Sauvignon, which forms the backbone of many of its wines. However, Merlot is more widely planted, and accounts for nearly half of all acreage. Cabernet Franc, Petit Verdot and Malbec are also significant here. Most Bordeaux wines are blends of two or more of these varieties.

The most widely planted white grape variety in Bordeaux is the Sémillon, followed closely by the Sauvignon Blanc. Muscadelle, Colombard and Ugni Blanc account for most of the remaining white production. Like the reds, most white Bordeaux is a blend of two or more varieties.

The Médoc remains the most important Bordeaux appellation. Cabernet Sauvignon is dominant here, accounting for the sturdy structure and long aging potential of classic Médoc clarets. Four major subregions of the Médoc are held in high regard; each has its own distinctive style. Margaux is known for its delicate bouquet and aristocratic svelteness; St.-Julien may be the best balanced, combining Margaux finesse with the classic characteristics of its neighbor Pauillac, known for its masculine cedar and cigar box aromas and powerful structure. St.-Estèphe, with the heaviest soil, produces the sturdiest and perhaps the most reliable claret, seeming to obtain a reasonable degree of concentration and depth even in difficult years.

In 1855, the best châteaux of the Médoc were classified into five levels, from first to fifth growth. The first growths, called the *premiers crus*, are perhaps the most famous wine names in the world: Lafite-Rothschild, Château Margaux, Latour, Mouton-Rothschild and Haut-Brion (although the latter is actually in the Graves). In recent years the quality of several lower classified growths has improved to the point where they can now challenge the first growths in every way but price. These so-called super-seconds include Léoville Las Cases, Ducru-Beaucaillou, Cos d'Estournal, Palmer (actually a third growth) and Léoville-Barton. Just below the classified growths are the many excellent *crus bourgeois*, several of which (Château Gloria and Château Chasse-Spleen, for instance) would almost certainly be ranked with the classified growths in the unlikely event of a reclassification.

Because it is close to the port of Bordeaux, the Médoc dominated the Bordeaux wine trade for centuries. In the last two decades, however, Saint-Emilion and Pomerol, on the so-called right bank of the Dordogne River, have achieved their rightful places alongside the great wines of the Médoc. Pomerol is dominated by Merlot. Its estates tend to be tiny, and demand for their best wines vastly outstrips supply. The most famous estate, Château Petrus, now sells its wines for more than any Médoc *premier cru*. Other top Pomerol properties include Trotanoy, L'Evangile,

La Conseillante, Lafleur, Vieux Château Certan, Clinet, and the microscopic Le Pin.

Saint-Emilion is a larger region than Pomerol, and the quality of its estates is more variable. Merlot is the most important grape, but here it is often blended with significant quantities of Cabernet Franc, Malbec and, less often, Cabernet Sauvignon. Unlike Pomerol, which has never had a classification, St.-Emilion was first classified in 1954, and had a subsequent reclassification in 1985. Its two top wines, Cheval Blanc and Ausone, are considered on a par with the Médoc first growths. Just below them are a dozen or so other fine estates that would rank with the better second and third growths of the Médoc. These include Figeac, Canon, Pavie, Magdelaine, and Clos Fourtet.

The Graves region, which surrounds the town of Pessac, a suburb of the city of Bordeaux, is unusual in that its reputation rests equally on the quality of its reds and whites. Many of the top estates, such as Haut-Brion, La Mission Haut-Brion, Domaine de Chevalier and Olivier produce exquisite whites from a blend of Sémillon and Sauvignon Blanc. Reds here rely more heavily on Merlot than do the wines of the Médoc, located just to the north. As a result, a red Graves tends to mature more quickly than a typical Médoc, though it shares the Médoc's robust structure.

Contained within the southern part of the Graves, the regions of Sauternes and Barsac produce one of the world's great sweet dessert wines, mostly from Sémillon, but with some Sauvignon Blanc used at certain estates. Like the great German late-harvest wines, the key to great Sauternes is the development of noble rot (*Botrytis cinerea*), which gradually draws water out of the grape, shriveling it and greatly concentrating the flavors of the grape. Among the wines of Sauternes, Château d'Yquem has no equal. However, great Sauternes are also made at Château Rieussec, Climens, Guiraud, Suduiraut and others.

The Abbey of St. Pièrre d'Hautvillers in Champagne; its cellar-master at the end of the 17th century was master blender Dom Pérignon.

Burgundy

No region has suffered so much for its fame as has Burgundy. Its name was appropriated by bulk producers to represent any generic red, and many were heavy and sweet. It was also a victim of its own abuses, as many producers let grape yields soar and allowed winemaking quality to slip in the years following World War II. But with yields firmly under control and a renewed commitment to conscientious cellar practices, there can be little doubt that today Burgundy is producing the best wines in its illustrious history.

The heart of Burgundy is the Côte d'Or, which at 20,000 acres, is less than a tenth the size of Bordeaux. The northern half of the Côte d'Or, the Côte de Nuits, specializes in red Burgundy, which is made exclusively from the Pinot Noir grape. The southern half of the Côte d'Or, the Côte de Beaune, produces both red and white Burgundy; the latter is usually made from Chardonnay, though other grape varieties, such as Pinot Blanc, are permitted. While red and white Burgundies are rarely as potent or strong as the great wines made elsewhere in the world, they are extraordinarily complex, and among the most avidly sought after by collectors of great wine.

The appellation system of Burgundy is complicated. At the top of the Burgundy hierarchy are the *grand cru* vineyards. The best known of these include Le Chambertin, Le Musigny, Romanée-Conti, Richebourg, La Tâche and Clos de Vougeot for red wines; Le Montrachet, Chevalier-Montrachet, Bâtard-Montrachet and Corton-Charlemagne for white wines. Classified below the *grands crus* are the *premier crus*, several of which produce wines that are virtually on par with *grands crus* and are usually less expensive. The best-known *premier crus* in the Côte de Nuits include Gevrey-

Chambertin le Cazetiers, Chambolle-Musigny Les Amoureuses, Chambolle-Musigny Les Charmes and Vosne-Romanée Les Suchots. In the Côte de Beaune, *premiers crus* include Beaune Clos des Mouches (white and red), Beaune Les Grèves (red), Pommard Les Epenots (red), Volnay Clos des Ducs (red), Meursault Charmes (white), Puligny-Montrachet Les Combettes (white) and Puligny-Montrachet Les Pucelles (white).

Somewhat confusingly, many of the *grands crus* have had their names appended to the nearby villages. Thus, the villages of Gevrey-Chambertin, Chambolle-Musigny, Vosne-Romanée, Puligny-Montrachet and Aloxe-Corton all produce wines under their names. While often quite good, these rarely have the depth and dimension of the *grands crus* or the *premiers crus*, which must come from a single vineyard.

Another point that should be emphasized is that most great Burgundy vineyards have more than one owner (Clos de Vougeot, for example, has nearly 80), and the range in quality between the best and the worst producers is enormous. The best way for consumers to assure themselves of a quality product is to consult a reliable wine publication (such as *Wine Spectator)* for ratings of individual producers' wines.

An important emerging region of Burgundy is the Côte Chalonnaise, which is developing a reputation for reasonably priced reds and whites that come close in style and quality to the wines of the Côte d'Or. The four major appellations of the Chalonnaise are Mercurey, Givry, Rully and Montagny. The first two are noted for their red wines, most of which are made exclusively from Pinot Noir (rather than the less exalted Gamay of Beaujolais). Both are more similar to the soft, fruity style of the Côte de Beaune than to the denser, earthier reds of the Côte de Nuits. While Mercurey is larger than Givry, the latter boasts several exceptionally fine vineyards—Cellier-aux-Moines and Domaine Thenard among them—which give it the stronger following among connoisseurs.

While Rully also makes good reds, both it and Montagny are better known for their whites, which are made from Chardonnay. Both are a distinct cut above the white wines of the Mâcon (also made from Chardonnay), and offer much of the taste of Côte de Beaune whites at fair prices. Classic, labor-intensive Burgundian techniques, such as barrel fermentation and lees stirring, are becoming more common here, further improving the flavor profiles of these wines. The best producers in the Chalonnaise include Rodet, Joblot, and Faiveley.

South of the Côte d'Or lie the highly productive regions of Beaujolais and Mâcon, both an excellent source of affordable everyday wines. Red Beaujolais is made from the vigorously fruity Gamay grape. The Mâcon wines are made largely from Chardonnay. Of particular distinction are the ten *crus* of Beaujolais, which offer greater complexity and concentration. The most prominent are Moulin-à-Vent, Fleurie, and Morgon. Many wine lovers find the debut of Beaujolais Nouveau, a grapey wine that is released the third Thursday of each November, a reason for special celebration.

The Rhône

Though they are often lumped together, the northern and southern regions of the Rhône are best viewed separately. Northern Rhône has a continental climate, with moderate summers. The southern Rhône is primarily Mediterranean, with much hotter summers. The wines of the north are firmly structured and tannic. The warmth of the south produces wines that are higher in alcohol, with a riper, softer edge. Vintages differ as well. For example, 1991 was mediocre at best in the south, while in the north it was well above average.

The major appellations of the north are Côte Rôtie, Hermitage, Crozes-Hermitage, St.-Joseph and Cornas for the reds; Condrieu for the whites. Hermitage, Crozes-Hermitage and St.-Joseph also make whites, primarily from Marsanne; Condrieu uses Viognier. All northern reds rely on the Syrah grape.

Châteauneuf-du-Pape, located in the southern Rhône, is without doubt the most famous appellation of the entire Rhône. The south also produces 80 percent of the region's Côtes-du-Rhône. Though inexpensive, Côtes-du-Rhône can be very good, in styles ranging from grapey Beaujolais types to serious wines that could almost pass for Châteauneuf-du-Papes. In the south, the major grape varieties include Grenache, Mourvèdre, Cinsault, Syrah and Cournoise. In recent years, Grenache has been de-emphasized in favor of the more complex Mourvèdre and Syrah. White grapes are less important in the south than in the north. However, Roussanne and Marsanne produce small cuvées of superb whites in Châteauneuf-du-Pape.

The historic château of Pichon-Lalande, in the Pauillac region of Bordeaux.

Other French Regions

The Loire is known for its crisp white wines; the best known is probably Muscadet, which is made from the Muscadet grape, sometimes called the *melon de Bourgogne*. Muscadet is made to be drunk when it is young and vigorous, though a few examples, which are labeled *sur lie* (meaning aged on yeasty sediment) can improve with short-term aging. The Chenin Blanc grape also produces a number of distinctive Loire wines. The best known is Vouvray, which can range from bone dry to quite sweet, depending on the style chosen by the producer. However, the best dry whites of the Loire are Sancerre and Pouilly Fumé. Both are made from the Sauvignon Blanc grape, which produces an especially crisp, flinty style of wine quite unlike examples from Bordeaux and California.

Red Loire is a relative rarity, but a few interesting types are made. These include Chinon rouge, made from Cabernet Franc, and Sancerre rouge, made from Pinot Noir.

Alsace lies on the French-German border and utilizes the major German varietals, including Riesling, Gewürztraminer and Sylvaner. Unlike German wines, which tend to be off-dry or sweet, most Alsatian wines are dry. However, in especially ripe years, the region produces late harvest wines called *vendage tardive*, some of which can be sweet, and *sélections de grains nobles*, always sweet.

Champagne

Champagne is widely imitated around the world, but true Champagne can only come from the Champagne region of France. It must be made by the *méthode champenoise*, in which a secondary fermentation takes place in the bottle. Most Champagne is made from a blend of Pinot Noir, Pinot Meunier and Chardonnay; when only the latter is used, the Champagne is called a blanc de blancs. Most Champagne is a blend of different vintages, which helps ensure a consistently reliable product. In exceptional years, however, many houses produce a vintage-dated Champagne. While not necessarily better than non-vintage, vintage Champagne is usually more distinctive and commands a higher price. Most houses also produce a luxurious—and expensive—prestige cuvée (formerly called the *tète de cuvée)*. Dom Perignon is the best known, but it is rare to find a prestige cuvée that does not deliver the very best the house has to offer.

ABBAYE DE VALMAGNE

Coteaux du Languedoc 1991 • $10 • (03/15/94) • **87**
Coteaux du Languedoc 1989 • $10 • (10/31/92) • **72**
Coteaux du Languedoc 1988 • $12 • (08/31/91) • **80**
Coteaux du Languedoc White 1991 • $9 • (03/15/94) • **81**

ABEILLE DE FIEUZAL

Pessac-Léognan 1995: Silky berry, vanilla and spice aromas and flavors. Medium- to full-bodied, adding fine tannins and a medium finish. Second label of Château de Fieuzal. • $NA • (05/15/96) • **85-89** (BT)

ABELE, HENRI

Brut Champagne NV: Fruity, easy to drink and straightforward in style, showing apple and pear flavors and a hint of sweetness. A good but uncomplicated bottle of bubbly. 11,000 cases made. • $25 • (12/31/95) • **83**

Brut Champagne Grande Marque Impériale 1982: Classically yeasty and toasty, with creamy texture and rich flavors of vanilla, fig and grapefruit, complex and spicy, lovely, nicely crafted Champagne in a restrained, elegant style. • $29 • (07/31/87) • **90**

Brut Champagne Le Sourire de Reims 1986: Vibrant flavors and elegant texture, enjoyably mature but still fresh. Balanced toward the lean side, as crisp citrus notes and firm acidity are accented by subtle butter and vanilla. 2,275 cases made. • $85 • (11/30/95) • **89**

Brut Champagne Le Sourire de Reims NV • $24 • (07/31/87) • **79**

Brut Rosé Champagne Cuvée Reservé 1983: Crisp and fruity, with intensely focused apple and spice aromas and flavors that hint at nutmeg and almond on the finish. Drinkable now. • $50 • (03/31/92) • **88**

Brut Rosé Champagne Grande Marque Impériale 1982: Rich and creamy, with lots of almond and smoke notes to the basic pear and grapefruit flavors that linger through the finish, modifying themselves and becoming more complex on the aftertaste. A fine Champagne for drinking now. • $25 • (03/31/92) • **88**

Brut Rosé Champagne NV • $29 • (07/31/87) • **77**

ACACIAS, DOMAINE DES

Touraine Sauvignon 1992: For a simple wine, this offers a jumble of flavors—hints of butter and earth, celery and pear flavors, a bitter chalkiness on the finish. It lacks verve and snap. 500 cases made. • $10 • (10/31/94) • **76**

ACACIAS, LES

Brut Crémant de Bourgogne Cépage Chardonnay NV • $11 • (06/15/90) • **78**

ADAM, J.-B.

Alsace Kaefferkopf Cuvée Traditionnelle 1992: Pleasant earth and mineral aromas, and modest pear and orange flavors add up to a white wine with ample personality and good balance. • $16 • (11/15/94) • **84**

Brut Crémant d'Alsace Jean-Baptiste Adam NV: An aggressive mousse gives this a lively impression, revealing pear, citrus and herb notes on the palate. Clean and refreshing, with good depth of flavor. • $15 • (11/15/94) • **85**

Gewürztraminer Alsace Grand Cru Kaefferkopf Cuvée Jean-Baptist 1992: Polished, even restrained for this varietal, but makes a round impression on the palate. The flavors shift from spices to rose petals to almonds, it's clean and long. • $18 • (11/15/94) • **87**

Gewürztraminer Alsace Réserve 1993: Nicely perfumed, fruity and lively, this white is elegant, dry and refreshing. Drinkable now. • $12 • (09/15/95) • **83**

Key: SS—Spectator Selection. CS—Cellar Selection. BB—Best Buy. $NA—Price not available. (BT)—Barrel tasting. Ⓐ—Auction Price.
Dates in parentheses represent the issues in which the ratings were published.

Gewürztraminer Alsace Réserve 1992: A rather stale, dull-tasting wine with apple cider flavors and a cheesy aftertaste. Drinkable, but not much fun. • $12 • (11/15/94) • **74**

Muscat Alsace Réserve 1993: Quite flavorful but unusual, offering fragrant, floral aromas and bright notes of mint and peach that turn slightly nutty on the finish. Very fresh and tangy. • $10 • (09/15/95) • **84**

Pinot Blanc Alsace Réserve 1993: Dry and earthy, but intriguing. The funky aroma is somewhat difficult, but apricot and peach flavors emerge in the palate and linger on aftertaste, blending mineral accents. • $9 • (07/31/95) • **84**

Pinot Blanc Alsace Réserve 1992: Light, delicate flavors and smooth, solid texture make this floral-scented Pinot Blanc a real charmer. Thin layers of peach, apple, cream and spice lead to a lingering, soft finish. • $9 • (11/15/94) • **86**

Riesling Alsace Grand Cru Kaefferkopf Cuvée Jean-Baptist 1992: Clean and silky-textured, leaning toward the herbal, citrus end of the spectrum. It's austere but balanced, with enough concentration to match well with food. • $18 • (11/15/94) • **86**

Riesling Alsace Letzenberg Cuvée Jean-Baptiste 1992: Fresh, vibrant and refreshing, this offers expressive aromas and flavors of pine, petrol, peach and apple, all in harmony. Only medium-bodied, it still makes an impact, lively and clean. A great accompaniment for grilled white-fleshed fish. • $14 • (09/15/94) • **88**

Riesling Alsace Réserve 1993: Opulent for a Riesling and at an incredible price for its quality. This round wine offers ripe, almost earthy aromas and flavors of ripe peaches and apricots wrapped around a firm core of mineral character. Drinkable now and should improve with age. 4,000 cases made. • $9 • (09/15/95) BB • **88**

Riesling Alsace Réserve 1992: Round, friendly and just a bit dull, this wine offers orange, peach and melon flavors that are generous and simple. • $11 • (11/15/94) • **81**

Sylvaner Alsace Réserve 1993: This has a distinctive personality, fresh fruit and mineral nuances that make it complex. Has great balance and plenty of flavor interest. • $9 • (09/15/95) • **86**

Tokay Pinot Gris Alsace Cuvée Jean-Baptiste 1992: Noticeable sweetness softens this wine to the point of flabbiness, and the apple tart and vanilla flavors aren't lively enough to perk it up. It's round and simple. • $15 • (11/15/94) • **78**

Tokay Pinot Gris Alsace Cuvée Jean-Baptiste 1991 • $15 • (11/15/94) • **83**

Tokay Pinot Gris Alsace Réserve 1993: Good quality table wine featuring modest herb and mineral flavors. Well made, smooth but simple. • $12 • (09/15/95) • **81**

Tokay Pinot Gris Alsace Réserve 1992: A hint of late-harvest richness sweetens the pear and almond flavors in this soft, ripe white. Full-bodied and easy to drink, with menthol and spice notes on the finish. • $12 • (11/15/94) • **83**

AGASSAC, CHÂTEAU D'

Haut-Médoc 1989 • $20 • (03/15/92) • **88**

AIGLON, MAISON L'

Grand Réserve St.-Chinian 1990 • $6 • (07/15/92) BB • **83**

Vin de Pays d'Oc Grand Réserve 1992: Concentrated flavors of apple and pear are matched by a pleasant butteriness in this flavorful white. The underlaying acidity doesn't quite mesh in the end, though. 15,000 cases made. • $6 • (09/30/94) • **82**

AIGUELIERE, DOMAINE L'

Montpeyroux Côte Dorée Coteaux du Languedoc 1991 • $NA • (03/15/94) • **89**
Montpeyroux Côte Rousse Coteaux du Languedoc 1991 • $NA • (03/15/94) • **87**
Montpeyroux Coteaux du Languedoc 1991 • $12 • (03/15/94) • **86**
Montpeyroux Coteaux du Languedoc 1989 • $11 • (04/15/93) • **77**

AIGUEVILLE, CHÂTEAU D'

Côtes du Rhône 1987 • $5 • (01/31/89) • **73**
Côtes du Rhône 1984 • $4 • (10/15/87) • **68**

AIGUILLOUX, CHÂTEAU

Corbières 1991 • $7 • (03/15/94) • **83**

ALBRECHT, DOMAINE LUCIEN

Pinot Blanc Alsace 1993: Broad and soft, this lacks definition and depth, the apple and toast flavors are a bit dull and earthy. • $10 • (11/15/94) • **78**

ALESME-BECKER, CHÂTEAU MARQUIS-D'

Margaux 1985 • $19 • (06/30/88) • **84**
Margaux 1984 • $16 • (06/15/87) • **69**
Margaux 1983 • $15 • (12/31/86) • **84**

ALIGNE

Côtes du Rhône 1985 • $6 • (02/28/87) • **74**
Moulin-à-Vent 1985 • $12 • (03/15/87) • **55**

ALLEMAND, THIERRY

Cornas 1991 • $NA • (05/31/94) • **84**
Cornas Chaillot 1991 • $27 • (05/31/94) • **86**

ALOUETTES, CHÂTEAU LES

Bordeaux Kosher 1986 • $10 • (03/31/90) • **70**

ALQUIER, GILBERT

Faugères 1991 • $9 • (03/15/94) • **87**
Faugères 1990 • $9 • (03/15/94) • **84**
Faugères 1985 • $7 • (09/30/87) • **78**

ALQUIER, J.M. & F.

Les Bastides Réserve Faugères 1991 • $15 • (03/15/94) • **87**

AMBROISE, BERTRAND

Chardonnay St.-Romain 1993: Rather ripe, beautiful pear and sweet melon tones. Harmonious, clean mineral flavors and a round, sound finish. Drink now. • $17 • (05/15/95) • **85**
Clos Vougeot 1993: An awesome blockbuster, boasting layers of ripe fruit, mineral and spice character. Full in body and mega-tannic, but if you are patient this will bring huge returns of pleasure. Try in 2004. • $90 • (11/15/95) • **96**
Corton Le Rognet 1993: Monumental. Just as we remember a barrel sample earlier this year. Amazing red boasting masses of plum, currant and wood-scented dark chocolate and vanilla character. Full in body, adding loads of fine tannins and a long, elegant finish. Try in 2006. 80 cases made. • $75 • (11/15/95) • **97**
Corton Le Rognet 1992: Brilliant deep color and concentrated berry notes pick up some nice cedar and spice overtones, finishing with gravelly tannins that need time to soften. Flavors come through nicely. Try in 1997 or '98. 80 cases made. • $55 • (12/15/94) • **89**
Corton Le Rognet 1991: Firm, austere and light, but has bright raspberry and red currant flavors. Focused and lively on the finish, albeit a bit stemmy. Drinkable now. 225 cases made. • $49 Ⓐ • (01/31/94) • **85**
Corton Le Rognet 1990: Combining the beauty with the beast, this supercharged red is big yet delicate, with great, ripe berry characteristics and a lot of well-integrated wood notes. Try in 1998. • $60 • (12/15/92) • **94**
Corton Le Rognet 1989 • $45 • (01/31/92) • **93**
Corton Le Rognet 1988 • $43 • (11/30/90) • **92**
Corton Le Rognet 1987 • $38 • (03/31/90) • **90**
Corton-Charlemagne 1993: Rich and fat, showing pear, pineapple and toasted coconut flavors. Somewhat heavy-handed on the finish. Drinkable now. From a producer known for his great reds. • $60 • (05/15/95) • **87**
Côte de Nuits-Villages 1992: Lean and smooth, with a gamy component to the black cherry flavor. Finishes solid, drinkable now. • $19 • (12/15/94) • **79**
Côte de Nuits-Villages 1987 • $15 • (02/28/90) • **82**
Nuits-St.-Georges 1993: Very well crafted, featuring a nice use of new wood, medium body, soft tannins and medium toasted oak and berry finish. Better in 1999. • $40 • (11/15/95) • **86**
Nuits-St.-Georges 1992: Chunky, chewy tannins make it hard to find the flavors in this sturdy wine. Maybe better after 1997. • $NA • (12/15/94) • **77**
Nuits-St.-Georges 1991: Modest currant and tobacco aromas and flavors are light, simple and directly appealing. Polished and already drinkable. 375 cases made. • $28 Ⓐ • (01/31/94) • **83**
Nuits-St.-Georges 1990: Bright and lively, with an abundance of cherry, berry and earth aromas and flavors and chewy tannins. Drinkable now. • $38 • (12/15/92) • **89**
Nuits-St.-Georges 1989 • $30 • (01/31/92) • **90**
Nuits-St.-Georges En Rue de Chaux 1992: Perfumed and rather deep for a '92. Chewy and flavorful, delivering a ripe texture, with plum, currant and tobacco notes. Drinkable now. • $38 • (12/15/94) • **85**
Nuits-St.-Georges En Rue de Chaux 1991: Vibrant currant and wild berry aromas and flavors shade toward toast on the finish of this firm, juicy, charming wine. Drinkable now. 125 cases made. • $36 Ⓐ • (01/31/94) • **86**
Nuits-St.-Georges En Rue de Chaux 1990: Very rich, but shows restraint. Offers loads of black cherry and earth characteristics along with masses of silky tannins. Drink in 1997. • $48 • (12/15/92) • **90**
Nuits-St.-Georges En Rue de Chaux 1989 • $38 • (01/31/92) • **91**
Nuits-St.-Georges En Rue de Chaux 1988 • $40 • (05/15/91) • **93**
Nuits-St.-Georges Les Vaucrains 1993: Extremely smooth, offering lovely, velvety tannins and a solid core of fruit. Full in body, firm tannins and long, flavorful finish. Try after 2000. • $65 • (11/15/95) • **90**
Nuits-St.-Georges Les Vaucrains 1992: Deep and rich but extremely tannic. Oaky and concentrated with currant flavors. Too much green tannin for us, however. • $44 • (12/15/94) • **78**
Nuits-St.-Georges Les Vaucrains 1991: Attractive wild berry and wildflower aromas carry on in the flavors, showing a thin thread running through the firm tannins and echoing on the finish. Drinkable now. 50 cases made. • $39 Ⓐ • (01/31/94) • **85**
Nuits-St.-Georges Les Vaucrains 1990: Decadent, with rich earth, truffle and fruit aromas and flavors and lots of firm tannins, yet has a fine mouth-feel. Drinkable now to 1998. • $44 Ⓐ • (12/15/92) • **90**
Nuits-St.-Georges Les Vaucrains 1989 • $38 • (01/31/92) • **94**
Vosne-Romanée Aux Damaudes 1993: Elegant red, showing wood, plum, fruit and tannins in just the right proportions. Medium- to light-body, fine tannins and fresh finish. Drink in 1999. • $45 • (11/15/95) • **88**

AMEILLAUD, DOMAINE DE L'

Côtes du Rhône 1984 • $4 • (06/01/86) • **72**

AMIOT, DOMAINE PIERRE

Clos de la Roche 1988 • $75 • (03/15/91) • **86**
Clos de la Roche 1987 • $49 • (12/15/89) • **86**
Clos de la Roche 1982 • $28 • (06/16/85) SS • **93**
Gevrey-Chambertin Les Combottes 1988 • $64 • (03/15/91) • **89**
Gevrey-Chambertin Les Combottes 1987 • $42 • (12/15/89) • **88**
Morey-St.-Denis Aux Charmes 1982 • $18 • (07/01/85) • **88**
Morey-St.-Denis Les Ruchots 1988 • $57 • (02/28/91) • **80**

AMIOT, GUY

Chassagne-Montrachet 1993: An early-drinking '93, featuring apple, cream and chalk character, medium body and delicious vanilla, apple finish. • $NA • (05/15/95) • **85**
Chassagne-Montrachet Caillerets 1994: Lovely, medium-bodied '94, featuring enough spice, mineral and ripe fruit flavors to keep anybody happy. Modest intensity. • $50 • (05/31/96) • **85**
Chassagne-Montrachet Les Champs Gain 1994: Very intense and vibrant, as distinctive dried herb notes mingle with fresh lemon and

honey character. Medium body, long finish. Needs time, try in 1999. • $44 • (05/31/96) 90 • **89**

Chassagne-Montrachet Les Champs Gain 1993: Toasted oak and green apple flavors, medium in body, firm acidity and light, toasty finish. • $43 • (05/15/95) • **84**

Chassagne-Montrachet Clos St.-Jean 1994: Crisp and refeshing, but showing some body and character, ripe pear and honey and a slight vegetal note. Good concentration on the lively finish. Drinkable now. • $44 • (05/31/96) 86 • **87**

Chassagne-Montrachet Clos St.-Jean 1993: Chewy and chalky, quite smooth for a '93, showing lime, pear and green apple flavor. Try now. • $43 • (05/15/95) • **83**

Chassagne-Montrachet Les Macherelles 1994: Some concentrated ripe pear and apple flavors, inserting a basil, oregano touch for added complexity. Medium- to full-bodied, this *premier cru* tastes crisp and fresh. Drinkable now through 1998. • $39 • (05/31/96) • **86**

Chassagne-Montrachet Les Vergers 1994: Flavorful and seductive, offering pretty lemon, honey and herbal notes, medium body and a chewy, chalky texture. Lovely, pure and clean. Try in 1998. • $44 • (05/31/96) • **87**

Puligny-Montrachet Les Demoiselles 1994: Lovely, creamy texture, with some butter and herbal notes marrying nicely in this harmonious, full-bodied '94. Fresh dried herbs, toasted oak add complexity. Try in 1999. • $60 • (05/31/96) • **84**

FRANCE

AMIOT-BONFILS

Chassagne-Montrachet 1992: Toasty, smoky aromas combine with honey and pear on the palate to make a very flavorful white. Drinkable now. • $NA • (08/31/94) • **85**

Chassagne-Montrachet Les Caillerets 1991 • $36 • (10/15/93) • **87**

Chassagne-Montrachet Les Champgains 1991 • $36 • (10/15/93) • **85**

Chassagne-Montrachet Les Vergers 1992: A bit simple, with a nice balance of crisp lemon and apple flavors, with an earthy touch, and a rather smooth and round finish. 260 cases made. • $56 • (08/31/94) • **82**

Chassagne-Montrachet Les Vergers 1991 • $36 • (10/15/93) • **80**

Montrachet 1991 • $180 • (10/15/93) • **91**

Puligny-Montrachet Les Demoiselles 1992: A tightly-wound white Burgundy with ample pear and peach flavors that are held in check by firm acidity. Shows restraint now, but it should mellow out and become even more enjoyable after 1996. 100 cases made. • $65 • (08/31/94) • **91**

Puligny-Montrachet Les Demoiselles 1991 • $50 • (10/15/93) • **91**

AMOURIERS, DOMAINE DES

Vieilles Vignes Corbières 1991 • $8 • (03/15/94) • **82**

ANDRE, PIERRE

Aloxe-Corton 1993: Very light and papery. Not much there really. Short finish. 416 cases made. • $35 • (11/15/95) • **72**

Chassagne-Montrachet Chanvennes 1993: Light, diluted and watery, with weedy, strawlike, musty character. 1,000 cases made. • $25 • (11/15/95) • **73**

Châteauneuf-du-Pape 1990: Earthy, barnyardy overtones tend to obscure the fruit, but what's there is decent enough. Seems a little tired, but it's drinkable. • $21 • (04/15/93) • **77**

Châteauneuf-du-Pape 1988 • $23 • (03/31/91) • **84**

Châteauneuf-du-Pape White 1991 • $24 • (04/15/93) • **85**

Clos Vougeot 1993: Unusally dry tannins, adding a dry cherry component. Firm yet not fruity enough to hold up to the tannins. Tough finish. Buy if you must. • $70 • (11/15/95) • **77**

Corton-Charlemagne 1993: A bit dumb with earthy, overripe apple and candied character. Rather dull and metallic on the finish. 750 cases made. • $65 • (08/31/95) • **81**

Key: SS—Spectator Selection. CS—Cellar Selection. BB—Best Buy. $NA—Price not available. (BT)—Barrel tasting. Ⓐ—Auction Price.
Dates in parentheses represent the issues in which the ratings were published.

Corton-Charlemagne 1992: Simple and straightforward, showing stale fruit flavors that verge on cardboard notes. Modest apple and pear here. It's a shame to release such average Corton-Charlemagne. • $52 • (08/31/94) • **79**

Corton Clos du Roi 1985 • $45 • (07/15/88) • **88**

Corton Hautes Mourottes 1992: Very light, with a candied strawberry character dominating the modest flavors. Drinkable now. 233 cases made. • $36 • (12/15/94) • **74**

Corton Pougets 1993: A delicate red offering some pretty dried plum and berry character, light body and silky finish. Better in 1999. 500 cases made. • $48 • (11/15/95) • **84**

Corton Pougets 1985 • $45 • (07/15/88) • **90**

Gevrey-Chambertin Champlain 1993: Elegant, focused cherry and plum character, medium body, fine tannins and delicate finish. Better in 1999. 750 cases made. • $21 • (11/15/95) • **82**

Gevrey-Chambertin Champlain 1992: Bright and flavorful, a little chewy in tannins, but shows nice berry and currant flavors and a touch of mineral. Drinkable now. 750 cases made. • $21 • (12/15/94) • **82**

Ladoix Clos des Chagnots 1993: Delicate style, rather light and nicely supple, offering a minty, plummy character but not much structure. Drinkable now. 1,000 cases made. • $20 • (11/15/95) • **79**

Ladoix Le Rognet White 1992: A white with personality, chewy, with lively spice, herb and apple flavors that offer balance and a satisfying drinking experience. 333 cases made. • $17 • (08/31/94) • **83**

Mâcon-Villages Mâcon André 1994: Sour and odd: cardboard flavors taste flat and dull. Not recommended. Tasted twice, with consistent notes. 7,000 cases made. • $9 • (08/31/95) • **67**

Meursault 1993: Lean and austere revealing mineral, lime and grapefruit character. Light-bodied, hard acidity. 667 cases made. • $26 • (05/15/95) • **79**

Meursault Les Charmes 1993: A bit dull: apple, cider and vanilla aromas and flavors, with a short finish. 200 cases made. • $40 • (08/31/95) • **76**

Nuits-St.-Georges 1993: Straightforward and very light, tasting more like water than wine, adding a hint of strawberry and cherry notes. Dry, short finish. • $30 • (11/15/95) • **76**

Pommard Premier Cru 1993: Silky, pretty berry and chocolate character, medium body, light tannins and fresh fnish. Drinkable now. 750 cases made. • $38 • (11/15/95) • **80**

Pouilly-Fuissé Domaine des Vieilles Pierres 1993: Wet straw, herbal, tart flavors are a bit one-dimensional—clean and straightforward. Drink now. • $17 • (05/15/95) • **77**

Puligny-Montrachet 1993: Green, citrusy, herbal flavors dominate at first, finishing with slightly astringent honey and earth notes. Try now. 417 cases made. • $27 • (05/15/95) • **78**

Puligny-Montrachet Les Folatières 1993: Very steely mineral, floral and fruit character. Medium- to light-bodied, light finish. 500 cases made. • $37 • (05/15/95) • **79**

Puligny-Montrachet Les Folatières 1992: This tastes crisp. lively and fruity, with lime, grapefruit and apple flavors. Straightforward and solid. 1,000 cases made. • $28 • (08/31/94) • **85**

St.-Aubin Les Anges 1993: Attractive lemon, lime, cream and mineral aromas, but very light-bodied with a crisp, almost neutral finish. 500 cases made. • $20 • (05/15/95) • **79**

St.-Véran 1994: Some decent pear and lemon flavors, but also showing odd cardboard notes. Drying, slightly burning, finish. 5,000 cases made. • $9 • (08/31/95) • **73**

Santenay 1993: A straightforward Burgundy, somewhat disappointing for its lack of fresh fruit. Offers only modest flavors. Drinkable now. • $NA • (11/15/95) • **79**

Santenay Domaine du Prieuré Sainte Agathe 1993: A straightforward Burgundy, somewhat disappointing for its lack of fresh fruit. Offers only modest flavors. Drinkable now. 583 cases made. • $18 • (11/15/95) • **79**

Savigny-lès-Beaune Clos des Guettes 1993: A round and soft red offering plummy, tobacco character, medium body and tannins and smooth, succulent texture. Drinkable now, better in 1997. 1,000 cases made. • $25 • (11/15/95) • **82**

Savigny-lès-Beaune Clos des Guettes 1985 • $20 • (07/31/88) • **85**

Savigny-lès-Beaune Le Champier 1993: Soft, round lemony, creamy, earthy flavors, with a somewhat odd, papery note. Slight dilution. Drinkable now. 750 cases made. • $21 • (05/15/95) • **74**

ANDRON-BLANQUET, CHÂTEAU

St.-Estèphe 1995: A good '95 with a pleasant berry and cherry character, but slightly short on the finish. • $NA • (05/15/96) • **80-84** (BT)

St.-Estèphe 1994: Some very pretty smoke and berry aromas, but very lean and hard on the palate with a dry finish. • $NA • (06/30/95) • **75-79** (BT)

St.-Estèphe 1993: Light- to medium-bodied, delivering red berry flavors but also a slight herbaceous note. Some dilution on the finish. Drinkable now. 9,000 cases made. • $18 • (01/31/96) • **79**

St.-Estèphe 1990: A no-nonsense wine, with berry, cassis and light spice aromas and flavors and silky tannins. Drinkable now. 6,500 cases made. • $18 • (03/31/93) • **88**

ANGELUS, CHÂTEAU L'

St.-Emilion 1995: Deep and dark, sporting lots of chocolate, berry and vanilla character, medium-to-full body, lots of flavors and a medium finish. Like biting into a bar of chocolate. Almost classic in quality. • $NA • (05/15/96) • **90-94** (BT)

St.-Emilion 1994: Impressive '94. Surprisingly thick, rich, ripe and full-bodied for this vintage. Perfumey and exotic, packs in lots of toasted oak notes and violet-scented red-berry and blackberry flavors. Long, beautiful finish. • $60 • (05/15/96) • **90-94** (BT)

St.-Emilion 1993: As outstanding as we remember from barrel. Ripe and seductive, a full-bodied St.-Emilion that stands out for this vintage. Oozes with plum, red berry, chocolate, tobacco and smoke flavors. Beautiful texture, elegant tannins and an impressive finish. Try after 1998. 9,583 cases made. • $50 • (01/31/96) • **90**

St.-Emilion 1992: Extraordinarily good, one of the stars of this weakling vintage. Black cherry and berry flavors, full-bodied, velvety and fresh. Long, long finish. Drinkable now. • $34 • (04/15/95) • **89**

St.-Emilion 1991: Well-crafted with smoky, berry, earthy aromas and flavors. Medium-bodied, tannic and lean finish. Drinkable now. • $32 • (03/31/94) • **80**

St.-Emilion 1990: Giant wine with loads of toasted oak, meat, plum, black coffee character, tons of velvety tannins and a long, tannic finish. Needs time to mellow, drink after 1998. 12,000 cases made. • $67 Ⓐ • (03/31/93) • **93**

St.-Emilion 1989 • $67 Ⓐ • (03/15/92) • **94**

St.-Emilion 1988 • $43 Ⓐ • (03/31/91) • **93**

St.-Emilion 1987 • $27 • (05/15/90) • **85**

St.-Emilion 1986 • $27 • (06/30/89) • **94**

St.-Emilion 1985: Very concentrated, with plum and cassis character and a hint of nuts. It's full-bodied, with well-integrated tannins and loads of coffee and fruit on the finish. Drinkable now. • $35 • (10/15/94) • **89**

St.-Emilion 1983: Fully mature, a very pretty Bordeaux with tobacco, chocolate and berry character, medium-light body and a silky finish. Drink now. • $30 • (10/15/94) • **83**

St.-Emilion 1982 • $37 • (05/15/89) • **88**

St.-Emilion 1981: Well-made and straightforward. Mineral, tobacco and fruit aromas and flavors, medium body and delicate firm tannins with a silky texture. Drink now. • $22 • (10/15/94) • **84**

St.-Emilion 1979 • $30 • (10/15/89) • **82**

St.-Emilion 1962 • $45 • (11/30/87) • **68**

ANGERVILLE, MARQUIS D'

Volnay Caillerets 1992: Firm-textured, young and lively, needs time to develop. Has a rather lean profile but good depth of fruit and lingering, plummy, spicy finish. Drink now through 1998. • $30 • (05/15/95) • **87**

Volnay Champans Premier Cru 1953: Impressive and extremely youthful, brimming with fresh blackberry and black cherry flavors. A dark-colored wine that shows great harmony. • $NA • **92**

Volnay Clos des Ducs 1992: Well-balanced black cherry flavors are accented by smoky, leathery, spicy notes. Firm in tannins, brightened by acidity and long on the finish. Drink now through 1998. • $32 • (05/15/95) • **87**

Volnay Clos des Ducs 1988 • $47 • (10/31/93) • **88**

Volnay Clos des Ducs 1985 • $49 Ⓐ • (03/15/88) • **80**

Volnay En Champans 1993: Bright, fresh fruit flavors and assertive oak notes make this a big, showy Volnay. Has black cherry, clove and spice notes, all in balance, and the finish really lingers. • $29 • (05/15/96) • **90**

Volnay En Champans 1992: Firm in texture, fresh fruit flavor is supported by enough tannin and acidity to make it well balanced and appealing. Drinkable now. • $25 • (05/15/95) • **84**

Volnay Premier Cru 1993: Great fruit combines with intriguing, spicy accents for a full-flavored, complex, interesting Burgundy sporting lingering aftertaste. Elegant but concentrated, firmly tannic but not harsh. Tempting now, but best in 1999. • $20 • (05/15/96) • **92**

Volnay Taillepieds 1992: Quite concentrated for a light vintage, showing plenty of currant and black cherry flavors framed by firm tannins and lively acidity. Great balance and lingering finish. Drink through 1997. • $27 • (05/15/95) • **86**

ANGLUDET, CHÂTEAU D'

Margaux 1995: Delicious black cherry, berry and mineral character. Wonderfully silky tannins. Almost outstanding. • $NA • (05/15/96) • **85-89** (BT)

Margaux 1994: Delicate and fruity, with some decent red berry notes. Light to medium body, and it turns slightly austere on the finish. • $NA • (05/15/96) • **80-84** (BT)

Margaux 1993: Rather lean but some good black cherry and dried herb character. Medium-bodied with firm tannins and a light finish. • $30 • (01/31/96) • **80**

Margaux 1990: Vibrant and delicate, with refreshing fruit and lively tannins. Not a blockbuster, but it's fun to taste. Drinkable now. 12,500 cases made. • $22 • (03/31/93) • **86**

Margaux 1989 • $20 Ⓐ • (03/15/92) • **87**

Margaux 1988 • $20 • (02/28/91) • **85**

Margaux 1987 • $17 • (05/15/90) • **78**

Margaux 1986 • $29 • (11/30/89) • **90**

Margaux 1985 • $20 Ⓐ • (04/15/88) • **90**

Margaux 1983 • $26 Ⓐ • (10/15/86) • **93**

Margaux 1982 • $23 Ⓐ • (08/31/92) • **91**

Margaux 1961: This came on strong at first, with complex and intriguing aromas, but then it faded in the glass, turning lean and more simple. Its minerally, earthy character will appeal to many, however. Drink now. • $28 • (04/30/96) • **84**

ANSELME, PERE

Châteauneuf-du-Pape 1989 • $16 • (03/31/94) • **83**

Châteauneuf-du-Pape 1986 • $14 • (10/15/91) • **84**

Châteauneuf-du-Pape 1985 • $14 • (10/15/91) • **86**

Châteauneuf-du-Pape 1983 • $23 • (10/15/91) • **89**

Châteauneuf-du-Pape 1981 • $NA • (10/15/91) • **88**

Châteauneuf-du-Pape Clos-Bimard 1989 • $NA • (10/15/91) • **84**

Châteauneuf-du-Pape Cuvée Prestige Clos Bimard 1988 • $20 • (10/15/91) • **88**

Châteauneuf-du-Pape La Fiole 1990: Ripe and spicy, with strawberry and raspberry jamlike flavors that give it a light, fruity profile. The tannins don't really show until the finish, but they remind you that this is a young wine that can stand cellaring. Drinkable now. • $17 • (04/15/93) • **85**

Châteauneuf-du-Pape La Fiole 1984 • $12 • (10/31/87) • **88**

Châteauneuf-du-Pape La Fiole du Pape NV • $14 • (09/30/89) • **86**

Châteauneuf-du-Pape La Fiole du Pape Uno Bono Fiolo NV • $13 • (01/31/88) • **82**

Châteauneuf-du-Pape La Fiole Grand Cuvée 1984 • $13 • (10/31/87) • **74**

Côte-Rôtie Tête de Cuvée 1982 • $13 • (10/15/87) • **68**

Côtes du Rhône-Villages Marescal 1985 • $5 • (12/31/87) • **75**

Côtes du Rhône-Villages Seguret 1990 • $9 • (04/15/93) • **83**

Côtes du Rhône-Villages Seguret 1986 • $5 • (05/15/89) • **72**

Côtes du Ventoux 1991 • $7 • (06/15/93) BB • **84**

Crozes-Hermitage 1986 • $7 • (07/31/89) • **80**

Crozes-Hermitage 1983 • $7 • (10/15/87) BB • **84**

Gigondas 1989 • $14 • (04/15/93) • **78**

Merlot Vin de Pays des Coteaux d'Enserune NV • $5 • (07/15/89) • **78**

ANTOINE, PHILIPPE

Beaujolais-Villages 1988 • $5 • (05/31/89) • **77**
Beaujolais-Villages 1986 • $6 • (03/15/88) • **75**
Brouilly 1988 • $12 • (05/31/89) • **82**
Fleurie 1988 • $12 • (05/31/89) • **84**
Juliénas 1988 • $12 • (05/31/89) • **85**
Moulin-à-Vent 1988 • $12 • (05/31/89) • **88**
Régnié 1988 • $12 • (05/31/89) • **81**

AQUERIA, CHÂTEAU D'

Tavel Rosé 1993: This dry wine has some stuffing with good herb and dry-cherry flavors. A tangy finish gives it a nice snap. Pleasant, flavorful and fairly rich. • $12 • **84**

ARCAUTE, J.M.

Merlot Bordeaux 1993: 10,000 cases made. • $8 • **65**

ARCHAMBAULT, PIERRE

Sancerre Cave du Clos La Perrière 1993: Heavy, dull, clumsy, showing agressive herbal flavors and a light musty, earthy note. Food might help. Tasted twice, with consistent notes. • $14 • (12/15/95) • **75**
Sancerre Cave du Clos La Perrière 1992: Attractive citrus and grassy flavors and clean acidity draw you into this harmonious wine, but a lack of concentration leaves the wine faint and rather austere. Tasted twice. • $14 • (10/31/94) • **81**

ARCHE, CHÂTEAU D'

Sauternes 1990: Thick, lush and extremely impressive honey, lemon, vanilla and cream flavors. So sweet, it is a dessert in itself. Drinkable now or hold past 2000. • $31 • (04/15/95) • **93**
Sauternes 1989: Racy, sweet and tart, showing a lot of botrytis character and bitter orange marmalade, spice, dried apricot and honey flavors. Medium in body, a long, elegant finish. Drinkable now, but better after 1998. • $26 • (04/15/95) • **91**
Sauternes 1988: Exotic style, loads of new wood and spicy clove, vanilla and butter flavors. The medium body and sweetness end in a zingy finish. Better in 1998. • $25 • (04/15/95) • **88**
Sauternes 1987 • $32 • (06/15/90) • **85**
Sauternes 1986 • $23 • **93**
Sauternes 1983 • $29 • (01/31/88) • **93**

ARDECHOIS, VIGNERONS

Vin de Pays des Coteaux de l'Ardeche 1988 • $4 • (04/30/90) BB • **79**

ARLAUD

Bonnes Mares 1983 • $30 • (12/01/85) • **91**

ARLOT, DOMAINE DE L'

Clos du Châpeau 1989 • $24 • (01/31/92) • **83**
Côte de Nuits-Villages Clos du Châpeau 1988 • $21 • (03/31/91) • **80**
Nuits-St.-Georges 1993: Combines great, pure fruit flavors with spicy, oaky accents in a firm-textured, firmly tannic, nicely balanced package. Focused and enjoyable. Best in 1999. • $22 • (05/15/96) • **88**
Nuits-St.-Georges 1990: An interesting wine, with black truffle and berry flavors and silky tannins. Could use a little more concentration of fruit, seems somewhat alcoholic. Drinkable now. 250 cases made. • $33 • (12/15/92) • **79**

Key: SS—Spectator Selection. CS—Cellar Selection. BB—Best Buy. $NA—Price not available. (BT)—Barrel tasting. Ⓐ—Auction Price.
Dates in parentheses represent the issues in which the ratings were published.

Nuits-St.-Georges Clos de L'Arlot 1993: Leathery, smoky aromas and oaky, spicy, stemmy flavors. Not much fruit showing now. It's concentrated and quite tannic but still smooth, and has a long finish. Try after 2000. • $34 • (05/15/96) • **89**
Nuits-St.-Georges Clos de L'Arlot 1990: Very raisiny in flavor, but rather light in body. Offers decent fruit flavors, but seems rather light on the finish. Drinkable now. 800 cases made. • $45 • (12/15/92) • **78**
Nuits-St.-Georges Clos de L'Arlot 1989 • $48 • (01/31/92) • **78**
Nuits-St.-Georges Clos de L'Arlot 1988 • $43 • (03/31/91) • **87**
Nuits-St.-Georges Clos des Forêts St.-Georges 1993: Balanced like a tightrope walker. Really fruity and focused, bright and juicy in flavor, offering ripe cherry and strawberry notes accented by spice and smoke. Firmly tannic, but broad and chewy rather than tough in texture. Lively and long on the finish. Tempting now, but best in 1998. • $40 • (05/15/96) • **92**
Nuits-St.-Georges Clos des Forêts St.-Georges 1990: Traditional in style, with spicy, woody chocolate and fruit flavors, medium tannins and a long finish. Drinkable now. 1,400 cases made. • $49 • (12/15/92) • **87**
Nuits-St.-Georges Clos des Forêts St.-Georges 1989 • $55 • (01/31/92) • **90**
Nuits-St.-Georges Clos des Forêts St.-Georges 1988 • $53 • (03/31/91) • **85**
Nuits-St.-Georges Clos des Forêts St.-Georges 1987 • $43 • (03/31/90) • **83**

ARMAILHAC, CHÂTEAU D'

Pauillac 1995: Ripe and sweet, with lovely, succulent fruit. Moderate tannins on the finish, with the ripe, delicious fruit lasting straight through. • $NA • (05/15/96) • **85-89** (BT)
Pauillac 1994: Lovely and lush, with tobacco and berry aromas and flavors. The round tannins and rich, fruity finish make a nice tasting experience. Very good indeed. Almost outstanding. • $18 • (05/15/96) • **85-89** (BT)
Pauillac 1993: Beautifully balanced, boasting lovely currant, mineral and black cherry flavors, medium-to-full body, good complexity and well-integrated tannins. Should improve with age, try in 1999. • $25 • (01/31/96) • **89**
Pauillac 1992: Slightly one-dimensional, showing raspberry character and firm tannins, racy texture but somewhat aggressive. Drinkable now. • $20 • **80**
Pauillac 1991: An alluring smoky, nutty, fruity quality in this wine that has a soft, round mouthfeel. • $20 • (03/31/94) • **85**
Pauillac 1990: A pretty wine, with delicacy and good concentration of ripe fruit. There's plenty of tobacco, blackberry and brown sugar character and firm tannins. Drink after 1997. 18,000 cases made. • $22 • (03/31/93) • **89**
Pauillac 1989 • $22 Ⓐ • (03/15/92) • **94**
Pauillac 1985: Closed and tight with lots of grapey, berry, ripe fruit character. Full-bodied and alcoholic with full tannins. Try after 1997. • $24 • (10/15/94) • **91**

ARMAND, COMTE

Pommard Clos des Epeneaux 1993: Excellent concentration, but this dark-colored *premier cru* also tastes very woody at this stage, showing cedar, cigar box, chestnut and spice flavors and some fine cassis and cherry notes. A drying finish keeps it from scoring higher. Better in 2000? • $52 • **85**
Pommard Clos des Epeneaux 1990: Big and massive, packed to the brim with fruit and tannins. Shows elegance that bodes well for cellaring, drinkable now. 1,500 cases made. • $57 • (12/15/92) • **93**
Pommard Clos des Epeneaux 1989 • $50 • (11/30/92) • **82**
Pommard Clos des Epeneaux 1988 • $46 • (02/28/91) • **90**
Pommard Clos des Epeneaux 1987 • $41 • (08/31/90) • **81**
Pommard Clos des Epeneaux 1985 • $44 • (03/15/88) • **91**

ARNAULD, CHÂTEAU

Haut-Médoc 1995: A bit simple, but with some very good fruity notes and berry and cherry aromas and flavors. Medium-to-light body, with good tannins. • $NA • (05/15/96) • **80-84** (BT)
Haut-Médoc 1994: Fresh and fruity, offering elegant tannins, medium-to-light body and crisp finish. A bit simple. • $NA • **80-84** (BT)

Haut-Médoc 1993: A bit light and simple, but it offers some pretty currant and cherry flavors. Drinkable now. • $17 • (01/31/96) • **81**

Haut-Médoc 1992: Herb and cassis aromas and flavors accompany medium body, medium tannins and an herbal finish. • $11 • (04/15/95) • **78**

Haut-Médoc 1991: Pleasant plum, vanilla character with round texture and a light finish. • $11 • (03/31/94) • **77**

Haut-Médoc 1990: This offers an impressively chunky texture and well-focused herbal, tomato flavors. Drinkable now. 9,000 cases made. • $19 • (03/31/93) • **86**

Haut-Médoc 1989 • $14 • (03/15/92) • **88**

Haut-Médoc 1988 • $15 • (04/30/91) • **84**

Haut-Médoc 1987 • $13 • (11/30/89) • **79**

Haut-Médoc 1986 • $18 • (11/30/89) • **82**

Haut-Médoc 1985 • $15 • (02/15/88) • **82**

Haut-Médoc 1983 • $9 • (01/01/86) • **75**

Haut-Médoc 1982 • $17 • (11/30/89) • **71**

ARNOUX, ROBERT

Bourgogne Pinot Noir 1993: A core of blackberry, currant and earth. Has a sweet-tasting but somewhat hot and astringent finish. Drinkable now. • $18 • (11/15/95) • **79**

Clos de Vougeot 1993: Racy red sporting sleek tannins and loads of smoky, berry, raspberry character. Medium-bodied, finely tannic, a super fruity finish. Better in 2000. • $80 • (11/15/95) • **91**

Clos de Vougeot 1991: Ripe and chewy, leaning toward anise and spice in the otherwise sweet raspberry fruit, a stemmy note on the finish. Drinkable now, best from 1997. • $60 • (08/31/94) • **86**

Clos Vougeot 1988 • $70 • (03/15/91) • **78**

Echézeaux 1993: Beautiful plum and floral character, medium body, soft tannins and sweet fruit finish. Not a heavyweight but a joy to taste. • $80 • (11/15/95) • **89**

Echézeaux 1991: An appealing, lighter style displaying ample cherry and plum flavors, firm tannins, smooth texture and lingering finish. Drinkable now. • $72 • (05/31/95) • **87**

Echézeaux Grand Cru 1991: An appealing, lighter style Burgundy with ample cherry and plum flavors, firm tannins, smooth texture and lingering finish. Try now. • $72 • (05/31/95) • **87**

Nuits-St.-Georges 1991: Generous, fruity and easy to like, with good balance and firm tannins. Drinkable now, should improve through 1997. • $30 • (05/31/95) • **86**

Nuits-St.-Georges Les Corvées Pagets 1993: Delicate mocha, vanilla and berry character, medium body, soft tannins and a fresh finish. Better in 1999. • $55 • (11/15/95) • **81**

Nuits-St.-Georges Les Corvées Pagets 1991: Aromas of cinnamon and vanilla indicate lots of oak influence in this attractive, fruity but slightly tough red Burgundy. Drink now through 1997, when it should be softer. • $55 • (05/31/95) • **88**

Nuits-St.-Georges Les Poisets 1993: Rather meager but attractive spicy, fruity flavors, light-to-medium body, light tannins and fresh finish. Drink now. • $50 • (11/15/95) • **81**

Nuits-St.-Georges Les Poisets 1991: Generous in fruity, gamy flavors and balanced well by crisp acidity and firm tannins. A complete, enjoyable package that is developing an alluring, spicy aroma. Drink now. • $55 • (05/31/95) • **87**

Pinot Noir Bourgogne 1993: A solid little Burgundy showing fresh fruit flavors, velvety texture, firm tannins and good balance. Should improve through 1998. 900 cases made. • $18 • (05/15/96) • **85**

Romanée-St.-Vivant 1993: Seductively velvety, this soft-style, full-bodied red unfolds its charm in a cascade of rose petal, plum, mocha and spice flavors. It shows its pedigree in the seamless body and finish. Tempting now, but try to hold off until 1999. • $NA • (11/15/95) • **93**

Romanée-St.-Vivant 1991: There is dazzling flavor intensity in this seductively rich and fruity Burgundy. It has ample cherry and berry aromas, ripe black cherry flavors accented by oak, firm, fine tannins, lively acidity and a long, long finish. Tempting to drink now, but will improve through about 1999. • $210 • (05/31/95) • **92**

Romanée-St.-Vivant 1988 • $250 • (11/15/90) • **91**

Romanée-St.-Vivant Grand Cru 1991: There is dazzling flavor intensity in this seductively rich and fruity Burgundy. It has ample cherry and berry aromas, ripe black cherry flavors accented by oak and a long, long finish. Has firm, fine tannins and lively acidity. Drinkable now. • $210 • (05/31/95) • **92**

Vosne-Romanée 1992: Rather tough and tight now, but solid, chewy fruit flavors give it life and hints of vanilla add complexity. Try now. • $38 • (05/15/95) • **84**

Vosne-Romanée Les Chaumes 1993: Pretty plum, vanilla and cherry character, medium-to-light body, light tannins and soft finish. Better in 1999. • $55 • (11/15/95) • **88**

Vosne-Romanée Les Chaumes 1991: Firm-textured, young and tannic, needs time to develop, yet has enough fruit stuffing to age nicely. Tastes tight and closed, but should be ready to drink in 1997. • $50 • (05/31/95) • **89**

Vosne-Romanée Les Chaumes 1988 • $45 • (02/28/91) • **80**

Vosne-Romanée Les Hautes Maizières 1993: Nice and sweet, but quite light. Tastes of raspberries and strawberries, showing tannins that seem somewhat drying. Might be better in 1997. • $50 • (11/15/95) • **78**

Vosne-Romanée Les Hautes Mazières 1991: Elegant, well balanced and complete, exhibiting intrguing aromas of tea, spice and cherry, solid fruit flavors and a firm but smooth texture. Drink now through 1997. • $40 • (05/31/95) • **86**

Vosne-Romanée Les Suchots 1993: Some good ripe fruit character, but slightly diluted on the center palate. Medium in body and tannins and a short finish. Better in 1998. • $80 • (11/15/95) • **87**

Vosne-Romanée Les Suchots 1991: Nicely mature and complex, demonstrating the subtle bottle bouquet we look for in aged Burgundy, but with enough bright fruit and acidity to keep it balanced. Drink now through 1997. • $70 • (05/31/95) • **88**

Vosne-Romanée Les Suchots 1988 • $60 • (02/28/91) • **86**

Vosne-Romanée Les Suchots 1985 • $52 • (07/31/88) • **90**

ARROMANS, CHÂTEAU LES

Entre-Deux-Mers 1993: Fresh and clean, featuring grassy, dried-herb flavors and an austere, slightly short finish. • $8 • (05/31/95) • **79**

ARROSEE, CHÂTEAU L'

St.-Emilion 1989 • $40 Ⓐ • (04/30/92) • **93**

St.-Emilion 1988 • $21 Ⓐ • (03/15/91) • **94**

St.-Emilion 1987 • $28 • (05/15/90) • **82**

St.-Emilion 1986 • $36 • (02/15/89) • **87**

St.-Emilion 1985 • $46 Ⓐ • (02/29/88) • **85**

St.-Emilion 1983 • $25 Ⓐ • (05/16/86) • **87**

St.-Emilion 1982 • $46 Ⓐ • (05/15/89) • **91**

St.-Emilion 1970 • $50 • (05/15/93) • **90**

ARSAC, CHÂTEAU D'

Haut-Médoc 1989 • $9 • (03/15/92) • **82**

Haut-Médoc 1985 • $5 • (02/15/89) • **75**

ASPES, DOMAINE DES

Chardonnay Vin de Pays d'Oc 1992 • $NA • (03/15/94) • **82**

AUBEL

Brut Blanc de Blancs NV • $6 • (06/01/86) • **61**

AUBERT, DOMAINE MAX

Châteauneuf-du-Pape La Nonciature 1994: Straightforward and fruity, this was rushed to the market to be drunk young while it's still fresh. Soft tannins accompany the smooth texture. • $20 • (10/15/95) • **82**

Châteauneuf-du-Pape White La Nonciature 1994: A fresh, clean white sporting floral, nutty, fruity flavors and enough body to provide lingering aftertaste. Fine as a substitute for Chardonnay. • $22 • (10/15/95) • **85**

Côtes du Rhône Domaine de la Présidente 1994: A light, soft-textured red with cherry candy flavors and very little tannin. Simple and quaffable. • $10 • (11/15/95) • **79**

Côtes du Rhône Domaine de la Présidente Blanc de Blancs 1994: A substantial dry white Rhône offering subtle floral, figgy aromas and flavors, smooth, rich texture but only modest notes. • $10 • (09/30/95) • **82**

Côtes du Rhône-Villages Domaine de la Présidente Cairanne 1994: A crisp-feeling, light-bodied red with ample raspberry and currant flavors and lively acidity. Slightly tannic, but this tastes vibrant and fresh. • $12 • (11/15/95) • **83**

Côtes du Rhône-Villages Domaine de la Présidente Cairanne Goutillonnage 1994: Deep-colored, offering enough tannin to provide substance. Lots of rich fruit emerges and lingers on aftertaste. Drinkable now through 1997. 1,400 cases made. • $14 • (09/30/95) • **86**

AUBUISIERES, DOMAINE DES

Vouvray Le Bouchet Demi-Sec 1993: A pleasant, balanced blend of sweet and crisp, this offers honey, orange, spice and floral aromas and flavors, lively and clean. A great apéritif. • $14 • (12/15/95) • **87**

Vouvray Le Marigny Moelleux 1993: Open honey and spice aromas give way to a thick, sweet wine with intense vanilla and candied orange flavors. There's enough acidity for balance, and the wine lingers on the finish. Attractive now, it should improve with age. • $14 • (12/15/95) • **87**

Vouvray Le Marigny Sec 1993: Very austere for a Vouvray, this is light and very tart, finishing bone dry with a lemon-peel bitterness. There is some peachy fruit underneath. • $14 • (12/15/95) • **79**

AUGEY

Bordeaux 1993: Sturdy and simple, with rustic tannins, but enough berry and cherry show through to make it drinkable, especially with food. • $7 • (12/15/95) • **80**

Bordeaux 1991: Attractive cherry, spice and celery flavors. The tannins close in on the finish, but would soften with a meal. It's balanced, fresh and drinkable now. 25,000 cases made. • $6 • (11/15/94) • **79**

Bordeaux 1989 • $7 • (11/30/92) • **78**

Bordeaux White 1994: This has a nice, crisp balance and round texture and subtle flavors of fig, citrus and mineral that linger on the finish. • $7 • (02/29/96) • **84**

Bordeaux White 1992: Soft and easy to drink, with fresh fruit and herb flavors. Clean, if a bit lacking in concentration. Good value. 33,500 cases made. • $6 • (11/15/94) • **81**

AUJOUX, JEAN-MARC

Beaujolais-Villages RT Limited Edition 1993: Refreshing, light and crisp, with bright cherry flavor and a nip of tannin. It's simple but clean and quaffable. 2,000 cases made. • $7 • (06/30/94) • **79**

Beaujolais-Villages RT Limited Edition 1992: Soft, light-bodied and beginning to show maturity, offers typical cherry, spice and gamy flavors, but lacks depth and grip. 2,000 cases made. • $7 • (06/30/94) • **79**

Brouilly RT 1994: Pleasant spice and cinnamon notes add interest to this soft, fruity red. The cherry and berry flavors are ripe but simple, while gentle tannins supply structure. • $8 • (06/15/95) • **84**

Brouilly RT Limited Edition 1993: A will-o'-the-wisp. There's pleasant grapey freshness, then it almost evaporates on the palate, very light, with a refreshing tart streak. 300 cases made. • $8 • (06/30/94) • **80**

Brouilly RT Limited Edition 1992: The structure is good here—round and velvety, firm tannins, balanced acidity—but the strawberry flavors are simple, and the whole simply fades on the finish. 300 cases made. • $8 • (06/30/94) • **80**

Chiroubles RT 1994: Fleshy, pleasant cherry, smoke and light gamy flavors, but tart acidity makes it sharp. Better with food, such as sausage or pâté. • $9 • (07/31/95) • **79**

Chiroubles RT Limited Edition 1993: Fresh and vivacious, with bright berry and light smoky flavors, this is elegant and still has the exuberance of youth. Well-made and enticing. 300 cases made. • $9 • (06/30/94) • **84**

Chiroubles RT Limited Edition 1992: Light and elegant, vibrating with spicy, bright cherry and strawberry flavors, crisp acidity keeps it lively and fresh. An excellent example of the cru, and a great picnic wine, served lightly chilled. 300 cases made. • $9 • (06/30/94) • **87**

Fleurie RT 1994: There's good concentration here, offering fleshy fruit and muscular tannins, but the flavors are still closed, hinting at plum, spice and chocolate. Drinkable now. • $10 • (06/15/95) • **85**

Fleurie RT Limited Edition 1993: A voluptuous Beaujolais, stuffed with very ripe fruit, accented with spice, almost jammy, it's impressive but just misses elegance. Ambitious winemaking and attractive flavors, but a bit out of character for the region. 300 cases made. • $10 • (06/30/94) • **84**

Fleurie RT Limited Edition 1992: Right now it offers ripe plum and smoky flavors, firm tannins and a smoky finish, without much complexity. 300 cases made. • $10 • (06/30/94) • **82**

Juliénas RT 1994: Soft, modest strawberry and banana flavors and aromas and a slightly tannic finish. • $9 • (07/31/95) • **82**

Juliénas RT Limited Edition 1993: There's nice presence here, with silky texture and light but firm tannins, and the black cherry and plum flavors are pleasant. It could use more concentration, but it's balanced and quaffable now. 300 cases made. • $9 • (06/30/94) • **83**

Juliénas RT Limited Edition 1992: Pretty and light-bodied with appealing cherry and strawberry flavors, and enough stuffing to work with food, and it's still fresh and fruity. 300 cases made. • $9 • (06/30/94) • **84**

Mâcon-Villages 1994: Mineral and earth flavors give distinctive character, but it's lean and light, showing apple and lemon notes. 4,000 cases made. • $9 • (06/30/95) • **77**

Morgon RT 1994: Fresh and clean, sporting bright black cherry and light nutmeg flavors. The tannins are light, yet this is balanced and attractive now. • $8 • (07/31/95) • **83**

Morgon RT Limited Edition 1993: There's a tarry, licorice element that seems closer to the Rhône than most Beaujolais, the wine is rich, round and if it lacks vivacious fruit, makes up for it in concentration and structure. An intriguing wine, though a bit muted. 300 cases made. • $8 • (06/30/94) • **86**

Moulin-à-Vent RT 1994: Well-structured and balanced, this foursquare red isn't showing much fruit now. It's ripe and clean. • $10 • (07/31/95) • **83**

Moulin-à-Vent RT Limited Edition 1993: This rich wine combines ripe fruit, primarily black cherry and plum, with full tannins in a muscular structure that's characteristic of this cru at its best. It's concentrated and long in the finish and drinks well now. 300 cases made. • $10 • (06/30/94) • **86**

Moulin-à-Vent RT Limited Edition 1992: Drying out already. Earthy aromas give way to raisin flavors and a dry finish in this big but austere wine. Not much pleasure here. 300 cases made. • $10 • (06/30/94) • **76**

St.-Amour RT 1994: Simple tropical fruit and strawberry flavors and aromas. This is a light Beaujolais that needs to be served chilled. • $10 • (07/31/95) • **81**

St.-Amour RT Limited Edition 1993: A bruiser, muscular with ripe fruit, firm tannins and a heady spice note that lingers on the finish. Good depth, but it could use more definition. 300 cases made. • $10 • (06/30/94) • **82**

St.-Véran 1994: Crisp and pleasant, but seems a bit square and rough despite some nice pear, apple and wet earth flavors. Slightly diluted on the finish. 416 cases made. • $11 • (08/31/95) • **80**

AUPILHAC, DOMAINE D'

Vin de Pays du Mont Baudille Le Carignan 1992 • $8 • (03/15/94) • **88**
Vin de Pays du Mont Baudille White 1992 • $9 • (03/15/94) • **83**
Coteaux du Languedoc Montpeyroux 1992 • $9 • (03/15/94) • **87**

AUSONE, CHÂTEAU

St.-Emilion 1995: It's been decades since Ausone has made something like this. A spellbinding, full-bodied wine of great complexity—smoke, mineral, spice, fruit—it's got it all. • $NA • (05/15/96) • **95-100** (BT)

St.-Emilion 1994: One of the best of the '94s. An Ausone that delivers a wonderful combination of spices, fruit and wood in the aromas and flavors. Medium-to-full body and very well-integrated tannins. Super fine. • $100 • (05/15/96) • **90-94** (BT)

Key: SS—Spectator Selection. CS—Cellar Selection. BB—Best Buy. $NA—Price not available. (BT)—Barrel tasting. Ⓐ—Auction Price.
Dates in parentheses represent the issues in which the ratings were published.

FRANCE

St.-Emilion 1993: Features plenty of seductive toasted oak and sweet fruit character, medium body, delicate tannins and long vanilla, tobacco and plum finish. Delicious now, but better in 1997. • $90 • (01/31/96) • **88**
St.-Emilion 1990: An alluring wine with gorgeous plum, blackberry and toasted oak character, full silky tannins and a long rich finish. Still very tight, should be a long ager. Drink after 1998. 2,150 cases made. • $95 Ⓐ • (03/31/93) • **94**
St.-Emilion 1989 • $94 Ⓐ • (03/15/92) • **93**
St.-Emilion 1988: Beginning to evolve now, this mingles cherry and cranberry flavors with smoke, spice and leather notes. It has firm tannins and fresh acidity and finishes a bit rough and rustic. Drinkable now. 2,000 cases made. • $105 • (10/15/94) • **86**
St.-Emilion 1986: Firm and vivid, offering clear cherry, tobacco and cedar flavors backed by firm, round tannins, it blooms on the finish. Drink now or hold until 2000. 2,000 cases made. • $65 Ⓐ • (10/15/94) • **89**
St.-Emilion 1985: A deceptive wine still not giving much. Pure fruit aromas of raspberry and strawberry, full-bodied with fine tannins. Try after 1997. • $73 Ⓐ • (10/15/94) • **92**
St.-Emilion 1983: Big fruity wine with loads of raspberry, jam character. Full-bodied and tannic but round and medium in finish. Needs time. Only beginning to come out. Try after 1997. • $115 Ⓐ • (10/15/94) • **90**
St.-Emilion 1982 • $181 Ⓐ • (08/31/92) • **90**
St.-Emilion 1981: Solid, youthful wine with fresh character. Medium ruby color with berry, milk chocolate aromas. Medium body with firm tannins and lively fruit. Drink or hold. • $95 • (10/15/94) • **88**
St.-Emilion 1980 • $30 • (11/30/87) • **86**
St.-Emilion 1979 • $60 Ⓐ • (10/15/89) • **92**
St.-Emilion 1978 • $86 • (11/30/87) • **93**
St.-Emilion 1977 • $29 • (11/30/87) • **83**
St.-Emilion 1976 • $105 • (11/30/87) • **89**
St.-Emilion 1974 • $28 • (11/30/87) • **76**
St.-Emilion 1973 • $45 • (11/30/87) • **77**
St.-Emilion 1972 • $30 • (11/30/87) • **75**
St.-Emilion 1971 • $90 • (11/30/87) • **83**
St.-Emilion 1970 • $150 • (05/15/93) • **89**
St.-Emilion 1969 • $173 Ⓐ • (11/30/87) • **76**
St.-Emilion 1967 • $65 • (11/30/87) • **79**
St.-Emilion 1966 • $115 Ⓐ • (11/30/87) • **85**
St.-Emilion 1964 • $137 Ⓐ • (11/30/87) • **78**
St.-Emilion 1962 • $48 Ⓐ • (11/30/87) • **85**
St.-Emilion 1961: Probably on the down slope, as indicated by the smoky-brown color on the rim, but a rich taste experience anyway. Has aromas of earth and tobacco, with broad, chocolaty flavors and a smooth, melt-in-your-mouth texture. Drink through 2000. • $141 • (04/30/96) • **89**
St.-Emilion 1959 • $300 • (10/15/90) • **79**
St.-Emilion 1958 • $95 • (11/30/87) • **79**
St.-Emilion 1957 • $250 • (11/30/87) • **74**
St.-Emilion 1956 • $175 • (11/30/87) • **86**
St.-Emilion 1955 • $195 • (11/30/87) • **91**
St.-Emilion 1954 • $180 • (11/30/87) • **87**
St.-Emilion 1953 • $240 • (11/30/87) • **78**
St.-Emilion 1952 • $102 Ⓐ • (11/30/87) • **85**
St.-Emilion 1950 • $220 • (11/30/87) • **78**
St.-Emilion 1949 • $350 • (11/30/87) • **91**
St.-Emilion 1947 • $380 • (11/30/87) • **83**
St.-Emilion 1945 • $325 Ⓐ • (03/16/86) • **75**
St.-Emilion 1943 • $76 Ⓐ • (11/30/87) • **84**
St.-Emilion 1942 • $250 • (11/30/87) • **81**
St.-Emilion 1937 • $93 Ⓐ • (11/30/87) • **83**
St.-Emilion 1936 • $300 • (11/30/87) • **82**
St.-Emilion 1929 • $650 • (11/30/87) • **83**
St.-Emilion 1928 • $640 • (11/30/87) • **83**
St.-Emilion 1926 • $680 • (11/30/87) • **82**
St.-Emilion 1925 • $175 • (11/30/87) • **75**
St.-Emilion 1924 • $250 • (11/30/87) • **95**
St.-Emilion 1923 • $200 • (11/30/87) • **76**
St.-Emilion 1921 • $1,150 • (11/30/87) • **94**
St.-Emilion 1918 • $850 • (11/30/87) • **87**
St.-Emilion 1916 • $430 • (11/30/87) • **86**
St.-Emilion 1914 • $380 • (11/30/87) • **79**
St.-Emilion 1913 • $380 • (11/30/87) • **81**
St.-Emilion 1912 • $380 • (11/30/87) • **79**
St.-Emilion 1905 • $600 • (11/30/87) • **82**
St.-Emilion 1902 • $300 • (11/30/87) • **83**
St.-Emilion 1900 • $1,500 • (11/30/87) • **78**
St.-Emilion 1899 • $1,250 • (11/30/87) • **77**
St.-Emilion 1894 • $800 • (11/30/87) • **85**
St.-Emilion 1879 • $700 • (11/30/87) • **93**
St.-Emilion 1877 • $2,250 • (11/30/87) • **92**

AUSSELONS, DOMAINE LES

Côtes du Rhône Vinsobres 1987 • $8 • (06/30/90) • **75**

AUTARD, DOMAINE PAUL

Châteauneuf-du-Pape 1993: Fruity and focused, showing fresh, ripe raspberry and black cherry flavors that echo on the finish. Nicely balanced, elegant in texture, adding just a hint of tannin. 7,000 cases made. • $17 • (10/15/95) • **84**
Côtes du Rhône 1994: Tastes candied and bit oxidized, but has some good ripe plum and cherry fruit flavors. Lacks integration now, but could come together. Try now. 5,000 cases made. • $8 • (11/15/95) • **80**

AUVENAY, DOMAINE D'

Auxey-Duresses 1993: Impressive for the vintage. Quite rich, displaying apple, truffle, mushroom and cream character, medium-to-full body and a smooth texture. Drinkable now. • $35 • (05/15/95) • **86**
Auxey-Duresses 1991 • $38 • (10/15/93) • **82**
Auxey-Duresses Red 1989 • $42 • (01/31/92) • **88**
Corton-Charlemagne 1993: Solid and muscular, turning silky on the finish, delivering pear, vanilla bean and coconut flavors edged between smoky, toasty oak shadings. Woodiness should smooth out by 1998. From Lalou Bize-Leroy. • $NA • **88**
Meursault Les Narvaux 1992: Beautiful, with elegant yet very flavorful character, delivers attractive fig, toasted bread, honey and spice flavors and a lingering finish. Drinkable now. • $NA • (08/31/94) • **90**
Meursault Les Narvaux 1991 • $60 • (10/15/93) • **88**
Puligny-Montrachet Les Folatières 1993: Ripe and delicious. Deep yellow color, medium body, vanilla, lemon and lime flavors and toasted oak finish. Wonderful sweet fruit. From Lalou Bize-Leroy. • $NA • (08/31/95) • **86**
Puligny-Montrachet Les Folatières 1992: An exotic, rich, floral style of Puligny that smells like vanilla and ginger, tastes like honey, pear and nutmeg and has a long finish. Smooth and supple in texture. Very inviting. From Lalou Bize-Leroy. 170 cases made. • $96 • (08/31/94) • **90**
Puligny-Montrachet Les Folatières 1991 • $93 • (10/15/93) • **92**

AUVIGUE & REVEL

Pouilly-Fuissé Vieilles Vignes 1994: A middle-of-the road white, of light-to-medium body. Slightly awkward, offering stale aromas but some fresh, crisp fruit flavors. Could use more harmony. 916 cases made. • $24 • (05/31/96) • **77**

AUVIGUE, ANDRE

Pouilly-Fuissé Solutré 1994: Very good intensity of fruit, offering green apple, pineapple and pear notes. Clean and crisp, a medium-bodied white that delivers plenty of flavors. Drinkable now. • $18 • (05/31/96) • **85**

AUVIGUE, MAISON

Pouilly-Fuissé Solutré Vendanges Manuelles 1993: Tart and sharp. The lime, apple skin and grassy aromas and flavors round off on the finish, unfolding some decent, ripe pear, mineral and grapefruit flavors. Drinkable now. 2,083 cases made. • $14 • (05/15/95) • **80**
Pouilly-Fuissé Vieilles Vignes 1993: Good intensity, showing earthy, buttery, yeasty notes echoed on the palate. Lots of fresh lemon in the chewy, chalky finish. Try now. 813 cases made. • $22 • (05/15/95) • **83**

AYALA

Brut Blanc de Blancs Champagne 1988: Extremely appley, almost like cider. Full-bodied and velvety, showing fresh apple character and a crisp finish. Scored the same in August 1992 tasting. Drinkable now. 1,600 cases made. • $40 • (12/31/93) • **84**

Brut Blanc de Blancs Champagne 1985 • $33 • (12/31/90) • **90**

Brut Blanc de Blancs Champagne 1982: Dry, medium-bodied and pleasant in a fruity, slightly herbal style. Well-balanced with acid, and clean and refreshing on the finish. • $29 • (04/15/88) • **85**

Brut Champagne 1985 • $59 • (12/31/90) • **89**

Brut Champagne 1983: Simple, straightforward and uncomplicated, with dough, spice and vanilla flavors that are somewhat ponderous on the palate. A touch of caramel on the finish makes it more interesting. • $30 • (12/31/89) • **80**

Brut Champagne 1982: Full and nicely mature in style. Shows mature appley, slightly butterscotch y flavors and a smooth, mouth-filling texture. Very well made. • $27 • (04/15/88) • **86**

Brut Champagne NV: Smooth and rich but not heavy, marked by fresh, lively fruit flavors and nice touches of maturity in the vanilla and nutmeg accents. Combines great balance and enticing flavors. 42,000 cases made. • $31 • (12/15/94) • **89**

Brut Champagne Extra Quality NV • $28 • (12/31/87) • **78**

Brut Champagne Grand Cuvée 1985: A slightly herbal style of Champagne, with earthy aromas and full, lemony flavors. Crisp but round in texture. • $57 • (12/31/89) • **84**

Brut Champagne Grand Cuvée 1982: Nicely tart style with crisp, subdued citrus flavors and just a hint of maturity. Drinkable now. • $52 • (04/15/88) • **87**

Brut Rosé Champagne NV • $26 • (04/15/88) • **85**

Brut Rosé Champagne Extra Quality NV • $20 • (05/31/87) • **80**

AYDIE, CHÂTEAU D'

Madiran 1991: Pretty and sophisticated, round and soft, with plenty of plum, cassis, chocolate and cedar flavors. It's not heavy but has plenty of staying power, drinkable now. • $14 • (06/30/94) • **87**

AZO, HERVE

Chablis 1994: Attractive mineral and lemon aromas and flavors, medium body and lovely delicacy. 517 cases made. • $15 • **85**

Chablis Côte de Léchet 1994: Silky and of medium intensity and body, it has some attractive pear, apple and citrus flavors but lacks a bit of depth and concentration, turning very crisp on the finish. Drinkable now. • $20 • (05/31/96) • **82**

Chablis Côte de Léchet 1993: Rather dull and candied, with apple, cider and green character. Hard finish. 916 cases made. • $19 • (08/31/95) • **75**

Chablis Vaudevey 1994: Very intense, vibrant, zesty *premier cru.* Focused, earthy lime, avocado, pink grapefruit and grassy flavors. Light- to medium-bodied, it puckers the mouth on its clean, crisp finish. Drinkable now. • $20 • (05/31/96) • **83**

Chablis Vaudevey 1993: Very oaky style: smoky, toasty flavors and a thread of solid acidity run through it. A round and silky mouth-feel. For fans of woody wines. 1,333 cases made. • $20 • **83**

BACHELET, DOMAINE

Charmes-Chambertin 1990: Dense and chunky, like a rich raspberry sauce. Has plenty of tannins and fresh acidity, making it a wine to lay away for decades. Try in 1998. 175 cases made. • $53 • (12/15/92) • **94**

Charmes-Chambertin Vieilles Vignes 1986 • $43 • (07/15/89) • **87**

Côte de Nuits-Villages 1990: This charmer displays plenty of raspberry and sweet berry flavors and medium tannins. Drinkable now. • $18 • (12/15/92) • **84**

Key: SS—Spectator Selection. CS—Cellar Selection. BB—Best Buy. $NA—Price not available. (BT)—Barrel tasting. Ⓐ—Auction Price.
Dates in parentheses represent the issues in which the ratings were published.

Gevrey-Chambertin Les Corbeaux Vieilles Vignes 1986 • $30 • (07/15/89) • **83**

Gevrey-Chambertin Vieilles Vignes 1990: So seductive you can almost drink it now, with fresh raspberry and cherry flavors and a hint of toastiness. Really turns up the volume in the end. 400 cases made. • $43 • (12/15/92) • **91**

Gevrey-Chambertin Vieilles Vignes 1986 • $24 • (07/15/89) • **88**

BACHELET-RAMONET

Bâtard-Montrachet 1994: Has some elegance and a core of citrus, pear, herb and mineral flavors. But this medium-bodied white is very tart on aftertaste. Better in 1998? • $NA • (05/31/96) 79 • **79**

Chassagne-Montrachet Caillerets 1994: A serious, medium-bodied white Burgundy, delivering plenty of punchy character, mineral, wet earth and citrus flavors and a long finish. • $NA • (05/31/96) • **87**

Chassagne-Montrachet La Grande Montagne 1994: Clean, crisp and straightforward, a *premier cru* delivering modest mineral, green apple and vegetal flavors. Quite sharp, tart finish. • $NA • (05/31/96) • **80**

BAHANS HAUT-BRION, CHÂTEAU

Pessac-Léognan 1995: Loads of fruit in this wine that's bursting with berry and cherry character. Full body, and the full, velvety tannins last through a long finish. Almost outstanding. • $NA • (05/15/96) • **85-89** (BT)

Pessac-Léognan 1994: Lovely cherry and berry flavors mingle with a hint of brown sugar. Very typical Cabernet Sauvignon in nature. Good tannins and body, but a short finish. • $20 • (05/15/96) • **85-89** (BT)

Pessac-Léognan 1989 • $36 Ⓐ • (03/15/92) • **90**

Pessac-Léognan 1986 • $27 Ⓐ • (09/15/89) • **86**

BAHUAUD, DONATIEN

Muscadet de Sèvre et Maine Cuvée des Aigles 1992: Crisp, simple and light—nothing to fault nor to get excited about. The light green apple and lemon flavors are clean and fresh. • $6 • (10/31/94) • **80**

BAILLY, COMTE DE

Brut Crémant de Bourgogne 1983 • $8 • (10/15/86) • **70**

BAILLY, FRANCK & JEAN-FRANCOIS

Sancerre Chavignol 1992: This is a rich wine, with grassy aromas and full-bodied apple flavors, but an earthy note dulls it a bit. It lacks crispness and verve. • $16 • (10/31/94) • **79**

BALAC, CHÂTEAU

Haut-Médoc 1990: Full-bodied and fruity, offering nice cherry and raspberry flavors. Firm and fairly tannic, with good aromas. A sturdy Bordeaux that's best to drink now. • $12 • (09/15/93) • **85**

BALESTARD-LA-TONNELLE, CHÂTEAU

St.-Emilion 1989 • $28 • (03/15/92) • **85**

St.-Emilion 1988 • $25 • (04/30/91) • **91**

St.-Emilion 1982 • $24 Ⓐ • (08/31/92) • **82**

BALLAND, DOMAINE JEAN-PAUL

Sancerre 1994: Assertive, offering plenty of grassy, herbal flavors and very crisp acidity, adding lime and mineral notes on aftertaste. Textbook Loire Sauvignon Blanc, but could use more fruit to soften its hard edges. • $15 • (12/15/95) • **80**

Sancerre 1993: Full-bodied for a Sancerre, this rich wine offers mineral, herb and grapefruit flavors over a core of tart acidity. • $13 • (10/31/94) • **86**

BALLOT-MILLOT & FILS, R.

Meursault 1993: Somewhat hard but very lively, offering green apple, mineral and cream character, medium body, firm acidity and lean finish. 300 cases made. • $28 • (08/31/95) • **80**

Meursault-Charmes 1992: Simple, lean and a bit hollow, with a mint, herb and wet earth character, seems a bit diluted. 250 cases made. • $NA • (08/31/94) • **79**

Meursault Genevrières 1991 • $38 • (10/15/93) • **90**

Meursault Les Charmes 1993: Very intense earthy, ripe fruit character, medium body, high acidity and long finish. 100 cases made. • $45 • (08/31/95) • **84**

Meursault Les Criots 1992: Mature, tastes tired on the palate, with stale apple and earthy flavors. 250 cases made. • $38 • (08/31/94) • **73**

Meursault Les Criots 1991 • $33 • (10/15/93) • **83**

BALLUE-MONDON, CHÂTEAU

Bordeaux 1988 • $8 • (03/31/90) • **71**

BARA, PAUL

Brut Champagne 1988: Powerfully fruity, boasting apple and honey aromas, tight, tart flavors and ample acidity to keep it lively. • $45 • (11/30/95) • **90**

Brut Champagne 1986 • $45 • **87**

Brut Champagne 1982: Snappy and crisp. A straightforward Brut at first that develops some nice buttery and more complex touches in the glass. Fruity aromas with a good dose of peach. • $34 • (12/31/88) • **89**

Brut Champagne Comtesse Marie de France 1985: A wonderfully complete and complex bottle of bubbly that blends toasty, nutty aromas with figgy, appley, pearlike flavors in a seamless package. The texture is lively but velvety and the finish lingers nicely. • $58 • **90**

Brut Champagne Spécial Club Grand Cru 100% 1988: Elegant, crisp and stylish. Aromas are slightly toasty, flavors are lean, lemony and nutty. The texture and acidity is refreshing and appetizing. 500 cases made. • $49 • (12/31/94) • **85**

Brut Champagne Grand Cru 100% 1986: Vividly fruity, with peach and apricot flavors, but it clamps down on the finish. Seems a bit awkward, but has interesting cheese aromas and good complexity. 1,000 cases made. • $36 • (12/31/94) • **86**

Brut Champagne Réserve NV: Round and smooth but perhaps fading, slightly sweet flavors accented by nutty, vanilla nuances that turn somewhat flat on aftertaste. Tired, lackluster bubbles. • $42 • (12/31/95) • **79**

Brut Rosé Champagne NV: A straightforward, refreshing rosé, with modest cherry and vanilla flavors accented by cinnamon. Tasty, but short on the finish. 1,500 cases made. • $35 • (12/31/94) • **84**

BARANCOURT

Brut Blanc de Blancs Champagne Cramant Grand Cru NV • $30 • (12/31/90) • **85**

Brut Blanc de Blancs Champagne Cramant NV • $20 • (05/31/87) • **71**

Cuvée de Fondateurs Champagne 1985 • $NA • (12/31/90) • **90**

BARAT, MICHEL

Chablis 1994: Ripe tropical fruit character, medium-to-full body, apple and straw flavors, fresh yet balanced acidity and long finish. • $14 • **86**

Chablis Côte de Léchet 1994: Fresh, clean and vibrant, a lively *premier cru* showing grassy, citrus character. Light- to medium-bodied, adding subtle honey and mineral notes on the finish. Should go well with fish. • $16 • (05/31/96) • **83**

Chablis Côte de Léchet 1993: Racy apple, spice and honey aromas and flavors, medium body and acidity and a fresh finish. • $NA • **83**

Chablis Les Fourneaux 1994: Charming, smooth mouth-feel, silky texture and sweet-tasting fruit character. Reveals some honey, mineral, pear and apple flavors, but lacks a bit of harmony on the finish. Drinkable now. • $16 • (05/31/96) • **80**

Chablis Mont de Milieu 1994: Clean, crisp and very intense, offering assertive dried herb and vegetal flavors. Tightly made, full in body, a harsh white that may smooth on aging. For now, it's quite a challenge to taste. Better in 2000? • $16 • (05/31/96) • **87**

Chablis Mont de Milieu 1993: Lots of mineral, salty, chalky character. Medium in body and firm, with a fresh finish. • $NA • **86**

Chablis Vaillons 1994: Distinctive, ripe, medium-bodied, combining compacted mineral and honey character and tart, citric, grassy flavors. Tantalizing, electifies the palate. Should only gain upon aging, try in 1999. • $16 • (05/31/96) • **87**

Chablis Vaillons 1993: Clean and well crafted, tasting almost more like Sauvignon Blanc than Chardonnay. Lovely gooseberry, floral, grassy character and a crisp finish. • $NA • (08/31/95) • **82**

BARET, CHÂTEAU

Pessac-Léognan 1992: A little bit of berry and plum flavor, but still diluted and very light. • $12 • (04/15/95) • **73**

Pessac-Léognan 1991: A wine with focused black cherry and earthy aromas and flavors. Light body and silky texture. • $12 • (03/31/94) • **81**

Pessac-Léognan 1989 • $18 • (03/15/92) • **93**

Pessac-Léognan White 1993: Old-style, dull, slightly oxidized character. Medium-bodied and round, but slightly candied on the finish. • $19 • **78**

BARGE, GILLES

Côte-Rôtie 1991: A muscular wine, with firm tannins and straightforward fruit, but it's rather simple and short on the finish. Drinkable now. • $NA • (05/31/94) • **83**

Côte-Rôtie 1990: Still evolving, a traditional-style wine, showing game, pepper and spice flavors. The tannins are still firm, try now. • $NA • (05/31/94) • **86**

Côte-Rôtie 1989 • $30 • (04/15/93) • **83**

BARGE, PIERRE

Côte-Rôtie 1988 • $42 • (07/31/91) • **84**

BARJAC, GUY DE

Cornas 1985 • $17 • (10/15/88) • **81**

BAROLET, DR.

Aloxe-Corton Villamont Red 1952 • $59 Ⓐ • (08/31/90) • **92**

BARONNE, CHÂTEAU DE LA

Grenache en Vert Montagne d'Alaric Corbières 1991 • $12 • (03/15/94) • **84**

Montagne d'Alaric Corbières 1991 • $10 • (03/15/94) • **81**

Montagne d'Alaric Corbières 1990 • $NA • (03/15/94) • **83**

Vieilles Vignes Montagne d'Alaric Corbières 1991 • $9 • (03/15/94) • **85**

BAROUX, G.

Côtes du Rhône Château de Bourdines 1988 • $8 • (12/15/90) • **79**

BARRADIS, CHÂTEAU LE

Monbazillac 1988 • $20 • (07/15/91) • **76**

BARRAUD, DANIEL

Pouilly-Fuissé Cuvée Vieilles Vignes 1994: Somewhat mature already, featuring butterscotch and buttery flavors that seem heavy. Rich, fat, lacking a bit of freshness on the finish. Drinkable now. 416 cases made. • $28 • (05/31/96) • **80**

Pouilly-Fuissé Cuvée Vieilles Vignes 1993: Austere quality softens and delivers some lovely, ripe pear, butter and spice flavors. Quite fresh, even tart, finish. 417 cases made. • $28 • (05/15/95) • **84**

Pouilly-Fuissé La Roche 1994: Quite tight, offering a hint of complexity—butter, fig, pear and green apple. Fresh but slightly tart on the finish. 141 cases made. • $24 • (05/31/96) • **80**

Pouilly-Fuissé La Verchère 1994: Very pretty and attractive, a light- to medium-bodied white putting all the pieces together, from ripe tropical aromas to the citric crispness on aftertaste that keeps going, titillating the palate. 416 cases made. • $21 • (05/31/96) • **87**

BARRE, DOMAINE

Muscadet de Sèvre et Maine 1993: Crisp and lemony, goes down quick and clean. It's light-bodied and basically neutral, with tart green apple and citrus notes. • $9 • (10/31/94) • **82**
Muscadet de Sèvre et Maine Le Muscadet de Barré 1994: A crisp, straightforward Muscadet with good acidity, very modest fruit flavors, and a whiff of an earthy, briny character. • $9 • (11/15/95) • **79**

BARREYRES, CHÂTEAU

Haut-Médoc 1986 • $8 • (06/30/89) • **78**

BARROT, DOMAINE LUCIEN

Châteauneuf-du-Pape 1989 • $20 • (10/15/91) • **88**
Châteauneuf-du-Pape 1988 • $18 • (10/15/91) • **87**
Châteauneuf-du-Pape 1986 • $18 • (10/15/91) • **89**
Châteauneuf-du-Pape 1981 • $16 • (09/30/87) • **87**

BARRYES, CHÂTEAU

Haut-Médoc 1989 • $10 • (07/15/92) • **75**

BARTHOD, GHISLAINE

Bourgogne 1990 • $23 • (12/15/92) • **83**
Bourgogne 1988 • $20 • (03/31/91) • **82**
Chambolle-Musigny 1990: This solid red offers a round texture, perfumed aromas, a core of earth, tobacco and plum flavors and firm tannins. Drinkable now. • $25 • (12/15/92) • **87**
Chambolle-Musigny 1988 • $50 • (03/15/91) • **88**
Chambolle-Musigny Aux Beaux-Bruns 1990: Like a piece of art, this wine grows on you as it ripples across the palate, showing increasing plum, blackberry and smoke aromas and flavors and a silky texture. Very fine. Drink from 1997 to '99. • $50 • (12/15/92) • **93**
Chambolle-Musigny Les Beaux-Bruns 1988 • $45 • (02/28/91) • **83**
Chambolle-Musigny Les Charmes 1990: Exquisite, well structured and firm. Underneath the hard, tannic surface is a lovely core of lush berry, violet, plum and earth flavors that show breeding. Should be great in 1998. • $50 • (12/15/92) • **90**
Chambolle-Musigny Les Crâs 1990: Charming and supple. The pretty raspberry and cherry flavors make this pleasant enough to drink now, but it will improve with age. • $50 • (12/15/92) • **87**
Chambolle-Musigny Les Crâs 1988 • $45 • (02/28/91) • **87**
Chambolle-Musigny Les Véroilles 1990: Extremely firm, restrained and understated, with plum, cherry and forest underbrush notes that should show beautifully after a few years in the cellar. Drink in 1998. • $50 • (12/15/92) • **90**
Chambolle-Musigny Les Véroilles 1988 • $45 • (02/28/91) • **81**

BARTHOD-NOELLAT, G.

Chambolle-Musigny Charmes 1984 • $27 • (10/31/87) • **82**
Chambolle-Musigny Les Cras 1985 • $37 • (07/31/88) • **88**

BARTON & GUESTIER

Beaujolais St.-Louis 1995: Fresh flavors of black cherries and plums shine though this clean red. It's light but firm enough to match with food, and finishes with a pleasant spicy note. • $NA • **82**
Beaujolais St.-Louis 1994: Light and fresh. Simple grapey flavors and bright acidity make this a refreshing red. Serve slightly chilled. • $7 • (10/31/95) • **82**
Beaujolais St.-Louis 1993: Here's a light, fresh wine chock full of cherry, light banana and pepper flavors. It's simple and charming and will fade soon, without regrets. 180,000 cases made. • $7 • (06/30/94) • **82**
Beaujolais-Villages 1995: Spicy cinnamon and sandalwood aromas give this wine personality, on the palate, it's firm and a bit gamy. It's rather austere for Beaujolais, try with grilled meats. • $NA • **82**
Beaujolais-Villages 1993: Stale and tired. Not much life left, with only some stewed fruit flavors on the finish. 100,000 cases made. • $7 • (06/15/95) • **72**
Beaujolais-Villages 1988 • $9 • (05/31/89) • **77**
Beaujolais-Villages St.-Louis 1988 • $7 • (05/31/89) • **75**
Bordeaux 1988 • $6 • (03/31/90) • **78**
Bordeaux Fondation 1725 1990: Firm and flavorful, with generous red cherry, spice and cedar aromas and flavors. Finishes toasted and sweet. Drinkable now. • $9 • (03/15/93) • **82**
Bordeaux Fondation 1725 1989 • $9 • (07/31/91) • **75**
Bordeaux White Fondation 1725 1991 • $9 • (04/30/93) • **83**
Brouilly 1988 • $11 • (05/31/89) • **82**
Cabernet Sauvignon Bordeaux 1990: Firm-textured and somewhat austere, with a bit more tannin than the modest strawberry and cherry flavor might warrant. Drinkable now, however, with a slice of roast. • $6 • (11/30/92) • **78**
Cabernet Sauvignon Bordeaux 1988 • $6 • (02/15/90) • **73**
Cabernet Sauvignon Vin de Pays d'Oc 1994: Smooth raisin, spice and tobacco flavors. Seems very advanced for a 1994, but it's harmonious and the spice notes linger on aftertaste. • $6 • (10/31/95) • **80**
Cabernet Sauvignon Vin de Pays d'Oc 1993 44,000 cases made. • $6 • **55**
Chardonnay Vin de Pays d'Oc 1994: Smooth and creamy, plump with vanilla, coconut and melon flavors. It lacks crispness, though. • $9 • (12/15/95) • **82**
Chardonnay Vin de Pays d'Oc 1993: Fairly rich and buttery, with good apple and honeydew melon flavors. It is clean and well made, but without much of a finish. 54,000 cases made. • $6 • (11/30/94) BB • **83**
Châteauneuf-du-Pape 1992: Rustic game and barnyard aromas and flavors, with hints of chocolate and prunes and tough tannins. Lacks finesse and already mature. For fans of the traditional style. • $17 • (11/15/95) • **79**
Châteauneuf-du-Pape 1990: Tough and earthy, a rough-textured wine with austere, barklike flavors, offering little in the way of generosity. Try now. • $16 • (10/31/93) • **71**
Châteauneuf-du-Pape 1983 • $11 • (09/30/87) • **74**
Côtes du Rhône 1990 • $7 • (11/15/93) • **80**
Côtes du Rhône 1989 • $5 • (04/15/93) • **75**
Gevrey-Chambertin 1985 • $21 • (04/30/88) • **89**
Mâcon St.-Louis 1993: Rather rich and weighty. The creamy pear, apple and hazelnut character turns a bit harsh and dull on the short finish. Slight dilution. 1,666 cases made. • $7 • (08/31/95) • **78**
Mâcon St.-Louis 1991 • $8 • (03/31/93) BB • **83**
Mâcon-Villages 1993: Round and harmonious wet hay, mineral, wet earth and grass notes mingle with decent apple and pear flavors. • $NA • **81**
Margaux 1985 • $12 • (04/30/88) • **75**
Merlot Bordeaux 1990: Herbal and cedary at first, but some appealing raspberry and currant flavors take over on the finish. Drinkable now. 35,000 cases made. • $6 • (11/30/92) BB • **82**
Merlot Bordeaux 1988 • $6 • (02/15/90) BB • **84**
Merlot Vin de Pays d'Oc 1994: Solid and straightforward, featuring cherry, herb and chocolate flavors and enough tannin for grip. Not complex, but a modest complement for grilled meats. • $6 • (10/31/95) • **82**
Merlot Vin de Pays d'Oc 1993: A straightforward, medium-bodied Merlot with light tannins and pleasant plum and herb flavors. 78,000 cases made. • $6 • (02/28/95) • **81**
Moulin-à-Vent 1988 • $13 • (05/31/89) • **84**
Pommard 1985 • $21 • (11/30/87) • **81**
Pouilly-Fuissé 1992: Time in the bottle has lent attractive smoky, toasty notes, but it's soft, lacking firmness and depth. 25,000 cases made. • $16 • (03/31/95) • **79**
St.-Julien 1985 • $13 • (02/15/88) • **83**

Key: SS—Spectator Selection. CS—Cellar Selection. BB—Best Buy. $NA—Price not available. (BT)—Barrel tasting. Ⓐ—Auction Price.
Dates in parentheses represent the issues in which the ratings were published.

FRANCE

Sauternes 1985 • $12 • (05/31/88) • **75**

Vin de Pays du Jardin de la France Sauvignon Blanc 1993: Basic white wine. It's medium-bodied with neutral flavors and hints of nuts and herbs. Not offensive, but why bother? 22,000 cases made. • $6 • (10/31/94) • **76**

Vouvray 1993: This lively wine has a nice mix of honeyed sweetness and crisp acidity, with peach and mineral accents. It's not rich, but lingers on the finish. • $10 • (11/15/95) • **83**

BAS, CHÂTEAU

Cuvée Temple Coteaux d'Aix en Provence 1986 • $9 • • **61**

BASSAC, DOMAINE DE

Vin de Pays d'Oc 1992 • $5 • (03/15/94) • **85**

BASTIDE DAUZAC, LA

Margaux 1994: Tart and crisp, light-to-medium body, a strong herbal, asparagus character distracts from the black cherry flavors. Second label of Château Dauzac. • $NA • **70-74** (BT)

Margaux 1991: A good wine for this vintage with its silky mouthfeel, cherry flavors and slightly herbal character on finish. • $11 • (03/31/94) • **80**

BASTIDE, CELLIER DE LA

Entre-Deux-Mers 1994: Appealing balance in this just-so, grassy-styled white. A bit light on the finish and slightly aggressive, but it's fresh and crisp. • $8 • **82**

BASTOR-LAMONTAGNE, CHÂTEAU

Sauternes 1990: Impressively classy and focused, lemon, lime, tropical, dried apricot and toasted coconut flavors are presented in a seductive, velvety package. Drinkable now. • $25 • (04/15/95) • **92**

Sauternes 1989: Well made and concentrated, medium-bodied, built more for finesse than power, displaying lemon, honey and butterscotch flavors that offer zing and creaminess at the same time. • $33 • (04/15/95) • **88**

Sauternes 1988: Simple and light, offering modest lemon, honey and melon flavors, medium sweetness and a short finish. • $21 • (04/15/95) • **80**

Sauternes 1987 • $17 • (06/15/90) • **67**

Sauternes 1986 • $NA • (04/15/95) • **88**

Sauternes 1985 • $20 • (05/31/88) • **82**

Sauternes 1983 • $23 • (01/31/88) • **82**

BATACCHI, PHILIPPE

Clos de la Roche 1991: Very youthful, jammy and peppery, showing a dill edge to the anise, blackberry and currant aromas and flavors up front, turning crisp and lemony on the finish. Needs until 1997 to settle. 25 cases made. • $30 Ⓐ • (01/31/94) • **86**

Clos de la Roche 1990: A fruit bomb. Tastes like a barrel sample, with freshly crushed berry, lovely violet and vanilla notes and plenty of tannins to go along with the supple, delicious texture. Drink in 1997. 83 cases made. • $59 • (12/15/92) • **93**

Côte de Nuits-Villages 1990: Shows the essence of Burgundy fruit flavor, with oodles of black licorice, raspberry and cherry nuances and fine tannins. A joy to drink now. 200 cases made. • $20 • (12/15/92) • **88**

Fixin 1990: Absolutely delicious, with loads of licorice and berry flavors and velvety tannins. Drinkable now. 125 cases made. • $23 • (12/15/92) • **87**

Gevrey-Chambertin Jeune Rois 1991: Relatively dark in color and concentrated in flavor, offering bright cherry and currant aromas and flavors that linger on the finish. Drinkable now. 140 cases made. • $30 Ⓐ • (01/31/94) • **85**

Gevrey-Chambertin Les Evocelles 1991: Strangely floral, brightly fruity and light. Try now. 110 cases made. • $30 • (01/31/94) • **79**

Gevrey-Chambertin Les Evocelles 1990: Like a polished diamond, this wine shines with bright color and a vivid texture. Razor sharp, well made and satiny, offering ultraclean raspberry, cherry, plum and vanilla flavors and racy acidity to lengthen the finish. Drinkable now. 250 cases made. • $32 • (12/15/92) • **91**

Gevrey-Chambertin Les Jeunes Rois 1990: The essence of fruit, this tastes like a barrel sample it's so young and juicy, with full-throttle black cherry aromas and flavors and a beautiful round, fruity finish. An unusual wine. Drinkable now. 292 cases made. • $38 • (12/15/92) • **90**

Morey-St.-Denis Premier Cru 1991: Distinctive, almost bizarre, with odd, gamy, leathery notes. Drink now. 60 cases made. • $27 Ⓐ • (01/31/94) • **79**

Morey-St.-Denis Premier Cru 1990: Offers fruit, fruit and more fruit, this bubbles with raspberry flavors. So youthful and extracted it tastes like a barrel sample, but an underlying structure of fine tannins and lively acidity gives it a fresh finish. Drinkable now. 100 cases made. • $44 • (12/15/92) • **93**

BATAILLEY, CHÂTEAU

Pauillac 1992: Elegant, harmonious berry and light tobacco character, medium-to-light body, silky tannins and fresh finish. Try now. • $19 • (04/15/95) • **80**

Pauillac 1991: Some pretty tobacco, berry and herbal notes. Medium body with a very silky texture. • $19 • (03/31/94) • **83**

Pauillac 1989 • $19 Ⓐ • (03/15/92) • **81**

Pauillac 1988 • $30 • (04/30/91) • **90**

Pauillac 1982 • $32 Ⓐ • (08/31/92) • **86**

Pauillac 1970 • $30 Ⓐ • (05/15/93) • **88**

Pauillac 1961: A nicely mature wine with a fruity, spicy bouquet and enough fruit flavor to give it life. Turns a bit metallic and thin on the finish, however. Drink now. • $83 • (04/30/96) • **84**

Pauillac 1945: Smells better than it tastes, especially the way lively fruit blends with mature richness. Smoky at the edges, but taste is thin and watery. • $200 • (11/30/95) • **78**

BATARDIERE, DOMAINE DE LA

Muscadet de Sèvre et Maine 1994: Quite rich for a Muscadet, offering strong *sur lie* flavors of yeast and butter, citrus and pine notes and slight earthiness. Much going on, not all pleasant. • $8 • **74**

Muscadet de Sèvre et Maine 1992: A round wine with almond and pear flavors and good depth on the palate. The acidity is well-integrated and the wine is still fresh. It's smooth, clean and has enough weight to match up well with chicken on the grill. • $7 • (08/31/94) BB • **85**

BATISSE, CHÂTEAU LA

Haut-Médoc 1985 • $10 • (06/30/88) • **82**

BATISTE PERTOIS

Brut Blanc de Blancs Champagne Cuvée de Réserve NV: Straightforward, fruity and well balanced, with all its pieces in place. It smells appley and lemony, tastes reasonably rich and adds a clean, lingering finish. • $36 • **86**

Brut Blanc de Blancs Champagne Cuveé de Réserve Premier Cru NV • $33 • (12/31/92) • **80**

BAUGET-JOUETTE

Brut Blanc de Blancs Champagne 1988: Rich, smooth and complex with layers of spice, ginger, pear and toasty flavors that are creamy and smooth, staying with you on a long, flavorful finish. Delicious now. 1,000 cases made. • $51 • (12/31/93) • **92**

Brut Blanc de Blancs Champagne 1985: Ripe, smooth and elegant, with lively, creamy pear, spice and honeyed notes that are intense and focused, picking up a hint of hazelnut on the aftertaste. Complex and stylish, with a long finish. Drink now. 825 cases made. • $59 • (12/31/92) • **90**

Brut Champagne 1985: Broad, ripe, rich and flavorful, with mouthfilling pear, spice, vanilla and toast flavors that are intense and concentrated. A smooth, substantive Champagne, with flavors that linger. Drinkable now. 1,400 cases made. • $55 • (12/31/92) • **90**

Brut Champagne NV: Unusually yeasty-tasting, with a doughy character throughout. Soft and almost sweet. Drinkable, but won't appeal to everybody. 8,300 cases made. • $30 • (12/31/94) • **73**

Brut Champagne Grande Réserve 1988: Smooth, rich, creamy and spicy with tiers of pear, ginger, vanilla and toast flavors that are focused and lively, finishing with excellent length. Tasty now but capable of aging. Drinkable now. • $47 • (12/31/93) • **93**

Brut Champagne Grande Réserve NV • $45 • (12/31/92) • **83**

Brut Rosé Champagne NV: Deep color, open aromas of toast and plums and spicy vinous character are reminiscent of a light red Burgundy. Rich and deep. • $33 • (12/15/95) • **89**

BAULOS, CHÂTEAU

Bordeaux Prince Albert Poniatowski 1988 • $8 • (08/31/91) • **69**

BAUMARD, DOMAINE DES

Quarts de Chaume 1993: Sweet and spicy, this shows plenty of Botrytis character, along with ripe apple and candied pineapple flavors. It's rich, yet has bright acidity. Intense and concentrated enough to develop further in the bottle. • $27 • (12/15/95) • **88**

Savennières 1993: Fragrant with peach, honey and pine aromas, this follows through on the palate with generous ripe peach and light butter flavors. It's round and soft, balanced, with a lingering finish. • $14 • (12/15/95) • **85**

Savennières Clos du Papillon 1993: Firm and quite intense, this rich wine offers full flavors of peach, pineapple, grapefruit and an intriguing note of white chocolate. Good underlying acidity gives it backbone, drinkable now. • $14 • **88**

BEAU MAYNE

Bordeaux 1983 • $5 • (03/31/87) BB • **81**

BEAUCASTEL, CHÂTEAU DE

Châteauneuf-du-Pape 1992: A light, elegant version of Châteauneuf, with interesting leather and earth aromas, bright cherry and blackberry flavors and a lingering finish. Drink now. • $31 • (11/30/94) • **85**

Châteauneuf-du-Pape 1991: A solid wine, not as glorious as the top vintage, but still ripe and earthy. A leathery-barnyard component to the black cherry flavors, lingering on the finish. Try now. 10,000 cases made. • $25 • (03/31/94) • **89**

Châteauneuf-du-Pape 1990: Not as appealing as the '89, our Wine of the Year in 1991, but it's a generous, concentrated, intensely fruity Châteauneuf that blends mouthfilling flavors with complex cedar, spice and leather accents. Sturdy tannins and solid acidity mark this as a good candidate to cellar until 1997. Tasted twice. 17,000 cases made. • $40 • (03/15/93) • **92**

Châteauneuf-du-Pape 1989 • $47 • (10/15/91) CS • **97**

Châteauneuf-du-Pape 1988 • $32 • (10/15/91) • **90**

Châteauneuf-du-Pape 1987 • $21 • (11/30/89) • **83**

Châteauneuf-du-Pape 1986 • $33 • (10/15/91) • **91**

Châteauneuf-du-Pape 1985 • $38 • (10/15/91) • **91**

Châteauneuf-du-Pape 1984 • $22 • (11/30/89) • **89**

Châteauneuf-du-Pape 1983 • $48 • (10/15/91) • **90**

Châteauneuf-du-Pape 1982 • $30 • (11/30/89) • **92**

Châteauneuf-du-Pape 1981 • $50 • (10/15/91) • **96**

Châteauneuf-du-Pape 1980 • $38 • (11/30/89) • **83**

Key: SS—Spectator Selection. CS—Cellar Selection. BB—Best Buy. $NA—Price not available. (BT)—Barrel tasting. Ⓐ—Auction Price.
Dates in parentheses represent the issues in which the ratings were published.

Châteauneuf-du-Pape White 1992: A heady, full-bodied white, with pungent flavors of herb, apple, almond and tobacco. Soft and ripe in texture and ready to drink. • $32 • (11/30/94) • **84**

Châteauneuf-du-Pape White 1991 • $38 • (04/15/93) • **82**

Châteauneuf-du-Pape White Vieilles Vignes 1991 • $25 • (06/15/93) • **89**

Côtes du Rhône Coudoulet de Beaucastel 1990 • $40 • (04/15/93) • **67**

Côtes du Rhône White Coudoulet de Beaucastel 1993: Generous and fruity, with pear and grapefruit flavors, accented by fennel. Full-bodied, nicely tart and lively. • $22 • (11/30/94) • **84**

BEAUCLAIRE

Bordeaux 1989 • $7 • (06/15/93) BB • **81**

Bordeaux Supérieur 1988 • $6 • (12/31/90) • **79**

BEAU-SEJOUR BECOT, CHÂTEAU

St.-Emilion 1995: Rich berry, earth and chocolate aromas and flavors, medium body and tannins and a velvety texture. • $NA • (05/15/96) • **85-89** (BT)

St.-Emilion 1994: Full-bodied, solid, firm and muscular structure. Terrific flavors of cassis, sweet toasted oak and wet soil, stone character and long finish. Almost outstanding. • $NA • **85-89** (BT)

St.-Emilion 1993: Flavorful and quite firm, showing sweetness on the palate and some blackberry, roasted coffee bean, bark and tomato notes. Try in 1997 after it smooths out. • $25 • (01/31/96) • **86**

St.-Emilion 1988 • $21 • (06/30/91) • **87**

St.-Emilion 1986 • $22 • (07/31/89) • **79**

St.-Emilion 1982 • $25 • (05/15/89) • **85**

BEAU-SITE, CHÂTEAU

St.-Estèphe 1992: Herbal and light with cut-grass character. Light-bodied, light finish. Drinkable now. • $14 • **76**

St.-Estèphe 1991: Fresh and easy to drink with its cherry, spice and herb character. Light-bodied, light on the finish. • $13 • (03/31/94) • **78**

St.-Estèphe 1990: Attractive berry, spice and plum aromas and flavors, medium tannins and a long, silky finish. Drinkable now. 15,000 cases made. • $23 • (03/31/93) • **90**

St.-Estèphe 1989 • $20 • (03/15/92) • **90**

St.-Estèphe 1987 • $12 • (11/30/89) • **81**

St.-Estèphe 1986 • $18 • (11/30/89) • **86**

St.-Estèphe 1982 • $18 • (08/31/92) • **86**

St.-Estèphe 1970 • $36 • (05/15/93) • **82**

BEAU-VALLON, CHÂTEAU DU

St.-Emilion 1990: There's a resinous quality in the aromas accompanied by sweet, plummy flavors and a robust, slightly alcoholic constitution. Drinkable now. • $14 • (08/31/95) • **83**

St.-Emilion 1987 • $10 • (05/15/90) • **81**

St.-Emilion 1986 • $10 • (09/30/89) • **84**

St.-Emilion 1985 • $8 • (09/30/88) • **82**

BEAUDET, PAUL

Pouilly-Fuissé Domaine des Trois Tilleuls Vieilles Vignes 1994: Tightly wound earth, mineral, nutmeg and green apple notes. Quite lean and sharp on the finish, even a bit tough. Drinkable now or hold until 1997. 1,000 cases made. • $NA • (05/31/96) • **83**

BEAULT-FORGEOT

Mazis-Chambertin Hospice de Beaune Cuvée Madeleine-Collig 1980 • $56 • (07/01/84) • **91**

Nuits-St.-Georges Les Plateaux 1981 • $17 • (07/01/84) • **83**

BEAUMET

Blanc de Noirs Champagne 1988: Very simple and dominated by the bubbles. It's clean but lacks much character other than apple. Drink now. • $35 • (12/31/93) • **78**

Brut Blanc de Blancs Champagne NV • $30 • (12/31/90) • **85**

Brut Blanc de Blancs Champagne Cuvée Malakoff 1985: Vibrant and exotic. Lots of fresh and mysterious fruit in this, with orange, fig, and apple character, high acidity and loads of bubbles on the finish. Drinkable now. • $45 • (12/31/93) • **92**

Brut Blanc de Blancs Champagne Cuvée Malakoff 1982 • $41 • (12/31/90) • **91**

Brut Blanc de Blancs Champagne Cuvée Malakoff 1979 • $30 • (05/31/87) • **89**

Brut Blanc de Noirs Champagne 1985 • $30 • (12/31/90) • **90**

Brut Blanc de Noirs Champagne 1983: Firm, crisp and elegant, a flavorful wine centered around lemon and toast aromas and flavors, sharply focused, long and lively. White pepper and apple flavors are particularly appealing. A classy wine. • $30 • (12/31/89) • **89**

Brut Champagne 1988: Loads of foam and a large bead. Rather simple and short with some pear character, and fruity, but very light and thin. Tannic. Drink now. • $35 • (12/31/93) • **79**

Brut Champagne NV • $26 • (12/31/91) • **86**

Brut Rosé Champagne 1983: Firm and elegant, with spice and cherry aromas and flavors, a touch of smoke and a lively texture to make it interesting. One of the best of the vintage. 20,000 cases made. • $30 • (12/31/89) • **90**

Brut Rosé Champagne 1979 • $16 • (12/16/85) • **79**

BEAUMONT DES CRAYERES

Brut Blanc de Blancs Champagne Nostalgie 1985: A big, open and welcoming Champagne with lots of vanilla, apple and pear aromas and flavors. Full-bodied and rather round with a long, flavorful finish. Drinkable now. • $NA • (12/31/93) • **88**

Brut Champagne Cuvée Prestige NV • $NA • (12/31/91) • **82**

Brut Champagne Cuvée Réserve NV • $NA • (12/31/91) • **91**

Brut Champagne Nostalgie 1987: Strong, muscular fizz with intriguing aromas and flavors of smoke and fruit, quietly foamy, good acidity and a long finish. Drink now. • $NA • (12/31/93) • **86**

BEAUMONT, CHÂTEAU

Haut-Médoc 1995: Offers some nice red berry and cedar flavors, although new wood dominates the fruit now and imparts an overall lean character on the finish. • $NA • (05/15/96) • **80-84** (BT)

Haut-Médoc 1994: Attractive roasted nut and berry aromas and flavors, medium body, fine tannins and a medium finish. • $NA • (06/30/95) • **80-84** (BT)

Haut-Médoc 1993: Some decent currant and black cherry, but it's awfully dry and has a whiff of paper that's distracting. Bottle sickness? Tasted twice, with consistent notes. 35,000 cases made. • $13 • (01/31/96) • **79**

Haut-Médoc 1992: Some cherry character but rather light and diluted. Try now. • $11 • **76**

Haut-Médoc 1991: Attractive and aromatic with herbal and vanilla character, but light and having a slightly dry finish. • $11 • (03/31/94) • **77**

Haut-Médoc 1990: Extremely ripe and raisiny, with baked fruit, coffee flavors and big, soft tannins. A little overdone for us. Drinkable now. 30,000 cases made. • $13 • (03/31/93) • **80**

Haut-Médoc 1989 • $14 • (03/15/92) • **82**

Haut-Médoc 1988 • $15 • (07/15/91) • **82**

Haut-Médoc 1986 • $9 • (06/30/89) • **84**

Haut-Médoc 1985 • $14 • (04/30/88) • **74**

Haut-Médoc 1982 • $18 • (08/31/92) • **87**

BEAUREGARD, CHÂTEAU

Pomerol 1995: Pretty blackberry and vanilla aromas and flavors. Medium in body, medium-velvety tannins and a medium-chewy finish. • $NA • (05/15/96) • **85-89** (BT)

Pomerol 1994: Unctuous and seductive, full-bodied, with smooth, ripe tannins. Moderate intensity in its fruit and spicy, oaky character. Delicious and round on the finish. It just lacks the length to make it outstanding. • $20 • (05/15/96) • **85-89** (BT)

Pomerol 1993: Well made, delicious, medium-bodied, showing harmony between oak and fruit. Good amount of tannin and a sweet-tasting finish. Try in 1998. 4,167 cases made. • $26 • (01/31/96) • **87**

Pomerol 1988 • $36 • (07/31/91) • **90**

Pomerol 1986 • $24 • (06/15/89) • **87**

Pomerol 1982 • $23 Ⓐ • (08/31/92) • **87**

BEAUREGARD, CHÂTEAU DE

Coteaux du Languedoc 1989 • $5 • (12/15/91) BB • **81**

Coteaux du Languedoc 1986 • $3 • (05/31/88) BB • **85**

Pouilly-Fuissé 1994: Fat, rich and somewhat unfocused, showing a truffle, buttery and honeyed character that is seductive but doesn't quite pull through on the short finish. Drinkable now. From J. Burrier. 2,416 cases made. • $23 • (05/31/96) • **80**

Pouilly-Fuissé 1993: A middle-of-the-road Pouilly, offering modest fruit and a diluted finish. Try now. • $18 • (05/15/95) • **74**

BEAURENARD, DOMAINE DE

Châteauneuf-du-Pape 1991: Rings true for Châteauneuf-du-Pape, with its leathery, earthy edge, but shows cherry and plum flavors underneath and drinks OK. Ready now through 1997. Tasted twice, with consistent notes. 9,500 cases made. • $19 • (06/15/93) • **82**

Châteauneuf-du-Pape 1990: Firm in texture, with focused black cherry, blackberry and black pepper aromas and flavors, well-integrated tannins and lots of fruit echoing on the finish. Balanced and flavorful, drinkable now. 9,500 cases made. • $19 • (11/15/92) • **90**

Châteauneuf-du-Pape 1989 • $21 • (10/15/91) • **86**

Châteauneuf-du-Pape 1988 • $20 • (10/15/91) • **89**

Châteauneuf-du-Pape 1986 • $24 • (10/15/91) • **88**

Châteauneuf-du-Pape 1985 • $20 • (10/15/91) • **87**

Châteauneuf-du-Pape 1983 • $20 • (10/15/91) • **87**

Châteauneuf-du-Pape 1982 • $9 • (04/01/85) BB • **85**

Châteauneuf-du-Pape 1981 • $20 • (10/15/91) • **88**

Châteauneuf-du-Pape White 1991 • $21 • (04/15/93) • **82**

Châteauneuf-du-Pape White 1990 • $25 • (10/15/91) • **86**

Côtes du Rhône 1991 • $10 • (06/15/93) • **83**

Côtes du Rhône 1990 • $10 • (04/15/93) • **78**

Côtes du Rhône 1989 • $10 • (11/15/92) • **78**

BEAUSEJOUR-DUFFAU-LAGARROSSE, CHÂTEAU

St.-Emilion 1989 • $44 • (03/15/92) • **91**

St.-Emilion 1988 • $28 Ⓐ • (04/30/91) • **87**

St.-Emilion 1986 • $34 • (06/30/89) • **91**

St.-Emilion 1982 • $30 • (08/31/92) • **88**

St.-Emilion 1970 • $40 • (05/15/93) • **84**

BEAUSEJOUR, CHÂTEAU

Côtes de Castillon 1986 • $5 • (06/15/89) BB • **80**

St.-Emilion 1995: Well-crafted and that builds on your palate. Medium in body, ripe fruit and firm tannins. Long finish. Almost outstanding. • $NA • (05/15/96) • **85-89** (BT)

St.-Emilion 1994: Lovely chocolate and berry aromas and flavors. Medium in body, velvety tannins and a long finish. • $NA • (05/15/96) • **85-89** (BT)

St.-Emilion 1993: A joy to drink. Plenty of pleasant berry and cherry aromas and flavors and a hint of cocoa. Medium in body, fine tannins and long, fresh finish. Drinkable now. • $30 • (01/31/96) • **87**

St.-Emilion 1992: Firm and crisp young red featuring dried cherry and berry aromas and flavors, medium-to-light body, medium tannins and light finish. Drinkable now. • $7 • (04/15/95) • **80**

St.-Emilion 1990: Wild, exciting and classy, with round, polished texture and intense smoky, vanilla, grapey aromas and flavors. This property is really coming on strong. Drinkable in 1997. 3,000 cases made. • $50 • (03/31/93) • **95**

St.-Emilion 1961: A very corky bottle. • $NA • (04/30/96) • **55**

BEAUVOLAGE

Brut Blanc de Blancs Touraine Réserve 1989 • $24 • (01/31/92) • **83**
Brut Rosé Touraine Réserve NV • $29 • (01/31/92) • **84**
Brut Touraine Réserve 1989 • $24 • (01/31/92) • **84**
Brut Vouvray Suprême Cuvée Comtesse Anne 1985 • $39 • (01/31/92) • **80**
Cuvée Rouge et Noir Haut Poitou 1985 • $35 • (01/31/92) • **81**

BECKER, J.

Brut Blanc de Blancs Crémant d'Alsace Méthode Traditionelle NV: Rounder and creamier than many Alsace sparklers, this shows toasty, smoky notes to complement the apple and melon flavors. It's bold and assertive, with full body. 1,200 cases made. • $14 • (11/15/94) • **86**

Pinot Blanc Alsace 1992: A feather-pillow of a wine, soft and generous. Apple and lime flavors are delicate and light, appealing without much structure. 3,000 cases made. • $10 • (11/15/94) • **82**

Riesling Alsace 1992: Lemon and grapefruit are the dominant flavors in this light, keen white. It's very dry and a bit tart, light-bodied but nervy. Try with grilled fish. 2,000 cases made. • $11 • (11/15/94) • **83**

BEL-AIR, CHÂTEAU

Pomerol 1961: A good wine that's hanging in there with a firm, slightly tart texture, mature, roasted flavors and a short finish. Drink now. • $24 • (04/30/96) • **84**

BEL-AIR, CHÂTEAU DE

Lalande-de-Pomerol 1985 • $18 • (09/30/88) • **85**

BEL AIR, CHÂTEAU

Entre-Deux-Mers 1994: Lovely, delicate honey, grassy, vanilla aromas and flavors, medium-bodied, round and a flavorful finish. • $9 • (05/31/95) • **84**

Entre-Deux-Mers 1983: A wine slightly on its way down now. It shows cedar, ash, tobacco character, medium body and a light, slightly dry finish. Drink now. • $NA • **83**

Entre-Deux-Mers 1981: Very evolved color with leather, chestnut, cherry aromas and flavors. Light and delicate with a fresh finish but slightly astringent and diluted on finish. • $NA • **80**

BEL AIR, CHÂTEAU

Haut-Médoc 1988 • $15 • (04/30/91) • **85**
Haut-Médoc 1986 • $9 • (11/15/89) BB • **88**
Haut-Médoc 1985 • $5 • (03/15/88) BB • **80**
Haut-Médoc 1983 • $6 • (12/31/86) • **83**
Haut-Médoc 1981 • $6 • (05/01/84) • **72**

BEL EVEQUE, CHÂTEAU

Corbières 1991: Deep in color and rich in flavor, with a smooth texture and full body. It turns earthy on the finish. 4,800 cases made. • $12 • (02/28/95) • **82**

BEL-ORME-TRONQUOY-DE-LALANDE, CHÂTEAU

Haut-Médoc 1995: Rather attractive, bright, red berry notes. Vivid and fresh. Medium in body, it lacks a bit of depth, but the flavors are pretty. • $NA • (05/15/96) • **85-89** (BT)

Haut-Médoc 1994: Decent tobacco, cherry, berry character, but the finish is lean and hard. Could move up a notch next year. • $NA • **75-79** (BT)

Key: SS—Spectator Selection. CS—Cellar Selection. BB—Best Buy. $NA—Price not available. (BT)—Barrel tasting. Ⓐ—Auction Price.
Dates in parentheses represent the issues in which the ratings were published.

BELAIR, CHÂTEAU

St.-Emilion 1995: Beautifully crafted, rich, unctuous vanilla, spice, chocolate and ripe fruit character. Full-bodied, adding loads of tannins. • $NA • (05/15/96) • **85-89** (BT)

St.-Emilion 1994: Pleasant and light, showing some pretty cherry, plum and mint flavors. Short and a touch diluted on the finish. • $NA • (06/30/95) • **80-84** (BT)

St.-Emilion 1993: Soft and delicious, harmonious, quite light-bodied, showing anise, cherry and mocha flavors and supple tannins. Drinkable now. • $36 • (01/31/96) • **81**

St.-Emilion 1990: Offers plenty of floral, berry and rose aromas and flavors, medium-full tannins and a long, fresh finish. Drinkable in 1997. 4,000 cases made. • $35 • (03/31/93) • **90**

St.-Emilion 1989 • $37 • (03/15/92) • **89**
St.-Emilion 1986 • $26 • (03/31/90) • **82**

St.-Emilion 1985: Pretty, well crafted wine with strawberry, cherry flavors, medium body and a delicious finish. Drinkable now. • $NA • **86**

St.-Emilion 1982 • $39 Ⓐ • (08/31/92) • **92**
St.-Emilion 1970 • $49 • (05/15/93) • **88**

St.-Emilion 1961: Mature but lively, showing spicy, cedary, herbal flavors and modest fruit on a firm structure of tannins and acidity. Well balanced and very good to drink now through 2000. • $68 • (04/30/96) • **87**

St.-Emilion Grand Cru Classé 1990: Beautifully focused and balanced, with an ethereal intermingling of ripe fruit, full silky tannins and long, smoky finish. There's plenty of new oak here, but it's still fresh and elegant. • $45 • **93**

BELAIR-LAFAGE, CHÂTEAU

Côtes du Rhône Cuvée Privilège 1991 • $6 • (04/15/93) BB • **84**

BELCIER, CHÂTEAU DE

Côtes de Castillon 1990: Bright and vivid cherry and berry aromas and flavors are appealing in this light wine, with medium tannins and a silky finish. Drink now. • $NA • (03/31/93) • **84**

Côtes de Castillon 1985 • $5 • (06/30/88) • **76**

BELGRAVE, CHÂTEAU

Haut-Médoc 1995: A good red with a minty, earthy berry character. Good tannins and a silky finish. • $NA • (05/15/96) • **85-89** (BT)

Haut-Médoc 1994: Very extracted style presenting loads of tannins and fruit. Full in body and tough, perhaps a little coarse. Almost outstanding. • $NA • (06/30/95) • **85-89** (BT)

Haut-Médoc 1993: Some simple, pleasant cherry and earth character, medium body and tannins and short finish. Drinkable now. • $20 • (01/31/96) • **81**

Haut-Médoc 1991: A lanky wine with very pretty black cherry and toasted oak flavors, couched in fine tannins. • $14 • (03/31/94) • **80**

Haut-Médoc 1988 • $28 • (07/31/91) • **79**
Haut-Médoc 1986 • $16 • (03/31/90) • **81**

BELIN, JULES

Nuits-St.-Georges Les St.-Georges 1943 • $NA • (08/31/90) • **91**

BELLAND, ADRIEN

Corton Grèves 1982 • $17 • (09/01/85) • **87**
Santenay Comme 1987 • $22 • (11/15/90) • **78**
Santenay Comme 1982 • $25 • (08/01/85) CS • **91**

BELLAND, ROGER

Chassagne-Montrachet Morgeot-Clos Pitois 1994: Chewy, rich crème brûlée, toasted coconut, pear and citrus combination. Of medium-to-full body, this *premier cru* packs good flavors that stay on the lingering finish. Drinkable now. 250 cases made. • $NA • (05/31/96) • **86**

Puligny-Montrachet Champ Gain 1994: Ripe and fat, delivering lots of apple, fig and date notes. Full in body and flavor, it tastes just a bit rough, caramelized and hot on the finish. Better in 1998. 200 cases made. • $NA • (05/31/96) • **85**

BELLE PERE & FILS

Crozes-Hermitage 1990 • $20 • (02/28/93) • **90**
Crozes-Hermitage Les Pierrelles 1991 • $17 • (05/31/94) • **84**
Hermitage 1991: Ripe berry, chocolate and meaty flavors mingle in this muscular yet gentle wine. This is concentrated and chewy. Drink now. Tasted twice. • $40 • (05/31/94) • **90**
Hermitage 1990: Broad, fleshy, spicy and seductive, this smooth-textured wine offers layers of currant, raspberry, plum, chocolate and violet aromas and flavors. Silky enough to drink now, but has enough stuffing to improve through 1997 to 2000. 200 cases made. • $46 • (04/15/93) • **93**

BELLEGRAVE-VAN DER VOORT, CHÂTEAU

Pauillac 1989 • $20 • (09/15/93) • **85**
Pauillac 1988 • $20 • (08/31/91) • **83**
Pauillac 1986 • $19 • (10/31/91) • **80**

BELLERIVE, CHÂTEAU

Bordeaux Supérieur 1985 • $7 • (11/15/87) • **70**
Bordeaux Supérieur 1982 • $8 • (12/16/85) • **72**
Médoc 1986 • $4 • (02/15/89) • **79**

BELLEVUE LA FORET, CHÂTEAU

Côtes du Frontonnais 1985 • $6 • (11/15/87) • **72**

BELLEVUE-FIGEAC, CHÂTEAU

St.-Emilion 1993: Light and fresh but rather weedy, offering dried herb and red fruit character. Soft and easy to drink now. • $28 • (01/31/96) • **79**

BENJAMIN DE BEAUREGARD, LE

Pomerol 1991: Light and herbal with a chocolate flavor, but very diluted on the finish. • $12 • (03/31/94) • **75**

BERARD PERE & FILS

Côte-Rôtie Cuvée Prestige 1986 • $29 • (08/31/92) • **80**
Crozes-Hermitage Cuvée Prestige 1989 • $15 • (08/31/92) • **71**
Hermitage Cuvée Prestige 1986 • $29 • (08/31/92) • **72**

BERGAT, CHÂTEAU

St.-Emilion 1991: Simple and attractive with a good core of fruit and silky tannins. • $13 • (03/31/94) • **80**
St.-Emilion 1990: A wine of moderation, with lovely earthy, tobacco, berry aromas and flavors and medium tannins. Drinkable now. 1,100 cases made. • $19 • (03/31/93) • **86**

BERLIQUET, CHÂTEAU

St.-Emilion 1983 • $12 • (12/31/86) • **90**

BERLOUP

Coteaux du Languedoc 1992 • $9 • (03/15/94) • **80**

BERNADOTTE, CHÂTEAU

Pauillac 1987 • $20 • (11/30/89) • **79**
Pauillac 1986 • $20 • (11/30/89) • **92**
Pauillac 1985 • $19 • (03/31/88) • **89**
Pauillac 1983 • $14 • (02/15/87) • **90**

BERNARD, DOMAINE MICHEL

Côtes du Rhône Domaine de la Serrière 1987 • $7 • (03/15/91) • **77**
Côtes du Rhône Les Domaniaes 1993: A tired-tasting, simple red with stale aromas and thin body. Tasted twice, with consistent notes. 5,000 cases made. • $6 • (12/31/95) • **68**

BERNARD, DOMAINE PAUL

Fleurie Red 1990 • $13 • (10/31/91) • **87**

BERNARD, GUY

Côte-Rôtie 1988 • $30 • (10/15/90) • **78**

BERTAGNA

Chambertin 1991: Light and chewy, a crisp, straightforward wine that offers modest strawberry and spice aromas and flavors, finishing tannic enough to need until 1997. • $NA • (01/31/94) • **85**
Clos St.-Denis 1993: This shows loads of wild berry, mushroom and smoke character. Full- to medium-bodied, sporting fine tannins and a long, toasted oak finish. Better in 2000. • $71 • (05/15/96) • **90**
Clos de Vougeot 1993: Lovely, rich plum, berry and vanilla aromas and flavors, medium body, fine tannins, good acidity and long finish. Very good winemaking here. Try in 2000. • $90 • (05/15/96) • **88**
Clos de Vougeot 1991: Crisp and light, has a vaguely minty strawberry character and an austere, citrusy finish. • $NA • (01/31/94) • **77**
Nuits-St.-Georges Aux Murgers 1990: Compact but restrained, showing plenty of black cherry and tar aromas and flavors and round, ripe tannins. Try in 1997. • $NA • (12/15/92) • **89**
Nuits-St.-Georges Aux Murgers 1985 • $41 • (02/28/89) • **85**
Vosne-Romanée Les Beaux Monts Bas 1985 • $35 • (10/15/88) • **82**
Vougeot Clos de la Perrière 1993: A bit lean but some good, clean berry and cedar aromas and flavors, fine tannins and fresh finish. Better in 1998. • $58 • (05/15/96) • **86**
Vougeot Clos de la Perrière 1991: Crisp, light and diluted. Drinkable now. • $NA • (01/31/94) • **78**
Vougeot Clos de la Perrière 1990: An attractive wine that gives lovely plum and cherry intensity and plenty of ripe tannins. Drinkable now. • $NA • (12/15/92) • **85**
Vougeot Clos de la Perrière 1985 • $40 • (04/15/89) • **87**
Vougeot Les Crâs 1985 • $30 • (03/31/88) • **85**

BERTHEAU, DOMAINE

Bonnes Mares 1987 • $55 • (06/15/90) • **89**
Chambolle-Musigny 1987 • $25 • (06/15/90) • **80**
Chambolle-Musigny Les Amoureuses 1987 • $50 • (06/15/90) • **84**
Chambolle-Musigny Les Charmes 1987 • $35 • (06/15/90) • **81**

BERTINERIE, CHÂTEAU

Premières Côtes de Blaye Red 1988 • $10 • (07/15/90) • **85**

BESSIERE, DANIEL

Coteaux du Languedoc 1987 • $5 • (09/30/89) BB • **83**
Faugères 1987 • $6 • (09/15/89) • **73**
Minervois 1986 • $6 • (09/15/89) BB • **81**
St.-Chinian 1987 • $6 • (08/31/89) • **79**

BESSIN, JEAN-CLAUDE

Chablis 1992: The buttery aromas and flavors don't have much fruit to back them up, so it comes off as one-dimensional and thin despite the appealing texture. 2,000 cases made. • $18 • (11/15/94) • **79**

BEYCHEVELLE, CHÂTEAU

St.-Julien 1995: Sleek and racy with steely tannins and good fruit. Full-bodied but compact. Could use a bit more fruit to be outstanding—but very close. • $NA • (05/15/96) • **85-89** (BT)
St.-Julien 1994: Attractive and flavorful, with lovely currant and toasted oak notes mingling together, medium-to-full body, it delivers spice and sweet fruit in satisfying doses. Well-integrated tannins. • $21 • (05/15/96) • **85-89** (BT)
St.-Julien 1993: Rather hollow '93, offering some decent berry, cherry and mint flavors and silky tannins but lacking in body. Slightly disappointing for this estate. Drinkable now. 25,000 cases made. • $25 • (01/31/96) • **80**
St.-Julien 1992: Well-presented Bordeaux, showing berry and cherry aromas and flavors, medium body, fine tannins and a long, delicious finish. Drinkable now. • $23 • (04/15/95) • **82**
St.-Julien 1991: A well-made, sexy wine that delivers lovely aromas of violet, smoke and blackberry. Stands out among the 1991s with its silky texture and good intensity. • $25 • (03/31/94) • **85**
St.-Julien 1990: Beautifully integrated, with sweet fruit, silky tannins and crisp acidity. Lovely raspberry and tobacco character on the finish, but it's a little light. Drink after 1996. 25,000 cases made. • $34 • (03/31/93) • **87**
St.-Julien 1989 • $47 Ⓐ • (03/15/92) • **95**
St.-Julien 1988 • $26 Ⓐ • (04/30/91) • **93**
St.-Julien 1987 • $29 • (05/15/90) • **79**
St.-Julien 1986 • $41 Ⓐ • (05/31/89) • **93**
St.-Julien 1985: Stylish wine with vanilla, spicy, cherry aromas and flavors, very silky texture and a long vanilla finish. Drink now or hold. • $45 • (10/15/94) • **91**
St.-Julien 1984 • $24 • (05/15/87) • **78**
St.-Julien 1983: Very fresh and clean wine but rather lean with berry fruit character, medium body and firm tannins. Drink now. • $NA • **84**
St.-Julien 1982 • $62 Ⓐ • (08/31/92) • **89**
St.-Julien 1981: A little past its prime but some rich, herbal, berry character. Soft and delicate on finish. • $27 • **80**
St.-Julien 1979 • $23 Ⓐ • (10/15/89) • **92**
St.-Julien 1978 • $28 Ⓐ • (12/31/89) • **86**
St.-Julien 1971 • $44 • (12/31/89) • **85**
St.-Julien 1970 • $39 Ⓐ • (05/15/93) • **90**
St.-Julien 1967 • $37 • (12/31/89) • **83**
St.-Julien 1962 • $40 Ⓐ • (11/30/87) • **95**
St.-Julien 1961: Depth of flavor makes this firmly textured wine special. It has enticing earthy, tobaccolike aromas, ripe fruit flavors, just enough tannin and a lingering finish. Still cruising, so drink through 2005. • $134 • (04/30/96) • **89**
St.-Julien 1959 • $102 Ⓐ • (10/15/90) • **80**
St.-Julien 1948 • $175 • (12/31/89) • **92**
St.-Julien 1945: Looks and tastes old and fragile, still showing some lovely floral and strawberry notes. A little drying but still sound. • $380 • **82**
St.-Julien 1929 • $232 Ⓐ • (12/31/89) • **95**

BEYER, LEON

Gewürztraminer Alsace 1993: Exuberant floral and spicy aromas are matched by full body and strong fruit flavors in this classic Gewürztraminer. Distinctive, almost meaty in character, and long on the finish. 6,000 cases made. • $15 • (11/15/94) • **86**
Gewürztraminer Alsace 1992: Dry, full-bodied and packed with spice, rose petal and apricot flavors that are well defined and long-lasting on the finish. Balanced, fresh and assertive in style. 6,000 cases made. • $15 • (11/15/94) • **87**
Gewürztraminer Alsace Cuvée des Comtes d'Eguisheim 1993: Very aromatic and full-bodied, showing lively acidity and delicious, intriguing, dry flavors of honey, pear, mineral and spice that linger nicely on the finish. 2,000 cases made. • $32 • (09/15/95) • **87**
Gewürztraminer Alsace Réserve 1993: The rose petal and grapefruit aromas give way to simpler fruit cocktail flavors and a soft finish. Good, but straightforward. 2,000 cases made. • $20 • (09/15/95) • **82**
Pinot Blanc Alsace 1994: Smooth, medium-bodied and well balanced, showing earth and mineral notes and an underlying lemony acidity. Not showy, but flavorful in a subtle way. 20,000 cases made. • $10 • (09/15/95) • **83**
Pinot Blanc Alsace 1993: There's good depth of flavor in this round, soft wine. Orange, melon and vanilla notes marry nicely and follow through on the long finish, the wine is well-balanced and fresh. 20,000 cases made. • $10 • (11/15/94) • **87**
Pinot Blanc Alsace 1991 • $14 • (06/15/93) • **81**
Riesling Alsace 1993: Subdued flavors of apricot, grapefruit and lime really expand as you sip, and the lively acidity make this a good quality, refreshing Riesling. 6,000 cases made. • $14 • (11/15/94) • **85**
Riesling Alsace 1992: An intriguing blend of citrus and mineral flavors, with an earthy edge that adds depth. It's light-bodied, but has intensity and nerve, assertive acidity wants food for balance. 6,000 cases made. • $14 • (11/15/94) • **85**
Riesling Alsace Cuvée des Comtes d'Eguisheim 1993: A bone-dry Riesling showing dried apricot and smoke aromas, lemon flavors and taut, lean texture. It's appetizing and nicely austere. 300 cases made. • $33 • (09/15/95) • **84**
Tokay Pinot Gris Alsace 1993: This has lots of body yet not much flavor. Acceptable quality, but simple. 10,000 cases made. • $13 • (09/15/95) • **77**
Tokay Pinot Gris Alsace 1992: Lean, with hints of bitterness and earth on the palate, this wine offers smoke and herbal flavors, distinctive and bracing but a bit austere. It's smooth and quite crisp. 6,000 cases made. • $14 • (11/15/94) • **83**

BICHERON, DOMAINE DU

Blanc de Blancs Crémant de Bourgogne NV • $12 • (03/31/90) • **84**

BICHOT, ALBERT

Aloxe-Corton 1983 • $18 • (11/30/86) • **68**
Beaune 1988 • $15 • (08/31/90) • **82**
Beaune Bressandes 1986 • $24 • (07/31/88) • **80**
Beaune Hospices de Beaune Cuvée Guigone-de-Salins 1989 • $68 • (01/31/92) • **83**
Beaune Teurons 1992: Shows very light, floral, stemmy flavors more than fruit. Drinkable now. • $NA • (12/15/94) • **77**
Bourgogne Le Bourgogne Bichot Pinot Noir 1985 • $8 • (11/15/87) • **81**
Bourgogne Château de Dracy Pinot Noir 1989 • $9 • (06/15/92) • **82**
Bourgogne Château de Dracy Pinot Noir 1988 • $8 • (02/28/90) • **68**
Bourgogne Château de Dracy Pinot Noir 1986 • $6 • (12/31/88) • **76**
Bourgogne Château de Montpatey Pinot Noir 1989 • $10 • (06/15/92) BB • **85**
Bourgogne Croix St.-Louis Pinot Noir 1989 • $9 • (06/15/92) BB • **83**
Bourgogne Croix St.-Louis Pinot Noir 1986 • $6 • (10/31/88) • **77**
Bourgogne Pinot Noir 1993: Quite satisfying for immediate consumption, sporting relatively ripe fruit flavors. A touch of burning on the finish keeps it from scoring higher. • $12 • (11/15/95) • **82**
Brouilly 1984 • $7 • (02/01/86) • **81**
Chablis Premier Cru 1994: Honeyed, sweet and easy to appreciate, this is quite delicious now. Shows some ripe pear and a citrus touch. Drinkable now. Tasted twice, with consistent notes. 1,083 cases made. • $21 • (05/31/96) • **84**
Chassagne-Montrachet 1994: Straightforward and lean. Some decent fruit flavors and good acidity, but it seems short and a bit diluted. 475 cases made. • $NA • (05/31/96) 78 • **78**
Chassagne-Montrachet Morgeots 1992: Earthy, woodsy aromas and flavors never cut past the chewy tannins. This is lean, with a little currant sneaking in on the finish. • $NA • (12/15/94) • **77**
Chassagne-Montrachet Premier Cru 1993: Clean and crisp vanilla, honey, cream and apple aromas and flavors. Slightly diluted finish. • $NA • (05/15/95) • **80**
Châteauneuf-du-Pape 1988 • $13 • (09/30/90) • **84**

Key: SS—Spectator Selection. CS—Cellar Selection. BB—Best Buy. $NA—Price not available. (BT)—Barrel tasting. Ⓐ—Auction Price.
Dates in parentheses represent the issues in which the ratings were published.

Châteauneuf-du-Pape 1987 • $10 • (03/15/90) • **82**
Châteauneuf-du-Pape 1986 • $9 • (11/30/88) • **86**
Châteauneuf-du-Pape 1985 • $12 • (11/15/87) • **86**
Corton Hospices de Beaune Cuvée Docteur-Peste 1989 • $100 • (01/31/92) • **88**
Corton-Charlemagne 1993: Polished and austere, delivering significant fruit and spice flavors in an elegant package. But it's as hard as nails now and could use a bit more generosity. • $NA • **85**
Côte de Beaune-Villages 1993: Some very light plum and tobacco character but light-bodied and drying on the finish. Drinkable now. • $15 • (11/15/95) • **74**
Côte de Nuits-Villages 1993: Light and simple with some decent berry and cedar aromas and flavors but not much else. Drinkable now. • $15 • (11/15/95) • **77**
Côtes de Duras 1989 • $6 • (03/31/92) BB • **81**
Côtes du Rhône 1987 • $3 • (11/15/88) • **72**
Côtes du Rhône 1985 • $5 • (12/15/87) • **75**
Côtes du Rhône Château d'Orsan 1989 • $7 • (06/15/92) • **74**
Echézeaux 1993: Intensely aromatic featuring dried fruit and plum character, medium body, fine tannins and fresh, crisp finish. Better in 1999. • $NA • (11/15/95) • **85**
Gevrey-Chambertin 1993: Fresh and easy, offering pleasant vanilla and dried cherry character, medium-to-light body, light tannins and fresh finish. Drink on release. • $30 • (11/15/95) • **81**
Gevrey-Chambertin 1983 • $13 • (02/01/86) • **58**
Gevrey-Chambertin Domaine du Clos Frantin 1992: Diluted and watery, with some modest red berry flavors. Short and tannic finish. • $NA • (12/15/94) • **78**
Grands Echézeaux Domaine du Clos Frantin 1993: Deep and ripe but also firm and hard at this stage, showing little charm. Tannic, but you can taste the sweetness of fruit underneath. Try after 2000. • $NA • **88**
Mâcon-Lugny 1994: Odd wine, tasting like cider. Has some fruit cocktail flavors and an astringent finish. Drink if you must. 2,166 cases made. • $NA • (05/31/96) 74 • **72**
Mâcon-Villages 1994: Hard to cozy up to this green, hard, herbal and tough white. Too lean for us. 5,000 cases made. • $10 • (05/31/96) • **75**
Meursault 1994: Round and supple, but also a bit hollow from lack of fruit. Hints of chestnut, coffee and spice. Drinkable now. 1,000 cases made. • $25 • (05/31/96) • **78**
Meursault 1993: Steely apple, pear, melon character. Medium in body, fresh acidity. Limited distribution. • $20 • (05/15/95) • **80**
Meursault Charmes 1993: Rather lean and light-bodied, demonstrating a strange character of mineral and peppermint, firm acidity. Limited distribution. • $30 • (05/15/95) • **77**
Monthelie 1993: Pretty black cherry flavor, medium body and a chewy texture on the finish. Drink on release. • $NA • (11/15/95) • **84**
Monthelie Hospices de Beaune Cuvée Lebelin 1985 • $52 • (10/15/87) • **86**
Nuits-St.-Georges Les Boudots Hospices de Nuits Cuvée Mesny de Boissea 1986 • $36 • (03/31/90) • **77**
Nuits-St.-Georges Les Maladières Hospices de Nuits 1986 • $33 • (02/28/89) • **75**
Nuits-St.-Georges Les Maladières Hospices de Nuits Cuvée Grangier 1986 • $30 • (03/31/90) • **80**
Nuits-St.-Georges Les Vignerondes Hospices de Nuits Cuvée 1986 • $40 • (02/28/89) • **85**
Pommard 1988 • $25 • (08/31/90) • **87**
Pommard 1986 • $20 • (09/15/89) • **79**
Pommard 1983 • $19 • (09/15/86) • **83**
Pommard Le Clos du Pavillon 1993: Some pretty fruit character on nose and palate but slightly diluted, adding an herbal edge to the aftertaste. Astringent. • $26 • (11/15/95) • **78**
Pommard Hospices de Beaune Cuvée Cyrot-Chaudron 1989 • $70 • (01/31/92) • **86**
Pommard Hospices de Beaune Cuvée Cyrot-Chaudron 1985 • $60 • (10/31/88) • **91**
Pouilly-Fuissé 1993: Green, herbal and tart, it tastes more like acid juice than white Burgundy. Modest fruit, drink if you must. 1,000 cases imported to U.S. (limited distribution). 1,000 cases made. • $17 • (05/15/95) • **72**
Puligny-Montrachet 1994: Light and diluted, showing a cardboard, watery character. 1,000 cases made. • $26 • (05/31/96) • **70**
Puligny-Montrachet Les Folatières 1993: Clean and crisp green apple, pear and basil flavors, quite steely in texture. Medium body and tart finish. Limited distribution. • $32 • (05/15/95) • **83**
St.-Véran 1994: Straightforward white, showing tons of citrusy flavors but not enough fruit concentration. While lean, it should still be a good match with shellfish. Drinkable now. 1,083 cases made. • $NA • (05/31/96) • **80**
Santenay 1986 • $12 • (10/15/89) • **78**
Santenay Les Gravières 1985 • $15 • (03/15/88) • **66**
Savigny-lès-Beaune 1986 • $10 • (10/15/89) • **81**
Savigny-lès-Beaune Hospices de Beaune Cuvée Fouquerand 1988 • $39 • (01/31/92) • **78**
Vin Rouge NV • $3 • (08/31/89) • **75**
Volnay 1988 • $25 • (08/31/90) • **84**
Volnay 1983 • $18 • (09/15/86) • **68**
Volnay Clos des Chânes 1992: Crisp and simple, showing enough berry flavor to balance the slightly chewy tannins. • $NA • (12/15/94) • **81**
Volnay Hospices de Beaune Cuvée Blondeau 1988 • $60 • (06/15/92) • **87**
Volnay Hospices de Beaune Cuvée Blondeau 1985 • $53 • (04/30/89) • **88**
Volnay Hospices de Beaune Cuvée Blondeau 1982 • $26 • (08/01/84) SS • **92**
Volnay Premier Cru 1993: Very clean and fresh dried cherry, wet earth and mineral flavors, medium-to-light body and a light finish. Drinkable now. • $25 • (11/15/95) • **83**
Vosne-Romanée Les Beaux Monts 1988 • $34 • (07/15/90) • **87**
Vosne-Romanée Les Malconsorts Domaine du Clos Frantin 1993: Chewy, firm and tannic, delivering pretty currant, raspberry and licorice flavors, medium body and medium intensity. Should glow by 2000. • $NA • (11/15/95) • **87**
Volnay-Santenots 1986 • $22 • (10/31/89) • **77**

BILLAUD-SIMON

Chablis 1994: Charming and delicious, sporting ripe pear, melon, fig and spice flavors. Medium body. Acidity manages to keep it lively on the finish. • $18 • **85**
Chablis Fourchaume 1994: Splendid *premier cru*, rich yet restrained, full-bodied and packed with dried herb, grassy, wet earth, stony, mineral character. Long, graceful, silky, honeyed finish. Drinkable now or hold until 2000. Tasted twice. 200 cases made. • $NA • (05/31/96) • **89**
Chablis Fourchaume 1993: Perfumed apple, spice and pie crust notes. Medium body, firm acidity and short finish. • $24 • **82**
Chablis Les Clos 1994: Beautiful, concentrated mineral, lemon and ripe fruit flavors. Youthful, zesty, very fresh, full-bodied, with a round, supple and elegant texture. The stony, wet earth notes are superb. Silky yet intense finish. Try in 2000. 250 cases made. • $45 • (05/31/96) • **92**
Chablis Les Clos 1993: Some round character perks through while well-defined lemon, pear and melon flavors come into focus on the long, crisp finish. Drinkable now. • $43 • **83**
Chablis Les Preuses 1994: Corked. Tasted twice, and both times corked. 233 cases made. • $NA • (05/31/96) • **60**
Chablis Les Preuses 1993: Citrusy, full of lemon and grapefruit flavors, showing a hint of honey and pear on the tart finish. • $43 • **80**
Chablis Mont de Milieu 1994: Gorgeous, silky *premier cru*, caressing the palate with mineral, pear, apple and ripe tropical fruit complexity. Medium to full in body, it delivers a long, harmonious finish. Delicious now through 2000. 2,000 cases made. • $24 • (05/31/96) • **90**
Chablis Mont de Milieu 1993: Intense, racy straw, spice and mineral character. Medium-bodied and lots of fruit flavor. Drinkable now. • $23 • **86**
Chablis Montée de Tonnerre 1994: Well made, solid and very intense, exploding in citrus, fruit and herb flavors. Full-bodied and quite silky on the palate, it turns very crisp on aftertaste, which shows pretty honey peeking through. Better in 1999. 1,666 cases made. • $23 • (05/31/96) • **87**
Chablis Montée de Tonnerre 1993: Tough, hard and somewhat lean for us, offering loads of lemon, green apple and grapefruit flavors and a chalky finish. • $23 • **80**
Chablis Tête d'Or 1994: Nice and simple, this light-bodied, standard Chablis is crisp, showing a citrus, green apple and mineral character and a lively, tart finish. Drinkable now. 500 cases made. • $19 • (05/31/96) • **79**

Chablis Vaillons 1994: Amazingly intense. Medium body, citrus, mineral and fruit character and firm, crisp finish, but there is an undercurrent of stony, wet earth and honey notes. Try in 1999. Tasted twice. 2,333 cases made. • $22 • (05/31/96) • **86**

Chablis Vaillons 1993: Intense aromas of straw and grass, medium body, dried herbs, honey and a fresh finish. Incredibly tart. Drinkable now. • $23 • **80**

Chablis Vaudésir 1994: Lively and flavorful, a juicy, intense *grand cru* boasting good amounts of lemon, honey, mineral, pineapple and ripe pear notes. Medium body, firm structure, crisp, balanced and sweet-tasting finish. Cellar until 1999. 416 cases made. • $38 • (05/31/96) • **90**

Chablis Vaudésir 1993: Somewhat disjointed, offering a hint of honey, pine nut and green apple. Turns odd and metallic on the lean finish. Not very appealing. • $42 • (08/31/95) • **78**

BILLECART-SALMON

Brut Blanc de Blancs Champagne 1983: Tart, lean, crisp and well balanced, very intense and concentrated, sharp around the edges. Drinkable now. • $50 • (12/31/89) • **88**

Brut Blanc de Blancs Champagne 1982: Nutty, floral style with medium body, nutty, appley flavors, with become st ronger and deeper on the finish. More fruit than most, but very enjoyable. • $43 • (05/31/87) • **86**

Brut Champagne 1986: Well-proportioned yet muscular Champagne. This shows plenty of toasty, strawberry character, medium body and fresh acidity. Drink now. 6,000 cases made. • $45 • (12/31/93) • **88**

Brut Champagne 1983: Tart, crisp, lean and concentrated with sharply focused, well-balanced lemon, spice, cherry and vanilla-coconut notes that are quite pleasing. Full-bodied, with a sense of finesse. • $47 • (12/31/89) • **89**

Brut Champagne NV • $28 • (12/31/91) • **86**

Brut Rosé Champagne NV • $28 • (12/16/85) • **80**

BINET

Blanc de Blancs Champagne 1988: Rather light and simple, showing good apple and canned peaches character and a light foamy finish. Drink now. • $NA • (12/31/93) • **81**

Brut Champagne 1988: It develops on your palate as you taste it. Lots of character. Complex aromas and flavors of cinnamon, vanilla, and melons. Full-bodied yet refreshing. A good Champagne for food. Drinkable now. • $NA • (12/31/93) • **89**

BIROT, CHÂTEAU DE

Premières Côtes de Bordeaux 1990: Lean and herbal, evolving spicy leather and cedar notes. It's well integrated and smooth, but lacks richness and breadth. Drinkable now. • $10 • (05/15/94) • **82**

BISTON-BRILLETTE, CHÂTEAU

Moulis 1995: Has lovely fruit and mineral aromas and flavors, with fine tannins and a silky finish. Lovely balance. • $NA • (05/15/96) • **85-89** (BT)

BITOUZET, PIERRE

Aloxe-Corton Valozières 1990 • $NA • (12/15/92) • **88**

Aloxe-Corton Valozières 1989 • $28 • (11/30/92) • **82**

Aloxe-Corton Valozières 1986 • $19 • (08/31/90) • **78**

Bourgogne White 1993: Sharp, tongue-twisting, citrusy white, revealing green-bean, earth and grapefruit character. Lean finish. Try with seafood. • $NA • (05/15/95) • **73**

Chablis Beauroy 1994: Rich and ripe, a full-bodied *premier cru* Chablis that turns to apple cider and seems heavy-handed on the finish. Will fall apart soon, becoming tart and astringent. • $NA • (05/31/96) • **74**

Key: SS—Spectator Selection. CS—Cellar Selection. BB—Best Buy. $NA—Price not available. (BT)—Barrel tasting. Ⓐ—Auction Price.
Dates in parentheses represent the issues in which the ratings were published.

Corton-Charlemagne 1994: Balanced and supple, full-bodied and silky, coating the mouth with its fruit, honey and spice character. Of medium intensity, it lacks a touch of complexity for a *grand cru*. Drinkable now. 250 cases made. • $50 • (05/31/96) 86 • **86**

Corton-Charlemagne 1993: Full-throttle, full-bodied wine, generous with tropical and ripe fruit flavors, mineral and spice. The color is already turning a bit gold, and this has a terrific, velvety finish. Try in 1998. • $NA • (08/31/95) • **88**

Corton-Charlemagne 1992: Pure, focused, vivid and ripe, quite charming and fruity, offering excellent balance. Medium-bodied. • $52 • (08/31/94) • **89**

Corton-Charlemagne 1991 • $77 • (05/15/93) • **87**

Pommard Platières 1993: Firm and tannic with a stout backbone, but rather lean in flesh. Medium body and finish, adding a lightly fruity aftertaste. Better in 1999. • $40 • (11/15/95) • **84**

Savigny-lès-Beaune 1993: Not big but fine and fresh, showing good dried cherry character and delicate tannins. Drinkable now. • $25 • (11/15/95) • **83**

Savigny-lès-Beaune Les Goudelettes White 1993: Ripeness balances refreshing citrus flavors. A light- to medium-bodied white, offering delicate pear, orange-peel, apple and lime notes. Delicious finish. Drinkable now. • $NA • (05/15/95) • **83**

Savigny-lès-Beaune Les Goudelettes White 1992: Simple and straightforward, with the round texture of a good white, but so light on modest fruit flavors it seems diluted. 320 cases made. • $20 • (08/31/94) • **77**

Savigny-lès-Beaune Les Lavières 1993: Light, rather simple, straightforward fruit and earth character. Short and slightly diluted on the finish. • $30 • (11/15/95) • **76**

Savigny-lès-Beaune Les Lavières 1990: This beautiful Savigny offers plenty of crushed raspberry flavors and earth notes against a relatively firm background of supple tannins. Drinkable now. • $NA • (12/15/92) • **88**

Savigny-lès-Beaune Les Lavières 1986 • $15 • (03/31/90) • **87**

Savigny-lès-Beaune Les Lavières 1985 • $19 • (03/15/88) • **67**

Savigny-lès-Beaune Les Talmettes White 1993 : Very odd wine. A '93 *premier cru* that smells like oatmeal, earth and salted peanuts. Sharp and crisp. 250 cases made. • $NA • (05/31/96) 73 • **73**

BITOUZET-PRIEUR

Meursault Les Corbins 1993: Racy and clean lemon, mineral, apple and cream aromas and flavors, medium body, very fruity and firm and a fresh finish. Drinkable now. 292 cases made. • $35 • (05/15/95) • **89**

Volnay Clos des Chênes 1987 • $36 • (12/31/90) • **80**

Volnay Pituies 1985 • $36 • (07/31/88) • **91**

BIZE & FILS, SIMON

Aloxe-Corton Le Suchot 1993: An elegant, multidimensional red that smells fruity, ripe and slightly oaky, then melts on your palate, blending cherry and berry and slightly earthy flavors into a gentle but firm texture. Tempting now, but best in 1998. • $24 • (05/15/96) • **90**

Aloxe-Corton Le Suchot 1991 • $28 Ⓐ • (01/31/94) • **77**

Bourgogne Les Perrières 1990 • $17 • (12/15/92) • **87**

Savigny-lès-Beaune 1990: Very elegant, ripe, round and attractive, with plum, earth and currant notes and a medium-long finish. Drinkable now. 208 cases made. • $20 • (12/15/92) • **85**

Savigny-lès-Beaune Aux Fournaux 1993: Not deeply fruity, but cedary and woodsy in flavor and sturdy-textured. Firmly tannic on the finish. • $25 • (05/15/96) • **82**

Savigny-lès-Beaune Aux Fournaux 1990: Brightly flavored, with plummy blueberry and cherry notes. Very closed in, but the firm finish is juicy and fruity. Drinkable now. 400 cases made. • $28 • (12/15/92) • **89**

Savigny-lès-Beaune Aux Grands Liards 1993: A lighter, leaner style of Burgundy, offering attractive herbal, smoky, cherrylike flavors, good balance and moderate tannins. Drink now while it's fresh. • $19 • (05/15/96) • **84**

Savigny-lès-Beaune Aux Grands Liards 1992: Mature, simple, revealing basic cherry and tea flavors and weak, watery texture. Drink now if you like this style. • $20 • (06/15/95) • **78**

Savigny-lès-Beaune Aux Grands Liards 1991: Light, earthy and modestly fruity. Drinkable now. 300 cases made. • $21 Ⓐ • (01/31/94) • **75**

Savigny-lès-Beaune Aux Grands Liards 1990: Pretty floral and spice notes and superfine tannins. Should make for excellent drinking now. 417 cases made. • $22 • (12/15/92) • **87**

Savigny-lès-Beaune Aux Guettes 1991: Earthy, rubbery and slightly astringent, has little charm. 150 cases made. • $30 Ⓐ • (01/31/94) • **67**

Savigny-lès-Beaune Aux Guettes 1990: Juicy and ripe, with attractive cherry, plum and earth characteristics that won't overwhelm you, but the balance makes for a nice wine. Drinkable now. 170 cases made. • $33 • (12/15/92) • **86**

Savigny-lès-Beaune Aux Vergelesses 1991: Light and simple, offers modest cherry notes and an earthy, slightly tannic finish. Drinkable now. 600 cases made. • $28 Ⓐ • (01/31/94) • **80**

Savigny-lès-Beaune Aux Vergelesses 1990: Very flattering, with attractive toast and smoke characteristics and masses of firm tannins, but feels a shade light in the middle and on the finish. Drinkable now. 125 cases made. • $29 • (12/15/92) • **90**

Savigny-lès-Beaune Aux Vergelesses 1989 • $27 • (01/31/92) • **87**

Savigny-lès-Beaune Aux Vergelesses Premier Cru 1992: Mature already, featuring almost sweet flavors of cherry, tea and brown sugar that linger on the finish. Light in tannins and acidity. Drinkable now. • $24 • (05/15/95) • **84**

Savigny-lès-Beaune Les Bourgeots 1991: Simple, earthy and drying on the finish. 1,500 cases made. • $20 Ⓐ • (01/31/94) • **72**

Savigny-lès-Beaune Les Bourgeots 1989 • $19 • (01/31/92) • **85**

Savigny-lès-Beaune Les Fournaux 1991: Tough, earthy, leathery shoe polish aromas and flavors kill this for us. 250 cases made. • $25 • (01/31/94) • **60**

Savigny-lès-Beaune Les Fournaux Premier Cru 1992: Very rustic and earthy leather and barnyard aromas, tealike flavors and not much fruit. Dry texture, short finish. • $NA • (06/15/95) • **78**

Savigny-lès-Beaune Les Marconnets 1993: Lots of fresh, lively fruit flavors in this smooth-textured, moderately tannic and well-balanced Burgundy. Hints of spice give it complexity. Fine to drink now through 1998. • $25 • (05/15/96) • **86**

Savigny-lès-Beaune Les Marconnets 1992: Fruity and flavorful, yet also very tart. It's lively and crisp on the palate but finishes vegetal and leathery. • $24 • (06/15/95) • **82**

Savigny-lès-Beaune Les Marconnets 1991: Gamy, toasty flavors overshadow the modest black cherry flavor in this meaty wine. Drinkable now. 180 cases made. • $30 Ⓐ • (01/31/94) • **80**

Savigny-lès-Beaune Les Marconnets 1990: Clever winemaking went into producing this delightful Savigny, where the toasty, smoky notes balance the berry flavors. Has fine tannins and a medium finish. Drinkable now. 300 cases made. • $33 • (12/15/92) • **90**

BLACHON, ROGER

St.-Joseph 1993: Round and fruity, this is a pleasant, early-drinking wine with ripe black cherry flavors and black pepper accents, light tannins and a clean finish. 3,500 cases made. • $17 • (11/15/95) • **84**

St.-Joseph 1990 • $15 • (04/15/93) • **84**

BLAIN-GAGNARD

Bâtard-Montrachet 1992: Exotic, ripe and rich with fruit flavor, layered with peach, apricot and honey, almost like a late-harvest wine. It is bold and fruity, backing off a bit on the finish. Very good, but not our favorite style of white Burgundy. • $90 • (08/31/94) • **89**

Chassagne-Montrachet La Boudriotte 1994: Elegant and almost delicate, this well-made, medium-bodied '94 shows substantial tropical fruit, grapefruit, mineral and lemon flavors. Lovely finish. 375 cases made. • $45 • (05/31/96) • **85**

Chassagne-Montrachet La Boudriotte 1993: Textbook Chassagne, exhibiting pineapple, chalk and mineral aromas and flavors, medium-bodied and crisp. Delicious to drink now. • $NA • (05/15/95) • **85**

Chassagne-Montrachet La Boudriotte 1992: Simple and straightforward, with coarse texture and some modest apple cider flavors. • $35 • (08/31/94) • **76**

Chassagne-Montrachet Caillerets 1994: Very supple and seductive honey, cream, toasted coconut and mineral flavors. Full in body and delicious to drink now. Doesn't overwhelm us by its intensity, but who's complaining? 200 cases made. • $45 • (05/31/96) • **87**

Chassagne-Montrachet Caillerets 1992: Earthy, toasty aromas combine with vivid, aggressive fruit flavors for a lively but rangy white Burgundy. • $35 • (08/31/94) • **81**

Chassagne-Montrachet Clos St.-Jean 1994: Round and smooth, soft, medium in body and intensity, offering some tropical fruit, citrus, apple and cream character. Fun and delicious now, but not much staying power on the relatively short finish. 125 cases made. • $45 • (05/31/96) • **85**

Chassagne-Montrachet Morgeot 1994: Very balanced and supple, featuring some intense citrus, dried herb, honey and mineral quality. Fresh, focused, well made and full-bodied. Silky finish. Needs until 1999 to show it all. 350 cases made. • $45 • (05/31/96) 90 • **90**

Criots-Bâtard-Montrachet 1994: Elegant yet very ripe, this medium- to full-bodied white delivers some rather intense citrus, honey and pear flavors. Rich but focused. 100 cases made. • $95 • (05/31/96) 86 • **86**

BLANC, GEORGES

Blanc de Blancs NV • $9 • (12/31/87) • **83**

Mâcon-Azé Domaine d'Azenay 1993: Subtle, delicate touch of butter, mineral, spice, mint and nutmeg complexity and a very crisp, lemony, harmonious finish. Drinkable now. 3,542 cases made. • $12 • **85**

Mâcon-Azé Fleur d'Azenay 1993: Clean, crisp and straightforward Chardonnay-light, tight and austere. Green apple, citrus and a touch of butter character. 4,167 cases made. • $10 • **80**

BLANCHET, BERNARD

Pouilly-Fumé Les Champs des Plantes 1994: Smells like a late-harvest wine, then turns tart, herbal and earthy. Awkward. • $15 • (04/30/96) • **75**

BLANCHET, FRANCIS

Pouilly-Fumé 1993: Like a field of hay and wildflowers, this is sunny, aromatic and pure. It has a nice balance of ripeness and crisp acidity, with vibrant fruit and a clean finish. A good food wine. 900 cases made. • $12 • (11/15/95) • **87**

Pouilly-Fumé 1991 • $13 • (07/31/93) • **86**

BLANCK FRERES

Gewürztraminer Alsace 1994: Spicy and extremely perfumed with good litchi nut and baked apple flavors. Interesting and forceful, with an intense finish marked by clove and nutmeg. • $10 • (02/29/96) • **87**

Pinot Blanc Alsace 1994: This has some body, but not a lot of punch, with only modest green apple and flavors. • $10 • (02/29/96) • **78**

Riesling Alsace 1994: Fresh and lively, with nice apple, mint and pineapple flavors that linger on the finish. Satisfying and delicious, it has some body as well. • $10 • (02/29/96) • **85**

Tokay Pinot Gris Alsace 1994: Fairly rich, with good melon and green peach flavors, and a nice honeyed quality as well. Laced with a distinctive earthiness. Not for everyone, but still tasty. • $10 • (02/29/96) • **84**

BLANCK, DOMAINE PAUL

Gewürztraminer Alsace 1991 • $12 • (07/31/93) • **88**

Tokay Pinot Gris Alsace Graffreben 1991 • $9 • (07/31/93) • **82**

BLANQUETIER, MAISTRE

Brut Blanquette de Limoux Le Berceau NV • $9 • (04/15/90) • **81**

BLANQUETTE DE LIMOUX

Brut Blanc de Blancs Blanquette de Limoux Cuvée Réservée NV • $9 • (05/31/87) • **70**

BLIN, H.

Brut Champagne NV • $18 • (12/31/91) • **85**

BLOMAC, CHÂTEAU DE

Minervois Cuvée Tradition 1991: Supple and clean, this soft red shows raspberry, plum, toast and licorice flavors. It's drinking well now. • $7 • (06/30/94) • **82**

Minervois Cuvée Tradition 1988 • $6 • (12/31/91) BB • **82**

BOCARD, GUY

Meursault-Charmes Premier Cru 1992: Rich, ripe and luscious, a white Burgundy that's saturated with flavors of honey, almonds, pear and vanilla. The texture is smooth and thick, with lots of body. Turns lighter on the finish. • $36 • (05/15/95) • **86**

BOILLOT & FILS, LUCIEN

Bourgogne 1990 • $14 • (12/15/92) • **86**

Gevrey-Chambertin Les Cherbaudes 1993: Wonderful finesse and loads of dried cherry character here. Medium in body, fine tannins and crisp acidity. Sweet fruit on the finish. Drink in 1999. • $40 • (11/15/95) • **88**

Gevrey-Chambertin Les Cherbaudes 1991: A sharp beam of raspberry and floral flavors shines through this light, lean wine. Crisply tannic. Drinkable now. • $34 Ⓐ • (01/31/94) • **82**

Gevrey-Chambertin Les Cherbaudes 1990: A firm wine, with pretty plum, cherry and herb flavors, medium body and a focused finish. Drinkable now. 175 cases made. • $35 • (12/15/92) • **85**

Gevrey-Chambertin Les Cherbaudes 1987 • $25 • (05/31/90) • **85**

Gevrey-Chambertin Les Corbeaux 1993: Unusually full-bodied for this group, dark-colored with massive tannins and sensational currant, black cherry and wild berry flavors. Long, chewy finish. Definitely needs until after 2000. • $40 • (11/15/95) • **87**

Gevrey-Chambertin Les Corbeaux 1990: Vivid in color and flavor, this sharp-edged wine delivers focused raspberry, cherry, herb and earth characteristics and fresh acidity. Drinkable now. 156 cases made. • $33 • (12/15/92) • **88**

Nuits-St.-Georges Les Pruliers 1993: Straightforward plum and cherry flavors, medium body and medium tannins. Try in 1999. • $40 • (11/15/95) • **85**

Nuits-St.-Georges Les Pruliers 1991: Pleasant strawberry and cherry flavors make this firm, mildly chewy wine pleasant and appealing. Finishes harmonious. Drinkable now. • $36 Ⓐ • (01/31/94) • **83**

Nuits-St.-Georges Les Pruliers 1987 • $25 • (07/15/90) • **88**

Pommard Les Croix Noires 1991: Light and simple. The strawberry aromas have appeal, but the watery flavors fade quickly into astringency. • $30 Ⓐ • (01/31/94) • **75**

Pommard Les Fremiers 1993: Marvelous Pommard, featuring nice concentration of clean, pure, beautiful red berry flavor that cascades on the palate. A bit of chocolate and mocha on the finish. Great now, but try after 2000. • $38 • (11/15/95) • **91**

Volnay Les Angles 1991: Light in color and lean, a layer of tannin allows only a glimpse of the cedary berry character underneath. Try now, but it will always be delicate. • $30 Ⓐ • (01/31/94) • **80**

Volnay Les Angles 1990: Layered with cherry, tobacco, plum and chestnut flavors, this well-crafted red is no blockbuster, but is quite elegant and refined, with a medium-long finish. Drinkable now. 600 cases made. • $32 • (12/15/92) • **87**

Volnay Les Angles 1985 • $33 • (07/15/88) • **86**

Volnay Les Brouillards 1993: Aromatic but could use a little more on the palate. Attractive plum, fruit, vanilla and leaf aromas and flavors, medium body and tannins and short finish. Better in 1999. • $37 • (11/15/95) • **87**

Volnay Les Brouillards 1991: Crisp, light and modest in flavor. Raspberry and strawberry notes lurk under fine tannins. Drinkable now. • $28 Ⓐ • (01/31/94) • **81**

Key: SS—Spectator Selection. CS—Cellar Selection. BB—Best Buy. $NA—Price not available. (BT)—Barrel tasting. Ⓐ—Auction Price.
Dates in parentheses represent the issues in which the ratings were published.

Volnay Les Brouillards 1990: Fun and interesting. Tastes like a bowl of raspberries, with a captivating texture and a firm, appealing finish. Drinkable now. 375 cases made. • $32 • (12/15/92) • **90**

Volnay Les Caillerets 1993: Lots going on here, offering intense flavors of ripe raspberries and sliced plums. Medium-bodied with a solid core of fruit, medium-to-full tannins and velvety texture. Try in 2000. • $38 • (11/15/95) • **91**

BOILLOT, HENRI

Bourgogne 1985 • $13 • (12/31/88) • **76**

BOILLOT, JEAN

Beaune Clos du Roi 1992: Light, definitely tannic, but showing just enough berry and black cherry flavor to balance the tough edge. Best from 1997. • $29 • (12/15/94) • **79**

Beaune Clos du Roi 1991: Firm and almost fleshy, with a solid core of currant and berry aromas and flavors and a twang of vegetal, earthy notes to give it personality. Drinkable now. • $32 Ⓐ • (01/31/94) • **81**

Beaune Les Epenottes 1992: Simple and chewy, a sturdy red with modest black cherry and spice flavors. Drinkable now. • $29 • (12/15/94) • **80**

Beaune Les Epenottes 1991: Light, firm and bright, with pretty raspberry, earth and mushroom aromas and flavors. Echoes fruit on the smooth, delicate finish. Drinkable now. • $32 Ⓐ • (01/31/94) • **83**

Nuits-St.-Georges Les Cailles 1992: Light and herbal, with a floral component overshadowing the modest berry flavors. Drinkable now. • $38 • (12/15/94) • **77**

Nuits-St.-Georges Les Cailles 1991: Light and refreshing, with modest strawberry flavor and fine tannins. Drinkable now. • $48 Ⓐ • (01/31/94) • **81**

Puligny-Montrachet 1994: Some nice tropical and citrus flavors, but also somewhat one-dimensional and square. Leaves you hungry for a bit more complexity. Very drinkable now, though. • $49 • (05/31/96) • **83**

Puligny-Montrachet Clos de la Mouchère 1994: Supple and honey-flavored *premier cru*, sporting a whiff of lemon and ripe pear. Medium-bodied, attractive and drinkable now. Very soft finish. • $44 • (05/31/96) • **85**

Puligny-Montrachet Les Perrières 1994: Straightforward and a bit thin, showing some odd leesy notes and buttery, butterscotch, green apple character. • $45 • (05/31/96) • **77**

Puligny-Montrachet Les Pucelles 1994: Beautifully crafted, clean and crisp, boasting loads of honey, lemon, toasted oak and ripe pear complexity. Medium to full in body, it's elegant and restrained, classy, racy and long on the finish. Try in 1999. • $45 • (05/31/96) • **90**

Savigny-lès-Beaune Les Lavières 1992: Light and smooth, with a modest band of cherry and tobacco flavors coming through the fine tannins. Best from 1996. • $27 • (12/15/94) • **82**

Savigny-lès-Beaune Les Lavières 1991: A pretty wine that's bright and open in texture, offering berry, cherry and floral aromas and flavors. Drinkable now. • $30 Ⓐ • (01/31/94) • **84**

Volnay Les Caillerets 1992: Delicate but focused, delivering intense flavors. Notes of tea leaf and black cherry, with a touch of smoky, spicy oak character that lingers nicely on the finish. • $36 • (12/15/94) • **83**

Volnay Les Caillerets 1991: Very pretty, elegant, smooth and polished, showing bright raspberry, vanilla and spice aromas and flavors. Echoes fruit and violet notes on the light, long finish. Drinkable now. • $44 Ⓐ • (01/31/94) • **86**

Volnay Les Chevrets 1992: Light and approachable, with modest black cherry and slightly gamy flavors. Drinkable now. • $34 • (12/15/94) • **80**

Volnay Les Chevrets 1991: Fresh, clean, simple and slightly toasty, showing a pleasant vanilla edge to the modest raspberry flavors. Delicate, graceful and stylish. Drinkable now. • $40 Ⓐ • (01/31/94) • **83**

Volnay Les Fremiets 1992: Firm, somewhat chewy, with modest black cherry flavors that finish a little sugary. Best after 1996. • $34 • (12/15/94) • **79**

Volnay Les Fremiets 1991: Lean and toasty, with a walnutty edge to the red cherry and raspberry flavors. An elegant wine that shows character in a modest frame. Drinkable now. • $40 Ⓐ • (01/31/94) • **84**

BOILLOT, JEAN-MARC

Bâtard-Montrachet 1991 • $114 • (10/15/93) • **87**

Beaune Les Montremenots 1992: Riper than most in this appellation. Delivers some intense blackberry and raspberry flavors but peters out a bit on the finish. Still, a good effort for '92. • $29 • (12/15/94) • **85**

Beaune Les Montrevenots 1993: Nice and round, sporting good, ripe fruit character, medium body and tannins which come together harmoniously on the finish. A bit too tannic, so wait until 2000. • $30 • (11/15/95) • **85**

Beaune Les Montrevenots 1991: Supple and concentrated, shows a lot more density and vibrancy than most 1991s. Scads of black cherry and blackberry flavors, shaded by earth and chocolate notes, make this cellar worthy. Try in 1997. • $30 • (01/31/94) • **88**

Beaune Les Montrevenots 1990: So concentrated you can almost cut it with a knife, but though massive it manages also to be elegant. Shows excellent intensity of berry flavors and supple tannins. Drinkable now to 1998. • $39 • (12/15/92) • **92**

Beaune Les Montrevenots 1988 • $37 • (05/15/91) • **88**

Bourgogne 1993: Nice concentration of ripe plum, cedar and earth flavors. Very compact and muscular, yet fruity. A bit dry and tannic now, so leave it until 1998. • $17 • (11/15/95) • **86**

Bourgogne 1990 • $19 • (12/15/92) • **88**

Pommard Les Jarollières 1993: Very harmonious now with cherry, earth, berry and meat character. Medium to full body, fine tannins and a long finish. Better in 1999. • $50 • (11/15/95) • **90**

Pommard Les Jarollières 1992: Succulent and complex, with interesting twists and turns. Layers of smoke, violet, spice and blackberry-boysenberry notes in a ripe, lovely wine with a firm, almost tart finish. Needs until 1997 to show it all. • $50 • (12/15/94) • **89**

Pommard Les Jarollières 1991: Tough in texture, but the blackberry and black cherry flavors are concentrated and dense enough to remain focused and show through the chewy tannins on the finish. Hold until 1998 to 2000. • $46 Ⓐ • (01/31/94) • **87**

Pommard Les Jarolières 1990: An exotic wine that seduces you with its multidimensional violet, red berry and plum flavors. Made in a full-bodied style that ends with loads of firm but fine tannins. Drinkable now to 1998. 50 cases made. • $67 • (12/15/92) • **94**

Pommard Les Saucilles 1991: Firm and focused, offering pleasingly dense berry flavors shaded by anise notes. Echoes fruit and spice on the finish. Drinkable now. • $NA • (01/31/94) • **85**

Pommard Les Saucilles 1990: So silky it melts in your mouth. Bright and lively, echoing raspberry and vanilla notes and ending with a long, smooth finish. Drinkable now to 1998. • $48 • (12/15/92) • **92**

Pommard Les Saucilles 1988 • $47 • (05/15/91) • **77**

Puligny-Montrachet 1994: Seductively ripe and honeyed, this sweet-tasting, medium-bodied Burgundy makes for attractive drinking now, offering pear, apple pie and cream character. Holds together nicely on the medium-long finish. • $37 • (05/31/96) • **86**

Puligny-Montrachet 1993: This has the classic creamy, buttery, pearlike aromas and flavors, backed by crisp acidity. It's promising, and may need time to come together. Try now. • $36 • (05/15/95) • **85**

Puligny-Montrachet 1992: Full-flavored and full-bodied, a ripe Burgundy with butter, butterscotch, citrus and spice flavors, quite supple, but the backbone of acidity keeps it together. Drinkable now. • $NA • (08/31/94) • **87**

Puligny-Montrachet 1991 • $35 • (10/15/93) • **83**

Puligny-Montrachet Champ-Canet 1994: Very ripe and nearly off-dry, its sweet apricot, pear and excessive honey flavors stand out. Full in body and unctuous almost to a fault, be prepared for something different here. Drinkable now. • $47 • (05/31/96) • **84**

Puligny-Montrachet Champ-Canet 1993: This is rich in flavor, full-bodied and with good depth and concentration. The pear, vanilla and hazelnut notes are supported by lively acidity, and they linger on the finish. • $46 • (05/15/95) • **88**

Puligny-Montrachet Champ-Canet 1991 • $54 • (10/15/93) • **82**

Puligny-Montrachet La Truffière 1993: Bright, fruity and straightforward, with flavors that remind us of pineapple and tangerine. Drink now while it's fresh. • $50 • (05/15/95) • **83**

Puligny-Montrachet La Truffière 1991 • $50 • (10/15/93) • **79**

Puligny-Montrachet Les Combettes 1994: Amazing balance and concentration for a '94, showing both finesse and power, beckoning you back for another sip. Ripe-tasting, honey- and mineral-scented, lemon-spiked nectar. Shows a deft hand at keeping things on track from start to finish. Try in 1997. • $62 • (05/31/96) • **93**

Puligny-Montrachet Les Combettes 1993: Fresh and lively honey, lemon and spice character. Medium in body and super clean, a lovely mineral, pear finish. • $54 • (05/15/95) • **86**

Puligny-Montrachet Les Combettes 1991 • $58 • (10/15/93) • **85**

Puligny-Montrachet Les Folatières 1994: A Burgundy inspired by Sauternes, sporting loads of honey, apricot and apple. No subtlety here, but we love this full-bodied, rich and ripe white. Drinkable now or hold until 1999. • $51 • (05/31/96) • **90**

Puligny-Montrachet Les Pucelles 1994: Total seduction, a low-acidity, soft, supple and very honeyed *premier cru*, featuring fig, date, apricot and ripe pear flavors. Could use some more intensity, but what a fun, unctuous, full-bodied Chardonnay to drink now—and fast. • $58 • (05/31/96) • **90**

Puligny-Montrachet Les Referts 1994: Sweet, honey-spiked white with apricot and peach character. Medium to full in body, it's delicious to drink now, may not have much staying power. • $47 • (05/31/96) • **87**

Puligny-Montrachet Les Referts 1993: A subtle, well-balanced white that keeps you coming back for more. Lightly fruity aromas lead to fresh and full fruit flavors accented by gorgeous butter and nutmeg on the finish. It's crisp and firm in texture. • $46 • (05/15/95) • **87**

Puligny-Montrachet Les Referts 1992: Ripe, round and generous, with oodles of pear, pineapple and lemon flavor, a smooth, creamy texture and a lingering, fruity finish. Very pure and focused, almost sweet, but with enough acidity to keep it fresh. Drinkable now. • $NA • (08/31/94) • **91**

Puligny-Montrachet Les Referts 1991 • $47 • (10/15/93) • **87**

Volnay 1993: Amazing for a village wine. Unbelievable. Essence of wild raspberries added to a hint of earth. Full in body and lots of tannins, which the ripe fruit seems to soften somewhat. Give it time, tempting now, but better in 1998. 550 cases made. • $30 • (11/15/95) • **93**

Volnay 1992: Crisp and light, with enough ripe berry flavors to get past the firm tannins. Drink now. • $29 • (12/15/94) • **83**

Volnay 1991: A layer of coarse tannins takes away from the otherwise ripe, sweet fruit flavors. Light in structure, finishing with a bitter almond edge. Drinkable now. • $NA • (01/31/94) • **80**

Volnay 1990: Amazingly good for a village wine. Full-bodied, showing a beautiful combination of fruit and new wood nuances and tons of plum, cherry and earth flavors. Firm, elegant tannins play a nice supporting role to the long, violet-scented, refined finish. Drinkable now. 150 cases made. • $40 • (12/15/92) • **92**

Volnay Carelle Sous La Chapelle 1993: Very fruity, showing good structure for medium-term aging. Attractive aromas of plums and melons are followed by medium body and tannin and a light finish. Better in 1999. • $42 • (11/15/95) • **89**

Volnay Carelle Sous La Chapelle 1992: Impressive structure for this vintage. Firm, youthful and vibrant, packed with ripe, sweet blackberry, boysenberry and violet flavors that lead to a tannic finish. Better after 1998. • $42 • (12/15/94) • **88**

Volnay Pitures 1993: Rich, ripe and lovely, quite solid, offering loads of well-defined red berry, plum and wet earth character and massive, supple tannins. Hold until at least 2000. • $42 • (11/15/95) • **92**

Volnay Pitures 1992: Crisp and focused, showing very pretty blackberry and floral aromas and flavors that echo nicely on the finish. • $NA • (12/15/94) • **85**

Volnay Pitures 1991: Crisp and lively, offering cedary currant flavors. Finishes chewy and a bit tannic. Try now. • $37 Ⓐ • (01/31/94) • **80**

Volnay Pitures 1990: Simply terrific, with toasty, smoky black cherry and earth aromas and flavors. Tastes almost sweet and offers almost everything you could want. Drinkable now to 1998. 75 cases made. • $55 • (12/15/92) • **94**

Volnay Le Ronceret 1991: A solid beam of fresh currant and blackberry aromas and flavors shines through a light veil of fine tannins. Firm, focused, elegant and true to form. Drinkable now. • $NA • (01/31/94) • **86**

BOILLOT, PIERRE

Volnay Santenots 1988 • $37 • (08/31/90) • **85**

Volnay Santenots 1987 • $37 • (06/15/90) • **86**

BOIRON, HENRI

Châteauneuf-du-Pape 1983 • $11 • (08/31/86) • **79**
Châteauneuf-du-Pape Les Relagnes 1984 • $13 • (11/15/87) • **76**

BOIS DAUPHIN, DOMAINE DU

Châteauneuf-du-Pape 1983 • $12 • (11/15/87) • **62**
Châteauneuf-du-Pape Cuvée de Boisdauphin 1990: Firm and focused, with generous black cherry, blackberry and toast aromas and flavors and hints of chocolate on the smooth finish. Drinkable now. • $19 • (04/15/93) • **87**

BOIS DE LA GARDE, CHÂTEAU DU

Côtes du Rhône 1989 • $8 • (05/31/91) • **83**
Côtes du Rhône 1988 • $7 • (10/31/90) BB • **82**

BOIS-VERT, CHÂTEAU

Bordeaux 1983 • $3 • (11/16/85) • **53**

BOISSET, JEAN-CLAUDE

Beaujolais 1993: Unstable, fizzy and sharp, too lean and awkward to take advantage of the pleasant, light berry flavors. • $6 • (06/30/94) • **76**
Beaujolais 1988 • $6 • (11/15/90) • **77**
Beaujolais-Villages 1993: Ripe and jammy, with notes of plum and banana, fresh and lively and has the grip to go with food. Lots of personality here. • $7 • (06/30/94) • **83**
Beaujolais-Villages 1988 • $7 • (11/15/90) • **76**
Bourgogne Confërie des Chevaliers du Tastevin 1989 • $7 • (06/15/92) • **76**
Bourgogne Pinot Noir 1993: Very light. Some OK red berry and earth character, but it's a touch diluted and one-dimensional, adding an astringent finish. • $NA • (11/15/95) • **74**
Bourgogne Pinot Noir Charles de France 1993: Shows only modest cherry, raspberry and strawberry notes, light body and color and delicate finish. Drink now. • $NA • (11/15/95) • **75**
Bourgogne Pinot Noir de Bourgogne 1992: A nicely balanced, modest style of Burgundy that's fruity and spicy in aroma, firm in texture and offers enough cherry and strawberry flavors. If only it didn't turn stemmy and murky on the finish. 1,500 cases made. • $9 • (11/30/94) • **82**
Bourgogne Tastevinage 1988 • $11 • (08/31/91) • **72**
Bourgogne White Chardonnay Charles de France 1992: Simple, refreshing, only a candied edge detracting from the lemony pear and spice flavors. Drinkable now. 20,000 cases made. • $8 • (02/28/94) • **78**
Bourgogne White Chardonnay Charles de France 1991 • $9 • (05/15/93) BB • **84**
Bourgogne White Chardonnay de Bourgogne, Charles de France 1993: A bit lean and green, yet showing pleasant mineral, chalk, pear and fig notes. It delivers good flavor intensity, but seems somewhat muted on the finish. • $10 • (08/31/95) • **81**
Bourgogne White Charles de France Chardonnay de Bourgogne 1992: Tastes mature for its age, with gobs of butter and oak that are heavy-handed. Try this wine if you like smoky and ripe fig flavors, but it lacks finesse. • $8 • **81**
Brouilly 1993: Lean and tart, offering some light berry flavor, but it's dominated by a musty, earthy note that reduces its appeal. • $9 • (06/30/94) • **77**
Cabernet Sauvignon Vin de Pays d'Oc 1994: The blackberry and chocolate flavors are ripe and appealing in this lush French wine, and the round tannins give support without astringency. The bargain price also adds to the appeal. Drinkable now. 7,500 cases made. • $6 • (10/31/95) BB • **85**

Key: SS—Spectator Selection. CS—Cellar Selection. BB—Best Buy. $NA—Price not available. (BT)—Barrel tasting. Ⓐ—Auction Price.
Dates in parentheses represent the issues in which the ratings were published.

Chablis 1994: Fresh, clean, crisp, fruity, shows floral, citrus and apple flavors. It's quite full-bodied, but subdued. 5,000 cases made. • $14 • (06/30/95) • **82**
Chablis 1992: Decent Chablis. Earthy, doughy aromas and spicy-herbal flavors make this light on fruit flavor, but it does linger nicely on the finish. • $11 • (11/15/94) • **80**
Chardonnay Vin de Pays d'Oc 1994: A fresh, ripe Chardonnay offering pleasant flavors of lemon, melon and light vanilla, harmonious and clean, though not very concentrated. Enjoy it now. 12,000 cases made. • $6 • (06/30/95) • **84**
Chardonnay Vin de Pays d'Oc 1993: Simple and resinous, with vanilla, apple and spice flavors that linger on the finish. 7,500 cases made. • $6 • (11/30/94) • **77**
Charmes-Chambertin 1993: Light and showing a sweet core of raspberry and strawberry notes, but it's somewhat diluted. Drink on release. 275 cases made. • $56 • (11/15/95) • **77**
Chassagne-Montrachet 1993: Some vanilla, dried apricot character but a diluted and light finish. Try now. 1,000 cases made. • $16 • (05/15/95) • **80**
Chassagne-Montrachet 1992: Crisp and straightforward, with apple, lemon and mineral flavors, a lively texture and a chalky finish. Tasted twice with consistant notes. • $16 • (08/31/94) • **82**
Chassagne-Montrachet Red 1993: Pleasant but light, deceptively seductive raspberry, cherry and wild berry flavors. Delicate texture, but the tannins are there to keep it going. 1,960 cases made. • $18 • (11/15/95) • **82**
Châteauneuf-du-Pape 1986 • $12 • (11/30/88) • **80**
Clos de Vougeot Red 1993: A rather light Pinot, offering some decent red berry flavor and dry, tannic structure. May be better in 1998? • $46 • (11/15/95) • **79**
Corton-Charlemagne 1991 • $48 • (02/28/94) • **90**
Côte de Beaune-Villages 1982 • $5 • (07/01/85) BB • **86**
Côte de Nuits-Villages 1983 • $13 • (02/01/86) • **78**
Côtes du Rhône 1992: Lean and thin for a Côtes du Rhône, with thin aromas and simple, watery fruit flavors. Light tannins. Drinkable but very simple. • $5 • (11/30/94) • **78**
Côtes du Rhône 1990 • $8 • (07/31/92) • **84**
Côtes du Rhône 1987 • $4 • (07/31/89) • **78**
Côtes du Rhône 1986 • $4 • (10/31/87) • **73**
Côtes du Rhône 1985 • $3 • (11/30/86) BB • **77**
Côtes du Rhône White 1992: A dry white that's adding some lightly nutty character to the simple, lean fruit flavor. • $5 • (10/15/94) • **79**
Côtes du Ventoux 1988 • $4 • (10/15/90) • **75**
Gevrey-Chambertin 1993: Rather light and weedy, offering some fruit but also a metallic edge. medium-to-light body and watery finish. 260 cases made. • $16 • (11/15/95) • **76**
Gevrey-Chambertin 1991: Displays nice cherry and anise aromas and flavors in a light, simple, chewy style. Drinkable now. • $NA • (01/31/94) • **82**
Gevrey-Chambertin 1990: A generously flavored Burgundy that's already losing its rough edges and getting ready to drink. It has earthy, plummy, minerallike flavors, moderate tannins and a touch of astringency on the finish. • $17 • **82**
Gevrey-Chambertin 1982 • $9 • (06/01/85) • **74**
Mâcon-Blanc-Villages 1994: Lavishly oaked, standing out with its full, ripe, sweet-tasting vanilla and toast notes. The wood may get tiring, slightly astringent finish. 10,000 cases made. • $8 • (08/31/95) • **80**
Mâcon-Blanc-Villages 1993: This light, slightly fizzy wine with crisp acidity offers simple fruit cocktail flavors. Good for spritzers. • $6 • **77**
Merlot Vin de Pays d'Oc 1994: Light and firm, with light, dry tannins, this offers more barnyard and earthy flavors than fruit. Not much pleasure here. • $6 • (10/31/95) • **75**
Meursault 1993: A bit one-dimensional, but it has some nice texture and a mineral note accompanying leaner citrusy, green and herbal flavors. Drink now. 3,500 cases made. • $16 • (05/15/95) • **81**
Meursault 1992: Clean and pleasant, showing some straightforward apple, pear and melon notes, a bit light and short. This bottle did not show as well as in a previous tasting. • $15 • (08/31/94) • **81**
Meursault 1991 • $50 • (10/15/93) • **87**
Morgon 1993: This shows earthy and peppery flavors along with ripe berry notes, it's lean but balanced and quite firm. A distinctive profile, but not one that gets the juices flowing. • $9 • (06/30/94) • **80**

Nuits-St.-Georges 1985 • $25 • (04/30/88) • **79**
Pommard 1985 • $28 • (04/30/88) • **78**
Pommard Rugiens 1985 • $33 • (03/15/88) • **76**
Pouilly-Fuissé 1994: Earth, pear and hard-candy flavors keep this off-balance, though not flawed, it lacks harmony and varietal character. 6,500 cases made. • $14 • (06/30/95) • **75**
Pouilly-Fuissé 1993: There's a nice buttery aroma, but the flavors are lean and a bit diluted, finishing with an herbal tang. It's well-crafted, but lacks fruit. • $13 • **79**
Puligny-Montrachet 1993: A straightforward white, quite light, diluted and short. 450 cases made. • $18 • (05/15/95) • **74**
Puligny-Montrachet 1992: Simple and light, showing modest, stale fruit flavors. Drinkable now. • $25 • (08/31/94) • **78**
Puligny-Montrachet 1991 • $55 • (10/15/93) • **86**
Rully 1992: This wine fails to balance its intensely ripe fruit and buttery oak flavors, and it turns coarse and tart on the finish. A top-heavy, simple wine that lacks an appealing core of flavors. • $8 • **76**
Rully White 1993: Clean and crisp, straightforward and easy to drink, presenting fresh apple and vanilla flavors and a slight metallic note. 35,000 cases made. • $11 • (06/30/95) • **81**
Rully White 1992: A pleasing, well-rounded Chardonnay with toasty aromas, solid flavors of pear and nutmeg and a lingering finish. Lively and well-balanced, too. 3,000 cases made. • $9 • (02/28/95) BB • **86**
Savigny-lès-Beaune 1993: Delicate and light-bodied, showing some pretty earth and sweet, ripe flavors and a slightly drying finish. Try in 1999. 4,600 cases made. • $12 • (11/15/95) • **82**
Syrah Vin de Pays d'Oc 1994: Licorice and gamy aromas say Syrah, and while the flavors are a bit lean and tannins somewhat dry, this is true to the variety. Straightforward and drinkable now. • $6 • (10/31/95) • **80**
Syrah Vin de Pays d'Oc 1993: Pungent blackberry jam aromas and similar flavors make this a strapping but not very tannic red. 7,500 cases made. • $6 • (02/28/95) • **77**
Volnay Clos des Chênes 1985 • $28 • (04/15/88) • **86**

BOIZEL

Brut Champagne 1988: This has an abundance of sliced apple character, lively acidity, and foam, but is slightly simple to be rated higher. Drink now. • $17 • (12/31/93) • **85**
Brut Champagne Joyau de France 1985: Gentle and delicious with a fine mousse and deep ripe apple and melon flavors. Crisp acidity yet round and caressing. Drink now. • $26 • (12/31/93) • **89**
Brut Champagne Réserve NV • $30 • (12/31/91) • **86**

BOKOBSA

Côtes du Rhône Cuvée du Centenaire 1986 • $6 • (02/28/90) • **68**

BOLLINGER

Brut Blanc de Noirs Champagne Vieilles Vignes Françaises 1986: Tastes good but older than it is, showing slightly baked aromas, caramel and pineapple flavors and exuberant effervescence. May not be for everyone, but those who favor mature Champagne will love this. • $219 • (12/31/95) • **86**
Brut Blanc de Noirs Champagne Vieilles Vignes Françaises 1981 • $NA • **84**
Brut Champagne Extra RD 1982: Roasted almond and toast aromas turn tight and austere on the palate, where the mature grapefruit and citrus flavors turn to hints of sherry. Drink up. Tasted three times, with consistent notes. • $100 • (11/15/91) • **87**
Brut Champagne Extra RD 1979 • $79 • (12/31/89) • **94**
Brut Champagne Extra RD 1976 • $59 • (04/15/88) • **88**
Brut Champagne Extra RD 1975 • $64 • (05/16/86) • **89**
Brut Champagne Grande Année 1988: Zesty, fruity, vivid and alive, packed with orange, lemon, honey and ginger flavors and with a creamy, smooth texture. Full-bodied, full-flavored, with great acidity and long-lasting on the finish. Fine to drink now. 16,667 cases made. • $60 • (12/31/94) • **91**
Brut Champagne Grand Année 1985: Classically styled, one of the all-time greats in standard vintage Champagne. Firm yet elegant, with plenty of smoke, apple and toast character, a fine, silky texture and great acidity. Drinkable now. Tasted three times, first two bottles were less good. 15,000 cases made. • $60 • (12/31/93) • **94**
Brut Champagne Grand Année 1983: Floral and grapefruit aromas and flavors make this crisp, medium-bodied wine lively and agreeable, but it's simple. A touch of ginger on the finish is especially appealing. • $43 • (12/31/89) • **86**
Brut Champagne Grand Année 1982: Rich, toasty and very assertive, high in extract and intensity with a heavy toasty flavor that compliments the pear and cherry flavors. Smoky flavors carry the finish. It's a rich style that may be to powerful for some. • $30 • (07/15/88) • **93**
Brut Champagne Special Cuvée NV: Exotic flavors and aromas make for an appealing mix. Rather light with the lemon, pear and ginger flavors, but a ripe aroma. The finish is fruity, spicy and lingering. 83,333 cases made. • $38 • (12/31/95) • **86**
Brut Rosé Champagne 1985: This slightly sweet, nicely aged Champagne has spicy citrus flavors accented by floral notes and a mature, nutty quality. Very good. 2,500 cases made. • $72 • (12/31/94) • **86**
Brut Rosé Champagne Grand Année 1985: Pale copper in color and delicate through and through, with modest cherry and bread dough aromas and flavors. Perhaps a bit metallic on the finish, but it would be enjoyable with food that isn't too rich. Drinkable now. • $60 • (11/15/91) • **85**
Brut Rosé Champagne Grand Année 1983: Rich, toasty and round, with a gentle structure, smooth texture, subtle flavors of strawberry, smoke and a touch of cherry. A nip of crisp lime on the finishkeeps it lively. • $50 • (12/31/89) • **89**
Brut Rosé Champagne Grand Année 1982: Toasty with cherry and spicy flavors but it lacks depth and finesse and the flavors lack persistence and depth. Still it's perfectly drinkable, finish ing with a slight metallic flavor. • $35 • (07/15/88) • **80**
Brut Rosé Champagne Grand Année 1979 • $40 • (12/16/85) • **94**

BON-PASTEUR, CHÂTEAU LE

Pomerol 1995: Subtle but exciting, it grows on you with its excellent red berry flavors and silky tannins. Smoke, toast, vanilla, mineral intensity. It butters the palate and ends in a long finish. • $NA • (05/15/96) • **90-94** (BT)
Pomerol 1993: Elegant, enticing, subtle berry and dark chocolate aromas and flavors. Medium in body, soft tannins and fresh, fruity finish. Drinkable now. 3,333 cases made. • $32 • (01/31/96) • **87**
Pomerol 1992: Pleasant, delicate vanilla, cherry and berry aromas and flavors, light body, silky tannins and a light finish. Drinkable now. • $21 • (04/15/95) • **81**
Pomerol 1990: Gorgeous, keeps you coming back for more. Has wonderful milk chocolate, roasted oak and fruit aromas and flavors and plenty of silky tannins. Drink in 1997. 3,000 cases made. • $33 • (03/31/93) • **93**
Pomerol 1989 • $38 Ⓐ • (04/30/92) • **88**
Pomerol 1988 • $23 • (02/28/91) • **85**
Pomerol 1987 • $22 • (05/15/90) • **81**
Pomerol 1986 • $46 Ⓐ • (06/15/89) • **92**
Pomerol 1985: Surprisingly fruity and elegant for this estate. The wine shows tobacco, cherry aromas and flavors. Medium body and a light delicate finish. Drink now. • $31 Ⓐ • **85**
Pomerol 1984 • $13 • (06/15/87) • **86**
Pomerol 1983: Well-crafted wine with a lovely combination of tobacco, vanilla, plum, peppery character. Medium bodied with firm tannins. Drink now or hold. • $24 Ⓐ • **88**
Pomerol 1982 • $130 Ⓐ • (08/31/92) • **94**
Pomerol 1981: Slightly overdone. Volatile with extremely ripe, raisiny character. Full-bodied and tannic with an astringent finish. Doesn't appear to be improving. Drying out. • $NA • **79**
Pomerol 1979 • $NA • (10/15/89) • **91**

BONALGUE, CHÂTEAU

Pomerol 1994: Powerful toast and coffee aromas and flavors are evidence of new oak, but the tannins don't have enough fruit behind them. Try now. • $28 • (12/15/95) • **80**

FRANCE

Pomerol 1993: The deft combination of oak and fruit are appealing. Coffee flavors mingle with blackberry, floral and light truffle notes. Generous but not overly tannic. • $27 • (12/15/95) • **86**

BONHOMME, CHÂTEAU DE

Minervois 1991 • $8 • (03/15/94) • **83**

BONNAIRE

Brut Blanc de Blancs Champagne Cramant 1985: Attractive in a fresh, pleasant style. Tastes fruity and delicate, with direct flavors of pear and lemon. • $42 • (12/31/89) • **83**
Brut Blanc de Blancs Champagne Cramant 1983: Creamy and well-balanced with all the rough edges smoothed off. • $38 • (02/29/88) • **87**
Brut Blanc de Blancs Champagne Cramant 1979 • $40 • (05/31/87) • **86**
Brut Blanc de Blancs Champagne Cramant NV • $30 • (12/31/89) • **90**
Brut Blanc de Blancs Champagne Premier Cru NV: A mineral, earthy character gives an extra dimension of richness that's backed up by pear and fruit flavors. Harmonious, firmly-structured and mature with a long finish that echoes honey and toast. • $40 • (12/31/94) • **90**

BONNAT, CHÂTEAU LE

Graves 1995: Pretty, medium- to full-bodied '95, showing a luscious red berry character with complex spice and oak flavors. You wish for a bit more complexity in the mid-palate and length on the finish. • $NA • (05/15/96) • **80-84** (BT)
Graves 1989 • $18 • (04/30/92) • **81**
Graves 1988 • $18 • (12/31/90) • **87**
Graves 1987 • $12 • (04/15/90) • **83**
Graves White 1988 • $17 • (03/31/90) • **84**

BONNEAU DU MARTRAY

Corton 1993: Solid Corton offering lovely plum and red berry flavors and a hint of oak, medium body, firm tannins and long, fresh finish. Better in 2000. • $45 • (11/15/95) • **88**
Corton 1985 • $62 • (10/15/88) • **91**
Corton-Charlemagne 1993: Firm and elegant, with a solid, racy structure. Enticing smoke, spice, mineral and pear flavors turn to beautiful cream and mineral on the finish. 4,041 cases made. • $60 • (08/31/95) • **88**
Corton-Charlemagne 1992: Lush, soft and inviting, a generous, ready-to-drink Corton that tastes like honey, pear and apricot, has an attractive, clean finish laced with moderate lime flavors. Drinkable now. Tasted twice. • $44 Ⓐ • (08/31/94) • **90**
Corton-Charlemagne 1991 • $NA • (10/15/93) • **89**

BONNEAU, HENRI

Châteauneuf-du-Pape Réserve des Celestins 1986 • $19 • (05/31/89) • **82**

BONNET, CHÂTEAU

Bordeaux 1989 • $9 • (07/15/92) • **79**
Bordeaux 1988 • $7 • (04/30/91) • **77**
Bordeaux 1987 • $7 • (04/15/90) • **79**
Bordeaux 1986 • $6 • (05/15/89) • **73**
Bordeaux 1983 • $4 • (05/01/86) • **72**
Bordeaux 1982 • $4 • (04/16/85) • **73**
Bordeaux 1981: Barely holding on. Another old style of wine with nutty, chestnut, berry character, medium body and a dry finish. • $NA • **78**
Bordeaux en Fûts de Chêne Réserve 1989 • $11 • (07/15/92) • **85**
Bordeaux Réserve 1995: Some decent berry flavors, but rather diluted and slightly herbal on the watery finish. • $NA • (05/15/96) • **75-79** (BT)
Bordeaux Réserve 1994: Seductively smooth and silky, showing black olive and red berry flavors, medium body and firm tannins on the finish. • $NA • (06/30/95) • **80-84** (BT)
Bordeaux Réserve 1993: Lovely, balanced plum, black cherry and vanilla aromas and flavors, medium body, fine tannins and fresh finish. Try now. • $10 • (01/31/96) • **82**
Bordeaux Réserve 1991: Shows some sweet, caressing fruit but slightly short, tough. • $10 • (03/31/94) • **77**
Bordeaux Réserve 1990: Straightforward, with pleasant tar, roasted nut and tomato character and medium-firm tannins. Drinkable now. 30,000 cases made. • $NA • (03/31/93) • **82**
Bordeaux Réserve 1988 • $11 • (07/15/91) • **78**
Bordeaux Vinifié en Fûts de Chêne 1992: Pleasant but diluted, presenting plum, slightly herbal character, medium-to-light-bodied. Drinkable now. • $8 • (04/15/95) • **78**
Bordeaux White 1992 • $NA • (06/15/94) • **83**
Entre-Deux-Mers 1994: Intense Sauvignon character, with grassy aromas and flavors, supported by lime accents. Medium-bodied, fresh in acidity and light on the finish. Tasted twice, with consistent notes. • $8 • (03/31/96) • **84**
Entre-Deux-Mers 1993: Always delicious. A fresh and easy-to-drink white showing grass and quince character, medium-to-light body and zingy finish. Drinkable now. • $8 • (05/31/95) • **80**
Entre-Deux-Mers 1992 • $7 • (08/31/93) BB • **82**
Entre-Deux-Mers 1991 • $7 • (05/15/93) • **78**
Entre-Deux-Mers Vinifié en Fûts Neuf 1992: Well made and balanced, featuring a subtle, grassy note and butter, orange and honey flavors. • $10 • (05/31/95) • **86**
Entre-Deux-Mers Vinifié en Fûts de Chêne 1993: Extremely refined vanilla, toasted oak, grass and melon character, medium body, fresh acidity and a lovely finish. • $10 • (05/31/95) • **85**
Graves 1985 • $5 • (04/15/88) BB • **84**

BONNIGAL, M.

Touraine Domaine la Prévötè Sauvignon de Touraine White 1993: There's not much varietal character in this tart, appley wine, but it's light, clean and refreshing. A simple but snappy wine. • $7 • (10/31/94) • **83**

BORDEAUX PRESTIGE, LE

Bordeaux 1985 • $9 • (09/30/88) • **80**

BORDES-QUANCARD, CHAI DE

Bordeaux Vieilli dans nos Chais 1990: Simple and spicy, with a strong cedary component to the basic herbal and cherry flavors. Drinkable now. • $10 • (03/15/93) • **78**

BORIE, CHÂTEAU LA

Côtes du Rhône Cuvée de Prestige 1985 • $6 • (07/15/87) • **74**
Côtes du Rhône Cuvée de Prestige 1983 • $4 • (03/16/85) BB • **87**

BOSC, DOMAINE DU

Vin de Pays de l'Herault Cépage Grenache Sec 1992 • $6 • (03/15/94) • **81**
Vin de Pays de l'Herault Cépage Viognier 1992 • $10 • (03/15/94) • **83**

BOSCQ, CHÂTEAU LE

Médoc 1988 • $20 • (04/30/91) • **84**
Médoc 1986 • $10 • (06/30/89) • **75**
Médoc 1983 • $8 • (01/01/86) • **70**
Médoc 1982 • $6 • (10/01/85) BB • **76**
St.-Estèphe 1995: Elegant and racy, yet showing good concentration of fruit, mint, spice and smoke character. Full-bodied with a good amount of supple, ripe tannins. Almost outstanding. • $NA • (05/15/96) • **85-89** (BT)

Key: SS—Spectator Selection. CS—Cellar Selection. BB—Best Buy. $NA—Price not available. (BT)—Barrel tasting. Ⓐ—Auction Price.
Dates in parentheses represent the issues in which the ratings were published.

BOSQUET DES PAPES

Châteauneuf-du-Pape 1989 • $18 • (10/15/91) • **85**
Châteauneuf-du-Pape 1988 • $18 • (10/15/91) • **83**
Châteauneuf-du-Pape 1986 • $18 • (10/15/91) • **90**
Châteauneuf-du-Pape 1985 • $18 • (10/15/91) • **86**
Châteauneuf-du-Pape 1984 • $17 • (11/15/87) • **91**
Châteauneuf-du-Pape 1983 • $NA • (10/15/91) • **86**
Châteauneuf-du-Pape 1981 • $NA • (10/15/91) • **93**
Châteauneuf-du-Pape White 1990: An early drinking, fresh style, though lean and steely. The melon and grape aromas follow through on the palate. Medium in acidity, with a lively finish. • $22 • (10/15/91) • **82**

BOUCHACOURT, ROLAND

Mâcon-Villages 1994: Light-bodied, with attractive flavors of pear and melon to offer a touch of ripeness, but it turns somewhat sour and diluted on the finish. 5,833 cases made. • $7 • **77**
Mâcon-Villages Château de Péronne 1994: Racy little white, showing some intensity of flavor including a pronounced grass and lime edge. Light-bodied, clean and very tart. Try with seafood. 4,583 cases made. • $7 • **80**

BOUCHARD AÎNÉ

Chambertin Clos de Bèze 1959 • $NA • (08/31/90) • **84**
Chambertin Clos de Bèze Domaine Marion 1989 • $NA • (01/31/92) • **88**
Chassagne-Montrachet 1991 • $NA • (10/15/93) • **83**
Corton-Charlemagne 1991 • $45 • (10/15/93) • **90**
Merlot Vin de Pays de l'Aude NV • $5 • (06/30/90) • **72**
Meursault 1991 • $19 • (10/15/93) • **88**
Puligny-Montrachet 1991 • $20 • (10/15/93) • **86**

BOUCHARD PERE & FILS

Aloxe-Corton 1992: Simple and appealing, with a bright core of black cherry flavor that echoes on the finish. Drinkable now. • $30 • (12/15/94) • **82**
Aloxe-Corton 1989 • $36 • (01/31/92) • **87**
Aloxe-Corton Domaines du Château de Beaune 1990 • $30 • (12/15/92) • **88**
Bâtard-Montrachet 1994: A medium-bodied Chardonnay showing pleasant fruit, toasted coconut and dried herb flavors. Picks up some intensity on the supple finish. • $96 • (05/31/96) 85 • **87**
Beaujolais-Villages Le Chamville 1993: Juicy strawberry and cherry flavors are up front here, round and balanced, in a clean, easy-drinking style. • $10 • (06/30/94) • **79**
Beaune Clos de la Mousse 1992: Firm in texture, chewy, with caramel and tobacco overtones to the modest berry flavor. Drinkable now. • $25 • (12/15/94) • **81**
Beaune Clos de la Mousse Domaines du Château de Beaune 1993: Extremely smooth, silky, young '93. Well-crafted plum, cherry and earth character, tannins sneaking up on the finish. Drinkable now, better in 1999. • $28 • (11/15/95) • **85**
Beaune Clos de la Mousse Domaines du Château de Beaune 1991: Tough, chewy and mature for the vintage. Drinkable now. 1,300 cases made. • $28 Ⓐ • (01/31/94) • **79**
Beaune Clos de la Mousse Domaines du Château de Beaune 1986 • $33 • (07/31/88) • **78**
Beaune Clos St.-Landry 1994: Very elegant, subtle and quite creamy. Lots of spice, nutmeg, pear, toasted bread, mineral and vanilla flavors. Some intensity on the finish. Try in 1999. • $32 • (05/31/96) 87 • **87**
Beaune Clos St.-Landry Domaines du Château de Beaune 1993: Honey, pear and vanilla aromas and flavors, medium body, firm acidity and a good core of fruit. Drink now or hold. • $31 • **86**
Beaune Clos St.-Landry Domaines du Château de Beaune 1992: Light but pleasant, simple and clean, with some modest apple, pear and mineral flavors. • $24 • (08/31/94) • **79**
Beaune Domaines du Château de Beaune Clos St.-Landry 1991 • $28 • (10/15/93) • **79**
Beaune Grèves Vigne de l'Enfant Jésus 1993: Light and delicate, pleasant and accessible now, featuring some plum, cherry, chocolate character. Disappointing for this vineyard site. 1,500 cases made. • $50 • (11/15/95) • **82**
Beaune Grèves Vigne de l'Enfant Jésus 1991: Lean and spicy, with a strong anise edge to the blackberry and black cherry aromas and flavors. Finishes juicy and bright. Drinkable now. 1,500 cases made. • $48 Ⓐ • (01/31/94) • **84**
Beaune Grèves Vigne de l'Enfant Jésus 1990: Smooth and generous, a supple, silky Beaune with caramel and tobacco notes playing against the polished raspberry and strawberry flavors. Delicious now, probably better in 1997. • $53 • **88**
Beaune Grèves Vigne de l'Enfant Jésus 1989: Rich and generous, graceful and polished, plush-textured, pouring out its floral, spice, vanilla, strawberry, raspberry and red plum flavors. Delicious now. • $59 • **91**
Beaune Grèves Vigne de l'Enfant Jésus 1988: Quite rich and youthful but also lean, hard and tannic, showing spice, tobacco and mineral flavors and a nice hint of raspberry. Not very charming at this stage. • $59 • **85**
Beaune Grèves Vigne de l'Enfant Jésus 1987: Light and charming, spicy, with a delicate texture and mature flavors of faded rose petal, caramel, raspberry and red currant. • $38 • **86**
Beaune Grèves Vigne de l'Enfant Jésus 1986: Mature, light and diluted, slightly earthy, with floral and stemmy aromas and flavors turning tight and tannic on the finish. Past its peak. • $46 Ⓐ • **79**
Beaune Grèves Vigne de l'Enfant Jésus 1985: Ripe, chewy and focused, black cherry, toast and spice flavors echo on the firm finish. Appealing now. • $32 Ⓐ • (02/28/95) • **89**
Beaune Grèves Vigne de l'Enfant Jésus 1983: Mature, showing all its charm now, with a soft, silky core of cinnamon, plum, earth and mineral character. Drying on the finish. • $34 • **82**
Beaune Marconnets 1992: Crisp, a little tannic, only a modest level of cherry flavor sneaking through on the finish. • $27 • (12/15/94) • **79**
Beaune Marconnets Domaines du Château de Beaune 1991: Barnyardy aromas and flavors . Nice vanilla- and spice-scented cherry flavor balances it relatively well. Drinkable now. 880 cases made. • $30 Ⓐ • (01/31/94) • **74**
Beaune Marconnets Domaines du Château de Beaune 1990: What a beauty. Solid as a rock and both firm and velvety, showing great complexity and tons of berry, plum and chocolate characteristics that come together on the almost sweet finish. Drink in 1997 or '98. • $28 • (12/15/92) • **93**
Beaune Marconnets Domaines du Château de Beaune 1989 • $39 • (01/31/92) • **90**
Beaune Marconnets Domaines du Château de Beaune 1986 • $24 • (07/31/88) • **83**
Beaune Marconnets Domaines du Château de Beaune 1985 • $35 • (01/31/89) • **89**
Beaune Premier Cru 1994: Subtle yet intense, elegant, full in body. Lots of finesse at first, shouting its full-throttle tropical fruit, lime, earth and toasted bread flavors on the lovely, supple and silky finish. Drinkable now or hold until 1998. • $28 • (05/31/96) 87 • **87**
Beaune Teurons Domaines du Château de Beaune 1993: Incredibly floral nose, medium body and tannins and a crisp finish. Open and delicious to drink now but will improve. 1,900 cases made. • $28 • (11/15/95) • **86**
Beaune Teurons Domaines du Château de Beaune 1991: Crisp and light, with focused blackberry and currant aromas and flavors that turn lean and slightly astringent on the finish. Try now. 900 cases made. • $29 Ⓐ • (01/31/94) • **80**
Beaune Teurons Domaines du Château de Beaune 1990: Quite forward and open for a '90. Light and pleasant, with clean, pretty chestnut and raspberry flavors. Drinkable now. • $30 • (12/15/92) • **84**
Beaune Teurons Domaines du Château de Beaune 1986 • $32 • (07/31/88) • **81**
Beaune Teurons Domaines du Château de Beaune 1985 • $35 • (01/31/89) • **85**
Beaune Teurons Domaines du Château de Beaune 1983 • $21 • (09/15/86) • **71**
Beaune Vigne de L'Enfant Jésus 1992: Solid quality in a well-balanced Burgundy that has straightforward fruit flavors, good structure and acidity and a clean finish. 1,500 cases made. • $40 • (10/31/94) • **86**

BOUCHARD PERE & FILS

Bourgogne Pinot Noir La Vignée 1992: Closer to water than wine, with a hint of strawberry character. • $NA • (12/15/94) • **70**
Bourgogne Chardonnay La Vignée 1991 • $10 • (10/15/93) • **84**
Chambertin 1986 • $78 • (07/31/88) • **81**
Chambertin Clos de Bèze 1989 • $92 • (01/31/92) • **92**
Chambertin Clos de Bèze 1988 • $82 • (04/30/91) • **89**
Chambertin Domaines du Château de Beaune 1990: A bit lean and not showing much. Lacks flesh and depth, but delivers pleasant strawberry and cherry characteristics. Drinkable now. • $NA • (12/15/92) • **88**
Chambolle-Musigny 1992: Middle-of-the-road Chambolle, with toasty, gamy, red berry flavors opening up to a firm-structured, tannic finish. • $32 • (12/15/94) • **79**
Chambolle-Musigny 1986 • $29 • (07/31/88) • **73**
Chambolle-Musigny Domaines du Château de Beaune 1990: Focused and a bit austere now, but plenty of wet earth, forest underbrush and plum characteristics make it a promising wine for the cellar. Try in 1998. • $NA • (12/15/92) • **86**
Chambolle-Musigny Domaines du Château de Beaune 1993: Delicate, pretty, medium-bodied, offering well-defined floral, earth, rose petal and currant flavors. Good tannin structure yet very supple finish. Best in 2000. 310 cases made. • $36 • (11/15/95) • **88**
Chassagne-Montrachet Red 1993: The wood brings out smoky, toasted flavors that blend nicely with black cherry and licorice notes. Beautiful, silky, ripe mouth-feel and soft finish. Better in 1998. • $25 • (11/15/95) • **87**
Chassagne-Montrachet Red 1990: A pleasant but straightforward wine that's quite light and one-dimensional, with cherry and herb flavors. Drinkable now. • $21 • (12/15/92) • **80**
Chassagne-Montrachet Red 1988 • $22 • (04/30/91) • **85**
Châteauneuf-du-Pape 1990: Bold and assertive, with cooked plum and smoke flavors and peppery accents. Full-bodied, tannic and well-balanced, drink now to 1997. • $16 • (04/15/93) • **83**
Châteauneuf-du-Pape 1985 • $11 • (09/30/87) • **82**
Chevalier-Montrachet 1993: Plenty of new wood here, shows firm acidity and lots of apple and mineral character. Medium-bodied, adding good fruit and a medium finish. Drink now. 1,900 cases made. • $93 • **86**
Chevalier-Montrachet 1991 • $106 • (10/15/93) • **91**
Chevalier-Montrachet Domaines du Château de Beaune 1992: It flies over the palate as delicately as a glider in the sky, leaving in its wake a trail of subtle, seamless flavors. Delicate with plenty of depth, offering focused lime, lemon, pear and toast flavors, with a creamy yet solid finish. • $81 • (08/31/94) • **94**
Clos de la Roche 1989 • $NA • (01/31/92) • **89**
Clos de Vougeot 1959 • $NA • (08/31/90) • **85**
Corton Le Corton Domaines du Château de Beaune 1991: Tough, astringent and thin, with modest fruit buried under the tannins. Unbalanced. 1,400 cases made. • $46 Ⓐ • (01/31/94) • **77**
Corton Le Corton Domaines du Château de Beaune 1990: Tightly knit, with loads of fruit and tannins, showing an impressive amount of black cherry and earth flavors and a round mouth-feel. • $50 • (12/15/92) • **91**
Corton Le Corton Domaines du Château de Beaune 1989 • $79 • (01/31/92) • **92**
Corton Le Corton Domaines du Château de Beaune 1988 • $77 • (03/31/91) • **91**
Corton Le Corton Domaines du Château de Beaune 1986 • $47 • (07/31/88) • **85**
Corton Le Corton Domaines du Château de Beaune 1983 • $37 • (09/15/86) • **83**
Corton Le Corton Grand Cru Domaines du Château de Beaune 1992: Nicely focused, fruity and smooth in texture, a young but promising red with firm tannins, great balance and just a touch of oak. Try now, or hold until 1998. 1,400 cases made. • $38 • (10/31/94) • **88**
Corton-Charlemagne 1994: Skillful winemaking stands behind this lovely, fresh and intense '94. Packs lemon, pear and honey flavors in wonderful proportions. Seductively voluptuous and full-bodied, adding a focused, long finish. Drinkable now or hold until 1999. • $60 • (05/31/96) • **91**
Corton-Charlemagne Domaines du Château de Beaune 1993: Distinctive mushroom and cream aromas and flavors, medium body, firm acidity and delicious finish. Lovely to drink now. 1,000 cases made. • $61 • **87**
Corton-Charlemagne Domaines du Château de Beaune 1992: Well-rounded and creamy, with a beam of lemon to cut through the richness. A bit plain for a Corton, yet the complexity of the vanilla, pear, and lime flavors will make any wine-drinker happy. • $50 • (08/31/94) • **89**
Côte de Beaune-Villages 1982 • $19 • (05/16/84) SS • **88**
Côte de Beaune-Villages Clos des Topes Bizot 1983 • $22 • (09/15/86) • **82**
Côte de Nuits-Villages 1990: Tastes like a pleasant, simple Beaujolais, with modest tannins and plenty of light fruit flavors. Drinkable now. • $NA • (12/15/92) • **78**
Côtes du Rhône 1989 • $8 • (07/15/91) BB • **82**
Côtes du Rhône Le Chamville 1993: Fairly herbal and a bit thin in the middle with only modest cherry and currant fruit flavors. Turns green and a little bitter on the finish. • $10 • **78**
Echézeaux 1991: Tight, chewy and a lot more concentrated than most '91s, showing earthy rose petal and toast-scented currant and berry flavors. A chunky wine that needs until 1997 or '98 to soften. 400 cases made. • $54 Ⓐ • (01/31/94) • **89**
Echézeaux 1990: Ripe, concentrated and complex, with tight currant, cherry and plum-tinged flavors that take on a pleasant, earthy edge on the finish, where the tight tannins kick in. Drinkable now. • $42 • (10/31/92) • **89**
Echézeaux 1989 • $62 • (01/31/92) • **88**
Gevrey-Chambertin 1993: Very good village wine. Lovely fruit and silky tannins. Medium-bodied, showing dark chocolate and berry character and a long, long aftertaste. Better in 1999. • $29 • (11/15/95) • **86**
Gevrey-Chambertin 1992: Delicate and verging on diluted. The wet earth, raspberry and black cherry character raises some interest. • $27 • (12/15/94) • **79**
Gevrey-Chambertin 1982 • $18 • (06/16/84) • **80**
Mâcon-Villages Le Chamville 1994: Subtle mineral, pear, apple and spice flavors develop in smooth little waves to a harmonious finish. Lacks a bit of intensity. • $11 • **82**
Meursault 1993: Crisp, smooth mineral character and citrusy, herbal notes. Long finish. Try now. • $26 • **84**
Meursault 1992: Rather tight Meursault, light- to medium-bodied, with fresh and clean character from green apple, herb and citrus flavors. • $20 • (08/31/94) • **83**
Meursault Les Charmes 1991 • $NA • (10/15/93) • **88**
Meursault Clos des Corvées de Citeaux 1991 • $45 • (10/15/93) • **88**
Meursault Les Genevrières 1994: Lovely, medium- to full-bodied, delivering a good amount of honey, apricot and ripe pear aromas and flavors. Lacks a bit of panache and intensity, but provides delicious drinking now. • $46 • (05/31/96) • **85**
Meursault Genevrières 1993: Relatively ripe and very delicious, featuring a polished, silky texture, zesty acidity and some attractive pear, honey and mineral flavors. Drink now. • $45 • (05/15/95) • **88**
Meursault Genevrières 1991 • $45 • (10/15/93) • **87**
Montrachet 1994: An elegant, distinguished wine with a sense of class. Has mineral, honey, cream, vanilla, spice and ripe fruit flavors in the right proportions, and an understated citrus intensity on the finish, which just builds and builds. • $185 • (05/31/96) • **94**
Montrachet Domaines du Château de Beaune 1993: Intense, generously flavored, vibrant and well made, offering floral, lime, dried herb character. Full-bodied. Needs time to soften its acidic edges, will be terrific. 300 cases made. • $181 • **88**
Nuits-St.-Georges 1983 • $21 • (09/15/86) • **68**
Nuits-St.-Georges Les Cailles 1959 • $90 • (08/31/90) • **87**
Nuits-St.-Georges Clos des Argillières 1990: A fruity style of Nuits, with ripe cherry and spice aromas and flavors and medium-hard tannins. Somewhat one-dimensional. Drinkable now. • $31 • (12/15/92) • **86**
Nuits-St.-Georges Clos-St.-Marc 1993: Rather light in structure but chewy on the finish, inserting fresh red berry and earth character. Ends slightly dry, could use more ripe fruit. Try in 1997. • $47 • **82**
Nuits-St.-Georges Clos-St.-Marc 1992: Light and a little wimpy, barely offering any of its strawberry flavors. This is a *premier cru*? • $43 • **73**

Key: SS—Spectator Selection. CS—Cellar Selection. BB—Best Buy. $NA—Price not available. (BT)—Barrel tasting. Ⓐ—Auction Price.
Dates in parentheses represent the issues in which the ratings were published.

Nuits-St.-Georges Clos St.-Marc 1991: Modest tobacco and plum flavors and hard tannins on the finish. Needs until 1998, but then what? • $45 • (01/31/94) • **75**

Nuits-St.-Georges Clos-St.-Marc 1989 • $59 • (01/31/92) • **89**

Nuits-St.-Georges Clos-St.-Marc 1985 • $53 • (02/28/89) • **87**

Nuits-St.-Georges Clos-St.-Marc 1983 • $33 • (09/15/86) • **74**

Nuits-St.-Georges La Richemone 1989 • $NA • (01/31/92) • **89**

Pommard 1992: Crisp, simple, tasting modestly of black cherry. • $35 • **79**

Pommard 1988 • $37 • (04/30/91) • **90**

Pommard 1983 • $23 • (09/15/86) • **74**

Pommard Clos du Pavillon 1989 • $NA • (01/31/92) • **92**

Pommard Premier Cru Domaines du Château de Beaune 1990: For being a blend of vineyards, this is unbelievable. Ripe, rich and firm, showing terrific breeding, with lovely, elegant, focused red berry flavors and superfine tannins. Drinkable now. • $39 • (12/15/92) • **94**

Pommard Premier Cru Domaines du Château de Beaune 1988 • $53 • (03/31/91) • **89**

Pommard Premier Cru Domaines du Château de Beaune 1986 • $41 • (07/31/88) • **87**

Puligny-Montrachet 1993 • $24 • **83**

Puligny-Montrachet 1991 • $32 • (10/15/93) • **85**

Puligny-Montrachet Les Chalumeaux 1991 • $NA • (10/15/93) • **82**

Puligny-Montrachet Les Folatières 1994: Soft and supple, offering medium body and intensity, it tastes of vanilla ice cream, honey and apple. Could use more concentration. Drinkable now. • $38 • (05/31/96) • **84**

Puligny-Montrachet Les Folatières 1993: Some citric, mushroom character. Medium-bodied and crisp, slightly earthy finish. A bit dull overall. • $36 • **79**

Puligny-Montrachet Les Pucelles 1994: Round and supple, balanced and harmonious honey, pear, vanilla and mineral character. Not very intense and quite soft on the finish, but makes for lovely drinking now. • $46 • (05/31/96) • **87**

Puligny-Montrachet Les Pucelles 1993: Fresh citric and mineral character, medium body, firm acidity and a clean finish. • $41 • **81**

Puligny-Montrachet Les Pucelles 1992: Subtly complex, still closed in aroma, but the flavors are clearly defined, and they grow on the finish. Reminds us of honey, hazelnut and pear, combined in a silky, seamless package. Try now. 75 cases made. • $30 • (08/31/94) • **88**

Puligny-Montrachet Les Pucelles 1991 • $NA • (10/15/93) • **91**

La Romanée Château de Vosne-Romanée 1993: Refined but closed in now, showing some nice concentration of red berry flavor and tannins that clamp down on the finish. Of medium body, with lovely rose petal and currant notes. Try in 1999. 330 cases made. • $120 • (11/15/95) • **90**

La Romanée Château de Vosne-Romanée 1992: Under the coarse tannins lies a nice thread of spice, tobacco and berry flavor that lingers on the chewy finish. Try in 1997 or 1998. • $118 • (12/15/94) • **85**

La Romanée Château de Vosne-Romanée 1986 • $83 Ⓐ • (07/31/88) • **91**

Savigny-lès-Beaune 1989 • $29 • (01/31/92) • **82**

Savigny-lès-Beaune Les Lavières Domaines du Château de Beaune 1990: Traditionally-styled, with mellow chestnut and cherry aromas and flavors and smooth tannins. Lacks intensity. Drinkable now. • $NA • (12/15/92) • **82**

Savigny-lès-Beaune Les Lavières Domaines du Château de Beaune 1988 • $29 • (04/30/91) • **83**

Savigny-lès-Beaune Les Lavières Domaines du Château de Beaune 1986 • $25 • (07/31/88) • **78**

Volnay Callierets Ancienne Cuvée Carnot Domaines du Château de Beaune 1992: A smooth and silky Burgundy with classic earthy, toasty, leathery aromas, polished fruit flavors and a good finish. Drinkable now. 1,500 cases made. • $29 • (10/31/94) • **85**

Volnay Caillerets Ancienne Cuvée Carnot Domaines du Château de Beaune 1991: Flavorful and smoky, this lean, firm-textured wine has flesh and style to frame the gamy, toasty, berryish aromas and flavors. Drinkable now. 1,500 cases made. • $37 • (01/31/94) • **85**

Volnay Caillerets Ancienne Cuvée Carnot Domaines du Château de Beaune 1990: Firm and tightly structured, with plenty of fruit to give it a velvety feel and intense, gamy cherry and tobacco flavors. The finish is loaded with tannins. Try in 1998. • $37 • (12/15/92) • **90**

Volney Caillerets Ancienne Cuvée Carnot Domaines du Château de Beaune 1989 • $52 • (02/29/92) CS • **94**

Volnay Caillerets Ancienne Cuvée Carnot Domaines du Château de Beaune 1988 • $47 • (03/31/91) • **87**

Volnay Caillerets Ancienne Cuvée Carnot Domaines du Château de Beaune 1986 • $34 • (07/31/88) • **83**

Volnay Caillerets Ancienne Cuvée Carnot Domaines du Château de Beaune 1985 • $44 • (01/31/89) • **87**

Volnay Chevret 1992: Light, but showing some ripe currant flavor that fades on the finish. Drinkable now. • $NA • **79**

Volnay Frémiets Clos de la Rougette 1992: Firm and a little chewy, with enough berry and currant flavor to keep it in balance. Drinkable now. • $38 • **82**

Volnay Frémiets Clos de la Rougeotte Domaines du Château de Beaune 1993: Light-to-medium body, showing some plummy, meaty flavors. A bit one-dimensional and dry on the finish. Try in 1998. 590 cases made. • $35 • **84**

Volnay Frémiets Clos de la Rougeotte Domaines du Château de Beaune 1990: An aromatic and open wine, with chestnut and cherry aromas and flavors that are not very intense, but show lovely balance. Try now or hold. • $NA • (12/15/92) • **86**

Volnay Frémiets Clos de la Rougeotte Domaines du Château de Beaune 1985 • $35 • (01/31/89) • **88**

Volnay Taillepieds 1992: Lean and crisply tannic, with a modest level of berry flavor that persists into the finish. Drinkable now. • $32 • **82**

Volnay Taillepieds Domaines du Château du Beaune 1991: Earthy, almost muddy in flavor. A chewy wine that has little charm and is drying on the finish. Drinkable now. 450 cases made. • $34 • (01/31/94) • **78**

Volnay Taillepieds Domaines du Château du Beaune 1990: Tight and hard as a rock when first tasted, deep, packed with vanilla, chocolate, plum and black cherry elements. Try now. • $34 Ⓐ • (12/15/92) • **92**

Volnay Taillepieds Domaines du Château du Beaune 1989 • $48 • (01/31/92) • **88**

Volnay Taillepieds Domaines du Château du Beaune 1988 • $50 • (03/31/91) • **88**

Vosne-Romanée Aux Reignots Château de Vosne-Romanée 1993: Firm and solid, muscular and full-bodied, featuring red berry, earth and mineral character. Some dryness on aftertaste makes us wonder how it will age. But try in 2006. • $51 • **88**

Vosne-Romanée Aux Reignots Château de Vosne-Romanée 1992: A beautifully perfumed but tightly wound red that will need until '96 or beyond to reach its peak. Has exotic leafy, earthy, meaty aromas, followed by tart cherry and plum flavors. Great finish, too. • $40 • (10/31/94) • **89**

Vosne-Romanée Aux Reignots Château de Vosne-Romanée 1991: Lean and simple, with a watery texture than cramps the modest berry flavors. Pleasant enough, but nothing special. Drinkable now. 750 cases made. • $51 • (01/31/94) • **80**

Vosne-Romanée Aux Reignots Château de Vosne-Romanée 1990: A more delicate Vosne, with game, berry and chestnut aromas and flavors and medium tannins. Drinkable now. • $53 • (12/15/92) • **85**

Vosne-Romanée Aux Reignots Château de Vosne-Romanée 1989 • $55 • (01/31/92) • **93**

Vosne-Romanée Aux Reignots Château de Vosne-Romanée 1986 • $50 • (07/31/88) • **89**

Vosne-Romanée Aux Reignots Château de Vosne-Romanée 1985 • $51 • (02/28/89) • **90**

BOUCHARD, PASCAL

Chablis 1994: Short and quite diluted, it smells and tastes of cardboard and odd earthy notes. • $18 • (05/31/96) • **71**

Chablis Beauroy 1994: Tight and flinty, showing only modest fruit flavors. Rather lean and a bit too crisp on the finish. Better in 1998? • $NA • (05/31/96) • **80**

Chablis Blanchots 1994: Supple, offering rich, ripe, soft texture, decent apple and pear components and nice mineral notes. Lacks a bit of concentration. • $NA • (05/31/96) • **85**

Chablis Les Clos 1994: Rich, ripe and lush but tasting somewhat rustic, with butterscotch, cedar and earth aromas and flavors. Slightly sour finish. • $45 • (05/31/96) • **74**

Chablis Les Clos 1993: Firm and citrusy, a steely Chablis that delivers character and personality in a lean frame. Drink with seafood. 100 cases made. • $NA • (08/31/94) • **83**

FRANCE

Chablis Fourchaume 1994: Quite woody but unctuous and solidly built. Packed with fresh, lemony, crisp character, this full-bodied '94 *premier cru* delivers honey, mineral, wet earth and lime flavors. A bit harsh on aftertaste. Try in 1999. • $36 • (05/31/96) • **85**

Chablis Mont de Milieu 1994: Fresh and rather vibrant, showing a grassy, slightly herbal character. Quite tart and long on the finish. May need until 1999 to be ready for drinking. • $36 • (05/31/96) • **88**

Chablis Mont de Milieu 1993: Mineral and dried herb aromas and flavors, medium body, crisp acidity and a long, spicy finish. 400 cases made. • $NA • (08/31/94) • **84**

Chablis Montmains 1994: Full-bodied and rather fat, delivering some citrus, apple and herb character. Seductive and silky at first, it turns a bit flat and sour on aftertaste. Drinkable now. • $36 • (05/31/96) • **78**

Chablis Vaudésir 1994: Good concentration and quite seductive at first, but then fell apart in the glass. Turned tart, adding a cardboard, dry finish. • $NA • (05/31/96) • **72**

BOUCHE PERE & FILS

Brut Champagne Cuvée Réservée NV • $20 • (01/31/92) • **87**

BOUCHE, DOMAINE

Côtes du Rhône La Truffière 1990 • $12 • (04/15/93) • **79**
Côtes du Rhône l'Amandier 1990 • $8 • (04/15/93) • **80**

BOUCHOTTE, VALENTIN

Savigny-lès-Beaune Hauts-Jarrons 1988 • $31 • (02/28/91) • **83**

BOUISSIERE, DOMAINE LA

Gigondas 1989 • $15 • (04/15/93) • **74**

BOULEY, DOMAINE JEAN-MARC

Pommard Les Rugiens 1987 • $34 • (11/15/90) • **63**
Pommard Les Rugiens 1985 • $30 • (10/31/88) • **92**
Volnay Caillerets 1985 • $27 • (10/15/88) • **90**
Volnay Clos des Chênes 1985 • $27 • (10/15/88) • **87**

BOULLAY, PIERRE

Sancerre Chavignol 1992 • $22 • (05/15/96) • **68**

BOUR, DOMAINE

Coteaux du Tricastin 1993: Like a Beaujolais in style, with fresh, light, candied fruit flavors and a soft, ready-to-drink texture. Try it chilled. • $10 • **81**

Coteaux du Tricastin 1990 • $8 • (06/15/93) • **76**

BOUREE PERE & FILS

Beaune Les Epenottes 1989 • $30 • (01/31/92) • **91**
Beaune Les Epenottes 1987 • $35 • (06/15/90) • **88**
Bonnes Mares 1985 • $85 • (05/31/88) • **91**
Bourgogne 1988 • $15 • (03/31/92) • **73**

Chambertin 1990: Not as concentrated as we would expect from a *grand cru*, but offers pleasant strawberry and earth characteristics and medium tannins nonetheless. Drinkable now. 125 cases made. • $85 • (12/15/92) • **84**

Chambertin 1987 • $100 • (05/31/90) • **90**
Chambertin 1985 • $81 Ⓐ • (05/31/88) • **92**
Chambolle-Musigny 1987 • $44 • (06/15/90) • **82**
Chambolle-Musigny Charmes 1987 • $56 • (06/15/90) • **82**
Charmes-Chambertin 1988 • $75 • (03/31/91) • **89**

Key: SS—Spectator Selection. CS—Cellar Selection. BB—Best Buy. $NA—Price not available. (BT)—Barrel tasting. Ⓐ—Auction Price.
Dates in parentheses represent the issues in which the ratings were published.

Charmes-Chambertin 1987 • $66 • (05/31/90) • **87**
Charmes-Chambertin 1985 • $68 • (05/31/88) • **88**

Clos de la Roche 1990: Graceful, with sumptuous earth, plum and cherry aromas and flavors and velvety tannins. Drinkable now. 125 cases made. • $70 • (12/15/92) • **90**

Clos de la Roche 1989 • $65 • (01/31/92) • **94**
Clos de la Roche 1988 • $85 • (03/31/91) • **91**
Clos de la Roche 1987 • $86 • (06/15/90) • **85**
Gevrey-Chambertin 1989 • $35 • (01/31/92) • **85**
Gevrey-Chambertin Les Cazetiers 1987 • $66 • (05/31/90) • **80**
Gevrey-Chambertin Les Cazetiers 1985 • $67 • (05/31/88) • **91**
Gevrey-Chambertin Clos de la Justice 1988 • $54 • (03/31/92) • **78**
Gevrey-Chambertin Clos de la Justice 1985 • $51 • (05/31/88) • **85**

Gevrey-Chambertin Le Clos St.-Jacques 1990: Extremely firm, with fresh mushroom, wet earth and berry aromas and flavors and toasty chestnut notes. Has plenty of acidity and firm tannins to warrant cellaring until 1997. 75 cases made. • $60 • (12/15/92) • **90**

Gevrey-Chambertin Le Clos St.-Jacques 1987 • $56 • (05/31/90) • **86**
Latricières-Chambertin 1959 • $NA • (08/31/90) • **98**
Morey-St.-Denis 1987 • $35 • (05/15/90) • **74**
Nuits-St.-Georges Les Vaucrains 1985 • $68 • (05/31/88) • **93**
Santenay Gravières 1985 • $30 • (05/31/88) • **88**
Vosne-Romanée 1987 • $44 • (07/15/90) • **68**

BOURGEOIS, HENRI

Pouilly-Fumé 1994: Lively, vibrant ripe pear and melon flavors and zippy, citrusy acidity. The herbal notes are downplayed in this round, muscular Sauvignon Blanc. Drinkable now. • $17 • (11/15/95) • **88**

Pouilly-Fumé 1991 • $17 • (09/15/93) • **84**

Pouilly-Fumé La Demoiselle de Bourgeois 1993: This wine is aromatic with the beautiful smoky note that gives Pouilly-Fumé its name, and ripe with pear and fig flavors to boot. It's round and soft on the palate, with a lingering fruity finish. Try now. • $22 • (11/15/95) • **88**

Sancerre Côtes des Monts Damnés 1991 • $22 • (09/15/93) • **85**

Sancerre Grande Réserve 1994: Thick on the palate, with sweet apple fruit and pie crust flavors, this resembles a New World Sauvignon Blanc more than a Loire. It's round and soft, and makes easy-drinking. • $17 • **81**

Sancerre Grande Réserve 1991 • $17 • (09/15/93) • **81**

Sancerre La Bourgeoise 1993: This pleasant wine shows freshness and good typicity in a balanced, unobtrusive style. Green apple and herbal flavors mingle over firm acidity, and a pretty floral note emerges on the lingering finish. • $25 • (11/15/95) • **85**

Sancerre La Bourgeoise 1991 • $25 • (11/30/92) • **88**

Sancerre La Bourgeoise 1990: Surprisingly rich for a Loire Pinot, this deep-colored wine has firm tannins and a smooth texture, with spicy cherry fruit and plenty of earthy and gamy flavors, finishing with accents of smoke and spice. Drinkable now. • $15 • **83**

Sancerre La Côte des Monts Damnés 1994: There's a resinous quality that runs through the lemon and pine flavors, plus some menthol. Turns slightly soft in the middle and tastes of marzipan on aftertaste. • $24 • (04/30/96) • **83**

Sancerre La Porte du Caillou 1992: Distinctive and unusual, showing ripe fruit aromas of banana and pear, then a rich, viscous mouth-feel with tropical fruit and spice flavors, saved from flabbiness by crisp acidity. Tastes more like New World Sauvignon Blanc than Sancerre. • $14 • (08/31/94) • **88**

Sancerre Le MD de Bourgeois 1992: Classically styled Sancerre. Herbaceous aromas are still young and snappy. On the palate this wine is softening a little, yet retaining firm acidity to counteract the rich texture and mineral and apple flavors. Harmonious and balanced and though drinking well now, will still improve in bottle. • $25 • (11/15/95) • **90**

Sancerre Le MD de Bourgeois 1991 • $25 • (11/30/92) • **86**

BOURGEOIS, RICHARD

Pouilly-Fumé 1994: A hard wine, with steely acidity but not much fruit, it's marred by earthy and cat's-pee notes. It has Loire Sauvignon character, but it's not much fun. 3,000 cases made. • $14 • **79**

Pouilly-Fumé 1993: Crisp and minerally; firm and focused but a bit austere. Some citrus flavors and very tart acidity with a short finish. 5,000 cases made. • $15 • (10/31/94) • **79**

Sancerre 1994: Typical herbal Sauvignon Blanc flavors are softened and amplified by pleasant creamy, melon notes, very fresh and lively. It's a modest wine that makes up in enthusiasm what it lacks in depth. 3,000 cases made. • $14 • **84**

Sancerre 1993: Pungent herbal and grapefruit aromas give way to ripe apple and citrus flavors, with a lean, crisp finish. A distinctive wine with sharp, fresh flavors that will marry well with grilled fish. 5,000 cases made. • $15 • (10/31/94) • **85**

BOURGEON, PAUL

Mâcon-Villages 1993: Grassy like a Sauvignon Blanc, showing loads of green, almost asparagus flavors. Unbelievably tart. • $NA • **77**

BOURGNEUF, CHÂTEAU

Pomerol 1995: Gorgeous blackberry, raspberry and licorice aromas and flavors, full body, medium-to-full tannins and long, fruity finish. Excellent. • $NA • (05/15/96) • **90-94** (BT)

Pomerol 1994: Exotically perfumed and very silkey, offering rose-pteal aromas and currant, olive, herb and chocolate flavors. Rich, full body, ripe and almost sweet-tasting finish. • $NA • **85-89** (BT)

Pomerol 1993: Somewhat overdone green bean and berry aromas and flavors. Medium-bodied, medium-to-light tannins and an herbal, dry finish. Drinkable now. • $23 • (01/31/96) • **81**

Pomerol 1990: A solid, racy wine, with complex aromas of tar, licorice, violets and ripe fruit which follow through on the palate. Excellent tannin structure. Drinkable in 1998. 5,000 cases made. • $23 • (03/31/93) • **94**

Pomerol 1989 • $32 • (03/15/92) • **90**

Pomerol 1988 • $19 • (06/30/91) • **90**

Pomerol 1985: Sometimes this estate really makes amazing wines. Massive, hedonistic wine with layer upon layer of tar, dark chocolate and fruit character. Full-bodied and super velvety. Try in 1998. • $NA • **92**

Pomerol 1983: Traditional styled wine with earthy, berry, chocolate character, medium-bodied with pretty of chocolate, berry flavors but rather light on the finish. Drink now. • $NA • **83**

Pomerol 1982 • $NA • (05/15/89) • **83**

Pomerol 1981: Rich and wonderful. At its peak. Overtly aromatic with tobacco, dried herbs and ripe fruit character. Medium body with beautiful silky texture and excellent intensity of tobacco, bitter chocolate flavors. Drink now. • $NA • **87**

BOURGOGNE ST.-VINCENT

Châteauneuf-du-Pape 1983 • $8 • (07/16/85) • **81**

BOURILLON-DORLEANS, DOMAINE

Vouvray Vielles Vignes 1992: This thick, full-bodied, concentrated wine is packed with buttery, vanilla, ripe pear and honey flavors. It's not sweet, but still rich and luscious, with an attractive malt and nutmeg finish. • $11 • **87**

BOUSCAT, CHÂTEAU LE

Bordeaux Grand Réserve 1990: Here's a harmonious, balanced wine with a solid core of black cherry and plum fruit, attractive accents of tobacco and herbs and a firm frame of tannins. It only lacks complexity. Drinkable now. 2,100 cases made. • $9 • (11/15/94) • **86**

Bordeaux White Grand Réserve 1992: An oaky style of white Bordeaux, with seductive aromas of toast and vanilla, but not much fruit flavor to back them up. Clean and balanced, but lacking richness and focus. 1,700 cases made. • $9 • (11/15/94) • **83**

BOUSCAUT, CHÂTEAU

Graves 1985 • $15 • (12/31/88) • **90**

Graves 1982 • $18 • (08/31/92) • **84**

Graves 1981 • $12 • (05/01/84) • **86**

Graves 1970 • $27 • (05/15/93) • **85**

Graves 1961: Considerable life left in this tangy, enticing Graves. It tastes fresh, lively, cranberrylike, even if it fades on the finish. Drink through 1998. • $NA • (04/30/96) • **85**

Pessac-Léognan 1994: Crisp and very firm, medium-bodied, delivering some pretty cassis and black olive flavors. Slightly dry on finish. Might be better at our next tasting. • $NA • **80-84** (BT)

Pessac-Léognan 1993: Straightforward tobacco and cherry character, medium-to-light body, light tannins and simple finish. Drinkable now. 10,833 cases made. • $25 • (01/31/96) • **82**

Pessac-Léognan 1990: Meaty and rich, with decadent smoky and berry aromas and flavors and velvety tannins. Drinkable now. 15,000 cases made. • $18 • (03/31/93) • **88**

Pessac-Léognan 1989 • $22 • (03/15/92) • **93**

Pessac-Léognan 1988 • $20 • (04/30/91) • **87**

Pessac-Léognan 1986 • $9 • (02/15/89) • **78**

Pessac-Léognan White 1994: Firm and crisp, with lovely, creamy apple and lime character. Medium body and firm acidity right through the finish, better in 1997. • $18 • (03/31/96) • **86**

Pessac-Léognan White 1992 • $NA • (06/15/94) • **77**

BOUSQUETTE, CHÂTEAU

St.-Chinian 1991 • $9 • (03/15/94) • **82**

St.-Chinian 1989 • $10 • (07/15/92) • **81**

St.-Chinian 1986 • $8 • (03/31/90) • **82**

BOUVERIE, LA

Costières de Nimes 1994: A good, fruity wine that's accented with some nice tobacco-like flavors. The fruit is dominated by fairly concentrated berry flavors. 12,000 cases made. • $6 • **82**

Costières de Nimes 1989 • $6 • (07/15/91) • **79**

Costières de Nimes White 1994: Pleasant and fruity, showing some nice buttery notes and almond and peach flavors that linger through the finish. 12,000 cases made. • $6 • (09/30/95) • **82**

Costières de Nimes White 1992: Ripe and interesting in flavor and aroma, blending herb, smoke, pepper and tart cherry. Full-bodied, but not too tannic. Drinkable now. 40,000 cases made. • $5 • (10/15/94) BB • **84**

Merlot Vin de Pays d'Oc Cuvée Spéciale 1993: Well made and well priced, this French red offers balanced black cherry, herb and spice flavors, firm but not overbearing tannins and a lingering, smoky finish. Drinkable now. 8,000 cases made. • $7 • (10/31/95) BB • **84**

Viognier Vin de Pays d'Oc Cuvée Spéciale 1993: A core of steely acidity gives this a refreshing intensity, along with clean, muted fruit flavors, it doesn't taste much like Viognier, though. 4,000 cases made. • $8 • (02/29/96) • **81**

BOUVET

Brut Rosé Excellence NV • $12 • (06/15/90) • **80**

Brut Rosé NV • $10 • (06/15/90) • **80**

Brut Saumur Ladubay Tresor NV • $44 • (10/15/88) • **81**

Brut Saumur Vintage Saphir 1992: Very fruity and fairly full-bodied, this has a blast of apple and spice flavor that makes it enjoyable. Well-balanced and refreshing, too. • $14 • (11/15/95) • **83**

Brut Saumur Saphir 1991: Light on the palate, but complex and nicely mature in flavor. Has an intriguing streak of vanilla, toasted almond and pear that lingers on the finish. • $14 • (11/15/95) • **85**

Brut Saumur Saphir 1988 • $14 • (01/31/92) • **82**

Brut Saumur Saphir 1985 • $12 • (06/15/90) • **84**

Brut Saumur Signature NV: Rather rich in flavor, with a nice, crisp texture and enough body to make it satisfying to drink. Has buttery nuances and solid appley flavors, with spicy accents that linger on the finish. • $12 • (11/15/95) • **84**

Rubi's NV • $10 • (06/15/90) • **72**

BOUYOT, CHÂTEAU

Barsac 1987 • $NA • (06/15/90) • **74**

BOUZEREAU & FILS, MICHEL

Meursault Genevriéres 1992: Vividly fruity, lively with flavor and acidity, making the pear, apple and spice flavors last a long time on the finish. It's smooth, pure and refined. • $NA • (08/31/94) • **88**

Meursault Le Tesson 1994: Attractive village wine, harmonious, supple and medium-bodied, offering lovely, focused ripe fruit character. A clean and authentic-tasting white Burgundy. Drinkable now. • $35 • (05/31/96) • **85**

Meursault Le Tesson 1992: Fairly ripe and rich, blending pear, hazelnut and vanilla flavors with an elegant, balanced finish. • $29 Ⓐ • (08/31/94) • **86**

Meursault Les Charmes 1994: Some exciting mineral and vanilla character in this medium-bodied white. Intense citrus, almond and butter character. Very well made and voluptuous on the finish. Try now and through 2000. • $45 • (05/31/96) • **90**

Meursault Les Genevrières 1994: Super Chardonnay, full-bodied yet refined and classy. Quite toasty, beautifully supple and smooth, boasting a lovely honey and ripe fruit character. Concentrated and silky on the perfectly balanced finish. Drinkable now. • $45 • (05/31/96) • **95**

Meursault Les Grands Charrons 1994: Soft and supple, very pleasant with honey, apricot, lemon and pear character. Seduces you with its sweet flavors and mineral texture. Delicious now. • $30 • (05/31/96) • **85**

Meursault Les Grands Charrons 1992: Pure, focused fruit, packed with intense pear, apple and grapefruit flavors that are laced with a touch of honey, lingers on the finish. More fruit intensity than most village Meursault. Try now. • $NA • (08/31/94) • **89**

Puligny-Montrachet Champ Gain 1994: Magnificent. Restrained and yet full of flavor, it melts like whipped double cream in your mouth. The symphony of flavors—vanilla, mineral, hazelnut, coconut, pear and lemon—marry flawlessly in this tightly wrapped, medium- to full-bodied white. Drinkable now. • $45 • (05/31/96) • **94**

BOXLER, ALBERT

Riesling Alsace Grand Cru Sommerberg 1992: This shows an elegant, mineral character reminiscent of Germany's Mosel. Delicate, even shy, it expands on the palate, with peach and floral notes, and finishes clean and long. Well made and expressive. • $25 • (09/15/94) • **90**

BOYD-CANTENAC, CHÂTEAU

Margaux 1985 • $27 Ⓐ • (04/15/88) • **90**

Margaux 1983 • $19 Ⓐ • (04/16/86) • **86**

Margaux 1982 • $29 Ⓐ • (08/31/92) • **90**

Margaux 1961: It tastes earthy, decadent and mature, like you'd expect in a 35-year-old wine. Good but lean in flavor. Drink now. • $31 • (04/30/96) • **84**

BRAC DE LA PERRIERE

Beaujolais-Villages Domaine de la Brasse 1995: Straightforward and pretty. A pleasant mix of cherry, spice and light banana notes gives this wine immediate appeal. It has enough structure to match with food, too. • $NA • **84**

BRANAIRE-DUCRU, CHÂTEAU

St.-Julien 1995: This shows a very good dose of ripe berry, smoke and vanilla aromas and flavors. Good tannins and a long finish. Almost outstanding. • $NA • (05/15/96) • **85-89** (BT)

St.-Julien 1994: Fairly round, with a nice, perfumey character and black currant and toasted oak flavors, though it ends a bit dry and short. • $NA • (05/15/96) • **80-84** (BT)

Key: SS—Spectator Selection. CS—Cellar Selection. BB—Best Buy. $NA—Price not available. (BT)—Barrel tasting. Ⓐ—Auction Price.
Dates in parentheses represent the issues in which the ratings were published.

St.-Julien 1993: Attractive berry, wet earth aromas and flavors, medium body, medium silky tannins and fresh finish. Try in 1997. • $25 • (01/31/96) • **85**

St.-Julien 1991: It shows some good tobacco and vanilla flavors. Drinkable now. • $22 • (03/31/94) • **80**

St.-Julien 1990: Sleek and pretty, with floral, mint and plum aromas and flavors and lovely, silky tannins. Drinkable in 1997. 20,000 cases made. • $25 • (03/31/93) • **90**

St.-Julien 1989 • $35 Ⓐ • (03/15/92) • **90**

St.-Julien 1985: A wine with lots of fresh fruit. The cherry, plum character is everywhere. It's medium bodied with firm tannins and a loverly cherry finish. Drink now or hold. • $NA • **87**

St.-Julien 1983: Very ripe style almost over done. A ruby, garnet edged color with very ripe almost raisin, fresh berry aromas and flavors. Medium bodied and firm tannins. Drinkable now. • $NA • **84**

St.-Julien 1982 • $41 Ⓐ • (08/31/92) • **90**

St.-Julien 1981: Slightly one dimensional, but still shows a lot of vivacity. Medium bodied with lovely soft texture and a long intense violet, berry, minty finish. Drink or hold. • $NA • **86**

St.-Julien 1970 • $42 • (05/15/93) • **90**

St.-Julien 1961: Just good, probably well past its glory. It has earthy, tobaccolike aromas and metallic flavors, with a tannic bite on the finish. Drink now. • $58 • (04/30/96) • **80**

St.-Julien 1959 • $80 Ⓐ • (10/15/90) • **86**

St.-Julien 1945 • $175 • (03/16/86) • **67**

BRANE-CANTENAC, CHÂTEAU

Margaux 1995: Bright and fruity, with earthy berry aromas and flavors. Medium- to light-bodied, with fine tannins. • $NA • (05/15/96) • **80-84** (BT)

Margaux 1994: Some attractive tobacco, cherry and blackberry character, medium body and tannins and a slightly short finish. • $NA • **80-84** (BT)

Margaux 1993: Some good berry and cherry character and a hint of black pepper. Medium-bodied, velvety tannins, polished finish. Try in 1998. • $25 • (01/31/96) • **85**

Margaux 1991: Slightly diluted, but some pretty berry and raspberry flavors finding harmony in the fine tannins. • $24 • (03/31/94) • **80**

Margaux 1990: This is solid yet very appealing, with ripe fruit and vanilla character, fine, well-integrated tannins and a long, refreshing, jammy finish. Drinkable in 1997. 29,000 cases made. • $28 • (03/31/93) • **91**

Margaux 1989 • $31 Ⓐ • (03/15/92) • **94**

Margaux 1988 • $42 • (08/31/91) • **76**

Margaux 1986 • $26 • (06/15/89) • **87**

Margaux 1985: Ripe and fruity with plenty of everything. Still a bit tough on the palate. Needs time to mellow. Try in 1998. • $NA • **88**

Margaux 1983: Pretty, elegant wine with spicy, fruit, toasted oak aromas and flavors. Medium bodied and silky, fresh aftertaste. Drink now. • $NA • **87**

Margaux 1982 • $29 Ⓐ • (08/31/92) • **88**

Margaux 1981: Another delicate wine at its peak with cedar, berry, spice character, medium/light body and a crisp finish. Drink now. • $NA • **82**

Margaux 1979 • $NA • (10/15/89) • **80**

Margaux 1970 • $26 Ⓐ • (05/15/93) • **87**

Margaux 1962 • $34 Ⓐ • (11/30/87) • **60**

Margaux 1961: A very mature bottle bouquet and a cherry-herb flavor makes it interesting, but it's on its way down, so drink now. • $63 • (04/30/96) • **84**

Margaux 1945 • $NA • (03/16/86) • **87**

BRANE, CHÂTEAU BARON DE

Margaux 1994: Light in color and body, offering modest raspberry and strawberry flavors and tannic finish. Second label of Château Brane-Cantenac. • $NA • (06/30/95) • **70**

Margaux 1989 • $NA • (03/15/92) • **89**

BRASSAC, CHÂTEAU

Bordeaux Supérieur 1986 • $5 • (08/31/88) BB • **80**

BREDIF, MARC

Chinon 1993: Mouthwatering. This ripe, juicy wine marries bright berry and plum flavors with attractive meaty and vanilla notes. It has good acidity and light tannins, balanced for drinking now. • $12 • **85**

Chinon 1992: Bottle age has softened the tannins in this light red, and added tobacco and cola notes to the black cherry fruit. It's balanced and clean, a good match for game birds or rich fish, such as salmon. At its peak now. 330,000 cases made. • $12 • (10/31/94) • **84**

Vouvray 1993: Classic Chenin Blanc flavors of honey, apple and beeswax are followed by a rich, broad texture. The lively, mineral finish is long, but needs until 1998 to soften. • $14 • (04/30/96) • **84**

Vouvray Vin Moelleux Nectar 1989: Still youthful, sporting apricot, honey and tangerine flavors and rich texture. The vibrant acidity keeps it from cloying. A dessert style from a great vintage, this will age forever. • $25 • (04/30/96) • **90**

Vouvray Vin Moelleux Nectar 1985 • $16 Ⓐ • (06/15/91) • **75**

BREGEON, ANDRE-MICHEL

Muscadet de Sèvre et Maine Sur Lie 1992: A year in bottle has softened this wine nicely, turning the citrus notes into rounder apple flavors, and a slight spritz keeps it refreshing. It's smooth and polished, as Muscadets go. 1,000 cases made. • $10 • (10/31/94) • **83**

BRETON, P.

Bourgueil Les Galichets 1993: Very Cabernet Franc in character, featuring leafy cedar and black currant flavors, all on a lean frame. Drinkable now. 480 cases made. • $15 • (05/15/96) • **84**

BRETONNIERE, YVES

Muscadet de Sèvre et Maine Domaine des 3 Versants, La Févrie 1993: Light-bodied and a bit green and bitter, like a slightly unripe grapefruit. A real palate cleanser. 2,500 cases made. • $8 • (10/31/94) • **77**

BREUIL, CHÂTEAU DU

Haut-Médoc 1992: Attractive, delicate currant, mint and cherry character, medium body, medium tannins and fresh, silky finish. Drinkable now. • $NA • **80**

BRIARE, BARON

Touraine Sauvignon de Sauvignon 1992: Past its prime, this dull white offers flavors of browned cut apple and vinegar. It lacks fruit and freshness. • $NA • **72**

BRICOUT

Brut Blanc de Blancs Champagne NV • $21 • (12/31/87) • **85**

Brut Champagne 1985: Overflowing with strawberry and fruit cocktail aromas and flavors, there is medium acidity with intense caramel and brandy flavors on the finish. A bit coarse for us. Drinkable now. 500 cases made. • $48 • (12/31/93) • **80**

Brut Champagne Carte d'Or 1988: Buttery, spicy aromas and robust, rather sweet flavors. Fun to taste, but could be better balanced. 55,000 cases made. • $26 • **86**

Brut Champagne Carte d'Or Prestige 1986: Tart and lemony, this lean, crisp style zings across the palate, but may be too lean for some. Picks up pretty honey and vanilla notes on the finish. Drink now. • $40 • (12/31/91) • **86**

Brut Champagne Carte d'Or Prestige 1983: Very dry, with floral, nutty aromas and flavors, it's crisp and austere on the finish, not at all generous, deep or smooth. • $25 • (12/31/89) • **75**

Brut Champagne Carte d'Or Prestige NV • $30 • (12/31/91) • **83**

Brut Champagne Carte Noire Réserve NV • $30 • (12/31/91) • **90**

Brut Champagne Cuvée Arthur Bricout NV • $62 • (12/31/93) • **86**

Brut Champagne Elegance de Bricout 1985 • $NA • (12/31/90) • **85**

Brut Champagne Elegance de Bricout 1982: Simple but spicy, with pleasant ginger-ale aromas and flavors, plus a nice touch of toast and vanilla, smooth and tasty. • $50 • (12/31/88) • **90**

Brut Rosé Champagne NV • $28 • (12/31/88) • **90**

BRIDAY, MICHEL

Rully Champ Clou 1987 • $16 • (12/31/90) • **68**

BRIGANDS, DOMAINE DE

Moulin-à-Vent 1993: Overripe flavors of stewed fruit and vegetables float in this awkward, diluted red, then close up as tannins shut down the finish. • $16 • (07/31/95) • **76**

BRILLETTE, CHÂTEAU

Moulis 1990: Polished and deep, with smoke, roasted nut and cedar aromas and flavors, medium tannins and a crisp finish. Drinkable now. 6,700 cases made. • $18 • (03/31/93) • **87**

Moulis 1989 • $17 • (03/15/92) • **86**

Moulis 1988 • $15 • (08/31/91) • **81**

Moulis 1987 • $15 • (11/30/89) • **72**

Moulis 1986 • $14 • (11/30/89) • **78**

Moulis 1982 • $19 • (11/30/89) • **85**

BRIOT, CHÂTEAU

Bordeaux 1985 • $4 • (05/15/87) • **75**

BROCARD, JEAN-MARC

Bourgogne Domaine Ste.-Claire 1994: Like biting into a lime. Amazing mouthpuckering intensity sears your palate with citrus and mineral notes. Tastes leesy and earthy now, could use more balance. Better in 1999. • $11 • (05/31/96) • **86**

Chablis Les Clos 1994: An odd, distinctive apple cider note. Advanced in both color and taste, it comes across as stripped of pure fruit flavors. • $NA • (05/31/96) • **76**

Chablis Malantes 1994: A super wine. Thick, rich, ripe and delicious, packed with honey, chalk, mineral and lemon. Full-bodied and seductive, lasts a long time on the delicious finish. Great now, but better in 2000. • $NA • (05/31/96) • **91**

Chablis Montmains 1994: Distinctive *premier cru* that's both seductive and odd at the same time. Lush, ripe, lovely lemon and honey character, full body, some smoky, earthy, matchstick flavors and long finish. Needs until 1999. • $NA • (05/31/96) • **87**

Chablis Vieilles Vignes Domaine Ste.-Claire 1994: Vibrant, mouthpuckering, electifying citrus, apple and honey flavors. Also ample earthiness. Of medium body, delivering a crisp but slightly one-dimensional finish. Better in 1999? • $NA • (05/31/96) • **85**

Chablis Vielles Vignes 1992: This wine shows mature aromas of smoke, honey and earth, with earth and mineral flavors battling tart green-apple acidity. Seems a bit advanced. • $20 • (03/31/95) • **79**

Sauvignon de St.-Bris Domaine Ste.-Claire 1994: Intense, fresh, clean, honeyed, dried herbal and grassy flavors. Lots of fruit here. Sparks fly on the palate as it cascades to a long, intense finish. Drinkable now. • $NA • (05/31/96) • **87**

BROCHARD, HUBERT

Sancerre 1994: Grapefruit and egg cream flavors give this white a curious sweet-and-sour appeal. It's fresh, but light and short. 3,000 cases made. • $19 • (05/31/96) • **81**

BROTTE, LAURENT CHARLES

Châteauneuf-du-Pape White 1993: Ripe, fruity and satisfying, marked by apple and pear notes and delivered with a smooth, rounded texture. The flavors even linger on the finish. 1,900 cases made. • $17 • (10/15/94) • **84**

Châteauneuf-du-Pape White 1992: Earthy and a touch bitter with tart grapefruit and pear flavors. Fruit wins out on the finish. • $17 • (04/30/94) • **82**
Côtes du Rhône-Villages Seguret 1990 • $5 • (04/15/93) • **79**
Côtes du Rhône-Villages Seguret 1986 • $6 • (09/30/89) BB • **80**
Gigondas 1990 • $10 • (03/31/94) • **86**
Viognier Vin de Pays d'Oc 1993: Has some body and good figgy flavors, but it is dominated by odd notes of onion and smoke. Turns harsh on the finish. 4,500 cases made. • $8 • (11/30/94) • **76**
Viognier Vin de Pays d'Oc 1992 • $5 • (08/31/93) • **77**
Viognier Vin de Pays d'Oc 1991 • $8 • (06/30/92) BB • **81**

BROUSTET, CHÂTEAU

Barsac 1990: Chewy and intense, providing plenty of toasted oak, tropical fruit, dried apricot and honey flavors, the burning finish seems slightly aggressive. Better after 1998. • $23 • **83**
Barsac 1988: Ripe and rich, with lots of almond, honey and vanilla aromas and flavors that are sweet and concentrated without being cloying. A bit earthy or moldy on the finish. Drinkable, but probably better after it settles down around 1995 to '98. • $4 Ⓐ • (03/31/91) • **83**

BROWN-LAMARTINE, CHÂTEAU

Bordeaux Supérieur 1994: Rather meager mineral, tobacco and cherry aromas and flavors, medium-to-light body, fine tannins and light finish. • $NA • **75-79** (BT)
Bordeaux Supérieur 1993: Some pretty red berry, anise and earth flavors could use a bit more concentration. Herbaceous note on the slightly dry finish. • $NA • (01/31/96) • **79**
Bordeaux Supérieur 1992: Not bad but rather lean. Light-bodied with dried cherry and herbs. Try now. • $NA • **76**

BRUCK, LIONEL J.

Bourgogne St.-Vincent Pinot Noir 1983 • $10 • (02/15/87) • **78**

BRUGNE, JEAN

Moulin-à-Vent Le Vivier 1991 • $12 • (06/15/94) • **86**

BRUMMELL

Blanc de Blancs Carte Noir NV • $7 • (06/15/90) • **79**

BRUN, GEORGES

Morgon Le Clachet 1991 • $10 • (06/15/94) • **87**

BRUN, JEAN-PAUL

Beaujolais Cuvée à l'Ancienne Domaine des Terres Dorées 1993: Stewed fruit and brown sugar aromas and flavors lack freshness. Tomato and herbal notes, dry finish. • $12 • (06/15/95) • **77**
Beaujolais Domaine des Terres Dorées 1992 • $9 • (06/15/94) • **85**
Beaujolais Domaine des Terres Dorées Cuvée Tradition 1993: Earthy and overripe, soft but rather dull. Cherry and strawberry flavors taste cooked, vegetal note on finish. Drink up. • $10 • **77**
Chardonnay Beaujolais Domaine des Terres Dorées 1993: Generous, showing rich, buttery Chardonnay character and just enough acidity to keep it firm and fresh. Enjoy with poultry and cream sauces. • $14 • (07/31/95) • **87**
Chardonnay Beaujolais Domaine des Terres Dorées 1992: Intriguing floral and citrus notes give this wine interest, but an earthy edge creeps into the finish. It's still firm, but lacks breadth. Try now. • $13 • **81**

Key: SS—Spectator Selection. CS—Cellar Selection. BB—Best Buy. $NA—Price not available. (BT)—Barrel tasting. Ⓐ—Auction Price.
Dates in parentheses represent the issues in which the ratings were published.

BRUNET, PATRICK

Fleurie Domaine de Robert 1992: A rich mix of intense strawberry and raspberry flavors and attractive smoky undertones lend complexity and appeal. Round but still firm. Try now. • $16 • (01/31/95) • **87**
Morgon Domaine de Robert 1992: This ripe, chewy wine offers plenty of blackberry and black cherry flavors backed by muscular tannins. It's harmonious and would make a good match with sausage or pate. • $14 • (01/31/95) • **86**

BRUSSET, DANIEL

Gigondas Les Hauts de Montmirail 1991 • $18 • (03/31/94) • **87**
Gigondas Les Hauts de Montmirail 1990 • $28 • (04/15/93) • **89**
Gigondas Les Hauts de Montmirail 1989 • $22 • (11/15/91) • **91**
Gigondas Les Hauts de Montmirail 1988 • $19 Ⓐ • (09/30/90) • **90**

BRUSSET, DOMAINE

Côtes du Rhône-Villages Cairanne Coteaux des Trabers 1990 • $11 • (04/15/93) • **71**
Côtes du Rhône-Villages Cairanne Coteaux des Trabers 1986 • $7 • (06/15/89) • **61**
Côtes du Rhône-Villages Coteaux des Trabers 1988 • $7 • (12/15/90) BB • **86**

BUCHERATS, DOMAINE DES

Juliénas 1992: Aged and spicy, almost like a Rioja with its vanilla and brown sugar flavors. Chocolate and coffee notes add to its appeal. Drink for its mature style. • $16 • **84**

BUFFET, DOMAINE F.

Pommard Rugiens 1985 • $40 • (10/15/88) • **88**
Volnay en Champane 1985 • $35 • (10/15/88) • **91**

BUNAN, DOMAINE

Bandol Red Château la Rouvière 1989: Pushes the limits of style, in its roasted, tobaccolike aromas and vivid plum and herb flavors. Firmly tannic, but mature tasting, ready to drink now. • $19 • (03/31/95) • **83**
Bandol Rosé Mas de la Rouvière 1993: Has plenty of texture and body, but not much flavor. Finishes hot. • $14 • (08/31/95) • **78**
Bandol Red Mas de la Rouvière 1990: Understated, supple and attractive. Not very aromatic, but soft, plush, chocolaty and good. The finish lingers and develops. Drinkable now. 917 cases made. • $15 • (03/31/95) • **87**
Bandol Blanc de Blancs Mas de la Rouvière 1993: Clean and fresh, round and full-bodied, with ripe apple and fig flavors, earthy and herbal components and a good, lingering finish. 1,250 cases made. • $12 • (03/31/95) • **84**

BURGAUD, BERNARD

Côte-Rôtie 1991: Fresh and focused, offering ripe black cherry flavors and an undercurrent of smoky roasted meat. It's smooth and accessible, drinkable now. • $36 • (05/31/94) • **87**
Côte-Rôtie 1990: Ripe, rich and balanced, with refreshing, citrusy acidity and all the ripe berry, wildflower and game aromas and flavors you could want. Smooths itself out on the finish, and the tannins are well-integrated. Should be best after 1997. 1,000 cases made. • $37 • (04/15/93) • **91**
Côte-Rôtie 1989 • $32 • (01/31/92) • **84**
Côte-Rôtie 1988 • $40 • (03/31/91) • **87**
Côte-Rôtie 1987 • $29 • (02/28/90) • **85**
Côte-Rôtie 1986 • $31 • (01/31/89) • **93**
Côte-Rôtie 1984 • $22 • (10/15/87) • **90**
Côte-Rôtie 1983 • $18 • (05/01/86) • **92**

BURGUET, ALAIN

Bourgogne 1992: Light and simple, a little chewy around the fine thread of raspberry that persists into the finish. • $15 • **82**
Bourgogne 1990 • $18 • (12/15/92) • **84**
Gevrey-Chambertin 1992: Extremely floral and distinctive with a modicum of fruit to keep it in balance. • $26 • **80**
Gevrey-Chambertin 1991: Well-defined if youthful berry and plum aromas and flavors show a moderate level of intensity and finish with a tobacco edge. Drinkable now. • $30 Ⓐ • (01/31/94) • **83**
Gevrey-Chambertin 1990: A vivid expression of Pinot Noir that's focused and charming. Not a blockbuster, but quite subtle, showing a range of cherry, currant, vanilla and earth flavors that come together to create an exciting, concentrated finish. Try in 1997. • $NA • (12/15/92) • **89**
Gevrey-Chambertin Vieilles Vignes 1991: A disappointment. Very crisp and tannic, almost green and stemmy. • $39 Ⓐ • (01/31/94) • **75**
Gevrey-Chambertin Vieilles Vignes 1990: Excellent quality for a Gevrey village wine. Offers lovely, bright, vivid cherry, blackberry and earth aromas and flavors and a solid core of well-integrated tannins and fruit. Drinkable now. • $43 • (12/15/92) • **90**
Gevrey-Chambertin Vieilles Vignes 1988 • $45 • (12/31/90) • **88**
Gevrey-Chambertin Vieilles Vignes 1986 • $33 • (07/15/89) • **84**

BURRIER, GEORGES

Chardonnay Mâcon-Villages 1994: Rich and honeyed with plenty of spice and ripe apple flavors. Lacks intensity and depth, but has some nice fennel and licorice notes. 2,000 cases made. • $10 • (05/31/96) • **84**
Pouilly-Fuissé 1994: Rich and flavorful, sporting loads of honey and spice. It also has very good green apple and citrus flavors wrapped together in an elegant style. Crisp and delicious. 2,400 cases made. • $18 • (05/31/96) • **86**

BUXY, CAVE DES VIGNERONS DE

Pinot Noir Bourgogne Grande Réserve 1985 • $7 • (06/30/88) • **75**
Pinot Noir Bourgogne Grande Réserve 1983 • $5 • (02/01/86) • **73**

CABANNE, CHÂTEAU LA

Pomerol 1991: More like water than wine. Clean and fruity, but very light. • $15 • (03/31/94) • **73**
Pomerol 1990: Restrained, early-maturing Pomerol, with pretty, silky tannins and fresh smoky, chocolate, black cherry character. Drinkable now. 5,000 cases made. • $27 • (03/31/93) • **87**
Pomerol 1989 • $20 Ⓐ • (03/15/92) • **92**
Pomerol 1982 • $23 • (08/31/92) • **84**
Pomerol 1961 • $NA • (04/30/92) • **77**

CABOCHE, DOMAINE DU PERE

Châteauneuf-du-Pape 1989 • $20 • (10/15/91) • **84**
Châteauneuf-du-Pape 1988 • $20 • (10/15/91) • **87**
Châteauneuf-du-Pape 1986 • $20 • (10/15/91) • **81**
Châteauneuf-du-Pape 1985 • $20 • (10/15/91) • **85**
Châteauneuf-du-Pape 1983 • $18 • (10/15/91) • **77**
Châteauneuf-du-Pape 1981 • $30 • (10/15/91) • **87**
Châteauneuf-du-Pape White 1990: Lively, fruity and interesting, with freshly sliced peach aromas and hints of almond. Medium-bodied, round and delicious, with a strawberries-and-cream flavor and an almond finish. • $20 • (10/15/91) • **85**

CABRIAC, CHÂTEAU DE

Corbières 1992 • $8 • (03/15/94) • **87**

CABRIERES, CHÂTEAU

Châteauneuf-du-Pape 1988 • $17 • (11/30/90) • **82**

CACHEUX, JACQUES

Echézeaux 1992: Lean and chewy, offering a modest level of berry and cigar-box flavors that finish narrow and with some finesse. • $NA • **83**
Vosne-Romanée Les Suchots 1992: A bit chewy, but the plum and currant flavors jump out of the glass. With a hint of tea and tobacco on the finish. Drinkable now. • $NA • **83**

CADEAUX

Brut Royal Crown NV: An easy-to-drink bubbly with mature flavors, a soft texture and a bit of sweetness. Simple but good. 60,000 cases made. • $9 • (02/28/95) • **80**

CADET-PIOLA, CHÂTEAU

St.-Emilion 1988 • $20 • (07/15/91) • **89**
St.-Emilion 1982 • $23 • (05/15/89) • **88**

CAILBOURDIN, DOMAINE A.

Pouilly-Fumé Cuvée de Boisfleury 1993: Rather disjointed, showing pungent herbal aromas, then round melon and lime flavors on the palate, then sharp and grassy notes again on the finish. Perhaps a few months in the bottle will smooth it out. • $17 • (10/31/94) • **81**
Pouilly-Fumé Les Cornets 1992: The herbal and grassy notes here are a bit exaggerated, and a lack of fresh acidity turns the overall profile earthy instead of bright. It has Sauvignon Blanc character, but in a minor key. • $18 • (10/31/94) • **81**
Pouilly-Fumé Les Cris 1994: Austere, showing very firm acidity and bare hints of apple and herb flavors. This makes a tough apéritif but would show better accompanying food. 2,660 cases made. • $19 • (06/15/96) • **80**
Pouilly-Fumé Les Cris 1993: Attractive aromas of smoke, pine and lime carry through on the clean, focused palate, with ripe yet crisp melon, herbal and citrus flavors, concentrated and long. Great typicity. A lively match with food. • $19 • (11/15/95) • **89**
Pouilly-Fumé Les Cris 1992: This light, grassy wine tastes more like Sancerre than do most Pouilly-Fumés. It's crisp and fresh with plenty of smoky, herbaceous, minerally notes; makes a great appetizer wine. • $19 • (08/31/94) • **87**

CAILLOT, ROGER

Pommard 1987 • $35 • (09/15/89) • **79**

CAILLOU, CHÂTEAU

Barsac 1991: Some appealing butterscotch, nut, lemon, pear and vanilla flavors. Not much depth, but it'll do as an apéritif. Drink now. • $NA • **83**
Barsac 1990: Fabulously balanced and fully botrytised, it shows alluring complexity, creamy texture, zippy acidity, caramel, honey and lemon flavors and an extremely long finish. • $NA • **92**
Barsac 1989: Fresh, medium-bodied white demonstrating attractive mineral notes and a lemon, honey character. Very creamy finish is supported by good acidity. Drinkable now. • $40 • **87**
Barsac 1988: Distinctive and straightforward, promoting some wet earth, mushroom, cedar and honey flavors. Drinkable now. • $39 • **84**
Barsac 1987 • $32 • (06/15/90) • **85**
Barsac Private Cuvée 1986: Powerful, yet exquisitely balanced, featuring toast, hazelnut, pineapple, apricot and cream flavors. Medium in body and sweetness. Try in 1999. • $NA • **92**
Barsac Private Cuvée 1983: Balanced, medium sweetness, good intensity. The toasty, smoky flavors and dried apricot, honey and spice notes come together on the silky finish. Should improve with age. • $NA • **89**

CAILLOU, DOMAINE DU

Châteauneuf-du-Pape 1990: Dense, concentrated and deeply colored, packing in plenty of fruit flavors and adding layers of gamy, earthy, woodsy accents to give it extra interest. Solid berry, plum and prune flavors carry it on the finish. Lots of fine tannins and great balance indicate it should age well through about 1998. • $19 • (04/15/93) • **89**

Châteauneuf-du-Pape 1988 • $22 • (03/31/91) • **86**

CAILLOU BLANC DU CHÂTEAU TALBOT

Bordeaux White 1994: An enchanting dry white Bordeaux. Complex mineral, apple, cream and fruit aromas and flavors. Fine acidity and a extremely long on the finish. Better in 1998. • $23 • (03/31/96) • **90**

CAILLOUX, LES

Châteauneuf-du-Pape 1990: A generous, spicy, berry-flavored wine with flavors that expand as you sip. Gentle for a Châteauneuf, with plenty of soft tannins and an easy texture. Great for drinking now through 1997. 1,500 cases made. • $24 • (04/15/93) • **88**

Châteauneuf-du-Pape 1988 • $18 • (10/15/91) • **88**

Châteauneuf-du-Pape 1986 • $18 • (10/15/91) • **79**

Châteauneuf-du-Pape 1985 • $16 • (10/15/91) • **82**

Châteauneuf-du-Pape 1983 • $55 • (10/15/91) • **88**

Châteauneuf-du-Pape 1981 • $30 • (10/15/91) • **76**

Châteauneuf-du-Pape White 1990: A serious wine, with good concentration, full-bodied, with honeydew melon and green apple aromas, ripe honey and melon flavors, an excellent backbone and a very rich finish. • $24 • (10/15/91) • **88**

Châteauneuf-du-Pape Cuvée Centenaire 1990: Big, muscular, ripe and velvety, this seductively smooth, many-layered wine offers plum, currant, cherry, toast and chocolate flavors in turn and finishes soft and exotic, with impressive length. A distinctive style. 350 cases made. • $24 • (04/15/93) • **93**

Châteauneuf-du-Pape Sélection Reflets 1986 • $18 • (05/31/89) • **89**

CAIRANNE, CAVE DES COTEAUX

Côtes du Rhône 1986 • $7 • (07/31/88) • **86**

Côtes du Rhône Domaine le Château 1985 • $6 • (08/31/87) BB • **85**

Côtes du Rhône Le Château a Cairanne 1987 • $7 • (12/15/89) • **77**

Côtes du Rhône Le Château a Cairanne 1986 • $6 • (07/31/88) BB • **82**

Côtes du Rhône-Villages 1988 • $6 • (02/28/90) BB • **81**

Côtes du Rhône-Villages Cairanne 1988 • $6 • (06/30/90) • **76**

CALABRE, CHÂTEAU

Montravel 1992 • $7 • (08/31/93) • **81**

CALAGE, CHÂTEAU DE

Coteaux du Languedoc 1991 • $7 • (03/15/94) • **80**

CALISSANNE, CHÂTEAU DE

Coteaux d'Aix en Provence Cuvée Prestige 1990 • $15 • (06/15/93) • **79**

Coteaux d'Aix en Provence Cuvée Prestige 1988 • $12 • (08/31/91) • **78**

CALON-SEGUR, CHÂTEAU

St.-Estèphe 1995: Could be the bargain of the vintage. Both seductive and muscular, this complex, rich, dark-colored, ripe, full-bodied Bordeaux delivers plenty of red berry, tar and toasted oak character in a well-integrated package. • $NA • (05/15/96) • **90-94** (BT)

St.-Estèphe 1993: Good '93 featuring sweet berry and tobacco character, medium body, firm tannins and slightly dry finish. Try now. • $25 • (01/31/96) • **84**

St.-Estèphe 1991: A bit lean, but some very nice tobacco and fruit aromas and flavors. Medium body and a short finish. • $21 • (03/31/94) • **82**

St.-Estèphe 1989 • $27 Ⓐ • (03/15/92) • **95**

St.-Estèphe 1988 • $25 Ⓐ • (07/15/91) • **85**

St.-Estèphe 1986 • $34 Ⓐ • (05/31/89) • **86**

St.-Estèphe 1985 • $25 Ⓐ • (05/31/88) • **88**

St.-Estèphe 1983 • $21 Ⓐ • (10/31/86) • **83**

St.-Estèphe 1982 • $61 Ⓐ • (08/31/92) • **87**

St.-Estèphe 1970 • $23 Ⓐ • (05/15/93) • **83**

St.-Estèphe 1962 • $NA • (11/30/87) • **70**

St.-Estèphe 1961: Call it a rough-hewn wine because of its tannic texture and chunky, obvious flavor components of fruit, butter and earth. But it's likable and enjoyable and seems to improve as you sip. Drink through 2000. • $146 • (04/30/96) • **86**

St.-Estèphe 1959 • $NA • (10/15/90) • **82**

St.-Estèphe 1945: One of the insider favorites of the vintage, this bottle was firm, smooth and polished, a beautifully balanced Calon that layers its spice, tobacco, black cherry and earthy-cedary notes on the finish. Might be losing it somewhat, but still graceful. • $475 • **90**

CAMENSAC, CHÂTEAU DE

Haut-Médoc 1995: Clean and fresh, with plenty of ultrafine tannins and a lovely complement of cherry and mineral notes. Very fresh finish. Almost outstanding. • $NA • (05/15/96) • **85-89** (BT)

Haut-Médoc 1994: Rather light and weedy, delivering some fruit, but just not enough to score higher. • $NA • (05/15/96) • **75-79** (BT)

Haut-Médoc 1989 • $16 • (03/15/92) • **86**

Haut-Médoc 1988 • $16 • (07/15/91) • **55**

Haut-Médoc 1986 • $14 • (06/30/89) • **83**

Haut-Médoc 1979 • $22 • (10/15/89) • **82**

Haut-Médoc 1970 • $35 • (05/15/93) • **87**

CAMPLAZENS, CHÂTEAU

Coteaux du Languedoc La Clape Sélection 1990 • $7 • (03/15/94) • **83**

CAMPREDON, CHÂTEAU DE

St.-Chinian 1990: Fully mature aromas are followed by black cherry, pepper and herbal flavors, but the wine lacks concentration and freshness. Drinkable now. Tasted twice with consistent notes. 4,000 cases made. • $7 • (06/30/94) • **78**

CANARD-DUCHENE

Brut Champagne Cuvée Bicentenaire NV • $29 • (11/15/91) • **87**

Brut Champagne Cuvée Spèciale de Charles VII NV • $75 • (12/31/89) • **85**

Brut Champagne Patrimoine 1983: Ripe and intense, somewhat alcoholic and soft in a style that manages to correct itself and find a modest equilibrium. After a glass or so the style begins to wear on you. • $42 • (12/31/89) • **80**

Brut Champagne Patrimoine NV • $34 • (12/31/91) • **85**

CANDELAY, CHÂTEAU

Bordeaux Supérieur 1986 • $5 • (06/15/89) • **78**

CANET, CHATEAU

Minervois Cuvée Elevée en Futs Grande Réserve 1988 • $6 • (05/31/90) • **69**

CANON, CHÂTEAU

Canon-Fronsac 1994: Light and delicate with berry herbal character and a light finish. • $NA • **75-79** (BT)

St.-Emilion 1995: Ripe, rich, full-bodied, this delicious '95 delivers a lot of good things, including tons of red berry, dried herb and spice wrapped in a silky texture. Very sweet and succulent despite the massive tannins. • $NA • (05/15/96) • **90-94** (BT)

St.-Emilion 1994: Rather light for Canon but some good cherry, berry and mineral character. Medium- to light-bodied, fine tannins, light finish. • $NA • (05/15/96) • **80-84** (BT)

Key: SS—Spectator Selection. CS—Cellar Selection. BB—Best Buy. $NA—Price not available. (BT)—Barrel tasting. Ⓐ—Auction Price.
Dates in parentheses represent the issues in which the ratings were published.

FRANCE

St.-Emilion 1993: Delicious, succulent chocolate, berry and cherry aromas and flavors. Medium- to light-bodied, adding delicate tannins and a fresh finish. Drinkable now. • $36 • (01/31/96) • **85**

St.-Emilion 1992: A bit austere and simple, revealing cherry, green pepper character, light body and a hard finish. Drinkable now. Tasted twice, with consistent notes. • $32 • **76**

St.-Emilion 1990: One of the best modern-day vintages of Canon. Everything is in just the right proportions. Medium- to full-bodied with fascinating, velvety earth and berry notes. Try in 1998. • $40 • **91**

St.-Emilion 1989: Rather closed and not giving much at this point of its evolution, but shows much promise. Lovely, perfumed, earthy, fruity character on nose and palate. Full in body and very firm fine tannins. Try in 1998. • $55 • **90**

St.-Emilion 1988: Solid Bordeaux featuring pretty fruit and firm tannins. A bit lean but has some very attractive cherry, berry and vanilla character. Try after 1997. • $42 • **88**

St.-Emilion 1987: Somewhat fading, but retaining herb, rosemary and fruit aromas and flavors. Medium-bodied, firmly tannic and slight dryness on the finish suggest drinking this now. • $30 • **86**

St.-Emilion 1986: Elegant and refined, offering lots of lovely aromas and flavors of cherry, berry and roasted meat. Full in body and very silky in tannins. Try in 1997. • $45 • **90**

St.-Emilion 1985: I have always thought highly of this wine. It's ripe and fleshy, offering up loads of fruit and medium tannins. Delicious now, but will improve. • $48 • (04/30/95) • **91**

St.-Emilion 1983: Slightly overdone for Canon with raisin-like aromas and flavors and very hard tannins. Can wait and see, but not much promise for it. Drinkable now. • $40 • **84**

St.-Emilion 1982: Always a blockbuster and one of the greatest wines ever produced from this estate. Layers of ripe berries and other fruits on the nose and palate, full in body and very rich, sporting lovely, velvety tannins and a long aftertaste. Delicious now but will improve for years to come. • $70 • **93**

St.-Emilion 1981: Not altogether a good bottle here. Medium-red in color with a garnet rim, showing some fruit but a rather grassy, herbal character. Other bottles have been close to outstanding. Drink now. • $28 • **82**

St.-Emilion 1980: Meager and more like a mature Burgundy. Rich aromas of mushroom, berry and herb very light finish. Drink now. • $19 • **79**

St.-Emilion 1979: Rather a brute for Canon. Full-bodied and very fruity but slightly hard and tannic. Still, you'll find plenty of beautiful berry, chocolate and earth character. Drinkable now. • $40 • **90**

St.-Emilion 1978: A quite complete wine and an excellent '78. Terrific aromas and flavors of cherry, earth and vanilla. Medium in body and very fruity long, velvety finish. • $50 • **91**

St.-Emilion 1977: Better than expected considering the appalling reputation of '77. Some plum, cedar character light-bodied and very simple. Drink now. • $18 • **74**

St.-Emilion 1976: Time is running out on this vintage. Almost raisiny, herbal aromas and flavors, but slightly dry and diluted on the finish. Drink now. • $25 • **81**

St.-Emilion 1975: Seems to need a bit more bottle age. Aromas of berries and licorice, medium body and ripe flavors. Drinkable now but better in two or three years. • $38 • **86**

St.-Emilion 1974: Way past it now. Garnet in color, brown sugar flavors and dry, almost watery character. • $20 • **62**

St.-Emilion 1973: Generously, this is drinkable despite volatile acidity and nail polish character. • $20 • **72**

St.-Emilion 1972: Surprisingly drinkable. Dusty in character some attractive fruit on the finish. Drink now. • $20 • **79**

St.-Emilion 1971: Other bottles of '71 have verged on outstanding in quality. This is only very good. Ripe, fruity, earthy character, firm tannins, slightly dry finish. • $45 • **85**

St.-Emilion 1970: Charming and delicious, offering cherry, berry and cedar aromas and flavors. Medium-bodied and soft with succulent fruit. Drink now. • $67 • **88**

St.-Emilion 1969: Good color for a '69, pleasant at first, but showing high volatile acidity. Drink if you must. • $25 • **74**

St.-Emilion 1967: Very elegant and lovely but already past its peak. Medium-bodied and fruity with a pleasing chocolate character on the finish. Drink now. • $65 • **83**

St.-Emilion 1966: Perhaps even better a few years ago. Still displays ripe fruit, cedar and pepper character throughout. Slightly dry finish, drink now. • $150 • **84**

St.-Emilion 1964: One of the best wines I have ever tasted from this vintage. Lovely and complete in every way full-bodied with plum and meat aromas and flavors and velvety tannins. Delicious, caressing finish. • $80 • **90**

St.-Emilion 1962: Reserved in nature, showing extremely attractive licorice, berry, chocolate and perfume character on both the nose and palate. Perfect to drink now. A fine, mature claret. • $175 • **91**

St.-Emilion 1961: Quite lively in texture, youthful and delicious in flavor. Has developed an enticing bottle bouquet, while still being packed with cherry and currant flavors. Quite full-bodied and quite long on the finish. Drink through 2010. • $58 • (04/30/96) • **90**

St.-Emilion 1960: Slightly dusty but some attractive berry, vanilla, roasted coffee character. Drink up. • $75 • **79**

St.-Emilion 1959: Fading a tiny bit but delicious all the same. Perhaps not a great bottle here. Attractive earth, berry and chocolate aromas and a medium-to-light finish. Drink up. • $200 • **86**

St.-Emilion 1958: Amazingly good for what is considered a weak vintage. Excellent color with terrific aromas of chocolate and fruit which follow through on the finish. • $80 • **89**

St.-Emilion 1957: Another example of a good wine from a questionable vintage. Medium in body with earth and berry aromas and flavors and a delicate finish. • $75 • **82**

St.-Emilion 1955: Just what you expect in an excellent glass of mature claret: lovely aromas and flavors of chocolate and ripe fruit, medium body and a long, silky, elegant finish. • $110 • **90**

St.-Emilion 1953: This really caresses with its ripe fruit and gentle tannins. Polished to near perfection after four decades. Medium-bodied and silky showing cherry, berry and light mushroom character. • $125 • **91**

St.-Emilion 1952: A bit hard, rather volatile, offering some interesting ripe berry, rose petal character. • $95 • **79**

St.-Emilion 1950: Somewhat volatile with intense varnish character. The concentrated ripe fruit makes it drinkable. • $190 • **76**

St.-Emilion 1949: This shows exotic fruit, raspberry and mushroom character on the nose and palate. Full in body and wonderfully silky. Classy wine here. • $375 • **92**

St.-Emilion 1948: Yet another fabulous Canon with loads of cherry, plum and floral character on the nose and palate. Lovely, velvety texture. • $375 • **90**

St.-Emilion 1947: Terrific. Bottled at the château and better than the merchant bottling. It shows intensely ripe fruit character, nut, plum, berry and earth flavors and a long, velvety finish. Wonderful to drink. • $550 • **93**

St.-Emilion 1945: Some people at the tasting absolutely raved about this wine, but the owners of the château and I found it slighty overdone and verging on a strange rubber character. Still, it is very darkly colored with loads of ripe fruit and highly extracted in tannins. • $475 • **84**

St.-Emilion 1943: Pretty licorice, fruit and berry aromas and flavors accompany fine tannins and a delicate finish. • $125 • **86**

St.-Emilion 1942: Not bad for a '42 which is less than a great year. Light and fruity, pleasing character and a berry finish. • $200 • **80**

St.-Emilion 1937: Very dry and tannic nonetheless, there's some pleasant cherry, nutty character. • $150 • **81**

St.-Emilion 1934: No longer a wine. Vinegar. • $175 • **50**

St.-Emilion 1933: Pleasant but really past its prime. Light in body, some fruit character and a dusty finish. • $160 • **77**

St.-Emilion 1929: Probably much better a decade or two ago, but who's complaining Lovely berry and fresh button mushroom aromas and flavors and a silky cedar finish. • $250 • **89**

St.-Emilion 1928: A glamorous old wine. Loads of mushroom character and an underlying fruitiness. It's medium-bodied and very silky with a long, delicate finish. • $300 • **87**

St.-Emilion 1926: Decent, mature red. Slightly volatile, offering enough fresh fruit to make it interesting. • $225 • **79**

St.-Emilion 1923: This is outstanding, with a bounty of violet, herb, berry character, medium body and an exceptionally long aftertaste. • $175 • **90**

St.-Emilion 1920: Still impressive, displaying ripe fruit, meaty aromas and flavors and a fresh finish. Slightly dry though. • $200 • **86**

St.-Emilion 1916: Rather cheesy and unclean but you have to like this wine. There's still plenty of fruit. • $175 • **79**

St.-Emilion English Bottling 1947: Incredibly ripe and youthful, featuring cherry and rose petal character, medium body, plenty of fruit and soft tannins on the finish. English bottling. • $NA • **90**

CANON-DE-BREM, CHÂTEAU

Canon-Fronsac 1994: Fresh, clean berry and olive character, medium body, firm tannins and a dried-herb finish. • $NA • **80-84** (BT)

Canon-Fronsac 1993: Rather simple herbal, berry and cherry character, medium-to-light body, light tannins and finish. Drinkable now. • $14 • (01/31/96) • **80**

Canon-Fronsac 1992: Light and fruity, revealing watery, mineral, cherry character. Drink if you must. • $13 • **75**

Canon-Fronsac 1990: Rich and opulent wine with plenty of attractive chocolate, berry character, round tannins and a long aftertaste. Drinkable now. 8,000 cases made. • $17 • (03/31/93) • **89**

Canon-Fronsac 1989 • $23 • (03/15/92) • **84**

Canon-Fronsac 1986 • $15 • (03/31/90) • **86**

Canon-Fronsac 1982 • $NA • (08/31/92) • **91**

CANON-LA-GAFFELIERE, CHÂTEAU

St.-Emilion 1995: Another great wine from this producer. Wonderful aromas of allspice, ripe fruit and vanilla, full body, silky tannins and long, exquisite finish. Layers and layers of fruit. Almost classic. • $NA • (05/15/96) • **90-94** (BT)

St.-Emilion 1994: A tannic but flavorful '94 that is tightly wound, showing a complex range of red berry flavors and an oaky, earthy character. A serious wine that has depth, full tannins and a long, firm finish. Almost outstanding. • $30 • (05/15/96) • **85-89** (BT)

St.-Emilion 1993: One of the great young wines we have tasted this year. A stupendous, silky, full-bodied red of great character and depth, deep color and tons of pure fruit. Layered with mineral, mint, blackberry and dried herb flavors. Long finish and well-integrated tannins make it tempting now, but try to wait until 2000. • $30 • (01/31/96) • **92**

St.-Emilion 1992: Polished tobacco, fruit and smoke character, medium-bodied, silky and a flavorful finish. Drinkable now. • $20 • **82**

St.-Emilion 1990: Combines power and elegance. It has the rich structure of a long-aging wine, yet the complexity is already elegant. Ripe fruit, cedar, licorice, violets, plums and minerals are all there. Tasted twice. Drinkable after 2000. 8,400 cases made. • $30 • (03/15/93) • **95**

St.-Emilion 1989 • $36 Ⓐ • (03/15/92) • **88**

St.-Emilion 1988 • $30 • (06/30/91) • **86**

St.-Emilion 1986 • $21 • (06/30/89) • **91**

St.-Emilion 1985: Supple wine with perfumed cherry, berry aromas and flavors. Medium bodied and nicely structured with a fresh finish. Drinkable now. • $NA • **86**

St.-Emilion 1983: Some pretty, ripe fruit but rather simple and old in style with chestnut, berry, coffee flavors. Drinkable now. • $NA • **82**

St.-Emilion 1981: Rather light, but showing rich flavors. Slightly decadent and medium in body with earthy, berry flavors and aromas, light tannins and a delicate finish. Drinkable now. • $NA • **82**

Canon-Fronsac 1990: A pretty wine, with loads of blackberry and licorice character and supple round tannins on the finish. Drinkable now. 4,000 cases made. • $18 • (03/31/93) • **85**

Canon-Fronsac 1989 • $24 • (03/15/92) • **82**

CANON MOUEIX, CHÂTEAU

Canon-Fronsac 1994: Light, fruity and simple, offering some berry flavors but a rather lean finish. • $NA • **75-79** (BT)

Canon-Fronsac 1993: Some decent fruit but slightly herbal. Medium in body, adding slightly aggressive tannins and a dried herb, berry finish. Better in 1998. • $18 • (01/31/96) • **81**

> **Key:** SS—Spectator Selection. CS—Cellar Selection. BB—Best Buy. $NA—Price not available. (BT)—Barrel tasting. Ⓐ—Auction Price.
> **Dates in parentheses represent the issues in which the ratings were published.**

Canon-Fronsac 1992: Very light cherry and berry flavors, light tannins and a slightly weedy finish. Drinkable now. • $14 • **78**

Canon-Fronsac 1990: An approachable wine, with an attractive berry, earthy character, round tannins and a soft finish. Drinkable now. 2,000 cases made. • $15 • (03/31/93) • **84**

Canon-Fronsac 1989 • $22 • (03/15/92) • **86**

CANORGUE, CHÂTEAU LA

Côtes du Lubéron 1990 • $10 • (04/15/93) • **84**

CANTELAUDE, CHÂTEAU

Haut-Médoc 1986 • $17 • (06/30/89) • **78**

CANTELYS, CHÂTEAU

Pessac-Léognan White 1994: Wonderfully crafted to show off its subtle honey, citrus, almond, vanilla and floral aromas and flavors. Medium to full in body, with firm acidty and a flavorful finish. Drinkable now, but can age. • $NA • (03/31/96) • **89**

CANTEMERLE, CHÂTEAU

Haut-Médoc 1995: Some decent blackberry and cherry aromas and flavors but rather simple, showing medium body and medium tannins. • $NA • (05/15/96) • **80-84** (BT)

Haut-Médoc 1994: Straightforward mineral and berry character, medium in body and fine tannins. • $NA • **80-84** (BT)

Haut-Médoc 1994: Light and watery, showing some berry character, but just too light to rate higher. • $17 • (05/15/96) • **75-79** (BT)

Haut-Médoc 1991: Attractive, velvety wine with a fruit and dried-herb character, medium body and medium finish. • $22 • (03/31/94) • **80**

Haut-Médoc 1990: A bit disappointing for this estate. Simple and fruity, with pleasant nutmeg, berry, grassy character and a light backbone of tannins. Drinkable now. 8,000 cases made. • $25 • (03/31/93) • **81**

Haut-Médoc 1989 • $35 • (03/15/92) • **91**

Haut-Médoc 1988 • $19 Ⓐ • (03/15/91) • **85**

Haut-Médoc 1987 • $21 • (05/15/90) • **87**

Haut-Médoc 1986 • $30 • (06/30/89) • **89**

Haut-Médoc 1985: Simple, early drinker with meaty, berry character, medium-bodied and medium tannins. Drinkable now. • $NA • **82**

Haut-Médoc 1984 • $17 • (06/15/87) • **85**

Haut-Médoc 1982 • $38 Ⓐ • (08/31/92) • **90**

Haut-Médoc 1981: A solid, one-dimensional wine with medium body, plummy character and a medium fruity finish. Drinkable now. • $NA • **85**

Haut-Médoc 1979 • $15 Ⓐ • (10/15/89) • **78**

Haut-Médoc 1970 • $25 Ⓐ • (05/15/93) • **88**

Haut-Médoc 1962 • $NA • (11/30/87) • **90**

Haut-Médoc 1961: Good but weakening. It has earthy, decadent aromas, and tomatolike flavors that give it breadth but little depth. Mature, drink now. • $66 • (04/30/96) • **84**

Haut-Médoc 1945 • $103 Ⓐ • (03/16/86) • **92**

CANTENAC-BROWN, CHÂTEAU

Margaux 1995: Well made, medium-to-full in body, packed with red fruit, blackberry and spice notes. Although intense, it manages to remain subtle. Solid backbone of ripe, supple tannins. Nearly outstanding. • $NA • (05/15/96) • **85-89** (BT)

Margaux 1994: Soft and attractive currant and olive notes. A lovely wine, medium- to full-bodied, ripe and firm. • $19 • **85-89** (BT)

Margaux 1993: Intense blackberry flavor and a hint of violets. Medium-bodied, very firm tannins and medium finish. Needs time, try in 1997. 15,000 cases made. • $23 • (01/31/96) • **85**

Margaux 1992: Delicate, beautiful, succulent, perfumed berry and raspberry aromas and flavors. Medium in body, a long aftertaste. Drinkable now. • $20 • (04/15/95) • **84**

Margaux 1991: Lots of fruit, with a hint of bell pepper. Medium-bodied and chewy, with a long aftertaste. • $23 • (03/31/94) • **82**

Margaux 1990: Big and powerful, with loads of tar, berry, chocolate character and velvety tannins. Drink in 1997. 15,000 cases made. • $24 • (03/31/93) • **92**
Margaux 1989 • $32 • (03/15/92) • **89**
Margaux 1988 • $25 • (04/30/91) • **89**
Margaux 1987 • $18 • (02/15/90) • **78**
Margaux 1984 • $19 • (05/15/87) • **85**
Margaux 1982 • $22 Ⓐ • (05/01/85) • **91**
Margaux 1981 • $17 Ⓐ • (03/01/85) • **91**
Margaux 1970 • $26 Ⓐ • (05/15/93) • **83**
Margaux 1961: Turning frail in its old age, but still well balanced. It has subtle, earthy aromas and lean flavors with a short finish. Drink now. • $39 • (04/30/96) • **82**
Margaux 1959 • $NA • (10/15/90) • **89**
Margaux 1945 • $NA • (03/16/86) • **75**

CANUET, CHÂTEAU

Margaux 1995: Very intense aromas and flavors of tar and some notes reminiscent of a black currant bush. Medium- to full-bodied, with loads of tannins on the finish. Slightly coarse. • $NA • (05/15/96) • **85-89** (BT)
Margaux 1994: A bit lean but some pretty mineral, mint and berry character on the nose and palate. Medium body, fine tannins and a fresh finish. • $NA • **80-84** (BT)
Margaux 1993: Very herbal with green pepper, bush character and a slightly metallic edge. 5,000 cases made. • $13 • (01/31/96) • **74**
Margaux 1992: Some decent plum flavors, but lean and slightly dry on the finish. Tasted twice, with consistent notes. Drinkable now. • $12 • (04/15/95) • **74**
Margaux 1991: Like tasting overcooked strawberry jam. Also weedy and green. Not pleasant. Tasted twice. • $12 • (03/31/94) • **69**
Margaux 1990: This wine is thick yet balanced, with concentrated raspberry and cassis character, soft, ripe tannins and luscious fruit on the finish. Not quite as concentrated as the barrel sample. From Jean-Michel Cazes. Drinkable now. • $18 • (03/31/93) • **89**
Margaux 1989 • $18 • (03/15/92) • **82**
Margaux 1987 • $13 • (05/15/90) • **74**
Margaux 1986 • $15 • (11/30/89) • **88**

CAP D'ANTIBES

Coteaux du Languedoc Picpoul de Pinet Grand Réserve 1991 • $7 • (06/15/93) • **81**

CAP DE MOURLIN, CHÂTEAU

St.-Emilion 1989 • $23 • (03/15/92) • **87**
St.-Emilion 1988 • $20 • (04/30/91) • **84**
St.-Emilion 1986 • $18 • (06/30/89) • **87**
St.-Emilion 1982 • $18 Ⓐ • (08/31/92) • **90**

CAPBERN-GASQUETON, CHÂTEAU

St.-Estèphe 1991: Clean and fruity but very watery. • $13 • (03/31/94) • **74**
St.-Estèphe 1989 • $27 • (03/15/92) • **84**
St.-Estèphe 1986 • $20 • (11/30/89) • **76**
St.-Estèphe 1985 • $23 • (08/31/88) • **85**
St.-Estèphe 1983 • $19 • (02/15/88) • **66**
St.-Estèphe 1982 • $22 • (11/30/89) • **83**

CAPENDU, CHÂTEAU

Corbières Cuvée Elevée en Futs Grande Réserve 1988 • $6 • (05/31/90) • **77**

CAPION, DOMAINE DE

Cabernet Sauvignon-Merlot Vin de Pays d'Oc 1989 • $9 • (01/31/92) • **77**
Syrah Vin de Pays d'Oc 1989 • $9 • (12/15/91) • **82**
Vin de Pays d'Oc 1991 • $9 • (03/15/94) • **81**

CAPLANE, DOMAINE DE

Sauternes 1985 • $11 • (09/30/88) • **81**

CAPTAIN-GAGNEROT

Clos Vougeot 1985 • $67 • (12/31/88) • **86**
Corton Les Renardes 1985 • $70 • (12/31/88) • **92**

CARBONNIEUX, CHÂTEAU

Graves 1985 • $20 • (11/30/88) • **87**
Graves 1982 • $26 • (08/31/92) • **83**
Graves 1970 • $33 • (05/15/93) • **84**
Graves 1961: A solid and attractive wine with flinty, earthy aromas, clean cherry flavors and a firm texture with ample tannins. A lingering finish, too. Drink through 2000. • $35 • (04/30/96) • **86**
Pessac-Léognan 1995: Softer than some '95s, it delivers a silky mouthfeel and lots of vivid red berry flavor. It only lacks a bit of length and complexity. • $NA • (05/15/96) • **80-84** (BT)
Pessac-Léognan 1994: Quite impressive, with good complexity of fruit and spice and some depth. Full-bodied, sweet and ripe, with full tannins and a silky texture. Succulent finish. Almost outstanding. Better than the '95 Carbonnieux. • $18 • (05/15/96) • **85-89** (BT)
Pessac-Léognan 1993: Crisp, lively, firmly tannic, this delivers cassis, earth and plum flavors but also a slight herbal note. Somewhat dry on the finish. Better in 1998. • $23 • (01/31/96) • **82**
Pessac-Léognan 1992: Interesting, delicate tobacco, cedar and berry aromas and flavors, medium- to light-bodied with medium tannins and a succulent finish. Drinkable now. • $17 • **84**
Pessac-Léognan 1991: Clean, lean and crisp with cherry character, light tannins and a refreshing finish. • $17 • (03/31/94) • **78**
Pessac-Léognan 1990: Subtle and balanced, with rich berry, mineral character, plenty of fruit and elegant tannins. This estate never makes showy wines, but they age well. Drinkable now. 22,000 cases made. • $19 • (03/31/93) • **87**
Pessac-Léognan 1989 • $26 • (03/15/92) • **85**
Pessac-Léognan 1988 • $20 • (02/28/91) • **86**
Pessac-Léognan 1987 • $15 • (05/15/90) • **80**
Pessac-Léognan 1986 • $18 • (09/15/89) • **87**
Pessac-Léognan White 1994: A stunner for Carbonneiux. Rich and powerful, yet reserved, loads of vanilla, apple, citrus and spice filling out this full-bodied, very intense white. Great class and balance. Superb winemaking. • $23 • (03/31/96) • **90**
Pessac-Léognan White 1993: Better than the '92. Crisp and elegant, showing mineral, new wood and apple aromas and flavors, medium in body and very crisp. Drinkable now. • $18 • (05/31/95) • **87**
Pessac-Léognan White 1992 • $20 • (06/15/94) • **84**

CARDINALE, LE

Brut NV • $5 • (06/15/90) BB • **80**

CARDONNE, CHÂTEAU LA

Médoc 1986 • $10 • (02/15/90) • **84**
Médoc 1985 • $12 • (12/31/88) • **83**
Médoc 1983 • $13 • (10/15/86) • **79**
Médoc 1982 • $20 • (08/31/92) • **86**

CARILLON, LOUIS

Puligny-Montrachet 1994: Solid, medium- to full-bodied, showing a core of grapefruit, ripe tropical fruit and lovely honey character. Very vivid and fresh yet ending in supple aftertaste. Built for aging, try in 1999. 1,666 cases made. • $35 • (05/31/96) • **87**
Puligny-Montrachet 1993: Firm, medium-bodied, lemon, lime and mineral character. Pleasant aftertaste. 400 cases imported to U.S. • $31 • **82**
Puligny-Montrachet 1992: Racy and well-made, a bracing Burgundy of medium body with vivid, distinct and refreshing grapefruit, fresh herb, and green apple flavors. Great intensity and length. Try now. 2,500 cases made. • $33 • (08/31/94) • **90**

Puligny-Montrachet Champ Canet 1993: Rich and opulent, featuring white truffle, honey and mineral aromas and flavors, medium body, fine acidity and long, tasty finish. Drinkable now. • $48 • **88**

Puligny-Montrachet Champ Canet 1992: A Puligny that will grow with age. Firm and flavorful, smelling of pears and peaches, tasting of vanilla and pear, with good balance and length on the finish. 340 cases made. • $43 • (08/31/94) • **90**

Puligny-Montrachet Les Perrières 1993: Pretty lemon and toasted oak aromas and flavors. Medium body, good acidity and a long, fresh finish. • $50 • **86**

Puligny-Montrachet Les Perrières 1992: Ripe, smooth and flavorful, with pineapple and pear notes that really fill it out, round in texture, showing nice lingering fruit flavors on the finish. 575 cases made. • $41 • (08/31/94) • **90**

CARLES, CHÂTEAU DE

Fronsac 1995: Lovely and harmonious, fairly rich, full-bodied and complex, delivering impressive red berry, chocolate and earth character. • $NA • (05/15/96) • **85-89** (BT)

Fronsac 1994: Loads of crushed grape, chocolate and earth character, full-to-medium body, firm tannins but short finish. A bit rustic. • $NA • **80-84** (BT)

Fronsac 1993: Straightforward dried cherry and wet earth aromas and flavors, medium body, silky tannins and fresh finish. Drinkable now. • $10 • (01/31/96) • **81**

CARMES-HAUT-BRION, CHÂTEAU LES

Graves 1961: A pleasant surprise that has fine balance, ripe but mature fruit flavors and a rich, easygoing texture. Drink now through 1998. • $50 • (04/30/96) • **86**

CARONNE-STE.-GEMME, CHÂTEAU

Haut-Médoc 1995: Lovely red berry and plum notes marry nicely with the spice, earth and mocha flavors. Medium-bodied, turning a bit dry on the finish. • $NA • (05/15/96) • **85-89** (BT)

CARRUADES DE LAFITE ROTHSCHILD

Pauillac 1995: Lovely, round wine with plenty of berry and chocolate aromas and flavors. Medium body, soft tannins and a fresh finish. • $NA • (05/15/96) • **85-89** (BT)

Pauillac 1994: Lovely perfume in this, but it's slightly hard yet. Medium-bodied and has good vanilla, tobacco and cherry notes and a decent finish. Could move up in the next tasting. • $20 • (05/15/96) • **80-84** (BT)

Pauillac 1993: Lively and crisp, medium- to light-bodied, offering some well-defined red berry flavors, but a bit one-dimensional and lean. Second label of Château Lafite Rothschild. Drinkable now. • $23 • (01/31/96) • **83**

Pauillac 1992: An attractive core of good fruit and spicy character, medium body and tannins and a short aftertaste. Drinkable now. • $17 • **84**

Pauillac 1989 • $34 Ⓐ • (03/15/92) • **89**

Pauillac 1983 • $14 • (10/31/86) • **88**

Pauillac 1982 • $34 Ⓐ • (08/31/92) • **92**

Pauillac 1967 • $NA • (11/30/87) • **82**

Pauillac 1964 • $24 Ⓐ • (11/30/87) • **81**

Pauillac 1962 • $NA • (11/30/87) • **75**

Pauillac 1961: The second label of Château Lafite Rothschild gives its big brother a run for the money in this vintage. An enticing, plush wine that is expansive in aroma and flavor, silky smooth in texture and fully mature. Drink through 2000. • $45 • (04/30/96) • **90**

Pauillac 1959 • $100 • (11/30/91) • **90**

Pauillac 1937 • $125 • (11/30/87) • **77**

Pauillac 1934 • $145 • (11/30/87) • **84**

Key: SS—Spectator Selection. CS—Cellar Selection. BB—Best Buy. $NA—Price not available. (BT)—Barrel tasting. Ⓐ—Auction Price.
Dates in parentheses represent the issues in which the ratings were published.

Pauillac 1902 • $530 • (11/30/87) • **80**

CARSIN, CHÂTEAU

Bordeaux White 1994: Classy fruit flavors and great balance make this a very good white wine. It has fig, citrus and mango flavors for a refreshing mix. 5,000 cases made. • $8 • (02/29/96) • **86**

Premières Côtes de Bordeaux 1993: This vivid red offers attractive plum, floral and spicy aromas and flavors. Nicely balanced, with modest structure. Drinkable now. • $8 • (12/15/95) • **83**

CARTEYRON, CHÂTEAU

St.-Emilion 1982 • $7 • (09/01/85) • **79**

CARTILLON, CHÂTEAU DU

Haut-Médoc 1995: A bit lean but showing some decent cherry and strawberry aromas and flavors. Light-bodied and light on the tannins. • $NA • (05/15/96) • **80-84** (BT)

Haut-Médoc 1993: Very diluted with some spice and pepper character. • $12 • (01/31/96) • **76**

Haut-Médoc 1991: Very watery and light. Maturing quickly. • $10 • (03/31/94) • **74**

CASSAN, DOMAINE DE

Côtes du Rhône-Villages Beaumes de Venise Cuvée St.-Christophe 1989 • $11 • (04/15/93) • **77**

CASTAGNIER, GUY

Bonnes Mares 1990: An alluring wine that shows remarkable harmony. Isn't as huge as some in this group, but the focused, packed berry, earth and smoke characteristics are seductive. Is almost sweet on the palate and velvety on the finish. Try around 1997 or '98. • $NA • (12/15/92) • **94**

Bonnes Mares 1989 • $67 • (01/31/92) • **91**

Bonnes Mares 1988 • $67 • (07/15/91) • **87**

Bonnes Mares 1986 • $50 • (04/15/89) • **91**

Chambolle-Musigny 1990: Aromatic and supple, with plenty of pretty raspberry, plum and earth flavors that form a harmonious texture on the firm finish. Drinkable now. • $NA • (12/15/92) • **87**

Chambolle-Musigny 1989 • $39 • (01/31/92) • **88**

Chambolle-Musigny 1986 • $31 • (07/15/89) • **84**

Charmes-Chambertin 1990: Offers beautiful fruit flavors, but is more one-dimensional than some others wines in this group. Still, it shows a solid structure of tannins, acidity and fruit. Drinkable now. • $NA • (12/15/92) • **89**

Charmes-Chambertin 1989 • $62 • (01/31/92) • **90**

Clos de la Roche 1990: Not a huge wine, but the racy structure, fresh acidity and elegant plum, berry and earth flavors offer plenty of pleasure. Drinkable now. • $NA • (12/15/92) • **90**

Clos de la Roche 1989 • $62 • (01/31/92) • **90**

Clos de la Roche 1988 • $63 • (07/15/91) • **91**

Clos de la Roche 1986 • $43 • (07/15/89) • **75**

Clos St.-Denis 1990: Graceful and balanced, a refined *grand cru*, with a fine tannin and fruit structure and lots of flavors, including earth, plum and raspberry. Drinkable now. • $NA • (12/15/92) • **93**

Clos St.-Denis 1989 • $62 • (01/31/92) • **91**

Clos St.-Denis 1988 • $63 • (07/15/91) • **89**

Clos St.-Denis 1986 • $43 • (07/15/89) • **84**

Clos de Vougeot 1990: Very fruity, with medium tannins, pleasant plum, cherry, vanilla and chocolate notes and firm tannins. Drinkable now. • $NA • (12/15/92) • **87**

Clos de Vougeot 1989 • $64 • (01/31/92) • **85**

Clos de Vougeot 1988 • $65 • (08/31/91) • **86**

Gevrey-Chambertin 1990: Smooth and round, with interesting forest underbrush and wet earth notes complementing the berry and cherry flavors on an elegant framework. Drinkable now. • $NA • (12/15/92) • **87**

Latricières-Chambertin 1990: Not as intensely fruity as others in this group, but shows a generous amount of earthy, ripe berry aromas and flavors and medium tannins. Drinkable now. • $NA • (12/15/92) • **89**
Latricières-Chambertin 1989 • $62 • (01/31/92) • **93**
Latricières-Chambertin 1988 • $63 • (07/15/91) • **93**
Mazis-Chambertin Mazy-Chambertin 1990: An elegantly made Mazis that displays good class and balance, with ripe cherry, blackberry and tobacco aromas and flavors. The finish shows fantastic harmony. Drink from 1998. • $NA • (12/15/92) • **94**
Mazis-Chambertin Mazy-Chambertin 1989 • $62 • (01/31/92) • **93**
Mazis-Chambertin Mazy-Chambertin 1988 • $63 • (07/15/91) • **91**
Morey-St.-Denis 1990: The crisp strawberry and raspberry aromas and flavors are bright and lively and the tannins are supple in this delicious wine that's drinkable now. • $NA • (12/15/92) • **85**
Morey-St.-Denis 1989 • $NA • (01/31/92) • **86**
Morey-St.-Denis 1986 • $28 • (07/15/89) • **66**

CASTELLANE, DE

Brut Blanc de Blancs Champagne 1981 • $33 • (04/15/88) • **84**
Brut Blanc de Blancs Champagne 1980 • $22 • (05/31/87) • **91**
Brut Blanc de Blancs Champagne Chardonnay 1983 • $NA • (12/31/90) • **90**
Brut Blanc de Blancs Champagne Chardonnay NV • $30 • (12/31/91) • **84**
Brut Champagne NV • $38 • (12/31/91) • **83**
Brut Champagne Cuvée Commodore 1981 • $50 • (04/15/88) • **87**
Brut Champagne Cuvée Florens de Castellane 1982 • $59 • (12/31/90) • **88**
Brut Rosé Champagne NV • $29 • (12/31/90) • **88**

CASTENET-GREFFIER, CHÂTEAU

Entre-Deux-Mers 1994: Not much to it, really: light pear and apple aromas and flavors, light body, light finish. • $8 • **77**

CATHERINE DE ST.-JUERY

Coteaux du Languedoc 1993: Concentrated, full-bodied and firmly tannic, showing deep color, peppery, berrylike flavors and a sense of intensity. Try now. • $8 • (03/31/95) • **84**
Coteaux du Languedoc 1992 • $8 • (03/15/94) BB • **87**
Coteaux du Languedoc 1991 • $8 • (06/15/93) • **80**
Coteaux du Languedoc 1990 • $8 • (10/31/92) BB • **85**

CATHIARD-MOLINIER

Nuits-St.-Georges Les Meurgers 1986 • $22 • (02/28/89) • **77**

CATTIER

Brut Champagne Chigny-Les-Roses Premier Cru 1988: A ripe style of Champagne with subtle apple, toasty, creamy character, medium body and a delicate finish. Drinkable now. • $35 • (12/31/93) • **87**
Brut Champagne Chigny-Les-Roses Premier Cru NV • $30 • (12/31/91) • **92**
Brut Champagne Clos du Moulin NV • $60 • (12/31/93) • **85**
Brut Champagne NV: Generous and fruity in style, easy to drink, may be best as an apéritif. Offers plenty of fresh apple, pear and lemon flavors subtly accented by almond and vanilla notes that linger on aftertaste. • $29 • **88**
Brut Rosé Champagne NV: The perfect choice for a romantic occasion. This pretty pink sparkler offers sweet vanilla and cream flavors with raspberry and piecrust accents that linger. • $40 • (12/15/95) • **90**

CAUZE, CHÂTEAU DU

St.-Emilion 1986 • $15 • (06/30/89) • **84**

CAYLA, CHÂTEAU

Premières Côtes de Bordeaux 1985 • $7 • (06/30/89) • **76**

CAYROU, CHÂTEAU DU

Cahors 1985 • $8 • (12/31/88) • **81**

CAZAL-VIEL, CHÂTEAU

St.-Chinian 1990 • $8 • (03/15/94) • **83**

CAZANOVE, CHARLES DE

Brut Champagne 1985: Good intensity of Pinot Noir character in this Champagne. It's full flavored with lots of character and good acidity. Drinkable now. 25,000 cases made. • $30 • (12/31/93) • **89**
Brut Champagne Millèsime 1989: A lush-textured, honey-flavored vintage Champagne that tastes smooth, creamy and fairly rich. Almost sweet, but not cloying, crisp acidity keeps it refreshing. 4,000 cases made. • $30 • (07/31/95) • **88**
Brut Champagne NV • $28 • (12/31/91) • **84**
Brut Champagne Ruban Azur NV • $32 • (12/31/91) • **87**
Brut Champagne Stradivarius 1989: Buttery, smooth and generous style of Champagne that has a full texture, ample fruit flavors and nice touches of complexity. Very appealing. 2,000 cases made. • $50 • (02/28/95) • **89**
Brut Champagne Stradivarius 1985: This wine locks in the flavors on your palate. Well defined with excellent structure, there's loads of creamy, pear, apple flavors and ripe acidity. Much better than when we tasted it in December 1991. Drinkable now. 20,000 cases made. • $50 • (12/31/93) • **91**

CAZIN, FRANCOIS

Cheverny Le Petit Chambord 1994: Gooseberry and melon characteristics are tempered by soft, floral notes. Firm, adding a moderate finish. Interesting. 500 cases made. • $12 • (05/15/96) • **84**
Cheverny Le Petit Chambord 1992: Citrus, herb and apple flavors are balanced and well-defined, and a pleasing mineral note comes out in the finish. It's crisp, refreshing and has good varietal character. • $10 • (10/31/94) • **85**

CECI, DOMAINE

Chambolle-Musigny Aux Echanges 1988 • $33 • (07/15/91) • **91**
Chambolle-Musigny Aux Echanges 1987 • $20 • (03/31/90) • **72**
Clos de Vougeot 1988 • $48 • (07/15/91) • **93**
Clos de Vougeot 1987 • $40 • (03/31/90) • **82**

CEDRE, CHÂTEAU DU

Cahors 1989 • $11 • (10/31/92) • **82**
Cahors 1988 • $10 • (08/31/91) • **83**
Cahors 1987 • $11 • (08/31/91) • **81**
Cahors Le Prestige 1988 • $14 • (08/31/91) • **84**
Cahors Le Prestige 1987 • $14 • (03/15/90) • **75**
Cahors Le Prestige 1985 • $9 • (12/31/88) • **80**

CEDRES, DOMAINE DES

Côtes du Rhône Pons Dominique 1986 • $10 • (03/31/90) • **82**

CELLIER DES BARONNIES

Côtes du Lubéron 1993: Fairly concentrated, with dried cherry and plum flavors and a lot of tannin. A rustic style, with a strong leathery component. • $NA • **81**
Vacqueyras 1990: Ripe, smooth, well balanced and fully mature, featuring smoke, leather, plum and pepper flavors and a lingering finish. Drinkable now. • $NA • (09/30/95) • **87**

CERTAN DE MAY, CHÂTEAU

Pomerol 1995: Powerful and rich, packed with everything you can expect in a top '95: loads of tannins, fruit, spice and toasted oak com-

FRANCE

plexity. One to lay down for years. Very exciting. • $NA • (05/15/96) • **95-100** (BT)

Pomerol 1994: Nice complexity and intensity of fruit and spice. Full-bodied, yet a bit austere in its hard tannins. Slightly drying on the finish but might come around. • $40 • (05/15/96) • **85-89** (BT)

Pomerol 1990: A big, ripe wine that maintains focus and complexity. It's chewy and firm, with notes of tobacco, black plums, meat and spice, the tannins are rich but not aggressive. Try now. 1,600 cases made. • $85 • (10/15/94) • **91**

Pomerol 1989: Enticing aromas of tobacco, roasted fruit and oak give way to muscular tannins and ripe plum, blackberry and herbal flavors on the palate. It's rich, balanced and accessible, but best after 1996. 1,600 cases made. • $65 • (10/15/94) • **89**

Pomerol 1988 • $67 Ⓐ • (06/30/91) • **90**

Pomerol 1986 • $58 Ⓐ • (09/15/89) • **93**

Pomerol 1985: Juicy with black cherry and tobacco flavors. It's full-bodied and velvety with plenty of fine tannins. Delicious now but best after 1996. • $86 Ⓐ • (10/15/94) • **90**

Pomerol 1983: This is a fruit bomb. Jumps out of the glass with wild herbs and ripe raspberry fruit, full-bodied with loads of fruit and tannins and a herbal finish that goes on and on. Still needs time to improve. Try after 1998. • $53 • (10/15/94) • **96**

Pomerol 1982 • $135 Ⓐ • (05/15/89) • **92**

Pomeral 1981: Ties for first place in this vintage. A blockbuster. Yet harmonious. Great dark color with layers of chocolate, olive, berry fruit character. Full-bodied and tannic yet very velvety. Long, long finish. Drink or hold for as long as you like. • $50 • (10/15/94) • **95**

Pomerol 1979 • $86 Ⓐ • (10/15/89) • **90**

CERTAN-GIRAUD, CHÂTEAU

Pomerol 1988 • $23 • (02/28/91) • **89**

Pomerol 1986 • $22 • (06/30/89) • **86**

Pomerol 1985 • $19 Ⓐ • (04/30/88) • **85**

Pomerol 1982 • $NA • (05/15/89) • **90**

Pomerol 1961: This was tight and closed at first, then opened up into a plush, cherry-scented claret with nice depth and round, smooth texture supported by just enough tannin. • $59 • (04/30/96) • **87**

CHABLISIENNE, LA

Chablis 1994: Elegant and racy almond, grapefruit and apple aromas and flavors, medium body and fresh finish. • $NA • (08/31/95) • **85**

Chablis Beauroy 1993: Classy, racy mineral, apple and flinty aromas and flavors. Medium body, fine acidity and a long, fresh finish. Drinkable now. • $NA • (08/31/95) • **87**

Chablis Blanchots 1993: Rather meager and acidic, offering some lemon, lime and vanilla aromas and flavors and a short finish. • $NA • (08/31/95) • **81**

Chablis Bougros 1993: Creamy vanilla and lemon character, medium body and toasted oak finish. A bit simple. • $NA • (08/31/95) • **82**

Chablis Côte de Léchet 1993: Oaky style, showing vanilla bean, lemon and mineral flavors. A crisp and vibrant finish. • $NA • (08/31/95) • **84**

Chablis Cuvée L.C. 1994: Well made, fresh and clean, packing more punch than some standard Chablis, offering apple and citrus flavors and a touch of pear. Light-to-medium body, very crisp finish. Drinkable now. • $23 • (05/31/96) • **81**

Chablis Fourchaume 1994: Lush, supple honey, pear and apple flavors and a full body. It delivers some lively lemon notes, but lacks a bit of complexity on the zesty yet slightly coarse finish. Drinkable now. • $30 • (05/31/96) • **84**

Chablis Fourchaume 1993: Impressively ripe pineapple and honey aromas, medium-to-full body, grapefruit, honey and cream character and a long, fresh finish. Better in 1997. • $NA • (08/31/95) • **86**

Chablis Grenouilles Château Grenouilles 1993: Some good ripeness, with apple, almond and cream aromas and flavors and a medium body. Vanilla and pineapple on the finish. Drinkable now. • $NA • (08/31/95) • **86**

Chablis Les Clos 1993: Flavorful and elegant, this medium-bodied grand cru Chablis offers fine acidity, plenty of apple and honey notes and a hint of vanilla. Perhaps slightly too oaky? • $NA • (08/31/95) • **86**

Chablis Les Preuses 1993: Delicious mineral, spice and almond aromas and flavors. Medium in body, fresh acidity and long, flavorful finish. Drinkable now. • $NA • (08/31/95) • **86**

Chablis Mont de Milieu 1994: Tight as nails, linear, one-dimensional. Might soften in time, but for now it's tough and tasting of cedar, dried herb and citrus flavors. Not much pleasure there. Hopefully better by 1999. • $30 • (05/31/96) • **83**

Chablis Mont de Milieu Les Domaines La Chablisienne 1993: Firm character, with a good amount of mineral, spice, toast, pear, cream and citrus flavors shaded by vanilla-scented oak. An elegant, long finish. • $NA • (08/31/95) • **86**

Chablis Montée de Tonnerre 1993: Flinty, spicy aromas and flavors, medium body, fresh fruit and pretty finish. • $NA • (08/31/95) • **84**

Chablis Premier Cru Vieilles Vignes 1993: Smooth, buttery and light-bodied. Has mineral, pear and honey flavors and a balanced, elegant finish, but could use some more intensity. • $NA • (08/31/95) • **84**

Chablis Vaudésir 1993: Provocatively oaky, but there's enough fruit to take it. Loads of spice, toast, smoke and pear flavors, with a showy and supple finish. Try in 1997. • $NA • (08/31/95) • **85**

CHAGALE, BARON

Brut Blanc de Blancs NV • $6 • (06/15/90) • **70**

CHAINIER SELECTION, PIERRE

Bourgueil 1985 • $7 • (09/30/88) • **78**

Chinon 1985 • $7 • (09/30/88) • **83**

CHAINTRE, CAVE DE

Mâcon-Fuissé 1994: Round, smooth and quaffably pleasant, but it lacks fresh intensity. Already golden in color, with some banana, citrus, pear and almond flavors. Drinkable now. • $NA • **79**

St.-Véran White 1994: Lovely peach, apricot and almost Viognier-like flavors shine in this smooth, elegant, light- to medium-bodied white. It's slightly diluted, though. • $NA • **82**

CHAIS BAUMIERE

Chardonnay Vin de Pays d'Oc 1994: This resembles an international-style Chardonnay, with vanilla, sweet melon and light apple flavors. Easy to quaff. 10,000 cases made. • $6 • (02/29/96) • **81**

Chardonnay Vin de Pays d'Oc 1991 • $NA • (03/15/94) • **85**

Merlot Vin de Pays d'Oc 1990 • $NA • (03/15/94) • **80**

Sauvignon Blanc Vin de Pays d'Oc 1994: A ripe-tasting, clean and fresh white with ample melon and citrus flavors. Soft and easy to drink. 8,000 cases made. • $6 • (02/29/96) • **81**

Sauvignon Blanc Vin de Pays d'Oc 1992 • $NA • (03/15/94) • **86**

Sauvignon Blanc Vin de Pays d'Oc 1991 • $NA • (03/15/94) • **84**

Syrah Vin de Pays d'Oc 1993: Very gamy and only modest fruit flavors. Soft and disjointed, adding a tannic finish. 6,000 cases made. • $6 • (05/15/96) • **78**

CHAIZE, CHÂTEAU DE LA

Brouilly 1993: Though light, this is firm and still fresh, with light cherry and berry flavors and a tannic backbone. The wine is balanced but slightly diluted. • $NA • **81**

Brouilly 1992: Fleshy but aging fast, shows some cherry flavor, but it's dominated by brown sugar and raisin notes, and lacks grip and crispness. Drink up. Tasted twice. • $10 • (06/30/94) • **75**

CHALET, CHÂTEAU DU

Bordeaux 1987 • $6 • (04/15/90) • **78**

Key: SS—Spectator Selection. CS—Cellar Selection. BB—Best Buy. $NA—Price not available. (BT)—Barrel tasting. Ⓐ—Auction Price.
Dates in parentheses represent the issues in which the ratings were published.

FRANCE

CHAMBERT-MARBUZET, CHÂTEAU

St.-Estèphe 1995: A '95 with a good level of fruit and toasted oak. The silky tannins and good, solid finish bode well for the future of this wine. • $NA • (05/15/96) • **85-89** (BT)

St.-Estèphe 1994: Distinctively minty with some plum and currant, dominated by wood now. Light-to-medium body, somewhat diluted on the finish. • $NA • **75-79** (BT)

St.-Estèphe 1993: Diluted, showing some decent wood, vanilla and plum character but very light. Drinkable now. 3,333 cases made. • $25 • (01/31/96) • **79**

St.-Estèphe 1992: Too much new wood, some decent fruit, but dominated and slightly dried out by the tannins. Drinkable now. • $15 • **76**

St.-Estèphe 1991: Pretty, sexy aromas and flavors accompanied by lots of new wood and cherry notes. Medium body, silky texture and a light finish. Second label of Haut-Marbuzet. • $14 • (03/31/94) • **83**

St.-Estèphe 1990: A bit one-dimensional, but it offers beautiful aromas and flavors of berry, vanilla, and cherry, medium tannins and plenty of sweet fruit on the finish. Drinkable now. 3,800 cases made. • $25 • (03/31/93) • **86**

St.-Estèphe 1987 • $18 • (11/30/89) • **79**

St.-Estèphe 1986 • $29 • (11/30/89) • **89**

St.-Estèphe 1985 • $32 • (06/30/88) • **87**

St.-Estèphe 1983 • $15 • (09/30/86) • **77**

St.-Estèphe 1982 • $30 • (11/30/89) • **88**

CHAMBERT, CHÂTEAU DE

Cahors 1986 • $12 • (08/31/89) • **87**

CHAMBLAIN, PAUL

Brut Blanc de Blancs NV • $6 • (06/15/90) • **74**

CHAMIREY, CHÂTEAU DE

Marsannay 1992: Smooth-textured Burgundy, with some decent vanilla, butter, apple and pear flavors, and a fresh finish. From Antonin Rodet. • $17 • (08/31/94) • **83**

Mercurey 1994: Pleasant and sweet-tasting, it's round and a bit simple, showing apricot, peach and pear flavors. • $20 • (05/31/96) • **80**

Mercurey Red 1991: Very crisp and moderately astringent, this tough little wine has charms that reveal themselves after several sips. Drinkable now. • $NA • (01/31/94) • **81**

CHAMOUX, JEAN-PIERRE

Pouilly-Fumé Les Chantlouettes 1993: Not much fruit here. Aromas of earth and herbs, slightly candied and vegetal flavors and a streak of lean acidity don't give much pleasure. • $15 • **78**

Pouilly-Fumé Les Chantalouettes 1992: Intriguing and distinctive. Complex aromas of spice, vanilla and almond draw you in, turning creamy on the palate, showing apple, honey and citrus flavors. It's broad and multifaceted, with good concentration. • $14 • (10/31/94) • **88**

CHAMPAGNON, LOUIS

Chénas Red 1984 • $7 • (05/01/86) • **75**

Moulin-à-Vent Red 1984 • $7 • (05/01/86) • **68**

CHAMPALOU

Vouvray 1993: With good focus and structure, this offers honeyed pear and pine flavors with an intriguing floral accent. 3,800 cases made. • $14 • (11/15/95) • **85**

Vouvray Cuvée Moelleuse 1994: Plenty of wet wool aromas, supported by citrus and tobacco, yet the flavors are basically one-dimensional. Lots of acidity and mineral character. Try after 2000. • $20 • (05/15/96) • **83**

CHAMPET, EMILE

Côte-Rôtie 1989 • $28 • (04/15/93) • **78**

Côte-Rôtie Côte Brune 1991: Rich and juicy, oozing with new oak. Classy, round and silky, with plenty of berry and plum flavors to balance the toast and vanilla. Drinkable now. • $32 • (05/31/94) • **87**

Côte-Rôtie Côte Brune 1990: Pure velvet, with extremely ripe raisin and prune flavors supported by full, round tannins. It's rich, but a bit rustic. Try now. • $33 • (05/31/94) • **89**

CHAMPS, JEANNE-MARIE DE

Corton Hospices de Beaune Cuvée Charlotte-Dumay 1985 • $76 • (10/15/88) • **87**

Nuits-St.-Georges Les Didiers Hospices de Nuits Cuvée Cabet 1988 • $26 Ⓐ • (09/30/90) • **83**

Nuits-St.-Georges Les Didiers Hospices de Nuits Cuvée Cabet 1985 • $53 • (03/15/88) • **96**

Nuits-St.-Georges Les Didiers Hospices de Nuits Cuvée Jacques Duret 1988 • $49 • (09/30/90) • **89**

Nuits-St.-Georges Les Terres Blanches 1988 • $39 • (07/15/91) • **90**

CHANDON DE BRIAILLES

Aloxe-Corton 1983 • $25 • (09/15/86) • **84**

Corton Blanc 1991 • $69 • (05/31/94) • **90**

Corton Bressandes 1991: Smoky, earthy aromas and fairly generous fruit flavors make this an accessible, easy-drinking Burgundy from a difficult vintage. The flavors are plummy, beefy and generous, and the texture is smooth. The finish, lingers, too. Drinkable now. • $53 • **85**

Corton Bressandes 1988 • $75 • (02/28/91) • **89**

Corton Bressandes 1986 • $43 • (02/28/90) • **88**

Corton Clos du Roi 1991: Tough, tannic and young, this Corton has smoky, earthy aromas, a tight texture laced with firm tannins, and tart, greenish flavors. You could admire it for its structure, but it's so light on fruit flavor that it becomes awkward and heavy handed. • $57 • **81**

Corton Clos du Roi 1986 • $27 Ⓐ • (02/28/90) • **85**

Corton Maréchaudes 1991: A sturdy but refined Burgundy with just enough fruit flavor to fill out the basically tannic framework. It starts out with seductively spicy oak aromas, goes into solid cherry flavors and finishes with spice and smoke. Drinkable now. • $44 • **85**

Corton White Corton 1991 • $69 • (05/31/94) • **90**

Pernand-Vergelesses Ile des Vergelesses 1991: This has a good core of cherry and raspberry flavors balanced by firm acidity and tannins, making for a complete, well-rounded red Burgundy. Solidly built. Drink now. • $28 • **84**

Pernand-Vergelesses Ile des Vergelesses 1988 • $35 • (02/28/91) • **83**

Savigny-lès-Beaune 1991: A rather tight Burgundy with stiff tannins and tart acidity but enough cherry and raspberry flavor to fill it out. • $21 • **83**

Savigny-lès-Beaune Les Fourneaux 1991: Fresh, flavorful and vibrant, with ample floral aromas, strawberry and cherry flavors and a clean, tannic finish. • $23 • **82**

Savigny-lès-Beaune Les Lavières 1991: A firm-textured, lean flavored Burgundy with raspberry and herbal accents and a touch of toasy oak. Moderate tannins and good acidity will make it a refreshing dinner time wine. • $26 • **84**

Savigny-lès-Beaune Les Lavières 1988 • $31 • (02/28/91) • **86**

CHANGROLLE, CHÂTEAU

Lalande-de-Pomerol 1982 • $6 • (12/16/84) • **78**

CHANSON PERE & FILS

Beaune Clos des Fèves 1988 • $35 • (08/31/90) • **84**

Beaune Clos des Fèves 1987 • $23 • (07/31/89) • **85**

Beaune Clos des Fèves 1985 • $25 • (01/31/89) • **92**

Beaune Clos des Marconnets 1986 • $20 • (05/31/89) • **81**

Bourgogne Cuvée Alexis Chanson 1994: Sweet-tasting and soft, showing distinctive mint, honey and ripe pear character. Light-bodied and ready to drink. • $10 • (05/31/96) • **79**

Chablis 1994: Clean and crisp, showing modest citrus, green apple and earth notes. Light in body, long finish. Good with simple dishes or shellfish. • $18 • (05/31/96) • **78**
Chablis Blanchots 1994: Offers some green apple, wet earth, herb and honey character. A bit tart and linear. Better in 1998? • $25 • (05/31/96) • **84**
Chablis Montmains 1994: Delicious and supple, this round, ready-to-drink Chablis offers some cream, lemon, ripe apple and honey character. A bit one-dimensional and the finish is very crisp. Drinkable now or hold until 1998. • $29 • (05/31/96) • **83**
Corton 1986 • $30 • (04/30/89) • **90**
Givry 1988 • $13 • (12/31/90) • **78**
Montagny Premier Cru 1994: Nicely made and satisfying, a medium-bodied '94 featuring good concentration of ripe fruit flavors in an elegant package. Stands out for its chewy honey, pear, caramel character. • $13 • (05/31/96) • **84**
Pernand-Vergelesses Les Vergelesses 1988 • $24 • (08/31/90) • **85**
Pernand-Vergelesses White 1994: Straightforward and simple, cardboard character. Short on flavors. • $16 • (05/31/96) 71 • **71**
Pouilly-Fuissé St.-Vincent 1994: Lively, vibrant, juicy, lemony flavor. Tasty, light-bodied white of modest character. Try now with oysters or other seafood. • $19 • (05/31/96) • **84**
Vosne-Romanée Suchots 1988 • $55 • (09/30/90) • **87**

CHANTE CIGALE

Châteauneuf-du-Pape 1989 • $14 • (10/15/91) • **84**
Châteauneuf-du-Pape 1988 • $18 • (10/15/91) • **89**
Châteauneuf-du-Pape 1986 • $18 • (10/15/91) • **89**

CHANTE PERDRIX, DOMAINE

Châteauneuf-du-Pape 1990: Enjoyable but odd, with walnutty, honey-like, peppery aromas and similar flavors. Likable, but so unusual with its oxidized character that it throws you for a loop. Tasted twice, with consistent notes. • $20 • (04/15/93) • **79**
Châteauneuf-du-Pape 1989 • $20 • (08/31/92) • **82**
Châteauneuf-du-Pape 1988 • $17 • (05/31/91) • **82**

CHANTE-PERDRIX, CAVE DE

St.-Joseph 1992 • $12 • (05/31/94) • **76**
St.-Joseph 1991 • $12 • (05/31/94) • **77**
St.-Joseph 1989 • $12 • (05/31/94) • **89**

CHANTEFLEUR

Cabernet Sauvignon Vin de Pays d'Oc 1994: Smooth, soft, offering raisin, light cherry and earth flavors, but though pretty well concentrated it appears tired already. 25,000 cases made. • $5 • (10/31/95) • **78**
Cabernet Sauvignon Vin de Pays d'Oc 1993: Simple but appetizing, showing fresh plum and cherry flavors and moderate tannins. 15,000 cases made. • $5 • (02/28/95) • **81**
Cabernet Sauvignon Vin de Pays de l'Ardèche 1991 • $5 • (06/15/93) BB • **81**
Cabernet Sauvignon Vin de Pays de l'Ardèche 1988 • $6 • (05/31/90) BB • **80**
Chardonnay Vin de Pays d'Oc 1994: From the vegetal aromas to the brown sugar finish, this wine lacks fruit and varietal character. There's little concentration and less appeal. 25,000 cases made. • $5 • (06/30/95) • **73**
Chardonnay Vin de Pays d'Oc 1993: This round, soft wine has an herbal note on the palate and sweet vanilla flavor on the finish. A nice apéritif. 15,000 cases made. • $5 • (01/31/95) • **79**
Chardonnay Vin de Pays d'Oc 1991 • $5 • (04/15/93) • **75**

Key: SS—Spectator Selection. CS—Cellar Selection. BB—Best Buy. $NA—Price not available. (BT)—Barrel tasting. Ⓐ—Auction Price.
Dates in parentheses represent the issues in which the ratings were published.

Merlot Vin de Pays d'Oc 1994: An odd combination of sweet berry and onion flavors, accompanied by drying tannins, mars this simple, fleshy red. 25,000 cases made. • $5 • (10/31/95) • **76**
Merlot Vin de Pays d'Oc 1993: A robust, fairly tannic and fruity red with jammy flavors and a nice bite to the texture. 15,000 cases made. • $5 • (02/28/95) • **82**
Merlot Vin de Pays d'Oc 1992 • $5 • (03/15/94) • **80**
Merlot Vin de Pays d'Oc 1991 • $5 • (03/15/93) BB • **81**
Merlot Vin de Pays d'Oc 1988 • $6 • (05/31/90) • **75**
Sauvignon Blanc Vin de Pays d'Oc 1993: Smooth, rather earthy, with hints of almonds and peaches. Basically neutral in character. 15,000 cases made. • $5 • (01/31/95) • **77**
Syrah Vin de Pays d'Oc 1993: A full-bodied, dry, tannic red with blackberry and black peppper flavors that persist on the finish. Good and solid, if a bit rough. 15,000 cases made. • $5 • (02/28/95) • **80**

CHANTEGRIVE, CHÂTEAU DE

Graves 1991: Very watery with dried cherry, vanilla aromas and flavors. • $11 • (03/31/94) • **72**
Graves 1990: This is an angular, muscular wine with good, rich fruit and solid tannins, but it's not giving much at the moment. Drink in 1997. • $14 • (03/31/93) • **87**
Graves 1989 • $20 • (03/15/92) • **88**
Graves 1982 • $20 • (08/31/92) • **88**
Graves Cuvée Edouard 1990: This wine shows aromas and flavors of cassis, smoke and a full yet fine tannin structure. Big and muscular. Drinkable now. • $16 • (03/31/93) • **88**
Graves Cuvée Edouard 1989 • $22 • (03/15/92) • **85**
Graves White 1993: Simple and clean, offering grassy, citric, appley character, medium body and crisp finish. • $10 • **83**
Graves White Cuvée Caroline 1992: Grassy style, but very polished. Some earth, dried-herb and honey flavors, beautifully textured, with a smooth, long finish. Drinkable now. • $20 • (05/31/95) • **88**

CHANTOVENT

Cabernet Sauvignon Prestige Vin de Pays d'Oc Prestige 1988 • $6 • (03/15/90) BB • **81**
Cabernet Sauvignon Prestige Vin de Pays d'Oc Prestige 1987 • $5 • (10/31/89) • **78**
Cabernet Sauvignon Prestige Vin de Pays d'Oc Prestige 1986 • $6 • (05/15/89) • **79**
Merlot Prestige Vin de Pays d'Oc Prestige 1989 • $7 • (06/15/93) • **76**
Merlot Prestige Vin de Pays d'Oc Prestige 1988 • $6 • (03/15/90) • **73**
Merlot Prestige Vin de Pays d'Oc Prestige 1986 • $6 • (05/15/89) • **69**

CHAPELLE DE LA MISSION-HAUT-BRION, LA

Pessac-Léognan 1995: Plenty of fruit in this one—grapey and delicious. It shows velvety tannins, medium-to-full body and a good finish. • $NA • (05/15/96) • **85-89** (BT)
Pessac-Léognan 1994: Lovely, silky tannins frame the tobacco, berry and chocolate flavors. Medium body, sweet fruit character and a nicely done finish. • $NA • (05/15/96) • **80-84** (BT)

CHAPOUTIER, M.

Cuvée de Belleruche Red 1989 • $13 • (06/15/92) • **82**
Châteauneuf-du-Pape Barbe Rac 1992: Full-bodied, round in texture and marked by ripe, soft flavors of prunes and tomatoes, firm tannins and a lingering finish. • $77 • (10/15/95) • **84**
Châteauneuf-du-Pape La Bernardine 1992: A full-bodied red with vague fruit flavors and pretty stiff tannins. Tastes a bit tired and watery in the middle, and turns astringent on the finish. • $26 • **77**
Châteauneuf-du-Pape La Bernardine 1990: Shows uncommon balance, proportion and finesse, offering lovely currant, cherry, chocolate and smoky oak flavors that are complex and luscious. The finish is long and complex, with soft but firm tannins. Tasty now, but can age through 1998. 8,000 cases made. • $16 • (08/31/92) SS • **90**
Châteauneuf-du-Pape La Bernardine 1989 • $20 • (08/31/91) • **84**
Châteauneuf-du-Pape La Bernardine 1988 • $17 • (12/31/91) • **81**

Châteauneuf-du-Pape La Bernardine 1985 • $25 • (03/15/90) • **89**
Châteauneuf-du-Pape La Bernardine 1983 • $15 • (06/01/86) • **81**
Châteauneuf-du-Pape White La Bernardine 1993: One of the more fruity, flavorful whites from Châteauneuf-du-Pape, showing fresh grassy, appley notes and a rich texture. Lingers on the finish, too. • $34 • (12/31/95) • **85**
Cornas 1991 • $32 • (05/31/94) • **86**
Cornas 1990 • $32 • (05/31/94) • **58**
Côte-Rôtie 1992: Fresh, with cherry and smoky flavors, but rather lean on the palate. Drinkable now. • $35 • (05/31/94) • **83**
Côte-Rôtie 1991: Smooth and youthful, a slightly chewy wine with fine tannins and a solid burst of leather-tinged cherry flavor. Drinkable now. • $37 • (10/31/93) • **85**
Côte-Rôtie 1990: An earthy style, with mulchy, green flavors-not quite ripe. Shows true Côte-Rôtie character, but at this stage the earthiness dominates. Drink after 1996. 5,000 cases made. • $41 • (05/31/94) • **80**
Côte-Rôtie 1989 • $30 • (07/31/91) • **86**
Côte-Rôtie 1988 • $27 • (11/15/91) • **84**
Côte-Rôtie Brune et Blonde 1992: From an off year in the Northern Rhône, but of interest and substance. Smoky, mineral accents and plummy, peppery flavors, good acidity, firm tannins and a lingering finish. • $48 • (12/31/95) • **87**
Côte-Rôtie Brune et Blonde 1990: Fresh and ebulliently flavorful, with lavishly black-pepper accented black cherry and raspberry aromas and flavors, hinting at vanilla and cedar on the finish. A solid wine, with a graceful sense of balance and refined tannins that put it at its best now to 1997. 4,000 cases made. • $35 • (11/15/92) • **90**
Côte-Rôtie La Mordorée 1992: Balanced but rather light, this marries smoky, earthy flavors with cherry and herbal notes. The tannins are firm and lean, offering some complexity for early drinking. • $93 • (10/15/95) • **83**
Côte-Rôtie La Mordorée 1991: Ripe and plump, with attractive flavors of plums, smoke and grilled meat. Full-bodied with silky tannins. Drinkable now. Tasted twice. • $87 • (05/31/94) • **86**
Côte-Rôtie La Mordorée 1990: A muscular wine that still achieves great elegance, with restrained ripe plum, tobacco and tar flavors. The tannins are huge, but the wine is balanced, try in 1999. • $87 • (05/31/94) • **91**
Côtes du Rhône 1987 • $9 • (12/31/91) • **79**
Côtes du Rhône Belleruche 1994: Bright and fruity, marked by cherry, berry and cider flavors and moderate tannins. Enough depth and body to be mouth-filling. Drinkable now. • $10 • (12/31/95) • **82**
Côtes du Rhône Belleruche 1993: Smoky and herbal with good, well-rounded ripe fruit flavors of plum and black cherry. It finishes with a nice note of chocolate. • $10 • **83**
Côtes du Rhône Cuvée de Belleruche 1990 • $11 • (11/30/92) • **77**
Côtes du Rhône Cuvée de Belleruche 1986 • $12 • (12/15/89) • **87**
Côtes du Rhône White Belleruche 1993: A tart wine, with lemony flavors and aromas. Turns somewhat bitter and thin on the finish. • $10 • **78**
Côtes du Rhône-Villages Rasteau 1990 • $14 • (04/15/93) • **79**
Côtes du Ventoux La Ciboise 1993: The fresh, herbaceous aroma is intriguing, but the simple, lean flavors aren't enough to keep this interesting. • $9 • **76**
Côtes du Ventoux La Ciboise 1990 • $7 • (04/15/93) • **76**
Crozes-Hermitage La Petite Ruche 1991 • $18 • (05/31/94) • **86**
Crozes-Hermitage Les Meysonniers 1993: Has great balance, fresh fruit flavors and spicy accents to add complexity. Not a blockbuster, but bright and lively. Drinkable now. • $22 • (12/31/95) • **85**
Crozes-Hermitage Les Meysonniers 1992: Intriguing aromas of licorice and black pepper give way to light fruit on the palate. Not concentrated but typical, well balanced with soft tannins. Drinkable now. • $20 • **84**
Crozes-Hermitage Les Meysonniers 1991 • $17 • (05/31/94) • **80**
Crozes-Hermitage White Les Meysonniers 1992 • $NA • (05/31/94) • **80**
Hermitage Chante-Alouette White 1991: A bruiser. An intense, oily wine that shows plenty of ripe pear and butter character, but lacking structure and balance. Drinkable now. • $38 • (05/31/94) • **82**
Hermitage Chante-Alouette White 1990 • $33 • (11/30/92) • **82**
Hermitage Ermitage De L'Orvée White 1991 • $80 • (05/31/94) • **79**
Hermitage Ermitage Le Pavillon 1992: Ambitious, offering plenty of ripeness, plenty of extraction and plenty of oak. Tough now, but cassis, smoke and bitter chocolate flavors promise to unwind after time in bottle. Try in 1997. • $109 • **87**
Hermitage Ermitage Le Pavillon 1991: Firm and focused, with concentrated black cherry, tobacco and spice aromas and flavors. Almost drinkable now, best from 1997. 450 cases made. • $102 • (05/31/94) • **87**
Hermitage Le Pavillon 1990: Dark, dense and concentrated. A firm-textured wine with a strong smoky character that threads through the powerful berry and spice flavors. The earthy notes are disturbing. Needs until1998. • $160 • (12/15/93) • **85**
Hermitage Le Pavillon NV • $60 • (01/31/89) • **88**
Hermitage Monier de la Sizeranne 1992: Smooth and supple for Hermitage, this shows plenty of ripe cherry flavors and appealing smoke and pepper notes. The tannins are firm, but they're well-integrated with the fruit. Drinkable now, better in 1997. • $45 • **87**
Hermitage Monier de la Sizeranne 1991: Chunky and tight, with a nice core of berry and spice flavors struggling to get past the fine tannins. Ends up balanced and promising fine things. Best from 1997. 10,000 cases made. • $42 • (05/31/94) • **86**
Hermitage Monier de la Sizeranne 1989 • $33 • (08/31/91) • **89**
Hermitage Monier de la Sizeranne 1988 • $25 • (12/31/91) • **85**
Hermitage Monier de la Sizeranne 1983 • $19 • (05/01/86) • **83**
Hermitage Monier de la Sizeranne 1981 • $10 • (11/01/84) • **88**
Hermitage Monier de la Sizeranne Grande Cuvée NV • $14 • (05/01/86) • **83**
Hermitage Monier de la Sizeranne Red 1990 • $28 • (08/31/92) • **91**
Hermitage White Chante-Alouette 1992: A very good white boasting honeyed, toasty aromas and attractive flavors of apricot and spice. Richly textured, full in body, almost unctuous, adding a late-harvest kind of complexity and lingering, seductive finish. • $40 • **88**
Hermitage White De L'Orée 1992: Goes for intensity, but stumbles on extreme tartness. Has buttery, honeylike aromas, apricot and honey flavors and a lingering but tart finish. Drink now. • $81 • **84**
Muscat de Beaumes-de-Venise 1993: Big and bold, full in body and thick-textured, emphasizing the slightly bitter side of Muscat's flavors. Reminds us of orange zest, bitter almond and apricot. • $13 • **86**
St.-Joseph Deschants 1992 • $20 • (05/31/94) • **88**
St.-Joseph Deschants 1991 • $20 • (05/31/94) • **79**
St.-Joseph Deschants 1990 • $20 • (04/15/93) • **83**
St.-Joseph Deschants White 1992 • $18 • (05/31/94) • **83**
St.-Joseph Deschants White 1991 • $18 • (05/31/94) • **78**

CHARBAUT FRERES

Brut Blanc de Blancs Crémant de Bourgogne 1986 • $15 • (01/31/92) • **80**
Brut Rosé Crémant de Bourgogne 1986 • $12 • (12/31/90) • **79**

CHARBAUT, A.

Brut Blanc de Blancs Champagne 1988: Tight, rich and beautifully focused with spicy pear, lemon and cedary notes that turn elegant and complex on a long, rich finish. Picks up hints of honey and toast on the finish. Delicious now but has the intensity and depth to age through 1996. 20,000 cases made. • $42 • (11/30/93) • **91**
Brut Blanc de Blancs Champagne 1987: Tastes off-dry, with perfumed, fruity aromas that turn soft and fleshy. Finishes with a coarseness and lack of finesse. Fails to impress, but it's certainly drinkable. Drink now. 10,000 cases made. • $42 • (08/31/92) • **76**
Brut Blanc de Blancs Champagne 1982: Deliciously rich and vivid, with layers of creamy cherry, toast, vanilla and spice flavors that are deep and concentrated. Plenty of pretty flavors on the aftertaste, too. Drink now to 1994. • $43 • (04/15/90) • **90**
Brut Blanc de Blancs Champagne 1979 • $34 • (05/31/87) • **96**
Brut Blanc de Blancs Champagne NV: Overripe flavors of pineapple and fig are salvaged by a nice creaminess. It comes off just a bit dull and awkward, though. 4,000 cases made. • $35 • (12/31/94) • **80**
Brut Blanc de Blancs Champagne Certificate 1985: Refreshing wine with appley, young aromas and flavors and a hint of toasted oak. Medium-bodied with lovely acidity and a long finish. Better than when tasted in August 1992. Drink now. 4,000 cases made. • $88 • (12/31/93) • **88**
Brut Blanc de Blancs Champagne Certificate 1982: Broad, rich, well-defined pear, vanilla, apple and spice notes, a full-bodied style that's attractive, with time it may display more complexity and finesse, but for now those are modest shortcomings. • $82 • (12/31/89) • **87**

Brut Blanc de Blancs Champagne Certificate 1979 • $80 • (07/15/88) • **92**

Brut Blanc de Blancs Champagne Certificate 1976 • $63 • (05/31/87) • **87**

Brut Champagne 1987: Refined Champagne with bright ripe apple, lemon-lime and light toast character, excellent acidity and a long flavorful finish. Another lovely apéritif. Much better now with a little bottle age since we reported on it in August '92. Drink now. 6,000 cases made. • $42 • (12/31/93) • **88**

Brut Champagne 1985 • $49 • (12/31/90) • **94**

Brut Champagne 1979 • $23 • (02/01/86) • **74**

Brut Champagne NV: A light, delicate, pleasing style of bubbly showing citrus, vanilla and fresh dough flavors. Has elegant, creamy texture too. Great as an apéritif. • $28 • (12/31/95) • **87**

Brut Champagne André Charbaut NV • $35 • (11/30/93) • **77**

Brut Champagne Cuvée de Réserve NV • $35 • (12/31/91) • **90**

Brut Champagne Extra Quality NV • $30 • (12/31/91) • **86**

Brut Champagne Gold Label NV: A different flavor spectrum-juniper, grapefruit, apple cider-makes this unsual. On the rough, rustic side, but with vivid, distinctive flavors. 20,000 cases made. • $28 • (12/31/94) • **82**

Brut Rosé Champagne NV: Shows a lot of Pinot Noir character in the cherry-berry aromas and nuances of spice and tea. Crisp but elegant in texture, with great balance and a lingering finish. 4,000 cases made. • $35 • (12/31/95) • **90**

Brut Rosé Champagne Certificate 1985: Soft, light and fruity, with pretty strawberry and watermelon flavors that turn delicate on the finish. Drinks well now. 4,000 cases made. • $85 • (08/31/92) • **85**

Brut Rosé Champagne Certificate 1982: Pretty orange salmon color, with plenty of Pinot Noir, strawberry and cherry flavors that are beginning to show signs of complexity and nuance. Ready in 1993. • $82 • (12/31/89) • **88**

Brut Rosé Champagne Certificate 1979 • $80 • (07/15/88) • **89**

Demi-Sec Champagne Sélection NV: Definitely sweet, but intriguingly flavorful, too. It has toasty, honey aromas and sweet, satisfying pear and peach flavors. Smooth and creamy in texture. 2,000 cases made. • $35 • (12/31/94) • **86**

Extra Dry Champagne NV • $22 • (12/31/88) • **87**

CHARDONNAY, CAVE DE

Mâcon-Chardonnay Chardonnay de Chardonnay 1991 • $10 • (03/31/93) • **80**

CHARLOPIN-PARIZOT

Charmes-Chambertin 1990: Tight and focused, with a bright beam of toasty berry and plum aromas and flavors. Tannins wrap the flavors tightly on the finish, but the fruit persists and keeps echoing. Drinkable now. • $70 • (08/31/92) • **92**

Clos St.-Denis 1990: Tough in texture but beautifully focused, with elegant currant and berry flavors and floral and vanilla notes on the long finish. The tough tannins will need until 1997 to '98 to smooth themselves out. • $76 • (08/31/92) • **89**

Gevrey-Chambertin 1985 • $22 • (11/30/87) • **64**

Gevrey-Chambertin Cuvée Vieilles Vignes 1990: Ripe, plush and generous, with a velvety smooth texture and beautifully articulated raspberry, black cherry and anise aromas and flavors intertwining through the long finish. Drinkable now. 150 cases made. • $40 • (04/30/92) • **90**

Gevrey-Chambertin Cuvée Vieilles Vignes 1989 • $75 • (11/15/91) • **88**

Gevrey-Chambertin Cuvée Vieilles Vignes 1988 • $31 • (12/31/90) • **79**

Marsannay en Montchenovoy 1990: Crisp and berrylike, but with enough flesh to bring out the smooth, polished texture. Balanced and appealing, with simple, refreshing flavors that are more like Beaujolais than Burgundy. Drinkable now. • $19 • (04/30/92) • **84**

Key: SS—Spectator Selection. CS—Cellar Selection. BB—Best Buy. $NA—Price not available. (BT)—Barrel tasting. Ⓐ—Auction Price.
Dates in parentheses represent the issues in which the ratings were published.

CHARLOPIN-PARIZOT, PHILIPPE

Charmes-Chambertin 1993: A pure, clean, "serious" red Burgundy that coats the palate with its silky texture. Quite smoky and toasty in character, featuring lots of wild berry and currant flavors and complex aftertaste. Full-bodied, it seduces from start to finish. Delicious now but should age beautifully well into the next century. • $94 • (05/15/96) • **94**

Clos St.-Denis 1993: Lovely clarity of berry and cherry character and a hint of mineral notes. Full, fine tannins and long, silky finish. Ultrafine Burgundy. Better in 2000. • $94 • (05/15/96) • **90**

Gevrey-Chambertin Cuvée Vieilles Vignes 1993: Almost outstanding, featuring lovely plum, earth and berry character, velvety tannins and a medium finish. Better in 1999. • $NA • **88**

CHARLOPIN, PHILIPPE

Chambertin 1990: Firm in texture and bold in flavor, with complex cedar- and smoke-scented currant, plum and berry flavors, all tightly packed and long on the finish. The tannins are well integrated, but this should be at its best in 1998. 100 cases made. • $90 • (08/31/92) • **94**

Chambertin 1989 • $35 • (11/15/91) • **91**

CHARMES-GODARD, CHÂTEAU LES

Côtes de Francs 1995: Offers some decent red berry and spice character, but hard tannins and pronounced oak notes taste a bit harsh and rustic now. • $NA • (05/15/96) • **80-84** (BT)

Côtes de Francs 1989 • $NA • (03/15/92) • **86**

Côtes de Francs White 1993: Refined and subtle, showing pear, cedar and apple character, medium body, firm acidity and well-integrated flavors. Drink now. • $NA • **84**

CHARMILLES, CHÂTEAU LES

Bordeaux Supérieur 1985 • $8 • (02/15/88) • **71**

CHARNAY, CAVE DE

Brut Crémant de Bourgogne NV: Has appealing buttery, nutty flavors, like a white Burgundy with bubbles. Full-bodied and fairly soft, with nice maturity. A good stand-in for Champagne. • $15 • **85**

CHARRON, CHÂTEAU DE

Bordeaux 1993: Herbaceous flavors dominate, with accents of black cherry and earth. Firm and straightforward. • $8 • (12/15/95) • **78**

Bordeaux 1991: Attractive cherry, spice and celery flavors. The tannins close in on the finish, but would soften with a meal. It's balanced, fresh and drinkable now. 3,900 cases made. • $7 • (11/15/94) • **79**

Bordeaux 1982 • $5 • (07/01/85) • **76**

Bordeaux White 1994: An unassuming white with subtle fig and citrus flavors and a short finish. Clean and simple. • $8 • (02/29/96) • **80**

Bordeaux White 1992: A soft, slightly sweet white with simple earth and herb flavors and a bland finish. 1,900 cases made. • $7 • (11/15/94) • **77**

CHARTREUSE, CHÂTEAU DE LA

Sauternes 1987 • $NA • (06/15/90) • **77**

Sauternes 1983 • $10 • (01/31/88) • **90**

CHARTRON & TREBUCHET

Auxey-Duresses 1994: Theatrical white. Full in body, sporting bursts of toasted oak, pie crust and pear character. Delicious in an up-front way, it peters out a bit on the finish. Still, very seductive. Drinkable now. 833 cases made. • $14 • (05/31/96) 85 • **85**

Auxey-Duresses 1993: Some nice round and ripe character and modest fruit flavors, the finish seems a bit one-dimensional. • $19 • **79**

Auxey-Duresses 1992: An oaky style, with enough pear and apple flavor to back up the toasty, buttery, spicy character obtained from aging in oak barrels. Has firm acidity, a smooth but restrained texture and a lingering finish. 250 cases made. • $18 • (07/31/94) • **85**

Auxey-Duresses 1991 • $15 • (10/15/93) • **81**

Bâtard-Montrachet 1993: Ripe and rich, offering honey, pear, butter and tropical fruit flavors. Medium-bodied, good use of oak on the toasty finish. Try now. • $95 • **88**

Bâtard-Montrachet 1992: Delivers all the richness and viscosity you expect from this elite appellation. Buttery, spicy aromas and ripe pear, honey and hazelnut flavors make this seductive and intriguing to drink. It combines ripe, delicious fruit flavors with layers of complexity on the long finish. Tempting to drink now, but should improve through 1997. 75 cases made. • $82 • (07/31/94) • **92**

Bâtard-Montrachet 1991 • $75 • (10/15/93) • **88**

Bourgogne 1993: Flavorful, but coarse, dominated by green apple flavors with a touch of fig. A simple, correct wine, that finishes with a spritzy quality. 4,500 cases made. • $12 • **80**

Bourgogne White Chardonnay 1994: Wonderful for a simple Bourgogne. Fresher than many '94s, sporting juicy, succulent, mouthpuckering flavors of lime, pear and ripe apple and a long finish. Drinkable now through 1998. 6,666 cases made. • $10 • (05/31/96) • **87**

Bourgogne White Chardonnay 1991 • $9 • (11/30/92) • **82**

Chassagne-Montrachet Clos St.-Marc 1992: Toasty, oaky aromas blend well with the bright lemon and apple flavors in this smooth-textured, well-balanced Chassagne. Tastes clean, flavorful and complete. Drinkable now. 875 cases made. • $30 • (07/31/94) • **85**

Chassagne-Montrachet Clos St.-Marc Monopole Les Vergers Premier Cru 1993: Crisp green apple, lime, mineral and stone flavors turn chewy and interesting on the tart finish. Drink now. • $33 • **85**

Chassagne-Montrachet Les Morgeots 1994: Impressive, very rich and ripe, packed with fig, apricot and honey flavors. Soft core, and very drinkable now. Not much length here, so better to consume it soon. 791 cases made. • $25 • (05/31/96) 88 • **89**

Chassagne-Montrachet Les Morgeots 1992: Young and tight, but the array of toasty, honeyed, pearlike flavors is backed by firm acidity. Starts out subtle, but gains in complexity through the finish. Drinkable now. • $22 • (08/31/94) • **87**

Chassagne-Montrachet Les Morgeots 1991 • $30 • (10/15/93) • **85**

Corton-Charlemagne 1993: A beautiful wine for the long term. Starts out very hard and crisp, but picks up cream, ripe pear and honey flavors on the palate and then sails to a long finish. Try after 1997. • $58 • **90**

Corton-Charlemagne 1992: Light for a Corton-Charlemagne, but it is elegant in texture and long-lasting on the finish. We could ask for more ripeness and fullness to the lemon and apple flavors, but the balance and harmony are inviting. 50 cases made. • $56 • (07/31/94) • **88**

Côte de Beaune-Villages 1988 • $16 • (02/28/91) • **79**

Hautes-Côtes de Beaune White 1991 • $11 • (10/15/93) • **78**

Mâcon-Villages 1994: Pleasantly ripe for a '94 Mâcon, showing pear, butter, peanut and honey character that turns smooth and lovely on the finish. Light to medium body, good for drinking now. 642 cases made. • $12 • **81**

Mercurey 1994: Clean, crisp and lively, showing some nice citrus, pear and apple flavors. A bit simple on the tart finish. 416 cases made. • $15 • (05/31/96) • **80**

Mercurey 1992: An incredibly spicey and oaky wine. The flavors of butter, fig and maple are appealing for their intensity. Certainly exaggerated and lacking harmony, but still a good wine that's meant to be drunk with a hearty meal. Drink now. 105 cases made. • $15 • **84**

Meursault 1994: Appealing butter, peach, toast and pear flavors accompanied by zingy citrus components that give it lots of life on the finish. You wish for a bit more "volume" and density. Drinkable now. 2,500 cases made. • $22 • (05/31/96) • **85**

Meursault 1993: Straightforward and fruity, displaying apple, pear and light vanilla flavors, medium body and simple finish. Drinkable now. • $19 • (05/15/95) • **84**

Meursault 1991 • $20 • (05/15/93) • **89**

Meursault Les Charmes 1993: Full-bodied and firm white Burgundy, featuring smoke, toast and pear flavors and lots of mineral character. It ends with a slightly herbal bite. 150 cases made. • $35 • (08/31/95) • **84**

Meursault Les Charmes 1991 • $28 • (10/15/93) • **87**

Montrachet White 1993: Round and attractive yet quite intense, delivering flavors of honey, toasted bread, marzipan, mango and spice. Should make for even better drinking in 1997. 50 cases made. • $200 • **87**

Pernand-Vergelesses 1994: A voluptuous, full-bodied '94 offering nice amounts of honey, peach and fig flavors. Lacks some length on the finish, but what's there is pleasant. 1,666 cases made. • $15 • (05/31/96) • **85**

Pernand-Vergelesses White 1993: Tart and very citrusy, displaying some pear notes. Extremely crisp, light finish. Drink now. • $19 • **79**

Pernand-Vergelesses White 1992: Buttery aromas, lean fruit flavors and a tight texture indicate the need for a little aging, try now, or hold into 1997. 625 cases made. • $18 • (07/31/94) • **82**

Pommard Les Epenots 1988 • $45 • (02/28/91) • **87**

Pouilly-Fuissé Domaine de la Chapelle 1993: This is an unusually deep-colored wine for a new '93, showing candied, butterscotch aromas, and rich viscous flavors. It will appeal to some people, but we find it a bit heavy handed. Drink immediately if this style appeals to you. 1,100 cases made. • $18 • **78**

Puligny-Montrachet 1994: Seductive village wine, creamy and lush, full-bodied and fat, boasting layers of toasted coconut, pear, pie crust and spice. Yet for all its opulence, it remains elegant on the long finish. Worth seeking out. Drinkable now and through 2000. 2,083 cases made. • $26 • (05/31/96) • **90**

Puligny-Montrachet 1993: Fresh lemon, mineral, honey character, medium body, firm acidity and light, fruity finish. • $31 • **84**

Puligny-Montrachet 1992: Rich, complex aromas and smooth, ripe flavors add up to a generous, well-proportioned wine. This has pear, hazelnut and butter flavors, a silky texture and a long finish. Combines freshness, complexity and concentration. 1,050 cases made. • $25 • (07/31/94) • **90**

Puligny-Montrachet 1991 • $26 • (10/15/93) • **86**

Puligny-Montrachet Les Referts 1994: Subtle and supple, showing nice fruit character, chewy, mineral, toasted flavors and medium body and intensity. Drinkable now. 250 cases made. • $29 • (05/31/96) 84 • **84**

Puligny-Montrachet Les Referts 1992: For fans of a complex but restrained style. Very aromatic, but fairly tight in texture and restrained in fruit flavor, yet it opens up and lets the flavors linger on the finish. • $28 • (08/31/94) • **90**

Puligny-Montrachet Les Referts 1992: For fans of a complex but restrained style. Very aromatic, but fairly tight in texture and restrained in fruit flavor, yet it opens up and lets the flavors linger on the finish. • $28 • (08/31/94) • **90**

Rully White La Chaume 1994: Textbook honey and tropical fruit flavors of medium intensity. Medium- to light-bodied, this tastes a bit one-dimensional on the crisp and fresh finish. 3,083 cases made. • $14 • (05/31/96) • **83**

Rully White La Chaume 1993: Sharp and crisp, green, herbaceous character, a mouth-puckering experience, clean and firm. Drink now. • $16 • **78**

Rully White La Chaume 1992: Tastes like a single-malt Chardonnay, with an intense oak flavor and aroma. The ripe fig and apple flavors stand up well to the butter and toast flavors of the oak, but it is quite a mouthful of wood in the end. 2,200 cases made. • $15 • **84**

Rully White La Chaume 1991 • $13 • (05/15/93) • **84**

Santenay 1994: Understated and superelegant, featuring solid mineral, wet earth and spice character backed by some dried herb and pear flavors. You can sense good aging potential here. Hold until 1999. 175 cases made. • $15 • (05/31/96) • **89**

St.-Aubin La Chatenière 1994: Balanced, harmonious pear, pie crust, cream and apple flavors topped by a touch of honey. Of medium body, this *premier cru* turns refreshingly lively on the finish. Drinkable now. 375 cases made. • $17 • (05/31/96) • **85**

St.-Aubin La Chatenière 1993: Harmonious white. The slight herbal character is muted by a hint of ripe fruit, a touch of toastiness and some hazelnut and cream flavors. Tart aftertaste, though. • $23 • **83**

St.-Aubin La Chatenière 1991 • $17 • (10/15/93) • **87**

St.-Aubin La Chatenière Premier Cru 1992: Fairly big-bodied and quite woody, it tastes of vanilla, spice and apple, and offers a round texture. Well-made for those who enjoy an oaky style of Chardonnay. • $18 • (08/31/94) • **83**

St.-Romain 1994: Some decent citrus, pear and apple flavors, but this medium-bodied white turns unfocused on the slightly sour finish. Drinkable now. 2,000 cases made. • $14 • (05/31/96) • **79**

St.-Romain 1993: A certain suppleness. Quite tart but also showing pear, honey, grass and subtle grapefruit flavors. Drinkable now. • $NA • **80**

St.-Romain 1992: A pleasantly aromatic and smooth-textured white Burgundy with buttery, appley flavors that are rather light. Light-bodied, too, with a short finish. Still, it's a good wine from a lesser district. 1,025 cases made. • $16 • (07/31/94) • **83**

St.-Romain 1991 • $13 • (10/15/93) • **87**

St.-Véran Château du Chasselas White 1994: Subtle oak shadings give it a vanilla bean flavor that marries nicely and smoothly with pear, melon, fig and spice notes. Atypical St.-Véran, but pleasant. Drink now. 350 cases made. • $15 • **80**

CHARTRON LA FLEUR

Bordeaux 1986 • $4 • (05/15/89) • **74**

CHARTRON, JEAN

Beaune Hospices de Beaune Cuvée Cyrot-Chaudron 1988 • $40 • (02/15/91) • **88**

Bourgogne Clos de la Combe 1990: Intense and firmly tannic, with ripe plum and currant flavors underneath. A bold, concentrated wine to drink now. • $11 • (03/31/92) • **85**

Chevalier-Montrachet 1991 • $90 • (10/15/93) • **89**

Chevalier-Montrachet Clos des Chevaliers 1993: Wonderful, creamy white Burgundy exhibiting loads of class. Pear, apple, toasted oak character, medium-to-full body, long finish. Better after 1996. • $112 • **90**

Chevalier-Montrachet Clos des Chevaliers 1992: This shows 1992 at its best—generous and harmonious. Extremely open and inviting with lots of flavors that mingle subtly and seamlessly and last a long time on the finish, blends pear, vanilla, nutmeg, toast and honey in a rich, seductive mix. The texture is wonderfully smooth, firmed up by fresh acidity, but thick enough to make the flavors really last. Drinkable now, but save it through 1997 or beyond if you like more maturity. 208 cases made. • $95 • (08/31/94) • **96**

Puligny-Montrachet Clos du Cailleret 1994: Fairly rich tropical fruit, pear and coconut character and creamy texture. Medium-bodied, very round and supple. Nice vibrancy on the finish. • $42 • (05/31/96) • **85**

Puligny-Montrachet Clos du Cailleret 1993: Intense and lively, but quite tart and austere, showing green, herbal flavors and a lot of green-apple notes. Might be better after 1996. • $42 • **82**

Puligny-Montrachet Clos du Cailleret 1992: Extremely spicy and flavorful, full of generous pear, vanilla, nutmeg and cinnamon in a broad, appealing style. Has a long finish, too. Delicious to drink now but there is no reason to think it won't age well through about 1997. • $34 • (08/31/94) • **90**

Puligny-Montrachet Clos du Cailleret 1991 • $40 • (10/15/93) • **90**

Puligny-Montrachet Clos de la Pucelle 1994: Supple, full-bodied and rather rich, sporting some lovely honey, pear, dried herb, toasted bread and lemon flavors. Good intensity from start to finish. Needs until 1998 to come together. • $NA • (05/31/96) • **88**

Puligny-Montrachet Clos de la Pucelle 1993: Interesting grapefruit, apple and mineral aromas which follow through on the palate. Medium body, high acidity and toasted oak finish. • $42 • (08/31/94) • **85**

Puligny-Montrachet Clos de la Pucelle 1992: Beautifully balanced, combines seductively spicy aromas of nutmeg and cinnamon with ripe pear and vanilla flavors that linger nicely on the finish. Tempting to drink now for its obvious charms, but it has the firm acidity to age and improve with time. • $36 • (08/31/94) • **89**

Puligny-Montrachet Clos de la Pucelle 1991 • $35 • (10/15/93) • **86**

Puligny-Montrachet Les Folatières 1994: Opulent and rich, but there's a lot of toasted oak dominating whatever fruit is there. Too much for us. Still, the lemon, apple and honey notes show underneath. Better in 1999. • $42 • (05/31/96) • **81**

Puligny-Montrachet Les Folatières 1993: Chewy and showy, presenting a mouthful of vivid earth, honey, stone and fruit character, still tart on the finish. Aging might improve, try after 1997. • $37 • **84**

Puligny-Montrachet Les Folatières 1992: A well-balanced, well-made Puligny with bright, focused fruit flavors accented by toasty oak and vanilla aromas. Its flavors turn a bit earthy and smoky on the finish. Try now. 225 cases made. • $35 • (07/31/94) • **86**

Puligny-Montrachet Les Folatières 1991 • $33 • (10/15/93) • **89**

CHASSE-SPLEEN, CHÂTEAU

Bordeaux White 1994: A very woody style with almond, vanilla and some tropical fruit. Medium body and acidity, showing lots of toasted oak on the finish. Better in 1997. • $NA • (03/31/96) • **85**

Bordeaux White 1993: New from one of the rising-star red-wine producers in the Médoc. Somewhat diluted, but some pretty vanilla, toasted oak and lemon aromas and flavors. Young vines. Drink now. • $NA • **80**

Moulis 1995: A racy red with excellent tannin structure. Decent fruit overall and good, minty berry notes on the finish. • $NA • (05/15/96) • **85-89** (BT)

Moulis 1994: A laudable effort for this vintage. Firm structure and the sweet red berry flavors show god depth. Delicious now, with well-integrated tannins that show promise. • $NA • (05/15/96) • **85-89** (BT)

Moulis 1993: Plenty of fruit in this one. Medium to full body, berry and cherry flavors, medium-to-full tannins and long finish. Better in 1998. 2,333 cases made. • $22 • (01/31/96) • **88**

Moulis 1992: Well-made Bordeaux, exhibiting focused cassis and vanilla character, medium body, silky tannins and a fine finish. Drink now. • $21 • **80**

Moulis 1991: Well-crafted wine with smoky, berry and gamy aromas and flavors. Medium-bodied with round, soft tannins. • $21 • (03/31/94) • **84**

Moulis 1990: This estate usually makes outstanding wines, and '90 is no exception. It's extremely elegant, with gorgeous spice and blackberry flavors and fine tannins. Very har-monious. Drink after 1996. 25,000 cases made. • $27 • (03/31/93) • **90**

Moulis 1989 • $30 • (03/15/92) • **95**

Moulis 1988 • $32 • (03/31/91) • **89**

Moulis 1987 • $15 • (02/15/90) • **78**

Moulis 1986 • $28 • (11/30/89) • **90**

Moulis 1985 • $28 • (05/15/88) • **86**

Moulis 1984 • $15 • (06/15/87) • **74**

Moulis 1983: Big and well-integrated wine with loads of fruit and tannins but long velvety finish. Drinkable now. • $24 • (10/15/94) • **90**

Moulis 1982 • $41 • (11/30/89) • **90**

Moulis 1981: Drinking beautifully with coffee, tobacco, chocolate character. Full-bodied and firm with silky tannins and a long rich finish. Drink now. • $29 • (10/15/94) • **88**

Moulis 1970 • $61 • (05/15/93) • **84**

Moulis 1961: Has plenty of structure, but the flavor profile is not for everyone. Odd aromas and flavors of pepper, anise and steak sauce make it less than ideal. Tart and tannic, too. Drink now. • $52 • (04/30/96) • **82**

CHASSE, MARQUIS DE

Bordeaux 1990: A hearty, tannic, full-bodied Bordeaux, with muted, ripe plum and dried cherry flavors and spicy, earthy notes giving it a nice smoky quality. Drinkable now through 1998. Tasted twice. 20,000 cases made. • $7 • (03/15/93) BB • **82**

Bordeaux Réserve 1993: Offers toast, coffee and tobacco aromas and flavors, with firm tannins and a chewy texture. Has concentration and a lingering finish. • $8 • (12/15/95) • **83**

Bordeaux White 1994: A basic, crisp and lean white wine that smells a bit grassy and tastes grapefruity. • $7 • (02/29/96) • **79**

Bordeaux White 1993: A straightforward, modestly flavorful white Bordeaux that has good balance and crispness, and a clean, lingering finish. Simple but good. • $7 • **82**

Bordeaux White 1991 • $7 • (04/30/93) BB • **83**

CHÂTEAU, DOMAINE DE

Côtes du Rhône 1990 • $10 • (04/15/93) • **78**

Côtes du Rhône-Villages Cairanne 1990 • $12 • (04/15/93) • **85**

Key: SS—Spectator Selection. CS—Cellar Selection. BB—Best Buy. $NA—Price not available. (BT)—Barrel tasting. Ⓐ—Auction Price.
Dates in parentheses represent the issues in which the ratings were published.

CHATELAIN, JEAN-CLAUDE

Pouilly-Fumé Domaine de St.-Laurent-l'Abbaye 1992: Firm, good structure and attractive flavors of peaches, melons and subtle herbs. It combines crisp acidity with good concentration, finishing clean and long. • $12 • (08/31/94) • **88**

Pouilly-Fumé Domaine de St.-Laurent-l'Abbaye 1992: A firm wine with good structure and attractive flavors of peaches, melons and subtle herbs. It combines crisp acidity with good concentration, finishing clean and long.\ • $12 • (08/31/94) • **88**

CHATENOY, DOMAINE DE

Menetou-Salon 1994: Made in a delicate style, this shows peach and floral aromas and flavors, light on the palate, balanced and lively. It's attractive, and not aggressively varietal in character. 10,000 cases made. • $12 • (11/15/95) • **83**

Menetou-Salon 1993: Ripe and soft, this offers green apple and herbal flavors and still maintains a good underlying acidity. Made in a rounder style, it's clean and generous. • $11 • (08/31/94) • **85**

Menetou-Salon Red 1992: The tart cherry, herb and spice aromas are true to Pinot Noir, but on the palate it's very light and quite vegetal. Lacks ripeness and concentration, try it slightly chilled. 500 cases made. • $15 • (11/15/94) • **77**

CHAUVENET, F.

Auxey-Duresses 1993: Simple and straightforward, some modest fruit character and plenty of citrus flavors on the tart finish. 800 cases made. • $19 • **76**

Auxey-Duresses Red Le Val 1989 • $NA • (01/31/92) • **79**

Beaune 1993: Simple, modest strawberry and earth character. Somewhat short and dry on the finish, ending on a paperish note. 2,170 cases made. • $24 • **70**

Beaune Clos des Mouches 1986 • $27 • (12/31/88) • **82**

Beaune Grèves 1989 • $30 • (01/31/92) • **91**

Beaune Grèves 1986 • $25 • (12/31/88) • **79**

Beaune Hospices de Beaune Rosseau-Deslandes 1980 • $36 • (06/16/86) • **91**

Beaune Les Grèves 1993: Pleasant, plummy earth and spice character, medium body, light tannins and cedary finish. Drink now. 300 cases made. • $29 • **80**

Beaune Les Grèves 1990: A charming wine that offers juicy currant, cinnamon and berry aromas and flavors and a supple texture that is enchanting. Drinkable now. • $35 • (12/15/92) • **89**

Beaune Theurons 1985 • $23 • (07/31/87) • **88**

Bienvenues-Bâtard-Montrachet White 1993: Perfectly clear, lovely apple, mineral and chalk character, medium body, firm acidity and lemony finish. 100 cases made. • $115 • **86**

Bourgogne 1990 • $NA • (12/15/92) • **80**

Bourgogne Pinot Noir Château Marguerite de Bourgogne 1993: Clean cherry, cedar and mocha aromas and flavors, medium-to-light body, soft tannins and fresh finish. One of the better wines from Chauvenet this year. Drink now. • $14 • **80**

Bourgogne Pinot Noir Château Marguerite de Bourgogne 1985 • $10 • (06/30/88) • **80**

Cabernet Sauvignon Vin de Pays d'Oc 1994: Polished and ripe, offering cassis and light tobacco notes and enough structure for food in a pretty, well-integrated package. Good for drinking now. 4,000 cases made. • $9 • (10/31/95) • **84**

Chambolle-Musigny 1993: Light, modest fruit flavors. A bit diluted in the finish. Drink chilled on release. • $37 • **78**

Chambolle-Musigny 1990: Packs a lot of nice flavors into a medium-bodied wine. Offers subtle raspberry and plum flavors touched by fresh acidity and lively tannins. Drinkable now. • $45 • (12/15/92) • **85**

Chambolle-Musigny Les Charmes 1982 • $33 • (04/30/87) • **83**

Chardonnay Vin de Pays d'Oc 1994: Though not flamboyant, this solid white is clean and vibrant with ripe fruit. Vanilla and hazelnut flavors mingle with melon and floral notes, and the citrusy acidity keeps it fresh. Good value in a French white. 7,000 cases made. • $8 • (12/15/95) • **86**

Charmes-Chambertin 1993: Unusually soft for the vintage, a medium-bodied red sporting cherry, earth and chocolate flavors and lush tannins. Already quite forward, tempting upon release. • $78 • **86**

Charmes-Chambertin 1986 • $65 • (07/31/88) • **90**

Charmes-Chambertin 1985 • $72 • (07/31/87) • **97**

Charmes-Chambertin 1983 • $24 • (09/15/86) • **88**

Chassagne-Montrachet 1993: Lean and steely Chassagne, displaying green, grassy, aggressive flavors and a tart finish. Try now. 1,000 cases made. • $32 • **83**

Clos St.-Denis 1990: A stunning beauty. Velvety and multidimensional, offering unique character and texture, with cigar box, violet, cedar and blackberry aromas and flavors and a decadent finish. Drinkable now. • $65 • (12/15/92) • **95**

Clos St.-Denis Red 1989 • $60 • (01/31/92) • **87**

Clos St.-Denis Red 1986 • $50 • (02/28/89) • **90**

Clos St.-Denis Red 1985 • $67 • (07/31/87) • **94**

Clos de Vougeot 1990: Muscular, big and chewy, a complex Clos de Vougeot that shows plenty of currant, wet earth, mushroom and smoke aromas and flavors. Will need until 1998 to 2000 to come around, but then it should be great. • $69 • (12/15/92) • **92**

Clos de Vougeot Red 1989 • $60 • (01/31/92) • **90**

Clos de Vougeot Red 1986 • $57 • (07/31/88) • **87**

Clos de la Roche 1990: Extremely ripe, with smoky cinnamon and brown sugar flavors that seem almost sweet on the delicious finish. Drinkable now. • $76 • (12/15/92) • **87**

Corton 1993: Has some dried cherry and smoky character but tastes of cardboard too. Medium- to light-bodied, firm tannins, short, papery finish. 150 cases made. • $54 • **78**

Corton 1990: Like a marble sculpture, has solid tannins, masses of fruit and covers your palate with blackberry and toasted oak flavors. Drinkable in 1997. • $60 • (12/15/92) • **94**

Corton 1989 • $50 • (01/31/92) • **93**

Corton 1986 • $50 • (07/31/88) • **87**

Corton 1985 • $53 • (07/31/87) • **96**

Corton Hospices de Beaune Docteur-Peste 1985 • $133 • (07/15/88) • **97**

Côte de Beaune-Villages 1985 • $16 • (07/31/87) • **84**

Echézeaux 1990: Closed and hard now, but underneath the tight structure lurk violet, red berry and currant flavors. Needs years to mold the steely tannins into something softer. Try now. • $62 • (12/15/92) • **91**

Echézeaux 1989 • $56 • (01/31/92) • **92**

Echézeaux 1985 • $47 • (07/31/87) • **89**

Gevrey-Chambertin Charreux 1985 • $33 • (10/15/87) • **88**

Gevrey-Chambertin Clos St.-Jacques 1989 • $45 • (01/31/92) • **89**

Gevrey-Chambertin Clos St.-Jacques 1986 • $35 • (07/31/88) • **85**

Gevrey-Chambertin Estournelles St.-Jacques 1990: While this is quite firm, it has more generosity and flesh than many Gevreys, offering enticing blueberry, black cherry and earth aromas and flavors and a focused finish. Drinkable in 1998. • $56 • (12/15/92) • **89**

Gevrey-Chambertin Estournelles St.-Jacques 1989 • $40 • (01/31/92) • **91**

Gevrey-Chambertin Estournelles St.-Jacques 1986 • $35 • (07/31/88) • **89**

Gevrey-Chambertin Lavaut St.-Jacques 1990: Quite generous for a *premier cru* Gevrey, a bit toasty and smoky, with a lovely structure and black cherry and currant characteristics showing on the appealing, smooth finish. Drinkable now. • $56 • (12/15/92) • **90**

Gevrey-Chambertin Lavaux St.-Jacques 1991: Earthy and simple, a bright beam of raspberry and anise flavors pokes through a pervasive earthy character. • $NA • (01/31/94) • **79**

Gevrey-Chambertin Lavaux St.-Jacques 1989 • $45 • (01/31/92) • **88**

Gevrey-Chambertin Lavaux St.-Jacques 1986 • $35 • (07/31/88) • **86**

Mâcon-Blanc-Villages Les Jumelles 1994: Ripe and firm fruit, almond and honey flavors. Light- to medium-bodied, adding an attractively bitter twist on the finish. Drink now. 4,000 cases made. • $8 • **83**

Mazis-Chambertin 1983 • $27 • (06/30/87) • **72**

Merlot Vin de Pays d'Oc 1994: This big red has grip and pleasant black cherry flavor, but strong barnyard notes detract on an astringent finish. 6,000 cases made. • $9 • (10/31/95) • **78**

Meursault Les Charmes 1993: A bit acidic, very crisp and tart, lean and hollow, could use more ripe fruit. • $47 • (05/15/95) • **77**

Monthélie 1990 • $21 • (12/15/92) • **84**

Monthélie Les Champs-Fulliot 1990 • $NA • (12/15/92) • **87**

Monthélie Les Champs-Fulliot 1989 • $20 • (01/31/92) • **81**

Nuits-St.-Georges 1993: Soft, silky vanilla, spice and plum aromas and flavors, medium body and tannins and crisp finish. Better in 1998. • $40 • **78**

Nuits-St.-Georges 1991: Very pretty raspberry and strawberry aromas turn light and astringent on the palate and barely peek through a veil of chewy tannins on the finish. Try now. • $NA • (01/31/94) • **81**

Nuits-St.-Georges Aux Chaignots 1990: Made in the old style, with chestnut, berry and spice aromas and flavors and round tannins. Slightly dry on the finish. Drinkable now. • $53 • (12/15/92) • **83**

Nuits-St.-Georges Les Chaignots 1989 • $45 • (01/31/92) • **91**

Nuits-St.-Georges Les Chaignots 1986 • $40 • (07/31/88) • **87**

Nuits-St.-Georges Les Perrières 1985 • $48 • (07/31/87) • **80**

Nuits-St.-Georges Les Plâteaux 1985 • $34 • (07/31/87) • **84**

Nuits-St.-Georges Les Plâteaux 1982 • $16 • (01/01/85) • **78**

Nuits-St.-Georges Les Pruliers 1990: An elegant Nuits, with beautiful fruit and fine tannins. Shows finesse and plenty of smoke, berry and earth aromas and flavors. Drinkable now. • $52 • (12/15/92) • **90**

Nuits-St.-Georges Les Pruliers 1989 • $45 • (01/31/92) • **88**

Pommard 1990: This lovely, medium-bodied wine offers raspberry and chestnut aromas and flavors and a fine, long finish. • $45 • (12/15/92) • **86**

Pommard Epenots 1989 • $45 • (01/31/92) • **94**

Pommard Epenots 1985 • $48 • (07/31/87) • **95**

Pommard Hospices de Beaune Cuvée Dames-de-la-Cha 1982 • $36 • (02/01/85) CS • **91**

Pommard Les Chanlins 1990: A bit tough at this stage and lacking finesse, but a distinctive wine, with smoky herbal and olive aromas and flavors. Drinkable now. • $59 • (12/15/92) • **87**

Pommard Les Chanlins 1989 • $45 • (01/31/92) • **86**

Pommard Les Chanlins 1986 • $40 • (07/31/88) • **90**

Puligny-Montrachet 1993: Steely and balanced, showing a polished core of green apple, pear and melon flavors. Vibrant finish. Try after 1996. 800 cases made. • $35 • **86**

Puligny-Montrachet Red 1985 • $16 • (06/15/87) • **81**

St.-Romain 1993: Very green and herbaceous, showing unpleasant, underripe character and a grassy finish. 1,000 cases made. • $19 • **70**

Santenay 1985 • $18 • (07/31/87) • **84**

Syrah Vin de Pays d'Oc 1994: Earthy and animal aromas lend funky character. Lean and dry on the palate without much fruit. Tough to like. 3,000 cases made. • $9 • (10/31/95) • **74**

Volnay Clos des Chênes 1990: Focused and racy, with plenty of cherry, plum and tobacco flavors in an elegant, medium-bodied style. Drinkable now. • $58 • (12/15/92) • **86**

Volnay Clos des Chênes 1989 • $40 • (01/31/92) • **90**

Volnay Premier Cru 1989 • $36 • (01/31/92) • **88**

Vosne-Romanée Les Suchots 1985 • $46 • (07/31/87) • **92**

CHAUVENET, JEAN

Nuits-St.-Georges Les Bousselots 1985 • $49 • (05/31/88) • **88**

CHAUVIN, CHÂTEAU

St.-Emilion 1988 • $20 • (06/30/91) • **84**

St.-Emilion 1986 • $15 • (06/30/89) • **75**

CHAVE, BERNARD

Crozes-Hermitage 1991 • $45 • (06/15/93) • **85**

Crozes-Hermitage 1988 • $14 • (02/15/91) • **78**

Crozes-Hermitage 1985 • $12 • (11/30/88) • **86**

Hermitage 1990: Firm and fleshy, with a nice array of grape, plum and earth aromas and flavors that extend into a rich finish. The tannins have it in a solid grip for now, but should soften by 1997. • $45 • (04/15/93) • **87**

Hermitage 1989 • $40 • (12/31/91) • **91**

Hermitage 1986 • $32 • (11/30/88) • **86**

Key: SS—Spectator Selection. CS—Cellar Selection. BB—Best Buy. $NA—Price not available. (BT)—Barrel tasting. Ⓐ—Auction Price.
Dates in parentheses represent the issues in which the ratings were published.

CHAVE, J.L.

Hermitage 1992: Balanced, even delicate aromas and flavors of cherry, game and eucalyptus, yet firm tannins promise long life. Not as muscular as Hermitage can be, but it covers all the bases. Drink now through 2000. • $50 • **88**

Hermitage 1991: Straightforward, with plenty of ripe, raisiny fruit. Has muscle and it's big, but dumb. Try now. • $50 • (05/31/94) • **85**

Hermitage 1990: Such rich fruit, jammed with plum, herb, licorice, meat, spice and tar flavors, that you almost overlook the muscular tannins and think you could drink it now. Don't. This wine is concentrated and built to age. Wild and distinctive, it's a beautiful representation of the northern Rhône at its best. Drink from 1997 to 2007. 2,500 cases made. • $63 • (05/31/94) CS • **96**

Hermitage 1987 • $48 • (06/30/90) • **89**

Hermitage 1984 • $29 • (08/31/87) • **89**

Hermitage 1980 • $40 • (05/01/86) • **83**

Hermitage White 1992: Buttery, nutty and raisin flavors—along with high alcohol—remind us of dry Sherry. The wine is heavy but flat, lacking fruit and freshness, and turns bitter on the finish. Tasted three times with consistent scores. 2,300 cases made. • $45 • **78**

St.-Joseph 1992 • $NA • (05/31/94) • **76**

CHAVY, PHILIPPE

Puligny-Montrachet Corvée des Vignes 1994: Clean and pretty, bursting with lovely fig, pear and toasted bread aromas. Of light-to-medium body, it enchants by a focused delivery and long, lively finish. • $30 • (05/31/96) • **87**

Puligny-Montrachet Les Nosroyes 1994: Rather subtle yet well made, showing its stuff slowly. Starts a bit green and vegetal, but picks up some toasted oak, honey and cream flavors on the rather tight and crisp finish. Better in 1998. • $30 • (05/31/96) • **84**

CHAZELLE, DOMAINE DES

Mâcon-Viré 1993: Balanced and attractive, subtle. The silky texture offers some almond, pear and apple tart flavors. A bit diluted. From Josette and Jean-Noël Chaland. • $12 • **80**

CHEFFIEUX, DOMAINE DE

St.-Joseph 1990 • $15 • (04/15/93) • **88**

CHENAS, CHÂTEAU DE

Moulin-à-Vent Red 1994: Lush vanilla and plum aromas give way to a generous palate of ripe fruit, full, soft tannins and a lick of acidity for balance. It's up-front pleasure, sweet and satisfying. • $13 • (10/31/95) • **87**

CHENE, DOMAINE DU

St.-Joseph 1992 • $20 • (05/31/94) • **72**

St.-Joseph Anais 1992 • $20 • (05/31/94) • **79**

St.-Joseph Anais 1991 • $20 • (05/31/94) • **82**

St.-Joseph Anais 1989 • $20 • (05/31/94) • **82**

CHEREAU, B.

Muscadet de Sèvre et Maine Cuvée des Ducs 1993: Light, crisp and delicate, offering apple and light melon flavors, with a hint of bread dough on the finish. It's clean and short. • $6 • (10/31/94) • **81**

CHERET-PITRES, CHÂTEAU

Graves 1993: A lean red that offers smoky cherry and light earthy flavors, showing some firm but well-integrated tannins. Not showy, but should improve through 1997. • $13 • (12/15/95) • **83**

CHERRIER

Sancerre 1992: Attractive grassy and herbal notes predominate in this fresh, lively wine, and tart grapefruit and lemon flavors keep it sunny and clean. A well-balanced, refreshing wine. • $17 • (10/31/94) • **86**
Sancerre Domaine Cherrier & Fils 1991 • $18 • (09/15/93) • **86**

CHERRIER & FILS, PIERRE

Sancerre Domaine de la Rossignole Cuvée Vieilles Vignes 1994: A basic white offering solid herbal and grassy flavors and some citrus as well. It has a clarity of flavor but lacks intensity. • $15 • (04/30/96) • **82**

CHESNAIE, CHÂTEAU DE LA

Muscadet de Sèvre et Maine Sur Lie 1993: Light floral and herbal aromas are attractive, and the wine has a bracing austerity on the palate, with lively grapefruit flavors. It's clean and very tart, refreshing with food. • $8 • (10/31/94) • **83**

CHEVAL BLANC, DOMAINE DE

Bordeaux 1985 • $5 • (05/15/88) • **78**

CHEVAL-BLANC, CHÂTEAU

St.-Emilion 1995: Succulent, concentrated and harmonious. A classy red delivering loads of everything. Firm backbone yet very ripe, subtle and elegant. Almost classic in quality. • $NA • (05/15/96) • **90-94** (BT)
St.-Emilion 1994: Wonderful finesse. Classy. Lovely chocolate, berry, cherry and vanilla flavors, fine tannins and a fresh finish. Improving every time we taste it. • $75 • (05/15/96) • **85-89** (BT)
St.-Emilion 1993: Gorgeous Cheval. Lovely, elegant plum, toasted oak, mineral and berry aromas and flavors give complexity to the medium body and silky tannins. The finish is fresh and lingering. Better in 1998. • $75 • (01/31/96) CS • **90**
St.-Emilion 1992: Slightly underwhelming for this estate, but some beautiful oak complements good berry, meat and fruit character. Light-to-medium bodied, light tannins and crisp finish. Drink now. • $65 • **80**
St.-Emilion 1990: Rich and racy, with toasted oak and nutty, ripe berry aromas and flavors, well-integrated tannins and a sweet fruit finish. Tasted twice. Drink after 1998. 12,000 cases made. • $182 Ⓐ • (03/31/93) • **91**
St.-Emilion 1989 • $114 Ⓐ • (03/15/92) • **90**
St.-Emilion 1988 • $63 Ⓐ • (12/31/90) CS • **93**
St.-Emilion 1987 • $42 Ⓐ • (02/15/91) • **82**
St.-Emilion 1986 • $122 Ⓐ • (02/15/91) • **93**
St.-Emilion 1985: Breathtaking elegance in this fine wine with lovely tobacco, tar, fruit character. It's full bodied with fine tannins and a fruity finish. Better after 1997. • $120 • (10/15/94) • **92**
St.-Emilion 1984 • $45 • (02/15/91) • **85**
St.-Emilion 1983: Bordeaux aficionados have known about this great wine for some time. The greatest Cheval Blanc of the 80s for us. It's amazing with great richness and harmony. Masses of wonderful complex character of lead pencil, tobacco and fruit. Full-bodied and super • $166 • (10/15/94) • **97**
St.-Emilion 1982 • $373 Ⓐ • (08/31/92) • **95**
St.-Emilion 1981: The first in a series of great wines from this estate in the 80s. The 81 shows loads of character with olive, berry, gamy, earthy flavors. Full-bodied and rich with velvety texture. Drink or hold. • $88 • (10/15/94) • **91**
St.-Emilion 1980 • $56 • (02/15/91) • **84**
St.-Emilion 1979 • $119 Ⓐ • (02/15/91) • **88**
St.-Emilion 1978 • $105 Ⓐ • (02/15/91) • **94**
St.-Emilion 1977 • $20 • (02/15/91) • **74**
St.-Emilion 1976 • $77 Ⓐ • (02/15/91) • **88**
St.-Emilion 1975 • $177 Ⓐ • (02/15/91) • **91**
St.-Emilion 1974 • $36 • (02/15/91) • **83**
St.-Emilion 1973 • $60 • (02/15/91) • **83**
St.-Emilion 1972 • $40 • (02/15/91) • **82**
St.-Emilion 1971 • $79 Ⓐ • (02/15/91) • **89**
St.-Emilion 1970 • $151 Ⓐ • (05/15/93) • **91**
St.-Emilion 1969 • $NA • (02/15/91) • **75**
St.-Emilion 1967 • $57 Ⓐ • (02/15/91) • **85**
St.-Emilion 1966 • $137 Ⓐ • (02/15/91) • **87**
St.-Emilion 1964 • $251 Ⓐ • (02/15/91) • **94**
St.-Emilion 1962 • $98 Ⓐ • (02/15/91) • **85**
St.-Emilion 1961: Beautiful to drink, and has plenty of life ahead of it. A very deep color, expansive and complex aromas, opulent, layered fruit flavors and a silky, elegant texture make it extraordinary. Ultrafine tannins and a long finish complete the package. Drink through 2010. • $506 • (04/30/96) • **93**
St.-Emilion 1960 • $74 Ⓐ • (02/15/91) • **81**
St.-Emilion 1959 • $316 Ⓐ • (02/15/91) • **90**
St.-Emilion 1958 • $200 • (02/15/91) • **86**
St.-Emilion 1955 • $230 Ⓐ • (02/15/91) • **94**
St.-Emilion 1953 • $359 Ⓐ • (02/15/91) • **87**
St.-Emilion 1952 • $360 • (02/15/91) • **91**
St.-Emilion 1951 • $150 • (02/15/91) • **76**
St.-Emilion 1950 • $280 • (02/15/91) • **89**
St.-Emilion 1949 • $936 • (02/15/91) • **84**
St.-Emilion 1948 • $450 • (02/15/91) • **97**
St.-Emilion 1946 • $470 • (02/15/91) • **87**
St.-Emilion 1945: Generous, ripe and chewy, very pretty from start to finish, supple and nicely rounded, glowing with plum, raspberry and spice flavors that remain gentle and elegant. Heady, somehow remaining elevated and elegant throughout. • $650 • **95**
St.-Emilion 1943 • $139 Ⓐ • (02/15/91) • **85**
St.-Emilion 1941 • $175 • (02/15/91) • **71**
St.-Emilion 1940 • $520 • (02/15/91) • **83**
St.-Emilion 1938 • $150 • (02/15/91) • **75**
St.-Emilion 1937 • $280 • (02/15/91) • **93**
St.-Emilion 1936 • $280 • (02/15/91) • **81**
St.-Emilion 1934 • $450 • (02/15/91) • **93**
St.-Emilion 1933 • $270 • (02/15/91) • **88**
St.-Emilion 1931 • $230 • (02/15/91) • **72**
St.-Emilion 1930 • $280 • (02/15/91) • **82**
St.-Emilion 1929 • $350 • (02/15/91) • **90**
St.-Emilion 1928 • $480 • (02/15/91) • **92**
St.-Emilion 1926 • $400 • (02/15/91) • **85**
St.-Emilion 1924 • $300 • (02/15/91) • **69**
St.-Emilion 1923 • $200 • (02/15/91) • **65**
St.-Emilion 1919 • $500 • (02/15/91) • **70**
St.-Emilion 1917 • $500 • (02/15/91) • **70**
St.-Emilion 1916 • $300 • (02/15/91) • **71**
St.-Emilion 1915 • $500 • (02/15/91) • **72**
St.-Emilion 1908 • $500 • (02/15/91) • **71**
St.-Emilion 1905 • $600 • (02/15/91) • **70**
St.-Emilion 1899 • $1,250 • (02/15/91) • **90**

CHEVALIER DE BEAUBASSIN

Cuvée Montgolfier NV • $4 • (03/31/88) • **79**
Nuits-St.-Georges 1985 • $31 • (04/30/88) • **84**

CHEVALIER DE MALLE

Bordeaux White 1992: Already at its peak (or slightly past it), offering wood, vanilla, honey, fruit character and a buttery finish. Tired, old-style dry Sauternes. • $NA • **79**

CHEVALIER DE RODILAN

Vin de Pays d'Oc 1994: This French red is loaded with tannins that are layered through its blackberry and plum flavors. It has an elegant aroma, with a spicy finish. Drinkable now. 10,000 cases made. • $6 • (12/31/95) BB • **84**
Chardonnay Vin de Pays d'Oc 1994: Straightforward and almost neutral, with adequate acidity but not much fruit. 10,000 cases made. • $6 • (12/15/95) • **77**
Merlot Vin de Pays d'Oc 1994: A good effort. Rich, vibrant and fresh with plenty of plum and berry flavors. Has good concentration, but a little short on the finish. 10,000 cases made. • $6 • (12/31/95) • **83**

CHEVALIER DE VEDRINES

Bordeaux 1985 • $6 • (06/30/88) • **77**

CHEVALIER DUCLA

Bordeaux 1986 • $5 • (05/15/89) BB • **80**

CHEVALIER PERE & FILS

Aloxe-Corton Red 1983 • $19 • (09/15/86) • **85**
Ladoix Les Corvées 1992: Inviting aromas, complex but light flavors of cherry, tea and spice, moderate tannins and acidity and a short finish. Drink now. 200 cases made. • $25 • (05/15/95) • **84**

CHEVALIER, CHÂTEAU DU

Montagne-St.-Emilion 1986 • $19 • (03/31/91) • **71**

CHEVALIER, DOMAINE DE

Graves 1985: Yet another outstanding wine from this estate. Extremely fine with wonderful cedar, cherry aromas and flavors. Full-bodied with a super tannin structure. Drink now or hold. • $66 • (10/15/94) • **91**
Graves 1983: Beautiful and elegant with ripe aromas and flavors of cherry and vanilla. Medium-bodied and firm with a fresh finish. Drinkable now. • $39 • (10/15/94) • **91**
Graves 1984 • $25 • (08/31/87) • **90**
Graves 1982: Mature, leaning toward vegetal flavors. Firm tannins give way to raisin, fennel and dill notes, then dry up on the finish. It lacks balance and freshness. This vintage of Chevalier is famously inconsistent, some bottles are good quality, most are average at best. • $42 • (10/15/94) • **79**
Graves 1981: One of the best of the 1981 Bordeaux. It fills your mouth with ripe berry flavor and layers of tobacco and chocolate character. Full-bodied and truly velvety, long and rich. Drinkable now. • $42 • (10/15/94) • **94**
Graves 1979 • $44 • (10/15/89) • **87**
Graves 1970 • $80 • (05/15/93) • **91**
Graves 1961: A distinct personality marks this firmly textured, densely layered Graves. It has herbal, toasty aromas, lively yet well-developed fruit flavors and a lingering finish. Has life ahead of it, so drink through 2005. • $249 • (04/30/96) • **90**
Graves 1959 • $100 • (10/15/90) • **97**
Graves 1945: Very old and oxidized. More tobacco than anything else. • $200 • **74**
Pessac-Léognan 1995: Offers plenty of sweet, ripe fruit and fine tannins. Not as rich as expected but shows wonderful finesse and length. • $NA • (05/15/96) • **85-89** (BT)
Pessac-Léognan 1994: Delicious wine with smoky, berry, cherry and tobacco aromas and flavors. Medium to full-bodied with medium tannins and a fruity finish. Almost outstanding. • $NA • **85-89** (BT)
Pessac-Léognan 1993: A very delicate style for this estate. Elegant, fresh and lively, offering plum and black cherry notes, fine tannins and crisp finish. Better in 1997. • $35 • (01/31/96) • **84**
Pessac-Léognan 1992: Lots of tobacco and some pretty plum, berry character. Medium in body, adding medium tannins and a cedary, mineral finish. • $30 • **80**
Pessac-Léognan 1991: Extremely well balanced wine with just enough fruit, toasted oak and fine tannins. Drinkable now. • $30 • (03/31/94) • **86**
Pessac-Léognan 1990: Rich and powerful, with meaty, smoky, earthy, berry character, tons of fruit and masses of soft, thick tannins. Drink after 1998. 5,000 cases made. • $42 • (03/31/93) • **92**
Pessac-Léognan 1989 • $59 • (03/15/92) • **96**
Pessac-Léognan 1988 • $40 • (07/15/91) • **91**
Pessac-Léognan 1986 • $36 • (06/15/89) • **89**

Key: SS—Spectator Selection. CS—Cellar Selection. BB—Best Buy. $NA—Price not available. (BT)—Barrel tasting. Ⓐ—Auction Price.
Dates in parentheses represent the issues in which the ratings were published.

Pessac-Léognan White 1994: Opulent ripe apple, cream and pie crust aromas and flavors. Full-bodied, intense and very long on the finish. A delicious white Bordeaux. • $75 • (03/31/96) • **91**
Pessac-Léognan White 1992: Better than a year ago. Full-throttled, toasty, barrel-fermented style, fresh and elegant, boasting terrific mineral and honey flavors. Polished yet powerful. Drink or hold. • $55 • (05/31/95) • **92**

CHEVALIER, GUY

Cabernet-Syrah Vin de Pays de l'Aude 1990 • $8 • (12/31/91) • **79**
Corbières La Coste 1990 • $9 • (03/15/94) • **81**
Corbières La Coste 1989 • $9 • (08/31/91) • **72**
Le Texas Vin de Pays de l'Aude 1989 • $9 • (07/15/91) • **74**

CHEVILLON, DENIS

Nuits-St.-Georges Les Chaignots 1987 • $33 • (07/15/90) • **87**
Nuits-St.-Georges Les Pruliers 1987 • $38 • (07/15/90) • **84**

CHEVILLON, ROBERT

Bourgogne 1989 • $16 • (01/31/92) • **77**
Nuits-St.-Georges 1992: Spicy, exotic aromas and flavors never quite lift off in this surprisingly mature-tasting but tannic wine. • $NA • **75**
Nuits-St.-Georges 1989 • $36 • (01/31/92) • **89**
Nuits-St.-Georges 1986 • $37 • (12/15/89) • **74**
Nuits-St.-Georges 1985 • $40 • (04/30/88) • **85**
Nuits-St.-Georges Les Bousselots 1992: Delivers some sweet plum and black cherry flavors, a ripe-tasting Burgundy that is already appealing. • $NA • **84**
Nuits-St.-Georges Les Cailles 1992: Medium-dark color, with nicely defined blackberry and currant flavors riding a layer of soft tannins to a gentle finish. Drink now. • $NA • **84**
Nuits-St.-Georges Les Cailles 1991: Ripe and perfumed, clean and crisp, with nicely defined currant and blackberry flavors that are stronger on the finish. Ends up crisp and juicy rather than broad. Give the tannins until 1997. 200 cases made. • $48 • (01/31/94) • **87**
Nuits-St.-Georges Les Chaignots 1992: Simple, light and watery, with a very modest strawberry flavor. • $NA • **70**
Nuits-St.-Georges Les Chaignots 1991: Enough black cherry and currant flavors balance the firm tannins in this modest wine. Crisp and flavorful. 650 cases made. • $38 • (01/31/94) • **84**
Nuits-St.-Georges Les Perrières 1992: Lean, modest and simple, with straightforward strawberry notes and a sharp finish. Not much here. • $NA • **73**
Nuits-St.-Georges Les Pruliers 1992: Round and appealing, with a ripe core of plum, currant and black cherry. This light-textured wine stays with you. A good effort in this vintage. • $NA • **84**
Nuits-St.-Georges Les Roncières 1992: Light, crisp and a little tannic for the modest level of citrusy strawberry flavors. Try now. • $NA • **78**
Nuits-St.-Georges Les Roncières 1991: Firm in texture, a densely flavorful wine that pours out its raspberry and currant flavors with vanilla-spicy overtones. Harmonious and elegant, this has the right stuff to develop well beyond 1999-2000. • $34 • (08/31/94) • **91**
Nuits-St.-Georges Les St.-Georges 1992: Starts off with some appealing strawberry, but it just dissipates on the chewy finish. • $NA • **78**
Nuits-St.-Georges Les St.-Georges 1991: A little tannic, but packed with violet scented currant and blackberry fruit, a mouthfilling wine on a lean frame, finishing chewy enough to want until 1998-2000. • $39 • (08/31/94) • **88**
Nuits-St.-Georges Les St.-Georges 1990: Ripe, chewy and concentrated, with densely packed violet, rose petal, black cherry, tobacco and floral notes, a great future ahead. • $63 • **92**
Nuits-St.-Georges Les St.-Georges 1989: Bright and complex, with nice strawberry and rose flavors that glow softly on the finish. • $53 • **86**
Nuits-St.-Georges Les St.-Georges 1988: Big and flavorful, with polished rose petal, toast and spicy oak notes. Youthful and tannic, so give this time to show it all. • $59 • **90**
Nuits-St.-Georges Les St.-Georges 1987: Round and chewy, generous, offering nicely focused plum, vanilla, spice and berry flavors. Finishes solidly with a tannic edge. • $43 • **88**

Nuits-St.-Georges Les St.-Georges 1986: Fully drinkable now yet quite chewy, offering good acidity but also tough tannins with only a modest level of rose and berry flavor sneaking in. • $55 • **82**

Nuits-St.-Georges Les St.-Georges 1985: This grows on you. Lean at first, it opens up and turns charming and seductively smooth, with ripe berry flavor and mature tobacco and brown sugar tones. • $75 • **89**

Nuits-St.-Georges Les St.-Georges 1983: Light and tight, firm-textured and mature, with spice, cinnamon and rose-scented strawberry flavors. It is drying a touch on the finish, so drink now. • $55 • **84**

Nuits-St.-Georges Les Vaucrains 1992: Decent currant and cherry flavors and a crisp style. Youthful, fresh and pleasant for drinking now. • $NA • **80**

Nuits-St.-Georges Les Vaucrains 1991: Dense and expansive, with a slightly herbal edge to the chunky raspberry, blackberry and spice aromas and flavors, a powerful wine buried under a thick layer of chewy tannins. Tightly wrapped now, it should be best from 2000. • $39 • (08/31/94) • **91**

Nuits-St.-Georges Les Vaucrains 1989 • $65 • (01/31/92) • **89**

CHEZE, DOMAINE

St.-Joseph 1991: Showing maturity now, this offers eucalyptus, leather, herbal and barnyard flavors but lacks fruit, the tannins are dry on the finish. It has complexity, but doesn't deliver much pleasure. • $NA • **78**

St.-Joseph White 1991 • $18 • (09/30/95) • **81**

St.-Joseph Cuvée Prestige de Caroline 1992 • $18 • (05/31/94) • **76**

St.-Joseph Cuvée Prestige de Caroline 1991 • $18 • (05/31/94) • **81**

CHEZEAUX, DOMAINE DES

Chambolle-Musigny Les Charmes 1985 • $75 • (06/15/88) • **91**

Griotte-Chambertin 1988 • $110 • (05/15/91) • **90**

Griotte-Chambertin 1985 • $150 Ⓐ • (06/15/88) • **91**

CHIDAINE, FRANCOIS

Brut Montlouis NV: A riper style, exhibiting honey and peach flavors. The finish is relatively dry and refreshing. • $14 • (06/15/96) • **83**

Montlouis Clos du Breuil 1993: Soft texture and light peach flavors are appealing, but a musty note dominates and turns the wine tough and somewhat sour. • $12 • (06/15/96) • **74**

Montlouis Les Tuffeaux 1993: Wet wool pervades the aroma, but the flavors are more in line—honey and beeswax. Straightforward and correct. • $13 • (05/15/96) • **84**

CHOFFLET-VALDENAIRE

Givry 1993: Ripe plum and black cherry notes mark this broadly textured, charming red. Nicely balanced, somewhat complex in flavor, moderately tannic. Drinkable now through 1998. 350 cases made. • $20 • (05/15/96) • **86**

Givry 1992: A good Burgundy whose flavors don't balance the nice bouquet. Expansive aromas of strawberry, cherry and spice are followed by lean, tough, unripe flavors and an astringent finish. 1,500 cases made. • $15 • **82**

CHOFFLET, JEAN

Givry Red 1985 • $12 • (11/15/87) • **70**

CHOPIN, A.

Côte de Nuits-Villages 1985 • $9 • (10/31/87) BB • **83**

Nuits-St.-Georges Aux Murgers 1988 • $28 • (07/15/90) • **91**

Nuits-St.-Georges Aux Murgers 1987 • $26 • (12/15/89) • **85**

Nuits-St.-Georges Aux Murgers 1986 • $29 • (10/15/88) • **78**

CHOPIN-GROFFIER

Chambolle-Musigny 1989 • $32 • (01/31/92) • **90**

Clos Vougeot 1993: Ah, attractive fruit flavors. Ripe, even fat, for the vintage, but also somewhat hot on the palate and finish that keeps it from scoring higher. Ripe plum and mint notes. Try in 1999. • $85 • **88**

Clos Vougeot 1992: Fresh and lively, a simple red with appealing currant and toasty, spicy notes that linger on the slightly chewy finish. Drink now. • $80 • **85**

Clos Vougeot 1991: This lean, sprightly, pretty wine shows modest cherry and berry flavors and hints of lime and anise on the finish. Has charm, but little depth. Drinkable now. 125 cases made. • $62 Ⓐ • (01/31/94) • **85**

Clos Vougeot 1990: What finesse. Despite the solid structure, it offers abundant black cherry, currant and plum flavors and manages to tame the massive, firm, long tannins. The finish is silky and enchanting. Try in 1997. • $70 • (12/15/92) • **94**

Clos Vougeot 1989 • $72 • (01/31/92) • **94**

Clos Vougeot 1988 • $70 • (05/15/91) • **87**

Côte de Nuits-Villages 1993: Pretty currant and cherry flavors. Quite tannic and firm. Medium in body, it seems a bit dry and tough on the finish now. Might be better in 1999. • $22 • **83**

Côte de Nuits-Villages 1992: Delicious, focused currant, black cherry and chestnut flavors, more concentrated than some premiers crus. At its peak now. • $18 • **82**

Nuits-St.-Georges 1993: Smooth and fruity, offering delicate aromas of rose petal, black cherry and earth and super, supple tannin structure. Better in 1997. • $45 • **79**

Nuits-St.-Georges 1991: Lean and tannic, but well defined, offering bright berry flavors at a modest level. Finishes a bit stemmy. Drinkable now. 250 cases made. • $33 Ⓐ • (01/31/94) • **83**

Nuits-St.-Georges 1990: A very elegant, very good village wine, with focused blackberry and chocolate aromas and flavors and very supple tannins. Drinkable now. • $43 • (12/15/92) • **89**

Nuits-St.-Georges 1989 • $32 • (01/31/92) • **91**

Nuits-St.-Georges Aux Chaignots 1990: An elegant wine, with excellent intensity. Offers plenty of smoke and raspberry aromas and flavors and firm tannins to back them up. Drinkable now. • $40 • (12/15/92) • **91**

Nuits-St.-Georges Les Chaignots 1993: Quite light and charming, delivering some earth, raspberry, cherry and rose petal notes. A bit dry on the lean finish. Try in 1997. • $60 • **82**

Nuits-St.-Georges Les Chaignots 1992: Appealing, balanced and focused on toasty and currant flavors that lead to a juicy finish. Needs a bit more concentration. Drinkable now. • $45 • **84**

Nuits-St.-Georges Les Chaignots 1991: A bit raw in texture and flavor, but comes together nicely on the palate, mixing smoke, toast and berry flavors harmoniously. Drinkable now, or hold into 1997. 125 cases made. • $40 Ⓐ • (01/31/94) • **86**

Nuits-St.-Georges Les Chaignots 1989 • $40 • (01/31/92) • **93**

Vougeot 1992: Smoky, toasty, gamy and quite interesting, a round-textured and flavorful 1992 that clamps down on the palate. Good complexity and length for this difficult vintage. • $35 • **84**

Vougeot 1991: Tough, astringent, cardboardy, possibly corky, especially because of the musty character on the finish. Has some nice raspberry and lemon flavors that belong to a good wine. • $NA • (01/31/94) • **79**

Vougeot 1990: It's hard to find a wine with better, brighter, livelier fruit than this, even in this vintage. The impressive toasted nut, plum, cherry and earth characteristics shine and there are plenty of firm tannins on the long finish. Drinkable now. • $44 • (12/15/92) • **93**

Vougeot 1988 • $32 • (05/15/91) • **92**

CHOPPIN, A.R.

Beaune Bressandes 1985 • $32 • (09/30/87) • **90**

Beaune Cent Vignes 1985 • $32 • (10/31/87) • **81**

Beaune Grèves 1985 • $32 • (09/30/87) • **79**

Beaune Teurons 1987 • $30 • (02/28/90) • **87**

Beaune Teurons 1985 • $32 • (10/31/87) • **87**

Beaune Toussaints 1987 • $30 • (02/28/90) • **83**

Savigny-lès-Beaune Vergelesses 1987 • $32 • (02/28/90) • **79**

Savigny-lès-Beaune Vergelesses 1985 • $25 • (10/31/87) • **87**

CHUSCLAN, CAVE DES VIGNERONS A

Côtes du Rhône Prieure St.-Julien 1985 • $4 • (12/31/87) BB • **79**

CINQUIN, PAUL

Régnié Domaine des Braves Red 1994: Aging well, this shows attractive dried cherry, herbal and toasty flavors, the tannins are still fresh, though this finish is a bit dry. A good food wine. • $10 • **84**

CISSAC, CHÂTEAU

Haut-Médoc 1995: Attractive perfume characterizes this one, with flavors of red berry, vanilla and strawberry. Good tannins and lots of sweet fruit on the finish. • $NA • (05/15/96) • **85-89** (BT)
Haut-Médoc 1992: Delicate, fine, succulent berry, cherry and smoke aromas and flavors, medium tannins and a medium finish. Drink now. • $14 • **81**
Haut-Médoc 1991: Slightly mature but pleasant and soft, with sweet berry fruit flavors. • $14 • (03/31/94) • **76**
Haut-Médoc 1990: This is a solid wine in a lovely aromatic style with black cherry, minty, vanilla character and medium-intense tannins. Drinkable now. 25,000 cases made. • $18 • (03/31/93) • **88**
Haut-Médoc 1989 • $19 • (03/15/92) • **85**
Haut-Médoc 1987 • $14 • (11/30/89) • **81**
Haut-Médoc 1986 • $12 Ⓐ • (11/30/89) • **79**
Haut-Médoc 1985 • $12 • (07/31/88) • **79**
Haut-Médoc 1982 • $21 Ⓐ • (11/30/89) • **81**
Haut-Médoc 1961: Fully mature, and exotic in flavor, showing a good fruit core enhanced by a bottle bouquet of spice, cola and leather. Drink through 1998. • $36 • (04/30/96) • **88**

CITRAN, CHÂTEAU

Haut-Médoc 1995: Lots of new wood in this, but plenty of berry and raspberry accents support it. Medium to full body, fine tannins and a fruity finish. Almost outstanding. • $NA • (05/15/96) • **85-89** (BT)
Haut-Médoc 1994: Some decent berry and cherry aromas and flavors, medium, slightly dry tannins and a short finish. Not as good as last time. Too dry. • $NA • (05/15/96) • **80-84** (BT)
Haut-Médoc 1993: No-nonsense '93 featuring decent tobacco and cherry character. Medium-to-light in body, light tannins and fresh finish. • $20 • (01/31/96) • **80**
Haut-Médoc 1991: Surprisingly good considering the vintage. Velvety texture, delicate currant and toast notes, medium body and finish. • $13 • (03/31/94) • **84**
Haut-Médoc 1990: Not as great as the '89, but a seductive wine with attractive vanilla, black cherry aromas and flavors, medium tannins, lovely balance and a long, fresh finish. Drinkable now. 42,000 cases made. • $20 • (03/31/93) • **86**
Haut-Médoc 1989 • $20 • (03/15/92) • **93**
Haut-Médoc 1988 • $20 • (04/30/91) • **91**
Haut-Médoc 1983 • $12 • (04/01/86) • **82**
Haut-Médoc 1982 • $12 • (04/01/85) • **78**
Haut-Médoc 1961: Has turned brown in color, thin and weak in taste, with vegetal, tealike flavors. Apparently well past its prime. • $22 • (04/30/96) • **77**

CLAIR, BRUNO

Bourgogne White 1992 • $19 • **69**
Chambertin Clos de Bèze 1991: Ripe and elegant, a dark, dense wine in an airy frame, beaming its currant, black cherry and tobacco flavors right through the long finish. Drinkable now. 185 cases made. • $78 Ⓐ • (01/31/94) • **91**
Chambertin-Clos de Bèze 1990: Very complex, with a symphony of coffee, licorice, tobacco, plum, earth and cedar notes, a full-bodied structure and great intensity on the finish. Drinkable now. 188 cases made. • $70 • (12/15/92) • **93**

Key: SS—Spectator Selection. CS—Cellar Selection. BB—Best Buy. $NA—Price not available. (BT)—Barrel tasting. Ⓐ—Auction Price.
Dates in parentheses represent the issues in which the ratings were published.

Corton-Charlemagne 1993: Very ripe mango and vanilla aromas and flavors. Full-bodied and quite rich. A lovely creamy, appley finish. Drinkable now. • $76 • **88**
Gevrey-Chambertin 1993: Really flavorful, smooth, easy to like, featuring cherry and strawberry notes accented by licorice. Attractive, medium-bodied and basically ready to drink. • $47 • (05/15/96) • **86**
Gevrey-Chambertin Cazetiers 1991: Ripe, pretty and delicate, showing an impressive concentration of currant, raspberry and floral aromas and flavors. Finishes firm and elegant. Drinkable now. 251 cases made. • $53 Ⓐ • (01/31/94) • **87**
Gevrey-Chambertin Clos du Fonteny 1991: Artfully expressed currant, black cherry and anise aromas and flavors persist on the finish of this crisp, lively, light wine. Drinkable now. 219 cases made. • $42 Ⓐ • (01/31/94) • **86**
Gevrey-Chambertin Clos du Fonteny 1990: This multidimensional, complex wine delivers superb intensity, with raspberry, earth and cigar box aromas and flavors. Shows a lot of elegance and the finish goes on and on. A great Gevrey. Drinkable now. • $45 • (12/15/92) • **92**
Gevrey-Chambertin Les Cazetiers 1990: A solid wine, with ripe berry aromas and flavors and very firm acidity. Built for aging, try in 1997. 200 cases made. • $55 • (12/15/92) • **89**
Gevrey-Chambertin Les Cazetiers 1989 • $61 • (01/31/92) • **89**
Gevrey-Chambertin Premier Cru Clos du Fonteney Monopole 1992: A tart and tannic wine with bright raspberry flavors accented by chocolate. It stays tight and closed through the finish. Drink now, before the fruit fades. • $50 • (05/15/95) • **83**
Marsannay 1992: Tastes just like a chocolate-raspberry dessert without the sweetness. Fascinating, but not what we look for in Burgundy. • $19 • (05/15/95) • **83**
Marsannay 1988 • $16 • (11/15/91) • **80**
Marsannay Les Grasses Têtes 1993: Really ripe and flavorful, relatively soft in tannins, offering black cherry and chocolate notes, full body, smooth texture and a fruity finish. • $25 • (05/15/96) • **86**
Marsannay Les Grasses Têtes 1990: A light-styled, delicious wine, with straightforward plum and earth flavors and light tannins. Drinkable now. • $28 • (12/15/92) • **80**
Marsannay Les Longeroies 1992: Firm-textured, tannic, lean but impressive. Attractive cherry and raspberry flavors fight through on the finish, showing promise for the future, best to drink now through '98. • $23 • (05/15/95) • **85**
Marsannay Les Longeroies 1990: Firm and one-dimensional, with vivid strawberry flavors and a touch of herbs. Drinkable now. • $18 • (12/15/92) • **83**
Marsannay Les Longeroies 1989 • $18 • (01/31/92) • **87**
Marsannay Les Vaudenelles 1993: Quite rich, thick and chocolaty, delivering ripe fruit and herbal flavors and relatively soft tannins. Enjoy it now through 1998. • $22 • (05/15/96) • **85**
Marsannay Les Vaudenelles 1992: A sturdy Pinot Noir. This is tart, cranberry flavored, accented by smoky oak. Attractive, but not deep or concentrated. Drink now. • $21 • (05/15/95) • **81**
Marsannay Les Vaudenelles 1989 • $18 • (01/31/92) • **81**
Marsannay Rosé Pinot Noir 1993: A dry, smooth rose, elegant in texture, light in flavor, with touches of cherry and strawberry to give it life. • $16 • (05/15/95) • **83**
Morey-St.-Denis 1985 • $20 • (05/15/88) • **73**
Morey-St.-Denis En La Rue de Vergy 1994: Round and pleasant, as the lemon tart, pie crust and vanilla flavors mingle nicely in this harmonious, lively '94. Drinkable now. • $40 • (05/31/96) • **84**
Morey-St.-Denis en La Rue de Vergy 1991: Firm and focused. Lively blackberry and currant flavors bounce through this juicy wine. A layer of crisp tannins will need until 1997 to smooth out. 310 cases made. • $33 Ⓐ • (01/31/94) • **86**
Morey-St.-Denis En La Rue de Vergy 1990: This serious village wine offers tons of jammy raspberry, blueberry and spice flavors and is almost sweet on the palate, with ripe fruit and velvety tannins. Drinkable now. • $37 • (12/15/92) • **90**
Morey-St.-Denis En La Rue de Vergy 1989 • $36 • (01/31/92) • **90**
Savigny-lès-Beaune La Dominode 1991: More generous than most '91 Savignys. Black cherry and vanilla aromas and flavors keep singing on the finish. A soft wine, drinkable now. 399 cases made. • $32 Ⓐ • (01/31/94) • **86**

FRANCE

Savigny-lès-Beaune La Dominode 1990: A class act. Tastes like a raspberry reduction sauce and is so concentrated it nearly jumps out of the glass. A joy to taste, with rich raspberry and chocolate characteristics and tons of firm tannins. Drinkable now. • $32 • (12/15/92) • **92**

Savigny-lès-Beaune La Dominode 1989 • $24 Ⓐ • (01/31/92) • **89**

Savigny-lès-Beaune La Dominode 1985 • $24 • (03/15/88) • **80**

Vosne-Romanée Les Champs Pedrix 1991: Bright and flavorful. Earthy, decadent edge to the herbal black cherry character at the core and crisp, somewhat tart finish. Try now. 214 cases made. • $28 Ⓐ • (01/31/94) • **81**

Vosne-Romanée Les Champs Pedrix 1989 • $30 • (01/31/92) • **91**

CLAIR, FRANCOISE & DENIS

Puligny-Montrachet La Garenne 1994: If you think all '94s are soft and supple, think again. This one demonstrates a solid, incredibly intense core of lime, grapefruit and fresh pineapple flavors that are backed by earth and mineral complexity. Mouthpuckering yet elegant. Needs time. 125 cases made. • $44 • (05/31/96) • **89**

St.-Aubin Les Murgers des Dents de Chien 1994: Pure, clean and well-structured *premier cru*, showing crisp texture and ripe pear, citrus, mineral, ginger and dried herb complexity. Medium-bodied, smooth and silky on the vanilla- and spice-flavored finish. Better in 1999. Terrific accomplishment in this appellation. 333 cases made. • $27 • (05/31/96) • **90**

Santenay Clos de la Comme 1990: Light, earthy and flavorful, with woodsy, mushroomy overtones to the modest black cherry and raspberry flavors. Finishes soft and supple. Drinkable now. • $26 • (02/15/93) • **81**

Santenay Clos de la Comme 1988 • $25 • (06/15/92) • **85**

Santenay Clos de Tavannes 1990: Lean and tight, with a hint of vinegar in the sharply focused cherry flavors. Tight and tough on the finish. Drinkable now to 1997. • $29 • (02/15/93) • **83**

CLAIR, LOUIS

Santenay Gravières Domaine de L'Abbay 1985 • $17 • (10/15/87) • **88**

CLAIRAC, CHÂTEAU

Premières Côtes de Blaye Red 1985 • $4 • (04/15/88) • **76**

CLAIREFONT, CHÂTEAU DE

Margaux 1993: Sweet and fruity, offering modest licorice, currant and cherry flavors, rather light body and supple tannins. Second label of Château Prieuré-Lichine. Drink on release. • $15 • (01/31/96) • **79**

Margaux 1985 • $9 • (04/30/88) • **79**

CLAIRFONT, DOMAINE DE

Vin de Pays de Vaucluse Red 1991 • $6 • (10/31/92) BB • **82**

CLAPE, A.

Cornas 1991 • $24 • (05/31/94) • **87**

Cornas 1990 • $26 • (04/15/93) • **87**

Cornas 1986 • $19 Ⓐ • (01/31/89) • **88**

Cornas 1984 • $13 • (08/31/87) • **78**

CLARKE, CHÂTEAU

Listrac 1990: A very ripe, somewhat rustic wine with raisin, leather and earthy flavors in an ample frame. It's chewy and rich, but drinkable now. 17,500 cases made. • $15 • (11/15/94) • **83**

Listrac 1989 • $16 • (03/15/92) • **85**

Listrac 1988 • $18 • (04/30/91) • **81**

Listrac 1986 • $17 • (11/15/89) • **90**

Listrac 1982 • $13 • (10/15/86) • **68**

CLAVEL, DOMAINE

Coteaux du Languedoc La Méjanelle 7ème Printemps des Comédiens 1991 • $7 • (03/15/94) • **86**

CLAVERIE, CHÂTEAU LA

Côtes de Francs 1990: A light, everyday wine, with delicate, simple strawberry character and light, smooth tannins. Drinkable now. • $19 • (03/31/93) • **80**

Côtes de Francs 1989 • $21 • (03/15/92) • **88**

CLEMANCEY FRERES

Fixin Les-Hervelets 1985 • $21 • (04/30/88) • **71**

CLEMENT PICHON, CHÂTEAU

Haut-Médoc 1995: A good amount of berry and blackberry flavors, with a light note of tar. Velvety tannins and it stays chewy on the finish. An honest, though somewhat simple, wine. • $NA • (05/15/96) • **80-84** (BT)

Haut-Médoc 1994: Spicy and meaty, offering herbal, raisiny character, medium to full body, rustic tannins and earthy finish. • $NA • **80-84** (BT)

Haut-Médoc 1993: Attractively smooth, showing some nice red berry flavor and a hint of gamy, earthy character, sweet-tasting finish and supple tannins. Drinkable now. • $15 • (01/31/96) • **80**

Haut-Médoc 1991: Weedy and diluted with strawberry flavor and grassy character. Tasted twice. • $12 • (03/31/94) • **68**

Haut-Médoc 1988 • $15 • (08/31/91) • **78**

Haut-Médoc 1987 • $14 • (11/30/89) • **73**

Haut-Médoc 1986 • $11 • (11/30/89) • **85**

CLEMENT, ABEL

Côtes du Rhône 1993: Tannic and overdone with candied cherry and plum flavors and aromas. The resinous flavors make this a heavy-handed wine. • $8 • **77**

Côtes du Rhône 1990 • $7 • (04/15/93) • **72**

Côtes du Rhône 1988 • $6 • (02/28/90) BB • **80**

Côtes du Rhône 1985 • $5 • (01/31/87) BB • **78**

CLEMENT, BERNARD & PIERRE

Sancerre 1994: Clean, and rather neutral, but rather lean and tart, this white offers light herbal and piney flavors but finishes short. Serviceable but not much fun. • $14 • **80**

Sancerre 1993: 7,500 cases made. • $15 • **58**

Sancerre 1992: The sunny, generous fruit flavors of apple and peach are braced by bright herbal and floral notes. It's well-defined, refreshing and even delicate in its assertive way, keeps you coming back for more. 10,000 cases made. • $13 • (08/31/94) • **89**

CLERAY, CHÂTEAU DU

Muscadet de Sèvre et Maine Carte D'Or Sur Lie 1992: A pronounced earthy note mars this light-bodied white, which lacks the acidity and fruit to overcome it. Finishes bitter. • $6 • (10/31/94) • **74**

Muscadet de Sèvre et Maine Réserve du Cléray Sur Lie 1992: Fresh pear and grapefruit flavors enliven this ripe, round Muscadet, yet it's still crisp and lively. It shows good concentration and a nice balance of fruit and acidity. • $12 • (08/31/94) • **85**

Muscadet de Sèvre et Maine Sauvion du Cléray Sur Lie 1992: An earthy undertone runs through this soft-textured yet very dry white, making it austere and a little bitter on the finish. • $7 • (10/31/94) • **78**

Muscadet de Sèvre et Maine Sur Lie 1993: The deep gold color and strong vanilla and butter aromas are untraditional but appealing, with perfumed honey flavors and silky body. Is this a special American cuvée? It will please fans of oak flavors. 5,000 cases made. • $7 • **83**

CLERC & FILS, HENRI

Beaune Chaume Gaufriot 1985 • $29 • (11/15/88) • **81**

CLERC MILON, CHÂTEAU

Pauillac 1995: Always a winner: Clerc shows its stuff. Full body and loads of fine tannins and a very long finish of minty berry and cassis. Almost as good as Mouton. • $NA • (05/15/96) • **90-94** (BT)

Pauillac 1994: Racy and classy, with plenty of fruitiness and black cherry character. Medium to full body, fine tannins and a long finish full of vanilla, spice and mineral overtones. One of the best values of this vintage. • $23 • (05/15/96) • **90-94** (BT)

Pauillac 1993: Clerc Milon is a sure bet for a very good wine in any vintage. Impressive medium to full body, tobacco, cherry, tar and chestnut character, velvety tannins and medium finish. Needs time, try in 1998. • $24 • (01/31/96) • **89**

Pauillac 1992: Solid yet very polished, exhibiting currant, berry and tobacco character, medium-to-full body, refined tannins and a long, velvety finish. • $22 • **88**

Pauillac 1991: A balanced, supple wine, with lovely blackberry, vanilla complexity, sweet and ripe. Tasted twice. • $22 • (03/31/94) • **85**

Pauillac 1990: A seamless wine with great character, offering cigar, tobacco, cedar, and rich plum flavors. Full-bodied yet well balanced, with lovely, full, silky tannins and a long finish. Drink after 2000. 13,000 cases made. • $30 • (03/31/93) • **94**

Pauillac 1989 • $33 • (03/15/92) • **96**

Pauillac 1988 • $26 • (04/30/91) SS • **94**

Pauillac 1986 • $38 Ⓐ • (05/31/89) • **97**

Pauillac 1985 • $47 Ⓐ • (05/15/88) • **91**

Pauillac 1984 • $18 • (06/15/87) • **78**

Pauillac 1983: Muscular and dense wine with ripe fruit, gamy, toasted oak aromas and flavors. Full bodied with loads of ripe fruit and round tannins. Very good drink but could use a little more time. Better after 1997. • $17 • (10/15/94) • **87**

Pauillac 1982 • $41 Ⓐ • (08/31/92) • **90**

Pauillac 1981: Lively and well-balanced. Attractive aromas of spice and cedar give way to cherry, tobacco and cedar flavors, braced by brisk tannins. Still fresh, it's drinkable now but will soften further in the bottle. • $25 • **88**

Pauillac 1961: A poor showing, possibly due to a bad bottle. This has odd cooked and buttery aromas, an awkward, tough feel to it and a sweet-seeming finish. • $NA • (04/30/96) • **76**

CLERGET, GEORGES

Vosne-Romanée Les Violettes 1986 • $23 • (08/31/89) • **71**

CLERGET, MICHEL

Chambolle-Musigny 1986 • $23 • (08/31/89) • **78**

Chambolle-Musigny 1985 • $38 • (05/15/88) • **73**

Chambolle-Musigny Les Charmes 1986 • $33 • (08/31/89) • **76**

Chambolle-Musigny Les Charmes 1985 • $41 Ⓐ • (05/15/88) • **83**

Echézeaux 1986 • $31 • (08/31/89) • **85**

Echézeaux 1985 • $51 • (07/31/88) • **82**

CLERGET, RAOUL

Prestige de Raoul Clerget NV • $3 • (07/15/88) • **79**

CLERGET, YVON

Bourgogne 1990 • $15 • (12/15/92) • **82**

Key: SS—Spectator Selection. CS—Cellar Selection. BB—Best Buy. $NA—Price not available. (BT)—Barrel tasting. Ⓐ—Auction Price.
Dates in parentheses represent the issues in which the ratings were published.

Pommard Les Rugiens 1990: Surprisingly light, showing simple strawberry and cherry aromas and flavors. Drinkable now. 200 cases made. • $48 • (12/15/92) • **79**

Volnay 1990: Nice, juicy and flavorful, offering berry and earth notes. Attractive in an elegant way. Drinkable now. 330 cases made. • $34 • (12/15/92) • **84**

Volnay Clos du Verseuil 1990: Fresh but light, this medium-bodied wine offers good berry flavors and lively tannins. Drinkable now. 330 cases made. • $42 • (12/15/92) • **84**

Volnay Les Caillerets 1990: Elegance defines this Volnay. Lovely black currant, mint and chestnut aromas and flavors are presented in a subtle package, ending with round tannins. Drinkable now. 125 cases made. • $45 • (12/15/92) • **86**

Volnay Premier Cru 1990: Velvety and perfumed, with lovely black currant, mint and cherry notes, silky texture and a supple finish. Drinkable now. 225 cases made. • $37 • (12/15/92) • **87**

CLIMENS, CHÂTEAU

Barsac 1991: Attractively sweet and lush, showing some zingy lemon, honey and spice flavors and a smooth finish. Drink as an apéritif. • $NA • **86**

Barsac 1990: Classy, both solid and seductive, featuring a velvety texture and subtle, spicy, toasty butterscotch, lemon and honey character. Hard to resist now, it has the stuffing to improve past 1999. • $67 • **93**

Barsac 1989: High-wired, super-focused, seductively creamy and beautifully balanced. The beam of lemon, honey, spice, pear and melon flavor shines through to a fresh, long finish. Tempting now, better after 1997. • $68 • **93**

Barsac 1988: Extremely polished and complex, showing beautiful dried herb, grass, honey and pine flavors. Has a long finish, medium body and just-so sweetness. Drinkable now. • $49 • **91**

Barsac 1986: Gorgeous, ripe, and rich, oozing with tropical, honey and mineral flavors that take off like a heat-seeking missile on the finish. Tempting now but better after 1998. • $51 • **94**

Barsac 1983: Perfectly balanced between acidity and the sweet, honey and cream character that coats the palate. Bravo! Drinkable now. • $50 • **92**

CLINET, CHÂTEAU

Pomerol 1995: Fabulously rich berry, prune, blackberry and wet earth character. Full in body, loads of velvety tannins and a long finish. • $NA • (05/15/96) • **90-94** (BT)

Pomerol 1994: Loads of tobacco, cedar and berry come through the full tannins, which end up with a mouthpuckering finish. • $70 • (05/15/96) • **85-89** (BT)

Pomerol 1993: Exciting and solid all the way through, showing super depth of color and character. Ripe, rich complexity and mineral, earth, currant and plum flavors. It's sweet-tasting and coats your mouth with supple and elegant tannins. A pleasure to drink now, but should improve for years. Try after 1999. • $40 • (01/31/96) • **90**

Pomerol 1992: Clinet does it again in a weak year. Lots of new wood, cherry and raspberry aromas and flavors, medium body, firm tannins and slightly dry finish. Drinkable now. • $30 • **85**

Pomerol 1991: Consider it very good for this vintage: dark color, big and chewy, with vanilla and milk chocolate aromas and flavors, medium body and a clean finish. • $32 • (03/31/94) • **85**

Pomerol 1988 • $56 • (02/28/91) • **92**

Pomerol 1986 • $29 • (09/15/89) • **78**

Pomerol 1985 • $50 • (04/30/88) • **91**

Pomerol 1982 • $38 • (05/15/89) • **78**

Pomerol 1970 • $39 • (05/15/93) • **84**

Pomerol 1961: A fully mature Pomerol with wild aromas and flavors that are earthy, meaty and, yes, fruity too. A silky texture and all that complexity overcome a slightly metallic finish. Drink through 2000. • $33 • (04/30/96) • **88**

CLOCHERS DU HAUT-MEDOC, LES

Haut-Médoc 1983 • $7 • (06/15/87) • **60**

CLOS, DOMAINE DU

Frantin Grands Echézeaux 1993: Deep and ripe but also firm and hard at this stage, showing little charm. Tannic, but you can taste the sweetness of fruit underneath. Try after 2000. From Albert Bichot. • $60 • (11/15/95) • **88**

Frantin Vosne-Romanée Aux Malconsorts 1993: Chewy, firm and tannic, delivering pretty currant, raspberry and licorice flavors, medium body and medium intensity. Should glow by 2000. From Albert Bichot. • $50 • (11/15/95) • **87**

CLOS DE L'ABBAYE

Bourgueil 1986 • $16 • (08/31/89) • **86**

CLOS L'ABEILLEY

Sauternes 1990: Delicate and easy to drink, featuring vanilla, toast and pineapple flavors, medium body and sweetness and a rather hot finish. Could be better in 1996. Second label from Château de Rayne-Vigneau. • $NA • (04/15/95) • **84**

CLOS DES CAZAUX, DOMAINE LE

Vacqueyras Cuvée des Templiers 1983 • $11 • (01/31/87) • **83**

CLOS DU CLOCHER, CHÂTEAU

Pomerol 1994: Plum and black cherry aromas give way to more herbal and tobacco flavors. It's polished, but light-bodied and on the austere side, with firm tannins. Try now. • $29 • (12/15/95) • **84**

Pomerol 1993: Fresh, open aromas of blackberry and vanilla give way to round flavors of ripe fruit and spices. A velvety texture adds appeal, while ripe tannins add structure. Pleasant now through 1997. • $28 • (12/15/95) • **86**

Pomerol 1985 • $20 • (02/29/88) • **88**

Pomerol 1982 • $33 • (05/15/89) • **83**

CLOS L'EGLISE

Pomerol 1995: Big and chewy, featuring impressive fruit and spice, chocolate and oak-scented flavors. Full-bodied but a bit angular and rough on the finish. In time could rate outstanding. • $NA • (05/15/96) • **85-89** (BT)

Pomerol 1994: Smooth and round, featuring nice fruit character. Medium-bodied, velvety and well structured. • $NA • **85-89** (BT)

Pomerol 1993: Muscular and slightly rustic, featuring loads of firm tannins and cherry, berry, dried fruit character. Full to medium in body and a long, somewhat dry finish. Better in 1998. • $25 • (01/31/96) • **85**

Pomerol 1988 • $26 • (06/30/91) • **83**

Pomerol 1986 • $33 • (02/15/90) • **86**

Pomerol 1982 • $29 • (05/15/89) • **88**

Pomerol 1961 • $75 • (04/30/92) • **68**

Pomerol 1945: Earthy, animal flavors add grace notes to the dark cherry and toast character in this foursquare, solid Pomerol. Still a little tannic, but better to drink soon. • $230 • **84**

CLOS FOURTET

Pomerol 1945: Sweet flavors, but drying tannins keep it from being as charming as its potential. The earthy, slightly decadent edge persists on a long finish, but so do the sweet strawberry and lime notes. • $280 • **81**

St.-Emilion 1995: An attractive red with enticing berry, cherry and smoky nuances. Medium-bodied, with fine tannins and a fresh finish. • $NA • (05/15/96) • **85-89** (BT)

St.-Emilion 1994: Wonderfully crafted berry, cherry and vanilla flavors and fine tannins. Medium in body and solid, sporting an elegant structure. • $NA • (05/15/96) • **85-89** (BT)

St.-Emilion 1993: Light in color and body, showing plum, dried herb and toasted oak notes. Somewhat lean on the finish, but a pleasant glass of wine. Drinkable now. • $25 • (01/31/96) • **82**

St.-Emilion 1992: A decent core of plum, cherry and berry flavor, medium-to-light body, light tannins and a short finish. Drink now. • $17 • **78**

St.-Emilion 1990: Rich and fleshy, with a bounty of black cherry and smoky tobacco character, velvety tannins and a long, long finish. Drink in 1997. 5,000 cases made. • $30 • (03/31/93) • **90**

St.-Emilion 1989 • $28 • (03/15/92) • **89**

St.-Emilion 1988 • $27 • (10/31/91) • **86**

St.-Emilion 1986 • $41 • (06/30/89) • **80**

St.-Emilion 1982 • $20 Ⓐ • (08/31/92) • **83**

St.-Emilion 1970 • $29 • (05/15/93) • **85**

St.-Emilion 1961: A good but not great wine with aromas and flavors reminiscent of olives, cherries and beef. Drink through 2000. • $45 • (04/30/96) • **84**

St.-Emilion 1945 • $280 • (03/16/86) • **68**

CLOS FRANTIN, DOMAINE DU

Chambertin 1989 • $73 • (01/31/92) • **88**

Chambertin 1986 • $63 • (02/28/89) • **90**

Clos de Vougeot 1992: Very light, almost watery, with just a touch of sweet plum flavor before the tannins kick in on the finish. Try in 1997. • $NA • **77**

Clos de Vougeot 1989 • $56 • (01/31/92) • **91**

Clos de Vougeot 1987 • $56 • (07/15/90) • **85**

Clos de Vougeot 1986 • $37 • (11/30/88) • **87**

Corton 1990: Crisp, tart and earthy, with less breadth than Corton should have, offering tightly reined-in cherry and spice flavors that fade quickly behind a layer or two of tannin. Needs until 1997 to '99 to soften, but then what? • $53 • (11/30/92) • **81**

Corton 1989 • $58 • (01/31/92) • **86**

Corton-Charlemagne 1993: Polished and austere, delivering significant fruit and spice flavors in an elegant package. But it's hard as nails now and could use a bit more generosity. From Albert Bichot. • $NA • (08/31/95) • **85**

Echézeaux 1992: A distinctive minty character runs through this firm-textured, nicely focused Echézeaux that echoes its berry and herb flavors on the tough finish. Best from 1997. • $NA • **87**

Echézeaux 1990: Firm in texture and focused in flavor, with generous plum, currant and blackberry aromas and flavors tightly wrapped in a moderate veil of tannin. Drinkable now. • $42 • (11/30/92) • **88**

Echézeaux 1989 • $45 • (01/31/92) • **93**

Echézeaux 1986 • $30 • (11/30/88) • **90**

Echézeaux 1985 • $37 • (09/15/87) • **96**

Gevrey-Chambertin 1990: Tart and lively, with a greenish streak running through the bright raspberry and toast aromas and flavors. Drinkable now. • $28 • (11/30/92) • **84**

Gevrey-Chambertin 1989 • $29 • (01/31/92) • **84**

Gevrey-Chambertin 1988 • $37 • (07/15/90) • **87**

Gevrey-Chambertin 1987 • $20 • (03/31/90) • **82**

Grands Echézeaux 1989 • $56 • (01/31/92) • **90**

Grands Echézeaux 1987 • $56 • (07/15/90) • **86**

Grands Echézeaux 1986 • $60 • (02/28/89) • **87**

Nuits-St.-Georges 1990: Light and fruity, with ripe plum and currant flavors that turn dry and leathery on the finish. A simple, pleasing wine, but doesn't have any extra dimensions. Drinkable now. • $29 • (11/30/92) • **81**

Nuits-St.-Georges 1989 • $29 • (02/29/92) • **91**

Nuits-St.-Georges 1986 • $20 • (11/15/88) • **82**

Nuits-St.-Georges 1983 • $18 • (02/01/86) • **83**

Richebourg 1989 • $117 • (01/31/92) • **95**

Richebourg 1986 • $100 • (08/31/89) • **88**

Vosne-Romanée 1990: Earthy, woody and stalky, with little aroma and flavors that show only a modest level of fruit. Drinkable now. • $28 • (11/30/92) • **78**

Vosne-Romanée 1989 • $30 • (01/31/92) • **89**

Vosne-Romanée 1986 • $19 • (12/31/88) • **80**

Vosne-Romanée 1985 • $29 • (10/15/87) • **91**

Vosne-Romanée Les Malconsorts 1992: Lean, almost crisp, with little fruit to balance the hard tannins. The finish suggests it might improve with cellaring until 1997. • $NA • **79**

Vosne-Romanée Les Malconsorts 1990: A bit austere and reined in, but the moderate tannins are holding back lovely plum, berry and spice aromas and flavors. Remains subtle and elegant through the finish. Drinkable now. • $37 • (11/30/92) • **86**

Vosne-Romanée Les Malconsorts 1987 • $30 • (07/15/90) • **88**

Vosne-Romanée Les Malconsorts 1986 • $35 • (10/31/88) • **79**

Vosne-Romanée Les Malconsorts 1985 • $55 • (09/30/87) • **95**

CLOS HAUT-PEYRAGUEY, CHÂTEAU

Sauternes 1990: Exotically charming, gingersnap flavors complementing the lemon, vanilla bean and wet earth character of this medium-bodied, very sweet, well-balanced Sauternes. Try around 1997. • $NA • (04/15/95) • **90**

Sauternes 1989: A distinctive, earthy touch makes it a bit rustic, pretty orange-peel, honey and melon flavors come through on the balanced finish. Drink now or hold until 1997. • $30 • (04/15/95) • **86**

Sauternes 1988: Very attractive, featuring a fresh, grassy edge to complement the tropical fruit and butterscotch flavors. Medium-bodied and accessible, try now. • $26 • (04/15/95) • **88**

Sauternes 1987 • $21 • (06/15/90) • **83**

Sauternes 1986 • $23 • (04/15/95) • **89**

CLOS DES JACOBINS, CHÂTEAU

St.-Emilion 1995: Rather light and forward for the vintage, featuring grapey, earthy and green aromas and flavors and a light finish. • $NA • (05/15/96) • **75-79** (BT)

St.-Emilion 1994: Quite opulent yet firm, ripe, seductive and balanced. Currant, black olive, tobacco, toasted oak flavors, silky texture and long finish. One to watch. Sample variation noted. • $NA • **80-84** (BT)

St.-Emilion 1993: Smooth and round, offering delicious ripe tannins, toasty character and blackberry flavors. Medium body and intensity. Drinkable in 1997. • $25 • (01/31/96) • **85**

St.-Emilion 1991: Rather weedy, smoky and herbaceous, with light body and astringent finish. Tasted twice with consistent notes. • $20 • (03/31/94) • **77**

St.-Emilion 1990: Light and simple, with stewed tomato and stemmy aromas and flavors and light tannins. Disappointing. Drinkable now. 3,500 cases made. • $35 • (03/31/93) • **77**

St.-Emilion 1989 • $45 • (03/15/92) • **85**

St.-Emilion 1988 • $26 • (04/15/91) • **90**

St.-Emilion 1987 • $24 • (05/15/90) • **73**

St.-Emilion 1986 • $34 • (06/30/89) • **94**

St.-Emilion 1985 • $31 • (09/30/88) • **89**

St.-Emilion 1984 • $20 • (05/15/87) • **83**

St.-Emilion 1982 • $NA • (08/31/92) • **82**

St.-Emilion 1981: Surprisingly good. Chewy and concentrated with plenty of fruit. There's plenty of meaty, smoky, ripe fruit character that goes on and on. Drink now. • $NA • **85**

CLOS J. KANON

St.-Emilion 1987 • $10 • (05/15/90) • **77**

St.-Emilion 1986 • $17 • (11/15/89) • **91**

CLOS LABARDE

St.-Emilion 1986 • $15 • (06/30/89) • **82**

CLOS LARCIS

St.-Emilion 1995: Soft and easy, sporting some artichoke and berry aromas and flavors, medium body, round tannins and medium finish. • $NA • (05/15/96) • **80-84** (BT)

St.-Emilion 1994: Lean and silky, with good berry and strawberry accents in a light- to medium-bodied wine. • $NA • (05/15/96) • **80-84** (BT)

St.-Emilion 1993: Light, simple, fruity and slightly diluted. A bit disappointing for this estate. Drinkable now. • $14 • (01/31/96) • **79**

Key: SS—Spectator Selection. CS—Cellar Selection. BB—Best Buy. $NA—Price not available. (BT)—Barrel tasting. Ⓐ—Auction Price.
Dates in parentheses represent the issues in which the ratings were published.

St.-Emilion 1992: Better than expected. Elegant and drinkable, featuring cassis, berry and mint aromas and flavors, medium body, medium tannins and light finish. Drink now. • $12 • **83**

St.-Emilion 1991: Rather lean, but has some interesting black olive and berry aromas and flavors. • $12 • (03/31/94) • **78**

St.-Emilion 1990: A delicate and refined wine, with pretty vanilla and berry aromas and flavors and soft, refined tannins. Drinkable now. • $25 • (03/31/93) • **85**

St.-Emilion 1989 • $28 • (03/15/92) • **92**

CLOS DU MARQUIS

St.-Julien 1988 • $16 Ⓐ • (10/31/91) • **80**

St.-Julien 1987 • $12 • (05/15/90) • **79**

St.-Julien 1986 • $19 Ⓐ • (09/15/89) • **84**

St.-Julien 1985 • $89 Ⓐ • (09/30/88) • **84**

CLOS MARSALETTE

Pessac-Léognan 1995: Rich, intense and full-bodied, it's packed with sweet-tasting red currant, cedar, tobacco and toasted oak. Well made and quite hard now, the massive tannins will need years to smooth out, but the wait should reward the patient collector. Almost outstanding. • $NA • (05/15/96) • **85-89** (BT)

Pessac-Léognan 1993: Straightforward dark chocolate, berry and cherry aromas and flavors, medium body, firm tannins and short finish. Needs time to open, try in 1997. • $NA • (01/31/96) • **84**

CLOS DU MONT-OLIVET

Châteauneuf-du-Pape 1990: Tight and complex, offering crushed pepper, plum and currant flavors that are a bit rough around the edges. Finishes with gripping tannins that hang on. Drinkable now. • $20 • (04/15/93) • **83**

Châteauneuf-du-Pape 1989 • $20 • (02/28/93) • **86**

Châteauneuf-du-Pape 1988 • $19 • (10/15/91) • **88**

Châteauneuf-du-Pape 1986 • $17 • (10/15/91) • **87**

Châteauneuf-du-Pape 1985 • $20 • (10/15/91) • **92**

Châteauneuf-du-Pape 1983 • $28 • (10/15/91) • **86**

Châteauneuf-du-Pape 1982 • $12 • (03/16/86) • **91**

Châteauneuf-du-Pape 1981 • $30 • (10/15/91) • **87**

Châteauneuf-du-Pape White 1990: Has an impressive fruit and earth character, with pear, almond and melon aromas, rich, fruity flavors, a mineral, earthy character and a fresh finish. • $20 • (10/15/91) • **86**

CLOS NAUDIN, DOMAINE DU

Vouvray Moelleux 1989 • $34 • (04/30/91) • **83**

Vouvray Moelleux Réserve 1989 • $54 • (03/31/91) • **89**

Vouvray Sec 1992: Beautiful aromas of honey and spice indicate presence of "noble rot." Apple, mineral and honey flavors linger on aftertaste. Try now. 6,000 cases made. • $16 • (11/15/95) • **88**

CLOS NOIR

Clos de la Roche 1992: Crisp, fresh, lightweight, like biting into a fresh bunch of currants, distinctive floral nuances add to the fruit. Best after 1996. • $NA • **86**

Côte de Nuits-Villages Preaux 1992: A little tough in texture, with woodsy, toasty, slightly herbal flavors. • $NA • **79**

Gevrey-Chambertin Jeunes Rois 1992: Firm in texture but not too tannic, showing some nice floral and currant flavors that persist on the solid finish. Best from 1997. • $NA • **84**

Morey-St.-Denis 1992: Light and floral in aroma, a nice bead of raspberry flavor carrying through the smooth finish. Drinkable now. • $NA • **85**

CLOS DE L'ORATOIRE

St.-Emilion 1995: Marked by extreme finesse and grace, yet amazingly concentrated and powerful, this exhilarating, full-bodied, ripe, silky, harmonious '95 delivers tons of red- and blackberry flavors and nice spice notes. The finish goes on and on. • $NA • (05/15/96) • **90-94** (BT)

St.-Emilion 1994: Solid, big and full-bodied, well crafted and silky, this delivers a lot of earthy berry and oak character. There is just a hint of dilution on the finish, but it's impressive for this vintage nonetheless. • $NA • (05/15/96) • **85-89** (BT)
St.-Emilion 1993: Impressively ripe, featuring loads of raspberry, wet earth and dark chocolate character, medium to full body, velvety tannins and long finish. Not quite as great as we remember, but very good indeed. From the same producers as Château Canon-La Gaffelière. 4,654 cases made. • $25 • (01/31/96) • **88**
St.-Emilion 1992: Delicate chocolate, tobacco and fruit character, medium-to-light body and a succulent finish. Drink now. • $19 • **81**
St.-Emilion 1990: Port-like, with masses of berry, chocolate and cedar aromas and flavors, thick and velvety, with an excellent tannin structure and a long, long finish. From the owners of Château Canon-La Gaffelière. Drink in 1998. 3,700 cases made. • $28 • (03/31/93) • **94**
St.-Emilion 1982 • $NA • (05/15/89) • **78**

CLOS DE L'ORATOIRE DES PAPES

Châteauneuf-du-Pape 1985 • $10 • (07/31/88) • **87**

CLOS DE PAULILLES, LES

Collioure 1989 • $20 • **80**
Robert Doutres Banyuls 1989 • $17 • **72**

CLOS DES PAPES

Châteauneuf-du-Pape 1990: Thick and tannic, with lots of plum and pepper flavors and a chewy texture. Drinkable now. • $30 • (04/15/93) • **85**
Châteauneuf-du-Pape 1989 • $20 • (10/15/91) • **86**
Châteauneuf-du-Pape 1988 • $19 • (10/15/91) • **86**
Châteauneuf-du-Pape 1986 • $18 • (10/15/91) • **74**
Châteauneuf-du-Pape 1985 • $NA • (10/15/91) • **89**
Châteauneuf-du-Pape 1983 • $NA • (10/15/91) • **88**
Châteauneuf-du-Pape 1981 • $NA • (10/15/91) • **87**
Châteauneuf-du-Pape White 1990: A good, classic Châteauneuf blanc. Fresh mineral, spice and apple aromas open to medium-bodied, blanched almond and mineral flavors. Has nice concentration and a smooth finish. • $25 • (10/15/91) • **85**

CLOS RENE, CHÂTEAU

Pomerol 1988 • $24 • (04/30/91) • **88**
Pomerol 1986 • $22 • (06/15/89) SS • **94**
Pomerol 1985 • $NA • **86**
Pomerol 1983 • $NA • **89**
Pomerol 1982 • $32 Ⓐ • (05/15/89) • **87**
Pomerol 1981 • $NA • **80**
Pomerol 1962 • $35 • (11/30/87) • **60**
Pomerol 1959 • $50 • (10/15/90) • **88**
Pomerol 1945: Delicate, smooth and elegant, still lively, showing plum, spice, coffee and tea leaf notes that remain sweet and silky through the finish. Very fine, almost ethereal. Cruse bottling. • $175 • **88**

CLOS ROCHE BLANCHE

Sauvignon Touraine 1994: Pungent herbal, even weedy aromas give way to more neutral flavors, lean and crisp, that cleanse the palate, then disappear. • $9 • (12/15/95) • **80**

CLOS ST.-MICHEL

Châteauneuf-du-Pape 1990: Earthy, gamy, leathery flavors dominate the fruit in this medium-weight, problematic wine. Too gamy for us. • $16 • (11/15/92) • **76**
Châteauneuf-du-Pape White 1991: Ripe and spicy, with floral pear and vanilla notes. Ultimately it's simple and enjoyable, but nothing special. Drink now. • $15 • (12/15/92) • **81**
Châteauneuf-du-Pape Cuvée Réserve 1989 • $17 • (11/15/92) • **85**

CLOS ST.-PONCIAN

St.-Chinian 1990 • $NA • (03/15/94) • **80**

CLOS STE.-NICOLE

Cabernet Sauvignon French-California Cuvée NV • $5 • (10/31/89) • **77**
Merlot French-California Cuvée NV • $5 • (10/31/89) • **79**

CLOS TRIGUEDINA

Cahors 1983 • $11 • (02/28/91) • **80**
Cahors Prince Probus 1985 • $17 • (02/28/91) • **82**
Cahors Prince Probus 1983 • $14 • (12/31/88) • **79**

CLOSEL, DOMAINE DU

Savennières Cuvée Spéciale 1993: This clean white is soft and appealing, with peach and apple flavors and accents of citrus and beeswax, giving an impression of sweet fruit on the palate but finishing crisp. • $17 • **83**
Savennières Cuvée Spéciale 1992: Imagine an apple tart glazed with honey and lemon. This wine has the same richness and intensity of flavor, but it's still tight and young. It's concentrated, balanced and long, with a trace of sweetness to balance the firm acidity, and a long beeswax and honey finish. 2,600 cases made. • $14 • (08/31/94) • **92**

CLOTTE, CHÂTEAU LA

St.-Emilion 1985 • $27 • (05/15/88) • **87**
St.-Emilion 1983 • $12 • (05/16/86) • **68**

CLUSEL, DOMAINE

Côte-Rôtie 1988 • $36 • (11/15/91) • **87**

CLUSEL, GILBERT

Côte-Rôtie La Vialliere 1986 • $23 • (04/15/89) • **85**

CLUSEL ROCH, DOMAINE

Côte-Rôtie 1991: Lush and supple, with layers of ripe fruit, roasted meat and licorice, balanced with firm tannins. Drinkable now. • $40 • (05/31/94) • **85**
Côte-Rôtie 1990: Gorgeous berry, vanilla and spice aromas and flavors wind themselves around your palate as this smooth, generous wine opens up and shows what it has. Elegant, ripe, rich and subtle, this keeps pumping out the berry and chocolate flavors on the supple finish. Tempting now but should be at its best after 1997. 500 cases made. • $40 • (04/15/95) • **80**
Côte-Rôtie Les Grandes Places 1991: Rich and smooth yet firm, offering flavors of crushed berries, spice and game. A solid wine, try now. Tasted twice. • $50 • (05/31/94) • **90**
Côte-Rôtie Les Grandes Places 1990: Powerful for this vintage. It's reserved, but shows plummy, gamy, spicy flavors with full tannins. Built for aging, drink after 1996. • $50 • (05/31/94) • **91**

CLUSIERE, CHÂTEAU LA

St.-Emilion 1982 • $20 • (05/15/89) • **88**
St.-Emilion 1970 • $28 • (05/15/93) • **86**

COCHE-DURY, J.-F.

Auxey-Duresses Red 1987 • $30 • (02/28/90) • **87**
Bourgogne Pinot Noir 1987 • $25 • (02/28/90) • **79**
Corton-Charlemagne 1993: A blockbuster with the finesse to seduce the most demanding aficionados of top white Burgundy. Voluptuous, supple and intense as can be, this opulent crowd-pleaser delivers plenty of toasted oak, apple, citrus and mineral character. Brilliant winemaking at work here. Try in 2001. • $170 • (05/31/96) CS • **99**

Corton-Charlemagne 1992: Fabulous balance, showing rich, round and creamy texture, but it stays the course with racy acidity and elegance. Lots of depth and complexity, with honey, hazelnut, nectarine and smoke flavors. Drinkable now. • $170 • (08/31/94) • **93**

Meursault 1993: Seductive white Burgundy, balanced, intense and full-bodied. Youthful-tasting, as tons of toasted oak, tropical fruit and grapefruit flavors go on and on. Try in 1999. • $45 • (05/31/96) • **93**

Meursault 1992: Full-blown, flavorful and aromatic, with a rich texture, lots of honey accents and a lingering finish. Has a beautifully complex aroma of butter, toasted almonds and dried apricots. Try now. • $NA • (08/31/94) • **90**

Meursault 1987 • $30 • (02/28/90) • **80**

Meursault Les Perrières 1993: Iron fist in a velvet glove, this powerful white caresses the palate despite its amazing fruit intensity. Silky and concentrated citrus, toasted bread and mineral complexity. Full in body, the finish keeps pounding it on. Try in 2000. • $80 • (05/31/96) • **95**

Meursault Les Perrières 1992: Complex, lovely, silky texture. It's a bit earthy, but also honey-flavored and ripe. Excellent backbone and a classy, racy finish. Don't touch until 1997. • $83 • **93**

Meursault Les Rougeots 1993: Well crafted, intense and balanced, full in body, pumping out citrus, toasted oak, butter, honey and wet stone flavors in great intensity. Thick and fresh, very long on the slightly earthy finish. Drinkable now. • $60 • (05/31/96) • **92**

Meursault Les Rougeots 1992: A big wine, chewy yet polished, providing tons of butter, butterscotch, mineral, honey and chalk flavors and an earthy touch on the finish. The texture is smooth and silky. Try after 1998. • $NA • **93**

Meursault Les Rougeots 1991 • $52 • (10/15/93) • **91**

COFFINET, FERNAND

Chassagne-Montrachet 1991: Extremely toasty, buttery aromas aren't backed up by much fruit flavor in this stylish but underachieving Chardonnay. The flavors are a bit dull, lacks harmony, at least at this age. • $27 • (07/31/94) • **83**

COING DE ST.-FIACRE, CHÂTEAU DU

Muscadet de Sèvre et Maine Sur Lie 1993: Ripe, full flavors move from apple to melon and pear. It's generous, round on the palate and long in the finish. Though plenty crisp for food, it isn't dominated by acidity. • $8 • (08/31/94) BB • **85**

COLIN, MADAME FRANCOIS

Puligny-Montrachet Les Demoiselles 1993: Well-defined and ripe, exhibiting a beam of green apple, herb and citrus character and classy finish. Better after 1997. • $NA • **89**

COLIN, MARC

Chassagne-Montrachet 1994: A bit lean, but hinting at mint, butter, earth and cedar. Light- to medium-bodied, adding some richness on the ginger-flavored finish. • $35 • (05/31/96) 84 • **84**

Chassagne-Montrachet 1993: A very clean white demonstrating freshly cut apple, light honey and spice character, medium-to-light body and crisp acidity. Drinkable now. • $32 • **82**

Chassagne-Montrachet 1992: Big and rangy, buttery in aroma, full of pear and orange flavors and backed by firm acidity. Very lively and straightforward. 210 cases made. • $20 • (08/31/94) • **84**

Chassagne-Montrachet Les Ancégnières 1991 • $30 • (10/15/93) • **86**

Chassagne-Montrachet Les Caillerets 1994: Balanced, delicious, supple hazelnut, caramel and spice character. Shows some sparks, medium body and a lemony finish. Drinkable now. • $45 • (05/31/96) • **85**

Chassagne-Montrachet Les Caillerets 1993: A rich and buttery Chassagne, showing pedigreed, complex intensity from the dried-herb, honey and mineral notes. Long finish. Drinkable now. • $40 • **87**

Key: SS—Spectator Selection. CS—Cellar Selection. BB—Best Buy. $NA—Price not available. (BT)—Barrel tasting. Ⓐ—Auction Price.
Dates in parentheses represent the issues in which the ratings were published.

Chassagne-Montrachet Les Caillerets 1992: Closed, tight and young, but underneath are great characteristics of lemon, pear, vanilla and spice that begin to open up on the finish. Drinkable now. • $32 • (08/31/94) • **86**

Chassagne-Montrachet Les Caillerets 1991 • $38 • (10/15/93) • **86**

Chassagne-Montrachet Les Champs Gain 1994: Straightforward and a touch green, of medium body and intensity, offering some dried herb, lemon and apple flavors. Try now through 1998. • $40 • (05/31/96) • **85**

Chassagne-Montrachet Les Champs-Gains 1993: Lean, decent honey, green apple and chalk character, medium body and steely finish. • $40 • **84**

Chassagne-Montrachet Les Champs-Gains 1991 • $38 • (10/15/93) • **85**

Chassagne-Montrachet Vide Bourse 1994: Vibrant and lively honey, lemon, cream, mineral, spice and pie crust character. Of medium body, this *premier cru* is well structured and elegant, showing enough concentration to warrant aging until 1999. • $38 • (05/31/96) 90 • **90**

Montrachet 1994: A blockbuster with satiny mouth-feel, this full-bodied, full-throttled white Burgundy is a class act. Rich and thick, backed by toasted hazelnut, mineral, cedar, ripe fruit and long, restrained, citrus-spiked finish. Try in 2001. 2,916 cases made. • $200 • (05/31/96) • **96**

Montrachet 1993: Masses of fruit, tasting of lime, pineapple and honey as well as freshly crushed grapes. Medium-to-full body and a long, long finish. Better after 1996. • $200 • **90**

Montrachet 1991 • $150 • (10/15/93) • **89**

Puligny-Montrachet La Garenne 1994: Tight and a bit hard now, medium-bodied, featuring some pear, floral and butterscotch flavors. Seems somewhat short and lacking in fruit. • $45 • (05/31/96) • **83**

Puligny-Montrachet Le Trézin 1994: Hard, unyielding and showing nothing on the nose right now, but on the palate are mineral, vanilla, cream and ripe pear flavors that are delightful. Try in 1999. • $40 • (05/31/96) • **85**

Puligny-Montrachet Le Trézin 1993: Sleek, clean mineral and honey character, medium-to-light bodied, adding crisp acidity. • $38 • **84**

Puligny-Montrachet Le Trézin 1991 • $35 • (10/15/93) • **84**

Puligny-Montrachet Les Garennes 1993: Bubbling with freshly crushed grape character. Medium body and medium richness, apple and cream notes on the finish. • $42 • **85**

Puligny-Montrachet Les Garennes 1991 • $40 • (10/15/93) • **86**

St.-Aubin En Remilly White 1994: Lean and very tart, showing modest apple cider flavors and a short finish. • $24 • (05/31/96) 73 • **73**

St.-Aubin En Remilly White 1993: Surprisingly smooth, ripe and velvety, butterscotch and toast flavors mingling with lime, chalk and citrus notes. Tight, try after 1996. • $23 • **83**

St.-Aubin En Remilly White 1992: Interesting, but the smoky, earthy flavors dominate the modest apple and pear notes, for fans of a funky style. 410 cases made. • $14 • (08/31/94) • **80**

St.-Aubin En Remilly White 1991 • $30 • (10/15/93) • **86**

St.-Aubin La Chatenière White 1994: Tart and slightly paperish, as a cardboard taste takes away from whatever else might be in this *premier cru*, including its mineral, apple character. • $24 • (05/31/96) • **76**

St.-Aubin La Chatenière White 1993: Grassy style, but what's there shows finesse and class, sweet pea, green apple and lime flavors. A bit too tart and austere on the finish. • $24 • **83**

St.-Aubin La Chatenière White 1991 • $30 • (10/15/93) • **82**

St.-Aubin Le Charmois 1994: Soft, supple and pleasant *premier cru*, showing apricot, honey, apple and pear flavors, medium body and intensity and a touch of citrus keeping the finish alive. Drinkable now or hold until 1997. • $24 • (05/31/96) • **85**

St.-Aubin Les Combes White 1991 • $30 • (10/15/93) • **85**

St.-Aubin Les Cortons White 1994: Powerful but ungenerous. Somewhat too cedary and of medium body, it offers nice citrus, apple and honey flavors. Tough as nails on the finish. A good choice with seafood. • $24 • (05/31/96) • **85**

St.-Aubin Les Cortons White 1993: Pretty, approachable toasted oak, vanilla and pear character and a medium, slightly acidic finish. Drink now. • $24 • **81**

St.-Aubin Les Cortons White 1991 • $30 • (10/15/93) • **84**

COLIN, PIERRE

Bâtard-Montrachet 1994: Understated greatness. Very sharply focused and tightly wound. Give it time to fully deliver its mineral, stony, flinty, vanilla flavors. Super elegance. Very austere, but what pleasure in store for the patient collector! Try after 2000. • $NA • (05/31/96) • **94**

Bâtard-Montrachet 1993: Impressive mineral, spice and citric character. Medium-bodied and superfresh, crisp, tart finish. • $120 • **86**

Bâtard-Montrachet 1992: A real class act. It's generous and toasty in aroma, rich in flavor, expertly balanced and long on the finish. The pear, honey, vanilla and hazelnut flavors are vivid but blend subtly and gracefully for an overall effect of harmony. Drinkable now. • $50 • (08/31/94) • **95**

Bâtard-Montrachet 1991 • $90 • (10/15/93) • **90**

COLIN-DELEGER, MICHEL

Chassagne-Montrachet 1993: Fresh, simple apple and honey aromas and flavors. Medium in body, some chalky character, rather short on the finish. • $NA • **83**

Chassagne-Montrachet 1991 • $30 • (10/15/93) • **86**

Chassagne-Montrachet En Remilly 1994: Seductive and charming, boasting tons of ripe pear and apple flavors. Rich honey, cream and dried herb complexity. Voluptuous mouth-feel and amazing silkiness. Needs time, try in 1999. 408 cases made. • $40 • (05/31/96) • **93**

Chassagne-Montrachet En Remilly 1991 • $36 • (10/15/93) • **87**

Chassagne-Montrachet La Maltroie 1993: Well-balanced, pretty pear, pineapple and nut flavors, silky texture. Rounder than most. Try now. • $44 • **84**

Chassagne-Montrachet La Maltroie 1991 • $36 • (10/15/93) • **88**

Chassagne-Montrachet Les Chaumées 1994: Toasty, round, supple, ripe fig, melon and pear character. Would rate higher if it wasn't for a somewhat hollow mid-palate. Drinkable now. 783 cases made. • $40 • (05/31/96) • **83**

Chassagne-Montrachet Les Chaumées 1992: Beautifully made, balanced and harmonious, showing some pretty, ripe honey, apple and pear flavors, it's got a lot going for it. • $45 • (08/31/94) • **87**

Chassagne-Montrachet Les Chaumées 1991 • $36 • (10/15/93) • **84**

Chassagne-Montrachet Les Chenevottes 1994: Lovely elegance in this full- to medium-bodied white Burgundy. Melts in the mouth with silky mineral, vanilla, cream, pear and tropical fruit character. Very subtle finish. Drinkable now. 570 cases made. • $45 • (05/31/96) 90 • **89**

Chassagne-Montrachet Les Chenevottes 1993: Focused and a bit green, apple mingling with asparagus flavors, slightly diluted finish. • $42 • **83**

Chassagne-Montrachet Les Chenevottes 1992: An expressive, balanced and medium-bodied white, with plenty of toasty, buttery and pear flavors backed by some mouth-puckering, lemon character that kicks in on the intense finish. • $36 • (08/31/94) • **88**

Chassagne-Montrachet Les Chenevottes 1991 • $36 • (10/15/93) • **86**

Chassagne-Montrachet Les Vergers 1994: Round, supple and flavorful, there is an interesting piney, resinous character mingling with the honey and pear notes. A bit tart on the finish now. Might be better in 1998. 708 cases made. • $40 • (05/31/96) • **84**

Chassagne-Montrachet Les Vergers 1993: Fresh apple and cream flavors show a hint of mineral. Medium in body and lightly buttery, appley, coconut finish. Drink now. • $44 • **85**

Chassagne-Montrachet Les Vergers 1992: Good intensity, rather chewy, showing some lime, vanilla and butter notes backed with vibrant pineapple flavors. Lively and smooth, yet crisp, medium-bodied. • $40 • (08/31/94) • **86**

Chassagne-Montrachet Les Vergers 1991 • $36 • (10/15/93) • **88**

Chassagne-Montrachet Morgeot 1994: Totally voluptuous and enchanting, oozing honey, ripe apricot and pear. Full in body and seductive. Drinkable now and into 1998. 583 cases made. • $40 • (05/31/96) 88 • **88**

Chassagne-Montrachet Morgeot 1993: Beautiful and subtle, focused apple, mineral and chalk flavors and the class you expect from fine white Burgundy. Should be better after 1997. • $44 • **89**

Chassagne-Montrachet Morgeot 1991 • $36 • (10/15/93) • **86**

Chevalier-Montrachet 1993: Good concentration, displaying pineapple and vanilla character, medium body, plenty of fruit and well-integrated acidity. Try after 1996. • $NA • **88**

St.-Aubin En Charmois White 1993: A touch of mineral and lime and round texture make for appealing drinking in this well-made and focused white, but it's austere and short on the finish. • $24 • **80**

St.-Aubin Les Combes White 1993: Quite ripe, complex, lush and focused, showing lovely honey, floral, mineral and herb flavors. Tight now, but potential to improve through 1997. • $NA • **87**

COLLECTION FOLLE EPOQUE

Bordeaux Supérieur 1989 • $9 • (11/30/92) • **75**

COLLET, JEAN

Chablis 1994: Loads of apple, apricot and cream character. Medium body, fresh, ripe acidity and a delicious finish. • $NA • **85**

Chablis Mont de Milieu 1994: Perfumed and easy, a bit simple and staightforward. Slightly harsh and drying on the finish. Drinkable now. • $25 • (05/31/96) • **75**

Chablis Montée de Tonnerre 1994: Overly oaked. Somewhat rustic and odd-tasting in its caramel, butterscotch and crème brûlée flavors. Drinkable now. • $NA • (05/31/96) • **76**

Chablis Montée de Tonnerre 1993: Firm with a good amount of oak, quite tart and crisp. Fruit salad, candied, grapefruit and minty notes. Tart finish. • $NA • **82**

Chablis Montmains 1994: Very intense *premier cru*, tight and mouth-puckering, offering limelike flavors, full body, good concentration and tons of dried herb, honey, wet earth and mineral character that give it silkiness. Cellar until at least 2000. • $20 • (05/31/96) • **85**

Chablis Montmains 1993: Blanched almond, apple and lemon character, medium body, fresh acidity and a white pepper finish. • $NA • **84**

Chablis Vaillons 1994: Fresh, vibrant and lively, a light-bodied premier cru sporting lovely, grassy notes reminisicent of crisp Sauvignon Blanc. Balanced finish. Drinkable now. • $20 • (05/31/96) • **81**

Chablis Vaillons 1993: Very unusual and distinctive, showing ripe character as grass and honey flavors mingle attractively. A white you won't get tired of drinking. • $NA • **85**

Chablis Valmur 1994: Ripe and rich honey, wet earth and lemon character. Quite chewy and chalky, full-bodied, presenting plenty of personality but lacking a bit of finesse. Try in 1998. • $50 • (05/31/96) • **87**

Chablis Valmur 1993: Attractive honey, grapefruit, butterscotch and lemon flavors. Medium body, crisp acidity and a long, long finish. • $NA • **85**

COLLIN & BOURISSET

Pouilly-Fuissé Domaine Tranchand 1994: Quite a nice mouth-feel in this one, showing complex mineral and wet earth components that kick in on the finish and compensate for the lack of intense fruit. Drinkable now. 666 cases made. • $16 • (05/31/96) • **84**

COLOMBETTE, DOMAINE LA

Chardonnay Vin de Pays d'Oc 1991 • $8 • (03/15/94) • **85**

Sauvignon Blanc Vin de Pays des Coteaux du Libron 1992 • $8 • (03/15/94) • **85**

Sauvignon Blanc Vin de Pays des Coteaux du Libron 1991 • $7 • (08/31/93) • **81**

COLOMBIER, DOMAINE DU

Crozes-Hermitage 1992 • $12 • (05/31/94) • **76**

Crozes-Hermitage Cuvée Gaby 1992 • $15 • (05/31/94) • **80**

Hermitage 1991: Pretty, and accessible for Hermitage, with berry and coffee notes and supple tannins. Balanced, but lacks concentration, drinkable now. • $28 • (05/31/94) • **83**

COLOMBIER-MONPELOU, CHÂTEAU

Pauillac 1988 • $15 • (10/31/91) • **75**

COLOMBO, JEAN-LUC

Cornas Les Ruchets 1991 • $35 • (05/31/94) • **82**

Cornas Les Ruchets 1989 • $45 • (11/15/91) • **89**

Cornas Les Ruchets 1988 • $45 • (10/15/91) • **87**

Cornas Les Ruchets 1987 • $45 • (11/15/91) • **75**

Cornas Terres Brûlées 1992: Round, fresh, nicely interwoven flavors of plum, game, smoke and pepper, concentrated but not hard, and a long, fruity finish. Well made, boasting sophistication and panache. Drink now. • $30 • **89**

Côtes du Rhône 1993: Large, appealing, full of ripe plum and berry notes and a smoky element. Fairly rich leather and barnyard aromas and flavors, as well as some green olive on the finish. • $13 • (09/30/95) • **86**

Côtes du Rhône 100% Syrah 1993: Lively, fruity aromas and flavors, nice leathery and spicy notes are interwoven with ripe plum and cherry flavors. Drinkable now, but there's no rush. • $18 • (09/30/95) • **86**

Les Collines de Laure Vin de Table Français 1993: Peppery, vegetal and lean-tasting, simple and already mature. Tasted twice, with consistent notes. • $18 • (12/31/95) • **76**

COMBE DES DAMES, LA

Bordeaux 1985 • $6 • (03/15/88) • **74**

COMBE, PIERRE

Côtes du Rhône-Villages Domaine des Richards 1990 • $7 • (10/15/91) BB • **89**

Côtes du Rhône-Villages Domaine des Richards 1987 • $4 • (01/31/89) • **78**

Vacqueyras Domaine des Richards 1989 • $9 • (10/15/91) • **86**

COMBIER, DOMAINE

Crozes-Hermitage 1992: Big and hearty, scented with herbs and pepper, flavored with beef, tomato and ripe plum notes that thin out on the finish. Moderately tannic, but easy to drink now. • $14 • (10/15/94) • **85**

Crozes-Hermitage 1991 • $17 • (05/31/94) • **86**

Crozes-Hermitage Clos des Grives 1992: A velvety, new-oak flavor smooths the rough edges in this intense, full-bodied red. Peppery, roasted and ripe raspberry flavors well up and linger on the finish. Drinkable now through 1998. 400 cases made. • $20 • (10/15/94) • **87**

Crozes-Hermitage Clos des Grives 1991 • $25 • (05/31/94) • **84**

Crozes-Hermitage Clos des Grives 1990 • $20 • (04/15/93) • **92**

COMMANDERIE DU BONTEMPS

Bordeaux 1961: An extremely rare bottle, blended from top growths of the Médoc and Graves, though the sum seems less than the parts. It has intriguing, complex aromas, rather lean but solid fruit flavors and good length. Drink now. • $NA • (04/30/96) • **85**

COMMANDERIE, CHÂTEAU LA

Pomerol 1995: Solid, chunky, featuring firm and rich tannins, loads of berry, cherry flavor and long finish. • $NA • (05/15/96) • **85-89** (BT)

Pomerol 1991: Herbal and fruity, but rather watery. Tasted twice with consistent notes. • $15 • (03/31/94) • **72**

St.-Emilion 1994: A bit hard but some attractive berry, mineral aromas and flavors. Medium bodied with medium tannins and a fresh finish. • $NA • **80**

St.-Emilion 1993: Elegant and quite firm, offering a decent core of plum, red berry, tobacco, cedar and chocolate notes. Of medium body, it's a bit one-dimensional. Drinkable now. • $15 • (01/31/96) • **83**

St.-Emilion 1989 • $19 • (03/15/92) • **92**

St.-Emilion 1988 • $15 • (10/31/91) • **79**

St.-Emilion 1983 • $11 • (01/01/86) • **79**

CONFRERIES, CHÂTEAU LES

Bordeaux 1985 • $3 • (02/15/88) • **75**

Key: SS—Spectator Selection. CS—Cellar Selection. BB—Best Buy. $NA—Price not available. (BT)—Barrel tasting. Ⓐ—Auction Price.
Dates in parentheses represent the issues in which the ratings were published.

CONFURON, JEAN-JACQUES

Chambolle-Musigny 1989 • $35 • (11/30/92) • **81**

Chambolle-Musigny Premier Cru 1991: Light in texture but ripe in flavor, showing floral, prune and currant aromas and flavors, finishing firm and crisp, almost with a lime edge. Drinkable now. • $37 Ⓐ • (01/31/94) • **86**

Chambolle-Musigny Premier Cru EP 1993: Amazing quality for a *premier cru*. Subtle, complex red with great reservation. Full in body, offering chocolate, mineral and berry character, full tannins and long finish. Superb. Try after 2000. 15 cases made. • $60 • **94**

Clos Vougeot Red 1993: Tough now, a wine with a future. Dried cherry and dried herb flavors, medium to full body, firm tannins and a long, spicy, tannic finish. Better in 2000. • $85 • **90**

Clos Vougeot Red 1991: Displays a firm texture, a moderate level of anise-scented raspberry flavor and a bit of chewiness on the finish. Drinkable now. • $60 Ⓐ • (01/31/94) • **85**

Côte de Nuits-Villages Les Vignottes 1989 • $16 • (11/30/92) • **84**

Nuits-St.-Georges Aux Boudots 1989 • $32 • (11/30/92) • **81**

Nuits-St.-Georges Les Chaboeufs 1993: Firm and hard at this stage, medium-bodied, a mineral, earthy character blanketing the pretty currant and black cherry notes. Needs time, try in 1999. • $60 • **89**

Nuits-St.-Georges Les Chaboeufs 1989 • $32 • (11/30/92) • **83**

Nuits-St.-Georges Les Fleurières 1989 • $26 • (11/30/92) • **69**

Nuits-St.-Georges Les Fleurières LD 1993: A well-made, fresh, medium-bodied Nuits, sporting enticing plum, currant, toast and spice character. Loads of tannins clamp down on the finish, so give it until 2000. • $45 • **90**

Romanée-St.-Vivant 1993: Not as big as expected from this grand cru, but impressive. Very fresh citrus, berry and plum aromas and flavors, medium body and fine tannins. Better in 1999. • $150 • **89**

Romanée-St.-Vivant 1989 • $113 • (10/31/92) • **90**

Vosne-Romanée Les Beaux Monts 1993: Smelling this is like walking into a flower shop. Better than his Romanée-St.-Vivant. Lovely perfumes and fabulous concentration of fruit, adding loads of tannins and an ultralong, fruity finish. Superb potential. Better after 2000. • $63 • **94**

CONFURON-COTETIDOT, J.

Chambolle-Musigny 1993: Very flavorful, quite thick and rich, chunky texture. Lots of coffee, smoke, cassis and pepper notes and a chewy finish. Slightly rustic village wine. Try in 2000. • $NA • **88**

Chambolle-Musigny 1992: Light but smooth and supple, with an herbal edge to the modest berry notes. Finishes with a little more flavor than most 1992 Chambolles. • $38 • **83**

Chambolle-Musigny 1991: Simple and coarse, fruity enough to be pleasant, but has little Pinot or Chambolle character. • $41 Ⓐ • (01/31/94) • **74**

Chambolle-Musigny 1989 • $32 • (11/30/92) • **89**

Clos de Vougeot 1993: Very smoky, almost meaty, showing loads of berry, cassis and ripe fruit character, medium to full body, loads of velvety tannins and a long finish. Delicious now, but better in 2000. • $NA • **89**

Clos de Vougeot 1991: Supple and generous, this elegant wine features spicy, toasty chocolate, black cherry and blackberry aromas and flavors. Finishes smooth and delicate, echoing fruit and spice. Drinkable now. • $65 Ⓐ • (01/31/94) • **86**

Clos de Vougeot 1989 • $60 • (09/15/92) • **91**

Echézeaux 1993: Disappointing wine from this producer. Rather earthy and raisiny and a slightly watery finish. Disjointed. Drinkable now. • $NA • **81**

Echézeaux 1991: Looks and feels tired already, offers more gamy, toasty aromas and flavors than fruit. • $65 Ⓐ • (01/31/94) • **79**

Echézeaux 1990: A hard wine that needs time, but the texture and concentration are superb enough to provide a seductive, round mouth-feel. Has subdued raspberry and vanilla flavors and a long finish. Try in 1998. • $65 • (12/15/92) • **91**

Echézeaux 1989 • $1 Ⓐ • (10/31/92) • **83**

Gevrey-Chambertin 1993: Deep-colored village wine, sporting pure cassis and black currant flavors. Sweet-tasting, as a wet earth component adds complexity. Don't expect showy opulence, just a beam of crisp, youthful, well-defined fruit. • $NA • (05/15/96) • **94**

Nuits-St.-Georges 1993: Excellent village wine that bursts with vibrant cassis and currant flavors and a toasty, if slightly tart, finish. This medium-bodied Burgundy will be pretty but not showy in aging. Try around 2000. • $NA • **89**
Nuits-St.-Georges 1992: Unusual for its aromas that are difficult to describe. Has a cinnamon-scented, red berry character, with some spice notes and a tart, crisp finish. Appealing and drinkable now. • $38 • **84**
Nuits-St.-Georges Premier Cru 1993: Super personality, bursting with bright cassis and Syrahlike flavors. Very peppery, medium to full body, long, delicious finish. Try in 2000. • $NA • **89**
Nuits-St.-Georges Premier Cru 1991: Light and airy, showing pleasant currant and vanilla aromas and flavors. Drinkable now. • $47 Ⓐ • (01/31/94) • **77**
Nuits-St.-Georges Premier Cru 1990: Has a wonderful mouth-feel, with velvety tannins and concentrated, beautiful ripe plum and tobacco characteristics. Drinkable now. • $28 • (12/15/92) • **91**
Vosne-Romanée 1993: What happened here? Rather light and weedy showing some fruit cassis flavors, but medium-bodied at best and a weedy finish. Not very exciting. • $NA • **80**
Vosne-Romanée 1992: Sharp and tart, with floral, gamy, peppery notes that give it some character. Ends a bit short. • $34 • **78**
Vosne-Romanée 1990: Big and bulky, with loads of fruit and tannins. An impressive wine, but lacks a bit of finesse. Drinkable now. • $30 • (12/15/92) • **84**
Vosne-Romanée 1989 • $27 • (10/31/92) • **89**
Vosne-Romanée Les Suchots 1993: A middle-of-the-road '93, delivering some decent mocha, red berry and smoke flavors. Lacks a bit of depth and complexity. Quite crisp on the finish. Try it in 1999. • $NA • **84**
Vosne-Romanée Les Suchots 1991: A crisp, toasty, austere wine that features an anise tinge to the basic black cherry aromas and flavors. Turns herbal on the finish. Drinkable now. • $NA • (01/31/94) • **81**
Vosne-Romanée Les Suchots 1990: This light-textured Vosne is pleasant, offering modest cherry and strawberry flavors, but has a rather short finish. Sweet in flavor and round, but shows odd stewed tomato notes. Drinkable now. • $44 • (12/15/92) • **83**

CONSEILLANTE, CHÂTEAU LA

Pomerol 1995: Pretty, medium-bodied '95, with a sweet, ripe and supple character. Nice red berry, cedar and tobacco flavors, but lacks a bit of complexity and depth. • $NA • (05/15/96) • **85-89** (BT)
Pomerol 1994: Some decent berry and vanilla aromas and flavors. A bit one-dimensional. • $60 • (05/15/96) • **80-84** (BT)
Pomerol 1992: This entry has always been disappointing. Very light and fresh, diluted, offering floral and strawberry aromas and flavors. Tasted twice, with consistent notes. Drink now. • $35 • **77**
Pomerol 1990: Pure fruit in this wine shows the true personality of the estate. Enticing aromas of nutmeg, cinnamon and fruit give way to rich, silky tannins. Drink after 1997. 5,000 cases made. • $110 Ⓐ • (03/31/93) • **94**
Pomerol 1989 • $96 Ⓐ • (03/15/92) • **92**
Pomerol 1988 • $48 • (03/31/91) • **90**
Pomerol 1987 • $35 • (05/15/90) • **86**
Pomerol 1986 • $59 • (06/15/89) • **93**
Pomerol 1985 • $54 Ⓐ • (02/29/88) • **93**
Pomerol 1984 • $26 • (03/31/87) • **93**
Pomerol 1983 • $38 Ⓐ • (11/15/86) • **84**
Pomerol 1982 • $120 Ⓐ • (08/31/92) • **87**
Pomerol 1981: Good mature red garnet color with meaty, berry, earthy aromas and flavors. Still rather fresh with a firm backbone of tannins and lovely chocolate, earthy flavors. Drink now. • $50 • **88**
Pomerol 1970 • $54 Ⓐ • (05/15/93) • **94**
Pomerol 1962 • $55 • (11/30/87) • **60**
Pomerol 1961: Has all the right components of a nicely mature Bordeaux: complex aromas, rich and mouth-filling fruit flavors and texture that's still firm. Drink now through 2002. • $114 • (04/30/96) • **87**
Pomerol 1959 • $150 • (10/15/90) • **88**
Pomerol 1945: Vibrant berry, spice and lemon notes leap from this delicate Pomerol, becoming more powerful as it hits the finish. Sound and complex, adding lovely earthy overtones. • $650 • **88**

CORBILLIERES, DOMAINE DES

Touraine Sauvignon 1992 • $8 • (09/15/93) • **82**

CORBIN, CHÂTEAU

St.-Emilion 1986 • $15 • (06/30/89) • **88**
St.-Emilion 1985 • $15 • (05/31/88) • **86**

CORBIN-MICHOTTE, CHÂTEAU

St.-Emilion 1995: Lovely soft wine with an abundance of cherry, berry and vanilla aromas and flavors. Medium body and velvety tannins on the finish. Harmonious. • $NA • (05/15/96) • **85-89** (BT)
St.-Emilion 1988 • $15 • (07/15/91) • **72**
St.-Emilion 1961: Tastes delicious and easygoing, with spicy, toasty aromas, a smooth, supple texture and attractive fruit. Very pleasant to drink now through 2000. • $NA • (04/30/96) • **86**

CORCIA

Chambolle-Musigny 1992: Delicate with very pretty raspberry and spicy oak flavors on a frame that remains smooth and silky through the finish. Just a touch of tannin on the aftertaste. • $22 • **83**
Clos de Vougeot 1992: Plummier than most, with a nice beam of currant and spice pushing through the firm tannins. Has richness, smokiness and style, then finishes a little short. Best from 1998. • $42 • **88**
Nuits-St.-Georges 1992: Lean and a little spicy, with modest berry and currant flavors that narrow down on the finish. • $22 • **79**
Vosne-Romanée 1992: Tough and chewy but finishing with enough finesse to be worth cellaring until 1997. Leathery in both texture and flavor, it only hints at currant on the finish. • $26 • **80**

CORDEILLAN-BAGES, CHÂTEAU

Pauillac 1995: Another elegant, seductive '95. Rich, ripe and balanced, with lovely red- and blackberry character backed by supple, sweet tannins and spicy, slightly smoky flavors. • $NA • (05/15/96) • **90-94** (BT)
Pauillac 1994: More concentrated than the '93 but coarser. Black cherry, tobacco and slightly green character, medium body, medium velvety tannins and dry finish. Tasted twice, with consistent notes. • $NA • **80-84** (BT)
Pauillac 1992: Holds together beautifully on the palate, displaying plum, chocolate and light tobacco character, medium body and finish and medium, velvety tannins. Drinkable now. • $18 • **85**
Pauillac 1991: Very nicely crafted. It has the character of tobacco, smoke and bitter chocolate, with medium body. Firm but slightly astringent on finish. • $16 • (03/31/94) • **83**
Pauillac 1990: A deep, dark giant, with smoky, cassis aromas and flavors and tons of fruit and tannins. Doesn't show much now but it's all there. Drinkable in 2000. 900 cases made. • $33 • (03/31/93) • **95**
Pauillac 1989 • $24 • (03/15/92) • **96**

CORDIER PERE & FILS

Pouilly-Fuissé Les Vignes Blanches 1994: Lots of character here, well made and smooth. Plenty of buttery, baked apple pie and herb flavors and a hint of toasty aromas. Balanced finish. Worth seeking out and cellaring until 1998. 500 cases made. • $34 • (05/31/96) • **87**
Pouilly-Fuissé Les Vignes Blanches 1993: Charming, ripe, seductively crisp pear, mango, apricot and pineapple flavors stay focused on the supple, chalky finish. 500 cases made. • $22 • **87**
Pouilly-Fuissé Lot No.1 1994: Serious Pouilly here. Focused and well constructed, showing earth, mineral, spice, fig and honey complexity. Good fruit intensity and finishing with smooth finesse. Buy a case and enjoy! 833 cases made. • $21 • (05/31/96) • **88**
Pouilly-Fuissé Lot No. 1 1993: Excellent concentration of fruit, medium-bodied, flavorful. Ripe pear, apple, honey and mineral notes turn to a lovely, fresh lime finish. Drinkable now. 833 cases made. • $19 • **87**
Pouilly-Fuissé Lot No. 2 1994: Intensely crisp, citrusy and quite lean. Somewhat herbal, offering a touch of honey. Slightly one-dimensional. Should do well with shellfish. 1,666 cases made. • $21 • (05/31/96) • **82**

FRANCE

Pouilly-Fuissé Lot No. 2 1993: Super-intense, crisp and tart. Ripe yet vibrant palate showing pear, apple, honey and tropical fruit flavors. Medium-bodied, try after 1996. 500 cases made. • $19 • **86**

Pouilly-Fuissé Vieilles Vignes 1994: Crisp, sharp and tart, in an uncompromisingly citrusy style. For those who love intense Chardonnay, sporting herbal and oregano flavors. Not for everyone, but delightful with mussels or oysters. 500 cases made. • $30 • (05/31/96) • **84**

Pouilly-Fuissé Vieilles Vignes 1993: Clean, crisp pear, green apple skin and honey flavors unfold almost sweetly on the finish. Medium in body. Try with seafood. 500 cases made. • $22 • **85**

CORDIER, JEAN

Rouge NV • $3 • (12/31/90) • **75**

CORMEIL-FIGEAC, CHÂTEAU

St.-Emilion 1988 • $20 • (04/30/91) • **85**
St.-Emilion 1986 • $12 • (06/30/89) • **75**

CORNEAU, DOMAINE PAUL

Pouilly-Fumé Les Foltières 1992: Light pear and melon notes are pleasant, on the whole the wine is earthy and diluted, finishing with tired vegetal flavors. • $12 • (10/31/94) • **77**

CORNU, EDMOND

Aloxe-Corton 1991 • $24 Ⓐ • (01/31/94) • **78**
Aloxe-Corton Les Moutottes 1987 • $35 • (12/31/90) • **83**
Bourgogne 1990 • $15 • (12/15/92) • **85**

Chorey-lès-Beaune Les Bons Ores 1993: Crisp, odd, earthy, herbal character. May be at a strange phase now, only to improve later. Still quite lean and lacking some fruit. Try in 1997. 583 cases made. • $20 • **81**

Chorey-lès-Beaune Les Bons Ores 1992: Aromatic and attractive, with a minty, velvety currant character, good color and medium body. A pleasant, flavorful '92. Try now. 150 cases made. • $17 • **85**

Corton Bressandes 1993: Supple red of medium intensity and body, a bit closed now, but showing some pretty plum and red berry character. 183 cases made. • $57 • **87**

Corton Bressandes 1992: Lean and bright, with focused raspberry, spice and vanilla flavors that linger on the narrow finish. Try now. • $43 • **81**

Corton Bressandes 1991: Smooth, elegant and lovely, the beautifully defined black cherry and raspberry flavors are refined through the lithe finish. Best around 1998. 200 cases made. • $48 Ⓐ • (01/31/94) • **88**

Corton Bressandes 1990: A solid Corton, with smoky, earthy plum aromas and flavors and very firm tannins. A well-made wine to drink in 1997. 200 cases made. • $60 • (12/15/92) • **89**

Corton Bressandes 1987 • $53 • (12/31/90) • **90**

Ladoix 1993: Some sweet, pretty fruit character features light plum aromas and flavors, medium to light body, light tannins and a fresh finish. Drink now. 608 cases made. • $22 • **82**

Ladoix 1992: A pretty wine, with medium body, good fruit and a smooth finish. The raspberry and blackberry flavors are delicious. 38 cases made. • $18 • **80**

Ladoix 1991: Earth, anise and tar aromas and flavors turn tough and bitter on the finish. The fruit comes in to make it more appealing. Drinkable now. 583 cases made. • $18 Ⓐ • (01/31/94) • **81**

Ladoix 1987 • $18 • (02/28/91) • **78**

Ladoix Les Carrières 1993: A beauty, showing supple texture and delicious complexity of smoke, earth, plum and currant, medium body, well-integrated tannins and good power on the finish. Try in 1999. 375 cases made. • $27 • **89**

Ladoix Les Carrières 1992: Light but chewy, with the tannins and earthy-mineral notes more prominent than the prune flavor. Try now. 38 cases made. • $22 • **78**

Key: SS—Spectator Selection. CS—Cellar Selection. BB—Best Buy. $NA—Price not available. (BT)—Barrel tasting. Ⓐ—Auction Price.
Dates in parentheses represent the issues in which the ratings were published.

Ladoix Les Corvées 1992: Flavorful currant, raspberry and violet notes. Dark color, but relatively light texture. Attractively built. Drink now. 38 cases made. • $25 • **84**

Ladoix Les Corvées 1991: Light, smooth and simple, with appealing currant and cooked berry flavors. Drinkable now. 167 cases made. • $24 Ⓐ • (01/31/94) • **79**

Savigny-lès-Beaune 1993: Rather hard red does not give much on the palate of firm tannins and crisp acidity, but has some good fruit underneath. Medium-bodied, sweet fruit finish. Try in 1997. 375 cases made. • $22 • **85**

Savigny-lès-Beaune 1992: Light and simple, a modest level of black cherry and floral flavors giving it some class. Drinkable now. 50 cases made. • $18 • **81**

CORSIN

Mâcon-Villages 1994: Delicious, racy, well-defined lime, hay, butter and honey notes. Round yet vibrant, it sparks with life and a long finish. Drink now. • $12 • **86**

St.-Véran White 1994: Impressively structured, silky-textured, showing depth and complexity and super layers of mineral, wet hay, pear, spice and melon. Very smooth, almond-flavored finish. • $15 • **87**

St.-Véran White 1993: Youthful yet creamy-textured, with rich, buttery overtones. Provides some mineral notes on the somewhat astringent finish. • $NA • **83**

CORTENAY, JACQUES

Châteauneuf-du-Pape 1985 • $8 • (09/30/87) BB • **85**

COS-D'ESTOURNEL, CHÂTEAU

St.-Estèphe 1995: Extremely appealing and exotic, smelling of cassis bush. Vibrant and vivid, with a laser-sharp beam of ripe, red berry, vanilla, spice and earth flavors. Medium- to full-bodied, it reminds us a bit of Cos d'Estournel of the late '80s, with unctuous texture and a milky character. • $NA • (05/15/96) • **90-94** (BT)

St.-Estèphe 1994: Bold yet silky and extremely well made. A seductive, full-bodied beauty that's packed with well-defined red berry, plum and toast flavors. • $NA • **90-94** (BT)

St.-Estèphe 1993: Cos-d'Estournel never lets you down in a vintage. Pretty blackberry character hints of mocha and chocolate. Medium-bodied, adding velvety tannins and toasted oak finish. Drinkable now, but better in 1998. • $33 • (01/31/96) • **88**

St.-Estèphe 1992: Impressive for the vintage, displaying a wonderful silky texture and plenty of blackberry and tobacco character. Drinkable now. • $26 • **87**

St.-Estèphe 1991: One of the best wines of the vintage. Well focused, with lots of chunky fruit. The vanilla, tobacco and chocolate flavors go on and on. Delicious now. • $31 • (03/31/94) • **88**

St.-Estèphe 1990: Like eating chocolate mousse, this wine delivers loads of chocolate, cherry and berry flavors and soft, round tannins. The '89 was better. Drinkable now. 30,000 cases made. • $72 Ⓐ • (03/31/93) • **90**

St.-Estèphe 1989 • $46 Ⓐ • (03/15/92) • **95**
St.-Estèphe 1988 • $36 Ⓐ • (07/15/91) CS • **95**
St.-Estèphe 1987 • $23 • (05/15/90) • **81**
St.-Estèphe 1986 • $62 Ⓐ • (05/15/90) • **92**

St.-Estèphe 1985: Not giving much now but racy in style with dried cherry, tobacco character. Full bodied, full body, lots of silky tannins. Needs time still. Try after 1997. • $55 • **92**

St.-Estèphe 1984 • $22 • (05/15/90) • **81**

St.-Estèphe 1983: Dense and powerful with tobacco, cherry, vanilla aromas and flavors. Full bodied and very firm with a long finish. Needs time. Try after 1998. • $37 • (10/15/94) • **91**

St.-Estèphe 1982 • $112 Ⓐ • (08/31/92) • **93**

St.-Estèphe 1981: A big, chewy traditional styled wine. Dense red color with green tobacco, pruny, berry character. Full bodied and thick with a chewy slightly dry finish. Drink now. • $32 • (10/15/94) • **87**

St.-Estèphe 1980 • $33 • (05/15/90) • **83**
St.-Estèphe 1979 • $35 Ⓐ • (05/15/90) • **92**
St.-Estèphe 1978 • $38 Ⓐ • (05/15/90) • **93**

St.-Estèphe 1977 • $30 • (05/15/90) • **85**
St.-Estèphe 1976 • $43 • (05/15/90) • **84**
St.-Estèphe 1975 • $37 Ⓐ • (05/15/90) • **88**
St.-Estèphe 1973 • $31 • (05/15/90) • **82**
St.-Estèphe 1971 • $48 • (05/15/90) • **91**
St.-Estèphe 1970 • $51 Ⓐ • (05/15/93) • **85**
St.-Estèphe 1969 • $26 Ⓐ • (05/15/90) • **58**
St.-Estèphe 1967 • $22 Ⓐ • (05/15/90) • **82**
St.-Estèphe 1966 • $36 Ⓐ • (05/15/90) • **74**
St.-Estèphe 1964 • $65 • (05/15/90) • **84**
St.-Estèphe 1962 • $80 • (05/15/90) • **79**
St.-Estèphe 1961: Beautifully spicy, evolved aromas and layered flavors of fruit and cedar make this delicious to drink. Falls just short of outstanding. Has firm tannins and a lingering finish. Drink through 2002. • $173 • (04/30/96) • **89**
St.-Estèphe 1960 • $85 • (05/15/90) • **79**
St.-Estèphe 1959 • $230 • (10/15/90) • **90**
St.-Estèphe 1958 • $95 • (05/15/90) • **89**
St.-Estèphe 1956 • $60 • (05/15/90) • **79**
St.-Estèphe 1955 • $175 • (05/15/90) • **90**
St.-Estèphe 1954 • $80 • (05/15/90) • **81**
St.-Estèphe 1953 • $51 Ⓐ • (05/15/90) • **91**
St.-Estèphe 1952 • $90 • (05/15/90) • **95**
St.-Estèphe 1950 • $100 • (05/15/90) • **86**
St.-Estèphe 1949 • $195 Ⓐ • (05/15/90) • **80**
St.-Estèphe 1947 • $330 • (05/15/90) • **91**
St.-Estèphe 1945: Smells musty, drying finish. Possibly corky, but not pleasant anyway. • $400 • **67**
St.-Estèphe 1943 • $220 • (05/15/90) • **85**
St.-Estèphe 1942 • $110 • (05/15/90) • **78**
St.-Estèphe 1937 • $143 Ⓐ • (05/15/90) • **64**
St.-Estèphe 1934 • $150 • (05/15/90) • **88**
St.-Estèphe 1929 • $390 • (05/15/90) • **92**
St.-Estèphe 1928 • $341 Ⓐ • (05/15/90) • **90**
St.-Estèphe 1926 • $300 • (05/15/90) • **77**
St.-Estèphe 1924 • $300 • (05/15/90) • **82**
St.-Estèphe 1921 • $200 • (05/15/90) • **65**
St.-Estèphe 1920 • $350 • (05/15/90) • **93**
St.-Estèphe 1917 • $250 • (05/15/90) • **73**
St.-Estèphe 1905 • $250 • (05/15/90) • **65**
St.-Estèphe 1904 • $210 • (05/15/90) • **63**
St.-Estèphe 1899 • $700 • (05/15/90) • **87**
St.-Estèphe 1898 • $500 • (05/15/90) • **72**
St.-Estèphe 1890 • $330 • (05/15/90) • **69**
St.-Estèphe 1870 • $1.250 • (05/15/90) • **90**
St.-Estèphe 1869 • $1,250 • (05/15/90) • **82**

COS-LABORY, CHÂTEAU

St.-Estèphe 1995: Subtle, full-bodied '95, offering exuberant floral, cassis and spice flavors. While attractive, it lacks a bit of length on the finish. • $NA • (05/15/96) • **85-89** (BT)
St.-Estèphe 1994: Big, chewy and very tannic, full-bodied and dark-colored, with plum, black currant and spicy, toasted oak flavors. Drying on the finish, but time might smooth that out. • $19 • (05/15/96) • **85-89** (BT)
St.-Estèphe 1993: Nice and pleasant, a soft red that will make for pleasant drinking in the short term. Attractive chocolate, currant and mineral flavors. Drinkable now. 7,000 cases made. • $20 • (01/31/96) • **80**
St.-Estèphe 1992: Polished red berry and cedar character unfolds in a silky texture on your palate, medium-bodied. • $20 • **85**
St.-Estèphe 1991: Very nice spice and fruit character for this vintage. Medium-bodied and velvety, but slightly diluted. • $20 • (03/31/94) • **83**
St.-Estèphe 1990: A textbook wine for the appellation, with spicy, meaty fruit character, full tannins and a long, juicy finish. Don't touch this for a decade. Drink in 2000. 6,700 cases made. • $25 • (03/31/93) • **94**
St.-Estèphe 1989 • $18 • (03/15/92) • **93**
St.-Estèphe 1988 • $20 • (04/30/91) • **85**
St.-Estèphe 1985 • $16 • (04/30/88) • **87**
St.-Estèphe 1984 • $12 • (06/15/87) • **73**
St.-Estèphe 1983 • $9 • (05/16/86) • **86**
St.-Estèphe 1982 • $NA • (08/31/92) • **86**

St.-Estèphe 1961: Here's a very mature '61 that tastes roasted, herbal and beefy. Little fruit is left. • $NA • (04/30/96) • **75**

COSTE, DOMAINE DE LA

Cuvée Sélectionnée Saint Christol Coteaux du Languedoc 1993: A sturdy, hearty red that reminds us of a Côtes du Rhône with its peppery, grapey flavor profile and moderate tannins. 2,000 cases made. • $7 • (03/31/95) • **82**
Cuvée Sélectionnée Saint Christol Coteaux du Languedoc 1991: A serious red wine and a good value, too. Has lots of color, concentration and length. The black cherry and red-beet flavors have depth, and the structure of acid and tannins is firm. Drink now through 1998. 2,000 cases made. • $8 • **85**
St.-Christol Coteaux du Languedoc 1991 • $8 • (03/15/94) • **85**

COSTE-CAUMARTIN

Bourgogne 1993: Lean but pretty, the tannins balanced by some nice red licorice, currant and earth flavors. Seems to clamp down on the finish. Better wait until 1999. • $18 • **83**
Bourgogne 1990 • $16 • (12/15/92) • **88**
Bourgogne 1989 • $15 • (01/31/92) • **87**
Pommard 1993: Appealing but lighter than some of these Pommards, showing decent raspberry and cherry notes. A bit short on the finish. Better in 1998? 500 cases made. • $37 • **80**
Pommard 1991: Lean and flavorful, but an annoying streak of stalkiness. Try now. 1,083 cases made. • $30 Ⓐ • (01/31/94) • **79**
Pommard 1990: A monumental, fantastic Pommard that tastes like chocolate mousse with raspberry sauce. Extremely firm, tannic and full-bodied, will reward patient collectors. Try now. 1,250 cases made. • $28 • (12/15/92) • **94**
Pommard 1987 • $21 • (11/15/90) • **76**
Pommard Clos des Boucherottes 1993: Pretty, freshly crushed raspberry, blueberry and blackberry flavors. Subtle and seductive, adding a delicious, smooth, juicy finish of massive, well-integrated tannins. Try in 1999. 716 cases made. • $42 • **90**
Pommard Clos des Boucherottes 1992: Ripe and generous, with some nice blackberry, tobacco and spice flavors and tannin on the finish. Drinkable now. 833 cases made. • $35 • **87**
Pommard Clos des Boucherottes 1991: Bright, lively and light in texture. Nicely balances the raspberry and toasty oak aromas and flavors and finishes light but harmonious. Drinkable now. 583 cases made. • $38 Ⓐ • (01/31/94) • **83**
Pommard Clos des Boucherottes 1990: Ripe but focused, this has a massive structure yet manages to remain elegant. A wine to put away for decades. From an exclusive vineyard owned only by Coste-Caumartin. Drinkable 1997 to 2000. 650 cases made. • $37 • (12/15/92) • **95**
Pommard Clos des Boucherottes 1989 • $38 • (01/31/92) • **92**
Pommard Les Fremiers 1993: Not big but delicious. Wonderfully perfumed berry and dried cherry aromas and flavors. Medium in body, firm tannins and fruity finish. Better in 1999. • $NA • (05/15/96) • **88**
Pommard Les Fremiers 1992: Light and crisp, showing modest berry and floral flavors that persist on the finish. Drinkable now. 667 cases made. • $31 • **81**
Pommard Les Fremiers 1991: A light, appealing style that features modest raspberry and lemon aromas and flavors. Finishes with polish and style. Drinkable now. 500 cases made. • $33 Ⓐ • (01/31/94) • **85**
Pommard Les Fremiers 1990: This massive wine is bursting with everything, loaded with raspberry and earth characteristics and firm tannins. Drinkable now. 550 cases made. • $32 • (12/15/92) • **94**
Pommard Les Fremiers 1989 • $35 • (01/31/92) • **92**
Pommard Les Fremiers 1987 • $26 • (11/15/90) • **79**
Pommard Les Vignots 1992: Crisp in texture, with modest raspberry flavors that finish tight and slightly tannic. Drinkable now. 267 cases made. • $26 • **78**

COTAT, PAUL

Sancerre Chavignol La Grande Côte 1991 • $30 • (09/15/93) • **88**

FRANCE

Sancerre Chavignol Réserve des Monts Damnés 1992: Drink this with stir-fried vegetables, that's what it tastes like, with celery, herbal and light citrus flavors. It's a full-bodied wine, but lacks fruit and delicacy. • $15 • (10/31/94) • **77**
Sancerre Red Chavignol 1989 • $21 • (09/30/92) • **79**

COTE MONTPEZAT, CHÂTEAU

Côtes de Castillon 1993: Supple and elegant, featuring a stony, mineral, berry character, medium body and soft finish. Drink now. • $NA • **83**

COTE ROL, CHÂTEAU

St.-Emilion 1995: Some pretty fruit, but it seems a bit diluted. Medium body, fine tannins and pronounced spice, mocha, toast and red berry flavors. Somewhat dry on the finish. • $NA • (05/15/96) • **80-84** (BT)

COTTIN

Chambolle-Musigny 1990: Firm in texture, with a light stream of berry and spice flavors nosing through the tannins. Hints at stemminess on the finish. Needs until 1998 to soften. • $22 • (06/15/93) • **83**

COUCHEROY, CHÂTEAU

Pessac-Léognan 1993: Subtle plum, milk chocolate, dried herb and berry character, medium body, soft tannins and long, succulent finish. Drinkable now. • $11 • (01/31/96) • **84**
Pessac-Léognan White 1994: Round and creamy, offering pear, apple and lemon flavors in a medium-bodied frame offset by moderate acidity. Plenty of pear in the aftertaste. • $10 • (03/31/96) • **83**
Pessac-Léognan White 1991 • $9 • (05/15/93) BB • **85**

COUDERT, FERNAND

Fleurie Clos de la Roilette 1993: Ripe and maturing, presenting stewed cherry and rhubarb aromas and flavors in a lush yet still tannic structure. Tasty, but lacks the clean, fresh fruitiness one expects in Beaujolais. • $17 • (06/15/95) • **81**
Fleurie Clos de la Roilette 1992 • $15 • (06/15/94) • **88**
Fleurie Clos de la Roilette 1991 • $13 • (07/31/92) • **85**

COUFRAN, CHÂTEAU

Haut-Médoc 1995: Delicious: a solid core of fruit and tannins in this. Medium- to full-bodied, with plenty of vanilla character and a long, flavorful finish. • $NA • (05/15/96) • **85-89** (BT)
Haut-Médoc 1994: Some attractive plum and currant aromas and flavors, medium body and tannins and a slightly diluted finish. • $NA • **80-84** (BT)
Haut-Médoc 1992: Fresh blackberry, slightly herbal aromas and flavors, light-bodied, light finish. Drink now. • $12 • **81**
Haut-Médoc 1991: Pretty black cherry and spice aromas and flavors, but light-bodied and slightly dry on the finish. • $12 • (03/31/94) • **78**
Haut-Médoc 1990: Luscious and ripe. This is rich, almost Port-like, with loads of plummy, berry aromas and flavors and a long, ripe finish. Drink in 1997. 34,000 cases made. • $17 • (03/31/93) • **88**
Haut-Médoc 1989 • $14 • (03/15/92) • **89**
Haut-Médoc 1988 • $15 • (04/30/91) • **84**
Haut-Médoc 1987 • $12 • (11/30/89) • **81**
Haut-Médoc 1986 • $15 • (11/30/89) • **82**
Haut-Médoc 1985 • $22 • (06/30/88) • **85**
Haut-Médoc 1982 • $24 • (08/31/92) • **85**

COUHINS-LURTON, CHÂTEAU

Pessac-Léognan White 1992 • $NA • (06/15/94) • **87**

Key: SS—Spectator Selection. CS—Cellar Selection. BB—Best Buy. $NA—Price not available. (BT)—Barrel tasting. Ⓐ—Auction Price.
Dates in parentheses represent the issues in which the ratings were published.

Pessac-Léognan White 1991 • $20 • (03/31/94) • **78**

COUILLAUD, LES FRERES

Chardonnay Vin de Pays du Jardin de la France Domaine La Morinière 1995: Broad aromas and flavors of ripe apple, peach and butter are the hallmarks of this soft, easy-drinking white. There's good complexity and a moderate finish. • $8 • (05/15/96) • **85**
Chardonnay Vin de Pays du Jardin de la France Domaine Trois Frères 1994: Very ripe honey and lanolin flavors. It's rich, yet the finish is just a touch bitter. 5,000 cases made. • $8 • (05/15/96) • **80**
Muscadet de Sèvre et Maine Château la Morinière 1992: This anonymous white is simple and balanced but lacks definition and fruit, turning a bit earthy on the finish. • $NA • (10/31/94) • **78**
Muscadet de Sèvre et Maine Sur Lie Château La Morinière 1994: Surprising depth and freshness, delivering almond and green apple flavors that segue into a firm, slightly bitter finish. Well made. • $10 • (05/15/96) • **85**
Muscadet de Sèvre et Maine Sur Lie Château La Morinière 1993: Bracing and nicely balanced, this has crisp lemon and apple flavors, accented by buttery, minerallike nuances on the finish. A light, smooth and well-made wine. • $10 • (11/15/95) • **85**
Muscadet de Sèvre et Maine Sur Lie Domaine La Morinière 1994: Developed flavors of pine and herb are matched by a firm structure. Drink this with oysters or light seafood. • $9 • (05/15/96) • **83**
Muscadet de Sèvre et Maine Sur Lie Domaine La Morinière 1993: This is very tart and lean in flavor and tight in texture. Its lemon and green-apple flavors are shaded slightly by a briny, minerally aftertaste. • $9 • (11/15/95) • **81**
Vin de Pays du Jardin de la France Chardet White 1995: A nutty, creamy, buttery note dominates, detracting from the freshness, but there's depth and balance. Good as a summertime quaff. Chardonnay and Muscadet. • $9 • (05/15/96) • **82**
Vin de Pays du Jardin de la France Chardet White 1994: Smooth but crisp, with fresh fruit flavors rounded out by almond and nutmeg accents on the finish. It tastes lively and clean, but with enough body and richness. • $9 • (11/15/95) • **84**
Vin de Pays du Jardin de la France Domaine Bernier White 1992: This soft, easy-drinking wine has a mix of fruit cocktail flavors and a sheen of vanilla that lends an almost sweet note to the finish. Appealing at first, it becomes cloying on the second glass. • $8 • (10/31/94) • **78**
Vin de Pays du Jardin de la France Domaine Couillaud White 1992: Smooth and full-bodied, with vanilla and butter notes that blend well with the apple and peach flavors. It's soft and well integrated, not complex or long, but appealing. • $10 • (10/31/94) • **84**
Vin de Pays du Jardin de la France Domaine Morinère Chardonnay White 1994: Crisp and lemony on one hand, creamy and buttery on the other, but it doesn't come together as it should. Tastes rather sour, lacks balance and harmony. • $7 • (11/15/95) • **77**
Vin de Pays du Jardin de la France Domaine Morinière Chardonnay White 1993: A nicely balanced, lean Chardonnay with subtle butter, vanilla and almond aromas, similar flavors and a crisp, clean finish. • $7 • (11/15/95) • **82**
Vin de Pays du Jardin de la France Domaine Morinière White 1992: Crisp, balanced and moderately fruity, with ripe apple and light vanilla flavors, this wine is appealing but not rich or distinctive. A pleasant apéritif wine. • $NA • (10/31/94) • **81**
Vin de Pays du Jardin de la France Domaine Trois Fréres White 1992: Here's the lowest common denominator of Chardonnay. It has some butter and apple flavors, but it's austere and short. • $NA • (10/31/94) • **79**

COUJAN, DOMAINE DE

1990 • $7 • (03/15/94) • **86**
Rolle Vin de Pays des Coteaux du Murviel 1992 • $7 • (03/15/94) • **84**

COULY-DUTHEIL

Chinon Clos de L'Echo 1989: This is about as big as a Loire red gets. It has a deep, young color, open aromas of smoke, meat and plums, and it's firm on the palate, with plenty of plum and tobacco flavors. It's distinctive and rich. Drinkable now. • $NA • (10/31/94) • **88**

Chinon Domaine Rene Couly 1993: Fresh with the virtues of youth: clean blackberry and herb flavors, light tannins and crisp acidity. Smoke and cocoa accents add interest. This is for drinking young, try it slightly cool. • $12 • (10/31/94) • **84**

Chinon Domaine de Versailles 1981 • $13 • (03/15/87) • **86**

Chinon La Diligence 1993: Good concentration here, with a dark garnet color, vivid smoke and blueberry aromas, and good concentration with firm tannins and acidity. There's enough fruit to make it tasty now. • $NA • (10/31/94) • **87**

Chinon Les Gravieres d'Amador Abbe de Turpenay 1993: Clean and straightforward, with cherry and light herbal flavors, soft tannins and a fresh, very dry finish. It's balanced and vivid, without aiming for too much weight or complexity. Drink now. • $NA • (10/31/94) • **86**

Chinon Les Gravieres d'Amador Abbe de Turpenay 1986 • $10 • (04/30/88) • **72**

Chinon Les Gravieres d'Amador Abbe de Turpenay 1985 • $9 • (02/28/87) • **86**

Chinon Rosé René Couly 1993: Pale pink color, dry and refreshing, with light strawberry and peach flavors. It's clean and uncomplicated-a good apéritif. • $NA • (10/31/94) • **83**

Saumur Champigny La Vigneronne Red 1985 • $10 • (02/15/87) • **87**

COUR PAVILLON, LA

Bordeaux 1986 • $7 • (02/28/91) • **77**

Bordeaux 1985 • $6 • (07/15/88) • **67**

Bordeaux 1983 • $7 • (08/31/87) • **68**

COURBEROC

Merlot Vin de Pays d'Oc 1990 • $6 • (03/15/94) • **84**

Syrah SCV Les Vignerons du Progrè Vin de Pays d'Oc 1990 • $6 • (03/15/94) • **82**

COURCEL, DOMAINE DE

Pommard Clos des Epeneaux 1985 • $37 • (04/30/88) • **89**

Pommard Grand Clos des Epenots 1993: Lovely and distinctive, featuring tons of chocolate and mocha flavors. The smooth, round mouthfeel is followed by a supple, subtle, lasting finish. Tempting now, but better in 1999. • $33 • **88**

Pommard Les Rugiens 1993: Attractively lush and earthy, offering an intense, concentrated red berry, chocolate, mocha complexity. Smoky and toasty on the long finish. Tempting now, but better in 1999. • $42 • **90**

Pommard Rugiens 1985 • $32 Ⓐ • (04/30/88) • **92**

COUROULU, DOMAINE LE

Vacqueyras 1992: Ripe plum, smoky and herbal aromas and flavors are expressive and fresh, the wine is light but graceful, with light tannins and focused fruit. Drinkable now. 10,000 cases made. • $10 • (10/31/95) • **86**

Vacqueyras 1990 • $10 • (04/15/93) • **83**

Vacqueyras 1985 • $8 • (01/31/89) BB • **83**

COURSODON, PIERRE

St.-Joseph 1992 • $NA • (05/31/94) • **78**

St.-Joseph 1991 • $NA • (05/31/94) • **85**

COURTADE, LA

Côtes de Provence Red 1990 • $24 • (06/15/93) • **76**

COURTEILLAC, DOMAINE DE

Bordeaux Supérieur 1993: Simple and fruity, showing some berry character but appearing slightly herbal on the finish. Drinkable now. • $NA • (01/31/96) • **79**

Bordeaux White Cuvée Antholien 1994: A solid white with apple, lime, lemon and vanilla aromas and flavors. Fine acidity and a lovely vanilla-apple finish that goes on and on. Try in 1997. • $NA • (03/31/96) • **88**

Bordeaux White Cuvée Antholien 1993: A well-made white with plenty of interesting grapefruit and grassy character. Fine acidity and a fresh finish. Delicious. • $NA • (03/31/96) • **86**

COURTESSES, DOMAINE DE

Pouilly-Fuissé 1993: Oddly mature already, but silky and buttery on the palate. Sherry-like aromas, rose-petal, honey, mushroom flavors. Try now. 833 cases made. • $NA • **79**

Pouilly-Fuissé Cuvée Vieilles Vignes 1993: Floral notes border on eau-de-vie apricot character or sweet perfume, lean and hard in the mouth. 417 cases made. • $NA • **70**

COURTIAL, MICHEL

Cornas 1989 • $15 • (05/31/94) SS • **91**

Crozes-Hermitage 1991 • $8 • (05/31/94) • **83**

Crozes-Hermitage 1990 • $8 • (05/31/94) • **82**

Hermitage 1991: Elegant and broadens on the palate, showing black cherry, mint and licorice flavors, with firm tannins. Drink now. • $NA • (05/31/94) • **87**

Hermitage White 1990: Round and simple, with pear and anise flavors, it's a bit diluted and earthy on the finish. From the Tain cooperative.-TM • $NA • (05/31/94) • **76**

St.-Joseph 1991 • $12 • (05/31/94) • **75**

COUSPAUDE, CHÂTEAU LA

St.-Emilion 1995: Diluted and light, with some fruit showing, but it's earthy and strange. Barely acceptable. • $NA • (05/15/96) • **965**

COUTET, CHÂTEAU

Barsac 1992: A pretty, medium-sweet white, showing attractive lemon, spice and wax character and an easy-to-like finish. • $NA • **81**

Barsac 1991: Lightly sweet, domineering oak flavors. Not really what we expect here, but it has some decent vanilla and toasty coconut character. Drink now. • $NA • **80**

Barsac 1990: Racy and elegant, quite floral, demonstrating some spicy, buttery, lime and juicy flavors that keep it fresh on the finish. Medium body and sweetness. Drinkable now. • $NA • **89**

Barsac 1989: Lush and viscous, very sweet, showing ripe tropical fruit and lemon flavors and a burning sensation on the finish that reflects good concentration. Drinkable now. • $29 • **90**

Barsac 1988: Extraordinary complexity and finesse are the hallmarks of this earth-scented, butter-laced, honeyed, lemon-flavored gem. The finish seems to never end thanks to all that great acidity. Better after 1998. • $47 • **91**

Barsac 1987 • $27 • (06/15/90) • **80**

Barsac Cuvée Madame 1989: Super-sweet, super-ripe, but not any better than the regular bottling. Dark color with a brilliant gold hue and very intense aromas of butterscotch, vanilla, honey and apricot. Tasted twice, with consistent notes. Drinkable now, but better after 1996. • $190 • **90**

Barsac Cuvée Madame 1988: Lots of botrytis and spice character and ripe fruit here, quality is about the same as the regular bottling. Medium-to-full-bodied, very sweet, round texture, butterscotch aftertaste. Drink now. • $175 • **91**

COUVENT, CHÂTEAU LE

St.-Emilion 1982 • $13 • (06/16/86) • **78**

COUVENT DES JACOBINS

St.-Emilion 1989 • $28 • (04/30/92) • **89**

St.-Emilion 1988 • $28 • (03/31/91) • **81**

St.-Emilion 1985 • $27 • (03/31/88) • **84**

St.-Emilion 1983 • $27 • (03/16/86) • **95**

FRANCE

COYEUX, DOMAINE DE

Muscat de Beaumes-de-Venise 1992: Fairly rich fig and apricot flavors make this a good dessert wine. Full-bodied and balanced, it offers plenty of spirit but not much punch. • $20 • **84**

CROCHET, GILLES

Sancerre la Grange aux Dimes 1992: Ripe fig and honey flavors give this a round, New World style, attractive and rather soft, though citrus flavors emerge on the finish. It's a big wine that wants drinking now. • $12 • (11/15/95) • **87**

CROCHET, LUCIEN

Sancerre 1994: Nicely assertive herbal notes in the aroma, which carry through to the finish, keep this running on all pistons. Rich, intense, grassy flavors and zippy acidity. 800 cases imported. • $16 • (06/15/96) • **87**

Sancerre 1993: Typical Sancerre flavors of herbs, citrus and tart apple complement an earthy, cheesy edge that undermines the fruit. Old in style, exaggerated, extreme. • $15 • **82**

Sancerre 1992: Quintessential Sauvignon Blanc: high-intensity and classic flavors in an elegant, subtle style. The citrus, grapefruit and mineral elements are balanced and clean, the acidity is bracing without sharpness. Great with food. 2,500 cases made. • $15 • (08/31/94) • **90**

Sancerre La Croix du Roy 1994: Herbal in style, sporting firm, focused flavors of green apple and lemon. Racy, focused, zippy acidity and a touch of elegance. • $18 • (06/15/96) • **86**

Sancerre Le Chêne 1994: There's a hint of peach here that, combined with herb and mineral, makes Sancerre so seductive. Balanced and elegant, adding harmonious aftertaste. 1,000 cases imported. • $19 • (05/15/96) • **88**

CROCK, CHÂTEAU LE

St.-Estèphe 1995: A pleasant wine that offers some good earthy berry and cassis character. Medium to light body, light tannins and a fresh finish. • $NA • (05/15/96) • **80-84** (BT)

St.-Estèphe 1987 • $16 • (11/30/89) • **79**

St.-Estèphe 1986 • $21 • (11/30/89) • **92**

St.-Estèphe 1985 • $18 • (02/15/88) • **79**

St.-Estèphe 1983 • $9 • (12/16/85) • **81**

St.-Estèphe 1982 • $20 • (11/30/89) • **80**

CROISIERE

Sparkling Peche NV • $9 • **86**

CROIX, CHÂTEAU LA

Pomerol 1988 • $19 • (07/31/91) • **82**

Pomerol 1985 • $25 • (05/15/88) • **93**

Pomerol 1983 • $14 • (11/30/86) • **84**

Pomerol 1982 • $30 • (05/15/89) • **89**

Pomerol 1981 • $14 • (05/01/89) • **72**

Pomerol 1979 • $11 • (04/01/84) • **60**

CROIX DU CASSE, CHÂTEAU LA

Pomerol 1995: Very silky vanilla and berry character and a fine, refreshing finish. • $NA • (05/15/96) • **85-89** (BT)

Pomerol 1994: Delicious and harmonious, sweet-tasting and ripe, this full-flavored '94 is impressive for its concentrated red berry, tar, dried herb and earth character. Only a slightly diluted impression in the mid-palate keeps it from scoring outstanding. • $26 • (05/15/96) • **85-89** (BT)

Pomerol 1993: Rather lean and hard, showing an earthy, slightly strange character. • $24 • (01/31/96) • **78**

Pomerol 1985 • $25 • (05/15/88) • **82**

CROIX DE FIGEAC, CHÂTEAU LA

St.-Emilion 1993: Light and herbaceous, featuring some red fruit and slightly aggressive tannins. • $NA • (01/31/96) • **76**

CROIX-DE-GAY, CHÂTEAU LA

Pomerol 1995: Attractive, flavorful and full-bodied. Toasted oak mingles nicely with the red- and blackberry character, shows smooth, silky texture despite the impressive tannic structure. You wish perhaps for a bit more class on the slightly herbaceous finish. • $NA • (05/15/96) • **85-89** (BT)

Pomerol 1994: Good berry, tobacco and vanilla character, medium to light body, medium tannins and light finish. Could move up after bottling. • $NA • (05/15/96) • **80-84** (BT)

Pomerol 1993: Lovely, silky chocolate and berry character and smooth tannins. Medium body and finish. Delicious to drink now. • $20 • (01/31/96) • **85**

Pomerol 1992: Better than we remember from barrel. Subtle raspberry and toasted oak aromas, medium-to-light-bodied, delivering firm fruit and slightly hard tannins and acidity. Succulent finish. Drink now. • $17 • **82**

Pomerol 1991: A pleasing wine with roasted nut, cherry and tomato aromas and flavors. Medium body, silky texture and a quick finish. • $17 • (03/31/94) • **78**

Pomerol 1990: As usual, it's big, thick and rich with loads of nutmeg, berry and ripe fruit character. Long in the aftertaste, with extremely velvety tannins. Drink in 1998. 5,000 cases made. • $28 • (03/31/93) • **94**

Pomerol 1989 • $27 • (03/15/92) • **88**

Pomerol 1988 • $30 • (06/30/91) • **89**

Pomerol 1985: Big, bruiser of a wine with masses of super ripe fruit, roasted nut, rich raspberry aromas and flavors. Full bodied with loads of ripe tannins and a long, long finish. Try after 1998. • $24 • **91**

Pomerol 1983: Well-crafted wine with pretty, tobacco, berry character. Medium bodied with medium and a long silky finish. Delicious now. • $NA • **87**

Pomerol 1982 • $27 Ⓐ • (05/15/89) • **91**

Pomerol 1981: Medium ruby/garnet color with pretty tobacco, chocolate aromas and flavors. Medium body and silky with a herbal, slightly edgy, tobacco finish. Past its peak. Tasted twice. Drink now. • $NA • **79**

Pomerol 1961: This is old but still fun to drink. Its color is turning to brown, it has slightly cooked or maderized aromas, but then it turns soft, rich and almost sweet on the palate. Drink now. • $NA • (04/30/96) • **82**

Pomerol 1945 • $NA • (03/16/86) • **70**

CROIX DE GIRON, CHÂTEAU LA

Bordeaux Supérieur 1986 • $5 • (05/15/89) • **76**

CROIX DE MILLORIT, CHÂTEAU LA

Côtes de Bourg 1986 • $9 • (05/15/91) • **79**

CROIX ST.-JEAN, CHÂTEAU LA

Bordeaux Supérieur 1986 • $6 • (11/30/88) BB • **81**

CROIX SENAILLET, DOMAINE DE LA

St.-Véran White 1994: Pleasant and well made, light-bodied but balanced, featuring creamy yet fresh texture, some lovely fruit character and crisp finish. Nice as an apéritif. • $NA • **80**

Key: SS—Spectator Selection. CS—Cellar Selection. BB—Best Buy. $NA—Price not available. (BT)—Barrel tasting. Ⓐ—Auction Price.
Dates in parentheses represent the issues in which the ratings were published.

FRANCE

CROIZET-BAGES, CHÂTEAU

Pauillac 1995: Refined and racy. Lovely '95, bright and vivid, with an abundance of cassis, good acidity and ripe tannins, although it turns slightly dry on the finish. • $NA • (05/15/96) • **85-89** (BT)
Pauillac 1994: A bit simple. Pretty plum flavors and medium-fine tannins. Medium in body and fresh finish. • $NA • **80-84** (BT)
Pauillac 1993: More water than wine, this diluted Bordeaux tastes of stewed tomatoes and bell pepper. • $25 • (01/31/96) • **74**
Pauillac 1988 • $28 • (08/31/91) • **73**
Pauillac 1986 • $15 • (06/30/89) • **78**
Pauillac 1982 • $26 • (08/31/92) • **82**
Pauillac 1970 • $45 • (05/15/93) • **85**
Pauillac 1962 • $60 • (11/30/87) • **83**
Pauillac 1961: A very good, smooth-textured and mature Bordeaux that offers complex cedary aromas and rather light but long-lasting fruit flavors. Drink through 1998. • $37 • (04/30/96) • **85**

CROQUE-MICHOTTE, CHÂTEAU

St.-Emilion 1982 • $25 • (05/15/89) • **83**

CRU DE COUDELET

Côtes du Rhône 1987 • $12 • (12/15/89) • **76**
Côtes du Rhône 1986 • $15 • (09/30/88) • **84**
Côtes du Rhône 1985 • $12 • (04/30/88) • **85**

CRUZEAU, CHÂTEAU DE

Graves 1985 • $9 • (06/15/88) BB • **85**
Graves 1982 • $26 • (08/31/92) • **91**
Pessac-Léognan 1995: Ripe and medium in body, delivering nice plum, spice and toasted oak flavors that are quite intense. • $NA • (05/15/96) • **85-89** (BT)
Pessac-Léognan 1994: Quite sweet and ripe, but with an undertow of herbal flavors that may not appeal to everybody. Fair extraction, with firm tannins on the slightly dry finish that has good notes of berry. Not as good as a barrel sample tasted earlier. • $NA • (05/15/96) • **80-84** (BT)
Pessac-Léognan 1993: Pretty cherry, chocolate and berry aromas and flavors, medium body, medium to light silky tannins and fresh finish. Drinkable now. • $14 • (01/31/96) • **83**
Pessac-Léognan 1992: Lean, short in fruit and tough in tannins. Drink now. • $12 • **75**
Pessac-Léognan 1990: A wine with rich flavors of cassis, plum, blackberry and oak. There are masses of tannins to boot. Drink in 1998. 15,000 cases made. • $16 • (03/31/93) • **91**
Pessac-Léognan 1989 • $14 • (03/15/92) • **86**
Pessac-Léognan 1988 • $14 • (02/28/91) • **87**
Pessac-Léognan 1986 • $10 • (06/30/89) • **87**
Pessac-Léognan 1981: Good color red with very ripe fruity style but drying and alcoholic on finish. Drink now. • $NA • **79**
Pessac-Léognan White 1994: Plenty of character in this one. The grapefruit, celery and honey aromas and flavors are set off against crisp acidity. Long and delicious on the finish. • $12 • (03/31/96) • **86**
Pessac-Léognan White 1992 • $NA • (06/15/94) • **77**

CUILLERON

Condrieu Les Chaillets Vieilles Vignes 1993 • $45 • (05/31/94) • **85**
St.-Joseph 1983 • $13 • (02/16/86) • **76**
St.-Joseph Cuvée de la Côte 1987 • $16 • (11/30/90) • **80**
St.-Joseph Cuvée Prestige 1991 • $20 • (05/31/94) • **82**

CURE-BON-LA-MADELAINE, CHÂTEAU

St.-Emilion 1982 • $30 • (05/15/89) • **84**

CURSON, CHÂTEAU

Crozes-Hermitage 1989 • $17 • (07/15/91) • **89**

CUVEE LES BASTIDES

Faugères 1990 • $NA • (03/15/94) • **87**

CUVEE DU BELVEDERE

Châteauneuf-du-Pape Le Boucou 1986 • $16 • (01/31/89) • **86**
Châteauneuf-du-Pape Le Boucou 1985 • $18 • (02/15/88) • **93**
Châteauneuf-du-Pape Le Boucou 1983 • $16 • (11/15/87) • **62**

CUVEE DES ERMITES

NV • $7 • (01/31/92) • **78**

CUVEE PIERRE ROUGE

Red 1990 • $7 • (06/30/92) • **78**

CYPRES DE CLIMENS

Barsac 1992: Light and easy, featuring pine, pineapple, honey and grass flavors, quite pleasant as a clean and slightly sweet ap(E1)ritif. Drink now. Second label from Château Climens. • $NA • **83**

DAGUENEAU, DIDIER

Maudit 1990 • $50/500ml • (09/30/93) • **84**
Pouilly-Fumé Buisson Menard 1993: Striking, seductive aromas of toast and herbs give way to a firm palate stuffed with lime, pineapple and melon flavors, bookended by toasty oak and razor-sharp acidity. It's powerful and keeps you coming back for more. Drinkable now. 800 cases made. • $40 • (11/15/95) • **92**
Pouilly-Fumé Buisson Menard 1992: This big wine is bright and lively, thanks to firm acidity and vivid herbal, pine and grapefruit flavors. It's firm and fresh, and finishes cleanly. A tasty wine in the classic style. 800 cases made. • $34 • (08/31/94) • **87**
Pouilly-Fumé En Chailloux 1994: Floral and spice aromas are followed by whopping acidity that lends an overall lean, citrus character. Try in 1997, or accompanying food. • $26 • (05/15/96) • **83**
Pouilly-Fumé En Chailloux 1993: Good fruit intensity gives this wine a juicy appeal. Flavors of melon, peach and orange mingle on the broad palate, vibrant and fresh, and linger on the finish. A good example of the traditional style. • $33 • **86**
Pouilly-Fumé En Chailloux 1992: Round and ripe, this wine shows tropical fruit and fairly strong vegetal flavors, full-bodied and mellow on the palate and a clean, minerally finish. A big wine but a bit flabby. We expected more from this top producer. 3,000 cases made. • $27 • (10/31/94) • **82**
Pouilly-Fumé Pur Sang 1993: New World style, stuffed with tropical fruit and vanilla flavors, this mingles coconut and pineapple notes in a ripe, yet still crisp and lively wine. A Chardonnay drinker will love it. 1,200 cases made. • $38 • (11/15/95) • **89**
Pouilly-Fumé Pur Sang 1992: New oak is the dominant element here, from the rich aromas of butter and vanilla to the spicy, coconut notes on the palate. But the almost austere, herbal-accented fruit keeps it true to Sauvignon Blanc, with plenty of concentration and acidity to balance the wood. It's harmonious and drinkable now. 1,400 cases made. • $34 • (08/31/94) • **90**
Pouilly-Fumé Silex 1994: New oak delivers vanilla notes and rounded character, but there's still fresh, herbal fruit underneath. Good depth here and a lingering finish. • $49 • (05/15/96) • **88**
Pouilly-Fumé Silex 1992: Vivid and rich, this wine shows a beautifully-integrated marriage of toasty oak and ripe, fresh fruit. Taut acidity carries the vanilla and butter notes, while peach, citrus and melon flavors follow through on the long finish. Should develop well in the bottle. 700 cases made. • $45 • (08/31/94) • **91**

DALEM, CHÂTEAU

Fronsac 1990: This is a shapely, aromatic wine, with lovely flavors of black cherry and berry and silky tannins, but a little short on the finish. Drinkable now. • $20 • (03/31/93) • **86**

DAME, CHÂTEAU DE LA

Margaux 1988 • $15 • (02/15/91) • **86**

DAMOY, PIERRE

Chambertin Red 1993: A big Chambertin, medium- to full-bodied, delivering silky tannins and long finish that tastes of strawberry and raspberry jam. Try after 2000. • $69 • **91**

Chambertin Clos de Bèze Red 1993: Elegant, attractive vanilla, plum and raspberry aromas, medium body, fine tannins and sweet, candied fruit finish. Better in 2000. • $55 • **91**

Chapelle-Chambertin 1993: Can red Burgundy get silkier than this? A beauty to behold, featuring enormous concentration and superb currant and earth flavors. Massively tannic, but fruit supports the whole edifice. Try in 2000. • $57 • **91**

Gevrey-Chambertin Clos Tamisot LD 1993: Well crafted and silky, full in body. Earth and red berry flavors add some plum and mint. There is enough delicious fruit to balance the massive tannins. Cellar until past 2000. • $30 • **89**

DAMPIERRE, COMTE AUDOIN DE

Brut Champagne Grande Année 1983: A very complete and enjoyable Champagne. Tastes dry, it's almost delicate in texture, with mature flavors of toast, vanilla and honey. Rich in spice and fruit flavors, with a lingering finish. • $32 • (12/31/90) • **89**

DARD & RIBO

Crozes-Hermitage 1990 • $17 • (04/15/93) • **86**

DARGENT

Brut Blanc de Blancs Côtes du Jura 1984 • $10 • (03/31/88) • **82**

Brut Blanc de Blancs Côtes du Jura Chardonnay 1988 • $11 • (06/15/90) • **83**

Brut Côtes du Jura 1992: A disjointed wine, with pineapple and grapefruit flavors and a slightly bitter finish. Refreshing, but not very satisfying. 100,000 cases made. • $11 • **76**

Brut Rosé Côtes du Jura 1984 • $10 • (03/31/88) • **86**

Brut Rosé Côtes du Jura Pinot Noir 1990: Mature red-wine flavors give this dry rosé some lively fruit character. Tart on the finish with some nice spice flavors. 100,000 cases made. • $11 • **80**

DARVIOT, YVES

Beaune Clos des Mouches White 1993: Pretty apple and cream aromas and flavors. Medium in body, showing loads of toasted coconut and vanilla character and a delicate, fruity finish. • $NA • **86**

Beaune Clos des Mouches White 1992: Rich and oily texture, toasty and smoky, with modest spice, vanilla and pear flavors and a subtle finish. • $43 • (08/31/94) • **84**

DASSAULT, CHÂTEAU

St.-Emilion 1988 • $17 • (07/15/91) • **83**

St.-Emilion 1982 • $20 • (05/15/89) • **90**

DAUNY, NICOLE & CHRISTIAN

Sancerre Clos du Roy 1993: The grapefruit and light grassy flavors have a creamy element in this soft, fruity wine. It lacks the assertiveness of many Sancerres, but it's round and easy to drink 2,200 cases made. • $17 • (10/31/94) • **82**

Key: SS—Spectator Selection. CS—Cellar Selection. BB—Best Buy. $NA—Price not available. (BT)—Barrel tasting. Ⓐ—Auction Price.
Dates in parentheses represent the issues in which the ratings were published.

DAUPHINE, CHÂTEAU DE LA

Fronsac 1995: Full in body, solid, extremely appealing, showing lovely fruit, spice and chocolate complexity and firm but ripe tannins on the long finish. • $NA • (05/15/96) • **85-89** (BT)

Fronsac 1994: Interesting crushed-fruit character and a light, herbal, earthy finish. • $NA • **75-79** (BT)

Fronsac 1993: Enjoyable milk chocolate and berry character. Medium in body, delicate tannins and delicious finish. Drinkable now. • $22 • (01/31/96) • **82**

Fronsac 1992: Somewhat fruity, but slightly metallic and hard. Cherry, berry finish. Drink now. • $17 • **75**

Fronsac 1990: A traditional-style Fronsac, with tomato and herbal character and hard, tight tannins. Drinkable now. 4,500 cases made. • $17 • (03/31/93) • **81**

Fronsac 1989 • $15 • (03/15/92) • **80**

Fronsac 1985 • $20 • (09/30/88) • **84**

DAUVISSAT, JEAN

Chablis Les Preuses 1994: Disappointing *grand cru*. Silky mineral and earth character, but toasted oak flavors take away somewhat from the taste of pure *terroir*. Full-bodied, fat, rich and ripe, but a bit overdone. Hot finish distracts. Better in 2000? 208 cases made. • $45 • (05/31/96) • **81**

Chablis Séchet 1994: Very fat and somewhat overdone, a sweet-tasting, superripe white featuring pear, honey, chalk, lemon, crème brûlée character. Very toasty, slightly burning finish. Drinkable now. 150 cases made. • $23 • (05/31/96) • **80**

Chablis Vaillons 1994: Flavorful and full-bodied, sporting ripe fruit and mineral character, this luscious, silky *premier cru* delivers harmony and lots of pleasure. A subtle stony, toasty note on the long finish adds to its complexity. Try in 1999. 475 cases made. • $24 • (05/31/96) • **90**

Chablis Vaillons Vieilles Vignes 1994: An oaky style of Chablis, showing cedar, toffee, honey, spice, vanilla and mineral notes. Full body, seductive texture and toasted bread flavors on the finish. Needs time, so try in 1999. 208 cases made. • $30 • (05/31/96) • **85**

DAUVISSAT, RENE & VINCENT

Chablis 1994: Quite young and intense, it's difficult to taste now but offers some fine pear, mineral, green apple and honey flavors and grassy, green notes. Very reductive, "icebox" kind of wine. Better in 1999? 750 cases made. • $NA • (05/31/96) • **86**

Chablis La Forêt 1994: Distinctively milky and "lactic" in taste, bordering on cork. Upon opening up, however, it reveals lovely mineral, cream, vanilla and pear notes and fresh citrus flavors. Try to decant before serving. Drinkable now. 2,916 cases made. • $NA • (05/31/96) • **87**

Chablis La Forêt 1992 • $28 • (02/28/94) • **89**

Chablis Les Clos 1994: Great wine. Ripe and lush, but boasting a solid backbone of mineral, chalk, stone, citrus, honey, cedar and wet earth character. Full in body yet elegant, adding an extremely intense and long searing finish. A pure, clean *grand cru* that delivers the goods. Try in 2000. Tasted twice, with consistent notes. 833 cases made. • $60 • (05/31/96) CS • **93**

Chablis Les Clos 1993: Intense, racy and elegant, featuring freshly cut apple, almond and vanilla character. Medium-bodied, balanced and a little closed. Needs time, better in 1997. 1,000 cases made. • $61 • **87**

Chablis Les Clos 1992 • $46 • (02/28/94) • **86**

Chablis Les Preuses 1994: Supple, harmonious, ripe, rich, almost soft texture. Lots of honey, pear and apple and a long, smooth finish. Drinkable now or try in 1999. 500 cases made. • $60 • (05/31/96) • **89**

Chablis Les Preuses 1993: Chablis of the vintage? Extremely well made, showy yet elegant, so silky it melts in the mouth. Concentrated, complex, boasting tropical, pear and mineral flavors and a delicious finish. 500 cases made. • $61 • **89**

Chablis Les Preuses 1992 • $46 • (02/28/94) • **83**

Chablis Séchet 1994: Racy and seductive *premier cru*. Full- to medium-bodied, offering a silky, mineral texture that coats the mouth. Ends on a fresh lime, honey and wet earth note. Try in 1999. 500 cases made. • $32 • (05/31/96) • **90**

Chablis Séchet 1993: A clean machine, slim, straight as an arrow, with spice, green apple, citrus flavors. Chablis at its steeliest, yet honey and truffle hints perk through. Needs time, try in 1998. 500 cases made. • $32 • **86**

Chablis Séchet 1992 • $28 • (04/15/94) • **86**

Chablis Vaillons 1994: Gorgeous and balanced to a T. Full-bodied, offering a crisp undertow of lemon that contrasts with chalk, mineral, honey and wet earth notes. The chewy, full and silky finish goes on and on. Bravo! Try in 1999. 750 cases made. • $32 • (05/31/96) • **91**

Chablis Vaillons 1993: Pretty apple, banana and vanilla character, medium body, ripe fruit flavors and crisp finish. Drinkable now. 833 cases made. • $32 • **85**

Chablis Vaillons 1992 • $28 • (02/28/94) • **87**

DAUVISSAT-CAMUS, DOMAINE

Chablis La Forest 1991 • $25 • (06/30/93) • **85**

Chablis Les Clos 1991 • $40 • (06/30/93) • **87**

Chablis Vaillons 1991 • $25 • (06/30/93) • **88**

DAUZAC, CHÂTEAU

Margaux 1995: Plenty of berry, cherry and mineral aromas and flavors, showing good character, but a little light on the finish. • $NA • (05/15/96) • **85-89** (BT)

Margaux 1994: Delicious and better than most '94s, with some sweet, lush fruit backing the spicy, smoky oak flavors. Has well-integrated, ripe tannins. • $21 • (05/15/96) • **85-89** (BT)

Margaux 1993: More ripe fruit than in many '93s, offering red berry, plum, tobacco and chocolate flavors, medium body and nice, silky tannins. Try in 1999. • $24 • (01/31/96) • **86**

Margaux 1992: Surprisingly ripe for the vintage, offering plum and currant character, medium body, silky tannins and a tobacco, cassis finish. • $17 • (04/15/95) • **84**

Margaux 1990: A plump wine, with an abundance of plum and berry flavors and soft, round tannins. Easy to drink, try now. 15,000 cases made. • $23 • (03/31/93) • **85**

Margaux 1989 • $26 • (03/15/92) • **90**

Margaux 1988 • $20 • (06/30/91) • **90**

Margaux 1985 • $21 • (09/30/88) • **87**

Margaux 1985 • $21 • **87**

Margaux 1982 • $28 • (08/31/92) • **91**

DAVENAY, CHÂTEAU DE

Montagny White Premier Cru 1993: Rich and ripe with nutmeg and green apple flavors. Well rounded and balanced, this is all up-front, delivering loads of acidity and moderate intensity. • $NA • (04/30/96) • **84**

DAVRIL, CHÂTEAU

Bordeaux 1987 • $5 • (09/30/89) • **79**

DECELLE, CHÂTEAU LA

Coteaux du Tricastin 1989 • $7 • (07/15/91) BB • **82**

DEHOURS

Brut Champagne Réserve NV • $NA • (12/31/91) • **87**

Demi-Sec Champagne NV • $30 • (12/31/91) • **84**

DEISS, DOMAINE MARCEL

Gewürztraminer Alsace Mittelwihr 1992: This lively, intensely flavored Gewürz adds an extra dimension of herb and mineral to the abundant peach, apple and spice notes. Has great concentration and a distinctive profile. • $25 • (09/30/94) • **89**

Pinot Blanc Alsace Bergheim 1992: This crisp-textured, enjoyable Pinot Blanc has vivid floral aromas and straightforward apple and melon flavors. It's dry, and rather lean on the finish. • $12 • (11/15/94) • **81**

DELAGOUTTIERE, GILBERT

St.-Nicolas de Bourgueil Red 1987 • $9 • (12/31/88) • **82**

DELAMOTTE

Blanc de Blancs Champagne 1982: Delicious and soft on the palate, but finishes tart and slightly astringent . Nutmeg and honey flavors are vivid. Enjoyable but slightly out of balance . • $28 • (04/15/88) • **84**

Blanc de Blancs Champagne NV • $24 • (12/31/87) • **79**

Brut Blanc de Blancs Champagne 1985: Very austere, steely style of Champagne. A great oyster fizz. It's squeaky clean with light pineapple and dough aromas and flavors, light-bodied with crisp acidity and a fresh finish. Similar score given in December 1991. Drink now. • $50 • (12/31/93) • **85**

Brut Blanc de Blancs Champagne NV: Subtle and mellow, with an intriguing nutty aroma. It has mature flavors that are dominated by toasty, buttery components. Very harmonious from beginning to end, with a long finish. Perfect as an apéritif with its luscious pear flavors. • $28 • (12/31/94) • **91**

Brut Champagne NV • $30 • (12/31/91) • **85**

Brut Rosé Champagne NV • $38 • (12/31/91) • **88**

Rosé Champagne Spècial NV • $28 • (12/31/87) • **91**

DELAPORTE, DOMAINE VINCENT

Sancerre 1995: Young and aromatic, dominated by grapey flavors and herbal, fresh-cut grass notes. Nice concentration, but needs some time to settle down. • $23 • (04/30/96) • **83**

Sancerre 1993: This bright, fruity wine offers pear and apple flavors in a soft, rounded package that's light on herbal and grassy notes. It's simple and easy to drink. • $NA • (10/31/94) • **82**

Sancerre 1992: Accents of butterscotch and nutmeg add interest to this ripe, fruity wine. The classic herbal and citrus notes draw breadth and richness from contact with the lees before bottling, the wine finishes round and soft. • $20 • (10/31/94) • **86**

Sancerre Chavignol 1991 • $22 • (07/31/93) • **85**

DELARCHE PERE & FILS, MARIUS

Corton-Charlemagne 1993: Distinctive beeswax, apple and lime character, medium body, plenty of new wood and a long, crisp finish. Aftertaste is rather candied. Drinkable now. • $NA • **81**

Corton Les Renardes 1990: Pleasantly fruity, with tasty currant and black cherry-scented flavors that turn spicy. Finishes with firm tannins and a splash of vanilla from the oak. Drinkable now. • $49 • (06/15/93) • **87**

Pernand-Vergelesses 1989 • $15/375ml • (04/30/91) • **82**

Pernand-Vergelesses Ile des Vergelesses 1990: Smells attractive, with a bouquet of fruit aromas, and turns elegant and spicy on the palate, with layers of plum and cherry flavors and a smooth, silky texture. Drinkable now. • $28 • (06/15/93) • **87**

Pernand-Vergelesses Ile des Vergelesses 1985 • $23 • (10/15/88) • **89**

Pernand-Vergelesses Les Vergelesses 1990: A pleasant wine that's crisp and focused, with bright cherry and strawberry-tinged flavors framed by toasty, cedary oak notes. Turns tannic on the finish. Drinkable now. • $25 • (06/15/93) • **84**

DELAS

Châteauneuf-du-Pape 1985 • $17 • (10/31/87) • **91**

Châteauneuf-du-Pape 1983 • $18 • (10/15/91) • **72**

Châteauneuf-du-Pape Cuvée de Haute Pierre 1989 • $16 • (10/15/91) • **90**

Châteauneuf-du-Pape Cuvée de Haute Pierre 1988 • $17 • (10/15/91) • **86**

Châteauneuf-du-Pape Cuvée de Haute Pierre 1986 • $20 • (10/15/91) • **86**

Châteauneuf-du-Pape Cuvée de Haute Pierre 1985 • $20 • (10/15/91) • **86**

■ ■ ■ ■

Châteauneuf-du-Pape Les Calcerniers 1993: A chewy wine with cassis, licorice and gamy flavors over firm tannins, this has good focus in an accessible style. Drinkable now. • $20 • **84**
Châteauneuf-du-Pape White Cuvée de Haute Pierre 1990: A rather traditional style, with earthy almond flavors. Full-bodied, with almond and honey aromas, very ripe flavors verging on raisins and a spicy almond finish. • $21 • (10/15/91) • **80**
Châteauneuf-du-Pape White Les Calcerniers 1991: This is going over the hill fast. It has toasty, nutty aromas, little fruit flavor and a sherry-like finish. Too mature for most people to enjoy. 9,000 cases made. • $22 • **74**
Condrieu 1991 • $45 • (05/31/94) • **87**
Condrieu Viognier 1992: Perfumed toasty new oak dominates this silky white, overshadowing the distinctive Viognier fruit, which emerges only in hints of spice and rose petals. It lacks acidity for freshness, and finishes a bit bitter. It's exotic, but lacks balance. • $40 • **78**
Cornas Chante-Perdrix 1991 • $28 • (05/31/94) • **86**
Cornas Chante-Perdrix 1990 • $28 • (09/30/93) • **88**
Crozes-Hermitage 1985 • $7 • (12/15/87) • **78**
Crozes-Hermitage Les Launes 1990: Rich, ripe, concentrated cassis and blackberry flavors are accented by appealing tobacco and mint. This solid red has good aging potential, drink now or hold through 1997. 8,000 cases made. • $12 • **89**
Crozes-Hermitage Les Launes White 1993: This cheerful wine is stuffed with sweet vanilla, peach and almond flavors, with a soft texture and a light piney finish. Well-integrated and distinctive. • $12 • **83**
Crozes-Hermitage Les Launes White 1992: An intriguing apricot aroma makes this dry, smooth white Rhône memorable. Subtle flavors of honey and spice add interest. It's mature, so drink now. 1,500 cases made. • $12 • (09/30/95) • **82**
Côte-Rôtie Seigneur de Maugiron 1991: A supple wine with fresh cherry, chestnut and barnyard flavors. Accessible but not complex. Drinkable now. • $36 • (05/31/94) • **81**
Côte-Rôtie Seigneur de Maugiron 1990: Firm and earthy, with a spicy streak that is more prominent than the fruit, finishing almost lean and austere. Needs until 1998 to soften. • $36 • (09/30/93) • **84**
Côtes du Rhône St.-Esprit 1993: A meaty wine in a full-blown style with nice notes of spice, herb and plum. Ripe and ready to drink, this isn't a wine for the faint of heart. 18,000 cases made. • $9 • **83**
Côtes du Rhône St.-Esprit 1988 • $6 • (12/15/90) BB • **84**
Côtes du Rhône St.-Esprit 1985 • $5 • (12/15/87) BB • **80**
Côtes du Ventoux Val Muzols 1993: Dried out and leathery, with only modest dried cherry and plum flavors. Overdone and heavy-handed, this wine lacks depth. 15,000 cases made. • $8 • **76**
Hermitage Cuvée Marquise de la Tourette 1991: Almost overripe, with raisin flavors and tough tannins. Compact and a bit hard. Try now. • $35 • (05/31/94) • **84**
Hermitage Cuvée Marquise de la Tourette 1990: This solid, firm-textured wine offers a broad beam of plum, berry, anise and tobacco aromas and flavors that extend into a focused finish. The tannins need until 1997 to 2000 to soften. • $36 • (09/30/93) • **88**
Hermitage Les Bessards 1990: Thick and chewy, offering rich tar, leather and game flavors typical of Syrah, muscular tannins and ripe plum notes. Powerful and concentrated, but a bit rustic. Drink in 1997. 291 cases made. • $75 • **89**
Hermitage White Cuvée Marquise de la Tourette 1992: Ripe and luscious, with honey aromas and flavors, along with almond and smoky notes. New oak adds interest to the soft melon fruit flavors. Full-bodied and round, it needs food for balance. • $30 • **85**
Hermitage White Cuvée Marquise de la Tourette 1991: Fresh and clean, offering almond and pear flavors on a light frame, it's simple but correct. Try it now as an apéritif or with grilled fish. • $30 • (05/31/94) • **80**
Merlot Vin de Pays d'Oc 1993: Smooth drinking and nicely flavored, with blackberry and cherry accents and light tannins. Rich fruit, appealing texture, and drinkable now. • $9 • (07/31/95) • **83**
St.-Joseph Cuvée Francois de Tournon 1991 • $NA • (05/31/94) • **79**

Key: SS—Spectator Selection. CS—Cellar Selection. BB—Best Buy. $NA—Price not available. (BT)—Barrel tasting. Ⓐ—Auction Price.
Dates in parentheses represent the issues in which the ratings were published.

Viognier Vin de Pays d'Oc 1993: A thin and unbalanced wine with exaggerated flavors of banana and watermelon. 2,000 cases made. • $9 • (03/31/95) • **73**

DELAUNAY, EDOUARD

Bourgogne Pinot Noir En Fleur 1993: Light, delicate, modest fruit flavors. Drink now through 1997. 5,000 cases made. • $15 • **78**
Clos de Vougeot Red 1993: Very light for this appellation, delivering a slightly weedy, metallic character, medium to light body, medium tannins and short finish. Drink now. 100 cases made. • $85 • **73**
Côte de Beaune-Villages 1993: Light, lean, modest strawberry and raspberry character, light tannins and rather short finish. Try now. • $18 • **79**

DELBECK

Brut Champagne Heritage NV • $NA • (12/31/91) • **84**

DELETANG, DOMAINE

Touraine Sauvignon de Touraine White 1993: Fresh herbal and lemon aromas and flavors give this wine character and typicity. It's very dry and crisp and the herbal note carries through on the finish. A good picnic wine. • $10 • (10/31/94) • **83**

DELMAS, BERNARD

Brut Blanquette de Limoux NV • $14 • (03/31/90) • **79**

DEMERAULMONT, CHÂTEAU

St.-Estèphe 1988 • $10 • (08/31/91) BB • **82**

DEMESSEY

Mâcon-Villages 1994: Straight-as-an-arrow style that grows on you as it warms up in the glass. Lean, crisp, well-defined citrus, gooseberry and grass character and a mouth-puckering finish. Try now. 1,666 cases made. • $12 • **83**
Pouilly-Fuissé 1994: Rich and rather fat, it appears too mature for our taste, adding a cooked apple note that distracts from otherwise nice tropical fruit flavors. • $20 • (05/31/96) • **78**
Pouilly-Fuissé 1993: Intensely tart and crisp, fresh lime and herb flavors. The finish is lean and green. Drink now. 1,667 cases made. • $18 • **78**

DERVIEUX-THAIZE, A.

Côte-Rôtie Côte Blonde la Garde Cuvée Réservée 1988 • $42 • (08/31/91) • **79**

DERVIN, MICHEL

Brut Champagne NV • $20 • (12/31/92) • **85**

DESCHAMPS, DOMAINE CLAUDINE

Gevrey-Chambertin Bel-Air 1985 • $28 • (03/31/88) • **87**

DESCHAMPS, MARC

Pouilly-Fumé Les Champs de Cri Les Loges 1994: Quite complex, featuring mineral, apple, menthol and a hint of peach, round and direct in its appeal. 600 cases imported. • $18 • (05/15/96) • **84**

DESCHAUX, LUCIEN

Beaujolais Le Vieux Presbytère 1994: Light-bodied even for Beaujolais, this supple wine shows light cherry flavors with a hint of spice. Chill it for easy quaffing now. • $NA • **79**
Beaujolais-Villages Le Vieux Presbytère 1994: A year in bottle has polished this wine and added chocolate and tea notes to the basic core of

cherry fruit. Though not as fruity as a typical Beaujolais, it developed well. • $NA • **84**

Bordeaux 1990: A bit tough around the edges, its astringency putting the brakes on otherwise good herb and currant Bordeaux flavors. Drinkable now with hearty food. Tasted twice. • $6 • (01/31/92) • **75**

Bordeaux White 1991: A basically tight and austere wine that has developed some attractively nutty, toasty flavors that make it interesting. It's mature and ready to drink now. • $8 • (11/15/94) • **83**

Brut Chardonnay Vin Mousseux NV: Simple and light with fruit cocktail flavors. Tastes off-dry, and has an onion note on the finish. • $8 • **80**

Châteauneuf-du-Pape Le Vieux Abbé 1992: A fruity, accessible, forward style of Châteauneuf, with cherry, raspberry and leather aromas, appealing fruit flavors and a smooth texture. Drink now. • $14 • (10/15/94) • **83**

Châteauneuf-du-Pape Le Vieux Abbé 1990: Soft and lighter than most Châteauneuf-du-Papes, almost Burgundian in style, with plenty of appealing strawberry, raspberry and spice aromas and flavors, finishing velvety. Drinkable now. • $13 • (11/15/92) • **86**

Châteauneuf-du-Pape Le Vieux Abbé 1987 • $10 • (12/31/91) • **82**

Côtes du Rhône Le Vieux Presbytère 1991: Spicy and rich, with pleasant plum and cherry flavors. Some nice cinnamon notes linger on the finish, but beginning to fade. Drink now. • $8 • (10/15/94) • **83**

Côtes du Ventoux La Cuvée du Chanoine 1990 • $5 • (01/31/92) • **75**

Côtes du Ventoux Le Vieux Presbytère 1989 • $6 • (12/31/91) BB • **80**

Graves White 1991: A robust white Graves, with buttery, earthy flavors and a smooth texture. Full-bodied and assertive, but it could use more fruit. • $9 • (11/15/94) • **82**

Muscadet de Sèvre et Maine 1992: Diluted and tart, showing hints of fennel flavor but lacking fruit and roundness. Very light and fading rapidly. • $11 • (10/31/94) • **77**

Médoc 1990: A simple, sturdy red, with pruny aromas and flavors that turn toward cherry and toast on the finish. Drinkable now. 3,500 cases made. • $8 • (01/31/92) BB • **80**

Rosé d'Anjou 1992: A full-bodied rosé that's quite sweet, with strawberry jam flavors that turn cloying on the finsh. A bit heavy and candied. • $7 • (11/15/94) • **77**

DESMEURE

Crozes-Hermitage Domaine des Remizières 1991 • $26 • (05/31/94) • **83**

Crozes-Hermitage Domaine des Remizières Cuvée Particulair 1986 • $8 • (05/31/89) BB • **84**

Hermitage Domaine des Remizières 1986 • $19 • (04/15/89) • **68**

DESMIRAIL, CHÂTEAU

Margaux 1994: Not much there really: plummy, bubblegum character, light body and a tannic finish. • $NA • **75-79** (BT)

Margaux 1993: Good core of ripe berry, cherry and tobacco flavors. Medium body and tannins and a soft finish. Better in 1997. • $23 • (01/31/96) • **83**

Margaux 1991: Clean and easy to drink. Light body and cherry flavors, a slightly watery finish. • $16 • (03/31/94) • **78**

Margaux 1990: An excellent wine, with a beautiful core of plum and black cherry flavors, fine tannins and a firm backbone. Very pretty. From the owners of Château Brane-Cantenac. Drinkable now. 4,000 cases made. • $27 • (03/31/93) • **91**

Margaux 1989 • $27 • (03/15/92) • **86**

Margaux 1986 • $22 • (06/30/89) • **90**

Margaux 1981: Cracking up a bit now with raisin, herbal, berry character, medium body and a soft finish. Tasted twice with consistent notes. Drink now. • $NA • **78**

DESSERRE, DOMAINE

Chinon 1987 • $9 • (12/31/88) • **86**

DESTIEUX, CHÂTEAU

St.-Emilion 1988 • $19 • (06/30/91) • **81**

St.-Emilion 1985 • $14 • (03/31/88) • **84**

DESVIGNES, LOUIS-CLAUDE

Morgon Côte du Py Red 1993: Ripe cassis and earthy flavors are attractive, but tannins dominate the slightly diluted fruit. This big Morgon may dry out before it softens. Try now. • $16 • **83**

Morgon Javernieres Red 1993: Barnyard aromas are off-putting, and linger on the palate, which shows earth and leather flavors under thick tannins. Extraction here, but not much grace. • $17 • **79**

DEURRE, DOMAINE DE

Côtes du Rhône-Villages Vinsobres 1989 • $9 • (08/31/92) • **84**

DEUTZ

Brut Blanc de Blancs Champagne 1990: Wonderfully fruity and vibrant in flavor, although somewhat tight because of crisp apple, lemon and grapefruit notes. Tasty to drink now. • $45 • **89**

Brut Blanc de Blancs Champagne 1988: A broad-textured Champagne that's lively and intense, with toasty pear, pine and slightly vinegary flavors. Finishes crisp and lemony. Drink now. • $37 Ⓐ • (11/30/92) • **83**

Brut Blanc de Blancs Champagne 1985 • $53 Ⓐ • (12/31/90) • **83**

Brut Blanc de Blancs Champagne 1982 • $39 • (05/31/87) • **90**

Brut Blanc de Noirs Champagne Cuvée Marie-Damarisse NV: Has a lot of red wine character. Crisp and lively in texture, lean but satisfying in flavor, distinguished by intriguing cherry and meaty flavors and accented by toast and vanilla 6,000 cases made. • $25 • **87**

Brut Champagne 1988: Super-clean and powerful, yet elegant, showing subtle toasty, fruity character, medium body and a firm acid structure. Delicious. It's improved with bottle age since we last tasted it about a year ago. Drink now or hold. 10,000 cases made. • $35 • (12/31/93) • **89**

Brut Champagne 1985 • $40 • (12/31/90) • **83**

Brut Champagne NV • $25 • (11/30/92) • **88**

Brut Champagne 150 Anniversaire NV • $50 • (12/31/88) • **89**

Brut Champagne Classic NV: Openly fruity, with easy-going flavors, crisp acidity and a touch of sweetness on the short finish. 63,000 cases made. • $25 • **82**

Brut Champagne Cuvée Lallier Gold Lack NV • $33 • (12/31/90) • **80**

Brut Champagne Cuvée Porsche NV: Fresh fruit flavor defines this clean, straightforward, smooth bubbly. It has apple and citrus notes and a dry, lingering finish. Enticing subtlety. 100 cases made. • $35 • **86**

Brut Champagne Cuvée William Deutz 1988: Very fruity, broad and creamy-textured, offering exuberant pear and pineapple notes and subtle accents of vanilla and spice. Has a blast of flavor, then fades on the finish. • $69 • **86**

Brut Champagne Cuvée William Deutz 1985: This shows intense vanilla and apple aromas and flavors, it has a full body but is rather rough on the finish, with searing acidity. Needs time. Similar score given in December 1992. 3,500 cases made. • $60 • (12/31/93) • **85**

Brut Champagne Cuvée William Deutz 1982: Elegant and yeasty, with lemon, spice and toast flavors and a slightly coarse texture on the finish. • $61 • (12/31/89) • **85**

Brut Champagne Cuvée William Deutz 1979 • $47 • (07/16/85) • **90**

Brut Champagne Georges Mathieu 1982: Attractive for its pretty pear, cherry and vanilla notes, well balanced, deep and full-bodied, with plenty of richness and concentration and a full, fruity aftertaste. • $40 • (12/31/89) • **89**

Brut Champagne Georges Mathieu Réserve 1985: Very firm and well-balanced, offering just enough crisp fruit flavor to back up the firmness. It has touches of earthy complexity, but stays basically straightforward in style. • $46 • (12/31/90) • **86**

Brut Champagne de Noirs Cuvée Marie-Damarisse NV • $20 • (10/31/93) • **86**

Brut Rosé Champagne 1988: Tastes like it's already heading over the hill. Drink now. Tasted twice, with consistent notes. 3,500 cases made. • $40 • (12/31/92) • **74**

Brut Rosé Champagne 1985: A Rosé that's delicious and assertive. Firm, well structured and showing good Pinot Noir flavors of cherry and strawberry, with hints of spice for seasoning. • $46 • (12/31/90) • **88**

Brut Rosé Champagne 1982 • $35 • (12/31/87) • **86**

Brut Rosé Champagne 1981 • $27 • (12/16/85) • **67**

Brut Rosé Champagne Cuvée Marie-Damarisse NV: A round, assertive sparkler showing mature flavors of toast and ripe berries. Full-bodied and dry on the finish, rich but a bit heavy. • $25 • (12/15/95) • **85**

DEUX RIVES, LES

Corbières 1992 • $7 • (03/15/94) • **80**

DEUX ROCHES, DOMAINE DES

Mâcon-Villages 1994: Richer than most '94 Mâcons, offering a smooth, buttery texture and picking up apple, pear, spice and melon flavors on the silky finish. 5,000 cases made. • $13 • **85**
St.-Véran 1994: Well crafted, balancing a touch of sweet-tasting wood with ripe melon, pear and fig flavors. At this stage it's woodier than most traditional St.-Vérans but finishes harmoniously. • $NA • **85**
St.-Véran Les Terres Noires 1994: Tastes more like Meursault than St.-Véran with all the round, seductive pear, smoke and sweet vanilla character from wood. Turns slightly astringent on the finish. 1,666 cases made. • $17 • **82**

DEVAUX, VVE. A.

Brut Champagne Grande Réserve NV • $NA • (12/31/91) • **88**

DEVOY, DOMAINE DU

Lirac White 1991 • $10 • (06/15/93) • **75**

DEYDIER & FILS, DOMAINE JEAN

Châteauneuf-du-Pape 1993: A tannic red wine with good but straightforward fruit flavors and a tough finish. Has more structure than flavor, but may just need cheese to balance it out. • $20 • **82**
Châteauneuf-du-Pape Les Clefs D'Or 1983 • $16 • (10/31/87) • **78**
Châteauneuf-du-Pape White 1994: Light and simple, with fruit candy aromas and earthy flavors, this lacks depth and freshness. Possibly corky. • $22 • **68**
Côtes du Rhône 1993: Brings out leathery, peppery aromas and ripe fruit flavors of the Grenache grape. Moderately tannic, well balanced, smells and tastes nicely mature already, so drink soon. • $13 • (09/30/95) • **85**
Côtes du Rhône 1990 • $12 • (04/15/93) • **82**

DEYREM-VALENTIN, CHÂTEAU

Margaux 1995: Solid intensity of fruit with plenty of smoky, spicy berry character. Medium body, fine tannins and a long, silky finish. • $NA • (05/15/96) • **85-89** (BT)

DIANE DE BELGRAVE

Haut-Médoc 1993: Weedy and unripe. Second label of Château Belgrave. Drink as soon as possible. • $NA • (01/31/96) • **75**

DICONNE, JEAN-PIERRE

Meursault Les Luchets 1993: A bit simple but the flavors are quite tropical, featuring chalky, smoky, toasty, oaky notes, firm texture and vibrant, tart, lemony finish. • $NA • (08/31/95) • **84**
Meursault Les Narvaux 1993: Lean in texture, with intense citrus character, numbs your palate with acidity. Modest tropical fruit, green apple and pear flavors. • $NA • (08/31/95) • **83**

DIEBOLT-VALLOIS

Brut Rosé Champagne Cramant NV • $21 • (10/31/87) • **89**

Key: SS—Spectator Selection. CS—Cellar Selection. BB—Best Buy. $NA—Price not available. (BT)—Barrel tasting. Ⓐ—Auction Price.
Dates in parentheses represent the issues in which the ratings were published.

DILIGENT, FRANCOIS

Brut Champagne Carte Blanche NV • $NA • (12/31/91) • **83**

DILLON, CHÂTEAU

Haut-Médoc 1995: Quite impressive for its sheer intensity of pure cassis and dried herb character, but it's slightly lean in texture. The finish is a bit dry and slightly metallic. • $NA • (05/15/96) • **80-84** (BT)

DIMERIE, CHÂTEAU DE LA

Muscadet de Sèvre et Maine 1994: There'a a note of maturity here that brings out herbal and petrol elements. Still, it's balanced and lively. Drink up. • $7 • (05/15/96) • **83**

DOCTEUR PARCE

Domaine du Mas Blanc Cuvée Collioure 1991: Modest fruit flavors and accents of leather and spice make this an interesting, though light, red to drink now. • $21 • **81**
Domaine du Mas Blanc Rimage Banyuls 1991: Pruny, smoky flavors and sweetness give this dessert wine ripe character. Rather coarse and tannic, though. • $27 • **78**

DOISY-DAENE, CHÂTEAU

Bordeaux White 1993: Not a bad dry white from this sweet-wine producer. Lime, citrus and vanilla character, medium body, fine acidity and lemony, vanilla finish. Drink now. • $15 • **82**
Sauternes 1991: Attractive and sharp, well made, light-to-medium-bodied but featuring pretty honey, almond, spice and pineapple flavors. Drinkable now. • $NA • (04/15/95) • **85**
Sauternes 1988: A bit grassy, medium-bodied and medium-sweet, but the vanilla bean, honey and pineapple flavors unfold harmoniously to a clean finish. Drinkable now, but might be better after 1998. • $35 • (04/15/95) • **87**
Sauternes 1986 • $35 • (04/15/95) • **89**
Sauternes 1985: Tastes light and watery, more like a sweet Chenin Blanc than a classic Sauternes. It's sugary with a touch of apricot and tobacco flavors but it's not very concentrated and lacks depth. • $24 • (05/31/88) • **73**
Sauternes 1983 • $31 Ⓐ • (01/31/88) • **73**

DOISY-VEDRINES, CHÂTEAU

Sauternes 1992: Sweet and sour, but interesting, offering orange-peel, marmalade, grapefruit and spice notes and a slightly bitter finish. Drink now. • $NA • (04/15/95) • **79**
Sauternes 1990: Intriguing lime, floral, tropical character, fresh and delicious, medium weight and sweetness. Age should improve it—try now through 1998. • $38 • (04/15/95) • **88**
Sauternes 1989: This subtle white grows on you, showing lovely tropical, toasted coconut and lemon flavors that blend together harmoniously on the intense, long, sweet finish. Drink now or hold through the '90s. • $50 • (04/15/95) • **91**
Sauternes 1988: Super-charged, incredibly intense Sauternes, exploding with tons of dried apricot, tropical and lemon flavors whistling through your palate to a long, long finish. Bravo! Don't touch until after 2000. • $32 • (04/15/95) • **93**
Sauternes 1986 • $52 • (12/31/89) • **86**

DOMINIQUE, CHÂTEAU LA

St.-Emilion 1995: Nicely packed, with well-defined red berry and spice character, this is almost Burgundian in its earthiness. But it's a bit rustic on the long finish. • $NA • (05/15/96) • **85-89** (BT)
St.-Emilion 1994: Attractive dried herb, olive, tar and currant flavors. Medium-bodied and rather complex, but just a bit short on the seductive and supple finish. • $35 • (05/15/96) • **85-89** (BT)

St.-Emilion 1993: Firm and racy chocolate, berry and cherry aromas and flavors, medium body, fine tannins and crisp finish. This needs a year or two of bottle age, try in 1997. • $30 • (01/31/96) • **87**

St.-Emilion 1992: Soft and succulent, medium body and tannins and plenty of black olive, black cherry and vanilla character. Drink now. • $18 • **83**

St.-Emilion 1991: A wine with refined tobacco and fruit flavors and an elegant tannin structure to harmonize with the fruit. • $18 • (03/31/94) • **80**

St.-Emilion 1990: Has loads of toasted new oak character and ripe fruit aromas and full, almost dry tannins. A little clumsy. Drinkable now. 7,000 cases made. • $35 • (03/31/93) • **88**

St.-Emilion 1989 • $33 Ⓐ • (03/15/92) • **91**

St.-Emilion 1988 • $25 • (06/30/91) • **86**

St.-Emilion 1986 • $40 Ⓐ • (06/30/89) • **95**

St.-Emilion 1985 • $30 • (03/31/88) • **83**

St.-Emilion 1983 • $28 Ⓐ • (05/16/86) • **88**

St.-Emilion 1982 • $45 Ⓐ • (08/31/92) • **79**

St.-Emilion 1979 • $27 • (10/15/89) • **81**

St.-Emilion 1961 • $NA • (04/30/96) • **85**

DONA, CELLIER DE LA

Côtes du Roussillon-Villages 1988 • $8 • (10/15/90) BB • **85**

DONA BAISSAS, CHÂTEAU

Côtes du Roussillon-Villages 1990 • $8 • (03/31/92) • **79**

Côtes du Roussillon-Villages 1988 • $7 • (10/15/90) • **77**

DONATS, CHÂTEAU LES

Premières Côtes de Blaye Red 1989 • $9 • (11/30/92) • **78**

DOPFF AU MOULIN

Gewürztraminer Alsace White 1992: Fruity and flavorful, full-bodied and lively in texture, marked by a milky overtone to the peach and grapefruit flavors. Has a lingering finish that adds an extra dimension. • $14 • (11/15/94) • **85**

Riesling Alsace White 1992: Light and fresh, showing grapefruit, nutmeg and pine tar flavors, crisp and tart. It's refreshing, but rather simple and short. • $11 • (11/15/94) • **80**

DOUDET-NAUDIN

Chablis 1994: Quite ripe and rich for a village Chablis, sporting lemon, cedar, honey, crème brûlée and toasted bread flavors. Very crisp, tart, medium-long finish. Try in 1999. • $NA • (05/31/96) • **86**

Chablis Montmains 1994: Magnificent, well-defined lemon and honey flavors served up with digital clarity in a full-bodied, fresh package. The creamy texture coats your mouth yet it remains balanced and electrifying. Long and very crisp finish. Tempting now, but better in 2000. • $NA • (05/31/96) • **90**

Corton Renardes 1945 • $NA • (08/31/90) • **86**

Savigny-lès-Beaune Domaine Doudet 1993: A bit lean but offering some decent berry, mineral and plum character, medium to light body, firm, slightly dry tannins and short finish. Drinkable now. • $18 • **80**

Vosne-Romanée Les Suchots 1993: Rather light and watery, delivering stewed tomato and weedy character, light body and tannins and a dry finish. • $36 • **76**

DOUELLES, LES

Bordeaux 1982 • $3 • (10/01/85) BB • **79**

DOURTHE, PIERRE

Bordeaux Numero 1 1993: Plenty of cassis and berry character, medium to full body, silky tannins and fruity finish. A serious merchant blend for the vintage. Drinkable now. • $9 • (01/31/96) • **83**

Bordeaux Numero 1 1990: There's plenty of ripe, fresh fruit-black currant, plum, cherry-and a full complement of tar, licorice and cedar accents. Not a blockbuster, but extremely well made. Drinkable now. • $9 • (05/15/94) BB • **88**

Bordeaux White Numero 1 1993: Extreme example of the grassy style, revealing aggesive herbal and vegetal notes. But it's flavorful and shows personality. • $9 • **80**

Bordeaux White Numero 1 1992: This is a rich-textured, full-bodied white with grapefruit, mineral and almond flavors. It could have more fruit flavor to fill out its large frame. Good but bit heavy. • $9 • **82**

DOZON, DOMAINE

Chinon Clos du Saut au Loup Cuvée Alexandre 1991: The mature tobacco and dried fruit aromas are attractive but it's lost on the palate, leaving chalky, earthy flavors and drying tannins. • $15 • (10/31/94) • **75**

DRAPPIER

Brut Blanc de Blancs Champagne NV • $NA • **91**

Brut Blanc de Blancs Champagne Signature NV • $46 • (11/30/92) • **83**

Brut Champagne Carte d'Or 1989: Packs in lots of concentrated flavors, yet maintains its elegance and finesse, with spicy pear, vanilla, toast and light cherry notes, finishing with a smooth, creamy texture. Drink now through 1996. • $35 • (12/31/93) SS • **92**

Brut Champagne Carte d'Or 1988: Crisp and austere, with tart ginger, pear and citrus flavors that are tightly wound. Has attractive aromas, hinting at vanilla and nutmeg, and an earthy finish. Drinkable now. • $44 • (11/30/92) • **86**

Brut Champagne Carte d'Or NV: Creamy, smooth and has figgy, spicy aromas and rich flavors of pear, vanilla and hazelnut that linger nicely on the finish. Slightly sweet, generous and supple in texture. 30,000 cases made. • $29 • **87**

Brut Champagne Collection Cuvée General Charles de Gaulle 1988: Firm and intense with a tight core of crisp, spicy, toasty flavors with hints of pear and perfume, finishing with a touch of lime. Drink now through 1996. • $48 • (12/31/93) • **89**

Brut Champagne Collection Cuvée General Charles de Gaulle 1986: Complex and engaging, with a pretty range of toast, pear, citrus and spice flavors that are neatly woven together. Finishes with subtle hints of ginger and spice. Drink now. 500 cases made. • $56 • (11/30/92) • **91**

Brut Champagne Cuvée Maurice Chevalier NV • $45 • (11/30/92) • **87**

Brut Champagne Grande Sendrée 1985: Tart and intense, but a sharp, earthy edge holds the focused lime and citrus flavors on a tightrope. Turns chalky and hard on the finish, perhaps with time this will be more palatable. Drink now. • $58 • (11/30/92) • **86**

Brut Rosé Champagne Val des Demoiselles 1981 • $23 • (12/16/85) • **72**

Brut Rosé Champagne Val des Demoiselles NV: A full-flavored, multi-dimensional rosé with ripe cherry and peach flavors accented by mineral and chalk notes on the dry finish. Could be a little smoother. 1,000 cases made. • $34 • **85**

Demi-Sec Champagne NV • $34 • (11/30/92) • **90**

DROIN, JEAN-PAUL

Chablis Les Clos 1994: Rather opulent, ripe and intense, offering some crisp lemon, honey and pear character, medium to full body and long but somewhat rough finish. Better in 1998? Tasted twice, with consistent notes. 416 cases made. • $45 • (05/31/96) • **85**

Chablis Les Clos 1993: Big, young, steely, balanced and intense, offering mineral, apple and melon flavors, medium body and long, spicy finish. Try in 1997. 590 cases made. • $40 • **86**

Chablis Montmains 1994: Beautifully made, elegant and extremely fresh and vibrant. Like wet stone, boasting tons of citrus, ripe pear and pineapple flavors. Its chewy texture and a touch of subtle, toasted oak add complexity. Built for the cellar, try in 1999. Tasted twice, with consistent notes. 208 cases made. • $28 • (05/31/96) • **91**

Chablis Montmains 1993: Lovely, spicy mineral, apple and honey character, medium body, fine acidity and fresh finish. 590 cases made. • $24 • **84**

Chablis Montée de Tonnerre 1994: Crisp and fresh citrus, grassy, green apple, honey and mineral character. Medium- to light-bodied, a prototypical Chablis that's a bit coarse on the finish. Tasted twice, with consistent notes. 1,000 cases made. • $30 • (05/31/96) • **84**

Chablis Montée de Tonnerre 1993: Pretty in an elegant style. Medium-bodied, with a creamy apple and spice character. Crisp finish. 1,200 cases made. • $26 • **85**

Chablis Vaillons 1994: Intriguing, charming and intense, featuring gooseberry, floral, grassy, wet earth and dried herb character. Medium-bodied and nicely ripe, very crisp and fresh. Try in 1999. Tasted twice, with consistent notes. 1,250 cases made. • $28 • (05/31/96) • **85**

Chablis Vaillons 1993: Firm mineral, steely and earthy aromas and flavors, medium body, hard acidity and light finish. A bit short. 3,200 cases made. • $24 • **81**

Chablis Vaudésir 1994: Fat, rich, quite heavy, overdone. Full-bodied and quite matured, as evidenced by its yellow color. Drinkable now. Tasted twice, with consistent notes. 416 cases made. • $45 • (05/31/96) • **75**

Chablis Vaudésir 1993: Classically steely Chablis-lots of citrus and green apple notes. But a hint of flinty mineral, honey and spice character adds complexity on the firm and elegant finish. 600 cases made. • $40 • **85**

Chablis Vosgros 1993: Beautifully made, exhibiting mineral, chalk, green apple and pear character and good concentration. It ends in a long, stylish finish. 375 cases made. • $24 • **87**

DROUHIN, JOSEPH

Aloxe-Corton 1990 • $33 • (12/15/92) • **88**
Aloxe-Corton 1989 • $27 • (01/31/92) • **89**
Aloxe-Corton 1986 • $25 • (04/30/89) • **83**
Aloxe-Corton 1985 • $23 • (11/15/87) • **90**

Bâtard-Montrachet 1993: Crisp lime, honey and pear flavors in a vibrant package. Drink now. Very clean finish. • $105 • **86**

Bâtard-Montrachet 1992: Generous and supple, charming and almost ready to drink, with creamy vanilla bean, peach, pear and toast flavors laced with some honey and hazelnut notes. Drinkable now. • $120 • (08/31/94) • **92**

Bâtard-Montrachet 1991 • $110 • (10/15/93) • **87**

Beaujolais-Villages 1994: A muddled wine with herbal flavors and aromas, though there is still some appealing berry flavors and a spicey finish. • $NA • (06/15/95) • **77**

Beaune Clos des Mouches 1994: Showing good intensity in its relatively lean package, this medium-bodied white offers ripe apple, lime and a touch of mineral character. Somewhat linear and one-dimensional. Better in 1998? • $60 • (05/31/96) 84 • **84**

Beaune Clos des Mouches 1993: Good straightforward Pinot offering berry and cherry character, medium body, light tannins and crisp finish. Better in 1997. • $50 • **86**

Beaune Clos des Mouches 1992: Quite tannic and rough, more like a 1991 than a '92, but has some sweet, ripe fruit below the tight, hard tannins. Fans of this wine know it ages well, might be better after 1996. • $33 • **84**

Beaune Clos des Mouches 1991: Fresh and fruity, showing lots of appealing strawberry and red cherry aromas and flavors. Very bright and appealing for its beautifully defined fruit and substantial length. Drinkable now. • $37 Ⓐ • (01/31/94) • **86**

Beaune Clos des Mouches 1990: A joy to taste. Gorgeous, smooth, round, supple and full of crisp, focused raspberry, earth and currant aromas and flavors. Ravishing to drink in 1997. 1,800 cases made. • $52 • (12/15/92) • **93**

Beaune Clos des Mouches 1989 • $40 • (02/29/92) • **92**
Beaune Clos des Mouches 1988 • $50 • (02/15/91) • **88**
Beaune Clos des Mouches 1987 • $47 • (06/15/90) • **83**

Beaune Clos des Mouches White 1993: This fresh white Burgundy has honey, mineral and apple character. Medium-bodied and crisp, long, clean finish. • $48 • **85**

Beaune Clos des Mouches White 1992: Racy, with lovely, silky texture and smoky, toasty, lemon and pear flavors, all in good proportions, medium-bodied, focused and classy, with a gorgeous, minerally finish. Try now. Tasted twice. • $55 • (08/31/94) • **90**

Beaune Clos des Mouches White 1991 • $52 • (10/15/93) • **87**

Beaune Grèves 1992: Very light and crisp, with modest strawberry and floral notes. Drinkable now. • $25 • **80**

Beaune Grèves 1991: Light, firm and modestly flavorful, with a pleasant ring of toasty, cedary berry aromas and flavors that persist on the finish. Drinkable now. • $28 Ⓐ • (01/31/94) • **82**

Beaune Grèves 1989 • $47 • (01/31/92) • **88**
Beaune Grèves 1959 • $90 • (08/31/90) • **80**

Beaune Hospices de Beaune Cuvée Maurice Drouhin 1990: Focused and elegant, offering a nicely-crafted texture, raspberry and earth aromas and a smooth, refined finish. Drinkable now • $NA • (12/15/92) • **88**

Bonnes Mares 1993: Vibrant, steely Burgundy sporting bright cherry and plum aromas, medium body, clean fruit flavors and fine tannins. Drink in 1998. • $100 • **88**

Bonnes Mares 1992: Lithe, appealing berry and floral aromas and flavors, silky and generous on the palate right through the lean, supple finish. Should be best around 1997. • $64 • **86**

Bonnes Mares 1991: Lean, almost delicate, with a minty, rose petal edge to the strawberry and raspberry fruit, which persists on the finish. A fragile wine with subtle flavors and substantial length. Tannins are beautifully integrated. • $76 Ⓐ • (01/31/94) • **89**

Bonnes Mares 1990: The lovely complexity grows on you, from the forest, wet earth and underbrush aromas to the silky blackberry flavors. Has an excellent backbone of tannins, and the intensity on the long finish is almost perfect. Drink in 1998. • $91 • (12/15/92) • **93**

Bonnes Mares 1989 • $99 • (01/31/92) • **93**
Bourgogne Pinot Noir Laforàt 1989 • $9 • (04/30/91) BB • **85**
Bourgogne Pinot Noir Laforàt 1988 • $10 • (03/31/91) BB • **84**
Bourgogne Pinot Noir Laforàt 1987 • $8 • (06/15/89) • **78**
Bourgogne Pinot Noir Laforàt 1985 • $8 • (11/15/87) • **78**
Bourgogne Pinot Noir Laforàt 1983 • $7 • (11/01/85) • **71**

Brouilly 1995: This silky wine is flush with fruit, showing lots of plum and black cherry flavors with attractive chocolate and banana accents. There's just enough tannin for grip. • $16 • **86**

Brouilly 1994: Black cherry and light tomato notes mingle in this soft, round Brouilly. It's straightforward but shows some depth. • $13 • (06/15/95) • **82**

Brouilly 1993: Ripe and plush showing generous plum and berry flavors, round and soft, with good presence on the palate and a lingering finish. A solid, well-made Beaujolais, bigger than many Brouillys. 4,500 cases made. • $12 • (06/30/94) • **86**

Chablis 1994: Loads of delicious flavors range from ripe apple to minerals. Medium to full in body and a good finish. • $19 • (08/31/95) • **84**

Chablis Domaine de Vaudon 1994: Lemon, spice and almond aromas and flavors. Medium body, good fruit and a long, rich finish. • $24 • (08/31/95) • **85**

Chablis Les Clos 1994: Rich and lively honey, lemon, pear and toasted oak notes and a touch of mineral character. Of medium to full body, it's delicious now but will improve upon cellaring. Best to try in 1999. Tasted twice, with consistent notes. • $45 • (05/31/96) • **90**

Chablis Les Clos 1993: Very intense, sporting spice and mineral character, searing acidity, medium body and a flavorful finish. Better in 1997. • $45 • (08/31/95) • **87**

Chablis Premier Cru 1994: Crisp and tight, somewhat grassy like a Sauvignon Blanc, adding hints of ripe pear, tropical fruit and honey character. Very clean, attractive, sweet-tasting, balanced finish. Drinkable now or try in 1997. • $25 • (05/31/96) • **84**

Chablis Secher 1993: Nicely made, it shows a grassy yet also ripe character and some honey, pear and green apple. Very crisp. Tempting now, but better in 1997. • $25 • (08/31/95) • **85**

Chablis Vaudésir 1994: A Chablis *grand cru* that rivals a top Montrachet. Unbelievable intensity and elegance. Offers mineral, earth, honey and toasted bread character as well as searing fruit and citrus flavors. Full-bodied but refined, one of the best white Burgundies of the vintage. Long and intense finish. Don't touch until 2001. Tasted twice, with consistent notes. • $44 • (05/31/96) • **94**

Chablis Vaudésir 1993: Appealingly spicy, a pleasing and rather ripe Chablis sporting citrusy and toasty flavors on a lean frame. • $45 • (08/31/95) • **83**

Key: SS—Spectator Selection. CS—Cellar Selection. BB—Best Buy. $NA—Price not available. (BT)—Barrel tasting. Ⓐ—Auction Price.
Dates in parentheses represent the issues in which the ratings were published.

FRANCE

Chambertin 1993: Wonderful and well made, medium in body, with a full-throttle tannic structure and plenty of ripe fruit flavors. Drink in 2000. • $119 • **91**
Chambertin 1992: Lean and a little leafy-stemmy in character, but with enough strawberry flavor to save it. Drink now. • $74 • **79**
Chambertin 1991: Crisp and light, its rose petal-scented raspberry flavors bouncing through the delicate frame, picking up some smoky, meaty notes on the finish. Best by 1997. • $84 Ⓐ • (01/31/94) • **86**
Chambertin 1990: Muscular yet harmonious, velvety and intense, with beautiful ripe plum, earth and cherry flavors and a hint of smoke. Drink in 1997. • $113 • (12/15/92) • **91**
Chambertin 1989 • $114 • (01/31/92) • **90**
Chambertin 1988 • $83 • (02/15/91) • **94**
Chambertin 1986 • $80 • (02/28/89) • **90**
Chambertin 1985 • $107 • (11/15/87) • **95**
Chambolle-Musigny 1992: Crisp and nicely focused, a lighter style with appealing raspberry and anise flavors that linger on the delicate finish. Drinkable now. • $25 • **82**
Chambolle-Musigny 1991: Light, almost watery, with extremely modest strawberry and citrusy aromas and flavors. Drinkable now. • $29 Ⓐ • (01/31/94) • **75**
Chambolle-Musigny 1990: Bright and vivid, with subtle leaf, plum, mushroom and wet earth flavors that grow into an interesting finish. Try in 1997. • $36 • (12/15/92) • **87**
Chambolle-Musigny 1989 • $41 • (01/31/92) • **91**
Chambolle-Musigny 1986 • $27 • (07/31/88) • **88**
Chambolle-Musigny 1985 • $33 • (11/15/87) • **93**
Chambolle-Musigny Les Amoureuses 1992: A good effort for '92. Smoky, gamy, red berry flavors blend with floral notes in a complex, supple, ripe wine. Has appealing concentration and a medium-long finish. Try now. • $55 • **85**
Chambolle-Musigny Les Amoureuses 1991: Light, almost watery, with barely discernible currant flavors that sneak in on the finish. Drinkable now. • $67 Ⓐ • (01/31/94) • **77**
Chambolle-Musigny Les Amoureuses 1990: A classy, well-knit wine that's extremely seductive, with lovely vanilla, earth, smoke and berry aromas and flavors dancing across the palate and a beautiful, silky finish. Drinkable now. 250 cases made. • $80 • (12/15/92) • **93**
Chambolle-Musigny Les Amoureuses 1988 • $76 • (12/31/90) • **87**
Chambolle-Musigny Les Amoureuses 1955 • $250 • (08/31/90) • **65**
Chambolle-Musigny Les Baudes 1991: Delicate but flavorful and amazingly long on the finish, showing delicious currant, blackberry and anise aromas and flavors that remain silky and smooth through the finish. Drinkable now. • $39 Ⓐ • (01/31/94) • **86**
Chambolle-Musigny Les Baudes 1989 • $52 • (01/31/92) • **89**
Chambolle-Musigny Les Feusselottes 1989 • $55 • (01/31/92) • **92**
Chambolle-Musigny Les Hauts Doix 1990: Tight and elegant, with lovely, focused chocolate and berry flavors. A medium-bodied, firmly tannic wine to drink in 1997. • $53 • (12/15/92) • **88**
Chambolle-Musigny Les Sentiers 1989 • $55 • (01/31/92) • **92**
Chambolle-Musigny Premier Cru 1993: Somewhat hollow on the palate, showing decent plum and dried cherry character and medium body. It could use a bit more fruit on the finish. Better in 1999? • $45 • **87**
Chambolle-Musigny Premier Cru 1991: Light in texture, a pretty wine with appealing raspberry and vanilla aromas and flavor. Drinkable now. • $33 Ⓐ • (01/31/94) • **83**
Chambolle-Musigny Premier Cru 1989 • $50 • (01/31/92) • **89**
Charmes-Chambertin 1993: Attractive berry and vanilla character, but it's still somewhat disappointing for a *grand cru*. Medium in body, delivering sweet fruit and a very delicate finish. Better in 1999. • $84 • **85**
Charmes-Chambertin 1991: Supple and elegant, a smooth-textured wine that offers a moderate lovel of blackberry and spice aromas and flavors that persist into a crisp finish, hinting at smoke and toast. Try in 1997. • $59 Ⓐ • (01/31/94) • **87**
Charmes-Chambertin 1990: Opulent and sensational, with ripe fruit flavors that ooze from the glass. Not only does it have amazing fruit, but the tannins are equally impressive and are in near-perfect balance. Drink in 1998. • $81 • (12/15/92) • **96**
Charmes-Chambertin 1989 • $80 • (01/31/92) • **92**
Charmes-Chambertin 1988 • $65 • (11/15/90) • **93**
Charmes-Chambertin 1986 • $60 • (02/28/89) CS • **91**
Charmes-Chambertin 1985 • $60 • (11/15/87) • **89**
Chassagne-Montrachet 1994: Straightforward green apple, vegetal and dried herb notes. Tart finish. • $38 • (05/31/96) 78 • **78**
Chassagne-Montrachet 1993: Chalky, fruity character and relatively rich texture, offering mineral and stone qualities and clean finish. A laudable effort. Try now. • $32 • **85**
Chassagne-Montrachet 1991 • $28 • (10/15/93) • **86**
Chassagne-Montrachet Red 1990: Straightforward Chassagne. Light and pleasant, with one-dimensional berry and earth aromas and flavors. Drinkable now. • $22 • (12/15/92) • **84**
Chassagne-Montrachet Red 1989 • $23 • (01/31/92) • **87**
Chassagne-Montrachet Marquis de Laguiche White 1994: Some nice intensity here, a fresh, medium-bodied white that delivers appealing, ripe fruit flavors. Harmonious and drinkable now. • $54 • (05/31/96) 81 • **81**
Chassagne-Montrachet Marquis de Laguiche White 1993: Green and tart apple, grapefruit and herb flavors and crisp finish. Could use a bit more ripe fruit, maybe time will make it smoother. Try now. • $42 • **84**
Chassagne-Montrachet Marquis de Laguiche White 1992: A nicely fruity and fresh white Burgundy, with focused grapefruit, apple and lime flavors that give it life and zest. Clean and vibrant. • $42 • (08/31/94) • **85**
Chassagne-Montrachet Marquis de Laguiche White 1991 • $40 • (10/15/93) • **85**
Chassagne-Montrachet Morgeot Red 1991: Light ande spicy, showing a nice balance of strawberry and raspberry fruit with an overlay of sweet oak. Enjoyable to drink now. • $20 Ⓐ • (01/31/94) • **82**
Chassagne-Montrachet Morgeot White 1991 • $40 • (10/15/93) • **85**
Chiroubles 1995: A mouthwatering wine, with vivid plum and light chocolate flavors, supple on the palate yet firm in the finish. Bright and balanced, with a juicy finish. • $17 • **86**
Chiroubles 1993: This hearty wine is stuffed with black cherry fruit and firm tannins, if it lacks the elegance characteristic of the cru, it's still rich and flavorful. 900 cases made. • $12 • (06/30/94) • **83**
Chorey-lès-Beaune 1993: Fine and clean, featuring zingy berry and plum character, light tannins and a fresh finish. Not big, but delicious. Drink now. • $20 • **83**
Chorey-lès-Beaune 1992: Light in body and texture, but showing a focused beam of clean, pure raspberry and currant. A good effort in a difficult vintage. • $16 • **83**
Clos de la Roche 1991: A succulent beam of spicy raspberry flavor picks up black pepper notes on the finish. Light, charming and a bit watery in texture. Drinkable now. • $49 Ⓐ • (01/31/94) • **85**
Clos de la Roche 1990: Pretty and delicate, with a bounty of raspberry flavors and refreshing acidity. Delivers a focused feeling along with ripe tannins. Try now. • $69 • (12/15/92) • **89**
Clos de la Roche 1989 • $77 • (01/31/92) • **88**
Clos de la Roche 1988 • $73 • (02/15/91) • **93**
Clos de la Roche 1986 • $53 • (07/15/89) • **83**
Clos de la Roche 1985 • $60 • (11/15/87) • **97**
Clos de Vougeot 1992: A delicate Burgundy with pretty raspberry and vanilla flavors that linger on the sweet finish. Tannins are very fine. Drinkable now. • $44 • **85**
Clos de Vougeot 1991: Light, elegant and soft in texture, very fine tannins and a bright beam of delicate raspberry and strawberry flavors runs through to the finish. Might develop into a real beauty with aging until 1997 to '99. • $62 Ⓐ • (01/31/94) • **86**
Clos de Vougeot 1990: Opulent, with a hard-as-nails undertow that sweeps across the palate, then turns smooth and velvety on the focused finish, with lovely currant, raspberry, cherry and smoke notes. Drinkable in 1998. • $71 • (12/15/92) • **91**
Clos de Vougeot 1988 • $85 • (02/15/91) • **90**
Clos de Vougeot 1986 • $55 • (04/15/89) • **86**
Clos de Vougeot 1985 • $38 Ⓐ • (11/15/87) • **94**
Clos St.-Denis 1989 • $76 • (01/31/92) • **91**
Corton 1991: Tough, earthy and solid, pretty currant and plum flavors lurk behind a wave of gritty tannins and minerally, mushroomy notes. Try in 1997. • $42 Ⓐ • (01/31/94) • **84**
Corton 1990: Very velvety, with plenty of attractive blackberry and earth aromas and flavors and firm, almost steely tannins. Drinkable now to 1998. • $58 • (12/15/92) • **88**
Corton 1985 • $48 • (11/15/87) • **92**

Corton Bressandes 1993: Delicious and beautifully crafted violet, vanilla and ripe fruit character, full body, silky tannins and long, fresh finish. Better in 2000. • $70 • **93**
Corton Bressandes 1988 • $60 • (11/15/90) • **92**
Corton Bressandes 1986 • $45 • (04/30/89) • **90**
Corton-Charlemagne 1991 • $55 • (10/15/93) • **89**
Côte de Beaune 1992: Light and crisp, but with a solid core of berry that keeps sailing through the finish to liven it up. • $18 • **81**
Côte de Beaune-Villages 1986 • $13 • (06/15/89) • **78**
Côte de Beaune-Villages 1985 • $14 • (11/15/87) • **85**
Côte de Nuits-Villages 1990: Crisp and fresh, with attractive berry and earth aromas and flavors and a medium tannin structure. Drinkable now. • $20 • (12/15/92) • **82**
Côte de Nuits-Villages 1985 • $19 • (11/15/87) • **86**
Echézeaux 1991: A lithe, lively mouthful of anise-scented currant and blackberry flavors, which are much more appealing and distinctive than the earthy aromas. Intense enough on the finish to warrant cellaring until 1998. • $49 Ⓐ • (01/31/94) • **87**
Echézeaux 1990: Effusively aromatic and flavorful, solid and seductive. The raspberry and earth characteristics are beautiful on the long finish. Drinkable in 1997. 175 cases made. • $69 • (12/15/92) • **91**
Echézeaux 1988 • $60 • (11/15/90) • **93**
Echézeaux 1986 • $60 • (07/31/88) • **92**
Fleurie 1995: Smoky, gamy aromas give way to ripe plum flavors on the palate, with very firm tannins that dominate the finish. This is a big wine that sacrifices balance for extraction. Try in early 1997. • $19 • **84**
Fleurie 1994: Harmonious but light. Berry and cherry flavors are juicy and fresh, but the structure is more like a Brouilly. Pleasant and lively, drink now. • $13 • (06/15/95) • **84**
Gevrey-Chambertin 1992: Light and fragrant, charming and delicate, emphasizing bright currant and strawberry flavors that linger nicely on the palate. Drinkable now. • $24 • **84**
Gevrey-Chambertin 1991: Crisp and lively, showing a nice streak of cherry and spice aromas and flavors. Drinkable now. • $25 Ⓐ • (01/31/94) • **81**
Gevrey-Chambertin 1990: Very attractive and seductive, with almost sweet flavors. Shows good intensity of berry, cherry and earth notes that develop into a focused beam on the finish. Drinkable now. • $36 • (12/15/92) • **88**
Gevrey-Chambertin 1986 • $27 • (02/28/89) • **83**
Gevrey-Chambertin 1985 • $33 • (11/15/87) • **91**
Gevrey-Chambertin Champeaux 1991: Light and spicy, featuring anise and earth overtones to the modest raspberry flavors. Finishes tough. Try in 1997. • $37 Ⓐ • (01/31/94) • **80**
Gevrey-Chambertin Champeaux 1990: Boasts the quintessential, round, lush, ripe texture of many wines from this vintage. Elegant yet rich, with sweet berry, red licorice and black cherry flavors that are smooth and velvety on the long, flavorful finish. Drinkable now. • $70 • (12/15/92) • **91**
Gevrey-Chambertin Lavaux St.-Jacques 1989 • $70 • (01/31/92) • **86**
Gevrey-Chambertin Les Cazetiers 1989 • $70 • (01/31/92) • **91**
Grands Echézeaux 1992: Simple and sturdy, crisp, with tart berry and citrus notes that ring on the narrow, tannic finish. May be best from 1997. • $74 • **80**
Grands Echézeaux 1991: Oh, how seductive. Bright, youthful and focused, with delicious currant, vanilla and toast flavors and extremely well-integrated, smooth tannins. Bravo. • $85 • **93**
Grands Echézeaux 1990: Chewy and focused, makes up in fruit what it lacks in overall complexity. Offers plenty of plum and berry characteristics, but the finish is a bit lacking in intensity for this appellation. Try now. 150 cases made. • $102 • (12/15/92) • **90**
Grands Echézeaux 1989 • $114 • (01/31/92) • **91**
Grands Echézeaux 1988 • $85 • **88**
Grands Echézeaux 1987 • $40 • **90**
Grands Echézeaux 1986 • $55 • **84**
Grands Echézeaux 1985 • $75 • **86**

Key: SS—Spectator Selection. CS—Cellar Selection. BB—Best Buy. $NA—Price not available. (BT)—Barrel tasting. Ⓐ—Auction Price.
Dates in parentheses represent the issues in which the ratings were published.

Grands Echézeaux 1983 • $55 • **79**
Griotte-Chambertin 1991: Very pretty, light and elegant, offering nicely focused black cherry, cola and coffee flavors that echo on the long finish. Stylish, has the finesse and tannins to age through 1998. • $63 Ⓐ • (01/31/94) • **88**
Griotte-Chambertin 1990: The essence of Burgundy, with enticing crushed fruit, berry, tea and cedar aromas and flavors, masses of ultra-fine tannins and fresh acidity. Drinkable in 1997. 250 cases made. • $84 • (12/15/92) • **94**
Griotte-Chambertin 1989 • $90 • (01/31/92) • **91**
Griotte-Chambertin 1988 • $81 • (11/15/90) • **91**
Griotte-Chambertin 1986 • $81 • (07/31/88) • **92**
Griotte-Chambertin 1985 • $68 • (11/15/87) • **95**
Juliénas 1994: Distinctive and rich, with a perfumed aroma, if you like mint, this is your wine. It also has some nice strawberry and spice flavors that carry through to the finish. • $NA • **85**
Juliénas 1993: This vivid, juicy wine begins with bright strawberry and menthol aromas, continues with layers of ripe fruit and spice on the palate, and lingers pleasantly on the finish. If you open one bottle, have another on hand. 1,800 cases made. • $12 • (06/30/94) • **88**
Ladoix 1993: Very nicely made, delicate yet containing good ripe fruit. Unpretentious, neither opulent nor full-bodied, it tingles the palate with well-defined flavors. Drink in 1998. • $20 • **81**
Ladoix 1991: Light and crisp, a decent level of currant flavor emerges nicely on the palate. Finishes soft and surprisingly generous. Drinkable now. • $17 Ⓐ • (01/31/94) • **83**
Latricières-Chambertin 1991: Lean, supple and delicate, displaying pretty currant and blackberry flavors, a smooth texture and a narrow finish. A bit short on finesse, but long on attractive flavors. Try now. • $59 Ⓐ • (01/31/94) • **85**
Latricières-Chambertin 1988 • $72 • (02/15/91) • **87**
Maranges Premier Cru 1993: Straightforward Pinot showing cherry, light earth character and medium-fine tannins. Not much to talk about but delicious all the same. Drinkable now. • $20 • **84**
Maranges Premier Cru 1990: A no-nonsense, simple Burgundy, with plummy, earthy aromas and flavors and medium tannins. Drinkable now. • $19 • (12/15/92) • **83**
Maranges Première Cru 1989 • $20 • (01/31/92) • **85**
Mazis-Chambertin 1989 • $86 • (01/31/92) • **92**
Mercurey 1985 • $17 • (11/15/87) • **83**
Meursault 1994: Appealing but light-bodied, offering citrus and pineapple flavors. Clean, crisp, not much complexity. Drinkable now. • $37 • (05/31/96) • **82**
Meursault 1993: A very good Meursault, showing toast, honey and citrus flavors. Built on a lean frame, lots of acidity. Might be better after 1997. • $30 • **85**
Meursault Perrières 1994: Focused mineral and lemon flavors give this a bit of subtlety. Of medium body, it's fresh and clean on the straightforward finish. • $52 • (05/31/96) • **84**
Meursault Perrières 1993: A refined Meursault, not big, displaying well-defined fruit, acidity and structure, medium-bodied. • $38 • **85**
Meursault Perriéres 1992: Well-made white that offers some lovely honey, toast, apple and pear notes along with a touch of coffee. Very delicate and gracious with good acidity. Try now. Tasted twice. • $40 • (08/31/94) • **88**
Meursault Perrières 1991 • $42 • (10/15/93) • **88**
Monthelie 1991 • $17 Ⓐ • (01/31/94) • **78**
Montrachet Marquis de Laguiche 1993: A crowd charmer: big, buttery and stylish. Oozes cream, toasted coconut, apple and spice notes. Full-bodied and tempting to drink now, but will be better in 1998. • $225 • **90**
Montrachet Marquis de Laguiche 1992: Great finesse is the hallmark of this Montrachet. Well-balanced, very supple, gorgeous, offers some honey, nut, pear and grapefruit flavors, with a touch of mineral and vanilla notes on the lingering, subtle finish. Should be fabulous in 1998 and thereafter. • $162 Ⓐ • (08/31/94) • **94**
Montrachet Marquis de Laguiche 1991 • $175 • (10/15/93) • **92**
Morey-St.-Denis 1993: A rather delicate Burgundy, showing medium to light body, light, dry tannins and light finish. Better in 1999. • $NA • **81**
Morey-St.-Denis 1990: Charms you with its effusive raspberry, cherry and strawberry aromas and flavors, delicious texture and smooth finish. Drinkable now. • $33 • (12/15/92) • **88**

Morey-St.-Denis Clos Sorbè 1993: A shining star that's delicate, offering loads of fine tannins and crisp fruit, medium body, lively acidity and refreshing finish. Better in 1998. • $43 • **87**
Morey-St.-Denis Clos Sorbè 1989 • $45 • (01/31/92) • **86**
Morey-St.-Denis Monts-Luisants 1988 • $38 • (02/28/91) • **92**
Morgon 1993: Firm and focused, this throws a strong beam of ripe cherry, strawberry and plum flavors, along with an earthy note that adds complexity. It's tight and tannic, and though drinking well now it may benefit from a bit more time in bottle. 2,200 cases made. • $12 • (06/30/94) • **86**
Moulin-à-Vent 1994: Elegant floral, cherry and spice flavors over firm yet balanced tannins. It makes attractive drinking now. • $16 • **84**
Moulin-à-Vent 1993: Abundant fruit and firm, though unobtrusive, tannins give this vibrancy and presence. There are strawberry and cherry flavors, along with mint and cedar notes, and it is fresh and lively. Good drinking now. 2,800 cases made. • $13 • (06/30/94) • **85**
Musigny 1993: A bit disappointing for such a renowned grand cru. Silky, well-structured red offering plum, raspberry and oak character but appearing a little too light. Medium in body, firm tannins and light finish. Try in 1999. • $130 • **88**
Musigny 1991: Light, elegant, seductive and flavorful, displaying gorgeous currant, blackberry and floral aromas and flavors that are beautifully defined and delicate through the long finish. The tannins should soften by 1997 or '98. • $98 • (01/31/94) • **88**
Musigny 1990: A magical wine that's incredibly smooth for being so young. Has an abundance of plum, earth and chocolate aromas and flavors and a backbone of massive, velvety tannins. A pleasure to taste now, should be a pleasure to drink around 1998. • $129 • (12/15/92) • **95**
Nuits-St.-Georges 1986 • $25 • (04/30/89) • **86**
Nuits-St.-Georges 1985 • $29 • (11/15/87) • **92**
Nuits-St.-Georges Les Boudots 1990: Attractive, with cinnamon and berry aromas and flavors, silky tannins and a juicy finish. Drinkable now. • $57 • (12/15/92) • **88**
Nuits-St.-Georges Les Boudots 1989 • $70 • (01/31/92) • **80**
Nuits-St.-Georges Les Roncières 1986 • $38 • (04/30/89) • **85**
Nuits-St.-Georges Les Roncières 1985 • $38 • (11/15/87) • **93**
Pernand-Vergelesses 1994: Crisp, even tart, this citrus-tasting white is attractively clean but lacks a bit of depth and interest. Should go well with shellfish, though. • $24 • (05/31/96) • **83**
Pernand-Vergelesses 1990: An eye-opener, with pretty, lively, bright fruit flavors on a super-supple framework that sings on the round finish. Drinkable now. • $21 • (12/15/92) • **87**
Pernand-Vergelesses 1985 • $17 • (11/15/87) • **91**
Pommard 1992: Bright and fragrant, crisp on the palate and simple, with appealing strawberry flavor. Best now. • $25 • **83**
Pommard 1991: Firm and chunky, showing solid yet delicate raspberry and black cherry aromas and flavors. Charming and satisfying. Drinkable now. • $27 Ⓐ • (01/31/94) • **84**
Pommard 1990: Pleasant but light for this appellation. Medium-bodied, with herbal, gamy flavors in an easy-to-drink style. Drinkable now. • $36 • (12/15/92) • **82**
Pommard 1989 • $43 • (01/31/92) • **85**
Pommard 1986 • $27 • (04/30/89) • **87**
Pommard 1985 • $33 • (11/15/87) • **93**
Pommard 1981 • $28 • (09/01/84) • **83**
Pommard Epenots 1993: Lovely, vivid raspberry and blackberry character, medium body and tannins and clean finish. Better in 1999. • $35 • **85**
Pommard Epenots 1991: Light, charming and simple, with raspberry and lingonberry aromas and flavors. Has enough of a light tannic bite on the finish to try now.Ⓐ • $36 Ⓐ • (01/31/94) • **83**
Pommard Epenots 1990: Seductive and beautiful, with berry and earth flavors unfolding like soft waves. Offers a caressing texture on the firm finish and shows an appealing herbal character, too. Drinkable in 1998. • $48 • (12/15/92) • **91**
Pommard Epenots 1989 • $56 • (01/31/92) • **89**
Pommard Epenots 1986 • $40 • (07/31/88) • **83**
Pommard Epenots 1985 • $41 • (11/15/87) • **95**
Pommard Rugiens 1989 • $56 • (01/31/92) • **87**
Puligny-Montrachet 1994: Lovely from first sip to last, both fresh and unctuous. Of medium body, it delivers some ripe apple, dried herb, cream and honey flavors. Crisp, slightly grassy finish. Drinkable now. • $39 • (05/31/96) • **87**
Puligny-Montrachet 1993: Clean and fresh, perhaps a bit modest on the palate, sporting tart acidity and green apple finish. Drinkable now. • $32 • **81**
Puligny-Montrachet 1991 • $30 • (10/15/93) • **86**
Puligny-Montrachet Clos de la Garenne 1992: Refined, classy and tart, this slowly unfolds its secrets. Wonderful complexity, with good acidity and terrific apple, honey, hazelnut and mineral notes that seem so racy. Try with lobster or scallops. Try now. • $43 • (08/31/94) • **92**
Puligny-Montrachet Clos de la Garenne 1991 • $42 • (10/15/93) • **88**
Puligny-Montrachet Les Folatières 1994: A full-bodied white offering lots of personality and chewy, rich, mineral character. Clever winemaking here, and just the right proportions of toasted oak, honey and ripe fruit flavors. Sculpted with a deft hand from start to finish. Try in 1999. • $54 • (05/31/96) • **91**
Puligny-Montrachet Les Folatières 1993: Racy mineral, apple and honey character, medium body, firm acidity and sleek finish. Drink now. • $42 • **84**
Puligny-Montrachet Les Folatières 1991 • $42 • (10/15/93) • **85**
Puligny-Montrachet Les Pucelles 1993: Not bad for the vintage, providing some honey, herb and pie-crust character, medium body, medium fruit and crisp acidity. • $50 • **84**
Puligny-Montrachet Les Pucelles 1991 • $42 • (10/15/93) • **91**
Romanée-St.-Vivant 1992: Smooth and satisfying, spicy and ripe, displaying blackberry, black cherry and currant flavors that linger enticingly with a smoky edge on the finish. Tannins are a little drying, drink now. • $80 • **89**
Romanée-St.-Vivant 1991: Crisp and polished, this lean, smooth-textured wine displays creamy raspberry, strawberry and vanilla aromas and flavors, but not exactly in profusion. Finishes a bit austere and citrusy. Should be best after 1996. • $90 Ⓐ • (01/31/94) • **86**
Romanée-St.-Vivant 1989 • $94 • (01/31/92) • **92**
St.-Amour 1995: Strong spicy and herbal notes add interest to this supple, fruity red. The black cherry flavors are supported by firm tannins. A well-made wine with character. • $19 • **86**
St.-Aubin 1994: Terrific quality for a simple village wine from this appellation. Ripe yet elegant, intense, full in body, delivering plenty of spice, citrus and pear flavors. Restrained, but in a few years it should turn harmonious and exciting. Try in 1999. • $22 • (05/31/96) • **90**
Santenay 1990: Bright, lean and racy. Delivers nice black cherry and raspberry aromas and flavors, but turns a bit astringent and herbal on the finish. Drinkable now. • $22 • (12/15/92) • **83**
Santenay 1989 • $44 • (01/31/92) • **87**
Santenay 1985 • $17 • (11/15/87) • **88**
Santenay Beaurepaire 1991: Light and smooth, refreshingly straightforward, shades its raspberry flavor with spice and tobacco overtones. A bit astringent on the finish. Drinkable now. • $17 Ⓐ • (01/31/94) • **81**
Savigny-lès-Beaune 1993: Quite sweet-tasting, a light-bodied red to enjoy sooner rather than later. Delivers some nice raspberry, cherry and strawberry flavors. Try now through 1997. • $25 • **80**
Savigny-lès-Beaune 1992: Crisp and more than a little tannic, tight, with a narrow band of strawberry and spice. May be best from 1997. • $16 • **80**
Savigny-lès-Beaune 1991: Crisp, clean and lively, with a pretty thread of raspberry flavor. Drinkable now. • $18 Ⓐ • (01/31/94) • **83**
Savigny-lès-Beaune 1990: A straightforward fruit bomb. Very juicy, with ripe strawberry and earth flavors. A wine for early drinking. • $22 • (12/15/92) • **84**
Savigny-lès-Beaune 1989 • $23 • (01/31/92) • **87**
Savigny-lès-Beaune 1985 • $25 • (11/15/87) SS • **91**
Savigny-lès-Beaune 1981 • $16 • (09/01/84) • **79**
Volnay 1992: A light but appealing Volnay, with an oak-scented layer atop the floral raspberry flavors. Has a tart but satisfying finish. • $21 • **81**
Volnay 1990: Solid as a rock, this distinctive Volnay delivers plenty of berry and earth aromas and flavors, but needs time. Try now to 1998. • $33 • (12/15/92) • **90**
Volnay 1985 • $29 • (11/15/87) • **88**
Volnay Chevret 1993: Elegant for early drinking. Lovely, sweet and silky, featuring pretty violet flavors and somewhat short finish. Better than a barrel sample tasted earlier this year. • $38 • **88**
Volnay Chevret 1991: Light and fragrant, modest raspberry and strawberry aromas and flavors persist on the simple finish. Drinkable now. • $26 Ⓐ • (01/31/94) • **81**
Volnay Chevret 1989 • $50 • (01/31/92) • **90**

FRANCE

Volnay Clos des Chênes 1991: Floral and delicate, showing a violet edge to the currant and toast aromas and flavors. Finishes warm. Try now. • $32 Ⓐ • (01/31/94) • **81**
Volnay Clos des Chênes 1990: This classy Volnay offers loads of gamy, earthy berry characteristics and full, velvety tannins that explode on the finish. Drinkable now to 1997. • $42 • (12/15/92) • **93**
Volnay Clos des Chênes 1989 • $50 • (01/31/92) • **91**
Volnay Clos des Chênes 1988 • $45 • (02/15/91) • **85**
Volnay Clos des Chênes 1987 • $30 • (06/15/90) • **85**
Volnay Clos des Chênes 1986 • $31 • (04/30/89) • **80**
Vosne-Romanée 1993: Totally ready to drink now. Decent plum, cedar and tobacco flavors, medium body and light tannins. • $38 • **82**
Vosne-Romanée Les Beaumonts 1989 • $70 • (01/31/92) • **91**
Vosne-Romanée Les Beaumonts 1988 • $46 Ⓐ • (03/31/91) • **80**
Vosne-Romanée Les Beaumonts 1985 • $31 Ⓐ • (11/15/87) • **93**
Vosne-Romanée Les Petits-Monts 1990: Beautiful, showing round tannins and lots of pretty smoke, blackberry and cherry flavors. Drinkable now. 75 cases made. • $NA • (12/15/92) • **90**
Vosne-Romanée Les Suchots 1990: Substantially ripe and very appealing, not showy, but quite a mouthful, with black cherry and dark chocolate aromas and flavors and silky tannins on the long finish. Drinkable now. 225 cases made. • $58 • (12/15/92) • **86**
Vosne-Romanée Les Suchots 1989 • $70 • (01/31/92) • **89**
Vosne-Romanée Les Suchots 1988 • $57 • (02/28/91) • **90**
Vosne-Romanée Les Suchots 1985 • $42 • (11/15/87) • **94**

DROUHIN, ROBERT

Clos de Vougeot Red 1989 • $88 • (01/31/92) • **89**

DROUHIN-LAROZE

Bonnes Mares 1993: Shockingly light for a Bonnes Mares. Some decent fruit flavors but rather diluted, showing light body and tannins and slightly watery finish. Drinkable now. • $62 • **78**
Bonnes Mares 1992: Light, almost watery, with modest raspberry and cola notes that fade on the caramel-tinged finish. Drinkable already. 583 cases made. • $50 • **77**
Bonnes Mares 1988 • $81 • (12/31/90) • **93**
Bonnes Mares 1987 • $38 • (03/31/90) • **89**
Chambertin Clos de Bèze 1993: Light and pleasant but also quite diluted, showing decent strawberry, raspberry and cherry notes. Drinkable now. • $68 • **81**
Chambertin Clos de Bèze 1992: Very light and watery, only a wispy character rising above the level of simple raspberry notes. Drinkable now. 416 cases made. • $60 • **78**
Chambertin Clos de Bèze 1988 • $88 • (12/31/90) • **92**
Chambertin Clos de Bèze 1987 • $40 • (03/31/90) • **90**
Chambertin Clos de Bèze 1985 • $110 • (10/15/88) • **92**
Chapelle-Chambertin 1992: Very firm and chewy, with nicely focused strawberry and raspberry notes playing on a lean frame. The fruit persists on the mildly tannic finish. Try in 1997. 83 cases made. • $45 • **84**
Chapelle-Chambertin 1988 • $68 • (12/31/90) • **88**
Clos de Vougeot 1993: Firm and lovely, showing excellent tannin structure. Unfolds red berry and mineral flavors nicely, offering a harmonious, lingering finish. Try in 2000. • $62 • **89**
Clos de Vougeot 1992: Sturdy with lightish flavors of wild berry and anise, finishing a little coarse. May be better after 1996. 333 cases made. • $50 • **78**
Clos de Vougeot 1988 • $81 • (12/31/90) • **89**
Clos de Vougeot 1987 • $38 • (03/31/90) • **79**
Clos de Vougeot 1985 • $60 • (10/15/88) • **88**
Gevrey-Chambertin Clos Prieur 1988 • $44 • (12/31/90) • **88**
Gevrey-Chambertin Lavaux St.-Jacques 1993: Straightforward and a bit tired, showing modest red berry and earth notes. Slightly drying on the diluted finish. • $38 • **77**
Gevrey-Chambertin Lavaux-St.-Jacques 1988 • $44 • (12/31/90) • **80**

Key: SS—Spectator Selection. CS—Cellar Selection. BB—Best Buy. $NA—Price not available. (BT)—Barrel tasting. Ⓐ—Auction Price.
Dates in parentheses represent the issues in which the ratings were published.

Latricières-Chambertin 1993: Some simple, pleasant cherry and plum character and a hint of vanilla, but surprisingly light and diluted. Drink now. • $52 • **80**
Latricières-Chambertin 1992: Extremely light, watery and barely showing some raspberry notes that manage to linger on the simple finish. Give it until 1997. 167 cases made. • $45 • **77**
Latricières-Chambertin 1988 • $68 • (12/31/90) • **91**
Latricières-Chambertin 1987 • $36 • (03/31/90) • **88**
Mazis-Chambertin 1985 • $47 • (10/15/88) • **90**

DROUIN, BEATRICE & JEAN-MICHEL

Pouilly-Fuissé Domaine des Gerbeaux 1994: Clean, crisp, buttery, fruity character softens the hard edges. Of light to medium body, this middle-of-the-road Pouilly should go well with food. Drinkable now. • $NA • (05/31/96) • **81**
Pouilly-Fuissé Domaine des Gerbeaux Cuvée Préstige 1994: Crisp Pouilly of wet hay, slight herbal, mineral and green apple character. Light to medium in body, it turns slightly tart on the finish. Better in 1998. • $16 • (05/31/96) • **84**

DUBOEUF, GEORGES

Beaujolais 1991 • $7 • (07/31/92) • **81**
Beaujolais 1990 • $6 • (09/30/91) BB • **84**
Beaujolais 1989 • $10 • (06/15/92) • **87**
Beaujolais Château de la Plume 1990 • $6 • (10/31/91) BB • **84**
Beaujolais Flower Label 1994: Robust for a Beaujolais, this shows round plum and grapey flavors and a mild jolt of tannin. Spice and bubblegum flavors linger on the finish. • $7 • (06/15/95) • **81**
Beaujolais-Villages 1991 • $7 • (07/31/92) • **82**
Beaujolais-Villages 1990 • $7 • (09/15/91) BB • **87**
Beaujolais-Villages 1989 • $8 • (11/15/90) BB • **87**
Beaujolais-Villages 1988 • $8 • (05/31/89) • **83**
Beaujolais-Villages 1986 • $6 • (07/31/87) • **84**
Beaujolais-Villages Château de la Grande Grange 1994: Good strawberry and cherry flavors dominate this medium-bodied wine. It has moderate tannins and a nice dried-fruit finish. • $8 • (06/15/95) • **82**
Beaujolais-Villages Château de la Grande Grange 1993 • $7 • (06/30/94) • **73**
Beaujolais-Villages Château de la Grande Grange 1990 • $7 • (09/15/91) BB • **82**
Beaujolais-Villages Château de Varennes 1995: Mouthfilling flavors of plums and cherries are vivid in this firm red. It's clean and fresh, round in texture but with a firm backbone of tannin. • $NA • **84**
Beaujolais-Villages Château de Varennes 1994: Fruity and exuberant with a nice touch of richness and spice. Appealling plum and cherry flavors makes this a delicious quaff. Drink slightly chilled. • $8 • (06/15/95) • **86**
Beaujolais-Villages Château de Varennes 1993: Fresh and clean with good grip and pretty red cherry and smoky flavors. It's balanced and quaffable. • $8 • (06/30/94) • **84**
Beaujolais-Villages Château des Vierres 1995: Ripe black cherry and grapey flavors give this wine appeal, it has a nice balance of spice and tannin. It's bright and fruity, with some depth. • $NA • **84**
Beaujolais-Villages Château des Vierres 1994: Moderately rich and flavorful, with good strawberry flavors and a slightly green quality. The tropical, banana flavors linger on the finish. • $8 • (06/15/95) • **83**
Beaujolais-Villages Château des Vierres 1993: Full-bodied for a Beaujolais-Villages, with firm tannins and crisp acidity, but the fruit isn't very expressive, it's serious but a bit heavy for our taste. • $7 • (06/30/94) • **82**
Beaujolais-Villages Château des Vierres 1990 • $7 • (11/15/91) • **79**
Beaujolais-Villages Domaine du Granit Bleu 1995: Ripe fruit and round tannins give this wine a good texture on the palate, with plenty of plum fruit accented with smoky, gamy notes. Crisp acidity keeps it lively. Drink now or hold. • $NA • **85**
Beaujolais-Villages Domaine du Granit Bleu 1994: Moderately rich and tannic, with appealing spice and plum flavors, this wine also has a tropical fruit component that begins in the aroma and carries through to the finish. • $8 • (06/15/95) • **84**

Beaujolais-Villages Domaine du Granit Bleu 1993: Generous cherry and plum flavors and a plush texture make this easy to drink and easy to like. It's round and full of fruit. • $7 • (06/30/94) • **85**

Beaujolais-Villages Flower Label 1995: Straightforward and firm, this sturdy red has balance and structure, but the black cherry flavors are muted now. Give it till late 1996 to open up. • $NA • **83**

Beaujolais-Villages Flower Label 1994: Tropical flavors and aromas are matched by some nice strawberry flavors. It has good structure, richness and moderate tannins. There's also some good spice on the lingering finish. 250,000 cases made. • $7 • (06/15/95) BB • **87**

Beaujolais-Villages Flower Label 1993: A big wine that adds pepper and mineral notes to the cherry flavor, along with moderate tannins. It's a bit blunt, but still very agreeable. • $7 • (06/30/94) BB • **84**

Beaujolais White 1991 • $9 • (11/30/92) • **81**

Bourgogne Blanc Flower Label White 1992: Rather awkward, featuring a touch of grassiness, medium body and apple, pear and cut grass flavors. Fresh finish. • $9 • **68**

Brouilly 1991 • $9 • (07/31/92) • **82**

Brouilly 1990 • $9 • (09/15/91) • **81**

Brouilly 1988 • $11 • (05/31/89) • **83**

Brouilly 1986 • $9 • (07/31/87) • **90**

Brouilly 1985 • $9 • (12/15/86) • **82**

Brouilly Château de Nervers 1995: Round and quite rich, this shows good concentration for a Brouilly, with ripe plum, chocolate and light chocolate flavors. Delicious now, it should improve well into 1997. • $NA • **87**

Brouilly Château de Nervers 1994: Polished, firm, even a bit hard, this offers black cherry, light chocolate and herbal flavors on a tannic frame. • $10 • (06/15/95) • **85**

Brouilly Château de Nervers 1993: Firm tannins and ripe fruit give this a firm, well-integrated character that promises good development. It's fruity but not frivolous. Drinkable now. • $9 • (06/30/94) • **86**

Brouilly Château de Nervers 1992 • $8 • (12/15/93) • **83**

Brouilly Château de Nervers 1990 • $9 • (09/15/91) • **82**

Brouilly Château de Nervers 1988 • $11 • (05/31/89) • **89**

Brouilly Château de Pierreux 1994: Subtle chocolate and coffee flavors add complexity to this ripe, firm Brouilly. The plum and black cherry notes are ripe, and the wine is balanced and long. This is rich enough to accompany a meal and is drinkable now. • $10 • (06/15/95) • **88**

Brouilly Château de Pierreux 1993: Bright raspberry and herbal notes dominate this light, vibrant Brouilly. Fresh and zippy, it sings a simple two-note song. • $9 • (06/30/94) • **79**

Brouilly Château de Pierreux Comte de Toulgoët 1995: Alluring aromas of ripe fruit, toast and spice give way to a big, meaty wine with ripe fruit, round tannins and a pleasant gamy note. Shows the serious side of Beaujolais, but drinkable now. • $NA • **87**

Brouilly Domaine des Nazins 1990 • $9 • (09/15/91) • **87**

Brouilly Flower Label 1995: Perfumed with berry and floral aromas, this light, silky wine is bright and fruity. Perfect for summer afternoon quaffing. • $NA • **86**

Brouilly Flower Label 1994: There's real flair here, floral and bright berry notes giving immediate appeal and crisp acidity keeping it taut and fresh. No blockbuster but lots of personality. 50,000 cases made. • $9 • (06/15/95) • **86**

Brouilly Flower Label 1993: Velvety texture and forward fruit give this immediate appeal. It shows soft blackberry and black cherry flavors with pretty smoky accents, and melts in your mouth. • $8 • (06/30/94) BB • **87**

Chardonnay Vin de Pays d'Oc 1994: A touch of oak adds interest, and toasty flavors that complement the apple flavor. It's clean and well-balanced. A classy wine for the appellation. Slight bottle variation noted. • $7 • (07/31/95) • **86**

Chardonnay Vin de Pays d'Oc 1993: Medium-bodied, with fig and pear flavors and spicy overtones. Simple and refreshing, with good varietal character. Enjoy it now for its liveliness. • $6 • (09/15/94) • **84**

Chardonnay Vin de Pays d'Oc (Flower Label) 1992 • $6 • (03/15/94) BB • **85**

Chasan Vin de Pays d'Oc 1994: The floral aromas and soft peach flavors are pleasant in this soft, simple white. Shows some delicacy and would make a good apéritif. • $6 • (07/31/95) • **80**

Châteauneuf-du-Pape 1990: Smoky and tannic but austere, showing prune, orange peel and leather flavors. Dry and astringent on the finish, drinkable now. • $12 • (04/15/93) • **82**

Chénas 1991 • $8 • (07/31/92) BB • **83**

Chénas 1990 • $8 • (09/15/91) • **88**

Chénas 1988 • $10 • (05/31/89) • **85**

Chénas 1986 • $8 • (07/31/87) • **85**

Chénas 1985 • $9 • (12/15/86) • **81**

Chénas Domaine des Darroux 1994: A bit lean, revealing some berry and cherry flavors. Workmanlike, though not distinctive. 3,000 cases made. • $9 • **79**

Chénas Domaine des Darroux 1993: Exuberant fruit backed by muscular tannins give this a distinctive amplitude and make it a natural with food. It's balanced and big. • $8 • (06/30/94) BB • **88**

Chénas Flower Label 1994: Lush and well structured, featuring chewy plum and cherry flavors and a nice shot of spice. Exuberant, lingering finish. 13,000 cases made. • $9 • **85**

Chénas Flower Label 1993: Dense and tannic, offers rich plum flavor but not much breadth. It's closed and tight right now but may bloom in 1995. • $7 • (06/30/94) • **84**

Chiroubles 1992 • $9 • (12/15/93) • **80**

Chiroubles 1991 • $9 • (07/31/92) • **82**

Chiroubles 1990 • $9 • (09/15/91) • **88**

Chiroubles 1988 • $11 • (05/31/89) • **84**

Chiroubles 1986 • $9 • (07/31/87) • **87**

Chiroubles 1985 • $9 • (12/15/86) • **78**

Chiroubles Château de Javernand 1995: Supple yet thick-textured, this spicy red offers bright cherry and smoky flavors, vivid and rich. It's a bit heavy for a Chiroubles, but shows good balance nonetheless. • $NA • **85**

Chiroubles Château de Javernand 1994: Cherry and cinnamon flavors mingle in this clean, balanced Beaujolais, which offers crisp acidity and firm tannins to match the ripe fruit. 6,000 cases made. • $9 • **85**

Chiroubles Château de Javernand 1993: Enticing aromas of cherry, spice and spring flowers carry through on the palate, with focused flavors and a vibrant spiciness. Vivid with good balance and delicious fruit. • $9 • (06/30/94) • **87**

Chiroubles Château de Javernand 1992 • $9 • (12/15/93) • **82**

Chiroubles Domaine Desmures Père et Fils 1990 • $9 • (10/31/91) • **79**

Chiroubles Domaine Desmures 1994: Ripe and round, this big-style Chiroubles delivers soft plum, smoke and spice flavors, adding some depth and a pleasant, chewy mouth-feel. 2,000 cases made. • $9 • **84**

Chiroubles Domaine Desmures 1993: Strawberry is the dominant flavor element in this bright, light-bodied Chiroubles. It's jammy and forward, and a nice pepper note comes out in the finish. Vibrant and even a bit aggressive. • $9 • (06/30/94) • **86**

Chiroubles Domaine Desmures 1992 • $9 • (12/15/93) • **80**

Chiroubles Flower Label 1995: Typical Chiroubles — light, bright and pretty. Cherry, citrus and smoky flavors suffuse the palate, then fade quickly, leaving somewhat dry tannins. • $NA • **83**

Chiroubles Flower Label 1994: Fresh and delicate berry and herb notes, slightly green, surrounding a firm core of light tannins. Overall impression is somewhat meager. 20,000 cases made. • $9 • **79**

Chiroubles Flower Label 1993: Ripe and rich for this cru, with plum and smoky flavors and good grip. Perhaps it sacrifices a bit of elegance for power. • $8 • (06/30/94) • **85**

Côte de Brouilly 1991 • $9 • (07/31/92) • **84**

Côte de Brouilly 1990 • $9 • (11/15/91) • **76**

Côte de Brouilly 1986 • $9 • (07/31/87) • **90**

Côte de Brouilly Domaine de la Feuillée 1995: Juicy black cherry and plum flavors are bright and balanced in this typical Beaujolais. It's light enough to serve as an apéritif, but firm enough for food. • $NA • **85**

Côte de Brouilly Domaine de la Madone 1990 • $9 • (09/15/91) • **77**

Côte de Brouilly Flower Label 1995: A polished, silky wine with attractive floral and cherry notes. A bit subdued right now, but it shows good balance. • $NA • **84**

Côte de Brouilly Flower Label 1994: The flavors here are pretty, ranging from floral to cherry to spice, but the wine lacks concentration and the tannins are a bit green. 20,000 cases made. • $9 • **80**

Côte de Brouilly Flower Label 1993: Chunky, and not as fresh as many '93s, this shows maturing black cherry and earthy flavors. It has enough tannic grip to go with food, but lacks verve. • $8 • (06/30/94) • **80**

DUBOEUF, GEORGES

Côte-Rôtie Domaine de la Rousse 1991: Vivid aromas of violets and berries, ripe and round on the palate, with a finish that echoes sweet vanilla. Rich and drinkable now. From Georges Duboeuf. • $NA • (05/31/94) • **87**
Côte-Rôtie Domaine de la Rousse 1989 • $24 • (02/28/93) • **82**
Côte-Rôtie Domaine de la Rousse 1988 • $18 • (07/31/91) • **87**
Côtes du Rhône 1992 • $5 • (11/15/93) BB • **80**
Côtes du Rhône 1991 • $6 • (02/28/93) BB • **85**
Côtes du Rhône 1990 • $8 • (12/31/91) BB • **84**
Côtes du Rhône 1989 • $6 • (10/15/90) BB • **80**
Côtes du Rhône Domaine des Aires Vieilles 1994: This wine has loads of black cherry and berry fruit flavors, but not much structure to back it up. Simple and straightforward. • $6 • **78**
Côtes du Rhône Domaine des Aires Vieilles 1992 • $6 • (04/30/94) • **82**
Côtes du Rhône Domaine des Moulins 1994: Ripe and round with good plum and spice flavors, but still a bit simple in the end. Cassis notes linger on the tannic finish. • $6 • **81**
Côtes du Rhône Domaine des Moulins 1993: A young, dark and tannic Rhône, with peppery, herbal, dried fruit aromas, but flavors that thin out on the finish. It's hearty and impressive, but it needs more richness and depth. Drink now. • $6 • (11/30/94) • **82**
Côtes du Rhône White 1992 • $6 • (04/30/94) BB • **84**
Côtes du Ventoux 1994: Soft and fruity, with modest berry and plum flavors. This is a simple and serviceable wine that you may want to serve slightly chilled. • $6 • **80**
Crozes-Hermitage 1990 • $8 • (04/15/93) • **83**
Crozes-Hermitage 1988 • $9 • (01/31/91) • **85**
Domaine de Bordeneuve Vin de Pays d'Oc 1993: You can almost taste the southern French sun here, with the wine's dark color, flavors of ripe plums and grilled meat and firm tannins. Enjoy this simple, vivid red in its youth. • $5 • (09/15/94) • **83**
Fleurie 1992 • $9 • (12/15/93) • **83**
Fleurie 1991 • $11 • (07/31/92) • **87**
Fleurie 1990 • $11 • (09/15/91) • **89**
Fleurie 1988 • $15 • (05/31/89) • **89**
Fleurie 1986 • $10 • (07/31/87) • **87**
Fleurie 1985 • $10 • (12/15/86) • **69**
Fleurie Château des Déduits 1995: Quite rich, yet still elegant, this ripe wine offers plum and black cherry fruit flavors with notes of toast and smoke. Concentrated yet supple, it's a good match with food. • $NA • **86**
Fleurie Château des Déduits 1994: Big-boned and fruity, this has rich tannins, ripe plum fruit and a spicy finish. • $12 • (06/15/95) • **87**
Fleurie Château des Déduits 1993: Fresh and grapey, with plenty of fruit, this is a Beaujolais meant to be enjoyed now for its smooth character and youthful flavor. Tasted twice. • $10 • (06/30/94) • **83**
Fleurie Château des Déduits 1992 • $9 • (12/15/93) • **85**
Fleurie Château des Déduits 1990 • $11 • (10/31/91) • **87**
Fleurie Clos des Quatre Vents 1994: Velvet evening-gown of a wine, harmonious and elegant, sophisticated. Floral, ripe plum, cassis and spice flavors, light, well-integrated tannins. Delicious to drink now. 6,000 cases made.. • $12 • (06/15/95) • **88**
Fleurie Clos des Quatre Vents 1993: There are full-flavored black currant, herbal and smoky notes here, but it's rough and ready, with biting tannins. Aggressive but enjoyable. • $10 • (06/30/94) • **83**
Fleurie Domaine des Quatre Vents 1993: This sturdy Fleurie has balance and body, but lacks expressive fruit. The black cherry flavor has less punch than the tannin. Well-made but not distinctive. • $10 • (06/30/94) • **82**
Fleurie Domaine des Quatre Vents 1992 • $9 • (12/15/93) • **81**
Fleurie Flower Label 1995: Fresh and well-balanced, this vibrant red marries black cherry, floral and spicy notes with firm tannins and clean acidity in an appealing wine that will marry well with food. • $NA • **86**
Fleurie Flower Label 1994: Opulent, rich and round, from dark color through spicy aromas to ripe plum and cassis flavors, character and concentration. Delicious now. 25,000 cases made. • $11 • (06/15/95) • **89**

Key: SS—Spectator Selection. CS—Cellar Selection. BB—Best Buy. $NA—Price not available. (BT)—Barrel tasting. Ⓐ—Auction Price.
Dates in parentheses represent the issues in which the ratings were published.

Fleurie Flower Label 1993: More fruit complexity than most Gamays, with plenty of structure to back it up. The flavors run from black currant to raspberry, smoke to spice, and the wine is clean and balanced. Good drinking now. • $9 • (06/30/94) BB • **88**
Fleurie Grand Pre 1993: Round and fruity, voluptuous and alluring, with plenty of plum and blackberry flavors. There's not much structure, but the abundant fruit doesn't need it. • $10 • (06/30/94) • **86**
Fleurie La Madone 1994: Supple, ripe, balanced, concentrated, harmonious. The black cherry and cassis flavors are attractive, and there's just enough tannin to maintain firmness and help it match with food. 4,500 cases made. • $12 • (06/15/95) • **88**
Gigondas 1989 • $12 • (01/31/92) • **84**
Gigondas 1988 • $10 • (09/30/90) • **79**
Grenache Rouge Vin de Pays d'Oc 1992: A light, simple quaffing wine with some pleasant strawberry and tea flavors but almost no backbone. Try it slightly chilled. • $5 • (11/30/94) • **77**
Juliénas 1992 • $8 • (12/15/93) • **84**
Juliénas 1991 • $9 • (07/31/92) • **84**
Juliénas 1990 • $9 • (09/15/91) • **86**
Juliénas 1986 • $9 • (07/31/87) • **84**
Juliénas Château de Poupets 1993: Ripe and soft with generous plum flavors that are flavorful and immediately appealing. Enjoy it now with cold cuts and fruit. • $9 • (06/30/94) • **85**
Juliénas Domaine de la Seigneurie 1990 • $9 • (10/31/91) • **84**
Juliénas Domaine de la Seigneurie de Juliénas 1993: Though soft and velvety, this round Julienas is a bit hollow, with some plum flavors and a short finish. It's simple and seems mature already. • $9 • (06/30/94) • **80**
Juliénas Domaine de la Seigneurie de Juliénas 1992 • $8 • (12/15/93) BB • **85**
Juliénas Domaine des Mouilles 1992 • $8 • (12/15/93) • **82**
Juliénas Flower Label 1994: Fairly rich, demonstrating a hint of chocolate and good tropical and berry flavor components. Fruity and easy to drink, spicy finish. 31,000 cases made. • $9 • **84**
Juliénas Flower Label 1993: Simple and straightforward, with cherry and smoke flavors and firm tannins. It's sturdy but not very expressive. • $8 • (06/30/94) • **79**
Mâcon-Lugny Chardonnay Fête des Fleurs 1994: Good concentration and clean, varietal fruit give this wine depth and appeal, which underscore its value. The fruit flavors run from apple to melon to pear, with just enough oak for structure and acidity for balance. Well made. 10,000 cases made. • $8 • (06/30/95) BB • **86**
Mâcon-Villages 1994: Tart but fresh, showing some exotic banana and coconut flavors that marry nicely with the apple, pear and melon notes. Turns a bit green on the slightly drying finish. • $NA • **83**
Mâcon-Villages 1991 • $9 • (11/30/92) • **80**
Mâcon-Villages Domaine les Chenevières 1994: Straightforward apple flavor and a fat palate feel are strengths, but there's little complexity or depth. It's clean and offers easy drinking now. • $8 • (06/30/95) • **81**
Mâcon-Villages Flower Label 1994: Despite pleasant apple, herbal and pear flavors, earthy aromas and a chalky texture pull this wine down. It has some richness but lacks finesse. • $8 • (06/30/95) • **79**
Mâcon-Villages Glen Carlou Chard Réserve 1994: This wine has the richness and expressive flavors of a pineapple cream pie — lots of sweet, toasty oak, plenty of ripe, tropical fruit and a long finish of fruit and smoke. It has enough concentration to age, but it's irresistable now. • $NA • **89**
Merlot Domaine de Bordeneuve Vin de Pays d'Oc 1994: Dark and tannic, with attractive aromas and flavors of smoke, cherry and herbs. Has enough complexity of flavor, but firm with tannins. Try now. • $7 • (07/31/95) • **84**
Merlot Vin de Pays d'Oc 1994: Deep in color, smoky and herbal in aroma, with modest plum and licorice flavors and moderate tannins. Enjoyable and drinkable now. • $7 • (07/31/95) • **83**
Morgon 1992 • $8 • (12/15/93) • **84**
Morgon 1991 • $9 • (07/31/92) • **86**
Morgon 1990 • $9 • (09/15/91) • **80**
Morgon 1988 • $11 • (05/31/89) • **87**
Morgon 1986 • $9 • (07/31/87) • **88**
Morgon 1985 • $10 • (12/15/86) • **87**

Morgon Domaine Bellevue 1994: Fragrant, expressive, lively black cherry and violet flavors, chewy yet balanced on the palate. Good depth and concentration. Drinkable now. 7,000 cases made. • $10 • **88**

Morgon Domaine Bellevue 1993: Ripe raspberries shine through this rather rustic Morgon, accented by herbal and smoky notes. Though a bit clumsy, it has concentration and vivacity. • $9 • (06/30/94) • **84**

Morgon Domaine des Versauds 1992 • $8 • (12/15/93) • **83**

Morgon Flower Label 1994: Attractive combination of round fruit and firm tannins, fine expression of the appellation. Chewy, offering fresh, ripe plum flavors and gamy, spicy accents. Drinkable now. 50,000 cases made. • $9 • (06/30/95) BB • **87**

Morgon Flower Label 1993: Smooth, solid and flavorful. Attractive black cherry and blackberry flavors are backed by gentle tannins in this straightforward wine. • $8 • (06/30/94) • **83**

Morgon Jean Descombes 1994: Light barnyardy aromas start this off, but earthy fruit and spice flavors come together and present a rich, firm Morgon. Excellent concentration and *goût de terroir*. 9,000 cases made. • $11 • **88**

Morgon Jean Descombes 1993: Seductive blackberry aromas combined with a hint of chocolate on the palate and moderate tannins give this immediate appeal, yet its flesh and concentration suggest it may be better in a year. Tasted twice. • $9 • (06/30/94) • **85**

Morgon Jean Descombes 1992 • $8 • (12/15/93) • **82**

Morgon Jean Descombes 1990 • $9 • (09/30/91) BB • **87**

Morgon Jean Descombes 1988 • $12 • (05/31/89) • **90**

Moulin-à-Vent 1992 • $10 • (12/15/93) • **87**

Moulin-à-Vent 1991 • $10 • (08/31/92) • **85**

Moulin-à-Vent 1990 • $11 • (09/15/91) • **84**

Moulin-à-Vent 1988 • $13 • (05/31/89) • **87**

Moulin-à-Vent 1986 • $10 • (07/31/87) SS • **92**

Moulin-à-Vent 1985 • $10 • (12/15/86) • **87**

Moulin-à-Vent Aged in Oak 1991: Here's a winner. Bottle age has given this wine rich, exotic mature flavors of tobacco, cedar, plums and prunes, it's big but silky, firm but well-integrated, with a core of tannins that support but never intrude. Though it lacks the grapey freshness characteristic of young Beaujolais, it has only grown over time. • $11 • (06/30/94) SS • **91**

Moulin-à-Vent Domaine de la Tour du Bief 1994: Toasty new oak dominates now, spicy vanilla, black cherry and berry flavors. Balanced, velvety texture. Drink now. 7,000 cases made. • $12 • **86**

Moulin-à-Vent Domaine de la Tour du Bief 1993: Though still a bit disjointed, this shows all the elements: alluring aromas, full tannins, ripe plum flavor and a long finish. It should develop well. • $10 • (06/30/94) • **87**

Moulin-à-Vent Domaine de la Tour du Bief 1992 • $10 • (12/15/93) • **85**

Moulin-à-Vent Domaine des Rosiers 1994: Not your typical Beaujolais, but very tasty, sweet, toasty oak and bright blackberry flavors and a firm yet velvety texture. It's lively and distinctive. Try now. 15,000 cases made. • $12 • **87**

Moulin-à-Vent Domaine des Rosiers 1993: Rich and dense, with a nice balance of ripe plum flavor and smoky new oak. There's good concentration and fresh fruit. It's still young and raw, raspy with tannin, but will settle down, drinkable now. • $10 • (06/30/94) BB • **89**

Moulin-à-Vent Domaine des Rosiers 1992 • $10 • (12/15/93) • **86**

Moulin-à-Vent Domaine des Rosiers 1990 • $11 • (09/15/91) • **85**

Moulin-à-Vent Flower Label 1994: Fragrant cherry and berry aromas, rich yet supple on the palate, offering vibrant fruit and light toasty flavors. It's balanced, clean and drinking well now. 25,000 cases made. • $11 • **87**

Moulin-à-Vent Flower Label 1993: Toasty, chocolate flavors are attractive in this velvety, medium-bodied Beaujolais, but the black cherry loses some vividness in the exchange. Not typical, but will appeal to fans of new wood. • $9 • (06/30/94) • **86**

Moulin-à-Vent New Barrel 1988 • $13 • (05/31/89) • **93**

Moulin-à-Vent Oak Aged 1993: Starts slow and astringent, but adds nice fruit and spice flavors. Cherry, plum and nutmeg notes linger on the finish. Well structured and fairly rich. Bottle variation noted. 8,000 cases made. • $11 • **85**

Pouilly-Fuissé 1994: Difficult to like, as matchstick, earthy aromas and flavors dominate from start to finish. Where is the fruit? Tastes like it's just been bottled. 25,000 cases made. • $15 • (05/31/96) • **75**

Pouilly-Fuissé 1992: Pungent and earthy, but once those flavors blow off, pear and spice emerge. The earthy notes never quite disappear, but they fold in nicely on the finish. Ready now. • $11 • (09/15/93) • **84**

Pouilly-Fuissé 1991 • $14 • (08/31/92) • **84**

Pouilly-Fuissé Clos Reissier 1994: Attractive flavors of pineapple, lemon ream and light earth run through this balanced, lively Mâcon. Not rich but still manages good intensity, displaying deft use of oak. 2,000 cases made. • $17 • (06/30/95) • **84**

Pouilly-Fuissé Clos Reissier 1993: A complex and flavorful, reasonably priced wine with toasty, smoky aromas, ripe flavors of fig, pear, butterscotch and walnut, followed by a long finish. This is seductive, smooth and distinctive. • $13 • **88**

Pouilly-Fuissé Flower Label 1994: A rich, ripe wine with plenty of new oak, this offers tropical fruit flavors with nuances of pineapple, mango and spice, along with plenty of sweet vanilla and hazelnut accents. It's a bulldozer, and may not age well, but it makes an impact now. • $16 • (06/30/95) • **86**

Pouilly-Fuissé Flower Label 1993: Rich but not flashy, this is a solidly built wine with slightly toasty aromas, pear and nutmeg flavors and a lasting finish. Well-balanced, smooth textured and appealing overall. • $12 • **84**

Pouilly-Fuissé Oak-Aged 1994: A showy Pouilly, as smoky, toasty notes from oak barrels give a buttery feel to this medium-bodied white. Nicely balanced citrus flavors maintain focus on the round finish. Drinkable now or try in 1998. 5,000 cases made. • $17 • (05/31/96) • **87**

Régnié 1995: This is supple, yet shows concentration, with black cherry and smoky flavors, good balance and firm underlying tannins. It will bloom with food. • $8 • **85**

Régnié 1992 • $7 • (12/15/93) • **81**

Régnié 1991 • $8 • (07/31/92) BB • **86**

Régnié 1990 • $8 • (09/15/91) • **81**

Régnié 1988 • $8 • (05/31/89) • **83**

Régnié Château de Ponchon 1994: Nicely proportioned, with good berry and plum flavors, and a hint of chocolate. Simple, but satisfying. 3,000 cases made. • $8 • (07/31/95) • **82**

Régnié Château de Ponchon 1993: Tart acidity gives this a real edge, marked by effusive berry and strawberry flavors. It's tight and lean, begging for a ham sandwich with sharp mustard. • $8 • (06/30/94) • **82**

Régnié Domaine des Buyats 1994: Intense plum and cherry aromas and flavors. There are also hints of banana and interesting herbal notes throughout this well-made Beaujolais. 4,000 cases made. • $8 • (07/31/95) • **85**

Régnié Domaine des Buyats 1993: This chunky wine offers firm structure and ripe fruit, though it lacks expressiveness and delicacy. Good with food, but not that interesting on its own. • $8 • (06/30/94) • **82**

Régnié Domaine du Potet 1995: Distinctive. Attractive floral and bell pepper aromas give way to ripe flavors of chocolate and cherries, thick on the palate with good underlying tannins. It's juicy and rich. • $NA • **87**

Régnié Domaine du Potet 1994: A spicy aroma is followed up some rich fruit flavors of plum, cherry and strawberry. Fairly light, though it still has some nice intensity. 3,500 cases made. • $8 • (07/31/95) • **86**

Régnié Domaine du Potet 1993: Firm tannins get in the way in this solid, rather dull Regnie. There's some black cherry and plum flavor, but it seems earth-bound and heavy. • $8 • (06/30/94) • **79**

Régnié Domaine du Potet 1992 • $7 • (12/15/93) • **81**

Régnié Domaine du Potet 1990 • $8 • (09/30/91) BB • **85**

Régnié Flower Label 1994: Simple and fruity, revealing tropical flavors and aromas. It's lively, though not particularly intense, adding a good, clean finish. 20,000 cases made. • $8 • (07/31/95) • **83**

Régnié Flower Label 1993: An exotic flavor profile offers cassis, mint and citrus notes and firm tannins. A bigger Beaujolais that needs six months in the bottle to round it out. • $7 • (06/30/94) • **85**

St.-Amour 1992 • $9 • (12/15/93) • **85**

St.-Amour 1991 • $11 • (07/31/92) • **83**

St.-Amour 1990 • $11 • (09/15/91) • **87**

St.-Amour 1986 • $9 • (07/31/87) • **87**

St.-Amour 1985 • $8 • (12/15/86) • **83**

St.-Amour Domaine de la Pirolette 1995: Raspberry and floral notes distinguish this from a typical Beaujolais, adding interest to the cherry fruit. The tannins are firm but well-integrated, and the wine should improve through 1997. • $NA • **87**

St.-Amour Domaine de la Pirolette 1993: Raspberry, stawberry and menthol flavors run through this sinuous, concentrated Beaujolais. It's focused and long, with a distinctive character. • $10 • (06/30/94) • **87**

St.-Amour Domaine de la Pirolette 1994: Rich and full-bodied, demonstrating appealing plum and tropical flavors, fruity aromas and a slightly spicy finish. 4,000 cases made. • $12 • (07/31/95) • **85**

St.-Amour Domaine de la Pirolette 1993: Raspberry, strawberry and menthol flavors run through this sinuous, concentrated Beaujolais. It's focused and long, with a distinctive character. • $10 • (06/30/94) • **87**

St.-Amour Domaine des Pins 1992 • $9 • (12/15/93) • **83**

St.-Amour Domaine des Pins 1990 • $11 • (09/15/91) • **82**

St.-Amour Flower Label 1995: Ripe and round, this shows rich plum flavors with smoky notes and well-integrated tannins that give polish to the texture. It's not dramatic, but it's easy to like. • $NA • **84**

St.-Amour Flower Label 1994: Fresh and fruity with a bit of a tang. Cherry and red plum flavors and some orange peel to boot, beautiful aromas and good, clean finish. 22,000 cases made. • $11 • (07/31/95) • **84**

St.-Amour Flower Label 1993: Lively and vivid with plenty of black cherry and bright berry flavors, it's fresh and bracing. Mouthwatering, with enough body to go with a meal. • $9 • (06/30/94) BB • **87**

St.-Joseph 1988 • $11 • (11/30/90) • **76**

St.-Véran 1994: Tropical fruit and buttery flavors stand out in this exuberant wine, which still has a crisp core of citrusy acidity. It doesn't go very deep, but offers harmony and even elegance in a fruit-driven style. • $9 • (06/30/95) • **86**

St.-Véran Domaine de la Batie 1993: Fresh, fruity and straightforward, on the light-bodied side, with a smooth texture and simple, grapey flavors. Uncomplicated. • $8 • **79**

St.-Véran Domaine St.-Martin 1994: Smooth and round, light but well proportioned. Medium intensity and some decent fruit character. A bit diluted. 1,000 cases made. • $9 • **79**

Sauvignon Blanc Vin de Pays du Jardin de la France 1995: Flat and rather dull, this white shows ripe apple and banana flavors in a waxy testure, but it lacks varietal personality. A disappointment from an otherwise reliable producer. • $7 • (06/15/96) • **76**

Sauvignon Vin de Pays d'Oc 1994: Basically neutral in flavor, but rugged and has enough body and acidity to hold its own with food. Simple and straightforward - a good refresher. • $6 • (07/31/95) • **81**

Syrah Vin de Pays d'Oc 1994: Like a Cotes du Rhône but fresher. Deep in color, smoky and peppery in aroma but mild in flavor. Light on tannins, easy to drink. • $6 • **82**

Syrah Vin de Pays d'Oc 1992 • $5 • (03/15/94) • **83**

Syrah Vin de Pays d'Oc Rosé 1994: Banana and watermelon are the predominant aromas, and the flavors are surprisingly concentrated-full of spicy raspberry and cherry. Finishes dry. • $6 • (08/31/95) • **85**

DUBOIS, JEAN-LUC

Chorey-lès-Beaune 1990: Ripe and fruity, with rich black cherry and currant-scented flavors that pick up traces of mineral and spice on the finish. The tannins are fleshy and firm, making the wine drinkable now. • $30 • (06/15/93) • **87**

Ladoix La Combe 1990: Hard-edged and tannic, with an earthy lime- and currant-scented flavor profile. The tannins turn gritty and chewy. Drinkable now. • $19 • (06/15/93) • **84**

DUBREUIL-FONTAINE PERE & FILS, P.

Corton Les Bressandes 1993: Plenty of ripe fruit here. Medium to full in body, featuring medium- velvety tannins and a long, spicy finish.Better in 2000. • $NA • (05/15/96) • **88**

Corton Les Bressandes 1992: Not a big wine but firm in texture, turning supple on the finish and echoing some very pretty raspberry, currant and floral flavors. • $57 • **85**

Key: SS—Spectator Selection. CS—Cellar Selection. BB—Best Buy. $NA—Price not available. (BT)—Barrel tasting. Ⓐ—Auction Price.
Dates in parentheses represent the issues in which the ratings were published.

Corton Les Bressandes 1991: Clean and nicely focused, shining a beam of currant and blackberry flavors. Hints at anise and toast on the finish. A mini version of a fine Corton, should be best around 1997. 250 cases made. • $50 Ⓐ • (01/31/94) • **88**

Corton Les Bressandes 1990: Very elegant, with ripe blackberry and earth aromas and flavors and firm tannins. Drinkable now. • $59 • (12/15/92) • **89**

Corton Les Bressandes 1985 • $50 • (01/31/89) • **86**

Corton Les Bressandes 1982 • $24 • (10/16/85) • **85**

Corton Le Clos du Roi 1993: Well made and harmonious, showing some lovely, complex mocha, spice and red berry notes. Sweet-tasting and flavorful, this medium-bodied *grand cru* is quite subtle and elegant. Try in 1999. • $NA • **87**

Corton Le Clos du Roi 1992: Lean and lithe, a little chewy from tannin, but the slightly gamy floral, blackberry and blueberry flavors persist into a solid finish. Harmonious Corton that is approachable now, better after 1996. • $60 • **87**

Corton Le Clos du Roi 1991: Harmonious, seamless and elegant, displaying sparks of ripe currant, plum, berry, anise and mint notes and a bit of gaminess, as well. Complex, showing more than the usual generosity on the finish. The tannins are present, but not harsh. Best after 1998. 450 cases made. • $52 Ⓐ • (01/31/94) • **90**

Corton Le Clos du Roi 1990: Pure fruit extract, with tons of raspberry, tobacco and vanilla flavors. Combines superb concentration of fruit and tannins. Drinkable in 1997. • $61 • (12/15/92) • **93**

Corton Le Clos du Roi 1989 • $63 • (01/31/92) • **92**

Corton Le Clos du Roi 1987 • $34 • (12/31/90) • **85**

Corton Le Clos du Roi 1985 • $49 • (07/15/88) • **90**

Corton Le Clos du Roi 1982 • $25 • (09/16/85) • **86**

Corton Le Perrières 1993: Delicious plum, berry and cherry flavors cascade to a long, velvety finish. Hard not to drink this one now, although it should improve past 1998. • $NA • **88**

Corton-Charlemagne 1992: Full-bodied, heavy and a bit vague, with some hazelnut, pine nut and lemon flavors that lead to a clean finish. • $61 • (08/31/94) • **84**

Pernand-Vergelesses 1994: You can taste *terroir* in the wet earth and mineral notes, but it's rather lean, lacking a bit of ripe fruit. Drinkable now. 333 cases made. • $56 • (05/31/96) • **80**

Pernand-Vergelesses 1993: Sprightly and clean, delivering refreshing acidity and firm tannins. Not generous, but shows some very good fruit and a delicious finish. Drinkable now. • $NA • (05/15/96) • **85**

Pernand-Vergelesses 1991: Lean and chewy, a small wine, with modest cherry flavors and well-modulated tannins. Drinkable now. 675 cases made. • $33 Ⓐ • (01/31/94) • **82**

Pernand-Vergelesses White 1992: A spicy flavor, lively texture and good acidity give this wine some presence. It's crisp, clean, and tastes of apples and nutmeg. • $NA • (11/15/94) • **82**

Pernand-Vergelesses Clos Berthet Monopole White 1992: A bit earthy and quite woody, simple, with modest fruit flavors. • $30 • (08/31/94) • **79**

Pernand-Vergelesses Ile des Vergelesses 1993: Some nice fruit, but it's a bit disjointed. Somewhat tart in texture, lacking focus, one-dimensional, finish slightly diluted. • $NA • **77**

Pernand-Vergelesses Ile des Vergelesses 1990: Firm and focused, with juicy, delicious berry and earth characteristics. Tightly built and succulent on the long finish. Drinkable now. • $37 • (12/15/92) • **88**

Pernand-Vergelesses Ile des Vergelesses 1989 • $40 • (01/31/92) • **84**

Pernand-Vergelesses Ile des Vergelesses 1982 • $18 • (10/16/85) • **78**

Pommard Les Epenots 1990: Extremely silky, flowing over the palate and leaving a sense of lightness. A joy to drink, with lots of chocolate and raspberry nuances. Drinkable now. • $59 • (12/15/92) • **91**

Savigny-lès-Beaune Aux Vergelesses 1993: Relatively light and straightforward, showing some cherry and strawberry flavors and earthy complexity. Try now through 1998 for everyday drinking. • $NA • **81**

Savigny-lès-Beaune Aux Vergelesses 1990: Straightforward Savigny, with pleasant chestnut and strawberry notes. An early-maturing style, with medium tannins and a light finish. Drinkable now. • $25 • (12/15/92) • **81**

Savigny-lès-Beaune Les Vergelesses 1992: Firm and focused, turning supple on the finish, shows slightly gamy black cherry and floral aromas and flavors. Drinkable now. • $25 • **81**

Savigny-lès-Beaune Les Vergelesses 1991: Modest, showing pretty black cherry and raspberry flavors and a bit of toastiness to add an extra dimension. Drinkable through 1997. 667 cases made. • $22 Ⓐ • (01/31/94) • **82**

Savigny-lès-Beaune Les Vergelesses 1985 • $24 • (01/31/89) • **88**

DUCHET, DOMAINE

Beaune Cent-Vignes 1985 • $27 • (03/15/88) • **85**

DUCLA, CHÂTEAU

Bordeaux 1988 • $7 • (08/31/91) • **74**

Bordeaux Cuvée Extrème 1988 • $11 • (07/15/92) • **83**

DUCLUZEAU, CHÂTEAU

Listrac 1993: Light, diluted with tomato, weedy, a hint of fruit on the palate. • $12 • (01/31/96) • **77**

Listrac 1987 • $7 • (11/30/89) • **79**

Listrac 1986 • $11 • (11/30/89) • **83**

Listrac 1982 • $16 • (08/31/92) • **81**

DUCOIN, CHARLES

Brut Champagne Carte Blanche NV: Clean but simple. It has modest grapefruit and pineapple flavors and a contrasting, sweet-tart balance. 3,000 cases made. • $20 • **81**

DUCRU-BEAUCAILLOU, CHÂTEAU

St.-Julien 1995: Stunning for its concentration of pure, racy flavors, which blend cassis and spicy oak notes in a seamless package. Massive, supple, ripe tannins. Full-bodied and rich, adding a long finish. Best Ducru in two decades. • $NA • (05/15/96) • **95-100** (BT)

St.-Julien 1993: Somewhat disappointing for this estate. Decent berry and plum flavors and firm tannins, although a slight tomato character takes away from the overall quality. Drinkable on release. • $33 • (01/31/96) • **81**

St.-Julien 1992: Lean, racy mint and berry character but very short on the finish. Tasted twice, with consistent notes. Drinkable now. • $28 • **79**

St.-Julien 1991: Nice black cherry and tobacco flavors, quite velvety in the mouth. Drinkable now. • $31 • (03/31/94) • **83**

St.-Julien 1990: A little clumsy now. Tough and muscular, with loads of fruit hidden underneath the sharp tannins. Needs time to mellow. Tasted twice. Drinkable after 1998. 17,000 cases made. • $40 Ⓐ • (03/31/93) • **89**

St.-Julien 1989 • $53 Ⓐ • (10/15/92) • **91**

St.-Julien 1988 • $30 • (10/15/92) • **92**

St.-Julien 1987 • $26 • (10/15/92) • **83**

St.-Julien 1986 • $52 Ⓐ • (06/30/89) • **91**

St.-Julien 1985 • $48 Ⓐ • (10/15/94) • **90**

St.-Julien 1984 • $31 • (08/31/87) • **87**

St.-Julien 1983 • $39 Ⓐ • (10/15/94) • **87**

St.-Julien 1982 • $71 Ⓐ • (08/31/92) • **93**

St.-Julien 1981 • $40 Ⓐ • (10/15/94) • **89**

St.-Julien 1980 • $23 • (05/01/84) CS • **88**

St.-Julien 1979 • $29 • (10/15/89) • **87**

St.-Julien 1978 • $53 • (05/01/85) • **91**

St.-Julien 1970 • $79 • (05/15/93) • **91**

St.-Julien 1962 • $49 • (11/30/87) • **80**

St.-Julien 1961 • $233 Ⓐ • (04/30/96) • **92**

St.-Julien 1959 • $230 Ⓐ • (10/15/92) • **92**

St.-Julien 1958 • $100 • (10/15/92) • **83**

St.-Julien 1957 • $85 • (10/15/92) • **77**

St.-Julien 1955 • $140 • (10/15/92) • **87**

St.-Julien 1953 • $240 • (10/15/92) • **88**

St.-Julien 1952 • $160 • (10/15/92) • **81**

St.-Julien 1949 • $220 • (10/15/92) • **90**

St.-Julien 1945 • $550 • (10/15/92) • **95**

St.-Julien 1934 • $190 • (10/15/92) • **82**

St.-Julien 1929 • $166 • (10/15/92) • **83**

St.-Julien 1928 • $250 • (10/15/92) • **88**

St.-Julien 1924 • $200 • (10/15/92) • **80**

St.-Julien 1898 • $450 • (10/15/92) • **97**

St.-Julien 1887 • $450 • (10/15/92) • **89**

St.-Julien 1867 • $950 • (10/15/92) • **92**

DUFOULEUR PERE & FILS

Beaune Champs Pimonts 1991: A fruity Burgundy that's crisp and lively in balance and has plenty of black cherry flavor to keep it interesting. Turns lean on the finish. Drinkable now. • $17 • (05/31/95) • **84**

DUFOULEUR, LOIS

Beaune Champs Pimont 1991: Firmly tannic and tight enough to bury the otherwise appealing anise- and tar-scented currant flavors until the finish. Worth cellaring until 1997 or '98. • $NA • (01/31/94) • **85**

Beaune Clos du Roi 1991: Tough and chewy, but offers a mouthful of juicy currant, plum, mushroom and spicebox aromas and flavors. Finishes crisp and lemony. Try in 1997. • $31 Ⓐ • (01/31/94) • **85**

Beaune Les Cent Vignes 1991: Velvety, refined and flavorful, offering a nice range of prune, coffee and currant aromas and flavors. Finishes soft and generous, with finely integrated tannins. Has enough muscle to take it through 1997 or '98. • $34 Ⓐ • (01/31/94) • **86**

DUGAT, CLAUDE

Charmes-Chambertin 1993: Lovely sweet fruit character here, offering medium body, plum, smoke, mineral flavors, medium tannins and a silky finish. Better in 1999. 25 cases made. • $90 • **90**

Gevrey-Chambertin 1993: Great village wine! Beautifully made up, locating everything in the right place. Medium- to full-bodied, with loads of fine tannins, a hint of wood and an abundance of berry and cherry character. Try in 2000. • $40 • **90**

Gevrey-Chambertin Lavaux St.-Jacques 1993: How to describe greatness? This is profound, ripe and rich, but shows restraint and elegance, too. As silky as it gets in this vintage, with a thread of currant, smoke, earth and plum flavors that marry seamlessly on the inspiring finish. Try in 2000. • $65 • **92**

Gevrey-Chambertin Premier Cru 1993: Impressive and showy Gevrey, featuring plenty of color, raspberry character, a hint of new wood, medium to full body, fine tannins and long, long finish. Better in 2000. • $50 • **91**

DUHART-MILON ROTHCHILD, CHÂTEAU

Pauillac 1995: Spicy character, with a hint of orange zest. Medium-bodied, with good, velvety tannins and a long, sweet finish. • $NA • (05/15/96) • **85-89** (BT)

Pauillac 1994: A bit tough on the palate, but it does have some pretty berry, strawberry and vanilla aromas and flavors. Medium body and firm tannins. Could rate very good in a later tasting. • $36 • (05/15/96) • **80-84** (BT)

Pauillac 1993: Nice, velvety texture, but slightly green bean and herbal in nature. Medium body and tannins, adding a long finish. Perhaps better with time, try in 1997. • $25 • (01/31/96) • **80**

Pauillac 1992: Fresh, light, diluted, showing berry, cherry and vanilla aromas and flavors. Light-bodied, fruity finish. Drink now. • $22 • **76**

Pauillac 1990: Black cherry and plum aromas leap from the glass and follow through on the palate with mint, tar and chocolate accents. It's focused, lively and firm, with plenty of concentration. Hard to resist now, but it will improve with aging, try in 1998. 13,000 cases made. • $25 • (10/15/94) • **92**

Pauillac 1989 • $25 • (03/15/92) • **90**

Pauillac 1988 • $24 • (08/31/91) • **88**

Pauillac 1987 • $22 • (05/15/90) • **79**

Pauillac 1986 • $26 • (05/31/89) • **90**

Pauillac 1985 • $27 • (10/15/94) • **93**

Pauillac 1983 • $24 • (10/15/94) • **89**

Pauillac 1982 • $49 • (08/31/92) • **91**

Pauillac 1981 • $26 • (10/15/94) • **87**

Pauillac 1979 • $20 Ⓐ • (10/15/89) • **86**

DUJAC, DOMAINE

Bonnes Mares 1987 • $31 Ⓐ • (03/31/90) • **91**

Bonnes Mares 1986 • $34 Ⓐ • (04/15/89) • **85**

Chambolle-Musigny 1993: Flavorful, complex and intriguing, the smoky, leafy, tealike notes inviting you back for another sip. Open, generous, smooth, moderately tannic. Drinkable now through 2000. • $37 • (05/15/96) • **86**

Chambolle-Musigny Les Gruenchers 1987 • $47 • (03/31/90) • **93**

Chambolle-Musigny Les Gruenchers 1986 • $48 • (07/31/88) • **76**

Chambolle-Musigny Les Gruenchers 1985 • $43 • (03/31/88) • **74**

Charmes-Chambertin 1991: Aromas are earthy and gamy, but flavors of currant and berry balance them, finishing lean and citrusy. Drinkable now. 300 cases made. • $71 Ⓐ • (01/31/94) • **83**

Charmes-Chambertin 1990: A luxurious wine, with impressive raspberry, violet and cedar aromas and flavors. Is in near-perfect harmony with the fruit and tannins. Drinkable now. 300 cases made. • $75 • (12/15/92) • **92**

Charmes-Chambertin 1989 • $72 • (01/31/92) • **90**

Charmes-Chambertin 1988 • $60 • (03/31/91) • **85**

Charmes-Chambertin 1986 • $50 • (07/31/88) • **85**

Charmes-Chambertin 1985 • $100 • (03/15/88) • **95**

Clos de la Roche 1991: Crisp in texture, with warm, earthy, gamy shades to the solid currant and cherry flavors, all of which plays clearly across the palate. A bit shy in the middle, but has the style and firmness to age well through 1997. 500 cases made. • $77 Ⓐ • (01/31/94) • **88**

Clos de la Roche 1990: Clever winemaking brings you this distinctive, smoky, toasty, gamy Burgundy, with a satiny texture that packs in the firm tannins. Not big, but very rich. Drinkable now. 750 cases made. • $83 • (12/15/92) • **92**

Clos de la Roche 1989 • $80 • (01/31/92) • **89**

Clos de la Roche 1988 • $75 • (03/31/91) • **90**

Clos de la Roche 1987 • $53 • (03/31/90) • **86**

Clos de la Roche 1986 • $56 • (07/31/88) • **79**

Clos de la Roche 1985 • $85 • (03/15/88) • **95**

Clos St.-Denis 1993: Yummy, suave, plush-textured, as its fruity, spicy flavors seem sweet and really linger on the finish. Not too tannic to drink now and through 2000, and utterly delicious. • $79 • (05/15/96) • **91**

Clos St.-Denis 1992: A lush and broad-tasting Burgundy with ample chocolate and vanilla flavors framing the core of plum and cherry. It's intriguingly toasty in aroma, and remains interesting through the finish. • $66 • (05/15/95) • **87**

Clos St.-Denis 1991: Toasty and earthy on the nose, but elegant berry, spice and game flavors persist into a lean finish. Seems a bit mature for a '91. Drinkable now. 233 cases made. • $77 Ⓐ • (01/31/94) • **86**

Clos St.-Denis 1990: A very distinctive wine that stands out with seductive, smoky, toasty bacon and game characteristics, but it's also surprisingly delicate for a '90 *grand cru*, showing plenty of solid tannins. Drinkable now. 350 cases made. • $83 • (12/15/92) • **90**

Clos St.-Denis 1989 • $80 • (01/31/92) • **91**

Clos St.-Denis 1987 • $58 • (03/31/90) • **85**

Clos St.-Denis 1986 • $56 • (07/31/88) • **89**

Clos St.-Denis 1985 • $89 • (03/15/88) • **91**

Echézeaux 1991: Light but ripe, offering a nice bead of currant and blackberry flavors shaded by anise, cedar and tobacco notes that keep ringing on the finish. Try now. 250 cases made. • $81 Ⓐ • (01/31/94) • **86**

Echézeaux 1990: Elegant, toasty and complex. Kicks in with nice tea, strawberry and roasted nut flavors on the delicate finish. Drinkable now. 850 cases made. • $88 • (12/15/92) • **91**

Echézeaux 1988 • $70 • (03/31/91) • **90**

Echézeaux 1987 • $56 • (05/15/90) • **82**

Echézeaux 1986 • $52 • (04/30/89) • **89**

Gevrey-Chambertin Aux Combottes 1993: Nicely fruity and easy in texture yet firmly tannic, this is elegant, almost soft in the middle but has grip on aftertaste. Almost ready to drink, try in 1997 to 2000. • $65 • (05/15/96) • **88**

Gevrey-Chambertin Aux Combottes 1991: Crisp and spicy, showing earthy, oaky overtones to the raspberry and currant aromas and flavors. Graceful, drinkable now. 267 cases made. • $63 Ⓐ • (01/31/94) • **84**

Gevrey-Chambertin Aux Combottes 1990: This distinctive red Burgundy is seductive despite the firm, hard core of tannins and fruit, showing chocolate, berry, smoke and spice flavors and a lovely, toasty finish. A well-made wine to drink around 1997. 350 cases made. • $67 • (12/15/92) • **92**

Gevrey-Chambertin Aux Combottes 1989 • $65 • (01/31/92) • **86**

Gevrey-Chambertin Aux Combottes 1988 • $54 • (03/31/91) • **86**

Gevrey-Chambertin Aux Combottes 1987 • $42 • (05/31/90) • **80**

Morey-St.-Denis 1993: Very smooth, harmonious, mellow and rich in flavor, the ample fruit accented by spicy, woodsy notes. Tempting now for its silky texture, but can age through at least 1999. • $37 • (05/15/96) • **88**

Morey-St.-Denis 1992: Intriguing toasty aromas that flirt with funk followed by ripe, broad fruit flavors make this a distinctive and satisfying experience. Cherry and cranberry are smoothed over by lavish, oaky notes, all coming together in a lingering finish. Drink now. • $31 • (05/15/95) • **88**

Morey-St.-Denis 1991: Displays more citrusy lime aromas and flavors than red fruit, although it picks up light raspberry notes on the finish. Drinkable now. 775 cases made. • $38 Ⓐ • (01/31/94) • **84**

Morey-St.-Denis 1990: Raspberry, spice and earth aromas and flavors make this a pretty Pinot Noir to drink now. 1,400 cases made. • $41 • (12/15/92) • **87**

Morey-St.-Denis 1989 • $40 • (01/31/92) • **84**

Morey-St.-Denis 1987 • $23 • **74**

DULUC, CHÂTEAU

St.-Julien 1991: Feels supple in the mouth, but ends with an astringent finish and bell pepper flavors. Second label of Branaire. • $14 • (03/31/94) • **77**

St.-Julien 1989 • $NA • (03/15/92) • **84**

DUMAS, DOMAINE LAURENT

Beaujolais-Villages 1992: Big for the vintage, shows ripe fruit and firm tannins, with floral, smoky, meaty accents that add depth and interest. It's still young and firm. • $10 • (06/30/94) • **83**

Fleurie 1992: The cassis and tobacco flavors aren't typical of Beaujolais, but they're appealing in this round, firm wine. A vegetal note detracts a bit, but overall the balance and structure are sound. • $16 • (06/30/94) • **83**

DUPLESSIS-FABRE, CHÂTEAU

Moulis 1989 • $9 • (03/15/92) • **88**

Moulis 1987 • $7 • (11/30/89) • **71**

Moulis 1986 • $7 • (11/30/89) • **74**

Moulis 1982 • $10 • (11/30/89) • **79**

DUPLESSIS, CHÂTEAU

Moulis 1993: Light and watery, showing only modest fruit and dry tannins. • $11 • (01/31/96) • **76**

DUPLESSY, CHÂTEAU

Premières Côtes de Bordeaux Red 1985 • $6 • (05/31/88) • **75**

DURAND-LAPLAGNE, CHÂTEAU

St.-Emilion 1982 • $7 • (09/16/85) • **79**

Key: SS—Spectator Selection. CS—Cellar Selection. BB—Best Buy. $NA—Price not available. (BT)—Barrel tasting. Ⓐ—Auction Price.
Dates in parentheses represent the issues in which the ratings were published.

DURBAN, DOMAINE DE

Muscat de Beaumes-de-Venise 1993: A delicious, exuberant, full-bodied, sweet wine that tastes peachy, adding lively acidity and lingering finish. • $18 • **85**
Muscat de Beaumes-de-Venise 1992 • $20 • (10/31/93) • **85**
Muscat de Beaumes-de-Venise 1988 • $15 • (03/31/91) • **86**

DURDILLY, PIERRE & PAUL

Beaujolais Les Grandes Coasses 1990 • $7 • (09/30/91) • **74**

DURFORT-VIVENS, CHÂTEAU

Margaux 1994: Raspberry, smoke and mineral aromas and flavors, medium body, firm tannins and medium finish. • $NA • **80-84** (BT)
Margaux 1993: Slightly one-dimensional but featuring some attractive mint, rosemary, cherry character. Medium body, firm tannins and medium finish. Drink in 1997. • $23 • (01/31/96) • **84**
Margaux 1991: A well-focused wine with a lovely mixture of smoke and berry notes, medium body and silky texture. • $20 • (03/31/94) • **83**
Margaux 1990: Delicate and sure-footed, with lovely cherry and vanilla aromas and flavors, silky tannins and sweet fruit on the finish. Drinkable now. 5,500 cases made. • $22 • (03/31/93) • **88**
Margaux 1989 • $28 • (03/15/92) • **92**
Margaux 1988 • $40 • (08/31/91) • **73**
Margaux 1986 • $25 • (06/15/89) • **90**
Margaux 1982 • $NA • (08/31/92) • **90**
Margaux 1981 • $NA • **74**

DURIEU, DOMAINE

Châteauneuf-du-Pape 1989 • $17 • (10/15/91) • **85**
Châteauneuf-du-Pape 1988 • $16 • (10/15/91) • **86**
Châteauneuf-du-Pape 1986 • $16 • (10/15/91) • **89**
Châteauneuf-du-Pape 1985 • $14 • (10/15/91) • **79**
Châteauneuf-du-Pape 1984 • $13 • (11/15/87) • **78**
Châteauneuf-du-Pape 1983 • $NA • (10/15/91) • **82**
Châteauneuf-du-Pape 1981 • $NA • (10/15/91) • **90**
Côtes du Rhône-Villages 1988 • $6 • (03/15/91) • **78**

DUVAL-LEROY

Brut Blanc de Blancs Champagne Chardonnay NV • $30 • (12/31/91) • **88**
Brut Champagne NV • $NA • (12/31/91) • **89**
Brut Champagne Fleur de Champagne NV • $25 • (12/31/91) • **87**
Cuvée des Roys Champagne 1985 • $NA • (12/31/90) • **84**

DUVERGEY-TABOUREAU

Mâcon-Villages 1994: Well made, clean and crisp, offering some pear, melon and fig flavors in a style rather ripe for the vintage. Pleasant and accessible now. 471 cases made. • $14 • **81**
St.-Véran 1993: Some buttery and mineral flavors but it turns dry, herbaceous and tough in the palate and on the clumsy, slightly burning finish. 1,000 cases made. • $16 • **79**

DUVERNAY

Rully Les Cloux 1988 • $18 • (12/31/90) • **82**

ECARD, MAURICE

Savigny-lès-Beaune Aux Serpentières 1993: This well-made '93 *premier cru* bursts with ripe red berry flavors and refined, smoky, toasty character. Supple mouth-feel, yet rich and complex. Full in body and very silky finish. Tempting now, but better in 1999. • $94 • (05/15/96) • **93**
Savigny-lès-Beaune Les Peuillets 1989 • $25 • (11/15/91) • **87**
Savigny-lès-Beaune Les Serpentières 1989 • $25 • (11/15/91) • **88**
Savigny-lès-Beaune Les Serpentières 1987 • $17 • (10/15/89) • **80**

EGLISE-CLINET, CHÂTEAU L'

Pomerol 1990: Soft and ripe, showing a definite ring of mintiness to complement the sweet currant and blackberry flavors. Remains solid through the finish. Needs until 1997 to settle down. • $45 Ⓐ • (06/15/93) • **86**
Pomerol 1989 • $45 • (08/31/92) • **96**
Pomerol 1988 • $47 • (12/31/90) • **91**
Pomerol 1987 • $22 • (02/15/90) • **83**
Pomerol 1986 • $55 Ⓐ • (06/15/89) • **91**
Pomerol 1985 • $70 Ⓐ • (02/29/88) • **93**
Pomerol 1983 • $19 • (03/16/86) • **88**
Pomerol 1982 • $53 Ⓐ • (05/15/89) • **87**
Pomerol 1981 • $NA • **87**
Pomerol 1961 • $30 • (04/30/96) • **88**

EGLISE, DOMAINE DE L'

Pomerol 1992: Delicate berry, cherry, and strawberry aromas and flavors, light-bodied and firm, slightly thin. Drinkable now. • $18 • **80**
Pomerol 1991: Soft and delicious. A tobacco and fruit character, medium body and a silky finish. • $18 • (03/31/94) • **82**
Pomerol 1990: A smooth and attractive wine, with lovely tobacco, chocolate and tomato aromas and flavors and a light, silky finish. Drinkable now. 3,500 cases made. • $37 • (03/31/93) • **87**
Pomerol 1989 • $33 • (03/15/92) • **93**
Pomerol 1961 • $NA • (04/30/96) • **87**

EGLY-OURIET

Brut Champagne Grand Cru Millesime 1986: Starts out bold and rich, with nut, almond and yeast aromas, but turns stylish and elegant on the palate, offering hints of almond, pear and spice flavors. Elegant, graceful and delicious to drink now. 4,100 cases made. • $40 • (06/15/93) • **90**
Brut Rosé Champagne Grand Cru NV • $30 • (06/15/93) • **87**

ELLNER

Brut Blanc de Blancs Champagne NV • $32 • (07/31/89) • **90**
Brut Champagne 1982: An earthy, perfumey style, with a rich, intense, fleshy texture and peach-tinged toast and almond flavors, smooth and elegant. • $38 • (07/31/89) • **91**
Brut Champagne Réserve NV • $30 • (07/31/89) • **87**

ENCLOS, CHÂTEAU L'

Pomerol 1989 • $24 • (04/30/92) • **82**
Pomerol 1988 • $20 • (03/15/91) • **85**
Pomerol 1986 • $20 • (06/15/89) • **92**
Pomerol 1984 • $20 • (03/31/87) • **83**
Pomerol 1982 • $43 Ⓐ • (05/15/89) • **86**
Pomerol 1945 • $100 • (03/16/86) • **78**

ENGARRAN, CHÂTEAU DE L'

Blanc de Blancs Vin de Pays d'Oc 1992 • $7 • (03/15/94) • **80**
Vin de Pays des Collines de La Moure 1990 • $7 • (03/15/94) • **84**

ENGEL, RENE

Clos Vougeot 1992: Behind a light burr of tannin there's a nice thread of black cherry, smoke and slightly pruny flavor that persists into an elegant finish. Drinkable now. • $NA • **86**
Clos Vougeot 1989 • $66 • (11/15/91) • **85**
Clos Vougeot 1988 • $37 Ⓐ • (03/15/91) • **91**
Clos Vougeot 1986 • $50 • (11/30/88) • **81**
Clos Vougeot 1985 • $75 Ⓐ • (10/15/87) • **85**
Clos Vougeot 1983 • $30 • (02/16/86) • **80**
Echézeaux 1992: More generous with its fruit than most '92s, but it's on a small scale and gets a little astringent on the finish. The currant and berry flavors carry through. May be best after 1996. • $NA • **83**

Echézeaux 1989 • $47 • (11/15/91) • **89**
Echézeaux 1988 • $41 Ⓐ • (03/31/91) • **92**
Echézeaux 1986 • $38 • (11/30/88) • **78**
Echézeaux 1985 • $32 • (10/15/87) • **90**
Grands Echézeaux 1989 • $75 • (11/15/91) • **90**
Grands Echézeaux 1986 • $50 • (11/30/88) • **71**
Grands Echézeaux 1985 • $43 • (10/15/87) • **86**
Vosne-Romanée 1992: Lean and earthy, with very little fruit to balance. Drinkable, but charming only if you like such flavors. • $NA • **76**
Vosne-Romanée 1989 • $34 • (11/15/91) • **85**
Vosne-Romanée 1988 • $30 • (07/15/90) • **81**
Vosne-Romanée 1986 • $29 • (02/28/89) • **75**
Vosne-Romanée 1985 • $24 • (10/15/87) • **77**
Vosne-Romanée 1983 • $19 • (02/16/86) • **67**
Vosne-Romanée Les Brûlées 1989 • $35 • (11/15/91) • **87**
Vosne-Romanée Les Brûlées 1988 • $45 • (02/28/91) • **89**
Vosne-Romanée Les Brûlées 1986 • $32 • (10/31/88) • **68**
Vosne-Romanée Les Brûlées 1985 • $28 • (10/15/87) • **85**
Vosne-Romanée Les Brûlées 1983 • $22 • (03/16/86) • **78**

ERMITAGE DE PIC ST.-LOUP

Coteaux du Languedoc Pic Saint Loup 1992 • $6 • (03/15/94) • **83**

ESMONIN, FREDERIC

Gevrey-Chambertin Clos Prieur 1993: Like inhaling a Havana cigar, so strong are the tobacco flavors here. But thankfully it turns to currant and other red berry notes, and the structure is solid. Try in 2000. 830 cases made. • $30 • **86**
Gevrey-Chambertin Les Corbeaux 1990: This funky wine has flavors that stretch from herb, vegetal and olive notes to ripe currant. Clumsy, with a green touch to the flavors. Drinkable now. • $39 • (10/31/92) • **82**
Gevrey-Chambertin Les Corbeaux 1989 • $42 • (03/31/92) • **88**
Gevrey-Chambertin Estournelles-St.-Jacques 1993: Pretty plum and berry character, medium body, fine tannins and a fresh finish. Drinkable now. 350 cases made. • $40 • **84**
Gevrey-Chambertin Estournelles St.-Jacques 1989 • $42 • (03/31/92) • **86**
Gevrey-Chambertin Lavaux St.-Jacques 1990: Has a tart, green edge to the raspberry and cherry notes. The tight, narrow band of flavors has had time to evolve and develop. Drinkable now. • $39 • (10/31/92) • **83**
Gevrey-Chambertin Lavaux St.-Jacques 1989 • $42 • (03/31/92) • **88**
Griotte-Chambertin 1989 • $80 • (03/31/92) • **92**
Mazis-Chambertin Mazy-Chambertin 1990: A light, pleasantly fruity wine, with ripe plum and prune flavors framed by toasty oak notes. Finishes with light tannins. Drinkable now. 100 cases made. • $71 • (10/31/92) • **83**
Mazis-Chambertin Mazy-Chambertin 1989 • $80 • (03/31/92) • **89**
Ruchottes-Chambertin 1993: Beautiful tea leaf and berry aromas and flavors, medium body and tannins and a fresh finish. Better in 1997. 200 cases made. • $65 • **90**
Ruchottes-Chambertin 1990: This smooth, fleshy wine has soft, ripe plum and cherry notes that are elegant and lively. Finishes with a lively aftertaste and firm but well-integrated tannins. Drinkable now. 100 cases made. • $71 • (10/31/92) • **86**
Ruchottes-Chambertin 1989 • $80 • (03/31/92) • **91**

ESMONIN, MICHEL

Gevrey-Chambertin 1993: Light and pleasant, showing some decent sweet strawberry, raspberry and stewed tomato flavors, medium body and velvety texture. Try now through 1998. • $29 • **83**
Gevrey-Chambertin Clos St.-Jacques 1993: Seductive, beautiful plum, vanilla and berry flavors. Medium-bodied, offering ultrafine tannins and a long, succulent finish. Delicious now, but better in 1999. • $64 • **89**
Gevrey-Chambertin Clos St.-Jacques 1987 • $44 • (03/31/90) • **87**
Gevrey-Chambertin Estournelles St.-Jacques 1988 • $40 • (03/31/91) • **84**

Key: SS—Spectator Selection. CS—Cellar Selection. BB—Best Buy. $NA—Price not available. (BT)—Barrel tasting. Ⓐ—Auction Price.
Dates in parentheses represent the issues in which the ratings were published.

Mazis-Chambertin Mazy-Chambertin 1991: Ripe and generous, a little chewy but showing enough smoky berry and tomato flavors to bode well. Should be best from 1997. • $48 • (08/31/94) • **85**
Ruchottes-Chambertin 1991: Lean and distinctly herbal and leafy, a sturdy wine with a modest level of cherry fruit to balance the earthy notes. Best from 1997. • $48 • (08/31/94) • **82**

ESPERANCE, CHÂTEAU L'

Bordeaux 1986 • $7 • (09/30/89) • **77**

ESPERANCE, DOMAINE DE L'

Côtes du Rhône 1990 • $11 • (04/15/93) • **78**

ESPIGOUETTE, DOMAINE DE L'

Côtes du Rhône Vieilles Vignes 1993: Strong backbone of acidity and tannins. Plum and black cherry are accented by coffee and spice notes. Drinkable now. 3,000 cases made. • $9 • (09/30/95) • **88**
Côtes du Rhône-Villages Plan de Dieu 1993: A good, robust wine with plenty of stuffing. It has plenty of blackberry and black cherry flavors that are framed by tannins. Drinkable now. 1,500 cases made. • $10 • **84**
Syrah Côtes du Rhône Vieilles Vignes 1993: This Rhône stretches the boundaries of style, with its earthy, smoky, decadent aromas and flavors. If you like reds funky and reasonably tannic, this is for you. Ready to drink. 600 cases made. • $10 • **79**

ESTOURNEL, MAITRE-D'

Bordeaux 1990: Ripe in flavor, showing simple plum and currant nuances and a firm texture. Drinkable now. • $9 • (11/30/92) • **81**
Bordeaux 1989 • $9 • (11/30/92) • **76**
Bordeaux 1988 • $9 • (11/30/92) • **81**
Bordeaux 1985 • $7 • (05/31/88) • **84**
Bordeaux White 1993: A nice, clean, crisp white Bordeaux that has zingy grapefruit flavors and a refreshing balance. • $9 • (02/29/96) • **84**
Bordeaux White 1991 • $9 • (09/15/93) • **75**

ETANG DES COLOMBES, CHÂTEAU

Corbières 1991 • $8 • (03/15/94) • **80**
Corbières Bicentenaire Vieilles Vignes 1991 • $10 • (03/15/94) • **80**
Corbières Cuvée du Bicentenaire 1986 • $9 • (03/31/91) • **77**
Corbières Cuvée du Bicentenaire 1985 • $6 • (04/15/88) • **73**

EVANGILE, CHÂTEAU L'

Pomerol 1995: Absolutely fabulous with layer upon layer of wonderful fruit. Full body, full, silky tannins and a stupendous finish. This is one of the big success stories of the vintage. • $NA • (05/15/96) • **95-100** (BT)
Pomerol 1994: What a treat to find such a lovely wine. The superfine tannins marry well with the ripe berry and chocolate aromas and flavors. Medium to full body and there's plenty of richness to fill it out. • $85 • (05/15/96) • **90-94** (BT)
Pomerol 1993: Perhaps not as great as some people think, but it offers delicious berry, green tobacco and fruit aromas and flavors. Medium-bodied, firm tannins and crisp finish. Tasted twice, with consistent notes. Better in 1997. • $65 • (01/31/96) • **87**
Pomerol 1990: A beautifully polished wine, with well-integrated oak and fruit character and superfine tannins. A class act. Drink after 1997. 4,500 cases made. • $83 Ⓐ • (03/31/93) • **92**
Pomerol 1989 • $60 Ⓐ • (03/15/92) • **92**
Pomerol 1988 • $47 • (06/30/91) • **87**
Pomerol 1986 • $44 Ⓐ • (09/15/89) • **88**
Pomerol 1985 • $92 Ⓐ • (02/29/88) • **92**
Pomerol 1984 • $75 • (02/15/87) • **79**
Pomerol 1983 • $52 Ⓐ • (10/15/94) • **92**
Pomerol 1982 • $169 Ⓐ • (05/15/89) • **93**
Pomerol 1981 • $52 • (10/15/94) • **82**
Pomerol 1961 • $552 Ⓐ • (04/30/96) • **83**
Pomerol 1945 • $600 • **87**

FABAS, CHÂTEAU

Minervois 1986 • $5 • (09/15/89) • **72**

FADEZE, DOMAINE LA

Terret Blanc Vin de Pays de l'Herault 1991 • $7 • (06/15/93) BB • **82**

FAIVELEY, J.

Beaune Champs-Pimont 1989 • $34 • (01/31/92) • **90**
Beaune Champs-Pimont 1985 • $36 • (03/15/88) • **86**
Bourgogne Joseph Faiveley 1990 • $11 • (12/15/92) • **85**
Bourgogne Joseph Faiveley 1989 • $12 • (01/31/92) • **84**
Bourgogne Joseph Faiveley 1979 • $8 • (04/16/86) BB • **75**
Bourgogne White Georges Faiveley 1992: Firm and solid, with a focused band of ripe pear, spice, mineral and vanilla bean flavors, light- to medium-bodied, subtle and attractive. • $16 • (08/31/94) • **85**
Bourgogne White Georges Faiveley 1991 • $14 • (10/15/93) • **85**
Chambertin-Clos de Bèze 1993: Thick, rich, smoky, exotic and packed with flavor. This is an all-out taste experience backed by firm tannins, chewy texture, lively acidity and long finish. Needs until at least 1999 to show its best. • $113 • (05/15/96) • **91**
Chambertin-Clos de Bèze 1992: Very light and astringent, with a modest level of earthy, slightly gamy, vaguely berryish flavors. Try now. 542 cases made. • $92 • **78**
Chambertin-Clos de Bèze 1991: Thin, tough and tannic, although berry and currant flavors struggle through the astringent finish. An extreme style. 151 cases made. • $89 Ⓐ • (01/31/94) • **78**
Chambertin-Clos de Bèze 1990: Very appealing, with a sumptuous texture, tobacco, coffee and berry aromas and flavors and a smoky finish. An alluring wine that should be ready to drink around 1998. 500 cases made. • $130 • (12/15/92) • **93**
Chambertin-Clos de Bèze 1989 • $63 Ⓐ • (01/31/92) • **90**
Chambertin-Clos de Bèze 1987 • $70 • (03/31/90) • **83**
Chambertin-Clos de Bèze 1986 • $58 Ⓐ • (07/15/89) • **88**
Chambertin-Clos de Bèze 1985 • $105 • (03/15/88) • **96**
Chambolle-Musigny 1989 • $34 • (01/31/92) • **85**
Chambolle-Musigny 1985 • $45 • (05/15/88) • **89**
Chambolle-Musigny 1981 • $24 • (05/01/86) • **88**
Chambolle-Musigny La Combe d'Orveau 1992: A chewy style of Chambolle that's a bit rough and tough. Has pleasant aromas and flavors, but finishes a bit green and dry. May be better after 1996. 125 cases made. • $56 • **77**
Chambolle-Musigny Les Fuées 1992: Light, smooth and floral, a little short on fruit but the delicate berry flavors are pleasant and drinkable now. • $56 • **81**
Chambolle-Musigny Les Fuées 1991: Chewy, with juicy berry and plum flavors that never quite overcome the thick layers of tannin. Way out of balance, but may come around by 1998. 50 cases made. • $49 Ⓐ • (01/31/94) • **83**
Chambolle-Musigny Les Fuées 1990: Wonderful plum and black cherry flavors fold nicely into the earth and tobacco notes in this harmonious, medium-bodied, refined wine. Drinkable now. • $36 Ⓐ • (12/15/92) • **89**
Charmes-Chambertin 1992: Light and chewy, with some ripe currant and spice flavors sneaking into the lean, tannic finish. May be best after 1997. 525 cases made. • $74 • **83**
Charmes-Chambertin 1991: A lean and elegant wine, firm and chewy, a bit earthy at first, but then the currant and blackberry flavors come coursing through and keep vibrating through the finish. Has enough intensity and finesse to age through 2000 at least. 75 cases made. • $75 Ⓐ • (01/31/94) • **92**
Chassagne-Montrachet 1991 • $35 • (10/15/93) • **83**
Clos de la Roche 1986 • $55 • (07/15/89) • **82**
Clos de la Roche 1985 • $105 Ⓐ • (03/15/88) • **78**
Clos de Vougeot 1992: Lean and tough, an astringent red that tastes more of forest underbrush than fruit, and it's too soon for that. 584 cases made. • $68 • **74**
Clos de Vougeot 1991: Crisp, flavorful and tightly wound, showing a lean core of blackberry and plum flavors and a layer of fine tannins that needs until 1997 or '98 to begin to soften. 175 cases made. • $63 Ⓐ • (01/31/94) • **86**
Clos de Vougeot 1990: A graceful wine, with earth and berry characteristics, masses of fine tannins and a truly gorgeous finish. Try in 1997. 500 cases made. • $50 Ⓐ • (12/15/92) • **92**
Clos de Vougeot 1989 • $41 Ⓐ • (01/31/92) • **85**
Corton-Charlemagne 1992: Stylish, with lots of vibrant lemon, vanilla and toast flavors, shows excellent length. Not a grand, opulent style of Burgundy, but very fresh despite the oak. • $62 • (08/31/94) • **91**
Corton-Charlemagne 1991 • $96 • (10/15/93) • **86**
Corton Clos des Cortons 1992: Lean and tannic, with some pretty floral and berry flavors struggling to get past the layer of toughness. A roll of the dice, but try it in 1999. 967 cases made. • $62 • **85**
Corton Clos des Cortons 1991: Tough, tannic and drying on the palate, with a thin strand of juicy currant flavor. The tannins require cellaring until 1998. 250 cases made. • $63 Ⓐ • (01/31/94) • **83**
Corton Clos des Cortons 1990: Offers an enormous amount of fruit to back up the tannins, even though it's pretty hard on the palate. Made for aging, try in 1997 or '98. 1,000 cases made. • $86 • (12/15/92) • **90**
Corton Clos des Cortons 1989 • $68 • (01/31/92) • **91**
Corton Clos des Cortons 1988 • $120 • (03/31/91) • **90**
Corton Clos des Cortons 1987 • $50 • (03/31/90) • **92**
Corton Clos des Cortons 1985 • $100 • (03/15/88) • **79**
Echézeaux 1993: Vividly fruity, distinctive and elegant, as a lively strawberry flavor runs from aromas through the lingering finish. Absolutely delicious and seductive. Firm enough in tannins to suggest cellaring until at least 1998. • $56 • (05/15/96) • **91**
Echézeaux 1991: Tough, tannic and lean, with little to offset the tannins. Might improve by 1997. 125 cases made. • $68 Ⓐ • (01/31/94) • **77**
Echézeaux 1990: Has a lovely structure and coats your mouth with silky red berry and plum flavors that echo on the firm finish with violet and earth notes. Drinkable in 1997. 350 cases made. • $71 Ⓐ • (12/15/92) • **91**
Echézeaux 1989 • $53 Ⓐ • (01/31/92) • **89**
Echézeaux 1987 • $53 • (03/31/90) • **80**
Echézeaux 1985 • $74 • (03/31/88) • **89**
Echézeaux 1981 • $40 • (05/01/86) • **68**
Fixin 1989 • $21 • (01/31/92) • **85**
Gevrey-Chambertin 1989 • $34 • (01/31/92) • **87**
Gevrey-Chambertin 1985 • $38 • (04/15/88) • **90**
Gevrey-Chambertin Les Cazetiers 1992: Lean and spicy, a juicy red that keeps its anise and currant flavors coming on the narrow finish. Try now. • $NA • **80**
Gevrey-Chambertin Les Cazetiers 1991: Awkward, hard and a little bitter. Drinkable now. 175 cases made. • $33 Ⓐ • (01/31/94) • **79**
Gevrey-Chambertin Les Cazetiers 1990: Lovely rose petal, violet and raspberry aromas and flavors are charming, and fresh mushroom and wet earth notes emerge on the firm finish. Drinkable now. 900 cases made. • $49 • (12/15/92) • **89**
Gevrey-Chambertin Les Cazetiers 1989 • $47 • (01/31/92) • **89**
Gevrey-Chambertin Les Cazetiers 1988 • $57 • (03/31/91) • **89**
Gevrey-Chambertin Les Cazetiers 1985 • $53 • (03/31/88) • **92**
Gevrey-Chambertin La Combe Aux Moines 1989 • $47 • (01/31/92) • **87**
Gevrey-Chambertin Les Marchais 1992: Hats off to this village Gevrey for its focused, bright flavors that zero in beautifully on raspberry, black cherry and chestnut. The lingering finish suggests holding it until 1997. • $NA • **85**
Gevrey-Chambertin Les Marchais 1990: A great wine that will take time to come around. Hard as marble now, this firm, tannic, racy red is full of berry, cherry and earth aromas and flavors. Not for the fainthearted. Try in 1998. 450 cases made. • $45 • (12/15/92) • **92**
Latricières-Chambertin 1992: Lean and tightly wound, with modest cherry and currant flavors struggling to get past the chewy tannins. Tough, needs until 2000. 584 cases made. • $70 • **81**
Latricières-Chambertin 1991: An earthy tobacco note drowns out the modest fruit character in this tough-textured, chunky wine. An echo of blackberry saves it on the finish. Give it until 2000. 125 cases made. • $69 Ⓐ • (01/31/94) • **87**
Latricieres-Chambertin 1989 • $53 Ⓐ • (01/31/92) • **89**
Latricières-Chambertin 1985 • $77 • (03/15/88) • **88**
Mazis-Chambertin 1991: A nice streak of currant, plum and violet aromas and flavors hangs on at the finish of this crisp, focused wine. Modest in tannins and drinkable now. 175 cases made. • $69 Ⓐ • (01/31/94) • **85**

Mazis-Chambertin 1990: Ripe and seductive, with rich plum, berry and tobacco aromas and flavors. Drinkable in 1998. 500 cases made. • $52 Ⓐ • (12/15/92) • **91**

Mazis-Chambertin 1989 • $46 Ⓐ • (01/31/92) • **95**

Mazis-Chambertin 1985 • $91 Ⓐ • (03/15/88) • **92**

Mercurey Clos des Myglands 1985 • $20 • (04/30/88) • **75**

Mercurey Clos des Myglands 1981 • $11 • (06/16/86) • **68**

Mercurey Clos du Roy 1993: Rugged, full-bodied, cedary, mature flavors, good concentration and very firm tannins. Drinkable now through 1997. • $25 • (05/15/96) • **84**

Mercurey Clos du Roy 1988 • $22 • (03/31/91) • **84**

Mercurey Clos du Roy 1985 • $23 • (04/30/88) • **81**

Mercurey Domaine de la Croix Jacquelet 1988 • $18 • (03/31/91) • **81**

Meursault 1991 • $32 • (10/15/93) • **86**

Meursault Les Poruzots 1991 • $37 • (10/15/93) • **87**

Morey-St.-Denis Clos des Ormes 1990: Impressively bright and delicious, the essence of a fine Pinot Noir. Very ripe and almost sweet, with plum and raspberry flavors and a succulent finish. Try now. • $12 Ⓐ • (12/15/92) • **92**

Morey-St.-Denis Clos des Ormes 1989 • $44 • (01/31/92) • **88**

Musigny Le Musigny 1949 • $NA • (08/31/90) • **92**

Nuits-St.-Georges 1990: Lacks extra dimension, but shows beautiful fruit flavors and firm tannins. Drinkable now. 1,500 cases made. • $36 • (12/15/92) • **85**

Nuits-St.-Georges 1989 • $33 • (01/31/92) • **83**

Nuits-St.-Georges 1985 • $40 • (03/15/88) • **90**

Nuits-St.-Georges Aux Chaignots 1992: Light and simple, with a bitter edge sneaking in past the modest berry flavors. Try now. • $NA • **76**

Nuits-St.-Georges Aux Chaignots 1990: Vibrant and well constructed, with lovely raspberry and berry aromas and flavors and velvety tannins. Drinkable now. 300 cases made. • $48 • (12/15/92) • **90**

Nuits-St.-Georges Clos de la Maréchale 1992: Light and crisp, offering a nice thread of raspberry and strawberry flavors. Try now. • $NA • **80**

Nuits-St.-Georges Clos de la Maréchale 1991: Tough, astringent and dryingly tannic. Try in 1997. 1,200 cases made. • $33 Ⓐ • (01/31/94) • **78**

Nuits-St.-Georges Clos de la Maréchale 1990: A sweet, solid red Burgundy from a pedigreed producer, with cinnamon, licorice and berry characteristics and round, ripe tannins. Drinkable now. 4,000 cases made. • $36 Ⓐ • (11/30/92) • **90**

Nuits-St.-Georges Clos de la Maréchale 1989 • $25 Ⓐ • (01/31/92) • **85**

Nuits-St.-Georges Clos de la Maréchale 1988 • $25 Ⓐ • (03/15/91) • **76**

Nuits-St.-Georges Clos de la Maréchale 1985 • $51 • (03/15/88) • **85**

Nuits-St.-Georges Clos de la Maréchale 1982 • $20 • (05/01/86) • **84**

Nuits-St.-Georges Les Damodes 1992: Bright, crisp and lively, with appealing strawberry and red cherry flavors that echo on the finish. Drinkable now. • $NA • **80**

Nuits-St.-Georges Les Damodes 1990: A vivid wine, with super-focused plum and spice aromas and flavors. The tannins are fine and elegant. Drinkable now. 300 cases made. • $45 • (12/15/92) • **91**

Nuits-St.-Georges Les Damodes 1989 • $45 • (01/31/92) • **90**

Nuits-St.-Georges Les Damodes 1988 • $52 • (03/31/91) • **85**

Nuits-St.-Georges Les Lavières 1992: Tough and tannic, hiding its modest black cherry and spice flavors under the tannins. • $NA • **78**

Nuits-St.-Georges Les Porêts St.-Georges 1992: Tough and simple, with bitter, leafy accents playing off the modest black cherry flavor. Try now. • $NA • **79**

Nuits-St.-Georges Les Porêts St.-Georges 1991: Dull and flat, the earthy flavors fall short of full maturity. Finishes diluted. 200 cases made. • $37 Ⓐ • (01/31/94) • **76**

Nuits-St.-Georges Les Porêts St.-Georges 1989 • $42 • (01/31/92) • **84**

Nuits-St.-Georges Les Porêts St.-Georges 1985 • $47 Ⓐ • (03/15/88) • **76**

Nuits-St.-Georges Les St.-Georges 1992: Light and a little chewy, with extremely modest red cherry flavors lurking in the background. Try now. 150 cases made. • $62 • **77**

Nuits-St.-Georges Les St.-Georges 1991: Shows earthy raspberry character on a firm structure. The fruit fades. Drinkable now. 75 cases made. • $62 Ⓐ • (01/31/94) • **79**

Key: SS—Spectator Selection. CS—Cellar Selection. BB—Best Buy. $NA—Price not available. (BT)—Barrel tasting. Ⓐ—Auction Price.
Dates in parentheses represent the issues in which the ratings were published.

Nuits-St.-Georges Les St.-Georges 1989 • $28 Ⓐ • (01/31/92) • **92**

Nuits-St.-Georges Porrets St.-Georges 1993: A big, assertive, promising Burgundy delivering lots of body, seemingly sweet fruit flavors, very firm tannins and lingering aftertaste. Tough to drink now, but it should be excellent in time, try from 1998 to 2003. • $43 • (05/15/96) • **90**

Nuits-St.-Georges Porrets St.-Georges 1990: Chewy and rich, manages to pack in a lot of fruit flavors, firm tannins and abundant spice, cherry and oak notes. Drinkable now to 1998. 800 cases made. • $45 • (12/15/92) • **90**

Pommard Les Chaponnières 1990: Truly elegant, with succulent fruit, vanilla, raspberry and earth aromas and flavors and an elegant finish. Drinkable now to 1998. 125 cases made. • $65 • (12/15/92) • **90**

Pommard Les Chaponnières 1989 • $50 • (01/31/92) • **90**

Rully 1986 • $18 • (06/15/89) • **83**

Vosne-Romanée 1989 • $35 • (01/31/92) • **88**

FAIZEAU, CHÂTEAU

Montagne-St.-Emilion 1983 • $9 • (11/15/87) • **75**

Montagne-St.-Emilion Sélection Vieilles Vignes 1995: Another full-bodied winner, with well-defined, fresh, grapey, zingy red berry character. Quite firm and angular at this stage, but it pumps out the flavors at the end. • $NA • (05/15/96) • **85-89** (BT)

Montagne-St.-Emilion Vieilles Vignes 1994: Clean, straightforward cherry and vanilla aromas and flavors. Medium in body, good tannins. • $NA • **80-84** (BT)

Montagne-St.-Emilion Vieilles Vignes 1993: Delicious now, showing chocolate, berry and cherry aromas and flavors, silky texture and fruity finish. Not big, but offers some good fruit. Drinkable now. • $15 • (01/31/96) • **84**

Montagne-St.-Emilion Vieilles Vignes 1992: Aromatic mint, earth and cherry aromas and flavors, but light body and finish. Drink now. • $NA • **78**

Montagne-St.-Emilion Vieilles Vignes 1991: A nice little wine, with a core of light-bodied cherry, plum and tobacco notes. • $12 • (03/31/94) • **80**

Montagne-St.-Emilion Vieilles Vignes 1990: From the owners of Château La Croix-de-Gay. A decadent wine, with raspberry syrup, chocolate and cedar aromas and flavors, full, velvety tannins and a rich finish. Drinkable in 1997. • $15 • (03/31/93) • **89**

FARAUD, MICHEL

Gigondas Domaine du Cayron 1988 • $14 • (10/15/91) • **89**

Gigondas Domaine du Cayron 1985 • $16 • (11/30/88) • **93**

FARGUES, CHÂTEAU DE

Sauternes 1988: Wonderfully spicy orange marmalade, cedar and pine-nut flavors, full-bodied and very sweet. Drinkable now. • $75 • **88**

FAURE, CHÂTEAU JEAN

St.-Emilion 1983 • $17 • (03/31/87) • **87**

St.-Emilion 1982 • $14 • (11/16/85) • **85**

FAURIE-PASCAUD, CHÂTEAU

Bordeaux 1986 • $5 • (06/30/88) • **79**

FAURIE, BERNARD

Hermitage 1991: Bitter chocolate and berries burst out in this ripe wine. Very firm on the palate and long on the finish. Try now. • $26 • (05/31/94) • **88**

Hermitage 1990: This is velvety, with full, round tannins, black pepper, licorice and thick raisin flavors. It's closed now, but concentrated, try after 1996. • $30 • (05/31/94) • **89**

FAURY, PHILIPPE

Condrieu 1993: This tastes simple for a wine from such an exclusive district. Drinkable, but not well balanced. It may need more time for the opposing citrus and creamy flavors to harmonize. Comes off sharp in texture and awkward in flavor. 1,500 cases made. • $28 • **78**

St.-Joseph 1993: A basically lean, dry white wine whose buttery, spicy aromas don't get much follow through from the simple, watery flavors. • $15 • **76**

FAUST, SERGE

Brut Champagne Cuvée de Réserve à Vandières NV • $33 • (12/31/90) • **86**

FAUTERIE, DOMAINE DE

Cornas 1991 • $NA • (05/31/94) • **84**

St.-Joseph 1991 • $17 • (04/15/93) • **82**

St.-Joseph 1990 • $13 • (08/31/92) • **80**

FAVRAY, CHÂTEAU

Pouilly-Fumé 1992: Green apple and fresh cream aromas follow through on the palate in this clean, zingy Pouilly-Fumé. It's light and refreshing and would make a good apéritif. 300 cases made. • $16 • (08/31/94) • **87**

FAVREAU, YANNICK

Pomerol 1993: Firm, interesting toasted oak, berry, dried herb character, medium body, solid tannins and medium finish. A négociant wine from a Belgian merchant. Mostly the second wine of Château Le Pin. Better in 1999. • $NA • (02/29/96) • **86**

FAYOLLE

Hermitage Les Diognières 1991: Concentrated but a bit rustic, with hard tannins and barnyard notes. It shows some berry and plum flavors. Try now. • $NA • (05/31/94) • **82**

Hermitage Les Diognières 1990: Closed with hard tannins, but shows some tar and berry flavors. Time may pull it together, try after 1996. • $NA • (05/31/94) • **84**

FERE, CHARLES DE

Brut Chardonnay Tradition NV: A refreshing bottle of bubbly with crisp, lean apple and lemon flavors and a lively feel from effervescence and generous acidity. • $10 • (10/31/95) • **81**

Brut Tradition NV • $12 • (11/30/91) • **82**

Brut Blanc de Blancs NV • $10 • (01/31/92) • **79**

Brut Blanc de Blancs Réserve NV: Frothy, bland-tasting and just slightly sweet. Not much to get excited about, but at least it tastes clean. • $7 • (10/31/95) • **78**

Brut Rosé NV • $10 • (06/15/90) • **70**

FERRAND, CHÂTEAU

Pomerol 1995: Decent balance of fruit and fine tannins, with herbal berry and earthy notes. • $NA • (05/15/96) • **80-84** (BT)

FERRANDE, CHÂTEAU

Graves 1981 • $7 • (03/16/85) • **75**

FERRATON PERE

Crozes-Hermitage La Matinière 1990 • $16 • (04/15/93) • **89**

Crozes-Hermitage La Matinière 1988 • $14 • (06/30/90) • **85**

Hermitage Cuvée les Miaux 1990: Polished and balanced, but lacking a bit in concentration. Black cherry and smoked-meat flavors, with soft tannins. Drinkable now. • $NA • (05/31/94) • **86**

FERRAUD & FILS, PIERRE

Beaujolais-Villages Cuvée Ensorceleuse 1988 • $10 • (05/31/89) • **81**

Brouilly Domaine Rolland 1992: There are rich plum and licorice flavors in this ripe, round Brouilly, but earthy and gamy notes are overtaking them. A pretty big wine, but it needs to be drunk now. • $12 • (06/30/94) • **76**

Brouilly Domaine Rolland 1988 • $16 • (05/31/89) • **84**

Chénas Cuvée Jean-Michel 1988 • $10 • (05/31/89) • **89**

Chénas Côte Remont 1992: This big Beaujolais has the structure to keep it going, with fresh plum and intriguing spicy flavors on a firm-frame. This cru is generally hard in its youth, and that's paying off now. • $12 • (06/30/94) • **83**

Chiroubles Domaine de la Chapelle du Bois 1988 • $12 • (05/31/89) • **79**

Côte de Brouilly 1988 • $16 • (05/31/89) • **83**

Côte de Brouilly Domaine Rolland 1992: Brawny with good structure, this offers mature plum, black cherry and chocolate flavors, with just a hint of earthiness in the finish. • $12 • (06/30/94) • **80**

Fleurie 1988 • $15 • (05/31/89) • **87**

Fleurie Château de Grand Pre 1988 • $16 • (05/31/89) • **86**

Fleurie Domaine du Clos des Garands 1992: Ripe and almost jammy, has plenty of strawberry and cherry flavor, but lacks freshness and verve. A big, but tiring, Beaujolais. • $14 • (06/30/94) • **80**

Juliénas 1988 • $12 • (05/31/89) • **73**

Mâcon-Villages 1994: Crisp, sharp and light-bodied, showing wet hay, lemon and green apple flavors of medium intensity. Good balance on the juicy finish. 667 cases made. • $9 • **79**

Morgon Domaine de l'Eveque 1988 • $16 • (05/31/89) • **89**

Moulin-à-Vent 1988 • $16 • (05/31/89) • **83**

Régnié 1988 • $10 • (05/31/89) • **81**

Régnié Cuvée Antoine Ferraud 1992: A bit tired already, light and slightly bitter, tastes of strawberries and oversteeped tea. Drink soon. • $12 • (06/30/94) • **75**

St.-Amour 1988 • $12 • (05/31/89) • **85**

St.-Amour Château du Chapître 1992: Silky and a bit sweet, this maturing wine shows black cherry, smoky and herbal flavors. It's straightforward and balanced, drink soon. • $12 • (06/30/94) • **79**

St.-Véran 1994: Sparkling with life and vibrant citrus character, this light-to medium-bodied white delivers intense lemon, grapefruit and pear notes. Could use a more complex finish. 1,083 cases made. • $10 • **84**

FERRET, J.-A.

Pouilly-Fuissé Les Ménétrières 1993: Supple and honeyed, harmonious and enchanting, delivering some lovely mineral, wet earth character underneath the opulent pear and apple flavors. Long, lemony finish suggests it will hold until 1999. 150 cases imported. • $45 • (05/31/96) • **90**

Pouilly-Fuissé Tête de Cru 1994: Beautiful white, both thick and crisp, delivering a blend of honey and citrus character. Turns somewhat lean and green on the finish. Better in 1998? 150 cases imported. • $40 • (05/31/96) 84 • **85**

Pouilly-Fuissé Tête de Cuvée 1993: Impressively silky and creamy texture and butterscotch, yeasty aromas and flavors. Lots of intense lemon, lime and pear character on the immensely pleasing, velvety finish that goes on and on. Drinkable now. • $35 • **90**

Pouilly-Fuissé Tournant de Pouilly 1994: Simply gorgeous. Rich, unctuous and supple, yet it's not overdone, boasting toasted coconut, spice, honey and hazelnut. Full body, electrifying flavors and a long finish. Try now and through 1999. 100 cases imported. • $45 • (05/31/96) • **93**

FERRIERE, CHÂTEAU

Margaux 1995: A great surprise of the vintage. All finesse and length, a wonderful, seamless wine boasting berry, licorice and spice aromas and flavors, loads of fruit and a long, silky finish. Almost classic. • $NA • (05/15/96) • **90-94** (BT)

Margaux 1994: Elegant, refined and delicate berry character and fine tannins. • $20 • (05/15/96) • **85-89** (BT)

Margaux 1993: Good sweetness of fruit here. Mint, dried herb and plum aromas and flavors, medium body and tannins and silky finish. Better in 1998. 2,917 cases made. • $NA • (01/31/96) • **87**

Margaux 1992: Smooth and silky plum and cherry flavors, but slightly one-dimensional and short. Drinkable now. • $NA • (04/15/95) • **81**

FESSY, SYLVAIN

Brouilly Domaine de Chavannes 1985 • $8 • (12/15/86) • **87**
Côte de Brouilly Domaine de Chavannes 1985 • $8 • (12/15/86) • **72**
Fleurie La Roilette 1991: Mature now, showing ripe berry and raisin flavors, with hints of earth and chocolate that give it pleasing complexity. Though still firm, it's beginning to fade, drink now. 4,000 cases made. • $15 • (06/30/94) • **82**
Juliénas Cuvée Michel Tête 1986 • $7 • (12/31/87) • **71**
Juliénas Cuvée Michel Tête 1985 • $8 • (12/15/86) • **86**
Morgon Cuvée André Gauthier 1991: Tired and fading. The stewed fruit and vegetal flavors testify to a wine heading downhill. • $15 • (06/30/94) • **71**
Morgon Cuvée André Gauthier 1986 • $7 • (12/31/87) • **74**
Morgon Cuvée André Gauthier 1985 • $8 • (12/15/86) • **76**
Pouilly-Fuissé Cuvée Gilles Guérrin 1991 • $17 • (02/28/94) • **76**

FEUILLATTE, NICHOLAS

Brut Champagne Palmes d'Or 1985: For a long-aged Champagne, this is still quite fresh and lively, showing just enough of an exotic, mature character to make the wait worthwhile. It blends solid citrus and apple flavors with accents of vanilla and almond. 2,000 cases made. • $80 • (12/15/94) • **88**
Brut Champagne Premier Cru Réserve Particuliére NV: A note of maturity makes this assertive and complex. Has nutty, earthy aromas, apple and mushroom flavors and a lingering, vanilla-accented finish. It tastes round, complete and satisfying. 90,000 cases made. • $18 • **86**
Brut Rosé Champagne Premier Cru NV: Exotic, mature and rich for a rosé, with cherry and cassis accents to the vivid fruit flavors. Bold, smooth and imposing, well-integrated and complex, with a lingering finish. 8,000 cases made. • $23 • (12/15/94) • **88**

FEVRE, WILLIAM

Chablis 1994: Crisp and quite oaky, with some lemon, green apple, wet earth and celery flavors. Very tart finish. Perhaps better in 1998. 666 cases imported. • $16 • (05/31/96) • **79**
Chablis Bougros 1994: Great harmony in this subtle, seductive white Burgundy that unfolds its charm with graceful flavors of toasted nuts, butter, honey, lemon and ripe fruit. Full-bodied and creamy, with a powerful, intense finish. Tempting now, but wait until 1999. 400 cases imported. • $35 • (05/31/96) • **93**
Chablis Bougros 1993: Very appealing mineral, straw, truffle, spice and honey flavors are backed by fresh acidity and end on a pretty finish. Medium body. 250 cases made. • $35 • **85**
Chablis Les Clos 1994: Like a ballerina dancing Swan Lake. Full of sinewy finesse, it tip-toes along the palate with amazing grace. Full-bodied, with compact mineral, earth, honey, vanilla, pear and cream flavors. Great harmony on the finish. Tempting now, but better in 2000. 416 cases imported. • $35 • (05/31/96) • **92**
Chablis Les Clos 1993: A Chablis with some oak. Slightly toasty and smoky, with ripe-tasting pear, green apple and spice notes. Too bad it's somewhat astringent on the finish. 250 cases made. • $32 • **85**
Chablis Grenouilles 1994: Tight, hard, and solidly structured. A *terroir* wine that has notes of wet earth and mineral. Big and almost rustic, a *grand cru* with tons of personality but also a sense of balance, with good concentration of fruit and honey notes. Try in 1999. From Domaine de la Maladière. 100 cases imported. • $35 • (05/31/96) • **88**
Chablis Montmains 1994: A distinctive Chablis with a lactic, milky component that may not be for everyone. Pear tart, vanilla and cream notes. Soft, lush and ripe, it begs to be drunk soon. Tasted twice, with consistent notes. 150 cases imported. • $22 • (05/31/96) • **83**

Key: SS—Spectator Selection. CS—Cellar Selection. BB—Best Buy. $NA—Price not available. (BT)—Barrel tasting. Ⓐ—Auction Price.
Dates in parentheses represent the issues in which the ratings were published.

Chablis Montmains 1993: Firm and full-bodied, the proverbial steely Chablis, offering plenty of lemon, grapefruit and melon flavors. Tart but long, long finish. 300 cases made. • $22 • **85**
Chablis Montée de Tonnerre 1994: A silky beauty.This full-bodied, ripe and oak-treated Chablis seduces you with its smooth texture, round mouth-feel and terrific combination of mineral, toasted bread, cedar, vanilla, cream and fruit flavors. Elegant and focused on the finish. Try in 1998. 300 cases imported. • $25 • (05/31/96) • **91**
Chablis Les Preuses 1994: Ripe, rich and harmonious, with a distinctive floral note. Medium- to full-bodied, with lovely honey and ripe fruit flavors and a long, intense finish. An elegant, balanced and lovely wine through and through. Try in 1998. 300 cases imported. • $35 • (05/31/96) • **87**
Chablis Vaillons 1994: Ripe and supple, you can taste the obvious oaky influence in the vanilla, cream and butter, which should marry nicely over time with the apple, honey and citrus flavors. Well made and crisp. 200 cases imported. • $25 • (05/31/96) • **84**
Chablis Vaudésir 1994: Classy, racy and subtle, a connoisseur's wine. Not an opulent style and it's very tight and closed now, but the mineral quality and an attractive, pronounced oaky, vanilla character show through. A lemony note emerges on the long finish. Try in 1998. 100 cases imported. • $35 • (05/31/96) • **94**

FEYTIT-CLINET, CHÂTEAU

Pomerol 1995: A bit rustic but delivering some good fruit, earthy undertones, medium body and hard tannins. Wait and see how this evolves. • $NA • (05/15/96) • **80-84** (BT)
Pomerol 1994: Subtle, classy, supple structure, medium body, ripe fruit and complex character. • $NA • **85-89** (BT)
Pomerol 1985 • $30 • (04/30/88) • **88**
Pomerol 1983 • $13 • (07/16/86) • **70**
Pomerol 1982 • $37 Ⓐ • (05/15/89) • **91**

FIEFS DE LAGRANGE, LES

St.-Julien 1995: Lovely, bright red berry character. Medium-bodied, offers good finesse and acidity, with chewy tannins. Second label of Lagrange. • $NA • (05/15/96) • **80-84** (BT)
St.-Julien 1993: Full of life and zingy character, a delicious, medium-bodied St.-Julien worth seeking out, featuring soft tannins and cassis, blackberry and mint flavors. Lovely to drink now. • $16 • (01/31/96) • **85**
St.-Julien 1991: A delicate wine that turns a bit astringent on the finish, delivering some alluring floral, red berry and tobacco flavors. • $13 • (03/31/94) • **79**
St.-Julien 1990: An elegant wine, with a lovely balance of blackberry, tobacco flavors and soft, silky tannins. Not a blockbuster, but well proportioned. Drinkable now. • $18 • (03/31/93) • **88**
St.-Julien 1988 • $17 • (04/30/91) • **92**
St.-Julien 1983 • $10 • (05/01/86) • **85**

FIEUZAL, CHÂTEAU DE

Pessac-Léognan 1995: Harmonious essence of blackberry and chocolate. Full in body, loads of smoky, berry character and long, velvety finish. Nearly outstanding. • $NA • (05/15/96) • **85-89** (BT)
Pessac-Léognan 1994: An elegant wine with fine tannins and cherry, berry and strawberry aromas and flavors. Medium to full body and a delicate finish. • $25 • (05/15/96) • **85-89** (BT)
Pessac-Léognan 1993: Delicious raspberry and blackberry aromas and flavors. Medium-bodied and succulent, adding fine tannins and a sweet fruit finish. Better in 1997. • $25 • (01/31/96) • **87**
Pessac-Léognan 1992: Some good fruit but rather aggressive, showing gravel, meat and green bean character. Medium-bodied and slightly hard and dry. • $20 • **82**
Pessac-Léognan 1991: Not as good as expected. A lean wine with white pepper and cherry aromas and flavors, medium body and a light finish. Tasted twice. • $14 • (03/31/94) • **79**
Pessac-Léognan 1990: A powerful wine, with masses of tar, berry and earthy character, gripping tannins and sweet fruit on the finish. Drink after 1998. 7,500 cases made. • $29 • (03/31/93) • **92**
Pessac-Léognan 1989 • $32 • (03/15/92) • **95**

Pessac-Léognan 1988 • $33 • (04/30/91) • **91**
Pessac-Léognan 1987 • $18 • (05/15/90) • **81**
Pessac-Léognan 1986 • $23 • (06/30/89) • **90**
Pessac-Léognan White 1994: Creamy vanilla, lemon and grapefruit aromas and flavors. Medium body, fine tannins and a long finish. Very fruity and rich. • $NA • **90-94** (BT)
Pessac-Léognan White 1993: Polished and racy, highlighting plenty of lemon, grass and gooseberry aromas and character, full body, great acidity and a very long finish. The flavors last for minutes on the palate. Try after 1996. • $40 • (05/31/95) • **91**
Pessac-Léognan Blanc 1992: Several points better than a year ago. Plenty of crushed fruit and wonderful apple and toasted oak character. Still young, firm acidity and long finish. Drinkable now. • $40 • (05/31/95) • **89**
Graves 1985 • $24 • (10/15/94) • **90**
Graves 1983 • $25 • (10/15/94) • **85**
Graves 1982 • $22 • (08/31/92) • **82**
Graves 1981. • $24 • (10/15/94) • **88**
Graves 1979 • $NA • (10/15/89) • **83**

FIGARO

Vin de Pays de l'Herault 1993: Broad and soft texture, simply fruity and peppery in flavor, with earthy, leathery accents. 8,500 cases made. • $5 • (03/31/95) • **79**

FIGEAC, CHÂTEAU

St.-Emilion 1995: Racy and vibrant, showing some lovely smoky, currant, earth character. Supple tannins on the crisp finish. • $NA • (05/15/96) • **90-94** (BT)
St.-Emilion 1994: Aromatic and subtle, with currant, plum, toasted oak and earth flavors. Well-integrated tannins, though a touch light on the mid-palate. • $32 • (05/15/96) • **80-84** (BT)
St.-Emilion 1993: Elegant and subtle, showing a good amount of toasty, vanilla-flavored new wood and a combination of herbal-scented Merlot character with cassis, earth and plum. Supple tannins. Try in 1997. • $33 • (01/31/96) • **87**
St.-Emilion 1990: Tantalizing, with beautiful aromas of chocolate, vanilla and berry that carry through to the long, clean finish. Round and juicy. Drink after 1997. 12,500 cases made. • $45 • (03/31/93) • **92**
St.-Emilion 1989 • $48 Ⓐ • (03/15/92) • **93**
St.-Emilion 1988 • $45 • (06/30/91) • **93**
St.-Emilion 1987 • $35 • (10/31/91) • **83**
St.-Emilion 1986 • $51 • (10/15/94) • **84**
St.-Emilion 1985 • $51 Ⓐ • (10/15/94) • **90**
St.-Emilion 1984 • $30 • (03/31/87) • **83**
St.-Emilion 1983 • $46 Ⓐ • (10/15/94) • **91**
St.-Emilion 1982 • $110 Ⓐ • (08/31/92) • **90**
St.-Emilion 1981 • $44 • (10/15/94) • **87**
St.-Emilion 1980 • $30 • (05/01/85) • **90**
St.-Emilion 1979 • $31 Ⓐ • (10/31/91) • **88**
St.-Emilion 1978 • $34 Ⓐ • (10/31/91) • **89**
St.-Emilion 1976 • $46 • (10/31/91) • **87**
St.-Emilion 1975 • $44 Ⓐ • (10/31/91) • **78**
St.-Emilion 1971 • $75 • (10/31/91) • **84**
St.-Emilion 1970 • $75 Ⓐ • (05/15/93) • **90**
St.-Emilion 1966 • $38 Ⓐ • (10/31/91) • **85**
St.-Emilion 1964 • $110 • (10/31/91) • **93**
St.-Emilion 1962 • $90 • (10/31/91) • **85**
St.-Emilion 1961 • $105 Ⓐ • (04/30/96) • **90**
St.-Emilion 1955 • $250 • (10/31/91) • **96**
St.-Emilion 1953 • $150 • (10/31/91) • **86**
St.-Emilion 1952 • $48 Ⓐ • (10/31/91) • **85**
St.-Emilion 1950 • $220 • (10/31/91) • **91**
St.-Emilion 1949 • $271 Ⓐ • (10/31/91) • **99**
St.-Emilion 1947 • $620 • (10/31/91) • **93**
St.-Emilion 1945 • $300 • (10/31/91) • **96**
St.-Emilion 1943 • $150 • (10/31/91) • **90**
St.-Emilion 1942 • $125 • (10/31/91) • **85**
St.-Emilion 1939 • $125 • (10/31/91) • **83**
St.-Emilion 1937 • $125 • (10/31/91) • **69**
St.-Emilion 1934 • $160 • (10/31/91) • **79**
St.-Emilion 1929 • $400 • (10/31/91) • **98**
St.-Emilion 1926 • $300 • (10/31/91) • **87**
St.-Emilion 1924 • $350 • (10/31/91) • **88**
St.-Emilion 1911 • $400 • (10/31/91) • **78**
St.-Emilion 1906 • $350 • (10/31/91) • **78**
St.-Emilion 1905 • $430 • (10/31/91) • **95**

FIGEAT, COLETTE

Pouilly-Fumé 1992: A strong smoky aroma lends distinctive character, it's bold and firm on the palate, with green apple and mineral flavors. This has presence, though it may be a bit austere for some. • $18 • (10/31/94) • **85**
Pouilly-Fumé Les Loges 1993: This full-bodied wine has good acidity but isn't showing much fruit, apart from light citrus notes, and the finish is earthy and dull. It's muscular, but lacks definition. • $18 • (10/31/94) • **77**

FILHOT, CHÂTEAU

Sauternes 1991: Fresh and lively, revealing floral notes and vibrant, grassy, unripe apricot flavors, lightly sweet on the crisp finish. Drink as an apéritif. • $NA • (04/15/95) • **80**
Sauternes 1990: Pleasant, light-bodied, offering decent concentration of lemon, pear, melon and earth flavors, a bit short on the finish. • $29 • (04/15/95) • **81**
Sauternes 1989: A light style, supplying attractive lilac, honeycomb, butterscotch, lemon and grass flavors. Drinkable now. Good as apéritif. • $27 • (04/15/95) • **85**
Sauternes 1988: Clean and fresh lemon, spicy character, light and moderately sweet. Drinkable now. • $25 • (04/15/95) • **84**
Sauternes 1987 • $19 • (06/15/90) • **68**
Sauternes 1986 • $19 • (12/31/89) • **83**
Sauternes 1983 • $33 • (04/15/95) • **87**
Sauternes 1980 • $11 • (05/01/84) • **80**
Sauternes Crème de Tête 1990: Unbelievably rich and unctuous, thick, ripe and creamy, quite sugary, sporting an orange flavor to accent the botrytis character. Drinkable now. • $NA • (04/15/95) • **90**

FILLIATREAU, L.

Saumur Champigny La Grande Vignolle Red 1992: Clean and straightforward, a pleasant, medium-bodied red, with berry and lightly herbal, smoky flavors. Drinkable now and would be a refreshing counterpoint to hearty fish dishes. • $13 • (11/15/94) • **84**

FINES ROCHES, CHÂTEAU DES

Châteauneuf-du-Pape 1989 • $20 • (05/31/92) • **81**
Châteauneuf-du-Pape 1986 • $14 • (09/30/90) • **85**
Châteauneuf-du-Pape 1985 • $12 • (10/31/87) • **80**
Châteauneuf-du-Pape 1984 • $12 • (09/30/87) • **89**

FLEUR CRAVIGNAC, CHÂTEAU LA

St.-Emilion 1990: Ripe and concentrated, but overall it's simple and clumsy. Drink up. 2,000 cases made. • $18 • (08/31/95) • **76**

FLEUR, CHÂTEAU LA

St.-Emilion 1995: Attractive wild berry aromas and flavors added to a complex of vanilla, mineral and spice. Full-bodied, showing great, fine tannins and a long finish. Approaching outstanding quality. • $NA • (05/15/96) • **85-89** (BT)
St.-Emilion 1994: Very light and lean, some decent fruit flavors but rather dry on the finish. • $NA • **75-79** (BT)
St.-Emilion 1993: Succulent and soft, featuring silky tannins and plenty of berry, plum and tobacco character. Medium body and finish. Drinkable now. • $17 • (01/31/96) • **85**
St.-Emilion 1992: Decent color but slightly weedy plum, dried herb character, light-bodied and lean. Drink now. • $14 • **77**

St.-Emilion 1990: Decadent, with plenty of earth, tar, tobacco and cherry character and assertive tannins. A little rough around the edges. Drinkable in 1997. 2,500 cases made. • $22 • (03/31/93) • **89**
St.-Emilion 1989 • $18 • (03/15/92) • **84**
St.-Emilion 1986 • $14 • (02/15/90) • **82**

FLEUR-CARDINALE, CHÂTEAU

St.-Emilion 1995: Aromatic mocha, spice and smoke notes back up the red berry flavor. Very supple and smooth. Lacks a bit of concentration in the mid-palate. • $NA • (05/15/96) • **85-89** (BT)
St.-Emilion 1993: Well-proportioned '93, showing medium body, smooth tannins and attractive mineral, plum and cedar flavors. A Bordeaux that delivers finesse more than loads of character. Drinkable now. • $NA • (01/31/96) • **84**

FLEUR-PETRUS, CHÂTEAU LA

Pomerol 1995: Bright and fresh raspberry and cherry character, medium to full body and a delicious, silky tannin finish. Almost outstanding. • $NA • (05/15/96) • **85-89** (BT)
Pomerol 1994: Very good chocolate and berry character, medium body and slightly angular tannins on the finish. • $33 • (05/15/96) • **85-89** (BT)
Pomerol 1993: Nicely balanced. Medium- to light-bodied and elegant with medium intensity and a very attractive core of sweet fruit. Supple tannins add to the pleasurable taste. Try in 1997. • $39 • (01/31/96) • **86**
Pomerol 1992: Better than when we tasted it in barrel. Attractive leather, berry and light plum aromas and flavors, subtle, complex palate and light body. Drink now. • $34 • **84**
Pomerol 1990: The flavors build on the palate with luscious cassis, olive and berry flavors and medium tannins. Drink after 1997. 2,300 cases made. • $70 • (03/31/93) • **90**
Pomerol 1989 • $70 • (03/15/92) • **88**
Pomerol 1986 • $46 • (02/15/90) CS • **93**
Pomerol 1985 • $50 • (10/15/94) • **90**
Pomerol 1983 • $44 • (10/15/94) • **86**
Pomerol 1982 • $103 Ⓐ • (08/31/92) • **90**
Pomerol 1981 • $50 • (10/15/94) • **86**
Pomerol 1961 • $150 • (04/30/96) • **89**
Pomerol English Bottled 1959 • $150 • (10/15/90) • **92**
Pomerol 1945 • $300 • (03/16/86) • **63**

FLEUR-POURRET, CHÂTEAU LA

St.-Emilion 1995: Tightly knit, with a solid backbone of firm but ripe tannins, it delivers plenty of bitter chocolate, blackberry and red berry character. Long, tannic finish. • $NA • (05/15/96) • **85-89** (BT)
St.-Emilion 1992: Rather aggressive tobacco, herbal, stewed tomato character, medium in body and metallic on the finish. Drink now. • $NA • **78**
St.-Emilion 1990: A very pretty, early maturing wine, with tobacco, cedar, ripe fruit aromas and flavors and medium-light tannins. Drinkable now. 2,500 cases made. • $23 • (03/31/93) • **86**
St.-Emilion 1989 • $NA • (03/15/92) • **82**

FLEUR-ST.-GEORGES, CHÂTEAU LA

Lalande-de-Pomerol 1990: This is a slinky wine, with intense aromas and flavors of raspberries and ripe fruit, silky tannins and a slightly dry finish. Drink after 1996. • $NA • (03/31/93) • **88**

FLEUR DE GAY, CHÂTEAU LA

Pomerol 1995: Bright, lively and delicious, medium-bodied, with wonderful, grapey, red berry character and a harmonious finish. Tasted twice, with consistent notes. • $NA • (05/15/96) • **85-89** (BT)

Key: SS—Spectator Selection. CS—Cellar Selection. BB—Best Buy. $NA—Price not available. (BT)—Barrel tasting. Ⓐ—Auction Price.
Dates in parentheses represent the issues in which the ratings were published.

Pomerol 1994: Lovely, rich, sweet fruit character and smoky oak, medium to full tannins and a velvety finish. • $82 • (05/15/96) • **85-89** (BT)
Pomerol 1993: An amazing '93. Gorgeous, full-bodied Pomerol of great intensity and harmony, bursting with pure fruit—from well-tuned, toasty flavors to mocha, blackberry, black olive, truffle and plum notes. A brilliant, seamless finish. Drinkable now but will age very well. • $50 • (01/31/96) CS • **94**
Pomerol 1992: Impressive blackberry, tobacco and toasted oak aromas and flavors. Medium-bodied and rather chewy, offering medium, velvety tannins and a fruity, vanilla finish. • $40 • **85**
Pomerol 1991: Delicious and opulent with the toasted oak, plum and chocolate character, medium body and long, velvety, flavorful finish. • $40 • (03/31/94) • **85**
Pomerol 1990: A brooding monster of a wine with great concentration of ripe fruit and fine tannins. The finish goes on and on. Drink after 1998. 2,000 cases made. • $75 • (03/31/93) • **95**
Pomerol 1989 • $117 Ⓐ • (03/15/92) • **98**
Pomerol 1988 • $67 Ⓐ • (06/30/91) • **94**
Pomerol 1986 • $53 Ⓐ • (10/31/89) CS • **95**
Pomerol 1985 • $65 • (10/15/94) • **92**
Pomerol 1982 • $75 • (05/15/89) • **88**

FOLIE, LA

Brut Blanc de Blancs Réserve NV • $5 • (06/15/90) • **63**

FOMBRAUGE, CHÂTEAU

St.-Emilion 1990: Round and spicy, with lots of earthy, gamy flavors that rob the wine of any charm or fruit. • $20 • (02/28/94) • **74**
St.-Emilion 1988 • $14 Ⓐ • (11/30/92) • **85**
St.-Emilion 1986 • $19 • (06/30/89) • **86**
St.-Emilion 1985 • $25 • (05/15/88) • **87**

FONBADET, CHÂTEAU

Pauillac 1995: Quite woody, offering medium-intense fruit flavors that seem for now to be dominated by oak. A bit dry on the finish. • $NA • (05/15/96) • **80-84** (BT)
Pauillac 1988 • $16 • (08/31/91) • **89**
Pauillac 1982 • $16 • (08/01/85) • **86**

FONPLEGADE, CHÂTEAU

St.-Emilion 1992: Lean cherry, herbal character, medium-to-light body and hard, metallic tannins. • $16 • **77**
St.-Emilion 1990: Rich and chunky, with loads of smoky, tobacco, sweet fruit character, soft tannins and a luscious cedar finish. Drink after 1997. 7,500 cases made. • $25 • (03/31/93) • **90**
St.-Emilion 1988 • $18 • (06/30/91) • **85**
St.-Emilion 1982 • $NA • (05/15/89) • **77**
St.-Emilion 1961 • $NA • (04/30/96) • **86**

FONREAUD, CHÂTEAU

Bordeaux White Le Cygne 1993: New white from a red estate. Light, fresh and straightforward, showing lemon, lime and light mineral character. • $NA • **79**
Listrac 1992: Pleasant plum and green bean flavors, light body and finish. Drinkable now. • $15 • **76**
Listrac 1990: A no-frills wine, with focused tar and berry character and solid tannins. Drinkable now. 20,500 cases made. • $16 • (03/31/93) • **83**
Listrac 1988 • $15 • (04/30/91) • **82**

FONROQUE, CHÂTEAU

St.-Emilion 1995: Racy berry, cherry and vanilla aromas and flavors, full body, fine tannins and long, long finish. Impressive. Nearly outstanding. • $NA • (05/15/96) • **85-89** (BT)

St.-Emilion 1994: Some pretty berry, herb character, medium body, lean and slightly hard tannin structure. Could move up next year. • $NA • **75-79** (BT)

St.-Emilion 1993: Pretty chocolate and berry character, medium to light body and soft, silky tannins. Drinkable now. • $19 • (01/31/96) • **83**

St.-Emilion 1992: Fresh and crisp, more like a decent Loire red. Light-bodied, cherry, earth character. Drinkable now. • $16 • **78**

St.-Emilion 1990: A real sleeper. Huge, with tons of tobacco, floral and berry character. It's thick yet agile, with very silky tannins and a long finish. Drinkable in 1998. 6,500 cases made. • $28 • (03/31/93) • **94**

St.-Emilion 1989 • $24 • (03/15/92) • **88**

St.-Emilion 1985 • $23 • **86**

St.-Emilion 1982 • $21 • (08/31/92) • **89**

St.-Emilion 1981 • $NA • **88**

FONSALETTE, CHÂTEAU DE

Côtes du Rhône Réservé 1992: An elegant, mature red that has subtle complexity in its fruity, spicy flavors, adding a long finish. It's smooth and supple in texture and ready to drink. • $30 • (09/30/95) • **85**

Côtes du Rhône Réservé 1991: There's a richness and apparent sweetness to the fruit flavors in this full-bodied, dark-colored red that make it special. Has chocolate, pepper and smoke accents for interest. Tannic, but drinkable now through 1997. • $25 • (11/30/94) • **87**

Côtes du Rhône Réservé 1989 • $20 • (11/30/92) • **88**

Côtes du Rhône Réservé 1985 • $16 • (09/30/88) • **87**

Côtes du Rhône Réservé White 1991: Nicely mature and rich, with nutty, buttery, vanilla aromas and figgy flavors that linger on the finish. Full-bodied, smooth-textured. Great to drink now, but don't save it too long. • $22 • (10/15/94) • **86**

Syrah Côtes du Rhône Réservé 1990 • $25 • (04/15/93) • **88**

FONT DE MICHELLE, DOMAINE

Châteauneuf-du-Pape 1990: Tight and focused, with appealing black cherry and toast aromas and flavors shaded by black pepper and bitter chocolate notes that persist on the finish. Try now. 2,000 cases made. • $17 • (04/15/93) • **82**

Châteauneuf-du-Pape 1989 • $18 • (10/15/91) • **83**

Châteauneuf-du-Pape 1988 • $21 • (10/15/91) • **86**

Châteauneuf-du-Pape 1986 • $20 • (10/15/91) • **89**

Châteauneuf-du-Pape 1985 • $20 • (10/15/91) • **84**

Châteauneuf-du-Pape 1983 • $25 • (10/15/91) • **85**

Châteauneuf-du-Pape 1981 • $20 • (10/15/91) • **88**

FONT DU LOUP, CHÂTEAU DE LA

Châteauneuf-du-Pape 1989 • $50 • (04/15/93) • **87**

FONT VILLAC

St.-Emilion 1989 • $14 • (11/30/92) • **81**

FONT-SANE, DOMAINE DE

Côtes du Ventoux 1990 • $8 • (04/15/93) • **80**

Gigondas 1990 • $15 • (04/15/93) • **82**

Gigondas 1985 • $13 • (01/31/89) • **86**

FONTAINE-GAGNARD

Bâtard-Montrachet 1994: Fresh and lively, with fig, citrus, mineral, toast aromas and flavors. Focused and smooth on the finish. 141 cases made. • $90 • (05/31/96) • **86**

Bourgogne 1993: Nice concentration, offering currant, violet, mineral and wet earth flavors that make your palate pay attention. Long, well-balanced finish. Delicious now but should improve through 1997. • $14 • **88**

Chassagne-Montrachet 1994: Simple and crisp, with apple cider flavors and a slightly green, astringent character. 550 cases made. • $40 • (05/31/96) 74 • **74**

Chassagne-Montrachet 1993: A big, burly, dark-colored, solid red Burgundy, offering medium tannins and smoky, earthy, blackberry flavors. Impressive, and should improve by cellaring until 1998. • $23 • **87**

Chassagne-Montrachet Red 1985 • $16 • (12/31/88) • **85**

Chassagne-Montrachet Caillerets 1994: This medium-bodied wine shows some tart, apple cider flavors along with notes of dried herbs. Tasted twice, with consistent notes. 200 cases made. • $46 • (05/31/96) • **79**

Chassagne-Montrachet Les Chenevottes 1994: A distinctive white, both ripe and a bit tough, showing some pear, citrus and onion peel flavors. Full-bodied, with a vegetal, honeyed character on the rather intense finish. Hold off until 1997 at least. 30 cases made. • $46 • (05/31/96) • **84**

Chassagne-Montrachet La Boudriotte 1994: Attractively supple and relatively ripe, with a lovely honey, pear, pie crust, lemon and mineral character. Medium to full body, lacks intensity, but it's lush and silky on the finish. 308 cases made. • $46 • (05/31/96) • **86**

Chassagne-Montrachet Red Clos St.-Jean 1992: A lot of wine in a small frame, but it needs time for the ripe blackberry and anise flavors to poke through the fine tannins. Best after 1996. • $32 • **85**

Chassagne-Montrachet La Grande Montagne 1994: Hard, lemony and tough to taste now, this *premier cru* shows little opulence. Well structured, with lots of lime, dried herb and mineral notes. A bit harsh on the finish. Perhaps better in 1998. 125 cases made. • $46 • (05/31/96) • **84**

Chassagne-Montrachet La Maltroie 1994: You can taste the full Burgundian treatment in this. Fairly rich, with a chewy character and lots of toasted oak notes. Nicely balanced, with tropical fruit and lemon flavors on the finish. Enjoy now or in 1997. 308 cases made. • $46 • (05/31/96) • **85**

Chassagne-Montrachet Les Vergers 1994: Supple, round and distinctively appley, a focused but rather simple Chardonnay with a hint of mineral character on the crisp finish. 191 cases made. • $46 • (05/31/96) • **83**

Chassagne-Montrachet Morgeot 1994: Soft and supple, with a touch of honey and lime, this full-bodied but somewhat one-dimensional Chardonnay should be drunk now. 116 cases made. • $46 • (05/31/96) • **82**

Chassagne-Montrachet Red Morgeot 1993: A beauty from start to finish. Dishes out the pure, concentrated fruit flavors in buckets. Cassis, black cherry and earth aromas are amazing. Silky texture. Delicious now, but can hold for years. • $27 • **89**

Criots-Bâtard-Montrachet 1994: Very rich, thick and ripe, tasting of apricot, peach and ripe pear, oozing with honey character. Full-bodied and coats your mouth, but has a supple finish. Distinctive and delicious now. 166 cases made. • $90 • (05/31/96) 88 • **88**

Volnay 1992: A little more dense than most, with slightly gamy blackberry and currant flavor that persists on the solid finish. Best after 1996. • $48 • **85**

Volnay Clos des Chànes 1993: Sleek and racy, sporting a solid core of fruit and steely tannin. Smoky, earthy character. Medium in body and tannins and fresh finish. This needs some cellaring, try in 2000. • $43 • **90**

FONTAINE, CHÂTEAU LA

Fronsac 1993: A robust wine that combines good structure with plenty of flesh and spicy fruit. The finish is lingering. Drink now. 4,000 cases made. • $9 • (08/31/95) • **85**

FONTANCHE, CHÂTEAU DE

St.-Chinian Cuvée Grand Veneur 1990 • $7 • (07/15/92) BB • **81**

FONTANELLES, DOMAINE DES

Sauvignon Blanc Vin de Pays d'Oc 1993: This fresh, lively wine shows typical and appealing grapefruit and herbal flavors in a lighter style. It's clean and bright, but lacks a bit of concentration. 3,000 cases made. • $7 • (09/30/94) • **82**

Shiraz-Syrah Vin de Pays d'Oc 1993: Very fruity, as grape, blueberry and cherry flavors end on a tannic, drying finish. Awkward. 4,000 cases made. • $7 • (05/15/96) • **77**

FRANCE

FONTENIL, CHÂTEAU

Fronsac 1995: Well made, seductive, succulent, ripe, full-bodied, sporting pure cassis character, fine tannins and spicy complexity. Velvety, long finish. Almost outstanding. • $NA • (05/15/96) • **85-89** (BT)
Fronsac 1994: Quite delicious, bursting with cassis flavors. Medium body, crisp, fresh character. • $NA • **85-89** (BT)
Fronsac 1993: A bit rustic in style, offering some pretty ripe berry and raspberry aromas and flavors. Medium to light body, velvety tannins and light finish. Drinkable now. 4,083 cases made. • $12 • (01/31/96) • **83**
Fronsac 1990: A classy red showing great winemaking. Fills your mouth with plum and black cherry flavors and silky tannins. From Michel Rolland. Drinkable now. 3,500 cases made. • $17 • (03/31/93) • **91**
Fronsac 1986 • $14 • (02/15/90) • **76**
Fronsac 1985 • $14 • (09/30/88) • **87**

FONTJUN, DOMAINE DU

St.-Chinian 1990 • $5 • (07/15/92) • **76**

FONTSAINTE, DOMAINE DE

Corbières Réserve la Demoiselle 1990 • $10 • (03/15/94) • **85**
Corbières Réserve la Demoiselle 1986 • $7 • (08/31/89) • **77**
Corbières Réserve la Demoiselle 1984 • $8 • (10/31/87) • **83**

FOREAU

Vouvray Domaine du Clos Naudin 1994: The deep color and butterscotch aromas combined with a dry, tart profile create a study in contrast. An angular, austere style. 300 cases made. • $16 • (04/30/96) • **81**
Vouvray Domaine du Clos Naudin 1993: The moderate sweetness balances the acidity and plays off the ripe tangerine, peach and apple notes. Appealing now through 1998. 200 cases imported. 200 cases made. • $18 • (04/30/96) • **85**

FOREY PERE & FILS

Bourgogne 1993: Quite chewy at this stage, with decent fruit flavors. Square and tough, it turns a little dry on the one-dimensional finish. Try now. • $12 • **79**
Echézeaux 1993: A super *grand cru* boasting loads of raspberry, plum and smoke character, medium to full body, fine tannins and lovely, fruity finish. Better in 2000. • $45 • **91**
Echézeaux 1990: A rich, ripe, well-structured wine that's seductive, refined and powerful. Packs in concentrated raspberry, earth and smoke aromas and flavors that echo on the long finish. Drinkable in 1997. 121 cases made. • $65 • (12/15/92) • **92**
Echézeaux 1989 • $NA • (01/31/92) • **90**
Nuits-St.-Georges 1993: Straightforward Pinot, showing light, modest structure and some decent licorice and black cherry flavors. A bit diluted on the finish. • $24 • **82**
Nuits-St.-Georges Les Perrières 1993: Very firm and not giving much. Medium-bodied, sporting solid tannins and a long spicy, plummy finish. Needs time, try in 1999. • $33 • **85**
Nuits-St.-Georges Les Perrières 1990: A mellow Nuits, with attractive cherry, berry and chestnut aromas and flavors and medium tannins. Drinkable now. 162 cases made. • $40 • (12/15/92) • **79**
Nuits-St.-Georges Les Perrières 1989 • $NA • (01/31/92) • **89**
Vosne-Romanée 1993: Wonderfully aromatic violets and plums follow through on the palate. Medium- to full-bodied, adding fine tannins and a fresh finish. Better in 2000. • $26 • **88**
Vosne-Romanée 1990: Quite straightforward, with game, strawberry and earth aromas and flavors, medium body and firm tannins. Drinkable now. 460 cases made. • $30 • (12/15/92) • **85**
Vosne-Romanée 1989 • $NA • (01/31/92) • **85**
Vosne-Romanée Les Gaudichots 1993: Rather sensational. Beautiful, well-defined fruit sets this one on fire, boasting lovely, ripe currant and black cherry character. Smoothly structured, it envelops the palate in seductive flavors. Tempting now, better after 2000. • $45 • **92**

FORGE, LA

Côtes du Lubéron 1989 • $7 • (11/15/91) • **79**

FORNEROT, JEAN-CHARLES

Chassagne-Montrachet Red La Maltroie 1985 • $19 • (07/31/89) • **86**
Chassagne-Montrachet Red Les Champs Gain 1985 • $19 • (07/31/89) • **83**
St.-Aubin Les Perrières 1985 • $15 • (07/31/89) • **82**

FORTANT DE FRANCE

Cabernet Sauvignon Vin de Pays d'Oc 1993: A robust, enjoyable Cabernet that is firm-textured, full-flavored and fairly tannic. • $7 • (02/28/95) • **83**
Cabernet Sauvignon Vin de Pays d'Oc 1990 • $7 • (03/15/94) • **82**
Cabernet Sauvignon Vin de Pays d'Oc 1988 • $6 • (04/30/91) • **70**
Chardonnay Vin de Pays d'Oc 1994: A ripe, generous wine with melon and honey flavors and just enough acidity to keep it taut. Spicy, nutmeg notes add interest. • $8 • (12/15/95) • **84**
Chardonnay Vin de Pays d'Oc 1993: Packs a punch with its good apple and peach flavors. Crisp and lively, with a good acidity and a clean finish. • $8 • (11/30/94) • **83**
Chardonnay Vin de Pays d'Oc 1992 • $7 • (03/15/94) • **84**
Chardonnay Vin de Pays d'Oc 1991 • $7 • (03/15/94) • **86**
Merlot Rosé Vin de Pays d'Oc 1994: Simple and fruity, showing berry and banana flavors and aromas. Pleasant, though not very exciting. • $7 • (09/30/95) • **78**
Merlot Vin de Pays d'Oc 1994: Appealing blackberry and smoke aromas carry through on the soft, full palate, though lean tannins on the finish detract. Ripe and flavorful. • $7 • (10/31/95) • **83**
Merlot Vin de Pays d'Oc 1993: Typical Merlot, from the herbal aromas to flavors of tomato, plum and tobacco. Moderately tannic. • $7 • (02/28/95) • **79**
Merlot Vin de Pays d'Oc 1992: This fresh, clean Merlot shows plum and cherry flavors with a pleasant herbal accent, it's medium-bodied, with moderate, well-integrated tannins. Not that expressive, but well balanced and accessible now. • $7 • (09/15/94) • **82**
Merlot Vin de Pays d'Oc 1991 • $7 • (03/15/94) • **81**
Merlot Vin de Pays d'Oc 1990 • $7 • (03/15/94) • **83**
Merlot Vin de Pays d'Oc 1988 • $6 • (05/31/91) • **70**
Sauvignon Blanc Vin de Pays d'Oc 1994: A very neutral white wine that's clean in flavor and sturdy in texture, but lacks fruit flavor. • $7 • (02/29/96) • **78**
Sauvignon Blanc Vin de Pays d'Oc 1993: This fresh white has bright, fruity flavors and a rich texture without much complexity. It makes pleasant quaffing now. • $7 • (01/31/95) • **83**
Sauvignon Blanc Vin de Pays d'Oc 1992 • $7 • (03/15/94) • **84**
Sauvignon Blanc Vin de Pays d'Oc 1991 • $6 • (08/31/93) • **78**
Syrah Rosé Vin de Pays d'Oc 1994: Dry and earthy, its flavors dominated by dried cherry and spice. Seems very full-bodied. • $7 • (09/30/95) • **80**
Syrah Vin de Pays d'Oc 1991 • $7 • (03/15/94) • **82**
Syrah Vin de Pays d'Oc 1993: Simple candied flavors and aromas dominate this proto-wine. Drink chilled. • $7 • **75**
Viognier Vin de Pays d'Oc 1992 • $8 • (03/15/94) • **83**

FORTIA, CHÂTEAU

Châteauneuf-du-Pape 1983 • $14 • (12/31/87) • **87**
Châteauneuf-du-Pape Tête de Cru 1988 • $22 • (06/15/93) • **78**
Châteauneuf-du-Pape Tête de Cru 1985 • $22 • (05/31/92) • **81**

FORTNUM & MASON

Charmes-Chambertin English Bottling 1947 • $NA • (08/31/90) • **94**

Key: SS—Spectator Selection. CS—Cellar Selection. BB—Best Buy. $NA—Price not available. (BT)—Barrel tasting. (A)—Auction Price.
Dates in parentheses represent the issues in which the ratings were published.

FORTS DE LATOUR, LES

Pauillac 1995: Lots of tannin in this. Full-bodied, with plenty of berry flavor and a long, tannic finish. Second label of Latour. • $NA • (05/15/96) • **85-89** (BT)
Pauillac 1994: Good doses of berry, cherry and cassis come out with the fine tannins, although the finish is a bit light. Almost very good. Second label of Latour. • $26 • (05/15/96) • **80-84** (BT)
Pauillac 1993: Some good berry, cherry character, but rather lean and slightly hard with firm tannins. Better in 1998. • $28 • (01/31/96) • **83**
Pauillac 1992: Pretty minty, berry, mineral character, medium-bodied, fine tannins and fresh finish. Drink now. • $22 • **80**
Pauillac 1991: Simple and straightforward. The fruit is dominated by cherry, a light, slightly green finish. Second label of Latour. • $23 • (03/31/94) • **78**
Pauillac 1990: Draws you into the glass with enticing plum, blackberry, vanilla and coconut aromas and flavors. Full-bodied yet balanced with an abundance of soft tannins, but not aggressive. Drinkable in 2000. • $34 • (03/31/93) • **94**
Pauillac 1989 • $NA • (03/15/92) • **91**
Pauillac 1985 • $54 • (08/31/91) • **87**
Pauillac 1983 • $32 • (10/15/90) • **85**
Pauillac 1982 • $58 • (08/31/92) • **93**
Pauillac 1981 • $NA • **86**
Pauillac 1979 • $35 Ⓐ • (10/15/89) • **87**

FORTUNE, DOMAINE

Beaujolais-Villages 1994: Spicy cinnamon aromas add interest to this firm, fruity red, which offers grapey, cherry flavors and modest tannins. Fresh yet well structured. 1,800 cases made. • $9 • (10/31/95) • **84**

FOUGERAY, DOMAINE

Bonnes Mares 1991: Ripe in flavor and chewy in texture, a supple wine with concentrated black cherry and slightly gamy aromas and flavors. Nicely formed if a bit shy on muscle or richness. An appealing wine, drinkable now. • $NA • (01/31/94) • **87**
Marsannay St.-Jacques 1991: Tough in texture and light, the plummy flavors never quite get off the ground. Try now. • $NA • (01/31/94) • **77**

FOURCAS-DUPRE, CHÂTEAU

Listrac 1995: A fruity '95 with wet earth, mineral and cassis character. Good tannins and slightly steely on the finish. • $NA • (05/15/96) • **80-84** (BT)
Listrac 1992: Displays some earth and black cherry character and mineral nuances, but a very short finish. Drink now. • $15 • **79**
Listrac 1991: Astringent and angular. Interesting cherry flavor, but short, fading out too quickly. • $15 • (03/31/94) • **74**
Listrac 1990: A traditional-style wine with earthy, smoky character, round tannins and a smoky finish. Drinkable now. 22,000 cases made. • $17 • (03/31/93) • **82**
Listrac 1989 • $25 • (03/15/92) • **86**
Listrac 1988 • $22 • (04/30/91) • **83**
Listrac 1983 • $9 • (10/31/86) • **89**
Listrac 1982 • $NA • (08/31/92) • **79**

FOURCAS-HOSTEN, CHÂTEAU

Listrac 1995: Flavorful. Rich, ripe, grapey, and full-bodied, tasting of crushed wild berries, black currants and grapes. Very pure and vivid and judiciously oaked. Supple tannins. Needs a touch more elegance to be outstanding. • $NA • (05/15/96) • **85-89** (BT)
Listrac 1992: Very one-dimensional, offering berried, slightly alcoholic character, medium body, soft tannins and light finish. Drink now. • $15 • **76**
Listrac 1991: Stylish and lean, but just average. Has a fruity, slightly herbal character. • $15 • (03/31/94) • **79**
Listrac 1990: A tough wine with a compact fruit and tannin structure but some rich berry and cherry flavors underneath. Drinkable now. 20,000 cases made. • $20 • (03/31/93) • **85**
Listrac 1989 • $19 • (03/15/92) • **87**
Listrac 1988 • $13 • (07/15/91) • **82**
Listrac 1986 • $14 • (11/15/89) • **79**
Listrac 1983 • $16 • (10/15/86) • **83**
Listrac 1982 • $18 • (08/31/92) • **90**
Listrac 1961 • $26 • (04/30/96) • **81**

FOURCAS-LOUBANEY, CHÂTEAU

Listrac 1988 • $17 • (02/28/91) • **83**

FOURNAS-BERNADOTTE, CHÂTEAU

Haut-Médoc 1988 • $18 • (06/15/91) • **76**

FRANC BIGAROUX, CHÂTEAU

St.-Emilion 1988 • $24 • (07/31/91) • **91**

FRANC-MAYNE, CHÂTEAU

St.-Emilion 1995: Rather austere berry, earthy character. Medium in body, firm tannins and a sharp finish. • $NA • (05/15/96) • **80-84** (BT)
St.-Emilion 1994: Round and harmonious, with some nicely expressed fruit character, full body and full, supple tannins. A bit short and diluted at the end, though. • $18 • (05/15/96) • **80-84** (BT)
St.-Emilion 1993: A no-nonsense '93 featuring cherry, light dried herb and berry aromas and flavors, medium body, medium to light tannins and fresh finish. Drinkable now. • $20 • (01/31/96) • **81**
St.-Emilion 1992: Firm, decent fruit but rather austere and herbal, medium-to-light-bodied, delivering green pepper and slightly metallic character. • $17 • **79**
St.-Emilion 1991: Pleasant black cherry and bitter chocolate aromas and flavors, medium body and a silky texture. • $15 • (03/31/94) • **82**
St.-Emilion 1990: A succulent wine, with rich berry, white pepper aromas and flavors, firm tannins and a long, polished finish. From Jean-Michel Cazes. Drink after 1997. 2,700 cases made. • $23 • (03/31/93) • **91**
St.-Emilion 1989 • $28 • (03/15/92) • **94**
St.-Emilion 1988 • $15 • (07/15/91) • **83**

FRANCE, CHÂTEAU DE

Pessac-Léognan 1993: A vivid white offering orange-peel, vanilla and pear character, medium in body and long, flavorful finish. • $NA • **85**
Pessac-Léognan 1992: Lovely young white offering pineapple, mineral and vanilla character. Medium in body and crisp, lively, fruity finish. Drinkable now. • $NA • (05/31/95) • **87**
Pessac-Léognan 1991: A wine with nice clean berry, fruit and tree bark flavors. Light tannins and a rather short, dry finish. • $13 • (03/31/94) • **78**
Pessac-Léognan 1990: Not a big wine, but enjoyable. Delicate in style, with spicy, cherry, autumnal aromas and flavors and silky tannins. Drinkable now. 16,000 cases made. • $20 • (03/31/93) • **85**
Pessac-Léognan 1989 • $22 • (03/15/92) • **89**
Pessac-Léognan 1988 • $18 • (02/28/91) SS • **92**
Graves 1982 • $NA • (08/31/92) • **79**

FREJAU, DOMAINE LOU

Châteauneuf-du-Pape 1988 • $17 • (03/31/91) • **82**
Châteauneuf-du-Pape 1986 • $16 • (01/31/89) • **87**
Côtes du Rhône 1986 • $8 • (05/31/89) • **73**

FUISSE, CHÂTEAU

Pouilly-Fuissé 1994: Light to medium body, with modest fruit flavors. Rather smooth and approachable, though it lacks a bit of character and turns slightly herbal on the finish. • $NA • (05/31/96) • **78**
Pouilly-Fuissé Le Clos 1994: If you like them silky, this is your type. Well crafted, lots of fig, pear and butter flavors, it seduces you with its remarkable harmony. Enjoy now through 1998. • $34 • (05/31/96) • **89**

Pouilly-Fuissé Les Combettes 1994: Fairly opulent, fresh and lively, yet also smooth, offering some floral, honey and ripe apple flavors. Good concentration, with an unctuous mouth-feel, mineral, rose petal and apricot notes come out on the long, harmonious finish. Drinkable now, or try in 1998. • $34 • (05/31/96) • **89**

Pouilly-Fuissé Vieilles Vignes 1994: What a beauty. A well-sculpted wine built for finesse, charming you with its layers of citrus, honey and floral notes. It pulsates with complexity, showing good depth on the long, lovely finish. Drinkable now through 1998. • $44 • (05/31/96) • **90**

FUMET-PEYROUTAS, CHÂTEAU

St.-Emilion 1985 • $7 • (07/31/88) BB • **84**

FUSSIACUS

Pouilly-Fuissé Vieilles Vignes 1993: Intense but tart, light-to-medium in body, plenty of citrus, green apple flavors and a touch of mineral character. Turns somewhat astringent on the finish. Drinkable now. • $NA • **80**

GAFFELIERE, CHÂTEAU LA

St.-Emilion 1988 • $38 • (04/30/91) • **84**
St.-Emilion 1982 • $29 • (08/31/92) • **93**
St.-Emilion 1979 • $34 • (10/15/89) • **81**
St.-Emilion 1962 • $60 • (11/30/87) • **88**
St.-Emilion 1961 • $69 Ⓐ • (04/30/96) • **79**
St.-Emilion 1959 • $95 • (10/15/90) • **82**
St.-Emilion 1945 • $140 • (03/16/86) • **85**

GAGNARD, JEAN-NOEL

Bâtard-Montrachet 1993: One of the best wines of the vintage. Wonderful, fresh, classy vanilla, honey and cream aromas and flavors. Medium in body, lovely, long finish. • $100 • **90**

Bâtard-Montrachet 1992: Ripe, fruity and grand. Full of bold apricot, pineapple and pear flavors, with great intensity and a long, long finish. Still a bit tight with acidity, not showing its full potential. Drinkable now. • $100 • (08/31/94) • **94**

Chassagne-Montrachet Clos de la Maltroye 1993: Perfumed apple, mineral, flint character, flavors following through on the palate. Steely and slightly hard finish. Drinkable now. • $33 • **85**

Chassagne-Montrachet Les Caillerets 1993: A bit green and hard, revealing fresh-cut apple and honey flavors and steely character. Medium-bodied, high acidity. • $50 • **82**

Chassagne-Montrachet Les Caillerets 1992: Youthful but very promising, with vanilla and hazelnut flavors held in tightly by a lemon, grapefruit acidity. Has mineral and earth accents, and a long finish. • $47 • (08/31/94) • **87**

Chassagne-Montrachet Les Champs Gains 1993: Austere and tart but offering some complexity, toasty, mineral flavors persist on the medium-long finish. • $33 • **80**

Chassagne-Montrachet Les Chenevottes 1993: Floral and lime flavors are grassy and tart, but it's clean and has a juicy finish. Try now. • $33 • **83**

Chassagne-Montrachet Les Chenevottes 1992: Subtle and pretty, a medium-bodied Chassagne with a toast, hazelnut and lemon character, offers appealing, lean and clean flavors. • $36 • (08/31/94) • **85**

Chassagne-Montrachet Les Masures 1993: Wonderfully put together, displaying vanilla, toasted oak and apple character, medium body, fresh fruit and crisp finish. Drink now. • $30 • **85**

Chassagne-Montrachet Les Masures 1992: Crisp and lean in flavor, with green apple and citrus notes, backed by a fairly full body and a lively finish. • $30 • (08/31/94) • **82**

Chassagne-Montrachet Red 1990: Ripe and fruity, with peppery berry flavors that run close to Beaujolais, but the finish shows a sturdy frame of oak and tannins. Drinkable now. • $50 • (11/30/92) • **84**

Chassagne-Montrachet Red Morgeot 1990: Light in texture, but firm and flavorful, with lively raspberry, red cherry and mineral aromas and flavors that remain smooth and silky through the finish. Drinkable now. Tasted twice. • $25 • (02/15/93) • **86**

Chassagne-Montrachet Red Morgeot 1989 • $25 • (11/15/91) • **87**
Chassagne-Montrachet Red Morgeot 1988 • $20 • (12/31/90) • **86**
Chassagne-Montrachet Red Morgeot 1985 • $18 • (11/30/87) • **79**

Santenay Clos de Tavannes 1990: Light and zippy, with a bright beam of raspberry and tar aromas and flavors. Straightforward and nicely balanced, drinkable now. • $16 • (11/30/92) • **80**

Santenay Clos de Tavannes 1989 • $25 • (11/15/91) • **85**
Santenay Clos de Tavannes 1988 • $25 • (11/15/90) • **84**

GAGNEROT & FILS, FRANCOIS

Corton-Charlemagne 1994: Soft and supple, a honeyed Chardonnay that is full-bodied and rather rich, with some nice pear, date and mineral notes. Very ripe finish bordering on sweet. Ready to drink now. • $36 • (05/31/96) 85 • **84**

Ladoix White Les Gréchons 1994: A simple, straightforward, basic Chardonnay that delivers some pear, apple and citrus flavors without much complexity. Somewhat light-bodied, try with seafood or as an apéritif. • $NA • (05/31/96) 80 • **80**

GAILLARD, PIERRE

Côte-Rôtie Côte Brune et Blonde 1990: Intense and focused, with tart cherry, earth and toast flavors that turn peppery on the finish. Soft and fleshy, but supported by enough tannin to warrant cellaring. Drinkable now. • $30 • (04/15/93) • **86**

Côte-Rôtie Côte Brune et Blonde 1989 • $28 • (10/15/91) • **89**
Côte-Rôtie Côte Brune et Blonde 1988 • $30 • (11/30/90) • **90**
Côte-Rôtie Côte Brune et Blonde 1987 • $24 • (08/31/89) • **82**
Côte-Rôtie Côte Brune et Blonde 1986 • $25 • (11/30/88) • **86**
St.-Joseph Clos de Cuminaille 1990 • $20 • (04/15/93) • **87**
St.-Joseph Clos de Cuminaille 1988 • $15 • (12/31/90) • **87**
St.-Joseph Clos de Cuminaille 1987 • $14 • (03/15/90) • **87**

GALET DES PAPES, DOMAINE DU

Châteauneuf-du-Pape 1989 • $21 • (08/31/92) • **88**

Châteauneuf-du-Pape Vieilles Vignes 1990: A strong current of ashy bitterness runs through this otherwise ripe, almost raisiny wine, making it a bit unpleasant. • $28 • (09/30/93) • **76**

GALICHETS, LES

Bourgueil 1992: Vivid raspberry and black cherry flavors are appealing, but leather and earthy notes loom like stormclouds on the horizen. It's a gamble. • $NA • (10/31/94) • **75**

GALLULA, LIONEL

Cabernet Sauvignon Vin de Pays d'Oc 1992: This ripe, concentrated red shows plum, tar and menthol flavors, but the tannins are a bit hard and there's a green note in the finish. It may soften and deepen by late 1994. • $8 • (09/15/94) • **82**

Chardonnay Vin de Pays d'Oc 1992: Strong, buttery flavors turn a bit harsh on the finish, the modest apple and pear flavors pale in comparison. • $8 • (11/30/94) • **78**

Merlot Vin de Pays d'Oc 1992: Soft and fleshy, this simple wine is inoffensive but lacks freshness and fruit, with faint notes of cherry and fresh herbs. • $8 • (11/30/94) • **77**

GAMAGE, CHÂTEAU

Entre-Deux-Mers 1994: Fresh, steely white presenting light grass and apple aromas and flavors. Slightly short and earthy on the finish. • $8 • **79**

Key: SS—Spectator Selection. CS—Cellar Selection. BB—Best Buy. $NA—Price not available. (BT)—Barrel tasting. Ⓐ—Auction Price.
Dates in parentheses represent the issues in which the ratings were published.

GAMBIER, JEAN

Bourgueil Domaine del Galluches Cuvée Ronsard 1993: There is structure and intensity in this red, showing cherry and plum flavors and just a hint of herbs. Sufficient concentration and length warrant aging until 1997. • $13 • (05/15/96) • **88**

GARAUDET, JEAN

Beaune Red Le Clos des Mouches 1990: Crisp and focused, with berry, cherry and currant flavors and nice toast and vanilla overtones. The modest, well-integrated tannins don't get in the way. Drinkable now. • $35 • (08/31/92) • **87**
Beaune Red Le Clos des Mouches 1989 • $32 • (11/15/91) • **91**
Beaune Red Le Clos des Mouches 1988 • $40 • (11/15/90) • **86**
Bourgogne Passe-tout-grains 1990: A very reasonably priced Burgundy that includes Gamay grapes. A strong beam of currant flavor runs through this fruity-smelling, tightly textured wine. Drinkable now. • $10 • (06/15/92) • **84**
Monthelie 1990 • $25 • (08/31/92) • **85**
Monthelie 1989 • $22 • (11/15/91) • **86**
Monthelie 1988 • $23 • (11/15/90) • **88**
Pommard 1988 • $37 • (11/15/90) • **88**
Pommard 1987 • $25 • (09/15/89) • **88**
Pommard Les Charmots 1990: Fragrant and enticing, bursting with oak-scented, ripe currant, berry and plum aromas and flavors that turn spicy on the long finish. Tannins rush in on the palate, meaning this will need from now to 1999 to settle down, but the fruit intensity is there. 100 cases made. • $48 • (08/31/92) • **91**
Pommard Les Charmots 1988 • $46 • (11/15/90) • **90**
Pommard Les Charmots 1987 • $30 • (09/15/89) • **88**
Pommard Les Noizons 1990: Firm and focused, with generous currant and plum aromas and flavors that persist into a long, lively finish. The tight structure needs from now to 1998 to settle down, but the flavors warrant it. • $40 • (08/31/92) • **88**
Pommard Noizons 1989 • $34 • (11/15/91) • **91**

GARAUDET, PAUL

Bourgogne 1994: Has an interesting chalky, mineral character, but also a reductive, "ice box" flavor that's hard to like. Quite creamy in texture, with a crisp finish. 266 cases made. • $NA • (05/31/96) • **80**
Meursault Vieille Vigne 1994: Well crafted and very exciting. Excellent concentration of fruit, mineral and earth notes that coat the mouth. Ripe and fresh, the silky texture is pure seduction. The intense, lingering finish needs time to soften, try in 1999. 570 cases made. • $26 • (05/31/96) • **89**
Monthelie Les Champs Fulliot 1994: A middle-of-the-road '94 that's balanced but lacking in flavor. Somewhat lighter in body, it offers some modest lemon, earth and mineral flavors. A bit dull on the finish. 95 cases made. • $20 • (05/31/96) • **79**
Puligny-Montrachet 1994: Quite woody, with a hint of mineral, vanilla and butter. It's silky in texture, though lacking a bit in fruit flavors and somewhat short on the finish. 73 cases made. • $27 • (05/31/96) • **81**

GARDE, CHÂTEAU LA

Pessac-Léognan 1995: Bright cherry and wet earth aromas and flavors, medium body, fine tannins and a fresh finish. Delicious. • $NA • (05/15/96) • **85-89** (BT)
Pessac-Léognan 1994: Elegant and enticing smoke, tobacco and red berry flavors. Supple, complex, smooth, medium in body. Almost outstanding. • $NA • **85-89** (BT)
Pessac-Léognan Réserve de Château 1993: Pretty, plummy Bordeaux showing plenty of vanilla and fruit character, medium body, fine tannins and fresh finish. Drinkable now. • $17 • (01/31/96) • **83**
Pessac-Léognan Réserve de Château 1991: A touch of green character but plenty of plum and vanilla flavors. Medium body and velvety texture. • $13 • (03/31/94) • **78**
Pessac-Léognan White Réserve de Château 1994: Round and rich, with loads of ripe apple, honey and melon flavors in a full-bodied package. Moderate acidity and a lovely, fruity finish. • $16 • (03/31/96) • **87**

GARDINE, CHÂTEAU DE LA

Châteauneuf-du-Pape 1990: Firm and fleshy, bursting with clearly articulated berry, cherry, tobacco and spice aromas and flavors, hinting at pepper on the solid finish. Drinkable now. • $24 • (09/30/93) • **87**
Châteauneuf-du-Pape 1989 • $25 • (10/15/91) • **95**
Châteauneuf-du-Pape 1988 • $33 • (10/15/91) • **85**
Châteauneuf-du-Pape 1986 • $17 • (10/15/91) • **90**
Châteauneuf-du-Pape 1985 • $15 • (12/31/87) • **87**
Châteauneuf-du-Pape 1984 • $15 • (12/31/87) • **78**
Châteauneuf-du-Pape 1983 • $25 • (10/15/91) • **89**
Châteauneuf-du-Pape 1981 • $NA • (10/15/91) • **86**
Châteauneuf-du-Pape Cuvée des Générations 1990: Rich, supple and smooth, with a wonderful band of spicy currant, berry and tobacco aromas and flavors. All of it remains in balance and finishes generous and fleshy. Drinkable now, but should be fine through 2000. • $38 • (09/30/93) • **89**
Châteauneuf-du-Pape Cuvée des Générations 1989 • $38 • (02/28/93) CS • **94**
Châteauneuf-du-Pape Cuvée des Générations 1985 • $NA • (10/15/91) • **92**
Châteauneuf-du-Pape White 1990: Somewhat atypical, but well-made. It's difficult to tell if the fruit will emerge from the new wood. Shows blanched almond, vanilla and fruit aromas. Full-bodied, with lots of new wood flavor, a firm backbone and a toasty finish. Very tight and closed in. Try now. • $20 • (10/15/91) • **86**
Côtes du Rhône-Villages Benjamin Brunel 1990 • $14 • (09/30/93) • **82**

FRANCE

GAUBY, DOMAINE

Côtes du Roussillon 1991 • $7 • (03/15/94) • **82**
Côtes du Roussillon-Villages Vieilles Vignes 1991 • $9 • (03/15/94) • **85**

GAUDET, JEAN

Morgon 1988 • $10 • (05/31/89) • **87**
Régnié Domaine de la Grange-Barjot 1993: Quite rich and fresh, offering round, spicy plum, cherry and nutmeg flavors and light, firm tannins. Pretty berry notes linger on the finish. • $12 • (07/31/95) • **84**

GAUDRY, DOMAINE DENIS

Pouilly-Fumé Coteaux du Petit Boisgibault 1995: Fresh, youthful aromas of herbs and almonds, followed by flavors of citrus and herb with tropical nuances. Rich texture, but lively acidity keeps it focused. • $19 • (04/30/96) • **85**
Pouilly-Fumé Coteaux du Petit Boisgibault 1993: Clean, balanced and soft as a pillow. The flavors are restrained but elegant, with pear, almond and herbal notes, lightbodied and crisp without excessive acidity or grassiness. A pretty wine for drinking now. • $NA • (10/31/94) • **87**
Pouilly-Fumé Coteaux du Petit Boisgibault 1992: Fresh as a sea breeze. Intense and vivid, offering crisp lemon-lime and light herbal notes with a nervy acidity that gives it lift and elegance. It's fresh, clean and maintains good focus through a long finish. 15,000 cases made. • $16 • (08/31/94) • **90**
Pouilly-Fumé Coteaux du Petit Boisgibault 1991 • $16 • (09/15/93) • **88**

GAUNOUX, JEAN-MICHEL

Corton Les Renardes 1990: Simple and straightforward for a *grand cru*, with modest strawberry, earth and cherry aromas and flavors and a somewhat dull finish. Try now. • $60 • (12/15/92) • **74**
Volnay Le Clos des Chênes 1990: Firm, fruity and medium-bodied, offering plenty of elegance in the raspberry and tea leaf aromas and flavors that echo on the lovely, long finish. Drinkable now. • $NA • (12/15/92) • **90**

GAUTHIER, REMY

Volnay Santenots 1985 • $27 • (03/15/88) • **87**

GAVOTY, DOMAINES

Côtes de Provence Cuvée Clarendon 1987 • $8 • (03/31/90) • **72**

GAY, CHÂTEAU LE

Pomerol 1995: Sleek and racy Pomerol boasting plenty of berry, cherry and mineral character and fine tannins. Wonderful Le Gay. • $NA • (05/15/96) • **90-94** (BT)

Pomerol 1994: Medium-bodied, offering angular tannins and a very good level of berry, cherry and vanilla character. • $NA • (05/15/96) • **85-89** (BT)

Pomerol 1993: Somewhat disappointing for Le Gay. Fresh and clean dried cherry and berry aromas and flavors, medium in body, sleek tannins and crisp finish. Slightly one-dimensional. Drinkable now. • $29 • (01/31/96) • **80**

Pomerol 1992: Shockingly light. Clean, revealing some fruit, but really watery. Drink if you must. • $22 • **73**

Pomerol 1990: Absolutely massive, with tons of exotic ripe raspberry flavor and velvety tannins. Thick and rich yet has great balance. Drink in 2000. 2,000 cases made. • $49 • (03/31/93) • **96**

Pomerol 1989 • $43 Ⓐ • (03/15/92) • **91**

Pomerol 1988 • $23 Ⓐ • (04/30/91) • **83**

Pomerol 1986 • $27 • **94**

Pomerol 1985 • $30 • **90**

Pomerol 1983 • $28 • **93**

Pomerol 1982 • $40 Ⓐ • (05/15/89) • **89**

Pomerol 1970 • $75 • (05/15/93) • **83**

Pomerol 1961 • $73 • (04/30/96) • **82**

GAZIN, CHÂTEAU

Pomerol 1995: Lovely berry, cherry and smoke aromas and flavors, medium body, fine tannins and fresh finish. • $NA • (05/15/96) • **85-89** (BT)

Pomerol 1994: Really impressive for the vintage, better than its '95. Muscular and racy, boasting loads of toasted oak, berry and cherry character and classy tannins. • $NA • (05/15/96) • **90-94** (BT)

Pomerol 1993: Pretty Merlot character here, offering tobacco, cherry and olive aromas and flavors, medium to full body, good fruit and a medium-tannic finish. Better in 1997. • $30 • (01/31/96) • **87**

Pomerol 1992: Slightly disappointing after various good barrel samples. Cherry, plum, tomato aromas and flavors, medium-to-light body, slightly hard finish. Tasted twice. Drinkable now. • $24 • **78**

Pomerol 1991: Pretty aromas matched by cherry, toasted oak and good fruit flavors, but a little bitter on finish. Drinkable now. • $24 • (03/31/94) • **81**

Pomerol 1990: An attractive, well-made wine. It shows rich plum, tar and berry aromas with ripe berry and chocolate flavors, medium-soft tannins and a light finish. Drinkable now. 8,500 cases made. • $32 • (03/31/93) • **88**

Pomerol 1989 • $27 Ⓐ • (03/15/92) • **91**

Pomerol 1988 • $27 Ⓐ • (06/30/91) • **87**

Pomerol 1985 • $21 • (09/30/88) • **90**

Pomerol 1983 • $NA • **89**

Pomerol 1982 • $31 Ⓐ • (08/31/92) • **93**

Pomerol 1981 • $NA • **79**

Pomerol 1970 • $32 Ⓐ • (05/15/93) • **80**

Pomerol 1961 • $55 • (04/30/96) • **84**

Pomerol 1945 • $220 • **83**

GEANTET-PANSIOT

Bourgogne Pinot Fin 1992: Attractively fruity in flavor, and well-balanced for drinking now. Shows exuberant cherry and raspberry aromas and flavors, good freshness and acidity, and a bit of spice on the finish. Moderately tannic, drinkable now. 300 cases made. • $16 • (11/30/94) • **85**

Charmes-Chambertin 1993: Elegant, caressing, velvety texture. Medium- to full-bodied, adding a sweet berry, cherry, earthy, mineral finish. Seductive. Better in 2001. • $60 • (05/15/96) • **90**

Gevrey-Chambertin Poissenot 1993: Super *premier cru* boasting lots of depth and complexity. Chewy character, as tons of cassis and other red berry flavors fan out on the palate, adding a touch of wet earth. There's *terroir interoir* written all over it from start to finish. A beauty. Try now through 2002. • $45 • (05/15/96) • **90**

GEISWELLER & FILS

Bourgogne 1990 • $NA • (12/15/92) • **86**

GELIN & MOLIN

Fixin Clos du Châpitre Domaine Marion 1985 • $25 • (04/30/88) • **82**

GELIN, GERARD

Beaujolais-Villages Domaine des Nugues 1989 • $8 • (11/15/90) BB • **86**

GELIN, PIERRE

Chambertin Clos de Bèze 1985 • $77 • (03/15/88) • **84**

Fixin Clos Napolèon 1985 • $25 • (04/30/88) • **76**

Gevrey-Chambertin 1985 • $25 • (04/15/88) • **93**

Gevrey-Chambertin 1982 • $19 • (03/16/85) • **80**

Mazis-Chambertin 1985 • $25 • (03/15/88) • **90**

GENILLON, DOMAINE DE

Morgon Le Terrain Rouge 1994: Ripe, fleshy yet slightly rustic, this thick Beaujolais shows jammy plum and licorice flavors but lacks finesse. 1,000 cases made. • $10 • **82**

GENTAZ-DERVIEUX

Côte-Rôtie Côte Brune Cuvée Réservée 1990: Firm in texture, with earthy, barnyardy aromas and flavors and enough ripe blackberry and cherry notes to bring it around. A distinctive wine that lovers of old-style Rhônes will especially like. Drink after 1997. Tasted twice. • $55 • (04/15/93) • **85**

Côte-Rôtie Côte Brune Cuvée Réservée 1987 • $40 • (06/30/90) • **73**

GEOFFROY, ALAIN

Chablis Beauroy 1994: Fat, ripe and a bit overdone, with butterscotch, cedar and pear flavors that lack finesse. 3,875 cases made. • $20 • (05/31/96) • **77**

Chablis Beauroy 1993: A bit light and thin, but it shows some lovely honey and mineral aromas and flavors. Medium-bodied and steely, showing a lemony character and fresh finish. • $19 • **81**

GEOFFROY, DOMAINE

Gevrey-Chambertin Clos Prieur 1987 • $29 • (03/31/90) • **93**

Gevrey-Chambertin Clos Prieur 1986 • $29 • (07/15/89) • **89**

Gevrey-Chambertin Les Champeaux 1986 • $36 • (07/15/89) • **85**

Gevrey-Chambertin Les Escorvées 1986 • $26 • (07/15/89) • **79**

Mazis-Chambertin 1987 • $48 • (03/31/90) • **92**

GERARD, FRANCOIS

Côte-Rôtie 1988 • $36 • (07/31/91) • **70**

Côte-Rôtie 1987 • $30 • (10/15/90) • **77**

GERIN, J.M.

Condrieu 1992 • $29 • (04/30/94) • **86**

Key: SS—Spectator Selection. CS—Cellar Selection. BB—Best Buy. $NA—Price not available. (BT)—Barrel tasting. Ⓐ—Auction Price.
Dates in parentheses represent the issues in which the ratings were published.

Côte-Rôtie 1991: Rich yet supple, with vivid plum, game and spice flavors. This shows skillfull winemaking. Try now. • $NA • (05/31/94) • **88**

Côte-Rôtie Champin le Seigneur 1992: Solid and balanced, showing firm tannins wrapped around ripe berry and meaty flavors. Well made. • $32 • (05/31/94) • **88**

Côte-Rôtie Champin le Seigneur 1991: Solid, generous in its berry flavor, with a leathery edge, finishing broad and sturdy. Drinkable now. 2,200 cases made. • $27 • (05/31/94) • **84**

Côte-Rôtie Les Grandes Places 1992: Well built but approachable. Elegant and offers chocolate, spice, blackberry and floral notes. The tannins are supple, drinkable now. • $45 • (05/31/94) • **86**

Côte-Rôtie Les Grandes Places 1991: A generous dose of new wood adds an extra dimension, but it's already rich with exotic berry, violet and smoke flavors. Lush, silky, irresistible, try now. • $45 • (05/31/94) • **92**

GERMAIN, HENRI

Blanc de Blancs Champagne 1988: This producer always makes excellent Chardonnay-based Champagnes. Uplifting wine that makes you want to take another sip. Fresh and clean with beautiful apple, creamy character, medium body and a fresh finish. Drink now or age. • $NA • (12/31/93) • **90**

Brut Champagne 1990: An elegant, focused Champagne that has intriguing, toasty, almondlike aromas. Its exuberant fruit flavors are accented by spice, and the finish is lingering and complex. Great to drink now for its fascinating fruit, but it should improve through 1997. 10,000 cases made. • $39 • (12/15/95) • **91**

Brut Champagne 1988: Ripe and fresh with layers of fruit interspersed with toast and earth. Full-bodied and steely with a crisp finish. Slightly coarse. Drink now. • $NA • (12/31/93) • **87**

Brut Champagne NV: Combines great style in the aroma with substance of fruit flavors: aromas of vanilla, toast and bread dough, cherry and slightly earthy tones. Good depth. 40,000 cases made. • $25 • (12/15/95) • **89**

Brut Champagne President NV • $NA • (12/31/93) • **88**

Brut Champagne President Germain NV: A crisp, lean, well-focused Champagne with apple tart flavors and refreshing balance. Elegant, almost austere, but fine in this style. 20,000 cases made. • $35 • (12/15/95) • **87**

Brut President Germain Grand Cru Chardonnay 1988: Combines ample fruit flavors with some nuances of age for a complex, intriguing wine with a smooth texture. Distinctive and harmonious, managing to blend opulent notes with an elegant mouth-feel. 3,000 cases made. • $60 • (12/15/95) • **90**

Brut Rosé Champagne NV: Vividly fruity and boasts lots of spicy Pinot Noir flavor. Nicely balanced, distinctive and fresh. 10,000 cases made. • $30 • (12/15/95) • **87**

Chassagne-Montrachet Morgeot 1993: Delicious ripe apple, tropical fruit and vanilla character, medium to full body, fine acidity and toasted oak finish. Drinkable now. • $NA • **86**

Chassagne-Montrachet Morgeot 1992: Vivid and fruity in flavor, with crisp grapefruit and orange notes, a lively texture and good balance overall. Drinkable now. 260 cases made. • $39 • (08/31/94) • **85**

Meursault Les Charmes 1993: Impressive, classy mineral, apple, pineapple and toasted oak character, medium body, racy acidity and long, solid fresh and fruity finish. Drinkable now. • $43 • (08/31/95) • **89**

Meursault Les Charmes 1992: Earthy, herbal flavors and a rough texture make this less than exciting for us. It has some lemon and green-apple notes, but a short finish. 270 cases made. • $40 • (08/31/94) • **77**

Meursault Les Chevalières 1993: Elegant and racy apple, cream and chalk character, medium body, fresh acidity and flavorful finish. • $NA • (08/31/95) • **87**

Meursault Le Limozin 1993: Rather thick and flavorful, showing apple, mango and cream character. Full-bodied and round, with well-integrated acidity but a rather short finish. Drink now. • $33 • (08/31/95) • **87**

Meursault Le Limozin 1992: A chewy, dense and racy Meursault with lots of personality, shows delicious fruit character, with focused toast, lime, mineral, grapefruit and honey notes. Should improve with age. • $33 • (08/31/94) • **90**

GERMAIN, JACQUES

Beaune Les Boucherottes 1990: Cherry and strawberry flavors ripple across the palate and come together with silky tannins in this intense, bright, juicy wine. Drinkable now to 1997. 333 cases made. • $42 • (12/15/92) • **89**

Beaune Les Cents-Vignes 1990: Big, chewy and muscular, with cinnamon and raspberry notes and ample fruit to balance the vanilla-scented new oak flavors. Has a solid tannic backbone. Drinkable now to 1997. 250 cases made. • $46 • (12/15/92) • **91**

Beaune Aux Crâs 1992: Light in texture, but the berry and spice flavors come together nicely on the finish for a delicate Beaune that is at its best now. • $NA • **83**

Beaune Aux Cras 1991: Crisp, focused and delicate, with brightly expressed raspberry and black cherry aromas and flavors that linger on the finish. Try now. 417 cases made. • $33 • (01/31/94) • **85**

Beaune Aux Cras 1990: Fleshy and quite impressive, delivering plenty of violet, vanilla, plum and cherry notes and a lot of ripe fruit flavors, but it's a little short on the finish to warrant an outstanding rating. Drinkable now. 417 cases made. • $46 • (12/15/92) • **89**

Beaune Aux Crâs 1989 • $48 • (01/31/92) • **90**

Beaune Les Teurons 1992: A little more flavor from this vintage than most, centering around gamy black cherry and toasty, spicy notes on the finish. Drinkable now. • $NA • **84**

Beaune Les Teurons 1991: Light but chewy, with a modest level of ripe cherry flavor and an astringent finish. Try now. 583 cases made. • $33 Ⓐ • (01/31/94) • **79**

Beaune Les Teurons 1990: Classy and seductive, with just the right balance of concentrated fruit flavor to compensate for the vanilla-tinged new oak nuances. Plum and berry notes sail across the palate to a seductive, long finish. Drinkable now to 1997. 667 cases made. • $48 • (12/15/92) • **91**

Beaune Les Teurons 1989 • $50 • (01/31/92) • **92**

Beaune Les Teurons 1988 • $42 • (02/15/91) • **90**

Beaune Les Teurons 1986 • $33 • (07/31/88) • **70**

Beaune Les Vignes-Franches 1992: Elegant, smooth and very light. Shows good berry and cherry flavors, but they turn short on the supple finish. Try now. • $NA • **78**

Beaune Les Vignes-Franches 1991: Lean and lively, showing nice raspberry and currant flavors underneath a layer of fine tannins and mineral notes. Drinkable now. 333 cases made. • $30 Ⓐ • (01/31/94) • **86**

Beaune Les Vignes-Franches 1990: There's wonderful finesse in this wine, showing a concentrated core of sweet-tasting tar, spice and berry flavors, fine tannins and a long finish. Drinkable now to 1998. 333 cases made. • $46 • (12/15/92) • **91**

Beaune Les Vignes-Franches 1989 • $45 • (01/31/92) • **91**

Chorey-Côte-de-Beaune Château de Chorey-lès-Beaune 1989 • $24 • (01/31/92) • **84**

Chorey-lès-Beaune Chateau de Chorey-lès-Beaune 1992: Straight forward and a bit diluted, with modest strawberry and currant flavors and a short finish. • $NA • **76**

Chorey-lès-Beaune Château de Chorey-lès-Beaune 1991: Crisp and simple, a decent level of currant and vanilla flavor fading on the astringent finish. 1,250 cases made. • $20 Ⓐ • (01/31/94) • **78**

Chorey-lès-de-Beaune Château de Chorey-lès-Beaune 1990: Firm and chewy, showing an elegant texture and lively raspberry characteristics. Drinkable now. 1,833 cases made. • $24 • (12/15/92) • **85**

Chorey-lès-Beaune Château de Chorey-lès-Beaune 1986 • $16 • (07/31/89) • **80**

GERMAIN, JEAN

Chardonnay Côtes du Jura 1993 • $11 • **67**

GERMAIN, MARIE-PIERRE

Aloxe-Corton Les Vercots 1989 • $NA • (01/31/92) • **88**

GERMAIN, THIERRY

Saumur Champigny Terres Chades Domaine des Roches Neuves 1992: Quite ripe, this mouthfilling wine shows plum, smoke and attractive herbal flavors, smooth and rich, with a lingering licorice finish. It's subtle, but has well-defined character. Drinkable now. 8,000 cases made. • $13 • **86**

GERMAINE, H.

Blanc de Blancs Crémant Champagne 1983 • $24 • (12/31/90) • **89**
Blanc de Blancs Crémant Champagne 1982 • $53 • (05/31/87) • **77**
Brut Champagne NV • $28 • (12/31/91) • **88**

GIRARD, DOMAINE

Sancerre La Garenne 1994: Chalky texture underlies flavors of fig and gooseberry, followed by a roundness that adds to its appeal. Drinkable now. 650 cases made. • $17 • (05/15/96) • **87**
Sancerre La Garenne 1993: Delicate yet expressive, this offers herbal, pine and floral notes, with ripe pear fruit and crisp acidity. It's clean and well-made. • $13 • (11/15/95) • **85**
Sancerre La Garenne 1992: Here's a muscular wine with firm acidity. It's very dry, with mineral notes on the palate and an appealing tangerine finish. A bit austere, but it shows good structure and balance. • $14 • (10/31/94) • **87**

FRANCE

GIRARD, ROBERT

Châteauneuf-du-Pape Cuvée du Belvedere Le Boucou 1990: Lean and earthy, with modest raspberry and spice aromas and flavors, bordering on chalky at the edges. Seems more mature than its actual age. Drinkable now. • $19 • (04/15/93) • **81**

GIRARDIN, ALETH

Beaune Clos des Mouches 1993: Beautifully crafted red offering wood, fruit and tannins in just the right proportions. Medium in body, medium silky tannins and a long, fresh finish. Try in 1999. • $48 • **90**
Beaune Clos des Mouches 1988 • $36 • (07/15/91) • **71**
Pommard Charmots 1988 • $44 • (07/15/91) • **87**

GIRARDIN, ARMAND

Pommard Charmots 1993: Bold and wonderful berry, raspberry and vanilla character, full body and tannins, yet refined and caressing. Long aftertaste. Try in 2000. • $60 • **91**
Pommard Epenots 1993: Super concentration and structure, full body, loads of tannins, rich tobacco, gamy, meaty, fruity character and long, long finish. Better after 2000. • $60 • **90**

GIRARDIN, DOMAINE JEAN

Santenay Clos Rousseau Château de la Charrière 1987 • $25 • (02/28/91) • **87**
Santenay Comme Château de la Charrière 1987 • $25 • (02/28/91) • **83**
Santenay Comme Château de la Charrière 1986 • $23 • (10/15/89) • **80**

GIRARDIN, VINCENT

Chassagne-Montrachet Morgeot Vieilles Vignes 1993: The wood, acidity and fruit are not very well integrated. Diluted, green finish. 417 cases made. • $34 • **75**
Meursault Les Narvaux 1993: Plenty of buttery, doughy, lemony aromas, but modest and fruity on the palate. Drink now. 417 cases made. • $29 • (05/15/95) • **81**
Santenay Clos de la Confrérie 1993: Harmonious and crisp, round mouth-feel. Shows a caressing, creamy character as well as vibrant lime and grapefruit notes. Could use more fruit concentration, tart finish. Drinkable now. • $NA • **83**

Key: SS—Spectator Selection. CS—Cellar Selection. BB—Best Buy. $NA—Price not available. (BT)—Barrel tasting. Ⓐ—Auction Price.
Dates in parentheses represent the issues in which the ratings were published.

Savigny-lès-Beaune Les Vermonts Dessus 1993: Quite austere but clean and crisp, adding a hint of honey amidst the green apple skin, lemon rind and grass flavors. Drink now. 917 cases made. • $23 • **80**

GISCOURS, CHÂTEAU

Margaux 1995: Classy wine, with an impressively firm backbone. Refined, elegant and full-bodied, it delivers nice concentration of fruit and tobacco along with mineral notes for complexity. The finish is intense but it's marked by high acidity. Almost outstanding. • $NA • (05/15/96) • **85-89** (BT)
Margaux 1994: Elegant, refined berry, cherry, vanilla and cedar character, medium tannins and a long, fresh finish. • $NA • (05/15/96) • **85-89** (BT)
Margaux 1993: Sleek and racy, featuring some lovely cassis, cedar and black cherry flavors. Medium body, supple tannins. Drink in 1997. 3,500 cases made. • $24 • (01/31/96) • **86**
Margaux 1991: A wine with an herbal berry character, medium body and a slightly diluted finish. • $24 • (03/31/94) • **78**
Margaux 1990: Complete and expressive, with intense black cherry, plum, tobacco character, fine silky tannins and a long, lively finish. Drink in 1997. 33,000 cases made. • $35 • (03/31/93) • **92**
Margaux 1989 • $27 Ⓐ • (03/15/92) • **92**
Margaux 1988 • $23 Ⓐ • (04/30/91) • **89**
Margaux 1986 • $24 Ⓐ • (06/15/89) • **83**
Margaux 1985 • $35 • (09/30/88) • **86**
Margaux 1983 • $28 Ⓐ • (05/01/89) • **78**
Margaux 1982 • $26 Ⓐ • (08/31/92) • **88**
Margaux 1981 • $12 • (06/01/84) • **82**
Margaux 1980 • $NA • (02/16/84) • **80**
Margaux 1979 • $34 • (10/15/89) • **87**
Margaux 1978 • $39 Ⓐ • (02/16/84) • **87**
Margaux 1976 • $45 • (02/16/84) • **83**
Margaux 1970 • $62 Ⓐ • (05/15/93) • **86**
Margaux 1964 • $55 • (02/16/84) • **89**
Margaux 1962 • $33 • (11/30/87) • **68**
Margaux 1961 • $100 • (04/30/96) • **80**

GLANA, CHÂTEAU DU

St.-Julien Vieilles Vignes 1995: Soft and pretty, delivering smoke, berry and cherry aromas and flavors, medium body and soft character. Early drinker. • $NA • (05/15/96) • **80-84** (BT)
St.-Julien Vieilles Vignes 1994: Pretty black cherry, mineral and berry aromas and flavors. Medium in body, firm tannins and fresh finish. • $NA •(06/30/95) • **80-84** (BT)
St.-Julien 1990: This thick, husky wine shows loads of tobacco, blackberry and redwood character, full, velvety tannins and a succulent finish. It lacks a bit of finesse, though. Drink in 1997. 17,000 cases made. • $20 • (03/31/93) • **88**
St.-Julien 1989 • $NA • (03/15/92) • **87**
St.-Julien 1987 • $NA • (11/30/89) • **81**
St.-Julien 1986 • $17 • (11/30/89) • **84**
St.-Julien 1982 • $NA • (11/30/89) • **85**

GLEON MONTANIE, CHÂTEAU

Cuvée Spéciale Corbières 1990 • $11 • (03/15/94) • **87**
Cuvée Tradition Corbières 1990 • $9 • (03/15/94) • **85**

GLORIA, CHÂTEAU

St.-Julien 1994: Lots of things going on here. Full-bodied, showing loads of cassis and wild berry flavors, this packs a wallop. Ripe, sweet tannins finish this off. • $NA • (05/15/96) • **90-94** (BT)
St.-Julien 1994: Lovely berry character in this minty and fruity St.-Julien offering fine tannins and a fresh finish. Well crafted for this vintage. • $22 • (05/15/96) • **85-89** (BT)
St.-Julien 1992: Beautiful tobacco and currant aromas and flavors, a polished palate, medium-to-light body and fine tannins. Much better than the '91. • $17 • **84**

St.-Julien 1991: Delicate red berry and raspberry aromas and flavors. This medium-bodied wine shows light tannins and a slightly drying finish. Tasted twice with consistent notes. • $19 • (03/31/94) • **77**

St.-Julien 1990: Understated, with plum, vanilla and new oak flavors and silky, racy tannins. A firm and sleek wine. Drink in 1997. 16,000 cases made. • $20 • (03/31/93) • **89**

St.-Julien 1989 • $23 Ⓐ • (10/15/92) • **89**
St.-Julien 1988 • $18 • (10/15/92) • **88**
St.-Julien 1987 • $15 • (10/15/92) • **75**
St.-Julien 1986 • $23 • (10/15/92) • **89**
St.-Julien 1985 • $35 Ⓐ • (10/15/92) • **90**
St.-Julien 1984 • $14 • (10/15/92) • **79**
St.-Julien 1983 • $24 • (10/15/92) • **83**
St.-Julien 1982 • $48 Ⓐ • (10/15/92) • **87**
St.-Julien 1981 • $18 Ⓐ • (10/15/92) • **83**
St.-Julien 1979 • $16 • (10/15/92) • **85**
St.-Julien 1978 • $26 Ⓐ • (10/15/92) • **74**
St.-Julien 1976 • $24 • (10/15/92) • **86**
St.-Julien 1975 • $24 Ⓐ • (10/15/92) • **83**
St.-Julien 1971 • $39 • (10/15/92) • **86**
St.-Julien 1970 • $33 Ⓐ • (10/15/92) • **88**
St.-Julien 1967 • $28 • (10/15/92) • **84**
St.-Julien 1966 • $55 • (10/15/92) • **87**
St.-Julien 1964 • $50 • (10/15/92) • **81**
St.-Julien 1962 • $55 • (10/15/92) • **79**
St.-Julien 1961 • $135 • (10/15/92) • **91**
St.-Julien 1960 • $NA • (10/15/92) • **71**
St.-Julien 1948 • $NA • (10/15/92) • **85**

GOBET, P.

Chiroubles 1994: Fresh and crisp, typical for Chiroubles, offering strawberry flavors while earth and vanilla accents add a bit of complexity. Light tannins provide grip. 2,000 cases made. • $10 • **85**

GOERG, PAUL

Brut Blanc de Blancs Champagne NV: Very inviting, rich and creamy in texture, sporting delicate, mouth-filling effervescence. Slightly sweet from generous flavors of fruit, vanilla and spice that linger nicely on the finish. • $27 • **87**

Brut Champagne Cuvée du Centenaire NV: Vibrant and lively, packed with fruit flavor and supported by firm acidity. Subtle notes of toast and spice lend complexity and clean notes linger on the finish. • $50 • **86**

Brut Champagne Millésimé 1989: Not sweet, but almost like a dessert in style. It has lovely vanilla, chocolate and banana notes carried on rich, creamy texture. Not long on the finish, but very flavorful and appealing. • $34 • **88**

Brut Champagne Tradition NV: Generous fruit in the aroma and flavors, but it leans toward a rustic, mature style that won't be for everyone. • $27 • **82**

Brut Rosé Champagne NV: This has very deep color, an aggressive mousse and even light tannins, yet doesn't offer the fruit to match, adding pale toast and plum notes. It's assertive but lacks grace. • $32 • (12/15/95) • **84**

GOFFRETEAU, CHÂTEAU

Bordeaux 1989 • $8 • (05/15/91) BB • **84**
Bordeaux Supérieur 1988 • $6 • (02/28/91) BB • **81**
Bordeaux Supérieur 1986 • $6 • (06/15/89) BB • **82**

GOISOT

Bourgogne Aligoté 1994: Amazing quality for a Bourgogne Aligoté. An exciting and electrifying marriage of honey, lemon, earth and mineral flavors. Solidly structured, its texture is silky, and it's clean, fresh, slightly grassy and appealingly sweet on the finish. From Domaine du Corps de Garde. • $NA • (05/31/96) • **88**

Bourgogne Côtes d'Auxerre Chardonnay 1994: Supple and honeyed—a delight to taste. Kicks in with refreshing lemon, lightly grassy and underripe apricot notes on the pure, clean, long finish. Not very complex perhaps, but a delicious white for drinking now through 1997. • $NA • (05/31/96) • **87**

Bourgogne Côtes d'Auxerre Chardonnay Domaine du Corps de Garde 1994: Both lush and elegant, this beauty packs loads of honey, mineral and ripe fruit flavors. Balanced, full-bodied and silky, it has a backbone of fresh citrus to cut through the sweetness and a very long finish. Drinkable now or wait to see what develops. • $NA • (05/31/96) • **92**

Sauvignon de Saint-Bris 1994: Charming, fresh and fruity, a light to medium-bodied '94 that is pleasing, laced with lemon and honey notes of moderate intensity. Balanced and a joy to drink now. From Domaine du Corps de Garde. • $NA • (05/31/96) • **84**

GOMBAUDE-GUILLOT, CHÂTEAU

Pomerol 1982 • $NA • (05/15/89) • **83**

GOMERIE, CHÂTEAU LA

St.-Emilion 1995: Some decent fruit but a little thin. Medium body and tannins and light finish. Second label of Château Beau-Séjour Bécot. • $NA • (05/15/96) • **80-84** (BT)

GONET, MICHEL

Brut Blanc de Blancs Champagne Chardonnay Grand Crus 1988: A very rich style, almost too rich. It shows overripe apple and steely aromas and flavors, medium body and a tart finish. Drinkable now. • $NA • (12/31/93) • **82**

Brut Blanc de Blancs Champagne Club de Viticulteurs 1985: This is a very opulent, almost oxidized style with a toasted nut and apple aroma and flavor. It's full-bodied and rich with a long crisp finish. Perfect with fish or white meat dishes. Drinkable now or hold. • $NA • (12/31/93) • **84**

Brut Rosé Champagne NV • $21 • (12/16/85) • **89**

GOSSET

Brut Champagne Excellence NV: Smooth-textured and slightly sweet, this is easy to like, tastes like Chardonnay and should be a crowd-pleaser. 25,000 cases made. • $36 • **86**

Brut Champagne Grande Millésime 1985: Mature in flavor, with rich, nutty spice, cherry and plum flavors and a creamy texture. Has good depth, richness and concentration, with lemony flavors that linger. Ready to drink now. • $72 • (04/30/91) • **89**

Brut Champagne Grande Millésime 1983: As rich and intense as expected. Great aromas and flavors of bread dough and apples with a hint of coconut, medium-bodied with intense green apple flavors, medium and crisp acidity and a flavorful finish. Tasted three times. Drinkable now. • $75 • (12/31/93) • **90**

Brut Champagne Grande Millésime 1982: Layers of toast, pear, citrus, nutmeg and creamy vanilla nuances are right on the mark for this vintage Champagne that's rich and complex. The finish brings all the flavors together for a complex encore. Drink now to 1993. 4,200 cases made. • $60 • (12/31/90) • **90**

Brut Champagne Grande Millésime 1979 • $45 • (07/15/87) • **96**

Brut Champagne Grande Réserve NV • $50 • (12/31/93) • **87**

Brut Champagne Réserve NV • $27 • (12/31/91) • **88**

Brut Rosé Champagne 1982: Fruity and tart with strawberry, banana and spicy flavors that are lively and refreshing on the palate. It's well balanced, offering depth and some complexity, finishing dry. • $75 • (12/31/88) • **88**

Brut Rosé Champagne NV • $37 • (12/31/90) • **85**

Brut Rosé Champagne Grand Rosé 1988: There's plenty of fruit in this rosé, almost jammy flavors of cherries and plums, yet it's lively and fresh, with an attractive pie crust finish. Intense and focused. 1,250 cases made. • $60 • (12/15/95) • **90**

FRANCE

GOUBARD, MICHEL

Pinot Noir Bourgogne Côte Chalonnaise Mont-Avril 1989 • $10 • (03/15/93) • **77**

GOUBERT, DOMAINE LES

Côtes du Rhône 1986 • $6 • (03/31/88) • **78**

Côtes du Rhône-Villages Beaumes de Venise 1987 • $9 • (07/31/89) • **81**

Côtes du Rhône-Villages Beaumes de Venise 1985 • $9 • (04/30/88) • **80**

Côtes du Rhône-Villages Sablet 1985 • $8 • (04/30/88) • **76**

Gigondas 1989: Not for the faint-of-heart. A rustic, compact wine with plenty of tannins and flavors of prune and dried cherry. The cigar-box aromas are almost overpowering. Packs quite a punch. Drinkable from 1996 to 2000. • $13 • (10/15/94) • **87**

Gigondas 1986 • $13 • (03/15/90) • **81**

Gigondas 1985 • $11 • (04/30/88) • **89**

Gigondas Cuvée Florence 1989: Rich, luscious and finely textured, with loads of sweet plum and cherry flavors. Quite lively, with nice touches of honey and vanilla. The long finish is dominated by coffee flavors. Drinkable from 1996 through 2000. • $23 • (10/15/94) • **87**

Gigondas Cuvée Florence 1986 • $24 • (04/30/88) • **92**

GOUGES, HENRI

Nuits-St.-Georges 1991: Firm and relatively fleshy for the vintage, has spicy cherry aromas and flavors and a tannic, slightly bitter finish. Drinkable in 1997. 500 cases made. • $30 Ⓐ • (01/31/94) • **83**

Nuits-St.-Georges 1990: Round and rich, with attractive, spicy berry flavors and plenty of velvety tannins. Drinkable now. 100 cases made. • $40 • (12/15/92) • **88**

Nuits-St.-Georges 1986 • $30 • (07/31/88) • **84**

Nuits-St.-Georges Clos des Porrets Premier Cru 1985: A super Nuits, with lush character and sweet taste, but it's also firm in structure. Great concentration. Tempting now, will last through 1997. • $NA • **92**

Nuits-St.-Georges Clos des Porrets Premier Cru 1976: Shows good fruit intensity, with vanilla and floral notes. It's quite lean and finishes hard, with green, unripe notes. • $NA • **85**

Nuits-St.-Georges Clos des Porrets Premier Cru 1971: Wonderful balance, showing the ripe, sweet fruit character typical for this vintage. Appealing cinnamon and spice notes come in on the round and seductive finish. • $NA • **93**

Nuits-St.-Georges Clos des Porrets Premier Cru 1953: Fantastic wine, with a firm backbone and lovely, focused fruit. Still youthful. A *premier cru,* but it rivals the quality of a *grand cru.* • $NA • **93**

Nuits-St.-Georges Clos des Porrets Premier Cru 1949: Smells a bit odd at first, with leathery, dusty notes, but after a while, the appealing sweet, ripe fruit character laced with chocolate notes emerge forcefully. Lingers on the finish. • $NA • **90**

Nuits-St.-Georges Clos des Porrets Premier Cru 1943: Past its peak. Light color, with some modest cherry flavors and a tough, hard finish. • $NA • **75**

Nuits-St.-Georges Clos des Porrets St.-Georges 1991: Solid, straightforward, crisp and juicy. Needs until 1997 or '98 to soften. 625 cases made. • $40 Ⓐ • (01/31/94) • **81**

Nuits-St.-Georges Clos des Porrets St.-Georges 1990: Very intense, with loads of cherry, earth and plum aromas and flavors and a super tannin structure. The finish goes on and on. Drinkable in 1997. 100 cases made. • $58 • (12/15/92) • **92**

Nuits-St.-Georges Clos des Porrets St.-Georges 1989 • $45 • (01/31/92) • **87**

Nuits-St.-Georges Les Chaignots 1986 • $40 • (07/31/88) • **90**

Nuits-St.-Georges Les Pruliers 1991: Slightly decadent berry and currant flavors balance the earthy, citrusy notes that emerge on the moderately tannic finish. Try now. 625 cases made. • $40 Ⓐ • (01/31/94) • **81**

Nuits-St.-Georges Les Pruliers 1990: Extremely well toned, with hard tannins covering the lovely, ripe fruit flavors. Nonetheless, it shows pretty black cherry and earth notes. Drinkable now to 1998. 130 cases made. • $58 • (12/15/92) • **90**

Nuits-St.-Georges Les Pruliers 1989 • $45 • (01/31/92) • **86**

Nuits-St.-Georges Les Pruliers Premier Cru 1969: A bit herbal in character, but the structure is firm and lovely. The chocolate and cinnamon notes are appealing. • $NA • **85**

Nuits-St.-Georges Les St.-Georges 1991: Tough and chewy, offering more earthy, barklike flavors than modest berry notes. Needs until 1997. 375 cases made. • $44 Ⓐ • (01/31/94) • **77**

Nuits-St.-Georges Les St.-Georges 1990: Very distinguished. A dense, rich Nuits, with raspberry, earth and spice characteristics and a wonderful velvety texture. Drinkable now. 75 cases made. • $60 • (12/15/92) • **92**

Nuits-St.-Georges Les St.-Georges 1989 • $49 • (01/31/92) • **89**

Nuits-St.-Georges Les St.-Georges 1985 • $45 • (02/15/88) • **68**

Nuits-St.-Georges Les St.-Georges Premier Cru 1992: Soft and appealing at first, but turns a bit green on the finish, showing tough tannins. Has more character than many '92 red Burgundies. From a site known to produce long-aging wines of *grand cru* quality. Try in 1997. • $NA • **86**

Nuits-St.-Georges Les St.-Georges Premier Cru 1991: Beautiful intensity and character, but also a bit green and hard. Definitely needs until 1997 or beyond to soften. More concentrated than the '92. • $44 • **88**

Nuits-St.-Georges Les St.-Georges Premier Cru 1983: Showing its age-hard, drying and slightly bitter-with some woody and wet earth flavors. • $NA • **81**

Nuits-St.-Georges Les St.-Georges Premier Cru 1972: Rich and ripe, lacking balance and tasting a bit too sweet, but with mature truffle, mushroom and smoked bacon flavors. • $NA • **84**

Nuits-St.-Georges Les St.-Georges Premier Cru 1964: A great, silky red Burgundy at its peak. Gorgeous and sweet on the palate, with vanilla and spice notes following on the extraordinary round finish. • $NA • **92**

Nuits-St.-Georges Les St.-Georges Premier Cru 1959: Starts out tasting ripe and rich, but turns dry on the finish. Has nice cinnamon and cherry flavors. • $NA • **81**

Nuits-St.-Georges Les St.-Georges Premier Cru 1955: Beautiful balance, with sweet fruit character and cinnamon notes. Clean as a whistle and delicious. • $NA • **93**

Nuits-St.-Georges Les St.-Georges Premier Cru 1937: Maybe a bad bottle. The color is impressively dark, but it smells mature and tastes of citrus and dried herbs. • $NA • **79**

Nuits-St.-Georges Les St.-Georges Premier Cru 1926: Old and past its time, with drying chestnut and caramel flavors. • $NA • **68**

Nuits-St.-Georges Les Vaucrains 1991: Firm, spicy and straightforward, showing an aromatic currant and anise character. Finishes lean, simple and a bit tannic. Drinkable now. 375 cases made. • $44 Ⓐ • (01/31/94) • **80**

Nuits-St.-Georges Les Vaucrains 1990: A beautiful Nuits, with plummy, earthy characteristics and an excellent intensity of fruit and tannins. Well balanced and focused, drinkable now. 75 cases made. • $60 • (12/15/92) • **91**

Nuits-St.-Georges Les Vaucrains 1989 • $49 • (01/31/92) • **90**

Nuits-St.-Georges Les Vaucrains Premier Cru 1990: Silky and beautifully balanced. Has a quite round and supple texture. Try now. • $60 • **88**

Nuits-St.-Georges Les Vaucrains Premier Cru 1989: Holding up beautifully, shows that Gouges made age-worthy wines even in a supple year like '89. Quite tannic and closed in, with ripe, intense flavors and an appealing, oily mouth-feel. Try in 1997. • $49 • **89**

Nuits-St.-Georges Les Vaucrains Premier Cru 1961: Rather lean, but shows good intensity and finesse offers smoked bacon and gamy flavors. • $NA • **87**

GOULAINE, MARQUIS DE

Muscadet de Sèvre et Maine Cuvée du Millénaire Sur Lie 1994: A basic, straightforward white with earthy aromas, modest citrus flavors, and a crisp texture. 6,000 cases made. • $10 • (11/15/95) • **79**

Muscadet de Sèvre et Maine Cuvée du Millénaire Sur Lie 1993: A simple wine that shows typical apple and citrus flavors, dull, earthy notes lack spark and length. 6,000 cases made. • $10 • (10/31/94) • **77**

Key: SS—Spectator Selection. CS—Cellar Selection. BB—Best Buy. $NA—Price not available. (BT)—Barrel tasting. Ⓐ—Auction Price.
Dates in parentheses represent the issues in which the ratings were published.

Muscadet de Sèvre et Maine Sur Lie 1994: Round on the palate, yet quite crisp, this shows typical pear and leesy flavors with a hint of soapiness on the finish. It's bright but lacks depth. 40,000 cases made. • $7 • **78**

Muscadet de Sèvre et Maine Sur Lie 1993: Hints of nuts and spice give this an appealing complexity. It's crisp and firm but not overly tart, with more substance than many Muscadets. Nicely balanced and round. 30,000 cases made. • $7 • (08/31/94) BB • **84**

GOULART, ROGER

Brut Champagne NV • $12 • • **68**

GOULET, GEORGE

Blanc de Blancs Crémant Champagne 1982: Maturity and a bit of complexity give it interest. Tart, lean in flavor and well balanced, with lemon and toasty aromas, lemon and nutmeg flavors and a long finish. • $30 • (07/31/88) • **86**

Brut Blanc de Blancs Champagne Cuvée G NV • $26 • (07/31/88) • **74**

Brut Champagne 1982: Rich and mature with ginger, toast, lemon and spice flavors that are rich and round on the palate, smooth and full with more depth and complexity than you find in most Champagnes. • $30 • (07/31/88) • **90**

Brut Champagne NV • $21 • (07/31/88) • **83**

Brut Champagne Cuvée du Centenaire 1982: Deep and firm, classicly structured with lean, crisp acidity and delicate lemon, toast and spicy ginger flavors. Good length. • $47 • (07/31/88) • **87**

Brut Rosé Champagne 1982: A hearty, complex rose with attractive Pinot Noir aromas and flavors. Lots of cherry, spice and plum flavors come through. Finish is long and fruity. • $31 • (07/31/88) • **85**

GOUR DE CHAULE, DOMAINE DU

Gigondas 1986 • $13 • (09/15/90) • **90**

GOURGAZAUD, CHÂTEAU DE

Minervois 1991: Light in flavor for a wine that's so dark in color. Has moderate tannins and modest cherry and herb notes. Drinkable now. • $8 • **79**

GRAILLOT, ALAIN

Crozes-Hermitage 1993: Young and almost raw, this shows potential, as concentrated cassis flavor is enhanced by smoky, licorice accents and firm tannins. Drinkable now. • $15 • **85**

Crozes-Hermitage 1992 • $14 • (05/31/94) • **84**

Crozes-Hermitage 1991 • $15 • (05/31/94) • **79**

Crozes-Hermitage 1990 • $17 • (04/15/93) • **88**

Crozes-Hermitage 1989 • $14 • (03/31/91) • **88**

Crozes-Hermitage 1986 • $9 • (04/15/89) • **88**

Crozes-Hermitage Blanc 1991 • $17 • (04/15/93) • **82**

Crozes-Hermitage La Guiraude 1992 • $18 • (05/31/94) • **80**

Crozes-Hermitage La Guiraude 1991 • $18 • (05/31/94) • **84**

Hermitage 1990: Muscular and powerful, with masses of plum, black cherry and spice flavors. The rich tannins are beautifully integrated and the wine has great balance. Drink after 1997. • $45 • (05/31/94) • **90**

St.-Joseph 1993: Earthy and animal aromas place this firmly in the Rhône, but on the palate it's rather light, with cherry flavors and a short finish. Though lacking concentration, it makes pleasant drinking now. • $17 • **80**

St.-Joseph 1992 • $18 • (05/31/94) • **80**

St.-Joseph 1991 • $18 • (05/31/94) • **86**

GRAND-BARRAIL-LAMARZELLE FIGEAC, CHÂTEAU

St.-Emilion 1986 • $15 • (06/30/89) • **72**

St.-Emilion 1982 • $25 Ⓐ • (05/15/89) • **85**

GRAND CAUMONT, CHÂTEAU DU

Corbières 1990 • $10 • (03/15/94) • **83**

GRAND CHARIOT

Corbières 1990 • $NA • (03/15/94) • **81**

GRAND CHEMIN, CHÂTEAU

Côtes de Bourg 1989 • $9 • (11/30/92) • **79**

Côtes de Bourg 1985 • $8 • (06/15/89) • **76**

GRAND CLARET, CHÂTEAU

Premières Côtes de Bordeaux 1988 • $7 • (07/31/91) • **78**

GRAND CLOS, DOMAINE DU

Bourgueil 1985 • $9 • (09/30/87) • **83**

GRAND CRES, DOMAINE DU

Corbières 1990 • $10 • (06/15/93) • **82**

GRAND-CORBIN-DESPAGNE, CHÂTEAU

St.-Emilion 1961 • $14 • (04/30/96) • **84**

St.-Emilion 1945 • $NA • (03/16/86) • **70**

GRAND IMPERIAL

Brut NV • $4 • (06/15/90) • **76**

GRAND MAISON, DOMAINE DE

Pessac-Léognan 1986 • $8 • (04/15/90) • **80**

GRAND-MAYNE, CHÂTEAU

St.-Emilion 1995: Rich, delicious blackberry, cherry, milk chocolate and tobacco character. Full-bodied and very velvety, showing intense fruit and round tannins. • $NA • (05/15/96) • **90-94** (BT)

St.-Emilion 1989 • $22 • (03/15/92) • **93**

St.-Emilion 1988 • $15 • (07/15/91) • **87**

St.-Emilion 1986 • $16 • (06/30/89) • **87**

GRAND MOULIN, CHÂTEAU

Haut-Médoc 1983 • $6 • (04/16/86) • **63**

GRAND ORMEAU, CHÂTEAU

Lalande-de-Pomerol 1985 • $16 • (05/31/88) • **88**

GRAND-PONTET, CHÂTEAU

St.-Emilion 1995: Lovely, sweet berry and vanilla aromas and flavors, medium to full body, round tannins and a long, ripe fruit finish. • $NA • (05/15/96) • **85-89** (BT)

St.-Emilion 1993: Big, solid peppery, gamy, tobacco aromas and flavors, full to medium body, hard tannins and long finish. Try this in 1999. • $22 • (01/31/96) • **86**

St.-Emilion 1988 • $21 • (07/15/91) • **86**

St.-Emilion 1961. • $NA • (04/30/96) • **82**

GRAND PREBOIS, DOMAINE DU

Côtes du Rhône 1990 • $9 • (11/30/92) • **80**

GRAND-PUY-DUCASSE, CHÂTEAU

Pauillac 1995: Some decent fruit in this—plenty of berry and cherry aromas and flavors. Moderate tannins and a slightly tough finish. Could move up a notch next year. • $NA • (05/15/96) • **80-84** (BT)
Pauillac 1989 • $23 • (04/30/92) • **86**
Pauillac 1988 • $21 • (04/30/91) • **89**
Pauillac 1986 • $21 Ⓐ • (06/30/89) • **85**
Pauillac 1985 • $19 • (02/29/88) • **90**
Pauillac 1961 • $43 • (04/30/96) • **87**

GRAND-PUY-LACOSTE, CHÂTEAU

Pauillac 1995: Loads of bright berry, cassis and violet aromas and flavors in this one. Full body and a solid core of fruit and tannins. A nice, long finish. • $NA • (05/15/96) • **90-94** (BT)
Pauillac 1994: Impressive berry, currant and spice aromas, medium to full body, ripe fruit character and fine tannins. Almost outstanding. • $NA • **85-89** (BT)
Pauillac 1993: Good fruit, some elegant currant notes, a slightly herbal character and well-integrated tannins. Nice to drink now but should improve until at least 1997. • $25 • (01/31/96) • **85**
Pauillac 1992: Light and earthy, berry-flavored, but rather short and diluted. Tasted twice, with consistent notes. Drink now. • $24 • **76**
Pauillac 1991: Straightforward green tobacco and fruit aromas and flavors, medium tannins and a very light finish. • $24 • (03/31/94) • **82**
Pauillac 1990: A big, up-front wine with intense aromas of cedar, tobacco, cassis and berries that carry through on the palate and lots of tannins to back it all up. As big as the great '82. Drink after 1998. 27,500 cases made. • $26 • (03/31/93) • **95**
Pauillac 1989 • $22 Ⓐ • (03/15/92) • **91**
Pauillac 1988 • $28 • (04/30/91) • **90**
Pauillac 1987 • $18 • (05/15/90) • **77**
Pauillac 1986 • $31 Ⓐ • (05/31/89) • **88**
Pauillac 1985 • $37 Ⓐ • (10/15/94) • **90**
Pauillac 1984 • $15 • (10/15/87) • **83**
Pauillac 1983 • $30 • (10/15/94) • **84**
Pauillac 1982 • $72 Ⓐ • (08/31/92) • **95**
Pauillac 1981: Excellent dark color accompanying plummy, floral and lead pencil aromas and flavors. Muscular for the vintage with ripe tannins and peppery, fruity tones. Drinkable now. • $28 • (10/15/94) • **88**
Pauillac 1979 • $29 Ⓐ • (10/15/89) • **88**
Pauillac 1970 • $35 Ⓐ • (05/15/93) • **90**
Pauillac 1961 • $150 • (04/30/96) • **86**
Pauillac 1945 • $400 • (03/16/86) • **80**

GRAND-ROMAINE, DOMAINE

Gigondas 1990 • $13 • (04/15/93) • **85**
Gigondas 1989 • $16 • (08/31/91) • **87**
Gigondas Medaille d'Argent 1990 • $16 • (01/31/92) • **85**
Gigondas Medaille d'Or 1990 • $16 • (01/31/92) • **87**

GRAND TINEL, DOMAINE DU

Châteauneuf-du-Pape 1989 • $15 • (10/15/91) • **88**
Châteauneuf-du-Pape 1988 • $17 • (10/15/91) • **87**
Châteauneuf-du-Pape 1986 • $20 • (10/15/91) • **86**
Châteauneuf-du-Pape 1985 • $23 • (10/15/91) • **75**
Châteauneuf-du-Pape 1983 • $25 • (10/15/91) • **87**
Châteauneuf-du-Pape 1981 • $27 • (10/15/91) • **89**
Châteauneuf-du-Pape 1990: A fat, soft wine made from very ripe fruit, somewhat tiring to drink. Shows typical fig, pineapple and tropical fruit aromas and very ripe, tropical fruit flavors, and has a full-bodied, thick, oily texture. • $18 • (10/15/91) • **81**

Key: SS—Spectator Selection. CS—Cellar Selection. BB—Best Buy. $NA—Price not available. (BT)—Barrel tasting. Ⓐ—Auction Price.
Dates in parentheses represent the issues in which the ratings were published.

GRAND VERDUS, CHÂTEAU LE

Bordeaux Supérieur 1988 • $7 • (10/31/91) BB • **80**

GRANDES-MURAILLES, CHÂTEAU

St.-Emilion 1989 • $NA • (03/15/92) • **88**
St.-Emilion 1982 • $NA • (05/15/89) • **81**

GRANDIN

Brut Ingrandes-Sur-Loire NV: A soft, earthy-smelling bubbly with simple apple and honey flavors. Slightly sweet. • $8 • (01/31/96) • **79**
Brut Ingrandes-Sur-Loire Cuvée de Réserve NV: Fresh and fruity, if uncomplicated, with flavors that remind us of pineapple and apricot. Clean and reasonably crisp. • $11 • (01/31/96) • **82**

GRANDS CHENES, CHÂTEAU LES

Médoc Cuvée Préstige 1995: One of our discoveries of the vintage. Racy, rich and elegant, yet packed with intense, deep cassis and plum character and lots of toast, vanilla, mocha and oak flavors. Medium-to-full-bodied, solid, ripe tannins. Almost outstanding. • $NA • (05/15/96) • **85-89** (BT)

GRANDS JAYS, CHÂTEAU LES

Bordeaux Supérieur 1986 • $6 • (05/15/89) • **77**

GRANGE CLINET, CHÂTEAU LA

Premières Côtes de Bordeaux 1993: Supple and shows off fresh berry flavors and hints of nutmeg. Has the polish of Bordeaux without much depth. 6,000 cases made. • $8 • (12/15/95) • **80**

GRANGE DE QUATRE SOUS, LA

Les Serrotes Vin de Pays d'Oc 1991 • $9 • (03/15/94) • **85**

GRANGEON, DOMAINE ALAIN

Châteauneuf-du-Pape 1986 • $16 • (01/31/89) • **77**

GRANGEOTTE, CHÂTEAU LA

Bordeaux 1993: Bright black cherry and firm underlying tannins give this good definition and balance. Drinkable now. • $9 • (12/15/95) • **81**
Bordeaux 1991: Cherry and cedar aromas and flavors are appealing, but on the palate it's lean, tannic and lacks concentration. Drinkable now. 4,250 cases made. • $7 • (11/15/94) • **79**

GRANGES, CHÂTEAU LES

Haut-Médoc 1990: An appealing wine with straightforward cherry flavors and silky tannins. Drinkable now. • $NA • (03/31/93) • **83**

GRAS, ALAIN

Auxey-Duresses Red 1993: More lean than opulent, but give it until 1997. Crisp acidity, firm texture and massive but round tannins. Offers plenty of fresh, red berry flavor topped by mocha, chocolate and spice notes. • $20 • **86**
Auxey-Duresses Red 1992: A dark-colored 1992, with attractive pepper, currant and blackberry flavors presented in a smooth package. Enjoy now through 1997. • $23 • **85**
Auxey-Duresses Red 1990: Focused but quite chewy, this medium-bodied wine offers a lot of tobacco and strawberry flavors and a smoky finish. Drinkable now. • $29 • (12/15/92) • **85**
St.-Romain Red 1993: Nicely balanced, from fresh fruit character to smooth tannins. The round mouth-feel offers some crisp red berry flavors and an earthy touch on the finish. • $18 • **84**

St.-Romain Red 1992: Crisp in texture, with coarse tannins and modest currant flavors. • $21 • **78**
St.-Romain Red 1990: A firm wine, with plenty of intense characteristics. Shows a good dose of tobacco, black cherry and smoke flavors that lead to a finish supported by a solid backbone of tannins. Drinkable now. • $24 • (12/15/92) • **86**
St.-Romain White 1994: Crisp and slightly herbal, with a reductive, "ice-box" sort of character. Chewy and a bit tart on the finish, with a touch of a mineral, minty, earthy flavor. • $22 • (05/31/96) • **75**

GRATIEN

Brut Saumur NV • $9 • (06/15/90) • **83**

GRATIEN, ALFRED

Brut Champagne 1985: Like spring time in the glass with floral, apple and honey character, super fresh acidity and a long lively finish. Soft texture. Great apéritif wine. Drink now but will improve. • $55 • (12/31/93) • **92**
Brut Champagne 1983: Fascinating Champagne with a sensual vanilla, toasty, oak and fruit character. Full bodied with loads of flavor and well-integrated acidity. Drink now but will improve. • $55 • (12/31/93) • **92**
Brut Champagne 1979 • $28 • (09/16/85) • **92**
Brut Champagne Cuvée Paradis NV • $85 • (12/31/93) • **95**
Brut Champagne NV • $23 • (11/01/85) • **93**
Rosé Champagne NV • $24 • (10/01/85) • **81**

GRATIEN & MEYER

Brut Saumur Cuvée Renaissance NV: This may be a white sparkling wine, but it tastes of red grapes. Plum and red cherry character reflects richness, and fruit flavors are nicely balanced by some toasty notes. It finishes clean and smooth. 10,000 cases made. • $19 • (04/30/96) • **86**
Brut Saumur Fleur de Lys NV: Full of honey, fig and caramel flavors, it tastes mature and somewhat soft, adding a toasty, honeyed finish. 50,000 cases made. • $13 • (04/30/96) • **83**
Demi-Sec Saumur Délice NV: A sweet style showing some honey and pear flavors that fold into a nice, soft bubbly. Would be good as an after-dinner treat accompanying fresh fruit. 50,000 cases made. • $13 • (04/30/96) • **85**
Demi-Sec Saumur Noir de Noirs Cardinal NV: A full-bodied red sparkling wine offering loads of currant, herb and plum flavors. Aromas are wonderfully fruity, but the character turns slightly astringent and falls short on aftertaste. Not for the faint of heart. 50,000 cases made. • $13 • (04/30/96) • **83**

GRAVE A POMEROL, CHÂTEAU LA

Pomerol 1995: This offers some very good vanilla, spice, herb and red berry character. • $NA • (05/15/96) • **85-89** (BT)
Pomerol 1993: Lovely black cherry and chocolate character, medium body, velvety tannins and a long cocoa, fruity finish. Drinkable now. • $28 • (01/31/96) • **87**
Pomerol 1992: At its peak, with pretty, velvety tobacco, chocolate and berry aromas and flavors, medium body and soft finish. Not to hold, drink now. • $NA • **80**
Pomerol 1990: Extremely pretty, with coffee, berry aromas and flavors and rich, round tannins. Subtle and balanced in style. Drink in 1997. 2,500 cases made. • $28 • (03/31/93) • **92**
Pomerol 1989 • $35 • (03/15/92) • **88**
Pomerol 1986 • $36 Ⓐ • (03/31/90) • **89**
Pomerol 1983: Traditional styled wine with rather advanced ruby, garnet color with earthy, berry character and a slight nuttiness. Medium bodied and soft with a light finish. Drink now. • $NA • **84**
Pomerol 1982 • $NA • (08/31/92) • **86**
Pomerol 1981: Simple and light. Attractive delicate wine with tobacco, chocolate, herbal character, medium body and a light slightly diluted finish. Drink now. • $NA • **80**
Pomerol 1979 • $NA • (10/15/89) • **90**
Pomerol 1970 • $NA • (05/15/93) • **90**

GRAVE, CHÂTEAU DE LA

Bordeaux Supérieur 1988 • $8 • (07/15/90) BB • **82**
Côtes de Bourg 1982 • $5 • (02/16/85) • **70**
Côtes de Bourg 1981 • $4 • (02/16/85) • **74**
Minervois 1990 • $7 • (03/15/94) • **82**

GREFFET, MARC

Pouilly-Fuissé 1993: Clean and flavorful, medium in body, presenting wet hay, green apple and lime tones and a tart finish. Drinkable now. 583 cases made. • $NA • **82**

GREFFIERE, CHÂTEAU DE LA

Mâcon-la Roche Vineuse Vieilles Vignes 1993: Crisp and fresh, offering dried herb, green apple and cream flavors and a touch of mineral character on the tart finish. • $12 • **80**

GRESSIER-GRAND-POUJEAUX, CHÂTEAU

Moulis 1993: Loads of new wood but the fruit also comes through. Ripe and delicious, sporting fine tannins and a slightly dry finish. Drinkable now. • $16 • (01/31/96) • **85**
Moulis 1961 • $NA • (04/30/92) • **84**

GREYSAC, CHÂTEAU

Médoc 1995: Silky, refined style delivering lovely raspberry and cherry aromas and flavors. Sports medium tannins and finish. • $NA • (05/15/96) • **85-89** (BT)
Médoc 1994: Firm and tight, demonstrating good tannins and plenty of berry, red-fruit character. Medium body, short finish. • $NA • **80-84** (BT)
Médoc 1990: A no-nonsense wine, with good character, nice ripe fruit flavors and round tannins. Drinkable now. 35,000 cases made. • $12 • (03/31/93) • **84**
Médoc 1989 • $12 • (03/15/92) • **79**
Médoc 1988 • $15 • (04/30/91) • **87**
Médoc 1986 • $10 • (11/30/89) • **85**
Médoc 1985 • $9 • (12/31/88) • **77**
Médoc 1983 • $8 • (07/31/87) • **65**
Médoc 1982 • $18 • (08/31/92) • **88**
Médoc 1981 • $8 • (06/01/84) • **77**

GRILLE, CHÂTEAU DE LA

Chinon 1987 • $18 • (08/31/91) • **77**

GRINOU, CHÂTEAU

Bergerac White 1992 • $8 • (08/31/93) • **82**

GRIPA, BERNARD

St.-Joseph 1992 • $NA • (05/31/94) • **77**
St.-Joseph Le Berceau 1992 • $NA • (05/31/94) • **83**

GRIPPAT, J.L.

St.-Joseph 1991 • $22 • (05/31/94) • **78**
St.-Joseph Vignes de l'Hospice 1991 • $NA • (05/31/94) • **83**
St.-Joseph Vignes de l'Hospice 1990 • $32 • (05/31/94) • **85**

GRIVAULT, ALBERT

Meursault 1994: Talented winemaking. This creamy wine has aromas that seduce with their yeasty, pie crust and lemony character. Focused and tightly wound now, the citrus and honey notes should fully emerge by 1999. 633 cases made. • $25 • (05/31/96) • **88**

Meursault 1992: Quite showy for the vintage. Rich and flavorful, with lovely honey, peach and tropical flavors. Silky and balanced, with good acidity throughout. • $28 • (08/31/94) • **88**

Meursault Clos des Perrières 1992: Soft, ripe and fat, showy and exuberant, offers exotic peach, dried apricot and honey flavors and a lush, mellow character. Tastes like botrytis. Drinkable on release. 400 cases made. • $80 • (08/31/94) • **87**

Meursault Les Perrières 1994: Elegant and focused, with a good combination of mineral, vanilla, pear, honey and citrus flavors. Caresses the palate with its silky texture. A lovely wine that drinks well now but should age. 716 cases made. • $39 • (05/31/96) • **90**

GRIVOT, JEAN

Chambolle-Musigny La Combe d'Orvaux 1987 • $47 Ⓐ • (06/15/90) • **85**

Clos de Vougeot 1993: A powerful, delicious red Burgundy that features awesome black cherry and black currant flavors shaded by toasty, smoky oak. It's all wrapped in firm but smooth texture and followed up by lingering, fruity aftertaste. Has a great future ahead, try in 1999. 650 cases made. • $45 • (05/15/96) CS • **92**

Clos de Vougeot 1988 • $70 • (04/30/91) • **85**

Clos de Vougeot 1985 • $62 • (04/30/88) • **81**

Echézeaux 1993: An exotic and enticing Burgundy combining concentrated fruit with spicy, oaky accents that dance and linger on the finish. Reminiscent of cherry, berry, cinnamon and smoke, adding really firm tannins, lively acidity and fine overall balance. Drink in 1999. 200 cases made. • $45 • (05/15/96) • **92**

Nuits-St.-Georges Les Boudots 1993: A handsome Burgundy that's stylish and sturdy at the same time. Offers solid fruit flavors, smoky, earthy accents, firm tannins and lingering aftertaste. Has great balance and should be best in 1999. 300 cases made. • $32 • (05/15/96) • **90**

Nuits-St.-Georges Les Boudots 1990: Mellow and slightly premature, showing pleasant roasted nut and berry aromas and flavors and medium tannins. Drinkable now. • $NA • (12/15/92) • **79**

Nuits-St.-Georges Les Boudots 1989 • $NA • (01/31/92) • **77**

Nuits-St.-Georges Les Boudots 1988 • $54 • (04/30/91) • **87**

Nuits-St.-Georges Les Charmois 1987 • $47 • (07/15/90) • **81**

Nuits-St.-Georges Les Pruliers 1988 • $53 • (04/30/91) • **89**

Nuits-St.-Georges Les Pruliers 1987 • $55 • (07/15/90) • **71**

Nuits-St.-Georges Les Roncières 1987 • $55 • (07/15/90) • **88**

Richebourg 1993: Intense, deep and smoldering, a young, powerful red that's closed in aroma but expansive and impressive in flavor. It has focused dried cherry, black cherry and currant flavors, extremely firm tannins, but enough fruit to balance them out. Aristocratic. Needs until at least 2000 to mellow. 100 cases made. • $128 • (05/15/96) • **96**

Richebourg 1990: Rather hard and austere, packing in plenty of black cherry, tea, herb and spice aromas and flavors and an iron backbone of tannins. A sour finish is slightly distracting. Needs time to come around, try from 1998. 150 cases made. • $NA • (12/15/92) • **84**

Richebourg 1989 • $NA • (01/31/92) • **93**

Vosne-Romanée 1993: Hearty, flavorful, tannic, well structured, delivering tastes of currant, pepper and cherry. Tightens up with tannins on the finish. Best to drink in 1999. 300 cases made. • $22 • (05/15/96) • **88**

Vosne-Romanée 1990: Smells and tastes of old redwood, has high acidity and lacks freshness. Not recommended. • $NA • (12/15/92) • **69**

Vosne-Romanée 1985 • $31 • (04/30/88) • **87**

Vosne-Romanée Les Beaumonts 1989 • $NA • (01/31/92) • **75**

Vosne-Romanée Les Beaux Monts 1993: A deep, dark Burgundy that has concentrated, intense, ripe fruit notes, luscious oaky accents and a sense that it's still tight and youthful. Great balance between its firm acidity, tight tannins and ample hoard of flavors. Best to wait until 2000. 300 cases made. • $32 • (05/15/96) • **94**

Vosne-Romanée Les Beaux Monts 1990: An odd, disappointing wine that's prematurely aging, showing a brown edge. Medium-bodied, with modest caramel, chestnut and tomato flavors. • $NA • (12/15/92) • **76**

Key: SS—Spectator Selection. CS—Cellar Selection. BB—Best Buy. $NA—Price not available. (BT)—Barrel tasting. Ⓐ—Auction Price.
Dates in parentheses represent the issues in which the ratings were published.

Vosne-Romanée Les Suchots 1993: Slightly austere, showing firm tannins and some fruit, but could use a bit more concentration. Touches of acidity on the finish. Drinkable now. • $NA • **85**

GROFFIER, ROBERT

Bonnes Mares 1989 • $79 • (01/31/92) • **81**

Bonnes Mares 1988 • $80 • (11/15/90) • **90**

Bonnes Mares 1987 • $67 • (07/31/89) • **89**

Bourgogne 1989 • $14 • (01/31/92) • **78**

Chambertin Clos de Bèze 1987 • $45 • (07/31/89) • **88**

Chambolle-Musigny Amoureuses 1988 • $66 • (11/15/90) • **93**

Chambolle-Musigny Amoureuses 1987 • $51 • (08/31/89) • **86**

Chambolle-Musigny Amoureuses 1986 • $50 • (02/28/89) • **84**

Chambolle-Musigny Les Hauts-Doix 1987 • $33 • **65**

Chambolle-Musigny Les Sentiers 1988 • $45 • (11/15/90) • **89**

Chambolle-Musigny Les Sentiers 1987 • $37 • (08/31/89) • **87**

Chambolle-Musigny Les Sentiers 1986 • $36 • (02/28/89) • **90**

Gevrey-Chambertin 1986 • $27 • (02/28/89) • **85**

GROLET, CHÂTEAU LA

Côtes de Bourg 1989 • $9 • (08/31/91) • **82**

Côtes de Bourg 1985 • $5 • (05/15/88) • **69**

GROS, A.-F.

Bourgogne Hautes Côtes de Nuits 1993: Already browning at the edges, it tastes of brown sugar and cooked fruit. Fat and ripe, leaving a hot, astringent mouth-feel. • $20 • **75**

Bourgogne Hautes Côtes de Nuits 1992: Light and fruity, nicely polished and offers a pleasant strawberry and spice character. Drinkable now. 1,042 cases made. • $22 • **81**

Bourgongne Hautes Côtes de Nuits 1989 • $19 • (06/15/92) • **78**

Bourgogne Hautes Côtes de Nuits 1988 • $22 • (03/31/91) • **80**

Clos Vougeot Le Grand Maupertuis 1989 • $NA • (01/31/92) • **90**

Echézeaux 1993: Rather light and disapponting for this *grand cru* and producer. Elegant and fruity, adding fine tannins and racy acidity on aftertaste. Better in 1998? Tasted twice, with consistent notes. • $84 • **83**

Echézeaux 1992: Open-textured with graceful berry, currant and floral aromas and flavors, a little touch of hay on the nose adding a distinctive note. Drinkable now. 108 cases made. • $106 • **83**

Echézeaux 1991: Light and crisp, has simple berry and cedar aromas and flavors and a citrusy finish. Try in 1997. 100 cases made. • $70 Ⓐ • (01/31/94) • **76**

Echézeaux 1990: Ripe and rich, showing almost sweet fruit flavors. Isn't giving much now, but offers hints of excellence. Try in 1997. 120 cases made. • $90 • (12/15/92) • **90**

Echézeaux 1988 • $84 • (02/15/91) • **91**

Richebourg 1992: An open and generous style, offering black cherry, root beer and toast aromas and flavors that linger on the supple finish. Approachable now. • $NA • **86**

Richebourg 1990: Exotic and very aromatic, with toast, smoked bacon and ginger aromas and flavors and a focused, long finish. Drinkable in 1998. 90 cases made. • $180 • (12/15/92) • **94**

Richebourg 1989 • $130 • (01/31/92) • **97**

Richebourg 1988 • $190 • (02/15/91) • **97**

Vosne-Romanée Aux Réas 1993: Enticingly sweet-tasting, featuring a ripe raspberry character that is quite soft at first, but with enough solid tannins below. Try this medium-bodied red around 1999. • $44 • **87**

Vosne-Romanée Aux Réas 1992: Has clean and focused fruit flavors with a smoky, red berry character, but it's diluted and short on the finish. 583 cases made. • $47 • **79**

Vosne-Romanée Aux Réas 1991: A light, pretty, anise-scented wine built around raspberry and vanilla flavors. Finishes with charm and echoes fruit. Drinkable now. 275 cases made. • $35 Ⓐ • (01/31/94) • **83**

Vosne-Romanée Aux Réas 1990: Light and delicate, with modest raspberry and cherry flavors and a light finish. An early drinking wine, drink now. Tasted twice, with consistent notes. Drinkable now. 200 cases made. • $40 • (12/15/92) • **79**

Vosne-Romanée Aux Réas 1988 • $41 • (02/28/91) • **71**

Vosne-Romanée Maizières 1993: Light, delicate chestnut, berry and cherry character, medium to light body, light tannins and fresh finish. Better in 1998. • $50 • **87**

GROS, ANNE & FRANÇOIS

Bourgogne 1992: Relatively ripe and quite light, the flavors remaining nicely focused on the raspberry, currant and cherry flavors. Drink young. 583 cases made. • $NA • **80**

Bourgogne 1990 • $17 • (12/15/92) • **84**

Bourgogne Pinot Noir 1993: Very light, straightforward red berry flavor, a bit dry on the finish. You wish for more concentration. Drink through 1997. • $13 • **81**

Chambolle-Musigny 1992: Lean in texture, with tightly focused raspberry and rose petal flavors that persist into a light finish. Drinkable now. 375 cases made. • $NA • **83**

Chambolle-Musigny La Combe d'Orveau 1993: Pretty Burgundy, offering some good tannic structure and currant and blackberry flavors in sizable amounts. Long finish. Needs time to smooth out, try in 2000. • $29 • **88**

Chambolle-Musigny La Combe d'Orveau 1990: A toasty wine that offers nice, sweetish fruit notes, but mostly shows distracting, odd gooseberry and citrus aromas and flavors that simply don't match the high quality we've come to expect from this fine producer. Tasted twice. Try now. • $40 • (12/15/92) • **72**

Clos Vougeot Le Grand Maupertuis 1993: Laser-sharp definition of red berry flavor that zooms in with crystal clarity. As supple as the '93s come, medium-bodied, the fresh acidity carrying it on to a very long finish. Tempting now, but try after 2000. • $55 • **95**

Clos Vougeot Le Grand Maupertuis 1992: A ripe style that features plenty of currant, black cherry, vanilla and spicy oak flavors that flow together beautifully on the supple finish. Has enough tannin to want until 1997, but it's close to drinkable now. 333 cases made. • $NA • **88**

Clos Vougeot Le Grand Maupertuis 1991: Firm in texture but polished, showing off the modest black cherry and toast flavors to their best advantage. Drinkable now. 400 cases made. • $58 Ⓐ • (01/31/94) • **82**

Clos Vougeot Le Grand Maupertuis 1990: Magic grace and power embody this Clos Vougeot. Superbly concentrated, with tons of currant, cherry and smoke complexity and a stunning, velvety yet firm finish. Drinkable in 1998. 350 cases made. • $75 • (12/15/92) • **95**

Richebourg 1993: Extremely vivid and intoxicating plum and raspberry character, medium to full body, medium velvety tannins and fresh finish. Try in 2000. • $100 • **91**

Richebourg 1992: Focused and flavorful, crisp-textured, with fresh currant, vanilla and spice overtones playing on the slightly tannic finish. Give it until 1997. 208 cases made. • $NA • **86**

Richebourg 1991: Spicy, elegant and smoothly polished, the ripe currant, prune and spice flavors have chocolate and cream overtones. Graceful, harmonious and almost drinkable now, but has the goods to improve through 1998 to 2000. 200 cases made. • $100 Ⓐ • (01/31/94) • **89**

Richebourg 1990: Amazingly rich, ripe and firm, the fruit just erupts like a volcano. Offers marvelous plum, currant and violet aromas and flavors and a touch of toasted bread and vanilla on the complex, supple finish. Drinkable in 1998. 240 cases made. • $130 • (12/15/92) • **97**

Vosne-Romanée 1993: Lovely, elegant green tobacco and plum aromas and flavors, medium body, fine tannins and supple texture. Deliciously fruity finish. Better in 1999. • $40 • **88**

Vosne-Romanée 1992: Simple, charming and velvety, with appealing plum and currant flavors that linger on the soft finish. Drinkable now. 150 cases made. • $NA • **82**

Vosne-Romanée 1991: Firm and flavorful, a light, complex wine that paints an appealing profile of raspberry, black cherry, rose petal and anise aromas and flavors. Finishes toasty and spicy, with a lingering splash of fruit. Drinkable now. 200 cases made. • $32 Ⓐ • (01/31/94) • **86**

GROS, JEAN

Bourgogne 1990 • $16 • (12/15/92) • **81**

Clos de Vougeot 1992: Chunky in texture, somewhat overripe perhaps, with prune and anise flavors that pick up a little black cherry on the finish. Tannins need until 1997. • $NA • **83**

Clos Vougeot 1991: Ripe, cedary and sturdy, the watery flavors manage to pick up berry and hazelnut tones on the finish. Not too tannic. Drinkable now. 75 cases made. • $80 Ⓐ • (01/31/94) • **81**

Nuits-St.-Georges 1993: Tastes diluted, with vanilla, nail polish and slightly vegetal character, medium to light body and short finish. Drink if you must. • $32 • **79**

Nuits-St.-Georges 1991: Excessively earthy, muddy, decadent aromas and flavors ruin this one for us. • $NA • (01/31/94) • **67**

Nuits-St.-Georges 1990: A fresh, bright Nuits, with attractive berry and earth characteristics and velvety tannins. Somewhat simple. Try now. 192 cases made. • $30 • (12/15/92) • **85**

Nuits-St.-Georges 1989 • $39 • (01/31/92) • **87**

Nuits-St.-Georges 1988 • $42 • (02/28/91) • **81**

Nuits-St.-Georges 1985 • $36 • (07/31/88) • **85**

Richebourg 1993: Vibrant fruit on the palate really impresses. Intense aromas of currant, mocha, game and plum. Very smooth, showing velvety texture, fine tannins and long finish. Try in 2000. 83 cases made. • $160 • **94**

Richebourg 1992: Ripe, generous and supple, with spice, cinnamon and caramel overtones to the currant and raspberry flavors. Finishes smooth and sweet. Drinkable now. 83 cases made. • $150 • **88**

Richebourg 1991: An exotic wine, with dramatic wild berry, anise and coffee aromas. Spreads out on the palate to reveal more currant, plum and chocolate nuances. Smooth, polished, elegant and seductive, tempting now, but should be at its best after 1997. 140 cases made. • $149 Ⓐ • (01/31/94) • **92**

Richebourg 1990: Spellbinding, with smoke, ginger, spice and berry aromas and flavors. Full-bodied *grand cru*, with velvety texture and a firm, very long finish that's unforgettable. Drinkable in 1998. 183 cases made. • $150 • (12/15/92) • **94**

Richebourg 1989 • $180 • (01/31/92) • **98**

Richebourg 1988 • $190 • (02/28/91) • **98**

Richebourg 1987 • $170 • (03/31/90) • **95**

Vosne-Romanée 1993: Attractive, velvety texture is somewhat raisiny. Perhaps slightly overdone? Full-bodied with intense tar and fruit character and medium tannins. Try in 1999. Scored lower than a barrel sample tasted earlier this year. 708 cases made. • $35 • **89**

Vosne-Romanée 1992: A delicate, soft Vosne-Romanée that brings out some oak-scented vanilla notes along with red berry flavors. Light-bodied and ready to drink. 667 cases made. • $35 • **78**

Vosne-Romanée 1989 • $39 • (01/31/92) • **90**

Vosne-Romanée 1988 • $38 • (02/28/91) • **90**

Vosne-Romanée 1987 • $32 • (04/30/90) • **89**

Vosne-Romanée Clos des Réas 1993: Alluring aromas of vanilla, currant and raspberry follow through on the palate. Medium- to full-bodied with silky tannins and a fresh finish. Drink in 1999. • $60 • **91**

Vosne-Romanée Clos de Réas 1991: Distinctive, showing more cedar and earth than fruit. A bit diluted. Drinkable now. 720 cases made. • $53 Ⓐ • (01/31/94) • **78**

Vosne-Romanée Clos des Réas 1990: Very subtle, with gamy, roasted berry characteristics that build on the palate. Finely structured and finishes long and rich. From a vineyard exclusively owned by this producer. Drinkable now. 917 cases made. • $48 • (12/15/92) • **93**

Vosne-Romanée Clos des Réas 1989 • $70 • (01/31/92) • **92**

Vosne-Romanée Clos des Réas 1988 • $50 • (02/28/91) • **94**

Vosne-Romanée Clos des Réas 1987 • $44 • (04/30/90) • **93**

Vosne-Romanée Clos des Réas 1986 • $36 • (02/28/89) • **90**

Vosne-Romanée Clos des Réas 1985 • $58 • (07/31/88) • **87**

GROS, MICHEL

Bourgogne Hautes Côtes de Nuits 1993: Simple and bubbling with fruit. Medium body, plum and crushed strawberry flavors, light tannins and a fresh finish. Drink now. • $16 • **82**

Bourgogne Hautes Côtes de Nuits 1989 • $NA • (01/31/92) • **82**

Chambolle-Musigny 1993: Amazing quality for a village wine, showing lovely elegance, solid structure, medium to full body, lots of mocha and red berry character, silky tannins and long, fruity finish. One to age, try after 2000. 108 cases made. • $35 • **91**

Côte de Nuits-Villages 1990: Extremely elegant, with lovely, delicate berry, raspberry and earth aromas and flavors and silky tannins. Drinkable now. • $NA • (12/15/92) • **85**
Hautes Côtes de Nuits 1987 • $14 • (02/28/90) • **78**
Vosne-Romanée 1991: Tough, cedary and earthy, minimizing the fruit to show more toasty, spicy character. Drinkable now. 125 cases made. • $36 Ⓐ • (01/31/94) • **76**
Vosne-Romanée Clos de la Fontaine 1993: Fresh, lively mocha, coffee, cherry, earth and spice flavors. Balanced and crisp on the smoky, toasty, sweet-tasting finish. Tempting to drink now, but should improve past 1998. • $NA • **87**

GROS FRERE & SOEUR

Bourgogne Hautes Côtes de Nuits 1993: Some good berry flavor and a hint of cedar, but slightly short on the finish. Drink now. • $15 • **80**
Bourgogne Hautes Côtes de Nuits 1992: Light and crisp, with strawberry flavors clicking in delicately. • $NA • **79**
Bourgogne Hautes Côtes de Nuits 1989 • $NA • (01/31/92) • **82**
Clos Vougeot Musigni 1992: Pretty, drinkable and flavorful, showing meaty, vanilla-scented blueberry and raspberry notes that never quite get revved up. • $NA • **85**
Clos Vougeot Musigni 1991: Crisp, austere and sharply focused. Lean raspberry, currant and black cherry flavors shade toward toastiness on the finish. An elegant wine that needs until 1997 or '98 to soften. 300 cases made. • $75 Ⓐ • (01/31/94) • **86**
Clos Vougeot Musigni 1990: Big and chewy, what impresses you first are all those smoky, toasty flavors. Packed with plum and cherry notes and loads of firm tannins. Hold until 1997. 300 cases made. • $68 Ⓐ • (12/15/92) • **93**
Clos Vougeot Musigni 1989 • $80 Ⓐ • (01/31/92) • **91**
Clos Vougeot Musigni 1988 • $95 • (03/31/91) • **92**
Clos Vougeot Musigni 1985 • $102 • (03/31/88) • **75**
Côte de Nuits-Villages 1990: Shows very good density of fruit and medium tannins along with attractive, ripe plum and cedar notes on the finish. Try now. • $18 •(12/15/92) • **86**
Grands Echézeaux 1993: A beautiful wine that sneaks up on you with its wonderful fruit character. Refreshing plum, berry and currant aromas follow through on the palate. Fine tannins. Better in 2000. • $69 • **93**
Grands Echézeaux 1992: Elegant, its silky texture supporting a nice beam of currant and blackberry flavor, shaded with touches of anise and mint around the edges. Drinkable now. • $NA • **87**
Grands Echézeaux 1991: Firm and crisp, this lighter, elegant style offers modest, tobacco-scented berry and currant aromas and flavors and a light, appealing finish. Drinkable now. 300 cases made. • $75 Ⓐ • (01/31/94) • **85**
Grands Echézeaux 1990: Very delicate and refined, well balanced and offering plenty of pretty strawberry, violet, vanilla and chocolate aromas and flavors. Quite supple. Drinkable in 1997. 400 cases made. • $85 • (12/15/92) • **91**
Grands Echézeaux 1989 • $80 • (01/31/92) • **92**
Grands Echézeaux 1985 • $75 • (03/31/88) • **71**
Richebourg 1993: Beautifully crafted, opulent red sporting fine tannins, succulent plum flavors and a long, silky finish. Better in 2000. • $110 • **94**
Richebourg 1992: Nuances of mocha and spice add to the fine, delicate thread of berry flavor, finishing creamy and smooth. Nicely fashioned, tasty to drink already. • $NA • **86**
Richebourg 1991: Polished and elegant. Bright raspberry and strawberry flavors shine through overtones of rose petal, vanilla and violet. Harmonious and supple, should be at its best from 1998. 300 cases made. • $100 Ⓐ • (01/31/94) • **90**
Richebourg 1990: A seductive wine, with tons of bright violet, licorice, black cherry, vanilla and earth characteristics. The finish is restrained and firm. Drinkable in 1997 to 2000. 350 cases made. • $150 • (12/15/92) • **96**
Richebourg 1989 • $180 • (01/31/92) • **95**

Key: SS—Spectator Selection. CS—Cellar Selection. BB—Best Buy. $NA—Price not available. (BT)—Barrel tasting. Ⓐ—Auction Price.
Dates in parentheses represent the issues in which the ratings were published.

Richebourg 1988 • $192 • (02/28/91) • **91**
Vosne-Romanée 1993: Ripe and rich Burgundy, featuring wild chestnut, mocha, blackberry and plum character, medium to full body, fine tannins and a lovely, silky finish. Better in 1999. • $35 • **91**
Vosne-Romanée 1992: Light and spicy, smooth-textured, with a touch of chocolate on the finish. Drinkable now. • $NA • **80**
Vosne-Romanée 1991: Nicely articulated raspberry and cherry flavors persist on the finish, remaining delicate and appealing. Drinkable now. 450 cases made. • $35 Ⓐ • (01/31/94) • **84**
Vosne-Romanée 1989 • $39 • (01/31/92) • **91**
Vosne-Romanée 1988 • $46 • (03/31/91) • **89**
Vosne-Romanée 1985 • $35 • (04/15/88) • **70**

GROSSOMBRE, CHÂTEAU

Entre-Deux-Mers 1994: Grassy and fresh, fruity and lively, exhibiting dried-herb, melon and pear character. • $8 • **80**

GROSSOT, JEAN-PIERRE

Chablis 1994: Possibly the best village Chablis of this vintage? Shows plenty of harmony and character. The oak shows through with its vanilla and spice notes but doesn't dominate the juicy fruit flavors and lovely honey character. Delicious now, but should be even better after 1998. 1,666 cases made. • $17 • (05/31/96) • **89**
Chablis 1992: Finesse and power mingle beautifully in this charm. Harmonious blend of distinctive mineral, lemon, pear and herb flavors. The texture is silky and the finish sophisticated. A winner from start to finish. • $NA • (07/31/94) • **88**
Chablis Les Fourneaux 1994: Great winemaking: mellow and lush, packed with flavors ranging from citrus to honey, mineral to cream. Comes together beautifully on a silky yet long and refreshing finish. Drinkable now through 2000. 583 cases made. • $22 • (05/31/96) • **91**
Chablis Les Fourneaux 1993: Alluring mineral, apple and spice aromas and flavors, medium body, crisp acidity and flavorful finish. Drinkable now. 900 cases made. • $20 • **86**
Chablis Mont de Milieu 1994: A pure, full-bodied white Burgundy: straight as an arrow, bursting with mineral, citrus, floral, apricot and honey flavors. Quite rich and silky, but the finish is intense and mouthpuckering. Needs until 1998 to settle down. 458 cases made. • $25 • (05/31/96) • **88**
Chablis Mont de Milieu 1993: Nicely balanced and quite supple, showing lemon, mineral and earth flavors. Surprisingly forward for a '93. Drink now. 500 cases made. • $29 • **85**
Chablis Vaucoupin 1994: Total seduction: full to medium body, zipping along on the palate while leaving a trace of well-defined, intense fruit. Packed with lemon, honey, ripe pear, apricot and mineral flavors. Harmonious and simply too delicious not to hunt down. Minutes-long finish. Tempting now and through 2000. 441 cases made. • $25 • (05/31/96) • **91**
Chablis Vaucoupin 1993: Clean and fresh, supplying toasted oak, honey and apple aromas and flavors, medium body and fresh finish. 600 cases made. • $23 • **84**

GROTHE, CAVES JEAN

Pouilly-Fumé Acacia 1994: Loads of mineral character are accented by green plum, herb and a leesy quality. Very dry and stony. Needs food. • $16 • (05/15/96) • **84**
Pouilly-Fumé Acacia 1993: A fresh, fruity wine with pleasant citrus and green apple flavors without much herbaceousness. Good acidity keeps it crisp. Refreshing and quaffable.\ • $NA • (10/31/94) • **83**
Sancerre Acacia 1994: Extremely herbal, as lime and a touch of tartness seem out of sync. Try with food. • $15 • (05/15/96) • **83**
Sancerre Acacia 1993: This delicate, floral white offers bright gooseberry and light apple flavors, with crisp, almost chalky acidity firm on the finish. It's clean and balanced, drinking well now. • $14 • (11/15/95) • **85**
Sancerre Acacia 1992: Ripe fruit balances the crisp herbal notes in this clean, balanced wine. It's easygoing and delicate, with grapefruit and mineral flavors, mouthwatering and very fresh. • $15 • (10/31/94) • **85**

GRUAUD-LAROSE, CHÂTEAU

St.-Julien 1995: Disappointing for Gruaud-Larose. Bright berry and cherry character on the nose and palate. Firm tannins and fresh finish. A bit simple and light. • $NA • (05/15/96) • **80-84** (BT)
St.-Julien 1994: Rather supple and light, with some decent red berry and plum flavors. Quite succulent on the finish. • $33 • (05/15/96) • **80-84** (BT)
St.-Julien 1993: A seductive beauty. Medium in body, lovely, silky tannins and plenty of minty, cherry, berry character. Delicious now but will improve with age. • $30 • (01/31/96) • **88**
St.-Julien 1992: Tobacco, toasted oak and very fruity character, medium-bodied, medium tannins and a silky finish. Drinkable now. • $25 • **85**
St.-Julien 1991: Chewy and rich with a black cherry and currant character. Almost full-bodied, with a lovely supple texture. • $25 • (03/31/94) • **85**
St.-Julien 1990: A wine with lovely ripe fruit and an attractive tobacco and smoke character. It shows good tannin structure and a long finish. Well proportioned. Drink after 1997. 32,000 cases made. • $35 • (03/31/93) • **90**
St.-Julien 1989 • $36 Ⓐ • (03/15/92) • **93**
St.-Julien 1988 • $27 Ⓐ • (03/31/91) • **84**
St.-Julien 1987 • $26 • (02/28/91) • **83**
St.-Julien 1986 • $59 Ⓐ • (02/28/91) • **89**
St.-Julien 1985: A lovely Gruaud but not as great as expected. No nonsense '85 with spicy cedar, tobacco flavors, medium/full body, medium tannins and a rather short finish. Time will tell. Tasted twice with consistent notes. Drink now. • $40 • (10/15/94) • **87**
St.-Julien 1984 • $21 • (02/28/91) • **83**
St.-Julien 1983: Solid, intense wine. Roasted coffee, cassis aromas and flavors with lovely ripe fruit finish. Well-built with firm tannins. Drinkable but better after 1998. • $36 • (10/15/94) • **90**
St.-Julien 1982 • $83 Ⓐ • (08/31/92) • **94**
St.-Julien 1981: Polished, big wine. Dark colored with rich and opulent aromas and flavors and loads of tobacco, cedary, berry character. Drink now or hold. • $43 • (10/15/94) • **91**
St.-Julien 1980 • $25 • (02/28/91) • **83**
St.-Julien 1979 • $33 Ⓐ • (02/28/91) • **89**
St.-Julien 1978 • $36 Ⓐ • (02/28/91) • **91**
St.-Julien 1977 • $33 • (02/28/91) • **71**
St.-Julien 1976 • $NA • (02/28/91) • **85**
St.-Julien 1975 • $34 Ⓐ • (02/28/91) • **89**
St.-Julien 1974 • $28 • (02/28/91) • **63**
St.-Julien 1973 • $22 • (02/28/91) • **76**
St.-Julien 1971 • $31 • (02/28/91) • **85**
St.-Julien 1970 • $41 Ⓐ • (05/15/93) • **86**
St.-Julien 1969 • $16 Ⓐ • (02/28/91) • **50**
St.-Julien 1968 • $19 Ⓐ • (02/28/91) • **65**
St.-Julien 1967 • $33 • (02/28/91) • **78**
St.-Julien 1966 • $34 Ⓐ • (02/28/91) • **87**
St.-Julien 1964 • $70 • (02/28/91) • **88**
St.-Julien 1962 • $95 • (02/28/91) • **94**
St.-Julien 1961: Has this château's characteristic earthy style, seeming almost pungent on first whiff, but it also packs plenty of ripe, sweet-seeming fruit flavor. In very solid condition, full-bodied but well balanced, firm with tannins. Drink through 2005. • $203 • (04/30/96) • **90**
St.-Julien 1959 • $201 • (02/28/91) • **85**
St.-Julien 1957 • $65 • (02/28/91) • **78**
St.-Julien 1955 • $150 • (02/28/91) • **87**
St.-Julien 1953 • $195 • (02/28/91) • **88**
St.-Julien 1952 • $157 • (02/28/91) • **85**
St.-Julien 1950 • $175 • (02/28/91) • **83**
St.-Julien 1949 • $225 Ⓐ • (02/28/91) • **85**
St.-Julien 1947 • $285 • (02/28/91) • **88**
St.-Julien 1945 • $365 Ⓐ • (02/28/91) • **96**
St.-Julien 1943 • $94 Ⓐ • (02/28/91) • **83**
St.-Julien 1937 • $150 • (02/28/91) • **87**
St.-Julien 1934 • $150 • (02/28/91) • **83**
St.-Julien 1929 • $550 • (02/28/91) • **85**
St.-Julien 1928 • $500 • (02/28/91) • **94**
St.-Julien 1926 • $180 • (02/28/91) • **95**
St.-Julien 1924 • $250 • (02/28/91) • **89**
St.-Julien 1921 • $250 • (02/28/91) • **87**
St.-Julien 1920 • $300 • (02/28/91) • **85**
St.-Julien 1918 • $323 Ⓐ • (02/28/91) • **78**
St.-Julien 1907 • $255 • (02/28/91) • **72**
St.-Julien 1906 • $300 • (02/28/91) • **85**
St.-Julien 1899 • $600 • (02/28/91) • **83**
St.-Julien 1893 • $500 • (02/28/91) • **78**
St.-Julien 1887 • $400 • (02/28/91) • **71**
St.-Julien 1878 • $500 • (02/28/91) • **83**
St.-Julien 1870 • $521 Ⓐ • (02/28/91) • **87**
St.-Julien 1865 • $1,800 • (02/28/91) • **65**
St.-Julien 1844 • $NA • (02/28/91) • **85**
St.-Julien 1834 • $NA • (02/28/91) • **83**
St.-Julien 1819 • $NA • (02/28/91) • **89**

GRUET

Brut Champagne 1988: Seems a little thin but has some decent lemon, herbal character, medium bodied and a light finish. Drink now. 8,500 cases made. • $30 • (12/31/93) • **82**

GUERIN, ANDRE

Pouilly-Fuissé La Roche No. 1 1994: An odd wine, packing tons of intense citrus flavors that lead to a long, long finish, but it's also excessively earthy, with a slight aroma of burnt matches. Drinkable now through 1998. • $NA • (05/31/96) • **83**

GUERIN, MME. R.

Pouilly-Fuissé La Roche Sélection Vieilles Vignes Cuvée No. 1 1994: Well crafted, with a chewy, chalky character and mineral, honey, citrus and floral notes throughout. A bit rough on the finish now, so give it until about 1997 to smooth out. 200 cases made. • $NA • (05/31/96) • **86**

GUERIN, RENE

Pouilly-Fuissé La Roche 1993: Well made and solid, medium-bodied, displaying earth, wet straw and chalk character and some attractive lemon and pear flavors. Not for everyone. Drinkable now. 292 cases made. • $20 • **83**
Pouilly-Fuissé La Roche 1992: Smooth and complete, with lemon and pear flavors accented by a hint of toasty oak, balanced by a creamy texture. • $20 • (11/15/94) • **83**
Pouilly-Fuissé La Roche Oak-aged Cuvée No. 2 1994: Tart and odd-tasting—like onions—with some citrus and herbal flavors. Lean and not for everyone. 150 cases made. • $19 • (05/31/96) • **75**
Pouilly-Fuissé La Roche Sélection Vieilles Vignes 1991 • $21 • (03/31/93) • **76**
Pouilly-Fuissé La Roche Sélection Vieilles Vignes No. 2 1994: Rich and clean, with good concentration of apricot, fig, citrus and pear flavors, along with a bitter almond note on the long, intense finish. Tart now but give it some time, try in 1997. 500 cases made. • $21 • (05/31/96) • **86**

GUERIN, THIERRY

Mâcon-Villages 1991 • $12 • (05/15/93) • **82**
Pouilly-Fuissé Clos de France 1994: Fat and rich, with a lush character. Some nice honey, herb and green apple flavors, but this medium- to full-bodied white turns a bit herbaceous on the finish. May improve by 1997. 150 cases made. • $22 • (05/31/96) • **82**
Pouilly-Fuissé Clos de France 1993: Medium in body, revealing earth, wet straw, butter and herb notes. Drinkable now. 100 cases made. • $23 • **79**
Pouilly-Fuissé La Roche 1994: Tastes a bit odd, at least at this stage, with earthy, burnt match aromas that detract from the citrus and green apple flavors. Light to medium body, lacks focus. 250 cases made. • $19 • (05/31/96) • **78**
Pouilly-Fuissé La Roche Vieilles Vignes 1994: Intense—in a word—summarizes this wine. Crisp and tart, with honeydew, pear, lemon and

mineral flavors. It's focused from start to finish. Drinkable now, or try in 1998. 250 cases made. • $22 • (05/31/96) • **85**

St.-Véran Clos des Pierres Brûlées 1994: A honeyed, sweet-tasting wine that is, in the end, pretty straightforward. Light to medium body, and delivers some earth and spice notes. But short on the finish. 833 cases made. • $13 • (05/31/96) • **79**

GUFFENS-HEYNEN

Mâcon-Pierreclos En Chavigne Cuvée Bois Neuf 1990: Ripe, generous and decidedly toasty, with a sturdy backbone of acidity to balance the ripe currant and berry flavors. A toasty, smoky edge emerges on the finish. More complex than what you might expect from a red Mâcon. Drinkable now. • $18 • (08/31/92) • **82**

Pouilly-Fuissé Clos des Petits-Croux 1994: Deliciously seductive and offering substantial concentration. Shows silky texture and a lot of complexity, hinting at toasted bread, hazelnut, ripe pear, lemon and honey. Extremely flavorful now through 1998. • $34 • (05/31/96) • **92**

Pouilly-Fuissé Clos des Petits-Croux 1992: This could pass for a little Montrachet, with its rich, ripe, powerful character. Extremely toasty and buttery, the opulent texture coating your mouth, long, fresh, citrus-flavored finish. Try after 1996. • $NA • **93**

Pouilly-Fuissé Deuxième Tri 1993: Clever winemaking here. Seductively toasty, this chiseled white unfolds its butter, mineral, pear, apple and fresh herb notes, picking up intensity on the long, lemon-flavored finish. Try after 1996. • $43 • **90**

Pouilly-Fuissé La Roche 1994: A beauty, offering the full-blown white Burgundy treatment, as tons of ripe fruit flavors are backed by toasted hazelnut, smoke, honey, lemon, spice and butter characteristics that just keep going on the long finish. Full-bodied and silky, but it's somewhat more intense than the Clos des Petits-Croux, so try in 1999. Tasted twice, with consistent notes. • $40 • (05/31/96) • **93**

GUIBON, CHÂTEAU

Bordeaux 1989 • $8 • (07/15/92) • **75**

Entre-Deux-Mers 1994: Vibrant, fetauring a core of lime, pear and herb flavors and a distinctively grassy, zingy finish. • $6 • **82**

Entre-Deux-Mers 1992 • $5 • (09/15/93) • **79**

Entre-Deux-Mers 1991 • $5 • (05/15/93) BB • **82**

GUICHARDE, DOMAINE DE LA

Côtes du Rhône 1988 • $7 • (03/15/91) BB • **84**

GUIGAL, E.

Châteauneuf-du-Pape 1990: A solid, chunky style that packs in rich currant, earth, mineral and spicy flavors into a long, full, persistent finish. A lot of win, finishing with firm tannins. Best between 1996 and 2002. 10,000 cases made. • $20 • (03/15/94) • **89**

Châteauneuf-du-Pape 1988 • $20 • (11/30/90) • **90**

Châteauneuf-du-Pape 1986 • $19 • (03/15/90) • **87**

Châteauneuf-du-Pape 1985 • $18 • (10/15/88) • **87**

Châteauneuf-du-Pape 1983 • $29 • (11/30/87) • **87**

Condrieu 1994: An enticing, floral-spicy aroma and charming pear and apricot flavors make this delicious and refreshing. Has enough body for a smooth texture and lingering, fruity finish. • $45 • (12/31/95) • **88**

Condrieu La Doriane 1994: A serious style of Viognier that smells toasty and oaky, tastes rather restrained and smoky at first, then opens up with pear, floral and vanilla flavors that linger on the finish. Should improve through 1997. • $50 • (12/31/95) • **87**

Condrieu Viognier 1992 • $35 • (04/30/94) • **89**

Condrieu Viognier 1991 • $45 • (09/30/92) • **90**

Côte-Rôtie Côtes Brune et Blonde 1991: Soft and pretty, packed with black cherry fruit, lovely now but should close soon and re-emerge for drinking now through 2003. • $35 • (11/15/95) • **88**

Key: SS—Spectator Selection. CS—Cellar Selection. BB—Best Buy. $NA—Price not available. (BT)—Barrel tasting. Ⓐ—Auction Price.
Dates in parentheses represent the issues in which the ratings were published.

Côte-Rôtie Côtes Brune et Blonde 1990: Made in a traditional style. Round and soft, with meaty, gamy, woodsy flavors. The tannins are soft, drink now or hold. Not as good as in an earlier tasting. • $214 • (11/15/95) • **88**

Côte-Rôtie Côtes Brune et Blonde 1989: Lovely flavors of black cherry, pepper and spice are well-integrated but hard tannins mute the fruit right now, robbing it of richness. Give it until 1998 to soften. • $30 • (11/15/95) • **88**

Côte-Rôtie Côtes Brune et Blonde 1988: Well-focused and harmonious, if not as big as 1989 and '90, this shows black cherry, licorice and pepper notes in a lean, firm style. Drinkable now, but better in 1997. • $151 • (11/15/95) • **89**

Côte-Rôtie Côtes Brune et Blonde 1987: Soft and spicy, with cedar, tobacco, cherry and raisin notes, this is mature now. • $28 • (11/15/95) • **84**

Côte-Rôtie Côtes Brune et Blonde 1986: An intriguing mix of firm tannins and lush fruit, with blackberry, vanilla, black pepper and spice flavors. Drinkable, but better in 1997. • $345 • (11/15/95) • **88**

Côte-Rôtie Côtes Brune et Blonde 1985 • $50 • (11/15/95) • **55**

Côte-Rôtie Côtes Brune et Blonde 1984: Fading now, this silky wine mingles raisin, brown sugar and tobacco notes. Drink up. • $28 • (11/15/95) • **79**

Côte-Rôtie Côtes Brune et Blonde 1983: Ripe, thick and tannic. The vanilla and floral aromas are still young, and the plum and sweet licorice flavors promise long development. Drinkable now, but better in 1998. • $41 • (11/15/95) • **90**

Côte-Rôtie Côtes Brune et Blonde 1982: Maturing now, this is perfumed with spice and cedar, with raisin and black pepper flavors on the palate. Drink now. • $32 • (11/15/95) • **87**

Côte-Rôtie Côtes Brune et Blonde 1980: Light and beginning to dry out, this still gives pleasure, with cherry and cedar notes. Drink now. • $40 • (11/15/95) • **81**

Côte-Rôtie Côtes Brune et Blonde 1979: A big wine, but a bit hollow. Chocolate and prunes are the main flavors, firm but short. Drink now. • $45 • (11/15/95) • **83**

Côte-Rôtie Côtes Brune et Blonde 1978: Disappointing for such a heralded vintage. The sweet cherry, cedar and spicy flavors have only a trace of dry leather, showing surprising elegance. Drink now. • $90 • (11/15/95) • **84**

Côte-Rôtie Côtes Brune et Blonde 1976: Quite rich and ripe, this is mature now, with cherry, raisin and licorice flavors. • $49 • (11/15/95) • **85**

Côte-Rôtie Côtes Brune et Blonde 1971: A strong note of rubber detracts here, and underneath are only metallic and vegetal flavors. Yet Randall Grahm loved it! • $75 • (11/15/95) • **72**

Côte-Rôtie Côtes Brune et Blonde 1969: The animal and leather notes say Syrah, but the brown sugar and mushroom flavors say drink up. Perhaps a less than perfect bottle. • $100 • (11/15/95) • **78**

Côte-Rôtie Côtes Brune et Blonde 1966: Light and beginning to dry out, yet still attractive, with spice, cedar and truffle notes. Drink now. • $125 • (11/15/95) • **83**

Côte-Rôtie Côtes Brune et Blonde 1964: On the downward track now, but still showing thick, ripe fruit, and sweet rather than dry on the finish. Drink up. (375ml). • $100 • (11/15/95) • **83**

Côte-Rôtie Côtes Brune et Blonde 1962 • $85 • (11/15/95) • **89**

Côte-Rôtie Côtes Brune et Blonde 1961: Very impressive. Still youthful in color, it offers rich plum, prune and spice flavors, with a sweet finish tinged with tobacco. Delicious, but drink soon. Made by Etienne Guigal. • $100 • (11/15/95) • **90**

Côte-Rôtie Côtes Brune et Blonde Hommage Ö Etienne Guigal 1989: A tribute to Marcel's father. Lovely vanilla and blueberry flavors are sweet and attractive, but it's tannic and a bit lean on the palate. • $NA • (11/15/95) • **85**

Côte-Rôtie Côtes Brune et Blonde La Pommiäre 1990: A special one-time bottling. Intense yet balanced, lush with oak and oozing with plum, licorice and gamy flavors. A real beauty. • $NA • (11/15/95) • **94**

Côte-Rôtie La Landonne 1991: A blockbuster. This has it all: explosive aromas of toast, coffee and plums, great concentration on the palate and plenty of oak to match the ripe fruit. The long finish echoes a smoky, gamy and chocolaty character. This is luscious, balanced and delicious now, but it should still improve for a decade or more. 700 cases made. • $150 • (11/15/95) • **97**

Côte-Rôtie La Landonne 1990: Lush and velvety, rich with the vanilla and toast flavors of new oak and a ripe blackberry and plum character. It's closed now, but big, try in 1998. 500 cases made. • $135 • (11/15/95) • **94**

Côte-Rôtie La Landonne 1989: Rich and aromatic. The ripe plum, chocolate, toast and spice flavors are concentrated and harmonious, the firm tannins promise long life. Hard now, it should begin to open in 1999. • $165 • (11/15/95) • **94**

Côte-Rôtie La Landonne 1988: Very oaky, but then, it's still very young, with sweet plum and licorice flavors that go on and on. Has the classic La Landonne tannic structure, and should be better in 1998. • $190 • (11/15/95) • **94**

Côte-Rôtie La Landonne 1987: Lighter in character than most La Landonnes, this shows plum flavors with spice and licorice accents. Drink now. • $175 • (11/15/95) • **89**

Côte-Rôtie La Landonne 1986: A big wine in a big vintage. This is meaty, with dark chocolate and plum flavors and muscular tannins. Try in 1997. • $190 (11/15/95) • **91**

Côte-Rôtie La Landonne 1985: One of the greatest northern Rhône wines ever made. Intense, concentrated and beautifully balanced, it's packed with characteristic gamy, tar, plum, spice and vanilla flavors. Luscious now, it may live forever. • $340 • (11/15/95) • **100**

Côte-Rôtie La Landonne 1984: Earthy and dry. The truffle and tobacco notes are attractive, but the prune fruit is thick and dull. Drink now. • $125 • (11/15/95) • **78**

Côte-Rôtie La Landonne 1983: Very rich, and very ripe, this is packed with tannins and flavors of plum, black pepper and game. Still needs time to harmonize, try in 2000. • $290 • (11/15/95) • **92**

Côte-Rôtie La Landonne 1982: Maturity has given this a complex earthy character of spice, coffee and prune flavors, sweet and firm. Drink now through 1998. • $225 • (11/15/95) • **88**

Côte-Rôtie La Landonne 1981: The core of plum fruit is still strong, buttressed by tobacco and earth flavors, with spice accents. Drink now through 2000. • $140 • (11/15/95) • **86**

Côte-Rôtie La Landonne 1980: Earthy and tannic, this is fresher than La Mouline, with plum and cherry flavors, but heavy and a bit coarse. Drink now through 2000. • $195 • (11/15/95) • **84**

Côte-Rôtie La Landonne 1979: Still fresh, this balanced wine marries ripe plum and fragrant spice notes. Lovely now, it should hold through 2000. • $240 • (11/15/95) • **88**

Côte-Rôtie La Landonne 1978: The first vintage of this cru shows its character but — in this bottle, anyway — not quite the class to come. Rich prune and coffee flavors are thick and sweet and very tannic. Drink now or try in 1997. • $380 • (11/15/95) • **89**

Côte-Rôtie La Mouline 1991: Beautiful oak is the dominant element here. Features plenty of spicy, chocolaty and smoky flavors and gorgeous, ripe cherry and berry notes, but lacks concentration to balance the oak. This is almost supple, with a spicy, tannic finish. 400 cases made. • $150 • (11/15/95) • **90**

Côte-Rôtie La Mouline 1990: Irresistible. This lush, concentrated wine is spilling over with gorgeous raspberry, floral, toast and smoky flavors, it's intense, lively and long. Delicious now, but better after 2000. • $180 • (11/15/95) • **98**

Côte-Rôtie La Mouline 1989: Velvety, concentrated and beautifully balanced. The raspberry fruit and vanilla oak marry seamlessly and ride effortlessly over rich tannins. An ager, try in 2000. • $160 • (11/15/95) • **95**

Côte-Rôtie La Mouline 1988: Ripe and concentrated, without being overly tannic, this seductive wine offers raspberry, cherry and vanilla flavors and a long, elegant finish. Drinkable now, but better in 1998. • $190 • (11/15/95) • **95**

Côte-Rôtie La Mouline 1987: Extraordinary effort for a difficult vintage. This is lush with toasty oak and ripe with blackberry and licorice flavors. Drink now through 2000. • $170 • (11/15/95) • **91**

Côte-Rôtie La Mouline 1986: Very firm and still young. The toasty, spicy oak flavors are in beautiful balance with the lush bery and plum notes. Delicious now, it should improve through 2000. • $200 • (11/15/95) • **94**

Côte-Rôtie La Mouline 1985: Vivid, concentrated and complete, this gorgeous wine is rich with kirsch, floral, vanilla and raspberry flavors that go on forever. Lovely now, but better after 2000. • $350 • (11/15/95) • **97**

Côte-Rôtie La Mouline 1984: Still lively, this has rich, extracted flavors of plums, berries and chocolate. Drinking well now, it should hold through 1998. • $140 • (11/15/95) • **87**

Côte-Rôtie La Mouline 1983: Concentrated and complex. The plum, black pepper and spicy Syrah flavors are backed by chocolate and vanilla notes from the oak, still coming together and headed for a long future. Try in 1998. • $290 • (11/15/95) • **93**

Côte-Rôtie La Mouline 1982: Sweet and lush, with tobacco and coffee notes and some raisin fruit over tannins that are a bit dry in the finish. Drink now. • $210 • (11/15/95) • **87**

Côte-Rôtie La Mouline 1981: Bright and balanced, this shows spicy, cedar notes along with fresh cherry fruit, with a long, graceful finish. Drink now through 2000. • $175 • (11/15/95) • **88**

Côte-Rôtie La Mouline 1980: Firm, thick and a bit dry, this offers dark flavors of chocolate and truffles. A cloudy color suggests that other bottles might be better. • $230 • (11/15/95) • **83**

Côte-Rôtie La Mouline 1979: Firm, if a bit dry, this is still generous, with flavors of roasted prunes, chocolate and spices. Drink now. • $225 • (11/15/95) • **85**

Côte-Rôtie La Mouline 1978: Corked. • $290 • (11/15/95)

Côte-Rôtie La Mouline 1977: A pleasant surprise from a weak vintage. Light yet firm, it shows gamy, spice and tobacco flavors. Drink now. • $225 • (11/15/95) • **86**

Côte-Rôtie La Mouline 1976: Thickly tannic, even a bit clumsy, this still shows abundant sweet cherry flavors and fragrant tobacco and toasty notes, with a long finish. Drink now through 1998. • $400 • (11/15/95) • **87**

Côte-Rôtie La Mouline 1975 • $NA • (03/15/90) • **75**

Côte-Rôtie La Mouline 1974: Mature and beautifully balanced, this mingles tobacco, chocolate and cherry flavors with a hint of earthiness. Drink now. • $250 • (11/15/95) • **86**

Côte-Rôtie La Mouline 1973: Still muscular, but beginning to turn to flab, this offers cedar, mushroom and light cherry fruit flavors. Drink up. • $240 • (11/15/95) • **78**

Côte-Rôtie La Mouline 1972: Controversial, a whiff of volatile acidity charmed some tasters but put off others, with its lifted cherry and brown sugar flavors. Drink up. • $NA • (11/15/95) • **75**

Côte-Rôtie La Mouline 1971: Atypically soft and light, with cedar and spicy flavors and a touch of dried cherries. Drink up. • $350 • (11/15/95) • **79**

Côte-Rôtie La Mouline 1970: Spicy, with attractive tobacco and pepper notes, but also a bit vegetal, it's beginning to fade. • $300 • (11/15/95) • **82**

Côte-Rôtie La Mouline 1969: Extraordinary life and intensity for its age. Still young in color, it offers plum, chocolate and spice flavors, round and firm. Drinking well now, it should hold through 2000. • $700 • (11/15/95) • **91**

Côte-Rôtie La Mouline 1968: Rich, ripe and mature. Chocolate, prune and coffee flavors give this wine an earthy appeal. Drink now. • $300 • (11/15/95) • **84**

Côte-Rôtie La Mouline 1967: Fully mature, this is soft yet still generous wine offers a peppery Syrah bite, with cedar, raisin and cherry notes. • $400 • (11/15/95) • **85**

Côte-Rôtie La Mouline 1966: Earthy and nutty, with some fading plum fruit, this is rather light and drying out. The first vintage for La Mouline, those who had tasted other bottles recently claimed it's better than this. • $700 • (11/15/95) • **81**

Côte-Rôtie La Turque 1991: A lush and polished wine that marries vivid fruit with plenty of new oak. This is alluring and has great concentration, balance and elegance. The ripe flavors of raspberry, smoke, black pepper, sage and licorice are complex and well integrated. Tempting now, but it will improve with bottle age, try in 1997. 300 cases made. • $150 • (11/15/95) • **93**

Côte-Rôtie La Turque 1990: Beautiful and lush. The floral, vanilla and blueberry flavors are distinctive and concentrated, if the oak is dominant now, the fruit is ripe and lively. Try in 1997. • $230 • (11/15/95) • **95**

Côte-Rôtie La Turque 1989: A bit out of character for La Turque, with meaty and tobacco notes, but still rich and spicy. The earliest-drinking of the crus in this big vintage, try now. • $170 • (11/15/95) • **91**

FRANCE

Côte-Rôtie La Turque 1988: Exotic floral and spice notes add interest to the vanilla and plum flavors, the wine is vivid and rich but the dominant flavor is oak. Try in 1997. • $250 • (11/15/95) • **92**

Côte-Rôtie La Turque 1987: Silky and sweet, the blackberry fruit is still fresh and lush, backed by toast and chocolate flavors from the oak. Lovely drinking now. • $240 • (11/15/95) • **89**

Côte-Rôtie La Turque 1986: The most delicate of the crus in this vintage, it shows lovely tobacco and floral notes, with plenty of toasty oak on the palate. Drink now through 2000. • $325 • (11/15/95) • **92**

Côte-Rôtie La Turque 1985: The first vintage of La Turque. Lush and haunting, this is vivid with blueberry, plum, vanilla and floral notes. Amazing concentration considering the vines were planted in 1981. Drink now through 2010. • $460 • (11/15/95) • **95**

Côtes du Rhône 1992: Smooth and well-structured with pleasant herbal and plum flavors. It finishes with a nice spicey note. Try now. • $11 • **83**

Côtes du Rhône 1991: A lively Rhône, with plenty of plum, cherry and spice flavors. It has good acidity to match the fruit, as well as a pleasant gameyness. Firmly textured and flavorful. Drink now. 100,000 cases made. • $10 • (10/15/94) • **85**

Côtes du Rhône 1990 • $10 • (04/15/93) • **85**

Côtes du Rhône 1989 • $12 • (08/31/92) • **85**

Côtes du Rhône 1988 • $12 • (07/15/91) • **81**

Côtes du Rhône 1986 • $9 • (02/28/90) • **84**

Côtes du Rhône 1985 • $8 • (09/30/88) • **85**

Côtes du Rhône 1984 • $7 • (12/15/87) • **84**

Côtes du Rhône 1982 • $6 • (05/01/86) • **85**

Côtes du Rhône 1981 • $5 • (05/01/84) • **86**

Côtes du Rhône 1980 • $4 • (05/01/84) • **85**

Côtes du Rhône White 1994: Vibrant, floral and elegant, featuring herbal flavors and earthy aromas, full body, good structure and length. • $11 • (09/30/95) • **84**

Côtes du Rhône White 1992 • $9 • (04/30/94) • **79**

Côtes du Rhône White 1991 • $10 • (04/15/93) • **85**

Côtes du Rhône Rosé 1994: Subtle watermelon and spicy berry aromas are followed by dried cherry and cola. Fruity, adding a touch of sweetness. • $11 • (09/30/95) • **80**

Gigondas 1991: Maturing now, this offers spicy berry and light leather flavors on a supple frame, with chocolate and floral notes on the finish. It's not complex but well-integrated. Drink now. • $16 • (11/15/95) • **83**

Gigondas 1990 • $15 • (03/15/94) • **84**

Gigondas 1988 • $15 • (03/31/91) • **85**

Gigondas 1986 • $17 • (11/30/90) • **87**

Gigondas 1985 • $17 • (09/30/88) SS • **91**

Gigondas 1984 • $15 • (11/30/87) • **86**

Gigondas 1983 • $18 • (07/31/87) • **91**

Hermitage 1990: Beautiful aromas of raspberry and cedar follow through on the lush, full palate. It's intense and well crafted, with a long, rich finish. Start drinking now. 5,000 cases made. • $35 • (05/31/94) • **93**

Hermitage 1989 • $33 • (04/15/93) • **91**

Hermitage 1988 • $41 • (12/31/91) • **83**

Hermitage 1987 • $29 • (01/31/91) • **86**

Hermitage 1986 • $34 • (02/28/90) • **92**

Hermitage 1985 • $34 • (04/15/89) • **92**

Hermitage 1983 • $34 • (04/30/87) • **87**

Hermitage 1982 • $29 • (05/01/86) • **91**

Hermitage 1980 • $50 • (09/01/84) • **91**

Hermitage 1978 • $74 • (03/15/90) • **91**

Hermitage 1976 • $60 • (03/15/90) • **80**

Hermitage 1969 • $100 • (03/15/90) • **84**

Hermitage 1966 • $100 • (03/15/90) • **90**

Hermitage 1964 • $100 • (03/15/90) • **93**

Hermitage White 1991: Ripe, smooth and generous, with spice, pear, hazelnut and vanilla notes. A complex aftertaste keeps reiterating the flavors. 3,000 cases made. • $25 • (04/30/94) • **85**

Key: SS—Spectator Selection. CS—Cellar Selection. BB—Best Buy. $NA—Price not available. (BT)—Barrel tasting. Ⓐ—Auction Price.
Dates in parentheses represent the issues in which the ratings were published.

Hermitage White 1990: Earthy and a bit funky, but solid. Has rich, cheesy pear and vanilla flavors giving it character. Has a long aftertaste. Drink now. • $27 • (09/30/92) • **81**

Rhône Hermitage 1991: A tight, tannic, unevolved red that needs time to develop. Good, deep color, lean fruit flavors, very firm tannins and a bit of a lingering finish. Try now. • $39 • (12/31/95) • **84**

Tavel 1994: A generous, dry rosé with fresh strawberry and watermelon flavors and plenty of body. Smooth and rich in texture, with a lingering finish. • $11 • (12/31/95) • **85**

GUILBAUD, HERITIERS

Muscadet de Sèvre et Maine Clos de Beauregard Sur Lie 1993: Very dry, light, modestly fruity, with some tart apple and lemon flavors. Quite tight and crisp in texture. • $8 • (11/15/95) • **79**

Muscadet de Sèvre et Maine Clos de Beauregard Sur Lie 1992: Appealing aromas of apples, butter and herbs give way to round, fresh fruit on the palate, marred just a bit by a slightly sour finish, which might not matter so much with food. • $8 • (08/31/94) • **84**

GUILLEMOT, PIERRE

Savigny-lès-Beaune Jarrons 1990: Offers plenty of good fruit flavors and tannins, but just doesn't have the concentration, length and class of its 1990 brethren. Drinkable now. 150 cases made. • $24 • (12/15/92) • **83**

Savigny-lès-Beaune Serpentières 1990: Emphasizes the fruit more than the wood, with bright cherry and raspberry notes playing nicely against a subtle, toasty background. The finish is solid, with firm tannins. Drinkable now. 375 cases made. • $24 • (12/15/92) • **89**

GUILLOT CLAUZEL, CHÂTEAU

Pomerol 1993: One of the "finds" of the vintage. Delicious dark chocolate, berry and cherry character, medium body, firm tannins and long, succulent finish. Needs time, try in 1998. • $NA • (01/31/96) • **88**

GUIRAUD, CHÂTEAU

Bordeaux White 1993: Odd, seems disjointed, a bit diluted and light, offering modest fruit. Dry Sauternes. • $12 • **73**

Bordeaux White 1992: Typical dry Sauternes, offering spicy botrytised and orange-peel aromas. Very dry and slightly harsh, yet intriguing all the same. Not everyone's glass, but interesting. • $12 • **83**

Sauternes 1992: Rich and mouth-filling, offers bitter orange marmalade flavors and a hint of tropical notes and acidity. The finish is a bit heavy. Try now. • $NA • (04/15/95) • **84**

Sauternes 1990: Stunning Sauternes displaying great balance and smooth, creamy texture. Rich and ripe, it oozes dried apricot, almond, acacia, honey and spice flavors leading to a long, vibrant finish. Try now or after 1999. • $56 • (04/15/95) • **96**

Sauternes 1989: This full-bodied Sauternes stretches the limits of botrytis. Offers loads of beeswax, almost moldy aromas, yet it is fresh and zingy with plenty of honey, spice, toast and lemon flavors. Try in 1998. • $65 • (04/15/95) • **92**

Sauternes 1988: Elegant and well made, exhibiting medium body and sweetness. Nutmeg, clove and thyme flavors play against honey, melon and oak-scented vanilla notes. Ready to drink. • $52 • (04/15/95) • **87**

Sauternes 1987 • $NA • (06/15/90) • **72**

Sauternes 1986: A fabulous, exotic blockbuster of great balance and harmony, tasting of orange slices and chocolate, honey and cream, leading to an intense finish. Tempting now but built for aging. • $48 • (04/15/95) • **93**

Sauternes 1983: Perfect to drink now, the razor-sharp focus of citrus, dried fruit and almond flavors blending with honey, marzipan and spice. Excellent intensity on the long finish. • $39 • (04/15/95) • **89**

Sauternes Le Dauphin 1987 • $11 • (12/31/89) • **72**

GUIRAUD-CHEVAL-BLANC, CHÂTEAU

Côtes de Bourg 1989 • $6 • (11/30/92) • **77**

GUITTON, JEAN

Beaune Les Sizies 1986 • $19 • (05/31/89) • **69**
Savigny-lès-Beaune Les Hauts-Jarrons 1986 • $16 • **68**
Savigny-lès-Beaune Les Peuillets 1986 • $16 • **71**

GURGUE, CHÂTEAU LA

Margaux 1995: Rich, round berry, tobacco and cherry character, medium to full body, plenty of tannins and velvety finish. Almost outstanding. • $NA • (05/15/96) • **85-89** (BT)
Margaux 1994: Lovely, subtle, well-made '94, with perfumey black currant and toasted oak flavors. Medium-bodied, sweet-tasting and delicious. Quite delicate on the finish. • $NA • (05/15/96) • **85-89** (BT)
Margaux 1993: Good concentration of fruit for the vintage, offering flavors of dried herb, plum and berry. Medium-bodied, medium tannins, fruity finish. From the owners of Château Chasse-Spleen. Better in 1998. • $21 • (01/31/96) • **85**
Margaux 1991: A lovely, silky texture and shows some refinement. Good raspberry notes, fruity, earthy aromas and flavors, followed up by a long finish. • $17 • (03/31/94) • **84**
Margaux 1990: A vivid, raffish, balanced Margaux, with sweet berry, spicy aromas and flavors, fine tannins and a lively finish. Drinkable now. 5,000 cases made. • $27 • (03/31/93) • **87**
Margaux 1989 • $30 • (03/15/92) • **92**
Margaux 1988 • $34 • (04/30/91) • **90**
Margaux 1987 • $13 • (05/15/90) • **81**
Margaux 1986 • $23 • (11/30/89) • **85**
Margaux 1985 • $19 • (02/15/88) • **90**
Margaux 1983 • $10 • (01/01/86) • **90**
Margaux 1982 • $24 • (11/30/89) • **85**

GUY, BERNARD

Côte-Rôtie 1992: Delicate and vivid berry and cherry flavors add light, smoky accents. Not a blockbuster, but subtle and elegant. Drinkable now. 1,000 cases made. • $30 • **87**
Côte-Rôtie 1990: Lighter in color and texture than most Rhônes. This is a simple wine, with straightforward strawberry and currant flavors. Finishes modestly for such a good vintage. Drinkable now. Tasted twice, with consistent notes. • $30 • (04/15/93) • **80**
Côte-Rôtie 1987 • $25 • (08/31/89) • **87**
Côte-Rôtie 1986 • $29 • (09/30/88) • **89**

GUYARD, ALAIN

Vosne-Romanée Aux Réas 1987 • $29 • (07/15/90) • **71**

GUYON, ANTONIN

Meursault Les Charmes-Dessus 1994: Like a piece of great art, carefully constructed to deliver a harmonious whole. Very focused, full in body, intense and elegant. Hold until at least 1998. Bravo! 350 cases made. • $32 • (05/31/96) • **92**
Pernand-Vergelesses 1994: A crisp, fresh, light-bodied white with a grassy, citrusy character and green apple flavors, showing real personality. Tastes almost like a Sauvignon Blanc on the clean, lingering finish. 375 cases made. • $20 • (05/31/96) • **82**

GUYOT, JEAN-CLAUDE

Pouilly-Fumé Fumé de Pouilly Sauvignon Blanc 1992: Maturing now, somewhat hollow, this offers smoke and petrol aromas, rather shy melon and herb flavors and softening acidity. • $NA • **79**
Pouilly-Fumé Les Loges 1993: The deep color and honey aroma suggest maturity, yet this is still quite firm. It offers some nice flavors without a lot of complexity. Drinkable now. • $17 • (04/30/96) • **84**

HAEGELEN-JAYER

Chambolle-Musigny 1988 • $39 • (05/15/91) • **73**
Clos de Vougeot 1993: Lots of chewy, plummy, flavorful personality here, fresh, vibrant but also full-bodied. A wine to sink your teeth into. Tannic and somewhat rustic, but who cares? Try in 1999. • $NA • **89**
Clos de Vougeot 1988 • $69 • (05/15/91) • **73**
Clos de Vougeot 1985 • $64 • (04/15/88) • **90**
Echézeaux 1988 • $61 • (08/31/91) • **67**
Nuits-St.-Georges Les Damodes 1988 • $39 • (05/15/91) • **89**

HAMELIN, THIERRY

Chablis Beauroy 1994: Polished and elegant, this lovely wine caresses the palate with its silky yet crisp texture. Very seductive, showing lemon, apple and pear flavors and a hard-to-describe earthy character. Melts in the mouth. Subtle finish, too. Drinkable now, but can age. • $NA • (05/31/96) • **89**
Chablis Vau Ligneau 1994: Delicious from start to finish. A focused beam of lemon, apple, honey and spice flavors carries this concentrated and subtle yet intense *premier cru* to a long finish. Drinkable now, but can age. • $NA • (05/31/96) • **90**

HAMM, MAISON

Brut Champagne Réserve Premier Cru NV • $22 • (12/31/91) • **90**

HANTEILLAN, CHÂTEAU

Haut-Médoc 1991: Pleasant but short on the palate. Herbal, light and lean. • $15 • (03/31/94) • **75**
Haut-Médoc 1990: Traditional-style Bordeaux, with tomato and herbal aromas and flavors and soft, round tannins. Drinkable now. 35,000 cases made. • $17 • (03/31/93) • **81**
Haut-Médoc 1989 • $14 • (03/15/92) • **77**
Haut-Médoc 1987 • $13 • (11/30/89) • **75**
Haut-Médoc 1986 • $15 • (11/30/89) • **81**
Haut-Médoc 1982 • $18 • (08/31/92) • **86**

HAURET LALANDE, DOMAINE DU

Graves White 1992: Nicely crafted pear, light oak and melon character, medium in body, fine acidity and an attractive, grassy finish. • $NA • **83**

HAUT BOMMES, CHÂTEAU

Sauternes 1987 • $NA • (06/15/90) • **74**

HAUT BRETON LARIGAUDIERE, CHÂTEAU

Margaux 1985 • $16 • (02/15/88) • **82**

HAUT DES TERRES BLANCHES, DOMAINE DU

Châteauneuf-du-Pape 1989 • $16 • (05/31/92) • **84**
Châteauneuf-du-Pape 1988 • $16 • (07/15/91) • **85**
Châteauneuf-du-Pape Réserve du Vatican 1983 • $12 • (09/30/87) • **88**

HAUT POITOU

Haut Poitou Cabernet 1986 • $6 • (10/31/88) • **79**

HAUT SARPE, CHÂTEAU

St.-Emilion 1988 • $91 • (06/30/91) • **83**
St.-Emilion 1982 • $20 • (05/15/89) • **87**
St.-Emilion 1979 • $12 Ⓐ • (04/01/84) • **78**
St.-Emilion 1970 • $30 • (05/15/93) • **89**

HAUT-BAGES-AVEROUS, CHÂTEAU

Pauillac 1995: Elegant, fine tannins and plenty of berry, cherry and spice character. • $NA • (05/15/96) • **85-89** (BT)

Pauillac 1994: Very tannic, slightly herbal character. Medium-bodied and hard. Slightly out of balance. • $NA • **75-79** (BT)
Pauillac 1993: Nicely textured blackberry and vanilla character, but green bean flavors detract from the overall quality. Second label of Château Lynch-Bages. 10,000 cases made. • $19 • (01/31/96) • **79**
Pauillac 1992: Unripe grapes lend a dill, green bean character. Second label from Château Lynch-Bages. Drink if you must. • $17 • **71**
Pauillac 1991: Some decent ripe fruit, but a bit too herbal on the finish. The second label of Château Lynch-Bages. • $16 • (03/31/94) • **79**
Pauillac 1990: Extremely well crafted, with mint, berry and cassis aromas and flavors and loads of velvety tannins. A spicy, juicy wine. Drink in 1998. • $22 • (03/31/93) • **91**
Pauillac 1989 • $26 • (03/15/92) • **90**
Pauillac 1988 • $20 • (04/30/91) • **93**
Pauillac 1987 • $15 • (11/30/89) • **85**
Pauillac 1986 • $21 • (11/30/89) • **90**
Pauillac 1985 • $17 • (04/30/88) • **82**
Pauillac 1982 • $25 • (08/31/92) • **81**
Pauillac 1979 • $18 • (10/15/89) • **84**

HAUT-BAGES-LIBERAL, CHÂTEAU

Pauillac 1995: Vivid aromas and flavors give spark to this cassis-scented, medium- to full-bodied '95. Turns slightly hard on the tannic finish. Time will tell how it develops. • $NA • (05/15/96) • **85-89** (BT)
Pauillac 1994: Extremely well made, very firm. Vivid black cherry, violet and licorice character, medium body and long finish. • $NA • **85-89** (BT)
Pauillac 1993: Lively cherry, berry and vanilla aromas and flavors, medium body, lovely tannins and long, fresh finish. Needs some time, try in 1998. • $22 • (01/31/96) • **84**
Pauillac 1992: A bit one-dimensional, but offers currant and berry character, medium body, firm tannins and short finish. Drink now. • $17 • **79**
Pauillac 1991: Supple and well-made with lovely fruity, tobacco character, medium body and fine tannins. • $17 • (03/31/94) • **84**
Pauillac 1990: Lean in texture, but definitely ripe in flavor, with berry, black currant and herb aromas and flavors cutting right through the fine tannins. Finishes solid. Drinkable now. • $22 • (06/15/93) • **83**
Pauillac 1989 • $17 Ⓐ • (03/15/92) • **89**
Pauillac 1988 • $19 Ⓐ • (03/15/91) • **88**
Pauillac 1986 • $38 Ⓐ • (05/31/89) • **91**
Pauillac 1985 • $32 • (04/30/88) • **88**
Pauillac 1984 • $19 • (06/15/87) • **67**
Pauillac 1983 • $18 • (05/01/86) • **67**
Pauillac 1959 • $55 • (10/15/90) • **85**

HAUT-BAILLY, CHÂTEAU

Graves 1985: This estate continues to produce classy, fine wines and the '85 is no different. Cherry tobacco chocolate aromas and flavors. Full bodied and very firm with wonderful tannins and long voluptuous finish. Drink or hold. • $28 • (10/15/94) • **91**
Graves 1984 • $19 • (06/15/87) • **87**
Graves 1983 • $27 • (04/16/86) • **86**
Graves 1981 • $30 • (06/01/84) • **87**
Graves 1979 • $35 • (10/15/89) • **84**
Graves 1961: Firm and fruity, with mature enough aromas and flavors to make it intriguing, but not advanced enough to indicate old age. Drink now or hold through 2005. • $44 • (04/30/96) • **88**
Graves 1945 • $200 • (03/16/86) • **94**
Pessac-Léognan 1995: Pretty, well-balanced Bordeaux offering good fruit, medium tannins and a fresh finish. • $NA • (05/15/96) • **85-89** (BT)
Pessac-Léognan 1994: Good level of fruit and firm tannins, but slightly herbal on the finish. Not as good as in earlier tastings. • $NA • (05/15/96) • **80-84** (BT)

Key: SS—Spectator Selection. CS—Cellar Selection. BB—Best Buy. $NA—Price not available. (BT)—Barrel tasting. Ⓐ—Auction Price.
Dates in parentheses represent the issues in which the ratings were published.

Pessac-Léognan 1993: This shows some potential. Medium in body, medium-silky tannins and a long cherry, chocolate and black olive aftertaste. Give it a year or two. Try in 1997. 11,917 cases made. • $30 • (01/31/96) • **86**
Pessac-Léognan 1992: Solid and well balanced, exhibiting tobacco, mineral, berry and tar aromas and flavors. Full-bodied and firm yet not aggressive. Tasted twice, with consistent notes. Delicious now but will improve. • $25 • **87**
Pessac-Léognan 1990: A solid Cabernet character, with plenty of herbal cassis character, silky tannins and a smoky finish. Drink after 1996. 11,000 cases made. • $28 • (03/31/93) • **88**
Pessac-Léognan 1989 • $28 Ⓐ • (03/15/92) • **92**
Pessac-Léognan 1988 • $35 • (04/30/91) • **94**
Pessac-Léognan 1986 • $23 • (06/15/89) • **91**
Pessac-Léognan 1983: Loads of fruit in this wine with plum, chocolate character and hint of toasted oak. Full-bodied but still shows a very refined tannin structure. Drink now but better after 1997. • $27 • **91**
Pessac-Léognan 1982: Rather traditional styled for this estate. Medium red with a garnet hue it shows chestnut, berry aromas and flavors but an underlying freshness of cherry, fruit character. Drink now. • $42 • **84**
Pessac-Léognan 1981: This wine is very harmonious and subtle with attractive leathery, spice, cedar character, medium body and a delicate, fruity finish. Drink now. • $30 • **87**

HAUT-BATAILLEY, CHÂTEAU

Pauillac 1993: Attractive black cherry and currant aromas and flavors, medium body, firm tannins and a slightly simple finish. Drinkable now. • $23 • (01/31/96) • **84**
Pauillac 1992: Sleek, well-made Bordeaux offering cherry, plum and raspberry aromas and flavors, medium body, fine tannins and a medium finish. Drink now. • $17 • **80**
Pauillac 1991: Light and slightly weedy but some pleasant berry fruit character and a light smoky finish. • $17 • (03/31/94) • **79**
Pauillac 1990: Weak for the vintage. What happened? 7,500 cases made. • $23 • (03/31/93) • **84**
Pauillac 1989 • $26 • (03/15/92) • **87**
Pauillac 1988 • $19 Ⓐ • (08/31/91) • **87**
Pauillac 1987 • $17 • (05/15/90) • **86**
Pauillac 1986 • $23 • (05/31/89) • **85**
Pauillac 1985 • $24 • (11/30/88) • **81**
Pauillac 1983: Big, lumbering wine. Thick and full with rich coffee, prune, chestnut aromas and flavors. Full bodied and rather fat with round tannins and a soft finish. Drink now. • $NA • **85**
Pauillac 1982 • $45 Ⓐ • (08/31/92) • **93**
Pauillac 1981: Elegant and crisp with pretty aromatic cedar, tobacco, cassis character in a firm and solid package of ripe fruit. Drink now or hold. • $NA • **87**
Pauillac 1979 • $28 • (10/15/89) • **82**
Pauillac 1970 • $34 Ⓐ • (05/15/93) • **88**
Pauillac 1961: This tastes broad, ripe and mature, with meaty, herbal flavors, a seductively soft texture and long finish. Drink now through 2000. • $52 • (04/30/96) • **87**

HAUT-BEAUSEJOUR, CHÂTEAU

St.-Estèphe 1995: Rich and full-bodied, as plenty of ripe tannins and chewy character make this a mouthful. Offers substantial earth, mocha, mineral, berry and floral complexity. Somewhat austere on the finish now. • $15 • (05/15/96) • **85-89** (BT)

HAUT-BERGERON, CHÂTEAU

Sauternes 1992: Absolutely delicious, exhibiting loads of honey, spice and dried apricot character, full-bodied, sweet and very rich. Drinkable now. • $NA • (04/15/95) • **87**
Sauternes 1991: Already past its peak, but offers some decent dried-fruit, apricot and coconut character, full-bodied texture and a slightly dry and short finish. Drinkable now. • $NA • (04/15/95) • **83**
Sauternes 1990: A real star, exploding orange-peel, spice, dried apricot and honey flavors. Despite its rich, unctuous character, balance is

impeccable, the long, cleansing finish going on forever. Try now. • $NA • (04/15/95) • **93**

Sauternes 1989: Big, powerful and rich, full-bodied, loads of sweet, thick honey character. Very spicy, leading to a honey and raisin finish. Drinkable now. • $NA • (04/15/95) • **90**

Sauternes 1988: Rather lean and austere, showing some interesting honey, spice, woody character. Disappointing. Sweet but slightly flat finish. • $NA • (04/15/95) • **79**

Sauternes 1987 • $NA • (06/15/90) • **81**

Sauternes 1986 • $NA • (04/15/95) • **92**

HAUT-BERNAT, CHÂTEAU

Puisseguin-St.-Emilion Vieilli en Fûts de Chêne Red 1992: Tastes like a decent Côtes du Rhône. Fruity, gamy, earthy, tomato character, medium in body and round. Drink now. • $NA • **79**

HAUT-BRION, CHÂTEAU

Graves 1985: Back on form with the '85 after a slightly less grand '83, this is a gorgeous, harmonious wine. Beautiful ripe fruit, tobacco aromas and flavors. Full bodied and velvety with a fine rich finish. Try after 1998. • $80 • (10/15/94) • **95**

Graves 1984 • $53 • (07/31/87) • **80**

Graves 1983: Wonderful to drink now with rich, already mature character. This wine is flavor intensive with decadent character of lead pencil, tobacco, chocolate and mint. Very fine tannins. Drink now. • $86 • (10/15/94) • **88**

Graves 1982 • $120 • (08/31/92) • **99**

Graves 1981: The smoke and menthol aromas are attractive, but the wine flattens out on the palate, with gripping tannins and cooked, vegetal flavors. The finish is short. It's distinctive, but beginning to stagger. Tasted many times. • $NA • (10/15/94) • **82**

Graves 1979 • $95 • (11/15/91) • **92**

Graves 1978 • $105 • (11/15/91) • **96**

Graves 1975 • $110 • (11/15/91) • **92**

Graves 1974 • $37 • (11/15/91) • **74**

Graves 1971 • $130 • (11/15/91) • **85**

Graves 1970 • $NA • (05/15/93) • **93**

Graves 1966 • $190 • (11/15/91) • **94**

Graves 1962 • $160 • (11/15/91) • **93**

Graves 1961: A stunning vintage for Haut-Brion, giving a dazzling combination of perfect ripeness and maturity in flavor. It has concentration, depth, complexity and a mouth-filling but lively texture. The flavors are exotic without becoming extreme, evoking chocolate, pepper, ripe fruit and tobacco. Difficult to imagine it getting much better, but there's no hurry, either. Drink through 2010. • $442 • (04/30/96) • **97**

Graves 1959 • $430 • (11/15/91) • **98**

Graves 1949 • $550 • (11/15/91) • **95**

Graves 1945 • $850 • (11/15/91) • **99**

Pessac-Léognan 1995: An elegant wine of great finesse. A complex Haut-Brion that has wonderfully silky tannins and a long, caressing finish. Medium to full body, with lots of sweet fruit in the aftertaste. • $NA • (05/15/96) • **90-94** (BT)

Pessac-Léognan 1994: Fine and elegant, with lovely fruit character. Full-bodied and very fine, showing hints of tobacco, chocolate, mushroom—you name it, it's there. Perhaps even better than the 1995. • $80 • (05/15/96) • **90-94** (BT)

Pessac-Léognan 1993: Fabulous for the vintage. Wonderful aromas of violet, ripe fruit and toasted oak. Medium- to full-bodied, boasting loads of raspberry and vanilla flavors, medium tannins and a long, succulent finish. Better in 1998. • $72 • (01/31/96) • **91**

Pessac-Léognan 1992: Refined and delicious, offering mineral, berry, cherry and toasted oak flavors, medium-to-light body, fine tannins and a long finish. Drink now. • $60 • **87**

Pessac-Léognan 1991: Well-crafted, complex wine with classy use of oak, ripe fruit and a silky texture. Beautiful to drink now. • $65 • (03/31/94) • **87**

Pessac-Léognan 1990: The essence of Graves, with great concentration but no rough edges. The fruit and tannins are rich yet fully integrated, and the tobacco and cedar notes are classic for this estate. Drink after 2000. 12,000 cases made. • $76 • (04/30/93) • **96**

Pessac-Léognan 1989 • $135 • (03/15/92) • **97**

Pessac-Léognan 1987 • $48 • (10/15/90) • **90**

Pessac-Léognan 1986 • $78 • (06/30/89) • **92**

Pessac-Léognan White 1994: A ripe, rich, full-bodied white that has lots of character and offers plenty of honey, nutmeg and spice flavors that don't quit on the toasty finish. Almost more like a *grand cru* white Burgundy than a Pessac-Léognan. Delicious now, but will improve through at least 1999. 500 cases made. • $250 • (03/31/96) • **96**

Pessac-Léognan White 1993: As complex as a great Puligny-Montrachet, boasting toasty, honey flavors coming in waves and a flawless texture, round, smooth and velvety. You want to drink and enjoy this one now, but it should improve with age. • $55 • (05/31/95) • **92**

Pessac-Léognan White 1992: Still somewhat young and wild, but exhibiting very, very good aromas of coconut, lime and tropical fruit, medium body and high acidity, the ripe flavors come through. • $65 • (05/31/95) • **88**

HAUT-CADET, CHÂTEAU

St.-Emilion 1981 • $6 • (04/01/85) • **73**

HAUT-COLAS NOUET, CHÂTEAU

Bordeaux Supérieur 1985 • $4 • (11/15/87) • **71**

HAUT-CORBIN, CHÂTEAU

St.-Emilion 1995: Very fine indeed. Medium body, refined tannins and well-focused berry, cherry and mineral character. • $NA • (05/15/96) • **85-89** (BT)

St.-Emilion 1994: Good fruit and concentration, displaying velvety texture, medium body, firm tannins and a medium finish. • $NA • **85-89** (BT)

St.-Emilion 1991: A bit weedy and stewed, but some sweet fruit shows through. Medium body and astringent finish. • $16 • (03/31/94) • **76**

St.-Emilion 1990: A gorgeous wine with a beautiful mix of exotic fruit and earth flavors on the nose and palate. The tannins are fine and well proportioned. Drinkable now. 2,500 cases made. • $18 • (03/31/93) • **91**

St.-Emilion 1989 • $26 • (03/15/92) • **89**

HAUT-COUTELIN, CHÂTEAU

St.-Estèphe 1982 • $13 • (02/15/88) • **81**

HAUT-FAUGERES, CHÂTEAU

St.-Emilion 1988 • $17 • (04/30/92) • **84**

HAUT-GARDERE, CHÂTEAU

Graves 1985 • $15 • (07/31/88) • **77**

Pessac-Léognan 1995: Firm, fruity earth and berry character, firm tannins and medium, slightly austere finish. • $NA • (05/15/96) • **80-84** (BT)

Pessac-Léognan 1986 • $11 • (09/30/89) • **81**

HAUT-LAGRANGE, CHÂTEAU

Pessac-Léognan 1995: Firm and fruity, showing solid backbone of tannins and steely finish. Somewhat closed. Wait and see. • $NA • (05/15/96) • **85-89** (BT)

Pessac-Léognan 1994: Round and soft, revealing some decent fruit, quite light-structured, yet tannic. Might move up a quality notch later. • $NA • **75-79** (BT)

Pessac-Léognan 1993: Rather simple tobacco, slightly herbal, fruity aromas, medium to light body, light tannins and short finish. Drinkable now. 2,166 cases made. • $17 • (01/31/96) • **81**

Pessac-Léognan 1992: A mouthful but rather herbal, displaying medium-to-full body, medium tannins and a flavorful tobacco, cherry and bell pepper finish. • $14 • **81**

Pessac-Léognan 1991: Very silky and caressing wine. Cherry, strawberry aromas and flavors and fine tannins. • $14 • (03/31/94) • **83**

Pessac-Léognan White 1994: A subtle, medium-bodied white with grapefruit, mineral and spice character, even showing a grassy side. Delicious finish. Has some finesse. • $NA • (03/31/96) • **85**

Pessac-Léognan White 1993: Attractive mineral, light flinty, vanilla character, medium-bodied and slightly one-dimensional. • $NA • **83**

Pessac-Léognan White 1992: Subtle and refined vanilla, honey, pear and floral aromas and flavors. Medium-bodied, similar character on the palate. Drinkable now. • $NA • **84**

HAUT-MAILLET, CHÂTEAU

Pomerol 1990: A pretty wine, with lovely berry and chocolate aromas and flavors, medium tannins and a flavorful, fruity, cedary finish. Drinkable now. • $25 • (03/31/93) • **88**

HAUT-MALLET, CHÂTEAU

Bordeaux Supérieur 1987 • $7 • (04/15/90) • **76**

HAUT-MARBUZET, CHÂTEAU

St.-Estèphe 1995: Exuberant and perfumed, featuring rose petal, cassis and earth character, medium body, smooth tannins and long, tightly knit, chewy finish. • $NA • (05/15/96) • **85-89** (BT)

St.-Estèphe 1994: Beautiful chocolate, berry and vanilla aromas and flavors. Medium-bodied, soft tannins and a sweet fruit finish. • $NA • **85-89** (BT)

St.-Estèphe 1993: Delicious fresh cherry, berry and vanilla aromas and flavors, medium body and round tannins. Drinkable now. 23,077 cases made. • $33 • (01/31/96) • **85**

St.-Estèphe 1992: Currant, thyme and vanilla flavors, medium body, fine tannins and a delicate finish. Drink now. • $17 • **83**

St.-Estèphe 1991: Pleasing and supple, with a spicy, vanilla and fruit character, medium body and a soft finish. • $16 • (03/31/94) • **84**

St.-Estèphe 1990: An extremely pretty, perfumed wine with velvety tannins and rich spicy, blueberry flavors. Not a huge wine, but it's gorgeous. Drink after 1997. 18,500 cases made. • $32 • (03/31/93) • **92**

St.-Estèphe 1989 • $35 Ⓐ • (03/15/92) • **90**

St.-Estèphe 1988 • $32 • (12/31/90) • **91**

St.-Estèphe 1987 • $20 • (05/15/90) • **85**

St.-Estèphe 1986 • $31 • (11/30/89) • **92**

St.-Estèphe 1985: Drinking beautifully now with loads of new wood but delicious and round with plummy, tobacco, chocolate character. Drink now or hold. • $26 • (10/15/94) • **88**

St.-Estèphe 1983: A wonderful glass of wine with a palate full of fruit and sophisticated wood character. Full bodied and rich with super soft tannins and an array of cedar, tobacco, licorice, ripe fruit character. Drink now or hold. • $25 • (10/15/94) • **90**

St.-Estèphe 1982 • $59 Ⓐ • (08/31/92) • **90**

St.-Estèphe 1981: This wine shows great clarity in fruit character. Elegant and fine with solid fruit and fine tannins. Excellent winemaking. Drink or hold. • $24 • (10/15/94) • **90**

St.-Estèphe 1979 • $30 • (10/15/89) • **85**

St.-Estèphe 1962 • $50 • (11/30/87) • **70**

St.-Estèphe English Bottled 1959 • $60 • (10/15/90) • **83**

HAUT-MAZIERES, CHÂTEAU

Bordeaux 1993: Attractive berry and spicy aromas give way to fresh fruit flavors backed by a pleasant toasty accent. It's light but balanced and firm enough for food. • $9 • (12/15/95) • **83**

Bordeaux 1990: Ripe fruit and judicious use of oak make for chewy concentration and age-worthiness. It's firm and a bit austere now, but balanced and fresh: a mini-Pauillac. Good value. Drinkable now. 6,250 cases made. • $10 • (11/15/94) • **87**

Bordeaux White 1993: If you like the spice that new oak adds, you'll like this very aromatic, very high-profile and interesting white wine. It has solid fig and mango flavors and good balance. Drink through 1997. • $10 • (02/29/96) • **87**

Bordeaux White 1991: A very good wine from an off vintage. Clean, balanced, complex and developing an intriguing maturity. It blends toast, fig, coconut and pineapple flavors in a harmonious mix that lingers long on the finish. Keeps you coming back for more. 1,250 cases made. • $10 • (11/15/94) • **89**

HAUT-NOUCHET, CHÂTEAU

Pessac-Léognan 1994: Light, herbaceous and disappointing, diluted finish. • $NA • **70-74** (BT)

Pessac-Léognan 1993: Rather light, offering some dried cherry and berry character and a hint of herbs. Light-bodied, light tannins and short finish. Drinkable now. • $NA • (01/31/96) • **78**

Pessac-Léognan White 1994: Interesting almond, spice and grapefruit notes set up in a medium-bodied style with moderate acidity and a fruity finish. • $NA • (03/31/96) • **85**

Pessac-Léognan White 1993: Attractive dried apricot and honey aromas and flavors. Nice body, acidity and finish to round it all out. • $NA • (03/31/96) • **83**

HAUT-REDON, CHÂTEAU

Bordeaux 1994: Bordeaux flavors and Beaujolais structure. The fresh plum and grape flavors have herbal and smoky accents. 4,000 cases made. • $9 • (12/15/95) • **83**

HAUT-RIAN, CHÂTEAU

Entre-Deux-Mers 1994: Super-fresh apple and pear character, light-to-medium body and a spritzy, delicate finish. • $8 • **80**

Entre-Deux-Mers 1993: Satisfying, zesty white offering a hint of complexity, melon, lemon and honey flavors and light-to-medium body. • $8 • **80**

Premières Côtes de Bordeaux 1988 • $7 • (05/15/90) • **81**

HAUTE GALINE, DOMAINE

Minervois 1991 • $7 • (03/15/94) • **83**

HAUTERIVE LE HAUT, CHÂTEAU

Corbières 1993: Pretty black cherry flavors are spiced by cinnamon and orange peel accents in this soft, attractive red. Not big, but it has a distinctive personality. Drink now. • $10 • (10/31/95) • **85**

Corbières 1990 • $10 • (03/15/94) • **88**

HAUTS DE BRAME, CHÂTEAU LES

St.-Estèphe 1986 • $22 • (03/31/91) • **80**

HAUTS DE SMITH

Pessac-Léognan 1993: Some attractive black cherry and berry character but slightly diluted in the mid-palate. Medium to light in body, light tannins and rather short finish. Drinkable now. • $NA • (01/31/96) • **79**

Pessac-Léognan White 1994: Lovely richness of fruit in this one. Medium to full on the palate, with tropical fruit, vanilla and citrus flavors. Fine acidity and long on the finish. Drinkable now, but can age. • $NA • (03/31/96) • **89**

HAUTS-CONSEILLANTS, CHÂTEAU LES

Lalande-de-Pomerol 1993: Spice, tobacco and plum flavors give this appeal and balance; firm tannins lend structure. Drinkable now. • $19 • (12/15/95) • **84**

Key: SS—Spectator Selection. CS—Cellar Selection. BB—Best Buy. $NA—Price not available. (BT)—Barrel tasting. Ⓐ—Auction Price.
Dates in parentheses represent the issues in which the ratings were published.

FRANCE

HAUX, CHÂTEAU DE

Bordeaux White 1994: An unusual but appealing white Bordeaux that's bright and fragrant, with honey, vanilla and apricot flavors and plenty of richness. 4,166 cases made. • $10 • (02/29/96) • **84**

HEIDSIECK, CHARLES

Brut Blanc de Blancs Champagne NV • $33 • (12/31/90) • **84**
Brut Blanc de Blancs Champagne Brut de Chardonnay 1981 • $30 • (05/31/87) • **78**
Brut Champagne 1985: This continues to be a winner after we tasted it in fall '90. A big and flamboyant Champagne with lots of character. Full-bodied with very toasted smoke and fruity character but fresh acidity. Excellent food Champagne or for at the end of a meal. Drink now. • $35 • (12/31/93) • **91**
Brut Champagne 1983: A Champagne with uncommon character, this mature wine is round, creamy and generous on the palate, with all sorts of honey, toast and earth aromas and flavors. A rich, full-bodied, heady style of Champagne. • $41 • (03/31/91) • **90**
Brut Champagne 1982: Powerful, rich and memorable. Extremely intense with toasty, smoky and nutty (walnuts come to mind) flavors. Long, yeasty finish that is wonderful. A surprisingly fine Champagne at half the price of the prestige cuvées. • $40 • (12/31/88) • **93**
Brut Champagne Blanc des Millénaires 1983: A beautifully rich, creamy, expansive Champagne with abundant pear and apple flavors accented by vanilla and toast. This is a great example of a vintage Champagne at its peak: mature but still lively, generous and long on the finish. 3,000 cases made. • $55 • (12/31/95) • **92**
Brut Champagne Millésime 1983: Beautiful flavors of rich, toasty, pear, apple and spice, with a fine structure that keeps the flavors lingering on the finish. An impressive package that's ready to drink now. • $38 • (12/31/89) • **87**
Brut Champagne Réserve NV: A big, full-bodied, rich style of Champagne that starts with powerfully toasty, mature aromas and follows with broad flavors of baked apples and vanilla, a light but rich texture and a lingering, creamy finish. • $37 • (12/31/95) • **91**
Brut Rosé Champagne 1985: Rich, satisfying, smooth and subtle, with mouth-filling flavors of apple and pear, accented by vanilla and spice, balanced with its creamy, broad texture. 33,345 cases made. • $40 • (12/15/94) • **89**
Brut Rosé Champagne 1983: Pale, delicate and creamy in texture, with lots of toasty overtones to the modest berry and vanilla aromas and flavors. Smooth and flavorful without sacrificing delicacy. • $49 • (03/31/91) • **89**
Brut Rosé Champagne 1982: Hangs together wonderfully well. Prominent Pinot Noir character mingles nicely with toasty, assertive and crisp flavors. Balanced, complex, lush and clean. • $40 • (12/31/88) • **91**
Brut Rosé Champagne 1976 • $25 • (12/16/85) • **61**

HEIDSIECK MONOPOLE

Brut Champagne Diamant Bleu 1985: So smooth, so fine, it's a joy to drink. There are layers of tropical fruit, smoke and coconut with medium body and firm acidity. Drink now. • $85 • (12/31/93) • **92**
Brut Champagne Diamant Bleu 1982 • $70 • (11/30/87) • **89**
Brut Champagne Diamant Bleu 1979 • $39 • (05/16/86) • **93**
Brut Champagne Diamant Rosé 1982 • $85 • (11/30/87) • **90**
Brut Champagne Dry Monopole 1985 • $NA • (12/31/90) • **90**
Brut Champagne Dry Monopole 1982 • $43 • (12/31/88) • **88**
Brut Champagne Dry Monopole NV • $31 • (12/31/91) • **82**
Brut Rosé Champagne 1983: Dry and cherryish, but lacks the richness and texture one expects from a Rosé Champagne, leaving it coarse and simple. • $40 • (12/31/89) • **75**
Brut Rosé Champagne 1982: Good balance with distinctive earthy style. Meaty flavors with hint of cherries. Crisp finish. • $43 • (12/31/88) • **84**
Brut Rosé Champagne 1979 • $27 • (12/16/85) • **72**
Extra Dry Champagne NV • $38 • (11/30/92) • **82**

HELENE, CHÂTEAU

Corbières Cuvée Tradition 1990 • $7 • (03/15/94) • **83**

HENRI DE GRAMEY

Brut Saumur NV: Clean and simple, offering modest fig, honey and apple notes. A bit soft, but flavorful and easy to drink. 50,000 cases made. • $10 • (04/30/96) • **80**

HENRIOT

Brut Blanc de Blancs Champagne de Chardonnay NV • $NA • (12/31/90) • **85**
Brut Champagne 1988: This is really expressive with distinctive raspberry and cream aromas and flavors, medium body and acidity and a flavorful finish. Drink now. • $39 • (12/31/93) • **88**
Brut Champagne Cuvée Baccarat 1983: You can't not like the intense toasty, apple character in this one. It's got very good acidity, slight tannin pucker, and rich fruit. • $NA • (12/31/93) • **88**
Brut Champagne Cuvée du Soleil NV • $27 • (12/31/87) • **70**
Brut Champagne NV • $21 • (07/01/86) • **86**
Brut Champagne Souverain NV • $40 • (12/31/91) • **86**
Brut Rosé Champagne 1981 • $28 • (07/01/86) • **93**

HER, DOMAINE MORIN

Chinon 1986 • $7 • (12/31/88) • **78**

HERARD, PHILIPPE

Brut Blanc de Blancs NV • $9 • (06/15/90) • **74**

HERBEAUX, CHÂTEAU DES

Chambertin 1990: Rich, ripe and concentrated without losing a sense of lightness and deftness, melding the spicy, toasty nuances of oak with a supple beam of blackberry, currant and black cherry flavors. Showing a lot of complexity already, but should be fine through 1997. • $75 • (02/15/93) • **89**
Chambertin 1988 • $75 • (12/31/90) • **87**
Clos Vougeot 1988 • $65 • (11/30/90) • **86**
Musigny 1988 • $75 • (12/31/90) • **83**
Volnay Santenots 1988 • $36 • (11/30/90) • **88**

HERESZTYN-BAILLY, R.

Gevrey-Chambertin 1986 • $20 • (07/15/89) • **86**
Gevrey-Chambertin Les Goulots 1986 • $28 • (10/15/89) • **82**

HERESZTYN, BERNARD

Gevrey-Chambertin Les Goulots 1988 • $44 • (07/15/91) • **90**

HERESZTYN, STANISLAS

Gevrey-Chambertin 1987 • $25 • (03/31/90) • **83**
Gevrey-Chambertin Les Champonnets 1988 • $37 • (12/31/90) • **82**

HERITIER-GUYOT, L'

Auxey-Duresses 1994: An odd wine that has a perfumey, floral, butterscotch character that is somewhat balanced by a nice chewy, chalky texture and mineral notes. It turns rather lean on the finish, though. 125 cases made. • $18 • (05/31/96) 80 • **80**
Bourgogne 1994: Some modest fruit flavors, but mostly quite tart and lean. 300 cases made. • $12 • (05/31/96) • **77**
Chambolle-Musigny 1993: Diluted and light, tasting like it was cut with water, showing a filter-pad, cardboard flavor on the finish. Drink if you must. • $30 • **74**

Chassagne-Montrachet 1994: It's Burgundian, with a toasty, honeyed complexity, but it lacks fruit concentration. Short and a bit diluted despite the full body and texture. Tastes a little candied on the finish. 125 cases made. • $28 • (05/31/96) 79 • **80**

Clos de Vougeot 1993: Rather lean and hard, showing game, leather and fruit aromas and flavors, medium body and tough tannins. Better in 1999? • $35 • **84**

Clos de Vougeot 1988 • $51 • (03/15/93) • **76**

Corton Les Renardes 1993: Rather straightforward plum, berry and light cedar character, medium body, light tannins and a fresh finish. • $60 • **86**

Côte de Nuits-Villages 1993: Rather firm, tannic and quite dry, medium-bodied. Hopefully currant and black cherry flavors will balance tannins in the future. Try in 1999. • $15 • **83**

Gevrey-Chambertin Les Cazetiers 1993: Tannic and structured on the palate, featuring a good core of red berry flavor. Quite tasty and ripe, medium-bodied, rather hard at this stage. Try in 1998. • $45 • **84**

Hautes Côtes de Nuits 1994: Very fresh and intense, with a nice lemony, zesty character. Some green apple, grapefruit and dried herb flavors and somewhat short on the finish. 551 cases made. • $13 • (05/31/96) • **79**

St.-Romain 1994: A sharp, vibrant, assertive white that tastes like a delicious Sauvignon Blanc—a bit grassy and herbal, with a tangy note on the long, fruity, lively finish. 175 cases made. • $16 • (05/31/96) • **86**

Vougeot Clos Blanc de Vougeot 1994: Very pretty and nicely balanced, with apricot, floral, honey and lemon notes. Focused on the clean, fresh finish. A lively wine to enjoy now through 1998. 786 cases made. • $40 • (05/31/96) • **89**

Vougeot Les Cras 1er 1993: Lean and tannic with some fruit, but it's hot and burning on the palate. Out of balance. Drink if you must. • $35 • **77**

HERMITAGE, CHÂTEAU

Pomerol 1982 • $NA • (05/15/89) • **83**

HERMITE, DOMAINE DE L'

Hermitage 1983 • $9 • (05/01/86) • **88**
Hermitage 1980 • $13 • (05/01/86) • **84**

HERRICK, JAMES

Chardonnay Vin de Pays d'Oc 1992 • $NA • (03/15/94) • **86**

HERZOG

Cabernet Sauvignon Vin de Pays d'Oc 1988 • $6 • (03/15/90) • **67**
Cabernet Sauvignon Vin de Pays d'Oc NV • $7 • (03/31/91) • **88**
Merlot Vin de Pays d'Oc NV • $7 • (03/31/91) • **75**

HEZ, CLOS DU

Graves White 1992: Simple, sour and difficult to like, yielding modest citrus and artichoke flavors. • $NA • **73**

HORTE, CHÂTEAU DE L'

Corbières Réserve Spéciale 1991 • $9 • (03/15/94) • **83**

HORTUS, DOMAINE DE L'

Coteaux du Languedoc 1991 • $8 • (03/15/94) • **83**

Key: SS—Spectator Selection. CS—Cellar Selection. BB—Best Buy. $NA—Price not available. (BT)—Barrel tasting. Ⓐ—Auction Price.
Dates in parentheses represent the issues in which the ratings were published.

HUET, S.A.

Vouvray Clos du Bourg Sec 1993: A wine with good intensity and verve. Clean and crisp, it has rich flavors of melon and tangerine that linger on the finish. Not complex but delightful drinking. • $18 • **85**

HUGEL

Alsace Gentil Hugel 1993: A spicy, floral-tasting white that's exuberant and fresh, quite dry and refreshing. Solid, flavorful and interesting. • $10 • (11/15/94) • **86**

Alsace Gentil Hugel 1992: A subtly flavored white wine with an appealing richness of texture. It's smooth and broad, with light apple flavors and a good finish. • $9 • (11/15/94) • **83**

Gewürztraminer Alsace White 1992: A lighter style with pretty floral aromas and bright, peachy flavors. • $15 • (11/15/94) • **84**

Pinot Blanc Alsace Cuvée Les Amours White 1991: A modestly proportioned wine that is smooth, light, and showing herbal and appley flavors. • $11 • (11/15/94) • **79**

Pinot Noir Alsace Jubilée Réserve Personnelle 1990: Solid-quality, medium-bodied Pinot Noir that's soft in tannins and flavored with cherry, bacon and smoke. Comparable to a dry Beaujolais or village wine from the Côte de Beaune. • $29 • (11/15/94) • **81**

INSTITUT PASTEUR, DOMAINE DE L'

Côte de Brouilly 1988 • $10 • (05/31/89) • **84**

ISSAN, CHÂTEAU D'

Margaux 1995: Rich and round, sporting delicious wild berry and chocolate aromas and flavors. Full-bodied, plenty of round tannins and long finish. Unctuous. • $NA • (05/15/96) • **90-94** (BT)

Margaux 1994: Very fine and elegant for the vintage, featuring berry, cherry and a hint of vanilla. Light finish. • $NA • (05/15/96) • **80-84** (BT)

Margaux 1993: Nicely made, smooth, showing anise, currant and black cherry character. Enjoy now, but it lacks some length on the finish. • $25 • (01/31/96) • **83**

Margaux 1990: Impressive concentration but lacks finesse. A big, burly wine, with prune, raisin and earth character, rich, round tannins and a long finish. Wait and see, drinkable in 1998. 12,000 cases made. • $19 • (03/31/93) • **86**

Margaux 1989 • $34 • (03/15/92) • **84**
Margaux 1988 • $22 Ⓐ • (04/30/91) • **88**
Margaux 1987 • $20 • (05/15/90) • **76**
Margaux 1986 • $25 Ⓐ • (06/15/89) • **83**
Margaux 1985 • $28 Ⓐ • (04/15/88) • **88**
Margaux 1984 • $19 • (03/31/87) • **86**
Margaux 1983 • $31 Ⓐ • (04/16/86) • **91**
Margaux 1982 • $27 Ⓐ • (08/31/92) • **88**

JABOULET AINE, PAUL

Châteauneuf-du-Pape 1983 • $10 • (10/15/91) • **85**

Châteauneuf-du-Pape Les Cèdres 1990: Big and oaky, with layers of rich chocolate, oak and currant flavors seasoned by hints of spice. Drink after 1997. • $63 Ⓐ • (08/31/92) • **87**

Châteauneuf-du-Pape Les Cèdres 1989 • $36 Ⓐ • (10/15/91) • **88**
Châteauneuf-du-Pape Les Cèdres 1988 • $13 Ⓐ • (10/15/91) • **86**
Châteauneuf-du-Pape Les Cèdres 1986 • $17 Ⓐ • (10/15/91) • **87**
Châteauneuf-du-Pape Les Cèdres 1985 • $34 Ⓐ • (10/15/91) • **88**
Châteauneuf-du-Pape Les Cèdres 1981 • $NA • (10/15/91) • **86**
Cornas 1990 • $29 • (11/30/92) • **82**

Côte-Rôtie Les Jumelles 1991: Not a blockbuster, but pretty, with subtle berry, game and licorice flavors, balanced and soft. Drinkable now. • $35 • (05/31/94) • **86**

Côte-Rôtie Les Jumelles 1989 • $38 • (02/28/93) • **81**
Côte-Rôtie Les Jumelles 1985 • $35 • (09/30/88) • **93**

Côtes du Rhône Parallèle 1993: A full-bodied, deep-flavored, sturdy Rhône with ample blackberry, pepper and smoke flavors. It's tannic and dry, but best to drink soon. • $9 • **83**

Côtes du Rhône Parallèle 45 1992 • $9 • (04/30/94) • **83**

Côtes du Rhône Parallèle 45 1990 • $9 • (08/31/92) • **88**
Côtes du Rhône Parallèle 45 1988 • $6 • (12/15/89) • **84**
Côtes du Rhône Parallèle 45 1985 • $6 • (04/30/88) • **73**
Côtes du Ventoux 1993: Earthy and leathery, including a wallop of tannin as well. Full-bodied, rich plum and chocolate flavors, needs some time to smoothen. • $7 • (09/30/95) • **85**
Côtes du Ventoux 1990 • $18 • (04/15/93) • **82**
Crozes-Hermitage Domaine de Thalabert 1992: Jammy blackberry flavor and sweet, toasty oak give this red immediate appeal and a character reminiscent of Australian Shiraz. Drinkable now. • $22 • **85**
Crozes-Hermitage Domaine de Thalabert 1991 • $16 • (05/31/94) • **88**
Crozes-Hermitage Domaine de Thalabert 1989 • $18 • (07/15/91) • **90**
Crozes-Hermitage Domaine de Thalabert 1988 • $15 • (10/15/90) • **83**
Crozes-Hermitage Domaine de Thalabert 1987 • $10 • (03/31/90) • **83**
Crozes-Hermitage Domaine de Thalabert 1986 • $16 • (09/30/88) • **88**
Crozes-Hermitage Domaine de Thalabert 1985 • $22 • (09/30/88) • **85**
Crozes-Hermitage Les Jalets 1992: Pretty blackberry is the dominant note here, adding light, earthy accents and moderate tannins. It's clean and balanced. Drink now. • $14 • **84**
Crozes-Hermitage Les Jalets 1990 • $14 • (03/31/94) • **88**
Crozes-Hermitage Mule White 1991 • $15 • (11/30/92) • **86**
Gigondas 1989 • $18 • (07/15/91) • **84**
Hermitage La Chapelle 1991: Voluptuous, smooth, intriguing, offering the smoky, toasty notes of new wood and ripe cherry and plum flavors. Polished yet concentrated, try now. • $50 • (05/31/94) • **90**
Hermitage La Chapelle 1990: Bold, ripe and powerful, with a solid, rich core of mineral, currant, plum and cedar flavors that are remarkably complex, smooth and polished, with fine but firm tannins. Elegant, refined and tasty to drink now, but sure to age. 9,400 cases made. • $62 • (08/31/92) • **95**
Hermitage La Chapelle 1989 • $55 • (08/31/91) CS • **93**
Hermitage La Chapelle 1988 • $45 • (03/31/91) • **92**
Hermitage La Chapelle 1986 • $35 • (11/15/89) • **89**
Hermitage La Chapelle 1985 • $50 • (11/15/89) • **93**
Hermitage La Chapelle 1984 • $31 • (11/15/89) • **80**
Hermitage La Chapelle 1983 • $90 • (11/15/89) • **94**
Hermitage La Chapelle 1982 • $64 • (11/15/89) • **89**
Hermitage La Chapelle 1981 • $44 • (11/15/89) • **83**
Hermitage La Chapelle 1980 • $59 • (11/15/89) • **79**
Hermitage La Chapelle 1979 • $62 • (11/15/89) • **86**
Hermitage La Chapelle 1978 • $180 • (11/15/89) • **98**
Hermitage La Chapelle 1976 • $65 • (11/15/89) • **87**
Hermitage La Chapelle 1975 • $50 • (11/15/89) • **81**
Hermitage La Chapelle 1974 • $90 • (11/15/89) • **85**
Hermitage La Chapelle 1973 • $70 • (11/15/89) • **89**
Hermitage La Chapelle 1972 • $150 • (11/15/89) • **90**
Hermitage La Chapelle 1971 • $140 • (11/15/89) • **85**
Hermitage La Chapelle 1970 • $175 • (11/15/89) • **93**
Hermitage La Chapelle 1969 • $200 • (11/15/89) • **92**
Hermitage La Chapelle 1967 • $150 • (11/15/89) • **83**
Hermitage La Chapelle 1966 • $270 • (11/15/89) • **95**
Hermitage La Chapelle 1964 • $220 • (11/15/89) • **93**
Hermitage La Chapelle 1962 • $250 • (11/15/89) • **91**
Hermitage La Chapelle 1961 • $725 • (11/15/89) • **100**
Hermitage La Chapelle 1959 • $500 • (11/15/89) • **77**
Hermitage La Chapelle 1955 • $330 • (11/15/89) • **88**
Hermitage La Chapelle 1953 • $550 • (11/15/89) • **90**
Hermitage La Chapelle 1952 • $480 • (11/15/89) • **77**
Hermitage La Chapelle 1949 • $450 • (11/15/89) • **77**
Hermitage La Chapelle 1944 • $800 • (11/15/89) • **93**
Hermitage La Chapelle 1937 • $800 • (11/15/89) • **50**
Hermitage Le Chevalier de Sterimberg White 1994: Surprisingly delicate for white Hermitage, marrying melon, citrus and vanilla flavors in a well-balanced, clean package. Though not exuberantly fruity, it matches with poultry and meaty fish. • $37 • **87**
Hermitage Le Chevalier de Sterimberg White 1991: 2,200 cases made. • $37 • **71**
Hermitage Le Pied de la Côte 1991: Alluring spice, berry and smoke aromas lead to firm, focused flavors of ripe fruit, licorice and black pepper. Clean, vibrant and concentrated, adding firm tannins and long, fruity finish. A very traditional style. Drinkable now, but better in 1997. • $30 • **90**
Muscat de Beaumes-de-Venise Vin Doux Naturel 1993: An extremely concentrated and intense dessert wine that reminds us of Gewürztraminer in the power of its floral, spicy flavors. Wows you with unctuous texture and sweetness and has enough fruit flavor and lively acidity to keep it all in balance. • $22 • **90**
Muscat de Beaumes-de-Venise Vin Doux Naturel 1986 • $17 • (10/15/88) • **84**
St.-Joseph Le Grand Pompée 1992 • $15 • (05/31/94) • **84**
St.-Joseph Le Grand Pompée 1985 • $12 • (10/15/88) • **86**
Vacqueyras 1990: A blockbuster boasting loads of sweet plum, dried cherry and tobbacolike flavors. Fully mature and balanced, ripe and well rounded, adding soft tannins and some spice notes on the finish. Big, lush and ready to drink now. • $14 • (09/30/95) • **90**

JACOB, ROBERT & RAYMOND

Corton-Charlemagne 1994: A big, serious and distinctive '94 that's smoky and intense. Tightly structured, this full-bodied, racy wine shows at this stage only a bit of its powerful mineral, floral, fruit and toast flavors. Try in 2000. • $NA • (05/31/96) • **93**

JACQUART

Brut Blanc de Blancs Champagne NV • $25 • (12/31/90) • **85**
Brut Champagne 1983: Charming flavor and finesse, with toast, ginger, pear and spice flavors and a long, lingering aftertaste. Drink now to 1993. • $43 • (04/15/90) • **88**
Brut Champagne 1982: Crisp, toasty and delicate with spicy pear, yeast and fruity flavors, fine structure and lively acidity that carries the flavors. • $39 • (12/31/88) • **90**
Brut Champagne NV • $24 • (12/31/88) • **83**
Brut Champagne La Cuvée Renommée 1982: Creamy and delicate, more vanilla and toast than fruit, but there's enough of a thread of concentration to carry through to a long, lovely finish. • $64 • (12/31/88) • **90**
Brut Champagne Sélection NV • $24 • (11/30/92) • **88**
Brut Rosé Champagne La Cuvée Renommée 1982: Salmon color, delicate texture, soft structure, with nuances of tea, berry and toast, dry and clean. Flavorful. • $74 • (12/31/88) • **88**
Brut Rosé Champagne NV • $38 • (12/31/88) • **90**
Extra Dry Champagne NV • $23 • (12/31/88) • **89**

JACQUES DE MERIAL

Vin de Pays des Bouches du Rhône 1993: A mature and rustic wine that tastes slightly oxidized, but still tastey. It's flavors are dominated by spice, leather and herbal notes. • $NA • **79**
Vin de Pays des Bouches du Rhône White 1993: Apple and light earthy flavors mingle in this simple, crisp wine. Though not complex, it has enough weight to stand up to food. • $NA • **79**

JACQUES, DOMAINE PIERRE

Chardonnay Vin de Pays d'Oc 1993: There are toasty and nutty accents to the pear and mineral flavors in this firm, smooth wine. Still lively, though a bit short. 10,000 cases made. • $8 • (12/15/95) • **83**

JACQUES-BLANC, CHÂTEAU

St.-Emilion Cuvée du Maitre 1988 • $23 • (04/30/91) • **78**

JACQUESON, RENE

Gevrey-Chambertin Le Fonteny 1990: Smells okay, but turns leathery and bitter on the palate, finishing with little grace or charm. Drinkable now. 308 cases made. • $24 • (06/15/93) • **72**

JACQUESSON

Blanc de Blancs Champagne NV • $45 • (12/31/91) • **87**
Brut Blanc de Blancs Champagne 1990: Subtle spice and citrus flavors make this crisp, dry wine a refreshing taste experience. It gains complexity and interest on the finish. 6,250 cases made. • $30 • **87**

Brut Blanc de Blancs Champagne NV: A big, fruity, forward Champagne that has vigorous flavors of grapefruit, pear and honey, with creamy accents. Bold, crisp and straightforward. 4,167 cases made. • $27 • **85**
Brut Champagne Degorge Tardive 1975 • $64 • (12/31/93) • **90**
Brut Champagne Perfection 1988: A creamy, light delicate vintage Champagne with a fine structure. Medium bodied with elegant acidity, light frothy foam and a long lightly toasted finish. Drink now. • $35 • (12/31/93) • **89**
Brut Champagne Perfection 1985 • $33 • (12/31/90) • **84**
Brut Champagne Perfection NV • $28 • (12/31/91) • **87**
Brut Champagne Signature 1985: Not giving you much now but with time it will. A very firm wine with super clean, apple fruit aromas and flavors and a hint of toast, medium body and fine acidity on the finish. Drink now. • $50 • (12/31/93) • **88**
Brut Champagne Signature 1979 • $34 • (07/31/87) • **93**
Brut Rosé Champagne Perfection NV: A wonderfully spicy, different style, packed with aromas and flavors of ginger, cinnamon and nutmeg that linger on the finish. Combines bold flavor with elegant texture. Unique and appealing. 2,500 cases made. • $27 • (12/31/94) • **91**
Brut Rosé Champagne Signature 1989: A complete, focused rosé that adds strawberry and cherry nuances on top of the solid structure and fruit flavor. Doughy, spicy touches add complexity, especially on the finish. 833 cases made. • $48 • (12/15/94) • **89**

FRANCE

JADOT, LOUIS

Auxey-Duresses Domaine du Duc de Magenta 1993: Tart and citrusy, tasting like a Chablis, showing green apple, toast, spice and honey flavors that come together nicely on the crisp finish. Try after 1996. • $18 • **86**
Auxey-Duresses Domaine du Duc de Magenta 1991 • $16 • (10/15/93) • **84**
Bâtard-Montrachet 1993: Racy and impressively mineral in character. Velvety and medium in body, toast, pear and honey flavors linger on the finish. Tempting now but will last for years. • $87 • **88**
Beaujolais Jadot 1993: It's fragrant and jammy in aroma, but turns very lean and dry on the palate. Simple in taste, acceptable in quality. • $8 • **77**
Beaujolais Jadot 1990 • $9 • (09/30/91) BB • **85**
Beaujolais Jadot 1989 • $6 • (11/15/90) • **79**
Beaujolais-Villages 1992: Firm with straightforward cherry and gamy flavors, round but simple. It's at its peak, so drink now. • $10 • (06/30/94) • **78**
Beaujolais-Villages 1991 • $9 • (07/31/92) • **80**
Beaujolais-Villages-Jadot 1995: Brawny for a Beaujolais. The meaty texture and firm tannins show promise, but the fruit is a bit buried and overall the wine is clumsy. Try in late 1996. • $10 • **81**
Beaujolais-Villages-Jadot 1994: Tastes like a light Pinot Noir, offering some spice and chocolate notes. Fruit flavors are dominated by plum and cherry, which linger on the finish. • $10 • (06/15/95) • **84**
Beaune Boucherottes 1989 • $38 • (01/31/92) • **90**
Beaune Boucherottes 1988 • $33 • (03/31/91) • **92**
Beaune Boucherottes 1985 • $30 • (03/15/88) • **91**
Beaune Bressandes 1986 • $28 • (05/31/89) • **90**
Beaune Bressandes 1985 • $35 • (03/15/88) • **87**
Beaune Chouacheux 1991: Tough and astringent, a modest wine, with weak anise and berry aromas and flavors. Shows more earthy notes than fruit on the finish. Try now. • $17 Ⓐ • (01/31/94) • **78**
Beaune Clos de Couchereaux 1993: Good intensity of dried herb and plum aromas and flavors. Medium in body, adding firm tannins and a slightly one-dimensional finish. Better in 1999. • $25 • **87**
Beaune Clos des Couchereaux 1992: Smells ripe and generous but gets tight and tannic enough to overshadow the black cherry and toast flavors. May be better after 1996. • $19 • **81**
Beaune Clos des Couchereaux 1988 • $35 • (03/31/91) • **90**
Beaune Clos des Couchereaux 1985 • $34 • (03/15/88) • **91**
Beaune Clos des Ursules 1993: More elegant than chunky, this is a delight to taste now, showing its core of plum, cedar and red berry flavors. Turns slightly chewy on the finish, so keep until 1998. • $35 • (11/15/95) • **88**
Beaune Clos des Ursules 1992: Flavorful and solid, kicking in on the finish with a layer of tannins and red berry flavors. Drinkable now. • $29 • **85**
Beaune Clos des Ursules 1991: A big disappointment. Usually among the best Beaune *premiers crus*, this is thin and mildly astringent. • $23 Ⓐ • (01/31/94) • **75**
Beaune Clos des Ursules 1990: Very seductive, with lovely intensity, super berry flavors and nicely integrated tannins. Drinkable now to 1998. • $44 • (12/15/92) • **91**
Beaune Clos des Ursules 1989 • $73 Ⓐ • (02/29/92) • **91**
Beaune Clos des Ursules 1988 • $56 Ⓐ • (03/31/91) • **91**
Beaune Clos des Ursules 1987 • $30 • (06/15/90) • **81**
Beaune Clos des Ursules 1986 • $33 • (03/15/89) • **88**
Beaune Clos des Ursules 1985 • $44 Ⓐ • (03/15/89) • **91**
Beaune Clos des Ursules 1983 • $67 Ⓐ • (03/15/89) • **93**
Beaune Clos des Ursules 1980 • $26 • (03/15/89) • **83**
Beaune Clos des Ursules 1978 • $47 • (03/15/89) • **89**
Beaune Clos des Ursules 1976 • $29 Ⓐ • (03/15/89) • **85**
Beaune Clos des Ursules 1973 • $40 • (03/15/89) • **86**
Beaune Clos des Ursules 1971 • $70 • (03/15/89) • **78**
Beaune Clos des Ursules 1969 • $120 • (03/15/89) • **90**
Beaune Clos des Ursules 1966 • $41 Ⓐ • (03/15/89) • **90**
Beaune Clos des Ursules 1964 • $90 • (03/15/89) • **86**
Beaune Clos des Ursules 1962 • $90 • (03/15/89) • **79**
Beaune Clos des Ursules 1961 • $125 • (03/15/89) • **88**
Beaune Clos des Ursules 1959 • $160 • (03/15/89) • **98**
Beaune Clos des Ursules 1957 • $110 • (03/15/89) • **89**
Beaune Clos des Ursules 1954 • $75 • (03/15/89) • **81**
Beaune Clos des Ursules 1952 • $100 • (03/15/89) • **87**
Beaune Clos des Ursules 1949 • $175 • (03/15/89) • **86**
Beaune Clos des Ursules 1947 • $175 • (03/15/89) • **95**
Beaune Clos des Ursules 1945 • $250 • (03/15/89) • **84**
Beaune Clos des Ursules 1937 • $175 • (03/15/89) • **92**
Beaune Clos des Ursules 1933 • $200 • (03/15/89) • **80**
Beaune Clos des Ursules 1928 • $200 • (03/15/89) • **97**
Beaune Clos des Ursules 1926 • $200 • (03/15/89) • **88**
Beaune Clos des Ursules 1923 • $175 • (03/15/89) • **78**
Beaune Clos des Ursules 1919 • $300 • (03/15/89) • **90**
Beaune Clos des Ursules 1915 • $400 • (03/15/89) • **95**
Beaune Clos des Ursules 1911 • $300 • (03/15/89) • **81**
Beaune Clos des Ursules 1906 • $NA • (03/15/89) • **92**
Beaune Clos des Ursules 1904 • $NA • (03/15/89) • **88**
Beaune Clos des Ursules 1895 • $NA • (03/15/89) • **80**
Beaune Clos des Ursules 1887 • $NA • (03/15/89) • **90**
Beaune-Grèves Le Clos White 1994: Tasty, flavorful, full-blown style of Chardonnay, with ripe pear, butter and spice galore. It gives you lots of wine for your buck. Verges on being overdone, but lovely all the same. • $38 • (05/31/96) 86 • **86**
Beaune Grèves White 1993: A mouthful but somewhat dull on the palate, vanilla, apple and chalk aromas and flavors. Medium in body. Drink now. • $36 • **82**
Beaune Grèves White 1991 • $32 • (10/15/93) • **90**
Beaune Hospices de Beaune Cuvée Dames-Hospitalier 1985 • $85 • (03/15/88) • **90**
Beaune Hospices de Beaune Cuvée Nicolas-Rolin 1985 • $85 • (03/15/88) • **92**
Beaune Les Avaux 1990: Lively and fresh, with lovely plum and cherry aromas and flavors. Behind the subtle texture lurks nice concentration and a large dose of refined tannins. Drinkable now. • $28 • (12/15/92) • **87**
Beaune Les Chouacheux 1986 • $24 • (05/31/89) • **85**
Beaune Les Chouacheux 1985 • $30 • (03/15/88) • **91**
Beaune Premier Cru 1991: A firm, tannic, solidly built Burgundy whose enticing aromas remind us of cedar and tobacco and whose flavors are like black cherry and spices. But it turns tannic and tight on the finish, with a green, astringent taste. Drinkable now. • $19 • **84**
Beaune Premier Cru 1988 • $26 • (06/15/93) • **83**
Beaune Premier Cru 1987 • $28 • (09/15/92) • **81**
Beaune Teurons 1991: Light and green, with an astringent edge to the earthy flavors. Drinkable now. • $NA • (01/31/94) • **76**

Key: SS—Spectator Selection. CS—Cellar Selection. BB—Best Buy. $NA—Price not available. (BT)—Barrel tasting. Ⓐ—Auction Price.
Dates in parentheses represent the issues in which the ratings were published.

Bonnes Mares 1991: Firm and focused, a layer of fine tannins framing a core of currant, black cherry and toast flavors that persist into a generous finish. Has the intensity to keep developing through 1997 at least. • $51 Ⓐ • (01/31/94) • **87**

Bonnes Mares 1990: Big and chewy, this muscular monster of a wine has plenty of earth, chocolate, berry and cherry aromas and flavors and a firm backbone of tannins. Try in 1998. • $75 • (12/15/92) • **91**

Bonnes Mares 1988 • $65 • (03/15/91) • **88**

Bonnes Mares 1987 • $52 • (06/15/90) • **91**

Bonnes Mares 1986 • $57 • (04/15/89) • **89**

Bonnes Mares 1985 • $78 • (03/15/88) • **95**

Bourgogne 1990 • $NA • (12/15/92) • **77**

Bourgogne Chardonnay Cuvée Réserve Spéciale White 1991 • $16 • (05/15/93) • **82**

Bourgogne Chardonnay White 1991 • $13 • (07/31/93) • **78**

Bourgogne Pinot Noir 1989 • $NA • (01/31/92) • **83**

Bourgogne Pinot Noir 1985 • $11 • (04/30/88) • **78**

Bourgogne Pinot Noir Jadot 1993 • $11 • **50**

Bourgogne Pinot Noir Jadot 1992: Good for a basic red Burgundy. Ripe and spicy in aroma, plummy and cherrylike in flavor and firm and moderately tannic in texture. • $11 • (11/30/94) • **83**

Bourgogne Pinot Noir Jadot 1989 • $12 • (06/15/93) • **76**

Brouilly 1995: Supple and fresh. The black cherry flavors are subdued but clean, balanced by firm, discrete tannins. A well-balanced, understated wine. • $15 • **84**

Brouilly 1993: Clean, crisp and lean. Not much fruit flavor but it's well balanced, dry and refreshing. • $10 • **78**

Brouilly 1992: There's pleasant cherry flavor in this straightforward, solid Beaujolais. It has a firm structure but not much embroidery. • $12 • (06/30/94) • **79**

Brouilly 1987 • $8 • (07/15/88) • **81**

Chambertin Clos de Bèze 1993: Sleek and racy Burgundy. Vivid black cherry, mineral character. Medium-bodied, adding an abundance of fine tannins and a long, fresh finish. Better in 2000. • $87 • **90**

Chambertin Clos de Bèze 1992: A solid Burgundy offering smoke, berry and floral flavors and a chalky edge that ends up feeling chunky and tannic. Might have enough to improve through 1997 or 1998. • $70 • **86**

Chambertin Clos de Bèze 1991: Brilliantly focused, with currant, violet and raspberry flavors packed into a lean and elegant frame, finishing long and seductive. Tannins need until 1998 to soften. • $60 • **91**

Chambertin Clos de Bèze 1990: Supple, concentrated and classy with plum, currant and prune flavors. Tannins clamp down on the finish, but time will make for great drinking in a few years. • $105 • **92**

Chambertin Clos de Bèze 1989: Satisfying, maturing Burgundy, with ripe red berry flavors and a toasty and slightly nutty edge. Pretty to drink now. • $100 • **88**

Chambertin Clos de Bèze 1988: A lovely red showing medium concentration, more elegant than opulent, with red berry and floral flavors. Ready to drink. • $90 • **88**

Chambertin Clos de Bèze 1987: A sensational '87. Seductive and elegant, a touch light, with a narrow, focused beam of ripe berry and currant flavor sliding through the fine tannins. • $65 • **88**

Chambertin Clos de Bèze 1986: Light and mature, with orange peel, mint and berry flavors. Elegant but fading a bit on the drying finish. • $63 • **85**

Chambertin Clos de Bèze 1985: Firm and focused, spanking-clean and youthful-tasting, impeccably balanced, offering grapey spice, berry and slightly jammy flavors on a silky texture. • $113 • **88**

Chambertin Clos de Bèze 1983: Shows very mature, earthy aromas and flavors and coarse, slightly bitter tannins, but brown sugar notes along with the sweet finish offer some compensation. • $55 • **83**

Chambolle-Musigny 1993: Some good red fruit character but could use a little more concentration. Light to medium body, medium tannins and slightly dry finish. Better in 1998. • $28 • **84**

Chambolle-Musigny 1992: Very light and stalky, only modest raspberry flavors sneaking in to add a little charm. Drinkable now. • $26 • **77**

Chambolle-Musigny 1991: Crisp and citrusy, with modest raspberry fruit poking through the fine layer of tannins, echoing berry and cherry on the light finish. Drinkable now. • $22 Ⓐ • (01/31/94) • **84**

Chambolle-Musigny 1990: Elegant, beautiful and extremely aromatic, with lovely plum, raspberry and chocolate notes. Shows a ripe, almost sweet character, firm tannins and a long finish. Drinkable in 1998. • $30 • (12/15/92) • **91**

Chambolle-Musigny 1986 • $30 • (07/15/89) • **78**

Chambolle-Musigny 1985 • $27 Ⓐ • (05/15/88) • **91**

Chambolle-Musigny Les Feusselottes 1991: Delicate, aromatic, a noseful of berry, floral and gamy aromas, adding a bit more ripeness in the flavors to offset the layer of fine tannins. Try in 1997. • $31 Ⓐ • (01/31/94) • **83**

Chapelle-Chambertin 1988 • $75 • (03/15/91) • **93**

Chapelle-Chambertin 1985 • $54 • (03/15/88) • **90**

Chassagne-Montrachet 1992: Nice and harmonious, with a lovely flavor spectrum, showing some vanilla, apple tart and honey notes that make it a fine, if not very complex, drink. • $23 • (08/31/94) • **86**

Chassagne-Montrachet 1991 • $25 • (10/15/93) • **86**

Chassagne-Montrachet Morgeot Clos de la Chapelle Domaine du Duc de Magenta 1988 • $20 • (03/31/91) • **85**

Chassagne-Montrachet Morgeot Clos de la Chapelle Domaine du Duc de Magenta 1986 • $18 • (10/31/89) • **77**

Chassagne-Montrachet Morgeot Clos de la Chapelle Domaine du Duc de Magenta 1985 • $19 • (04/15/88) • **83**

Chassagne-Montrachet Morgeot Duc de Magenta 1993: Some pretty vanilla, toasted oak and green apple character. Medium-bodied and slightly sharp but well crafted. Drink now. • $30 • **82**

Chassagne-Montrachet Morgeot Duc de Magenta 1991 • $28 • (10/15/93) • **84**

Chevalier-Montrachet Les Demoiselles 1993: Classy and round, promoting some green apple, mineral and dried-herb flavors and good intensity on the finish. Drink after 1996. • $103 • **89**

Chevalier-Montrachet Les Demoiselles 1992: Good concentration. Tight and restrained, it holds back now and tastes somewhat woody and closed-in. Medium-bodied, with vanilla, pear and apple flavors, and some excellent mineral notes on the finish. Should improve with cellaring, drinkable now. • $93 • (08/31/94) • **91**

Chevalier-Montrachet Les Demoiselles 1991 • $93 • (10/15/93) • **87**

Clos St.-Denis 1993: Surprisingly light for a *grand cru*. Delicate Pinot offering cherry, vanilla and tobacco aromas and flavors, medium to light body, fine tannins and fruity finish. Better in 1998. • $62 • **82**

Clos St.-Denis 1992: Light and crisp, with a smoky, gamy edge to the modest black cherry flavors, finishing with a wee touch of bitterness. Drinkable now. • $58 • **80**

Clos de Vougeot 1993: A big wine in a beautiful package. From the deep color, through the perfumey spice, mint and game aromas, to the rich plum fruit, sweet oak and full tannins, this promises pleasure for the future. It's balanced and deep, already showing some complexity. • $NA • **92**

Clos Vougeot 1992: Firm and chewy, lean, with modest tobacco and berry flavors, hinting at spice on the finish. Drinkable now. • $42 • **80**

Clos Vougeot 1991: Only modest berry and anise aromas and flavors. Light and astringent, turning stemmy on the finish. • $37 Ⓐ • (01/31/94) • **77**

Clos Vougeot 1990: Long and flavorful, like a fine cigar, this is full of classy tobacco, plum and current flavors that echo on an extremely solid finish. Drinkable now to 1999. 175 cases made. • $55 • (12/15/92) • **91**

Clos Vougeot 1989 • $74 • (01/31/92) • **87**

Clos Vougeot 1988 • $68 • (11/15/91) • **73**

Clos Vougeot 1986 • $50 • (04/15/89) • **87**

Clos Vougeot 1985 • $85 • (03/31/88) • **82**

Corton-Charlemagne 1993: Seductive, creamy, silky texture, sporting nice pear, fig and mineral flavors and a very elegant finish. Drink now. • $59 • **89**

Corton-Charlemagne 1992: Terrific, both smooth and chewy, delivering tons of character and flavor. Its butter, caramel, hazelnut and pear flavors fold into a cream-accented finish that's topped by a smoky accent and goes on and on. • $56 • (08/31/94) • **93**

Corton-Charlemagne 1991 • $NA • (10/15/93) • **84**

Corton Pougets 1993: Balanced and deeply satisfying, a full-bodied red that's both delicate and ripe, showing pretty red berry and earth flavors. Try in 2000. • $46 • **92**

Corton Pougets 1992: Smooth and balanced, with a nice core of caramel-tinged berry flavors. Drinkable now. • $40 • **83**

JADOT, LOUIS

Corton Pougets 1991: Richly aromatic, but the tannins tend to overshadow the modest wild berry flavor until the finish, where the fruit echoes nicely. Needs until 1997 or '98. • $34 Ⓐ • (01/31/94) • **86**
Corton Pougets 1990: A fruit bomb, with a refined structure of cherry and earth flavors and a spicy, smoky, firm, long finish. Drinkable now. • $50 • (12/15/92) • **90**
Corton Pougets 1989 • $64 • (01/31/92) • **93**
Corton Pougets 1988 • $61 • (03/31/91) • **93**
Corton Pougets 1987 • $41 • (06/15/90) • **87**
Corton Pougets 1986 • $42 • (04/30/89) • **86**
Corton Pougets 1985 • $52 • (03/15/88) • **89**
Côte de Beaune-Villages 1990: Smooth and supple, with plum, cherry and smoke flavors bringing out the classic Pinot Noir structure of this round, elegant wine. Drinkable now. • $15 • (12/15/92) • **87**
Côte de Beaune-Villages 1989 • $19 • (08/31/92) • **84**
Côte de Beaune-Villages 1986 • $15 • (06/15/89) • **78**
Côte de Beaune-Villages 1985 • $17 • (04/15/88) • **79**
Fixin 1993: Sleek and well made. Great for a wine from this rather obscure appellation. Ripe plum and mineral aromas and flavors, medium body, fine backbone of tannins and fresh finish. Drink now through 1998. • $18 • **87**
Fixin 1990: Lovely, with attractive, smoky, meaty licorice and fruit aromas and flavors and fresh tannins and acidity. Drinkable now. • $15 • (12/15/92) • **85**
Fixin 1989 • $21 • (01/31/92) • **88**
Fleurie 1994: Firm tannins deliver stucture, but tend to dominate the black cherry and licorice flavors right now. This Fleurie is fresh and complete and will show better accompanied by food. • $13 • (10/31/95) • **85**
Fleurie 1993: Flavorful but very tight and dry Fleurie. Has good raspberry and cherry tones, firm tannins and an overall austerity that not everybody will like. • $11 • **81**
Fleurie 1992 • $13 • (06/15/94) • **84**
Fleurie 1987 • $11 • (07/15/88) • **79**
Fleurie 1983 • $9 • (11/01/85) • **68**
Gevrey-Chambertin 1986 • $25 • (07/15/89) • **77**
Gevrey-Chambertin Clos St.-Jacques 1992: A polished wine with character and complexity. Very well crafted, with smooth tannins and gorgeous black cherry flavors. Just short of outstanding because it lacks the extra dimensions on the finish. • $44 • **88**
Gevrey-Chambertin Clos St.-Jacques 1991: Offers Bardolino-like strawberry and cherry aromas and flavors and a nice burst of fruit on the finish. Light, simple and drinkable now. • $80 Ⓐ • (01/31/94) • **80**
Gevrey-Chambertin Clos St.-Jacques 1990: Round, smooth and quite decadent, with lots of flavors—earth, mushroom, berry and cedar—adding excitement to this medium-bodied, elegant wine. Drinkable now. • $48 • (12/15/92) • **90**
Gevrey-Chambertin Clos St.-Jacques 1989 • $22 Ⓐ • (01/31/92) • **90**
Gevrey-Chambertin Clos St.-Jacques 1988 • $52 • (03/15/91) • **88**
Gevrey-Chambertin Clos St.-Jacques 1986 • $44 • (07/15/89) • **84**
Gevrey-Chambertin Clos St.-Jacques 1985 • $75 Ⓐ • (03/31/88) • **94**
Gevrey-Chambertin Estournelles St.-Jacques 1993: Full-bodied, featuring plenty of tannin structure and nice blackberry and wet earth character. Just short of outstanding because it's a bit one-dimensional. Better in 1998? • $48 • **89**
Gevrey-Chambertin Estournelles St.-Jacques 1988 • $50 • (03/15/91) • **91**
Gevrey-Chambertin Estournelles St.-Jacques 1986 • $40 • (07/15/89) • **87**
Gevrey-Chambertin Estournelles St.-Jacques 1985 • $41 • (03/31/88) • **86**
Griotte-Chambertin 1990: Powerful yet refined, with beautiful raspberry and spice aromas and flavors and a silky tannin mouth-feel. Drinkable now. • $70 • (12/15/92) • **91**
Griotte-Chambertin 1988 • $75 • (03/15/91) • **94**
Griotte-Chambertin 1987 • $50 • (07/15/90) • **80**
Juliénas 1987 • $8 • (07/15/88) • **80**
Mâcon-Lugny Jadot Les Petites Pierres 1993: Dominated by earthy and mineral flavors, adding some honey, green apple and spice notes as well. Fairly intense, showing good depth and a modest finish. • $8 • **83**

Key: SS—Spectator Selection. CS—Cellar Selection. BB—Best Buy. $NA—Price not available. (BT)—Barrel tasting. Ⓐ—Auction Price.
Dates in parentheses represent the issues in which the ratings were published.

Mâcon-Lugny Jadot Les Petites Pierres 1991 • $8 • (05/15/93) • **76**
Mâcon-Villages La Fontaine 1991 • $10 • (11/30/92) • **83**
Mâcon-Viré 1991 • $8 • (07/31/93) • **80**
Marsannay 1986 • $11 • (06/15/89) • **77**
Marsannay White 1992: Quite intense, but also bulky and a bit disjointed now; it needs a year or so to come around. Good acidity, with some toast, grapefruit and lime flavors. Try now. Tasted twice. • $NA • (08/31/94) • **83**
Mazis-Chambertin 1990: A massive wine built for aging, with tons of hard tannins, but has plenty of ripe plum, berry and earth notes underneath the tough surface. Try in 1998. • $70 • (12/15/92) • **90**
Mazis-Chambertin 1987 • $50 • (05/31/90) • **92**
Meursault 1991: Decent quality, with earthy, buttery flavors but not much fruit. Balanced toward the heavy side. • $24 • (11/15/94) • **78**
Meursault-Charmes 1992: Delicious and quite subtle, with vivid and bright pear, vanilla and mineral flavors, below the seductive creamy texture, this reveals good backbone and structure. Not showy, just classy. • $35 • (08/31/94) • **89**
Meursault Perrières 1994: Both supple and crisp, playing on contrasts in its attractive, ripe, smooth and creamy package. Honey, dried herb and ripe pear notes. Delicous now, but might be better in 1997. • $38 • (05/31/96) • **89**
Meursault Perrières 1993: Subtle Meursault boasting a lovely palate which unfolds with toasted coconut, apple, mineral and cream character. Medium-bodied and very long on the finish. Good now but wait a couple of years. • $37 • **90**
Meursault Perrières 1991 • $NA • (10/15/93) • **88**
Monthelie 1990 • $18 • (12/15/92) • **86**
Monthelie 1989 • $21 • (01/31/92) • **87**
Morgon 1992 • $12 • (06/15/94) • **86**
Morgon 1990 • $12 • (09/30/91) • **83**
Moulin-à-Vent 1993: Starts out smooth and tasty, but turns tough and tannic on the finish. Probably best to drink now for its fresh cranberry and currant flavors. • $11 • **82**
Moulin-à-Vent 1992 • $13 • (06/15/94) • **87**
Moulin-à-Vent 1990 • $15 • (09/30/91) • **79**
Moulin-à-Vent 1987 • $11 • (07/15/88) • **83**
Musigny Le Musigny 1986 • $70 • (04/15/89) • **77**
Musigny Le Musigny 1985 • $74 • (03/31/88) • **88**
Nuits-St.-Georges 1985 • $30 • (04/15/88) • **91**
Nuits-St.-Georges Clos des Corvées 1992: Straightforward, with modest strawberry and raspberry flavors. Light but also offers a hint of ripe currant on the smooth finish. • $28 • **80**
Nuits-St.-Georges Clos des Corvées 1990: An elegant Nuits, with pleasant black cherry and plum characteristics, medium tannins and a fresh finish. Drinkable now. • $36 • (12/15/92) • **85**
Nuits-St.-Georges Clos des Corvées 1989 • $56 • (01/31/92) • **85**
Nuits-St.-Georges Clos des Corvées 1988 • $49 • (02/28/91) • **89**
Nuits-St.-Georges Clos des Corvées 1987 • $35 • (04/30/90) • **84**
Nuits-St.-Georges Clos des Corvées 1986 • $37 • (04/30/89) • **83**
Nuits-St.-Georges Clos des Corvées 1985 • $46 • (03/15/88) • **96**
Nuits-St.-Georges Les Boudots 1991: Firm and flavorful. Features simple currant and toast aromas and flavors and a balanced, harmonious finish. Drinkable now. • $26 Ⓐ • (01/31/94) • **84**
Nuits-St.-Georges Les Boudots 1988 • $49 • (02/28/91) • **88**
Nuits-St.-Georges Les Boudots 1986 • $38 • (04/30/89) • **85**
Nuits-St.-Georges Les Boudots 1985 • $42 • (03/15/88) • **75**
Pernand-Vergelesses 1985 • $18 • (04/15/88) • **85**
Pernand-Vergelesses Clos de la Croix de Pierre 1993: Easygoing red sporting delicate floral, berry character and medium-fine tannins. Drinkable now. • $19 • **84**
Pernand-Vergelesses Clos de la Croix de Pierre 1992: Bright, generous and a little chewy, but there's a solid core of silky berry underneath that persists into the finish. • $18 • **84**
Pernand-Vergelesses Clos de la Croix de Pierre 1991: A bit raw in texture, but youthful and lively, displaying concentrated red currant and raspberry flavors and a chewy finish. Fresh and appealing. Drinkable now. • $15 Ⓐ • (01/31/94) • **83**
Pernand-Vergelesses Clos de la Croix de Pierre 1990: Just lovely, with plenty of pretty cherry, strawberry and wet earth notes on the palate. Has round tannins. Nothing big or terribly complex, but fun to drink now. • $18 • (12/15/92) • **88**

FRANCE

Pernand-Vergelesses Clos de la Croix de Pierre 1989 • $21 • (01/31/92) • **86**

Pernand-Vergelesses Clos de la Croix de Pierre 1988 • $17 • (03/31/91) • **86**

Pernand-Vergelesses Clos de la Croix de Pierre 1987 • $15 • (11/15/90) • **79**

Pernand-Vergelesses Clos de la Croix de Pierre 1986 • $17 • (07/31/89) • **85**

Pernand-Vergelesses Clos de la Croix de Pierre 1985 • $18 • (04/15/88) • **83**

Pernand-Vergelesses White 1991 • $16 • (10/15/93) • **81**

Pommard 1988 • $36 • (03/31/91) • **83**

Pommard Chaponnières 1985 • $39 • (03/15/88) • **91**

Pommard Grands Epenots 1989 • $50 • (01/31/92) • **88**

Pommard Grands Epenots 1988 • $38 • (03/31/91) • **86**

Pommard Les Arvelets 1990: So closed now that it doesn't yield much at first but kicks in near the finish, with tons of fine tannins and sweet, ripe fruit flavors that go on and on. Try now to 1998. • $42 • (12/15/92) • **90**

Pouilly-Fuissé 1993: Rich, robust and well-structured, dominated by pear and fig flavors and a hint of apricot. Solid and well-made, with a nice touch of butter on the end. It has a good acidity that balances well with the generous fruit flavors. The finish is refreshing. • $18 • **87**

Pouilly-Fuissé 1991 • $18 • (03/31/93) • **80**

Pouilly-Fuissé Cuvée Réserve Spéciale 1993: Showy butter and sweet vanilla flavors boast of oak influence, but the wine underneath is modest, with light lemon and green apple notes. • $23 • (03/31/95) • **82**

Pouilly-Fuissé Cuvée Réserve Spéciale 1991 • $22 • (07/31/93) • **88**

Puligny-Montrachet 1994: A bit rustic, showing chestnut aromas and drying finish. • $34 • (05/31/96) • **72**

Puligny-Montrachet 1993: Sharp and solid, this crystal-like wine seduces with its challenging, tightly-wound core of citrus, lime and dried herb character. Nice concentration of mineral and honey flavors on the long finish. • $NA • **86**

Puligny-Montrachet Cailleret 1991 • $40 • (10/15/93) • **91**

Puligny-Montrachet Clos de la Garenne Duc de Magenta Monopo 1992: Seductive, gorgeous Puligny of seamless, smooth and creamy texture that coats your mouth. The vanilla, mineral and pear flavors, laced by a touch of smoke and hazelnut, are full-bodied but elegant. • $33 • (08/31/94) • **92**

Puligny-Montrachet Les Folatières 1993: Lively mineral, apple and lime aromas and flavors, medium body and fresh acidity. • $33 • **86**

Puligny-Montrachet Les Perrières 1994: Thick, rich and almost oily in texture, though it still manages to remain elegant and structured. Tons of ripe fruit, including pear, apricot and ripe apple, adding a touch of honey, mineral and chalk. Somewhat tart on the finish now, but give it time. • $38 • (05/31/96) • **91**

Régnié 1994: Candied cherry flavors and slightly harsh tannins detract from the pleasure in this firm, rustic red. • $12 • (10/31/95) • **78**

Régnié 1993: Very dry, very lean, tart and somewhat tannic. Where is the fruit? Clean, but not much fun to drink. • $9 • (07/31/95) • **78**

Régnié 1992: Soft and reserved, this wine has good balance and supple cherry flavors in a straightforward style. Tasty, but without much Beaujolais character. • $11 • (06/30/94) • **79**

Romanée-St.-Vivant 1993: Very fine fruit and tannin structure. Not a big wine, but significant for its sleek and racy style. Try in 1999. • $135 • **88**

Ruchottes-Chambertin 1988 • $75 • (03/15/91) • **91**

St.-Aubin 1994: A very accessible '94, with a round, smooth texture and a touch more intensity than many other village wines. Has grapefruit, apple, almond and herbal notes. Drinkable now through 1997. • $19 • (05/31/96) • **83**

St.-Véran La Chapelle White 1993: A smooth, soft texture and light buttery flavors make this an agreeable if simple wine. Tasted twice. • $13 • (11/15/94) • **80**

St.-Véran La Chapelle White 1991 • $13 • (11/30/92) • **83**

Santenay Clos de Malte 1994: Straightforward and crisp, with some decent green apple flavors. But tart on the finish. • $17 • (05/31/96) • **78**

Santenay Clos de Malte 1993: Both delicate and firm, sporting earth and nicely defined Pinot Noir fruit flavors ranging from cherry to raspberry. Sizable amount of tannins. Good to drink now, better in 1997. • $16 • **85**

Santenay Clos de Malte 1990: Juicy and flavorful, offering focused black cherry, earth and plum characteristics and an elegant, fruity finish. Drinkable now. • $18 • (12/15/92) • **87**

Savigny-lès-Beaune 1994: Soft and pleasing, with some toasted coconut, pineapple and spice flavors. It caresses the palate with its silkiness but could use just a bit more intensity and concentration. Drinkable now. • $20 • (05/31/96) • **84**

Savigny-lès-Beaune La Dominode 1992: Focused and firm, with a modest undercurrent of black cherry flavor that expands a bit on the finish. Drinkable now. • $16 • **82**

Savigny-lès-Beaune La Dominode 1990: A delightful wine that's not huge by any stretch of the imagination, but crafted in just the right proportions, evolving from cherry and berry flavors to chocolate and earth notes. Has firm, supple tannins. Drinkable now. • $23 • (12/15/92) • **88**

Volnay 1992: Crisp and aromatic, showing enough spicy black cherry flavors to finish nicely. Drinkable now. • $26 • **83**

Volnay 1990: This solid wine offers fresh, focused raspberry and strawberry flavors that are full and rich along with caressing tannins. Drinkable now. • $28 • (12/15/92) • **87**

Vosne-Romanée 1991: Fresh and crisp, offering a nice core of black cherry flavor and pleasant rose petal and walnut shadings. Fresh and smooth on the finish. Drinkable now. • $21 Ⓐ • (01/31/94) • **83**

Vosne-Romanée 1990: Displays stunning balance in a village wine, with alluring violet, berry and chocolate flavors, fine tannins and a long, delicious finish. Drinkable now. • $30 • (12/15/92) • **92**

Vosne-Romanée 1989 • $40 • (01/31/92) • **89**

Vosne-Romanée 1985 • $33 • (03/31/88) • **86**

Vosne-Romanée Les Suchots 1993: Not quite as great as when tasted from barrel in spring of 1995. Still lovely and elegant, showing attractive plum character, delicate tannins, medium body and medium-silky texture. Better in 2000. • $46 • **88**

Vosne-Romanée Les Suchots 1991: Lean, crisp and modest, centered around a thread of raspberry flavor and hints of chocolate and cedar on the finish. Drinkable now. • $34 Ⓐ • (01/31/94) • **81**

Vosne-Romanée Les Suchots 1990: Well made and pretty. More open and accessible than some wines, offering lovely cherry, strawberry and earth aromas and flavors and good intensity on the finish. Drinkable now. 225 cases made. • $49 • (12/15/92) • **88**

JAFFELIN

Aloxe-Corton 1993: What a shame. Starts out fruity but then turns very papery and dry. Drink in 2000. • $20 • **74**

Aloxe-Corton 1992: Interesting floral and rhubarb overtones to strawberry and watermelon flavors. A lean and lively village Aloxe. • $19 • **81**

Aloxe-Corton 1989 • $27 • (01/31/92) • **89**

Auxey-Duresses 1993: Disappointing, lean and herbal, showing asparagus and metallic character. Not much wine here. Light color, watery. • $12 • **74**

Auxey-Duresses 1991: Light and simple, with appealing currant flavor to cut through the firm tannins. Drinkable now. • $12 Ⓐ • (01/31/94) • **79**

Auxey-Duresses 1990: Fresh and lively, with crushed raspberry characteristics. Elegant and rather light, but the violet, smoke and cherry flavors are attractive. Drinkable now. 200 cases made. • $16 • (12/15/92) • **84**

Auxey-Duresses 1989 • $16 • (01/31/92) • **85**

Auxey-Duresses White 1992: Lively, showing a subtle and focused band of apple, pear and peach flavors backed by some mineral and crisp citrus notes. • $13 • (08/31/94) • **82**

Bâtard-Montrachet 1993: Classy, racy and quite delicate, delivering good complexity of honey, chalk and pear notes. While wonderfully silky on the palate, it finishes firm and hard. Needs time to soften, try in 1997. • $70 • **88**

Beaujolais-Villages Domaine de Riberolles 1994: Weedy and herbal flavors give this wine a dried-out quality. Lean, with little fruit. 14,000 cases made. • $8 • (06/15/95) • **76**

Beaujolais-Villages Domaine de Riberolles 1993: There's as much Beaujolais character as fresh fruit in this silky red, with its bright cherry notes and long finish. It's elegant and graceful. 20,000 cases made. • $7 • (06/30/94) • **84**

Beaujolais-Villages Domaine de Riberolles 1987 • $7 • (04/15/89) • **79**

JAFFELIN

Beaune Champs-Pimont 1993: Simple and one-dimensional, delicate but also a bit diluted. Short finish. • $19 • **73**
Beaune Champs-Pimont 1992: Light and lean, with a bead of bright berry flavor that shines through to the finish. Drinkable now. • $22 • **82**
Beaune Champs-Pimont 1991: Light, floral and distinctive, with blackberry and black cherry flavors at the core, plus shades of iris, jasmine and lime adding zing to the finish. Drinkable now. • $22 Ⓐ • (01/31/94) • **85**
Beaune Champs-Pimont 1990: A succulent, ripe style of Beaune, packed with ripe plum, cherry and earth notes. Seduces you with its velvety texture and supple tannins. Drinkable now. 200 cases made. • $25 • (12/15/92) • **90**
Beaune du Châpitre 1986 • $18 • (12/31/88) • **77**
Beaune Hospices de Beaune Cuvée Clos des Avaux 1986 • $65 • (12/31/88) • **85**
Beaune Les Bressandes 1990: Flavorful and juicy, showing pretty plum, raspberry, cherry and earth aromas and flavors. All the parts are very much in balance in this supple, medium-bodied wine. Try now. 300 cases made. • $27 • (12/15/92) • **87**
Beaune Les Bressandes 1989 • $28 • (01/31/92) • **85**
Beaune Les Champimonts 1989 • $27 • (01/31/92) • **89**
Beaune Les Champimonts 1983 • $18 • (09/15/86) • **68**
Bourgogne du Chapitre 1993: Starts out round and pretty, light in body, medium intensity, but then turns slightly forward, diluted and vegetal on the finish. Try on release. • $10 • **78**
Bourgogne du Chapitre 1993: Fruity and straightforward, quite light, revealing modest pear, apple and a hint of honey-tropical character. Drinkable now. • $10 • (05/15/95) • **77**
Bourgogne du Châpitre 1990 • $11 • (12/15/92) • **82**
Bourgogne Hautes Côtes de Beaune 1993: Simple Burgundy showing floral, strawberry aromas and flavors and a slightly dry finish. Drink now. • $12 • **79**
Bourgogne Hautes Côtes de Beaune 1992: Light in texture, but a fine thread of raspberry and currant jam flavors show through and persist into the finish. • $13 • **80**
Bourgogne Pinot Noir 1989 • $10 • (01/31/92) • **83**
Brouilly 1994: Light and simple, this offers tart cherry and herb flavors, fresh and a touch dry on the finish. 3,000 cases made. • $12 • **78**
Brouilly 1993: The light color and earthy aromas are warnings, borne out on the muddy, earthy palate. This lacks life and freshness, a disappointment for the vintage. 1,000 cases made. • $12 • (06/30/94) • **77**
Brouilly 1992: Already past its prime. Earthy aromas give way to overly sweet, silky vanilla and plum flavors. It lacks freshness and life. Drink up. 2,000 cases made. • $11 • (06/30/94) • **72**
Chambertin Le Chambertin 1986 • $65 • (12/31/88) • **89**
Chambertin Le Chambertin 1983 • $48 • (04/16/86) • **93**
Chambolle-Musigny 1993: One-dimensional with some attractive fruit character, but rather light and diluted on the finish. Drink in 1997. • $24 • **78**
Chambolle-Musigny 1989 • $28 • (01/31/92) • **89**
Chambolle-Musigny 1988 • $32 • (12/31/90) • **88**
Chambolle-Musigny 1983 • $21 • (03/16/86) • **81**
Charmes-Chambertin 1990: Portlike, with an abundance of ripe berry flavors, full tannins and a superlong finish. The ripe fruit keeps you coming back for more. Try now. 100 cases made. • $55 • (12/15/92) • **92**
Charmes-Chambertin 1989 • $66 • (01/31/92) • **87**
Charmes-Chambertin 1986 • $45 • (12/31/88) • **77**
Chassagne-Montrachet 1992: A well-knit core of solid red berry and supple tannins. Drinkable now. • $16 • **83**
Chassagne-Montrachet 1990: Smooth and round in the mouth and firm on the finish, this balanced wine offers attractive toast and berry aromas and flavors. Drinkable now. 200 cases made. • $16 • (12/15/92) • **85**
Chassagne-Montrachet 1989 • $18 • (01/31/92) • **86**
Chassagne-Montrachet Les Vergers White 1992: Clean, with pear, spice and apple flavors, showing a touch of vanilla and toast notes on the fresh, zesty finish. • $30 • (08/31/94) • **84**
Chorey-Côte-de-Beaune 1989 • $13 • (01/31/92) • **75**

Key: SS—Spectator Selection. CS—Cellar Selection. BB—Best Buy. $NA—Price not available. (BT)—Barrel tasting. Ⓐ—Auction Price.
Dates in parentheses represent the issues in which the ratings were published.

Clos de Vougeot 1990: This pleasant, chocolate-scented Clos de Vougeot delivers more finesse than power, but seems a bit frugal with the fruit. Medium-bodied, with a medium finish. Try now. 150 cases made. • $55 • (12/15/92) • **86**
Clos de Vougeot 1989 • $60 • (01/31/92) • **89**
Clos de Vougeot 1986 • $45 • (12/31/88) • **77**
Clos de Vougeot 1985 • $49 • (06/15/88) • **96**
Clos St.-Denis 1989 • $53 • (01/31/92) • **94**
Corton 1989 • $54 • (01/31/92) • **91**
Corton 1986 • $45 • (12/31/88) • **87**
Corton 1983 • $45 • (04/01/86) • **91**
Corton-Charlemagne 1991 • $NA • (10/15/93) • **85**
Côte de Beaune-Villages 1989 • $14 • (01/31/92) • **82**
Côte de Nuits-Villages Red 1989 • $15 • (01/31/92) • **84**
Echézeaux 1989 • $60 • (01/31/92) • **91**
Echézeaux 1986 • $45 • (12/31/88) • **86**
Echézeaux 1983 • $30 • (05/01/86) • **90**
Fixin 1993: Very light and weedy with stewed tomatoes and beans. Drink if you must. • $17 • **76**
Fixin 1989 • $18 • (01/31/92) • **85**
Fleurie 1993: This silky-textured Beaujolais carries a needle of acidity and a peppery bite along with cranberry and cherry flavors. It's light for the appellation. 500 cases made. • $15 • (06/30/94) • **81**
Fleurie 1985 • $9 • (12/15/86) • **85**
Gevrey-Chambertin 1992: Light overall, with a smooth texture and a pleasant thread of black cherry and tobacco flavors. Drinkable now. • $24 • **82**
Gevrey-Chambertin 1989 • $30 • (01/31/92) • **88**
Gevrey-Chambertin 1988 • $25 • (08/31/91) • **88**
Gevrey-Chambertin 1986 • $49 • (02/28/89) • **85**
Gevrey-Chambertin 1983 • $17 • (10/01/85) • **77**
Gevrey-Chambertin Lavaut St.-Jacques 1990: Wonderfully intense fruit flavors lend class and charm to this solid wine. Has a great backbone of acidity and tannins. Drinkable in 1997. 100 cases made. • $42 • (12/15/92) • **91**
Gevrey-Chambertin Lavaux St.-Jacques 1989 • $40 • (01/31/92) • **81**
Ladoix Côte de Beaune 1989 • $13 • (01/31/92) • **85**
Mâcon-Villages 1994: Looks and tastes as if aging quickly: Chocolate, bark and caramel flavors mingle with pear and apple. Drink fast, if you have some. 1,666 cases made. • $9 • **75**
Meursault 1993: Clean and tart, tightly wrapped around citrus, green apple and herb flavors. Very crisp, mouth-puckering finish. Where is the opulence of Meursault? • $18 • (05/15/95) • **82**
Meursault Les Cras 1992: Intense and concentrated, with grapefuit and pineapple flavors accented by mineral and earth notes on the finish. Has lots of fruit, good balance and a tightly-knit texture. Try now. • $34 • (08/31/94) • **88**
Meursault Les Genevrières 1993: Round and silky texture adding lively honey, citrus and floral aromas and flavors. Some mineral character surfaces on the tart finish. Drinkable now. • $25 • (05/15/95) • **85**
Montagny White 1992: A crisp, grassy style, refreshing, with some apple, citrus notes. Still, it's quite light. • $12 • (08/31/94) • **80**
Monthelie 1990 • $17 • (12/15/92) • **88**
Monthelie 1989 • $19 • (01/31/92) • **87**
Monthelie 1986 • $15 • (06/15/89) • **79**
Morey-St.-Denis Les Ruchots 1989 • $30 • (01/31/92) • **86**
Morgon 1994: Lean and tart, displaying some nice raspberry and cherry flavors and fruity aromas, in the end it's a bit thin. 2,000 cases made. • $11 • **81**
Morgon 1993: Ripe fruit gains an added dimension with a dusty, attractively earthy note that gives finesse and length to this dense, polished wine. 500 cases made. • $12 • (06/30/94) • **88**
Moulin-à-Vent Red 1985 • $9 • (12/15/86) • **89**
Nuits-St.-Georges 1993: Very light, both in color and body, offering very modest strawberry and raspberry flavors. Lacks fruit and tastes dry on the short finish. • $25 • **74**
Nuits-St.-Georges 1992: More Beaujolais than Nuits-St.-Georges, with tart raspberry and strawberry flavors on a very light frame. • $25 • **79**
Nuits-St.-Georges 1989 • $27 • (01/31/92) • **83**
Nuits-St.-Georges 1986 • $28 • (02/28/89) • **80**
Nuits-St.-Georges 1983 • $19 • (09/15/86) • **72**
Nuits-St.-Georges Les Damodes 1989 • $36 • (01/31/92) • **90**

Pernand-Vergelesses 1993: Delicious for early drinking, showing berry, cedar and earth aromas and flavors. Medium-bodied with smooth texture and a caressing finish. Can hold. • $14 • **82**
Pernand-Vergelesses 1991: Light and crisp, has appealing strawberry flavor and a fresh, tart finish. Drinkable now. • $13 Ⓐ • (01/31/94) • **80**
Pernand-Vergelesses 1990: Pleasant in a down-to-earth sort of way, with good cherry, herb and chocolate flavors complementing the firm tannins. Try now. 200 cases made. • $16 • (12/15/92) • **85**
Pernand-Vergelesses 1989 • $19 • (01/31/92) • **86**
Pommard 1991: Behind the chunky tannins lies a core of ripe currant and black cherry flavors shaded by floral and cedar notes. Try now. • $20 Ⓐ • (01/31/94) • **83**
Pommard 1990: Seductive, with lots of raspberry and earth characteristics, lovely, silky tannins and a flavorful finish. Drinkable now. 200 cases made. • $30 • (12/15/92) • **89**
Pommard 1989 • $33 • (01/31/92) • **85**
Pommard 1986 • $26 • (04/30/89) • **79**
Pommard 1985 • $38 • (03/15/88) • **89**
Pommard 1983 • $19 • (09/15/86) • **81**
Puligny-Montrachet 1993: Clean and racy mineral and spice character, medium body and fresh acidity. • $20 • **84**
Puligny-Montrachet 1991 • $30 • (10/15/93) • **86**
Puligny-Montrachet Sous Le Puits 1991 • $NA • (10/15/93) • **86**
Romanée St.-Vivant 1990: Harmony is the code word here. Supple and focused, with a racy character and tons of lovely raspberry, cherry and earth aromas and flavors. Is smooth and just great on the finish. Drinkable now to 1998. 150 cases made. • $75 • (12/15/92) • **93**
Romanée-St.-Vivant 1989 • $80 • (01/31/92) • **91**
Rully 1986 • $13 • (06/15/89) • **77**
Rully White 1992: Tart and lean, the narrow band of grapefruit, lemon and floral notes lively and focused. Overall, pleasant and straightforward. • $14 • (08/31/94) • **81**
St.-Aubin 1989 • $14 • (01/31/92) • **84**
St.-Aubin Premier Cru White 1992: Light but balanced, offering a good harmony of toasty, vanilla-flavored wood notes and decent apple and citrus flavors. • $13 • (08/31/94) • **81**
St.-Aubin White 1991 • $NA • (10/15/93) • **80**
St.-Romain White 1993: Straightforward and clean, delivering modest fruit flavors on a tart, crisp, light frame. Drink now. • $12 • **77**
St.-Romain White 1991 • $NA • (10/15/93) • **80**
St.-Véran White 1994: Distinctive, offering more fruit intensity than some St.-Vérans but showing a rustic, drying character on the rough finish. 833 cases made. • $10 • **76**
Santenay 1990: Jammy, chewy and pretty, with raspberry, cherry and earth aromas and flavors and round tannins. Drinkable now. 300 cases made. • $16 • (12/15/92) • **85**
Santenay 1989 • $17 • (01/31/92) • **85**
Santenay Clos Rousseau 1993: Elegant, refined, silky texture. Subtle earth, red berry and mocha flavors lead to a ripe finish. Try in 1998. • $17 • **84**
Santenay La Maladière 1990: Nicely structured, with lively raspberry, vanilla and cherry aromas, silky tannins and a racy finish. 400 cases made. • $19 • (12/15/92) • **84**
Santenay La Maladière 1989 • $20 • (01/31/92) • **82**
Santenay La Maladière 1988 • $21 • (08/31/91) • **84**
Santenay La Maladière 1985 • $22 • (03/15/88) • **84**
Savigny-lès-Beaune 1989 • $18 • (01/31/92) • **85**
Volnay 1993: One of the few good wines from Jaffelin this year. Juicy cherry and chestnut aromas and flavors, medium to light body, slightly dry tannins and fresh finish. Better in 1998. • $24 • **86**
Volnay 1992: Simple and a little chewy, generous with its rustic berry and slightly candied flavors. • $20 • **79**
Volnay 1991: The light thread of raspberry and spice aromas and flavors is marred only by a greenish tinge on the finish. Lean and crisp, drinkable now. • $20 • (01/31/94) • **81**
Volnay 1990: Pretty, elegant and seductive, with subtle notes that kick in with sweet, ripe cherry and plum flavors on the silky finish. Drinkable now. 200 cases made. • $24 • (12/15/92) • **85**
Volnay 1989 • $29 • (01/31/92) • **89**
Volnay 1988 • $30 • (08/31/91) • **88**
Volnay 1986 • $27 • (04/30/89) • **86**
Volnay 1985 • $30 • (03/15/88) • **88**
Volnay 1983 • $17 • (10/16/85) • **92**
Vosne-Romanée 1989 • $29 • (01/31/92) • **86**
Vosne-Romanée 1986 • $30 • (02/28/89) • **79**

JALOUSIE-BEAULIEU, CHÂTEAU

Bordeaux Supérieur 1985 • $7 • (12/31/88) • **70**

JAMELLES, LES

Cabernet Sauvignon Vin de Pays d'Oc 1994: Solid black cherry, tobacco and black olive notes and firm tannins. Rich, sturdy, well integrated if not complex. 6,000 cases made. • $7 • (10/31/95) • **84**
Cabernet Sauvignon Vin de Pays d'Oc 1993: Appealing fruit flavors and firm tannins make this a good, straightforward Cabernet to drink tonight. 6,000 cases made. • $7 • (02/28/95) • **82**
Chardonnay Vin de Pays d'Oc 1994: Vanilla and pineapple aromas are promising, but on the palate, this shuts down. Firm, smooth texture but little fruit, with a slightly bitter finish. 12,000 cases made. • $7 • (12/15/95) • **80**
Chardonnay Vin de Pays d'Oc 1993: Apple and butter flavors dominate this simple wine. A pleasant pineapple note chimes in before a tart finish. 10,000 cases made. • $7 • **81**
Chardonnay Vin de Pays d'Oc 1992 • $7 • (02/28/94) • **74**
Cinsault Vin de Pays d'Oc 1994: The aromas are strawberry and cherry in this soft, fruity rosé. Medium bodied, in a fruity style. 2,000 cases made. • $7 • **81**
Cinsault Vin de Pays d'Oc 1993: A touch of sweetness in this wine wine is matched by pleasant strawberry and cherry flavors. A good alternative to white Zinfandel. 2,000 cases made. • $7 • **80**
Marsanne Vin de Pays d'Oc 1993: Faded and stale, like a bouquet of flowers abandoned in a hot room for weeks. 2,000 cases made. • $8 • (02/29/96) • **72**
Marsanne Vin de Pays d'Oc 1992 • $8 • (02/28/94) • **80**
Merlot Vin de Pays d'Oc 1994: Ripe, fleshy, sporting jammy prune and chocolate flavors and firm tannins on aftertaste. Sacrifices elegance for power, but comes up a bit short on the finish. 20,000 cases made. • $7 • (10/31/95) • **82**
Merlot Vin de Pays d'Oc 1993: Bright fruit makes this appealing, but the tough, biting tannins knock it off balance. 20,000 cases made. • $7 • (02/28/95) • **77**
Merlot Vin de Pays d'Oc 1991 • $7 • (07/31/93) • **84**
Mourvèdre Vin de Pays d'Oc 1993: Light cherry and tea flavors accompany drying tannins to suggest that this is on the downward slope. 2,000 cases made. • $7 • (10/31/95) • **75**
Muscat Sec Vin de Pays d'Oc 1994: Vibrant aromas of peaches, roses and spice follow through on the palate, though the flavors are a bit diluted—a more successful perfume than wine. • $8 • (02/29/96) • **78**
Rolle Vin de Pays de l'Ile de Beauté 1994: This tart, neutral white has faint overtones of herbs and chemicals. Refreshing but not very pleasant. • $8 • (02/29/96) • **75**
Syrah Vin de Pays d'Oc 1994: Ripe, almost jammy, this offers pleasant blackberry, licorice and tar flavors and round, lush tannins, adding an attractive smoky finish. Drinkable now. 10,000 cases made. • $7 • (10/31/95) • **84**
Syrah Vin de Pays d'Oc 1992: Mature and mellow red but full-bodied. Light in tannins, with modest plum and herb flavors. 10,000 cases made. • $7 • (07/31/95) • **80**
Syrah Vin de Pays d'Oc 1991 • $7 • (03/31/94) • **84**
Viognier Vin de Pays d'Oc 1994: Clean and round, with some apple flavors that are simple and fresh, but the chief virtue here is inoffensiveness. 2,500 cases made. • $12 • (02/29/96) • **78**
Viognier Vin de Pays d'Oc 1993: Simple and fruity, with loads of apple, peach and melon flavors. A nice lingering finish is dominated by vanilla and spice. 2,500 cases made. • $12 • (11/30/94) • **81**
Viognier Vin de Pays d'Oc 1992 • $13 • (02/28/94) • **82**

JAMET, JEAN-PAUL ET JEAN-LUC

Côte-Rôtie 1991: Concentrated yet balanced, with ripe raspberry and tar flavors on a solid frame and a rich, smoky finish. A combination of intensity and poise. Drinkable now. • $39 • (05/31/94) • **90**

FRANCE

Côte-Rôtie 1990: Try this rich and luscious wine with roast lamb studded with rosemary; the flavors will marry beautifully. It's big and expressive, but still needs time to open. • $39 • (05/31/94) • **92**
Côte-Rôtie 1988 • $49 • (06/15/93) • **78**

JAMET, JOSEPH

Côte-Rôtie 1985 • $33 • (04/15/89) • **88**

JANIN, PAUL

Beaujolais-Villages Domaine des Vignes des Jumeaux 1992: Still fresh, this light red offers cherry and smoky flavors typical of Gamay. It's very soft. • $9 • (06/30/94) • **80**
Moulin-à-Vent 1985 • $13 • (10/31/87) • **85**
Moulin-à-Vent 1983 • $9 • (11/01/85) • **83**
Moulin-à-Vent Domaine des Vignes du Tremblay 1991: Big for a Beaujolais, ripe and concentrated, deep plum flavors, smoke and chocolate notes, firm tannins. Well-balanced. Drinkable now. • $16 • (01/31/95) • **89**

JANODET, JACKY

Morgon 1991 • $12 • (06/15/94) • **90**
Moulin-à-Vent 1991 • $13 • (06/15/94) • **84**
Moulin-à-Vent Domaine les Fines Graves 1992: Fading now, this wine veers between stewed fruit and metallic flavors, thin texture and tough tannins. Drink up. 1,050 cases made. • $17 • (07/31/95) • **74**

JASMIN

Côte-Rôtie 1992: Pretty and silky, but isn't showing much yet. The berry, chocolate and spice flavors come out on the finish. Try now. • $42 • (05/31/94) • **84**
Côte-Rôtie 1991: A bit lean, but some pretty spice and black pepper notes are hiding under the tannin. Tasted twice. • $43 • (05/31/94) • **82**
Côte-Rôtie 1990: Not big, but elegant and balanced, with spicy cherry and raspberry flavors and soft tannins. Try now. Tasted twice. • $45 • (05/31/94) • **86**
Côte-Rôtie 1988 • $32 • (12/31/90) • **89**
Côte-Rôtie 1987 • $30 • (06/30/90) • **90**

JAU, CHÂTEAU DE

Côtes du Roussillon 1988 • $6 • (08/31/91) • **75**
Vin de Pays des Côtes Catalanes Le Jaja de Jau 1993: This light, fruity red makes pleasant summertime quaffing, with fresh cherry and strawberry flavors, soft tannins and a peppery kick. Try it slightly chilled. Tasted twice. 25,000 cases made. • $7 • (09/15/94) • **83**

JAVILLIER, PATRICK

Bourgogne Cuvée de Forgets White 1993: Attractively ripe and supple, light-to-medium-bodied, showing a vivid streak of lemon, apple and mineral character, juicy finish. Enjoy now. • $19 • **83**
Bourgogne Cuvée de Forgets White 1991 • $19 • (10/15/93) • **86**
Bourgogne Cuvée Oligocène 1994: Fresh and crisp, with some apple and mineral flavors, but it doesn't really show much and even seems a bit hollow. Somewhat one-dimensional on the finish. 416 cases made. • $23 • (05/31/96) • **80**
Bourgogne Cuvée Oligocène White 1993: Solid and well made, showing supple texture yet a good backbone of lime, pear and green apple flavors and long, slightly rough finish. Drinkable now. • $23 • **85**
Meursault Clos du Cromin 1993: The minerally, creamy texture delivers fine toast, hazelnut and butter character on a narrow frame. Drinkable now. • $38 • (05/15/95) • **87**
Meursault Clos du Cromin 1991 • $33 • (10/15/93) • **88**

Key: SS—Spectator Selection. CS—Cellar Selection. BB—Best Buy. $NA—Price not available. (BT)—Barrel tasting. Ⓐ—Auction Price.
Dates in parentheses represent the issues in which the ratings were published.

Meursault Les Casses-Têtes 1994: Focused and of moderate intensity, hinting at honey and mineral to set off the apricot, pear and ripe apple flavors. Subtle finish. 83 cases made. • $39 • (05/31/96) • **83**
Meursault Les Casses-Têtes 1993: Quite racy, lovely balance between vibrant acidity and toast, honey, hazelnut and pear flavors. Medium in body, crisp finish. Drinkable now. • $38 • (05/15/95) • **86**
Meursault Les Casses-Têtes 1992: Nice, smooth and moderately intense, with some ripe-tasting honey, coffee and vanilla bean flavors, ends with a tangy touch of citrus. • $30 • (08/31/94) • **85**
Meursault Les Casses-Têtes 1991 • $33 • (10/15/93) • **90**
Meursault Les Cloux 1993: A fruit bomb of a wine, ripe and lush, sporting tiers of tropical fruit, mineral, smoke and toasty oak flavors and a chalky finish. Great complexity. • $40 • (08/31/95) • **85**
Meursault Les Cloux 1991 • $33 • (10/15/93) • **89**
Meursault Les Narvaux 1992: Big and rich, showy and full-bodied, has plenty of toast, pineapple and grapefruit flavors, all backed by a core of good acidity. Long-lasting finish bodes well for the future. Try now. • $35 • (08/31/94) • **92**
Meursault Les Narvaux 1991 • $33 • (10/15/93) • **91**
Meursault Les Tillets 1993: Polished and sophisticated, this wonderfully smooth, full-bodied and complex Meursault has loads of mineral, tropical fruit and citrus flavors. Honey and hazelnut emerge gracefully on the finish. Try in 1997. 300 cases made. • $38 • (08/31/95) • **89**
Meursault Les Tillets 1992: Full-bodied, flavorful Meursault, it hits you with its baked pear, toast and honey flavors that are broad, lush and ripe. Drinkable now. 833 cases made. • $33 • (08/31/94) • **89**
Meursault Les Tillets 1991 • $33 • (10/15/93) • **89**
Puligny-Montrachet Les Levrons 1994: Rich, ripe and full-bodied, oozing caramel, spice, mineral, toasted coconut and ripe pear flavors. Not too intense, but who is complaining? Silky and well made. Drinkable now through 1997. 100 cases made. • $NA • (05/31/96) • **90**
Puligny-Montrachet Les Levrons 1993: Distinctive and seductive, displaying lush, creamy texture and lime, butterscotch, toast, hazelnut, honey and pear flavors. Supple and ripe, round mouth-feel. Try now. • $38 • **87**
Savigny-lès-Beaune Les Montchenevoy 1993 : Tart and crisp, with a mineral, lime and spice character that makes it attractive. The tartness intensifies on the lean finish, but should go well with shellfish. 350 cases made. • $29 • (05/31/96) • **82**

JAYER, HENRI

Echézeaux 1988 • $59 Ⓐ • (05/15/91) • **94**
Echézeaux 1987 • $115 • (05/15/91) • **87**
Echézeaux 1986 • $160 • (05/15/91) • **88**
Echézeaux 1985 • $264 Ⓐ • (05/15/91) • **96**
Echézeaux 1982 • $150 • (06/16/86) • **94**
Echézeaux 1981 • $100 • (05/15/91) • **82**
Echézeaux 1980 • $220 • (05/15/91) • **89**
Echézeaux 1979 • $175 • (05/15/91) • **92**
Echézeaux 1978 • $440 • (05/15/91) • **91**
Echézeaux 1976 • $400 • (05/15/91) • **90**
Echézeaux 1972 • $300 • (05/15/91) • **81**
Echézeaux 1970 • $300 • (05/15/91) • **80**
Echézeaux 1969 • $550 • (05/15/91) • **91**
Richebourg 1987 • $280 • (05/15/91) • **87**
Richebourg 1986 • $350 • (05/15/91) • **93**
Richebourg 1985 • $625 • (05/15/91) • **99**
Richebourg 1980 • $300 • (05/15/91) • **88**
Richebourg 1979 • $290 • (05/15/91) • **93**
Vosne-Romanée Cros Parantoux 1988 • $180 • (05/15/91) • **93**
Vosne-Romanée Cros Parantoux 1987 • $85 • (05/15/91) • **86**
Vosne-Romanée Cros Parantoux 1986 • $105 • (05/15/91) • **87**
Vosne-Romanée Cros Parantoux 1985 • $230 • (05/15/91) • **95**
Vosne-Romanée Cros Parantoux 1980 • $175 • (05/15/91) • **89**
Vosne-Romanée Cros Parantoux 1978 • $310 • (05/15/91) • **94**
Vosne-Romanée Les Beaumonts 1988 • $160• (05/15/91) • **89**
Vosne-Romanée Les Brûlées 1987 • $100 • (05/15/91) • **85**
Vosne-Romanée Les Brûlées 1986 • $105 • (05/15/91) • **90**
Vosne-Romanée Les Brûlées 1985 • $300 • (05/15/91) • **93**
Vosne-Romanée Les Brûlées 1980 • $185 • (05/15/91) • **88**
Vosne-Romanée Les Brûlées 1979 • $150 • (05/15/91) • **88**

Vosne-Romanée Les Brûlées 1978 • $310 • (05/15/91) • **92**
Vosne-Romanée Les Brûlées 1976 • $250 • (05/15/91) • **81**
Vosne-Romanée Les Brûlées 1972 • $250 • (05/15/91) • **87**

JAYER, J.

Echézeaux 1988 • $100 • (03/15/91) • **91**
Nuits-St.-Georges Les Lavières 1985 • $38 • (03/15/88) • **88**
Vosne-Romanée Les Rouges 1985 • $44 • (03/15/88) • **80**

JAYER-GILLES, ROBERT

Bourgogne Hautes Côtes de Beaune 1993: Exciting, vibrant, medium-bodied red, featuring perfumy, rose petal, currant, smoky flavors folded into the wood and impressive tannin structure. Try in 2000. • $22 • **90**
Bourgogne Hautes Côtes de Beaune 1990: Shows impressive concentration, with a deep color and violet and vanilla flavors. A clever wine that feels smooth at first, but has too much new oak for our taste, giving the wine an astringent finish. Drinkable now. 700 cases made. • $24 • (12/15/92) • **80**
Bourgogne Hautes Côtes de Beaune 1989 • $24 • (01/31/92) • **84**
Bourgogne Hautes Côtes de Beaune 1988 • $26 • (05/15/91) • **88**
Bourgogne Hautes Côtes de Nuits 1993: Full-blown, earthy, ripe, rich, plummy red berry character. Seductive now, featuring lots of personality in a rustic way. Quite chewy as it adds peppery notes on the finish. Try now through 2000. • $22 • **88**
Bourgogne Hautes Côtes de Nuits 1992: Light and fruity, with a tantalizing overlay of spicy oak to the currant and plum flavors. Simple and inviting, drinkable now. • $23 • **82**
Bourgogne Hautes Côtes de Nuits 1989 • $24 • (01/31/92) • **86**
Bourgogne Hautes Côtes de Nuits White 1993: Smooth and sophisticated, lovely mineral, chalky, lemony character. Closed up and difficult to judge now, finishing somewhat rough, but give it the benefit of the doubt. Try now. • $20 • **87**
Bourgogne Hautes Côtes de Nuits Blanc 1989 • $32 • (01/31/92) • **87**
Côte de Nuits-Villages 1993: Gorgeous, melts in the mouth, like a reduced blackberry and wine sauce. It delivers the essence of flavors in a silky, medium-bodied package. Ripe tannins make this drinkable now but better in 1999. • $36 • **90**
Côte de Nuits-Villages 1992: Immediately attractive for its aromatic, spicy, currant and berry character, but turns simple in flavor and light in texture. Drinkable now. • $28 • **82**
Côte de Nuits-Villages 1991: Marked by spicy, sweet oak, this offers enough ripe currant and blackberry flavors to keep it in balance. Try now. 300 cases made. • $29 Ⓐ • (01/31/94) • **82**
Côte de Nuits-Villages 1990: A superb, massive wine for this appellation, offering tons of smoky berry and earth characteristics and silky tannins. Drinkable now. 650 cases made. • $34 • (12/15/92) • **90**
Echézeaux 1992: Has the ripe fruit and rich texture that are missing in so many '92s, layering the berry, spice and delicate herbal flavors. Tannins are firm enough to want until 1997. • $110 • **89**
Echézeaux 1989 • $101 • (01/31/92) • **94**
Echézeaux 1982 • $23 • (11/01/85) • **58**
Echézeaux Du Dessus 1993: Superb concentration of exotic blackberries and raspberries and a good dose of smoky oak. Full in body with velvety tannins and long, wild-fruit finish. Try after 2000. • $135 • **95**
Echézeaux Du Dessus 1991: Smooth, polished, silky and elegant, unfolding raspberry, smoke, toast, game and plum flavors that persist into a long, luscious finish. Has scratchy tannins to lose, but the goods to age through 1998 to 2000. 200 cases made. • $85 Ⓐ • (01/31/94) • **91**
Echézeaux du Dessus 1990: Superintense and gorgeous in texture, this powerful wine is also delicate, with violet, game, berry and earth nuances that are so well integrated they feel like cream on the palate. Drinkable in 1997. 200 cases made. • $100 • (12/15/92) • **97**
Nuits-St.-Georges Les Damodes 1993: An explosion of currant and berry aromas and flavors. Full-bodied with toasted oak and fruit, velvety tannins and long finish. Better in 2000. • $85 • **92**
Nuits-St.-Georges Les Damodes 1992: Lithe, very pretty spicy oak aromas and blackberry and currant flavors are settling nicely into a firm framework. The lingering finish shows more spice notes. • $70 • **85**
Nuits-St.-Georges Les Damodes 1991: Smooth, round and generous, offering spicy, toasty new oak, currant and blackberry aromas and flavors. Captures the maximum of this vintage for this appellation. Drinkable now through 1997. 50 cases made. • $55 Ⓐ • (01/31/94) • **88**
Nuits-St.-Georges Les Haut Poirets 1993: Breathtaking wine. Amazing concentration of wild fruit. Full-bodied, adding full, velvety tannins and a finish that lingers for minutes. Hold this until 2005. • $70 • **93**
Nuits-St.-Georges Les Hauts Poirets 1992: Packs a lot of spicy, tobacco-scented fruit on a modest frame. Warm and toasty, but finishing austerely as the fine tannins clamp down. Try now. • $58 • **84**
Nuits-St.-Georges Les Haut Poirets 1991: Distinctively toasty and spicy, this ripe, round wine has a generous component of black cherry, currant and prune flavors that extends into a polished finish. Drinkable now. 125 cases made. • $48 Ⓐ • (01/31/94) • **86**
Nuits-St.-Georges Les Hauts Poirets 1990: Unbelievable structure in a Nuits. A giant wine, with a huge amount of fruit and tannins, but shows elegance and refinement at the same time. Made for long-term aging, try 1998 to 2000. 125 cases made. • $48 • (12/15/92) • **97**

JEAN, PIERRE

Bordeaux Supérieur 1989 • $9 • (07/15/92) • **79**
Bordeaux Supérieur 1988 • $8 • (07/31/91) • **75**
St.-Emilion 1988 • $10 • (06/30/91) • **85**

JESSIAUME PERE & FILS

Santenay Gravières 1988 • $21 • (03/31/91) • **86**

JESSY, DE

Extra Dry NV • $9 • (06/15/90) • **81**

JOBARD, CHARLES & REMI

Bourgogne Chardonnay 1994: A standout for its different flavors. Intense butterscotch, toast and citrus flavors. Very round and silky on the long finish. Excellent quality for a simple Bourgogne. • $20 • (05/31/96) • **85**
Meursault Les Chevalières 1994: Clean and fresh, with good intensity, likeable citrus and melon flavors and youthful finish. Drinkable now. • $32 • (05/31/96) • **84**
Meursault Les Genevrières 1994: Very seductive, very honeyed and very balanced. Elegant and understated grapefruit and ripe pear flavors. Amazing fullness and harmony, with a mineral component to die for. Super-long finish. Drinkable now through 2000. • $45 • (05/31/96) • **93**

JOBARD, FRANÇOIS

Bourgogne Blanc 1993 : Fresh and crisp, with a tart apple cider character. Very tight now and somewhat lighter in body, but it turns refreshingly clean and lemony on the finish. • $NA • (05/31/96) • **80**
Meursault 1993 : A lovely, well-made and nicely balanced white that marries its ripe fruit and sweet honey character to the citrus and mineral notes. This is delicious now. • $NA • (05/31/96) • **88**
Meursault Blagny 1991 • $45 • (05/31/94) • **87**
Meursault Charmes 1991 • $47 • (05/31/94) • **89**
Meursault En la Barre 1991: An overly mature wine, with few fruit flavors remaining. What apple and fig flavors are there turn a bit harsh and oxidized on the finish. Tasted twice with consistent notes. • $NA • **78**
Meursault Genevrières 1993 : Very rich and ripe, with tons of tropical fruit, apricot, peach and floral aromas and flavors. A bit rustic, turning a little coarse on the finish, but this full-bodied wine certainly isn't boring. May be better in 1999. Tasted twice, with consistent notes. • $NA • (05/31/96) • **85**
Meursault Genevrières 1992: Fat and ripe, quite silky, exhibiting spicy, honeyed character and a lovely blend of toasty hazelnut and pear flavors. Ready to drink. • $50 • (08/31/94) • **87**
Meursault Genevrières 1991 • $47 • (05/31/94) • **88**
Meursault Poruzots 1993: Lots going on here, with spice, pineapple, toasted oak and a good amount of citrus flavor. Rich but not overdone

to make a very focused and lively wine. Try in 1998. • $NA • (05/31/96) • **89**

Meursault Poruzots 1992: Honey, hazelnut, chalk, almond character, silky-textured, showing ripe flavors on the long finish. Should improve with age, given this producer's track record. Tasted twice, with consistent notes. • $50 • **89**

Meursault Poruzots 1991 • $47 • (05/31/94) • **86**

JOBLOT

Givry Clos de la Servoisine 1989 • $25 • (01/31/92) • **88**

Givry Clos du Cellier aux Moines 1989 • $25 • (01/31/92) • **90**

Givry Clos du Cellier aux Moines 1988 • $26 Ⓐ • (12/31/90) • **84**

JOGUET, CHARLES

Chinon Clos de la Dioterie Vieilles Vignes 1993: Licorice and herbal aromas give way to flavors of plum, coffee and earth in this round red. Though it has ripe flavors, it seems a bit light, but may simply need time to show its best. • $26 • **82**

Chinon Clos de la Dioterie Vieilles Vignes 1992: Raspberry and smoke flavors mingle with accents of herbs and grilled meat in this intense wine. Good structure, vibrant acidity and firm tannins. Tasty now. 250 cases made. • $25 • (10/31/94) • **88**

Chinon Clos du Chêne Vert 1993: Big for a Loire red, this round, velvety wine mingles plum, smoky and gamy flavors with balance and complexity, and licorice and smoke linger on the finish. A solid, well-made wine. Drinkable now. • $24 • **88**

Chinon Cuvée des Varennes du Grand Clos 1986 • $15 • (04/30/88) • **82**

Chinon Cuvée du Clos de la Dioterie 1986 • $21 • (12/31/88) • **89**

Chinon les Varennes du Grand Clos 1993: Ripe and lively, with berry, plum and spicy flavors, this is firm without heaviness, elegant yet still has grip. It's clean and well-integrated. Drink now. • $24 • **85**

JOILLOT, JEAN-LUC

Bourgogne Tastevinage 1985 • $15 • (06/30/88) • **84**

JOLIET, JEHAN

Fixin Clos de la Perrière 1985 • $25 • (07/31/88) • **90**

JOLIVET, PASCAL

Pouilly-Fumé 1994: This has plenty of apple and herb and some interesting smoke, nut and clove notes that create a complex, well-balanced whole. • $17 • (05/15/96) • **86**

Pouilly-Fumé La Grande Cuvée 1994: Pronounced herbal and mineral flavors give this full-bodied, firm wine a distinctive, if somewhat austere, character that carries through on the long finish. Try with smoked fish or white meats. • $22 • (06/15/96) • **88**

Pouilly-Fumé La Loge Aux Moines 1994: Herbs, minerals and stone fruits mark this austere and slightly tart white, which finishes with a bite. • $23 • (05/15/96) • **82**

Sancerre 1994: Round and somewhat heavy-handed, showing some appealing green plum and gooseberry flavors though there's a hint of matchstick as well. Finishes on an herbal note. • $17 • (04/30/96) • **80**

Sancerre Château du Nozay 1994: A basket of herb seasonings, adding dashes of salt. Flavors are dominated by thyme and basil, featuring raw acidity and an off-putting finish. • $21 • (04/30/96) • **78**

Sancerre Domaine du Colombier 1989 • $23 • (08/31/92) • **75**

Sancerre La Grande Cuvée 1994: Awkward and out of balance, showing candied and herbal flavors. The finish tastes earthy and overdone. Tasted twice, with consistent notes. • $21 • (06/15/96) • **74**

Key: SS—Spectator Selection. CS—Cellar Selection. BB—Best Buy. $NA—Price not available. (BT)—Barrel tasting. Ⓐ—Auction Price.
Dates in parentheses represent the issues in which the ratings were published.

JOLY, N.

Savennières Becherelle 1992: Typical peach and mineral aromas give way to clean, crisp flavors that open up on the palate. It's not huge, but has good intensity and still needs time to open. • $20 • **86**

Savennières-Roche-aux-Moines Clos de la Bergerie 1992: Maturing now, this offers mineral and earthy aromas, with ripe pear and vanilla flavors. It has good body, and just enough acidity to carry the round, soft flavors. • $23 • **84**

JONQUEYRES, CHÂTEAU

Bordeaux Supérieur 1995: A well-crafted wine with lovely silky tannins and a delicious aftertaste of berry and mineral. • $NA • (05/15/96) • **85-89** (BT)

Bordeaux Supérieur 1992: Licorice aromas and flavors are consistent throughout this wine. Has a chewy texture, but it's still a bit simple. 12,000 cases made. • $10 • (08/31/95) • **81**

Bordeaux Supérieur Cuvée Vieilles Vignes 1988 • $12 • (03/31/91) • **65**

JONQUIERES, CHÂTEAU

Corbières 1991 • $7 • (03/15/94) • **81**

JOSMEYER

Auxerrois Alsace 1991 • $NA • **83**

Gewürztraminer Alsace Cuvée des Folastries White 1992: A mouthful of fruit flavor fills out this spicy, floral-scented white. It tastes just off-dry, full in body, rich in texture, with a lingering finish. • $15 • (11/15/94) • **85**

Pinot Blanc Alsace Mise du Printemps White 1992: Exuberant lime, floral and mineral flavors, with hints of vanilla and spice. The texture is lively and refined, carrying the flavors into a long finish. • $12 • (11/15/94) • **84**

Riesling Alsace Le Kottabe White 1992: Earth, peach and petrol aromas mark this lean, apple-flavored Riesling. It's refreshing and bracing, but we would appreciate more concentration. • $14 • (11/15/94) • **84**

Tokay Pinot Gris Alsace Le Fromenteau White 1992: Earthy, mineral aromas and lean fruit flavors give this smooth-textured white a quiet personality. • $14 • (11/15/94) • **80**

JOUGLA, DOMAINE DES

St.-Chinian 1990 • $9 • (03/15/94) • **84**

St.-Chinian 1986 • $6 • (05/15/89) • **76**

JUGE, MARCEL

Cornas 1986 • $23 • (11/30/90) • **83**

Cornas Coteaux 1986 • $21 • (02/10/91) • **78**

Cornas Cuvée C 1986 • $25 • (06/15/89) • **85**

Cornas Cuvée S C 1986 • $30 • (06/15/89) • **87**

JUILLOT, MICHEL

Bourgogne White 1994: Light and straightforward, showing modest fruit flavors. Seems a bit diluted. 1,500 cases made. • $14 • (05/31/96) 74 • **74**

Corton-Charlemagne 1994: Corked. 316 cases made. • $94 • (05/31/96) • **76**

Corton Perrieres 1988 • $54 • (08/31/92) • **75**

Côte Chalonnaise 1990: Simple, straightforward red Burgundy, with an earthy edge to the modest cherry and spice flavors. Finishes dry and a bit austere. Drinkable now. 800 cases made. • $13 • (10/31/92) • **80**

Mercurey 1994: Rich and unctuous, with a lot of character. Full-bodied, with honey, toasted oak and a chalky, chewy character. Could use a bit more fruit, but it's definitely ready now. 1,583 cases made. • $23 • (05/31/96) • **86**

Mercurey 1989 • $21 • (08/31/92) • **75**

Mercurey Clos Tonnerre 1989 • $24 • (08/31/92) • **85**

Mercurey Les Champs Martins 1989 • $24 • (08/31/92) • **84**

JURAT, CHÂTEAU LE

St.-Emilion 1995: A bit lean and lacking in fruit but some decent mineral and berry flavors. • $NA • (05/15/96) • **75-79** (BT)
St.-Emilion 1994: Like drinking pure grape juice. Full-bodied and quite thick, presenting berry, grapey flavors and a long, velvety finish. • $NA • **85-89** (BT)
St.-Emilion 1991: A decent wine with a cherry and berry character, smooth texture and light finish. • $14 • (03/31/94) • **76**

JUSTICES, CHÂTEAU LES

Sauternes 1991: Features some good body and sweetness with honey and lemon character, but appears slightly herbal on the finish. Drinkable now. • $NA • (04/15/95) • **81**
Sauternes 1990: An impressive balance of toasted oak, honey and lemon aromas and flavors, medium-bodied and sweet, fresh finish. Needs time to develop, try in 1997. • $NA • (04/15/95) • **87**
Sauternes 1989: Plenty of ripe fruit character, showing powerful raisin aromas and flavors of orange, vanilla, cream and honey; long, long finish. Drinkable now. • $23 • (04/15/95) • **91**
Sauternes 1988: Enchanting lemon, vanilla and honey aromas and flavors, medium body, medium sweetness and a coffee, lightly spicy finish. Drinkable now. • $38 • (04/15/95) • **86**
Sauternes 1987 • $24 • (06/15/90) • **75**
Sauternes 1986: Light and easy to drink showing lime and vanilla aromas and flavors, medium sweetness and a light finish. Drinkable now. • $20 • (04/15/95) • **79**
Sauternes 1983: Always a disappointment. Flat and unbalanced. Not very pleasant. Tasted twice, with consistent notes. • $18 • (04/15/95) • **65**

KIENTZLER, ANDRE

Pinot d'Alsace Alsace White 1993: The expressive pear, floral and light earth aromas and flavors are attractive, tart citrus notes complement tight, firm texture. Better with food than as an apéritif. • $11 • (09/15/95) • **84**
Pinot d'Alsace Alsace White 1992: A hint of spritz lends a perky, vivacious character. The flavors are simple and a bit green, with grapefruit and herb notes, it finishes crisp and fresh. • $11 • (11/15/94) • **81**
Riesling Alsace Réserve White 1993: Characteristic floral and mineral aromas follow through on the palate in this taut, vibrant Riesling. The peach and citrus flavors are crisp and tart and could use some time to unwind. • $13 • (08/31/95) • **86**
Riesling Alsace Réserve White 1992: A Riesling in the German style, soft and delicate. It shows light floral and mineral notes, light body and a clean finish, but lacks intensity. A nice apéritif. • $13 • (11/15/94) • **82**
Tokay Pinot Gris Alsace Réserve Particulière White 1992: Rich and somewhat blowsy, showing perfumed aromas of peach and lilac, honeyed flavors of almond, biscuit and pear and a long, spicy finish. Ripe but a bit cloying. • $NA • (11/15/94) • **87**

KIRWAN, CHÂTEAU

Margaux 1995: Complex, multilayered, full-bodied, this one is a cascade of tobacco, red berry, mineral, smoky flavors. Quite woody at this stage. • $NA • (05/15/96) • **90-94** (BT)
Margaux 1994: Lavishly oaked, but also has a good dose of sweet fruit. A bit diluted, but delicate and rather appealing. • $22 • (05/15/96) • **80-84** (BT)
Margaux 1993: One of the better Kirwans in quite a while. Wonderfully aromatic tobacco, earth and red fruit character and hints of smoky oak. Medium in body, medium-fine tannins and fresh finish. Better in 1997. • $20 • (01/31/96) • **86**
Margaux 1992: Weedy, artichoke flavors, rather simple tobacco and chocolate character, medium tannins and finish. • $22 • **78**
Margaux 1990: A vivacious wine, with lots of ripe fruit, tobacco and cedar character, well-integrated tannins and a long finish. A vast improvement over the '89. Drinkable now. 11,300 cases made. • $28 • (03/31/93) • **90**
Margaux 1989 • $32 • (03/15/92) • **87**
Margaux 1988 • $28 • (04/30/91) • **87**
Margaux 1986 • $25 • (06/30/89) • **82**
Margaux 1985 • $27 • (02/15/89) • **90**
Margaux 1983 • $22 • (07/16/86) • **86**
Margaux 1970 • $50 • (05/15/93) • **86**
Margaux 1945: Very smoky, almost like creosote, very old, but offering a sweetness that carries the finish nicely. Bottled by J. Lyons of London. • $175 • **82**

KLUG

Cabernet Sauvignon Merlot Vin de Pays d'Oc Selection des Grands Chais 1994: This is thin and herbal, with modest dill and dried cherry flavors. A touch of richness, but overall tired and over-the-hill. 4,000 cases made. • $7 • (12/31/95) • **78**
Cabernet Sauvignon Merlot Vin de Pays Selection des Grands Chais d'Oc 1993: A kiss of sweet oak flavor lends some appeal to a basically lean and mature red. 4,000 cases made. • $7 • (07/31/95) • **79**
Chardonnay-Sauvignon Blanc Vin de Pays d'Oc Sélection des Grands Chais 1994: Combines ample fruit flavors and a fairly rich texture for a solid, straightforward character. 4,000 cases made. • $7 • (02/29/96) • **81**
Chardonnay-Sauvignon Blanc Vin de Pays d'Oc Séléction des Grands Chais 1993: The bottle mimics the Empire State Building, but the wine fails to reach its heights. It's ripe and soft, with floral and melon flavors that turn slightly cloying on the finish. 4,000 cases made. • $7 • (07/31/95) • **79**
Chardonnay Vin de Pays d'Oc Sélection des Grands Chais 1994: A lively, well-rounded white with fresh acidity and ripe melon and peach flavors. It's soft and clean. 4,000 cases made. • $7 • (02/29/96) • **82**
Merlot Vin de Pays d'Oc Selection des Grands Chais 1994: Tough and tannic, with earthy aromas. The modest plum and berry flavors are quickly overwhelmed by earthiness and astringency. 4,000 cases made. • $7 • (12/31/95) • **75**

KREVEL

K de Krevel Montravel 1991 • $16 • (08/31/93) • **78**

KREYDENWEISS, MARC

Auxerrois Alsace Kritt Klevner 1992: Ripe, sweet flavors of honey, peach and baked apple are layered delicately over a soft, silky texture. Has length, but sweetness overrides flavor. 350 cases made. • $18 • (11/15/94) • **82**
Gewürztraminer Alsace Kritt White 1992: Sweet and honeyed, yet clean and lively. This is botrytis-styled, with apricot and peach flavors that blend and linger nicely on the finish. Good acidity and balance. 650 cases made. • $19 • (11/15/94) • **87**
Gewürztraminer Alsace Kritt Sélection de Grains Nobles White 1992: One of the thickest, richest wines we have ever encountered. It has an amazingly viscous texture and coats your mouth like a fruity version of molasses. The flavors are good but they pale in comparison to the voluptuous feel of the wine. 20 cases made. • $NA • **92**
Pinot Blanc Alsace Kritt White 1992: Rich and ripe from the aroma of honey to the peach and pineapple flavors to the lingering, fruity finish. Silky texture, vibrant acidity and beautiful balance. 660 cases made. • $14 • (11/15/94) • **87**
Riesling Alsace Andlau White 1992: A vivacious wine, this offers vivid peach, tart lime, spice and floral notes, clean and long on the finish. It's light-bodied and very crisp, balanced on the acidic side, it would go well with rich food. 800 cases made. • $15 • (11/15/94) • **86**
Riesling Alsace Grand Cru Andlau White 1993: This has zippy acidity, with mineral and floral flavors, but not much depth. It finishes on a fairly earthy note. • $18 • (02/29/96) • **81**
Riesling Alsace Grand Cru Kastelberg White 1993: Earthy and mineral in character, with some body, but not much flavor. Fades on the finish, with a touch of bitterness. • $34 • (02/29/96) • **78**
Riesling Alsace Grand Cru Wiebelsberg 1993: Ripe apple flavors and a foxy note run through this medium-bodied Riesling. Short finish. Good, but somewhat flabby. • $28 • (05/15/96) • **82**

Riesling Alsace Grand Cru Wiebelsberg #1 White 1992: An exotic aroma of pear and clove gives way to honey and hazelnut, well balanced and concentrated. A bit atypical for a Riesling, but attractive nonetheless. 250 cases made. • $NA • (11/15/94) • **87**

Riesling Alsace Grand Cru Wiebelsberg #2 White 1992: A fresh, straightforward wine with crisp acidity that lacks much fruit character right now. The structure is good, but the flavor range is narrow, with plenty of green apple and lime. 400 cases made. • $25 • (11/15/94) • **84**

Tokay Pinot Gris Alsace Grand Cru Moenchberg 1993: Rich and flavorful, with green peach, pineapple and nutmeg flavors. It is a well-balanced and fresh wine that is focused and flavorful. • $32 • (02/29/96) • **85**

Tokay Pinot Gris Alsace Grand Cru Moenchberg Vendange Tardive 1992: A grand late harvest wine that is rich, sweet and thick with pear and vanilla flavor. Has good balance and a long finish, satisfying, focused and layered with fruit. 75 cases made. • $30 • (11/15/94) • **87**

Tokay Pinot Gris Alsace Grand Cru Moenchberg White 1992: Sweet, supple, offering pear and melon flavors with spicy, honeyed accents. It's appealing, but lacks concentration and enough acidity for balance. 400 cases made. • $30 • (11/15/94) • **84**

Tokay Pinot Gris Alsace Lerchenberg White 1992: Spicy vanilla and toasted almond flavors jump out of the glass with this vibrant wine, which has enough acidity to carry significant sweetness and finishes clean. A showy wine that's ready now. 300 cases made. • $NA • **89**

Tokay Pinot Gris Alsace Moenchberg Vendange Tardive White 1992: A grand dessert wine that is rich, sweet and thick with flavor. This pear and vanilla-accented Pinot Gris has good balance and a long finish. Satisfying, focused and layered with fruit. 75 cases made. • $NA • (11/15/94) • **87**

White Alsace Clos du Val d'Eléon 1992: This has a lightly nutty, figgy aroma, smooth texture and lively peach notes. Crisp, bracing and well balanced, with enough flavor to keep it interesting. 650 cases made. • $24 • (11/15/94) • **85**

KRITER

Blanc de Blancs Brut de Brut 1985 • $9 • (06/15/90) • **57**
Brut Blanc de Blancs Extra Leger 1983 • $6 • (05/31/87) • **83**
Brut Blanc de Blancs Imperial 1983 • $12 • (06/15/90) • **57**
Brut Rosé NV • $9 • (06/15/90) • **71**
Demi-Sec Délicatesse NV • $12 • (06/15/90) • **83**
Demi-Sec NV • $9 • (06/15/90) • **71**

KRUG

Brut Blanc de Blancs Champagne Clos du Mesnil 1985: Classy, bright gold color, toasty, butterscotchy aromas, a rich, buttery texture and lots of honey, vanilla and lemon flavors that linger on the finish. • $229 • (12/31/95) • **92**

Brut Blanc de Blancs Champagne Clos du Mesnil 1983: Good example of a mature Champagne. Full-bodied, assertive flavor and intriguingly nutty in character, showing lingering walnut, cider and mushroom notes. Some will love this, but it's not for everyone. • $229 • **88**

Brut Blanc de Blancs Champagne Clos du Mesnil 1982 • $150 • (12/31/90) • **84**

Brut Blanc de Blancs Champagne Clos du Mesnil 1981 • $140 • (12/31/90) • **87**

Brut Blanc de Blancs Champagne Clos du Mesnil 1980 • $100 • (05/31/87) • **80**

Brut Champagne 1985: Elegant, refined, and firmly fruity, showing complex aromas of toast, fig, almond and pear, backed by ripe apple, fig and nut flavors and supported by refreshing acidity. This is focused in flavor and harmonious in balance, an outstanding Champagne. 6,000 cases made. • $130 • (12/31/94) • **94**

Brut Champagne 1982: If you like your Champagne very mature, drink this. Superbly rich with bread dough and vanilla and ripe fruit aromas and flavors. Full bodied yet fine with mature and rich flavors. Drink now. • $130 • (12/31/93) • **90**

Key: SS—Spectator Selection. CS—Cellar Selection. BB—Best Buy. $NA—Price not available. (BT)—Barrel tasting. Ⓐ—Auction Price.
Dates in parentheses represent the issues in which the ratings were published.

Brut Champagne 1981 • $105 • (08/31/92) • **88**
Brut Champagne 1979 • $120 • (08/31/92) • **84**
Brut Champagne 1976 • $142 • (08/31/92) • **92**
Brut Champagne 1973 • $530 • (08/31/92) • **92**
Brut Champagne 1971 • $200 • (08/31/92) • **87**
Brut Champagne 1969 • $370 • (08/31/92) • **89**
Brut Champagne 1966 • $210 • (08/31/92) • **89**
Brut Champagne 1964 • $230 • (08/31/92) • **95**
Brut Champagne 1962 • $250 • (08/31/92) • **96**
Brut Champagne 1961 • $210 • (08/31/92) • **82**
Brut Champagne 1959 • $280 • (08/31/92) • **92**
Brut Champagne 1955 • $260 • (08/31/92) • **92**
Brut Champagne 1953 • $300 • (08/31/92) • **89**
Brut Champagne 1952 • $300 • (08/31/92) • **91**
Brut Champagne 1949 • $330 • (08/31/92) • **85**
Brut Champagne 1947 • $450 • (08/31/92) • **98**
Brut Champagne 1945 • $500 • (08/31/92) • **93**
Brut Champagne 1942 • $500 • (08/31/92) • **90**
Brut Champagne 1938 • $500 • (08/31/92) • **91**
Brut Champagne 1937 • $950 • (08/31/92) • **96**
Brut Champagne 1929 • $1,500 • (08/31/92) • **94**
Brut Champagne 1928 • $1,500 • (08/31/92) • **95**
Brut Champagne Clos de Mesnil 1981 • $NA • **87**
Brut Champagne Grand Cuvée NV • $80 • (12/31/93) • **88**
Brut Rosé Champagne NV • $115 • (12/31/89) • **93**

KUENTZ-BAS

Gewürztraminer Alsace Cuvée Tradition White 1992: A full, soft style that has plenty of honey, peach and spice flavor on a smooth texture. Round and clean, full of nice flavors. 400 cases made. • $13 • (11/15/94) • **83**

Gewürztraminer Alsace Réserve Personelle White 1992: Pleasant, rich-tasting and soft in texture. Seems slightly sweet, with spicy almond and peach flavors. Easy to enjoy. 400 cases made. • $16 • (11/15/94) • **83**

Pinot Blanc Alsace Cuvée Tradition White 1992: Intense and delicate, with vivid, balanced peach, orange and herb flavors, long and clean on the finish. Good freshness and depth, try with Vietnamese or Thai cuisine. 1,200 cases made. • $11 • (11/15/94) • **86**

Tokay Pinot Gris Alsace Cuvée Tradition White 1992: Soft and easy-drinking, with pleasant pear, smoke and butter flavors and just enough acidity to keep it lively on the long finish. 300 cases made. • $12 • (11/15/94) • **85**

Tokay Pinot Gris Alsace Réserve Personelle White 1992: A lively blend of grapefruit and vanilla, lemon and butter in this vivid, soft, smooth-textured white. Ripe character and a sweet-seeming finish add to the picture. 300 cases made. • $15 • (11/15/94) • **83**

L DE LA LOUVIERE

Pessac-Léognan 1995: A bit rustic, but some good berry and earthy character shows through. Slightly herbal on the finish. • $NA • (05/15/96) • **80-84** (BT)

Pessac-Léognan 1994: Firm and tannic, showing black olive, herbal character and medium body. It has good concentration but seems a bit drying on the finish. • $NA • **80-84** (BT)

Pessac-Léognan 1993: Fresh and vibrant, sporting a feeling of juicy, grapey fruit on the palate and ending in nice, crisp acidity. Shows some tomato, herb, plum and mocha aromas and flavors. Drinkable now. • $15 • (01/31/96) • **80**

Pessac-Léognan White 1994: Wild, ripe flavors that focus on grapefruit, tropical fruit and grassy notes. Good, pleasant acidity and a long finish. Second wine of La Louvière. If you love great Loire whites, try this. • $14 • (03/31/96) • **87**

Pessac-Léognan White 1993: Flavorful and jumping with varietal character, showing lovely citrus, grassy, melon notes, light-to-medium body and a long, juicy finish. Second label from Château La Louvière. • $15 • (05/31/95) • **86**

Pessac-Léognan White 1992 • $NA • (06/15/94) • **80**

L'ECU, DOMAINE DE

Muscadet de Sèvre et Maine Sur Lie 1992: Unusually thick-bodied, maintaining the high acidity characteristic of the region, yet it's neutral in flavor with only faint echoes of melon and apple. Made from organic grapes. • $NA • (10/31/94) • **81**

LA GARENNE, DOMAINE DE

Mâcon-Azé 1993: Mature, gold-colored, seems to be losing its fruit. Tart and astringent, with a bitter lime edge on the finish. From Perinet and Renoud-Grappin. • $NA • **74**

Pomerol 1994: A beautiful wine with silky tannins and vanilla, berry cherry character. Medium bodied with a medium finish. • $NA • **85-89** (BT)

LA PORCII

Chardonnay Vin de Pays d'Oc 1992: A big, rich wine with toast, butter and fig flavors, it's deep, soft and ready to drink. Oak lovers will appreciate it, but it could use more fruit for balance. 6,500 cases made. • $10 • (01/31/95) • **84**

LABAT, CHÂTEAU

Haut-Médoc 1981 • $7 • (04/01/85) • **72**

LABEGORCE, CHÂTEAU

Margaux 1995: Thick, rich, ripe, concentrated and seductive. Balanced and full-bodied, delivering tons of red berry, tar and earth character. Melts like butter, but it has a lot of sweet fruit and solid tannins. Almost outstanding. • $NA • (05/15/96) • **85-89** (BT)

Margaux 1991: Light and diluted, with tobacco and tomato aromas and flavors. • $14 • (03/31/94) • **74**

Margaux 1990: A wine made from overripe grapes with a rather stewed fruit character. Full-bodied and raisiny with full tannins. Drinkable now. 11,000 cases made. • $20 • (03/31/93) • **82**

Margaux 1987 • $13 • (03/31/91) • **77**

Margaux 1986 • $15 • (02/15/90) • **86**

Margaux 1982 • $20 • (08/31/92) • **88**

LABEGORCE-ZEDE, CHÂTEAU

Margaux 1995: Solid and racy, with sleek tannins and plenty of spicy berry and cherry flavors. Stays flavorful through the finish. Almost outstanding. • $NA • (05/15/96) • **85-89** (BT)

Margaux 1992: A polished Bordeaux providing good color and berry and raspberry aromas, but slightly diluted on the finish. Drink now. • $14 • (04/15/95) • **79**

Margaux 1991: A solid wine with a refined berry and smoke character, medium body and velvety tannins. • $14 • (03/31/94) • **84**

Margaux 1990: Subtle, with aromas of cinnamon, tobacco, and plums that follow through to the palate. Ultrafine tannins. Drinkable now. 9,500 cases made. • $22 • (03/31/93) • **89**

Margaux 1989 • $20 • (03/15/92) • **86**

Margaux 1988 • $20 • (04/30/91) • **83**

Margaux 1987 • $16 • (11/30/89) • **84**

Margaux 1986 • $22 • (11/30/89) • **91**

Margaux 1985 • $38 Ⓐ • (02/29/88) • **84**

Margaux 1983 • $15 • (10/15/86) • **88**

Margaux 1982 • $21 • (11/30/89) • **87**

LABET & N. DECHELETTE, J.

Clos Vougeot Château de la Tour 1991: Light and affable, showing a decent level of berry flavor and an overlay of earthy, stalky notes. Tries hard to be likable, and mostly succeeds. Drinkable now. • $60 Ⓐ • (01/31/94) • **84**

Clos Vougeot Château de la Tour 1990: Overflowing with pure raspberry and cherry flavors, this has a very ripe texture, lots of velvety tannins and a long, beautiful finish. Tastes like a barrel sample and needs time to come around, try after 1997. • $65 • (12/15/92) • **94**

Clos Vougeot Château de la Tour 1988 • $56 • (11/30/90) • **91**

Clos Vougeot Château de la Tour 1987 • $50 • (02/15/91) • **84**

Clos Vougeot Château de la Tour 1985 • $60 • (06/15/88) • **90**

Clos Vougeot Château de la Tour 1979 • $40 • (09/01/84) • **66**

LABET, PIERRE

Beaune Aux Coucherias 1990: An elegant Beaune that's supple and lovely, with plenty of earthy plum characteristics and well-integrated tannins. A joy to drink now. • $35 • (12/15/92) • **88**

Beaune Clos des Monsnières 1994: A bit odd, with a perfumey, floral character. Modest fruit intensity and some cardboard notes. • $26 • (05/31/96) • **70**

Beaune Clos des Monsnières 1993: Lovely ripe strawberry character in this slightly simple but well-structured red which features firm tannins and a medium body of fruit. Try in 1998. • $20 • **87**

Beaune Clos des Monsnières 1991: Extremely earthy, with anise and mud aromas and flavors, never becomes charming or shows much fruit. • $25 Ⓐ • (01/31/94) • **70**

Beaune Clos des Monsnières 1990: Stylish, aromatic and beautiful, with ripe, appealing plum, earth and chocolate flavors lingering on the firm but round finish. Drinkable now. • $30 • (12/15/92) • **89**

Beaune Coucherias 1993: Convoluted style, showing ripe, slightly raisiny character and a dry, tannic finish. Perhaps better in time • $26 • **73**

Beaune Coucherias 1992: Light and pleasant, with some attractive licorice, smoke, spice and red berry flavors around a tannic core that needs time to smooth out. • $26 • **80**

Beaune Coucherias 1991: Woody and harsh, with little roundness of fruit to relieve the tough texture. Finishes mercifully short. • $32 Ⓐ • (01/31/94) • **66**

Bourgogne Pinot Noir 1993: Pleasantly juicy and vibrant, showing some plum, currant and earth flavors. Tannins creep up on the finish. Try from now until 1998. • $14 • **84**

Savigny-lès-Beaune Aux Vergelesses 1994: Attractive, pleasant, moderate intensity, with a nice tropical character in its banana, pear and apple flavors. Lacks concentration, but nice all the same. • $34 • (05/31/96) • **84**

LABOROTTE, LA

Cornas 1991 • $NA • (05/31/94) • **82**

LABOURE-ROI

Bonnes Mares 1990: What a disappointment for a *grand cru*. Firm in texture, with a modest level of cherry and toast flavors peeking through the veil of tannin. Needs until 1997 to '99 to soften. 106 cases made. • $56 • (06/15/93) • **78**

Bonnes Mares 1989 • $55 • (08/31/92) • **92**

Bourgogne 1988 • $12 • (03/31/91) • **83**

Bourgogne Chardonnay White 1991 • $7 • (10/15/93) • **86**

Bourgogne Pinot Noir 1993: A bit earthy but some decent berry and cherry aromas and flavors, medium body and dry tannins. • $9 • **80**

Bourgogne Pinot Noir 1989 • $8 • (08/31/92) • **83**

Bourgogne White 1993: Seems advanced for its age, presenting oaky, drying, grassy flavors. • $8 • **70**

Bourgogne White 1992: Ripe, with exaggerated varietal flavors of sweet apple and fig. It lacks freshness and turns flat on the finish. A dull wine that has little concentration. 7,500 cases made. • $8 • **76**

Chablis 1994: Fresh and lovely, showing ripe, sweet character, light to medium body, a grassy, lemony note and sweet-tasting finish. • $19 • **84**

Chablis Fourchaume 1993: Ripe tropical fruit, apple and spice character, medium body and lots of toasted oak. Perhaps slightly overwooded on the finish. • $17 • **82**

Chablis Les Clos 1993: A bit mean right now with hard, searing acidity, loads of oak and lemony finish. Medium-bodied, somewhat disjointed and rather disappointing for such a great vineyard. • $NA • **80**

Chambertin 1989 • $55 • (08/31/92) • **84**

Chambertin Clos de Bèze 1989 • $60 • (08/31/92) • **84**

Chambolle-Musigny 1991: A healthy dose of oak adds attractive vanilla and brown sugar notes to the cherry and strawberry flavors in this

FRANCE

silky wine. It's harmonious, lean and tannic. Drinkable now through 1997. • $30 • (01/31/95) • **85**

Chambolle-Musigny 1990: Light in texture but generous in flavor, with appealing raspberry, earth and spice aromas and flavors that persist into a firm, focused finish. Drinkable now. 1,600 cases made. • $20 • (06/15/93) • **84**

Chambolle-Musigny 1988 • $35 • (02/28/91) • **86**

Chambolle-Musigny Domaine Cottin 1989 • $30 • (03/31/92) • **76**

Charmes-Chambertin 1993: Crisp, well-defined, lovely red berry flavors, medium body and massive but nicely integrated tannins. Needs time, try after 1997 to '98. • $59 • **86**

Charmes-Chambertin 1990: Ripe, generous and flavorful, with an odd anise edge to the basic berry and cherry flavors. Smooth and round, turning a bit soft and watery on the finish. Drinkable now. 125 cases made. • $45 • (06/15/93) • **85**

Chassagne-Montrachet 1992: An oaky, stiff-textured white with appley and buttery aromas, woody-buttery flavors and vanilla on the finish. • $NA • (08/31/94) • **81**

Chassagne-Montrachet 1991 • $20 • (10/15/93) • **86**

Chassagne-Montrachet Cailleret 1993: Sort of showy, lots of toasted oak character mingling with the lemon and apple flavors. Rather lean and tart, a bit too woody for us. • $25 • **84**

Chassagne-Montrachet Les Morgeots White 1991 • $26 • (10/15/93) • **83**

Chassagne-Montrachet White 1993: Subtle green apple, honey and toasted oak aromas and flavors. Medium-bodied and fresh with a honeyed finish. Slight dilution. Drink now. • $23 • **85**

Clos de Vougeot 1993: Good, silky texture with medium and fine tannins, but slightly herbal and weedy on the finish. Disappointing for this appellation. Try now through 1998. • $57 • **80**

Clos de Vougeot 1990: A firm, focused wine that's lighter in style and elegant, offering strawberry, orange peel and cherry aromas and flavors. Finishes tight and a bit astringent. Drinkable now. 165 cases made. • $44 • (06/15/93) • **83**

Corton-Charlemagne 1993: Hard as a rock. Tart, firm and muscular, showing a tight core of mineral, lime and green apple flavors and elegance on the finish. Try after 1997. • $52 • **82**

Corton-Charlemagne 1991 • $50 • (10/15/93) • **87**

Côtes du Rhône Domaine des Pervanches 1992: This is a tart, simple wine that's also has a nice peppery quality. The plum flavors are subdued. Drink now. • $7 • **83**

Crozes-Hermitage 1991 • $9 • (06/15/93) • **86**

Echézeaux 1993: Fresh and crisp, medium-bodied, showing lively, vivid flavors and silky texture. A touch of chocolate and mocha adds complexity to the raspberry and currant notes. Try now through 2000. • $54 • **89**

Echézeaux 1990: This is an Echézeaux? Light, simple and firm in texture, with little intensity. Drinkable now, but boring. 210 cases made. • $36 • (06/15/93) • **80**

Gevrey-Chambertin 1993: Amazingly refined for a simple village wine, offering vibrant plum, currant and earth aromas. Medium in body, solid fruit and long, silky finish. Better in 1998. • $22 • **87**

Gevrey-Chambertin 1991: There's plenty of fruit here, ripe blackberry and plum flavors, in a round, almost jammy structure, with spicy oak and chocolate notes. It lacks subtlety, but has good concentration. Drinkable now. • $22 • (01/31/95) • **85**

Gevrey-Chambertin 1990: Firm in texture, with solid black cherry and currant flavors that try to get past the gravelly tannins and succeed in part. Drinkable now. 1,600 cases made. • $20 • (06/15/93) • **83**

Gevrey-Chambertin 1988 • $35 • (12/31/90) • **81**

Mâcon-Blanc-Villages 1994: Interesting roasted pine nut, grapefruit and pear flavors. Crisp, but slightly diluted and astringent finish. 9,000 cases made. • $10 • **79**

Mâcon-Blanc-Villages 1991 • $7 • (07/31/93) • **78**

Mazis-Chambertin 1990: Tough and tannic, with more earthy, stemmy flavors than fruit, although hints of nice strawberry and spice come through on the finish. Drinkable now. 106 cases made. • $29 • (06/15/93) • **79**

Key: SS—Spectator Selection. CS—Cellar Selection. BB—Best Buy. $NA—Price not available. (BT)—Barrel tasting. Ⓐ—Auction Price.
Dates in parentheses represent the issues in which the ratings were published.

Meursault 1993: Plenty of mineral, apple, floral, citrus character. Medium in body, tart acidity and herbal finish. • $22 • (05/15/95) • **82**

Meursault 1992: Rich, ripe and well-made Meursault, delivering a lush character, with toast, butter, hazelnut and wet earth flavors that all add up to fine complexity. • $NA • (08/31/94) • **87**

Meursault 1991 • $19 • (10/15/93) • **87**

Montagny White 1993: Nice and lush, supple. Offers some ripe pineapple, pear and green apple flavors and turns lemony and crisp on the finish. • $NA • **83**

Nuits-St.-Georges 1993: Simple and very light with some fruit, but rather weedy and dry on the finish. • $27 • **75**

Nuits-St.-Georges 1991: An attractive wine with flavors that blend smoky oak and spicy fruit. It's on the light side, stylish and smooth, with a fresh, lingering finish. Drinkable now. • $28 • (01/31/95) • **86**

Nuits-St.-Georges 1990: Tight and firm, but a floral, plummy cherry edge and crisp tannins remind you that this a young, unevolved wine. Drinkable now. 1,500 cases made. • $20 • (06/15/93) • **86**

Pinot Noir Bourgogne 1991: Fresh and fruity, offering appealing strawberry, black cherry and spice aromas and flavors that persist on the soft finish, where it echoes a touch of stemminess. Drinkable now. 1,500 cases made. • $7 • (06/15/93) • **83**

Pommard 1993: Crisp and fresh, showing good intensity of blackberry flavor on a relatively lean frame. Clean as can be, but you wish for some more concentration. Try on release. • $24 • **84**

Pommard 1991: Solid and a bit rustic, this wine shows ripe black cherry and attractive earthy flavors, with fair concentration leading to a lingering, but slightly dry finish. Drinkable now through 1997. • $24 • (01/31/95) • **85**

Pommard 1990: Young, tight and compact, with spicy plum and cherry aromas. Firm and tannic, too, but the core of fruit flavor needs time to evolve. Drinkable now through 1997. 1,000 cases made. • $20 • (06/15/93) • **85**

Pommard Les Bertins 1993: Captivating fruit, tasting like freshly crushed raspberries and cherries and adding a light mineral character. Medium in body, tannins and finish. Better in 1998. • $29 • **86**

Pommard Les Bertins 1985 • $29 • (03/15/88) • **79**

Pouilly-Fuissé 1991 • $12 • (07/31/93) • **88**

Puligny-Montrachet 1993: Vivid golden color, vibrant, demonstrates mostly grapefruit flavors and a hint of honey. Elegant, juicy finish. • $24 • **84**

Puligny-Montrachet 1991 • $22 • (10/15/93) • **85**

Puligny-Montrachet Les Chalumeaux 1993: Medium-bodied, quite green, grassy and aggressive, offering some lime, green apple and herb flavors. Try after 1996. • $30 • **81**

Richebourg 1990: Light in color and intensity, this is pleasant enough, but simple and fruity. The strawberry and spice notes are nice, but it's more like a simple Chassagne than an exalted Richebourg. 180 cases made. • $71 • (06/15/93) • **84**

St.-Véran White 1994: Too oaky, tasting more of freshly cut wood boards than wine, but the sweet vanilla shadings and pear and citrus flavors finish nicely. 25,000 cases made. • $8 • **77**

St.-Véran White 1993: Gentle, nicely balanced, presenting lime, earth, wet straw and green apple flavors and a lively, fresh finish. • $9 • **83**

Vosne-Romanée 1991: This gentle, mellow wine offers attractive cherry, spice and toast flavors. Soft and subtle, it's drinkable now. • $23 • (01/31/95) • **83**

LABRY, DOMAINE A. & B.

Auxey-Duresses 1992: Pretty, floral aromas and bright cherry and strawberry flavors distinguish this red of firm texture and medium body. Drink now, while it's charming and delicious. 1,500 cases made. • $16 • (05/15/95) • **87**

LACHESNAYE, CHÂTEAU

Haut-Médoc 1992: Light and earthy with tobacco, watery, cherry character. • $18 • **70**

Haut-Médoc 1990: Well crafted, with rich, earthy, cherry aromas and flavors and a wonderful balance of silky tannins. The finish is long. Drinkable now. • $17 • (03/31/93) • **88**

FRANCE

LACOSTE-BORIE

Pauillac 1993: Medium-bodied but rather diluted plum, herbal, metallic character. • $19 • (01/31/96) • **75**

Pauillac 1990: Plenty of smoky, ripe raspberry aromas and fruit and a smooth texture with integrated tannins. A wine for early drinking. Try now. • $14 • (03/31/93) • **87**

Pauillac 1989 • $15 • (03/15/92) • **89**

Pauillac 1988 • $19 • (04/30/91) • **89**

Pauillac 1986 • $15 • (06/30/89) • **84**

Pauillac 1983 • $7 • (06/15/87) • **75**

LADAU, CHÂTEAU DE

Coteaux du Languedoc 1991 • $NA • (03/15/94) • **82**

LADOUCETTE, DE

Pouilly-Fumé 1993: This white has subtle green plum, mineral and herb notes that carry through from start to the long, mouthwatering finish. Appealing for its subtlety and grace. Drink through 1997. • $25 • (04/30/96) • **87**

Pouilly-Fumé 1992: A rich wine with mature flavors and aromas that are dominated by peach, honey and citrus. Full-bodied and balanced, it is definitely on the softer side with an herbal note on the finish. Drink now. • $23 • (12/31/95) • **85**

Pouilly-Fumé 1991: A big wine beginning to show its age. Butter and vanilla aromas and flavors wrap around a core of apple and herbal notes, the finish mingles citrus and honey. It's muscular and quite rich. Tasted twice. • $24 • (10/31/94) • **84**

Pouilly-Fumé Baron de L 1992: Wet stones and an herb garden are the predominant notes, adding nuances of citrus and chalk. Rich and complex, this is nearing its peak but balanced for drinking into 1998. • $54 • (04/30/96) • **87**

LAFARGE, MICHEL

Bourgogne 1989 • $19 • (01/31/92) • **85**

Bourgogne Pinot Noir 1992: Modest and straightforward, with some strawberry and plum flavors. • $20 • **72**

Bourgogne Pinot Noir 1990 • $18 • (12/15/92) • **82**

Meursault 1992: Simple and straightforward. Shows plenty of lime, grapefruit and green apple flavors, but overall it seems rather dull. Tasted twice with similar results. 180 cases made. • $NA • (08/31/94) • **78**

Volnay 1992: Crisp and lively, with modest berry and floral flavors kicking in on the finish. • $35 • (12/15/94) • **80**

Volnay 1991: Crisp, light, simple and straightforward. An earthy, drying note takes the edge off the fruit. Drinkable now. 333 cases made. • $38 Ⓐ • (01/31/94) • **77**

Volnay 1990: Well made and subtle, with a sense of elegance despite the intensity from the deeply concentrated earth, ripe black cherry and plum flavors. The finish is beautiful and smooth. Drinkable now. • $43 • (12/15/92) • **90**

Volnay 1989 • $41 • (01/31/92) • **88**

Volnay 1987: Lovely, silky and delicious for its rose-petal-scented strawberry and raspberry flavors. Supple and plush in texture. • $52 • **88**

Volnay 1986: Floral aromas. A little chewy but has a nice, narrow beam of plum and currant flavors that linger on the finish. Slightly drying on the finish. • $39 • **87**

Volnay 1985: Very mature, slightly decadent, finishing smooth and complex, echoing plum, berry and earthy tobacco flavors. Subtle, supple and appealing now. • $75 • **89**

Volnay 1983: Mature and a bit tired, with rose petal, plum, spice and prune aromas and flavors. Still chewy and tannic, a little coarse. The flavors echo on the finish. • $NA • **82**

Volnay Clos des Chênes 1993: Not quite as exciting as his Clos du Château des Ducs, yet lovely, fruity and intensely flavored nonetheless. Medium to full body, zingy acidity, turns silky on the finish. Approachable now, but probably will improve. • $94 • **88**

Volnay Clos des Chênes 1992: Very pretty, with polished blackberry and black cherry character, turning spicy and crisp on the finish. Drinkable now. • $65 • (12/15/94) • **85**

Volnay Clos des Chênes 1991: Delicious and supple, with superbly focused floral, raspberry and strawberry flavors and fine tannins. Ready to enjoy now. • $62 • **92**

Volnay Clos des Chênes 1990: Ripe and rich, bursting with currant and blackberry, then becoming a little chewy on the finish. Youthful, exuberant and flavorful without being heavy. Better after 1998. • $75 • **94**

Volnay Clos de Chênes 1989 • $67 • (01/31/92) • **95**

Volnay Clos de Chênes 1988 • $65 • (07/15/91) • **90**

Volnay Clos du Château des Ducs 1993: Vibrant and lovely cherry and plum flavors and a hint of bark. Medium in body, adding soft tannins, sweet fruit and succulent finish. Better in 1999. • $65 • **93**

Volnay Clos du Château des Ducs 1992: Light, a little chewy, but the ripe black cherry flavors and tobacco and earth overtones persist into the finish. Drinkable now. • $65 • (12/15/94) • **83**

Volnay Clos du Château des Ducs 1991: A firm, chunky, solid wine that features generous raspberry, anise and currant aromas and flavors. Finishes with depth, a sense of refinement and elegance. Drinkable now. 333 cases made. • $62 Ⓐ • (01/31/94) • **86**

Volnay Clos du Château des Ducs 1991: Crisp and enjoyable, offering nice currant notes that narrow on the lean, citrusy finish. Try now. 200 cases made. • $62 Ⓐ • (01/31/94) • **85**

Volnay Clos du Château des Ducs 1990: Just gorgeous, with startling violet, tobacco, red berry and earth aromas that are echoed on the palate. The tannins are refined yet firm enough to warrant cellaring this beauty until 1997 or '98. This vineyard site is a monopole, meaning that only Lafarge makes wine from it. 325 cases made. • $75 • (12/15/92) • **95**

Volnay Clos du Château des Ducs 1989 • $67 • (01/31/92) • **94**

Volnay Clos du Château des Ducs 1988 • $65 • (07/15/91) • **90**

Volnay Premier Cru 1988 • $44 • (07/15/91) • **87**

Volnay Vendanges Sélectionées 1992: Bright and aromatic, but it turns crisp and not very generous in flavor. May be better after 1996. • $40 • (12/15/94) • **81**

Volnay Vendanges Sélectionées 1991: Light and tart, displays pretty raspberry and floral aromas and flavors and a bite of tannin on the finish. Try in 1997. 415 cases made. • $40 Ⓐ • (01/31/94) • **82**

LAFAURIE-PEYRAGUEY, CHÂTEAU

Sauternes 1992: Very impressive for the vintage. Medium-bodied and medium-sweet, showing tropical, mineral, lemon and honey flavors that offer plenty of pleasure on the pretty finish. Drinkable now. • $NA • (04/15/95) • **86**

Sauternes 1991: Very sweet and soft, displaying an opulent texture and some cedar, caramel and butterscotch flavors. Drinkable now. • $NA • (04/15/95) • **80**

Sauternes 1990: Gorgeous, classy, appealing creamy texture, lemon, honey and dried apricot flavors, medium body and sweetness and a long finish. Drink now or hold through the decade. • $43 • (04/15/95) • **90**

Sauternes 1989: Unforgettable, packs it in and doesn't pull punches, displaying chewy, bold, toasted oak character and honey, spice, dried apricot and pineapple flavors that end in a fresh finish. Best after 1998. • $50 • (04/15/95) • **94**

Sauternes 1988: Elegant yet intense, medium-bodied, offers plenty of refined toast, vanilla, butter, honey, lemon-pie and spice flavors and a long, long finish. Try in 1998. • $45 • (04/15/95) • **89**

Sauternes 1987 • $27 • (06/15/90) • **87**

Sauternes 1986: Creamy and buttery with custard, spice and oaky flavors that are very sweet and rich. Drinkable now or in the next three to five years. • $30 • (12/31/89) • **86**

Sauternes 1985: Rich and complex, with hazelnut, ginger and orange overtones to the classic fig and tobacco Sauternes flavors. Earthy and sophisticated, long and elegant. Easily one of the best Sauternes of this vintage. • $32 • (09/30/88) • **92**

Sauternes 1983: A vibrant, beautifully balanced wine, lingering on the finish, with good acidity to keep you coming back for more. Medium gold, with lots of ripe apple, pear, spice, delicacy, depth and a fair amount of wood. • $40 • (01/31/88) • **91**

LAFFITTE-CARCASSET, CHÂTEAU

St.-Estèphe 1981 • $7 • (03/16/85) • **74**

LAFITE ROTHSCHILD, CHÂTEAU

Pauillac 1995: As good as the great Lafites of the late '80s. Incredibly complex, with loads of fruit character—from plum to berry to black cherry. Goes on and on with its licorice and mineral notes. Full-bodied, with plenty of rich fruit and ripe tannins. Fabulous. • $NA • (05/15/96) • **95-100** (BT)
Pauillac 1994: Intense aromas of coffee, vanilla, tobacco and cherry. Full-bodied and very racy, with loads of cherry, plum and vanilla flavors that sing through the finish. A big, bruising Lafite in the old style—very much like the '61. • $80 • (05/15/96) • **90-94** (BT)
Pauillac 1993: Very polished and well-crafted black cherry, toast, earth and mineral flavors, all in nice proportions. Medium body, supple tannins. Slightly disappointing for Lafite. Try in 1998. Tasted twice, with consistent notes. • $72 • (01/31/96) • **86**
Pauillac 1992: A real achievement for the vintage, boasting plenty of fruit, tobacco and dark chocolate character. Full-bodied and velvety, impressive richness of ripe tannins. Better after 1996. • $65 • **89**
Pauillac 1991: A balanced, supple wine, with lovely blackberry, complex vanilla and ripe sweetness. Tasted twice with consistent notes. • $60 • (03/31/94) • **85**
Pauillac 1990: Amazing length. It goes on and on, with minty plum and cassis aromas and flavors and ultrafine tannins. Superb. Drink after 1999. 25,000 cases made. • $153 Ⓐ • (03/31/93) • **97**
Pauillac 1989 • $113 Ⓐ • (03/15/92) • **95**
Pauillac 1988 • $104 Ⓐ • (11/30/91) • **94**
Pauillac 1987 • $46 Ⓐ • (11/30/91) • **88**
Pauillac 1986 • $141 Ⓐ • (11/30/91) • **96**
Pauillac 1985: Almost as great as the 1982. Dense, luscious wine with amazingly deep plum, blackberry chocolate aromas and flavors. Full bodied and full tannins. A wine with terrific future. Better after 1998. • $95 • (10/15/94) • **95**
Pauillac 1984 • $39 Ⓐ • (11/30/91) • **87**
Pauillac 1983: Another excellent vintage for Lafite. Extremely fresh, with lovely blackberry and cassis character, a medium body and full tannins. Needs time. Try after 1996. • $90 • (10/15/94) • **91**
Pauillac 1982 • $243 Ⓐ • (08/31/92) • **97**
Pauillac 1981: Delicious, ripe and silky, solid Lafite. Tobacco and berry aromas and flavors. Has medium body with fine tannins and a medium finish. Tasted twice with consistent notes. Drinkable now. • $95 • (10/15/94) • **88**
Pauillac 1980 • $38 Ⓐ • (11/30/91) • **86**
Pauillac 1979 • $88 Ⓐ • (11/30/91) • **92**
Pauillac 1978 • $92 Ⓐ • (11/30/91) • **94**
Pauillac 1977 • $29 Ⓐ • (11/30/91) • **87**
Pauillac 1976 • $152 Ⓐ • (11/30/91) • **88**
Pauillac 1975 • $139 Ⓐ • (11/30/91) • **71**
Pauillac 1974 • $56 • (11/30/91) • **89**
Pauillac 1973 • $30 Ⓐ • (11/30/91) • **87**
Pauillac 1972 • $31 Ⓐ • (11/30/91) • **82**
Pauillac 1971 • $52 Ⓐ • (11/30/91) • **87**
Pauillac 1970 • $138 Ⓐ • (05/15/93) • **89**
Pauillac 1969 • $25 Ⓐ • (11/30/91) • **80**
Pauillac 1968 • $19 Ⓐ • (11/30/91) • **61**
Pauillac 1967 • $42 Ⓐ • (11/30/91) • **80**
Pauillac 1966 • $120 Ⓐ • (11/30/91) • **84**
Pauillac 1965 • $45 • (11/30/91) • **73**
Pauillac 1964 • $101 Ⓐ • (11/30/91) • **87**
Pauillac 1963 • $50 • (11/30/91) • **69**
Pauillac 1962 • $124 Ⓐ • (11/30/91) • **93**
Pauillac 1961: A really good, suave example of Lafite from a vintage in which it often tastes harsh and unyielding with tannins. This bottle blends spicy, nutmeglike aromas with abundant fruit flavors and meaty undertones. It is plenty firm and tannic, but not overly so. The finish is exceptionally long, too. Drink through 2010. • $713 • (04/30/96) • **94**
Pauillac 1960 • $90 • (11/30/91) • **92**
Pauillac 1959 • $489 Ⓐ • (11/30/91) • **94**
Pauillac 1958 • $59 Ⓐ • (11/30/91) • **77**
Pauillac 1957 • $150 • (11/30/91) • **87**
Pauillac 1956 • $83 Ⓐ • (11/30/91) • **85**
Pauillac 1955 • $173 Ⓐ • (11/30/91) • **94**
Pauillac 1954 • $85 Ⓐ • (11/30/91) • **82**
Pauillac 1953 • $314 Ⓐ • (11/30/91) • **94**
Pauillac 1952 • $185 • (11/30/91) • **90**
Pauillac 1951 • $150 • (11/30/91) • **78**
Pauillac 1950 • $177 Ⓐ • (11/30/91) • **91**
Pauillac 1949 • $357 Ⓐ • (11/30/91) • **87**
Pauillac 1948 • $600 • (11/30/91) • **61**
Pauillac 1947 • $240 Ⓐ • (11/30/91) • **74**
Pauillac 1946 • $214 Ⓐ • (11/30/91) • **79**
Pauillac 1945: Magnificent, complex aromas of cedar, spice and currant swirl elegantly through the lean frame. Exudes class and silky finesse as it builds toward the finish. A touch of lime intrudes on aftertaste, and it ends up being sharp after time in the glass. • $NA • **90**
Pauillac 1944 • $380 • (11/30/91) • **63**
Pauillac 1943 • $320 • (11/30/91) • **87**
Pauillac 1942 • $320 • (11/31/91) • **80**
Pauillac 1941 • $500 • (11/30/91) • **69**
Pauillac 1940 • $700 • (11/30/91) • **85**
Pauillac 1939 • $320 • (12/15/88) • **78**
Pauillac 1938 • $225 • (11/30/91) • **83**
Pauillac 1937 • $300 • (11/30/91) • **81**
Pauillac 1934 • $420 • (11/30/91) • **90**
Pauillac 1933 • $200 • (11/30/91) • **80**
Pauillac 1931 • $550 • (11/30/91) • **77**
Pauillac 1929 • $725 Ⓐ • (11/30/91) • **87**
Pauillac 1928 • $674 Ⓐ • (11/30/91) • **66**
Pauillac 1926 • $400 • (11/30/91) • **89**
Pauillac 1925 • $200 • (11/30/91) • **56**
Pauillac 1924 • $474 Ⓐ • (11/30/91) • **88**
Pauillac 1923 • $300 • (11/30/91) • **75**
Pauillac 1922 • $325 • (11/30/91) • **64**
Pauillac 1921 • $500 • (12/15/88) • **77**
Pauillac 1920 • $700 • (11/30/91) • **94**
Pauillac 1919 • $254 Ⓐ • (11/30/91) • **76**
Pauillac 1918 • $238 Ⓐ • (11/30/91) • **80**
Pauillac 1917 • $500 • (11/30/91) • **75**
Pauillac 1916 • $350 • (11/30/91) • **71**
Pauillac 1914 • $560 • (11/30/91) • **58**
Pauillac 1913 • $500 • (11/30/91) • **82**
Pauillac 1912 • $850 • (11/30/91) • **69**
Pauillac 1911 • $443 Ⓐ • (11/30/91) • **83**
Pauillac 1910 • $460 Ⓐ • (11/30/91) • **69**
Pauillac 1909 • $500 • (11/30/91) • **73**
Pauillac 1908 • $600 • (11/30/91) • **86**
Pauillac 1907 • $700 • (11/30/91) • **64**
Pauillac 1906 • $350 • (11/30/91) • **90**
Pauillac 1905 • $500 • (11/30/91) • **88**
Pauillac 1904 • $660 • (11/30/91) • **84**
Pauillac 1903 • $352 Ⓐ • (11/30/91) • **68**
Pauillac 1902 • $950 • (11/30/91) • **80**
Pauillac 1901 • $700 • (11/30/91) • **74**
Pauillac 1900 • $3,500 • (11/30/91) • **79**
Pauillac 1899 • $NA • (12/15/88) • **78**
Pauillac 1898 • $700 • (12/15/88) • **79**
Pauillac 1897 • $1,400 • (12/15/88) • **81**
Pauillac 1896 • $800 • (12/15/88) • **79**
Pauillac 1895 • $2,050 • (12/15/88) • **89**
Pauillac 1894 • $1,500 • (11/30/91) • **71**
Pauillac 1893 • $950 • (12/15/88) • **84**
Pauillac 1892 • $1,300 • (11/30/91) • **72**
Pauillac 1891 • $797 Ⓐ • (11/30/91) • **70**
Pauillac 1890 • $1,100 • (12/15/88) • **83**
Pauillac 1889 • $950 • (12/15/88) • **85**

Key: SS—Spectator Selection. CS—Cellar Selection. BB—Best Buy. $NA—Price not available. (BT)—Barrel tasting. Ⓐ—Auction Price.
Dates in parentheses represent the issues in which the ratings were published.

Pauillac 1888 • $550 • (12/15/88) • **82**
Pauillac 1887 • $1,500 • (11/30/91) • **67**
Pauillac 1886 • $299 Ⓐ • (12/15/88) • **88**
Pauillac 1882 • $800 • (12/15/88) • **82**
Pauillac 1881 • $750 • (11/30/91) • **66**
Pauillac 1880 • $1,500 • (12/15/88) • **82**
Pauillac 1879 • $2,800 • (12/15/88) • **83**
Pauillac 1878 • $1,900 • (12/15/88) • **83**
Pauillac 1877 • $2,500 • (12/15/88) • **88**
Pauillac 1876 • $2,500 • (12/15/88) • **84**
Pauillac 1875 • $608 Ⓐ • (12/15/88) • **91**
Pauillac 1874 • $2,500 • (12/15/88) • **84**
Pauillac 1870 • $3,500 • (11/30/91) • **92**
Pauillac 1869 • $3,500 • (11/30/91) • **87**
Pauillac 1868 • $3,500 • (11/30/91) • **91**
Pauillac 1865 • $400 Ⓐ • (11/30/91) • **50**
Pauillac 1864 • $5,500 • (12/15/88) • **84**
Pauillac 1858 • $4,000 • (12/15/88) • **96**
Pauillac 1848 • $8,500 • (12/15/88) • **92**
Pauillac 1846 • $9,000 • (12/15/88) • **83**
Pauillac 1844 • $6,500 • (12/15/88) • **84**
Pauillac 1832 • $9,000 • (11/30/91) • **78**
Pauillac 1806 • $25,000 • (12/15/88) • **83**

LAFITTE, CHARLES

Brut Champagne Tête de Cuvée NV • $NA • (12/31/91) • **84**

LAFLEUR, CHÂTEAU

Pomerol 1995: Loads of racy, sleek and fast tannins, very good concentration and silky finish. Needs a bit more concentration to be outstanding. Wait and see next year. • $NA • (05/15/96) • **85-89** (BT)
Pomerol 1994: This medium-bodied '94 is almost outstanding, featuring pretty berry and chocolate character. Just a bit angular at this stage. • $NA • (05/15/96) • **85-89** (BT)
Pomerol 1993: Bracing wine for the vintage, featuring firm tannins and ripe berry and cherry aromas and flavors. Medium- to full-bodied, closed finish. Better in 1999. • $180 • (01/31/96) • **88**
Pomerol 1992: Refined currant and tobacco flavors, medium body, silky texture and a medium, fruity finish. Drinkable now. • $140 • **88**
Pomerol 1990: Dense, sweet and rich, with several layers of chewy tannins to shed, but plenty of opulent cherry, currant and tobacco flavors showing through. Wait until 2005 or 2010. • $200 • (05/15/94) • **95**
Pomerol 1989 • $190 • (05/15/94) • **93**
Pomerol 1988 • $140 Ⓐ • (03/31/94) • **91**
Pomerol 1986 • $181 Ⓐ • (03/31/94) • **94**
Pomerol 1985: Gorgeous wine. Sheer, luxurious wine with minty, licorice and fruit character and a sexy silky texture. Better after 1996. • $170 • (10/15/94) • **91**
Pomerol 1983 • $181 Ⓐ • (05/15/94) • **94**
Pomerol 1982 • $382 Ⓐ • (03/31/94) • **93**
Pomerol 1981: Decadent and rich like always. Shows loads of ripe, mature fruit on the finish. Full in body yet compacted and firm with an excellent backbone of ripe tannins. Drinkable now. • $120 • (10/15/94) • **92**
Pomerol 1979 • $225 • (05/15/94) • **88**
Pomerol 1978 • $174 Ⓐ • (05/15/94) • **82**
Pomerol 1975 • $468 Ⓐ • (05/15/94) • **78**
Pomerol 1973 • $140 • (05/15/94) • **78**
Pomerol 1971 • $220 Ⓐ • (05/15/94) • **85**
Pomerol 1970 • $275 • (05/15/94) • **86**
Pomerol 1967 • $275 • (05/15/94) • **67**
Pomerol 1966 • $362 Ⓐ • (05/15/94) • **85**
Pomerol 1964 • $300 • (05/15/94) • **87**
Pomerol 1962 • $325 • (05/15/94) • **86**
Pomerol 1961: Big and bold, a full-bodied, fully-fleshed-out Pomerol that matched Petrus in this tasting. It has great concentration, lots of body, firm tannins and layers of deep, mouth-filling fruit flavors that are still lively and fresh. Beautiful to drink now, but should be fine through 2010. • $715 • (04/30/96) • **93**
Pomerol 1959 • $550 • (05/15/94) • **87**
Pomerol 1955 • $276 Ⓐ • (05/15/94) • **50**
Pomerol 1953 • $650 • (05/15/94) • **85**
Pomerol 1952 • $650 • (05/15/94) • **87**
Pomerol 1950 • $2,000 • (05/15/94) • **91**
Pomerol 1949 • $2,100 • (05/15/94) • **80**
Pomerol 1947 • $979 Ⓐ • (05/15/94) • **98**
Pomerol 1945 • $2,500 • (05/15/94) • **88**
Pomerol English Bottling 1952 • $375 • (05/15/94) • **79**

LAFLEUR-DU-ROY, CHÂTEAU

Pomerol 1982 • $28 • (05/15/89) • **83**
Pomerol 1970 • $85 • (05/15/93) • **85**

LAFLEUR-GAZIN, CHÂTEAU

Pomerol 1995: Rich berry, cherry, earthy character. Medium body, tannins and finish. Delicious. • $NA • (05/15/96) • **85-89** (BT)
Pomerol 1993: Delicious milk chocolate, berry and cherry aromas and flavors, medium body, delicate tannins and fresh finish. Drinkable now. • $24 • (01/31/96) • **85**
Pomerol 1990: Round and generous, with an abundance of rich fruit and soft tannins. The character goes from earthy to licorice. Drinkable now. 3,500 cases made. • $30 • (03/31/93) • **90**
Pomerol 1989 • $NA • (03/15/92) • **87**
Pomerol 1945 • $NA • (03/16/86) • **58**

LAFON, DOMAINE DES COMTES

Meursault 1992: Showy, ripe and almost sweet, with layers of butter, honey, vanilla and pear flavors that expand on the finish. Drink now through 1997. • $48 • (05/15/95) • **88**
Meursault Clos de la Barre 1992: A silky, smooth Burgundy that's full-bodied and plays variations on its carmel, butterscotch, coffee and spice notes. It also delivers some refreshing lemon character and a chalky, mineral quality that gives it depth and interest. Drinkable now. • $55 • **90**
Meursault Les Charmes 1992: What a beauty! Brilliant winemaking here. It pushes the envelope with seductive toasted hazelnut, pear, pie crust, honey and earth flavors in perfectly balanced proportions. This is what white Burgundy is all about. Awesome now but should taste great for years. • $75 • (08/31/94) • **93**
Meursault Les Genevrières 1992: Showy and unctuous, full-throttled, full-bodied white Burgundy that's amazingly ripe, rich and fat. Delivers tons of honey, toasted coconut, spice, pear and apricot flavors, but stays fresh and vibrant on the finish. Drinkable now through 1999. • $75 • **94**
Meursault Les Perrières 1993: Classy white Burgundy, boasting a leesy character that's bursting with exciting lemon, honey, toasted bread and pie crust flavors. Extremely well made, tightly wrapped, focused and concentrated, right through the long, searing finish. Better in 2000. • $80 • (05/31/96) • **93**
Meursault Perrières 1992: A full-blown, full-bodied, ripe and rich white Burgundy that's packed with toasted oak, pear, spice and caramel flavors. For those who love this fat style. Turns to truffle and mushroom flavors on the chewy, intense finish. Better in 1998. • $80 85 • **90**
Monthelie-les-Duresses 1992: A stylish red from a lesser village in Burgundy. It has attractive spicy, cedary, chocolaty aromas, good cherry and berry flavors and a lean, tart, rather tannic finish. Drinkable now. • $25 • (05/31/95) • **84**
Montrachet 1994: Mind-boggling, full-throttle white Burgundy that not only delivers amazing toast, butterscotch, honey and ripe fruit complexity, but also kicks in on the finish with awesome intensity. Creamy, silky texture and overall balance are simply magical. Drinkable now or age until the next century. 100 cases made. • $350 • (05/31/96) • **98**
Montrachet 1990 • $413 • (10/15/93) CS • **100**
Volnay 1992: Lively and approachable, its raspberry and strawberry flavors on a lean frame, slightly candied finish. Drinkable now. • $NA • **85**
Volnay 1991: Earthy, smoky aromas and flavors characterize this light, slightly astringent wine. Shows a touch of berry and a bit more complexity than most. Drinkable now. • $54 Ⓐ • (01/31/94) • **83**

Volnay Clos des Chânes 1993: Interesting '93, as some earthy, minty, red berry notes marry into an elegant package. Of medium body, it's flavorful and sweet-tasting, adding a long, exuberant finish. Try in 2000. • $NA • **88**

Volnay En Champans 1993: A bit simple for the vintage, delivering black cherry and wet earth aromas and flavors. Medium-bodied, light tannins, light finish. Drinkable now. • $NA • **85**

Volnay-Santenots Les Santenots du Milieu 1993: A red of distinction. Loads of fruit but also fascinating mineral and spice character. Full body, fine tannins and long, long finish. Needs time, better in 2001. • $NA • (05/15/96) • **93**

Volnay-Santenots Les Santenots du Milieu 1992: A sweet-tasting beauty, packed with red berry, earth and mineral character, remaining tight now but should improve and soften upon aging until 2001. Somewhat dry on the finish. Massive tannins and long, long finish. One of the best red Burgundies we've tasted from the difficult '92 vintage. • $NA • **90**

LAFON-ROCHET, CHÂTEAU

St.-Estèphe 1995: Solid as a rock. Loads of wild blackberry and cherry flavor and minty character. Full yet very fine tannins. Long, long finish. Superb all around. • $NA • (05/15/96) • **90-94** (BT)

St.-Estèphe 1994: Attractive black cherry and mineral aromas and flavors. Medium-bodied, fine tannins and simple finish. • $NA • **80-84** (BT)

St.-Estèphe 1993: Attractive and quite beefy, showing loads of tobacco, cassis and wet earth character. Full in body, it coats your mouth with massive but supple tannins. This one needs time, try in 2000. 15,200 cases made. • $23 • (01/31/96) • **88**

St.-Estèphe 1992: Bright and vivid, interesting currant character. Medium in body with firm tannins but slightly astringent on the finish. Drinkable now. • $18 • **84**

St.-Estèphe 1991: Simple, light and fruity, with pleasant berry and cherry flavors and a slightly dry finish. • $18 • (03/31/94) • **78**

St.-Estèphe 1990: Traditional St.-Estèphe, with spicy, earthy and berry aromas and flavors, firm tannins and a rich finish. No frills but well made. Drinkable now. 12,000 cases made. • $21 • (03/31/93) • **89**

St.-Estèphe 1989 • $31 Ⓐ • (03/15/92) • **92**

St.-Estèphe 1982 • $86 Ⓐ • (08/31/92) • **90**

St.-Estèphe 1970 • $27 Ⓐ • (05/15/93) • **80**

St.-Estèphe 1961 • $80 • (03/16/86) • **58**

St.-Estèphe 1945 • $100 • (03/16/86) • **75**

LAFOND, COMTE

Sancerre 1992: Wonderfully mature, rich, complex and well focused, boasting aromas and flavors to match. It's bursting with ripe fig, tobacco, quince and citrus notes and plenty of acidity. Lingering finish, drink now through 1997. • $23 • (04/30/96) • **89**

LAFRAN-VEYROLLES, DOMAINES

Bandol 1983 • $NA • (08/31/86) • **67**

LAGARENNE, CHÂTEAU

Bordeaux Supérieur 1988 • $8 • (07/31/90) • **82**

LAGET, DOMAINE FRANCOIS

Châteauneuf-du-Pape 1985 • $14 • (09/30/87) • **71**

Châteauneuf-du-Pape 1984 • $14 • (12/31/87) • **76**

Châteauneuf-du-Pape 1983 • $12 • (09/30/87) • **89**

Key: SS—Spectator Selection. CS—Cellar Selection. BB—Best Buy. $NA—Price not available. (BT)—Barrel tasting. Ⓐ—Auction Price.
Dates in parentheses represent the issues in which the ratings were published.

LAGRANGE, CHÂTEAU

Pomerol 1995: A bit light and easy, offering some decent fruit notes. Somewhat one-dimensional. • $NA • (05/15/96) • **80-84** (BT)

Pomerol 1994: Rather exotic, sporting lots of coconut, toasted oak and vanilla flavors, medium body and firm tannins. • $NA • (05/15/96) • **85-89** (BT)

Pomerol 1993: Delicious and round, showing gamy, earthy, red berry character. Medium in body, medium-velvety tannins and a fruity finish. Drinkable now. • $29 • (01/31/96) • **83**

Pomerol 1992: Evolving more quickly than we thought. Light in body and diluted, showing dried-herb and berry flavors. • $24 • **75**

Pomerol 1990: Dense and powerful, with a breathtaking aftertaste of blackberries, chocolate and earth. Superb wine with harmonious structure to easily take you into the next century. Drinkable in 2000. 3,000 cases made. • $30 • (03/31/93) • **95**

Pomerol 1989 • $29 • (03/15/92) • **87**

Pomerol 1982 • $30 • (05/15/89) • **84**

St.-Julien 1995: Very elegant for Lagrange, featuring pretty, perfumed blackberry and mineral aromas and flavors, full body, fine tannins and long, succulent finish. • $NA • (05/15/96) • **90-94** (BT)

St.-Julien 1994: Round texture, with fine tannins and fresh fruit flavors. A good, solid wine. Delicious. • $24 • (05/15/96) • **85-89** (BT)

St.-Julien 1993: A very good St.-Julien from this consistent property, really caressing your palate in velvety tannins. Medium body and pretty berry, vanilla, toasted oak character. Better in 1997. • $25 • (01/31/96) • **89**

St.-Julien 1992: Extremely well made, exhibiting a lovely balance of round, supple tannins and vivid berry and cherry flavors. Medium body and tannins and a fruity finish. Drinkable now. • $20 • **87**

St.-Julien 1991: A lovely wine for this vintage, with smoky blackberry and tobacco flavors. An elegant, medium-bodied wine that delivers velvety texture with its fine tannins. • $24 Ⓐ • (03/31/94) • **86**

St.-Julien 1990: Like a Rodin sculpture: rugged yet well-defined. It shows concentrated cassis, berry and dark chocolate flavors, rich tannins and a long, opulent finish. Drink after 1998. 22,500 cases made. • $30 • (03/31/93) • **95**

St.-Julien 1989 • $29 • (03/15/92) • **95**

St.-Julien 1986 • $33 • (02/15/90) • **86**

St.-Julien 1985: The first outstanding quality Lagrange from its new regime. A distinctive wine with dark chocolate, prune aromas and flavors. Full body and big with lots of silky tannins. Needs time. Try after 1997. • $32 • (10/15/94) • **91**

St.-Julien 1983: Very good and straightforward with lead pencil, plum and berry character, medium body and very firm tannins. Drink now. • $28 • (10/15/94) • **88**

St.-Julien 1982 • $36 • (08/31/92) • **89**

St.-Julien 1981: From the old days at this estate. Still, a pretty, old-fashioned Bordeaux with medium body, firm texture and fruity, chestnut character. Drink now. • $23 • (10/15/94) • **85**

St.-Julien 1970 • $44 • (05/15/93) • **84**

St.-Julien 1961: A firmly textured, nicely fruity Bordeaux that starts with mature, earthy aromas, then turns clean and snappy on the palate and finish. Drink now through 2000. • $47 • (04/30/96) • **86**

LAGRAVE PARAN, CHÂTEAU

Bordeaux 1989 • $8 • (02/28/91) • **79**

Bordeaux 1988 • $6 • (07/15/90) • **82**

Bordeaux 1987 • $7 • (05/15/90) • **80**

LAGREZETTE, CHÂTEAU

Cahors 1992: Densely flavored, tannic, dark in color, showing attractive oaky accents of vanilla and cinnamon. Robust and concentrated, should gain some complexity with time. Try after 1996. 5,000 cases made. • $12 • (03/31/95) • **86**

Cahors 1990: Deep color and intriguing anise and smoky aromas promise more than this delivers right now, on the palate it's smooth and firm, but lacking in fruit. Still, there's some concentration. 10,000 cases made. • $10 • (09/15/94) • **83**

Cahors 1989: There's plenty to like here, from the deep, youthful color to the long, complex finish. Appealing aromas of tobacco and roasted fruit lead to plum, licorice and smoky flavors. It's smooth, concentrated and well-balanced. Drinkable now. • $10 • **88**

LAGUNE, CHÂTEAU LA

Haut-Médoc 1990: A wine to linger over. The aromas are opulent with new oak and ripe fruit, a rich, concentrated palate offers cherry, current, cedar and licorice flavors. It's full-bodied yet graceful, beautifully structured and seamless, with a long fruity finish. Drinkable now. 25,000 cases made. • $24 Ⓐ • (10/15/94) • **95**
Haut-Médoc 1989 • $27 Ⓐ • (03/15/92) • **86**
Haut-Médoc 1988 • $17 Ⓐ • (04/30/91) • **91**
Haut-Médoc 1987 • $20 • (05/15/90) • **89**
Haut-Médoc 1986 • $34 Ⓐ • (06/30/89) • **89**
Haut-Médoc 1985: Elegant and fresh with a minty, berry character. Medium-bodied and delicious to drink now. • $25 • (10/15/94) • **89**
Haut-Médoc 1984 • $15 Ⓐ • (03/31/87) • **86**
Haut-Médoc 1983: Extremely well crafted with a firm, polished structure. Grapey, vanilla and chocolate aromas and flavors with a full body and long caressing finish. Drinkable now. • $28 • (10/15/94) • **91**
Haut-Médoc 1982 • $62 Ⓐ • (08/31/92) • **94**
Haut-Médoc 1981: Super-fine, with tobacco, chocolate, vanilla and fruit aromas and flavors. Full-bodied yet reserved, followed by a long silky finish. Drinkable now. • $25 • (10/15/94) • **91**
Haut-Médoc 1979 • $29 • (10/15/89) • **86**
Haut-Médoc 1970 • $46 Ⓐ • (05/15/93) • **87**
Haut-Médoc 1962 • $34 Ⓐ • (11/30/87) • **80**
Haut-Médoc 1961: A ripe, almost sweet fruitiness is the hallmark of this broadly flavored, smoky-tasting, richly textured wine. Reminds you of an aged Burgundy. Drink now through 2000. • $83 • (04/30/96) • **88**
Haut-Médoc 1945 • $200 • (03/16/86) • **87**

LAISSUS, CHÂTEAU

Vieilles Vignes Côte de Brouilly 1994: Tea and tobacco notes have emerged with bottle age in this polished, yet still firm red. The black cherry flavors are ripe and linger on the finish. • $NA • **84**

LAJOLIE

Cabernet Sauvignon Vin de Pays d'Oc 1987 • $6 • (10/31/88) • **78**

LALANDE, DOMAINE

Sauvignon Blanc Vin de Pays d'Oc 1992 • $8 • (08/31/93) • **79**

LALANDE-BORIE, CHÂTEAU

St.-Julien 1993: Vivid, polished '93 offering mint, berry and vanilla aromas and flavors, medium body, sleek tannins and long, silky finish. Delicious. • $18 • (01/31/96) • **85**
St.-Julien 1991: Decent texture and a lean structure, with red berry and stewed tomato flavors. • $14 • (03/31/94) • **77**
St.-Julien 1990: This delivers plenty of plummy tobacco character and velvety tannins with an attractive smoky, fruity finish. Drinkable in 1997. • $19 • (03/31/93) • **90**
St.-Julien 1989 • $17 • (03/15/92) • **88**
St.-Julien 1988 • $17 • (04/30/91) • **87**
St.-Julien 1987 • $15 • (11/30/89) • **81**
St.-Julien 1986 • $17 • (11/30/89) • **91**
St.-Julien 1982 • $17 • (08/31/92) • **91**

LALEURE-PIOT

Bourgogne Passetoutgrain 1993: Vibrant red featuring sliced plum and citrus character, medium body, crisp acidity and light tannin structure. Drinkable now. • $15 • **84**
Chorey-lès-Beaune Les Champs Longs 1993: Brilliant, vivid dried cherry, raspberry and wet earth character, medium body and tannins and a long, crisp finish. Better in 1999. • $17 • **87**
Corton Bressandes 1993: Tight and not giving much at this stage, yet featuring some fine tannins and ripe fruit. Medium to full body and a short finish. Give it time, try after 2000. • $51 • **91**
Corton Bressandes 1990: Voluptuous, with loads of smoky black cherry aromas and flavors and velvety tannins. Drinkable now. • $NA • (12/15/92) • **90**
Corton-Charlemagne 1994: Decent apple and toasted oak flavors. Very tart and a bit short on the finish. • $70 • (05/31/96) • **75**
Corton Le Rognet 1993: Nicely balanced between plum, earth and red berry notes. Medium in body, well-integrated tannins. The finish is ripe and long but a touch alcoholic. Try in 1999. • $47 • **89**
Côte de Nuits-Villages 1990: Extremely high in volatile acidity, with aromas of paint thinner and nail polish remover. What a shame, since it also shows an amazing amount of rich fruit flavor. Not recommended. • $NA • (12/15/92) • **65**
Pernand-Vergelesses 1994: Lean and crisp, with only modest fruit flavors and little length. • $28 • (05/31/96) • **78**
Pernand-Vergelesses Ile des Vergelesses 1993: Soft at first, offering a currant, vanilla and smoke character before tannins tighten on the palate and finish. Medium body and good concentration. Try in 2000. • $33 • **85**
Pernand-Vergelesses Ile des Vergelesses 1990: Offers loads of fruit, a very round texture with glorious currant, cherry and earth notes. Drinkable now. • $NA • (12/15/92) • **90**
Pernand-Vergelesses Les Vergelesses 1993: Some good floral, dried cherry aromas but rather muted in the palate, adding hard tannins and short aftertaste. Perhaps better after a year or two of bottle age, try in 1997. • $24 • **84**
Pernand-Vergelesses Les Vergelesses 1992: Open-textured with appealing wild berry and plum flavors. Rustic in style but generous enough. Drinkable now. • $27 • **83**
Pernand-Vergelesses Les Vergelesses 1990: Juicy and ripe, combining lovely black cherry, herb and tar notes and fine tannins. The finish goes on and on. Drinkable now. • $NA • (12/15/92) • **89**
Pernand-Vergelesses Premier Cru 1994: A solid, muscular, full-bodied floral white that has tons of flavors—oak, cedar, apple, pear and mineral. A bit rough and tumble, like a hammer hitting you over the head, but it has personality. Try in 1998. • $34 • (05/31/96) • **88**
Pernand-Vergelesses Premier Cru 1993: Lively acidity and fresh fruit but rather one-dimensional. Medium to light body and firm tannins. Drinkable now. • $22 • **84**
Savigny-lès-Beaune Les Vergelesses 1993: Not a big wine but has lovely bright fruit character. Medium-bodied, adding firm tannins and medium aftertaste of dried cherries and minerals. Better in 1998. • $25 • **86**

LAMARCHE, DOMAINE FRANCOIS

Clos de Vougeot 1987 • $55 • (09/30/90) • **86**
Clos de Vougeot 1985 • $48 • (10/15/88) • **90**
Echézeaux 1987 • $48 • (09/30/90) • **87**
Vosne-Romanée La Grande Rue 1987 • $68 • (09/30/90) • **91**
Vosne-Romanée La Grande Rue 1985 • $60 • (10/15/88) • **89**
Vosne-Romanée Malconsorts 1985 • $44 • (10/15/88) • **84**
Vosne-Romanée Suchots 1985 • $36 • (10/15/88) • **91**

LAMARQUE, CHÂTEAU DE

Haut-Médoc 1992: Very light and diluted with cherry, earthy character and a light finish. Drink now. • $13 • **74**
Haut-Médoc 1991: Elegant yet simple. Delivers ripe fruit in a lean-structured wine. • $13 • (03/31/94) • **80**
Haut-Médoc 1990: A firm and well-structured wine, with a solid tannin backbone and fresh cherry and herbal character. Drinkable now. 25,000 cases made. • $18 • (03/31/93) • **86**
Haut-Médoc 1989 • $26 • (03/15/92) • **89**
Haut-Médoc 1988 • $20 • (04/30/91) • **86**
Haut-Médoc 1987 • $10 • (11/30/89) • **74**
Haut-Médoc 1986 • $18 • (11/30/89) • **75**
Haut-Médoc 1982 • $18 • (08/31/92) • **82**

LAMARTINE, CHÂTEAU

Bordeaux Supérieur 1991: Clean, steely wine with plum and cherry aromas and flavors, medium tannins and a short finish. Tasted twice. • $10 • (03/31/94) • **78**

Bordeaux Supérieur 1990: Fresh and fruity, but slightly simple and diluted. Drinkable now. • $NA • (03/31/93) • **79**

Bordeaux Supérieur 1984 • $9 • (05/15/87) • **76**

LAMBRAYS, DOMAINE DES

Clos des Lambrays 1993: Very classy *grand cru*, showing lively raspberry, wild berry, cassis and toasted oak flavors that marry nicely with firm tannins. Rather sweet and ripe, chewy. Long finish. Cellar until 1999. • $NA • **89**

LAMOTHE, CHÂTEAU

Sauternes 1988: Light and fruity, with appealing nectarine and earth aromas and flavors that are a bit grassy, smoothing out on the finish. Drinkable now. • $16 • (03/31/91) • **84**

Sauternes 1986: Has complexity and subtlety in a medium-weight framework, ripe and round without being overblown. Smooth and well balanced for drinking now. • $29 • (12/31/89) • **85**

LAMOTHE DE HAUX, CHÂTEAU

Bordeaux White 1994: A basic, medium-bodied white Bordeaux that has onion and mineral flavors. • $8 • (02/29/96) • **78**

LAMOTHE-CISSAC, CHÂTEAU

Haut-Médoc 1987 • $10 • (11/30/89) • **74**

Haut-Médoc 1986 • $12 • (11/30/89) • **69**

LAMOTHE-DESPUJOLS, CHÂTEAU

Sauternes 1987 • $NA • (06/15/90) • **84**

LAMOTHE-GUIGNARD, CHÂTEAU

Sauternes 1992: Smooth but slightly unbalanced, showing some spicy apricot and honey flavors and a somewhat alcoholic finish. Drinkable now. • $NA • (04/15/95) • **78**

Sauternes 1990: Impressively unctuous, powerful and exotic, good acidity backing up the ripe, rich marmalade, spice, honey and dried apricot flavors. A mouth-filling Sauternes that should age for decades but is tempting now. • $30 • (04/15/95) • **92**

Sauternes 1989: Flashy and enticing, round, thick and velvety, offering full-throttle tropical flavors backed by some vanilla and lemon notes. Lacks a bit of acidity. Drinkable now. • $25 • (04/15/95) • **88**

Sauternes 1988: Quite mature already and very sweet. Ripe, rich and thick, displaying dried apricot, honey and butterscotch character, though falling a bit short on the finish. • $35 • (04/15/95) • **87**

Sauternes 1987 • $23 • (06/15/90) • **77**

Sauternes 1986: Wonderfully balanced, presenting a grassy, lime edge that cuts through the ripe, rich, oily texture. Distinctive and harmonious, yet serious enough to postpone drinking until after 2000. • $30 • (04/15/95) • **92**

Sauternes 1983: A racy, clean-as-a-whistle Sauternes that graciously unfolds its spice, clove, honey and smoke flavors. Needs another five to ten years to show it all. • $NA • (04/15/95) • **92**

LANCON PERE & FILS

Châteauneuf-du-Pape Domaine de la Solitude 1983 • $14 • (12/31/87) • **58**

Key: SS—Spectator Selection. CS—Cellar Selection. BB—Best Buy. $NA—Price not available. (BT)—Barrel tasting. Ⓐ—Auction Price.
Dates in parentheses represent the issues in which the ratings were published.

LANDAT, CHÂTEAU

Haut-Médoc 1987 • $7 • (11/30/89) • **73**

LANDAY, CHÂTEAU

Haut-Médoc 1982 • $6 • (02/16/85) • **77**

Haut-Médoc 1981 • $6 • (02/16/85) • **72**

LANDEREAU, CHÂTEAU

Bordeaux Supérieur 1985 • $6 • (02/15/88) • **81**

LANESSAN, CHÂTEAU

Haut-Médoc 1992: Some decent body but just too unripe, presenting stewed tomato, green bean character. Drink if you must. • $15 • **73**

Haut-Médoc 1990: Polished and smooth, with lovely aromas and flavors of cherry and earth and very velvety tannins. Drinkable now. 3,000 cases made. • $16 • (03/31/93) • **86**

Haut-Médoc 1989 • $20 • (03/15/92) • **85**

Haut-Médoc 1988 • $20 • (07/31/91) • **80**

Haut-Médoc 1985 • $16 Ⓐ • (04/30/88) • **87**

Haut-Médoc 1982 • $23 Ⓐ • (08/31/92) • **91**

LANGE, CHÂTEAU

Sauternes 1987 • $NA • (06/15/90) • **78**

LANGLOIS-CHÂTEAU

Brut Crémant de Loire Langlois: Plenty of acidity here, featuring chalky texture and flavors dominated by citrus notes and some earthy nuances. A bit coarse, but it has character, though the finish falls slightly short. • $14 • (04/30/96) • **84**

Brut Crémant de Loire NV • $11 • (07/15/88) • **84**

Chinon Château de Rivière 1992: Rustic, with an earthy tinge to the raspberry and herb flavors, the astringent finish lacks grace. • $11 • (10/31/94) • **77**

Pouilly-Fumé Les Pierrefeux 1994: Fresh and lively, but rather neutral in flavor. It lacks generosity. • $18 • (04/30/96) • **78**

Rosé Saumur Crémant NV • $11 • (07/15/88) • **86**

Sancerre Château de Fontaine-Audon 1994: Assertively herbal grapefruit, lemon and grass flavors. It's lean and tart and tastes a bit green on the finish. • $18 • (04/30/96) • **78**

Sancerre Château de Fontaine-Audon 1992: Pungent herbaceous aromas give way to mineral and light peach flavors, crisp and dry on the palate. A slight earthiness detracts a bit, but the wine is stylish and focused. • $16 • (10/31/94) • **83**

Saumur 1993: Plenty of red berry flavors punctuate the smoky, herbal scent. Fresh and lively for current drinking. • $11 • (05/15/96) • **84**

Saumur White 1994: Granny Smith apples and beeswax flavors are buoyed by firm acidity that suggests giving this white a little time to smooth out. Very good depth and concentration here. • $11 • (05/15/96) • **85**

LANGOA BARTON, CHÂTEAU

St.-Julien 1995: Pretty violet, berry and cherry aromas and flavors, medium body, fine tannins and a fresh finish. • $NA • (05/15/96) • **85-89** (BT)

St.-Julien 1994: Well-made red offering fine tannins, medium fruit and a fresh finish. • $NA • (05/15/96) • **85-89** (BT)

St.-Julien 1993: Very good berry and cherry flavor and a hint of new wood. Medium in body with medium-firm tannins and light finish. Better in 1998. • $25 • (01/31/96) • **86**

St.-Julien 1991: Soft, simple and fruity, with black cherry and chocolate notes. A bit dry. • $18 • (03/31/94) • **77**

St.-Julien 1990: A balanced, refined wine with everything in the right proportions. Vanilla, cherry and plum character and fine tannins are all there. Drinkable in 1997. 7,000 cases made. • $27 • (03/31/93) • **91**

St.-Julien 1989 • $25 • (03/15/92) • **94**

St.-Julien 1988 • $20 • (07/15/91) • **86**
St.-Julien 1985 • $26 Ⓐ • (06/15/88) • **91**
St.-Julien 1983: Another fresh wine with medium ruby color and a fine perfume of berries and cherries. Not a blockbuster but its elegance in fresh fruit and fine tannins is impressive. Drink now. • $NA • **87**
St.-Julien 1982 • $31 • (08/31/92) • **91**
St.-Julien 1981: Straightforward wine with cherry, spicy, mushroom character, medium body and a fruity finish. Drink now. • $NA • **83**
St.-Julien 1970 • $50 • (05/15/93) • **85**
St.-Julien 1961 • $115 • (03/16/86) • **63**
St.-Julien 1945 • $250 • (03/16/86) • **71**

LANGOUREAU, SYLVAIN

Meursault La Pièce Sous Le Bois 1992: Quite soft and harmonious, it delivers some pleasant butter, vanilla and pear flavors, ending with a toasty note on the finish. • $32 • (08/31/94) • **85**
St.-Aubin Les Remilly White 1992: Crisp and simple, with modest apple, pear and spice notes. Seems a bit advanced for such a young wine. • $17 • (08/31/94) • **77**

LANSON

225th Anniversary Cuvée 1981 • $43 • (10/15/88) • **89**
225th Anniversary Spècial Cuvée 1980 • $43 • (11/30/86) • **95**
Blanc de Blancs Champagne 1983: Not for everyone, this well-aged Champagne has intriguing aromas of ripe Brie, and flavors of toast, fig, vanilla and apple, followed by a tart finish. • $NA • **85**
Brut Champagne 1988: Tastes like a fresh, lively, concentrated Chardonnay with bubbles. Has good acidity and a lingering finish. Drinkable now. Tasted twice. • $39 • **89**
Brut Champagne 1985: A super Champagne. Wonderfully focused and well balanced, with focused lemon and apple aromas, sweet, ripe lemon flavor and hints of dough. Medium-bodied, with a creamy mouth-feel. 40,000 cases made. • $37 • (12/31/90) • **93**
Brut Champagne 1983: Young, intense, rich and lively, with good depth of flavor and lemon, spice and ginger nuances in an agressive style that needs food to offset some of the coarseness. Drink now. • $30 • (12/31/89) • **85**
Brut Champagne 1982: Toasty, rich and concentrated, offering elegance and finesse, complexity and suppleness, yeasty and with just a hint of Pinot Noir fruit. Finish is long and tasty. • $27 • (10/15/88) • **92**
Brut Champagne Black Label Cuvée NV • $24 • (12/31/88) • **88**
Brut Champagne Black Label NV • $35 • (12/31/91) • **87**
Brut Champagne Noble Cuvée de Lanson 1988: Generous and fruity in flavor, lively in balance but tart on the finish. The seductive aromas of vanilla and nutmeg are followed by crisp, appley flavors. • $NA • **88**
Brut Rosé Champagne 1982: A nicely made, light and delicate rose. Shy nose that reveals just a touch of cherry and spice. It feels elegant and smooth on the palate. Subtle wine with some smokiness on the finish. • $35 • (12/31/88) • **88**
Brut Rosé Champagne NV • $24 • (12/31/86) • **73**
Extra Dry Champagne Ivory Label NV • $19 • (12/31/88) • **86**
Extra Dry Champagne White Label NV • $19 • (12/31/88) • **70**

LAPELLETRIE, CHÂTEAU

St.-Emilion 1990: Lean and earthy, a simple wine with modest flavors and some nice spicy-toasty notes on the finish. Drinkable now. • $19 • (02/28/94) • **79**
St.-Emilion 1989 • $19 • (07/15/92) • **82**

LAPORTE, DOMAINE

Sancerre Domaine du Rochoy 1994: A solid white offering good herbal flavors and hints of green peach as well. It's well rounded and balanced with a clean, lingering finish marked by some mineral notes. • $15 • (04/30/96) • **84**
Sancerre Domaine du Rochoy 1993: Pungent herbaceous aromas proclaim this a Loire Sauvignon, while ripe pineapple and almond notes give it roundness and weight on the palate. It's a very dry wine with a definite point of view. • $17 • (11/15/95) • **88**
Sancerre Domaine du Rochoy 1992: An exotic wine, almost California-like in its ripe aromas and flavors of melon and honey, but there's an underlying acidity that keeps it refreshing. It's showy, but lacks complexity on the finish. • $16 • (10/31/94) • **85**
Sancerre Domaine du Rochoy 1991 • $18 • (09/15/93) • **85**

LARCIS-DUCASSE, CHÂTEAU

St.-Emilion 1995: Lots of berry, earth and coffee aromas and flavors. Medium body and good fruit on the finish. • $NA • (05/15/96) • **85-89** (BT)
St.-Emilion 1991: Simple and light, with notes of chive and berry. • $16 • (03/31/94) • **74**
St.-Emilion 1990: Harmonious and well proportioned, with lovely berry and cassis character, firm tannins and a crisp finish. Drinkable in 1997. 5,000 cases made. • $25 • (03/31/93) • **90**
St.-Emilion 1989 • $28 • (03/15/92) • **91**
St.-Emilion 1988 • $20 • (04/30/91) • **82**
St.-Emilion 1982 • $27 • (08/31/92) • **85**

LARGE, A.

Côte de Brouilly 1994: Pure, clean cherry flavor and light brown sugar notes are appealing in this fresh, vivid Beaujolais. A hint of spritz adds life, but may surprise some tasters. 1,000 cases made. • $10 • (10/31/95) • **84**

LARMANDE, CHÂTEAU

St.-Emilion 1995: Impressive, both refined and powerful, showing bright berry flavors and a smooth, silky texture. The finish is sweet and ripe yet firm, and it's very long. This has great potential. • $NA • (05/15/96) • **90-94** (BT)
St.-Emilion 1994: Surprisingly rich and round for this vintage, with plenty of berry, cherry and vanilla. Good character and velvety tannins. Impressive. Almost outstanding. • $26 • (05/15/96) • **85-89** (BT)
St.-Emilion 1993: Polished raspberry, toasted oak character, medium body, fine tannins and fresh finish. Better in 1998. • $24 • (01/31/96) • **87**
St.-Emilion 1992: Succulent and fruity, offering vanilla, cherry and mineral aromas and flavors, medium-to-light body, light tannins and fresh finish. Drink now. • $20 • **84**
St.-Emilion 1990: This dances across your palate with floral, vanilla, blackberry and black cherry flavors and superbly silky tannins. Exciting. Drink after 1998. 8,000 cases made. • $24 • (03/31/93) • **94**
St.-Emilion 1989 • $18 Ⓐ • (03/15/92) • **95**
St.-Emilion 1988 • $23 • (04/30/91) • **86**
St.-Emilion 1986 • $20 • (06/30/89) • **91**
St.-Emilion 1985: Well balanced and elegant with an alluring nose of flowers, raspberries and strawberries which follow through on the palate. Medium body and a fine texture. Drinkable now. • $23 • (10/15/94) • **89**
St.-Emilion 1983: Still very fresh and youthful with lovely bright fruit and toasted oak character. Full-bodied yet elegant, sporting a fine long finish. Drinkable now. • $21 • (10/15/94) • **88**
St.-Emilion 1982 • $29 Ⓐ • (08/31/92) • **82**
St.-Emilion 1981: Compacted and firm wine with very fresh cherry, berry and chocolate aromas and flavors, medium body and a long silky finish. Drink or hold. • $25 • (10/15/94) • **89**

LARMANDIER, GUY

Brut Blanc de Blancs Champagne Cramant NV • $27 • (05/31/87) • **92**
Brut Rosé Champagne NV • $20 • (12/31/89) • **84**

LAROCHE

Chablis 1994: Distinctive and balanced, with a minty, mineral character, grapefruit and green apple flavors, and a supple finish. More complex than many standard Chablis. • $15 • (05/31/96) • **81**
Chablis 1991 • $12 • (05/15/93) • **84**

Chablis Beauroy 1993: Pretty aromas of straw and freshly cut apples, medium body, firm acidity and a long, crisp finish. 250 cases made. • $19 • **84**

Chablis Cuvée Première 1993: Rather meager and mean, showing some lemon and mineral character, but very short. 1,000 cases made. • $17 • **79**

Chablis Grand Cru 1992: Lush, seductive Chardonnay exhibiting subtle butter and honey aromas, ripe fruit flavors and wonderfully elegant texture. Not the usually crisp, mineral style, but it tastes great. • $29 • **88**

Chablis Les Blanchots 1994: An elegant, subtle *grand cru,* packed with mineral, honey, vanilla and ripe fruit. It dances on the palate to a very harmonious tune. Full-bodied, it glides like silk to a long, gorgeous finish. Great winemaking in a super vineyard. Try after 1999. 100 cases made. • $40 • (05/31/96) • **92**

Chablis Les Blanchots 1993: A nice blend of green apple and toasted oak. Medium in body, quite firm, grassy character and a long, crisp finish. Try now. 150 cases made. • $37 • **85**

Chablis Les Blanchots Réserve de L'Obédiencerie 1994: Lovely, harmonious and rich. The beautiful butter, honey and mineral aromas and flavors seduce you from the start. Fat without being heavy, a powerful, silky, world-class Chardonnay. Try in 1998. 100 cases made. • $56 • (05/31/96) • **92**

Chablis Les Blanchots, Réserve de l'Obédiencerie 1993: Lovely resin and pine nut aromas and flavors, medium body, short finish and a hint of honey. Drink now. 100 cases made. • $56 • **81**

Chablis Les Clos 1994: Simply fantastic. Tight yet supple, balanced and packed with honey and ripe fruit that shows through the chalky, mineral, lemony character. Full-bodied and amazingly supple, with a very seductive finish. Try in 1999. 30 cases made. • $50 • (05/31/96) • **91**

Chablis Les Clos 1993: Firm, fresh mineral and toasted oak aromas and flavors, medium body and long finish. Drinkable now. 50 cases made. • $47 • **85**

Chablis Les Fourchaume 1993: Apple, mineral and honey aromas and flavors, medium body and long, spicy finish. 400 cases made. • $23 • **86**

Chablis Les Fourchaumes Vieilles Vignes 1994: Crisp and rather elegant, with some good fruit and mineral character. Has an attractive and lively finish that brings out lemon and a touch of honey. Try in 1997. 100 cases made. • $25 • (05/31/96) • **84**

Chablis Les Vaillons 1994: Light and refreshing, somewhat like lemonade, with a honey and pear character. Attractive wine for drinking now. 400 cases made. • $21 • (05/31/96) • **81**

Chablis Les Vaillons 1991 • $19 • (05/15/93) • **86**

Chablis Les Vaudevey 1994: A flavorful, ripe *premier cru,* with wet earth, citrus, vanilla and butter notes. Nicely balanced, with a crisp, pear- and honey-flavored finish. 400 cases made. • $18 • (05/31/96) • **85**

Chablis Les Vaudevey 1991 • $18 • (05/15/93) • **77**

Chablis Cuvée Première 1994: Clean and crisp, with hints of lime and a distinctive chalky, mineral character. Subtle, with a silky mouth-feel. • $NA • (05/31/96) • **83**

Chablis Cuvée Première 1991 • $15 • (06/30/93) • **76**

Chablis St.-Martin 1991 • $14 • (05/15/93) • **80**

Chablis St.-Martin Vieilles Vignes 1994: Lively and fruity, with a core of pear, green apple and wet earth. A well-balanced, typical Chablis. Light body and the finish is very crisp. 1,000 cases made. • $16 • (05/31/96) • **81**

Chablis Vaillons 1993: Straightforward Chablis, showing lots of citrus and some mint. Firm, tart and medium-bodied, should be good with seafood. 400 cases made. • $21 • **82**

Chablis Vaudevey 1993: Light but rather exotic, showing some floral, juniper and mint flavors. Smooth and balanced, but slightly diluted. 400 cases made. • $18 • **81**

Mâcon-Lugny 1994: Clean but simple. The green, tart and grassy character turns sour on the diluted finish. 1,200 cases made. • $10 • **75**

Mâcon-Villages 1994: Straightforward and attractive butter, wet hay and almond character. Light-bodied and a bit diluted. Drink now. 6,000 cases made. • $9 • **77**

Nuits-St.-Georges 1988 • $28 • (11/15/90) • **87**

Key: SS—Spectator Selection. CS—Cellar Selection. BB—Best Buy. $NA—Price not available. (BT)—Barrel tasting. Ⓐ—Auction Price.
Dates in parentheses represent the issues in which the ratings were published.

LAROQUE, CHÂTEAU

St.-Emilion 1983 • $13 • (02/15/88) • **64**

LAROSE-TRINTAUDON, CHÂTEAU

Haut-Médoc 1990: This wine is rather dull and slightly metallic in character with stemmy, earthy flavors and a light finish. Drinkable now. 80,000 cases made. • $12 • (03/31/93) • **75**

Haut-Médoc 1989 • $12 • (03/15/92) • **87**

Haut-Médoc 1988 • $9 • (04/30/91) • **84**

Haut-Médoc 1987 • $9 • (11/30/89) • **71**

Haut-Médoc 1986 • $10 • (11/30/89) • **78**

Haut-Médoc 1985 • $8 • (11/30/88) • **84**

Haut-Médoc 1983 • $13 • (10/15/86) • **73**

Haut-Médoc 1982 • $16 • (11/30/89) • **79**

Haut-Médoc 1979 • $15 • (10/15/89) • **76**

LARRIVET-HAUT-BRION, CHÂTEAU

Pessac-Léognan 1995: Succulent and vibrant, a vivid '95, bursting with cassis and crushed fruit. Full-bodied and harmonious, with massive but well-integrated tannins. Long finish and almost outstanding. • $NA • (05/15/96) • **85-89** (BT)

Pessac-Léognan 1994: Good berry and earth accents in this light- to medium-bodied red that features moderate tannins and a short finish. • $NA • (05/15/96) • **80-84** (BT)

Pessac-Léognan 1993: Pretty tobacco, smoke and toasted oak character. Medium in body, medium-soft tannins and medium aftertaste of red berries and chocolate. Delightful. • $19 • (01/31/96) • **86**

Pessac-Léognan 1992: Subtle and silky tobacco, tar and berry character, a good core of fruit and tannins, but short on the finish. Drink now. • $15 • **79**

Pessac-Léognan 1989 • $33 • (03/15/92) • **89**

Pessac-Léognan 1988 • $25 • (04/30/91) • **94**

Pessac-Léognan 1986 • $17 • (06/15/89) • **82**

Pessac-Léognan White 1994: Crisp and pretty, with honey and apple aromas and flavors, showing some grassy character too. Medium body, with clean fruit and a crisp finish. • $18 • (03/31/96) • **83**

Pessac-Léognan White 1993: Outscores the '92. Very subtle apple, pear and mineral character and a hint of chalkiness. Medium-bodied and round, fresh finish. • $17 • (05/31/95) • **87**

Pessac-Léognan White 1992: Not bad, toasted oak, lemon and dough aromas and flavors. Light-bodied, simple finish. Drink now. • $17 • **79**

LASCAUX, CHÂTEAU DE

Coteaux du Languedoc 1991 • $8 • (03/15/94) • **84**

Coteaux du Languedoc 1990 • $8 • (03/15/94) • **85**

LASCOMBES, CHÂTEAU

Margaux 1995: Full-bodied, delivering loads of blueberry and cherry aromas and flavors, lovely, velvety texture and long, sweet, succulent finish. Nearly outstanding. • $NA • (05/15/96) • **85-89** (BT)

Margaux 1993: Simple blackberry and cherry flavors and a delicate tannin structure. 20,000 cases made. • $26 • (01/31/96) • **80**

Margaux 1990: A rich wine, with leathery, berry, milk chocolate character, fine tannins and a long finish. Drinkable now. 26,500 cases made. • $22 • (03/31/93) • **86**

Margaux 1988 • $33 • (08/31/91) • **82**

Margaux 1983 • $36 Ⓐ • (02/15/88) • **84**

Margaux 1982 • $34 Ⓐ • (08/31/92) • **81**

Margaux 1981 • $31 • (05/16/85) • **85**

Margaux 1979 • $18 Ⓐ • (10/15/89) • **84**

Margaux 1961: Quite enjoyable to drink now, with solid fruit flavors, great balance, a lively texture and enough depth and length to make it satisfying. Can hold through 2000. • $51 • (04/30/96) • **86**

LASSALLE, J.

Brut Blanc de Blancs Champagne 1987: Shows how interesting and delicious vintage Champagne can become with age, even from an unheralded year. Tastes complex, offering doughy, buttery, figgy and almondlike flavors that turn leaner on the finish. Drink now. • $43 • **86**

Brut Blanc de Blancs Champagne 1986: Fresh and youthful for its age, this wine is harmonious and subdued with crisp citrus flavors that blend well with its buttery and toasty notes. Its creaminess gives it a nice subtlety and the finish is firm. Drinkable now. • $40 • **90**

Brut Champagne 1987: Nicely mature aromas clash with tight, sharp, acidic texture, making this an intriguing but lean taste experience. Drink now before it develops further. • $39 • **83**

Brut Champagne NV: A bold, distinctive style that smells toasty and buttery, tastes rich and mature and finishes with a lingering, nutty nuance. Seductive and satisfying. • $32 • (12/31/94) • **91**

Brut Champagne Cuvée Angeline 1987: Mature, interesting flavors of mushroom and nutmeg that are smooth and broad in texture. Has a good finish and complexity. 1,000 cases made. • $44 • **87**

Brut Champagne Special Club 1989: Complex flavors and a luxuriously rich texture make this a treat. It has apple tart flavors—notes of cinnamon, vanilla, lemon peel—with clean, fresh acidity and a lingering, creamy finish. It keeps bringing you back for more. 500 cases made. • $50 • **94**

Brut Champagne Special Club Premier Cru 1985: Gorgeously rich and almost fat in flavor, with butterscotch, pear and vanilla notes and a creamy, smooth texture. This is showy, round, easy to like and ready to drink. Melts in your mouth. 300 cases made. • $46 • (12/31/94) • **91**

Brut Rosé Champagne NV: Very doughy and yeasty-flavored with accents of vanilla. Not much fruit, but has sweet, candied notes. A creamy, smooth texture keeps it enjoyable. 1,500 cases made. • $35 • **83**

Brut Rosé Champagne Réserve des Grandes Années NV: Like a ballerina: well balanced, delicate and lean. Has nice spicy cherry and lightly smoky flavors. It may develop with time. • $40 • (12/15/95) • **89**

LASSARAT, ROGER

Pouilly-Fuissé Clos de France 1994: Crisp and tart, a lean-textured wine with some green apple and lime flavors. Very hard to enjoy now. 704 cases made. • $NA • (05/31/96) • **79**

Pouilly-Fuissé Clos de France 1993: Effusively fruity, crisp green apple, grapefruit and fresh herb flavors and a hint of pineapple. Austere at this stage but refreshing, clean finish. Drinkable now. 833 cases made. • $13 • **84**

Pouilly-Fuissé Cuvée Prestige 1994: Straightforward and extremely crisp, with lots of citrus flavors but not quite enough complexity. A bit lean and simple on the finish, but should make a good match with seafood. Could be better in 1997. 381 cases made. • $NA • (05/31/96) • **81**

Pouilly-Fuissé Cuvée Prestige 1993: Seems quite advanced for a 1993, demonstrating meat, lemon, hazelnut, marzipan, honey and dried-fruit flavors. Quite toasty and silky, somewhat hot on the very long finish. Drink now. • $NA • **84**

Pouilly-Fuissé Cuvée Prestige Vin Non Filtré 1993: Chalky, chewy Pouilly, offering a silky mouth-feel but also some cedary, woody, earthy components and more elegant spice and fruit flavors. Big finish. Drinkable now. • $NA • **85**

LASSIME, MARQUISE DE

Cépage Merlot Côtes de Gascogne 1991 • $5 • (10/31/92) • **76**

LATOUR A POMEROL, CHÂTEAU

Pomerol 1995: Lovely, elegant tannin structure complementing cherry and berry flavors and a mineral finish. • $NA • (05/15/96) • **85-89** (BT)

Pomerol 1994: Very ripe character on the nose of roasted coffee and berries. Full in body and tannins and a medium finish. Almost outstanding. • $NA • **85-89** (BT)

Pomerol 1993: Disappointing for this estate. Appealing now, showing crisp, light-bodied texture and some cherry, olive, dried herb and blackberry notes. Somewhat diluted. A barrel sample tasted earlier was much better. • $40 • (01/31/96) • **81**

Pomerol 1992: Firm and steely, showing cherry, raspberry and wet earth aromas and flavors, medium-to-light body, good tannins and fresh finish. Drink now. • $30 • **80**

Pomerol 1990: Muscular yet harmonious, showing tar, licorice and currant aromas and flavors. The firm tannins are well integrated, the flavors are ripe yet fresh and well balanced. It's drinkable now, but will be better in 1997. • $60 • (10/15/94) • **90**

Pomerol 1989 • $55 • (05/15/94) • **93**

Pomerol 1988: Balanced and still fresh, displaying black cherry and currant flavors in a lean, firm package. It's tightly focused and well defined, with good concentration and a clean finish, will show better in 1997. 3,500 cases made. • $29 Ⓐ • (10/15/94) • **90**

Pomerol 1986: Solidly built, the cherry and blackberry flavors are fresh, but aromas of smoke and cedar show maturity. Smooth and harmonious, though still a bit stiff with tannin. 3,500 cases made. • $50 • (10/15/94) • **86**

Pomerol 1985 • $40 Ⓐ • (05/15/94) • **90**

Pomerol 1983: Huge, rich wine for the vintage yet very fresh and youthful. The fruit jumps out of the glass with spicy, plum, cedar character. Full bodied with masses of fruit and tannins. Long, long finish. Needs some time. Better after 1997. • $75 • (10/15/94) • **92**

Pomerol 1982 • $144 Ⓐ • (05/15/94) • **94**

Pomerol 1981: A pretty, zingy Bordeaux, with fresh black cherry, berry and chocolate aromas and flavors, medium body and fine tannins. Drinkable now • $50 • (10/15/94) • **88**

Pomerol 1979 • $45 • (05/15/94) • **85**

Pomerol 1976 • $75 • (05/15/94) • **87**

Pomerol 1975 • $70 • (05/15/94) • **80**

Pomerol 1971 • $80 • (05/15/94) • **82**

Pomerol 1970 • $115 Ⓐ • (05/15/94) • **91**

Pomerol 1966 • $175 • (05/15/94) • **79**

Pomerol 1964 • $87 Ⓐ • (05/15/94) • **82**

Pomerol 1962 • $200 • (05/15/94) • **86**

Pomerol 1961: The best Pomerol in the tasting, a distinctive and powerful wine that managed to still be smooth and elegant. It tastes like something rich, beefy, even chocolaty, with integrated tannins and mature fruit flavors that fill the mouth and linger for minutes on the finish. Fabulous to drink now, but should hold through at least 2005. • $3,530 • (04/30/96) • **94**

Pomerol 1959 • $575 • (05/15/94) • **91**

Pomerol 1955 • $200 • (05/15/94) • **82**

Pomerol 1953 • $350 • (05/15/94) • **88**

Pomerol 1952 • $300 • (05/15/94) • **85**

Pomerol 1949 • $1,500 • (05/15/94) • **72**

Pomerol 1947 • $1,600 • (05/15/94) • **92**

Pomerol 1945 • $978 Ⓐ • (05/15/94) • **74**

LATOUR-GIRAUD

Meursault Clos du Cromin 1994: Fat and ripe, with some honey and floral notes. Tastes a bit overdone. Also slightly simple and astringent on the finish. • $NA • (05/31/96) • **75**

Meursault Les Genevrières 1994: Quite elegant and rather tightly built, with mineral, grapefruit and vanilla aromas and flavors, but it needs a bit more length and concentration. • $NA • (05/31/96) • **84**

Meursault Les Narvaux 1994: Some decent apple, pear and honey notes, adding chalky, chewy character on the finish. • $NA • (05/31/96) • **81**

Meursault Perrières 1993: Polished and austere, showing some floral, honey and mineral flavors, good concentration. The hard finish should soften with some bottle age, try after 1996. • $NA • (05/15/95) • **85**

Puligny-Montrachet Champ Canet 1994: Voluptous and rich, thick and full-bodied. This unctuous wine delivers some nice honey, toast and caramel flavors. A touch hard on the finish, though. • $NA • (05/31/96) • **85**

Puligny-Montrachet Champ Canet 1993: Some pear, appley, steely character. Medium-bodied, slightly candied. • $NA • (05/15/95) • **78**

LATOUR, CHÂTEAU

Pauillac 1995: One of the classiest and finest Latours made in a long time. Full-bodied, with masses of very fine tannins. It caresses your palate for minutes. Perhaps not the blockbuster one might expect, but it impresses you with its classiness. • $NA • (05/15/96) • **90-94** (BT)
Pauillac 1994: Round, rich and uncharacteristically friendly at this stage. Full-bodied and round, with a lovely range of earthy cherry and berry notes. Ripe tannins. • $80 • (05/15/96) • **90-94** (BT)
Pauillac 1993: Powerful and extremely balanced, a wine with guts and character, delivering seamless texture and mint, lead-pencil, currant, chocolate and slightly toasty character. Deep and full-bodied, yet the tannins are incredibly supple. Great soil and winemaking here. Try in 2000. • $70 • (01/31/96) • **91**
Pauillac 1992: Star of the vintage. Absolutely delicious vanilla, berry and currant flavors, very good intensity, medium body and medium-firm tannins. Very silky with a long finish. Drinkable now. • $65 • **89**
Pauillac 1991: Stretching the limits of this vintage. A complex wine with a major dose of new wood. Very silky and fine. Better after a little more time in the cellar. • $50 Ⓐ • (03/31/94) • **89**
Pauillac 1990 • $80 • **100**
Pauillac 1989 • $95 Ⓐ • (03/15/92) • **97**
Pauillac 1988 • $80 Ⓐ • (04/30/91) • **93**
Pauillac 1987 • $48 • (10/15/90) • **80**
Pauillac 1986 • $85 Ⓐ • (03/31/90) • **93**
Pauillac 1985: After a couple of less than superb years, 1985 puts Latour back with the best. A mouthful of mint, licorice, tar and vivid fruit and buttressed with velvety tannins. Excellent balance and grace, but better after 1997. • $90 • (10/15/94) • **94**
Pauillac 1984 • $37 Ⓐ • (03/31/87) • **92**
Pauillac 1983: Not as immense as one would expect, but very good all the same. Delicious, with dark chocolate and berry aromas and flavors, medium body and firm tannins. Drink now. • $75 • (10/15/94) • **89**
Pauillac 1982 • $280 Ⓐ • (08/31/92) • **94**
Pauillac 1981: Elegant and refined for Latour with cassis, tar, mint and tobacco character. It has a medium body and a fine silky finish. Drink now. • $90 • (10/15/94) • **89**
Pauillac 1979 • $72 Ⓐ • (03/31/90) • **90**
Pauillac 1978 • $102 Ⓐ • (03/31/90) • **94**
Pauillac 1976 • $62 Ⓐ • (03/31/90) • **87**
Pauillac 1975 • $109 Ⓐ • (03/31/90) • **93**
Pauillac 1971 • $77 Ⓐ • (03/31/90) • **84**
Pauillac 1970 • $342 Ⓐ • (05/15/93) • **93**
Pauillac 1967 • $58 Ⓐ • (03/31/90) • **79**
Pauillac 1966 • $234 Ⓐ • (03/31/90) • **93**
Pauillac 1965 • $135 • (03/31/90) • **74**
Pauillac 1964 • $200 Ⓐ • (03/31/90) • **86**
Pauillac 1963 • $150 • (03/31/90) • **77**
Pauillac 1962 • $250 • (03/31/90) • **92**
Pauillac 1961: The highest-rated wine out of 102 1961s tasted. Simply magnificent for its focus, texture, powerful fruit flavors and seeming agelessness. Has enticing aromas of cedar, mint and smoke, deep, deep flavors of cherry and currant and massive, but not harsh, tannins. Almost too young to fully enjoy, best to drink between, perhaps, 2000 and 2020. • $1,544 • (04/30/96) • **98**
Pauillac 1960 • $308 Ⓐ • (03/31/90) • **88**
Pauillac 1959 • $533 Ⓐ • (10/15/90) • **98**
Pauillac 1958 • $140 • (03/31/90) • **81**
Pauillac 1956 • $250 • (03/31/90) • **62**
Pauillac 1955 • $204 Ⓐ • (03/31/90) • **90**
Pauillac 1953 • $162 Ⓐ • (03/31/90) • **80**
Pauillac 1952 • $111 Ⓐ • (03/31/90) • **91**
Pauillac 1950 • $103 Ⓐ • (03/31/90) • **79**
Pauillac 1949 • $831 Ⓐ • (03/31/90) • **94**
Pauillac 1948 • $245 Ⓐ • (03/31/90) • **84**
Pauillac 1947 • $350 Ⓐ • (03/31/90) • **91**
Pauillac 1945 • $NA • (03/31/90) • **98**
Pauillac 1944 • $169 Ⓐ • (03/31/90) • **70**
Pauillac 1943 • $186 Ⓐ • (03/31/90) • **67**
Pauillac 1942 • $202 Ⓐ • (03/31/90) • **59**
Pauillac 1940 • $250 • (03/31/90) • **64**
Pauillac 1937 • $257 Ⓐ • (03/31/90) • **89**
Pauillac 1936 • $400 • (03/31/90) • **75**
Pauillac 1934 • $136 Ⓐ • (03/31/90) • **83**
Pauillac 1929 • $3,000 • (03/31/90) • **95**
Pauillac 1928 • $2,300 • (03/31/90) • **91**
Pauillac 1926 • $690 Ⓐ • (03/31/90) • **87**
Pauillac 1924 • $750 • (03/31/90) • **91**
Pauillac 1920 • $530 • (03/31/90) • **50**
Pauillac 1918 • $124 Ⓐ • (03/31/90) • **75**
Pauillac 1900 • $1,700 • (03/31/90) • **90**
Pauillac 1899 • $1,900 • (03/31/90) • **94**
Pauillac 1893 • $3,500 • (03/31/90) • **67**
Pauillac 1892 • $1,200 • (03/31/90) • **63**
Pauillac 1875 • $1,800 • (03/31/90) • **77**
Pauillac 1874 • $3,500 • (03/31/90) • **97**
Pauillac 1870 • $4,500 • (03/31/90) • **94**
Pauillac 1865 • $7,000 • (03/31/90) • **94**
Pauillac 1864 • $10,000 • (03/31/90) • **59**
Pauillac 1847 • $18,500 • (03/31/90) • **93**

LATOUR, LOUIS

Aloxe-Corton 1992: Light and sweet-tasting, supple and lean, with some modest raspberry and plum flavors. Seems a bit hot on the finish. Ready now. 1,800 cases made. • $19 • **80**
Aloxe-Corton 1955 • $NA • (08/31/90) • **85**
Aloxe-Corton Domaine Latour 1993: Delicate plum, berry and vanilla character, medium to light body, fine tannins and a fresh finish. Drink now. 2,500 cases made. • $21 • **82**
Aloxe-Corton Domaine Latour 1991 • $18 Ⓐ • (01/31/94) • **82**
Aloxe-Corton Domaine Latour 1990 • $22 • (12/15/92) • **84**
Aloxe-Corton Domaine Latour 1989 • $24 • (01/31/92) • **84**
Aloxe-Corton Les Chaillots 1985 • $37 • (04/15/88) • **76**
Beaune Domaine Latour 1993: Pretty apple, cream and honey flavors and a hint of oak on nose and palate. Medium-bodied, firm acidity and a long, long finish. Impressive for the appellation. Drink now. 250 cases made. • $30 • **86**
Beaune Domaine Latour 1991: Crisp texture, modest flavor, with watered down berry aromas and flavors. Drinkable now. 42 cases made. • $17 Ⓐ • (01/31/94) • **77**
Beaune Domaine Latour 1990: Elegant and well made, this round, smooth wine has perfumed, delicate aromas, medium body and chocolate, cedar and earth flavors. Drinkable now. 500 cases made. • $21 • (12/15/92) • **87**
Beaune Domaine Latour 1989 • $22 • (01/31/92) • **91**
Beaune Domaine Latour 1993: Rather light but enjoyable to drink, featuring soft tannins, delicate berry, cherry character and fresh finish. Drink now. 1,000 cases made. • $22 • **80**
Beaune Vignes Franches 1992: Very light and floral, an appealing red that finishes with a stemmy edge. 250 cases made. • $20 • **76**
Beaune Vignes Franches 1985 • $51 Ⓐ • (03/15/88) • **90**
Beaune Vignes Franches 1993: Delicate, easy-to-drink '93 which caresses your palate with fine tannins, although it's slightly light. Drinkable now. 583 cases made. • $26 • **80**
Bonnes Mares 1989 • $60 • (01/31/92) • **93**
Bourgogne Chardonnay White 1993: Quite hard and tart. Light-to-medium body, some decent fruit character, bitter almond, acidic finish. 5,833 cases made. • $10 • **73**
Bourgogne Cuvée Latour 1990 • $11 • (12/15/92) • **86**
Bourgogne Cuvée Latour 1989 • $NA • (01/31/92) • **80**
Bourgogne Pinot Noir 1992: Crisp in texture but watery in flavor, showing only modest strawberry accents on the light finish. 4,000 cases made. • $10 • **74**
Bourgogne Pinot Noir 1990 • $10 • (12/15/92) • **79**
Chablis 1994: Simple and chewy, with a chalky, wet earth, pear and pie crust character. A bit diluted. Tasted twice, with consistent notes. 4,750 cases made. • $18 • (05/31/96) • **76**

Key: SS—Spectator Selection. CS—Cellar Selection. BB—Best Buy. $NA—Price not available. (BT)—Barrel tasting. Ⓐ—Auction Price.
Dates in parentheses represent the issues in which the ratings were published.

Chablis Montmains 1994: Tart, sour and disappointing *premier cru*, with some modest mineral, earth and fruit flavors. Medium-bodied, it turns a bit harsh on the finish. Tasted twice, with consistent notes. 633 cases made. • $25 • (05/31/96) • **76**

Chambertin Cuvée Hèritiers Latour Red 1989 • $90 • (01/31/92) • **78**

Chambertin Cuvée Hèritiers Latour Red 1985 • $76 • (03/15/88) • **95**

Chambertin 1993: Surprisingly weak dried cherry and wet earth character. Medium-bodied, fine tannins and a sweet fruit finish. Drinkable now. 200 cases made. • $102 • **84**

Chardonnay Vin de Pays des Coteaux de l'Ardeche 1993: Soft and dull, this round wine offers some nutty, vanilla flavors but there's not much fruit, and it fades quickly on the finish. Drink up. • $NA • (04/30/95) • **77**

Charmes-Chambertin 1985 • $50 • (03/15/88) • **85**

Chassagne-Montrachet 1994: Focused and lively, with an assertive vegetal component. Light to medium body, with hints of honey, spice, dried herb and wet earth. Good intensity and richness on the finish. Drinkable now through 1998. 3,333 cases made. • $34 • (05/31/96) 82 • **82**

Chassagne-Montrachet 1993: Clean citrus and apple character, light and delicate on the palate, adding a crisp vanilla finish. 1,750 cases made. • $32 • **82**

Chassagne-Montrachet 1992: Mellow and tasty, with nut and honey flavors, good balance and smooth texture. Solid and satisfying. 2,400 cases made. • $26 • (08/31/94) • **82**

Chassagne-Montrachet 1991 • $24 • (07/31/93) • **88**

Chassagne-Montrachet Les Chenevottes 1994: Focused and somewhat angular, offering little right now, but there are some interesting mineral, toasty oak, ripe pear and apple flavors. 500 cases made. • $37 • (05/31/96) • **85**

Chassagne-Montrachet Les Chenevottes 1993: Attractive cream, apple and honey aromas and flavors, medium body, firm acidity and long, toasted oak and fruit finish. • $35 • **86**

Chevalier-Montrachet Les Demoiselles 1994: Ripe and relatively intense, featuring some lovely, sweet-tasting honey, apricot and pear flavors and a drop of mineral character. Medium in body and quite delicate. Try in 1999. 241 cases made. • $148 • (05/31/96) • **85**

Corton Château Corton Grancey 1992: Light in color and flavor, with appealing strawberry and mint aromas and taste notes. Simple and drinkable. • $NA • **80**

Corton Château Corton Grancey 1990: Not made in a big style, but the intensity is there, with mint and milk chocolate notes, a very creamy, supple mouth-feel and smooth, round finish. Develops in the glass. Tasted twice. Drinkable now. 800 cases made. • $43 • (12/15/92) • **89**

Corton Château Corton Grancey 1989 • $48 • (01/31/92) • **89**

Corton Château Corton Grancey 1985 • $46 • (03/15/88) • **89**

Corton Château Corton Grancey 1959 • $NA • (08/31/90) • **89**

Corton Château Corton Grancey 1953 • $NA • (08/31/90) • **91**

Corton Château Corton Grancey 1947 • $NA • (08/31/90) • **85**

Corton Clos de la Vigne au Saint 1985 • $43 • (03/15/88) • **89**

Corton Corton Grancey 1993: Sleek and racy berry, plum and vanilla character. Very fresh on the palate with fine tannins. Drink in 1999. 1,250 cases made. • $43 • **88**

Corton Domaine Latour 1991: Basic cherry flavors have an anise edge in this light, spicy wine. Finishes on the crisp side, echoing fruit. Drinkable now. 117 cases made. • $29 Ⓐ • (01/31/94) • **84**

Corton Domaine Latour 1990: Incredibly light for this appellation, with a weak color, premature aromas and flavors and a diluted finish. Drinkable now. • $35 • (12/15/92) • **70**

Corton Domaine Latour 1985 • $38 • (03/15/88) • **90**

Corton-Charlemagne 1994: Distinctive and a bit rustic. Very intense, with excellent concentration of lime, dried herb, smoke, cream and honey notes. Hard to judge at this stage, try in 1998. 4,166 cases made. • $78 • (05/31/96) 91 • **90**

Corton-Charlemagne 1993: Muscular honey, toasted oak and mineral aromas and flavors, medium to full body, fine acidity and long, tasty finish. • $70 • **88**

Corton-Charlemagne 1992: Very seductive but also quite earthy now and difficult to assess. But we love the honeyed, ripe richness and racy, tight beam of hazelnut, toffee, vanilla and fruit flavors. There is a toasty, smoky and complex finish. • $60 • (08/31/94) • **90**

Côte de Beaune-Villages 1990: Simple and a little green, falling short of the overall quality of this vintage. 4,000 cases made. • $16 • (12/15/92) • **78**

Echézeaux 1985 • $49 • (03/15/88) • **87**

Gevrey-Chambertin 1992: Balanced and pretty, offering some complexty, with tar, rose petal, raspberry and cherry flavors. It's light, but also silky and appealing. Ready now. 900 cases made. • $27 • **84**

Gevrey-Chambertin 1990: Straightforward and earthy, with wet earth, hay and barnyardy notes underneath the modest cherry flavors. Drinkable now. 2,000 cases made. • $32 • (12/15/92) • **78**

Gevrey-Chambertin 1989 • $35 • (01/31/92) • **87**

Gevrey-Chambertin 1985 • $36 • (10/15/88) • **77**

Meursault 1994: Vibrant, zesty, with a grassy, green apple character, but rather lean on the finish. 7,500 cases made. • $30 • (05/31/96) • **79**

Meursault 1993: A medium-bodied white demonstrating mineral, apple and some asparagus flavors, crisp, lightly fruity finish. 4,166 cases made. • $27 • (05/15/95) • **83**

Meursault 1991 • $24 • (10/15/93) • **80**

Meursault Château de Blagny 1993: Ready to drink, showing apple and mushroom aromas and flavors, medium body and simple finish. 2,900 cases made. • $34 • (08/31/95) • **81**

Meursault Goutte d'Or 1992: Lush, exotic and ripe in flavor, generous and silky in texture and very long-lasting on the finish. Has fine balance, but it leans toward the fat and full-blown style. 350 cases made. • $31 • (08/31/94) • **89**

Meursault Les Gouttes d'Or 1994: Distinctive chestnut and cedar flavors mingle with a touch of honey and lime in this rather straightforward Chardonnay. A bit disjointed now, but try in 1997. 500 cases made. • $40 • (05/31/96) • **80**

Meursault Les Gouttes d'Or 1993: Rich and smooth, supple, delivering some nice mineral, tropical fruit and pear flavors and a hint of honey and toasted oak on the sweet-tasting finish. Drinkable now. 500 cases made. • $37 • (08/31/95) • **86**

Montagny La Grande Roche 1994: A vibrant and exciting *premier cru* from a minor appellation, with intense flavors of dried herb, fresh basil, honey and grapefruit. Juicy, though it turns a bit herbal and short on the finish. 11,666 cases made. • $13 • (05/31/96) • **84**

Montrachet 1994: Distinctive chalky, smoky, chewy character and good intensity. Of medium to full body, it delivers plenty of crisp citrus and mineral notes. Very fresh on the long finish. Better in 1999. Tasted twice. 233 cases made. • $230 • (05/31/96) • **86**

Montrachet White 1993: Massive, rich and ripe-surprisingly opulent for the vintage. Loads of coconut, tropical fruit and smoke flavors. Extremely silky on the palate, adding a long, long finish. • $195 • • **90**

Montrachet White 1992: Builds on a solid base of flavors and adds layers as you drink it. Quite lively and exotic, has some inviting flavors of ginger, hazelnut, pear, coconut and pineapple. Ripe and full-bodied, delicious now. • $170 • (08/31/94) CS • **95**

Mâcon-Lugny Les Genièvres 1993: Expressive and vibrant, this light-bodied, bone-dry Mâcon titillates the palate using clean flavors—lemon, lime, apple and spice—that end on a juicy finish. Drink with seafood. 33,333 cases made. • $11 • **83**

Nuits-St.-Georges 1993: Light Nuits delivers some ripe fruit character but remains sligthly diluted in texture. Drink now. 500 cases made. • $31 • **78**

Nuits-St.-Georges 1991: Hints of cherry and spice liven up this light, elegant style. Finishes clean and modestly tannic, echoing fruit and spice. Drinkable now. 42 cases made. • $28 Ⓐ • (01/31/94) • **84**

Pernand-Vergelesses 1994: Oaky and fat, with some modest honey, pear and pie crust aromas and flavors. Could use some more fruit. 383 cases made. • $20 • (05/31/96) • **78**

Pommard 1993: Delicate and delicious now. Medium in body, featuring game and berry character, medium tannins and fresh finish. 500 cases made. • $28 • **82**

Pommard Epenots 1992: Crisp and nicely focused, showing more flavor than aroma at this point, echoing raspberry and spice on the finish. 50 cases made. • $32 • **83**

Pommard Epenots 1991: Youthful color, light and fragrant, with pleasant strawberry and floral notes on the finish. A little citrusy but lively. A bit less ripeness than the '90. • $32 • **85**

LATOUR, PIERRE

Pommard Epenots 1990: An extremely silky, beautiful wine for drinking early. Shows pretty vanilla, chocolate and raspberry notes and supple tannins on the finish. Drinkable now. 300 cases made. • $37 • (12/15/92) • **85**
Pommard Epenots 1989: Nice faded-rose color and subtle flavors. A light wine with graceful raspberry, currant and floral notes that play delicately on the finish. • $38 • **85**
Pommard Epenots 1988: Maturing, with a hint of fruit. Seems a bit dry and has a lean finish. Drink soon. • $38 • **81**
Pommard Epenots 1987: Browning at the edge, seems a little tired and diluted, with cinnamon flavors and gamy, wet-earth notes. Beginning to fade on the palate, but still good. • $30 • **81**
Pommard Epenots 1986: Brownish edges signal an older wine, and it tastes mature and drying on the finish. Modest cinnamon, spice and red berry flavors. • $35 • **82**
Pommard Epenots 1985 • $46 • (03/15/88) • **89**
Pommard Epenots 1983: Lean and mature, showing its age, but delicate and appealing. Some nicely focused berry and spice flavors are hiding in the background. • $35 • **84**
Pouilly-Fuissé 1994: Good fruit but one-dimensional. Offers plenty of pear, apple and even a touch of tropical fruit character. It's round and sweet-tasting, but turns slightly herbal on the finish. 12,500 cases made. • $21 • (05/31/96) • **81**
Pouilly-Fuissé 1993: A clean and straightforward Pouilly, offering some wet earth, green apple character and good acidity. Medium body, medium length. Drink now. 16,667 cases made. • $15 • **80**
Puligny-Montrachet 1994: Sharp and tart, with a green, earthy character. Modest fruit. 5,000 cases made. • $35 • (05/31/96) • **72**
Puligny-Montrachet 1993: Impressive village wine offering good concentration of toasted oak, apple and pear character, medium body and richness and a lovely coconut finish. 4,250 cases made. • $34 • **84**
Puligny-Montrachet 1992: Supple and generous village wine, with ripe pear and a hint of honey laced with mineral and vanilla flavors. Drinkable now. 4,000 cases made. • $27 • (08/31/94) • **87**
Puligny-Montrachet 1991 • $27 • (10/15/93) • **85**
Puligny-Montrachet La Garenne 1993: Delicious mineral, apple and spice aromas and flavors. Medium body, well-integrated acidity and a long finish. 750 cases made. • $36 • (08/31/95) • **85**
Puligny-Montrachet Les Folatières 1994: Round and smooth, with a mineral and green apple character. Somewhat lighter in body and a bit short and simple. Tasted twice, with consistent notes. 750 cases made. • $45 • (05/31/96) • **79**
Puligny-Montrachet Les Folatières 1993: Extremely fresh apple, truffle and honey aromas and flavors. Full-bodied, fine acidity and a long, tasty finish. Drinkable now. 500 cases made. • $39 • (08/31/95) • **86**
Puligny-Montrachet Les Folatières 1992: Distinctively earthy, nutty and buttery in style. Solid and firm in texture, complex in flavor and very long-lasting on the finish. Drinkable now through 1997. 780 cases made. • $34 • (08/31/94) • **89**
Romanée St.-Vivant Les Quatre Journaux 1993: Elegant, delicious cassis and berry aromas and flavors, medium body, silky tannins and a long, fruity finish. Better in 2001. • $NA • **89**
Romanée-St.-Vivant Les Quatre Journaux 1992: Delicate, with floral, slightly herbal overtones to the focused thread of raspberry and green tobacco flavor. Finishes a little chewy. Drinkable now. 200 cases made. • $120 • **81**
Romanée St.-Vivant Les Quatre Journaux 1990: Very pleasing, with a lot of milk chocolate, raspberry and vanilla aromas and flavors. A very delicate style, with good intensity on the soft finish. Try now. 300 cases made. • $139 • (12/15/92) • **89**
Romanée-St.-Vivant Les Quatre Journaux 1989 • $140 • (01/31/92) • **93**
Romanée-St.-Vivant Les Quatre Journaux 1985 • $99 • (03/15/88) • **98**
Romanée-St.-Vivant Les Quatre Journaux 1953 • $NA • (08/31/90) • **94**
St.-Véran White 1994: Smooth and round, tasting ripe and sweet, offering pear, melon and cream flavors. Lacks a bit of vibrancy. Enjoy now. 2,500 cases made. • $11 • **83**
Santenay 1989 • $NA • (01/31/92) • **80**

Key: SS—Spectator Selection. CS—Cellar Selection. BB—Best Buy. $NA—Price not available. (BT)—Barrel tasting. Ⓐ—Auction Price.
Dates in parentheses represent the issues in which the ratings were published.

Savigny-lès-Beaune 1992: Light, crisp and simple, with modest raspberry and tobacco flavors. Drinkable now. 1,200 cases made. • $13 • **78**
Savigny-lès-Beaune 1991: Light, simple and pleasant. Drinkable now. 100 cases made. • $13 Ⓐ • (01/31/94) • **79**
Savigny-lès-Beaune 1989 • $NA • (01/31/92) • **84**
Vosne-Romanée Beaumonts 1985 • $36 • (03/15/88) • **86**

LATOUR, PIERRE

Volnay 1953 • $NA • (08/31/90) • **86**
Volnay 1952 • $NA • (08/31/90) • **90**

LAUNAY, CHÂTEAU

Entre-Deux-Mers 1994: Light and straightforward, presenting a bread dough, melon character and some pear flavors. • $9 • **79**

LAURENS

Blanc de Blancs Blanquette de Limoux Clos des Demoiselles 1986 • $11 • (12/31/90) • **81**
Brut Blanc de Blancs Blanquette de Limoux Tête de Cuvée 1988 • $15 • (11/30/92) • **82**

LAURENS, DOMAINE J.

Brut Blanc de Blancs Blanquette de Limoux 1988 • $10 • (11/30/92) • **80**

LAURENT, DOMINIQUE

Beaune Premier Cru Vieilles Vignes 1993: Pretty, plummy red featuring velvety tannins and a hint of vanilla on aftertaste. Medium in body and tannins and an easy finish. Drinkable now. • $NA • **86**
Bonnes Mares 1992: Very ripe, smooth, generous and supple with gorgeous violet, currant and berry flavors that persist on the long finish, accented by a touch of spicy oak. • $NA • **90**
Chambertin Clos de Bèze 1992: A laudable effort, ripe and delicate, supple and stylish, unusual for this vintage. It carries focused blackberry, black cherry, mint and toasty oak flavors, finishing with a satisfying silkiness. Approachable now, but best from 1997. • $125 • **91**
Charmes-Chambertin 1992: Starts off ripe and generous, offering lovely raspberry, cedar and toast flavors that become rich and seductive on the finish. Gets somewhat tannic. Try in 1997. • $62 • **87**
Clos Vougeot 1993: What can we say? Packed to the rim with fruit. Full body and tannins and a kaleidoscope of black cherry and red berry flavors. Long finish. Give this time, better in 2003. • $NA • (05/15/96) • **94**
Gevrey-Chambertin Vieilles Vignes 1993: Profound, caressing and superbly crafted, boasting tons of red berry, spice and wood-scented character. Cascades through your palate to a long, exquisite, delicate, toasty, smoky finish. Supple and silky, amazing quality for a village wine. Tempting now but better in 2000. • $NA • (05/15/96) • **95**
Mazis-Chambertin 1993: Wine of the vintage? From very old vines, this is a monumental red Burgundy of superb length. Amazingly complex aromas of black and red berries, mineral and cedar. Full in body and packed with tannins, it might be approachable around 2002 and then should age for two decades. • $117 • (05/15/96) • **98**
Nuits-St.-Georges Les Vaucrains 1993: Thick, rich and packed with flavors, it's more like Cabernet than Pinot. Impressive mint, berry and plum aromas and flavors, full body and tannins and long finish. Needs time, try in 2003. • $NA • **89**
Pommard Les Epenots 1993: An electrifying *premier cru* packed with personality. Very chewy and full-bodied, it delivers tons of harmony and delicious mocha, cassis and wild berry flavors. Given time this should offer gobs of pleasure. Long, crisp finish. Try in 2000. • $85 • (05/15/96) • **93**
Pommard Vieilles Vignes 1993: This beautiful '93 combines crisp aromas of cassis and black currant typical of the vintage with a slight toast, mocha, coffee complexity. Seductive, chewy, minerally, earthy, spicy character. Long, flavorful finish. Try in 2000. • $48 • (05/15/96) • **93**

Ruchottes-Chambertin 1993: A big mouthful here: full-bodied and loads of fruit. Berry, plum, pineapple, the flavor sensations go on and on. Velvety tannins and long finish. Amazing. Better in 2006. • $117 • (05/15/96) • **96**

Volnay 1993: Dark-colored, brooding, difficult to taste. Overly vibrant and crisp cassis and black cherry flavors. Seems a bit tart and rustic, but it has substantial fruit concentration. Better in 2000? • $NA • **86**

Vosne-Romanée 1993: Rather lean, but very good plum and berry character. Medium body, somewhat one-dimensional flavors and hard tannins. Needs time, better in 1999. • $NA • **86**

LAURENT-PERRIER

Brut Champagne 1988: Promises a little more on the nose than the palate. If you want a super dry fizz, this is it. Very clean and focused flavors, high acidity and a crisp finish. Tasted twice. Drink now. 100,000 cases made. • $46 • (12/31/93) • **86**

Brut Champagne 1985 • $40 • (12/31/90) • **87**

Brut Champagne 1983: Shows the maturity you might expect from a 1983, but this was an excellent vintage for Champage and this one offers a rich and earthy core of toasty pear and pineapple, finishing with a long, flavorful finish. Packs in lots of flavor. A special drinking 50,000 cases made. • $40 • (11/30/93) • **93**

Brut Champagne 1982: Just lovely. A subdued elegance gives way on the finish to a lively, creamy and complex aftertaste that lingers on. Lots of attractive dough and yeast aromas and flavors; it's both creamy and crisp. A class act all the way. • $95 • (12/31/88) • **93**

Brut Champagne NV • $30 • (10/31/93) • **86**

Brut Champagne Cuvée Grand Siècle 1982: Sophisticated, youthful and complex. A lovely wine in the lighter style. Smooth and creamy, ripe and concentrated, it is intense without being heavy. Layers of honey, vanilla and pear. • $72 • (12/31/88) • **92**

Brut Champagne Cuvée Grand Siècle 1979 • $87 • (02/15/88) • **90**

Brut Champagne Cuvée Ultra Brut NV • $40 • (11/30/93) • **83**

Brut Champagne Cuvée Ultra Brut Cuvée Sans Dosage NV: Bold and assertive, featuring enticing toasty, nutty aromas backed by fresh acidity and satisfying citrus flavors. Texture is firm but rich and mouth-filling. Creamy vanilla notes linger on the finish. 2,000 cases made. • $41 • (11/30/95) • **90**

Brut Champagne Grand Siècle 1985: Incredibly fine and intense with grapefruit, vanilla, toast aromas and flavors and all perfectly integrated. An absolute joy to drink today. Continues to improve in the bottle. • $109 • (12/31/93) • **92**

Brut Champagne L.P. NV: A vibrant Brut that pairs high-toned cream, vanilla and butter aromas with zesty fruit flavors and lively acidity. It's focused, harmonious and lush, staying sprightly on the lingering finish. 400,000 cases made. • $32 • (11/30/95) • **90**

Brut Rosé Champagne Cuvée Rosé Brut NV: Smoky, toasty aromas give way to crisp, clean flavors of raspberry and watermelon in this elegant and slightly exotic rosé. 30,000 cases made. • $42 • (12/15/95) • **85**

Brut Rosé Champagne Grand Siècle Cuvée Alexandra 1982: Pretty salmon color, with rich, toasty, elegant and complex spice, cherry, toast and nutmeg flavors that are broad and expansive, finishing with a cherry and spice aftertaste. • $125 • (12/31/89) • **91**

Extra Dry Champagne NV • $30 • (10/31/93) • **89**

LAURETAN, CHÂTEAU

Bordeaux 1986 • $5 • (05/15/89) • **79**

LAURETTE, CHÂTEAU

Ste.-Croix-de-Mont 1985 • $8 • (09/30/88) • **78**

LAURIOL

Côtes de Francs 1986 • $8 • (06/15/89) • **73**

Côtes de Francs 1985 • $6 • (06/30/88) • **78**

LAVANTUREUX, ROLAND

Chablis 1991 • $16 • (05/15/93) • **88**

LAVERNETTE, CHÂTEAU DE

Pouilly-Fuissé Cuvée Jean-Jacques de Boissieu 1993: Tight and rather austere, chalky, green, grassy flavors and rock-hard texture. Might be better after 1996. • $NA • **81**

LAVILLE BERTROU, CHÂTEAU

Minervois 1991 • $9 • (03/15/94) • **82**

Minervois 1990 • $9 • (06/15/93) • **77**

Minervois 1988 • $8 • (08/31/91) • **76**

LAVILLE HAUT BRION, CHÂTEAU

Pessac-Léognan 1994: Soft and attractive, of moderate intensity, with some nice mineral, earth, pear, litchi and lime overtones. Quite rich and lovely on the succulent finish. • $100 • (03/31/96) • **86**

Pessac-Léognan 1993: Young and oaky now, but there's very good intensity of green apple, lemon, lime and vanilla character underneath. Needs time, try after 1996. • $55 • (05/31/95) • **89**

Pessac-Léognan 1992: A bit hard, showing some intense fruit and acid structure on the nose and palate. Rather mature in character and disappointing for Laville. Tasted twice, with consistent notes. • $60 • **84**

LAY STRUCTURE

Touraine 1990: Tannic and harsh, the dark color can't hide the lack of fruit. Not too old or drying out, just hard and simple. • $12 • (11/15/94) • **78**

LEBEGUE-BICHOT

Chambertin Clos de Bèze 1945 • $305 • (08/31/90) • **96**

LECHENEAUT

Chambolle-Musigny 1993: Compact Chambolle showing plenty of thick fruit but also slight barnyard character. Medium- to full-bodied, adding silky tannins and a pretty plum, berry finish. Try in 2000. • $48 • **88**

Chambolle-Musigny Premier Cru 1993: A beautiful, full-bodied red Burgundy to dream about. Ripe yet full of finesse, its well-defined plum, currant, earth and rose petal flavors unfold graciously. Firm structure of supple tannins. Don't touch until 2004. • $68 • **93**

Clos de la Roche 1993: Round and sweet-tasting, a lovely, medium-bodied wine with currant, raspberry and black cherry flavors. Great, crisp intensity on the long, chewy finish. Try in 1999. • $90 • **91**

Clos de la Roche 1992: Striving for delicacy and grace, this pretty wine shows floral, spicy oak nuances to the fine thread of raspberry flavor that extends into the finish. • $70 • **88**

Nuits-St.-Georges 1992: Crisp, light and modestly fruity, with just a hint of currant flavor to brighten it. Drinkable now. • $26 • **78**

Nuits-St.-Georges Les Cailles 1992: Soft and medium-bodied, delivering some enticing cinnamon, toast, vanilla, plum and black cherry flavors that last on the finish. Ready now. • $39 • **82**

Nuits-St.-Georges Les Damodes 1993: Sleek and exciting, it bursts with fresh floral, currant, spice, black cherry and lightly toasted flavors. Medium- to full-bodied, adding an underpinning of acidity and a long, chewy finish. Try in 2000. • $68 • **93**

Nuits-St.-Georges Les Damodes 1992: Smooth and appealing, with a spicy edge to the currant flavor and a slightly astringent finish. Tasty now. • $35 • **83**

Nuits-St.-Georges Premier Cru 1993: Big, chunky Nuits delivering spice, vanilla and fruit notes, full body, medium tannins and long, tasty finish. Try in 2000. • $60 • **90**

LECHERE

Brut Blanc de Blancs 1985: Intense and earthy, with ripe pear and fruit cocktail flavors that turn slightly bitter on the finish. Drink now. Tasted twice. • $44 • (05/15/92) • **78**
Brut Blanc de Blancs Champagne Cuvée Orient Express NV • $45 • (12/31/90) • **86**
Brut Blanc de Blancs Champagne Grand Cru 1983: A complex, focused wine, with more style than charm. Firm and concentrated, featuring earthy lemon, nutmeg and cedar flavors that extend into a long finish. An austere style, with character and complexity. 500 cases made. • $90 • (05/15/92) • **92**
Brut Blanc de Blancs Champagne NV • $25 • (12/31/87) • **89**
Brut Blanc de Blancs Champagne Première Cru NV • $42 • (12/31/91) • **91**
Brut Champagne Première Cru NV • $37 • (12/31/91) • **90**
Brut Champagne Première Cru Orient Express NV • $49 • (03/31/92) • **88**
Brut Rosé Champagne Première Cru Orient Express NV • $54 • (03/31/92) • **90**

LECLERC, PHILIPPE

Bourgogne Les Bons Bâtons 1992: Firm, ripe and spicy, marked by new oak nuances around a generous core of ripe currant and black cherry. Drinkable now. • $18 • **80**
Bourgogne Les Bons Bâtons 1988 • $22 • (08/31/91) • **64**
Chambolle-Musigny Les Babillaires 1992: Light and delicate, carrying a pound of oak and more barrel flavors than fruit, finishing with a wash of spice and vanilla. Try now. • $45 • **79**
Gevrey-Chambertin 1984 • $26 • (07/15/87) • **90**
Gevrey-Chambertin Champeaux 1990: Rich and oaky, isn't everyone's glass of wine, but offers loads of cedar, tobacco box, plum and leather flavors in a tightly wrapped package that contains extremely firm tannins. From a producer who prides himself on aging his wines for about two and a half years in new oak barrels before bottling them unfiltered. Needs until 1998. • $50 • (12/15/92) • **91**
Gevrey-Chambertin Combes aux Moines 1992: Spicy, chewy and a little drying from too much tannin, but the toast and prune notes manage to be heard over the din. May be best after 1996. • $72 • **82**
Gevrey-Chambertin Combes aux Moines 1991: Firm, oaky, spicy and pruny, with a tough, tannic finish. Not very likable. • $83 Ⓐ • (01/31/94) • **73**
Gevrey-Chambertin Combes aux Moines 1990: Fleshy and rich, with bold plum, berry and oak characteristics and a sweet aftertaste of ripe fruit. Has a lot of power. Drinkable now. 375 cases made. • $70 • (12/15/92) • **92**
Gevrey-Chambertin Combes aux Moines 1987 • $68 • (05/31/90) • **76**
Gevrey-Chambertin Combes aux Moines 1985 • $70 • (10/15/88) • **92**
Gevrey-Chambertin En Champs 1992: Those who like oaky Burgundies will like the clean character in this. It shows enticing violet, blueberry, black cherry flavors. Try in 1997. • $42 • **84**
Gevrey-Chambertin En Champs 1991: Shows a bit more oak than the light cherry flavor might warrant, but finishes with nice, ripe sweetness. Firm and chewy. Drinkable now. • $40 • (01/31/94) • **80**
Gevrey-Chambertin La Combe aux Moines 1988 • $72 • (07/15/91) • **82**
Gevrey-Chambertin La Combe aux Moines 1984 • $42 • (08/31/87) • **82**
Gevrey-Chambertin Les Cazetiers 1992: Oak-dominated, with drying tannins and modest fruit flavors. Too much oak for such a light vintage. Might be better after 1998. • $68 • **73**
Gevrey-Chambertin Les Cazatiers 1991: An oaky style that works in enough pruny currant flavors to stay balanced. Hard tannins need until 1997 to 2000 • $75 Ⓐ • (01/31/94) • **79**
Gevrey-Chambertin Les Cazetiers 1990: Very traditional in style and a bit woody, with chestnut, cedar and plum aromas and flavors and a chunky texture. Aged for about two and a half years in oak casks and not filtered. Drinkable now. 375 cases made. • $65 • (12/15/92) • **85**
Gevrey-Chambertin Les Cazetiers 1988 • $66 • (07/15/91) • **82**

Key: SS—Spectator Selection. CS—Cellar Selection. BB—Best Buy. $NA—Price not available. (BT)—Barrel tasting. Ⓐ—Auction Price.
Dates in parentheses represent the issues in which the ratings were published.

Gevrey-Chambertin Les Cazetiers 1987 • $63 • (05/31/90) • **85**
Gevrey-Chambertin Les Cazetiers 1985 • $64 • (10/15/88) • **89**
Gevrey-Chambertin Les Cazetiers 1984 • $38 • (08/31/87) • **83**
Gevrey-Chambertin Les Cazetiers 1982 • $21 • (11/16/85) • **68**
Gevrey-Chambertin Les Champeaux 1991: Ripe, pruny and definitely woody, this frankly oaky style has enough chocolaty plum and spice flavors to balance the toastiness. Wait until 1997 to 2000. • $65 Ⓐ • (01/31/94) • **84**
Gevrey-Chambertin Les Champeaux 1985 • $55 • (10/31/88) • **79**
Gevrey-Chambertin Les Platières 1992: Light and simple, with modest strawberry and raspberry flavors, and a short, drying, oaky finish. • $39 • **76**
Gevrey-Chambertin Les Platières 1991: Thin and woody. Drink now. • $43 Ⓐ • (01/31/94) • **72**
Gevrey-Chambertin Les Platières 1990: Big and chewy, with plenty of everything in the chocolate, plum, berry and oak aromas and flavors. Elegance isn't this wine's speciality, but if you want character, this is for you. Try in 1997. • $35 • (12/15/92) • **90**
Gevrey-Chambertin Les Platières 1989 • $44 • (10/31/92) • **81**
Gevrey-Chambertin Les Platières 1988 • $40 • (07/15/91) • **74**
Gevrey-Chambertin Les Platières 1987 • $35 • (05/31/90) • **81**
Gevrey-Chambertin Les Platières 1985 • $38 • (10/15/88) • **90**

LECLERC, RENE

Gevrey-Chambertin Combes aux Moines 1985 • $41 Ⓐ • (10/31/88) • **82**

LECLERC-BRIANT

Brut Champagne 1979 • $31 • (03/15/88) • **85**
Brut Champagne Cuvée Wolfgang Mozart 1983: Has nice, mature nutty, spicy and toasty aromas and similar flavors that dance around a central thread of lemon and vanilla, making this an interesting wine, but it could show a little more finesse. • $60 • (12/31/91) • **85**
Brut Champagne Divine 1985: Crisp and elegant, with lively lemon, vanilla and butter aromas and flavors with hints of pear, all held together in a neat package that focuses the flavors on the finish. • $45 • (12/31/91) • **89**
Brut Champagne Extra NV: Rather sweet and earthy style that has the right creamy texture, but its flavors and balance go awry. Smoky aroma, peachy flavor, chalky finish. • $25 • **79**
Brut Champagne Réserve NV • $23 • (03/15/88) • **80**
Brut Champagne Spécial Club 1983: Full-bodied, goes down easy, with plenty of fruit and a touch of coarseness. But overall it's balanced, with lemon, apple and toast notes. Young and lively, ready to drink. 1,800 cases made. • $35 • (12/31/89) • **83**
Brut Rosé Champagne NV • $28 • (03/15/88) • **84**
Brut Rosé Champagne Rubis Rosé de Noirs 1989: This has the crimson color of Cold Duck, and nearly the same grapey fruitiness, though finishing crisp and dry. Exuberant fruit, lacking sophistication and depth. • $29 • (12/15/95) • **83**
Sparkling Champagne Cuvée Divine 1988: Combines subtlety and power for an elegant, lively, flavorful Champagne. Complex aromas of lemon, vanilla and bread dough are followed by solid fruit notes and a seductive echo of the aromas on aftertaste. 2,000 cases made. • $50 • • **92**

LEFLAIVE, DOMAINE

Bâtard-Montrachet 1994: Both supple and quite lively, this medium-bodied '94 shows a nice blend of honey, citrus and tropical flavors. Crisp, slightly hot and coarse finish. Better in 1999? Tasted twice. • $140 • (05/31/96) • **83**
Bâtard-Montrachet 1991 • $120 • (10/15/93) • **93**
Bienvenues-Bâtard-Montrachet 1994: Elegant and stylish, this medium-bodied, racy white offers understated citrus, pear, and mineral flavors that intensify on the long, structured, focused and vibrant finish. Should age nicely, try in 1998. • $125 • (05/31/96) • **89**
Bienvenues-Bâtard-Montrachet White 1991 • $100 • (10/15/93) • **93**
Chevalier-Montrachet 1993 : Brilliant winemaking here. A gorgeous, full-bodied white Burgundy that manages to deliver tons of lemon, honey and pear flavors in a seductive package, yet it's fresh and draws

FRANCE

you back for more. Intense finish. Delicious now, but could age for years. • $165 • (05/31/96) • **95**

Chevalier-Montrachet 1991 • $150 • (10/15/93) • **88**

Chevalier-Montrachet Grand Cru 1992: A clearly outstanding wine that's chock full of flavor and liberally spiced with toasty oak. This is a full-bodied, white Burgundy. The lingering, expanding aftertaste is a hallmark of quality. • $155 • (05/15/95) • **93**

Puligny-Montrachet 1992: Very subtle in flavor, but firm and smooth in texture, with hints of pear and toasty oak coming out on the lingering finish. Not obvious, but it grows in interest as you sip. • $49 • (05/15/95) • **87**

Puligny-Montrachet Clavoillon 1993: A beauty from start to finish. Standing out for its amazingly vibrant character, this superbly focused white needs to age a few years to fully integrate the layers of citrus, mineral and toasted oak that tantalize the palate. Long aftertaste. • $70 • (05/31/96) • **92**

Puligny-Montrachet Clavoillon 1992: A flamboyant, ripe and seductive style of Chardonnay, with plenty of fruit flavor accented by intriguing notes of butter, vanilla, nutmeg and toast. Firm with acidity, full-bodied and long on the finish. Appealing now, but better to wait until 1997. 300 cases made. • $65 • (05/15/95) • **92**

Puligny-Montrachet Clavoillon 1991 • $65 • (10/15/93) • **87**

Puligny-Montrachet Les Combettes 1992: This river runs deep and wide. The aromas are peachy and pearlike, the flavors full of apricot, nutmeg and hazelnut that linger and expand on the finish. It's expansive and concentrated, smooth as velvet, and hard to resist. Drink now through 1998. • $83 • (05/15/95) • **91**

Puligny-Montrachet Les Combettes 1991 • $80 • (10/15/93) • **87**

Puligny-Montrachet Les Folatières 1993: Beautiful, distinctive, amazing chalk and mineral character, sporting notes of citrus and wet earth. Thick but fresh, this full-bodied white coats your palate while remaining structured and focused. Delicious now, but better in 2000. • $95 • (05/31/96) • **91**

Puligny-Montrachet Les Folatières 1991 • $80 • (10/15/93) • **92**

Puligny-Montrachet Les Pucelles 1993: A class act. Full-bodied and ripe, but also fresh and vibrant, with a silky, creamy mouth-feel and complex honey, oregano, basil, vanilla and mineral notes. Clear, clean and wonderfully focused, this has a smooth, supple finish that goes on and on. • $100 • (05/31/96) • **92**

Puligny-Montrachet Les Pucelles 1992: A stylish wine with a nice buttery, nutty character and subtle fruit flavors of apple and lime. The texture is smooth and silky and the flavors seem to expand on the finish. May need time. Good now, but should improve through 1997. • $86 • (05/15/95) • **89**

Puligny-Montrachet Les Pucelles 1991 • $85 • (10/15/93) • **87**

LEFLAIVE FRERES, OLIVIER

Bâtard-Montrachet 1993: Crystal clear, offering apple and cream aromas and flavors and a hint of coconut on the finish. Medium body and fine acidity. Well made. Drinkable now. 75 cases made. • $100 • **88**

Bâtard-Montrachet 1992: Immensely pleasing and well crafted, boasting a silky texture and freshly cut mushroom, ripe pear and butter notes. Drink now or hold past 1996. • $100 • **92**

Bienvenues-Bâtard-Montrachet White 1992: Seductive and silky, all the pieces in the right places, showing complex white truffle and honey flavors that are so enchanting. Long, polished finish. Great now, but will improve through 1997. • $85 • **92**

Bonnes Mares 1987 • $50 • (09/30/90) • **88**

Bourgogne Chardonnay White 1992: Coarse and sour, with a nutty quality that overwhelms the apple and spice flavors. Simple and uninspired, with a slightly bitter finish. • $9 • **76**

Bourgogne Les Sétilles White 1993: Straightforward and simple, offering modest fruit flavors and slight dilution. Drink now. • $NA • **72**

Bourgogne Les Sétilles White 1991: A crisp and refreshing white wine with enough apple and grapefruit flavors to make it interesting. Just slightly on the green side, but should be fine at the table. • $15 • (11/15/94) • **82**

Bourgogne Pinot Noir 1992: Modest plum and strawberry aromas, matched with smoky, spicy flavors and a dry, tannic finish add up to a typical, solid Burgundy. Drink now while the fruit lasts. • $9 • (11/30/94) • **82**

Charmes-Chambertin 1989 • $60 • (01/31/92) • **88**

Charmes-Chambertin 1986 • $50 • (07/31/88) • **88**

Chassagne-Montrachet 1993: Pretty little wine offering creamy, appley character, medium body and firm acidity. Try now. • $NA • **81**

Chassagne-Montrachet 1992: Light-bodied, with a delicate raspberry, floral and smoky character. A bit diluted on the finish. • $NA • **77**

Chassagne-Montrachet 1991: Perhaps a bit on the oaky side, but the ripe black cherry and raspberry flavors shine through. May always be lean. Drinkable now. 700 cases made. • $15 Ⓐ • (01/31/94) • **84**

Chassagne-Montrachet 1990: Firm and aromatic, delivering a subtext of barklike, herbal, vegetal, vanilla and cinnamon flavors. Very distinctive, but a bit lean. Drinkable now. 600 cases made. • $17 • (12/15/92) • **85**

Chassagne-Montrachet 1986 • $26 • (02/29/88) • **89**

Chassagne-Montrachet 1985 • $32 • (10/31/88) • **83**

Chassagne-Montrachet Morgeot 1993: Lean and meager, the crisp, fresh texture delivering little pleasure. Modest cherry, earth notes. Firm tannins don't help. • $34 • **79**

Chassagne-Montrachet Morgeot White 1993: Appealing and ready to drink, this smoky, toasty and lush Burgundy offers some modest chalk, mineral and fruit flavors. 75 cases made. • $38 • **84**

Chassagne-Montrachet Morgeot White 1992: Clean-tasting, well-balanced and harmonious. Its pear, orange, vanilla and spice flavors are lean but complex. Tight and well-knit. Drink now through 1997. • $45 • (08/31/94) • **85**

Chevalier-Montrachet 1992 : Rich, ripe and a bit overdone, with cooked apple, honey and butter flavors. Very soft on the finish. • $NA • (05/31/96) 79 • **80**

Clos St.-Denis 1989 • $56 • (01/31/92) • **93**

Clos de la Roche 1989 • $63 • (03/15/93) • **82**

Corton Bressandes 1986 • $45 • (07/31/88) • **88**

Corton-Charlemagne 1993: Clean and fresh, offering zingy acidity, medium body, toasted oak, lime and apple flavors and crisp finish. Not big, but delicious. 75 cases made. • $75 • **85**

Corton-Charlemagne 1992: Firm and tart, hinting of honey and hazelnut, rather lean, displaying green apple, pear and a touch of mineral on the finish. May be better after 1996. Tasted twice, with consistent notes. • $65 • **85**

Givry Red 1988 • $16 • (10/31/92) • **76**

Mercurey White 1993: Lively and vibrant, light-bodied, featuring zingy acidity and green apple, citrus and herb character. The finish is lean but juicy. Drink now. • $NA • **80**

Meursault 1993: Lean now, but offering good mineral, pear and apple character and citrusy notes. Should gain roundness after cellaring for a couple of years; try in 1997. • $NA • **85**

Meursault 1992: Delicate and elegant, with moderate fruit flavors and a silky texture, but you wish it had more intensity. Drinkable now. 530 cases made. • $32 • (08/31/94) • **82**

Meursault 1991 • $27 • (10/15/93) • **86**

Meursault Les Perrières 1993: Stylish, offering plenty of ripe lemon and pineapple character, medium to full body and fine acidity. 125 cases made. • $42 • (08/31/95) • **88**

Meursault Les Perrières 1992: Nicely balanced, with subtle spice, vanilla and pear flavors braced by good acidity. The sort of wine you want to drink a lot of. 128 cases made. • $45 • (08/31/94) • **87**

Meursault Les Poruzots 1991 • $38 • (10/15/93) • **88**

Meursault Perrières 1991 • $40 • (10/15/93) • **88**

Monthelie 1991 • $19 Ⓐ • (01/31/94) • **80**

Monthelie Premier Cru 1990 • $19 • (12/15/92) • **82**

Montrachet White 1993: A beauty, featuring pie crust, apple and citrus aromas and flavors, medium body, fine acidity and finish shaded by toasted oak. Drinkable now. 25 cases made. • $180 • **89**

Montrachet White 1992: Quite fat, demonstrating a rich texture and lots of pear, mineral and honey flavors. Medium-bodied, perfect to drink now. • $175 • **87**

Montrachet White 1991 • $150 • (10/15/93) • **91**

Morey-St.-Denis 1989 • $30 • (01/31/92) • **87**

Pommard 1993: A bit lean but some vivid cherry and mineral character. Medium-bodied with fine tannins and a long, crisp finish. Better in 1999. • $32 • **84**

Pommard 1992: A delicate Pommard, with a tannic underpinning that makes it last on the finish. Light in texture and offering only modest strawberry, raspberry and cherry flavors. Try now. • $NA • **84**
Pommard 1990: A concentrated village wine that's rich, ripe and supple, packed with wild raspberry, leaf and earth aromas and flavors. Coats your mouth and leaves a lasting impression on the elegant finish. Drinkable now through 1998. 500 cases made. • $30 • (12/15/92) • **92**
Pommard 1989 • $32 • (01/31/92) • **84**
Pommard Epenots 1993: A lean '93 with some berry, herbal character. Better in 1998? Medium-bodied with firm tannins and a light fruity finish. Leflaive's village Pommard is better. • $46 • **82**
Pommard Epenots 1990: A delight to smell, this toasty wine offers terrific smoke, game and plum aromas and flavors that come across gracefully on the lovely, supple finish. Drinkable now. 125 cases made. • $35 • (12/15/92) • **90**
Pommard Epenots 1989 • $40 • (01/31/92) • **88**
Pommard Rugiens 1993: Tough red, offering loads of tannins and hot fruit, full body, substantial raspberry and cherry character and a hint of earth. Slightly overdone. Needs time to mellow, try in 2000. • $48 • **86**
Pommard Rugiens 1992: Nicely focused, medium-bodied, with pretty blackberry, boysenberry and violet notes. Firm but slightly lean on the finish. Might improve some by 1997. • $NA • **84**
Pommard Rugiens 1991: Tough, astringent and very lean. Try now. 200 cases made. • $37 Ⓐ • (01/31/94) • **77**
Pommard Rugiens 1990: A class act. Muscular yet supple and well constructed, oozing with intense, concentrated black cherry, fleshy, ripe fruit flavors and smoky, chocolaty undertones that come together on the firm but supple finish. Drinkable now. 100 cases made. • $35 • (12/15/92) • **91**
Puligny-Montrachet 1993: Very clean and fresh Chardonnay displaying apple, mineral character, fresh acidity and a medium, creamy finish. • $NA • **85**
Puligny-Montrachet 1992: Solid and straightforward, firm, medium-bodied, with good balance and moderate fruit intensity, delivers some honey and pear flavors and a moderate-long finish. Drinkable now. 600 cases made. • $38 • (08/31/94) • **84**
Puligny-Montrachet 1991 • $30 • (10/15/93) • **83**
Puligny-Montrachet Champ Canet 1993: Ripe and lush style, quite smoky and toasty, offering dried herb, mineral and pear flavors. A bit heavy-handed on the finish. 100 cases made. • $40 • (08/31/94) • **81**
Puligny-Montrachet Champ Gain 1993: Very lively, sporting honey, mineral and cream character, medium body, fine acidity and a zingy finish. Drinkable now. 125 cases made. • $35 • **86**
Puligny-Montrachet Les Champs-Canet 1992: A very good white that features toast, butter and vanilla-like flavors that are nicely supported by firm acidity. The texture is full but a bit tight, and the finish is lingering. Try now. 100 cases made. • $50 • (08/31/94) • **86**
Puligny-Montrachet Les Champs-Canet 1991 • $NA • (10/15/93) • **90**
Puligny-Montrachet Les Folatières 1993: Well-made Burgundy in a relatively lean package. What's there is quite delicious, offering mineral, pear and lightly toasted bread flavors. Smooth finish and ready to drink. 225 cases made. • $42 • **86**
Puligny-Montrachet Les Folatières 1992: A distinctively oaky, smoky aroma and tightly-wound flavors of apple, grapefruit and mint make for a big, bold, square-jawed wine that will need time to mellow. Has good fruit concentration and a lingering aftertaste. 100 cases made. • $52 • (08/31/94) • **90**
Puligny-Montrachet Les Folatières 1991 • $38 • (10/15/93) • **87**
Puligny-Montrachet Premier Cru Les Champs Gains 1991: A complex but subtle white Burgundy that smells toasty and buttery, tastes like pear and hazelnut and stays with you on the finish. Nicely balanced. • $40 • (11/15/94) • **84**
Rully 1990: Crisp in texture, with a definite woody, spicy character that obscures the modest core of fruit. Drinkable now. Tasted three times. • $20 • (11/30/92) • **80**
Rully Premier Cru 1994: An ager. Amazing concentration of mineral, citrus, tropical fruit and pear flavors that are exciting to taste. Appears "reductive" at first (like stale ice), but after a while it reveals great depth and length. Don't touch till after 2000. 400 cases made. • $19 • (05/31/96) • **91**
St.-Aubin En Remilly 1994: A fat, supple wine that oozes ripe fruit and honey. Full-bodied and chalky, this *premier cru* delivers some toast, pear and pie crust flavors. Nice, long finish. Try in 1997. 300 cases made. • $22 • (05/31/96) • **87**
St.-Aubin En Remilly White 1993: Attractive mineral, spice and toasted oak character, medium body and a light, fruity finish. • $NA • **83**
St.-Aubin En Remilly White 1991 • $20 • (10/15/93) • **86**
St.-Aubin En Remilly White Premier Cru 1991: Very stylish, with toasty, buttery aromas, subtle fruit flavors and a lingering finish. Earthy, nutty nuances add to its complexity and appeal. • $23 • (11/15/94) • **85**
St.-Aubin Sur Gamay White 1991 • $20 • (10/15/93) • **84**
St.-Romain 1994: Crisp and lively, with sharp, earthy flavors of dried herbs and green apple. Rather lean. 200 cases made. • $18 • (05/31/96) • **79**
St.-Romain White 1993: Crisp, citrusy white Burgundy, offering green apple, orange-peel and cream flavors. A bit green on the finish. Drink now. • $NA • **76**
St.-Romain White 1991 • $15 • (10/15/93) • **85**
Santenay 1993: A lean machine, light-bodied and somewhat odd at this stage, tasting of sausage, cherry and spice flavors. Drink now. • $20 • **79**
Santenay 1986 • $17 • (07/31/88) • **81**
Santenay Les Gravières 1990: Bright and clean, with an elegant texture and nice plum, tobacco and black cherry flavors. A bit short on the finish. Drinkable now. 300 cases made. • $17 • (12/15/92) • **85**
Volnay 1992: Light and supple, showing a nice core of smoky berry flavors that just make it to the finish. • $NA • **81**
Volnay 1991: Light, bright and polished. Vanilla-scented raspberry and anise aromas and flavors persist delicately on the finish. Drinkable now. 150 cases made. • $36 Ⓐ • (01/31/94) • **84**
Volnay 1990: An exquisite wine, with finesse and a silky texture. It's thick and light, yet also supple and tannic, oozing with toasty currant, cherry and game aromas and flavors. Drinkable now. 125 cases made. • $36 • (12/15/92) • **92**
Volnay 1989 • $38 • (01/31/92) • **92**
Volnay 1987 • $27 • (08/31/90) • **78**
Volnay 1986 • $28 • (07/31/88) • **89**
Volnay Frémiets 1993: Beautiful, vivid and ripe, sporting a gorgeous core of plum and red berry flavors and silky texture. Tannins creep up on the finish, so should need until 2000 to show it all. • $42 • **93**

LEGER-PLUMET, BERNARD

Pouilly-Fuissé Domaine des Gerbaux Fût de Chêne 1992: Sensational Pouilly, featuring earthy, buttery, lime-flavored, mineral character, a solid backbone that turns remarkably harmonious on the palate and a long, intense and fresh finish. Drink now to 1997. • $NA • **90**
Pouilly-Fuissé Les Chailloux 1993: Fresh and clean, steely texture and wet hay, green apple, chalky flavors. Could provide more round opulence on the finish. Drink with seafood. 2,033 cases made. • $20 • **82**

LEGRAS, R & L

Brut Blanc de Blancs Champagne Cuvée St.-Vincent 1976 • $33 • (05/31/87) • **85**
Brut Blanc de Blancs Champagne Grand Cru NV • $23 • (12/31/92) • **90**
Brut Blanc de Blancs Champagne NV • $32 • (12/31/91) • **85**
Brut Blanc de Blancs Champagne Présidence 1982: Nicely concentrated flavors, with hints of ginger, lemon and apple, on a fairly elegant framework, make this a wine worth paying attention to. • $29 • (05/31/87) • **85**

LEGROS, FRANCOIS

Chambolle-Musigny Les Noirots 1990: Firm and tight, with a core of black cherry, earth, cedar and currant flavors that is focused and complex. Tight and tannic, drinkable now. • $40 • (03/15/93) • **88**
Chambolle-Musigny Les Noirots 1989 • $30 • (11/15/91) • **92**
Nuits-St.-Georges Aux Bousselots 1990: Dry, chewy and tannic, with a solid core of cherry and raspberry flavors that is stiff with tannins and

Key: SS—Spectator Selection. CS—Cellar Selection. BB—Best Buy. $NA—Price not available. (BT)—Barrel tasting. Ⓐ—Auction Price.
Dates in parentheses represent the issues in which the ratings were published.

tightly wound. The finish offers a glimpse of hope and complexity, with spicy oak and fruit nuances. Drinkable now. • $39 • (03/15/93) • **87**

Nuits-St.-Georges Les Perrières 1990: Shows lots of currant and black cherry-scented flavors up front, but turns tart and lean on the finish, where the tannins become more evident. Drinkable now. • $39 • (03/15/93) • **88**

Nuits-St.-Georges Les Perrières 1989 • $29 • (11/15/91) • **87**

Vougeot Les Crâs 1990: Starts out with generous black cherry and currant-scented flavors, but then the tannins kick in and it tightens up. Can try it now. • $45 • (03/15/93) • **87**

LEJEUNE

Bourgogne 1990 • $18 • (12/15/92) • **85**

Bourgogne Passetoutgrain 1993: Crisp, decent core of plum, cherry and currant flavors and a silky, ready-to-drink mouth-feel. Somewhat hot and raisiny on the finish. Try now. • $13 • **80**

Pommard 1993: Rather light and fruity, offering an interesting aroma and flavors of pineapple and berry, fine tannins and a delicate fruit finish. Better in 1999. • $NA • **84**

Pommard Les Argillières 1993: Not as good as the sample we tasted in the fall. Some decent fruit but rather mature already, showing nutty, earthy aromas and flavors. Drinkable now. • $NA • (05/15/96) • **81**

Pommard Les Argillières 1991: Tough and drying, showing sweet cherry and currant notes. 400 cases made. • $36 Ⓐ • (01/31/94) • **77**

Pommard Les Argillières 1990: So huge and tannic we wonder if it's not overdone. Offers substantial fruit, but also a lot of new wood, with impressive vanilla, milk chocolate and fruit characteristics. Let the monster tannins sort themselves out uncork around 2000. 580 cases made. • $40 • (12/15/92) • **88**

Pommard Les Poutures 1993: Racy, earthy berry and plum aromas and flavors. Medium-bodied, fine tannins and velvety texture on finish. Best in 2000. Better than we remember a previous sample. • $NA • **87**

Pommard Les Poutures 1991: Cherry flavor, but is watery at the core and finishes with more oak than fruit. Try now. 450 cases made. • $32 Ⓐ • (01/31/94) • **75**

Pommard Les Rugiens 1993: Oaky, smoky, toasty *premier cru*, featuring tons of mocha, spice and pepper. The red berry flavor below will carry this full-bodied but supple red forward until at least 2000. • $NA • **86**

Pommard Les Rugiens 1990: If you are a chocoholic, this is for you. Smells and tastes like chocolate mousse, with smoky raspberry and sweet fruit flavors. The firm but refined tannins take over on the long finish. Drinkable now. 150 cases made. • $49 • (12/15/92) • **92**

Pommard Les Rugiens 1993: Delicious flavors. Not the biggest of wines, but some fine tannins, medium body and a tasty gamy and berry finish. Better in 1998. 125 cases made. • $65 • **83**

Pommard Les Rugiens 1991: Woody, spicy notes characterize this firm-textured, dryingly tannic wine. Try now. 80 cases made. • $52 Ⓐ • (01/31/94) • **79**

LEJEUNE, DOMAINE LENZ MOSER

Bourgogne 1993: Tight and dry, tannins being outplayed by the fruit. Lacks ripeness. Very hard finish. Better in 2000? • $14 • **76**

LEMENICIER, JACQUES

Cornas 1990 • $16 • (04/15/93) • **75**

LEON, CHÂTEAU

Côtes de Bordeaux 1983 • $5 • (11/15/86) • **79**

LEONARD DE ST.-AUBIN

Beaujolais-Villages 1995: Supple and spicy. Bright cherry and citrus notes are accented by spicy, smoky notes in this understated wine that blooms on the finish. A bit more sophisticated than many Beaujolais-Villages. • $NA • **85**

Chambolle-Musigny 1993: Solid, flavorful, fairly fruity, rather soft and easy on the tannins. A modestly proportioned red that's pleasant but closed in. 500 cases made. • $30 • (05/15/96) • **84**

Chassagne-Montrachet 1994: An exaggerated style, the ripe honey and spice notes almost overpowering this white. It tastes a bit candied, but still pleasant. Flavors soften somewhat on the finish. 600 cases made. • $26 • (05/31/96) • **84**

Gevrey-Chambertin 1993: A stiff-textured, tightly structured Burgundy showing flavors that tend toward the lean, herbal side. Intense but not expansive. Drink in 1998. 1,250 cases made. • $26 • (05/15/96) • **84**

Gevrey-Chambertin 1985 • $25 • (11/30/87) • **66**

Meursault 1992: A basic white Burgundy that tantalizes you with spicy aromas, but turns rather thin and lean on the palate. • $NA • (11/15/94) • **78**

Nuits-St.-Georges 1993: Tight, tannic and not especially fruity at this stage, showing lean, slightly green flavors and tough texture. 1,400 cases made. • $26 • (05/15/96) • **78**

Nuits-St.-Georges 1985 • $25 • (11/30/87) • **71**

Pommard 1993: Firmly textured, almost tough, difficult to enjoy now, but may not mellow with age. The aromas are resinous, oaky and earthy and the flavors slightly herbal. Try in 1999. 1,200 cases made. • $27 • (05/15/96) • **85**

Pouilly-Fuissé 1993: A hard white, with mineral and asparagus flavors but not much fruit, fading quickly. 8,000 cases made. • $12 • (03/31/95) • **76**

Puligny-Montrachet 1994: A stylish, well-constructed white that's fairly rich, sporting ripe apple and spice flavors. It has modest intensity and an aftertaste loaded with vanilla. 1,750 cases made. • $27 • (05/31/96) • **86**

Puligny-Montrachet 1992: If a wine can be suave, this is. It has toasty, spicy, oaky aromas, a smooth texture and long, buttery aftertaste. Not overtly fruity, but with plenty of nut, coffee and honey flavors. 1,250 cases made. • $24 • (11/15/94) • **87**

Volnay 1993: Intriguing, spicy-smelling, smooth and supple, featuring ripe fruit flavors and exotic nuances of cinnamon and smoke. Nicely concentrated and long on the finish, firmly tannic but impeccably balanced. Drink in 1999. 650 cases made. • $26 • (05/15/96) • **89**

LEOVILLE BARTON, CHÂTEAU

St.-Julien 1995: Like the '94, a well-styled wine of extracted fruit and tannins. Full body and tannins and long, vanilla finish. Complex, subtle and delicious. • $NA • (05/15/96) • **90-94** (BT)

St.-Julien 1994: One of *the* wines of the vintage. Super well-made '94, as good as the '95. Fine berry, vanilla and mineral aromas and flavors. Medium body, fine tannins and long, silky finish. • $44 • (05/15/96) • **90-94** (BT)

St.-Julien 1993: Léoville Barton continues to move up. Bright berry flavor and a lovely, silky tannin structure. Wonderful ripe fruit and long, delicious finish. Very well made. • $30 • (01/31/96) • **88**

St.-Julien 1991: Supple and pretty, showing soft plum and currant notes that end with a velvety finish, though it's a bit short. Could use more cellar time, drinkable now. • $23 • (03/31/94) • **84**

St.-Julien 1990: Sleek and racy, with plum, raspberry and earthy aromas and flavors, silky tannins and a wonderfully long finish. Drink after 1998. 22,000 cases made. • $48 Ⓐ • (03/31/93) • **93**

St.-Julien 1989 • $33 Ⓐ • (03/15/92) • **94**

St.-Julien 1988 • $29 Ⓐ • (03/31/91) • **91**

St.-Julien 1987 • $20 • (05/15/90) • **80**

St.-Julien 1986 • $36 Ⓐ • (05/31/89) • **90**

St.-Julien 1985: The beginning of a new era at this estate. Wonderfully crafted, with vibrant black currant, cedar and vanilla aromas and flavors, medium body and a succulent finish. Drinkable now. • $32 • (10/15/94) • **90**

St.-Julien 1983: Beautiful wine with wonderful subtlety and finesse. Complex aromas and flavors of tobacco, plum and berries, full-bodied yet reserved and silky. Drink or hold. • $37 • (10/15/94) • **90**

St.-Julien 1982 • $58 Ⓐ • (08/31/92) • **90**

St.-Julien 1981: A fine mature claret with frshness. Excellent red, ruby color with subtle aromas of cherry and green tobacco. This wine shows vivid fruit flavors with mineral undertones and a fine silky texture of tannins. Delicious now but should improve. • $31 • **88**

St.-Julien 1970 • $45 Ⓐ • (05/15/93) • **88**

St.-Julien 1962 • $80 • (11/30/87) • **70**

St.-Julien 1961: A beautifully balanced, elegant wine that just keeps on improving in the glass. It has earthy, herbal aromas, light but focused

FRANCE

fruit flavors and a firmly tannic texture that's just right. Drink through 2002. • $140 • (04/30/96) • **87**
St.-Julien 1959 • $125 • (10/15/90) • **85**
St.-Julien 1945 • $340 • (03/16/86) • **73**

LEOVILLE LAS CASES, CHÂTEAU

St.-Julien 1992: Slightly disappointing at this juncture. Berry, vanilla and earth character, medium body, soft tannins and light finish. Drinkable now. • $35 • **84**
St.-Julien 1991: A mouthful of fruit in this full-bodied red, featuring masses of mint, berry and cherry flavors, velvety tannins and long finish. One of the best '91s. Really delicious for the Médoc in an off year. Better in 1998. • $38 • (02/29/96) • **89**
St.-Julien 1988 • $46 Ⓐ • (02/15/92) • **95**
St.-Julien 1987 • $NA • (02/15/92) • **88**
St.-Julien 1986 • $86 Ⓐ • (02/15/92) • **95**
St.-Julien 1985: Impressively rich wine. Dense and thick with black color, super opulent character of cassis, tar, berry. It goes on and on. Try after 1998. • $56 • (10/15/94) • **94**
St.-Julien 1984 • $33 • (02/15/92) • **85**
St.-Julien 1983: Deceptive which shows extremely gamy, roasted, ripe fruit character, medium body and a silky mouth feel. Drink or hold. • $42 • (10/15/94) • **87**
St.-Julien 1982 • $168 Ⓐ • (08/31/92) • **94**
St.-Julien 1981: Lovely round and soft wine with a good backbone of ripe tannins. Very aromatic with plum, spice, cherry character. Full bodied and a lovely cedar, fruity finish. • $45 • (10/15/94) • **88**
St.-Julien 1980 • $20 • (02/15/92) • **82**
St.-Julien 1979 • $36 Ⓐ • (02/15/92) • **89**
St.-Julien 1978 • $55 Ⓐ • (02/15/92) • **87**
St.-Julien 1977 • $20 • (02/15/92) • **78**
St.-Julien 1976 • $28 Ⓐ • (02/15/92) • **83**
St.-Julien 1975 • $60 Ⓐ • (02/15/92) • **88**
St.-Julien 1971 • $66 • (04/01/86) • **76**
St.-Julien 1970 • $41 Ⓐ • (05/15/93) • **87**
St.-Julien 1966 • $61 Ⓐ • (02/15/92) • **86**
St.-Julien 1964 • $53 Ⓐ • (02/15/92) • **88**
St.-Julien 1962 • $41 Ⓐ • (02/15/92) • **81**
St.-Julien 1961: Not as great as you would hope from Las Cases, but a very good and well-balanced bottle with ample fruit flavor and solid tannins. Drink through 2002. • $168 • (04/30/96) • **85**
St.-Julien 1959 • $127 Ⓐ • (02/15/92) • **80**
St.-Julien 1955 • $190 • (02/15/92) • **81**
St.-Julien 1953 • $225 • (02/15/92) • **87**
St.-Julien 1952 • $165 • (02/15/92) • **73**
St.-Julien 1950 • $165 • (02/15/92) • **73**
St.-Julien 1948 • $165 • (02/15/92) • **65**
St.-Julien 1947 • $141 Ⓐ • (02/15/92) • **86**
St.-Julien 1945: Deep, dark and remarkably vibrant, showing layers of black cherry, plum and silky spice flavors. A little chewy, powerful up front and gentle on the finish. Feels like it still can improve. • $600 • **89**
St.-Julien 1928 • $450 • (02/15/92) • **94**

LEOVILLE POYFERRE, CHÂTEAU

St.-Julien 1995: Amazing, it offers a mouthful of extracted, concentrated, sweet fruit character and loads of silky, ripe tannins. A big wine that manages to remain refined. • $NA • (05/15/96) • **90-94** (BT)
St.-Julien 1994: Well-made, classy berry, cherry and vanilla character. This offers medium tannins and a fresh finish. • $29 • (05/15/96) • **85-89** (BT)
St.-Julien 1991: Some fine complexity here, with beautiful smoky, red berry and vanilla flavors, but it doesn't have much length. Drinkable now. • $23 • (03/31/94) • **81**

Key: SS—Spectator Selection. CS—Cellar Selection. BB—Best Buy. $NA—Price not available. (BT)—Barrel tasting. Ⓐ—Auction Price.
Dates in parentheses represent the issues in which the ratings were published.

St.-Julien 1990: A chewy wine, with impressively rich aromas and flavors of ripe plums, tobacco, cedar and earth and attractive velvety tannins. Drinkable in 1998. 18,500 cases made. • $31 • (03/31/93) • **92**
St.-Julien 1989 • $42 • (03/15/92) • **90**
St.-Julien 1988 • $21 Ⓐ • (07/15/91) • **81**
St.-Julien 1987 • $24 • (05/15/90) • **86**
St.-Julien 1986 • $24 • (05/31/89) • **86**
St.-Julien 1985 • $25 Ⓐ • (04/30/88) • **92**
St.-Julien 1984 • $25 • (10/15/87) • **85**
St.-Julien 1983 • $28 Ⓐ • (03/01/86) • **83**
St.-Julien 1982 • $53 Ⓐ • (06/01/85) • **89**
St.-Julien 1981 • $25 • (06/01/84) • **88**
St.-Julien 1970 • $23 Ⓐ • (05/15/93) • **85**
St.-Julien 1961: A very good St.-Julien that has elegance and finesse in a nicely balanced package of soft texture and good fruit flavor. Drink now through 1998. • $65 • (04/30/96) • **85**
St.-Julien 1945 • $210 • (03/16/86) • **80**

LEPITRE, ABEL

Brut Champagne 1986: Rather simple and very vinous and chewy with earthy fruity aromas and flavor, medium body and a fruity finish. Very foamy texture. Drink now. • $NA • (12/31/93) • **84**
Brut Champagne 1985: A wine for meditation and sipping. Very mature style verging on sparkling sherry. Medium bodied with rich fruit, light acidity and a long rich finish. Drink now. • $NA • (12/31/93) • **84**

LEQUIN-ROUSSOT

Chassagne-Montrachet Morgeot 1985 • $24 • (05/31/88) • **86**
Corton Les Languettes 1985 • $39 • (07/15/88) • **86**
Nuits-St.-Georges 1985 • $39 • (04/15/88) • **75**
Santenay 1987 • $15 • (11/15/90) • **76**
Santenay 1985 • $18 • (05/31/88) • **78**
Santenay La Comme 1985 • $24 • (05/31/88) • **85**

LEROY

Auxey-Duresses Les Clous 1988 • $52 • (05/15/91) • **85**
Bourgogne d'Auvenay 1988 • $15 • (04/30/91) • **87**
Bourgogne d'Auvenay 1986 • $17 • **84**
Bourgogne d'Auvenay 1985 • $12 • (03/31/88) • **73**
Bourgogne Leroy 1990: Chunky and earthy, with spice and berry flavors and a good concentration of fruit and tannins on the finish. Drinkable now. • $18 • (12/15/92) • **86**
Bourgogne Leroy 1989 • $18 • (01/31/92) • **85**
Bourgogne Leroy White 1992: Light and tart, offering very crisp texture and some straightforward citrus, floral, wet hay and apple flavors. Very firm on the finish. Drinkable now. Tasted twice with identical results. 8,000 cases made. • $19 • (08/31/94) • **80**
Bourgogne White 1993: Delicious, easygoing white, offering apple, cream and mineral character, medium body and pretty finish. • $15 • (08/31/95) • **83**
Chambertin 1993: Wonderfully sexy, soft and silky, featuring pretty plum and vanilla character, medium body, ultrafine tannins and sweet fruit finish. Better in 1999. 72 cases made. • $500 • **95**
Chambertin 1992: Lean, accessible, nicely focused, a sharp beam of black cherry, toast and spice flavors shining through. Smooth tannins make it drinkable already, may be best from 1997. • $266 • **88**
Chambertin 1991: An extreme wine, lean in structure but silky and polished, exotic in flavor, featuring an array of spices both sweet and sharp around a fine thread of floral berry and black cherry fruit. A stylish wine that needs until 1998 or 2000. Tasted three times. 75 cases made. • $257 Ⓐ • (01/31/94) • **88**
Chambertin 1990: Remarkably balanced and harmonious, this is complex, tightly knit, big and massive, with tons of toasted, roasted wood and game characteristics. Also delivers tobacco box, smoke, plum and cherry flavors on the ripe, very elegant finish. Drinkable in 1998. 169 cases made. • $456 Ⓐ • (12/15/92) • **96**
Chambertin 1989 • $212 Ⓐ • (01/31/92) • **93**
Chambolle-Musigny Les Charmes 1993: Lovely, elegant berry, vanilla and spice character, medium body, fine tannins and light, fresh finish.

FRANCE

Better in 1999. A bit less impressive than a barrel sample tasted earlier this year. 24 cases made. • $200 • **90**

Chambolle-Musigny Les Charmes 1992: Sweet and ripe at first, but it ends a bit diluted. Modest raspberry and currant notes with a gamy, smoky edge. Drink soon. • $NA • **79**

Chambolle-Musigny Les Fremières 1993: Generous and seductively flavorful, offering ripe plum, currant, black cherry and chocolate. Same quality level as a barrel sample tasted in the spring of 1995. Tempting now, but hold until 2000. 24 cases made. • $125 • **88**

Chambolle-Musigny Les Fremières 1992: Decidedly gamy, but backed up with a decent quotient of black cherry flavor, all of which lingers on the smooth finish. Drinkable now. • $NA • **83**

Chambolle-Musigny Les Fremières 1991: A lithe, lean wine that seems earthy at first, but the blackberry and currant fruit comes bursting through as the flavors emerge wrapped in a blanket of fine tannins. Try in 1997. 48 cases made. • $74 Ⓐ • (01/31/94) • **87**

Chambolle-Musigny Les Fremières 1990: Has everything in unbelievable amounts: concentration, fruit, color, tannins and suppleness. Stands out with its rich character of grilled, toasted oak, violet, raspberry and chocolate aromas and flavors. Will need years before the new oak and fruit flavors melt together harmoniously. Drinkable in 1999 or 2000. 143 cases made. • $79 • (12/15/92) • **94**

Chambolle-Musigny Les Fremières 1989 • $80 • (01/31/92) • **94**

Clos de la Roche 1993: Big and beautiful, boasting voluptuous blackberry and vanilla character, full body, silky tannins and long, sweet finish. Better in 2000. Rated just a notch below a barrel sample earlier this year. 72 cases made. • $325 • **94**

Clos de la Roche 1992: A good red Burgundy that is fruity, moderately tannic and tart. Medium-bodied, lively cherry and raspberry flavors. Drinkable now. • $196 • (05/15/95) • **84**

Clos de la Roche 1991: Earthy, floral and flavorful, offering a core of solid blackberry and currant underneath a layer of slightly gamy, musty, smoky violet character. Tough and chewy on the finish, but juicy at the core. May be best after 1998. 237 cases made. • $124 Ⓐ • (01/31/94) • **90**

Clos de la Roche 1990: Leaves you speechless. Shows such concentration, grace and beauty, it's obviously the work of an artist. Complex vanilla, violet, plum and blackberry flavors are cut with razor-sharp acidity, and it shows a smoky, toasty aftertaste. The considerable fruit balances new oak. Drinkable in 1999 or 2000. 218 cases made. • $289 Ⓐ • (12/15/92) • **97**

Clos de la Roche 1989 • $148 Ⓐ • (01/31/92) • **94**

Clos de Vougeot 1993: Stupendous. So balanced it's difficult not to drink this one now. Lovely spice, mocha and fruit character. Full-bodied, adding velvety tannins and a long, savory finish. Better in 2000. • $250 • **96**

Clos de Vougeot 1992: Not flashy, but it packs a lot of flavor into a lean frame, showing ripe blackberry, currant, anise and floral character that maintains its balance and focus through the lingering finish. Best from 1998. • $100 • **90**

Clos de Vougeot 1991: Highly distinctive, offering layers of earthy flavors. Mineral and mushroom notes shade the core of black cherry, currant and blackberry that extends into a rich, finely tannic finish. Best after 1998. 75 cases made. • $181 • (01/31/94) • **90**

Clos de Vougeot 1990: A full-blown Clos de Vougeot that's been given the full-blown new oak treatment. Stands out in this group, with its violet, raspberry and plum characteristics and massive, hard tannins. Drinkable in 1999. 400 cases made. • $155 Ⓐ • (12/15/92) • **97**

Clos de Vougeot 1989 • $88 Ⓐ • (01/31/92) • **95**

Clos de Vougeot 1988 • $89 Ⓐ • (04/30/91) • **89**

Corton Bressandes 1992: Ripe, chewy and distinctive, packing a fair amount of blackberry and currant flavors into a solid frame. Has overtones of anise and earth that echo on the tannic finish. Best from 1997. • $83 • **91**

Corton-Charlemagne 1993: Solid and muscular, turning silky on the finish, delivering pear, vanilla bean and coconut flavors edged between smoky, toasty oak shadings. Wood should smooth out by 1998. • $150 • (08/31/95) • **88**

Corton-Charlemagne 1991 • $116 • (10/15/93) • **92**

Corton Renardes 1993: A Corton with finesse. Pretty blackberry, toasted oak and smoke flavors, solid fruit, firm tannins and long, succulent finish. Better in 2000. Same quality and score as a barrel sample tasted earlier this year. 169 cases made. • $185 • **92**

Corton Renardes 1991: A crisp, sharply pleated wine that folds in raspberry, violet, vanilla and anise aromas and flavors and coats your mouth with fruit and tannins on the finish, while remaining elegant, classy and focused. Try now. 121 cases made. • $100 Ⓐ • (01/31/94) • **90**

Corton Renardes 1990: If you like the violet and vanilla flavors from masses of new oak and fruit, this is for you. Refined, with enough fruit to back up the tannins. Drinkable in 1998 to 2000. 167 cases made. • $111 • (12/15/92) • **92**

Corton Renardes 1989 • $117 • (01/31/92) • **95**

Gevrey-Chambertin Les Combottes 1993: Provides lots of strawberry, vanilla and cherry character, medium body and tannins and soft finish. Better in 1999. Same quality as we remember in a barrel sample earlier this year. 24 cases made. • $220 • **89**

Gevrey-Chambertin Les Combottes 1992: Has a little more distinction than most, folding its violet, berry and currant flavors into a nice package. Drinkable now. • $83 • **86**

Gevrey-Chambertin Les Combottes 1991: Distinctively earthy and floral. Violet and rose petal aromas and flavors and a lively array of berry and passion fruit swirl across the palate and into the firm finish. Needs until 1997. 48 cases made. • $100 Ⓐ • (01/31/94) • **88**

Gevrey-Chambertin Les Combottes 1990: A beautiful Gevrey, with great concentration and elegant, toasty raspberry and vanilla characteristics. Like many from this appellation, it's very firm but offers more flesh than most on the finish. Drinkable in 1997 or '98. 144 cases made. • $111 • (12/15/92) • **92**

Gevrey-Chambertin Les Combottes 1989 • $68 Ⓐ • (01/31/92) • **93**

Latricières-Chambertin 1993: Loads of personality. Full in body, offering a core of earth, currant, chocolate, leather and plum. Slightly rough finish. Try in 1999. As good as we rated a barrel sample in the spring of '95. 48 cases made. • $325 • **91**

Latricières-Chambertin 1992: Crisp and chewy, with enough body to deliver some complexity, gamy currant notes predominate now. Flavors echo nicely on the finish, but this doesn't quite live up to its name. Best after 1996. • $155 • **86**

Latricières-Chambertin 1991: Earthy notes keep peering through the currant and berry aromas and flavors in this chewy, hard-textured wine. Offers a real mouthful of as-yet unfocused flavor, has the stuffing to be worth cellaring until 1999 or 2000. Tasted twice. 73 cases made. • $181 Ⓐ • (01/31/94) • **89**

Latricières-Chambertin 1990: Pure fruit, with laser-guided flavors that engulf your taste buds. Offers masses of violet, fruit and berry characteristics and ultrafine tannins and acidity. Superb. Try in 1998. 195 cases made. • $204 • (12/15/92) • **96**

Latricières-Chambertin 1989 • $151 Ⓐ • (01/31/92) • **93**

Musigny 1993: Explosive and superbly crafted, packing black currant, plum, earth and toast flavors. Full-bodied with enormous intensity and concentration. Needs until 2005 to show it all. 72 cases made. • $500 • **97**

Musigny 1992: Light and supple, with a nice range of berry and smoked bacon notes finishing with a little grip of fine tannin. May be best after 1997. • $NA • **89**

Musigny 1991: Earthy up front, featuring fine tannins, nicely articulated blackberry, wild berry and game aromas and flavors and a crisp, refined finish. Very firm in texture. Should be best after 1999. 50 cases made. • $439 Ⓐ • (01/31/94) • **91**

Nuits-St.-Georges 1993: Excellent, intense aromas and flavors of spice, plum and berry. Medium in body, firm tannins. Less than outstanding because of somewhat short finish. Not showing its true potential right now? Try in 1999. 267 cases made. • $110 • **89**

Nuits-St.-Georges Au Bas de Combe 1992: A full-blown style that stretches the boundaries of Burgundy with coffee, raisin and chocolate flavors that are practically sweet. Appealing, if unusual. Drink now. • $63 • (05/15/95) • **82**

Nuits-St.-Georges Au Bas de Combe 1991: A firm, chewy mouthful of anise- and tobacco-scented currant and wild berry flavors. Tighter and earthier than most, yet seems youthful and exuberant. Give it until 1998 to 2000. Tasted twice. 24 cases made. • $58 Ⓐ • (01/31/94) • **90**

Nuits-St.-Georges Au Bas de Combe 1990: Shows clever winemaking, a pretty Burgundy, with plum, spice and toasted oak aromas and flavors and a fine tannin structure. Not as big as some, but very well balanced. Drinkable now. 48 cases made. • $58 • (12/15/92) • **88**

Nuits-St.-Georges Aux Allots 1992: Stylish, concentrated and flavorful, unfolding its delicious currant and smoky tobacco character into a long and appealing finish. Drinkable now. • $55 • **87**

Nuits-St.-Georges Aux Allots 1991: Firm and focused, offering a lovely streak of ripe currant, blackberry and spicy oak aromas and flavors. Finishes harmonious and balanced enough to age through 1997 or '98. Tasted twice. 121 cases made. • $40 Ⓐ • (01/31/94) • **85**

Nuits-St.-Georges Aux Allots 1990: Spectacular, with amazing concentration of fruit and tannins. A smoky, toasty violet and spice component surfaces from the glass, and it shows wonderful harmony. Drinkable now to 1998. 142 cases made. • $67 • (12/15/92) • **95**

Nuits-St.-Georges Aux Allots 1989 • $75 Ⓐ • (01/31/92) • **92**

Nuits-St.-Georges Aux Allots 1988 • $84 Ⓐ • (04/30/91) • **89**

Nuits-St.-Georges Aux Boudots 1990: A huge wine, with tons of spice, violet and berry flavors and masses of full tannins. Appears to be built to last for decades, but try around 1998 to see how it's coming around. 460 cases made. • $108 • (12/15/92) • **94**

Nuits-St.-Georges Aux Boudots 1989 • $117 • (01/31/92) • **95**

Nuits-St.-Georges Aux Boudots 1988 • $230 • (04/30/91) • **93**

Nuits-St.-Georges Aux Lavières 1992: Dark-colored, plush in texture, toasty-earthy in aroma and nicely accented by vanilla and chocolate from oak aging. Fruit is modest but clean, a rich, round package. • $63 • (05/15/95) • **87**

Nuits-St.-Georges Aux Lavières 1991: A narrow beam of violet-scented currant and berry flavors is shaded by smoky, toasty, earthy notes. Crisp and focused, drinkable now. 121 cases made. • $59 Ⓐ • (01/31/94) • **83**

Nuits-St.-Georges Aux Lavières 1990: Shows great breeding, with tons of ripe, spicy fruit flavors, ripe tannins and toasty oak notes. Extremely well made. Drinkable in 1997. 168 cases made. • $59 • (12/15/92) • **94**

Nuits-St.-Georges Aux Lavières 1989 • $75 • (01/31/92) • **89**

Nuits-St.-Georges Aux Lavières 1988 • $84 • (04/30/91) • **82**

Nuits-St.-Georges Vigne Rondes 1993: Just as we remember a barrel sample earlier this year—wonderfully aromatic nutmeg and fruit character, medium body, supple tannins and spicy aftertaste. Better in 2000. 217 cases made. • $185 • **91**

Nuits-St.-Georges Aux Vigne Rondes 1990: A gorgeous Nuits that's extremely concentrated and firm, boasting beautiful, gamy plum and black cherry characteristics along with masses of charred, toasty new oak notes that will need time to soften. Amazingly balanced for such a big wine. Tasted twice. Try in 1998 to 2000. 150 cases made. • $100 • (12/15/92) • **95**

Nuits-St.-Georges Les Boudots 1992: Tight and beautifully structured, packs spicy, violet-scented blackberry, currant and vanilla flavors onto a lithe and racy frame. Sweet tannins need until 1997 to 1999 to sort themselves out. • $79 • **90**

Nuits-St.-Georges Les Boudots 1991: Oddly aromatic, offering plenty of barnyard, mineral and currant aromas and flavors. May be better in 1997. Tasted three times. 219 cases made. • $93 Ⓐ • (01/31/94) • **83**

Nuits-St.-Georges Les Vigne Rondes 1993: Defines harmony. Purple-colored and thick with currant, spice and lightly toasted flavors. Tastes sweet, ripe and supple, showing restraint and elegance. As good as a barrel sample tried earlier this year. Better in 1998. 24 cases made. • $185 • **95**

Nuits-St.-Georges Les Vigne Rondes 1992: Smooth and well made, dark in color and tastes of currant and black cherry, with an appealing balance and toasty character. • $79 • **85**

Nuits-St.-Georges Les Vigne Rondes 1991: Dark and dense, this peppery, spicy, cedary wine has enough intense currant and blackberry flavors to carry it through 1998 to 2000, when it should be at its best. Tasted twice. 73 cases made. • $93 • (01/31/94) • **87**

Nuits-St.-Georges Les Vignes Rondes 1989 • $53 Ⓐ • (01/31/92) • **92**

Pommard Les Vignots 1993: Exuberant, lovely, freshly crushed grape flavors. Tight and firm now, boasting an intriguing blend of pure cassis and some earthy notes. Long finish. Try after 2000. Even better than barrel sample tasted earlier this year. 437 cases made. • $94 • **92**

Pommard Les Vignots 1992: A lovely Pommard: blackberry and boysenberry flavors laced with violet and a hint of minty, gamy complexity. Medium-bodied, satisfying, with supple tannins. Try now. • $57 • **85**

Pommard Les Vignots 1991: Earthy, barnyardy aromas and flavors hit you first, but rich currant and blackberry flavors come through and keep singing through the long, rich finish. Remarkably intense for the vintage. Drinkable now. Tasted twice. 292 cases made. • $44 Ⓐ • (01/31/94) • **89**

Pommard Les Vignots 1990: Exotically seductive, with amazing violet, rose petal, raspberry and currant aromas. The essence of fruit blooms in this wine and the flavors linger on the remarkably classy finish. This defines great Burgundy. Drinkable now or in the next century. 262 cases made. • $74 • (12/15/92) • **97**

Pommard Les Vignots 1989 • $70 Ⓐ • (01/31/92) • **96**

Pommard Les Vignots 1988 • $84 • (04/30/91) • **88**

Pommard Trois Follots 1990: A sensual wine that oozes with concentrated raspberry extract and more than a hint of wood. The intense flavors ripple across the palate to a long, impressive finish. Drinkable now. 24 cases made. • $69 • (12/15/92) • **95**

Richebourg 1993: Superfine and classy, the epitome of silkiness. Full in body yet reserved and firm-structured, delivering loads of red berry and vanilla character and a long finish. Better after 2000. • $500 • **96**

Richebourg 1992: Bright, generous and supple, with layers of berry, mineral and subtle spice nuances, concentrated and remarkably approachable. Has a clarity of flavor that needs until 1997 or 1998 to begin showing. • $210 • **91**

Richebourg 1991: Firmly tannic and tough, showing undercurrents of cherry and currant bubbling beneath a layer of tannins and stalky, floral violet notes, but the breeding is evident. Needs until at least 2000 or 2001. 146 cases made. • $267 Ⓐ • (01/31/94) • **90**

Richebourg 1990: Massive and gorgeous, with tons of violet, plum and raspberry aromas and flavors and so many toasty, smoky, vanilla-flavored new oak nuances that it almost masks the fruit now. Very firm and solid despite its perfumed, immediate appeal. Don't touch until the turn of the century. 240 cases made. • $299 • (12/15/92) • **98**

Richebourg 1989 • $206 Ⓐ • (01/31/92) • **96**

Romanée-St.-Vivant 1993: Exotic and thick, featuring wild berry, floral, mint and spice character, full body, masses of fruit and a long, vanilla-spice finish. Better after 2000. 72 cases made. • $500 • **95**

Romanée-St.-Vivant 1992: A lot of violet and spice character runs through the subtle aromas and flavors, glowing with sweet blackberry and currant notes on the supple finish. Drinkable now. • $210 • **91**

Romanée-St.-Vivant 1991: Dramatic, earthy and elegant, packed with blackberry and currant flavors shaded by truffle and violet overtones. The fruit persists on the supple finish. A chewy layer needs until 1997 or '98. Tasted twice. 175 cases made. • $267 Ⓐ • (01/31/94) • **91**

Romanée-St.-Vivant 1990: Wild, beautiful and classy, a wine that stands out for its deep color. The refined violet, vanilla, blueberry and raspberry flavors burst out of the glass, delivering a lot of character in a restrained, supple package. Drinkable in 2000. 240 cases made. • $299 • (12/15/92) • **97**

Romanée-St.-Vivant 1989 • $197 Ⓐ • (01/31/92) • **95**

Romanée-St.-Vivant 1988 • $431 Ⓐ • (04/30/91) • **95**

Savigny-lès-Beaune Les Narbantons 1993: Nice fruit here but also an earthy component that gives it character and may not be for everyone. Still, the currant, plum and wet earth flavors are well integrated. Try in 1999. 169 cases made. • $70 • **89**

Savigny-lès-Beaune Les Narbantons 1992: Light and supple, with complex gamy, earthy berry and black cherry flavors that hint at anise on the finish. Best after 1996. • $40 • **85**

Savigny-lès-Beaune Les Narbantons 1991: Delicate and subtle, yet impressively concentrated, featuring plenty of brilliantly articulated black cherry, currant and toast aromas and flavors that echo on the supple finish. Drinkable now. 194 cases made. • $44 Ⓐ • (01/31/94) • **89**

Savigny-lès-Beaune Les Narbantons 1990: Big, well-crafted and muscular, lacking in finesse what it makes up in power, with loads of new oak and tannins and plenty of roasted coconut, vanilla and raspberry flavors. Drinkable now. 288 cases made. • $138 Ⓐ • (12/15/92) • **92**

Savigny-lès-Beaune Les Narbantons 1989 • $65 • (01/31/92) • **91**

Key: SS—Spectator Selection. CS—Cellar Selection. BB—Best Buy. $NA—Price not available. (BT)—Barrel tasting. Ⓐ—Auction Price.
Dates in parentheses represent the issues in which the ratings were published.

Volnay 1992: Crisp in texture but plays out its ripe berry and slightly gamy flavors nicely. Drinkable now. • $NA • **83**
Volnay Santenots 1993: Like great sex: exciting at first and relaxing in the end. Full-bodied and very voluptuous, boasting loads of berry, smoky, chocolate character. Full, velvety tannins and a long finish. Better after 2000. 97 cases made. • $185 • **96**
Vosne-Romanée Aux Réas 1990: Out of this world. A kaleidoscope of aromas and flavors, offering red berry, toasted oak, chocolate, spice and fully integrated tannins. Will improve for decades. Drinkable now. 48 cases made. • $58 • (12/15/92) • **97**
Vosne-Romanée Les Beaux Monts 1993: An extremely refined yet full-bodied and very powerful red. Bold aromas of licorice, berry, vanilla and currant follow through on the palate. Silky tannins, but it remains rather closed? Try after 2000. 362 cases made. • $185 • **94**
Vosne-Romanée Les Beaux Monts 1992: A little coarse in tannins, but the plummy, grapey flavors are good. • $90 • **85**
Vosne-Romanée Les Beaux Monts 1991: Tough and chewy, this earthy, gamy wine emerges with a distinctive violet scent, a solid core of currant and berry flavors and a tight, hard finish. Drinkable now. 292 cases made. • $100 Ⓐ • (01/31/94) • **91**
Vosne-Romanée Les Beaux Monts 1990: What else do you want in a Burgundy? It's both powerful and delicate, with lovely, enchanting spice, plum, vanilla and black currant flavors that cascade across the palate, showing endless complexity. Drinkable now. 775 cases made. • $200 Ⓐ • (12/15/92) • **95**
Vosne-Romanée Les Beaux Monts 1989 • $83 Ⓐ • (01/31/92) • **92**
Vosne-Romanée Les Beaux Monts 1988 • $74 Ⓐ • (04/30/91) • **93**
Vosne-Romanée Les Brûlées 1993: The essence of fruit, featuring loads of plum, cherry and strawberry character, full body, substantial velvety tannins and a long, long finish. Better after 2000. 24 cases made. • $185 • **93**
Vosne-Romanée Les Brûlées 1992: More flavorful than most Vosne-Romanées, delivering some interesting gamy, smoky flavors to enhance the lovely, focused boysenberry and blackberry flavors. Ready now. • $83 • **85**
Vosne-Romanée Les Brûlées 1989 • $111 Ⓐ • (01/31/92) • **94**
Vosne-Romanée Les Genevrières 1992: This emphasizes oak over fruit flavors, showing vanilla, chocolate and maple syrup overtones and some black cherry underneath. Enticing and rich, but balanced for drinking now before the fruit dries up. • $61 • (05/15/95) • **84**
Vosne-Romanée Les Genevrières 1991: Very firm and chewy, earthy at first, turning smooth and relatively fruity beneath several layers of chunky tannins. Shows blackberry, currant and plum flavors and finishes tight and polished. Tasted twice. Drinkable now. 121 cases made. • $57 Ⓐ • (01/31/94) • **90**
Vosne-Romanée Les Genevrières 1990: Like a slow-burning fuse on your palate: The ripe fruit, firm tannins and toasted oak characteristics build to the finish. Shows great winemaking. Drinkable now. 364 cases made. • $61 • (12/15/92) • **95**
Vosne-Romanée Les Genevrières 1989 • $75 • (01/31/92) • **91**

LESCALLE, CHÂTEAU

Bordeaux Supérieur 1986 • $8 • (06/30/89) • **81**

LESCURE, CHANTAL

Beaune Les Chouacheux 1989 • $19 • (08/31/92) • **88**
Clos de Vougeot 1990: Light, watery and simple, with little flavor other than a touch of strawberry and earth. Drinkable now. 110 cases made. • $44 • (06/15/93) • **76**
Clos de Vougeot 1989 • $45 • (08/31/92) • **82**
Nuits-St.-Georges Les Damodes 1990: Lean, tough and leathery, with currant and cherry flavors buried beneath. Time may benefit this wine, but it may always retain its chewy edge. Drinkable now. 226 cases made. • $25 • (06/15/93) • **80**
Pommard Les Bertins 1990: Thin and hollow, disappointing for a 1990, lacking richness and flavor. A narrow band of plum and leather flavors turns green and tannic on the finish. Drinkable now. 497 cases made. • $22 • (06/15/93) • **76**
Pommard Les Bertins 1989 • $25 • (08/31/92) • **87**
Pommard Les Bertins 1988 • $22 Ⓐ • (11/30/90) • **88**

Vosne-Romanée Les Suchots 1990: Lean and focused, with a bright, sharp beam of currant and berry flavors reined in by hard-edged tannins and acidity. A simple wine that's drinkable now. 381 cases made. • $26 • (06/15/93) • **81**
Vosne-Romanée Les Suchots 1989 • $25 • (08/31/92) • **89**

LESTAGE, CHÂTEAU

Listrac 1990: A perky wine, with complex aromas and flavors of chocolate, cherry, spice and cedar, it has lively tannins and fresh acidity. Drinkable now. • $18 • (03/31/93) • **88**
Listrac 1988 • $20 • (08/31/91) • **82**

LESTAGE-SIMON, CHÂTEAU

Haut-Médoc 1987 • $13 • (11/30/89) • **74**
Haut-Médoc 1986 • $13 • (11/30/89) • **85**
Haut-Médoc 1982 • $15 • (11/30/89) • **84**

LEYDET-FIGEAC, CHÂTEAU

St.-Emilion 1985 • $18 • (09/30/88) • **84**

LEYRAT

Pineau des Charentes Grande Réserve Sélection Robert Hass NV • $23 • (03/31/91) • **82**

LEZONGARS, CHÂTEAU

Premières Côtes de Bordeaux 1985 • $7 • (11/15/87) • **72**

LICHINE, ALEXIS

Bordeaux 1986 • $4 • (03/31/89) • **70**
Bordeaux Premier de Lichine 1993: A bit of a leafy-berry character reminiscent of Cabernet Franc, but the finish is tough and tannic. • $6 • (08/31/95) • **77**
Cabernet Sauvignon Vin de Pays d'Oc 1993: An herbal-scented, plum-flavored, tough-textured red that is simple and sturdy. Drinkable now. • $6 • (07/31/95) • **80**
Chardonnay Vin de Pays d'Oc 1993: Ripe and round, this blowsy white has attractive pear, honey and earth notes but lacks structure and finesse. 5,000 cases made. • $6 • (06/30/95) • **77**
Merlot Vin de Pays d'Oc 1993: An average-quality red wine with decent fruit and herb flavors and mild tannins. • $6 • (07/31/95) • **78**

LIGER-BELAIR

Beaune Les Avaux 1947 • $NA • (08/31/90) • **87**

LIGNIER, GEORGES

Bonnes Mares 1987 • $75 • (03/31/90) • **92**
Chambolle-Musigny 1987 • $32 • (06/15/90) • **77**
Clos de la Roche 1987 • $55 • (03/31/90) • **90**
Clos de la Roche 1985 • $63 • (03/15/88) • **85**
Clos St.-Denis 1987 • $49 • (05/15/90) • **89**
Clos St.-Denis 1985 • $54 • (03/15/88) • **91**
Gevrey-Chambertin 1987 • $29 • (05/31/90) • **84**
Gevrey-Chambertin Les Combottes 1987 • $34 • (05/31/90) • **87**
Morey-St.-Denis 1987 • $25 • (05/15/90) • **82**
Morey-St.-Denis 1985 • $23 • (03/15/88) • **82**
Morey-St.-Denis Clos des Ormes 1987 • $32 • (05/15/90) • **88**
Morey-St.-Denis Clos des Ormes 1985 • $28 • (03/15/88) • **86**

LIGNIER, HUBERT

Clos de la Roche 1990: Round, velvety, stylish and wonderful, with gorgeous wild strawberry and raspberry flavors and hints of wood. Drinkable now. 250 cases made. • $90 • (12/15/92) • **92**

Morey-St.-Denis 1990: Focused, distinctive and pleasant, with menthol, cedar and black currant flavors that come across as sharp and lively. Drinkable now. • $36 • (12/15/92) • **86**

Morey-St.-Denis Premier Cru 1990: Subtle and ripe, with round flavors making it succulent. Has red licorice, smoke and raspberry aromas and flavors and a juicy finish. Drinkable now. • $36 • (12/15/92) • **88**

LILIAN LADOUYS, CHÂTEAU

St.-Estèphe 1995: Delicious, sweet, ripe fruit flavors and plenty of cassis character. Medium in body, adding fine tannins and a sleek, racy finish. • $NA • (05/15/96) • **85-89** (BT)

St.-Estèphe 1994: A fairly lean '94 that has a decent streak of earthy red berry and plum aromas and flavors. A bit short and dry on the finish. • $NA • (05/15/96) • **80-84** (BT)

St-Estèphe 1993: Some decent red berry flavor on a rather lean frame, drawing a slight toasty character from the oak. Elegant tannins make it pleasant drinking now. • $NA • (01/31/96) • **82**

LIONNET, JEAN

Cornas 1987 • $23 • (03/31/90) • **90**
Cornas 1986 • $23 • (01/31/89) • **87**
Cornas Cuvée Rochepertuis 1988 • $28 • (01/31/91) • **83**
Cornas Domaine de Rochepertuis 1991 • $23 • (05/31/94) • **80**
Cornas Domaine de Rochepertuis 1990 • $23 • (05/31/94) • **89**

Côtes du Rhône Cépage Syrah 1992: Robust, full-bodied and flavorful, if not refined. It has smoky, cherrylike, leathery flavors, full body and a ripe, lingering finish. 4,500 cases made. • $15 • (10/15/94) • **83**

Côtes du Rhône Cépage Syrah 1990 • $16 • (08/31/92) • **88**
Côtes du Rhône Cépage Syrah 1986 • $10 • (09/30/88) • **79**

LIOT, CHÂTEAU

Barsac 1988: Sweet, clean and modestly flavorful, with pear, pineapple and peach notes. Drinkable now. • $25 • (11/15/91) • **84**

Barsac 1986: Rich and fairly concentrated, showing lots of toast and spice notes gracing the pear and honey aromas and flavors, long and elegant on a medium-weight frame. Try now. • $22 • (12/31/89) • **87**

Barsac 1985: A good value with vivid flavors, even if not quite as magnificent as the bightly earthy flavors. Balance keeps it from being cloying. • $9 • (05/31/88) • **84**

Barsac 1983 • $11 • (04/01/86) • **56**

Sauternes 1993: A light-and-easy Sauternes displaying lemony, lightly sweet character. Drinkable now. • $NA • (04/15/95) • **82**

Sauternes 1990: Pretty apéritif-styled Sauternes displaying creamy, pear character. Light in body and medium sweet, leading to a light finish. Drinkable now. • $23 • (04/15/95) • **81**

Sauternes 1989: Lively character and polished flavors of honey, cream and spice, medium sweetness and a fresh finish. Drinkable now. • $29 • (04/15/95) • **84**

Sauternes 1988: Fresh, straightforward pear, apple and honey aromas and flavors, medium-to-light body, medium sweetness and a light finish. Drinkable now. • $50 • (04/15/95) • **86**

LIQUIERE, CHÂTEAU DE LA

Faugères 1992 • $8 • (03/15/94) • **85**

LIVERSAN, CHÂTEAU

Haut-Médoc 1995: Disappointing for this estate. Some decent fruit, but it turns slightly weedy and metallic on the finish. Tasted twice, with consistent notes. • $NA • (05/15/96) • **75-79** (BT)

Haut-Médoc 1993: Some very good berry, cherry and almond flavors, medium body and tannins and a firm, slightly short finish. Better in 1998. • $15 • (01/31/96) • **85**

Key: SS—Spectator Selection. CS—Cellar Selection. BB—Best Buy. $NA—Price not available. (BT)—Barrel tasting. Ⓐ—Auction Price.
Dates in parentheses represent the issues in which the ratings were published.

Haut-Médoc 1990: This is very rich and fruity, with alluring aromas and flavors of tobacco, cassis and vanilla and a fine tannin structure. Better in 1997. 15,000 cases made. • $19 • (03/31/93) • **89**

Haut-Médoc 1989 • $18 • (03/15/92) • **87**
Haut-Médoc 1988 • $15 Ⓐ • (07/31/91) • **87**
Haut-Médoc 1985 • $11 Ⓐ • (04/30/88) • **90**
Haut-Médoc 1982 • $24 • (08/31/92) • **85**

Haut-Médoc 1961: A soft, simple Bordeaux that tastes buttery, feels smooth and plush but lacks depth. Drink now. • $29 • (04/30/96) • **84**

LOGIS DE LA GIRAUDIERE

Anjou Rouge de Cépage Cabernet 1989 • $8 • (08/31/91) • **80**

LONES, DOMAINE DES

Coteaux du Tricastin 1988 • $11 • (05/31/91) • **84**
Coteaux du Tricastin 1986 • $7 • (10/15/88) • **82**

LONG-DEPAQUIT, A.

Chablis 1994: A bit hard and meager, but showing some decent lemon, apple and almond aromas and flavors and light finish. From Albert Bichot. • $NA • **81**

Chablis Les Blanchots 1994: Silky and supple, with ripe fruit, mineral and vanilla character. For enjoying now, gives a lot of pleasure, though a bit soft on the finish. Domaine owned by Albert Bichot. 200 cases made. • $NA • (05/31/96) • **88**

Chablis Les Clos 1994: Nice finesse but hard as nails now, with apple, apricot and citrus flavors. Lovely mineral character. Medium to full body, it zings with acidity and will need time, better in 1998. Domaine owned by négociant Albert Bichot. 416 cases made. • $30 • (05/31/96) • **90**

Chablis Les Clos 1993: Pretty honey, mineral and spice character, medium body, firm acidity and long, fresh finish. • $NA • **85**

Chablis Les Vaillons 1994: Flavorful and crisp, with citrus, mineral and chalk accents overlaying the fruit flavors. Lacking a bit on opulence and complexity. Tasted twice, with consistent notes. Domaine owned by Albert Bichot. 2,250 cases made. • $23 • (05/31/96) • **80**

Chablis Les Vaillons 1992: An earthy aroma and ripe, full flavors make this a robust, rich textured Chardonnay. Rather soft and almost sweet, it's appealing for current consumption. • $17 • **81**

Chablis Les Vaucopins 1992: Appealing in flavor, soft and smooth in texture, a sophisticated Chablis that's marked by accents of toast, butterscotch and ripe apple. Supple and lingering on the finish. • $17 • **84**

LOUBIERE, CHÂTEAU LA

Pomerol 1983 • $15 • (06/16/86) • **77**
Pomerol 1982 • $13 • (05/15/89) • **88**

LOUDENNE, CHÂTEAU

Bordeaux White 1993: Some decent grassy fruit but slightly candied. Old style of simple white Bordeaux. • $13 • **75**

Bordeaux White 1992: Old Sémillon character with honey and a touch of plastic. Almost completely past its sell-by date. • $13 • **70**

Médoc 1992: Very light and watery, some decent strawberry, tobacco character finishes rather green and unripe. • $15 • **73**

Médoc 1991: Earthy character to the currant flavor, with a lean, light-bodied structure. Pleasant to drink now. • $12 • (03/31/94) • **80**

Médoc 1990: A very ripe wine, with mature fruit aromas and flavors that verge on raisins, well-integrated, medium tannins, long finish. Drinkable now. 25,000 cases made. • $17 • (03/31/93) • **87**

Médoc 1989 • $13 • (03/15/92) • **81**
Médoc 1988 • $10 • (08/31/91) • **82**
Médoc 1987 • $10 • (11/30/89) • **75**
Médoc 1986 • $12 • (11/30/89) • **74**
Médoc 1985 • $14 • (11/30/88) • **75**
Médoc 1982 • $NA • (08/31/92) • **88**
Médoc 1981 • $11 • (09/01/84) • **84**

FRANCE

LOUVIERE, CHÂTEAU LA

Graves 1985 • $16 • (06/30/88) • **87**
Graves 1983 • $16 • (11/30/86) • **78**
Graves 1982 • $25 • (08/31/92) • **91**
Pessac-Léognan 1995: A very special Bordeaux of great depth and intense spice, mineral and berry character. Thick and rich, it remains subtle and elegant thanks to the smooth, silky texture and round, seductive finish. • $NA • (05/15/96) • **90-94** (BT)
Pessac-Léognan 1994: Some decent fruit in this medium-bodied '94, but it tastes a bit herbal and is somewhat short. Disappointing for this château. • $22 • (05/15/96) • **75-79** (BT)
Pessac-Léognan 1993: Medium-bodied, pretty red, offering anise, currant and plum flavors and a fresh, crisp finish. There are some firm tannins, but this should make for nice drinking around 1997. • $23 • (01/31/96) • **85**
Pessac-Léognan 1992: Plenty of body, offering spice, dried herbs, tobacco and berry on the nose and palate. Drinkable now. • $20 • **80**
Pessac-Léognan 1991: Another disappointment. Surprisingly sweet, ripe fruit for this vintage, with black cherry and tobacco notes and an herbaceous finish. • $20 • (03/31/94) • **79**
Pessac-Léognan 1990: Seductively powerful, with tons of lovely oak and ripe fruit, full tannins and a long, luscious finish. Drinkable in 1998. 18,750 cases made. • $21 • (03/31/93) • **94**
Pessac-Léognan 1989 • $22 • (03/15/92) • **91**
Pessac-Léognan 1988 • $24 • (08/31/91) SS • **92**
Pessac-Léognan 1986 • $30 • (06/15/89) • **91**
Pessac-Léognan 1985: Slightly overdone. Big and raisiny with masses of fruit and tannins but the alcohol dominates at this point. Try after 1997. • $NA • **83**
Pessac-Léognan 1983: Very ripe wine with coffee, chocolate, violet character, full body and firm tannins but slightly cooked and bitter on finish. Tasted twice. Better with time? • $NA • **82**
Pessac-Léognan 1981: A harmonious, caressing wine definitely at or slightly past its peak. Medium ruby/garnet color with chocolate-cedar aromas, medium body with a soft texture, light integrated tannins and a delicate chocolate, earthy finish. Drink as soon as possible. • $NA • **83**
Pessac-Léognan White 1994: Powerful and intense, plenty of grassy apple and celery aromas and flavors in this one. Full body and lively acidity. The fresh, fruity finish rounds it out. Chewy and rich. Forget the Loire, drink this. • $25 • (03/31/96) • **91**
Pessac-Léognan White 1993: So fresh it's like a barrel sample: full of freshly crushed fruit aromas and intense, grassy pear and vanilla flavors. This is medium-bodied, with firm acidity and a long finish. Drinkable now. 6,000 cases made. • $22 • (05/31/95) • **90**
Pessac-Léognan White 1992 • $22 • (06/15/94) • **84**
Pessac-Léognan White 1991 • $18 • (09/15/93) • **83**

LUC, CHÂTEAU DE

Corbières 1990 • $5 • (07/15/92) • **84**

LUCAT, CHÂTEAU DE

Bordeaux Supérieur 1982 • $4 • (10/01/85) • **71**

LUGNY, CAVE DE

Mâcon-Lugny Les Charmes 1994: Vibrant and fresh, this balanced white offers layers of green apple, pear and honey flavors in a medium-bodied package. Slightly fizzy. 80,000 cases made. • $9 • **84**

LUPE-CHOLET

Aloxe-Corton 1985 • $18 • (03/15/88) • **84**
Beaune Avaux 1986 • $NA • (07/31/88) • **89**
Bourgogne Chardonnay Comtesse de Lupé White 1994: Light, tart, slightly diluted, with modest fruit flavors. • $NA • (05/31/96) • **73**
Bourgogne Clos de la Roche 1986 • $10 • (07/31/88) • **78**
Bourgogne Clos de Lupé 1993: Light and hard with a slightly veggie character. Not much joy here. • $12 • **73**
Bourgogne Clos de Lupé 1992: Tart, sharp and lean, with a lemony, herbal character. • $NA • **77**
Bourgogne Clos de Lupé 1985 • $15 • (03/31/88) • **79**
Bourgogne Hautes Côtes de Beaune 1987 • $10 • (04/15/90) • **78**
Bourgogne Pinot Noir Comte de Lupé 1989 • $7 • (01/31/92) • **86**
Chablis Château de Viviers 1994: Enjoyable, medium-bodied, ripe and fruity. Offers honey, pear and spice flavors. • $NA • (08/31/95) • **82**
Chablis Vaucoupin, Château de Viviers 1993: Elegant and smooth, offering some mineral, spice and green apple flavors. Crisp finish. • $NA • (08/31/95) • **83**
Chambolle-Musigny 1992: Soft, light and charming, with smooth, appealing licorice, currant and raspberry flavors. A slightly stemmy edge on the finish. Ready now. • $NA • **83**
Chambolle-Musigny 1986 • $20 • (07/31/88) • **81**
Chassagne-Montrachet 1994: Crisp and tightly built, not showing much now in terms of fruit, but the chalky, mineral character is appealing and suggests it might age well. It shows some good concentration, with almond, pear and pie crust flavors. Try in 1998. • $NA • (05/31/96) • **85**
Crozes-Hermitage 1987 • $8 • (03/31/90) • **83**
Côte de Nuits-Villages 1992: Pleasant but a bit simple, modest currant and cherry flavors peeking through the cedar and chestnut. Short finish and a bit diluted. • $NA • **79**
Gevrey-Chambertin Lavaux St.-Jacques 1983 • $27 • (11/30/86) • **59**
Mâcon-Villages 1994: A white with modest spicy, creamy fruit flavors. Shows some crisp, citrusy notes on the finish, too. Drinkable now. • $NA • (05/31/96) 76 • **77**
Meursault 1994: Slightly tart and lean, with a hint of ripe pear and honey. • $NA • (05/31/96) • **79**
Monthélie 1983 • $9 • (09/15/86) • **69**
Nuits-St.-Georges Château Gris 1992: Very firm and tannic for such light flavors. It falls short on the fruit until the berry note on the finish. May be better after 1997. • $NA • **78**
Nuits-St.-Georges Château Gris 1987 • $38 • (03/31/90) • **84**
Nuits-St.-Georges Château Gris 1986 • $33 • (07/31/88) • **86**
Nuits-St.-Georges Château Gris 1985 • $39 • (02/15/88) • **88**
Nuits-St.-Georges Château Gris 1983 • $24 • (06/16/86) • **77**
Nuits-St.-Georges Château Gris 1er 1993: A little meager, but showing some pretty spice, berry and vanilla character, medium to light body, fine tannins and short finish. Better in 1999? • $35 • **82**
Nuits-St.-Georges Les Vignes Rondex Hospice de Nuits 1986 • $NA • (07/31/88) • **91**
Pommard Les Boucherottes 1983 • $19 • (06/16/86) • **86**
Puligny-Montrachet 1994: A pleasant surprise from Lupé-Cholet. Light to medium body, offering up a touch of vanilla, spice and honey. Elegant and subtle. Try in 1997. Tasted twice, with consistent notes. • $NA • (05/31/96) • **84**
Savigny-lès-Beaune Les Serpentières 1985 • $17 • (03/15/88) • **83**
Volnay 1986 • $NA • (07/31/88) • **91**

LUQUET, ROGER

Mâcon Clos de Condemine 1994: Round and smooth. Shows some decent fruit but lacks panache, despite its almond, pear and green apple character. Needs more intensity. 2,916 cases made. • $9 • **79**
Pouilly-Fuissé 1994: Odd and flat, with earthy, funky, almost cheesy flavors. It shows some ripe fruit underneath, with a fine, fresh finish. Perhaps in an awkward stage now. 2,083 cases made. • $16 • (05/31/96) • **81**
Pouilly-Fuissé 1993: Light, tangy and refreshing. This fresh white Burgundy has lively acidity, simple fruit flavors and hints of spice on the finish. 2,500 cases made. • $12 • (11/15/94) • **81**
Pouilly-Fuissé Clos du Bourg 1994: Attractive and earthy, with pear, pineapple and citrus flavors touched by a white pepper note that adds some spice. The sweet-tasting finish gives it a touch of richness. 708 cases made. • $19 • (05/31/96) • **85**
Pouilly-Fuissé Clos du Bourg 1993: Delivers intense lime, earth, orange blossom and wet straw flavors. Its round, supple and oily texture is impressive, leading to a long, vibrant finish. Drinkable now. 708 cases made. • $20 • **86**

St.-Véran White 1994: Interesting but not exciting. Offers slightly earthy truffle, citrus and pear character. Quite chalky and dry on the finish. 4,166 cases made. • $10 • **80**

LURTON, J & F

Chardonnay Vin de Pays d'Oc 1991 • $5 • (06/15/93) • **76**

LUSSAC, CHÂTEAU DE

Lussac-St.-Emilion 1982 • $6 • (05/01/84) • **73**

LYNCH-BAGES, BLANC DE

Bordeaux White 1994: A wonderful, well-made white with beautiful honey, vanilla, cream and apple character. Full body, fine acidity and delicious now, yet it's still holding something back for the future. • $40 • (03/31/96) • **90**
Bordeaux White 1992 • $30 • (06/15/94) • **86**

LYNCH-BAGES, CHÂTEAU

Bordeaux Blanc de Lynch Bages 1993: Impressive white, with a taste of the earth accompanying mineral, pear and papaya flavors. The texture is velvety yet tight and focused. Try now through 1997. • $28 • (05/31/95) • **88**
Pauillac 1995: Racy and succulent, with tons of cassis and blackberry character. Lightly smoky and plummy, medium- to full-bodied, with velvety tannins and elegant, crisp, very long finish. • $NA • (05/15/96) • **90-94** (BT)
Pauillac 1994: An earthy character, with some spicy blackberry and plum flavors of moderate intensity and supple tannins. • $35 • (05/15/96) • **85-89** (BT)
Pauillac 1993: Not big, but a lovely, harmonious Lynch-Bages featuring blackberry, cherry and vanilla aromas and flavors, medium body, fine tannins and fresh finish. Better in 1998. 35,000 cases made. • $33 • (01/31/96) • **87**
Pauillac 1992: Attractive, modest plum and cherry character, medium body and tannins and a firm finish. Drinkable now. • $28 • **81**
Pauillac 1991: Like silk in your mouth with its cassis and fruit flavors. Medium-bodied with a fine finish. Better in 1995. • $25 • (03/31/94) • **86**
Pauillac 1990: Big-boned, with plenty of flesh, this wine shows loads of plum, tar and smoke character and full, velvety tannins. Highly extracted. Drink after 1998. 35,000 cases made. • $58 Ⓐ • (03/31/93) • **94**
Pauillac 1989 • $71 Ⓐ • (03/15/92) • **98**
Pauillac 1988: Powerful aromas of roasted fruit, smoke and toast change gears on the palate, which is as fresh and elegant as it is concentrated, with cherry, plum, tar and toast flavors. Firm tannins kick in on the finish, giving it good grip. Has the stuffing and balance to age for years. 25,000 cases made. • $58 Ⓐ • (10/15/94) • **97**
Pauillac 1987 • $27 • (02/15/90) • **86**
Pauillac 1986 • $50 Ⓐ • (10/31/89) • **94**
Pauillac 1985: Our wine of the year in 1988. Muscular but shapely, with fabulous toasted oak, berry and currant on the palate. It's full-bodied and has a long, long finish. Tasted twice. Second bottle better. Try after 1997. • $60 • (10/15/94) • **97**
Pauillac 1984 • $27 • (10/31/89) • **87**
Pauillac 1983: Impressive finesse for the vintage, with beautiful, fresh tobacco, cedar and coffee aromas and flavors. Full-bodied and very silky with a fine, long finish. Drinkable now • $39 • (10/15/94) • **90**
Pauillac 1982 • $106 Ⓐ • (08/31/92) • **91**
Pauillac 1981: Rich and zingy with masses of character, featuring licorice, ripe cherry and chocolate aromas and flavors. A full, silky Bordeaux with a long ripe fruit finish. Tasted twice, better the second time. Drinkable now. • $41 • (10/15/94) • **90**
Pauillac 1980 • $24 • (10/31/89) • **88**
Pauillac 1979 • $28 Ⓐ • (10/31/89) • **87**
Pauillac 1978 • $37 Ⓐ • (10/31/89) • **92**
Pauillac 1977 • $25 • (10/31/89) • **78**
Pauillac 1976 • $55 • (10/31/89) • **70**
Pauillac 1975 • $46 Ⓐ • (10/31/89) • **90**
Pauillac 1973 • $15 Ⓐ • (10/31/89) • **82**
Pauillac 1971 • $28 • (10/31/89) • **67**
Pauillac 1970 • $151 Ⓐ • (05/15/93) • **90**
Pauillac 1967 • $23 Ⓐ • (10/31/89) • **79**
Pauillac 1966 • $53 Ⓐ • (10/31/89) • **90**
Pauillac 1964 • $38 Ⓐ • (10/31/89) • **76**
Pauillac 1962 • $90 • (10/31/89) • **94**
Pauillac 1961: Smooth-textured, almost sweet in its fruity flavors, with earthy, leathery accents that are intriguing and typical for Lynch-Bages. May be past its prime, but not by much, still packs a lot of pleasure. Drink through 2000. • $317 • (04/30/96) • **88**
Pauillac 1960 • $55 • (10/31/89) • **76**
Pauillac 1959 • $118 Ⓐ • (10/15/90) • **95**
Pauillac 1958 • $60 • (10/31/89) • **79**
Pauillac 1957 • $95 • (10/31/89) • **88**
Pauillac 1955 • $250 • (10/31/89) • **92**
Pauillac 1954 • $75 • (10/31/89) • **74**
Pauillac 1953 • $75 Ⓐ • (10/31/89) • **77**
Pauillac 1952 • $140 • (10/31/89) • **83**
Pauillac 1949 • $175 • (10/31/89) • **84**
Pauillac 1947 • $350 • (10/31/89) • **90**
Pauillac 1945 • $130 Ⓐ • (03/16/86) • **65**
Pauillac 1945: Broad and rich, despite some astringency and volatility on the finish, but shows a nice core of freshness and life, echoing prune, currant and spice. Second bottle less lively. • $500 • **85**
Pauillac Danish Bottled 1945 • $250 • (10/31/89) • **80**

LYNCH, KERMIT

Beaujolais 1990 • $10 • (09/15/91) • **83**
Côtes du Rhône 1985 • $9 • (01/31/89) • **83**

LYNCH, MICHEL

Bordeaux 1993: A light, herbal '93 showing tomato and berry character. • $10 • (01/31/96) • **76**
Bordeaux 1988 • $8 • (10/31/91) • **76**
Bordeaux 1983 • $6 • (10/15/87) • **75**
Bordeaux White 1994: Lovely and elegant, with honey, strawberry, rose petal and apricot aromas and flavors. Medium body, fine acidity and a fresh finish. • $8 • (03/31/96) • **84**
Bordeaux White 1993: A bit hard and metallic, some decent appley, citrusy, steely character. Too tart on the finish. • $8 • **78**
Bordeaux White 1992: Seems slightly tired, presenting vanilla and candied apple character, medium body and short finish. • $8 • **74**

LYNCH-MOUSSAS, CHÂTEAU

Pauillac 1991: Very herbal character with brown sugar aromas and flavors. A little overchaptalized. • $16 • (03/31/94) • **73**
Pauillac 1990: A wine with spicy tobacco and chocolate character and medium fruit and tannins. Not one to lay down for too long. Drinkable now. 12,500 cases made. • $18 • (03/31/93) • **87**
Pauillac 1989 • $18 • (03/15/92) • **90**
Pauillac 1988 • $25 • (08/31/91) • **85**
Pauillac 1986 • $18 • (06/30/89) • **86**
Pauillac 1982 • $22 Ⓐ • (08/31/92) • **81**
Pauillac 1961: A sturdy Bordeaux that's holding its own. It has roasted, peppery aromas, a tannic, crisp texture and ample fruit flavors. Drink now through 1998. • $21 • (04/30/96) • **84**
Pauillac 1959 • $115 • (10/15/90) • **86**

LYONNAT, CHÂTEAU DU

Lussac-St.-Emilion 1985 • $13 • **64**

Key: SS—Spectator Selection. CS—Cellar Selection. BB—Best Buy. $NA—Price not available. (BT)—Barrel tasting. Ⓐ—Auction Price.
Dates in parentheses represent the issues in which the ratings were published.

M & G

Côte de Beaune-Villages 1987 • $20 • (03/31/91) • **73**
Gevrey-Chambertin 1987 • $40 • (03/31/91) • **73**

MACHARD DE GRAMONT

Aloxe-Corton Les Morais 1985 • $34 • (07/15/88) • **80**
Beaune Les Chouacheux 1985 • $34 • (05/31/88) • **89**
Chorey-lès-Beaune Les Beaumonts 1985 • $22 • (07/31/88) • **84**
Pinot Noir Bourgogne Domaine de la Vierge Romaine 1985 • $13 • (06/30/88) • **81**
Nuits-St.-Georges Les Allots 1987 • $30 • (07/15/90) • **82**
Nuits-St.-Georges Les Allots 1985 • $35 • (05/31/88) • **86**
Nuits-St.-Georges Les Damodes 1990: Smoky and spicy aroma, leading to generous fruit tones, very firm tannins and tough but flavorful finish. Fine depth and concentration, needs time to mature. Drink in 1997. • $48 • (05/31/95) • **89j**
Nuits-St.-Georges en la Perrière Noblot 1985 • $41 • (05/31/88) • **89**
Nuits-St.-Georges Les Hauts Poirets 1985 • $41 • (06/15/88) • **84**
Nuits-St.-Georges Les Hauts Pruliers 1988 • $37 • (07/15/91) • **88**
Nuits-St.-Georges Les Hauts Pruliers 1987 • $32 • (04/30/90) • **85**
Nuits-St.-Georges Les Hauts Pruliers 1986 • $22 • (12/15/89) • **77**
Nuits-St.-Georges Les Hauts Pruliers 1985 • $36 • (02/15/88) • **90**
Nuits-St.-Georges Les Vallerots 1985 • $47 • (05/31/88) • **78**
Savigny-lès-Beaune Les Guettes 1985 • $25 • (07/31/88) • **89**
Vosne-Romanée Les Réas 1988 • $32 • (07/15/91) • **89**

MACMAHON, MARQUIS DE

Chassagne-Montrachet Abbaye de Morgeot 1992: Tough and tight, with an odd earthy note along with some apple, mineral and vanilla flavors. Seems astringent on the finish. Drinkable now. • $NA • (08/31/94) • **77**
Meursault Les Meix Chavaux 1992: Mellow, smooth and supple, a bit earthy, with nice but modest pear, vanilla and grapefruit flavors. Ready to drink. • $NA • (08/31/94) • **83**
Puligny-Montrachet La Garenne 1992: Too earthy to our taste, but it also displays some hazelnut, smoke and apple flavors. Drinkable now. • $NA • (08/31/94) • **79**

MADELEINE, CHÂTEAU LA

Pomerol 1985 • $10 • (03/15/88) • **56**

MADER

Gewürztraminer Alsace 1992: Apricot and light honey flavors and a thick texture make this a rather sweet, forward wine that's probably showing all it has right now. • $14 • (11/15/94) • **84**
Riesling Alsace 1992: Serviceable but uninspired with vaguely citrus flavors, tough acidity and an almost bitter finish. Might improve. • $14 • (11/15/94) • **78**
Riesling Alsace Grand Cru Rosacker 1992: Lean and herbal, this tart, austere wine focuses on a narrow range of mineral and citrus flavors, and finishes very dry. Unyielding now, it may unwind with time in the bottle. Drinkable now. • $17 • (11/15/94) • **84**
Tokay Pinot Gris Alsace 1992: Silky and honeyed, this marries almond and light vegetal flavors in a soft, round balance of sweetness and clean acidity. It's open and ready to drink now. • $14 • (11/15/94) • **86**

MAGDELAINE, CHÂTEAU

St.-Emilion 1995: Delicious spice and red berry character, full body and lots of personality, yet very harmonious on the toasty finish. • $NA • (05/15/96) • **85-89** (BT)
St.-Emilion 1994: Shows more intensity than most '94s, medium body, firm tannins and some vanilla, chocolate and spice character mingling with the red berry flavors. • $NA • (05/15/96) • **85-89** (BT)
St.-Emilion 1993: Wonderful, vibrant perfumes of flowers and fruit. Medium-bodied, medium to light tannins and crisp finish. Drinkable now. • $36 • (01/31/96) • **85**
St.-Emilion 1992: Soft and drinkable, presenting tobacco, berry and plum character, medium body, gentle tannins and a slightly herbal finish. • $32 • **80**
St.-Emilion 1990: A big, extracted wine, with loads of fruit and full tannins. Drinkable in 1997. 3,800 cases made. • $36 Ⓐ • (03/31/93) • **90**
St.-Emilion 1989 • $38 Ⓐ • (03/15/92) • **88**
St.-Emilion 1988 • $27 Ⓐ • (10/31/91) • **81**
St.-Emilion 1986 • $48 • (02/15/90) • **94**
St.-Emilion 1985 • $45 • **86**
St.-Emilion 1983 • $NA • **87**
St.-Emilion 1982 • $68 Ⓐ • (08/31/92) • **91**
St.-Emilion 1981 • $NA • **86**
St.-Emilion 1979 • $27 Ⓐ • (10/15/89) • **89**
St.-Emilion 1970 • $90 • (05/15/93) • **92**
St.-Emilion 1961 • $107 • (04/30/96) • **90**
St.-Emilion 1959 • $150 • (10/15/90) • **89**
St.-Emilion 1945 • $250 • **76**

MAGNEAU, CHÂTEAU

Graves 1987 • $12 • (05/15/90) • **78**

MAGNI, DOMAINE

Châteauneuf-du-Pape 1990: Tough and earthy, a big, hearty wine, with more green olive and cedar flavors than fruit. Finishes astringent and slightly bitter. Try now. • $17 • (08/31/92) • **73**

MAGNIEN, HENRI

Gevrey-Chambertin 1985 • $25 • (10/15/87) • **81**
Gevrey-Chambertin 1983 • $18 Ⓐ • (02/01/86) • **68**
Gevrey-Chambertin 1982 • $12 • (07/01/85) • **89**
Gevrey-Chambertin Les Cazetiers 1985 • $35 • (10/15/87) • **88**
Gevrey-Chambertin Les Cazetiers 1983 • $22 Ⓐ • (12/16/85) • **72**
Gevrey-Chambertin Les Cazetiers 1982 • $16 • (05/01/84) • **80**
Gevrey-Chambertin Premier Cru 1985 • $29 • (10/15/87) • **80**

MAGNOL, CHÂTEAU

Haut-Médoc 1983 • $9 • (07/31/87) • **77**
Haut-Médoc 1981 • $8 • (08/31/87) • **69**

MAILLARD PERE & FILS

Corton White 1994: Hard and a bit unyielding, with decent fruit flavors and a mineral background, but a touch one-dimensional on the finish. • $NA • (05/31/96) • **81**

MAIRE, JEAN

Blanc de Blancs Champagne Cuvée Elysée 1985: Another great aperitif. This has an intense character of cream, vanilla and fruit, yet, it's delicate with excellent acidity. Starting to fade a bit since we tasted it three years ago. Drink now. • $33 • (12/31/93) • **88**
Brut Blanc de Blancs Champagne NV • $NA • (12/31/90) • **77**
Brut Blanc de Noirs Champagne 1988: Very easy-to-like Champagne. It's round and soft with rich fruit and pie crust aromas and flavors. Long finish. Drink now. • $43 • (12/31/93) • **87**
Brut Champagne 1988: Another clean, delicate and appley vintage Champagne although slightly one dimensional, medium bodied and fruity with a fresh clean finish. Drink now. • $33 • (12/31/93) • **87**
Brut Champagne 1985 • $NA • (12/31/90) • **75**
Brut Champagne NV • $NA • (12/31/91) • **83**

MAISON-BLANCHE, CHÂTEAU

Montagne-St.-Emilion 1985 • $13 • (02/15/89) • **80**

MAISON BLANCHE, DOMAINE DE

Chablis Blanchot Cuvée Vieille Vigne 1994: Supple—even soft—with loads of honey, apricot, ripe pear and pie crust flavors. Not much backbone here, but this is delicious and ready to drink now. • $NA • (05/31/96) • **84**

Chablis Mont de Milieu Cuvée Vieille Vigne 1994: Crisp and straightforward, with some lemon, honey and pear flavors. Light-to-medium body, and makes for nice drinking now. A touch diluted on the finish, though. • $NA • (05/31/96) • **80**

Chablis Mont de Milieu Cuvée Vieille Vigne 1993: Very steely mineral, white pepper and lemon character. Medium body, crisp acidity and flavorful finish. From Billaud-Simon. • $NA • (08/31/94) • **86**

Quincy 1993: A straightforward wine with apple and crisp lemon flavors, it's refreshing without being complex. Drink as an apéritif or with a picnic. • $15 • **82**

Quincy 1992: Melon and ripe apple flavors come through in this round white. Underlying acidity is softened by buttery and slightly earthy notes. It lacks the vivacity of the best Loire Sauvignons, but offers an accessible charm. • $12 • (10/31/94) • **84**

MAISON DE LAMARTINE

Beaujolais-Villages 1993: An awkward, muddled Beaujolais that smells eggy, tastes ripe at first but then turns tight and tart on the finish. • $10 • (01/31/95) • **71**

Moulin-à-Vent 1993: Aromatic and flavorful, but it turns too tight, tart and tannic on the finish to fully enjoy now. Ample black cherry and raspberry flavors give it life. 280 cases made. • $15 • (01/31/95) • **83**

MAISON-NEUVE, CHÂTEAU

Montagne-St.-Emilion 1985 • $7 • (03/15/88) • **78**

MALAGAR, CHÂTEAU

Bordeaux White 1993: Slightly flat "white." Offering some decent ripe fruit, but lacking freshness. • $NA • **78**

Premières Côtes de Bordeaux 1992: Interesting black pepper, spice, green bean character, medium body, medium tannins and light finish. Drink now. • $NA • **78**

MALANDES, DOMAINE DES

Chablis Montmains 1993: Interesting apricot and mineral aromas and flavors. Medium body, fresh acidity and clean finish. Delicious, crisp style. • $NA • **83**

MALARTIC-LAGRAVIERE, CHÂTEAU

Pessac-Léognan 1995: Rather light and straightforward in this group. A bit green, herbal and tart, with slightly dry tannins. This medium-bodied '95 offers some modest complexity in what (at least now) is a rather disjointed package. • $NA • (05/15/96) • **80-84** (BT)

Pessac-Léognan 1994: Not as good as the '93. Pretty plum and berry character, medium in body, fine, delicate tannins and light, fruity finish. • $NA • **80-84** (BT)

Pessac-Léognan 1993: A bit lean but some good tobacco and cherry character, medium body, firm tannins and medium finish. Better in 1997. 833 cases made. • $25 • (01/31/96) • **83**

Pessac-Léognan 1989 • $24 • (03/15/92) • **85**

Pessac-Léognan 1988 • $32 • (07/15/91) • **84**

Pessac-Léognan 1986 • $18 • (06/15/89) • **90**

Graves 1982 • $34 Ⓐ • (08/31/92) • **92**

Graves 1970 • $32 • (05/15/93) • **85**

Key: SS—Spectator Selection. CS—Cellar Selection. BB—Best Buy. $NA—Price not available. (BT)—Barrel tasting. Ⓐ—Auction Price.
Dates in parentheses represent the issues in which the ratings were published.

Pessac-Léognan White 1994: Lovely and rich, with grapefruit, pear and honey character that comes out in a full-bodied package. Loads of fruit flavors, moderate acidity and a long, fruity aftertaste. Better in 1997. • $25 • (03/31/96) • **90**

MALESCASSE, CHÂTEAU

Haut-Médoc 1995: Medium-bodied, showing decent plum, tar, smoke and red berry character. Fairly ripe, but turns a bit dry on the finish. • $NA • (05/15/96) • **80-84** (BT)

Haut-Médoc 1994: Rich, ripe and seductive, full-bodied, showing currant and tobacco flavors, sweet-fruit character and smooth yet plentiful tannins. • $NA • **85-89** (BT)

Haut-Médoc 1993: Some vanilla, dried herb and berry character, slightly lean. Fine tannins, medium body and short finish. Drink in 1997. • $17 • (01/31/96) • **83**

Haut-Médoc 1991: Herbal, diluted and seems rather advanced in age for this vintage, but has pretty mint notes. • $13 • (03/31/94) • **78**

Haut-Médoc 1989 • $13 • (03/15/92) • **84**

Haut-Médoc 1987 • $9 • (11/30/89) • **74**

Haut-Médoc 1986 • $9 • (11/30/89) • **88**

Haut-Médoc 1982 • $18 • (11/30/89) • **82**

MALESCOT-ST.-EXUPERY, CHÂTEAU

Margaux 1990: Despite a definite gamy edge, this meaty wine has a silky texture and a nice range of currant, coffee and cedar flavors to its credit. Best now through 2000. • $24 • (02/28/94) • **87**

Margaux 1989 • $27 • (03/15/92) • **87**

Margaux 1988 • $20 • (04/30/91) • **89**

Margaux 1986 • $29 • (06/15/89) • **88**

Margaux 1985 • $18 Ⓐ • (09/30/88) • **87**

Margaux 1983 • $22 • (09/30/86) • **82**

Margaux 1981 • $14 Ⓐ • (05/01/89) • **87**

Margaux 1962 • $80 • (11/30/87) • **65**

Margaux 1961 • $62 Ⓐ • (04/30/96) • **85**

Margaux 1959 • $150 • (10/15/90) • **87**

Margaux 1945 • $200 • **79**

MALIGNY, CHÂTEAU DE

Chablis 1992: Fairly rich and soft for a Chablis, going from earthy, buttery aromas to nutty, smoky butterscotch flavors. Could use more fruit. 4,000 cases made. • $15 • (11/15/94) • **77**

Chablis Fourchaume Premier Cru 1992: Fruity and fresh, but not very representative of Chablis. Just a good white wine with apple and pear notes that turns a bit soft on the finish. 4,000 cases made. • $16 • **81**

MALLE, CHÂTEAU DE

Sauternes 1991: Rich and ripe for the vintage, offering date, fig and orange notes, creamy texture and a seductively tart, marzipan-flavored finish. • $NA • (04/15/95) • **85**

Sauternes 1990: Electrifying spice, tropical and dried apricot flavors deliver lots of pleasure. Very sweet, yet a long, fresh finish. What can we say? Buy it and try after 2000, but waiting is difficult. • $30 • (04/15/95) • **95**

Sauternes 1989: Fresh and floral style, appealingly focused vanilla, honey and toast character. Good balance, medium body and sweetness. Drinkable now. • $28 • (04/15/95) • **88**

Sauternes 1988: Elegant, focused and well balanced, offering finesse, medium sweetness and body and lovely citrus, honey and quince flavors. Drinkable now. • $23 • (04/15/95) • **88**

Sauternes 1987 • $15 • (06/15/90) • **81**

Sauternes 1986 • $43 • (04/15/95) • **94**

Sauternes 1981 • $13 • (08/31/86) • **84**

MALLERET, CHÂTEAU DE

Haut-Médoc 1991: Soft and smooth, with attractive herb and light bell pepper aromas and flavors, light tannins and soft finish. • $13 • (03/31/94) • **79**

Haut-Médoc 1989 • $NA • (03/15/92) • **90**
Haut-Médoc 1981 • $6 • (03/01/85) • **77**

MALMAISON, CHÂTEAU

Moulis 1991: Rather lean and watery despite some pleasant fruit and almond notes. Tasted twice. • $14 • (03/31/94) • **71**
Moulis 1990: A property on the rise. This is a thick wine with elegance, it has focused berry and plum aromas and flavors and a velvety tannin structure. Drinkable now. • $14 • (03/31/93) • **89**
Moulis 1989 • $16 • (03/15/92) • **85**

MALTROYE, CHÂTEAU DE LA

Chassagne-Montrachet Boudriottes Red 1985 • $17 • (10/15/88) • **86**
Chassagne-Montrachet Clos St.-Jean Red 1985 • $19 • (10/15/88) • **89**
Chassagne-Montrachet Clos St.-Jean Red 1983 • $13 • (11/16/85) • **65**
Chassagne-Montrachet Grandes Ruchottes 1993: Straightforward, modest fruit flavors and a diluted finish. 167 cases made. • $40 • **77**
Chassagne-Montrachet Morgeot Vieille Vigne 1993: Tart, tight and ungenerous, presenting lime, citrusy flavors and lean texture. Not much there. 417 cases made. • $35 • **78**

MANCIAT-PONCET

Pouilly-Fuissé Les Crays 1994: A prototype for '94 white Burgundy: laced with a thread of pretty honey and fruit, nicely fresh and crisp on the finish. Lovely and light-bodied, drinkable on release as an apéritif or with light dishes. 2,500 cases made. • $18 • (05/31/96) • **84**
Pouilly-Fuissé Les Crays 1993: Crisp lemon and pear flavors blend together nicely, adding a hint of honey and floral notes on the juicy finish. A touch diluted, drinkable now. 2,550 cases made. • $17 • **83**

MANCIAT, JEAN

Mâcon-Villages Franclieu 1993: Tart and crisp, showing loads of citrus flavors. Austere and difficult to warm up to. A bit simple. 583 cases made. • $13 • **74**
Mâcon-Villages Franclieu Cuvée Spéciale 1993: A round, lemony note and light-to-medium body. Plenty of wet hay, green pea and green apple flavors. Austere finish. 75 cases made. • $14 • **79**

MANN, ALBERT

Auxerrois Alsace Vieilles Vignes 1992: A sulfury, earthy aroma with dry, almost neutral flavor make this uninspired and awkward. It does have good acidity. • $12 • (11/15/94) • **77**
Gewürztraminer Alsace Grand Cru Furstentum Cuvée Victoria 1993: Easygoing, fruity, sweet and full-bodied, adding soft texture, plenty of peach and apricot flavor and a lingering finish. Tastes clean and fresh. 75 cases made. • $36 • (09/15/95) • **86**
Tokay Pinot Gris Alsace Grand Cru Hengst 1993: A fruity, supple dry white, smooth in texture and reminiscent of ripe pears and apples. Clean, well balanced, lively acidity and lingering finish. 200 cases made. • $22 • (09/15/95) • **87**

MANUEL, DOMAINE RENE

Bourgogne White 1993: Toast, hazelnut, honey and pear aromas are well defined—and echoed on the palate—but the wine turns hard, tart and herbal on the finish. • $11 • **84**
Meursault Clos de la Baronne 1993: Clean and well defined but tart and lacking in body, offering some modest fruit and herbal character. • $25 • (05/15/95) • **79**
Meursault Clos de la Baronne 1991 • $21 • (10/15/93) • **91**
Meursault Clos les Bouchères 1993: Vivid and well defined, rather steely, offering mostly lime, lemon and grapefruit flavors and also hints of mineral and honey on the vibrant finish. Try now. • $44 • (05/15/95) • **85**
Meursault Clos les Bouchères 1992: Rich in aroma, full-bodied and ripe in flavor, with loads of pineapple, honey, and peach notes, layered with butter, toast and hazelnut. Very long-lasting on the finish. Try now. • $NA • (08/31/94) • **91**
Meursault Red Clos de la Baronne 1988 • $18 • (03/31/91) • **79**

MARBUZET, CHÂTEAU DE

St.-Estèphe 1995: A bit herbal yet some impressive concentration of fruit and firm tannins. Full-bodied and rich, but green bean character on the finish mars the overall quality. • $NA • (05/15/96) • **80-84** (BT)
St.-Estèphe 1994: Fairly soft and slightly diluted, though it still delivers some sweet fruit and ripe tannins. An early-drinking '94. • $NA • (05/15/96) • **80-84** (BT)
St.-Estèphe 1993: Some good concentration of fruit but rather herbal and grassy with a metallic edge. • $20 • (01/31/96) • **78**
St.-Estèphe 1992: Tobacco and cassis aromas and flavors, medium body, firm tannins and a stone, berry, slightly herbal finish. Drinkable now. • $16 • **78**
St.-Estèphe 1990: Full-bodied and tannic, with loads of currant and black cherry flavors, rich, spicy notes, plenty of stuffing and a long, flavorful finish accented by chocolate and coffee. Drinkable now. • $19 • (09/15/93) • **86**
St.-Estèphe 1989 • $21 • (03/15/92) • **89**
St.-Estèphe 1988 • $17 • (07/15/91) SS • **92**
St.-Estèphe 1987 • $14 • (11/30/89) • **80**
St.-Estèphe 1986 • $16 • (11/30/89) • **86**
St.-Estèphe 1985 • $21 • (06/30/88) • **87**
St.-Estèphe 1983 • $22 • (10/15/86) • **91**
St.-Estèphe 1982 • $22 • (11/30/89) • **86**

MARCHAND-GRILLOT & FILS

Gevrey-Chambertin 1990: Firm and aromatic, offering a beam of raspberry, red cherry and tobacco aromas and flavors. Smooth in texture, finishing with a nice touch of herb. Try now. • $20 • (06/15/93) • **84**
Gevrey-Chambertin Petite Chapelle 1986 • $30 • (10/15/89) • **76**

MARCHAND, CLAUDE

Chambolle-Musigny 1986 • $32 • (07/15/89) • **85**
Charmes-Chambertin 1986 • $50 • (07/15/89) • **92**
Gevrey-Chambertin 1987 • $22 • (07/15/90) • **81**
Gevrey-Chambertin 1986 • $28 • (07/15/89) • **89**
Morey-St.-Denis 1987 • $30 • (09/30/90) • **80**
Morey-St.-Denis Clos des Ormes 1987 • $30 • (09/30/90) • **69**
Morey-St.-Denis Clos des Ormes 1986 • $33 • (07/15/89) • **85**

MARCHAND, JEAN-PHILIPPE

Charmes-Chambertin 1987 • $60 • (12/31/90) • **76**
Gevrey-Chambertin Les Combottes 1987 • $30 • (07/15/90) • **82**

MARCHIVE, LYNE & JEAN-BERNARD

Chablis 1994: Terrific village Chablis, showing ripe pear, melon and spice notes and a sweet-tasting finish that is both crisp and clean. Well done. From Domaine des Malandes. • $NA • **85**

MARCOUX, DOMAINE DE

Châteauneuf-du-Pape 1988 • $24 • (10/15/91) • **82**
Châteauneuf-du-Pape 1986 • $20 • (10/15/91) • **84**
Châteauneuf-du-Pape 1983 • $25 • (10/15/91) • **87**
Châteauneuf-du-Pape 1981 • $30 • (10/15/91) • **85**
Châteauneuf-du-Pape Special Cuvée 1990: Smells ripe and jammy, with lots of cherry and plum-scented characteristics that come through on the palate. Big, firm and tannic, a rustic style that will require patience. Cellar through 1996. 200 cases made. • $22 • (08/31/92) • **88**
Châteauneuf-du-Pape Vieilles Vignes 1989 • $30 • (10/15/91) • **95**
Côtes du Rhône 1989 • $8 • (08/31/92) • **82**

MARDON, DOMAINE

Quincy 1992: A soft wine with melon flavors and marked celery and herbal notes, it's a bit rustic and dull. Easy to drink, but it lacks snap. • $13 • (10/31/94) • **79**

MARGAUX, CHÂTEAU

Margaux 1995: Perhaps the wine of the vintage: very close indeed. Layers of wonderful raspberry, cherry and fruit. Full-bodied and compact yet elegant, with lots of finesse. The fine tannins go on and on. • $NA • (05/15/96) • **95-100** (BT)
Margaux 1994: A beautifully aromatic Margaux that has an abundance of cherry, vanilla and cedar aromas and flavors. Medium to full body and extremely well-integrated tannins. Long and fresh on the finish. • $85 • (05/15/96) • **90-94** (BT)
Margaux 1993: Château Margaux is back after a weak '92. Big for the vintage, featuring loads of new oak to provide a smoky, toasty taste. Attractive currant, black cherry and rose petal character. Medium-bodied, exotic and ripe. Somewhat hard now, and you wish for a bit more concentration, but time should turn it into a lovely wine. Try in 1999. • $72 • (01/31/96) • **90**
Margaux 1992: Elegant but somewhat light for Château Margaux. Fresh and delicious black cherry and raspberry aromas and flavors, medium-to-light body, firm tannins and light finish. Tasted three times, with consistent notes. Drink now. • $65 • **81**
Margaux 1991: A little disappointing, but a pretty wine to smell and taste. Impressive fruit and wood accented by silky tannins, but slightly dry and herbaceous on the finish. • $41 Ⓐ • (03/31/94) • **85**
Margaux 1990: A seductive, tantalizing wine with gorgeous aromas and flavors of tobacco, cedar, berry and cassis, superb soft tannins and a long, long finish. Drink after 1998. 25,000 cases made. • $400 Ⓐ • (03/31/93) • **96**
Margaux 1989 • $106 Ⓐ • (03/15/92) CS • **99**
Margaux 1988 • $61 Ⓐ • (03/31/91) CS • **97**
Margaux 1987 • $50 Ⓐ • (05/15/90) • **87**
Margaux 1986 • $154 Ⓐ • (12/15/89) • **98**
Margaux 1985: Young, exuberant and exciting. Fabulously well integrated with raspberry, mint and violet character. Full-bodied with loads of fine tannins. Try after 1998. • $100 • (10/15/94) • **95**
Margaux 1984 • $26 Ⓐ • (07/15/87) • **91**
Margaux 1983 • $161 Ⓐ • (10/15/94) • **98**
Margaux 1982 • $305 Ⓐ • (08/31/92) • **95**
Margaux 1981 • $181 Ⓐ • (10/15/94) • **95**
Margaux 1980 • $66 • (07/15/87) • **80**
Margaux 1979 • $97 Ⓐ • (12/15/89) • **91**
Margaux 1978 • $124 Ⓐ • (12/15/89) • **92**
Margaux 1977 • $323 Ⓐ • (07/15/87) • **75**
Margaux 1976 • $59 Ⓐ • (07/15/87) • **81**
Margaux 1975 • $64 Ⓐ • (07/15/87) • **88**
Margaux 1971 • $76 • (07/15/87) • **77**
Margaux 1970 • $59 Ⓐ • (05/15/93) • **88**
Margaux 1967 • $22 Ⓐ • (07/15/87) • **84**
Margaux 1966 • $117 Ⓐ • (07/15/87) • **90**
Margaux 1964 • $79 Ⓐ • (07/15/87) • **86**
Margaux 1962 • $240 • (12/15/89) • **86**
Margaux 1961: Mature, smooth and finely textured, showing a beautiful bottle bouquet, ample fruity, meaty flavors and firm but integrated tannins. Elegant compared to some of the vintage's blockbusters, and a joy to drink now through 2005. • $431 Ⓐ • (04/30/96) • **92**
Margaux 1959 • $280 Ⓐ • (10/15/90) • **93**
Margaux 1957 • $200 • (07/15/87) • **90**
Margaux 1955 • $170 • (07/15/87) • **79**
Margaux 1953 • $556 Ⓐ • (12/15/89) • **84**
Margaux 1952 • $500 • (07/15/87) • **85**
Margaux 1950 • $600 • (07/15/87) • **89**

Key: SS—Spectator Selection. CS—Cellar Selection. BB—Best Buy. $NA—Price not available. (BT)—Barrel tasting. Ⓐ—Auction Price.
Dates in parentheses represent the issues in which the ratings were published.

Margaux 1949 • $220 Ⓐ • (07/15/87) • **95**
Margaux 1947 • $326 Ⓐ • (07/15/87) • **96**
Margaux 1945 • $654 Ⓐ • (03/16/86) • **90**
Margaux 1943 • $430 • (07/15/87) • **78**
Margaux 1937 • $340 • (07/15/87) • **82**
Margaux 1934 • $240 Ⓐ • (07/15/87) • **88**
Margaux 1929 • $232 Ⓐ • (07/15/87) • **83**
Margaux 1928 • $864 Ⓐ • (07/15/87) • **73**
Margaux 1926 • $300 • (07/15/87) • **77**
Margaux 1924 • $230 • (07/15/87) • **73**
Margaux 1923 • $330 • (07/15/87) • **81**
Margaux 1920 • $420 • (07/15/87) • **79**
Margaux 1918 • $87 Ⓐ • (07/15/87) • **80**
Margaux 1917 • $300 • (07/15/87) • **62**
Margaux 1909 • $480 • (07/15/87) • **65**
Margaux 1908 • $530 • (07/15/87) • **85**
Margaux 1905 • $800 • (07/15/87) • **64**
Margaux 1900 • $3,200 • (07/15/87) • **93**
Margaux 1899 • $1,700 • (07/15/87) • **94**
Margaux 1898 • $1,600 • (07/15/87) • **75**
Margaux 1893 • $148 Ⓐ • (07/15/87) • **95**
Margaux 1892 • $750 • (07/15/87) • **80**
Margaux 1887 • $426 Ⓐ • (07/15/87) • **81**
Margaux 1870 • $3,300 • (07/15/87) • **89**
Margaux 1868 • $2,000 • (07/15/87) • **69**
Margaux 1865 • $5,000 • (07/15/87) • **97**
Margaux 1864 • $3,500 • (07/15/87) • **98**
Margaux 1848 • $10,000 • (07/15/87) • **95**
Margaux 1847 • $25,000 • (07/15/87) • **96**
Margaux 1791 • $NA • (07/15/87) • **97**
Margaux 1771 • $NA • (07/15/87) • **99**

MARILYN MERLOT

Merlot Vin de Pays de l'Aude 1987 • $6 • (03/15/90) • **77**

MARIS, DOMAINE

Minervois Carte Noire 1990 • $9 • (03/15/94) • **80**
Minervois J. Maris Cuvée Prestige 1990 • $9 • (03/15/94) • **86**

MARJOSSE, CHÂTEAU

Bordeaux 1995: Light, herbal, disappointing, this light-bodied '95 lacks ripe fruit. Dry finish. • $NA • (05/15/96) • **70-74** (BT)
Bordeaux 1993: Light and slightly dry, showing some cherry, dried herb and earth flavor and a hint of tomato. Drinkable now. • $NA • (01/31/96) • **80**
Bordeaux 1992: Clean but rather herbal and spicy, offering light body and tannins and a watery finish. Drinkable now. • $NA • **75**
Bordeaux Elève en Fûts de Chêne 1993: Displays attractive, perfumed, fruity character, medium body, medium-to-light tannins and light finish. Made by the winemaker at Château Cheval Blanc. Drinkable now. • $NA • **80**
Entre-Deux-Mers 1994: Tasting this is like eating a puree of pears. Medium-bodied, with straightforward flavors and good acidity. • $NA • (03/31/96) • **85**

MAROT, CHÂTEAU

Bergerac 1988 • $7 • (08/31/91) • **79**

MAROTTE, CHÂTEAU

Bordeaux 1986 • $3 • (04/30/88) • **70**

MARSAC-SEGUINEAU, CHÂTEAU

Margaux 1983 • $9 • (09/30/86) • **68**

MARSAU, CHÂTEAU

Côtes de Francs 1995: Pretty, flavorful, medium- to full-bodied '95, showing nice cassis, mocha and toasted oak character. Although quite tannic, it's rather delicate and subtle. • $NA • (05/15/96) • **85-89** (BT)

Côtes de Francs 1994: Fruity, supple and attractive, sporting medium body and complexity. • $NA • **80-84** (BT)

MARTIN, JEAN-JACQUES

Beaujolais-Villages 1993: A mature wine with prune and stewed fruit flavors and aromas. Spicey flavors and tannins linger on the finish. • $NA • (06/15/95) • **80**

Beaujolais-Villages 1992: Fresh and vivid, with a broader palate of flavors than Beaujolais usually shows: cherry, green pepper, smoke and licorice. A bit disjointed, but still lively. Drink now. • $10 • (06/30/94) • **83**

Juliénas 1993: Dried-out fruit flavors and barnyardy aromas make this hard to like. Astringent on the finish. • $14 • **72**

Juliénas 1992 • $14 • (06/15/94) • **85**

Pouilly-Fuissé Les Chevrières 1994: Simply superb, with lots of crisp citrus flavors up front, turns silky and creamy as it glides to a smooth finish. Lovely apricot, lemon, honey and fig flavors from start to finish. Delicious now, but should improve into 1998. • $NA • (05/31/96) • **89**

St.-Amour 1993: Earthy aromas give way to stewed flavors that include prunes, tomatoes and a little spice. A little tired, but still enjoyable. • $NA • (07/31/95) • **80**

St.-Amour 1992: Dark and muscular, has ripe plum and gamy flavors underpinned by firm tannins, along with a burnt finish. Clumsy now, it may come together with more time in the bottle. • $15 • (06/30/94) • **78**

MARTINOLLES, DOMAINE DE

Brut Blanquette de Limoux 1990 • $10 • (03/31/92) • **84**

Brut Blanquette de Limoux 1989 • $9 • (03/31/92) BB • **83**

Brut Blanquette de Limoux 1986 • $11 • (03/31/92) • **78**

Brut Blanquette de Limoux NV • $8 • (04/15/90) BB • **84**

Brut Crémant de Limoux 1989 • $10 • (11/30/92) • **81**

Chardonnay Vin de Pays de l'Aude 1991 • $8 • (04/15/93) • **77**

MAS BLANC, DOMAINE DU

Banyuls Vendanges Tardives 1982 • $26 • (02/28/91) • **80**

Banyuls Vieilles Vignes 1982 • $27 • (02/28/91) • **82**

Banyuls Vieilles Vignes 1976 • $40 • (02/28/91) • **85**

Collioure Cuvée Cosprons Levants 1988 • $21 • (03/31/91) • **82**

MAS CHAMPART

Coteaux du Languedoc 1991 • $8 • (03/15/94) • **83**

St.-Chinian 1991 • $8 • (03/15/94) • **84**

MAS CREMAT, DOMAINE DU

Côtes du Roussillon 1991 • $9 • (03/15/94) • **83**

MAS DE DAUMAS GASSAC

Vin de Pays de l'Herault 1990 • $28 • (10/31/92) • **87**

Vin de Pays de l'Herault 1989 • $25 • (12/15/91) • **83**

Vin de Pays de l'Herault 1987 • $23 • (10/31/89) • **85**

Vin de Pays de l'Herault 1986 • $25 • (12/15/88) • **81**

Vin de Pays de l'Herault Haute Vallée du Gassac 1992 • $25 • (03/15/94) • **90**

Vin de Pays de l'Herault Haute Vallée du Gassac 1991 • $28 • (03/15/94) • **87**

Vin de Pays de l'Herault Haute Vallée du Gassac 1989 • $28 • (03/15/94) • **93**

Vin de Pays de l'Herault Haute Vallée du Gassac Blanc de Raisins de Blancs 1993 • $38 • (03/15/94) • **89**

Vin de Pays de l'Herault Haute Vallée du Gassac Blanc de Raisins de Blancs 1991 • $38 • (03/15/94) • **90**

MAS DE GOURGONNIER

Coteaux d'Aix en Provence Les Baux de Provence 1990 • $11 • (03/15/93) • **80**

Coteaux des Baux en Provence 1983 • $3 • (12/16/85) • **70**

Coteaux des Baux en Provence Coteaux d'Aix 1984 • $5 • (03/15/87) BB • **82**

Coteaux des Baux en Provence Les Baux de Provence 1988 • $8 • (04/30/91) • **79**

MAS DE LA ROUVIERE

Bandol 1983 • $NA • (08/31/86) • **65**

Bandol 1982 • $NA • (08/31/86) • **73**

Bandol 1979 • $NA • (08/31/86) • **80**

MAS DES BRESSADES

Cabernet-Syrah Vin de Pays du Gard 1990 • $13 • (04/15/93) • **83**

MAS JULLIEN

Coteaux du Languedoc Les Cailloutis 1991 • $10 • (03/15/94) • **84**

Coteaux du Languedoc Les Depierre 1991 • $10 • (03/15/94) • **83**

MAS STE.-BERTHE

Coteaux d'Aix en Provence 1989 • $7 • (07/15/92) • **68**

Coteaux d'Aix en Provence Cuvée Louis David 1990 • $16 • (07/15/92) • **81**

Coteaux d'Aix en Provence Cuvée Tradition 1992: Promising roasted aromas are followed by greener, leaner fruit flavors. Interesting but limited. Drink now. 5,000 cases made. • $10 • (03/31/95) • **80**

MASSON-BLONDELET, DOMAINE J.-M.

Pouilly-Fumé 1992: Clean and straightforward, this quaffable wine balances fruit and herbs in a soft, refreshing style. It's well-made, balanced and typical. • $12 • (10/31/94) • **85**

Pouilly-Fumé Les Bascoins 1993: This bold, rich wine offers herbal, melon and light vanilla flavors, full-bodied and firm, with a clean finish of limes and hay. It's muscular but harmonious, drinkable now. • $15 • (11/15/95) • **90**

Pouilly-Fumé Les Bascoins 1991: Atypically soft, this reminds us of buttered toast spread with orange marmalade. It seems a bit disjointed right now, despite its appealing components. • $13 • (10/31/94) • **83**

MATHIEU, DOMAINE

Châteauneuf-du-Pape 1990: A ripe, complex wine, with broad, rich, leathery plum, earth and spice flavors that are full-bodied and chocolaty on the finish. Has a good dose of alcohol, too, but is balanced and fun to drink now through 1998. 2,000 cases made. • $15 • (11/30/92) • **87**

Châteauneuf-du-Pape 1989 • $18 • (08/31/92) • **87**

Châteauneuf-du-Pape White 1991 • $18 • (06/15/93) • **81**

MATIBAT, DOMAINE DE

Cabernet Sauvignon Vin de Pays d'Oc 1991 • $6 • (04/15/93) • **72**

MATROT, DOMAINE JOSEPH

Chardonnay Bourgogne 1993 • $15 • **67**

Chardonnay Bourgogne 1991 • $14 • (10/15/93) • **88**

Meursault 1993: Simple in flavor, slightly earthy even, turning dull on the finish. There's not much to get excited about. Tasted twice. • $26 • (05/15/95) • **74**

Meursault 1991 • $29 • (10/15/93) • **88**

Meursault Blagny 1993: Attractive Meursault showing lovely apple and pear aromas and flavors, medium body and firm acidity. Tasted twice. 567 cases made. • $34 • **83**

Meursault Blagny 1991 • $43 • (10/15/93) • **86**

FRANCE

Meursault Les Charmes 1993: Not much more than a generic white wine, from the vaguely earthy aromas to almost neutral flavors. Gets a bit nice and spicy on the finish, but where's the fruit? • $37 • (05/15/95) • **77**
Meursault Les Charmes 1992: Ripe and lush, with texture like cream, and wonderful mineral, caramel, apple and pear flavors. Seductive, with excellent acidity, grows in complexity as it comes in contact with the air. From a producer known to make long-aged wines. Tasted three times. • $33 • (08/31/94) • **89**
Meursault Les Charmes 1991 • $45 • (10/15/93) • **91**
Meursault Les Chevalières 1993: Hard at first but then begins to sing, flashing a distinctive mineral character that dominates from start to the seductively smooth finish. Try after 1996. 167 cases made. • $23 • (05/15/95) • **87**
Meursault Les Chevalières 1992: Round, ripe and intense, this is difficult to evaluate. Tastes reductive and a bit of cardboard, but the content of a bottle opened for hours turned seductive, silky and incredibly minerally. • $25 • (05/15/95) • **87**
Meursault Les Chevalières 1991 • $45 • (10/15/93) • **89**
Puligny-Montrachet Les Chalumeaux 1991 • $45 • (10/15/93) • **85**

MATROT, PIERRE

Chardonnay Bourgogne 1994: A round, smooth, ready-to-drink Burgundy that has decent fruit flavors and toasty aromas. • $17 • (05/31/96) • **81**
Meursault 1992: Quite complex and very silky, exceptional finesse, with a solid core of pear, mineral, vanilla and white pepper flavors. Smooth and round finish. From a producer whose wines need time to show it all. • $20 • (08/31/94) • **88**
Puligny-Montrachet Les Chalumeaux 1992: Well-balanced and modestly flavored, with butter, green apple and vanilla flavors that linger a bit on the finish. May need some time for the tart fruit component to blend in. A wine with a good track record for improving with age, drinkable now. • $30 • (08/31/94) • **85**
Puligny-Montrachet Les Chalumeaux 1991 • $32 • (10/15/93) • **90**
Puligny-Montrachet Les Combettes 1991 • $35 • (10/15/93) • **87**

MAU, YVON

Bordeaux Officiel du Bicentenaire de la Revolution Francaise 1986 • $4 • (06/30/89) • **72**
Sauvignon Gris Bordeaux 1992 • $7 • (09/15/93) • **74**

MAUCAILLOU, CHÂTEAU

Moulis 1992: Light and diluted, with strawberry, tobacco, herbal character. Drink now. • $14 • **73**
Moulis 1988 • $14 • (07/31/91) • **82**
Moulis 1985 • $18 • (08/31/88) • **88**
Moulis 1983 • $16 • (03/15/87) • **87**
Moulis 1982 • $25 • (11/30/89) • **90**
Moulis 1981 • $14 • (10/01/85) • **88**

MAUCOIL, CHÂTEAU

Châteauneuf-du-Pape Réserve Suzeraine 1985 • $13 • (11/15/87) • **86**

MAUME

Charmes-Chambertin 1988 • $60 • (07/15/91) • **86**
Gevrey-Chambertin 1993: Seductive and distinguished, showing lots of pure, lively cassis, black cherry and wild berry character. It expands on the palate, adding coffee, spice, mocha and cedar notes. Very complex and full-bodied. Try in 2000. • $NA • (05/15/96) • **90**
Gevrey-Chambertin 1987 • $25 • (03/31/90) • **77**
Gevrey-Chambertin En Pallud 1987 • $36 • (03/31/90) • **80**

> **Key:** SS—Spectator Selection. CS—Cellar Selection. BB—Best Buy. $NA—Price not available. (BT)—Barrel tasting. Ⓐ—Auction Price.
> **Dates in parentheses represent the issues in which the ratings were published.**

Gevrey-Chambertin Lavaux St.-Jacques 1993: Very pure and vibrant cassis and currant character, lovely floral, rose petal complexity, medium body, wet earth notes and lingering finish. Could use a bit more opulence and body. Slightly drying aftertaste. • $NA • **86**
Gevrey-Chambertin Lavaux St.-Jacques 1991: Lean and tight, with a fine beam of raspberry and cherry fruit poking through the layer of tannins. Give it until 1998. • $40 • (08/31/94) • **84**
Gevrey-Chambertin Lavaux St.-Jacques 1987 • $45 • • **62**
Gevrey-Chambertin Premier Cru 1991: Ripe, with an open texture, a generous wine that floats across the palate, showing plum, black cherry and spice with an herbal edge on the finish. Tannins are not obtrusive. Drinkable now. • $28 • (08/31/94) • **87**
Mazis-Chambertin 1991: Lean and chewy, showing a lot of tea leaf and herbal notes around a tannic core of dark fruit and spice. Remains astringent on the finish. Try after 1998. • $59 • (08/31/94) • **82**
Mazis-Chambertin 1987 • $56 • (03/31/90) • **74**

MAUVINON, CHÂTEAU

St.-Emilion 1983 • $10 • (11/30/86) • **87**

MAX, ROBERT

Pommard 1982 • $16 • (12/16/84) • **82**

MAXIM'S

Brut Champagne NV • $NA • (12/31/91) • **85**

MAXIME GODET

Brut Champagne Cuvée Speciale Premier Cru NV: Lean and crisp in flavor. A nicely doughy aroma accents lemon and apple notes. Tasted twice. 5,000 cases made. • $NA • **84**

MAYARD, JEAN-LUC

Châteauneuf-du-Pape Domaine du Galet des Papes 1992: Aging fast, showing mature and complex aromas of earth, leather and spice, with decent fruit flavors underneath, full body and good finish. • $23 • **82**
Châteauneuf-du-Pape Domaine du Galet des Papes Vieilles Vignes 1992: Decent flavor, soft in balance, offering prune and herb accents. Drinkable now. • $32 • **81**

MAYNE DES CARMES, CHÂTEAU

Sauternes 1989: An earthy character influences the fig, honey and walnut flavors in this medium-weight wine. Good if you don't mind a little funkiness. The finish is modest and slightly bitter. • $20 • (06/30/92) • **83**

MAYNE-DAVID, CHÂTEAU

Côtes de Castillon 1985 • $6 • (02/28/87) BB • **81**

MAYNE, CHÂTEAU LE

Puisseguin-St.-Emilion 1982 • $7 • (12/01/85) • **64**

MAZERIS-BELLEVUE, CHÂTEAU

Canon-Fronsac 1990: This wine is extremely firm, with full tannins and exotic cassis, berry and earth aromas and flavors. Drinkable in 1997. 5,000 cases made. • $15 • (03/31/93) • **88**

MAZERIS, CHÂTEAU

Canon-Fronsac 1994: Beautiful, ripe fruit and very round tannins. Dark-colored and chewy, smoke, berry and tobacco character. • $NA • **85-89** (BT)

Canon-Fronsac 1993: Some berry and chocolate flavors, yet too light and diluted to be anything but average. Drinkable now. • $19 • (01/31/96) • **78**

Canon-Fronsac 1990: Very rip—perhaps too ripe—with meaty, raisin and plum flavors and a dry tannic finish, this wine has rich flavors. Drinkable now. • $13 • (05/15/94) • **80**

MAZEROLLE, CHÂTEAU LA

Bordeaux 1990: Soft, supple, dry and modestly tannic, with flavors reminiscent of cherry pie, offering spicy red cherry and butter aromas and flavors. A tasty, harmonious wine, drinkable now. 5,000 cases made. • $9 • (03/15/93) BB • **87**

MELLOT, DOMAINE ALPHONSE

Sancerre Domaine La Moussière 1994: Ripe and exaggerated style, delivering flavors of honey and marzipan, some good concentration and balance and a lingering finish. Not for everyone. • $20 • (04/30/96) • **83**

Sancerre Domaine La Moussière 1991 • $16 • (07/31/93) SS • **91**

MELOTERIE, DOMAINE DE LA

Vouvray Demi-Sec 1989 • $9 • (06/15/91) • **87**

MEO-CAMUZET, DOMAINE

Bourgogne 1990: Throws a lot of fruit at you, with pretty berry, cherry and raspberry flavors and a slight citrus edge. Ripe and balanced, a tasty mouthful of Pinot Noir. Ready now. • $20 • (06/15/93) • **85**

Bourgogne 1989 • $23 • (11/15/91) • **83**

Bourgogne Passe-tout-grains 1992: Hats off to this exotic wine packed with floral, violet and boysenberry flavors. Refreshes the palate with more pure, clean fruit than many other '92s. • $NA • **83**

Bourgogne Passe-tout-grains 1990: A ripe, bold style that gushes with raspberry, cherry and currant flavors framed by smoky oak and firm, drying tannins. Still, on the finish you taste a rich core of fruit. Drinkable now. • $17 • (03/31/92) • **86**

Bourgogne Passe-tout-grains 1989 • $17 • (07/15/91) • **84**

Clos de Vougeot 1993: Perhaps not as concentrated as expected from this top winery. Sleek and silky mocha, fruit, vanilla and spice character, medium body, fine tannins and long, crisp finish. Better in 1999. • $55 • **88**

Clos de Vougeot 1992: Very pretty ripe flavors on a supple frame, the blackberry and spice hinting at chocolate on the smooth finish. Drinkable now. • $57 • **88**

Clos de Vougeot 1991: A dissappointment, light and fruity, showing some pleasent raspberry and anise aromas and flavors, narrowing on the finish. Drinkable now. 650 cases made. • $77 • (01/31/94) • **83**

Clos de Vougeot 1990: Serves up nice supple berry and currant flavors, but they're not as bright and lively as we've found in most 1990s. Tannins are smooth and easy on the finish. Ready now through 1997. Tasted twice. • $77 • (09/30/93) • **84**

Clos de Vougeot 1989 • $91 • (11/15/91) CS • **94**

Clos de Vougeot 1988 • $95 • (11/30/90) • **92**

Clos de Vougeot 1986 • $55 • (11/30/88) • **91**

Clos de Vougeot 1985 • $105 • (03/31/88) • **93**

Corton 1992: Manages to focus its generous beam of blackberry and currant flavors through layers of spicy oak and very fine-grained tannins. Supple and beautifully crafted, it rises above the vintage. Approachable now, best from 1997. • $57 • **91**

Corton 1989 • $76 • (11/15/91) • **93**

Corton 1986 • $50 • (10/31/88) • **89**

Corton Clos Rognet 1991: There's a lot to like in this wine even though it's a lighter style. Spice and ripe cherry flavors are framed by toasty, buttery, smoky oak notes, giving the finish depth and complexity. Drinkable now. 125 cases made. • $73 • (01/31/94) • **89**

Corton Clos Rognet 1990: Elegant and spicy, with a pretty core of ripe black cherry and raspberry flavor that turns smooth and silky on the finish. Delicious now. 150 cases made. • $68 • (06/15/93) • **89**

Nuits-St.-Georges 1992: Gorgeous fruit unfolds with a cascade of violet, currant and black cherry flavors. Elegant, smooth and drinkable. Could only use a bit more concentration. Tempting now, but better after 1996. • $33 • **86**

Nuits-St.-Georges 1990: Ripe and spicy, with a definite touch of new oak to add complexity to the ripe plum and black cherry flavors. Has a smooth, elegant finish. Drinkable now. • $38 • (02/15/93) • **88**

Nuits-St.-Georges 1989 • $52 • (11/15/91) • **92**

Nuits-St.-Georges 1988 • $50 • (11/30/90) • **91**

Nuits-St.-Georges 1987 • $42 • (12/15/89) • **86**

Nuits-St.-Georges 1986 • $32 • (11/15/88) • **90**

Nuits-St.-Georges Aux Boudots 1993: Pretty Burgundy, sporting loads of peppery, spicy, fruity character, although slightly short on the finish. Medium in body, fine tannins. Try in 2000. • $60 • **90**

Nuits-St.-Georges Aux Boudots 1992: Firm, chewy and solid, with dark berry and spicy prune flavors lurking underneath a layer of fine tannins. Try after 1996. • $54 • **85**

Nuits-St.-Georges Aux Boudots 1991: Firm in texture and modest in intensity, serving up appealing aromas and flavors that emerge harmoniously on the finish. 175 cases made. • $62 Ⓐ • (01/31/94) • **84**

Nuits-St.-Georges Aux Boudots 1990: A balance of rich, plummy flavors and spicy, toasted oak notes gives this wine finesse, intensity and complexity. Lively and luscious on the finish. Drinkable now. 250 cases made. • $68 • (02/15/93) • **91**

Nuits-St.-Georges Aux Boudots 1989 • $81 • (11/15/91) • **90**

Nuits-St.-Georges Aux Boudots 1988 • $80 • (11/30/90) • **92**

Nuits-St.-Georges Aux Boudots 1987 • $56 • (12/15/89) • **88**

Nuits-St.-Georges Aux Boudots 1986 • $46 • (11/15/88) • **92**

Nuits-St.-Georges Aux Murgers 1993: Lots of wood in this brooding, dark-colored Burgundy. Plenty of plum, chestnut and currant flavors, full body, a fresh core and solid tannins. Try in 1999. • $60 • **93**

Nuits-St.-Georges Aux Murgers 1992: Pretty berry and vanilla flavors rise past the chewy tannins in this medium-bodied, deep-colored wine. It just needs time to settle down—best from 1997. • $54 • **86**

Nuits-St.-Georges Aux Murgers 1991: Smooth in texture and attractive, showing fresh currant and wild berry flavors that keep echoing on the finish, nicely shaded by spicy oak. Should be fine through 1997. 275 cases made. • $62 Ⓐ • (01/31/94) • **88**

Nuits-St.-Georges Aux Murgers 1990: A firm wine that offers generous, clear black cherry, raspberry and spice aromas and flavors. Solid, with pure, focused flavors balanced by enough acidity and tannin. Drinkable now to 1998. 375 cases made. • $68 • (02/15/93) • **90**

Nuits-St.-Georges Aux Murgers 1989 • $81 • (11/15/91) • **94**

Nuits-St.-Georges Aux Murgers 1988 • $80 • (11/30/90) • **91**

Nuits-St.-Georges Aux Murgers 1987 • $56 • (12/15/89) • **93**

Nuits-St.-Georges Aux Murgers 1986 • $48 • (11/15/88) • **92**

Nuits-St.-Georges Aux Murgers 1985 • $73 • (04/15/88) • **90**

Richebourg 1993: Simply fabulous. Like an iron fist in a velvet glove, this seduces yet displays a firm side. Very sweet-tasting and ripe, boasting superb currant, mint and black cherry flavors. Goes on and on. Bravo! Try after 2000. • $175 • **94**

Richebourg 1992: Supple, stylish, generous and bursting with delicious currant and raspberry notes layered under violet and spicy oak tones. It keeps pouring out the flavor on a long, polished finish. Delicious now. • $NA • **91**

Richebourg 1991: Firm and focused, a polished, youthful wine with creamy currant, spice and chocolate aromas and flavors in refined proportions. Has elegance if not effusiveness. Drinkable now, but best from 1997. 100 cases made. • $219 • (01/31/94) • **90**

Richebourg 1990: A stunning 1990 that packs in a wonderful range of ripe, delicious fruit and combines it with elegance, finesse and grace. Deeply colored, with tiers of black cherry, currant and raspberry-scented flavors that pick up spicy anise and cedar notes. Impeccably balanced, long, rich and concentrated. A sheer joy to drink now, but should age through the decade with ease. 125 cases made. • $242 • (06/15/93) • **97**

Richebourg 1989 • $270 • (11/15/91) • **97**

Richebourg 1988 • $253 • (11/30/90) • **96**

Richebourg 1987 • $165 • (12/15/89) • **96**

Richebourg 1986 • $160 • (10/31/88) • **90**

Richebourg 1985 • $235 • (03/31/88) • **97**

Vosne-Romanée 1992: Sharp and tart. The pretty rose petal, black currant and smoky, toasty flavors are clean and pure, but it could use a bit more concentration. • $33 • **80**

Vosne-Romanée 1991: A decent core of cherry and currant flavors turns intense and concentrated, with toasty, smoky oak and a rich, full finish. Not a blockbuster; drinkable now. 175 cases made. • $36 • (01/31/94) • **89**

Vosne-Romanée 1990: Long and lavish, with many threads of nutmeg- and vanilla-scented blackberry, plum and currant aromas and flavors weaving together through the elegant finish. A polished wine that's flavorful and generous without weight. Drinkable now. • $36 • (02/15/93) • **93**

Vosne-Romanée 1989 • $47 • (11/15/91) • **91**

Vosne-Romanée 1988 • $50 • (12/31/90) • **87**

Vosne-Romanée 1987 • $35 • (12/15/89) • **90**

Vosne-Romanée 1986 • $30 • (10/31/88) • **88**

Vosne-Romanée Aux Brûlées 1993: Beautifully crafted red offering crushed raspberry and plum character. Full-bodied yet silky and sophisticated, caressing your palate. Try in 2000. • $75 • **93**

Vosne-Romanée Aux Brûlées 1992: With more density and color than most '92s, this is almost exuberantly fruity and generous, showing bright currant, berry and spicy oak aromas and flavors. Drinkable now. • $72 • **85**

Vosne-Romanée Aux Brûlées 1991: Silky and flavorful, an earthy edge to the pretty blackberry and cherry flavors and shades of chocolate and cedar add extra dimensions. An elegant wine, with impressive length. Drinkable now. 137 cases made. • $73 Ⓐ • (01/31/94) • **89**

Vosne-Romanée Aux Brûlées 1990: Supple, forward and fruity, with an amazing range of spicy cherry, raspberry and currant flavor that's pure and delicious, picking up toasty oak notes in the background. Complex, concentrated, young and vibrant. The tannins barely show on the long, full finish. Drinkable now. 225 cases made. • $81 • (06/15/93) • **93**

Vosne-Romanée Aux Brûlées 1989 • $91 • (11/15/91) • **94**

Vosne-Romanée Aux Brûlées 1988 • $84 • (11/30/90) • **89**

Vosne-Romanée Aux Brûlées 1987 • $63 • (12/15/89) • **95**

Vosne-Romanée Les Chaumes 1993: Magnificent. Supple yet full of vibrant currant, raspberry and violet notes and a touch of earth. Quite ripe and sweet, but it needs time. Try in 2004. • $70 • **93**

Vosne-Romanée Les Chaumes 1992: Richer than most in this vintage, with a smoky, toasty character to the currant and black cherry. Flavors persist on the finish and the tannins are in balance. • $43 • **86**

Vosne-Romanée Les Chaumes 1990: Ripe, focused, generous, supple, spicy and complex, with currant, raspberry, chocolate and spice aromas and flavors. Chewy and tannic enough to wait until 1998, but it's concentrated enough to be drinkable now. 240 cases made. • $55 • (02/15/93) • **94**

Vosne-Romanée Les Chaumes 1989 • $62 • (01/31/92) • **91**

Vosne-Romanée Les Chaumes 1986 • $38 • (12/31/88) • **83**

Vosne-Romanée Les Chaumes 1985 • $80 • (03/31/88) • **92**

Vosne-Romanée Cros-Parantoux 1992: Well-defined fruit, focusing on raspberry and currant, in a smooth wine with supple tannins and toasty character. It's good, but doesn't approximate the *grand cru* character as it usually does. Tasted twice. • $73 • **85**

Vosne-Romanée Cros-Parantoux 1991: Subtle and elegant, showing plenty of blackberry, vanilla and toast aromas and flavors up front and on the finish, although it takes a dip in the middle. Drinkable now. 75 cases made. • $73 Ⓐ • (01/31/94) • **88**

Vosne-Romanée Cros-Parantoux 1990: A tremendous wine for this price. Amazingly ripe, complex and elegant, with tiers of black cherry, currant, raspberry and spice aromas and flavors. Shows tremendous balance between elegance and concentration, suppleness and structure, intensity and finesse. Picks up toasted oak notes and fine tannins on the finish. Drinkable now. 100 cases made. • $81 • (06/15/93) • **99**

Vosne-Romanée Cros-Parantoux 1989 • $91 • (11/15/91) • **95**

Vosne-Romanée Cros-Parantoux 1988 • $84 • (11/30/90) • **94**

Vosne-Romanée Cros-Parantoux 1987 • $63 • (12/15/89) • **95**

Key: SS—Spectator Selection. CS—Cellar Selection. BB—Best Buy. $NA—Price not available. (BT)—Barrel tasting. Ⓐ—Auction Price.
Dates in parentheses represent the issues in which the ratings were published.

Vosne-Romanée Cros-Parantoux 1986 • $60 • (07/31/88) • **93**

MERCEY, DOMAINE DU CHÂTEAU DE

Mercurey 1983 • $10 • (05/01/86) • **56**

MERIC, CHÂTEAU

Graves 1989 • $16 • (07/15/92) • **77**

Graves 1988 • $17 • (04/30/91) • **76**

MERODE, PRINCE FLORENT DE

Aloxe-Corton 1987 • $30 • (02/28/91) • **87**

Aloxe-Corton Premier Cru 1990 • $37 • (12/15/92) • **86**

Corton Les Bressandes 1993: Pretty Corton, not for long aging but very pleasant now. Shows plum, cedar and cream character, medium body, soft tannins and medium finish. 457 cases made. • $37 • **86**

Corton Les Bressandes 1992: A little chewy, but the berry and spice flavors slide in on the chunky finish. Best after 1996. 500 cases made. • $35 • **81**

Corton Les Bressandes 1991: Shows off spicy, toasty oak and cherry and plum flavors underneath that are simple but bright. Ready now. 500 cases made • $32 • (01/31/94) • **84**

Corton Les Bressandes 1990: Not as concentrated in fruit as some, but shows a solid backbone of tannins and pleasant fruit characteristics. Try now. 200 cases made. • $54 • (12/15/92) • **85**

Corton Les Bressandes 1989 • $56 • (11/30/92) • **84**

Corton Les Bressandes 1987 • $45 • (03/31/91) • **92**

Corton Les Bressandes 1986 • $38 • (08/31/89) • **84**

Corton Les Bressandes 1985 • $52 • (02/15/88) • **93**

Corton Le Clos du Roi 1993: Very solid and closed. Knocks you over the head. Full body, medium tannins and a muscular finish. Give it time, try after 2000. 220 cases made. • $44 • **88**

Corton Le Clos du Roi 1992: Ripe and chewy, with fresh, youthful berry and currant flavor that lingers on the supple finish. Give it until 1997. 242 cases made. • $42 • **86**

Corton Le Clos du Roi 1991: Firm and focused, showing some nice currant and blackberry flavors shaded by anise and toast on the velvety finish, fading a little on the aftertaste. Drinkable now. 337 cases made. • $38 • (01/31/94) • **84**

Corton Le Clos du Roi 1990: As velvety as wines get in Corton, melts in your mouth, with lovely chocolate, raspberry and cherry aromas and flavors and a smoky, toasty, vanilla-flavored finish that is supple and delicious. Should be great sooner than most, try now. 95 cases made. • $64 • (12/15/92) • **90**

Corton Le Clos du Roi 1987 • $44 • (03/31/90) • **87**

Corton Le Clos du Roi 1986 • $49 • (08/31/89) • **80**

Corton Maréchaudes 1993: Firm, vibrant and fruity, featuring lots of cherry character and fresh acidity. Rather lean but delicious. Try in 1999. 194 cases made. • $32 • **87**

Corton Maréchaudes 1992: Relatively light and pleasant, with a decent level of berry flavor sneaking in on the chewy finish. Best from 1997. 216 cases made. • $32 • **82**

Corton Maréchaudes 1990: Fruity and flavorful, the blend of earth, strawberry and cherry notes makes for pleasant drinking. Not as big as the best, but offers enough depth to please most Burgundy lovers. Drinkable now. 250 cases made. • $49 • (12/15/92) • **86**

Corton Maréchaudes 1987 • $36 • (08/31/90) • **88**

Corton Maréchaudes 1986 • $33 • (08/31/89) • **82**

Corton Maréchaudes 1985 • $49 • (03/15/88) • **81**

Corton Les Renardes 1993: Light, pleasant, delicate red berry and floral notes and a crisp but fresh and lively finish. Might be better in 1998. 194 cases made. • $37 • **85**

Corton Les Renardes 1992: Supple and nicely focused, with raspberry and blackberry notes that keep singing on the smooth finish. Not powerful but showing nice flavors. Best in 1997. 212 cases made. • $35 • **82**

Corton Les Renardes 1991: Simple and spicy, offering earthy cherry and currant notes. A lighter style that's best to enjoy now, while the fruit is showing. 205 cases made. • $32 • (01/31/94) • **85**

Corton Les Renardes 1990: How much more refined can a Corton get? You can taste the finesse. The violet, raspberry and earth characteristics just go on and on at the end, when the supple but long finish kicks

in. Try whenever you've got a chance. 90 cases made. • $54 • (12/15/92) • **94**
Corton Les Renardes 1987 • $36 • (03/31/90) • **92**
Corton Les Renardes 1986 • $38 • (08/31/89) • **76**
Ladoix Les Chaillots 1993: A surprise from this rather unheralded village. Marvelous pure fruit from start to finish, boasting an excellent tannin structure, medium body and currant, vanilla and cream flavors. Try after 2000. 631 cases made. • $17 • **90**
Ladoix Les Chaillots 1992: Light and tight, hinting at currant at first, but fading quickly. A small wine with small flavors. 658 cases made. • $21 • **76**
Ladoix Les Chaillots 1991: Crisp in texture, but a nice beam of currant and spice flavors opens up on the finish. Drinkable now. 1,100 cases made. • $28 Ⓐ • (01/31/94) • **81**
Ladoix Les Chaillots 1990: Shows the essence of fruit, and so refined that the flavors linger. Ripe without being overblown, seducing you with its focused black cherry, blackberry and plum aromas and flavors. Drinkable now. 550 cases made. • $23 • (12/15/92) • **88**
Ladoix Les Chaillots 1987 • $18 • (11/15/90) • **77**
Ladoix Les Chaillots 1986 • $18 • (08/31/89) • **74**
Ladoix Hautes Mourottes White 1991 • $45 • (11/15/93) • **83**
Pommard Clos de la Platière 1993: Chunky Pommard, offering plenty of thick fruit and tannins, medium to full body, excellent backbone and long finish. Seems deceptively simple now and needs time, try in 1999. 583 cases made. • $31 • **88**
Pommard Clos de la Platière 1992: Crisp in texture, with modest black cherry flavor poking through the firm tannins. Best after 1996. 542 cases made. • $31 • **79**
Pommard Clos de la Platière 1991: Firm and focused, with juicy black cherry, longonberry and ceder aromas and flavors, finishing lean and flavorful. Drinkable now. 1,200 cases made. • $35 • (01/31/94) • **82**
Pommard Clos de la Platière 1990: Full of finesse despite the concentrated character and solid tannins. Focused and well made, delivering plenty of red berry, violet and smoke aromas and flavors and refined tannins. Drinkable now. 475 cases made. • $48 • (12/15/92) • **90**
Pommard Clos de la Platière 1989 • $48 • (11/30/92) • **86**
Pommard Clos de la Platière 1987 • $36 • (08/31/90) • **76**
Pommard Clos de la Platière 1986 • $35 • (07/31/89) • **86**
Pommard Clos de la Platière 1985 • $45 • (03/15/88) • **94**
Pommard Clos de la Platière 1984 • $23 • (02/15/88) • **71**

MESTRE-MICHELOT

Chardonnay Bourgogne 1993: Lean, hard and a bit green, displaying decent citrus and apple flavors. Bitter, herbal notes kick in on the finish. Drink if you must. • $NA • **74**
Meursault Genevrières 1993: Very attractive mineral, apple and pineapple notes and a touch of toasted oak. Medium-bodied, exhibiting solid fruit and flinty aftertaste. Drink now. • $NA • (05/15/95) • **89**
Meursault Le Limozin 1993: A tart Meursault that tastes quite green but also shows some decent lime, honey and grapefruit flavors. Might be better in 1997. • $NA • (05/15/95) • **82**
Meursault Le Limozin 1992: Lovely and complex, medium-bodied, shows toast, butter, peach and mineral flavors, all in a smooth and vibrant package, deliciously lingering finish. Drinkable now. • $38 • (08/31/94) • **89**
Meursault Le Limozin 1991 • $NA • (10/15/93) • **88**
Meursault Le Porusot 1992: Ripe and opulent in style, luxurious and flavorful, piling honey and pineapple on top of hazelnut, toast and butter. Lush in texture, but not too fat. A forward style that is very enjoyable now. • $NA • (08/31/94) • **89**
Meursault Le Porusot 1991 • $NA • (10/15/93) • **85**
Meursault Sous la Velle 1993: Quite tight and hard now but shows excellent potential. Toast, dried-herb and green apple flavors come together refreshingly on the finish. Hold until after 1997. • $NA • **85**

METAIREAU, LOUIS

Muscadet de Sèvre et Maine Sur Lie Cuvée One 1993: Tart acidity keeps this wine crisp as light apple and pear fruit flavors are appealing, if short. A bit long in the tooth for Muscadet, though. • $14 • (06/15/96) • **80**

METAIRIE, LA

Corbières 1989 • $7 • (12/15/91) • **78**

MEULIERE, CHÂTEAU DE LA

Premières Côtes de Bordeaux 1988 • $9 • (02/28/91) • **76**

MEUNIER ST.-LOUIS, CHÂTEAU

Corbières 1991 • $NA • (03/15/94) • **87**

MEUNIER, DOMAINE DU

Côtes de Gascogne 1985 • $5 • (05/31/88) • **72**

MEURGEY, GEORGES

Vouvray 1992: The apple and honey flavors are attractive but rather simple and dull in this rich, slightly sweet wine. It's straightforward, well-made without complexity. • $7 • **81**

MEURGEY, HENRI

Chassagne-Montrachet Clos de la Boudriotte Red 1985 • $40 • (10/31/88) • **88**

MEURSAULT, CHÂTEAU DE

Beaune Les Cent-Vignes 1985 • $31 • (02/28/90) • **87**
Beaune Premier Cru 1992: On the light side, but pleasant in flavor and smooth in texture. Hints of smoke and mineral add to the currant cherry flavors, and the finish lingers nicely. Drink now. • $26 • (05/15/95) • **83**
Pinot Noir Bourgogne du Château 1992: A sturdy, rather simple red Burgundy that is medium-bodied, moderately tannic and greenish in flavor. Best to drink now. • $13 • (05/31/95) • **82**
Pinot Noir Bourgogne du Château 1988 • $16 • (01/31/92) • **82**
Savigny-lès-Beaune Savigny du Domaine 1992: Simple and mature tasting, with plum, honey and apricot flavors, mild tannins and a sense of sweetness. Drink now. • $20 • (05/15/95) • **79**
Volnay Clos des Chênes 1992: A heavy dose of oak makes this at once supple and overdone. Tastes almost sweet, with vanilla, maple syrup and butter flavors. Appealing to some, but not our style. • $30 • (05/15/95) • **78**
Volnay Clos des Chênes 1988 • $47 • (07/15/91) • **87**

MEYER-FONNE

Gewürztraminer Alsace Cuvée Réservée 1992: Shows characteristic spice and almond flavors, balanced but lacks stuffing, turning a bit hollow on the palate. Tasted twice. • $15 • (11/15/94) • **78**
Gewürztraminer Alsace Réserve Particulière 1993: Ripe, rich and smooth, offering plenty of peach and honey flavors. Seems sweet at first but finishes dry. Still fairly full-bodied and assertive. • $18 • (09/15/95) • **85**
Gewürztraminer Alsace Réserve St.-Urbain 1993: Pleasant, soft, supple and very fruity, with just enough acid to keep in balance. Bold flavors—peach, grapefruit, honey—make it attractive. • $20 • (09/15/95) • **87**
Muscat Alsace 1992: Bold aromas of honey and flowers edge into the barnyard here, the light-bodied wine is bone dry and clean, with orange zest, menthol and herbal flavors. Plenty of flavors, but not much harmony. • $13 • (11/15/94) • **80**
Pinot Blanc Alsace 1993: True-to-type Pinot Blanc, dry and full-bodied, tasting like melons, almonds and minerals, adds fine tangy acidity and a lingering finish. 2,500 cases made. • $10 • (07/31/95) • **86**
Pinot Blanc Alsace 1992: Fresh and smooth, this attractive wine offers orange, cream and melon flavors in a balanced package with lively acidity. Hints of almond add interest on the finish. • $10 • (11/15/94) • **85**
Riesling Alsace 1992: A Mosel-style austerity and mineral quality don't mesh well with the rather soft balance of this Riesling. Floral notes add a bit of intrigue. • $13 • (11/15/94) • **80**

FRANCE

Riesling Alsace Grand Cru Wineck-Schlossberg 1993: Want a big, assertive Riesling? Try this full-bodied, brightly fruity and firmly acidic white. Vanilla, almond and honey aromas are followed by green peach and lemon flavors and a crisp finish. May mellow by 1997. • $28 • (09/15/95) • **85**

Riesling Alsace Kaefferkopf 1993: Fruity in flavor and smooth-textured, filled out by ripe pear and apple notes that fade on the finish. Satisfying, if not too complex. • $25 • (09/15/95) • **84**

Riesling Alsace Vendange Tardive Vielles Vignes 1992: Pretty apricot and vanilla aromas give way to sweet flavors of apricot and honey, with an underlying acidity to give it balance. Almost Californian in its rich, straightforward fruitiness. Drinking nicely now. • $25 • (08/31/95) • **85**

Riesling Alsace Vignoble de Katzenthal 1993: A straightforward Riesling offering soft texture, modest apple and peach flavors and tart finish. • $18 • (09/15/95) • **82**

Sylvaner Alsace 1993: Fresh and lively, a full-flavored white showing apple and lemon notes accented by mineral and earth tones. • $10 • (09/15/95) • **85**

Tokay Pinot Gris Alsace Cuvée Réservée 1992: Ripe flavors and generous texture make this an easy-going, fruity Tokay Pinot Gris. There are pear, vanilla and peach notes, with adequate acidity to back them up. • $14 • (11/15/94) • **83**

Tokay Pinot Gris Alsace Réserve Particulière 1993: Rich and seductive, with nutty, smoky aromas and flavors along with ripe pear notes and a long, almost sweet finish. It's opulent, though not powerful, balanced for drinking now. • $17 • (08/31/95) • **87**

MEYNEY, CHÂTEAU

St.-Estèphe 1995: Racy, well-made red featuring plenty of tannins, fruit and acidity, medium to full body and medium finish. • $NA • (05/15/96) • **85-89** (BT)

St.-Estèphe 1994: Some nice plum and red berry flavors make up the supple core of fruit, couched in fine tannins. Overall a bit short and a touch diluted, though. • $18 • (05/15/96) • **80-84** (BT)

St.-Estèphe 1993: Meyney is always a winner. Lovely mint, berry, cherry and vanilla aromas and flavors, medium body, silky tannins and fresh finish. Better in 1998. • $17 • (01/31/96) • **86**

St.-Estèphe 1992: Very polished and silky tobacco, mint, currant and vanilla aromas and flavors. Medium in body. Drink now. • $15 • **83**

St.-Estèphe 1991: A fruity wine with a hint of herbs and bell pepper. Medium-bodied with a light finish. • $15 • (03/31/94) • **79**

St.-Estèphe 1990: A beautiful wine, with cassis, berry and citrus aromas and flavors, medium tannins and a long, crisp finish. Drinkable now. 25,000 cases made. • $15 • (03/31/93) • **90**

St.-Estèphe 1989 • $30 Ⓐ • (03/15/92) • **93**

St.-Estèphe 1988 • $17 • (03/15/91) • **88**

St.-Estèphe 1987 • $14 • (05/15/90) • **87**

St.-Estèphe 1986 • $31 Ⓐ • (11/30/89) • **88**

St.-Estèphe 1985 • $16 • **92**

St.-Estèphe 1984 • $11 • (05/15/87) • **79**

St.-Estèphe 1983 • $18 • **87**

St.-Estèphe 1982 • $23 • (08/31/92) • **91**

St.-Estèphe 1981 • $NA • **79**

St.-Estèphe 1979 • $18 • (10/15/89) • **87**

St.-Estèphe 1961 • $47 • (04/30/96) • **83**

MICHAUD, ALAIN

Brouilly Prestige de Vieilles Vignes 1993: Thick and rather harsh, good concentration, but flavors of tobacco, brandied cherry and herb are heavy for Beaujolais. Lacks freshness. • $17 • (06/15/95) • **79**

Key: SS—Spectator Selection. CS—Cellar Selection. BB—Best Buy. $NA—Price not available. (BT)—Barrel tasting. Ⓐ—Auction Price.
Dates in parentheses represent the issues in which the ratings were published.

MICHAUD, DOMAINE J.F.

Beaujolais Le Toléron 1994: Round and soft, this marries fresh black cherry flavors, an appealing smoky note and enough tannins to deliver good character for a simple Beaujolais. 2,000 cases made. • $8 • (10/31/95) • **83**

MICHEL, LOUIS

Chablis 1994: Straightforward, light and fruity. The texture is nicely silky, and a mineral, green apple note is pleasant. 2,966 cases made. • $20 • (05/31/96) • **80**

Chablis 1992 • $19 • (09/15/93) • **87**

Chablis Les Clos 1994: Smells a bit musty and tastes a little dry on the finish, but it also offers some decent fruit, butterscotch and citrus flavors. Tasted twice, with consistent notes. 208 cases made. • $45 • (05/31/96) • **74**

Chablis Les Clos 1993: Very crisp white featuring high acidity and plenty of green apple, mineral and parsley flavors. Try now. • $40 • (08/31/95) • **83**

Chablis Grenouilles 1994: A sexy *grand cru* that's a monument to hedonism. Ripe, rich and full-bodied, this silky, quintessential Chardonnay is packed with honey, apricot, peach, lemon, tropical fruit and mineral flavors. Drinkable now through 1999. 275 cases made. • $45 • (05/31/96) • **93**

Chablis Grenouilles 1993: Unusually ripe for a 1993 Chablis, showing some nice mineral, straw, honey and pear complexity and a delicate, elegant finish. • $NA • (08/31/95) • **86**

Chablis Montée de Tonnerre 1994: Rich but not overly ripe, showing some class, with a stony, wet earth, flinty, lemony character and a long finish. Unyielding now, but an intense *premier cru* that has the backbone to age. Better in 1998. 2,216 cases made. • $28 • (05/31/96) • **86**

Chablis Montée de Tonnerre 1993: Some good mineral and flinty character, but slightly dull on the herbal finish. Medium-bodied and flavorful. • $23 • (08/31/95) • **81**

Chablis Montmain 1994: An uncompromising Chablis, tight and hard as nails, but showing a nice concentration of mineral, wet earth, honey, herb, citrus and green apple flavors. Straight as an arrow. Better in 1999. Tasted twice, with consistent notes. 3,050 cases made. • $24 • (05/31/96) • **86**

Chablis Montmains 1993: Simple and clean milk, mineral and apple aromas and flavors, medium body and short finish. • $23 • (08/31/95) • **80**

Chablis Vaillons 1994: Impressive, though tightly structured and hard as nails now. The flinty apple and wet earth aromas and flavors are ripe yet subtle. An assertive mineral character fills the mouth. Will need time, try in 1999. 1,000 cases made. • $24 • (05/31/96) • **93**

Chablis Vaudésir 1994: Supple and pleasant, with notes of wet earth and a distinctive *goût de terroir* that links it to the soil. The mineral flavors come through in this full-bodied, honeyed, solidly built *grand cru.* Wonderful, silky, long finish. Try in 1998. 683 cases made. • $42 • (05/31/96) • **90**

Chablis Vaudésir 1993: Rather meager straw, honey and apple character, medium to light body and crisp acidity. • $40 • (08/31/95) • **82**

MICHEL, R.

Cornas Cuvée des Coteaux 1991 • $16 • (05/31/94) • **89**

Cornas La Geynale 1991 • $20 • (05/31/94) • **82**

MICHELE, ROBERT

Muscadet de Sèvre et Maine Les Trois Fils 1994: A neutral white that's showing zippy acidity but not much else. 500 cases made. • $7 • (05/15/96) • **77**

Muscadet de Sèvre et Maine Les Trois Fils 1993: This clean, crisp wine shows firm acidity and green apple flavors with a tangy citrus finish. Very refreshing, a good shellfish wine. • $NA • (10/31/94) • **84**

Vouvray Les Trois Fils 1993: There are pretty floral and peachy flavors here, enlivened by lemony acidity, but an earthy note detracts. It's got good weight on the palate, and finishes dry. 2,800 cases made. • $7 • (11/15/95) • **82**

MICHELOT-BUISSON

Bourgogne White 1991 • $NA • (10/15/93) • **80**
Meursault Charmes 1992: Bold with lots of personality, the winemaker is stretching here, putting the pedal to the floor. Chewy and flavorful, it tastes a bit tough, youthful and even a bit coarse now, but it turns supple and gracious after awhile in the glass. • $57 • (08/31/94) • **91**
Meursault Les Charmes 1991 • $NA • (10/15/93) • **68**
Meursault Clos St.-Felix 1993: Well-defined mineral, spice and honey aromas and flavors, medium body, firm acidity and long, fresh, fruity finish. • $NA • **87**
Meursault Les Genevrières 1991 • $NA • (10/15/93) • **87**
Meursault Les Narvaux 1993: Interesting use of wood here, loads of green apple character. Medium body and a slightly dull, tart finish. • $NA • **80**
Meursault Les Perrières 1993: Fine, delicate cream, apple and pear aromas and flavors, medium body and smooth texture. Crisp finish. Drinkable now. • $NA • **84**
Meursault Les Perrières 1991 • $NA • (10/15/93) • **85**

MICHELOT, ALAIN

Nuits-St.-Georges 1988 • $39 • (07/15/91) • **91**
Nuits-St.-Georges 1982 • $17 • (05/01/84) • **86**
Nuits-St.-Georges Les Cailles 1988 • $54 • (05/15/91) • **83**
Nuits-St.-Georges Les Cailles 1982 • $19 • (07/16/85) • **90**
Nuits-St.-Georges Aux Chaignots 1988 • $56 • (05/15/91) • **90**
Nuits-St.-Georges Les Champs-Perdrix 1986 • $30 • (12/15/89) • **81**
Nuits-St.-Georges Les Porrets-St.-Georges 1988 • $56 • (05/15/91) • **83**
Nuits-St.-Georges Les Richemone 1988 • $54 • (05/15/91) • **89**
Nuits-St.-Georges Les Vaucrains 1988 • $56 • (05/15/91) • **87**
Nuits-St.-Georges Les Vaucrains 1986 • $30 • (12/15/89) • **88**

MICHELOT, C.

Meursault Les Charmes 1993: A bit too woody for us, but some decent fruit and crisp acidity underneath it all. • $NA • (05/15/95) • **78**
Meursault Les Grands Charrons 1992: Seductive and as smooth-textured as a Chardonnay gets, with exotic tangerine, mineral and pear flavors backed by well-integrated acidity. Great length. Try now. • $NA • (08/31/94) • **90**
Meursault Les Grands Charrons 1991 • $NA • (10/15/93) • **86**
Puligny-Montrachet 1993: Odd wine, revealing some strange, volatile, paint thinner flavors that seem unappealing. Very woody. • $NA • **70**

MICHELOT, DOMAINE

Meursault Clos du Cromin 1994: A well-crafted, supple Burgundy, showing a seductive core of toasted oak, pineapple, coconut and spice flavors. The silky texture carries through on the finish. Drinkable now through 1998. • $38 • (05/31/96) • **85**
Meursault Clos St.-Félix 1994: Elegant and subtle, with some mineral, pear and tropical flavors. It's pleasant to drink now, but seems a touch short on the finish. • $35 • (05/31/96) • **83**
Meursault Les Charmes 1994: Smooth and supple, a light- to medium-bodied '94 that's ready to drink, with pleasant pear, spice, vanilla, honey and toasted hazelnut flavors. • $50 • (05/31/96) • **85**
Meursault Les Grands Charrons 1994: Round, supple and toasty. An attractive Chardonnay that shows some apple and spice flavors and a smooth finish. Lacks complexity, though. • $38 • (05/31/96) • **81**
Meursault Les Narvaux 1994: As smooth as cream, this full-bodied Burgundy caresses the palate with its lush character. Overflowing with flavors—honey, vanilla, spice, toasted pine nuts and pie crust—it shows staying power on the long, balanced finish. Drinkable now or try in 1997. • $40 • (05/31/96) • **87**
Meursault Les Perrières 1994: Supple and creamy, with ripe pear, mineral and loads of honey flavors. A full-bodied, showy Chardonnay, with notes of toasted bread on the finish. Drinkable now through 1997. • $60 • (05/31/96) • **85**
Meursault Le Porusot 1994: A full-bodied wine in a forward, opulent style, offering pleasing doses of honey, fig, and almond. The finish is supple and very round but a touch short. • $40 • (05/31/96) • **83**
Meursault Sous la Velle 1994: Supple and elegant, a round, silky Burgundy with tons of toasted bread and coconut flavors along with some pear and apple notes. Could use a bit more fruit concentration. Still, very seductive and pleasant now. • $30 • (05/31/96) • **85**

MICHELOT, G.

Meursault 1994: Attractive from start to finish, with seductive lemon, pie crust, toasted bread and ripe pear flavors. It's full-bodied yet also manages to be elegant and refreshing. Long finish. Amazing quality for a simple village wine. • $NA • (05/31/96) • **90**
Meursault 1993: Showy and toasty, smooth, sporting a lively edge and lean frame. Somewhat short, could use more fruit concentration. Drinkable now. • $NA • (05/15/95) • **83**
Meursault Clos du Cromin 1993: Honey, nut, pear and earth character, medium body, substantial crispness and a long, fresh finish. Tempting now but better after 1997. • $NA • (05/15/95) • **86**
Meursault Clos du Cromin 1992: Gorgeous, jumping with complexity and beautiful aromas, rich and elegant, with fig, vanilla, pear and honey notes, each flavor more distinctive than the last. Delicious now. • $38 • (08/31/94) • **91**
Meursault Clos du Cromin 1991 • $NA • (10/15/93) • **85**
Meursault Les Grands Charrons 1993: Delicious honey, nut and floral aromas and good taste, but this is still quite austere, grassy, herbal finish. Drinkable now. • $NA • (05/15/95) • **84**
Puligny-Montrachet Les Folatières 1991 • $NA • (10/15/93) • **87**

MICHELOT, JEAN

Pommard 1987 • $33 • (08/31/90) • **78**
Pommard 1985 • $29 • (04/30/88) • **87**
Pommard 1983 • $21 • (06/16/86) • **78**

MILHAU-LACUGUE, CHÂTEAU

St.-Chinian 1990 • $8 • (03/15/94) • **83**

MILLE, CHÂTEAU DE

Côtes du Lubéron 1985 • $8 • (12/15/88) • **83**

MILLEGRAND, CHÂTEAU

Minervois 1988 • $5 • (04/30/90) • **77**

MILLOT, JEAN-MARC

Echézeaux 1993: Clean and fresh, offering very good intensity of berry, cherry and cedar character. Medium body, fine tannins, medium finish. Drink in 1999. • $NA • **86**

MINET, REGIS

Pouilly-Fumé Vieilles Vignes 1993: Lively and pleasant, this fresh white offers pear, citrus and mineral flavors, clean and crisp. Well-focused, if a bit narrow, a good food wine. Tasted twice with consistent notes. 2,500 cases made. • $14 • **84**
Pouilly-Fumé Vieilles Vignes 1992: Notes of earthiness and grilled nuts predominate in this soft, rather dull wine. It lacks typicity and life, and finishes short. 800 cases made. • $13 • (10/31/94) • **77**

MIOLANE, RENE

Beaujolais-Villages Cuvée des Chasseurs 1992: It's plump and round, and ripe cherry and plum flavors are appealing, but a stewed, stemmy note detracts from the pleasure. • $9 • (06/30/94) • **78**

MISSEREY, P.

Nuits-St.-Georges Les Vaucrains 1988 • $35 • (08/31/92) • **83**

MISSION-HAUT-BRION, CHÂTEAU LA

Pessac-Léognan 1995: Big and solid, loads of berry, black cherry, mint and licorice showing through. Full-bodied and powerful—highly tannic at this stage. Almost classic. • $NA • (05/15/96) • **90-94** (BT)
Pessac-Léognan 1994: Tight for the moment, but underneath are rich, ripe berry and chocolate aromas and flavors. Medium- to full-bodied, fine tannins and long, caressing finish. Almost outstanding. • $NA • **85-89** (BT)
Pessac-Léognan 1994: Plenty of cherry, tobacco and raspberry aromas and flavors. Moderate tannins and a fresh finish. Almost outstanding. • $62 • (05/15/96) • **85-89** (BT)
Pessac-Léognan 1993: Superbly elegant, supple and lush, featuring mineral, mint, cassis, dried herb, cedar and plum complexity, soft tannins and a seductive finish. Very tempting now, but will benefit with cellaring until about 1998. • $60 • (01/31/96) • **89**
Pessac-Léognan 1992: Slightly disappointing, yet good nonetheless. Focused core of dried cherry and berry character, medium-bodied and fruity, demonstrating silky texture. Drinkable now. • $44 • **84**
Pessac-Léognan 1991: Fine, firm, and elegant wine with tobacco, red berry aromas and flavors, medium body and tannins, long finish. • $45 • (03/31/94) • **85**
Pessac-Léognan 1990: Excellent winemaking is evident here. A big wine with wonderful wet stone, berry and leafy aromas and flavors and ultrafine tannins. Drink after 1996. 7,000 cases made. • $65 • (03/31/93) • **95**
Pessac-Léognan 1989 • $100 • (03/15/92) • **96**
Pessac-Léognan 1988 • $65 • (11/15/91) • **90**
Pessac-Léognan 1987 • $41 • (11/15/91) • **84**
Pessac-Léognan 1986 • $51 • (11/15/91) • **97**
Graves 1985 • $70 • (10/15/94) • **90**
Graves 1984 • $55 • (11/15/91) • **85**
Graves 1983 • $83 • (10/15/94) • **93**
Graves 1982 • $152 Ⓐ • (08/31/92) • **97**
Graves 1981 • $58 Ⓐ • (11/15/91) • **87**
Graves 1980 • $22 Ⓐ • (11/15/91) • **86**
Graves 1979 • $58 Ⓐ • (11/15/91) • **86**
Graves 1978 • $117 Ⓐ • (11/15/91) • **94**
Graves 1975 • $351 Ⓐ • (11/15/91) • **90**
Graves 1974 • $26 Ⓐ • (11/15/91) • **87**
Graves 1973 • $52 • (11/15/91) • **80**
Graves 1972 • $50 • (11/15/91) • **77**
Graves 1971 • $87 • (11/15/91) • **91**
Graves 1970 • $211 Ⓐ • (05/15/93) • **90**
Graves 1969 • $32 • (11/15/91) • **84**
Graves 1968 • $60 • (11/15/91) • **67**
Graves 1967 • $85 • (11/15/91) • **89**
Graves 1966 • $191 Ⓐ • (11/15/91) • **93**
Graves 1965 • $100 • (11/15/91) • **76**
Graves 1964 • $105 Ⓐ • (11/15/91) • **91**
Graves 1963 • $100 • (11/15/91) • **78**
Graves 1962 • $121 Ⓐ • (11/15/91) • **90**
Graves 1961: A truly classic Bordeaux that epitomizes complexity and distinction in a red wine. Well-defined but beautifully integrated aromas and flavors of cedar, earth, tobacco, chocolate and plum make it memorable, while a lively, firm texture keeps it fresh to drink. A fabulous taste experience from start to lingering finish. Drink through 2010. • $558 • (04/30/96) • **96**
Graves 1960 • $140 • (11/15/91) • **84**
Graves 1959 • $450 • (11/15/91) • **94**
Graves 1958 • $180 • (11/15/91) • **83**
Graves 1957 • $165 • (11/15/91) • **85**
Graves 1956 • $210 • (11/15/91) • **87**
Graves 1955 • $863 Ⓐ • (11/15/91) • **89**
Graves 1954 • $375 • (11/15/91) • **86**
Graves 1953 • $422 Ⓐ • (11/15/91) • **93**
Graves 1952 • $310 • (11/15/91) • **98**
Graves 1950 • $350 • (11/15/91) • **79**
Graves 1949 • $624 Ⓐ • (11/15/91) • **95**
Graves 1948 • $600 • (11/15/91) • **98**
Graves 1947 • $700 • (11/15/91) • **100**
Graves 1946 • $700 • (11/15/91) • **85**
Graves 1945 • $850 • **96**
Graves 1944 • $350 • (11/15/91) • **78**
Graves 1943 • $450 • (11/15/91) • **88**
Graves 1942 • $275 • (11/15/91) • **83**
Graves 1941 • $250 • (11/15/91) • **81**
Graves 1940 • $330 • (11/15/91) • **82**
Graves 1939 • $350 • (11/15/91) • **87**
Graves 1938 • $190 • (11/15/91) • **81**
Graves 1937 • $200 • (11/15/91) • **88**
Graves 1936 • $200 • (11/15/91) • **62**
Graves 1935 • $575 • (11/15/91) • **85**
Graves 1934 • $500 • (11/15/91) • **86**
Graves 1933 • $475 • (11/15/91) • **74**
Graves 1931 • $375 • (11/15/91) • **70**
Graves 1929 • $900 • (11/15/91) • **100**
Graves 1928 • $460 Ⓐ • (11/15/91) • **84**
Graves 1926 • $375 • (11/15/91) • **59**
Graves 1924 • $550 • (11/15/91) • **89**
Graves 1921 • $600 • (11/15/91) • **85**
Graves 1919 • $600 • (11/15/91) • **85**
Graves 1918 • $550 • (11/15/91) • **83**
Graves 1916 • $350 • (11/15/91) • **82**
Graves 1914 • $500 • (11/15/91) • **65**
Graves 1904 • $600 • (11/15/91) • **85**
Graves 1899 • $850 • (11/15/91) • **92**
Graves 1895 • $700 • (11/15/91) • **99**
Graves 1888 • $1,000 • (11/15/91) • **95**
Graves 1877 • $1,000 • (11/15/91) • **93**

MOC ET BARIL

Cabernet d'Anjou 1994: Smells and tastes funky and oxidized with dried fruit flavors. Peppery on the finish. • $7 • (09/30/95) • **76**
Cabernet d'Anjou Rosé 1992: Off-dry with crisp acidity, combining berry, tea and celery flavors. Has vivacity but an odd vegetal character. • $7 • (10/31/94) • **78**

MOËT & CHANDON

Brut Champagne Cuvée Dom Pérignon 1988: A beautiful wine with a long finish. At first sip this is sharp and crisp, showing lime and citrus flavors, but it turns a bit earthy on the palate and develops yeasty, chalky notes. Try in 1997. • $89 • **91**
Brut Champagne Cuvée Dom Pérignon 1985: Another great bottle of DP. Aromatic and exciting, with straw, lemon-lime and apple character, medium body and a fruity and crisp finish. Drink now or hold. • $52 Ⓐ • (12/31/93) • **91**
Brut Champagne Cuvée Dom Pérignon 1983. • $79 Ⓐ • (05/15/92) • **95**
Brut Champagne Cuvée Dom Pérignon 1982 • $103 Ⓐ • (10/15/88) • **93**
Brut Champagne Cuvée Dom Pérignon 1980 • $76 Ⓐ • (09/15/86) SS • **94**
Brut Champagne Cuvée Dom Pérignon 1978 • $195 • (05/16/86) • **88**
Brut Champagne Cuvée Dom Pérignon 1976 • $150 • (10/15/95) • **87**
Brut Champagne Cuvée Dom Pérignon 1973 • $175 • (10/15/95) • **90**
Brut Champagne Cuvée Dom Pérignon 1969 • $225 • (10/15/95) • **89**
Brut Champagne Cuvée Dom Pérignon 1966 • $250 • (10/15/95) • **85**
Brut Champagne Cuvée Dom Pérignon 1962 • $200 • (10/15/95) • **79**
Brut Champagne Cuvée Dom Pérignon 1959 • $300 • (10/15/95) • **84**
Brut Champagne Impérial 1990: Complex and interesting aroma, very firm, crisp, almost austere in flavor, but showing a restrained fruitiness that's attractive. Toasty, smoky, spicy aromas and lemon and grapefruit flavors are its hallmarks. • $48 • (11/30/95) • **89**
Brut Champagne Impérial 1988: So slick and clean. The best standard vintage Moet we have had in years. A solid wine. This wine perfectly marries the ripe fruit and toasty character. Full bodied and refined with a long silky texture. A perfect Champagne for drinking now but will age for years to come. • $35 • (12/31/93) SS • **91**

Key: SS—Spectator Selection. CS—Cellar Selection. BB—Best Buy. $NA—Price not available. (BT)—Barrel tasting. Ⓐ—Auction Price.
Dates in parentheses represent the issues in which the ratings were published.

Brut Champagne Impérial 1986: Earthy, grassy aromas and flavors lack depth, but the structure is crisp and refreshing. Drinkable now. • $40 • (03/31/92) • **77**
Brut Champagne Impérial 1985 • $57 • (12/31/90) • **87**
Brut Champagne Impérial 1983 • $42 • (12/31/89) • **69**
Brut Champagne Impérial 1982 • $52 • (04/15/88) • **84**
Brut Champagne Impérial 1980 • $58 • (03/16/85) • **91**
Brut Champagne Impérial NV: Rich and inviting, smooth and creamy, with toasty aromas, full fruit flavors and a hint of honey. Apple, melon and caramel flavors come to mind. Full-blown and ready to drink. • $32 • (12/31/94) • **88**
Brut Rosé Champagne Cuvée Dom Pérignon 1982: A beautifully mature, mellow Champagne that has lots to offer the serious connoisseur. Almost Burgundian in flavor, with mushroom, spice and almond accents to the core of honey and cherry. The flavors linger and blend on the finish. • $130 • (12/31/94) • **92**
Brut Rosé Champagne Cuvée Dom Pérignon 1978 • $89 • (10/15/86) • **90**
Brut Rosé Champagne Cuvée Dom Pérignon 1975 • $310 • (12/16/85) • **93**
Brut Rosé Champagne Impérial 1990: The copper color, nutty aromas and vanilla and earthy flavors suggest an older wine. Not much fruit or depth here. • $47 • (12/15/95) • **82**
Brut Rosé Champagne Impérial 1988: Pale salmon in color and soft and fleshy in texture, with smoke and spicy cherry flavors that turn mature on the finish. Balanced and easy to drink for those who like dry, mature rosés. Drink now. Tasted twice. • $34 • (06/15/93) • **85**
Brut Rosé Champagne Impérial 1986 • $43 • (03/31/92) • **83**
Brut Rosé Champagne Impérial 1983 • $40 • (12/31/89) • **88**
Brut Rosé Champagne Impérial 1982 • $36 • (04/15/88) • **90**
Brut Rosé Champagne Impérial 1978 • $55 • (12/16/85) • **70**
Demi-Sec Champagne NV: Honey, apple and melon flavors are generous and clean in this slightly sweet sparkler. Though not complex or deep, it makes a pleasant quaff. • $36 • (12/15/95) • **84**
Extra Dry Champagne White Star NV: Tastes like a late-harvest wine, with somewhat sweet flavors of pear, honey and nuts. Tends toward heaviness in balance, but it's soft, creamy-textured and good. • $36 • **83**

MOILLARD

Aloxe-Corton Les Affouages 1989 • $NA • (01/31/92) • **83**
Bâtard-Montrachet 1994: Deliciously rich and concentrated, intensely spicy, boasting loads of clove and nutmeg notes supported by ripe apple and pear flavors. It has a lingering finish of vanilla and butterscotch. 118 cases made. • $85 • (05/31/96) • **90**
Beaune 1990: Ripe and firm, showing plum and red berry flavors and a good backbone, but lacking a bit of flesh despite the mouth-coating tannins that strike on the finish. Drinkable now. 1,100 cases made. • $26 • (12/15/92) • **87**
Beaune 1983 • $10 • (10/16/85) • **68**
Beaune Les Grèves Domaine Thomas-Moillard 1990: Impressive concentration and length make this a wine that stays with you for a long time. Tastes like freshly sliced plums, with intense flavors, firm tannins and a very long finish. Drinkable now. 400 cases made. • $40 • (12/15/92) • **91**
Beaune Les Grèves Domaine Thomas-Moillard 1989 • $28 • (01/31/92) • **89**
Beaune Les Grèves Domaine Thomas-Moillard 1986 • $14 • (12/31/88) • **80**
Beaune Les Grèves Domaine Thomas-Moillard 1985 • $25 • (03/15/87) • **89**
Beaune Les Grèves Domaine Thomas-Moillard 1984 • $12 • (02/15/87) • **87**
Beaune Hospices de Beaune Cuvée Clos des Avaux 1988 • $80 • (08/31/91) • **88**
Bonnes Mares Domaine Thomas-Moillard 1986 • $45 • (11/15/88) • **86**
Bonnes Mares Domaine Thomas-Moillard 1984 • $35 • (05/31/87) • **92**
Bourgogne Hautes Côtes de Beaune Les Alouettes 1990: Very light and simple, with pleasant earth and cherry flavors and light tannins on the rather short finish. Drinkable now. 450 cases made. • $16 • (12/15/92) • **79**
Bourgogne Hautes Côtes de Beaune Les Alouettes 1989 • $17 • (01/31/92) • **83**
Bourgogne Hautes Côtes de Beaune Les Alouettes 1988 • $15 • (07/15/91) • **83**
Bourgogne Hautes Côtes de Nuits Les Hameaux 1986 • $11 • (12/31/88) • **81**
Bourgogne Hautes Côtes de Nuits Les Vignes Hautes 1989 • $NA • (01/31/92) • **84**
Bourgogne Passe-tout-grains Notre Dame des Ceps 1990: Light and simple, with modest cherry and tobacco aromas and flavors, hinting at stemminess on the finish. • $9 • (08/31/91) • **75**
Brouilly Château Belliard 1990 • $13 • (09/15/91) • **82**
Chablis Communaux d'Aronce 1994: Clever winemaking: soft and skillfully laced with wood to give harmony and balance. Offers notes of apple and dried herb, plus a vanilla, butterscotch and honey component. Enjoy this now. A pleasant surprise from this négociant. Tasted three times, with consistent notes. • $22 • (05/31/96) • **85**
Chablis Communaux d'Aronce 1992 • $25 • (11/15/93) • **82**
Chambertin 1984 • $42 • (05/31/87) • **76**
Chambertin Clos de Bèze 1984 • $42 • (05/31/87) • **80**
Chambertin Clos de Bèze 1983 • $60 • (09/16/85) CS • **93**
Chambolle-Musigny 1984 • $15 • (11/30/86) • **89**
Chardonnay Bourgogne Hautes-Côtes de Beaune Les Alouettes 1994: Crisp, featuring some nice honey and spice flavors, good richness and a straightforward finish. 3,000 cases made. • $15 • (05/31/96) • **82**
Chardonnay Bourgogne Tradition 1994: Simple, smelling and tasting of apple juice, adding a slightly bitter finish. 3,800 cases made. • $12 • (05/31/96) • **78**
Charmes-Chambertin 1990: Ripe and chewy, with an earthy streak running through the plum and berry flavors, which echo on the finish. Drinkable now. • $35 • (12/31/93) • **84**
Charmes-Chambertin 1985 • $55 • (05/31/88) • **94**
Chassagne-Montrachet Morgeot 1985 • $15 • (05/31/87) • **84**
Châteauneuf-du-Pape Jean et Jean-Paul Versino 1987 • $15 • **63**
Chiroubles 1990 • $13 • (09/15/91) • **84**
Clos de Vougeot 1984 • $32 • (05/31/87) • **90**
Clos de Vougeot 1983 • $45 • (10/16/85) CS • **95**
Corton-Charlemagne 1991 • $60 • (10/15/93) • **80**
Corton Clos des Vergennes 1990: Supple and rich, with round, ripe red berry, chocolate and earth characteristics. Drinkable now to 1998. 500 cases made. • $53 • (12/15/92) • **89**
Corton Clos des Vergennes 1989 • $40 • (01/31/92) • **89**
Corton Clos des Vergennes 1985 • $36 • (05/31/87) • **92**
Corton Clos des Vergennes 1983 • $19 • (10/01/85) • **88**
Corton Le Clos du Roi Domaine Thomas-Moillard 1989 • $41 • (01/31/92) • **85**
Corton Le Clos du Roi Domaine Thomas-Moillard 1984 • $24 • (05/31/87) • **87**
Côtes du Rhône Les Violettes 1991 • $7 • (08/31/92) BB • **81**
Côtes du Rhône Les Violettes 1990 • $7 • (10/15/91) BB • **82**
Côtes du Rhône Les Violettes 1989 • $7.50 • (05/31/91) BB • **85**
Côtes du Rhône Les Violettes 1988 • $6 • (08/31/89) BB • **84**
Côtes du Rhône Les Violettes 1985 • $4.50 • (11/15/86) BB • **85**
Côtes du Rhône Les Violettes White 1992 • $8 • (07/31/93) • **82**
Echézeaux 1990: Tough and tannic, a very ripe wine that gets soft in the middle and never quite allows its flavors to open up. Finishes with a bite of prune and smoke. Drinkable now. • $45 • (12/31/93) • **81**
Echézeaux 1985 • $47 • (04/15/88) • **94**
Echézeaux 1984 • $30 • (11/15/86) SS • **96**
Fixin 1989 • $NA • (01/31/92) • **88**
Fixin Clos d'Entre Deux Velles 1989 • $28 • (01/31/92) • **86**
Fixin Clos d'Entre Deux Velles 1985 • $16 • (05/31/87) • **79**
Fixin Clos d'Entre Deux Velles 1984 • $11 • (11/30/86) • **78**
Fixin Clos de la Perrière 1990: A lively wine, with focused fruit flavors, well-integrated tannins and plenty of attractive berry, earth and spice nuances. Drinkable now. 900 cases made. • $30 • (12/15/92) • **85**
Fixin Clos de la Perrière 1986 • $18 • (02/28/89) • **85**
Fixin Clos de la Perrière 1983 • $12 • (10/16/85) • **78**
Fixin Confrérie des Chevaliers du Tastevin 1988 • $19 • (08/31/91) • **84**
Fleurie Château du Vivier 1990 • $17 • (09/15/91) • **91**
Fleurie Grumage 1985 • $8 • (12/15/86) • **81**

Gevrey-Chambertin 1990: Pleasant and smooth, with a pretty berry and milk chocolate component. Medium-bodied and rather soft. Try now. 4,125 cases made. • $33 • (12/15/92) • **85**
Gevrey-Chambertin 1987 • $20 • (03/31/90) • **66**
Grands Echézeaux 1984 • $39 • (05/31/87) • **90**
Hautes Côtes de Nuits 1983 • $6 • (11/01/85) • **76**
Juliénas Bois de la Salle 1990 • $13 • (09/15/91) • **81**
Ladoix Côte de Beaune 1989 • $NA • (01/31/92) • **85**
Meursault 1994: Powerful, tightly wound, featuring exotic flavors of mineral and orange peel, pear and apple. The finish is fairly restrained. 1,500 cases made. • $29 • (04/30/96) • **85**
Meursault Les Charmes 1994: Rich and aromatic, boasting good length and body. Ripe pear and apple flavors are highlighted by buttery and spicy notes. It has a firm backbone of acidity and the butterscotch lingers on the finish. 52 cases made. • $37 • (04/30/96) • **89**
Meursault Les Charmes 1991 • $45 • (10/15/93) • **83**
Meursault Clos du Cromin 1994: An overripe style, as honey and spice notes wrap around a decent core of apple and pear flavors. Finishes on a sharp, cheesy note. 545 cases made. • $28 • (05/31/96) • **82**
Morey-St.-Denis Monts Luisants 1991: Lean, austere, almost stemmy in flavor, with just enough spicy, earthy fruit-tinged flavor to make it drinkable. Drinkable now. 900 cases made. • $30 • (03/15/94) • **76**
Morey-St.-Denis Monts Luisants 1990: Racy and lively, with focused vanilla, tobacco and berry notes that offer plenty of concentration. Has nice intensity on the firm finish. Drinkable in 1997. 500 cases made. • $33 • (12/15/92) • **90**
Morey-St.-Denis Monts Luisants 1989 • $28 • (01/31/92) • **89**
Morey-St.-Denis Monts Luisants 1988 • $30 • (12/15/90) • **91**
Morey-St.-Denis Monts Luisants 1985 • $21 • (05/31/87) • **87**
Morgon Domaine du Crêt de Ruyère 1990 • $13 • (09/15/91) • **86**
Moulin-à-Vent Château du Vivier 1990 • $16 • (09/30/91) • **82**
Musigny 1984 • $38 • (05/31/87) • **92**
Nuits-St.-Georges Clos de Thorey Domaine Thomas-Moillard 1991: Dull and flat; the earthy flavors fall short of full maturity. Finish is diluted. 1,900 cases made • $40 • (01/31/94) • **77**
Nuits-St.-Georges Clos de Thorey Domaine Thomas-Moillard 1990: Rather austere and aggressive in an old style. Harsh and slightly acidic, with drying tannins on the finish. Try now. 2,150 cases made. • $50 • (12/15/92) • **79**
Nuits-St.-Georges Clos de Thorey Domaine Thomas-Moillard 1989 • $35 • (01/31/92) • **89**
Nuits-St.-Georges Clos de Thorey Domaine Thomas-Moillard 1988 • $50 • (12/31/90) • **89**
Nuits-St.-Georges Clos de Thorey Domaine Thomas-Moillard 1987 • $27 • (12/15/89) • **88**
Nuits-St.-Georges Clos de Thorey Domaine Thomas-Moillard 1986 • $28 • (11/15/88) • **78**
Nuits-St.-Georges Clos de Thorey Domaine Thomas-Moillard 1985 • $38 • (05/31/87) • **89**
Nuits-St.-Georges Clos de Thorey Domaine Thomas-Moillard 1984 • $24 • (05/31/87) • **84**
Nuits-St.-Georges Clos de Thorey Domaine Thomas-Moillard 1983 • $19 • (09/16/85) • **84**
Nuits-St.-Georges Hospices de Nuits Cuvée Jacques Duret 1988 • $68 • (08/31/91) • **89**
Pinot Noir Bourgogne 1985 • $7 • (03/31/88) • **78**
Pinot Noir Vin de Pays d'Oc Hugues le Juste 1994: Hearty dried plum and cherry flavors. A bit thin in the middle and tannic on the finish. 1,400 cases made. • $9 • (05/15/96) • **77**
Pommard Clos des Epeneaux 1985 • $45 • (06/30/88) CS • **92**
Pommard Rugiens 1990: An attractive and elegant wine that lacks the concentration of many Pommards, yet it's delicious, with raspberry and smoke aromas and flavors. Can be drunk earlier than many from this vintage, drinkable now. 200 cases made. • $50 • (12/15/92) • **86**
Pommard Rugiens 1985 • $40 • (06/30/88) • **85**

Key: SS—Spectator Selection. CS—Cellar Selection. BB—Best Buy. $NA—Price not available. (BT)—Barrel tasting. Ⓐ—Auction Price.
Dates in parentheses represent the issues in which the ratings were published.

Pouilly-Fuissé Domaine Greffet 1994: Well-balanced grapefruit and licorice flavors characterize this fairly rich white that finishes with a touch of honey. 1,720 cases made. • $22 • (05/31/96) • **84**
Puligny-Montrachet 1994: Buttery and full-bodied, offering spicy flavors and aromas. Lots of ripe pear, apple and honey notes lead to a finish of butterscotch and vanilla that is not overpowering. 860 cases made. • $30 • (05/31/96) • **86**
Puligny-Montrachet Les Perrières 1994: Bright pear and apple flavors are framed by some nice, toasty notes. Restrained, but still packs plenty of punch. The crisp finish should prove a good match for a cream sauce. 139 cases made. • $39 • (05/31/96) • **87**
Régnié Domaine de Reyssiers 1990 • $12 • (09/30/91) • **66**
Romanée-St.-Vivant 1984 • $42 • (05/31/87) • **87**
Rully 1989 • $14 • (08/31/91) • **82**
Savigny-lès-Beaune Domaine Thomas-Moillard 1990: Very perfumed, with lovely berry nuances. Almost sweet on the palate, adding a ripe, firm, supple finish. Drinkable now. 450 cases made. • $20 • (12/15/92) • **88**
St.-Amour Domaine des Pins 1990 • $16 • (09/15/91) • **86**
St.-Joseph 1988 • $15 • (08/31/91) • **85**
St.-Véran Domaine de la Verchère 1994: Stylistically akin to American Chardonnay in its ripe apple and pear flavors. This white has a nice, honeyed quality that runs throughout, but could be richer and more concentrated. 1,910 cases made. • $12 • (05/31/96) • **82**
Syrah Vin de Pays d'Oc Hugues le Juste 1994: Youthful and basic grapey and berry flavors and aromas. Lingering finish. 22,000 cases made. • $7 • (05/15/96) • **79**
Vacqueyras 1989 • $9 • (10/15/91) • **77**
Volnay Clos des Chênes 1985 • $32 • (07/15/88) • **89**
Volnay Clos des Chênes 1983 • $15 • (12/01/85) • **75**
Vosne-Romanée Malconsorts Domaine Thomas-Moillard 1989 • $60 • (01/31/92) • **93**
Vosne-Romanée Malconsorts Domaine Thomas-Moillard 1988 • $50 • (03/31/91) • **88**
Vosne-Romanée Malconsorts Domaine Thomas-Moillard 1987 • $30 • (08/31/89) • **91**
Vosne-Romanée Malconsorts Domaine Thomas-Moillard 1986 • $29 • (10/31/88) • **88**
Vosne-Romanée Malconsorts Domaine Thomas-Moillard 1985 • $47 • (07/31/88) • **95**
Vosne-Romanée Malconsorts Domaine Thomas-Moillard 1984 • $28 • (05/31/87) • **80**

MOINGEON

Savigny-lès-Beaune 1992: Light and crisp, a simple red with distinct floral overtones to the light strawberry flavors. • $NA • **80**
Vosne-Romanée Suchots 1992: A little earthy or gamy around the edges, but the forceful berry flavors finish with some grace. • $NA • **80**
Vougeot Les Cras 1992: Simple and light, with modest currant and cherry flavors. A bit short on the finish. Drinkable now. • $NA • **77**

MOMMESSIN

Aloxe-Corton 1991 • $16 Ⓐ • (01/31/94) • **80**
Aloxe-Corton 1990 • $20 • (12/15/92) • **91**
Aloxe-Corton Les Valozières 1989 • $28 • (01/31/92) • **88**
Auxey-Duresses Red 1989 • $13 • (01/31/92) • **82**
Beaujolais-Villages 1994: A good, well-rounded wine, though a bit tannic on the finish. It offers moderate fruit flavors of strawberry and red plum. 15,000 cases made. • $8 • (06/15/95) • **83**
Beaujolais-Villages 1992: Silky and straightforward, revealing cherry, brown sugar and light cola flavors. Still hanging in there, but time to drink it. • $7 • **79**
Beaujolais-Villages Château de Montmelas 1988 • $9 • (05/31/89) • **78**
Beaujolais-Villages Château du Carra 1994: Fruity and youthful, with a dollop of tannin and spice. Strawberry and banana flavors put their stamp on this medium-bodied wine. 6,000 cases made. • $8 • (06/15/95) • **83**
Beaune 1993: Clean and well-defined red berry, floral, plummy character. Solid and perhaps a bit dry on the finish, but the tannins should soften with time. Try after 1998. 683 cases made. • $23 • **85**

Beaune 1989 • $18 • (01/31/92) • **90**

Beaune Les Cent-Vignes 1993: Well-crafted red showing a charming use of new wood, medium body and tannins and ripe fruit. Delicious now, but better in 1999. 316 cases made. • $30 • **89**

Beaune Les Cent-Vignes 1992: Tannins are somewhat coarse but the black cherry flavor tastes ripe. Toasty, anise-like overtones add a nice touch. Drinkable now. 625 cases made. • $26 • **83**

Beaune Les Cent-Vignes 1990: Wonderfully balanced, refined and smooth, with gorgeous plum and earth aromas and flavors and firm, supple tannins. Drinkable now. • $20 • (12/15/92) • **90**

Beaune Les Cent-Vignes 1989 • $23 • (01/31/92) • **86**

Bonnes Mares 1993: Well-defined cherry, vanilla and tobacco flavors and a hint of tea leaf. Medium-bodied, adding velvety tannins and long, sweet fruit finish. Drink in 1999. • $80 • **89**

Brouilly 1995: Sweet cherry and dried cherry flavors give this light, firm wine a slightly candied character, but vibrant acidity keeps it fresh. The tannins are a bit dry on the finish. • $14 • **82**

Brouilly 1994: Clean and fruity, this offers bright simple flavors of cherry, banana and hard candy. It's friendly, but not complex. 5,000 cases made. • $10 • (06/15/95) • **82**

Brouilly Château de Briante 1995: A light wine with an earthy edge to the simple cherry fruit, with drying tannins that emerge on the finish. Shows personality in a rustic style. • $14 • **81**

Brouilly Château de Briante 1994: A soft, spicy wine with ripe berry and cinnamon flavors. It's appealing, but could use more concentration. 8,000 cases made. • $11 • (06/15/95) • **82**

Brouilly Château de Briante 1988 • $12 • (05/31/89) • **81**

Cabernet Sauvignon Vin de Pays d'Oc 1993: Black cherry, herbal and smoky aromas lead to a light, smooth, well-integrated palate. This doesn't show much fruit, but it's balanced and drinking well now. 11,000 cases made. • $6 • (10/31/95) • **82**

Chablis 1994: Crisp, even green, this straightforward, almost neutral wine lacks fruit flavor, finishing with a hard, mineral note. • $NA • **73**

Chablis Fourchaumes 1994: A supple, honeyed, easy-to-drink '94. Lacks a strong backbone, but smooth enough to enjoy now. • $24 • (05/31/96) • **82**

Chambolle-Musigny 1992: Supple and accessible, with some modest red berry flavors, but watery and dry on the finish. Try now. 667 cases made. • $32 • **77**

Chambolle-Musigny 1990: Pleasant but slightly one-dimensional, with lots of pretty raspberry, plum and earth aromas and flavors. Drinkable now. • $22 • (12/15/92) • **86**

Chambolle-Musigny Premier Cru 1993: Beautiful plum, dried cherry and mineral character, medium to full body, silky tannins and fresh, fruity finish. Better in 2000. • $45 • **88**

Chardonnay Vin de Pays d'Oc 1994: Crisp apple and light vanilla flavors keep this on the straight and narrow. Not much complexity, but will make a discreet partner with food. 16,000 cases made. • $6 • (12/15/95) • **84**

Charmes-Chambertin 1993: Light perhaps for a *grand cru*, but some very firm tannins and mineral, dried cherry character run through and through. Medium-bodied. Try in 1999. • $68 • **85**

Charmes-Chambertin 1992: Lean, crisp and chewy, but there's a nice core of raspberry and floral character that persists into the modest finish. Try in 1997. • $NA • **82**

Charmes-Chambertin 1990: Overflowing with raspberry, strawberry and other fruit flavors and has all the tannins you expect with such great concentration. Built to age, try in 1999. • $45 • (12/15/92) • **96**

Charmes-Chambertin 1985 • $45 • (02/15/88) • **83**

Chassagne-Montrachet 1993: Lovely, balanced apple, toasted oak and mineral aromas and flavors. Medium-to-full-bodied, fresh acidity and medium finish. 550 cases made. • $24 • **85**

Chassagne-Montrachet 1992: A toasty, buttery aroma, backed by crisp, reasonably appley flavors adds up to a complete, satisfying white. The flavors linger nicely on the finish, too. 500 cases made. • $26 • (08/31/94) • **84**

Chassagne-Montrachet Morgeot 1993: Elegant apple, coconut and pear aromas and flavors. Medium in body, fine acidity and fresh finish. 250 cases made. • $25 • **85**

Châteauneuf-du-Pape Clos des Brusquières 1993: Good, but on the lean side, featuring smoky aromas, tart cherry flavors and a slightly unripe sensation on the finish. Moderately tannic. • $17 • **80**

Chiroubles Château de Raousset 1988 • $12 • (05/31/89) • **83**

Clos de Tart 1993: Distinctively smoky and toasty, sporting lovely, silky texture and nice wood. The finish is a bit diluted and alcoholic. Could use more fruit concentration. Try in 1999. • $86 • **84**

Clos de Tart 1992: Lean and spicy, delicate, exhibiting cedar and vanilla grace notes to the basic currant flavor, finishes with a sweet edge. May be best from 1997. • $99 • **85**

Clos de Tart 1991: Strikingly earthy and spicy on the nose, picking up black cherry and currant on the palate. The tannins give a drying walnut character on the finish. A tough wine that needs until 1998 to emerge. 700 cases made. • $73 Ⓐ • (01/31/94) • **87**

Clos de Tart 1990: Unique, fascinating and well structured, offering crushed black pepper aromas and flavors that run like a thread through the bright berry and smoke characteristics. A beauty of a wine that should hit its stride around 1997. • $96 • (12/15/92) • **95**

Clos de Tart 1989 • $52 • (01/31/92) • **92**

Clos de Tart 1985 • $77 Ⓐ • (02/15/88) • **91**

Clos de Tart 1950 • $125 • (08/31/90) • **78**

Corton-Charlemagne 1992: Dense, round and ripe, with pronounced tropical and honeyed flavors coating your mouth, it gains complexity with lush, sweet fruit and some mineral, apple and citrus notes. Drinks almost like a dry dessert wine. • $70 • (08/31/94) • **89**

Corton Les Grèves 1989 • $45 • (01/31/92) • **91**

Côte de Beaune-Villages 1985 • $13 • (02/15/88) • **85**

Côte de Nuits-Villages 1985 • $17 • (07/31/88) • **85**

Côtes du Rhône 1986 • $4 • (04/30/88) BB • **82**

Côtes du Rhône Château de Domazan 1993: An awkward wine that starts out soft and fruity, but then tightens up. Raspberry and plum are the dominant flavors. • $7 • **78**

Côtes du Ventoux 1993: A wine with some character that's dominated by leather, plum and berry flavors and a touch of spice. Altogether, nicely balanced and fairly mature. Drink now. • $6 • **84**

Crozes-Hermitage 1992: Supple, with herbal and vegetal aromas and flavors and light cherry fruit, this is balanced and drinkable but doesn't show much depth. • $11 • **79**

Echézeaux 1979 • $18 • (02/16/86) • **86**

Fixin 1989 • $15 • (01/31/92) • **87**

Fleurie 1995: Black cherry and spicy flavors are appealing, but the wine is a bit light for Fleurie, and finishes tannic and dry. May soften by late 1996. • $16 • **82**

Fleurie 1994: Elegant and seductive, this is ripe, supple and pretty. The flavors range from floral to cinnamon to black cherry, harmonious and delicate. This isn't big, but it's attractive. 5,000 cases made. • $12 • (06/15/95) • **87**

Fleurie 1992: Maturing nicely, this shows tobacco, dried cherry and spice flavors and firm structure. No longer the grapey stereotype of Beaujolais, still fresh but has gained complexity. 5,000 cases made. • $12 • **85**

Fleurie 1988 • $14 • (05/31/89) • **87**

Fleurie Clos de la Roilette 1995: A chunky wine with firm tannins, this red shows more gamy and earthy flavors than fruit, and finishes a bit dry. Might soften with food. • $16 • **81**

Fleurie Clos de la Roilette 1994: Fresh and lively, this offers cherry, light spice and herbal flavors. It has a firm backbone, but could use more flesh. 1,500 cases made. • $12 • (06/15/95) • **84**

Gevrey-Chambertin 1991: Light-textured, with gamy currant aromas and somewhat watery flavors. Drinkable now. 500 cases made. • $22 Ⓐ • (01/31/94) • **78**

Gevrey-Chambertin 1985 • $25 • (02/15/88) • **90**

Gevrey-Chambertin Lavaux St.-Jacques 1990: Rather complex, with fresh mushroom, vanilla and berry flavors that are tightly wrapped around firm tannins now, but it should grow into a subtle, velvety wine with age. Try in 1997. • $45 • (12/15/92) • **90**

Gevrey-Chambertin Lavaux St.-Jacques 1989 • $45 • (01/31/92) • **85**

Gevrey-Chambertin Premier Cru 1993: An attractive core of raspberry and cherry notes. Fresh and relatively light, it offers nice pleasure now. • $45 • **83**

Gevrey-Chambertin Premier Cru 1992: Lean and chewy, a strong anise component running through the modest currant flavors. Drinkable now. 792 cases made. • $42 • **81**

MOMMESSIN

Gigondas 1993: Combines intense, lively fruit flavors and firm tannins. Peppery nuances furnish complexity and the finish is lingering. Tempting to drink now, but should improve through 1997. • $14 • **87**

Juliénas Domaine de la Conseillere 1988 • $11 • (05/31/89) • **81**

Mâcon-Villages 1994: Simple and coarse, a rustic white that gives more pain than pleasure. What happened? 12,500 cases made. • $11 • (05/31/96) • **70**

Maranges 1989 • $13 • (01/31/92) • **87**

Merlot Vin de Pays d'Oc 1993: Soft, round, typical black cherry and light herbal flavors, reminiscent of a Bordeaux petit château in character. It's drinking well now. 19,000 cases made. • $6 • (10/31/95) • **83**

Meursault 1993: Lovely pineapple and coconut aromas and flavors, medium-to-full body, fine acidity and fresh finish. Delicious. 850 cases made. • $24 • **85**

Meursault 1992: Quite ripe and rich, with fruit all over the place, and a round texture packed with grapefruit, lemon, pineapple and butter-toast flavors. Delivers character, if not much finesse. • $25 • (08/31/94) • **88**

Meursault Les Charmes 1992: Broad, ripe and quite aromatic, this gold-colored wine shows some floral, honey and pear flavors that are appealingly rich but seems to peter out a bit on the finish. Given the good acidity, it may improve with age. Try now. 208 cases made. • $34 • (08/31/94) • **87**

Meursault Les Criots 1993: Wonderful tropical fruit and toasted oak character, medium-to-full body, fresh acidity and long, flavorful finish. 200 cases made. • $25 • **88**

Meursault Premier Cru 1993: Open and rich but also a bit heavy-handed, showing ripe melon, pear, green apple, mineral, and wet earth flavors. Harmonious on the finish. Drinkable now. 300 cases made. • $40 • **85**

Morey-St.-Denis La Forge 1993: Light and a bit diluted, featuring modest red berry, tobacco and earth flavors and short finish. Drink now. • $57 • **81**

Morgon 1994: Intense, ripe black cherry and cassis flavors enliven this lean, but still firm, Morgon. Drinkable now. 4,000 cases made. • $10 • **84**

Morgon 1988 • $10 • (05/31/89) • **86**

Morgon Domaine de Lathevalle 1994: Ripe and polished, very round cassis and coffee flavors. Tannins show extraction and depth-rich and earthy. Drinkable now. 5,000 cases made. • $10 • **88**

Moulin-à-Vent 1994: Fruity and supple yet intense, showing almost jammy blackberry and black cherry flavors. It's spicy and lean for a Moulin-à-Vent, but still attractive. 4,000 cases made. • $12 • **85**

Moulin-à-Vent 1992: A year in bottle has improved this. Still firm, fresh and fruity, boasting velvety plum and berry flavors supported by toasty oak, lingering finish. Drinkable now. 4,000 cases made. • $11 • **88**

Moulin-à-Vent Domaine de Champ de Cour 1994: Rich plum and cassis flavors, coffee and toast accents from new oak, plenty of tannin, deep color. Concentrated yet vibrant. Try now. 4,000 cases made. • $12 • **89**

Moulin-à-Vent Domaine de Champ de Cour 1988 • $13 • (05/31/89) • **91**

Nuits-St.-Georges Aux Chaignots 1993: Pretty rose petal, raspberry and currant notes. Medium-bodied, well crafted, adding a sweet-tasting, delicious finish. Almost ready upon release, but try in 1997. • $57 • **87**

Nuits-St.-Georges Aux Chaignots 1992: Lean and firm, with a nice thread of currant and vanilla flavors weaving through the fine tannins. Drink now or hold. 400 cases made. • $45 • **82**

Nuits-St.-Georges Aux Chaignots 1990: Rich as olive oil, with beautiful fruit. This viscous red has loads of raspberry and cedar characteristics and fine, silky tannins. Drinkable now to 1998. • $29 • (12/15/92) • **90**

Nuits-St.-Georges Les Vaucrains 1989 • $45 • (01/31/92) • **90**

Nuits-St.-Georges Premier Cru 1991: Firm, tannic and aromatic, offering peppery, spicy currant and chocolate flavors that sneak in at a modest level. Drinkable now. 150 cases made. • $28 Ⓐ • (01/31/94) • **83**

Pinot Noir Bourgogne 1983 • $5 • (02/16/86) • **61**

Pommard 1993: Relatively soft and accessible Pommard, showing a sweet- and ripe-tasting character. Clean and pure Pinot Noir flavors on the medium-long finish. 1,083 cases made. • $35 • **84**

Pommard 1989 • $28 • (01/31/92) • **88**

Key: SS—Spectator Selection. CS—Cellar Selection. BB—Best Buy. $NA—Price not available. (BT)—Barrel tasting. Ⓐ—Auction Price.
Dates in parentheses represent the issues in which the ratings were published.

Pommard Premier Cru 1993: Diluted and watery with some berry character, but rather metallic and weedy. 375 cases made. • $40 • **76**

Pouilly-Fuissé 1994: Excellent effort from this négociant. Intensely citrusy, with a backdrop of mineral notes that adds nice complexity. This full-bodied Burgundy packs a wallop of pear, honey and apricot flavors. Try after 1997 when the searing intensity has subsided. 4,416 cases made. • $25 • (05/31/96) • **88**

Pouilly-Fuissé 1993: Youthful and flavorful, a light-to-medium-bodied white presenting plenty of lime, grapefruit and butter notes. Clean and crisp finish. 5,833 cases made. • $18 • **84**

Pouilly-Fuissé Château Pouilly 1993: Simple and straightforward, showing modest grapefruit and apple notes and a somewhat minerally finish. Drink now. 1,917 cases made. • $20 • **76**

Puligny-Montrachet 1993: A bit hard, but some good fruit and nut character on the nose and palate, medium in body, good acidity, nutty finish. 700 cases made. • $27 • **84**

Puligny-Montrachet 1992: A flavorful, well-made Chardonnay; delivers lovely tropical, citrus, pear and apple flavors. Tastes more like an international-style Chardonnay than distinctive Burgundy, but it makes for nice drinking all the same. Try now. 625 cases made. • $27 • (08/31/94) • **85**

Puligny-Montrachet La Garenne 1992: Austere, earthy and green-tasting, with tons of super-tart apple flavors. Sharp, but the acidity, at least, makes it fresh. 166 cases made. • $36 • (08/31/94) • **77**

Puligny-Montrachet Les Folatières 1993: Delicious apple pie and tropical fruit character. Medium-bodied, good acidity and loads of fruit on the finish. 350 cases made. • $40 • **86**

St.-Amour Domaine de Monreve 1988 • $12 • (05/31/89) • **84**

St.-Aubin 1990: A light style that's a bit harsh, with stemmy, vegetal aromas and flavors and brown sugar and cinnamon notes on the finish. Drinkable now. • $NA • (12/15/92) • **77**

St.-Véran Domaine de l'Evèque 1994: Decent and simple, with the fresh taste of lemonade. This light-bodied white makes for a quaffable drink on a hot summer day. 3,333 cases made. • $14 • (05/31/96) • **79**

Santenay Clos Rousseau 1993: Dark-colored and firm, this chewy red features cherry pit, earth and wild berry flavors. Try now. 800 cases made. • $26 • **84**

Santenay Clos Rousseau 1992: Crisp in texture and aromatic, with cherry flavor that tightens a little on the finish. Tasty now. 792 cases made. • $23 • **80**

Santenay Clos Rousseau 1990: You can taste the soil in this one, wet earth and mineral components play nicely against plum and red berry flavors. Has lovely balance and a round mouth-feel. A wine with character. • $14 • (12/15/92) • **86**

Savigny-lès-Beaune 1993: Impressive concentration yet a bit overextracted on the finish. Nice plum and red berry character, but the lean, tannic texture makes you wonder how it will age. Try in 2000. 1,160 cases made. • $21 • **87**

Savigny-lès-Beaune 1992: Lean in texture, modest in flavor, featuring more black cherry than anything else. Has a sugary edge. Drinkable now. 1,330 cases made. • $19 • **78**

Savigny-lès-Beaune 1991: Has a firm texture, herbal and floral overtones to the crisp, green plum character. Drinkable now. 500 cases made. • $16 Ⓐ • (01/31/94) • **79**

Savigny-lès-Beaune 1990: Wild and exotic, bursting at the seams with tons of round fruit flavors, loads of wild berry characteristics, hints of violets, earth and blueberries and well-integrated tannins to boot. Worth seeking out. Drinkable now. • $14 • (12/15/92) • **90**

Savigny-lès-Beaune 1985 • $17 • (07/31/88) • **80**

Syrah Vin de Pays d'Oc 1993: Soft, rather light and simple berry flavors are maturing already. A bit tough and short. 8,000 cases made. • $6 • (10/31/95) • **79**

Volnay Taillepieds 1993: Juicy cherry, mushroom and plum character, medium body and tannins and a dry finish. Delicious now, but better in 1998. 316 cases made. • $40 • **80**

Volnay Taillepieds 1992: Crisp in texture, ripe and generous, centering around smoky berry flavor and a floral note on the finish. Best after 1996. 542 cases made. • $29 • **84**

Volnay Taillepieds 1991: Ripe and focused, with a tarry, anise edge to the concentrated currant and berry aromas and flavors. Shaded on the finish by a nice hint of mint. Has character and style, drinkable now. 150 cases made. • $23 Ⓐ • (01/31/94) • **85**

Volnay Taillepieds 1990: Incredibly concentrated, with phenomenal amounts of fruit extract. Needs time to show it all, but the plum, tobacco and black cherry aromas and flavors stay with you for a long time on the firm finish. Drinkable now to 1998. • $23 • (12/15/92) • **92**

Volnay 1985 • $80 • (03/15/88) • **91**

Vosne-Romanée 1993: Attractive berry, chestnut and almond character but slightly meager in structure. Light- to medium-bodied, light tannins. Drink now. • $40 • **81**

Vosne-Romanée 1992: Light and simple, with modest strawberry and cherry aromas and flavors that offer a touch of ripe, sweet notes on the finish. 483 cases made. • $49 • **80**

Vosne-Romanée Aux Brûlées 1989 • $38 • (01/31/92) • **89**

Vosne-Romanée Les Suchots 1990: This concentrated Vosne is bursting with plum, cherry and vanilla flavors and is round and supple on the intense finish. Drinkable now. • $35 • (12/15/92) • **91**

Vosne-Romanée Premier Cru 1993: Exuberantly plummy character, medium body, fine tannins and a long, fruity finish. Try in 1999. • $46 • **87**

MONBOUSQUET, CHÂTEAU

St.-Emilion 1995: A property on the rise. This is thick and rich, with a lovely violet character and notes of berry, tar and clove. Full-bodied with good concentration, yet an underlying silkiness and elegance remains. Impressive. • $NA • (05/15/96) • **90-94** (BT)

St.-Emilion 1994: Lovely rich chocolatey berry and vanilla character, medium to full body, velvety tannins and a fruity finish. Almost outstanding. • $18 • (05/15/96) • **85-89** (BT)

St.-Emilion 1993: Caresses your palate. Impressive color, concentration and fruit, full- to medium-bodied, round tannins and a long aftertaste of toasted oak, chocolate and berries. Drinkable now, but better in 1997. • $23 • (01/31/96) • **88**

MONBRISON, CHÂTEAU

Margaux 1995: Built like a sprinter, very racy. Complex and flavorful, full-bodied, with plenty of smoky, mineral and red- and blackberry character. Firm tannins. • $NA • (05/15/96) • **85-89** (BT)

Margaux 1994: Supple and pretty. Light- to medium-bodied and one-dimensional, licorice, currant and cherry flavors. • $NA • **80-84** (BT)

Margaux 1993: A bit disappointing. Short and herbal, adding some blackberry and green bean character. Drinkable now. • $26 • (01/31/96) • **75**

Margaux 1992: Perfumed, mineral and grassy character, light-bodied and light finish. Drink now. • $21 • **77**

Margaux 1991: Simple, straightforward, with cherry flavors and aromas that have a toasted oak character, medium body. • $14 • (03/31/94) • **81**

Margaux 1990: Luscious and elegant, with a bounty of ripe blackberry, licorice and tobacco character and well-integrated tannins. One of the very best cru bourgeois. Drink after 1997. 5,500 cases made. • $22 Ⓐ • (03/31/93) • **91**

Margaux 1989 • $28 • (03/15/92) • **93**

Margaux 1988 • $16 Ⓐ • (02/28/91) • **92**

Margaux 1987 • $20 • (05/15/90) • **85**

Margaux 1986 • $23 • (11/30/89) • **92**

Margaux 1985 • $23 • (10/15/94) • **90**

Margaux 1984 • $15 • (05/15/87) • **78**

Margaux 1983 • $20 • (10/15/94) • **86**

Margaux 1982 • $22 • (11/30/89) • **90**

Margaux 1981 • $19 • (10/15/94) • **82**

MONCAUT, CHARLES

Fleurie 1984 • $6 • (12/01/85) • **74**

Nuits-St.-Georges Les Argillières 1984 • $32 • (06/15/87) • **90**

Vosne-Romanée Cuvée Particulière 1983 • $16 • (09/15/86) • **62**

MONCONTOUR, CHÂTEAU

Brut Touraine Tête de Cuvée 1993: The pleasant texture is rich and creamy, but flavors are herbal and somewhat austere. This will make a good mixer for cocktails and punches. • $13 • (06/15/96) • **77**

Brut Vouvray 1994: This crisp sparkler offers grapefruit and tart apple flavors and hints of creaminess. A simple but refreshing quaff for a summer afternoon. • $16 • (06/15/96) • **83**

Vouvray 1993: A refreshing white with pleasant apple cider aromas and applesauce flavors that are simple but appealing. Try this on a porch swing some summer day. 10,000 cases made. • $12 • (06/15/96) • **82**

MONGEARD-MUGNERET

Bourgogne 1993: Harmonious, with fruit balancing the tannins nicely. Fresh, pretty floral and cherry flavors. Try now through 1998. • $16 • **83**

Bourgogne 1992: Light and crisply tannic, only a modest level of strawberry sneaking in. 875 cases made. • $14 • **79**

Bourgogne 1989 • $9 • (01/31/92) • **85**

Bourgogne Hautes Côtes de Nuits 1993: Lots of personality here. Medium to light body, ripe, silky tannins and very good red berry, earthy concentration. Pretty finish. Try now through 1998. • $17 • **85**

Bourgogne Hautes Côtes de Nuits 1992: Crisp, light and simple, with modest strawberry flavors. 358 cases made. • $15 • **76**

Bourgogne Hautes Côtes de Nuits 1989 • $16 • (01/31/92) • **77**

Clos de Vougeot 1993: Like eating chocolate mousse. Full in body, delivering loads of velvety tannins and a long aftertaste of mocha, chocolate and fruit. Somewhat earthy, but delicious. Better after 2000. • $71 • **93**

Clos de Vougeot 1992: Light and chewy with tannin and a greenish edge to the berryish flavors. Modest, should be at its best around 1997. 308 cases made. • $61 • **80**

Clos de Vougeot 1991: Crisp, light and a bit more astringent than we'd like in such a delicate wine. Herbal, floral berry flavors extend into a long but fragile finish. Drinkable now. • $45 Ⓐ • (01/31/94) • **83**

Clos de Vougeot 1989 • $77 • (01/31/92) • **87**

Clos de Vougeot 1987 • $53 • (05/15/90) • **81**

Clos de Vougeot 1986 • $56 • (07/31/89) • **87**

Echézeaux 1993: Seductive and elegant, sporting alluring plum, raspberry and mineral aromas and flavors. Medium- to full-bodied with fine tannins and a sweet, really fine fruit finish. Try in 2000. • $50 • **91**

Echézeaux 1992: A little green around the edges, tart and astringent enough to take the charm away from the modest berry flavors. Try in 1997. 1,058 cases made. • $44 • **78**

Echézeaux 1984 • $28 • (02/15/88) • **68**

Echézeaux Vieille Vigne 1993: Amazing intensity of vivid flavors. Ripe plum, black cherry, minty taste. Of medium body, it shows finesse despite the massive, supple tannins. Long and flavorful finish. Try after 2000. • $60 • **92**

Echézeaux Vieille Vigne 1991: Ripe and gamy, has a toasty edge to the supple plum and wild berry aromas and flavors and hints at vanilla bean and coffee on the spicy finish. Smooth and round enough to be tempting now, but should be best around 1997. • $43 Ⓐ • (01/31/94) • **90**

Echézeaux Vieille Vigne 1989 • $59 • (01/31/92) • **93**

Echézeaux Vieille Vigne 1988 • $61 • (02/15/91) • **88**

Echézeaux Vieille Vigne 1987 • $42 • (05/15/90) • **86**

Echézeaux Vieille Vigne 1986 • $44 • (08/31/89) • **90**

Fixin 1992: Straightforward and tart, a bit herbal and fresh-tasting. A light-bodied Burgundy ends on a zesty raspberry note. Drinkable now. 533 cases made. • $20 • **79**

Fixin 1991: Earthy, a bit jammy and simple. The flavors are decent, but the texture is watery. Drinkable now. • $18 Ⓐ • (01/31/94) • **77**

Fixin 1990: Light in color, with weedy dill and earthy strawberry flavors that thin out on the finish. Turns barnyardy on the aftertaste. Drinkable, but there are better 1990s. 500 cases made. • $26 • (03/15/93) • **77**

Fixin 1989 • $25 • (01/31/92) • **83**

Fixin 1986 • $19 • (10/15/89) • **84**

Grands Echézeaux 1993: Not as good as its two Echézeaux, but delivers very good concentration of ripe plum and mint flavor and firm tannins. Medium in body, a bit forward. Try in 1999. • $100 • **87**

Grands Echézeaux 1992: Earth and barnyard aromas predominate in this tough-textured red, barely fruity enough to balance. Might improve by 1997. 633 cases made. • $75 • **80**

Grands Echézeaux 1991: Ripe and elegant, offering a generous array of gamy, toasty, rose petal-scented currant, black cherry and plum aromas

FRANCE

and flavors that extends into a chewy finish. Needs until 1998 or 2000 to sort out the tannins. 600 cases made. • $68 Ⓐ • (01/31/94) • **91**
Grands Echézeaux 1989 • $95 • (01/31/92) • **93**
Grands Echézeaux 1987 • $65 • (05/15/90) • **85**
Grands Echézeaux 1986 • $73 • (08/31/89) • **92**
Grands Echézeaux 1955: Delicate, lean structure and light color, with good, ripe, intense flavors. • $NA • **82**
Grands Echézeaux 1953: A fat, rich, ripe, vanilla-scented Burgundy. Smooth and round, only showing a bit less finesse than Gouges' 1953 and less fruit than d'Angerville's 1953. • $NA • **87**
Nuits-St.-Georges Aux Boudots 1989 • $49 • (01/31/92) • **84**
Nuits-St.-Georges Aux Boudots 1987 • $32 • (04/30/90) • **81**
Nuits-St.-Georges Aux Boudots 1984 • $23 • (02/15/88) • **78**
Richebourg 1993: Lush and velvety, sporting well-defined currant, plum and tobacco character and firm finish. A well-made, medium-bodied Burgundy that should last and improve until around 2000. • $110 • **88**
Richebourg 1992: Lean and earthy, a watery red showing only simple underbrush and cherry flavors that fade on the finish. Try now. 117 cases made. • $134 • **77**
Richebourg 1991: A strong, earthy anise streak runs through the berry and toast aromas and flavors in this crisp, firm, focused Burgundy. Nicer on the palate than on the nose. Drinkable now. • $117 Ⓐ • (01/31/94) • **88**
Richebourg 1989 • $95 • (01/31/92) • **92**
Richebourg 1987 • $102 • (08/10/90) • **90**
Richebourg 1985 • $123 • (03/15/88) • **92**
Savigny-lès-Beaune 1993: Better than the winery's premiers crus due to less wood in aging. Medium body, silky tannins and a long finish of sweet, ripe red berries. Drink now through 1997. • $22 • (11/15/95) • **87**
Savigny-lès-Beaune Les Narbantons 1993: Lightly smoky, a delicate style of Pinot Noir, offering some toast, leather and cherry flavors. Light- to medium-bodied, nicely balanced. Drink now through 1997. • $26 • **83**
Savigny-lès-Beaune Les Narbantons 1992: A touch of sweet, ripe fruit peeks through in this light-bodied, lively wine. A bit short on the finish. 617 cases made. • $23 • (11/15/95) • **80**
Savigny-lès-Beaune Les Narbantons 1991: Narrow and lean, but has pretty cherry and spice aromas and flavors. Finishes a touch earthy. Drinkable now to 1997. • $21 Ⓐ • (01/31/94) • **81**
Savigny-lès-Beaune Les Narbantons 1990: A good but bizarre wine that's marred by dry, bitter tannins that overshadow the modest plum and cherry flavor profile. Perhaps with time it will be more appealing. Drinkable now. 550 cases made. • $33 • (06/15/93) • **80**
Savigny-lès-Beaune Les Narbantons 1989 • $28 • (01/31/92) • **78**
Vosne-Romanée 1992: Lean and chewy, tightly tannic, with only modest currant flavors hovering in the background, features tobacco and tea on the finish. 983 cases made. • $29 • **79**
Vosne-Romanée 1991: A firm, flavorful, crisp-textured wine, with toasty berry and spice aromas and flavors that echo nicely on the finish. Drinkable now. • $26 Ⓐ • (01/31/94) • **84**
Vosne-Romanée 1989 • $34 • (01/31/92) • **85**
Vosne-Romanée 1986 • $26 • (08/31/89) • **79**
Vosne-Romanée En Orveaux 1993: Relatively light, showing some modest red berry flavor and tannin structure. Serve chilled upon release. • $40 • **82**
Vosne-Romanée En Orveaux 1992: A modest Vosne-Romanée, with some cherry and banana flavors complemented by light toasty notes. Very simple. 475 cases made. • $36 • **78**
Vosne-Romanée En Orveaux 1991: This crisp-textured wine offers a fascinating range of blackberry, leaf and lime aromas and flavors and more citrus than anything else on the finish. Smells better than it tastes. Drinkable now. • $32 Ⓐ • (01/31/94) • **82**
Vosne-Romanée En Orveaux 1989 • $43 • (01/31/92) • **94**
Vosne-Romanée En Orveaux 1987 • $35 • (07/15/90) • **62**
Vosne-Romanée En Orveaux 1986 • $34 • (08/31/89) • **82**
Vosne-Romanée En Orveaux 1985 • $32 • (03/15/88) • **82**
Vosne-Romanée En Orveaux 1984 • $18 • (02/15/88) • **68**
Vosne-Romanée Les Petits Monts 1987 • $35 • (04/30/90) • **74**
Vosne-Romanée Les Suchots 1987 • $35 • (06/15/90) • **82**
Vougeot Les Cras 1989 • $NA • (01/31/92) • **93**

MONMOUSSIN

Brut Touraine Etoile 1986 • $13 • (12/31/90) • **82**
Brut Touraine Monmousseau 1983 • $11 • (02/15/88) • **79**
Brut Vouvray Cuvée du Centenaire 1983 • $11 • (01/31/88) • **69**
Extra Dry Vouvray 1985 • $13 • (12/31/90) • **81**

MONNIER, DOMAINE RENE

Beaune Les Cent Vignes 1985 • $25 • (10/31/87) • **89**
Meursault Les Charmes 1992: A core of focused, pure fruit flavor makes this refreshing and tasty to drink. It layers subtle vanilla and honey accents on top of generous pear and pineapple for a satisfying mixture that lingers on the finish. Drinkable now through 1997. 408 cases made. • $40 • (08/31/94) • **89**
Meursault Les Chevalières 1992: Beautiful intensity in this steely, vibrant white, closed and not showing much now, with appealing mineral, lime and apple flavors. Try now. • $25 • (08/31/94) • **86**
Pommard Les Vignots 1985 • $30 • (11/15/88) • **89**
Pommard Les Vignots 1982 • $17 • (07/01/85) • **81**
Puligny-Montrachet Les Folatières 1992: Earthy, toasty aromas and tart, citrus flavors, a chewy texture and short, clean finish. Solid but nothing special. • $40 • (08/31/94) • **82**

MONPATEY, CHÂTEAU DE

Chardonnay Bourgogne Marquis d'Espés 1993: Odd, lean, extremely citrusy and high in acidity. Shows modest green apple skin and lime flavors. Drink now. From Albert Bichot. • $10 • **72**

MONPERTUIS, DOMAINE DE

Châteauneuf-du-Pape 1990: Ripe and intense, with spicy, peppery plum and black cherry-tinged flavors that turn a bit leathery on the finish. Firmly tannic, drinkable now. Tasted three times, with significant bottle variation. 2,000 cases made. • $16 • (04/15/93) • **83**
Châteauneuf-du-Pape 1987 • $14 • (06/30/90) • **83**
Châteauneuf-du-Pape 1986 • $18 • (09/30/89) • **73**

MONT BELAIR, CHÂTEAU

St.-Emilion 1989 • $12 • (11/15/91) • **81**

MONT-REDON, CHÂTEAU

Châteauneuf-du-Pape 1990: Fleshy and lively, a complex wine with a generous range of spicy, peppery overtones wrapped around solid cherry and plum flavors. A delicious wine that keeps itself in balance while showing plenty of muscle. Firm enough to wait until 1997. • $23 • (09/30/93) • **91**
Châteauneuf-du-Pape 1989 • $31 Ⓐ • (08/31/92) • **79**
Châteauneuf-du-Pape 1988 • $22 • (10/15/91) • **83**
Châteauneuf-du-Pape 1986 • $17 • (10/15/91) • **85**
Châteauneuf-du-Pape 1985 • $25 • (10/15/91) • **90**
Châteauneuf-du-Pape 1984 • $11 • (09/30/87) • **92**
Châteauneuf-du-Pape 1983 • $25 • (10/15/91) • **88**
Châteauneuf-du-Pape 1981 • $30 • (10/15/91) • **90**
Châteauneuf-du-Pape White 1993: Dry and nearly austere in flavor, yet intriguing. On the surface a bare-bones white with very little fruit, but has an appealingly crisp balance and a rich texture. • $23 • (10/15/94) • **83**
Châteauneuf-du-Pape White 1990 • $21 • (04/15/93) • **83**
Côtes du Rhône 1993: A bold wine on the rustic side that suffers from too much earthiness. The extremely dried cherry and plum flavors are appealing, but a stale quality mars this wine. • $10 • **78**
Côtes du Rhône 1992: Rich and round, fruity and full-bodied, meaty in flavor and texture. Tannic, but ready to drink now. • $9 • (10/15/94) • **85**
Côtes du Rhône 1990 • $9 • (08/31/92) • **78**

Key: SS—Spectator Selection. CS—Cellar Selection. BB—Best Buy. $NA—Price not available. (BT)—Barrel tasting. Ⓐ—Auction Price.
Dates in parentheses represent the issues in which the ratings were published.

MONT TAUCH, LES PRODUCTEURS DU

Corbières 1991 • $7 • (03/15/93) • **81**
Fitou 1990 • $8 • (04/15/93) • **74**
Fitou 1985 • $6 • (04/15/89) • **79**
Vin de Pays du Torgan Le Sanglier 1991 • $6 • (04/15/93) BB • **83**

MONT VERRIER, DOMAINE DU

Beaujolais-Villages 1988 • $10 • (05/31/89) • **76**

MONTAUDON

Brut Champagne 1988: Straightforward wine and slightly rough with loads of baked apple character and a foamy texture. Full bodied with good acidity and a fruity finish. Drink now. • $25 • (12/31/93) • **84**
Brut Champagne M NV • $25 • (12/31/91) • **90**

MONTFORT, CHÂTEAU DE

Vouvray 1994: Tart and rather earthy, not fitting Vouvray's typical profile, except for the thick texture and honeyed notes on aftertaste. It's young and perhaps will soften. • $9 • **77**

MONTHELIE-DOUHAIRET, DOMAINE

Bourgogne Aligoté 1994: Crisp and a bit green, even a bit disjointed, but it's fresh, with decent herb, citrus and green apple flavors. Should go well with oysters or grilled fish. 300 cases made. • $14 • (05/31/96) • **80**
Meursault 1994: A hard wine that doesn't show much now, but there is a chalky, chewy mineral character that signals depth and good aging potential. Could use a bit more fruit. Try in 1997. 100 cases made. • $34 • (05/31/96) • **84**
Meursault Les Cras 1992: Very thin in texture, light on flavor, leaning toward sour. Basic white wine that could be from almost anywhere. • $37 • (11/15/94) • **74**
Meursault Les Santenots 1994: Shows some personality. A bit coarse, but it delivers decent tropical fruit, apple and pear flavors. 175 cases made. • $34 • (05/31/96) • **82**
Monthelie 1994: Quite round but straightforward, with some caramel, butter and pear flavors. Harmonious and crisp on the delicate finish. 125 cases made. • $20 • (05/31/96) • **83**
Monthelie 1985 • $16 • (06/30/88) • **81**
Monthelie Clos le Meix Garnier 1992: Tough and awkward, starting out nice with cherry and strawberry aromas, but tannic and rather bitter on the finish, with tobacco and smoke flavors. • $23 • (10/31/94) • **76**
Monthelie Les Duresses 1994: Subtle and balanced, showing some chalky lime, mineral and honey flavors, but a hint of a green, herbal character detracts from it. We wish for more harmony and length on the finish. Perhaps better in 1997. 125 cases made. • $31 • (05/31/96) • **84**
Monthelie Les Duresses Premier Cru 1992: An exotic flavor of anise accents the modest pear and apple notes in this smooth-textured, nicely balanced white Burgundy. Complete and harmonious. • $34 • (11/15/94) • **84**
Volnay En Champans 1993: Full-blown currant juice, a reduction of fruit. Wonderfully concentrated layers of raspberry character. Full-bodied with velvety tannins, sweet fruit and very long finish. Try in 2000. • $44 • **93**
Volnay En Champans Premier Cru 1992: Crisp, tart and fruity, with cherry and cranberry flavors, firm tannins and a dry finish. A sturdy, well-structured wine to drink now through 1997. • $38 • (10/31/94) • **82**
Volnay En Champans 1985 • $25 • (07/15/88) • **87**

MONTMIRAIL, CHÂTEAU DE

Côtes du Rhône 1991 • $9 • (06/15/93) • **78**
Gigondas Cuvée de Beauchamp 1990 • $13 • (04/15/93) • **75**
Gigondas Cuvée de Beauchamp 1985 • $14 • (09/30/88) • **78**
Gigondas Cuvée de Beauchamp 1983 • $11 • (11/30/86) • **90**
Vacqueyras Cuvée de L'Ermite Red 1990 • $11 • (04/15/93) • **82**

MONTPATEY, CHÂTEAU DE

Chardonnay Bourgogne 1994: More water than wine. Diluted and thin, tasting a bit of cardboard. From Albert Bichot. 1,667 cases made. • $10 • (05/31/96) • **70**
Chardonnay Bourgogne Marquis d'Espiès 1993: Odd, lean, extremely citrusy and high in acidity. Shows modest green apple skin and lime flavors. Drink now. From Albert Bichot. • $10 • (05/15/95) • **72**

MONTROSE, CHÂTEAU

St.-Estèphe 1995: Not as exciting as expected from this estate, although it's still a beautiful wine that offers good, minty berry, cherry and cassis aromas and flavors. Refined tannins and a fruity finish. Tasted twice, with consistent notes. • $NA • (05/15/96) • **85-89** (BT)
St.-Estèphe 1994: Refined for this vintage. A bit lean, but has some good mineral, berry, cherry and mint aromas and flavors, moderate tannins and light finish. • $40 • (05/15/95) • **85-89** (BT)
St.-Estèphe 1993: Fabulous for a '93. Montrose continues to make excellent wines regardless of the vintage. Rich and elegant tobacco, cherry, smoke, toasted oak character, medium to full body, fine tannins and long, flavorful finish. Better in 1998. 21,250 cases made. • $38 • (01/31/96) • **90**
St.-Estèphe 1992: Well crafted and nicely textured, offering cassis, tobacco and cherry character. Medium-bodied and soft, a fruity finish. Drinkable now. • $28 • **86**
St.-Estèphe 1991: Soft, supple and pretty. A harmonious wine with berry, cherry and spice notes and an attractive finish. Tasted twice with consistent notes. • $28 • (03/31/94) • **85**
St.-Estèphe 1990: A polished, concentrated wine, with intense cherry, raspberry, vanilla and tobacco aromas and flavors, velvety tannins and a long, rich finish. Drink after 1997. 22,000 cases made. • $154 Ⓐ • (03/31/93) • **94**
St.-Estèphe 1989 • $55 Ⓐ • (03/15/92) • **95**
St.-Estèphe 1988 • $27 Ⓐ • (03/31/91) • **87**
St.-Estèphe 1987 • $18 Ⓐ • (02/15/90) • **80**
St.-Estèphe 1986 • $53 Ⓐ • (05/15/89) SS • **96**
St.-Estèphe 1985 • $33 • (10/15/94) • **89**
St.-Estèphe 1984 • $14 • (03/31/87) • **88**
St.-Estèphe 1983 • $30 • (10/15/94) • **85**
St.-Estèphe 1982 • $56 Ⓐ • (08/31/92) • **92**
St.-Estèphe 1981 • $26 Ⓐ • (12/01/84) • **90**
St.-Estèphe 1979 • $24 Ⓐ • (10/15/89) • **81**
St.-Estèphe 1970 • $95 • (04/01/86) • **80**
St.-Estèphe 1970 • $84 Ⓐ • (05/15/93) • **87**
St.-Estèphe 1962 • $100 • (11/30/87) • **90**
St.-Estèphe 1961 • $210 • (04/30/96) • **85**
St.-Estèphe 1959 • $140 • (10/15/90) • **90**
St.-Estèphe 1945 • $576 Ⓐ • (03/16/86) • **79**

MONTUS, CHÂTEAU

Madiran 1985 • $10 • (04/15/89) • **79**
Madiran Cuvée Prestige 1989 • $30 • (07/15/92) • **85**
Madiran Elevée en Füts de Chêne 1989 • $17 • (07/15/92) • **77**

MONTVIEL, CHÂTEAU

Pomerol 1995: Big and rich chocolate, berry and cherry aromas and flavors and medium-soft tannins. Delicious. • $NA • (05/15/96) • **85-89** (BT)

MORDORÉE, DOMAINE DE LA

Côtes du Rhône 1992: Fruity in aroma, but very dry and lean in flavor with tart cherry and smoke accents and firm tannins. Rather rustic, spare, almost austere. A good wine but we would like more ripeness and depth. 2,200 cases made. • $8 • (11/30/94) • **82**
Côtes du Rhône 1988 • $5 • (02/28/90) • **68**
Lirac 1986 • $11 • (09/30/88) • **88**

MOREAU

Chablis 1994: Plenty of mineral, spice and flinty character, medium body and fresh acidity. Drinkable now. • $13 • **82**

Chablis 1992: Here is a rather rich-textured Chardonnay with flavors that lean toward earth and mineral rather than fruit. It's full-bodied but could use more concentration and length. • $13 • **78**

Chablis Les Clos 1994: Better tighten your seat belt for this wild, savage ride. Aficionados will appreciate the uniqueness of this complex, extravagant, full-bodied *grand cru*. Distinctively earthy, with intense honey, citrus, chalk and mineral flavors, the finish is so long it burns a hole in our palate. Bravo! • $40 • (05/31/96) • **92**

Chablis Les Clos 1993: Chablis in the classic style, showing extremely crisp mineral and chalk character and a ripe pear, grassy, herbal edge. Tart finish now, try in 1997. • $47 • **85**

Chablis Les Clos des Hospices 1994: An incredibly elegant, silky *grand cru*. Laced with honey, earth, ripe pear and mineral aromas. Focused, medium to full body, it offers flavors of toasted bread, wet earth and mineral that adds to its attraction, keeping balanced on the finish. Try in 1999. • $48 • (05/31/96) • **89**

Chablis Les Clos des Hospices 1993: Distinctive earth, butter and white pepper flavors. Creamy texture, medium body and pleasant finish. • $55 • **84**

Chablis Moreau 1994: Attractively balanced and shows a few layers of fruit, but it's tart. • $15 • (05/31/96) • **79**

Chablis Vaillons 1994: An interesting wine that delivers a lot of crisp, citrusy, minty, mineral character. Has lots of personality and a chewy texture. Harsh and a little bitter on the finish at this stage, perhaps better in 1997. • $22 • (05/31/96) • **83**

Chablis Vaillons 1993: Mineral, apple and cream character is slightly short on the finish. • $25 • **83**

Chablis Vaillons Cuvée Préstige Guy Moreau 1994: A bit rustic, with some cedar, earth, honey and cardboard flavors. Where is the fruit? Only a touch of lemon on the short, drying finish. Tasted twice, with consistent notes. What happened? • $25 • (05/31/96) • **74**

Chablis Valmur 1994: Elegant and multi-dimensional, this seductive, ripe, rich beauty coats the palate with its silky texture. The mineral, spice, lemon and fruit flavors are charming, as is the fresh finish. Give it time to develop its full complexity, try in 1998. • $39 • (05/31/96) • **91**

Chablis Valmur 1993: There is some fruit here, and the wine is round and ripe, with earthy, lemony and spicy flavors. But it seems a bit short. • $47 • **81**

Chablis Vaudésir 1994: A *grand cru* in a distinctively earthy style. Very ripe, almost soft, with deliciously chewy mineral and ripe pear flavors. Full-bodied and kicks in with a long, lemony, rather subtle finish. Try in 1997. • $39 • (05/31/96) • **88**

Chablis Vaudésir 1993: Mineral and spice notes accompany apple and pear aromas and flavors. Medium body, fresh acidity and long finish. • $47 • **85**

Chardonnay Vin de Pays d'Oc 1993: A basic white that is pleasant enough, but lacks excitement. The green apple flavors are straightforward, with a little grapefruit tang. • $6 • (11/30/94) • **80**

Merlot Vin de Pays de Cassan 1992: Solid fruit notes are rounded out by spicy accents in this fully mature red. Drink now for its smooth texture and cherry-plum flavors. • $6 • (02/28/95) • **83**

MOREAU, BERNARD

Chassagne-Montrachet Morgeot La Cardeuse 1986 • $16 • (12/31/88) • **61**

MORETEAUX, DOMAINE JEAN

Bourgogne Pinot Noir Les Clous 1985 • $9 • (11/15/87) • **77**

Côte de Beaune-Villages 1983 • $8 • (03/16/86) • **63**

Key: SS—Spectator Selection. CS—Cellar Selection. BB—Best Buy. $NA—Price not available. (BT)—Barrel tasting. Ⓐ—Auction Price.
Dates in parentheses represent the issues in which the ratings were published.

MOREY-BLANC

Meursault Les Charmes 1992: Modestly-proportioned white, with some pear, vanilla, butter and toast notes. Well-balanced but on a modest scale. • $57 • (08/31/94) • **83**

Meursault Les Narvaux 1992: A bit traditional and rustic, showing straightforward fruit and a touch of butter, but it's sturdy and lacking finesse. • $40 • (08/31/94) • **79**

MOREY-COFFINET, MICHEL

Chassagne-Montrachet 1994: Fat and somewhat flat, tasting of overripe apples more than anything. It's still lush and rich but a bit overdone for us. Drinkable now. 200 cases made. • $24 • (05/31/96) • **76**

Chassagne-Montrachet 1992: Ripe, buttery aromas give way to simple, earthy flavors and an earthy finish, making this an awkward, old-fashioned style. • $25 • (07/31/94) • **78**

Chassagne-Montrachet Caillerets 1994: Ripe and rich, with a caramel, baked apple, cinnamon and spice character. The toasted oak notes dominate the fruit now, but this is a full-bodied and rather showy white with a very long finish. A wine to enjoy now through 1998. 225 cases made. • $34 • (05/31/96) 88 • **88**

Chassagne-Montrachet La Romanée 1994: A beautifully crafted, medium- to full-bodied white that's incredibly supple and creamy in texture, with a solid mineral character. Has some hints of basil and oregano, wet earth and apple flavors. Harmonious and elegant, it beckons for another sip. Terrific. 233 cases made. • $37 • (05/31/96) 89 • **88**

Chassagne-Montrachet Caillerets 1992: Straightforward simple style of white Burgundy that doesn't have much fruit in the aromas or flavors. It tastes light and dilute, only a lingering lemon and mineral character gives it life. • $36 • (07/31/94) • **78**

Chassagne-Montrachet La Romanée 1992: This rich, satisfying white Burgundy has butterscotch and custard aromas followed by lemon, apple and floral flavors that expand and linger on the finish. Nicely balanced. Drinkable now. • $39 • (07/31/94) • **87**

MOREY, ALBERT

Bâtard-Montrachet 1992: Strikes a nice balance between ripe, spicy pear and vanilla flavors, but it doesn't have all the extra dimensions. Young and awkward, still it's a nice glass of Bâtard. • $114 • (02/28/94) • **85**

MOREY, BERNARD

Chassagne-Montrachet Red 1990: Crisp and firm, with tight, ripe strawberry, oak and spice flavors and anise and currant notes that linger on the finish. A young wine with firm tannins, drinkable now. 130 cases made. • $28 • (06/15/93) • **85**

Chassagne-Montrachet Red 1989 • $23 • (11/30/92) • **81**

Chassagne-Montrachet Red 1987 • $20 • (10/31/89) • **75**

Chassagne-Montrachet Les Baudines 1993: Lean mineral and apple aromas and flavors, light body, crisp finish. 75 cases imported. • $35 • **81**

Chassagne-Montrachet Les Baudines 1992: Tight and crisp with vanilla, pear and apple notes that are intense and lively, but it lacks body and depth. Drinkable now. • $34 • (02/28/94) • **87**

Chassagne-Montrachet Les Baudines 1991 • $43 • (05/15/93) • **86**

Chassagne-Montrachet Caillerets 1993: Clean and well-made mineral and honey aromas and flavors, medium body and good texture. Drinkable now. • $35 • **86**

Chassagne-Montrachet Caillerets 1992: Doesn't quite taste ripe. It's a crisp and lean style with tart acidity and a narrow band of pear and spice flavors, clipped on the finish. Drinkable now. • $33 • (02/28/94) • **81**

Chassagne-Montrachet Les Embazées 1993: Superbly crafted, exhibiting a subtle mineral, apple and melon character and lovely, silky texture. Good now but better in 1997. • $35 • **89**

Chassagne-Montrachet Les Embazées 1992: A low-key style with muted spice and pear flavors that come up short on the finish. Drinkable now. • $33 • (02/28/94) • **84**

Chassagne-Montrachet Les Embazées 1991 • $43 • (05/15/93) • **85**

Chassagne-Montrachet Morgeot 1993: Honey, lemon and mineral character galore and a slight grassiness. Medium body and finish, high acidity. Drinkable now. • $35 • **83**

Chassagne-Montrachet Morgeot 1992: Ripe and supple with spicy pear, honey and nutmeg flavors that run deep and complex. Has the depth and concentration to age. Drink now through 1997. • $33 • (02/28/94) • **89**

Chassagne-Montrachet Morgeot 1991 • $43 • (05/15/93) • **83**

Chassagne-Montrachet Vieilles Vignes 1993: Toast, apple, pear and chalk flavors are quite tight and hard now, but show a round mouthfeel. Lovely, steely. Try in 1997. • $NA • **86**

Chassagne-Montrachet Vieilles Vignes 1992: A wine with uninteresting, simple flavors that don't taste ripe or intense. Watery finish. Drinkable now. • $29 • (02/28/94) • **80**

Santenay Grand Clos Rousseau 1987 • $24 • (10/15/89) • **87**

St.-Aubin Le Charmois 1992: Smooth and creamy, with intense, focused spice, hazelnut and pear flavors. Finishes with good length, drinkable now. • $23 • (02/28/94) • **83**

St.-Aubin Le Charmois 1991 • $30 • (06/15/93) • **85**

MOREY, DOMAINE MARC

Beaune Les Paules 1988 • $24 • (08/31/90) • **85**

Beaune Les Paules 1985 • $15 • (12/31/88) • **84**

Bâtard-Montrachet 1993: Impressive concentration. Layers of ripe fruit and fresh acidity, full body, wonderful cream, apple and mineral flavors and extremely long aftertaste. Drinkable now. 15 cases made. • $110 • **89**

Bâtard-Montrachet 1992: Big-volumed Burgundy, with gorgeous, complex honey, pear, peach, lemon and toast character in extremely well-proportioned amounts, subtle yet deep, it melts like butter in the palate and picks up intensity on the finish. • $92 • (08/31/94) • **93**

Chassagne-Montrachet 1994: Quite supple and attractive, backed by vanilla, apple, pear, cream and mineral flavors. The oak flavors are a bit too pronounced, but it's nicely round on the finish. 79 cases made. • $33 • (05/31/96) • **85**

Chassagne-Montrachet 1992: Woody, buttery flavors dominate this clean, solidly-built Chassagne. Drinkable now. • $30 • (08/31/94) • **83**

Chassagne-Montrachet Caillerets 1993: Fat and rich, harmonious, sporting a chalk, mineral, pineapple, vanilla and ripe fruit character. Almost outstanding. • $35 • **89**

Chassagne-Montrachet Les Chenevottes 1994: Thick and opulent, this showy, full-bodied white Burgundy delivers lots of toasted coconut, caramel, pear and butter flavors. Turns very oaky on the rich finish. Needs time to come together, try in 1997. Tasted twice, with consistent notes. 500 cases made. • $40 • (05/31/96) • **86**

Chassagne-Montrachet Les Chenevottes 1992: Rather bold and gold-colored Chassagne, with butterscotch, butter and pear flavors, it is round and ready to drink, with a silky, somewhat mature texture. • $35 • (08/31/94) • **84**

Chassagne-Montrachet Les Vergers 1994: Round and supple yet fresh. Approachable now, it's seductive without being overdone. Enjoy the lovely, unctuous mix of honey, lime, butter, cream and mineral flavors that caress your palate. Whoa! 516 cases made. • $40 • (05/31/96) 90 • **90**

Chassagne-Montrachet Morgeot 1994: Rich yet elegant, with loads of honey, fresh fig and date flavors, but also enough lemon and grapefruit notes to give this full-bodied wine a sense of balance. The nutmeg and spice add complexity to the finish. 141 cases made. • $48 • (05/31/96) • **87**

Chassagne-Montrachet Morgeot 1993: Lovely, very showy young white presenting nut, apple and pear aromas and flavors, medium body, ripe fruit and round finish. Drink now. • $35 • **86**

Chassagne-Montrachet Morgeot 1992: Ripe and buttery in flavor, rich and smooth in texture, yet lively and well-balanced with acidity. • $36 • (08/31/94) • **85**

Chassagne-Montrachet En Virondot 1994: Like eating a waffle with maple syrup. Soft, sweet and fun to drink now. Lots of honey, pear, pie crust and doughy flavors. Not much length, but this will open up by 1997. 1,083 cases made. • $40 • (05/31/96) • **85**

Chassagne-Montrachet En Virondot 1993: Fresh and zesty, a vibrant, straightforward white that bubbles with life but little depth. Shows some pear, melon and salty flavors. Drink now. • $35 • **80**

Chassagne-Montrachet En Virondot 1992: Seductive, full-bodied and silky with excellent balance, the flavors wrap around a tight core of pear, grapefruit and honey. It remains fresh and crisp on the finish. Drinkable now. • $35 • (08/31/94) • **90**

Puligny-Montrachet Les Pucelles 1994: Distinctive for its attractive, chewy, chalky texture, a mouthful of a wine, with mineral and floral qualities in its honey and pear flavors. Full-bodied and a bit soft. Drinkable now or try in 1997. 166 cases made. • $60 • (05/31/96) • **86**

Puligny-Montrachet Les Pucelles 1993: Quite young, exhibiting very good concentration of fruit and fresh acidity, medium body and earthy mineral finish. • $50 • **87**

Puligny-Montrachet Les Pucelles 1992: A seductively rich, fat style with abundant, ripe flavors of pear, honey, cream and vanilla. If richness is your goal, you can't do much better than this. Full-bodied, drinkable now through 1997. • $53 • (08/31/94) • **90**

MOREY, PIERRE

Bourgogne White 1992: Simple and lean, clean but neutral, showing just a hint of apple, smoke and lemon flavors. • $19 • (08/31/94) • **78**

MORIN, GERARD

Sancerre 1993: Well made and harmonious, featuring typical gooseberry, light herb and mineral flavors, crisp acidity and long, firm finish. A great white for food. • $14 • **87**

MOROT, ALBERT

Beaune Les Bressandes 1990: Very mellow, with nice, subtle toast and smoke notes bracketed between earth, chestnut and cherry flavors. Round and supple on the finish. Drinkable now. • $38 • (12/15/92) • **86**

Beaune Les Bressandes 1988 • $30 • (03/31/91) • **87**

Beaune Les Cent-Vignes 1991: Tough, astringent, earthy and bitter. A decadent wine, with little freshness or charm. • $28 Ⓐ • (01/31/94) • **73**

Beaune Les Cent-Vignes 1988 • $30 • (04/30/91) • **91**

Beaune Les Grèves 1988 • $32 • (07/15/91) • **86**

Beaune Les Marconnets 1990: A bit simple but good, showing modest strawberry, earth, wet hay and plum aromas and flavors, medium body and supple tannins. Drinkable now. • $38 • (12/15/92) • **84**

Beaune Les Teurons 1991: Gamy, ashy aromas and flavors add a layer of complexity to the modest cherry flavors. Finish is tough and earthy. • $28 Ⓐ • (01/31/94) • **78**

Beaune Les Teurons 1990: Ripe and juicy, with pretty plum and berry notes that don't offer much length, but certainly give a lot of pleasure. Drinkable now. • $39 • (12/15/92) • **85**

Beaune Les Teurons 1988 • $20 Ⓐ • (07/15/91) • **80**

Beaune Les Toussaints 1991: A quiet wine, offering modest berry and chocolate aromas and flavors and a bite of tannin on the light finish. Drinkable now. • $28 Ⓐ • (01/31/94) • **79**

Beaune Les Toussaints 1990: Pleasant and approachable, with nice chestnut and berry notes and a light, velvety finish. Drinkable now. • $38 • (12/15/92) • **84**

Savigny-lès-Beaune Vergelesses 1991: Bright raspberry flavor enlivens this modest, sharply focused wine. Crisp and light, drinkable now. • $26 • (01/31/94) • **82**

Savigny-lès-Beaune Vergelesses La Bataillère 1988 • $26 • (03/31/91) • **86**

MORTET & FILS

Bourgogne Les Charmes au Châtelain 1990 • $NA • (12/15/92) • **87**

Chambertin 1990: Sleek, beautiful and extremely pretty, with sweet cherry and wild berry aromas and flavors and fine tannins, but could be more concentrated on the finish. Drinkable now. 75 cases made. • $92 • (12/15/92) • **86**

Chambolle-Musigny Aux Beaux Bruns 1990: Supple and balanced, with plenty of cherry, raspberry and chocolate flavors. Shows finesse on the finish. Drinkable now. • $45 • (12/15/92) • **90**

Clos de Vougeot 1990: Wonderfully intense, with smoke, plum and earth characteristics. The ripe, rich flavors lead to a focused, firm and extremely seductive finish. Drinkable in 1998. 175 cases made. • $NA • (12/15/92) • **94**

Gevrey-Chambertin 1990: Effusively aromatic and starts out firm on the palate, but the violet, cherry and chocolate flavors open up and come together nicely on the flavorful finish. Give it time, try from 1997. • $NA • (12/15/92) • **90**

Gevrey-Chambertin Champeaux 1990: A seductive wine that bursts with pure raspberry, bright cherry and spice flavors. Smooth tannins. Drinkable now. • $45 • (12/15/92) • **91**

Gevrey-Chambertin Clos Prieur 1990: Shows good depth and great class, with beautiful blackberry, black cherry and spice flavors that stay with you on the intense, firm finish. Drinkable in 1998. • $38 • (12/15/92) • **93**

MORTET, CHARLES

Bourgogne 1989 • $14 • (01/31/92) • **87**
Bourgogne 1986 • $15 • (06/15/89) • **79**
Chambertin 1989 • $68 • (01/31/92) • **94**
Chambertin 1987 • $69 • (03/31/90) • **87**
Chambertin 1986 • $62 • (02/28/89) • **91**
Chambertin 1985 • $64 • (06/15/88) • **90**
Chambolle-Musigny Aux Beaux Bruns 1989 • $34 • (01/31/92) • **89**
Clos de Vougeot 1989 • $47 • (01/31/92) • **86**
Clos de Vougeot 1986 • $43 • (04/15/89) • **84**
Gevrey-Chambertin 1989 • $25 • (01/31/92) • **88**
Gevrey-Chambertin 1988 • $35 • (02/15/91) • **89**
Gevrey-Chambertin 1987 • $28 • (03/31/90) • **86**
Gevrey-Chambertin 1986 • $24 • (02/28/89) • **87**
Gevrey-Chambertin Clos Prieur 1989 • $30 • (01/31/92) • **88**
Gevrey-Chambertin Clos Prieur 1988 • $41 • (02/15/91) • **91**
Gevrey-Chambertin Clos Prieur 1987 • $32 • (03/31/90) • **83**
Gevrey-Chambertin Clos Prieur 1986 • $30 • (02/28/89) • **84**
Gevrey-Chambertin Clos Prieur 1985 • $29 • (07/31/88) • **92**
Gevrey-Chambertin Champeaux 1989 • $34 • (01/31/92) • **90**
Gevrey-Chambertin Champeaux 1988 • $46 • (03/15/91) • **87**
Gevrey-Chambertin Champeaux 1987 • $36 • (03/31/90) • **81**
Gevrey-Chambertin Champeaux 1986 • $33 • (02/28/89) • **86**

MORTET, DENIS

Bourgogne Les Charmes au Chatelain 1993: Like freshly crushed raspberries and black cherries. Full- to medium-bodied, adding firm tannins and a long, fresh finish. Better in 1998. • $15 • **88**

Bourgogne Les Charmes au Chatelain 1992: Delicious, with a ripe core of currant and black cherry flavors and a touch of vanilla, all presented in a sophisticated package. • $NA • **83**

Chambertin 1993: Super well-crafted Burgundy, offering lovely wild berry, plum and currant character and a hint of vanilla. Medium in body, loads of tannins and long, sweet fruit finish. Better in 1999. • $115 • **94**

Chambertin 1992: Very pretty, with an appealing rose petal accent to the blackberry and raspberry flavors up front, fades a little on the finish. Drinkable now. • $NA • **85**

Chambertin 1991: Lean and focused, a spicy wine with a fine thread of black cherry and earth aromas and flavors, sharply focused and elegant on the finish. Try in 1997. • $91 Ⓐ • (01/31/94) • **86**

Chambolle-Musigny Aux Beaux Bruns 1993: Seductive ripe fruit, tobacco and toasted oak notes, medium to full body, silky tannins and long, flavorful aftertaste. Better in 2000. • $43 • **91**

Chambolle-Musigny Aux Beaux Bruns 1992: Charming and delicate, with enough currant and red berry flavors to make it interesting. Supple and elegant finish. Try soon. • $NA • **84**

Chambolle-Musigny Aux Beaux Bruns 1991: A delicate wine that shows little distinction. Drinkable now. • $46 Ⓐ • (01/31/94) • **78**

Key: SS—Spectator Selection. CS—Cellar Selection. BB—Best Buy. $NA—Price not available. (BT)—Barrel tasting. Ⓐ—Auction Price.
Dates in parentheses represent the issues in which the ratings were published.

Clos de Vougeot 1993: Blockbuster Burgundy featuring complex aromas and flavors of plum, vanilla and spice. Super fruity, followed by a super finish. Great backbone of tannins. Try after 2000. • $80 • **94**

Clos de Vougeot 1992: Impressive for its pure fruit, tightly structured with firm, fine tannins and a beam of lovely currant and berry flavor that lingers on the finish. Give it until 1997. • $NA • **88**

Clos de Vougeot 1991: Light, fragrant, simple and direct, offering a narrow beam of raspberry and earth aromas and flavors. Drinkable now. • $63 Ⓐ • (01/31/94) • **81**

Gevrey-Chambertin 1993: Impressive village wine that's wonderfully floral and fruity. Medium body, fine tannins and a long, succulent finish. Delicious to taste, but will age for many years to come. Better in 2000. • $42 • **90**

Gevrey-Chambertin 1992: Light but quite delicious, with a sweet core of clean raspberry and cherry flavors and a supple, crisp finish. Well made and juicy. • $NA • **84**

Gevrey-Chambertin 1991: Light, fresh and agreeable, showing earthy strawberry aromas and flavors. Finishes earthy. Drinkable now. • $33 Ⓐ • (01/31/94) • **78**

Gevrey-Chambertin En Champs Vieille Vigne 1993: Impressively dark-colored, sporting a lovely ripe berry, plum character on the nose. Surprisingly delicate finish. Medium in body, adding silky tannins and vanilla, cherry aftertaste. Try in 1999. • $50 • **90**

Gevrey-Chambertin Champeaux 1993: Well-crafted cherry and vanilla aromas and flavors, medium body, fine tannins and sweet, fruity finish. Drinkable now. • $58 • **90**

Gevrey-Chambertin Champeaux 1992: A sturdy red with straightforward currant and floral flavors that persist into a chunky finish. Best from 1997. • $NA • **83**

Gevrey-Chambertin Champeaux 1991: Light, refreshing and charming, serving up spicy raspberry and strawberry flavors and a hint of anise on the smooth finish. Drinkable now. • $46 Ⓐ • (01/31/94) • **84**

Gevrey-Chambertin Clos Prieur 1991: Smooth, supple, flavorful and medium in weight, displaying appealing currant and blackberry flavors. Drinkable now. • $40 Ⓐ • (01/31/94) • **85**

Gevrey-Chambertin Lavaux-St.-Jacques 1993: Intensely fruity, featuring dried cherry and mineral character, medium body, fine tannins and a long, fruity finish. Better in 1999. • $58 • **90**

Gevrey-Chambertin En Motrot 1993: A silky, medium-bodied Gevrey, bursting with fresh, grapey and ripe red berry flavors. Touches of earth persist on the finish. Well-defined structure and beautiful texture should make this a delight to drink in 2000. • $46 • **90**

Gevrey-Chambertin Au Vellé 1993: A lovely, silky red featuring very good color and plenty of dried cherry, plum, chocolate character, medium body, fine tannins and crisp finish. Better in 2000. • $46 • **88**

Marsannay Les Longeroies Red 1993: Impressive red from this village, sporting lovely, ripe berry, smoke, mint and vanilla aromas and flavors. Medium-bodied and very silky. Better in 1998. • $30 • **89**

MORTET, THIERRY

Bourgogne 1993: Beautifully fruity, offering firm acidity and moderate tannins. Drinkable now. • $NA • (05/15/96) • **84**

Chambolle-Musigny Aux Beaux Bruns 1993: Vivid, bright and lively, featuring moderate tannins, smooth texture and fresh fruit flavors lightly accented by spice. Very good example of an elegant Chambolle. Drinkable through 1998. • $58 • (05/15/96) • **87**

Gevrey-Chambertin Clos Prieur 1993: A medium-rich red offering lovely, velvety texture and lots of cherry, berry and cedar character. Better in 2000. • $NA • (05/15/96) • **88**

MOUCHET, CHÂTEAU DE

Montagne-St.-Emilion 1961 • $NA • (04/30/96) • **87**

MOUEIX, A.

Fronsac 1985 • $9 • (09/30/88) • **83**
St.-Emilion 1981 • $7 • (09/01/85) • **78**

MOUEIX, JEAN-PIERRE

Merlot Bordeaux Christian Moueix 1993: Not much on the nose and the fruit flavors lack depth. A smooth texture punctuated by a hint of spice and plum on the finish. • $10 • (08/31/95) • **79**
Merlot Bordeaux Christian Moueix 1990: Sweet, toasty new oak is the dominant flavor in this round but tannic wine. There's cherry fruit, but it's not concentrated enough for balance. A tasty but slightly unbalanced effort. • $10 • (11/15/94) • **82**
Merlot Bordeaux Christian Moueix 1989 • $9 • (11/30/92) • **83**
Merlot Bordeaux Christian Moueix 1988 • $9 • (11/30/92) • **76**
St.-Emilion 1989 • $13 • (06/15/93) • **74**
St.-Emilion 1988 • $13 • (04/30/92) • **82**

MOUEIX, MAISON

Bordeaux 1988 • $6 • (01/31/92) BB • **81**

MOUJAN, CHÂTEAUX DE

Coteaux du Languedoc 1987 • $4 • (08/31/89) • **80**

MOULIN AUX MOINES, DOMAINE DU

Auxey-Duresses Red 1983 • $10 • (03/15/87) • **76**

MOULIN BOUSQUET, CHÂTEAU

Corbières 1990 • $NA • (03/15/94) • **82**

MOULIN DE BEL-AIR, CHÂTEAU

Médoc 1989 • $NA • (03/15/92) • **77**

MOULIN DE CITRAN, CHÂTEAU

Haut-Médoc 1991: Decent cherry, currant and tobacco flavors, but light and simple. • $13 • (03/31/94) • **78**
Haut-Médoc 1989 • $14 • (03/15/92) • **80**

MOULIN DE DUHART

Pauillac 1993: Some decent fruit yet also lacking definition. Offers plum, blackberry and wet earth notes, but tastes slightly diluted on the finish. Drinkable now. • $16 • (01/31/96) • **79**
Pauillac 1990: Horsy, gamy flavors dominate this wine, but if you don't mind that, it's drinkable. • $14 • (02/28/94) • **75**
Pauillac 1989 • $20 • (12/31/92) • **84**

MOULIN DE LA BRIDAN, CHÂTEAU DU

St.-Julien 1983 • $11 • (04/01/86) • **76**

MOULIN DE LAUNAY, CHÂTEAU

Entre-Deux-Mers 1993: Lovely and fresh, featuring pear, slightly grassy character, medium body, soft texture and light finish. • $8 • **80**

MOULIN DE PEYRONIN, CHÂTEAU DU

Bordeaux 1989 • $10 • (07/15/92) • **76**
Bordeaux 1986 • $10 • (03/31/90) • **73**

MOULIN DU CADET, CHÂTEAU

St.-Emilion 1995: Lovely, solid spice, toasted oak and red berry flavors mingle harmoniously. Lots of ripe tannins. • $NA • (05/15/96) • **85-89** (BT)
St.-Emilion 1994: Shows some decent fruit and a ripe, almost sweet character. Light- to medium-bodied, slightly tough tannins on the finish. • $NA • **80-84** (BT)
St.-Emilion 1993: Light, simple, attractive berry flavor and delicate, sweet fruit character on the finish. Drinkable now. • $NA • (01/31/96) • **79**
St.-Emilion 1992: Light color and a mint, cedar, fruit aroma. Like a weak Rioja. • $NA • **70**
St.-Emilion 1990: There's plenty of fruit in this wine, with intense raspberry and berry aromas and flavors, silky tannins and a long finish. Drink after 1997. 1,800 cases made. • $NA • (03/31/93) • **91**
St.-Emilion 1989 • $NA • (03/15/92) • **86**

MOULIN HAUT-LAROQUE, CHÂTEAU

Fronsac 1990: A big, rich wine, with beautiful aromas and flavors of toasted oak and raspberries and round, velvety tannins. Drink after 1996. 6,000 cases made. • $14 • (03/31/93) • **89**
Fronsac 1986 • $11 • (11/15/89) • **78**

MOULIN RICHE, CHÂTEAU

St.-Julien 1987 • $18 • (11/30/89) • **79**
St.-Julien 1986 • $20 • (11/30/89) • **88**
St.-Julien 1985 • $20 • (06/15/88) • **83**
St.-Julien 1982 • $22 • (11/30/89) • **90**

MOULIN ROUGE, CHÂTEAU

Haut-Médoc 1987 • $12 • (11/30/89) • **74**
Haut-Médoc 1986 • $14 • (11/30/89) • **87**
Haut-Médoc 1983 • $10 • (07/31/87) • **83**
Haut-Médoc 1982 • $13 • (11/30/89) • **80**

MOULIN-MEYNEY, CHÂTEAU DU

Bordeaux 1986 • $6 • **62**

MOULIN-PEY LABRIE, CHÂTEAU

Canon-Fronsac 1990: Rich and thick, with smoky, cherry, earthy character, full, silky tannins and a long, flavorful finish. Drink after 1996. • $16 • (03/31/93) • **88**

MOULIN-RICHE, CHÂTEAU

St.-Julien 1995: Fresh, crisp, vivid cassis and wild berry flavors, firm tannins and medium body, finishing a touch tart. • $NA • (05/15/96) • **80-84** (BT)

MOULIN-ST.-GEORGES, CHÂTEAU

St.-Emilion 1995: Amazingly seductive. Like tasting crème de cassis, full in body, melting in the mouth and cascading over the palate to a seamless finish. Supple, ripe tannins. Could rate outstanding in our next tasting. • $NA • (05/15/96) • **85-89** (BT)

MOULIN-TACUSSEL, DOMAINE

Châteauneuf-du-Pape 1990: Buttery oak and ripe blueberry and blackberry flavors combine for a sweet-seeming, rich-tasting wine, with a full, chocolaty finish. Full-bodied and moderately tannic, built for drinking now or aging through 1997. • $19 • (04/15/93) • **88**

MOULINE, CHÂTEAU LA

Moulis 1988 • $20 • (02/15/91) • **81**

MOULINET, CHÂTEAU

Pomerol 1992: A steely Pomerol, displaying earth, mineral and cherry aromas and flavors, light-bodied, firm, short finish. • $16 • **79**
Pomerol 1988 • $17 • (07/31/91) • **88**
Pomerol 1982 • $10 • (05/15/89) • **87**

FRANCE

MOUSSET, LOUIS

Châteauneuf-du-Pape 1982 • $6 • (12/16/84) • **75**
Côtes du Rhône 1983 • $2.50 • (12/16/84) BB • **81**
Gigondas 1983 • $6 • (12/01/84) • **75**

MOUTON-BARONNE-PHILIPPE, CHÂTEAU

Pauillac 1988 • $25 • (04/30/91) • **90**
Pauillac 1986 • $23 • (05/31/89) • **93**
Pauillac 1985 • $24 • (05/15/88) SS • **91**
Pauillac 1984 • $18 • (06/15/87) • **64**
Pauillac 1983 • $17 • (03/01/86) • **88**
Pauillac 1982 • $37 • (08/31/92) • **88**
Pauillac 1981 • $25 • (06/01/84) • **81**
Pauillac 1970 • $31 Ⓐ • (05/15/93) • **86**
Pauillac 1961 • $125 • (04/30/96) • **88**
Pauillac 1945 • $390 • (03/16/86) • **80**

MOUTON-CADET

Bordeaux 1990: A fresh, firm wine with attractive cherry and licorice notes. This has enough muscle to match hearty dishes. Drinkable now. Much better than a bottle tasted earlier. • $10 • **84**
Bordeaux 1989 • $8 • (07/15/92) BB • **84**
Bordeaux 1988 • $9 • (04/30/91) BB • **81**
Bordeaux 1987 • $7 • (04/15/90) • **79**
Bordeaux 1986 • $7 • (02/15/89) BB • **81**
Bordeaux 1985 • $6 • (05/15/88) BB • **80**
Bordeaux NV: Pleasant and refreshing with nice strawberry flavors and aromas. A Bordeaux rosé with clean flavors and a spicy finish. • $10 • **82**
Bordeaux White 1992: Brightly fruity, with pear, melon and slightly herbal flavors and good richness and body. Attractive and generous in flavor, yet well balanced with acidity. • $10 • (11/15/94) • **84**

MOUTON-ROTHSCHILD, CHÂTEAU

Pauillac 1995: Seduces you with its wonderful cassis, berry, vanilla and mint aromas and flavors. Full body, ultrafine tannins and a long, caressing finish. It's hard to resist even at this stage. • $NA • (05/15/96) • **95-100** (BT)
Pauillac 1994: Mouton shows wonderful elegance in its '94, with plenty of tobacco, mint and cassis character and ultrafine, ripe tannins. A complex and enjoyable wine. • $85 • (05/15/96) • **90-94** (BT)
Pauillac 1993: Mouton comes through again. Impressive '93, deep in color and full-bodied, boasting plenty of currant, black cherry, mint and toast character. Well crafted, showing depth for this vintage. Give the tannins some time to mellow. Try in 2000. • $72 • (01/31/96) • **90**
Pauillac 1992: Impressive. Beautiful plum, berry, tobacco, cedar and toasted oak aromas and flavors, medium body and tannins and a succulent finish. Drinkable now. • $65 • **88**
Pauillac 1991: Incredibly fine and subtle for the vintage with tobacco, black currant and berry aromas and flavors, medium body and a long flavorful, silky finish. Drink or hold. • $49 Ⓐ • (03/31/94) • **89**
Pauillac 1990: Seductive, with plum, smoke and vanilla aromas and flavors, full, silky tannins and a long, rich finish. Still quite backward, needs time to unwind. Drink after 1998. 25,000 cases made. • $104 Ⓐ • (05/15/93) CS • **95**
Pauillac 1989 • $130 Ⓐ • (03/15/92) • **99**
Pauillac 1988 • $89 • (04/30/91) • **100**
Pauillac 1987 • $58 Ⓐ • (05/15/90) • **89**
Pauillac 1986 • $245 Ⓐ • (05/15/91) • **97**
Pauillac 1985 • $118 Ⓐ • (10/15/94) • **96**
Pauillac 1984 • $55 Ⓐ • (03/31/87) • **92**
Pauillac 1983 • $78 Ⓐ • (10/15/94) • **94**
Pauillac 1982 • $344 Ⓐ • (08/31/92) • **95**

Key: SS—Spectator Selection. CS—Cellar Selection. BB—Best Buy. $NA—Price not available. (BT)—Barrel tasting. Ⓐ—Auction Price.
Dates in parentheses represent the issues in which the ratings were published.

Pauillac 1981 • $63 Ⓐ • (10/15/94) • **91**
Pauillac 1980 • $85 • (06/16/86) • **67**
Pauillac 1979 • $63 Ⓐ • (10/15/89) • **96**
Pauillac 1978 • $78 Ⓐ • (05/15/91) • **92**
Pauillac 1977 • $100 • (06/16/86) • **68**
Pauillac 1976 • $68 Ⓐ • (06/16/86) • **85**
Pauillac 1975 • $90 Ⓐ • (05/15/91) • **89**
Pauillac 1974 • $48 Ⓐ • (06/16/86) • **67**
Pauillac 1973 • $65 Ⓐ • (06/16/86) • **75**
Pauillac 1972 • $40 Ⓐ • (06/16/86) • **55**
Pauillac 1971 • $61 Ⓐ • (06/16/86) • **78**
Pauillac 1970 • $134 Ⓐ • (05/15/93) • **96**
Pauillac 1969 • $90 Ⓐ • (06/16/86) • **78**
Pauillac 1968 • $77 Ⓐ • (06/16/86) • **64**
Pauillac 1967 • $49 Ⓐ • (06/16/86) • **87**
Pauillac 1966 • $161 Ⓐ • (05/15/91) • **88**
Pauillac 1965 • $236 Ⓐ • (06/16/86) • **61**
Pauillac 1964 • $73 Ⓐ • (06/16/86) • **84**
Pauillac 1963 • $434 Ⓐ • (06/16/86) • **77**
Pauillac 1962 • $186 Ⓐ • (05/15/91) • **93**
Pauillac 1961: Subtle in flavor, silky in texture and still firm with tannins, this Mouton is clearly outstanding in quality. Elegance, not richness, is its hallmark, and the mélange of spice-earth-fruit flavors is nearly mature. Drink now through 2005. • $775 • (04/30/96) • **92**
Pauillac 1960 • $215 Ⓐ • (06/16/86) • **84**
Pauillac 1959 • $621 Ⓐ • (05/15/91) • **98**
Pauillac 1958 • $284 Ⓐ • (06/16/86) • **68**
Pauillac 1957 • $117 Ⓐ • (06/16/86) • **86**
Pauillac 1956 • $2000 • (06/16/86) • **85**
Pauillac 1955 • $395 Ⓐ • (05/15/91) • **95**
Pauillac 1954 • $886 Ⓐ • (06/16/86) • **81**
Pauillac 1953 • $595 Ⓐ • (05/15/91) • **94**
Pauillac 1952 • $616 Ⓐ • (06/16/86) • **90**
Pauillac 1951 • $709 Ⓐ • (06/16/86) • **84**
Pauillac 1950 • $276 Ⓐ • (06/16/86) • **83**
Pauillac 1949 • $882 Ⓐ • (05/15/91) • **87**
Pauillac 1948 • $539 Ⓐ • (06/16/86) • **87**
Pauillac 1947 • $1200 • (05/15/91) • **75**
Pauillac 1946 • $5800 • (06/16/86) • **77**
Pauillac 1945 • $2500 • **94**
Pauillac 1944 • $354 Ⓐ • (06/16/86) • **86**
Pauillac 1943 • $266 Ⓐ • (06/16/86) • **78**
Pauillac 1940 • $530 • (06/16/86) • **77**
Pauillac 1939 • $500 • (06/16/86) • **55**
Pauillac 1938 • $500 • (06/16/86) • **73**
Pauillac 1937 • $440 • (05/15/91) • **91**
Pauillac 1936 • $280 Ⓐ • (06/16/86) • **63**
Pauillac 1934 • $243 Ⓐ • (05/15/91) • **90**
Pauillac 1933 • $300/375ml • (06/16/86) • **78**
Pauillac 1929 • $736 Ⓐ • (05/15/91) • **75**
Pauillac 1928 • $806 Ⓐ • (05/15/91) • **89**
Pauillac 1926 • $800 • (06/16/86) • **65**
Pauillac 1925 • $1100 • (06/16/86) • **40**
Pauillac 1924 • $1750 • (06/16/86) • **69**
Pauillac 1921 • $500 • (05/15/91) • **80**
Pauillac 1920 • $700 • (06/16/86) • **75**
Pauillac 1919 • $600 • (05/15/91) • **79**
Pauillac 1918 • $562 Ⓐ • (05/15/91) • **83**
Pauillac 1916 • $420 • (06/16/86) • **67**
Pauillac 1914 • $550 • (06/16/86) • **65**
Pauillac 1912 • $400 • (06/16/86) • **62**
Pauillac 1910 • $400 • (05/15/91) • **76**
Pauillac 1909 • $1200 • (06/16/86) • **65**
Pauillac 1908 • $1200 • (06/16/86) • **50**
Pauillac 1907 • $850 • (06/16/86) • **50**
Pauillac 1906 • $800 • (06/16/86) • **66**
Pauillac 1905 • $970 • (05/15/91) • **88**
Pauillac 1900 • $1500 • (05/15/91) • **90**
Pauillac 1899 • $1500 • (06/16/86) • **82**
Pauillac 1888 • $1100 • (06/16/86) • **60**
Pauillac 1886 • $1200 • (06/16/86) • **60**

Pauillac 1881 • $1380 • (06/16/86) • **74**
Pauillac 1878 • $521 Ⓐ • (05/15/91) • **99**
Pauillac 1874 • $660 Ⓐ • (05/15/91) • **95**
Pauillac 1870 • $3500 • (05/15/91) • **87**
Pauillac 1869 • $1700 • (06/16/86) • **40**
Pauillac 1867 • $2100 • (06/16/86) • **40**

MUGNERET-GIBOURG

Bourgogne 1992: An overlay of sweet oak gives this a little extra class, with berry and currant notes threaded through the fine texture. • $NA • **80**
Bourgogne 1990: • $18 • (12/15/92) • **86**
Bourgogne 1989 • $17 • (06/15/92) • **82**
Echézeaux 1992: Firm and chewy, almost crisp, with smoke and toast notes adding some extra dimension to the strawberry and raspberry flavors. A little short, but it might pick up a bit more finesse by 1997. • $NA • **82**
Echézeaux 1991: Firm and crisp, featuring pretty rose petal-scented currant and raspberry aromas and flavors and hints of smoke on the finish. Has style, but seems a bit watery. Try now. • $68 Ⓐ • (01/31/94) • **85**
Echézeaux 1990: Like satin, this wine caresses the palate with intense red berry, violet and earth flavors, yet has a real iron backbone that leads to a sophisticated, supple finish. Shows wonderful finesse. Try in 1997. 250 cases made. • $66 • (12/15/92) • **93**
Echézeaux 1989 • $62 • (04/30/92) • **88**
Echézeaux 1988 • $70 • (11/15/90) • **89**
Echézeaux 1987 • $50 • (10/15/89) • **93**
Echézeaux 1986 • $55 • (11/30/88) • **83**
Echézeaux 1985 • $57 • (02/29/88) • **93**
Echézeaux 1984 • $32 • (03/15/87) • **85**
Vosne-Romanée 1993: Simple, rather light and clean berry, cherry and almond aromas and flavors, medium to light body, light tannins and diluted finish. Drinkable now. • $NA • **83**
Vosne-Romanée 1992: Light color, light body and some decent red berry flavors about sums it up. Delicate and easy to drink, but a bit diluted. • $NA • **79**
Vosne-Romanée 1991: Crisp, focused and lively, showing toasty, anise-scented berry flavors and a juicy, fresh finish. Drinkable now. • $400 Ⓐ • (01/31/94) • **83**
Vosne-Romanée 1989 • $34 • (04/30/92) • **81**
Vosne-Romanée 1988 • $34 • (12/31/90) • **64**
Vosne-Romanée 1987 • $30 • (10/15/89) • **90**
Vosne-Romanée 1986 • $33 • (07/31/88) • **84**
Vosne-Romanée 1985 • $33 • (02/29/88) • **85**

MUGNERET-GOUACHON, B.

Echézeaux 1985 • $29 • (12/31/88) • **91**

MUGNERET, GEORGES

Chambolle-Musigny Les Feusselottes 1992: Light and fruity, pleasant raspberry and strawberry flavors echoing on the simple finish. Drinkable now. • $NA • **83**
Chambolle-Musigny Les Feusselottes 1989 • $47 • (04/30/92) • **87**
Chambolle-Musigny Les Feusselottes 1988 • $54 • (11/15/90) • **86**
Chambolle-Musigny Les Feusselottes 1987 • $41 • (10/15/89) • **92**
Chambolle-Musigny Les Feusselottes 1986 • $45 • (11/15/88) • **90**
Clos Vougeot 1991: Very light and delicate, with a bright beam of raspberry flavor. Simple and easy to drink, echoing the lively fruit on the long finish. • $90 Ⓐ • (01/31/94) • **83**
Clos Vougeot 1990: Crisp and sharp, with intense berry characteristics that deliver plenty of focused cherry, smoke and toast flavors and a mouth-puckering finish. Try in 1997. 150 cases made. • $89 • (12/15/92) • **91**
Clos Vougeot 1988 • $90 • (11/15/90) • **84**
Clos Vougeot 1987 • $68 • (10/15/89) • **91**
Clos Vougeot 1986 • $73 • (11/30/88) • **90**
Nuits-St.-Georges Aux Chaignots 1993: A bit earthy but solid, offering loads of cherry and blackberry character, medium to full body, fine tannins and long, fresh finish. Better in 2001. • $NA • **88**
Nuits-St.-Georges Aux Chaignots 1992: Light in color, light in aroma and light in flavor, with only a touch of raspberry flavor on the finish. Drinkable now. • $NA • **79**
Nuits-St.-Georges Aux Chaignots 1991: Crisp and almost austere. Pleasant strawberry and milk chocolate flavors struggle to rise above a modest level. Drinkable now. • $50 Ⓐ • (01/31/94) • **80**
Nuits-St.-Georges Aux Chaignots 1990: Elegant and round, with pretty raspberry, chestnut and berry aromas and flavors, medium tannins and a charming finish. Drinkable now. 325 cases made. • $45 • (12/15/92) • **88**
Nuits-St.-Georges Aux Chaignots 1989 • $43 • (04/30/92) • **86**
Nuits-St.-Georges Aux Chaignots 1988 • $47 • (11/15/90) • **80**
Nuits-St.-Georges Aux Chaignots 1987 • $41 • (10/15/89) • **87**
Nuits-St.-Georges Aux Chaignots 1986 • $40 • (11/15/88) • **89**
Nuits-St.-Georges Aux Chaignots 1984 • $26 • (03/15/87) • **89**
Ruchottes-Chambertin 1992: Lean and tight, showing some cherry flavor at the core, but the overlay of herbal, stalky character is too much. May be better after 1996. • $NA • **74**
Ruchottes-Chambertin 1990: An impressive *grand cru*, with delicate, sweet berry and earth aromas and flavors and a finish that goes on and on. The tannin and fruit structure is truly beautiful, with great balance and harmony. Drinkable in 1997. 300 cases made. • $78 • (12/15/92) • **93**
Ruchottes-Chambertin 1989 • $66 • (04/30/92) • **91**
Ruchottes-Chambertin 1988 • $69 • (11/15/90) • **92**
Ruchottes-Chambertin 1987 • $44 • (10/15/89) • **93**
Ruchottes-Chambertin 1986 • $45 • (11/15/88) • **91**
Ruchottes-Chambertin 1985 • $150 • (02/15/88) • **92**
Ruchottes-Chambertin 1984 • $34 • (03/15/87) • **83**
Ruchottes-Chambertin 1982 • $26 • (09/01/85) SS • **92**

MUGNERET, GERARD

Nuits-St.-Georges Aux Boudots 1988 • $48 • (02/28/91) • **76**
Nuits-St.-Georges Aux Boudots 1987 • $40 • (07/15/90) • **88**
Vosne-Romanée 1988 • $37 • (02/28/91) • **86**
Vosne-Romanée 1987 • $32 • (07/15/90) • **79**
Vosne-Romanée Les Suchots 1988 • $57 • (02/28/91) • **84**
Vosne-Romanée Les Suchots 1987 • $42 • (07/15/90) • **82**

MUGNERET, RENE

Vosne-Romanée 1985 • $27 • (04/30/88) • **90**
Vosne-Romanée 1983 • $16 • (11/16/85) • **73**
Vosne-Romanée 1982 • $17 • (07/16/85) • **86**

MUGNIER, JACQUES-FREDERIC

Bonnes Mares 1993: Gorgeous—a joy to drink. Ample, seductive, rich in dark fruit flavors including black cherry and currant, plush-textured and long on the finish. Firm tannins, lively acidity, wonderful balance. Tempting now, but better in 1998. • $90 • (05/15/96) • **92**
Chambolle-Musigny 1993: Rich, ripe fruit and ample, rounded texture make this an appealing, broad, generous Burgundy. Fairly tannic, slightly astringent, could use until at least 1998 to soften. • $39 • (05/15/96) • **88**
Chambolle-Musigny 1989 • $41 • (01/31/92) • **91**
Chambolle-Musigny 1988 • $96 Ⓐ • (05/15/91) • **86**
Chambolle-Musigny Les Amoureuses 1993: Rather closed, offering only medium concentration of black cherry, red berry and currant flavors. Still, quite an elegant structure although at this stage the tannins seem dry. Better in 2000. • $100 • **85**
Chambolle-Musigny Les Amoureuses 1989 • $62 • (01/31/92) • **90**
Chambolle-Musigny Les Amoureuses 1988 • $80 • (05/15/91) • **86**
Chambolle-Musigny Les Fuées 1993: A purely luscious, plush-textured, young red boasting generous fruit flavors, moderate tannins and lingering finish. Pleasurable to drink now and through 1999. • $69 • (05/15/96) • **90**
Chambolle-Musigny Les Fuées 1988 • $60 • (05/15/91) • **89**
Musigny 1989 • $125 • (01/31/92) • **88**

FRANCE

MULTIER, J.Y.

Syrah Côtes du Rhône Cèpage 1990 • $15 • (06/15/92) • **85**
Syrah Côtes du Rhône Cèpage 1988 • $10 • (12/15/90) • **74**

MUMM, G.H.

Brut Blanc de Blancs Champagne Mumm de Cremant NV: Assertive and stylized Champagne. Full-flavored for a blanc de blancs, adding heady aromas of smoke and toast and modest earthy, smoky notes that linger somewhat on the aftertaste. • $40 • **87**
Brut Champagne Cordon Rouge 1988: Bold and brassy, aromas reminding us of butter and caramel. Expressive flavors are smoky and doughy, leading to a dry finish. Mature and ready to drink now. • $36 • **88**
Brut Champagne Cordon Rouge 1985: A fruit bomb. Tastes like chocolate covered cherries. Full bodied with a velvety texture. Excellent acidity and a long flavorful finish. Would work well with dessert. Much better than we remembered from other tastings. Drinkable now but will improve with age • $35 • (12/31/93) • **90**
Brut Champagne Cordon Rouge 1982: • $37 • (12/31/88) • **85**
Brut Champagne Cordon Rouge 1979 • $55 • (02/16/86) • **93**
Brut Champagne Cordon Rouge NV: A nicely frothy but off-balance bubbly, with simple flavors that don't harmonize well. Milky, buttery accents clash with tart, lemon notes. 450,000 cases made. • $24 • **78**
Brut Champagne Grand Cordon 1985: Mellow and mature, a late-release 1985 that is definitely ready to drink. Flavors of apple and toast and nuts are its main attributes, and its buttery, caramel-like finish lingers. • $99 • **85**
Brut Champagne René Lalou 1985: A Champagne-lover's Champagne, from the toasty, nutty, smoky aromas to the lively fruit flavor to the lingering aftertaste. It has great balance-crisp enough but still creamy and luxurious in texture. There are "bigger" Champagnes, but few that have this much finesse. A marvelous improvement in the bottle since an earlier tasting. • $50 • **92**
Brut Champagne René Lalou 1982: Lots of toasty, yeasty complexity in a delicate, medium-bodied wine, soft around the edges but firmly anchored by a streak of lemony acidity. Beautifully balanced. • $55 • (09/30/88) • **90**
Brut Champagne René Lalou 1979 • $56 • (05/16/86) • **95**
Brut Rosé Champagne Cordon Rosé 1988: Mature and dry in style, with toasty aromas and earthy, mineral flavors that turn astringent and lean on the finish. 5,000 cases made. • $35 • **83**
Brut Rosé Champagne Cordon Rosé 1985: A colorful wine, both literally and in the flavor department, with hints of walnut, toast, orange peel, cherry and earth. A bit tart on the finish. • $100 • (01/31/92) • **86**
Brut Rosé Champagne Cordon Rosé 1983 • $30 • (12/31/89) • **81**
Brut Rosé Champagne Cordon Rosé 1982 • $30 • (12/31/88) • **83**
Brut Rosé Champagne Cordon Rose NV: A round, fruity rosé with ripe flavors of cherry and strawberry. Fresh and clean, well integrated and lively. Not at all heavy. • $35 • (12/15/95) • **88**
Extra Dry Champagne NV • $43 • (12/31/91) • **84**
Extra Dry Champagne Carte Classique NV: Attractive, sporting enough sweetness to take the edge off, but not a dessert wine. It combines apple, pear, butter and vanilla notes and good acidity, flavors lingering on the finish. • $22 • **86**
Extra Dry Champagne Cordon Vert NV • $43 • (01/31/92) • **86**

MURE

Brut Crémant d'Alsace Réserve NV • $7 • (06/15/90) • **79**
Crémant d'Alsace Réserve NV • $12 • (05/31/87) • **65**
Gewürztraminer Alsace Côte de Rouffach 1991 • $12 • (06/15/93) • **79**
Gewürztraminer Alsace Grand Cru Vorbourg Clos St.-Landelin 1993: This is high-class Gewürztraminer, with the complexity of a great white Burgundy and unmistakable richness and flavor of its own variety. It smells toasty and buttery, tastes ripe and creamy and turns honeylike on the finish. Try as an apéritif. 1,100 cases made. • $21 • (08/31/95) • **91**
Gewürztraminer Alsace Grand Cru Vorbourg Clos St.-Landelin 1992: Poached pears come to mind with this thick-textured, off-dry white, heavy and mature for its age, lacking varietal character. 1,400 cases made. • $17 • (11/15/94) • **79**
Gewürztraminer Alsace Grand Cru Vorbourg Clos St.-Landelin 1991: Orange and apricot aromas hint at Muscat while the flamboyant fruit flavors continue the theme. It's round, still fresh, focused and distinctive, if not in a typical style. • $19 • (11/15/94) • **86**
Muscat Alsace Grand Cru Vorbourg Clos St.-Landelin 1994: Essence of Muscat. Pungent and raisiny green apricot and apple flavors. It's very dry, showing floral aromas and very good richness. • $26 • (05/15/96) • **85**
Muscat Alsace Grand Cru Vorbourg Clos St.-Landelin 1993: Aromas are beautiful—orange blossom, lilac, crème brûlée—but the flavors are less expressive in this light, dry Muscat that ends slightly bitter. • $15 • (09/15/95) • **84**
Muscat Alsace Grand Cru Vorbourg Sélection de Grains Nobles Clos St.-Landelin 1991: An exotic and distinctive dessert wine with a vivid, straightforward apricot character in the aroma, flavor and finish. It's sweet, thick in texture and delicious. 125 cases made. • $60 • (11/15/94) • **88**
Muscat Alsace Grand Cru Vorbourg Vendanges Tardives Clos St.-Landelin 1992: A wine that non-wine lovers will love. Exuberant in aroma and packed with slightly sweet flavors of mandarin orange, almond and banana. It has a smooth texture and lingering finish that give it some flair. • $30 • (11/15/94) • **84**
Pinot Blanc Alsace Clos St.-Landelin 1993: Lean, refreshing, but not very rich style of Pinot Blanc. It has good acidity, rather green flavors and a short finish. • $14 • (09/15/95) • **82**
Pinot Blanc Alsace Clos St.-Landelin 1992: A modestly flavored Pinot Blanc with some pineapple and honey flavors in a straightforward package. Good, but nothing special. • $14 • (11/15/94) • **78**
Pinot Blanc Alsace Côte de Rouffach 1991 • $10 • (06/15/93) • **76**
Pinot Noir Alsace Clos St.-Landelin Vielle en Pièces de Chêne 1993: Toasty, smoky, oaky aromas and flavors dominate the black cherry and herbal notes, light-bodied but tannic. Good varietal character and ripeness for Alsace. Drinkable now. 900 cases made. • $25 • (09/15/95) • **84**
Riesling Alsace Côte de Rouffach 1991 • $11 • (06/15/93) • **79**
Riesling Alsace Grand Cru Vorbourg Clos St.-Landelin 1994: Intense and spicy, offering vibrant acidity and concentrated fruit flavors. Delicate, rich apple and grapefruit notes and a touch of almond on the finish. • $19 • (05/15/96) • **86**
Riesling Alsace Grand Cru Vorbourg Clos St.-Landelin 1993: Ripe and tasty, but in a different flavor spectrum than usual. It offers apple, melon and mango and these notes are backed by good acidity. Very good, if not classic Riesling. • $15 • (09/15/95) • **85**
Riesling Alsace Grand Cru Vorbourg Sélection de Grains Nobles Clos St. Landelin 1991: Sweet, rich and flavored with banana and coconut. This is a Pina Colada of a wine. Tasty, well balanced, long on the finish. 175 cases made. • $75 • (11/15/94) • **85**
Sylvaner Alsace Clos St.-Landelin Cuvée Oscar 1994: Pleasant and firm citrus and litchi-fruit flavors. A bit lean but still satisfying, and ends on a mineral note. • $12 • (05/15/96) • **84**
Sylvaner Alsace Clos St.-Landelin Cuvée Oscar 1993: Sturdy, well balanced, pleasantly floral in aroma, fairly full-bodied, offering apple and bitter almond flavors and good lemony acidity. 300 cases made. • $12 • (09/15/95) • **83**
Tokay Pinot Gris Alsace Grand Cru Vorbourg Clos St.-Landelin 1994: An archetypal Tokay Pinot Gris that's rich and broad-flavored. Elegant, well balanced, luscious, appealing peach flavors and a hint of grapefruit on the finish. • $23 • (05/15/96) • **88**
Tokay Pinot Gris Alsace Grand Cru Vorbourg Clos St.-Landelin 1992: Muscular, showing impressive focus and freshness. With ripe pear and cream flavors, it still has enough acidity to keep crisp and lively. There's good balance and enough concentration to age well. • $NA • (09/15/94) • **90**
Tokay Pinot Gris Alsace Grand Cru Vorbourg Vendanges Tardives Clos St.-Landelin 1992: Ripe in flavor but light on its feet. Fairly mature

Key: SS—Spectator Selection. CS—Cellar Selection. BB—Best Buy. $NA—Price not available. (BT)—Barrel tasting. Ⓐ—Auction Price.
Dates in parentheses represent the issues in which the ratings were published.

butter and pecan aromas lead to sweet vanilla and piecrust notes and finish with a touch of honey. 275 cases made. • $35 • (11/15/94) • **85**

MUSSY, DOMAINE

Beaune Epenottes 1993: Some decent plum and berry flavor, but rather light and slightly diluted on the finish. Drinkable now. • $26 • **78**

Beaune Epenottes 1992: Simple, modest and diluted, with some decent raspberry and strawberry flavors. Drink up. • $32 • **74**

Beaune Epenottes 1991: Firm, focused and sturdy, with youthful plum, currant and tar aromas and flavors and echoes of ripe plum on the spicy finish. Supple and rich. Drinkable now. • $34 Ⓐ • (01/31/94) • **88**

Beaune Epenottes 1986 • $28 • (05/31/89) • **86**

Beaune Les Montrevenots 1993: Lovely rose petal and berry character, medium body and firm tannins. Not big but deliciously fresh. Better in 1998. • $26 • **84**

Beaune Les Montrevenots 1992: Firm in texture, with just enough raspberry and currant flavor to balance the tannins. Finish is a little sugary. Drinkable now. • $32 • **79**

Beaune Les Montrevenots 1991: Sturdy and flavorful, with an exotic cigar, tobacco and mineral edge to the currant and plum flavors. Finishes earthy and a bit chewy, but broad enough to suggest aging until 1997. • $34 Ⓐ • (01/31/94) • **86**

Beaune Les Montrevenots 1990: Elegant, but unyielding and rather lean and mean, with pretty berry and cherry aromas and flavors and a hint of herb. Lacks flesh. Drinkable now. • $45 • (12/15/92) • **87**

Beaune Les Montrevenots 1986 • $28 • (05/31/89) • **86**

Pommard 1993: Distinctive style, gamy and barnyardy, adding some odd salami notes. A bit drying on the finish. • $34 • **82**

Pommard 1992: Supple and generous, with raspberry and toast flavors that linger on the finish. Drinkable now. • $38 • **84**

Pommard 1991: Chunky and simple, a nice, curranty wine that veers off toward lime on the finish. Drinkable now. • $41 Ⓐ • (01/31/94) • **81**

Pommard 1986 • $32 • (04/30/89) • **66**

Pommard 1985 • $35 • (10/15/88) • **86**

Pommard Les Epenots 1993: Medium- to light-bodied red that lacks depth and complexity. Some raspberry and strawberry flavors and a short, slightly dry finish. • $45 • **79**

Pommard Les Epenots 1992: A supple Pommard that gains some complexity as the blackberry, prune and raspberry flavors unfold into a rather short finish. Try now. • $49 • **82**

Pommard Les Epenots 1991: Tries to be elegant, but comes up a little short. The unripe berry flavors never quite smooth out. Try now. • $54 Ⓐ • (01/31/94) • **80**

Pommard Les Epenots 1990: Very well made in a subtle, refined style, with round, supple cherry characteristics graced by silky tannins. Drinkable now. • $50 • (12/15/92) • **86**

Pommard Premier Cru 1993: Smells somewhat like a barnyard but rich fruit lies under it all. Medium body and tannins and peppery finish. Tastes more like Rhône than Burgundy. • $38 • **79**

Pommard Premier Cru 1991: Tough in texture, offering a broad array of prune, mushroom and berry aromas and flavors. Finishes softer than many '91s. Tannic, but drinkable now. • $NA • (01/31/94) • **83**

Pommard Premier Cru 1986 • $35 • (04/30/89) • **86**

Volnay 1993: Rather earthy and funky showing some good red fruit character, but it's light-bodied with a slightly bitter finish. Try in 1997. • $NA • **79**

Volnay 1992: Balanced but on the light side, showing some decent red berry flavors and a tannic edge on the finish. Drinkable now. • $NA • **77**

Volnay 1991: Ripe and exotic, with a violet and spicebox edge to the thick, concentrated plum and currant aromas and flavors. Offers a real mouthful of flavor on the finish. Try now. • $34 Ⓐ • (01/31/94) • **86**

MUTS, CHÂTEAU LES

Côtes de Bergerac 1983 • $6 • (11/15/86) • **80**

MYLORD, CHÂTEAU

Entre-Deux-Mers 1994: Appley, grassy aromas and character complement a fine, steely, racy texture and medium aftertaste. • $8 • **78**

Entre-Deux-Mers 1993: Grassy, appley character and a touch of tropical fruit, but light and slightly diluted on the finish. • $8 • **79**

MYRAT, CHÂTEAU DE

Barsac 1991: A bit earthy, offering lemon, spice and mineral character, quite crisp, moderately sweet and rich, but somewhat flat on the finish. Drinkable now. • $NA • (04/15/95) • **80**

NADDEF, PHILIPPE

Gevrey-Chambertin 1988 • $25 • (07/15/91) • **80**

Gevrey-Chambertin 1987 • $19 • (03/31/90) • **86**

Gevrey-Chambertin 1985 • $25 • (04/15/88) • **94**

Gevrey-Chambertin Les Cazetiers 1987 • $35 • (03/31/90) • **88**

Gevrey-Chambertin Champeaux 1987 • $28 • (03/31/90) • **90**

Gevrey-Chambertin Champeaux 1985 • $29 • (03/31/88) • **80**

Mazis-Chambertin 1988 • $60 • (07/15/91) • **69**

Mazis-Chambertin 1987 • $22 Ⓐ • (03/31/90) • **89**

Mazis-Chambertin Vieilles Vignes 1991: Firm and chewy, with anise and mint flavors dominating the chunky berry and currant fruit, finishing with enough tannin to want until 1998-2000 to soften the blocky edges. • $48 • (08/31/94) • **89**

NAIRAC, CHÂTEAU

Barsac 1992: Sweet, yet tasting like bitter orange liqueur. Some may like it, but not us. • $NA • **75**

Barsac 1991: A serious effort, providing dried apricot, honey and fig flavors that continue nicely on the finish. Drink now or try after 1996. • $NA • **84**

Barsac 1990: An intense, medium-to-full-bodied sweet wine with real grip, showing off its apricot, orange-peel, honey, toast and butter flavors accompanied by lots of panache. Explodes on the finish. Should be even better after 1998. • $31 • **90**

Barsac 1989: Fresh and elegant, lavishly oaked and toasted, showing vanilla, chocolate and honey flavors, medium-bodied, medium-sweet, relatively austere. Better after 1996? • $38 • **87**

Barsac 1988: Full-bodied, balanced, well-made Barsac, with just the right amount of new wood, ripe fruit and botryitis character. Better after 1998. • $30 • **91**

Barsac 1987 • $31 • (06/15/90) • **81**

Barsac 1983 Dominated by oak-scented vanilla now, but incredibly fresh and youthful, with spice, floral and honey character. Medium-sweet, fresh finish. Drinkable now. • $33 • **87**

NARDIQUE LA GRAVIERE, CHÂTEAU

Entre-Deux-Mers 1994: Flat, dull and one-dimensional, yielding only a slight hint of fruit. • $8 • **72**

Entre-Deux-Mers 1993: Very grassy and herbal, giving vibrant acidity that might soften with bottle age. But it's quite aggressive now. • $8 • **79**

NATTER, HENRY

Sancerre Cuvée de la Grange de Montigny 1992: Complex and harmonious, this has well-integrated mineral, melon, herbal and honey notes, it's round and generous yet still crisp and clean, with a long, fruity finish. Drinkable now. • $18 • (11/15/95) • **88**

Sancerre Domaine de Montigny 1993: Mixing smooth-textured ripe peach and marzipan flavors with crisp, citrusy acidity gives this wine a distinctive style, soft yet bright and fruity. It would make a good apéritif. • $15 • **83**

Sancerre Domaine de Montigny 1992: A big wine with good balance, blending pear and apple flavors with herbal and celery notes in a smooth, harmonious package. It's subtle and smooth, without rough edges or great depth. • $14 • (10/31/94) • **85**

Sancerre Red Domaine de Montigny 1990: A ripe vintage and a dollop of new oak combine to offer a wine with dark color, firm tannins, black cherry flavor and an attractive toastiness. Still fresh, but it should be drunk before the wood overwhelms the fruit. • $15 • (10/31/94) • **84**

Sancerre Rosé Domaine de Montigny 1992: A pale rosé that combines a full, dry, spicy palate with a touch of new oak. It's pleasant and subtly fruity. • $15 • (08/31/95) • **81**

NAUDIN-FERRAND, HENRI

Bourgogne Aligoté 1994: Crisp and straightforward, with modest fruit flavors. Tart finish. 2,916 cases made. • $NA • **76**

Bourgogne Hautes-Côtes de Beaune 1994: Zingy acidity holds it together, and the peach, apricot, mineral, wet earth and pear flavors are lovely. No oak character, but it's subtle, elegant and delicious. A great effort for this appellation. 845 cases made. • $NA • **88**

NENIN, CHÂTEAU

Pomerol 1990: A pretty, restrained wine, with plum, tobacco and berry notes and silky tannins. Drinkable now. 10,000 cases made. • $25 Ⓐ • (03/31/93) • **88**

Pomerol 1986 • $22 • (06/30/89) • **84**

Pomerol 1982 • $31 Ⓐ • (05/15/89) • **89**

Pomerol 1970 • $24 Ⓐ • (05/15/93) • **84**

Pomerol 1961: This bottle had a relatively low fill, but what an elegant wine came out of it. An exotic and complex bottle bouquet is mirrored in the smooth, rich fruit flavors. It has a velvety texture backed by firm tannins and followed by a nicely lingering finish. Drink through 2000. • $47 • (04/30/96) • **91**

Pomerol 1959 • $100 • (10/15/90) • **88**

Pomerol 1945: Decadent, spoilage aromas. Still tannic, falling apart, drying. Army-Navy bottling. • $250 • **71**

NERTHE, CHÂTEAU DE LA

Châteauneuf-du-Pape 1991 • $25 • **85**

Châteauneuf-du-Pape 1990: Deep, intense and finely polished, with loads of plum, spice and leather flavors. Rich, chewy and well balanced. Dried cherry and chocolate flavors linger on the long finish. Drink now through 1998. • $25 • (10/15/94) • **89**

Châteauneuf-du-Pape 1989 • $25 • (10/15/91) • **87**

Châteauneuf-du-Pape 1988 • $25 • (10/15/91) • **88**

Châteauneuf-du-Pape 1986 • $18 • (10/15/91) • **87**

Châteauneuf-du-Pape 1985 • $17 • (10/15/91) • **86**

Châteauneuf-du-Pape 1983 • $25 • (10/15/91) • **88**

Châteauneuf-du-Pape 1981 • $30 • (10/15/91) • **94**

Châteauneuf-du-Pape Cuvée des Cadettes 1990: Ripe and rich on the palate, more flavorful than aromatic, offering cedary, toasty notes in the aromas and focused plum and currant flavors on a round, smooth texture. Drink now. • $50 • (04/15/93) • **89**

Châteauneuf-du-Pape Cuvée des Cadettes 1989 • $30 • (10/15/91) • **88**

Châteauneuf-du-Pape Cuvée des Cadettes 1988 • $30 • (10/15/91) • **89**

NEVEU, ANDRE

Sancerre Les Longues Fins 1992: This distinctive wine marries earthy, nutty, toasty aromas with ripe pear and light vanilla flavors. Showing a round, mature character. • $15 • (10/31/94) • **82**

Sancerre Le Manoir 1991 • $17 • (09/15/93) • **86**

NICOLAS

Beaujolais-Villages 1989 • $8 • (11/15/90) BB • **82**

Bonnes Mares 1959 • $NA • (08/31/90) • **75**

Cabernet Sauvignon Vin de Pays d'Oc Maison Nicolas Réserve 1993: Herbaceous, green bean flavors characterize this light wine with dry tannins. Simple and tough. 32,000 cases made. • $6 • (10/31/95) • **78**

Chardonnay Vin de Pays d'Oc Maison Nicolas Réserve 1994: This smooth wine has a nice lanolin mouth-feel that makes it generous and creamy, the attractive melon and lightly spicy flavors just could use more crispness. 32,000 cases made. • $6 • (12/15/95) • **83**

Chardonnay Vin de Pays d'Oc Réserve 1992 • $6 • (03/15/94) • **81**

Merlot Vin de Pays d'Oc Maison Nicolas Réserve 1993: The plum and chocolate flavors have good concentration in this fresh-tasting French Merlot, and the tannins have mellowed, which allows the fruit to linger on the finish. A harmonious wine that doesn't break the bank. 32,000 cases made. • $6 • (10/31/95) BB • **84**

Pouilly-Fumé 1993: Rich, but top-heavy and lacking verve, this opens with intense aromas of butter and vanilla, and follows through with honeyed, fig flavors. Not your typical Loire Sauvignon Blanc. 5,000 cases made. • $9 • **81**

Sancerre 1993: Deep gold color and buttery aromas are atypical. Awkward, unfocused flavors. Tasted twice, with consistent notes. 5,000 cases made. • $9 • **77**

Vouvray 1993: Attractive aromas of wildflower honey give way to a smooth texture on the palate, with honey, melon and light citrus flavors. It has some richness and just a touch of sweetness. 7,000 cases made. • $6 • (11/15/95) • **83**

NICOLE, CUVEE

Puligny-Montrachet 1992: An extreme style of white Burgundy that tastes like honey and nectarine in a full-bodied package. It tastes sweet and thick like a dessert wine, then finishes on the tart side. 200 cases made. • $40 • (05/15/95) • **84**

NICOT, CHÂTEAU

Haut-Benauge 1984 • $4 • (11/16/85) • **69**

NIELLON, MICHEL

Bâtard-Montrachet 1994: Voluptuous, supple, ripe fig, pineapple and toasted oak flavors. Needs time to let oak marry the fruit. Quite intense on its lingering finish. Try in 1999. • $135 • (05/31/96) • **88**

Bâtard-Montrachet 1993: Lovely, well crafted and smoother than most '93s, boasting honey, butter and vanilla flavors, medium-bodied, balanced, delicious and quite ripe. Try after 1996. • $122 • **88**

Chassagne-Montrachet 1994: Well made and seductive, with pure, clean fruit flavors that caress your palate. Light to medium body, with mineral, vanilla and pear notes. It shows a round and supple yet fresh finish. • $45 • (05/31/96) • **88**

Chassagne-Montrachet 1993: A touch of complexity emerges shyly, some grassy notes mingle attractively with honey, almond, and lime flavors. Hard now, but has an artist's signature all over it. Try after 1996. • $38 • **86**

Chassagne-Montrachet 1992: A full and rich white Burgundy, with bacon and pear aromas and smooth, generous texture along with good fruit on the finish. Lively and vibrant, drinkable now. • $32 • (08/31/94) • **86**

Chassagne-Montrachet Les Champs Gain 1994: Rather rich and ripe, with supple, lush honey, lemon, toast and apricot aromas and flavors. This full-bodied '94 is a mouthful. Clean, focused and has a lovely round finish. Drinkable now through 1998. • $55 • (05/31/96) • **85**

Chassagne-Montrachet Les Champs Gain 1993: Interesting nut, toasted oak and fruit aromas and flavors, but slightly short on the finish. Drinkable now. • $46 • **83**

Chassagne-Montrachet Clos de la Maltroie 1994: Beams out a focused ray of lemon and honey, presented in a solid, full-bodied frame that beckons you for another sip. Fresh, vibrant and well crafted. Better still in 1998. • $NA • (05/31/96) • **90**

Chassagne-Montrachet Clos de la Maltroie 1993: Green, grassy, honey notes blend nicely with lime and citrusy flavors and a hint of mineral on the finish. Still, it's tough going now, try after 1996. • $NA • **88**

Chassagne-Montrachet Clos de la Maltroie 1992: Appealing, fat and ripe, with hazelnut and marzipan flavors, a bit soft and definitely ready to drink. • $NA • (08/31/94) • **87**

Chassagne-Montrachet Clos St.-Jean 1994: A rich, voluptuous and distinctive *premier cru*, with complex flavors of dried herb, honey and tropical fruit. Lovely, full-bodied and very ripe in character. Drinkable now, but it should be nice in 1998. • $NA • (05/31/96) • **89**

Key: SS—Spectator Selection. CS—Cellar Selection. BB—Best Buy. $NA—Price not available. (BT)—Barrel tasting. Ⓐ—Auction Price.
Dates in parentheses represent the issues in which the ratings were published.

Chassagne-Montrachet Clos St.-Jean 1993: Pretty fresh pear and delicate chalky character. Medium-to-light body, fresh acidity. Try now. • $NA • **84**

Chassagne-Montrachet Clos St.-Jean 1992: A Chassagne with character and personality, showing plenty of silky spice, nutmeg, toast, pear and butter flavors that marry well on the sophisticated finish. Deft winemaking here. • $NA • (08/31/94) • **88**

Chevalier-Montrachet 1994: A blockbuster that delivers tons of flavor. Rich coconut, citrus, cream, honey and ripe fruit strike the palate in this full-bodied, very concentrated and intense wine. Well crafted and generous on the long finish. Tempting now, but should age through 2000. • $135 • (05/31/96) • **92**

Chevalier-Montrachet 1993: Very good concentration for the vintage, with enticing mineral, apple and pear character, medium body and fresh finish. Try after 1996. • $122 • **88**

NOBILIS

Minervois 1990 • $NA • (03/15/94) • **87**

NOBLE, DOMAINE LA

Merlot Vin de Pays de l'Aude 1991 • $7 • (06/15/93) • **77**
Merlot Vin de Pays de l'Aude 1990 • $7 • (03/31/92) • **73**

NOUVEAU, CLAUDE

Santenay White 1994: Straightforward, crisp and light-bodied, with green apple, rose petal and herbal flavors. Refreshing and quite intense. Clean and tart on the finish. 500 cases made. • $NA • **78**

OGEREAU, DOMAINE

Anjou-Villages Red 1990: Aromas of smoke, tar and roasted fruit leap from the glass in this deep-colored red. It's not overly tannic or full-bodied, but the flavors are rich and ripe, with light berry notes under the smoke, spice and herbs. • $NA • (10/31/94) • **85**

OGIER & FILS, A.

Châteauneuf-du-Pape Grande Cuvée 1985 • $22 • (06/15/93) • **76**

OGIER, MICHEL

Côte-Rôtie 1990: Firm and tannic, with appealing black cherry and violet aromas and flavors. Subtle, with nuances of toast, hazelnut and vanilla. Needs until 1997 to soften the tannins. 350 cases made. • $42 • (04/15/93) • **88**

Côte-Rôtie 1988 • $38 • (11/15/91) • **87**

OLEK-MERY

Chinon Cuvée des Tireaux 1993: Youthful and vibrant, from the spicy, clove aromas to the concentrated red currant flavors. A Loire red of substance and complexity. • $18 • (05/15/96) • **87**

OLIVIER, CHÂTEAU D'

Graves 1981 • $14 • (10/16/85) • **86**
Graves 1982 • $21 • (08/31/92) • **90**
Graves 1983 • $23 • (05/01/89) • **92**
Graves 1985 • $20 • (02/15/89) SS • **93**

Pessac-Léognan 1995: Plenty of medium-bodied earthy, berry, herbal character adds to decent fruit but a slightly austere finish. Tasted twice, with consistent notes. • $NA • (05/15/96) • **80-84** (BT)

Pessac-Léognan 1994: Very good berry and cherry character and fine tannins. Not big but appealing. Better than its '95. • $NA • (05/15/96) • **85-89** (BT)

Pessac-Léognan 1993: Very grapey, offering wet earth, berry and cherry aromas and flavors, medium body and tannins and a slightly coarse finish. Needs some time, try in 1997. 9,333 cases made. • $23 • (01/31/96) • **85**

Pessac-Léognan 1992: A good amount of cherry and violet character, firm tannins and vibrant fruit. Drink now. • $18 • **83**

Pessac-Léognan 1990: Firm, focused and elegant, this is a solid wine, with a wide band of cherry, spice, tobacco and olive aromas and flavors. Finishes smooth in texture. Drinkable now. 8,500 cases made. • $20 • (12/31/92) • **90**

Pessac-Léognan 1989 • $23 • (03/15/92) SS • **95**
Pessac-Léognan 1988 • $25 • (02/15/91) • **91**

Pessac-Léognan White 1994: Thick and rich, with loads of apple and lime aromas and flavors, distinguished by a grassy character. Full-bodied and fruity, a touch of fine acidity opening it up. (Estimated price) • $16 • (03/31/96) • **90**

Pessac-Léognan White 1993: Well made, exhibiting balanced, subtle honey, butter and pear flavors. You only wish for a bit more concentration. • $16 • **85**

Pessac-Léognan White 1992 • $15 • (06/15/94) • **80**

OLLIEUX, CHÂTEAU LES

Corbières 1988 • $5 • (11/30/90) BB • **80**

ORMES-DE-PEZ, CHÂTEAU LES

St.-Estèphe 1995: Has lots of tannins and ripe fruit,but slightly disjointed at the moment. Difficult to judge. • $NA • (05/15/96) • **85-89** (BT)

St.-Estèphe 1994: Softer and more supple than some '94s, but tastes light with a slightly diluted feel. Attractive plum and red berry character, some smoky, spicy notes to add complexity and firm tannins. • $16 • (05/15/96) • **80-84** (BT)

St.-Estèphe 1993: Wonderful polish to this red, adding a core of ripe, red berry flavor. Medium-bodied, harmonious mouth-feel and an extremely elegant, supple finish. Delicious now, but better in 1997. 15,000 cases made. • $19 • (01/31/96) • **87**

St.-Estèphe 1992: Decent licorice, spice and cedar character, light body, light tannins. Drink now. • $17 • **78**

St.-Estèphe 1991: Very fruity and pleasant with berry and cherry aromas and flavors, medium tannins and a light finish. • $15 • (03/31/94) • **82**

St.-Estèphe 1990: A monstrous wine, with huge amounts of cherry and toasted oak flavors and velvety tannins. Quite hard on the palate, but the very long finish suggests greatness. From Jean-Michel Cazes. Drinkable in 1998. 12,500 cases made. • $22 • (03/31/93) • **93**

St.-Estèphe 1989 • $24 • (03/15/92) • **86**
St.-Estèphe 1988 • $21 • (04/30/91) • **88**
St.-Estèphe 1987 • $15 • (05/15/90) • **83**
St.-Estèphe 1986 • $22 Ⓐ • (11/30/89) • **87**
St.-Estèphe 1985 • $27 Ⓐ • (04/30/88) • **89**
St.-Estèphe 1983 • $17 • (10/15/86) • **86**
St.-Estèphe 1982 • $43 Ⓐ • (08/31/92) • **84**

St.-Estèphe 1961: A subtle, beautifully balanced and mature St.-Estèphe with fine tannins for a silky texture and flavors that linger on the finish. Drink through 2000. • $55 • (04/30/96) • **87**

ORMES-SORBET, CHÂTEAU LES

Médoc 1988 • $20 • (04/30/91) • **84**

ORMESSON, DOMAINE D'

Vin de Pays d'Oc 1992 • $NA • (03/15/94) • **87**
Vin de Pays d'Oc 1991 • $NA • (03/15/94) • **83**
Vin de Pays d'Oc 1985 • $4 • (04/15/89) • **77**

ORMIERES, CHÂTEAU

Minervois 1991 • $7 • (03/15/94) • **83**

ORSAN, CHÂTEAU D'

Côtes du Rhône 1988 • $6 • **61**
Côtes du Rhône 1987 • $4 • (11/15/88) • **77**
Côtes du Rhône 1986 • $4 • (02/29/88) BB • **81**
Côtes du Rhône 1985 • $6 • (12/15/87) • **79**

OSTANGE, DOMAINE D'

Mâcon 1993: Good, straightforward Chardonnay, light in body and bone-dry, showing well-defined, crisp lime, mineral and green apple flavors and a fresh finish. From Noël Perrin. • $NA • (08/31/95) • **82**

OSTERTAG, DOMAINE

Riesling Alsace Vignoble d'Epfig 1992: This assertive wine opens with attractive petrol and steely aromas and the palate is firm, with green apple and mineral notes. By the finish, however, the acidity is almost overwhelming, suggesting it needs time to soften. Try now. • $18 • (11/15/94) • **81**

OTT, DOMAINES

Bandol Cuvée Marine 1993: Pale salmon color, with earthy, mineral aromas and candied flavors. An austere style that combines dryness with high alcohol. Not for everyone. • $20 • (08/31/95) • **81**

Bandol Rosé Cuvée Marine 1989 • $19 • (07/15/91) • **79**

Côtes de Provence 1989 • $25 • (07/15/92) • **84**

Côtes de Provence 1987 • $22 • (05/31/91) • **78**

Côtes de Provence Clair de Noirs 1993: Aromas of dried fruit and herbs yield to a juicy, fruity-tasting wine that finishes hot. Austere, and the alcohol disturbs the balance. • $25 • **81**

Côtes de Provence La Déesse 1993: The herb and dried cherry notes are strung on a lean, dry frame here. • $20 • (08/31/95) • **77**

Côtes de Provence Rosé Clair de Noirs 1990 • $20 • (06/30/92) • **73**

Côtes de Provence Rosé Clair de Noirs 1987 • $19 • (07/15/89) • **83**

Côtes de Provence Rosé Clair de Noirs 1986 • $18 • (07/31/88) • **80**

Côtes de Provence La Victoire 1992: Awkward and bitter with a medicinal taste and an off-putting herbaceousness. The aroma is sulphury. • $18 • **73**

OUDINOT

Brut Blanc de Blancs Champagne 1988: Extremely fruity style of blanc de blancs. The nose and palate is dominated with apple, lime and banana character, full-bodied with steely acidity. Drinkable now. • $29 • (12/31/93) • **88**

Brut Blanc de Blancs Champagne NV • $25 • (12/31/90) • **74**

Brut Blanc de Noirs Champagne 1988 • $29 • (12/31/93) • **88**

Brut Champagne 1985 • $28 • (12/31/90) • **90**

Brut Rosé Champagne 1983 • $25 • (12/31/89) • **88**

PABIOT, DIDIER

Pouilly-Fumé Coteaux des Loges 1992: Fresh and balanced citrus and apple flavors outweigh the herbal notes. There are nice floral and smoky accents and a clean, fruity finish. • $17 • (10/31/94) • **86**

PABIOT, DOMINIQUE

Pouilly-Fumé Les Cerisottes 1993: Round, and relatively soft, this shows apple, light vegetal and honey notes; it's ripe but lacks concentration and verve. 8,000 cases made. • $15 • **78**

PABIOT, J.A.D

Pouilly-Fumé Domaine des Chantebines 1993: Smoky aromas dominate the nose, but step back on the palate to allow lean, lemony acidity and rather delicate peach and mineral flavors to shine. It's firm but not a body-builder, and harmonious. • $16 • (11/15/95) • **86**

Pouilly-Fumé Prestige de Vieilles Vignes 1993: Ripe and muscular, showing round, rather blunt flavors of pear and melon and a firm acid backbone. It's not subtle or complex but would stand up to food. • $23 • (11/15/95) • **85**

PABIOT & FILS, JEAN

Pouilly-Fumé Les Cerisottes 1992: Firm and tart, showing rustic earth, apple and anise flavors. It lacks delicacy and definition. 10,000 cases made. • $14 • (10/31/94) • **76**

PADERE, CHÂTEAU DE

Buzet 1986 • $5 • (12/15/88) • **79**

PAILLARD, BRUNO

Brut Blanc de Blancs Champagne 1983 • $40 • (05/31/87) • **94**

Brut Blanc de Blancs Champagne 1975 • $42 • (05/31/87) • **70**

Brut Blanc de Blancs Champagne Chardonnay Réserve Privée NV: Charming and light, with fruity, toasty aromas, a gentle but mouth-filling texture and flavors of fig and vanilla that linger on the finish. Tasted twice. 2,500 cases made. • $30 • **86**

Brut Blanc de Blancs Crémant NV • $36 • (12/31/90) • **85**

Brut Champagne 1985 • $35 • (12/31/93) • **93**

Brut Champagne Première Cuvee NV: Lots of strong bass notes in this Champagne: toasty, yeasty, red berry flavors, firm and full-bodied in style. A good match with a meal. • $25 • (12/15/95) • **88**

Brut Rosé Champagne Première Cuvee NV: Delicate and crisp, showing attractive strawberry, dried fig, light vanilla and floral notes, it's light-bodied but expressive. A beautiful apéritif. • $35 • (12/15/95) • **90**

PAILLET-QUANCARD, CHÂTEAU DE

Premières Côtes de Bordeaux 1990: Tart, earthy and unpleasant, a wine with very little meat on its bones. For those who like austere Bordeaux only. 11,000 cases made. • $14 • (06/15/93) • **76**

PAJOT, CHÂTEAU

Sauternes 1983 • $8 • (01/31/88) • **62**

PALLIERES, DOMAINE LES

Gigondas 1988 • $20 • (08/31/92) • **79**

Gigondas 1986 • $21 • (11/15/91) • **79**

Gigondas 1984 • $14 • (09/30/89) • **86**

Gigondas 1983 • $15 • (01/31/89) • **88**

Gigondas 1982 • $11 • (05/31/87) • **89**

Gigondas 1981 • $11 • (03/15/87) • **90**

PALME, CHÂTEAU LA

Côtes du Frontonnais 1988 • $7 • (07/31/91) • **63**

PALMER, CHÂTEAU

Margaux 1995: Wonderfully made, pretty Bordeaux boasting loads of bright berry and cherry flavor and soft tannins. Medium- to full-bodied and round, adding a fruity finish. All finesse. • $NA • (05/15/96) • **90-94** (BT)

Margaux 1994: Lots of pretty fruit and expensive oak showing in this wine. Moderate tannins and a silky finish. Almost outstanding. • $NA • (05/15/96) • **85-89** (BT)

Margaux 1993: Supersilky wine featuring toasted oak, berry and cherry character, medium body, fine tannins and delicate finish. Needs time, better in 1997. • $40 • (01/31/96) • **88**

Margaux 1992: Light and fruity, offering some pretty cherry and plum character, but straightforward and short on the finish. Drink now. • $38 • **80**

Margaux 1991: This estate is always very good in a mediocre vintage. Lovely character of vanilla, cherry and berry, firm tannins and a long, silky finish. Drinkable now. • $38 • (03/31/94) • **87**

Key: SS—Spectator Selection. CS—Cellar Selection. BB—Best Buy. $NA—Price not available. (BT)—Barrel tasting. (A)—Auction Price.
Dates in parentheses represent the issues in which the ratings were published.

Margaux 1990: Gives more in flavor than in aroma at the moment, but excellent. It's chunky for a Margaux, with loads of plummy cedar flavors and full, soft tannins. Drink after 1996. 16,000 cases made. • $42 Ⓐ • (03/31/93) • **91**
Margaux 1989 • $91 Ⓐ • (03/15/92) • **95**
Margaux 1988 • $39 Ⓐ • (02/28/91) CS • **96**
Margaux 1987 • $31 • (05/15/90) • **84**
Margaux 1986 • $41 Ⓐ • (06/15/89) • **94**
Margaux 1985: Greatness in subtlety. Clearly focused black cherry and vanilla character. It's full-bodied with medium tannins and a juicy, fruity finish. Drink now. • $60 • (10/15/94) • **91**
Margaux 1984 • $30 • (10/15/87) • **84**
Margaux 1983: Some people always thought this was better than the '82 Palmer. Sorry. An outstanding wine nonetheless. Firm and solid wine with great dark color and fresh fruit plum aromas and flavors with a hint of new wood. Firm finish. Drink now. • $563 • **90**
Margaux 1982 • $68 Ⓐ • (08/31/92) • **92**
Margaux 1981: Always a delicious wine. Soft and elegant with perfumed cherry, strawberry, cedar box character, fine tannins and a silky finish. Drink now. • $46 • **89**
Margaux 1980 • $19 • (05/01/85) • **86**
Margaux 1979 • $51 Ⓐ • (10/15/89) • **90**
Margaux 1978 • $65 Ⓐ • (05/01/85) • **81**
Margaux 1970 • $135 Ⓐ • (05/15/93) • **91**
Margaux 1962 • $80 Ⓐ • (11/30/87) • **80**
Margaux 1961: A mouth-watering example of Palmer that outshines châteaus with higher classifications. It displays a broad palette of flavors that blend and enhance the elegant, lively texture and lingering finish. In a word, it has finesse. Drink through 2005. • $563 • (04/30/96) • **93**
Margaux 1959 • $307 Ⓐ • (10/15/90) • **98**
Margaux 1945: Firm, still somewhat chewy in tannin, but tightly packed with black cherry, anise and toast flavors that remain on the long, long finish. A solid '45 featuring style and enough grace to make up for the chewiness. • $500 • **91**

PAPE, CHÂTEAU LE

Pessac-Léognan 1990: An elegant austerity pervades this wine. It blends ripe black currant aromas and flavors with a lean texture. Drinkable now. • $16 • (08/31/95) • **83**

PAPE CLEMENT, CHÂTEAU

Graves 1985 • $NA • **90**
Graves 1983 • $NA • **84**
Graves 1982 • $33 • (02/01/85) • **84**
Graves 1981 • $NA • **73**
Graves 1979 • $20 • (10/15/89) • **84**
Graves 1970 • $66 • (05/15/93) • **84**
Graves 1962 • $120 • (11/30/87) • **90**
Graves 1961: A ripe-tasting, chewy-textured wine that is lively despite its years and offers deep plummy flavors that make you come back for another sip. Drink through 2000. • $560 • (04/30/96) • **88**
Graves 1959 • $100 • (10/15/90) • **80**
Pessac-Léognan 1995: Round, rich, earthy berry and wild mushroom character, full body, soft tannins and long finish. Best Pape Clément in years. • $NA • (05/15/96) • **90-94** (BT)
Pessac-Léognan 1994: Plenty of lovely spice, berry and vanilla aromas and flavors. Moderate tannins, but slightly dry. Not quite as good as in an earlier tasting. • $32 • (05/15/96) • **80-84** (BT)
Pessac-Léognan 1993: Elegant, light- to medium-bodied, showing some nice fruit and meaty, gamy character that's quite appealing. Firm tannins, so try in 1998. • $38 • (01/31/96) • **84**
Pessac-Léognan 1992: Subtle aromas of berry, tobacco and stones follow through on the palate, light-bodied. Tasted twice, with consistent notes. Drink now. • $26 • **79**
Pessac-Léognan 1990: No holds barred on this wine. It's packed with decadent, earthy fruit aromas and flavors and loads of tannins. Drinkable in 1998. 11,000 cases made. • $47 • (03/31/93) • **92**
Pessac-Léognan 1989 • $43 • (03/15/92) • **88**
Pessac-Léognan 1988 • $40 • (12/31/90) • **93**
Pessac-Léognan 1987 • $24 • (05/15/90) • **84**
Pessac-Léognan 1986 • $36 • (06/30/89) • **92**
Pessac-Léognan White 1994: Can a white get more harmonious than this? Sensational from start to finish, building slowly from the perfectly balanced honey, citrus, earth and mineral complexity to an extended, long finish. It's all presented with a remarkably smooth mouth-feel. Great now, but better with cellaring until at least 1999. (Estimated price) • $50 • (03/31/96) • **96**
Pessac-Léognan White 1993: Fine mineral, cream, apple and grapefuit character, medium-bodied and very solid, leading to a long finish. Drinkable now. • $50 • (05/31/95) • **88**
Pessac-Léognan White 1992 • $NA • (06/15/94) • **87**

PAPES, CAVES DES

Châteauneuf-du-Pape 1988 • $14 • (10/31/93) • **83**
Côtes du Rhône 1993: Ripe, round and easy-drinking with rich, plummy flavors and a hint of chocolate and spice. A sturdy and flavorful wine that's ready to drink now. 25,000 cases made. • $7 • **83**
Côtes du Rhône 1990 • $6 • (10/31/93) • **81**
Côtes du Rhône Domaine des Jonquiers 1990 • $7 • (04/30/94) • **81**
Côtes du Rhône White 1993: Not much going on here. Thin and overly herbal, with unappealing earthy flavors. 25,000 cases made. • $7 • **74**
Gigondas 1988 • $13 • (10/31/93) • **78**

PAQUET, FRANCOIS

Mâcon-Lugny Cépage Chardonnay, Cuvée St.-Denis Tradition 1993: Clean, crisp wet hay, green apple and citrus are quite tart and unyielding, but light, fresh and dry. 1,916 cases made. • $9 • (08/31/95) • **78**
Mâcon Blanc-Villages Cépage Chardonnay 1994: A pleasant, fresh, sharp and tart character, mingling quince, pear and apple notes. Juicy, clean and vibrant finish. 3,000 cases made. • $9 • (08/31/95) • **79**
Mâcon Blanc-Villages Cépage Chardonnay 1993: Light and straightforward, showing grapefruit, hay and a slight salty, fishy and cardboard taste on the finish. Diluted. 3,000 cases made. • $9 • (08/31/95) • **70**

PAQUET, JEAN-PAUL

Pouilly-Fuissé Domaine de Fuissiacus Vieilles Vignes 1994: What happened? Dull-tasting, quite diluted, showing a cardboard note and only modest fruit flavors. • $15 • (05/31/96) • **72**
Pouilly-Fuissé Domaine Les Vieux Murs 1994: Basic Chardonnay, with a tart core of green apple, earth and citrus flavors. Somewhat light, with a crisp finish. • $NA • (05/31/96) • **78**

PARAZA, CHÂTEAU DE

Minervois 1985 • $6 • (02/29/88) • **80**
Minervois Cuvée Spéciale 1988 • $7 • (05/31/91) • **67**
Minervois Cuvée Spéciale 1986 • $6 • (10/15/88) • **76**

PARENCHERE, CHÂTEAU DE

Bordeaux Supérieur 1986 • $9 • (06/30/89) • **81**

PARENT

Beaune Les Epenotes 1993: A delicate '93 that won't knock your socks off but is fun to drink now, featuring silky tannins, medium body of fruit and fresh finish. Can hold until 1998. 416 cases made. • $57 • **85**
Beaune Les Epenotes 1991: Extremely light and medicinal in aroma, tasting watery and musty. 833 cases made. • $NA • (01/31/94) • **69**
Beaune Les Epenotes 1990: This pretty wine wraps nicely around a core of spice, chestnut, cinnamon and berry flavors and offers a ripe, almost sweet nuance and a silky finish. Drinkable now • $NA • (12/15/92) • **85**
Corton Les Renardes 1993: Elegant, distinguished Corton featuring lovely cedar, berry and plum character. Not a big wine but really pretty. Smooth tannins and fresh finish. Drink in 1999. 125 cases made. • $62 • **90**

■ ■ ■ ■

PARIGOT PERE & FILS

Corton Les Renardes 1992: Has light, grapey, peppery and herbal flavors, but seems diluted. Not very interesting. 125 cases made. • $76 • **74**

Corton Les Renardes 1990: Smells and tastes of strawberries, but where is the beef? Lacks character, but makes for pleasant *grand cru* drinking. Drinkable now. • $NA • (12/15/92) • **83**

Monthelie Les Champs Fulliot 1992: Very pretty, spicy berry and currant flavors open up a little just before the coarse tannins clamp down on the finish. Try now. • $NA • **81**

Pommard 1982 • $18 • (11/01/85) • **83**

Pommard Les Chanlins 1993: Soft and gentlemanly, somewhat light but pleasant, offering plum and red berry flavor and a dry finish. Tasted twice, with consistent notes. 10 cases imported. 10 cases made. • $47 • **78**

Pommard Les Chaponnières 1993: Succulent and soft chocolate, berry and tobacco character and medium tannins. Delicious now, but better in 1998. 375 cases made. • $50 • **86**

Pommard Les Chaponnières 1992: Crisp and spicy, with a gamy edge to the lean blackberry flavor. Best after 1996. 375 cases made. • $50 • **80**

Pommard Les Chaponnières 1991: This solid wine has a chewy texture, chunky tannins and nicely defined black cherry and earth aromas and flavors. Try now. 292 cases made. • $NA • (01/31/94) • **82**

Pommard Les Chaponnières 1990: A traditional style, with distinctive, earthy leaf, mushroom and chestnut aromas and flavors and an unexciting finish. Drinkable now. • $NA • (12/15/92) • **81**

Pommard Les Epenots 1993: Delightful aromas of raspberries and strawberries, with well-integrated, smooth tannins. Good acidity. Try now and through 1997. Not as good as a barrel sample tasted earlier this year. 833 cases made. • $57 • **87**

Pommard Les Epenots 1992: Ripe yet delicate, medium-bodied, with decent strawberry, raspberry and red licorice flavors that turn sweet on the supple finish. Drinkable now. 417 cases made. • $70 • **83**

Pommard Les Epenots 1991: Nicely defined blackberry and black cherry aromas and flavors make this smooth, polished and supple. Drinkable now. 333 cases made. • $NA • (01/31/94) • **83**

Pommard Les Epenots 1990: Well crafted and silky, with raspberry and cherry characteristics that will give lots of pleasure after a couple of years in the cellar. Try now. • $NA • (12/15/92) • **89**

Pommard Les Epenots 1959 • $NA • (08/31/90) • **94**

Pommard Les Rugiens 1992: Lean in structure but supple enough to show its generous blackberry and raspberry flavor nicely, echoing toast and spice as well. Best from 1997. • $NA • **86**

PARIGOT PERE & FILS

Beaune Les Grèves 1987 • $26 • (02/28/90) • **88**

Pommard Les Charmots 1987 • $28 • (07/31/89) • **87**

Pommard Les Charmots 1985 • $34 • (06/15/87) CS • **93**

PASCAL, JEAN

Pommard La Chanière 1986 • $30 • (10/15/88) • **78**

PASCAUD-VILLEFRANCHE, CHÂTEAU

Sauternes 1986 • $24 • (12/31/89) • **78**

Sauternes 1983 • $10 • (01/31/88) • **65**

PASSAT, ANDRE

Côte-Rôtie 1985 • $25 • (10/15/87) • **88**

PATACHE D'AUX, CHÂTEAU

Médoc 1995: Succulent, grapey, freshly crushed wild berry and currant flavors. This is sheer fruit from start to finish, unadorned by oak. Tastes delicious. • $NA • (05/15/96) • **85-89** (BT)

Key: SS—Spectator Selection. CS—Cellar Selection. BB—Best Buy. $NA—Price not available. (BT)—Barrel tasting. Ⓐ—Auction Price.
Dates in parentheses represent the issues in which the ratings were published.

Médoc 1994: Supple, full tannins and the red berry notes are appealing, but it still tastes a bit watery and light, marred by an herbal character. • $NA • (05/15/96) • **75-79** (BT)

Médoc 1988 • $17 • (04/30/91) • **80**

Médoc 1982 • $20 • (05/01/85) • **83**

PATISSIER, G.

St.-Amour Vignoble Les Poulets 1994: Though round and fresh it isn't showing much character, with simple grapey flavors and a short finish. Agreeable, but not memorable. • $13 • /10/31/95 •**81**

PATISSIER, P.

Juliénas 1994: You can sink your teeth into this one. Generous, lush, ripe plum, meat and smoke flavors and plenty of tannin for backbone. Concentrated and balanced, drink now. 1,500 cases made. • $10 • (10/31/95) • **88**

PATRIARCHE PERE & FILS

Bourgogne-Hautes Côtes de Nuits Cuvée Varache 1989 • $11 • (01/31/92) • **81**

Côtes du Rhône-Villages Cuvée Leblanc-Vatel 1985 • $5 • (08/31/89) • **77**

PAUILLAC DE CHÂTEAU LATOUR

Pauillac 1995: Delicious cherry, dried berry, and vanilla aromas and flavors. Medium body, fine tannins and a light finish. • $NA • (05/15/96) • **80-84** (BT)

Pauillac 1994: A lovely, round, easy-drinking red that offers good tobacco and berry character. Third label of Latour. • $NA • (05/15/96) • **80-84** (BT)

Pauillac 1990: Shows interesting decadent aromas and flavors of earth, berries, and chocolate, with round and soft tannins. A big, rustic style. Drink after 1998. • $29 Ⓐ • (03/31/93) • **89**

PAVELOT, JEAN-MARC

Pernand-Vergelesses Les Vergelesses 1991: Fresh and aromatic, showing nice raspberry flavor and hints of spices and earth on the finish. Drinkable now. • $NA • (01/31/94) • **81**

Savigny-lés-Beaune 1994: Rather lean and crisp, showing some citrus and dried herb flavors, the lime notes dominate the slightly astringent finish. 350 cases made. • $NA • (05/31/96) • **79**

Savigny-lès-Beaune 1993: Lovely high acidity, freshly crushed fruit character, medium body and a long, delicate finish. Drinkable now. • $22 • **85**

Savigny-lès-Beaune 1992: Sparkling with bright raspberry, floral and cherry flavors presented in a tight package. A bit bitter on the lean finish, but the aromas are enchanting. • $NA • **84**

Savigny-lès-Beaune 1991: Crisp and light, the modest berry flavors fade into citrus on the finish. Drinkable now. • $20 Ⓐ • (01/31/94) • **80**

Savigny-lès-Beaune 1990: Firm, ripe and juicy, this is immediately appealing for its fine raspberry flavors, lively tannins and good acid balance. Try now. • $22 • (12/15/92) • **89**

Savigny-lès-Beaune 1986 • $18 • (10/15/89) • **84**

Savigny-lès-Beaune La Dominode 1993: Very harmonious core of lovely plum, blackberry and smoke character and a succulent finish. Medium body, high acidity, medium tannins. Tempting now, but should improve past 1999. • $28 • **90**

Savigny-lès-Beaune La Dominode 1992: Light and crisp, simple, with appealing raspberry flavor that lingers nicely on the finish. • $NA • **86**

Savigny-lès-Beaune La Daminode 1991: Crisp and citrusy. A modest level of currant tries to sneak in on the finish. Drinkable now. • $27 Ⓐ • (01/31/94) • **78**

Savigny-lès-Beaune Aux Gravains 1993: Solid Pinot fruit, strawberry, currant and cherry aromas and flavors, medium body, firm tannins and long finish. Drinkable now. • $30 • **89**

Savigny-lès-Beaune Aux Gravains 1992: Crisp and tight, focused berry flavors pushing through the firm tannins. Best from 1997. • $NA • **80**

FRANCE

Savigny-lès-Beaune Aux Gravains 1991: This crisp, flavorful style displays a greenish, lemony edge to the basic currant and plum aromas and flavors. Finishes tight and tannic. Try now. • $24 Ⓐ • (01/31/94) • **81**

Savigny-lès-Beaune Aux Guettes 1993: Well made, lively and vibrant, offering delicious currant, plum and earth character, medium body, massive, supple tannins and a juicy, high-acidity finish. Try after 2000. • $28 • **90**

Savigny-lès-Beaune Aux Guettes 1992: Smooth and velvety, with a generous beam of black cherry and toasty spice flavors shining through. Drinkable now. • $NA • **85**

Savigny-lès-Beaune Aux Guettes 1991: Light, fruity and silky, showing attractive raspberry, blackberry and delicate spice character. Finishes smooth and refined. Drinkable now. • $24 Ⓐ • (01/31/94) • **86**

Savigny-lès-Beaune Aux Guettes 1990: A stunning wine. Focused and concentrated, with blueberry, violet and currant flavors in perfect harmony with the supple tannins. The finish is seductive. Worth the hunt. Drinkable now to 2000. • $33 • (12/15/92) • **92**

Savigny-lès-Beaune Aux Guettes 1986 • $22 • **64**

Savigny-lès-Beaune Aux Guettes 1985 • $20 • (02/15/88) • **89**

Savigny-lès-Beaune Les Narbantons 1993: Vivid, lively, crisp, medium-bodied red sporting lovely acidity and a long, slightly woody but flavorful finish. Drinkable now. • $29 • **87**

Savigny-lès-Beaune Les Narbantons 1992: Crisp and somewhat earthy, with a gamy streak running through the floral cherry flavors. • $NA • **82**

Savigny-lès-Beaune Les Narbantons 1991: A nice beam of raspberry and strawberry flavors shines on into the delicate finish of this light, pleasant wine. Has enough tannin to keep through 1997, but is fresh and drinkable now. • $24 Ⓐ • (01/31/94) • **84**

PAVIE, CHÂTEAU

St.-Emilion 1995: Lovely, luscious red delivering loads of grapey, chocolaty and raspberry aromas and flavors. Medium- to full-bodied with medium-soft tannins. • $NA • (05/15/96) • **85-89** (BT)

St.-Emilion 1994: Rather light for Pavie. Delicate fresh plum, berry and cherry character and crisp finish. • $NA • **80-84** (BT)

St.-Emilion 1994: Light and simple, with modest red berry character and a lean texture. • $29 • (05/15/96) • **75-79** (BT)

St.-Emilion 1993: Full-bodied and delicious from start to finish, showing good depth of fruit and lovely harmony. Exciting flavors of black olive, wet earth and blackberry. Smoky, silky finish. Drink in 1997. • $45 • (01/31/96) • **88**

St.-Emilion 1992: Delicate and delicious, pretty and silky, offering toasted oak, light coffee and raspberry aromas and flavors, medium body and tannins and firm finish. Drinkable now. • $30 • **82**

St.-Emilion 1990: A steamroller of a wine with tons of extract. The toffee, floral and plum aromas and flavors keep coming. Superb tannin structure. Better than the '89. Drink after 1998. 12,000 cases made. • $38 • (03/31/93) • **94**

St.-Emilion 1989 • $36 Ⓐ • (03/15/92) • **90**

St.-Emilion 1988 • $34 Ⓐ • (03/31/91) • **89**

St.-Emilion 1987 • $35 • (05/15/90) • **82**

St.-Emilion 1986 • $35 Ⓐ • (06/30/89) • **93**

St.-Emilion 1985: Yet another winner from Pavie. Caresses the palate and defines elegance. Lovely mint, berry and chocolate character. Full-bodied yet very refined. Better after 1997 • $33 • (10/15/94) • **91**

St.-Emilion 1983: Extremely well polished and fresh with plummy, toasted oak character. Medium-bodied with medium silky tannins and a long delicate finish. Drinkable now. • $27 • (10/15/94) • **90**

St.-Emilion 1982 • $54 Ⓐ • (08/31/92) • **94**

St.-Emilion 1981: Delicious, ripe and exotic, with earthy, meaty and fruity character. Big and solid, lots of fresh, velvety fruit and a long chewy finish. Drink now and enjoy. • $27 • (10/15/94) • **89**

St.-Emilion 1979 • $NA • (10/15/89) • **86**

St.-Emilion 1970 • $26 Ⓐ • (05/15/93) • **89**

St.-Emilion 1961: Very mature, simple in flavor and still tannic in texture. It has aromas of herbs and beef broth and tired flavors. Drink now. • $130 • (04/30/96) • **78**

PAVIE-DECESSE, CHÂTEAU

St.-Emilion 1994: Lots of finesse here as vanilla, cherry and berry character contribute to a caressing texture. Improving. • $NA • (05/15/96) • **85-89** (BT)

St.-Emilion 1993: A pleasant, lively core of plum, cassis, mineral and dried herb flavors, medium body and firm tannins. Needs time to show it all, try in 1998. • $24 • (01/31/96) • **85**

St.-Emilion 1992: Well made. Beautiful perfumes of violets and raspberries, medium body and very round tannins, gorgeous fruit character. Drink now or hold for a few years. • $19 • **84**

St.-Emilion 1990: A chunky wine, with loads of strawberry, earth, toasted oak and mint aromas and flavors, velvety tannins and a long finish. Drink after 1997. 4,800 cases made. • $22 • (03/31/93) • **93**

St.-Emilion 1989 • $29 • (03/15/92) • **90**

St.-Emilion 1988 • $16 Ⓐ • (03/31/91) • **94**

St.-Emilion 1986 • $21 Ⓐ • (06/30/89) • **93**

St.-Emilion 1985: Superb, elegant raspberry and blackberry aromas and flavors. Full-bodied yet held back, with fine tannins and a long, flavorful finish. Better after 1997. • $22 • (10/15/94) • **91**

St.-Emilion 1983: Extremely graceful with velvety texture and lots of fresh fruit. It shows alluring plum, blackberry and green tobacco character and firm tannins. Drinkable now. • $26 • (10/15/94) • **91**

St.-Emilion 1982 • $30 • (08/31/92) • **89**

St.-Emilion 1981: Sound wine with concentrated fruit flavors and a wonderful freshness. Full bodied and rich with chocolate, berry flavors and a long velvety finish. Drink or hold. • $22 • (10/15/94) • **88**

St.-Emilion 1961: Strikingly fresh, vital and firm-textured for a 35-year-old wine. Its pluses are the bright cherry flavors and good acidity. Very drinkable and refreshing, if not exactly rich in character. Drink through 2002. • $51 • (04/30/96) • **87**

PAVIE-MACQUIN, CHÂTEAU

St.-Emilion 1995: Pure chocolate, berry and cherry character. Full in body and luscious, superfine, integrated tannins. Harmonious and seductive. Very impressive indeed. • $NA • (05/15/96) • **90-94** (BT)

St.-Emilion 1994: Lots of sweet fruit here, adding fine tannins and a chocolate, vanilla and berry finish. • $35 • (05/15/96) • **85-89** (BT)

St.-Emilion 1993: Pretty St.-Emilion. Medium in body, featuring lovely cassis, wild berry and black cherry notes. Lots of fruit here, but it could use a year or so for the tannins to smooth out. Better in 1998. • $18 • (01/31/96) • **86**

St.-Emilion 1991: A floral, fresh wine with light body and a refreshing finish, simple and straightforward. • $15 • (03/31/94) • **78**

St.-Emilion 1982 • $NA • (05/15/89) • **89**

PAVILLON BLANC DU CHÂTEAU MARGAUX

Bordeaux 1994: Full-bodied and a bit on the heavy side. Plenty of honey and fruit flavors, but turns bitter and overripe on the finish. • $NA • (03/31/96) • **78**

PAVILLON LA CROIX FIGEAC, CHÂTEAU

St.-Emilion 1995: Very pretty cassis bush, plum and herb flavors, adding firm, slightly dry tannins. • $NA • (05/15/96) • **80-84** (BT)

PAVILLON ROUGE DU CHÂTEAU MARGAUX

Margaux 1994: Beautiful berry, cherry and raspberry aromas and flavors. Medium bodied with silky tannins and a smoky finish. Bit short. • $NA • **80-84** (BT)

Margaux 1989 • $40 Ⓐ • (04/30/92) • **87**

Margaux 1988 • $30 • (04/30/91) • **88**

Margaux 1987 • $19 • (05/15/90) • **79**

Margaux 1986 • $22 Ⓐ • (06/30/89) • **84**

Margaux 1985 • $38 • (04/15/88) SS • **93**

Margaux 1983 • $36 • (06/30/87) • **80**

Margaux 1982 • $69 Ⓐ • (07/15/87) • **85**

Margaux 1981 • $26 • (07/15/87) • **87**

Margaux 1980 • $20 • (07/15/87) • **76**

Margaux 1979 • $29 Ⓐ • (07/15/87) • **78**
Margaux 1916 • $NA • (07/15/87) • **63**

PAVILLON-MERCUROL, DOMAINE DU

Crozes-Hermitage 1991 • $NA • (05/31/94) • **85**
Crozes-Hermitage 1990 • $NA • (05/31/94) • **88**
Crozes-Hermitage 1989 • $45 • (05/31/94) • **85**

PAYSAGE

Merlot Vin de Pays d'Oc Caillou Vineyards 1993: A brownish color and tired, tealike flavors make it dull. 3,000 cases made. • $10 • (03/31/95) • **73**
Red Vin de Pays d'Oc Galet Vineyards 1993: Light, simple cherry flavor and soft tannins. It's balanced and adds a pleasant, spicy finish. Drink now. 5,000 cases made. • $10 • (10/31/95) • **80**
White Vin de Pays d'Oc Galet Vineyard 1993: A simple white showing good balance and modest apple and citrus flavors. 2,000 cases made. • $10 • (03/31/95) • **78**

PECH DE JAMMES, CHÂTEAU

Cahors 1989: A lively red, offering bright acidity and firm tannins, but the ripe cherry and berry flavors are a bit subdued. It's clean and refreshing, but needs food to soften and round it out. 6,200 cases made. • $8 • (09/30/94) • **81**
Cahors 1988 • $10 • (09/30/92) • **81**
Cahors 1987 • $9 • (06/30/90) • **78**
Cahors 1983 • $9 • (10/15/88) • **77**

PECH REDON, CHÂTEAU DE

Coteaux du Languedoc La Clape 1991 • $10 • (03/15/94) • **84**
Coteaux du Languedoc La Clape Cuvée Réserve 1991 • $10 • (03/15/94) • **81**

PEDAUQUE, LA REINE

Chassagne-Montrachet 1993: Rather straightforward, green and diluted, revealing modest fruit flavor. 25 cases made. • $26 • **76**
Chassagne-Montrachet 1992: Lively, crisp and well-balanced, showing lime, mineral and creamy vanilla flavors. Solid and straightforward. 260 cases made. • $22 • (08/31/94) • **82**
Corton Les Renardes 1993: Starts out rather lean and crisp, showing a hint of wet earth, cedar, plum and red berry flavor, and picks up ripe character on the smooth but slightly hot finish. • $50 • **83**
Corton-Charlemagne 1993: Some nice fruit underneath, but not showing optimally at this point. Seems a bit flat and dull, although well-knit texture carries the wine. Might be better after 1996. 25 cases imported. • $55 • **83**
Corton-Charlemagne 1992: Straightforward and rather simple, with modest apple, lemon and earth flavors, offers a crisp taste but also some stale fruit flavors that distract. • $52 • (08/31/94) • **83**
Gevrey-Chambertin 1993: A bit lean on the palate but some pretty berry, cherry character. Medium-bodied, medium tannins and lean finish. Better in 1998. • $25 • **79**
Meursault Les Charmes 1992: Round and supple, this well-made Meursault delivers pretty pear, peach, vanilla and cream flavors, and the finish is long, but it lacks a bit of volume and concentration in the middle. Drinkable now. 200 cases made. • $29 • (08/31/94) • **85**
Mâcon-Villages Coupées 1994: Already showing gold color and mature flavors, this is aging quickly and ungraciously. Flat, dull and uninteresting flavors dominate. 1,667 cases made. • $9 • **70**
Nuits-St.-Georges 1993: Light and diluted, showing only modest red berry flavor. Not much here. Disappointing. • $25 • **75**

Key: SS—Spectator Selection. CS—Cellar Selection. BB—Best Buy. $NA—Price not available. (BT)—Barrel tasting. Ⓐ—Auction Price.
Dates in parentheses represent the issues in which the ratings were published.

Pommard 1993: Pretty crushed raspberry and a hint of earth but it's slightly light, adding firm tannins and delicate finish. Drink in 1999. • $30 • **80**
Pouilly-Fuissé Griselles 1993: Rather round and supple, revealing grapefruit and green apple flavors, but a bit one-dimensional. 600 cases made. • $15 • **79**
Puligny-Montrachet Les Folatières 1993: Interesting green apple skin and cream notes, medium body and tart finish. Try now. 25 cases made. • $32 • **80**

PEDESCLAUX, CHÂTEAU

Pauillac 1986 • $18 • (02/15/90) • **79**

PEGAU, DOMAINE DU

Châteauneuf-du-Pape Cuvée Réservée 1991: Plum and berry notes are accented by spice, mint and leather nuances lingering on the firmly tannic finish. Tempting to drink now or save through 1998. 4,000 cases made. • $20 • **89**
Châteauneuf-du-Pape Cuvée Réservée 1989 • $22 • (04/15/93) • **85**
Châteauneuf-du-Pape Cuvée Réservée 1988 • $17 • (11/15/91) • **88**

PELLE, DOMAINE HENRY

Menetou-Salon Morogues 1995: Delicious peach and smoke flavors are the highlights that interplay with crisp acidity to create an interesting complexity. Lovely now. • $16 • (05/15/96) • **87**
Menetou-Salon Morogues 1994: Bracing aromas of gooseberry and herbs enliven this crisp, lean white. Citrus fruit flavors are bright and clean, the wine isn't deeply concentrated, but it shows good typicity. • $15 • (11/15/95) • **84**
Menetou-Salon Morogues 1993: Vivid aromas of pine, fresh herbs and citrus are followed by crisp, clean grapefruit and pine flavors. It's nervy, balanced and direct. • $15 • (08/31/94) • **87**
Menetou-Salon Morogues Clos des Blanchais 1995: Herb and melon aromas and flavors are complemented by a hint of nuttiness in this exubrant, lively white. Drink now through 1997. • $19 • (05/15/96) • **85**
Menetou-Salon Morogues Clos des Blanchais 1994: Ripe apple flavors marry well with firm acidity in this relatively rich Sauvignon Blanc. It has good concentration, but a toasty, earthy note detracts from the fruit. • $17 • (11/15/95) • **82**
Menetou-Salon Morogues Clos des Blanchais 1993: Focused and expressive, this shows clean, typically Loire flavors — grassy, herbaceous, citrus — in a polished frame. A year in bottle has rounded out the wine, it's lipsmacking now. 1,700 cases made. • $19 • (11/15/95) • **87**
Menetou-Salon Morogues Clos des Blanchais 1992: Rich with a solid core of pear and melon, kept fresh by tart acidity, full-bodied, yet still lively and refreshing. A food-friendly wine that's round and inviting on its own. 15,000 cases made. • $14 • (08/31/94) • **87**
Menetou-Salon Red Morogues 1994: This light Pinot Noir shows nicely varietal spice and cherry aromas, on the palate it's lean and a bit tart, but still fresh with cherry and light earthy flavors. 2,500 cases made. • $15 • (12/15/95) • **81**
Menetou-Salon Red Morogues 1987 • $11 • (07/15/89) • **85**
Sancerre La Croix au Garde 1995: Lean and lively, offering the right balance between honeydew melon and herbal flavors and mouthwatering acidity. • $18 • (05/15/96) • **85**
Sancerre La Croix au Garde 1994: Crisp and straightforward, this shows mainly herbal flavors, with a creamy note that adds some richness to the light-bodied, almost neutral palate. No offense here, but not much excitement. • $18 • **81**
Sancerre La Croix au Garde 1993: A focused, tangy wine that offers mineral and grapefruit flavors in a tart, balanced frame. There's not much fruit evident, but the clean austerity is taut and refreshing. • $17 • (10/31/94) • **86**
Sancerre La Croix au Garde 1991 • $15 • (09/15/93) • **83**
Sancerre Red La Croix au Garde 1994: Firm tannins and crisp acidity in this moderately rich Pinot Noir, showing some varietal spicy, earthy flavors. Fresh and clean but lacks fruit in the middle. 1,500 cases made. • $18 • **80**

FRANCE

PELLERIN

Brouilly 1987 • $8 • (04/15/89) • **83**

PELOUX, DU

Châteauneuf-du-Pape 1986 • $12 • (04/15/89) • **85**
Côtes du Rhône 1986 • $4 • (05/15/89) • **75**
Côtes du Rhône-Villages 1986 • $5 • (05/15/89) • **78**

PENNAUTIER, CHÂTEAU DE

Cabardès 1989 • $7 • (12/15/91) • **75**

PENSEES DE LAFLEUR

Pomerol 1995: Thick and silky concentration of ripe fruit, tasting of prune, plum and spice. A smooth mouthful. Delicately smoky on the finish. Second label of Château Lafleur. • $NA • (05/15/96) • **85-89** (BT)
Pomerol 1994: Very ripe, almost raisiny mint and berry character. Medium to full body, velvety tannins and slightly coarse finish. • $NA • **85-89** (BT)

PERENNE, CHÂTEAU

Premières Côtes de Blaye 1989 • $9 • (03/31/91) • **78**
Premières Côtes de Blaye 1986 • $7 • (06/30/89) • **82**
Premières Côtes de Blaye 1985 • $7 • (02/15/88) • **80**
Premières Côtes de Blaye 1982 • $5 • (11/16/85) BB • **79**

PERNIN-ROSSIN, A.

Vosne-Romanée 1986 • $31 • (02/28/89) • **61**

PERNOT, PAUL

Beaune Les Teurons 1990: Crisp and focused, with bright, vibrant black cherry, wild berry and toast aromas and flavors that remain intense and elegant right through the long finish. Has the raw material to develop well through 2000. 85 cases made. • $33 • (04/30/92) • **90**
Beaune Les Teurons 1988 • $33 • (03/31/91) • **86**
Meursault-Blagny La Pièce sous le Bois 1990: Tart, thin and woody, with a spurt of fruit at the very end that lifts it into the respectable range. • $33 • (04/30/92) • **79**

PERON, JULES

Saumur Red 1993: This is clean and fresh, with plenty of raspberry, cherry and black pepper flavors, soft tannins and good balance. A pleasant wine for early drinking. • $6 • (11/15/94) • **83**
Saumur White 1992: A crisp, lively, still-youthful white wine with attractive apple and honey flavors, a smooth texture and light, but lingering finish. • $6 • **84**

PERRET, ANDRE

St.-Joseph Les Grisières 1992 • $13 • (05/31/94) • **77**

PERRIER, JOSEPH

Brut Blanc de Blancs Champagne Cuvée Royale NV • $37 • (12/31/90) • **88**
Brut Champagne 1985 • $37 • (12/31/90) • **82**
Brut Champagne 1979 • $22 • (10/01/85) • **87**
Brut Champagne NV • $19 • (11/16/85) • **92**
Brut Champagne Cuvée Josephine 1985: A well-made wine with classic flavors of apples and toast that shows plenty of fruit and acidity but lacks the intensity to be outstanding. Drink now. • $NA • (12/31/93) • **89**
Brut Champagne Cuvée Josephine 1982 • $100 • (12/31/90) • **93**
Brut Champagne Cuvée Royale 1985: Enjoyable vintage bubbly with pleasant cookie dough and apple aromas and flavors, good acidity and a long flavorful finish. Slightly better than in fall 1990. Drink now. • $38 • (12/31/93) • **86**
Brut Champagne Cuvée Royale 1982 • $32 Ⓐ • (12/31/89) • **89**
Brut Champagne Cuvée Royale NV • $32 • (12/31/92) • **86**
Brut Rosé Champagne Cuvée Royale NV • $45 • (12/31/92) • **85**

PERRIER, PASCAL

St.-Joseph Domaine de Gachon 1990 • $19 • (04/15/93) • **90**

PERRIER-JOUET

Brut Champagne 1955 • $NA • (10/15/87) • **90**
Brut Champagne 1947 • $NA • (10/15/87) • **85**
Brut Champagne 1928 • $NA • (10/15/87) • **97**
Brut Champagne 1914 • $NA • (10/15/87) • **55**
Brut Champagne 1911 • $104 Ⓐ • (10/15/87) • **95**
Brut Champagne 1900 • $NA • (10/15/87) • **97**
Brut Champagne 1893 • $NA • (10/15/87) • **80**
Brut Champagne 1825 • $NA • (10/15/87) • **95**
Brut Champagne NV: Sweet, smooth and ripe-tasting, with honey and apple flavors. But they turn thick and chalky on the finish. Flavorful, but a bit off balance. • $24 • **83**
Brut Champagne Blason de France NV • $40 • (12/31/93) • **92**
Brut Champagne Fleur de Champagne 1988: One of the best flower bottles vintages in years. Textbook top notch Champagne with fruity, light toasted aromas and flavors, full body yet a fine underlying acidity. Very long finish. Better now. • $80 • (12/31/93) • **91**
Brut Champagne Fleur de Champagne 1985: • $75 • (12/31/90) • **86**
Brut Champagne Fleur de Champagne 1983 • $65 • (12/31/89) • **88**
Brut Champagne Fleur de Champagne 1982 • $65 • (12/31/88) • **88**
Brut Champagne Fleur de Champagne 1979 • $50 • (02/01/86) • **93**
Brut Champagne Grand Brut NV: A broad, rich, ripe-tasting Champagne whose flavors are reminiscent of pear, almond and caramel. Full-bodied and assertive, though smooth-textured and leaning toward sweetness in balance. • $27 • **88**
Brut Champagne Réserve Cuvée 1988: A fresh vintage Champagne with vibrant aromas and flavors of lemons, pears, and shortbread cookies, medium body and a refreshing finish. Large bead and foamy texture. Drinkable now. • $35 • (12/31/93) • **87**
Brut Rosé Champagne Fleur de Champagne 1988: Very dry, very vivid and showing crisp, lean flavors of cherry, spice and orange. It's sophisticated, elegant and taut in character. • $95 • (12/15/95) • **87**
Brut Rosé Champagne Fleur de Champagne 1986: Wonderfully mature and distinctive, reminding us of a well-aged Burgundy, but with a refreshing effervescence that keeps it light and lively. Dry, and elegant. For special occasions. • $90 • **92**
Brut Rosé Champagne Fleur de Champagne 1985 • $70 • (12/31/89) • **88**
Brut Rosé Champagne Fleur de Champagne 1982 • $57 • (11/15/87) • **89**
Brut Rosé Champagne Fleur de Champagne 1978 • $55 • (12/16/85) • **90**
Extra Dry Champagne Cuvée Spéciale NV • $30 • (12/31/92) • **84**

PERRIERE, DOMAINE

Vin de Pays de l'Aude Les Amandiers 1990 • $5 • (10/31/92) BB • **80**
Vin de Pays de l'Aude Les Amandiers 1988 • $4 • (04/15/90) • **77**

PERROT-MINOT, HENRI

Chambolle-Musigny 1990: Crisp and austere with red cherry and earthy notes. Firmly tannic, try in 1997. 460 cases made. • $32 • (03/15/94) • **82**
Chambolle-Musigny La Combe d'Orveau 1991: Austere, with rubbery, acrid flavors that mar what little black cherry fruit exists. 250 cases made. • $45 • (03/15/94) • **74**
Charmes-Chambertin 1991: Aromatic, with spicy, toasty, chocolate nuances to the core of black cherry and berry fruit. Firm in texture, needing until 1997 or 1998 to settle in. 800 cases made. • $50 • (03/15/94) • **85**
Morey-St.-Denis La Riotte 1992: Supple, broad and easygoing, featuring soft tannins, good acidity and fairly bright cherry and berry flavors. Appealing to drink now. • $35 • **86**

Morey-St.-Denis La Riotte 1990: Light and smooth, offering a range of plum, cola and herb aromas and flavors that finish with a ring of fruit. Drinkable now. 200 cases made. • $40 • (12/31/93) • **86**

Morey-St.-Denis En la Rue de Vergy 1992: The fruit flavors really come out as you sip this solid, ripe, firmly textured Burgundy. It is focused, with well-balanced acidity and moderate tannins, and the fruit lingers on the finish. Drinkable now. 600 cases made. • $27 • (05/15/95) • **89**

Morey-St.-Denis En la Rue de Vergy 1990: Dark in color, rich in flavor with spicy black cherry, plum and raspberry fruit, picking up a floral note with the oak and tannins a little heavy handed. Drinkable now. 580 cases made. • $25 • (03/15/94) • **87**

PERVENCHES, DOMAINE DES

Côtes du Rhône 1990 • $5 • (07/31/93) BB • **83**

PESQUIER, DOMAINE DU

Côtes du Rhône 1991 • $10 • (06/15/93) • **82**
Côtes du Rhône 1990 • $10 • (04/15/93) • **83**
Gigondas 1990 • $15 • (04/15/93) • **86**
Gigondas 1989 • $15 • (04/15/93) • **83**

PETIT-FAURIE-DE-SOUTARD, CHÂTEAU

St.-Emilion 1988 • $20 • (04/30/91) • **82**
St.-Emilion 1986 • $15 • (06/30/89) • **80**

PETIT-FIGEAC, CHÂTEAU

St.-Emilion 1995: Firm and fruity but slightly austere. Medium-bodied, offering firm tannins and a slightly green finish. • $NA • (05/15/96) • **80-84** (BT)

St.-Emilion 1993: Pretty, focused red berry, currant and tobacco aromas and flavors, medium body, medium-silky tannins and fresh finish. Drinkable now. • $22 • (01/31/96) • **83**

St.-Emilion 1992: Some good fruit tinged with wet earth. Medium-bodied and very firm, a decent finish. Drink now. • $18 • **80**

St.-Emilion 1990: Seductive, with everything in proportion: black cherry and berry aromas and flavors with soft yet firm tannins. Beautiful. Drinkable now. • $24 • (03/31/93) • **90**

St.-Emilion 1989 • $21 • (03/15/92) • **90**

PETIT-PUCH, CHÂTEAU DU

Entre-Deux-Mers 1994: Some cream, grass and celery character, medium body, crisp acidity and light finish. Drink now. • $8 • **79**

PETIT-VILLAGE, CHÂTEAU

Pomerol 1995: Beautiful, succulent wine with bright flavors and a perfumed, floral character. Rich, ripe and supple, with sweet tannins that coat your mouth. Very seductive finish. • $NA • (05/15/96) • **90-94** (BT)

Pomerol 1994: Impressive concentration of fruit and tannins. Full-bodied, delivering loads of vanilla and oak and an herbal, berry, cherry character. But a bit coarse. • $36 • (05/15/96) • **85-89** (BT)

Pomerol 1993: Sleek and well-crafted Pomerol offering red berry, toasted oak and a hint of smokiness. Medium in body, fine tannins and fresh finish. Drinkable now. 4,500 cases made. • $35 • (01/31/96) • **86**

Pomerol 1992: Velvety chocolate, cedar and fruit character, medium in body, impressive texture and medium finish. Drinkable now. • $34 • **84**

Pomerol 1991: A bit aggressive with its berry, chocolate and herb character and hard tannins. Tasted twice, with consistent notes. • $22 • (03/31/94) • **75**

Pomerol 1990: A showy wine with velvety-textured tannins and rich fruit. This has no rough edges. Drinkable in 1997. 3,900 cases made. • $47 • (03/31/93) • **92**

Pomerol 1989 • $46 • (03/15/92) • **88**
Pomerol 1985 • $NA • **90**
Pomerol 1983 • $NA • **86**
Pomerol 1982 • $86 Ⓐ • (08/31/92) • **91**
Pomerol 1981 • $NA • **77**
Pomerol 1959 • $NA • (10/15/90) • **86**

PETIT CHEVAL, LE

St.-Emilion 1988 • $35 • (03/31/91) • **89**

PETITE EGLISE, LA

Pomerol 1986 • $15 • (09/15/89) • **78**

PETRUS, CHÂTEAU

Pomerol 1995: Lots of everything here. Loads of smoke, berry, cherry and chocolate aromas and flavors. Full body, soft tannins and fresh finish. Really impressive, could move up to classic quality next year. • $NA • (05/15/96) • **90-94** (BT)

Pomerol 1994: A very good Pétrus, but not as good as the glorious '93. Loads of coconut, vanilla and berry aromas. Offers lovely sweet fruit and medium tannins. • $290 • (05/15/96) • **85-89** (BT)

Pomerol 1993: A truly classic Pétrus and comparable to the '88, '86 and '82. Showy and impressive with excellent use of new oak. It delivers loads of toasty coconut and chocolate flavors balanced by plum and blackberry notes. Incredible concentration for the vintage. Supple, long finish. Try after 2000. • $225 • (01/31/96) CS • **95**

Pomerol 1992: Not great but very good. Lovely finesse and good backbone of tannins and fruit. Medium-bodied and silky, featuring a berry, tobacco and mineral finish. Drinkable now. • $300 • **88**

Pomerol 1990: An aristocratic wine, almost as good as the awesome '89. Expressive and sophisticated, with wonderful aromas of ripe fruit and vanilla and a palate of extremely silky tannins and superb fruit concentration. Drink after 1999. 4,000 cases made. • $594 Ⓐ • (03/31/93) • **98**

Pomerol 1989: A Rolls Royce of a wine. Explosive and opulent; perhaps as great as the 1961. Big and powerful, with super-rich berry, tobacco, and olive flavors and full, round, ripe tannins. Will go on for decades; try after 1999. • $460 • (03/15/92) • **100**

Pomerol 1988 • $379 Ⓐ • (08/31/91) • **94**
Pomerol 1987 • $181 Ⓐ • (02/15/91) • **85**
Pomerol 1986 • $299 Ⓐ • (02/15/91) • **96**

Pomerol 1985: Another superb bottle from Pétrus. Solid as a rock with mint, raspberry, cherry and tar character, full body and firm tannins. Needs time. Try after 1998. • $400 • (10/15/94) • **93**

Pomerol 1984 • $153 Ⓐ • (02/15/91) • **83**

Pomerol 1983: What you'd expect from such a legendary estate. Wonderful palate impression with silky, rich fruit. Plenty of blackberry, chocolate character, full body and a medium finish. Needs time. Try after 1997. • $290 • (10/15/94) • **93**

Pomerol 1982 • $878 Ⓐ • (08/31/92) • **94**

Pomerol 1981: Big and very ripe, almost raisiny. Mouth coating fruit with ripe tannins but a little clumsy to be outstanding. Drink now or hold. • $280 • (10/15/94) • **89**

Pomerol 1980 • $163 Ⓐ • (02/15/91) • **86**
Pomerol 1979 • $246 Ⓐ • (02/15/91) • **90**
Pomerol 1978 • $279 Ⓐ • (02/15/91) • **89**
Pomerol 1976 • $237 Ⓐ • (02/15/91) • **86**
Pomerol 1975 • $483 Ⓐ • (02/15/91) • **93**
Pomerol 1973 • $182 Ⓐ • (02/15/91) • **78**
Pomerol 1971 • $546 Ⓐ • (02/15/91) • **94**
Pomerol 1970 • $740 Ⓐ • (05/15/93) • **89**
Pomerol 1968 • $150 Ⓐ • (02/15/91) • **79**
Pomerol 1967 • $268 Ⓐ • (02/15/91) • **87**
Pomerol 1966 • $560 Ⓐ • (02/15/91) • **93**
Pomerol 1964 • $718 Ⓐ • (02/15/91) • **94**
Pomerol 1962 • $480 Ⓐ • (02/15/91) • **94**

Pomerol 1961: A rich and opulent vintage of Pomerol's most acclaimed wine. It tastes subdued at first, but then the flavors warm up and turn

Key: SS—Spectator Selection. CS—Cellar Selection. BB—Best Buy. $NA—Price not available. (BT)—Barrel tasting. Ⓐ—Auction Price.
Dates in parentheses represent the issues in which the ratings were published.

deep and nicely mature. The texture is thick and chewy without being tough and the finish is long. • $4,869/1.5L • (04/30/96) • **93**

Pomerol 1959 • $520 Ⓐ • (02/15/91) • **96**
Pomerol 1958 • $242 Ⓐ • (02/15/91) • **85**
Pomerol 1955 • $292 Ⓐ • (02/15/91) • **91**
Pomerol 1953 • $403 Ⓐ • (02/15/91) • **92**
Pomerol 1952 • $468 Ⓐ • (02/15/91) • **89**
Pomerol 1950 • $1,300 • (02/15/91) • **99**
Pomerol 1949 • $1,450 • (02/15/91) • **98**
Pomerol 1948 • $1,150 • (02/15/91) • **91**
Pomerol 1947 • $2,350 • (02/15/91) • **97**
Pomerol 1945: Very firm and focused, chewy in texture. Flavors seem disharmonious, chunky rather than elegant. Solid, with herbal, minty overtones to the black cherry notes, but not elevated. Some thought this just needed more time! • $3,750 • **88**

PEU DE LA MORIETTE, DOMAINE LE

Vouvray Moelleux Cuvée Exceptionelle 1989 • $19 • (06/15/91) • **80**

PEYRAUD, CHÂTEAU

Premières Côtes de Blaye 1993: Soft and light, showing light berry and green pepper flavors on a modest frame. Drinkable now. • $9 • (12/15/95) • **79**
Premières Côtes de Blaye 1989 • $8 • (03/31/91) • **80**

PEZ, CHÂTEAU DE

St.-Estèphe 1995: A reserved style. Wonderfully elegant tannins, medium to full body and plenty of blackberry and cherry flavors on the finish. • $NA • (05/15/96) • **85-89** (BT)
St.-Estèphe 1990: A wine overflowing with berry and raspberry flavor. Structurally it's elegant and fine, with firm tannins and excellent length. Drinkable in 1998. 12,000 cases made. • $20 • (03/31/93) • **93**
St.-Estèphe 1989 • $21 • (03/15/92) • **89**
St.-Estèphe 1988 • $19 • (06/15/91) • **83**
St.-Estèphe 1986 • $21 Ⓐ • (06/30/89) • **90**
St.-Estèphe 1985 • $22 • **89**
St.-Estèphe 1983 • $NA • **88**
St.-Estèphe 1982 • $22 • (08/31/92) • **93**
St.-Estèphe 1981 • $NA • **88**
St.-Estèphe 1961: A California style of Bordeaux that features very ripe, pruney flavors that still seem youthful and rich. It has a lively balance despite the ripeness, and plenty of body. Drink through 2000. • $NA • (04/30/96) • **85**

PHELAN-SEGUR, CHÂTEAU

St.-Estèphe 1995: Plenty of black cherry, berry and spice in this one. Medium to full body, fine tannins and a silky texture. • $NA • (05/15/96) • **85-89** (BT)
St.-Estèphe 1994: Has silky texture and good fruit, but it could use a little more concentration. • $20 • (05/15/96) • **80-84** (BT)
St.-Estèphe 1993: Elegant cherry, berry and milk chocolate aromas and flavors, medium body, fine tannins and delicate finish. Drinkable now. • $20 • (01/31/96) • **84**
St.-Estèphe 1992: A lovely core of fruit, medium body, velvety tannins and succulent finish. Drinkable now. • $17 • **85**
St.-Estèphe 1991: A classy wine with a subtle character of berry and wet earth. It is medium-bodied with firm tannins and has a good core of fruit flavors. • $15 • (03/31/94) • **85**
St.-Estèphe 1990: A wine with rich, spicy vanilla, berry and chocolate aromas and flavors and round, rich tannins. Better than the '89. Drinkable in 1997. 24,000 cases made. • $20 • (03/31/93) • **91**
St.-Estèphe 1989 • $23 • (03/15/92) • **85**
St.-Estèphe 1988 • $20 • (07/15/91) • **87**
St.-Estèphe 1987 • $16 • (11/30/89) • **82**
St.-Estèphe 1986 • $20 • (11/30/89) • **86**
St.-Estèphe 1982 • $34 Ⓐ • (08/31/92) • **91**
St.-Estèphe 1970 • $26 Ⓐ • (05/15/93) • **84**
St.-Estèphe 1961: Mature and lean in profile, notable for its cherry flavors and smooth, balanced texture on the palate. Solid and fine to drink now. • $42 • (04/30/96) • **84**

PHILIPPE, JEAN

Brut Blanquette de Limoux 1986 • $11 • (06/15/90) • **80**
Brut Blanquette de Limoux NV • $9 • (01/31/88) • **80**

PHILIPPONNAT

Brut Blanc de Blancs Champagne 1980 • $26 • (05/31/87) • **92**
Brut Blanc de Blancs Champagne Cuvée Première 1980 • $39 • (12/31/88) • **89**
Brut Blanc de Blancs Champagne Grand Blanc 1985 • $40 • (12/31/90) • **87**
Brut Champagne Clos des Goisses 1986: A very floral, fruity Champagne and rather feminine in style. Light, medium bodied with crisp acidity and good pineapple character and medium finish. Drink now. • $NA • (12/31/93) • **87**
Brut Champagne Clos des Goisses 1985: A bold, assertive Champagne with great aromas of toast, nutmeg and walnut, and lots of apple, fig and nut flavors. Very dry, firmly acidic, full-bodied, but nicely balanced out by the generous fruit component and utterly plush in texture. Drink now. 1,500 cases made. • $90 • **92**
Brut Champagne Clos des Goisses 1982 • $89 • (12/31/88) • **84**
Brut Champagne Grand Blanc 1988: This Chardonnay based wine gives everything on the finish. Needs time. Intensely fruity with peaches and apple aromas and flavors, excellent acidity and a long finish. Try now. • $NA • (12/31/93) • **90**
Brut Champagne Grand Blanc 1986: Unctuous and concentrated, with strong, toasty aromas and beautifully mature flavors dominated by almond and smoke. Very assertive and bold, with a finish that comes off a bit astringent. 4,000 cases made. • $49 • **89**
Brut Champagne Grand Blanc 1982 • $38 • (12/31/88) • **84**
Brut Champagne Le Reflet NV: Soft, appealing and somewhat sweet, the peach and vanilla flavors accented by almond and butter. Stays fruity and refreshing on the finish. • $40 • (07/31/95) • **83**
Brut Champagne Royale Réserve NV: A generous Champagne that leans toward an overripe style, showing apple, pear and honey flavors and soft texture. It's good and rich, but drink well chilled. • $29 • **83**
Brut Rosé Champagne NV • $26 • (12/16/85) • **72**
Brut Rosé Champagne Réserve NV: Focused and intense, this rosé is chock-full of vanilla, strawberry and piecrust flavors. Lively on the palate and long in the finish. Bright and alluring. • $32 • (12/15/95) • **90**

PIADA, CHÂTEAU

Barsac 1991: Wonderfully harmonious and elegant, buttery, creamy and slightly honeyed, to drink, not just to sip. Try as an apéritif, but hold off until after 1996. • $NA • **86**
Barsac 1990: Super-ripe and unctuous botrytis character. Extremely sweet without being cloying, offering tons of spicy, dried apricot, lemon and honey flavors which thickly coat your mouth. Try to keep for the next century. Tasted twice, with consistent notes. • $NA • **93**
Barsac 1989: Creamy and wonderfully harmonious, you can't go wrong here, marzipan, honey, nut and lemon flavors add up to a great drink. Better after 1997. Tasted twice, with consistent notes. • $NA • **91**
Barsac 1988: Nicely focused intensity, offering medium body and sweetness and caramel, wet earth, fig, dried apricot and toast flavors in satisfying amounts. Drinkable now. • $NA • **87**
Barsac 1987 • $35 • (03/31/91) • **86**
Barsac 1986 • $NA • **83**
Barsac 1983. • $11 • **84**

PIALADE, LA

Côtes du Rhône 1991: This is a nicely-balanced, spicey wine that is well-crafted. It has flavors redolent of dried cherries and is reminiscent of an Amarone. Ready to drink now. • $14 • (11/30/94) • **82**

PIAUGIER, DOMAINE DE

Côtes du Rhône-Villages Sablet Montmartel 1990 • $10 • (04/15/93) • **84**
Gigondas 1990 • $15 • (04/15/93) • **88**

PIBARNON, CHÂTEAU DE

Bandol 1990 • $23 • (04/15/93) • **80**
Bandol 1987 • $17 • (03/15/90) • **75**
Bandol 1985 • $17 • (10/15/88) • **79**
Bandol 1984 • $NA • (08/31/86) • **70**
Bandol 1982 • $9 • (10/01/85) • **75**

PIBRAN, CHÂTEAU

Pauillac 1995: Very tight and hard at the time we tasted this, it showed good depth of fruit, but the tannins seemed a bit dry. Medium- to full-bodied, with lots of cassis and subtle mineral and toasted oak flavors. • $NA • (05/15/96) • **80-84** (BT)
Pauillac 1994: Impressive concentration, but herbaceous, green-bean character detracts slightly from the quality. Tough tannins. • $NA • **80-84** (BT)
Pauillac 1993: Some decent concentration but rather herbal and green, showing bell pepper character. Disappointing. Drinkable now. • $19 • (01/31/96) • **78**
Pauillac 1992: Some decent fruit and grassy flavors, but rather hard and tannic. Drink now. • $15 • **75**
Pauillac 1991: Rich and quite powerful for this vintage with its good tannins. But slightly herbaceous on the finish. • $15 • (03/31/94) • **82**
Pauillac 1990: Incredibly rich yet elegant. It overflows with ripe blackberries, tobacco and chocolate, backed up with velvety tannins. Drinkable in 2000. 4,000 cases made. • $25 • (03/31/93) • **93**
Pauillac 1989 • $25 • (03/15/92) • **95**
Pauillac 1987 • $16 • (11/30/89) • **85**
Pauillac 1986 • $18 • (11/30/89) • **88**
Pauillac 1982 • $18 • (11/30/89) • **90**

PICARD, JEAN-PAUL

Sancerre 1992: Austere and earthy. This dull, flat wine lacks fruit, with musty and vegetal flavors dominant. Tasted twice with consistent notes. 20,000 cases made. • $14 • (10/31/94) • **72**
Sancerre Cuvée Prestige 1993: Aggressive herbal, mineral and gooseberry aromas give way to softer pear and light earthy flavors on the firm palate. It's a real old-style Sancerre, unapologetic and appealing. 1,000 cases made. • $17 • (11/15/95) • **86**

PICCINI

Minervois 1992 • $8 • (06/30/94) • **75**

PICHON, CHÂTEAU

Haut-Médoc 1985 • $13 • (08/31/88) • **85**

PICHON, PHILIPPE

St.-Joseph 1988 • $22 • (11/15/91) • **76**

PICHON-LONGUEVILLE-BARON, CHÂTEAU

Pauillac 1995: Extremely silky and well made, a supple, rich, sweet-tasting '95 that has an opulent texture and delivers a mouthful of cassis, subtle toasted oak and plum flavors. Very impressive. • $NA • (05/15/96) • **90-94** (BT)
Pauillac 1994: Very distinctive, bursting with earthy, smoky berry flavors and notes of tar and mineral. The tannins are full and velvety. It delivers a lot, and has a long, firm finish. Impressive for this vintage. Almost outstanding. • $28 • (05/15/96) • **85-89** (BT)
Pauillac 1993: Stylish, well-defined red berry, mineral, smoke and toast flavors, adding some herbal notes. Medium in body, well balanced, with a crisp but satisfying and lingering finish. Try in 1998. 25,000 cases made. • $33 • (01/31/96) • **85**
Pauillac 1992: Impressive violet and berry aromas precede a polished, smooth texture and chocolate, toasted oak character on the finish. Very tannic, perhaps too much? Drink after 1996. • $28 • **84**
Pauillac 1991: Solid as rock. Well-structured and very balanced with lovely reserved violet, berry character, firm tannins and a long, slightly herbaceous finish. Drink now. • $27 • (03/31/94) • **84**
Pauillac 1990: Massive. It's showing smoky, berry, plum aromas and flavors, huge tannins and a long finish. Drink after 2000. 20,000 cases made. • $38 Ⓐ • (03/31/93) • **94**
Pauillac 1989 • $60 Ⓐ • (03/15/92) • **98**
Pauillac 1988 • $39 Ⓐ • (03/31/91) SS • **95**
Pauillac 1987 • $25 • (10/15/90) • **88**
Pauillac 1986 • $58 Ⓐ • (05/31/89) • **97**
Pauillac 1985: Class was back with Baron at this stage. Caressing wine with silky texture and loads of coffee, toasted oak and berry character. Better after 1997. • $40 • (10/15/94) • **90**
Pauillac 1984 • $23 • (09/30/88) • **78**
Pauillac 1983: Not up to today's standard for this estate, but it's a friendly wine with lovely cassis and berry aromas and flavors, medium body and a light fruity finish. Drink now. • $34 • (10/15/94) • **85**
Pauillac 1982 • $39 Ⓐ • (08/31/92) • **92**
Pauillac 1981: Plenty of flavor but lacks breeding. Fresh and vivid tobacco and chocolate character. Drink now. • $33 • (10/15/94) • **85**
Pauillac 1980 • $17 • (09/30/88) • **79**
Pauillac 1979 • $22 Ⓐ • (10/15/89) • **88**
Pauillac 1978 • $27 Ⓐ • (09/30/88) • **80**
Pauillac 1977 • $13 • (09/30/88) • **76**
Pauillac 1976 • $30 • (09/30/88) • **73**
Pauillac 1975 • $35 • (09/30/88) • **74**
Pauillac 1974 • $15 • (09/30/88) • **78**
Pauillac 1973 • $27 • (09/30/88) • **78**
Pauillac 1972 • $13 • (09/30/88) • **68**
Pauillac 1971 • $31 • (09/30/88) • **71**
Pauillac 1970 • $28 Ⓐ • (05/15/93) • **84**
Pauillac 1969 • $25 • (09/30/88) • **78**
Pauillac 1967 • $18 Ⓐ • (09/30/88) • **80**
Pauillac 1966 • $26 Ⓐ • (09/30/88) • **80**
Pauillac 1964 • $37 Ⓐ • (09/30/88) • **88**
Pauillac 1962 • $65 • (09/30/88) • **88**
Pauillac 1961: Still solid in its texture and fruit flavors, this has picked up butter and caramel aromas from long aging. Appealing but apparently starting to slide. • $106 • (04/30/96) • **85**
Pauillac 1960 • $50 • (09/30/88) • **81**
Pauillac 1959 • $39 Ⓐ • (10/15/90) • **94**
Pauillac 1958 • $95 • (09/30/88) • **79**
Pauillac 1957 • $110 • (09/30/88) • **76**
Pauillac 1955 • $135• (09/30/88) • **81**
Pauillac 1954 • $95 • (09/30/88) • **80**
Pauillac 1953 • $150 • (09/30/88) • **80**
Pauillac 1952 • $120 • (09/30/88) • **84**
Pauillac 1950 • $150 • (09/30/88) • **83**
Pauillac 1949 • $175 • (09/30/88) • **87**
Pauillac 1947 • $135 • (09/30/88) • **80**
Pauillac 1945: Mature, with lots of anise and smoke woven through the slightly raisiny flavor. Earthy, animal notes intrude on the finish. Except for the barnyard qualities it's fine, adding chewy tannins. • $400 • **82**

PICHON-LONGUEVILLE-LALANDE, CHÂTEAU

Pauillac 1995: Gorgeous. Amazing harmony, with plenty of depth and great concentration of cassis, wild berry, vanilla and spice notes. What

Key: SS—Spectator Selection. CS—Cellar Selection. BB—Best Buy. $NA—Price not available. (BT)—Barrel tasting. Ⓐ—Auction Price.
Dates in parentheses represent the issues in which the ratings were published.

lovely, silky texture. Get your hands on at least a case of this. • $NA • (05/15/96) • **95-100** (BT)

Pauillac 1994: A well-made and fairly opulent '94 that's lavishly oaked and toasty, with a lean band of fruit underneath. Rather long but somewhat dry on the finish. • $40 • (05/15/96) • **85-89** (BT)

Pauillac 1993: Very lovely, supple and seductive, offering some pretty cassis and toast flavors, all presented in a sleek package. Quite racy, but clearly lacking the concentration and length of an outstanding wine. Start drinking now and through 1999. • $33 • (01/31/96) • **88**

Pauillac 1992: Pretty cherry and tobacco aromas and flavors, medium body and medium tannins, presenting some lovely black cherry, toasted oak character. Drinkable now. • $28 • **85**

Pauillac 1991: Solid, with very good berry and light herbal aromas and flavors, a fine mouthfeel of velvety tannins. Drink now. • $29 • (03/31/94) • **85**

Pauillac 1990: A seductive, exciting wine, it's hard not to drink it now. Has a harmonious silky texture with minty, berry and cassis aromas and flavors and ultrafine tannins. Drink after 1998. 33,500 cases made. • $55 Ⓐ • (03/15/93) SS • **97**

Pauillac 1989 • $58 Ⓐ • (03/15/92) • **92**

Pauillac 1988 • $45 Ⓐ • (04/30/91) • **91**

Pauillac 1987 • $31 Ⓐ • (02/15/90) • **87**

Pauillac 1986 • $65 Ⓐ • (05/31/89) • **97**

Pauillac 1985: This is a joy to taste. Great silky texture. Wonderful aromas and flavors of ripe black currants, with new oak backed up by velvety tannins. Better after 1996. • $55 • (10/15/94) • **92**

Pauillac 1984 • $22 Ⓐ • (01/31/87) CS • **94**

Pauillac 1983: Super wine with a great integration of ripe fruit, fine tannins and wonderful fruit. There's a palate full of flavors — minty, smoky, berry, vanilla and fruit. Drink or hold. • $46 • (10/15/94) • **92**

Pauillac 1982 • $163 Ⓐ • (08/31/92) • **97**

Pauillac 1981: A graceful wine that waltzes across your palate. Complex aromas and flavors of plum, chocolate and berries. Full bodied and silky with plenty of flavor at the end. Drink or hold. • $59 • (10/15/94) • **89**

Pauillac 1980 • $32 Ⓐ • (05/01/85) • **92**

Pauillac 1979 • $59 Ⓐ • (05/01/85) • **90**

Pauillac 1978 • $71 Ⓐ • (05/01/85) • **91**

Pauillac 1970 • $95 Ⓐ • (05/15/93) • **89**

Pauillac 1962 • $65 • (11/30/87) • **85**

Pauillac 1961: An elegant, subtle but complex wine that is understated in its mature spice and fruit flavors. Easy and smooth in texture, nicely balanced. Drink now through 2000. • $121 • (04/30/96) • **87**

Pauillac 1959 • $137 Ⓐ • (10/15/90) • **97**

Pauillac 1945: Very light-colored and fragile in texture, but it picks up some richness and echoes currant and spicy vanilla on the finish. • $450 • **87**

PICHOT, J.-C.

Vouvray Demi-Sec Domaine Le Peu de la Moriette 1995: Complex enigma of a white that combines apple and honey, grapefruit and earth, a touch of sweetness with searing acidity. Kind of like lemon meringue. Try in 1999. • $13 • (05/15/96) • **87**

Vouvray Molleux Domaine Le Peu de la Moriette 1995: There's little fruit flavor in this soft, simple white, just a sugary sweetness that cloys after the second sip. Stick with apple juice. • $18 • (06/15/96) • **75**

PICQUE-CAILLOU, CHÂTEAU

Graves 1982 • $NA • (08/31/92) • **78**

PIERRIERE, CHÂTEAU LA

Côtes de Castillon 1986 • $6 • (12/31/88) • **77**

PIGNAN

Châteauneuf-du-Pape Réservé 1991: This wine is a very ripe style with raisiney and prune-like flavors. Simple, with good concentration and some heavy-duty tannins. There is a hint of bittersweet chocolate on the finish. • $28 • (10/15/94) • **83**

Châteauneuf-du-Pape Réservé 1989 • $27 • (08/31/92) • **83**

Châteauneuf-du-Pape Réservé 1988 • $30 • (10/15/91) • **82**

Châteauneuf-du-Pape Réservé 1986 • $29 • (10/15/91) • **83**

Châteauneuf-du-Pape Réservé 1985 • $38 • (08/31/87) SS • **95**

Châteauneuf-du-Pape Réservé 1983 • $38 • (10/15/91) • **85**

Châteauneuf-du-Pape Réservé 1981 • $35 • (10/15/91) • **94**

Châteauneuf-du-Pape Réservé 1980 • $30 • (10/15/86) • **87**

PILLOT, FERNAND

Chassagne-Montrachet 1994: Good power and decent concentration, giving a rich feel in the mouth, but the slightly vegetal flavors of this well-structured white may not be quite everyone's taste. • $NA • (05/31/96) • **85**

Chassagne-Montrachet Morgeot 1994: Ripe yet very fresh, with a green, dried herb character along with honey, butterscotch and pear flavors. Long, intense and exotically sweet-tasting on the mouth-puckering finish. Drinkable now, but can age. • $NA • (05/31/96) • **85**

Chassagne-Montrachet Morgeot 1993: Fresh and clean mineral, spice and honey flavors. Medium-bodied, lightly fruity, crisp finish. • $33 • **84**

Chassagne-Montrachet Les Grandes Ruchottes 1994: Rather intense and nicely creamy, with some dried herb, fresh basil, pear and honey flavors. It's crisp, with a floral character. Try in 1998. • $NA • (05/31/96) • **88**

Chassagne-Montrachet Les Grandes Ruchottes 1993: Lovely pear, honey and chalk aromas and flavors, medium body and a mineral, glycerin texture. • $37 • **84**

Chassagne-Montrachet Les Vergers 1994: Beautiful, round, supple, full-bodied and seductive, with a dried herb character that adds complexity to the honey and ripe fruit flavors. More powerful than elegant, with a long finish. Solid. • $NA • (05/31/96) • **90**

Chassagne-Montrachet Les Vergers 1993: A good amount of almond, spice and honey character. Medium-to-full-bodied, straightforward yet fairly rich fruit flavors. Drink now. • $30 • **85**

Chassagne-Montrachet Vide Bourse 1994: Unctuous, overflowing with ripe, rich honey, herb and lime flavors. Seductive from start to finish, this full-bodied premier cru remains fresh on the long finish. A beauty. • $NA • (05/31/96) • **90**

Chassagne-Montrachet Vide Bourse 1993: Vibrant, lemony and honeyed, pleasant, delivering plenty of zest but not much depth. Try now. • $32 • **85**

Puligny-Montrachet 1994: Pulls no punches. Extremely intense, hinting at green apricot, with wonderful floral and mineral notes that tantalize the palate. A searing, slightly vegetal finish. • $NA • (05/31/96) • **88**

PILLOT, JEAN

Chassagne-Montrachet 1994: Odd wine, both crisp and ripe, with some sweet-tasting pear, apple, honey and citrus flavors. Very supple, yet almost dull on the finish. A disappointment from this fine producer. 416 cases made. • $25 • (05/31/96) • **80**

Chassagne-Montrachet 1992: A bit too funky for our tastes, with smoky-earthy aromas, mineral, honey and grapefruit flavors and a crisp finish. • $NA • (08/31/94) • **80**

Chassagne-Montrachet Caillerets 1994: Silky and delicious at first, it offers sweet-tasting pear, honey and honeydew melon flavors. Round and a bit unfocused on the finish. 83 cases made. • $42 • (05/31/96) • **85**

Chassagne-Montrachet Caillerets 1993: Some subtle apple, cream and toasted oak character. Lean style. • $50 • **80**

Chassagne-Montrachet Les Champs Gain 1994: Lively and crisp, mingling citrus, wet earth and honey flavors in a rather tight package. Charming from start to finish, with a very fresh finish that should keep this going through 1997. 150 cases made. • $32 • (05/31/96) • **85**

Chassagne-Montrachet Les Champs Gain 1992: Ripe and rich, with a lush texture that's kept in check with a good backbone of acidity, offers a mouthful of pear, vanilla, honey and grapefruit flavors. Worth the search, drinkable now. • $32 • (08/31/94) • **90**

Chassagne-Montrachet Les Chenevottes 1994: Rich and creamy, with lush hazelnut and tropical fruit flavors. Full-bodied and has lots of personality, this puts on quite a show. Needs until 1998 for its slightly rough finish to smooth out. 175 cases made. • $30 • (05/31/96) • **87**

FRANCE

Chassagne-Montrachet Les Chenevottes 1993: Relatively light and very tart, austere, delivering some green apple, dried-herb character. • $35 • **81**

Chassagne-Montrachet Les Chenevottes 1992: Charming Chassagne, quite thick in texture, showing an unctuous lime and honey character that seduces you and begs for another sip. Balanced and vibrant with a pear and toasty note on the finish. • $30 • (08/31/94) • **89**

Chassagne-Montrachet Les Macherelles 1994: A well-crafted and highly focused *premier cru,* delivering its gorgeous lemon, honey and mineral flavors with digital clarity. Somewhat fuller in body, it has more intensity than most '94s. Should improve with age. • $NA • (05/31/96) • **88**

Chassagne-Montrachet Les Macherelles 1993: Harmonious, smooth texture, good mineral, chalk and class. A lovely Chassagne, tart and hard but with enough concentration. Bravo! Better after 1996. • $NA • **87**

Chassagne-Montrachet Les Vergers 1994: Gorgeous, silky, elegant, a little fuller in body, offering a cascade of mineral, vanilla, pear and earth flavors. Subtle yet powerful, it tastes as smooth as double cream. Try this in 2000. 175 cases made. • $32 • (05/31/96) • **93**

Chassagne-Montrachet Morgeot 1994: A lovely, full-bodied '94, bursting with honey, pear and apple pie flavors. Stays the course with a lemony character that gives it structure. Fabulous drinking now, but will last through 1998. 200 cases made. • $NA • (05/31/96) • **89**

Chassagne-Montrachet Morgeot 1992: Vivid and ripe in flavor, showing the peach and honey notes of Botrytis. Full-bodied and technically dry, but seems to be sweet. An enjoyable but noticeably different style. Drinkable now. • $37 • (08/31/94) • **83**

Puligny-Montrachet 1994: Crisp, fresh and mineral, with a ripe mouthfeel. Very well built for a village wine. Could use a bit more fruit concentration, but it has finesse. 250 cases made. • $NA • (05/31/96) • **85**

Puligny-Montrachet 1993: Clean and fresh steel, mineral and spice character, medium body, firm acidity and a racy finish. • $30 • **82**

Puligny-Montrachet 1992: Earthy but elegant, of medium body, chewy and mouth-puckering, and packing plenty of grapefruit, pineapple, pear and mineral flavors. Fresh and delicious now, it should improve with aging until at least 1997. • $26 • (08/31/94) • **87**

PILLOT, PAUL

Chassagne-Montrachet Red Clos St.-Jean 1986 • $23 • (02/28/90) • **84**

Chassagne-Montrachet Red Clos St.-Jean 1985 • $24 • (11/15/88) • **86**

PIN, CHÂTEAU LE

Pomerol 1995: Supersexy and seductive red featuring berry, chocolate and cherry aromas and flavors. Medium to full body, silky tannins and long, succulent, berry finish. Caresses your palate. Almost classic. • $NA • (05/15/96) • **90-94** (BT)

Pomerol 1994: Great class. As good as the '95. Lovely berry and cherry flavors accompany plenty of new wood. Medium to full body, racy tannins and a long, sweet, fruit finish. Delicious. • $NA • (05/15/96) • **90-94** (BT)

Pomerol 1993: Delicious Le Pin. Exotic and flashy, sporting lots of new wood which lends a smoky, toasted oak character to the berry notes. Medium in body, delicate tannins and fruity finish. Drinkable now. • $300 • (01/31/96) • **90**

Pomerol 1992: The biggest disappointment of the vintage. Why bottle such a wine? Very light and watery with milk chocolate, berry and vanilla character. Tasted twice. Drink now. • $150 • **74**

Pomerol 1990: Rich, concentrated, supple and exotic, with brilliant articulated currant and red plum at the core, layered with chocolate and spice. tempting now, best from 2004. • $929 Ⓐ • (03/31/94) • **94**

Pomerol 1989 • $250 Ⓐ • (05/15/94) • **94**

Pomerol 1988 • $230 Ⓐ • (05/15/94) • **95**

Pomerol 1986 • $200 Ⓐ • (05/15/94) • **93**

Pomerol 1985: The wine of the vintage and the greatest Le Pin ever made. It's so thick and rich that you could almost mold it with your hands. Unbelievable aromas and flavors of crushed fruit, the essence of currants. Full-bodied with masses of velvety tannins. Better after 2000, but it may still be too young then. • $220 • (10/15/94) • **98**

Pomerol 1983: Exciting and vivacious. Gorgeous aromas and flavors of coffee, plum, chocolate and toasted oak. Full-bodied and velvety with a fresh, rich fruit aftertaste and fine tannins. Drinkable now. • $200 • (10/15/94) • **91**

Pomerol 1982 • $320 • (05/15/94) • **95**

Pomerol 1981: Rich and wonderful with ripe, minty aromas and flavors and hints of chocolate, tobacco and berry. Solid backbone of tannins and a long finish. Drinkable now. • $200 • (10/15/94) • **91**

Pomerol 1979 • $550 Ⓐ • (05/15/94) • **90**

PINEDE, DOMAINE DE LA

Châteauneuf-du-Pape 1990: Spicy, earthy, gamy flavors tend to dominate this robust wine, but sweet, raisiny notes sneak through on the finish. An interesting wine that may not improve with age. 3,500 cases made. • $15 • (04/15/93) • **78**

PINTEY, CHÂTEAU DU

Bordeaux Supérieur 1988 • $11 • (08/31/91) • **75**

Bordeaux Supérieur 1986 • $8 • (12/10/90) • **70**

PIPER-HEIDSIECK

Brut Champagne 1985: Another straightforward fizz with strawberry, toasty character, medium body and very crisp acidity. Tasted twice. May be better now. 57,400 cases made. • $36 • (12/31/93) • **85**

Brut Champagne 1982 • $32 • (12/31/88) • **86**

Brut Champagne Cuvée Brut NV: A good, appealing Champagne, featuring ample fruit flavor, crisp acidity and doughy-yeasty accents to make it interesting. Turns lean on the finish. • $30 • (12/31/95) • **85**

Brut Champagne Rare 1985: Amazing balancing act between richness and freshness. Shows mature flavors but it has the structure to age. Intense aromas and flavors of smoke, fruit and nuts. Medium bodied with great acidity and long flavorful finish. Much, much better than in the past. 20,600 cases made. • $80 • (12/31/93) • **93**

Brut Champagne Rare 1979 • $34 Ⓐ • (03/15/87) • **89**

Brut Champagne Rare 1976 • $66 • (08/01/85) • **88**

Brut Champagne Sauvage 1985: A beautifully integrated and mature tasting wine, with roasted and toasty aromas. It is full-bodied with vanilla and lemon flavors and a finish full of honey. Stylish and satisfying. • $35 • **90**

Brut Champagne Sauvage 1982 • $35 • (12/31/93) • **76**

Brut Rosé Champagne 1982: Nice, creamy texture. Lush and soft, with tart cherry aromas. Off-dry Rose with mature Pinot Noir character and some touches of smoke and oak. The finish is rather pleasant and long. • $38 • (12/31/88) • **84**

Brut Rosé Champagne NV: Has the taste of authenticity, with a provocative style that reminds us of an aged red Burgundy. Earthy, leathery aromas, well-seasoned, meaty flavors and echoes of cherry and spice on the long finish. Exciting and unique. 9,000 cases made. • $30 • (11/30/94) • **93**

Extra Dry Champagne NV: Very fruity, slightly sweet, refreshing and straightforward, offering melon and pineapple flavors and a hint of toasty-doughy character. • $30 • (12/31/95) • **83**

PITRAY, CHÂTEAU DE

Côtes de Castillon 1992: Spicy cherry and plum flavors are framed by firm tannins. It's medium-bodied, straightforward and simple, but balanced and rich enough for food. • $8 • (11/15/94) • **80**

Côtes de Castillon 1990: Rough, straightforward and tannic, with modest spice and anise flavors. Pleasant plum and cherry notes partially offset its basic austerity. May have smoothed out by now. 5,000 cases made. • $9 • (03/15/93) • **80**

Côtes de Castillon 1988 • $7 • (02/28/91) BB • **83**

Côtes de Castillon 1986 • $6 • (09/30/89) BB • **81**

Key: SS—Spectator Selection. CS—Cellar Selection. BB—Best Buy. $NA—Price not available. (BT)—Barrel tasting. Ⓐ—Auction Price.
Dates in parentheses represent the issues in which the ratings were published.

PLACE D'ARGENT

Cabernet Sauvignon Vin de Pays de l'Aude 1985 • $5 • (04/15/89) • **78**
Merlot Vin de Pays de l'Aude 1987 • $5 • (04/30/90) • **77**
Merlot Vin de Pays de l'Aude 1985 • $5 • (12/15/88) BB • **80**

PLAGNAC, CHÂTEAU

Médoc 1995: Light and watery, featuring modest fruit and weak tannin structure. Disappointing. • $NA • (05/15/96) • **75-79** (BT)
Médoc 1993: Why bottle this? Smells and tastes of stewed tomatoes and bell pepper, watery and short. • $11 • (01/31/96) • **70**
Médoc 1991: Bell pepper character dominates this wine, but some decent sweet fruit and its round texture show through. • $11 • (03/31/94) • **78**
Médoc 1989 • $12 • (03/15/92) • **88**
Médoc 1988 • $8 • (04/30/91) • **79**
Médoc 1987 • $8 • (11/30/89) • **77**
Médoc 1986 • $9 • (11/30/89) • **82**
Médoc 1985 • $9 • (08/31/88) • **68**

PLAIMONT

Colombelle Vin de Pays des Côtes de Gascogne 1994: Thick-textured and tart, mingling light apple and strong vegetal flavors. 25,000 cases made. • $6 • (02/29/96) • **76**

PLAISANCE, CHÂTEAU

Premières Côtes de Bordeaux Cuvée Spéciale Red 1989 • $13 • (01/31/92) • **86**

PLANERES, CHÂTEAU

Côtes du Roussillon 1989 • $7 • (04/15/93) • **78**
Côtes du Roussillon White 1994: Richly-textured and rustic, but it's appealing, with flavors of pears, almonds and herbs that linger on the finish. • $8 • (02/29/96) • **82**

PLANTEY, CHÂTEAU

Pauillac 1989 • $NA • (03/15/92) • **78**

PLANTIERS DU HAUT-BRION, LES

Graves 1974 • $24 • (03/31/89) • **80**

PLINCE, CHÂTEAU

Pomerol 1995: Beautiful, delivering tons of sweet fruit, spice, mocha and earth complexity. Full in body, solid, rich, ripe tannins and a long, silky finish. Almost outstanding. • $NA • (05/15/96) • **85-89** (BT)
Pomerol 1994: A nice little wine that's light- to medium-bodied, but slightly short and simple. • $NA • **75-79** (BT)
Pomerol 1993: Some decent body but the stewed tomato and herbal nature takes away from the quality. • $24 • (01/31/96) • **78**
Pomerol 1990: This is rich and concentrated, but a bit overripe and overoaked, with plum and cherry flavors accented by bitter chocolate, coffee and prune notes. Drinkable now. • $25 • **82**
Pomerol 1982 • $NA • (05/15/89) • **92**

PLOYEZ-JACQUEMART

Brut Blanc de Blancs Champagne 1988: An insider's wine. Ultrafine Champagne with great acidity and wonderful appley, vanilla fruit, it's medium bodied and superfirm with a creamy texture. Drink now or age. 670 cases made. • $42 • (12/31/93) • **93**
Brut Champagne Extra Quality NV • $28 • (11/30/92) • **89**
Brut Champagne Liesse d'Harbonville 1989: Exotic wine that bombards your palate with exotic fruit character. A big wine but not heavy. Mango, papaya, and pineapple aromas and flavor, full body, rich foam, full acidity, and long flavorful finish. Drink now. 450 cases made. • $65 • (12/31/93) • **90**
Brut Champagne Liesse d'Harbonville 1985: A very dry and lively style with fresh lemon, apple and light toasty character, medium body and long refreshing finish. Fine texture. Excellent apéritif. Tasted twice. Drink now. 225 cases made. • $65 • (12/31/93) • **89**

PLUMET HERITIERS, HENRI

Pouilly-Fuissé Clos du Chalet Pouilly 1994: Both fat and crisp, this mouthful of a wine delivers plenty of character with its pineapple, salted peanut and citrus flavors. Needs time to smooth out, try in 1998. • $NA • (05/31/96) • **85**
Pouilly-Fuissé Clos du Chalet Pouilly 1993: Surprisingly brownish color for a 1993. Shows some cacao, cedar, green apple aromas and flavors, slightly short finish. Drink now. • $NA • **79**

POCE, CHÂTEAU DE

Brut Crémant de Loire 1982 • $12 • (07/31/88) • **84**
Brut Touraine Crémant de Blancs NV • $11 • (10/15/88) • **81**

POINTE, CHÂTEAU LA

Pomerol 1995: Wonderful ripe, sweet tannins and plenty of red fruit character. Medium- to full-bodied, finely tannic and finishing long. • $NA • (05/15/96) • **90-94** (BT)
Pomerol 1994: Sweet and round, with good tannins and a lovely aftertaste full of cherry, berry and chocolate notes. • $NA • (05/15/96) • **85-89** (BT)
Pomerol 1992: Interesting aromas and flavors of nutmeg, fruit and bread dough, medium-to-light-bodied. Drink now. • $19 • **78**
Pomerol 1990: Attractive cherry, raspberry character and firm tannins give this wine appeal, but it's a little short on the finish. Drinkable now. 9,000 cases made. • $27 • (03/31/93) • **86**
Pomerol 1989 • $17 Ⓐ • (03/15/92) • **95**
Pomerol 1988 • $13 Ⓐ • (07/31/91) • **83**
Pomerol 1986 • $21 • (06/15/89) • **90**
Pomerol 1982 • $31 Ⓐ • (08/31/92) • **84**
Pomerol 1970 • $29 Ⓐ • (05/15/93) • **88**
Pomerol 1962 • $35 • (11/30/87) • **80**
Pomerol 1961: Mature but still vital, with complex fruit flavors accented by mineral and tea notes. It has a dense, tannic texture and a dry finish. Drink through 2000. (Tasted in magnum.) • $39 • (04/30/96) • **85**
Pomerol 1945: Very mature, complex, decadent aromas are fascinating to smell, but the tannins are a bit too astringent to let the last wisps of berry flavor show through. • $250 • **80**

POIRON, HENRI

Muscadet de Sèvre et Maine Sur Lie Château des Grandes Noëlles 1993: Floral notes add interest to the light lemon and green apple flavors. It's light-bodied, crisp and has a pleasing delicacy. • $9 • (08/31/94) • **84**

POL ROGER

Brut Blanc de Blancs Champagne Blanc de Chardonnay 1986: Even better than the very good 1985 blanc de blancs from Pol Roger. Super fresh and crisp like freshly cut pineapple. It's medium bodied with vivacious, sparkling flavors. Drink now. • $63 • (12/31/93) • **90**
Brut Blanc de Blancs Champagne Blanc de Chardonnay 1985: A toasty, complex bubbly, with plenty of winy character, showing buttery, smoky overtones to the crisp apple and lemon flavors. Has layers of flavor wrapped in a tight package. A stylish wine that's drinkable now. • $62 • (01/31/92) • **89**
Brut Blanc de Blancs Champagne Blanc de Chardonnay 1982 • $50 • (12/31/90) • **91**
Brut Blanc de Blancs Champagne Blanc de Chardonnay 1979 • $41 • (12/31/90) • **84**

Brut Champagne 1988: This is fresh and frankly fruity, featuring orange, apple and lemon flavors accented by light, toasty notes. Clean, pleasant and straightforward. • $50 • **86**

Brut Champagne 1986: This Champagne shows a lovely nose of toast and apple but the palate seems slightly tired and short. For lovers of old Champagne. Tasted twice. Drink now. • $48 • (12/31/93) • **83**

Brut Champagne 1979 • $23 • (09/01/85) • **90**

Brut Champagne NV: A bold, flavorful Champagne that is fully mature, with buttery, nutty flavors and lots of body. If you like a robust, developed style of bubbly, this is for you. • $37 • (12/15/95) • **86**

Brut Champagne Cuvée Sir Winston Churhill 1985: A classic, elegant Champagne that is beautifully balanced, complex in aroma and flavor, but still lively and youthful in texture. Hints of lime, fig, butter, nutmeg and vanilla combine for a complete taste experience. Harmonious and beguiling. • $100 • **96**

Brut Champagne Cuvée Sir Winston Churchill 1982 • $63 • (04/15/90) • **92**

Brut Champagne Extra Cuvée de Réserve 1982: Toasty, buttery and perfumed aromas turn smoky and earthy on the palate, picking up complex mineral and pear flavors and a tannic texture, but it finishes OK. Not for everyone, but the style grows on you. Drink now. • $30 • (12/31/90) • **82**

Brut Champagne Réserve 1985: • $35 • (12/31/90) • **86**

Brut Champagne Réserve NV • $32 • (11/15/91) • **87**

Brut Rosé Champagne 1988: An elegant marriage of fruit and toast gives this vibrancy and depth. The flavors range from cherry and raspberry to smoke and toast, with a long, crisp finish. Delicious now, but should improve in the bottle. • $52 • (12/15/95) • **92**

Brut Rosé Champagne 1986: A complete, well-balanced, flavorful rosé that has fresh fruit flavors accented by spice. It's mouth-filling, vibrant and harmonious overall. • $53 • (12/15/94) • **88**

Brut Rosé Champagne 1985 • $50 • (01/31/92) • **89**

Brut Rosé Champagne 1982 • $34 • (12/31/88) • **80**

Brut Rosé Champagne 1979 • $28 • (12/16/85) • **88**

Brut Rosé Champagne 1975 • $33 • (12/16/85) • **67**

POMMARD, CHÂTEAU DE

Pommard 1993: Solid core of berry and raspberry flavor, full body, long tobacco and dried cherry finish and full yet fine tannins. Better in 2000. • $36 • **88**

Pommard 1992: Light and lean, with a nice strawberry and spice streak that echoes on the finish. Best after 1996. • $NA • **82**

Pommard 1991: Tough and astringent, a medium-weight wine with light-weight flavors. Picks up a touch of oak on the finish. Drinkable now. 3,500 cases made. • $40 Ⓐ • (01/31/94) • **82**

Pommard 1990: Bright, lively, juicy and extremely flavorful. Not as tannic as some Pommards in this vintage, but has plenty of pretty raspberry, cherry and earth flavors. Drinkable now. • $60 • (12/15/92) • **88**

Pommard 1989 • $65 • (01/31/92) • **86**

Pommard 1988 • $53 • (09/15/92) • **87**

Pommard 1979 • $49 Ⓐ • (09/01/85) • **88**

POMMERY

Brut Champagne 1985 • $40 • (12/31/90) • **87**

Brut Champagne 1982: Delicate style with plenty of charm and complexity. It's very toasty and creamy with rich honey and very delicate nuances. The finish is long and smooth with plenty of complexity. At the price a relative bargain. • $24 • (02/15/88) • **93**

Brut Champagne NV • $23 • (12/31/87) • **79**

Brut Champagne Royal NV: Soft and simple, showing candied fruit flavors of caramel apple and a short, sweet finish. Balance could be better. • $22 • **79**

Brut Rosé Champagne NV: Attractive, spicy cherry and raspberry aromas give way to a very foamy palate, with ripe berry flavors and light toasty accents on the finish. It's clean and fresh. • $29 • (12/15/95) • **88**

Key: SS—Spectator Selection. CS—Cellar Selection. BB—Best Buy. $NA—Price not available. (BT)—Barrel tasting. Ⓐ—Auction Price.
Dates in parentheses represent the issues in which the ratings were published.

PONIATOWSKI, PRINCE

Vouvray Clos Baudoin 1993: Intriguing aromas of spice and honey give way to lively fruit flavors that mingle peach, apple, spice and citrus, rich yet crisp. It's vivid and fresh, a nice apéritif. • $16 • **85**

PONNELLE, PIERRE

Beaune Les Grèves 1993: Attractive dried cherry and floral character, medium body, medium-firm tannins and crisp, lively finish. Drinkable now. • $21 • **82**

Bonnes Mares 1993: Light red, offering modest fruit character and structure and touches of ripe cherry and raspberry flavors. Amazingly bad for a grand cru. • $66 • **76**

Bonnes Mares 1990: Smooth in texture, moderately tannic and almost mature tasting, with black cherry and raspberry flavors accented by chocolate and cedar. It seems ready to drink now, before the fruit starts to fade. • $56 • **86**

Chambolle-Musigny Les Argillières 1991: Fragrant, with lovely floral raspberry aromas, but the flavors weaken and thin out. Try in 1997. • $NA • (01/31/94) • **79**

Clos de Vougeot 1993: Light and easy, offering some straightforward raspberry and strawberry notes. Quite diluted on the rather dry finish. What happened? • $57 • **77**

Clos de Vougeot 1991: Extremely earthy and barnyardy, although it's so crisp and narrow it hardly matters. • $NA • (01/31/94) • **72**

Clos de Vougeot 1990: Smooth, fruity and flavorful, well-balanced and appealing. It may not be the best Clos de Vougeot, but it's a spicy, nicely polished Burgundy that's astringent on the finish, but ready to drink now. • $48 • **86**

Corton Le Clos du Roi 1993: Very fresh, crisp, vibrant cherry character and hints of earth, added to fine tannins and a citric finish. Could use some more fruit. • $43 • **82**

Corton Le Clos du Roi 1990: A full-flavored, cedary and earthy Burgundy that's assertive in aroma, tannic in texture and a bit dry on the finish. Mineral and chalk aromas mingle with coffee, cherry and spice flavors. Drinkable now. • $36 • **84**

Côte de Beaune Les Pierres Blanches 1993: Fresh, vibrant, well-defined fruit flavors unhindered by woody notes. Extremely juicy, light-to-medium-bodied. Drinkable now. • $14 • **83**

Côte de Beaune Les Pierres Blanches 1992: A fresh, fruity red with lots of cherry and strawberry flavors, soft tannins and piney, herbal accents. Generous in flavor, easy in texture, ready to drink now. • $11 • **81**

Fixin Les Hervelets 1959 • $NA • (08/31/90) • **94**

Mâcon-Villages 1993: Straightforward flavors of apple and grapefruit are lifted by crisp acidity in this easy-drinking wine. It has a few rough edges, but clean varietal character. • $8 • **80**

Mazoyères-Chambertin 1991: Earthy, mushroomy aromas and flavors almost mask the berry flavors, and the forest underbrush aromas and flavors will not appeal to many. Distinctive enough to warrant cellaring until 1997. • $NA • (01/31/94) • **82**

Musigny 1990: Earthy, bitter and thin, with a metallic edge that hurts the finish. 50 cases made. • $125 • (12/31/93) • **71**

Pouilly-Fuissé 1993: Aromatic and delicate, this silky, polished wine offers melon and smoky flavors with hints of apricots and herbs. Not a blockbuster, but it has good integration and balance. • $14 • (05/31/94) • **86**

Vougeot White 1991 • $18 • (10/15/93) • **86**

Vougeot White Le Village Clos du Prieuré 1993: Straightforward white, revealing only modest fruit flavors and a diluted finish. • $19 • **77**

PONSOT, CHRISTINE

Coteaux du Tricastin 1994: Thin, light and easy drinking with modest raspberry flavors. Becomes a little astringent on the finish. • $NA • **79**

Coteaux du Tricastin 1993: A good, fruity wine with lush berry and cherry flavors. It is medium-bodied, with a peppery aroma and tannins on the finish. • $NA • **83**

Côtes du Rhône 1994: Light, spicey and fruity with modest raspberry and cherry flavors. This is a simple and satisfying wine, with a good dash of pepper flavors. • $NA • **81**

Côtes du Rhône-Villages 1994: Fairly tight and tannic with modest cherry and berry flavors. It's in a rustic style with not much in the middle. • $NA • **79**

PONSOT

Chambolle-Musigny Les Charmes 1988 • $58 • (04/30/91) • **92**
Chambolle-Musigny Les Charmes 1985 • $75 • (06/15/88) • **94**
Chapelle-Chambertin 1991: Smoky, gamy, barnyardy flavors pick up enough sweet fruit to balance this otherwise smooth wine better on the palate, but it's not for the faint of heart. • $65 • (08/31/94) • **80**
Clos de la Roche 1992: Firm in texture, but the sandalwood-scented currant flavor comes through, finishing tight and tannic. Needs until 1997 to resolve the tannins, but has enough concentration to promise nice things. • $102 • **88**
Clos de la Roche 1984 • $48 • (02/15/88) • **73**
Clos de la Roche 1959: Remarkably opulent and generous, still youthful and showing no sign of a brown edge in its color. The tannins are sweet and smooth, but it still has a firm backbone that gives it depth and structure. Ponsot said it was undrinkable during the first 20 years. • $NA • **94**
Clos de la Roche Cuvée Vieilles Vignes 1990: Bold, rich, complex and concentrated, a tight, yet polished, highly extracted style. Packs in lots of currant, black cherry, toast and chocolate flavors that gently unfold on the long, full finish. Has rich tannins, but they're smooth and polished. Drinkable now. 500 cases made. • $150 • (03/15/93) • **92**
Clos de la Roche Cuvée Vieilles Vignes 1988 • $185 • (05/15/91) • **88**
Clos de la Roche Cuvée Vieilles Vignes 1985 • $200 • (06/15/88) • **90**
Clos de la Roche Cuvée William 1988 • $150 • (05/15/91) • **89**
Clos St.-Denis Cuvée Vieilles Vignes 1988 • $165 • (07/15/91) • **85**
Gevrey-Chambertin Cuvée de l'Abeille 1991: Lean and tannic, with a beam of prune and black cherry fruit poking through the layer of chewiness. Hints at menthol and tobacco on the finish. A stylish wine, best from 1998. • $30 • (08/31/94) • **83**
Griotte-Chambertin 1991: Comes off as lean and simple, a spicy wine with cinnamon overtones to the modest currant and raisin flavors, smoky on the finish. Best from 1997. • $38 • (08/31/94) • **83**
Griotte-Chambertin 1988 • $150 • (05/15/91) • **89**
Latricières-Chambertin 1988 • $150 • (05/15/91) • **91**
Morey-St.-Denis 1990: Smells effusively fruity, with lots of plum, raspberry and black cherry aromas and similar flavors that follow through on the palate, picking up supple, generous floral notes. A wonderful array of fruit makes this delicious to drink now and at its peak in 1997. 200 cases made. • $68 • (03/15/93) • **91**
Morey-St.-Denis Monts Luisants 1988 • $40 • (04/30/91) • **85**
Morey-St.-Denis White Monts Luisant Vieilles Vignes 1992: Tart and lean, the lemon-lime flavors cleanse and refresh the palate, a bit smoky and toasty on the finish. 520 cases made. • $59 • (08/31/94) • **81**

PONTALLIER JOHNSON

Merlot Bordeaux 1982 • $8 • (10/15/87) • **77**

PONTET-CANET, CHÂTEAU

Pauillac 1995: Firm and solid berry and cherry aromas and flavors and a light earthiness. Medium body, tannins and finish. • $NA • (05/15/96) • **85-89** (BT)
Pauillac 1994: Very perfumey, showing some good depth and complexity to its black currant, plum, toasted oak notes. Tight, firm finish. Good potential here. Almost outstanding. • $27 • (05/15/96) • **85-89** (BT)
Pauillac 1993: One of the best Pontet-Canets in years. Lovely black cherry, raspberry, mint and mineral aromas and flavors, medium body, sleek, racy tannins and long, caressing texture. Better in 1998. 21,000 cases made. • $23 • (01/31/96) • **89**
Pauillac 1992: Straightforward, featuring cherry and berry aromas. Medium-bodied with some good tobacco character, medium tannins and a light finish. Drinkable now. • $16 • **82**
Pauillac 1991: A pretty wine with bark, tobacco and fruit notes. Medium body and a velvety finish. • $16 • (03/31/94) • **80**
Pauillac 1990: This one tried to do too much, it's clumsy and out of balance. Intense aromas of blackberry and vanilla do not prepare you for the massive amount of astringent tannins. An interesting wine, but will it ever come around? 30,000 cases made. • $29 • (03/31/93) • **82**
Pauillac 1989 • $17 Ⓐ • (03/15/92) • **89**
Pauillac 1986 • $31 Ⓐ • (05/31/89) • **89**
Pauillac 1982 • $25 Ⓐ • (08/31/92) • **90**
Pauillac 1970 • $19 Ⓐ • (05/15/93) • **84**
Pauillac 1961: Has the vintage's tight, firm character in spades. It may need more time, but the fruit may not last. Best to drink now through 1998. • $92 • (04/30/96) • **87**
Pauillac 1945: Smells better than it tastes. Rich, almost decadent aromas of prune, spice and hints of black cherry, but flavors thin quickly and dry out on the finish. • $250 • **79**

PONTIFICAL, DOMAINE

Châteauneuf-du-Pape 1990: Compares to hot Texas chili in its smoky, meaty flavor and full body. Quite tannic and rustic in texture, with plenty of heat on the finish. Not for the faint of palate, but a good, solid wine to drink now to 1998. 600 cases made. • $22 • (04/15/93) • **83**

POTENSAC, CHÂTEAU

Médoc 1988 • $12 Ⓐ • (10/31/91) • **80**
Médoc 1987 • $13 • (05/15/90) • **72**
Médoc 1986 • $16 • (11/30/89) • **86**
Médoc 1983 • $15 Ⓐ • (10/15/86) • **75**

POTHIER-EMONIN

Volnay 1986 • $24 • (04/30/89) • **85**

POTHIER-RIEUSSET

Beaune Les Boucherottes 1989 • $28 • (11/30/92) • **88**
Beaune Les Boucherottes 1988 • $35 • (11/30/90) • **88**
Beaune Les Boucherottes 1986 • $19 • (05/31/89) • **88**
Bourgogne 1986 • $10 • (06/15/89) • **79**
Bourgogne 1985 • $7 • (06/30/88) BB • **83**
Meursault Les Caillerets 1993: Lovely tropical fruit, fig and toasted oak aromas. Medium-bodied and firm with steely acidity and a touch of vanilla on the finish. Drinkable now. • $NA • **84**
Pommard 1989 • $32 • (11/30/92) • **82**
Pommard 1986 • $25 • (09/15/89) • **76**
Pommard Clos de Verger 1989 • $44 • (11/30/92) • **83**
Pommard Clos de Verger 1986 • $33 • (09/15/89) • **87**
Pommard Les Epenots 1989 • $49 • (11/30/92) • **82**
Pommard Les Rugiens 1989 • $49 • (11/30/92) • **84**
Pommard Les Rugiens 1986 • $35 • (09/15/89) • **72**
Volnay 1985 • $34 Ⓐ • (02/15/88) • **93**

POUGET, CHÂTEAU

Margaux 1995: Straightforward Cabernet character of cassis and earth. A moderate wine that has a short finish. • $NA • (05/15/96) • **80-84** (BT)
Margaux 1990: Makes you want to dive into the glass. A beautiful wine, with sexy aromas and flavors of vanilla, raspberry and spice and fine tannins. Drinkable in 1997. 3,500 cases made. • $22 • (03/31/93) • **91**
Margaux 1983 • $11 • (02/15/87) • **86**
Margaux 1970 • $NA • (05/15/93) • **84**

POUILLY, CHÂTEAU

Pouilly-Fuissé 1994: An uplifting wine, with a well-knit structure. Shows character, a good blend of citrus, honey, fig, spice and floral flavors. It's clean and well made. Drinkable now through 1998. From Canal Ducomet and Mommessin. 2,166 cases made. • $27 • (05/31/96) • **85**

POUJEAUX, CHÂTEAU

Moulis 1995: This shows a solid core of fruit and fine tannins, with plenty of minty berry and blackberry character. Fine tannins and a fresh finish. Almost outstanding. • $NA • (05/15/96) • **85-89** (BT)
Moulis 1994: Smells delicious, anticipating the wild berry, black currant and violet flavors. A bit angular now, and it turns slightly dry on the finish. • $NA • (05/15/96) • **80-84** (BT)
Moulis 1992: Lean and slightly herbal, presenting stone, mineral and fruit character, medium body and firm tannins. Drinkable now. • $15 • **78**
Moulis 1991: Delicate and elegant, with ripe berry and chocolate aromas and flavors. Silky finish. • $15 • (03/31/94) • **83**
Moulis 1990: Round and rich, with a delicious smoky, earthy, berry character and velvety tannins. Drinkable now. 20,000 cases made. • $20 • (03/31/93) • **88**
Moulis 1989 • $21 • (03/15/92) • **90**
Moulis 1988 • $15 • (02/28/91) • **88**
Moulis 1987 • $15 • (05/15/90) • **74**
Moulis 1986 • $19 • (11/30/89) • **88**
Moulis 1985 • $18 • (09/30/88) • **87**
Moulis 1983 • $19 • (10/31/86) • **79**
Moulis 1982 • $22 • (08/31/92) • **85**

FRANCE

POUMEY, CHÂTEAU

Pessac-Léognan 1995: Supple and delicious, this full-bodied '95 delivers an explosion of red berry intensity, good acidity and a long finish; too bad it also comes with a distracting astringent and herbaceous note. • $NA • (05/15/96) • **80-84** (BT)

POUSSE D'OR, DOMAIN DE LA

Pommard Les Jarolières 1993: Slightly disappointing for Pousse d'Or. Clean and fresh but somewhat lean in fruit. Medium-bodied, adding firm tannins and a fresh finish. Drink in 1999. • $65 • **85**
Pommard Les Jarolières 1992: Ripe, spicy and complex, rich and deep, with blackberry, vanilla and slightly herbal notes on the crisp finish. Drinkable now. 833 cases made. • $57 • **88**
Pommard Les Jarolières 1991: Crisp and distinctive, showing a streak of green stalkiness running through the modest blackberry flavors. Drinkable now. • $50 Ⓐ • (01/31/94) • **80**
Pommard Les Jarolières 1988 • $27 Ⓐ • (08/31/91) • **88**
Pommard Les Jarolières 1986 • $45 • (04/30/89) • **70**
Pommard Les Jarolières 1985 • $39 • (03/15/88) • **87**
Santenay Clos de Tavannes 1993: Lovely rose petal and crushed raspberry aromas and flavors. Medium in body, long finish, delivering itself slowly while unfolding layers of pure, silky fruit. • $40 • **87**
Santenay Clos de Tavannes 1991: Firm in texture, but the solid band of currant and blackberry character finishes open and appealing. A real mouthful of flavor. Drinkable now. • $26 Ⓐ • (01/31/94) • **84**
Santenay Clos de Tavannes 1989 • $29 • (01/31/92) • **91**
Santenay Clos de Tavannes 1988 • $28 • (08/31/91) • **83**
Santenay Clos de Tavannes 1986 • $27 • (06/15/89) • **78**
Santenay Clos de Tavannes 1985 • $22 • (03/15/88) • **67**
Santenay Les Gravières 1992: Open-textured and showing nice nuances of smoke and toast on modest, dark berry flavors. Drinkable now. • $28 • **81**
Volnay Les Caillerets 1993: Nice fruit here, but the finish is quite dry. Maybe it's just in an odd phase and needs quiet cellaring. Blackberry, plum and wet earth flavors. Hold until at least 1999. • $53 • **85**
Volnay Les Caillerets 1992: Nicely gamy, almost funky, backed by appealing boysenberry and black currant flavors. The aromas are spectacular but could use a bit more length on the crisp finish. Drinkable now. • $49 • **85**
Volnay Les Caillerets 1988 • $49 • (08/31/91) • **85**
Volnay Les Caillerets 1985 • $35 • (03/15/88) • **90**

Key: SS—Spectator Selection. CS—Cellar Selection. BB—Best Buy. $NA—Price not available. (BT)—Barrel tasting. Ⓐ—Auction Price.
Dates in parentheses represent the issues in which the ratings were published.

Volnay Les Caillerets-Clos des 60 Ouvrées 1993: Succulent red, offering good concentration of fruit character. Medium in body, it has solid tannins but ends on a seductive, seamless finish. Try this charmer in 2000. • $60 • **89**
Volnay Les Caillerets-Clos des 60 Ouvrées 1992: Ripe and aromatic, a bit tight and crisp on the palate but generous with blackberry and black cherry notes. Needs until 1997 to soften. • $53 • **86**
Volnay Les Caillerets-Clos des 60 Ouvrées 1990: A high-wire act of a wine that's elegant and firm, with loads of beautiful raspberry and earth flavors that gain depth on the gorgeous, supple finish. Drinkable now. 1,250 cases made. • $62 • (12/15/92) • **91**
Volnay Les Caillerets-Clos des 60 Ouvrées 1987 • $29 • (06/15/90) • **82**
Volnay Les Caillerets-Clos des 60 Ouvrées 1986 • $41 • (04/30/89) • **83**
Volnay Les Caillerets-Clos des 60 Ouvrées 1985 • $39 • (03/15/88) • **86**
Volnay Clos de l'Audignac 1989 • $45 • (01/31/92) • **92**
Volnay Clos de la Bousse d'Or 1993: Fills your mouth with fruit and tickles your palate with tannins. Pretty Pinot, tasting of plums and sliced oyster mushrooms. Medium body, medium-fine tannins, silky finish. • $70 • **88**
Volnay Clos de la Bousse d'Or 1992: Lean but nicely focused, with ripe, smoky berry and tobacco flavors that linger on the crisp finish. Drinkable now. • $61 • **86**
Volnay Clos de la Bousse d'Or 1991: A bright, flavorful, smooth-textured wine, featuring modest tannins and a nice beam of blackberry and raspberry aromas and flavors. Hints at chestnut on the finish. Delicate and drinkable now. • $55 Ⓐ • (01/31/94) • **86**
Volnay Clos de la Bousse d'Or 1990: From a great vintage, this beautiful Burgundy almost has it all. Firm yet supple, packed with lovely raspberry, earth and chocolate aromas and flavors that end with a super-long finish. Drinkable now. 1,375 cases made. • $75 • (11/30/92) CS • **93**
Volnay Clos de la Bousse d'Or 1989 • $60 • (01/31/92) • **90**
Volnay Clos de la Bousse d'Or 1986 • $46 • (04/30/89) • **75**

POUSSIE, LA

Sancerre 1994: Typical Sancerre flavors of herbs, hay and citrus give this white a nervy appeal. It's somewhat light and short on the finish, but still packs lots of pleasure. • $22 • (06/15/96) • **85**

PRADEAUX, CHÂTEAU

Bandol 1986 • $18 • (10/31/90) • **83**
Bandol Réserve 1981 • $NA • (08/31/86) • **58**

PREISS-HENNY

Gewürztraminer Alsace Château de Mittelwihr 1992: On the heavy side, with lots of body and texture, but light flavors that are pleasant but don't balance out the wine. Good and sturdy overall. • $13 • (11/15/94) • **82**

PRIEUR, JACQUES

Beaune Clos de la Féguine 1993: Ripe fruit but a tough wine, adding loads of tannins which verge on being dry. Medium in body and a solid core of fruit. Better in 1999. • $30 • **88**
Chambertin 1993: A retaste and still it doesn't stun us. Good amounts of stuffing with earth and berry aromas and flavors, velvety tannins and cedary finish. Better in 1998. • $NA • **89**
Chevalier-Montrachet 1994: Satiny, balanced and attractive, a full-bodied white that delivers plenty of pear tart, peach, honey and toasted pine nut character. Like whipped cream in your mouth, but it shows a solid structure with plenty of lemon flavors on the long, refreshing finish. 45 cases made. • $150 • (05/31/96) • **93**
Chevalier-Montrachet 1993: Terrific potential shows in this handsome wine. Hard and closed now, it's still remarkably harmonious and delivers nice concentration, with mineral, vanilla, pear and spice flavors in fine proportions. Try in 1998. 50 cases made. • $130 • **90**
Clos Vougeot 1993: An absolute blockbuster, offering masses of fruit and tannins, full body and long, long finish. Needs loads of time, better after 2000. • $54 • **92**

Clos Vougeot 1991: Firm, flavorful and light in texture, with crisp tannins and ripe, barnyard-scented berry and black cherry aromas and flavors. Has elegance. Try now. • $NA • (01/31/94) • **85**

Corton Les Bressandes 1993: Very woody, almost tasting like a Rioja with all that vanilla. But the flavors are ripe, delivering supple tannins. Try in 2000. • $70 • **88**

Corton Les Bressandes 1992: A chewy, flavorful, serious wine that packs pretty, violet-tinged blackberry and currant flavors onto a lean frame, with hints of gaminess around the edges. Best from 1997. • $NA • **89**

Corton Les Bressandes 1991: Ripe currant and toasty blackberry aromas and flavors pick up a touch of bark on the finish. Fresh, aromatic and supple, echoes fruit without the harsh tannins of some '91s. Drinkable now. • $NA • (01/31/94) • **87**

Corton-Charlemagne 1993: Vivid aromas of apple, cream, oak and hints of minerals. Medium-bodied and very crisp. Loads of new wood-perhaps a little too much. 83 cases made. • $68 • **84**

Meursault Clos de Mazeray 1994: Amazingly concentrated and elegant. This class act walks a tightrope between the intense citrus flavors and the subtle honey and toast character that comes through on the long, racy finish. Try in 1998. 525 cases made. • $35 • (05/31/96) • **90**

Meursault Clos de Mazeray 1993: Delectable chalk, lemon and mineral aromas and flavors, medium body, fine acidity and long finish. Drink now. 625 cases made. • $34 • (08/31/95) • **85**

Meursault Clos de Mazeray 1992: A bit odd and simple, a bit earthy and musty, with decent fruit in the middle. 833 cases made. • $32 • (08/31/94) • **75**

Meursault Les Perrières 1994: Nice and supple, with some pretty tropical fruit, fig and pear flavors. It's smooth and drinkable now. 83 cases made. • $70 • (05/31/96) • **85**

Meursault Les Perrières 1993: Wonderfully fresh and clean apple and cream aromas and flavors. Medium body, well-integrated acidity and a long, rich finish. 70 cases made. • $52 • (08/31/95) • **86**

Meursault Les Perriéres 1992: Big and powerful, opulent and showy, it shows more muscle than most '92s. A bit woody now, but time should help smooth out the rough edges. Bursts with classy smoke, toast, floral, peach, honey and orange-peel flavors. Good acidity and a very long finish • $45 • (08/31/94) • **92**

Meursault Red Clos de Mazeray 1993: Nice blend of wood and fruit, featuring nuances of mocha, spice and vanilla and red berry flavor. Plenty of tannins, but a bit lean. Try in 1997. • $30 • **82**

Meursault Red Clos de Mazeray 1991: Simple, crisp, straightforward and light in weight, with modest earthy, spicy cherry character. Drinkable now. • $NA • (01/31/94) • **80**

Montrachet 1993: Wine of the vintage? Vibrant and electrifying, boasting layers of ripe fruit. Shows wonderful freshness and harmony, full body and toasted oak, honey and tropical fruit character. The finish goes on and on. 167 cases made. • $208 • **92**

Montrachet 1992: A class act worth lining up around the block to taste. Massive, muscular and quite woody. Good acidity, formidable fruit concentration and a layer of toasty character make it a serious candidate for the wine of the vintage. Needs time, try in 1998 and beyond. • $200 • (08/31/94) • **97**

Musigny 1993: A blockbuster that's hard on the surface and full-bodied, revealing underneath a silky core of ripe plum, blackberry and mineral character that won't let go on the mile-long finish. It would be a waste to drink this before 2005. • $63 • **94**

Musigny 1992: Light and very pretty, with vanilla grace notes to the smooth-textured thread of raspberry, strawberry and mocha flavors. Graceful enough to drink already. • $NA • **85**

Musigny 1991: Distinctive and aromatic, earthy, gamy anise notes play over a chorus of currant and black cherry flavors. A complex wine, with a smooth texture and a good future. May be best after 1997. • $NA • (01/31/94) • **89**

Puligny-Montrachet Les Combettes 1994: Oozing with volptous, unctuous honey, apricot and toasted hazelnut flavors. Full body, borders on nectar with a soft texture. Great to gobble up now. Stays quite fresh on the finish despite its richness. 375 cases made. • $50 • (05/31/96) • **90**

Puligny-Montrachet Les Combettes 1993: A bit lean, showing apple, mineral and lime character, medium body, tart acidity and medium finish. Drinkable now. 320 cases made. • $44 • **83**

Puligny-Montrachet Les Combettes 1992: Flawless, with unbelievable intensity yet great subtlety, this medium-bodied beauty is shining with pure, focused fruit, blending nicely into the toasty oak flavors. Better after 1998. Tasted twice. 500 cases made. • $NA • (08/31/94) • **92**

Volnay En Champans 1993: Pleasant mix of fruit, tobacco and cedar character. Medium-bodied with medium tannins and a crisp finish. Better in 1998. • $36 • **88**

Volnay En Champans 1992: Ripe and aromatic, with a stalky edge to the blackberry, currant and spice flavors. Drinkable now. • $NA • **85**

Volnay Santenots 1993: Lovely clarity and finesse, medium body, fresh berry flavor, ultrafine tannins and long, long finish. Better in 1999. • $34 • **91**

Volnay-Santenots 1992: Beautifully aromatic, with a tannic underpinning. A vanilla-scented, lavishly oaked and solidly built Volnay that offers red berry notes and a lingering finish. • $NA • **85**

Volnay-Santenots 1991: Light, lively and especially attractive for its anise-scented currant and berry aromas and spicy flavors that extend into a polished finish. Drinkable now, better in 1997. • $NA • (01/31/94) • **85**

Volnay-Santenots Clos des Santenots 1993: Amazingly silky, boasting mouth-coating ripe tannins, medium body and beautiful mineral, earth, currant and plum flavors. The wood is surprisingly well integrated for a red wine from this estate. Better than a barrel sample tasted earlier this year. • $37 • **90**

PRIEURE, CHÂTEAU DE

Premières Côtes de Bordeaux 1985 • $4 • (05/31/88) • **71**

PRIEURE, CHÂTEAU DU

Côtes du Rhône 1993: A seductive wine with a nice soft texture. The sweet plum and spice flavors make it enticing, though not particularly complex or intense. • $8 • **82**

PRIEURE, CHÂTEAU LE

St.-Emilion 1995: Solid, tight blackberry, cherry and mineral aromas and flavors. Medium- to full-bodied, fine tannins and rich finish. Almost outstanding. • $NA • (05/15/96) • **85-89** (BT)

PRIEUR-BRUNET

Beaune Clos du Roi 1991: Ripe currant flavor fights a losing battle against the coarse tannins in this chunky, straightforward wine. Try now. • $34 Ⓐ • (01/31/94) • **80**

Beaune Clos du Roi 1990: Light, smooth and supple, offering plenty of raspberry and cherry flavors, hints of spice and toast, smooth-textured tannins and a long finish. Drinkable now. • $32 • (02/15/93) • **86**

Beaune Clos du Roi 1988 • $30 • (12/31/90) • **82**

Chassagne-Montrachet Red Morgeot 1991: Coarse and chewy in texture, with a nice beam of raspberry-cherry fruit poking through the gravelly tannins. Drinkable now. • $29 Ⓐ • (01/31/94) • **82**

Chassagne-Montrachet Red Morgeot 1988 • $17 • (11/15/90) • **83**

Meursault Les Charmes 1993: Delicious and elegant premier cru, offering apple, cream and stone aromas and flavors, medium body, fine acidity and tasty finish. • $NA • **87**

Meursault Les Chevalières 1993: Some decent mineral and lemon character but it's slightly grassy, adding dried herbs and high acidity. Drinkable now. • $NA • (08/31/95) • **80**

Pommard La Platière 1991: Generous, polished raspberry and strawberry flavors carry through to a smooth, delicate finish. A light, supple wine that is drinkable now. • $40 Ⓐ • (01/31/94) • **82**

Pommard La Platière 1990: Light and fruity, with generous strawberry and raspberry aromas and flavors that stay with you on the finish and remain smooth and velvety. Drinkable now. • $40 • (02/15/93) • **85**

Santenay La Comme 1991: Earthy, jammy, tarry and slightly bitter, with only modest fruit poking through. Try now. • $21 Ⓐ • (01/31/94) • **78**

Santenay La Maladière 1991: A crisp, spicy wine that displays bright strawberry and vanilla flavors and smoky tobacco notes on the focused finish. Delicate, drinkable now. • $21 Ⓐ • (01/31/94) • **80**

Santenay La Maladière 1990: Light and delicate, with modest red cherry and spice aromas and flavors and an earthy, crisp finish. Drinkable now. • $23 • (02/15/93) • **77**
Santenay La Maladière 1988 • $20 • (11/15/90) • **80**
Volnay-Santenots 1990: Firm and focused, with dark cherry, currant and spice aromas and flavors. Finishes with significant but well-integrated tannins. Drinkable now. • $35 • (02/15/93) • **85**
Volnay-Santenots 1988 • $35 • (11/30/90) • **85**
Volnay-Santenots Clos des Santenots 1991: Spicy and oaky for such a lean, light wine. Polished to a gleam to show off modest berry and vanilla aromas and flavors. Drinkable now. • $NA • (01/31/94) • **83**

PRIEURE DES MOURGES, CHÂTEAU DU

St.-Chinian 1991 • $10 • (03/15/94) • **86**

PRIEURE DE ST.-JEAN DE BEBIAN

Coteaux du Languedoc 1989 • $23 • (06/30/92) • **77**

PRIEURE-LICHINE, BLANC DU CHÂTEAU

Bordeaux 1992: New white from a well-known red-wine producer. New-world style of thyme, dried-herb, lemon and tropical fruit character. Medium in body and firm, long, exotic finish. Drinkable now. • $17 • **84**

PRIEURE-LICHINE, CHÂTEAU

Margaux 1995: Gorgeous '95, velvety yet brimming with bright red- and blackberry character. Exotic, with perfumed, floral, mineral notes, it's seductive and full-bodied, a wine that beckons you to sip and sip again. • $NA • (05/15/96) • **90-94** (BT)
Margaux 1994: Some decent fruit shows through, with toasted oak and spice coming through on the palate, but slightly austere and drying. • $24 • (05/15/96) • **80-84** (BT)
Margaux 1993: Fresh, simple black cherry and berry character. Medium-bodied, medium tannins and light finish. Drinkable now. • $23 • (01/31/96) • **81**
Margaux 1992: Elegant and silky tobacco, mint and cherry aromas and flavors, medium in body and fine tannins. Drinkable now. • $15 • **82**
Margaux 1991: An attractive, supple mouthful, with no-nonsense tobacco and red berry flavors, leading into a light finish. • $15 • (03/31/94) • **84**
Margaux 1990: A beautiful wine, with raspberry, cherry, plum and smoke aromas and flavors, medium tannins and a long finish. Drinkable now. 25,000 cases made. • $20 • (03/31/93) • **86**
Margaux 1989 • $25 • (03/15/92) • **86**
Margaux 1988 • $18 Ⓐ • (04/30/91) • **90**
Margaux 1987 • $15 • (02/15/90) • **78**
Margaux 1986 • $32 Ⓐ • (06/15/89) • **92**
Margaux 1985 • $25 • (02/15/88) • **82**
Margaux 1984 • $14 • (11/30/86) • **80**
Margaux 1983 • $54 Ⓐ • (04/16/86) • **96**
Margaux 1982 • $38 Ⓐ • (08/31/92) • **83**
Margaux 1981 • $30 • (11/01/84) • **86**
Margaux 1959 • $50 • (10/15/90) • **80**

PRIEURE-ROCH

Bourgogne Grand Ordinaire 1991: Light and spicy, with a bit of a sweaty, vegetal edge to the modest strawberry aromas and flavors. Finishes tart and lean. Drinkable, but not immediately appealing. • $16 • (06/15/93) • **74**
Clos de Vougeot 1990: Firm and focused, with a modest beam of raspberry and tobacco aromas and flavors. Lean and a bit tannic on the finish. Drinkable now. • $65 • (06/15/93) • **83**

Key: SS—Spectator Selection. CS—Cellar Selection. BB—Best Buy. $NA—Price not available. (BT)—Barrel tasting. Ⓐ—Auction Price.
Dates in parentheses represent the issues in which the ratings were published.

Vosne-Romanée Les Clous 1990: Warm and spicy, with chocolaty, toasty plum and prune aromas and flavors. Full-bodied and moderately tannic, finishing with a slightly overripe edge. Could be fleshier, but has promise. Drinkable now. • $30 • (06/15/93) • **85**
Vosne-Romanée Hautes Maizières 1990: Light, lean and simple, showing a narrow range of raspberry and spice aromas and flavors. Silky in texture and finishes smoothly. Drinkable now. • $50 • (06/15/93) • **82**

PRIEURS DE LA COMMANDERIE, CHÂTEAU

Pomerol 1995: Very herbal berry and burnt wood character. Not very pleasant. • $NA • (05/15/96) • **70-74** (BT)
Pomerol 1985 • $27 • (09/30/88) • **93**
Pomerol 1983 • $25 • (09/30/86) • **79**

PROSPER-MAUFOUX

Aloxe-Corton 1982 • $27 • (06/15/92) • **79**
Beaujolais-Villages 1994: Light with some herbal notes. Faint strawberry flavors are not enough to keep this wine interesting. Finishes chalky. • $10 • (06/15/95) • **74**
Beaujolais-Villages 1993: Pleasant cherry and grapey aromas give way to harsh, tart, lean flavors. It lacks the fruity generosity we expect from Beaujolais. • $9 • **76**
Beaujolais-Villages 1992: Straightforward and solid, the plum and cherry flavors are firm, if not complex, and still fresh. A silky, easy-drinking quaff. Tasted twice. • $9 • (06/30/94) • **81**
Beaujolais-Villages 1991 • $9 • (07/31/92) • **80**
Brouilly 1994: Attractive cherry and spice aromas give way to light, rather thin flavors of cherries and herbs. There's not much structure to this simple wine. • $12 • (06/15/95) • **78**
Brouilly 1993: Light and simple, showing some pleasant berry and floral notes. Diluted and short. More like a Nouveau. • $10 • **77**
Brouilly 1992: Very light, silky and delicate, showing raspberry and cedar flavors that are mature and still appealing. Drink lightly chilled, as an aperitif. • $11 • (06/30/94) • **80**
Brouilly 1991 • $12 • (08/31/92) • **59**
Chassagne-Montrachet Les Chenevottes 1993: Interesting anise, grapefruit and grass flavors. The austere finish hints of mineral notes. • $30 • **82**
Chassagne-Montrachet Les Chenevottes 1992: Elegant and subtle, with a round texture that showcases some mineral, grapefruit, apple and pear flavors. 300 cases made. • $25 • (08/31/94) • **84**
Châteauneuf-du-Pape 1988 • $16 • (05/31/92) • **81**
Côtes du Rhône 1990 • $8 • (06/15/92) BB • **84**
Côtes du Rhône 1989 • $9 • (05/31/91) • **84**
Côtes du Rhône 1988 • $6 • (06/30/90) • **79**
Côtes du Rhône 1987 • $6 • (06/15/89) • **74**
Côtes du Rhône White 1993: Simple, slightly floral, with apple flavor. Just enough body to make it smooth on the palate. Dry and austere. • $8 • (10/15/94) • **76**
Gigondas 1985 • $11 • (04/30/88) • **65**
Moulin-à-Vent 1991 • $12 • (06/15/94) **86**
Muscat de Beaumes-de-Venise NV • $18 • (07/15/91) • **85**
Pouilly-Fuissé 1993: Balanced, with some richness on the palate, featuring light floral and mineral notes, but lacking ripe fruit and flavor intensity. • $16 • (03/31/95) • **79**
Puligny-Montrachet 1993: Very steely and fresh lemon, grass and apple character, medium body and a light finish. • $29 • **79**
Puligny-Montrachet 1992: Round and smooth, its butterscotch and buttery flavors are almost overwhelming. Also shows some honey, apple and spice notes. Drinkable now. 600 cases made. • $22 • (08/31/94) • **84**
Puligny-Montrachet Les Folatières 1993: Slightly candied gingerbread and apple aromas and flavors, medium body, fruit cocktail notes and hard acidity. • $34 • **79**
Puligny-Montrachet Les Folatières 1992: Has an overripe, cidery aroma, nutty flavor and nutty, oxidized finish. Tastes as if something went wrong. Fully mature already. 150 cases made. • $30 • (08/31/94) • **70**
Puligny-Montrachet Hameau de Blagny 1993: Nutty, strange-tasting, cardboard flavors. A bit heavy on the finish. • $30 • **70**
St.-Amour 1992• $12 • (06/15/94) • **85**

FRANCE

Santenay Les Gravières 1985 • $17 • (10/15/89) • **85**

PROTHEAU & FILS, MAURICE

Mercurey White Les Ormeaux 1993: An earthy, minerally component runs through this fairly tight white. It has some very good apple and citrus flavors which linger on the finish and are joined by honey and spice. 2,500 cases made. • $17 • **85**

Rully Red La Chatalienne 1990: Lean and crisp, with drying tannins that barely allow the tart cherry and plum flavors to come out. Seems unbalanced. Drinkable now. • $14 • (06/15/93) • **74**

Rully White 1992: A thick, buttery-tasting Chardonnay with a broad, smooth texture, lots of vanilla and fig flavor and a lingering finish. Balanced on the soft, fat side. Drink now. • $8 • (02/28/95) • **84**

Rully White Les Fromanges 1993: Intense, rich and flavorful, tasting of honeydew melon and a splash of citrus. Notes of clove and cardamom linger on the finish. 3,600 cases made. • $13 • **85**

PROVENQUIERE, DOMAINE LA

Chardonnay Vin de Pays d'Oc 1992 • $7 • (03/15/94) • **85**

PRUNIER

Auxey-Duresses Red Clos du Val 1987 • $25 • (11/15/89) • **84**

Auxey-Duresses White 1994: Some intriguing floral and chalky aromas, a chewy texture and decent grapefruit and apple flavors. Rather lean, but focused. 279 cases made. • $NA • (05/31/96) 81 • **80**

Chassagne-Montrachet Red 1990: Lean and earthy, with a metallic edge to the modest strawberry flavors. Comes off as simple and dull. • $16 • (06/15/93) • **77**

Meursault 1994: Round and fat, but lacks class, with slightly funky character. Harsh finish. 104 cases made. • $NA • (05/31/96) 75 • **77**

Puligny-Montrachet La Garenne 1994: Opulent, showy and seductive. This is a lush, full-bodied white Burgundy with loads of toasted coconut, pineapple, spice and crème brûlée flavors that continue on long through the finish. 50 cases made. • $NA • (05/31/96) • **87**

St.-Aubin White Premier Cru 1994: Ripe and has a touch of honey and almond in it, but an odd note of varnish and overly butterscotchy character is surprising. Not for everyone. 291 cases made. • $NA • (05/31/96) • **78**

PUGET, DOMAINE DU

Cabernet Sauvignon Vin de Pays de l'Aude 1991: Herbal and bell pepper flavors dominate this soft, easy-drinking wine. It's straightforward and unexciting. 9,000 cases made. • $6 • (06/30/94) • **78**

Cabernet Sauvignon Vin de Pays de l'Aude 1989 • $5 • (09/30/92) BB • **83**

Merlot Vin de Pays de l'Aude 1991: Barnyard aromas overlay the raspberry flavors, and there's a mean tannic pinch in the finish. Not much grace here. 7,000 cases made. • $6 • (06/30/94) • **73**

Merlot Vin de Pays de l'Aude 1990 • $6 • (06/15/93) • **78**

Merlot Vin de Pays de l'Aude 1989 • $5 • (06/30/92) • **77**

Merlot Vin de Pays de l'Aude 1988 • $4 • (06/30/90) • **76**

PULIGNY-MONTRACHET, CHÂTEAU DE

Côte de Nuits-Villages 1990: Lean and spicy, with more oak and nutmeg characteristics than the modest strawberry flavor can take. Could be livelier. • $21 • (08/31/92) • **78**

Côte de Nuits-Villages 1988 • $17 • (03/31/91) • **82**

Meursault Les Perrières 1994: Balanced and flavorful, fairly full-bodied and has nicely proportioned lemon, honey and pear flavors. No flaws, but it could be a bit punchier in its fruit. 166 cases made. • $16 • (05/31/96) • **84**

Meursault Les Perrières 1991 • $36 • (02/28/94) • **87**

Meursault Le Porusot 1993: Delicate and flavorful, a crisp Meursault that hints of honey, toasted coconut, pear and hazelnut notes and delivers a polished finish. Try now. 192 cases made. • $30 • **88**

Meursault Le Porusot 1992: Flavorful and refined at the same time, fruity and ripe but not too showy, with ample pear, honey and mineral flavors held in nicely by vibrant acidity. It expands on the finish, promising a great drinking experience after 1996. 390 cases made. • $30 • (08/31/94) • **92**

Meursault Le Porusot 1991 • $34 • (02/28/94) • **86**

Monthelie 1990 • $21 • (08/31/92) • **84**

Monthelie 1988 • $16 • (11/15/90) • **77**

Monthelie White 1991 • $17 • (02/28/94) • **72**

Pommard 1990: The light color and tight texture keep the spicy rhubarb and strawberry flavors under wraps. A light, delicate style of Burgundy. Drinkable now. • $40 • (08/31/92) • **79**

Pommard 1988 • $34 • (08/31/90) • **83**

Puligny-Montrachet 1994: Ripe and full-bodied, loaded with honey and citrus flavors. Tastes round and flavorful, with an appealing toffee and toasted nut character. Lacks just a bit of punch on the finish. 750 cases made. • $16 • (05/31/96) • **86**

Puligny-Montrachet 1993: Crisp and tart now, but it has the potential to evolve into a smoother, rounder wine, with some honey, lemon and mineral notes. Try now. 667 cases made. • $26 • **84**

Puligny-Montrachet 1992: Broad and ripe flavors dominate in this round wine, shows some good pear, honey and coffee notes. 800 cases made. • $26 • (08/31/94) • **87**

Puligny-Montrachet Les Folatières 1994: Fresh, crisp and flavorful, this clean Chardonnay provides some good apple, pear and citrus flavors. A touch diluted and short on the finish, though. 250 cases made. • $20 • (05/31/96) • **82**

Puligny-Montrachet Les Folatières 1993: Flavorful, medium-bodied white, featuring vibrant lime character and hints of honey and chalk on the finish. Drink now through 1997. 250 cases made. • $36 • **83**

Puligny-Montrachet Les Folatières 1992: A very stylistic white Burgundy that emphasizes buttery, creamy, hazelnut flavors accented by pear and honey on the finish. Rather lean and tight in the middle, but long on the aftertaste. 280 cases made. • $34 • (08/31/94) • **89**

Puligny-Montrachet Les Perrières 1993: Well-structured Puligny offering toasted oak and apple flavors, medium body, firm acidity and medium finish. Drinkable now. • $NA • **85**

St.-Aubin En Remilly 1994: A soft, supple, full-bodied and honey-scented *premier cru,* with ripe pear and toasted oak flavors. Creamy texture and delicious now. 333 cases made. • $11 • (05/31/96) • **85**

St.-Aubin En Remilly 1990: Light and spicy, with a crisp texture and modest vanilla-scented strawberry and nutmeg aromas and flavors. • $25 • (08/31/92) • **79**

St.-Aubin En Remilly White 1993: Very distinctive toast, caramel, spice and honey aromas, turning incredibly tart and austere on the hard finish. Might be better after 1996. 417 cases made. • $16 • **83**

St.-Romain White 1991 • $15 • (02/28/94) • **78**

PUY-BLANQUET, CHÂTEAU

St.-Emilion 1995: Big and tannic but a bit rustic with coarse tannins and raisiny flavors. Wait and see. • $NA • (05/15/96) • **80-84** (BT)

St.-Emilion 1994: Attractive cranberry aromas and flavors, medium to light body, medium tannins and fruity finish. An early drinker. • $NA • **80-84** (BT)

St.-Emilion 1993: Some decent cherry and chocolate character, but slightly aggressive with a metallic edge. Drinkable now. • $15 • (01/31/96) • **78**

St.-Emilion 1990: Quite a jammy wine, with raspberry, blackberry and tobacco flavors, medium tannins and a short finish. Drinkable in 1997. • $13 • (03/31/93) • **87**

St.-Emilion 1989 • $14 • (03/15/92) • **90**

St.-Emilion 1983 • $12 • (12/31/86) • **76**

PUY-SERVAIN, CHÂTEAU

Montravel Sec 1991 • $9 • (08/31/93) • **84**

PUYGUERAUD, CHÂTEAU

Côtes de Francs 1995: Elegant and refined, with fine tannins and a silky finish. Has a good dose of fruit on the palate that lasts through the finish. But it's tight and closed now. • $NA • (05/15/96) • **85-89** (BT)

Côtes de Francs 1994: Supple and pleasant, showing modest fruit flavors and light to medium body. • $NA • **75-79** (BT)

Côtes de Francs 1993: A light Bordeaux, showing strawberries and cherries, light tannins and light color. Drink on release. • $18 • (01/31/96) • **80**

Côtes de Francs 1990: A simple and fresh wine, with attractive tomato, herbal aromas and flavors and light tannins. Drinkable now. • $18 • (03/31/93) • **81**

Côtes de Francs 1989 • $18 • (03/15/92) • **83**

Côtes de Francs 1986 • $12 • (06/15/89) • **84**

Côtes de Francs 1985 • $9 • (06/30/88) • **83**

Côtes de Francs 1983 • $8 • (10/16/85) • **82**

QUILLA, DOMAINE DE LA

Muscadet de Sèvre et Maine Sur Lie 1993: Crisp, clean and lightly fruity, but basically neutral in character. It has some pleasant citrus and pear character-tart and refreshing. • $9 • (08/31/94) • **84**

R DE RIEUSSEC

Bordeaux White 1994: Electrifying wine, scorching with intensity, offering earth, mineral, grapefruit and lime flavors. Full-bodied and opulent, only it seems a bit oxidized on the finish, which drags down the score. • $10 • (03/31/96) • **84**

Bordeaux White 1993: Disappointing. Fresh and clean apple and pear character, light body and crisp finish. The dry white from Sauternes' Château Rieussec. Drink now. • $8 • **79**

RABASSE CHARAVIN, DOMAINE

Côtes du Rhône 1985 • $6 • (08/31/87) BB • **81**

RABAUD-PROMIS, CHÂTEAU

Sauternes 1991: Clean, delicate and attractive mineral, earth, pineapple and honey flavors, all presented in good proportions, not very sweet and quite light, but it's got some nice flavors. Drinkable now. • $NA • (04/15/95) • **82**

Sauternes 1990: Fresh and clean, quite light in this company but focused, revealing lively hay, earth, mineral and lemon flavors that offer good length but not much opulence. Try in 1997. • $NA • (04/15/95) • **88**

Sauternes 1989: Rich and ripe, exhibiting a creamy texture and lots of butter, lemon and wet hay flavors, but it lacks that something that comes from more botrytis. Medium length. • $30 • (04/15/95) • **86**

Sauternes 1988: Elegant and full-bodied, exhibiting a burst of botrytis character, impressive structure and spicy, dried apricot, honey, caramel and lemon flavors and a long finish. Tempting now, better in 1998. • $35 • (04/15/95) • **93**

Sauternes 1987 • $22 • (06/15/90) • **83**

Sauternes 1986 • $28 • (04/15/95) • **84**

Sauternes 1983 • $51 • (04/15/95) • **91**

RAFFAULT, OLGA

Chinon Les Picasses 1990: This jammy Chinon mingles strawberry, raisin and cinnamon flavors, with almost volatile acidity and a drying finish. Enjoyable but precarious. • $16 • (10/31/94) • **77**

Key: SS—Spectator Selection. CS—Cellar Selection. BB—Best Buy. $NA—Price not available. (BT)—Barrel tasting. Ⓐ—Auction Price.
Dates in parentheses represent the issues in which the ratings were published.

RAGOTIERE, CHÂTEAU DE LA

Muscadet de Sèvre et Maine 1992 • $NA • **82**

Muscadet de Sèvre et Maine Sur Lie 1992: The aromas have evolved into pleasant butter and vanilla notes, and the wine is smooth and round. It lacks the sharp edge of acidity, but is still fresh and fruity. • $9 • (08/31/94) • **84**

RAHOUL, CHÂTEAU

Graves 1988 • $18 • (08/31/91) • **80**

Graves 1986 • $18 • (12/31/90) • **83**

RAIMBAULT, CLAUDE & REMY

Sancerre 1992: A clean, lean wine with herbal and grassy flavors. It has a refreshing tartness but the flavors are simple and short. Tasted twice. 800 cases made. • $15 • (10/31/94) • **78**

RAMAGE LA BATISSE, CHÂTEAU

Haut-Médoc 1990: Pretty raspberry and cherry aromas and flavors and light tannins. Drinkable now. 25,000 cases made. • $18 • (03/31/93) • **84**

Haut-Médoc 1989 • $15 • (03/15/92) • **88**

Haut-Médoc 1987 • $12 • (11/30/89) • **82**

Haut-Médoc 1986 • $14 • (11/30/89) • **82**

Haut-Médoc 1982 • $11 • (11/30/89) • **68**

RAMILLADE, LA

Côtes du Rhône 1982 • $5 • (11/01/85) BB • **84**

RAMONET

Bâtard-Montrachet 1993: Distinctive menthol character, but it's subdued and balanced by concentrated fruit flavors. Thick, full-bodied, silky and harmonious. This is a delicious wine with great intensity and class. Try in 2000. • $140 • (05/31/96) • **94**

Bâtard-Montrachet 1992: A big wine with a lot going for it, quite rough and tumble now, but it should grow into a handsome gem. Shows plenty of mineral, toasted oak and honey flavors and a long, firm finish. Try after 1997. • $NA • **94**

Chassagne-Montrachet Caillerets 1992: Exotic and quite minty, with floral, honey, acacia and pink grapefruit notes just bursting from the glass. Shows wonderful balance between acidity and the ripe flavors. Tempting now, but better after 1997. • $52 • **91**

Chassagne-Montrachet Morgeot 1992: Very flavorful and well crafted, showing chalk, mineral, green apple, smoke, toast and honey flavors. Good complexity leads to an earthy touch on the finish. Try after 1996. • $50 • **86**

Chassagne-Montrachet Les Ruchottes 1993: Distinctive and exotic, fat, rich and intense. It has notes of mint along with a floral, herbal, rose petal character and very ripe pear flavors. A full-bodied white that has a lot of personality. Try after 2000. • $75 • (05/31/96) • **90**

Chassagne-Montrachet Les Ruchottes 1992: Quite tart and austere, showing good fruit concentration and an exotic touch of spearmint. Flavorful, vibrant dried-herb and spice flavors, well-made finish. Better after 1997. • $68 • **87**

Chassagne-Montrachet Les Vergers 1992: Wonderful Chassagne, extremely closed now, smelling of freshly crushed fruit and balanced with cream, lime and earth flavors. A youthful beauty that needs until at least 1998 to show it all. • $NA • **91**

Montrachet 1992: A big, chunky, brooding white Burgundy, all muscle, offering tons of earth, mineral, mushroom, butter and honey flavors and a long, rich and unforgettable finish. Will smooth out with age, try after 1998. • $268 • **95**

Montrachet 1991: Bright and lemony, lively and concentrated. This remains incredibly light on its feet, despite tip-toeing through some canny moves. Echoes of honey, pear, mineral and spice. Beautifully made, long and enticing. Try in 1997 or 1998. • $375 • **91**

Puligny-Montrachet Champ Canet 1993: Distinctive and beautifully rich. An opulent wine that first comes across as very earthy and

FRANCE

yeasty, then it opens up to full-throttle on the lemon, beef jerky and tropical fruit flavors. The freshness comes through on the long finish. Try in 1999. • $75 • (05/31/96) • **90**

RAPET PERE & FILS

Bourgogne en Bully 1988 • $19 • (03/31/91) • **80**

Corton-Charlemagne 1994: Distinctively minty, with dried herb and pear flavors. Lots of intensity and a slightly vegetal note on the finish. Seems hard and unyielding now, but has enough going on to improve by 1998. 250 cases made. • $70 • (05/31/96) 85 • **86**

Pernand-Vergelesses 1994: Good intensity for a village wine, with vibrant fresh herb, grapefruit and apple flavors and an earthy character. Somewhat lighter in body, but it kicks in on the long finish. A bit tart, but delicious now. 250 cases made. • $21 • (05/31/96) • **85**

Pernand-Vergelesses 1988 • $31 • (02/28/91) • **79**

Pernand-Vergelesses Premier Cru 1994: Assertive, even aggressive, and the fruit flavors are modest. Hard to cozy up to this rather green wine. Could get better by 1997. 250 cases made. • $30 • (05/31/96) • **79**

RASPAIL, CHÂTEAU

Gigondas 1989 • $15 • (11/30/92) • **78**

RASPAIL-AY, DOMAINE

Gigondas 1990 • $20 • (04/15/93) • **80**

Gigondas 1989 • $19 • (04/15/93) • **83**

Gigondas 1988 • $19 • (11/15/91) • **79**

Gigondas 1986 • $15 • (01/31/89) • **92**

Gigondas Réserve 1993: A concentrated, polished and beautifully balanced Rhône. This has oodles of lively black cherry flavors and no new oak. Vibrant and satisfying. Delicious now and it has the nicely tannic structure to improve through at least 1997. • $20 • **90**

RATEAU, PIERRETTE & JEAN-CLAUDE

Beaune Clos des Mariages 1988 • $25 • (01/31/92) • **77**

RAUSAN-SEGLA, CHÂTEAU

Margaux 1992: Extremely well made, blackberry, cherry and tobacco flavors unfolding on the nose and palate. Medium-bodied and very velvety in texture, fine tannins. Drinkable now. • $30 • **86**

Margaux 1990: A traditional-style Bordeaux, with redwood, tea and ripe plum aromas and flavors and plenty of soft, round tannins. Drinkable now. 16,000 cases made. • $38 • (03/31/93) • **87**

Margaux 1989 • $44 • (03/15/92) • **88**

Margaux 1988 • $35 • (03/15/91) • **92**

Margaux 1986 • $82 Ⓐ • (09/15/89) • **87**

Margaux 1985 • $34 Ⓐ • (05/31/88) • **92**

Margaux 1982 • $30 Ⓐ • (08/31/92) • **88**

Margaux 1981 • $23 • (10/16/84) • **86**

Margaux 1979 • $24 Ⓐ • (10/15/89) • **69**

Margaux 1970 • $37 Ⓐ • (05/15/93) • **89**

Margaux 1961: A smooth, firm-textured, opulently flavored claret with smoky, cherrylike flavors that thin out on the finish. Drink through 1998. • $50 • (04/30/96) • **84**

Margaux 1945: Firm and still a little chunky and chewy, solid, featuring typical '45 power and tenacity. Still lively, somewhat lacking in depth. • $425 • **83**

RAUZAN, CHÂTEAU

Entre-Deux-Mers 1994: Distinctively grassy, offering melon, lime and dried-herb flavors, light body and vibrant finish. • $7 • **80**

Entre-Deux-Mers Fleur 91 1991 • $7 • (11/30/92) • **82**

RAUZAN-DESPAGNE, CHÂTEAU

Entre-Deux-Mers 1994: Fresh and appley, showing lovely, crisp acidity, creamy texture and loads of pear and melon character. Drink now. • $8 • **82**

RAUZAN-GASSIES, CHÂTEAU

Margaux 1995: Elegant and nice flavor up front, with a zesty, crisp backbone of acidity, some tobacco, cedar and red berry, but the tannins turn a bit dry and astringent on the finish. Lacks the concentration and sheer opulence of some '95s. • $NA • (05/15/96) • **80-84** (BT)

Margaux 1994: Light and diluted, straightforward strawberry and cherry flavors. Not much there. • $NA • **70-74** (BT)

Margaux 1993: Light and slightly diluted, offering some decent black cherry, earth and mineral flavors. A bit lean on the finish. Drinkable now. • $25 • (01/31/96) • **77**

Margaux 1988 • $35 • (08/31/91) • **85**

Margaux 1986 • $25 • (06/30/89) • **88**

Margaux 1982 • $32 Ⓐ • (08/31/92) • **84**

Margaux 1970 • $24 Ⓐ • (05/15/93) • **87**

Margaux 1961: A solid, square-shouldered Bordeaux. It tastes broad and fairly rich, with a plush texture, plenty of fruity, smoky flavors and enough firm tannin to give it a nice grip. Drink through 2000. • $51 • (04/30/96) • **85**

Margaux 1959 • $75 • (10/15/90) • **73**

Margaux 1945 • $300 • (03/16/86) • **91**

RAUZAN-SEGLA, CHÂTEAU

Margaux 1995: Sleek and racy berry, cassis and tar aromas and flavors. Full body and tannins and long, velvety finish. Almost too much, but wait and see. • $NA • (05/15/96) • **90-94** (BT)

Margaux 1994: Bright berry flavor, fine tannins, medium body, caressing texture and light finish. • $40 • (05/15/96) • **85-89** (BT)

Margaux 1993: Lovely, elegant, medium-bodied '93. Well crafted, polished and delivering lots of finesse, showing its red fruit character and a touch of toasty oak notes. Drinkable now or hold until 1998. • $33 • (01/31/96) • **87**

RAVATYS, CHÂTEAU DES

Brouilly 1988 • $10 • (05/31/89) • **78**

RAVAUT, GASTON & PIERRE

Aloxe-Corton 1985 • $35 • (07/31/88) • **88**

Corton Hautes Mourottes 1985 • $46 • (07/31/88) • **92**

Ladoix La Corvée 1985 • $26 • (07/31/88) • **88**

RAVENEAU, JEAN-MARIE

Chablis Blanchots 1992: Subtle, seductive honey, lime, cream and mineral flavors fan out on the palate. Beautifully silky and ready to drink now, but should hold through 1997. • $58 • **90**

Chablis Chapelot 1992: Harmonious and elegant, creamy texture, still a bit closed, layers of complex truffle, earth, mineral and pear flavors. Not a blockbuster, delicious now, but better after 1997. • $40 • **89**

RAVIER, SIMONE & OLIVIER

Côte de Brouilly Domaine de la Pierre Bleue 1994: Soft in texture, yet still lightly tannic on the finish, this wine has mellowed with age and now shows candied fruit and brown sugar flavors. Drink now. • $9 • **79**

RAYAS, CHÂTEAU

Châteauneuf-du-Pape Réservé 1993: A soft wine with round raspberry, chocolate and light herbal flavors, this lacks the concentration for aging but makes pleasant drinking now. Tasted twice with consistent notes. • $60 • **82**

Châteauneuf-du-Pape Réservé 1990: Dense and powerful, with a strange salty edge to the peppery, spicy black currant, raisin and black cherry aromas and flavors and hints of juniper and cedar on the finish. Seems raw and unformed at this stage, but has the pieces to come together into a full-bodied, muscular wine by 1997. 2,000 cases made. • $117 Ⓐ • (04/15/93) • **90**

Châteauneuf-du-Pape Réservé 1989 • $82 Ⓐ • (11/15/92) • **87**

Châteauneuf-du-Pape Réservé 1988 • $77 Ⓐ • (10/15/91) • **90**

Châteauneuf-du-Pape Réservé 1986 • $58 • (12/15/89) • **88**

Châteauneuf-du-Pape Réservé 1985 • $41 • (07/31/88) • **93**

Châteauneuf-du-Pape Réservé 1983 • $75 • (10/15/91) • **89**

RAYMOND-LAFON, CHÂTEAU

Sauternes 1991: Pretty and sweet. Delivers little length, tastes like an ice wine and shows some decent lemon, vanilla and honey. Try as an apéritif. • $NA • (04/15/95) • **80**

Sauternes 1990: Stands out in this crowd because of its stylish lilac, violet, floral, rose petal scents that delight from start to finish, medium-to-full body and sweetness plus a long finish. Better in 1998. • $53 • (04/15/95) • **90**

Sauternes 1989: Pretty floral, lilac and lemon flavors, turning a bit short on the finish. • $52 • (04/15/95) • **87**

Sauternes 1988: Attractively balanced and distinctively floral, lilac notes marrying nicely with the orange-peel, melon and honey flavors. Medium- to full-bodied. Drinkable now. • $60 • (04/15/95) • **91**

Sauternes 1987 • $58 • (04/15/95) • **86**

Sauternes 1986 • $53 • (04/15/95) • **87**

Sauternes 1983 • $58 Ⓐ • (01/31/88) • **93**

RAYNE-VIGNEAU, CHÂTEAU DE

Gemme de Rayne-Vigneau Bordeaux White 1991: Fat, rich, oaky and showy, but it seems tired and oxidized and tastes of cooked apple. • $NA • **79**

Le Sac de Rayne-Vigneau Bordeaux White 1992: Playful wine, crisp and fruity, showing honey, grass and lime character and fine acidity. Good dry white from a Sauternes estate. • $NA • **81**

Sauternes 1992: Attractive almond, apricot and lemon character and a relatively straightforward finish. Drinkable now. • $NA • (04/15/95) • **82**

Sauternes 1991: Lovely Sauternes, of medium sweetness and body, offering seductive, long-lasting honey, pear, floral and buttery flavors, carried by sharp acidity on the finish. Worth seeking out. • $NA • (04/15/95) • **85**

Sauternes 1990: Very fruity, zingy and racy, showing lovely lilac, floral and orange-peel flavors, medium body and sweetness, quite fresh. • $30 • (04/15/95) • **88**

Sauternes 1988: Beautifully crafted and creamy-textured, displaying lovely pineapple, honey, mineral and wet earth character that unfolds its complexity to a long, balanced finish. Tempting now, better in 1997. • $34 • (04/15/95) • **90**

Sauternes 1987 • $25 • (06/15/90) • **77**

Sauternes 1986 • $49 • **91**

Sauternes 1983 • $27 Ⓐ • (01/31/88) • **77**

REBOURSEAU, HENRI

Clos de Vougeot 1983 • $25 • (11/16/85) • **49**

RECTOIRE, DOMAINE DE LA

Collioure Cuvée I 1990 • $34 • (10/31/92) • **85**

Key: SS—Spectator Selection. CS—Cellar Selection. BB—Best Buy. $NA—Price not available. (BT)—Barrel tasting. Ⓐ—Auction Price.
Dates in parentheses represent the issues in which the ratings were published.

REDDE, MICHEL

Pouilly-Fumé La Moynerie 1994: A mix of mineral, apple and light creamy flavors keeps this wine interesting, and vibrant acidity offsets a light earthy note. It's clean and firm. • $16 • (11/15/95) • **85**

Pouilly-Fumé La Moynerie 1993: Dark, earthy aromas of smoke, coffee and toast give way to firm flavors of pine, herbs and lime. Try now. • $16 • (11/15/95) • **86**

Pouilly-Fumé La Moynerie 1992: Delicate floral and mineral aromas are enticing, but on the palate the wine is soft and a bit hollow, with light peach and herbal flavors but lacking vivacity. An apéritif wine. • $16 • (10/31/94) • **81**

Sancerre Les Tuilières 1993: Good intensity of lively, crisp green apple and ripe grapefruit flavors, refreshing acidity and a long mineral finish. It's complete, shows typical characteristics, drinkable now. • $17 • (08/31/94) • **88**

REMOISSENET PERE & FILES

Beaune Les Grèves 1988 • $38 • (11/30/90) • **90**

Bonnes Mares 1988 • $80 • (12/31/90) • **84**

Bonnes Mares 1985 • $88 • (03/15/88) • **82**

Chambertin 1985 • $100 • (03/15/88) • **91**

Clos de la Roche 1985 • $72 • (03/15/88) • **91**

Echézeaux 1985 • $73 • (03/15/88) • **75**

Givry du Domaine Thénard 1988 • $19 • (03/31/91) • **68**

Givry du Domaine Thénard 1985 • $18 • (04/30/88) • **77**

Mercurey Clos Fortoul 1988 • $17 • (03/31/91) • **83**

Nuits-St.-Georges Aux Argillats 1985 • $34 • (10/15/88) • **87**

Nuits-St.-Georges Aux Boudots 1964 • $70 • (11/10/90) • **70**

Richebourg 1985 • $138 • (03/15/88) • **91**

Vosne-Romanée Clos des Réas 1949 • $138 • (08/31/90) • **95**

Vosne-Romanée Les Suchots 1985 • $75 • (03/15/88) • **91**

REMORIQUET, GILLES

Nuits-St.-Georges 1982 • $19 • (07/16/85) • **84**

REMORIQUET, HENRI & GILLES

Nuits-St.-Georges Rue de Chaux 1985 • $22 • (07/31/88) • **81**

REMPARTS DE BASTOR, LES

Sauternes 1991: Very light and moderately sweet, a decent apéritif, revealing a bitter almond, honey and wet earth character. Tasted twice, with consistent notes. Second label from Château Bastor-Lamontagne. • $NA • (04/15/95) • **78**

RENJARDE, DOMAINE DE LA

Côtes du Rhône-Villages 1991 • $10 • (04/30/94) • **85**

Côtes du Rhône-Villages 1990 • $11 • (11/15/92) • **87**

RENJARDIERE, DOMAINE DE LA

Côtes du Rhône 1983 • $4 • (03/16/86) BB • **84**

RESERVE DE LA COMTESSE

Pauillac 1988 • $26 • (03/15/91) • **88**

Pauillac 1987 • $18 • (05/15/90) • **82**

Pauillac 1986 • $30 • (05/31/89) • **90**

Pauillac 1983 • $21 • (03/01/86) • **82**

RESERVE ST.-CHANELLE

Chardonnay Vin de Pays d'Oc 1992 • $NA • (03/15/94) • **81**

RESERVE ST.-MARQUIS

Chardonnay Vin de Pays de l'Aude 1992 • $7 • (03/15/94) • **82**

RESERVE ST.-MARTIN

Cabernet Sauvignon Vin de Pays de l'Aude 1989 • $7 • (10/31/92) • **77**
Chardonnay Vin de Pays d'Oc Gold Cuvée 1992 • $8 • (03/15/94) • **82**
Marsanne Corbières 1991 • $7 • (06/30/92) • **75**
Marsanne Vin de Pays d'Oc 1992 • $8 • (03/15/94) • **81**
Merlot Vin de Pays d'Oc 1991 • $7 • (03/15/94) • **80**
Merlot Vin de Pays d'Oc 1990 • $7 • (09/30/92) BB • **81**
Mourvèdre Minervois 1989 • $8 • (12/31/91) BB • **80**
Mourvèdre Vin de Pays d'Oc 1991 • $7 • (03/15/94) • **83**
Syrah Vin de Pays d'Oc 1991 • $7 • (03/15/94) • **82**
Syrah Vin de Pays d'Oc 1990 • $7 • (09/30/92) • **79**
Vin de Pays de l'Aude Sélection Rouge Cuvée No. 3 1990 • $4 • (09/30/92) • **78**
Viognier Vin de Pays d'Oc 1992 • $8 • (03/15/94) • **80**

RESPIDE MEDEVILLE, CHÂTEAU

Graves 1985 • $12 • (02/29/88) • **85**

RESPLANDY

Merlot Vin de Pays d'Oc 1990 • $6 • (10/31/92) • **77**
Merlot Vin de Pays d'Oc 1989 • $6 • (06/30/92) • **79**

REVERDY, HIPPOLYTE

Sancerre 1994: Herb and mineral aromas and flavors dissolve in a crisp, clean presentation. Lively and bracing, if not terribly complex. • $15 • (05/15/96) • **84**

Sancerre 1992: Fresh, clean and balanced, this wine shows appealing citrus and herbal flavors in a light, almost delicate frame. It's fresh and appealing. 1,200 cases made. • $15 • (10/31/94) • **84**

REVERDY, JEAN

Sancerre Vignoble de la Reine Blanche 1994: Ripe and rich herb, green plum and fig notes are nicely integrated. There's also a mineral quality that coats your mouth as flavors resonate on the finish. Can accompany fish or chicken. 4,000 cases made. • $16 • (04/30/96) • **88**

Sancerre Vignoble de la Reine Blanche 1993: This fruity wine resembles California more than typical Sancerre, with round, ripe pineapple, peach and waxy flavors. There's enough acidity to balance an impression of sweetness and the wine finishes clean and dry. 2,100 cases made. • $17 • (10/31/94) • **84**

REVEREND, DOMAINE DU

Corbières 1990 • $NA • (03/15/94) • **82**

REY, DOMAINE DU

Vin de Pays des Côtes de Gascogne 1991 • $7 • (08/31/92) • **80**

REYNARDIERE, DOMAINE DE LA

Faugères 1991 • $7 • (03/15/94) • **83**

REYNIER, CHÂTEAU

Bordeaux Supérieur 1983 • $3 • (10/16/85) BB • **83**
Entre-Deux-Mers 1984 • $3 • (12/16/85) • **62**

RICAUD, CHÂTEAU DE

Loupiac 1986 • $17 • (12/31/89) • **80**

RICHEAUME, DOMAINE

Cabernet Sauvignon Côtes de Provence 1988 • $15 • (10/31/90) • **75**
Syrah Côtes de Provence 1988 • $15 • (10/31/90) • **73**

RICHEMONT

Chardonnay Vin de Pays d'Oc 1994: Exuberant aromas of tropical fruit and vanilla give this French white an almost Australian character, which follows through on the round, nearly sweet palate. It's not sophisticated, but a good example of a popular style at a good price. 15,000 cases made. • $6 • (12/15/95) • **85**

Merlot Vin de Pays d'Oc 1993: Black olive and herbal flavors give this a distinctive personality. Fleshy and firmly tannic, but needing more fruit for balance and winding up somewhat clumsy. Try now. • $6 • (10/31/95) • **81**

Sauvignon Blanc Vin de Pays d'Oc 1994: Soft and round in texture, with ripe, clean fruit flavor that reminds us of Chardonnay. • $6 • (02/29/96) • **82**

Syrah Vin de Pays d'Oc 1993: There's plenty of ripe blackberry flavor here, soft and almost sweet on the palate. It resembles an Australian Shiraz, without the weight. Drinkable now. • $6 • (10/31/95) • **83**

RICHETERRE, CHÂTEAU

Margaux 1986 • $13 • (02/15/89) • **78**

RIEUSSEC, CHÂTEAU

Sauternes 1993: Rich, ripe and sweet like orange marmalade, yet exhibiting terrific acidity and exotic dry apricot, date, and chocolate flavors. Seductive and fabulously concentrated. Tempting now, but should be great through 2000. 2,000 cases made. • $NA • (04/15/95) • **92**

Sauternes 1992: Racy, well made and classy, quite light, but what's there is super, featuring pretty floral, honey, cream and nut flavors. • $NA • (04/15/95) • **85**

Sauternes 1991: Great for the vintage. Deep amber color, showing cedar, honey, orange-peel and spice character. Medium-bodied and quite sweet, long finish. Already perfect to drink. • $NA • (04/15/95) • **88**

Sauternes 1990: Richly textured and velvety, offering plenty of butterscotch, toasted oak, lime and tropical flavors that caress your palate. Great now, but should hold until 1999. • $58 • (04/15/95) • **92**

Sauternes 1989: Well proportioned and delicately built, delivering plenty of honey, spice and earth-mineral flavors. Drinkable now. • $62 • (04/15/95) • **89**

Sauternes 1988: Splendid, elegant, intensely spicy botrytis fruit character, rich and fat, kept in balance by an undertow of lemon-laced acidity. Drink now or can hold until 1998. • $55 • (04/15/95) • **91**

Sauternes 1987 • $32 • (06/15/90) • **89**
Sauternes 1986 • $50 • (04/15/95) • **89**
Sauternes 1985 • $38 • (05/31/88) • **86**
Sauternes 1983 • $48 Ⓐ • (01/31/88) • **94**
Sauternes 1982 • $13 • (02/01/85) • **86**
Sauternes 1981 • $14 • (12/01/84) • **90**

RION, ARMELLE & BERNARD

Chambolle-Musigny Les Echésaux 1992: Where is the fruit? This is more water than wine, with light floral, raspberry, strawberry and cherry notes. Ready now. 225 cases made. • $24 • **75**

Nuits-St.-Georges 1992: Light and earthy, with a sour edge to the red berry flavors that turn musty on the finish. 195 cases made. • $32 • **74**

Nuits-St.-Georges Les Damodes 1992: Fresh and youthful, quite light, but with enough raspberry and cherry flavors to make it appealing. It's for drinking early. 216 cases made, 75 imported to the United States. • $35 • **83**

Vosne-Romanée 1992: Light, earthy and herbal, with more tea leaf and tobacco flavors than fruit. Smooth texture though. Drinkable now. 325 cases made. • $24 • **77**

RION, DANIEL

Chambolle-Musigny Aux Beaux Bruns 1991: An odd but distinctive wine. Drinkable now. 100 cases made. • $43 Ⓐ • (01/31/94) • **76**

Chambolle-Musigny Aux Beaux Bruns 1989 • $45 • (01/31/92) • **89**
Chambolle-Musigny Aux Beaux Bruns 1988 • $37 • (01/31/91) • **87**
Chambolle-Musigny Aux Beaux Bruns 1986 • $39 • (04/15/89) • **86**

RION, DANIEL

Chambolle-Musigny Aux Beaux Bruns 1985 • $33 • (03/31/88) • **88**
Chambolle-Musigny Les Charmes 1993: Elegant, perfumed red offering lovely vanilla, plum and berry aromas and flavors, medium body and tannins and soft, caressing finish. Better after 2000. • $63 • **92**
Chambolle-Musigny Les Charmes 1991: Floral and minty, almost menthol-like overtones. Medium-weight, modestly tannic, ultimately simple and straightforward. Drinkable now. 120 cases made. • $70 Ⓐ • (01/31/94) • **84**
Clos Vougeot 1993: Giant wine. Greatest Clos Vougeot we have ever tasted. Mint, spice, dried herb and red berry flavor, full body, tons of tannins and a long, silky finish. Amazing even for this vintage. Try after 2000. 225 cases made. • $90 • **97**
Clos Vougeot 1992: Aromatic and more flavorful than most, packed with floral, mint, currant and blackberry notes, hinting at smoke on the chewy finish. Tannins want until 1997. 150 cases made. • $90 • **89**
Clos Vougeot 1991: Offers a firm texture and a strong floral, minty tinge to the narrow band of jammy berry flavors. Well crafted for the vintage and tannic enough to want until at least 1997. 90 cases made. • $85 Ⓐ • (01/31/94) • **87**
Clos Vougeot 1990: As classy as it gets in Burgundy. A great balancing act of power and elegance, boasting seductive black cherry, currant, smoke and earth flavors that take you for a memorable ride. Try to resist until 1998. 100 cases made. • $100 • (12/15/92) • **97**
Clos Vougeot 1989 • $94 • (01/31/92) • **92**
Clos Vougeot 1988 • $53 Ⓐ • (01/31/91) • **92**
Clos Vougeot 1986 • $70 • (04/15/89) • **90**
Côte de Nuits-Villages 1993: Aromatic and seductive, offering rose petal, floral, perfumy, wet earth notes, medium body and tannins and excellent balance. Nice drinking from now through 1998. • $17 • **87**
Côte de Nuits-Villages 1990: Shows lots of class in the smoky berry and earth flavors and silky tannins. Drinkable now. 600 cases made. • $25 • (12/15/92) • **85**
Côte de Nuits-Villages 1986 • $15 • (07/31/88) • **81**
Nuits-St.-Georges 1986 • $31 • (04/30/89) • **85**
Nuits-St.-Georges 1985 • $28 • (03/15/88) • **85**
Nuits-St.-Georges Aux Lavières 1991: Firm, almost fleshy, with a generous beam of berry and minty oak flavors. Drinkable now. 250 cases made. • $35 Ⓐ • (01/31/94) • **86**
Nuits-St.-Georges Aux Lavières 1988 • $33 • (02/15/91) • **93**
Nuits-St.-Georges Aux Lavières 1987 • $21 • (04/30/90) • **87**
Nuits-St.-Georges Aux Vignerondes 1993: Can Nuits get much better than this? The well-defined red berry flavors blend in spice and earth, unfolding beautifully to a long, refined but firm finish. A class act that's tempting now, but try to hold off until 2000. • $50 • **94**
Nuits-St.-Georges Aux Vignerondes 1992: Aromas and flavors with a minty underbrush character pervade this chewy, medium-weight wine. Pretty berry flavors finally emerge on the finish. Drinkable now. 200 cases made. • $NA • **84**
Nuits-St.-Georges Aux Vignerondes 1991: Minty and exotic, showing distinctive herbal over tones to the basic berry flavors in a medium-weight, otherwise straightforward wine. Drinkable now. 200 cases made. • $52 Ⓐ • (01/31/94) • **84**
Nuits-St.-Georges Aux Vignerondes 1990: Superbly made, with great elegance. Has gorgeous flavors that show an array of mint, raspberry and cherry nuances, a fantastic tannin structure and great elegance. Drinkable now. 220 cases made. • $70 • (12/15/92) • **92**
Nuits-St.-Georges Aux Vignerondes 1989 • $63 • (01/31/92) • **93**
Nuits-St.-Georges Aux Vignerondes 1988 • $54 • (01/31/91) • **92**
Nuits-St.-Georges Aux Vignerondes 1987 • $35 • (04/30/90) • **95**
Nuits-St.-Georges Aux Vignerondes 1986 • $43 • (04/30/89) • **88**
Nuits-St.-Georges Aux Vignerondes 1985 • $40 • (03/15/88) • **91**
Nuits-St.-Georges Clos des Argillières 1993: Lots of ripe fruit character, almost verging on raisins. Full in body, adding ripe, rich tannins and a long spicy, berry aftertaste. Try in 2000. • $50 • **88**
Nuits-St.-Georges Clos des Argillières 1992: Lean and crisp, bright but a little shy, with a minty component to the berry and currant flavors. Fine tannins need until 1997 to settle. 250 cases made. • $55 • **85**

Key: SS—Spectator Selection. CS—Cellar Selection. BB—Best Buy. $NA—Price not available. (BT)—Barrel tasting. Ⓐ—Auction Price.
Dates in parentheses represent the issues in which the ratings were published.

Nuits-St.-Georges Clos des Argillières 1991: Light but nicely balanced, showing a pleasant range of raspberry, strawberry and mint aromas and flavors. Drinkable now. 300 cases made. • $52 • (01/31/94) • **82**
Nuits-St.-Georges Clos des Argillières 1990: A delicious wine, with gorgeous aromas of violets, rose petals and black currants. Medium-bodied, with sweet, ripe fruit flavors and a fine tannin structure. 600 cases made. • $52 Ⓐ • (12/15/92) • **93**
Nuits-St.-Georges Clos des Argillières 1989 • $63 • (01/31/92) • **91**
Nuits-St.-Georges Clos des Argillières 1988 • $48 • (01/31/91) HR • **91**
Nuits-St.-Georges Clos des Argillières 1987 • $36 • (04/30/90) • **92**
Nuits-St.-Georges Clos des Argillières 1986 • $47 • (04/30/89) • **90**
Nuits-St.-Georges Clos des Argillières 1985 • $75 • (03/15/88) • **94**
Nuits-St.-Georges Les Grandes Vignes 1993: Just super, and as good as a barrel sample earlier this year. Tight and silky, boasting solid fruit, firm tannins and plenty of alluring cherry, mineral character. Needs time, try in 1999. • $32 • **93**
Nuits-St.-Georges Les Grandes Vignes 1992: Light and a little chunky, but the grapey currant flavor makes it appealing. Drinkable now. 300 cases made. • $36 • **81**
Nuits-St.-Georges Les Grandes Vignes 1990: Extremely fruity, with gorgeous rose petal, berry and violet aromas and flavors, a refined tannin structure and long finish. Drinkable now. • $42 • (12/15/92) • **92**
Nuits-St.-Georges Les Grandes Vignes 1989 • $38 • (01/31/92) • **88**
Nuits-St.-Georges Les Hauts Pruliers 1993: Slightly one-dimensional in plum flavor but a solid red, delivering medium body, firm tannins and fruity finish. Better in 1999. • $50 • **88**
Nuits-St.-Georges Les Hauts Pruliers 1991: Light and fragrant, the lively currant and floral aromas and flavors remain fresh and crisp through the finish. Drinkable now. 200 cases made. • $54 Ⓐ • (01/31/94) • **84**
Nuits-St.-Georges Les Hauts Pruliers 1990: Not a big wine, but shows beautiful fruit aromas and flavors. Violet, floral and currant characteristics practically jump out of the glass. Drinkable now. 190 cases made. • $70 • (12/15/92) • **90**
Nuits-St.-Georges Les Hauts Pruliers 1989 • $63 • (01/31/92) • **92**
Nuits-St.-Georges Les Hauts Pruliers 1988 • $54 • (01/31/91) • **91**
Nuits-St.-Georges Les Hauts Pruliers 1987 • $35 • (04/30/90) • **91**
Nuits-St.-Georges Les Hauts Pruliers 1986 • $45 • (04/30/89) • **91**
Nuits-St.-Georges Les Hauts Pruliers 1985 • $43 • (03/15/88) • **88**
Vosne-Romanée 1993: Extremely rich raspberry and dried herb aromas and flavors. Medium- to full-bodied, silky tannins, long finish. Try in 1999. • $32 • **90**
Vosne-Romanée 1991: Crisp, focused, light and lean, has earthy anise-scented berry flavors along with nice rose petal shadings on the finish. Drinkable now. 650 cases made. • $35 Ⓐ • (01/31/94) • **83**
Vosne-Romanée 1990: This incredibly complex village wine shows wonderful rose, raspberry and oak aromas. Full-bodied, with silky, fine tannins and great finesse. Drinkable now. 500 cases made. • $42 • (12/15/92) • **91**
Vosne-Romanée 1989 • $37 • (01/31/92) • **89**
Vosne-Romanée 1987 • $21 • (04/30/90) • **89**
Vosne-Romanée 1986 • $31 • (04/30/89) • **87**
Vosne-Romanée 1985 • $28 • (02/29/88) • **78**
Vosne-Romanée 1983 • $19 • (02/01/86) • **63**
Vosne-Romanée Les Beaux Monts 1993: A princess of a wine, graceful and royal, showing plenty of class. Flavors are well defined, quite ripe and sweet, offering black currant character that fans out on the palate. Pure, silky, long finish. Try after 2000. • $50 • **92**
Vosne-Romanée Les Beaux Monts 1992: Bright and flavorful, a little short on concentration, but shades its currant and berry tones with hints of rose petal and spice. Drinkable now. 400 cases made. • $56 • **86**
Vosne-Romanée Les Beaux-Monts 1991: A narrow beam of blackberry and black cherry flavors runs through the veil of tannins in this decidedly fruity wine. Drinkable now. 420 cases made. • $52 Ⓐ • (01/31/94) • **84**
Vosne-Romanée Les Beaux Monts 1990: Aromatic, ripe and concentrated, showing superb, deep, rich plum, spice and berry flavors that are focused and elegant. Has a long, delicious finish. Drinkable now. 250 cases made. • $70 • (12/15/92) • **92**
Vosne-Romanée Les Beaux Monts 1989 • $63 • (01/31/92) • **90**
Vosne-Romanée Les Beaux Monts 1988 • $48 • (02/15/91) • **92**
Vosne-Romanée Les Beaux Monts 1986 • $43 • (04/30/89) • **91**

Vosne-Romanée Les Beaux Monts 1985 • $55 • (02/29/88) • **95**

Vosne-Romanée Les Chaumes 1993: Superfine, delivering classy plum, mint and mineral flavors and aromas, full body, fine tannins and a long, elegant finish. Superb. Try in 2000. • $50 • **93**

Vosne-Romanée Les Chaumes 1992: Firm in texture and brimming with floral, violet-tinged currant flavors, it never becomes supple but has the concentration to improve through around 1997. 180 cases made. • $58 • **84**

Vosne-Romanée Les Chaumes 1991: Dense in texture and concentrated, pumping out ripe berry, currant and floral flavors and finishing with a distinct touch of mint. Tannic and needs time to settle down, try in 1998. • $54 • **91**

Vosne-Romanée Les Chaumes 1990: Powerful and beautifully structured, with a solid backbone of tannins, ripe, floral flavors run deep in this superbly crafted Burgundy. Try in 1998 or even 2000. • $70 • **93**

Vosne-Romanée Les Chaumes 1989: Normally this wine is much better. Bad bottle? Firm and tannic, with a lean band of berry and floral flavor that fades a little on the pleasant but light finish. • $63 • **85**

Vosne-Romanée Les Chaumes 1988: Gorgeous, full of violet, currant and berry flavors that just unfold in multiple layers. Intense and delicate, this supple and elegant Vosne defines balance. • $54 • **91**

Vosne-Romanée Les Chaumes 1987: Lovely, with a fine bead of blackberry and floral flavors. Just touches of dilution and tannins clamp down on the finish, but the fruit is holding up fine. • $35 • **88**

Vosne-Romanée Les Chaumes 1986: Mature and plummy, showing old cedar notes and finishing with chewy and drying tannins. Past its peak. • $54 • **84**

Vosne-Romanée Les Chaumes 1985: Ripe and lush, at its peak, delivering a great deal of smooth and supple character, with currant, tobacco and slightly smoky notes beaming through the tannins. • $60 • **91**

Vosne-Romanée Les Chaumes 1983: Mature, "old wine" nose, with underbrush, currant and mint character. Dry finish. • $36 • **82**

RION, MICHELE & PATRICE

Bourgogne Les Bons Bâtons 1993: Effusively aromatic, featuring vibrant currant, smoke and spice flavors that won't stop on the delicious, silky finish. Shows both finesse and power. Tempting now, should keep well through 1998. • $15 • **88**

Chambolle-Musigny Les Cras 1993: Vivid crushed berries through and through. Aromatic with a lovely rich palate of ripe fruit, rose and mint and firm tannins. A wine to age. Try in 2000. • $38 • **90**

Chambolle-Musigny Les Cras 1992: Extremely minty and floral, an aromatic Burgundy that's light and a little too tannic for the modest berry flavor. Try now. • $NA • **78**

RION PERE & FILS

Chambolle-Musigny Les Lavrottes 1987 • $31 • **67**

Clos Vougeot Red 1987 • $48 • (11/15/90) • **86**

Nuits-St.-Georges Aux Murgers 1987 • $31 • (03/31/90) • **79**

RIPEAU, CHÂTEAU

St.-Emilion 1982 • $18 • (05/15/89) • **88**

St.-Emilion 1961: Not luscious, but respectable for its powerful, smoky aromas and rather severe flavors. The balance is tight and a bit tart. Drink now. • $19 • (04/30/96) • **84**

ROBERT, DOMAINE DE

Fleurie 1983 • $8 • (12/16/85) • **85**

ROBERT, DOMAINE

Brut Blanc de Blancs Blanquette de Limoux 1986 • $8 • (06/15/90) • **78**

Brut Blanc de Blancs Blanquette de Limoux 1983 • $8 • (01/31/88) • **77**

ROBERT-DENOGENT

Pouilly-Fuissé Les Carrons 1994: Straightforward and a bit angular, with a cinnamon-spice character and green apple flavors. A bit one-dimensional on the finish. • $34 • (05/31/96) • **80**

Pouilly-Fuissé La Croix 1994: Lemony and crisp, a lean wine with green, herbaceous flavors and no fruit. • $23 • (05/31/96) • **75**

Pouilly-Fuissé Cuvée Claude Denogent 1994: Straightforward, with minor-league citrus and fruit aromas and flavors. A light wine that's fresh and should make a pretty good companion for seafood. • $28 • (05/31/96) • **80**

Pouilly-Fuissé Cuvée Claude Denogent Vieilles Vignes 1993: Showy, ripe and rich, displaying a chalky, chewy texture, honey and hazelnut flavors lack a bit of vibrancy. Drink now or hold until 1997. 333 cases made. • $28 • **85**

Pouilly-Fuissé Les Reisses Vieilles Vignes 1994: Straightforward, with a lot of citrus and a touch of cinnamon and spice. Fairly lean and tart, but still enjoyable. • $24 • (05/31/96) • **80**

Pouilly-Fuissé Les Reisses Vieilles Vignes 1993: There is some decent fruit but it's disjointed, with pronounced wet hay, herbal, and asparagus flavors. Not very attractive. 500 cases made. • $25 • **74**

Pouilly-Fuissé Vieilles Vignes 1993: Lemon, herbal, wet earth character, medium-bodied, good acidity. A cardboard note is slightly distracting on the finish. Drink now. 667 cases made. • $NA • **79**

ROBIN, CHÂTEAU

Côtes de Castillon 1993: Light and plummy red showing light tannins and a hint of tomatoes. Drinkable now. • $NA • (01/31/96) • **79**

ROBLET-MONNOT, F

Volnay Les Caillerets 1989 • $37 • (11/15/93) • **85**

ROC DE CAMBES, CHÂTEAU LE

Côtes de Bourg 1990: Earthy, gamy, smoky aromas and flavors shoulder past the modest fruit, making this an odd wine that few will like. • $16 • (06/15/93) • **68**

ROC MIGNON D'ADRIEN, CHÂTEAU

Bordeaux Supérieur 1989 • $6 • (02/28/91) BB • **82**

ROCHELLE, DOMAINE DE LA

Moulin-à-Vent 1988 • $10 • (05/31/89) • **91**

ROCHEMORIN, CHÂTEAU DE

Graves 1985 • $14 • (06/15/88) • **85**

Graves 1982 • $22 • (08/31/92) • **90**

Graves 1981: A lanky rather one-dimensional fresh fruit and chocolate character, medium body and very firm taninns. Drink now. • $NA • **83**

Pessac-Léognan 1995: Slightly herbal and diluted, though some berry character shows through. It's rather light and short on the finish. • $NA • (05/15/96) • **75-79** (BT)

Pessac-Léognan 1994: Thin and rather diluted, showing some fruit character and an herbal finish. • $NA • (05/15/96) • **75-79** (BT)

Pessac-Léognan 1993: Subtle and elegant, medium- to light-bodied, featuring an appealing touch of cassis, wet earth and dried herbs. Delicious now. • $14 • (01/31/96) • **84**

Pessac-Léognan 1992: Extremely herbal and hard with aggressive tannins and vegetal character. • $13 • **72**

Pessac-Léognan 1991: Rather green with weak artichoke and tomato aromas and flavors. • $13 • (03/31/94) • **72**

Pessac-Léognan 1990: The earthy, meaty, mineral character and firm tannins make this a typical traditional Pessac-Léognan. Drinkable in 1997. 4,000 cases made. • $12 • (03/31/93) • **89**

Pessac-Léognan 1989 • $16 • (03/15/92) • **88**

Pessac-Léognan 1986 • $15 • (06/15/89) • **84**

Pessac-Léognan White 1994: Fresh and clean, with a spicy, grassy apple character. Medium-bodied and fresh with acidity. A lively white. • $13 • (03/31/96) • **84**

Pessac-Léognan White 1992: Shows better than a year ago, providing lots of fresh apple, grass and mineral aromas and flavors, medium body, firm acidity and medium finish. A bit rustic. • $18 • **83**

Pessac-Léognan White 1991 • $17 • (03/31/94) • **82**

ROCHER, CHÂTEAU DU

St.-Emilion 1983 • $11 • (05/15/87) • **73**

ROCHER BELLEVUE FIGEAC, CHÂTEAU

St.-Emilion 1995: Supple, ripe and sweet-tasting, quite silky and creamy, with grapey, red berry, cinnamon and spice character. Full-bodied with soft tannins, but a bit forward. • $NA • (05/15/96) • **85-89** (BT)

St.-Emilion 1994: This shows lots of plum and berry character, medium-bodied. Velvety tannins and long, flavorful finish. Sample variation noted. • $NA • **85-89** (BT)

St.-Emilion 1991: Very odd aromas of salami and earth, but the palate is fresh and fruity. • $12 • (03/31/94) • **73**

St.-Emilion 1990: Obviously made from high-yield grapes. A wine with light grassy, berry, almost watery flavors and a light tannin structure. Drinkable now. 3,500 cases made. • $15 • (03/31/93) • **79**

St.-Emilion 1988 • $18 • (04/30/91) • **87**

ROCHES NEUVES, DOMAINE DES

Saumur-Champigny 1992: Cherry, raspberry and light herbal flavors mingle nicely. Supple, fresh and delicate, with enough body to carry the flavors through the finish. Drink it young to enjoy the fruit. • $13 • (11/15/94) • **81**

Saumur-Champigny Terres Chaudes 1992: Ripe and generous for the vintage, round and fruity, offering pleasant black cherry and blackberry flavors. Lush and velvety on the palate. It's balanced and accessible. • $20 • (11/15/94) • **85**

RODET, ANTONIN

Beaujolais-Villages Rodet 1988 • $8 • (11/15/90) • **75**

Chambolle-Musigny 1993: Somewhat raisiny but an impressive concentration of ripe fruit. Medium- to full-bodied, adding chewy tannins and a tarry, berry-flavored aftertaste. Slightly overdone. Better in 2000. • $30 • **84**

Chassagne-Montrachet La Grande Montagne 1994: A seductively ripe *premier cru* that's smooth and supple, but a touch unfocused in the aromas. Appealing apricot, ripe pear, mineral and honey flavors, it coasts the mouth with its creamy, silky texture. 128 cases made. • $48 • (05/31/96) • **84**

Chassagne-Montrachet Morgeot 1994: A bit rustic, with some chestnut aromas. Modest grapefruit, honey and tropical notes. Tastes a bit diluted and short. 256 cases made. • $43 • (05/31/96) • **79**

Corton-Charlemagne 1992: A super-ripe, super-charged style of Corton that comes across as thick, rich, almost cloying. A bit extreme for us, with all those butter, apple and honey flavors. Drinkable now. • $NA • (08/31/94) • **88**

Gevrey-Chambertin 1986 • $25 • (07/15/90) • **86**

Gevrey-Chambertin Les Cazetiers 1993: Some good berry and fruit character but rather light, delivering elegant tannins and an easy finish. Drinkable now. • $45 • **84**

Gevrey-Chambertin Lavaut St.-Jacques 1982 • $35 • (06/30/87) • **92**

Meursault Les Perrières 1994: Seductively supple and honeyed, showing some buttery, pie crust flavors along with toasted hazelnut and pear. Creamy in texture, a little fuller in body, and harmonious for drinking now. 76 cases made. • $53 • (05/31/96) • **86**

Key: SS—Spectator Selection. CS—Cellar Selection. BB—Best Buy. $NA—Price not available. (BT)—Barrel tasting. Ⓐ—Auction Price.
Dates in parentheses represent the issues in which the ratings were published.

Meursault Les Perriéres 1992: The fruit flavors are bright and clean in this well-proportioned and modest Meursault. Elegant, creamy-textured and enjoyable, with a lingering, lightly toasty finish. Tasted twice. • $NA • (08/31/94) • **84**

Meursault Rodet 1992: Smells attractive with rich butter, butterscotch, vanilla and peach flavors, and a round texture to go with it, but you are left wanting a bit more fruit in the mid-palate. • $NA • (08/31/94) • **85**

Nuits-St.-Georges Roncière 1993: Chunky spice and plum aromas and flavors, medium to full body, firm tannins and long, succulent finish. Better in 1999. • $45 • **88**

Puligny-Montrachet Le Cailleret 1994: Rich, ripe and full-bodied, showing creamy, milky coconut aromas and flavors. May seem a bit overdone and too soft to some, but has its appeal. Good drinking now. 148 cases made. • $53 • (05/31/96) • **84**

Puligny-Montrachet Hameau de Blagny 1994: A bit lean and fruitless, offering only modest citrus, spice and honey flavors and a short finish. The wood dominates. 144 cases made. • $45 • (05/31/96) • **78**

Rully Red Château de Rully 1991: Lean and lively, offering a bright thread of wild berry and currant flavor that extends into a silky finish. Appealing to drink now. • $NA • (01/31/94) • **83**

Rully White Château de Rully 1992: It's maturing fast, with earthy, cheesy notes along with some modest apple and pear flavors. • $16 • (08/31/94) • **77**

Volnay-Santenots 1993: Overdone really. Concentrated but lacks finesse. Raisin, plum and mushroom aromas and flavors. Medium-bodied and a bit alcoholic. Try in 1998. • $35 • **84**

Vosne-Romanée 1993: Quite distinctive, showing mint, wet earth, plum and mineral flavors. A bit too raisiny to be truly classy, but it offers plenty of ripe character. Medium in body and tannins. Try around 1998. • $30 • **86**

ROEDERER, LOUIS

Brut Blanc de Blancs Champagne 1990: Beautifully fresh, focused and appealing, featuring lots of lemony, doughy, spicy flavors, crisp acidity and tangy finish. Very youthful, clean and elegant. Should improve through 1997. • $40 • **88**

Brut Blanc de Blancs Champagne 1983 • $45 • (12/31/90) • **83**

Brut Blanc de Blancs Champagne 1979 • $39 • (05/31/87) • **94**

Brut Champagne 1988: Powerfully fruity, lively in texture, featuring cherry and almond extract flavors and firm acidity. A bold Champagne that grabs you on the first sip, but fades a bit on aftertaste. • **85**

Brut Champagne 1985 • $50 • (12/31/90) • **85**

Brut Champagne 1982 • $45 • (12/31/88) • **93**

Brut Champagne NV • $25 • (05/16/86) • **82**

Brut Champagne Brut Premier NV: Harmonious and elegant in style, sporting lots of vibrant fruit flavor and just enough doughy, toasty nuances to make it intriguing. Has everything in just the right proportions, including a lingering finish. • $25 • (11/30/95) • **89**

Brut Champagne Cristal 1988: Intriguing and complex, with enticing aromas of fig, butter and toast, backed by mouth-filling flavors of pear, cream and apple. Long on the finish, too. Gorgeous, refined and balanced. Drinkable now through 1997. 50,000 cases made. • $100 • **93**

Brut Champagne Cristal 1986: A chewy and flavorful wine with lemon, berry, almond character, high acidity and a bitter almond finish. Tasted twice with consistent notes. Drinkable now. • $100 • (12/31/93) • **89**

Brut Champagne Cristal 1985 • $132 • (05/15/92) • **85**

Brut Champagne Cristal 1983 • $120 • (12/31/89) • **88**

Brut Champagne Cristal 1982 • $106 • (09/30/87) • **92**

Brut Champagne Cristal 1981 • $120 • (05/16/86) • **91**

Brut Rosé Champagne 1989: A lean, well-balanced, dry rosé, with a light salmon color and hints of cherry in the otherwise straightforward fruit flavors. 4,200 cases made. • $40 • **85**

Brut Rosé Champagne NV • $37 • (12/16/85) • **79**

Brut Rosé Champagne Cristal 1979 • $87 • (12/16/85) • **69**

ROGER, DOMAINE JEAN-MAX

Sancerre Cuvée G.C. 1992: Pungent with herbal notes of chive and eucalyptus, this wine falls in the traditional style, with lean grapefruit

and grassy flavors. It's a tart, refreshing wine that needs food for balance. • $15 • (10/31/94) • **83**
Sancerre Cuvée G.C. 1991 • $19 • (09/15/93) • **80**

ROGUE, LA

Bandol 1987 • $11 • (11/30/90) • **83**

ROLAND, CHÂTEAU

St.-Emilion 1986 • $12 • (06/30/89) • **79**

ROLLAND, CHÂTEAU

Barsac 1987 • $NA • (06/15/90) • **77**

ROLLAND-MAILLET, CHÂTEAU

St.-Emilion 1995: Bright cherry and mineral aromas and flavors in this, though it's a little light on the finish and it could use a bit more fruit. • $NA • (05/15/96) • **80-84** (BT)

ROLLET, CATHERINE & PASCAL

Pouilly-Fuissé Domaine de la Chapelle 1994: Fairly rich, fresh tropical character, with pineapple, fig, coconut and pear flavors. Nicely balanced and very attractive now. 116 cases made. • $16 • (05/31/96) • **85**
Pouilly-Fuissé Domaine de la Chapelle 1993: Ripe and pleasant, delivering pear, floral, honey and fresh herb notes. A supple palate turns tart on the intense finish at this stage. Drinkable now. 125 cases made. • $15 • **85**
Pouilly-Fuissé Domaine de la Chapelle Vieilles Vignes 1994: Vibrant, lively and attractive, with spice, honey and wet hay notes. A little light and lacks power, but it's ready to drink now. 533 cases made. • $19 • (05/31/96) • **85**
Pouilly-Fuissé Domaine de la Chapelle Vieilles Vignes 1993: Remarkable, understated yet powerful. Unfolds its subtle lemon, honey, melon, pear and mineral character in one seductive wave after another. Lush, smooth texture creams your mouth, the finish is supple. Try now. 400 cases made. • $19 • **90**

ROMANECHE-THORINS

Moulin-à-Vent Château des Jacques 1985 • $10 • (03/15/88) • **81**

ROMANEE-CONTI, DOMAINE DE LA

Echézeaux 1993: Super vanilla, coffee, berry character, quite oaky and more like a Bordeaux than a Burgundy, but how can we fault it? Well structured and refined. Better in 2000. • $95 • (05/15/96) • **90**
Echézeaux 1992: Ripe but light-bodied, with pleasant spice, brown sugar, cinnamon and strawberry aromas and flavors. Light tannins and a tart finish. Disappointing. Drinkable now. • $52 • **79**
Echézeaux 1991: Smooth, ripe and opulent, layering the currant, black cherry and raspberry fruit with grace notes of spice and toast. Intense in flavor and refreshingly balanced with a thread of acidity, this is approachable now but should be at its best after 1999. 1,474 cases made. • $95 • (08/31/94) CS • **93**
Echézeaux 1990: Smooth, polished and velvety, a richly layered wine with marvelous plum, blackberry, vanilla, toast and spice aromas and flavors that linger on the finish. Graceful and deep. Perhaps best around 2000 to 2005. 1,446 cases made. • $182 Ⓐ • (12/31/93) CS • **94**
Echézeaux 1989 • $114 • (10/31/92) • **90**
Echézeaux 1988 • $158 Ⓐ • (04/30/91) • **92**
Echézeaux 1987 • $53 Ⓐ • (09/30/90) • **92**
Echézeaux 1986 • $79 Ⓐ • (08/31/89) • **92**
Echézeaux 1985 • $176 Ⓐ • (02/29/88) • **96**
Echézeaux 1984 • $68 • (02/28/87) • **90**
Echézeaux 1983 • $67 Ⓐ • (11/30/86) • **63**
Echézeaux 1952 • $96 • (08/31/90) • **97**
Grands Echézeaux 1993: Solid and fairly tannic, featuring plum, black cherry and earth character. Rather lean, with mocha, spice and toast notes on the woody finish. Lacks the supple structure of some top '93s, and the color was a bit lighter. Time should soften its taut personality, try in 2005. • $135 • **88**
Grands Echézeaux 1992: Attractive and delicate berry, cherry, violet and vanilla aromas with brown sugar and cinnamon flavors. Medium-to-light body, with soft tannins and a light finish. Drinkable now. • $79 • **84**
Grands Echézeaux 1991: Firm in texture but it promises to become an opulent wine. The spicy, violet-scented black cherry and currant flavors rolling across the palate in waves. Finishes ripe, smooth and gracefully balanced with refreshing acidity. 799 cases made. • $150 • (08/31/94) • **93**
Grands Echézeaux 1990: Smooth and polished, with jammy raspberry notes adding complexity and richness to the basic plum and currant flavors. Feels soft and generous, but it has the intensity and length to want cellaring until 1998 or 1999. 914 cases made. • $160 • (12/31/93) CS • **94**
Grands Echézeaux 1989 • $111 Ⓐ • (10/31/92) • **93**
Grands Echézeaux 1988 • $153 Ⓐ • (04/30/91) • **92**
Grands Echézeaux 1987 • $81 Ⓐ • (09/30/90) • **89**
Grands Echézeaux 1986 • $133 Ⓐ • (08/31/89) • **94**
Grands Echézeaux 1985 • $323 Ⓐ • (02/29/88) • **94**
Grands Echézeaux 1984 • $88 • (02/28/87) • **88**
Grands Echézeaux 1983 • $99 Ⓐ • (11/30/86) • **64**
Grands Echézeaux 1942 • $230 • (08/31/90) • **93**
Richebourg 1993: Austere and tough in texture now, showing a dry, tannic edge. Offers compacted blackberry, dry cherry and vanilla character, accompanied by a somewhat green flavor. This is a closed wine that needs time to come together. Try in 2005. • $190 • (05/15/96) • **90**
Richebourg 1992: Elegant and light-bodied, the attractive berry, cherry and violet notes mingle with the cinnamon and brown sugar flavors. A pretty finish makes this quite smooth and seductive. Drinkable now. • $96 • **83**
Richebourg 1991: Lean in texture, modest in scope, with more tea leaf and underbrush flavors than fruit, although it finishes with a prune edge. Maybe best from 1997. 1,187 cases made. • $190 • (08/31/94) • **80**
Richebourg 1990: Ripe and tannic, but smoothly polished, offering several layers of spice, fruit and toast, centered around a tight core of plum and currant flavor. Has richness and elegance to spare but needs until 1998. Tasted twice, with the first bottle showing a decidedly earthy edge. 1,315 cases made. • $310 Ⓐ • (12/31/93) • **91**
Richebourg 1989 • $214 Ⓐ • (10/31/92) • **90**
Richebourg 1988 • $216 Ⓐ • (04/30/91) • **94**
Richebourg 1987 • $72 Ⓐ • (09/30/90) • **93**
Richebourg 1986 • $141 Ⓐ • (08/31/89) • **94**
Richebourg 1984 • $102 • (02/28/87) • **91**
Richebourg 1983 • $163 Ⓐ • (11/30/86) • **52**
Richebourg 1954 • $175 • (08/31/90) • **88**
Richebourg 1947 • $750 • (08/31/90) • **65**
Romanée-Conti 1993: Savage, muscular and tightly knit, this offers pure Pinot fruit. Has a full range of cassis, black cherry, mineral and vanilla notes, but it also shows an austere, underripe edge of spicy, tobacco and leafy flavors. With its tough tannins and good length, this is an outstanding "masculine" red Burgundy that has the power and potential to improve into the next century. • $850 • (05/15/96) • **94**
Romanée-Conti 1992: A solid core of fruit and tannins in a medium-bodied wine. Plum, berry and mushroom aromas and flavors, with hints of violet, brown sugar and cinnamon. Enough tannins on the finish to cellar until 1997. • $600 • **85**
Romanée-Conti 1991: Smooth, elegant and intense enough to keep the leafy, smoky berry and black cherry flavors rolling through the polished finish. Harmonious and concentrated, should be best from 2000. 420 cases made. • $800 • (08/31/94) • **93**
Romanée-Conti 1990: Densely packed, with earthy, tarry and spicy overtones running through the powerful plum, currant and berry flavors, all wrapped in several layes of fine tannins. Give it until 2000. 620 cases made. • $750 • (12/31/93) CS • **93**
Romanée-Conti 1989 • $850 • (10/31/92) • **97**
Romanée-Conti 1987 • $608 Ⓐ • (09/30/90) • **89**
Romanée-Conti 1986 • $553 Ⓐ • (08/31/89) • **95**
Romanée-Conti 1985 • $1,080 • (01/31/90) • **100**
Romanée-Conti 1984 • $640 • (01/31/90) • **94**
Romanée-Conti 1983 • $750 • (01/31/90) • **78**
Romanée-Conti 1982 • $638 Ⓐ • (01/31/90) • **85**

Romanée-Conti 1979 • $660 Ⓐ • (01/31/90) • **90**
Romanée-Conti 1978 • $520 Ⓐ • (01/31/90) • **95**
Romanée-Conti 1975 • $780 • (01/31/90) • **82**
Romanée-Conti 1964 • $605 Ⓐ • (01/31/90) • **98**
Romanée-Conti 1963 • $555 Ⓐ • (01/31/90) • **50**
Romanée-Conti 1959 • $1,800 • (01/31/90) • **68**
Romanée-Conti 1953 • $2,100 • (01/31/90) • **93**
Romanée-Conti 1937 • $1,950 • (01/31/90) • **50**
Romanée-Conti 1935 • $400 • (01/31/90) • **50**
Romanée-Conti 1934 • $2,100 • (01/31/90) • **66**
Romanée-Conti 1929 • $2,400 • (01/31/90) • **50**
Romanée St.-Vivant 1993: Closed and tough, featuring tannic, austere character that's almost rustic. Offers plenty of redberry and blackberry flavors. Seems somewhat awkward and off-balance now, but it's a big wine and the potential is there. Try in 2005. • $135 • (05/15/96) • **92**
Romanée St.-Vivant 1992: Soft and supple, but very light and diluted. Offers modest fruit flavors with brown sugar and herbal accents. Not much to taste. A brownish edge signals that this is maturing quickly. Drink up fast. • $73 • **74**
Romanée St.-Vivant 1991: Ripe and generous, a fairly smooth-textured wine with nicely integrated tannins, a smoky edge to the currant and berry flavors. Tasty and balanced for cellaring until 1997. 1,548 cases made. • $120 • (08/31/94) • **88**
Romanée St.-Vivant 1990: Firm and flavorful, with a strong toasty-smoky edge to the earthy currant and plum aromas and flavors, finishing with a polished core of flavor poking through the veil of chewy tannins. Best in 1998. • $175 • (12/31/93) • **90**
Romanée St.-Vivant 1989 • $118 Ⓐ • (10/31/92) • **91**
Romanée St.-Vivant 1987 • $82 Ⓐ • (09/30/90) • **89**
Romanée St.-Vivant 1986 • $195 • (08/31/89) • **98**
Romanée St.-Vivant 1985 • $201 Ⓐ • (02/29/88) • **88**
Romanée St.-Vivant 1984 • $36 Ⓐ • (02/28/87) • **96**
Romanée St.-Vivant 1983 • $96 Ⓐ • (11/30/86) • **66**
La Tâche 1993: A superb tasting experience: this really builds on the palate. Elegant yet showing some richness, full of lovely plum, berry and vanilla notes. The tannins are refined in this medium- to full-bodied La Tâche, but the finish is still very tannic, try it in 2006. • $270 • (05/15/96) • **94**
La Tâche 1992: Smooth and supple in texture, medium to light in body. This delivers lovely cherry and strawberry aromas and a hint of earthiness in the spice and mocha flavors. Finishes light with fine tannins. Drinkable now. • $139 • **84**
La Tâche 1991: A gentle wine with seductive violet-scented currant, blackberry and spice flavors that swirl across the palate in profusion, echoing chocolate on the finish. Beautifully balanced, harmonious and concentrated enough to want at least until 1999-2000. 1,428 cases made. • $295 • (08/31/94) CS • **95**
La Tâche 1990: Tough and tight, an immensely concentrated wine, with plum and currant at the core plus shades of toast and exotic spices, all wrapped in a layer of tannin that will need until 2000 to open up. Until then, it's not showing enough to be able to predict where it's going. 2,005 cases made. • $428 Ⓐ • (12/31/93) • **91**
La Tâche 1989 • $368 Ⓐ • (10/31/92) • **91**
La Tâche 1987 • $231 Ⓐ • (09/30/90) • **92**
La Tâche 1986 • $420 Ⓐ • (08/31/89) CS • **98**
La Tâche 1985 • $605 Ⓐ • (02/29/88) • **98**
La Tâche 1984 • $150 • (02/28/87) • **95**
La Tâche 1983 • $336 Ⓐ • (11/30/86) • **61**

ROMANIN, CHÂTEAU

Les Baux de Provence Coteaux d'Aix-en-Provence 1990 • $17 • (02/15/93) • **80**
Coteaux d'Aix-en-Provence 1991: Lean and a bit tough, with tart acidity and nutty flavors-past its prime. May still work with grilled fish. • $8 • (07/31/95) • **77**

Key: SS—Spectator Selection. CS—Cellar Selection. BB—Best Buy. $NA—Price not available. (BT)—Barrel tasting. Ⓐ—Auction Price.
Dates in parentheses represent the issues in which the ratings were published.

ROMEFORT, CHÂTEAU

Médoc 1990: Smooth and supple, a polished wine with nicely rounded plum and cherry aromas and flavors, hinting at fresh leather on the finish. Drinkable now. • $10 • (02/28/94) • **84**

ROMER DU HAYOT, CHÂTEAU

Sauternes 1988: Drinkable, but flawed and flat tasting. Tasted twice. • $122 • (04/30/91) • **72**
Sauternes 1986 • $22 • (12/31/89) • **78**
Sauternes 1983 • $19 • (01/31/88) • **72**
Sauternes 1982 • $13 • (10/16/85) • **82**

RONCEE, DOMAINE DU

Chinon 1993: Light-bodied and soft, offering round, ripe fruit for drinking now. Just enough tannin for grip, with a nice, smoky note on the finish. Gentle and accommodating. Tasted twice. • $12 • (10/31/94) • **84**

ROPITEAU FRERES

Bienvenues-Bâtard-Montrachet 1993: Vivid apple and mineral aromas and flavors. Medium body, racy acidity and chalky finish. Well constructed. • $105 • **86**
Bourgogne Hautes-Côtes de Nuits 1993: Light and short, this tastes like it was cut with water, offering only modest strawberry and earth flavors. • $12 • **72**
Chassagne-Montrachet 1993: Straightforward apple and mineral character, medium-bodied, medium finish. More like a Mâcon. Drinkable now. • $28 • **82**
Chassagne-Montrachet Red 1993: Soft and ripe, a bit light, but featuring enticing, sweet-tasting licorice and red berry flavors. Drink on release. • $17 • **80**
Côte de Beaune-Villages 1993: Rather thin berry and tobacco character, but very light and dry on the finish. Drink now. • $13 • **75**
Côte de Nuits-Villages 1993: Delicate, sweet-tasting character and modest strawberry and cherry flavors. A bit light on the drying finish. • $14 • **77**
Criots-Bâtard-Montrachet 1993: Pretty mushroom, cream and apple aromas and flavors. Medium body and finish, with good acidity. Drink now. • $105 • **85**
Gevrey-Chambertin 1993: Middle-of-the-road Burgundy with a slight dilution, showing only modest raspberry, cherry and strawberry flavors. Drinkable now. • $23 • **79**
Mâcon-Villages Les Chanterelles 1994: Medium in body, round and silky, nicely ripe, hinting at wet earth, pear, melon and prosciutto ham. Astringent on the finish. 1,666 cases made. • $9 • **79**
Meursault 1993: Crisp and lean-framed, presenting a citrusy edge and dried herbs, honey, mineral and hints of hazelnut playing in the background. Try after 1996 to 1997. Tasted twice, with consistent notes. • $27 • (05/15/95) • **85**
Meursault Les Perrières 1993: Vivid apple, mineral and cream aromas and flavors, medium body and a medium-long, fruity aftertaste. Tasted twice, with consistent notes. • $36 • **86**
Meursault Red 1993: Somewhat light and short, showing a lightish color. Decent Pinot Noir flavors, but vegetal notes appear on the diluted finish. Drink now. Serve chilled. • $16 • **78**
Pinot Noir Bourgogne 1993: Light and a bit lean, delivering modest raspberry and cherry flavors. Still somewhat dry at this stage. Drinkable now. • $9 • **79**
Pommard 1993: Good level of gamy fruit character but slightly green on the meaty finish. Medium in body and velvety tannins. Better in 2000. • $25 • **80**
Puligny-Montrachet Champ Gain 1993: Subtle and elegant, a medium-bodied Burgundy shaded by spice and vanilla flavors. Turns firm and chalky on the delicate but long finish. • $35 • **85**
St.-Véran 1994: Straightforward, fresh and pleasant, offering some pear, apple and wet hay flavors and light-to-medium body. 833 cases made. • $11 • **80**
Santenay 1993: Light- to medium-bodied, compacted and well defined, featuring delicious cherry, smoke and earth character. Drink slightly cool and enjoy this '93 for what it's straightforward, fruity style. • $16 • **85**

Viognier Vin de Pays d'Oc 1994: A neutral white that is balanced and drinkable but lacks the flamboyant flavors characteristic of good Viognier. 4,500 cases made. • $11 • (02/29/96) • **76**

Volnay Clos des Chênes 1993: Not very good. Has some fruit, but very papery and mushroomy. Better in 1999. • $30 • **75**

Vosne-Romanée 1993: Weedy, resembling cabbage. Light. Where's the fruit? • $26 • **74**

ROPITEAU-MIGNON

Meursault 1992: Seems mature, with some nutty, apple pie, vanilla notes, ending with a chewy, almost rustic finish. Bottled by Vaucher. • $NA • (08/31/94) • **79**

Meursault Les Gouttes d'Or 1993: Starts off well showing mineral, apple and honey character but finishes slightly grassy. Medium body, tart acidity. Drinkable now. • $32 • (05/15/95) • **81**

ROQUE, CHÂTEAU LA

Coteaux du Languedoc 1990 • $9 • (02/15/93) • **75**

Coteaux du Languedoc Pic St.-Loup 1992 • $10 • (03/15/94) • **86**

Coteaux du Languedoc Pic St.-Loup 1991 • $7 • (03/15/94) • **82**

Coteaux du Languedoc Pic St.-Loup Cupa Numismae 1990 • $10 • (03/15/94) • **86**

ROQUE SESTIERE

Corbières Blanc Vieilles Vignes 1992 • $NA • (03/15/94) • **86**

ROQUEBRUN, CHÂTEAU

Coteaux du Languedoc 1992 • $NA • (03/15/94) • **82**

ROQUEFORT, CHÂTEAU

Bordeaux 1993 • $10 • **55**

ROQUEGRAVE, CHÂTEAU

Médoc 1983 • $6 • (04/01/86) • **63**

ROQUENEGADE, DOMAINE DE

Cabernet Sauvignon Vin de Pays de l'Aude 1991 • $8 • (03/15/94) • **87**

ROQUES, CHÂTEAU DES

Vacqueyras Cuvée de Noe 1986 • $7 • (12/15/89) BB • **88**

ROQUETTE, DOMAINE DE LA

Châteauneuf-du-Pape 1992: Smooth, mature and interesting to drink, from the woodsy aromas through the herb and currant flavors to the plush texture. Drink now through 1997. • $20 • **85**

Châteauneuf-du-Pape 1990: Firm and flavorful, with roasted meat, earth and blackberry flavors and a solid dose of crisp tannins on the finish. Drinkable now. • $15 • (06/15/93) • **83**

Châteauneuf-du-Pape 1989 • $17 • (10/15/91) • **86**

Châteauneuf-du-Pape 1988 • $17 • (10/15/91) • **86**

Châteauneuf-du-Pape 1986 • $18 • (10/15/91) • **85**

Châteauneuf-du-Pape 1985 • $13 • (07/31/88) SS • **90**

ROSE FIGEAC, CHÂTEAU LA

Pomerol 1982 • $25 • (05/15/89) • **85**

ROSIERE, DOMAINE LA

Syrah Coteaux des Baronnies 1988 • $6 • (02/28/90) • **78**

ROSSI, G.

Chénas En Guinchay 1994: Firm and bigger-boned than most Beaujolais, and also more austere, featuring ripe plum flavor and licorice notes in a red that's more serious than fun. Try with food. • $9 • **86**

ROSSIGNOL, PHILIPPE

Côte de Nuits-Villages 1985 • $10 Ⓐ • (07/31/88) • **89**

Gevrey-Chambertin 1987 • $23 • (05/31/90) • **69**

Gevrey-Chambertin Les Corbeaux 1993: Subtle and delicious, this harmonious *premier cru* coats your mouth with sweet-tasting, red berry flavors. Silky mouth-feel and wet earth, leather, plum, cedar, toast and spice character. It turns a bit tannic on the finish now, so don't touch until 2000. • $NA • **89**

Gevrey-Chambertin Les Corbeaux Cuvée Vieilles Vignes 1993: This shows a very refined style of elegant tannins, fresh fruit and long, lingering finish. Medium in body with plenty of fruit and perfume. Delicious now, but should improve well into the next century. • $NA • (05/15/96) • **90**

ROSSIGNOL-FEVRIER

Volnay 1988 • $32 • (03/31/91) • **92**

ROSSIGNOL-TRAPET

Beaune Les Teurons 1993: Plenty of currant character, medium body, firm tannins and long, sweet fruit finish. Better in 1997. 483 cases made. • $33 • **90**

Beaune Les Teurons 1992: Pleasant but light-bodied, with black cherry, fig and chocolate mousse flavors. Drinkable now. 416 cases made. • $30 • **83**

Beaune Les Teurons 1991: Firm and flavorful, with blackberry, anise and caramel aromas and flavors. Looks a bit mature, but tastes fine. Drinkable now. 267 cases made. • $27 Ⓐ • (01/31/94) • **81**

Beaune Les Teurons 1990: A well-crafted Burgundy that does justice to this fine vintage. So lively and young it practically jumps from the glass, with exciting, bright berry and toast characteristics. The finish is supple yet firm. Drinkable now. 30 cases made. • $46 • (12/15/92) • **91**

Chambertin 1993: Pretty, focused plum and red berry character, medium body, firm tannins and medium fruity finish. Better in 1999. 541 cases made. • $77 • **90**

Chambertin 1992: Lean and silky, with a gamy edge to the cherry and tobacco flavors, a bit tannic, but the sweet flavors underneath bode well. Best from 1997. • $NA • **87**

Chambertin 1991: Delicate, elegant wine, silky and brimming with currant and berry flavors, finishing refined and adding a touch of spice to the fruit. Drinkable now. 1,058 cases made. • $58 Ⓐ • (01/31/94) • **87**

Chambertin 1990: A beauty of a wine that offers a mouthful of big, gorgeous flavors, rich texture and velvety finish. Packed to the brim with black currant, raspberry and toast characteristics. Wonderfully balanced and built for long aging. Drinkable in 1998 to 2000. 50 cases made. • $106 • (12/15/92) • **95**

Chapelle-Chambertin 1993: Very well-made dried cherry and earth aromas, medium body, full, almost dried tannins and a medium fruity finish. Better in 1999. 541 cases made. • $77 • **87**

Chapelle-Chambertin 1992: Lean and chewy with very little flavor to compensate, finishing with a bitter bite. Hard to tell if this will improve, try now or in 1997. 167 cases made. • $56 • **79**

Chapelle-Chambertin 1991: Velvety and rich, an elegant wine that plays its complex flavors one card at a time, until the table is filled with plum, currant, blackberry, tobacco and coffee flavors piling up on one another. Everything comes together into a delicious finish. Tannins could use unitl 1998-2000 to do their best. 100 cases made. • $49 Ⓐ • (01/31/94) CS • **94**

Chapelle-Chambertin 1990: Has incredible harmony, a dense fruit and tannin structure and an amazing balance of refined smoke, berry, tobacco and raspberry characteristics. Drinkable in 1998. 35 cases made. • $83 • (12/15/92) • **95**

Gevrey-Chambertin 1993: Distinctive minty, lead-pencil, plummy character and medium body. Quite forward and accessible now, it's round yet intense. Should improve until 1999. 1,916 cases made. • $28 • **87**

Gevrey-Chambertin 1992: Simple, crisp and a little stemmy, but the modest berry flavors carry through on the finish. 2,083 cases made. • $26 • **79**

Gevrey-Chambertin 1991: Light, fruity and agreeable, with a lean structure and pretty floral, strawberry and red currant aromas and flavors. Approachable now. 62 cases made. • $23 Ⓐ • (01/31/94) • **84**

Gevrey-Chambertin Petite Chapelle 1993: Solid and fragrant, offering substantial dried cherry and plum character and a complement of fine tannins. Medium body and finish. Better in 1999. 191 cases made. • $43 • **88**

Gevrey-Chambertin Petite Chapelle 1992: Gamy, earthy aromas and flavors narrow down to a solid core of fruit that fades as the drying tannins clamp down on the finish. 208 cases made. • $39 • **82**

Gevrey-Chambertin Petite Chapelle 1991: Crisp and simple. Nice currant flavor comes in to save it on the tight, tannic finish. Drinkable now. 417 cases made. • $33 Ⓐ • (01/31/94) • **80**

Gevrey-Chambertin Petite Chapelle 1990: So intense it takes you aback, with earthy black cherry and violet aromas and flavors along with a stemmy, vegetal note and an extremely well-focused finish. Try around 1997. 25 cases made. • $21 Ⓐ • (12/15/92) • **90**

Latricières-Chambertin 1993: Fabulous Burgundy. Wonderful color and concentration of dried cherry and plum aromas. Full-bodied and very firm, featuring a solid core of fruit and fine tannins. Better in 2000. 191 cases made. • $64 • **92**

Latricières-Chambertin 1992: Light but balanced, with a modest level of earthy, slightly gamy black cherry flavor. Drinkable already, but the tannins could use until 1997. 250 cases made. • $56 • **86**

Latricières-Chambertin 1991: Lean, velvety and earthy, playing its mushroomy currant, berry and tobacco aromas and flavors over a chewy background. Nicely focused and long, has finesse and more muscle than most '91s. Drink around 1998. 37 cases made. • $49 Ⓐ • (01/31/94) • **90**

Latricières-Chambertin 1990: Incredibly exciting, with violet, plum, earth and smoke aromas and flavors, loads of ripe fruit characteristics and velvety tannins. A great wine to drink from 1998. 25 cases made. • $83 • (12/15/92) • **97**

ROSTAING, RENE

Côte-Rôtie 1990: Smooth and polished up front before the tannins weigh in. Hints of earth, mineral and black cherry flavors stay with you. Ready now. • $31 • (05/31/94) • **84**

Côte-Rôtie Côte Blonde 1987 • $40 • (06/30/90) • **86**

ROTHSCHILD, BARONS EDMOND & BENJAMIN

Haut-Médoc 1987 • $24 • (03/31/91) • **75**

Haut-Médoc 1986 • $48 • (03/31/91) • **76**

ROTHSCHILD, BARON PHILIPPE DE

Cabernet Sauvignon Vin de Pays d'Oc 1994: Dominated by herbal aromas and flavors. Medium-bodied and fairly well balanced, finishing with a hint of chocolate and spice. • $10 • (12/31/95) • **83**

Chardonnay Vin de Pays d'Oc 1994: Floral and vanilla aromas give way to lemon custard flavors in this smooth, balanced white. Tropical fruit accents add interest, but it finishes short. • $10 • (12/15/95) • **84**

Graves White 1992: This is an aromatic and nicely full-bodied white that turns lean in flavor with herb and mineral notes. • $11 • (11/15/94) • **80**

Médoc 1989 • $11 • (11/15/94) HR • **89**

Merlot Vin de Pays d'Oc 1994: A workmanlike wine with modest chocolate, cherry and plum flavors. Well balanced and still a bit tannic. It finishes on an astringent note. • $10 • (12/31/95) • **82**

St.-Emilion 1985 • $11 • (09/30/88) • **85**

Sauternes 1991: Soft and easy to drink, with fresh fruit and herb flavors. Clean, if a bit lacking in concentration. Good value. • $25 • (11/15/94) • **85**

Sauvignon Blanc Vin de Pays d'Oc 1994: Nicely balanced and smooth, with modest fruit flavors and nice, fresh acidity. Appealing for its crispness. • $10 • (02/29/96) • **82**

ROTHSCHILD, DOMAINES BARONS DE

Pauillac Réserve Spéciale 1987 • $12 • (12/31/90) • **81**

Pauillac Réserve Spéciale NV • $12 • (02/15/90) • **85**

ROTY, JOSEPH

Bourgogne Cuvée de Pressonier 1992: Light and juicy, with a minty raspberry and strawberry character. Has a fresh texture. Drinkable now. • $NA • **80**

Bourgogne White Grande Ordinaire Cuvée Philippe Roty 1992: Light and simple, with crisp tannins that are more than the fruit can absorb. • $NA • **73**

Charmes-Chambertin Cuvée de Très Vieilles Vignes 1992: Firm in texture, with a narrow range of agreeable cherry and toast flavors that echo lightly on the finish. Best from 1997. • $135 • **82**

Gevrey-Chambertin 1992: Firm in texture, with a nice thread of pure, ripe currant flavor running through the tannins. Drinkable now. • $48 • **84**

Gevrey-Chambertin Clos Prieur 1992: Firm in texture and solid in flavor, with smoky black cherry and currant flavors packed in. Aromatic and drinkable now. • $50 • **83**

Gevrey-Chambertin Cuvée des Champs-Chenys 1992: Awfully tannic for the modest level of fruit, a distinctive overlay of spicy vanilla adding a little extra. Give it until 1997 to sort out the tannins. • $NA • **83**

Gevrey-Chambertin Fonteny 1992: Delicate, round and smooth. Has good character, showing roasted chestnut, toast and black cherry flavors and solid tannins. • $72 • **85**

Griotte-Chambertin 1992: Light in texture, showing more oak flavor than fruit, but the raspberry notes in the background suggest this will develop decently through 1997. • $200 • **83**

Marsannay Red Les Ouzeloy 1992: The oak dominates here, its toasty vanilla flavors mingling with some decent currant and black cherry notes. Should be better after 1996. • $NA • **80**

Mazis-Chambertin 1992: Has much more intensity and character than do most in this vintage, unfolding smoke, mint, currant and blackberry flavors through a veil of fine tannins. Best from 1998. • $200 • **88**

ROUFFLIAC, CHÂTEAU DE

St.-Emilion 1985 • $15 • (09/30/88) • **89**

ROUGET, CHÂTEAU

Pomerol 1990: A frank, supple wine with open cherry, herbal and chocolate flavors, this gives plenty of pleasure now. It has good balance and definition. Drink now through 2000. 5,500 cases made. • $29 • **88**

Pomerol 1982 • $28 • (05/15/89) • **86**

Pomerol 1961: A nicely balanced, cedary smelling, mature Bordeaux that's deep in color, with dried cherry flavors and dry texture. Drink through 2000. • $51 • (04/30/96) • **85**

Pomerol 1945: Very pleasant surprise. Looks, smells and tastes like a spicy, youthful Pomerol, still alive and glowing with delicious black cherry, sweet spice and tea leaf flavors that keep echoing on the finish. • $400 • **87**

ROUGET, EMMANUEL

Echézeaux 1993: Stunning from start to finish, seamless in its silky texture, exotic and bursting with rose, violet, toast and spice character.

Key: SS—Spectator Selection. CS—Cellar Selection. BB—Best Buy. $NA—Price not available. (BT)—Barrel tasting. Ⓐ—Auction Price.
Dates in parentheses represent the issues in which the ratings were published.

FRANCE

Big and full-bodied, it remains extremely racy. Sensational, really. Tempting now, but better in 2001. • $80 • (05/15/96) • **95**

Echézeaux 1991: Smooth and elegant, a polished wine with beautiful black cherry and berry flavors, plus a light herbal note on the finish. Tannins are deftly integrated, making the wine almost drinkable now. Best from 1998. • $87 • (08/31/94) • **89**

Echézeaux 1988 • $81 • (11/15/90) • **96**

Echézeaux 1987 • $55 • (03/31/90) • **88**

Echézeaux 1986 • $55 • (12/31/88) • **87**

Nuits-St.-Georges 1993: Exuberant, ripe and delicious village wine, featuring lovely, sweet-tasting plum, spice and smoke flavors. Full-bodied, even chewy, adding supple tannins and a balanced finish. Well made. Try in 2000. • $NA • (05/15/96) • **90**

Nuits-St.-Georges 1989 • $48 • (11/15/91) • **86**

Nuits-St.-Georges 1987 • $32 • (03/31/90) • **86**

Savigny-lès-Beaune 1993: Crushed fruit flavors, wild berries and flowers point the way to wonderful character and medium tannins. Not a red of great class, but absolutely delicious. Better in 1999. • $NA • **89**

Vosne-Romanée 1993: Rather earthy and light, delivering some berry and cherry character and meaty highlights, but it's only medium- to light-bodied and lacks punch. Drinkable now. • $NA • **83**

Vosne-Romanée 1989 • $48 • (11/15/91) • **91**

Vosne-Romanée 1987 • $32 • (03/31/90) • **91**

Vosne-Romanée Les Beaux Monts 1993: Not giving it all at the moment but shows potential. Medium- to full-bodied, voluptuous, adding fine tannins and a long, flavorful finish. Better in 2001. • $55 • (05/15/96) • **91**

Vosne-Romanée Les Beaux Monts 1986 • $40 • (12/31/88) • **89**

Vosne-Romanée Cros Parantoux 1993: Racy, sleek *premier cru*, showing digital definition in every aspect of its flavor components. Loaded with sweet-tasting red berry character, and just a touch of wood and spice for added complexity. Very long, focused finish. Try in 2000. • $72 • (05/15/96) • **95**

Vosne-Romanée Cros Parantoux 1989 • $83 • (11/15/91) • **94**

ROULOT, GUY

Chardonnay Bourgogne 1994: A quite fresh, light-bodied white with some crisp green apple flavors and pleasant chalky notes. • $19 • (05/31/96) • **80**

Chardonnay Bourgogne 1993: A touch more ripeness than many generic Bourgognes, lightly flavored by pear and pink grapefruit notes. The finish is tart and lean, but balanced. Drink now. 750 cases made. • $19 • **80**

Chardonnay Bourgogne 1991 • $18 • (10/15/93) • **86**

Meursault Les Charmes 1994: Impressive, very muscular and tightfisted, with lots of fruit. Shows lovely mineral, earth, toasted bread and vanilla notes. Concentrated flavors linger on the finish. Try in 1999. • $63 • (05/31/96) • **92**

Meursault Les Charmes 1991 • $48 • (10/15/93) • **85**

Meursault Les Luchets 1994: More intense than many other '94s, this balanced white delivers a citrus zing. Very pretty, focused and elegant, with pineapple, toasted pinenut and honey flavors. Try in 1998. • $36 • (05/31/96) • **88**

Meursault Les Luchets 1992: Focused and intense, with toast, lime and pear flavors, elegant and keenly balanced, the steely finish needing time to show all it has. A sophisticated wine with everything in place. • $32 • (08/31/94) • **90**

Meursault Les Luchets 1991 • $34 • (10/15/93) • **85**

Meursault Les Meix Chavaux 1993: Extremely steely and fresh style, featuring almond, apple and pear aromas and flavors. Medium in body and long, racy finish. Should improve with bottle age, try in 1997. 250 cases made. • $37 • (08/31/95) • **87**

Meursault Les Meix Chavaux 1991 • $34 • (10/15/93) • **87**

Meursault Les Perrières 1992: Vibrant yet seductively creamy, this supple but firm Meursault shows how good '92 is. Packed with pear, apple and grapefruit, you sense its future potential with the vanilla, butter and butterscotch character surfacing on the toasty finish. 116 cases made. • $58 • (08/31/94) • **91**

Meursault Le Tesson Clos de Mon Plaisir 1994: Lovely, round, ripe and supple, with lots of fresh tropical fruit, mineral and toasty flavors. Elegant on the lingering, near-flawless finish. Try in 1998. • $13 • (05/31/96) • **91**

Meursault Le Tesson Clos de Mon Plaisir 1993: Complex and delicious, tart but harmonious, featuring flavors of dried herb, honey, lime and green apple. Try after 1996. 459 cases made. • $52 • **88**

Meursault Le Tesson Clos de Mon Plaisir 1992: Well made and tightly wound around a core of vibrant acidity and ripe flavors that peek through in this elegant, firm Meursault. Try now. • $40 • (08/31/94) • **87**

Meursault Le Tesson Clos de Mon Plaisir 1991 • $36 • (10/15/93) • **86**

ROUMIER, CHRISTOPHE

Charmes-Chambertin 1992: Tannins are a bit coarse but there is finesse behind them, showing notes of ripe currant and faded roses that linger on the finish. Worth cellaring until 1997 or 1998. • $55 • **88**

Charmes-Chambertin 1990: Offers loads of fruit and raspberry, pepper and earth characteristics. The superb depth is bolstered by a solid tannin structure. Drinkable in 1998. 87 cases made. • $105 • (12/15/92) • **93**

Ruchottes-Chambertin 1992: Light and pretty, simple, with bright raspberry flavor and a mushroomy, toasty edge. Has some style and grace, folding its fine tannins in on the finish. Drinkable now. • $58 • **85**

Ruchottes-Chambertin 1991: Has a lot of flavor, but feels remarkably delicate and silky. The currant and anise aromas and flavors almost glow against the supple texture. Finishes long and delicately chewy. Accessible now, but should be best after 1998. 84 cases made. • $58 Ⓐ • (01/31/94) • **90**

Ruchottes-Chambertin 1990: An awesome wine, with amazing density of ripe fruit and tannins, yet it remains incredibly balanced and shows wonderful finesse. Don't touch this until the turn of the century. 87 cases made. • $80 • (12/15/92) • **97**

Ruchottes-Chambertin 1989 • $70 • (01/31/92) • **94**

ROUMIER, G.

Bonnes Mares 1992: Lean and tannic, squeezing just a bit of currant and blackberry flavor between the spicy, cedary notes. Best after 1997. • $58 • **82**

Bonnes Mares 1991: Very firm and tannic, but the youthful flavors have the zing of blackberry, currant and anise flavors that remain lively through the finish, echoing currant. Has the stuff to age through 1998-2000 at least. 265 cases made. • $45 Ⓐ • (01/31/94) • **91**

Bonnes Mares 1990: Hard as granite, this is sculpted with an eye toward the 21st century. Packed to the brim with plum, blackberry, chocolate, smoke and earth aromas and flavors and burns with intensity on the extremely firm finish. Try around 2000. 550 cases made. • $100 • (12/15/92) • **96**

Bonnes Mares 1989 • $46 Ⓐ • (01/31/92) • **93**

Chambolle-Musigny 1992: Firm-textured but light in flavor, a tight little red that offers modest berry and toast notes lasting to the finish. Drinkable now. • $24 • **79**

Chambolle-Musigny 1991: Light and tart, with a nice beam of currant flavor running across a racy, citrusy streak. Drinkable now. 1,060 cases made. • $22 Ⓐ • (01/31/94) • **80**

Chambolle-Musigny 1990: Velvety and quite plummy, with dark chocolate and black cherry characteristics, medium body and a supple, ripe finish. Drinkable now. • $28 • (12/15/92) • **88**

Chambolle-Musigny 1989 • $38 • (01/31/92) • **90**

Chambolle-Musigny 1988 • $30 • (07/15/91) • **89**

Chambolle-Musigny 1985 • $26 • (02/15/88) • **87**

Chambolle-Musigny Les Amoureuses 1992: Charming and crisp in texture, its pretty raspberry and vanilla flavors lingering delicately on the finish. Approachable now. • $48 • **84**

Chambolle-Musigny Les Amoureuses 1991: Has beautifully defined currant and berry aromas and flavors that carry straight through the finish, a soft-textured wine that has some fine tannins. Drinkable now. 100 cases made. • $48 Ⓐ • (01/31/94) • **85**

Chambolle-Musigny Les Amoureuses 1990: Impressive intensity draws you into this remarkable wine that's closed now, but it offers excellent blackberry, cherry and earth flavors and a firm texture that will require until at least 1998 to smooth out. 225 cases made. • $55 • (12/15/92) • **92**

Chambolle-Musigny Les Amoureuses 1989 • $62 • (01/31/92) • **88**

Clos Vougeot 1992: A middle-of-the-road Burgundy that shows some nice currant and blackberry flavor and earthy, drying tannins, wait until 1997. • $48 • **79**

Clos Vougeot 1991: Light, fragrant, lean and somewhat austere, featuring a modest level of black cherry and toast aromas and flavors. Drinkable now. 62 cases made. • $45 Ⓐ • (01/31/94) • **84**

Clos Vougeot 1990: Just what you would expect from Clos Vougeot in an outstanding vintage, with lots of firm tannins and ripe berry and spice characteristics. Drinkable in 1997. • $65 • (12/15/92) • **92**

Clos Vougeot 1989 • $62 • (01/31/92) • **87**

Morey-St.-Denis Clos de La Bussière 1992: A Burgundy that grows on you—slight in aroma, but offering some sweet, ripe black cherry flavors, a welcome tannic edge and a lingering finish. Drinkable now. • $24 • **84**

Morey-St.-Denis Clos de La Bussière 1991: Crisp and delicate, showing lovely raspberry and currant flavors, but it's tight and hard enough to want until 1997 to soften. The flavors keep singing on the finish, so it's worth the wait. 416 cases made. • $22 Ⓐ • (01/31/94) • **85**

Morey-St.-Denis Clos de La Bussière 1990: Shows plenty of intensity, with vivid raspberry, spice and smoke characteristics. A full-bodied wine, with a long finish built on firm tannins. Drinkable now. • $53 • (12/15/92) • **89**

Morey-St.-Denis Clos de La Bussière 1989 • $38 • (01/31/92) • **85**

Morey-St.-Denis Clos de La Bussière 1988 • $30 • (07/15/91) • **83**

Morey-St.-Denis Clos de La Bussière 1985 • $27 • (04/30/88) • **92**

Musigny 1992: Lean and tight, with plum and strawberry flavors that kick in with the spicy oak notes. A generous finish also has a lot of fine tannins that need until 1997 to soften. • $NA • **90**

Musigny 1991: Tough and chewy. Has modest blackberry and currant flavors, toasty, ashy overtones and a crisp but watery finish. A disappointment. Tasted twice. 37 cases made. • $85 Ⓐ • (01/31/94) • **78**

Musigny 1989 • $95 • (01/31/92) • **96**

ROUMIER, HERVE

Chambolle-Musigny 1986 • $29 • (08/31/89) • **82**

Chambolle-Musigny Les Amoureuses 1985 • $65 • (03/31/88) • **89**

Clos Vougeot 1986 • $NA • • **64**

ROUMIEU-LACOSTE, CHÂTEAU

Barsac 1990: A wine with a great future. Deceptively subtle, racy, exhibiting lemon, spice, orange, vanilla and butterscotch character. Full-bodied, and a sweet yet very compacted and firm, long, long finish. Try after 1998. • $22 • (04/15/95) • **91**

ROUSSEAU, ARMAND

Chambertin 1992: Delicate and appealing, with seductive, spicy, oak-scented raspberry, strawberry and rose petal aromas and flavors that linger on the supple finish. Tannins are submerged, making this drinkable already. • $NA • **88**

Chambertin 1991: A fairly big, chewy wine for the vintage, shading its ripe currant and plum fruit with a definite component of sweet, spicy oak, finishing with a pruny edge, a tannic bite and enough muscle to want until 1998 or 2000. • $130 • (01/31/94) • **91**

Chambertin 1990: A solid wine that's not giving much now. Has a satiny texture and fine, toasted, gamy violet and berry aromas and flavors. All the elements are in place for excellence, time will tell exactly how great it will be. Try in 1998. 825 cases made. • $150 • (12/15/92) • **92**

Chambertin 1988 • $201 • (05/15/91) • **93**

Chambertin 1985 • $49 Ⓐ • (03/15/88) • **97**

Chambertin-Clos de Bèze 1992: Delicate and spicy, juicy enough, with lightish black cherry and rose petal flavors that reverberate on the finish. Tannins are nicely integrated, making it best from 1997. • $NA • **88**

Chambertin-Clos de Bèze 1991: Light and elegant, featuring a smooth, polished beam of currant and plum aromas and flavors, shaded with cola and coffee notes, a fresh youthful style that needs until 1997 or 1998 to build up some depth. • $35 • (01/31/94) • **88**

Chambertin-Clos de Bèze 1990: Impressively concentrated, packed with bright flavors. Shows ripe fruit, smoke and earth notes on the extremely long finish. An exciting wine that takes off like a rocket. Drinkable in 1998. 450 cases made. • $135 • (12/15/92) • **95**

Chambertin-Clos de Bèze 1989 • $135 • (01/31/92) • **93**

Chambertin-Clos de Bèze 1988 • $188 • (05/15/91) • **95**

Charmes-Chambertin 1985 • $63 • (10/15/88) • **86**

Clos de la Roche 1992: Smooth and delicate, with a nice core of blackberry and floral aromas and flavors that echo on the appealing finish. Harmonious, should be at its best after 1996. • $NA • **88**

Clos de la Roche 1991: Lithe, elegant and lean, lovely raspberry flavors up front edge toward currant and vanilla on the long, long finish. Not as concentrated as it could be, but stylish and persistant. • $75 • (01/31/94) • **89**

Clos de la Roche 1990: A round, rich, ripe and intense wine that delivers grace and pleasure, with plum, berry and smoke aromas and flavors. Drinkable in 1997. • $78 • (12/15/92) • **92**

Clos de la Roche 1988 • $75 • (05/15/91) • **91**

Gevrey-Chambertin 1989 • $NA • (01/31/92) • **88**

Gevrey-Chambertin Le Clos St.-Jacques 1992: Firm and chewy, spicy, with a little ripe currant flavor lurking in the background. Drinkable now. • $NA • **78**

Gevrey-Chambertin Le Clos St.-Jacques 1991: A light, uncomplicated, lean mouthful of red raspberry and red currant flavors, with a light bite of tannin on the finish. Drinkable now. • $75 • (01/31/94) • **82**

Gevrey-Chambertin Le Clos St.-Jacques 1990: A supple 1990, with a firm core of solid tannins and enough fruit to compensate for the tannic backbone. A well-integrated wine, with lots of raspberry, mushroom and wet earth flavors. Drinkable in 1997. • $85 • (12/15/92) • **90**

Gevrey-Chambertin Le Clos St.-Jacques 1989 • $95 • (01/31/92) • **90**

Gevrey-Chambertin Le Clos St.-Jacques 1985 • $85 • (10/15/88) • **92**

Mazis-Chambertin Mazy Chambertin 1992: Very light and floral, with a touch of raspberry and strawberry flavor sneaking in on the palate. The finish picks up a little, suggesting that 1997 or 1998 would be about right. • $NA • **82**

Mazis-Chambertin Mazy Chambertin 1991: Supple and exotic, a mouthful of wild berry, black cherry, spice and earth notes comes together into an opulent, toasty finish. A graceful wine that cascades its flavors seductively, then hits the tannin mark on the finish. Needs until 1997 or '98. • $75 • (01/31/94) • **90**

Mazis-Chambertin Mazy-Chambertin 1990: Ripe and chewy, with concentrated plum, black cherry and toast characteristics and a gorgeous finish. A monster wine that needs time to come around, try in 1999. • $75 • (12/15/92) • **93**

Mazis-Chambertin Mazy-Chambertin 1989 • $80 • (01/31/92) • **90**

Mazis-Chambertin Mazy-Chambertin 1985 • $63 • (10/15/88) • **85**

Ruchottes-Chambertin Clos des Ruchottes 1992: Lean and very light with a pleasant ring of raspberry and hints of black cherry. Tannins are hardly present. Drinkable already, but better in 1997. Tasted twice. • $NA • **84**

Ruchottes-Chambertin Clos des Ruchottes 1991: Lean and firm, opening out into a broad finish that rides a crescendo of currant, plum and blackberry flavors along with a few coffee and spice notes. Stylish and more intense than most '91s. • $NA • (01/31/94) • **89**

Ruchottes-Chambertin Clos des Ruchottes 1990: A well-toned monster, with a huge amount of ripe raspberry, cherry and earth aromas and flavors and tons of refined tannins. Goes on and on and on. A wine to welcome in the new century. • $80 • (12/15/92) • **96**

Ruchottes-Chambertin Clos des Ruchottes 1989 • $85 • (01/31/92) • **90**

ROUSSEAU, JEANNE

Beaujolais 1994: This light red offers ripe strawberry and cherry flavors, it's soft and simple. A pleasant quaff. Try it chilled. • $7 • (06/15/95) • **78**

Pouilly-Fuissé 1994: Solid white that offers lemon, apricot and pie-crust flavors in a crisp, delicate package. It's clean and tangy. • $13 • (06/30/95) • **83**

Key: SS—Spectator Selection. CS—Cellar Selection. BB—Best Buy. $NA—Price not available. (BT)—Barrel tasting. Ⓐ—Auction Price.
Dates in parentheses represent the issues in which the ratings were published.

ROUSSELLE, CHÂTEAU LA

Fronsac 1990: Hard and steely, a wine with an excellent backbone of sharp tannins but a little thin in fruit. • $NA • (03/31/93) • **83**

ROUTAS, CHÂTEAU

Agrippa Coteaux Varois 1992: A rich wine vivid with heat and extract. Firm tannins structure ripe plum, black pepper and minty flavors; it's concentrated but rustic. Drinkable now. 500 cases made. • $11 • (06/30/94) • **86**

Coteaux Varois 1993: Fresh and grapey, seems barely out of the cradle, yet it's balanced and firm enough to marry well with simple food. 4,000 cases made. • $7 • (11/30/94) • **82**

Coteaux Varois 1992: After an earthy note blows off, the wine shows herbal and black pepper flavors, medium body and soft tannins. It's accessible, but doesn't make much of a statement. 3,000 cases made. • $7 • **82**

Infernet Coteaux Varois 1993: Clean, lively and gutsy, with nice bright fruit flavors and a crisp, moderately tannic texture. Has an appealing, appetizing sense of balance. 3,500 cases made. • $11 • (03/31/95) • **85**

Infernet Coteaux Varois 1992: A straightforward wine with firm tannins, this has muscle but lacks breadth despite its concentration. The flavors are blackberry, smoke and grape jam. Drinkable now. 5,000 cases made. • $8 • (06/30/94) • **83**

Lilli Coteaux Varois 1992: Modest raspberry and vanilla flavors come together to make for an oaky rosé. Dry and flavorful but not particularly complex. Try it with salad. 500 cases made. • $10 • (06/30/94) • **81**

Luc Sorin Coteaux Varois 1993: Extremely intense, tannic and oaky, from the cedary aromas to the chocolate, vanilla and black cherry flavors and woody, lingering finish. Try after 1996. 2,000 cases made. • $15 • (03/31/95) • **87**

Luc Sorin Coteaux Varois 1992: So silky and polished it seems almost thin at first, but then the rich tannins, black cherry and licorice flavors come through. A blend of Cabernet Sauvignon and Syrah. 1,000 cases made. • $11 • (06/30/94) • **87**

Pyramus Coteaux Varois 1993: A spicy white, with modest green apple and fig flavors. Straightforward and refreshing, with a fairly alcoholic finish. 800 cases made. • $8 • (11/30/94) • **83**

Pyramus Coteaux Varois 1992: Appealingly fruity with nice pear and apple flavors and a touch of lemon. Lush and viscous, with a hint of earthiness in the aroma. A pleasant balance of fruit and body. A good picnic wine. 3,000 cases made. • $8 • (09/15/94) • **83**

Rouvière Coteaux Varois 1993: A simple rosé with modest berry flavors and an astringent finish. Herbal notes dominate the aroma. Drink with food. 3,000 cases made. • $7 • **79**

Rouvière Coteaux Varois 1992: Spicy with strawberry and raspberry flavors, but in a typically austere style. No hint of sugar in this rosé, while well balanced, the flavors aren't particularly powerful. 8,000 cases made. • $7 • **83**

ROUVIER SELECTIONS

Côte-Rôtie 1990: Ripe, with floral, raspberry and vanilla flavors, it's full and long, firm and very well balanced. Try now. • $30 • (05/31/94) • **89**

Crozes-Hermitage 1991 • $12 • (05/31/94) • **85**

ROUX, ARMAND

Bordeaux Verdillac 1989 • $7 • (01/31/92) • **71**

Bordeaux Verdillac 1988 • $6 • (07/15/90) BB • **79**

Brut Blanc de Blancs Carousel NV: This tastes good but light from the creamy aromas to the vanilla and tutti-frutti flavors to the short finish. 100,000 cases made. • $8 • **82**

Côtes du Lubéron Red La Forge 1989 • $6 • (04/15/93) BB • **80**

Côtes du Rhône La Berberine 1994: Fresh and fruity, almost like Beaujolais with its abundant berry flavors accented by black pepper. It has light tannins and should be drunk while it's fresh. 10,000 cases made. • $8 • (12/31/95) • **83**

Côtes du Rhône La Berberine 1988 • $7 • (10/31/90) BB • **81**

Echézeaux 1959 • $110 • (08/31/90) • **94**

Picpoul de Pinet Coteaux du Languedoc 1994: An assertive wine that offers flavors of almonds, smoke and figs and a tart, acidic core. It has personality without refinement. 50,000 cases made. • $7 • (02/29/96) • **80**

Richebourg 1959 • $130 • (08/31/90) • **91**

Volnay Hospices de Beaune Général Muteau 1959 • $115 • (08/31/90) • **91**

ROUX PERE & FILS

Chardonnay Bourgogne 1994: Subtle yet intense. It's restrained but what's there is focused: spice, butter, melon and toasted pine nuts. Lovely, long, clean and focused finish. 3,333 cases made. • $NA • (05/31/96) • **87**

Chassagne-Montrachet 1994: Nicely structured, smooth and ripe on the palate, offering good pineapple, honey, mineral and citrus flavors in nice proportions. 375 cases made. • $NA • (05/31/96) 85 • **85**

Chassagne-Montrachet 1993: Riper and richer than most, providing honey, woody, apple-tart flavors. Made in an accessible, creamy style, but could show more concentration. Drink now. 417 cases made. • $28 • **84**

Chassagne-Montrachet Red Clos St.-Jean 1983 • $13 • (09/16/85) • **86**

Meursault Clos des Poruzots 1994: Packed with reductive, dry ice aromas, it gets better as it airs, developing some vanilla and mineral notes that are very seductive. Full-bodied and silky, with intense lime on the finish. Not for everyone, but enjoyable. 125 cases made. • $NA • (05/31/96) • **84**

Puligny-Montrachet Les Enseignères 1994: Light body, modest fruit flavors, it manages a certain understated harmony until the astringent finish. 208 cases made. • $NA • (05/31/96) • **76**

Puligny-Montrachet Les Enseignères 1993: Quite tough, but offering some decent, ripe honey, green apple and mineral notes. Long, earth-tasting finish. Drinkable now. 333 cases made. • $28 • **85**

St.-Aubin White La Chatenière 1992: Rich and smooth, with some honey, walnut and apple flavors, quite lush in texture, but we could only wish for a bit more fruit intensity in this enjoyable white Burgundy. • $NA • (08/31/94) • **84**

St.-Aubin White Les Cortons 1994: Assertive and crisp, with some honey, almond and cedar aromas and flavors. Fresh and juicy, though it may strike some as a touch hollow in the mid-palate. 833 cases made. • $NA • (05/31/96) • **83**

St.-Aubin White Les Cortons 1993: Candied, cooked apple taste and some toasty, wet hay character. Sour finish, oxidized? 667 cases made. • $21 • **77**

St.-Aubin White Les Cortons 1992: Nice, modest white Burgundy with subtle pear, vanilla, butter and walnut flavors and a very smooth, pleasant texture. • $NA • (08/31/94) • **82**

St.-Aubin White Les Pucelles 1994: Rustic, tart and simple, with modest fruit flavors and a lean finish. 2,000 cases made. • $NA • **73**

Santenay 1985 • $21 • (10/31/87) • **83**

Volnay En Champans 1988 • $35 • (03/31/90) • **86**

Volnay En Champans 1985 • $25 • (03/15/87) • **92**

ROUX, CHARLES

Côtes du Rhône-Villages Rasteau 1985 • $10 • (02/28/90) • **89**

ROY PERE & FILS

Gevrey-Chambertin Clos Prieur 1988 • $35 • (12/31/90) • **68**

Gevrey-Chambertin Vieilles Vignes 1988 • $30 • (12/31/90) • **72**

ROYER, CHARLES

Brut Champagne Sélections de Propriétaires NV • $NA • (12/31/91) • **84**

ROYES, DOMAINE DES

St.-Joseph 1991 • $NA • (05/31/94) • **78**

RUDEL, COMTE DE

Entre-Deux-Mers 1993: Some decent pear and apple aromas and flavors, but fading slightly on the palate. • $9 • **79**

FRANCE

RUET

Brouilly Cuvée Spéciale 1993: Sweet fruit tastes a bit stewed, plenty of spice and even raisin flavors, but the finish is tart. Lacks balance. • $15 • (06/15/95) • **78**

RUINART

Brut Blanc de Blancs Champagne 1988: An assertive style with ripe flavors. Fairly rich and buttery, with toast and honey to boot. Lively, with apple and pineapple flavors and a good finish. Fresh for its age. 600 cases made. • $80 • **87**

Brut Blanc de Blancs Champagne Dom Ruinart 1988: A fully mature style of Champagne that smells earthy and nutty, tastes creamy and custardlike. It's fun to drink now for its abundance of flavor, but we wouldn't cellar it. • $93 • (12/15/95) • **87**

Brut Blanc de Blancs Champagne Dom Ruinart 1986: Super rich and toasty Champagne in an elegant and refined style. Full-bodied with apple, vanilla and lemon character, intense acidity and a medium finish. Drink now. • $83 • (12/31/93) • **90**

Brut Blanc de Blancs Champagne Dom Ruinart 1985 • $83 • (12/31/93) • **95**

Brut Blanc de Blancs Champagne Dom Ruinart 1983 • $60 • (12/31/90) • **87**

Brut Blanc de Blancs Champagne Dom Ruinart 1982 • $61 • (12/31/90) • **90**

Brut Blanc de Blancs Champagne Dom Ruinart 1981 • $61 • (12/31/89) • **90**

Brut Blanc de Blancs Champagne Dom Ruinart 1979 • $39 • (10/31/86) • **91**

Brut Blanc de Blancs Champagne Dom Ruinart 1978 • $40 • (05/16/86) • **87**

Brut Blanc de Blancs Champagne Dom Ruinart 1976 • $30 • (10/01/84) • **84**

Brut Champagne 1988: Seriously rich Champagne with structure and flavor of a Meursault. Fine bubbles and acidity and a long flavorful finish. Powerful and rich. Drinkable now. • $46 • (12/31/93) • **92**

Brut Champagne 1986: Another very rich and ripe wine with a fine foamy texture, toasted, vanilla, apple flavors, medium body and a long fresh finish. Tasted twice. Drink now. • $46 • (12/31/93) • **87**

Brut Champagne NV: A beautifully complex aroma of toast, nuts, figs and bread dough make this especially intriguing. It is dry, lean and crisp, but picks up again on the finish, showing lingering, creamy, mature flavors. 3,500 cases made. • $30 • **89**

Brut Champagne R de Ruinart 1988: This is wonderfully mature and complex, from the smoky, nutty aromas through the lingering, subtle finish. It's a bit austere in texture, but makes up for it in the intriguing, elegant blend of fruit and mature flavors—a rare quality and a pleasant find. Great to drink now, or cellar through 1998. • $50 • **94**

Brut Champagne R de Ruinart NV: Here is a great white wine that happens to be bubbly. It has terrific fruit flavors accented by intriguing coffee, vanilla, tobacco and mushroom notes, all wrapped in one smooth-textured, full-bodied package. A bold style that would go well with dinner. • $37 • **91**

Brut Rosé Champagne NV: Generous, flavorful, fruity and complex. This rosé has toasty, buttery aromas, cherry flavors and a dry but lingering finish. 150 cases made. • $56 • **86**

Brut Rosé Champagne Dom Ruinart 1986: A flavorful, mature bubbly that combines distinctive Pinot Noir character with nuances of age. Slightly sweet and round, with a spicy, peachy finish. • $109 • (12/15/95) • **87**

Brut Rosé Champagne Dom Ruinart 1985: Easy-going, smooth and mouth-filling, with a creamy texture and flavors of pear, apple and cherry. It has the toasty, doughy, almond nuances that we look for in an aged bubbly. 200 cases made. • $96 • (12/15/94) • **89**

Brut Rosé Champagne Dom Ruinart 1979 • $80 • (09/30/88) • **92**

Brut Rosé Champagne Dom Ruinart 1978 • $40 • (09/30/86) • **91**

Brut Rosé Champagne Dom Ruinart 1976 • $60 • (12/16/85) • **61**

Brut Rosé Champagne R de Ruinart NV: Beautifully mature and suave, showing the benefits of age without giving up the lively texture and well-defined fruit flavors of youth. Spicy, slightly earthy and lingers on aftertaste. • $59 • **86**

RULLY, CHÂTEAU DE

Rully White 1994: A solid village wine with a crisp core of lemon, pear, wet earth and ripe apple flavors, though it seems a bit green on the finish. Drinkable through 1997. From Antonin Rodet. • $20 • (05/31/96) • **81**

SABON & FILS, DOMAINE ROGER

Châteauneuf-du-Pape 1988 • $20 • (09/30/90) • **88**

Châteauneuf-du-Pape Cuvée Prestige 1988 • $23 • (09/30/90) • **85**

Châteauneuf-du-Pape Cuvée Réserve 1988 • $20 • (09/30/90) • **80**

Côtes du Rhône 1989 • $12 • (11/15/91) • **70**

Côtes du Rhône 1988 • $11 • (10/31/90) • **79**

SABONITE, LA

Vin de Table Français Red NV • $5 • (09/30/88) BB • **85**

SADE, MARQUIS DE

Brut Blanc de Blancs Champagne NV: Fruity, with nice accents of toast and fig. A good, Chardonnay-like aroma with a crisp, citrusy finish. Balanced and refreshing. • $NA • **87**

Brut Blanc de Blancs Champagne Grand Cru NV • $35 • (03/31/92) • **85**

Brut Champagne NV: An assertive, bold style, with toasty, earthy, doughy aromas and toasted-almond and butter flavors. A bit rough-textured, though, and short on the finish. • $25 • **82**

Brut Champagne Private Réserve 1988: Spicy and aromatic, with yeasty flavors and aromas. Aggressive at first, but it settles down, with pleasant butter, toast and almond notes. Firm and well balanced, with a citrusy finish. • $NA • **88**

Brut Champagne Private Réserve 1985: The simple, lemony aromas and flavors have intensity, but little finesse. There's rosemary on the finish, making the wine a little odd. • $48 • (03/31/92) • **79**

Brut Champagne Private Réserve 1981 • $56 • (12/31/90) • **89**

SAGET, GUY

Pouilly-Fumé Les Loges 1992: Buttery and spicy with plump fruit that shows a touch of oak. It's soft and sunny, but lacks the nervy acidity that usually characterizes this appellation. 10,000 cases made. • $11 • (10/31/94) • **84**

Sancerre Sélection Première Vieilles Vignes 1992: Toasty, vanilla aromas and rich, buttery flavors. Underneath, the flavors show citrus and herbal notes and crisp acidity. It's a solid, well-made wine with intense, attractive flavors. Some will argue that it's not Sancerre. 5,000 cases made. • $12 • (10/31/94) • **87**

SAIER

Clos des Lambrays 1990: An earthy wine, with tart, leafy mineral and limestone flavors that dominate more than the black cherry notes. Tight and firm. Drinkable now. 1,750 cases made. • $73 • (03/15/93) • **80**

Clos des Lambrays 1989 • $68 • (11/15/91) • **85**

Clos des Lambrays 1988 • $75 • (03/31/91) • **91**

Clos des Lambrays Domaine des Lambrays 1985 • $55 • (02/15/88) • **78**

Mercurey Les Champs Martins 1988 • $17 • (08/31/91) • **80**

Mercurey Les Champs Martins 1985 • $20 • (03/31/88) • **83**

Mercurey Les Chenelots 1988 • $17 • (04/30/91) • **67**

ST.-ANDRE, CHÂTEAU

Châteauneuf-du-Pape 1988 • $16 • (11/30/90) • **87**

Key: SS—Spectator Selection. CS—Cellar Selection. BB—Best Buy. $NA—Price not available. (BT)—Barrel tasting. (A)—Auction Price.
Dates in parentheses represent the issues in which the ratings were published.

ST.-ANDRE-CORBIN, CHÂTEAU

St.-Georges-St.-Emilion 1995: Muscular berry and cassis aromas and flavors, loads of coarse tannins and thick, oily texture. • $NA • (05/15/96) • **80-84** (BT)

St.-Georges-St.-Emilion 1994: Not too serious but soft, supple and delicious, offering crushed red berries and a fresh finish. • $NA • **80-84** (BT)

St.-Georges-St.-Emilion 1993: Slightly rough red berry, metallic, steely character and a dry, lean finish. • $15 • (01/31/96) • **77**

St.-Georges-St.-Emilion 1990: A big, velvety wine, with loads of berry and cherry character, soft tannins and a lingering aftertaste of berries. Drinkable in 1997. • $15 • (03/31/93) • **88**

St.-Georges-St.-Emilion 1989 • $15 • (04/30/92) • **91**

St.-Georges-St.-Emilion 1986 • $22 • (03/31/90) • **77**

ST.-AURIOL, CHÂTEAU

Corbières 1991 • $10 • (03/15/94) • **82**

ST.-BONNET, CHÂTEAU

Médoc 1985 • $6 • (04/15/88) • **79**

ST.-CESAIRE

Vin de Pays des Bouches-du-Rhône NV • $4 • (06/30/90) • **72**

ST.-CHARLES, DOMAINE

Beaujolais-Villages Château du Bluizard 1988 • $8 • (11/15/90) BB • **82**

ST.-CHRISTOPHE, CHÂTEAU

Médoc 1985 • $6 • (07/31/88) BB • **82**

ST.-DESIRAT, CAVE DE

St.-Joseph 1992: Interesting notes of licorice and toasted nuts give this wine character, but dry tannins dominate the light cherry fruit. Drinkable now, but a bit lean. 8,000 cases made. • $14 • **78**

Syrah Vin de Pays des Collines Rhodaniens 1993: Smells just like black pepper and tastes light and green. Drinkable, but too lean. 8,000 cases made. • $8 • (07/31/95) • **76**

ST.-ESTEVE, CHÂTEAU

Corbières 1992 • $6 • **80**

ST.-ESTEVE D'UCHAUX, CHÂTEAU

Côtes du Rhône 1989 • $9 • (11/15/91) • **80**

Côtes du Rhône Grand Réserve 1989 • $12 • (11/15/91) • **83**

Côtes du Rhône-Villages 1989 • $10 • (11/15/91) • **84**

ST.-EULALIE, DOMAINE

Minervois 1992: Cherry and earthy flavors mingle in this soft, supple wine. It's accessible, but lacks spark. Drink now. • $8 • **78**

Minervois 1991 • $9 • (03/15/94) • **82**

ST.-FLORIN, CHÂTEAU

Entre-Deux-Mers 1993: It smells earthy, tastes vegetal and watery. Very simple. • $7 • (02/29/96) • **75**

ST.-GAYAN, DOMAINE

Côtes du Rhône 1988 • $8 • (10/31/90) • **75**

Côtes du Rhône 1985 • $6 • (04/30/88) • **75**

ST.-GEORGES, CHÂTEAU

St.-Georges-St.-Emilion 1990: Offers plenty of ripe, concentrated, stewed plum flavors in a style that is rustic and slightly astringent. The finish is long. • $23 • (08/31/95) • **86**

St.-Georges-St.-Emilion 1988 • $18 • (04/30/92) • **73**

St.-Georges-St.-Emilion 1986 • $14 • (07/15/90) • **87**

St.-Georges-St.-Emilion 1985 • $11 • (07/31/89) • **87**

ST.-GEORGES, DOMAINE

Corbières 1990 • $8 • (03/15/94) • **82**

Corbières Grand Millésime 1990 • $8 • (06/15/93) • **73**

Corbières Grand Millésime Elevé en Fûts de Chêne 1988 • $8 • (07/15/92) • **81**

ST.-JAMES, CHÂTEAU

Corbières 1992 • $8 • (03/15/94) • **80**

Viognier Vin de Pays d'Oc 1992 • $13 • (03/15/94) • **88**

ST.-JEAN DE L'ARBORISIER, DOMAINE

Coteaux du Languedoc 1992 • $NA • (03/15/94) • **84**

ST.-JOVIAN

Bordeaux 1985 • $4 • (05/15/88) • **75**

Bordeaux Supérieur 1988 • $5 • (07/31/91) BB • **80**

Cabernet Sauvignon Bordeaux 1986 • $4 • (07/31/88) • **78**

Merlot Bordeaux 1986 • $5 • (05/15/89) • **76**

ST.-LAURENT, CHÂTEAU

Corbières Réserve Privée 1991 • $7 • (06/15/93) • **78**

ST.-LAURENT-L'ABBAYE, DOMAINE DE

Pouilly-Fumé 1994: Fresh apple and pear flavors keep this wine user-friendly, it's ripe and round, without aggressive acidity. A pleasant apéritif wine for drinking now. • $17 • **83**

ST.-LOUIS, DOMAINE

Chardonnay Vin de Pays d'Oc 1991 • $9 • (03/15/94) • **87**

Syrah Vin de Pays d'Oc 1992 • $7 • (03/15/94) • **82**

ST.-LUC, DOMAINE

Coteaux du Tricastin 1993: Fruity, generous and simply delicious. This medium-bodied red goes down easily because of its light tannins and ample cherry and berry flavors. • $8 • (12/31/95) • **84**

Coteaux du Tricastin 1989 • $7 • (12/31/91) BB • **83**

Coteaux du Tricastin 1988 • $11 • (08/31/91) • **77**

Coteaux du Tricastin White 1994: A very dry white wine that's clean, but has a sweet-tart balance. The fruit cocktail flavors are supported by firm acidity. • $9 • (12/31/95) • **79**

Syrah Coteaux du Tricastin Elevé en Fût de Chêne 1993: A gutsy, flavorful little red with focused fruit flavors and enough spicy, earthy nuances to make it interesting. Moderately tannic, but drink soon for its freshness. • $14 • (12/31/95) • **85**

ST.-MARC, CHÂTEAU

Barsac 1987 • $NA • (06/15/90) • **69**

ST.-MARTIN DE LA GARRIGUE, DOMAINE

Coteaux du Languedoc 1992 • $10 • (03/15/94) • **85**

ST.-PIERRE, LES CAVES

Châteauneuf-du-Pape Clefs des Prelats 1988 • $13 • (01/31/91) • **87**
Côte-Rôtie Marquis de Tournelles 1987 • $23 • (01/31/91) • **84**
Côtes du Rhône-Villages Les Lissandres 1988 • $7 • (12/15/90) BB • **84**
Hermitage Tertre des Carmes 1988 • $23 • (12/31/90) • **88**

ST.-PIERRE, CHÂTEAU

St.-Julien 1995: Big, rich, full-bodied blockbuster, with loads of fruit and toasted oak complexity. Very powerful, yet super silky and concentrated. This is well made. • $NA • (05/15/96) • **90-94** (BT)
St.-Julien 1994: Some pretty fruit here as well as fine tannins and pronounced, toasted oak. • $26 • (05/15/96) • **80-84** (BT)
St.-Julien 1993: Pleasant red berry and cherry character, medium body, medium to light tannins and fresh finish. Drinkable now. • $22 • (01/31/96) • **85**
St.-Julien 1992: Quite a mouthful of tobacco and plum flavor, medium-bodied and ripe, ending in a long, velvety finish. Drink now. • $18 • **87**
St.-Julien 1991: Well crafted, with a solid core of fruit. It doesn't show much now, but the blackberry flavor marries nicely with the oak. Drinkable now. • $17 • (03/31/94) • **84**
St.-Julien 1990: Made in a restrained style, but there's gorgeous fruit with chocolate, berry and plum character and compact, velvety tannins. Drinkable in 1997. 8,000 cases made. • $26 • (03/31/93) • **92**
St.-Julien 1989 • $21 Ⓐ • (10/15/92) • **91**
St.-Julien 1988 • $27 • (10/15/92) • **88**
St.-Julien 1987 • $17 • (10/15/92) • **80**
St.-Julien 1986 • $24 • (10/15/92) • **90**
St.-Julien 1985 • $23 • (10/15/92) • **87**
St.-Julien 1984 • $12 • (10/15/92) • **79**
St.-Julien 1983 • $24 • **79**
St.-Julien 1982 • $28 • (10/15/92) • **83**
St.-Julien 1981 • $24 • **86**
St.-Julien 1979 • $24 • (10/15/92) • **77**
St.-Julien 1978 • $28 • (10/15/92) • **83**
St.-Julien 1975 • $20 • (10/15/92) • **72**
St.-Julien 1970 • $45 • (10/15/92) • **84**
St.-Julien 1969 • $15 • (10/15/92) • **70**
St.-Julien 1962 • $55 • (10/15/92) • **72**
St.-Julien 1961 • $95 • (10/15/92) • **74**
St.-Julien 1959 • $90 • (10/15/92) • **75**

ST.-ROBERT, CHÂTEAU

Graves White Cuvée Poncet-Deville 1992: Impressive toasted oak, honey, lemon and light tropical fruit flavors, medium-bodied and round with a long, intensely flavored finish. Drinkable now. • $NA • **85**

ST.-SAUVEUR, DOMAINE

Côtes du Ventoux 1990 • $6 • (08/31/92) • **79**
Côtes du Ventoux 1988 • $4 • (10/15/91) BB • **83**
Muscat de Beaumes-de-Venise Vin Doux Naturel 1988 • $17 • (03/31/91) • **80**

ST.-SEVE, CHÂTEAU

Médoc 1985 • $6 • (11/15/87) • **70**

ST.-SULPICE, CHÂTEAU

Bordeaux 1988 • $7 • (08/31/91) BB • **81**
Bordeaux 1982 • $6 • (05/15/87) • **73**

Key: SS—Spectator Selection. CS—Cellar Selection. BB—Best Buy. $NA—Price not available. (BT)—Barrel tasting. Ⓐ—Auction Price.
Dates in parentheses represent the issues in which the ratings were published.

STE.-ANNE, DOMAINE

Bordeaux 1987 • $5 • (05/15/90) • **77**
Côtes du Rhône-Villages Cuvée Notre-Dame des Cellettes 1987 • $7 • (01/31/89) • **80**
Syrah Côtes du Rhône 1990 • $20 • (04/15/93) • **82**

STE.-MAIRE, CHÂTEAU

Entre-Deux-Mers Cuvée Madlys 1993: Clean, lively and straightforward, displaying a buttery note that softens the citrusy edge. • $10 • **80**

STE.-PAULE, DOMAINE

Corbières 1990 • $9 • (03/15/94) • **83**

STE.-TULALIE, DOMAINE

Minervois 1991 • $NA • (03/15/94) • **85**

SALENTE, DOMAINE DE

Sauvignon Vin de Pays d'Oc 1992 • $NA • (03/15/94) • **84**
Vin de Pays d'Oc Cuvée Spéciale 1990 • $NA • (03/15/94) • **85**
Viognier Vin de Pays d'Oc 1992 • $NA • (03/15/94) • **82**

SALES, CHÂTEAU DE

Pomerol 1995: Lovely, soft tannins and plenty of chocolate and berry character. Fresh, subtle finish. • $NA • (05/15/96) • **85-89** (BT)
Pomerol 1986 • $23 • (06/30/89) • **86**
Pomerol 1985 • $22 • (06/30/88) • **87**
Pomerol 1982 • $32 Ⓐ • (05/15/89) • **88**

SALLE DE COEURS

Cabernet Sauvignon Vin de Pays d'Oc 1994: A tough wine. Earthy notes dominate the black cherry flavors, and hard tannins overwhelm the fruit. It has concentration but lacks polish, try decanting well in advance of serving. 5,000 cases made. • $8 • **77**
Merlot Vin de Pays d'Oc 1994: Ripe plum, meat and tomato flavors offer roundness without much stuffing, and a lean streak of tannin dominates the finish. Best accompanying food. 5,000 cases made. • $8 • (10/31/95) • **81**

SALLE DE POUJEAUX, CHÂTEAU LA

Moulis 1989 • $15 • (03/15/92) • **85**

SALON

Brut Blanc de Blancs Champagne Le Mesnil 1983: Elegant and firm, with lemon and grapefruit flavors that are balanced by a luscious, creamy texture. It's still crisp and lively for an aged Champagne and has a long, delicate finish. Drink now or cellar through 1997. • $NA • (11/30/94) • **93**
Brut Blanc de Blancs Champagne Le Mesnil 1982: Every time we taste this wine with love it even more. High volume, high intensity wine. They pulled out all the stops to get the most fruit and vanilla flavors, fine acidity and long finish. At its peak. A Cellar Selection in December 1991. Drink now. 4,000 cases made. • $100 • (12/31/93) • **95**
Brut Blanc de Blancs Champagne Le Mesnil 1979 • $108 • (12/31/88) • **92**
Brut Blanc de Blancs Champagne Le Mesnil 1976 • $110/1.5L • (12/31/88) • **91**

SALVARD, DOMAINE DU

Cheverny White 1993: A charming, light, fragrant wine with floral, spicy aromas, ripe fruit flavors and a clean finish. 5,400 cases made. • $9 • **82**

FRANCE

Cheverny White 1992: This is lean and aggressive, with pine and grapefruit flavors and a very dry finish plus a hint of earthiness. If you like it austere, this is your style. 600 cases made. • $9 • (10/31/94) • **78**

SANG DES CAILLOUX, DOMAINE LE

Vacqueyras 1993: Deep color, inviting aromas and thick tannins, a robust, hearty young Rhône. Peppery, tobaccolike flavors linger on aftertaste. Needs time to soften. Tasted twice, with consistent notes. 6,000 cases made. • $13 • (09/30/95) • **86**

Vacqueyras 1990 • $12 • (04/15/93) • **83**

SANTA DUC, DOMAINE

Côtes du Rhône 1990 • $11 • (04/15/93) • **78**

Gigondas 1990 • $21 • (04/15/93) • **80**

SARDA-MALET, DOMAINE

Côtes du Roussillon 1986 • $7 • (10/15/90) • **60**

SARTRE, CHÂTEAU LE

Pessac-Léognan 1995: Shows some pretty fruit and texture, but it's a bit lighter than some in this group, with an herbaceous character that makes it somewhat disjointed. • $NA • (05/15/96) • **75-79** (BT)

Pessac-Léognan 1993: Good cherry, berry and chocolate aromas and flavors, medium body and tannins and a crisp finish. Better in 1997. • $18 • (01/31/96) • **84**

Pessac-Léognan 1992: Short and lean but has a certain elegance, delivering berry, dried-herb and mineral flavor. Drink now. • $14 • **79**

Pessac-Léognan 1991: Round and delicate, with black olive and herbal notes, medium body, but diluted on the finish. • $14 • (03/31/94) • **77**

Pessac-Léognan 1990: An elegant wine, with perfumed berry aromas and fine fruit and tannins. Drinkable now. 2,000 cases made. • $19 • (03/31/93) • **87**

Pessac-Léognan White 1994: Lovely, full-bodied white, with a chalky, buttery, earthy character. Quite soft, smooth and accessible now. Shows smoky pear and mineral notes on the long, toasty finish. • $18 • (03/31/96) • **90**

Pessac-Léognan White 1993: Fresh, exotic, wild gooseberry and vanilla aromas and flavors, medium body and a long, zingy, dried apricot finish. From the makers of Château Carbonnieux. Drink now. • $13 • (05/31/95) • **88**

Pessac-Léognan White 1992: Well balanced, displaying fresh lemon and apple flavor, medium acidity and a crisp finish. Drink now. • $NA • **82**

SAUGERE, LYLIANE

Côte-Rôtie La Colline d'Argent 1991: Nicely balanced and harmonious, smooth-textured and keeps the tannins well modulated, offering berry and spice flavors. Drinkable now. 1,100 cases made. • $27 • (05/31/94) • **86**

Hermitage 1992: Ripe and chunky, showing good ripeness for the vintage, sweet plum, earth and black pepper flavors and muscular tannins. Gutsy, it matches well with grilled beef. Drink now through 1999. • $32 • **86**

Hermitage 1991: Ripe and luscious, this shows classic Syrah flavors of spice, licorice and game, plenty of ripe blackberry on the palate and a healthy dollop of new oak which adds complexity. Still very young and tannic, it will benefit from time in the bottle. Try in 1997. • $32 • **90**

Hermitage La Côte des Seigneurs 1990: A tough, sturdy and hard-edged young wine that's backward and closed, but once the spicy, leathery, black cherry and mineral flavors begin to emerge, it's gorgeous. The tannins are substantial, but also fine and balanced. Hands off until 1997 to 2000. 660 cases made. • $26 • (04/15/94) • **91**

SAULT, DOMAINE DU

Corbières 1988 • $5 • (07/15/92) • **78**

SAUMAIZE-MICHELIN, ROGER

Mâcon-Villages Les Sertaux 1993: Rather fat and heavy-handed, tasting of caramel, butter, pear, cream and lemon. Somewhat simple and dull on the finish. • $NA • **76**

Pouilly-Fuissé Clos de la Roche 1994: An elegant white that has pineapple flavors mingling harmoniously with the creamy texture. Subtle and crisp on the finish. Try in 1997. 750 cases made. • $NA • (05/31/96) • **84**

Pouilly-Fuissé Les Ronchevats 1994: Bursting with citrus and lime flavors, but it manages to stay nicely focused. An uncompromising, crisp style that should be wonderful with fish. A touch of mineral and honey on the finish. Drinkable now through 1998. 250 cases made. • $NA • (05/31/96) • **85**

SAUMAIZE, JACQUES

Pouilly-Fuissé La Roche 1994: Tasty and attractive, tasting almost like pear gelato, both creamy and fruity. Fresh and crisp, but not tart, on the lovely finish. Try with oysters or shellfish now through 1998. • $17 • (05/31/96) • **87**

Pouilly-Fuissé Vieilles Vignes 1994: Quite likeable and ready to drink, a straightforward white that has decent spice, citrus, apple and honey flavors. Turns creamy on the sweet-tasting finish. • $16 • (05/31/96) • **84**

SAUMAIZE, ROGER

Pouilly-Fuissé 1991 • $22 • (09/15/93) • **83**

Pouilly-Fuissé Clos de la Roche 1991 • $25 • (09/15/93) • **88**

Pouilly-Fuissé Les Ronchevats 1991 • $26 • (09/15/93) • **88**

Pouilly-Fuissé Vigne Blanche 1994: Nicely made, with a round, citrus-honey character. It's crisp and enjoyable now, but should be better in 1998. 1,000 cases made. • $NA • (05/31/96) • **85**

St.-Véran White 1993: Maturing fast. Tastes woody. Vanilla bean and butterscotch flavors seem flat and dull on the finish. • $NA • **77**

SAUTEJEAU, MARCEL

Muscadet de Sèvre et Maine Sur Lie Réserve 1992: Vanilla and butter flavors make this distinctive and much rounder and softer than most Muscadets, with accompanying honeydew and anise notes. Enough acidity here to keep it crisp. • $11 • (08/31/94) • **84**

SAUVAGE, CHÂTEAU

Premières Côtes de Bordeaux Red 1986 • $9 • (04/15/90) • **81**

SAUVION & FILS

Muscadet de Sèvre et Maine Sur Lie Carte d'Or 1995: The melon and marzipan flavors are balanced by moderate acidity, keeping this white fresh and lively. Enjoyable now. 25,000 cases made. • $7 • (05/15/96) • **84**

Muscadet de Sèvre et Maine Sur Lie Château du Cléray 1995: Fresh and crisp, showing a hint of creaminess on the palate. Melon and herb flavors linger on the finish. Just what to look for in a Muscadet. 10,000 cases made. • $9 • (05/15/96) • **85**

Muscadet de Sèvre et Maine Sur Lie Château du Cléray Réserve du Cléray 1994: Crisp in texture, clean and lemony in flavor. Just what you need to wash down some oysters or clams. Not a fancy wine, but a good mealtime drink. • $13 • (11/15/95) • **83**

Muscadet de Sèvre et Maine Sur Lie Sauvion du Cléray 1995: A ripe, exotic style, that delivers loads of peach and grilled almond aromas and flavors. Not typical perhaps, yet it makes a very intriguing value nonetheless. 18,000 cases made. • $7 • (05/15/96) BB • **86**

Muscadet de Sèvre et Maine Sur Lie Sauvion du Cléray 1994: Pleasant, but on the earthy side of the flavor spectrum. Its melon notes are rounded off by smoky nuances, crisp texture and clean, fruity finish. • $9 • (11/15/95) • **84**

SAUZET, DOMAINE ETIENNE

Bâtard-Montrachet 1993: Harmonious *grand cru*, with everything in the right place. Round, silky texture is backed up by firm acidity and nice amounts of honey, fruit and spicy-smoky flavors. Unusually ripe and honeyed for this vintage. Tempting now, better around 1997. • $123 • **90**

Bâtard-Montrachet 1992: This is tight and subtle for a *grand cru*, revealing its pear, honey and hazelnut flavors slowly as you sip it. Very elegant, balanced and harmonious, with no sharp edges but with a sense of restraint. Drinkable now. • $127 • (08/31/94) • **91**

Bâtard-Montrachet 1991 • $121 • (10/15/93) • **93**

Bienvenues-Bâtard-Montrachet 1993: Extremely well crafted, both subtle and powerful, the sort of wine that shows its pedigree from start to finish. Wonderfully concentrated, boasting a silky core and lots of mineral, pear and lightly toasted oak flavors. Superb. Can age for years. • $123 • **91**

Bienvenues-Bâtard-Montrachet 1992: All dressed up and ready for a night on the town. A very buttery, butterscotch-flavored white that's grand in scope, bold and rich in flavor and lingering on the finish. It's thick, almost sweet, yet balanced nicely with fruity, fresh acidity. Combines elegance and richness at the same time. • $127 • (08/31/94) • **94**

Chassagne-Montrachet 1993: Quite ripe, distinctive, silky texture. Mineral, pear and apple flavors come together nicely on the medium-long finish. Drinkable now. • $41 • **85**

Chevalier-Montrachet 1993: Complex aromas and flavors of straw, apple and mineral and a hint of spice. Medium- to full-bodied, long finish. Needs time. Try after 1996. 15 cases made. • $159 • **88**

Chevalier-Montrachet 1992: Substantial and ripe-tasting, full-bodied and bold, with peach and pear flavors, firm acidity and a vanilla note that lasts on the finish. Drinkable now through 1998. • $114 Ⓐ • (08/31/94) • **92**

Montrachet 1993: Subtle yet rich apple, honey, vanilla and cream aromas and flavors, medium body, firm acidity and a long finish. Better in 1997. • $220 • **90**

Puligny-Montrachet 1993: Flavorful and quite ripe honey, hazelnut and earth flavors are knitted nicely together. Medium-bodied, vibrant, long finish. • $42 • **86**

Puligny-Montrachet 1992: Clean, crisp and flavorful, this straightforward, medium-bodied Burgundy delivers decent tart lime, apple, and honey flavors. Try now. 2,150 cases made. • $46 • (08/31/94) • **84**

Puligny-Montrachet 1991 • $45 • (10/15/93) • **86**

Puligny-Montrachet Champ Canet 1993: Lots going on here: gorgeous texture of fruit and creamy acidity, medium-to-full body and honey, apple and mineral finish. • $68 • **88**

Puligny-Montrachet Champ Canet 1992: Bold and full of fruit flavor, this complex Puligny delivers a symphony of flavors, from pineapple and peach to vanilla, toast and hazelnut. Firm, almost chewy in texture, the richness lingering on the finish. Drinkable now. 560 cases made. • $68 • (08/31/94) • **93**

Puligny-Montrachet Champ-Canet 1991 • $64 • (10/15/93) • **90**

Puligny-Montrachet La Garenne 1993: Lovely balance of lemon, mineral and honey character. Medium-bodied, fresh finish. • $63 • **85**

Puligny-Montrachet La Garenne 1992: Exotic and tropical, with pineapple, guava and mango flavors mingling with the lime and apple notes. This medium-bodied white is ripe, soft and very appealing, showing enough crisp flavors to hold it all together on the medium-intense finish. • $62 • (08/31/94) • **88**

Puligny-Montrachet La Garenne 1991 • $58 • (10/15/93) • **93**

Puligny-Montrachet Les Combettes 1993: Round and rather rich, but also quite oaky, showing herb, spice and vanilla flavors and some chalky notes on the finish. Try after 1997. • $79 • **87**

Puligny-Montrachet Les Combettes 1992: Lively and rich, packed with ripe pineapple, pear and honey flavors. It makes for a deep, chewy-textured, fully ripe style of white Burgundy. Enjoy now for its opulence, or age through about 1997. 825 cases made. • $79 • (08/31/94) • **88**

Puligny-Montrachet Les Combettes 1991 • $74 • (10/15/93) • **90**

Key: SS—Spectator Selection. CS—Cellar Selection. BB—Best Buy. $NA—Price not available. (BT)—Barrel tasting. Ⓐ—Auction Price.
Dates in parentheses represent the issues in which the ratings were published.

Puligny-Montrachet Les Folatières 1993: Well-presented cream, apple and lemon character, medium-to-light body, firm acidity and a fresh finish. • $79 • **85**

Puligny-Montrachet Les Folatières 1992: Racy in character and built for aging. A firmly fruity and crisp Puligny with ample peach and pear flavors, a lively fresh finish and hints of butter and honey. • $68 • (08/31/94) • **91**

Puligny-Montrachet Les Referts 1993: Rich coconut, pear, and relatively ripe fruit character, medium-to-full body and fresh acidity on the finish. • $NA • **86**

Puligny-Montrachet Les Referts 1992: Butter and nut flavors add complexity to the basic tart apple flavors, for this straightforward and enjoyable Puligny. Leans toward the green side. 725 cases made. • $62 • (08/31/94) • **85**

Puligny-Montrachet Les Referts 1991 • $58 • (10/15/93) • **86**

SAVOYE, DOMAINE R.

Régnié 1994: Nice combination of fresh fruit and firm tannins is undercut by some dilution on the palate. It's straightforward but a bit dull. 2,000 cases made. • $9 • (10/31/95) • **81**

SCHLUMBERGER, DOMAINES

Gewürztraminer Alsace Fleur de Guebwiller 1991: Elegant and appealing, medium-bodied, vibrant. Nicely mature aromas and firm acidity, lively apricot and herb flavors linger and expand on the finish. 8,300 cases made. • $16 • **88**

Pinot Blanc Alsace 1993: Exotic accents of honey and pineapple feature this especially ripe and fruity-tasting Pinot Blanc. It's almost like Chardonnay, as its buttery notes linger on the finish. 22,500 cases made. • $10 • (07/31/95) BB • **87**

Pinot Blanc Alsace 1992: Coconut and almond flavors mingle in this rich, fat wine. The flavors are bold but a bit dull, it lacks the crispness to carry its weight. An exaggerated style that fans of honey and vanilla will find appealing. • $10 • (11/15/94) • **82**

Pinot Gris Alsace 1992: Smooth and fat, offering tropical flavors of papaya and tangerine and a rich butter note. Rather low in acidity, drink while it's young and fresh. 2,770 cases made. • $15 • (09/15/95) • **83**

Pinot Gris Alsace 1991: Smooth and creamy texture, plus vanilla and butter flavors, make this taste like a plush Chardonnay. May lack a bit of fruit and acidity, but it's fun to drink. • $15 • (11/15/94) • **82**

Sylvaner Alsace 1992: Light and simple, offering pleasant floral aromas and soft flavors of melon and almond, a bit diluted on the finish. • $9 • (11/15/94) • **78**

SCHOFFIT, DOMAINE

Gewürztraminer Alsace Grand Cru Clos Saint-Théobald Rangen de Thann 1993: Glowing gold color and heady honey aromas are the tip-off to great richness, concentration and body. It's sweet but sublime, like a Sauternes or German auslese. So ripe, but so clean, fresh and pure in flavor. Drink now through at least 2000. 100 cases made. • $38 • (08/31/95) • **90**

Gewürztraminer Alsace Grand Cru Rangen de Thann Clos Saint-Théobald 1991: Concentrated and rich. This smooth, well-integrated wine oozes with flavors of peach, melon, spice and butter. Well balanced and so rich it tastes a bit sweet, finishing with echoes of marzipan and honey. Drinkable now. • $39 • (09/30/94) • **91**

Pinot Blanc Alsace Auxerrois Cuvée Caroline 1993: Very ripe and rich, slightly sweet, packed with pear and peach flavors that are clean and fresh. Balanced toward the soft side, though. 1,000 cases made. • $12 • (07/31/95) • **84**

Riesling Alsace Grand Cru Rangen de Thann Clos Saint-Théobald 1992: Lush as a down comforter, offers honey, dried apricot and banana flavors with plenty of spice and sweetness. Drinking well now. Dry, but would be a tough match for food. • $39 • (09/15/94) • **88**

Riesling Alsace Harth 1992: Generous, offering a good balance of crisp acidity and slight sweetness, with peach, apple and grapefruit flavors. Lively and clean. • $19 • (11/15/94) • **85**

Riesling Alsace Harth Cuvée Prestige 1993: Ripe and full-bodied, offering apple tart aromas and flavors. Reminiscent of pears, apples and honey. Well balanced and complex enough to maintain interest on the finish. 1,000 cases made. • $16 • (07/31/95) • **88**

Tokay Pinot Gris Alsace Grand Cru Clos Saint-Théobald Rangen de Thann 1993: Not as opulent as the deep gold color would lead you to believe. Lingering smoky and apricotlike flavors, thick-textured but not too sweet. Bright acidity keeps it lively. 100 cases made. • $38 • (09/15/95) • **87**

SCHYLER, ALFRED

Médoc 1985 • $8 • (06/30/88) • **72**

SEGLA

Margaux 1995: Slightly one-dimensional blackberry character and firm tannins. Second wine of Château Rauzan-Ségla. • $NA • (05/15/96) • **80-84** (BT)

Margaux 1993: Polished black cherry and wet earth character on the nose and palate. Medium body, firm tannins and fresh finish. Drinkable now. • $NA • (01/31/96) • **83**

SEGONZAC, CHÂTEAU

Premières Côtes de Blaye 1986 • $9 • (06/30/89) • **79**

Premières Côtes de Blaye 1985 • $9 • (02/15/88) • **85**

SEGUIN, HERVE

Pouilly-Fumé 1992 • $14 • (09/15/93) • **87**

SEGUR, CHÂTEAU

Haut-Médoc 1988 • $15 • (12/31/90) • **82**

Haut-Médoc 1982 • $6 • (04/16/85) • **75**

SELOSSE, JACQUES

Brut Blanc de Blancs Champagne 1986: A very popular insiders' Champagne in France right now. A ripe, richly styled bubbly with intense flavors. Very intense ripe apple, almost apricot and dough, yeast aromas and flavors, it's full-bodied with a round and silky texture. Long finish. Drink now. • $NA • (12/31/93) • **89**

SELTZ

Gewürztraminer Alsace Réserve 1992: Soft and sweet, tasting like apple cider and cheese, with canned fruit flavors thrown in. Very simple. 15,000 cases made. • $15 • (11/15/94) • **74**

Pinot Blanc Alsace 1992: Made in a delicate style, this offers grapefruit and hazelnut flavors in a clean, almost austere frame. It's crisp yet still soft. 15,000 cases made. • $9 • (11/15/94) • **82**

Sylvaner Alsace Zotzenberg 1992: Snappy acidity gives this a pleasant grip, but there's not much fruit to add interest, it feels better than it tastes. An herbal note comes out on the finish. 5,000 cases made. • $13 • (11/15/94) • **80**

Tokay Pinot Gris Alsace Réserve 1992: Round texture and ripe flavors make this agreeably soft and lush to drink now. It has almond aromas, pear tones and a clean, slightly sweet finish. 5,000 cases made. • $15 • (11/15/94) • **82**

SENARD, DANIEL

Aloxe-Corton Valozières 1991 • $38 Ⓐ • (01/31/94) • **68**

Corton Bressandes 1991: Light and floral almost to an extreme, showing more violet and irislike character than fruit. Finishes austere. • $65 Ⓐ • (01/31/94) • **77**

Corton Bressandes 1990: A muscular wine, with lots of fruit aromas and flavors. Drinkable now. • $NA • (12/15/92) • **88**

Corton Clos de Meix 1992: Extremely minty and vegetal, bitingly tannic, with flavors of cedar and blackberry that can barely make themselves heard over the tannic din. Try in 1999. • $38 • **81**

Corton Clos des Meix 1990: Big, chewy and complex, this is a monster of a wine, filled with berry, spice and floral characteristics. Has a ripe, rich mouth-feel, firm tannins and a long, supple finish. Try around 1997. • $NA • (12/15/92) • **93**

Corton Clos du Roi 1992: A firm, ripe, chunky wine, with sweet black cherry and currant flavors that persist on the chewy finish. Tannins need until 1997. • $52 • **85**

Corton Clos du Roi 1991: Chunky, ripe currant flavors struggle against a wall of earthy, tarry tannins. Finishes austere. Try in 1997. • $65 Ⓐ • (01/31/94) • **79**

Corton En Charlemagne 1992: Firm in texture, with floral overtones to the currant and blackberry flavors. Gets a little chewy on the finish, but worth cellaring until 1997. • $52 • **84**

Corton En Charlemagne 1991: Soft, supple and straightforward. The anise-scented wild berry flavors are a bit diluted when they get to the finish. Drinkable now. • $65 Ⓐ • (01/31/94) • **81**

Corton En Charlemagne 1990: Superfirm, but so full of beautiful fruit flavors that it coats the tannins. Beautifully crafted. Drink from 1997 or '98. • $NA • (12/15/92) • **93**

Corton Le Clos du Roi 1990: Extremely well made, with plenty of raspberry, earth and spice flavors and a lovely, supple structure. Compact and concentrated. Drinkable in 1997 or '98. • $55 • (12/15/92) • **93**

SENECHAUX, DOMAINE DES

Châteauneuf-du-Pape 1985 • $17 • (10/15/88) • **85**

SENEJAC, CHÂTEAU

Haut-Médoc 1988 • $14 • (04/30/91) • **78**

SENEZ, CHRISTIAN

Brut Champagne 1988: Decent, light and frothy, with modest candied pear character. Drink now. • $NA • (12/31/93) • **81**

Brut Champagne 1987: Decent, offering straightforward apple and melon aromas and flavors, but is rather aggressive and foamy in texture and very high in acidity. Drinkable now. • $NA • (12/31/93) • **84**

Brut Champagne NV: Like drinking a pear tart. Vivid, sweet fruit flavors combine with heavy vanilla and clove accents. An attention-getting but extreme style. 20,000 cases made. • $20 • (07/31/95) • **80**

SEPTIMANIE

Maury Mascotte NV: Medium sweet and high in alcohol, this has good plummy flavors and a nutty, tannic finish. But it's coarse in texture and simple in flavor. • $15 • (01/31/95) • **80**

SERAFIN PÈRE & FILS

Charmes-Chambertin 1993: Like an Olympic sprint champion: light on its feet yet very muscular, bursting out of the starting block with amazing grace. Tons of blackberry, floral and earth character. Don't even touch until the next century. Sensational! • $90 • **96**

Charmes-Chambertin 1992: Shows what could be done in 1992 with a little luck and hard work. Impressive intensity of spicy raspberry and juniper flavors persist into a pure, lively finish. Nicely-integrated tannins. Best from 1997 or 1998. • $50 • **89**

Charmes-Chambertin 1989 • $43 Ⓐ • (01/31/92) • **92**

Gevrey-Chambertin 1990: An elegant, refined Pinot Noir, with terrific, toasty black currant and cherry flavors that echo on the vivid, silky finish. Drinkable now. • $45 • (12/15/92) • **89**

Gevrey-Chambertin 1988 • $35 • (03/31/91) • **92**

Gevrey-Chambertin Le Fonteny 1993: Wonderful clarity of ripe fruit, fragrant and vivid. Medium-bodied, adding fine tannins and lovely vanilla flavors. Delicious now, but will age for many years to come. • $65 • **91**

Gevrey-Chambertin Le Fonteny 1992: Its spicy, earthy, tobacco, currant and plum flavors get revved up, but there are some rough tannins to lose, perhaps by 1997 or 1998. • $40 • **85**

Gevrey-Chambertin Le Fonteny 1990: A focused Gevrey that's more elegant than generous, offering currant, black cherry and modest cinnamon flavors. Drinkable now. 150 cases made. • $63 • (12/15/92) • **87**
Gevrey-Chambertin Le Fonteny 1989 • $50 • (01/31/92) • **86**
Gevrey-Chambertin Le Fonteny 1988 • $50 • (05/15/91) • **92**
Gevrey-Chambertin Le Fonteny 1987 • $38 • **70**
Gevrey-Chambertin Les Cazetiers 1993: Quite chunky layers of green tobacco, cherry and berry character, offering fine tannins, medium-to-full body and dried cherry, vanilla finish. Drink in 1998. • $70 • **91**
Gevrey-Chambertin Les Cazetiers 1992: Good character and intensity prevails, with deep black cherry and raspberry flavors that turn chewy and tannic on the lingering, juicy finish. Needs until 1997. • $44 • **86**
Gevrey-Chambertin Les Cazetiers 1990: Beautifully aromatic, lively and vivid, with bright blackberry, violet, rose petal and mushroom flavors. Shows excellent intensity of well-balanced tannins and acidity. Drinkable in 1997. 200 cases made. • $56 • (12/15/92) • **91**
Gevrey-Chambertin Les Cazetiers 1989 • $54 • (01/31/92) • **89**
Gevrey-Chambertin Les Cazetiers 1988 • $53 • (05/15/91) • **91**
Gevrey-Chambertin Vieilles Vignes 1993: Some good berry and plum character but slightly light on the finish. Medium in body with firm tannins. A bit one-dimensional. Drink in 1998. • $55 • **85**
Gevrey-Chambertin Vieilles Vignes 1992: Shows some spicy new oak character and just barely enough berry and currant flavor to balance it. Firm enough to want until 1997. • $35 • **84**
Gevrey-Chambertin Vieilles Vignes 1990: A bit ungenerous now on the palate, but the aromas are pretty, with cinnamon, earth, berry and slightly vegetal notes. Drinkable now. • $50 • (12/15/92) • **87**
Gevrey-Chambertin Vieilles Vignes 1989 • $45 • (01/31/92) • **92**
Gevrey-Chambertin Vieilles Vignes 1987 • $35 • (03/31/90) • **91**

SERRE DE LAUZIERE

Côtes du Rhône-Villages 1988 • $7 • (10/31/90) • **78**

SERRE, CHÂTEAU LA

St.-Emilion 1995: A delicious '95 that builds on the palate, with intense cassis, raspberry and spicy oak character, velvety and rich, delivering supple and ripe tannins as it rolls to a wonderful, long finish. Almost outstanding. • $NA • (05/15/96) • **85-89** (BT)
St.-Emilion 1994: Some attractive fruit flavors—predominantly plum and currant—in a medium-bodied package of fairly supple texture. But it's slightly diluted on the finish. • $NA • (05/15/96) • **80-84** (BT)
St.-Emilion 1990: It's easy to like this wine. Very attractive, with perfumed floral and rose aromas and an elegant, silky texture of sweet berry and floral flavors. Medium tannins hold it all together. Drinkable now. 3,000 cases made. • $22 • (03/31/93) • **88**
St.-Emilion 1988 • $18 • (06/15/91) • **80**
St.-Emilion 1985 • $15 • (05/15/88) • **91**

SERVEAU, DOMAINE B.

Bourgogne 1989 • $10 • (01/31/92) • **83**
Bourgogne 1985 • $13 • (11/15/87) • **76**
Chambolle-Musigny 1989 • $27 • (01/31/92) • **83**
Chambolle-Musigny Les Amoureuses 1991: Soft and appealing, a bit watery at the center, but shows nicely defined blackberry, currant, vanilla and toast aromas and flavors that keep echoing on the finish. Drinkable now. 150 cases made. • $55 Ⓐ • (01/31/94) • **80**
Chambolle-Musigny Les Amoureuses 1990: Very closed and unyielding, showing excellent breeding and class. The vivid fruit and firm tannins are good guarantees that this will deliver great pleasure after some cellaring. Try in 1997 or '98. 150 cases made. • $68 • (12/15/92) • **91**
Chambolle-Musigny Les Amoureuses 1989 • $50 • (01/31/92) • **85**
Chambolle-Musigny Les Amoureuses 1988 • $66 • (02/28/91) • **84**
Chambolle-Musigny Les Amoureuses 1985 • $75 • (06/15/88) • **91**

Key: SS—Spectator Selection. CS—Cellar Selection. BB—Best Buy. $NA—Price not available. (BT)—Barrel tasting. Ⓐ—Auction Price.
Dates in parentheses represent the issues in which the ratings were published.

Chambolle-Musigny Les Chabiots 1991: Smooth and silky, with gamy, meaty overtones to the currant and berry fruit at the center. Fades a bit on the finish, but charming. 300 cases made. • $30 Ⓐ • (01/31/94) • **84**
Chambolle-Musigny Les Chabiots 1990: Light and pleasant, with pretty but modest strawberry, milk chocolate and cream aromas and flavors and a smooth, silky finish. Drinkable now. 250 cases made. • $35 • (12/15/92) • **85**
Chambolle-Musigny Les Chabiots 1989 • $30 • (01/31/92) • **79**
Chambolle-Musigny Les Chabiots 1988 • $39 • (02/28/91) • **86**
Chambolle-Musigny Les Chabiots 1987 • $30 • (06/15/90) • **78**
Chambolle-Musigny Les Chabiots 1985 • $39 • (06/15/88) • **90**
Chambolle-Musigny Les Chabiots 1984 • $23 • (04/15/87) • **91**
Chambolle-Musigny Les Sentiers 1991: Light, watery, stemmy and citrusy, not very likeable. 100 cases made. • $30 Ⓐ • (01/31/94) • **73**
Chambolle-Musigny Les Sentiers 1990: Bright, plummy and ripe, with hints of earth, strawberry and violet flavors and a smooth, focused texture. Drinkable now. 125 cases made. • $35 • (12/15/92) • **88**
Chambolle-Musigny Les Sentiers 1989 • $30 • (01/31/92) • **93**
Chambolle-Musigny Les Sentiers 1988 • $39 • (02/28/91) • **79**
Morey-St.-Denis Les Sorbets 1991: Tough, tannic and sturdy, offering simple currant flavors and chunky, drying tannins. Drinkable now. 500 cases made. • $30 Ⓐ • (01/31/94) • **82**
Morey-St.-Denis Les Sorbets 1990: Good but a bit simple, with modest strawberry and plum notes and a hint of chestnut on the finish. 50 cases made. • $35 • (12/15/92) • **80**
Morey-St.-Denis Les Sorbets 1989 • $30 • (01/31/92) • **86**
Morey-St.-Denis Les Sorbets 1988 • $35 • (02/28/91) • **88**
Morey-St.-Denis Les Sorbets 1987 • $30 • (05/15/90) • **83**
Morey-St.-Denis Les Sorbets 1985 • $39 • (06/15/88) • **88**
Morey-St.-Denis Les Sorbets 1984 • $22 • (03/15/87) • **87**
Nuits-St.-Georges Châines Carteaux 1991: Firm in texture and modest in intensity, serving up appealing aromas and flavors that emerge harmoniously on the finish. 100 cases made. • $32 Ⓐ • (01/31/94) • **78**
Nuits-St.-Georges Châines Carteaux 1990: Distinctive, rich and round, with impressive plum, berry and leaf aromas and plenty of round tannins. Tasted twice. Drinkable in 1998. 83 cases made. • $46 • (12/15/92) • **91**
Nuits-St.-Georges Châines Carteaux 1988 • $39 • (03/31/91) • **84**
Nuits-St.-Georges Châines Carteaux 1985 • $39 • (06/15/88) • **86**

SIAURAC, CHÂTEAU

Lalande-de-Pomerol 1994: Fresh berry, wet-earth character, medium body, firm tannins and lean finish. Could move up a notch. • $NA • **75-79** (BT)
Lalande-de-Pomerol 1993: Light and weedy, slightly aggressive, showing some fruit but a very short aftertaste. Drinkable now. • $19 • (01/31/96) • **77**
Lalande-de-Pomerol 1990: Voluptuous and offers plenty of appealing ripe plum and cassis flavors, accented by smoke and herbs. It's a bit diluted, perhaps, but has freshness and firm tannins; enjoy now. • $19 • (05/15/94) • **84**

SIGALAS RABAUD, CHÂTEAU

Sauternes 1986: Simple, sweet and fruity, with a touch of oxidation that takes away from the quality. • $42 • (12/31/89) • **77**
Sauternes 1985: Very smooth and honey-like but somewhat light compared to great years. Has tasty pear and rich honey flavors and a long finish. Drinkable now. • $41 • (07/15/88) • **82**
Sauternes 1983: A bit rough around the edges, but all the elements are there to age into a great wine. Deep gold, with flavors that lean to pineapple and resin, framed with oak. Big and concentrated, like pineapple syrup magically transformed into wine. • $24 • (01/31/88) • **88**

SIGAUT, HERVE

Chambolle-Musigny 1992: Light, juicy and modest, more Beaujolais than Burgundy. This is almost washed out, with straightforward strawberry and raspberry flavors. • $NA • **82**
Chambolle-Musigny Les Sentiers 1992: Very light and fragrant, more Beaujolais than Burgundy, with candied strawberry flavors echoing on the finish. Drinkable now. • $NA • **81**

SIGNAC, CHÂTEAU

Côtes du Rhône 1990 • $9 • (11/30/92) BB • **84**

SILVER CLOUD

Brut Blanc de Blancs Blanquette de Limoux 1985 • $9 • (04/15/90) • **85**

SIMARD, CHÂTEAU

St.-Emilion 1970 • $NA • (05/15/93) • **84**

SIMIAN, CHÂTEAU

Châteauneuf-du-Pape 1989 • $19 • (08/31/92) • **84**
Châteauneuf-du-Pape 1988 • $20 • (07/15/91) • **86**
Côtes du Rhône 1989 • $11 • (11/30/92) • **78**

SIMIANE, MARQUIS DE

Côtes du Rhône 1990 • $7 • (04/15/93) • **72**

SIMONNET-FEBVRE

Chablis Les Clos 1994: Burns a hole in your palate from its sheer intensity. Ripe, rich, full-bodied, packed with complex flavors of earth, toast, butter, mineral, honey and ripe pear. This delivers an unforgettable mouth-feel. Lush, round, long and intense on the finish. Try in 2000. • $NA • (05/31/96) • **95**
Chablis Mont de Milieu 1994: Beautiful white, silky and full-bodied, sporting chewy mineral aromas and sweet flavors of honey, ripe pear and apple pie. Though rich, it's elegant on the long, delicious finish. Try in 1999. • $NA • (05/31/96) • **91**

SIRAN, CHÂTEAU

Margaux 1995: A big wine to watch. Powerful, rich, full-bodied, with tons of tannins and fruit, it makes up in sheer power what it lacks in finesse. Very extracted and concentrated, with a velvety mouth-feel. Time should tame it. • $NA • (05/15/96)• **90-94** (BT)
Margaux 1994: Decent fruit, fine tannins and a berry, raspberry finish. • $NA • (05/15/96) • **80-84** (BT)
Margaux 1993: Very elegant black cherry, mint and berry aromas and flavors, medium body, fine tannins and fresh finish. Better in 1998. • $22 • (01/31/96) • **85**
Margaux 1991: Subtle complexity of berry, cherry and vanilla flavors and aromas, medium tannins and long aftertaste. • $15 • (03/31/94) • **84**
Margaux 1990: Rich and thick, this wine shows a restrained fruit and tannin structure but kicks in on the finish. Drinkable in 1997. 10,000 cases made. • $22 • (03/31/93) • **90**
Margaux 1989 • $25 • (03/15/92) • **88**
Margaux 1988 • $19 • (06/30/91) • **88**
Margaux 1985 • $15 • (09/30/88) • **90**
Margaux 1982 • $30 • (08/31/92) • **89**

SIRIUS

Bordeaux 1988 • $15 • (08/31/91) • **77**

SIRUGUE & FILS, JEAN-LOUIS

Côte de Nuits-Villages Clos de la Belle Marguerite 1993: Light-bodied, pleasant and nicely balanced between dry, ripe tannins and black cherry and wet earth notes. Better in 1998. • $15 •(11/15/95) • **83**
Côte de Nuits-Villages Clos de la Belle Marguerite 1990: An old style, with green, hard tannins that make the plum and currant-scented flavors taste tight and lean. Drinkable now. 2,000 cases made. • $10 • (06/15/93) • **82**
Côte de Nuits-Villages Clos de la Belle Marguerite 1988 • $16 • (03/31/91) • **83**
Gevrey-Chambertin 1993: Pretty, easy-to-drink Pinot delivering berry, cherry and chocolate character. Medium-bodied, with light, delicate fruit and medium-fine tannins. Try now. From Labouré-Roi. • (11/15/95) • $25 • **83**
Gevrey-Chambertin 1989 • $20 • (08/31/92) • **80**

SMITH-HAUT-LAFITTE, CHÂTEAU

Graves 1985 • $15 • (11/30/88) • **89**
Graves 1982 • $18 • (08/31/92) • **81**
Graves 1981 • $18 • (06/01/84) • **79**
Graves 1979 • $20 • (10/15/89) • **69**
Pessac-Léognan 1995: Magnificently elegant, full-bodied '95, showing great finesse of flavors, aromas and tannic structure. It butters the palate with fine, ripe, rich tannins. • $NA • (05/15/96) • **90-94** (BT)
Pessac-Léognan 1994: Medium-to-light body, showing fine tannins and a fresh berry, smoky aftertaste. • $26 • (05/15/96) • **80-84** (BT)
Pessac-Léognan 1993: Lots of great new wood here but just enough fruit to balance it out. Medium in body and tannins and a firm finish. Better in 1997. • $25 • (01/31/96) • **86**
Pessac-Léognan 1992: Lovely berry, tobacco and chocolate character, medium body and medium, velvety tannins. Good finish. Drink now. • $17 • **84**
Pessac-Léognan 1991: Very agreeable wine with ripe berry and smoky chocolate behind its fruit character. Medium body and a subtle finish. • $17 • (03/31/94) • **83**
Pessac-Léognan 1990: Superbly crafted. A wine with lush, velvety tannins and gorgeous plummy, earthy, vanilla notes. This estate is on the rise. Try in 1998. 13,000 cases made. • $22 • (03/31/93) • **93**
Pessac-Léognan 1989 • $19 • (03/15/92) • **91**
Pessac-Léognan 1987 • $15 • (05/15/90) • **84**
Pessac-Léognan White 1994: Lively and fresh, with well-defined grapefruit, lilac, honey and orange peel flavors. Medium-bodied and wonderfully harmonious, showing depth and length on the lightly toasty finish. • $37 • (03/31/96) • **90**
Pessac-Léognan White 1993: Not quite as impressive as the '92, but still very good. Lovely, clean, grassy, mineral and vanilla character, medium body, medium intensity and fine finish. Drink now. • $30 • (05/31/95) • **86**
Pessac-Léognan White 1992 • $30 • (06/15/94) • **88**
Pessac-Léognan White 1991 • $30 • (03/31/94) • **86**

SOCIANDO-MALLET, CHÂTEAU

Haut-Médoc 1995: A wine with bright berry and red fruit character and plenty of smokey oak. Full-bodied and very chewy, with a long finish. Almost outstanding. • $NA • (05/15/96) • **85-89** (BT)
Haut-Médoc 1994: Elegant tannins and a good amount of fruit, medium to light body and delicate finish. Not up to the quality we expected from our first tasting. • $24 • (05/15/96) • **80-84** (BT)
Haut-Médoc 1993: Polished and gorgeous, showing finesse and power, amazingly well-integrated tannins, full body and layers of currant, black cherry and plum flavors. Supple, tasty finish. Tempting now, but will improve until 1998. • $25 • (01/31/96) • **88**
Haut-Médoc 1992: So polished, so fine, this estate is nearly always producing fabulous wines. Medium body, delicate tannins and pretty berry and mint flavors, medium finish. Drinkable now. • $20 • **87**
Haut-Médoc 1991: A superbly crafted wine for this vintage. Supple in texture, but a little lean and short on the finish. • $17 • (03/31/94) • **85**
Haut-Médoc 1990: This estate nearly always makes outstanding wine. This one is vibrant, with vivid cherry and vanilla character and loads of tannins, yet it remains well balanced. Drink after 1997. 18,500 cases made. • $29 Ⓐ • (03/31/93) • **91**
Haut-Médoc 1989 • $28 Ⓐ • (03/15/92) • **90**
Haut-Médoc 1988 • $26 • (03/31/91) • **87**
Haut-Médoc 1987 • $15 • (05/15/90) • **88**
Haut-Médoc 1986 • $29 Ⓐ • (11/30/89) • **94**
Haut-Médoc 1985 • $33 Ⓐ • (10/15/94) • **91**
Haut-Médoc 1984 • $11 • (03/31/87) • **84**
Haut-Médoc 1983 • $15 • (10/15/94) • **92**
Haut-Médoc 1982 • $40 Ⓐ • (08/31/92) • **92**
Haut-Médoc 1981 • $23 • (10/15/94) • **88**

SOCIANDO-MALLET, LA DEMOISELLE DE

Haut-Médoc 1992: Pretty tobacco, cherry and berry aromas and flavors with modest body and firm, slightly green tannins. Amazing for a second label in such a weak year. Drink now. • $17 • **80**
Haut-Médoc 1989 • $21 • (03/15/92) • **84**

SOLITUDE, DOMAINE DE LA

Châteauneuf-du-Pape 1992: Spicy and smooth, but about to go over the hill already. Drink now if you like tea, vanilla and brown sugar flavors accented by a hint of fruit. • $22 • **79**
Châteauneuf-du-Pape 1990: Soft and generous, with fleshy plum, spice, tobacco and currant flavors and elegant earth shadings. Finishes long and smooth, with lush but firm tannins. Drinkable now. • $27 • (04/15/93) • **89**
Châteauneuf-du-Pape 1989 • $19 • (05/31/92) • **86**
Châteauneuf-du-Pape White 1992: A nearly neutral tasting white wine with substantial body due to the alcohol but little flavor interest. • $22 • **76**
Côtes du Rhône 1993: A spicey and exaggerated style that works since it is backed up by some good dried plum and cherry fruit flavors. Rich and concentrated with good balance and a nice finish that's accented by chocolaty notes. Drink now. • $12 • **84**

FRANCE

SOLITUDE, DOMAINE DE LA

Pessac-Léognan 1993: Light and somewhat diluted, offering modest cherry, dried herb and chocolate flavors. Drink on release. • $18 • (01/31/96) • **77**
Pessac-Léognan White 1993: Delicious and refined apple, grapefruit and mineral character, medium in body, featuring rich texture and a lively finish. New from the producers of Domaine de Chevalier. Drinkable now. • $15 • (05/31/95) • **86**
Pessac-Léognan White 1994: This really builds on the palate. Subtle aromas of cream, apricot and honey open up to a full palette of flavors. Medium-bodied, with a very lively finish. Delicious. From the producers of Domaine de Chevalier. Better in 1997. • $15 • (03/31/96) • **90**

SORIN, DOMAINE

Côtes de Provence 1994: Ripe, rich, velvety textured, offering sweet blackberry, tar, tobacco and light vanilla flavors and good concentration. Try now. Tasted twice, with consistent notes. 3,300 cases made. • $13 • (10/31/95) • **86**

SORREL, H.

Hermitage 1991: Fresh and straightforward, with floral, berry and vanilla notes. It's pleasant and accessible now. Tasted twice. • $25 • (05/31/94) • **83**
Hermitage 1990: Crisp and unexpectedly earthy, with lime and citrus flavors and little richness or generosity. The tannins clamp down on the finish. Age could bring it around, try from 1998. • $35 • (04/15/93) • **82**
Hermitage 1985 • $29 • (07/31/88) • **87**
Hermitage Le Gréal 1991: Expressive aromas of dark chocolate, raisins and plums carry through the richness. Full-bodied, though the finish is a bit dry now. Try now. Tasted twice. • $45 • (05/31/94) • **88**
Hermitage Le Gréal 1990: Ripe, round and aromatic, loaded with generous currant, blackberry, spice and vanilla characteristics. Spicy and toasty on the solid finish, echoing cedar, tar and black pepper notes. Shows a lot of potential, ready to open up with cellaring until 1997 or '98. • $44 • (04/15/93) • **89**
Hermitage Le Gréal 1988 • $49 • (11/15/91) • **88**
Hermitage Le Gréal 1983 • $19 • (05/01/86) • **84**
Hermitage Le Gréal 1980 • $25 • (05/01/86) • **74**

Key: SS—Spectator Selection. CS—Cellar Selection. BB—Best Buy. $NA—Price not available. (BT)—Barrel tasting. Ⓐ—Auction Price.
Dates in parentheses represent the issues in which the ratings were published.

Hermitage Le Vignon 1988 • $36 • (08/31/91) • **77**

SOUDARS, CHÂTEAU

Haut-Médoc 1995: A lot of new oak in this medium-bodied wine, it could use a little more fruit to balance the wood. • $NA • (05/15/96) • **80-84** (BT)
Haut-Médoc 1994: Light and one-dimensional, revealing silky texture and racy tannins but lacking a bit of fruit. • $NA • **80-84** (BT)
Haut-Médoc 1992: Good color, but very herbal and hard, somewhat aggressive finish. Drink now. • $15 • **74**
Haut-Médoc 1991: A light, elegant claret, with black cherry flavors. Slightly diluted on the finish. • $15 • (03/31/94) • **79**
Haut-Médoc 1990: A pretty wine, with perfumed, spicy aromas, cherry and spice flavors and firm tannins, but it's slightly diluted. Drinkable now. 10,000 cases made. • $18 • (03/31/93) • **84**
Haut-Médoc 1989 • $15 • (03/15/92) • **85**
Haut-Médoc 1988 • $15 • (04/30/91) • **88**
Haut-Médoc 1987 • $12 • (11/30/89) • **77**
Haut-Médoc 1986 • $13 • (11/30/89) • **79**

SOUFRANDISE, DOMAINE DE LA

Pouilly-Fuissé 1993: Refined and velvety, yet solid. Shows straightforward grapefruit, wet straw and green apple flavors. Drink now. 583 cases made. • $23 • **86**
Pouilly-Fuissé Domaine La Soufrandise Vieilles Vignes 1994: Quite civilized, with a smooth, round and lush texture, offering butter and pear notes. But the finish leaves a bitter, astringent lingering note. Starts better than it ends. • $25 • (05/31/96) 78 • **78**

SOUFRANDISE, DOMAINE DE V

Mâcon-Fuissé 1993: Ripe pear, fig and mineral complexity. Light body, with a clean, crisp and delicious finish. From Françoise and Nicolas Melin. • $NA • **84**

SOUMADE, DOMAINE LA

Côtes du Rhône-Villages Rasteau 1986 • $11 • (02/28/90) • **82**
Côtes du Rhône-Villages Rasteau Cuvée Réservee 1982 • $5 • (10/31/87) • **69**

SOURS, CHÂTEAU DE

Bordeaux 1995: Intensely fruity, medium in body and featuring good cassis and wild berry backed by subtle oak flavors. A bit light, but providing firm tannins and juicy aftertaste. • $NA • (05/15/96) • **80-84** (BT)

SOUTARD, CHÂTEAU

St.-Emilion 1989 • $27 • (09/15/93) • **87**
St.-Emilion 1985 • $23 Ⓐ • (05/15/88) • **85**
St.-Emilion 1982 • $31 Ⓐ • (05/15/89) • **84**
St.-Emilion 1961 • $22 • (04/30/96) • **85**

SPARR, PIERRE

Brut Crémant d'Alsace Réserve NV: This sparkler is bone-dry, even austere, showing hints of fig and almond on the finish. It's clean and sharp, with pinpoint bubbles. Very refreshing, a good apéritif. 20,000 cases made. • $15 • (11/15/94) • **84**
Chasselas Alsace Vielles Vignes 1992: Attractive floral aromas lead to peach and grapefruit flavors in this dry, delicate wine. With refreshing acidity and soft flavors, it has enough charm to while away a summer afternoon. 1,200 cases made. • $8 • (11/15/94) • **83**
Gewürztraminer Alsace Carte d'Or 1993: Light for a Gewürztraminer, perfumed with apple, mint and spice. Has elegant texture, good acidity and tastes floral on the finish. • $11 • (09/15/95) • **84**
Gewürztraminer Alsace Catre d'Or 1992: Lively, fruity and fresh, with zesty lemon and orange flavors and great balance. Firm acidity keeps

it clean and helps the flavors linger on the finish. 30,000 cases made. • $10 • (11/15/94) • **85**

Gewürztraminer Alsace Réserve 1992: Clean, elegant and refined. The subtle peach and spice flavors are nicely supported by crisp acidity as they linger and mingle on the finish. Very good quality. 2,000 cases made. • $12 • (11/15/94) • **87**

Pinot Blanc Alsace Diamant d'Alsace Réserve 1992: Lime and floral aromas don't follow through on the palate, which is crisp, austere and a bit earthy. 35,000 cases made. • $8 • (11/15/94) • **78**

Pinot Blanc Alsace Diamant d'Alsace Réserve 1991 • $14 • (07/31/93) • **77**

Pinot Blanc Alsace Vielles Vignes 1992: A bit tough and awkward with earthy, garlicky aromas, muted fruit flavors and a nutty finish. 1,000 cases made. • $12 • (11/15/94) • **74**

Pinot Gris Alsace Carte d'Or 1993: A sturdy, dry white showing apple and pear flavors accented by floral undertones. Nicely balanced and tangy. • $11 • (09/15/95) • **83**

Pinot Gris Alsace Carte d'Or 1992: Expressive yet subtle, generous, exhibiting pear, honey and butter flavors. Soft and clean, balanced and easy to drink. 10,000 cases made. • $10 • (11/15/94) • **84**

Pinot Gris Alsace Réserve 1992: Firm and intense yet not heavy-handed, offering well-defined almond, anise and pear flavors brightened by crisp acidity. Try with tarragon-scented chicken or pork. 1,000 cases made. • $12 • (11/15/94) • **86**

Riesling Alsace Carte d'Or 1993: Great balance and subtle fruit make this lively and elegant. It has delicate apple aromas and rather lean, lemony flavors. • $10 • (09/15/95) • **85**

Riesling Alsace Carte d'Or 1992: Smooth texture, with integrated flavors of apple, peach and grapefruit and a long finish. Drinkable now. 20,000 cases made. • $9 • (09/15/94) BB • **88**

Riesling Alsace Réserve 1992: Starts out soft and inviting, not a typical Riesling, but becomes vibrant and crisp. It is well balanced with menthol flavors and a refreshing finish. 1,500 cases made. • $11 • (11/15/94) • **84**

STUART, MARIE

Brut Blanc de Blancs Champagne 1979 • $25 • (12/31/87) • **87**
Brut Blanc de Blancs Champagne NV • $19 • (12/31/87) • **85**
Brut Champagne Cuvée de la Reine NV • $26 • (12/31/87) • **84**
Brut Champagne NV • $22 • (12/31/87) • **82**
Brut Rosé Champagne NV • $23 • (12/31/87) • **80**
Extra Dry Champagne NV • $19 • (12/31/87) • **74**

SUDUIRAUT, CHÂTEAU DE

Sauternes 1990: Beautiful and alluring, harmonious and full-bodied, it caresses the palate with lovely dried fruit, toasted oak and vanilla flavors. Very sweet, but in balance. Delicious now, better after 1998. • $46 • (04/15/95) • **93**

Sauternes 1989: Exotically perfumed violet and rose petals burst on your palate, accompanied by dried apricot, lemon and honey flavors. Gorgeous and subtle, glowing on the finish. • $48 • (04/15/95) • **92**

Sauternes 1986: Ripe and golden, with buttered pear and pineapple aromas and long, honeyed fruit flavors. Lacks the roundness that should come with age. Drinkable now. • $35 • (12/31/89) • **85**

Sauternes 1985 • $20 Ⓐ • (11/30/88) • **81**
Sauternes 1984 • $22 • (11/30/88) • **81**
Sauternes 1983 • $44 • (04/15/95) • **88**
Sauternes 1982 • $29 Ⓐ • (11/30/88) • **83**
Sauternes 1979 • $30 • (11/30/88) • **86**
Sauternes 1978 • $22 • (11/30/88) • **78**
Sauternes 1976 • $41 Ⓐ • (11/30/88) • **77**
Sauternes 1975 • $63 • (11/30/88) • **84**
Sauternes 1972 • $25 • (11/30/88) • **77**
Sauternes 1970 • $34 Ⓐ • (11/30/88) • **81**
Sauternes 1969 • $70 • (11/30/88) • **88**
Sauternes 1959 • $159 Ⓐ • (11/30/88) • **93**
Sauternes 1928 • $300 • (11/30/88) • **90**

Sauternes Crème de Tête 1989: An amazing, full-bodied Sauternes with the texture of double cream, cascading its exotic blend of orange-peel, thyme, dried-herb and honey flavors to a long finish. Drink now or hold until after 1998. • $160 • (04/15/95) • **96**

Sauternes Cuvée Madame 1982 • $140 • (11/30/88) • **90**

Coteaux du Tricastin White 1994: A very dry white that's clean and has a sweet-tart blaance. The fruit-cocktail flavors are supported by firm acidity. • $9 • (12/31/95) • **79**

SOURS, CHÂTEAU DE

Bordeaux Supérieur 1986 • $7 • (09/30/89) • **78**

TAILHAS, CHÂTEAU

Pomerol 1988 • $20 • (04/30/91) • **91**
Pomerol 1982 • $15 • (05/15/89) • **82**

TAILLEFER, CHÂTEAU

Pomerol 1992: Rather lean and tart, sporting berry, earthy, slightly metallic character. Light-bodied, hard tannins. Drinkable now. • $19 • **77**

Pomerol 1988 • $22 • (06/30/91) • **87**
Pomerol 1985 • $24 • (06/30/88) • **81**
Pomerol 1982 • $23 • (05/15/89) • **85**

TAILLEVENT

Brut Blanc de Blancs Champagne 1985: Floral and earthy, with a touch of bitterness on the finish. The pear, vanilla and spice flavors are elegant and balanced. Ready to drink now. • $49 • (11/15/91) • **84**

Brut Blanc de Blancs Champagne 1983: Lean and compact, it has lemon and spice flavors along with a coarse, metallic quality that detracts a bit. Despite that, there's good intensity and concentration of flavor. • $33 • (12/31/89) • **82**

Brut Champagne Grande Réserve NV • $43 • (11/15/91) • **88**
Brut Rosé Champagne Phantom of the Opera NV • $32 • (12/31/89) • **82**
Rosé Champagne Grande Réserve NV • $56 • (11/15/91) • **88**

TAIN L'HERMITAGE, CAVE DE

Cornas Michel Courtial 1986 • $11 • (07/31/89) • **89**
Crozes-Hermitage Michel Courtial 1986 • $6 • (05/15/89) • **77**
Hermitage 1986 • $15 • (07/15/89) • **82**
Hermitage Michel Courtial 1986 • $15 • (03/31/90) • **89**
St.-Joseph Michel Courtial 1986 • $8 • (07/31/89) • **79**

TAITTINGER

Brut Blanc de Blancs Champagne Comtes de Champagne 1986: Opulent showy Champagne with grapefruit, marzipan aromas and flavors, medium body and fresh acidity. Tasted twice with consistent notes. Drink now. • $95 • (12/31/93) • **87**

Brut Blanc de Blancs Champagne Comtes de Champagne 1985 • $96 • (12/31/90) • **92**

Brut Blanc de Blancs Champagne Comtes de Champagne 1983 • $92 • (12/31/90) • **93**

Brut Blanc de Blancs Champagne Comtes de Champagne 1982 • $83 • (12/31/89) • **95**

Brut Blanc de Blancs Champagne Comtes de Champagne 1981 • $78 • (04/15/88) • **93**

Brut Blanc de Blancs Champagne Comtes de Champagne 1979 • $65 • (05/31/87) • **92**

Brut Blanc de Blancs Champagne Comtes de Champagne 1976 • $95 • (05/16/86) • **83**

Brut Champagne 1988: Smooth and elegant, with a tight, complex core of spice, pear, hazelnut and vanilla flavors that turns creamy and supple on the finish, where it delivers finesse and grace. Smells toasty and doughy. Drinkable now. • $48 • (09/30/93) • **89**

Brut Champagne 1985 • $50 • (12/31/90) • **89**
Brut Champagne 1983 • $38 • (12/31/89) • **84**
Brut Champagne NV • $26 • (12/31/87) • **89**
Brut Champagne Artist Collection Arman 1981 • $87 • (05/31/87) CS • **92**

Brut Champagne Artist Collection Hartung 1986: Crisp, firm and elegant with a sharply focused beam of pear, spice, vanilla and ginger notes that are rich and concentrated. Finishes with a burst of flavor that stays with you on a long, full finish. Drinkable now. • $140 • (10/31/93) • **92**

Brut Champagne Artist Collection Imai 1988: Solid, well-made, elaborately packaged Champagne with great balance, crisp texture and lively citrus fruit flavors. A bit of doughy complexity comes out on the finish. Drinkable now. • $150 • (02/28/95) • **88**

Brut Champagne Artist Collection Lichtenstein 1985: A wine with style and personality, characterized by spicy, toasty, pear-accented flavors. Medium-bodied, offering persistent, harmonious flavors on the finish. 8,000 cases made. • $150 • (05/15/92) • **89**

Brut Champagne Artist Collection Masson 1982: A mature wine, with impressive depth, offering plenty of toasty, spicy notes around a core of pear and hazelnut flavors that keeps unfolding through the long finish. Despite all the flavor intensity, it has delicacy and creamy smoothness. 8,000 cases made. • $125 • (05/15/92) • **94**

Brut Champagne Artist Collection Vieira da Silva 1983: They don't get a whole lot better than this. Extremely flavorful and rich, packed with pear, hazelnut, toast and butter notes that linger on the finish. The powerful fruit flavor and firm acidity give it great strength on the palate. • $120 • (05/15/92) • **94**

Brut Champagne Comtes de Champagne 1988: Crisp and lean, with pretty aromas and flavors of flowers, spices and peaches. Charming and light as an apéritif. Tasted twice. • $97 • **84**

Brut Champagne La Française NV: An elegant Champagne that's on the light side in body, but plenty of fruit and spice flavors hold your interest. It combines lemon, apple and vanilla notes for an attractive package. • $41 • **88**

Brut Champagne Millésime 1989: Easy-going and smooth-textured, with spicy, doughy aromas. It's light, rather soft and has mellow citrus and vanilla flavors that linger on the finish. • $50 • **88**

Brut Champagne Millésime 1986: Crisp and fruity, with lively pear, citrus and vanilla shadings that are focused and refreshing. A vibrant youthful wine that drinks well now. • $47 • (08/31/92) • **85**

Brut Champagne Millésime 1982: Toasty dough aromas give way to rich yet elegant fruit with hints of honey, citrus and pear flavors that are nicely knit. Finish is crisp and clean. • $38 • (12/31/88) • **89**

Brut Champagne Réserve NV • $24 • (05/16/86) • **73**

Brut Rosé Champagne Comtes de Champagne 1991: A clean, refreshing, crisp rosé that's lean in profile but has enough spicy, buttery, mineral accents to achieve some complexity. • $120 • (12/15/95) • **87**

Brut Rosé Champagne Comtes de Champagne 1986: Tight, firm and complex, with focused black cherry, smoke and vanilla flavors that are bright and pleasing. Turns elegant and crisp on the finish, inviting you back for another sip. Drinks well now. • $110 • (06/15/93) • **89**

Brut Rosé Champagne Comtes de Champagne 1985: A full-flavored, dry Rosé with bracing acidity, great Pinot Noir flavors and a clean, crisp finish. Its red-wine flavor and slightly rough texture would make it a better choice with dinner rather than as an apéritif. • $110 • (05/15/92) • **88**

Brut Rosé Champagne Comtes de Champagne 1982: Rich, complex and delicate, pretty to look at, and even better to sip. The fruit is fresh and enticing with spicy cherry, Pinot Noir, nutmeg and spice flavors, all wrapped up in a pretty package. Long, satisfying aftertaste. Drink now. • $140 • (12/31/89) • **92**

Brut Rosé Champagne Comtes de Champagne 1981 • $88 • (04/15/88) • **94**

Brut Rosé Champagne Comtes de Champagne 1976 • $240 • (12/16/85) • **90**

Brut Rosé Champagne Cuvée Prestige NV: Ripe and bold, rich with its plum, spice and chocolate flavors carried on an exuberant mousse. It's distinctive and sturdy enough to stand up to food. • $48 • (12/15/95) • **87**

TALBOT, CHÂTEAU

St.-Julien 1995: Delicious red berry character and medium body, adding a hint of toasted oak and spice and smooth tannins. Pleasant but slightly dry on the finish. • $NA • (05/15/96) • **85-89** (BT)

St.-Julien 1994: Better than the '95 Talbot. Round and fruity, with lovely vanilla, chocolate and berry character. Good concentration for the vintage. • $24 • (05/15/96) • **85-89** (BT)

St.-Julien 1993: Ripe, lush red berry and plummy character. Medium-bodied, quite soft and delicious now, adding a seductive lead-pencil, mint, currant character and smooth finish. Drinkable now. 27,500 cases made. • $25 • (01/31/96) • **86**

St.-Julien 1992: Disappointingly lean and hard, revealing some decent plum and berry character but a rather metallic finish. Drink if you must. Tasted twice, with consistent notes. • $20 • **75**

St.-Julien 1991: A little disappointing. Decent chocolate, tobacco and black cherry flavors, but the finish is short and astringent. Tasted twice with consistent notes. • $22 • (03/31/94) • **78**

St.-Julien 1990: Like eating a reduced raspberrysause. Rich and thick, With tons of fruit and velvety tannins, yet it's perfectly balanced. Drink after 1988. 23,500 cases made. • $24 Ⓐ • (03/31/93) • **93**

St.-Julien 1989 • $32 Ⓐ • (03/15/92) • **90**

St.-Julien 1988 • $21 Ⓐ • (03/15/91) • **90**

St.-Julien 1987 • $19 • (05/15/90) • **85**

St.-Julien 1986 • $51 Ⓐ • (05/31/89) • **91**

St.-Julien 1985 • $40 Ⓐ • (10/15/94) • **90**

St.-Julien 1984 • $19 • (05/15/87) • **80**

St.-Julien 1983 • $39 Ⓐ • (10/15/94) • **90**

St.-Julien 1982 • $92 Ⓐ • (05/01/89) • **88**

St.-Julien 1981 • $32 Ⓐ • (10/15/94) • **85**

St.-Julien 1979 • $31 Ⓐ • (10/15/89) • **84**

St.-Julien 1962 • $43 Ⓐ • (11/30/87) • **55**

St.-Julien 1961 • $101 • (04/30/96) • **88**

St.-Julien 1959 • $NA • (10/15/90) • **86**

St.-Julien 1945 • $325 • (03/16/86) • **81**

TALMARD, DOMAINE

Mâcon-Villages Macon-Chardonnay 1993: Soft and simple, straightfoward and lacking interest, with light vanilla and clean apple and peach flavors. Drinkable now. • $10 • (06/30/95) • **78**

TALMONT, CHÂTEAU

Bordeaux 1989 • $8 • (02/28/91) • **74**

TALUAU, JOEL & CLARRISE

St.-Nicolas de Bourgueil Cuvée du Domaine Red 1993: Bright berry and vanilla aromas give way to a light, polished wine with plenty of fruit, along with black pepper and vanilla accents, and just enough tannin for grip. A pretty wine for drinking now. • $15 • **83**

St.-Nicolas de Bourgueil Red 1985 • $12 • (04/15/88) • **71**

TANESSE, CHÂTEAU

Premières Côtes de Bordeaux 1994: Straightforward and one-dimensional, a bit diluted and herbal, showing modest anise and red berry flavors. • $NA • **75-79** (BT)

Premières Côtes de Bordeaux 1992: Decent earthy, tobacco, fruity character and a slightly weedy finish. Drink now. • $NA • **79**

Premières Côtes de Bordeaux White 1993: Smells of butter and butterscotch with some melon notes, but tastes a bit dull. • $NA • **76**

TARDY, JEAN

Clos de Vougeot 1987 • $49 • (03/31/90) • **70**

TARIN, JULIEN

Brut Champagne NV • $25 • (02/15/87) • **78**

TATOUX, DOMAINE J.

Brouilly Garnache 1994: Clean, fresh, sweet cassis flavors are firm and focused, balanced by enough tannin to match well with food. 1,200 cases made. • $10 • **84**

Key: SS—Spectator Selection. CS—Cellar Selection. BB—Best Buy. $NA—Price not available. (BT)—Barrel tasting. Ⓐ—Auction Price.
Dates in parentheses represent the issues in which the ratings were published.

TAUPENOT-MERME, DOMAINE

Chambolle-Musigny 1990: Fragrant, elegant and delightful to drink. This has pretty aromas of cherry, spice and roses, with flavors to match. Nicely balanced and drinkable now. 600 cases made. • $22 • (11/30/94) • **90**
Charmes-Chambertin 1990: Packed with flavor and firmly balanced with tannins and acidity. This offers ripe, focused cherry and currant flavors and meaty, earthy accents that keep it interesting through the long finish. 150 cases made. • $58 • (11/30/94) • **91**
Gevrey-Chambertin Bel Air 1990: A rustic, traditional wine, quite advanced for a 1990, with earthy, vegetal flavors and firm tannins. It could use more fruit character. Drinkable now. 150 cases made. • $30 • (01/31/95) • **81**
Morey-St.-Denis 1990: Lively, fruity and flavorful, starting with fresh berry and attractive brie aromas, followed by ripe cherry flavors and firm tannins. There's a bit of astringency on the finish, but the fruit lasts, too. 600 cases made. • $22 • (11/30/94) • **88**

TAYAC, CHÂTEAU

Côtes de Bourg 1990: Lean, toasty and austere, with a narrow band of currant and smoke aromas and flavors and a firm, tart finish. Drinkable now. • $12 • (06/15/93) • **78**
Côtes de Bourg 1988 • $10 • (01/31/92) • **78**

TEMPIER, DOMAINE

Bandol 1984 • $15 • (12/15/87) • **79**
Bandol 1983 • $30 Ⓐ • (08/31/87) • **78**
Bandol 1981 • $NA • (08/31/86) • **73**
Bandol Cuvée Spéciale La Migoua 1987 • $22 • (10/31/90) • **86**
Bandol Cuvée Spéciale La Tourtine 1987 • $22 • (10/31/90) • **82**

TERME, CHÂTEAU MARQUIS DE

Margaux 1988 • $23 • (04/30/91) • **92**
Margaux 1986 • $23 • (06/30/89) • **79**
Margaux 1961 • $NA • (04/30/96) • **82**

TERRASSE, CHÂTEAU LA

Bordeaux Supérieur 1989 • $8 • (03/31/91) • **79**
Bordeaux Supérieur 1986 • $8 • (06/30/89) • **76**
Bordeaux Supérieur 1985 • $6 • (11/15/87) • **78**
Bordeaux Supérieur 1982 • $4 • (11/16/85) • **74**
Bordeaux Supérieur La Terrasse sur la Rivière 1993: Pleasing black currant and plum flavors plus a dash of herbs and tobacco and medium body add up to a tasty wine for drinking now. • $9 • (08/31/95) • **85**

TERRASSES DE GUILHEM, LES

Vin de Pays de l'Herault Un Vin Comme Autrefois 1993 • $7 • (03/15/94) • **84**

TERRE FERME, DOMAINE DE

Châteauneuf-du-Pape 1989 • $20 • (08/31/92) • **88**

TERREBRUNE, DOMAINE DE

Bandol 1982 • $NA • (08/31/86) • **60**

TERREFORT-QUANCARD, CHÂTEAU DE

Bordeaux 1989 • $14 • (12/31/92) • **81**

TERREY-GROS-CAILLOUX, CHÂTEAU

St.-Julien 1987 • $12 • (11/30/89) • **85**
St.-Julien 1986 • $20 • (11/30/89) • **87**

TERTRE, CHÂTEAU DU

Margaux 1991: A bit too herbal and diluted to rate higher, but there are some pretty cherry and chocolate flavors. • $17 • (03/31/94) • **77**
Margaux 1989 • $29 • (03/15/92) • **90**
Margaux 1988 • $30 • (06/30/91) • **86**
Margaux 1986 • $22 • (06/15/89) • **89**
Margaux 1985 • $26 Ⓐ • (06/30/88) SS • **93**
Margaux 1983 • $24 • (07/16/86) • **91**
Margaux 1982 • $29 Ⓐ • (08/31/92) • **80**

TERTRE DAUGAY, CHÂTEAU

St.-Emilion 1989 • $29 • (04/30/92) • **83**
St.-Emilion 1988 • $20 • (04/30/91) • **85**

TERTRE ROTEBOEUF, CHÂTEAU LE

St.-Emilion 1990: Ripe and generous, with a streak of tannin that keeps the spicy, tobacco-scented black cherry flavors from showing well. Needs until 1997 to soften. • $76 Ⓐ • (06/15/93) • **83**
St.-Emilion 1989 • $79 Ⓐ • (03/15/92) • **93**
St.-Emilion 1988 • $56 Ⓐ • (06/15/91) • **90**
St.-Emilion 1987 • $25 • (02/15/90) • **83**
St.-Emilion 1986 • $39 • (06/30/89) • **90**
St.-Emilion 1985 • $61 Ⓐ • (06/30/88) • **89**
St.-Emilion 1983 • $35 • (05/16/86) • **81**
St.-Emilion 1982 • $30 • (09/16/85) • **85**

TETE, MICHEL

Juliénas Domaine du Clos du Fief Cuvée Prestige 1993: Full-bodied and fairly rich, raisiny and plummy flavors are laced with brown sugar and spice. Still has some energy to it. • $20 • **83**
Juliénas Domaine du Clos du Fief 1992 • $16 • (06/15/94) • **90**

TEYSSIER, CHÂTEAU

Montagne-St.-Emilion 1995: Amazing concentration of fruit but seems very acidic. Disjointed at this point. Full-bodied, offering full tannins, loads of fruit and piercing acidity. • $NA • (05/15/96) • **80-84** (BT)
Montagne-St.-Emilion 1994: Lots of pretty fruit and tannins, full-bodied and good length. A bit dry on the finish, though. If it smooths out, may rate higher in our next tasting. • $NA • **80-84** (BT)
Montagne-St.-Emilion 1993: Rather one-dimensional, showing dark cherry character, medium body, high acidity and fresh, slightly dry finish. • $NA • (01/31/96) • **78**

THEVENET, JEAN

Mâcon Clessé Domaine de la Bongran Cuvée Tradition 1993: Great harmony, round and smooth, yet remaining fresh and crisp. Balances its honey, floral and yeasty notes with great agility, and the finish is as silky as whipped cream. Bravo! • $NA • (05/31/96) • **92**
Mâcon Viré Domaine Emilian Gillet Quintaine 1993: Well crafted, intense and concentrated, full of citrus, honey, pear and ripe apple character. Full bodied and steeped through with flavor. Worth holding until 1998. • $20 • (05/31/96) • **89**
Mâcon Viré Domaine Emilian Gillet Quintaine 1992: Very exotic, with pleasingly decadent, seductive apricot, honey and blanched almond flavors backed up by crisp texture. Somewhat fuller in body and off-dry on the surprising finish. Long and harmonious. Drinkable now or try in 1998. • $20 • (05/31/96) • **90**

THEVENET, JEAN-CLAUDE

Mâcon-Villages 1994: Lively and vibrant lime, wet hay and grass notes carry over to the juicy, long finish. Somewhat tart, but seafood with a rich sauce should make a delicious match. 1,250 cases made. • $10 • **84**
St.-Véran Clos de l'Ermitage, Cuvée Vieilles Vignes White 1994: Deep, intense, smooth, medium-bodied, round and minerally, offering crisp

FRANCE

citrus flavors and pear and green apple notes. Drinkable now. 1,250 cases made. • $16 • **87**

THEVENOT-MACHAL, JACQUES

Volnay Santenots 1988 • $36 • (11/15/90) • **89**

THIBERT PERE & FILS

Pouilly-Fuissé 1994: Extremely well made, clean and focused, this sings with intense, nicely integrated spice and ripe fruit flavors. Terrific finish. 1,416 cases made. • $15 • (05/31/96) • **88**

Pouilly-Fuissé Vieilles Vignes 1994: Fresh, clean and well made. This is focused, medium bodied and has citrus, green apple, honey and cream flavors. Very likeable. 466 cases made. • $16 • (05/31/96) • **86**

Pouilly-Fuissé Vignes Blanches 1994: Like biting into a slice of lime. Tart, crisp and unyielding, with just a hint of earth and butterscotch. It might work with the appropriate food. 350 cases made. • $14 • (05/31/96) • **79**

THIEULEY, CHÂTEAU

Bordeaux White 1994: Interesting grapefruit, apple and grass character, medium bodied and fresh, displaying an aftertaste of freshly-cut apples. Drink now. • $NA • **80**

Bordeaux White Cuvée Francis Courselle 1994: Simple and straightforward, showing some melon and pear notes. Wood gives the impression of dilution, not much better than regular bottling. • $NA • **80**

THOMAS

Pouilly-Fuissé 1994: Delicious for drinking now. Not very intense and somewhat diluted, it still provides lots of pleasure, as its honey touches make a perfect apéritif. Light-bodied and balanced, featuring some citrus, pear and apricot notes on the finish. 833 cases made. • $17 • (05/31/96) • **84**

Pouilly-Fuissé 1993: Extremely crisp, well-defined fruit, lots of wet hay, green apple, lime and fresh herb notes and a vibrant finish. Light-to-medium body. 813 cases made. • $18 • (05/15/95) • **81**

Pouilly-Fuissé Vieilles Vignes 1994: A beautiful, flavorful white, with plenty of ripe pear, toasted pine nut and butter notes along with a citrusy finish that is long and vibrant. Full-bodied and quite opulent, though it falls short of outstanding because it needs a tad more focus. 208 cases made. • $25 • (05/31/96) • **88**

St.-Véran 1994: Fresh, elegant and fruity, delivering pretty citrus, pear and tropical fruit flavors. Buttery on the palate, smooth and creamy on the finish. 1,250 cases made. • $12 • (08/31/95) • **85**

St.-Véran Vieille Vigne Cuvée Préstige 1994: St.-Véran of the vintage? Classy and sweet tasting, featuring a creamy mouth-feel, delicious mineral, citrus, pear, chive and sweet pea flavors, medium body and long finish. 1,250 cases made. • $16 • (08/31/95) • **88**

THOMAS, CLAUDE

Sancerre Chavignol Les Monts Damnés 1994: Soft herbal and green apple flavors keep this characteristic of Sancerre, but it's diluted and lacks acidity for firmness. 400 cases made. • $20 • (06/15/96) • **78**

Sancerre Les Monts Damnés 1993: It may not be classic Sancerre, but it sure is tasty. Appealing aromas of spice and vanilla give way to rich, round flavors of figs, pineapple, vanilla and honey, yet it retains an attractive nervy delicacy. A maverick stand-out in the appellation. • $15 • **88**

Sancerre Les Monts Damnés 1992: Extremely herbal and vegetal, this wine is loaded with what the British refer to as "cat's-pee" flavors. An exaggerated style that may put off many Sauvignon Blanc fans. Tasted twice with consistent notes. • $NA • (10/31/94) • **71**

Key: SS—Spectator Selection. CS—Cellar Selection. BB—Best Buy. $NA—Price not available. (BT)—Barrel tasting. Ⓐ—Auction Price.
Dates in parentheses represent the issues in which the ratings were published.

THOMAS, LUCIEN

Sancerre Clos de la Crèle 1992: A smooth, rich wine, with focused apple, citrus and vanilla flavors, bigger than many '92s, finishing tart and clean. It shows more muscle than delicacy, and can stand up to a wide range of fish and white meat dishes. • $18 • (10/31/94) • **86**

Sancerre Clos de la Crèle 1991 • $14 • (09/15/93) • **73**

Sancerre Cuvée Lucien Thomas 1991 • $21 • (09/15/93) • **83**

THOMAS PAUL

Sancerre Chavignol Les Comtesses Grande Réserve de Notre Vignoble 1994: This tasty wine offers a nice balance of ripe fruit, lively acidity and rich texture. Well-defined lemon, melon and hay notes linger on the finish. • $19 • (06/15/96) • **88**

Sancerre Chavignol Les Comtesses Grande Réserve de Notre Vignoble 1993: Unusually broad and thick, sporting honey and buttery aromas, very ripe apple and melon flavors and a hint of exotic spices. Not typical, but appealing. • $21 • (11/15/95) • **86**

THOMAS-MOILLARD

Chardonnay Bourgogne Hautes-Côtes de Nuits 1994: Modest depth and decent acidity, offering good grapefruit and gooseberry flavors. It has a nice touch of spice on the finish. 2,530 cases made. • $14 • (05/31/96) • **81**

Corton-Charlemagne 1994: Extremely buttery-tasting, sporting very good acidity and concentration. It has tropical notes of banana and melon and a spicy finish. Falls slightly short, but still packs plenty of flavor. 194 cases made. • $60 • (05/31/96) • **87**

THORIN

Beaujolais-Villages 1988 • $7 • (05/31/89) • **79**

Châteauneuf-du-Pape 1986 • $13 • (11/30/88) • **87**

Côtes du Rhône L'Escalou 1987 • $6 • (01/31/89) • **67**

Moulin-à-Vent Château des Jacques 1988 • $16 • (05/31/89) • **88**

Pommard 1986 • $24 • (02/28/90) • **75**

THOU, DOMAINE LE

Merlot Vin de Pays d'Oc 1990 • $10 • (03/15/94) • **82**

TIGNY, DE

Saumur Champigny Château de Chaintres 1992: Round and smooth, with firm tannins, chocolate and menthol flavors dominating the modest fruit. It's fresh but a bit dull. 10,000 cases made. • $10 • (11/15/94) • **79**

TIJOU, PIERRE-YVES

Coteaux du Layon-Chaume Cuvée Clémentine 1993: Incredibly rich aromas of honey and apricot, followed by moderately sweet spiced apple notes. The finish is elegant and minerally, adding a bitter almond aftertaste. • $20 • (05/15/96) • **89**

Savennières Clos des Perrières 1993: Piercing scent of honey, apple and beeswax and a touch of mineral. Vibrant and youthful, the lean, intense flavors suggest plenty of life ahead. Try in 1998. • $17 • (05/15/96) • **85**

TIMBERLAY, CHÂTEAU

Bordeaux Supérieur 1991: Extremely herbaceous wine with smoky, asparagus character. Light body and finish. • $10 • (03/31/94) • **70**

Bordeaux White 1993: Smells OK, but very tart on the palate, straightforward, diluted, woody and flat. • $8 • **73**

TINEL, F.

Pouilly-Fumé Genetin 1993: Pleasant richness and intensity underscore smoky, ripe peach notes that unfold into a firm, lingering finish. Give this until 1997. Best with food. 2,500 cases made. • $17 • (05/15/96) • **86**

Pouilly-Fumé Genetin 1992: Round, soft and fruity, this shows pear, sweet pea and light grassy flavors. It's generous, clean, pleasant and direct. 2,500 cases made. • $15 • (10/31/94) • **84**

TINEL-BLONDELET, F.

Pouilly-Fumé L'Arret Buffatte 1993: Inviting aromas of ripe apples and spices follow through on the round palate. This has enough acidity for crispness, but it's delicate and soft as a pillow. 1,000 cases made. • $18 • (10/31/94) • **83**

TIREGAND, CHÂTEAU DE

Pécharmant 1985 • $8 • (10/31/88) • **82**

TOLLOT-BEAUT

Aloxe-Corton 1993: Very good structure complements delicious floral, rose petal, currant and plum aromas and flavors. A bit tough now, try in 1997. • $29 • **86**

Aloxe-Corton 1992: Round and spicy, light and pleasant, showing peppery red berry notes in balance with a hint of oak. Ready to drink. 1,308 cases made. • $27 • **82**

Aloxe-Corton 1991 • $28 • (01/31/94) • **82**

Aloxe-Corton 1990 • $38 • (12/15/92) • **93**

Aloxe-Corton 1989 • $60 Ⓐ • (01/31/92) • **90**

Aloxe-Corton 1985 • $29 Ⓐ • (03/15/88) • **89**

Aloxe-Corton Les Vercots 1993: Well crafted, round and smooth, delicious, delivering mocha, vanilla and currant character. So supple it melts in the mouth, but has enough tannin structure to hold until 1999. • $37 • **89**

Beaune Clos du Roi 1993: Decent plum and berry character, but just slightly herbal. Medium-bodied with medium tannins and a silky finish. Try in 1998. • $35 • **88**

Beaune Clos du Roi 1992: A pretty wine, with raspberry and cherry flavors playing against the chestnut and sweet-oak notes on the supple finish. Easy to drink. 525 cases made. • $30 • **85**

Beaune Clos du Roi 1991: A bright, flavorful, harmonious wine, with well-defined currant and blackberry flavors shaded by toast and vanilla notes and a touch of anise. May be best in 1997. 517 cases made. • $30 Ⓐ • (01/31/94) • **87**

Beaune Clos du Roi 1990: A beauty of a wine, complex and refined, with bright violet, vanilla, tea and red berry aromas and flavors that grow and grow in the glass. Nicely structured, with firm tannins. Drinkable now. • $48 • (12/15/92) • **90**

Beaune Clos du Roi 1988 • $53 • (02/28/91) • **86**

Beaune Clos du Roi Premier Cru 1989 • $52 • (01/31/92) • **91**

Beaune Grèves 1993: Very good chocolate, berry and raspberry character, medium body, velvety tannins and a fresh finish. Better in 1999. • $35 • **87**

Beaune Grèves 1992: Juicy and oak-scented, comes across as light and shows modest fruit flavors and a short, crisp finish. 283 cases made. • $30 • **79**

Beaune Grèves 1991: Lean and focused, with a delicate, bright beam of currant, blackberry and anise aromas and flavors that fades on finish. Drinkable now. 283 cases made. • $30 Ⓐ • (01/31/94) • **82**

Beaune Grèves 1990: Beautifully crafted, with wonderful plum, toast and berry characteristics and perfectly integrated tannins. Isn't enormously concentrated, but what it has is fantastic. Drinkable now. • $40 • (12/15/92) • **92**

Beaune Grèves 1989 • $44 • (01/31/92) • **90**

Bourgogne White 1993: Subtle and elegant, showing some nice mineral, lemon, vanilla, apple and chalk flavors shaded by sweet oak notes. Tart finish, but given time it may flesh out. 458 cases made. • $15 • **84**

Bourgogne White 1992: Vibrant acidity and seductive toasty, smoky and honeyed notes. Ends with some spice, pear and vanilla accents. A bit woody. Drinkable now. Tasted twice. • $15 • (08/31/94) • **85**

Bourgogne White 1991 • $15 • (10/15/93) • **82**

Chorey-Côte-de-Beaune 1993: Elegant and pure, a crystal-clear red offering plum, currant and touches of smoke on the crisp finish. Tempting now, but should hold until 1999. • $18 • **87**

Chorey-Côte-de-Beaune 1992: Light texture, showing toast, raspberry and prune aromas and flavors, finishing a little earthy. Try now. 3,000 cases made. • $15 • **83**

Chorey-Côte-de-Beaune 1990: Well crafted and velvety, with plenty of action. Offers plum, redwood and vanilla flavors and tobacco and toast notes on the finish. Drinkable now. • $26 • (12/15/92) • **86**

Chorey-Côte-de-Beaune 1989 • $28 • (01/31/92) • **87**

Chorey-Côte-de-Beaune 1985 • $18 • (04/15/88) • **83**

Chorey-lès-Beaune 1988 • $25 • (12/31/90) • **88**

Corton 1993: A well-crafted red boasting lovely vanilla, ripe berry and currant aromas and flavors, medium body, velvety tannins and fresh, long finish. Better in 2000. • $57 • **91**

Corton 1992: Light and fragrant, with appealing raspberry and strawberry flavors that fade a little on the sweet finish. A delicate style that is drinkable now. 250 cases made. • $45 • **82**

Corton 1990: Bubbling over the rim of the glass with fruit, this seductive, luscious wine has opulent blackberry and smoke characteristics. Drinkable now to 1998. • $56 • (12/15/92) • **94**

Corton 1989 • $67 • (01/31/92) • **90**

Corton 1986 • $45 • (08/31/89) • **87**

Corton 1985 • $75 • (03/15/88) • **97**

Corton Bressandes 1993: Beautiful, fresh and crisp red Burgundy, showing lovely vanilla, plum, raspberry, currant flavors and an enticing earthy component. Hard now, but give it until 2000. • $57 • **90**

Corton Bressandes 1992: Relatively simple and direct, showing less oak than usual, but flavors focus nicely on raspberry, currant and vanilla. The finish is smooth and elegant. Approachable now. 400 cases made. • $45 • **85**

Corton Bressandes 1991: Light and crisp, with bright anise-scented raspberry and strawberry flavors shining through the finish. A bit tight at the end, but nicely balanced overall. Drinkable now through 1998. 408 cases made. • $45 Ⓐ • (01/31/94) • **88**

Corton Bressandes 1990: Red Burgundy doesn't get much better than this. Complex, ripe, lavish and dense, with deep black cherry, blackberry, vanilla and violet flavors that linger on the finish. Tempting now but will remain great for years. • $40 • **96**

Corton Bressandes 1989 • $58 • **94**

Corton Bressandes 1988 • $59 • **92**

Corton Bressandes 1987 • $33 • **86**

Corton Bressandes 1986 • $40 • **83**

Corton Bressandes 1985 • $75 • **88**

Corton Bressandes 1983 • $40 • **83**

Corton Le Corton 1991: Beautifully articulated fruit flavors course through this elegant, brilliantly focused, supple wine. Much more generous than most '91s. A gorgeous mouthful that lingers. Drinkable now. 267 cases made. • $45 Ⓐ • (01/31/94) • **91**

Corton Les Bressandes 1990: A multidimensional Corton, with a solid structure and elegant fruit flavors. Has plenty of vanilla, earth and ripe cherry characteristics. Drinkable in 1997. • $40 • (12/15/92) • **91**

Corton-Charlemagne 1993: Impressive for the vintage. Extremely well made, boasting cream, mineral, coconut and apple flavors, medium-to-full body and a long, crisp finish. 110 cases made. • $70 • **90**

Corton-Charlemagne 1992: A tart and firm style of Corton. Appealingly toasty and fresh, with bright and lively flavors accented by butter and ripe fruit notes, delivers a sharp, refreshing lime edge on the vanilla-scented finish. • $70 • (08/31/94) • **92**

Corton-Charlemagne 1991 • $85 • (10/15/93) • **87**

Savigny-lès-Beaune Lavières 1993: Extremely attractive. Vibrant aromas of cherry and tobacco follow through on the palate. Medium-bodied and a silky texture. Try in 1998. • $25 • **90**

Savigny-lès-Beaune Lavières 1992: Firm in texture with nicely focused, spicy cherry flavor echoing on the slightly tannic finish. Drinkable now. 1,200 cases imported. • $24 • **84**

Savigny-lès-Beaune Lavières 1991: Light and crisp, offering simple raspberry and strawberry flavors in modest proportions. 983 cases made. • $22 Ⓐ • (01/31/94) • **82**

Savigny-lès-Beaune Lavières 1990: Delightfully complex, starting with raspberry, chocolate and plum flavors in a combination that beckons

you back for more and ending with a toasty, refined finish. Drinkable now. • $35 • (12/15/92) • **90**
Savigny-lès-Beaune Lavières 1989 • $38 • (01/31/92) • **90**

TOMAZE, CHÂTEAU LA

Anjou Villages Cuvée des Lys 1990: Round and smooth on the palate, this offers grapey and black pepper flavors that turn a bit tannic on the finish. It's ripe and balanced. 1,000 cases made. • $10 • **83**

TONNELLE, CHÂTEAU LA

Haut-Médoc 1987 • $12 • (11/30/89) • **76**
Haut-Médoc 1986 • $11 • (11/30/89) • **70**
Haut-Médoc 1985 • $10 • (02/15/89) • **77**
Premières Côtes de Blaye 1990: A soft, simple, agreeable red that's full of herb and tomato flavors and shows hints of plum and cherry as well. Moderately tannic, smooth and drinkable now. 4,000 cases made. • $8 • (03/15/93) • **81**

TOQUES & CLOCHERS

Chardonnay Sélection 1991 • $18 • (03/15/94) • **84**
Chardonnay Terroir d'Autan 1991 • $NA • (03/15/94) • **86**
Chardonnay Terroir Haute Vallée 1991 • $NA • (03/15/94) • **85**
Chardonnay Terroir Méditerranean 1991 • $NA • (03/15/94) • **89**
Chardonnay Terroir Océanique 1991 • $NA • (03/15/94) • **85**

TORTOCHOT, DOMAINE

Chambertin 1985 • $90 • (12/31/88) • **94**

TOUMALIN, CHÂTEAU

Canon-Fronsac 1990: Very light and simple for the vintage, with some cherry flavor but not much else. Drinkable now. 3,500 cases made. • $14 • (03/31/93) • **74**

TOUR, CHÂTEAU DE LA

Bordeaux Supérieur 1995: Medium- to full-bodied, featuring red berry and blackberry flavors, quite fresh and vivid, but ending on a slightly short finish. Could use a bit more opulence. • $NA • (05/15/96) • **85-89** (BT)
Bordeaux Supérieur 1992: This simple wine offers cherry fruit, along with earthy and weedy notes, and light tannins. It's balanced and drinkable, but meager. Drinkable now. • $8 • (11/15/94) • **77**
Bordeaux Supérieur Réserve du Château 1994: Very firm, sporting fine, slightly hard tannins, medium body and a delicious tobacco, cherry character. • $NA • **80-84** (BT)
Bordeaux Supérieur Réserve du Château 1993: Medium-bodied, tasting slightly herbaceous, with herbal and tomato flavors and some dry tannins. • $15 • (01/31/96) • **79**

TOUR, CHÂTEAU DE LA

Clos Vougeot 1993: Pleasant and already quite attractive. Mineral, earth and currant character makes this enticing. Rather tannic, sweet-tasting and well done. Lacks a bit of class and depth. Try in 1999. • $53 • **84**
Clos Vougeot 1992: Ripe and generous, with a spicy edge to the chunky currant and black cherry flavors which are nicely polished without discernible oak. Approachable now, but best from 1997. • $51 • **87**

TOUR-BALADOZ, CHÂTEAU

St.-Emilion 1995: Lively, vibrant cassis and wild berry notes, bracketed by subtle spice and smoky oak flavors, make this an appealing medium- to full-bodied Bordeaux. Lacks a bit of elegance on the slightly short finish. • $NA • (05/15/96) • **85-89** (BT)
St.-Emilion 1985 • $12 • (02/29/88) • **82**

TOUR-DE-BESSAN, CHÂTEAU LA

Margaux 1989 • $NA • (03/15/92) • **87**

TOUR-DE-BY, CHÂTEAU LA

Médoc 1995: Plenty of bright cherry, berry and cassis aromas and flavors. Fine tannins and plenty of sweet fruit on the finish. Delicious. • $NA • (05/15/96) • **85-89** (BT)
Médoc 1992: Stewed tomato, herbal character. Diluted. • $11 • **73**
Médoc 1991: Very herbal, light and bitter. Astringent finish. • $11 • (03/31/94) • **74**
Médoc 1990: A traditional-style Bordeaux, with earth, leather, berry character and slightly overripe fruit on the finish. It has medium tannins with a soft texture. Drinkable now. 39,000 cases made. • $12 • (03/31/93) • **82**
Médoc 1989 • $19 • (03/15/92) • **85**
Médoc 1988 • $13 • (06/15/91) • **86**
Médoc 1987 • $10 • (11/30/89) • **79**
Médoc 1986 • $12 • (11/30/89) • **80**
Médoc 1983 • $18 • (10/16/85) • **78**
Médoc 1982 • $20 • (08/31/92) • **85**
Médoc Cuvée Prestige 1982 • $20 • (08/31/92) • **89**

TOUR-GRAND-FAURIE, CHÂTEAU

St.-Emilion 1985 • $9 • (02/15/89) • **79**

TOUR-HAUT-BRION, CHÂTEAU LA

Graves 1985 • $30 • (02/15/89) • **86**
Graves 1983 • $25 • (03/15/87) • **90**
Graves 1981 • $33 • **85**
Graves 1979 • $30 • (11/15/91) • **85**
Graves 1975 • $175 • (11/15/91) • **84**
Graves 1970 • $150 • (05/15/93) • **85**
Graves 1966 • $175 • (11/15/91) • **84**
Graves 1964 • $110 • (11/15/91) • **83**
Graves 1962 • $60 • (11/30/87) • **85**
Graves 1961: A wonderful minty, cedary character marks this mature but still lively wine. It has enough of a chewy texture to keep it lively, and solidly fruity, meaty flavors to keep it satisfying. Drink through 2000. • $NA • (04/30/96) • **88**
Graves 1959 • $190 • (11/15/91) • **84**
Graves 1958 • $150 • (11/15/91) • **85**
Graves 1957 • $125 • (11/15/91) • **86**
Graves 1955 • $300 • (11/15/91) • **87**
Graves 1953 • $300 • (11/15/91) • **86**
Graves 1950 • $230 • (11/15/91) • **50**
Graves 1947 • $630 • (11/15/91) • **91**
Graves 1945: Sweet and silky, very mature, even a bit raisiny, but elegant and finely textured. Has length and finesse. • $650 • **85**
Graves 1943 • $230 • (11/15/91) • **85**
Graves 1940 • $190 • (11/15/91) • **83**
Graves 1929 • $500 • (11/15/91) • **85**
Graves 1928 • $300 • (11/15/91) • **68**
Pessac-Léognan 1995: A solid wine that's tannic and slightly austere, but it expresses a good level of Cabernet character, with good concentration of fruit. Muscular wine. • $NA • (05/15/96) • **85-89** (BT)
Pessac-Léognan 1994: Good levels of ripe berry, cherry and raspberry come out in this medium-bodied red that has nice, even tannins and a light finish. • $29 • (05/15/96) • **85-89** (BT)
Pessac-Léognan 1990: Big and extracted, with earth, cassis and cedar character and muscular tannins. Weighty. Try in 1998. 2,500 cases made. • $35 • (03/31/93) • **93**
Pessac-Léognan 1989 • $44 • (03/15/92) • **95**
Pessac-Léognan 1988 • $30 • (06/15/91) CS • **91**
Pessac-Léognan 1987 • $22 • (05/15/90) • **87**

Key: SS—Spectator Selection. CS—Cellar Selection. BB—Best Buy. $NA—Price not available. (BT)—Barrel tasting. (A)—Auction Price.
Dates in parentheses represent the issues in which the ratings were published.

Pessac-Léognan 1986 • $NA • **50**

TOUR-DU-HAUT-MOULIN, CHÂTEAU

Haut-Médoc 1988 • $20 • (04/30/91) • **88**
Haut-Médoc 1987 • $15 • (11/30/89) • **80**
Haut-Médoc 1986 • $16 • (11/30/89) • **90**
Haut-Médoc 1985 • $15 • (02/15/89) • **84**
Haut-Médoc 1982 • $16 • (11/30/89) • **84**

TOUR-DU-MIRAIL, CHÂTEAU

Haut-Médoc 1987 • $10 • (11/30/89) • **83**
Haut-Médoc 1986 • $12 • (11/30/89) • **79**
Haut-Médoc 1982 • $9 • (11/30/89) • **79**

TOUR-DU-PIN-FIGEAC, CHÂTEAU LA

St.-Emilion 1988 • $24 • (07/15/91) • **77**
St.-Emilion 1982 • $21 • (05/15/89) • **88**

TOUR-DU-PIN-FIGEAC-BELIEVIER, CHÂTEAU LA

St.-Emilion 1989 • $24 • (04/30/92) • **83**
St.-Emilion 1982 • $22 • (05/15/89) • **82**

TOUR-PRIGNAC, CHÂTEAU

Médoc 1989 • $9 • (07/15/92) • **75**

TOUR-ST.-BONNET, CHÂTEAU LA

Médoc 1995: Very pretty, distinctive, sweet-tasting plum, red berry and somewhat minty character. Tannins are firm and the finish a bit harsh and inelegant now. • $NA • (05/15/96) • **80-84** (BT)
Médoc 1985 • $13 Ⓐ • (06/30/88) • **83**

TOUR DE L'ANGE, CHÂTEAU DE LA

Bordeaux 1991: Light and pleasant with cherry, chocolate aromas and flavors, light tannins and a simple finish. • $10 • (03/31/94) • **78**

TOUR DE BELLEGARDE, CHÂTEAU

Bordeaux Supérieur 1986 • $4 • (05/15/89) • **77**

TOUR BLANCHE, CHÂTEAU LA

Sauternes 1990: Delicious and drinkable now, offering spice, ginger and pepper flavors and attractive hints of pear, melon and honey that might go well with Asian food. • $56 • (04/15/95) • **88**
Sauternes 1989: Intense and exotic, ripe and rich botrytis flavors explode on the palate to a long finish. Very sweet and full in body, it packs in the spice, white pepper, cream, coffee, quince and dried apricot notes. • $49 • (04/15/95) • **92**
Sauternes 1988: Big and ripe, very sweet and full in body, with lots of tropical fruit, a lovely, creamy texture and some caramel, apricot and butter flavors. Long finish. Try in 1998. • $32 • (04/15/95) • **89**
Sauternes 1987 • $23 • (06/15/90) • **82**
Sauternes 1986 • $26 • (04/15/95) • **84**
Sauternes 1985 • $32 • (07/15/88) • **85**
Sauternes 1983 • $32 • (04/15/95) • **88**

TOUR BOISEE, DOMAINE LA

Minervois 1990 • $8 • (03/15/94) • **82**
Minervois Cuvée Marie-Claude 1990 • $11 • (03/15/94) • **88**

TOUR CALON, CHÂTEAU

Montagne-St.-Emilion 1990: There are some concentrated plummy, spicy, fruitcake aromas, however, the ripe, stewed flavors result in a dull, flat taste. • $13 • (08/31/95) • **82**
Montagne-St.-Emilion 1989 • $13 • (11/30/92) • **78**
Montagne-St.-Emilion 1986 • $10 • (09/30/89) • **81**

TOUR CARNET, CHÂTEAU LA

Haut-Médoc 1995: Loads of fruit in this one. Medium-to-full body, with lots of rich berry, blackberry and raspberry flavors. The tannins are velvety. • $NA • (05/15/96) • **85-89** (BT)
Haut-Médoc 1992: This has good body but is a bit too herbal and green to be better than average, medium tannins. Drink now. • $17 • **76**
Haut-Médoc 1991: Very weak, but fair brown sugar and plum character. • $15 • (03/31/94) • **71**
Haut-Médoc 1989 • $24 • (03/15/92) • **92**
Haut-Médoc 1988 • $15 • (08/31/91) • **82**
Haut-Médoc 1985 • $22 • (12/31/88) • **71**
Haut-Médoc 1983 • $13 • (02/29/88) • **69**
Haut-Médoc 1945 • $130 • (03/16/86) • **88**

TOUR FIGEAC, CHÂTEAU LA

St.-Emilion 1982 • $22 • (05/15/89) • **89**

TOUR HAUT-CAUSSAN, CHÂTEAU

Médoc 1992: Polished although lean, medium-bodied, fresh currant character and sleek texture. Drink now. • $14 • **82**
Médoc 1991: An attractively aromatic wine, with cherry aroma and flavor, a smoky character, light body, mild tannins and a short finish. • $14 • (03/31/94) • **81**
Médoc 1990: A lively wine, with vivid aromas and flavors of tobacco, cherries and cinnamon and ripe, round tannins. Polished and well structured. Drinkable now. 10,500 cases made. • $17 • (03/31/93) • **89**
Médoc 1989 • $20 • (03/15/92) • **87**
Médoc 1988 • $13 • (07/15/91) • **79**
Médoc 1987 • $11 • (11/30/89) • **80**
Médoc 1986 • $14 • (11/30/89) • **88**
Médoc 1984 • $10 • (02/15/88) • **80**
Médoc 1982 • $16 • (08/31/92) • **90**

TOUR LEOGNAN, CHÂTEAU LA

Pessac-Léognan 1990: This shows good winemaking, with well-focused fruit and tannins. Drinkable in 1997. • $21 • (03/31/93) • **87**
Pessac-Léognan 1986 • $11 • (02/15/89) • **85**

TOUR MARTILLAC, CHÂTEAU LA

Graves 1985 • $19 • (08/31/88) • **87**
Pessac-Léognan 1995: Lovely, silky texture and quite delicate, almost light, with the fruit up front. It's a pleasure to taste now, but we wish for a bit more depth. Could move up to "very good" in our next tasting. • $NA • (05/15/96) • **80-84** (BT)
Pessac-Léognan 1994: Big, muscular, extracted, meaty black cherry, spice, berry and earth flavors and a long, tannic finish. Borderline outstanding, let's see next year. Tasted twice, with consistent notes. • $NA • **85-89** (BT)
Pessac-Léognan 1993: Some nice ripeness in this medium- to full-bodied '93, as attractive plum, cherry and currant flavors linger on the plate. Supple tannins. Try in 1997. • $18 • (01/31/96) • **83**
Pessac-Léognan 1992: Green tobacco, cedar and berry aromas and flavors, medium-to-light body, light tannins and a toasted oak finish. Drink now. • $15 • **83**
Pessac-Léognan 1991: Elegant and aromatic, with a vanilla and cherry character, medium body and light, dry finish. • $15 • (03/31/94) • **78**
Pessac-Léognan 1990: Starts off slowly but then builds on the palate. It offers rich tar, berry and earth character and big tannins. Drinkable in 1999. 8,000 cases made. • $25 • (03/31/93) • **91**

Pessac-Léognan 1988 • $24 • (02/28/91) • **88**
Pessac-Léognan 1986 • $15 • (02/15/90) • **90**
Pessac-Léognan White 1994: Complex aromas and flavors of tropical fruit, almonds, vanilla and cream. Has fine acidity but full body and a long finish. Lovely now. Better than when we tasted it a year ago. • $30 • (03/31/96) • **89**
Pessac-Léognan White 1993: Round and straightforward, although a little dull, shows mineral and pear aromas and flavors. Not as good as the '92. • $20 • **82**
Pessac-Léognan White 1992 • $25 • (06/15/94) • **85**
Pessac-Léognan White 1991 • $20 • (03/31/94) • **85**

TOUR DE MIRAMBEAU, CHÂTEAU

Entre-Deux-Mers 1994: Rather ripe, tasting of sweet fruit and mineral notes, quite lovely, balanced and flavorful. • $NA • **82**

TOUR DE MONS, CHÂTEAU LA

Margaux 1992: Not much fruit here, some strawberry and cherry character, but very diluted. Drinkable now. • $15 • (04/15/95) • **75**
Margaux 1991: A simple and firm wine with medium body and tannins. A pleasant cherry character. Drinkable now. • $15 • (03/31/94) • **82**
Margaux 1990: A well-toned wine, with plenty of tobacco, cedar and plum aromas and flavors, loads of fruit extract and balanced silky tannins. Drinkable in 1997. 10,000 cases made. • $20 • (03/31/93) • **89**
Margaux 1989 • $25 • (03/15/92) • **88**
Margaux 1986 • $19 • (11/30/89) • **90**
Margaux 1982 • $18 Ⓐ • (08/31/92) • **88**
Margaux 1945 • $200 • (03/16/86) • **89**

TOUR DU PIN, CHÂTEAU LA

St.-Emilion 1982 • $12 • (05/01/85) • **81**

TOUR DU ROC, CHÂTEAU

Haut-Médoc 1989 • $13 • (06/15/93) • **71**
Haut-Médoc 1987 • $10 • (11/30/89) • **74**
Haut-Médoc 1986 • $11 • (11/30/89) • **76**
Haut-Médoc 1982 • $12 • (11/30/89) • **84**

TOURELLES, DOMAINE DES

Gigondas 1989 • $16 • (08/31/92) • **81**

TOURELLES DE LONGUEVILLE

Pauillac 1995: Elegant and relatively concentrated, with cassis flavors bracketed by tobacco and spice notes. A well-made, velvety, medium-bodied '95 that races over the palate to a long finish. • $NA • (05/15/96) • **85-89** (BT)
Pauillac 1994: Typical of '94, emphasizing the spice more than the fruit flavors, although this has some decent red berry and plum accents. A touch diluted and slightly herbal, though. Second label of Château Pichon-Longueville-Baron. • $20 • (05/15/96) • **80-84** (BT)
Pauillac 1993: Modest fruit but also a bit herbaceous, medium body, firm texture, somewhat dry finish. Try now and through 1997. 10,000 cases made. • $20 • (01/31/96) • **78**
Pauillac 1992: Not bad texture but weedy, green and slightly metallic. Drink if you must. • $16 • **70**
Pauillac 1991: Loads of green peppers, medium-bodied with a velvety texture. • $16 • (03/31/94) • **78**
Pauillac 1990: A well-knit wine, with ripe cassis, berry and tobacco character, lush tannins and an opulent finish. Drinkable in 1998. • $24 • (03/31/93) • **90**
Pauillac 1989 • $27 • (03/15/92) • **94**

Key: SS—Spectator Selection. CS—Cellar Selection. BB—Best Buy. $NA—Price not available. (BT)—Barrel tasting. Ⓐ—Auction Price.
Dates in parentheses represent the issues in which the ratings were published.

TOURIER, PAUL

Puligny-Montrachet Champ Gain 1993: Tight and tart, showing modest pear and almond flavors. Not particularly rich or intense and turns a bit astringent on the finish. Might smooth out in another year. 1,295 cases made. • $26 • (04/30/96) • **82**

TOURNONS, CELLIER DES

Pouilly-Fuissé Rocqenvert 1994: Good finesse here, showing a touch of wet earth, herb and smoke. Turns somewhat sharp and tart on the finish. May be better in 1997. 166 cases made. • $19 • (05/31/96) • **83**

TOURS, CHÂTEAU DES

Brouilly 1995: This is rich and weighty for Brouilly. The plum and black cherry flavors are ripe and deep, but an earthy note detracts a bit. It needs food to soften the firm tannins, and should improve into 1997. 30,000 cases made. • $14 • **86**
Brouilly 1993: Round and full, with bright, deep blackberry and meaty flavors, offering good structure and depth. A wine for rich food. 25,000 cases made. • $12 • (06/30/94) • **86**
Côtes du Rhône 1989 • $12 • (03/15/91) • **80**
Côtes du Rhône Réserve 1993: Vibrant and fruity aroma, nicely peppery in flavor, well balanced and moderately tannic. Distinctive, jammy fruit and spice nuances linger on the finish. • $12 • (09/30/95) • **86**
Côtes du Rhône Réserve 1992: A dried cherry aroma, musty flavors and dry, tannic finish don't add up to much fun. Possibly corky? • $10 • (11/30/94) • **76**
Côtes du Rhône Réserve 1990 • $12 • (04/15/93) • **81**
Vacqueyras Réserve 1991 • $15 • (03/31/94) • **85**
Vacqueyras Réserve 1990 • $16 • (04/15/93) • **79**
Vacqueyras Réserve 1989 • $15 • (10/15/91) • **85**

TOURS, DOMAINE DES

Vin de Pays de Vaucluse 1993: A pleasantly fruity, well-balanced red with soft tannins and an appealing, smooth texture. Fresh and delightful. • $8 • **84**
Vin de Pays de Vaucluse 1990 • $7 • (04/15/93) BB • **82**
Vin de Pays de Vaucluse 1989 • $8 • (03/31/91) • **78**

TOURS, MARQUIS DES

Bordeaux 1988 • $5 • (02/28/91) • **78**

TRAPET, DOMAINE

Gevrey-Chambertin 1991: Crisp and lively, a tough-textured wine with ripe currant fruit sneaking in on the finish. • $23 • (03/15/94) • **80**
Latricières-Chambertin 1991: Soft and velvety, a ripe wine with a green streak running through it, probably best around 1997. • $49 • (03/15/94) • **85**

TRAPET, JEAN & JEAN-LOUIS

Chambertin 1993: Loads of lovely, ripe berry, cherry and earth aromas and flavors. Medium- to full-bodied, velvety tannins and fresh finish. Needs time, better in 2000. • $NA • (05/15/96) • **92**
Chapelle-Chambertin 1993: Rich, ripe and flavorful red berry, plum and toasted oak notes, which turn somewhat tart on the finish. A bit tough now, but after 2000 it should be a joy to drink. • $NA • **87**
Gevrey-Chambertin 1993: Loads of cedar, spice and red berry character and long, chewy finish in this full-bodied red. Lacks a bit of class to rate higher because it's slighty rough on aftertaste. • $NA • **85**
Latricières-Chambertin 1993: Medium-bodied red showing vibrant, clean red berry flavors, earthy, chewy character and toasty, rather crisp finish. Try in 1999. • $NA • **86**

TRAPET, LOUIS

Chambertin 1988 • $111 • (07/15/91) • **92**

Chambertin 1987 • $75 • (05/31/90) • **91**
Chambertin 1985 • $101 • (03/15/88) • **88**
Chambertin Cuvée Vieilles Vignes Red 1988 • $119 • (07/15/91) • **89**
Chapelle-Chambertin 1988 • $84 • (07/15/91) • **89**
Chapelle-Chambertin 1985 • $64 • (03/15/88) • **84**
Chapelle-Chambertin Réserve Jean Trapet 1987 • $62 • (03/15/91) • **79**
Gevrey-Chambertin 1988 • $40 • (07/15/91) • **81**
Gevrey-Chambertin 1987 • $30 • (07/15/90) • **74**
Gevrey-Chambertin 1985 • $40 • (05/31/88) • **79**
Latricières-Chambertin 1988 • $84 • (07/15/91) • **84**
Latricières-Chambertin 1987 • $62 • (05/31/90) • **88**
Marsannay Red 1987 • $17 • (03/31/91) • **78**

TREMBLAY, GERARD

Chablis 1994: Falls flat on flavor and depth. Green apple notes add some spice and a touch of sweetness. • $14 • (05/31/96) • **79**
Chablis Fourchaume 1994: Fairly soft, minerally flavors and an aroma that's redolent of honey. Green apple and green plum notes dominate this nicely balanced white. • $18 • (05/31/96) • **83**

TRENEL & FILS

Beaujolais-Villages 1990 • $10 • (09/15/91) • **81**
Beaujolais-Villages 1988 • $9 • (05/31/89) • **78**
Chénas 1988 • $14 • (05/31/89) • **86**
Chiroubles 1988 • $12 • (05/31/89) • **83**
Côte de Brouilly 1990 • $15 • (09/15/91) • **82**
Fleurie 1988 • $14 • (05/31/89) • **86**
Morgon Côte de Py 1988 • $17 • (05/31/89) • **92**
Moulin-à-Vent La Rochelle 1988 • $17 • (05/31/89) • **90**
Régnié 1988 • $12 • (05/31/89) • **83**
St.-Amour 1988 • $15 • (05/31/89) • **87**

TREVALLON, DOMAINE DE

Les Baux Coteaux d'Aix en Provence 1987 • $18 • (03/31/90) • **78**
Les Baux Coteaux d'Aix en Provence 1986 • $21 • (04/15/89) • **87**
Les Baux Coteaux d'Aix en Provence 1985 • $48 Ⓐ • (02/29/88) • **82**

TRIBUT, LAURENT

Chablis 1994: A clean, crisp and lively Chablis that is well made and focused on apple, pear and mineral flavors. Silky, oaky finish. Straightforward but delicious. • $22 • (05/31/96) • **82**
Chablis Beauroy 1994: Overdone and showing too much new oak, the vanilla and caramel dominate the fruit flavors. A bit disjointed and tart on the finish. • $30 • (05/31/96) • **78**
Chablis Côte de Léchet 1994: An elegant and polished *premier cru* with a pronounced new oak character. It delivers some nice flavors of mineral, toasted pine nuts, citrus and smoke, with a hint of honey on the finish. Try in 1997. • $30 • (05/31/96) • **84**

TRICHARD, BENOIT

Moulin-à-Vent Red 1990 • $12 • (08/31/92) • **85**

TRIGNON, CHÂTEAU DU

Côtes du Rhône Viognier 1993: Labelled as a Viognier, this is a middle of the road white wine, with fairly fresh, floral aromas and a smooth texture. • $17 • **78**
Côtes du Rhône-Villages Rasteau 1993: A flat-tasting wine that smells and tastes a bit varnishy. The fruit flavors are dominated by plum and dried cherry with a hint of spice. • $13 • **72**
Côtes du Rhône-Villages Rasteau 1986 • $9 • (12/15/90) • **80**

TRIMBACH

Alsace Alsace Pinot Blanc 1992: Fairly crisp and light, with earthy aromas, mineral and honey flavors. Very dry and a bit chalky on the finish. • $9 • **79**
Gewürztraminer Alsace 1992: Beautifully ripe and rich in style, with aromas of honey and butter, notes of peach and pineapple and a pleasingly thick texture that helps the flavors persist on the aftertaste. • $14 • (11/15/94) • **85**
Pinot Gris Alsace Réserve Personelle 1992: Round and slightly sweet, plump, smoky and easy to drink, but fading into simple sweetness on the finish. It would be an awkward match with food, not the traditional Trimbach style. Tasted twice, with consistent notes. • $26 • (09/15/95) • **80**
Pinot Gris Alsace Réserve 1992: Muscular and austere, this shows earth, anise and orange peel flavors. Firm acidity enlivens the palate, the finish is a bit rough. It's intense and may improve with time. • $14 • (11/15/94) • **82**
Riesling Alsace 1992: Pleasant enough, but rather neutral in character, offering floral aromas and crisp citrus and light peach flavors. An easy-drinking white that won't offend or astonish. • $11 • (11/15/94) • **82**

TRIMOULET, CHÂTEAU

St.-Emilion 1990: Luscious fruit flavors are blended with a rich array of spicy notes. A seamless, supple texture adds to the complexity of the cherry, plum and blackberry flavors. Well balanced, with a touch of gaminess on the finish. Drinkable now. 8,000 cases made. • $20 • (09/15/93) • **86**
St.-Emilion 1988 • $16 • (06/15/91) • **91**
St.-Emilion 1982 • $15 • (05/15/89) • **81**

TRINITE VALROSE, CHÂTEAU

Bordeaux Supérieur Ile de Patiras 1988 • $7 • (08/31/91) • **78**
Bordeaux Supérieur Ile de Patires 1985 • $6 • (11/15/87) • **71**

TRINQUEVEDEL, CHÂTEAU DE

Rosé 1992: Austere on the nose, with some dried cherry, leather and herb, but dull and lacking finish. • $NA • **75**

TROCARD, CHÂTEAU

Bordeaux Supérieur 1988 • $8 • (01/31/92) BB • **83**

TROISGROS, CAVE LA

Bordeaux 1989 • $9 • (05/15/91) • **82**

TROLLAT, RAYMOND

St.-Joseph 1992 • $15 • (05/31/94) • **83**
St.-Joseph 1991 • $15 • (05/31/94) • **88**

TRONQUOY-LALANDE, CHÂTEAU

St.-Estèphe 1995: Plenty of rich and grapey aromas and flavors in this. It focuses on fruit on the finish. • $NA • (05/15/96) • **85-89** (BT)
St.-Estèphe 1994: Attractive plum and smoke aromas and flavors, medium body, silky tannins and medium finish. Very well made. • $NA • **85-89** (BT)
St.-Estèphe 1993: Clean, fresh, simple mint, berry and cherry aromas and flavors. More like a light Loire red. Drinkable now • $21 • (01/31/96) • **79**
St.-Estèphe 1991: Very fruity, but one-dimensional aromas and flavors of strawberry and cherry. Medium body, light tannins. • $17 • (03/31/94) • **79**
St.-Estèphe 1988 • $14 • (07/15/91) • **84**
St.-Estèphe 1987 • $13 • (11/30/89) • **84**
St.-Estèphe 1986 • $15 • (11/30/89) • **92**
St.-Estèphe 1982 • $20 • (11/30/89) • **86**

TROPLONG-MONDOT, CHÂTEAU

St.-Emilion 1995: A blockbuster: dark color, deep and firm, with loads of cedar, red berry, mineral, vanilla and earthy aromas and flavors. It's

FRANCE

sweet and ripe, but the tannins are massive and will require some time to mellow. Almost classic. • $NA • (05/15/96) • **90-94** (BT)

St.-Emilion 1994: Silky texture, intense berry, smoky character, medium tannins and slightly austere finish. Almost outstanding. Not quite as great as last year. Wait and see after bottling. • $49 • (05/15/96) • **85-89** (BT)

St.-Emilion 1993: One of the rising stars of the Right Bank. Sleek and racy, sporting fine tannins, plenty of beautiful currant and berry flavors, medium body, firm tannins and long finish. Better in 1998. • $35 • (01/31/96) • **88**

St.-Emilion 1992: Complex aromas of dark chocolate, tobacco and fruit. Very velvety vanilla, grape and chocolate flavors. Medium-to-full body, medium finish. Drinkable now. • $20 • **88**

St.-Emilion 1991: Beautiful, aromatic wine with a plum and chocolate character. Medium-bodied, but a very light finish. • $20 • (03/31/94) • **81**

St.-Emilion 1990: A showy wine, with appealing aromas and flavors of violets, vanilla and fruit and ultrafine tannins. If you like new wood, you will like this St.-Emilion. Drinkable in 1997. 10,000 cases made. • $30 • (03/31/93) • **91**

St.-Emilion 1989 • $26 • (03/15/92) • **89**
St.-Emilion 1988 • $31 Ⓐ • (07/15/91) • **85**
St.-Emilion 1986 • $20 • (06/30/89) • **88**
St.-Emilion 1985 • $21 • (06/30/88) • **88**
St.-Emilion 1961 • $37 • (04/30/96) • **85**

FRANCE

TROTANOY, CHÂTEAU

Pomerol 1995: An outstanding Trotanoy featuring wonderful finesse and refinement, medium-to-full body, medium fruit and a long mineral, mint finish. Caresses your palate. • $NA • (05/15/96) • **90-94** (BT)

Pomerol 1994: An impressive 1994 that has very fine tannins and plenty of berry and cherry flavors accompanied by a hint of mineral. A bit more fruit on the finish would make it outstanding. • $39 • (05/15/96) • **85-89** (BT)

Pomerol 1993: Complex and subtle with lots going on in the glass. Not a huge wine, but has wonderful berry, chocolate, earth and mineral character. Medium in body and tannins, adding a long, delicious finish. Better in 1999. • $50 • (01/31/96) CS • **91**

Pomerol 1992: Ultraclean raspberry and floral character, medium to light body, crisp acidity and fresh finish. A little one-dimensional. Drink now. • $42 • **82**

Pomerol 1990: Supple, generous and polished, with a slight tarry note adding interest to the ripe plum and cedar flavors. Has length and balance, but seems less powerful than in a tasting in Bordeaux last year. Best from 2000. • $46 Ⓐ • (05/15/94) • **92**

Pomerol 1989 • $43 Ⓐ • (05/15/94) • **90**
Pomerol 1988 • $42 Ⓐ • (05/15/94) • **87**
Pomerol 1987 • $27 Ⓐ • (05/15/94) • **84**
Pomerol 1986 • $56 Ⓐ • (05/15/94) • **82**
Pomerol 1985 • $64 Ⓐ • (05/15/94) • **81**
Pomerol 1983 • $41 Ⓐ • (05/15/94) • **88**
Pomerol 1982 • $298 Ⓐ • (05/15/94) • **95**
Pomerol 1981 • $61 Ⓐ • (05/15/94) • **91**
Pomerol 1979 • $50 Ⓐ • (05/15/94) • **89**
Pomerol 1978 • $46 Ⓐ • (10/15/88) • **83**
Pomerol 1975 • $163 Ⓐ • (05/15/94) • **83**
Pomerol 1971 • $178 Ⓐ • (05/15/94) • **86**
Pomerol 1970 • $157 Ⓐ • (05/15/94) • **88**
Pomerol 1967 • $105 • (05/15/94) • **82**
Pomerol 1966 • $153 Ⓐ • (05/15/94) • **85**
Pomerol 1964 • $185 • (05/15/94) • **83**
Pomerol 1962 • $160 • (05/15/94) • **82**
Pomerol 1961 • $920 Ⓐ • (05/15/94) • **94**
Pomerol 1959 • $430 • (05/15/94) • **93**
Pomerol 1955 • $245 Ⓐ • (05/15/94) • **90**
Pomerol 1953 • $300 • (10/15/88) • **86**
Pomerol 1952 • $190 • (05/15/94) • **85**
Pomerol 1949 • $1,450 • (05/15/94) • **92**
Pomerol 1947 • $800 • (05/15/94) • **92**
Pomerol 1945 • $1,550 • (05/15/94) • **94**
Pomerol 1934 • $450 • (05/15/94) • **83**
Pomerol 1928 • $600 • (10/15/88) • **95**
Pomerol 1926 • $900 • (05/15/94) • **86**
Pomerol 1924 • $600 • (05/15/94) • **79**

TROTTEVIEILLE, CHÂTEAU

St.-Emilion 1992: Light and slightly unripe herbal, berry, watery character. Drink if you must. • $18 • **71**

St.-Emilion 1991: Somewhat mature flavors, but a lovely tobacco and cherry character. Soft and round. • $18 • (03/31/94) • **82**

St.-Emilion 1990: Deceptive wine that starts out slowly on the palate but then kicks in on the finish with tobacco, cedar, vanilla and berry aromas and flavors and a long, velvety finish. Drinkable in 1997. 4,500 cases made. • $29 • (03/31/93) • **91**

St.-Emilion 1989 • $44 • (03/15/92) • **90**
St.-Emilion 1988 • $51 • (04/30/91) • **85**
St.-Emilion 1982 • $24 Ⓐ • (08/31/92) • **89**
St.-Emilion 1962 • $30 • (11/30/87) • **75**

TROUBADOUR

Merlot Vin de Pays de l'Aude 1987 • $5 • (08/31/89) • **76**

TRUCHOT, JACKY

Charmes-Chambertin Vieilles Vignes 1991: Firm, chewy and lean in texture, a strong menthol note dominating the modest berry fruit. Try now. • $50 • (08/31/94) • **85**

TUILERIE, CHÂTEAU DE LA

Costières du Gard 1986 • $4 • (06/30/88) • **74**
Costières du Gard 1985 • $6 • (02/15/87) BB • **77**

TUQUE BEL-AIR, DOMAINE LA

Côtes de Castillon 1985 • $8 • (09/30/88) • **72**

TURCAUD, CHÂTEAU

Entre-Deux-Mers 1994: Fresh but a bit one-dimensional, delivering some grass, pear and citrus flavors. Slightly aggressive, yet fun. • $8 • **80**

Entre-Deux-Mers 1993: Some decent grassy, steely character, but rather short and light on the finish. • $8 • **78**

TURCKHEIM

Pinot Noir Alsace Cuvée à l'Ancienne 1988 • $25 • (10/31/91) • **82**
Pinot Noir Alsace Cuvée Réserve 1989 • $15 • (10/31/91) • **80**
Pinot Noir Alsace Rouge de Turckheim 1988 • $40 • (10/31/91) • **77**

UCCM

Chardonnay Vin de Pays d'Oc 1992 • $NA • (03/15/94) • **81**

USSEGLIO, DOMAINE RAYMOND

Châteauneuf-du-Pape 1990: Bright and appealing. A light style of Châteauneuf-du-Pape that features spicy red plum, cherry and black pepper aromas and flavors. Drinkable now. • $16 • (04/15/93) • **85**

VACHET-ROUSSEAU, G.

Gevrey-Chambertin 1988 • $30 • (12/31/90) • **85**
Gevrey-Chambertin 1983 • $16 • (05/01/86) • **64**

Key: SS—Spectator Selection. CS—Cellar Selection. BB—Best Buy. $NA—Price not available. (BT)—Barrel tasting. Ⓐ—Auction Price.
Dates in parentheses represent the issues in which the ratings were published.

VAISSE, DOMAINE A.

A. Vaisse Fleurie Grille-Midi 1994: Attractive floral, berry and spice aromas promise more complexity than usual Beaujolais and the palate delivers, offering rich, structured black cherry and smoke flavors. 1,000 cases made. • $12 • **87**

VAL D'ORBIEU

Chardonnay Vin de Pays d'Oc Réserve St. Martin 1994: Ripe, fruity and simple, offering vanilla and melon flavors in a soft, round, straightforward style with earthy accents. 30,000 cases made. • $8 • (12/15/95) • **81**

Marsanne Vin de Pays d'Oc Réserve St. Martin 1994: Marsanne makes great whites in Hermitage, here it's round and generous, with floral and melon flavors. Not profound, but it brings you back for another sip. 15,000 cases made. • $7 • (02/29/96) • **83**

Merlot Vin de Pays d'Oc Réserve St. Martin 1993: A barnyard aroma is unpleasant, but on the palate plum and light bell pepper flavors come through, brisk tannins giving it grip. Drink now. 25,000 cases made. • $7 • (11/30/94) • **77**

Muscat de St.-Jean-de-Minervois Petit Grains NV: A blast of fresh fruit and plenty of richness make this a satisfying sweet wine. Vivid apricot, banana and almond flavors give it depth and appeal. 10,000 cases made. • $14 • (01/31/95) • **87**

Vin de Pays d'Oc La Cuvée Mythique 1990: At first glance this could be mistaken for a Graves, with its tobacco and cedar aromas and polished, supple texture. If it lacks the concentration of a first-class Bordeaux, it still has fruit, balance and length. A well-made wine. Drinkable now. 30,000 cases made. • $NA • (06/30/94) • **88**

VAL JOANIS, CHÂTEAU

Côtes du Lubéron 1992: Effusively spicey and fairly concentrated with interesting juniper berry and caraway flavors. Very mature and ready to drink, it finishes with a good dose of dried fruit flavors. A good job for a tough vintage. 46,000 cases made. • $8 • **84**

Côtes du Lubéron 1988 • $7 • (06/30/90) BB • **82**

Côtes du Lubéron White 1993: On the light side, with herbal and oniony flavors and aromas. There's enough ripe pear and almond flavors to make it interesting, but just barely. 25,000 cases made. • $8 • **79**

Côtes du Lubéron Les Griottes 1990: Delicious, mature red, offering plenty of nice plum and cherry flavors. There's a spicy element that runs through it as well. Ready to drink. 3,500 cases made. • $15 • (09/30/95) • **87**

Côtes du Lubéron Les Merises Fût de Chêne 1994: Not much on the nose, but flavors are reminiscent of dried cherries and currants. Full-bodied and dry. • $10 • (09/30/95) • **79**

Côtes du Lubéron Rosé 1993: A bright, fruity, berry character and a touch of spice offset the firm, dry texture. It is balanced for matching with light summer food. 25,000 cases made. • $8 • (08/31/95) • **85**

VALADE, CHÂTEAU LA

Fronsac 1986 • $5 • (05/15/89) BB • **81**

VALANDRAUD, CHÂTEAU DE

St.-Emilion 1995: This estate gets better and better. A seductive wine that caresses your palate with velvety tannins. Full-bodied, loads of smoky berry, cherry and chocolate character. Fabulous. • $NA • (05/15/96) • **90-94** (BT)

St.-Emilion 1994: International style: warm and caressing with an abundance of gamy, toasted oak aromas and flavors. Full-bodied and tannic yet round and impressive. But is it Bordeaux? Tasted twice, with consistent notes. • $NA • **85-89** (BT)

St.-Emilion 1993: Newcomer to the Right Bank and making a lot of noise. Beautifully aromatic red berry, vanilla and tobacco character. Medium-bodied and very soft, featuring round tannins and medium finish. Drinkable now, but better in 1997. 350 cases made. • $95 • (01/31/96) • **89**

VALETTE, DOMAINE

Mâcon-Chaintré Vieilles Vignes 1994: A work of art. This blends its crisp acidity nicely into creamy, butterscotch flavors. Fat yet restrained, seductive and full-bodied. Extremely long finish. Delicious now, but even better in 1999. 1,166 cases made. • $NA • (05/31/96) • **91**

Mâcon-Chaintré Vieilles Vignes 1993: Succulent and fresh, with a slightly earthy, wet hay character. Excellent intensity of lime, pear and green apple. A bit grassy on the long, juicy finish. • $11 • **84**

Pouilly-Fuissé Le Clos de Monsieur Noly 1993: Lots of buttery, toasty flavors play against citrusy, pineapple and other tropical notes. Medium-bodied, both velvety and firm. Hold until 1996. 1,000 cases made. • $24 • **88**

Pouilly-Fuissé Le Clos de Monsieur Noly Vieilles Vignes 1993: Flavorful, fresh and supple, offering lemon, honey, pear and spice notes. Medium in body; drinkable now. • $29 • **88**

Pouilly-Fuissé Clos Reyssié 1993: Smooth, round, spicy, silky, a solid frame. Grapefruit and tropical fruit notes emerge on the intense finish. Enjoy with fish. 333 cases made. • $26 • **88**

Pouilly-Fuissé Clos Reyssié 1992: Quite distinctive butterscotch aromas and fresh lime, wet hay flavors. Creamy smooth texture and long finish offer a hint of honey, hazelnut, mature complexity. Drink now. • $NA • **87**

Pouilly-Fuissé Clos Reyssié Réserve Particulière 1993: Exquisite, silky and harmonious, fresh and fruity, showing creamy, pear tart, mineral flavors that caress the palate. Medium-bodied, faultless finish. Drinkable now. 167 cases made. • $33 • **89**

Pouilly-Fuissé Clos Reyssié Réserve Particulière 1991: Lush, medium-bodied, offering silky-mouth feel and butter, lemon and mineral notes. A burnt-butter character of cooked fruit keeps it from scoring higher. Drink now. • $NA • **85**

VALLONGUE, CHÂTEAU DE

Coteaux d'Aix en Provence Les Baux 1988 • $11 • (12/15/91) • **73**

VALLONNIERES, CHÂTEAU DES

Côtes du Rhône 1990 • $8 • (06/15/92) • **83**

VALLOUIT, L. DE

Châteauneuf-du-Pape 1989 • $16 • (12/31/91) • **77**

Côte-Rôtie 1989 • $30 • (01/31/92) • **89**

Côte-Rôtie 1985 • $20 • (10/15/87) • **75**

Gigondas 1989 • $13 • (01/31/92) • **89**

Hermitage 1983 • $12 • (05/01/86) • **79**

St.-Joseph Red 1989 • $13 • (01/31/92) • **76**

St.-Vincent 1990 • $7 • (06/15/92) BB • **82**

Vin de Pays des Collines Rhodanienn Les Sables 1989 • $6 • (12/31/91) BB • **81**

Vin de Pays des Collines Rhodanienn Les Sables 1988 • $4 • (06/30/90) BB • **78**

VALMAISON

Bordeaux Philibert Bourgeois 1992: Light and soft, with some interesting flavors of chocolate, spice and plum. Modest, a bit diluted, with little tannin. • $5 • (11/15/94) • **78**

VANNIERES, CHÂTEAU

Bandol 1986 • $15 • (09/15/89) • **67**

Bandol 1983 • $NA • (08/31/86) • **80**

Côtes de Provence La Provence de Vannières 1986 • $15 • (08/31/89) • **80**

VARICHON & CLERC

Blanc de Blancs 1992: Lively texture and nicely fruity character at reasonable rates. This well-balanced French sparkling wine reminds us a lot of Chardonnay. It has fresh apple and pear flavors accented by

FRANCE

vanilla, leading into a lingering finish. 10,000 cases made. • $10 • (12/15/95) • **86**
Blanc de Blancs 1989 • $9 • (03/31/92) BB • **87**
Brut Blanc de Blancs NV • $7 • (12/31/89) BB • **87**
Brut Blanc de Blancs Black Orchid Cuvée Speciale NV • $8 • (03/31/92) • **77**
Brut Blanc de Blancs Trocadero NV: Light and simple, the flavors turning syrupy on the finish. 20,000 cases made. • $7 • (12/15/95) • **79**
Brut Rosé 1992: Rather sweet and very grapey, tasting like candied cherries and sugar. Quaffable but simple. 2,000 cases made. • $10 • (12/15/95) • **79**
Demi-Sec NV • $7 • (01/31/90) BB • **82**

VATAN, ANDRE

Sancerre Les Charmes Domaine des P'tits Perriers 1991 • $18 • (09/15/93) • **74**

VATAN, EDMOND

Sancerre Clos La Néore 1994: Round but dull, marrying earth and light pineapple flavors with hints of menthol. Not your usual Sauvignon Blanc profile, and a bit musty. • $NA • (06/15/96) • **76**
Sancerre Clos La Néore 1993: An infusion of oak gives this a Graves-like character, with marzipan and vanilla aromas and flavors that complement the appley, earthy and mineral notes. A rich wine with vibrant acidity that finishes very dry, it draws you back for another sip. Drinkable now • $19 • (11/15/95) • **88**
Sancerre Clos La Néore 1992: With delicate pine and floral aromas and light herbal and peach flavors, this is a fresh, vivacious wine, crisp and refreshing. A good apéritif. • $20 • (10/31/94) • **84**

VAUCHER

Corton-Charlemagne 1992: Great breeding in this does Corton proud. The butter, hazelnut, vanilla and pear flavors unfold in a subtle package that offers length. Try now. • $NA • (08/31/94) • **91**
Puligny-Montrachet 1992: Elegant and flavorful, with a ripe core of honey, pear, apple and citrus flavors, not very big or opulent, but very attractive finish. • $NA • (08/31/94) • **88**

VAUDIEU, CHÂTEAU DE

Châteauneuf-du-Pape 1984 • $13 • (11/15/87) • **72**

VAUDON, DOMAINE DE

Chablis 1994: Lemon, spice and almond aromas and flavors. Medium-bodied, good fruit and a long, rich finish. From Joseph Drouhin. • $NA • **85**

VAUFUGET, DOMAINE DE

Vouvray 1992: Apple cider flavors and light vegetal notes run through this sweet, light-bodied wine. It has appeal, but not much depth. 4,000 cases made. • $8 • **81**

VENOGE, DE

Blanc de Blancs Champagne 1983: Very heavy and rich buttery style with loads of toasty, ripe apple character. Slightly out of balance, full-bodied, thick and rather soft with a decadently rich finish. A mature blanc de blancs. Not a wine to keep. Drink now. • $40 • (12/31/93) • **84**
Brut Blanc de Blancs Champagne NV • $38 • (12/31/90) • **86**
Brut Champagne 1988: A rather restrained style of Champagne with very fresh fragrant aromas and flavors and a lively finish. Sophisticated apéritif. Drink now or hold. • $40 • (12/31/93) • **88**

Key: SS—Spectator Selection. CS—Cellar Selection. BB—Best Buy. $NA—Price not available. (BT)—Barrel tasting. Ⓐ—Auction Price.
Dates in parentheses represent the issues in which the ratings were published.

Brut Champagne 1985 • $38 • (12/31/90) • **86**
Brut Champagne Champes des Princes 1985: Like double cream in your mouth. This is very, very rich with ripe fruit and vanilla aromas and flavors, excellent acidity and a long ripe fruit finish. Fantastic. Drink now or hold. • $60 • (12/31/93) • **92**
Brut Champagne Cordon Bleu NV • $22 • (12/31/91) • **84**
Rosé Champagne Crémant NV • $26 • (12/31/88) • **88**

VERDIGNAN, CHÂTEAU

Haut-Médoc 1995: Rich, ripe and fairly concentrated, offering some pure cassis bush flavors and lovely spice and mocha notes. Solidly structured tannins will need time to soften. • $NA • (05/15/96) • **85-89** (BT)
Haut-Médoc 1994: Some good fruit here but also lots of tannins. Medium-bodied and hard, mineral, berry finish. Could move up a notch next year. • $NA • **80-84** (BT)
Haut-Médoc 1992: Clean and lightly fruity, showing firm tannins and a light, slightly herbal finish. Too diluted. Drink now. • $14 • **75**
Haut-Médoc 1991: A wine with good silky texture, medium body and very light cherry flavor. • $14 • (03/31/94) • **80**
Haut-Médoc 1990: A very aromatic wine with attractive black cherry and roasted nut aromas and fruity flavors, the tannins are firm but the finish is light. Drinkable now. 30,000 cases made. • $17 • (03/31/93) • **85**
Haut-Médoc 1989 • $17 • (03/15/92) • **90**
Haut-Médoc 1988 • $15 • (04/30/91) • **86**
Haut-Médoc 1987 • $15 • (11/30/89) • **78**
Haut-Médoc 1986 • $15 • (11/30/89) • **76**
Haut-Médoc 1985 • $15 • (02/15/88) • **81**
Haut-Médoc 1983 • $13 • (04/01/86) • **69**
Haut-Médoc 1982 • $16 • (08/31/92) • **80**

VERDILLAC

Bordeaux 1993: Clumsy. The light berry and prune flavors are diluted and dominated by raspy tannins. Not much pleasure. 35,000 cases made. • $7 • (12/15/95) • **76**
Bordeaux 1990: A fairly light Bordeaux that's fruity and supple, showing fresh raspberry flavors, modest tannins and nice accents of vanilla and leather. Ready to drink now. 12,000 cases made. • $7 • (09/15/93) BB • **83**
Bordeaux 1989 • $8 • (11/30/92) • **77**
Bordeaux White 1994: Very bland, with little aroma or flavor, but it tastes clean. 60,000 cases made. • $7 • (02/29/96) • **76**
Bordeaux White 1992 • $7 • (09/15/93) • **77**

VERGE, ROGER

Fleurie 1986 • $9 • (12/31/87) • **76**
Juliénas 1986 • $9 • (12/31/87) • **83**
Moulin-à-Vent 1986 • $12 • (12/31/87) • **79**

VERGER, DOMAINE LE

Chablis 1994: Well-defined almond and straw character, medium body and acidity and a fresh finish. • $NA • **84**

VERGET

Bâtard-Montrachet 1993: Quite ripe and forward, golden-colored, showing delicious apple, pear and grapefruit flavors. Very drinkable now, might be better in 1997. • $130 • (08/31/95) • **86**
Bâtard-Montrachet 1992: If you want a great bottle of wine for tonight, go for this. It's white Burgundy at its peak. Rich and seductive in flavor, broad in texture with a deep gold color, marked by toasty, smoky aromas, pear and nutmeg flavors and a spicy, long-lasting finish. • $125 • (08/31/94) • **93**
Chablis Montée de Tonnerre 1994: Explodes with intense flavors, but this full-bodied '94 seems a bit disjointed now. Oak flavors dominate over the crisp apple and pear notes. Very lemony and sharp on the mouthpuckering finish. Lacks finesse, and way too oaky. • $28 • (05/31/96) • **79**

Chassagne-Montrachet 1993: Has the ripe fruit and buttery qualities we look for in white Burgundy. Very aromatic, nicely flavorful and smooth, but turning tart and tight on the finish. Drinkable now. • $23 • (05/15/95) • **84**

Chassagne-Montrachet 1991 • $33 • (02/28/93) • **83**

Chassagne-Montrachet Les Champs Gains 1993: Dull-tasting and coarse in texture, this doesn't offer much pleasure. It has apple-skin flavors and a muddy finish. • $25 • (05/15/95) • **74**

Chassagne-Montrachet Morgeot 1992: Combines a buttery, toasty aroma with bright pear and citrus flavors and accents of honey and vanilla. Tangy and long on the finish. Drinkable now. • $44 • (08/31/94) • **87**

Chassagne-Montrachet Morgeot Cuvée Vieille Vigne 1993: Beautiful velvet texture and mineral undertones give it a lot of class. Solid backbone, grapefruit, hazelnut and honey character. Drinkable now. Tasted twice. • $39 • **89**

Chassagne-Montrachet Premier Cru 1994: Nicely made, showing good balance. Somewhat fuller-bodied, with pear, dried herb, honey, lime, hazelnut and apple pie flavors. Lacks the intensity to climb into the outstanding category. Drinkable now, but can age, too. • $27 • (05/31/96) • **87**

Chassagne-Montrachet La Romanée 1994: Excellent intensity for a '94. Mingles honey, lime, mineral and dried herb flavors. Great focus and clarity. You can bet this solid wine will age beautifully, try in 1998. • $50 • (05/31/96) • **92**

Chassagne-Montrachet La Romanée 1993: Solid and deep yet also smooth, boasting mineral, apple and toast flavors. A bite on the finish, better wait until after 1996. Tasted twice. 375 cases made. • $45 • (05/15/95) • **88**

Chassagne-Montrachet La Romanée 1992: Vivid and vibrant, it's quite tart, with lemon, grapefruit and toast flavors. Try now. • $50 • (08/31/94) • **86**

Chassagne-Montrachet La Romanée 1991 • $45 • (02/28/93) • **84**

Corton-Charlemagne Cuvée Vieilles Vignes 1994: Impressively intense, racy and sharply focused—like drinking nectar. Has a lovely honey, lime, pear and mineral character, unctuous while keeping a fresh mouth-feel. Tempting now, but better in 1998. Tasted twice, with consistent notes. • $57 • (05/31/96) • **92**

Meursault 1993: Toasty, buttery accents lend extra interest to this crisp, lemon- and grapefruit-flavored Chardonnay. It is lean and elegant in texture, very bracing but not full-bodied. • $23 • (05/15/95) • **84**

Meursault 1991 • $33 • (01/31/93) • **84**

Meursault Casse-Tête 1993: Quite grassy and intense, offering dried-herb, citrus and lime flavors and a hint of honey. Lean now, but give it some time, try in 1997. Tasted twice with consistent notes. 583 cases made. • $28 • (05/15/95) • **86**

Meursault Les Charmes Cuvée Vieilles Vignes 1994: Exemplifies '94, showing both the finesse and power of this vintage. Great lemon, honey and pie crust aromas and flavors. Medium-bodied and very clean, a well-crafted wine that kicks in with a long finish. • $52 • (05/31/96) • **91**

Meursault Genevriéres 1992: Extremely buttery and oaky in aroma, but backed by firm fruit flavors and acidity. An ambitious, heavy style that will need time to show how successful it can be. Try after 1996. • $50 • (08/31/94) • **87**

Meursault Les Genevrières Hospices de Beaune 1994: Fat, showy and almost overdone, oozing ripe and rich flavors. Full-bodied, this crowd-pleaser offers a symphony of toasted bread, butter, ripe fruit and citrus notes. Very creamy and silky in texture, adding honey-laced, ripe aftertaste. Enjoy now. Tasted twice, with consistent notes. • $35 • (05/31/96) • **90**

Meursault Les Porusot 1994: Decadent yet harmonious, balancing its ripe flavors nicely on the citrusy background to beckon you back for another sip. Well structured, it delivers its honey, grapefruit and toast flavors with great elegance. Enjoy it now through 2000. • $44 • (05/31/96) • **92**

Meursault Les Porusot 1993: Surprisingly silky for the vintage, showing apple, pear and mineral flavors and a touch of honey that kicks in on the refined finish. Drinkable now. 117 cases made. • $42 • (05/15/95) • **90**

Meursault Les Rougeots 1994: Clean and crisp, with lively character, delivering some nice citrus, manderine orange and spice flavors. Fresh, vibrant and lovely from start to finish. Drinkable now through 1998. • $31 • (05/31/96) • **86**

Montrachet 1994: Racy, subtle and refined, it ends with a bang, delivering the whole scope of white Burgundy complexity, from very toasted hazelnut and bread flavors to ripe fruit, honey, mineral and lemon character. Medium- to full-bodied, silky and seductive, adding a very long finish. Terrific now, but better in 2001. • $160 • (05/31/96) • **96**

Pouilly-Fuissé 1993: Distinctive butter, toast and butterscotch aromas, super-intense, citrusy flavors on the palate and a chalky, chewy, long finish. 1,250 cases made. • $17 • (05/15/95) • **89**

Pouilly-Fuissé 1992: Rich, ripe and extremely attractive, delivering lots of toasted oak, hazelnut, lime and fresh pineapple flavors. A pleasure to drink now, seductive, long finish. 2,083 cases made. • $17 • **90**

Pouilly-Fuissé Tête de Cuvée 1994: Creamy up-front, followed by notes of citrus, this is full of contrasts. Very appealing and you can feel the winemaking talent. Good concentration on the long finish. Try in 1998. • $25 • (05/31/96) • **89**

Puligny-Montrachet Les Enseignères 1994: Focused, restrained and harmonious, shows spice, toasted oak, cream and nice fruit flavors. It all comes together on a fresh, seductive finish. Delicious now, but better in 1998. • $33 • (05/31/96) • **89**

Puligny-Montrachet Les Enseignères 1993: Sharp and steely, toasty, buttery, pear flavors soften the hard edges somewhat. Medium-bodied, providing a touch of honey on the vibrant finish. 625 cases made. • $29 • **86**

Puligny-Montrachet Les Pucelles 1993: A rather delicate Puligny, showing some lovely hazelnut, honey and apple flavors, light-to-medium body and a vibrant finish. Drink now. Tasted twice, with consistent notes. 367 cases made. • $47 • (05/15/95) • **85**

Puligny-Montrachet Sous Le Puits 1994: Soft yet refreshing, providing a supple, delicious drinking experience. Mingles honey and pear flavors with citrus and ginger. Tasted twice, with consistent notes. • $38 • (05/31/96) • **86**

Puligny-Montrachet Sous Le Puits 1992: Stylish, exuberant and lively, with tons of toast, butter and pear flavors. Its vibrant lime and lemon character keeps it in check, and leads to a crisp finish that gives it length and—for sure—a long life in the cellar. Drinkable now. • $38 • (08/31/94) HR • **93**

Puligny-Montrachet Sous le Puits 1991 • $37 • (01/31/93) • **86**

St.-Aubin Premier Cru 1994: Crisp and quite tart, light-to-medium body, with nicely focused citrus and green apple flavors, followed by a hint of honey and mineral on the finish. • $18 • (05/31/96) • **82**

St.-Aubin Premier Cru 1993: Mineral, ripe fruit flavors are diminished only by a slight, cooked-apple quality. Drink now. Tasted twice. 1,125 cases made. • $19 • (05/15/95) • **84**

St.-Romain 1994: Zingy and vibrant, with a core of lemon and green apple. Light-bodied and very crisp but clean and fresh on the somewhat grassy finish. • $17 • (05/31/96) • **80**

St.-Romain 1991 • $15 • (06/15/93) • **84**

VERHAEGHE & FILS

Château du Cédre Cahors 1991: Not for the faint of heart. A big, concentrated red with a cedary aroma, lots of tannin and an astringent finish. Has enough cherry and berry flavor to fill out the rustic texture. • $11 • (03/31/95) • **81**

VERNAY, GEORGES

Côte-Rôtie 1991: Ripe and luscious, with jammy cherry and smoke flavors in a supple, rustic style. Drinkable now. • $30 • (05/31/94) • **84**

VERNAY, VEUVE DU

Brut Blanc de Blancs NV • $7 • (11/30/91) BB • **82**

VERNEDE, CHÂTEAU LA

Coteaux du Languedoc 1990 • $9 • (06/15/93) • **75**

VERSET, NOEL

Cornas 1993: Charming for a Cornas, this offers intriguing floral and berry flavors, balanced and fresh, as firm tannins emerge on the finish. Hard now, but better to drink by 1997. 700 cases made. • $24 • **85**
Cornas 1987 • $23 • (03/31/90) • **88**
Cornas 1986 • $22 Ⓐ • (01/31/89) • **86**

VESSELLE, GEORGES

Brut Champagne Cuvée Juline Grand Cru NV • $NA • (12/31/93) • **87**
Brut Champagne Grand Cru 1986: Extremely fruity, off-beat style of Champagne with pineapple and peach character, medium bodied with a fine foam and a tart, appley finish. Drink now. 825 cases made. • $NA • (12/31/93) • **85**
Brut Champagne Zero Grand Cru 1986: Bold style not for casual sipping. Big and powerful Champagne with butterscotch and ripe fruit character, full body and a long flavorful finish. Delicious now. 825 cases made. • $NA • (12/31/93) • **89**
Brut Rosé Champagne de Noirs NV • $30 • (12/16/85) • **53**

VEUVE AMIOT

Brut Saumur Cuvée Haute Tradition NV • $13 • (03/31/90) • **78**

VEUVE CLICQUOT

Brut Champagne 1982: Rich in flavor and full-bodied, with lots of earthy, yeasty character, depth of flavor and crisp balance despite the full flavors. A real mouthful. • $47 • (05/31/87) SS • **93**
Brut Champagne 1979 • $50 • (12/16/85) • **88**
Brut Champagne Gold Label 1983: Attractive fig, peach, toast and vanilla flavors are rich, deep and complex, with a smooth texture and a long, full finish that keeps echoing the fruitiness. Drink now. 98,000 cases made. • $42 • (12/31/90) • **90**
Brut Champagne Gold Label 1982: Straightforward and full of vibrant, youthful fruit flavors. Crisp with apple aromas and flavors with just a hint of complex nut and butter tones on the finish. • $37 • (12/31/88) • **85**
Brut Champagne Gold Label Vintage Réserve 1985: A bold, toasty style, packed with tiers of spice, nut and mature pear and citrus flavors that are tight, focused, dry and austere. Remarkably complex and well balanced, showing richness, depth and complexity. Ready now. • $52 • (09/30/93) • **92**
Brut Champagne La Grande Dame 1988: Vivid, lively and fruity, offering bright acidity, flavors of baked apple and cinnamon and enough body and texture to carry it. Tangy and generous on the finish. Tasted twice, with consistent notes. • $100 • (12/15/95) • **86**
Brut Champagne La Grande Dame 1985: Like a wild horse. Tons of potential. It's extremely exuberant and lively. Full-bodied with masses of lemon, toast and apple character. It shows great acidity and long finish. Tasted twice. • $100 • (12/31/93) • **94**
Brut Champagne La Grande Dame 1983: Smooth and elegant, with intense ginger, pear and toast aromas and flavors and a velvety texture, long and fragrant on the finish. A complex wine that gets better with every sip. Much better than a bottle tasted earlier. • $79 • (12/31/89) • **92**
Brut Champagne La Grande Dame 1979 • $61 • (05/16/86) • **96**
Brut Champagne Réserve 1988: Bold and distinctive, with assertive aromas, a firm, slightly astringent texture and ample flavors of walnut, apple and spice. Drinkable now. • $50 • (07/31/95) • **89**
Brut Champagne Vintage Réserve 1985: Shows some age yet remains fresh on the finish. Firm and delicious with dough and fruit character and a long finish. Fine bead and texture. We gave it a 92 in 9/30/93. Always excellent. Drink now. • $50 • (12/31/93) • **90**
Brut Rosé Champagne 1983: Focused strawberry and ginger cookie aromas and flavors hang nicely on a medium-weight, generous frame. Focused flavors turn broad and expansive on the finish. • $47 • (12/31/89) • **86**
Brut Rosé Champagne 1979 • $35 • (07/16/86) • **89**
Brut Rosé Champagne 1978 • $60 • (12/16/85) • **82**
Brut Rosé Champagne Réserve 1985: Beautiful pale salmon in color, with earthy cherry and smoke aromas and flavors that are just a touch bitter. Finishes crisp and delicate. Drinkable now. Tasted twice, with consistent notes. • $60 • (11/30/92) • **85**
Demi-Sec Champagne NV: A big, blowsy sparkler offering plenty of sweetness but not much fruit. This is best suited for punch. • $40 • (12/15/95) • **78**

VIALE, DOMAINE GABRIEL

Crozes-Hermitage 1990 • $8 • (06/15/93) • **82**

VIDAL-FLEURY, J.

Cornas 1990 • $27 • (05/31/94) • **80**
Cornas 1989 • $10 • (06/15/92) • **81**
Cornas 1988 • $20 • (01/31/91) • **85**
Crozes-Hermitage 1990 • $10 • (05/31/94) • **87**
Crozes-Hermitage 1988 • $13 • (12/31/90) • **86**
Crozes-Hermitage 1986 • $10 • (05/31/88) • **78**
Crozes-Hermitage 1985 • $11 • (10/31/87) CS • **92**
Côte-Rôtie 1990: Dense but not exuberant. Tastes like chocolate-covered raspberries. It's velvety and ripe. Try now. • $30 • (05/31/94) • **88**
Côte-Rôtie La Chatillon 1990: Powerfully aromatic, with lush raspberry, plum, vanilla and licorice flavors. Very concentrated and balanced. Reserved now, try in 1998. • $42 • (05/31/94) • **92**
Côte-Rôtie Côte Blonde La Chatillonne 1988 • $42 • (03/15/94) • **87**
Côte-Rôtie Côte Blonde La Chatillonne 1984 • $26 • (10/31/87) • **73**
Côte-Rôtie Côtes Brune et Blonde 1989 • $28 • (03/15/94) • **87**
Côte-Rôtie Côtes Brune et Blonde 1988 • $30 • (10/15/90) • **88**
Côte-Rôtie Côtes Brune et Blonde 1985 • $25 • (03/15/90) • **90**
Côte-Rôtie Côtes Brune et Blonde 1945 • $NA • (03/15/90) • **85**
Côte-Rôtie Côtes Brune et Blonde 1934 • $NA • (03/15/90) • **85**
Côtes du Rhône 1990 • $8 • (04/30/94) BB • **85**
Côtes du Rhône 1988 • $9 • (12/15/90) • **85**
Côtes du Rhône 1985 • $7 • (10/31/87) BB • **88**
Côtes du Ventoux 1990: Strives for complexity, with soft, silky earth, currant, black cherry and tar notes and tannins that muscle their way to the forefront. Drinkable now. 8,000 cases made. • $7 • (06/30/94) BB • **84**
Gigondas 1985 • $13 • (10/31/87) • **86**
Hermitage 1985 • $22 • (10/31/87) • **89**
Hermitage 1945 • $NA • (03/15/90) • **80**
Hermitage 1937 • $NA • (03/15/90) • **91**
St.-Joseph 1990 • $14 • (05/31/94) • **85**
St.-Joseph 1988 • $14 • (01/31/91) • **84**
Vacqueyras 1990 • $9 • (03/31/94) BB • **86**
Vacqueyras 1988 • $14 • (12/15/90) • **89**

VIE-MAGNE, DOMAINE

Crozes-Hermitage 1990: Plump and supple, this is already showing the maturity of classic Syrah game and earth flavors but the fruit, though ripe, lacks freshness. Drinkable now. 2,800 cases made. • $10 • **84**

VIEILLE CURE, CHÂTEAU LA

Fronsac 1995: Well-made and attractive, medium-bodied '95 with fresh grapey, berry character, spice and mineral complexity. Quite sweet and ripe, with chocolate coming out on the tannic finish. • $NA • (05/15/96) • **85-89** (BT)
Fronsac 1994: Fine silky, peppery, berry character, medium body and a light finish. Much better than the '93. • $NA • **80-84** (BT)
Fronsac 1993: Attractive cherry and cracked black pepper flavors, light-to-medium body, firm tannins and light, slightly dry finish. Drinkable now. • $19 • (01/31/96) • **79**

Key: SS—Spectator Selection. CS—Cellar Selection. BB—Best Buy. $NA—Price not available. (BT)—Barrel tasting. Ⓐ—Auction Price.
Dates in parentheses represent the issues in which the ratings were published.

Fronsac 1992: Deep red color and dried cherry and herb character, light-bodied and firm with some decent fruit but a short finish. Drink now and hurry. • $15 • **79**
Fronsac 1990: Tightly knit. It's rich but not giving much with steely tannins. Needs time, try in 1997. 7,000 cases made. • $19 • (03/31/93) • **88**
Fronsac 1989 • $16 • (03/15/92) • **88**
Fronsac 1988 • $19 • (10/31/91) • **81**
Fronsac 1987 • $14 • (05/15/90) • **82**
Fronsac 1986 • $15 • (05/15/91) • **81**
Fronsac 1985 • $15 • (12/31/88) • **88**
Fronsac 1982 • $15 • (08/31/92) • **84**

VIEILLE FERME, LA

Côtes du Lubéron White 1993: A simple, enjoyable white wine with basic apple flavors and good acidity. Refreshing in a straightforward style. • $7 • (11/30/94) • **81**
Côtes du Lubéron White 1992 • $7 • (04/30/94) • **76**
Côtes du Lubéron White 1991 • $6 • (11/30/92) • **77**
Côtes du Rhône Réserve 1992: Touches of spicy, meaty complexity add interest to this solidly fruity, full-bodied, moderately tannic red. It blends blackberry, smoke and pepper notes for an intriguing profile. 215,000 cases made. • $10 • (11/30/94) BB • **85**
Côtes du Rhône Réserve 1990 • $8 • (08/31/92) BB • **87**
Côtes du Rhône Réserve 1989 • $9 • (03/15/91) BB • **87**
Côtes du Rhône Réserve 1988 • $7 • (12/15/90) BB • **84**
Côtes du Rhône Réserve 1987 • $6 • (06/15/89) BB • **80**
Côtes du Rhône Réserve 1985 • $7 • (11/15/88) BB • **85**
Côtes du Rhône Réserve White 1993: A simple, enjoyable white, with basic apple flavors and good acidity. Refreshing in a straightforward style. 49,600 cases made. • $10 • (11/30/94) • **81**
Côtes du Rhône Réserve White 1992 • $9 • (04/30/94) • **76**
Côtes du Rhône Réserve White 1991 • $8 • (11/30/92) • **80**
Côtes du Ventoux 1992: Agreeably jammy in flavor, full-bodied, peppery and fresh. A good, solid mouthful of wine for current drinking. • $7 • (11/30/94) • **84**
Côtes du Ventoux 1990 • $7 • (04/15/93) • **78**
Côtes du Ventoux 1988 • $8 • (06/30/90) • **78**
Côtes du Ventoux 1987 • $5 • (06/15/89) BB • **81**
Côtes du Ventoux 1986 • $6 • (10/15/88) BB • **83**
Côtes du Ventoux Le Mont 1993 • $7 • **87**

VIEILLE JULIENNE, DOMAINE DE LA

Châteauneuf-du-Pape 1990: A tight, tannic wine, with potential for aging. Already has a complex aroma, but the stiff texture and intense fruit will need time to open up for maximum enjoyment. Currant, black cherry, cedar, earth and spice flavors make it fascinating to sip. Best to cellar until at least 1998. 6,000 cases made. • $17 • (04/15/93) • **91**
Châteauneuf-du-Pape 1978 • $20 • (11/15/87) • **67**
Châteauneuf-du-Pape 1972 • $20 • (11/15/87) • **73**

VIEILLES PIERRES, DOMAINE DES

Pouilly-Fuissé Vieilles Vignes Elevé en Fût de Chêne 1993: Well made, medium in body, showing supple texture, some butter, mushroom, wet earth, pear flavors and fresh lemon notes. Long finish. Drink now. • $NA • **87**
Pouilly-Fuissé Vieilles Vignes La Roche 1993: Very fresh, young and intense, light-bodied but bursting with floral, peach, pineapple, green apple and pear flavors. Juicy finish. Drink now. • $NA • **85**

VIENOT, CHARLES

Beaujolais-Villages 1993: Big but slightly dumb, with an earthy note that masks the round plum flavors. It lacks the lightness and grace we like in Beaujolais. • $8 • (06/30/94) • **77**
Bourgogne 1985 • $9 • (06/15/89) • **78**
Bourgogne 1983 • $6 • (12/16/85) • **75**
Bourgogne 1982 • $6 • (11/01/85) • **52**
Bourgogne Clos Le Village 1992: Fairly ripe and concentrated with some nice apple and fig flavors. This is a middle-of-the-road wine with some structure that indicates it may age well. It turns buttery on the finish, drink now or wait until 1995. • $9 • **82**
Bourgogne Clos Le Village 1991 • $8 • (10/15/93) • **83**
Chassagne-Montrachet 1991: Youthful, fruity and chewy, but the earthy, gamy aromas and flavors rob it of some charm. • $NA • (01/31/94) • **77**
Corton Maréchaudes 1985 • $57 • (07/15/88) • **84**
Côte de Nuits-Villages Cuvée Roi de Saxe 1993: Disappointing, showing light fruit character, diluted mid-palate and short, paperish finish. • $15 • **71**
Gevrey-Chambertin 1985 • $32 • (04/30/88) • **87**
Hautes-Côtes de Beaune 1992: A good, basic red Burgundy with solid cherry flavors, some smoky accents and good balance. Soft tannins and smooth texture make it drinkable now. • $11 • (10/31/94) • **83**
Mâcon-Villages 1993: A round wine with earthy, butter and fig flavors, more assertive than complex, it can stand up to grilled fish and birds. • $8 • **82**
Mercurey 1985 • $12 • (04/30/88) • **85**
Pommard 1985 • $33 • (04/30/88) • **81**
Pouilly-Fuissé 1993: Enticing aromas of smoke, toast and pears pull you into this wine, but there's not much fruit on the palate. Still, good acidity and deft use of wood give it verve and a pleasant, citrusy finish. • $13 • **83**

VIEUX-CHÂTEAU-CERTAN

Pomerol 1995: Racy and firm raspberry, cherry and vanilla character. Medium body, good fruit and beautiful mid-palate of grapey accents. Clearly outstanding. • $NA • (05/15/96) • **90-94** (BT)
Pomerol 1994: A well-made '94 with subtle berry, tobacco, oak, mineral and tar flavors. Has enough fruit to balance the tannins, and a harmonious, long finish makes this quite attractive. • $52 • (05/15/96) • **85-89** (BT)
Pomerol 1993: Supple mocha, plum and red berry flavors and a slightly herbaceous character which slightly detracts from the overall quality. Medium in body and tannins. Drinkable now. Tasted twice, with consistent notes. • $40 • (01/31/96) • **82**
Pomerol 1992: Disappointing, already at its peak. Some very soft plum and berry character. Tasted twice, with consistent notes. Drink now. • $39 • **75**
Pomerol 1990: Lovely and ripe, with milk chocolate and plum flavors, soft, velvety tannins and a long, peppery finish. Still, we expected more after the strong '89. Drink after 1997. 6,000 cases made. • $61 Ⓐ • (03/31/93) • **89**
Pomerol 1989 • $46 Ⓐ • (03/15/92) • **91**
Pomerol 1988 • $39 Ⓐ • (03/31/91) • **91**
Pomerol 1987 • $24 Ⓐ • (05/15/90) • **84**
Pomerol 1986 • $65 Ⓐ • (06/15/89) • **93**
Pomerol 1985: A pretty, ripe style with cherry, berry and tobacco aromas and flavors. Full-bodied and fruity with firm tannins and a fresh finish. Better after 1996. • $58 • (10/15/94) • **90**
Pomerol 1983: Well crafted with black olive, tar and ripe fruit character, medium body and silky well-integrated tannins. Drinkable now • $39 • (10/15/94) • **90**
Pomerol 1982 • $62 Ⓐ • (08/31/92) • **85**
Pomerol 1981: Delicious and gentle, displaying solid red color with a garnet edge. Lovely, rich tobacco, milk chocolate and fruit character. Has a full body, soft velvety texture and rich flavors. Drinkable now. • $45 • (10/15/94) • **87**
Pomerol 1979 • $34 Ⓐ • (10/15/89) • **87**
Pomerol 1970 • $40 Ⓐ • (05/15/93) • **94**
Pomerol 1962 • $70 • (11/30/87) • **60**
Pomerol 1961: Cuts a leaner figure than the other top Pomerols, but it is still very flavorful for a fully mature claret. Has a pleasant softness to the texture and lightness in body that makes it a pleasure to drink. • $134 Ⓐ • (04/30/96) • **86**
Pomerol 1959 • $190 • (10/15/90) • **91**
Pomerol 1945 • $500 Ⓐ • (03/16/86) • **50**

VIEUX CHÂTEAU GAUBERT

Graves White 1991 • $16 • (07/31/93) • **85**

VIEUX CHÂTEAU GUIBEAU

St.-Emilion 1982 • $8 • (09/16/85) • **80**

VIEUX CHENE, DOMAINE DU

Vin de Pays de Vaucluse 1990 • $7 • (01/31/92) • **77**
Vin de Pays de Vaucluse 1988 • $NA • • **80**

VIEUX DONJON, LE

Châteauneuf-du-Pape 1990: Warm, ripe and peppery-tasting, with leathery, earthy accents to the plum and currant flavors. Solid, flavorful and hearty, drink now or hold. 1,100 cases made. • $26 • (04/15/93) • **86**
Châteauneuf-du-Pape 1989 • $17 • (10/15/91) • **85**
Châteauneuf-du-Pape 1988 • $16 • (10/15/91) • **85**
Châteauneuf-du-Pape 1986 • $15 • (10/15/91) • **88**
Châteauneuf-du-Pape 1985 • $16 • (02/15/88) • **79**
Châteauneuf-du-Pape 1984 • $14 • (10/31/87) • **79**
Châteauneuf-du-Pape 1981 • $NA • (10/15/91) • **89**

FRANCE

VIEUX-FERRAND, CHÂTEAU

Pomerol 1982 • $NA • (05/15/89) • **82**

VIEUX GABRIAN, CHÂTEAU

Bordeaux Supérieur 1988 • $11 • (04/30/91) • **84**

VIEUX LAZARET, DOMAINE DU

Châteauneuf-du-Pape 1989 • $16 • (10/15/91) • **85**
Châteauneuf-du-Pape 1986 • $14 • (01/31/89) • **89**
Châteauneuf-du-Pape 1985 • $12 • (10/15/91) • **82**
Châteauneuf-du-Pape White 1990: Light and refreshing, an early-drinking wine that's good, but nothing special. Clean, fresh aromas of peach and apple follow through to a light, refreshing palate and a fresh finish. • $16 • (10/15/91) • **81**

VIEUX SARPE, CHÂTEAU

St.-Emilion 1982 • $NA • (05/15/89) • **83**

VIEUX TELEGRAPHE, DOMAINE DU

Châteauneuf-du-Pape 1990: Thick, chewy and full-bodied, with juniper, cedar and dried currant flavors. A muscular and focused Rhône, with an intriguing flavor profile, but too tough to warm up to at this young age. Everything is in balance, though, so it's a good bet to cellar until at least 1997. 15,000 cases made. • $23 • (02/28/93) SS • **89**
Châteauneuf-du-Pape 1989 • $53 Ⓐ • (10/15/91) • **87**
Châteauneuf-du-Pape 1988 • $22 Ⓐ • (10/15/91) • **85**
Châteauneuf-du-Pape 1987 • $32 • (09/30/90) • **81**
Châteauneuf-du-Pape 1986 • $23 Ⓐ • (10/15/91) • **90**
Châteauneuf-du-Pape 1985 • $30 • (10/15/91) • **82**
Châteauneuf-du-Pape 1984 • $16 Ⓐ • (09/30/87) • **89**
Châteauneuf-du-Pape 1983 • $29 Ⓐ • (10/15/91) • **85**
Châteauneuf-du-Pape 1981 • $35 • (10/15/91) • **80**
Châteauneuf-du-Pape Vieux Mas des Papes 1993: Smells and tastes like cherries accented by herbs and spices. Full-bodied, rich, moderately tannic, well balanced. Drink now through 1997. Second wine of Vieux Télégraphe. • $17 • **86**
Châteauneuf-du-Pape White 1990: A round, caressing style that's fatter and oilier than some, with pungent banana and melon aromas, a round mouth-feel and tropical fruit flavors. Spicy and fruity on the finish. • $20 • (10/15/91) • **86**

VIEUX-ROBIN, CHÂTEAU

Médoc 1995: Steely and slightly tough, showing plenty of berry and earthy fruit nuances. Moderate tannins, but slightly coarse on the finish. • $NA • (05/15/96) • **85-89** (BT)

VIGNELAURE, CHÂTEAU

Coteaux d'Aix en Provence 1981 • $10 • (10/01/84) • **89**

VIGNERONS D'IGE, LES

Mâcon-Igé 1994: Lovely Chardonnay. Medium in body and intensity, showing mineral, green apple and pear character. Balanced and delicious, smooth finish. • $NA • **84**
Mâcon-Igé 1993: Silky texture, but seems hollow and diluted, cardboard character dominates the fruit flavors. Disappointing, short finish. • $NA • **73**
Mâcon-Igé Château London 1994: A rather neutral white, disclosing only bits of pear, apple and mineral character. Clean, light, short finish. Somewhat diluted. • $10 • **77**
Mâcon-Igé Château London 1993: Some decent ripe fruit blends nicely with a grassy, wet hay, bitter almond and citrus character. • $10 • (08/31/94) • **78**
St.-Véran White 1994: Flat and dull—no fruit. Bad from start to finish, showing a cardboard box character. Tasted twice, with consistent notes. • $NA • **62**

VIGNERONS DE MANCEY, CAVE DES

Bourgogne Cuvée Spéciale Vieille en Fûts de Chêne 1993: Rather lean-flavored, tight and tannic in texture, delivering earthy, herbal tones and an astringent finish. 3,000 cases made. • $9 • (05/15/96) • **79**
Mâcon-Villages Vieilles Vignes 1994: Intense but also quite sour. Lemon, lime and wet hay flavors turn grassy on the finish. 4,167 cases made. • $9 • (08/31/94) • **76**

VIGNERONS DE RASTEAU, CAVE DES

Côtes du Rhône Cuvée Réservé 1989 • $8 • (04/15/93) • **78**

VIGNERONS DES COTEAUX DE ST.-JEAN, LES

Coteaux du Languedoc 1992 • $7 • (03/15/94) • **83**
Vin de Pays de l'Herault Cuvée des Capitelles NV • $6 • (03/15/94) • **84**

VIGNOBLE DE LA JASSE

Côtes du Rhône 1986 • $8 • (12/15/89) • **79**

VILLA BEL AIR

Graves 1995: Quite thick, rich and full-bodied, with nice red fruit character, but you wish for more class in the slightly rustic, weedy finish. • $NA • (05/15/96) • **75-79** (BT)
Graves 1994: Light, diluted and disappointing, modest fruit flavors. • $NA • **70-74** (BT)
Graves 1993: Light, simple black olive and fruit character, medium body and slightly metallic tannins. Drinkable now. • $NA • (01/31/96) • **78**
Graves 1992: Very, very herbal, showing hard tannins and a slightly metallic character. • $NA • **70**
Graves White 1994: A reserved style that isn't giving up much at the moment, but plenty of fruit shows through. Medium-to-full on the

Key: SS—Spectator Selection. CS—Cellar Selection. BB—Best Buy. $NA—Price not available. (BT)—Barrel tasting. Ⓐ—Auction Price.
Dates in parentheses represent the issues in which the ratings were published.

palate, with honey, apple and grapefruit flavors and firm acidity. Better in 1997. • $14 • (03/31/96) • **84**

Graves White 1993: Much better than the '92. Young and fresh, displaying pear puree, mineral and light vanilla on the nose and palate. Medium-bodied, light finish. • $NA • **84**

Graves White 1992 • $NA • (06/15/94) • **79**

VILLADIERE, CHÂTEAU

St.-Emilion 1982 • $8 • (09/01/85) • **75**

VILLAINE, A. & P. DE

Bourgogne La Digoine Bouzeron 1989 • $17 • (11/15/91) • **84**

Côte Chalonnaise Bouzeron La Digoine 1990: Stylish, forward and spicy, with generous blackberry, raspberry and currant flavors folded together with a nice touch of oak. Lean in texture, focused in flavor and drinkable now. A good value for '90 Burgundy. 2,000 cases made. • $16 • (11/30/92) • **87**

VILLAMONT, HENRI DE

Bourgogne Pinot Noir 1989 • $11 • (03/31/91) • **78**

Chambolle-Musigny 1988 • $39 • (02/15/91) • **83**

Mâcon-Villages 1994: Where is the beef? More water than wine in this disappointing, diluted white. Offers (very) modest fruit. • $NA • **70**

St.-Véran Clos de l'Ermitage White 1994: Good intensity, with vibrant citrus and green apple character, but it ends on a slightly sour note. • $NA • **79**

Savigny-lès-Beaune Le Village 1988 • $18 • (03/31/91) • **80**

VILLARS, CHÂTEAU

Fronsac 1990: A very aromatic wine, with a gamy, earthy, cherry character, medium tannins and short finish. Drinkable now. 11,000 cases made. • $17 • (03/31/93) • **83**

Fronsac 1989 • $16 • (06/15/93) • **78**

VILLEGEORGE, CHÂTEAU

Haut-Médoc 1993: Light and rather pleasant, but lacks concentration and tastes a bit diluted on the finish. Drink. • $NA • (01/31/96) • **79**

Haut-Médoc 1991: A little more to it than many of the others in this tasting. Lovely vanilla and fruit aromas and flavors, medium body and a silky finish. • $13 • (03/31/94) • **81**

Haut-Médoc 1989 • $14 • (03/15/92) • **79**

Haut-Médoc 1982 • $18 • (08/31/92) • **84**

Haut-Médoc 1981: Delicious, ripe wine with chocolate, prune, berry character. Full-bodied with loads of fruit and very velvety tannins. Drink now. • $NA • **86**

VILLEMAJOU, CLOS DE

Corbières 1988 • $6 • (04/30/90) • **78**

Corbières 1985 • $7 • (05/31/90) • **71**

VILLEMAURINE, CHÂTEAU

St.-Emilion 1995: Light and fruity and some decent flavors, but seems diluted for the vintage. • $NA • (05/15/96) • **75-79** (BT)

St.-Emilion 1994: Some decent fruit, but rather thin and slightly herbal. • $NA • (05/15/96) • **75-79** (BT)

St.-Emilion 1993: Bright, vibrant red berry character, light body and fresh finish. More like a Loire red. • $16 • (01/31/96) • **79**

St.-Emilion 1992: Firm and lightly fruity showing toasted oak and cherry character, light-to-medium body, light tannins and a slightly diluted finish. Drink now. • $13 • **79**

St.-Emilion 1991: Another delicate wine with plum and cherry flavors and a light finish. • $13 • (03/31/94) • **77**

St.-Emilion 1990: Understated but grand. A wine with floral, perfumed fruit aromas and flavors, lots of new oak character and fine, silky tannins. Drinkable in 1997. 3,800 cases made. • $28 • (03/31/93) • **92**

St.-Emilion 1989 • $30 • (03/15/92) • **93**

St.-Emilion 1982 • $40 • (08/31/92) • **93**

VILLENEUVE CHÂTEAU CANTEMERLE

Haut-Médoc 1994: Surprisingly light, Pinot aromas, weedy, plummy flavors, light tannins and finish. • $NA • **75-79** (BT)

VILLENEUVE, ARNAUD DE

Côtes du Roussillon-Villages 1991 • $9 • (03/15/94) • **85**

VILLERAMBERT, CHÂTEAU JULIEN

Minervois Cuvée Trianon 1989 • $15 • (12/15/91) • **73**

VILLOTTE, CHÂTEAU

Bordeaux 1993: Lean and supple, with light cherry flavors and a hint of chocolate. • $8 • (12/15/95) • **79**

Bordeaux 1991: A medium-bodied red with plenty of tannin, but falls short on fruit. A bit hollow and bitter. 2,250 cases made. • $7 • (11/15/94) • **77**

Bordeaux White 1994: A soft, pleasant white wine with modest pear, vanilla and citrus flavors. Fairly rich in texture, but simple. • $8 • (02/29/96) • **79**

Bordeaux White 1992: Drinkable, but soft, slightly sweet and innocuous. Simple stuff. 8,300 cases made. • $7 • (11/15/94) • **77**

VINCENT, J.J.

Mâcon-Villages Pièce d'Or 1992: A good, ripe-tasting Macon with ample fruit flavors, smooth texture and plenty of body. It has good concentration and texture, but not much finesse. • $7 • **82**

Pouilly-Fuissé 1993: Delicate and crisp, light-to-medium-bodied, offering clean green apple, grapefruit and butter flavors. Drink now. From the producer of Château Fuissé. 1,667 cases made. • $12 • **84**

Pouilly-Fuissé 1992: A basic, lean, slightly earthy tasting wine that's decent quality but nothing special. The flavors are herb and mineral and the finish is earthy and vegetal. • $11 • **77**

St.-Véran 1992: A fairly full-bodied, smooth-textured wine marked by attractive vanilla and butter aromas that melt into the modest fruit flavors and linger on the finish. Good value, too. • $9 BB • **85**

VINCENT, M.

Pouilly-Fuissé Château Fuissé 1993: A bit astringent and herbal but showing vibrant, well-defined Granny Smith apple and pear flavors. Drinkable now. 6,667 cases made. • $24 • **85**

Pouilly-Fuissé Château Fuissé 1992: A ripe and lively white wine with floral, buttery and orangelike flavors and a creamy texture. Stays interesting and satisfying on the finish. • $37 • (11/15/94) • **86**

Pouilly-Fuissé Château Fuissé Les Brûlés 1993: A lovely Pouilly, offering smooth texture and succulent, fruity, floral notes. It butters your mouth with mineral flavors and a long, solid finish. Drinkable now. 250 cases made. • $30 • **90**

Pouilly-Fuissé Château Fuissé Le Clos 1993: Polished and smooth, a creamy, medium-bodied white that delivers lightly toasted, honeyed, mineral, pear and grapefruit notes and a pretty, chalky finish. Drinkable now. 500 cases made. • $30 • **88**

Pouilly-Fuissé Château Fuissé Les Combettes 1993: Classy, rich and well balanced, supple, packing good concentration of fruit. The mineral, pear, honey, floral and light toast flavors are exquisite, subtle finish. Drinkable now. 250 cases made. • $30 • **90**

Pouilly-Fuissé Château Fuissé Vieilles Vignes 1993: Remarkably velvety, mineral character that you must taste to believe. Subtle, medium-bodied, fruity and firm, sporting toast, honey, pear and grapefruit flavors and a harmonious finish. Drinkable now. 1,667 cases made. • $35 • **90**

Pouilly-Fuissé Château Fuissé Vieilles Vignes 1992: Vividly fruity, lively and refreshing. It reminds us of grapefruit, pineapple and banana, rounded out by a creamy, lingering finish. Drinkable now. • $50 • (11/15/94) • **86**

St.-Véran 1992: Lean, crisp, modestly flavorful white wine that's well-balanced and reminds us of apples and lemons. A good, serviceable dinner wine. • $15 • **83**

VINS DE ROQUEBRUN, CAVE LES

Cuvée Roches Noires Macération St.-Chinian 1991 • $9 • (03/15/94) • **85**
Prestige St.-Chinian 1991 • $8 • (03/15/94) • **80**
Tradition St.-Chinian 1991 • $7 • (03/15/94) • **82**

VIOLET, CHÂTEAU

Sauternes 1987 • $NA • (06/15/90) • **79**

VIOLETTE, CHÂTEAU LA

Pomerol 1995: A bit tough, but there are some decent berry flavors and an earthy character to keep it interesting. Medium-to-light body, sleek tannins and a short finish. • $NA • (05/15/96) • **80-84** (BT)
Pomerol 1982 • $25 • (05/15/89) • **88**
Pomerol 1979 • $35 • (10/15/89) • **79**

FRANCE

VIORNERY, GEORGES

Côte de Brouilly 1990 • $13 • (10/31/91) • **88**

VIRE, CAVE DE

Mâcon-Viré 1994: Exotic and ripe, with some body and weight to it—grass, honey, pear and floral character. Extremely well made and a pleasure to drink now. • $NA • **84**
Mâcon-Viré Cuvée Spéciale 1994: Wild Mâcon that's distinctively, intensely grassy, featuring gooseberry, raspberry and rose petal notes. Medium-bodied and rather ripe, spice and nutmeg on the finish adding complexity. Drink now. • $NA • **85**
Mâcon-Viré Fûts de Chêne Neufs 1992: Silky-textured, medium in body, a maturing wine with an impressively round and rich mouth-feel. An earthy component distracts from honey, hazelnut and butterscotch flavors. • $NA • **82**
Mâcon-Viré Grande Réserve 1994: Grassy, like a pure Sauvignon Blanc. Has mineral, herb and wet hay notes, but also good intensity of green apple and pear flavors. • $NA • **84**

VIRELY-ROUGEOT

Pommard 1992: An odd salty flavor and an astringent texture makes this difficult to like. 1,000 cases made. • $25 • (05/15/95) • **73**

VITALLIS, CHÂTEAU

Pouilly-Fuissé Vieilles Vignes 1993: A bit too tart for us, offering substantial citrusy flavors, but it has vibrant, juicy character. Lean and hard, steely finish lends itself to seafood. Try now. 2,333 cases made. • $25 • **82**

VIVIERS, CHÂTEAU DE

Chablis Blanchots 1994: Light, supple and easy-drinking. Lacks the complexity and depth for the cellar, but it offers nice honey, pear and ripe apple flavors for enjoying right away. From Lupé-Cholet. • $NA • (05/31/96) • **80**
Chablis Vaillons 1994: Fresh and attractive lemon, honey, pear and apple flavors. Medium-bodied and deliciously crisp on the finish. Try in 1998. From Lupé-Cholet. • $NA • (05/31/96) • **86**
Chablis Vaucopins 1994: Quite ripe, though slightly lighter in body, with intense citrus, green apple and grassy flavors. Hints of mineral on the crisp finish. Try in 1998. From Lupé-Cholet. • $NA • (05/31/96) • **84**

VIVONNE, DOMAINE DE LA

Bandol 1981 • $NA • (08/31/86) • **68**

VOARICK, DOMAINE MICHEL

Aloxe-Corton 1993: Traditional, quite intense, full-bodied, featuring currant, spice and raisiny character. Some tough tannins will need until 2000 to come around. A bit overdone for us. • $30 • **82**
Aloxe-Corton 1990 • $26 • (12/15/92) • **79**
Corton Les Bressandes 1990: Extremely traditional in style. Medium-bodied, with rather high acidity and a diluted finish. Not worth the price, but it's drinkable now. • $36 • (12/15/92) • **73**
Corton Clos du Roi 1993: Portlike masses of raisin, berry and tar, full body and tannins and a slightly alcoholic finish. Overdone? Better in 2000. • $60 • **85**
Corton Clos du Roi 1990: Quite disappointing. Tastes like cherry juice and lacks concentration and complexity, but does show pleasant sweetness and modest smokiness. Drinkable now. • $36 • (12/15/92) • **75**
Corton Renardes 1993: Loads of raisin, dried fruit and spice character. Could use a bit more finesse. Full in body, medium tannins and short finish. Needs time to open, try in 2000. • $60 • **86**
Pernand-Vergelesses 1993: Extremely ripe dried cherry, pepper and black cherry character verges on being raisiny. Full-bodied and slightly overdone, it could use more finesse. Drink or hold until 1998. • $20 • **85**
Romanée St.-Vivant 1990: An odd wine, with cherry, strawberry and earth aromas and flavors, but is a bit sour on the finish. Has good fruit, but lacks balance. The off-side of this wine is more obvious as it stays in the glass. Not recommended. • $76 • (12/15/92) • **69**

VOCORET & FILS

Chablis 1994: Decent fruit in this lively village Chablis—lots of citrus, green apple, and dried herb character. Unfortunately, it turns sour on the finish. 10,000 cases made. • $14 • (05/31/96) • **78**
Chablis Blanchot 1994: Awesome power: ripe, rich, full-bodied and unctuous. This firm, tightly-built *grand cru* has lots of personality, the lightly grassy, dried herb notes mingle well with the honey, ripe pear, mineral, chalk and wet earth aromas and flavors. It makes for quite an intense wine experience. 833 cases made. • $42 • (05/31/96) • **92**
Chablis La Forêt 1994: Good intensity of dried herb, green apple and mineral notes. Clean, crisp and very lively, with a fresh finish. 2,500 cases made. • $19 • (05/31/96) • **84**
Chablis Montée de Tonnerre 1994: Fresh and very crisp, with wonderful focus in its fruit flavors. Has a touch of mineral, but basically, it's tight and zesty. Try in 1997. Tasted twice, with consistent notes. 833 cases made. • $20 • (05/31/96) • **84**
Chablis Vaillon 1994: Tight and crisp, with mineral, honey and apple character. Subtle yet intense, delivering some delicious ripe flavors on the balanced finish. Shows good potential, try in 1998. 2,500 cases made. • $20 • (05/31/96) • **86**

VOGE, ALAIN

Cornas 1991 • $25 • (05/31/94) • **86**
Cornas Cuvée Barriques 1990 • $25 • (04/15/93) • **87**
Cornas Cuvée Vieilles Vignes 1990 • $27 • (05/31/94) • **83**
Cornas Cuvée Vielles Vignes 1989 • $32 • (04/15/93) • **83**
Cornas Vieilles Vignes 1991 • $27 • (05/31/94) • **86**

VOGUE, COMTE GEORGES DE

Bonnes Mares 1993: A beauty, boasting clean, pure, subtle currant, black cherry and mint flavors. Elegant structure of silky tannins. Tight and closed in, it's not giving much now, try in 2000. 466 cases made. • $115 • **94**
Bonnes Mares 1992: Supple and generous, with gorgeous raspberry, currant and vanilla flavors, fine-textured tannins and a juicy finish. A

Key: SS—Spectator Selection. CS—Cellar Selection. BB—Best Buy. $NA—Price not available. (BT)—Barrel tasting. Ⓐ—Auction Price.
Dates in parentheses represent the issues in which the ratings were published.

stylish wine that is nice now but should be best in 1996 or 1997. 583 cases made. • $85 • **88**

Bonnes Mares 1991: Deep in color and flavor, a wine that shows both power and elegance, muscular up front and more delicate on the finish. Flavors run toward ripe currant, chestnut and black cherry, echoing cherry on the finish, framed with fine tannins. Try in 1997. 250 cases made. • $90 Ⓐ • (01/31/94) • **93**

Bonnes Mares 1990: A classy, monumental wine, with an impressive deep color and spellbinding complexity. The concentration takes your breath away as the plum, blackberry, raspberry and vanilla flavors coat your palate. Try in 1998. 500 cases made. • $66 Ⓐ • (12/15/92) • **99**

Bonnes Mares 1989 • $93 • (01/31/92) • **94**

Bonnes Mares 1988 • $65 Ⓐ • (03/31/91) • **89**

Bonnes Mares 1987 • $73 • (07/15/90) • **87**

Bonnes Mares 1979 • $48 • (11/16/84) • **88**

Bonnes Mares 1976 • $56 Ⓐ • (11/16/84) • **90**

Bonnes Mares 1972 • $125 • (11/16/84) • **79**

Bonnes Mares 1971 • $91 Ⓐ • (11/16/84) • **88**

Bonnes Mares 1959 • $179 • (11/16/84) • **83**

Bonnes Mares 1955 • $285 • (11/16/84) • **91**

Bonnes Mares 1949 • $500 • (11/16/84) • **90**

Bonnes Mares Avery Bottling 1959 • $NA • (11/16/84) • **87**

Bonnes Mares Grivolet 1934 • $NA • (11/16/84) • **82**

Chambolle-Musigny 1993: Sleek, fine, focused plum and fruit character, medium body and tannins and a crisp, lively finish. Better in 2000. 833 cases made. • $60 • **88**

Chambolle-Musigny 1992: Firm, chewy and trying hard to show currant and spice flavors behind it all, but it comes up a little short. Approachable now, best from 1996. 917 cases made. • $45 • **83**

Chambolle-Musigny 1991: Light and fragrant, a silky mouthful of lovely currant, blackberry and earthy flavors, which persist nicely on the finish. Drinkable now. 250 cases made. • $47 Ⓐ • (01/31/94) • **88**

Chambolle-Musigny 1990: Impressively structured, showing a lot of concentration, with masses of wood, plum, cherry and berry flavors. A serious Chambolle village wine for the cellar. Try in 1998. 917 cases made. • $45 • (12/15/92) • **90**

Chambolle-Musigny 1989 • $44 • (01/31/92) • **89**

Chambolle-Musigny Les Amoureuses 1993: A blockbuster, dark in color, delivering beautiful cranberry, vanilla and plum aromas, full body and masses of fruit and tannins. Try after 2000. 200 cases made. • $125 • **94**

Chambolle-Musigny Les Amoureuses 1992: Light and fragrant, showing some ripe raspberry and currant flavors on the delicate framework. Finishes with a touch of tannin. Drinkable now. 250 cases made. • $85 • **83**

Chambolle-Musigny Les Amoureuses 1991: Has beautifully defined currant and berry aromas and flavors that carry straight through the finish, a soft-textured wine that has some fine tannins, drinkable now. 100 cases made. • $90 Ⓐ • (01/31/94) • **87**

Chambolle-Musigny Les Amoureuses 1990: An ager, well crafted, showing great extract of berry and plum flavors and a lot of elegance despite masses of firm tannins. Try in 1998. 250 cases made. • $66 • (12/15/92) • **94**

Chambolle-Musigny Les Amoureuses 1989 • $93 • (01/31/92) • **93**

Chambolle-Musigny Les Amoureuses 1988 • $93 • (02/28/91) • **89**

Chambolle-Musigny Les Amoureuses 1987 • $74 • (03/31/90) • **87**

Chambolle-Musigny Les Amoureuses 1971 • $85 • (11/16/84) • **86**

Chambolle-Musigny Les Amoureuses 1970 • $55 • (11/16/84) • **78**

Musigny 1992: Tough and narrow, bright and floral, showing a nice thread of tart berry and spice character, finishes with tight, chalky tannins that will need until 1998 to 2000 to soften. 1,167 cases made. • $100 • **85**

Musigny 1953 • $200 • (11/16/84) • **81**

Musigny 1952 • $200 • (11/16/84) • **85**

Musigny 1949 • $600 • (11/16/84) • **98**

Musigny 1945 • $1,600 • (11/16/84) • **96**

Musigny 1937 • $650 • (11/16/84) • **93**

Musigny 1934 • $600 • (11/16/84) • **95**

Musigny Cuvée Vieilles Vignes 1993: Tough-as-nails, assertive *grand cru.* Full in body featuring ripe fruit and loads of tannins that need time to open. Try in 2006. 1,000 cases made. • $140 • **96**

Musigny Cuvée Vieilles Vignes 1991: Elegant, flavorful and earthy at first, but bursts with delicious currant and blackberry flavors that extend into a long, inviting finish. The fruit is sharply articulated and the fine tannins wrap it into a neat package. Worth cellaring through 2000. 916 cases made. • $134 Ⓐ • (01/31/94) CS • **91**

Musigny Cuvée Vieilles Vignes 1990: A monument. Brilliant, deep and stylish, delivering supple and intense currant, spice, vanilla and violet flavors. Firm finish. Start trying it in 1998, or even 2000. • $140 • **100**

Musigny Cuvée Vieilles Vignes 1989 • $134 • (01/31/92) • **96**

Musigny Cuvée Vieilles Vignes 1988 • $96 Ⓐ • (02/28/91) • **90**

Musigny Cuvée Vielles Vignes 1987: Light in texture and flavor, a bit simple for this appellation with just a touch of dilution, but some nice, spicy notes add interest to the supple strawberry character. • $105 • **87**

Musigny Cuvée Vieilles Vignes 1986: Crisp and a little chewy but still stylish, showing its grand cru breed with spice, toast and black cherry flavors sneaking through on the narrow finish. • $100 • **87**

Musigny Cuvée Vieilles Vignes 1985: Light and chewy, with a distinctive anise edge to the smoky orange peel and berry flavors, developing maturity and showing some nice perfumes. • $103 Ⓐ • **87**

Musigny Cuvée Vieilles Vignes 1979 • $114 • (11/16/84) • **87**

Musigny Cuvée Vieilles Vignes 1976 • $74 Ⓐ • (11/16/84) • **86**

Musigny Cuvée Vieilles Vignes 1972 • $122 • (11/16/84) • **80**

Musigny Cuvée Vieilles Vignes 1971 • $150 Ⓐ • (11/16/84) • **90**

Musigny Cuvée Vieilles Vignes 1969 • $220 • (11/16/84) • **65**

Musigny Cuvée Vieilles Vignes 1966 • $173 Ⓐ • (11/16/84) • **92**

Musigny Cuvée Vieilles Vignes 1962 • $550 • (11/16/84) • **90**

Musigny Cuvée Vieilles Vignes 1961 • $184 Ⓐ • (11/16/84) • **93**

Musigny Cuvée Vieilles Vignes 1959 • $440 • (11/16/84) • **89**

Musigny Cuvée Vieilles Vignes 1957 • $255 • (08/31/90) • **95**

VOILLAND, LEON

Beaune Clos du Roy 1945 • $NA • (08/31/90) • **90**

VOLPATO-COSTAILLE

Chambolle-Musigny 1988 • $34 • (02/28/91) • **78**

VOLPATO, JEAN-CLAUDE

Bourgogne Passe-tout-grains 1988 • $13 • (03/31/91) • **73**

VOULTE-GASPARETS, CHÂTEAU LA

Corbières 1990 • $10 • (03/15/94) • **85**

VRAI CAILLOU, CHÂTEAU

Entre-Deux-Mers 1993: Vanilla-scented notes accompany a buttery, cedary character. Well made, velvety finish. • $8 • **81**

VRANKEN

Brut Champagne Demoiselle 1986: A lot of potential here. Tightly knit with very good fruit concentration, fine acidity and a fresh clean finish. Needs time to develop. Well-made. From Champagne Vranken. Drinkable now. • $NA • (12/31/93) • **89**

Brut Champagne Demoiselle Téte de Cuvée 1989: Smooth, elegant and creamy-textured, offering subtle Chardonnay notes and a lingering finish. The flavors seem to expand and turn delicately nutty and honey-like as you sip. 33,333 cases made. • $40 • (01/31/96) • **90**

Brut Champagne Demoiselle Tête de Cuvée NV • $NA • (12/31/93) • **86**

Brut Champagne Grande Cuvée NV • $NA • (12/31/91) • **86**

Champagne Demoiselle Grande Cuvée NV: Aromatic and mellow in character, sporting nutty, toasty, lemony flavors and a nice sense of lightness in texture and body. Crisp and refreshing on the finish, too. 58,000 cases made. • $27 • (01/31/96) • **89**

VRAYE-CROIX-DE-GAY, CHÂTEAU LA

Pomerol 1995: Beautiful from start to finish. Elegant and powerful, a brooding, ink-colored, seamless '95 boasting well-defined, earthy red fruit and blackberry flavors. • $NA • (05/15/96) • **90-94** (BT)

WEINBACH, DOMAINE

Gewürztraminer Alsace Altenbourg Cuvée Laurence 1993: Oodles of pear, apple, honey and spice flavors. Sweet enough to drink with cheese and fruit desserts. 330 cases made. • $37 • (09/15/95) • **85**

Gewürztraminer Alsace Clos des Capucins Réserve Personnelle 1991 • $23 • (06/15/93) • **81**

Gewürztraminer Alsace Cuvée Laurence 1992: Very thick and quite sweet, this wine leans towards a late-harvest style. There are apple, peach, butter and honey flavors, but the main impression is textural. Best for dessert. • $40 • (11/15/94) • **85**

Gewürztraminer Alsace Cuvée Théo 1993: Exuberant and flavorful, sporting pronounced floral, meaty, spicy aromas, smooth, soft texture and an almost sweet finish. Strong in bouquet, but easy on the palate. 620 cases made. • $23 • (09/15/95) • **86**

Gewürztraminer Alsace Cuvée Théo 1992: Fruity and slightly sweet, this offers flavors of ripe apple, pear, banana and honey. It's soft and gentle on the palate, an easy-drinking apéritif style. • $27 • (11/15/94) • **83**

Gewürztraminer Alsace Grand Cru Furstentum Cuvée Laurence 1993: Smoky, almost charred aroma gives way to sweet flavors of candied oranges and peaches. Soft and viscous. Tasted twice with consistent notes. 350 cases made. • $42 • (09/15/95) • **84**

Gewürztraminer Alsace Grand Cru Furstentum Cuvée Laurence 1992: Soft and slightly sweet, this wine starts off a bit earthy but luscious peach and pineapple flavors emerge on the palate and the finish is clean and delicate. An easy-drinking wine for a summer afternoon. • $44 • (11/15/94) • **85**

Riesling Alsace Clos des Capucins Réserve Personnelle 1991 • $22 • (06/15/93) • **81**

Riesling Alsace Cuvée Ste. Catherine 1992: Powerful and concentrated. This rich, ripe Riesling is chock-full of apricot, orange and honey flavors, and the slight sweetness is in perfect balance with its firm structure. A big wine with a long future. • $34 • (09/15/94) • **91**

Riesling Alsace Cuvée Théo 1993: Typical Riesling character, taut and intense-vivid aromas of peach and smoke, lively flavors of apple and mineral and a dry, bracing texture. Drinkable now. 600 cases made. • $23 • (07/31/95) • **89**

Riesling Alsace Cuvée Théo 1992: A gentle, aromatic wine with a hint of sweetness. It has pleasant floral aromas and it's soft and fruity on the palate. A good apéritif, but it might be a bit cloying with food. Drink now. • $24 • (11/15/94) • **79**

Riesling Alsace Grand Cru Schlossberg Cuvée Ste. Catherine 1993: Apple and apricot flavors are ripe but crisp and enlivened by citrusy acidity. It's straightforward, clean, bright, harmonious and lively, adding good varietal typicity. Tasted twice, with consistent notes. 340 cases made. • $38 • (09/15/95) • **86**

Riesling Alsace Grand Cru Schlossberg Cuvée Ste. Catherine 1992: Enticing aromas of apricot, cream and honey give way to a round, polished palate showing ripe apple, melon, spice and honey flavors. Beautifully balanced and generous with a long finish. • $42 • (09/15/94) • **89**

Tokay Pinot Gris Alsace Cuvée Ste. Catherine 1992: Silky and honeyed, this wine marries almond and light vegetal flavors in a soft, round balance of sweetness and clean acidity. It's open and ready to drink now. • $34 • (11/15/94) • **87**

Tokay Pinot Gris Alsace Cuvée Ste. Catherine 1992: Silky and honeyed, this wine marries almond and light vegetal flavors in a soft, round balance of sweetness and clean acidity. It's open and ready to drink now. • $34 • (11/15/94) • **87**

WILDMAN & SONS, FREDERICK

Brut Vouvray NV • $7 • **85**

Key: SS—Spectator Selection. CS—Cellar Selection. BB—Best Buy. $NA—Price not available. (BT)—Barrel tasting. Ⓐ—Auction Price.
Dates in parentheses represent the issues in which the ratings were published.

WILLI'S WINE BAR

Crozes-Hermitage Cuvée Anniversaire 1980-1990 1988 • $11 • (03/31/91) • **70**

WILLM, ALSACE

Crémant Alsace NV: A light, soft sparkler with a foamy mousse, this gives an impression of slight sweetness and a canned fruit cocktail note to the peach and melon flavors. Quaffable, but lacks sophistication. • $15 • (11/15/94) • **79**

Gewürztraminer Alsace 1993: Subtle and refined for a Gewürz, with subdued spice aromas, polished apple and mint flavors and a lingering finish. Very smooth in texture, too. • $11 • (11/15/94) • **85**

Pinot Blanc Alsace 1993: A smooth, flavorful wine with notes of peach and hazelnut, this has enough underlying acidity to keep it lively, but gives a round, full feeling without tartness. Easy to drink, best as an apéritif. • $8 • (11/15/94) • **83**

Riesling Alsace 1993: A simple, straightforward Riesling with green apple and honey flavors and a rather short, cidery finish. • $10 • (11/15/94) • **78**

WOLFBERGER

Crémant d'Alsace NV • $12 • (07/31/89) • **83**

YON-FIGEAC, CHÂTEAU

St.-Emilion 1990: An understated wine, with ripe fruit and toasted nut aromas and flavors, medium tannins and a succulent finish. Drinkable now. 7,500 cases made. • $24 • (03/31/93) • **86**

St.-Emilion 1982 • $25 • (05/15/89) • **87**

YQUEM, CHÂTEAU D'

Sauternes 1989: A majestic Yquem, exhibiting solid backbone and masses of toasted coconut, honey, spice and dried apricot character. Sweet but not very thick, with a long aftertaste. The new oak dominates now, try after 1999. • $200 • (04/15/95) • **97**

Sauternes 1988: Big and showy, rich and ripe, featuring sweet mango, pineapple and lime character. Full in body, with a long finish that reins in honey, dried apricot and toasted vanilla flavors. Drink or hold until at least 1998. • $200 • (04/15/95) • **94**

Sauternes 1987 • $130 • (04/15/95) • **88**
Sauternes 1986 • $130 • (04/15/95) • **95**
Sauternes 1985 • $112 Ⓐ • (12/15/93) • **91**
Sauternes 1984 • $150 • (12/15/93) • **90**
Sauternes 1983 • $260 • (04/15/95) • **98**
Sauternes 1982 • $118 Ⓐ • (12/15/93) • **91**
Sauternes 1981 • $240 • (12/15/93) • **87**
Sauternes 1980 • $143 Ⓐ • (12/15/93) • **84**
Sauternes 1979 • $317 Ⓐ • (12/15/93) • **85**
Sauternes 1978 • $280 Ⓐ • (12/15/93) • **80**
Sauternes 1976 • $261 Ⓐ • (12/15/93) • **92**
Sauternes 1975 • $339 Ⓐ • (12/15/93) • **97**
Sauternes 1971 • $275 Ⓐ • (12/15/93) • **90**
Sauternes 1970 • $173 Ⓐ • (12/15/93) • **84**
Sauternes 1967 • $543 Ⓐ • (12/15/93) • **81**
Sauternes 1966 • $208 Ⓐ • (12/15/93) • **84**
Sauternes 1962 • $284 Ⓐ • (12/15/93) • **85**
Sauternes 1961 • $351 Ⓐ • (12/15/93) • **83**
Sauternes 1959 • $637 Ⓐ • (12/15/93) • **93**
Sauternes 1958 • $330 Ⓐ • (12/15/93) • **88**
Sauternes 1957 • $489 Ⓐ • (12/15/93) • **85**
Sauternes 1955 • $553 Ⓐ • (12/15/93) • **78**
Sauternes 1953 • $902 Ⓐ • (12/15/93) • **80**
Sauternes 1950 • $395 Ⓐ • (12/15/93) • **88**
Sauternes 1949 • $803 Ⓐ • (12/15/93) • **91**
Sauternes 1948 • $593 Ⓐ • (12/15/93) • **92**
Sauternes 1947 • $811 Ⓐ • (12/15/93) • **90**
Sauternes 1945 • $1,200 • (12/15/93) • **95**
Sauternes 1943 • $538 Ⓐ • (12/15/93) • **83**

Sauternes 1942 • $452 Ⓐ • (12/15/93) • **87**
Sauternes 1937 • $974 Ⓐ • (12/15/93) • **94**
Sauternes 1934 • $643 Ⓐ • (12/15/93) • **88**
Sauternes 1928 • $775 Ⓐ • (12/15/93) • **92**
Sauternes 1924 • $678 Ⓐ • (12/15/93) • **86**
Sauternes 1921 • $2,100 • (12/15/93) • **97**
Sauternes 1900 • $2,200 • (12/15/93) • **97**
Sauternes 1893 • $2,500 • (12/15/93) • **73**
Sauternes 1874 • $3,000 • (12/15/93) • **98**
Sauternes 1870 • $4,000 • (12/15/93) • **83**
Sauternes 1865 • $4,000 • (12/15/93) • **73**
Sauternes 1858 • $4,000 • (12/15/93) • **55**
Sauternes 1847 • $15,000 • (12/15/93) • **99**

ZIND-HUMBRECHT, DOMAINE

Gewürztraminer Alsace Clos Windsbuhl Hunawihr 1993: Very distinctive and attractive. Rich in fruit, creamy in texture, full-bodied but lively in balance. It has the classic rose petal and grapefruit aromas and flavors and a nicely lingering finish. 400 cases made. • $40 • (08/31/95) • **90**

Gewürztraminer Alsace Clos Windsbuhl Hunawihr 1992: Some soft, fruity bottle bouquet is already developing. Toasty, smoky aromas and an appealing grapefruity bitterness of Gewürz. 400 cases made. • $40 • (09/15/95) • **86**

Gewürztraminer Alsace Grand Cru Goldert 1993: Bold and opulent but dry, combining smoky aromas, ripe pear and honey flavors and a long-lasting nutty, mineral character on the finish. Very full-bodied and assertive, yet well-balanced by acidity. Drinkable now through 2000. 300 cases made. • $35 • (08/31/95) • **92**

Gewürztraminer Alsace Grand Cru Goldert Gueberschwihr 1992: Clean and well-balanced, made in a dry style that complements food. A tasty wine that offers ripe melon and almond flavors with a hint of black pepper in the finish. May show better with time. • $32 • (11/15/94) • **86**

Gewürztraminer Alsace Grand Cru Hengst Wintzenheim 1993: Heady aromas of rose petal, earth and grapefruit mark this as a classic Gewürztraminer. Bold flavors, full body and lingering fruit on the finish. It's assertive, concentrated and dry. Tempting now, but should improve through 1997. 500 cases made. • $35 • (08/31/95) • **90**

Gewürztraminer Alsace Grand Cru Hengst Wintzenheim 1992: Delicacy and muscle mingle in this dry wine. The aromas are gentle, floral and lemony, but the palate is big, even austere, with grapefruit, mineral and almond flavors. It's not a showboat, but has impressive intensity. Will show better with time. • $32 • (09/30/94) • **89**

Gewürztraminer Alsace Gueberschwihr 1992: Middle of the road wine, with subdued flavors and a smooth but lively texture. Pleasant, but we would like to taste more fruit. • $20 • (11/15/94) • **81**

Gewürztraminer Alsace Heimbourg Turckheim 1993: Thick in texture, honey- and nut-flavored, very ripe and opulent style. Practically a dessert wine, adding apricot, pineapple and spice for bold taste experiences. 350 cases made. • $35 • (09/15/95) • **88**

Gewürztraminer Alsace Heimbourg Turckheim 1992: Thick and soft as a feather mattress, rich as syrup, yet it's completely dry. Intense flavors of spice, nuts and rose petals are complex and balanced and echo on the long finish. Though not an easy match with a meal, it's a superb wine in its own right. • $32 • (11/15/94) • **91**

Gewürztraminer Alsace Herrenweg Turckheim 1993: Very solid, well-balanced Gewürz with delicious pear and grapefruit flavors accented by spice. Smooth texture and lively acidity get more interesting with each sip. 1,000 cases made. • $25 • (08/31/95) • **89**

Gewürztraminer Alsace Herrenweg Turckheim 1992: Bone-dry, using crisp acidity to carry well-defined flavors of ripe apple, spice and bitter almonds, full-bodied, concentrated and balanced, with great intensity. • $22 • (09/30/94) • **90**

Gewürztraminer Alsace Turckheim 1992: A Gewürztraminer of a different color, literally. From the green-tinged hue, to the toasty aromas, smoky-herbal flavors and lively acidity, this is an unusual and distinctive Gewurz. A bit heavy with smoke on the finish, but overall a good taste experience. • $19 • (11/15/94) • **82**

Gewürztraminer Alsace Wintzenheim 1993: Bold flavors and opulent texture make this imposing. Has flavors of walnut and grapefruit, an appealing touch of bitterness and lots of body. It's dry, however, and should be great with grilled fish, roast pork or ham. 400 cases made. • $20 • (08/31/95) • **90**

Gewürztraminer Alsace Wintzenheim 1992: A distinctive and concentrated Gewürztraminer that blends intense herb, mineral, toast, rose petal and fruit in a tight frame of acidity. The flavors linger on the finish, turning toasty and complex. • $17 • (09/30/94) • **89**

Muscat Alsace 1992: An austere wine, dry and bitter, with intense earthy, herbal, smoky and mineral flavors and a bone-dry finish. Striking but not particularly appealing. • $19 • (11/15/94) • **77**

Muscat Alsace Grand Cru Goldert Gueberschwihr 1993: Ripe and flavorful, richly textured, somewhat sweet, showing tangy acidity and apricot and floral notes that linger on the finish, turning honeyed and spicy. 150 cases made. • $30 • (09/15/95) • **87**

Pinot Alsace d'Alsace 1993: Wonderfully rich and velvety-textured, boasting lots of fruit flavor accented by subtle earth and mineral aromas. It has great depth, concentration and balance. Pear and apricot notes expand on the finish. • $17 • (07/31/95) • **91**

Pinot Alsace d'Alsace 1992: Ripe and fruity tasting, almost sweet, with plenty of pear, orange and hints of vanilla flavors. Balanced toward the fat, soft side, with a clean finish. • $16 • (11/15/94) • **83**

Riesling Alsace Clos Häuserer 1993: Lots of satisfying flavor, distinctive, well-balanced, smells of peach and mint, tastes like apple and peach accented by pine. Lively texture makes it light but lasting on the palate. 350 cases made. • $28 • (09/15/95) • **87**

Riesling Alsace Clos Häuserer 1992: Packed with flavor, but not heavy-handed, this features ripe apricot, pine and spice notes, with vibrant acidity and a clean, fresh finish. Exuberant and young, it should benefit from aging. • $23 • (09/15/94) • **89**

Riesling Alsace Clos Windsbuhl Hunawihr 1993: This has very good peachy, appley aromas, and rather austere peach and mineral flavors that tend to expand as you sip. A modestly proportioned but well-balanced Riesling that should improve through 1997. 200 cases made. • $40 • (09/15/95) • **86**

Riesling Alsace Grand Cru Brand Turckheim 1993: Distinguished, offering lots of fruit flavor accented by subtle mineral and savory notes, all wrapped in a full-bodied, rich-textured package. Lingering finish, too. 200 cases made. • $40 • (07/31/95) • **89**

Riesling Alsace Grand Cru Brand Turckheim 1992: A generous wine with good balance. Peach and floral aromas lead to a round, slightly sweet palate with peach, orange and honey flavors. Good acidity keeps it refreshing, though. • $34 • (11/15/94) • **87**

Riesling Alsace Grand Cru Clos St.-Urbain Rangen de Thann 1993: This is Riesling on a grand scale: bold, rich and assertive, a vivid yellow-gold color and an ample palate, enhanced by the great, smooth texture and extended finish. Packed with peach, apple and pineapple flavors, accented with honey and vanilla. 200 cases made. • $64 • (09/15/95) • **92**

Riesling Alsace Grand Cru Clos St.-Urbain Rangen de Thann 1991: This lean wine is still somewhat hard, with petrol, orange peel and tea flavors over firm acidity. It's well-integrated and focused. • $40 • (11/15/94) • **87**

Riesling Alsace Herrenweg Tuckheim 1993: A complex, satisfying and exotic style-ripe flavors, full body and lively texture. Bright pear and apple notes are accented by almond and butter. 400 cases made. • $25 • (07/31/95) • **88**

Riesling Alsace Herrenweg Turckheim Vieilles Vignes 1992: An intriguing marriage of tart and sweet, this wine shows mandarin orange, pineapple and honey flavors wrapped around a core of bracing acidity. It's vivid, firm and bright, with a long fruity finish. Drink now. • $22 • (11/15/94) • **87**

Riesling Alsace Turckheim 1992: Rich, full-blown flavors of ripe apples and pears are braced by vivid, crisp acidity for a racy, lively effect. Tastes satisfying and refreshing now. • $18 • (11/15/94) • **86**

Riesling Alsace Wintzenheim 1993: Ripe and enticing in flavor, sporting rich peach and pineapple notes and an earthy accent. Fruitiness builds and lingers on the finish, fine balance and harmony. Drinkable now. 500 cases made. • $17 • (07/31/95) SS • **89**

Tokay Pinot Gris Alsace Clos Jebsal Selection de Grains Nobles 1991: If they use motor oil in heaven, maybe it's like this: viscous, incredibly rich, thick and sweet, perfumed with jasmine, orange peel and the spice of botrytis. It's still young, but hard to believe it'll improve, try now. 70 cases made. • $375 • (08/31/95) • **93**

FRANCE

ZIND-HUMBRECHT, DOMAINE

Tokay Pinot Gris Alsace Clos Jebsal Turckheim 1993: Gorgeous flavor and velvety texture. A dessert wine that is abundantly ripe and rich, dripping with honey, butter and peach notes that are luscious on the palate and long-lasting in the finish. 350 cases made. • $55 • (07/31/95) • **92**

Tokay Pinot Gris Alsace Clos Jebsal Turckheim Vendange Tardive 1992: Rich and quite sweet, with pretty floral, vanilla and almond aromas and flavors. Straightforward and still young, but firm acidity promises improvement. Drink now through 1997. 250 cases made. • $54 • (08/31/95) • **89**

Tokay Pinot Gris Alsace Clos Jebsal Turckheim Vendange Tardive 1991: Not candied, but candylike, with white chocolate, honey and orange-cream flavors. It's intense, thick and sweet, but straightforward. What it lacks in complexity it makes up in shameless appeal. 80 cases made. • $60 • (08/31/95) • **90**

Tokay Pinot Gris Alsace Clos Windsbuhl Hunawihr 1993: Elegantly fruity, soft and supple, harmonious in balance, slightly sweet and quite long on the finish. Has bright apricot, pear and honey flavors. 350 cases made. • $55 • (07/31/95) • **89**

Tokay Pinot Gris Alsace Clos Windsbuhl Hunawihr Vendange Tardive 1991: A real wild card: from the neon orange color to the marzipan and toast aromas through the oily texture to the sweet flavors of dried pineapple and honey. Intense and unusual, this is a rich wine to dazzle and stump your friends. Drink now. 150 cases made. • $60 • (08/31/95) • **92**

Tokay Pinot Gris Alsace Grand Cru Rangen de Thann Clos St.-Urbai 1992: Sharp focus and outstanding character mark this luscious wine. It's deep in color and full-bodied, with pear, almond and hazelnut flavors and a firm, almost abrasive acidity that promises long life. Rich, and though very ripe the finish is dry. Great concentration, built for aging. • $NA • (09/15/94) • **92**

Tokay Pinot Gris Alsace Heimbourg Turckheim 1993: Robust and assertive in flavor, rather sweet, very full-bodied and packed with earthy, nutty, smoky notes. Vibrant acidity keeps lemon, pear and peach tones lively as they linger on the finish. Drinkable now, but should improve through at least 1997. 400 cases made. • $40 • (07/31/95) CS • **92**

Tokay Pinot Gris Alsace Heimbourg Turckheim Selection de Grains 1991: Extremely sweet and incredibly concentrated, with thick but light texture. Complex aromas of toast, crème brûlée and apricot, flavors of honey, vanilla, pear and peach. The finish is clean, long and expansive. Delicious now, but should improve through at least 1998, if you can stand to wait. 75 cases made. • $300 • (09/30/94) • **95**

Tokay Pinot Gris Alsace Rotenberg Wintzenheim Selection de Grains Nobles 1991: Balanced and clean, this rich but zesty wine offers lime and honey flavors, both firm acidity and marked sweetness. It finishes on a pleasant, bitter almond note. Has character and should develop well in the bottle. • $300 • (08/31/95) • **94**

Tokay Pinot Gris Alsace Vieilles Vignes 1993: Very smooth, very flavorful, very distinctive. Made in a late-harvest style, featuring opulent apple, spice and nut character, assertive but seamless, backed by firm acidity. Great with foie gras or Muenster cheese. 300 cases made. • $34 • (07/31/95) • **89**

Tokay Pinot Gris Alsace Vieilles Vignes 1991: Smoke and toast notes dominate this rich, thick Tokay Pinot Gris, along with orange peel and nut flavors. It's very ripe and full-bodied, but vibrant acidity enlivens the almost viscous palate, and it finishes dry. Showing some maturity now, it should still age well. A success in a difficult vintage. 1,000 cases made. • $32 • (09/15/94) • **91**

Key: SS—Spectator Selection. CS—Cellar Selection. BB—Best Buy. $NA—Price not available. (BT)—Barrel tasting. Ⓐ—Auction Price.
Dates in parentheses represent the issues in which the ratings were published.

Germany

In marked contrast to their tongue-twisting names and complicated official nomenclature, the sensory appeal of German wines is instantaneous. Combining abundant fruit with lively, refreshing crispness, German wines have a knack for charming the palates of novices and experts in equal measure.

The Riesling is the most important German grape variety and produces most of its greatest wines. However, very good, often great wines are made from the Gewürztraminer, Scheurebe and Sylvaner grapes.

1. Mosel-Saar-Ruwer
2. Nahe
3. Rheingau
4. Rheinhessen
5. Pfalz

GERMAN WINE CLASSIFICATIONS

German wines are divided into seven levels of quality based on ripeness and natural sugar levels. Kabinetts are the entry level of the so-called "QmP" wines, the respected category of German wines made from grapes that reach a minimum level of natural ripeness without chaptalization (the addition of sugar prior to fermentation). Most Kabinetts are moderately sweet, with a tangy acidity at the finish. (Tasty wines are made in a similar style in the lower "QbA" category, but these are targeted at a less critical mass audience.)

The remaining categories are arranged by ascending order of natural sugar levels at harvest. Just above Kabinett is Spätlese, which means late harvest. Generally richer than Kabinett, Spätlese can be particularly successful when made in the very dry "trocken" style or the slightly less dry "halbtrocken" style. These are the German wines that are most similar to white table wines produced elsewhere, though they maintain a true distinctiveness.

Auslese, made from specially selected bunches of late harvest grapes, is almost always sweet. Beerenauslese is made from selected individual grapes, usually affected by "noble rot." Rarest of all is Trockenbeerenauslese, an intensely sweet wine made only from shriveled grapes affected by noble rot. The latter two types rank among the greatest sweet wines in the world, and can age for decades.

GERMAN WINE REGIONS

German wine regions produce distinctive styles of wines owing to their unique conditions of soil and climate. Most of the important regions are located in what used to be called West Germany.

Rheingau. This is Germany's most aristocratic wine region, and historically its finest. Yet sometimes it's the most disappointing. A number of long-time estate owners are content to rest on their laurels; despite high prices, they don't deliver a quality commensurate with the region's reputation. Fortunately, a younger generation of Rheingau producers is leading a quality revolution. And at its best, no region packs more vitality into its product: powerful wines noted for their longevity.

Mosel-Saar-Ruwer. One regional name encompasses all three vineyard areas, which produce Rieslings noted for their fruity acidity. The Middle Mosel (Mittelmosel) is perhaps the most famous wine region of Germany, and encompasses the familiar Piesporter Michelsberg and Bernkasteler Doktor (though many less renowned wines offer better value). Ruwer and Saar wines tend to be steelier and harder than Mosels, though in years of great ripeness they excel.

Vineyards belonging to the Rheinhessen estate of Gunderloch, overlooking the Rhein near the town of Nackenheim.

Nahe. Perhaps the best buy in Germany, the wines of the Nahe fall between the Rheingau and Mosel in style, with much of the power of the former and the raciness of the latter. Wines from famous vineyards in the Nahe can be undervalued compared to the better known Mosels and Rheingaus. Supplies are short for some Nahes at this time—if you spot a bottle or two of the fabulous Staatsdomaine or Crusius wines, snap them up.

Rheinhessen. Nierstein has the best vineyards of Rheinhessen, and the wines have a distinctive flavor of smoked meat. Ripeness levels run high here compared with the rest of Germany, so Kabinetts and other light wines are less common.

Rheinpfalz. The southernmost of the well-known German regions and possibly the most exciting today. Its wines tend to be rich and earthy, with generous fruit. Many of the lighter wines are bottled in full liter bottles in the Rheinpfalz, often at very attractive prices.

CHOOSING GERMAN WINES

Vintage quality varies vastly from year to year in Germany. Also, since many great vineyards have several owners, consumers must look for growers who are meticulous about quality and who own the most favored sites of certain vineyards. No region can consistently be said to produce the best wines. Also, while the classifications that have been made in the German wine laws are useful, they are not infallible, and consumers must never rely on classification alone to make a buying decision.

A reliable path is to choose the wines recommended by a respected wine publication, such as *Wine Spectator*. In addition, you can seek out shops where there are specialists with expertise in the sometimes arcane field of German wines. Developing a relationship with a reliable merchant or salesperson can be invaluable.

BIFFAR, JOSEF

Riesling Auslese Pfalz Deidesheimer Kalkofen 1992 • $25 • (11/30/93) • **91**
Riesling Auslese Pfalz Wachenheimer Altenburg 1993: This shows an abundance of honey, spice and ripe fruit character. Full- to medium-bodied and sweet with acidity retaining the freshness. 67 cases made. • $30 • (11/30/94) • **87**
Riesling Auslese Trocken Pfalz Deidesheimer Kalkofen 1993: Round and fruity with an attractive, slightly sweet character not unlike fruit cocktail. Drinkable now. 67 cases made. • $25 • (11/30/94) • **84**
Riesling Auslese Trocken Pfalz Ruppertsberger Reiterpfad 1992 • $NA • (11/30/93) • **86**
Riesling Kabinett Pfalz Deidesheimer Kieselberg 1994: A crisp, clean Riesling with lots of mineral and earth character. Medium to light body, almost dry and fresh acidity to liven it up. Delicious now. • $15 • (11/30/95) • **86**
Riesling Kabinett Pfalz Deidesheimer Kieselberg 1993: Very sweet for a kabinett, with the spicy fruit character and acidity slightly disjointed. Drinkable now. 133 cases made. • $12 • (11/30/94) • **84**
Riesling Spätlese Pfalz Deideshiemer Grainhübel 1994: A lovely, rich and spicy Riesling that has every element of flavor expected in this category. Medium-bodied, excellent concentration and a very long, spice-and-mineral finish. Drinkable now, but will reward patience. • $29 • (11/30/96) • **90**
Riesling Spätlese Pfalz Deidesheimer Herrgottsacker 1992 • $16 • (11/30/93) • **88**
Riesling Spätlese Pfalz Wachenheimer Altenburg 1993: Extremely fresh and clean and also extremely sweet. Drink with dessert. Medium-bodied, medium acidity, and a bit of lemon, spice on the finish. Drink now or hold. 100 cases made. • $18 • (11/30/94) • **87**
Riesling Spätlese Pfalz Wachenheimer Goldbachel 1993: Very elegant, featuring plenty of lemon and spice character. Extremely clean and crisp with a long, citric finish. 100 cases made. • $18 • (11/30/94) • **87**
Riesling Spätlese Trocken Pfalz Deidesheimer Mäushölle 1992 • $18 • (11/30/93) • **82**
Riesling Spätlese Trocken Pfalz Wachenheimer Gerümpel 1994: The intense citrus, white peach and mineral aromas and flavors are matched by a racy balance that makes this full-bodied wine seem deceptively light and crisp. Best now. • $NA • (11/30/95) • **87**
Riesling Trockenbeerenauslese Pfalz Deidesheimer Kieselberg 1994: Lovely, creamy marzipan aromas and flavors, with a full and sweet palate, keep this in the very good range. Could be more concentrated and opulent for this category, though. The long finish has some caramel notes. Drinkable now, or try holding off to develop. • $107 • (11/30/95) • **87**

BISCHOFLICHES PRIESTERSEMINAR

Riesling Auslese Mosel Dhron Hofberger 1992 • $25 • (11/30/93) • **82**
Riesling Kabinett Halbtrocken Saar-Ruwer Ayler Kupp 1992 • $NA • (11/30/93) • **79**
Riesling Kabinett Mosel Trittenheimer Apotheke 1992 • $12 • (11/30/93) • **72**

BLUE NUN

Liebfraumilch Pfalz 1993: A soft and fruity white with plenty of citrus and peach flavors and some honey on the finish. Easy to drink. • $6 • (12/15/95) • **81**

BREUER, GEORG

Riesling Auslese Gold Cap Rheingau Rüdesheimer Bischofsberg 1993: Very ripe with plenty of spicy, slightly raisiny character. Full-bodied and quite sweet yet fresh on the finish. Drinkable now. • $NA • (11/30/94) • **86**
Riesling Beerenauslese Rheingau Rüdesheimer Bischofsberg 1993: Slightly exaggerated style showing maple syrup, honey, spice and sweet fruit character. Full in body and very thick with a long finish. Somewhat volatile. Drinkable now. • $NA • (11/30/94) • **86**
Riesling Beerenauslese Rheingau Rüdesheimer Bischofsberg 1992 • $123 • (11/30/93) • **79**
Riesling Kabinett Rheingau Charta Rüdesheimer Berg Schlossberg 1992 • $22 • (11/30/93) • **84**
Riesling QbA Rheingau Berg Schlossberg Charta 1993: Simple Riesling with pleasant spice and lemon aromas and flavors, light body and a tart finish. • $NA • (11/30/94) • **82**
Riesling QbA Rheingau Charta-Wein 1992 • $13 • (11/30/93) • **84**
Riesling QbA Rheingau Rauenthaler Nonnenberg Charta 1993: A bit dull. Full-bodied and dry with some decent apple and earth flavors and a short finish. • $NA • (11/30/94) • **82**
Riesling QbA Rheingau Rüdesheimer Berg Schlossberg Charta 1993: Simple Riesling with pleasant spicy, lemon aromas and flavors, light-bodied and a tart finish. Drink now. • $NA • **82**
Riesling Spätlese Rheingau Charta Rauenthaler Nonnenberg 1992 • $22 • (11/30/93) • **86**
Riesling Trockenbeerenauslese Rheingau Rüdesheimer Bischofsberg 1993: Tastes older than it is, displaying focused spice and butterscotch aromas and flavors. Full-bodied and sweet with an interesting caramel, ripe fruit finish. Drinkable now. • $NA • (11/30/94) • **87**

BURKLIN-WOLF, DR.

Muskateller Auslese Trocken Pfalz 1993: Unusually big, rich, dry wine for Germany. Perfect for spicy food. Intense aromas of grapefruit and cream follow through to the palate. Full-bodied, dry, and quite oily. Delicious now. • $22 • (11/30/94) • **87**
Muskateller Trockenbeerenauslese Pfalz Wachenheimer Luginsland 1992 • $75 • (11/30/93) • **95**
Riesling Beerenauslese Pfalz Wachenheimer Goldbächel 1994: A beautiful beerenauslese that delivers caramel, cream and dried apricot aromas and flavors. Full-bodied and very sweet, with smooth texture and a long, flavorful finish. Drinkable now, but it should reward patience. • $75 • (11/30/95) • **92**
Riesling Kabinett Pfalz 1993: Sweet, simple and spicy with pleasant fruit character and a medium finish. Drinkable now. • $13 • (11/30/94) • **83**
Riesling Kabinett Pfalz 1992 • $14 • (11/30/93) • **78**
Riesling Kabinett Pfalz Ruppertsberger Gaisböhl 1994: Promises more than it delivers. Fresh fruit cocktail and lemon character, light body, juicy and appealing, but it ends up rather simple and short. Drinkable now. • $18 • (11/30/95) • **83**
Riesling Kabinett Pfalz Wachenheimer Rechbächel 1994: Very fresh citrus, pear and mineral aromas and flavors. Full of fruit on the palate. Elegant acidity and quite a long, clean finish. Drinkable now, but will age well. • $17 • (11/30/95) • **87**
Riesling Kabinett Rheinpfalz 1993: A tightly wound, aggressively crisp Riesling with ample fruit flavor that's reined in by acidity. Apple, peach and herb flavors linger on the finish. Drink now. 4,800 cases made. • $13 • (11/30/94) • **83**
Riesling Kabinett Rheinpfalz 1991 • $9 • (12/15/92) • **83**
Riesling Kabinett Rheinpfalz Ruppertsberger Gaisböhl 1991 • $15 • (12/15/92) • **82**
Riesling Kabinett Rheinpfalz Wachenheimer Rechbächel 1991 • $12 • (12/15/92) • **84**
Riesling QbA Pfalz Forster 1994: Perhaps a bit big and rich for a QbA, though its plentiful ripe peach and grapefruit character still has its appeal. This is medium-sweet and full-bodied. Only a somewhat simple finish takes it down a peg. Drinkable now. • $14 • (11/30/95) • **85**
Riesling QbA Rheinpfalz 1993: Tart, dry, verging on sour, with simple green-apple flavors and a mouth-puckering finish. 4,800 cases made. • $12 • (11/30/94) • **76**
Riesling Spätlese Pfalz Wachenheimer Altenburg 1994: Peach, coconut and lemon aromas and flavors, medium body and a lively balance between its fresh acidity, fruit and moderate sweetness. Long, clean finish. Drinkable now, but can also age. • $20 • (11/30/95) • **85**
Riesling Spätlese Pfalz Wachenheimer Gerümpel 1993: A terrific off-dry wine, made to go with food. Rich and wonderful, featuring loads of spice and honey character, a full body and long, rich finish. Fine winemaking here. • $18 • (11/30/94) • **91**
Riesling Spätlese Pfalz Wachenheimer Gerümpel 1994: Rather developed, with pine, petrolic and apple aromas and flavors. Medium-bodied and lightly sweet, with a fruity finish. Drinkable now. • $20 • (11/30/95) • **83**

Riesling Spätlese Pfalz Wachenheimer Gerümpel 1992 • $19 • (11/30/93) • **63**

Riesling Spätlese Rheinpfalz Wachenheimer Rechbächel 1991 • $21 • (12/15/92) • **87**

Riesling Spätlese Trocken Pfalz Wachenheimer Altenberg 1993: A subtle, dry, fruity wine with grapefruit, creamy character and a fresh crisp finish. Delicious now to drink. • $19 • (11/30/94) • **84**

Riesling Spätlese Trocken Pfalz Wachenheimer Goldbächel 1994: Lush apricot, citrus and smoke aromas and flavors make this easy to enjoy. Full-bodied, with lots of juicy fruit flavors. It could do with a bit more structure on the finish, though. Drinkable now. • $22 • (11/30/95) • **87**

Riesling Trockenbeerenauslese Pfalz Forster Kirchenstück 1994: An extremely rich, lush Riesling that exhibits complex raisin flavors. Full-bodied and sweet, but with lots of concentration and an excellent structure of acidity. Long and powerful on the finish. A classic that will last; try in 2000. • $211 • (11/30/95) • **96**

Scheurebe Auslese Rheinpfalz Wachenheimer Mandelgarten 1991 • $24 • (12/15/92) • **92**

Scheurebe Beerenauslese Rheinpfalz 1991 • $120 • (12/15/92) • **93**

Weissburgunder Kabinett Trocken Rheinpfalz 1991 • $11 • (12/15/92) • **83**

Weissburgunder QbA Trocken Pfalz 1993: Fresh, clean and rather neutral, with lemon and light pie-crust aromas and flavors. Medium body, very dry and a fresh, crisp finish. • $15 • (11/30/94) • **82**

Weissburgunder Spätlese Trocken Pfalz 1992 • $16 • (11/30/93) • **69**

CASTELL, FURST ZU

Kerner Kabinett Franken Schloss Castell QmP 1993: Crisp, lemony and herbal in flavor, with zingy acidity that keeps it fresh, even on the finish. A fine thirst quencher that should be versatile with food. 4,800 cases made. • $14 • (11/30/94) • **82**

Müller-Thurgau QbA Franken 1993: This wine has good weight and body, but unusual herb and mineral flavors. Acceptable, but basically heavy and undistinguished. 3,600 cases made. • $11 • (11/30/94) • **78**

Riesling Spätlese Franken Casteller Schlossberg QmP 1993: Nicely balanced and flavorful despite its light body. The peach, floral and apple flavors fill your mouth and linger on the finish. Draws you back for another sip. 2,400 cases made. • $23 • (11/30/94) • **85**

CHRISTOFFEL, JOH. JOS.

Riesling Auslese Gold Cap Mosel-Saar-Ruwer Urziger Würzgarten Five Stars 1994: A deceptive wine: only medium in body, but intense and beautifully balanced, developing its richness on the finish that is packed with melon and mineral flavors. Drinkable now, better with age. • $NA • (11/30/95) • **87**

Riesling Auslese Gold Cap Mosel-Saar-Ruwer Urziger Würzgarten Four Stars 1994: Very grapey and fresh, but more like a regular auslese than a special bottling. Fresh passion fruit and grape aromas and flavors, medium body and very lively acidity. Becomes fuller on the finish. Drinkable now. • $39 • (11/30/95) • **85**

Riesling Auslese Mosel-Saar-Ruwer Erdener Treppchen 1994: Far too light for this category, but a very attractive glass of wine nonetheless. Fresh apple flavors, racy acidity and a very clean finish. Drinkable now, but can age, too. • $31 • (11/30/95) • **83**

Riesling Auslese Mosel-Saar-Ruwer Urziger Würzgarten 1994: A lively, light auslese with honey, lime, apple and spice character. Light to medium in body, lightly sweet, with firm acidity and a fresh finish. Drinkable now, but can age. • $21 • (11/30/95) • **84**

Riesling Auslese Mosel-Saar-Ruwer Urziger Würzgarten Two Stars 1994: An appealing glass of Mosel Riesling, but nothing special among the others of this vintage. Fresh lemon and herbal character, medium-bodied, nicely sweet, with a light finish. Drinkable now. • $NA • (11/30/95) • **83**

Riesling Beerenauslese Mosel-Saar-Ruwer Urziger Würzgarten 1994: Smells and tastes like cooked pears. Clean, ripe, sweet fruit flavors, but needs more depth and richness for this category. Drinkable now. • $NA • (11/30/95) • **84**

Riesling Spätlese Mosel-Saar-Ruwer Erdener Treppchen 1994: Very attractive white peach character, medium body and only a touch of sweetness. A short but clean finish. Drinkable now. • $17 • **83**

Riesling Spätlese Mosel-Saar-Ruwer Urziger Würzgarten 1994: Very clean and well defined apple and spice flavors with a creamy character. Firm acidity, medium body and moderately sweet. Delicious now. • $17 • (11/30/95) • **85**

CHRISTOFFEL ERBEN, JOH. JOS.

Riesling Auslese Gold Cap Mosel Four Stars Urziger Würzgarten 1992 • $31 • (11/30/93) • **90**

Riesling Auslese Mosel Erdener Treppchen 1993: A lovely auslese exhibiting clove, honey and melon character. It's full-bodied and sweet with fresh acidity and a fruity finish. Drinkable now. • $22 • (11/30/94) • **87**

Riesling Auslese Mosel Erdener Treppchen 1992 • $18 • (11/30/93) • **82**

Riesling Auslese Mosel Urziger Würzgarten 1993: Subtle yet lively with delicate floral, lemon, mineral character and very intense acidity. Medium-bodied and sweet with a very crisp finish. Drinkable now. • $25 • (11/30/94) • **85**

Riesling Auslese Mosel Urziger Würzgarten 1992 • $20 • (11/30/93) • **84**

Riesling Auslese Mosel Urziger Würzgarten Three Stars 1993: Very good but not at the superior level we expect in special-designation wine. Fresh and lively showing honey, melon and apple character. Medium in body and good acidity with a fresh finish. Drinkable now. • $31 • (11/30/94) • **86**

Riesling Eiswein Mosel Urziger Würzgarten 1993: Electrified with super-lively acidity. Full-bodied yet very fresh featuring lemon-lime flavors and a long, sweet, honey finish. Delicious now but will improve with age. • $65 • (11/30/94) • **90**

Riesling Eiswein Mosel Urziger Würzgarten 1992 • $43 • (11/30/93) • **87**

Riesling Kabinett Mosel-Saar-Ruwer Erdener Treppchen 1994: Textbook Riesling. Very fresh melon and apple aromas, followed by clean flavors. Light body and a crisp, medium finish. Drinkable now. • $14 • (11/30/95) • **83**

Riesling Kabinett Mosel-Saar-Ruwer Urziger Würzgarten 1994: A good wine that could rate higher if it had more personality. This is quite developed and round, with a somewhat jammy character in its peach flavor. Medium-bodied, medium-sweet, but just falls a bit short on the finish. • $NA • (11/30/95) • **82**

Riesling Spätlese Mosel Erdener Treppchen 1992 • $14 • (11/30/93) • **84**

Riesling Spätlese Mosel Urziger Würzgarten 1993: Lively, elegant and clean with plenty of carbon dioxide, apple and spice character. Medium in body and lightly sweet, crisp finish. Drinkable now but much better with age. • $15 • (11/30/94) • **87**

Riesling Spätlese Mosel Urziger Würzgarten 1992 • $10 • (11/30/93) • **88**

CRUSIUS & SOHN, HANS

Riesling Auslese Gold Cap Nahe Traisener Rotenfels 1992 • $46 • (11/30/93) • **75**

Riesling Auslese Nahe Schlossböckelheimer Felsenberg 1994: Lovely essence of ripe tropical fruit makes this an easy wine to enjoy. Big and powerful, though perhaps a little simple at the finish. Drinkable now, or age for more depth. • $NA • (11/30/95) • **87**

Riesling Auslese Nahe Traisener Rotenfels 1992 • $34 • (11/30/93) • **84**

Riesling Auslese Trocken Nahe Traiser Bastei 1994: A delicious dry German wine. Lots of mineral and apple character. Medium-bodied, with well-integrated acidity. Long, fresh finish that has honey notes chiming in. • $NA • (11/30/95) • **88**

Riesling Beerenauslese Nahe Traiser Rotenfels 1994: A rich, very sweet Riesling with some nice honey aromas and flavors, but marred by some odd, musty notes, perhaps from bad botrytis? • $NA • **79**

Riesling Eiswein Nahe Traisener Rotenfels 1992 • $195 • (11/30/95) • **94**

Riesling Kabinett Halbtrocken Nahe Traiser Rotenfels 1994: A lightweight compared with others in this category, but it's clean and fresh, with enough fruit to make an appealing summer drink. Has a clean finish. Drinkable now. • $NA • (11/30/95) • **84**

Riesling QbA Halbtrocken Nahe 1992 • $11 • (11/30/93) • **78**

Key: SS—Spectator Selection. CS—Cellar Selection. BB—Best Buy. $NA—Price not available. (BT)—Barrel tasting. Ⓐ—Auction Price.
Dates in parentheses represent the issues in which the ratings were published.

GERMANY

Riesling QbA Trocken Nahe Traiser Rotenfels 1994: An old-fashioned, slightly earthy wine that only shows modest fruit on its light frame. There is just enough flavor to make it pleasant drinking. • $NA • (11/30/95) • **80**

Riesling Spätlese Halbtrocken Nahe Schlossböckelheimer Felsenberg 1992 • $20 • (11/30/93) • **86**

Riesling Spätlese Nahe Niederhäuser Felsensteyer 1994: Very fresh lemon and pine needle bouquet, medium body, high acidity, and just enough fruit to balance. A tart finish. Drinkable now. • $NA • (11/30/95) • **85**

Riesling Spätlese Nahe Schlossböckelheimer Felsenberg 1994: Very fresh and rich for this category. A big wine that offers lots of fruit and flesh. Also shows lots of acidity on the finish. Drinkable now. • $NA • (11/30/95) • **87**

Riesling Spätlese Trocken Nahe Traiser Rotenfels 1994: Some decent apple and mineral character comes through, but it's slightly light on the finish. Medium body and a light finish. • $NA • (11/30/95) • **81**

Riesling Trockenbeerenauslese Nahe Traiser Bastei 1994: Canned pineapple aromas and flavors, medium body and sweet. The acidity and fruit don't quite balance the sweetness. Short finish. Drink now. • $NA • (11/30/95) • **80**

Weissburgunder QbA Trocken Nahe Traiser 1994: Rather light, neutral and tart, but not too acidic or aggressive. The finish is short and very simple. • $NA • (11/30/95) • **79**

DARTING, KURT

Rieslaner Beerenauslese Pfalz Dürkheimer Nonnengarten 1992 • $17 • (11/30/93) • **86**

Rieslaner Trockenbeerenauslese Pfalz Ungsteiner Bettelhaus 1992 • $28 • (11/30/93) • **92**

Riesling Auslese Pfalz Ungsteiner Herrenberg 1992 • $16 • (11/30/93) • **87**

Riesling Kabinett Pfalz Dürkheimer Hochbenn 1992 • $8 • (11/30/93) • **83**

Riesling Spätlese Pfalz Ungsteiner Bettlehaus 1992 • $9 • (11/30/93) • **85**

DEINHARD

Mosel-Saar-Ruwer Bereich Bernkastel 1993: A tangy, fruity, lean Riesling that's slightly sweet and tart at the same time. Has herbal, peppery aromas and tart grapefruit flavors. • $13 • (11/30/94) • **78**

Mosel-Saar-Ruwer Green Label 1992: An awkward, earthy tasting wine that's unappealing. Herbal, lemon and earth flavors followed by a sweet finish make for a jumble. • $7 • (11/30/94) • **73**

Pinot Blanc White Pfalz 1992: This is clean and fresh, with subtle aromas and flavors that remind us of herbs, minerals and almonds. Good, refreshing and well balanced. • $7 • (11/30/94) • **82**

Riesling Kabinett Mosel-Saar-Ruwer Piesporter Goldtröpfchen 1991: Very crisp and lean, with green-apple flavors accented by smoke and mineral. It's flavorful, but within a narrow spectrum. Clean and austere overall. • $10 • (08/31/94) • **81**

Riesling Kabinett Mosel-Saar-Ruwer Wehlener-Sonnenuhr 1991: The crisp lemon, lime and grapefruit flavors give this focus and flavor. It is lean but distinctive, and has a lingering finish. Drinkable now. • $15 • (08/31/94) • **84**

Sparkling Brut Lila Vin Mousseux NV • $8 • (01/31/93) • **82**

Sparkling Riesling Lila Imperial NV • $7 • (08/31/89) BB • **81**

DIEL, SCHLOSSGUT

Nahe Victor 1992 • $37 • (11/30/93) • **86**

Nahe Victor 1991 • $39 • (12/15/92) • **85**

Riesling Auslese Gold Cap Nahe 1994: More like a good spätlese than an auslese. Ripe pear flavor, rich and succulent, but too superficial for this level. Medium body and a short finish. Drinkable now. • $NA • (11/30/95) • **83**

Riesling Auslese Gold Cap Nahe 1993: Wonderfully concentrated yet a surprising amount of elegance. Full-bodied and sweet with lovely pineapple and tropical fruit character. Long, flavorful finish. Drinkable now or hold. • $86 • (11/30/94) • **92**

Riesling Auslese Gold Cap Nahe 1992 • $55 • (11/30/93) • **93**

Riesling Auslese Nahe Dorsheimer Goldloch 1992 • $37 • (11/30/93) • **91**

Riesling Auslese Nahe Dorsheimer Pittermännchen 1993: Extremely fresh and fruity, exhibiting appley, flinty aromas and flavors. Full-bodied and sweet with a long, spicy, crisp finish. Drinkable now. • $40 • (11/30/94) • **91**

Riesling Beerenauslese Nahe BA Gold Cap 1994: This would have been better as a top auslese. Very nice honey aromas and flavors, but it's more pretty than powerful. Medium-bodied, with a somewhat simple finish that holds it back. • $NA • (11/30/95) • **87**

Riesling Beerenauslese Nahe Gold Cap 1993: Terrific sweet wine. Super-intense, showing botrytis and spicy, dried orange peel aromas and flavors. Full-bodied and overflowing with sweet, ripe fruit character. Long, long finish. Drinkable now but better after 1997. Made for aging. • $158 • (11/30/94) • **94**

Riesling Eiswein Nahe 1994: Very intense citrus aromas, but only a touch of honey character that would make this more typical of a beerenauslese. Yet this is full-bodied and very sweet, with marvelous acidity to cut through the richness and make the long finish very clean. • $142 • (11/30/95) • **90**

Riesling Eiswein Nahe 1993: Full, voluptuous style with lovely honey, syrup and spice character. Full in body and round with super-sweet flavors. Delicious now but can improve with age for years to come. • $191 • (11/30/94) • **93**

Riesling Eiswein Nahe 1992 • $104 • (11/30/93) • **93**

Riesling Eiswein Nahe 1991 • $176 • (12/15/92) • **89**

Riesling Kabinett Nahe Dorsheimer Goldloch 1994: Very fresh and lively, with a captivating balance of ripe citrus and white peach flavors and racy acidity. Medium-bodied, beautiful balance and a long, very clean finish. Drinkable now or hold.• $23 • (11/30/95) • **87**

Riesling Kabinett Nahe Dorsheimer Goldloch 1993: Extremely versatile, on its own or with food. Very flavor-intensive showing lemon and light spice character. Medium in body and fresh. Long finish. Drinkable now. • $21 • (11/30/94) • **89**

Riesling Kabinett Nahe Dorsheimer Pittermännchen 1994: Very fresh and lively, with nice tart peach and lemon aromas and flavors, but may be a little too sweet and simple for some. Drinkable now. • $23 • (11/30/95) • **84**

Riesling Kabinett Nahe Dorsheimer Pittermännchen 1991 • $21 • (12/15/92) • **82**

Riesling QbA Nahe 1994: Completely Mosel in style. Lovely peach and citrus aromas, medium body and extremely juicy, the racy acidity giving the finish an extra kick. Drinkable now. • $12 • (11/30/95) • **86**

Riesling QbA Nahe Dorsheimer Goldloch 1991 • $22 • (12/15/92) • **79**

Riesling Spätlese Halbtrocken Nahe Dorsheimer Goldloch 1992 • $27 • (11/30/93) • **89**

Riesling Spätlese Nahe Dorsheimer Goldloch 1994: A disappointing performance for this winery. A nicely fruity wine, but it tastes like a simple QbA. Medium body, medium sweetness, medium everything, except for a short finish. Drinkable now. • $30 • (11/30/95) • **80**

Riesling Spätlese Nahe Dorsheimer Goldloch 1991 • $29 • (12/15/92) • **90**

Riesling Spätlese Nahe Dorsheimer Pittermännchen 1994: A slightly candied character, with some good fruit showing, but becomes rather cloying on the finish. Medium-bodied and sweet, with moderate acidity. Drinkable now, or allow to age. • $30 • (11/30/95) • **83**

Riesling Spätlese Nahe Dorsheimer Pittermännchen 1993: Incredibly fresh and exciting with loads of fruit and super-fine, crisp acidity. Medium body, medium sweetness, a captivating aftertaste of apricots and apples. Drinkable now. • $28 • (11/30/94) • **90**

Riesling Spätlese Nahe Dorsheimer Pittermännchen 1992 • $27 • (11/30/93) • **89**

Riesling Spätlese Nahe Dorsheimer Pittermännchen 1991 • $29 • (12/15/92) • **83**

Weissburgunder QbA Trocken Nahe 1991 • $28 • (12/15/92) • **79**

DONNHOFF, H.

Riesling Auslese Gold Cap Nahe Niederhäuser Hermannshöhle 1992 • $16 • (11/30/93) • **95**

Riesling Auslese Gold Cap Nahe Oberhäuser Brücke 1993: Like a bowl full of fruit displaying lovely, candied orange spice character. Medium-bodied and sweet with fresh acidity and flavors. Drinkable now. • $35 • (11/30/94) • **90**

Riesling Auslese Nahe Niederhäuser Hermannshöhle 1994: Rich, if rather simple peach and baked apple aromas and flavors on a first impression, but this is a rather deceptive wine that has an elegant, racy core.Try now. • $34 • (11/30/95) • **86**

Riesling Auslese Nahe Niederhäuser Hermannshöhle 1993: Delicate, with lovely apple and honey character. Medium-bodied and medium-sweet, very good acidity and a long, fresh, mineral finish. Drinkable now. • $29 • (11/30/94) • **89**

Riesling Auslese Nahe Oberhäuser Brücke 1994: Very fine apricot and honey aromas, medium body but very intense flavors, with an almost electric balance of fruit, sweetness and acidity. A very long, piquant finish. Better in 1997. • $33 • (11/30/95) • **89**

Riesling Eiswein Nahe Oberhäuser Brücke 1994: Packed full of dried fruit flavor and an acidity that almost burns your palate with electricity. Very concentrated and extremely long and intense on the finish. A wine to age into 2000. • $127 • (11/30/95) • **94**

Riesling Eiswein Nahe Oberhäuser Brücke 1992 • $NA • (11/30/93) • **96**

Riesling Eiswein Nahe Oberhäuser Felsenberg 1993: Textbook ice wine. Amazing intensity of sweet and sour character. Full-bodied yet refined with lemon, lime, dried fruit character. Long, long finish. Drinkable or hold. • $135 • (11/30/94) • **92**

Riesling Kabinett Halbtrocken Nahe Oberhäuser Felsenberg 1992 • $NA • (11/30/93) • **86**

Riesling Kabinett Nahe Niederhauser Hermannshöhle 1993: Rich, more like a Spätlese. Full-bodied, sweet yet very fresh apricot, peach character and a long crisp finish. Delicious. Drinkable now. • $13 • (11/30/94) • **88**

Riesling Kabinett Nahe Oberhäuser Leistenberg 1994: A fairly standard Riesling—flavors of apple and spice in a medium-bodied, medium-sweet package that has a light finish. Drinkable now. • $15 • (11/30/95) • **82**

Riesling Spätlese Halbtrocken Nahe Niederhäuser Hermannshöhle 1992 • $13 • (11/30/93) • **89**

Riesling Spätlese Nahe Niederhäuser Hermannshöhle 1994: Very lemony and lively, but a little one-dimensional. Medium body, quite high acidity, and a tart finish. Drinkable now. • $23 • (11/30/95) • **83**

Riesling Spätlese Nahe Niederhäuser Hermannshöhle 1993: Delicate, subtle wine with melon, apple aromas and flavors. Medium-bodied and medium-sweet with a firm texture and sweet fruit. Drinkable now or hold. • $19 • (11/30/94) • **88**

Riesling Spätlese Nahe Niederhäuser Hermannshöhle 1992 • $13 • (11/30/93) • **88**

Riesling Spätlese Nahe Oberhäuser Brücke 1994: Round and rich, exhibiting its lemon, apple and pear character well. Full-bodied and medium-sweet, with lots of fruit and a complement of acidity. Drinkable now, or try aging a few years. • $23 • (11/30/95) • **85**

Riesling Spätlese Nahe Oberhäuser Brücke 1993: Rather plain and tart with some decent fruit character but light on the finish. Drinkable now. • $18 • (11/30/94) • **80**

Riesling Spätlese Nahe Oberhäuser Brücke 1992 • $12 • (11/30/93) • **86**

Riesling Trockenbeerenauslese Nahe Niederhäuser Hermannshöhle 1994: Fabulous balance. An indisputable classic with everything in the right place. Honey, green apple, almond, dried fruit flavors, layers of fruit. Wonderfully integrated, with high acidity and intense sweetness. Buy it if you can find it. Drink and enjoy, or hold in the cellar for posterity. • $168 • (11/30/95) • **96**

EBERBACH, STAATSWEINGUTER, KLOSTER

Riesling Kabinett Rheingau Rauenthaler Baiken 1994: On the tart side, with herbally apple flavors. A bit awkward and cloying on the finish. 2,000 cases made. • $14 • (11/30/95) • **79**

Riesling Rheingau Steinberger 1994: An austere, serious wine to be enjoyed with food. Well-structured, with mineral, apple and peach flavors and good acidity. 4,000 cases made. • $14 • (11/30/95) • **85**

Key: SS—Spectator Selection. CS—Cellar Selection. BB—Best Buy. $NA—Price not available. (BT)—Barrel tasting. Ⓐ—Auction Price.
Dates in parentheses represent the issues in which the ratings were published.

ECKEL, GEBRUDER

Riesling Kabinett Pfalz Wachenheimer Mandelgarten 1992 • $8 • (11/30/93) • **64**

Riesling QbA Pfalz Wachenheimer Mandelgarten 1992 • $7 • (11/30/93) • **79**

ESER, AUGUST

Riesling Auslese Rheingau Oestricher Doosberg 1992 • $41 • (11/30/93) • **92**

Riesling Kabinett Halbtrocken Rheingau Oestricher Lenchen 1993: Boring and flabby with sulfur and candied fruit character. Off-dry. • $15 • (11/30/94) • **73**

Riesling Kabinett Halbtrocken Rheingau Oestricher Lenchen 1992 • $14 • (11/30/93) • **84**

Riesling Kabinett Rheingau Oestricher Lenchen 1993: One of the more lively Kabinetts we've had this year from the Rheingau. It shows fresh spicy, pie crust flavors and a crisp acidity. Slightly sweet. Drink now. • $15 • (11/30/94) • **85**

Riesling Kabinett Rheingau Rauenthaler Rothenberg 1992 • $15 • (11/30/93) • **85**

Riesling Spätlese Halbtrocken Rheingau Oestricher Doosberg 1993: Very balanced yet lively. Young and vivacious with lemon and spice flavors and excellent acidity. Drinkable now. • $20 • (11/30/94) • **87**

Riesling Spätlese Rheingau Oestricher Lenchen 1993: Clean and round with spicy, lemon, fruit character. Medium-bodied, sweet with a fruity finish. Drinkable now. • $20 • (11/30/94) • **85**

Riesling Spätlese Rheingau Oestricher Lenchen 1992 • $19 • (11/30/93) • **89**

Riesling Spätlese Rheingau Rauenthaler Rothenberg 1993: Squeaky-clean style of spätlese with loads of lemon and mineral aromas and flavors. Medium in body, medium-sweet and a long, crisp finish. • $21 • (11/30/94) • **87**

Riesling Spätlese Rheingau Rauenthaler Rothenberg 1992 • $19 • (11/30/93) • **88**

Riesling Spätlese Trocken Rheingau Hallgartener Schönhell 1992 • $19 • (11/30/93) • **77**

FITZ-RITTER

Gewürztraminer Spätlese Rheinpfalz Dürkheimer Abtsfronhof 1992: A lovely, flavorful wine with classic aromas of spice and litchee. This wine is dominated by grapefruit flavors, and is slightly effervescent. Full-bodied and rich, with a good spicy finish. A Gewürztraminer in the crisp style. • $16 • (08/31/94) • **86**

Gewürztraminer Spätlese Trocken Pfalz Dürkheimer Abstsfronhof QmP 1992: Exotic and zesty, showing floral, fruity aromas, apricot and peach flavors and great balance. Very open and exuberant in flavor, yet nicely dry in texture and lingering on the finish. • $NA • (11/30/94) • **85**

Grauburgunder Kabinett Trocken Pfalz Wachenheimer Mandelgarten Grauer Burgunder 1994: Basically lean and tart with apple and butter aromas. Crisp and grapefruity on the palate and finish. Needs food. • $13 • (12/15/95) • **82**

Rheinpfalz Wachenheimer Mandelgarten 1992: Green peach flavors with floral aromas. Full-bodied but tastes unripe, with an astringent finish. Hard to like. • $12 • (08/31/94) • **78**

FRIEDRICH-WILHELM-GYMNASIUM

Riesling Kabinett Mosel-Saar-Ruwer Graacher Himmelreich 1994: Nice and fresh. Slightly spritzy and has a zippy acidity. Apple flavors are complemented by a touch of spice. • $NA • (11/30/95) • **84**

Riesling QbA Mosel-Saar-Ruwer Falkensteiner Hofberg 1991 • $9 • (01/31/93) • **82**

GALLAIS, LE

Riesling Auslese Gold Cap Mosel-Saar-Ruwer Wiltinger Braune Kupp 1994: Beautiful dried apricot and sweet floral aromas lead through to a full, very sweet palate brimming with honey and fruit. Lively acidity makes the long finish very clean. Drinkable now. From Egon Müller. • $NA • (11/30/95) • **91**

Riesling Auslese Mosel-Saar-Ruwer Wiltinger Braune Kupp 1994: A fresh and fruity white, but it lacks the concentration and richness to truly qualify in this category. Medium-bodied and moderately sweet, with a light finish. Drinkable now. From Egon Müller. • $75 • (11/30/95) • **84**

Riesling Beerenauslese Mosel-Saar-Ruwer Wiltinger Braune Kupp 1994: Not as sweet as some BA in this vintage but terrific. Full-bodied and moderately sweet, with loads of lemon, apple and dried apricot flavors. Very long on the finish. Drinkable now, or hold in the cellar. • $NA • **90**

Riesling Beerenauslese Saar-Ruwer Wiltinger Braune Kupp 1993: Wonderful. Super-thick and intense with honey, syrup, orange and citric character. Masses of fruit, incredibly sweet. It goes on and on. Drinkable now or hold. From Egon Müller • $NA • (11/30/94) • **95**

Riesling Kabinett Mosel-Saar-Ruwer Wiltinger Braune Kupp 1994: Rather feeble. Steely character, apple and baby powder aromas. Light body, lightly sweet and light finish. • $22 • (11/30/95) • **79**

Riesling Spätlese Mosel-Saar-Ruwer Wiltinger Braune Kupp 1994: Has strong waxy, lemony aromas and flavors, but the high acidity is too one-sided. Medium-bodied and very sleek, though slightly aggressive on the finish. Perhaps better in 1997. • $34 • (11/30/95) • **82**

GRAFF, CARL

Riesling Kabinett Mosel-Saar-Ruwer 1994: Light, almost delicate and slightly sweet, with crisp apple, peach and floral aromas and flavors. Just what you want in a kabinett. • $6 • (12/15/95) • **84**

Riesling Kabinett Mosel-Saar-Ruwer 1993: A lean, tart Riesling with lemon and green-apple flavors. Not a casual sipper. Because of its ultra-crispness and subtle flavors, it needs food. 2,400 cases made. • $8 • **83**

Riesling QbA Mosel-Saar-Ruwer Ürziger Schwarzlay 1994: Fresh, fruity, nearly dry, with smoky citrus aromas, straightforward fruit flavors and a lively texture. • $5 • (12/15/95) • **81**

Riesling Kabinett Mosel Urziger Würzgarten 1992 • $8 • (11/30/93) BB • **84**

Riesling QbA Mosel-Saar-Ruwer Urziger Schwarzlay 1993: Floral and peachy in flavor, slightly sweet, with a smooth texture and short finish. Fruity and straightforward. 2,400 cases made. • $7 • **81**

Riesling Spätlese Halbtrocken Mosel Erdener Prälat 1992 • $NA • (11/30/93) • **83**

Riesling Spätlese Mosel Urziger Würzgarten 1992 • $10 • (11/30/93) • **87**

Riesling Spätlese Mosel-Saar-Ruwer Erdener Treppchen 1994: Nicely balanced and fruity, with a pleasant sweetness and firm texture. • $9 • (12/15/95) • **84**

Riesling Spätlese Mosel-Saar-Ruwer Erdener Treppchen 1992: Has some of the traditional German Riesling attributes, but comes off clumsy, especially on the finish. Smoky, metallic and sweet but stale fruit flavors don't add up to much enjoyment. 4,200 cases made. • $10 • **78**

GRANS-FASSIAN

Riesling Auslese Gold Cap Mosel Trittenheimer Apotheke 1992 • $55 • (11/30/93) • **88**

Riesling Auslese Mosel Trittenheimer Apotheke 1993: Vivacious with floral-verging-on-grassy melon character. Full-bodied and sweet, very crisp acidity on the finish. Drinkable now. 166 cases made. • $35 • **86**

Riesling Auslese Mosel Trittenheimer Apotheke 1992 • $20 • (11/30/93) • **90**

Riesling Auslese Mosel Trittenheimer Apotheke Three Stars 1993: Swampy and green with asparagus, grassy character. Sweet and cloying. Tasted twice. Forget it. 75 cases made. • $73 • (11/30/94) • **68**

Riesling Beerenauslese Mosel Trittenheimer Apotheke 1993: Loads of concentrated sweet fruit, but a slightly strange asparagus character detracts from the overall quality. Not much future. 37 cases made. • $200 • (11/30/94) • **84**

Riesling Eiswein Mosel 1993: Fabulous wine. Shakes you to the bone with wildly sweet honey, fruity character and well-integrated acidity. Wonderfully long finish. Drinkable now. • $250 • (11/30/94) • **93**

Riesling Eiswein Mosel 1992 • $NA • (11/30/93) • **93**

Riesling Kabinett Mosel Trittenheimer Altärchen 1993: Tasting this is like biting into a green apple. Medium-bodied and lightly sweet with very fresh acidity. But not much else. Drinkable now. 416 cases made. • $17 • (11/30/94) • **83**

Riesling Kabinett Mosel Trittenheimer Altärchen 1992 • $11 • (11/30/93) • **70**

Riesling QbA Mosel 1992 • $9 • (11/30/93) • **73**

Riesling Spätlese Mosel Piesporter Goldtröpfchen 1993: Strange, with gooseberry and canned asparagus aromas and unripe flavors. Tasted twice. Drinkable now. 333 cases made. • $24 • (11/30/94) • **72**

GRÜNHÄUSER, MAXIMIN

Riesling Auslese Gold Cap Saar-Ruwer Abtsberg Fuder No. 83 1993: A steely auslese, with lemon and mineral character. Medium-bodied, medium sweetness and a fresh finish. Drinkable now. 100 cases made. • $59 • (11/30/94) • **88**

Riesling Auslese Gold Cap Saar-Ruwer Herrenberg Fuder No. 75 1993: Beautifully made auslese but perhaps not at gold cap level. Medium- to full-bodied with sweet, apple, melon character. Steely acidity. Drinkable now. 100 cases made. • $52 • (11/30/94) • **88**

Riesling Eiswein Saar-Ruwer Abtsberg 1993: Enchanting tension between sweetness and acidity. Intense mango and papaya aromas and flavors, full-bodied and concentrated, with electrifying acidity. Better after 2000. 20 cases made. • $360 • (11/30/94) • **90**

Riesling Eiswein Saar-Ruwer Herrenberg 1993: Some very good ripe fruit character and just a hint of eiswein features. Medium- to full-body, with lovely sweetness and a fresh, spicy finish. Drinkable now or hold. 50 cases made. • $124 • (11/30/94) • **87**

Riesling Kabinett Mosel-Saar-Ruwer Herrenberg 1993: Assertive fruit flavors, lively acidity and a touch of sweetness make this a bold wine. It's appley in flavor and crisp in texture. 1,200 cases made. • $20 • (11/30/94) • **83**

Riesling Kabinett Saar-Ruwer Abtsberg 1993: Intensely fruity, very ripe and round for a kabinett from this region. Medium body and sweetness, shows apple and mineral character and a long, fruity finish. 1,000 cases made. • $22 • (11/30/94) • **87**

Riesling QbA Mosel-Saar-Ruwer 1993: Crisp, fruity and lively. A refreshing Riesling that smells piney, tastes like grapefruit and apple and stays crisp on the finish. 1,800 cases made. • $16 • (11/30/94) • **84**

Riesling Spätlese Mosel-Saar-Ruwer Abtsberg 1993: Definitely sweet, but packed with enough fruit flavor and backed with enough refreshing acidity to keep it well-balanced. Reminds us of pineapple, peach and grapefruit all the way through the lingering finish. 600 cases made. • $27 • **86**

Riesling Spätlese Saar-Ruwer Abtsberg 1993: Plenty of apple, mineral and spice. Medium body and sweetness, with a fruity finish. 500 cases made. • $26 • (11/30/94) • **86**

GUNDERLOCH

Grauburgunder Spätlese Trocken Rheinhessen 1991 • $22 • (12/15/92) • **90**

Riesling Auslese Gold Cap Rheinhessen Nackenheimer Rothenberg 1994: A giant compared with others in this category, yet this is impeccably balanced, fully concentrated and extremely sophisticated. Waves of flavor roll over the palate and lead to an astonishingly long finish. Drinkable now, but can age. • $59 • **90**

Riesling Auslese Gold Cap Rheinhessen Nackenheimer Rothenberg 1993: Another luscious dessert Auslese with terrific honey, spice and crème brûlée aromas and flavors. Full-bodied and very sweet yet refreshing on the finish. Drinkable now. • $48 • (11/30/94) • **92**

Riesling Auslese Gold Cap Rheinhessen Nackenheimer Rothenberg 1992 • $45 • (11/30/93) • **91**

Riesling Auslese Rheinhessen Nackenheimer Rothenberg 1994: Lots of ripe apricot aromas and flavors. This is medium-bodied, but has a rich texture, which lightens up on the finish. Drinkable now. • $33 • **86**

Riesling Auslese Rheinhessen Nackenheimer Rothenberg 1993: This is packed with flavor, peach, mango and tropical fruit character overflowing from the glass. Full in body and sweet, leading to a long, captivating finish of fruit and mineral tones. Drinkable now. Tasted twice. • $30 • (11/30/94) • **91**

Riesling Auslese Rheinhessen Nackenheimer Rothenberg 1991 • $30 • (12/15/92) • **87**

Riesling Beerenauslese Rheinhessen Nackenheim Rothenberg 1992 • $74 • (11/30/93) • **99**

Riesling Beerenauslese Rheinhessen Nackenheimer Rothenberg 1994: Has a bit of a mushroom character, but will make an impressive botrytized wine with a little more time in the bottle. Very rich, very sweet and a long, lush and creamy finish. • $96 • **90**

Riesling Beerenauslese Rheinhessen Nackenheimer Rothenberg 1993: Honey in flavor and approaching olive oil in texture. This is a ripe and wonderful beerenauslese with loads of lemon, spice and hay character. Super-sweet. • $90 • (11/30/94) • **90**

Riesling Kabinett Rheinhessen Jean-Baptiste 1993: More like a spätlese than a kabinett. Full-bodied and very rich, with a spicy honey and fruit character and a long, spicy finish. Plenty of crisp acidity. • $14 • (11/30/94) • **89**

Riesling Kabinett Rheinhessen Jean-Baptiste 1992 • $13 • (11/30/93) • **88**

Riesling Kabinett Rheinhessen Jean-Baptiste 1991 • $14 • (12/15/92) • **89**

Riesling Kabinett Rheinhessen Nackenheimer Rothenberg Jean-Baptiste 1994: Stands out among the other '94s for its freshness, elegance and intensity. Medium body, racy acidity and a long, extremely clean finish. Drinkable now, but will reward patience. • $15 • (11/30/95) • **88**

Riesling QbA Trocken Rheinhessen 1994: A crisp and clean, dry German wine with floral and apple aromas and flavors. Medium-bodied, with high acidity and a slightly aggressive finish. Drinkable now. • $12 • (11/30/95) • **84**

Riesling QbA Trocken Rheinhessen Nackenheimer 1991 • $11 • (12/15/92) • **87**

Riesling Spätlese Rheinhessen Nackenheimer Rothenberg 1994: A stunning explosion of fruit yet exhibits great elegance. Medium-bodied, with a perfect balance of refreshing acidity and subdued sweetness, going into a very long, clean finish. Drinkable now, or allow a little age. 350 cases made. • $21 • (11/30/95) • **90**

Riesling Spätlese Rheinhessen Nackenheimer Rothenberg 1993: Vibrant, with an impressively fruity, melon and cantaloupe character. Full-bodied yet very fresh, clean and elegant. Fine winemaking here. • $19 • (11/30/94) • **90**

Riesling Spätlese Rheinhessen Nackenheimer Rothenberg 1992 • $17 • (11/30/93) SS • **92**

Riesling Spätlese Rheinhessen Nackenheimer Rothenberg 1991 • $18 • (12/15/92) • **91**

Riesling Spätlese Trocken Rheinhessen Nackenheimer Rothenberg 1992 • $22 • (11/30/93) • **89**

Riesling Spätlese Trocken Rheinhessen Nackenheimer Rothenberg 1991 • $25 • (12/15/92) • **87**

Riesling Trockenbeerenauslese Rheinhessen Nackenheimer Rothenberg 1994: Is this wine? Or should you spread it on toast? Whatever it is, it's stupendous. Like pure honey and molasses, with a sweetness to match. Dark amber, somewhat orange-hued nectar that offers complex flavors: pure, dried fruits, burnt almond, brown sugar. The finish extends beyond expectation. This will last, hold on until 2005. • $NA • (11/30/95) • **95**

Riesling Trockenbeerenauslese Rheinhessen Nackenheimer Rothenberg 1992 • $153 • (11/30/93) • **100**

GUNTRUM, LOUIS

Gewürztraminer Auslese Trocken Rheinhessen Oppenheimer Sackträger 1992 • $20 • (11/30/93) • **85**

Riesling Auslese Rheinhessen Oppenheimer Herrenberg 1992 • $20 • (11/30/93) • **83**

Riesling Kabinett Rheinhessen Niersteiner Bergkirche 1992 • $10 • (11/30/93) • **80**

Riesling Spätlese Halbtrocken Rheinhessen Niersteiner Heiligenbaum 1992 • $12 • (11/30/93) • **80**

Scheurebe Trockenbeerenauslese Rheinhessen Oppenheimer Herrenberg 1992 • $NA • (11/30/93) • **88**

Silvaner Eiswein Rheinhessen Oppenheimer Herrenberg 1992 • $NA • (11/30/93) • **69**

Key: SS—Spectator Selection. CS—Cellar Selection. BB—Best Buy. $NA—Price not available. (BT)—Barrel tasting. (A)—Auction Price.
Dates in parentheses represent the issues in which the ratings were published.

HAAG, FRITZ

Riesling Auslese Gold Cap Mosel Brauneberger Juffer-Sonnenuhr 1992 • $80 • (11/30/93) • **90**

Riesling Auslese Mosel Brauneberger Juffer-Sonnenuhr 1992 • $180 • (11/30/93) • **94**

Riesling Auslese Mosel Brauneberger Juffer-Sonnenuhr Nr. 18 1992 • $34 • (11/30/93) • **82**

Riesling Auslese Mosel Brauneberger Juffer-Sonnenuhr Nr. 6 1992 • $26 • (11/30/93) • **87**

Riesling Auslese Mosel-Saar-Ruwer Brauneberger Juffer-Sonnenuhr Long Gold 1991 • $314 • (12/15/92) • **91**

Riesling Kabinett Mosel Brauneberger Juffer-Sonnenuhr 1992 • $15 • (11/30/93) • **83**

Riesling Kabinett Mosel-Saar-Ruwer Brauneberger Juffer-Sonnenuhr Nr. 8 1991 • $29 • (12/15/92) • **84**

Riesling Kabinett Mosel-Saar-Ruwer Brauneberger Juffer-Sonnenuhr Nr. 5 1991 • $17 • (12/15/92) • **88**

Riesling Spätlese Mosel Brauneberger Juffer-Sonnenuhr 1992 • $20 • (11/30/93) • **88**

Riesling Spätlese Mosel-Saar-Ruwer Brauneberger Juffer-Sonnenuhr Nr. 10 1991 • $33 • (12/15/92) • **86**

Riesling Spätlese Mosel-Saar-Ruwer Brauneberger Juffer-Sonnenuhr Nr. 3 1991 • $25 • (12/15/92) • **87**

HAAG, WILLI

Riesling Auslese Gold Cap Mosel Brauneberger Juffer-Sonnenuhr 1992 • $NA • (11/30/93) • **85**

Riesling Auslese Mosel Brauneberger Juffer-Sonnenuhr Nr. 10 1992 • $26 • (11/30/93) • **87**

Riesling Auslese Mosel Brauneberger Juffer-Sonnenuhr Nr. 5 1992 • $NA • (11/30/93) • **84**

Riesling Kabinett Mosel Brauneberger Juffer Nr. 11 1992 • $9 • (11/30/93) • **74**

Riesling Kabinett Mosel Brauneberger Juffer Nr. 7 1992 • $9 • (11/30/93) • **84**

Riesling Spätlese Mosel Brauneberger Juffer-Sonnenuhr 1992 • $12 • (11/30/93) • **83**

HAART, REINHOLD

Riesling Auslese Gold Cap Mosel Piesporter Goldtröpfchen 1993: Shows tons of character. Very dense, featuring lots of botrytis, spice, fruity aromas and flavors. Thick, full-bodied and oily with a classy undercarriage of acidity. Drinkable now but will improve for many years. • $81 • (11/30/94) • **94**

Riesling Auslese Gold Cap Mosel Piesporter Goldtröpfchen 1992 • $48 • (11/30/93) • **92**

Riesling Auslese Mosel Piesporter Goldtröpfchen 1992 • $35 • (11/30/93) • **90**

Riesling Auslese Mosel-Saar-Ruwer Piesporter Goldtröpfchen 1994: A textbook auslese and an outstanding achievement for this vintage. Crushed grape, honey and melon aromas and flavors. Medium body and a long, luscious finish. Drinkable now. • $44 • (11/30/95) • **90**

Riesling Auslese Mosel Wintricher Ohligsberg 1993: Rich and mouthfilling with loads of honey and spice character. Full in body, sweet, long aftertaste. Drinkable now. • $28 • (11/30/94) • **89**

Riesling Beerenauslese Mosel-Saar-Ruwer Piesporter Goldtröpfchen 1994: Marvelous honey and peach aromas and flavors, very full and sweet, with a laser beam of acidity shooting through it. The very long, racy finish keeps coming back at you. Better still in 1998. • $NA • (11/30/95) • **94**

Riesling Kabinett Mosel Piesporter Goldtröpfchen 1993: Undeveloped, displaying extremely pronounced lemon and mineral character on the nose and palate. Medium-bodied and off-dry with fresh acidity. Drinkable now. • $16 • (11/30/94) • **87**

Riesling Kabinett Mosel Piesporter Goldtröpfchen 1992 • $15 • (11/30/93) • **86**

Riesling Kabinett Mosel-Saar-Ruwer Piesporter Goldtröpfchen 1994: Absolutely delicious. A beautifully balanced Riesling with floral, apple and honey aromas and flavors. Medium-bodied and very fresh, with crisp acidity and a long finish that brings out apple and spice notes. Drinkable now. • $18 • (11/30/95) • **88**

Riesling Spätlese Mosel Piesporter Domherr 1993: Plenty of character here. Medium in body and medium-sweet, with a long aftertaste of cantaloupe and spice. Drinkable now. • $22 • (11/30/94) • **86**

Riesling Spätlese Mosel Piesporter Goldtröpfchen 1993: Pretty, round-textured, mineral and ripe apple aromas and flavors. Medium-bodied and medium in sweetness with a fruity finish. Drinkable now. • $25 • (11/30/94) • **86**

Riesling Spätlese Mosel Piesporter Goldtröpfchen 1992 • $20 • (11/30/93) • **88**

Riesling Spätlese Mosel-Saar-Ruwer Piesporter Domherr 1994: An intense wine with a sweet-sour character. Medium body, moderate sweetness and a spicy finish. Drinkable now. • $24 • (11/30/95) • **88**

Riesling Spätlese Mosel-Saar-Ruwer Piesporter Goldtröpfchen 1994: Stunning, explosive peach and floral character. Concentrated, elegant and in perfect balance, with a long, extremely clean finish. Drinkable now or hold off to allow some development. • $27 • (11/30/95) • **87**

Riesling Trockenbeerenauslese Mosel Piesporter Goldtröpfchen 1993: Wonderfully harmonious for being so concentrated and sweet. Full-bodied, with honey, marzipan and spice flavors followed by a long, vibrant finish. Delicious now but will improve greatly upon cellaring. • $NA • (11/30/94) • **95**

HENKELL

Sparkling Trocken Feinertrockner Sekt NV • $10 • (10/15/88) • **72**

HEYL ZU HERRNSHEIM

Rheinhessen Baron von Heyl 1993: Soft and slightly sweet, a smooth-textured wine with subtle melon, almond, vanilla and caramel flavors. Enjoyable, but on the heavy side. 2,400 cases made. • $10 • **80**

Riesling Auslese Rheinhessen Niersteiner Pettenthal 1994: Meager for this vintage: some decent apple, spice and mineral aromas, but just not enough on the palate to warrant more attention. Light to medium body, with a fresh finish. • $26 • (11/30/95) • **80**

Riesling Auslese Rheinhessen Niersteiner Pettenthal 1993: Very ripe and rich, with honey, marzipan and spice character on the nose and palate. Full-bodied, sweet and long on the finish. Delicious now. • $20 • (11/30/94) • **88**

Riesling Auslese Rheinhessen Niersteiner Pettenthal 1992 • $24 • (11/30/93) • **80**

Riesling Kabinett Rheinhessen Niersteiner Rehbach 1992 • $12 • (11/30/93) • **81**

Riesling Kabinett Rheinhessen Schloss Mathildenhof 1994: Quite a subtle wine, though it gives off plenty of peach aroma. Medium-bodied, with nice peach and spice flavors, but doesn't have great depth or length. Drinkable now. • $14 • (11/30/95) • **84**

Riesling Kabinett Rheinhessen Schloss Mathildenhof 1993: A bright and well-balanced Riesling with fresh apple and peach flavors, good acidity and a clean, fruity finish. 1,200 cases made. • $12 • (11/30/94) • **84**

Riesling QbA Rheinhessen Baron von Heyl 1994: Subtle mineral, apple and flint character runs through this wine. Light to medium in body and lightly sweet, with a delicate finish. Drinkable now. • $10 • (11/30/95) • **84**

Riesling Spätlese Halbtrocken Rheinhessen Niersteiner Pettenthal 1994: Nice peach and citrus flavors make this medium-bodied wine very appealing. Not much depth behind it, but the balance of fruit, alcohol and acidity is right on. Drinkable now. • $19 • (11/30/94) • **87**

Riesling Spätlese Mittelrhein Niersteiner Olberg 1993: Very developed and sweet in style for a new wine but it shows some wonderfully delicious honey, melon, and spice character. Drink now. • $18 • (11/30/94) • **85**

Riesling Spätlese Rheinhessen Niersteiner Brudersberg 1992 • $17 • (11/30/93) • **79**

Riesling Spätlese Rheinhessen Niersteiner Pettenthal 1993: Pleasant, fresh and clean with pie crust flavor, light mineral character, medium body and a fresh finish. 1,200 cases made. • $17 • **83**

Riesling Spätlese Rheinhessen Niersteiner Pettenthal 1992 • $17 • (11/30/93) • **82**

Riesling Spätlese Trocken Rheinhessen Niersteiner Hipping 1992 • $17 • (11/30/93) • **77**

Riesling Spätlese Trocken Rheinhessen Niersteiner Pettenthal 1994: Chewy and grapey, this white shows an impressive concentration of honey, apple and cherry aromas and flavors. Full-bodied and rich, with moderate acidity and a long finish. Delicious now. • $22 • (11/30/95) • **87**

Riesling Spätlese Trocken Rheinhessen Niersteiner Pettenthal 1993: Disappointing. Fat, bland, flabby, with an earthy, fruity, slightly bitter character and a short finish. Organically produced. • $19 • (11/30/94) • **76**

Silvaner QbA Rheinhessen Niersteiner Rosenberg 1993: Shows an interesting leafy character with almond and honey notes. Full-bodied and alcoholic, with a long, oily finish. A bit coarse. Organically produced. • $12 • (11/30/94) • **80**

Silvaner QbA Trocken Rheinhessen Niersteiner Rosenberg 1994: A delicious dry wine with mineral and lemon character. Full body, well-integrated acidity and a grapey finish. Drinkable now. • $16 • (11/30/95) • **85**

HOHE DOMKIRCHE

Riesling Spätlese Halbtrocken Saar-Ruwer Avelsbacher Altenberg 1992 • $NA • (11/30/93) • **78**

Riesling Spätlese Saar-Ruwer Scharzhofberger 1992 • $NA • (11/30/93) • **83**

HOVEL, VON

Riesling Auslese Gold Cap Saar-Ruwer Oberemmeler Hütte 1993: Very pretty, with a peach, apricot and honey character. Full-bodied yet very balanced, with fresh acidity and a long, crisp finish. Drinkable now or hold. • $90 • (11/30/94) • **90**

Riesling Auslese Saar-Ruwer Oberemmeler Hütte 1993: Fresh and very sweet, with a mineral character and citrus notes. Medium-bodied and fresh, with a long, sweet finish. Drinkable now or hold. • $23 • (11/30/94) • **84**

Riesling Eiswein Saar-Ruwer Oberemmeler Hütte 1993: Beautifully balanced, with fresh peach, apple and honey flavors and a hint of eiswein spiciness. Medium- to full-bodied with very ripe fruit but has an underlying freshness from the acidity. • $NA • (11/30/94) • **91**

Riesling Kabinett Mosel-Saar-Ruwer Oberemmeler Hütte 1994: Exactly what we look for in a kabinett. Very fresh, lively apple and spice aromas and flavors, medium body and a clean finish. Drinkable now. • $13 • (11/30/95) • **85**

Riesling Kabinett Mosel-Saar-Ruwer Scharzhofberger 1994: A big kabinett. Peach and cream aromas, medium body and quite sweet on the palate. This is a bit fat and lush, getting diffuse on the finish. Drinkable now. • $NA • (11/30/95) • **82**

Riesling Kabinett Saar-Ruwer Balduin Von Hövel 1993: Plenty of body, with apple pie aromas and flavors. Medium-bodied and fruity, with an appley aftertaste. • $9 • (11/30/94) • **83**

Riesling Kabinett Saar-Ruwer Oberemmeler Hütte 1993: A rich and delicious kabinett, with ripe apple, spice and mineral character. Medium-bodied and rather soft, with a long, fruity finish. Lovely to drink now. • $12 • (11/30/94) • **87**

Riesling Kabinett Saar-Ruwer Oberemmeler Hütte 1992 • $12 • (11/30/93) • **80**

Riesling Kabinett Saar-Ruwer Scharzhofberger 1992 • $12 • (11/30/93) • **80**

Riesling QbA Saar-Ruwer Balduin Von Hövel 1992 • $9 • (11/30/93) • **76**

Riesling Spätlese Mittelrhein Oberemmeler Hütte 1993: Packed with fruit. An amazing achievement in a Spätlese. Medium- to full-bodied, medium-sweet and a long ripe fruit finish. Absolutely delicious. Drinkable now. • $15 • (11/30/94) • **90**

Riesling Spätlese Mosel-Saar-Ruwer Oberemmeler Hütte 1994: A textbook Saar Riesling that delivers plenty of peach and floral character embraced by fresh acidity. Medium in body and sweetness. Delicious now. • $16 • (11/30/95) • **81**

Riesling Spätlese Mosel-Saar-Ruwer Scharzhofberger 1994: Lush citrus and pineapple flavors mingle with the crisp acidity, though, it lacks the personality for a higher score. Medium body and sweetness, with a clean finish. Drinkable now. • $16 • (11/30/95) • **84**

Riesling Spätlese Saar-Ruwer Oberemmeler Hütte 1992 • $16 • (11/30/93) • **82**
Riesling Spätlese Saar-Ruwer Scharzhofberger 1992 • $16 • (11/30/93) • **83**

JOHANNISBERG, SCHLOSS

Riesling Auslese Rheingau Rosalack 1993: Strange aromas of paint. Tasted twice with consistent notes. Forget it. 50 cases imported to U.S. 333 cases made. • $90 • (11/30/94) • **68**
Riesling Beerenauslese Rheingau Rose-Godlack 1992 • $NA • (11/30/93) • **60**
Riesling Eiswein Rheingau 1992 • $NA • (11/30/93) • **85**
Riesling Kabinett Rheingau 1992 • $NA • (11/30/93) • **75**
Riesling Kabinett Rheingau Rotlack 1993: Simple and dry with melon and mineral flavors, medium body and tart finish. 2,500 cases made. • $22 • (11/30/94) • **80**
Riesling QbA Rheingau 1993: Incredibly lemony with high tart acidity and fresh, light, fruity finish. Bone-dry. Not for everyone. Tasted twice. Drinkable now. 1,000 cases imported to United States. • $17 • **81**
Riesling Spätlese Rheingau 1993: Petrol, spice, and ripe fruit aromas and flavors. Medium-bodied and slightly sweet with a bitter finish. Tasted twice. • $NA • (11/30/94) • **79**
Riesling Spätlese Rheingau 1992 • $NA • (11/30/93) • **75**
Riesling Spätlese Trocken Rheingau 1992 • $NA • (11/30/93) • **71**
Riesling Spätlese Trocken Rheingau Grunlack 1993: Rather difficult to judge at this stage. A dry style, with very earthy, ripe fruit aromas and flavors. Drinkable now. • $28 • (11/30/94) • **84**
Riesling Trockenbeerenauslese Rheingau Goldlack 1993: One of the greatest wines from this estate in a long time. Incredibly viscous. Very youthful and fresh, exhibiting masses of spice, honey and dried fruit aromas and flavors. Extremely concentrated with a thick, syrupy texture. Drink or age for as long as you like. 10 cases made. • $300 • (11/30/94) • **96**

JOHANNISHOF

Riesling Auslese Rheingau Johannisberger Hölle 1992 • $27 • (11/30/93) • **81**
Riesling Kabinett Rheingau Charta 1993: A dry white for serious German wine lovers. Very crisp and mouth-puckering, but there's a good amount of lemon and apple flavor with a hint of minerals on the finish. Drinkable now. • $16 • (11/30/94) • **87**
Riesling Kabinett Rheingau Johannisberger Goldatzel 1993: Rich in style with peach and light earth character, medium body and a slightly sweet finish. • $14 • (11/30/94) • **87**
Riesling Kabinett Rheingau Johannisberger Vogelsang 1993: Plenty of body and richness and unique white pepper character, but slightly dull at the finish. Suffering from bottle sickness. • $12 • (11/30/94) • **82**
Riesling Kabinett Rheingau Johannisberger Vogelsang 1992 • $15 • (11/30/93) • **79**
Riesling Spätlese Rheingau Johannisberger Goldatzel 1993: Pleasing aromas and flavors of freshly sliced peaches. Medium in body and very sweet with a fruity finish. • $20 • (11/30/94) • **88**
Riesling Spätlese Rheingau Johannisberger Goldatzel 1992 • $22 • (11/30/93) • **82**
Riesling Spätlese Rheingau Johannisberger Klaus 1993: Good Spätlese with plenty of fruit and character. Medium-bodied, medium-sweet with attractive, spice and pie crust flavors. Drink now. • $18 • (11/30/94) • **85**
Riesling Spätlese Rheingau Johannisberger Klaus 1992 • $21 • (11/30/93) • **84**

JOST, TONI

Riesling Auslese Gold Cap Mittelrhein Bacharacher Hahn 1993: A wonderful sweet wine, but perhaps not quite up to the gold cap level. Full-bodied and very rich, with honey and tropical fruit flavors and a long finish. Drink or hold. • $37 • (11/30/94) • **88**

Key: SS—Spectator Selection. CS—Cellar Selection. BB—Best Buy. $NA—Price not available. (BT)—Barrel tasting. Ⓐ—Auction Price.
Dates in parentheses represent the issues in which the ratings were published.

Riesling Auslese Mittelrhein Bacharacher Hahn 1992 • $26 • (11/30/93) • **90**
Riesling Auslese Mittelrhein Wallufer Walkenburg 1993: A beauty, rich and luscious yet fine. Delicate ripe fruit and floral aromas and flavors with a touch of spice. Medium body and sweet on the palate. Drinkable now. • $NA • (11/30/94) • **89**
Riesling Kabinett Mittelrhein Bacharacher Hahn 1993: Loads of character with its spices, fruit and creamy flavors lasting through the long, crisp finish. Medium-bodied, sweet and fresh. Drink now or hold. • $14 • (11/30/94) • **87**
Riesling Kabinett Mittelrhein Bacharacher Hahn 1992 • $13 • (11/30/93) • **73**
Riesling Spätlese Halbtrocken Mittelrhein Bacharacher Hahn 1992 • $14 • (11/30/93) • **76**
Riesling Spätlese Mittelrhein Bacharacher Hahn 1993: Lovely and balanced, with perfume, pear and melon aromas and flavors. Medium-bodied and sweet, with good acidity and a fruity finish. Drink now or hold. • $15 • (11/30/94) • **86**
Riesling Spätlese Mittelrhein Bacharacher Hahn 1992 • $14 • (11/30/93) • **88**
Riesling Spätlese Mittelrhein One Star Bacharacher Hahn 1992 • $15 • (11/30/93) • **85**
Riesling Spätlese Mittelrhein Wallufer Walkenburg 1993: Very appealing varietal bouquet with fresh aromas and flavors of lemon curd and fruit. Medium-bodied and sweet. Drink now. • $15 • (11/30/94) • **85**
Riesling Trockenbeerenauslese Mittelrhein Bacharacher Hahn 1993: Subtle yet thick and rich, with a wonderful honey and dried-fruit character. Full-bodied and sweet, with good acidity and a long, flavorful finish. Drink or hold. • $NA • (11/30/94) • **90**

KARLSMUHLE

Riesling Auslese Long Gold Cap Saar-Ruwer Lorenzhofer 1993: Closed and hard right now but some excellent ripe fruit and ample acidity. Full-bodied and linear in structure. Drinkable now. • $31 • (11/30/94) • **88**
Riesling Auslese Saar-Ruwer Lorenzhöfer 1993: A clean, fresh auslese that's medium in body and sweetness. Has a steely, lemony, lightly mineral finish. A bit light. • $22 • (11/30/94) • **84**
Riesling Eiswein Saar-Ruwer Lorenzhöfer 1993: Slightly buttery, with very sweet flavors and high acidity, but it's rather one-dimensional and the buttery finish detracts. • $68 • (11/30/94) • **81**
Riesling Kabinett Saar-Ruwer Lorenzhöfer Mäuerchen 1993: Extremely fresh and fruity, reminiscent of uncooked apple pie and a slightly smoky character. It's medium-bodied, with a very lively acidity. Drinkable now. • $14 • (11/30/94) • **89**
Riesling Kabinett Saar-Ruwer Lorenzhöfer Mäuerchen 1992 • $13 • (11/30/93) • **84**
Riesling QbA Halbtrocken Saar-Ruwer Lorenzhöfer 1992 • $10 • (11/30/93) • **84**
Riesling QbA Saar-Ruwer Lorenzhöfer 1992 • $10 • (11/30/93) • **85**
Riesling Spätlese Halbtrocken Saar-Ruwer Kaseler Kehrnagel 1992 • $14 • (11/30/93) • **87**
Riesling Spätlese Halbtrocken Saar-Ruwer Lorenzhofer Felsay 1993: Exceedingly fresh wine with sliced apple, melon aromas and flavors. Medium-bodied, lightly sweet with a firm acidity. Drinkable now. • $16 • (11/30/94) • **84**
Riesling Spätlese Saar-Ruwer Kaseler Nies'chen 1993: A well-made, sophisticated spätlese, with an attractive mineral, spice and fruit character. Medium-bodied and lightly sweet with a lovely, fresh aftertaste. • $16 • (11/30/94) • **89**

KAUER, RANDOLPH

Riesling Spätlese Halbtrocken Mittelrhein Bacharacher Kloster Fürstental 1992 • $NA • (11/30/93) • **90**
Riesling Spätlese Trocken Mittelrhein Bacharacher Kloster Fürstental 1992 • $NA • (11/30/93) • **84**

KERPEN, HERIBERT

Riesling Auslese Mosel Bernkasteler Bratenhöfchen 1992 • $20 • (11/30/93) • **89**
Riesling Auslese Mosel Wehlener Sonnenuhr 1992 • $35 • (11/30/93) • **90**
Riesling Auslese Mosel Wehlener Sonnenuhr Two Stars 1992 • $22 • (11/30/93) • **90**
Riesling Eiswein Mosel Bernkasteler Bratenhöfchen 1992 • $NA • (11/30/93) • **88**
Riesling Kabinett Mosel Wehlener Sonnenuhr 1992 • $12 • (11/30/93) • **83**
Riesling Spätlese Halbtrocken Mosel Wehlener Sonnenuhr 1992 • $11 • (11/30/93) • **83**

KESSELER, AUGUST

Riesling Kabinett Rheingau 1993: Bright and fresh with floral, spice and light earth character. Light body, lively on the palate and a slightly sweet finish. Just right. • $NA • (11/30/94) • **86**
Riesling QbA Rheingau 1993: Pretty aromas of mineral, flowers and spice are followed up by delicate, light, sweet flavors. Light-bodied and delicious. • $NA • (11/30/94) • **85**
Riesling Spätlese Rheingau 1993: Light yet enjoyable with spicy, earthy character but a slightly weak aftertaste. Medium to light body, a little sweetness, pretty fruit and delicate finish. • $NA • (11/30/94) • **83**
Riesling Spätlese Trocken Rheingau Rüdesheimer Berg Roseneck 1993: Fresh, simple and spritzy, with apple flavor and a slightly grassy character. Medium body, dry, with a crisp, mineral finish. • $NA • (11/30/94) • **84**

KESSELSTATT, REICHSGRAF VON

Riesling Auslese Gold Cap Mosel-Saar-Ruwer Piesporter Goldtrîpfchen 1994: A good auslese, but rather light for gold cap. Medium body, moderately sweet, with a honey-, herb- and spice-flavored finish. Drinkable now. • $NA • (11/30/95) • **84**
Riesling Auslese Mosel Bernkasteler Doctor 1992 • $56 • (11/30/93) • **85**
Riesling Auslese Mosel Josephshöfer 1993: More like an excellent spätlese than an auslese. Super-ripe, displaying loads of spice and peach character. Medium- to full-bodied with sweet, intense flavors. Drinkable now. • $NA • (11/30/94) • **90**
Riesling Auslese Mosel Josephshöfer 1992 • $54 • (11/30/93) • **89**
Riesling Auslese Mosel-Saar-Ruwer Kaseler Nies'chen 1994: A very fresh wine that shows off its white peach, spice and mineral aromas and flavors. A beautifully balanced, medium-bodied Riesling with a long, clean, delicate finish. Drinkable now. • $NA • (11/30/95) • **87**
Riesling Auslese Mosel-Saar-Ruwer Scharzhofberger 1994: Bright citrus aromas and flavors, medium body and moderate sweetness. Indeed, medium everything, with a clean finish. Drinkable now. • $NA • (11/30/95) • **82**
Riesling Auslese Mosel Wiltinger Braunfels 1993: Ripe and slightly developed aromas and flavors but attractive, sweet cantaloupe and dried-apricot character. • $NA • (11/30/94) • **86**
Riesling Eiswein Saar-Ruwer Scharzhofberger 1993: Perplexing wine starts off slowly, jumps in to fifth gear but finishes in third. Still, well-made and fresh with ripe fruit and wonderful spiciness, sweetness. • $NA • (11/30/94) • **89**
Riesling Kabinett Mosel Piesporter Goldtröpfchen 1993: Thick, rich, oozing with freshly crushed grape character and a hint of dry ice. Medium-bodied and delicately sweet. Fresh finish. Drinkable now. • $NA • (11/30/94) • **88**
Riesling Kabinett Mosel-Saar-Ruwer Josephshöfer 1994: This is really fresh. Loads of apple, melon and peach rise out of the glass and onto the palate. Medium-bodied and off-dry, with a fresh finish. Drink now, or try aging a few bottles. • $NA • (11/30/95) • **86**
Riesling Kabinett Mosel-Saar-Ruwer Ockfener Bockstein 1994: Quite rich, but it lacks excitement. Medium-bodied and medium-sweet, with peach and melon flavors. Though, overall it's a bit dull and finishes short and flat. • $13 • **82**
Riesling Kabinett Mosel-Saar-Ruwer Piesporter Goldtröpfchen 1994: A lovely, straightforward kabinett with flinty apple and melon aromas and flavors. Medium to light body, lightly sweet and light on the finish. • $NA • (11/30/95) • **85**
Riesling Kabinett Mosel-Saar-Ruwer Scharzhofberger 1994: A rich, beautifully balanced kabinett. Fresh, tart peach and citrus aromas and flavors, medium body and sweetness, with a very clean, delicate finish. Drinkable now, but can age well. • $NA • (11/30/95) • **86**
Riesling Kabinett Saar-Ruwer Kaseler Nies'chen 1992 • $NA • (11/30/93) • **85**
Riesling Kabinett Saar-Ruwer Scharzhofberger 1992 • $NA • (11/30/93) • **85**
Riesling QbA Mosel-Saar-Ruwer Piesporter Goldtröpfchen 1994: Appealing to drink now, with loads of melon and mineral aromas and flavors. Medium body, medium-sweet and round, with a crisp, light finish. • $NA • (11/30/95) • **85**
Riesling Spätlese Mosel Josephshöfer 1992 • $20 • (11/30/93) • **89**
Riesling Spätlese Mosel Piesporter Goldtröpfchen 1993: Fresh with ripe apple and apricot aromas and flavors. Medium in body and lightly sweet, balanced acidity and a light finish. 333 cases made. • $NA • (11/30/94) • **86**
Riesling Spätlese Mosel Piesporter Goldtröpfchen 1992 • $23 • (11/30/93) • **87**
Riesling Spätlese Mosel-Saar-Ruwer Josephshöfer 1994: Ripe white peach character and beautiful balance. A model spätlese that matches its richness with an elegant style. Drinkable now, or after some age. • $NA • (11/30/95) • **87**
Riesling Spätlese Mosel-Saar-Ruwer Piesporter Goldtröpfchen 1994: Ripe, full, and spicy, but lacks the structure and depth to back it up. Light-bodied and unremarkable. • $NA • (11/30/95) • **78**
Riesling Spätlese Mosel-Saar-Ruwer Scharzhofberger 1994: Fresh and fruity, with floral, apple and spice aromas and flavors. Medium body and pleasantly sweet, but somewhat lean on the finish. Drinkable now, but can age. • $NA • (11/30/95) • **85**
Riesling Spätlese Saar-Ruwer Scharzhofberger 1993: Loads of fresh, ripe fruit and beautifully balanced. Clean and medium-bodied and medium-sweet with a fresh finish. Drinkable now or hold. • $NA • (11/30/94) • **87**
Riesling Trockenbeerenauslese Mosel-Saar-Ruwer Scharzhofberger 1994: A marvelous trockenbeerenauslese that carries off its rich dried fruit and sweet floral aromas and flavors with beautiful balance and elegance. Long and clean on the finish. This will improve, try in 1998. • $NA • (11/30/95) • **91**

KLEIN, WEINGUT

Kerner Spätlese Rheinhessen Niersteiner Olberg 1991: An appealing, floral-flavored wine with a bit of sweetness balanced by good acidity. Fairly simple but enjoyable. • $13 • (08/31/94) • **80**
Müller-Thurgau Kabinett Trocken Rheinhessen Niersteiner Spiegelberg 1992: A serious, dry Müller-Thurgau. It's a rich wine with nice, concentrated fruit flavors and a lingering finish. Appealing aromas of bread dough and apples. A good value at $10 for this one-liter bottle. • $10 • (08/31/94) • **86**
Riesling Kabinett Halbtrocken Rheinhessen Niersteiner Bildstock 1991: This is tart, taut and Teutonic. Austere to the point of being difficult to like. Only for fans of a very lean, tart style. Thin on flavor. • $11 • (08/31/94) • **76**
Riesling Kabinett Rheinhessen Niersteiner Bildstock 1992: Enticing peachy, floral aromas give way to a crisp and appealing Riesling. Seems dry, but still fairly concentrated. A nice apple note runs throughout this wine, and it has a nice clean finish. • $11 • (08/31/94) • **83**
Riesling Spätlese Rheinhessen Niersteiner Rehbach 1991: A light but decent Riesling with enough crisp apple and grapefruit flavors to give it life. Balanced toward the lean, tart side, but still enjoyable. • $15 • (08/31/94) • **81**

KNYPHAUSEN, BARON ZU

Riesling Kabinett Rheingau Erbacher 1994: A soft texture and a hint of sweetness make this an easy-drinking but simple white with a bit of peach flavor. • $11 • (12/15/95) • **80**
Riesling Kabinett Rheingau Erbacher 1992 • $13 • (11/30/93) • **82**

GERMANY

Riesling QbA Rheingau 1993: Slightly unripe flavors of green apples and earth. Thin and slightly diluted. Sweet finish. 300 cases made. • $10 • (11/30/94) • **72**

Riesling Rheingau 1994: An unusual Riesling that combines peppery aromas with green apple flavors and a tart finish. • $7 • (12/15/95) • **78**

Riesling Spätlese Rheingau Hattenheimer Wisselbrunnen 1994: Soft, sweet and modestly flavored, with apple and butter notes. Generous in texture, but fades quickly on the finish. • $18 • (12/15/95) • **82**

KNYPHAUSEN, FREIHERR ZU

Riesling Auslese Rheingau Hattenheimer Wisselbrunnen 1992 • $44 • (11/30/93) • **90**

Riesling Auslese Rheingau Kiedricher Sandgrub 1993: A wine with a lot of character but slightly aggressive. Spicy, fruity and honeyed with obvious botrytis tones. Medium-bodied and sweet with a thick raisiny finish. Drinkable now or hold. 1,200 cases made. • $24 • (11/30/94) • **83**

Riesling Beerenauslese Rheingau Erbacher Michelmark 1993: Seductive, displaying butter, honey and caramel aromas and flavors. It's full-bodied, rich and succulent with lively acidity on the finish. Tasted twice, second bottle much better. Drinkable now. 350 cases made. • $88 • (11/30/94) • **90**

Riesling Kabinett Rheingau Erbacher 1993: A rich-tasting, slightly sweet Riesling with plenty of mellow flavors of honey, ripe apple and spice. Smooth and delicious. 1,200 cases made. • $12 • (11/30/94) • **83**

Riesling Kabinett Rheingau Erbacher Macrobrunn 1993: Very strange character, with cotton candy aromas and flavors and a bitter finish. • $NA • (11/30/94) • **74**

Riesling Kabinett Rheingau Erbacher Steinmorgen 1993: Clean and fresh flavors that are slightly herbaceous in character. Medium in body and lightly sweet with a fresh finish. 300 cases made. • $14 • (11/30/94) • **80**

Riesling QbA Rheingau 1993: A balanced, fresh, modestly fruity Riesling with earthy aromas and a clean finish. Slightly sweet, just enough to make it smooth. 2,400 cases made. • $10 • (11/30/94) • **79**

Riesling Spätlese Rheingau Erbacher Marcobrunn 1992 • $24 • (11/30/93) • **83**

Riesling Spätlese Rheingau Hattenheimer Wisselbrunnen 1993: Beautifully ripe aromas of honey, peach and pineapple are followed by flavors that turn lean on the finish in this sweet, late-harvest style of Riesling. 600 cases made. • $21 • (11/30/94) • **81**

Riesling Spätlese Trocken Rheingau Hattenheimer Wisselbrunnen 1992 • $20 • (11/30/93) • **81**

Riesling Trockenbeerenauslese Rheingau Erbacher Michelmark 1992 • $230 • (11/30/93) • **95**

KOEHLER-RUPRECHT

Gewürztraminer Auslese Pfalz Kallstadter Steinacker 1994: Hot and burning, with a spicy, burnt almond character. Too dry. Full-bodied and rich, but not much pleasure. • $NA • (11/30/95) • **78**

Gewürztraminer Spätlese Pfalz Kallstadter Steinacker 1992 • $NA • (11/30/93) • **81**

Muskateller Auslese Pfalz Kallstadter Saumagen 1992 • $NA

Muskateller Beerenauslese Pfalz Kallstadter Saumagen 1992 • $NA • (11/30/93) • **84**

Muskateller Kabinett Trocken Pfalz Kallstadter Saumagen 1992 • $NA • (11/30/93) • **79**

Muskateller Trockenbeerenauslese Pfalz Kallstadter Saumagen 1994: Very intense raisin, honey and spice aromas and flavors. Extremely full-bodied and very sweet, but beautifully balanced. An outstanding Muskateller that will improve into 1998. • $NA • (11/30/95) • **94**

Riesling Auslese Pfalz Kallstadter Saumagen 1994: A big, voluptuous wine with lots of stuffing. Full-bodied and weighty, though it doesn't have quite enough sweetness for the ideal balance. A big punch of flavor at the end brings it back alive, however. Drinkable now, or try it with some age. • $NA • (11/30/95) • **88**

Key: SS—Spectator Selection. CS—Cellar Selection. BB—Best Buy. $NA—Price not available. (BT)—Barrel tasting. Ⓐ—Auction Price.
Dates in parentheses represent the issues in which the ratings were published.

Riesling Auslese Pfalz Kallstadter Saumagen 1993: Not your typical straightforward Auslese. This is racy, closed up with steely acidity yet rich and ripe character. Medium- to full-bodied, sweet and elegant. Drinkable now. • $28 • (11/30/94) • **89**

Riesling Auslese Pfalz Kallstadter Saumagen 1992 • $NA • (11/30/93) • **90**

Riesling Beerenauslese Pfalz Kallstadter Saumagen 1994: Intensely floral, almost like rose essence, this is very big and powerful showing much less sweetness than most others in this category. Lots of honey flavors on the palate lead to a long, chunky finish. Drink now, or age. • $NA • (11/30/95) • **89**

Riesling Beerenauslese Pfalz Kallstadter Saumagen 1993: More auslese in weight and character than a BA, but it still shows pretty spice, lemon and sweet fruit notes. • $NA • (11/30/94) • **84**

Riesling Beerenauslese Pfalz Kallstadter Saumagen 1992 • $NA • (11/30/93) • **92**

Riesling Kabinett Halbtrocken Pfalz Kallstadter Steinacker 1994: Off-dry and plenty of flavor, but just a little lighter than the flavors suggest. Nice spice, almond and earth aromas, though, and a clean finish. Drinkable now. • $NA • (11/30/95) • **83**

Riesling Kabinett Pfalz Kallstadter Steinacker 1994: Pleasantly balanced, grapey and spicy, showing off its pineapple character. Medium-bodied, off-dry, with lovely harmony between the fruit and acidity. Drinkable now. • $NA • (11/30/95) • **85**

Riesling Kabinett Pfalz Kallstadter Steinacker 1993: Unusual spicy, orange, lemon aromas and flavors. Medium-bodied and off-dry with a long spicy finish. Crisp and clean. Drinkable now. • $12 • (11/30/94) • **87**

Riesling Spätlese Halbtrocken Pfalz Kallstadter Saumagen 1994: Very appealing, ripe peach and honeysuckle character and succulent mouth-feel make this medium-bodied dry white easy to enjoy. Drinkable now. • $NA • (11/30/95) • **86**

Riesling Spätlese Halbtrocken Pfalz Kallstadter Saumagen 1993: Big yet lively showing spice and pie crust aromas and flavors. Full in body and off-dry with an abundance of ripe fruit character. Refreshing finish. Delicious. • $16 • (11/30/94) • **89**

Riesling Spätlese Pfalz Kallstadter Saumagen 1994: Quite rich and delivers lots of ripe fruit flavors. Full-bodied and succulent, only a hint of sweetness and a long, creamy finish. Drinkable now or try aging a few years. • $NA • (11/30/95) • **87**

Riesling Spätlese Pfalz Kallstadter Saumagen 1993: Very good Pfalz Spätlese with mineral, earthy fruity aromas and flavors. Full- to medium-bodied with a round and fruity texture. Medium-sweet and a clean finish. Drinkable now. • $19 • (11/30/94) • **89**

Riesling Trockenbeerenauslese Pfalz Kallstadter Saumagen 1994: A voluptuous, thick and buttery Riesling, with lovely honey, almond and lemon rind aromas and flavors. Full body, sweet and round, with a chewy texture. Drinkable now, but age will treat this well. • $NA • (11/30/95) • **90**

Scheurebe Beerenauslese Pfalz Kallstadter Saumagen 1994: Has very rich caramel accents. Big and powerful, but not as lively or succulent as many others from this vintage. The dried apricot flavors echo long on the finish. Drinkable now, or hold off for more development. • $NA • (11/30/95) • **87**

KREUSCH, LEONARD

Mosel-Saar-Ruwer Piesporter Michelsberg 1993: Simple grapefruit and green apple flavors dominate this simple and straightforward wine. Delicate on the finish. • $8 • (08/31/94) • **79**

Mosel-Saar-Ruwer Zeller Schwarze Katz 1993: Sweet, with moderate apple and grapefruit flavors. A touch of earthiness doesn't add to the appeal of this wine. • $8 • (08/31/94) • **78**

Riesling Auslese Mosel-Saar-Ruwer Piesporter Goldtröpfchen 1992: Ripe and tasty Riesling, with sweet apple and peach flavors, and hints of mint and mineral. Very solid in quality, smooth and fruity in taste. • $13 • (08/31/94) • **84**

Riesling Auslese Mosel-Saar-Ruwer Piesporter Michelsberg 1992: A delicate, beautifully balanced wine, but light for an Auslese. Complex aromas of peaches and flowers give way to full fruit flavors accented by mineral and floral notes. Firm enough with acidity that it hardly tastes sweet. • $12 • (08/31/94) • **85**

Riesling Kabinett Mosel-Saar-Ruwer Bernkasteler Kurfürstlay 1992: Dull and unexciting with a sour streak. The finish is slightly herbal. A green wine without much appeal. • $8 • (08/31/94) • **74**

Riesling Kabinett Mosel-Saar-Ruwer Piesporter Michelsberg 1992: Some peach and apple flavors try to show through, but this is a rough, lean, simple wine. An odd aroma reminds us of sulfur. Tasted twice, with consistent notes. • $9 • (08/31/94) • **68**

Riesling QbA Mosel-Saar-Ruwer Piesporter Goldtröpfchen 1992: A soft, neutral wine with flavors typical of this vintage. Smooth textured, apparently low in acidity but with a clean finish. Has fairly light peach and apple flavors. • $9 • (08/31/94) • **80**

Riesling Spätlese Mosel-Saar-Ruwer Bernkasteler Kurfürstlay 1992: A solid wine with minerally aromas and peach and apple flavors. Clean and well-made with a good, crisp finish. Good for a summer picnic. • $9 • (08/31/94) • **82**

Riesling Spätlese Mosel-Saar-Ruwer Piesporter Goldtröpfchen 1992: Simple and sweet. Tastes like apple juice and lacks finesse. An awkward wine. • $11 • (08/31/94) • **76**

Riesling Spätlese Mosel-Saar-Ruwer Piesporter Michelsberg 1992: Smells fishy and tastes watery, simple and sour. An empty and off-putting wine. Tasted twice, with consistent notes. • $10 • (08/31/94) • **60**

KUNSTLER, FRANZ

Riesling Auslese Rheingau Hochheimer Hölle 1993: Exciting auslese with intense peach and spice aromas and flavors. Medium body yet very rich character and a long aftertaste. • $44 • (11/30/94) • **90**

Riesling Auslese Rheingau Hochheimer Hölle 1992 • $42 • (11/30/93) • **94**

Riesling Auslese Rheingau Hochheimer Hölle 1991 • $43 • (12/15/92) • **90**

Riesling Auslese Rheingau Hochheimer Reichestal 1992 • $48 • (11/30/93) • **92**

Riesling Auslese Trocken Rheingau Hochheimer Hölle 1992 • $42 • (11/30/93) • **88**

Riesling Beerenauslese Rheingau Hochheimer Hölle 1994: Vibrant crushed fruit aromas and flavors seem to leap out of the glass. Full-bodied and very concentrated, with high acidity and a racy finish. Just short of outstanding now, but age may change that, try in 2000. • $104 • (11/30/95) • **89**

Riesling Kabinett Halbtrocken Rheingau 1993: A dry style that has a lovely presence of lemon, light mineral character, medium body, impressive balance, and a fresh finish. Dry. Drink now. • $13 • (11/30/94) • **85**

Riesling Kabinett Rheingau Hochheimer Herrenberg 1994: A bit too much of a canned fruit cocktail character in this. Medium-bodied and very sweet. Has a round texture, but an almost sickly sweet finish. • $17 • (11/30/95) • **77**

Riesling Kabinett Rheingau Hochheimer Herrenberg 1993: Slightly out of balance between sweetness and acidity. Canned fruit cocktail flavors, but some decent on the finish. • $15 • (11/30/94) • **79**

Riesling QbA Halbtrocken Rheingau 1994: Very ripe lemon aromas and flavors-almost like a lemon pie. Medium body and good concentration, though a little one-dimensional. Has a clean, simple finish. Drink now. • $14 • (11/30/95) • **86**

Riesling QbA Halbtrocken Rheingau 1992 • $11 • (11/30/93) • **80**

Riesling QbA Rheingau Charta Hochheimer Hofmeister 1991 • $19 • (12/15/92) • **85**

Riesling Spätlese Rheingau Charta Hochheimer Hölle 1991 • $29 • (12/15/92) • **87**

Riesling Spätlese Rheingau Hochheimer Herenberg 1994: Extremely fresh and lively, with subtle peach, floral and mineral aromas and flavors. Medium body, good concentration and a long, racy finish. Drinkable now. • $30 • (11/30/95) • **90**

Riesling Spätlese Rheingau Hochheimer Herenberg 1993: Lively and flavorful wine with spicy, apple and almond character. It's medium-bodied and medium-sweet with a fresh aftertaste. Drink now. • $27 • (11/30/94) • **85**

Riesling Spätlese Rheingau Hochheimer Reichstal 1991 • $19 • (12/15/92) • **85**

Riesling Spätlese Trocken Rheingau Hochheimer Hölle 1994: Extremely fresh grapefruit and peach aromas and flavors. Full-bodied and beautifully balanced. Layers of fruit and refreshing acidity and a long, elegant finish. Drinkable now. • $30 • (11/30/95) • **88**

Riesling Spätlese Trocken Rheingau Hochheimer Stielweg 1994: A solid dry Riesling that shows floral, apple and chalky character. Medium-bodied, with a lovely balance of acidity and mineral flavors. Drinkable now. • $30 • (11/30/95) • **87**

Riesling Spätlese Trocken Rheingau Hochheimer Stielweg 1993: Fresh and lemony with attractive yet light mineral character. Medium-bodied, dry and very crisp finish. Delicious now. • $28 • (11/30/94) • **84**

Riesling Spätlese Trocken Rheingau Hochheimer Stielweg 1992 • $26 • (11/30/93) • **85**

Riesling Spätlese Trocken Rheingau Hochheimer Stielweg 1991 • $29 • (12/15/92) • **85**

Riesling Trockenbeerenauslese Rheingau Hochheimer Hölle 1994: A classy dessert wine that delivers lots of dried apricot and raisin aromas. Very full and sweet, with lovely acidity and a long, clean finish. Drinkable now, but try aging. • $428 • (11/30/95) • **90**

Riesling Trockenbeerenauslese Rheingau Hochheimer Hölle 1992 • $NA • (11/30/93) • **94**

LAUERBURG, J.

Riesling Spätlese Mosel Bernkasteler Bratenhöfchen 1992: A young crisp wine that seems awkward at first, but the nice appley flavors give way to a smooth finish. Strong mineral flavors are distinctive and tastey. Not for the faint of heart. Try now. • $16 • (08/31/94) • **85**

Riesling Spätlese Mosel-Saar-Ruwer Bernkasteler Bratenhöfchen 1993: Has typical Mosel aromas of pine, smoke and flowers, backed by ripe apple and butter flavors. Turns a bit candied on the finish, but may improve with time. • $17 • (12/15/95) • **83**

LEITZ, JOSEF

Riesling Auslese Rheingau Rüdesheimer Berg Schlossberg 1994: Bubbling over with pineapple and tropical fruit character. Medium to full body and pleasantly sweet. An intriguing finish brings out notes of mango. Drinkable now. • $38 • (11/30/95) • **88**

Riesling Kabinett Halbtrocken Rheingau Rüdesheimer Berg Schlossberg 1993: Challenging, not typical. Extremely fresh and young with honeycomb, spice and sawdust character. Medium in body and very crisp. Drinkable now. • $20 • (11/30/94) • **87**

Riesling Kabinett Halbtrocken Rheingau Rüdesheimer Kirchenpfad 1994: Elegant and has a lovely softness. Medium-bodied and round, with lemon and light spice flavors. Delicious. • $16 • (11/30/95) • **83**

Riesling Kabinett Halbtrocken Rheingau Rüdesheimer Kirchenpfad 1993: Big and slightly atypical for this quality level. Good intensity of dried apricot and spice on the nose and palate. Medium-bodied and off-dry, lovely finish. Drinkable now. • $14 • (11/30/94) • **87**

Riesling Kabinett Rheingau Rüdesheimer Bischofsberg 1993: Pretty, packed with fruit. Medium in body and slightly sweet, loads of peach and floral character. Long finish. • $NA • (11/30/95) • **87**

Riesling Kabinett Rheingau Rüdesheimer Bischofsberg 1992 • $9 • (11/30/93) • **89**

Riesling Kabinett Trocken Rheingau Rüdesheimer Berg Rottland 1992 • $9 • (11/30/93) • **82**

Riesling Spätlese Rheingau Rüdesheimer Berg Rottland 1994: A rich wine that offers lots of almond, earth and baked apple character. Medium body and modest sweetness, but rather simple finish. Drinkable now. • $NA • (11/30/95) • **84**

Riesling Spätlese Rheingau Rüdesheimer Berg Rottland 1993: Textbook spätlese with plenty of pretty, spicy, pie crust character. Medium-bodied and medium in sweetness, firm acidity and a fruity, round finish. • $20 • (11/30/94) • **89**

Riesling Spätlese Rheingau Rüdesheimer Berg Schlossberg 1992 • $14 • (11/30/93) • **88**

Riesling Spätlese Rheingau Rüdesheimer Kirchenpfad 1992 • $14 • (11/30/93) • **90**

Riesling Spätlese Trocken Rheingau Rüdesheimer Berg Rottland 1993: Subtle with very good intensity of dried apricot and citrus flavor. Medium body, dry and a delicate, crisp finish. Drinkable now. • $NA • (11/30/94) • **88**

Riesling Spätlese Trocken Rheingau Rüdesheimer Berg Rottland 1992 • $14 • (11/30/93) • **86**

LIESER, SCHLOSS

Riesling Auslese Mosel Lieser Niederberg-Helden 1993: A deceptive wine with a lovely balance of sweet, creamy fruit and crisp acidity. Long aftertaste of melons and apples. Delicious to drink now but will improve with age. • $22 • (11/30/94) • **88**

Riesling Auslese Mosel Lieser Niederberg-Helden Two Stars 1993: Absolutely delicious and bubbling over with crushed fruit character. Medium- to full-bodied with sweet, melon, apple flavors. Fine acidity. Drinkable now. • $30 • (11/30/94) • **89**

Riesling Spätlese Mosel Lieser Niederberg-Helden 1993: Standard, good quality Mosel with fresh apple and mineral aromas and flavors. Medium-bodied and sweet with a delicate finish. • $16 • (11/30/94) • **84**

LINGENFELDER

Riesling Auslese Halbtrocken Pfalz Freinsheimer Goldberg 1993: Extremely spicy, rich and round, showing lovely, opulent flavors. Full in body and lightly sweet. Delicious as an apéritif or accompanying food. 200 cases made. • $18 • (11/30/94) • **90**

Riesling Auslese Trocken Pfalz Freinsheimer Goldberg 1993: Plenty of tropical fruit, vanilla and spice character. Full-bodied and dry with a round mouth-feel and very good finish. • $15 • (11/30/94) • **86**

Riesling Spätlese Pfalz Grosskarlbacher Osterberg 1993: Perplexing wine with an excellent delicate rose petal, floral aroma but it's rather thick and and very rich on the palate with ripe fruit and an oily finish. Drinkable now. 1,000 cases made. • $15 • (11/30/94) • **87**

Scheurebe Kabinett Trocken Pfalz Grosskarlbacher Burweg 1993: A delicious dry wine, with lovely floral, hay and apple notes. A little more delicate in flavors than aroma. Medium-bodied and balanced. 300 cases made. • $13 • (11/30/94) • **85**

Scheurebe Spätlese Pfalz Freinsheim 1993: Very intense, like a top late-harvest Alsace Pinot Gris. Full body, medium sweetness, with loads of ripe, spicy, almond and toast notes. Very long aftertaste. Drinkable now or hold. 300 cases made. • $16 • (11/30/94) • **91**

LOOSEN, DR.

Riesling Auslese Gold Cap Mosel Erdener Prälat 1993: Bursting with fruit, thick and honey-like in both texture and flavors. Loads of apple and floral nuances. Full in body, sweet yet very crisp. Drinkable now. • $61 • (11/30/94) • **94**

Riesling Auslese Gold Cap Mosel-Saar-Ruwer Erdener Prälat 1994: Delivers what you expect from a gold cap auslese. Yellow in color, with dried fruit, spice and orange peel in the aromas and flavors. Full body and very sweet palate, with a long, crisp finish. Excellent aging potential. Better in 1997 or later. • $65 • (11/30/95) • **93**

Riesling Auslese Gold Cap Mosel-Saar-Ruwer Urziger Würzgarten 1994: Beautifully balanced, with penetrating flavors of lemon, lime and cream, even buttressed by a hint of pie crust. Sweet and medium-bodied, but with crisp acidity. Drinkable now. • $47 • (11/30/95) • **91**

Riesling Auslese Long Gold Cap Mosel Erdener Prälat 1993: Supercharged Mosel. Deep yellow in color with very, very ripe fruit, honey aromas and flavors. High-tension acidity with the sweet-and-sour character of a top-class ice wine. Superb. Undeveloped. Drinkable now.(auction bottling). • $225 • (11/30/94) • **96**

Riesling Auslese Long Gold Cap Mosel-Saar-Ruwer Erdener Prälat 1994: A great beerenauslese in all but name. Formidable, intense dried fruit aromas and flavors, very full and sweet, but impeccably balanced. Waves of honey flavors pour over the palate. Has the presence to age into 2000. • $NA • (11/30/95) • **95**

Riesling Auslese Mosel Erdener Prälat 1992 • $35 • (11/30/93) CS • **95**

Riesling Auslese Mosel-Saar-Ruwer Erdener Prälat 1994: This is the real thing: Rich and beautiful dried apricot, honey and lemon character supported by a hint of earth. Full-bodied, medium sweetness and a long, flavorful finish. Drinkable now, but try aging. • $44 • (11/30/95) • **92**

Riesling Auslese Mosel-Saar-Ruwer Graacher Himmelreich 1991 • $35 • (12/15/92) • **92**

Riesling Auslese Mosel-Saar-Ruwer Urziger Würzgarten 1994: Impressive, big and ripe, with tropical fruit, pineapple and honey aromas and flavors. A full-bodied, medium-sweet Riesling that has lovely rich fruit character. Drinkable now. • $34 • (11/30/95) • **91**

Riesling Auslese Mosel-Saar-Ruwer Wehlener Sonnenuhr 1991 • $28 • (12/15/92) • **91**

Riesling Auslese Mosel Wehlener Sonnenuhr 1993: Delicious rich auslese with loads of fruit on the palate and sweet, spicy, mineral flavors. Full-bodied, crisp acidity, long finish. Drinkable now. • $31 • (11/30/94) • **91**

Riesling Auslese Mosel Wehlener Sonnenuhr 1992 • $23 • (11/30/93) CS • **93**

Riesling Beerenauslese Mosel Wehlener Sonnenuhr 1992 • $377 • (11/30/93) • **96**

Riesling Eiswein Mosel-Saar-Ruwer Erdener Prälat 1991 • $537 • (12/15/92) • **94**

Riesling Kabinett Mosel Erdener Treppchen 1993: Lots of carbon dioxide with lemon, apple and mineral notes on the nose and palate. Medium in body, medium-sweet and an attractive balance of acidity on the finish. Drinkable now. • $15 • (11/30/94) • **88**

Riesling Kabinett Mosel Erdener Treppchen 1992 • $14 • (11/30/93) • **88**

Riesling Kabinett Mosel-Saar-Ruwer Erdener Prälat 1991 • $24 • (12/15/92) • **87**

Riesling Kabinett Mosel-Saar-Ruwer Erdener Treppchen 1994: A big, rich kabinett, but it doesn't quite pull it off in the end. A medium-bodied wine with intense cake, spice and baked apple aromas and flavors that are only slightly sweet, but it's a little too soft on the finish. • $17 • (11/30/95) • **85**

Riesling Kabinett Mosel-Saar-Ruwer Erdener Treppchen 1991 • $16 • (12/15/92) • **89**

Riesling Kabinett Mosel-Saar-Ruwer Wehlener Sonnenuhr 1994: A marvellous wine, but almost too much for this category. The very seductive peach and dried apricot character is supported by its lovely rich texture. Drinkable now, but will be interesting to age. • $16 • (11/30/94) • **88**

Riesling Spätlese Mosel Erdener Prälat 1992 • $25 • (11/30/93) • **93**

Riesling Spätlese Mosel Erdener Treppchen 1992 • $18 • (11/30/93) • **91**

Riesling Spätlese Mosel-Saar-Ruwer Erdener Treppchen 1994: Very lush, complex peach and spice aromas followed by fully concentrated and beautifully balanced layers of fruit flavor. This has high acidity, but is very well integrated, and drives though to a long, powerful finish. Drinkable now. • $27 • (11/30/95) • **90**

Riesling Spätlese Mosel-Saar-Ruwer Urziger Würzgarten 1994: Wonderful ripe peach and apricot aromas and flavors with excellent concentration. Not terribly sweet, but full of flavor. Drinkable now. • $29 • (11/30/95) • **89**

Riesling Spätlese Mosel-Saar-Ruwer Urziger Würzgarten 1991 • $23 • (12/15/92) • **91**

Riesling Spätlese Mosel-Saar-Ruwer Wehlener Sonnenuhr 1991 • $21 • (12/15/92) • **87**

Riesling Spätlese Mosel Urziger Würzgarten 1993: Very impressive for the vintage showing vivacious fruit character throughout. Medium-to full-bodied with sweet, ripe apple and apricot flavors, fine acidity and a long aftertaste. Delicious now. • $25 • (11/30/94) • **92**

Riesling Trockenbeerenauslese Mosel-Saar-Ruwer Urziger Würzgarten 1994: Spellbinding noble rot character in this classic Riesling. Golden almond in color. Massive and very sweet, with loads of burnt almond, dried apricot and exotic spice flavors. This can go on and on, better in 2000. • $NA • (11/30/95) • **96**

Riesling Trockenbeerenauslese Mosel-Saar-Ruwer Wehlener Sonnenuhr 1991 • $53 • (12/15/92) • **97**

Riesling Trockenbeerenauslese Mosel Wehlener Sonnenuhr 1993: The essence of raisins in this incredibly ripe monster. Dark yellow-red-amber in color with dried raisin aromas and flavors. Syrupy consistency and very sweet, fruity character. Long, sweet but fresh finish. Drinkable now but better in 1998. • $NA • (11/30/94) • **93**

Key: SS—Spectator Selection. CS—Cellar Selection. BB—Best Buy. $NA—Price not available. (BT)—Barrel tasting. (A)—Auction Price.
Dates in parentheses represent the issues in which the ratings were published.

LOWENSTEIN, FURST

Riesling Beerenauslese Rheingau 1994: Is this really a beerenauslese? With its medium body and modest richness, this could easily be taken for standard auslese. Rather light for this category, but still good overall. Short and candied finish. Drinkable now. From Schloss Vollrads. • $NA • (11/30/95) • **83**

Riesling Kabinett Trocken Rheingau 1992 • $NA • (11/30/93) • **72**

MERKELBACH, ALFRED

Riesling Auslese Mosel Erdener Treppchen Nr. 11 1992 • $11 • (11/30/93) • **84**

Riesling Auslese Mosel Urziger Würzgarten 1992 • $NA • (11/30/93) • **86**

Riesling Spätlese Mosel Erdener Treppchen Nr. 6 1992 • $11 • (11/30/93) • **86**

Riesling Spätlese Mosel Kinheimer Rosenberg 1992 • $9 • (11/30/93) • **84**

Riesling Spätlese Mosel Urziger Würzgarten 1992 • $10 • (11/30/93) • **86**

Riesling Spätlese Mosel Urziger Würzgarten Nr. 10 1992 • $10 • (11/30/93) • **83**

MESSMER

Riesling Auslese Pfalz Burrweiler Schäwer 1992 • $12 • (11/30/93) • **85**

Riesling Kabinett Pfalz Burrweiler Schlossgarten 1992 • $7 • (11/30/93) • **82**

Riesling Spätlese Trocken Pfalz Burrweiler Schäwer 1992 • $NA • (11/30/93) • **81**

Riesling Trockenbeerenauslese Pfalz Burrweiler Schäwer 1992 • $42 • (11/30/93) • **94**

Weissburgunder Beerenauslese Pfalz Burrweiler Schlossgarten 1992 • $23 • (11/30/93) • **86**

MILZ

Riesling Auslese Gold Cap Mosel Trittenheimer Leiterchen 1992 • $49 • (11/30/93) • **76**

Riesling Auslese Mosel Trittenheimer Apotheke 1992 • $22 • (11/30/93) • **84**

Riesling Auslese Mosel Trittenheimer Felsenkopf 1992 • $25 • (11/30/93) • **83**

Riesling Eiswein Mosel Trittenheimer Felsenkopf 1992 • $NA • (11/30/93) • **90**

Riesling Spätlese Mosel Neumagener Nusswingert 1992 • $15 • (11/30/93) • **84**

Riesling Spätlese Mosel Piesporter Hofberger 1992 • $15 • (11/30/93) • **89**

MOSELLAND

Riesling Kabinett Mosel-Saar-Ruwer Graacher Himmelreich 1992: Simple and straightforward with pleasant apple and peach flavors. An easy-to-drink wine with nice acidity, though it lacks concentration. • $9 • (08/31/94) • **79**

Riesling Kabinett Mosel-Saar-Ruwer Zeltinger Himmelreich 1992: Simple with green apple flavors and a tart finish. Light and unexciting. Nice fruity aromas, but an awkward wine overall. • $8 • (08/31/94) • **77**

Riesling Spätlese Mosel-Saar-Ruwer Graacher Himmelreich 1992: A good middle-of-the-road wine with strong peachy aromas and flavors. Typical for the vintage with appealing, but soft, fruit flavors. The finish is appley and minerally. • $10 • (08/31/94) • **82**

MULLER, EGON

Riesling Auslese Gold Cap Mosel-Saar-Ruwer Scharzhofberger 1994: A marvelously rich, honeyed wine that is full of dried fruit flavors. Full and very sweet, with zingy acidity and a long, lush finish. Drinkable now. • $NA • (11/30/95) • **90**

Riesling Auslese Gold Cap Saar-Ruwer Scharzhofberger 1993: Spellbinding concentration, with masses of lemon, spice, mineral and ripe fruit. Full-bodied and a honeyed character. Amazing ripeness and acidity. This is built for aging. Drinkable now or hold. • $58 • (11/30/94) • **95**

Riesling Auslese Gold Cap Saar-Ruwer Scharzhofberger 1992 • $49 • (11/30/93) • **93**

Riesling Auslese Mosel-Saar-Ruwer Scharzhofberger 1994: Loads of intense grapefruit character in this. Medium to full in body, with ripe fruit flavors and a crisp finish. Lovely balance. • $129 • **89**

Riesling Auslese Mosel-Saar-Ruwer Scharzhofberger 1991 • $103 • (12/15/92) • **81**

Riesling Auslese Mosel-Saar-Ruwer Scharzhofberger Gold Cap 1991 • $358 • (12/15/92) • **90**

Riesling Auslese Mosel-Saar-Ruwer Wiltinger Braune Kupp 1991 • $79 • (12/15/92) • **89**

Riesling Auslese Saar-Ruwer Scharzhofberger 1993: Absolutely massive flavors of honey, melon, lemon and spice. Full-bodied, with a hint of botrytis and fine acidity. Superb wine here. Drink or hold as long as you like. • $58 • (11/30/94) • **93**

Riesling Auslese Saar-Ruwer Scharzhofberger 1992 • $44 • (11/30/93) • **90**

Riesling Beerenauslese Mosel-Saar-Ruwer Scharzhofberger 1994: With the high acidity, this could almost be an eiswein. Very intense citrus and pineapple aromas and flavors, full body and very sweet, but the acidity balances superbly. Better in 1997. • $NA • (11/30/95) • **93**

Riesling Beerenauslese Mosel-Saar-Ruwer Scharzhofberger 1991 • $NA • (12/15/92) • **94**

Riesling Beerenauslese Saar-Ruwer Scharzhofberger 1993: Takes your breath away with its intense fruit and acidity. Full-bodied and very sweet, yet the lemon, mineral and spice flavors remain powerful. Has a long, long finish. Superb. Try now. • $NA • (11/30/94) • **98**

Riesling Eiswein Saar-Ruwer Scharzhofberger 1992 • $169 • (11/30/93) • **95**

Riesling Kabinett Mosel-Saar-Ruwer Scharzhofberger 1994: A straightforward Riesling: round-textured and easy-drinking, with apple and melon character. Medium body, sweet-tasting and soft on the finish. Could use a bit more depth. • $NA • (11/30/95) • **82**

Riesling Kabinett Mosel-Saar-Ruwer Scharzhofberger Nr. 11 1991 • $26 • (12/15/92) • **82**

Riesling Kabinett Mosel-Saar-Ruwer Scharzhofberger Nr. 12 1991 • $28 • (12/15/92) • **88**

Riesling Kabinett Saar-Ruwer Scharzhofberger 1993: A kabinett with fuller body. Has a lemony, mineral character, rather sweet and round. Drinkable now or hold. • $NA • (11/30/94) • **84**

Riesling Kabinett Saar-Ruwer Scharzhofberger 1992 • $24 • (11/30/93) • **82**

Riesling QbA Mosel-Saar-Ruwer Scharzhofberger 1994: A wine for hot summer days. Simple lime and green apple aromas and flavors in a light-bodied, off-dry wine. Tart finish. Drinkable now. • $NA • (11/30/95) • **79**

Riesling Spätlese Mosel-Saar-Ruwer Scharzhofberger 1994: Very good intensity of flavor in this wine—peach, apple, melon and a hint of spice. Medium body, with high acidity and enough sweetness to pull it off. Drinkable now. • $NA • (11/30/95) • **87**

Riesling Spätlese Mosel-Saar-Ruwer Scharzhofberger 1991 • $35 • (12/15/92) • **87**

Riesling Spätlese Mosel-Saar-Ruwer Wiltinger Braune Kupp 1991 • $31 • (12/15/92) • **82**

Riesling Spätlese Saar-Ruwer Scharzhofberger 1993: Generously fruity with peach, melon and mineral aromas and flavors. Medium body and sweetness with a fresh, round mouth-feel. Drinkable now or hold. • $NA • (11/30/94) • **86**

Riesling Spätlese Saar-Ruwer Scharzhofberger 1992 • $33 • (11/30/93) • **86**

MULLER, RUDOLF

Sparkling Mosel-Saar-Ruwer Mosel-Riesling Sekt 1986 • $7 • (10/15/88) • **84**

Sparkling Mosel-Saar-Ruwer Splendid Sektkellerei Gold NV • $6 • (06/30/87) • **66**

GERMANY

MULLER-CATOIR

Gewürztraminer Eiswein Rheinpfalz Haardter Herrenletten 1991 • $130 • (12/15/92) • **93**

Muskateller Eiswein Pfalz Haardter Bürgergarten 1993: Has exciting, brilliantly intense flavors, yet shows great finesse. Full-bodied and very sweet, but the wonderful acidity makes it fresh and delicate. Could drink it now, but it's built for aging. • $73 • (11/30/94) • **92**

Muskateller Kabinett Halbtrocken Pfalz Gelber Haardter Bürgergarten 1994: A big, juicy white that has lots of flavor. Intense almond and grapefruit character, medium body and sweetness, with a full finish. Drinkable now. • $23 • (11/30/95) • **87**

Muskateller Kabinett Trocken Rheinpfalz Gelber Haardter Bürgergarten 1991 • $18 • (12/15/92) • **86**

Rieslaner Auslese Pfalz Auslese Mussbacher Eselshaut 1994: Stunning honey and dried peach character shows through this big, concentrated Rieslaner. It has an elegance that makes it easy to drink, even with its very high acidity. Drinkable now, but can age well. • $30 • (11/30/95) • **93**

Rieslaner Spätlese Pfalz Mussbacher Eselshaut 1993: More like an Auslese. This is very rich with a dark yellow color and loads of ripe apple, orange aromas and flavors. Full-bodied and very sweet with a long spicy, honey finish. Drink now. 97 cases made. • $26 • (11/30/94) • **89**

Rieslaner Spätlese Trocken Rheinpfalz Mussbacher Eselshaut 1991 • $26 • (12/15/92) • **90**

Rieslaner Trockenbeerenauslese Pfalz Mussbacher Eselshaut 1994: A somewhat herbaceous note detracts from this otherwise rich and succulent sweet wine. You can't fault its balance or style. Falls just shy of outstanding. Drinkable now. • $75 • (11/30/95) • **89**

Rieslaner Trockenbeerenauslese Pfalz Mussbacher Eselshaut 1992 • $44 • (11/30/93) • **97**

Riesling Beerenauslese Pfalz Mussbacher Eselshaut 1992 • $35 • (11/30/93) • **95**

Riesling Eiswein Pfalz Haardter Herenletten 1992 • $42 • (11/30/93) • **90**

Riesling Eiswein Rheinpfalz Haardter Herzog 1991 • $122 • (12/15/92) • **92**

Riesling Kabinett Halbtrocken Pfalz Haardter Herrenletten 1994: A juicy and appealing medium-bodied white that shows citrus and almond character, but it lacks a bit of life and length. Drinkable now. • $21 • (11/30/95) • **82**

Riesling Kabinett Pfalz Haardter Bürgergarten 1994: Very appealing, subtle peach aromas and flavors make this a truly elegant wine that delivers all you expect from a Rhein kabinett. Good length and a dry-ish aftertaste. Drinkable now, but can also age. • $21 • (11/30/95) • **87**

Riesling Kabinett Pfalz Haardter Bürgergarten 1993: Rich and oily with spicy, bread dough aromas and flavors. Medium- to full-bodied and a long, rich finish. Off-dry. 105 cases made. • $17 • (11/30/94) • **85**

Riesling Kabinett Rheinpfalz Haardter Bürgergarten 1991 • $16 • (12/15/92) • **84**

Riesling Spätlese Halbtrocken Pfalz Gimmeldinger Mandelgarten 1992 • $16 • (11/30/93) • **93**

Riesling Spätlese Halbtrocken Pfalz Haardter Herzog 1993: Gorgeous, opulent style of off-dry Riesling exhibiting spicy, creamy, honey aromas and flavors. Full-bodied and quite oily with a fresh finish. 113 cases made. • $24 • (11/30/94) • **91**

Riesling Spätlese Pfalz Gimmeldinger Mandelgarten 1994: The ripe peach, honey and citrus aromas and flavors are difficult to resist. A medium-bodied spätlese with tiers of flavor. Fresh and elegant on the finish. Drinkable now. • $29 • (11/30/95) • **88**

Riesling Spätlese Trocken Pfalz Gimmeldinger Mandelgarten 1993: A very good, full-bodied, spicy dry wine with plenty of fruit to support the alcohol. Well-integrated acidity and a fresh finish. 36 cases made. • $23 • (11/30/94) • **88**

Riesling Spätlese Trocken Rheinpfalz Haardter Bürgergarten 1991 • $22 • (12/15/92) • **86**

Key: SS—Spectator Selection. CS—Cellar Selection. BB—Best Buy. $NA—Price not available. (BT)—Barrel tasting. (A)—Auction Price.
Dates in parentheses represent the issues in which the ratings were published.

Scheurebe Kabinett Pfalz Haardter Mandelring 1993: Big, boisterous and rich. Loads of spicy, exotic fruit. Full-bodied and off-dry, with a long, fruity finish. 124 cases made. • $19 • (11/30/94) • **87**

Scheurebe Kabinett Rheinpfalz Haardter Mandelring 1991 • $16 • (12/15/92) • **88**

Scheurebe Spätlese Pfalz Haardter Mandelring 1994: Lovely ripe peach and passion fruit aromas and flavors pour out of this full-bodied wine. Masses of fruit on a medium-sweet frame with excellent acidity and a long, lively finish. Drinkable now, but can age. • $28 • (11/30/95) • **88**

Scheurebe Spätlese Trocken Pfalz Haardter Mandelring 1992 • $14 • (11/30/93) • **89**

NAGLER, DR. HEINRICH

Riesling Kabinett Halbtrocken Rheingau Rüdesheimer Berg Rottland 1992 • $12 • (11/30/93) • **83**

Riesling Kabinett Rheingau Rüdesheimer Berg Roseneck 1992 • $12 • (11/30/93) • **85**

Riesling Spätlese Rheingau Rüdesheimer Berg Roseneck 1992 • $16 • (11/30/93) • **78**

Riesling Spätlese Trocken Rheingau Rüdesheimer Berg Schlossberg 1992 • $16 • (11/30/93) • **85**

NEIPPERG, GRAF VON

Rotwein QbA Württemberg 1993: This deep-colored, spicy wine has attractive peppery and herbal flavors with a tannic intensity that seems due more to extraction than ripeness. 1,800 cases made. • $10 • (03/31/95) • **80**

Schwarzriesling Neipperger Schlossberg 1992: The color of strong tea, this shows spicy, leathery, vegetal and light berry flavors in a light-bodied wine. Made from Pinot Meunier. 1,200 cases made. • $14 • (03/31/95) • **78**

NICOLAY, PETER

Riesling Auslese Mosel Erdener Prälat 1992 • $26 • (11/30/93) • **87**

Riesling Auslese Mosel-Saar-Ruwer Erdener Prälat 1994: Delicious and rich, with lots of peach and melon aromas. Full-bodied and medium-sweet, though it lacks a little punch on the finish. Drinkable now, but can age. From Dr. Pauly-Bergweiler. • $35 • (11/30/95) • **86**

Riesling Auslese Mosel-Saar-Ruwer Urziger Goldwingert 1994: Lovely peach and mineral aromas, medium body and quite sweet, but enough acidity and extract balances it out. Drinkable now. From Dr. Pauly Bergweiler. • $NA • (11/30/95) • **84**

Riesling Beerenauslese Mosel Urziger Würzgarten 1992 • $72 • (11/30/93) • **90**

Riesling Spätlese Mosel-Saar-Ruwer Erdener Prälat 1991 • $23 • (03/31/93) • **81**

Riesling Spätlese Mosel-Saar-Ruwer Urziger Goldwingert 1994: Creamy white peach and lime aromas and flavors. Medium body and moderate sweetness, but lacks depth on the finish. Drinkable now. From Dr. Pauly-Bergweiler. • $NA • (11/30/95) • **85**

PAULY-BERGWEILER, DR.

Riesling Auslese Mosel Bernkasteler Alte Badstube am Doctorberg 1992 • $32 • (11/30/93) • **85**

Riesling Auslese Mosel Bernkasteler Lay 1993: Big and rich although it has a slilght resinous edge. Full-bodied and sweet with a long peach finish. • $NA • (11/30/94) • **80**

Riesling Auslese Mosel-Saar-Ruwer Bernkasteler Alte Badstube am Doctorberg 1991 • $50 • (03/31/93) • **83**

Riesling Auslese Mosel-Saar-Ruwer Bernkasteler Lay 1994: A lovely white that ought to have been sold as a top spätlese. Medium-bodied, good structure, with plenty of sweetness and acidity. Drinkable now, but can age. • $21 • (11/30/95) • **86**

Riesling Beerenauslese Mosel Bernkasteler Alte Badstube am Doctorberg 1993: This would be a fine Auslese but seems a little out of place as a BA. Still there's some very good citrus, ripe peach character and sweet fruit. Drinkable now. • $55 • (11/30/94) • **85**

Riesling Beerenauslese Mosel-Saar-Ruwer Bernkasteler Badstube 1994: Pleasant lemon and spice flavors, but a bit light for a beerenauslese.

GERMANY

Medium body and sweetness, with a crisp finish. Drinkable now. • $NA • (11/30/95) • **84**

Riesling Beerenauslese Mosel-Saar-Ruwer Bernkasteler Lay 1994: Wonderful honey, peach, cream and almond flavors in a medium-bodied package that has real concentration. A very long finish shows off intense peach flavors. Better in 1997. • $33 • (11/30/95) • **90**

Riesling Eiswein Mosel Graacher Himmelreich 1992 • $NA • (11/30/93) • **86**

Riesling Eiswein Mosel-Saar-Ruwer Graacher Himmelreich 1991 • $60 • (01/31/93) • **89**

Riesling Kabinett Mosel Bernkasteler Alte Badstube am Doctorberg 1993: Pretty, fresh flavors and crisp acidity in this white. Medium-bodied and fruity with apple pie, raspberry character. • $NA • (11/30/94) • **81**

Riesling Kabinett Mosel Bernkasteler Alte Badstube am Doctorberg 1992 • $16 • (11/30/93) • **84**

Riesling Kabinett Mosel-Saar-Ruwer Bernkasteler Alte Badstube am Doctorberg 1994: A very pleasant kabinett to enjoy now. Lots of fresh fruit and a lively balance of crisp acidity and modest sweetness, only it turns simple on the finish. • $25 • (11/30/95) • **82**

Riesling Kabinett Mosel-Saar-Ruwer Bernkasteler Alte Badstube am Doctorberg 1991 • $23 • (03/31/93) • **78**

Riesling Kabinett Mosel-Saar-Ruwer Brauneberger Juffer 1991 • $16 • (03/31/93) • **75**

Riesling Kabinett Mosel-Saar-Ruwer Wehlener Sonnenuhr 1994: Extremely fresh and lively, but the tart peach and pear aromas are nothing special. Light body, refreshing acidity and modest depth on the finish. Drinkable now, but may improve with age. • $NA • (11/30/95) • **83**

Riesling Spätlese Mosel Bernkasteler Alte Badstube am Doctorberg 1992 • $21 • (11/30/93) • **84**

Riesling Spätlese Mosel-Saar-Ruwer Bernkasteler Alte Badstube am Doctorberg 1994: Some real depth and concentration in this balances the sweet palate. Medium body, fresh acidity and full of flavor. A substantial finish keeps your attention. Drinkable now, interesting to age. • $27 • (11/30/95) • **86**

Riesling Spätlese Mosel-Saar-Ruwer Bernkasteler Badstube 1994: Simple aromas and flavors of green apple mix with juicy melon notes. The soft acidity and medium body make this immediately appealing. • $24 • (11/30/95) • **85**

Riesling Spätlese Mosel-Saar-Ruwer Bernkasteler Doctor 1994: Very floral, creamy and appealing. Medium body and sweetness, supple acidity and a fairly long finish. Drinkable now, but can age. • $47 • (11/30/95) • **85**

Riesling Trockenbeerenauslese Mosel Bernkasteler Alte Badstube am Doctorberg 1993: Not a typical TBA in richness, but delicious nonetheless. Intense citrus, honey and raisin character. Medium-bodied and medium in concentration with a sweet, rich finish. • $70 • (11/30/94) • **84**

Riesling Trockenbeerenauslese Mosel-Saar-Ruwer Bernkasteler Badstube am Doctorberg 1994: More like an eiswein that has incredibly harsh acidity. Full-bodied and very intense, with buttered popcorn, lemon and lime aromas and flavors. Very sweet. Perhaps will improve with bottle age, try in 2000. • $NA • (11/30/95) • **86**

PAZEN, WEINGUT HERBERT

Riesling Hochgewächs Mosel-Saar-Ruwer Zeltinger Himmelreich 1991 • $9 • (01/31/93) • **81**

Riesling Kabinett Mosel-Saar-Ruwer Zeltinger Himmelreich 1991 • $11 • (01/31/93) • **83**

PETERSHOF, WEINGUT

Riesling Kabinett Mosel-Saar-Ruwer Eitelsbacher Marienholz 1994: A little on the sweet side. Nice peach and apple flavors finish with an earthy accent. 300 cases made. • $8 • (11/30/95) • **80**

Riesling Spätlese Mosel-Saar-Ruwer Eitelsbacher Marienholz 1994: 400 cases made. • $10 • (11/30/95) • **0**

PFEFFINGEN

Riesling Auslese Pfalz Ungsteiner Hönigsäckel 1993: Very fresh and bubbling over with clove honey, apple, and pear character with a hint of dough. medium-bodied, sweet and fresh on the finish. Drink now. 835 cases made. • $23 • (11/30/94) • **88**

Riesling Kabinett Trocken Pfalz Ungsteiner Hönigsäckel 1992 • $13 • (11/30/93) • **84**

Riesling Spätlese Halbtrocken Pfalz Ungsteiner Herrenberg 1992 • $17 • (11/30/93) • **83**

Riesling Spätlese Trocken Pfalz Ungsteiner Herrenberg 1993: We have never tasted wine like this. Rich and dry with licorice, fruity character. Very attractive off-dry wine but not for everyone. Drinkable now. • $18 • (11/30/94) • **83**

Riesling Spätlese Trocken Pfalz Ungsteiner Herrenberg 1992 • $21 • (11/30/93) • **87**

Riesling Spätlese Trocken Pfalz Ungsteiner Weilberg 1992 • $18 • (11/30/93) • **82**

Scheurebe Auslese Pfalz Ungsteiner Herrenberg 1993: Dramatic, rich and spicy. Full-bodied and sweet, but doesn't quite come through on the finish. • $32 • (11/30/94) • **84**

Scheurebe Spätlese Pfalz Ungsteiner Herrenberg 1992 • $17 • (11/30/93) • **85**

PRUM, JOH. JOS.

Riesling Kabinett Mosel Urzinger Würzgarten 1993: Slightly better on the nose than the palate with typical Mosel mineral and lemon aromas. Medium body, light sweetness and aftertaste. • $12 • (11/30/94) • **83**

Riesling Kabinett Mosel Wehlener Sonnenuhr 1993: Thick and earthy with aromas of ash and fruit. medium-bodied, lightly sweet and fruity but dull on the finish. Bottle sickness. Drink now. • $19 • (11/30/94) • **81**

Riesling Spätlese Mosel-Saar-Ruwer Wehlener Sonnenuhr 1991: Light in body, but tightly structured and full of flavor. This shows how underrated the best 1991 Mosel Rieslings are. The complex, tart peach, rhubarb and floral aromas follow through on the palate where the racy acidity masks most of the sweetness. Drinkable now. • $NA • (03/31/94) • **88**

Riesling Spätlese Mosel Wehlener Sonnenuhr 1993: Wonderfully fresh with ripe apple and melon aromas and flavors. Medium-bodied, medium-sweet, crisp finish. Delicious now. • $27 • (11/30/94) • **86**

REINHARTSHAUSEN, SCHLOSS

Rheingau Chard SpT Erbacher Reinhell 1994: Rather mature, with caramel and pie crust aromas. Full-bodied and rich, yet crisp. Rather simple, but has plenty of character. Soft finish. Drink now. • $NA • (11/30/95) • **84**

Riesling Auslese Rheingau Erbacher Schlossberg 1993: Nicely textured Auslese with round and sweet flavors. Pleasant with its lemon, fruit, and honey character. Drink now. • $NA • **85**

Riesling Auslese Rheingau Erbacher Siegelsberg 1992 • $NA • (11/30/93) • **88**

Riesling Auslese Rheingau Hattenheimer Wisselbrunnen 1992 • $NA • (11/30/93) • **90**

Riesling Beerenauslese Rheingau Erbacher Marcobrunn 1992 • $NA • (11/30/93) • **84**

Riesling Beerenauslese Rheingau Hattenheimer Wisselbrunnen 1994: A magnificent bouquet of honey and dried fruit emanates from the glass. Full body, lusciously sweet, with a long finish. Needs some time yet to develop fully, try in 2000. • $NA • (11/30/95) • **89**

Riesling Beerenauslese Rheingau Hattenheimer Wisselbrunnen 1993: Underdeveloped at this stage. Intense aromas and flavors of honey, caramel and mushrooms, it's full in body and rich with a long, sweet, crisp finish. Better after 1997. Tasted twice. • $NA • (11/30/94) • **83**

Riesling Eiswein Rheingau Erbacher Michelmark 1993: Rather dull and lacking in true eiswein character. A good glass of sweet wine but where's the sweet and sour intensity you expect? Drink now. • $NA • (11/30/95) • **84**

Riesling Kabinett Halbtrocken Rheingau Hattenheimer Wisselbrunnen 1992 • $NA • (11/30/93) • **83**

Riesling Kabinett Halbtrocken Rheingau Kiedricher Sandgrub 1993: Lots of flavor in this dry wine, good match for light food. Lemon rind and peach character with fresh acidity and a flavorful finish. Drinkable now. • $NA • (11/30/94) • **86**

Riesling Spätlese Halbtrocken Rheingau Erbacher Schlossberg 1992 • $NA • (11/30/93) • **83**

Riesling Spätlese Rheingau 1993: Perhaps not as rich and intensely flavored as some in our tasting but still showing pretty, white peach and almond character. Light in body with balanced acidity. Drinkable now. • $NA • (11/30/94) • **82**

Riesling Spätlese Rheingau Erbacher Marcobrunn 1994: A big mouthful of peach flavor without any trace of heaviness. The fruit, sweetness and acidity are seamlessly integrated, and it's long and elegant on the finish. Drinkable now, but can age. • $NA • (11/30/95) • **85**

Riesling Spätlese Rheingau Hattenheimer Wisselbrunnen 1994: Pleasant, delicate style of spätlese, with mineral and pear character. Medium-bodied, lightly sweet, with pleasing flavors. Will improve with age. • $NA • (11/30/95) • **86**

Riesling Spätlese Trocken Rheingau Erbacher Marcobrunn 1992 • $NA • (11/30/93) • **81**

RHEINART

Riesling Auslese Mosel-Saar-Ruwer Ayler Kupp 1994: Disjointed, with herbal with onion flavors and aromas. Too funky. 200 cases made. • $12 • (11/30/95) • **72**

Riesling Kabinett Mosel-Saar-Ruwer Ockfener Bockstein 1994: An awkward wine with slightly dull, green apple flavors. 400 cases made. • $7 • (11/30/95) • **78**

Riesling Spätlese Mosel-Saar-Ruwer Ayler Kupp 1994: The modest green apple flavors are overshadowed by herbal notes. 300 cases made. • $9 • (11/30/95) • **77**

Riesling Spätlese Mosel-Saar-Ruwer Ockfener Bockstein 1994: A bit awkward. Has an odd, nut and herb taste. (First bottle flawed — 65 points). 500 cases made. • $9 • (11/30/95) • **75**

RICHTER, MAX FERD.

Riesling Auslese Mosel Graacher Domprobst 1993: Pretty, ripe, sweet fruit in this white displaying apricot and apple character. Medium body, medium acidity and a long, sweet finish. 222 cases made. • $28 • (11/30/94) • **87**

Riesling Auslese Mosel Graacher Domprobst 1992 • $23 • (11/30/93) • **84**

Riesling Auslese Mosel-Saar-Ruwer Brauneberger Juffer 1994: Extremely fresh and charming, with plenty of peach and citrus character, but a bit light-bodied for this category. The high acidity makes the finish rather tart. Drinkable now, or try aging. • $NA • (11/30/95) • **85**

Riesling Auslese Mosel-Saar-Ruwer Brauneberger Juffer-Sonnenuhr Two Stars 1994: Attractive ripe apple and pear aromas and flavors, but nowhere near enough depth to make it as a top auslese. Really flimsy at the finish. Drinkable now. • $NA • (11/30/95) • **79**

Riesling Auslese Mosel-Saar-Ruwer Veldenzer Elisenberg 1994: Quite rich and succulent but, oddly, a bit plain. Medium body and the sweetness tends to dominate the fruit. Drinkable now. • $31 • (11/30/95) • **83**

Riesling Auslese Mosel Veldenzer Elisenberg 1993: Round and fine with delicate cream, apple, spice character. Medium-bodied and medium-sweet with a fresh finish. Drink now or hold. 333 cases made. • $20 • (11/30/94) • **87**

Riesling Beerenauslese Mosel Brauneberger Juffer-Sonnenuhr 1993: Wonderful finesse in a very concentrated Riesling. Super-sweet and thick with fabulous honey, spicy, creamy character. Full-bodied yet elegant and a long, crisp finish. Drinkable now. 28 cases made. • $140 • (11/30/94) • **93**

Riesling Eiswein Mosel Mülheimer Helenenkloster 1993: Impressive clarity of fruit, brilliantly fresh with lemon, floral and spice character. Full in body yet very crisp and a long, clean finish. 55 cases made. • $120 • (11/30/94) • **90**

Key: SS—Spectator Selection. CS—Cellar Selection. BB—Best Buy. $NA—Price not available. (BT)—Barrel tasting. Ⓐ—Auction Price.
Dates in parentheses represent the issues in which the ratings were published.

Riesling Eiswein Mosel Mülheimer Helenenkloster 1992 • $NA • (11/30/93) • **79**

Riesling Kabinett Mosel Wehlener Sonnenuhr 1992 • $13 • (11/30/93) • **77**

Riesling Kabinett Mosel-Saar-Ruwer Brauneberger Juffer 1994: An attractive wine with a creamy character to its apple, melon and mineral aromas and flavors. Medium body and sweetness, with a light finish. Drink now or try holding in the cellar. • $NA • (11/30/95) • **84**

Riesling Kabinett Mosel-Saar-Ruwer Graacher Himmelreich 1994: Lovely peach character wrapped around a good structure. Good acidity, medium body and moderately sweet fruit flavor. Drinkable now. • $NA • (11/30/95) • **85**

Riesling Kabinett Mosel Wehlener Sonnenuhr 1993: Traditional, very sweet style of Kabinett with creamy, apple character. Rather simple and almost cloying, however. 278 cases made. • $15 • (11/30/94) • **82**

Riesling Spätlese Mosel Brauneberger Juffer 1992 • $15 • (11/30/93) • **83**

Riesling Spätlese Mosel Brauneberger Juffer-Sonnenuhr 1993: Very rich and sweet for a spätlese with honey and spice aromas and flavors. Medium-bodied, spicy aftertaste. Drinkable now. 222 cases made. • $19 • (11/30/94) • **87**

Riesling Spätlese Mosel Brauneberger Juffer-Sonnenuhr 1992 • $16 • (11/30/93) • **85**

Riesling Spätlese Mosel-Saar-Ruwer Brauneberger Juffer-Sonnenuhr 1994: Wonderful intensity of fruit: the floral, apple and melon character shows nicely. Light to medium in body, lightly sweet, with a fine acidity and a long, long finish. • $NA • (11/30/95) • **86**

Riesling Spätlese Mosel-Saar-Ruwar Graacher Domprobst 1994: Intense peach and mineral character makes this medium-bodied, lightly sweet Riesling extremely attractive, but the firm core of acidiy also gives it good aging potential, and makes the long finish very clean. Drink or hold. • $NA • (11/30/95) • **86**

Riesling Spätlese Mosel-Saar-Ruwer Wehlener Sonnenuhr 1994: Good concentration of ripe fruit for this vintage. Plenty of pie crust, apple and pear aromas and flavors packed into a medium-bodied package. Drinkable now, or try it after some aging. • $NA • (11/30/95) • **86**

Riesling Trockenbeerenauslese Mosel Brauneberger Juffer-Sonnenuhr 1992 • $300 • (11/30/93) • **94**

SAARSTEIN, SCHLOSS

Riesling Auslese Gold Cap Saar-Ruwer Serriger Schloss Saarsteiner 1993: Big and beautiful, with loads of ripe apple, pie crust and toast. Full-bodied and very rich, with a long, sweet, fruity finish. Drinkable now. 33 cases made. • $96 • (11/30/94) • **90**

Riesling Auslese Saar-Ruwer Serriger Schloss Saarsteiner 1993: Very big and rich for an auslese. Loads of ripe melon, cantaloupe and mineral aromas and flavors. Full-bodied and spicy, with a spritzy finish. Drinkable now. 111 cases made. • $29 • (11/30/94) • **90**

Riesling Auslese Saar-Ruwer Serriger Schloss Saarsteiner 1992 • $35 • (11/30/93) • **69**

Riesling Beerenauslese Saar-Ruwer Serriger Schloss Saarsteiner 1993: (Auction wine). A showy style, with ripe apricot, spice and lemon aromas and flavors. Full-bodied and round, very ripe fruit and a long, sweet, spicy finish. Quite enjoyable now. 33 cases made. • $NA • (11/30/94) • **94**

Riesling Eiswein Saar-Ruwer Serriger Schloss Saarsteiner 1993: A beautiful eiswein, with an elegant sweet-and-sour character and citrus on the long finish. Loads of spiciness coupled with sweet fruit and lively acidity. Drinkable now or hold. 33 cases made. • $114 • (11/30/94) • **90**

Riesling Eiswein Saar-Ruwer Serriger Schloss Saarsteiner 1992 • $NA • (11/30/93) • **92**

Riesling Kabinett Saar-Ruwer Serriger Schloss Saarsteiner 1993: Very, very tart, with a green apple character and full acidity on the finish. Interesting, but it needs time. Drinkable now. 1,225 cases made. • $12 • (11/30/94) • **85**

Riesling Kabinett Saar-Ruwer Serriger Schloss Saarsteiner 1992 • $11 • (11/30/93) • **70**

Riesling QbA Trocken Saar-Ruwer 1992 • $9 • (11/30/93) • **85**

Riesling Spätlese Saar-Ruwer Serringer Schloss Saarsteiner 1993: Clean and simple, with a pleasant apple character yet very sweet. Light finish. 333 cases made. • $18 • (11/30/94) • **82**

Riesling Spätlese Saar-Ruwer Serriger Schloss Saarsteiner 1992 • $17 • (11/30/93) • **88**

ST. ANTONY

Riesling Auslese Rheinhessen Niersteiner Hipping 1993: Great dessert wine. Wonderful dried apricot and super-ripe fruit aromas and flavors. Close to beerenauslese quality. Full-bodied, spicy, fruity and very sweet, yet the terrific acidity keeps it very fresh. Drinkable now. • $46 • (11/30/94) • **90**

Riesling Spätlese Saar-Ruwer Niersteiner Orbel 1993: Big and full-bodied with masses of spicy, mineral character. Medium-sweet and spicy on the finish with a slightly bitter aftertaste. Drink now. • $NA • (11/30/94) • **86**

Riesling Spätlese Trocken Rheinhessen Niersteiner Olberg 1993: Wonderful with food. Dry and massive like a top-notch Alsace Riesling, showing loads of spicy, dried apricot aromas and flavors. Excellent acidity and exceptionally intense character. Drinkable now. • $28 • (11/30/94) • **91**

Riesling Spätlese Trocken Saar-Ruwer Niersteiner Olberg 1993: Excellent for food. Dry and massive like a top-notch Alsace Riesling, with loads of spicy, dried apricot aromas and flavors. Excellent acidity and exceptionally intense character. Drink now or hold. • $NA • (11/30/94) • **91**

SALM-DALBERG, PRINZ ZU

QbA Nahe 1994: Clean, fresh and lively, with herbal and citrus flavors, a hint of sweetness, medium body and soft texture. • $7 • (12/15/95) • **80**

Riesling Auslese Nahe Wallhauser Johannisberg 1993: Good balance of honey, spicy character with just the right amount of sweetness and acidity to assure early drinking enjoyment. Drink now. 45 cases made. • $29 • (11/30/94) • **87**

Riesling Eiswein Nahe Schloss Wallhausen 1993: Wonderful, ripe almost burnt character with dried fruit, light maple syrup aromas and flavors. Full-bodied and super sweet with a soft texture. Drink now or hold. 28 cases made. • $110 • (11/30/94) • **91**

Riesling Kabinett Nahe Schloss Wallhausen 1994: Clean, fruity and fresh, with lively acidity and apple and citrus flavors to make it interesting. Nearly dry. • $13 • **84**

Riesling Kabinett Nahe Schloss Wallhausen 1993: Lovely grapefruit flavor in a fresh, crisp style. Full-bodied, off-dry, elegant and long on the palate. Delicious. Drinkable now. 378 cases made. • $13 • (11/30/94) • **89**

Riesling Spätlese Halbtrocken Nahe Schloss Wallhausen 1993: Very clean and pleasant with lovely lemon and spice aromas. Medium body and crisp finish. 211 cases made. • $18 • (11/30/94) • **85**

Riesling Spätlese Nahe Schloss Wallhausen 1993: Not giving much on the nose and palate. Full-bodied and lightly sweet but rather neutral on the finish. Drinkable now. 233 cases made. • $18 • (11/30/94) • **82**

Riesling Spätlese Nahe Wallhäuser Johannisberg 1994: A generous, full-flavored Riesling that's sweet but well balanced and marked by ripe, nutty apple and melon notes. • $15 • (12/15/95) • **85**

SCHAEFER, WILLI

Riesling Auslese Gold Cap Mosel Graacher Domprobst 1993: Classy and seamless offering layers of silky, sweet, ripe fruit. Full-bodied with fabulous honey, apple, creamy flavors. Long, long finish. Drinkable now. 25 cases made. • $47 • (11/30/94) • **92**

Riesling Auslese Mosel Graacher Domprobst 1993: Some real concentration in this very rich auslese, showing spice, ripe apple and apricot aromas and flavors. Full in body and packed with fruit all the way to the finish. Drinkable now. 29 cases made. • $NA • (11/30/94) • **91**

Riesling Auslese Mosel Graacher Domprobst 1992 • $22 • (11/30/93) • **87**

Riesling Auslese Mosel Graacher Himmelreich 1992 • $18 • (11/30/93) • **85**

Riesling Beerenauslese Mosel Graacher Domprobst 1993: Lively, sticky and sweet, displaying loads of lemon, lime and honey character. Full-bodied with a wonderfully long, sweet finish. Drinkable now. 62 cases made. • $43 • (11/30/94) • **94**

Riesling Beerenauslese Mosel Graacher Domprobst 1992 • $76 • (11/30/93) • **94**

Riesling Hochgewächs Mosel Graacher Domprobst 1992 • $9 • (11/30/93) • **78**

Riesling Kabinett Mosel Graacher Domprobst 1993: Surprisingly round and soft for a Mosel, with apple skin character. Medium in body and medium-sweet with a fruity finish. 200 cases made. • $13 • (11/30/94) • **82**

Riesling Kabinett Mosel Graacher Domprobst 1992 • $12 • (11/30/93) • **83**

Riesling Spätlese Mosel Graacher Domprobst 1993: Sweet, spicy, fruity character, medium body, medium acidity and a fresh finish. Drinkable now. (auction wine). 48 cases made. • $14 • (11/30/94) • **87**

Riesling Spätlese Mosel Graacher-Domprobst 1992 • $13 • (11/30/93) • **83**

SCHLEINITZ, VON

Riesling Auslese Mosel Koberner Uhlen 1992 • $18 • (11/30/93) • **79**

Riesling Auslese Mosel Koberner Weisenberg 1992 • $15 • (11/30/93) • **82**

Riesling Kabinett Mosel Koberner Weisenberg 1992 • $8 • (11/30/93) • **82**

Riesling QbA Halbtrocken Mosel Koberner Uhlen 1992 • $NA • (11/30/93) • **72**

Riesling Spätlese Halbtrocken Mosel Koberner Weisenberg 1992 • $9 • (11/30/93) • **78**

SCHMITT SCHENK

Riesling Auslese Mosel-Saar-Ruwer Longuicher Maximiner Herrenberg 1994: Appealing and fruity, with nice apple and apricot flavors. Slight sweetness is offset by a pleasantly spicy finish. 150 cases made. • $14 • **83**

Riesling Kabinett Mosel-Saar-Ruwer Bernkasteler Badstube 1994: Focused, with moderately concentrated green apple flavors and a hint of peach. Finish is a little tart. 400 cases made. • $9 • **82**

Riesling Kabinett Mosel-Saar-Ruwer Graacher Himmelreich Spätlese 1994: On the dry side, but plenty of apple flavor in a just-firm-enough structure. Slightly tart finish. 300 cases made. • $12 • **82**

Riesling Kabinett Mosel-Saar-Ruwer Trittenheimer Altarchen 1994: Sturdy, with green apple flavors and an earthy accent. Medium body and concentration. 200 cases made. • $9 • **81**

Riesling Kabinett Mosel-Saar-Ruwer Urziger Würzgarten 1994: Nicely smooth and ripe. Has balanced, well-defined apple and apricot flavors, would serve well as an apéritif. Finishes with a touch of honey. 250 cases made. • $9 • **85**

Riesling Spätlese Mosel-Saar-Ruwer Bernkasteler Badstube 1994: Has an earthy streak running through the good apple flavors. Nice acidity. Finish has a lime accent. 300 cases made. • $12 • **83**

Riesling Spätlese Mosel-Saar-Ruwer Erdener Treppchen 1994: A mouth-watering wine, showing luscious, rich apricot flavors and good concentration. Fairly sweet, but with a nice acidity. Honey notes on the finish. 250 cases made. • $12 • **87**

Riesling Spätlese Mosel-Saar-Ruwer Urziger Würzgarten 1994: Soft and rich, with enough acidity to keep the sweetness in check. Appealing baked apple and spice flavors and a lingering finish. 150 cases made. • $11 • **83**

SCHMITT SOHNE

Kabinett Mosel-Saar-Ruwer Wehlener Sonnenuhr Kabinett 1994: A sweet wine with faintly fruity flavors. Has an unpleasant foxy aroma. • $6 • (11/30/95) • **74**

Liebfraumilch Pfalz 1994: Soft and sweet, a simple wine with nice floral aromas, green apricot flavors and an earthy finish. • $4 • (11/30/95) • **79**

Mosel-Saar-Ruwer Bernkasteler Kurfürstlay Auslese 1993: A soft, simple wine with moderate apple and tangerine flavors. The flavors are clean, however, with a hint of rich sweetness on the finish. • $9 • (08/31/94) • **81**

Mosel-Saar-Ruwer Piesporter Michelsberg 1993: This is a fairly neutral wine, with moderate tangerine and apple flavors. Light and refreshing, but nothing exciting. • $5 • (08/31/94) • **80**

Mosel-Saar-Ruwer Zeller Schwarze Katz 1993: Peach and apple flavors dominate this solid and cleanly-made wine. Its acidity adds some nice zip and makes for a good, slightly-sweet quaff. • $5 • (08/31/94) BB • **82**

Niersteiner Gutes Domtal QbA Rheinhessen 1994: Ripe and balanced, with floral aromas and baked apple flavors. Finishes on a nicely spicy note. • $5 • (11/30/95) • **82**

Piesporter Goldtröpfchen Spätlese Mosel-Saar-Ruwer 1994: A bit candied and a little thin on the apple flavors. • $12 • (11/30/95) • **78**

Piesporter Michelsberg QbA Mosel-Saar-Ruwer 1994: Earthy, with nice green apple flavors. A bit sour on the finish. • $5 • (11/30/95) • **76**

Piesporter Michelsberg Spätlese Mosel-Saar-Ruwer 1994: Well-focused, with solid apricot and apple flavors, and a nice mineral note as well. Falls a bit short on the finish, but attractive nonetheless. • $8 • (11/30/95) • **83**

Riesling Auslese Mosel-Saar-Ruwer Schmitt Söhne 1993: Tastes mature for its age, with a hint of petrol. Peach and apple flavors otherwise dominate this fairly sweet and clumsy wine. The finish is a bit cloying. • $9 • (08/31/94) • **79**

Riesling Kabinett Mosel-Saar-Ruwer Piesporter Goldtröpfchen 1993: Firm, with moderate peach and apple flavors. A citrus note runs throughout this cleanly-made wine, which gives it a nice crispness. • $7 • (08/31/94) • **81**

Riesling Spätlese Mosel-Saar-Ruwer Piesporter Goldtröpfchen 1993: Pleasant and rich, with ripe peach and apple flavors and a good finish. The fruity aromas give way to a well-made Riesling. Flavorful and satisfying. • $9 • (08/31/94) • **84**

Schmitt Sohne Kabinett Riesling Mosel-Saar-Ruwer 1994: Austere and a bit astringent, with tarragon-like flavors and aromas. Tastes green. • $6 • (11/30/95) • **73**

Schmitt Sohne Spätlese Riesling Mosel-Saar-Ruwer 1994: Good, crisp apple flavors, nice acidity and a slightly herbal accent. Understated finish. • $7 • (11/30/95) • **81**

Zeller Schwarze Katz Mosel-Saar-Ruwer 1994: Oniony aromas and flavors dominate the moderately sweet flavors. • $5 • (11/30/95) • **75**

SCHONBORN, SCHLOSS

Riesling Auslese Rheingau Erbacher Marcobrunn 1993: Candied orange and marzipan flavors turn slightly bitter on the rather simple finish. Full-bodied and somewhat alcoholic. • $38 • (11/30/94) • **75**

Riesling Auslese Rheingau Erbacher Marcobrunn 1992: Just what you want from an Auslese: ripe, fruity aromas, a smooth, viscous texture, and a lingering, honeyed, but crisp finish. It is concentrated and distinctive, beginning with the deep gold color and continuing through the aftertaste. Tempting now, but hold. • $68 • (08/31/94) • **88**

Riesling Auslese Rheingau Geisenheimer Mäuerchen 1991 • $40 • (12/15/92) • **88**

Riesling Auslese Rheingau Rüdesheimer Berg Schlossberg 1993: Rather big, cloying and clumsy. Thick and sweet with bitter, fruity aftertaste. • $25 • (11/30/94) • **77**

Riesling Eiswein Rheingau Hattenheimer Nussbrunnen 1991 • $150 • (12/15/92) • **90**

Riesling Kabinett Rheingau 1992: An austerely textured, but concentrated wine with good apple and peach flavors. Well-made and flavorful with a good lingering finish that's dominated by mineral flavors. Weighty and powerful. Not just a simple quaffer. • $12 • (08/31/94) • **87**

Riesling Kabinett Rheingau Erbacher Marcobrunn 1991 • $22 • (12/15/92) • **86**

Riesling Kabinett Rheingau Hattenheimer Pfaffenberg 1991 • $15 • (12/15/92) • **85**

Riesling QbA Halbtrocken Rheingau 1991 • $9 • (12/15/92) • **86**

Riesling Spätlese Halbtrocken Rheingau Hattenheimer Pfaffenberg 1991 • $20 • (12/15/92) • **83**

Riesling Spätlese Rheingau 1992: Not the best-balanced Riesling, but it has an appealing green-apple flavor. Average quality. Its tart fruit flavor doesn't mesh well with the sugary finish. • $20 • (08/31/94) • **78**

Riesling Spätlese Rheingau Erbacher Marcobrunn 1992: A well-balanced and interesting wine with ample fruit in the aromas and flavors, plus crisp acidity and a sense of restraint that gives it elegance. Reminds us of grapefruit and apricot. Off-dry. • $24 • (08/31/94) • **85**

Riesling Spätlese Rheingau Erbacher Marcobrunn 1991 • $30 • (12/15/92) • **84**

Riesling Spätlese Rheingau Hattenheimer Nussbrunnen 1991 • $22 • (12/15/92) • **87**

Riesling Spätlese Rheingau Hattenheimer Pfaffenberg 1993: More like a very good Auslese with a bounty of spicy, ripe fruit character. Full-bodied and sweet with a medium finish. Drinkable now. • $NA • **85**

Riesling Spätlese Rheingau Hattenheimer Pfaffenberg 1992: Generous in fruit, with grapefruity aromas and peachy-appley flavors. It is soft and sweet on the palate, with a short finish. Tasty and easy to drink. • $20 • (08/31/94) • **83**

Riesling Spätlese Rheingau Rüdesheimer Bischofsberg 1993: A sweeter spätlese with marzipan and fruit flavors, medium body and very sweet finish. Quite simple. • $21 • (11/30/94) • **78**

Riesling Spätlese Trocken Rheingau Hattenheimer Pfaffenberg 1991 • $22 • (12/15/92) • **75**

Riesling Trockenbeerenauslese Rheingau 1993: Not as big as some TBAs but a deliciously rich and exciting glass of dessert wine. Medium- to full-bodied with spicy honey flavors and a long, sweet finish. Drinkable now. • $NA • (11/30/94) • **89**

Riesling Trockenbeerenauslese Rheingau Hattenheimer Pfaffenberg 1992: Pungent aromas of roasted nuts, honey and a hint of truffles are intriguing. On the palate, the wine is rich and luscious, extremely sweet, but we'd like a bit more fruit and acid to keep it lively. A down comforter of a wine. • $325 • (11/30/93) • **81**

SCHUBERT, C. VON

Riesling Auslese Mosel-Saar-Ruwer Abtsberg 1991 • $35 • (12/15/92) • **83**

Riesling Auslese Mosel-Saar-Ruwer Maximin Grünhäuser Abtsberg 1994: An attractive auslese with pie crust, apple and honey character. Medium body and acidity, with a fresh finish. Delicious now. • $45 • (11/30/95) • **85**

Riesling Auslese Mosel-Saar-Ruwer Maximin Grünhäuser Abtsberg Fuder No. 47 1994: A bit disappointing to come from this winery. The fresh grapey, citrus character hardly has the depth and concentration you expect even from a regular auslese, let alone a special bottling. Modest structure and length. Drinkable now. • $67 • (11/30/95) • **84**

Riesling Auslese Mosel-Saar-Ruwer Maximin Grünhäuser Herrenberg 1994: Disappointing. Rather simple and mediocre for this category. Superficial and light, with modest fruit, soft acidity and no real depth. Drinkable now. • $NA • (11/30/95) • **80**

Riesling Auslese Mosel-Saar-Ruwer Maximin Grünhäuser Herrenberg Fuder No. 45 1994: Very fresh but complex floral, mineral and tart peach aromas and flavors. Medium body, but good intensity, and a long, racy finish. Drinkable now. • $58 • (11/30/95) • **87**

Riesling Auslese Saar-Ruwer Maximin Grünhäuser Abtsberg 1992 • $40 • (11/30/93) • **90**

Riesling Auslese Saar-Ruwer Maximin Grünhäuser Herrenberg 1992 • $33 • (11/30/93) • **91**

Riesling Eiswein Mosel-Saar-Ruwer Herrenberg 1991 • $120 • (12/15/92) • **86**

Riesling Kabinett Mosel-Saar-Ruwer Abtsberg 1991 • $18 • (12/15/92) • **84**

Riesling Kabinett Mosel-Saar-Ruwer Herrenberg 1991 • $17 • (12/15/92) • **84**

Riesling Kabinett Mosel-Saar-Ruwer Maximin Grünhäuser Abtsberg 1994: Extremely fresh and brimming with fruit. Light-bodied yet delivers a wealth of fruit aromas, very refreshing acidity and a touch of sweetness. Almost dry on the finish. Drinkable now, but could also take a little age. • $21 • (11/30/95) • **85**

Riesling Kabinett Mosel-Saar-Ruwer Maximin Grünhäuser Bruderberg 1994: Vibrant aromas that show a spicy, fruity character. Medium body and sweetness, firm acidity, but it becomes a little muddled on the finish. • $21 • (11/30/95) • **83**

Riesling Kabinett Mosel-Saar-Ruwer Maximin Grünhäuser Herrenberg 1994: A no nonsense spätlese. Extremely fresh chopped parsley and apple aromas, brimming with fruit flavor, and the tart acidity makes the medium finish very clean. Drinkable now, but try aging. • $21 • (11/30/95) • **85**

Riesling Kabinett Saar-Ruwer Maximin Grünhäuser Abtsberg 1992 • $21 • (11/30/93) • **87**

Key: SS—Spectator Selection. CS—Cellar Selection. BB—Best Buy. $NA—Price not available. (BT)—Barrel tasting. Ⓐ—Auction Price.
Dates in parentheses represent the issues in which the ratings were published.

Riesling Kabinett Trocken Mosel-Saar-Ruwer Maximin Grünhäuser Abtsberg 1994: A bit shocking for a kabinett. A bone-dry, medium-bodied white with mineral and apple flavors and a very dry finish. Drinkable now. • $22 • (11/30/95) • **83**

Riesling QbA Mosel-Saar-Ruwer Maximin Grünhäuser 1994: Pleasant drinking, if still a bit yeasty. Fresh grass and green apple character, light and quite sweet, but it's clean. Could use a bit more depth on the finish. • $16 • (11/30/95) • **82**

Riesling QbA Mosel-Saar-Ruwer Maximin Grünhäuser Abtsberg 1994: Amazing for a QbA. Full of crushed grape and melon character. Medium-bodied, off-dry and fresh, with a bounty of flavors. Crisp and long on the finish. Drinkable now. • $16 • (11/30/95) • **87**

Riesling QbA Saar-Ruwer Maximin Grünhäuser Abtsberg 1992 • $18 • (11/30/93) • **84**

Riesling QbA Trocken Mosel-Saar-Ruwer Maximin Grünhäuser Herrenberg 1994: Fresh and lively, but a bit lean. The citrus and mineral aromas and flavors are not quite matched by enough flesh and body to balance it out. Very tart finish. • $17 • (11/30/95) • **80**

Riesling Spätlese Mosel-Saar-Ruwer Abtsberg 1991 • $22 • (12/15/92) • **87**

Riesling Spätlese Mosel-Saar-Ruwer Maximin Grünhäuser Abtsberg 1994: A big mouthful of fruit without a hint of heaviness. Beautiful peach, melon and passion fruit character, very lively acidity and a long, racy finish. Drinkable now, but can age. • $27 • (11/30/95) • **89**

Riesling Spätlese Mosel-Saar-Ruwer Maximin Grünhäuser Herrenberg 1994: A bit modest for this quality level. Tart apple and peach aromas, light body and only modest depth. The high acidity makes it a bit angular at the finish. Drinkable now. • $25 • (11/30/95) • **82**

Riesling Spätlese Saar-Ruwer Maximin Grünhäuser Abtsberg 1992 • $26 • (11/30/93) • **90**

Riesling Trockenbeerenauslese Mosel-Saar-Ruwer Maximin Grünhäuser Abtsberg 1994: Not huge, but a solid trockenbeerenauslese. Rich with toffee, butter-brickle and honey character. Medium to full body, very sweet, with a long finish that opens up almond, honey and vanilla nuances. Drinkable now, but try aging. • $220 • (11/30/95) • **88**

SELBACH, J & H

Riesling Hochgewächs Halbtrocken Mosel-Saar-Ruwer 1991 • $7 • (01/31/93) • **75**

Riesling Kabinett Mosel-Saar-Ruwer Piesporter Goldtröpfchen 1991 • $11 • (01/31/93) • **81**

Riesling QbA Mosel-Saar-Ruwer Bereich Bernkastel 1991 • $6 • (01/31/93) • **81**

Riesling QbA Mosel-Saar-Ruwer Piesporter Michelsberg 1991 • $8 • (01/31/93) • **84**

SELBACH-OSTER

Riesling Auslese Gold Cap Mosel Zeltinger Sonnenuhr 1992 • $29 • (11/30/93) • **80**

Riesling Auslese Mosel Lieser Niederberg-Helden Two Stars 1993: Absolutely delicious and bubbling over with crushed fruit character. Medium- to full-bodied with sweet, melon, apple flavors. Fine acidity. Drinkable now. • $30 • (11/30/94) • **89**

Riesling Auslese Mosel-Saar-Ruwer Wehlener Sonnenuhr 1994: This is just what you look for in a top auslese, but will so rarely find in 1994. Lovely peach and melon aromas and flavors, the acidity exactly balancing the sweetness and very long and clean on the finish. • $34 • (11/30/95) • **90**

Riesling Auslese Mosel-Saar-Ruwer Zeltinger Schlossberg 1994: Very fresh and exotic spicy Riesling. Full-bodied, with elegant acidity and perfectly balanced sweetness. The long finish ripples with fruit. Drinkable now, but try it with some age. • $37 • (11/30/95) • **87**

Riesling Auslese Mosel-Saar-Ruwer Zeltinger Sonnenuhr One Star 1994: Characteristic auslese: honey, apple and dried apricot aromas and flavors. Medium body, with a long, spicy finish. Drinkable now, but can take a little age as well. • $39 • (11/30/95) • **88**

Riesling Auslese Mosel Zeltinger Sonnenuhr 1993: Intense yet subtle with citrus and floral aromas and flavors. Medium in body, rich apricot notes, modest sweetness and a fresh finish. Drinkable now. 67 cases made. • $25 • (11/30/94) • **88**

Riesling Auslese Mosel Zeltinger Sonnenuhr 1992 • $28 • (11/30/93) • **88**

Riesling Auslese Mosel Zeltinger Sonnenuhr Three Stars 1993: A big and rich style, full-bodied and round with opulent, ripe fruit and spice flavors. Medium finish. 25 cases made. • $29 • (11/30/94) • **90**

Riesling Beerenauslese Mosel-Saar-Ruwer Zeltinger Sonnenuhr 1994: Shows some mushroom notes now, but stunning concentration of fruit and just enough sweetness to balance the vibrant acidity. The finish is very long and complex. Real aging potential, better in 1998 and for decades afterwards. • $83 • (11/30/95) • **93**

Riesling Beerenauslese Mosel Zeltinger Sonnenuhr 1993: Big, ripe and very sweet with a raisiny, spicy character. A full-bodied and voluptuous style, long, sweet finish. Drinkable now. 40 cases made. • $73 • (11/30/94) • **89**

Riesling Eiswein Mosel Zeltinger Schlossberg 1992 • $61 • (11/30/93) • **86**

Riesling Kabinett Mosel-Saar-Ruwer Bernkasteler Badstube 1994: Not only very sweet in taste, but this even smells heavy and sweet. Full-bodied, rather heavy and over-blown for this category, and turns dull on the finish. • $14 • (11/30/95) • **78**

Riesling Kabinett Mosel Wehlener Sonnenuhr 1993: Good straightforward Mosel. Fresh and off-dry with lemon and apple aromas and flavors. Light in body and firm acidity. • $12 • (11/30/94) • **85**

Riesling Kabinett Mosel Wehlener Sonnenuhr 1992 • $11 • (11/30/93) • **84**

Riesling QbA Trocken Mosel-Saar-Ruwer Zeltinger Schlossberg 1991 • $12 • (01/31/93) • **82**

Riesling Spätlese Mosel Zeltinger Schlossberg 1992 • $14 • (11/30/93) • **83**

Riesling Spätlese Mosel Zeltinger Sonnenuhr 1993: A lovely silky wine with aromas and flavors of cream, apple and melons. Medium-bodied and medium-sweet with just the right amount of acidity. Drinkable now. 225 cases made. • $16 • (11/30/94) • **88**

Riesling Spätlese Mosel Zeltinger Sonnenuhr 1992 • $11 • (11/30/93) SS • **90**

Riesling Spätlese Mosel-Saar-Ruwer Wehlener Sonnenuhr 1994: A dull wine with some apple and banana aromas and flavors. Medium body, with a light finish. • $18 • (11/30/95) • **78**

Riesling Spätlese Mosel-Saar-Ruwer Zeltinger Schlossberg 1994: Has some lovely mineral and apple flavors, but not much after that. Medium-bodied and pleasantly sweet, but an extremely short aftertaste. Drinkable now. • $NA • (11/30/95) • **83**

Riesling Trockenbeerenauslese Mosel Zeltinger Sonnenuhr 1993: Another outstanding TBA, caramel, honey, spice and orange peel aromas and flavors abound. Full in body, very fruity and incredibly thick with a long, sweet, syrupy finish. Drinkable now. 14 cases made. • $168 • (11/30/94) • **92**

SICHEL

Bereich Bernkastel Mosel-Saar-Ruwer 1993: Interesting smoky, earthy, floral aromas, simple fruit flavors, soft texture and short finish. • $8 • (12/15/95) • **78**

Piesporter Michelsberg Mosel-Saar-Ruwer 1993: Average stuff: earthy, smoky aromas, simple fruit-juice flavors and soft texture. • $8 • (12/15/95) • **76**

Pinot Gris Pfalz 1993: A distinctive, very dry white with an intriguing, doughy aroma, unusual mineral flavors and a bitter-almond finish. • $8 • (12/15/95) • **82**

Pinot Noir Rotwein Pfalz Dornfelder 1992: A generic red, showing good color and a pleasant, soft chewiness in the mouth, but there's little fruit or character. • $6 • (03/31/95) • **77**

Riesling Pfalz 1993: This Riesling is austere, with herbal, smoky aromas and crisp grapefruit flavors. Off-dry. • $8 • (12/15/95) • **80**

Riesling Rheingau Bereich Johannisberg 1993: This is smoky and earthy in aroma, amply fruity and sweet in flavor and rather soft in texture. • $8 • (12/15/95) • **82**

Riesling Spätlese Mosel-Saar-Ruwer Piesporter Goldtröpfchen 1994: A friendly, easy-going wine that's sweet and fruity-tasting, but vague and simple in character. • $14 • (12/15/95) • **82**

Riesling White Pfalz 1993: Evolved aromas of petrol and pine show some maturity in this dry Riesling. There's good typicity, but lacks the fruit to balance the earth and petrol flavors. • $6 • (08/31/95) • **80**

Trockenbeerenauslese Pfalz Kirschheimer Kreuz 1990: An opulent, thick-textured, but light in alcohol dessert wine that's enjoyable but already mature. Has interesting apricot, prune and nut flavors. • $30 • (12/15/95) • **84**

White Mosel-Saar-Ruwer Zeller Schwarze Katz 1993: Light and pleasant, with peachy, smoky aromas and similar flavors. A touch of honey on the finish. • $8 • (12/15/95) • **81**

SICHEL SOHNE

Mosel Piesporter Michelsberg QbA 1992: This wine has herbal and mineral flavors with pungent, spicy aromas. Fairly light, and a bit awkward, with a stale-sweet finish. • $8 • (08/31/94) • **78**

Rheinpfalz Kirchheimer Kreuz Beerenauslese 1992: A simple, rather neutral wine, this shows light honey and herbal flavors with only modest sweetness and little acidity. Pleasant but not distinctive. • $14 • (11/30/93) • **77**

Riesling QbA Rheingau Bereich Johannisberg 1992: Classic petrol aromas give way to a crisp, austere wine, with just a touch of sweetness. Good mineral and spice flavors. Drinkable now. • $8 • (08/31/94) • **84**

SIMMERN, LANGWERTH VON

Riesling Auslese Rheingau Erbacher Marcobrunn 1991 • $59 • (12/15/92) • **86**

Riesling Auslese Rheingau Hattenheimer Nussbrunnen 1993: Imposing aromas and flavors of lemon curd and spice. Full-bodied and sweet with good acidity and a flavorful finish. • $NA • (11/30/94) • **87**

Riesling Auslese Rheingau Hattenheimer Nussbrunnen 1991 • $110 • (12/15/92) • **89**

Riesling Auslese Rheingau Rauenthaler Baiken 1992 • $68 • (11/30/93) • **84**

Riesling Beerenauslese Rheingau Erbacher Marcobrunn 1992 • $NA • (11/30/93) • **83**

Riesling Beerenauslese Rheingau Erbacher Marcobrunn 1991 • $152 • (12/15/92) • **89**

Riesling Eiswein Rheingau Eltviller Sonnenberg 1991 • $129 • (12/15/92) • **89**

Riesling Kabinett Halbtrocken Rheingau Kiedricher Sandgrub 1992 • $12 • (11/30/93) • **86**

Riesling Kabinett Rheingau Eltviller Sonnenberg 1992 • $14 • (11/30/93) • **84**

Riesling Kabinett Rheingau Erbacher Marcobrunn 1991 • $15 • (12/15/92) • **85**

Riesling Kabinett Rheingau Hattenheimer Nussbrunnen 1991 • $14 • (12/15/92) • **83**

Riesling Kabinett Rheingau Kiedricher Sandgrub 1993: Slightly dull lemon, earthy character. Light-bodied and delicately sweet with a light finish. • $NA • (11/30/94) • **82**

Riesling Kabinett Rheingau Rauenthaler Baiken 1993: Shockingly poor considering this estate's reputation. Some unclean flavors, light-bodied and slightly sweet. Tasted twice. • $NA • (11/30/94) • **70**

Riesling QbA Rheingau Hattenheimer Nussbrunnen 1991 • $11 • (12/15/92) • **82**

Riesling Spätlese Rheingau Erbacher Marcobrunn 1993: If you love marzipan, drink this. An explosion of sweet almond paste with some fruit and good acidity. A little too much for us, however. Strange bottle. • $NA • (11/30/94) • **80**

Riesling Spätlese Rheingau Hattenheimer Mannberg 1992 • $22 • (11/30/93) • **85**

Riesling Spätlese Rheingau Hattenheimer Mannberg 1991 • $20 • (12/15/92) • **89**

Riesling Spätlese Rheingau Hattenheimer Nussbrunnen 1993: Rather soft and straightforward with spice and fruit character, medium-to-light body and a light finish. • $NA • (11/30/94) • **81**

Riesling Spätlese Rheingau Hattenheimer Nussbrunnen 1992 • $30 • (11/30/93) • **87**

Key: SS—Spectator Selection. CS—Cellar Selection. BB—Best Buy. $NA—Price not available. (BT)—Barrel tasting. Ⓐ—Auction Price.
Dates in parentheses represent the issues in which the ratings were published.

Riesling Spätlese Rheingau Rauenthaler Baiken 1991 • $26 • (12/15/92) • **84**

Riesling Trockenbeerenauslese Rheingau Hattenheimer Nussbrunnen 1993: This may have been better marketed as a BA but it's outstanding anyway. Loads of botrytis, spice and ripe fruit character. Very sweet and full-bodied with a silky, very long finish. Tasted twice, first bottle volatile and harsh. Better after 2000. • $NA • (11/30/94) • **90**

STAATLICHEN WEINBAUDOMANEN

Riesling Eiswein Nahe Niederhäuser Hermannsberg 1992 • $NA • (11/30/93) • **91**

Riesling Kabinett Halbtrocken Nahe Schlossböckelheimer Felsenberg 1992 • $NA • (11/30/93) • **84**

Riesling Kabinett Nahe Schlossböckelheimer Kupfergrube 1992 • $NA • (11/30/93) • **83**

Riesling QbA Nahe Schlossböckelheimer Kupfergrube 1992 • $NA • (11/30/93) • **81**

Riesling Spätlese Nahe Niederhäuser Hermannsberg 1992 • $NA • (11/30/93) • **87**

STAATLICHER HOFKELLER WURZBURG

Kabinett Franken Hoffkeller 1993: Firm, dry and flavorful with a nice concentration of apple, lime and mineral flavors and some earthy and spicy notes. 4,000 cases made. • $14 • (11/30/94) • **84**

Silvaner Kabinett Trocken Franken Würzburger Stein 1993: Dry, and moderately concentrated with nutty and earthy flavors and a hint of honey. Pungent to the nose. • $14 • (11/30/94) • **81**

STAATSWEINGUTER

Riesling Auslese Gold Cap Rheingau Erbacher Marcobrunn 1993: Well made with a little spice and honey character but loads of ripe fruit. Delicious in a more elegant style. • $NA • (11/30/94) • **87**

Riesling Auslese Rheingau Steinberger 1993: Clean and fruity with spicy botrytis character but it could use a little more weight to it. Medium-bodied, medium-sweet and a spicy finish. Drink now. • $NA • (11/30/94) • **84**

Riesling Beerenauslese Rheingau Rauenthaler Baiken 1993: Beautiful, with fascinating caramel and lemon flavors. Very sweet and clean, full body, fresh acidity and long finish. Drinkable now. • $NA • (11/30/94) • **92**

Riesling Kabinett Rheingau Rauenthaler Baiken 1993: Another simple fresh wine with light floral, lemon character. Light-bodied and slightly sweet with a crisp finish. Drinkable now. • $NA • (11/30/94) • **81**

Riesling Spätlese Rheingau Erbacher Marcobrunn 1993: An interesting green apple and lavender character in this white, more like a kabinett than a spätlese. Medium- to light-bodied and medium-sweet, with a light finish. • $NA • (11/30/94) • **83**

Riesling Spätlese Rheingau Hochheimer Domdechaney 1993: Loads of mineral and spice. Medium-bodied and medium-sweet with a fresh, crisp finish. • $NA • (11/30/94) • **86**

THANISCH (MULLER-BURGGRAEFF), DR. H.

Riesling Auslese Mosel-Saar-Ruwer Bernkasteler Doctor 1994: Very fresh and lively, but is this really an auslese? Medium body and decent sweetness, with plenty of fruit, but this is more like a spätlese. Drinkable now. • $NA • (11/30/95) • **84**

Riesling Auslese Mosel-Saar-Ruwer Brauneberger Juffer-Sonnenuhr 1994: A blend of ripe fruit and high acidity, medium body and moderate sweetness. A nice, medium finish. Drinkable now. • $NA • (11/30/95) • **84**

Riesling Auslese Mosel-Saar-Ruwer Graacher Himmelreich 1994: Perhaps not what would be expected from an auslese, though this is a nice, medium-bodied, medium-sweet wine with fresh acidity and a clean finish. Drinkable now. • $NA • (11/30/95) • **85**

Riesling Beerenauslese Mosel-Saar-Ruwer Bernkasteler Doctor 1994: A wine that would be better as an auslese: some richness, but only medium body, with little depth or length. Drinkable now. • $NA • **82**

Riesling Kabinett Mosel-Saar-Ruwer Bernkasteler Badstube 1994: Like drinking a fresh fruit salad. Very clean but ultimately rather simple and light-bodied. Medium sweet and a bit short at the finish. • $NA • (11/30/95) • **82**

Riesling Kabinett Mosel-Saar-Ruwer Bernkasteler Doctor 1994: Tight, lean and lemony. A light, simple wine with just enough fruit to carry it through to the light, tart finish. • $NA • (11/30/95) • **82**

Riesling Kabinett Mosel-Saar-Ruwer Wehlener Sonnenuhr 1994: An unusually dry, substantial kabinett that has lots of depth. Aromas and flavors of fresh-cut peach and citrus. This is tight and chewy, with a long, intense finish. Drinkable now. • $NA • (11/30/95) • **85**

Riesling Spätlese Mosel-Saar-Ruwer Bernkasteler Graben 1994: Some apple and apricot character in this one, but it doesn't show enough depth on the finish. Medium body. • $NA • (11/30/95) • **82**

Riesling Spätlese Mosel-Saar-Ruwer Wehlener Sonnenuhr 1994: Has pretty peach and apple aromas and flavors, but a little boring on the finish. Medium-bodied and clean. Drinkable now. • $NA • (11/30/95) • **82**

THANISCH, DR. H.

Riesling Auslese Gold Cap Mosel Bernkasteler Doctor 1993: Not up to par. Little light for a special designation Auslese. Beautiful apple, creamy and floral character on the nose but lacking a bit of fruit concentration on the palate. Drinkable now. • $211 • (11/30/94) • **85**

Riesling Auslese Gold Cap Mosel Bernkasteler Doctor 1992 • $NA • (11/30/93) • **91**

Riesling Kabinett Mosel Bernkasteler Badstube 1993: Racy with an attractive intensity of mineral and apple character. Medium in body and medium-sweet with a spicy finish. Drinkable now. • $NA • (11/30/94) • **85**

Riesling Kabinett Mosel Bernkasteler Badstube 1992 • $13 • (11/30/93) • **78**

Riesling Kabinett Mosel Bernkasteler Doctor 1992 • $27 • (11/30/93) • **85**

Riesling Kabinett Mosel Wehlener Sonnenuhr 1992 • $10 • (11/30/93) • **78**

Riesling Spätlese Mosel Bernkasteler Doctor 1993: A delicious spätlese featuring plenty of peach, apple, creamy character on the nose and palate. Medium in body and round-textured with a medium-sweet finish. • $39 • (11/30/94) • **86**

Riesling Spätlese Mosel Bernkasteler Doctor 1992 • $43 • (11/30/93) • **84**

Riesling Spätlese Mosel Brauneberger Juffer 1992 • $18 • (11/30/93) • **69**

Riesling Spätlese Mosel Lieserer Niederberg-Helden 1992 • $12 • (11/30/93) • **81**

TYRELL

Riesling Auslese Gold Cap Mosel-Saar-Ruwar Eitelsbacher Karthäuserhofberg Füder No. 41 1994: Intense dried peach and spice aromas with a touch of dried fruit. Medium-bodied and very sweeet, with marvelous ripe fruit flavors and a very long, juicy finish. Drinkable now, but can age. • $NA • (11/30/95) • **90**

Riesling Auslese Gold Cap Mosel-Saar-Ruwer Eitelsbacher Karthäuserhofberg Füder No. 19 1994: Tasting this is like biting into a ripe honeydew melon. Medium body and sweetness, with delicious fruit flavors and a crisp finish. Drinkable now, but this can age. • $52 • **86**

Riesling Auslese Gold Cap Saar-Ruwer Eitelsbacher Karthäuserhofberg 1993: Doesn't have the weight of a Gold Cap. Yet it shows pretty fresh fruit and a pleasant sweetness with a medium body and a medium finish. Drink now. • $80 • **85**

Riesling Auslese Gold Cap Saar-Ruwer Eitelsbacher Karthäuserhofberg Füder No. 43 1993: Plenty of fresh-crushed fruit character and sweetness. Medium-to-full body, with mineral and licorice flavors and a sweet finish. Drink or hold. • $NA • (11/30/94) • **88**

Riesling Auslese Mosel-Saar-Ruwer Eitelsbacher Karthäuserhofberg 1994: As a top spätlese, great. But as an auslese? Still, this is clean and fresh, with lovely honey, pie crust and apple character. Medium body and lightly sweet, showing crisp acidity to balance. Drinkable now. • $35 • **85**

Riesling Auslese Saar-Ruwer Eitelsbacher Karthäuserhofberg 1993: Steely and fresh, with bubbly melon and fruit character. Medium-to-full body, medium sweetness and a fresh, crisp finish. Drinkable now. • $33 • (11/30/94) • **88**

Riesling Auslese Saar-Ruwer Eitelsbacher Karthäuserhofberg 1992 • $31 • (11/30/93) • **84**

Riesling Auslese Saar-Ruwer Eitelsbacher Kathäuserhofberg Füder No. 30 1993: Medium-weight for an auslese. Yet it shows attractive fresh fruit and pleasant sweetness, with medium body and finish. • $80 • (11/30/94) • **85**

Riesling Eiswein Saar-Ruwer Eitelsbacher Karthäuserhofberg Füder No. 34 1993: More like a big spätlese than a proper eiswein. Medium-to-light body, a fresh lemon and apple character and a sweet finish. • $NA • (11/30/94) • **83**

Riesling Kabinett Halbtrocken Saar-Ruwer Eitelsbacher Karthäuserhofberg 1992 • $14 • (11/30/93) • **83**

Riesling Kabinett Mosel-Saar-Ruwer Eitelsbacher Karthäuserhofberg 1994: Lots of apple and peach aromas flow from this medium-bodied, slightly sweet wine. Clean acidity gives the finish an extra push. Drinkable now or try aging. • $17 • **85**

Riesling Kabinett Saar-Ruwer Eitelsbacher Karthäuserhofberg 1993: Crystal clear and fresh, with delicate apple and melon aromas and flavors. Light-bodied, barely sweet, with fresh, fruity acidity. Pleasing finish although very crisp. Drinkable now. • $15 • (11/30/94) • **88**

Riesling QbA Halbtrocken Saar-Ruwer Eitelsbacher Karthäuserhofberg 1992 • $11 • (11/30/93) • **83**

Riesling QbA Mosel-Saar-Ruwer Eitelsbacher Karthäuserhofberg 1994: Appealing floral and melon character makes this wine very easy to enjoy. Light-bodied and plenty of flavor. A supple finish, too. Drinkable now. • $14 • **83**

Riesling Spätlese Mosel-Saar-Ruwer Eitelsbacher Karthäuserhofberg 1994: Extremely fresh and vibrant, but a little bottle sick. Marvelously lively fruit and refreshing acidity, but not terribly concentrated. Drinkable now, maybe better with age. • $23 • **84**

Riesling Spätlese Saar-Ruwer Eitelsbacher Karthäuserhofberg 1993: Extremely fresh wine with vivid peach, melon character. Medium-bodied and slightly sweet, this wine is a live wire with crisp acidity and jazzy fruit flavors. Tasted twice. Second bottle much better. Drinkable now or hold. • $20 • (11/30/94) • **86**

Riesling Spätlese Saar-Ruwer Eitelsbacher Karthäuserhofberg 1992 • $19 • (11/30/93) • **80**

VALCKENBERG

Madonna Bereich Wonnegau Rheinhessen 1994: An attractive white blend from Germany that offers generous aromas of apricot and pineapple, lots of fruit flavor and lingering hints of honey and apricot on the finish. Nicely balanced with fresh acidity, at an agreeable price. 3,200 cases made. • $7 • (12/15/95) • **86**

Pfalz Dornfelder 1992: Hard to believe this comes from a northern vineyard-it's so deep-colored and ripe with fruit. Still it's simple and the finish is short. 1,200 cases made. • $8 • (03/31/95) • **79**

Pinot Blanc QbA Rheinhessen 1993: A light, almost delicate white wine with floral, peachy aromas and pleasant fruit flavors. Light-bodied and easy to drink. 1,000 cases made. • $7 • (11/30/94) • **82**

Pinot Blanc Rheinhessen 1994: A tart, bracing, dry Pinot Blanc with vivid grapefruit flavor and firm acidity. Smells ripe and exotic, turns leaner on the palate, but has depth. • $6 • (12/15/95) • **83**

Rheinhessen 1994: Average quality Riesling. It has tinny aromas, simple flavors of canned fruit and a tart finish. • $6 • (12/15/95) • **79**

Rheinhessen Madonna Bereich Wonnegau Kabinett QmP 1993: A soft-textured, easy going sweet wine with aromas that remind us of Gewürztraminer but that doesn't deliver much fruit on the palate. 7,500 cases made. • $7 • (11/30/94) • **77**

Riesling Kabinett Rheinhessen 1993: Simple and a bit flat in texture, with weak apple and mineral flavors. Not bad, but not interesting either. 1,200 cases made. • $7 • (11/30/94) • **78**

VOLLMER, HEINRICH

Pinot Blanc Kabinett Trocken Mosel-Saar-Ruwer Ellerstadter Kirchenstück 1991 • $9 • (01/31/93) • **81**

VOLLRADS, SCHLOSS

Riesling Auslese Rheingau 1994: A lovely, rich and creamy wine that offes some spicy botrytis character. Full-bodied but a little softer in texture. Good length. Drinkable now. • $55 • (11/30/95) • **85**
Riesling Kabinett Halbtrocken Rheingau 1994: The green apple and grass aromas have some appeal, but it's very light, lean and tart, with an aggressively acidic finish. Like a cheap Italian white. • $17 • (11/30/95) • **77**
Riesling Kabinett Halbtrocken Rheingau 1992 • $10 • (11/30/93) • **74**
Riesling Kabinett Rheingau 1994: What we expect from this estate: a real live wire with plenty of fruit and a very fresh style. Medium-bodied, with good balance, but just a slightly short, crisp finish. Drinkable now. • $17 • (11/30/95) • **85**
Riesling Kabinett Trocken Rheingau Blausilber 1993: Rather advanced in character with candy, cookie, slightly rubbery notes. Medium-bodied, dry, soft-textured. • $13 • (11/30/94) • **79**
Riesling QbA Halbtrocken Rheingau 1992 • $8 • (11/30/93) • **73**
Riesling QbA Halbtrocken Rheingau Grunsilber 1993: Extremely disappointing for this estate. Seems slightly contrived with sweet and sour character and an overall lack of freshness. Drinkable now. • $9 • (11/30/94) • **77**
Riesling QbA Rheingau 1994: A disappointing Riesling from this estate. Rather candied and odd, with a cloying canned fruit cocktail character. Light-bodied and sweet. • $13 • (11/30/95) • **75**
Riesling QbA Rheingau Grungold 1993: Simple and earthy showing slightly candied flavors. Medium body and light sweetness with a fruity finish. • $NA • (11/30/94) • **76**
Riesling QbA Trocken Rheingau 1992 • $8 • (11/30/93) • **67**
Riesling QbA Trocken Rheingau Grunsilber 1993: Disappointing. Intense mineral aromas but turns to rubbery acidic character. Very dry. Could use more fruit. • $9 • (11/30/94) • **79**
Riesling Spätlese Halbtrocken Rheingau 1992 • $15 • (11/30/93) • **80**
Riesling Spätlese Halbtrocken Rheingau Rosasilber 1993: A dud. Fat, hard and spicy with botrytis character. Full-bodied and flabby with a bitter finish. Drinkable now. • $17 • (11/30/94) • **75**
Riesling Spätlese Rheingau Rosagold 1993: Very clean and fresh with blanched almond, fruity character, but it fizzles out on the finish. Medium- to light-bodied and medium-sweet. • $17 • (11/30/94) • **81**

WAGNER, DR. HEINZ

Riesling Auslese Gold Cap Saar-Ruwer Three Stars Saarburger Rausch 1993: A top-class auslese: stunning honey, floral, spice character. It's medium-bodied and oily, with waves of flavors that keep rolling over your palate. Drinkable now or hold. • $30 • (11/30/94) • **91**
Riesling Auslese Saar-Ruwer Saarburger Rausch 1993: Undeveloped yet, with a lovely, silky texture and loads of apple, mineral and lemon. Full-bodied and rich, with plenty of mineral and fruit flavors on the finish. Drinkable now. • $17 • (11/30/94) • **90**
Riesling Eiswein Saar-Ruwer Saarburger Rausch 1993: An extremely sweet style, which masks its true character. Medium-bodied and and lightly spicy. Almost cloying finish. • $NA • (11/30/94) • **83**
Riesling Kabinett Saar-Ruwer Ockfener Bockstein 1993: Like a spätlese. Loads of apple pie and mineral aromas and flavors. Medium-to-full body, medium sweetness and packed with fruit and fine acidity. Slightly simple finish. Drinkable now or hold. • $11 • (11/30/94) • **87**
Riesling Kabinett Saar-Ruwer Ockfener Bockstein 1992 • $11 • (11/30/93) • **80**
Riesling Kabinett Saar-Ruwer Saarburger Rausch 1993: Rather candied and already somewhat mature, with a fruity character. Extremely sweet aftertaste. • $11 • (11/30/94) • **78**
Riesling Kabinett Saar-Ruwer Saarburger Rausch 1992 • $11 • (11/30/93) • **83**
Riesling QbA Saar-Ruwer Ockfener Bockstein 1992 • $NA • (11/30/93) • **84**
Riesling QbA Saar-Ruwer Saarburger Raush 1992 • $NA • (11/30/93) • **83**

Key: SS—Spectator Selection. CS—Cellar Selection. BB—Best Buy. $NA—Price not available. (BT)—Barrel tasting. Ⓐ—Auction Price.
Dates in parentheses represent the issues in which the ratings were published.

Riesling Spätlese Saar-Ruwer Ockfener Bockstein 1993: Nicely fruity, medium-bodied and sweet, with a pleasant apple and melon character. Light caramel finish. • $13 • (11/30/94) • **82**
Riesling Spätlese Saar-Ruwer Ockfener Bockstein 1992 • $16 • (11/30/93) • **78**
Riesling Spätlese Saar-Ruwer Saarburger Rausch 1992 • $15 • (11/30/93) • **85**

WALLHAUSEN, SCHLOSS

Riesling Auslese Nahe Wallhäuser Johannisberg 1992 • $29 • (11/30/93) • **85**
Riesling Beerenauslese Nahe 1992 • $75 • (11/30/93) • **86**
Riesling Eiswein Nahe 1992 • $59 • (11/30/93) • **83**
Riesling Kabinett Nahe 1992 • $14 • (11/30/93) • **84**
Riesling Spätlese Nahe 1992 • $17 • (11/30/93) • **82**
Riesling Spätlese Nahe Roxheimer Berg 1992 • $16 • (11/30/93) • **84**

WEGELER-DEINHARD

Riesling Auslese Mosel Bernkasteler Doctor 1993: Rich auslese showing honey, peach and spice character. Full in body yet very elegant and balanced with a crisp finish. Delicious now but will improve with age. 172 cases made. • $60 • (11/30/94) • **89**
Riesling Auslese Mosel Bernkasteler Doctor 1992 • $51 • (11/30/93) • **80**
Riesling Auslese Mosel-Saar-Ruwer Wehlener Sonnenuhr Geheimrat J 1994: Really intense and concentrated: just as expected of a top auslese. Has a very pronounced, flinty-mineral character, modest sweetness, medium body and a long, clean finish. Drinkable now, but will take to aging. • $NA • (11/30/95) • **90**
Riesling Auslese Mosel Wehlener Sonnenuhr 1992 • $30 • (11/30/93) • **86**
Riesling Auslese Pfalz Forster Ungeheuer 1993: This is round and delicious with all the spice, bread crust, apple, honey character we like in an auslese. Full-bodied and medium-sweet with a spicy finish. Drinkable now. 127 cases made. • $27 • (11/30/94) • **90**
Riesling Auslese Pfalz Forster Ungeheuer 1992 • $25 • (11/30/93) • **83**
Riesling Auslese Rheingau 1993: Interesting wine but already fully mature with sweet fruit, roasted almond character. Medium-bodied, medium-sweet and a spicy finish. Drinkable now. • $NA • (11/30/94) • **82**
Riesling Auslese Rheingau Geisenheimer Rothenberg 1992 • $28 • (11/30/93) • **79**
Riesling Auslese Rheingau Oestricher Lenchen 1993: Reasonably well-made auslese with spicy, pie crust, apple character. Medium-bodied and medium-sweet with a fruity finish. Drinkable now. 550 cases made. • $30 • (11/30/94) • **83**
Riesling Auslese Rheingau Winkeler Hasensprung Geheimrat J 1994: A big, honeyed wine. Full body, rich texture, firm acidity and stunning concentration. A full, intense finish that opens up to mineral and honey notes. Better in 1997. • $NA • (11/30/95) • **91**
Riesling Beerenauslese Mosel-Saar-Ruwer Bernkasteler Doctor Geheimrat J 1994: Smooth and caressing on the palate, but not quite enough concentration to reach the outstanding mark for this category. Full body, medium sweetness, with spice, mineral and apricot flavors and long finish. Drinkable now, or try aging. • $NA • (11/30/95) • **89**
Riesling Beerenauslese Rheingau Oestricher Lenchen 1993: Strange slightly maderized aromas and flavors with some interesting ripe fruit character. Tasted twice. 38 cases made. • $75 • (11/30/94) • **78**
Riesling Beerenauslese Rheingau Oestricher Lenchen Geheimrat J 1994: Very rich dried apricot character, but rather mature, full-bodied and high in alcohol. A strange dessert wine for Germany. Also a bit blunt on the finish. • $NA • (11/30/95) • **82**
Riesling Eiswein Rheingau Geisenheimer Rothenberg 1992 • $70 • (11/30/93) • **90**
Riesling Eiswein Rheingau Oestricher Lenchen 1992 • $70 • (11/30/93) • **87**
Riesling Eiswein Saar-Ruwer Kaseler Nies'chen 1993: Wonderful balance of spicy, ripe fruit, honeyed sweetness and high acidity. A textbook eiswein. Full-bodied and sweet, with loads of fruit and a long, spicy finish. Drinkable now or hold. • $NA • (11/30/94) • **89**
Riesling Kabinett Mosel 1992 • $13 • (11/30/93) • **82**
Riesling Kabinett Mosel-Saar-Ruwer Bernkasteler Graben Geheimrat J 1994: Lots of mineral character in this wine. Medium body and

GERMANY

sweetness, with acacia and melon flavors and a soft, round finish. • $13 • (11/30/95) • **84**

Riesling Kabinett Mosel Wehlener Sonnenuhr 1993: A little dull and not giving much on the nose, but there are some pleasant creamy, apple flavors. Medium body, medium-sweet with a short aftertaste. 544 cases made. • $16 • (11/30/94) • **81**

Riesling Kabinett Pfalz 1993: Slightly better than the Forster Ungeheuer. Extremely focused offering wonderful spicy, mineral, fruity character. Medium-bodied and lightly sweet with a fresh finish. 255 cases made. • $12 • (11/30/94) • **89**

Riesling Kabinett Pfalz 1992 • $12 • (11/30/93) • **84**

Riesling Kabinett Pfalz Forster Ungeheuer 1993: Bigger than a Kabinett, more like a spätlese. Medium- to full-bodied with sweet rich fruit and a medium finish. A little ponderous and heavy in style. Drinkable now. 178 cases made. • $15 • (11/30/94) • **85**

Riesling Kabinett Rheingau Oestricher Lenchen Geheimrat J 1994: This has full grapefruit and pineapple aromas and flavors, showing plenty of extract. Medium body, medium-sweet, with a long and juicy finish. Drinkable now. • $13 • (11/30/95) • **86**

Riesling Kabinett Rheingau Rüdesheimer Berg Rottland 1993: Dull. Disappointing for this producer. Another premature dry wine with smoky, earthy, fruity character. Medium-bodied and soft. Tasted twice with consistent notes. Drinkable now. 300 cases made. • $15 • (11/30/94) • **75**

Riesling Kabinett Rheingau Rüdesheimer Berg Rottland 1992 • $15 • (11/30/93) • **84**

Riesling Spätlese Mosel 1992 • $18 • (11/30/93) • **69**

Riesling Spätlese Mosel Bernkasteler Doctor 1993: Very disappointing. Rather flat and unexciting with appley, earthy flavors. Tasted twice. Drinkable now. 344 cases made. • $55 • (11/30/94) • **78**

Riesling Spätlese Mosel Wehlener Sonnenuhr 1992 • $20 • (11/30/93) • **60**

Riesling Spätlese Mosel-Saar-Ruwer Berncasteler Doctor Geheimrat J 1994: Not a huge wine, but classy and racy. Elegant style, with loads of mineral, mint and melon aromas and flavors. An off-dry, medium-bodied white with fine acidity and a long, fresh finish. Delicious now, but will take to a little age. • $NA • (11/30/95) • **87**

Riesling Spätlese Mosel-Saar-Ruwer Wehlener Sonnenuhr Geheimrat J 1994: A lovely, elegant wine that offers mineral and lemon aromas and flavors. Lightly sweet, with fine acidity and a long, crisp finish. Needs some time to show what it can offer. • $NA • (11/30/95) • **88**

Riesling Spätlese Mosel Wehlener Sonnenuhr 1993: Pleasant and soft with attractive flavors of peaches and cream. Medium body, light sweetness and finish. Could use a little more of an aftertaste. 756 cases made. • $20 • (11/30/94) • **83**

Riesling Spätlese Pfalz 1992 • $15 • (11/30/93) • **87**

Riesling Spätlese Pfalz Forster Ungeheuer 1993: Exciting, sweeter-styled, full-bodied spätlese with masses of spice, mineral and licorice character. It really goes straight for your taste buds. 1,260 cases made. • $19 • (11/30/94) • **88**

Riesling Spätlese Pfalz Forster Ungeheuer 1992 • $17 • (11/30/93) • **89**

Riesling Spätlese Rheingau Rüdesheimer Berg Rottland 1993: Good for food with cream sauces. Thick and rich with creamy, apricot, spicy character, full body, off-dry and a soft finish. Drink now. 133 cases made. • $20 • (11/30/94) • **84**

Riesling Spätlese Rheingau Rüdesheimer Berg Rottland 1992 • $20 • (11/30/93) • **80**

Riesling Spätlese Rheingau Rüdesheimer Berg Rottland Geheimrat J 1994: This is beautifully balanced. Ripe apple, spice and mineral aromas and flavors come through the medium-bodied frame, and continue on to a long, almost dry finish. Drinkable now, but try aging this. • $NA • (11/30/95) • **87**

Riesling Trockenbeerenauslese Pfalz Deidesheimer Herrgottsacker Geheimrat J 1994: More like caramel than wine. An outstanding, intensely spicy, smoky almond and honey character. Full body, honey-like texture, good acidity and a long, sweet finish. Still a little coarse on the finish. Drinkable now. • $NA • (11/30/95) • **92**

WEIL, ROBERT

Riesling Auslese Gold Cap Rheingau Kiedricher Gräfenberg 1994: This is actually a declassified beerenauslese, but who cares? Enveloping honey and dried aromas and flavors pour out in waves. This is full-bodied, sweet and beautifully balanced. Will improve in bottle, try in 1997. • $NA • (11/30/95) • **92**

Riesling Auslese Gold Cap Rheingau Kiedricher Gräfenberg 1993: This is definitely a beerenauslese hiding as an auslese. Super-thick and rich displaying masses of decadent, ripe honey flavor. Full-bodied and very sweet with fine acidity. So good. Drinkable now. 50 cases made. • $NA • **94**

Riesling Auslese Gold Cap Rheingau Kiedricher Gräfenberg 1992 • $159 • (11/30/93) • **93**

Riesling Auslese Rheingau Kiedricher Gräfenberg 1994: A lovely, elegant auslese with plenty of spice, honey and mineral character and a hint of almond. Medium-bodied, very sweet and spicy, with a light finish. Drinkable now. • $78 • (11/30/95) • **87**

Riesling Auslese Rheingau Kiedricher Gräfenberg 1992 • $53 • (11/30/93) • **90**

Riesling Beerenauslese Rheingau Kiedricher Gräfenberg 1994: This could easily pass for a trockenbeerenauslese. Still very undeveloped, but it already has the feel of enormously concentrated dried fruit flavor. Very full and very sweet, with stunning acidity and a huge finish. A classic. • $141 • **96**

Riesling Beerenauslese Rheingau Kiedricher Gräfenberg 1993: Much too young now, but sensational. Amazing concentration of fruit, with captivating aromas and flavors of honey and apricot. Full-bodied, super-sweet and thick. Better to try after 1998. 40 cases made. • $242 • (11/30/94) • **95**

Riesling Beerenauslese Rheingau Kiedricher Gräfenberg 1992 • $329 • (11/30/93) • **95**

Riesling Kabinett Rheingau 1994: A little dull, in spite of the pineapple flavor and spritzy quality. Medium-bodied, only slightly sweet, drably, one-dimensional on the finish. Drinkable now. • $19 • (11/30/95) • **82**

Riesling Kabinett Rheingau 1993: Wonderfully fresh wine with sliced peach, lemon aromas and flavors. Light-bodied and slightly sweet with a light floral finish. Drink now. • $17 • (11/30/94) • **85**

Riesling Kabinett Rheingau 1992 • $16 • (11/30/93) • **83**

Riesling Spätlese Rheingau 1992 • $21 • (11/30/93) • **86**

Riesling Spätlese Rheingau Kiedricher Gräfenberg 1994: Zingy lime and lemon flavors and a flinty character. Medium body, lively acidity and a lemony finish. Drinkable now. • $32 • (11/30/95) • **86**

Riesling Spätlese Rheingau Kiedricher Gräfenberg 1993: This is a spätlese suited for dessert, exhibiting masses of spice, botrytis and honey character. Medium- to full-bodied and very sweet with firm acidity and a long finish. 292 cases made. • $26 • (11/30/94) • **90**

Riesling Trockenbeerenauslese Rheingau Kiedricher Gräfenberg 1994: Great class in such a thick and sweet wine. Massive yet elegant. Full body, very sweet, with great acidity and a long finish that reveals notes of dried apricot, honey and orange peel. Drinkable now, but ageworthy. • $291 • (11/30/95) • **95**

Riesling Trockenbeerenauslese Rheingau Kiedricher Gräfenberg 1993: Another fabulous wine from Weil. Super-thick like olive oil and rich with honey, dried apricot and spice character. Full in body and very, very sweet. Enormous. Drinkable now. 40 cases made. • $250 • (11/30/95) • **95**

Riesling Trockenbeerenauslese Rheingau Kiedricher Gräfenberg 1992 • $218 • (11/30/93) • **96**

WEINGART, ADOLF

Riesling Auslese Mittelrhein Bopparder Hamm Feuerlay 1992 • $13 • (11/30/93) • **86**

Riesling Auslese Trocken Mittelrhein Bopparder Hamm Ohlenberg 1992 • $12 • (11/30/93) • **80**

Riesling Hochgewächs Mittelrhein Bopparder Hamm Feuerlay 1992 • $8 • (11/30/93) • **79**

Riesling Kabinett Halbtrocken Mittelrhein Bopparder Hamm Ohlenberg 1992 • $8 • (11/30/93) • **78**

Riesling Spätlese Mittelrhein Bopparder Hamm Ohlenberg 1992 • $9 • (11/30/93) • **84**

WERNER'SCHES, DOMDECHANT

Riesling Auslese Rheingau Hochheimer Domdechaney 1993: Not much of an auslese. Thin and short on fruit. Medium-bodied and medium-sweet. Some spicy flavors. • $NA • (11/30/94) • **76**

Riesling Auslese Rheingau Hochheimer Kirchenstück 1992 • $NA • (11/30/93) • **86**

Riesling Beerenauslese Rheingau Hochheimer Domdechaney 1992 • $NA • (11/30/93) • **80**

Riesling Eiswein Rheingau Hochheimer Domdechaney 1992 • $NA • (11/30/93) • **84**

Riesling Kabinett Halbtrocken Rheingau Hochheimer Stein 1992 • $11 • (11/30/93) • **69**

Riesling Kabinett Rheingau Hochheimer Hölle 1992 • $12 • (11/30/93) • **83**

Riesling Spätlese Halbtrocken Rheingau Hochheimer 1993: Textbook spätlese with lovely peach, apricot and spice aromas and flavors. Medium-to-full body, crisp acidity and slightly bitter aftertaste. Drinkable now. • $NA • (11/30/94) • **87**

Riesling Spätlese Rheingau Hochheimer Domdechaney 1992 • $18 • (11/30/93) • **84**

Riesling Spätlese Trocken Rheingau Hochheimer Domdechaney 1993: Another for early drinking. Lovely aromas of peaches and dried apricot follow through on the palate. Medium-bodied, dry, rather soft texture. Slightly bitter aftertaste. • $NA • (11/30/94) • **82**

ZILLIKEN

Riesling Auslese Gold Cap Saar-Ruwer Saarburger Rausch 1993: A fine, elegant auslese, with peach, apple and mineral aromas and flavors. Full-bodied and very firm, with fresh acidity and fruit on the aftertaste. Drinkable now or hold. • $NA • (11/30/94) • **91**

Riesling Auslese Long Gold Cap Saar-Ruwer Saarburger Rausch 1993: A terrific dessert wine, with racy spicy, mineral and sweet fruit character. Full-bodied and sweet yet with an impressive undercarriage of steely acidity. Built for aging. Try now or hold. • $114 • (11/30/94) • **93**

Riesling Auslese Mosel-Saar-Ruwer Saarburger Rausch 1994: A decent auslese with loads of flinty, mineral and apple aromas and flavors. Medium body and sweetness and very fruity on the finish. Drinkable now. • $34 • (11/30/95) • **84**

Riesling Auslese Saar-Ruwer Saarburger Rausch 1993: Beautiful and classy, with understated ripe peach and apple flavors. Medium-bodied, medium sweetness and a long, floral, fruity finish. Drink or hold. • $35 • (11/30/94) • **90**

Riesling Beerenauslese Mosel-Saar-Ruwer Saarburger Rausch 1994: Interesting almond and overripe apple character, but without the richness or concentration of a beerenauslese. Medium-bodied and very sweet, turning rather simple on the finish. Drinkable now. • $NA • (11/30/95) • **84**

Riesling Beerenauslese Saar-Ruwer Saarburger Rausch 1993: Very racy style of BA, more like an eiswein, with loads of ripe lemon and orange character. Full-bodied yet delicate and balanced, with a long, fresh finish. Drinkable now. • $NA • (11/30/94) • **93**

Riesling Kabinett Mosel-Saar-Ruwer Saarburger Rausch 1994: Typical and unexciting. Very crisp lemon and peach character. Medium to light body, rather dry, highly acidic and is light and slightly too tart on the finish. • $15 • (11/30/95) • **81**

Riesling Kabinett Saar-Ruwer Ockfener Bockstein 1992 • $13 • (11/30/93) • **80**

Riesling Kabinett Saar-Ruwer Saarburger Rausch 1993: Shows plenty of fresh-crushed fruit character with a hint of toasted almonds. Medium sweetness and a crisp finish. Drinkable now. • $13 • (11/30/94) • **87**

Riesling Kabinett Saar-Ruwer Saarburger Rausch 1992 • $14 • (11/30/93) • **81**

Riesling QbA Halbtrocken Mosel-Saar-Ruwer 1994: A model QbA: fresh and vibrant, with apple and mineral aromas and flavors. Medium-bodied and dry, with medium acidity and a crisp finish. • $10 • (11/30/96) • **85**

Riesling QbA Halbtrocken Saar-Ruwer 1992 • $11 • (11/30/93) • **78**

Riesling Spätlese Mosel-Saar-Ruwer Ockfener Bockstein 1994: A wine that promises more than it gives. Medium body, carrying nice peach and spice flavors, but a short finish. • $19 • (11/30/95) • **82**

Riesling Spätlese Mosel-Saar-Ruwer Saarburger Rausch 1994: A very good spätlese that delivers plenty of spicy and fruity aromas and flavors. Medium-bodied, not too sweet, with a fresh mineral finish. Drinkable now, or age a little. • $20 • (11/30/96) • **86**

Riesling Spätlese Saar-Ruwer Saarburger Rausch 1993: A sweet and steely style. Medium-bodied, sweet and fruity. A little simple and closed now, but it should develop more with age. Drinkable now. • $18 • (11/30/94) • **85**

Riesling Spätlese Saar-Ruwer Saarburger Rausch 1992 • $18 • (11/30/93) • **85**

Key: SS—Spectator Selection. CS—Cellar Selection. BB—Best Buy. $NA—Price not available. (BT)—Barrel tasting. Ⓐ—Auction Price.
Dates in parentheses represent the issues in which the ratings were published.

Italy

Italy makes more wine than any other country, but today its reputation rests not on quantity but on quality. Although Italy's greatest wines still come from the familiar regions of Piedmont and Tuscany, many fine new areas are emerging. These newer regions include Apulia, Friuli, Tentino-Alto Adige, Basilicata and Sicily, to name but a few.

Although Cabernet Sauvignon and Chardonnay are increasingly gaining favor throughout Italy, they still represent a relatively small portion of production. The soul of Italian wine will still be found in its indigenous grape varieties, such as the Nebbiolo, Barbera, Dolcetto, and Sangiovese for reds, and the Trebbiano and Malvasia for whites. These native varieties allow Italy to offer an unparalleled breadth and variety of flavor profiles.

For many years white wine was an afterthought in this country of red wine lovers. But that is changing rapidly as its whites improve. Indeed, Italy is rapidly improving the quality of its winemaking overall. When these improvements are combined with its fine vineyards and a favorable climate, it is easy to see why the Italians have now become formidable competitors in the world marketplace. Indeed, Italy's greatest wines are on a par with the best of France and the United States, and its everyday wines offer great value.

1. **Piedmont (Piemonte): Barbera, Dolcetto**
2. **Verona: Bardolino, Soave, Valpolicella**
3. **Trentino/Alto Adige**
4. **Friuli-Venezia**
5. **Tuscany**
6. **Umbria: Orvieto**
7. **The Marches: Verdicchio**
8. **Abruzzi: Montepulciano d'Abruzzo**

THE DOC SYSTEM

Unlike France and to an increasing extent the United States, Italy does not have an appellation system that is easy to understand. What it does have is a an older system of DOCs (*denominazioni di origine controllata*), over which has been superimposed a newer system of DOCG (the G stands for *Garantita,* and theoretically indicates a superior standard of wine quality). Over 250 different DOC and DOCG wines have been created, each with its own detailed rules and regulations covering such items as allowable grape varieties, acceptable yields, vineyard quality, soil type, geographic boundaries and minimum standards for aging.

Yet, too often, the ossified DOC rules have hindered rather than advanced the cause of Italian wine quality. While producers could get by simply by meeting the minimum standards of the DOC, creative winemakers found themselves stymied by rules that inhibited experiments with grape types, aging, the use of *barriques* (small wooden casks, typically made of French oak), and other winemaking techniques. The major consequence has been a plethora of so-called *vini da tavola,* unsanctioned wines that do not meet the official standards of the DOC/DOCG. At many estates, these wines surpass the level of the DOC wines in price and in quality. As a reflection of this trend and the growing dissatisfaction with the DOC system, a new law was passed in 1992. Ultimately this law will have the effect of scuttling the existing system in favor of one that emphasizes geographic origin and wine quality above such formalities as grape blends, alcohol levels, and minimum aging requirements.

ITALIAN WINE REGIONS

It's been said that there's no such thing as Italian food, only Italian regional cuisines. Much the same can be said of Italian wine. The Piedmontese don't make wine like the Tuscans, who don't make wine like the Apulians, and so on. The key to sorting out the differences is understanding the unique climate and soils of Italy's many regions, ranging from the Alpine hills in the North to the bottom of the boot in the south. But winemaking philosophies and traditions play a large part.

Tuscany

Tuscany epitomizes in many ways the blend of art and science that characterizes Italian winemaking. Though the Tuscan landscape still looks like the background of the *Mona Lisa*, things are changing rapidly behind the graceful facades of her ancient *castelli* and wineries.

At the heart of Tuscany, in terms of both geography and importance is the Chianti zone, which produces one of the first five wines to have been accorded the rank of DOCG status. Chianti ranges in style from soft, fruity and quaffable to deeply colored, tannic and ageworthy. At the core of all Chianti is the incredibly adaptable Sangiovese grape. Although it is cultivated throughout much of Italy, only in Tuscany does it achieve its classic style: a delicate, aromatic wine of warmth and depth, with an almost ethereal astringency on the finish.

Chianti Classico, which can only come from the strictly defined Classico zone, is the most structured and ageworthy Chianti. The Classico Riserva designation is reserved for its best wines, which have been aged in oak for a minimum statutory period (until recently three years, now reduced to 18-24 months). In the past, Chianti Classico tended to be show amber highlights fairly early in its development, but this style is rapidly being displaced in favor of one that is more vigorously fruity and displays an almost Merlot-like red/purple glow when young. Most of the famous Chianti producers have their centers of operation in the Classico zone. Among the top are Antinori, Ruffino, Fonterutoli, Felsina, Fontodi and Ama. Although the Gallo Negro ("Black Rooster") neck seal is still a well-known fixture in Chianti, several of the best known producers are not members of that consortium and have chosen to rely solely on brand image.

On a level with Chianti Classico is the much smaller Chianti Rufina zone (not to be confused with the Ruffino winery, in Classico), located in the hills east of Florence. Its most famous name is the Marchesi de' Frecobaldi, known for its Castello di Nippozano, Montesodi and Remole bottlings. Other top producers include Selvapiana and Villa Vetrice. The Rufina zone also surrounds the area called Pomino, an old DOC that was resurrected through the efforts of the Marchesi de' Frescobaldi, which owns all the vineyards. Pomino is a curiosity because, historically, it has relied heavily on French grapes for blends. The red Pomino made from Cabernet, Sangiovese and Merlot may be the best, but some excellent Chardonnay-based whites are made here as well.

The other Chianti zones—Colli Fiorentino, Pisani, Colli Senesi, Colli Aretini and Montalbano—offer distinct styles. The latter encompasses the Carmignano district, which like Pomino, has a centuries old-history of blending in substantial portions of Cabernet Sauvignon. Capezzana and Ambra are well-known. The other Chianti regions are not generally *riserva* producers, but they do make appealingly soft and fruity everyday wines meant to be drunk very young.

In southern Tuscany is Brunello di Montalcino, which along with Barolo, produces Italy's most acclaimed—and often its most expensive—traditional red wine. The only permissible grape for this DOCG is the Brunello, a potent clone of the Sangiovese. The austere, will-age-forever style of Brunello pioneered by Biondi-Santi seems destined for the endangered species list, as modern tastes—and modern wine critics—seem to prefer a less dauntingly structured wine with greater fruit and grapey extract. But it's all a bit unsettled now, as no one seems quite sure whether the *riservas* (extra rich wines put out in the best years) will outlast the more classic, somewhat leaner *normale* bottlings. Certainly the wines of the top producers, such as Tenuta Caparzo, Poggio Antico, Costanti, and others, seem to have the stuffing to age for decades. Note that for the budget-conscious or the impatient, Rosso di Montalcino, made from young vines and released in a fruitier style after minimal aging, may be the best choice from this region.

East of Montalcino, Vino Nobile di Montepulciano is trying set itself out from the crowd. Also made from the local clone of the Sangiovese, it combines much of the austere power of a Brunello with the rounder fruitiness of a Chianti Riserva. But that makes it sound better than it is. At least for the time

The Piedmont estate of Gaja, producer of world-famous Barbarescos.

being, Vino Nobile di Montepulciano has yet to justify its premium asking price.

Tuscany is also the place that started the *vino da tavola* movement, and has consistently provided the most fertile hot-bed for experimentation, discovery, and the free borrowing of ideas and techniques from winemakers around the world. The wines that have resulted are known as super-Tuscans. The best of these are now considered in a class with the top *crus* of Burgundy, Bordeaux and California—and are priced accordingly. Two different approaches predominate, of which the most popular relies either partly or wholly on Cabernet Sauvignon vinified in a Bordelais style using small oak barrels. Examples of this type include Sassicaia and Sammarco. The more original contributions are the super-Tuscans that have brought the indigenous Sangiovese to its ultimate expression, a supple core of warm fruit wrapped in an ethereal cloud of bright tannins. Made without the white grapes of traditional Chianti, and sometimes spiced up with a pinch or two of Cabernet, these extraordinary wines have no parallel outside of Tuscany. Some of the best are Fontalloro, Flaccianello, and Acciaiolo.

Piedmont

With its own dialect, unique winemaking philosophy, and vintages that bear little correlation to the rest of Italy, Piedmont, in Northwestern Italy, is a world apart both culturally and oenologically. Yet it would be difficult to name a region where the art of the winemaker flourishes more profoundly than amidst its fog-draped hills. Like Burgundy, Piedmont's greatness flows from the precarious balance of nature, in which the threat of disaster always looms in even the greatest vintages. This is a northerly limit for the production of great red wine, and only in the years when nature's tempestuous moods are moderated do its greatest wines live up to their reputation.

Barolo, sometimes called the king of Piedmont reds, is made from 100 percent Nebbiolo. The mist-shrouded hills of the Barolo region gave the Nebbiolo its name—from *nebbia*, meaning fog. Barolo is a wine of immense size and dimension. Even more than the great wines of Bordeaux and Burgundy, it demands cellaring. When mature, Barolo is brick orange, with aromas of truffles and smoke, and potent earth and tar flavors. Top producers include

Conterno (Aldo), Altere, Crubo Giacosa, Pio Cesare, Sandrone, and Einaudi.

Barbaresco is almost as long-lived and can be every bit as grand as Barolo. Not quite possessed of Barolo's immense strength, Barbaresco is more supple and elegant, making it ready to drink a bit sooner. The leading exponent of Barbaresco has been Angelo Gaja, who until recently did not even produce Barolo. Spurred on by Gaja, other Barbaresco producers now also make fine wine, the best of which may be the single-vineyard bottlings of Produttori del Barbaresco.

Two other good choices include Nebbiolo d'Alba and Nebbiolo delle Langhe. The first is made outside the Barolo and Barbaresco zone of Langhe. Not subject to a long minimum-aging requirement, most Nebbiolo d'Alba is fruitier and less forbidding than Barolo or Barbaresco, and quite delicious. Nebbiolo delle Langhe, which is made in the zone, is usually declassified Barolo or Barbaresco. Both Nebbiolos can offer exceptional value. Look for wines made by leading Barolo and Barbaresco producers.

Gattinara is from the north of Piedmont, on the other side of Turin from Alba. The Novara-Vercelli hills are its home. This wine should rival Barolo and Barbaresco. Due to inconsistent winemaking, however, it rarely does. At its best, Gattinara is the Margaux of Piedmont, exquisitely delicate and deeply flavored, with a bouquet of truffles, black plum and violets. The producers Vallana, Travaglini, and Dessilani can be excellent.

Budget-conscious lovers of Gattinara should seek out the wines of the myriad villages around the Novara-Vercelli hills. The best is Spanna, taken from the local name for the Nebbiolo grape. Spanna can be superb, rivaling Gattinara at half the cost.

Barbera and Dolcetto are also excellent Piedmont reds. Deliciously fruity in their youth, most are intended for early consumption.

The Cortese may be Italy's finest native white grape. It is responsible for Gavi, Gavi di Gavi, and Cortese di Gavi. Another fine Piedmont white is made from the Muscat-like Arneis grape. It is finely scented and tart. And of course, Chardonnay is making its appearance here, sometimes in a full, oaky style that calls to mind a Meursault.

UP-AND-COMING REGIONS

With prices of wines from Tuscany and the Piedmont on the rise, importers are increasingly turning to more obscure areas of Italy. Here are some of the most promising:

Apulia. On the heel of the Italian boot, Apulia is a sunny area that enjoys a moderating influence from the sea. Salice Salentino is a rich, often rustic red that can have real character—perhaps too much character for some palates. A lighter version called Rosso del Salento is also making a name for itself.

Valtellina. The Valtellina reds are a wholly different interpretation of Nebbiolo. Though complex, they are far lighter than the Piedmontese Nebbiolos. They shine with food; alone, they seem stingy. The leading wines are from the villages of Grumello, Inferno, Sassella and Valgella. Perhaps the best is Sfursat, a potent wine made from dried grapes and eminently suitable as a replacement for Port with strong cheese. The leading producers are Rainoldi and Nino Negri.

Sicily. Sicily has proven its potential for bulk production of flavorful, if not terribly complex, red and white table wines. Corvo's top bottlings, as well as those of other producers such as Regaleali, suggest that there is also great quality potential here.

Sardinia. Another out-of-the-way island, Sardinia produces wines with a gentle ripeness and smooth fruit. The white, made from the obscure Vermentino grape, may have the potential to be the next Pinot Grigio, in terms of mass acceptance and sales.

Abruzzo. This promising region has been plagued by gross overproduction, which has obscured the potential for much better wines if yields are kept under control. Done well, Montepulciano d'Abruzzo (Montepulciano is the grape) can produce a sort of ripe, almost Rhône-like cousin of Chianti.

Veneto. The predominant red grape in this region is Corvina, which is typically blended with Rondinella, Molinara and Negrara to produce Valpolicella and Bardolino. The ultimate expression of the Corvina grape is Amarone, which requires extensive drying of the grapes on open racks to concentrate the must sufficiently to create a wine of monumental character. Bertani, Anselmi and now even Bolla have shown that—aside from the traditional Amarones—there is a lot of unexploited potential for serious Valpolicella and Bardolino, made with far more intensity than the common versions, which are quite light. The same is true of Soave, made mostly from Garganega and Trebbiano.

Friuli. Although Cabernet Franc, with its distinctive peppery/herbal character, is best known as a major grape of the French districts St.-Emilion and Chinon, it has been cultivated in the Collio region of Friuli for well over a century. The Friuli interpretation emphasizes subtle aromatics allied with a complex, light body. Friuli also makes Merlots that have an abundance of bright fruit, a clean, dry finish and an herbal, almost grassy delicacy unique to this region. Adding Cabernet Sauvignon to the blend accents the herbal notes on the bouquet, and complements the round red-fruit notes of the Merlot grape.

Friuli (and the neighboring region of Trentino-Alto Adige) also have shown a knack for producing refreshing, surprisingly complex white wines. German varietals, such as Riesling, Sylvaner, Muller-Thurgau and Gewürztraminer, thrive in the cool, high-altitude vineyards found in these regions. Most are made in a dry, zesty style, often showing a distinctive smokiness on the nose. Sauvignon Blanc and Tocai Friulano (unrelated to the Tokaji of Hungary), show more power and intensity. Some are vinified in wood casks, giving an even richer, firmer wine.

The villa at Antnori, a leading Chianti Classico producer.

Another excellent variety is the Pinot Grigio. Although its huge commercial success has made it ubiquitous throughout Italy, Pinot Grigio has always been taken quite seriously in Friuli. Often it is vinified with extended skin contact, which allows it to take on an appealing coppery tinge and extraordinary intensity. Finally, the indigenous Ribolla Gaialla should not be overlooked. Dry and quite lemony, its firm acidity make it a perfect match with calamari.

ITALIAN VARIETAL WINES

Increasingly in Italy, as in France, grape varieties are getting top billing on wine labels. Below is a quick run-through of the leading types.

Sangiovese. Arguably Italy's most important grape, this mainstay of Chianti is becoming an important variety on its own. It tends to produce mid-weight, often quite fruity wines, with a characteristic tart, clean finish.

Pinot Grigio. This white grape is the same as Alsace's Pinot Gris, except that in Italian hands it sells like hot-cakes. Perhaps this is because Italy vinifies it in a light, fresh style with lots of soft fruit. Most of the best comes from Friuli, but it is increasingly being made successfully in other locales as well.

Merlot. Of all the classic Bordeaux varietals, Merlot appears to be the greatest commercial success. Often coupled with a regional name, such as Merlot del Piave, the Italians vinify it in a clean, fresh style so that it comes out something like a lightly herbal Chianti. Prices tend to be reasonable.

Chardonnay. Though a few very serious producers, such a Gaja, vinify a Chardonnay that tastes like a Meursault, most Italian Chardonnay is made in the style of a Pinot Grigio. This means little or no wood, and lots of cold-fermented, apple-like crispness up front.

Barbera. The best known examples of this red—from Alba and Asti in the Piedmont—can approach Barolo and Barbaresco in power, though rarely in finesse. Increasingly, experiments with low yields and new wood aging suggest star potential.

Dolcetto. Sometimes referred to as the Beaujolais of Italy, Dolcetto can be a very attractive wine when vinified in a grapey purple *nouveau* style. Like Barbera, its real future may lie in experiments with lower yields and barrel aging.

Trebbiano. Now beginning to make a name for itself as a single variety, this is the white grape that was once added to Chianti. It is also a component of many other popular Italian whites, such as Soave and Orvieto. Experiments in California have shown that with the right yields and careful vinification, Trebbiano can be made into a potent wine that can even take barrel fermentation.

ABBAZIA DI ROSAZZO

Chardonnay Colli Orientali del Friuli 1993: Brightly fruity, a simple, direct wine with appealing Golden Delicious apple fruit, finishing exceedingly tart. 750 cases made. • $19 • (01/31/95) • **79**
Colli Orientali del Friuli Verduzzo 1986 • $22 • (10/15/88) • **83**
Pignolo 1987 • $36 • (06/30/91) • **85**
Pignolo 1985 • $22 • (09/15/88) • **86**
Pinot Grigio Colli Orientali del Friuli 1994: Dry, fresh, lively and bracing. This has good balance, with firm acidity, bright but lean fruit flavors and a lingering, fruity finish. Lots of zip. • $20 • (06/15/96) • **87**
Pinot Grigio Colli Orientali del Friuli 1993: Extremely tart and crisp, this lean Pinot is steely, with pear, apple and lemon flavors. 833 cases made. • $19 • (01/31/95) • **79**
Ribolla Gialla Colli Orientali del Friuli Red 1990 • $21 • (01/31/92) • **76**
Ribolla Gialla Colli Orientali del Friuli White 1993: Simple and light, with modest apple, lemon notes. Short. 833 cases made. • $19 • (01/31/95) • **75**
Ronco dei Roseti 1987 • $35 • (07/15/91) • **87**
Ronco dei Roseti 1986 • $22 • (03/15/89) • **85**
Ronco dei Roseti 1983 • $20 • (09/15/88) • **87**
Ronco della Abbazia 1988 • $11/375ml • (07/15/91) • **73**
Sauvignon Colli Orientali del Friuli 1993: Fresh and appealing, flavors centered around apple and citrus, hinting at grapefruit on the finish. 750 cases made. • $18 • (01/31/95) • **83**

ABBAZIA DI VALLE CHIARA

Dolcetto d'Ovada 1990 • $11 • (04/30/93) • **80**
Dolcetto d'Ovada 1989 • $13 • (07/15/91) • **79**
Torre Albarola Red 1988 • $24 • (01/31/92) • **87**

ABBONA, MARZIANO & ENRICO

Barbera d'Alba Vigneto Ravera 1990 • $11 • (06/15/94) • **55**
Barolo 1986 • $30 • (12/15/92) • **81**
Barolo Vigneto Terlo Ravera 1990: Intense, tart fruit flavors, with plenty of tannin besides. A traditional style, with cranberry and raspberry flavors and strong aromas. Try in 1997. 1,800 cases made. • $25 • (07/31/95) • **85**
Barolo Vigneto Terlo Ravera 1989: An aroma of toasted oak gives this Barolo an attractive French accent to go along with the solid ripe fruit flavors of the Nebbiolo grape. It has depth, complexity and a lingering finish. Drinkable now through 2000. • $23 • (10/31/94) • **89**
Chardonnay 1992: Smooth textured but thin in flavor. The vanilla and honey aromas aren't backed up by much fruit, and it fades quickly on the finish. • $9 • (02/28/95) • **78**
Dolcetto di Dogliani Papa Celso 1992 • $13 • (06/15/94) • **84**
Dolcetto di Dogliani Vigneto Doriolo 1993: Cherry, black pepper and light earthy flavors are well integrated. Soft and accessible, the finish a bit dry, but flavors lingering. Drinkable now. 5,000 cases made. • $11 • (07/31/95) • **83**
Nebbiolo d'Alba 1990 • $14 • (06/15/94) • **89**
Riviera di Ponente Pigato White 1992: A fragrant, floral, richly textured wine with ample citrus and spice flavors. Not crisp, but lush and clean. • $16 • (02/28/95) • **85**
Roero Arneis White 1992: Subtle flavors and a lush texture make this a serious white wine. Ripe peach and apricot flavors are accented by butter and vanilla, lingering on the finish. • $14 • (02/28/95) • **86**

ACCOMASSO & FIGLIO, GIOVANNI

Barolo Vigneto Rocchette 1985 • $24 • (01/31/92) • **75**
Nebbiolo delle Langhe 1982 • $14 • (07/31/89) • **65**

Key: SS—Spectator Selection. CS—Cellar Selection. BB—Best Buy. $NA—Price not available. (BT)—Barrel tasting. Ⓐ—Auction Price.
Dates in parentheses represent the issues in which the ratings were published.

ADANTI

D'Arquata Montefalco 1985 • $7 • (07/31/88) • **84**
Sagrantino d'Arquata Montefalco 1983 • $13 • (10/15/88) • **77**

AIOLA

Chianti Classico 1993: A simple '93 Chianti. Refreshingly fruity with berry and cherry aromas and flavors, crisp acidity and a light finish. Serve chilled. • $13 • (10/31/95) • **80**
Chianti Classico 1991 • $NA • (10/31/93) • **85**
Chianti Classico 1990 • $11 • (09/15/92) • **81**
Chianti Classico Riserva 1988 • $18 • (09/15/92) • **79**
Logaiolo 1991: Light and disappointing with some berry, cherry character but diluted on the finish. • $18 • (10/31/95) • **75**
Logaiolo 1990 • $NA • (10/31/93) • **83**

AJA, L'

Chianti Classico 1993: Quite aromatic wine with lovely raspberry notes that beckon you to drink it. Modest plum and strawberry character. Light-bodied with a light finish. Drinkable now. • $NA • (10/31/95) • **81**
Chianti Classico 1991 • $NA • (10/31/93) • **82**

ALBOLA, CASTELLO D'

Acciaiolo 1990: Elegant and ambitiously oaky, with modest plum and cherry flavors and a good wallop of spice. Supple tannins and a lingering caramel finish. Drinkable now. • $35 • (07/31/95) • **84**
Acciaiolo 1988 • $40 • (09/15/91) • **88**
Chianti Classico 1992: Very light and diluted with mint, strawberry and pepper notes. Drinkable now. 70,000 cases made. • $9 • (02/28/95) • **74**
Chianti Classico 1991 • $9 • (10/31/94) • **80**
Chianti Classico 1990 • $9 • (09/15/92) • **76**
Chianti Classico 1988 • $10 • (09/15/91) • **89**
Chianti Classico 1986 • $7 • (11/30/89) • **85**
Chianti Classico Riserva 1990: Very traditional style, black pepper and cedar aromas and flavors but slightly dry on the finish. Drink as soon as possible. 6,000 cases made. • $13 • (02/28/95) • **79**
Chianti Classico Riserva 1988 • $15 • (10/31/93) • **80**
Chianti Classico Riserva 1985 • $12 • (11/30/89) • **76**
Pinot Grigio Aquileia 1993 • $9 • (12/15/94) • **77**

ALERAMICI, MARCHESATO DEGLI

Brunello di Montalcino 1990: Beautifully balanced Brunello featuring berry, rose and mineral aromas and flavors. Medium-bodied with fine tannins and a fresh finish. Delicious now. • $NA • (10/31/95) • **86**
Rosso di Montalcino 1993: Good berry, chocolate and a hint of chestnut on the nose and palate, medium body, light tannins and fresh finish. Drink now. • $NA • (10/31/95) • **81**

ALLEGRINI

La Poja 1986 • $55 • (09/15/92) • **86**
Recioto della Valpolicella Amarone 1985 • $28 • (09/15/92) • **84**
Recioto della Valpolicella Classico Amarone Superiore 1980 • $13 • (12/31/87) • **85**
Soave Classico Superiore Cortegiara 1991 • $14 • (09/15/92) • **76**
Valpolicella Classico 1991 • $11 • (09/15/92) • **78**
Valpolicella Classico 1990 • $11 • (09/15/92) • **82**
Valpolicella Classico La Grola 1988 • $18 • (09/15/92) • **82**
Valpolicella Classico Superiore La Grola 1990: The deep color and aromas of licorice, coffee and raisins suggest Amarone, with unusually muscular tannins and very ripe fruit. Admirably concentrated and balanced. Drinkable now through 1997. • $16 • (12/15/95) • **88**
Valpolicella Classico Superiore Palazzo Della Torre 1990: A firm red that shows mature flavors of coffee, tobacco and dried fruit, but it's still fresh, with good grip and a clean finish. • $13 • (12/15/95) • **84**
Valpolicella Classico Superiore Palazzo Della Torre 1988 • $16 • (09/15/92) • **78**

ITALY

Valpolicella Classico Superiore Palazzo Della Torre 1986 • $16 • (09/15/92) • **85**
Valpolicella Classico Superiore Palazzo Della Torre 1983 • $7 • (12/31/87) • **78**

ALTARE, ELIO

Barbera d'Alba 1991 • $15 • (11/15/93) • **82**
Barbera d'Alba 1989 • $13 • (03/15/91) • **91**
Barbera d'Alba 1988 • $10 • (03/31/90) • **84**
Barbera d'Alba 1987 • $12 • (08/31/89) • **92**
Barolo 1991: Round, open, delicious berry, cherry, leather and chocolate character. Medium-bodied with soft tannins and a delicious finish. 175 cases made. • $30 • (10/31/95) • **85**
Barolo 1990: Crisp in texture and lavishly tannic, with a modest level of concentration to the berry flavor. Very drying tannins could be a problem. Try in 1997. • $40 • (10/31/94) • **81**
Barolo 1988 • $32 • (10/31/93) • **85**
Barolo 1985 • $24 • (01/31/90) • **92**
Barolo 1982 • $13 • (06/30/87) • **88**
Barolo Vigna Arborina 1982 • $15 • (09/15/87) • **87**
Barolo Vigneto Arborina 1990: Big, muscular and extraordinarily well balanced, packed with black cherry, tar, rose petal and blackberry flavors that seem to enrich with each sip, echoing fruit and mineral notes on the harmonious finish. Not flashy, but elegant and powerful enough to wait until 1998 to 2002 to settle down. • $45 • (10/31/94) • **93**
Barolo Vigneto Arborina 1989: Tough and tart, a tightly closed wine that shows a nice spurt of blackberry flavor that sneaks between the layers of tannin on the finish. Drink after 1996. 320 cases made. • $45 • (10/31/93) • **85**
Barolo Vigneto Arborina 1988 • $42 • (10/31/93) • **88**
Cabernet Sauvignon La Villa 1992 • $NA • (10/31/94) • **89**
Dolcetto d'Alba 1988 • $10 • (03/31/90) • **82**
Dolcetto d'Alba 1987 • $9 • (02/28/89) • **90**
Nebbiolo Vigna Arborina 1987 • $32 • (09/15/90) • **84**
Nebbiolo Vigna Arborina 1986 • $20 • (02/28/89) • **90**
Nebbiolo Vigna Larigi 1987 • $28 • (05/31/90) • **89**
Nebbiolo delle Langhe 1988 • $10 • (03/31/90) • **81**
Nebbiolo delle Langhe 1987 • $9 • (07/31/89) • **85**
Piedmont 1989 • $12 • (07/15/91) • **85**
Vigna Arborina 1992 • $40 • (10/31/94) • **85**
Vigna Larigi 1992 • $40 • (10/31/94) • **91**

ALTESINO

Alte d'Altesi 1990: Very stylish wine with an abundance of green tobacco and fruity character in a full-bodied package. Needs time to come around. Made from Cabernet Sauvignon and Sangiovese. Try now. 1,100 cases made. • $34 • (10/31/93) • **86**
Alte d'Altesi 1988 • $35 • (09/15/91) • **92**
Alte d'Altesi 1987 • $35 • (01/31/92) • **69**
Alte d'Altesi 1986 • $32 • (07/15/89) • **85**
Brunello di Montalcino 1990: Very perfumed tobacco and violet aromas. Medium in body, adding fine tannins and a long, tobacco and cherry finish. Rather meager compared to the Montosoli. Delicious now. Tasted twice, with consistent notes. • $45 • (10/31/95) • **87**
Brunello di Montalcino 1988: A complex wine with a hint of spice in the aromas of tobacco, chocolate and red fruit. Medium body, with excellent fruit intensity and tannins. Long finish. Tasted three times. Try now. 2,500 cases made. • $28 • (04/30/94) • **91**
Brunello di Montalcino 1982 • $22 • (09/15/86) • **85**
Brunello di Montalcino 1981 • $22 • (09/15/86) • **80**
Brunello di Montalcino Montosoli 1990: One of "the" greatest Brunellos ever made. Very muscular with loads of polished tannins and fruit. Full-bodied and powerful, boasting gravel, mineral and berry character. Needs time, try after 2000. • $60 • **98**
Brunello di Montalcino Montosoli 1988 • $37 • (04/30/94) • **92**
Brunello di Montalcino Riserva 1988: Extremely fruity, with a thick, rich mouth-feel. Gorgeous aromas of cassis, strawberry and blackberry follow through on the palate accompanied by fine tannins and a medium finish. Not as good as the single-vineyard Montosoli, but outstanding all the same. Drinkable now. • $50 • (10/31/94) • **90**
Palazzo Altesi 1990: Always a beautiful glass of wine. Lovely chocolate, cedar and licorice aromas and flavors, medium body, well-integrated tannins and long finish. Made from Sangiovese. Drinkable in 1997. 1,100 cases made. • $26 • (10/31/93) • **89**
Palazzo Altesi 1988 • $26 • (09/15/91) • **90**
Palazzo Altesi 1987 • $25 • (01/31/92) • **78**
Palazzo Altesi 1985 • $23 • (10/31/90) • **82**
Palazzo Altesi 1983 • $17 • (02/15/88) • **88**
Riserva Red 1983 • $29 • (11/30/89) • **86**
Rosso di Altesino 1989 • $8 • (01/31/92) BB • **86**
Rosso di Montalcino 1993: Ripe and rather generous, sporting some green tobacco, smoke and plum character and medium body. Turns a bit dry on the crisp finish. Drink now. • $17 • **80**
Rosso di Montalcino 1992 • $15 • (04/30/94) • **81**
Rosso di Montalcino 1991 • $15 • (04/30/94) • **84**
Rosso di Montalcino 1988 • $15 • (07/15/91) • **73**
Rosso di Montalcino 1986 • $10 • (07/15/89) • **80**
Vigna Altesino 1985 • $32 • (09/30/90) • **91**
Vigna Altesino 1983 • $26 • (01/31/90) • **84**

AMA, CASTELLO DI

Chianti Classico 1993: A light and diluted Chianti for this normally top-notch producer. Modest fruit flavors, lacking concentration, and a bit dry on the finish. Tasted twice, with consistent notes. 17,000 cases made. • $15 • (10/31/95) • **78**
Chianti Classico 1992: Pretty and well made with vanilla, mint and cherry character. Light-bodied and fruity, but rather short on the finish. Drinkable now. 16,000 cases made. • $15 • (02/28/95) • **85**
Chianti Classico 1990 • $16 • (09/15/92) • **81**
Chianti Classico Castello di Ama 1988 • $18 • (04/15/91) • **87**
Chianti Classico Castello di Ama 1987 • $9 • (11/30/89) • **87**
Chianti Classico Castello di Ama 1986 • $8 • (01/31/89) • **87**
Chianti Classico Vigneto Bellavista 1992: Lovely perfumed wine for the vintage with berry, violet and grape character. Medium- to light-bodied with fine tannins and a fresh finish. Tasted twice, with consistent notes. 1,000 cases made. • $25 • **82**
Chianti Classico Vigneto Bellavista 1991: A real beauty, featuring vanilla, cherry, berry and coffee aromas and flavors. Medium in body, fine silky tannins and a smoky mocha finish. Drinkable now. 800 cases made. • $25 • **87**
Chianti Classico Vigneto Bellavista 1990: Rich and full-bodied yet very elegant. This is deeply colored with violet, raspberry and a touch of dried herbs. Delicious now. 1,100 cases made. • $38 • **91**
Chianti Classico di Ama Vigneto Bellavista 1988 • $34 • (09/15/92) • **90**
Chianti Classico di Ama Vigneto Bellavista 1986 • $36 • (11/30/89) • **90**
Chianti Classico di Ama Vigneto Bellavista 1985 • $30 • (07/31/89) • **94**
Chianti Classico di Ama Vigneto Bellavista 1983 • $25 • (12/15/87) • **90**
Chianti Classico Vigneto Bertinga 1990: Stupendous Chianti. Masses of berry and black cherry flavors. Full-bodied and fabulous, it fills your mouth with grapey, chocolatey notes and ripe tannins. Drinkable now. 1,100 cases made. • $34 • (02/28/95) • **93**
Chianti Classico di Ama Vigneto Bertinga 1988 • $34 • (09/15/92) • **89**
Chianti Classico Vigneto La Casuccia 1992: Another fresh and fruity wine with berry, violet and cherry character. Medium- to light-bodied with fresh acidity and a light tannic finish. Drinkable now. 1,000 cases made. • $25 • **82**
Chianti Classico Vigneto La Casuccia 1991: Delicious toasted oak and ripe blackberry flavors. Medium-bodied and firm with silky tannins and a medium finish. Drinkable now. 800 cases made. • $25 • **86**
Chianti Classico Vigneto La Casuccia 1990: An impressive bounty of fruit and tannins, yet well integrated. Very aromatic, exhibiting berry, cassis and wet earth character, medium-to-full body, fine tannins and a long, fruity finish. Drinkable now. 1,100 cases made. • $38 • **93**
Chianti Classico Vigneto La Casuccia Riserva 1990 • $36 • (09/15/92) • **85**
Chianti Classico Vigneto La Casuccia Riserva 1986 • $40 • (11/30/89) • **87**
Chianti Classico Vigneto La Casuccia Riserva 1985 • $40 • (09/15/91) • **89**
Chianti Classico Vigneto San Lorenzo 1990: Solid and firm with cassis, berry and mint aromas and flavors. Full body and full tannins, but fruity and succulent on the finish. Try in 1997. 1,000 cases made. • $34 • **90**
Chianti Classico Vigneto San Lorenzo 1988 • $34 • (09/15/92) • **91**

AMBRA

Chianti Classico Vigneto San Lorenzo 1986 • $36 • (11/30/89) • **84**
Chianti Classico Vigneto San Lorenzo 1985 • $32 • (11/30/89) • **86**
Colline di Ama 1986 • $9 • (11/15/87) • **82**
Merlot Vigna l'Apparita 1990: This is Italy's greatest Merlot. A wine with vivid blackberry and tar aromas and flavors, a full-bodied, polished palate of velvety tannins and long finish. Drinkable now. 1,170 cases made. • $40 • (10/31/93) • **92**
Merlot Vigna l'Apparita 1988 • $NA • (09/15/91) • **93**
Merlot Vigna l'Apparita 1986 • $NA • (11/30/89) • **87**
Merlot Vigna l'Apparita 1985 • $NA • (11/30/89) • **92**
Vigna Il Chiuso 1992: Old and rustic style of Pinot Noir, turning to brown sugar and licorice, with the fruit fading quickly. Astringent finish. Very disappointing from this reputable producer. Tasted twice, with consistent notes. 900 cases made. • $25 • (10/31/95) • **73**
Vigna Il Chiuso 1991: Incredibly flavorful Pinot Noir exhibiting peppersteak, berry and fruit quality, full body, medium tannins and finish. Delicious now but will improve with age. 1,000 cases made. • $25 • (02/28/95) • **88**
Vigna Il Chiuso 1988 • $25 • (09/15/91) • **90**
Vigna Il Chiuso Castello di Ama 1990: A fresh and fruity Pinot Noir in the style of a good village Côte d'Or Burgundy. Medium-bodied with silky tannins and a medium finish. Drinkable now. 200 cases made. • $34 • (10/31/93) • **85**
Vigna l'Apparita 1992: Another well-crafted, refined wine with fresh berry, blackberry and light oak aromas and flavors. Medium-bodied with fine tannins and a fruity finish. Made from Merlot. Drink or hold. 1,000 cases made. • $60 • **88**
Vigna l'Apparita 1991: As good as the '90. Ripe blackberry, cassis and toasted oak aromas and flavors bubble over. Full-bodied and very silky, impressive fruit and a medium finish. 100% Merlot. Try after 1997. 1,100 cases made. • $60 • **92**

AMBRA

Barco Reale 1985 • $7 • (04/15/88) • **76**
Carmignano 1986 • $13 • (05/15/89) • **80**
Carmignano 1985 • $11 • (04/15/88) • **83**
Carmignano 1984 • $8 • (12/31/87) • **79**
Carmignano 1983 • $9 • (07/16/86) BB • **88**

ANGELO, D'

Aglianico del Vulture 1985 • $18 • (09/15/89) • **70**

ANSELMI

Cabernet Sauvignon Realda 1989 • $28 • (12/15/92) • **84**
Cabernet Sauvignon Realda 1988 • $28 • (09/15/92) • **78**
Capitel Foscarino Soave Classico 1992: This sings a good bass note for a white wine, showing mature smoky, buttery aromas and solid pear and mint flavors. Nicely crisp in texture, harmonious and satisfying to drink. 950 cases made. • $18 • (05/31/95) • **86**
Recioto della Valpolicella 1985 • $19 • (06/30/91) • **86**
Recioto di Soave I Capitelli 1992: A soft, luscious dessert wine boasting wonderful creamy, buttery, nutty flavors that are complex and intriguing. Very sweet and concentrated, and long on the finish. 800 cases made. • $35 • (04/30/96) • **90**
Recioto di Soave I Capitelli 1989 • $35 • (09/15/92) • **94**
Recioto dei Capitelli 1988 • $34 • (09/15/92) CS • **95**
Soave Classico Sanvincenzo 1993: Really puts some interest in a too-often bland type of wine. Nicely balanced and intriguing in flavor, this has the expansive aromas—pear, pineapple, toasted almond—yet stays rather light and lively on the palate. 28,000 cases made. • $9 • (05/31/95) BB • **86**
Soave Classico Superiore 1991 • $9 • (09/15/92) • **83**

Key: SS—Spectator Selection. CS—Cellar Selection. BB—Best Buy. $NA—Price not available. (BT)—Barrel tasting. (A)—Auction Price.
Dates in parentheses represent the issues in which the ratings were published.

Soave Classico Superiore Capitel Croce 1991: Harsh smoke and vegetal aromas and flavors are too much for us, though settling down on the finish, it isn't pleasurable. 2,000 cases made. • $14 • (04/30/96) • **76**
Soave Classico Superiore San Vincenzo 1994: Butter and honey flavors overlay the pear and banana in this Soave. It has intensity and some length, adding a sweet, smoky finish. 7,500 cases made. • $9 • (04/30/96) • **84**

ANTINORI

Borro della Sala 1993 • $13 • (10/31/94) • **77**
Borro della Sala Castello della Sala 1991 • $13 • (09/15/93) • **88**
Borro della Sala 1993 • $13 • (10/31/94) • **77**
Campogrande Orvieto Classico 1993 • $8 • (10/31/94) • **82**
Cervaro della Sala Castello della Sala 1993: Oak dominates flavors of toast, butterscotch and vanilla, but there's enough sweet melon to keep it honest. A heavy wine that needs food, it will please fans of wood-aging. • $22 • **84**
Cervaro della Sala Castello della Sala White 1992: An international-style Chardonnay that shows off its oak-aging in buttery, toasty flavors and rich texture. Has crisp acidity and ample fruit yet maintains lightness. • $22 • (05/31/95) • **89**
Chardonnay Castello della Sala 1994: Bright, fresh and peachlike in flavor, nicely accented by toasty oak, with good depth and a lingering aftertaste. Crisp acidity makes it especially refreshing. • $8 • (02/29/96) • **86**
Chianti Classico 1988 • $11 • (09/15/91) • **86**
Chianti Classico Badia a Passignano 1993: Delicious and impressively concentrated for the vintage. Grapey, chocolatey, herbal aromas and flavors, medium-bodied and juicy, leading to a light finish. Drinkable now. 35,000 cases made. • $9 • (02/28/95) • **83**
Chianti Classico Badia a Passignano 1991 • $9 • (10/31/93) • **84**
Chianti Classico Badia a Passignano 1990 • $NA • (10/31/93) • **92**
Chianti Classico Badia a Passignano Riserva 1991: Excellent concentration of fruit with minty, chocolate, berry, toasted oak character. Medium to full body, plus fine, polished tannins and a long finish. Drinkable now or age. 5,000 cases made. • $30 • **89**
Chianti Classico Badia a Passignano Riserva 1990: A richly flavored, firmly tannic, many layered Chianti that's very young. It blends crisp raspberry flavors with rich chocolate and vanilla accents. Drinkable now. 5,000 cases made. • $30 • (02/28/95) • **89**
Chianti Classico Badia a Passignano Riserva 1988 • $30 • (04/30/94) • **88**
Chianti Classico Pèppoli 1993: Wonderfully perfumed wine with flowers and raspberry aromas. Medium- to light-bodied with fresh flavors and a light finish. Drinkable now. 15,000 cases made. • $16 • (10/31/95) • **82**
Chianti Classico Pèppoli 1991 • $NA • (10/31/93) • **82**
Chianti Classico Pèppoli 1990 • $14 • (09/15/92) • **86**
Chianti Classico Pèppoli 1988 • $19 • (09/15/91) • **88**
Chianti Classico Pèppoli 1987 • $22 • (05/15/90) • **83**
Chianti Classico Pèppoli 1986 • $41 • (07/15/89) • **90**
Chianti Classico Pèppoli 1985 • $16 • (05/31/88) • **92**
Chianti Classico Riserva 1985 • $9 • (10/15/89) • **89**
Chianti Classico Riserva 1982 • $10 • (11/30/89) • **87**
Chianti Classico Santa Cristina 1985 • $6 • (10/31/88) BB • **90**
Chianti Classico Tenute Marchese Antinori Riserva 1991: Firm yet rich wine with tobacco, cherry and earth aromas and flavors. Medium body. Ripe, firm tannins and a silky finish. Drinkable now. 16,000 cases made. • $22 • **87**
Chianti Classico Tenute Marchese Antinori Riserva 1990: Slightly overdone, ripe berry and a hint of cooked rhubarb. Medium-bodied and soft with a flavorful finish. Tasted twice, with consistent notes. Drinkable now. 16,000 cases made. • $22 • (02/28/95) • **85**
Chianti Classico Tenute Marchese Riserva 1989 • $22 • (10/31/93) • **82**
Chianti Classico Tenute Marchese Riserva 1988 • $22 • (04/30/94) • **85**
Chianti Classico Tenute Marchese Riserva 1987 • $22 • (09/15/92) • **85**
Chianti Classico Tenute Marchese Riserva 1985 • $21 • (10/31/91) • **88**
Chianti Classico Tenute Marchese Riserva 1983 • $16 • (11/30/89) • **90**
Chianti Classico Tenute Marchese Riserva 1982 • $16 • (05/31/89) • **90**
Chianti Classico Tenute Marchese Riserva 1980 • $16 • (09/15/87) • **90**
Chianti Classico Villa Antinori Riserva 1990: Modest cherry and plum flavors with a firm backbone and good structure. It has some leathery

and earthy notes as well. Still, it's fairly simple. 80,000 cases made. • $12 • (07/31/95) • **82**

Chianti Classico Villa Antinori Riserva 1989: A smooth, moderately tannic structure supports a generous core of fresh cherry flavor. Smoky, rustic nuances add character. • $12 • **82**

Chianti Classico Villa Antinori Riserva 1988 • $11 • (09/15/92) • **79**

Chianti Classico Villa Antinori Riserva 1987 • $11 • (11/30/91) • **82**

Chianti Classico Villa Antinori Riserva 1983 • $9 • (03/31/89) • **79**

Nature Spumante NV • $18 • (12/31/86) • **68**

Orvieto Classico Campogrande 1993 • $8 • (10/31/94) • **82**

Pinot Nero Castello della Sala Vigneto Consola 1990 • $NA • (10/31/93) • **84**

Rosso di Montepulciano La Braccesca 1993: Very tannic, making it slightly disjointed at this stage. Minty, berry character, medium body, astringent finish. Drink now. • $11 • **80**

Santa Cristina 1993: Always an excellent value. Light-bodied and fresh, with fragrant raspberry and black cherry character and a clean finish. Drink now. 90% Sangiovese. • $7 • (02/28/95) • **84**

Santa Cristina 1992 • $7 • (07/31/94) • **83**

Santa Cristina 1991 • $7 • (06/30/93) BB • **84**

Santa Cristina 1990 • $7 • (12/15/92) • **79**

Santa Cristina 1989 • $7 • (07/15/91) • **80**

Santa Cristina 1988 • $6 • (01/31/91) BB • **85**

Santa Cristina 1987 • $6 • (04/30/89) BB • **81**

Solaia 1991: What a beautiful wine! A classy Tuscan vino da tavola with a crisp character, but there are plenty of lovely, earthy cassis and sweet, ripe plum flavors. Delicious from start to finish. Watch for the tannins, better in 1998. 5,000 cases made. • $65 CS • **90**

Solaia 1990: The greatest vintage of Solaia to date, its aftertaste goes on for minutes. A marvelous balance between power and finesse. Full-bodied and rich, exhibiting layers of fruit yet the tannins are incredibly well integrated. Better after 1998. 5,000 cases made. • $65 • (02/28/95) CS • **97**

Solaia 1989 • $65 • (11/15/93) • **88**

Solaia 1988 • $95 • (11/15/93) • **97**

Solaia 1987 • $39 Ⓐ • (11/15/93) • **88**

Solaia 1986 • $52 Ⓐ • (11/15/93) • **90**

Tenuta Belvedere Guado al Tasso 1992: Silky, ripe, a delicious wine that delivers layers of tobacco, coffee, blackberry and earth flavors. Long, seamless, seductive finish. Drink now through 1997. • $NA • **86**

Tenuta Belvedere Guado al Tasso 1990: Debut red wine from Piero Antinori in Bolgheri. Pure silk here with gorgeous smoke, chestnut, meat and berry aromas and flavors, medium body and supple, long finish. Drinkable now. 800 cases made. • $NA • (02/28/95) • **89**

Tignanello 1991: Well-crafted with berry, violet and vanilla aromas and flavors. Medium-bodied with fine tannins and a delicate finish. Made from Sangiovese and Cabernet Sauvignon. Drink now. 23,000 cases made. • $38 • (10/31/95) • **86**

Tignanello 1990: Possibly the greatest Tignanello ever. Wonderfully aromatic, showing plum, coffee, leather, smoke and vanilla. It is ripe and subtle, full-bodied and richly tannic. Has a long, long finish. Try after 1997. 23,000 cases made. • $39 • (02/28/95) CS • **92**

Tignanello 1989 • $33 • (11/15/93) • **86**

Tignanello 1988 • $42 • (11/15/93) • **95**

Tignanello 1987 • $37 • (11/15/93) • **87**

Tignanello 1986 • $40 • (11/15/93) • **87**

Tignanello 1985 • $45 • (11/15/93) • **88**

Tignanello 1983 • $45 • (11/15/93) • **88**

Tignanello 1982 • $37 • (07/15/87) CS • **91**

Villa Antinori 1993 • $8 • (10/31/94) • **82**

Vino Nobile di Montepulciano La Braccesca 1992: Full-bodied, generous and firm-textured wine with grilled meat, tobacco and red berry character. Quite tannic, so try after 1997. • $18 • (10/31/95) • **86**

ANTONIOLO

Gattinara 1988 • $18 • (10/15/94) • **83**

Gattinara Vigneto Castelle 1988 • $22 • (10/15/94) • **85**

ANTONUTTI

Poggio Alto 1986 • $15 • (04/15/90) • **86**

AQUINO, GAETANO D'

Chianti Riserva 1988 • $10 • (09/15/92) • **82**

ARCENO, VILLA

Chianti Classico 1990 • $NA • (10/31/93) • **83**

ARGIANO

Brunello di Montalcino 1990: Seductively round, full in body and flavorful, it bursts with floral, violet, red berry and milk chocolate notes. Excellent backbone of supple tannins. Drink now. • $35 • (10/31/95) • **90**

Brunello di Montalcino 1988: A traditional estate on a roll. A beautifully integrated wine, with bright and clean fruit flavors of plums and blackberries, a hint of oak, lovely tannins and a long finish. Approachable, but better after 1996. 5,000 cases made. • $29 • (04/30/94) • **91**

Brunello di Montalcino 1979 • $11 • (09/15/86) • **77**

Brunello di Montalcino Riserva 1988: A lovely, traditional Brunello, though not as good as the regular Argiano bottling. This is big, ripe and smoky, with soft tannins. Very concentrated with a long, velvety finish but also a slight bite. Try in 1997. • $26 • (10/31/94) • **88**

Brunello di Montalcino Riserva 1985 • $42 • (12/15/92) • **88**

Brunello di Montalcino Riserva 1978 • $12 • (09/15/86) • **68**

Brunello di Montalcino Riserva 1977 • $13 • (09/15/86) • **67**

Rosso di Montalcino 1993: Very good chocolate, berry and toasted oak aromas and flavors, medium body, soft tannins and a delicious finish. Drinkable now. • $19 • (10/31/95) • **85**

Rosso di Montalcino 1992 • $13 • (10/31/94) • **77**

Rosso di Montalcino 1991 • $18 • (04/30/94) • **82**

ARGIOLAS

Turriga 1989: Subtle and harmonious. Attractive cedar, spice and cherry aromas lead to round flavors of cherry and chocolate and a fruity finish. Drinkable now. • $22 • (05/31/95) • **89**

ARMANI, AZIENDA AGRICOLA

Chardonnay Trentino Vigneto Capitel 1991 • $14 • (05/31/93) • **82**

Pinot Grigio Valdadige Vigneto Corvara 1991 • $14 • (06/30/93) • **83**

ARNALDO CAPRAI

Grecante Grechetto 1993 • $12 • (10/31/94) • **85**

Montefalco 1991: Thick, with flavors of earth, spice and prunes. Sturdy, but lacks definition and grace. Drinkable now, but may soften in 1997. 7,500 cases made. • $10 • **81**

Sagratino di Montefalco 1988: Smooth and thick, with dark flavors of chocolate, coffee and plums. Mature now, and a bit dry on the finish. It has more strength than grace, try with rich, meat dishes. 1,400 cases made. • $15 • **84**

ARPA CLASSICA

Sangiovese di Romagna 1985 • $4 • (12/31/87) • **70**

ARRIGONI, B.

Chianti Putto 1987 • $4 • (11/30/89) • **78**

ASCHERI, CANTINE GIACOMO

Barbaresco 1992: Already mature, with light cherry and almond aromas and flavors and medium to light body. Drink as soon as possible. 500 cases made. • $20 • (10/31/95) • **75**

Barolo Vigna Farina 1991: Round and easy berry, chestnut and a hint of cheese on nose and palate. Medium in body, adding soft tannins and finish. Drink now. 625 cases made. • $30 • (10/31/95) • **79**

AVIGNONESI

Aleatico Red 1990: Distinctive and lightly sweet, made to go with cheese. Like a fresh Port. Wonderfully aromatic rose petals, berries and spices. Medium-bodied. Drinkable now. 500 cases made. • $28 • (02/28/95) • **86**
Desiderio 1988 • $39 • (12/15/92) • **85**
Grifi 1990: As good now as when we tasted this Tuscan powerhouse in barrel. Loads of fruit with a jammy character and a hint of vanilla. Full-bodied and tannic, but very closed. Built for aging, try after 1998. 2,500 cases made. • $36 • (02/28/95) • **91**
Grifi 1988 • $32 • (11/15/93) • **93**
Grifi 1987 • $27 • (11/15/93) • **87**
Grifi 1986 • $30 • (11/15/93) • **88**
Grifi 1985 • $40 • (11/15/93) • **90**
Grifi 1983 • $30 • (11/15/93) • **90**
Grifi 1982 • $10 • (06/16/85) • **87**
Merlot 1991: Very good wine with cherry, tobacco, and vanilla character. Medium- to full-bodied with firm tannins and a medium smoky, berry finish. Drinkable now. 1,600 cases made. • $36 • **88**
Merlot 1990: Not as great as expected from our barrel-tasting results in 1993. Still, pleasant chocolate and plum character, medium body, light tannins and succulent finish. Tasted twice, with consistant notes. Drinkable now. 2,167 cases made. • $55 • (02/28/95) • **86**
Merlot 1989 • $36 • (10/31/93) • **82**
Pinot Nero di Valdicapraia 1990: Absolutely wonderful aromas of berry, tobacco and cigar box. Palate is less impressive. Medium-bodied and firm with tobacco and berry character and a slightly short finish. Drink now. • $NA • **86**
Rosso di Montepulciano 1993: Light and disappointing, very diluted. Modest strawberry and raspberry notes. Quite forward already. Somewhat dry on the finish. Tasted twice, with consistent notes. • $NA • (10/31/95) • **74**
Rosso di Montepulciano 1991 • $12 • (11/15/93) • **80**
Rosso di Montepulciano 1990 • $12 • (12/15/92) • **84**
Rosso di Montepulciano 1989 • $12 • (04/30/91) • **83**
Tuscany Red 1988 • $45 • (09/15/91) • **93**
Vin Santo 1984 • $75 • (01/31/93) • **92**
Vin Santo 1977 • $18 • (10/01/85) • **92**
Vino Nobile di Montepulciano 1992: Weedy and tired, light-bodied, with tobacco and tomato notes. Fading fast. Tasted twice, with consistent notes. 5,800 cases made. • $20 • (10/31/95) • **76**
Vino Nobile di Montepulciano 1990: Distinctive meaty, mineral aromas give way to round flavors of chocolate, cedar and dried black fruit. Though muted, it's well integrated and concentrated. • $22 • (02/29/96) • **85**
Vino Nobile di Montepulciano 1988 • $22 • (12/15/92) • **86**
Vino Nobile di Montepulciano 1985 • $12 • (02/15/88) • **86**
Vino Nobile di Montepulciano 1981 • $7 • (10/01/85) • **86**
Vino Nobile di Montepulciano 1980 • $6 • (07/01/85) • **85**
Vino Nobile di Montepulciano Riserva 1988 • $24 • (11/15/93) • **87**
Vino Nobile di Montepulciano Riserva Grandi Annate 1990: One of the last '90s to come out and delicious. Very silky and refined wine with tobacco, cedar and berry aromas and flavors. Medium-bodied with medium tannins and a long, succulent finish. Tasted twice, with consistent notes. Drinkable now or can be cellared. 1,000 cases made. • $36 • **89**

AZELIA

Barolo Bricco Fiasco 1989: This is an elegant wine with nice smooth tannins and mellow fruit flavors. Clean, well-balanced and full of black cherry and cranberry fruit. May be best to drink in 1997. • $24 • (10/31/94) • **85**
Barolo Bricco Fiasco 1985 • $30 • (07/15/91) • **81**
Barolo Bricco Punta 1982 • $23 • (11/15/88) • **92**

Key: SS—Spectator Selection. CS—Cellar Selection. BB—Best Buy. $NA—Price not available. (BT)—Barrel tasting. Ⓐ—Auction Price.
Dates in parentheses represent the issues in which the ratings were published.

Cascina Nuova 1986 • $8 • (12/31/87) • **78**
Dolcetto d'Alba 1987 • $7 • (03/15/89) • **85**
Dolcetto d'Alba Bricco dell'Oriolo 1989 • $9 • (07/15/91) • **79**

BADIA A COLTIBUONO

Cancelli 1993: Has the whole palette of Tuscan flavors—spice, cherry, olive, herb—in an elegant package of acidity and firm tannins. It's lean and mature, so drink soon. 5,000 cases made. • $8 • (12/31/95) • **85**
Cancelli 1990 • $7 • (10/31/93) • **78**
Chianti Cetamura 1990 • $8 • (10/31/93) • **78**
Chianti Cetamura 1988 • $7 • (12/15/90) BB • **82**
Chianti Classico 1987 • $8 • (11/30/89) • **85**
Chianti Classico Riserva 1990: Fresh, dried cherry and berry aromas and flavors, medium body and tannins and a silky finish. Tasted twice, with consistent notes. Drinkable now. • $25 • (02/28/95) • **85**
Chianti Classico Riserva 1988: Well matured, showing attractive aromas of earth, leather and spice. Dried cherry flavors and firm tannins give it a firm finish. Drink now. • $20 • (07/31/95) • **84**
Chianti Classico Riserva 1987 • $15 • (09/15/92) • **84**
Chianti Classico Riserva 1985 • $16 • (09/15/91) • **90**
Chianti Classico Riserva 1983 • $15 • (11/30/89) • **78**
Chianti Classico Riserva 1982 • $13 • (07/31/88) • **88**
Coltibuono Rosso 1986 • $6 • (07/31/88) • **81**
Sangioveto 1988 • $40 • (10/31/93) • **94**
Sangioveto 1985 • $30 • (11/30/89) • **85**
Sangioveto 1983 • $20 • (11/30/89) • **84**
Sangioveto 1982 • $20 • (11/30/89) • **87**
Sangioveto 1981 • $21 • (09/15/87) • **87**

BAGGIOLINO, FATTORIA

Chianti Colli Fiorentini 1993: Light, fresh and easy to drink, more like a wine spritzer. Disappointing. Tasted twice, with consistent notes. • $NA • (02/28/95) • **72**
Chianti Colli Fiorentini 1992: Good fruit, peppery, berry character and a supple mouth-feel. Drinkable now. • $NA • **83**
Chianti Colli Fiorentini 1990 • $NA • (10/31/93) • **86**
Chianti Colli Fiorentini Riserva 1991 • $NA • (10/31/93) • **85**
Chianti Colli Fiorentini Riserva 1990: Full power, full-blown style. Perhaps a little too much. But there's interesting prune and berry character and intense, velvety tannin structure. Drinkable now. • $NA • **87**
Poggio Brandi 1993: A generous, full-bodied wine, but slightly overdone. Very concentrated with loads of gamy, peppery character. A bit drying on the palate. Made from Sangiovese and Ciliegiolo. Try after 1997. • $NA • (10/31/95) • **85**
Poggio Brandi 1990: Distinctive Sangioveto- and Ciliegolo-based red displaying pepper, game and berry aromas and flavors, medium body, medium tannins and fresh finish. Drinkable now. 1,000 cases made. • $26 • **86**
Poggio Brandi 1986 • $19 • (08/31/91) • **86**
Poggio Brandi 1985 • $19 • (09/15/89) • **84**

BAIOCCHI, CANTINE

Vino Nobile di Montepulciano 1986 • $15 • (03/15/91) • **87**
Vino Nobile di Montepulciano Riserva 1985 • $10 • (11/30/89) • **85**

BANFI, CASTELLO

Asti Spumante NV • $13 • (05/15/93) • **81**
Belnero 1992: Elegant wine with flower, rose and leather aromas. Medium-bodied with firm tannins and a fresh finish. Made from Pinot Noir. Drinkable now. 1,500 cases made. • $28 • (10/31/95) • **85**
Belnero 1990: An agreeable Italian Pinot Noir that is smooth and polished in texture and nicely fruity in flavor, with light herb and olive accents. Has modest tannins and is ready to drink now. 1,400 cases made. • $30 • (02/28/94) • **83**
Brachetto d'Acqui 1992 • $16 • (05/15/93) • **87**
Brunello di Montalcino 1990: A wonderful Brunello boasting mineral, violet, berry and cherry character and a hint of new oak. Full-bodied and powerful, adding loads of tannins and a very long finish. One to

cellar for a long time, try in 1999. Better than a sample reviewed earlier in New York. • $30 • (10/31/95) • **93**
Brunello di Montalcino 1986 • $32 • (12/31/92) CS • **91**
Brunello di Montalcino 1985 • $30 • (10/15/90) • **92**
Brunello di Montalcino 1982 • $28 • (12/15/87) • **89**
Brunello di Montalcino 1981 • $23 • (03/31/87) CS • **92**
Brunello di Montalcino 1980 • $20 • (09/15/86) • **90**
Brunello di Montalcino 1979 • $18 • (04/16/85) SS • **90**
Brunello di Montalcino Poggio all'Oro 1985 • $37 • (12/15/91) CS • **92**
Brunello di Montalcino Poggio all'Oro Riserva 1988 • $32 • (10/31/94) • **90**
Cabernet Sauvignon Tavernelle 1988 • $23 • (09/15/91) • **87**
Cabernet Sauvignon Tavernelle 1985 • $23 • (03/31/93) • **83**
Cabernet Sauvignon Tavernelle 1984 • $18 • (01/31/88) • **89**
Cabernet Sauvignon Tavernelle 1982 • $15 • (08/01/85) • **88**
Chardonnay Fontanelle 1993: This complex and distinctive Chardonnay from Italy blends toasty, spicy oak aromas with ample fruit and nutty nuances to make a concentrated, focused, nicely balanced whole. Long on the finish and thoroughly enticing. 1,200 cases imported. • $17 • (02/29/96) • **91**
Chianti 1987 • $7 • (11/30/89) BB • **85**
Chianti Classico Riserva 1989 • $10 • (05/15/94) • **79**
Chianti Classico Riserva 1988 • $10 • (05/15/93) • **80**
Chianti Classico Riserva 1985 • $9 • (05/15/90) • **86**
Chianti Classico Riserva 1982 • $7 • (12/15/87) • **83**
Chianti Classico Riserva 1981 • $7 • (08/31/86) • **80**
Colvecchio 1992: A rather unpleasant stewed-fruit character, full-bodied and extracted but very dry on the finish. Dumb and out of balance. Syrah. Perhaps better after 1997. 2,200 cases made. • $25 • (02/28/95) • **78**
Colvecchio 1991: Fresh boysenberry and currant aromas in this Syrah, medium-bodied with tobacco, vanilla and fruit flavors and fine tannins. Slightly better than the '90. Drinkable now. 1,800 cases made. • $25 • (02/28/95) • **87**
Colvecchio 1990: A soft and round wine showing attractive berry, cedar and chocolate character, medium-bodied and velvety with a medium finish. Made from Syrah. Drinkable now. 1,600 cases made. • $30 • (10/31/93) • **85**
Fontanelle 1991: A full-bodied Chardonnay in the international style: plenty of toasty, creamy oak, ripe tropical fruit flavors, lemony acidity. It doesn't say Tuscany, but it does say flavor. 6,700 cases made. • $15 • (06/15/94) • **84**
Mandrielle 1992: Elegant violet, cassis, berry and toasted oak character, full-to-medium body, silky tannins and a ripe fruit finish. Made from Merlot. Drinkable now. 3,500 cases made. • $25 • (02/28/95) • **89**
Mandrielle 1990: Beautiful aromas of pepper, game and fruit, medium body, soft tannins and a delicious aftertaste. Drink this Merlot now. 1,500 cases made. • $25 • (02/28/95) • **87**
Rosso di Montalcino 1992 • $9 • (10/31/94) • **80**
Rosso di Montalcino Centine 1993: Medium-bodied Rosso, both crisp and generous, featuring ripe, sweet-tasting plum, black cherry and lemon rind flavors that end on a medium to long finish. 40,000 cases made. • $8 • (10/31/95) • **83**
Rosso di Montalcino Centine 1992 • $10 • (04/30/94) • **73**
Rosso di Montalcino Centine 1991 • $10 • (04/30/94) • **77**
Rosso di Montalcino Centine 1990 • $8 • (03/31/93) • **82**
Rosso di Montalcino Centine 1989 • $8 • (12/15/92) • **81**
Rosso di Montalcino Centine 1988 • $8 • (12/15/91) BB • **81**
Rosso di Montalcino Centine 1987 • $8 • (06/15/90) BB • **85**
Rosso di Montalcino Centine 1986 • $7 • (11/30/89) BB • **87**
Rosso di Montalcino Centine 1985 • $7 • (11/30/87) BB • **88**
Rosso di Montalcino Centine 1983 • $7 • (04/30/87) BB • **89**
San Angelo 1993 • $10 • (06/15/94) • **80**
Serena 1991 • $13 • (06/15/94) • **81**
Spumante Brut 1987 • $17 • (05/15/93) • **76**
Spumante Brut 1986 • $20 • (03/31/92) • **83**
Spumante Brut 1985 • $16 • (06/30/90) • **81**
Spumante Brut 1984 • $14 • (03/31/88) • **90**
Spumante Brut 1982 • $13 • (12/31/86) • **88**
Summus 1988 • $NA • (09/15/91) • **87**
Summus Tuscany 1990: Impressive texture, silky tannins, concentrated fruit and wonderful aromas and flavors of berry, mint, tar and tobacco. Made from Sangiovese, Cabernet Sauvignon and Syrah. Better in 1997. 3,000 cases made. • $40 • (10/31/93) • **92**
Tavernelle 1992: Polished and refined, with blackberry, dried herb and mint character, medium body, fine tannins and long berry finish. Made from Cabernet Sauvignon. Better in 1997. 2,500 cases made. • $20 • (10/31/95) • **88**
Tavernelle 1991: Sneaks up on you with plum, berry and tobacco aromas and flavors. Medium-bodied and very firm in tannins, sporting a long, tobacco finish. Cabernet Sauvignon. Drinkable now. 4,000 cases made. • $22 • (02/28/95) • **86**
Tavernelle 1990: Offering pretty cedar, berry and floral aromas, it's medium-bodied, soft and round with a ripe fruit finish. Made from Cabernet Sauvignon. Drinkable now. 3,500 cases made. • $23 • (10/31/93) • **85**
Tavernelle 1989 • $23 • (10/31/93) • **84**

BARACCO DE BARACHO

Barolo 1988 • $26 • (06/30/93) • **77**

BARBERINO

Chianti Alaura 1994: • $6 • **69**

BARBI

Secco Orvieto Classico 1992 • $8 • (10/31/94) • **84**

BARBI, FATTORIA DEI

Brunello di Montalcino 1990: Wonderfully fresh and finely structured plum, violet and berry character. Full-bodied and silky and a crisp, refreshing finish. Better in 1997. • $26 • (10/31/95) • **88**
Brunello di Montalcino 1988: Fresh and rather simple, with a pretty cherry and smoke character, medium body and moderate tannins. Tasted twice with consistent notes. • $30 • (04/30/94) • **81**
Brunello di Montalcino 1982 • $20 • (03/15/89) • **78**
Brunello di Montalcino 1981 • $20 • (09/15/86) • **85**
Brunello di Montalcino Blue Label 1986 • $28 • (08/31/91) • **84**
Brunello di Montalcino Blue Label 1981 • $20 • (01/31/91) • **81**
Brunello di Montalcino Riserva 1988: Not as good as the Vigna del Fiore. This is a bit one dimensional, in a chunky style, with clean berry flavor, firm tannins and a refreshing finish. Drinkable now. • $35 • (10/31/94) • **85**
Brunello di Montalcino Riserva 1985 • $46 • (11/30/91) • **87**
Brunello di Montalcino Riserva 1977 • $20 • (09/15/86) • **86**
Brunello di Montalcino Vigna del Fiore 1988: Excellent potential here, but not giving much now. Some beautiful aromas of plums, cherry and dark chocolate. Full-bodied and firm structured. Needs time. Try after 1997. • $NA • (04/30/94) • **90**
Brunello di Montalcino Vigna del Fiore Riserva 1988: Starting to close up but very harmonious now for its full body and loads of fruit and fine tannins. Long blackberry finish. Better after 1997. • $48 • (10/31/94) • **90**
Brusco dei Barbi 1992: Impressive black cherry, mushroom and meat character, medium-to-light body, light tannins and a fresh finish. Drinkable now. 5,000 cases made. • $10 • (02/28/95) • **83**
Brusco dei Barbi 1988 • $12 • (09/15/91) • **86**
Brusco dei Barbi 1986 • $9 • (04/30/89) • **79**
Brusco dei Barbi 1985 • $9 • (10/15/88) • **85**
Bruscone 1990: Extremely fine and approachable, plum, chestnut and chocolate aromas and flavors, medium-bodied, medium tannins and a delicious finish. 100 percent Sangiovese. Drinkable now. • $12 • **86**
Bruscone di Barbi 1990 • $NA • (10/31/93) • **87**
Bruscone dei Barbi 1988 • $27 • (09/15/91) • **84**
Orvieto Classico 1992 • $8 • (10/31/94) • **84**
Rosso di Montalcino 1993: Deliciously fruity and soft, medium in body, adding round tannins and a long grapey, berry and cherry finish. Drinkable now. • $14 • (10/31/95) • **85**
Rosso di Montalcino 1992 • $12 • (10/31/94) • **85**
Rosso di Montalcino 1991 • $9 • (04/30/94) • **80**
Vigna del Fiore Red 1982 • $22 • (03/15/89) • **64**

BARONE

Cabernet Piave 1993: Though it's firm and balanced, there's not much fruit. It has some vanilla, light berry and citrus flavors. Drinkable now. 6,000 cases made. • $5 • (01/31/96) • **78**

Chardonnay 1993: A simple, slightly green Chardonnay that's overtly tart. Serviceable white wine but without any varietal character. 10,000 cases made. • $5 • (02/28/95) • **75**

Merlot Piave 1994: A light, simple red that offers modest cherry flavors. 15,000 cases made. • $5 • (02/29/96) • **79**

Merlot Piave 1993: Maturing, this shows brown sugar, strawberry and citrus flavors in a lean structure. 15,000 cases made. • $5 • (06/15/96) • **77**

Pinot Grigio 1994: Soft and buttery, this has some pleasant vanilla and coconut flavors, but lacks acidity for freshness. Easy to drink but a bit cloying. 40,000 cases made. • $5 • (04/30/96) • **78**

Pinot Grigio 1993: Think of this as uncomplicated refreshment. Very dry and crisp, clean but simple flavors. 40,000 cases made. • $5 • (05/31/95) • **77**

BARTOLI, MARCO DE

Marsala Superiore Vigna La Miccia 1985 • $16 • (03/31/90) • **87**

Moscato di Pantelleria 1987 • $16 • (03/31/90) • **87**

BASSE, CASE

Soldera Intistiei 1987 • $68 • (01/31/92) • **87**

BATASIOLO, BENI DI

Barbaresco 1990: Crisp and chewy, modest, with plenty of tannin and a spicy vanilla edge to the berry flavors, finishing citrusy. Best after 1997. Tasted twice. • $22 • (10/31/94) • **80**

Barbaresco 1989: A little chewy, with pleasant strawberry fruit, but then it turns musty and austere on the finish. Tasted twice. • $18 • (10/31/94) • **72**

Barbera d'Alba 1992 • $NA • (10/31/94) • **76**

Barbera d'Alba 1991 • $10 • (11/15/93) • **82**

Barbera d'Alba 1988 • $11 • (04/15/91) • **88**

Barbera d'Alba Sovrana 1990: Lean, hard, tannic and tart, showing definite herbal-earthy overtones to the modest cherry flavors. Very tight and tough now, maybe better around 1997. RT • $18 • **79**

Barolo 1991: The black cherry, cigar and minty flavors are attractive in this light-bodied, yet quite tannic red. It's fresh, and drinking well now. • $22 • (10/31/95) • **82**

Barolo 1990: Tightly tannic and chewy, with muddy cherry flavors that never quite brighten up. Tasted twice. • $22 • (10/31/94) • **78**

Barolo 1989: Crisp and almost overly mature, a light-colored, lighter style of Barolo that offers modest raspberry, anise and earth aromas and flavors. Drink after 1996. 8,750 cases made. • $18 • (10/31/93) • **81**

Barolo 1988 • $25 • (10/31/94) • **85**

Barolo 1985 • $15 • (03/31/90) • **84**

Barolo Bofani 1988 • $34 • (10/31/93) • **66**

Barolo Boscareto 1990: Tannic and tough, a hard-edged wine with menthol and tobacco flavors that obscure the fruit. 1,100 cases made. • $NA • (10/31/93) • **74**

Barolo Boscareto 1989: Very firm and tannic, with anise- and tobacco-scented berry and tar aromas and flavors, finishing tough and unyielding. There is enough fruit buried under the tannin to make it worth cellaring until 1998 if you like the style. 1,100 cases made. • $32 • (10/31/93) • **84**

Barolo Boscareto 1988 • $34 • (10/31/93) • **85**

Barolo La Corda della Briccolina 1990: Ripe, round, rich and supple, with tarry vanilla, blackberry, black cherry and currant flavors. Seems to pick up momentum on the long finish, folding in some rose petal and anise notes. Chunky tannins pervade, but it's a blockbuster. Give it until 2000 to 2005. Tasted twice. • $40 • (10/31/94) • **94**

Barolo La Corda della Briccolina 1989: Totally disarming, a gorgeous array of rose petal and anise-scented raspberry, vanilla and strawberry aromas and flavors extending through a supple finish that wraps its fine tannins smoothly around the warm fruit and spice. Drink now. 725 cases made. • $38 • (10/31/93) • **94**

Barolo La Corda della Briccolina 1988 • $38 • (10/31/93) • **90**

Barolo La Corda della Briccolina 1987 • $35 • (01/31/92) • **84**

Barolo Riserva 1986 • $22 • (12/15/92) • **81**

Barolo Riserva 1982 • $17 • (03/31/90) • **79**

Barolo Vigneto Bofani 1989: Distinctively floral, offering a definite violet note that runs through the aromas and flavors, smoothly integrating its wild berry and plum fruit with spicy floral overtones. A focused, lively red that has charm. Approachable now, best from 1997. • $25 • (10/31/94) • **90**

Barolo Vigneto Boscareto 1989: Ripe and inviting, with tannins that come off as coarse around a supple core of caramel and black cherry flavors. Drink it with hearty food. • $28 • (10/31/94) • **82**

Dolcetto d'Alba 1990 • $13 • (10/31/92) • **77**

Dolcetto d'Alba 1989 • $12 • (02/15/92) • **84**

Dolcetto d'Alba 1988 • $11 • (12/31/90) • **85**

Moscato d'Asti 1991 • $15 • (05/15/93) • **83**

Moscato d'Asti 1989 • $14 • (07/15/91) • **85**

BAVA

Barbaresco 1982 • $23 • (04/30/91) • **83**

Barbera d'Asti 1985 • $13 • (03/15/91) • **87**

Barbera d'Asti Cocconato 1990 • $10 • (04/30/93) • **75**

Barolo 1985 • $19 • (04/30/91) • **83**

BEL COLLE

Barbera d'Alba Le Masche 1989 • $15 • (10/31/92) • **86**

Barolo Riserva 1982 • $15 • (03/31/90) • **85**

Barolo Vigna Monvigliero 1985 • $20 • (10/15/90) • **87**

Dolcetto d'Alba 1986 • $7 • (04/15/88) • **80**

Dolcetto d'Alba Altavilla 1990 • $12 • (10/31/92) • **81**

Dolcetto d'Alba Madonna Como 1990 • $14 • (10/31/92) • **79**

BELLAVISTA

Brut Cuvée Franciacorta NV: Toasty and nutty, with some lemon and grapefruit flavors and a slightly vegetal aroma. A bit astringent on the finish. Tasted twice. 30,000 cases made. • $25 • **79**

Brut Gran Cuvée Franciacorta 1982 • $27 • (12/31/86) • **84**

Lombardy Solesine 1986 • $30 • (05/15/89) • **92**

Spumante Brut Cuvée NV • $18 • (12/31/86) • **82**

BERA

Asti Spumante NV • $15 • (07/15/91) • **83**

Asti Spumante Cascina Palazzo NV • $18 • (05/15/93) • **82**

Moscato d'Asti 1992 • $15 • (05/15/93) • **82**

Moscato d'Asti NV • $14 • (07/15/91) • **84**

BERETTA, CECILIA

Soave Classico Terre di Brognoligo 1993: Honey and vanilla flavors are appealing at first but then a bit cloying in this soft white. Coconut and floral notes add some interest. 400 cases made. • $8 • (04/30/96) • **80**

Valpoicella Classico Terre di Cariano della Amarone 1985: Not your average Amarone, but a distinctive, fruity and vibrant red table wine. Great balance, lively cherry flavors and ample accents of spice and vanilla from oak aging. Drink now through at least 1997. 200 cases made. • $26 • (09/30/95) • **89**

Valpolicella Superiore Roccolo di Mizzole 1992: Sweet and spicy, bursting with black cherry, licorice, mint and toasty oak flavors, enlivened by tart acidity. Has enough tannin for grip, but should be drunk now. 400 cases made. • $8 • (12/15/95) • **84**

Key: SS—Spectator Selection. CS—Cellar Selection. BB—Best Buy. $NA—Price not available. (BT)—Barrel tasting. Ⓐ—Auction Price.
Dates in parentheses represent the issues in which the ratings were published.

ITALY

BERLUCCHI, GUIDO

Brut Cuvée Imperiale 1981 • $15 • (12/31/86) • **80**
Brut Cuvée Impériale NV • $17 • (05/15/93) • **82**
Cuvée Imperiale NV • $13 • (09/15/89) • **81**
Cuvée Imperiale Pas Dose NV • $13 • (12/31/86) • **75**
Max Rosé Cuvée Imperiale NV • $17 • (05/15/93) • **81**

BERSANO

Asti Spumante Dolce NV: Pleasant orange and grapefruit flavors carry enough acidity to balance sweetness in this fresh, rather lean sparkler. Not as sweet as some, it would complement fruit and nut desserts. 21,600 cases made. • $13 • (10/31/95) • **83**
Barbaresco 1991: Light-bodied and rather simple, with cherry and light vegetal flavors. It's smooth and compact, but lacks depth. 10,800 cases made. • $16 • (10/31/95) • **78**
Barbaresco 1983 • $7 • (01/31/89) • **79**
Barbaresco 1975 • $NA • (09/15/88) • **76**
Barbaresco 1971 • $NA • (09/15/88) • **78**
Barbaresco 1964 • $NA • (09/15/88) • **85**
Barbera d'Asti 1992: Light-bodied, silky and rather simple. Attractive black cherry and cassis flavors have a slight earthy edge. It's soft and drinking well now. • $NA • (10/31/95) • **80**
Barbera d'Asti 1987 • $9 • (03/15/91) • **80**
Barolo 1991: Light on fruit, but with tough tannins, this is a bit clumsy. It shows soft, almost stewed cherry flavors, with tar and earth accents. 24,400 cases made. • $18 • (10/31/95) • **78**
Barolo 1985 • $10 • (10/15/90) • **79**
Barolo 1983 • $9 • (11/15/88) • **81**
Barolo 1974 • $NA • (09/15/88) • **79**
Barolo 1971 • $NA • (09/15/88) • **77**
Barolo 1964 • $NA • (09/15/88) • **80**
Barolo Cascina Badarina 1990: Still fresh, with a deep, youthful color. Exuberant aromas of coffee, spice and plum lead to ripe plum and tar flavors. Has a strong tannic backbone and is well balanced. Approachable now, but try in 1997. 750 cases made. • $30 • (10/31/95) • **87**
Castellengo 1986 • $16 • (04/15/91) • **88**
Dolcetto d'Alba 1994: Comes off a little harsh, with a slight vinegary taste. The flavors are dominated by dried cherry and cedar notes. 7,750 cases made. • $12 • (10/31/95) • **78**
Gavi 1994: Very simple, watery in flavor and somewhat cheesy in character. 17,750 cases made. • $11 • **71**

BERTANI

Bardolino Classico Superiore 1990 • $9 • (09/15/92) • **84**
Catullo 1990 • $12 • (11/15/94) • **79**
Catullo 1986 • $13 • (09/15/92) • **81**
Catullo 1984 • $9 • (02/15/89) • **86**
Catullo 1983 • $9 • (06/30/88) • **81**
Le Lave Veneto 1993: An attempt at a serious style with loads of buttery flavors that are reminiscent of a California Chardonnay. Not much fruit, though it is balanced. An indulgence to the gods of oak. • $18 • (06/15/96) • **87**
Recioto della Valpolicella Classico Superiore Amarone 1985: Juicy and still quite young with loads of vanilla and dried cherry flavors. Rich and well rounded, with great texture. Finishes on a nice leathery and gamy note. Delicious to drink now though you could age it for a few more years. • $45 • (06/15/96) • **90**
Recioto della Valpolicella Classico Superiore Amarone 1983 • $40 • (11/15/94) • **87**
Recioto della Valpolicella Classico Amarone Superiore 1980 • $40 • (09/15/92) • **87**
Soave Classico Superiore Le Lave 1991: A healthy dose of oak imparts vanilla, melon and honey flavors. Acidity is somewhat low, yet the wine is still appealing. Not a typical Soave, but worth a try. • $15 • (04/30/96) • **85**
Valpolicella Valpantena Secco-Bertani 1992: This is powerful for a Valpolicella, yet retains the smoky, cherry flavors typical of the appellation. The tannins are softening, yet still firm, try it with grilled meats. 16,000 cases made. • $10 • (06/15/96) BB • **87**
Valpolicella Valpantena Secco-Bertani 1988 • $9 • (11/15/94) • **76**
Valpolicella Valpantena Secco-Bertani 1987 • $9 • (09/15/92) • **73**

BERTELLI, A.

Barbera d'Asti Giarone 1990 • $NA • (10/31/94) • **78**
Giarone 1991 • $NA • (10/31/94) • **78**
I Fossaretti 1985 • $34 • (12/31/90) • **92**
Montetusa 1990 • $NA • (10/31/94) • **80**

BIBBIANO, TENUTA

Chianti Classico Montornello 1993: Gorgeous black currant and crushed raspberry aromas. Medium-bodied with light tannins and a medium berry, currant finish. Drinkable now, can be cellared. • $NA • (10/31/95) • **85**
Chianti Classico Vigna del Capannino 1990: Delicate and fruity with raspberry and cherry aromas and flavors, medium body and a hint of mint. Drinkable now. • $NA • (02/28/95) • **86**

BIGI

Vigneto Torricella Secco Orvieto Classico 1993: Light and refreshing, with character. Juicy apple and pear flavors with almond accents give substance, crisp acidity keeps it lively. A nice apéritif. 10,000 cases made. • $9 • **85**
Vino Nobile di Montepulciano 1985 • $12 • (11/30/90) • **81**
Vino Nobile di Montepulciano Riserva 1982 • $9 • (01/31/88) • **77**
Vino Nobile di Montepulciano Riserva 1980 • $8 • (09/01/85) • **84**

BINDELLA

Vallocaia 1990: Has deep color and firm tannins, but the flavors are rather lean, so you should drink it before it fades. Good, but could use more fruit. 800 cases made. • $23 • (11/30/94) • **82**
Vallocaia 1989 • $25 • (11/30/94) • **89**
Vino Nobile di Montepulciano 1990: This shows polish and refinement for this region, but the herbal and earthy flavors are as evident as the cherry notes. Still firm, and it drinks well now. 3,300 cases made. • $14 • (02/29/96) • **83**
Vino Nobile di Montepulciano Riserva 1990: Elegant and polished, this smooth red offers tobacco and licorice aromas and flavors, ripe plum and meaty notes joining in on the palate. Still firm and drinkable now, but it should improve through 1998. • $22 • (02/29/96) • **89**
Vino Nobile di Montepulciano Riserva 1985 • $27 • (10/31/90) • **68**

BIONDI-SANTI

Brunello di Montalcino 1988: Surprisingly light, but improves with at least six hours of decanting. Very traditional, with plummy, nutty, cheesy aromas. Tasted five times. Better after 1999. • $65 • (04/30/94) • **81**
Brunello di Montalcino Riserva 1988: A very good riserva but failing this estate's reputation. Pretty chestnut, berry and truffle aromas and flavors, with medium body and good tannins. A bit lean on the finish and very dry. • $145 • (10/31/94) • **87**
Brunello di Montalcino Il Greppo 1983 • $66 • (11/30/89) • **91**
Brunello di Montalcino Il Greppo 1982 • $45 • (10/15/88) • **92**
Brunello di Montalcino Il Greppo 1981 • $53 • (09/15/86) • **93**
Brunello di Montalcino Il Greppo 1980 • $40 • (09/15/86) • **88**
Brunello di Montalcino Il Greppo 1978 • $45 • (09/15/86) • **70**
Brunello di Montalcino Riserva 1985 • $180 • (03/31/92) • **82**
Brunello di Montalcino Riserva 1982 • $80 • (10/15/88) CS • **94**
Rosso di Montalcino Il Greppo 1984 • $22 • (01/31/90) • **82**

BIONDI-SANTI, IOCOPO

Sassoalloro Red 1991: A very good debut from the son of the owner of Brunello's Biondi-Santi. Impressive balance of fruit and fine tannins. Silky mouth feel, although slightly herbal in flavor with hints of rosemary and cherry. Drink now or hold. • $NA • **87**

BOATINA, LA

Merlot Collio 1993: This deep-colored, tannic and full-bodied red has pruny, garlicky aromas and flavors that aren't very appealing. 1,000 cases made. • $11 • (06/15/96) • **75**
Pinot Grigio Collio 1994: An intriguing mix of grapefruit and honey flavors jump-starts this big, bold Pinot Grigio. Full-bodied yet crisp, it can stand up to rich foods. Drinkable now. 8,000 cases made. • $12 • (04/30/96) • **87**
Sauvignon Collio 1992: Definitely tart and herbal in flavor, with a stale quality on the finish. Drinkable but not much to write home about. 2,500 cases made. • $13 • **73**
Verduzzo 1989 • $17 • (01/31/92) • **84**

BOCCE, FATTORIA LE

Chianti Classico 1993: Fresh and delicious '93 Chianti with red berry, dried cherry and a hint of tobacco. Medium-bodied with light tannins and crisp finish. Drinkable now. • $9 • (10/31/95) • **84**
Chianti Classico 1992: Offers straightforward aromas and flavors, medium-to-light body, fresh acidity and a grapey, citric finish. Drinkable now. 25,000 cases made. • $9 • (02/28/95) • **80**
Chianti Classico 1991 • $13 • (10/31/93) • **81**
Chianti Classico 1990 • $11 • (09/15/92) • **90**
Chianti Classico Riserva 1991: Rather light with some berry, dried herb character but light and drying on the finish. Drink immediately. • $14 • **84**
Chianti Classico Riserva 1990: Pleasant to drink now with its soft cherry, slightly herbal character, medium body and flavorful finish. 8,333 cases made. • $15 • (02/28/95) • **85**
Chianti Classico Riserva 1988 • $16 • (09/15/92) • **86**
Vigna del Paladino Red 1990 • $NA • (10/31/93) • **84**

BOLLA

Bardolino 1990 • $8 • (01/31/92) • **79**
Bardolino 1982 • $5 • (10/31/88) • **74**
Bardolino Classico 1993 • $7 • (10/31/94) • **81**
Bardolino Classico 1991 • $8 • (09/15/92) • **81**
Chardonnay 1994: A bit heavy-handed. Buttery, candylike flavors overwhelm the fruit, and it turns bitter on the finish. • $6 • (02/29/96) • **73**
Chardonnay 1993: Light and crisp, this has pleasant mineral, flinty flavors on a lean frame, with enough apple fruit for balance. It's refreshing but simple. 90,000 cases made. • $7 • (06/30/95) • **81**
Creso 1987 • $33 • (03/31/93) • **86**
Creso 1986 • $33 • (03/31/93) • **87**
Merlot Piave 1994: Light and fresh, showing pretty berry and cherry flavors along with bright acidity and light tannins. It's fruity and refreshing, drinkable now. • $8 • (01/31/96) • **82**
Merlot Piave 1993 • $7 • (10/31/94) • **83**
Pinot Grigio 1994: Soft and round, this offers expressive mineral, earth and butter flavors, but not much fruit to back them up. It's straighforward and finishes short. • $6 • (10/31/95) • **78**
Pinot Grigio 1993: Tastes out of balance. The buttery nuances of aroma and flavor conflict with the tart, green fruit on the palate and watery finish. Comes off as sweet-sour. 55,000 cases made. • $7 • **72**
Recioto di Soave 1990 • $NA • (09/15/92) • **83**
Recioto Valpolicella Classico Amarone 1986 • $18 • (10/31/94) • **85**
Recioto della Valpolicella Amarone 1985 • $22 • (09/15/92) • **85**
Sangiovese di Romagna 1994: Simple and fruity, with some nice raspberry and pepper flavors. Fresh, with a good, clean finish. 33,000 cases made. • $6 • (02/29/96) • **82**
Soave Classico 1993 • $7 • (10/31/94) BB • **85**
Soave Classico 1992 • $8 • (06/15/94) • **75**
Soave Classico 1991 • $8 • (09/15/92) • **75**
Soave Classico Froscà 1991 • $NA • (09/15/92) • **77**

Key: SS—Spectator Selection. CS—Cellar Selection. BB—Best Buy. $NA—Price not available. (BT)—Barrel tasting. (A)—Auction Price.
Dates in parentheses represent the issues in which the ratings were published.

Valpolicella 1990 • $8 • (09/15/92) • **75**
Valpolicella 1986 • $6 • (12/15/89) • **71**
Valpolicella 1985 • $5 • (10/31/88) • **77**
Valpolicella Classico 1993: 470,000 cases made. • $7 • **76**
Valpolicella Classico Amarone 1988: All the pieces fall together in this mature wine. It has mushroomy aromas and dried cherry flavors with plenty of leather to boot. Well-balanced and almost chewy, with licorce and tea notes on the finish. Tempting now, but will last through 2000. 14,500 six-bottle cases made. 14,500 cases made. • $18 • (06/15/96) CS • **91**
Valpolicella Classico Vigneti di Jago 1987 • $13 • (09/15/92) • **81**
Valpolicella Classico Vigneti di Jago 1986 • $12 • (12/31/90) • **78**
Valpolicella Vigneti di San Vito 1990 • $NA • (09/15/92) • **78**

BOLLINI

Cabernet Sauvignon Grave del Friuli 1989: Lean in texture, sparse in flavor. Thin and simple, probably past its prime. • $12 • (02/28/95) • **74**
Cabernet Sauvignon Grave del Friuli 1987 • $11 • (12/15/92) • **76**
Cabernet Sauvignon Grave del Friuli 1983 • $6 • (07/31/87) • **73**
Cabernet Sauvignon Trentino Reserve Selection 1989 • $15 • (04/30/94) • **80**
Chardonnay Trentino Reserve Selection 1992: Fat and a little chewy, packed with flavor but leans heavily toward wood and minimizes the fruit, picking up a little peach and apple on the finish. • $16 • (01/31/95) • **83**
Chardonnay Trentino 1993: Light and lean, with burnt-ash edge to the modest green apple and spice flavors. • $8 • (01/31/95) • **78**
Chardonnay Trentino 1992 • $8 • (04/30/94) • **80**
Merlot Reserve Selection Trentino 1991: • $14 • **90**
Merlot Reserve Selection Trentino 1990 • $15 • (04/30/94) • **86**
Merlot Trentino 1992: Lean in texture, herbaceous in aroma and flavor. Simple and drinkable. Not very tannic. • $8 • (02/28/95) • **77**
Pinot Grigio Grave del Friuli Reserve Selection 1994: Fresh in aroma, figgy in flavor, fruity enough to be satisfying, yet on the light side in body and texture. • $8 • (06/15/96) • **84**
Pinot Grigio Reserve Selection Grave del Friuli 1993: Smooth and subtle, revealing light mineral and melon flavors. Good but simple. • $13 • (07/31/95) • **80**
Pinot Grigio Reserve Selection Grave del Friuli 1992: Has a touch of oak, which doesn't seem to balance well with the sweet pear and peach-centered fruit, drying on the finish. • $13 • (01/31/95) • **83**
Pinot Grigio Trentino 1993: Pleasant to drink on the green-apple side of the flavor spectrum. Modest concentration, charming. • $9 • **81**
Pinot Grigio Trentino 1992 • $8 • (04/30/94) • **82**

BOLOGNA, GIACOMO

Barbera Bricco dell'Uccellone 1991: Light, floral style of Barbera, a touch of rose petal adding extra appeal to the spicy berry flavors. Has a little bite of tannin, but it's drinkable now. • $47 • **82**
Barbera Bricco dell' Uccellone 1988 • $45 • (03/15/91) • **91**
Barbera Bricco dell' Uccellone 1987 • $45 • (03/15/91) • **88**
Barbera Bricco dell' Uccellone 1986 • $38 • (03/15/91) • **89**
Barbera Bricco dell' Uccellone 1985 • $33 • (08/31/89) • **88**
Barbera Bricco della Bigotta 1988 • $40 • (03/15/91) • **92**
Barbera Bricco della Bigotta 1987 • $34 • (03/15/91) • **88**
Barbera Bricco della Bigotta 1986 • $34 • (03/15/91) • **88**
Barbera d'Asti Bricco della Bigotta 1991: Bright in flavor, a little chewy in texture, but the strawberry, plummy, slightly jammy flavors balance nicely against a grace note of cedar. A tasty Barbera now. • $NA • **83**
Brachetto d'Acqui 1987 • $16 • (03/31/90) • **84**

BONARDI

Asti Spumante NV • $9 • (02/15/87) • **76**
Moscato d'Asti NV • $12 • (03/31/90) • **81**

BONFIO, FEDERICO

Chianti Le Poggiolo Riserva 1985 • $11 • (03/31/90) • **76**
Chianti Le Poggiolo Riserva 1982 • $7 • (11/15/87) • **73**

Chianti Le Portine Riserva 1985 • $9 • (03/31/90) • **85**
Chianti Le Portine Riserva 1982 • $9 • (11/15/87) • **79**
Chianti Proprietor's Reserve 1985 • $15 • (03/31/90) • **85**

BORDINO, CASCINA

Dolcetto d'Alba 1988 • $9 • (03/31/90) • **84**

BORGHETTI, VILLA

Valpolicella Classico 1989 • $7 • (04/30/92) • **78**

BORGIANNI

Chianti Classico 1982 • $3 • (04/01/85) • **71**

BORGO DELLE ROSE

Pinot Grigio Grave del Friuli 1994: A deep gold color and butter-vanilla flavors make this taste barrel-aged. It's different, but could use more lively fruit flavors to back up the full body. 5,000 cases made. • $9 • (06/15/96) • **83**

BORGO MAGREDO

Cabernet Sauvignon Grave del Friuli 1994: Modest cherry and bell pepper flavors dominate. Juicy and flavorful, with a note of black pepper on the finish. 2,000 cases made. • $8 • (06/15/96) • **82**
Cabernet Sauvignon Grave del Friuli 1990: A simple, basic Cabernet that tastes like beef bouillon and green beans. Palatable, but not much fun. • $NA • (02/28/95) • **72**
Chardonnay Grave del Friuli 1994: Fruity, floral and slightly buttery. A fresh, mouth-filling Chardonnay that's clean and refreshing. 10,000 cases made. • $8 • (02/29/96) • **82**
Chardonnay Grave del Friuli 1992: A bit rounder and richer than most wines of this region, showing a touch of butter and honey to accent the crisp, appley flavors. Clean and fresh on the finish. • $NA • **83**
Merlot Grave del Friuli 1994: Extremely vegetal, with an earthy quality as well. Thin and shows awkward, stewed flavors. 5,000 cases made. • $8 • (02/29/96) • **75**
Pinot Grigio Grave del Friuli 1994: Pungent herbal and smoky aromas give character to this white. It turns a bit softer on the palate, finishing in almond and light honey tones. 10,000 cases made. • $8 • (04/30/96) • **84**
Pinot Grigio Grave del Friuli 1991: Lean but distinctive. A crisply textured, mature-tasting white that has herbal aromas, mineral flavors and a smoky note on the finish. • $NA • **82**
Refosco Grave del Friuli 1994: Acceptable but simple, offering vegetal flavors and a sense of sweetness. Soft and not tannic. 1,000 cases made. • $8 • (04/30/96) • **77**
Sauvignon Grave del Friuli 1994: Grapefruit and herbal aromas are true to the varietal, and on the palate this is clean, fruity and refreshing. Well made in the Loire style. 4,000 cases made. • $8 • (04/30/96) • **85**
Sauvignon Grave del Friuli 1991: Very dry, lean and spicy tasting. This is a refreshing, light, subtle white wine that will be fine at the dinner table. • $NA • **80**
Tocai Friulano Grave del Friuli 1994: Flavors of mandarin orange, honey and herb mingle in this soft, appealing white. It's not big, but has enough acidity to keep it lively. 2,000 cases made. • $7 • (04/30/96) • **84**
Tocai Friulano Grave del Friuli 1991: A dry, smooth, nearly mature white wine with simple fruit flavors. Doesn't make much of a statement, but it's of decent quality. • $NA • **78**

BORGO SCOPETO, TENUTA

Chianti Classico 1992: Rather astringent and earthy, decent dried-cherry flavor and a hint of salami. • $NA • **78**
Chianti Classico 1991 • $10 • (10/31/94) • **79**
Chianti Classico Riserva 1990: There's plenty of upfront fruit here, with black cherry, plum and tobacco notes and a velvety mouthfeel, then the wine turns tannic and lean on the finish. Try now. 850 cases made. • $22 • (10/31/94) • **83**

BORGO, VILLA DEL

Chardonnay 1993: Very lean and tart, with a sour lemon edge that is not attractive. 8,400 cases made. • $8 • (01/31/95) • **74**
Pinot Grigio 1993: Crisp with lively lime, grapefruit and apple flavors that linger on the finish. Very light but fresh. 8,400 cases made. • $8 • (01/31/95) • **79**

BORGOGNO, GIACOMO

Barbera d'Alba 1990 • $10 • (06/15/94) BB • **88**
Barolo 1988 • $20 • (06/15/94) • **88**

BORTOLUZZI

Chardonnay Isonzo 1994: Pretty aromas of lemon and vanilla give way to discreet yet generous flavors of peach and butter. It's fresh and flavorful, in a delicate style. 1,000 cases made. • $15 • (06/15/96) • **84**
Pinot Grigio Isonzo 1994: A zesty, lively white wine with melon and cucumber flavors and good balance. 4,000 cases made. • $15 • (06/15/96) • **82**
Sauvignon Isonzo 1994: Good peach and herbal flavors make for an appealing mix. A medium-bodied white wine with some nice spicy notes on the finish. Very quaffable. 1,000 cases made. • $15 • (06/15/96) • **83**
Sauvignon Isonzo 1991 • $14 • (09/15/93) • **88**

BOSCAINI

Bardolino Classico Superiore Le Canne 1985 • $6 • (07/31/88) BB • **82**
Chardonnay Alto Adige Colle dell'Imperatore Vigneti di Cornaiano 1994: A heavy jolt of oak adds vanilla and caramel aromas and flavors to this fleshy wine, appealing but lacking in acidity. For fans of a bolder, heavier style of Chardonnay. • $11 • (06/15/96) • **82**
Lugana Lunatio 1991 • $12 • (12/15/92) • **81**
Pinot Grigio Valdadige La Cros 1991 • $12 • (09/15/92) • **80**
Pinot Grigio Alto Adige Castel Firmiano Vigneti di Cornaiano 1994: Burnt caramel and honey aromas follow through on the dull, brassy palate, all the way to a cloying finish. • $11 • (06/30/96) • **70**
Recioto della Valpolicella Classico Amarone Marano 1988 • $23 • (09/15/92) • **83**
Santo Stefano de le Cane 1988 • $15 • (09/15/92) • **80**
Soave Classico Monteleone 1991 • $10 • (09/15/92) • **78**
Soave Classico Monteleone Vigneti di Costeggiola 1994: Canned fruit flavors and aromas with a touch of herb. It has some richness as well. • $9 • (06/15/96) • **79**
Valpolicella Classico Superiore Marano 1990 • $10 • (09/15/92) • **81**
Valpolicella Classico Superiore Marano 1985 • $6 • (09/15/88) BB • **81**

BOSCARELLI

Chianti Colli Senesi 1986 • $8 • (01/31/89) • **78**
Chianti Colli Senesi 1984 • $6 • (09/15/87) • **72**
Rosso di Montepulciano 1992: Soft and rich, with black cherry flavors accented by an earthy note. Turns a little astringent on the finish. 2,083 cases made. • $14 • (08/31/95) • **82**
Tuscany 1985 • $30 • (02/15/89) • **92**
Tuscany 1983 • $29 • (06/30/88) • **85**
Vino Nobile di Montepulciano 1990: Inviting plum and cigar aromas give way to a balanced, integrated wine that offers lively plum, herb and licorice flavors. The concentrated fruit matches well with the firm tannins and promises long life. Cellar until 1997. 1,500 cases made. • $22 • (02/29/96) • **89**
Vino Nobile di Montepulciano 1981 • $10 • (07/01/86) • **71**
Vino Nobile di Montepulciano Riserva 1985 • $15 • (06/15/90) • **76**
Vino Nobile di Montepulciano Riserva 1981 • $11 • (10/31/86) • **70**

BOSCO, CASTIGLIONE DEL

Brunello di Montalcino 1990: Light and advanced, showing some leather and cedar character but very dry on the finish. Fading quickly. • $NA • **76**

Brunello di Montalcino 1979 • $14 • (04/30/87) • **93**
Rosso di Montalcino 1988 • $11 • (07/15/91) • **82**

BOSCO, TENUTA IL

Pinot Nero Oltrepò Pavese 1988 • $9 • (06/30/91) • **81**

BOSCOROTONDO, VILLA

Chianti Classico 1990 • $NA • (09/15/92) • **81**

BOSSI, CASTELLO DI

Chianti Classico 1993: A fun wine tasting of sweet, fresh plums, then picking up some fig, cassis and cherry flavors. Ripe and tannic on the finish. Try now. • $NA • **84**
Chianti Classico Riserva 1991: Already taking on a more mature cedar, tobacco and coffee character, indicating it's at or just past its peak. Medium body and very soft. Drinkable now. • $NA • **79**
Corbaia 1990: A really fascinating and beautifully balanced red that is tannic, but has enough spice, cedar, cherry and cranberry flavors to fill it out. Firm with acidity and built for aging through at least 1998. 1,000 cases made. • $32 • (12/31/95) • **89**
Corbaia 1988: Silky wine with tobacco, truffle and fruit aromas and flavors. Medium-bodied with fine tannins and a medium aftertaste. Drinkable now. • $NA • **84**

BRANCAIA

Brancaia 1991: Plenty of chestnut and black cherry aromas and flavors, medium-bodied and medium tannins. Drink now. • $NA • **86**

BRENTA D'ORO

Asti Spumante Vezza d'Alba NV • $7 • (05/31/87) • **79**

BREZZA

Barbera d'Alba Cannubi 1991 • $NA • (10/31/94) • **77**
Barolo Cannubi 1991: Delicious to drink now. Round and soft, offering ripe fruit and plenty of strawberry and cherry character. Medium-bodied with round tannins. • $30 • **86**
Barolo Cannubi 1990: Pretty aromas and flavors reminiscent of violets, fresh flowers and cherries. Full-bodied, with a rich gamy, minty, berry character. Full tannins and a long, minty finish. Better in 1997. • $40 • **88**
Barolo Cannubi 1989: Stylish and lavishly tannic, offering a supple core of spicy black cherry, floral and anise flavors. Finishes a little hot and sharp, give it until 2000 to 2003 to come together. • $NA • (10/31/94) • **88**
Dolcetto d'Alba San Lorenzo 1993: Vibrant dried cherry and berry aromas and flavors, medium body, fine tannins and a long, delicious finish. • $13 • **87**

BRIGL, JOSEF

Santa Maddalena 1986 • $6 • (10/15/88) • **75**

BROLIO, CASTELLO DI

Chianti Classico 1990 • $11 • (09/15/92) • **87**
Chianti Classico 1988 • $9 • (09/15/91) • **84**
Chianti Classico 1987 • $12 • (10/31/91) • **84**
Chianti Classico 1986 • $8 • (11/30/90) • **77**
Chianti Classico 1985 • $7 • (11/30/89) • **85**
Chianti Classico 1984 • $4 • (09/15/87) • **73**
Chianti Classico Riserva 1988 • $13 • (10/31/94) • **87**
Chianti Classico Riserva 1985 • $12 • (09/15/91) • **86**
Chianti Classico Riserva 1983 • $10 • (05/15/90) • **80**
Chianti Classico Riserva del Barone 1983 • $26 • (10/31/94) • **81**
Chianti Classico Riserva del Barone 1978 • $11 • (06/01/85) • **90**
Sangiovese Tuscany 1991 • $9 • (07/31/94) BB • **85**
Vin Santo Tuscany 1981 • $25 • (09/15/91) • **90**
Vin Santo Tuscany 1977 • $13 • (03/31/90) • **85**

BROTINI, VILLA

Chianti Classico Villa Brotini 1984 • $5 • (12/31/87) • **77**

BROVIA

Barbera d'Alba Sorí del Drago 1993: A lovely red, showing some mature mushroom flavors that blend nicely with the black cherry and currant notes. Fresh, crisp finish. 500 cases made. • $14 • **83**
Barolo 1990: A traditional Barolo: intense aromas and flavors of dried cherry, tomato and tar, with very firm tannins. Medium-bodied and a bit dry on the finish. Drinkable now, but will hold a bit. • $NA • **83**
Barolo 1989: A lighter style, showing a lithe core of cherry and raspberry flavor and some overtones of anise and tar. Tannins are somewhat crisp and drying. Best to wait until 1997. • $NA • (10/31/94) • **83**
Barolo Monprivato 1990: A lovely, clean red, packed with well-defined, delicious wild berry, tar, rose petal and violet flavors. You can't go wrong with this medium- to full-bodied Barolo. It should only improve with age, try in 1998. 208 cases made. • $44 • **88**
Barolo Monprivato 1989: Has weedy and anise aromas, with spicy cherry and tobacco flavors that narrow down to a sort of white-pepper bite on the finish. May be better after 1998. • $NA • (10/31/94) • **80**
Barolo Rocche dei Brovia 1989: Ripe and focused, with anise, black cherry and smoke flavors unfolding across the palate. Balanced and attractive, tannins are well integrated. Approachable now, but best from 1997. • $NA • (10/31/94) • **87**
Barolo Rocche dei Brovia 1988 • $30 • (10/31/93) • **82**
Dolcetto d'Alba Vignavillej 1993: Grapey chestnut and berry flavors, medium body and a light finish. 833 cases made. • $13 • **80**
Roero Arneis 1994: Crisp and fresh, a light-bodied white featuring some grapefruit, wet hay, orange and lemon peel flavors and medium acidity. Drinkable on release. 333 cases made. • $14 • **80**

BRUGNANO

Chianti Colli Fiorentini 1986 • $5 • (01/31/89) BB • **85**

BRUGO

Gattinara 1986: Mature but still lively and silky, offering cherry, nutmeg and vanilla aromas and flavors. Finishes a bit dry but with lingering fruit. Balanced and graceful. Drinkable now. 3,000 cases made. • $15 • (07/31/95) • **86**
Spanna del Piemonte 1990: Pungent barnyard aromas and a dry, tannic texture don't add up to much enjoyment. Astringent and bitter on the finish. 7,000 cases made. • $8 • (02/28/95) • **72**
Spanna del Piemonte 1987: • $NA • **67**

BUON DONNO

Chianti Classico 1993: Simple and straightforward, with cherry and mineral notes and a light finish. Slightly diluted. • $NA • **79**
Chianti Classico 1992: Very light and watery with candied watermelon flavors. • $NA • **70**

BUONASERA, VILLA

Chianti Classico 1993: A strange cherry and oyster mushroom character in the aromas and palate. Light-bodied, with light tannins and a slightly dry finish. Tasted twice, with consistent notes. • $NA • **78**
Chianti Classico Riserva 1991: An odd wine that has some rubbery aromas and flavors. Offers some ripeness and supple texture, but what happened? Tasted twice, with consistent notes. • $NA • **69**

Key: SS—Spectator Selection. CS—Cellar Selection. BB—Best Buy. $NA—Price not available. (BT)—Barrel tasting. (A)—Auction Price.
Dates in parentheses represent the issues in which the ratings were published.

BURATI

Asti Spumante NV • $6 • (03/15/89) • **75**

CA' BIANCA

Barbaresco Cascina Roncaglie Riserva 1988: Dried-out and tired, this wine has only modest cinnamon and plum flavors. Thin and astringent on the finish. Hard to like. Tasted twice with consistent notes. • $20 • (02/28/95) • **64**

Barolo Cascina Denegri 1988 • $29 • (11/30/94) • **83**

Barolo Riserva Cascina Denegri 1985 • $30 • (06/15/94) • **88**

CA' DE MONTE

Barbera d'Asti 1992 • $7 • **88**

Barolo 1990: Concentrated and intense, from the intriguingly complex aromas to the rich fruit flavors to the firm, tannic texture. Has cherry, cranberry and spice flavors that expand on the finish. Drink now through 2000. 4,000 cases made. • $16 • (02/28/95) • **88**

Dolcetto d'Alba 1993: Cherry and nutmeg flavors brightened by lively acidity. A brisk and light-bodied red that's fresh and ready to drink. 3,000 cases made. • $8 • (07/31/95) • **83**

Gavi 1993: A smooth and modestly fruity white, with banana and fig flavors and a hint of vanilla on the finish. Straightforward. 3,000 cases made. • $8 • (02/28/95) • **82**

Moscato d'Asti NV: Sweet, honeyed and herbaceous, with extremely youthful flavors, like just-pressed grape juice. Appealingly fresh and fruity, but simple. 4,000 cases made. • $8 • (07/31/95) • **80**

CA' DEI GANCIA

Barolo Cannubi 1990: Supple, ripe and generous, silky, with beautiful mahogany-scented black cherry, blackberry, rose petal and anise flavors that keep weaving through. Seductive and supple, this also has a veil of tannin that can use until 1998 to 2001 to dissolve. • $65 • (10/31/94) • **93**

Barolo Cannubi 1989: This stunning wine is rippling with layers and layers of dense, exuberant black cherry, violet, blackberry, tar and vanilla aromas and flavors. Muscular at the core, but sweet and supple through the extraordinary finish. A great wine in any context. The tannins are so refined you could drink it now, but has the stuff to age past 2000. 825 cases made. • $65 • (10/31/93) • **96**

Il Defino 1991: Slightly austere, but showing some pretty nutty, berry aromas and flavors. Medium in body, dry tannins and a good finish. • $NA • **81**

CA' DEL BOSCO

Chardonnay Franciacorta 1991 • $33 • (05/31/93) • **85**

Franciacorta 1992: An earthy wine marked by vegetal flavors. It has modest tannins and stewed fruit flavors. • $NA • (02/29/96) • **78**

Franciacorta 1988 • $11 • (01/31/92) • **81**

Franciacorta 1987 • $16 • (12/31/90) • **77**

Franciacorta 1985 • $11 • (09/15/88) • **83**

Franciacorta Brut NV: Strives for complexity. This has straightforward, crisp fruit flavors shaded by vanilla and butter on the finish. The texture is smooth and appealing. • $NA • (07/31/95) • **84**

Franciacorta Crémant NV • $46 • (12/31/91) • **90**

Franciacorta Dosage Zero NV : A dry, light bubbly with applelike flavors, a good, smooth texture and a short finish. Pleasant and straightforward in character. • $NA • (07/31/95) • **83**

Franciacorta Rosé NV • $42 • (12/31/91) • **83**

Franciacorta Satèn NV: A bright gold color and assertive toasty, doughy flavors make this a bold bottle of bubbly. It adds grace notes of almond, butter, pear and lemon, for a well-integrated, richly flavored taste experience. • $NA • (07/31/95) • **89**

Franciacorta White 1992: Mature and mellow in aroma, but tight and lean in flavor and texture. Not for everyone. 8,640 cases made. • $20 • (02/29/96) • **81**

Franciacorta White 1991 • $16 • (05/31/93) • **81**

Maurizio Zanella 1991: Rich and opulent, with loads of spice, chocolate and plum flavors. Tannic, but not overpowering. A generous wine with a smooth finish. Drinkable now through 1998. 1,515 cases made. • $40 • (02/29/96) • **88**

Maurizio Zanella 1990 • $34 • (07/31/93) • **85**

Maurizio Zanella 1988 • $32 • (09/30/91) • **93**

Maurizio Zanella 1987 • $40 • (12/31/90) • **88**

Maurizio Zanella 1985 • $38 • (09/15/88) • **92**

Pinot Nero Pinero 1988 • $50 • (01/31/92) • **83**

Pinot Nero Pinero 1987 • $69 • (06/15/90) • **82**

CA' NEUVA

Dolcetto di Dogliani 1990 • $16 • (10/31/92) • **81**

CA' NOVA, LA

Barbaresco 1986 • $15 • (10/31/90) • **87**

CA'ROME

Barbaresco 1990: Focused and flavorful, with a supple beam of rose-scented raspberry, anise and vanilla aromas and flavors that persist on the finish. Tannins are in balance. 900 cases made. • $30 • (10/31/93) • **85**

Barbaresco 1989: Crisp and fruity, with a streak of anise running through the lean black cherry fruit, smooth and drinkable. Should be fine through 1997. 950 cases made. • $30 • (10/31/93) • **85**

Barbaresco 1985 • $28 • (01/31/90) • **88**

Barbaresco Maria di Brun 1990: Stylish and a little chewy, the blackberry, currant and licorice flavors brightening up on the palate and lasting into the solid finish, echoing fruit and toast. • $40 • (10/31/94) • **89**

Barbaresco Maria di Brun 1989: A beautifully crafted wine, with more spicy anise and tar aromas and flavors than fruit, smoothly integrated and nicely focused. A bit tough in tannins, it might be best from 1997. 390 cases made. • $43 • (10/31/93) • **86**

Barbaresco Maria di Brun 1985 • $37 • (01/31/90) • **92**

Barolo 1985 • $35 • (10/15/90) • **89**

Barolo Rapet 1990: Lean in structure, bright in flavor, with appealing raspberry, rose petal and spice notes. Drinkable now. Tasted twice. • $35 • (10/31/94) • **87**

Barolo Rapet 1989: Light and crisp, an austere wine with black cherry and floral flavors, modest tannins that don't really get in the way now. Could develop a little more complexity by 1998. • $32 • (10/31/94) • **82**

Barolo Rapet 1988 • $36 • (10/31/93) • **83**

Barolo Vigna Rionda 1988 • $32 • (10/31/93) • **68**

Dapruvé 1989 • $24 • (04/15/94) • **80**

CA'VIT

Cabernet Sauvignon Riserva Trentino 1989: A mature, meaty tasting Cabernet with mineral accents to the lean herb and tomato flavors. Acceptable quality. 2,400 cases made. • $8 • (02/28/95) • **78**

Merlot Riserva Trentino 1991: Well-balanced and complex, in a Bordeaux style. A deeply flavored red that blends ripe plum, tomato and tobacco flavors with good acidity and modest tannins. Enjoy now. 3,600 cases made. • $8 • (02/28/95) • **85**

Riserva Teroldego Rotaliano 1991: Vanilla and butter flavors dominate this otherwise straightforward red. Could use more fruit and freshness. 3,100 cases made. • $8 • (02/28/95) • **77**

CACCHIANO, CASTELLO DI

Chianti Classico 1993: Crisp and fresh, with vibrant character, offering plenty of cassis and cherry flavors, though a bit one-dimensional and drying on the finish. • $13 • **80**

Chianti Classico 1992: Earthy, strawberry, weedy character, light and dry finish. 8,000 cases made. • $10 • **74**

Chianti Classico 1991 • $14 • (10/31/93) • **87**

Chianti Classico 1990 • $14 • (10/31/93) • **87**

Chianti Classico 1988 • $14 • (09/15/91) • **90**

Chianti Classico 1986 • $8 • (05/15/90) • **86**

Chianti Classico 1985 • $10 • (10/31/88) • **87**

Chianti Classico 1983 • $6 • (09/15/87) • **73**
Chianti Classico Millennio Riserva 1990: An explosion of ripe fruit offering complex nuances of tobacco, dried herbs and berries. Full-bodied and delicious with fine tannins and a long, flavorful finish. Drinkable now. 2,200 cases made. • $17 • **89**
Chianti Classico Millennio Riserva 1988 • $18 • (09/15/92) • **86**
Chianti Classico Millennio Riserva 1985 • $18 • (09/15/90) • **80**
RF 1990: Very Burgundian in style, displaying ripe raspberry and truffle aromas and flavors, medium body, medium tannins and a long, long, outstanding finish. Drinkable now. 800 cases made. • $25 • **90**
RF 1988 • $20 • (09/15/91) • **90**
RF 1986 • $16 • (06/15/90) • **85**
Rosso 1993: Round and ripe, a soft-tasting wine that offers plenty of plum, blackberry and black cherry flavors. Firm finish. Drink after '97. • $25 • **84**

CAFAGGIO, VILLA

Chianti Classico 1993: Fresh and delicious with berry, cherry and a hint of earth on the nose and palate. Medium- to light-bodied, light tannins and a soft finish. • $9 • **82**
Chianti Classico 1992: • $NA • **84**
Chianti Classico 1990 • $14 • (10/31/93) • **82**
Chianti Classico 1989 • $13 • (09/15/92) • **84**
Chianti Classico 1988 • $10 • (11/30/90) • **83**
Chianti Classico 1987 • $9 • (09/15/89) • **86**
Chianti Classico 1986 • $9 • (03/31/90) • **89**
Chianti Classico 1985 • $8 • (05/31/88) • **84**
Chianti Classico 1983 • $11 • (09/15/87) • **91**
Chianti Classico 1982 • $4 • (10/16/85) • **66**
Chianti Classico Riserva 1990: A classy riserva showing lovely cherry and game aromas and flavors, medium body, fine tannins and fresh acidity. Drinkable now. 1,500 cases made. • $17 • **87**
Chianti Classico Riserva 1988 • $18 • (09/15/92) • **91**
Chianti Classico Riserva 1986 • $18 • (12/15/90) • **86**
Chianti Classico Riserva 1985 • $13 • (09/15/91) • **91**
Chianti Classico Riserva 1983 • $10 • (05/31/88) • **80**
Cortaccio 1990: Superfocused, excellent concentration of berry, mint and vanilla aromas and flavors, full body and tannins followed by a crisp finish. Made from Cabernet Sauvignon. Try in 1997. • $32 • (10/31/93) • **91**
San Martino 1990: Gloriously perfumed aromas of violet, vanilla and cedar follow through to a medium-bodied palate with silky tannins and a lively finish. Made from Sangiovese. Drinkable now. • $31 • (10/31/93) • **89**
San Martino 1985 • $20 • (09/30/89) • **79**
Solatio Basilica 1990: Loads of finesse in this one. Very focused wine with attractive cherry, vanilla, pie crust character, medium body and velvety tannins. Made from Sangiovese. Drinkable now. • $32 • (10/31/93) • **87**
Solatio Basilica 1985 • $20 • (08/31/91) • **83**

CALCINAIA, VILLA

Chianti Classico 1992: Light, simple and grapey, fresh, with a delicate aftertaste. Drink immediately. 10,000 cases made. • $8 • **73**
Chianti Classico Riserva 1990: Very ripe and concentrated showing a slightly raisiny, earthy, berry character. Full-bodied, long, fruity aftertaste. Drinkable now. • $NA • **84**
Chianti Colli Senesi Geminiano 1994: A lovely, perfumy character. Medium body, firm tannins and a slightly short finish. Drinkable now. • $NA • **81**
Teodoro 1993: A middle-of-the-road Tuscan red. Medium body with some mint, plum and earth flavors. Smooth finish but also a bit short and diluted. • $NA • **80**

Key: SS—Spectator Selection. CS—Cellar Selection. BB—Best Buy. $NA—Price not available. (BT)—Barrel tasting. Ⓐ—Auction Price.
Dates in parentheses represent the issues in which the ratings were published.

CALDI, LUIGI

Barbera d'Asti 1985 • $7 • (07/31/89) • **78**
Gattinara 1982 • $12 • (01/31/90) • **69**

CALISSANO, LUIGI

Villa Meriggi Gavi 1994: A sturdy Gavi with some depth and length to the melony, earthy flavors. • $10 • (02/29/96) • **81**

CALMASINO

Bardolino 1990 • $NA • (09/15/92) • **79**

CALO & SONS, MICHELE

Vigna Spano 1990: Cedar, walnut and mushroom flavors run through this rich, mature wine, while tart acidity keeps it lively. It's rustic, and though there's some complexity, the wine lacks harmony. Drink now. • $20 • (05/31/95) • **81**

CAMIGLIANO, CASTELLO DI

Brunello di Montalcino 1990: Ripe and fresh smoky, leathery, cherry character. Medium in body. Delicious and supple, finishing crisply. Drink now. • $NA • **85**
Brunello di Montalcino 1988: A big Brunello with masses of fruit and tannins, but not aggressive in any way. Full-bodied with raspberry and chestnut aromas and flavors and a long, flavorful finish. Tasted twice. Better after 1996. • $NA • (04/30/94) • **89**
Chianti Colli Senesi 1985 • $3 • (12/15/87) • **77**
Chianti Colli Senesi 1983 • $2 • (05/16/85) BB • **82**
Riserva 1977 • $11 • (08/01/85) • **85**
Rosso di Montalcino 1993: Elegant Rosso of medium body, fine tannins, fresh acidity and plummy black cherry character. Drink now. • $NA • **81**
Rosso di Montalcino 1991 • $NA • (04/30/94) • **80**
Tuscany 1980 • $8 • (09/15/86) • **72**

CAMPACCI

Chianti Classico 1993: Juicy but a bit simple, with strawberry and raspberry flavors. Light-bodied and light on the finish. Drinkable now. • $NA • **79**

CAMPOGIOVANNI

Brunello di Montalcino 1990: This producer goes from strength to strength. A sensational wine, fresh and vibrant, offering marvelous blackberry, blueberry and black cherry flavors that linger for a long, long time on the palate. Sophisticated, supple, smooth finish. Better after 1999. Tasted twice, with consistent notes. 5,500 cases made. • $33 • **95**

CAMPRIANO

Chianti Colli Senesi 1994: Vibrant, fresh and fruity with berry and watermelon character. Light-bodied with light tannins and a fresh finish. Serve slightly chilled. • $NA • **83**

CANALETTO

Chardonnay 1994: A pretty wine, this shows floral and almond aromas and flavors with a silky, polished texture. It's a bit soft and perfumy for food, but makes an appealing apéritif. • $6 • (06/15/96) • **83**
Chardonnay delle Tre Venezie 1993: Smoky, oaky flavors pervade this enjoyable, but lightly fruity white. 50,000 cases made. • $6 • **82**
Merlot Veneto 1994: A light red structured like a rosé, offering plummy flavor and pleasant, smoky accents, but it tastes diluted. • $6 • (06/15/96) • **79**

Merlot del Veneto 1993: A light red with smoky aromas, subtle cherry flavors and soft tannins. Average, modest stuff. 50,000 cases made. • $6 • (07/31/95) • **78**

Montepulciano d'Abruzzo 1993: Soft and easy-going, with fresh strawberry flavors. Fresh, light, and medium-bodied. A supple and dry red wine. 50,000 cases made. • $6 • (03/31/95) • **83**

Pinot Grigio delle Tre Venezie 1994: Smooth, light-bodied and has a soft texture. Offers light melon flavors and a short finish. 60,000 cases made. • $6 • (07/31/95) • **80**

Pinot Grigio delle Tre Venezie 1993: An accent of vanilla enhances this otherwise straightforward white. 60,000 cases made. • $6 • **79**

CANALICCHIO DE SOTTO

Le Gode de Montosoli 1988: Supercharged wine, with intense fruit aromas and flavors. It is full-bodied, with full, hard tannins. A wine built for aging. From Primo Pacenti. Don't touch it until after 1997. • $NA • (04/30/94) • **90**

Rosso di Montalcino 1991 • $NA • (04/30/94) • **85**

CANALICCHIO DI SOPRA

Brunello di Montalcino 1990: Elegant, firm, silky tannins and rich fruit. Medium- to full-bodied, sporting mineral, berry and cherry flavors and a fine finish. Drinkable now. • $45 • **88**

Brunello di Montalcino 1988: Seems dominated by oak. It shows lovely ripe fruit character with full body, but it is slightly too dry and astringent on the palate. Try now. • $36 • (04/30/94) • **80**

Brunello di Montalcino Le Gode di Montosoli Riserva 1988: A vibrant, concentrated wine with lovely ripe fruit character, medium tannins and a crisp finish. Not as good as the normal bottling. Drink now or hold. • $35 • (10/31/94) • **88**

Brunello di Montalcino Riserva 1988: Extremely ripe wine with plenty of black cherry, earthy character. Full bodied and velvety with a long flavorful finish. From Franco e Rosildo Pacenti. Drink now. • $NA • (10/31/94) • **88**

Rosso di Montalcino 1993: Beautiful Rosso and a lot of wine for the buck. Impressive depth and layers add to an earthy, leathery, plummy character. Fine tannins, crisp finish. Drink now. • $19 • **88**

Rosso di Montalcino 1991 • $NA • (04/30/94) • **82**

CANDIDO, FRANCESCO

Salice Salentino Riserva 1988 • $8 • (07/31/93) BB • **84**

CANTALUPO, ANTICHI VIGNETI DI

Ghemme Collis Breclemae 1985 • $25 • (01/31/92) • **81**

CAPACCIA, PODERE

Chianti Classico 1990 • $NA • (10/31/93) • **84**
Chianti Classico 1988 • $NA • (09/15/91) • **89**
Chianti Classico Riserva 1988 • $NA • (09/15/92) • **86**
Chianti Classico Riserva 1985 • $NA • (09/15/91) • **88**
Querciagrande 1990 • $NA • (10/31/93) • **88**

CAPANNA

Brunello di Montalcino 1990: Round and easy berry, cherry and tobacco aromas and flavors, medium body and soft, light finish. Drink now. • $NA • **83**

Brunello di Montalcino 1988: A rather perplexing and rustic style, with a full body, very fruity character, but an underlying earthiness and dryness on the finish. Tasted three times. • $NA • (04/30/94) • **84**

Brunello di Montalcino Riserva 1988: Complex, showing aromas and flavors of berry, truffles and fruit. Mouth filling texture with wonderful full, round tannins, lovely ripe fruit and a long finish. Drinkable now. • $NA • (10/31/94) • **90**

Rosso di Montalcino 1993: Delicious cherry, berry and mineral aromas and flavors. Medium in body and soft tannins. Drink now. • $NA • (10/31/95) • **82**

Rosso di Montalcino 1992 • $NA • (04/30/94) • **79**
Rosso di Montalcino 1991 • $NA • (04/30/94) • **80**

CAPANNA FATTOI

Brunello di Montalcino Riserva 1988: This really builds on your palate. Incredibly young and fresh, with superbly concentrated cherry flavor and ultrafine tannins. Drinkable now, but better with some bottle age, try after 1997. • $NA • (10/31/94) • **92**

CAPANNELLE

Barrique 1988 • $NA • (10/31/93) • **86**
Tuscany 1988 • $NA • (10/31/93) • **85**

CAPARZO

Brunello di Montalcino 1990: Wonderful Brunello that's drinkable now. Beautiful and fruity, offering medium body, fine tannins and a long, caressing finish. • $36 • **91**

Brunello di Montalcino 1988: Extremely well-structured wine that needs time to show you what it has got. Full-bodied yet very fine and firm, with round tannins and a fresh finish. Try it after 1996. 5,000 cases made. • $30 • (04/30/94) • **91**

Brunello di Montalcino 1985 • $34 • (07/15/91) • **83**
Brunello di Montalcino 1982 • $31 • (09/15/86) • **95**
Brunello di Montalcino 1981 • $18 • (09/15/86) • **90**
Brunello di Montalcino 1980 • $23 • (09/15/86) • **88**

Brunello di Montalcino La Casa 1990: Big and thick, this powerhouse of a wine packs in a lot of flavors: plum, blackberry, earth and cedar. Impressive, seamless, with a silky texture and supple tannins. Tempting now, but better after 2000. 1,500 cases made. • $72 CS • **95**

Brunello di Montalcino La Casa 1988 • $60 • (04/30/94) • **94**
Brunello di Montalcino La Casa 1985 • $53 • (07/15/91) • **88**
Brunello di Montalcino La Casa 1982 • $50 • (11/30/89) • **67**
Brunello di Montalcino La Casa 1981 • $50 • (06/15/90) • **83**
Brunello di Montalcino La Casa 1979 • $27 • (09/15/86) • **89**

Brunello di Montalcino Riserva 1988: A blockbuster, with tons of ripe fruit and tannins-massive yet restrained. A beautifully focused blackberry and plum character and well-knit full tannins. Not quite as good as the La Casa single-vineyard Brunello from this estate, but who's quibbling? Better after 1998. • $55 • (10/31/94) • **92**

Brunello di Montalcino Riserva 1981 • $23 • (06/15/90) • **70**

Cà del Pazzo 1992: Shows finesse. Dried herb, berry and fruit character, medium body and fine tannins. Made from Cabernet Sauvignon. Drink now. 2,500 cases made. • $28 • **87**

Cà del Pazzo 1990: Rich and earthy style with a round and creamy texture. Plenty of ripe fruit, berry and chocolate character. Made from Sangiovese and Cabernet Sauvignon. Drinkable now. 2,800 cases made. • $25 • (10/31/93) • **86**

Cà del Pazzo 1987 • $24 • (08/31/91) • **85**
Cà del Pazzo 1985 • $28 • (05/15/90) • **77**

Rosso di Montalcino 1993: Very fresh berry and strawberry aromas and flavors, light to medium body, light tannins and a crisp finish. Drink now. • $13 • **83**

Rosso di Montalcino 1991 • $15 • (04/30/94) • **85**
Rosso di Montalcino 1988 • $14 • (04/30/91) • **81**
Rosso di Montalcino 1986 • $10 • (09/30/89) • **86**

Rosso di Montalcino La Caduta 1993: Beautiful wine from a single vineyard, featuring aromas of raspberries and chocolate, medium body, fresh fruit, fine tannins and grapey, mineral notes on the finish. Drinkable now. • $18 • **87**

Rosso di Montalcino La Caduta 1991 • $NA • (04/30/94) • **83**

CAPEZZANA

Barco Reale 1993: An herbal note runs through this and the dominant flavors are cranberry and green cherry. Fairly tight and still tannic, needs smoothing out. Drink now. 2,700 cases made. • $10 • (07/31/95) • **84**

Barco Reale 1987 • $12 • (07/15/91) • **78**
Carmignano 1986 • $15 • (07/15/91) • **81**

Carmignano Barco Reale 1994: Disappointing but still drinkable; with strawberry, rhubarb character but a light and slightly weedy finish. Tasted twice, with consistent notes. • $NA • **75**
Carmignano Riserva 1990: Some good ripe fruit, but it tastes like it was overly aged in old oak, it's dry and slightly tired on the finish. What a shame. Tasted twice, with consistent notes. 3,083 cases made. • $28 • **74**
Carmignano Riserva 1985 • $25 • (07/15/91) • **83**
Carmignano Villa di Capezzana Red 1989: Bright acidity lends elegance, but it's beginning to fade. Sweet fruit and mushroom flavors are followed by an astringent finish. Drink up. 10,656 cases made. • $12 • (08/31/95) • **82**
Chianti Montalbano 1994: A fresh wine that bubbles over with crushed berry character. Light-bodied, with light tannins and a crisp finish. Delicious chilled. 7,775 cases made. • $8 • **81**
Chianti Montalbano 1993: Firmly structured, with lots of strawberry and cherry flavors. Finishes a little earthy, but still appealing. 8,880 cases made. • $8 • (07/31/95) • **84**
Chianti Montalbano 1983 • $6 • (09/15/86) BB • **83**
Chianti Montalbano Conte Contini Bonacossi 1990 • $9 • (09/15/92) • **81**
Chianti Montalbano Conte Contini Bonacossi 1988 • $8 • (10/31/91) • **79**
Ghiaie della Furba 1990: Loads of olive and berry character. Good dark color, with plenty of fruit in aromas and on the palate, but slightly herbal. Medium-bodied, with sweet fruit and a long, minty, soft finish. Better in 1997. • $NA • **86**
Ghiaie della Furba 1988 • $34 • (12/15/92) • **69**
Ghiaie della Furba 1987 • $30 • (12/15/91) • **79**
Ghiaie della Furba 1985 • $20 • (01/31/90) • **91**
Sangiovese Conti Contini 1993: A flavorful cherry and plum palate is layered with tobacco and spice. Fresh and lively, with well-integrated tannins. Plenty of stuffing here, drink now. • $9 • (10/31/95) • **86**
Vin Santo di Carmignano 1981 • $16 • (10/31/86) • **68**

CAPPELLANO

Barbera d'Alba Vigneto Gabutti 1992 • $NA • (10/31/94) • **79**
Barolo 1991: Rather diluted, featuring some decent cherry character but light body and a dry finish. Drink now. • $NA • **78**
Barolo 1990: Firm and focused, with modest black olive-scented black cherry and tomato flavors, an unsual and distinctive wine that is polished enough to drink now. Probably best from 1998. • $NA • (10/31/94) • **85**
Barolo 1989: Ripe and supple, not big, but generous with its mocha, raspberry and black cherry flavors. Gets a little chewy with tannins on the finish. Should be best from 1997. Not as impressive as the barrel sample was last year, but well done. • $NA • (10/31/94) • **86**
Barolo 1988 • $32 • (10/31/93) • **91**
Barolo Gabutti 1991: Vibrant, lovely aromatic qualities of chocolate and cherry follow through on the palate. Medium-bodied with fine tannins and a fresh finish. Drinkable now. • $42 • **86**
Barolo Gabutti 1990: Superbly crafted, with excellent clarity of its mint, berry and cherry aromas and flavors. Full-bodied, fine tannins and a long finish. Better in 1998. • $42 • **90**
Barolo Gabutti 1989: Ripe and generous, bursting with black cherry, currant and anise flavors beneath a thin layer of chewy tannins, echoing chocolate and tar on the long finish. A powerful red that keeps unfolding with each additional sip. Tempting now, but has a great future, give it until 1999 to settle down. • $NA • (10/31/94) • **93**
Barolo Gabutti 1989: Ripe and generous, bursting with black cherry, currant and anise flavors beneath a thin layer of chewy tannins, echoing chocolate and tar on the long finish. A powerful wine that keeps unfolding with each additional sip. Tempting now. • $NA • (10/31/94) • **93**

CAPRILI

Rosso di Montalcino 1986 • $10 • (01/31/89) • **78**

Key: SS—Spectator Selection. CS—Cellar Selection. BB—Best Buy. $NA—Price not available. (BT)—Barrel tasting. Ⓐ—Auction Price.
Dates in parentheses represent the issues in which the ratings were published.

CARATELLO

Chianti Classico 1991 • $9 • (10/31/93) • **79**
Chianti Classico 1988 • $9 • (12/15/90) • **77**
Chianti Classico 1986 • $6 • (01/31/89) • **68**
Chianti Classico 1983 • $4 • (08/31/86) • **70**
Chianti Classico 1982 • $3 • (03/01/86) BB • **85**

CARLO, S.

Brunello di Montalcino 1983 • $23 • (06/15/90) • **86**
Rosso di Montalcino 1986 • $10 • (07/15/89) • **82**

CAROBBIO

Chianti Classico 1992: Already at its peak. Supple and soft with mint, berry and plum aromas and flavors, light-bodied and attractive. Drinkable now. • $NA • **80**
Chianti Classico 1990 • $NA • (10/31/93) • **90**
Chianti Classico Riserva 1991: Gorgeous wine with dark purple color, bursting with vibrant boysenberry and cassis. A balanced beauty to drink now or hold until '97. • $NA • **87**
Chianti Classico Riserva 1990: Stylish, terrific black truffle, blackberry and light toasted vanilla aromas and flavors. Full-bodied yet refined with a long silky finish. Drinkable now. • $NA • **89**

CARPINETO

Chianti Classico 1993: Obviously oaky, with a big vanilla component and spiciness. A good quaff, but hard to believe it's Chianti. Modest cherry and plum flavors. Drink now. 30,000 cases made. • $10 • (10/31/95) • **82**
Chianti Classico 1992: Attractive, supple Chianti featuring plummy, smoky, cherry character, light body and a long aftertaste. Drinkable now. 25,000 cases made. • $9 • (02/28/95) • **83**
Chianti Classico 1988 • $12 • (09/15/91) • **87**
Chianti Classico Riserva 1990: Very firm and solid with complex berry, mineral and plum character. Full in body and tannins but quite refined and elegant. Drinkable now. 8,000 cases made. • $13 • **87**
Chianti Classico Riserva 1988 • $14 • (09/15/92) • **85**
Chianti Classico Riserva 1985 • $19 • (09/15/91) • **89**
Farnito 1991: Pretty Cabernet Sauvignon displays plum, cassis and dried herb character, medium body, velvety tannins and a flavorful finish. Delicious now. 2,000 cases made. • $18 • **87**
Farnito 1990: Like eating blueberry sorbet. Boasting wonderful aromas of fruit, olives and violets, it's full in body with caressing, velvety tannins and a fruity finish. Made from Cabernet Sauvignon. Drinkable in 1997. • $18 • (10/31/93) • **93**
Farnito White 1993: Simple in flavor and appeal, with some buttery, earthy notes. 1,000 cases made. • $20 • (02/29/96) • **76**

CARRETTA

Barolo Poderi Cannubi 1988 • $23 • (03/31/93) • **75**
Barolo Poderi Cannubi 1985 • $26 • (01/31/92) • **82**
Barolo Poderi Cannubi 1980 • $14 • (09/15/87) • **62**
Bianco del Poggio 1993: An aggressive, toasty flavor dominates this medium-bodied white. There's enough acidity for balance, but not much fruit, finishing with a sweet, vanilla note. • $9 • (04/30/96) • **82**
Nebbiolo d'Alba Bric Paradiso 1990 • $19 • (04/30/93) • **82**
Nebbiolo d'Alba Bric Paradiso 1989 • $15 • (07/31/92) • **78**
Nebbiolo d'Alba Bric Tavoleto 1988 • $15 • (07/31/92) • **75**
Quercia Bric 1990 • $21 • (03/31/93) • **87**
Quercia Bric 1989 • $20 • (01/31/92) • **84**

CASAL THAULERO

Abbazia di Propezzano 1986 • $19 • (07/15/91) • **89**
Montepulciano d'Abruzzo 1993: A robust, hearty red with lots of cherry flavor, crisp acidity and firm tannins. Drink now while it's fresh. 250,000 cases made. • $6 • (02/29/96) • **82**
Montepulciano d'Abruzzo 1989 • $6 • (06/30/91) BB • **81**

Montepulciano d'Abruzzo 1988 • $5 • (05/31/90) BB • **80**
Montepulciano d'Abruzzo 1983 • $6 • (06/30/87) BB • **86**

CASALOSTE

Chianti Classico 1993: Fresh and easygoing red, with spicy, earthy strawberry aromas and flavors. Medium to light body and crisp, with a long finish. • $NA • **79**

CASANOVA DI NERI

Brunello di Montalcino 1990: Classy Brunello. Plenty of wonderful mineral, currant, berry and cherry character in this one. Full body, ultrafine tannins and succulent flavors that build on the finish. Drinkable now. • $33 • **90**
Brunello di Montalcino 1988: Slightly overdone, traditional style that masks the ripe, sweet black cherry flavor. Full-bodied with velvety tannins, but a slightly dry finish. Drinkable now. • $27 • (04/30/94) • **82**
Brunello di Montalcino Riserva 1988: Massive, with tons of extremely ripe fruit. The tar and plum aromas jump out of the glass leading to a juicy, tannic finish. Superbly concentrated. Drink now, but much better after 1997. • $NA • (10/31/94) • **92**
Rosso di Montalcino 1993: Big and rich Rosso-almost raisiny-showing loads of fruit and flavor, medium tannins and a long grapey, berry finish. Drink now. • $NA • **84**
Rosso di Montalcino 1991 • $14 • (04/30/94) • **84**

CASASLTE, E.

Vino Nobile di Montepulciano 1983 • $9 • (11/30/87) • **86**

CASCINACASTLE'T

Passum 1984 • $25 • (12/31/88) • **61**

CASCINETTA

Moscato d'Asti 1992 • $11 • (05/15/93) • **81**
Moscato d'Asti 1991 • $11 • (05/15/93) • **81**
Moscato d'Asti 1987 • $9 • (12/31/90) • **80**

CASELLO, IL

Brunello di Montalcino 1982 • $18 • (07/31/88) • **84**
Brunello di Montalcino 1981 • $15 • (10/31/87) • **84**

CASETTA

Barbera d'Alba Vigna Lazaretto 1990: An extremely flavorful but overblown style, that emphasizes tomato, beet and celery flavors. 6,000 cases made. • $10 • **77**
Barbera d'Alba Vigna Lazaretto 1987 • $9 • (03/15/91) BB • **89**

CASISANO-COLOMBAIO

Brunello di Montalcino 1990: Loads of rose petal and berry and a hint of tobacco. Medium in body, fine tannins and succulent finish. Drink now. • $NA • **87**
Rosso di Montalcino 1993: Light and fresh strawberry, cherry character, light body and a light, diluted finish. Drink now. • $NA • **78**

CASTELCOSA

Picolit 1983 • $NA • (09/15/88) • **83**
Refosco 1985 • $NA • (09/15/88) • **82**

CASTELGIOCONDO

Brunello di Montalcino 1990: Youthful violet, mineral and blackberry aromas and flavors. Full-bodied and very rich, adding velvety tannins and a long, minty finish. From Frescobaldi. Better in 1998. • $30 • **92**
Brunello di Montalcino Riserva 1988: A muscular Brunello with fine structure and cherry, raspberry, red pepper character. Full-bodied, yet lots of ripe fruit and rather lean on the finish. Needs time to open up, better after 1997. • $NA • (10/31/94) • **90**
Rosso di Montalcino Campo ai Sassi 1993: Lean and light-bodied, offering nice cherry, earth, mineral and smoke complexity. Fresh, crisp finish. Serve slightly chilled and enjoy. From Frescobaldi. • $NA • **83**
Rosso di Montalcino Campo ai Sassi 1992 • $NA • (10/31/94) • **79**

CASTELGREVE

Chianti Classico 1993: An easy-drinking Chianti with a gamy character and fresh berry and mushroom notes. Light-bodied, fine tannins and a delicious, succulent finish. • $10 • **80**
Chianti Classico 1992: Good concentration of fruit, although slightly herbal. Nice, silky texture and a crisp finish. Drinkable now. 220,000 cases made. • $9 • **82**
Chianti Classico 1991 • $9 • (10/31/93) • **82**
Chianti Classico 1990 • $10 • (09/15/92) • **78**
Chianti Classico Riserva 1991: Soft- and round-textured wine with cherry, spice and leather aromas and flavors. Medium body. Ripe fruity finish. Drinkable now. • $13 • **82**
Chianti Classico Riserva 1990: An elegant red offering tobacco, chocolate and blueberry aromas and flavors. Medium-bodied and fresh on the palate. Drinkable now. 20,000 cases made. • $12 • **85**

CASTELL'IN VILLA

Chianti Classico 1990 • $NA • (10/31/93) • **84**
Chianti Classico 1988 • $13 • (09/15/91) • **88**
Chianti Classico 1986 • $13 • (09/15/90) • **79**
Chianti Classico 1985 • $12 • (06/30/89) • **86**
Chianti Classico 1983 • $7 • (09/15/87) • **87**
Chianti Classico Riserva 1988 • $NA • (10/31/93) • **79**
Chianti Classico Riserva 1985 • $NA • (09/15/91) • **83**
Chianti Classico Riserva 1982 • $18 • (11/30/90) • **86**
Santacroce 1988 • $NA • (10/31/93) • **92**

CASTELLARE DI CASTELLINA

Bianco 1992 • $8 • (10/31/94) • **85**
Chianti Classico 1993: A simple and easy-drinking Chianti with cherry, berry and floral aromas and flavors, light body and a light finish. • $18 • **80**
Chianti Classico 1991 • $12 • (10/31/93) • **81**
Chianti Classico 1990 • $14 • (09/15/92) • **82**
Chianti Classico 1989 • $14 • (09/15/92) • **82**
Chianti Classico 1988 • $13 • (11/30/90) • **82**
Chianti Classico 1987 • $11 • (11/30/89) • **81**
Chianti Classico 1986 • $11 • (10/15/89) • **82**
Chianti Classico 1985 • $11 • (03/31/88) • **85**
Chianti Classico Riserva 1991: Ripe yet elegant, with loads of boysenberry, plum and cassis aromas and flavors. Medium body and supple tannins, packed with fruit. Lovely to drink now. • $21 • **85**
Chianti Classico Riserva 1990: Firm and crisp, pretty cherry, raspberry and mint aromas and flavors. Tasted twice, with consistent notes. Drinkable now. 600 cases made. • $20 • **84**
Chianti Classico Riserva 1988 • $23 • (09/15/92) • **83**
Chianti Classico Riserva 1986 • $11 • (11/30/89) • **86**
Chianti Classico Riserva 1985 • $17 • (09/15/91) • **77**
Coniale di Castellare 1988 • $35 • (09/15/91) • **92**
Coniale di Castellare 1987 • $31 • (10/31/90) • **87**
I Sodi di S. Niccolo 1991: Vibrant, fresh wine that needs time to come around due to the high acidity. Intense dried cherry and raspberry aromas and flavors. Medium-bodied. Fine tannins with a little bite on the finish. Try after 1997. • $42 • **87**
I Sodi di S. Niccolo 1990: Gorgeous plum, cassis and berry character. Medium-bodied and delicious, fine tannins and crisp finish. Drinkable now. 700 cases made. • $36 • **88**
I Sodi di San Niccolò 1988 • $35 • (09/15/91) • **88**
I Sodi di San Niccolò 1987 • $32 • (04/15/91) • **86**
I Sodi di San Niccolò 1986 • $25 • (11/30/89) • **94**

CASTELLI MARTINOZZI

I Sodi di San Niccolò 1985 • $25 • (05/31/88) • **96**
I Sodi di San Niccolò 1983 • $20 • (05/31/88) • **87**
I Sodi di San Niccolò 1982 • $20 • (09/15/87) • **89**
I Sodi di San Niccolò 1981 • $20 • (09/15/87) • **87**
Spartito 1990: Simple, sturdy, round and a little spicy from oak. A standard-issue white wine that's drinkable enough, but displays only modest distinction. Drinkable now. 600 cases made. • $20 • (09/15/93) • **82**
Vin Santo 1984 • $28/375ml • (09/30/90) • **88**

CASTELLI MARTINOZZI

Brunello di Montalcino 1988: Rather light and fruity with an earthy character on the nose and palate. A wine for early drinking. Tasted twice. • $NA • (04/30/94) • **79**
Rosso di Montalcino 1991 • $NA • (04/30/94) • **84**

CASTELLUCCIO

Le More 1992: A good, solid wine with integrated tannins and a core of black cherry flavor. It has lively acidity, firm texture and good balance. Drink now through 1997. • $19 • (02/29/96) • **85**
Ronco dei Ciliegi 1990: Fairly enjoyable, but a bit tired. Drinkable now if you like a mature, vegetal-tasting wine. • $35 • (02/29/96) • **77**
Ronco della Simia 1991: A bit thin and unfocused, with harsh tannins and modest plum and cherry flavors. Turns astringent on the finish. • $35 • (02/29/96) • **75**
Ronco delle Ginestre 1990: Mature and plummy, with some tannins hanging on as well. It finishes with some spicy notes, but is a bit astringent. • $27 • (02/29/96) • **79**

CASTELVECCHI

Chianti Classico Riserva 1982 • $13 • (05/15/90) • **85**

CASTELVECCHIO

Cabernet Franc 1991: A bold but lean-tasting red with peppery aromas and flavors, firm tannins and an astringent finish. Has more structure than flavor or finish. • $15 • (06/15/96) • **79**
Sauvignon 1993: Smells a bit volatile and resinous, with herbal and candied flavors. Finishes on a cloying note. • $13 • (06/15/96) • **77**

CAVALCHINA

Bardolino Chiaretto 1991 • $NA • (09/15/92) • **78**
Bianco di Custoza 1993: Fresh and bright, a light, narrow beam of a wine that accents its apple flavors with hints of mineral and vanilla. • $10 • (01/31/95) • **80**
Bianco di Custoza 1991 • $NA • (09/15/92) • **79**
Cabernet Sauvignon Vigneto del Falcone 1988 • $NA • (09/15/92) • **82**
Cabernet Vigneto del Falcone La Prendina 1989 • $NA • (09/15/92) • **88**
Le Pergole del Sole 1990 • $NA • (09/15/92) • **79**

CAVALIERI, FATTORIA DEI

Podere Cavalieri Verdicchio di Matelica 1992: Resinous flavors dominate this old style Verdicchio. Tastes somewhat oxidized with aromas verging on the herbal. 350 cases made. • $10 • (03/31/95) • **77**

CAVALOTTO

Barbaresco Vigna San Giuseppe Riserva 1985 • $22 • (02/28/91) • **90**
Barolo 1991: An attractive, delicate wine with berry and lightly earthy aromas and flavors. Medium-bodied, with a long, fresh finish. From Bricco Boschis. Drinkable now. • $29 • **82**
Barolo 1988 • $NA • (10/31/94) • **87**

Key: SS—Spectator Selection. CS—Cellar Selection. BB—Best Buy. $NA—Price not available. (BT)—Barrel tasting. Ⓐ—Auction Price.
Dates in parentheses represent the issues in which the ratings were published.

Barolo Riserva Bricco Boschis 1990: In a traditional style, but impressive. Wonderful almond, berry, black pepper and chocolate aromas and flavors. Full-bodied and rich, with fine tannins and a long, flavorful finish. Drink now or age a few years. • $39 • **87**
Barolo Vigna S. Giuseppe 1988 • $15 • (10/31/93) • **77**
Dolcetta d'Alba Mallera 1987 • $10 • (03/15/89) • **83**

CAVICCHIOLI

Malvasia Ca'Violi NV: The bubbles are the most prominent part of this sparkler, it lacks fruit and sweetness and carries a light earthy note. Simple and rather dull. • $NA • (10/31/95) • **78**

CECCHI

Capitolare di Cardisco Spargolo Red 1991: Polished and refined, with cherry, violet, mint and light oak aromas and flavors. Medium-bodied with medium tannins and a fresh finish. Better after 1997. 250 cases made. • $29 • **89**
Chianti 1986 • $5 • (01/31/89) • **80**
Chianti Classico 1993: Like a Beaujolais Nouveau, fresh and fruity, with strawberry and raspberry flavors. Very light. Serve chilled. 110,000 cases made. • $7 • **80**
Chianti Classico 1992 • $8 • (10/31/94) BB • **86**
Chianti Classico 1990 • $11 • (09/15/92) • **85**
Chianti Classico 1986 • $7 • (07/15/89) • **86**
Chianti Classico Masser Pietro di Teuzzo 1990 • $NA • (10/31/93) • **84**
Chianti Classico Teuzzo 1993: Firm and refreshing with dried cherry, berry character. Medium- to light-bodied with fine tannins and a fresh finish. Drinkable now. • $NA • **81**
Chianti Classico Villa Cerna Riserva 1990: Overly mature, with woody, spicy, cooked aromas and tart flavors like balsamic vinegar. 9,000 cases made. • $15 • (02/28/95) • **76**
Sangiovese di Toscana 1993: Firm structure, with cranberry and currant flavors. Fairly rich, concentrated and tart on the finish. 55,000 cases made. • $6 • (07/31/95) • **82**
Spargolo Predicato di Cardisco 1988 • $36 • (10/31/93) • **89**
Spargolo Predicato di Cardisco 1985 • $36 • (01/31/92) • **78**
Spargolo Predicato di Cardisco 1983 • $25 • (03/15/91) • **75**
Spargolo Predicato di Cardisco 1982 • $12 • (09/30/89) • **68**
Vino Nobile di Montepulciano 1991: Plum and black cherry flavors balance earth and leather notes. The fruit keeps it pleasant and builds up some complexity in this chunky, firm wine. 21,000 cases made. • $12 • (02/29/96) • **83**
Vino Nobile di Montepulciano 1987 • $13 • (03/31/92) • **77**
Vino Nobile di Montepulciano 1983 • $9 • (05/15/89) • **77**

CELLA

Asti Spumante NV • $7 • (01/31/88) • **77**

CELLOLE

Chianti Classico Riserva 1990: Beautiful, firm mushroom, berry and tobacco aromas and flavors. Try now. • $NA • **87**

CENNATOIO

Chianti Classico 1993: Lovely cherry, raspberry aromas that follow through on the palate. Medium-bodied with sweet fruit and a hint of pepper. Medium-crisp finish. • $13 • **85**
Chianti Classico 1992: Fresh and clean with some berry, cherry character. Too diluted. Average quality. 2,800 cases made. • $12 • **76**
Chianti Classico 1990 • $10 • (10/31/93) • **83**
Chianti Classico Riserva 1990: A very pretty Chianti riserva with floral, ripe berry aromas and flavors, medium body, silky tannins and a crisp, fruity finish. Drinkable now. 1,050 cases made. • $17 • **87**
Etrusco 1991: Complex Sangiovese featuring berry, meat, mint, vanilla and toast character. Medium-bodied with loads of tannins yet it's reserved and fine. Better after 1997. 300 cases made. • $26 • **88**
Etrusco 1990 • $11 • (10/31/93) • **89**

Rosso Fiorentino 1991: Better than the '90? A solid Cabernet showing mint, herb and currant aromas and flavors, medium body, supple tannins and a delightful finish. Drinkable now. 300 cases made. • $26 • **87**
Rosso Fiorentino 1990 • $10 • (10/31/93) • **83**

CERBAIA

Brunello di Montalcino 1988: Easy and soft, with earthy plum and berry aromas and flavors, medium tannins and a light finish. Tasted twice. Try now or hold. • $NA • (04/30/94) • **82**
Rosso di Montalcino 1991 • $NA • (04/30/94) • **84**

CERBAIOLA

Brunello di Montalcino Salvioni 1986 • $60 • (12/15/92) • **93**

CERBAIONA

Brunello di Montalcino 1988: Some pretty, but earthy, fruit aromas and flavors, medium tannins and short finish. Tasted twice. Drinkable on release. • $50 • (04/30/94) • **80**
Brunello di Montalcino 1985 • $60 • (11/30/91) • **71**
Rosso di Montalcino 1988 • $21 • (01/31/92) • **82**

CEREQUIO

Barolo 1982 • $19 • (11/15/88) • **91**
Barolo 1979 • $13 • (07/31/89) • **69**
Barolo Riserva 1980 • $13 • (07/31/89) • **80**

CERETTO

Arneis Blangé White 1991 • $19 • (05/31/93) • **87**
Barbaresco 1981 • $9 • (05/16/86) • **58**
Barbaresco Asij 1991: Light, watery mineral and chestnut character and drying on the finish. Why bottle this? Tasted twice, with consistent notes. Drink now. • $23 • **74**
Barbaresco Asij 1990: Spicy and herbal, modest in the fruit department, sort of green and crisp rather than generous. Maybe better after 1997. Tasted twice. • $23 • (10/31/94) • **80**
Barbaresco Asij 1989: Smooth and spicy, with a gentle core of raspberry, tar and cedar flavor running into a layer of tannins on the finish. 2,900 cases made. • $23 • (10/31/93) • **85**
Barbaresco Asij 1988 • $23 • (10/31/93) • **77**
Barbaresco Asij 1987 • $22 • (07/15/91) • **86**
Barbaresco Asij 1985 • $15 • (01/31/90) • **64**
Barbaresco Bricco Asili 1990: Austere and earthy, light in texture, adding some appealing violet and rose petal notes to the modest berry flavors, a little drying on the finish. Tasted twice. • $61 • (10/31/94) • **79**
Barbaresco Bricco Asili 1989: Firm and flavorful, a powerful shot of anise-scented raspberry and blackberry fruit, making for a sturdy wine with well-defined Nebbiolo fruit. Tannins are still tough. Best after 1996. 700 cases made. • $61 • (10/31/93) • **87**
Barbaresco Bricco Asili 1988 • $61 • (10/31/93) • **75**
Barbaresco Bricco Asili 1987 • $42 • (04/30/91) • **89**
Barbaresco Bricco Asili 1986 • $35 • (04/15/90) • **85**
Barbaresco Bricco Asili 1985 • $35 • (08/31/89) • **89**
Barbaresco Bricco Asili 1984 • $15 • (09/15/88) • **80**
Barbaresco Bricco Asili 1982 • $54 • (09/15/88) • **87**
Barbaresco Bricco Asili 1978 • $NA • (03/01/86) • **90**
Barbaresco Bricco Asili 1976 • $NA • (09/15/88) • **89**
Barbaresco Bricco Asili 1974 • $NA • (03/01/86) • **90**
Barbaresco Bricco Asili Fasêt 1990: Light in texture but generous in flavor, offering a nice range of mint, berry and currant notes, spicy and fruity on the smooth finish. Tannins are smoothly integrated. Approachable now. Tasted twice. • $44 • (10/31/94) • **86**
Barbaresco Bricco Asili Fasêt 1989: Simple and chunky, with modest spicy cherry flavors, finishing with a gritty texture and little intensity, more mature than other 1989's. May be best after 1996. 1,250 cases made. • $44 • (10/31/93) • **82**
Barbaresco Bricco Asili Fasêt 1988 • $44 • (10/31/93) • **79**
Barbaresco Bricco Asili Fasêt 1987 • $31 • (07/15/91) • **89**
Barbaresco Bricco Asili Fasêt 1985 • $31 • (01/31/90) • **87**
Barbera d'Alba Piana 1993: A touch of mint adds some complexity to cherry and raspberry flavors. Medium-bodied, offering a crisp side, but the balance and smoothness are there. 833 cases made. • $17 • **83**
Barbera d'Alba Piana 1991 • $17 • (11/15/93) • **76**
Barbera d'Alba Piana 1990 • $17 • (04/30/93) • **70**
Barbera d'Alba Piana 1989 • $18 • (10/31/92) • **87**
Barolo Bricco Rocche Bricco Rocche 1990: Light in color, smooth and rich, showing maturity in texture and flavor, a bit sharp on the finish, but the orange peel and plum character comes through. Approachable now. Tasted twice. • $100 • (10/31/94) • **88**
Barolo Bricco Rocche Bricco Rocche 1986 • $110 • (04/30/91) • **89**
Barolo Bricco Rocche Bricco Rocche 1985 • $103 • (03/31/90) • **86**
Barolo Bricco Rocche Bricco Rocche 1982 • $100 • (09/15/88) • **91**
Barolo Bricco Rocche Bricco Rocche 1980 • $60 • (03/01/86) • **90**
Barolo Bricco Rocche Brunate 1989: Firm and chewy, but offering a good dose of cherry and tar flavors that persist winningly on the finish. Tannins are at the forefront now, however. Try after 1997. 2,100 cases made. • $44 • (10/31/93) • **86**
Barolo Bricco Rocche Brunate 1988 • $44 • (10/31/93) • **81**
Barolo Bricco Rocche Brunate 1986 • $40 • (04/30/91) • **80**
Barolo Bricco Rocche Brunate 1985 • $41 • (01/31/90) • **92**
Barolo Bricco Rocche Brunate 1983 • $37 • (07/31/89) • **85**
Barolo Bricco Rocche Brunate 1979 • $42 • (03/01/86) • **86**
Barolo Bricco Rocche Brunate 1978 • $39 Ⓐ • (09/15/88) • **86**
Barolo Bricco Rocche Brunate 1967 • $100 • (10/20/87) • **90**
Barolo Bricco Rocche Prapò 1989: Rich, ripe and spicy, almost raisiny, but with a bitter edge like an Amarone, big and tough rather than elegant. Don't touch until 1998-2000. 1,100 cases made. • $54 • (10/31/93) • **82**
Barolo Bricco Rocche Prapò 1988 • $54 • (10/31/93) • **84**
Barolo Bricco Rocche Prapò 1986 • $50 • (02/28/91) • **91**
Barolo Bricco Rocche Prapò 1985 • $50 • (03/31/90) • **78**
Barolo Bricco Rocche Prapò 1983 • $31 • (07/31/89) • **86**
Barolo Bricco Rocche Prapò 1978 • $95 • (03/01/86) • **95**
Barolo Bricco Rocche Prapò 1976 • $80 • (09/15/88) • **82**
Barolo Bricco Rocche Prapò 1971 • $100 • (10/30/87) • **88**
Barolo Brunate 1990: Tannic and chewy, watery at the center, picking up a hint of minty berry flavor to make it drinkable, best after 1997. Tasted twice. • $44 • (10/31/94) • **77**
Barolo Cannubi 1971 • $NA • (03/01/86) • **85**
Barolo Prapò 1990: Bright and spicy, with a lively thread of sweet raspberry and strawberry fruit shaded by a strong anise note, echoing vanilla and mint on the finish. Tannins are nicely integrated, promising best things for 1998-2000. • $54 • (10/31/94) • **88**
Barolo Zonchera 1991: Shamefully dry. Too much wood. Medium-bodied with tons of woody, cedary flavors and a hint of fruit in the aftertaste. Dry finish. Tasted twice with consistent notes. • $23 • (10/31/95) • **76**
Barolo Zonchera 1989: A lean wine with generous black cherry, anise and other spices reverberating on the palate, echoing plum and tar on the finish. Tannins are sweet and well integrated. A little better than when tasted in 1993. • $23 • (10/31/94) • **88**
Barolo Zonchera 1988 • $23 • (10/31/93) • **87**
Barolo Zonchera 1987 • $23 • (08/31/91) • **86**
Barolo Zonchera 1985 • $16 • (06/15/90) • **82**
Barolo Zonchera 1984 • $16 • (09/15/88) • **83**
Barolo Zonchera 1982 • $16 • (06/30/87) • **90**
Barolo Zonchera 1980 • $16 • (02/16/86) SS • **96**
Cabernet Sauvignon La Bernardina 1991: Blockbuster of a red, lavishly oaked and massively tannic, extremely deep in color and fairly fruity, too. Tastes like vanilla, chocolate, blackberry and raspberry with tarry, peppery accents and a lush, oak-aged texture. Tempting now, but best after 1997. • $26 • (02/28/95) • **93**
Chardonnay La Bernardina 1993: An exaggerated but attractive style of Chardonnay, very oaky in flavor, but with abundant peach and apricot notes underneath. A toasty hazelnut character lingers on the finish. Drinkable now through 1998. • $24 • (02/29/96) • **87**
Chardonnay La Bernardina 1992: A very developed, nutty, oaky white that's near full maturity and flamboyant. Has subtle fruit, crisp acidity and a lingering finish. • $24 • (02/29/96) • **86**

ITALY

Dolcetto d'Alba Rossana 1994: Pretty, easy to drink, with plenty of raspberry and violet character. Light- to medium-bodied, with light tannins and a crisp finish. Knock it back with pizza. Drinkable now. 4,167 cases made. • $17 • (10/31/95) • **81**
Dolcetto d'Alba Rossana 1990 • $18 • (10/31/92) • **83**
Dolcetto d'Alba Rossana 1989 • $16 • (04/30/91) • **79**
Dolcetto d'Alba Rossana 1987 • $12 • (03/15/89) • **86**
Dolcetto d'Alba Rossana 1985 • $8 • (12/31/87) • **74**
Dolcetto d'Alba Vigna 1985 • $11 • (03/15/89) • **77**
Nebbiolo d'Alba Lantasco 1990 • $19 • (04/30/93) • **87**
Nebbiolo d'Alba Lantasco 1989 • $16 • (10/31/92) • **81**
Nebbiolo d'Alba Lantasco 1988 • $18 • (04/30/91) • **81**

CERNA, VILLA

Chianti Classico 1990 • $NA • (09/15/92) • **89**
Chianti Classico 1988 • $9 • (09/15/91) • **89**
Chianti Classico Riserva 1991: Rather short and simple, with some decent cherry and berry notes. Light body and a light finish. Drinkable now. • $19 • **79**
Chianti Classico Riserva 1988 • $NA • (09/15/92) • **88**
Chianti Classico Riserva 1985 • $16 • (09/15/91) • **87**
Chianti Classico Riserva 1983 • $8 • (03/31/89) BB • **84**
Vigneto La Gavina 1988 • $NA • (09/15/91) • **91**

CERRO, FATTORIA DEL

Chianti Colli Senesi 1987 • $5 • (07/31/89) • **74**
Rosso di Montepulciano 1992 • $9 • (07/31/94) • **83**
Vino Nobile di Montepulciano 1990: A rustic style that's not for us. Tight, tannic, astringent and tough. The fruit flavors are drying up already and the color is turning mature. Tasted twice, with consistent notes. 16,600 cases made. • $14 • (02/28/95) • **74**
Vino Nobile di Montepulciano Riserva 1988 • $16 • (07/31/94) • **85**
Vino Nobile di Montepulciano Vigneto Antica Chiusina 1990: Attractive plum and licorice aromas give way to a ripe, firm palate full of cherry, anise, clove and smoke flavors. Drinkable now. • $19 • (02/29/96) • **87**

CESARE E FIGLI, FRANCO

Amarone della Valpolicella Il Bosco Valpolicella 1988: A traditional style Amarone that layers nutty, spicy accents over good fruit flavors for a mellow-tasting but full-bodied taste experience. Soft in texture. 812 cases made. • $30 • (09/30/95) • **85**
Barolo Vigna Cerretta 1990: Floral and black cherry aromas give way to supple flavors of cherry, spice and tobacco, firm tannins kick in on the finish. A dusty note detracts from the light, almost sweet profile of the wine. • $NA • (10/31/95) • **79**

CESARE, PIO

Barbaresco 1991: Very pretty for the vintage, featuring flavors of dark chocolate, berry and dried cherry. A little hot and alcoholic, but some good silky texture and richness. Drink now. 8,000 cases made. • $32 • **82**
Barbaresco 1990: Smooth and inviting, a round, concentrated Barbaresco, redolent of rose petals and tar. It keeps its tannins buried beneath a mouthful of rich blackberry, black cherry, licorice and spice flavors. Approachable now, but best from 1997 or 1998. • $28 • (10/31/94) • **89**
Barbaresco 1989: Light in body, firm in texture, finally seems delicate, with a touch of licorice and cinnamon to the black cherry flavor. Drinkable now. • $NA • (10/31/94) • **81**
Barbaresco 1988 • $34 • (10/31/93) • **83**
Barbaresco Il Bricco Riserva 1990: Ripe and fleshy, showing sweet vanilla, bright black cherry and licorice flavors. The round tannins are well integrated and the finish is long and fruity. Harmonious and should improve through 2000. 500 cases made. • $52 • (10/31/95) • **88**

Key: SS—Spectator Selection. CS—Cellar Selection. BB—Best Buy. $NA—Price not available. (BT)—Barrel tasting. Ⓐ—Auction Price.
Dates in parentheses represent the issues in which the ratings were published.

Barbaresco Riserva 1989 • $34 • **58**
Barbaresco Riserva 1980 • $16 • (12/16/85) • **68**
Barbera d'Alba 1991 • $10 • (10/31/94) • **86**
Barbera d'Alba 1989 • $17 • (10/15/93) • **83**
Barbera d'Alba 1987 • $12 • (04/15/91) • **81**
Barbera d'Alba 1985 • $12 • (11/15/88) • **78**
Barolo 1990: Aromatic and generous, a broad-textured wine that puts a minty-eucalyptus edge to the ripe core of black cherry and berry flavors. Tannins seem well integrated. Should be at its best from 1998-1999. • $28 • (10/31/94) • **88**
Barolo 1989: The proportions are modest, but the cinnamon-spice berry and vanilla flavors are charming and the tannins do not intrude too far. A lighter style that is charming rather than powerful. Approachable now. • $28 • (10/31/94) • **86**
Barolo 1988 • $28 • (10/31/93) • **83**
Barolo 1987 • $27 • (12/15/92) • **82**
Barolo 1985 • $41 • (05/15/91) • **89**
Barolo 1983 • $33 • (09/15/88) • **88**
Barolo 1982 • $36 • (09/15/88) • **91**
Barolo 1981 • $25 • (09/15/88) • **87**
Barolo 1978 • $18 • (09/15/88) • **85**
Barolo 1974 • $40 • (09/15/88) • **77**
Barolo 1971 • $38 • (09/15/88) • **80**
Barolo Ornato 1990: Deep in color and tremendously rich in aroma and flavor, a supple package that oozes with licorice, plum, berry and black cherry notes. The tannins are beautifully integrated, gently supporting the whole show of fresh flavors. Awfully tempting to drink now, but try to hold off until 1997 to 2001. • $41 • (10/31/94) • **95**
Barolo Ornato 1988 • $NA • (10/31/93) • **90**
Barolo Ornato Riserva 1985 • $48 • (05/15/91) • **91**
Barolo Riserva 1982 • $31 • (11/15/88) • **86**
Barolo Riserva 1980 • $19 • (02/15/87) • **72**
Barolo Riserva 1978 • $28 • (10/01/84) SS • **89**
Chardonnay 1992 • $16 • (11/30/93) • **81**
Chardonnay del Piemonte 1994: A smooth, serious Chardonnay with complex flavors of pear, hazelnut and toast and a lingering finish. Subtle yet concentrated. In the style of a white Burgundy. 1,600 cases made. • $11 • (02/29/96) • **88**
Chardonnay del Piemonte 1993: A solid Chardonnay that is fruity and generous, with ample pear and spice flavors that linger on the crisp finish. • $10 • (02/28/95) • **84**
Chardonnay del Piemonte 1992: Has a bit of white Burgundy character in the nicely earthy, spicy aromas backed by good pear and citrus flavors. Has a broad, appealing texture. Tasted twice with consistent notes. 1,000 cases made. • $16 • (02/28/95) • **82**
Cortese di Gavi White 1994: Clean, crisp and well balanced, with fresh, light fruit flavors. • $17 • (02/29/96) • **84**
Cortese di Gavi White 1993: Appetizing and complex, with aromas of fig and toasted almond, deep but subtle flavors of peach and fig, great acidity and a lingering finish. • $16 • (02/28/95) • **87**
Dolcetto d'Alba 1992: Attractive plum and floral aromas, with some depth to the plum and cherry flavors, but it finishes a bit hollow and dry. Still pleasurable, though. • $10 • (07/31/95) • **83**
Nebbiolo 1983 • $8 • (02/16/86) • **88**
Ornato 1983 • $16 • (03/31/88) • **82**
Piedmont 1991 • $18 • (10/31/92) • **81**
Piedmont 1985 • $10 • (10/31/86) • **71**
Piodilei 1991 • $34 • (06/15/94) • **88**
Rosso del Piemonte 1989 • $12 • (01/31/92) • **83**

CESARI

Amarone della Valpolicella Il Bosco 1988: Traditional-style Amarone layering nutty, spicy accents over good fruit flavors for a mellow-tasting but full-bodied experience. Soft in texture. 812 cases made. • $30 • (09/30/95) • **85**

CESARI, UMBERTO

Riserva Sangiovese di Romagna 1992: Firm and moderately tannic, with an nice core of cherry flavors. Simple, but solid. 80,000 cases made. • $10 • (02/29/96) • **83**

CHERUBIN

Piedmont 1990 • $11 • (10/31/92) • **89**

CHIARLO, MICHELE

Asti Spumante NV: Full-bodied for an Asti, with heavy, rather dull flavors of candied orange and pineapple. Very sweet and a bit clumsy. • $12 • (12/15/95) • **79**

Asti Spumante Granduca NV • $13 • (12/15/92) • **70**

Barbaresco 1992: Smooth and well-made red licorice, cherry, raspberry character and some earthy notes. Very pleasant texture and light to medium body. 1,250 cases made. • $24 • **81**

Barbaresco 1990: Ripe and generous enough to carry the flavors through the finish, a smooth-textured wine that allows the black cherry and berry flavors to open up. Drinkable now. • $25 • (10/31/94) • **85**

Barbaresco 1989: Light and appealing, with simple raspberry and anise aromas and flavors, finishing just a bit tough. 2,000 cases made. • $23 • (10/31/93) • **81**

Barbaresco 1988 • $23 • (10/31/93) • **85**

Barbaresco Rabajà 1990: Ripe and generous, a smooth-textured wine, polished and appealing for its blackberry, currant and licorice flavors, an open-textured wine that shows off its flavors winningly. Drinkable now. • $48 • (10/31/94) • **90**

Barbaresco Rabajà 1989: Smooth, elegant and generous, with lovely vanilla-scented cherry and blackcurrant aromas and flavors that persist on the harmonious finish. Beautifully defined flavors and supple texture mark this as something special. Almost drinkable now. 330 cases made. • $48 • (10/31/93) • **91**

Barbaresco Rabajà 1988 • $48 • (10/31/93) • **90**

Barbera d'Asti 1993 • $9 • (10/31/94) • **85**

Barbera d'Asti 1991 • $9 • (06/15/94) • **79**

Barbera d'Asti 1990 • $9 • (10/15/93) BB • **91**

Barbera d'Asti Superiore 1990 • $22 • (06/30/93) • **87**

Barbera d'Asti Superiore 1986 • $18 • (03/15/91) • **86**

Barbera d'Asti Superiore Valle del Sole 1990: This is rich, concentrated and full-flavored, with a surplus of fruit and sweet vanilla on the palate. Elegant and perfumed, a nice roasted flavor running through it. The finish resonates with plum, cherry and sweet spice flavors. • $20 • (07/31/95) • **90**

Barbera d'Asti Superiore Valle del Sole 1988 • $19 • (10/31/92) • **83**

Barbera d'Asti Superiore Valle del Sole 1987 • $19 • (02/15/92) • **84**

Barbera d'Asti Valle del Sole 1989 • $19 • (10/15/93) • **86**

Barilot 1990 • $25 • (10/31/94) • **85**

Barilot 1987 • $31 • (06/15/94) • **86**

Barilot 1986 • $31 • (12/15/92) • **73**

Barolo 1991: Clean, fruity and well made, showing good acidity and some mineral, black cherry, tar and floral notes. Intriguing and quite delicious. Drink on release or hold for a couple of years. 6,667 cases made. • $24 • (10/31/95) • **85**

Barolo 1990: Ripe and easy in flavor, even if it might be a little hot on the finish. There's a minty edge to the plum and apricot. The tannins can use until 1999 or 2000 to sort themselves out. • $25 • (10/31/94) • **85**

Barolo 1989: Rich and spicy, with a strong thread of anise and toast aromas and flavors, finishing sweet and ripe, echoing blackberry, plum, cherry and spice flavors on the long finish. Approachable now despite the tannins, making it a real crowd pleaser, delicious to drink early as well as after 2000. 5,400 cases made. • $22 • (10/31/93) • **91**

Barolo 1988 • $23 • (10/15/93) SS • **92**

Barolo 1987 • $22 • (12/15/92) • **86**

Barolo Brunate 1990: Rich, broad, generous and distinctively minty, with supple texture and a foundation of berry and plum flavors to play against the mint and rose petal notes that dominate. Delicious enough to drink now, but it should be at its best after 1999. • $47 • (10/31/94) • **92**

Barolo Brunate 1989: Smooth, polished and delicious, with a lovely range of violet, black cherry, blackberry and pepper aromas and flavors. Not too tannic. Drink now. 300 cases made. • $47 • (10/31/93) • **89**

Barolo Brunate 1988 • $47 • (10/31/93) • **89**

Barolo Cannubi 1991: Beautiful violet and toasted oak character follows through on the palate. Medium in body, fine tannins and long, flavorful finish. Drinkable now. 166 cases made. • $60 • **86**

Barolo Cannubi 1990: Earthy and tough, showing a vegetal edge to the modest black cherry notes. May never come around. Tasted twice. • $56 • (10/31/94) • **74**

Barolo Cerequio 1991: Big and rich, sporting loads of berry, mint and cherry aromas and flavors, medium to full body, fine tannins and long, tasty finish. Very round and delicious now. Available only in California. 583 cases made. • $60 • **88**

Barolo Cerequio 1990: Distinctively minty and rich, silky in texture, with currant and berry flavors in ample concentration to finish sweet and elegant. Tannins are fine enough in texture to melt into the sweet fruit at the end. Approachable now, but promises better things by 2000. • $56 • (10/31/94) • **93**

Barolo Cerequio 1989: Very ripe and concentrated, sporting enough raspberry, plum, tar and rose petal flavor to bury the formidable tannins. A big wine, high in alcohol, high in extract. Give it until 1998-2000 to settle down. 800 cases made. • $54 • (10/31/93) • **87**

Barolo Cerequio 1988 • $54 • (10/31/93) • **90**

Barolo Granduca 1985 • $20 • (02/28/91) • **89**

Barolo Riserva 1988 • $30 • **76**

Barolo Rocche di Castiglione 1990: Minty, earthy flavors predominate in this chewy-textured wine, echoing raisin and licorice on the finish. Tannins are a little tough. Best from 1999. • $47 • (10/31/94) • **85**

Barolo Rocche di Castiglione 1989: Supple and elegant, a big, gentle wine that unfolds its plum, black cherry and anise flavors smoothly. With its fine tannins, this makes a seductive package that calls immediately for another sip. Pretty aromas and flavors make this especially attractive. 300 cases made. • $44 • (10/31/93) • **90**

Barolo Rocche di Castiglione 1988 • $44 • (10/31/93) • **89**

Barolo Rocche di Castiglione Riserva 1985 • $43 • (01/31/92) • **88**

Barolo Rocche di Castiglione Riserva 1983 • $30 • (02/28/91) • **78**

Barolo Vigna Cerequio 1988 • $57 • (03/31/93) • **88**

Barolo Vigna Rionda 1990: Distinctively floral, offering a definite violet note that runs through the aromas and flavors, smoothly integrating its wild berry and plum notes with spicy overtones. A focused, lively red that has charm. Approachable now, best from 1997. • $47 • (10/31/94) • **90**

Barolo Vigna Rionda di Serralunga 1990: The densely packed flavors on a lean frame show plenty of anise- and earth-scented cherry notes. (Barrel sample.) 330 cases made. • $NA • (10/31/93) • **982**

Barolo Vigna Rionda di Serralunga 1989: Fleshy, generous and flavorful, with an attractive core of black cherry and raspberry fruit, hitting some anise and tar notes on the finish. Tannins are well integrated. Drinkable now. 250 cases made. • $47 • (10/31/93) • **89**

Barolo Vigna Rionda di Serralunga 1988 • $47 • (10/31/93) • **85**

Barolo Vigna Rionda di Serralunga Riserva 1986 • $45 • (12/15/92) • **84**

Barolo Vigna Rionda di Serralunga Riserva 1985 • $39 • (02/28/91) • **81**

Barolo Vigna Rionda di Serralunga Riserva 1983 • $36 • (02/28/91) • **87**

Barolo Vigna Rionda di Serralunga Riserva 1982 • $32 • (01/31/90) • **89**

Countacc 1990 • $52 • (10/31/94) • **87**

Dolcetto d'Alba 1993: Fruity and refreshing berry, floral, grapey character, medium body, soft tannins and fresh finish. • $NA • **82**

Gavi 1993 • $13 • **67**

Gavi Fornaci di Tassarolo 1991 • $51 • (11/30/94) • **87**

Granduca Superiore 1989 • $10 • (02/15/92) • **84**

Moscato d'Asti Nivole 1994: A sweet, slightly bubbly white sporting delicate fruit flavors and an easy-drinking texture. Probably best with dessert. • $9 • (04/30/96) • **85**

CHIESA DI S. RESTITUTA, LA

Brunello di Montalcino 1988: Attractive raspberry and wild mushroom aromas and flavors, medium body, medium tannins and a light, dry finish. Try now. 2,000 cases made. • $32 • (04/30/94) • **85**

Brunello di Montalcino 1982 • $23 • (03/15/89) • **56**

Brunello di Montalcino Vigna S. Pietro Riserva 1988: Rather traditional, with a chestnut and berry character, medium body and aggressively dry tannins. Some good fruit, but too much wood on the finish. Drinkable now. • $NA • (10/31/94) • **83**

Chiesa S. Restituta 1990 • $NA • (10/31/93) • **94**

Rosso di Montalcino 1992 • $NA • (10/31/94) • **83**

Rosso di Montalcino 1991 • $14 • (04/30/94) • **83**

Rosso di Montalcino 1986 • $9 • (05/31/88) • **83**

CHIONETTI

Dolcetto di Dogliani Briccolero 1989 • $16 • (04/30/91) • **87**
Dolcetto di Dogliani San Luigi 1993: Fruity and easy, sporting a round, soft texture, grapey, berry character and light finish. Drink now. • $NA • **81**

CIABOT BERTON

Barbera d'Alba Bricco San Biagio 1993: A joyful wine with coconut, cherry, berry and vanilla aromas and flavors, full body, fine tannins and long, flavorful finish. • $NA • **86**
Barolo 1991: Like a mediocre, aged Beaujolais Nouveau. Not much there except water, a taste of burnt rubber and a hint of cherry and mint. • $NA • **71**
Barolo 1990: Soft, lush and ready to drink. Rather complex, with some chestnut, blackberry, licorice and smoke flavors and a gamy, roasted meat finish. Still tannic but opening up now. • $NA • **80**
Dolcetto d'Alba Rutuin 1993: A mouthful of delicious grapey, violet character. Medium in body, adding fine tannins and long finish. • $NA • **84**

CIACCI PICCOLOMINI D'ARAGONA

Brunello di Montalcino 1990: Fabulous, traditional Brunello di Montalcino offering great color and masses of mint, berry, mineral and nut aromas and flavors. Full in body and tannins, huge. Needs time, try after 1999. • $35 • **93**
Brunello di Montalcino 1984 • $25 • (06/15/90) • **91**
Brunello di Montalcino Riserva 1988: Extremely ripe and velvety, with plum, earth and cedar flavors, full body and a long, long finish. It massages your palate. Drinkable now. • $50 • (10/31/94) • **91**
Rosso di Montalcino 1992 • $15 • (10/31/94) • **80**
Rosso di Montalcino 1988 • $16 • (04/30/91) • **82**
Rosso di Montalcino Vigna della Fonte 1993: Mineral, chestnut, berry and grapey aromas and flavors, medium to full body, firm tannins and long finish. A well-structured red. Drinkable now. • $17 • **87**
Rosso di Montalcino Vigna della Fonte 1991 • $16 • (04/30/94) • **81**
Vigna di Pianrosso 1988: Intensely fruity yet harmonious. Pretty aromas and flavors of coffee, plums and black cherry, with full body, full tannins and a velvety finish. Try now. • $40 • (04/30/94) • **88**

CIELO

Merlot 1992 • $5 • (10/31/94) • **82**
Pinot Grigio 1993: Clean, crisp and elegant, will be good as an apéritif. This has lively apple and floral flavors, a smooth texture and a clean finish. 14,000 cases made. • $5 • (05/31/95) • **83**

CIGLIUTI, FRATELLI

Barbaresco Serraboella 1986 • $20 • (08/31/89) • **86**
Barbera d'Alba Serraboella 1993: A bit thin but showing some alluring grapey, cherry aromas and flavors. Light body and finish. • $NA • **80**
Barbera d'Alba Serraboella 1989 • $15 • (11/30/91) • **87**
Dolcetto d'Alba Serraboella 1993: Crisp and juicy, light- to medium-bodied, showing some cheesy, smoked salami flavors and a rather austere finish. • $NA • **78**

CILNIA, VILLA

Chianti Colli Aretini 1990 • $10 • (01/31/92) • **86**
Chianti Colli Aretini 1989 • $10 • (04/30/91) • **85**
Chianti Colli Aretini 1988 • $10 • (04/15/91) • **89**
Chianti Colli Aretini 1987 • $8 • (10/15/89) • **76**
Chianti Colli Aretini 1986 • $9 • (05/31/89) BB • **87**
Chianti Colli Aretini Riserva 1986 • $18 • (10/31/91) • **76**
Le Vignacce 1988 • $24 • (09/15/91) • **89**
Le Vignacce 1986 • $19 • (11/30/89) • **90**
Le Vignacce 1985 • $20 • (07/15/89) • **88**
Vocato 1986 • $11 • (05/15/89) • **86**

CINCIOLE, LE

Chianti Classico 1993: Nicely crafted, medium-bodied wine with the taste of pure Sangiovese. Bursts with well-defined blackberry, wild berry and violet notes. Crisp and vivid. Fine tannins. Drink now or hold for aging. • $NA • **88**

CINZANO

Cinzano Asti NV: Pretty orange and spice aromas carry Cinzano Asti through on the soft and foamy palate. Enough acidity balances the sweetness, making this a light, pleasant apéritif or dessert wine that's well priced. • $9 • (10/31/95) BB • **85**
Sauvignon Blanc Dry NV • $7 • (12/31/86) • **83**
Pas Dose 1983 • $30 • (12/31/86) • **78**
Pinot Nature NV • $7 • (12/31/86) • **84**

CISPIANO

Chianti Classico 1990 • $NA • (10/31/93) • **85**

CITRA

Montepulciano d'Abruzzo 1985 • $4 • (07/31/87) • **79**
Montepulciano d'Abruzzo Rubino 1979 • $5 • (07/31/87) • **65**

CLEMENTE & FIGLI, GUASTI

Barbaresco 1978 • $20 • (01/31/92) • **84**
Barbera del Monferrato 1990 • $8 • (04/30/93) • **79**
Barcarato 1989 • $27 • (03/31/93) • **88**
Barolo 1985 • $27 • (01/31/92) • **81**
Moscato d'Asti 1991 • $12 • (05/15/93) • **82**

CLERICO

Arte 1992 • $26 • (10/31/94) • **86**
Arte 1989 • $30 • (12/15/92) • **89**
Arte 1988 • $26 • (02/28/91) • **90**
Arte 1987 • $22 • (01/31/90) • **78**
Arte 1986 • $22 • (02/15/89) • **88**
Arte 1985 • $22 • (01/31/88) • **91**
Barbera d'Alba 1991 • $15 • (11/15/93) • **80**
Barbera d'Alba 1990 • $14 • (12/15/92) • **84**
Barbera d'Alba 1988 • $12 • (03/15/91) • **84**
Barbera d'Alba 1987 • $8 • (08/31/89) • **85**
Barbera d'Alba 1985 • $8 • (11/30/87) • **84**
Barolo 1984 • $13 • (08/31/88) • **85**
Barolo Briccoto Bussia 1990: Supple and generous, showing a lot of rose petal and anise on the nose, the currant and blackberry flavor coming through on the palate between the fine-textured tannins. Tasted twice. • $40 • (10/31/94) • **90**
Barolo Ciabot Mentin Ginestra 1991: A well-made, tightly wrapped wine that offers mineral, black cherry and wet earth character. Well-defined flavors and good length. Supple and subtle yet crisp. • $30 • **85**
Barolo Ciabot Mentin Ginestra 1990: Massive, mouth-drying tannins make this an austere wine, but it has subtle anise, tar and raspberry flavors that struggle—ultimately unsuccessfully—to get past the tannins at the end. Finishes a little short. Maybe better by 2000. • $40 • **84**
Barolo Ciabot Mentin Ginestra 1989: Firm and nicely structured, with a solid beam of black cherry and smoke aromas and flavors packed behind a thick layer of fine tannins. Very tightly packed, this has the concentration to develop well through 2000 at least. 1,100 cases made. • $45 • (10/31/93) • **92**
Barolo Ciabot Mentin Ginestra 1988 • $45 • (10/31/93) • **89**
Barolo Ciabot Mentin Ginestra 1985 • $40 • (04/15/90) CS • **92**

Key: SS—Spectator Selection. CS—Cellar Selection. BB—Best Buy. $NA—Price not available. (BT)—Barrel tasting. Ⓐ—Auction Price.
Dates in parentheses represent the issues in which the ratings were published.

ITALY

Barolo Ciabot Mentin Ginestra 1983 • $19 • (12/15/87) • **88**

Barolo Pajana 1991: Quite classy for this vintage, showing beautiful rose petal, tar, black cherry and impressive mineral character. Medium body and shows nice intensity on the crisp finish. Try in 1997. • $28 • **84**

Barolo Pajana 1990: Nicely aromatic and flavorful, with a hard edge of tannin and acidity and a supple core of anise-scented wild berry flavors that battle the tannins to a standstill on the finish. Needs until 2000-2005. • $40 • (10/31/94) • **90**

Barolo Vigna Bricotto della Bussia 1980 • $8 • (09/01/85) BB • **86**

Dolcetto d'Alba 1994: Lovely, delicious, floral red offering medium body, fine tannins and fresh, flowery finish. • $13 • **85**

Piedmont 1987 • $7 • (08/31/88) • **87**

Piedmont 1986 • $7 • (12/31/87) • **80**

Piedmont 1984 • $4 • (09/15/87) • **68**

COCORA ORTONA

Farnese Montepulciano d'Abruzzo 1992: Well-balanced and dominated by interesting blackberry and prune flavors. A fairly tannic wine that becomes astringent on the finish. 20,000 cases made. • $5 • (03/31/95) • **82**

COGNO, ELVIO

Barbera d'Alba Poggio Petorchino Bricco del Merlo 1991: Still tight, despite its age. Nice, concentrated cherry flavors and pleasant crispness. Well structured and full-bodied. Drinkable now. 300 cases made. • $15 • (07/31/95) • **85**

Piedmont 1984 • $5 • (02/16/86) • **82**

COL D'ORCIA

Brunello di Montalcino 1990: Elegant tobacco, berry and mineral aromas and flavors, medium body and tannins and a silky finish. Drinkable now. Slightly disappointing. Tasted twice, with consistent notes. • $NA • **87**

Brunello di Montalcino 1988 • $30 • (04/30/94) • **86**

Brunello di Montalcino 1985 • $23 • (11/30/90) • **88**

Brunello di Montalcino 1979 • $24 • (09/15/86) CS • **94**

Brunello di Montalcino Riserva 1988: Rich and ripe without being heavy, a meaty, gamy, opulent style. Full in body and very silky, with rich tobacco and berry notes and a long, flavorful finish. Drinkable now. • $27 • (10/31/94) • **90**

Brunello di Montalcino Riserva 1981 • $22 • (07/31/88) • **89**

Brunello di Montalcino Riserva 1978 • $18 • (09/15/86) • **65**

Ghiaie Bianche Chardonnay White 1992: An elegant wine with balance and structure. There's plenty of toasty oak, but the ripe, tropical fruit flavors hold their own. It's fresh and clean. 1,000 cases made. • $19 • (06/30/95) • **88**

Olmaia Red 1990: The Château Latour of Italy. Stupendous masses of cherry, berry and mint character and loads of tannins. It's super-concentrated yet shows refined tannins. Truly superb. Better after 1997. • $19 • (02/28/95) • **96**

Poggio al Vento 1988: Harmonious wine with a lovely balance of ripe berry and fruit flavors with a gamy character, firm tannins and a long finish. Better after 1997. • $NA • (04/30/94) • **92**

Poggio al Vento Riserva 1982 • $40 • (04/15/91) • **89**

Rosso di Montalcino 1993: Light, slightly herbal, quite diluted. A minor Rosso that turns a bit too sharp and tart on aftertaste. Tasted twice, with consistent notes. • $NA • **74**

Rosso di Montalcino 1992 • $11 • (10/31/94) • **81**

Rosso di Montalcino 1991 • $11 • (04/30/94) • **78**

Rosso di Montalcino 1988 • $9 • (04/30/91) • **84**

Rosso di Montalcino 1985 • $7 • (06/30/88) • **80**

Rosso di Montalcino 1983 • $6 • (06/30/87) • **76**

COLI

Chianti 1987 • $6 • (11/30/89) • **76**

COLLA, PODERI

Barbera d'Alba 1993: Simple red offering black cherry and tobacco aromas and flavors. Medium in body, soft texture and light finish. • $NA • **82**

COLLAVINI

Cabernet Collio Trebes 1993: Peppery, chalky, earthy aromas make this seem rustic at first, but it has good concentration of raspberry and cherry flavors on the palate and good length on the finish. Call it a meaty, traditional style of red. 4,000 cases made. • $12 • (05/31/96) • **86**

Cabernet Grave del Friuli Roncaccio 1993: Tastes ripe and full-bodied, with lots of cherry and berry flavor and not too much tannin. Enjoy now. 4,000 cases made. • $9 • (06/15/96) • **82**

Cabernet Grave del Friuli Roncaccio 1991: Mature and meaty-tasting, nice in aroma, but turning lean and somewhat astringent on the palate. Drink soon. 35,000 cases made. • $8 • (02/28/95) • **82**

Cabernet Sauvignon Grave del Friuli 1984 • $8 • (04/15/90) BB • **85**

Chardonnay Grave del Friuli dei Sassi Cavi 1994: Silky, and slightly sweet with vanilla, this has an immediate appeal, but the simple pineapple flavor and a slightly cloying finish make it a one-glass wine. 12,000 cases made. • $9 • (06/15/96) • **78**

Chardonnay Grave del Friuli dei Sassi Cavi 1992 • $7 • (12/15/94) • **73**

Il Grigio Brut NV • $11 • (05/15/92) • **83**

Merlot Collio Pubrida 1993: Firm-textured and somewhat tannic, this modestly flavored red is simple, but fine to drink now with hearty foods. 3,000 cases made. • $12 • (06/15/96) • **79**

Merlot Grave del Friuli Campo Olivio 1993: A basic, simple red with modest fruit flavors and light tannins. 4,500 cases made. • $9 • (06/15/96) • **78**

Merlot Grave del Friuli Campo Olivio 1991: Dry and austere, but with enough fruit flavor to flesh it out. Has raspberry, tomato and herb accents and light tannins. Drink now. 45,000 cases made. • $7 • (02/28/95) • **80**

Picolit Colli Orientali del Friuli 1993: Sweet, with nice flavors of ripe peach and honey. Finishes on a pleasant citrusy note. 120 cases made. • $40 • (06/15/96) • **83**

Pinot Grigio 1994: Sweet vanilla aromas are pleasant, but that's about the only flavor, except for hints of grapefruit. It's clean, very firm and refreshing, though. 10,000 cases made. • $9 • (06/15/96) • **80**

Pinot Grigio Grave del Friuli Borgo Armenti 1993 • $7 • (12/15/94) • **82**

Refosco Grave del Friuli Piduncolo Rosso 1994: Rather lean and earthy in flavor. Minerally, tart and light overall. 7,500 cases made. • $9 • (06/15/96) • **79**

Ribolla Gialla Colli Orientali del Friuli Turian 1994: A well-balanced wine with good apple and butter flavors. Some nice interplay between fruit, texture and acidity. 300 cases made. • $15 • (06/15/96) • **82**

Romandolo Colli Orientali del Friuli 1993: Very sweet, with plenty of honey and apple flavors. There's a nice touch of clove and butterscotch as well. Medium-bodied and balanced. 1,100 cases made. • $17 • (05/31/96) • **84**

Roncaccio Cabernet Grave del Friuli 1991: Mature, meaty-tasting Cabernet that's nice in aroma, but turns lean and a bit astringent on the palate. Good, but drink it soon. 35,000 cases made. • $8 • (02/28/95) • **82**

Schioppettino Colli Orientali del Friuli Turian 1993: An agreeable, modestly flavorful wine with herbal, plummy accents and moderate tannins. Drink while it's fresh. 300 cases made. • $20 • (06/15/96) • **83**

COLLE BERETO

Il Cénno 1990: Enticing but very young and unevolved. Like a Bordeaux in its spicy, oaky aromas, deep, dark fruit flavor, firm tannins and lingering finish. It's a bit stiff to drink now, but should improve through at least 1997. 50 cases made. • $27 • (12/31/95) • **91**

COLLE DI TREQUANDA, IL

Chianti 1993: Very fresh, featuring strawberry, light earth and cherry character, light body and a grapey finish. From Fattoria dei Barbi. Drinkable now. • $NA • **80**

Chianti 1990 • $NA • (10/31/93) • **86**

COLLE, IL

Brunello di Montalcino 1990: Nice complexity here, showing some mineral, truffle, mint, tobacco and floral notes that are enticing. Very approachable and lovely now, but on the light side. • $NA • **85**

Rosso delle Colline Lucchesi 1986 • $7 • (03/31/90) • **81**

Rosso di Montalcino 1993: Ripe and nicely balanced, sporting some black cherry, currant and plum flavors and medium to light body. Fine tannins on the elegant, crisp finish make this a smooth drink now. • $NA • **83**

COLLINE, LE

Barbaresco Riserva Spéciale 1979 • $15 • (07/31/87) • **79**

Gattinara Monsecco 1976 • $5 Ⓐ • (08/31/87) • **74**

COLMELLO DI GROTTA

Chardonnay Isonzo 1994: A pleasant mix of sweet and smoky aromas gives way to crisp, rather austere flavors of toast and grapefruit. Assertive and should open up with food. 850 cases made. • $13 • (06/15/96) • **83**

Pinot Grigio Isonzo 1994: Crisp and flavorful, with tangy notes that remind us of lemon and melon. Well-balanced, lively and fresh. 850 cases made. • $13 • (06/15/96) • **84**

Sauvignon Isonzo 1994: Canned peach flavors with a touch of butter and spice dominate this medium-bodied wine. Turns a bit astringent on the finish. 400 cases made. • $13 • (06/15/96) • **79**

COLOGNOLE

Chianti Rufina 1993: Light and simple, with some berry and cherry aromas and flavors, but rather light and diluted on the finish. • $8 • **78**

Chianti Rufina Riserva 1993: Lovely wine with loads of cassis bush, plum, wild berry and dried herb flavors. Good length with a medium-tannic finish. Delicious to drink now. • $12 • **85**

COLOMBAIA, LA

Recioto della Valpolicella Amarone 1979 • $12 • (07/01/86) • **80**

COLOSI

Malvasia delle Lipari Passito di Salina 1989 • $20 • (03/31/92) • **81**

COLUE, TENUTE

Barbaresco 1990: A spicy aroma gives way to a firm, focused wine dominated by cherry flavors. Fairly tannic and tart, but well balanced. Drinkable now through 1997. • $20 • (10/31/94) • **82**

Barbera d'Alba 1992: A very rustic style, with dried cherry and stewed plum flavors. A little dull and a bit astringent, but quaint. • $10 • (07/31/95) • **82**

Barolo 1989: Extremely tannic but flavorful, with loads of cherry, currant and plum. Not for the faint of heart. It has a nice touch of spice, but you'll have to wait at least a decade more to see if this wine will come into balance. • $20 • (10/31/94) • **83**

CONCADORO

Chianti Classico 1990 • $NA • (10/31/93) • **88**

Chianti Classico Riserva 1990: Old-style, slightly herbal, green olive and fruit flavors, light-bodied and dry. Tasted twice, with consistent notes. • $NA • **74**

Key: SS—Spectator Selection. CS—Cellar Selection. BB—Best Buy. $NA—Price not available. (BT)—Barrel tasting. Ⓐ—Auction Price.
Dates in parentheses represent the issues in which the ratings were published.

CONCILIO

Merlot Trentino 1990 • $10 • (12/15/92) • **70**

CONSORZIO VITICOLTORI DEL VULTURE

Aglianico del Vulture 1982 • $6 • (09/15/88) BB • **84**

CONTE BALDUINO

Extra Brut Riccadonna Sparkling 1981 • $14 • (12/31/86) • **78**

CONTERNO, ALDO

Barbera d'Alba 1993: Crisp and slightly green, featuring lemony, herbaceous, cherry character, medium body and a somewhat tart finish. • $NA • **80**

Barbera d'Alba Conca Tre Pile 1990 • $22 • (04/30/93) • **91**

Barbera d'Alba Conca Tre Pile 1989 • $21 • (10/31/92) • **91**

Barolo 1991: Very traditional with good fruit and a hint of salt on the palate. It's slightly dry and hard, showing medium body, firm tannins and short finish. Drink now. 1,500 cases made. • $62 • **81**

Barolo Bricco Bussia Vigna Cicala 1988 • $52 • (10/31/93) • **93**

Barolo Bricco Bussia Vigna Cicala 1985 • $67 Ⓐ • (06/15/90) • **90**

Barolo Bricco Bussia Vigna Cicala 1982 • $63 Ⓐ • (09/15/87) • **86**

Barolo Bricco Bussia Vigna Colonnello 1988 • $57 • (03/31/93) • **90**

Barolo Bricco Bussia Vigna Colonnello 1985 • $40 • (06/15/90) • **84**

Barolo Bussia Soprana 1989: Firm in texture, with lots of fine tannins and a persistent bead of raspberry, cherry and strawberry fruit, shaded by anise and tar. A familiar style of Barolo that approaches drinkability. Best after 1996. 1,429 cases made. • $42 • (10/31/93) • **86**

Barolo Bussia Soprana 1988 • $46 • (10/31/93) • **87**

Barolo Bussia Soprana 1985 • $40 • (09/15/90) • **87**

Barolo Bussia Soprana 1983 • $25 • (09/15/88) • **85**

Barolo Bussia Soprana 1982 • $33 • (09/15/87) • **85**

Barolo Bussia Soprana 1980 • $35 • (09/15/88) • **86**

Barolo Bussia Soprana 1978 • $64 • (09/15/88) • **92**

Barolo Bussia Soprana 1974 • $60 • (09/15/88) • **90**

Barolo Bussia Soprana 1971 • $50 • (09/15/88) • **87**

Barolo Granbussia 1990: Youthful and lively, tons of sweet fruit, licorice, rose petal and violet notes. A lovely, smooth, supple wine with depth and character. A crowd pleaser that's worth seeking out. Delicious now, but should hold out for years. 500 cases made. • $120 • **90**

Barolo Granbussia 1982 • $NA • (09/15/88) • **93**

Barolo Riserva Granbussia 1985 • $75 • (12/15/92) • **85**

Barolo Vigna Cicala 1990: A tannic wine that comes through with some pretty raspberry, chocolate and anise flavors, finishing balanced and appealing. Approachable now, best from 1997. Tasted twice. • $NA • (10/31/94) • **83**

Barolo Vigna Colonello 1990: A chewy wine with generous, concentrated flavors, tarry and smoky up front, with a grace note of sage to the basic berry and black cherry flavors. Tannins coat the mouth, but so do the flavors. Seems to have enough in reserve to improve through 2000. • $NA • (10/31/94) • **92**

Barolo Vigna Colonello 1989: Crisp and focused, with layers of mineral, earth and tar streaking through the firm black cherry and slightly tart flavors. A steely, firm wine that needs a long time to come around. 434 cases made. • $52 • (10/31/93) • **89**

Barolo Vigna Colonello 1988 • $52 • (10/31/93) • **87**

Bussia Soprana 1990 • $18 • (10/31/92) • **84**

Chardonnay Langhe Bussiador 1991 • $28 • (05/31/93) • **83**

Dolcetto d'Alba 1987 • $12 • (09/15/90) • **84**

Dolcetto d'Alba 1985 • $10 • (05/15/87) • **77**

Dolcetto d'Alba Bussia 1993: Licorice and black cherry flavors show good ripeness and taste almost sweet. Of medium body, it's a delight to drink. 1,417 cases made. • $20 • **85**

Il Favot 1992 • $NA • (10/31/94) • **89**

Il Favot 1988 • $32 • (03/31/93) • **89**

Nebbiolo delle Langhe Bussia Conca Tre Pile 1985 • $13 • (11/15/88) • **85**

Nebbiolo Il Favot 1983 • $13 • (05/31/90) • **84**

Nebbiolo Il Favot NV • $10 • (05/31/90) • **83**

ITALY

CONTERNO, GIACOMO

Barbera d'Alba 1992 • $15 • (11/15/93) • **82**
Barbera d'Alba Cascina Francia 1991 • $15 • (11/15/93) • **81**
Barolo 1985 • $23 • (04/15/90) • **87**
Barolo 1983 • $23 • (09/15/88) • **88**
Barolo 1982 • $25 • (09/15/88) • **90**
Barolo Cascina Francia 1989: Firm and crisply focused, with raspberry, plum and currant aromas and flavors, finishing round and with a touch of vanilla and anise. Has generosity and elegance without excessive tannin. Almost drinkable now, best after 1996. • $NA • (10/31/93) • **86**
Barolo Cascina Francia 1988 • $40 • (10/31/93) • **82**
Barolo Monfortino Reserva 1982 • $57 • (06/30/87) • **91**
Barolo Riserva Speciale 1978 • $40 • (09/15/88) • **83**
Barolo Riserva Speciale 1970 • $NA • (09/15/88) • **88**
Barolo Vigna Rionda 1990: Simple, chunky and tough, with lots of tannin and a moderate level of juicy raspberry fruit. Finishes tough and lean. 3,000 cases made. • $40 • (10/31/93) • **979**
Dolcetto d'Alba 1994: A bit more muted than some of the other exuberant '94 Dolcettos, adding traces of tobacco along with the typical red berry flavor. More tannic backbone than others. Drinkable now. • $NA • (10/31/95) • **85**

CONTERNO FANTINO

Barbera d'Alba Vignota 1993: Extremely tart and crisp, with herbaceous green character that delivers an austere mouth-feel. 1,100 cases made. • $16 • **76**
Barbera d'Alba Vignota 1992 • $NA • (10/31/94) • **86**
Barbera d'Alba Vignota 1991 • $14 • (11/15/93) • **78**
Barbera d'Alba Vignota 1990: A flamboyant style. Loads of jammy black cherry and cassis with very high acidity makes this rich and flavorful. Lush and firmly-structured. Drink now. 1,100 cases made. • $15 • (07/31/95) • **87**
Barbera d'Alba Vignota 1989 • $20 • (03/15/91) • **86**
Barolo Sorì Ginestra 1991: Appealing mineral and floral aromas and flavors. Medium in body, adding fine tannins and a light, fresh finish. Drink now. 360 cases made. • $32 • **84**
Barolo Sorì Ginestra 1990: Rich, ripe and generous, a huge mouthful of seductive, pure fruit, balanced and supple right through the finish. Tannins are smoothly integrated into the berry, black cherry, anise, rose petal and violet flavors that seem to fan out over the palate. Delicious now, but has a great future, target 2000 to 2005. • $40 • (10/31/94) • **96**
Barolo Sorì Ginestra 1989: An earthy, austere wine with more tar and cedar than fruit, although the sweet cherry flavors on the finish come as a relief and promise improvement through 1997. 1,150 cases made. • $31 • (10/31/93) • **83**
Barolo Sorì Ginestra 1988 • $30 • (10/31/93) • **80**
Barolo Sorì Ginestra Riserva 1982 • $24 • (01/31/90) • **84**
Barolo Vigna del Gris 1990: Ripe, almost jammy, displaying beautiful wet earth, strawberry and vanilla aromas and flavors that glide smoothly across the palate. Tannins are beautifully integrated, making for a seductive Barolo that should be at its best from 1998 to 2000. • $36 • (10/31/94) • **93**
Barolo Vigna del Gris 1989: Smooth and generous, a beautifully polished wine that exudes black cherry, raspberry and tobacco aromas and flavors, turning slightly floral on the aftertaste. Tannins intrude on the finish, but this remains elegant and promises great things by 1997. 550 cases made. • $29 • (10/31/93) • **88**
Barolo Vigna del Gris 1988 • $28 • (10/31/93) • **80**
Dolcetto d'Alba Bricco Bastia 1994: Lovely raspberry and black cherry notes and just enough tannic backbone to accompany food. Fruity and flavorful finish. 1,500 cases made. • $15 • **85**
Monprá 1992: Quite enticing at first, sporting currant, spice and mint notes. But it's somewhat diluted and on the light side, with a bit too much wood showing through. 500 cases made. • $35 • **80**
Monprá 1991 • $35 • (10/31/94) • **86**
Monprà 1990 • $32 • (04/15/94) • **88**
Monprá 1989 • $30 • (10/31/92) • **87**
Monprá 1988 • $27 • (03/15/91) • **91**

Nebbiolo delle Langhe Ginestrino 1990: A nicely mature red with an enticing bottle bouquet of fruit and floral notes, smooth texture, ripe, easy-going flavors and mild tannins. Drink now. 850 cases made. • $19 • (02/28/95) • **85**

CONTI BRANDOLINI D'ADDA

Merlot Grave del Friuli Vistorta 1992: Very flavorful and densely textured, featuring ample oak influence, ripe, juicy fruit, a firm feel on the palate, abundant but fine tannins and lingering finish. Tempting now, or save through 1998. 1,000 cases made. • $14 • (04/30/96) • **88**
Vistorta Grave del Friuli 1991: 1,000 cases made. • $14 • **11**

CONTI D'ATTIMIS

Brunello di Montalcino Ferrante 1983 • $35 • (09/30/90) • **88**
Chianti Classico Ermanno 1987 • $11 • (09/15/90) • **82**
Chianti Classico Ermanno Riserva 1985 • $13 • (09/15/90) • **84**
Chianti Classico Odorico 1988 • $10 • (11/30/90) • **78**
Vino Nobile di Montepulciano Varnero 1987 • $14 • (09/15/90) • **75**

CONTI FORMENTINI

Cabernet Franc Collio 1994: This smooth, clean, focused red has fresh, bright flavors of black cherry accented by black pepper. Moderate tannins, generous flavors and good balance make it pleasing to drink now. • $13 • (05/31/96) • **86**
Ribolla Gialla Collio 1994: An overdone style dominated by clove and ripe apple flavors. Not for the faint of heart. • $13 • (06/15/96) • **79**

CONTRATTO

Asti Fermentazione Naturale NV • $8 • (10/31/86) • **75**
Barolo 1983 • $10 • (03/31/90) • **75**
Barolo 1979 • $9 • (09/30/86) • **76**
Barolo del Centenario Riserva 1978 • $18 • (05/16/86) • **86**
Brut Classico Disgorgment Winter 1989 NV • $10 • (06/15/90) • **82**
Brut Classico Riserva Degorgement Spring 1981 • $19 • (12/31/86) • **64**
Classico Reserve NV • $15 • (12/31/86) • **60**

CONVENTI, BORGO

Chardonnay Colle Russian Collio 1992: Crisp and citrusy, with lemon and lime overtones to the basic apple flavor, simple and appealing. 750 cases made. • $18 • (01/31/95) • **82**
Chardonnay Collio 1991: Seems a little tired, with more orange peel and butterscotch character than fruit, shows some style but finishes a little short. Drinkable, but not special. 1,100 cases made. • $18 • (01/31/95) • **80**
Merlot Collio 1987 • $15 • (03/31/89) • **84**
Pinot Bianco Collio 1993: Quite intense but a bit simple, with tart lemon, grapefruit rinds and earthy flavors. Very crisp finish. 800 cases made. • $14 • (01/31/95) • **78**
Pinot Grigio Collio 1993: A pretty wine. More ripeness than most in this group, with almond, pear and apple flavors, rather seductive, with a touch of spritz and spice. 3,000 cases made. • $15 • (01/31/95) • **82**
Ribolla Gialla Collio 1993: Lean and austere, a tight little wine with more mineral character than fruit. 500 cases made. • $14 • (01/31/95) • **80**
Sauvignon Collio 1993: Very crisp and vegetal, with more asparagus and green pepper than fruit. A distinctive style not everyone will like. 1,900 cases made. • $15 • (01/31/95) • **82**
Sauvignon Collio 1992: Distinctive, with interesting honey, grass and lemon flavors, well-balanced. 1,800 cases made. • $15 • (01/31/95) • **83**

COPPO, LUIGI

Barbera d'Asti Camp du Rouss 1993: Effusively fruity, with a delicious orange peel component that gives this a nice zest. Good acidity, soft and supple. Smells young and tastes delicious. • $15 • (07/31/95) • **86**
Barbera d'Asti Camp du Rouss 1991 • $13 • (10/31/94) • **75**
Barbera d'Asti Camp du Rouss 1990 • $13 • (10/31/94) • **85**

Barbera d'Asti Camp du Rouss 1988 • $21 • (03/15/91) • **88**
Barbera d'Asti Camp du Rouss 1986 • $19 • (03/31/90) • **87**
Barbera d'Asti Pomorosso 1990 • $33 • (10/31/94) • **90**
Barbera d'Asti Pomorosso 1989 • $30 • (10/31/94) • **79**
Barbera d'Asti Pomorosso 1987 • $41 • (03/15/91) • **90**
Barbera d'Asti Pomorosso 1986 • $41 • (03/15/91) • **84**
Barbera Le Taccole 1994: Simple and fruity, with bright strawberry and raspberry flavors and aromas. • $11 • (07/31/95) • **79**
Chardonnay Piemonte Monteriolo 1992: Made in a buttery, spicy style that's appealing, but it could use more fruit to back up the richness. 200 cases made. • $39 • (02/29/96) • **82**
Dolatto d'Alba 1989 • $11 • (07/15/91) • **81**
Mondaccione 1990 • $30 • (10/31/94) • **83**
Mondaccione 1988 • $34 • (01/31/92) • **73**
Mondaccione 1987 • $13 • (03/31/90) • **87**
Moscato d'Asti 1991 • $17 • (05/15/93) • **86**
Moscato d'Asti Moncalvina 1993: Sweet, fresh and tasty. A spicy, peach-flavored bubbly that is soft in texture and short on the finish. • $12 • (07/31/95) • **83**

CORDERO DI MONTEZEMOLO, PAOLO

Barbera d'Alba 1992 • $18 • (10/31/94) • **85**
Barolo 1990: Crisp in texture, a lean red with well-modulated tannins, showing a little tar and smoke to go along with the orange peel and berry flavors. Approachable now. • $40 • (10/31/94) • **82**
Barolo 1988 • $NA • (10/31/93) • **81**
Barolo 1980 • $20 • (12/15/87) CS • **91**
Barolo Enrico VI 1990: Lively, elegant and concentrated, billowing with black cherry, raspberry and anise flavors, smoothly integrated under slightly chewy tannins. Hold until at least 1997. • $40 • (10/31/94) • **91**
Barolo Enrico VI 1989: An attractive wine with an unusual (for Barolo) vegetal, herbal edge to the otherwise ripe and supple cherry and tar flavors at the core. Intense enough to want until 1997 or 1998. 1,000 cases made. • $NA • (10/31/93) • **88**
Barolo Enrico VI 1988 • $NA • (10/31/93) • **78**
Barolo Enrico VI 1983 • $20 • (09/15/88) • **86**
Barolo Enrico VI 1982 • $20 • (09/15/88) • **88**
Barolo Enrico VI 1981 • $25 • (09/15/88) • **88**
Barolo Enrico VI 1980 • $NA • (09/15/88) • **85**
Barolo Monfalletto 1984 • $NA • (09/15/88) • **88**
Barolo Monfalletto 1983 • $17 • (02/28/89) • **85**
Barolo Monfalletto 1980 • $11 • (01/31/87) • **91**
Barolo Monfalletto 1979 • $33 • (09/15/88) • **82**
Barolo Monfalletto 1978 • $NA • (09/15/88) • **84**
Barolo Monfalletto 1977 • $NA • (09/15/88) • **69**
Barolo Monfalletto 1975 • $NA • (09/15/88) • **77**
Barolo Monfalletto 1973 • $NA • (09/15/88) • **65**
Barolo Monfalletto 1971 • $NA • (09/15/88) • **85**
Dolcetto d'Alba Monfalletto 1994: Grapey and flowery offering delicious fruit, medium body, fine tannins and long, flavorful finish. • $NA • **81**

CORINO

Barbera d'Alba Vigna Giachini 1989 • $14 • (11/30/91) • **91**
Barbera d'Alba Vigna Pozzo 1990 • $30 • (11/15/93) • **92**
Barolo Vigna Giachini 1991: Crisp and a bit austere, with a lemony, tart and dry finish. Has some modest red berry flavors, but a bit lean. • $30 • **79**
Barolo Vigna Giachini 1990: Lavishly tannic, but underneath the texture seems rich and almost oily, offering plenty of anise-scented black cherry flavors. Solidly built, it needs to shed some tannins. Try in 2000-2005. • $45 • (10/31/94) • **90**
Barolo Vigna Giachini 1988 • $45 • (10/31/93) • **93**

Key: SS—Spectator Selection. CS—Cellar Selection. BB—Best Buy. $NA—Price not available. (BT)—Barrel tasting. (A)—Auction Price.
Dates in parentheses represent the issues in which the ratings were published.

Barolo Vigneto Rocche 1991: Modest amounts of tar and rose petal flavors, seems smooth yet structured, with a good bite of lively acidity. Too bad it turns austere and drying on the finish. • $NA • **79**
Barolo Vigneto Rocche 1990: Bright and spicy, a beautifully focused and lively wine with minty currant and raspberry flavors that keep dancing on the finish. Has very fine tannins and, though drinkable now, enough weight to carry it through 2000. • $45 • (10/31/94) • **91**
Dolcetto d'Alba Vigna Giachini 1990 • $14 • (03/31/93) • **84**

CORNACCHIA, BARONE

Montepulciano d'Abruzzo 1992: A rustic, ripe red wine with leathery and peppery flavors. Flirts with vinegary and overly earthy components. Still, a fairly gutsy red. 15,000 cases made. • $8 • (03/31/95) • **81**
Montepulciano d'Abruzzo 1988 • $5 • (12/31/90) • **78**

CORREGGIA, MATTEO

Barbera d'Alba Bricco Marun 1993: Wonderful milk chocolate, mint, berry and vanilla aromas and flavors. Medium in body, round, ripe tannins and long, tasty finish. 200 cases made. • $30 • **86**
Barbera d'Alba Bricco Marun 1990 • $20 • (10/31/94) • **86**
Barbera d'Alba Marun 1991 • $29 • (10/31/94) • **83**
Bracchetto Langhe 1992 • $12 • (10/31/94) • **82**
Nebbiolo d'Alba La Val dei Preti 1993: Rather serious Nebbiolo, smooth and pretty, featuring a slight licorice, minty, cherry character, medium body and some decent, sweet fruit. 200 cases made. • $28 • **85**
Nebbiolo d'Alba La Val dei Preti 1992: Harmonious, adding a touch of mint and cherry. It's smooth, decent, but somewhat light and diluted. 200 cases made. • $28 • **81**
Nebbiolo d'Alba La Val dei Preti 1991: Lean and lively, a pretty wine with floral strawberry and vanilla aromas and flavors, nicely balanced to finish harmoniously. • $19 • **86**

CORTE SANT'ALDA

Recioto della Valpolicella Amarone 1986 • $19 • (09/15/92) • **85**
Recioto della Valpolicella Amarone Metius 1986 • $23 • (09/15/92) • **79**
Valpolicella 1991 • $9 • (09/15/92) • **83**
Valpolicella 1988 • $11 • (09/15/92) • **82**
Valpolicella Metius 1988 • $17 • (09/15/92) • **85**
Valpolicella Superiore 1993: Made in a beefier style than traditional Valpolicella, this has ripe blackberry and tar flavors and round, firm tannins. It's fruity and still fresh. 5,000 cases made. • $10 • (06/15/96) • **85**

CORTE VECCHIA

Recioto della Valpolicella Classico Amarone 1985 • $19 • (09/15/92) • **83**
Valpolicella Classico 1988 • $9 • (09/15/92) • **83**

CORTESE, GIUSEPPE

Barbaresco 1982 • $19 • (12/15/88) • **85**
Barbaresco Rabajà 1986 • $19 • (09/15/90) • **89**
Barbaresco Rabajà 1983 • $18 • (01/31/90) • **75**
Barbaresco Rabajà 1981 • $12 • (08/31/89) • **72**
Barbera d'Alba 1989 • $11 • (07/15/91) • **86**
Barbera d'Alba 1988 • $9 • (03/15/91) • **86**
Dolcetto d'Alba 1991 • $15 • (12/15/92) • **84**
Dolcetto d'Alba 1990 • $12 • (02/15/92) • **71**
Dolcetto d'Alba 1989 • $9 • (12/31/90) • **83**
Dolcetto d'Alba 1988 • $8 • (03/31/90) • **78**
Nebbiolo delle Langhe 1990 • $15 • (07/31/92) • **83**
Nebbiolo delle Langhe Vigna in Rabajà 1988 • $13 • (02/28/91) • **80**

CORTI, FATTORIA LE

Chianti Classico 1993: Not as good as the '92. Some pretty cherry, raspberry flavors make this an interesting, easy, pizza and pasta wine. Serve slightly chilled and enjoy. • $NA • **81**
Chianti Classico 1992: Decent fruit and a slightly herbal character. Light-bodied and crisp. Drinkable now. • $11 • **79**

Chianti Classico 1990 • $14 • (10/31/93) • **85**
Masso Tondo 1985 • $20 • (04/30/89) • **86**

CORTILE, IL

Chianti Colli Fiorentini 1990 • $NA • (10/31/93) • **79**

CORVO

Brio White 1993: Clean, simple, slightly sweet, with a sugared grapefruit flavor. Drinkable, but quite unusual. 25,000 cases made. • $9 • (10/31/95) • **77**

Duca di Salaparuta Duca Enrico 1984 • $27 • (09/15/89) • **92**
Duca Enrico 1987 • $38 • (11/30/94) • **89**
Rosso 1985 • $5 • (09/15/88) • **71**

Terre D'Agala 1989: Dry and reticent, this thick-bodied wine shows earthy, prune and coffee flavors but hard tannins take over and shut down the finish. It's ripe but rustic. Drinkable now. • $11 • (05/31/95) • **80**

COSI

Pinot Grigio Valdadige 1993: Age has softened and blurred this ripe, round wine. Hints of honey and grilled nuts are pleasant, but the fruit is fading without a firm backbone of acidity. 10,000 cases made. • $10 • (06/15/96) • **80**

COSTALUNGA

Recioto di Soave 1989 • $NA • (09/15/92) • **74**

COSTANTI, CONTI

Brunello di Montalcino 1990: Best wine ever made by Costanti. It's bursting at the seams with fresh fruit. Layers of violet, rose petal and red berry are balanced by lovely oak. Could age a bit more, but tempting now. Try in 1998. • $54 • **93**

Brunello di Montalcino 1988: Understated and well made. Very lively wine, black cherry flavor, with a wet earth and licorice character. Full-bodied with silky tannins and firm backbone of acidity. Try now. • $45 • (04/30/94) • **88**

Brunello di Montalcino 1987 • $40 • (12/15/92) • **88**
Brunello di Montalcino 1982 • $32 • (07/31/88) • **81**
Brunello di Montalcino 1981 • $20 • (09/15/86) • **80**
Brunello di Montalcino 1980 • $17 • (09/15/86) • **89**

Brunello di Montalcino Riserva 1988: Fresh blackberry, licorice and mint aromas and flavors in a medium bodied package, with medium tannins and a delightful finish. Drink now. • $NA • (10/31/94) • **89**

Rosso di Montalcino 1993: Pretty floral, berry and cherry aromas and flavors. Medium-bodied and very fruity, showing fine tannins and a crisp finish. Drinkable now. • $NA • **85**

Rosso di Montalcino 1991 • $21 • (04/30/94) • **81**

Vermiglio 1991: Straightforward and uncomplicated with some decent red berry flavor up front and a light finish. Tasted twice, with consistent notes. • $NA • **80**

Vermiglio 1981 • $7 • (10/31/86) • **79**

D'ANGELO (AGLIANICO)

Aglianico del Vulture 1991: Aromas of roasted coffee, menthol and black cherry highlight this robust red. The tannins are sufficient to warrant hearty food. 10,000 cases made. • $15 • (01/31/96) • **84**

Canneto 1991: Robust and chewy, from the deep color and cooked plum aromas to the tar and licorice flavors. It's balanced, in a forceful, masculine style. Drinkable now. 500 cases made. • $25 • (01/31/96) • **85**

Vigna Caselle Riserva Aglianico del Vulture 1990: Rich, ripe fruit aromas with nuances of menthol and mineral mark this lively, flavorful wine. It starts off supple, then turns tannic. The finish lingers. 5,000 cases made. • $20 • (01/31/96) • **85**

D'ANGELO, DARIO

Montepulciano d'Abruzzo 1993: A fruity, medium-bodied red wine with fresh berry flavors and a hint of licorice. Easy-to-drink, with a simple finish. • $4 • (03/31/95) • **82**

DAL FORNO ROMANO

Recioto della Valpolicella Amarone Vigneti del Monte Lodoletta 1987 • $47 • (09/15/92) • **89**

Valpolicella Superiore 1987 • $20 • (09/15/92) • **86**
Valpolicella Superiore 1986 • $20 • (04/30/92) • **84**

DE FORVILLE

Barbaresco 1981 • $14 • (02/16/86) • **63**
Vigneto Loreto 1989 • $12 • (02/28/91) • **81**

DEI

Vino Nobile di Montepulciano Riserva 1985 • $13 • (04/15/90) • **85**

DELIZIA, LA

Charme di Krizia NV: A rather coarse-textured and simple tasting sparkling wine with herb and fruit-cocktail flavors. 10,000 cases made. • $18 • **77**

Le Delizie di Krizia Red 1989: A lean wine with dried-out fruit flavors and a murky finish. Complex, with a lot of vegetal flavors, this is wine that's almost over the hill. 7,500 cases made. • $18 • **75**

Le Delizie di Krizia White 1992: They pulled out all the stops in making this butterscotch and vanilla-scented wine, but there's not much fruit flavor in thia Sauvignon Blanc-Chardonnay blend. 7,500 cases made. • $18 • **78**

DESSILANI

Barbera 1990 • $8 • (10/31/92) BB • **83**
Barbera del Piemonte 1986 • $7 • (03/15/91) BB • **87**
Caramino Riserva 1985 • $13 • (09/15/90) • **79**

Spanna 1990: A streak of earthy flavor marks this otherwise hearty, peppery, fruity red. Not too tannic. Good to drink now if you like a rustic style of wine. 30,000 cases made. • $9 • (02/28/95) • **79**

Spanna Riserva 1988: A fruity, crisp and well-balanced red with lively cranberry and cherry flavors, moderate tannins and a lingering, fruity finish. 5,500 cases made. • $11 • (02/28/95) • **83**

DIEVOLE

Broccato 1987 • $19 • (12/15/91) • **86**
Chianti Classico 1990 • $10 • (09/15/92) • **85**
Chianti Classico 1988 • $13 • (09/15/91) • **85**
Chianti Classico Dieulele 1990 • $24 • (10/31/93) • **84**
Chianti Classico Dieulele 1988 • $22 • (04/15/91) • **91**
Chianti Classico Riserva 1988 • $18 • (09/15/92) • **88**
Chianti Classico Vigna Campi Nuovi 1988 • $15 • (04/15/91) • **82**
Chianti Classico Vigna Campi Nuovi 1987 • $10 • (11/30/90) • **84**
Chianti Classico Vigna Petrignano 1988 • $12 • (01/31/92) • **84**
Chianti Classico Vigna Sessina 1988 • $12 • (01/31/92) • **84**
Chianti Classico Villa Dievole 1987 • $8 • (12/15/90) • **83**

DONNA VALENTINA

Brut NV • $7 • (12/15/92) • **79**

DORIGO, GIROLAMO

Merlot Montsclapade Colli Oriental del Friuli 1985 • $10 • (04/15/88) • **80**
Montsclapade 1987 • $25 • (02/15/91) • **84**
Pinot Nero Montsclapade Colli Orientali del Friuli 1985 • $10 • (04/15/88) • **70**

ITALY

DRAGO, CASCINO

Bricco del Drago Vigna delle Mace 1987 • $17 • (01/31/92) • **75**
Bricco del Drago Vigna delle Mace 1986 • $22 • (01/31/92) • **81**
Bricco del Drago Vigna delle Mace 1985 • $22 • (01/31/89) • **79**
Bricco del Drago Vigna delle Mace 1982 • $14 • (11/30/87) • **84**
Campo Romano 1990 • $14 • (01/31/92) • **73**

DRI, GIOVANNI

Refosco Colli Orientali del Friuli 1986 • $11 • (09/15/89) • **82**

EINAUDI, LUIGI

Barbera Langhe 1992 • $13 • (10/31/94) • **78**
Barolo 1991: Good intensity here, with cherry, raspberry, mineral and earth aromas and flavors. Offers good complexity. The finish mingles some mushroom notes in with nice sweet flavors. 858 cases made. • $37 • **81**
Barolo 1989: Earthy, anise, mulch-like flavors, showing more cedar and chestnut than fruit. Tough and tannic, with a stalky, vegetal edge. Not appealing. Tasted twice. • $43 • (10/31/94) • **71**
Barolo 1988 • $30 • (12/15/92) • **83**
Barolo 1982 • $23 • (06/30/87) • **81**
Dolcetto di Dogliani 1993: Round and simple berry and cherry flavors and a light finish. 7,350 cases made. • $12 • **80**
Dolcetto di Dogliani 1990 • $11 • (10/31/92) • **87**
Dolcetto di Dogliani 1983 • $7 • (09/30/86) • **58**
Dolcetto di Dogliani Vigna Tecc 1993: Clean and lovely, crisp and youthful, licorice, blackberry and cherry flavors unfolding nicely. Of light to medium body, the long, juicy finish cleanses your palate. 2,100 cases made. • $16 • **84**
Nebbiolo 1991: Mature fruity-spicy flavors, a smooth texture and light tannins make it fine to drink now. 900 cases made. • $17 • (02/28/95) • **79**
Nebbiolo delle Langhe 1992 • $16 • **78**
Nebbiolo delle Langhe 1983 • $8 • (07/01/86) • **70**

EMMA, CASA

Chianti Classico 1993: Classy wine with violet, mint, cherry aromas and flavors. Medium-bodied with fine tannins and a light silky finish. Drinkable now or hold. • $NA • **85**
Chianti Classico 1992: Earthy aromas, decent fruit underneath. Medium-to-light body and crisp finish. Drinkable now. • $NA • **77**
Chianti Classico 1991 • $NA • (10/31/93) • **83**
Chianti Classico Riserva 1990: More delicate and fresh in style, with plum and cherry aromas and flavors, medium body, silky tannins and a zesty, fruity finish. Drinkable now. • $NA • **87**

ENDRIZZI

Pinot Grigio Trentino 1994: A simple, generic-tasting white wine with fruit cocktail flavors and a rather soft, heavy texture. 2,500 cases made. • $17 • (06/15/96) • **75**

ENO-FRIULIA

Cabernet Sauvignon Collio 1988 • $12 • (07/15/91) • **76**
Chardonnay 1995: Light and crisp, this lemony wine has some pear and earthy flavors. Try with light, simple dishes. 5,000 cases made. • $12 • (06/15/96) • **79**
Chardonnay Collio 1993: Light, lean and more than a little earthy, a crisp Mâcon-like wine with lively character, hitting at lemony mineral note on the finish. 15,000 cases made. • $11 • (01/31/95) • **83**
Merlot Collio 1988 • $12 • (04/30/91) • **82**

Key: SS—Spectator Selection. CS—Cellar Selection. BB—Best Buy. $NA—Price not available. (BT)—Barrel tasting. Ⓐ—Auction Price.
Dates in parentheses represent the issues in which the ratings were published.

Pinot Bianco 1995: Clean and refreshing, with good peach flavors and aromas. There's enough concentration and vitality to make it good to drink with food. 2,000 cases made. • $12 • (06/15/96) • **84**
Pinot Bianco Collio 1993: Smooth and harmonious, if a little green and herbal, a lively wine with simple flavors. 3,333 cases made. • $11 • (01/31/95) • **80**
Pinot Grigio 1995: Tart and tingly. This is more a wake-up call than a wine, with gum-numbing acidity but little fruit. 35,000 cases made. • $12 • (06/15/96) • **78**
Pinot Grigio Collio 1993: Shows a bit more buttery, silky texture than most, with lovely lime accent topped by pear, apple and vanilla notes along with an intriguing cigar-box note. 13,000 cases made. • $11 • (01/31/95) • **81**
Sauvignon 1995: Peachy and spicy with a touch of richness. Balanced, though not particularly powerful. Crisp and cleanly-made. 6,000 cases made. • $12 • (06/15/96) • **83**
Tocai Friulano Collio 1993: Quite lovely, with a superb focused beam of lime, honey, earh and mineral flavors that sing on the palate. Turns a bit earthy when it warms up in the glass, but it's still nice. 4,000 cases made. • $11 • (01/31/95) • **88**

EQUIPE 5

Brut NV • $15 • (12/31/86) • **78**
Brut Riserva NV • $20 • (12/31/86) • **83**

ETTORE, GERMANO

Barolo 1991: Lovely, firm Barolo offering dried cherry and wet earth character. Medium- to light-bodied with hard tannins and a mineral spice finish. Drink now. • $NA • **81**

FALESCO

Merlot di Aprilia Aprilia 1993: This is firm and shows more tannin than fruit now, but it has weight and the ripe blackberry, herb and mint flavors are coming through. Drinkable now. • $13 • (01/31/96) • **84**

FANTI

Brunello di Montalcino 1990: Wonderfully perfumed strawberry, cassis bush character. Medium-bodied and soft with a fruity finish. Drink now. • $NA • **87**
Brunello di Montalcino 1988: Thick and velvety with a rustic, earthy, ripe fruit character. Tasted twice. From San Filippo. Drink now. • $NA • (04/30/94) • **79**
Rosso di Montalcino 1993: Enticing violet and rose petal aromas without enough character to fight off the wood, although what's there is ripe and delicious. Just a bit dry on the finish. Drinkable now. • $NA • **84**
Rosso di Montalcino 1991 • $NA • (04/30/94) • **82**

FANTINEL

Cabernet Sauvignon Grave del Friuli 1985 • $7 • (07/31/87) • **80**
Merlot Grave del Friuli 1985 • $7 • (07/31/87) • **83**

FARALTA

Rosso del Friuli-Venezia Giulia 1986 • $13 • (04/15/90) • **74**

FARINA, REMO

Recioto della Valpolicella Classico Amarone 1983 • $13 • (03/31/90) • **70**

FARINA, STEFANO

Barbaresco 1989: Ripe and raisiny, with a tight, tannic texture. A bit earthy, the flavors are already on the dull side. 1,700 cases made. • $15 • (10/31/94) • **79**
Barolo 1990: Drinkable despite its youth. Medium body, nice plum and dried cherry flavors with orange peel notes that give it zest. The aroma

is dominated by menthol and eucalyptus. 2,500 cases made. • $18 • (07/31/95) • **88**

Barolo 1989: A rich and flavorful Barolo that focuses on fruit: cherry, currant and strawberry accents give it depth and complexity. Has a fine balance between acidity, tannins and fruit, and a long finish. Drink now through 2000. 2,500 cases made. • $16 • (06/15/94) • **90**

Chianti La Ginestra 1992 • $6 • (02/28/94) • **77**

Dolcetto d'Alba 1991 • $10 • (06/15/94) • **78**

Pinot Grigio 1992: A very simple white wine with onion and almond flavors. 42,000 cases made. • $6 • **74**

FARNESE

Montepulciano d'Abruzzo 1993: Smooth, spicy, almost plush in texture, with good cherry flavors and nice balance. An Italian red that is easy to enjoy now. 75,000 cases made. • $5 • (02/29/96) BB • **85**

FARNETA, TENUTA

Bongoverno 1988 • $31 • (12/15/92) • **85**

Bongoverno 1986 • $30 • (09/30/91) • **87**

Chianti 1990 • $6 • (09/15/92) • **78**

Chianti di Collalto 1989 • $7 • (10/31/91) BB • **81**

Chianti di Collalto 1988 • $6 • (12/15/90) BB • **88**

Chianti Villa Farneta 1988 • $14 • (10/31/91) • **79**

Selezione di Bongoverno 1990: Smooth and lush, with good chocolate and spice flavors that linger on the finish. Fairly tannic but a nice core of currant and plum flavors. Solid, plenty of flavor and drinkable now. 1,000 cases made. • $25 • (10/31/95) • **87**

FARNETELLA, CASTELLO DI

Chianti Colli Senesi 1992: As good as its '91. Lovely for the vintage, with flavors of currant, dried cherry and dried herb. Light-bodied and crisp on the finish. Drinkable now. 7,000 cases made. • $10 • **81**

Chianti Colli Senesi 1991: A beautiful red showing lively floral and plum aromas and flavors, light-to-medium body and a citric finish. Drinkable now. 7,000 cases made. • $10 • **81**

FASSATI

Vino Nobile di Montepulciano Riserva 1985 • $22 • (11/30/89) • **86**

Vino Nobile di Montepulciano Riserva 1978 • $8 • (07/01/86) • **73**

FASTELLI

Brunello di Montalcino 1988: Not much going for this. Cherry and chestnut aromas and flavors, medium body and tannins. From Paradiso di Fastelli. • $NA • (04/30/94) • **77**

Rosso di Montalcino 1991 • $NA • (04/30/94) • **76**

FAURY, PHILIPPE

Barbera d'Alba Bricco Boschis 1991: Tart and lemony, sharp-edged but it has tremendous intensity. The berry, citrus and toasty flavors really fly. Needs until 1997-98 to settle down. • $NA • **84**

Barolo Dedicato a Claus Riedel 1990: Lovely tobacco, coconut and cherry aromas and flavors. Medium to full body, round tannins and a long, flavorful finish. Drinkable now, but can age. • $NA • **86**

Chianti 1994: A straightforward, fruity Chianti with light tannins and a crisp finish. Pleasant glass of wine. Drinkable now. • $NA • **80**

Chianti Classico 1993: Rather light and forward and in an old style. Cherry and cedar aromas and flavors, soft tannins and a succulent finish. • $NA • **79**

Chianti Classico 1991: A bit hard, tight and over-oaked. Plenty of attractive raspberry, earthy, tobacco character and loads of new wood. Medium-bodied, medium tannins and a crisp finish. From La Sala. Try now. • $NA • **81**

Chianti Colli Fiorentini Riserva 1991: Fresh and crisp, a wine with lovely red berry fruit in a medium-bodied package. The well-defined flavors (boysenberry, cassis, black cherry) carry to a long finish. • $NA • **85**

Rosso di Montalcino 1993: Impressively big, inky, generous and full-bodied, yet remaining elegant and rather fresh on the palate, with tons of plum, cherry and prune. Would score higher if not so raisiny. • $NA • **84**

Vigna del Bosco 1992: A triumph for a 1992. Big, burly, thick and chewy. Dark-colored, ripe and sweet wine, with complex tobacco, chestnut, cedar, smoky, blackberry flavors. Well-integrated tannins. Made from Syrah. Try after 1997. • $NA • **90**

FAUSTO GEMME

Gavi 1993: A refreshing but lean wine with good acidity and subtle fig and almond flavors. • $11 • (02/28/95) • **81**

Gavi La Merlina 1993: Easy-going, straightforward white wine with modest floral flavors and a good, crisp texture. • $12 • (02/28/95) • **79**

FAZI-BATTAGLIA

Brut NV • $10 • (12/31/86) • **82**

Verdicchio dei Castelli di Jesi 1993: Refreshing, with grapefruit and lemon flavors. Floral aromas framed by a nice tropicality. A bit soft and simple, but attractive. • $10 • (03/31/95) • **83**

FELLUGA, LIVIO

Cabernet Franc Collio 1988 • $15 • (06/30/91) • **84**

Cabernet Franc Collio 1986 • $14 • (09/15/88) • **75**

Esperto Colli Orientali del Friuli 1994: The bright, crisp texture of this wine is appealing, but the mix of flavors—pineapple, herbs, fennel—doesn't exactly say Chardonnay. Still, it's fresh and clean. • $14 • (10/31/95) • **80**

Merlot Colli Orientali del Friuli 1993: Generous and rich, with bright plum and cherry flavors that are nicely accented by vanilla and nutmeg notes. Well balanced and smooth, the tannins firm but not overpowering. • $17 • (02/29/96) • **85**

Merlot Collio 1988 • $16 • (07/15/91) • **84**

Picolit Colli Orientali del Friuli 1991: Very earthy, a sweet wine with more barnyard character than fruit or honey. Not appealing. • $66 • (01/31/95) • **68**

Pinot Grigio Colli Orientali del Friuli 1994: Bright, tart grassy, herbal and citrus flavors. Full-bodied marzipan notes add roundness to the very crisp acidity. Aftertaste of apple and almond. Needs food for balance. • $15 • (10/31/95) • **85**

Pinot Grigio Collio 1993: An odd wine, both perfumed and earthy that smells a bit funky. Not for everyone, but the round texture and the fruit character are quite attractive. Barrel sample. Might be much better after bottling. 15,000 cases made. • $15 • (01/31/95) • **76**

Pinot Grigio Collio 1992: Stale, tired and a bit earthy, with appley flavors, seems a bit oxidized. 15,000 cases made. • $15 • (01/31/95) • **71**

Terre Alte 1993: Full-bodied, offering pear, light herbal, sweet vanilla and toasty notes. It's rich, firm and stands up to food. • $30 • (04/30/96) • **84**

Terre Alte 1992: Crisp and fruity, lively with fresh apple and citrus aromas and flavors, finishing smooth and harmonious. 3,300 cases made. • $30 • (01/31/95) • **83**

Tocai Friulano Colli Orientali del Friuli 1993: Lovely floral and beeswax aromas carry through on the perfumed palate, where orange, honey and lime flavors add appeal. Not powerful or big, this still offers plenty of intensity. • $18 • (04/30/96) • **87**

Tocai Friulano Collio 1992: Very floral, perfumed wine, this smooth-textured wine delivers distinctive flavors. Lovely finish. 3,300 cases made. • $18 • (01/31/95) • **82**

FELLUGA, MARCO

Carantan 1990: A stew of meaty, vegetal, vinegary flavors makes this a complex but still rustic and rough-textured wine. Very tannic, too. 400 cases made. • $20 • (06/15/96) • **78**

Carantan 1988 • $36 • (04/30/92) • **88**

Merlot Collio 1993: Fairly concentrated fruit flavors and firm tannins will make this good to drink now through 1997 with meat, pasta or cheese dishes. • $11 • (06/15/96) BB • **82**

Molmatta 1994: Crisp and simple, with some delicacy as well. Tastes of baked apple and lemon. Finishes with bitter almond. • $14 • (06/15/96) • **82**

Moscato Rosa del Friuli 1993: A sweet, slightly fizzy red wine, disarmingly fruity and appealing, finishing clean and balanced. • $NA • (01/31/95) • **85**

Pinot Grigio Collio 1994: Good quality, but rather simple. A basic white with fairly full body and texture and hints of pear and fig. • $11 • (06/15/96) • **82**

Tocai Friulano Collio 1994: Modest and a bit candied, with pineapple and basil like flavors. An odd mix, but still likeable. • $11 • (06/15/96) • **77**

FELSINA, FATTORIA DI

Chianti Classico 1987 • $10 • (11/30/89) • **83**

Chianti Classico 1986 • $7 • (11/30/89) • **78**

Chianti Classico Berardenga 1992: A solid, peppery, woody red, offering vanilla, berry and raspberry flavors on a light-to-medium body. Drinkable now. 3,000 cases made. • $12 • **84**

Chianti Classico Berardenga 1991 • $9 • (10/31/93) • **85-89** (BT)

Chianti Classico Berardenga 1990 • $12 • (09/15/92) • **91**

Chianti Classico Berardenga 1988 • $13 • (09/15/91) • **89**

Chianti Classico Berardenga 1987 • $8 • (05/15/90) • **83**

Chianti Classico Berardenga 1986 • $7 • (12/15/88) • **72**

Chianti Classico Berardenga Rancia Riserva 1990: Fabulous, with loads of flavor and a tobacco like character. Full-bodied and concentrated, with masses of fruit and tannins. Has a long, long finish. Drinkable now. 3,000 cases made. • $28 • (02/28/95) SS • **93**

Chianti Classico Berardenga Riserva 1990: Polished like a fine jewel, it shines on the palate with tobacco, berry and light earth character. Medium-to-full body, super-fine tannins and fruit. Drinkable now. 9,000 cases made. • $18 • **90**

Chianti Classico Berardenga Riserva 1988 • $17 • (09/15/92) • **92**

Chianti Classico Berardenga Riserva 1985 • $15 • (09/15/91) • **86**

Chianti Classico Berardenga Riserva 1983 • $12 • (11/30/89) • **87**

Chianti Classico Berardenga Vigneto Rancia Riserva 1985 • $23 • (04/30/90) CS • **93**

Chianti Classico Berardenga Vigneto Rancia Riserva 1983 • $17 • (12/15/88) • **91**

Chianti Classico Riserva Berardenga 1993: Impressive for the vintage with loads of cherry, tobacco and vanilla character. Medium-bodied with firm tannins and a long finish. Lots of class. Drinkable now. • $NA • (01/31/96) • **87**

Fontalloro 1990: Gorgeous, voluptuous blackberry, chocolate and tobacco character, full body and a long, flavorful finish. Drinkable now. 2,500 cases made. • $38 • **91**

Fontalloro 1988 • $28 • (11/15/93) • **93**

Fontalloro 1986 • $30 • (11/15/93) • **89**

Fontalloro 1985 • $24 • (09/15/88) • **91**

Fontalloro 1983 • $33 • (11/15/93) • **88**

Fontalloro 1982 • $35 • (11/15/93) • **92**

Maestro Raro 1989 • $38 • (10/31/93) • **83**

Maestro Raro 1988 • $38 • (10/31/93) • **91**

FENOCCHIO, GIACOMO

Barolo Bussia 1990: Ripe tannins and lovely chocolate, berry and leather notes, medium body and flavorful finish. Drinkable now. • $20 • **85**

FENOCCHIO, RICCARDO

Barbera d'Alba Pianpolvere Soprano 1988 • $10 • (03/15/91) • **84**

Barbera d'Alba Pianpolvere Soprano 1987 • $10 • (03/15/91) • **75**

Barbera d'Alba Pianpolvere Soprano 1986 • $8 • (03/15/89) • **83**

Barbera d'Alba Pianpolvere Soprano 1985 • $15 • (03/15/91) • **86**

Barolo Pianpolvere Soprano 1990: A bit lean and tough, with tar, rose petal and black cherry notes and a mineral accent that adds interest. A bit dry on the finish. 452 cases made. • $40 • **79**

Barolo Pianpolvere Soprano 1989: Tough and stemmy, with a swampy component that robs the wine of its charm. Has some cherry fruit at the core, but it fades. Not our style. 750 cases made. • $33 • (10/31/93) • **67**

Barolo Pianpolvere Soprano 1988 • $30 • (10/31/93) • **80**

Barolo Pianpolvere Soprano 1984 • $15 • (07/31/89) • **62**

Barolo Pianpolvere Soprano 1982 • $26 • (07/31/89) • **74**

FERRARI

Brut NV • $20 • (05/15/93) • **86**

Brut de Brut 1981 • $22 • (05/31/87) • **84**

Brut de Brut NV • $16 • (12/31/86) • **90**

Brut Perlé 1985 • $30 • (12/31/90) • **88**

Brut Rosé Trento Metodo Classico 1988: Assertive toasty, smoky aromas carry through on the palate, where the mature flavors of bread dough and baked apples are firm and long. Clean and well focused. • $28 • (12/15/95) • **89**

Trento Brut Metodo Classico Sparkling NV: Well-rounded, modestly flavored sparkling wine that reminds us of a mini-Champagne. It has good balance, subtle fruit flavors and a lingering finish. • $26 • (07/31/95) • **85**

Trento Brut Rosé Sparkling 1988: A very pale rose that nonetheless packs lots of sophisticated flavor in a smooth-textured package. It has spicy, fruity, doughy aromas and subtle but delicious flavors that remind us of cherry, orange zest and mushrooms. Drink now. • $28 • **93**

FERRARI, GIULIO

Riserva del Fondatore 1982 • $50 • (12/31/90) • **86**

FERRERO, EREDI VIRGINIA

Barolo S. Rocco 1982 • $22 • (07/15/88) • **92**

Barolo S. Rocco Riserva 1979 • $19 • (07/31/89) • **67**

FERRO, VILLA DAL

Colli Berici La Rive Rosse 1989 • $NA • (09/15/92) • **73**

Pinot Bianco del Rocolo 1991 • $NA • (09/15/92) • **84**

Riesling del Veneto Busa Calcara 1991 • $NA • (09/15/92) • **81**

Sauvignon Colli Berici Monte Cavallo 1991 • $NA • (09/15/92) • **78**

Tocai Italico Costiera Grande Colli Berici 1991 • $NA • (09/15/92) • **70**

FEUDI DI SAN GREGORIO

Fiano di Avellino 1993: An intriguing white wine with some exotic spice and apple flavors that are reminiscent of a dry Gewurztraminer. Rich and flavorful, with a long finish. • $20 • (03/31/95) • **87**

Greco di Tufo 1993: Tart apricot and peach flavors dominate this very good, dry wine. Pleasantly earthy, with interesting spice nuances. A bit austere, with a lingering finish. • $16 • (03/31/95) • **85**

Taurasi 1991: Has a firm structure underneath the concentrated blackberry flavor with a hint of tar that turns floral on the finish. A bit austere now, but should improve. • $26 • (01/31/96) • **88**

FICINO, MARSILIO

Poggio Il Pino 1986 • $6 • (07/31/89) • **70**

FILIGARE, FATTORIA LE

Chianti Classico 1990 • $NA • (10/31/93) • **88**

Chianti Classico 1988 • $NA • (09/15/91) • **91**

Chianti Classico Riserva 1988 • $18 • (09/15/92) • **90**

Podere Le Rocce 1990 • $NA • (10/31/93) • **93**

Key: SS—Spectator Selection. CS—Cellar Selection. BB—Best Buy. $NA—Price not available. (BT)—Barrel tasting. (A)—Auction Price.
Dates in parentheses represent the issues in which the ratings were published.

FINI, BARONE

Cabernet Sauvignon Cabernello 1988 • $10 • (07/15/91) • **76**
Cabernet Sauvignon Cabernello 1985 • $9 • (04/15/88) • **85**
Pinot Grigio Valdadige 1993: Rather full-bodied, but without much fruit flavor. Appealing accents of smoke and nuts, though. • $10 • (07/31/95) • **77**

FIORIAE, LE

Chianti Classico 1992: Straightforward aromas and flavors of dried cherry and earth. Light body, crisp finish. Drinkable now. • $NA • **75**
Chianti Classico Riserva 1990: Rose-petal and fruit aromas and flavors here. Simple, medium-bodied and crisp but rather short on the finish. Drinkable now. • $NA • **80**

FIORINA, FRANCO

Barolo 1990 • $14 • (10/31/92) • **83**
Barolo 1989 • $13 • (04/30/91) • **83**
Barolo 1987 • $8 • (07/31/89) • **76**
Barolo 1982 • $22 • (05/31/88) • **79**
Freisa delle Langhe 1989 • $16 • (07/15/91) • **78**
Nebbiolo d'Alba 1985 • $9 • (08/31/88) • **80**

FOGNANO, FATTORIA DI

Chianti Colli Senesi 1985 • $6 • (05/15/89) • **67**
Vino Nobile di Montepulciano Riserva Talosa 1983 • $7 • (05/15/89) BB • **85**
Vino Nobile di Montepulciano Riserva Talosa 1981 • $8 • (05/15/89) • **76**

FOLONARI

Cabernet Sauvignon 1986 • $5 • **66**
Pinot Grigio 1993 • $6 • **82**
Soave 1991 • $7 • (09/15/92) • **79**

FONTANA CANDIDA

Chardonnay 1994: A clean, charming, smooth-textured Chardonnay that shows appealing apple and nutmeg flavors and great balance. • $8 • (02/29/96) • **84**
Frascati Superiore 1993: Crisp, lean and refreshing, with herbal aromas, appley flavors and a clean, short finish. • $9 • **79**
Merlot della Tre Venezie 1994: A polished wine that has a nice mix of smoky, herbal flavors of black cherry and shows balance between its bright acidity and light tannins. Drinkable now. • $8 • (01/31/96) • **83**
Pinot Grigio 1994: A simple white that goes down easy, this is light and crisp, showing pear and almond notes and an herbal finish. Best as an apéritif. • $5 • (04/30/96) • **80**
Pinot Grigio 1993: Subtle mineral and herb flavors give this some appeal, but though dry and clean it's simple. • $7 • **82**
Villa Fontana 1993: Light and soft, this offers strawberry and rasberry flavors without much depth or tannin. Crisp acidity holds it together, though, try it slightly chilled. Drink now. • $6 • (05/31/95) • **82**

FONTANAFREDDA

Asti NV: Simple, sweet jelly bean flavors carry a hint of soapiness in this sparkler, all froth and candy. Tastes like soda pop in its new bottle. • $12 • (10/31/95) • **76**
Asti The Royal Preserves NV • $11 • (01/31/88) • **86**
Barbaresco 1990: Ripe and plummy, a supple wine with firm tannins and plenty of cherry and plum fruit to sail into the finish. • $NA • (10/31/93) • **984**
Barbaresco 1989: An earthy style, mature already, showing truffle and mushroom grace notes to the soft berry flavors. Still a little tannic. Tasted twice. • $18 • (10/31/94) • **79**
Barbaresco 1988 • $12 • (10/31/93) • **75**
Barbaresco 1983 • $12 • (09/15/88) • **80**
Barbaresco 1982 • $NA • (09/15/88) • **81**
Barbaresco 1978 • $NA • (09/15/88) • **86**
Barbera d'Alba 1993: A light body and aftertaste accompany strawberry and cherry aromas and flavors. • $11 • **79**
Barbera d'Alba 1990: Interesting mature aromas of truffles and mushrooms. Flavors of dried cherries turn a bit astringent on the finish. Almost over the hill. 41,600 cases made. • $10 • (07/31/95) • **83**
Barbera d'Alba Vigna Raimondo 1990 • $9 • (11/15/93) • **78**
Barolo 1990: Hard and chewy, with some pretty raspberry and strawberry flavors underneath, echoing plum and tar on the finish. The fruit suggests it will be at its best after 1997 or 1998. • $16 • (10/31/94) • **89**
Barolo 1989: Lean, almost crisp in texture, with enough ripe, sweet plum and cherry notes to complement the smoky, tarry flavors and chewy tannins. Best from 1997 to 2000. Tasted twice. • $16 • (10/31/94) • **84**
Barolo 1988 • $13 • (10/31/93) • **85**
Barolo 1983 • $16 • (09/15/88) • **83**
Barolo 1982 • $16 • (09/15/88) • **84**
Barolo 1978 • $13 • (02/15/84) • **80**
Barolo di Serralunga d'Alba 1990: A medium-bodied Barolo with berry, strawberry and earthy character. Fine tannins but a slightly short finish. Drinkable now, but can age. 8,840 cases made. • $20 • **86**
Barolo Lazarito 1982 • $42 • (09/15/88) • **90**
Barolo San Pietro 1982 • $42 • (09/15/88) • **85**
Barolo Vigna Gattinera 1990: A bit of the old style, with a nutty, earthy mushroom and berry character. Medium-bodied and hot. A bit dry, but has some lovely almond flavors. Drinkable now. 404 cases made. • $39 • **81**
Barolo Vigna Gattinera 1989: Seems tired, earthy and volatile, only a chewy anise note and a smooth texture providing some pleasure. Not recommendable. Tasted twice. • $NA • (10/31/94) • **67**
Barolo Vigna La Delizia 1990: Lean but focused, with a green pepper edge to the raspberry flavors, finishing bright and lively. Not too tannic. • $NA • (10/31/93) • **982**
Barolo Vigna La Delizia 1989: Supple, round and generous, showing ripe raspberry, cherry, anise and vanilla flavors wrapped smoothly in a thin veil of fine-textured tannins. Elegant, charming and approachable with a lively core of fruit and acidity. Should continue to improve through 1997 to 2000. • $39 • (10/31/94) • **90**
Barolo Vigna La Rosa 1989: Earthy, gamy character runs through this firm-textured, old-fashioned, rustic wine, but it has enough modest berry fruit to be drinkable. Tasted twice. • $39 • (10/31/94) • **81**
Barolo Vigna La Rosa 1982 • $45 • (09/15/88) • **89**
Barolo Vigna La Villa 1989: Solid and chewy, muscular and tannic, with anise, smoke, blackberry and cherry flavors that reflect tar and floral notes on the long finish. Has a great future, open it around 2000 to 2005. • $39 • (10/31/94) • **91**
Barolo Vigna La Villa Paiagallo 1990: A very classy Barolo, with rose petal, mint, black cherry and tar aromas and flavors in a supple texture. A mature taste of mushroom comes through on the finish, which is rather polished. 383 cases made. • $39 • **85**
Barolo Vigna La Villa Paiagallo 1989: Lean and spicy, with more anise and tar character than fruit, but it has a classy feel to it, an austerity that stops short of astringency. Should be approachable by 1997. 350 cases made. • $NA • (10/31/93) • **85**
Barolo Vigna Lazzarito 1990: A nice, well-defined character shines through in this medium-bodied, polished Barolo that offers lovely tar, black cherry and toast flavors with good length. Still youthful, brimming with fine tannins. Try in 1998. 595 cases made. • $39 • **87**
Barolo di Serralunga 1989: A massive traditional-style Barolo with mushroomy aromas and raspberry, currant, anise and tar flavors. There is a layer of chunky tannins, should be at its best from 2000. • $20 • (10/31/94) • **89**
Barolo di Serralunga 1988 • $17 • (10/31/93) • **85**
Contessa Rosa NV • $5 • (12/31/86) • **68**
Di Treiso 1992 • $12 • (06/15/94) • **86**
Dolcetto d'Alba 1993: A light wine with smoky berry flavors that finish tart. The aroma is reminiscent of Pinot Noir. • $11 • (10/31/95) • **80**
Dolcetto d'Alba Di Treiso 1993: Medium-bodied and chewy, with nice cherry and berry flavors and aromas. Has structure and a fairly tannic finish. Drinkable now. • $NA • (10/31/95) • **84**
Dolcetto d'Alba Di Treiso 1992 • $12 • (06/15/94) • **86**

FONTERUTOLI, CASTELLO DI

Brancaia 1990: A radiant wine with class and finesse, offering beautiful aromas and flavors of vanilla, cedar, violets and berries. Full-bodied yet elegant, with fine tannins and acidity. 1,000 cases made. • $24 • (10/31/93) • **91**

Chianti Classico 1993: Firm and fruity, with dried cherry and a hint of spice on the nose and palate. Medium-bodied and crisp with silky tannins and a light finish. Drinkable now. Tasted twice, with consistent notes. 1,333 cases made. • $13 • **81**

Chianti Classico 1992: Impressive, offering delicious, fruity, crushed black pepper character, light-to-medium body, silky tannins and a fresh finish. Drinkable now. 17,000 cases made. • $13 • **85**

Chianti Classico 1991 • $13 • (10/31/93) • **88**

Chianti Classico 1990 • $13 • (09/15/92) • **89**

Chianti Classico 1988 • $14 • (11/30/90) • **85**

Chianti Classico 1987 • $11 • (11/30/89) • **90**

Chianti Classico 1986 • $11 • (01/31/89) • **85**

Chianti Classico 1985 • $11 • (11/30/89) • **88**

Chianti Classico Riserva 1983 • $15 • (11/30/89) • **88**

Chianti Classico Ser Lapo 1991: Big and rich wine that tastes more like Cabernet than Sangiovese. Full-bodied and round with green pepper, cherry and herbal character. Medium tannins and a short finish. A bit too herbal. 583 cases made. • $25 • **84**

Chianti Classico Ser Lapo Riserva 1990: Slightly disappointing for this producer. Floral, red berry aromas and flavors, medium-to-light body, silky tannins and a cherry finish. 6,400 cases made. • $26 • **86**

Chianti Classico Ser Lapo Riserva 1988 • $20 • (09/15/92) • **90**

Chianti Classico Ser Lapo Riserva 1986 • $25 • (11/30/90) • **88**

Chianti Classico Ser Lapo Riserva 1985 • $18 • (09/15/91) • **87**

Chianti Classico Ser Lapo Riserva 1983 • $15 • (01/31/89) • **88**

Concerto 1991: Ripe and rich with a crisp character that makes it very fresh. Enticing mineral, chocolate, red berry character. Beautiful supple texture and long, delicious finish. 416 cases made. • $30 • **88**

Concerto di Fonterutoli 1990: Well-crafted wine with lovely vanilla, berry and tobacco aromas and flavors, medium body and tannins and a long, flavorful finish. Made from Sangiovese and Cabernet Sauvignon. Drinkable now. 1,200 cases made. • $27 • (10/31/93) • **88**

Concerto di Fonterutoli 1986 • $35 • (03/15/91) • **87**

Concerto di Fonterutoli 1985 • $25 • (02/15/89) • **84**

Concerto di Fonterutoli 1983 • $15 • (11/30/89) • **86**

Siepi 1993: Like a top-growth Bordeaux. A monumental, exciting wine with purple-black color, full body and great concentration. Bursting with earthy cassis and mint flavors and fine tannins that need until 1998 to soften. From Sangiovese and Merlot. Tasted twice, with consistent notes. 83 cases made. • $30 • **94**

Siepi 1992: Big and powerful, for a 1992, and needs bottle age to soften its edges. Gorgeous aromas of crushed berries, coffee and toasted oak. Full-bodied, with full tannins and a long, ripe fruit finish. Made from Sangiovese and Merlot. Better after 1997. 83 cases made. • $30 • **90**

FONTEVINO

Brunello di Montalcino 1990: Slightly advanced, showing layers of flavor from berry to tobacco. Medium-bodied and silky with a long finish. Drink now. • $NA • **83**

Brunello di Montalcino Riserva 1988: A slightly oxidized style, with peppermint, berry and cedar notes, medium body and a rather dry finish. Drinkable now. • $NA • (10/31/94) • **79**

Rosso di Montalcino 1993: Smooth, round and crisp, an uncomplicated but very pretty little red sporting well-defined cherry and plum flavors. Turns surprisingly sweet and opulent on the delicious finish. • $NA • **85**

Key: SS—Spectator Selection. CS—Cellar Selection. BB—Best Buy. $NA—Price not available. (BT)—Barrel tasting. Ⓐ—Auction Price.
Dates in parentheses represent the issues in which the ratings were published.

FONTODI

Chianti Classico 1993: Always a winner despite the overall quality of the vintage. Vibrant, well-focused wine with violet, boysenberry and mineral aromas and flavors. Keeps going on the palate. Drinkable now. 7,000 cases made. • $12 • **86**

Chianti Classico 1992: Packs a lot for a '92 Chianti. Fresh berry, mint and plum aromas and flavors, medium-bodied and silky in texture. Drink and enjoy. 8,000 cases made. • $13 • **85**

Chianti Classico 1991 • $12 • (10/31/93) • **87**

Chianti Classico 1990 • $16 • (09/15/92) • **87**

Chianti Classico 1989 • $13 • (11/30/91) • **89**

Chianti Classico 1988 • $13 • (09/15/91) SS • **91**

Chianti Classico 1987 • $8 • (11/30/89) • **90**

Chianti Classico 1986 • $9 • (01/31/89) • **74**

Chianti Classico Al Sorbo 1990: A sophisticated, international style of Chianti displaying violet, ripe berry and vanilla character. Very refined and full in body, fine tannins. Drinkable now. 1,500 cases made. • $27 • **91**

Chianti Classico Riserva 1991: A wine to age. Superb for the vintage. Big and grapey with chocolate, berry character. Full-bodied and round with thick, soft tannins and a long finish. Drinkable now. 2,000 cases made. • $18 • **90**

Chianti Classico Riserva 1990: Seductive and gentle. A beauty, displaying cassis, rose petal, berry and perfume character, medium-to-full body, fine tannins and a long, flavorful finish. Drinkable now. 3,000 cases made. • $20 • **89**

Chianti Classico Riserva 1988 • $18 • (10/31/93) • **89**

Chianti Classico Riserva 1985 • $16 • (09/15/91) • **93**

Chianti Classico Riserva 1983 • $8 • (09/15/87) • **87**

Chianti Classico Riserva 1982 • $7 • (09/15/87) • **87**

Chianti Classico Vigna del Sorbo Riserva 1988 • $28 • (10/31/93) • **92**

Chianti Classico Vigna del Sorbo Riserva 1985 • $25 • (09/15/91) • **88**

Flaccianello 1990 • $35 • (11/15/93) • **90**

Flaccianello 1988 • $40 • (11/15/93) • **92**

Flaccianello 1987 • $35 • (11/15/93) • **88**

Flaccianello 1986 • $29 • (11/30/89) • **90**

Flaccianello 1985 • $38 • (11/15/93) • **90**

Flaccianello 1983 • $25 • (11/15/93) • **83**

Flaccianello 1982 • $35 • (11/15/93) • **85**

Flaccianello della Pieve 1991: On a par with the '90. Incredible amounts of cassis and vanilla aromas and flavors. Full- to medium-bodied and very well structured, focused berry character and firm tannins. This needs time. Try after 1997. 2,000 cases made. • $32 • **90**

Pinot Nero Case Via 1993: One of the few Tuscan Pinots that emulates Burgundy. Elegant red with black cherry and red fruit character. Medium-bodied with firm tannins and a flavorful finish. Delicious now. 250 cases made. • $35 • **87**

Pinot Nero Case Via 1992: Lovely Pinot showing raspberry and cherry flavors, medium body, light tannins and a fresh finish. Drinkable now. 350 cases made. • $30 • **83**

Pinot Nero Tuscany Case Via 1990: Exotic aromas and flavors of crushed cherries, berries and vanilla, medium-bodied with wonderful elegance and finesse. Drinkable now. 200 cases made. • $35 • (10/31/93) • **88**

Syrah Case Via 1992: A fresh, opulent Syrah with some chestnut, cassis, black cherry flavors. Vibrant and crisp. Supple tannins. Drink now. • $NA • **86**

Syrah Case Via 1991: Not as great as the '90, but excellent. Muscular, tight and well crafted, with vanilla, berry and coffee aromas and flavors. Medium-bodied, with velvety tannins and a long, flavorful finish. Drinkable now. 400 cases made. • $30 • **90**

Syrah Case Via 1990: The first commercial release of this wine. Superracy and exciting, it shows breathtaking crushed berry, currant and vanilla character, full body and tannins yet tempting elegance and a crisp finish. Made from 100 percent Syrah. Try in 1998. 250 cases made. • $28 • (10/31/93) • **93**

FORADORI

Granato di Mezzolombardo 1988 • $33 • (01/31/92) • **86**

Teroldego Rotaliano Vigneto Morei 1988 • $16 • (01/31/92) • **69**

FORTUNA, LA

Brunello di Montalcino 1990: Delicious, soft, sweet fruit. Medium- to light-bodied, adding fine tannins and a lemony, berry finish. Drink now. • $NA • **84**
Rosso di Montalcino 1993: Plenty of dried cherry and earthy character in this medium-bodied red, adding delicate tannins and a citric finish. • $NA • **82**

FOSSI

Chianti 1990 • $8 • (04/30/92) • **83**
Chianti 1988 • $8 • (10/31/91) BB • **84**
Chianti Classico Riserva 1985 • $18 • (09/15/91) • **82**
Vanti 1992: A little light, but still flavorful, showing cherry and leather notes. Simple, pleasant and reveals modest spice notes on the finish. 2,200 cases made. • $8 • (07/31/95) • **83**

FRANCESCO, CASA

Chianti Classico 1982 • $6 • (11/30/89) • **81**
Chianti Riserva 1988 • $8 • (12/15/92) • **80**
Chianti Riserva 1985 • $8 • (10/31/91) • **85**

FRANCO, NINO

Prosecco di Valdobbiadene Rustico 1987 • $12 • (12/31/91) • **79**

FRATTINA, VILLA

Vigneto Quartarezza Lison-Pramaggiore 1993 • $10 • (10/31/94) • **83**

FRESCOBALDI

Brunello di Montalcino Castelgiocondo 1988 • $30 • (04/30/94) • **85**
Brut 1985 • $12 • (12/31/90) • **86**
Capitolare di Biturica Mormoreto 1991: Very rich in aromas sporting green olive, berry character. Medium-bodied, extremely soft and caressing. Excellent winemaking here. • $32 • **90**
Capitolare di Biturica Mormoreto 1990: Big, powerful and raisiny Cabernet Sauvignon, crushed berry, tobacco and olive character. Full in body and highly concentrated. Drinkable now. • $32 • **88**
Chianti 1989 • $5 • (04/15/91) • **70**
Chianti 1988 • $5 • (11/30/89) BB • **85**
Chianti 1987 • $4 • (05/15/89) • **75**
Chianti 1986 • $3 • (12/15/87) • **75**
Chianti Rèmole 1994: A pleasant Chianti with berry and cherry aromas and flavors. Light body and a light finish. Drinkable now. 150,000 cases made. • $7 • **79**
Chianti Rèmole 1993: Simple and straightforward, with some modest strawberry and mushroom flavors. Seems advanced and quite diluted for such a young wine. • $7 • **74**
Chianti Rufina Castello di Nipozzano Riserva 1992: Quite lovely, with ripe plum and black cherry flavors giving it a sweet-tasting quality. A wonderful '92 Chianti that's worth seeking out for simple Italian dishes. Serve slightly chilled and enjoy. 45,000 cases made. • $14 • **85**
Chianti Rufina Castello di Nipozzano Riserva 1991 • $NA • (10/31/93) • **88**
Chianti Rufina Castello di Nipozzano Riserva 1990: A solid, fruity, forthright red with ample plum and berry flavors and firm tannins. It's fresh, lively and moderately tannic. Drink now. • $14 • (02/28/95) • **85**
Chianti Rufina Castello di Nipozzano Riserva 1989: Already maturing, showing spicy brown sugar and raisin aromas and flavors. Silky on the palate, with soft tannins. 416,000 cases made. • $14 • **80**
Chianti Rufina Castello di Nipozzano Riserva 1988 • $15 • (09/15/92) • **86**
Chianti Rufina Castello di Nipozzano Riserva 1986 • $11 • (09/15/90) • **82**
Chianti Rufina Castello di Nipozzano Riserva 1985 • $11 • (11/30/89) • **88**
Chianti Rufina Castello di Nipozzano Riserva 1983 • $10 • (11/30/89) • **89**
Chianti Rufina Montesodi 1990: Supercharged and very ripe, featuring masses of berry, prune, truffle character, full body, full velvety tannins and a long, long finish. • $32 • **91**
Chianti Rufina Montesodi 1988 • $32 • (10/31/94) CS • **90**
Chianti Rufina Montesodi 1985 • $35 • (09/15/91) • **90**
Chianti Rufina Montesodi 1982 • $31 • (12/15/88) • **86**
Chianti Rufina Montesodi Riserva 1991: Polished and refined with tobacco and cherry character. Medium body. Firm, verging on hard tannins and a crisp finish. Needs time to soften. Better after 1997. 5,000 cases made. • $32 • **86**
Chianti Rufina Rèmole 1993: Simple and attractive. Light in body, displaying meaty berry flavors and a fresh finish. Tasted twice, with consistent notes. Drinkable now. • $7 • **78**
Chianti Rufina Rèmole 1992 • $7 • (04/30/94) BB • **85**
Chianti Rufina Rèmole 1991 • $7 • (10/31/93) • **81**
Chianti Rufina Rèmole 1990 • $7 • (09/15/92) • **86**
Lamaione Castelgiocondo 1992: Amazing quality for a 1992. Black cherry and boysenberry aromas and flavors, full-to-medium body, silky tannins and cherry finish. Very harmonious Merlot. Drinkable now. 300 cases made. • $18 • **89**
Lamaione Castelgiocondo 1991: Excellent value. Loads of cassis, mineral and herbal character in this one. Racy and well made, displaying sleek tannins, medium body and a rich finish. Merlot from Frescobaldi. Drinkable now. • $18 • **90**
Mormoreto 1988 • $38 • (11/15/93) • **94**
Mormoreto 1986 • $38 • (11/15/93) • **91**
Mormoreto 1985 • $40 • (11/15/93) • **90**
Mormoreto 1983 • $40 • (11/15/93) • **90**
Mormoreto Predicato di Bitùrica 1988 • $30 • (11/30/89) • **93**
Mormoreto Predicato di Bitùrica 1983 • $34 • (02/15/89) • **88**
Pater Sangiovese di Toscana 1994: Fresh, simple and thoroughly delicious. Delicate fruit character with berry, strawberry flavors, light tannins and a crisp finish. • $NA • **81**
Pomino Tenuta di Pomino 1992: Some good berry, cassis flavors in this one but it's slightly herbal on the finish. Medium-bodied with medium tannins and a light finish. Drinkable now. 15,000 cases made. • $17 • **83**
Pomino Tenuta di Pomino 1991: Simple, straightforward Cabernet with berry and herbal aromas and flavors, medium body, light tannins and a fruity finish. Drinkable now. 15,000 cases made. • $17 • **80**
Pomino Tenuta di Pomino 1988 • $17 • (10/31/93) • **82**
Pomino Tenuta di Pomino 1986 • $14 • (01/31/90) • **87**
Pomino Tenuta di Pomino 1985 • $15 • (09/15/88) SS • **93**
Pomino Tenuta di Pomino Vin Santo 1981 • $20 • (10/15/88) • **87**
Rosso di Montalcino Campo al Sassi 1991 • $15 • (04/30/94) • **77**

FRIGGIALI, TENUTA

Brunello di Montalcino 1990: Vibrant fruity and milk chocolate character, full body, fine, powerful tannins and loads of fruit on the finish. This needs time, better in 1997. • $NA • **88**
Brunello di Montalcino 1988: Well-crafted wine with plenty of fruit and a hint of herbal aromas and flavors. Medium-bodied, medium tannins and a clean crisp finish. Drinkable now. • $NA • (04/30/94) • **87**
Rosso di Montalcino 1993: Slightly rustic red, featuring plenty of berry, smoky, strawberry character, full body, firm tannins and long, chewy, raisiny finish. • $NA • **82**
Rosso di Montalcino 1991 • $NA • (04/30/94) • **78**

FUGA, TENUTA LA

Brunello di Montalcino 1990: Rustic and traditional Brunello. A lot of chestnut flavors here, but the texture is supple and it tastes quite ripe and sweet. Drink now. • $NA • **81**
Rosso di Montalcino 1993: Somewhat hard and bitter plummy, stemmy and berry character. Medium in body, adding firm tannins and a medium finish. • $NA • **80**
Rosso di Montalcino 1992 • $NA • (04/30/94) • **79**

FULIGNI

Brunello di Montalcino 1990: Perhaps not as great as this producer's 1988 Brunello, but it's supple and smooth and outstanding. Sweet- and ripe-tasting, offering coffee, blackberry and black cherry flavors. Full-bodied, soft tannins. Drinkable now. 850 cases made. • $46 • **90**
Brunello di Montalcino Riserva 1988: Rich, mature and mouthfilling, a flavorful, smooth-textured red with plum, coffee, and tobacco flavors that linger nicely on the finish. Drink now. 240 cases made. • $54 • **89**

ITALY

Brunello di Montalcino Vigneti dei Cottimelli 1989: A handsome, rich and polished red wine that's complex in aroma, concentrated in flavor, smooth but firmly tannic in texture. A roasted, ripe, dried-fruit flavor is its hallmark. 580 cases made. • $39 • (11/30/94) • **88**

Brunello di Montalcino Vigneto dei Cottimelli Riserva 1988: The wine of the vintage, huge yet refined. Tons of raspberry, currant, vanilla and chocolate aromas and flavors. Full-bodied and massive, with loads of fruit and tannins, really caresses your palate. Better after 1998. • $NA • (10/31/94) • **95**

Rosso di Montalcino Ginestreto Vigneti dei Cottimelli 1993: Wonderful, big and rich, offering loads of fruit, hints of new wood, full body, gorgeous plum flavor and velvety tannin structure. A long, delicious finish. Better in 1997. 830 cases made. • $20 • **89**

Rosso di Montalcino Ginestreto Vigneti dei Cottimelli 1992 • $NA • (10/31/94) • **79**

Rosso di Montalcino Ginestreto Vigneti dei Cottimelli 1991 • $NA • (04/30/94) • **87**

Vigneti dei Cottimelli 1988: Superb winemaking here. This has deep, dark color and rich coffee and fruit aromas. Full-bodied, yet perfectly integrated, velvety tannins and ripe fruit flavors, finishing with a hint of oak. Drinkable now. • $NA • (04/30/94) • **91**

FURLAN CASTELCOSA

Pinot Grigio Castelcosa 1994: Exotic! Honey, pineapple and hard candy flavors give this wine more personality than appeal. Firm acidity holds it together, but there's little sense of grape variety or terroir. 6,000 cases made. • $10 • (06/15/96) • **80**

Tai 1994: Round and buttery, this shows sweet vanilla and lemon-lime flavors, intense yet not heavy at all. A lively apéritif that might be overshadowed by food. 800 cases made. • $14 • (06/15/96) • **83**

GABBIANO, CASTELLO DI

Ania 1986 • $30 • (12/15/92) • **72**

Ania 1985 • $30 • (01/31/90) • **93**

Ania 1983 • $25 • (07/15/87) • **83**

Ariella 1990: A deeply flavored, bold white wine with toasty, buttery aromas, pear- and fig-like flavors accented by smoke, and a long, minerallike finish. The flavors are beautifully articulated. • $19 • **91**

Chardonnay Ariella 1990: Ripe, smooth and silky, a toasty wine, with honey and spice overtones to the pear flavors. Nicely balanced, intense and focused, if a bit woody. • $19 • (04/30/94) • **84**

Chianti Classico 1990 • $9 • (04/30/94) • **81**

Chianti Classico 1987 • $7 • (11/30/89) • **81**

Chianti Classico 1986 • $7 • (05/31/89) BB • **82**

Chianti Classico 1985 • $7 • (02/15/88) • **72**

Chianti Classico 1983 • $6 • (05/31/87) BB • **85**

Chianti Classico 1982 • $6 • (01/01/86) • **68**

Chianti Classico Riserva 1990: Has generous, fruity aromas and flavors accented by hints of leather and herbs-in the classic Chianti style. Nicely crisp and definitely tannic. Drink now. • $15 • (02/28/95) • **86**

Chianti Classico Riserva 1985 • $19 • (04/30/94) • **82**

Chianti Classico Riserva 1983 • $19 • (09/15/92) • **78**

Chianti Classico Riserva 1982 • $11 • (07/31/88) • **84**

Chianti Classico Riserva Gold Label 1982 • $21 • (11/30/89) • **79**

Chianti Classico Riserva Gold Label 1981 • $18 • (02/15/88) • **81**

Chianti Classico Riserva Oro 1986 • $20 • (11/30/94) • **88**

Chianti Classico Titolato Gabbiano 1990 • $9 • (06/15/93) • **77**

Chianti Classico Titolato Gabbiano Riserva 1988 • $12 • (06/15/93) • **87**

Chianti Classico Titolato Gabbiano Riserva Gold Label 1985 • $20 • (06/15/93) • **82**

Il Cavaliere 1988 • $9 • (12/15/92) • **78**

Merlot 1988 • $55 • (07/15/91) • **86**

R & R 1986 • $38 • (01/31/91) • **90**

R & R 1985 • $30 • (03/31/90) • **91**

Sangiovese 1993 • $8 • **50**

Key: SS—Spectator Selection. CS—Cellar Selection. BB—Best Buy. $NA—Price not available. (BT)—Barrel tasting. Ⓐ—Auction Price.
Dates in parentheses represent the issues in which the ratings were published.

Vin Santo 1985 • $20 • (03/15/91) • **78**

GAGLIARDO, GIANNI

Barolo Batié 1990: Fruity, inviting and supple in texture, with lush cherry, cranberry, plum and nutmeg flavors and firm, well integrated tannins. Well-balanced, even elegant for a Barolo. Drink now through 1998. 1,000 cases made. • $28 • (06/15/94) • **87**

Barolo La Serra 1989: Deep-colored, very oaky in flavor and very tannic in texture. The heavy oak and tannins are holding down the fruit component, making it difficult to appreciate now. Should improve significantly with age, so try it after 1997. 1,000 cases made. • $26 • (06/15/94) • **85**

Barolo Preve 1990: A blockbuster that pours out masses of fruit and tannins-great structure. The spice, coffee and fruit flavors go on and on. Needs time, try in 1999. 2,500 cases made. • $35 • **91**

Dolcetto d'Alba 1994: Delicious dried cherry and strawberry aromas and flavors, medium to light body and fresh finish. Drink now. 12,000 cases made. • $13 • **82**

Neirole 1991 • $21 • (06/15/94) • **87**

GAIERHOF

Chardonnay Maso Poli 1992: Bright and floral, spicy like a Gewurztraminer, adding nice grace notes of green apple and butter, round and appealing. 1,300 cases made. • $12 • (01/31/95) • **82**

Maso Poli Sorni 1993: Light and simple, a crisp wine with modest green apple fruit and a hint of leafiness on the finish. Made from Nosiola (70 percent) and Muller-Thurgau. 2,000 cases made. • $12 • (01/31/95) • **78**

Nosiola Trentino 1993: Not much wine in this one, delicate, verging on watery. Light, short, diluted. Tasted twice. 3,500 cases made. • $15 • (01/31/95) • **74**

Pinot Grigio Maso Poli Atesino 1993: Nicely balanced, showing elegance with pear, vanilla, grapefruit, light but pleasant. 3,600 cases made. • $12 • (01/31/95) • **82**

Pinot Grigio Mosaico Atesino 1992: Light and supple, a smooth-textured wine with an earthy edge to the lemony pear flavors. 10,000 cases made. • $6 • (01/31/95) • **81**

Pinot Grigio Mosaico Torre di Luna Trentino 1993: Simple but direct, a fruity wine with straightforward pear, apple and citrus flavors. Sings a clear song, but no complexity. 7,000 cases made. • $10 • (01/31/95) • **81**

Teroldego Rotaliano 1988 • $11 • (09/30/91) • **75**

GAJA

Barbaresco 1991: Ripe, round, spicy and generous, melds its raspberry, plum and blackberry flavors with spicy oak and grace notes of violets. Stands out from the pack with its polished, refined character. Tasted twice. • $49 • (10/31/94) • **88**

Barbaresco 1990: A stunning wine, rich, ripe and supple, balanced with beautifully realized berry, red plum, vanilla and exotic spices, smoothly playing the fruit and toasty oak character off each other. A many layered wine that is approaching drinkability. 7,500 cases made. • $66 • (10/31/93) • **94**

Barbaresco 1989: Ripe, rich and generous, layering the smooth black cherry, blackberry, currant and plum fruit with spicy oak flavors. The tannins seem extreme, even for such a concentrated wine. Best to try in 1997. 5,200 cases made. • $60 • (10/31/93) • **88**

Barbaresco 1988 • $60 • (10/31/93) • **87**

Barbaresco 1986 • $47 • (01/31/90) CS • **92**

Barbaresco 1985 • $58 • (09/15/89) • **95**

Barbaresco 1983 • $53 • (09/15/89) • **93**

Barbaresco 1982 • $103 • (09/15/89) • **93**

Barbaresco 1981 • $110 • (09/15/89) • **90**

Barbaresco 1980 • $75 • (07/01/85) • **88**

Barbaresco 1979 • $130 • (09/15/89) • **89**

Barbaresco 1978 • $130 • (09/15/89) • **93**

Barbaresco 1976 • $130 • (09/15/89) • **91**

Barbaresco 1974 • $145 • (09/15/89) • **89**

Barbaresco 1971 • $156 • (09/15/89) • **86**

Barbaresco 1967 • $170 • (09/15/89) • **83**

Barbaresco 1964 • $195 • (09/15/89) • **87**
Barbaresco 1961 • $270 • (09/15/89) • **92**
Barbaresco Costa Russi 1990: Utterly gorgeous and seductive, supple on the palate, aromatic with vanilla- and anise-scented fruit, a bit tannic but glowing with raspberry, rose petal and currant flavors. Keeps singing away on the finish, harmonizing beautifully. 833 cases made. • $125 • (10/31/93) • **98**
Barbaresco Costa Russi 1989: Defines elegance with richness, a supple wine that offers cascades of cherry, currant, plum and vanilla flavors, sneaking in wonderful notes of anise, toast and spice, all of it so well integrated and harmonious that it's difficult to pick out the various pieces. Glorius stuff. Drink from 1997. 900 cases made. • $125 • (10/15/93) CS • **96**
Barbaresco Costa Russi 1988 • $110 • (10/31/93) • **92**
Barbaresco Costa Russi 1986 • $126 • (01/31/90) • **89**
Barbaresco Costa Russi 1985 • $100 • (12/15/88) • **96**
Barbaresco Costa Russi 1982 • $93 • (09/15/88) • **91**
Barbaresco Sorì San Lorenzo 1990: Elegant, ripe and polished, positively glowing with violet-tinged blackberry, currant and black cherry aromas and flavors, many-layered, complex and utterly seductive, a seamless wine that just melts across the palate. Nothing but greatness ahead. 830 cases made. • $139 • (10/31/93) • **96**
Barbaresco Sorì San Lorenzo 1989: Tough in texture, but ripe and toasty, offering lovely black cherry, plum and violet aromas and flavors, remaining generous and flavorful through the firm and elegant finish. Needs time to sort out the tannins, but everything is beautifully integrated and harmonious. Best after 1997. 900 cases made. • $139 • (09/15/93) • **98**
Barbaresco Sorì San Lorenzo 1988 • $125 • (10/31/93) • **93**
Barbaresco Sorì San Lorenzo 1986 • $106 • (01/31/90) • **91**
Barbaresco Sorì San Lorenzo 1985 • $102 • (12/15/88) • **96**
Barbaresco Sorì San Lorenzo 1983 • $99 • (09/15/88) • **90**
Barbaresco Sorì Tildìn 1990: Absolutely ranks with the finest wines in the world. Spicy, rich and concentrated, a laser beam of berry and plum flavor arcing through the smooth-textured tannins, shooting off sparks of anise, toasty vanilla and tar. An electric wine with power, polish subtlety and grace. 830 cases made. • $139 • (10/31/93) • **100**
Barbaresco Sorì Tildìn 1989: Ripe and succulent, so plush it is almost sweet, offering bright, lively plum, black cherry and raspberry fruit shaded with toast, sweet vanilla and spice overtones, an absolutely gorgeous wine that remains elegant and supple despite its muscular core. 890 cases made. • $139 • (10/15/93) CS • **96**
Barbaresco Sorì Tildìn 1988 • $125 • (10/31/93) • **93**
Barbaresco Sorì Tildìn 1986 • $109 • (01/31/90) • **93**
Barbaresco Sorì Tildìn 1985 • $125 • (09/15/89) • **98**
Barbaresco Sorì Tildìn 1983 • $97 • (09/15/89) • **88**
Barbaresco Sorì Tildìn 1982 • $140 • (09/15/89) • **94**
Barbaresco Sorì Tildìn 1981 • $150 • (09/15/89) • **87**
Barbaresco Sorì Tildìn 1979 • $225 • (09/15/89) • **89**
Barbaresco Sorì Tildìn 1978 • $220 • (09/15/89) • **90**
Barbaresco Sorì Tildìn 1973 • $156 • (09/15/89) • **88**
Barbaresco Sorì Tildìn 1971 • $200 • (09/15/89) • **91**
Barbaresco Sorì Tildìn 1970 • $220 • (09/15/89) • **78**
Barbera d'Alba 1992: Soft, round and silky, offering berry and light chocolate aromas and flavors and a light finish. 800 cases made. • $42 • **81**
Barbera d'Alba Vignarey 1990 • $40 • (10/15/93) • **89**
Barbera d'Alba Vignarey 1987 • $35 • (04/15/91) • **88**
Barbera d'Alba Vignarey 1986 • $27 • (03/15/91) • **88**
Barbera d'Alba Vignarey 1984 • $13 • (02/15/87) • **82**
Barolo Sperss 1991: Lovely and exotic flavors of roasted peanuts, blackberry and rose petal, it's rather lean perhaps, but it shows marvelous mineral character and a long, well-focused finish. 1,500 cases made. • $60 • **86**
Barolo Sperss 1989: Complex and fascinating, offering all sorts of floral, earthy overtones to the solid core of black cherry, blackberry and anise flavors. An intense wine that shows many facets, including a welcome whiff of vanilla and toast on the aftertaste. 2,700 cases made. • $60 • (10/31/93) • **96**
Barolo Sperss 1988 • $60 • (09/15/93) CS • **94**
Cabernet Sauvignon Darmagi 1988 • $60 • (12/15/92) • **92**
Cabernet Sauvignon Darmagi 1986 • $76 • (01/31/90) • **94**
Cabernet Sauvignon Darmagi 1985 • $70 • (03/15/89) CS • **94**
Cabernet Sauvignon Darmagi 1983 • $68 • (07/15/88) • **91**
Chardonnay Gaia & Rey 1994: Like a late-harvest Chardonnay with its honey, peach, apricot and floral aromas and flavors. Full-bodied and exuberant, it fills the palate with ripe fruit flavors and toasted oak notes. Could use a bit more length and depth. • $NA • **86**
Chardonnay Gaia & Rey 1992: Strong toasty flavors suggest coffee beans and walnuts, but good acidity and a lingering finish keep the wine appealing and fresh. Very heavily oaked, but still intriguing. • $NA • (08/31/95) • **84**
Chardonnay Gaia & Rey 1991: A sophisticated wine with deft use of oak, this offers elegant lemon, apricot, piecrust and spicy flavors, balanced and polished. Makes delicious drinking now. • $NA • (06/30/95) • **88**
Dolcetto Langhe 1994: Round and well made, a Dolcetto showing good depth and complexity, delicious red berry flavor and smooth texture. Drink now. 750 cases made. • $22 • **88**
Nebbiolo d'Alba Vignaveja 1985 • $30 • (02/15/89) • **87**
Nebbiolo d'Alba Vignaveja 1983 • $28 • (02/15/87) SS • **94**
Sito Moresco 1991 • $30 • (10/31/94) • **88**
Sitorey 1993: This Barbera is quite tasty and smooth, featuring mint, licorice and black cherry character and a crisp finish. 1,000 cases made. • $45 • **84**
Sitorey 1991 • $35 • (10/31/94) • **85**
Sorì Tildìn 1983 • $95 • (09/15/88) • **89**

GANCIA

Asti Spumante NV • $12 • (12/15/92) • **78**
Brut NV: A dry, delicate sparkling wine with subtle flavors and good balance. The lively texture keeps it fresh. • $11 • (02/28/95) • **83**
Brut Chardonnay NV • $11 • (12/31/90) • **82**
Crémant Gran Riserva NV • $15 • (12/31/86) • **82**
Extra Brut Sparkling NV • $6 • (12/31/86) • **82**
Gran Cuvée Sparkling NV • $11 • (12/31/86) • **85**
Pinot di Pinot NV • $12 • (12/31/86) • **80**
Spumante Brut Castello Gancia NV • $8 • (06/15/94) • **80**
Spumante dei Gancia NV • $10 • (12/31/86) • **85**

GAROFOLI

Classico Macrina Verdicchio dei Castelli di Jesi 1993: Citrus aromas and flavors and a hint of grassiness, crisp, clean and slightly nutty, with vivid acidity. Try with seafood. • $8 • (03/31/95) • **84**

GASPARINI, LOREDAN

Spumante Brut NV • $25 • (09/15/92) • **84**
Spumante Brut Riserva 1988 • $16 • (05/15/93) • **83**

GASTALDI

Dolcetto d'Alba Moriolo 1993: Impressive for all the vibrant fruit that remains in this medium-bodied red. Shows nice blueberry, raspberry and cherry flavors. The finish is crisp, lemony and rather lean. • $NA • **82**

GATTAVECCHI, CANTINA

Chianti Colli Senesi 1990 • $7 • (04/30/92) • **80**
Vino Nobile di Montepulciano 1990: Sweet chocolate and cherry flavors are bold but lack focus and refinement. This is thick yet simple, with tannins that dominate the finish. Try now. 2,000 cases made. • $14 • (02/29/96) • **80**
Vino Nobile di Montepulciano 1988 • $14 • (12/15/92) • **83**
Vino Nobile di Montepulciano Riserva 1985 • $11 • (11/30/89) • **81**

GEOGRAFICO

Brunello di Montalcino 1985 • $30 • (07/15/91) • **80**

Capitolare di Biturica Vigneti del Geografico Red 1990: Very well-crafted red featuring vanilla, berry and cherry aromas and flavors. Supple and round, lovely definition. • $NA • **88**
Chianti Classico 1993: Fresh and fruity wine with berry, cherry and citric character on the nose and palate. Drink and enjoy. • $9 • **83**
Chianti Classico 1992: Very fresh and grapey, displaying mint, mineral and light dried-herb character, light-to-medium body, fresh acidity and light tannins. Drinkable now. 2,000 cases made. • $10 • **82**
Chianti Classico 1991 • $10 • (10/31/93) • **82**
Chianti Classico 1990 • $12 • (09/15/92) • **87**
Chianti Classico 1988 • $9 • (11/30/91) • **78**
Chianti Classico Castello di Fagnano 1991 • $12 • (10/31/93) • **75**
Chianti Classico Castello di Fagnano 1989 • $9 • (01/31/92) • **70**
Chianti Classico Castello di Fagnano 1988 • $9 • (10/31/91) • **86**
Chianti Classico Contessa di Radda 1988 • $14 • (09/15/92) • **88**
Chianti Classico Contessa di Radda 1987 • $11 • (10/31/91) • **80**
Chianti Classico Tenuta Montegiachi Riserva 1986 • $15 • (10/31/91) • **79**
Predicato di Bitùrica 1986 • $21 • (08/31/91) • **85**
Vigneti del Geografico 1988 • $26 • (10/31/93) • **91**
Vino Nobile di Montepulciano Vigneti alla Cerraia 1986 • $15 • (07/15/91) • **85**

GERLA, LA

Birba 1990 • $NA • (10/31/93) • **87**
Birbante 1989 • $NA • (10/31/93) • **84**
Brunello di Montalcino 1990: Light and easy-drinking Brunello, a bit diluted, offering some strawberry, mint and cherry flavors. Lean wine, and short finish. Disappointing for this producer. • $NA • **84**
Brunello di Montalcino 1989 • $28 • **74**
Brunello di Montalcino 1988: A wine with vivid fruit aromas and flavors. It is full-bodied, with steely tannins and a crisp finish. Better after 1996. • $30 • (04/30/94) • **86**
Brunello di Montalcino Riserva 1988: Wonderfully integrated and polished. Perhaps a little heavy on the new wood, but beautiful aromas of black cherry and plum follow through on the palate. Full-bodied, with crisp acidity. Best after 1996 • $NA • (10/31/94) • **89**
Rosso di Montalcino 1991 • $12 • (04/30/94) • **84**

GHISOLFI ATTILO

Barbera d'Alba 1990 • $18 • (10/15/94) • **86**
Dolcetto d'Alba 1991 • $12 • (10/15/94) • **84**

GIACOSA FRATELLI

Barbaresco 1987 • $16 • (03/31/93) • **78**
Barbaresco 1986 • $17 • (07/15/91) • **87**
Barbaresco Suri Secondine 1986 • $12 • (10/31/90) • **72**
Barbera d'Alba Maria Gioana 1987 • $24 • (03/31/93) • **83**
Barbera d'Alba Maria Gioana 1986 • $22 • (03/15/91) • **86**
Barolo 1985 • $20 • (03/31/93) • **70**

GIACOSA, BRUNO

Barbaresco 1985 • $42 • (08/31/89) • **84**
Barbaresco 1983 • $24 • (07/31/87) • **88**
Barbaresco Asili 1990: Dense, full-bodied, a full-throated example of traditional Barbaresco, brimming with tar, rose petal and licorice aromas and flavors around a core of berry and currant fruit that lasts and last. Very distinctive, round and beautifully made. • $NA • (10/31/94) • **92**
Barbaresco Gallina 1990: Firm and concentrated, a chewy, chunky, traditional-style wine, earthy, complex, with licorice, berry and black cherry flavors coming forward at the center. Gets a little musty on the finish. Best from 1998. Tasted twice. • $NA • (10/31/94) • **86**

> **Key:** SS—Spectator Selection. CS—Cellar Selection. BB—Best Buy. $NA—Price not available. (BT)—Barrel tasting. Ⓐ—Auction Price.
> **Dates in parentheses represent the issues in which the ratings were published.**

Barbaresco Gallina 1989: Light in texture, with firm tannins and a modest level of anise-scented berry flavors, edging toward earth on the finish. 900 cases made. • $NA • (10/31/93) • **79**
Barbaresco Gallina di Neive 1986 • $40 • (08/31/91) • **88**
Barbaresco Santo Stefano 1990: Tough and chewy, a mouthful of earthy, mushroomy flavors that pick up a little olive and berry on the astringent finish. Tasted twice. • $NA • (10/31/94) • **83**
Barbaresco Santo Stefano 1988 • $55 • (10/31/93) • **60**
Barbaresco Santo Stefano di Neive 1986 • $62 • (08/31/91) • **83**
Barbaresco Santo Stefano di Neive 1982 • $57 • (09/15/88) • **92**
Barbaresco Santo Stefano di Neive Riserva 1985 • $60 • (08/31/91) • **77**
Barbaresco Santo Stefano di Neive Riserva 1982 • $60 • (09/15/88) • **90**
Barbera d'Alba 1993: Lots of licorice, black cherry and pepper in this medium-bodied, smooth, round, rather generous 1993. Barbera. Adds a slight minty character on the well-proportioned, soft, very approachable finish. • $17 • **82**
Barbera d'Alba Altavilla 1990 • $18 • (10/15/93) • **77**
Barbera d'Alba Altavilla d'Alba 1987 • $12 • (03/15/91) • **73**
Barbera d'Alba Altavilla d'Alba 1986 • $12 • (03/15/91) • **77**
Barolo 1990: Already a bit advanced, with an appealing character of minty, earthy black cherry and mushroom. Well made in a traditional style. There is fruit on the palate, but it seems to have dried out. • $NA • **84**
Barolo 1980 • $19 • (09/15/87) • **78**
Barolo 1978 • $31 • (09/16/84) • **88**
Barolo Collina Rionda 1989: Has a certain rustic charm, but the coarse texture and drying tannins don't do the spicy black cherry flavors justice. Drink it relatively soon with hearty food. • $NA • (10/31/94) • **78**
Barolo Collina Rionda di Serralunga 1985 • $50 • (04/30/91) • **86**
Barolo Falletto 1989: Spicy and exotic but rippingly tannic and biting, showing a lean line of floral berry flavor that picks up a little steam on the finish. May be better from 1997. Not the best from Giacosa in this vintage. Tasted twice. • $NA • (10/31/94) • **84**
Barolo Falletto 1988 • $50 • (10/31/93) • **68**
Barolo Le Rocche di Castiglione Falletto 1982 • $38 • (07/31/89) • **80**
Barolo Riserva 1982 • $65 • (01/31/90) • **72**
Barolo Rocche 1982 • $41 • (09/15/88) • **90**
Barolo Villero 1990: Relatively light, offering some sweet fruit and a vegetal edge that show more tobacco and olive flavors. Firm tannins, not too heavy. 1,400 cases made. • $48 • (10/31/93) • **978**
Barolo Villero 1989: Drinkable and generous, a spicy wine with caramel and tobacco notes to the mature cherry fruit that fades a little on the finish. • $NA • (10/31/94) • **81**
Barolo Villero 1988 • $39 • (10/31/93) • **70**
Barolo Villero di Castiglione 1983 • $29 • (01/31/89) • **85**
Dolcetto d'Alba 1989 • $12 • (02/28/91) • **88**
Plinet di Trezzo Tinella 1985 • $8 • (12/31/87) • **77**

GINI

Chardonnay Sorai 1992: Bright and harmonious, nicely balanced between the tropical fruit, nutmeg and creamy flavors, lively and appealing to drink now, with enough intensity to permit aging through 1997. • $NA • (01/31/95) • **88**
Col Foscarin 1989 • $22/375ml • (09/15/92) • **83**
Soave Classico La Frosca 1991 • $16 • (09/15/92) • **67**
Sauvignon Maciete Fumé 1993: Quite rich and ripe for this group; creamy, milky and juicy. An appealing, well-made wine that shows good zest on the finish. • $NA • (01/31/95) • **87**

GIOVANNI, ALMONDO

Roero Arneis Burigot White 1993: Lively and crisp, with grassy aromas and tempting flavors of orange zest and grapefruit. Has fine fruit and good balance. 1,600 cases made. • $14 • (02/28/95) • **84**

GIOVELLO

Pinot Grigio 1995: Fruity, bright flavors of green apple, peach and banana. Quite tart, and finishes with an earthy edge. More dramatic than impressive. 10,000 cases made. • $6 • **80**

GIRELLI, CASA

Chardonnay Trentino i Mesi 1994: Perfumed vanilla and floral aromas give way to firm flavors of melon, herb and toast in this delicate yet assertive white. Not showy, but makes you want another sip. • $9 • (06/15/96) • **85**

Chardonnay Trentino i Mesi 1993: Subtle smoky, buttery accents, presumably from oak barrels, give this otherwise straightforward white wine some interest. The finish is lingering, too. 2,300 cases made. • $9 • **84**

Moscato Rosa Trentino i Mesi 1991: An unusual and delicious style of dessert red that smells like roses and tastes of sweet plums. 333 cases made. • $29 • (06/15/96) • **84**

Müller Thurgau Trentino i Mesi 1993: Smooth in texture, melony in flavor and fairly full in body. A clean, fruity wine with presence. 1,300 cases made. • $9 • **82**

Pinot Grigio Trentino 1993: Light, crisp and straightforward, showing some simple but nice apple, grapefruit, mineral flavors, that end with a refreshing finish. • $NA • (01/31/95) • **78**

Pinot Grigio Trentino i Mesi 1995: Good varietal character in this lively white, offering fresh herbal and citrus flavors and vibrant acidity. It gets the juices flowing. • $9 • (06/15/96) • **85**

Pinot Grigio Trentino i Mesi 1993: A nearly neutral tasting white wine that is clean and innocuous. 3,000 cases made. • $9 • **78**

Pinot Nero i Mesi Trentino 1988 • $10 • (02/15/91) • **81**

GIRIBALDI, AZIENDA

Chardonnay delle Langhe Campo Fux Magna 1994: A quite distinctive Chardonnay that has the floral aroma of Alsace and rich fruit flavors accented by mineral and almond. It's dry but lingers on the finish. 12,900 cases made. • $13 • (02/29/96) • **85**

GLICINE, CANTINA DEL

Barbaresco 1985 • $27 • (08/31/91) • **75**

Piedmont 1989 • $13 • (11/30/91) • **79**

GONDI, MARCHESE

Chianti Rufina 1990 • $NA • (10/31/93) • **85**

GORELLI

Brunello di Montalcino 1990: Elegant and minty, sporting fine tannins and fresh fruit. Medium-bodied and round with toasted oak and a clean finish. Drinkable now. • $NA • **87**

Brunello di Montalcino 1988: A very ripe style, with a sweet berry, plum and smoke character. Full-bodied with full tannins. Needs time. Tasted twice. Try after 1998. • $NA • (04/30/94) • **87**

Rosso di Montalcino 1993: Lovely, new-style Rosso offering crushed berry and cherry aromas and flavors and a hint of new wood. Medium-bodied and soft, adding round tannins and fruity, vanilla finish. • $NA • **86**

Rosso di Montalcino 1992 • $NA • (10/31/94) • **80**

Rosso di Montalcino 1991 • $NA • (04/30/94) • **82**

GORETTI MINIATI

Apoteosi 1990 • $NA • (10/31/93) • **87**

Chianti Classico Il Palagio 1991 • $NA • (10/31/93) • **86**

Chianti Classico Il Palagio 1990 • $NA • (10/31/93) • **86**

GRASSO, ELIO

Barbera d'Alba Vigna Martina 1992: Smooth, round tomato, mint and fruit character, medium body and crisp finish. • $18 • **82**

Barbera delle Langhe Vigna Martina 1990 • $19 • (09/15/93) • **81**

Barolo 1991: Smooth and round, a drinkable Barolo that kicks in some tannins on the somewhat dry finish, but it shows decent cherry, currant and tar flavors. • $24 • **81**

Barolo Casa Maté 1990: Tannic and chewy, flavorful enough to show some tarry cherry notes underneath the thick layer of gravelly tannins, displaying spice and roses on the finish. Best from 2000. • $30 • (10/31/94) • **85**

Barolo Gavarini Vigna Chiniera 1990: Chewy with tannins, but it has some pleasant raspberry, cherry and vanilla flavors that come through and also follow on the finish. • $30 • (10/31/94) • **87**

Barolo Gavarini Vigna Rüncot 1988 • $30 • (09/15/93) • **84**

Barolo Gavarini Vigna Rüncot 1985 • $42 • (08/31/91) • **59**

Barolo Ginestra Vigna Casa Maté 1988 • $30 • (09/15/93) • **82**

Gavarini 1989 • $20 • (07/15/91) • **83**

Gavarini Vigna dei Grassi 1989 • $18 • (07/15/91) • **76**

Vigna Martina 1991: Deep in color, but tart and simple, a wine of modest proportions and a little more tannin than it seems to need. Maybe better after 1997, maybe not. RT • $19 • **77**

GRATTAMACCO

Tuscany 1990 • $NA • (10/31/93) • **93**

Tuscany 1989 • $NA • (10/31/93) • **86**

Tuscany 1988 • $NA • (09/15/91) • **87**

Tuscany 1986 • $25 • (12/15/92) • **72**

GRAVNER, FRANCESCO

Rujno-Northeast 1985 • $NA • (09/15/88) • **84**

GREPPONE MAZZI

Brunello di Montalcino 1990: Silky and refined, featuring plenty of ripe fruit, mint and roasted new oak character, medium to full body, fine tannins and long, slightly dry finish. Better in 1997. • $NA • **87**

Brunello di Montalcino 1982 • $NA • (09/15/86) • **90**

Brunello di Montalcino 1981 • $NA • (09/15/86) • **70**

Brunello di Montalcino Riserva 1988: A delicate, traditional Brunello, with a nice plummy, nutty character, light tannins and a crisp finish. Drinkable now. • $NA • (10/31/94) • **85**

Brunello di Montalcino Riserva 1986 • $33 • (12/15/92) • **84**

GRESY, MARCHESI DI

Barbaresco Camp Gros 1990: Chewy and tannic, but packed with bright strawberry and raspberry flavor that fills the medium-weight frame nicely. Needs to shed some tannins, best from 1997 or 1998. Not as good as last year. • $63 • (10/31/94) • **83**

Barbaresco Camp Gros 1989: Lean and biting, a mouthful of bitter tannins that never seems to get much fruit revved up to balance. Not as good as last year. • $61 • (10/31/94) • **73**

Barbaresco Camp Gros Martinenga 1990: Firm tannins and ripe cherry fruit haven't quite come together yet in this chunky, engaging wine. A bitter almond note adds an interesting edge to the finish. 670 cases made. • $60 • (10/31/93) • **90**

Barbaresco Camp Gros Martinenga 1989: Light and spicy, with a strong earthy, anise note that tamps down the fruit, finishing tannic. Maybe better after 1996. 630 cases made. • $60 • (10/31/93) • **78**

Barbaresco Camp Gros Martinenga 1988 • $60 • (10/31/93) • **82**

Barbaresco Camp Gros Martinenga 1985 • $73 • (01/31/89) • **92**

Barbaresco Camp Gros Martinenga 1983 • $85 • (09/15/88) • **88**

Barbaresco Camp Gros Martinenga 1982 • $26 • (09/15/88) • **89**

Barbaresco Camp Gros Martinenga 1979 • $40 • (09/15/88) • **88**

Barbaresco Gaiun Martinenga 1990: Earthy flavors stand out, the floral character dominating the lean core of raspberry. Scratchy tannins need until approximately 1998 to sort themselves out. Tasted twice. • $63 • (10/31/94) • **83**

Barbaresco Gaiun Martinenga 1989: Crisp, earthy and spicy, with a bittersweet chocolate character that smoothes out the slightly chewy edge to the cinnamon and strawberry flavors. Drinkable now, although the tannins can use until 1997 or 1998 to settle down. Much better than last year. • $61 • (10/31/94) • **86**

Barbaresco Gaiun Martinenga 1988 • $60 • (10/31/93) • **83**

Barbaresco Gaiun Martinenga 1986 • $96 • (09/15/90) • **90**

Barbaresco Gaiun Martinenga 1985 • $73 • (01/31/89) CS • **95**

Barbaresco Gaiun Martinenga 1983 • $83 • (09/15/88) • **84**
Barbaresco Gaiun Martinenga 1982 • $26 • (09/15/88) • **87**
Barbaresco Martinenga 1992: Light-bodied, subtle rose petal character and wet earth notes. Very accessible and drinkable now but quite diluted on the palate. 1,500 cases made. • $41 • **78**
Barbaresco Martinenga 1991: Elegant cherry and mineral aromas and flavors, light to medium body, fine tannins and long, tasty, slightly dry finish. 1,500 cases made. • $41 • **81**
Barbaresco Martinenga 1990: Very light and fruity, a delicate style with appealing strawberry and raspberry fruit, plus a touch of vanilla on the finish. Approachable now. Tasted twice. • $40 • (10/31/94) • **82**
Barbaresco Martinenga 1989: Very spicy and pretty on the nose, but the tannins clamp down big time and it comes off as bitey and cedary with just a hint of black cherry to rescue it. Tannins will never recede much, but it should be best from 1998. • $36 • (10/31/94) • **82**
Barbaresco Martinenga 1988 • $30 • (10/31/93) • **80**
Barbaresco Martinenga 1986 • $84 • (09/15/90) • **88**
Barbaresco Martinenga 1985 • $57 • (01/31/89) • **90**
Barbaresco Martinenga 1984 • $36 • (09/15/88) • **84**
Barbaresco Martinenga 1983 • $68 • (09/15/88) • **87**
Barbaresco Martinenga 1982 • $80 • (09/15/88) • **86**
Barbaresco Martinenga 1979 • $30 • (09/15/88) • **81**
Barbaresco Martinenga 1978 • $40 • (09/15/88) • **89**
Chardonnay Gresy 1993: A well-made Chardonnay featuring apple, toasted oak and coconut aromas and flavors, medium body, good acidity and ripe fruit finish. • $NA • **86**
Chardonnay Gresy 1992: Somewhat vegetal, appley, grassy character, medium in body, light finish. Not much to think about it. • $NA • **79**
Dolcetto d'Alba Monte Aribaldo 1994: Very fresh dried cherry and floral character and lovely refreshing acidity. Medium in body and a light finish. • $NA • **84**
Dolcetto d'Alba Monte Aribaldo 1993: Crisp and juicy, showing a lean texture and some modest cherry, raspberry and lemon flavors. • $NA • **80**
Monte Aribaldo 1986 • $8 • (10/31/88) • **81**
Nebbiolo Martinenga 1986 • $11 • (10/15/88) • **82**
Sauvignon Langhe 1994: Good, simple Sauvignon offering apple, grapefruit and light grassy character, medium to light body, fresh acidity and light finish. Young vines? • $NA • **81**
Villa Martis 1991: Light in color, a spicy wine that offers cherry and unusual grilled-meat flavors in small proportions. Tannins are obtrusive, but maybe better 1997-1998. A blend of Nebbiolo and Barbera. RT • $16 • **73**
Virtus 1991 • $25 • (10/31/94) • **83**

GRETOLE, PODERI DI

Chianti Classico 1990 • $9 • (10/31/93) • **83**
Chianti Classico 1989 • $9 • (12/15/92) • **82**
Chianti Classico 1988 • $8 • (10/31/91) BB • **82**
Chianti Classico Riserva 1988 • $11 • (10/31/93) • **86**
Chianti Classico Riserva 1986 • $11 • (10/31/91) • **83**

GREVEPESA

Chianti Classico Clemente VII 1993: Rather light and forward and in an old style. Cherry and cedar aromas and flavors, soft tannins and a succulent finish. • $NA • (01/31/96) • **79**

GREVEPESA, CASTELLI DEL

Chianti Classico Castelgreve Riserva 1988 • $9 • (09/15/92) • **79**
Chianti Classico Clemente VII 1988 • $8 • (09/15/92) • **81**
Chianti Classico Lamole 1990 • $NA • (10/31/93) • **76**
Chianti Classico Panzano 1988 • $11 • (09/15/92) • **84**
Chianti Classico Sant'Angiolo Vico Labate 1988 • $NA • (09/15/91) • **88**
Chianti Classico Vigna Elisa 1988 • $13 • (09/15/92) • **85**
Coltifredi Predicato di Cardisco 1988 • $21 • (10/31/93) • **85**

Key: SS—Spectator Selection. CS—Cellar Selection. BB—Best Buy. $NA—Price not available. (BT)—Barrel tasting. (A)—Auction Price.
Dates in parentheses represent the issues in which the ratings were published.

Magiòlo 1990 • $NA • (10/31/93) • **84**

GUERRIERI GONZAGA

San Leonardo 1986 • $33 • (12/15/92) • **86**
San Leonardo 1985 • $35 • (12/15/92) • **82**
San Leonardo 1983 • $35 • (12/15/92) • **79**

GUICCIARDINI, CASTELLO

Chianti Colli Fiorentini Il Cortile 1990: Bursting with tart cherry, herbs, sun-dried tomatoes and smoke. This is balanced, seductive, crisp and firm. Drinkable now. 30,000 cases made. • $8 BB • **88**
Chianti Colli Fiorentini Riserva 1986: Elegant, with complex black olive, plum and anise flavors. Shows good balance between firm tannins and bright acidity. Drinkable now. 4,166 cases made. • $10 • **88**
Colli Dell'Etruria Centrale Bianco della Gora 1992 • $7 • (06/15/94) • **72**
Colli Dell'Etruria Centrale Sassaia del Virginio 1992 • $8 • (06/15/94) • **74**
Tricorno 1987 • $18 • (07/31/94) • **86**

HAAS, FRANZ

Chardonnay Alto Adige 1993: Smoky and earthy in style, this crisp, austere wine makes no concessions to sweetness or even fruitiness yet manages to remain balanced and is a fine match for food. • $10 • (06/15/96) • **83**
Pinot Grigio Kris Alto Adige 1994: Smoky, herbal aromas give way to polished flavors of mineral, pear and light toast in this elegant, harmonious white. It's subtle but lively, with a pleasant hint of spritz. A value for an Italian white, and it's made for food. 8,500 cases made. • $10 • (10/31/95) BB • **87**

HAUNER, CARLO

Malvasia delle Lipari 1984 • $15 • (12/31/88) • **85**

I DUE CIPRESSI

Brunello di Montalcino 1990: This is a lovely autumnal wine that has wild mushroom, tobacco and meaty aromas and flavors. Medium body, ripe fruit character, round tannins and a rich finish. Drinkable now. 600 cases made. • $28 • **87**
Brunello di Montalcino 1989: Mature and soft, dominated by brown sugar flavors. Simple, with some chocolate notes, and ready to drink now. 600 cases made. • $28 • (07/31/95) • **82**
Rosso di Montalcino 1993: Elegant and pretty through and through. Tobacco, cherry and berry aromas and flavors. Medium-bodied and round, offering fine tannins and crisp finish. Try now. 800 cases made. • $14 • **84**
Rosso di Montalcino 1992: Rich, almost lush, with a taste of chocolate that carries through from beginning to end. Balanced and delicious now. 800 cases made. • $14 • (08/31/95) • **85**
Vino Nobile di Montepulciano 1992: Light and already mature, with tobacco and cherry aromas and flavors. Slightly diluted on the finish. 1,000 cases made. • $11 • **76**
Vino Nobile di Montepulciano 1991: Maturing now, this shows cherry, smoke and leather flavors on a lean, tannic frame. It turns bitter on the finish. 1,000 cases made. • $11 • (02/29/96) • **78**

I SODI

Chianti Classico 1992: Slightly odd sun-dried tomato aromas and flavors. Medium-to-light body, crisp finish. Drinkable now. • $NA • **78**

IL POGGIOLO, VILLA

Brunello di Montalcino 1990: Brick-brownish color suggests a slightly fading Brunello. It lacks fruit and tastes of mushroom, brown sugar and truffle. Drinkable but not pleasant. • $NA • (10/31/95) • **77**
Brunello di Montalcino Sassello 1990: Impressive intensity of tobacco, berry and toasted oak character. Full in body and round, with fine tan-

ITALY

nins and slightly dry finish. A bit too much wood. Drinkable now. • $NA • **86**

Carmignano Riserva 1985 • $16 • (05/15/90) • **80**

Rosso di Montalcino Sassello 1992: Fragrant and adds an element of earthiness to its ripe red cherry flavors. The texture is soft and appealing, but there are still some tannins on the finish. 300 cases made. • $14 • (08/31/95) • **86**

ILLUMINATI

Zanna Montepulciano d'Abruzzo 1988 • $15 • (07/31/94) • **79**

INFERNOTTO

Barolo 1990: A good example of Barolo from a great vintage. Clean, spicy aromas, and rich, meaty flavors make this an appealing wine to drink now. Moderately tannic, long on the finish. 4,167 cases made. • $9 • (02/28/95) • **85**

Chianti 1992: This is thin and tart, though it has some good, mature dried cherry flavors. Simple and already over the hill. • $4 • (07/31/95) • **78**

Chianti Classico 1992: A bit medicinal tasting. Already mature and browning, with simple dried cherry flavors. Dull and sugary on the finish. • $5 • (07/31/95) • **77**

Gavi 1992: • $6 • **61**

Merlot Grave del Friuli 1993: • $6 • **68**

Pinot Grigio Grave del Friuli 1993: Fruity but awkward, with simple fruit-cocktail flavors and a slightly sweet finish. • $6 • (07/31/95) • **75**

INNOCENTI, VITTORIO

Acerone 1990 • $10 • (10/31/93) • **78**

Acerone 1988 • $13 • (07/15/91) • **80**

Acerone 1985 • $9 • (09/15/89) • **78**

Chianti 1990 • $9 • (10/31/93) • **81**

Chianti 1987 • $7 • (05/15/90) BB • **83**

Chianti 1986 • $7 • (03/31/90) • **77**

Vino Nobile di Montepulciano 1988 • $13 • (11/15/93) • **85**

Vino Nobile di Montepulciano 1985 • $10 • (03/31/90) • **77**

ISOLE E OLENA

Antiche Tenute 1989 • $6 • (08/31/91) • **80**

Antiche Tenute 1988 • $6 • (09/15/89) BB • **83**

Antiche Tenute 1987 • $4 • (01/31/89) BB • **81**

Antiche Tenute 1986 • $5 • (11/15/88) • **78**

Cabernet Sauvignon Collezione de Marchi 1991: Wonderful aromas of mint, milk chocolate and fruit. Medium in body and very silky, long finish. Drinkable now. 760 cases made. • $30 • **90**

Cabernet Sauvignon Collezione de Marchi 1990: This continues to be one of the great Cabernets of Italy. Stunning, intense aromas and flavors of cassis, mint and tobacco, full-bodied and tannic yet soft and supple. A superb wine. Try in 1998. • $30 • (10/31/93) • **95**

Cabernet Sauvignon Collezione de Marchi 1988 • $40 • (09/15/91) • **94**

Cepparello 1991: Beautiful, succulent red displaying plum, grilled meat and tobacco aromas and flavors, medium body and a delicious finish. Drinkable now. • $28 • **86**

Cepparello 1990: Always superlative in fine vintages. Sleek and focused wine with vivid blackberry, tar and cedar character, full body and silky tannins. Super finish. Made from Sangiovese. Try in 1997. • $30 • (10/31/93) • **93**

Cepparello 1989 • $30 • (11/15/93) • **85**

Cepparello 1988 • $35 • (11/15/93) • **92**

Cepparello 1986 • $32 • (11/15/93) • **85**

Cepparello 1985 • $40 • (11/15/93) • **90**

Cepparello 1983 • $45 • (11/15/93) • **90**

Cepparello 1982 • $50 • (11/15/93) • **94**

Chianti Classico 1992: Not as good as expected. Strawberry, cherry and earth flavors. Very clean yet short on the finish. Drinkable now. 15,000 cases made. • $12 • **79**

Chianti Classico 1991 • $13 • (10/31/93) • **82**

Chianti Classico 1990 • $12 • (09/15/92) • **90**

Chianti Classico 1988 • $9 • (11/30/90) BB • **89**

Chianti Classico 1987 • $12 • (09/15/89) • **88**

Chianti Classico 1986 • $7 • (07/31/88) • **86**

Chianti Classico 1985 • $196 Ⓐ • (05/31/88) BB • **89**

Chianti Classico 1983 • $9 • (12/15/86) BB • **85**

Chianti Classico Riserva 1985 • $13 • • **68**

Collezione de Marchi l'Eremo 1990 • $NA • (10/31/93) • **89**

Collezione de Marchi l'Eremo 1988 • $NA • (09/15/91) • **90**

Vin Santo NV • $17/375ml • (03/31/90) • **93**

JERMANN

Capo Martino White 1992: Broad in texture but very tart, with pineapple and lemon flavors dominating, hinting at honey on the finish. Has intensity but seems like it needs time to develop. Drink now. 1,000 cases made. • $36 • (01/31/95) • **85**

Capo Martino in Ruttaris 1994: Smoke and apples mingle nicely in the aromas and flavors of this light but flavorful white, slightly bitter oak giving way to lively fruit on the finish. 1,250 cases made. • $42 • (06/15/96) • **80**

Chardonnay 1994: Earthy aromas and sweet, smoky flavors finish heavy and dull. It's assertive, but lacks freshness. 3,100 cases made. • $23 • (06/15/96) • **75**

Chardonnay 1992: Fruity, lively and intense, layering in some bright floral and spicy notes to the buttery green apple and apricot fruit. Oozes charm, even if it finishes less enthusiastically than it starts. 2,916 cases made. • $21 • (01/31/95) • **86**

Chardonnay Where the Dreams Have no End... 1994: An exuberant wine with vivid flavors of pineapple, melon and buttered toast, and enough acidity to keep them on their toes. It's sunny, bold, and very appealing. 1,250 cases made. • $44 • (06/15/96) • **88**

Chardonnay Where the Dreams Have no End... 1992: Elegant, spicy and supple, a harmonious wine with subtle nutmeg and vanilla grace notes to the pear and pineapple melody. A stylish wine that is tasty now, but it doesn't have the depth of the better vintages. 1,000 cases made. • $40 • (01/31/95) • **86**

Moscato Rosa del FVG Vigna Bellina 1989 • $26 • (03/15/91) • **81**

Moscato Rosa del FVG Vigna Bellina 1987 • $20 • (09/15/88) • **85**

Pinot Bianco 1993: A beautiful, exotic and racy wine, that delivers gorgeous fruit. Honey, lime, mineral and earth flavor marry superbly in this elegant and flavorful work of art. 1,500 cases made. • $20 • (01/31/95) • **89**

Pinot Bianco 1991 • $17 • (06/15/94) • **87**

Sauvignon 1994: Fairly rich, balanced and refreshing, with good peach flavors. This is a fruity wine that deliver the goods and finishes on a cinnamon note. 2,500 cases made. • $23 • (06/15/96) • **85**

Sauvignon 1993: Terrific Sauvignon, with a focused beam of lemon, apricot and grassy flavors, accented by some vanilla notes. Plays more on the fruit than on the grassy notes. 2,333 cases made. • $20 • (01/31/95) • **88**

Sauvignon 1992 • $19 • (06/15/94) • **88**

Traminer Aromatico 1994: This luscious wine is rich with apricot and honey flavors, full-bodied and spicy, yet still crisp. Not easy to match with food, but a rich apéritif. 800 cases made. • $24 • (06/15/96) • **85**

Vinnae da Vinnaioli 1994: A basic white with backbone and flavors dominated by grapefruit and green apple. Finishes with a hint of spice. 2,400 cases made. • $21 • (06/15/96) • **79**

Vinnae da Vinnaioli 1993: Lively and vibrant wine, of medium body, packed with excellent focus of lemon, pear, mineral flavors. Try now. 2,333 cases made. • $20 • (01/31/95) • **88**

Vintage Tunina 1994: Rich and crisp at once. Buttery, smoky flavors are lifted by lemony acidity, giving the wine a sweet and sour character that's slightly schizophrenic, yet appealing. 2,250 cases made. • $35 • (06/15/96) • **84**

Vintage Tunina 1993: Here's a big-boned, full-bodied white with more weight than flavor. The honey, butter and melon notes are harmonious

ITALY

and finish with an apricot sweetness. A rich wine for meaty fish. 3,200 cases made. • $35 • (06/15/96) • **86**

Vintage Tunina 1992: Not much on the nose, but the flavors are rich and inviting, balancing mineral and apple notes in harmony. Seems tightly closed at this point. 2,333 cases made. • $33 • (01/31/95) • **86**

LAGARIA

Pinot Grigio 1994: Earthy, smoky and herbal, this white is rich and round, but isn't showing much fruit. It gets more interesting on the finish. Try with food. 32,000 cases made. • $6 • (06/15/96) • **81**

LAGEDER, ALOIS

Cabernet Riserva Alto Adige/Südtirol 1989 • $15 • (03/31/94) • **80**

Chardonnay Alto Adige 1994: Discreet yet harmonious, this well-balanced wine offers firm acidity, typical apple and melon flavors and a clean finish. A nice match with white meat and fish. 10,000 cases made. • $11 • (06/15/96) • **84**

Chardonnay Alto Adige 1993: Crisp and lively, offering a generous serving of pear, peach and vanilla flavors that echo on the finish. 15,500 cases made. • $11 • (01/31/95) • **85**

Chardonnay Alto Adige/Südtirol 1991 • $11 • (11/30/93) • **82**

Chardonnay Löwengang Alto Adige 1993: Sweet oak is the dominant flavor here, on a clean background of crisp acidity and polished texture. Fresh, firm and appealing. • $31 • (06/15/96) • **84**

Chardonnay Löwengang Alto Adige 1991: Toasty, buttery style, lean in texture with a fine thread of banana and pear fruit weaving through the spicy oak flavors. Nicely balanced. 1,500 cases made. • $26 • (01/31/95) • **84**

Merlot Alto Adige 1994: A light, lean red wine with modest, clean fruit flavors and soft tannins. Straightforward. 4,000 cases made. • $13 • (06/15/96) • **81**

Merlot Alto Adige/Südtirol 1990 • $13 • (03/31/94) • **82**

Pinot Bianco Alto Adige 1993: Clean, light and simple, showing some tart lime, tangerine and grapefruit flavors — and little else. Very lean finish. 8,500 cases made. • $10 • (01/31/95) • **78**

Pinot Bianco Alto Adige/Südtirol 1991 • $11 • (09/30/93) • **78**

Pinot Bianco Alto Adige Haberlehof 1994: Fairly rich and enticing with good fig, pear and clove flavors. This is well balanced, with a creamy, spicy finish. 800 cases made. • $15 • (06/15/96) • **84**

Pinot Bianco Alto Adige Haberlehof 1992: An attempt to make a serious wine, but it tastes stale, like spoiled fruit, sweet and sour. 950 cases made. • $16 • (01/31/95) • **72**

Pinot Grigio Alto Adige 1994: Made in a mellow style, this full-bodied, slightly oily wine offers light pear and almond flavors, and could use a bit more acidity for freshness. It's plenty rich for food. 12,500 cases made. • $12 • (06/15/96) • **83**

Pinot Grigio Alto Adige 1993: Lovely wine, showing a lot of life and fresh character, lime galore that jumps out from the glass with notes of orange peel, apple skin and banana. Light and crisp. 18,000 cases made. • $10 • (01/31/95) • **82**

Pinot Grigio Alto Adige/Südtirol 1991 • $11 • (11/30/93) • **72**

Pinot Grigio Alto Adige/Südtirol Benefizuim Porer 1991 • $17 • (11/30/93) • **81**

Pinot Grigio Alto Adige Benefizium Porer 1994: New oak adds vanilla and butter flavors that are unusual for the region but sweetly appealing. Also offers lemon and pear flavors. It's well structured and long in the finish. 2,500 cases made. • $15 • (06/15/96) • **86**

Pinot Grigio Alto Adige Benefizium Porer 1992: Tart and lean, but with some appealing vanilla, milky, creamy flavors accented by lime notes. Shows good complexity, but very delicate. 1,750 cases made. • $16 • (01/31/95) • **83**

Sauvignon Terlaner 1991 • $13 • (09/15/93) • **89**

Sauvignon Terlaner Alto Adige 1993: Soft and slightly peppery, generous with its pear and vanilla flavors, finishing with a slight bite. 2,500 cases made. • $13 • (01/31/95) • **85**

Key: SS—Spectator Selection. CS—Cellar Selection. BB—Best Buy. $NA—Price not available. (BT)—Barrel tasting. Ⓐ—Auction Price.
Dates in parentheses represent the issues in which the ratings were published.

Sauvignon Terlaner Alto Adige Lehenhof 1994: Firm and juicy, with loads of green apple flavors framed by some spicy notes. Finishes with a nice touch of clove. 750 cases made. • $18 • (06/15/96) • **84**

LAMBERTI

Bianco di Custoza Orchidea Platino 1994: A slightly resinous white with an astringent finish. Piney and appley flavors dominate this medium-bodied wine, which also ends up quite dry as well. • $10 • (05/31/96) • **81**

Bianco di Custoza Orchidea Platino 1992 • $11 • (06/15/94) • **84**

Bianco di Custoza Orchidea Platino 1991 • $10 • (09/15/92) • **80**

Lugana Oro 1991 • $10 • (09/15/92) • **84**

Recioto della Valpolicella Amarone Corte Rubini 1990: A restrained style marked by dried plum and cherry flavors. Spicy and leathery with nice richness. Still tannic on the finish. Try in 1998. • $20 • (06/15/96) • **87**

Recioto della Valpolicella Amarone Corte Rubini 1985 • $19 • (09/15/92) • **80**

Vigneti di Ca' Bolcana Valpolicella 1991 • $9 • (09/15/92) • **74**

Vigneti di Fittà Soave Classico 1991 • $9 • (09/15/92) • **82**

LAMOLE DI LAMOLE

Chianti Classico 1991 • $14 • (10/31/93) • **86**

Chianti Classico 1990 • $12 • (09/15/92) • **73**

Chianti Classico 1988 • $12 • (09/15/91) • **90**

Chianti Classico Riserva 1988 • $17 • (09/15/92) • **82**

Chianti Classico Vigneto di Campolungo 1985 • $20 • (04/30/90) • **90**

LANCIOLA

Chianti Colli Fiorentini 1987 • $7 • (05/15/89) • **68**

LECCIA, CASTELLO LA

Chianti Classico 1991: Fresh and clean with lovely vanilla, berry and cherry aromas and flavors. Medium-bodied and silky. Drinkable now. 3,250 cases made. • $10 • **86**

Chianti Classico 1990 • $NA • (09/15/92) • **88**

LECCIAIA, LE

Brunello di Montalcino 1988: Fruity and simple, with light tannins and a sweet fruit finish. Pretty berry notes are slightly marred by a stewed character. Drink now. • $NA • (04/30/94) • **80**

Rosso di Montalcino 1991 • $NA • (04/30/94) • **78**

LEONARDINI

Asti Spumante NV: Tired and oxidized, with fruit-cocktail flavors and a buttery note that's not characteristic of Spumante. More like a mediocre Sherry with bubbles. • $8 • **73**

Cabernet Sauvignon 1991 • $6 • (11/15/94) • **78**

Merlot 1991 • $6 • (11/15/94) • **74**

Montepulciano d'Abruzzo 1991: Tart and fairly thin on the finish. Only modest cranberry flavors are discernible in this vinegary wine. • $5 • (03/31/95) • **73**

Valpolicella 1990 • $5 • (04/30/92) BB • **81**

LIBRANDI

Val di Neto Gravello 1989: Well-knit and appealing, this wine offers fresh cherry, spice and light herbal aromas and flavors in a firm yet approachable package. It's balanced and well-focused. Drink now. • $20 • (05/31/95) • **87**

LILLIANO

Anagallis 1990: A profusion of plum, boysenberry and cassis flavors. Medium-bodied and velvety, long, fruity finish. Drinkable now. • $25 • **88**

Anagallis 1987 • $25 • (12/15/92) • **85**
Anagallis 1985 • $34 • (03/31/90) • **86**
Chianti Classico 1993: This racy wine shows plenty of character, with well-defined blackberry, plum, black cherry flavors. Medium body. Intense finish. Drinkable now. • $NA • **87**
Chianti Classico 1990 • $11 • (09/15/92) • **89**
Chianti Classico 1988 • $10 • (11/30/90) • **81**
Chianti Classico 1987 • $8 • (11/30/89) • **86**
Chianti Classico 1986 • $7 • (05/15/89) • **70**
Chianti Classico 1985 • $6 • (10/31/87) • **74**
Chianti Classico Riserva 1990: A delicious, kind Chianti that makes you want to relax with it at dinner. Lovely plum, berry and truffle aromas and flavors, medium body and a soft finish. • $22 • **86**
Chianti Classico Riserva 1988 • $NA • (09/15/92) • **89**
Chianti Classico Riserva 1985 • $14 • (11/30/89) • **89**

LISINI

Brunello di Montalcino 1988: Seems overdone, showing raisiny, ripe fruit character. Full-bodied, incredibly tannic and dry on the finish. Tasted twice. Better after 1997. • $36 • (04/30/94) • **80**
Brunello di Montalcino 1985 • $33 • (08/31/91) • **81**
Brunello di Montalcino 1983 • $22 • (07/31/89) • **73**
Brunello di Montalcino 1982 • $25 • (01/31/89) • **84**
Brunello di Montalcino 1975 • $30 • (09/15/86) • **78**
Brunello di Montalcino Riserva 1988: A fruity red, with fine, silky tannins and a long, smoky finish that echoes cherry notes. Well crafted through and through. Drinkable now. • $NA • (10/31/94) • **86**
Rosso di Montalcino 1988 • $14 • (04/30/91) • **79**

LIVON

Refosco Colli Orientali del Friuli dal Peduncolo Rosso Riul 1988 • $11 • (01/31/92) • **79**
Schioppettino Red 1988 • $13 • (01/31/92) • **86**
Schioppettino Red 1987 • $18 • (04/15/90) • **81**

LOGGIA, FATTORIA LA

Chianti Classico Riserva 1990: A rich and decadent style, with plenty of black truffle and fruit concentration. Medium-bodied, round, soft-textured. Drinkable now. 4,500 cases made. • $17 • **85**
Nearco 1990 • $NA • (10/31/93) • **85**

LOSI, PAOLO & PIETRO

Chianti Classico Querciavalle 1990 • $10 • (07/31/94) • **85**

LUCIA, GALASSO

Don Giovanni di Giovanni Crosato Il Bianco 1994: Simple and rather tart, with grapefruit flavors. It has some body, but could use more punch. Finishes a bit short. 1,200 cases made. • $25 • (06/15/96) • **77**
Don Giovanni di Giovanni Crosato Il Rosso 1994: Generous, smooth-textured and oaky, with moderate tannins and fresh fruit flavors. Attractive and well balanced for drinking now. 800 cases made. • $25 • (05/31/96) • **85**

LUCIGNANO, FATTORIA DI

Chianti Colli Fiorentini 1990 • $7 • (04/30/92) BB • **85**
Chianti Colli Fiorentini 1987 • $6 • (06/30/89) • **76**

LUIANO

Chianti Classico Riserva 1978 • $6 • (08/31/86) • **71**

LUNGAROTTI

Bianco di Torgiano Torre di Giano 1995: Lean and crisp, its tart lemon and green apple flavors kept lively by a hint of spritz. Simple, but clean and refreshing. • $NA • **82**
Bianco di Torgiano Torre di Giano 1993: Lively and crisp in texture, light and lean in flavor, with enough peach and almond accents to give it interest. Appetizing and well-balanced. 100,000 cases made. • $9 • (05/31/95) BB • **84**
Cabernet Sauvignon 1983 • $18 • (05/15/91) • **85**
Cabernet Sauvignon 1979 • $11 • (02/15/87) • **79**
Chardonnay 1994: Fresh and fruity—simple, but clean. A bit soft in balance and light. • $11 • (02/29/96) • **79**
Chardonnay 1993: 25,000 cases made. • $11 • **77**
Chardonnay 1991 • $12 • (05/31/93) • **82**
Pinot Grigio 1994: Lemony acidity and toasty flavors highlight this relatively neutral wine. It's quite crisp and firm, and would show best with food. 8,000 cases made. • $13 • **82**
Pinot Grigio 1993: A good change of pace. An interesting but very dry and lean white with herb and grapefruit flavors, a touch of mineral to add complexity and a nicely austere finish. 8,000 cases made. • $10 • (05/31/95) BB • **87**
Pinot Grigio 1991 • $12 • (05/31/93) • **80**
San Giorgio 1985: Perfumed with cedar and spice, this rustic wine offers cherry, raisin and tobacco flavors in a firm structure. It's mature but balanced enough to hold for another year or two. 3,000 cases made. • $30 • (05/31/95) • **85**
San Giorgio 1982 • $34 • (07/15/91) • **77**
San Giorgio 1979 • $18 • (03/15/87) • **75**
San Giorgio 1978 • $19 • (04/16/85) • **84**
Spumante Brut NV • $23 • (03/15/89) • **82**
Torgiano Rubesco 1993: Soft and tasty. Cherry, berry and spicy flavors in a light, silky texture with just enough grip for food. Drinkable now. 80,000 cases made. • $11 • **84**
Torgiano Rubesco 1988 • $13 • (09/15/92) • **83**
Torgiano Rubesco 1987 • $11 • (05/15/91) • **83**
Torgiano Rubesco 1985 • $11 • (09/15/89) • **74**
Torgiano Rubesco 1979 • $8 • (01/01/86) • **77**
Torgiano Rubesco Monticchio Riserva 1982 • $25 • (09/15/92) • **71**
Torgiano Rubesco Monticchio Riserva 1980 • $27 • (07/15/91) • **84**
Torgiano Rubesco Monticchio Riserva 1978 • $23 • (09/15/89) • **82**
Torgiano Torre di Giano Il Pino White 1992: Thick, rich texture is appealing. Flavors are light, with vanilla and apple notes. Finish turns a bit chalky. Try with marinated, grilled dishes. 100,000 cases made. • $16 • **82**
Torgiano Torre di Giano 1989 • $11 • (07/15/91) • **83**
Torgiano Vino Santo 1991: Silky and medium-sweet with appealing vivacity. Brown color reflects the honey, toffee and orange-peel flavors. Drink it well-chilled after supper. 10,000 cases made. • $13 • **88**
Vin Santo 1988 • $15 • (07/31/93) • **84**
Vin Santo 1985 • $7 • (03/15/91) • **79**
Vin Santo 1983 • $9 • (03/15/89) • **81**

MACHIAVELLI

Chianti Classico Riserva 1986 • $16 • (10/31/91) • **84**
Chianti Classico Vigna di Fontalle Riserva 1990: Tobacco, ripe fruit and tar aromas and flavors, medium body and finish and racy, firm tannins. Already at its peak. • $NA • **84**
Chianti Classico Vigna di Fontalle Riserva 1988 • $21 • (10/31/93) • **87**
Chianti Classico Vigna di Fontalle Riserva 1985 • $NA • (09/15/91) • **91**

MACULAN

Breganze Rosso 1991 • $11 • (09/15/92) • **72**
Breganze di Breganze Bianco 1993: Soft and simple, showing hints of pleasant pear fruit. 10,000 cases made. • $5 • (01/31/95) • **79**
Brentino Red 1990 • $12 • (09/15/92) • **79**
Brentino Red 1986 • $9 • (03/31/89) • **85**
Cabernet Fratta Breganze 1990 • $39 • (09/15/92) • **92**
Cabernet Fratta Breganze 1986 • $29 • (03/31/89) • **92**
Cabernet Sauvignon Palazzotto 1987 • $30 • (01/31/92) • **82**
Cabernet Sauvignon Palazzotto 1986 • $19 • (03/31/89) • **71**
Cabernet Sauvignon Palazzotto Breganze 1990 • $24 • (09/15/92) • **77**
Chardonnay 1992: Bright, fresh and lovely, with a pleasant grassy edge to the melon, pear and spice flavors, a lighter style that balances har-

ITALY

moniously. A pretty wine that's appealing to drink now. 4,000 cases made. • $23 • (01/31/95) • **84**

Chardonnay 1991: Leans heavily on wood, with more green oak flavor than fruit. Not too appealing. 4,000 cases made. • $23 • (01/31/95) • **75**

Dindarello 1993: Sweet without being too rich, and spicy, carrying its pear, peach, honey and light acacia aromas and flavors lightly, floating nicely out of the glass to reveal its Orange Muscat origins. 1,500 cases made. • $14 • (01/31/95) • **87**

Dindarello 1991 • $28 • (09/15/92) • **84**

Dindarello 1989 • $24 • (07/15/91) • **84**

Torcolato 1990 • $44 • (09/15/92) • **87**

Torcolato 1988 • $35 • (04/15/91) • **91**

Torcolato 1985 • $15 • (03/31/89) • **84**

Torcolato 1983 • $29 • (11/15/87) • **82**

MADONNINA, LA

Chianti Classico 1988 • $NA • (09/15/91) • **84**

MALPAGA

Chardonnay Trentino 1994: A slightly sweet fruitiness gives this round wine immediate appeal. It's soft, with notes of peach, melon and vanilla, but it lacks the acidity for the long run. Enjoy now as an apéritif. 3,000 cases made. • $10 • (06/15/96) • **83**

Pinot Grigio Trentino 1994: A mouth-filling texture and rather ripe pear flavors make this a full-bodied, well-made white wine. Can handle the Chardonnay role before or during the meal. 3,400 cases made. • $10 • (06/15/96) • **84**

MALVIRA

Roero Arneis White 1992: Quite refreshing and vital, infused with apricot and peach flavors that linger nicely on the finish. Dry, nearly austere in balance, and intriguing. 3,300 cases made. • $15 • (02/28/95) • **86**

MALVOLTI, CARPENE

Spumante Brut 1982 • $14 • (12/31/86) • **75**

MANZANO

Vigna del Bosco 1992: A triumph for a 1992. Big, burly, thick and chewy. A dark-colored, ripe and sweet wine, with complex tobacco, chestnut, cedar, smoky, blackberry flavors. Well-integrated tannins. Made from Syrah. Try after 1997. • $NA • (01/31/96) • **90**

MANZONE

Barbera d'Alba Le Gramolere 1991: Green in flavor, lean in texture, with more bell pepper and olive character than fruit. Lacks charm. • $14 • **74**

Barbera d'Alba Le Gramolere 1990 • $18 • (11/15/93) • **90**

Barolo La Gramolere 1991: Tight and austere, with a backbone of refreshing, lemony, black cherry and mineral flavors. Lovely finish and medium length. 1,333 cases made. • $28 • **82**

Barolo La Gremolare 1990: Tough and tannic, with an earthy, barnyardy cast to the aromas rescued by a waft of cherry flavor that comes through on the palate. Chunky, could develop into something fine by 2000 to 2004. • $35 • (10/31/94) • **86**

Barolo La Gramolere 1989: Dark and dense, with a supple band of black cherry, tar and anise aromas and flavors that remain focused through the burr of tannin on the finish. Drinkable now. 900 cases made. • $35 • (10/31/93) • **89**

Barolo La Gramolere 1988 • $35 • (10/31/93) • **85**

Key: SS—Spectator Selection. CS—Cellar Selection. BB—Best Buy. $NA—Price not available. (BT)—Barrel tasting. Ⓐ—Auction Price.
Dates in parentheses represent the issues in which the ratings were published.

MARAI, FOSS

Cabernet Piave 1990 • $8 • (01/31/92) • **76**

Cabernet Sauvignon Piave Nono Gío 1992: Appealing in aroma, but it's tough in texture and just modest in fruit concentration. Shows the influence of oak barrels in the spicy, vanillalike aromas and chewy texture. • $38 • (06/15/96) • **82**

Prosecco di Valdobbiadene 1986 • $7 • (12/31/88) BB • **83**

Prosecco di Valdobbiadene NV: A lively, rather fruity sparkling wine with grapefruit flavors and a slight sweetness. • $12 • (06/15/96) • **82**

Prosecco di Valdobbiadene Cartizze NV: Fresh and fruity in flavor, light and frothy in texture. A tasty, elegant bubbly. • $25 • (06/15/96) • **84**

Spumante Brut Chardonnay NV • $8 • (03/15/89) BB • **84**

MARCA, LA

Cabernet Sauvignon Piave 1993: Hearty, superripe flavors of prune and blackberry make this a robust wine to enjoy now while it's fresh. Fairly light in tannins, but full-bodied. You won't balk at the price on this Italian red, either. 18,000 cases made. • $6 • (05/31/96) BB • **83**

Chardonnay Piave 1994: Light and simple, with apple and light butter flavors, this is pleasantly crisp but lacks character and depth. 22,000 cases made. • $6 • (06/15/96) • **78**

Merlot Novello del Veneto Piave 1995: Raspberry and tutti-fruiti flavors dominate this fresh wine. Light in tannins. • $6 • (02/29/96) • **80**

Merlot Novello del Veneto Piave 1994: Round, fruity and stuffed with ripe blackberry and light earthy flavors. Slightly jammy, with soft tannins. Drinkable now. • $6 • (01/31/96) • **83**

Merlot Piave 1993: A simple, mature style of red that is smooth in texture and light in flavor. 25,000 cases made. • $6 • **78**

Pinot Grigio Veneto 1994: The refreshment value is high here, but there's not enough flavor to keep your interest for long. It's firm, clean and neutral. 25,000 cases made. • $6 • (06/15/96) • **80**

MARCARINI

Barbaresco Campo Quadro 1989: Big, tannic and firm, carrying off nice spicy, tart cherry flavors and aromas. The concentrated fruit and woody flavors linger on the finish. Try after 1996. • $NA • (10/31/94) • **85**

Barbera d'Alba Ciabot Camerano 1988 • $18 • (03/15/91) • **90**

Barolo Brunate 1991: Dry and tough, struggling to bring out some fruit. It does offer some nice mineral and wet earth notes, though it's quite diluted on the finish. 2,777 cases made. • $26 • **77**

Barolo Brunate 1990: Ripe and exotic, layering some herbal notes of sage and basil between the blasts of Port-like berry and plum fruit. A big wine, it finishes with a final whack of alcohol. Give it until 2000-2004 to settle down. • $26 • (10/31/94) • **91**

Barolo Brunate 1989: Smooth and polished, with an elegant beam of raspberry, cherry, spice and rose petal lighting up the aromas and flavors, sweet tannins swarming over the finish. Still, the fruit shines through. Best to drink from 1997. 1,800 cases made. • $25 • (10/31/93) • **91**

Barolo Brunate 1988 • $27 • (10/31/93) • **85**

Barolo Brunate 1985 • $35 • (03/31/90) • **90**

Barolo Brunate 1983 • $23 • (09/15/88) • **89**

Barolo Brunate 1982 • $18 • (09/15/88) • **90**

Barolo Brunate 1979 • $29 • (09/15/88) • **88**

Barolo Brunate 1978 • $44 • (09/15/88) • **80**

Barolo Brunate 1971 • $60 • (09/15/88) • **89**

Barolo Brunate 1964 • $100 • (09/15/88) • **96**

Barolo La Serra 1991: Light to medium body shows earthy, smoky berry notes and a slightly cheesy character. Crisp and lemony. A bit light, simple and diluted. 1,156 cases made. • $26 • **77**

Barolo La Serra 1990: Bright, focused and very distinctive, with a floral, herbal-olive edge to the raspberry and spice flavors, moderately tannic. Approachable now, but best after 1997. • $26 • (10/31/94) • **88**

Barolo La Serra 1989: Nicely articulated fruit flavors call to mind cherry and raspberry, hinting at juniper and tar on the finish. Tannins are present but in check. Maybe best after 1996. 975 cases made. • $25 • (10/31/93) • **984**

Barolo La Serra 1988 • $27 • (10/31/93) • **77**

Barolo La Serra 1983 • $17 • (09/15/88) • **87**

Barolo La Serra 1982 • $18 • (09/15/88) • **91**

Barolo La Serra 1980 • $9 • (04/16/86) • **89**

Barolo La Serra 1978 • $18 • (09/16/84) • **79**

Dolcetto d'Alba Boschi di Berri 1989 • $23 • (04/30/91) • **89**

Dolcetto d'Alba Boschi di Berri 1988 • $17 • (03/31/90) • **86**

Dolcetto d'Alba Boschi di Berri 1987 • $13 • (03/15/89) • **89**

Dolcetto d'Alba Fontanazza 1991: Rich briar and earth aromas give way to full, soft tannins. However, it lacks fruit except for a hint of blackberry on the finish. Try now. 2,355 cases made. • $12 • (07/31/95) • **84**

Dolcetto d'Alba Fontanazza 1990 • $13 • (10/31/92) • **85**

Dolcetto d'Alba Fontanazza 1989 • $13 • (04/30/91) • **84**

Dolcetto d'Alba Fontanazza 1988 • $11 • (03/31/90) • **87**

Dolcetto d'Alba Fontanazza 1987 • $9 • (03/15/89) • **78**

Dolcetto d'Alba Fontanazza 1985 • $7 • (02/15/87) • **82**

Nebbiolo delle Langhe 1988 • $10 • (03/31/90) • **84**

Nebbiolo delle Langhe Lasarin 1989 • $9 • (04/30/91) • **84**

MARCHESI DI BAROLO

Barbaresco 1990: Earthy, toasty, with a fresh, bright beam of black cherry fruit shining through it. Moderately tannic, developing nicely. 3,750 cases made. • $18 • (10/31/93) • **88**

Barbaresco 1989: Lively, juicy style, with bright, crisp raspberry and blackberry fruit and a layer or two of herb and olive. Drinkable now. 3,750 cases made. • $18 • (10/31/93) • **87**

Barbaresco Montestefano 1991: Some decent dry cherry flavors, but quite tannic and dry. Shows little that's appealing or generous. Tough and hard. 290 cases made. • $20 • (10/31/95) • **77**

Barbaresco Rio Sordo 1988 • $18 • (01/31/92) • **86**

Barbera d'Alba 1990 • $10 • (10/15/93) • **70**

Barbera d'Alba Paiagallo 1990 • $12 • (10/15/93) • **76**

Barbera del Monferrato 1985 • $5 • (09/15/87) BB • **82**

Barbera del Monferrato Le Lune 1988 • $6 • (07/15/91) • **78**

Barolo 1991: Shows good fruit and body for this vintage. Medium-bodied, with a dried cherry and tobacco character. 21,000 cases made. • $20 • **83**

Barolo 1990: Very firm in texture, with leafy, forest-floor aromas and flavors and some ripe cherry notes. Tannins clamp down on the finish. • $15 • (10/31/94) • **79**

Barolo 1989: Ripe and flavorful, almost pruny in flavor, a full-bodied wine with dense black cherry and anise notes packed into the chunky texture. A gutsy wine that could use more finesse. Maybe best after 1997. 25,000 cases made. • $18 • (10/31/93) • **86**

Barolo 1988 • $18 • (10/31/93) • **88**

Barolo Brunate 1985 • $29 • (10/15/90) • **85**

Barolo Brunate 1982 • $14 • (02/15/89) • **89**

Barolo Cannubi 1989: Very firm and chewy, tightly closed at this point, with spice and earth flavors running through the focused plum and anise notes, tannins clamping down on the finish. Has plenty of character, but it can wait until 2000 to 2005 for balance. • $30 • (10/31/94) • **91**

Barolo Cannubi 1988 • $30 • (10/31/93) • **85**

Barolo Cannubi 1985 • $29 • (10/15/90) • **88**

Barolo Castel la Volta 1987 • $20 • (01/31/92) • **89**

Barolo Coste di Rosé 1985 • $29 • (10/15/90) • **86**

Barolo Riserva 1982 • $14 • (02/15/89) • **87**

Barolo Riserva 1978 • $20 • (02/28/89) • **86**

Barolo Sarmassa 1989: Distinctively minty and spicy, chewy with fine-textured tannins and intense black cherry, anise and tobacco flavors extending into a solid finish. May be best from 1997. Better than last year. • $35 • (10/31/94) • **88**

Barolo Sarmassa 1988 • $30 • (10/31/93) • **83**

Barolo Valletta 1985 • $29 • (10/15/90) • **88**

Dolcetto d'Alba Madonna di Como 1990 • $10 • (01/31/92) • **77**

Dolcetto d'Alba Madonna di Como 1989 • $9 • (12/31/90) BB • **88**

Dolcetto d'Alba Madonna di Como 1987 • $8 • (02/15/89) • **87**

MARCHISIO

Roero Vigneti Mongalletto 1987 • $10 • (03/31/90) • **78**

MARCIALLA, VILLA

Chianti Colli Fiorentini 1986 • $6 • (10/15/89) • **79**

MAREGA

Holbar Red 1991: Thick and rich, showing ripe tomato and blackberry flavors and a lively texture that's tart, almost effervescent. Tannic, but not harsh. Drinkable now through 1997. 150 cases made. • $22 • (04/30/96) • **85**

Holbar White 1991: Fully mature, this deeply-colored, rich white features intense aromas of caramel and bergamot, adding flavors of honey, pineapple and lime and a long, floral finish. Unusual and exciting. 550 cases made. • $22 • (04/30/96) • **88**

Malvasia Istriana 1992: Perfumed and exotic, this offers an intriguing blend of acacia, hazelnut, bitter orange and coconut flavors. Light and crisp, it would be terrific as an apéritif. 250 cases made. • $15 • (04/30/96) • **85**

Pinot Grigio 1993: Smoky and herbal aromas explode from the glass. Rich, even tannic, featuring grapefruit and smoke flavors. 275 cases made. • $15 • (04/30/96) • **86**

MARENGO-MARENDA, PODERI E

Dolcetto d'Alba Le Terre Forti 1992: Full-bodied, tart and moderately tannic, with smoky, meaty flavors that seem to show lots of oak influence. Good, even if the modest fruit flavors don't quite stand up to the oak. Drink now. • $11 • **82**

Dolcetto d'Alba Le Terre Forti 1990 • $12 • (01/31/92) • **84**

MARLUNGHE

Colli Euganei Bianco 1994: Perky, light-bodied, marrying assertive earth and lemon-lime flavors that settle down and turn creamy on the finish. Drink it cold. 3,300 cases made. • $10 • (06/30/96) • **79**

Fior d'Arancio Colli Euganei 1994: Sweet, fruity, figgy and fizzy. A simple but enjoyable sparkling wine. 1,600 cases made. • $14 • (06/15/96) • **80**

Merlot Colli Euganei 1994: Fresh, grapey aromas combine with a smooth texture and ample fruit flavor for a generous, easy-drinking Merlot. 1,100 cases made. • $11 • (05/31/96) • **84**

MARRONETO, IL

Brunello di Montalcino 1988: Simple and fruity Brunello in a traditional style. Stewed and earthy aromas and flavors, light tannins and finish. Tasted twice. Drink now. • $NA • (04/30/94) • **80**

MARTINENGO, RINO

Barbera d'Asti 1991: Good if you like dried fruit and leather. Aroma dominated by cloves, matched by a solid core of dried cherry. Concentrated and in a traditional style. Mature and drinkable now. • $11 • (07/31/95) • **84**

Barbera d'Asti Bricco del Donnaiolo 1991 • $35 • (06/15/94) • **88**

MARTINI & ROSSI

Asti Spumante NV: An exuberant mousse that carries expressive raisin, dried apple and bread dough flavors. It's quite sweet, but lacks vivacity. • $11 • (10/31/95) • **80**

Brut Riserva Montelera NV • $15 • (12/31/90) • **72**

Demi-Sec NV: Apple and earthy aromas give way to sweet apple flavors on the palate, surfing on a frothy mousse. Clean, it falls in between frankly sweet and dry. • $11 • (10/31/95) • **80**

MARTINI DI CIGALA

Chianti Classico San Giusto a Rentennano 1991 • $NA • (10/31/93) • **77**
Chianti Classico San Giusto a Rentennano 1990 • $16 • (10/31/93) • **85**
Chianti Classico San Giusto a Rentennano 1987 • $9 • (03/31/90) • **74**
Chianti Classico San Giusto a Rentennano 1986 • $8 • (01/31/89) • **79**
Chianti Classico San Giusto a Rentennano 1985 • $8 • (11/30/87) • **87**
Chianti Classico San Giusto a Rentennano 1983 • $6 • (09/15/87) • **80**
Chianti Classico San Giusto a Rentennano Riserva 1988 • $23 • (09/15/92) • **84**
Chianti Classico San Giusto a Rentennano Riserva 1985 • $17 • (11/30/89) • **91**
Chianti Classico San Giusto a Rentennano Riserva 1983 • $11 • (11/15/87) • **87**
Percarlo San Giusto a Rentennano 1990: A big, almost abrasive wine with masses of fruit and tannins. Somewhat dry on the finish from lots of wood. Time will tell whether it's outstanding. Made from Sangiovese. 450 cases made. • $37 • (10/31/93) • **87**
Percarlo San Giusto a Rentannano 1989 • $21 • (10/31/93) • **81**
Percarlo San Giusto a Rentennano 1986 • $24 • (11/30/89) • **88**
Percarlo San Giusto a Rentennano 1985 • $25 • (02/15/89) • **92**
Percarlo San Giusto a Rentennano 1983 • $13 • (09/15/87) • **77**
Vin Santo San Giusto a Rentennano 1982 • $18 • (12/31/88) • **96**
Vin Santo San Giusto a Rentennano 1981 • $25 • (12/31/87) • **89**

MARTINI, CONTI

Moscato di Mezzocorona 1991 • $23 • (05/31/93) • **87**

MASCARELLO, BARTOLO

Barbera d'Alba 1993: Grapey and stemmy raisin and tobacco character. A bit coarse but some lovely fruit. • $10 • **81**
Barolo 1991: Big for the vintage. A bit rustic, showing smoky, berry and gamy character, medium to full body, slightly drying tannins and rough finish. • $45 • **83**
Barolo 1989: Tough and bitterly tannic, like biting into a handful of walnut scraps, with wet earth and menthol overtones to the modest plum and prune fruit that's struggling to be heard over the noise. May be better in 2000. Tasted twice. • $NA • (10/31/94) • **76**
Barolo 1988 • $35 • (10/31/93) • **87**
Barolo 1983 • $27 • (05/31/88) • **88**
Dolcetto d'Alba 1993: Ripe fruit on the nose and palate supplements black cherry and licorice character, but it's a little dull on the finish. Drink now. • $10 • **81**

MASCARELLO & FIGLIO, GIUSEPPE

Barbaresco Marcarini 1988 • $32 • (10/31/93) • **94**
Barbaresco Marcarini 1985 • $30 • (08/31/89) • **85**
Barbera d'Alba Fasana 1987 • $10 • (03/15/91) • **80**
Barbera d'Alba Fasana 1985 • $9 • (11/30/87) • **85**
Barbera d'Alba Superiore Ginestra 1987 • $11 • (03/15/91) • **85**
Barbera d'Alba Superiore Santo Stefano di Perno 1987 • $13 • (09/15/90) • **83**
Barolo 1982 • $28 • (06/30/87) • **81**
Barolo 1978 • $19 • (09/16/84) • **91**
Barolo Belvedere 1985 • $42 • (06/15/90) CS • **93**
Barolo Bricco 1988 • $38 • (10/31/93) • **84**
Barolo Dardi 1982 • $18 • (09/15/87) • **87**
Barolo Monprivato 1990: An odd wine that smells of dried cherry but also like nail polish remover. Fruit masked by tannins and acidity. Dry finish. Tasted twice, with consistent notes. • $50 • **78**
Barolo Monprivato 1989: Light and lean in texture, with a walnut edge to the thread of raspberry fruit that runs through it, finishing fresh and lively. The tannins get in the way a bit, but the flavors remain appealing. Drinkable now. 800 cases made. • $42 • (10/31/93) • **85**
Barolo Monprivato 1988 • $42 • (10/31/93) • **82**
Barolo Monprivato 1986 • $47 • (07/15/91) • **88**
Barolo Monprivato 1985 • $53 • (06/15/90) • **86**
Barolo Monprivato 1983 • $28 • (09/15/88) • **86**
Barolo Monprivato 1982 • $29 • (09/15/88) • **89**
Barolo Monprivato 1981 • $23 • (09/15/88) • **84**
Barolo Monprivato 1980 • $23 • (09/15/88) • **76**
Barolo Monprivato 1979 • $28 • (09/15/88) • **83**
Barolo Monprivato 1978 • $42 • (09/15/88) • **86**
Barolo Monprivato 1974 • $90 • (09/15/88) • **91**
Barolo Monprivato 1971 • $73 • (09/15/88) • **81**
Barolo Monprivato 1970 • $60 • (09/15/88) • **80**
Barolo Monprivato Falletto 1983 • $23 • (07/31/89) • **80**
Barolo Santo Stefano di Perno 1985 • $35 • (10/15/90) • **94**
Barolo Villero 1983 • $17 • (10/15/88) • **77**
Dolcetto d'Alba Bricco 1993: Very colorful, dark ruby tones, but it adds an odd salami note atop the nice red berry flavors. Not for everyone. • $12 • **79**
Dolcetto d'Alba Bricco Falletto 1987 • $9 • (03/15/89) • **88**
Dolcetto d'Alba Bricco Ravera 1988 • $10 • (09/15/90) • **82**
Dolcetto d'Alba Gagliassi 1989 • $13 • (07/15/91) • **85**
Dolcetto d'Alba Gagliassi 1987 • $10 • (03/31/90) • **80**
Dolcetto d'Alba Gagliassi Monforte 1987 • $9 • (03/15/89) • **82**
Dolcetto d'Alba Grignolino del Monferrato Casalese Besso 1988 • $9 • (01/31/90) • **75**
Nebbiolo d'Alba San Rocco 1988 • $16 • (07/31/92) • **82**
Nebbiolo d'Alba San Rocco 1986 • $15 • (09/15/90) • **85**
Venora 1985 • $7 • (12/31/87) • **80**

MASCIARELLI

Montepulciano d'Abruzzo 1993: Fresh, lively and packed with fruit flavor. A bargain red from Italy that shows deep color, lots of cherry and berry notes, firm acidity and moderate tannins. 40,000 cases made. • $6 • (02/29/96) BB • **85**
Montepulciano d'Abruzzo 1992: Has loads of blackberry and blueberry fruit flavors, accented by nice earthy and meaty notes. It tastes chewy, dense and fairly well concentrated. A great bargain. 40,000 cases made. • $6 • (03/31/95) • **86**
Montepulciano d'Abruzzo Villa Gemma Riserva 1990: 1,000 cases made. • $20 • **79**

MASI

Amarone della Valpolicella Classico 1991: Very robust, flavorful and tannic, as sweet notes of caramel and honey accent the ripe, grapey, raisiny tones. • $28 • (04/30/96) • **85**
Amarone della Valpolicella Classico 1990: Ripe caramel aromas and flavors add to the complexity. This has better balance and more length than the 1991. • $25 • (05/31/96) • **86**
Amarone della Valpolicella Classico 1988: There's a hint of oxidation on the otherwise ripe fruit aromas, followed by flavors of prunes and dried cherries. Solid, but one-dimensional now. • $36 • (05/31/96) • **81**
Amarone della Valpolicella Classico Campolongo di Torbe 1988: Smoky, gamy, peppery aromas and flavors make this an assertive, if not funky, bottle of Amarone. Tannic, full-bodied, seemingly dry. Call it an adventure in taste. 875 cases made. • $53 • (04/30/96) • **84**
Amarone della Valpolicella Classico Mazzano 1988: The nose is a bit dull, offering pruny and woodsy notes. It's big yet clumsy, and the dried tomato and brown sugar flavors lack focus. • $54 • (05/31/96) • **84**
Amarone della Valpolicella Classico Serego Alighieri Vaio Armaron 1988: Very fragrant aromas of dried roses and cherries lead to a powerful, complex and flavorful young Amarone that's balanced and harmonious. Although delicious now for its exuberant fruit, it has another 20 years of development ahead. • $55 • (05/31/96) • **90**
Bardolino 1993: Very dry, lean-textured and peppery in flavor. It's thin, but lively and drinkable. • $15 • (04/30/96) • **78**
Bardolino Classico 1985 • $5 • (05/31/88) • **77**
Bardolino Classico 1984 • $5 • (05/15/87) BB • **80**
Bardolino Classico Superiore 1992 • $8 • (10/31/94) • **83**

Key: SS—Spectator Selection. CS—Cellar Selection. BB—Best Buy. $NA—Price not available. (BT)—Barrel tasting. Ⓐ—Auction Price.
Dates in parentheses represent the issues in which the ratings were published.

Bardolino Classico Superiore 1990 • $8 • (09/15/92) • **78**
Bardolino Classico Superiore 1988 • $9 • (05/15/91) BB • **82**
Bardolino Classico Superiore La Vegrona 1990: Mature, spicy aromas and rustic flavors characterize this lean, dry Bardolino. • $15 • (04/30/96) • **79**
Campo Fiorin 1988 • $15 • (09/15/92) • **79**
Campo Fiorin 1985 • $12 • (09/15/90) • **77**
Campo Fiorin 1983 • $7 • (05/15/89) BB • **81**
Campo Fiorin 1981 • $8 • (04/15/88) BB • **88**
Campo Fiorin Ripasso 1991: A flavorful, full-bodied, brooding style of red with ripe fruit accented by earth and mineral notes, a firm, tannic texture and an astringent finish. A bit tough, but we recommend drinking it now while the fruit flavor is good. • $14 • (05/31/96) • **84**
Campofiorin Ripasso 1990: Mature now, this offers flavors of coffee, earth, raisin and bitter herb. It's a bit murky, but soft and fairly rich. • $15 • (05/15/95) • **78**
Recioto della Valpolicella Amarone Campolongo 1983 • $26 • (04/15/88) • **85**
Recioto della Valpolicella Amarone Classico 1989 • $28 • (11/15/94) • **85**
Recioto della Valpolicella Amarone Classico 1988 • $28 • (09/15/92) • **81**
Recioto della Valpolicella Amarone Classico 1981 • $15 • (10/31/88) • **84**
Recioto della Valpolicella Amarone Classico Mazzano 1986 • $58 • (05/31/96) • **88**
Recioto della Valpolicella Amarone Classico Mazzano 1985 • $66 • (05/31/96) • **90**
Recioto della Valpolicella Amarone Classico Mazzano 1983 • $70 • (05/31/96) • **89**
Recioto della Valpolicella Amarone Classico Mazzano 1979 • $91 • (05/31/96) • **88**
Recioto della Valpolicella Amarone Classico Mazzano 1977 • $99 • (05/31/96) • **89**
Recioto della Valpolicella Amarone Classico Mazzano 1976 • $99 • (05/31/96) • **87**
Recioto della Valpolicella Amarone Classico Mazzano 1974 • $133 • (05/31/96) • **89**
Recioto della Valpolicella Amarone Classico Mazzano 1971 • $NA • (05/31/96) • **84**
Recioto della Valpolicella Amarone Classico Mazzano 1969 • $NA • (05/31/96) • **91**
Recioto della Valpolicella Amarone Classico Mazzano 1964 • $290 • (05/31/96) • **92**
Recioto della Valpolicella Amarone Classico Mazzano 1958 • $NA • (05/31/96) • **92**
Recioto della Valpolicella Amarone Classico Mazzano 1941 • $NA • (05/31/96) • **88**
Recioto della Valpolicella Amarone Mazzano 1980 • $26 • (10/31/88) • **88**
Recioto della Valpolicella Classico 1991 • $28 • (04/30/96) • **80**
Serégo Alighieri Bianco 1993: 6,000 cases made. • $14 • **55**
Soave Classico Col Baraca 1991 • $14 • (09/15/92) • **80**
Soave Classico Superiore 1994: Herbal and crisp, with oniony notes on the finish. A bit disjointed and awkward. • $9 • (06/15/96) • **79**
Soave Classico Superiore 1993 • $8 • (10/31/94) • **83**
Soave Classico Superiore 1991 • $8 • (09/15/92) BB • **84**
Toar 1992: An exotic red boasting oodles of flavor wrapped in a firm structure of acidity and moderate tannins. Fruit flavors are concentrated, accented by herb, pepper and mineral, finishing long. Drinkable now through 1998. 4,000 cases made. • $15 • (04/30/96) • **89**
Toar 1991: Lush fruit and soft tannins give this ripe wine appeal. It has taken on cedar and tobacco notes with maturity, but the berry and plum flavors are still fresh. At its peak now, but will hold. • $20 • (05/31/95) • **86**
Valpolicella 1993: This easy-drinking red is light and fresh, with little tannin and plenty of cherry flavor accented by licorice and mint. It's vivid yet still light on its feet. • $14 • (12/15/95) • **84**
Valpolicella Classico Superiore 1992 • $8 • (11/15/94) • **80**
Valpolicella Classico Superiore 1991 • $8 • (10/15/94) BB • **86**
Valpolicella Classico Superiore 1989 • $8 • (09/15/92) • **82**
Valpolicella Classico Superiore 1987 • $7 • (12/31/90) • **78**
Valpolicella Classico Superiore 1985 • $5 • (05/31/88) • **76**
Valpolicella Classico Superiore Serego Alighieri 1991: Nicely mature, spicy-tasting, featuring mellow aromas and rather lean fruit flavors. Good, solid quality. • $14 • (04/30/96) • **82**
Valpolicella Classico Superiore Serego Alighieri 1988 • $18 • (09/15/92) • **82**

MASI, RENZO

Chianti Paolo Masi 1991 • $6 • (06/15/93) • **79**
Chianti Rufina 1993 • $6 • (10/31/94) BB • **84**
Chianti Rufina Fattoria di Basciano 1991 • $9 • (10/31/93) • **78**
Chianti Rufina Fattoria di Basciano 1990 • $7 • (06/15/93) • **82**
Chianti Rufina Fattoria di Basciano 1990 • $8 • (10/31/93) • **88**

MASO CANTANGHEL

Pinot Nero Altesino Riserva 1988 • $33 • (02/15/91) • **84**

MASO POLI

Chardonnay 1991 • $12 • (05/31/93) • **86**

MASSA, LA

Chianti Classico 1993: Perfumed and elegant, with mineral, berry, cherry aromas and flavors. Medium to light body, with fresh tannins and finish. • $14 • **82**
Chianti Classico 1992: Pretty, crisp, medium-bodied dried cherry, smoke and berry flavors lead to a long finish. 1,450 cases made. • $12 • **84**
Chianti Classico 1990 • $NA • (10/31/93) • **89**
Chianti Classico Giorgio Primo 1992: Ripe yet crisp, a wine with good fruit concentration; plenty of well-defined cassis, violet, boysenberry and plum flavors. Well-integrated tannins. Fresh finish. Drinkable now. • $57 • **88**
Chianti Classico Riserva 1990: Bursting with fruit and loads of focused raspberry and berry aromas and flavors. Full-bodied yet very fine, resulting in a long, sumptuous finish. Drinkable now. 600 cases made. • $17 • **91**

MASSARA, FATTORIA

Barbera d'Alba 1990 • $12 • (12/15/92) • **86**
Barbera d'Alba 1987 • $7 • (09/15/90) • **74**
Barolo 1985 • $20 • (06/15/90) • **80**
Dolcetto d'Alba 1990 • $9 • (01/31/92) • **86**

MASSE DI GREVE, LE

Chianti Classico 1990 • $11 • (04/13/94) • **89**
Chianti Classico 1988 • $13 • (04/30/91) • **87**
Chianti Classico 1985 • $12 • (07/15/89) • **92**
Chianti Classico Riserva 1988 • $20 • (09/15/92) • **90**
Chianti Classico Riserva 1985 • $20 • (09/15/91) • **89**

MASSOLINO

Barbera d'Alba 1993: Lovely ripe cherry and violet character, medium body, crisp acidity and long, flavorful finish. • $NA • **84**
Barolo 1990: Medium concentration and a slight herbaceous note. Tastes a bit metallic, and the finish is tough. • $30 • **77**
Barolo Parafeda 1990: Polished and accessible, this elegant Barolo offers plenty of nice black cherry and floral notes. Seems to dry a bit on the finish. • $39 • **83**
Barolo Vigna Margheria 1990: Fairly generous and smooth, but it clamps down on the palate, turning very dry and almost metallic. Too bad because it starts out well. • $37 • **78**
Barolo Vigna Rionda 1990: Lovely and rich, with berry and milk chocolate aromas and flavors. Medium body, ripe, round tannins and a succulent finish. Drinkable now. • $40 • **85**
Dolcetto d'Alba Vigneto Barilot 1993: Lots of expressive and aromatic red berry flavor and a slight leesy, cheesy, smoked salami character. • $NA • **81**

MASTROBERARDINO

Avellanio 1992 • $10 • (07/31/94) • **77**
Avellanio 1991 • $12 • (03/31/93) • **83**
Avellanio 1989 • $11 • (07/15/91) • **87**
Greco di Tufo Vignadangelo 1991 • $19 • (03/31/93) • **82**
Greco di Tufo White 1991 • $19 • (03/31/93) • **83**
Lacryma Christi del Vesuvio 1991 • $15 • (07/31/93) • **84**
Lacryma Christi del Vesuvio 1989 • $14 • (07/15/91) • **89**
Mastro Rosso 1994: The cherry, raspberry aromas and flavors are attractive in this red, but they turn tart and astringent on the finish. • $10 • (01/31/96) • **79**
Plinius 1991 • $19 • (03/31/93) • **85**
Radici di Lapio Fiano di Avellino White 1992: Toasty, mature aromas add to an exotic character that is overlaid with smokiness. Ripe and rich, with tropical fruit flavors. Intriguing. 1,500 cases made. • $14 • (03/31/95) • **85**
Radici di Lapio Fiano di Avellino White 1991 • $33 • (03/31/93) • **85**
Radici Taurasi 1989: Mature aromas of cassis, cedar and tobacco predominate, followed by a rich, full-bodied palate. Has a sense of style, but it's austere and calls for food. • $20 • (01/31/96) • **87**
Radici Taurasi 1988 • $21 • (07/31/94) • **88**
Taurasi 1987 • $19 • (09/15/92) • **80**
Taurasi 1986 • $18 • (07/15/91) • **87**
Taurasi 1982 • $13 • (07/15/87) • **75**
Taurasi Riserva 1987 • $18 • (07/31/94) • **78**
Taurasi Riserva 1985 • $22 • (06/30/91) • **84**
Taurasi Riserva 1981 • $21 • (02/15/89) • **78**
Taurasi Riserva 1980 • $15 • (09/15/89) • **75**
Taurasi Riserva 1977 • $51 • (10/16/84) CS • **92**

MASTROJANNI

Brunello di Montalcino 1990: Big, ripe and full-bodied, this tannic monster still manages to show a lot of class. Offers tons of earth, red berry and black cherry notes. It's like a volcano waiting to erupt, so hold until at least 1998. • $27 • **94**
Brunello di Montalcino 1988: A rich and decadent style, with game, berry and wild aromas and flavors. Full-bodied with loads of fine tannins. Better after 1997. • $30 • (04/30/94) • **90**
Brunello di Montalcino 1982 • $17 • (06/15/90) • **87**
Brunello di Montalcino 1979 • $17 • (09/15/86) • **72**
Brunello di Montalcino Riserva 1988: A beautifully crafted Brunello that glides over your palate. Very fruity and fine, with silky tannins and a long, complete finish. Everything is there in the right proportions. Drinkable now. • $25 • (10/31/94) • **91**
Rosso di Montalcino 1991: There is maturity here and flavors of licorice and leather rather than fruit. A rustic style for drinking now. • $13 • (08/31/95) • **84**
Rosso di Montalcino 1987 • $10 • (07/15/91) • **79**

MATILDE, VILLA

Falerno Red 1983 • $5 • (05/15/87) • **76**

MAURO, PAOLA DI

Colle Picchioni 1986 • $15 • (03/31/90) • **80**
Vigna del Vassalle 1986 • $12 • (03/31/90) • **83**

MAZZI

Brurello di Montalcino Il Greppone Mazzi Riserva 1987 • $38 • (11/30/93) • **81**
Valpolicella Colle Crosetta 1988 • $17 • (09/15/92) • **82**
Valpolicella Poiega 1988 • $20 • (09/15/92) • **82**

Key: SS—Spectator Selection. CS—Cellar Selection. BB—Best Buy. $NA—Price not available. (BT)—Barrel tasting. Ⓐ—Auction Price.
Dates in parentheses represent the issues in which the ratings were published.

Valpolicella Poiega 1986 • $20 • (09/15/92) • **86**
Valpolicella Superiore 1988 • $12 • (09/15/92) • **79**

MAZZOLINO, TENUTA

Barbera Oltrepò Pavese 1990 • $11 • (04/30/92) • **82**
Barbera Oltrepò Pavese 1989 • $10 • (04/15/91) • **82**
Noir 1987 • $45 • (09/30/91) • **86**
Oltrepò Pavese 1990 • $14 • (01/31/92) • **77**

MEDICI ERMETE

Lambrusco Reggiano Concerto 1994: Beaujolais with bubbles. Deep ruby color and bright grapey flavors, with a pleasant hint of bitterness and dry finish. Refreshing for a summer afternoon. • $14 • (12/15/95) • **81**

MELINI

Chianti Borghi d'Elsa 1992: Tastes stale and earthy, offering only very modest cherry flavors. It seems rich, but not in flavor. • $13 • (07/31/95) • **74**
Chianti Borghi d'Elsa 1990 • $7 • (07/31/92) BB • **84**
Chianti Borghi d'Elsa 1989 • $6 • (10/31/91) • **81**
Chianti Classico 1987 • $7 • (04/30/90) • **80**
Chianti Classico 1986 • $6 • (10/31/88) BB • **83**
Chianti Classico 1985 • $5 • (07/31/88) BB • **82**
Chianti Classico Isassi 1990 • $10 • (10/31/93) • **83**
Chianti Classico Isassi 1989 • $9 • (09/15/92) • **81**
Chianti Classico Isassi 1988 • $8 • (09/15/91) • **89**
Chianti Classico Riserva Laborel 1990: A tart, aggressive Chianti, with cranberry and red cherry flavors and a texture that puckers the mouth. • $11 • (02/28/95) • **78**
Chianti Classico Riserva Laborel 1987 • $11 • (12/15/92) • **85**
Chianti Classico Riserva Laborel 1986 • $10 • (10/31/91) • **83**
Chianti Classico Riserva La Selvanella 1988 • $14 • (10/31/93) • **85**
Chianti Classico Riserva La Selvanella 1987 • $13 • (09/15/92) • **83**
Chianti Classico Riserva La Selvanella 1985 • $7 • (09/15/91) BB • **87**
Chianti Classico Riserva La Selvanella 1982 • $6 • (06/30/88) BB • **85**
Chianti Classico Vigneti La Selvanella 1990: Old-style red offering chestnut, berry and cherry aromas and flavors, medium body and soft tannins. Drinkable now. • $13 • **79**
Coltri Vigna 1 1986 • $20 • (12/15/92) • **85**
Coltri Vigna 2 1986 • $20 • (12/15/92) • **83**
Coltri Vigneto, Vineyard 1 Red 1990: Tannic, tightly wound, with tart fruit flavors and spicy, earthy accents. It's austere because of the tannins and sharp acidity. Tasty, but won't appeal to everybody. 1,250 cases made. • $20 • (12/31/95) • **85**
Vigneto Coltri, Vineyard 1 Red 1988 • $19 • (11/30/94) • **86**
Vigneto Coltri, Vineyard 2 Red 1990: Rich and enticing, with an exotic, spicy aroma, loads of fruit flavor and a smooth, firm texture. Shows a lot of oak influence in its toasty, herbal, chocolaty accents, but there are crisp cherry and berry flavors to flesh it all out. Has a great, lingering finish, too. Drinkable now through about 1998. 1,250 cases made. • $20 • (12/31/95) • **90**
Vigneto Coltri, Vineyard 2 Red 1988 • $19 • (11/30/94) • **90**
Vino Nobile di Montepulciano 1985 • $10 • (04/15/90) • **82**
Vino Nobile di Montepulciano Riserva 1983 • $7 • (06/30/88) • **74**

MEZZACORONA, CANTINE

Merlot Trentino 1993: A rich but rustic style of wine with earthy, spicy flavors, firm tannins and a short finish. • $8 • (06/15/96) • **81**
Merlot Trentino 1991 • $8 • (04/30/94) • **82**
Merlot Trentino 1990 • $8 • (09/15/92) • **81**
Pinot Grigio Trentino 1995: Bright, fresh and lively, if light and rather watery in flavor. • $8 • (06/15/96) • **82**
Pinot Grigio Trentino 1992 • $8 • (04/30/94) • **81**
Pinot Grigio Trentino Vigneto Zablani 1994: A satisfying and fruity Pinot Grigio in an Alsace style that's fresh and not too heavy; its floral and pear flavors linger on the finish. • $15 • (06/15/96) • **85**

Pinot Grigio Trentino Vigneto Zablani 1993: Lively acidity and clean banana and melon flavors make this refreshing and straightforward. Easy to enjoy. • $17 • **83**

Spumante Brut Rotari Riserva Trento 1991: A smooth and creamy-textured sparkler with light, clean, fruity flavors. Fresh and charming. • $13 • (06/15/96) • **85**

Teroldego Rotaliano Vigneto Sottodossi 1993: Here is a robust, tannic, rather tart red with lots of fruit flavor accented by peppery, earthy notes. Rough-edged and flavorful. • $15 • (06/15/96) BB • **83**

Teroldego Rotaliano Vigneto Sottodossi 1992: Almost like a Beaujolais. It's fresh, fruity, jammy in flavor, with soft tannins and a lush texture. Drink now. • $17 • (02/28/95) • **84**

Trentino Brut Rotari Riserva 1990: A well-rounded Italian bubbly that has ripe fruit and honey character, graced with a buttery note. Fairly complex and nicely balanced, with an appealing mix of apple and fig flavors. 20,000 cases made. • $10 BB • **85**

MIONETTO

Prosecco di Valdobbiadene NV: Very crisp sparkler with frothy, pinpoint bubbles, this is clean and extremely dry but lacks fruit; there are hints of citrus and earth. It would make a good mimosa. 5,000 cases made. • $11 • (10/31/95) • **82**

MIRAFIORE

Barbera d'Alba 1987 • $12 • (04/15/91) • **83**

MOCALI

Brunello di Montalcino 1990: Serious red featuring a solid backbone of tannins, accompanied by tobacco, black cherry and blackberry flavors. Stays fresh. Long, tannic finish. Delicious now, better in 1998. • $NA • **88**

MOCCAGATTA

Barbaresco Bric Balin 1992: Good concentration for the vintage, offering berry, mint and cherry character, medium body, fine tannins and silky finish. Slightly dry. Drinkable now. 250 cases made. • $28 • **83**

Barbaresco Bric Balin 1991: Smooth and elegant, a graceful red that merges its violet, currant and raspberry flavors with the sweet spiciness of new oak, finishing fresh and appealing. Approachable now, may be best around 1997. • $28 • (10/31/94) • **87**

Barbaresco Bric Balin 1990: Very ripe and concentrated, still very tannic but it plays out its blackberry, black cherry and rose petal aromas and flavors with finesse and elegance. Flavors keep humming on the finish. 212 cases made. • $31 • (10/31/93) • **93**

Barbaresco Bric Balin 1989 • $28 • (10/31/94) • **83**
Barbaresco Bric Balin 1988 • $28 • (10/31/93) • **89**
Barbaresco Bric Balin 1987 • $28 • (07/15/91) • **89**
Barbaresco Bric Basarin 1988 • $24 • (10/31/94) • **74**

Barbaresco Vigneto Basarin 1992: Some decent red berry flavor provides a modest taste of Barbaresco, but it's short, somewhat diluted and slightly drying on the finish. 200 cases made. • $26 • **79**

Barbaresco Vigneto Basarin 1991: A chewy red with a decent level of blackberry and currant flavor, finishing smoother than it starts. Maybe best from 1997. Tasted twice. • $24 • (10/31/94) • **85**

Barbaresco Vigneto Basarin 1990: Crisp and lively, with sharply focused berry flavors that persist on a long finish, not too tannic, but juicy with fresh acidity. 500 cases made. • $26 • (10/31/93) • **90**

Barbaresco Vigneto Basarin 1989 • $25 • (10/31/93) • **82**
Barbaresco Vigneto Basarin 1988 • $20 • (10/31/93) • **55**
Barbaresco Vigneto Basarin 1987 • $23 • (07/15/91) • **86**

Barbaresco Vigneto Cole 1992: Pretty rose petal and berry aromas. Medium-bodied, sporting firm tannins and a light finish. Somewhat diluted. Drink now. • $27 • **82**

Barbaresco Vigneto Cole 1991: Light and chewy with tannin, a modest level of cranberry and currant flavor sneaking in on the palate. A bit short on intensity, but appealing to drink through 1997. • $26 • (10/31/94) • **83**

Barbaresco Vigneto Cole 1990: Firm and focused, with a solid core of blackberry and black cherry fruit at the core and plenty of anise and tar overtones, finishing with muscle and a thwack of tannin. 250 cases made. • $33 • (10/31/93) • **88**

Barbaresco Vigneto Cole 1989: A pretty wine with smooth texture and well-integrated tannins, offering appealing black cherry and slightly minty edge to the smoke overtones. Has the concentration to improve through 1997. 240 cases made. • $27 • (10/31/93) • **89**

Barbaresco Vigneto Cole 1988 • $25 • (10/31/93) • **78**
Barbera Vigneto Basarin 1990 • $25 • (11/15/93) • **84**
Barbera d'Alba 1991 • $12 • (11/15/93) • **81**
Barbera d'Alba 1989 • $14 • (03/15/91) • **89**
Barbera d'Alba Vigneto Basarin 1991 • $NA • (10/31/94) • **80**
Dolcetto d'Alba Vigneto Buschet 1991 • $14 • (03/31/93) • **82**

MOLINO, MAURO

Acanzio 1989 • $15 • (01/31/92) • **85**
Barolo Vigna Conca 1986 • $29 • (02/28/91) • **87**
Barolo Vigna Conca 1985 • $25 • (03/31/90) • **82**
Dolcetto d'Alba 1989 • $14 • (02/28/91) • **87**
Dolcetto d'Alba 1988 • $12 • (03/31/90) • **82**
Nebbiolo delle Langhe 1989 • $12 • (07/31/92) • **83**
Nebbiolo delle Langhe 1988 • $12 • (03/31/90) • **84**
Pinotu 1989 • $20 • (08/31/91) • **84**

MONACESCA, FATTORIA LA

Verdicchio di Matelica 1992: Ripe and round, with almond and mineral flavors that add a nice complexity to this wine. The fairly vivid flavors linger on the finish. 4,000 cases made. • $13 • (03/31/95) • **85**

MONFORTESI, COLLI

Barolo 1982 • $15 • (04/30/87) SS • **92**

MONSANTO, CASTELLO DI

Chardonnay Fabrizio Bianchi 1993: Simple pine and tutti-frutti flavors, along with a tart, lean texture. Sharp and metallic in character. • $16 • (02/29/96) • **76**

Chianti Classico 1990 • $NA • (10/31/93) • **86**

Chianti Classico Riserva 1991: Has cherry and cedarlike flavors and aromas. A bit dry and astringent on the finish, but still appealing. Fully mature and drinkable now. • $NA • (10/31/95) • **82**

Chianti Classico Riserva 1988 • $23 Ⓐ • (09/15/92) • **86**
Chianti Classico Riserva 1987 • $16 • (12/15/92) • **68**
Chianti Classico Riserva 1986 • $15 • (04/15/91) • **85**
Chianti Classico Riserva 1985 • $10 • (11/30/89) • **89**
Chianti Classico Riserva 1982 • $10 • (02/15/88) • **72**
Chianti Classico Riserva 1981 • $10 • (12/15/87) • **67**
Chianti Classico Riserva 1979 • $9 • (11/01/84) • **83**
Chianti Classico Riserva Il Poggio Vineyard 1985 • $25 • (03/31/90) • **80**
Chianti Classico Riserva Il Poggio Vineyard 1983 • $23 • (11/30/89) • **86**
Chianti Classico Riserva Il Poggio Vineyard 1982 • $17 • (11/30/89) • **93**
Chianti Classico Riserva Il Poggio Vineyard 1981 • $19 • (11/30/89) • **82**
Chianti Classico Riserva Il Poggio Vineyard 1979 • $16 • (09/15/87) • **93**
Fabrizio Bianchi Vigneto Scanni 1988 • $30 • (10/31/93) • **85**
Fabrizio Bianchi Vigneto Scanni 1985 • $33 • (12/15/92) • **74**

Nemo 1990: Lovely balance of fruit and new wood. Aromas of violets, berries and toasted oak follow through on the palate. Medium body and fine tannins. Drink now or hold for a couple of years. • $29 • **88**

Nemo 1988 • $30 • (09/15/91) • **91**
Nemo 1986 • $33 • (12/15/92) • **84**
Nemo 1983 • $28 • (09/15/90) • **87**

Tinscvil 1990: Soft, supple, vibrant aromas of red berries and tanned leather, medium body and light, fruity finish. 75 percent Sangioveto and 25 percent Cabernet Sauvignon. Drinkable now. 1,000 cases made. • $21 • **81**

Tinscvil 1988 • $22 • (03/31/93) • **71**
Tinscvil 1986 • $32 • (01/31/93) • **83**
Tinscvil 1985 • $22 • (09/15/90) • **88**

MONSORDO

La Bernardina 1991: A blockbuster of a red wine, lavishly oaked and massively tannic, extremely deep in color and fairly fruity, too. Tastes like vanilla, chocolate, blackberry and raspberry with tarry, peppery accents and a lush, oak-aged texture. • $26 • (02/28/95) • **93**

MONTAGLIARI, FATTORIA DI

Chianti Classico La Quercia 1990 • $NA • (09/15/92) • **86**
Chianti Classico Riserva 1985 • $NA • (09/15/91) • **83**

MONTE ANTICO

Red 1991: A distinctive, deeply flavorful red that shows cranberry and dried cherry character, with tight acidity and very firm tannins. Hints of spice and oak develop as you sip. Should open up with time. 35,000 cases made. • $9 • (12/31/95) • **89**
Red 1990: A bit heavy and plodding, showing plum and stewed fruit flavors and aromas. Still tannic on the finish. Leaves an unfocused impression. 30,000 cases made. • $9 • (07/31/95) • **80**
Red 1985 • $6 • (06/30/88) • **85**
Red 1982 • $3 • (04/01/86) BB • **82**

MONTE BERNARDI

Chianti Classico 1993: The toasted oak and smoke flavors dominate the fruit. It may come around but time will tell. Try now. • $NA • **80**

MONTE ROSSA

Franciacorta Brut Sparkling NV • $NA • (12/31/86) • **90**
Franciacorta Non Docato Sparkling NV • $NA • (12/31/86) • **92**

ITALY

MONTE VERTINE

1983 • $20 • (02/15/87) • **83**
Il Novantuno di Sergio Manetti 1991: Very ripe plum flavor verging on prune, with sage and herb character. A massive Sangiovese supplying loads of fruit and tannins. Perhaps a little overdone. Better after 1997. • $NA • **89**
Il Sodaccio 1990: Perhaps not up to Monte Vertine's reputation, but delicious all the same. Delicate, light style of wine with orange peel and plum character, medium body, crisp acidity and a light finish. Drinkable now. 1,000 cases made. • $32 • (10/31/93) • **83**
Il Sodaccio 1988 • $35 • (09/15/91) • **91**
Il Sodaccio 1987 • $32 • (01/31/91) • **87**
Il Sodaccio 1986 • $30 • (09/30/89) • **90**
Il Sodaccio 1985 • $25 • (03/15/89) • **91**
Il Sodaccio 1983 • $20 • (02/15/87) • **93**
Le Pergole Torte 1992: Perhaps not up to Pergole Torte's usual outstanding quality but nevertheless a pretty wine, with wild berry and light tobacco character. Medium-bodied with medium-fine tannins and a fresh finish. Tasted twice, with consistent notes. • $46 • **86**
Le Pergole Torte 1990: Incredibly fresh and exotic with tobacco, chocolate and blackberry aromas and flavors, full body, velvety tannins and long, flavorful finish. Made from Sangioveto. Drinkable now. 900 cases made. • $45 • (10/31/93) • **91**
Le Pergole Torte 1988 • $45 • (11/15/93) • **93**
Le Pergole Torte 1987 • $45 • (11/15/93) • **86**
Le Pergole Torte 1986 • $45 • (11/15/93) • **86**
Le Pergole Torte 1985 • $50 • (11/15/93) • **91**
Le Pergole Torte 1983 • $50 • (11/15/93) • **86**
Le Pergole Torte 1982 • $17 • (07/16/86) • **90**
Le Pergole Torte 1981 • $12 • (07/16/85) • **87**

Key: SS—Spectator Selection. CS—Cellar Selection. BB—Best Buy. $NA—Price not available. (BT)—Barrel tasting. (A)—Auction Price.
Dates in parentheses represent the issues in which the ratings were published.

Le Pergole Torte Riserva 1990: This racy wine is full of finesse, with gorgeous aromas of raspberry, cedar and chocolate which follow through on the palate. Full body and tannins are wonderfully integrated. Try in 1998. 200 cases made. • $58 • (10/31/93) • **92**
Montevertine 1991: Elegant, delicate and balanced with fresh berry and strawberry flavors, silky tannins and a long finish. Drinkable now. 1,000 cases made. • $23 • **85**
Riserva 1990: A pretty early-drinking wine. Elegant and balanced with soft, supple texture and lovely, ripe raspberry, cherry and vanilla flavors. Made from Sangioveto and Canaiolo. Drinkable now. 1,200 cases made. • $30 • (10/31/93) • **86**
Riserva 1988 • $30 • (09/15/91) • **90**
Riserva 1987 • $30 • (03/15/91) • **91**
Riserva 1986 • $26 • (09/30/89) • **86**
Riserva 1982 • $18 • (02/15/87) • **84**
Riserva 1981 • $15 • (08/31/86) • **90**
Sangioveto 1985 • $17 • (08/31/88) • **89**
Sergio Manetti 1989 • $40 • (11/15/93) • **85**
Vin Santo NV • $20 • (02/15/87) • **89**

MONTE, VILLA DE

Chianti Rufina Riserva 1985 • $13 • (04/30/92) • **80**
Chianti Rufina Riserva 1979 • $16 • (04/30/92) • **81**

MONTEGIACHI, TENUTA

Chianti Classico Riserva 1990: A bit simple, but some lovely, intense, dried cherry and mineral aromas and flavors complement the medium-to-light body, firm tannins and crisp finish. Drinkable now. • $NA • **83**

MONTEGROSSI, CASTELLO DI

Chianti Classico 1988 • $15 • (09/15/91) • **91**
Chianti Classico 1986 • $8 • (07/15/89) • **89**
Chianti Classico 1985 • $5 • (09/15/88) • **86**
Vin Santo 1982 • $19 • (03/31/90) • **92**

MONTELLORI, FATTORIA

Chianti 1990 • $7 • (05/15/93) • **80**
Chianti Putto 1988 • $6 • (11/30/89) • **83**

MONTERSINO, VILLA

Barolo 1988 • $20 • (12/15/92) • **88**

MONTI, ANTONIO & ELIO

Montepulciano d'Abruzzo 1993: What a treat. An amazingly deep and intense wine for this region. It's packed with blackberry, herb, spice and smoke flavors, tannic but still smooth in texture. Drink through 1998. 3,000 cases made. • $10 • (02/29/96) • **88**
Montepulciano d'Abruzzo 1989 • $7 • (09/30/91) • **75**
Montepulciano d'Abruzzo 1988 • $6 • (02/15/91) BB • **83**

MONTIVERDI

Chianti Classico 1990 • $NA • (10/31/93) • **87**

MONTORI, CAMILLO

Montepulciano d'Abruzzo 1991 • $6 • (03/31/94) • **82**
Montepulciano d'Abruzzo 1987 • $8 • (03/31/90) • **80**

MONTRESOR

Fattoria di Cavalcaselle Bianco di Custoza 1994: An odd mix of fruit salad and musty flavors. It has some richness, but lacks harmony and finishes in a bitter note. 70,000 cases made. • $8 • (04/30/96) • **74**

Pinot Grigio la Colombaia Valdadige 1994: Mineral and citrus flavors give this white backbone; apple notes and a hint of butter provide roundness. It's an up-front wine for quaffing now. • $10 • (10/31/95) • **82**

MORBELLI

Carema 1982 • $21 • (11/30/89) • **87**

MOSCA

Bardolino 1993 • $5 • (11/15/94) • **80**
Pinot Grigio 1993: An aggressive white wine with herbal-earthy flavors, a sharp texture and tart finish. Serviceable, but too severe for us. 5,000 cases made. • $5 • **75**
Valpolicella 1993 • $5 • (10/31/94) • **82**

NARDI

Brunello di Montalcino 1990: Exotic and ripe, with spicy aromas and plenty of sweet plum and cherry flavors. Fine texture, supple tannins and some roasted notes on the finish. 4,200 cases made. • $25 • (07/31/95) • **86**
Brunello di Montalcino 1988: A well-made Brunello, with raspberry, leather and tar aromas and flavors. Full body, good tannins and a medium, slightly alcoholic finish. From Casale del Bosco. • $33 • (04/30/94) • **86**
Brunello di Montalcino Riserva 1988: Surprisingly light for a riserva. Shows some cedar and berry notes and light tannins on the finish. Drinkable now. • $36 • (10/31/94) • **79**
Rosso di Montalcino 1993: A medium-bodied red with moderate acidity that combines a touch of earth and leather with the aroma and flavor of cooked plums. Drink now. 3,500 cases made. • $13 • (08/31/95) • **84**
Rosso di Montalcino 1992 • $13 • (10/31/94) • **78**
Rosso di Montalcino European Panel 1993: Quite pretty and quite light, showing floral, cherry, earth and lemon flavors and crisp, fresh finish. Serve slightly chilled, with pizza and pasta. From Casale del Bosco. • $NA • **83**

NEGRI, NINO

Valtellina Superiore Le Botti d'Oro 1989: A severe style of red that is tannic and very dry. Has some cherry and cranberry flavor to give it life. • $13 • (02/28/95) • **77**
Valtellina Superiore Inferno 1990: A tight, dry red whose charming strawberry and cherry flavors aren't strong enough to flesh out the tannic, tart framework. • $13 • (02/28/95) • **78**
Valtellina Superiore Inferno 1989: Nebbiolo • $NA • **77**
Valtellina Superiore Riserva 1986: Age has brought it an attractive complexity, while it still retains lively fruit flavors that linger on the finish. Has great balance and a vivid flavor profile. • $20 • (02/28/95) • **86**

NEGRO

Barbera d'Alba Nicolon 1990 • $16 • (12/15/92) • **83**
Barbera d'Alba Nicolon 1989 • $12 • (03/15/91) • **88**

NEIRANO

Gavi 1994: A Gavi that offers something extra. This has great spicy aromas along with honey and baked apple flavors that linger on the finish. A firm, lively and full-bodied Italian white. 8,000 cases made. • $10 • (02/29/96) BB • **88**

NEIVE, CASTELLO DI

Barbaresco Santo Stefano 1990: Tight and chewy, aromatic, offers licorice, berry and tobacco flavors that glide nicely into the finish. A bit tannic, drink after 1997. Better than a sample tasted last year. • $20 • (10/31/94) • **88**
Barbaresco Santo Stefano 1989: Crisply focused and elegant, a refined wine with generous licorice-scented berry and tar aromas and flavors, firm and peppery on the finish.Tannins are well integrated. Drinkable now. 4,000 cases made. • $20 • (10/31/93) • **90**
Barbaresco Santo Stefano 1988 • $23 • (10/31/93) • **77**
Barbaresco Vigneto Santo Stefano 1988 • $25 • (12/15/92) • **75**
Barbaresco Vigneto Santo Stefano 1987 • $20 • (12/31/90) • **79**
Barbaresco Vigneto Santo Stefano 1982 • $27 • (09/15/88) • **86**
Barbera d'Alba Vigneto Messoirano 1988 • $11 • (07/15/91) • **83**
Barbera d'Alba Vigneto Messoirano 1987 • $11 • (04/15/91) • **69**
Dolcetto d'Alba Vigneto Basarin 1990 • $15 • (12/15/92) • **85**
Dolcetto d'Alba Vigneto Basarin 1989 • $12 • (02/28/91) • **80**
Dolcetto d'Alba Vigneto Basarin 1987 • $11 • (03/15/89) • **80**
Dolcetto d'Alba Vigneto Valtorta 1986 • $12 • (08/31/88) • **73**

NERVI, LUIGI & ITALO

Gattinara 1983 • $11 • (05/31/90) • **63**
Gattinara Vigneto Molsino 1983 • $15 • (05/31/90) • **68**
Gattinara Vigneto Valferana 1983 • $15 • (05/31/90) • **77**
Spanna 1988 • $9 • (07/15/91) • **80**

NICCOLINI

Chianti 1990 • $6 • (04/30/92) BB • **84**

NICODEMI, BRUNO

Montepulciano d'Abruzzo Dei Colli Venia 1984 • $5 • (11/15/87) • **74**

NICOLA, VILLA

Brunello di Montalcino 1985 • $32 • (11/30/90) • **91**
Brunello di Montalcino Riserva 1981 • $14 • (09/15/88) • **75**
Rosso di Montalcino 1988 • $15 • (01/31/91) • **89**

NITTARDI, CASANUOVA DI

Chianti Classico 1993: Vibrant Chianti with dried cherry and wet earth aromas and flavors. Medium-bodied with silky tannins and a long, fresh finish. Drinkable now or age. 2,500 cases made. • $12 • **85**
Chianti Classico 1990 • $NA • (09/15/92) • **80**
Chianti Classico Casanuova di Nittardi 1992: Extremely fresh and fruity with cherry, pepper and mint flavors and a juicy texture. Delicious now. • $NA • **82**
Chianti Classico Nittardi 1990 • $NA • (10/31/93) • **86**
Chianti Classico Nittardi Riserva 1990: Very ripe grapes produce a hot, almost pruny character. Full in body and a little aggressive but it shows plenty of fruit on the finish. Needs time, better after 1996. • $NA • **86**
Chianti Classico Riserva 1988 • $NA • (09/15/92) • **80**

NOARNA, CASTEL

Cabernet Vallagarina Vigna Romeo 1989 • $22 • (12/15/92) • **72**

NOZZOLE

Chardonnay Le Bruniche 1994: A good Chardonnay that's a bit heavy and simple, but it has a smooth texture. • $11 • (02/29/96) • **81**
Chardonnay Vigneto Le Bruniche 1992 • $10 • (04/30/94) • **84**
Chardonnay Vigneto Le Bruniche 1991 • $10 • (12/15/92) • **84**
Chianti Classico 1990 • $13 • (10/31/93) • **88**
Chianti Classico La Forra Riserva 1990: Very flavorful with tar, licorice and floral aromas, medium-to-full body, ripe fruit and tannins. Drinkable now. 5,000 cases made. • $22 • **86**
Chianti Classico La Forra Riserva 1988 • $20 • (09/15/92) • **82**
Chianti Classico La Forra Riserva 1985 • $21 • (09/15/92) • **84**
Chianti Classico La Forra Riserva 1982 • $20 • (10/31/91) • **77**
Chianti Classico Riserva 1991: Light and simple with cherry and earth aromas and flavors and a delicate, slightly diluted finish. Not up to par. Drinkable now. 20,000 cases made. • $12 • **77**

Chianti Classico Riserva 1990: A lovely glass of Chianti displaying coffee, tobacco, berry character, medium-to-light body and smoky flavors. Drinkable now. 20,000 cases made. • $12 • (02/28/95) • **85**
Chianti Classico Riserva 1989 • $12 • (10/31/93) • **82**
Chianti Classico Riserva 1988 • $14 • (09/15/92) • **81**
Chianti Classico Riserva 1986 • $9 • (10/31/91) • **83**
Chianti Classico Riserva 1985 • $13 • (09/15/91) • **88**
Chianti Classico Riserva 1981 • $7 • (10/31/87) • **72**
Il Pareto 1993: Always a winner. Subtle aromas of blackberry, mint and lightly toasted oak follow through to a terrific palate with refined tannins and medium body. Excellent potential. Made from Cabernet. Better in 1998. • $45 • **92**
Il Pareto 1990: An amazingly intense and flavorful red wine whose deep flavors of cherry, berry and plum are accented by hints of chocolate, cedar and currant. Finely textured in spite of massive tannins, firm but velvety. 1,000 cases made. • $41 • **96**
Il Pareto 1989 • $30 • (10/31/93) • **85**
Il Pareto 1988 • $28 • (06/15/93) • **91**

OBERTA, ANDREA

Barbera d'Alba Giada 1992: The full-bodied texture features some toasted coffee, tobacco, chocolate and truffle notes. Generous and round, delicious, well done. • $NA • **84**
Dolcetto d'Alba Vigneto San Francesco 1994: Rich for Dolcetto, offering dried cherry and wet earth aromas and flavors. Perhaps a bit too earthy. • $NA • **75**

OBERTO, LUIGI

Barolo Ciabot Berton 1988 • $28 • (12/15/92) • **85**
Dolcetto d'Alba Ciabot Berton 1993: Fresh, light and crisp, adding a slightly leesy character to lovely red berry flavors. Somewhat drying on the finish. • $NA • **79**
Dolcetto d'Alba Ciabot Berton 1990 • $12 • (03/31/93) • **83**
Nebbiolo delle Langhe 1988 • $16 • (07/31/92) • **78**
Nebbiolo delle Langhe Ciabot Berton 1988 • $12 • (03/31/93) • **82**

OCONE

Anglianico del Sannio Beneventano 1987: Fully mature, this light-bodied wine shows raisin and brown sugar flavors, but it's drying out. The flavors have some appeal but the wine is tired. Drink now. 4,000 cases made. • $17 • (05/31/95) • **78**

ODDERO

Barbaresco 1990: Tight, tough and herbal, with an unwelcome barnyard edge and little fruit to speak of, finishing dry. RT • $14 • **72**
Barbaresco 1989: Straightforward and flavorful, with focused raspberry, anise and tar aromas and flavors and a smooth, tasty finish. 1,500 cases made. • $15 • (03/31/93) • **85**
Barbaresco 1982 • $15 • (09/15/88) • **84**
Barbera d'Alba 1985 • $9 • (07/15/88) • **77**
Barolo 1991: Has some decent, sweet character, but mostly showing chestnut, smoke and tar flavors. Turns very dry on the finish. 4,165 cases made. • $17 • **79**
Barolo 1989: Muscular and chewy, showing a nice core of black cherry flavor covered with a thick layer of hard tannins that will probably never go away. • $16 • (10/31/94) • **82**
Barolo 1983 • $15 • (09/15/88) • **85**
Barolo 1982 • $14 • (09/15/88) • **92**
Barolo 1980 • $7 • (05/16/86) • **73**
Barolo Mondoca di Bussia Soprana 1990: Some decent licorice and cherry flavors, but touches of cheese, cedar and dried cherry pits make for a weird combination. Dirty old barrels? Tasted twice, with consistent notes. 833 cases made. • $30 • **69**

Key: SS—Spectator Selection. CS—Cellar Selection. BB—Best Buy. $NA—Price not available. (BT)—Barrel tasting. Ⓐ—Auction Price.
Dates in parentheses represent the issues in which the ratings were published.

Barolo Rocche di Bussia 1985 • $21 • (08/31/91) • **65**
Barolo Vigna Rionda 1990: Plain wet soil and mushroom character in aromas and flavors. From excellent grapes but poor winemaking technique. 833 cases made. • $30 • **72**
Nebbiolo delle Langhe 1990 • $NA • (10/31/94) • **79**

OLIVETO

Chianti 1990 • $6 • (03/31/93) • **79**

ORNELLAIA, TENUTA DELL'

Le Volte 1993: Better than the '92. Pretty and perfumed with light cherry and earth character, medium-to-light body, straightforward flavors, medium tannins and a chewy finish. Drinkable now. • $13 • **82**
Le Volte 1992: Decent quality, but buy the '93. Gamy aromas and flavors, light. Drinkable now. • $13 • **78**
Le Volte 1991 • $14 • (10/31/93) • **87**
Masseto 1992: Better than the 1990 or '91 Masseto. Deep and profound Merlot exhibiting intense berry, mint and cassis aromas and flavors. Full-bodied but very elegant and refined, wonderful silky tannins and succulent finish. Drinkable, but better after 1997. • $59 • **93**
Masseto 1991: A gem exploding with fruit. This has blackberry, tobacco and chocolate flavors. Full body, fine tannins and a long, fruity finish. Better after 1997. • $59 • **91**
Masseto 1990 • $NA • (10/31/93) • **90**
Masseto 1989 • $60 • (10/31/93) • **83**
Masseto 1988 • $NA • (09/15/91) • **90**
Ornellaia Tuscany 1992: A ripe, seductive, opulent texture with tobacco, black olives, dried herbs to give it some complexity. But it's a bit too herbal. Try after 1996. Tasted twice, with consistent notes. • $44 • **85**
Ornellaia Tuscany 1991: Pretty, well-made wine offering cassis and herb aromas and flavors, medium in body and tannins followed by a silky finish. Drinkable now. • $38 • **86**
Ornellaia Tuscany 1990: The greatest ever produced from this estate. It's a goliath of a wine with fruit and tannins almost bursting from the glass. Beautiful aromas and flavors of berries, herbs and vanilla, full body and tannins and tons of fruit. Try in 1998. • $42 • (11/15/93) • **96**
Ornellaia Tuscany 1989 • $30 • (11/15/93) • **87**
Ornellaia Tuscany 1988 • $50 • (11/15/93) • **93**
Ornellaia Tuscany 1987 • $46 • (11/15/93) • **88**
Ornellaia Tuscany 1986 • $55 • (11/15/93) • **92**
Ornellaia Tuscany 1985 • $50 • (11/15/93) • **87**

PACENTI, SIRO

Brunello di Montalcino 1990: Really caresses your palate with tobacco, berry and cedar character. Full in body, wonderfully ripe and round, featuring velvety tannins and a long, flavorful finish. Drinkable now. • $36 • **92**
Brunello di Montalcino 1988: A polished and delicious wine. Loads of ripe, plummy fruit aromas and flavors with a hint of toast and nuts. Full-bodied with velvety tannins and a long finish. From Pelagrilli. Better after 1996. 400 cases made. • $31 • (04/30/94) • **90**
Rosso di Montalcino 1993: Big and opulent, offering stunning quality for a Rosso-it's more like a Brunello-and boasting masses of plum, black cherry, cedar and dark chocolate flavors. Lush and generous finish. Drinkable now. • $18 • **90**
Rosso di Montalcino 1991 • $16 • (04/30/94) • **84**
Rosso di Montalcino 1989 • $14 • (04/30/92) • **87**

PADAELECTI

Brunello di Montalcino Riserva 1988: Medium intensity, beautiful cherry and chestnut character, medium tannins and a fruity finish. Delicious. Drinkable now. • $NA • (10/31/94) • **83**

PADELLETTI

Brunello di Montalcino 1990: Delicate, almost meager cherry and raspberry flavor and a hint of leather on the nose and palate. Medium in body, fine tannins and long finish. Drinkable now. • $NA • **85**

Brunello di Montalcino 1988: Lean and muscular, with lots of rich, ripe fruit, alcohol and balanced tannins. Flavorful finish. From Rigaccini. Try now. • $NA • (04/30/94) • **87**

PAGGIO

Pinot Grigio Alto Adige 1994: Expressive and distinctive. Unusual smoky and herbal aromas carry through on the ripe, yet firm, palate. It's clean and long. Not typical but worth a try. 5,000 cases made. • $8 • (06/15/96) • **86**

PAGLIAIA, VILLA LA

Chianti Classico 1991 • $NA • (10/31/93) • **86**

PAGLIARESE

Capitolare di Biturica Il Neri 1991: Sheer and beautiful with refined blackberry, vanilla and violet aromas and flavors. Medium-bodied with well-integrated tannins and a fresh finish. Drink or age. • $NA • **87**

Capitolare di Biturica Il Neri 1990: Beautifully crafted, offering silky blackberry, cherry and perfume character, medium body and a delicious finish. Drink now but will improve. • $NA • **88**

Chianti Classico 1993: Very attractive, succulent wine with vanilla, berry and wild cherry aromas and flavors. Medium-bodied and soft with fine tannins and a fresh finish. Drinkable now. • $NA • **86**

Chianti Classico 1992: Better than its '91. Well made, showing fine tannins, focused black cherry flavor, light-to-medium body and a fruity, light finish. Drinkable now. • $9 • **80**

Chianti Classico 1991 • $9 • (10/31/93) • **78**

Chianti Classico 1990 • $11 • (09/15/92) • **80**

Chianti Classico 1985 • $6 • (03/31/88) • **76**

Chianti Classico Boscardini Riserva 1981 • $9 • (05/31/88) • **82**

Chianti Classico Boscardini Riserva 1980 • $9 • (03/15/87) • **85**

Chianti Classico Riserva 1988 • $15 • (09/15/92) • **88**

Della Provincia di Siena Camerlengo 1991: Attractive Sangiovese with rose petal, violet aromas and black cherry flavors. Medium-bodied and quite seductive, showing a crisp texture on the sweet, ripe finish. Drinkable now or age. • $NA • **85**

PAITIN

Barbaresco Sor' Paitin 1991: Impressive cherry, black pepper and spice aromas and flavors, medium body, firm tannins and long, tasty finish. Drinkable now. 791 cases made. • $20 • **85**

PALAGIO, IL

Chianti Classico 1993: Mouth-puckering wine. Very fresh and lively with delicious dried cherry and citric flavors. Medium-bodied and a zingy finish with fine tannins. Drinkable now, but can cellar. • $NA • **82**

Chianti Classico 1992: Decent fruit but rather stemmy, grassy aftertaste. Light in body. Drinkable now. • $NA • **79**

Chianti Classico Riserva 1991: Plenty of life in this riserva, full of blackberry and licorice character and silky tannins. Medium-bodied, medium tannins and a lively finish. Delicious now. • $NA • **86**

Chianti Classico Riserva 1990: Delicious, intense aromas of dried cherries and licorice, wonderful ripe fruit flavors, medium-bodied and very soft. Drinkable now. • $NA • **86**

PALAZZETTA, LA

Brunello di Montalcino 1988: A straightforward wine with peppery, fruit aromas and flavors, medium body and slightly rustic tannins. From Fanti Flavio. Drink now. • $NA • (04/30/94) • **84**

Rosso di Montalcino 1991 • $14 • (04/30/94) • **83**

PALAZZO

Rosso di Montalcino 1993: Impressively big, inky, generous and full-bodied, yet remaining elegant and rather fresh on the palate, with tons of plum, cherry and prune. Would score higher if not so raisiny. • $NA • (10/31/95) • **84**

PALAZZONE, IL

Brunello di Montalcino 1990: Smooth and elegant, showing well-defined flavors of blackberry, black cherry and flowers. Supple tannins make for nice drinking now but it should improve. Better in 1998. • $NA • **88**

PALLAVICINI

Frascati Superiore 1993 • $9 • (10/31/94) • **83**

PANERETTA, CASTELLO DELLA

Chianti Classico 1992: Attractive plum, cherry, slightly herbal character. Light- to medium-bodied and fruity. Drinkable now. • $NA • **79**

Chianti Classico 1991 • $NA • (10/31/93) • **85**

Chianti Classico 1990 • $NA • (10/31/93) • **84**

Chianti Classico 1988 • $NA • (09/15/91) • **79**

Chianti Classico Riserva 1990: If you like excellent, mature Chianti, try this. A very autumnal wine with game, berry and truffle aromas, gentle texture and rich, leathery, cedary flavors. Delicious now. • $NA • **86**

Chianti Classico Riserva 1988 • $NA • (09/15/92) • **80**

Chianti Classico Riserva 1985 • $NA • (09/15/91) • **92**

Terrine 1990: Fresh and clean, with pie-crust, berry and cherry aromas and flavors, medium body and a crisp finish. Drinkable now. • $NA • **85**

PANIZZI

Vernaccia di San Gimignano 1992 • $19 • (06/15/94) • **82**

Vernaccia di San Gimignano Riserva 1991 • $26 • (06/15/94) • **85**

PANZANO

Chianti Classico Riserva 1985 • $NA • (09/15/91) • **86**

PARADISO, FATTORIA

Sangiovese di Romagna Riserva Superiore Vigna delle Lepri 1987 • $16 • (07/15/91) • **85**

Sangiovese di Romagna Riserva Superiore Vigna delle Lepri 1985 • $11 • **662**

PARADISO, IL

Brunello di Montalcino 1990: No paradise here. Smelling a bit funky and tasting a bit odd. Hard to recommend. Lean and earthy. • $NA • **70**

Rosso di Montalcino 1993: Soft and plummy, showing delicious flavors, medium body and light tannins. Crisp, lemony finish. Drink now. • $NA • **82**

Rosso di Montalcino 1991 • $NA • (04/30/94) • **82**

PARRINA

Riserva 1988 • $NA • (10/31/93) • **82**

PARUSSO

Barbera d'Alba 1988 • $12 • (03/15/91) • **85**

Barbera d'Alba Bricco di Pugnana 1990 • $20 • (10/15/93) • **91**

Barbera d'Alba Bricco di Pugnane 1989 • $18 • (10/31/92) • **88**

Barbera d'Alba Pugnane-Ornati 1992 • $17 • (10/31/94) • **75**

Barbera d'Alba Superiore 1989 • $11 • (10/31/92) • **84**

Barolo 1990: Ripe and plummy and focused, fires a bright shot of minerally currant and berry notes across the palate. Firm in texture, but not overly tannic, it has the sort of structure that makes the flavors sail smoothly. Approachable now, better around 1998 or 2000. • $27 • (10/31/94) • **90**

Barolo 1985 • $27 • (04/30/91) • **84**

ITALY

Barolo Bussia 1990: Herbal, peppery aromas and flavors predominate in this lean, crisply tannic wine. Finishes a little short. Maybe better after 1999. RT • $38 • **79**

Barolo Bussia 1989: Enormously tannic and chewy, with ripe, focused flavors of currant and blackberry plus an overlay of herb and floral notes. Powerful and lively, should be at its best after 2000. • $38 • (10/31/94) • **92**

Barolo Bussia-Rocche 1988 • $35 • (10/31/93) • **87**

Barolo Mariondino 1990: Extremely earthy, biting and sour. Tasted twice. • $32 • (10/31/94) • **68**

Barolo Mariondino 1989: Firm in texture but sweet and ripe in flavor, with rose-scented wild berry and anise aromas and flavors. Finishes with a swarm of fine tannins that needs until 1997. 390 cases made. • $30 • (10/31/93) • **87**

Barolo Mariondino 1988 • $25 • (10/31/93) • **90**

Barolo Mariondino 1986 • $23 • (04/30/91) • **83**

Bricco Rovella Red 1992: Light and tart, like a sour cherry candy, with a licorice edge to the crisp, modest fruit. A blend of what grapes? RT. • $15 • **76**

Dolcetto d'Alba 1994: Youthful and pretty, of light to medium body, showing lovely raspberry, wild berry, strawberry and cherry flavors. Lacks a bit of tannic structure, but sure is fun to drink. 2,000 cases made. • $12 • **80**

Mariondino 1991 • $11 • (10/31/94) • **80**

Mariondino 1990 • $14 • (10/31/92) • **86**

Nebbiolo delle Langhe 1988 • $11 • (07/31/92) • **79**

PASINI, VOLPE

Merlot Colli Orientali del Friuli Villa Volpe 1993: A peppery, firmly tannic, medium-bodied Merlot that's clean and refreshing if lean in flavor. 300 cases made. • $11 • (06/15/96) • **80**

Pinot Bianco Colli Orientali del Friuli Zuc di Volpe 1994: Canned fruit flavors and aromas don't make for much fun. 1,000 cases made. • $20 • (06/15/96) • **77**

Pinot Grigio Colli Orientali del Friuli Villa Volpe 1994: An interesting Pinot Grigio. This is flavorful—orange peel, banana and spice—has good balance and a lingering aftertaste. 4,100 cases made. • $11 • (06/15/96) • **84**

Pinot Grigio Colli Orientali del Friuli Zuc di Volpe 1994: An aromatic, but dry, lean style of Pinot Grigio that emphasizes spicy, orange peel flavors and a rather tight texture. Bracing. 2,500 cases made. • $20 • (06/15/96) • **84**

Refosco Colli Orientali del Friuli Zuc di Volpe 1990: After six years it still tastes tight and closed, with firm tannins, subdued fruit flavors and crisp acidity. A severe style of wine that may be best with cheese. 250 cases made. • $20 • (06/15/96) • **81**

Sauvignon Colli Orientali del Friuli Villa Volpe 1994: A bit dull and tastes of buttered popcorn on the finish. Inoffensive, but not very flavorful. 4,100 cases made. • $11 • (06/15/96) • **76**

PASOLINI

Chianti 1986 • $6 • (12/15/90) • **78**

Chianti 1985 • $5 • (09/15/88) • **79**

PASQUA, FRATELLI

Cabernet Sauvignon Marago 1989 • $13 • (09/15/92) • **83**

Recioto della Valpolicella Amarone Vigneti Casterna 1986 • $16 • (09/15/92) • **85**

Soave Classico Costalunga 1991 • $13 • (09/15/92) • **84**

Valpolicella Villa Borghetti 1989 • $7 • (09/15/92) • **79**

PASQUALE, VEGLIO

Barolo Vigna Batistot 1988 • $30 • (10/31/94) • **87**

Key: SS—Spectator Selection. CS—Cellar Selection. BB—Best Buy. $NA—Price not available. (BT)—Barrel tasting. Ⓐ—Auction Price.
Dates in parentheses represent the issues in which the ratings were published.

PASQUERO, ELIA

Barbaresco Sorì Paitin 1985 • $14 • (03/31/90) • **88**

Barbera d'Alba Sorì Paitin 1989 • $10 • (11/30/91) BB • **88**

Barbera d'Alba Sorì Paitin 1988 • $8 • (03/15/91) • **83**

Dolcetto d'Alba Sorì Paitin 1991 • $11 • (09/30/93) • **80**

PATERNOSTER

Aglianico del Vulture 1987 • $16 • (01/31/92) • **82**

Aglianico del Vulture Don Anselmo Riserva del Foudatore 1985 • $32 • (09/15/92) • **81**

PAVESE, LIVIO

Barbera d'Asti Superiore 1986 • $9 • (03/15/91) • **76**

Barolo Riserva Speciale 1978 • $12 • (09/16/84) • **90**

PECCHENINO

Dolcetto di Dogliani Pizabo 1994: Clean cherry, mineral and light tobacco character, medium body, fresh fruit and firm finish. Drink now. • $NA • **86**

PECORARI, FRANCESCO

Isonzo Lis Neris 1991: Unusually spritzy, with fresh blueberry and plum flavors. Not exactly a table wine, but appealing in its own right. Tasted twice, with consistent notes. 300 cases made. • $20 • (02/29/96) • **80**

Lis Neris 1990 • $20 • (10/15/94) • **89**

Picol 1992 • $15 • (09/30/94) • **82**

Picol-Sauvignon Isonzo 1994: This is a well-balanced wine with strong herbal flavors and some modest peach and green apple notes. Medium-bodied and assertive. 1,666 cases made. • $12 • (06/15/96) • **83**

Pinot Grigio Gris 1994: Strong herbal and vegetal components give this wine character, but it won't appeal to everyone. A sweet vanilla note adds some balance, and firm acidity holds it together. 500 cases made. • $12 • (06/15/96) • **81**

St. Jurosa Riserva 1992 • $20 • (09/30/94) • **88**

St. Jurosa White 1992: Somewhat foxy and cloying flavors turn earthy, harsh and a bit herbal on the finish. 1,000 cases made. • $15 • (06/30/96) • **75**

Sauvignon Isonzo 1994: Overly herbal and oniony. Tastes green and awkard and turns a bit bitter on the finish. 1,666 cases made. • $12 • (06/15/96) • **75**

Tal Luc 1992 • $20 • (09/30/94) • **84**

Tocai Friulano Isonzo 1994: This is a fairly soft wine with nice peach flavors and aromas. There's a bit of spice on the finish as well. 291 cases made. • $12 • (06/15/96) • **81**

Verduzzo Friulano Tal Lûc 1994: A bit of Alsace from Italy with nice spice and wild fruit flavors. Off-dry , but somewhat heavy handed. Plenty of buttery flavors to boot. • $20 • **85**

PELISSERO

Barbaresco 1992: Easy-drinking red showing cherry, berry and milk chocolate character, medium-to-light body, a crisp, light finish and delicate tannins. Drink now. • $NA • **82**

Barbaresco Vanotu 1991: Classy, mature and elegant, with lots of spicy, chocolaty accents to the solid, ripe berry and cherry flavors. Very firm tannins and acidity, but the fruit balances it out. Drinkable now. • $22 • (11/30/94) • **85**

Barbaresco Vanotu 1990: Rich, appealing cherry, plum and berry flavors and aromas. It is still quite tannic, but everything is in proportion. Nice licorice and chocolate notes echo on the long finish. • $NA • (11/30/94) • **87**

Barbaresco Vanuto 1991: Tannic and dry, lacking fruit, struggles to show some red berry character, but provides mostly a drying finish that's unlikely to smooth out. 833 cases made. • $19 • **76**

Barbera d'Alba Piani 1993: A brooding red, with black currant and dried cherry flavors. A lot of good fruit, but jammy and a little rustic. Finishes tart. • $12 • (07/31/95) • **84**

ITALY

Barbera d'Alba Ronchi 1990 • $11 • (04/30/93) • **87**
Dolcetto d'Alba Augenta 1993: Lush aromas of black cherry, chocolate and smoke give way to bright fruit and firm, light tannins. Clean and pretty. Drinkable now. • $12 • (07/31/95) • **84**
Dolcetto d'Alba Munfrina 1994: Wonderful berry, violet and grapey aromas and flavors. Medium in body, adding light tannins and a fruity, crisp finish. • $NA • **84**
Favorita Langhe 1993: Tired and a bit dirty tasting, a sweet-sour balance makes it awkward. Not much fun to drink. • $11 • (07/31/95) • **76**

PERTIMALI

Brunello di Montalcino 1982 • $25 • (01/31/88) • **77**
Brunello di Montalcino Riserva 1985 • $41 • (11/30/90) • **83**
Rosso di Montalcino 1987 • $13 • (01/31/91) • **84**

PESCAIA, LA

Brunello di Montalcino 1990: Brownish-colored, tasting simple and one-dimensional, like a weak Pinot Noir. Drink on release. • $NA • **79**
Brunello di Montalcino 1988: Big and ripe, with loads of raisin and dried plum character, full-bodied, full tannins and a slightly alcoholic finish. Slightly overdone. Try after 1996. • $NA • (04/30/94) • **80**
Rosso di Montalcino 1993: Rather diluted, offering some berry and chestnut character and light tannins. Drink now. • $NA • **78**
Rosso di Montalcino 1991 • $NA • (04/30/94) • **77**

PESCATORI, CASA DI

Red 1993: A touch rustic in its simple cherry, herb and brown sugar notes, followed by a slightly tannic finish. • $5 • (01/31/96) • **80**

PETRIOLO, FATTORIA

Merlot 1988 • $24 • (08/31/91) • **83**

PETROGNANO

Pomino 1993: Good red with berry, dried herb and cherry aromas and flavors. Medium-bodied with light tannins and a minty, berry finish. From the owners of Rufina's Selvapiana. Drinkable now. • $NA • **85**

PETROIO, FATTORIA DI

Chianti Classico 1993: Some nice fruit here. Elegant with licorice, plum and cassis flavors. Quite polished but lacks a bit of personality and length on the finish. • $NA • **80**
Chianti Classico 1992: Woolly, earthy, berry aromas and flavors, very light palate. Dry finish. • $NA • **73**
Chianti Classico 1991: Rather papery, cheesy and sour, with a short finish. This one is finished. Tasted twice, with consistent notes. From Lenzi. • $NA • **65**
Chianti Classico 1988 • $NA • (09/15/91) • **83**
Chianti Classico Cru Montetondo 1988 • $NA • (09/15/91) • **90**
Chianti Classico Riserva 1988 • $17 • (10/31/93) • **84**
Chianti Riserva 1990: Old-style Chianti, with grilled meat and berry aromas and flavors. Medium- to light-bodied, a little alcoholic. Drinkable now. • $NA • **79**
L'Unico di Petroio 1990 • $NA • (10/31/93) • **87**

PETROLO, FATTORIA

Chianti 1991 • $NA • (10/31/93) • **85**
Chianti 1990 • $NA • (10/31/93) • **80**
Chianti Colli Fiorentini 1993: Light and elegant, with cherry and tobacco aromas and flavors and a delicate finish. Serve slightly chilled. • $NA • **80**
Chianti Riserva 1991: Lovely but simple, a polished red displaying fresh chocolate and berry aromas and flavors, medium body and fruity finish. Drinkable now. • $NA • **84**

Torrione 1991: Very attractive Sangiovese featuring plum, berry and light herb aromas and flavors, medium-to-light body, clean fruit character, silky tannins and a light finish. Drink now. • $NA • **86**
Torrione 1990 • $NA • (10/31/93) • **90**

PIAN CORNELLO

Rosso di Montalcino 1991 • $NA • (04/30/94) • **80**

PIANPOLVERE SOPRANO

Barolo 1991: Delicious anise, berry and milk chocolate aromas and flavors. Medium body, soft tannins and a long, sweet finish. From Riccardo Fenocchio. Drinkable now. 470 cases made. • $32 • **84**
Dolcetto d'Alba 1993: A bit earthy but shows some pretty black cherry and dried fruit character. Medium in body and light finish. From Riccardo Fenocchio. 400 cases made. • $14 • **80**

PICCINI

Chianti 1991 • $6 • (06/15/93) • **75**
Chianti Classico 1992: Very clean and fruity, delicate cherry, light tar character. Light-bodied and fresh finish. Drinkable now. 10,000 cases made. • $7 • **79**
Chianti Classico 1990 • $8 • (06/15/93) • **79**
Chianti Classico Riserva 1990: Some decent ripe fruit character but rather tart and lean on the finish. Drink with food. • $10 • **79**

PICI, LE

Chianti Classico 1993: Like wine cut with water. Some strawberry character but very diluted. Tasted twice, with consistent notes. • $NA • **71**

PIEROPAN

La Colombare Recioto di Soave 1991: Ripe, lively apricot and peach notes. The sharp acidity and sweet flavors could marry better, however, and there's an earthy tone that detracts a bit. • $21 • (04/30/96) • **79**
La Colombare Recioto di Soave 1989 • $29 • (09/15/92) • **87**
Soave Classico 1991 • $9 • (09/15/92) • **83**
Soave Classico Superiore 1994: An oniony streak runs through this along with some green peach flavors. 1,100 cases made. • $12 • (06/15/96) • **80**
Soave Classico Superiore Vigneto Calvarino 1994: Lively and fresh, this has clean, citrusy acidity, round flavors of pear and hazelnut and a lingering finish. Balanced and well made. • $15 • (04/30/96) • **86**
Soave Classico Superiore Vigneto Calvarino 1991 • $13 • (09/15/92) • **85**
Soave Classico Superiore Vigneto la Rocca 1993: The lime, honey and almond flavors are appealing, but this is losing its zip. It's pleasant and soft, drinkable now. • $15 • (04/30/96) • **83**

PIERPAOLO PECORARI

Chardonnay Isonzo 1993: Soft and appealing, maybe a little sweet, but the pear and melon flavors come through nicely and balance with a touch of lemon on the finish. 650 cases made. • $16 • (01/31/95) • **83**
Chardonnay Isonzo 1991 • $19 • (12/15/92) • **84**
Pinot Bianco Fara Isonzo 1992: Distinctive and appealingly buttery and honeyed, it remains fresh through a grassy character that is attractive, harmonious and well-made. 100 cases made. • $18 • (01/31/95) • **85**
Pinot Bianco Isonzo 1993: Fresh and spicy, a simple wine with nicely defined pear and bitter almond flavors. 700 cases made. • $16 • (01/31/95) • **80**
Pinot Grigio Isonzo 1994: Strong weedy, earthy aromas and flavors make this an oddball. 800 cases made. • $18 • (06/15/96) • **75**
Pinot Grigio Isonzo 1993: Light, fresh and a bit simple with bitter almond, pear notes. 1,000 cases made. • $16 • (01/31/95) • **78**
Sauvignon Colaus Isonzo 1992: Very earthy on the nose, but rich and round in the mouth, an attempt to make a more complex wine that shows a lot more barrel flavor than most northeast Italian Sauvignons. 100 cases made. • $16 • (01/31/95) • **82**
Sauvignon Isonzo 1991 • $18 • (09/15/93) • **78**

Tocai Friulano Isonzo 1993: Soft and floral, a distinctive wine with pretty overtones of carnation and pepper to the basic apple fruit. 4,000 cases made. • $14 • (01/31/95) • **80**

PIETROSO

Brunello di Montalcino 1988 • $NA • (04/30/94) • **89**

PIEVE SANTA RESTITUTA

Brunello di Montalcino Rennina 1990: Thick and ripe, still quite tannic, offering plum, cedar, tobacco, black cherry, earth and chocolate flavors. Somewhat drying on aftertaste. Angelo Gaja's debut vintage in Montalcino. Perhaps better in 1998? • $NA • **85**

PIGHIN

Chardonnay Grave del Friuli 1993: Lean and green, marked by a pleasant note of sweet peas and flowers, finishing chalky and crisp. 9,000 cases made. • $10 • (01/31/95) • **80**
Pinot Grigio Collio 1993: Riper than most, this soft-texture Pinot Grigio offers a nutty, bread dough, pear character that is attractive. 4,500 cases made. • $16 • (01/31/95) • **80**
Pinot Grigio Collio 1992 • $18 • (04/30/94) • **86**
Pinot Grigio Grave del Friuli 1994: Fragrant floral, apple and almond aromas, bright, cheerful, lively and crisp. Though not complex, it has enough presence to stand up to food. • $16 • (10/31/95) • **84**
Pinot Grigio Grave del Friuli 1993: Bracing and fruity, a crisp white wine packed with apple and pineapple flavors. It's beautifully balanced and refreshing. • $11 • **83**
Pinot Grigio Grave del Friuli 1992 • $12 • (04/30/94) • **86**
Sauvignon Collio 1993: Smooth and generous, with a vanilla edge to the pear and slightly toasty flavors. 3,000 cases made. • $16 • (01/31/95) • **81**
Sauvignon Collio 1992: Fruity, lively and crisp, a fresh and satisfying white wine. Hints of vanilla and mineral flavors give it some extra interest, particularly on the finish. • $18 • **84**
Sauvignon Collio 1991 • $19 • (09/15/93) • **77**

PIONA

La Prendina Bianco 1992: Off-dry, with a sharp jab of acidity to keep the attractive pear and apple fruit in balance. A white blend aged in barrique. • $NA • (01/31/95) • **80**

PIRA

Barolo 1990: Interesting Barolo, with crisp acidity threading through it. Also has lots of milk chocolate and cherry flavors and a tannic finish. Needs to soften. Try in 1998. 1,250 cases made. • $40 • **85**

PLACIDO

Chianti 1989 • $6 • (07/15/91) • **76**

PLOZNER

Cabernet Sauvignon Bollini Grave del Friuli 1983 • $6 • (09/15/88) • **80**
Cabernet Sauvignon Grave del Friuli 1985 • $6 • (09/15/88) • **85**
Chardonnay Grave del Friuli 1994: Firm and rather austere, this polished white has good backbone but lacks fruit flavors. It's direct and clean, though, and might open up with food. 12,000 cases made. • $11 • (06/15/96) • **80**
Chardonnay Grave del Friuli 1992: Light and crisp, a lean wine with green apple and lemon fruit that wafts through the wine. 25,000 cases made. • $10 • (01/31/95) • **78**
Chardonnay Grave del Friuli 1991 • $8 • (11/30/93) • **82**
Chardonnay Grave del Friuli Barrique 1993: Thick and voluptuous, this shows rich, sweet oak and flavors of melon and coconut. It's harmonious, and has just enough acidity for balance. An exaggerated style, perhaps, yet appealing. 700 cases made. • $17 • (06/15/96) • **87**
Merlot Grave del Friuli 1993: The spicy, cedary aromas are attractive, but the flavors turn rather lean and earthy. Seems to be rapidly maturing. 3,000 cases made. • $9 • (06/15/96) • **77**
Merlot Grave del Friuli 1983 • $5 • (07/01/86) • **64**
Pinot Bianco Grave del Friuli 1993: Light and simple, showing some bright pear flavor, a nice drink on a modest scale. 2,500 cases made. • $10 • (01/31/95) • **82**
Pinot Grigio Grave del Friuli 1994: A well-balanced white that tastes fruity, focused and pure. The aromas and flavors are a blend of floral and citrus and the texture is lively. 15,000 cases made. • $12 • (06/15/96) • **85**
Pinot Grigio Grave del Friuli 1992: A soft, smooth-textured and some decent honey, citrus, and pear notes. Quite pleasant but lacks a bit of intensity. 25,000 cases made. • $11 • (01/31/95) • **79**
Pinot Grigio Grave del Friuli 1991 • $9 • (11/30/93) • **79**
Sauvignon Grave del Friuli 1993: Average wine that offers decent lime, grassy, pear flavors, and a tart, juicy finish. 2,500 cases made. • $10 • (01/31/95) • **78**
Tocai Friulano Grave del Friuli 1993: Hard-edged and green around the edges, showing little grace or charm. 2,500 cases made. • $9 • (01/31/95) • **74**

PODERE IL PALAZZINO

Chianti Classico 1990 • $16 • (10/31/93) • **90**
Chianti Classico 1988 • $16 • (09/15/91) • **90**
Chianti Classico 1987 • $12 • (03/31/90) • **67**
Chianti Classico 1986 • $9 • (01/31/89) • **86**
Chianti Classico 1985 • $11 • (11/30/87) SS • **93**
Chianti Classico 1983 • $5 • (09/16/85) • **78**
Chianti Classico Riserva 1987 • $15 • (12/15/92) • **85**
Chianti Classico Riserva 1985 • $22 • (09/15/91) • **88**
Chianti Classico Riserva 1983 • $21 • (11/15/87) • **80**
Chianti Classico Riserva 1981 • $6 • (04/16/86) • **69**
Grosso Sanese 1990: Harmonious wine with a seamless texture. Wonderful aromas and flavors of vanilla, violet and berry, fine tannins and solid acidity. Made from Sangiovese. From Alessandro e Andrea Sderci. Better in 1997. 575 cases made. • $35 • (10/31/93) • **93**
Grosso Sanese 1988 • $29 • (03/15/91) • **88**
Grosso Sanese 1987 • $25 • (11/30/89) • **90**
Grosso Sanese 1986 • $22 • (02/15/89) • **87**
Grosso Sanese 1985 • $13 • (12/15/87) • **94**

PODERE IL POGGIOLO

Brunello di Montalcino 1990: Brick-brownish color suggests a slightly fading Brunello. It lacks fruit and tastes of mushroom, brown sugar and truffle. Drink if you must. • $NA • **77**
Brunello di Montalcino 1985 • $34 • (11/30/90) • **93**
Brunello di Montalcino Riserva 1988: Light, with some berry, earthy fruit character, medium tannins and a diluted finish. Drink now. • $NA • (10/31/94) • **75**
Rosso di Montalcino 1991 • $NA • (04/30/94) • **78**
Rosso di Montalcino Sassello 1992: Fragrant and adds an element of earthiness to its ripe red cherry flavors. The texture is soft and appealing, but there are still some tannins on the finish. 300 cases made. • $14 • (08/31/95) • **86**

PODERE PETROIO

Chianti Classico Cru Montetondo 1990 • $NA • (10/31/93) • **86**

PODERINA, LA

Brunello di Montalcino 1990: Elegant and succulent berry, floral and cherry aromas and flavors, medium body, fine tannins and sweet, crisp finish. Drink now. • $NA • **86**

Key: SS—Spectator Selection. CS—Cellar Selection. BB—Best Buy. $NA—Price not available. (BT)—Barrel tasting. Ⓐ—Auction Price.
Dates in parentheses represent the issues in which the ratings were published.

ITALY

Brunello di Montalcino 1988: Big wine with loads of fruit, tannins and acidity, but extremely well focused on the palate. Silky tannins and a long, flavorful finish-highly refined. Drinkable now. • $32 • (04/30/94) • **91**

Brunello di Montalcino 1979 • $13 • (02/16/86) • **69**

Brunello di Montalcino Riserva 1988: Perhaps not up to the stellar quality of its regular '88 Brunello but a fine wine. Impressively fresh with cherry, watermelon character. Full bodied with refined tannins and a good long finish. Drink now. • $32 • (10/31/94) • **88**

Rosso di Montalcino 1983 • $6 • (12/01/85) BB • **87**

PODERUCCIO, IL

Brunello di Montalcino 1986 • $21 • (03/31/92) • **83**

I Due Cipressi 1985 • $22 • (04/15/91) • **91**

Rosso di Montalcino 1989 • $9 • (04/30/92) • **83**

Rosso di Montalcino I Due Cipressi 1988 • $9 • (04/30/91) • **83**

POGGERINO

Bugialla 1991: Amazing for a 1991, even better than the Bugialla '90. Nearly everything is in the right place. Exuberant aromas and flavors of mint, berry, chocoate and spice. Full body and full tannins, wonderful harmony. Tasted twice, with consistent notes. Try after 1996. • $NA • **93**

Bugialla 1990: Intensly fruity with masses of berry, raspberry, currant aromas and flavors, full tannins and a long and rich finish. • $20 • (10/31/93) • **91**

Chianti Classico 1993: Super well-made for a '93 Chianti. Elegant with a solid core of berry, cherry and violet fruit character. Medium body. Fine tannins and a long delicious finish. • $NA • **88**

Chianti Classico 1992: Delicious and round, showing plum, tar and a touch of earth character. Medium-bodied and velvety with a medium finish. Drinkable now. • $NA • **83**

Chianti Classico 1991 • $16 • (10/31/93) • **84**

Chianti Classico 1990 • $14 • (09/15/92) • **91**

Chianti Classico 1988 • $13 • (11/30/91) • **78**

Chianti Classico Riserva 1990: Fabulous, classy red showing ripe berry, violet, earth and mushroom flavors. Very complex and full in body yet velvety and harmonious. Drinkable now. • $NA • **91**

Chianti Classico Riserva 1988 • $20 • (09/15/92) • **85**

POGGIARELLO

Chianti Classico De Rham I Riservati 4 1985 • $6 • (10/31/88) BB • **83**

POGGIO A 'FRATI

Chianti Classico Riserva 1985 • $NA • (09/15/91) • **84**

POGGIO AL SOLE

Chianti Classico 1992: Exhibits perfumed cherry and raspberry character on the nose and palate, medium-to-light body, lovely texture and a clean finish. Drinkable now. • $NA • **84**

Chianti Classico 1988 • $NA • (09/15/91) • **91**

Chianti Classico Riserva 1990: Straightforward, pretty, ripe plum aromas and flavors, medium body and a silky, light finish. • $NA • **86**

Chianti Classico Riserva 1988 • $NA • (09/15/92) • **81**

Chianti Classico Riserva 1985 • $NA • (09/15/91) • **88**

POGGIO AL SORBO

Chianti Classico 1990 • $15 • (09/15/92) • **84**

Chianti Classico Riserva 1990: Rustic and somewhat prickly, showing plum, chestnut and earth aromas and flavors, light-to-medium body and light tannins. Drinkable now. 450 cases made. • $15 • **79**

Le Robbiaie 1991: Smoky, toasty aromas and a firm, tannic texture with lean, austere flavors. Has a green character on the palate and a finish that not everyone will like. 500 cases made. • $17 • (02/28/94) • **79**

POGGIO AL VENTO

Chianti Colli Senesi 1990 • $NA • (09/15/92) • **85**

POGGIO ALLE GAZZE

1991: Simple, lean and spicy, with a mild herbal edge to the modest apple notes, finishing with straightforward if modest flavor. Drinkable now. • $17 • (09/15/93) • **78**

POGGIO ANTICO

Altero 1990: Loads of cassis and berry character, but it's rather simple and straightforward with light body. Drinkable now. 500 cases made. • $33 • **82**

Brunello di Montalcino 1990: Delicious from start to finish, quite powerful. It's very ripe and very sweet-tasting and melts in the mouth, showing tons of plum, red berry and chocolate flavors. Give it until 1997 to come together. 3,750 cases made. • $42 • **91**

Brunello di Montalcino 1989: Spicy, rich and concentrated, with layers of cherry, nutmeg, game and leather flavors that blend for a complex taste experience. Lively, balanced, tannic, but drinkable now through 1999. 4,200 cases made. • $42 • (11/30/94) • **90**

Brunello di Montalcino 1988: Not as great as the 1985 from this producer, but wonderful all the same. Elegant style, with pretty cherry and licorice flavors, medium body and refined, silky tannins. Tasted twice. Drinkable now, but better after 1996. 2,500 cases made. • $35 • (04/30/94) • **91**

Brunello di Montalcino 1987 • $45 • (12/15/92) • **87**

Brunello di Montalcino 1986 • $40 • (08/31/91) • **91**

Brunello di Montalcino 1985 • $48 • (11/30/90) CS • **95**

Brunello di Montalcino 1982 • $62 Ⓐ • (11/30/89) • **92**

Brunello di Montalcino 1979 • $13 • (09/15/86) • **72**

Brunello di Montalcino Riserva 1988: Not as good as its normal Brunello but an attractive wine. Firm and racy with lovely truffle, olive, berry character. Medium- to full-bodied with sleek tannins, its rather lean and slightly dry on the finish. Tasted three times with consistent notes. • $56 • (10/31/94) • **85**

Brunello di Montalcino Riserva 1986 • $62 • (12/15/92) • **89**

Brunello di Montalcino Riserva 1985 • $55 • (08/31/91) • **93**

Rosso di Montalcino 1993: Sweet and ripe, elegant and floral, but quite light, with strawberry, raspberry and cherry flavors. Serve chilled. 1,450 cases made. • $25 • **83**

Rosso di Montalcino 1992 • $25 • (10/31/94) • **84**

Rosso di Montalcino 1991 • $24 • (04/30/94) • **83**

Rosso di Montalcino 1989 • $21 • (08/31/91) • **85**

POGGIO BONELLI

Chianti Classico 1990 • $NA • (10/31/93) • **88**

Chianti Classico Tramonto D'Oca 1990 • $NA • (10/31/93) • **89**

POGGIO DEGLI ULIVI

Brunello di Montalcino 1988: This is a big and peppery Brunello, built for aging, with full body, full tannins and ripe fruit. Try after 1997. • $NA • (04/30/94) • **88**

Rosso di Montalcino 1991 • $NA • (04/30/94) • **82**

POGGIO DI SOTTO

Rosso di Montalcino 1993: Big and disjointed, soft, offering tobacco, vanilla and berry aromas and flavors, medium body, round tannins and long, intense, earthy finish. • $NA • **83**

Rosso di Montalcino 1991 • $NA • (04/30/94) • **83**

POGGIO REALE

Chianti Rufina Riserva 1990: Beautiful mushroom, truffle and berry aromas and flavors, medium body, lovely, silky tannins and a long, long supple finish. Delicious now. • $NA • **88**

POGGIO SALVI

Brunello di Montalcino 1990: Very ripe and full-bodied, featuring an abundance of rich berry, cherry and plum aromas and flavors and a long, silky finish. Better in 1997. • $45 • **91**
Brunello di Montalcino 1988: A stylish Brunello, with lovely plum and mineral aromas and flavors and a fine, sleek structure of tannins and acidity. Drink now. • $42 • (04/30/94) • **88**
Brunello di Montalcino 1985 • $30 • (11/30/90) • **83**
Brunello di Montalcino 1981 • $20 • (10/15/88) • **88**
Brunello di Montalcino 1979 • $15 • (03/15/87) • **88**
Brunello di Montalcino Riserva 1988: Absolutely delicious wine with great class. Fabulous black cherry and chocolate character. Full-bodied and soft with fine tannins and a long flavorful finish. Drinkable now. • $45 • (10/31/94) • **90**
Brunello di Montalcino Riserva 1981 • $35 • (11/30/90) • **85**

POGGIO SAN POLO

Brunello di Montalcino 1989: A seamless wine with rich, plummy flavors and leathery aromas. Well structured and full-bodied, it is rounded out by supple tannins. Coffee and chocolate notes linger on the finish. This is still vibrant and ready to drink now through 1997. 450 cases made. • $24 • (07/31/95) • **91**
Rosso di Montalcino 1990: This is light and beginning to brown, but the aromas are enticing, suggesting mushroom, leather and spice. Fully mature now, the complex flavors lead into a long, lingering finish. Well made and from a great vintage. 600 cases made. • $15 • (08/31/95) • **88**

POGGIO, CASTELLO DEL

Barbera d'Asti 1989 • $9 • (12/15/92) • **80**
Barbera d'Asti 1988 • $9 • (10/31/91) BB • **85**

POGGIO, GIUSEPPE

Bricco Trionzo 1985 • $10 • (03/15/89) • **72**

POGGIOLINO, IL

Chianti Classico 1988 • $15 • (05/15/93) • **83**
Chianti Classico Riserva 1988 • $NA • (09/15/92) • **83**
Chianti Classico Riserva 1985 • $NA • (09/15/91) • **84**

POGGIOLO, IL

Brunello di Montalcino 1988 • $39 • (04/30/94) • **86**
Brunello di Montalcino Sassello 1988: A no-nonsense wine, with pretty cherry character on the nose and palate. Medium-bodied, soft tannins and a fruity, light finish. Drinkable now. • $NA • (04/30/94) • **83**
Rosso di Montalcino Sassello 1993: Papery, dry, almost like a corked bottle. Bad barrels? It's dry and the fruit is muted. Not recommended. Tasted twice, with consistent notes. • $NA • **65**

POGGIONE, IL

Brunello di Montalcino 1990: Beautiful, very ripe plum and berry aromas and flavors. Medium-bodied and soft, adding medium velvety tannins and a delicious finish. Drink now. • $NA • **87**
Brunello di Montalcino 1988: A wine in modest proportions but with vibrant fruit. It shows berry and smoke aromas and flavors. Medium body and tannins and a sweet, fruity finish. Drinkable now. • $42 • (04/30/94) • **86**
Brunello di Montalcino 1982 • $30 • (09/15/88) • **88**
Brunello di Montalcino 1981 • $28 • (09/15/86) • **93**

Key: SS—Spectator Selection. CS—Cellar Selection. BB—Best Buy. $NA—Price not available. (BT)—Barrel tasting. Ⓐ—Auction Price.
Dates in parentheses represent the issues in which the ratings were published.

Brunello di Montalcino Riserva 1988: Lovely finesse, showing perfumed, cherry aromas and flavors, with a long, silky finish and crisp acidity. Delicious plum and chocolate notes persist at the end. Drinkable now. • $48 • (10/31/94) • **90**
Brunello di Montalcino Riserva 1979 • $35 • (09/15/86) • **79**
Brunello di Montalcino Riserva 1978 • $35 • (07/01/84) SS • **92**
Rosso di Montalcino 1992: Vanilla, leather and sweet fruit mingle on the nose, followed by concentrated cherry flavors and a moderate finish. Has depth and richness, combining balance and style. 5,833 cases made. • $17 • (08/31/95) • **87**
Rosso di Montalcino 1991 • $18 • (04/30/94) • **82**
Rosso di Montalcino 1985 • $17 • (03/31/88) • **85**
Rosso di Montalcino European Panel 1993: A bit disappointing for this producer. Uncomplicated, quite light and even somewhat diluted, showing modest cherry, dried herb and cedar flavors. Slightly drying aftertaste. • $NA • **79**

POLIZIANO

Rosso di Montepulciano 1990 • $10 • (12/15/92) • **83**
Vino Nobile di Montepulciano 1989 • $13 • (03/31/93) • **84**
Vino Nobile di Montepulciano 1988 • $12 • (12/15/91) • **81**
Vino Nobile di Montepulciano 1987 • $12 • (03/15/91) • **84**
Vino Nobile di Montepulciano 1985 • $13 • (09/15/88) • **89**
Vino Nobile di Montepulciano Vigneto Caggiole Riserva 1988 • $23 • (06/30/93) • **82**

PONTI, LANZA GINORI

Vigna di Bugialla Poggerino 1988 • $17 • (01/31/92) • **84**

PORTA ROSSA, CANTINA DELLA

Barolo Riserva 1985 • $26 • (01/31/92) • **87**
Barolo Vigna Delizia Riserva 1982 • $25 • (08/31/91) • **87**
Diano d'Alba Vigna Bruni 1990 • $14 • (03/31/92) • **84**
Diano d'Alba Vigna Bruni 1988 • $25 • (02/15/91) • **85**

PRA

Recioto delle Fontane 1990 • $NA • (09/15/92) • **77**
Recioto delle Fontane 1989 • $NA • (09/15/92) • **80**
Soave Classico 1991 • $16 • (09/15/92) • **83**
Soave Classico Superiore 1992 • $12 • (10/31/94) • **86**
Soave Classico Vigneto Monte Grande 1991 • $18 • (09/15/92) • **85**

PRA' DI PRADIS

Pinot Grigio Collio 1994: Has more body than the typical Pinot Grigio. Floral aromas, pearlike flavors and a smooth, full texture make it satisfying. 550 cases made. • $16 • (06/15/96) • **84**
Tocai Friulano Collio 1994: A well-balanced and delicious wine that has a nice spicy element with some body as well. Taut and crisp with appealing ginger and apple flavors that linger. Reminiscent of viognier. 1,350 cases made. • $13 • (06/15/96) • **86**

PRATOLA, LE

Chianti Classico 1990 • $9 • (10/31/93) • **80**

PRINCIPE CORSINI

Chianti Classico Le Corti 1991 • $8 • (10/31/94) • **77**

PRODUTTORI DEL BARBARESCO

Barbaresco 1991: Extremely light, offering elegant berry and cherry aromas and flavors but not much else. Medium- to light-bodied, fine tannins, short finish. Drinkable now. 7,500 cases made. • $21 • **79**
Barbaresco 1989: Extremely tough and tannic, an inordinately chewy wine with anise and a thin thread of berry flavor to relieve the

onslaught. Will never be smooth. Try in 1997. 13,500 cases made. • $24 • (10/31/93) • **76**

Barbaresco 1988 • $24 • (10/31/93) • **84**
Barbaresco 1986 • $12 • (10/31/90) • **90**
Barbaresco 1985 • $12 • **74**
Barbaresco 1984 • $12 • (09/15/88) • **80**
Barbaresco 1983 • $17 • (09/15/88) • **85**
Barbaresco 1982 • $16 • (09/15/88) • **87**
Barbaresco 1979 • $17 • (09/15/88) • **90**

Barbaresco Asili 1990: Sweet, well made, offering cherry, currant, floral and tar flavors. But it's a bit lean overall and somewhat dry on the finish. What happened? As a barrel sample it was excellent. 1,200 cases made. • $35 • **81**

Barbaresco Asili 1989: A sturdy wine, aromatic with tar and cherries, with a hint of leather at the edge, firmly tannic, with a thread of elegance that suggests it might be fine after 1997. 1,175 cases made. • $32 • (10/31/93) • **85**

Barbaresco Asili 1988 • $32 • (10/31/93) • **88**
Barbaresco Asili Riserva 1985 • $27 • (10/31/90) • **92**
Barbaresco Asili Riserva 1982 • $22 • (09/15/88) • **89**

Barbaresco Moccagatta 1989: Powerful, full-bodied and very fruity in flavor. A young, high-powered, tannic and promising Barbaresco that will need cellaring until at least 1997 to begin to mellow. 1,154 cases made. • $29 • (10/31/94) • **87**

Barbaresco Moccagatta Riserva 1982 • $22 • (09/15/88) • **89**
Barbaresco Montefico Riserva 1982 • $22 • (09/15/88) • **85**
Barbaresco Montefico Riserva 1978 • $22 • (09/15/88) • **92**

Barbaresco Montestefano 1990: Tough in texture, with modest berry fruit and a bitter almond flavor that does not fade. 1,250 cases made. • $32 • (10/31/93) • **78**

Barbaresco Montestefano 1989: Very firm and chunky, with a solid beam of dried cherry, plum and tobacco aromas and flavors. Massive tannins may be too much for the level of intensity, but it delivers some real character. Try now. 1,250 cases made. • $32 • (10/31/93) • **87**

Barbaresco Montestefano 1988 • $32 • (10/31/93) • **89**
Barbaresco Montestefano Riserva 1985 • $25 • (10/31/90) • **82**
Barbaresco Montestefano Riserva 1982 • $22 • (09/15/88) • **88**

Barbaresco Ovello 1989: This young and tannic Barbaresco combines an attractively spicey, complex aroma with good, rather lean flavors of plum, smoke and anise. It's full-bodied, rough-textured, and will need until 1997 or later to near maturity. 1,315 cases made. • $29 • (10/31/94) • **85**

Barbaresco Ovello Riserva 1985 • $25 • (10/31/90) • **86**
Barbaresco Ovello Riserva 1982 • $22 • (09/15/88) • **86**
Barbaresco Paje Riserva 1982 • $22 • (09/15/88) • **91**

Barbaresco Pora 1989: Sturdy, full-bodied and tannic, with ripe plum and berry flavors and a bit of spice. Appealing, if rather basic compared to the best '89 Barbarescos. Drink now. 1,239 cases made. • $29 • (10/31/94) • **84**

Barbaresco Pora Riserva 1982 • $18 • (09/15/88) • **91**
Barbaresco Pora Riserva 1979 • $24 • (09/15/88) • **91**

Barbaresco Rabajà 1990: Fresh and focused dried cherry, berry and herb character, medium body, firm, slightly dry tannins and a sweet fruit finish. Better in 1998. 1,240 cases made. • $35 • **86**

Barbaresco Rabajà 1989: Smooth and well rounded at first, but its flavors are muted and turn very tannic on the finish. Lacks balance and harmony between the meaty flavors and tough texture. Best to drink after 1996. 1,168 cases made. • $33 • (10/31/94) • **82**

Barbaresco Rabajà Riserva 1982 • $22 • (09/15/88) • **89**

Barbaresco Rio Sordo 1990: A pretty Barbaresco from the great '90 vintage, and pedigree shows in sweet, harmonious tar, floral and cherry flavors. Slightly drying on the finish, though food should make it satisfying. 1,140 cases made. • $35 • **82**

Barbaresco Rio Sordo 1989: Subtly flavorful and well balanced, blending cinnamon, leather and anise aromas with nice, plummy flavors and a lingering finish. Drinkable now. 678 cases made. • $29 • (10/31/94) • **88**

Barbaresco Rio Sordo Riserva 1988 • $30 • (04/15/94) • **76**
Barbaresco Rio Sordo Riserva 1982 • $22 • (09/15/88) • **87**
Barbaresco Selezione del Trentennio '30' 1988 • $28 • (04/30/92) • **91**
Nebbiolo delle Langhe 1990 • $9 • (07/31/92) • **83**
Nebbioio delle Langhe 1988 • $9 • (02/28/91) • **82**

PROVENQUIERE, DOMAINE LA

Vigne Molin Lugana 1992 • $13 • • **84**

PRUNOTTO

Barbaresco 1991: Aromatic rose petal, tar and spice notes and some silky texture. Medium-bodied and a bit drying on the finish. 833 cases made. • $25 • **79**

Barbaresco 1990: Crisp and fruity, a little tannic but it shows some raspberry and brown sugar flavors that turn tart on the finish. Try in 1997. • $NA • (10/31/94) • **81**

Barbaresco 1989: Crisp and refreshing, a lively wine with bright raspberry and anise flavors that keep echoing on the finish with a touch of mushroom. Drinkable now, maybe best around 1997. • $21 • (10/31/94) • **85**

Barbaresco 1988 • $17 • (10/31/94) • **87**
Barbaresco 1987 • $27 • (03/31/92) • **70**

Barbaresco Monstefano 1990: Firm and chewy at first, but the berry and licorice flavors grow as this opens up, finishing with a bite of tannin that needs until 1998 to soften. Better than last year. • $NA • (10/31/94) • **85**

Barbaresco Montestefano 1989: Crisp and firm in texture, chewy and harmonious, with a lean, lithe line of berry, spicy and ever-so-slightly gamy flavors. Approachable now, but should be best after 1996. Much better than last year. • $35 • (10/31/94) • **85**

Barbaresco Montestefano 1987 • $37 • (03/31/92) • **76**
Barbaresco Montestefano 1986 • $37 • (12/31/90) • **86**
Barbaresco Montestefano 1985 • $29 • (03/31/90) • **87**
Barbaresco Rabajà Riserva 1982 • $19 • (07/31/87) • **81**
Barbera d'Alba 1991 • $11 • (11/15/93) • **74**
Barbera d'Alba 1987 • $9 • (03/31/90) • **85**
Barbera d'Alba 1985 • $8 • (07/15/88) • **81**
Barbera d'Alba 1983 • $6 • (07/15/87) BB • **89**
Barbera d'Alba Fiulot 1993 • $10 • (10/31/94) • **79**

Barbera d'Alba Fiulot 1992: Very light and simple, with a thread of strawberry and herb flavors, finishing a little watery. • $10 • **73**

Barbera d'Alba Pian Romualdo 1993: A delicious, silky-textured Barbera, medium in body, offering berry, grapey aromas and flavors. Drink now. • $22 • **85**

Barbera d'Alba Pian Romualdo 1991 • $19 • (10/31/94) • **77**
Barbera d'Alba Pian Romualdo 1990 • $19 • (10/31/94) • **81**

Barbera d'Alba Pian Romualdo 1989: Licorice and roasted chicory flavors dominate. Still firm for its age, with a lot of plum and cherry flavors. Well-structured and concentrated. 1,500 cases made. • $19 • (07/31/95) • **85**

Barbera d'Alba Pian Romualdo 1988 • $19 • (11/15/93) • **80**
Barbera d'Alba Pian Romualdo 1987 • $14 • (09/15/90) • **81**

Barolo 1991: Medium body, has an attractive silky character, showing a backbone of fine tannins. Has some nice cherry and chestnut, almost Pinot-like flavors, but a bit simple and drying on the finish. 2,500 cases made. • $27 • **80**

Barolo 1990: Nicely made, showing ripe fruit and spice balanced with fine tannins and sweet vanilla and floral notes chiming in on the finish. Approachable now, may be best from 1997. • $29 • (10/31/94) • **86**

Barolo 1989: Smooth, polished and lively, offering complex berry, spice and herbal flavors on a medium frame, finishing with a supple texture and range of cherry, cola and coffee notes that are very appealing. Drinkable now. 2,500 cases made. • $27 • (10/31/93) • **90**

Barolo 1988 • $27 • (09/30/93) • **93**
Barolo 1987 • $27 • (03/31/92) • **85**
Barolo 1985 • $31 • (03/31/90) • **82**

Barolo Bussia 1990: Ripe and chunky, shining a broad, concentrated beam of anise, black cherry and berry flavors through a veil of chewy tannins. Needs until 2000 to 2005 to sort out the tannins. • $NA • (10/31/94) • **88**

Barolo Bussia 1989: Classy, wearing its spicy, tarry black cherry and berry flavors inside a layer of fine tannins, with mineral and earth notes on the supple finish. Best from 1998 or 2000. • $37 • (10/31/94) • **89**

Barolo Bussia 1988 • $35 • (11/30/94) • **85**
Barolo Bussia 1986 • $39 • (03/31/92) • **78**
Barolo Bussia 1985 • $38 • (09/15/90) • **92**

ITALY

Barolo Bussia 1983 • $28 • (09/15/88) • **88**
Barolo Bussia 1982 • $30 • (09/15/88) • **91**
Barolo Bussia 1978 • $50 • (09/15/88) • **86**
Barolo Bussia 1974 • $65 • (09/15/88) • **80**
Barolo Bussia 1971 • $52 Ⓐ • (09/15/88) • **90**
Barolo Bussia 1967 • $49 • (09/15/88) • **82**
Barolo Bussia 1964 • $85 • (09/15/88) • **80**
Barolo Bussia 1961 • $110 • (09/15/88) • **91**
Barolo Cannubi 1990: Light in color and concentration, although there is enough earthy strawberry and raspberry flavor to come through on the finish against a layer of chewy tannins. • $NA • (10/31/94) • **81**
Barolo Cannubi 1989: Herbal, floral aromas and flavors give this lean, lithe red an unusual flair, shading the modest raspberry and strawberry notes. The fine tannins pick up a little edge on the finish, may be best from 1997 • $37 • (10/31/94) • **83**
Barolo Cannubi 1985 • $32 • (03/31/90) • **85**
Barolo Cannubi 1983 • $26 • (09/15/88) • **85**
Barolo Cannubi 1982 • $25 • (09/15/88) • **75**
Barolo Cannubi 1978 • $21 • (09/15/88) • **78**
Barolo Ginestra di Monforte d'Alba Riserva 1980 • $13 • (06/30/87) • **78**
Barolo Riserva 1980 • $12 • (06/30/87) • **65**
Dolcetto d'Alba 1990 • $11 • (09/30/93) • **80**
Dolcetto d'Alba 1989 • $11 • (02/15/92) • **83**
Dolcetto d'Alba 1985 • $10 • (03/15/89) • **84**
Gagliassi di Monforte Riserva 1985 • $12 • (03/15/89) • **88**
Mosesco 1990 • $15 • (09/30/93) • **82**
Nebbiolo d'Alba 1993: Soft, round, lovely berry, cherry and floral aromas and flavors, medium body and a simple finish. • $19 • **83**
Nebbiolo d'Alba Occhetti 1991: Lean and a little stemmy, a modest wine with little intensity to balance the tannin and acidity. RT • $16 • **74**
Nebbiolo d'Alba Occhetti 1990: Maturing and lean, showing dried cherry and tea flavors, with dry tannins. A bit tough but expressive, and would complement grilled or smoked meats. 2,200 cases made. • $17 • (07/31/95) • **82**
Roero 1986 • $10 • (06/30/88) • **82**
Roero 1985 • $9 • (07/31/87) • **88**

ITALY

PUIATTI

Chardonnay Collio 1995: Pale in the glass and light on the palate, this simple wine offers some crisp, green apple flavors, then vanishes. 5,000 cases made. • $18 • (06/15/96) • **78**
Chardonnay Collio 1993: Lean and minerally, with green apple and chalky flavors that finish smooth but without a lot of distinction. 10,000 cases made. • $15 • (01/31/95) • **83**
Merlot Collio 1989 • $26 • (01/31/92) • **78**
Pinot Bianco Collio 1995: Very young-tasting, with banana, vanilla and peach flavors. It is light, fresh and clean-tasting. 4,000 cases made. • $18 • (06/15/96) • **82**
Pinot Bianco Collio 1993: Smooth and ripe, with an vanilla edge to the bright pear and apple fruit, fresh and vibrant on the long finish. 2,500 cases made. • $15 • (01/31/95) • **87**
Pinot Bianco Collio 1991 • $20 • (09/30/93) • **87**
Pinot Grigio Collio 1995: Fresh and clean, but very light in flavor. Simple enjoyment in a dry, light-bodied wine. 8,000 cases made. • $18 • (06/15/96) • **78**
Pinot Grigio Collio 1993: Quite interesting, showing some complexity with all that butter, vanilla, creamy, milky flavors that make it a fun wine to drink. Feels smooth despite the crisp finish. 5,800 cases made. • $15 • (01/31/95) • **83**
Pinot Nero Collio 1989 • $26 • (09/15/92) • **70**
Sauvignon Collio 1995: Crisp and flavorful, with plenty of herb, peach and spicy notes. Very assertive and well-balanced. 5,000 cases made. • $18 • (06/15/96) • **84**
Sauvignon Collio 1993: A take-no-prisoners style, crisp and distinctive, showing plenty of pear, herb and licorice aromas and flavors, finishing bright anad citrusy. 5,800 cases made. • $15 • (01/31/95) • **88**
Sauvignon Collio 1991 • $21 • (09/15/93) • **89**

PUNSET

Barbaresco 1989: Beautifully complex aromas and harmonious flavors make this a winning wine that only needs time to bring out its best. It has cedar and tobacco aromas, fresh cherry and berry flavors and a lingering finish. Drinkable now. 1,675 cases made. • $17 • (06/15/94) • **90**
Barbera d'Alba 1990 • $14 • (04/30/93) • **87**
Chardonnay delle Langhe 1991 • $12 • (12/15/92) • **88**

PUPILLE, FATTORIA LE

Morellino di Scansano 1989 • $13 • (10/31/93) • **84**
Morellino di Scansano Riserva 1988 • $NA • (10/31/93) • **85**
Morellino di Scansano Riserva 1986 • $16 • (06/30/91) • **86**
Saffredi 1990: A deeply colored, oak-scented red with rich, opulent flavors of black cherry, tobacco and spice. It's tannic, but balanced. Best to wait until 1997. • $40 • (02/28/95) • **88**
Saffredi 1989 • $NA • (10/31/93) • **86**
Saffredi 1988 • $NA • (10/31/93) • **91**

QUERCE, FATTORIA LA

Chianti 1985 • $9 • (11/30/87) • **83**
Chianti Classico 1988 • $9 • (11/30/89) BT • **86**
Chianti Classico 1987 • $7 • (11/30/89) • **80**
Chianti Classico 1986 • $7 • (11/30/89) • **81**
Chianti Classico Caratello 1986 • $6 • (11/30/89) • **68**
Chianti Classico Caratello 1983 • $4 • (11/30/89) • **70**

QUERCECCHIO

Brunello di Montalcino 1990: Ripe but crisp with an interesting combination of black cherry, currant and tobacco flavors. Yet very hard and tannic, showing a funky chestnut character on the finish. Drink now. • $NA • **80**
Brunello di Montalcino 1988: A bit rustic and clumsy, with very ripe, almost raisiny, fruit, full body and round tannins. Not going anywhere. Tasted twice. • $NA • (04/30/94) • **79**
Brunello di Montalcino Riserva 1988: Herbal, spicy wine with fruity, peppery flavors. It's full bodied and concentrated with loads of tannins and a concentrated fruity finish. Slightly aggressive. Needs time to come around. Try after 1998. • $NA • (10/31/94) • **88**
Rosso di Montalcino 1993: Slightly tired chestnut, berry and tomato character. Medium-bodied and round, adding an herbal chocolate finish. Drink now. • $NA • **77**
Rosso di Montalcino 1991 • $NA • (04/30/94) • **81**

QUERCETO, CASTELLO DI

Chianti Classico 1992: Straightforward, with modest cherry and berry flavors that give way to a slightly astringent finish. A solid backbone of tannins. Drink now. 8,000 cases made. • $9 • (10/31/95) • **82**
Chianti Classico 1990 • $14 • (10/31/93) • **85**
Chianti Classico 1989 • $15 • (09/15/92) • **84**
Chianti Classico 1988 • $14 • (09/15/91) • **86**
Chianti Classico Il Picchio Riserva 1988 • $NA • (09/15/92) • **83**
Chianti Classico Riserva 1990: Well crafted, exhibiting mint, cassis, berry and cherry aromas and flavors. Medium-bodied and very fine with a long aftertaste. Drinkable now. • $14 • (02/28/95) • **87**
Chianti Classico Riserva 1988 • $19 • (09/15/92) • **86**
Chianti Classico Riserva 1985 • $16 • (11/30/89) • **91**
Chianti Classico Riserva Il Picchio 1990: Fresh despite its age, with loads of plum and cherry flavors that are modified by licorice and cedar notes. Well balanced, with plenty of backbone and a lingering finish. Delicious now. 1,500 cases made. • $27 • (10/31/95) • **88**
Cignale 1989 • $35 • (10/31/93) • **80**

Key: SS—Spectator Selection. CS—Cellar Selection. BB—Best Buy. $NA—Price not available. (BT)—Barrel tasting. Ⓐ—Auction Price.
Dates in parentheses represent the issues in which the ratings were published.

Cignale 1988: A gutsy red that's beginning to show the benefits of age. Has a very deep color, complex aromas, rich fruit and firm tannins. Nice, lingering finish, too. Drink now through about 1997. 480 cases made. • $40 • (02/28/95) • **87**
Cignale 1987: Tasty, robust and gaining complexity with age. It has spicy, smoky aromas, ripe berry and licorice flavors, and accents of nut and herb. Ready to drink now. 410 cases made. • $36 • (02/28/95) • **89**
Il Querciolaia 1988 • $40 • (09/15/91) • **88**
Il Querciolaia 1986 • $35 • (11/30/89) • **85**
Il Querciolaia 1985 • $30 • (02/15/89) • **85**
La Corte 1988: A rustic style, but it has some appealing plum and dried cherry flavors. A little tough on the finish. • $30 • (07/31/95) • **80**
La Corte 1985 • $20 • (11/30/89) • **93**
La Corte 1983 • $17 • (11/30/89) • **83**

QUERCIA, LA

Chianti Classico 1988 • $NA • (09/15/91) • **86**

QUERCIA AL POGGIO

Chianti Classico 1990 • $NA • (10/31/93) • **85**
Chianti Classico Riserva 1988 • $NA • (10/31/93) • **80**

QUERCIABELLA, FATTORIA

Camartina 1991: Big and thick with tobacco, cedar and berry character. Full-bodied with full tannins and a slightly astringent finish. May be better after 1996. Made from Cabernet and Sangiovese. • $NA • **85**
Chianti Classico 1988 • $13 • (09/15/91) • **90**
Chianti Classico Riserva 1991: Silky and soft with some nice spicy plum, dark chocolate flavors, but the tannins turn a bit drying on the finish. A wine with some depth. Drinkable now. • $NA • (10/31/95) • **84**
Chianti Classico Riserva 1988 • $20 • (09/15/92) • **90**
Chianti Classico Riserva 1985 • $17 • (09/15/91) • **89**

RAJA, LA

Gavi 1993 • $13 • (06/15/94) • **77**

RAMPOLLA, CASTELLO DEI

Chianti Classico 1992: Some decent fruit there, but rather weedy and has a tomato character. Light body and intensely herbal on the finish. Tasted twice, with consistent notes. 3,000 cases made. • $17 • **75**
Chianti Classico 1989 • $17 • (12/15/92) • **80**
Chianti Classico 1988 • $14 • (09/15/92) • **87**
Chianti Classico 1987 • $15 • (04/15/91) • **84**
Chianti Classico 1985 • $8 • (09/15/88) • **90**
Chianti Classico 1983 • $6 • (07/31/87) BB • **84**
Chianti Classico 1982 • $6 • (10/16/85) • **64**
Chianti Classico Riserva 1991: Ripe and quite opulent with a firm texture and good complexity. Tastes of tobacco, cedar, black cherry. Elegant finish. Needs a bit of time for the tannins to soften, so drink after 1996. 1,500 cases made. • $28 • **86**
Chianti Classico Riserva 1990: Well rounded and interesting, from the spicy, minty aroma to the satisfying fruit flavors to the vanilla-scented finish. Firm tannins, but drink now. • $25 • (02/28/95) • **88**
Chianti Classico Riserva 1988 • $19 • (05/15/93) • **88**
Chianti Classico Riserva 1985 • $46 Ⓐ • (04/30/90) • **81**
Sammarco 1991: Silky and fine with mineral and berry elements in the nose and palate. Medium-bodied, medium tannins, medium finish. Not as great as the '90 but still delicious. 2,500 cases made. • $58 • **87**
Sammarco 1990: Easily lives up to its reputation. Classy, thick and loaded with chewy tannins. This offers rich tobacco, cherry and berry flavors wrapped in toasty vanilla. Full body, full tannins-a wine for the cellar. Try in 1998. Better than a bottle reviewed earlier in New York. • $55 • **91**
Sammarco 1986 • $46 • (03/15/91) • **76**
Sammarco 1985 • $42 • (11/30/89) • **90**
Sammarco 1983 • $28 • (09/15/88) • **88**

RATTI, RENATO

Barbaresco 1990: Firm and chunky in texture, with a nice beam of bright raspberry and red cherry fruit that manages to pierce the blanket of tannins. A good bet to hold until 1998. • $26 • (10/31/94) • **85**
Barbaresco 1989: This is a lean wine with tired cherry, tomato and plum flavors. An odd rubbery note runs through the aroma all the way to the finish. 400 cases made. • $31 • (10/31/94) • **73**
Barolo 1990: Supple in texture, showing a nice range of sweet cherry, anise and chocolate aromas and flavors, finishing with a grip of heat that keeps it from being wishy-washy. Tannins are a little drying but not bitter. Best from 1997. • $31 • (10/31/94) • **85**
Barolo 1989: Chewy in texture, with a tobacco edge to the otherwise bright raspberry fruit, a sharp-edged wine with decent fruit at the core. Give it until 1998. Tasted twice. • $28 • (10/31/94) • **79**
Barolo 1985 • $27 • (09/15/90) • **85**
Barolo 1983 • $27 • (10/15/88) • **87**
Barolo 1982 • $28 • (06/30/87) CS • **93**
Barolo 1980 • $10 • (02/15/87) • **83**
Barolo 1979 • $9 • (01/01/86) • **89**
Barolo Conca Marcenasco 1988 • $NA • (10/31/93) • **78**
Barolo Marcenasco 1991: Soft, smooth and very drinkable. Delicious dried cherry flavors that have a slightly minty, smoky character. A bit one-dimensional but good. 500 cases made. • $33 • **84**
Barolo Marcenasco 1990: Rich and ripe, a cascade of rose petal, spice, currant, plum and anise aromas and flavors, wrapped in a fine-textured veil of tannins. Has character and intensity in spades, balanced for aging through 2000 and beyond. • $36 • (10/31/94) • **91**
Barolo Marcenasco 1989: Ripe and supple, generous with its black cherry, strawberry, anise and chocolate flavors. Not too tannic. Drinkable now, but concentrated enough to be best from perhaps 1998. 1,500 cases made. • $40 • (10/31/94) • **87**
Barolo Marcenasco 1988 • $NA • (10/31/93) • **84**
Barolo Marcenasco 1985 • $45 • (10/15/90) • **82**
Barolo Marcenasco 1982 • $37 • (06/30/87) • **90**
Barolo Marcenasco 1981 • $15 • (06/30/87) • **84**
Barolo Marcenasco Rocche 1989: Extremely tannic and tough, more aromatic than flavorful, offering some anise-scented strawberry and raspberry aromas and flavors. Finishes austere. Try after 1997. 375 cases made. • $NA • (10/31/93) • **81**
Barolo Marcenasco Rocche 1988 • $NA • (10/31/93) • **79**
Barolo Marcenasco Rocche 1983 • $30 • (01/31/89) • **86**
Barolo Marcenasco Rocche 1981 • $19 • (06/30/87) • **88**
Cabernet Sauvignon 1989 • $25 • (06/15/94) • **83**
Dolcetto d'Alba 1993: Ripe and round, marries its lush blackberry flavors with a light earthiness. Good balance of fruit and tannin, and impressive concentration. Drink now. 5,000 cases made. • $10 • (07/31/95) • **86**
Nebbiolo d'Alba 1993: Straightforward cherry, mineral character. Medium in body, fine tannins and a light finish. 100 cases made. • $18 • **82**
Nebbiolo d'Alba 1983 • $7 • (06/16/86) BB • **81**
Vigna Colombe 1985 • $9 • (02/28/87) • **90**
Villa Pattono 1989 • $18 • (10/31/94) • **83**

REGALEALI

Cabernet Sauvignon 1989 • $32 • (04/30/94) • **84**
Conte Tasca d'Almerita Red 1985 • $7 • (04/15/88) • **74**
Rosso 1987 • $11 • (12/15/89) • **77**
Rosso del Conte 1984 • $19 • (07/31/89) • **84**

RICASOLI, BARONE

Brolio Sangiovese 1993: Very crisp and clean, showing delicious berry and cherry aromas and flavors. Grab a pizza and enjoy. Drinkable now. 10,000 cases made. • $9 • (02/28/95) • **80**
Chianti 1994: A straightforward, fruity Chianti with light tannins and a crisp finish. Pleasant glass of wine. Drinkable now. • $NA • **80**
Chianti 1993: Straightforward cherry, game and earth aromas and flavors, light body and light, fruity finish. Drinkable now. • $7 • (02/28/95) • **79**

ITALY

Chianti 1989 • $7 • (04/15/91) BB • **83**
Chianti Classico 1993: Light, crisp and rather vibrant, displaying some well-defined raspberry, blackberry and wet earth flavors. But it's a bit diluted mid-palate. 80,000 cases made. • $8 • **81**
Chianti Classico Brolio 1990: Big-boned and a bit heavy-handed. This has earthy plum and chocolate flavors in a firm, alcoholic style that's concentrated but drinkable now. • $NA • **83**
Chianti Classico Brolio Riserva 1990: Very fresh profile of mint, berry, plum and tar. Medium-bodied and slightly lean, crisp finish. Barrel sample. Drinkable now. 4,000 cases made. • $13 • **85-89** (BT)
Chianti Classico Brolio Riserva 1988 • $13 • (10/31/94) • **87**
Chianti Classico Brolio Riserva del Barone 1983 • $26 • (10/31/94) • **81**
Chianti Classico Ricasoli Riserva 1983 • $8 • (11/30/89) • **83**
Chianti Classico Riserva 1990: Mature flavors of dried cherry and spice, with a fairly tannic finish. This offers some lively flavors up front, but drink up before they fade. • $12 • (10/31/95) • **82**
Chianti Classico San Ripolo 1988 • $9 • (10/31/91) BB • **84**
Chianti Classico San Ripolo 1987 • $10 • (04/15/91) • **79**
Chianti Ricasoli 1990 • $6 • (11/30/91) BB • **81**
Chianti Ricasoli 1987 • $6 • (11/30/89) • **79**
Chianti Ricasoli 1986 • $5 • (05/15/89) BB • **84**
Orvieto Classico 1994: Creamy almond and vanilla aromas are attractive in this firm, round wine. The peach and light earthy flavors are well balanced and will stand up to food. • $6 • **84**
Tremalvo Tuscany 1987 • $18 • (12/15/91) • **87**

RICCADONNA

Presidente Extra Seco NV • $5 • (12/31/86) • **75**
Riserva Privata 1981 • $13 • (12/31/86) • **68**

RIECINE

Chianti Classico 1992: Clean and fresh with simple dried cherry flavor and a touch of smokiness, light in body. Drinkable now. • $NA • **80**
Chianti Classico 1991 • $21 • (10/31/93) • **86**
Chianti Classico 1990 • $22 • (09/15/92) • **80**
Chianti Classico 1988 • $22 • (04/30/91) • **89**
Chianti Classico 1987 • $20 • (04/30/91) • **83**
Chianti Classico Riserva 1991: Muscular Chianti with minty, berry, black cherry and vanilla aromas and flavors. Medium-bodied with medium-fine tannins and a long finish. Drinkable now or can be aged. 250 cases made. • $35 • **88**
Chianti Classico Riserva 1990: A very good red showing delicious berry and meat character. Medium-bodied and fruity with medium tannins and finish. Drinkable now. • $NA • **88**
Chianti Classico Riserva 1988 • $24 • (09/15/92) • **82**
Chianti Classico Riserva 1985 • $19 • (09/15/91) • **87**
La Gioia 1991: The essence of crushed berries and violets. Full-bodied and very firm with an abundance of fruit and plenty of tannins. Made from Sangiovese. A wine to age: better after 1997. 250 cases made. • $42 • **89**
La Gioia 1990: Wonderfully refined, it has berry, tobacco and leather character. Medium-bodied with fine tannins and a long succulent finish. 250 cases made. • $45 • **90**
La Gioia di Riecine 1990: A lively wine with vivid black cherry and berry character, medium body, silky tannins and superfresh finish. Made from Sangiovese. Drinkable now. 375 cases made. • $45 • (10/31/93) • **89**
La Gioia di Riecine 1988 • $65 • (09/15/91) • **91**
La Gioia di Riecine 1987 • $45 • (04/30/91) • **82**

RIETINE

Chianti Classico 1992: Round and rather silky, a light-bodied red with some attractive plum, black cherry and minty notes. Well-done, smooth yet crisp finish. • $NA • **83**

Key: SS—Spectator Selection. CS—Cellar Selection. BB—Best Buy. $NA—Price not available. (BT)—Barrel tasting. (A)—Auction Price.
Dates in parentheses represent the issues in which the ratings were published.

Chianti Classico Riserva 1991: A maturing Chianti offering some mushroom aromas and plummy flavors that make for pleasurable drinking. Soft, supple and harmonious finish. • $NA • **84**
Tiziano Red 1990: Big and burly wine with loads of fruit and tar character. Full-bodied and thick with astringent tannins and a tar-flavored finish. A bit coarse-time will tell if this comes around. Try after 1997. • $NA • **85**

RIGHETTI, LUIGI

Amarone Capitel de' Roari Recioto della Valpolicella 1983 • $16 • (02/15/89) • **90**
Amarone della Valpolicella Classico Capitel de Roari 1990: A concentrated and intense red from this northern Italian appellation. This is packed with flavor, blending spicy, peppery nuances and full-bore fruit. Firm tannins, lots of body and a long, lingering finish. Drinkable now through 2000. 15,000 cases made. • $20 • (04/30/96) • **90**
Valpolicella Classico Superiore Campolieti 1993: Ripe and unusually concentrated for Valpolicella, with plum, licorice, coffee and toast aromas and flavors. The tannins are a bit light for the rich flavors, but it's still appealing. 25,000 cases made. • $10 • (12/15/95) • **85**

RINALDI & FIGLI, FRANCESCO

Barbaresco 1985 • $23 • (09/15/90) • **87**
Barbaresco 1983 • $16 • (01/31/89) • **79**
Barbera d'Alba 1993: Dark-colored, showing violet, black cherry and raspberry flavors. A bit more body than most '93 Barberas, but still quite crisp on the finish. • $13 • **85**
Barbera d'Alba 1991 • $12 • (09/30/93) • **86**
Barbera d'Alba 1989 • $13 • (10/31/92) • **89**
Barbera d'Alba 1987 • $10 • (03/15/91) • **87**
Barbera d'Alba 1986 • $9 • (02/15/89) • **88**
Barolo 1988 • $22 • (09/15/93) • **79**
Barolo 1986 • $38 • (07/15/91) • **83**
Barolo 1983 • $20 • (09/15/88) • **84**
Barolo 1982 • $50 • (09/15/88) • **83**
Barolo 1978 • $69 • (09/16/84) • **89**
Barolo Brunate Riserva 1988 • $30 • (10/31/93) • **71**
Barolo Cannubbio 1989: Lean in texture, with weedy, wild berry and tar aromas and flavors that turn a bit chunky and hard on the finish. Needs until 1997. • $30 • (10/31/93) • **976**
Barolo Cannubbio 1985 • $25 • (06/15/90) • **78**
Barolo Cannubbio 1982 • $16 • (10/31/87) • **75**
Barolo Cannubi 1990: Crisp and aromatic, spicy, with a lovely thread of berry flavor running through it. Finishes a little tight, but it has enough concentration to warrant cellaring until 1999. • $NA • (10/31/94) • **89**
Barolo Cannubi 1989: Firm in texture, with drying tannins, modest berry flavor and finishing with an earthy-anise fillip. Awkward at this stage, may be better after 1998. • $NA • (10/31/94) • **79**
Barolo La Brunata Riserva 1985 • $24 • (07/15/91) • **89**
Barolo La Brunata Riserva 1982 • $27 • (06/30/87) • **79**
Dolcetto d'Alba Roussot 1991 • $12 • (09/30/93) • **76**
Dolcetto d'Alba Roussot 1990 • $13 • (10/31/92) • **78**
Dolcetto d'Alba Roussot 1988 • $10 • (07/15/91) • **78**
Dolcetto d'Alba Roussot 1987 • $9 • (03/31/90) • **86**
Piedmont 1989 • $12 • (07/15/91) • **80**

RINALDI, GIOVANNI & BATTISTA

Barolo 1983 • $NA • (09/15/88) • **86**
Barolo 1982 • $NA • (09/15/88) • **84**

RINALDI, GIUSEPPE

Barolo 1990: With its drying tannins, this will need some smoothing with age, but the concentration of sweet, ripe raspberry and red cherry fruit is impressive enough. Keep your fingers crossed. 625 cases made. • $35 • (10/31/93) • **84-89**
Barolo 1989: Smooth, ripe and generous, a warm wine with sweet, almost opulent plum, chocolate and spice aromas and flavors, rich enough to

swing past the firm tannins, echoing fruit and oak on the finish. Tempting to drink now, best after 1996. 625 cases made. • $35 • (10/31/93) • **87**

Barolo Riserva Brunate 1989: Soft and relatively inviting, a lighter style of Barolo that adds a sweet touch of caramel and vanilla to the modest berry and herbal flavors. Approachable now. • $38 • (10/31/94) • **80**

RIPA, LA

Chianti Classico 1993: Cherry, watermelon and crushed raspberry aromas and flavors. Light body, light tannins and a watery finish. • $10 • **77**

Santa Brigida 1990: Disappointing for a '90. Rather weedy and green with a somewhat astringent finish. Made from Sangiovese and Cabernet Sauvignon. • $15 • **73**

RITRATTI

Pinot Grigio Trentino 1991: A white wine that has cheesy aromas, ripe but simple fruit flavors and an earthy finish. Average quality, not for everybody. 3,500 cases made. • $12 • **74**

Pinot Nero Trentino 1991: Has some Pinot Noir character, but it's lean and smoky tasting, austere overall. Sweet oak obscures the fruit. 1,800 cases made. • $12 • (02/28/95) • **78**

RIUNITE

Lambrusco Reggiano NV • $4 • (09/30/91) BB • **81**

RIVERA

Il Falcone Riserva Castel del Monte 1985 • $17 • (12/31/90) • **83**

RIVETTI & FIGLI, GIUSEPPE

Moscato d'Asti La Spinetta Bricco Quaglia 1991 • $15 • (05/15/93) • **80**

Moscato d'Asti La Spinetta Vigneto Biancospino 1992 • $15 • (05/15/93) • **88**

RIVETTI, FRATELLI

Barbera d'Alba Cairel 1990 • $12 • (06/15/94) • **82**

Nebbiolo d'Alba Vigneto rainè 1990 • $14 • (06/15/94) • **86**

RIZZARDI, GUERRIERI

Amarone Recioto della Valpolicella Classico 1990: Quite a mouthful from this rich, velvety and almost Port-like red. Loads of leather and tobacco flavors come through, and for its age it is still quite tannic and very concentrated. There are plenty of fruit flavors as well, which are by dominated dried cherry and plum. The finish is long and brings out good prune finish. • $22 • (06/15/96) • **90**

Amarone Recioto della Valpolicella Classico 1988 • $20 • (09/15/92) • **75**

Chardonnay di Val Lagarina 1991 • $9 • (09/15/92) • **74**

Classico Poiega Valpolicella 1988 • $9 • (12/15/89) • **82**

Classico Superiore Valpolicella 1987 • $6 • (03/31/90) • **79**

Costeggiola Soave Classico 1991 • $9 • (09/15/92) • **85**

Poiega Valpolicella Classico 1990 • $8 • (09/15/92) • **80**

Soave Classico 1994: Buttery aromas and flavors with some green apple mixed in. It has character, but ends up a bit cloying on the finish. • $8 • (06/15/96) • **82**

Soave Classico 1991 • $7 • (09/15/92) • **81**

Soave Classico Costeggiola 1994: A light and slighty sweet tasting white with appealing peach flavors and a hint of apricot and spice. Serve well-chilled. • $9 • (06/15/96) • **84**

Superiore Valpolicella Classico 1991 • $9 • (04/30/94) • **80**

Tacchetto Bardolino 1991 • $12 • (09/15/92) • **83**

Valpolicella Classico Superiore Villa Rizzardi Poiega 1993: Fragrant with cherry and smoky aromas, this light, crisp wine is balanced and still fresh, with just enough tannin to hold up to food. Well made and typical. • $7 • (06/15/96) • **85**

ROAGNA, ALFREDO & GIOVANNI

Barbaresco 1990: A strong menthol streak covers the fruit and makes this feel off. 1,500 cases made. • $30 • (10/31/93) • **969**

Barbaresco 1989: Earthy and a little funky, but the black cherry and plum flavors manage to ride to the fore on the palate, making for an exotic style that is impressive and distinctive. Drink after 1996. 1,500 cases made. • $30 • (10/31/93) • **87**

Barbaresco 1988: Extremely earthy and vegetal, too much for the modest berry fruit. RT • $33 • **72**

Barbaresco 1986 • $26 • (07/15/91) • **86**

Barbaresco 1985 • $37 • (08/10/90) • **87**

Opera Prima IV NV • $23 • (07/31/89) • **76**

Opera Prima Imbottigliato il 15 Novembre NV • $17 • (12/31/87) • **82**

ROCCA, ALBINO

Barbaresco Vigneto Brich Ronchi 1991: A little tannic, but the light flavors are charming, offering floral strawberry and anise character before the tannins start biting on the finish. • $23 • (10/31/94) • **83**

Barbaresco Vigneto Loreto 1991: Light and charming, floral at first, a supple thread of pleasant raspberry and strawberry flavor carrying through on the palate. Approachable now. • $22 • (10/31/94) • **82**

ROCCA, BRUNO

Barbaresco 1991: Remarkable ripe and generous, medium-bodied, smooth-textured, offering currant, blackberry and vanilla flavors that persist into a soft finish. • $42 • (10/31/94) • **86**

Barbaresco Rabajà 1992: Firm, fruity and ready to drink. Medium body and tannins and a long, silky texture complement tobacco and berry flavors. 1,000 cases made. • $40 • **80**

Barbaresco Rabajà 1989: Very pretty wine, offering gorgeous raspberry, floral and vanilla aromas and flavors, remaining smooth and elegant through the almost-delicate finish. A wine that caresses rather than powers its way over the palate. Delicious to drink already. Should be fine through 1998. 900 cases made. • $45 • (10/31/93) • **92**

Barbera d'Alba 1993: Delicious ripe fruit and milk chocolate aromas and flavors. Medium-bodied and soft, adding a long, sweet fruit finish. 500 cases made. • $20 • **86**

Barbera d'Alba 1991 • $22 • (10/31/94) • **88**

Fralù Red NV • $13 • (03/31/93) • **75**

Fralù da Vigneto Nebbiolo Red 1993: Very light and slightly diluted, offering some decent cherry and raspberry notes. Quite watery on the finish. 500 cases made. • $15 • **78**

ROCCA DELLE MACIE

Chianti Classico 1992: Modest bark and cherry aromas and flavors. Very light. 100,000 cases made. • $NA • **76**

Chianti Classico 1991 • $9 • (10/31/93) • **85**

Chianti Classico 1990 • $9 • (09/15/92) • **88**

Chianti Classico 1987 • $NA • (11/30/89) • **82**

Chianti Classico 1986 • $NA • (11/30/89) • **80**

Chianti Classico Riserva 1990: Quite mature, offering oatmeal and strawberry aromas and flavors. Light-bodied, modest fruit and tannins. Drinkable now. 14,500 cases made. • $13 • **75**

Chianti Classico Riserva 1985 • $14 • (09/15/91) • **77**

Chianti Classico Riserva di Fizzano 1987 • $NA • (11/30/89) • **89**

Chianti Classico Riserva di Fizzano 1985 • $NA • (11/30/89) • **88**

Chianti Classico Riserva di Fizzano 1982 • $16 • (03/31/89) • **87**

Chianti Classico Tenuta Sant'Alfonso 1992: Earthy and gamy with berry and cherry aromas and flavors. Crisp finish. Drinkable now. • $NA • **78**

Chianti Classico Tenuta Sant'Alfonso 1988 • $NA • (09/15/91) • **89**

Roccato 1990: Ripe, round and extremely balanced, a lush red showing meat, plum and earth flavors, medium round tannins and succulent finish. Drinkable now. 5,500 cases made. • $30 • **87**

Roccato 1988 • $NA • (09/15/91) • **90**

Rubizzo 1993: Decent licorice, mushroom, barnyard character. Light-bodied and fruity, but slightly astringent and aggressive on the finish. 13,000 cases made. • $10 • **77**

ITALY

Ser Gioveto 1990: A lighter style, with barnyard, berry and cherry character. Drinkable now. 4,400 cases made. • $16 • **82**
Ser Gioveto 1989 • $15 • (10/31/93) • **76**
Ser Gioveto 1987 • $NA • (11/30/89) • **90**
Ser Gioveto 1986 • $15 • (02/15/89) • **84**
Ser Gioveto 1985 • $15 • (11/30/89) • **88**

ROCCA DI CASTAGNOLI

Buriano 1990: A lovely, soft vino da tavola with plum and cedar aromas and flavors, medium body and tannins and delicate finish. Made from Cabernet Sauvignon. Drinkable now. 1,000 cases made. • $28 • (10/31/93) • **86**
Capraia 1990: Mature and ready to drink. A smoky, fruity Sangiovese, with cedar and berry aromas and flavors, medium body and soft tannins. 1,000 cases made. • $22 • (10/31/93) • **82**
Chianti Classico 1991: Already showing plenty of bottle age—maybe a bit too much. Plenty of game, leather and tobacco character. Medium body and a soft, slightly dry finish. 3,200 cases made. • $17 • **80**
Chianti Classico 1990: A nicely oaky, buttery aroma, and ripe, mellow flavors make this smooth and appealing. Has enough fruit flavor, good balance and lingering finish to make it satisfying. 4,000 cases made. • $14 • (02/28/95) • **86**
Chianti Classico Capraia Riserva 1988 • $NA • (09/15/92) • **84**
Chianti Classico Poggio A'Frati 1988 • $20 • (10/31/93) • **82**
Chianti Classico Poggio A'Frati Riserva 1990: Velvety and delicious with tobacco, mushroom, fruit character. Medium-bodied with medium tannins and a flavorful finish. Drinkable now or hold for cellaring. 5,400 cases made. • $22 • **87**
Chianti Classico Poggio A'Frati Riserva 1988 • $21 • (09/15/92) • **87**
Poggio A'Frati Tuscany 1990: A wonderfully pretty wine with floral, rose petal and violet notes on the nose and palate, full body, medium-silky tannins and a fruity, crisp finish. Made from Sangiovese. Drinkable now. 2,500 cases made. • $18 • (10/31/93) • **89**
Stielle 1991: Rich, ripe and wonderful with milk chocolate, violet, berry and tobacco aromas. Full-bodied and velvety with soft tannins and loads of fruit and toasted oak on the finish. Made from Sangiovese and Cabernet Sauvignon. Delicious now. 1,200 cases made. • $33 • **87**
Stielle 1990: Offers enticing truffle flavors and a smoky, wet earth character, followed by a touch of vanilla on the finish. A compact, elegant and firm wine that needs until at least 1998 to show it all. • $33 • (10/31/95) • **90**
Stielle 1988 • $28 • (10/31/93) • **82**
Stielle Tuscany 1990: This has great delicacy with pretty vanilla, violet and plum aromas and flavors, full body, smooth elegance and very silky tannins. Made from Sangiovese and Cabernet Sauvignon. 2,000 cases made. • $27 • (10/31/93) • **90**

ROCCA DI MONTEGROSSI

Chianti Classico 1991 • $NA • (10/31/93) • **76**
Chianti Classico 1990 • $16 • (10/31/93) • **88**
Chianti Classico Riserva 1987 • $17 • (05/15/93) • **78**

ROCCADORO

Chianti 1991 • $9 • (03/31/93) • **73**
Chianti Classico 1990 • $10 • (05/15/93) • **74**
Chianti Classico Riserva 1988 • $14 • (03/31/93) • **80**

ROCCHE COSTAMAGNA

Barbera d'Alba 1988 • $12 • (03/15/91) • **90**
Barbera d'Alba Rocche di la Morra 1992 • $NA • (10/31/94) • **78**
Barbera d'Alba Rocche di la Morra 1991 • $14 • (04/30/93) • **84**
Barbera d'Alba Rocche di la Morra 1990 • $17 • (10/31/92) • **86**

Key: SS—Spectator Selection. CS—Cellar Selection. BB—Best Buy. $NA—Price not available. (BT)—Barrel tasting. Ⓐ—Auction Price.
Dates in parentheses represent the issues in which the ratings were published.

Barolo Rocche di la Morra 1989: A deep, dark, aromatic, ripe tasting wine with plenty of body and tannins, ripe black cherry flavors and a subtle cedar and tobacco character on the finish. Combines power and complexity in a well-balanced style. Drink now through 2000. 1,350 cases made. • $20 • (10/31/94) • **89**
Barolo Rocche di la Morra 1988 • $26 • (12/15/92) • **87**
Barolo Rocche di la Morra 1985 • $25 • (02/28/91) • **72**
Barolo Rocchi di la Morra 1990: Crisp in texture, featuring a rich layer of black cherry and berry flavor, beautifully defined and spicy around the edges. Approachable, but it can use until 2000 to drop some tannins. • $NA • (10/31/94) • **89**
Barolo Vigneto Francesco 1990: Ripe and round, a smooth-textured wine that shows a gentle face of black cherry, anise and tar flavors on a supple frame. The flavors persist on the elegant finsih and the tannins are nicely integrated. Approachable now, best from 1998. • $NA • (10/31/94) • **90**
Dolcetto d'Alba 1993: A crisp, almost tart Dolcetto that offers some juicy red berry notes in its medium-bodied package. 917 cases made. • $13 • **81**
Piedmont 1989 • $12 • (04/30/91) • **83**
Roccardo Nebbiolo delle Langhe 1989 • $13 • (04/30/91) • **85**
Rocche delle Rocche 1990 • $17 • (03/31/93) • **81**

ROCCHE DEI MANZONI, PODERI

Barbera d'Alba Vigna La Cresta 1993: Very pretty berry, vanilla and cherry flavors. Medium-bodied and soft, adding a milk chocolate-flavored finish. Delicious Barbera d'Alba. • $NA • **85**
Barolo Riserva 1990: A sophisticated, generous, full-bodied Barolo with plenty of black cherry, toasted oak, spice and milk chocolate. Lots of things going on in this polished wine. Tempting now, but better in 1998. • $35 • **89**
Barolo Riserva 1989: Ripe and generous, with smooth tannins that allow the raspberry, tar and floral flavors to shine brightly. A bit alcoholic on the finish, but should grow through 1997 to 2000. • $NA • (10/31/94) • **88**
Barolo Riserva Vigna Big 1990: A big wine that has loads of toasted oak and ripe fruit, but maybe a bit too much new wood. Full body, full tannins and a slightly dry finish. Drinkable now, but can take some age. • $NA • **83**
Barolo Riserva Vigna Big 1989: Supple and ripe, unfolding its black cherry, anise and floral flavors gracefully. Nicely done, not too tannic, a bit hot and gamy on the finish. Best from 1998. • $NA • (10/31/94) • **87**
Barolo Riserva Vigna d'La Roul 1990: All the harmony you can ask for. Absolutely delicious and effused with the character of milk chocolate, cherry and violets. Full-bodied and velvety, with round tannins and a long, rich finish. Drinkable now, but can age. • $NA • **90**
Barolo Riserva Vigna d'La Roul 1989: Massive and richly tannic, layered with opulent black cherry, vanilla, coffee and exotic spice character, ultimately velvety and inviting on the long finish. Has several layers of tannin to lose but should be at its best after 1998. • $NA • (10/31/94) • **92**
Bricco Manzoni 1990 • $NA • (10/31/94) • **74**
Bricco Manzoni 1989: Tough and tart, a killer combination of astringency and acidity that makes it impossible to warm up to this Barbera-Nebbiolo blend. RT • $NA • **74**

RODANO

Chianti Classico 1993: Simple and straightforward, with berry and dried cherry accents. Medium body and a slightly dry, astringent finish. Try now. 5,000 cases made. • $13 • **78**
Chianti Classico 1990 • $10 • (10/31/93) • **87**
Chianti Classico Viacosta Riserva 1990: Very pretty, with boysenberry, violet and rose petal notes. Quite a mouthful of wine, silky at first but turns a bit drying on the finish. • $20 • **84**
Monna Claudia 1988: Delicious fruit, berry, floral and earth character. Medium-bodied with fine tannins and a medium finish. Better after 1997. • $NA • **86**

ROLAR

Asti Spumante NV • $7 • (05/15/93) • **71**

ROMAGNOLI

Famoso 1991: Swampy and musty, with an off-putting finish. Not recommended. Tasted twice, with consistent notes. 50,000 cases made. • $5 • (02/29/96) • **62**

ROMANDIOLA

Il Pavone D'Oro Superiore Sangiovese di Romagna 1993: A good, full-bodied wine with modest tannins. It is fruity and has some nice plum flavors and a touch of brown sugar. Mature and ready to drink. 1,100 cases made. • $7 • (02/29/96) • **84**

ROMITORIO, CASTELLO

Brio 1992: Solid fruit flavors and a firm texture make this a hearty, likeable red. Moderately tannic, nicely balanced with acidity and well-made. • $10 • (02/28/95) • **84**

Brunello di Montalcino 1988: Mellow and mature, a nicely aged red that smells spicy and oaky, tastes firm and fruity with loads of plum and dried cherry flavor. Lingering finish, too. Drink now. • $30 • (11/30/94) • **91**

Romito del Romitorio 1993: In a modern, international style, this is amazingly dark in color and rich in fruit. Full body and tannins, with loads of oak. It needs time to mello, try in 2000. Tasted twice, with consistent notes. • $25 • (01/31/96) • **91**

Romito del Romitorio 1992: Pure, unadorned fruit in a medium-bodied wine that's elegant and balanced. Lively acidity, bright flavors and a long finish. • $20 • (11/30/94) • **88**

RONCADE, CASTELLO DI

Villa Giustinian Vino da Tavola-Northeast 1988 • $13 • (10/15/94) • **85**

RONCHI, UMANI

Classico Casal di Serra Verdicchio dei Castelli di Jesi 1993: Sophisticated, toasty oak aromas and flavors lead to good acidity and modest apple and pear notes.
8,000 cases made. • $9 • (03/31/95) • **85**

Classico Villa Bianchi Verdicchio dei Castelli di Jesi 1993: An unusually buttery Verdicchio. Tastes mature for its age and gets a little thin on the finish. 15,000 cases made. • $8 • (03/31/95) • **81**

Cúmaro Rosso Cònero 1988 • $22 • (09/15/92) • **83**

Montepulciano d'Abruzzo 1989 • $5 • (02/15/91) • **75**

Montepulciano d'Abruzzo 1986 • $5 • **65**

Verdicchio del Castelli di Jesi Classico Villa Bianchi 1993: An unusually buttery Verdicchio. Tastes mature for its age and gets a little thin on the finish. 15,000 cases made. • $8 • (03/31/95) • **81**

RONCHI DI CIALLA

Refosco dal Peduncolo Rosso di Cialla Colli Orientali del Friuli 1983 • $23 • (03/31/89) • **79**

Schiopettino di Cialla Vino da Tavola-Northeast 1983 • $25 • (03/31/89) • **84**

RONCO DEI TASSI

Bianco Collio 1994: Fairly innocuous, with modest peach and canned fruit flavors. A slightly spicy finish. 650 cases made. • $18 • (06/15/96) • **77**

Bianco Collio 1993: Bright and fruity, a crisp-textured wine with generous pear, apple and spice flavors that echo nicely on the finish. 250 cases made. • $17 • (01/31/95) • **84**

Pinot Grigio Collio White 1993: Lovely wine, showing complexity and terrific harmony, with a bit of spice, pear, butter and citrus flavors, all in the right proportions. Smooth and ready to drink. 1,250 cases made. • $15 • (01/31/95) • **85**

Sauvignon Collio 1994: Well-made and refreshing, with good pineapple and spice flavors. Turns a bit cloying on the finish, but still attractive. 160 cases made. • $17 • (06/15/96) • **83**

Tocai Friulano Collio 1994: A bit heavy-handed, with a mix of peach and herbal flavors. Still, it has some backbone and a nice finish marked by a touch of spice. 650 cases made. • $18 • (06/15/96) • **80**

RONCO DEL GNEMIZ

Chardonnay Colli Orientali del Friuli 1991: Buttery, spicy style that emphasizes the wood flavors over the modest fruit. Has a pleasant hint of butter on the finish. 833 cases made. • $NA • (01/31/95) • **78**

Picolit Colli Orientali del Friuli White 1993: Lightly sweet, a simple wine with prominent oak overtones, especially in the nose. Finishes with some delicate sweetness, and a hint of pear. 83 cases made. • $38 • (01/31/95) • **78**

Pinot Grigio Colli Orientali del Friuli White 1993: A wine with a bite to it, showing a peppery side along with the green, celery and bitter almond flavors. Simple but sharp and crisp, tasting almost like grapefruit rinds on the finish. 416 cases made. • $16 • (01/31/95) • **80**

Rosso del Gnemiz Vino da Tavola-Northeast Red 1988 • $28 • (09/15/92) • **85**

Rosso Vino da Tavola-Northeast Red 1986 • $15 • (03/31/89) • **80**

Tocai Friulano Colli Orientali del Friuli 1994: Tastes mature, with vanilla and plenty of spice. The gooseberry flavors are a bit muted, but overall it's a satisfying quaff. • $18 • (06/15/96) • **82**

Tocai Friulano Colli Orientali del Friuli 1993: Very crisp and appealing, showing good backbone of acidity, with mineral, earth, lemon, pear flavors. Starts out lean, but it grows in the glass, gaining body and character. 249 cases made. • $16 • (01/31/95) • **83**

RONESCA, CA'

Sauvignon del Podere de Ipplis Colli Orientali del Friuli 1991 • $16 • (09/15/93) • **84**

ROSETI, DEI

Belconvento 1987 • $24 • (03/15/91) • **85**

Belconvento 1985 • $23 • (07/15/89) • **86**

Rosso di Montalcino 1988 • $13 • (01/31/91) • **87**

Rosso di Montalcino 1987 • $NA • **64**

Rosso di Montalcino 1985 • $9 • (07/15/89) • **78**

Brunello di Montalcino 1982 • $20 • (07/31/89) • **89**

Brunello di Montalcino 1979 • $10 • (08/31/86) • **88**

ROTARI

Spumante Brut Riserva 1988 • $10 • (05/15/93) • **84**

RUBENTINO

Chianti 1990 • $6 • (04/30/92) • **78**

Chianti Classico 1989 • $8 • (04/30/92) • **81**

RUFFINO

Cabreo Il Borgo 1993: Elegant, polished wine with wonderful crushed berry, violet aromas. Medium-bodied with round, silky tannins and long fresh finish. Made from Sangiovese and Cabernet Sauvignon. Drinkable now, can age. • $NA • **87**

Cabreo Il Borgo 1990 • $NA • (10/31/93) • **92**

Cabreo Il Borgo Predicato di Bitùrica 1988 • $NA • (09/15/91) • **90**

Cabreo Il Borgo Predicato di Bitùrica 1987 • $27 • (12/15/92) • **82**

Cabreo Il Borgo Predicato di Bitùrica 1985 • $21 • (09/30/89) • **90**

Chianti 1994: Light and simple, Beaujolais-like, with cherry and strawberry aromas and flavors and a fresh finish. Serve chilled. Lovely with pizza. • $NA • **80**

Chianti 1991 • $8 • (05/15/93) • **79**

Chianti 1990 • $8 • (01/31/92) • **77**

Chianti Classico 1987 • $7 • (04/30/90) BB • **83**
Chianti Classico 1984 • $5 • (11/30/86) • **78**
Chianti Classico Aziano 1992: Mature color, light structure and unripe flavors. Tasted twice, with consistent notes. 28,000 cases made. • $10 • **72**
Chianti Classico Aziano 1991 • $11 • (10/31/93) • **78**
Chianti Classico Aziano 1990 • $10 • (09/15/92) • **88**
Chianti Classico Aziano 1989 • $10 • (04/30/92) • **79**
Chianti Classico Aziano 1988 • $11 • (09/15/91) • **83**
Chianti Classico Aziano 1986 • $8 • (05/31/89) BB • **85**
Chianti Classico Aziano 1985 • $8 • (08/31/88) • **80**
Chianti Classico Ducale Oro (Gold Label) Riserva 1990: One of the last of the '90 riservas to come out and worth the wait. Dark-colored and rich with lovely fresh berry, minty and fruit character on the nose and palate. Medium-bodied with fine tannins and a long silky finish. Drinkable or age. • $25 • **90**
Chianti Classico Nozzole Vigneto La Forra Barrel 1987 • $NA • (11/30/89) BT • **88**
Chianti Classico Riserva Ducale 1990: A lively, mouth-cleansing red that's reaching a nice state of maturity. Has mellow aromas but bright fruit flavors. Tasted five times, significant bottle variation noted. 55,000 cases made. • $15 • (02/28/95) • **84**
Chianti Classico Ducale Gold Label Riserva 1988 • $25 • (09/15/92) • **87**
Chianti Classico Ducale Gold Label Riserva 1986 • $24 • (05/15/93) • **87**
Chianti Classico Ducale Gold Label Riserva 1983 • $22 • (11/30/89) • **84**
Chianti Classico Ducale Gold Label Riserva 1982 • $24 • (05/31/89) • **80**
Chianti Classico Ducale Gold Label Riserva 1979 • $23 • (09/30/86) • **70**
Chianti Classico Ducale Gold Label Riserva 1978 • $16 • (11/30/89) • **82**
Chianti Classico Ducale Gold Label Riserva 1977 • $38 • (09/16/85) • **89**
Chianti Classico Ducale Gold Label Riserva 1975 • $57 • (09/16/85) • **86**
Chianti Classico Ducale Gold Label Riserva 1971 • $61 • (09/16/85) • **85**
Chianti Classico Ducale Gold Label Riserva 1962 • $NA • (09/16/85) • **68**
Chianti Classico Ducale Gold Label Riserva 1958 • $144 • (09/16/85) • **82**
Chianti Classico Ducale Riserva 1989 • $14 • (04/30/94) • **83**
Chianti Classico Ducale Riserva 1988 • $15 • (09/15/92) • **82**
Chianti Classico Ducale Riserva 1987 • $14 • (09/15/92) • **86**
Chianti Classico Ducale Riserva 1986 • $16 • (10/31/91) • **89**
Chianti Classico Ducale Riserva 1985 • $13 • (09/15/91) • **90**
Chianti Classico Ducale Riserva 1981 • $9 • (10/31/86) • **66**
Chianti Classico Ducale Riserva 1979 • $23 • (09/16/85) • **80**
Chianti Classico Santedame 1993: A straightforward Chianti with a very light aftertaste. Light to medium body, some raspberry, wet earth and blackberry flavors. A bit short and diluted. • $NA • **79**
Chianti Classico Tenuta Santedame 1991 • $14 • (10/31/93) • **85**
Chianti Classico Tenuta Santedame 1990 • $14 • (10/31/93) • **87**
Chianti Classico Tenuta Santedame 1988 • $NA • (09/15/91) • **88**
Libaio 1991 • $10 • (12/15/92) • **78**
Nero del Tondo 1993: Pretty, aromatic wine with violet and strawberry aromas and flavors. Medium-bodied with light tannins and a fresh finish. Made from Pinot Noir. Drinkable now or can be aged. • $NA • **85**
Nero del Tondo 1988 • $18 • (09/15/91) • **88**
Romitorio 1993: In a modern, international style, this is amazingly dark in color and rich in fruit. Full body and tannins, with loads of oak. It needs time to mellow, try in 2000. Tasted twice, with consistent notes. • $NA • **91**
Spumante Monte Rossa Rosé NV • $18 • (05/15/93) • **80**
Torgaio Sangiovese 1992 • $10 • (10/31/93) • **83**
Torgaio Sangiovese di Toscana 1994: Another light, simple Sangiovese with fresh fruit and crisp acidity. Delicious. Serve well chilled. • $NA • **81**
Vino Nobile di Montepulciano Lodola Nuova 1991: Very aromatic with wild strawberry and floral notes. Medium-bodied with fine tannins and a delicate finish. Drinkable now. • $NA • **84**
Vino Nobile di Montepulciano Tenuta Lodola Nuova 1989 • $12 • (07/31/94) • **82**

Key: SS—Spectator Selection. CS—Cellar Selection. BB—Best Buy. $NA—Price not available. (BT)—Barrel tasting. Ⓐ—Auction Price.
Dates in parentheses represent the issues in which the ratings were published.

RUGGERI & C.

Prosecco di Valdobbiadene NV: A light but flavorful sparkling wine with fruity, herbal flavors and a soft texture. Just slightly sweet. 5,000 cases made. • $12 • (06/15/96) • **81**

RUGGERO, CASTEL

Chianti Classico 1993: Impressive for the vintage. Full of fresh berry, cherry aromas and flavors. Medium-bodied and silky with fine tannins and a medium finish. Delicious fruit. Drinkable or ageable. • $NA • **85**
Chianti Classico 1988 • $NA • (09/15/91) • **86**

RUSSIZ, VILLA

Cabernet Franc Collio 1986 • $15 • (09/15/88) • **83**
Merlot Collio 1989 • $27 • (04/30/92) • **86**
Merlot Collio 1986 • $14 • (09/15/88) • **80**
Pinot Bianco Collio 1993: Fresh and fruity, light in texture but effusive in flavor, easy to drink while it's fresh and lively. 800 cases made. • $18 • (01/31/95) • **83**
Pinot Grigio Collio 1993: Quite chewy and a bit earthy, with good intensity, showing white pepper, mineral, apple and bitter almond. A wine with character. 2,750 cases made. • $18 • (01/31/95) • **80**
Sauvignon Collio 1994: Very herbal, but with a nice dose of vanilla and peach flavors. Fairly rich and robust. It has a long-lasting and spicy finish. 1,600 cases made. • $19 • (06/15/96) • **85**
Sauvignon Collio 1993: Crisp and distinctive, racy and herbal on the nose, adding a little more fruit character as the flavors emerge, finishing balanced and harmonious. 1,833 cases made. • $18 • (01/31/95) • **86**
Sauvignon Collio 1991 • $20 • (09/15/93) • **78**
Tocai Friulano Collio 1993: Bright and zingy, flavors centered around citrus and pear, light and refreshing on the finish. 1,300 cases made. • $18 • (01/31/95) • **83**
Verduzzo 1987 • $NA • (09/15/88) • **76**

RUSSIZ SUPERIORE

Collio Rosso Riserva Degli Orzoni 1990: An extremely oaky tasting wine that may have the concentration of fruit to last until the overwhelming toast and vanilla flavors subside, but it's difficult to say. 400 cases made. • $30 • (06/15/96) BB • **83**
Merlot Collio 1993: Fresh, grapey, raspberrylike flavors make this generous and appealing. It is firm but smooth in texture, with a lingering fruity finish. • $18 • (05/31/96) • **86**
Pinot Bianco Collio 1993: Fresh and lively, a generous wine with appealing pear, spice and citrus aromas and flavors that echo on the lively finish. • $NA • (01/31/95) • **84**
Pinot Grigio Collio 1994: Floral aromas and nice citrus flavors make this medium-bodied white appealing. Fresh tasting and easy to drink. • $16 • (06/15/96) • **83**
Pinot Grigio Collio 1993: Straightforward and light, with tart and simple citrusy notes, green finish. • $NA • (01/31/95) • **78**
Riesling Italico Collio 1993: Fresh and crisp, with perfumed, jasmine aromas and good backbone of acidity. Very sharp, with lime and apricot notes. • $NA • (01/31/95) • **83**
Roncuz Colli Orientali del Friuli 1992: Earthy, sour, lean and mean, and not recommended. • $NA • (01/31/95) • **68**
Sauvignon Collio 1993: Clean, crisp and grassy, with some kiwi, apricot and celeri flavors. Well-made and appealing, but very tart and lemony. • $NA • (01/31/95) • **83**
Tocai Friulano Collio 1993: Simple, refreshing style, with a slightly spicy edge to the pear flavors. • $NA • (01/31/95) • **81**
Verduzzo Vino da Tavola-Veneto 1991: Lightly sweet, with spicy honey and apricot flavors in modest proportions. A pleasant wine that never quite revs up to something special. • $NA • (01/31/95) • **83**

SACCARDI

Chianti Classico 1990 • $10 • (10/31/94) BB • **87**
Chianti Classico 1987 • $10 • (05/15/90) • **75**
Chianti Classico 1985 • $6 • (11/30/87) BB • **89**

Chianti Classico Riserva 1988 • $13 • (10/31/94) • **85**
Chianti Classico Riserva 1983 • $12 • (05/15/90) • **87**
Chianti Classico Riserva 1981 • $9 • (11/30/87) • **81**

SAFFIRIO, JOSETTA

Barolo 1987 • $40 • (12/15/92) • **87**

SALA, LA

Campo All'Abero 1990: Wonderfully succulent cassis, berry and truffle aromas and flavors, full in body, medium velvety tannins and a ripe fruit finish. Delicious now but will improve. • $NA • **90**
Chianti Classico 1993: Already looking a bit mature for its amber tinge. Soft and round on the palate. Medium body and light finish. Perhaps a bit too much new wood. • $NA • **79**
Chianti Classico 1991: A bit hard, tight and over-oaked. Plenty of attractive raspberry, earthy, tobacco character and loads of new wood. Medium-bodied, medium tannins and a crisp finish. • $NA • (01/31/96) • **81**
Chianti Classico 1990 • $NA • (10/31/93) • **84**
Chianti Classico Riserva 1990: Deceptive, showing ripe plum and raspberry character with a hint of meat, medium body and tannins and lively acidity. Drinkable now. • $NA • **85**

SALCETINO

Chianti Classico 1991 • $NA • (10/31/93) • **78**

SALETTE, LE

Recioto della Valpolicella Amarone La Marega 1988 • $25 • (09/15/92) • **81**
Valpolicella Ca' Carnocchio 1989 • $NA • (09/15/92) • **81**
Valpolicella Classico I Progni 1991 • $12 • (09/15/92) • **72**
Valpolicella Classico Superiore I Progni 1989 • $12 • (09/15/92) • **79**

SALLE, CASTELLO DI

Montepulciano d'Abruzzo 1985 • $15 • (06/15/90) BB • **84**

SAMMICHELI

Chianti Classico 1990 • $9 • (03/31/93) • **78**

SAN FABIANO CALCINAIA

Cerviolo Rosso 1991: Cassis, berry and plum flavors add good definition to this full-bodied red, ripe and round tannins here. Drinkable now but better after 1996. • $15 • **88**
Cerviolo Rosso 1990 • $13 • (10/31/93) • **89**
Cerviolo Rosso 1988 • $14 • (12/31/92) • **81**
Cerviolo Rosso 1986 • $19 • (03/31/90) • **82**
Chianti Classico 1992: Some pretty fruit but rather diluted, with light body and tannins. Drinkable now. 5,833 cases made. • $11 • **76**
Chianti Classico 1991 • $12 • (10/31/93) • **84**
Chianti Classico 1990 • $9 • (10/31/93) • **85**
Chianti Classico 1988 • $12 • (09/15/91) • **89**
Chianti Classico 1988 • $12 • (09/15/91) • **84**
Chianti Classico Cellole 1990 • $11 • (10/31/93) • **86**
Chianti Classico Cellole 1988 • $15 • (09/15/91) • **83**
Chianti Classico Cellole Riserva 1988 • $16 • (09/15/92) • **87**
Chianti Classico Cellole Riserva 1985 • $13 • (11/30/89) • **91**
Chianti Classico Riserva 1988 • $NA • (09/15/92) • **85**
Chianti Classico Riserva 1985 • $NA • (09/15/91) • **84**

SAN FELICE

Belcaro 1991 • $13 • (06/30/93) • **81**
Brunello di Montalcino Campogiovanni 1988 • $36 • (04/30/94) • **90**
Brunello di Montalcino Campogiovanni 1986 • $28 • (11/30/91) • **92**
Brunello di Montalcino Campogiovanni 1985 • $24 • (09/30/90) • **85**
Brunello di Montalcino Campogiovanni 1982 • $27 • (07/31/88) CS • **92**
Chianti Classico 1993: Simple and straightforward. Pretty raspberry, cherry and leather aromas and flavors. Medium to light body, with fine tannins and a fresh finish. • $11 • **80**
Chianti Classico 1992: Fresh, juicy and crisp, showing berry, quince and stemmy aromas and flavors. Drinkable now. • $10 • **80**
Chianti Classico 1991 • $13 • (10/31/93) • **80**
Chianti Classico 1990 • $11 • (09/15/92) • **87**
Chianti Classico Campo del Civettino 1990 • $NA • (10/31/93) • **83**
Chianti Classico Campo del Civettino 1988 • $NA • (09/15/91) • **84**
Chianti Classico Il Grigio Riserva 1990: Another pretty Sangiovese offering blueberry, cherry, violet character, medium and delicate tannins and a crisp finish. Drinkable now. • $16 • **85**
Chianti Classico Il Grigio Riserva 1988 • $16 • (09/15/92) • **86**
Chianti Classico Il Grigio Riserva 1987 • $13 • (01/31/92) • **83**
Chianti Classico Il Grigio Riserva 1985 • $10 • (09/15/90) • **86**
Chianti Classico Il Grigio Riserva 1983 • $12 • (11/30/89) • **85**
Chianti Classico Il Grigio Riserva 1982 • $11 • (11/30/89) • **90**
Chianti Classico Il Poggio Riserva 1988 • $18 • (09/15/92) • **92**
Chianti Classico Poggio Rosso Riserva 1990: Delicious Chianti. Deep and complex aromas of flowers and wild berries. Full-bodied yet very fine, with black pepper, fruit and floral flavors and silky tannins. Drinkable now. • $24 • **90**
Chianti Classico Poggio Rosso Riserva 1987 • $23 • (06/30/93) • **68**
Chianti Classico Poggio Rosso Riserva 1986 • $24 • (01/31/92) • **86**
Chianti Classico Poggio Rosso Riserva 1985 • $20 • (09/15/91) • **85**
Chianti Classico Poggio Rosso Riserva 1983 • $17 • (11/30/89) • **87**
Chianti Classico Poggio Rosso Riserva 1982 • $15 • (09/15/90) • **81**
Chianti Classico Poggio Rosso Riserva 1981 • $15 • (11/30/89) • **87**
Chianti Classico Poggio Rosso Riserva 1978 • $14 • (03/15/87) • **73**
Chianti Classico Riserva Il Grigio 1991: Ripe, soft and lush, with lovely blackberry, boysenberry and plum flavors that caress the palate and linger on the supple, smooth finish. Very harmonious and seductive. Enjoy now. • $16 • **86**
Predicato di Bitùrica 1985 • $25 • (09/15/90) • **87**
Predicato di Bitùrica 1983 • $22 • (11/30/89) • **87**
Predicato di Bitùrica 1982 • $25 • (01/31/88) SS • **92**
Predicato di Bitùrica 1985 • $28 • (12/15/91) • **82**
Vigorello 1990 • $NA • (11/15/93) • **90-94** (BT)
Vigorello 1988 • $25 • (11/15/93) • **88**
Vigorello 1987 • $25 • (06/15/93) • **87**
Vigorello 1986 • $23 • (11/15/93) • **91**
Vigorello 1985 • $18 • (09/15/90) • **89**
Vigorello 1983 • $24 • (11/15/93) • **91**
Vigorello 1982 • $24 • (11/15/93) • **92**
Vigorello 1981 • $18 • (01/31/88) • **84**
Vigorello 1980 • $18 • (02/28/87) SS • **95**

SAN FILIPPO

Brunello di Montalcino 1990: This shows finesse with silky tannins and gamy, smoky, tobacco character, medium body and a fresh finish. Drink now. • $NA • **85**
Rosso di Montalcino 1987 • $11 • (04/30/91) • **68**

SAN FLORIANO, VIGNAIOLI DA

Pinot Bianco Collio 1994: Light pear and almond flavors give some character to this rather neutral white, but good body and firm acidity make it a discreet match for light dishes. 4,000 cases made. • $13 • (06/15/96) • **81**
Pinot Grigio Collio 1994: Has more substance than most Pinot Grigios, from the deeper color to the floral aromas to the lively fruit flavors. Rather full-bodied and smooth in texture. 4,000 cases made. • $13 • (06/15/96) • **84**
Tocai Friulano Collio 1994: Tastes a bit fishy and salty. A bizarre style. 4,000 cases made. • $13 • (06/15/96) • **70**

SAN GIORGIO

Brunello di Montalcino 1990: Fine and elegant, featuring silky tannins that tickle your palate and a wonderful cherry, mineral, salty character on aftertaste. Long in the mouth. Drinkable now. • $28 • (10/31/95) • **89**

Brunello di Montalcino 1988: Nicely matured, showing roasted coffee, dried cherry and plum flavors. A nice tar note carries through to the finish. Still a bit tannic, but drinkable with hearty food. 1,000 cases made. • $25 • (07/31/95) • **86**

SAN GUIDO, TENUTA

Bolgheri Sassicaia 1994: Very promising vintage for Sassicaia. Lovely, sweet, ripe fruit flavors. Deep-colored, full-bodied and thick, with loads of well-defined currant and black cherry flavors and massive but supple tannins. Barrel sample. • $NA • (07/31/96) • **90-94** (BT)

Sassicaia 1993: Elegant, offering medium intensity and body. Very tight and closed on the nose, but reveals supple black currant and wet earth complexity. Doesn't have quite the concentration or length to rate outstanding. • $NA • (07/31/96) • **86**

Sassicaia 1992: Wonderful aromas in this Sassicaia but it could use a bit more body. Some good berry and vanilla character but herbal and slightly unpleasant. Medium-bodied with medium tannins and a slightly short finish. Try after 1997. Tasted twice, with consistent notes. • $60 • (07/31/96) • **85**

Sassicaia 1991: Angular and quite hard now, with dried cherry, wet earth and black currant flavors. Lacks opulence and ripe fruit, turning slightly herbal and dry on the finish. Solidly built, it needs time for the tannins to soften. Try around 2002. • $57 • (07/31/96) • **81**

Sassicaia 1990: A sexy wine that has gained somewhat since 1993 when we rated it 90 points. Not as powerful as the '88, nor as rich as the '85, this is still prototypical Sassicaia for its great complexity. Offers mineral, lead pencil, tar, cassis and black olive notes, solid backbone and firm, elegant finish. • $90 • (07/31/96) • **93**

Sassicaia 1989: Pleasant example that makes for pretty drinking now and through 1998. Of medium body, it's supple and silky, with some tar, dried herb, mineral and cherry flavors. • $84 • (07/31/96) • **88**

Sassicaia 1988: The brute power of the '88 brings to mind Château Latour in top vintages. Full-bodied, it's firm and rock-solid yet tastes very silky thanks to sensational concentration of fruit. Loads of minerally, peppery character and blackberry and red berry flavors. Supercharged, intense, long finish. Try in 2003. • $99 • (07/31/96) • **97**

Sassicaia 1987: Delicate and clean, with pure, focused and direct raspberry, black cherry and black currant flavors. Quite elegant and of medium body, featuring some mineral and tar notes on the medium-intense finish. Delicious to drink now and through 1998. • $92 • (07/31/96) • **86**

Sassicaia 1986 • $65 • (11/15/93) • **91**

Sassicaia 1985: Unreal for its sheer hedonistic quality. Oozes rich and ripe fruit and sweet wood character, but doesn't taste overripe. Loaded with cassis and mineral flavors backed by tar and spice. Much thicker and darker in color than the '88, which is more elegant. In its history the winery has made no other Sassicaia with such massive tannins, yet the texture of the wine is supple. Made from very small yields. Tempting now but better in 2005. • $220 • (07/31/96) • **99**

Sassicaia 1984: Pleasant surprise from a disastrous, rainy year in Tuscany. Some sweet fruit, mineral and licorice flavors charm the palate, but a touch of chestnut distracts. Medium-bodied, slightly drying finish. • $NA • (07/31/96) • **82**

Sassicaia 1983: Beautifully balanced and quite seductive, showing some lovely cassis, mineral and tar character. Very supple. Drinkable now through 2000. • $88 • (07/31/96) • **88**

Sassicaia 1982: Rather intense, in a fresh way, reflecting perhaps the relatively high acidity in this wine from the start. Of medium to full body, it bursts with cassis and black cherry flavors and a touch of Sassicaia's characteristic mineral persona. Drinkable now. • $125 • (07/31/96) • **90**

Sassicaia 1981: From a lesser vintage in Tuscany, it's slightly drying now, but still ripe, rich and lovely, delivering a tar, iron, mineral, red and black fruit character. Nice harmony and power. Drinkable in 1998. • $120 • (07/31/96) • **89**

Sassicaia 1980: Light, watery and diluted vanilla and milk chocolate character. While smooth in texture and clean on the finish, this is a modest Sassicaia. Drinkable now. • $105 • (07/31/96) • **77**

Sassicaia 1979: Lovely and light, medium-bodied, caramel, mineral and black cherry character. From an average year in Tuscany, this '79 still shows that Sassicaia can age and turn out good wines even in difficult vintages. Drinkable now. • $102 • (07/31/96) • **83**

Sassicaia 1978: A huge red that should hold, even improve, for another decade. Deep, full-bodied, very ripe and complex. Tastes a bit savage, boasting earthy, dried herbal, salty, milky and red berry, dried fruit character. Still tannic and firm, adding a long, impressive finish. • $133 • (07/31/96) • **95**

Sassicaia 1977: Even though '77 was truly disappointing elsewhere in Tuscany, this Sassicaia is drinking nicely now, 19 years later. Very harmonious, offering soft texture, excellent blackberry character and a hint of tar. Somewhat lighter than the '75 and slightly short on the finish. • $NA • (07/31/96) • **85**

Sassicaia 1976: Even Sassicaia could not apparently escape the wet weather of this memorably bad vintage in Tuscany. It lacks harmony, having oxidized and developed a bitter orange character. Lean finish. • $79 • (07/31/96) • **65**

Sassicaia 1975: More than 20 years old, yet so intense you almost need an extinguisher to put out its fiery flavors. From a very good year in Tuscany, it's sweet, ripe and full-bodied, featuring complex mineral, earth and mint character. Impressively concentrated and silky-textured, revealing its age by a slight dryness on aftertaste. Drinkable soon. • $99 • (07/31/96) • **90**

Sassicaia 1974: From a year with excessive rainfall, it's quite soft yet still manages to offer pleasure, adding nice complexity of tobacco, wet earth, bitter chocolate, mineral and iron character. Drinkable now. • $NA • (07/31/96) • **83**

Sassicaia 1972: How Tenuta San Guido could produce such a delightful wine in a year that ranks among the most disastrous this century in Tuscany remains a mystery that goes to the heart of the Sassicaia legend. Inky, tarry, complex and medium-bodied, earthy, plummy and minty character and impressive finish. Would rate higher if not for a slight but distracting rustic chestnut aroma. • $NA • (07/31/96) • **85**

Sassicaia 1971: The first bottle showed hard, tough and lean character and a drying finish. The second was a more delicate wine, showing somewhat more fruit. Collectors should probably drink their '71s right away as they might be fading quickly. • $NA • (07/31/96) • **78**

Sassicaia 1970: A charmer that's supple, lush and silky, offering distinctive minty, red berry aromas and flavors and fresh character. Tuscany had good weather in 1970, yet this one tastes a touch diluted on the palate and finish. Drinkable now. • $NA • (07/31/96) • **83**

Sassicaia 1968: First bottle corked, second one medium-bodied, delicate and still fresh, showing a mineral, red berry, meat, spice character. Sassicaia's first commercial wine, this '68 (which includes some '67, '65 and '69) is a rare and expensive collector's item. • $550 • (07/31/96) • **88**

SAN LEONINO

Chianti Classico 1991 • $10 • (10/31/93) • **82**
Chianti Classico 1990 • $10 • (09/15/92) • **89**
Chianti Classico 1988 • $10 • (12/15/90) • **87**
Chianti Classico Riserva 1988 • $19 • (09/15/92) • **85**

SAN MICHELE

Chianti 1991: Thin and turns astringent on the finish. Where's the fruit? There's structure and texture, but no flavor. 40,000 cases made. • $7 • (07/31/95) • **75**

SAN PIETRO

Bardolino 1991 • $18 • (09/15/92) • **81**
Bianco di Custoza 1991 • $14 • (09/15/92) • **67**
Cabernet Sauvignon Refolà 1988 • $NA • (09/15/92) • **80**

Gavi 1993: A sweet-tart quality makes this odd. Drinkable, but its candylike flavors fight with aggressive lemony acidity and neither side wins. 4,000 cases made. • $12 • (02/28/95) • **75**

Gavi 1992 • $14 • (06/15/94) • **71**

Gavi Gazzaniga 1994: A crisp and subtly spicy white whose flavors lean toward herb and pepper. 4,000 cases made. • $14 • (02/29/96) • **81**

Key: SS—Spectator Selection. CS—Cellar Selection. BB—Best Buy. $NA—Price not available. (BT)—Barrel tasting. Ⓐ—Auction Price.
Dates in parentheses represent the issues in which the ratings were published.

SAN POLO IN ROSSO, CASTELLO DI

Cetinaia 1986 • $27 • (12/15/92) • **82**
Chianti Classico 1985 • $10 • (11/30/89) • **67**
Chianti Classico Riserva 1988 • $15 • (09/15/92) • **85**
Chianti Classico Riserva 1986 • $14 • (09/15/92) • **75**
Chianti Classico Riserva 1985 • $14 • (11/30/89) • **78**

SAN QUIRICO

Chianti Vecchione 1988 • $9 • (01/31/92) • **79**

SAN STEFANO

Moscato d'Asti 1990 • $17 • (01/31/92) • **88**

SAN VINCENTI

Chianti Classico 1990 • $NA • (10/31/93) • **68**
Chianti Classico Podere di Stignano 1991: Tired and dull, with only some modest tealike flavors. Very dry and rustic. • $13 • (10/31/95) • **74**
Chianti Classico Riserva Podere di Stignano 1988: Rustic stewed fruit flavors and a tannic finish. Mature and ready to drink now, though a little hollow in the middle and somewhat dried out. • $17 • (10/31/95) • **81**

SANDRONE, LUCIANO

Barbera d'Alba 1991 • $22 • (11/15/93) • **77**
Barolo 1984 • $14 • (08/31/88) • **82**
Barolo 1983 • $20 • (12/15/87) • **90**
Barolo 1982 • $15 • (06/30/87) • **94**
Barolo Cannubi Boschis 1991: A well-made, smooth, round Barolo that shows fine black cherry, rose petal and spice flavors. Quite austere, medium body and has the stuffing to age into 1997 and longer. • $NA • (10/31/95) • **84**
Barolo Cannubi Boschis 1990: Rich, ripe, round and utterly captivating, a powerful wine that wraps its rich fruit in plush textures. Berry, currant, black cherry, vanilla, spice and toasty flavors spill over the palate in a torrent of sweet richness. • $NA • **96**
Barolo Cannubi Boschis 1989: A mind-bending wine, deep, dark, dense and concentrated, a powerful wine with generous raspberry and cherry fruit, ample tannins smoothly integrated. Gorgeous rose- and tar-scented flavors carry through the finish. 680 cases made. • $50 • (10/31/93) CS • **95**
Barolo Cannubi Boschis 1988 • $50 • (10/31/93) • **92**
Barolo Cannubi Boschis 1986 • $34 • (12/31/90) • **89**
Barolo Cannubi Boschis 1985 • $30 • (01/31/90) • **92**
Barolo Le Vigne 1990: Firm, ripe, rich and elegant, a beautifully harmonious Barolo that practically melts in your mouth, displaying floral raspberry, vanilla and tobacco aromas and flavors balanced against a fine edge of lacy acidity. A plush wine that you can really sink into. Oh so tempting to drink now, but try to hold off until 1998. • $NA • (10/31/94) • **98**
Piedmont 1990 • $14 • (03/31/92) • **87**
Piedmont 1989 • $12 • (07/15/91) • **87**
Piedmont 1986 • $8 • (12/31/87) • **80**
Piedmont 1985 • $6 • (07/31/87) BB • **87**

SANGUINETO

Vino Nobile di Montepulciano Riserva 1980 • $9 • (10/31/86) • **86**

SANT'ANNA

Chianti Colli Senesi 1992: Decent fruit in there, but a bit light. Delicate berry, tobacco and cherry aromas and flavors lead to a light finish. Drinkable now. • $15 • **80**
Vigna Il Vallone 1992: Very flavorful and charming, a medium-bodied red showing some mint, blackberry and plum flavors. Made of Prugnolo Gentile and Cabernet Sauvignon. Try after 1997 to round some of the rough edges. • $23 • **86**

SANTA MARGHERITA

Cabernet Sauvignon Pramaggiore 1982 • $5 • (12/01/85) BB • **87**
Chardonnay del Veneto Orientale 1991 • $9 • (12/15/92) • **75**
Merlot Lison-Pramaggiore Selva Maggiore 1990 • $12 • (12/15/92) • **79**
Pinot Grigio Alto Adige 1994: Basically neutral in character, this lean white sneaks in some light lemony flavors, finishing soft and short. It's pleasant, but innocuous. • $13 • (06/15/96) • **80**

SANTA SOFIA

Bardolino Classico Superiore 1989 • $8 • (09/15/92) • **71**
Recioto della Valpolicella Classico Superiore Amarone 1986 • $28 • (10/31/94) • **82**
Recioto della Valpolicella Classico Superiore Amarone 1984 • $29 • (09/15/92) • **86**
Soave Classico Superiore 1993 • $9 • (10/31/94) • **84**
Valpolicella Classico Superiore 1992: Very light and silky, approaching a rosé in color and structure, with strawberry and tea flavors that perk up the palate, then slip away. Try it lightly chilled. • $8 • (12/15/95) • **80**
Valpolicella Classico Superiore 1989 • $8 • (09/15/92) • **78**
Valpolicella Classico Superiore Amarone 1988: A mature, full-bodied red featuring ample oaky aromas, tart cherry flavors, smooth texture and smoky finish. This is mellow and satisfying. • $30 • (09/30/95) • **85**

SANTA TRINITA

Chianti Classico 1988 • $NA • (09/15/91) • **86**

SANTANGELO

Colli del Moro Montepulciano d'Abruzzo 1992: A broad, amply flavored red that's generous, spicy, tannic but smooth enough to drink now while the cherry, blackberry and floral flavors stay fresh. 10,000 cases made. • $10 • (02/29/96) • **87**

SANTI

Bianco di Custoza I Frari 1991 • $8 • (09/15/92) • **84**
Pinot Grigio Vigneto Sortesele Trentino 1994: Fleshy and soft, with mineral, herb and light earthy flavors, this has good weight for a northern Italian white, but lacks fruit concentration and disappears on the finish. • $10 • (10/31/95) • **81**
Recioto della Valpolicella 1985 • $20 • (06/30/91) • **83**
Recioto della Valpolicella Amarone 1988 • $20 • (11/15/94) • **85**
Recioto della Valpolicella Amarone 1985 • $20 • (09/15/92) • **84**
Soave Classico Vigneti di Monteforte 1991 • $8 • (09/15/92) • **78**
Solane Valpolicella Classico 1993: Toast and vanilla flavors suggest oak aging, which is unusual for the region, but the plum and cherry flavors are ripe enough for balance. It shows some tannic structure and a pleasant, spicy finish. • $8 • (12/15/95) • **86**

SANTINA, VILLA

Chianti 1987 • $5 • (11/30/89) BB • **80**
Chianti Classico 1984 • $5 • (11/15/87) • **72**

SANTO STEFANO

Moscato d'Asti 1991 • $17 • (05/15/93) • **88**

SARDELLI, A.

Chianti Bartenura 1989 • $8 • (05/15/93) • **73**
Chianti Classico Bartenura 1987 • $9 • (03/31/91) • **70**

SARTORI

Bardolino Classico Superiore 1985 • $4 • (11/15/88) • **68**
Merlot Grave del Friuli 1989 • $6 • (12/15/92) • **80**
Merlot Grave del Friuli 1986 • $6 • (11/15/88) • **80**

Recioto della Valpolicella Classico Amarone Superiore 1982 • $11 • (11/15/88) • **79**
Valpolicella Classico Superiore 1990 • $6 • (09/15/92) • **80**
Valpolicella Classico Superiore 1985 • $4 • (11/15/88) BB • **80**

SASSETTI, LIVIO

Brunello di Montalcino 1988: Has everything you expect in a very good Brunello, with plenty of ripe fruit, full tannins and crisp acidity. From Pertimali. Even better after 1996. • $48 Ⓐ • (04/30/94) • **86**
Rosso di Montalcino 1991 • $17 • (04/30/94) • **78**

SASSO

Aglianico del Vulture 1985 • $11 • (03/15/89) • **83**

SAVIGNOLA PAOLINA

Chianti Classico Riserva 1990: Focused and well crafted, exhibiting ripe fruit and mushroom character, medium-to-full body and soft, velvety tannins. Delicious now but will improve with age. • $NA • **86**

SCAMPERLE

Amarone Recioto della Valpolicella Classico 1981 • $11 • (08/01/85) • **62**
Amarone Recioto della Valpolicella Classico 1978 • $9 • (09/01/84) • **77**

SCARLATTA

Montepulciano d'Abruzzo 1993: A hearty but simple red with moderate tannins, modest raspberry flavors and medium body. • $4 • (02/29/96) • **81**
Montepulciano d'Abruzzo Cerasuolo 1993: A chalky character is the common theme here, but there is enough cherry and vibrant acidity to balance it. Austere, yet with plenty of personality. • $4 • (08/31/95) • **83**

SCARPA

Barbaresco 1981 • $20 • (09/15/88) • **84**
Barbaresco 1979 • $20 • (09/15/88) • **90**
Barbaresco 1978 • $27 • (09/15/88) • **90**
Barbaresco 1974 • $30 • (09/15/88) • **89**
Barbaresco I Tetti di Neive 1978 • $27 • (03/15/87) • **83**
Barbera d'Asti 1985 • $12 • (08/31/89) • **88**
Barolo 1985 • $NA • (09/15/88) • **90**
Barolo 1982 • $NA • (09/15/88) • **88**
Barolo 1978 • $27 • (09/15/88) • **89**
Barolo Le Coste di Monforte 1978 • $27 • (03/15/87) • **81**

SCAVINO, PAOLO

Barbera d'Alba 1992: Beautifully crafted, this exciting beauty shows lush and youthful character. Exploding raspberry, currant and black cherry flavors are well defined. Bravo! Enjoy it now. • $13 • **88**
Barbera d'Alba 1991 • $30 • (10/31/94) • **87**
Barbera d'Alba 1990 • $40 • (10/15/93) • **89**
Barolo 1985 • $21 • (10/15/90) • **88**
Barolo 1983 • $NA • (09/15/88) • **85**
Barolo 1982 • $NA • (09/15/88) • **88**
Barolo Bric dël Fiasc 1990: Richly tannic but richly flavorful as well, a complex wine that cascades its licorice, black cherry, berry, tar and earth flavors across the palate, sweet and elegant on the finish beneath the layer of chewy tannins. Best to hold at least until 2000. • $45 • **93**
Barolo Bric dël Fiasc 1989: A luscious mouthful of wild berries, black cherry, toast and rose petal. Concentrated and exotic, a powerful wine with totally disarming aromas and flavors and remarkably supple texture. Layers and layers of personality make this a stellar candidate for cellaring until 1997 and beyond. 800 cases made. • $45 • (10/31/93) CS • **95**
Barolo Bric dël Fiasc 1988 • $45 • (10/31/93) • **87**
Barolo Bric dël Fiasc 1985 • $39 • (06/15/90) • **90**
Barolo Cannubi 1991: Classy fine tannins and plenty of mineral, spice and herb aromas and flavors, medium body, silky texture and medium finish. • $30 • **85**
Barolo Cannubi 1990: Has great presence, displaying an array of berry, anise, licorice, tar and rose petal notes through a lacy veneer of chewy tannins. A big wine with dramatic flavors, probably best after 1998 or 2000. 300 cases made. • $42 • (10/31/94) • **93**
Barolo Cannubi 1989: Supple, succulent and seductive, a remarkably smooth-textured, generous wine that plays its raspberry, plum, rose petal and tar notes against a background of vanilla and spice. A distinguished, elegant, opulent wine that is tempting to drink already but should improve 1998-2000. 280 cases made. • $45 • (10/31/93) • **94**
Barolo Cannubi 1988 • $45 • (10/31/93) • **86**
Barolo Cannubi 1985 • $30 • (01/31/90) • **74**
Barolo Riserva Rocche dell'Annunziata 1990: This is young and vibrant, with loads of fruit. Polished and modern. Has an earthy, minty berry character. Full-bodied, with chewy tannins. Better in 1997. • $65 • **90**
Dolcetto d'Alba Vigneto dël Fiasc 1994: Attractive raspberry, wild berry, lemon notes. Crisp and fresh, sporting medium body and a sweet mid-palate, this can accompany pizzas, salads, sandwiches. Good picnic wine that won't disappoint. • $13 • **84**

SCHIOPETTO

Pinot Bianco Collio 1994: Crisp and fruity, with some peach, almond and herbal flavors. Very typical wine for this region. A firm finish. • $24 • (06/15/96) • **84**
Pinot Bianco Collio 1993: Has an earthy, tobacco edge to the basic pear fruit, a simple wine with a touch of bitterness on the finish. Tasted twice. 1,750 cases made. • $23 • (01/31/95) • **79**
Pinot Grigio Collio 1993: Starts out earthy, but delivers good harmony and nice fruit, with floral, bitter almond, marzipan flavors. Tasted twice. 2,500 cases made. • $21 • (01/31/95) • **80**
Sauvignon Collio 1993: A bit earthy, a bit chewy and a bit short, it starts out better than it finishes, with vanilla, butter and nice grassy notes. As nice as they are, they are cut short on the finish. Tasted twice. 2,000 cases made. • $23 • (01/31/95) • **80**
Tocai Friulano Collio 1994: Young and simple, with good apple and peach flavors, and a hint of licorice as well. • $24 • (06/15/96) • **79**

SEBASTE

Barolo 1985 • $NA • (09/15/88) • **90**
Barolo 1984 • $NA • (09/15/88) • **85**
Barolo 1983 • $NA • (09/15/88) • **86**
Barolo 1982 • $NA • (09/15/88) • **91**
Barolo 1979 • $NA • (09/15/88) • **85**
Barolo Bussia 1988 • $30 • (06/15/94) • **87**
Barolo Bussia 1987 • $25 • (06/30/93) • **78**
Barolo Bussia Riserva 1984 • $17 • (07/31/89) • **84**
Barolo Bussia Riserva 1982 • $15 • (11/15/87) • **90**
Bricco Viole 1989 • $20 • (06/15/94) • **86**
Bricco Viole 1988 • $19 • (06/30/93) • **79**
Bricco Viole 1986 • $16 • (01/31/89) • **89**
Bricco Viole 1985 • $13 • (10/31/87) • **91**
Dolcetto d'Alba Monrobiolo di Bussia 1992 • $16 • (06/15/94) • **83**
Roero Arneis 1991 • $20 • (06/15/94) • **86**

SEGHESIO, RENZO

Barbera d'Alba 1989 • $12 • (11/30/91) • **81**
Barolo Bussia-Pianpolvere 1986 • $28 • (01/31/92) • **84**
Barolo Castelletto 1989: Exquisitely balanced, showing plenty of the spicy vanilla and toast character of small oak along with ripe raspberry and a touch of tobacco. Not a blockbuster, but beautifully made. Approachable now with food to balance the juicy acidity, best from 1998. • $NA • (10/31/94) • **88**

Key: SS—Spectator Selection. CS—Cellar Selection. BB—Best Buy. $NA—Price not available. (BT)—Barrel tasting. Ⓐ—Auction Price.
Dates in parentheses represent the issues in which the ratings were published.

ITALY

Barolo Vigneto La Villa 1991: Already mature Parmesan cheese and cherry character, medium body, light tannins and round finish. Not for holding but fun to drink now. • $NA • **81**
Dolcetto d'Alba Vigneto della Chiesa 1994: Nice, crisp red, offering a lemony touch and blueberry, raspberry flavors. Somewhat lean and austere on the slightly drying finish. • $NA • **79**
Piedmont 1989 • $12 • (11/30/91) • **77**
Piedmont 1988 • $9 • **78**
Ruri (Nebbiolo) 1989 • $14 • (01/31/92) • **84**

SELVAPIANA

Chianti Classico 1986 • $5 • (11/30/89) • **82**
Chianti Classico Riserva 1985 • $11 • (11/30/89) • **89**
Chianti Classico Riserva 1983 • $10 • (11/30/89) • **86**
Chianti Classico Riserva 1982 • $10 • (11/30/89) • **87**
Chianti Rufina 1992: Some pretty violet, berry and floral character in this light-bodied red. Tasted three times: two bottles high in volatile acidity. Drinkable now. • $10 • **82**
Chianti Rufina 1991 • $12 • (10/31/93) • **87**
Chianti Rufina 1990 • $13 • (09/15/92) • **92**
Chianti Rufina Bucerchiale Riserva 1988 • $21 • (09/15/92) • **85**
Chianti Rufina Bucerchiale Riserva 1985 • $19 • (09/15/90) • **91**
Chianti Rufina Riserva 1990: Very concentrated, with pepper, berry and meat aromas and flavors, full body, full tannins and crisp acidity. Long finish. Drinkable now. • $15 • **89**
Chianti Rufina Vigneto Bucerchiale 1990: Sleek and racy, built for aging. It's all there and incredibly compact with hints of black cherry, blueberry and firm tannins. Medium-to-full bodied. Great wine that needs time, better after 1997. • $20 • **92**
Chianti Rufina Vigneto Bucerchiale Riserva 1988 • $25 • (10/31/93) • **89**

SELVATICI, I

Chianti Colli Aretini 1990 • $NA • (10/31/93) • **85**
Predicato di Cardisco 1985 • $25 • (08/31/91) • **81**
Tuscany Claresco 1990 • $6 • (09/30/91) • **79**
Vin Santo Dessert 1984 • $16/ 375 ml • (04/30/91) • **89**

SELVOLE, FATTORIA DI

Barullo 1991: Elegant and beautifully crafted with raspberry and mineral character, medium body and fine, silky tannins. • $16 • **87**
Barullo 1990: Light and simple prune and herbal character. Delicate and easy to drink. Try on release. 100 cases made. • $15 • **78**
Chianti Classico 1993: Attractively light, crisp and easy-drinking, with some decent red berry notes and tannins. Serve slightly chilled. • $10 • **80**
Chianti Classico 1988 • $NA • (09/15/91) • **78**
Chianti Classico Lanfredini Castello di Selvole Riserva 1991: Deep, dark-colored, with intense aromas and flavors of black pepper, fruit and spice. Full-bodied and has full tannins with a minty, licorice finish. Slightly too jammy. Better after 1996. • $13 • **86**
Chianti Classico Lanfredini Riserva 1990: Rather dried out, exhibiting some nutmeg, cedar and tobacco character. Light in body. Drinkable now. 175 cases made. • $14 • **75**
Chianti Classico Lanfredini Riserva 1985 • $NA • (09/15/91) • **77**

SENZA NOME, VIGNA

Moscato d'Asti 1991 • $18 • (05/15/93) • **79**

SERENA, LA

Brunello di Montalcino 1988: Plenty of sweet, ripe fruit in this to soften the very good backbone of tannin. Full-bodied and velvety, with a toasty, fruity finish. Better after 1996. • $NA • (04/30/94) • **89**

SERTOLI SALIS, CONTI

Il Saloncello Red 1989 • $15 • (12/31/92) • **73**

SESTA, TENUTA DI

Brunello di Montalcino 1988: A muscular Brunello, lacking grace. Smoke, tar and ripe fruit aromas and flavors, drying tannins. Try after 1997. • $42 • (04/30/94) • **79**
Rosso di Montalcino 1991 • $NA • (04/30/94) • **75**

SETTIMO, AURELIO

Barolo Vigna Rocche 1982 • $19 • (05/31/88) • **83**
Barolo Vigna Rocche 1980 • $17 • (05/31/88) • **73**
Barolo Vigna Rocche 1979 • $25 • (05/31/88) • **67**

SOLA, CASA

Chianti Classico 1993: Delicate and fruity, with a dried herb and cherry character. Medium-to-light body, with fresh acidity and a light finish. • $NA • **81**

SOLDERA

Brunello di Montalcino 1990: A disappointment from this producer. Mature, seductive, sweet- and ripe-flavored red. Round and supple, quite advanced on the palate. Drink now. • $NA • **84**
Brunello di Montalcino 1988: One of the hot wines of the region. Intensely fruity with loads of character. A delicious gamy, meaty, fruity character. Medium-bodied with velvety tannins. From Casse Basse. Drink now. • $NA • (04/30/94) • **92**
Brunello di Montalcino 1985 • $90 • (07/15/91) • **89**

SOLE DEI BARBI

Rosso di Montalcino 1987 • $17 • (06/15/93) • **76**

SOLICHIATA

Torrepalino 1987 • $5 • (04/15/90) • **73**

SONNINO, FATTORIA

Cantinino Vigneto Fezzana 1990 • $NA • (10/31/93) • **85**
Cantinino Vigneto Fezzana 1988 • $NA • (10/31/93) • **83**
Chianti 1993: Attractive plum and floral character on the nose and palate. Light-bodied and very light finish. Drinkable now. • $NA • **79**
Chianti Castello di Montespertoli 1992: Lean and tart, showing some fruity, vanilla character. Light body and finish. Drinkable now. • $NA • **79**
Chianti Castello di Montespertoli 1991 • $NA • (10/31/93) • **80**
Chianti Castello di Montespertoli 1990 • $NA • (10/31/93) • **78**
Chianti Colli Fiorentini 1993: Impressive for the vintage. Full of fresh berry, cherry aromas and flavors. Medium-bodied and silky with fine tannins and a medium finish. Delicious fruit. Drinkable or ageable. • $NA • **85**
Sanleone 1993: Impressive debut. Ripe, rich and impressively flavorful, with loads of mint, blackberry and plum flavors. Attractively sweet Sangiovese-Merlot blend. Tannic enough to cellar until after 1997. • $NA • **88**

SONVICO

Barbera d'Asti Vigna d'Angelo 1992 • $NA • (10/31/94) • **83**
La Vigna di Sonvico 1991: Crisp, chewy style with some chunky berry flavors pushing against the layer of hard-edged tannin. Might have enough to be balanced when the tannins soften, around 1998-2001. • $NA • **85**

SORBAIANO

Montescudaio Rosso delle Miniere Red 1988 • $24 • (08/31/91) • **86**

SORTE, LA

Classico Soave 1992 • $6 • (06/15/94) • **81**

Superiore Valpolicella Classico 1991 • $6 • (10/15/94) • **83**

SPALLETTI

Chianti 1993: Firm and flavorful, with good cherry and almond flavors. Straightforward and fairly light, though with a stemmy quality in the aroma. Drink now. • $7 • (07/31/95) • **82**

Chianti 1992: Very light flavors of cherry and licorice. Tasted twice, with consistent notes. Drinkable now. • $NA • **77**

Chianti Rufina 1993: Attractive and flavorful. Medium body. Very plummy with a layer of raspberry and blackberry notes. Decent backbone of tannins. Crisp finish. Drinkable now. • $NA • **83**

Chianti Rufina Poggio Reale Riserva 1990: Soft and ready to drink. Medium body, some chestnut, plum and earth flavors and a touch diluted. A bit drying on the finish. Drinkable now. • $NA • **80**

Palazzo al Campo Red 1994: Well crafted, with berry, grape character. Medium-bodied with soft tannins and a grapey finish that's a bit simple. Drink on release. • $NA • **82**

SPERI

Valpolicella Classico Superiore Vigneto La Roverina 1993: This is rich for the region, with smoky plum and toasty flavors and good concentration. Maturing now, but still firm enough for food. 3,000 cases made. • $12 • (06/15/96) • **86**

Valpolicella Classico Superiore Vigneto La Roverina 1991 • $8 • (04/30/94) • **83**

STEFANO, S.

Chianti Classico 1993: Already tasting a bit mature and forward, with an odd mushroom and earthy note. Turns dry and slightly herbal on the finish. • $NA • **72**

STIVAL

Merlot del Veneto Orientale 1993: Disjointed and not very pleasant. A mix of tart acidity, sharp spritziness and earthy berry flavors. • $6 • (01/31/96) • **72**

Pinot Grigio del Veneto 1993: Awkward aromas and flavors of canned pineapple and apple cider suggest this wine is fading fast. Not much fruit or freshness. • $6 • (10/31/95) • **75**

STRACCALI

Chianti 1993: Loads of strawberry, stemmy character on the nose and palate. A bit aggressive and raw. Drinkable now. 30,000 cases made. • $7 • **73**

Chianti Classico 1992: Simple and delicious, strawberry and plum flavors. Light body and a fresh, fruity finish. Drinkable now. 16,650 cases made. • $NA • **79**

Chianti Classico 1991 • $NA • (10/31/93) • **83**

Chianti Classico 1990 • $6 • (09/15/92) • **79**

Chianti Classico Riserva 1990: Rather cheesy and dry but there's some decent ripe fruit. Perhaps better with food. 1,050 cases made. • $NA • **71**

Chianti Classico Riserva 1988 • $NA • (09/15/92) • **81**

Chianti Vernaiolo 1991 • $6 • (10/31/93) BB • **83**

STROZZI, GUICCIARDINI

Sodole Riserva 1985 • $16 • **60**

STRUZZIERO

Taurasi Riserva 1977 • $22 • (08/31/86) CS • **93**

Key: SS—Spectator Selection. CS—Cellar Selection. BB—Best Buy. $NA—Price not available. (BT)—Barrel tasting. Ⓐ—Auction Price.
Dates in parentheses represent the issues in which the ratings were published.

STURM

Pinot Grigio Collio 1994: A nutty, earthy flavor makes this stand out as a rustic white wine. Dry, fairly full-bodied. 1,000 cases made. • $14 • (06/15/96) • **77**

Refosco dal Peduncolo Rosso 1993: A frankly fruity red with oodles of berry and cherry flavors that linger on the finish. Slightly tannic and tart, best to drink now while it's fresh. 300 cases made. • $14 • (05/31/96) • **84**

Tocai Friulano Collio 1994: An awkward and unfocused wine with canned fruit flavors and aromas. 600 cases made. • $14 • (06/15/96) • **73**

SUBIDA DI MONTE

Pinot Grigio Collio 1994: A vibrant and lively wine with fresh fruit flavors, good crisp acidity and a lingering, fruity finish. Has good concentration and balance. 1,500 cases made. • $11 • (06/15/96) • **85**

SVEVO

Saracento Red 1991: The mahogany color and nutty flavors of this wine remind us of mediocre Sherry. It's flat, a bit sweet and dull. Drink up. 20,000 cases made. • $7 • (05/31/95) • **73**

TALENTI

Brunello di Montalcino Pian di Conte 1982 • $NA • (09/15/86) • **90**

Brunello di Montalcino Pian di Conte 1981 • $NA • (09/15/86) • **88**

Brunello di Montalcino Pian di Conte Riserva 1988: One of the best of the vintage. Truly elegant, with a plum and black cherry character. Full-bodied and fine tannins. A very sophisticated Brunello. Drinkable now. • $NA • (10/31/94) • **94**

Brunello di Montalcino Podere Pian di Conte 1990: A nicely maturing, ripe and sweet-tasting Brunello, showing very rich, plummy character and almost Port-like texture. Somewhat rustic and tannic, so try in 1998. • $NA • **88**

Brunello di Montalcino Podere Pian di Conte 1988: A tightly knit wine with excellent structure of ripe fruit, full, velvety tannins and long, rich finish. Best after 1996. • $40 • (04/30/94) • **90**

Rosso di Montalcino Podere Pian di Conte 1993: Light and crisp, with decent cherry, earth, cedar, chocolate flavors. Finishes somewhat dry and harsh. Serve chilled. Slightly disappointing from this producer. • $NA • **79**

Rosso di Montalcino Podere Pian di Conte 1992 • $NA • (10/31/94) • **79**

Rosso di Montalcino Podere Pian di Conte 1991 • $18 • (04/30/94) • **81**

TALOSA

Chianti Colli Senesi 1988 • $8 • (11/30/90) BB • **88**

Rosso di Montepulciano 1989 • $11 • (01/31/92) • **79**

Vino Nobile di Montepulciano Riserva 1988 • $16 • (07/31/94) • **84**

Vino Nobile di Montepulciano Riserva 1986 • $15 • (07/15/91) • **84**

Vino Nobile di Montepulciano Riserva 1983 • $8 • **79**

Vino Nobile di Montepulciano Riserva 1982 • $8 • (04/15/88) • **72**

TASSAROLO, CASTELLO DI

Gavi 1994: An average white that's soft and has earthy, vegetal flavors. • $14 • (02/29/96) • **76**

Gavi 1992: Exotic, full-flavored, stretching the boundaries of style. Has striking aromas of butter and citrus, ripe apricot nuances and a lingering finish. 5,830 cases made. • $11 • **86**

Gavi S 1993: An extreme style for Gavi, with plenty of new oak showing through in the toasty, nutty aromas and flavors that overshadow the fruit. • $14 • (02/29/96) • **82**

Gavi Vigneto Alborina 1991: Nicely mature, with honey and almond aromas to accent the basic fruit and herb flavors. Rich in texture and rather long on the aftertaste. • $33 • (02/29/96) • **85**

TAURINO, DR. COSIMO

Brindisi Patriglione 1981 • $14 • (12/31/90) • **85**

Brindisi Patriglione Riserva 1979 • $12 • (03/31/89) • **82**
Notarpanaro 1985 • $10 • (03/31/94) • **81**
Notarpanaro 1981 • $9 • (05/15/91) • **86**
Notarpanaro 1978 • $8 • (03/31/89) • **80**
Notarpanaro 1975 • $8 • (04/15/88) • **78**
Salice Salentino Riserva 1990: Begins with smoky barbecue aromas, followed by a fleshy, mouth-coating texture. The flavors lean toward stewed tomato and mineral. Drinkable now. • $9 • (01/31/96) • **82**
Salice Salentino Riserva 1988 • $8 • (03/31/94) • **80**
Salice Salentino Riserva 1986 • $8 • (01/31/92) BB • **84**
Salice Salentino Riserva 1985 • $8 • (02/15/91) BB • **85**
Salice Salentino Riserva 1983 • $6 • (12/15/89) BB • **81**
Salice Salentino Riserva 1982 • $6 • (03/31/89) BB • **82**
Salice Salentino Riserva 1981 • $6 • (03/31/88) BB • **81**
Salice Salentino Riserva 1980 • $5 • (12/15/87) BB • **84**
Salice Salentino Rosato 1989 • $9 • (03/31/92) • **82**
Salice Salentino Rosato 1988 • $7 • (03/15/91) BB • **84**
Salice Salentino Rosato 1987 • $6 • (12/31/89) BB • **84**

TEDESCHI

Capitel San Rocco 1988 • $NA • (09/15/92) • **78**
Capitel San Rocco 1983 • $11 • (02/15/89) • **84**
Recioto della Valpolicella Amarone Capitel Monte Olmi 1988 • $40 • (09/15/92) • **84**
Recioto della Valpolicella Capitel Monte Fontana 1988 • $NA • (09/15/92) • **85**
Soave Classico 1991 • $10 • (09/15/92) • **73**
Valpolicella Capitel del Nicalò 1989 • $14 • (09/15/92) • **82**

TENAGLIA, TENUTA LA

Grignolino del Monferrato Casalese 1991 • $24 • (06/30/93) • **81**

TERRABIANCA

Campaccio 1991: Very herbal wine dried thyme with loads of slightly unripe Cabernet character. Medium-bodied and round with a lovely texture but a bit too herbal and diluted on the finish. Made from Sangiovese and Cabernet Sauvignon. Drinkable now. • $NA • **80**
Campaccio 1990: Sexy, elegant wine with beautiful cedar, violet and berry aromas and flavors, medium body, lively acidity and fine tannins. Made from Sangiovese and Cabernet Sauvignon. Try in 1997. 2,200 cases made. • $20 • (10/31/93) • **88**
Campaccio Barriques 1991: A big wine but a bit rough with green bean and fruit character, full body and full, coarse tannins. Made from Sangiovese and Cabernet Sauvignon. Better after 1996. • $NA • **80**
Campaccio Barriques 1990: Cassis and herbal aromas and flavors, medium body and firm tannins, slightly underwhelming. Sangiovese 70 percent and Cabernet Sauvignon 30 percent. Drinkable now. 2,000 cases made. • $33 • **84**
Campaccio Barriques 1988 • $31 • (09/15/91) • **87**
Chianti Classico Riserva 1991: Pretty aromatic blackberry, violet character. Medium body. Fine tannins. Slightly diluted finish. • $NA • **84**
Chianti Classico Scassino 1992: Fresh, light cherry and berry character and a refreshing finish. • $12 • **78**
Chianti Classico Scassino 1991 • $16 • (10/31/93) • **85**
Chianti Classico Scassino 1990 • $13 • (09/15/92) • **90**
Chianti Classico Vigna della Croce Riserva 1990: This is wonderful accompanying food. Very pretty, firm and crisp, with plum, chestnut and berry aromas and flavors and a light, silky finish. Drinkable now. 2,000 cases made. • $17 • **87**
Chianti Classico Vigna della Croce Riserva 1988 • $25 • (09/15/92) • **88**
Chianti Classico Vigna della Croce Riserva 1985 • $NA • (09/15/91) • **87**
Piano del Cipresso 1990: This wine shows berry, peppery and gamy character and medium body and tannin structure. Made from Sangiovese. Drinkable now. 1,600 cases made. • $20 • (10/31/93) • **86**
Piano del Cipresso 1988 • $29 • (09/15/91) • **83**
Piano del Cipresso Barriques 1991: An earthy wine with minty, spicy character. Full-bodied with loads of fruit and tannins. Hint of oak. Quite thick and round. Made from Cabernet Sauvignon. Better after 1997. • $NA • **87**

TERRALE

Rosso 1994: Attractive, straightforward and has sweet plum and cherry flavors backed by vibrant acidity. Immediately appealing. 50,000 cases made. • $4 • (01/31/96) • **82**
Rosso 1993: Sweet fruit and soft tannins make this an appealing quaff. Cherry, raisin and spice flavors are fresh and graceful. Try it slightly chilled, drink now. 58,300 cases made. • $5 • (05/31/95) BB • **84**

TERRE FORTI, LE

Barbaresco 1982 • $19 • (09/15/90) • **77**

TERRICCI

Antiche Terre de'Ricci 1986 • $23 • (05/15/90) • **83**
Antiche Terre de'Ricci 1985 • $22 • (03/15/89) • **91**
Terricci 1986 • $20 • (09/30/91) • **67**

TERRICCIO, TENUTA DEL

Tassinaia 1993: Very stylish. Deeply colored, with intense chocolate, cinnamon and berry character. Full-bodied with wonderfully silky tannins and a long, caressing finish. Made from Cabernet Sauvignon and Merlot. Better after 1996. • $NA • **90**
Tassinaia 1992: An up-and-coming winery on the Tuscan coastline. A beautiful wine with mineral, berry, raspberry and mint aromas and flavors. Medium-bodied with delicate tannins and a silky finish. Drink now. • $NA • **86**

TERUZZI & PUTHOD

Vigna Peperino 1986 • $11 • (01/31/90) • **68**
Vigna Peperino 1985 • $11 • (10/31/88) • **92**

TIEFENBRUNNER

Cabernet Alto Adige 1987 • $9 • (03/31/89) • **84**
Cabernet Sauvignon Alto Adige Linticlarus 1992: Full-bodied, but with some rough edges. An exaggerated style that shows stewed plum and bell pepper flavors. It finishes on a smoky, tannic note. • $13 • (02/29/96) • **83**
Chardonnay Alto Adige 1994: Intense yet restrained, this nervy wine gives delicate floral and herbal aromas, crisp apple and lemon flavors and a light vanilla note on the finish. Not showy but very satsifying. • $11 • (06/15/96) • **86**
Chardonnay Alto Adige 1993: Light and bright, a tight little wine with pretty green apple fruit, even if it finishes a little short. 12,500 cases made. • $8 • (01/31/95) • **82**
Chardonnay Alto Adige Castel Turmhof 1993: Bright, fruity and refreshing, showing lively intensity of green apple and nectarine. A harmonious wine that echoes the fruit nicely on the finish. 2,100 cases made. • $11 • (01/31/95) • **85**
Chardonnay Alto Adige Linticlarus 1992: Light, crisp and refreshing, a juicy wine with pretty lemon, lime, floral and vanilla notes, opening up to apple and pear with a touch of spice on the finish. Pleasant to drink now. 950 cases made. • $15 • (01/31/95) • **84**
Gewürztraminer Alto Adige Castel Turmhof 1993: Beautifully defined varietal aromas and flavors on a pretty frame, singing its pear, grapefruit and rose-petal flavors in perfect harmony. 800 cases made. • $15 • (01/31/95) • **87**
Pinot Bianco Alto Adige 1993: A middle-of-the-road Pinot Bianco, with tart, simple citrus and apple flavors. Light and a bit diluted. 1,100 cases made. • $8 • (01/31/95) • **78**
Pinot Grigio Alto Adige 1994: Though lean, this clean white has good grip, with firm acidity and lingering flavors of lemon and hazelnut. A refreshing wine for food. • $10 • (06/15/96) • **84**
Pinot Grigio Alto Adige 1993: A well-made Pinot Grigio that delivers much pleasure, with focused pear, grapefruit, floral flavors, and lots of harmony. Light, delicious and quite smooth. 6,500 cases made. • $9 • (01/31/95) • **84**

TIEZZI, ENZO

Brunello di Montalcino 1990: Round and delicious berry, cedar and meat character. Full-bodied and soft, leading to a simple finish. Drink now. • $NA • (10/31/95) • **85**
Rosso di Montalcino 1993: Vivid cherry, lemon and berry aromas and flavors, medium body, elegant tannins and long, fresh finish. Drinkable now. • $NA • **85**

TIZZANO, CASTELLO DI

Chianti Classico Riserva 1982 • $18 • (07/15/89) • **78**

TOMMASI

Amarone Valpolicella Classico 1986 • $NA • (11/15/94) • **75**

TORRE GAIA

Il Dugentino 1986 • $5 • (09/15/88) • **82**

TORRE ROSAZZA

Chardonnay Colli Orientali del Friuli 1994: There's good structure here, richness and firmness, as smoky and toasty flavors add interest, yet not much fruit on the palate. Not a typical Chardonnay, but good with food. 3,000 cases made. • $11 • (04/30/96) • **81**
Merlot Colli Orientali del Friuli L'Altromerlot 1992: The opulent flavors here are reined in by a tight structure. This has loads of blueberry and plum flavors and a wallop of tannin besides. Well rounded, with a nice finish marked by chocolate and coffee notes. Try after 1997. 2,000 cases made. • $20 • (02/29/96) • **88**
Pinot Grigio Colli Orientali del Friuli 1994: Full-bodied and rich on the palate yet dry and crisp, this chewy white has ripe pear, mango and almond flavors and a smoky accent. Can stand up to richer dishes. 5,000 cases made. • $11 • (04/30/96) • **87**
Pinot Nero Colli Orientali del Friuli 1993: Polished fruit flavors, lively balance and slightly tannic texture make this an appealing and smooth red. 1,000 cases made. • $13 • (04/30/96) • **83**

TORRE TERZA

Rosso di Montalcino 1991 • $9 • (04/30/94) • **84**

TORRE, LA

Brunello di Montalcino 1990: Fruity, soft and a bit simple, offering pepper, tomato and cherry aromas and flavors, medium body and succulent finish. • $NA • **85**
Tuscany Red 1985 • $30 • (04/15/91) • **78**

TORREGIORGI

Barbaresco 1990: Ripe plum and licorice aromas give way to firm tannins and roasted fruit flavors. A traditional style. Drinkable now. • $NA • (10/31/95) • **82**

TORRESELLA

Merlot 1993: Earthy and herbaceous flavors dominate in this lean, firm red. Not showing much fruit now, but has some concentration. Drinkable now. • $9 • (01/31/96) • **81**
Merlot Lison-Pramaggiore Red 1986 • $5 • (10/31/88) • **79**
Pinot Grigio Veneto 1993: Almost neutral in character, this is clean and fresh but lacks fruit and depth. Try as a spritzer. • $9 • (04/30/96) • **78**
Sauvignon Blanc 1991 • $8 • (09/15/93) • **82**

Key: SS—Spectator Selection. CS—Cellar Selection. BB—Best Buy. $NA—Price not available. (BT)—Barrel tasting. Ⓐ—Auction Price.
Dates in parentheses represent the issues in which the ratings were published.

TOSCANE, VIGNE

Chianti Terre Toscane 1989 • $5 • (11/30/90) BB • **80**

TOSCOLO

Chianti Classico 1990 • $8 • (04/30/94) BB • **85**
Red Tuscan Table Wine Red 1986 • $4 • (01/31/89) • **79**

TOSTI

Asti Spumante NV: A sweet, spicy, minty, smooth-textured bubbly with a refreshing balance and distinctive flavors. A very good example of the style. • $9 • (07/31/95) • **86**
Brut Champenois NV • $12 • (12/15/92) • **82**

TRACOLLE

Chianti Classico 1993: Unclean and earthy, even hinting at salami. A slight fizziness to it and a dry finish. Tasted twice, with consistent notes. • $NA • **71**
Chianti Classico 1988 • $NA • (09/15/91) • **69**

TRAVAGLINI

Gattinara 1986 • $18 • (01/31/92) • **82**
Gattinara 1980 • $8 • (12/16/85) • **63**
Gattinara Numerata 1985 • $26 • (01/31/92) • **84**
Spanna 1988 • $10 • (07/15/91) • **83**

TRAVERSA

Barbaresco Sori Ciabot 1985 • $23 • (09/15/90) • **86**

TREROSE, TENUTA

Vin Santo 1986 • $33/ 375 ml • (07/31/93) • **89**
Vino Nobile di Montepulciano 1988 • $16 • (12/15/92) • **86**
Vino Nobile di Montepulciano 1986 • $16 • (07/15/91) • **80**
Vino Nobile di Montepulciano 1985 • $11 • (11/15/88) • **90**
Vino Nobile di Montepulciano Riserva 1985 • $19 • (07/15/91) • **85**
Vino Nobile di Montepulciano Simposio 1988 • $40 • (12/15/92) • **88**

UNTEREBNERHOF, TENUTA

Pinot Grigio Alto Adige 1994: Light-bodied and bland, soft and diluted, shows some pear flavors, but an earthy undertone detracts from the pleasure. 1,500 cases made. • $11 • (06/15/96) • **77**

UZZANO, CASTELLO DI

Chianti Classico 1988 • $NA • (09/15/91) • **87**
Chianti Classico Riserva 1985 • $NA • (09/15/91) • **85**

VADIAPERTI

Fiano di Avellino White 1993: Tart and crisp, with some green apple, almond and spice flavors. Refreshing, lively and dry as a bone, with a soft finish. • $17 • (03/31/95) • **84**
Greco di Tufo White 1993: Astringent, with only slight lemony flavors. A murky wine with a bitter finish. • $14 • (03/31/95) • **74**

VAJRA, G.D.

Barbera d'Alba 1992 • $NA • (10/31/94) • **81**
Barbera d'Alba Bricco delle Viole Riserva 1985 • $22 • (07/31/89) • **83**
Barbera d'Alba Vigneto Bricco delle Viole 1993: Round and rich grapey, rose petal aromas and flavors, medium body and light finish. • $35 • **82**
Barolo 1990: Earthy, musty, lacking in charm or much fruit character. Tasted twice. • $28 • (10/31/94) • **64**
Barolo 1988 • $NA • (10/31/93) • **85**
Barolo 1982 • $14 • (03/15/87) • **91**

Barolo Bricco delle Viole 1982 • $19 • (08/31/88) • **91**
Barolo Fossati Vineyard 1985 • $34 • (12/31/90) • **91**
Dolcetto d'Alba Coste & Fossati 1994: Grapey and firm with fine tannins. Medium-bodied and crisp and a long, fruity finish. Delicious now. • $19 • **85**

VAL DI SUGA

Brunello di Montalcino 1990: Wonderfully perfumed violet, berry and light cedar character, medium body and firm tannins. Drinkable now. • $NA • **86**
Brunello di Montalcino 1988: Rather traditional in style, with chestnut and berry aromas and flavors. Medium-bodied, but rather lean and slightly astringent. • $26 • (04/30/94) • **78**
Brunello di Montalcino Riserva 1988: A traditional style of Brunello: velvety tannins, intense, ripe fruit and an olive and tobacco character. Slightly bitter on the finish. Drinkable now. • $NA • (10/31/94) • **87**
Brunello di Montalcino Riserva 1986 • $27 • (11/30/93) • **87**
Brunello di Montalcino Riserva 1982 • $20 • (11/30/89) • **89**
Brunello di Montalcino Riserva 1978 • $14 • (03/15/87) • **67**
Brunello di Montalcino Vigna del Lago 1988: International in style with all its new French oak, but still fine and powerful. Vanilla and berry aromas and flavors, loads of fine tannins and excellent finish. Tasted four times. Try after 1997. 600 cases made. • $52 • (04/30/94) • **90**
Brunello di Montalcino Vigna del Lago 1987 • $NA • **70**
Brunello di Montalcino Vigna del Lago 1986 • $52 • (11/30/93) • **91**
Brunello di Montalcino Vigna del Lago 1985 • $52 • (07/15/91) • **90**
Brunello di Montalcino Vigna Spuntali 1988: Rich and spicy, with lush plum, cherry and chocolate flavors. Balanced and harmonious, though still with a good kick of tannins. Supple and drinkable now. 700 cases made. • $52 • (07/31/95) • **88**
Rosso di Montalcino 1993: Rustic and not totally clean, showing some pretty, ripe plum notes, but then turning somewhat murky and dry on the chestnut-flavored finish. • $NA • **77**
Rosso di Montalcino 1991 • $12 • (04/30/94) • **80**
Rosso di Montalcino 1988 • $10 • (04/30/91) • **87**
Rosso di Montalcino 1986 • $9 • (11/30/89) • **81**
Tuscany Red 1985 • $23 • (09/30/90) • **88**

VALDICAVA

Brunello di Montalcino 1990: Too bad its wet grass and mushroom character smells so funky, because the texture is smooth as can be, adding maturing berry, truffle and chestnut flavors. • $NA • **80**
Brunello di Montalcino 1988: A vivid wine, with red fruit aromas and hints of oak. It's medium-bodied, with medium firm tannins and a ripe fruit finish. Better after 1996. • $28 • (04/30/94) • **86**
Brunello di Montalcino Madonna del Piano Riserva 1988: Impressively concentrated with masses of fruit and plum character. But the masses of tannins and wood dry the finish slightly. Bit too much new wood? Drink now or hold. • $NA • (10/31/94) • **85**
Rosso di Montalcino 1993: Beautiful, perfumed cherry and violet aromas and flavors, medium body, soft tannins and a long, fruity finish. Drinkable now. • $NA • **84**
Rosso di Montalcino 1991 • $15 • (04/30/94) • **78**

VALENTINI

Montepulciano d'Abruzzo 1979 • $28 • (02/15/89) • **80**

VALERIA, S.

Chianti Classico Riserva 1985 • $NA • (09/15/91) • **78**

VALFIERI

Barbaresco 1989: Coarse, a little watery, lacking in personality and flavor, but it has some anise-scented cherry notes on the tannic finish. Try in 1997. 1,600 cases made. • $16 • (04/15/94) • **77**
Barbaresco 1986 • $12 • (09/15/90) • **82**
Barbaresco 1985 • $8 • (07/31/89) • **70**
Barbera d'Alba 1987 • $7 • (09/15/90) • **69**
Barolo 1990: Simple and tough, with prune flavors. It just might not have enough fruit to last until the tannins mellow. A blunt but flavorful wine. • $NA • (10/31/94) • **83**
Barolo 1985 • $13 • (10/15/90) • **90**
Dolcetto d'Alba 1992 • $10 • **67**
Piedmont 1988 • $8 • (12/31/90) • **81**
Piedmont 1987 • $5 • (03/15/89) • **78**

VALIANO

Chianti Classico 1992: Clean and crisp with berry and dried cherry flavors. Very light finish. Drinkable now. • $8 • **79**

VALLANA

Barbera 1988 • $7 • (03/31/90) • **80**
Barbera 1986 • $6 • (02/15/89) BB • **90**
Barbera del Piemonte 1990 • $9 • (10/31/92) • **79**
Barbera del Piemonte 1988 • $8 • (03/15/91) • **88**
Gattinara 1983 • $10 • (01/31/90) • **76**

VALLANIA

Cabernet Sauvignon Colli Bolognesi Terre Rosse Monte San Pietro 1986 • $18 • (09/30/91) • **66**
Sauvignon 1991 • $NA • (09/15/93) • **73**
Terre Rosse 1985 • $9 • (03/31/90) • **70**

VALLAROM

Cabernet Sauvignon Trentino 1988 • $27 • (12/15/92) • **80**
Pinot Nero Trentino 1990 • $25 • (07/31/93) • **74**

VALLE SELEZIONE ARALDICA

L'Araldo Collina Friulana 1985 • $20 • (05/15/91) • **84**

VALTELLINA, FATTORIA

Chianti Classico Giorgio Regni 1993: Delicious plum, cassis, smoke and earth flavors mingle nicely in this light- to medium-bodied, crisp Tuscan red. Refined tannins, but a bit short on the finish. Drinkable now. • $NA • **84**
Chianti Classico Giorgio Regni 1992: Amazingly good for the vintage. Quite rich, with meaty, smoky character, medium body, rich fruit and silky tannins. Ageable but better to drink now. • $13 • **86**
Chianti Classico Giorgio Regni 1990 • $NA • (10/31/93) • **90**
Chianti Classico Giorgio Regni 1988 • $19 • (09/15/91) • **83**
Chianti Classico Giorgio Regni Riserva 1990: Big, deep, brooding Chianti, concentrations of mint, cassis, berry and wet earth aromas and flavors. Yet so harmonious. Full in body but incredibly fine and well crafted. Monumental. Drinkable now. • $25 • **93**
Chianti Classico Giorgio Regni Riserva 1985 • $20 • (09/15/91) • **92**
Convivio Giorgio Regni 1991: Super-crafted, boasting fabulous vanilla, cherry, berry and chocolate character, medium-to-full body, full tannins and a long, long finish. Better after 1996. • $30 • **91**
Convivio Giorgio Regni 1990 • $NA • (10/31/93) • **93**

VASELLI

Santa Giulia 1988 • $10 • (01/31/92) • **83**
Santa Giulia Rosso NV • $19 • (01/31/92) • **80**

VECCHIA, VIGNA

Canvalle 1992: Some modest red berry fruit, but it's a rather simple medium-bodied wine and slightly diluted. Short finish. • $NA • **78**
Canvalle 1991: A bit too traditional and old tasting. Chestnut and cherry character with a light texture. A bit drying on the finish. Tasted twice, with consistent notes. • $NA • **78**
Chianti Classico 1993: Very light, with some pleasant cherry and berry flavors, but not much left on the finish. • $NA • **74**

Chianti Classico 1988 • $11 • (10/31/91) • **83**

Chianti Classico Riserva 1991: Rather mature and simple, with berry, tobacco and cedar character. Light body and slightly dry on the finish. • $NA • **76**

Chianti Classico Riserva 1990: Plum, prune and ham aromas and flavors, medium-bodied and soft, with a slightly diluted finish. Drinkable now. • $NA • **78**

Raddese 1990: Delicious up-front wine featuring raspberry, cherry and pepper character, medium body, good acidity, silky tannins and a long finish. Drinkable now. • $NA • **87**

VECCHIE TERRE DI MONTEFILI

Bruno di Rocca 1992: Soft and alluring wine with loads of crushed berries and fruit. Full-bodied with full, velvety tannins and a medium finish. Drink now or age. • $NA • **87**

Bruno di Rocca 1991: Beautifully complex aromas of herb, leather and spice add interest to the rich and concentrated flavors of cherry and raspberry. Moderately tannic, firmly acidic. • $40 • (11/30/94) • **87**

Bruno di Rocca 1990 • $NA • (10/31/93) • **89**

Bruno di Rocca 1989 • $NA • (10/31/93) • **87**

Chianti Classico 1993: Rich and round with blackberry and wet earth character. Medium-bodied with a velvety texture and a medium finish. Drinkable now, but can hold for the cellar. • $NA • **85**

Chianti Classico 1992: Pure fruit here, sage, berry and cherry aromas and flavors, medium body and a peppery finish. Drinkable now. • $20 • **85**

Chianti Classico 1990 • $20 • (10/31/93) • **86**

Chianti Classico 1988 • $20 • (09/15/91) • **90**

Chianti Classico 1986 • $14 • (04/30/90) • **85**

Chianti Classico Anfiteatro 1991: Electrifying wine, oozing with amazing cassis character. Medium- to full-bodied, it's ripe and fresh with round, polished texture and a long, lush finish. Tempting now, but better after 1996. • $32 • **90**

Chianti Classico Anfiteatro 1990: Big and impressive, rich in fruit and complex in aroma, showing a distinctive, meaty-gamy character that accents the solid black cherry and blackberry flavors. Tannic, full-bodied and young. Drinkable now. • $40 • (11/30/94) • **89**

Chianti Classico Anfiteatro Riserva 1988 • $24 • (09/15/92) • **89**

Chianti Classico Riserva 1985 • $NA • (09/15/91) • **90**

VENEGAZZU

Brut Loredan Gasparini 1988 • $14 • (12/15/92) • **78**

Brut di Venegazzu 1982 • $12 • (12/15/86) • **91**

Della Casa Red 1990 • $15 • (09/15/92) • **85**

Della Casa Red 1985 • $25 • (03/31/90) • **91**

Della Casa Red 1983 • $25 • (02/15/89) • **86**

Della Casa Red 1982 • $15 • (07/15/87) • **82**

Della Casa Red 1980 • $10 • (02/15/87) • **72**

Loredan Gasparini Capo di Stato 1992: Deep in color and fruit flavor, this is a grand, concentrated, oaky wine with a firm texture, well-integrated tannins and a lingering finish. Tempting to drink now, but should improve through at least 1998. 650 cases made. • $33 • (05/31/96) • **88**

Loredan Gasparini Capo di Stato 1990: Appealing aromas of toast, plum and herb presage a dry, hard red, very firm tannins. The flavors should soften and become more generous with a little age, though drinkable now. 1,172 cases made. • $33 • (05/15/95) • **83**

Loredan Gasparini Venegazzu della Casa 1992: The smoky bacon fat and black plum flavors say Merlot, the crisp structure with light tannins says Chile. Pleasant drinking now. 3,750 cases made. • $20 • (06/15/96) • **83**

Key: SS—Spectator Selection. CS—Cellar Selection. BB—Best Buy. $NA—Price not available. (BT)—Barrel tasting. Ⓐ—Auction Price.
Dates in parentheses represent the issues in which the ratings were published.

VERBENA

Brunello di Montalcino 1988: Ancient, rather weak wine of garnet color. Chestnut and earthy, ripe fruit aromas and flavors. • $NA • (04/30/94) • **75**

Rosso di Montalcino 1991 • $NA • (04/30/94) • **83**

VERBI, I

Brunello di Montalcino 1990: Big and rich with tobacco, spice and dried berry aromas and flavors. Full-bodied, round, offering velvety tannins and long aftertaste. A bit rustic and rough. Drink now. • $NA • **86**

Rosso di Montalcino 1993: Some ripe and sweet fruit here, but the cherry and plum flavors are slightly dominated by stewed tomato character. Harsh, dry finish. • $NA • **77**

VERDUNO, CASTELLO DI

Barbaresco Vigna Rabajà 1990: Light and charming, with strawberry and rose petal tones offering modest pleasures and not much richness or backbone. Drinkable now. • $NA • (10/31/94) • **80**

Barbera d'Alba Bricco del Cuculo 1993: Crisp, tart, medium-bodied, showing modest cherry and raspberry character but also some cheesy, leesy notes. • $NA • **79**

Barbera d'Alba Bricco del Cuculo 1992 • $NA • (10/31/94) • **80**

Barolo Vigna Massara 1990: Light in color, crisp and spicy, with a chestnut note that accompanies the modest berry flavors. An austere red that must age until 1998 or 2000. • $NA • (10/31/94) • **81**

VERRAZZANO, CASTELLO DI

Chianti Classico 1993: Lovely and quite opulent, showing vivid, clean cassis, plum, black cherry flavor that's sweet and ripe. A mouthful of a wine, medium- to full-bodied, with elegant tannins. Long finish. Drinkable now or age. • $9 • **86**

Chianti Classico 1992: Rich and delicious with loads of chocolate, cherry and vanilla character, medium body, medium velvety tannins and a long, flavorful finish. Drinkable now. 12,500 cases made. • $10 • **84**

Chianti Classico 1991 • $9 • (10/31/93) • **84**

Chianti Classico 1990 • $9 • (10/31/93) • **88**

Chianti Classico 1988 • $8 • (09/15/91) • **85**

Chianti Classico Cinquecentenario di Verrazzano Riserva 1985 • $NA • (09/15/91) • **83**

Chianti Classico Riserva 1991: Round and delicious with sweet, ripe fruit and a hint of spice on the palate. Medium body, medium tannins, soft finish. Drinkable now, will age well. • $9 • **86**

Chianti Classico Riserva 1988 • $NA • (09/15/92) • **84**

Sassello 1990 • $NA • (10/31/93) • **92**

VERSA, LA

Brut Metodo Classico 1982 • $NA • (12/31/86) • **83**

Extra Dry Cuvée Testarossa NV • $19 • (12/15/92) • **85**

VESCOVADO DI MURLO

Chianti 1991 • $7 • (09/15/92) • **80**

Chianti 1990 • $6 • (10/31/91) BB • **83**

VETRICE, VILLA DI

Chianti Classico 1991 • $8 • (10/31/93) • **75**

VIARTE, LA

Roi 1986 • $24 • (01/31/92) • **78**

VICCHIOMAGGIO, CASTELLO

Chianti Classico Petri Riserva 1991: Soft and smooth Chianti with decent plum, red berry. Medium body with a silky texture. A bit diluted and simple. Drinkable now. • $NA • **81**

ITALY

Chianti Classico Petri Riserva 1990: Slightly traditional in style, showing some lovely violet, berry and earthy aromas and flavors, medium-to light-bodied and a light finish. Drinkable now. • $NA • **85**
Chianti Classico Prima Vigna Riserva 1985 • $20 • (09/15/91) • **86**
Chianti Classico Riserva La Prima 1991: Very pretty, lively wine with cherry, watermelon and toasted oak character. Medium-bodied and fresh with a lively finish. Drinkable now. • $NA • **86**
Chianti Classico Riserva Petri del Castello Riserva 1988 • $NA • (09/15/92) • **87**
Chianti Classico San Jacopo 1991 • $NA • (10/31/93) • **80**
Chianti Classico San Jacopo 1990 • $NA • (10/31/93) • **87**
Ripa delle More 1991: Hard not to drink as much of this as possible. A beauty with rose petal, cherry, berry character. Medium-bodied with fine tannins and a long, fresh, minty finish. Drink or hold. • $NA • **88**
Ripa delle More 1990 • $NA • (10/31/93) • **91**

VIETTI

Barbaresco 1985 • $28 • (07/31/89) • **81**
Barbaresco 1982 • $15 • (07/31/87) • **84**
Barbaresco Della Localita' Rabajà 1986 • $18 • (10/31/90) • **87**
Barbaresco Masseria 1990: Lean and austere, with an oregano edge to the minty strawberry flavors. Very light and distinctive, finishing a little hard. Best from 1997. • $26 • (10/31/94) • **82**
Barbaresco Masseria 1989: This wine shows some elegance with its medium-bodied, almost silky texture, prominent tannins and a touch of spicy earthiness to the black cherry and blackberry flavors. A touch of sourness detracts from the finish. Best after 1996. 350 cases made. • $34 • (10/31/93) • **84**
Barbaresco Masseria 1988 • $34 • (10/31/93) • **78**
Barbera d'Alba Della Localita Scarrone 1987 • $11 • (08/31/89) • **86**
Barbera d'Alba Pian Romualdo 1991 • $20 • (11/15/93) • **83**
Barbera d'Alba Pian Romualdo 1990 • $20 • (11/15/93) • **85**
Barbera d'Alba Pian Romualdo 1989 • $19 • (11/30/91) • **83**
Barbera d'Alba Pianromualdo 1988 • $15 • (03/15/91) • **79**
Barbera d'Alba Scarrone 1992 • $15 • (10/31/94) • **85**
Barbera d'Alba Scarrone 1990 • $11 • (11/15/93) • **84**
Barbera d'Alba Scarrone 1989 • $13 • (03/15/91) • **85**
Barolo 1991: Attractive almond, chestnut and berry aromas and flavors, medium body, soft tannins and light finish. Ready now. • $30 • **84**
Barolo 1990: Very spicy, a mouthful of cinnamon and anise around a soft core of black cherry and plum flavors, modestly tannic and probably best to drink young. A little hot in the finish, too. • $NA • (10/31/94) • **82**
Barolo 1978 • $12 • (09/16/84) • **84**
Barolo Brunate 1990: Lean and crisp, with a narrow beam of floral and berry aromas and flavors. Tannins are a little chewy. Tasted twice. • $37 • (10/31/94) • **79**
Barolo Brunate 1989: Rich, creamy and spicy, an elegant wine that shows its vanilla and anise-scented raspberry and cherry flavors against a subtle background of spicy oak. Almost drinkable now it's so supple, and should be fine through 1998. 250 cases made. • $30 • (10/31/93) • **91**
Barolo Bussia Red 1990 • $11 • (11/30/91) • **85**
Barolo Bussia Red 1989 • $12 • (02/28/91) • **85**
Barolo Bussia 1982 • $20 • (09/15/87) • **89**
Barolo Della Localita Bussia Red 1987 • $11 • **75**
Barolo Lazzarito 1990: Smooth and inviting, an accessible red that displays creamy berry and chocolate flavors on a supple frame. Tannins are not intrusive, Drinkable now. • $37 • (10/31/94) • **85**
Barolo Rocche 1990: Shows beautiful fruit. Round and rich with fine tannins but has a slightly earthy character on the palate. Drinkable now. • $60 • **85**
Barolo Rocche 1989: Lean in structure, with a solid core of earthy, chocolaty, gamy flavors that seem to shoulder aside the modest raspberry notes. A stylish Barolo that should be best after 1997. • $40 • (10/31/94) • **83**
Barolo Rocche 1988 • $50 • (10/31/93) • **78**
Barolo Rocche 1982 • $60 • (07/31/89) • **85**
Barolo Rocche 1980 • $30 • (09/15/88) • **87**
Barolo Rocche 1979 • $NA • (09/15/88) • **79**
Barolo Rocche 1978 • $60 • (09/15/88) • **92**
Barolo Rocche 1971 • $70 • (09/15/88) • **86**
Barolo Rocche 1961 • $100 • (09/15/88) • **93**
Barolo Villero Riserva 1982 • $45 • (09/15/88) • **89**
Dolcetto d'Alba Bussia 1994: Clean and easy, offering tobacco and cherry character, medium body and a light finish. • $12 • **80**
Fioretto 1988 • $25 • (06/30/93) • **84**
Fioretto 1987 • $17 • (06/15/90) • **85**
Nebbiolo d'Alba San Michele 1983 • $7 • (09/15/87) • **69**
Piedmont della Localita Disa 1988 • $12 • (09/15/90) • **87**
Piedmont della Localita Disa 1985 • $7 • (09/15/87) • **74**

VIGNA VECCHIA

Canvalle 1990 • $NA • (10/31/93) • **91**
Chianti Classico 1991 • $NA • (10/31/93) • **79**
Chianti Classico 1990 • $12 • (10/31/93) • **74**

VIGNALE, FATTORIA

Chianti Classico 1988 • $NA • (09/15/91) • **85**
Chianti Classico Riserva 1988 • $11 • (09/15/92) • **86**
Chianti Classico Riserva 1985 • $NA • (09/15/91) • **88**

VIGNALTA

Alpinae 1990 • $24 • (09/15/92) • **85**
Cabernet Sauvignon Colli Euganei 1990 • $18 • (09/15/92) • **88**
Chardonnay 1994: Maturing rapidly, this shows a deep gold color, soft toasty and smoky aromas and flavors and sweet melon notes on the finish. It's appealing now, but catch it before it falls. 800 cases made. • $17 • (06/15/96) • **82**
Chardonnay 1992: Lean and spicy, a modest wine with floral apple flavors and a touch of toast on the finish. Drinkable now. 750 cases made. • $14 • (01/31/95) • **81**
Colli Euganei Rosso 1994: A nicely polished and fresh red that starts with enticing cinnamon and nutmeg aromas and leads to generous cherry and plum flavors that linger on the finish. Not too tannic, so drink now while it's fruity. 3,300 cases made. • $14 • (05/31/96) • **85**
Colli Euganei Rosso 1993: Wonderfully fruity and fresh in flavor, combining cherry and raspberry notes in a pure, well-balanced, easy-drinking style. Not too tannic, and nice fruit on the finish. 3,300 cases made. • $14 • (05/31/96) • **87**
Gemola 1993: Oak and fruit flavors are well integrated in this cherry- and berry-flavored red that is smooth in texture and moderate in tannins. Delicious to drink now. 1,300 cases made. • $18 • (05/31/96) • **86**
Gemola 1991: A wild, gamy edge to the fruit flavor gives this full-bodied, generous and chewy-textured red a distinctive character. It has good depth, concentration and length on the finish. Drinkable now through 1998. 1,300 cases made. • $18 • (05/31/96) • **89**
Gemola 1990 • $18 • (09/15/92) • **85**
Gemola 1988 • $22 • (09/30/91) • **81**
Merlot 1988 • $18 • (04/15/91) • **80**
Moscato Fior d'Arancio Apianae 1991: Smells like freshly cut pine, with a raisiny component that saves it. Lightly sweet for such a dark-colored wine. 350 cases made. • $22 • (01/31/95) • **76**
Pinot Bianco Colli Euganei 1994: The flavors are quite ripe, echoing of pear and banana, but there's a firm, underlying acidity. Though lacking harmony, it has punch. 1,000 cases made. • $12 • (04/30/96) • **81**
Pinot Bianco Colli Euganei 1993: Lean and citrusy, a lime edge to the simple apple fruit, finishing lively. 550 cases made. • $11 • (01/31/95) • **81**
Pinot Bianco Grand Cuvée 1991 • $16 • (09/15/92) • **68**
Sirio 1994: Made in a dry and extremely floral style. Redolent of violets and raisins. Finishes on a lean and almost severe note. 1,300 cases made. • $12 • (05/31/96) • **82**
Sirio 1993: Smooth, almost opulent, a spicy, floral wine with layers of citrus, pear and floral flavors that keep echoing on the finish. A dry Moscato. 850 cases made. • $10 • (01/31/95) • **85**
Zingarello 1993: Tastes like it's refermenting, sour and earthy. Not too pleasant. Tasted twice. 333 cases made. • $NA • (01/31/95) • **67**

VIGNAMAGGIO

1990 • $NA • (10/31/93) • **94**
Chianti Classico 1992: Vibrant berry, cherry and dried fruit aromas and flavors. Light-to-medium bodied with firm tannins and a fresh finish. Drinkable now. 2,800 cases made. • $14 • **84**
Chianti Classico 1990 • $13 • (09/15/92) • **90**
Chianti Classico 1988 • $17 • (09/15/91) • **85**
Chianti Classico 1986 • $12 • (05/15/90) • **85**
Chianti Classico 1985 • $11 • (08/31/88) • **86**
Chianti Classico Barrel 1988 • $NA • (11/30/89) • **88**
Chianti Classico Mona Lisa Riserva 1990: Very good but not equaling the 1988. Focused, ripe fruit yields mint and black cherry aromas and flavors. Medium- to full-bodied, medium tannins and crisp acidity. 3,000 cases made. • $17 • **88**
Chianti Classico Mona Lisa Riserva 1988 • $17 • (09/15/92) • **91**
Chianti Classico Mona Lisa Riserva 1986 • $20 • (10/31/91) • **88**
Chianti Classico Mona Lisa Riserva 1985 • $17 • (09/15/91) • **89**
Chianti Classico Riserva 1985 • $17 • (09/15/91) • **81**
Chianti Classico Riserva 1983 • $14 • (05/15/90) • **85**
Chianti Classico Riserva Barrel 1987 • $NA • (11/30/89) • **86**
Chianti Classico Riserva Barrel 1986 • $NA • (11/30/89) • **85**
Gherardino 1991: We have never had a wine with so much French green bean character. Full-bodied and concentrated but a bit too vegetal. • $NA • **79**
Gherardino 1990: Lovely, refined aromas and flavors of cassis, pepper and tobacco. Medium-bodied, medium tannins and a long, firm finish. Try after 1996. • $NA • **88**
Gherardino 1987 • $NA • (11/30/89) • **92**
Gherardino 1986 • $NA • (11/30/89) • **91**
Gherardino 1985 • $18 • (01/31/92) • **87**

VIGNE DAL LEON

Merlot 1989: A serious, nearly-mature red that has concentrated fruit flavors, but tannins that are still stiff even after all its aging. It may always be tough, so drink soon while the fruit lasts. • $15 • (05/31/96) • **85**
Pinot Bianco Colli Orientali del Friuli 1993: Tart and simple, with a mouthpuckering acidity, offers some modest apple, grapefruit and lime flavors. 500 cases made. • $16 • (01/31/95) • **78**
Sauvignon Colli Orientali del Friuli 1993: Fresh, clean and extremely juicy, a well-made vibrant, lively wine delivers lovely grassy flavors that typify Sauvignon. 500 cases made. • $16 • (01/31/95) • **84**
Tocai Friulano Colli Orientali del Friuli 1993: A racy, well-made wine that delivers good citrus and apple flavors. A bit short on the finish. 249 cases made. • $17 • (01/31/95) • **80**
Tullio Zamò 1991: A very buttery style with little fruit. Pleasant enough, but overdone at this stage. Drink if you like oakey flavors. • $20 • (05/31/96) • **80**
Tullio Zamò Vino da Tavola-Veneto 1991: Extremely woody, but the sweet vanilla-ice-cream, nutmeg and lemon flavors chime in nicely on the finish. Pinot Bianco and Tocai. 833 cases made. • $26 • (01/31/95) • **85**

VIGNOLE

Chianti Classico 1993: Bubbling over with fresh raspberry, watermelon character. A quick quaffer of a red. Medium- to light-bodied, light tannins and a crisp finish. • $NA • **83**
Chianti Classico 1992: Pretty, fruity Chianti displaying plum and floral notes, light body and a crisp finish. Drinkable now. • $NA • **82**
Chianti Classico 1990 • $NA • (10/31/93) • **85**
Chianti Classico 1988 • $NA • (09/15/91) • **90**
Chianti Classico Riserva 1990: Smells rotten. Prickly and sour. Major problem here. Tasted twice, with consistent notes. • $NA • **59**

Key: SS—Spectator Selection. CS—Cellar Selection. BB—Best Buy. $NA—Price not available. (BT)—Barrel tasting. Ⓐ—Auction Price.
Dates in parentheses represent the issues in which the ratings were published.

VILLA CERVIA

Montepulciano d'Abruzzo 1992: Peppery, fruity and concentrated with blackberry and currant flavors. Seems slightly sweet, with a good shot of tannin and fruit on the finish. Drinkable now. 10,000 cases made. • $4 • (03/31/95) BB • **84**

VILLA FIORE

Montepulciano d'Abruzzo 1993: An intensely fruity red with vibrant cherry and anise flavors, moderate tannins and a smooth texture. Fine to drink now. • $4 • (02/29/96) • **84**
Pinot Grigio Veneto 1993: Time in bottle has softened and flattened this white. It shows butter and coconut flavors and some richness, but little zing, losing interest after the first glass. • $4 • (04/30/96) • **76**

VILLA PIGNA

Rozzano 1990: Port-like aromas of chocolate and prunes give way to flavors of ripe plum and blackberry fruit and sweet oak. This big wine has attractive elements. 1,000 cases made. • $13 • (05/31/95) • **87**
Vellutato 1990: This combines thick texture with sharp focus, the flavors range from coffee and licorice to raisins and spice. It has enough tannin for grip, and a lingering finish. Drink now. 5,000 cases made. • $7 • (05/31/95) • **85**

VILLA ROCCA

Amarone Valpolicella Classico 1989 • $10 • (11/15/94) • **78**

VILLADORIA

Barbera d'Alba Superiore 1992: Smooth, fruity and shows smoky, light vanilla flavors, with soft tannins and moderate concentration. Not exciting, but easy to drink. • $NA • (10/31/95) • **82**
Barolo 1991: Lush blackberry and chocolate flavors run deep in this ripe, jammy wine. Bright, attractive and drinking well now, though it's not for the long run. • $NA • (10/31/95) • **86**
Barolo Riserva 1988: Maturing but still fragrant, with berry, spice and vanilla aromas that carry through to the velvety palate. Delicate for a Barolo, it has nice length on the finish. A lighter, well-integrated style. Drink now. • $NA • (10/31/95) • **85**
Barolo Riserva Spéciale 1978 • $14 • (08/31/86) • **73**
Piedmont 1987 • $6 • (03/15/89) • **65**

VILLALTA

Amarone Valpolicella Classico Single Vineyard 1988: An Amarone of decent quality that's marked by mushroomy aromas and earthy flavors. It tastes powerful, ripe and full-bodied. 500 cases made. • $18 • **80**
Amarone della Valpolicella Classico Single Vineyard I Communali 1991: A seductively fruity wine with plenty of prune, cherry and spice flavors. There is also a gamy flavor on the finish. Young and well balanced. Try in 2000. • $21 • (06/15/96) • **86**

VINATTIERRI

Rosso 1985 • $NA • (09/15/87) • **91**
Rosso 1983 • $14 • (09/15/87) • **84**
Rosso II 1986 • $18 • (08/31/91) • **84**
Rosso 1986 • $18 • (08/31/91) • **83**

VISTARENNI

Chianti Classico 1992: Light and quite complex with earthy, mushroomy aromas and flavors. Light in body and tannins, a fruity finish. Drinkable now. • $NA • **80**
Chianti Classico 1991 • $11 • (10/31/93) • **75**
Chianti Classico 1990 • $NA • (09/15/92) • **83**
Chianti Classico 1988 • $11 • (09/15/91) • **86**
Chianti Classico 1987 • $10 • (10/15/89) • **89**
Chianti Classico 1986 • $18 • (07/31/89) • **78**

Chianti Classico Riserva 1990: Huge and impressively concentrated with masses of fruit and tannins, yet seems a bit too jammy and almost raisiny on the nose and palate. Drinkable now. • $NA • **87**
Chianti Classico Riserva 1985 • $NA • (09/15/91) • **81**
Chianti Classico Vigneto Assòlo 1990 • $18 • (09/15/92) • **88**
Chianti Classico Vigneto Assòlo 1988 • $16 • (09/15/91) • **78**
Codirosso 1990: Multidimensional red showing rosemary, plum and berry aromas and flavors. Big and tough right now, firmly tannic. Closed and needs time, try after 1997. • $NA • **87**
Codirosso 1986 • $22 • (11/30/89) • **90**

VITICCIO

Chianti Classico 1993: A delicate style of red that has a dried cherry, berry and earthy character. Medium-to-light body, with fine tannins and a light finish. 11,800 cases made. • $10 • **80**
Chianti Classico 1991 • $10 • (10/31/93) • **83**
Chianti Classico 1990 • $11 • (09/15/92) SS • **90**
Chianti Classico 1988 • $10 • (04/30/92) • **81**
Chianti Classico 1987 • $9 • (04/30/90) • **78**
Chianti Classico 1986 • $8 • (03/31/89) BB • **88**
Chianti Classico 1984 • $5 • (11/15/87) • **74**
Chianti Classico Riserva 1991: Ripe and very crisp. Plenty of plum, spice and cassis character and a firm tannic backbone. Plenty of depth and character here. Try with a steak. Drinkable now or good for cellaring. 11,800 cases made. • $10 • **85**
Chianti Classico Riserva 1990: Intensely fruity, displaying violet and cherry aromas and flavors. Medium-bodied and very well polished with a gentle finish. A joy to drink now. • $NA • **87**
Chianti Classico Riserva 1988 • $15 • (09/15/92) • **88**
Chianti Classico Riserva 1985 • $11 • (11/30/89) • **85**
Chianti Classico Riserva 1983 • $12 • (11/30/89) • **80**
Chianti Classico Viticcio Riserva 1983 • $8 • (11/15/87) • **77**
Chianti Classico Viticcio Riserva 1982 • $8 • (11/15/87) • **84**
Chianti Classico Viticcio Riserva 1978 • $13 • (11/30/87) • **78**
Chianti Classico Viticcio Riserva 1975 • $14 • (11/15/87) • **71**
Monile 1991: Racy and gorgeous, offering vanilla, cherry, berry and raspberry aromas and flavors, medium body, fine tannins and a sweet fruit finish. Drinkable now. 1,065 cases made. • $33 • **90**
Prunaio 1990: A delightful wine with black cherry, berry and citrus aromas and flavors, medium body, silky tannins, fine acidity and a long, refreshing finish. Made from Sangiovese. • $34 • (10/31/93) • **90**
Prunaio 1988 • $28 • (03/31/92) • **88**
Prunaio 1986 • $19 • (03/31/90) SS • **92**
Prunaio 1985 • $18 • (04/30/89) • **88**

VITIGLIANO

Chianti Classico 1991 • $9 • (10/31/93) • **86**

VOERZIO, GIANNI

Barolo La Serra 1991: Rather big and full-bodied, a soft, lush style of Barolo, offering good character, some pretty cherry, mineral and currant flavors and sweet-tasting finish. Has a lot of personality. • $NA • **86**
Dolcetto d'Alba Ciabo della Luna 1994: Fresh and youthful, featuring a sweet-tasting core of plum, cherry and raspberry flavors. Smooth and delicious, with a fine-textured finish. Relatively light, try on release. • $NA • **84**

VOERZIO, ROBERTO

Barolo 1985 • $18 • (01/31/90) • **87**
Barolo 1983 • $15 • (09/15/88) • **88**
Barolo 1982 • $12 • (09/15/88) • **90**
Barolo La Serra 1991: Lovely mint, berry and cherry aromas and flavors, medium-to-full body, firm tannins and slightly dry finish. Better in 1998. • $NA • **85**
Barolo La Serra di La Morra 1982 • $12 • (07/31/87) • **91**
Dolcetto d'Alba Pria S. Francesco Croera 1994: This clean, dark red Dolcetto offers vibrant, luscious red berry flavor and some mineral, earth and wild berry character. Medium body, well-integrated tannins. Drink on release. • $NA • **86**
Nebbiolo delle Langhe Croera Fossati 1990 • $13 • (10/31/92) • **80**
Piedmont 1990 • $12 • (01/31/92) • **82**
Pria S. Francesco Croera 1991 • $12 • (10/31/92) • **81**
Priavino 1990 • $14 • (12/15/92) • **86**
Priavino 1988 • $11 • (12/31/90) • **87**
Vignaserra 1988 • $24 • (03/31/92) • **85**
Vignaserra 1987 • $18 • (08/31/91) • **85**

VOLPAIA, CASTELLO DI

Balifico 1991: Lovely cherry, tobacco and meat aromas. Full-bodied and tannic with a slightly dry finish. Will it come around with botttle age? We're not sure. Tasted twice, with consistent notes. Made from Sangioveto and Cabernet. • $26 • **83**
Balifico 1990: Voluminous wine that expands in your mouth with tar, coffee, berry and vanilla flavors. Full-bodied with a very velvety texture. Made from Sangiovese, Cabernet Sauvignon and Cabernet Franc. 1,200 cases made. • $27 • (10/31/93) • **90-94** (BT)
Balifico 1987 • $25 • (12/15/92) • **80**
Balifico 1986 • $19 • (04/30/89) • **83**
Balifico 1985 • $21 • (11/30/89) • **91**
Chianti Borgianni 1992: Full-bodied, with cherry and plum flavors. Simple and cleanly made, but nothing to get excited about. • $8 • (07/31/95) • **81**
Chianti Classico 1993: Round and generous. Well-made medium-bodied wine with lovely plum, cherry and mineral flavors. It's delicious to drink now. • $11 • **84**
Chianti Classico 1992: Modest berry, cherry character and refreshing finish. Tasted three times, with consistent notes. 10,000 cases made. • $10 • **76**
Chianti Classico 1991 • $11 • (10/31/93) • **80**
Chianti Classico 1990 • $16 • (09/15/92) • **88**
Chianti Classico 1989 • $12 • (09/15/92) • **79**
Chianti Classico 1988 • $14 • (09/15/91) • **85**
Chianti Classico 1987 • $16 • (11/30/89) • **85**
Chianti Classico 1986 • $10 • (03/31/90) • **75**
Chianti Classico 1985 • $10 • (06/30/89) SS • **90**
Chianti Classico 1983 • $8 • (09/15/87) • **88**
Chianti Classico Riserva 1991: Plenty of focused berry, cherry and a hint of mint on the nose and palate. Medium-bodied with silky tannins and a fresh finish. Drinkable now. • $14 • **84**
Chianti Classico Riserva 1990: A solid, very good riserva offering berry, licorace and tar character, medium body and a fresh finish. Drinkable now. 7,500 cases made. • $14 • (02/28/95) • **86**
Chianti Classico Riserva 1988 • $22 • (09/15/92) • **81**
Chianti Classico Riserva 1987 • $14 • (09/15/92) • **84**
Chianti Classico Riserva 1985 • $13 • (09/15/91) • **84**
Chianti Classico Riserva 1983 • $12 • (05/31/89) • **87**
Chianti Classico Riserva 1982 • $11 • (09/15/87) • **84**
Chianti Classico Riserva 1981 • $NA • (09/15/87) • **86**
Chianti Classico Riserva 1977 • $NA • (09/15/87) • **81**
Chianti Classico Riserva 1970 • $NA • (09/15/87) • **85**
Coltassala 1991: Lovely aromas of flowers, cherry and tobacco but the palate is a little too astringent. Medium-to-full body and a dry finish. Try after 1996. Tasted twice, with consistent notes. • $26 • **83**
Coltassala 1990: A sturdy, tannic young wine with complex aromas that are intriguing and distinctive, but a tough texture makes it difficult to enjoy now. Packed with cherry, olive, coffee and spice flavors that linger nicely on the finish. Try in 1998. 1,900 cases made. • $26 • (11/30/94) SS • **92**
Coltassala 1988 • $25 • (11/15/93) • **89**
Coltassala 1987 • $28 • (11/15/93) • **86**
Coltassala 1986 • $NA • (11/30/89) • **86**
Coltassala 1985 • $30 • (11/15/93) • **90**
Coltassala 1983 • $22 • (09/15/88) • **86**
Coltassala 1982 • $35 • (11/15/93) • **90**
Coltassala 1981 • $NA • (09/15/87) • **90**
Torniello 1990: Round and rich, with a spicy, toasty streak running through the pear, vanilla and honeyed smoothness, finishing long and

elegant. A graceful wine that shows restraint. Drinkable now. Tasted twice. • $18 • (12/15/92) • **85**

ZAMO & PALAZZOLO

Chardonnay Colli Orientali del Friuli 1993: Light and lively, with a distinctive ginger-spicy note to the flavors that would make this more appealing as an apéritif than with dinner. 500 cases made. • $15 • (01/31/95) • **81**

Pinot Grigio Colli Orientali del Friuli 1993: Perfumed, with some floral, apricot notes that are decent, but with a hard and tart edge. 833 cases made. • $15 • (01/31/95) • **76**

Pinot Grigio Colli Orientali del Friuli Villa Belvedere 1994: Sour barnyard flavors mar this firm white. Light almond and pear flavors underneath, but overall too earthy. • $17 • (06/30/96) • **72**

Tocai Friulano Colli Orientali del Friuli 1994: This wine has some structure and character. On the herbal side, with a slice of onion to boot, and some good peach flavors as well. • $17 • (06/15/96) • **82**

Tocai Friulano Colli Orientali del Friuli 1993: Fresh, crisp and lively, with vibrant lime, apple, and pear fruit, lean but appealing. 833 cases made. • $15 • (01/31/95) • **81**

Villa Belvedere Merlot Colli Orientali del Friuli 1993: Firm and fruity, with tart black cherry and strawberry flavors. Quite tannic, though balanced. A nice expression of pure fruit flavor. • $16 • (02/29/96) • **84**

ZEBRA, LA

Gavi 1994: Awkward-tasting: smells buttery and earthy and tastes like banana and vanilla. Not bad, but just not harmonious. 40,000 cases made. • $15 • (07/31/95) • **77**

ZEMMER, PETER

Chardonnay Alto Adige 1993: Lean and chalky, a simple, tart wine with only modest flavors. • $10 • (01/31/95) • **76**

Gewürztraminer Alto Adige 1995: Rose petals and spice flow from this rich, round wine, with enough lemony acidity to keep it food-friendly. Distinctive and intriguing. 2,000 cases made. • $10 • (06/15/96) • **84**

Gewürztraminer Alto Adige 1993: Smooth texture and peppery, with lots of vanilla and nutmeg flavors, but you wish for a bit more fruit. • $12 • (01/31/95) • **79**

Pinot Grigio Alto Adige 1995: This Italian white will wake up your taste buds. A crisp texture gives way to round flavors of pear and almond, but the citrus streak carries all the way through this balanced, refreshing wine. All that for so few dollars. 12,000 cases made. • $10 • (06/15/96) BB • **87**

Pinot Grigio Alto Adige 1993: Extremely tart and quite light, with some pear and blanched almond flavors, shows some decent round texture on the finish. • $10 • (01/31/95) • **79**

Pinot Grigio Alto Adige 1991 • $10 • (06/30/93) • **83**

Sauvignon Alto Adige 1993: Crisp and herbal, a nicely focused wine with a lean beam of licorice and pear flavor. • $NA • (01/31/95) • **81**

ZENATO

Amarone della Valpolicella Classico Signature Label 1983: Very pruny, with leathery and gamy flavors. Rich and well-rounded. Closed now and finishes fairly tannic and spicy. Try in 1998. • $35 • (06/15/96) • **88**

Bardolino Classico Superiore 1990 • $8 • (09/15/92) • **81**

Bardolino Classico Superiore 1989 • $7 • (07/15/91) • **78**

Bianco di Custoza 1991 • $11 • (09/15/92) • **81**

Bianco di Custoza Sole de Garda 1994: A wine with some punch to it, has good apple, unripe pear and some honey flavors. The finish is crisp, with a touch of almond. • $10 • (06/15/96) • **84**

Lugana Di San Benedetto 1994: Well-structured with good acidity and plenty of body. Tastes of fig and honey with a touch of spice. Pleasant and satisfying. • $10 • (05/31/96) • **84**

Lugana Di San Benedetto 1991 • $11 • (09/15/92) • **83**

Recioto della Valpolicella Classico Amarone 1988: Deep flavors, vibrant acidity, full-bodied and smooth. Fruit is accented by chocolate and vanilla on the lingering finish. • $25 • (09/30/95) • **86**

Recioto della Valpolicella Classico Amarone 1986 • $19 • (09/15/92) • **86**

Recioto della Valpolicella Classico Amarone 1981 • $11 • (03/15/89) • **81**

Soave Classico Superiore 1991 • $9 • (09/15/92) • **81**

Valpolicella Classico Superiore 1990 • $9 • (09/15/92) • **84**

Valpolicella Classico Superiore 1988 • $8 • (04/30/92) BB • **83**

Valpolicella Classico Superiore Ripassa 1992: Almost like Port in its deep, pruny, peppery tones. Very generous, well balanced, moderately tannic. Abundantly flavorful, nicely smooth and polished. • $15 • (04/30/96) • **87**

ZINGALE, VILLA

Chianti Riserva 1988 • $8 • (04/30/92) • **77**

ZONIN

Amarone Della Valpolicella Il Maso Valpolicella 1991: Suave and smooth, showing spicy, oaky accents to the seemingly sweet raspberry and cherry flavors. Coffee and chocolate notes add complexity. Nicely balanced for drinking now. 7,000 cases made. • $17 • (09/30/95) • **86**

Asti Spumante NV • $9 • (06/15/94) • **83**

Bardolino Classico 1991 • $7 • (09/15/92) • **82**

Berengario Barrel Aged 1989 • $24 • (03/31/93) • **85**

Berengario Barrel Aged 1988 • $30 • (01/31/92) • **84**

Bianco 1991 • $6 • (09/15/92) BB • **82**

Brut Blanc de Blancs NV • $12 • (12/31/91) • **88**

Brut Prosecco NV: A basic bubbly with vague herb and citrus flavors, a soft texture and dull finish. 4,000 cases made. • $11 • (06/15/96) • **78**

Chardonnay del Friuli Aquileia 1992 • $6 • (11/30/93) • **73**

Il Giangio Gambellara White 1991 • $8 • (09/15/92) • **82**

Il Maso Valpolicella Classico 1990 • $8 • (09/15/92) • **82**

Merlot Cabernet 1991 • $6 • (04/30/94) • **75**

Merlot Cabernet del Friuli 1992: A straightforward, nicely fruity red that's fresh and ready to drink. 48,000 cases made. • $6 • (02/28/95) • **82**

Merlot Cabernet del Friuli Aquileia 1990 • $7 • (09/15/92) • **74**

Merlot Cabernet del Friuli Le Vendemmie 1989 • $6 • (01/31/92) • **78**

Montepulciano d'Abruzzo 1993: A simple but adequate red wine with cherry and herb flavors and a lean texture. 100,000 cases made. • $6 • (02/29/96) • **79**

Montepulciano d'Abruzzo 1992: Cranberry and herbal flavors dominate this thin wine. Acceptable, but simple, with a slightly astringent finish. 95,000 cases made. • $6 • (03/31/95) • **77**

Montepulciano d'Abruzzo 1991 • $7 • (07/31/93) • **80**

Montepulciano d'Abruzzo 1990 • $7 • (09/15/92) BB • **83**

Montepulciano d'Abruzzo 1988 • $6 • (06/30/91) BB • **80**

Montepulciano d'Abruzzo 1987 • $4 • (03/31/90) • **78**

Montepulciano d'Abruzzo 1983 • $4 • (05/16/86) BB • **81**

Moscato d'Asti Gran Spumante NV • $7 • (05/15/93) • **74**

Pinot Grigio del Friuli Aquileia 1992 • $7 • (11/30/93) • **77**

Recioto della Valpolicella Amarone Il Maso 1988 • $16 • (09/15/92) • **82**

Recioto di Gambellara 1990 • $20 • (09/15/92) • **75**

Soave Classico 1991 • $7 • (09/15/92) • **80**

Valpolicella Amarone Il Maso 1990: Great buy for Amarone. Beautifully fruity and focused, a pure note of cherry-berry flavor harmonizing with subtle spicy, cedary accents. Smooth texture and rare sense of elegance. 2,000 cases made. • $16 • (09/30/95) • **89**

Key: SS—Spectator Selection. CS—Cellar Selection. BB—Best Buy. $NA—Price not available. (BT)—Barrel tasting. Ⓐ—Auction Price.
Dates in parentheses represent the issues in which the ratings were published.

ITALY

Portugal

Although Portugal produces a wide range of good red, white and rosé table wines, its reputation as a great wine-producing country is based on its production of Port, a sweet wine fortified with brandy. In recent years, however, the quality and value offered by Portugal's dry, unfortified wines has become more appreciated. Both Port and Portugal's other wines now merit the full attention of wine drinkers.

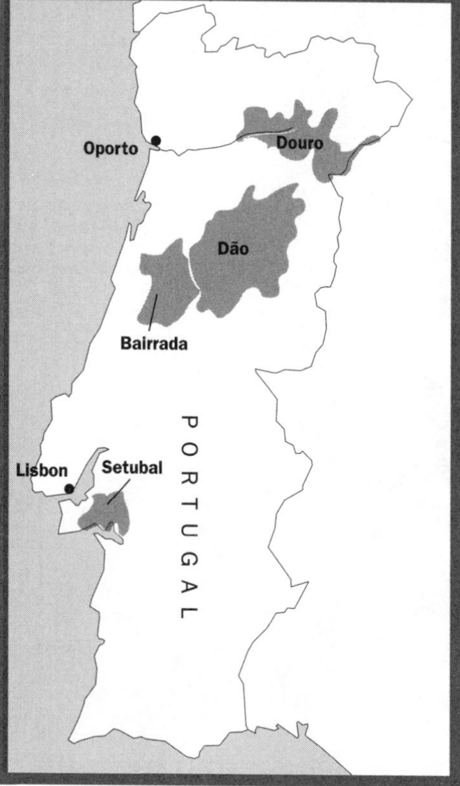

PORT

Although many inferior imitations are produced around the world, true Port comes only from a designated part of the Douro region of Portugal, centering on the city of Oporto. True Port is made in several styles, each with differing characteristics.

Most Ports are wood Ports, which simply means that all of the significant aging takes place in wood barrels before bottling. As a result, wood Ports are ready to drink upon release and do not require aging in the consumer's cellar. The two basic types of wood Ports are ruby Port and tawny Port. Both are usually blends of different vintages (and are thus designated non-vintage or NV). As the names suggest, a chief difference is the color. Ruby Port is red in color, offering vigorous fruit that tastes fresh and shows little evidence of oxidation. It tends to be a younger wine than tawny, and is intended to be enjoyed for its freshness, vivacity, and smoothness.

Tawny Port has a light orange/brown color and a more mature character than does ruby Port. The aromas and flavors typically display notes of caramel, orange peel and hazelnuts, as opposed to the red-fruit characteristics of ruby Port. Tawnies may be aged for many years, sometimes decades, in wood barrels before being bottled and released. Indeed, some shippers mark their tawnies with designations such as 10, 20 or 30 years, or older. Tawny Port is rarely powerful, but the flavors can have great length and depth. Indeed, a fine aged tawny is often a wine of great subtlety and complexity.

The most revered and collectible Port is vintage Port. Vintage Port is not considered a wood Port, although it does spend its first two years in wood casks. However, most of the aging of vintage Port takes place in the bottle, often over a period of decades in the cellars of collectors of this exquisite wine. Vintage Port is not made every year—only in the best years, when the grapes achieve a special ripeness and intensity. Port shippers will then "declare" a vintage, meaning that some of their production will be released with a vintage date, made in the unique style of vintage Port. The decision to declare a vintage is up to the individual Port house, but there tends to be a high degree of uniformity among the major houses.

A recent development has been the increasing availability of so called "single quinta" Ports. These are made exactly like vintage Ports, but are produced only in years that have not been "declared." Although they sell for significantly less than vintage Port, the quality is often very close, because the grapes that are used are carefully selected from the best vineyards owned or controlled by the house.

DRY PORTUGUESE WINES

Portugal's best known dry wine is Vinho Verde, which literally means "green wine." Vinho Verde can in fact be

Drawing barrel samples at the Taylor's Port lodge (warehouse) near Oporto. The wine is kept in 522-liter barrels for anywhere from two to 50 years.

red or white, as the "greenness" refers to the youth of the wine rather than its color, but most of the exports are white. White Vinho Verde, made primarily from the Loureiro grape and less often the Alvarinho, is a perfect apéritif wine, low in alcohol and nicely crisp. The red can be good, but is often rough around the edges.

Portugal's best known dry wine region is the Dão. Most Dão is red, but about a third is white. Dão reds age well. While vintage dates are not totally reliable, it is not unusual to find Dão reds drinking well after more than a decade in the bottle. Quality is improving markedly here as the influence of the old cooperatives fade. Wineries are now allowed to buy grapes directly from growers and vinify the wines themselves, which has dramatically raised the overall level of the wines. The term "garrafeira" means reserve, and often signifies the best quality wines of a producer.

The quality potential of the dry red wines of the Douro has long been recognized, even though they are overshadowed by the fame of Port. Red Douro is made from the same grapes as Port; unlike Port, the grapes are allowed to finish their fermentation in the normal way, without the addition of brandy (which arrests the fermentation of wines before all their sugar has turned to alcohol.) Douro reds take wood aging well. The most esteemed is Barca Velha—made by the Ferreira Port house—which is released only in the best vintages. White wines from the Douro can be pleasant, but they rarely satisfy as fully as the reds.

In recent years, other regions of Portugal have increased in prominence. The Barraida district, located between the Douro River and the Dão, makes fairly highly extracted, Rhône-like reds and lots of rather ordinary white intended for the domestic bulk market. While the principal red grape is the indigenous Baga, some experiments with Cabernet Sauvignon and Merlot have yielded impressive results.

Cabernet Sauvignon is also being planted alongside traditional varieties in the Sebutal district, until now best known for its sweet, Muscat-based wine. The Setubal firm of J.M. da Fonseca (unrelated to the Fonseca of Oporto) also makes an excellent dry red wine from the native Periquita grape.

Until recently the vast Alentejo region in Southern Portugal was known mostly for its light rosés. However, that has changed with the arrival of the Domaines Rothschild (Lafite), which is restoring an old estate called Quinta do Carmo. Its potent, wood-aged reds have received an excellent response.

ALIANÇA, CAVES

Alentejo Alabastro 1994: Light and fruity, dominated by strawberry and cherry flavors and featuring a menthol aroma that makes it somewhat eccentric. 14,000 cases made. • $8 • (03/31/96) • **78**

Alentejo Alabastro 1993: A good value. Bright, fresh cherry and berry flavors are accented by vanilla in this medium-bodied, lightly tannic red. Drink now for its freshness and charm. 10,000 cases made. • $7 • (04/30/95) • **84**

Bairrada 1991: An unusual sparkling wine with earthy, resinous aromas and dry, nutty flavors. Some will like it, but it's definitely out of the mainstream. • $8 • (02/28/95) • **78**

Bairrada Garrafeira 1984 • $10 • (04/15/94) • **78**

Bairrada Reserva 1992: Rustic and aggressive. Somewhat cedary plum and dried cherry flavors are pleasant but seem to be fading fast. Tasted twice, with consistent notes. 40,000 cases made. • $6 • (04/30/96) • **77**

Bairrada Reserva 1991: Spicy-smelling, simply flavored, smooth-drinking, full-bodied enough for most foods, and not too tannic to enjoy right now. • $6 • (04/30/95) • **80**

Bairrada Reserva 1990 • $6 • (03/31/94) BB • **86**

Bairrada Reserva 1989 • $5 • (06/15/93) • **79**

Bairrada Reserva 1987 • $5 • (07/15/91) • **77**

Beiras Aliança Garrafeira 1985 • $10 • (04/15/94) • **74**

Beiras Garrafeira 1985 • $8 • (06/15/93) • **76**

Beiras Garrafeira 1982 • $9 • (07/15/91) • **84**

Cabernet Sauvignon Beiras Galeria 1994: A punchy Cabernet offering plum and herb flavors and firm, tannic backbone. It's concentrated, if somewhat rustic. Drinkable now. 4,000 cases made. • $9 • (03/31/96) • **83**

Cabernet Sauvignon Beiras Galeria 1993: Sturdy and straightforward cherry and herb flavors and moderate tannins. Fine for drinking now, but nothing special. 8,000 cases made. • $10 • (04/30/95) • **79**

Cave do Duque NV • $4 • (04/15/94) • **78**

Dão Aliança Particular 1992: Full-bodied, tannic red showing decent plum flavors, though a bit earthy and gamy on the finish. 6,500 cases made. • $10 • (03/31/96) • **78**

Dão Garrafiera 1989: Attractive, clean, ripe flavors. Notes of plum, licorice and tar mingle in this soft, full-bodied red. Drinkable now with hearty food. 11,667 cases made. • $6 • (04/30/95) BB • **85**

Dão Reserva 1992: Spicy plum and black cherry flavors. Full in body, jammy, lots of gusto for an incredible price. Chocolate and coffee notes on the finish. 18,750 cases made. • $5 • (04/30/95) BB • **85**

Dão Reserva 1989 • $4 • (06/15/93) • **78**

Dão Vinho Tinto 1984 • $8 • (07/15/91) • **74**

Douro Foral 1992: Soft, velvety, sweet cherry and plum flavors. It has an earthy streak running through the middle, but it's still enjoyable. Drinkable now. 12,000 cases made. • $8 • (03/31/96) • **82**

Douro Foral 1991: Firm but polished and harmonious, with ripe fruit, licorice and black pepper flavors and barnyard aromas. Still young, but drinkable now. 7,083 cases made. • $5 • (04/30/95) BB • **86**

Douro Foral Garrafeira 1990: Aromas of cedar and cranberry, flavors of sweet currant, herb and eucalyptus. A firm Portuguese red table wine that's very tannic. Should have opened up by now. 5,833 cases made. • $6 • (04/30/95) BB • **87**

Douro Foral Garrafeira 1989: Rustic and tough, with overwhelming tannins and simple flavors of chocolate and plum. Some good elements, but unbalanced, bottom-heavy. 5,833 cases made. • $6 • (01/31/95) • **77**

Douro Foral Reserva 1992: Some nice, mature notes of dried cherry and currant, but still quite tannic and volatile. • $5 • (03/31/96) • **78**

Galeria 1991: Fresh and lively tasting, a bright young wine that preserves all the fruit flavor of the grapes. Moderate tannins and a smooth texture. Drinkable now. 9,000 cases made. • $10 • **83**

Palmela Aliança Particular 1991: Maturing raisin, brown sugar and light earth flavors, though smooth, it's a bit dry on the finish. Drinkable now. 5,000 cases made. • $10 • (03/31/96) • **77**

AVELEDA

Douro Charamba 1992: Deep color and lots of ripe fruit in this concentrated, very enjoyable and very inexpensive Portuguese red. Tannins and acidity carry the fruit into the lingering finish. Drinkable now. 8,000 cases made. • $5 • (04/30/95) BB • **86**

AVERY

Port Club NV • $9 • (03/31/88) • **77**

BACALHOA, QUINTA DA

Cabernet Sauvignon Terras do Sado 1992: Lively and firm, this bright red is chock-full of ripe blackberry, chocolate and light herbal flavors. Attractive now and it should continue to improve just a bit longer. • $14 • (03/31/96) • **85**

Cabernet Sauvignon Terras do Sado 1991: Soft in texture, ripe and chocolaty in flavor, with light tannins but plenty of body. Lots of fruit and generous accents of spice make the flavors intriguing. • $15 • **83**

BAIRRADA

Azeitao 1987 • $6 • (01/31/93) • **71**

BARROS

Tawny Port 20-year-old NV • $35 • (02/28/90) • **96**

Vintage Port 1991: Too light to be a good vintage Port. Medium purple to ruby in color, with delicate plum and chocolate aromas. Medium-bodied and medium-sweet, with delicate tannins and a light finish. Tasted twice with consistent notes. Try in or after 1997. • $NA • (07/31/94) **79**

Vintage Port 1987: Marks a return to the major leagues for Barros. Good purple color, with a very fresh, grapey, aromatic nose, medium- to full-bodied, with medium tannins and a balance of elegant fruit. No show-stopper, but has some class. • $28 • (01/01/90) • **81**

Vintage Port 1985: This is an early-drinking 1985 but it is nicely crafted all the same. Medium purple with a ruby hue, a very fresh and grapey nose, medium-bodied, with clean, fresh fruit flavors, medium tannins and a long finish. • $29 • (01/01/90) • **80**

Vintage Port 1983 • $30 • (01/01/90) • **76**

Vintage Port 1978 • $30 • (01/01/90) • **75**

Vintage Port 1974 • $40 • (01/01/90) • **74**

Vintage Port 1970 • $60 • (01/01/90) • **82**

BORBA, ADEGA COOPERATIVA DE

Alentejo 1992: Fruity, concentrated and fresh, almost sweet in its ripeness of flavor. Light in tannins, clean and ready to drink. 215,000 cases made. • $5 • (04/30/95) • **83**

Alentejo Borba 1994: Ripe, fruity style offering decent plum and cherry flavors. Not much complexity here, however, and the finish turns a bit coarse. 200,000 cases made. • $5 • (04/30/96) • **78**

Alentejo Borba 1991 • $5 • (04/15/94) BB • **82**

Alentejo Convento da Vila 1994: A fruit basket from Alentejo, but slightly disjointed. Red plum and currant flavors are dominant, without much behind them. 150,000 cases made. • $4 • (04/30/96) • **79**

Alentejo Convento da Vila 1992 • $4 • (04/15/94) • **78**

Alentejo Reserva 1989 • $9 • (04/15/94) • **77**

Alentejo Reserva 1988 • $7 • (04/15/94) • **80**

Alentejo Vila Morena 1994: Jammy and fruity, offering good blackberry and blueberry flavors, a touch of richness, some nice, spicy shadings and lively acidity. 120,000 cases made. • $5 • (04/30/96) • **82**

BORGES

Vintage Port 1985: This is so light and ready to drink that it is more like a ruby or a late-bottled vintage. Medium-to-light red, with simple aromas of cherries and chocolate, light-bodied and clean, with sweet cherry flavors and light tannins on the finish. • $15 • (05/01/90) • **70**

Vintage Port 1983 • $21 • (05/01/90) • **70**

Vintage Port 1982 • $30 • (05/01/90) • **79**

Vintage Port 1980 • $23 • (05/01/90) • **70**

Vintage Port 1979 • $22 • (05/01/90) • **65**

Vintage Port 1970 • $86 • (05/01/90) • **59**

BRIDÃO

Cartaxo 1991: Rustic and dull. From earthy aromas to musty flavors, this lacks fruit and vibrancy. Drink up. • $7 • (03/31/96) • **74**

BURMESTER

Port Quinta do Nova 1992: Not as great as from cask, but very good. Well-made Port showing grape-skin, berry and stem aromas, roasted peppery character, full body and plenty of tannins. Try in 1999. • $NA • **87**

Tawny Port 20-year-old NV • $40 • (02/28/90) • **95**

Vintage Port 1992: Roasted and ripe, sweet fruit flavors, medium body, round tannins and sweet finish. Drink in 1999. • $NA • **85**

Vintage Port 1991: As of 1994, was not showing as well as in a previous tasting. A bit spirited, with grape-skin and brandy aromas. Medium-bodied, with grapey flavors, medium sweetness, tannins and a silky finish. Tasted twice with consistent notes. Try after 1999. 1,500 cases made. • $NA • (07/31/94) • **86**

Vintage Port 1985: This is a great achievement for a 1985, perhaps one of the best wines of the vintage. Inky color, with berry and grape must aromas, full-bodied, with tons of fruit and tannin, very concentrated. Finish is extremely long. Outstanding. • $25 • (01/01/90) • **93**

Vintage Port 1984 • $NA • (01/01/90) • **84**

Vintage Port 1980 • $33 • (01/01/90) • **88**

Vintage Port 1977 • $31 • (01/01/90) • **82**

Vintage Port 1970 • $41 • (01/01/90) • **86**

Vintage Port 1963 • $131 • (01/01/90) • **83**

CÁLEM

Tawny Port 20 Años NV • $35 • (04/15/90) • **83**

Vintage Character Port Vintage Character NV • $16 • (03/15/94) • **79**

Vintage Port 1991: Early-drinking, harmonious and young, evolving more quickly than anticipated. Attractive floral and berry aromas and flavors. This shows medium-sweet fruit and fine tannins. Tasted three times with consistent notes.Try after 1997. 6,000 cases made. • $NA • (07/31/94) • **80**

Vintage Port 1985: The first vintage that brought Cálem attention. Deep purple, with an intense floral and licorice nose, full-bodied, good grip, a medium concentration of fruit flavors and a long finish. Very good potential. • $42 • (06/01/90) • **88**

Vintage Port 1983 • $40 • (06/01/90) • **84**

Vintage Port 1980 • $38 • (06/01/90) • **78**

Vintage Port 1977 • $56 • (11/01/89) • **69**

Vintage Port 1975 • $37 • (02/01/90) • **86**

Vintage Port 1970 • $50 Ⓐ • (11/01/89) • **80**

Vintage Port 1966 • $65 • (11/01/89) • **82**

Vintage Port 1963 • $85 • (12/01/89) • **82**

Vintage Port Quinta do Foz 1992: Better than the '91 Cálem blend. Aromatic plum, cherry character, medium in body and sweetness, sporting fine tannins and a medium finish. Try in 1999. • $NA • **86**

Vintage Port Quinta do Foz 1987: Made entirely from Cálem's Quinta do Foz, this young Port shows lots of fruit, with a rich and velvety mouth-feel. It will be an earlier drinker than the 1985. Purple, with ripe fruit and orange peel aromas, full-bodied, with lots of fruit flavors. • $28 • (06/01/90) • **84**

Vintage Port Quinta do Foz 1982 • $30 • (06/01/90) • **82**

CAMARATE, QUINTA DE

Azeitao 1986 • $10 • (01/31/93) • **77**

Ribatejo Falcoaria 1989: A tough and rather herbal tasting red that's drinkable but simple. The fruit component seems to be drying up already. 6,000 cases made. • $9 • **77**

Key: SS—Spectator Selection. CS—Cellar Selection. BB—Best Buy. $NA—Price not available. (BT)—Barrel tasting. Ⓐ—Auction Price.
Dates in parentheses represent the issues in which the ratings were published.

Ribatejo Terra de Lobos 1992: Young, tannic and flavorful, it packs a lot of punch in the fruit department. Well-balanced, but on the tight and firm side in texture. Drinkable now. 18,000 cases made. • $4 • **81**

CARDO, QUINTA DO

Douro Castelo Rodrigo 1989 • $7 • (12/31/90) BB • **84**

CARMO, QUINTA DO

Alentejo 1988 • $20 • (04/15/94) • **84**

Alentejo Vinho Tinto 1987 • $20 • (06/15/93) • **80**

CARVALHINHO, QUINTA DO

Bairrada Reserva 1991: Still fairly tannic, showing some modest plum and raisin flavors and spice on the finish, but overall this is a rather blunt red. • $10 • (04/30/96) • **78**

CARVALHO, RIBEIRO & FERREIRA

Bairrada Garrafeira 1980: The nicely developed aroma isn't backed up by much flavor. It turns lean and tough, especially on the finish. 8,000 cases made. • $8 • **77**

Dão C.R.&F. 1989: Bitter cherry and cranberry flavors and a varnishy character makes this a tough wine. • $NA • **76**

Dão Quinta do Serrado 1991: A restrained red, offering an earthy quality and plenty of tannins. The fruit flavors are dominated by cherry and cranberry and an herbal note as well. • $NA • **84**

Dão Quinta do Serrado 1990: Smoky, peppery aromas and hearty flavors of plum and spice are wrapped in a smooth package. A good, earthy style of red wine for drinking now. 4,200 cases made. • $7 • **82**

Douro Reserva 1990: Ripe, plummy fruit flavors are accented by earthy notes in this rather tannic, full-bodied red. A good wine for people who like a rustic style. • $NA • **83**

Ribatejo Serradayres 1993: Starts off lean but builds intensity with good blueberry, raspberry and cherry flavors. Medium-bodied and delicious, adding a nice touch of spice on aftertaste. Ready to drink now. • $6 • (03/31/96) • **83**

Ribatejo Serradayres 1989: A lean, mature red with some spicy bottle bouquet developing and enough fruit left to keep it interesting. Clean, firm in texture and moderately tannic. Drinkable now. 36,000 cases made. • $5 • **81**

Tràs-os-Montes Garrafeira 1990: Plum and herbal flavors are attractive, but a harsh, plastic note detracts and turns this red hard and dry on the finish. • $14 • (03/31/96) • **74**

CASA DE PANCAS

Chardonnay Estremadura Barrel Fermented 1994: Ripe and almost honeyed apple and cinnamon flavors. Somewhat coarse but firm, adding spicy aftertaste and a nice lemony note as well. 2,000 cases made. • $11 • (05/15/96) • **82**

CASA DE SANTAR

Dão 1990: Seems dried out and over the hill. Very tannic with only thin plum and cherry flavors. Not much fun. 40,000 cases made. • $7 • (03/31/96) • **72**

Dão Reserva 1992: Nice shades of vanilla and spice, lots of raspberry and cherry flavors and crisp finish. 4,000 cases made. • $10 • (03/31/96) • **82**

CASAL DE TONDA

Dão 1991: Ripe and gamy, this jammy wine is rich without subtlety or finesse. The licorice and plum flavors are marred by burnt, rubbery notes. Drinkable now. 1,200 cases made. • $9 • **77**

Dão Vinho Tinto 1990 • $8 • (04/15/94) BB • **85**

CAVES ALTOVISO

Dão Fastelo 1991: Attractive aromas of dried cherries and raisins give way to ripe fruit and firm tannins in this rustic red. Drinkable now. • $5 • (01/31/95) • **79**

CAVES DO BARROCAO

Bairrada Garrafeira 1988: You can work your way through tough tannins and earthy aromas to a core of cherry, raisin fruit. Or you can go on to the next wine. Better than a bottle tasted earlier. Drinkable now. • $10 • **75**

Bairrada Reserva 1990: Light and lean in flavor, with fresh fruit accented by vanilla and spice from aging in wood. Elegant and attractive, if simple in character. Drinkable now. • $7 • **82**

Dão Garrafeira 1980: A distinctive, mature wine worth trying. Tart and very lean in texture, but with nice strawberry and spice flavors that linger on the finish. Elegant and tasty, though still tannic. Drinkable now. • $13 • **85**

Dão Reserva 1990: A stiff texture and austere flavors are helped a bit by a floral, spicy aroma, but just a bit. It's simple and basic, with tough tannins. • $7 • **77**

CAVES VELHAS

Almeirim Garrafeira 1990: Simple and mature, featuring some good dried cherry and plum flavors. It has an appealing finish that's full of smoky, earthy notes. • $12 • (04/30/96) • **82**

Bairrada 1990: Hearty, nicely mature now, showing ripe plum and cherry flavors and earthy, spicy accents. Moderately tannic, smooth in texture. • $8 • **82**

Bairrada 1989: Abundant cherry and currant fruit keep this wine lively, despite rustic tannins. A solid wine and a good match for hearty food. Drinkable now. • $8 • **82**

Bairrada Garrafeira 1985: Cedary and spicy flavors make this interesting. Fully mature, ripe and round, it provides a good dose of supple tannins as well. Don't be put off by the gamy aromas. • $12 • (04/30/96) • **83**

Dão 1990: Well made and fruity, muscular tannins. Has the stuffing to age, showing cherry, licorice and black pepper flavors. Was a bit austere on last tasting, but try now. 3,500 cases made. • $8 •(04/30/95) BB • **86**

Dão 1989: A spicy note gives an extra flavor dimension to this attractive, fruity, well-balanced wine. The sophisticated fruit flavor is still rare in Portuguese table wines. Drinkable now. • $8 •**85**

Dão Reserva 1985: Round, soft cherry and cedar flavors are balanced, the tannins appear firm but a bit dry. This makes a good match with roast meats and should hold through 1997. • $10 • (04/30/95) • **85**

Ribatejo Garrafeira 1982: Going over the hill, but still hanging on. The interesting mature aromas aren't backed up by much fruit flavor at this advanced age. • $11 • **79**

Ribatejo Garrafeira 1980: An old, funky smelling wine that's been aged too long. The fruit flavors have faded, leaving only earthy notes. • $12 • **70**

Ribatejo Romeira 1987: A nicely mature red that has developed intriguing spice aromas while retaining good fruit flavors. Still fairly firm and tannic, but drink it now. • $7 • **83**

Ribatejo Romeira Garrafeira 1988: Smooth and supple, offering modest ripe cherry and plum flavors. A bit lacking in the mid-palate. Drink this soon before it dries out. • $12 • (04/30/96) • **80**

CERCA, CAVES DA

Vinho Verde Tâmega 1993: A good seafood wine. Dry and tart, but carrying enough apple and lemon flavors to make it lively and refreshing. 55,000 cases made. • $5 • (07/31/95) • **82**

CHAMPALIMAUD

Vintage Port 1982 • $20 • (02/01/90) • **86**

CHURCHILL

Late Bottled Port Traditional 1990: Clean and well crafted, with a raisiny, grapey character. A good unfiltered and fined wine, but slightly one-dimensional on the finish. Try now. 3,400 cases made. • $19 • (01/31/96) • **85**

Late Bottled Port Traditional 1988: A fairly big Port, with dried fruit flavors and some maple and hazelnut notes. Still has plenty of tannins so it may be best to drink in 1998. Chocolaty flavors linger on the finish. • $17 • (11/15/94) • **87**

Ruby Port VC Reserve NV: Big, rich and chocolaty, with prune and raisin notes. • $11 • (11/15/94) • **86**

Vintage Character Port Finest NV • $19 • (04/15/91) • **83**

Vintage Character Port Finest Reserve NV • $17 • (03/15/94) • **87**

Vintage Port 1991: This is impressive and the best vintage yet from this shipper. Thick and silky, with an earthy, berry and cherry character. Medium-bodied and medium-sweet with lovely flavors and a long finish. Try after 1999. 3,500 cases made. • $35 • (07/31/94) • **91**

Vintage Port 1985: This is an impressive wine on the palate, but I tasted it blind four times in early 1990 and a slightly odd, acetic nose showed three times. It doesn't seem to be getting any worse, however. Deep ruby-purple color, with earthy berry flavors, slightly volatile. • $39 • (02/01/90) • **81**

Vintage Port 1982 • $NA • (06/01/90) • **78**

Vintage Port Agua Alta 1992: Rustic monster of a wine, perhaps slightly overdone? Amazing concentration but slightly coarse, like crushed grapes in a lagar. Super raisin extract, almost dry, very tannic. Try in 2005. • $35 • **89**

Vintage Port Agua Alta 1987: Dense, fruity and backed by a solid grip of tannin and alcohol. The flavors lean toward berry and cherry, and taper off on the finish. Not a very sweet style. Should be best around 2000 to 2005. • $48 • (04/15/91) • **83**

Vintage Port Agua Alta 1983 • $22 • (07/01/90) • **69**

Vintage Port Fojo 1986: There are some attractive floral fruit flavors, but the nose has a slightly odd component. Medium purple, with a floral, perfumed, slight varnish nose, medium-bodied, with floral, earthy flavors, medium tannins and a good finish. • $NA • (02/01/90) • **78**

Vintage Port Fojo 1984 • $NA • (02/01/90) • **79**

CIMA

Ribatejo 1992: The unusual aromas of pepper and smoke take some getting used to, but it has good fruit flavors and a lingering finish. Enjoyable and different, for people who like gutsy red wines. • $6 • **82**

COCKBURN

Late Bottled Port 1987: This is dominated by fig and chocolate flavors that are nicely balanced. Has plenty of curves, lush and delicious. Smooth and ready to drink now. • $21 • (11/15/94) • **86**

Late Bottled Port Anno 1990: Typical for the vintage—slightly raisiny and roasted in character. Medium body and sweetness, with a big, fruity finish. Try this with Stilton cheese. • $17 • (01/31/96) • **85**

Ruby Port Fine NV • $10 • (03/31/88) • **85**

Ruby Port No. 25 NV • $8 • (03/31/88) • **85**

Tawny Port 10-year-old NV: A bit fiery but wonderfully elegant and silky. Medium body and sweetness with honey, walnut and light plum character. Well defined and balanced. 1,500 cases made. • $24 • (01/31/96) • **88**

Tawny Port 20-year-old NV • $35 • (02/28/90) • **86**

Tawny Port Directors' Reserve 20-year-old NV: Loads of sweet and creamy honey, toffee and vanilla aromas and flavors. Medium-bodied and medium in sweetness but slightly hot on the finish. • $43 • (01/31/96) • **86**

Vintage Character Port Special Reserve NV: Young, grapey and robust. Its flavors are dominated by raisin, plum and chocolate. Simple, straightforward and delicious, with a moderate grip. May be best right now. • $16 • (11/15/94) • **84**

Vintage Port 1991: A harmonious wine. Good, deep-purple color and fragrant raspberry and earthy aromas. Full-bodied yet reserved, with fine, full tannins and a long, delicious finish. Tasted twice with consistent notes.Try after 1998. 6,000 cases made. • $36 • (07/31/94) • **88**

PORTUGAL

Vintage Port 1985: Shows an abundance of thick, rich fruit and plenty of backbone. Very inky, dense color, with a rich, floral nose of berries and cherries. Full-bodied, medium sweet, with massive anise and cherry flavors and extremely well integrated tannins and acidity. • $16 Ⓐ • (06/01/90) • **90**
Vintage Port 1983 • $30 Ⓐ • (06/01/90) • **97**
Vintage Port 1975 • $21 Ⓐ • (01/01/90) • **77**
Vintage Port 1970 • $25 Ⓐ • (12/01/89) • **86**
Vintage Port 1967 • $19 Ⓐ • (12/01/89) • **85**
Vintage Port 1966 • $NA • (10/31/88) • **91**
Vintage Port 1963 • $47 Ⓐ • (12/01/89) • **88**
Vintage Port 1960 • $24 Ⓐ • (10/31/88) • **82**
Vintage Port 1958 • $NA • (11/01/89) • **84**
Vintage Port 1955 • $115 • (11/01/89) • **90**
Vintage Port 1950 • $43 Ⓐ • (11/01/89) • **76**
Vintage Port 1947 • $264 Ⓐ • (11/01/89) • **90**
Vintage Port 1935 • $174 Ⓐ • (02/01/90) • **92**
Vintage Port 1931 • $500 • (01/01/90) • **89**
Vintage Port 1927 • $272 Ⓐ • (12/01/89) • **91**
Vintage Port 1912 • $308 Ⓐ • (10/01/87) • **91**
Vintage Port 1908 • $271 Ⓐ • (10/01/87) • **89**
Vintage Port 1904 • $168 Ⓐ • (10/01/87) • **75**
Vintage Port 1896 • $400 • (02/01/90) • **82**
Vintage Port Quinta da Canias 1992: Better than Cockburn's 1991 blend, a single quinta to watch. Ripe, grapey berry and wet earth aromas and flavors, full body, medium sweetness, firm tannins and racy finish. Try in 2000. • $35 • **89**
Vintage Port Quinta do Tua 1987 • $28 • (06/15/93) • **89**

COTTO, QUINTA DO

Douro 1992: A delicious, hearty red wine with grapey, peppery aromas and flavors. It's smooth-textured, full-bodied and not too tannic. Drink now. • $10 • (04/30/95) • **88**
Douro 1991: A complex, earthy style that has lots of ripe fruit and flirts with decadence in its cedary, leathery aromas. It is rich, firmly tannic and concentrated. Drink now through 1997. • $10 • **87**
Douro Grande Escolha 1994: Thick and fruity, boasting blackberry and black plum flavors and aromas. It has big and strapping tannins and a dose of bittersweet chocolate and spice on the finish. Best to try in 1997. • $40 • (04/30/96) • **87**
Douro Grande Escolha 1990: A lush and distinctive Portugese red with ample oak accents and full, ripe flavors. It has richness, concentration, lots of fine-textured tannins and a lingering finish. Worth searching for. • $40 • (04/30/95) • **90**
Douro Grande Escolha 1987 • $18 • (12/31/90) • **81**
Douro Vinho Tinto 1987 • $9 • (04/30/91) • **74**

CRASTO, QUINTA DO

Vintage Port 1987: A balanced yet very simple wine. Shows improvement from earlier vintages. Deep purple, with a black pepper nose, medium-bodied, with medium tannins and very grapey, black pepper flavors. One-dimensional. • $NA • (01/01/90) • **80**
Vintage Port 1985: Short, simple and drinkable. Too light for a 1985. Medium ruby, with a light, grapey, Gamay-like nose, medium-bodied, with light tannins and a light, spicy finish. • $24 • (01/01/90) • **71**
Vintage Port 1978 • $NA • (01/01/90) • **70**
Vintage Port 1958 • $NA • (08/01/90) • **79**

CROFT

Tawny Port 20-year-old NV • $38 • (02/28/90) • **76**
Vintage Port 1991: Even better than I remember from prior tastings. The best Croft since 1966 and easily one of the best of the vintage. This shows terrific cassis and black fruit aromas and flavors. Full-bodied, thick and medium-sweet, massive, with loads of tannins. Try after 2002. 9,000 cases made. • $32 • (07/31/94) • **94**
Vintage Port 1985: This is evolving slightly more quickly than I expected, but there are still plenty of clean cherry notes on the nose and palate. Medium to deep ruby, with a slightly roasted-nut, cherry nose. Medium-bodied, with a well defined backbone and medium tannins. • $14 Ⓐ • (06/01/90) • **81**
Vintage Port 1982 • $13 Ⓐ • (04/01/90) • **69**
Vintage Port 1977 • $25 Ⓐ • (04/01/90) • **85**
Vintage Port 1975 • $18 Ⓐ • (10/31/88) • **80**
Vintage Port 1970 • $24 Ⓐ • (12/01/89) • **89**
Vintage Port 1966 • $29 Ⓐ • (12/01/89) • **90**
Vintage Port 1963 • $52 Ⓐ • (12/01/89) • **91**
Vintage Port 1960 • $70 • (09/01/89) • **90**
Vintage Port 1955 • $101 Ⓐ • (11/01/89) • **84**
Vintage Port 1950 • $170 • (04/01/90) • **77**
Vintage Port 1945 • $262 Ⓐ • (11/01/89) • **99**
Vintage Port 1935 • $146 Ⓐ • (02/01/90) • **93**
Vintage Port 1927 • $204 Ⓐ • (12/01/89) • **87**
Vintage Port Quinta da Roeda 1987: I tasted this Port just after it was blended and it was very impressive. But the last time I tasted it, it had an odd, "off" character on the nose and palate. Medium purple with a closed, slightly smoky nose, full-bodied, with grapey, earthy fruit flavors and medium tannins. • $NA • (02/01/90) • **79**
Vintage Port Quinta da Roeda 1983 • $22 • (02/01/90) • **85**
Vintage Port Quinta da Roeda 1980 • $27 • (02/01/90) • **75**
Vintage Port Quinta da Roeda 1978 • $24 • (02/01/90) • **83**
Vintage Port Quinta da Roeda 1967 • $60 • (01/01/90) • **85**

DA SILVA, C.

Vintage Port Presidential 1987: This is a solid 1987 with ample fruit and tannin to give it longevity. Medium purple, with a ripe raisin and tar nose, full-bodied, with full tannins and ripe fruit flavors. A little one-dimensional. • $NA • (02/01/90) • **80**
Vintage Port Presidential 1985: Seems short on grip and flesh for a 1985, but it's nonetheless a pleasant wine. Medium purple, with a perfumed cranberry nose, medium-bodied, with medium fruit flavors, rather delicate tannins and a light finish. • $30 • (02/01/90) • **78**
Vintage Port Presidential 1978 • $37 • (02/01/90) • **77**
Vintage Port Presidential 1977 • $39 • (02/01/90) • **72**
Vintage Port Presidential 1970 • $18 Ⓐ • (02/01/90) • **75**
White Presidential NV • $9 • (04/15/92) • **80**

DELAFORCE

Ruby Port Fine NV • $8 • (03/31/88) • **89**
Tawny Port His Eminence's Choice Reserve NV: Simple, straightforward Port offering tomato, fruit and plum character and a hint of honey. • $19 • (01/31/96) • **80**
Tawny Port Superb His Eminence's Choice NV • $9 • (04/16/85) • **86**
Vintage Character Port Vintage Character NV • $NA • (03/15/94) • **81**
Vintage Port 1992: Best Delaforce in more than a decade, very grapey, loads of floral character. Full-bodied and medium-sweet, boasting masses of velvety tannins. Tasting this is like getting a good back massage. Try in 2000. • $35 • **90**
Vintage Port 1985: A ripe and roasted style of Port. Medium ruby, with a raisiny, slightly burnt nose, medium-bodied, with silky, sweet fruit flavors and medium tannins. • $35 • (06/01/90) • **81**
Vintage Port 1982 • $27 • (06/01/90) • **69**
Vintage Port 1977 • $17 Ⓐ • (02/01/90) • **80**
Vintage Port 1975 • $43 • (02/01/90) • **76**
Vintage Port 1970 • $57 • (02/01/90) • **89**
Vintage Port 1966 • $65 • (02/01/90) • **85**
Vintage Port 1963 • $35 Ⓐ • (02/01/90) • **93**
Vintage Port Quinta da Corte 1991: Not a blockbuster, but well balanced. Pretty and elegant with medium-dark black purple color and plummy, slightly earthy aromas. Medium to full body and tannins with a medium aftertaste. Try after 1998. 1,800 cases made. • $29 • (07/31/94) • **87**
Vintage Port Quinta da Corte 1987: Classy and silky in the mouth, showing plenty of elegance and power. Deep purple, with a fresh

Key: SS—Spectator Selection. CS—Cellar Selection. BB—Best Buy. $NA—Price not available. (BT)—Barrel tasting. Ⓐ—Auction Price.
Dates in parentheses represent the issues in which the ratings were published.

black olive nose, full-bodied, with medium tannins and balanced tar and blackberry flavors. • $NA • (02/01/90) • **87**
Vintage Port Quinta da Corte 1984 • $NA • (02/01/90) • **84**
Vintage Port Quinta da Corte 1980 • $NA • (02/01/90) • **81**
Vintage Port Quinta da Corte 1978 • $24 • (02/01/90) • **80**

DIEZ HERMANOS

Vintage Port 1977 • $NA • (04/01/90) • **82**

DOM HERMANO

Ribatejo Reserva 1988: Not recommended. Smells and tastes swampy, and leaves a bad taste in your mouth. Tasted twice with consistent notes. • $7 • **62**

DOW

Tawny Port 10-year-old NV: Bright and beautiful honey, toffee, caramel and a touch of nuts. A vibrant, sweet Port of lovely, delicate structure. Can't put it down. • $23 • (01/31/96) • **89**
Tawny Port 20-year-old NV: Big and thick, offering loads of nut, toffee and crème brûlée character. Full-bodied and very sweet. Still shows grip but it's fresh and balanced with good acidity. • $42 • (01/31/96) • **89**
Tawny Port 30-year-old NV: Plenty of caramel, toffee and coffee aromas and flavors. Medium- to full-bodied, very sweet, smooth, succulent finish. Mellow tawny. • $73 • (01/31/96) • **89**
Tawny Port Boardroom NV: This shows some age in the nutty, slightly caramel character, but it's rather short and straightforward. • $18 • (01/31/96) • **82**
Tawny Port Fine Tawny NV: Simple, plummy, peppery, fruitcake aromas and flavors, medium body and sweetness and fruity finish. • $10 • (01/31/96) • **82**
Tawny Port Reserve Single Year 1982: Big and raisiny, sporting grapey, nut and plum character and a hint of earth. Slightly alcoholic. Full-bodied, very sweet, dried walnut finish. Needs some cheese to tame it. • $25 • (01/31/96) • **84**
Vintage Character Port AJ NV • $19 • (03/15/94) • **79**
Vintage Character Port AJS NV • $17 • (06/15/93) • **83**
Vintage Character Port NV • $10 • (03/31/88) • **89**
Vintage Port 1991: I have underrated this wine in the past, and when last tasted it still wasn't showing much at first. However, underneath the pretty fruit is a hard backbone of tannins. It has a full body with loads of fruit concentration and a long and tannic finish. Give it time. Tasted twice, second bottle better. Try after 2000. 6,500 cases made. • $42 • (07/31/94) • **91**
Vintage Port 1985: Fleshy and raw, bursting with fruit on the palate but may have closed up some. Deep dark ruby-purple, with intense tar and berry aromas, full-bodied, with ripe berry flavors, full tannins and a long finish. • $23 Ⓐ • (06/01/90) • **89**
Vintage Port 1983 • $20 Ⓐ • (06/01/90) • **94**
Vintage Port 1980 • $15 Ⓐ • (06/01/90) • **90**
Vintage Port 1977 • $37 Ⓐ • (04/01/90) • **94**
Vintage Port 1975 • $23 Ⓐ • (04/01/89) • **80**
Vintage Port 1972 • $36 • (01/01/90) • **79**
Vintage Port 1970 • $37 Ⓐ • (12/01/89) • **94**
Vintage Port 1966 • $50 Ⓐ • (12/01/89) • **94**
Vintage Port 1963 • $79 Ⓐ • (02/01/90) • **92**
Vintage Port 1960 • $32 Ⓐ • (02/01/90) • **88**
Vintage Port 1955 • $146 Ⓐ • (04/01/90) • **91**
Vintage Port 1950 • $150 • (11/01/89) • **86**
Vintage Port 1947 • $400 • (11/01/89) • **88**
Vintage Port 1945 • $277 Ⓐ • (11/01/89) • **89**
Vintage Port 1935 • $350 • (06/01/90) • **79**
Vintage Port 1934 • $350 • (06/01/90) • **84**
Vintage Port 1927 • $225 Ⓐ • (04/01/90) • **87**
Vintage Port Quinta do Bomfim 1992: Much better than from barrel. Perhaps better than Dow's blended 1991 vintage Port. This is big and concentrated, presenting masses of velvety tannins and intensely ripe violet, raspberry and cherry flavors. It goes on and on. Cellar until 2000. 2,200 cases made. • $30 • (06/30/95) • **92**
Vintage Port Quinta do Bomfim 1990: Firm and fleshy, with ripe black cherry, vanilla and coffee aromas and flavors. Shows a definite grip of tannin and alcohol on the finish, but in balance. A chewy wine that will need until 2000 to 2005 to sort itself out. • $31 • (01/31/93) • **86**
Vintage Port Quinta do Bomfim 1989: Powerful, full of marvelous fruit flavors, yet graceful enough to let them roll across the palate gently. Has the intensity and grip to age well. Expect it to keep developing through at least 2004 to 2010. 2,785 cases made. • $24 • (11/30/91) CS • **90**
Vintage Port Quinta do Bomfim 1987: Extremely impressive, with generous, rich black cherry notes. Deep inky purple, with ripe black cherry aromas, full-bodied, with full tannins and a great concentration of fruit flavors. Very well structured. • $NA • (02/01/90) • **86**
Vintage Port Quinta do Bomfim 1986: Very hard and closed when last tasted, but still showed good fruit flavors and potential. Very dark ruby with a black center, a grape and licorice nose, medium-bodied, with full, hard tannins, blackberry flavors and a closed finish. • $NA • (02/01/90) • **82**
Vintage Port Quinta do Bomfim 1984 • $NA • (02/01/90) • **86**
Vintage Port Quinta do Bomfim 1982 • $NA • (02/01/90) • **82**
Vintage Port Quinta do Bomfim 1979 • $28 • (02/01/90) • **81**
Vintage Port Quinta do Bomfim 1978 • $36 • (02/01/90) • **85**
Vintage Port Quinta do Bomfim 1965 • $NA • (06/01/90) • **87**

EIRA VELHA, QUINTA DA

Vintage Port 1987: A good all-around 1987 with excellent fruit and tannins. Dark ruby with a purple center, aromas of grape skins and bitter chocolate, medium- to full-bodied, with grape-skin flavors, medium to full tannins and a long finish. Very good potential. • $NA • (05/01/90) • **86**
Vintage Port 1982 • $NA • (03/01/90) • **81**
Vintage Port 1978 • $22 • (03/01/90) • **85**

ESPORAO

Alentejo Reguengos 1987: Light, simple, tired and sweet. Still drinkable but past its prime. Tasted twice. 37,000 cases made. • $10 • **72**
Reguengos Monte Velho 1992: This shows supple, fleshy texture and raisin, spice and light tobacco flavors. It's straightforward and accessible. • $7 • (03/31/96) • **82**

ESTEVA

Douro 1984 • $5 • (12/15/87) • **76**

FALCOARIA

Almeirim 1990: Ripe, almost sweet tasting, with plenty of plum and berry flavors. It has a firm, tannic structure and good acidity. 8,500 cases made. • $9 • **80**

FEIST

Vintage Port 1991: Light and simple. Medium to intense color, with aromas of berry and fruit. Pretty, round, sweet and fruity, with medium tannins and a light finish. Try after 1997. 1,500 cases made. • $NA • (07/31/94) • **83**
Vintage Port 1985: Light for a 1985, but the fruit is clean and pleasant on the palate. Light purple with some ruby, a nose of grapes and spices, medium-bodied, with sweet grape and watermelon flavors, light tannins and finish. • $25 • (01/01/90) • **72**
Vintage Port 1982 • $20 • (01/01/90) • **78**
Vintage Port 1978 • $22 • (01/01/90) • **78**

FERREIRA

Douro Barca-Velha 1983: There's still plenty of life left here in Portugal's most esteemed table wine. The plum and blackberry fruit flavors are ripe and fresh, the tannins are firm and the wine is balanced and long. It shows character and breed. Drink now or hold through 1997. • $35 • **89**
Ruby Port Superior NV • $7 • (03/31/88) • **83**

Tawny Port Duque de Bragança 20-year-old NV: Grapey and sweet, adding a murky, earthy note. This lacks freshness and definition on the palate. • $49 • (01/31/96) • **73**

Tawny Port Quinta do Porto 10-year-old NV: A bit astringent and volatile on the palate but some decent citrus and orange marmalade character. Medium-bodied, lightly sweet, hot finish. Lacks balance. • $25 • (01/31/96) • **81**

Vintage Port 1991: A deceptively fine Port here. Intense grapey, green tea and fruit aromas and flavors. This takes off slowly on the palate and then kicks in at the end. Excellent tannins on the finish, quite dry. Tasted twice, second bottle much better. Try after 1999. 2,000 cases made. • $19 • (07/31/94) • **91**

Vintage Port 1987: Well balanced, with delicious sweet fruit and a firm backbone. Inky color, with a very ripe raisin and grape nose, full-bodied, with sweet fruit flavors, medium tannins and a long finish. • $NA • (11/01/89) • **88**

Vintage Port 1985: A rich, sweet Port that grows in intensity on the palate. Medium to deep purple, with perfumed, earthy raspberry aromas, full-bodied, with very sweet, syrupy fruit flavors and medium tannins. Very round and luscious. • $29 • (11/01/89) • **87**

Vintage Port 1982 • $25 • (11/01/89) • **81**
Vintage Port 1980 • $32 • (11/01/89) • **80**
Vintage Port 1978 • $28 • (11/01/89) • **89**
Vintage Port 1977 • $49 • (11/01/89) • **86**
Vintage Port 1975 • $41 • (11/01/89) • **81**
Vintage Port 1970 • $45 • (04/01/89) • **86**
Vintage Port 1966 • $81 • (11/01/89) • **85**
Vintage Port 1963 • $25 Ⓐ • (10/31/88) • **90**
Vintage Port 1960 • $70 • (10/31/88) • **86**
Vintage Port 1955 • $50 Ⓐ • (11/01/89) • **85**
Vintage Port 1950 • $90 • (11/01/89) • **79**
Vintage Port 1945 • $121 Ⓐ • (11/01/89) • **81**
Vintage Port 1935 • $200 • (02/01/90) • **93**
Vintage Port Quinta do Seixo 1983 • $14 • (11/01/89) • **91**

FERREIRA, ANTONIO ESTEVES

Vinho Verde Alvarinho Soalheiro 1994: Rather generous in body and flavor, featuring smooth but crisp texture and a lingering finish. This white has good balance between acidity and body. • $15 • (04/30/96) • **84**

Vinho Verde Alvarinho Soalheiro 1993: Distinctive and grows on you. Aromas are a bit off, but the flavors are nicely juicy and orangelike and the finish is clean. 400 cases made. • $NA • (07/31/95) • **83**

FERREIRINHA

Douro Vinha Grande 1990: A solid, tannic red wine to drink now while the raspberry flavors are fresh and inviting. • $10 • **83**

FEUERHEERD

Vintage Port 1985: There is some fruit here but seemed extremely light on last tasting. Barely passable as a vintage. Medium ruby, with a light grape-skin nose, medium-bodied, with round, light tannins, clean fruit flavors and a very simple finish. • $NA • (01/01/90) • **72**

Vintage Port 1980 • $NA • (01/01/90) • **76**
Vintage Port 1977 • $17 • (01/01/90) • **69**
Vintage Port 1970 • $45 • (01/01/90) • **80**

FONSECA

Late Bottled Port 1989: Quite aggressive in its peppery raisin and fruit character and the tannin bite on the finish. Could still use a year or two of bottle age. • $18 • (01/31/96) • **85**

Late Bottled Port 1988: Spicy and somewhat spirity, offering attractive cherry and raisin flavors with tobacco and licorice accents. It's not too sweet, straightforward and clean. Drink or hold. • $17 • (11/15/94) • **84**

Key: SS—Spectator Selection. CS—Cellar Selection. BB—Best Buy. $NA—Price not available. (BT)—Barrel tasting. Ⓐ—Auction Price.
Dates in parentheses represent the issues in which the ratings were published.

Tawny Port 10-year-old NV: Portuguese paradox. Old and rich nut, tobacco and toffee flavors yet fresh, thick and fruity, adding a slight tannin bite. • $23 • (01/31/96) • **86**

Tawny Port 20-year-old NV: Disjointed, featuring some mature, nutty bark and honey character but also loads of fresh fruit, coffee and caramel flavors. Full in body, very sweet, rustic and rough finish. • $44 • (01/31/96) • **84**

Tawny Port 40-year-old NV: Very fruity style of old tawny sporting plum, brown sugar and butterscotch character. Medium-bodied, very sweet and a fresh finish. • $114 • (01/31/96) • **86**

Vintage Character Port Bin 27 NV • $16 • (03/15/94) • **85**

Vintage Port 1992: The best Fonseca since the perfect 1977. Intense cassis, violet and plum aromas. Full-bodied, medium sweet and bursting at the seams with fruit and tannins. A wine of great mass and concentration. Try in 2005. • $30 CS • **96**

Vintage Port 1991: Almost as good as the 1992 Fonseca. Wonderful, classy Port with superb balance. Super-dark and inky, featuring thick berry, tar and violet aromas and flavors. Sweet and silky with a long finish. Tasted twice with consistent notes. 3,000 cases made. • $NA • **93**

Vintage Port 1985: A hard, take-no-prisoners Port, extremely powerful and still closed when last tasted. Deep inky color, with concentrated blackberry and raisin aromas, full-bodied, with massive raisin flavors, a superb backbone and a very long finish. • $37 • (06/01/90) • **95**

Vintage Port 1983 • $34 • (06/01/90) • **90**
Vintage Port 1980 • $40 • (06/01/90) • **74**
Vintage Port 1977 • $60 • (04/01/90) • **100**
Vintage Port 1975 • $40 • (10/31/88) • **81**
Vintage Port 1970 • $65 • (12/01/89) • **96**
Vintage Port 1966 • $84 • (02/01/90) • **97**
Vintage Port 1963 • $162 • (12/01/89) • **98**
Vintage Port 1960 • $95 • (10/31/88) • **81**
Vintage Port 1955 • $200 • (08/01/88) • **96**
Vintage Port 1948 • $450 • (11/01/89) • **100**
Vintage Port 1945 • $500 • (11/01/89) • **91**
Vintage Port 1934 • $330 • (02/01/90) • **91**
Vintage Port 1927 • $430 • (12/01/89) • **100**

Vintage Port Guimaraens 1991: Wonderful and classy, with superb balance. Very dark and inky, featuring thick berry, tar and violet aromas and flavors. Sweet and silky with a long finish. Tasted twice with consistent notes. Try after 2002. 3,000 cases made. • $35 • (07/31/94) • **93**

Vintage Port Guimaraens 1987: Extremely racy and classy, well made, with an impressive fruit character and plenty of tannin. Deep purple, with a very ripe, grapey nose, full-bodied, with well integrated tannins and excellent berry and violet flavors. Long finish. • $NA • (02/01/90) • **90**

Vintage Port Guimaraens 1986: Tight, hard and closed when last tasted, but it has very good potential. Inky black-purple, with aromas of perfume and grapes, full-bodied, with tons of tannins and medium berry flavors. • $NA • (02/01/90) • **86**

Vintage Port Guimaraens 1984 • $NA • (02/01/90) • **85**
Vintage Port Guimaraens 1982 • $NA • (02/01/90) • **82**
Vintage Port Guimaraens 1978 • $35 • (02/01/90) • **80**
Vintage Port Guimaraens 1976 • $38 • (02/01/90) • **89**
Vintage Port Guimaraens 1974 • $40 • (01/01/90) • **84**
Vintage Port Guimaraens 1972 • $34 • (02/01/90) • **75**
Vintage Port Guimaraens 1968 • $40 • (02/01/90) • **84**
Vintage Port Guimaraens 1967 • $56 • (02/01/90) • **90**
Vintage Port Guimaraens 1965 • $64 • (02/01/90) • **89**
Vintage Port Guimaraens 1964 • $95 • (02/01/90) • **90**
Vintage Port Guimaraens 1962 • $70 • (02/01/90) • **88**
Vintage Port Guimaraens 1961 • $70 • (02/01/90) • **85**
Vintage Port Guimaraens 1958 • $90 • (02/01/90) • **88**

Vintage Port Quinta do Panascal 1987: A typical velvety example of the vintage. Medium purple, with cassis and tomato aromas, medium-bodied, with cassis flavors, medium tannins and a long finish. Well balanced. • $NA • (02/01/90) • **82**

Vintage Port Quinta do Panascal 1986: Very sweet, well-focused fruit flavors and a decent backbone. Medium purple, with earthy, wet leaf aromas, medium-bodied, with medium tannins and a slightly flabby finish. • $NA • (02/01/90) • **79**

Vintage Port Quinta do Panascal 1985: This was an improvement over the weak 1984. Deep ruby, with aromas of grapes and tar, full-bodied, with very hard, slightly harsh tannins and a lean, hard finish. Lacks balance. • $NA • (02/01/90) • **78**

Vintage Port Quinta do Panascal 1984 • $NA • (02/01/90) • **70**

Vintage Port Quinta do Panascal 1983 • $NA • (02/01/90) • **79**

FONSECA, JOSE MARIA DA

Alentejo 1987: This mature red has woody, spicy aromas, pruny, raisiny flavors and a tannic texture. Good in a very ripe style, but don't save it, drink now. 7,000 cases made. • $9 • **80**

Alentejo Garrafeira 1988: A mature but still fruity tasting red with spicy, pruny flavors and good balance. Drink now. 750 cases made. • $13 • **82**

Alentejo Garrafeira AP 1987: Massive and tannic in style, with flavors like Port. Has plenty of fruit flavor that is held in check by dense but fine tannins. Accented by spice and vanilla on the aroma and the finish. Concentrated and well-balanced. Drinkable now. 1,000 cases made. • $13 • **85**

Alentejo Morgado do Reguengo 1989: The tart acidity and tight tannins are softened a bit by spicy aromas and good fruit flavors. On the puckery side, but should be fine with rich meat and cheese dishes. 4,000 cases made. • $8 • **81**

Arrábida Garrafeira TE 1988: A tired, wornout wine with stewed aromas, brown sugar and smoke flavors, but little to give it life. Avoid. Tasted twice with consistent notes. • $NA • **67**

Dão Casa da Insua 1988: Dusty, herb and menthol aromas are followed by lean fruit flavors and a drying texture. Seriously out of whack. No fun to drink. Tasted three times with consistent notes. 1,200 cases made. • $9 • **76**

Dão Terras Altas 1990: A sturdy red wine that balances modest fruit flavor with firm tannins. Medium-bodied, somewhat spicy and herbal in aroma, with plummy, berrylike flavors. 70,000 cases made. • $7 • **79**

Dão Terras Altas 1987 • $7 • (11/15/91) • **69**

Garrafeira CO 1982 • $14 • (12/31/90) • **83**

Garrafeira RA 1982 • $14 • (12/31/90) • **88**

Pasmados 1984 • $7 • (04/30/91) BB • **83**

Periquita 1987 • $5 • (12/31/90) BB • **84**

Periquita Vintage Selection Unfiltered 1987 • $7 • (11/15/91) • **80**

Portalegre Morgado do Reguengo 1987 • $8 • (11/15/91) • **86**

Terras do Sado Pasmados 1989: Smooth in texture, mature in flavor, smoky in aroma, ready to drink now while the well-developed fruity and woodsy character lasts. 7,000 cases made. • $9 • **78**

Terras do Sado Periquita 1990: A nicely balanced, easy-to-drink red wine with moderate tannins, good fruit flavors and a touch of spicy complexity. Drink now. 90,000 cases made. • $7 BB • **84**

Terras do Sado Periquita Reserva 1984: Not as tired tasting as you would guess from the browning color, and it does have a solid raisin-prune flavor left, but still marginal in appeal. 1,100 cases made. • $9 • **70**

Terras do Sado Quinta de Camarate 1989: Barnyard and stale tobacco flavors dominate this tired, flabby wine. Tasted twice with consistent notes. 6,000 cases made. • $10 • **68**

Tinto Velho Requengos de Monsarax Colhei 1986 • $9 • (12/31/90) • **82**

FORUM PRIOR DO CRATO

Dão 1989: A very solid red that could use more time to develop. It has firm tannins, fresh and concentrated berry flavors and good balance. Drink now. • $9 • **82**

Planalto Mirandês 1990: Light yet tannic, with a sweet vegetal note that's a bit cloying. The berry, peppery flavors show some concentration. Drink now. • $7 • **78**

GILBERT

Vintage Port 1992: Pretty plum, meat and berry aromas and flavors. Medium-bodied, sweet and round, a pleasant finish. Drinkable now. • $NA • **85**

Vintage Port 1991: Not a big wine, but has some pretty cherry, raspberry and cedar character. Medium body and medium tannins, with a soft finish. Try after 1998. 500 cases made. • $NA • (07/31/94) • **85**

GOULD CAMPBELL

Late Bottled Port 1985 • $15 • (04/15/92) • **86**

Vintage Port 1991: Almost as thick as Graham and a favorite of the vintage. Racy and tannic with super dark color and loads of fruity, peppery aromas. Full-bodied yet reserved, quite dry with sleek tannins and a very long finish. Try after 2000. 500 cases made. • $35 • (07/31/94) • **92**

Vintage Port 1985: A good, standard 1985, quite lean and angular. Deep purple, with very grapey raspberry aromas, full-bodied, with medium tannins, sweet fruit and a slightly short finish. • $23 • (06/01/90) • **85**

Vintage Port 1983 • $31 • (06/01/90) • **90**

Vintage Port 1980 • $35 • (02/01/90) • **86**

Vintage Port 1977 • $29 Ⓐ • (02/01/90) • **93**

Vintage Port 1975 • $33 • (04/15/92) • **82**

Vintage Port 1970 • $54 • (02/01/90) • **88**

Vintage Port 1966 • $80 • (02/01/90) • **84**

GRAHAM

Ruby Port Fine NV • $7 • (03/31/88) • **74**

Ruby Port Six Grapes NV • $15 • (03/31/88) • **80**

Tawny Port 10-year-old NV: Complex orange peel, cedar and plum aromas and flavors are the hallmarks of this tawny. It has medium body and sweetness with a crisp, clean finish. Absolutely delicious to drink. Pure honey. • $24 • (01/31/96) SS • **91**

Tawny Port 20-year-old NV: Not as balanced as the 10-year-old. Really vibrant masses of honey, butterscotch and crème brûlée flavors. Medium-bodied, very fresh, long honey and orange peel finish. Slightly hot. • $45 • (01/31/96) • **88**

Tawny Port 30-year-old NV: Big and rich bitter chocolate, honey and almond character, medium body and sweetness and long, nutty finish. Slightly clumsy. • $75 • (01/31/96) • **87**

Tawny Port 40-year-old NV: Slightly atypical but showing plenty of character. More like a dry oloroso Sherry. Medium in body and sweetness, adding salty, nutty, hazelnut notes. Try with nuts, blue cheese or almond desserts. • $122 • (01/31/96) • **87**

Tawny Port Fine Tawny NV: Simple and earthy, showing some decent plum character, but rather boring. • $12 • (01/31/96) • **78**

Vintage Character Port Six Grapes NV • $21 • (03/15/94) • **81**

Vintage Port 1991: Getting better all the time in the bottle. Real blockbuster of a wine that sneaks up on you. Beautiful tar, grape and berry aromas and flavors. It's full-bodied, quite sweet and reserved, but kicks off at the end with loads of fruit and tannins. Tasted twice with consistent notes. Try after 2000. • $45 • (07/31/94) • **93**

Vintage Port 1985: What more could one want in a young vintage Port? It has great elegance and great power. Brilliant deep ruby-purple, with boysenberry and licorice aromas, full-bodied, very fleshy, with a firm backbone of tannins. • $42 • (06/01/90) • **96**

Vintage Port 1983 • $40 • (06/01/90) • **93**

Vintage Port 1980 • $42 • (06/01/90) • **90**

Vintage Port 1977 • $58 • (04/01/90) • **90**

Vintage Port 1975 • $49 • (02/01/89) • **78**

Vintage Port 1970 • $72 • (12/01/89) • **94**

Vintage Port 1966 • $88 • (12/01/89) • **93**

Vintage Port 1963 • $150 • (12/01/89) • **97**

Vintage Port 1960 • $80 • (10/31/88) • **88**

Vintage Port 1955 • $210 • (11/01/89) • **94**

Vintage Port 1954 • $160 • (02/01/90) • **91**

Vintage Port 1948 • $290 • (11/01/89) • **95**

Vintage Port 1945 • $510 • (11/01/89) • **95**

Vintage Port 1942 • $420 • (04/01/90) • **89**

Vintage Port 1935 • $400 • (04/01/90) • **94**

Vintage Port 1927 • $570 • (02/01/90) • **94**

Vintage Port Malvedos 1992: Impressively rich and concentrated aromas of currants and fruit, with hints of earth. Big and thick on the palate, showing masses of fruit and tannins. Almost as good as the Graham '91. This one is built for long aging, try in 2000. 3,000 cases made. • $39 • (06/30/95) • **91**

Vintage Port Malvedos 1988: Ripe, opulent and delicious. Beautifully peppery and fruity in flavor, with a silky smooth texture that belies its high alcohol and young age. A very long finish echoes black pepper and chocolate. Tempting to drink now for its fruitiness, but probably best after 2000. 7,000 cases made. • $26 • (01/31/91) HR • **93**

Vintage Port Malvedos 1987: Amazing richness and depth of sweet, chewy fruit flavors. Dark inky color, with intense blackberry and cherry aromas, full-bodied, with sweet grape and cherry flavors and an excellent balance of round, ripe tannins. A great density of ripe fruit. • $NA • (02/01/90) • **91**

Vintage Port Malvedos 1986: A medium-weight vintage Port, with very fine concentration of plum and anise aromas. Not quite so opulent on the palate, where the grip of tannin puts the brakes on any apparent richness, but the spicy finish suggests this is a good candidate for aging. • $20 • (03/31/90) • **84**

Vintage Port Malvedos 1984 • $NA • (02/01/90) • **83**

Vintage Port Malvedos 1982 • $NA • (02/01/90) • **90**

Vintage Port Malvedos 1979 • $NA • (02/01/90) • **74**

Vintage Port Malvedos 1978 • $34 • (02/01/90) • **82**

Vintage Port Malvedos 1976 • $31 • (02/01/90) • **74**

Vintage Port Malvedos 1968 • $50 • (02/01/90) • **70**

Vintage Port Malvedos 1965 • $58 • (02/01/90) • **79**

Vintage Port Malvedos 1964 • $54 • (02/01/90) • **82**

Vintage Port Malvedos 1962 • $62 • (02/01/90) • **89**

Vintage Port Malvedos 1961 • $65 • (02/01/90) • **87**

Vintage Port Malvedos 1958 • $65 • (02/01/90) • **79**

Vintage Port Malvedos 1957 • $70 • (02/01/90) • **84**

Vintage Port Malvedos 1952 • $125 • (11/01/89) • **85**

Vintage Port Malvedos Centenary 1990 • $32 • (01/31/93) • **82**

HOOPER

Tawny Port 20-year-old NV • $35 • (02/28/90) • **78**

Vintage Port 1985 • $20 • (06/01/90) • **80**

Vintage Port 1983 • $16 • (03/01/90) • **60**

Vintage Port 1982 • $18 • (05/01/90) • **68**

Vintage Port 1980 • $22 • (05/01/90) • **67**

HUTCHESON

Vintage Port 1991: An early-maturing Port with pretty fruit, medium-deep ruby color and plummy, earthy aromas. It has a medium body with sweet and velvety fruit, medium tannins and a light finish. From Barros, Almeida. Try after 1997. 1,000 cases made. • $19 • (07/31/94) • **81**

Vintage Port 1979 • $40 • (01/01/90) • **69**

Vintage Port 1970 • $50 • (01/01/90) • **79**

INFANTADO, QUINTA DO

Vintage Port 1992: The best ever made at this estate and one to watch in the future. Like a lagar full of grapes fermenting, big and powerful tar and raisin character. Full-bodied, sweet, tannic, in an extracted style. Try in 2000. • $35 • **90**

Vintage Port 1991: Deep and dark ruby, with wonderful dark chocolate and berry aromas and flavors. It's medium-bodied and quite sweet, with medium tannins and a fine finish. Try after 1998. • $25 • (07/31/94) • **85**

Vintage Port 1989: This sweet, fruity, agreeable Port offers lots of blackberry and cherry flavors and a smooth finish. Should be at its best now. 1,800 cases made. • $35 • (07/31/93) • **81**

Vintage Port 1985: Pleasant on the palate, this 1985 was quite forward as of 1990. Deep ruby, with a very ripe and roasted nose, medium-bodied with very sweet fruit flavors and a soft mouth-feel. • $33 • (07/01/90) • **76**

Vintage Port 1982 • $35 • (07/01/90) • **70**

Vintage Port 1978 • $NA • (07/01/90) • **75**

Key: SS—Spectator Selection. CS—Cellar Selection. BB—Best Buy. $NA—Price not available. (BT)—Barrel tasting. Ⓐ—Auction Price.
Dates in parentheses represent the issues in which the ratings were published.

JOÃO PATO

Bairrada 1991: Fresh, fruity, tart and juicy, a lip-smacking young wine with vibrant flavors that linger on the finish. Drink it now for its freshness and lively feel. 1,500 cases made. • $9 • **86**

JP VINHOS

Alentejo Herdade de Santa Marta 1993: Straightforward, fairly ripe plum, raspberry and sweet cherry flavors linger on the finish. A good quaff. • $9 • (03/31/96) • **83**

Alentejo Herdade de Santa Marta 1991 • $10 • (04/15/94) • **85**

Alentejo Tinto da Anfora 1991: Solid and lively, dominated by good raspberry and blueberry flavors and a nice, spicy finish. Drinkable now. • $10 • (03/31/96) • **84**

Alentejo Tinto da Anfora 1990 • $9 • (04/15/94) • **79**

Red Vinho de Mesa J.P. NV: This supple red offers light plum and bacon flavors. It's simple but will stand up to light dishes. 200,000 cases made. • $5 • (03/31/96) • **79**

Terras do Sado Quinta da Bacalhôa 1990 • $15 • (04/15/94) • **81**

Terras do Sado Quinta de Santo Amaro 1992 • $8 • (04/15/94) • **78**

KOPKE

Port Varsity NV • $6 • (03/31/88) • **72**

Tawny Port 20-year-old NV • $30 • (02/28/90) • **88**

Vintage Port 1991: Rather forward Port. Round and sweet berry and cherry character, medium to full body, sweet and soft tannins. From Barros, Almeida. May be drinkable now, or try after 1997. 1,700 cases made. • $NA • (07/31/94) • **82**

Vintage Port 1987: This is an elegant wine with good fruit and structure. Deep purple, with a rich, floral, grapey nose, full-bodied, with a good balance of medium tannins and sweet fruit flavors. • $24 • (01/01/90) • **86**

Vintage Port 1985: A dark horse that should finish among the top 1985s in years to come. Deep purple, with fresh blackberries and raspberries on the nose, full-bodied, with balanced tannins, a firm structure and a lovely finish. • $25 Ⓐ • (01/01/90) • **90**

Vintage Port 1983 • $23 • (01/01/90) • **85**

Vintage Port 1982 • $26 • (01/01/90) • **83**

Vintage Port 1980 • $13 Ⓐ • (01/01/90) • **71**

Vintage Port 1979 • $NA • (01/01/90) • **69**

Vintage Port 1978 • $29 • (01/01/90) • **70**

Vintage Port 1977 • $23 Ⓐ • (01/01/90) • **68**

Vintage Port 1975 • $28 • (01/01/90) • **82**

Vintage Port 1974 • $NA • (01/01/90) • **74**

Vintage Port 1970 • $25 Ⓐ • (01/01/90) • **82**

Vintage Port 1966 • $65 • (01/01/90) • **81**

Vintage Port 1960 • $65 • (01/01/90) • **87**

LAGOALVA, QUINTA DA

Ribatejo 1992: Coarse and a bit astringent. Extremely earthy and gamy aromas give way to plum and jam flavors. • $9 • (04/30/96) • **75**

Ribatejo 1991: Charming, almost sweet, like a fruit wine, packed with strawberry and cherry flavors. Unusual, but good, from the intense aroma through the easy texture and lingering fruity finish. • $7 • **83**

Ribatejo Cima 1992: Rustic, delivering plenty of hearty game, earth and ripe plum flavors. The finish kicks in some tobacco and cedary notes. Simple and satisfying. • $9 • (04/30/96) • **83**

Ribatejo Lagoalva de Cima 1991: Fresh, jammy-tasting and delicious. A medium-bodied, full-flavored red with lots of strawberry and cherry flavors and plenty of charm. Drink now. • $10 • **86**

MADREVINHOS

Cartaxo Três Hastins 1988 • $7 • (04/15/94) • **72**

MANDOS

Bairrada Reserva 1990: Light-bodied but aggressively dry, meager, marred by nail-polish and garlic aromas. Some fruit in the middle keeps it drinkable. • $6 • **73**

Dão Reserva 1989: There's a baked, musty note to this wine, like fruit left too long in the hot sun. There's some ripeness on the palate, but it's astringent on the palate, and short on the finish. Drink up. • $7 • **76**

MANGUALDE, ADEGA COOPERATIVA DE

Dão Foral D. Henrique Reserva 1990: Lots going on here, not all of it pleasant. The ripe fruit flavors and firm tannins are still fresh, but medicinal notes put us off. 10,000 cases made. • $5 • (01/31/95) • **78**

MARTINEZ

Tawny Port 20-year-old Directors NV • $25 • (02/28/90) • **93**

Vintage Port 1991: Round and delicious, but slightly forward compared to many. It shows a good balance of fruit, sweetness and tannins. Good aftertaste of minerals and fruit. Try after 1998. • $NA • (07/31/94) • **85**

Vintage Port 1987: Still very closed when last tasted, but round, ripe and rich, with extremely attractive fruit flavors and plenty of grip on the finish. Deep ruby with a purple center, aromas of flowers, milk chocolate and earth, full-bodied, with round tannins and a long finish. • $NA • (05/01/90) • **84**

Vintage Port 1985: A burly wine with muscles. Deep, dark ruby, with concentrated cherry aromas, full-bodied and tightly structured, with ripe tannins and rich cherry and earth flavors. • $35 Ⓐ • (06/01/90) • **89**

Vintage Port 1982 • $28 • (06/01/90) • **82**

Vintage Port 1975 • $40 • (02/01/90) • **75**

Vintage Port 1970 • $21 Ⓐ • (02/01/90) • **89**

Vintage Port 1967 • $56 • (02/01/90) • **93**

Vintage Port 1963 • $31 Ⓐ • (02/01/90) • **82**

Vintage Port 1955 • $120 • (11/01/89) • **86**

Vintage Port Quinta da Eira Velha 1992: Better than the declared '91 Martinez. Intense, very ripe fruit character, violet and floral tones. Full-bodied, lightly sweet, quite tough, adding firm tannins and long finish. Try in 2000. • $NA • **89**

MATO MIRANDA, QUINTA DE

Ribatejo 1992: Ripe, fairly rich and rustic, offering plenty of tannins. Flavors are dominated by cherry and coffee, inserting a shot of licorice on the finish. Best to drink soon. • $5 • (03/31/96) • **84**

MESSIA

Vintage Port 1985: An odd, slightly volatile, varnish nose detracts. I asked the winemaker about it and she said it was normally like that. Medium ruby with a light edge, violet and varnish aromas, medium-bodied, with simple fruit flavors and a short finish. • $20 • (02/01/90) • **67**

Vintage Port 1984 • $15 • (02/01/90) • **78**

Vintage Port 1982 • $13 • (02/01/90) • **72**

Vintage Port 1963 • $40 • (02/01/90) • **71**

Vintage Port Quinta do Cachão 1983 • $11 • (02/01/90) • **77**

Vintage Port Quinta do Cachão 1977 • $20 • (02/01/90) • **60**

Vintage Port Quinta do Cachão 1970 • $55 • (02/01/90) • **87**

Vintage Port Quinta do Cachão 1966 • $30 • (02/01/90) • **84**

MINHO, QUINTA DO

Vinha Verde 1994: Light and lean white, distinctive in flavor, showing crisp apple and grapefruit accents. Spritzy enough to keep it lively. • $7 • (04/30/96) • **82**

MORGAN (PORT)

Vintage Port 1985: Lacks class but is a good, rough and tough vintage to lay away. Deep purple-red, with ripe, almost raisiny aromas, full-bodied, with velvety, sweet plum flavors, full tannins and a long finish. • $NA • (02/01/90) • **85**

Vintage Port 1977 • $NA • (01/01/90) • **78**

Vintage Port 1970 • $NA • (02/01/90) • **88**

Vintage Port 1966 • $NA • (02/01/90) • **80**

Vintage Port 1963 • $NA • (02/01/90) • **86**

MURGAS, QUINTA DAS

Estremadura 1989: Mature red offering decent plum, chocolate and cherry flavors. It finishes on a dried fruit note. 4,000 cases made. • $8 • (04/30/96) • **79**

NAVEGA, ANTONIO AFONSO

Bairrada Quinta do Carvalhinho 1990: Ripe cassis and lush vanilla notes give this wine appeal, but it's a bit rustic and ill-defined. Drinkable now. • $NA • **80**

NIEPOORT

Douro Redoma 1991: A trip to the berry patch with plenty of blackberry, raspberry and blueberry flavors. Pleasantly rich, adding tannic aftertaste. Reminiscent of an old-style California Petite Sirah. • $12 • (03/31/96) • **85**

Tawny Port 10-year-old NV: Quite smooth and honeylike on the palate, medium-bodied and very sweet with a crisp finish. Slightly one-dimensional but really delicious. • $28 • (01/31/96) • **88**

Tawny Port 20-year-old NV: Incredibly sweet and unctuous. Medium in body with intense honey, truffle and caramel character and long, long aftertaste. Can't put it down. • $47 • (01/31/96) • **91**

Tawny Port 30-year-old NV: More like Sherry than Port with a rancid aroma yet also some pretty honey, burnt orange flavors. Viscous texture and smooth, but short. • $100 • (01/31/96) • **81**

Tawny Port Colheita 1985: Big, sweet tawny offering monolithic flavors of salted nuts, berries and dried plums, medium sweetness and fruity, clean finish. Great accompanying cheese and nuts. • $29 • (01/31/96) • **87**

Tawny Port Colheita 1983: Absolutely fabulous. One of the best tawnies we've had in a long time. An array of floral, dried fruit and nut character on the nose and palate. Medium in body and extremely smooth. Great balance. Mega-long finish. • $34 • (01/31/96) HR • **95**

Tawny Port Colheita 1978: Tasting this is like eating pure toffee. Medium-bodied and sweet, adding an assertive, rich finish. • $54 • (01/31/96) • **87**

Tawny Port Colheita 1976: Extremely intense-flavored tawny showing plum, honey and toffee character. Very sweet and packed with fruit. Rich, full-bodied, complex structure and great finish. • $60 • (01/31/96) • **93**

Tawny Port Colheita 1963: Thick, rich, complex flavors of honey, molasses and citrus. Full in body, very sweet, long, crisp finish. Extremely well balanced. • $160 • (01/31/96) • **91**

Tawny Port Fine Tawny NV: Interesting earthy, floral and fruity notes, medium-bodied, lightly sweet, adding a fruity, ironlike, earthy finish. • $17 • (01/31/96) • **84**

Vintage Character Port Vintage Character NV • $NA • (03/15/94) • **86**

Vintage Port 1992: This builds on your palate into super, well-constructed, balanced Port. Wonderful floral and fruit aromas, like walking into a lovely florist shop. Full in body, medium-sweet, loads of tannins and long, peppery, fruity finish. Give it time, try in 2003. • $33 • **90**

Vintage Port 1991: Slightly disappointing after the high preliminary marks last year, but it's still delicious. Attractive chocolate and berry aromas and flavors, fine tannins and a light, delicate finish. Tasted three times with consistent notes. Try after 1997. 1,700 cases made. • $NA • (07/31/94) • **85**

Vintage Port 1987: An impressive example of the vintage, with lots of power and backbone. Inky color, with a very intense, grapey, Syrah-like nose, full-bodied, with full, ripe tannins and plenty of sweet fruit flavors. Extremely long on the finish. • $17 Ⓐ • (11/01/89) • **91**

Vintage Port 1985: I have tasted some inspiring bottles of the 1985, but there may be some bottle variation. Nonetheless, it is a massive wine at its best. Deep purple, with a very jammy, grapey nose, full-bodied,

PORTUGAL

with lots of velvety, sweet fruit flavors and medium tannins. • $44 • (06/01/90) • **92**

Vintage Port 1983 • $16 Ⓐ • (06/01/90) • **84**
Vintage Port 1982 • $23 Ⓐ • (06/01/90) • **90**
Vintage Port 1980 • $16 Ⓐ • (06/01/90) • **87**
Vintage Port 1978 • $17 Ⓐ • (11/01/89) • **81**
Vintage Port 1977 • $50 • (04/01/90) • **89**
Vintage Port 1975 • $37 • (11/01/89) • **79**
Vintage Port 1970 • $55 • (01/01/90) • **93**
Vintage Port 1966 • $70 • (11/01/89) • **89**
Vintage Port 1963 • $90 • (11/01/89) • **90**
Vintage Port 1955 • $175 • (08/01/90) • **98**
Vintage Port 1945 • $250 • (02/01/90) • **97**
Vintage Port 1942 • $240 • (04/01/90) • **93**
Vintage Port 1927 • $300 • (04/01/90) • **97**

NOVAL, QUINTA DO

Tawny Port 20-year-old NV • $32 • (02/28/90) • **82**
Vintage Character Port Noval LB NV • $18 • (03/15/94) • **86**
Vintage Port 1991: Refined and well crafted. Dark purple, with fresh floral and grapey aromas and flavors. Medium body, medium sweetness and firm tannins. Try after 1999. 6,000 cases made. • $25 • (07/31/94) • **87**
Vintage Port 1987: This was not declared officially by Noval but about 1,200 cases were made. It is an exquisite wine with elegant, sweet fruit flavors. It reminds me of a top 1967. Excellent deep inky color, intense nose of blackberries and tar, full-bodied. • $30 • (01/01/90) • **89**
Vintage Port 1985: Very good, but seems a little stalky. It should come together with time. Medium ruby-purple, with a plum nose, full-bodied, with concentrated plum flavors, full tannins and a long finish. • $31 • (06/01/90) • **86**
Vintage Port 1982 • $36 • (06/01/90) • **78**
Vintage Port 1978 • $39 • (11/01/89) • **72**
Vintage Port 1977 • $50 • (10/31/88) • **78**
Vintage Port 1975 • $32 • (11/01/89) • **81**
Vintage Port 1970 • $60 • (11/01/89) • **89**
Vintage Port 1967 • $60 • (12/01/89) • **88**
Vintage Port 1966 • $75 • (12/01/89) • **91**
Vintage Port 1963 • $90 • (12/01/89) • **84**
Vintage Port 1960 • $84 • (11/01/89) • **82**
Vintage Port 1958 • $100 • (11/01/89) • **82**
Vintage Port 1955 • $100 • (08/01/90) • **88**
Vintage Port 1950 • $180 • (11/01/89) • **85**
Vintage Port 1947 • $200 • (11/01/89) • **93**
Vintage Port 1945 • $310 • (11/01/89) • **92**
Vintage Port 1942 • $200 • (04/01/90) • **86**
Vintage Port 1941 • $70 • (09/01/85) • **50**
Vintage Port 1938 • $110 • (09/01/85) • **71**
Vintage Port 1934 • $310 • (02/01/90) • **98**
Vintage Port 1931 • $850 • (11/01/89) • **99**
Vintage Port 1927 • $360 • (12/01/89) • **93**
Vintage Port Nacional 1987: This Port shows the essence of freshly crushed grapes. It is as dark as black ink, with a very closed nose, very full-bodied and extremely tannic, with masses of fruit flavors. • $145 • (01/01/90) • **94**
Vintage Port Nacional 1985: After a few rather weak years, this puts Nacional back on top. Very deep ruby-black, with ripe raisiny aromas, an abundance of fruit and tannins and an extremely thick and viscous finish. • $225 • (11/01/89) • **95**
Vintage Port Nacional 1982 • $130 • (11/01/89) • **86**
Vintage Port Nacional 1980 • $150 • (02/01/90) • **80**
Vintage Port Nacional 1978 • $160 • (11/01/89) • **77**
Vintage Port Nacional 1975 • $170 • (11/01/89) • **86**
Vintage Port Nacional 1970 • $300 • (11/01/89) • **98**
Vintage Port Nacional 1967 • $325 • (11/01/89) • **95**
Vintage Port Nacional 1966 • $310 • (11/01/89) • **98**

Key: SS—Spectator Selection. CS—Cellar Selection. BB—Best Buy. $NA—Price not available. (BT)—Barrel tasting. Ⓐ—Auction Price.
Dates in parentheses represent the issues in which the ratings were published.

Vintage Port Nacional 1964 • $250 • (11/01/89) • **84**
Vintage Port Nacional 1963 • $600 • (11/01/89) • **100**
Vintage Port Nacional 1962 • $350 • (11/01/89) • **86**
Vintage Port Nacional 1960 • $300 • (11/01/89) • **84**
Vintage Port Nacional 1950 • $650 • (11/01/89) • **90**
Vintage Port Nacional 1931 • $2,500 • (11/01/89) • **100**

OFFLEY

Late Bottled Port 1988: Fairly soft and grapey, with nice plum, chocolate and cherry flavors. The finish has a nice hint of pepper and a fair amount of grip. Drinkable now. 9,810 cases made. • $19 • (11/15/94) • **86**
Tawny Port 20-year-old Baron Forrester NV • $35 • (02/28/90) • **89**
Vintage Character Port Boa Vista Reserve NV • $14 • (03/15/94) • **75**
Vintage Port 1987: Simple, but has very good fruit structure. Dark purple, with grapey, floral aromas, full-bodied, with round, chewy fruit flavors, medium tannins and a long finish. • $NA • (01/01/90) • **84**
Vintage Port Boa Vista 1987: Very classy and well crafted. Deep inky color, very ripe black currant aromas, full-bodied, with plenty of racy fruit flavors, a tough backbone and a long finish. • $NA • (01/01/90) • **88**
Vintage Port Boa Vista 1985: Polished, with good fruit and backbone. Deep inky color, elegant perfumed nose, full-bodied, with silky, elegant fruit flavors, medium tannins and a long finish. • $31 • (06/01/90) • **89**
Vintage Port Boa Vista 1983 • $15 • (01/01/90) • **91**
Vintage Port Boa Vista 1982 • $23 • (06/01/90) • **84**
Vintage Port Boa Vista 1980 • $30 • (06/01/90) • **90**
Vintage Port Boa Vista 1977 • $18 Ⓐ • (01/01/90) • **88**
Vintage Port Boa Vista 1975 • $27 • (02/01/89) • **75**
Vintage Port Boa Vista 1972 • $36 Ⓐ • (02/01/89) • **79**
Vintage Port Boa Vista 1970 • $21 Ⓐ • (02/01/89) • **81**
Vintage Port Boa Vista 1966 • $45 • (02/01/89) • **90**
Vintage Port Boa Vista 1960 • $24 Ⓐ • (02/01/89) • **78**

OSBORNE

Vintage Port 1992: Loads of grape and berry aromas and flavors, medium body, medium sweetness, fine tannin structure and fresh finish. Try in 1999. • $28 • **88**
Vintage Port 1985: Well made, but much too light for such an excellent vintage. Medium ruby with a red hue, peppery aromas, medium-bodied, with elegant medium tannins and a light finish. • $20 • (02/01/89) • **76**
Vintage Port 1982 • $26 • (01/01/90) • **72**
Vintage Port 1970 • $50 • (01/01/90) • **77**
Vintage Port 1960 • $60 • (01/01/90) • **82**

PACO, QUINTA DO

Vinho Verde Paço de Teixeiró 1994: Strives for a generous, mature style of buttery and nutty aromas, but the flavors are somewhat too lean to balance it out. Still, a good white. • $11 • (04/30/96) • **81**

PANCAS, QUINTA DE

Alenquer 1990: A hearty red wine that's packed with fruit flavor and accented with spice. Tannic and full-bodied, but probably best to drink now while the fruit is fresh. 12,000 cases made. • $7 BB • **85**
Cabernet Sauvignon Alenquer Estate Bottled 1991: Round and polished, this fruity wine has good balance and bright flavors of plum and licorice. Cabernet Sauvignon-based, but it's not made for long aging, drink now. • $7 BB • **85**
Cabernet Sauvignon Estremadura Estate Bottled 1992: A deeply colored, ripe and flavorful red with solid cherry and berry flavors accented by spice. This is full-bodied and tannic but not harsh on the palate. • $NA • **83**

PARROTES, QUINTA DE

Alenquer 1992: Bright cherry flavor animates this round, fresh red, adding black pepper accents and light tannins. It has personality, if not much weight. • $7 • (03/31/96) • **83**

PORTUGAL

Alenquer 1991: The bright strawberry and cherry flavors remind us of Pinot Noir. This is easy-drinking, medium-bodied and charming, with plenty of fruit. • $NA • **84**
Alenquer Periquita 1990 • $6 • (04/15/94) BB • **83**

PASSADOURO, QUINTA DO

Vintage Port 1992: Not quite as great as when barrel-tasted last year. Ripe and roasted, medium-bodied and sweet, featuring round tannins and ripe fruit finish. Produced and bottled by Niepoort. Try in 1999. • $NA • **88**

PATO, LUIS

Bairrada 1988: A tannic, youthful and very flavorful red that is drinkable now. Packed with cranberry and raspberry flavor, difficult to say if more interesting flavors and a softer texture will emerge with time. 500 cases made. • $16 • **84**
Bairrada Oak Aged 1988: Rich, generous, almost chewy, with lots of raspberry and cranberry flavors backed by firm tannins and lively acidity. If you like assertive, robust reds, this is for you. Drink now. 500 cases made. • $17 • **85**
Bairrada Quinta do Ribeirinho Vinho Tinto 1990: Lively, juicy and fresh tasting, with plenty of fruit flavor and just enough tannin to give it a good bite. A straightforward style of wine to drink now. • $7 BB • **84**
Bairrada Vinhas Velhas 1990: Altogether agreeable. Smooth, well-rounded and flavorful, with ripe berry and plum flavors and a bit of vanilla from oak barrels to round it out. It even has a good finish. Drink now. 1,000 cases made. • $12 • **86**

PEDRA, QUINTA DA

Vinho Verde Alvarinho 1992 • $11 • (04/15/94) • **78**

PELLADA, QUINTA DA

Dão 1992: Ripe cherry, tomato and herb aromas and flavors are vibrant, accompanied by light, firm tannins and crisp acidity, could use depth and roundess. Drink now. • $10 • **80**

PEREIRA, MANUEL SALVADOR

Vinho Verde Alvarinho Dom Salvador 1994: Has excellent body and flavor for a normally lean white type. Combines fresh, floral, appley notes with crisp acidity and a nicely bitter finish that lingers. • $10 • (04/30/96) • **85**

PERIQUITA

Azeitao 1989 • $5 • (01/31/93) • **80**

PINTO, C.

Vinho do Porto Consolador NV • $7 • (03/31/88) • **78**

PINTOS DOS SANTOS, A.

Vintage Port 1985: May have matured too quickly in color and flavor. Medium ruby-red, with a spicy cherry nose, medium-bodied, with round, silky fruit flavors, light tannins and a light finish. • $NA • (01/01/90) • **69**
Vintage Port 1982 • $NA • (01/01/90) • **70**
Vintage Port 1980 • $NA • (01/01/90) • **70**
Vintage Port 1970 • $NA • (01/01/90) • **70**

POÇAS JUNIOR

Tawny Port 20-year-old NV • $35 • (02/28/90) • **89**
Vintage Port 1985: Hard and quite tough for a 1985, with lots of grapey, peppery flavors and a firm backbone, though it was still rather lean when last tasted. Purple with an inky center, black pepper nose, medium-bodied, with black pepper and fruit flavors, medium tannins and a hard finish. • $19 • (02/01/90) • **85**
Vintage Port 1975 • $42 • (02/01/90) • **74**
Vintage Port 1970 • $52 • (02/01/90) • **84**
Vintage Port 1963 • $100 • (02/01/90) • **82**
Vintage Port 1960 • $90 • (02/01/90) • **82**

POÇAS, PORTO

Vintage Port 1991: A medium-term Port with pretty fruit, medium-deep ruby color and perfumed cherry and blackberry aromas. Medium-bodied and very sweet with soft round texture, focused cherry and chocolate flavors and a medium finish. Try after 1997. • $NA • (07/31/94) • **84**

PORTA DA RAVESSA

Redondo 1990: A sturdy, straightforward red with generous plum flavors and moderate tannins. Good for drinking now. • $4 BB • **82**

PORTALEGRE

Alentejo 1990: Ripe, earthy tasting and full-bodied, with ample raspberry flavors. Fine for every day drinking with hearty food. 400 cases made. • $11 • **80**
Alentejo Conventual 1992: Some plum and cherry flavors struggle to the surface, but they're overwhelmed by earth and barnyard notes. 3,000 cases made. • $12 • (03/31/96) • **76**
Alentejo Conventual 1990 • $9 • (04/15/94) • **78**

PRIMAVERA, CAVES

Bairrada Colheita 1990: Round and fleshy, holding on to some cherry, meat and herb flavor, but the finish is dry and the future dim. • $5 • (03/31/96) • **76**
Dão 1989: Half of a nicely mature wine, with an attractively evolved bottle bouquet but austere flavors and a drying tannic texture. Browning in color, too. 35,000 cases made. • $5 • **74**

QUARLES HARRIS

Port Reserve Bottled in 1987 1940 • $70 • (01/31/88) • **96**
Ruby Port Club NV • $7 • (03/31/88) • **72**
Vintage Port 1985: Firm and well made, with a sufficient structure of fruit and tannin for long-term aging. Medium to deep ruby, light tomato and boysenberry nose, medium- to full-bodied, with medium tannins, spicy, peppery fruit flavors and a lingering finish. • $27 • (06/01/90) • **85**
Vintage Port 1983 • $31 • (02/01/90) • **89**
Vintage Port 1980 • $29 • (02/01/90) • **83**
Vintage Port 1977 • $43 • (02/01/90) • **89**
Vintage Port 1975 • $38 • (04/01/90) • **73**
Vintage Port 1970 • $52 • (02/01/90) • **89**
Vintage Port 1966 • $78 • (02/01/90) • **74**
Vintage Port 1963 • $95 • (02/01/90) • **85**

RAMOS-PINTO

Douro Duas Quintas 1991: Good but different. A concentrated and very fruity wine whose flavors are unusual and seemingly sweet-like prunes and nuts. 12,750 cases made. • $7 • **82**
Douro Duas Quintas Reserva 1992: Deliciously ripe and smooth, well crafted and integrated, offering loads of luscious plum, cherry and chocolate flavors, spicy aroma and lingering finish of blackberry jam. Drinkable now. • $16 • (03/31/96) • **86**
Douro Duas Quintas Reserva 1991: A good, middle-of-the-road quaff featuring plenty of jammy flavors. This would be fine to drink with barbecued foods, because of its nice, crisp acidity and lively fruit. • $16 • (03/31/96) • **84**
Ruby Port NV • $8 • (03/31/88) • **79**
Tawny Port 20-year-old Quinta Bom-Retiro NV • $39 • (02/28/90) • **84**
Tawny Port 30-year-old NV: Fabulous finish and plenty of walnut and toffee character. Full-bodied and incredibly sweet, offering a burnt

orange, nut flavor. Delicious old wine. 1,000 cases made. • $65 • (01/31/96) • **90**

Tawny Port Colheita 1937: Beautifully balanced old tawny boasting caramel, chocolate and nut character, full body and sweetness and long, long finish. Absolutely delicious. • $200 • (01/31/96) • **90**

Tawny Port Quinta da Ervamoira 10-year-old NV: Thick and very sweet maple syrup and toffee character, full body, long, walnut aftertaste. 5,000 cases made. • $25 • (01/31/96) • **86**

Tawny Port Quinta do Bom-Retiro 20-year-old NV: Fabulously complex and wonderful truffle, honey, cedar and tobacco box character. Medium to full in body, very sweet and a silky, opulent finish. Stunning. 2,000 cases made. • $48 • (01/31/96) HR • **93**

Tràs-os-Montes Quinta dos Bons Ares 1992: Polished and firm, this well-knit red offers plum, coffee and light earth flavors. Though not exuberantly fruity, it's harmonious and well balanced. Drinkable now. • $NA • **84**

Vintage Character Port Quinta da Urtiga NV • $17 • (03/15/94) • **86**

Vintage Port 1991: Big, fat, fruity style. Good, dark purple to ruby color. Grapey plum aromas, full-bodied and sweet, with a wonderfully smooth mouth-feel, loads of fruit and velvety tannins. Try after 1998. 5,500 cases made. • $26 • (07/31/94) • **86**

Vintage Port 1985: Very fine, though perhaps a little too elegant for longevity. Deep ruby, with incredibly fresh violet aromas, medium-bodied, with plenty of lovely, elegant, clean raspberry flavors, medium tannins and a balanced finish. • $37 • (11/01/89) • **85**

Vintage Port 1983 • $35 • (11/01/89) • **89**

Vintage Port 1982 • $15 Ⓐ • (11/01/89) • **79**

Vintage Port 1980 • $25 • (11/01/89) • **74**

Vintage Port 1970 • $85 • (11/01/89) • **81**

Vintage Port 1963 • $80 • (11/01/89) • **83**

REAL VINICOLA

Dão 1990: Tight and austere, revealing licorice and plum flavors. Finishes with a shot of tannins. • $NA • **79**

Douro Evel 1990: A distinctively spicy red that is full-bodied, ripe with fruit flavors and nicely balanced with moderate tannins and fresh acidity. Beginning to mature. Drink now. • $NA • **84**

REBELLO-VALENTE

Vintage Port 1985: Elegant and light for the vintage. Medium ruby, with a light raisin and black pepper nose, medium-bodied, with black pepper and fruit flavors and medium tannins. Lacks punch on the finish. • $33 • (06/01/90) • **81**

Vintage Port 1983 • $24 • (06/01/90) • **78**

Vintage Port 1980 • $41 • (02/01/90) • **80**

Vintage Port 1977 • $40 • (02/01/90) • **89**

Vintage Port 1975 • $53 • (02/01/90) • **75**

Vintage Port 1972 • $53 • (01/01/90) • **83**

Vintage Port 1970 • $50 • (02/01/90) • **92**

Vintage Port 1967 • $77 • (02/01/90) • **91**

Vintage Port 1966 • $60 • (02/01/90) • **82**

Vintage Port 1963 • $92 • (02/01/90) • **85**

Vintage Port 1960 • $55 • (11/01/88) • **85**

Vintage Port 1945 • $195 • (05/01/90) • **92**

Vintage Port 1942 • $140 • (02/01/85) • **75**

REGUENGOS DE MONSARAZ, COOPERATIVA

Alentejo Terras d'el Rei 1994: Youthful, modest flavors and little charm. Very jammy, showing light blackberry and raspberry notes. 250,000 cases made. • $4 • (04/30/96) • **78**

Alentejo Terras d'el Rei NV: This comes on like gangbusters, then seems to fade. Very flavorful, pungent blackberry and smoke flavors, moderate tannins and medium body. 500,000 cases made. • $4 • **80**

Key: SS—Spectator Selection. CS—Cellar Selection. BB—Best Buy. $NA—Price not available. (BT)—Barrel tasting. Ⓐ—Auction Price.
Dates in parentheses represent the issues in which the ratings were published.

Reguengos 1994: Luscious, featuring loads of exuberant blackberry and blueberry flavors framed by clove and cinnamon notes. Adds a touch of richness on the finish. A great bargain of a Portuguese red. 150,000 cases made. • $5 • (04/30/96) BB • **85**

Reguengos 1992: Vivid flavors of wild blackberry and chocolate make this an interesting red. It's medium-bodied, soft on tannins and ready to drink now. 126,500 cases made. • $5 • **84**

Reguengos 1990: An earthy aroma and muddy flavor mar this medium-bodied red. Pretty basic, dull stuff. • $5 • **71**

Reguengos Garrafeira dos Sócios 1990: Lots of vanilla and chocolate flavors, presumably from new oak barrels, make this a rich, almost sweet-tasting red. It's heavy on the oak, light on the tannins and good if you like this style. 6,300 cases made. • $12 • **83**

Reguengos Reserva 1990: A chalky, minerallike flavor brings this generally smooth red wine down to earth. It's medium-bodied, light in tannins and drinkable enough if you don't mind the earthy character. 9,400 cases made. • $8 • **78**

Reguengos Terras d'el Rei 1992: Soft and fruity with a hint of leather and spice in the aroma. Drink now while it's fresh. • $4 • **77**

Reguengos Terras d'el Rei Garrafeira 1987: A basic, simple red wine with ripe, pruny flavors and moderate tannins. • $10 • **77**

Reguengos Terras d'el Rei Reserva 1987: Mature and earthy in aroma and flavor, with enough fruit hanging in there to keep it drinkable. • $7 • **77**

ROBERTSON

Ruby Port Fine NV • $9 • (03/31/88) • **77**

Tawny Port 20-year-old Imperial NV • $33 • (02/28/90) • **81**

ROCHA

Vintage Port 1985: Beautifully focused cherry, nutmeg and exotic spice aromas and flavors carry through to the long, finely balanced finish, offering just the right hint of toast and spirit. A wine with elegance and grip that should age nicely through at least 2000. • $32 • (04/15/91) • **88**

Vintage Port 1977 • $19 • (04/30/91) • **81**

ROMANEIRA, QUINTA DA

Port Quinta das Liceiras 1992: Best ever from here. Very powerful wet earth and ripe fruit character. Medium- to full-bodied, medium sweet, exhibiting sleek tannins and a medium finish. Try in 1999. • $NA • **89**

Vintage Port 1987: Earthy and well structured, showing aging potential. Medium to deep purple, with earthy grape aromas, full-bodied, with lots of tannins and a good depth of earthy fruit flavors. • $NA • (01/01/90) • **81**

Vintage Port 1985: Very rustic in style. Medium ruby, with an earthy licorice nose, medium-bodied, with round tannins, good fruit flavors and some grip on the finish. • $29 • (01/01/90) • **78**

Vintage Port 1935 • $NA • (02/01/90) • **90**

ROQUEVALE

Alentejo Terras de Xisto 1990 • $5 • (04/15/94) • **77**

Alentejo Tinto da Talha 1992 • $7 • (04/15/94) • **79**

Redondo Vinho de Redondo 1990 • $6 • (04/15/94) • **77**

ROSA, QUINTA DE LA

Douro 1992: Bright cassis and raspberry fruit give this soft, fleshy wine appeal for current drinking. It's fresh and likeable. • $8 • **83**

Douro 1991: Ripe and jammy tasting with moderate tannins, a deep color and lasting fruit flavors. Young and exuberant, drink now for vitality. • $10 • **85**

Vintage Character Port Finest Reserve NV • $15 • (03/15/94) • **84**

Vintage Port 1992: Best La Rosa ever made. Very ripe, chocolaty, hot fruit character, medium body, racy tannins and long finish. Well integrated and elegant. Try in 2000. • $NA • **88**

Vintage Port 1991: Dark and inky, with green tea, tobacco and raspberry aromas. This is tight and tannic, with a sleek and steely structure.

May still need time. Tasted twice, second bottle much better. Try after 1998. 1,600 cases made. • $NA • (07/31/94) • **86**

Vintage Port 1988: Ripe and raisiny, with layers of currant, plum and anise flavors. Is also a bit hot, with chewy tannins and a hint of cedar on the aftertaste. Was rough-edged, but may be better now. • $18 • (04/15/92) • **85**

Vintage Port 1972 • $NA • (10/01/89) • **76**

Vintage Port 1966 • $NA • (10/01/89) • **82**

Vintage Port 1963 • $NA • (10/01/89) • **85**

Vintage Port 1960 • $NA • (10/01/89) • **88**

Vintage Port Feuerheerd Quinta de la Rosa 1927 • $NA • (12/01/89) • **87**

ROYAL OPORTO

Ruby Port NV • $7 • (03/31/88) • **68**

Tawny Port 20-year-old NV • $25 • (02/28/90) • **77**

Vintage Port 1987: A hard-edged, brandy-scented style of Port that comes through with enough plum and cherry flavors on the finish to suggest it should age well through 2001 to 2005. • $19 • (11/30/91) • **81**

Vintage Port 1985: This has some fruit but it is too evolved for a 1985. Medium ruby, with a grapey, raisiny nose, medium-bodied, with sweet, berry flavors and round tannins. Maturing quickly. • $16 Ⓐ • (06/01/90) • **71**

Vintage Port 1984 • $14 • (11/01/89) • **65**

Vintage Port 1983 • $14 • (06/01/90) • **76**

Vintage Port 1982 • $14 • (06/01/90) • **60**

Vintage Port 1980 • $20 • (06/01/90) • **60**

Vintage Port 1978 • $24 • (11/01/89) • **68**

Vintage Port 1977 • $30 • (11/01/89) • **74**

Vintage Port 1970 • $36 • (11/01/89) • **75**

Vintage Port 1967 • $30 • (11/01/89) • **72**

Vintage Port 1963 • $55 • (11/01/89) • **73**

Vintage Port 1871 • $NA • (11/01/89) • **98**

ROZES

Late Bottled Port 1985: Somewhat tired already for an '85. Shows tobacco, cedar and plum aromas and flavors, with cigar notes on the finish. Drink up. • $17 • (01/31/96) • **79**

Ruby Port Infanta Isabel 10-year-old NV: Clean and well made, featuring plum, almond and hazelnut character. Medium-bodied, not too sweet and has a focused, fruity, nutty aftertaste. • $20 • (01/31/96) • **85**

Vintage Port 1991: A relatively new face in Vintage Port and improving. The 1991 Rozes is elegant with solid berry and cherry aromas and flavors, medium body, medium sweetness and tannins and a sweet finish. Try after 1999. 5,000 cases made. • $23 • (07/31/94) • **87**

Vintage Port 1987: Elegant, lovely flavors, but early in maturing. Inky center with a ruby edge, a slight tar and cassis nose, full-bodied, with fresh, sweet, ripe raspberry flavors, firm tannins and a long, elegant, slightly nutty finish. • $NA • (06/01/90) • **86**

Vintage Port 1985: A good, rather chewy 1985 with a solid concentration of flavorful fruit and round tannins. Deep ruby with a red hue, pretty, light cherry aromas, full-bodied, with delicious, round, chewy fruit flavors, medium tannins and a sweet finish. Slightly simple. • $21 • (05/01/90) • **81**

Vintage Port 1982 • $NA • (06/01/90) • **75**

SAES, QUINTA DE

Dão 1992: There's a nice spiciness here, reminiscent of white pepper. Smooth, supple and round, delivering plum and dried cherry flavors which linger on the finish. • $10 • (04/30/96) • **82**

Dão 1990: Rich and meaty, with jammy plum and prune fruit flavors, this is straightforward, bright and lively. Drinkable now. Tasted twice, the other bottle was oxidized. • $9 • **84**

SANDEMAN

Ruby Port Fine NV • $8 • (03/31/88) • **78**

Tawny Port 20-year-old NV: A very well-aged tawny boasting wonderful honey, almond, nut and orange character. Medium-bodied and very sweet, delicate, silky texture and long, long finish. Tasted twice, with consistent notes. • $42 • (01/31/96) HR • **91**

Tawny Port 20-year-old Imperial NV • $29 • (02/28/90) • **87**

Tawny Port Royal NV • $13 • (01/01/85) • **76**

Vintage Character Port Founders Reserve NV • $17 • (03/15/94) • **81**

Vintage Port 1985: Elegant and balanced, but a little short on concentration. Medium ruby-purple, with a spicy plum nose, medium-bodied, with clean fruit flavors, medium tannins and finish. • $30 • (06/01/90) • **83**

Vintage Port 1982 • $36 • (06/01/90) • **82**

Vintage Port 1980 • $18 Ⓐ • (06/01/90) • **85**

Vintage Port 1977 • $28 Ⓐ • (06/01/90) • **85**

Vintage Port 1975 • $38 • (03/01/90) • **78**

Vintage Port 1970 • $30 Ⓐ • (03/01/90) • **83**

Vintage Port 1967 • $58 • (03/01/90) • **90**

Vintage Port 1966 • $75 • (07/15/90) • **90**

Vintage Port 1963 • $39 Ⓐ • (07/15/90) • **96**

Vintage Port 1960 • $26 Ⓐ • (07/15/90) • **79**

Vintage Port 1958 • $43 Ⓐ • (03/01/90) • **82**

Vintage Port 1957 • $NA • (10/01/88) • **85**

Vintage Port 1955 • $151 Ⓐ • (03/01/90) • **94**

Vintage Port 1950 • $170 • (03/01/90) • **87**

Vintage Port 1947 • $185 Ⓐ • (03/01/90) • **90**

Vintage Port 1945 • $201 Ⓐ • (03/01/90) • **95**

Vintage Port 1942 • $150 • (03/01/90) • **88**

Vintage Port 1935 • $320 • (03/01/90) • **92**

Vintage Port 1934 • $202 Ⓐ • (03/01/90) • **94**

Vintage Port 1927 • $30 • (03/01/90) • **92**

Vintage Port 1920 • $190 • (03/01/90) • **78**

Vintage Port 1917 • $175 • (03/01/90) • **88**

Vintage Port 1911 • $280 • (06/01/90) • **82**

Vintage Port 1908 • $320 • (03/01/90) • **75**

Vintage Port 1904 • $420 • (03/01/90) • **88**

Vintage Port 1896 • $400 • (03/01/90) • **81**

Vintage Port 1887 • $600 • (03/01/90) • **74**

Vintage Port 1870 • $700 • (03/01/90) • **98**

SÂO JOÃO, CAVES

Bairrada 1985: A lean, mature but dull wine with smoky, tarry aromas, modest fruit flavor and a tart finish. 15,000 cases made. • $6 • **78**

Bairrada Frei João 1989: Brownish-red color, vegetal aromas and thin flavors make this seem overly mature. Drinkable, but not much fun. 12,500 cases made. • $6 • **73**

Bairrada Frei João Reserva 1985: This deeply colored, nicely mature red has spicy, complex aromas, full fruit flavors and a lingering finish. At its peak of drinking pleasure in 1995. 3,500 cases made. • $13 • (04/30/95) • **85**

Bairrada Frei João Reserva 1983: Fully mature, with sweet cherry, tobacco and light mushroom flavors, it has balance and even grace. Drink now. 4,600 cases made. • $13 • **81**

Bairrada Reserva 1983: Fairly well preserved, and showing some complexities of flavor. A lean style with modest plum and cherry flavors and a crisp finish. 7,000 cases made. • $14 • **79**

Dão Porta dos Cavaleiros 1988: A good mix of plum and cherry gives way to a tough and tannic finish, mineral quality persists. 14,000 cases made. • $6 • **79**

Dão Porta dos Cavaleiros 1986: A very mature wine, from the brownish color to the spicy, leathery aromas and thinning but complex fruit flavors. Drink now. 15,000 cases made. • $6 • **80**

Dão Porta dos Cavaleiros 1984: The color is still deep in this wine, but the mature aromas and flavors show earthy and raisin flavors and the finish is dry. Drink up. 4,200 cases made. • $12 • (04/30/95) • **78**

Dão Porta dos Cavaleiros Reserva 1985: Attractively mature in aroma and flavor, with a spicy accent to the solid fruit character. Well-balanced, still vital, but gaining the complexity of age. Drink now. 8,000 cases made. • $12 • **85**

Dão Reserva 1985: Generous, mature aromas of plum, earth and vanilla make this an intriguing older wine. Smooth and fruity, complete and well balanced, lingering finish. 9,500 cases made. • $14 • **84**

SMITH WOODHOUSE

Port Oporto Portugal Bicentennial NV • $9 • (06/01/85) • **79**
Ruby Port Rich NV • $8 • (03/31/88) • **74**
Vintage Character Port Lodge Reserve NV • $15 • (06/15/93) • **82**
Vintage Port 1992: Wet earth, stemmy and ripe fruit character. Fresh, medium in body and sweetness, offering fine tannins and a medium finish. Drink in 1999. • $33 • **88**
Vintage Port 1991: Not showing as well as expected when last tasted, but very good nonetheless. Elegant and refined. Lovely and balanced with a silky finish. Medium-bodied, medium-sweet and fruity. Tasted twice with consistent notes. Try after 1998. 2,500 cases made. • $36 • (07/31/94) • **87**
Vintage Port 1985: I have tasted this blind with all the other big-name 1985s and it often holds its own. Medium deep ruby, with lovely violet aromas, full-bodied, with plenty of grip, full tannins and a powerful finish. • $33 • (06/01/90) • **89**
Vintage Port 1983 • $12 Ⓐ • (06/01/90) • **92**
Vintage Port 1980 • $33 • (06/01/90) • **90**
Vintage Port 1977 • $25 Ⓐ • (02/01/90) • **89**
Vintage Port 1975 • $40 • (02/01/90) • **80**
Vintage Port 1970 • $58 • (02/01/90) • **86**
Vintage Port 1966 • $75 • (02/01/90) • **83**
Vintage Port 1963 • $85 • (02/01/90) • **89**

SOGRAPE

Alentejo Vinha do Monte 1992: Here's a bruiser. Deeply colored, highly extracted, tannic and robust, showing some plum, prune and tobacco flavors. A good steak would tame it, or perhaps another year in bottle. 7,980 cases made. • $9 • (03/31/96) • **85**
Alentejo Vinha do Monte 1991: Mineral and cedar aromas and palate remind us of Bordeaux's Graves, rich, ripe plum and sweet currant flavors and plenty of tannin for backbone. Drink now or hold just a bit. • $9 • (04/30/95) • **86**
Bairrada Terra Franca 1985: Eight years is pushing the limit here. Stewed vegetal aromas and flavors dominate, and the finish is drying. Drink up. Tasted twice with consistent notes. • $7 • **72**
Dão Duque de Viseu 1992: A rich and deep Portuguese red that gives you lively plum flavor, supported by coffee and chocolate notes, good concentration and ripe tannins. It's fresh and more complex than most of its peers. Drinkable now and through 2000. 18,656 cases made. • $9 • (03/31/96) BB • **87**
Dão Duque de Viseu 1991: Slightly on the rustic side, sporting earthy and smoky notes and rude tannins, still offers concentration and sweet cherry flavor. Drink now. • $9 • **83**
Dão Duque de Viseu 1990: A smooth-textured, nicely balanced red wine with bright fruit flavors and a touch of oak. Harmonious and pleasant to drink now, since it's not too tannic. • $10 • **85**
Dão Grão Vasco 1992: Light-bodied but firm, this brisk red offers cherry, smoky and light herbal flavors. It's well knit and a good accompaniment for food. 300,000 cases made. • $5 • (03/31/96) • **81**
Dão Grão Vasco 1990: This average quality red wine has herbal, spicy aromas and modest fruit flavor. Decent and drinkable, but simple. • $7 • **77**
Dão Reserva 1985: A solidly flavorful, mature wine whose peppery, woody aromas and blackberry flavors will make for good, hearty drinking. Still tannic, but OK to drink now. • $11 • **83**
Douro Mateus 1990: This is not your father's Mateus. It's firm, still young, with herbal and tar notes. A bit lean, drink now. • $7 • **80**
Douro Mateus Signature 1992: Good dried cherry and earthy flavors and aromas. A pleasant, fully mature red that's ready to drink now. 20,204 cases made. • $6 • (04/30/96) • **80**
Douro Mateus Signature 1989: A soft and easy red wine with a low tannin level and generous fruit. Simple but good. 244,000 cases made. • $9 • **80**

Key: SS—Spectator Selection. CS—Cellar Selection. BB—Best Buy. $NA—Price not available. (BT)—Barrel tasting. Ⓐ—Auction Price.
Dates in parentheses represent the issues in which the ratings were published.

Douro Reserva 1992: Well made, concentrated, firmly tannic and rich with ripe black cherry flavor. Herb, vanilla and cedar notes linger on the finish. Pleasant now, it should be better in 1997. 7,090 cases made. • $10 • (03/31/96) • **85**
Douro Reserva 1990: Deep color and lively fruit testify to this wine's youth and concentration. It's big, with ripe plum and cassis flavors and plenty of tannin for backbone. Drinkable now. • $10 • (04/30/95) • **89**
Douro Reserva 1987: An elegant, modestly proportioned, mature red wine with cedary, spicy aromas and mellow raspberry flavors. • $11 • **83**
Douro Vila Regia 1990: Soft in texture but thick with seemingly sweet fruit flavors. Easy to drink but simple. • $7 • **78**
Vinho Verde Quinta de Azevedo 1993: Unusual, awkward. It smells ripe and peachy, tastes herbal and crisp, then turns so tart it makes your mouth pucker on the finish. • $7 • (07/31/95) • **75**

SOPÉ DA ENCOSTA

Ribatejo 1994: Fruity and simple. Raspberry flavors are reminiscent of a nouveau style. • $5 • (03/31/96) • **78**

SOUSELAS, ADEGA COOPERATIVA DE

Bairrada Reserva 1987: The cedary, almost musty aromas and tart, astringent cranberry flavors don't add up to much enjoyment for us. 19,000 cases made. • $5 • **75**

SYMINGTON

Vintage Port Quinta do Vesùvio 1990 • $45 • (01/31/93) • **83**

TAYLOR FLADGATE

Late Bottled Port 1989: A wonderful and very grapey LBV. Why waste a young vintage Port when this is available? Medium body and sweetness, with loads of currant and mint flavors. • $16 • (01/31/96) • **87**
Late Bottled Port 1988: Smooth, rich and flavorful, with a nice balance of fruit and spice. Plummy and raisiny, with spice flavors matched by chocolate notes. Fairly round and soft, but still has plenty of alcohol. Drinkable now. • $17 • (11/15/94) • **85**
Late Bottled Port Vintage 1986 • $16 • (06/15/93) • **83**
Port Special Club NV • $13 • (02/16/85) • **84**
Ruby Port Special NV • $8 • (03/31/88) • **78**
Tawny Port 10-year-old NV: Reduced flavors of toffee, tobacco and plum and hints of dried herbs. Impressively concentrated and sweet, adding a somewhat hot, peppery finish. Slightly unharmonious. Tasted twice, with consistent notes. • $22 • (01/31/96) • **84**
Tawny Port 20-year-old NV: • $42 • (01/31/96) • **84**
Tawny Port 30-year-old NV: Smells old but tastes much younger. Full body and very sweet plum, nut and chocolate flavors and sweet finish. Astringent, slightly volatile character detracts. • $81 • (01/31/96) • **81**
Tawny Port 40-year-old NV: Some pretty walnut, caramel and citric character, medium body and sweetness, round and smooth mouth-feel. Slightly short finish. • $102 • (01/31/96) • **86**
Vintage Character Port First Estate Lugar das Lages NV • $16 • (03/15/94) • **85**
Vintage Port 1992: The finest Taylor vintage since 1977 and a tribute to the firm's 300th anniversary. Powerful wet earth, grape, violet and berry aromas and flavors, full body, medium sweetness and long finish. Closing up quickly, try in 2000. • $37 • **95**
Vintage Port 1985: Extremely understated and closed, it starts out slowly but finishes quickly. Deep ruby-purple, with berry and cherry aromas and flavors, full-bodied, very tannic and hard. Great future. • $40 • (06/01/90) • **90**
Vintage Port 1983 • $35 • (06/01/90) • **89**
Vintage Port 1980 • $41 • (06/01/90) • **88**
Vintage Port 1977 • $70 • (04/01/90) • **98**
Vintage Port 1975 • $47 • (12/01/89) • **78**
Vintage Port 1970 • $70 • (12/01/89) • **98**
Vintage Port 1966 • $80 • (12/01/89) • **89**
Vintage Port 1963 • $140 • (12/01/89) • **97**
Vintage Port 1960 • $100 • (10/31/88) • **84**
Vintage Port 1955 • $200 • (11/01/89) • **88**

Vintage Port 1948 • $330 • (11/01/89) • **99**
Vintage Port 1945 • $525 • (11/01/89) • **97**
Vintage Port 1942 • $275 • (04/01/90) • **78**
Vintage Port 1938 • $265 • (04/01/90) • **79**
Vintage Port 1935 • $390 • (02/01/90) • **88**
Vintage Port 1927 • $350 • (12/01/89) • **95**
Vintage Port Quinta de Vargellas 1991: The greatest Vargellas ever produced. Offers an explosion of fruit flavor. Deep dark purple color, with amazing cassis and chocolate aromas. Thick and rich, medium-sweet, full tannins but racy and fine. Try after 2000. 4,000 cases made. • $NA • (07/31/94) • **94**
Vintage Port Quinta de Vargellas 1987: Rich, thick and concentrated, like pure crème de cassis. Deep purple, with a powerful nose of cassis and perfume, full-bodied, with masses of fruit flavors and plenty of tannins. A monumental wine. • $NA • (02/01/90) • **93**
Vintage Port Quinta de Vargellas 1986: Surprisingly tough and big for a 1986. Deep inky color, with an intense nose of anise and blackberries, full-bodied, with an excellent tannic backbone and long, rich violet and berry flavors on the finish. • $NA • (02/01/90) • **88**
Vintage Port Quinta de Vargellas 1984 • $NA • (02/01/90) • **87**
Vintage Port Quinta de Vargellas 1982 • $NA • (02/01/90) • **81**
Vintage Port Quinta de Vargellas 1978 • $34 • (02/01/90) • **85**
Vintage Port Quinta de Vargellas 1976 • $42 • (02/01/90) • **81**
Vintage Port Quinta de Vargellas 1974 • $36 • (02/01/90) • **78**
Vintage Port Quinta de Vargellas 1972 • $48 • (02/01/90) • **84**
Vintage Port Quinta de Vargellas 1969 • $50 • (02/01/90) • **85**
Vintage Port Quinta de Vargellas 1968 • $61 • (02/01/90) • **82**
Vintage Port Quinta de Vargellas 1967 • $50 • (02/01/90) • **82**
Vintage Port Quinta de Vargellas 1965 • $55 • (02/01/90) • **80**
Vintage Port Quinta de Vargellas 1964 • $50 • (07/01/90) • **75**
Vintage Port Quinta de Vargellas 1961 • $45 • (02/01/90) • **68**
Vintage Port Quinta de Vargellas 1958 • $55 • (02/01/90) • **68**

TEODOSIO, CAVES DOM

Bairrada Teodósio 1990: Nice balance, smooth texture, medium body, tart cherry flavors and moderate tannins, adding a nip of astringency on the finish. • $NA • **78**
Cartaxo Quinta do Bairro Falcão 1993: Fleshy black cherry and light earth flavors, soft and round. Straightforward but drinking well now. 5,600 cases made. • $7 • (03/31/96) • **82**
Cartaxo Quinta do Bairro Falcão 1992: This is straightforward, drinkable red wine that's been aged too long already for our tastes. Getting a bit brownish in color and thin in flavor. • $NA • **75**
Cartaxo Quinta do Bairro Falcão 1991: Generous and very fruity, with firm tannins and a lingering finish. It tastes bright and fresh. Drink now. 5,600 cases made. • $6 BB • **84**
Dão Cardeal 1991: Medium-bodied and mature in taste, sporting cherry and mineral flavors, smoky aroma and a slightly tannic finish. Drinkable now while it's still lively. • $6 • (03/31/96) • **84**
Dão Cardeal 1989: A well-balanced, mature wine with nice plum and cherry flavors and aromas. Full-bodied and a bit tannic, but still enjoyable. Finishes with some good spice flavors. • $5 • (04/30/95) • **85**
Dão Casaleiro 1990: Tastes and smells candied, with a sharp note of astringency on the finish. The flavors are dominated by a resinous taste. • $NA • **76**
Dão Casaleiro Garrafeira 1985: Distinctive olive and herbal flavors and aromas. Full-bodied and a little earthy, it's a good workmanlike red. • $NA • **83**
Dão Teodósio Garrafiera 1985: Full-bodied and fairly mature, but still fresh and vibrant, mint and spice flavors wrap around a solid core of plum and cherry. Long finish. • $9 • (04/30/95) • **86**
Estremoz Casaleiro Garrafeira 1992: An easy going, slightlty sweet red with simple fruit flavors and hints of brown sugar. Average quality. • $NA • **78**
Estremoz Casaleiro Garrafeira 1982: Distinctive and mature. A big old wine with attractive anise and olive flavors and plenty of tannin. Chewy and rich on the palate, the flavors linger on the finish. 6,700 cases made. • $9 • **84**
Estremoz Casaleiro Garrafeira Particular 1980: A brownish-red color and pungent aromas that remind us of motor oil and shoe polish aren't appetizing. The flavors are mature and leathery and the finish is astringent and tough. • $NA • **73**
Santarém Cabeça de Toiro Reserva 1991: Light and silky, this mature red shows cedar, tea and spice flavors and a slightly dry finish. Better accompanying food. 2,500 cases made. • $10 • (03/31/96) • **79**
Tomar Quinta de S. João Batista 1992: Mature and soft, this offers raisin, smoke and light herbal flavors in a supple, spicy package. Not rich but sweetly agreeable. 7,000 cases made. • $7 • (03/31/96) • **82**
Tomar Quinta de S. João Batista 1991: Rather rustic in flavor and coarse in style, this is a hearty, simple red with full body and fairly stiff tannins. • $NA • **76**
Vista do Vale NV: Drinkable, but rather tired and astringent. Has a dull, brownish red color and thin fruit flavors. • $NA • **74**

TERRA DE LOBOS

Ribatejo 1992: A tremendous value. Tastes like a rich Beaujolais, from the fresh, jammy aromas to the moderate tannins and lingering, fruity finish. Drink now while it's fresh. 16,800 cases made. • $5 • (04/30/95) • **86**

VAL DA FIGUEIRA, QUINTA DE

Vintage Port 1987: Extremely well crafted, with a firm structure of medium tannins, fresh strawberry flavors and a floral finish. The fruit and tannins are well integrated and focused on the palate. Great potential here for a new Douro shipper. • $NA • (02/01/90) • **83**

VALDARCOS, CAVES

Bairrada Garrafeira 1987: An interesting but lean and mature wine whose tart and astringent finish leaves a tough impression. Difficult to warm up to. • $NA • **79**
Bairrada Reserva 1989: A mature wine with herb and spice accents to the modest fruit character. Fairly lean and crisp in style, but it leans toward green, vegetal flavors. • $NA • **78**

VAN ZELLER

Vintage Port 1985: Not as good as the 1983, but it shows some power and robust fruit. It should be ready sooner than the 1983. Deep purple with a red hue, spicy raisin and plum nose, medium-bodied, with sweet raisin flavors that seem slightly burnt. Good tannic backbone. • $NA • (01/01/90) • **80**
Vintage Port 1983 • $38 • (01/01/90) • **84**
Vintage Port Quinta do Roriz 1985 • $NA • (07/01/90) • **87**
Vintage Port Quinta do Roriz 1983 • $22 • (07/01/90) • **84**
Vintage Port Quinta do Roriz 1970 • $NA • (07/01/90) • **86**
Vintage Port Quinta do Roriz 1960 • $NA • (07/01/90) • **83**

VASCONCELLOS

Vintage Port Butler & Nephew 1975 • $30 • (07/01/90) • **74**
Vintage Port Butler & Nephew 1970 • $45 • (07/01/90) • **76**
Vintage Port Gonzalez Byass 1970 • $50 • (06/01/90) • **81**
Vintage Port Gonzalez Byass 1963 • $82 • (07/01/90) • **87**

VELHAS, CAVES

Alentejo 1991 • $6 • (04/15/94) • **76**
Palmela Romeira 1990: Ripe fruit and soft tannins make this an attractive wine for drinking now. It tastes of black cherry, licorice and shows an attractive light herbal note in the finish. • $7 • (04/30/95) • **84**
Palmela Romeira 1989 • $7 • (04/15/94) • **76**

VESÚVIO, QUINTA DO

Vintage Port 1992: Fabulous Vesuvio, best ever, better than remembered and improving all the time. Amazing wet earth and ripe fruit character, full in body and very sleek, offering hard tannins and fresh flavors. Needs time to round off its rough edges, try in 2003. 1,962 cases made. • $49 • **94**

Vintage Port 1991: Loads of character in this one. You can almost smell the soil. Very powerful and impressive, with masses of tannins and medium sweetness. It shows opulent aromas and flavors of wet earth, green tea and berry. A tough young wine that needs to age. Tasted twice with consistent notes. Try after 2000. 1,300 cases made. • $48 • (07/31/94) • **91**

VIEIRA DE SOUSA

Vintage Port 1985: Pleasant flavors and aromas, but lacks depth and body. Medium ruby, with a light, earthy beet and berry nose, medium-bodied, with light tannins and advanced flavors. • $NA • (01/01/90) • **70**
Vintage Port 1980 • $NA • (01/01/90) • **70**
Vintage Port 1978 • $NA • (01/01/90) • **74**
Vintage Port 1970 • $NA • (01/01/90) • **71**

WARRE

Ruby Port Fine Selected NV • $8 • (03/31/88) • **84**
Tawny Port 20-year-old Nimrod NV • $38 • (02/28/90) • **84**
Tawny Port Reserve 1968: It's so sweet it hurts your teeth. Complex, tasty tawny boasting dried herb, flan and burnt sugar character and full body. Wild thing. • $65 • (01/31/96) • **88**
Tawny Port Sir William 10-year-old NV: Fresher style of 10-year-old Port offering nutty, grapey and cedar-spice character, medium body and sweetness and short, slightly hot finish. • $25 • (01/31/96) • **82**
Tawny Port Very Finest Rare Nimrod NV • $24 • (04/15/91) • **85**
Vintage Character Port Warrior Finest Reserve NV • $14 • (03/15/94) • **80**
Vintage Port 1991: This is feminine in style, with lovely berry and grapey aromas and flavors. The finish, however, is packed with fruit and tannins—it's got grip.Try after 2000. 6,000 cases made. • $35 • (07/31/94) • **91**
Vintage Port 1985: There is plenty of grip and backbone here. Deep purple, with concentrated grape and violet aromas, full-bodied, with huge grapey flavors, excellent backbone and a long finish. • $18 Ⓐ • (06/01/90) • **91**
Vintage Port 1983 • $16 Ⓐ • (06/01/90) • **88**
Vintage Port 1980 • $26 Ⓐ • (06/01/90) • **88**
Vintage Port 1977 • $32 Ⓐ • (04/01/90) • **92**
Vintage Port 1975 • $23 Ⓐ • (10/31/88) • **74**
Vintage Port 1970 • $34 Ⓐ • (12/01/89) • **88**
Vintage Port 1966 • $41 Ⓐ • (06/01/89) • **91**
Vintage Port 1963 • $65 Ⓐ • (12/01/89) • **92**
Vintage Port 1960 • $33 Ⓐ • (10/31/88) • **90**
Vintage Port 1958 • $53 Ⓐ • (11/01/89) • **81**
Vintage Port 1955 • $230 • (11/01/89) • **86**
Vintage Port 1947 • $214 Ⓐ • (11/01/89) • **88**
Vintage Port 1945 • $360 • (11/01/89) • **87**
Vintage Port 1934 • $285 • (02/01/90) • **87**
Vintage Port 1927 • $300 • (12/01/89) • **93**
Vintage Port 1900 • $430 • (11/01/89) • **79**
Vintage Port Quinta da Cavadinha 1992: A surprising improvement from the barrel tasting last year. It's solid, sleek and racy, featuring fine tannins and an ironlike backbone. Full-bodied, medium-sweet and reserved. This will age long, try in 2003. 2,100 cases made. • $26 • (06/30/95) • **91**
Vintage Port Quinta da Cavadinha 1987: This is quite hard for the normally delicate and fruity wines of Cavadinha. Deep purple, with very grapey, floral aromas, full-bodied, with a hard, tannic backbone and a short finish. Very good level of fruit flavors. May still need time. • $NA • (02/01/90) • **86**
Vintage Port Quinta da Cavadinha 1986: Very fleshy and elegant for a 1986 and as good as the impressive 1987. It may be one of the best 1986s. Excellent deep inky color, with a nose of tar and berries, full-bodied, with ripe, fleshy fruit flavors, full tannins and a gutsy finish. Good grip. • $NA • (02/01/90) • **85**
Vintage Port Quinta da Cavadinha 1984 • $NA • (02/01/90) • **81**
Vintage Port Quinta da Cavadinha 1982 • $NA • (02/01/90) • **86**
Vintage Port Quinta da Cavadinha 1979 • $25 • (07/31/90) • **82**
Vintage Port Quinta da Cavadinha 1978 • $28 • (02/01/90) • **83**

WIESE & KROHN

Tawny Port 20-year-old NV • $33 • (02/28/90) • **88**
Vintage Port 1985: This has attractive roasted coffee aromas and flavors in a more forward style than many of the top 1985s. Deep ruby with a purple edge, a bitter chocolate and coffee nose, full-bodied, with a velvety mouth-feel, medium tannins and a sweet finish. • $32 • (01/01/90) • **81**
Vintage Port 1984 • $20 • (01/01/90) • **86**
Vintage Port 1982 • $32 • (01/01/90) • **83**
Vintage Port 1978 • $37 • (01/01/90) • **84**
Vintage Port 1975 • $49 • (01/01/90) • **80**
Vintage Port 1970 • $75 • (01/01/90) • **74**
Vintage Port 1967 • $65 • (01/01/90) • **75**
Vintage Port 1965 • $100 • (01/01/90) • **85**
Vintage Port 1963 • $145 • (01/01/90) • **87**
Vintage Port 1961 • $125 • (01/01/90) • **85**
Vintage Port 1960 • $115 • (01/01/90) • **89**
Vintage Port 1958 • $180 • (01/01/90) • **87**

Key: SS—Spectator Selection. CS—Cellar Selection. BB—Best Buy. $NA—Price not available. (BT)—Barrel tasting. Ⓐ—Auction Price.
Dates in parentheses represent the issues in which the ratings were published.

Spain

With 3,500,000 acres, Spain has more vineyards under cultivation than Italy or France. Yet it makes only about half as much wine as Italy and 75 percent as much as France. Moreover, the style of its wine has remained staunchly nationalistic, reflecting the domestic preference for mellow, wood-aged red wines with a strong oak component and light tannins. Many of these wines are made from native grape varieties and vinified in a very traditional style.

However, things are changing. Alongside the traditional styles there is emerging a new breed of modern wines vinified in a fresher, fruitier style. These are becoming more popular, and are helping Spanish wine producers to compete more successfully in the world arena. The Spanish government has actively supported these developments, encouraging investment in new technologies and equipment, and helping its producers to explore world markets. With these efforts and much private initiative, Spain's back-seat position in western European winemaking should soon be a thing of the past.

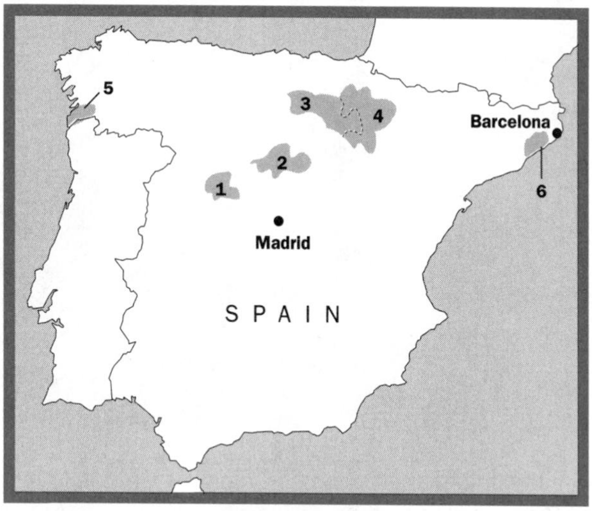

1. Rueda
2. Ribera del Duero
3. Rioja
4. Navarra
5. Rias Baixas
6. Penedès

SPAIN'S WINE REGIONS

Rioja

Spain has an excellent climate and a vast range of *terroirs* that are suitable for producing quality wines. Rioja is one region that has already made a name for itself. The modern history of Rioja dates back to the last century, when French vignerons from Bordeaux fled the phylloxera epidemic and set up house in this northerly region. As a result of their influence and techniques, the Rioja style offers a good deal of refinement. Basic Rioja, most often designated *crianza* (wood-aged), is marked by the vanilla and smoky tones of American oak overlaying the faintly earthy, spicy notes of the Tempranillo grape. Most *crianza* should be drunk within five years of the vintage. Above the *crianza* level are the reservas and gran reservas. Both are selections from the best vats of the harvest and are usually made only in better years. Gran reservas, which spend the most time in oak, can be profound, provided one has cultivated a taste for the traditional wood-dominated, autumnal flavors and aromas of older Rioja. The best Rioja producers include Marques de Riscal, Marques de Murrieta, Martinez Bujanda and CUNE.

Ribera del Duero

The Ribera del Duero region to the south of Rioja has for decades been producing wines that rival the world's best, including the legendary, fabulously rare and expensive Vega Sicilia, and the less expensive Pesquera.

While the average quality in this region is high, styles vary considerably. Vega Sicilia represents the traditional approach, using older wood barrels and extensive aging, and has similarities to Rioja. Recently, the more exuberant style epitomized by Pesquera has taken hold. Pesquera uses new French and American oak, and the flavor has more in common with a vigorous young Bordeaux than with Vega Sicilia. Other producers to watch are Alion and Ismael Arroyo.

Navarra

Next to Rioja is the Navarra district. Once known strictly for its rosés, it is now producing deeply pigmented, often exciting wines from Tempranillo, Grenache (here called Garnacha) and Cabernet.

The original winery of cava producer Raimat, which now makes Chardonnay and Cabernet Sauvignon as well.

Experimentation with Cabernet and Merlot has added herbal notes to the bouquet and flavors of Tempranillo-dominated wines, as well as a bit more authority on the finish.

Penedès

The Penedès region is home to two of Spain's most forward-thinking wineries, Torres and Jean León. The influence of Cabernet Sauvignon is strongly felt at both wineries, contributing a great deal to the superb Torres Coronas Black Label Reservas. However, the indigenous Tempranillo is still important here, as are Garnacha and Monastrell.

SPANISH WHITE WINES

The profile of Spanish white wines is changing. In the past these wines tended to be oxidized, tired, and suitable only for domestic consumption. Today, the whites are often fermented in stainless steel at cool temperatures. White Riojas and Ruedas, made from the native Viura grape, now emphasize lemony fruit and freshness, and Spanish Chardonnays are becoming quite good.

On the other hand, the traditional oak-aged style has certainly improved. Many fine Rioja reservas are fermented and aged in American oak. These offer genuine voluptuousness and power, and can be compared to some of the better premium whites of the Graves region of Bordeaux.

Some of the most impressive Spanish white wines come from Galicia, located just north of Portugal. The area's most exciting region now is the Rias Baixas. Its principal grape is the Albariño, which offers an intensity and complexity that calls to mind a French Hermitage blanc or an Alsace Riesling.

CAVA

One couldn't leave a discussion of Spanish wine without mentioning cava, Spain's immensely popular sparkling wine. Cava is made in some of the most technologically advanced, mechanized wineries anywhere in the world. It must spend a minimum of nine months in bottle, and many spend between one and three years. Penedès is the most important region for cava; indigenous grape varieties make up the bulk of the blends, which can be fresh and fruity—and much more affordable than Champagne.

ABADIA DEL ROBLE

La Mancha Fermin Ayuso 1990 • $6 • (12/15/92) BB • **81**

AGAPITO RICO, BODEGAS

Jumilla Carchelo 1993: Light on tannins but heavy on the smoky, pruny flavors. Hearty, and has the feel of a Beaujolais. Drink now. 3,000 cases made. • $6 • (12/15/94) • **82**

Monastrell Jumilla 1994: Firm and meaty, adding game and licorice flavors to the core of blackberry. It's got some concentration, but could use more liveliness. Mourvèdre. 6,000 cases made. • $6 • (04/30/96) • **83**

Monastrell Jumilla Carchelo 1995: Plum flavors have a slight, pleasant, bitter note in this firm, ripe red. It's somewhat alcoholic for balance, but fruit lingers on the finish. Made from Mourvèdre, plus some Merlot. 10,000 cases made. • $8 • (04/30/96) • **82**

Monastrell Jumilla Carchelo 1994: Vibrant and grapey, made in a fresh quaffing style. This has jammy fruit flavors and soft tannins, with a pleasant licorice hint. Made from Mourvèdre. Try slightly chilled. 5,000 cases made. • $7 • (04/30/95) • **81**

AGE

La Mancha Vega Serena 1993: A pleasant, easy-drinking red showing soft texture and simple, clean berry flavors. • $5 • (02/28/95) • **80**

Rioja Siglo 1993: A tasty white that blends mature, figgy aromas with intriguing fruity and floral flavors that linger on the finish. Silky in texture, too. • $6 • (02/28/95) • **85**

Rioja Siglo 1988 • $9 • (03/31/93) • **74**

Rioja Siglo Crianza 1991: Light and soft, this lacks backbone and definition. It has some jammy plum flavor, but plenty of earthiness, too. • $7 • (03/31/96) • **76**

Rioja Siglo Crianza 1990: A light, elegant style of Rioja that's dominated by sweet-seeming vanilla and cherry flavors. Smooth on the palate, lingering on the finish. Drink now. • $8 • (01/31/95) • **84**

Rioja Siglo Crianza 1989 • $7 • (04/15/94) • **84**

Rioja Siglo Gran Reserva 1984 • $12 • (03/31/93) • **84**

Rioja Siglo Reserva 1986: Holding up well: silky, traditional, showing coffee, spice and raisin flavors in a lean, soft frame. It matches well with food and has enough elegance to be enjoyed on its own. Drinkable now. • $10 • (03/31/96) • **85**

Rioja Siglo Reserva 1986: Silky and elegant, well balanced and firm, showing traditional Rioja vanilla, spice and coffee flavors plus a core of spicy cherry. Drinkable now. • $10 • (04/30/95) • **86**

Rioja Siglo Reserva 1985 • $10 • (03/31/93) • **77**

ALBET I NOYA

Cabernet Sauvignon Penedès 1993: Big, with more structure than grace. Has aggressive tannins and flavors of smoke, earth and raisins. Dries out on the finish. Ambitious, but harsh. 2,000 cases made. • $15 • **78**

Cabernet Sauvignon Penedès Collecció 1992: This thick, tannic wine has concentrated meaty, herbal, tobacco flavors, with roasty, oaky notes on the finish. Could use more fruit, but it's concentrated enough for rich food. Drinkable now. 3,000 cases made. • $14 • (04/30/95) • **83**

Penedès 1991 • $14 • (04/15/94) • **82**

Penedès Collecció 1993: Firm and fresh, balanced and concentrated, bright cherry and currant flavors and plenty of toasty oak. International style. Delicious now. 3,000 cases made. • $14 • (04/30/95) • **88**

Tempranillo Penedès 1993: An attractive marriage of sweet vanilla, oak and pretty cherry and blackberry flavors. Still young and fresh, bright and clean. Drinkable now, but should hold through 1998. 1,000 cases made. • $15 • **85**

ALELLA, MARQUES DE

Alella Clásico 1992 • $11 • (04/15/94) • **76**

ALION

Reserva Ribera del Duero 1991: An exciting new venture from the venerable Spanish estate of Bodegas Vega Sicilia. It's a rich, concentrated blockbuster that coats your mouth and lingers on your taste buds. Plenty of roasted and coffee nuances, almost jammy berry and black cherry and powerful yet silky tannins—this has it all. It promises great drinking in 1997 and beyond. 4,500 cases made. • $20 • (04/30/95) • **92**

AMEZOLA DE LA MORA, BODEGAS

Rioja Crianza Viña Amezola 1990: Pleasant coffee and cedar accents to the black cherry and strawberry flavors. A polished, elegant, traditional Rioja. It shows good balance and harmony. Drinkable now. • $10 • (04/30/95) • **85**

Rioja Reserva Señorio Amezola 1989: Beautiful aromas of spice, cedar and plum follow through on the voluptuous palate-sweet and jammy yet still balanced. Enjoyable now. • $13 • (04/15/95) • **87**

ARIENZO, MARQUES DE

Rioja 1987 • $7 • (03/31/92) • **84**

Rioja 1986 • $7 • (03/31/92) • **81**

Rioja 1985 • $8 • (03/15/90) • **78**

Rioja 1983 • $5 • (06/30/88) BB • **81**

Rioja Gran Reserva 1982 • $23 • (03/31/92) • **83**

Rioja Gran Reserva 1981 • $18 • (03/31/92) • **84**

Rioja Gran Reserva 1978 • $19 • (03/31/90) • **78**

Rioja Gran Reserva 1976 • $18 • (03/31/92) • **87**

Rioja Reserva 1985 • $12 • (03/31/92) • **84**

Rioja Reserva 1983 • $12 • (03/31/92) • **85**

Rioja Reserva 1981 • $12 • (07/31/89) • **83**

Rioja Reserva 1980 • $8 • (06/30/88) • **76**

ARROYO, BODEGAS ISMAEL

Ribera del Duero Mesoñeros de Castilla 1991: Dark and rich, with aging potential. Smoke and plum aromas give way to powerful flavors of plum, licorice and smoked bacon. Full-bodied with firm tannins. Not approachable yet, but should grow into a beauty. Try in 1997. 8,000 cases made. • $16 • **88**

Ribera del Duero Mesoñeros de Castilla 1986 • $6 • (04/30/88) • **60**

Ribera del Duero Mesoñeros de Castilla Crianza 1991: Exuberant aromas of coffee and ripe plum, surprising finesse characterizes this balanced, concentrated, youthful, firmly tannic red. Drink now or hold through 1998. 10,000 cases made. • $14 • (04/30/95) • **89**

Ribera del Duero Mesoñeros de Castilla Crianza 1990: Lush and velvety in texture, with focused flavors of black cherry and plum, accented by toast and chocolate notes from the oak barrels. Has a sense of grace despite the firm tannins. Lasts a long time on the finish. Drink now to 2000. 10,000 cases made. • $14 • **90**

Ribera del Duero Mesoñeros de Castilla Tinto 1991 • $7 • (04/15/94) • **78**

Ribera del Duero Val Sotillo Reserva 1990: Beautiful aromas of spice, game and leather, reminiscent of a top northern Rhone, give way to flavors of black cherry, spice and game in a surprisingly elegant package. The tannins are clean and firm, but not obtrusive. It's approachable now. 2,000 cases made. • $25 • (04/30/95) • **89**

Ribera del Duero Val Sotillo Reserva 1989: Impressive for its deep color and ripe fruit, accented by chocolate and spice notes. Velvety in texture, but tight tannins come out on the finish. Drink now through 1997. 2,000 cases made. • $27 • **87**

ARTADI

Alavesa Rioja 1987 • $6 • (04/30/88) • **80**

AZPILICUETA, BODEGAS FELIX

Rioja Gran Reserva 1982: Fading now, this shows brown sugar and tea flavors in light, silky texture. A traditional Rioja that needs drinking now. • $36 • (03/31/96) • **82**

BALBAS, BODEGAS

Ribera del Duero 1988 • $15 • (09/30/91) • **88**
Ribera del Duero 1987 • $14 • (09/30/90) • **81**
Ribera del Duero 1986 • $15 • (07/31/89) • **87**
Ribera del Duero 1985 • $13 • (09/15/88) • **83**
Ribera del Duero Reserva 1985 • $NA • (03/31/90) • **75**

BALBINO FERNANDEZ

Rioja Don Balbino Reserva 1987 • $NA • (04/15/94) • **82**

BARBADILLO, ANTONIO

Castillo de San Diego Viño de la Tierra de Cadiz Jerez 1994: Pleasant lemon and almond aromas give way to soft, light almond and vanilla flavors, with a slight soapy note on the finish. 25,000 cases made. • $6 • (07/31/95) • **78**
Castillo de San Diego Viño de la Tierra de Cadiz Jerez 1993: Earthy, fennel-like aromas and dry, austere flavors mark this very lean white. Good if you like lightness and simplicity. 244,000 cases made. • $6 • (03/31/95) • **80**

BARBIER, RENE

Cabernet Sauvignon Penedès 1987 • $7 • (04/15/94) BB • **84**
Cabernet Sauvignon Penedès 1981 • $5 • (03/31/90) • **74**
Cabernet Sauvignon Penedès Mediterranean Select 1990: Coffee and herbal flavors predominate in this chewy red. It's round, has some grip and a nice, fruity sweetness on the palate, but lacks focus. Drinkable now. 5,500 cases made. • $7 • (03/31/96) • **80**
Merlot Penedès Mediterranean Select 1992: Sweet vanilla oak dominates this round, supple red, also showing pleasant black cherry flavor and light coffee accents. It's quite rich, if a bit simple. 4,500 cases made. • $7 • (03/31/96) • **84**
Penedès 1982 • $3 • (01/31/87) • **77**
Penedès Family Reserve NV: Assertive earthy and cinnamon flavors add a feisty note to this smooth wine, the cherry fruit is soft and a bit cooked. Drinkable now. 11,000 cases made. • $6 • (04/15/94) • **75**
Penedès Mediterranean Red NV: A light, simple wine that almost disappears in your mouth, except for an unpleasant barnyard note. Other bottlings have shown much better. It's as drinkable now as it will ever be. 150,000 cases made. • $5 • **72**
Penedès Reserva 1978 • $4 • (03/31/90) • **77**
Priorato Clos Mogador 1991: An inky wine with great concentration on the palate. It's almost sweet with ripe fruit and buttressed with tannins like huge oak beams. Big and heady, it manages both power and balance. Approachable now. • $35 • (04/30/95) • **90**
Priorato Clos Mogador 1990: Rich and ripe, with plenty of sweet fruit and lush tannins. Blackberry, sweet vanilla and coffee flavors are just edging into maturity. Drinkable now. • $35 • **87**
Red Table Wine 1983 • $3 • (03/31/90) BB • **80**

BARCELO, HIJOS DE ANTONIO

Castilla y Leon Peñascal 1987 • $5 • (04/15/94) BB • **83**
Ribera del Duero Crianza 1990 • $8 • (04/15/94) • **73**
Ribera del Duero Reserva 1989 • $11 • (04/15/94) • **81**
Ribera del Duero Viña Mayor Cosecha 1994: Strong but harsh and tannic with smoke and barnyard flavors. Not much fruit or depth. Maybe time will soften it, try in 1997. • $NA • **78**
Ribera del Duero Viña Mayor Crianza 1991: A strong jolt of sweet vanilla from oak, accompanied by attractive cherry flavor. Has good texture and grip, drinkable now through 1997. • $8 • (04/30/95) BB • **86**
Ribera del Duero Viña Mayor Crianza 1990 • $7 • (02/15/92) BB • **83**
Ribera del Duero Viña Mayor Crianza 1989 • $9 • (12/15/93) • **83**

Key: SS—Spectator Selection. CS—Cellar Selection. BB—Best Buy. $NA—Price not available. (BT)—Barrel tasting. Ⓐ—Auction Price.
Dates in parentheses represent the issues in which the ratings were published.

Ribera del Duero Viña Mayor Crianza 1987 • $9 • (02/15/92) • **82**
Ribera del Duero Viña Mayor Tinto 1992 • $6 • (04/15/94) • **75**
Ribera del Duero Viña Mayor Tinto 1991 • $7 • (01/31/93) BB • **86**

BARCO, CASA

Viño de Mesa Tinto NV • $4 • (06/15/93) • **76**

BARON DE LEY

Rioja Reserva 1986 • $10 • (04/15/94) • **84**

BARON DE OÑA

Reserva Rioja 1989: Meaty, gamy flavors dominate the light cherry fruit. Thick and rather dull, especially on the finish. Not much pleasure here. • $15 • **76**

BERBERANA, BODEGAS

Marino NV: This lively, grapey red has some grip and freshness, though little depth, and can stand up to food. 75,000 cases made. • $6 • (04/30/96) • **78**
Rioja Carta de Oro Crianza 1989 • $8 • (08/31/93) • **85**
Rioja Carta de Oro Crianza 1988 • $10 • (03/31/92) • **78**
Rioja Carta de Oro Crianza 1987 • $10 • (03/31/92) • **87**
Rioja Carta de Oro Crianza 1986 • $8 • (03/31/90) • **81**
Rioja Carta de Oro Crianza 1985 • $6 • (07/31/89) • **78**
Rioja Carta de Plata 1989 • $8 • (03/31/92) • **77**
Rioja Carta de Plata 1988 • $7 • (09/30/91) BB • **83**
Rioja Carta de Plata 1987 • $7 • (12/15/90) BB • **84**
Rioja Carta de Plata 1986 • $6 • (05/15/89) BB • **88**
Rioja Carta de Plata 1985 • $6 • (10/31/88) BB • **89**
Rioja Gran Reserva 1983: Truffle, brown sugar and raisin flavors are graceful and appealing, yet the wine lacks zest and is a bit dry on the finish. A pretty, traditional wine, drink now. 30,000 cases made. • $15 • (01/31/96) • **85**
Rioja Gran Reserva 1982 • $24 • (11/30/91) • **88**
Rioja Gran Reserva 1980 • $18 • (10/31/88) • **82**
Rioja Gran Reserva 1975 • $13 • (03/31/92) • **88**
Rioja Gran Reserva 1973 • $20 • (03/31/92) • **89**
Rioja Preferido 1992 • $5 • (08/31/93) • **78**
Rioja Reserva 1988: Maturing well, fragrant with sweet vanilla, roses and strawberries, then silky and balanced on the palate, with sweet cherry and tea flavors. Well made in a traditional style. 58,000 cases made. • $11 • (01/31/96) • **87**
Rioja Reserva 1986 • $11 • (03/31/92) • **81**
Rioja Reserva 1985 • $13 • (03/31/92) • **82**
Rioja Reserva 1983 • $12 • (03/31/92) • **82**
Rioja Reserva 1982 • $20 • (03/31/92) • **85**
Tempranillo Crianza Rioja 1991: Traditional style Rioja, smooth and lean, with cola, herb and raisin flavors. Could be fresher, but it has character. Light and drinkable now. • $9 • (01/31/96) • **82**
Tempranillo d'Avalos Rioja 1994: Deep color, velvet texture, with flavors of smoke, tar and ripe blackberries. This seems more like Beaujolais than Rioja. Pleasant enough, but it's soft and a bit flabby. 40,000 cases made. • $8 • (01/31/96) • **80**
Tempranillo Dragon Label Rioja 1994: Ripe and round, with plenty of sweet vanilla oak flavors. Has enough cherry and light plum to keep it balanced. Very pleasant, though not much structure, so drink up. 40,000 cases made. • $10 • (06/30/96) BB • **86**
Tempranillo Dragon Label Rioja 1993: This features sweet vanilla and tart cherry flavors, spicy and soft on the palate. It's light but makes pleasant drinking now. 40,000 cases made. • $10 • (01/31/96) • **83**
Tempranillo Rioja 1992: Finely proportioned, with some nice spice and fruit components to its flavors. An upfront and brash wine that turns a bit astringent on the finsh. Drinkable now. 4,167 cases made. • $10 • (03/31/95) • **84**

BERONIA, BODEGAS

Rioja Crianza 1990: Polished and broad, not showing much now, but the cherry and chocolate flavors and firm tannins promise to bloom. Drinkable now. • $8 • (04/30/95) • **79**
Rioja Crianza 1989 • $8 • (04/15/94) • **77**
Rioja Gran Reserva 1981: Coffee, cola and dried berry flavors mingle in this dark, rich wine. It's still fresh, and still closed, but a lifted note suggests it won't benefit much from age. • $18 • (01/31/96) • **83**
Rioja Gran Reserva 1980: A delicate wine with the soft, light flavors of strawberry, tea and vanilla so characteristic of Rioja. Happily, it's still fresh, not drying out. Well-made in the classic style. Drinkable now. • $18 • (04/15/94) • **85**
Rioja Reserva 1985 • $11 • (04/15/94) • **80**
Rioja Reserva 1982 • $12 • (03/31/90) • **82**

BILBAINAS, BODEGAS

Rioja Viña Pomal 1983 • $8 • (06/30/90) • **79**
Rioja Viña Pomal Crianza 1990: Fresh and lively, firm yet elegant, sporting blackberry, tobacco and spice flavors that linger on the finish. Drinking well now. 18,000 cases made. • $13 • (03/31/96) • **85**
Rioja Viña Pomal Gran Reserva 1980 • $26 • (04/15/94) • **83**
Rioja Viña Pomal Gran Reserva 1978 • $20 • (03/31/90) • **88**
Rioja Viña Pomal Reserva 1988: This traditional-style Rioja shows tea, leather and dried cherry flavors, dry tannins and silky texture. It's lean and a bit earthy. Drinkable now. 3,000 cases made. • $29 • (03/31/96) • **80**
Rioja Viña Pomal Reserva 1985: Lots of toasty oak on the nose, then plenty of tannin on the palate, this wine has been nearly smothered in the barrel. But there's enough black cherry fruit to keep it alive. Drink now or hold. 17,000 cases made. • $12 • (04/15/94) • **84**

BLEDA

Jumilla Castillo Jumilla 1990 • $NA • (04/15/94) • **69**

BORJA, AGRICOLA DE

Borsao Campo de Borja 1993: Very fruity and rather light, with peppery aromas and raspberry-strawberry flavors. Drink it now while it's fresh. 40,000 cases made. • $4 • (03/31/95) • **81**

BRANAVIEJA, BODEGAS

Navarra Pleno 1988 • $6 • (12/15/90) BB • **85**

BRETON, BODEGAS

Rioja Dominio de Conte Reserva 1991: Aromatic with smoke and spices. Bright cherry and spicy flavors with firm tannins on the finish. Well-balanced and should improve through 1997. 3,000 cases made. • $26 • **87**
Rioja Dominio de Conte Reserva 1990: Gutsy aromas of chocolate and licorice give way to a light-bodied, crisp red offering tart cherry and light vanilla flavors, freshness and some intensity. Drinkable now. 1,365 cases made. • $24 • (01/31/96) • **84**
Rioja Loriñon 1993: Lean and has appealing fig and green apricot aromas and flavors, with a tart, citrusy finish. Clean and firm, with a distinct mineral quality. 1,000 cases made. • $9 • **83**
Rioja Loriñon Crianza 1991: Raspberry and vanilla aromas and flavors are appealing, but this red is a bit tart and tannic, lacking ripeness. Better accompanying food. Drinkable now. 20,000 cases made. • $10 • (03/31/96) • **81**
Rioja Loriñon Crianza 1990: Ripe cherry and plum flavors stretch out on an ample frame with good concentration and firm tannins. A traditional Rioja with spice and vanilla accents at an attractive price. Drinkable now. 8,000 cases made. • $9 • (04/15/95) • **86**
Rioja Loriñon Crianza 1989: Ripe plum fruit gives this chewy wine a juicy appeal, and there's plenty of spicy oak to back it up. It's balanced, firm and concentrated. • $9 BB • (04/15/95) • **87**
Rioja Loriñon Crianza 1988 • $10 • (01/31/92) • **83**
Rioja Loriñon Crianza 1985 • $9 • (03/31/90) • **85**
Rioja Loriñon Reserva 1989: Plum, spice and caramel flavors are appealing. Round, soft, and ripe, with soft tannins. Made in a traditional style and drinkable now. • $17 • (04/30/95) • **82**
Rioja Loriñon Reserva 1987 • $15 • (12/15/93) • **77**

BUJANDA, BODEGAS MARTINEZ

Rioja Conde de Valdemar Crianza 1992: A round wine with light tannins, plenty of vanilla and ripe plum and licorice flavors. It's soft enough for drinking now. • $10 • (01/31/96) • **82**
Rioja Conde de Valdemar Crianza 1991: Fairly complex, with appealing cedar and berry flavors and aromas, fringed by spice and sugar. Lively and appealing, it tastes like a Pinot Noir. 70,000 cases made. • $8 • (03/31/95) • **85**
Rioja Conde de Valdemar Gran Reserva 1987: Coffee and brown sugar flavors dominate, and some prune and vanilla notes show through, but it dries up on the finish. This is tiring, drink up. Better than a sample tasted last year. 1,500 cases made. • $20 • (01/31/96) • **83**
Rioja Conde de Valdemar Reserva 1990: Ripe, almost unctuous, with spice and cherry notes and a nearly floral aroma. Full-bodied, lively and delicious, its flavors carry to the finish. 35,000 cases made. • $12 • (04/30/95) • **89**
Rioja Crianza 1989: The jammy blackberry flavors and toasty oak give this wine a lush appeal, and the tannins are light enough to make it pleasant drinking now. It's clean and fresh. 90,000 cases made. • $9 BB • (04/15/94) • **85**
Rioja Fermentado en Barrica 1994: This has bold flavors of vanilla, honey and nuts, rich but dry, with a long finish. It's not heavy, though, and has the acidity to match well with food. Well crafted and distinctive. 3,500 cases made. • $14 • (02/29/96) • **88**
Rioja Gran Reserva 1985: Thick and chewy, with lots of jammy berry fruit, this is vivid, lush and long in the finish. An abundance of oak marries well with the ripe, juicy fruit. This may not be a typical Rioja, but it's tasty nonetheless. 15,000 cases made. • $21 • (04/15/94) • **90**
Rioja Reserva 1989: Ripe and round, with loads of sweet blackberry and vanilla flavors, this wine offers a fresh, lush style still rare in Rioja. Drink now or hold through 1997. 25,000 cases made. • $12 • (04/15/94) • **88**
Rioja Reserva 1987: Quite big for an '87, and showing lots of ripe, raisiny fruit, but gamy, coffee notes detract. Drinkable now. 30,000 cases made. • $12 • (04/15/94) • **79**

CACERES, MARQUES DE

Rioja 1993: Grapefruit and herbal flavors are refreshing. Clean, crisp and has enough body to stand up to food. Balanced and has some richness. • $7 • (07/31/95) • **84**
Rioja 1992: Plum and chocolate flavors have some concentration and enough tannin for structure. Not expansive or complex, but it's well knit. Drinkable now. • $12 • (03/31/96) • **83**
Rioja 1991: A good, solid, middle-of-the-road wine that delivers appealing plum and cherry flavors. Spicy and sugary notes come through on the finish. 357,000 cases made. • $10 • (03/31/95) • **84**
Rioja 1989 • $9 • (03/31/93) • **86**
Rioja 1987 • $9 • (03/31/92) • **88**
Rioja 1986 • $9 • (03/31/92) • **82**
Rioja 1985 • $9 • (03/31/90) • **80**
Rioja 1982 • $7 • (11/15/87) • **87**
Rioja 1981 • $5 • (11/01/85) BB • **88**
Rioja Antea Barrel Fermented 1992: A healthy shot of new oak adds appealing vanilla and pinelike flavors, but overwhelms the fresh but modest fruit. It's still crisp and clean, though. • $9 • **84**
Rioja Crianza 1990: Soft, smooth and easy going, almost as delicate as a good Pinot Noir, with good fruit flavor and light tannins. Drink now while it's fresh. • $10 • (04/15/94) • **84**
Rioja Crianza 1989: A light, smooth wine with vanilla and tea notes enhancing the cherry flavors in a traditional Rioja style. Slightly rough on the finish. 550,000 cases made. • $9 • (04/15/94) • **84**
Rioja Gran Reserva 1987: This smooth, velvety red is pleasant on the palate but lacks character. The muted flavors suggest black cherry and tobacco, but disappear on the short, tannic finish. • $25 • (03/31/96) • **83**

Rioja Gran Reserva 1986: This thick wine still shows ripe berry and prune flavors, but its sweet, jammy character lacks focus and finesse. Drinking nicely now, it probably won't improve. • $25 • (03/31/96) • **83**
Rioja Gran Reserva 1982 • $25 • (03/31/92) • **89**
Rioja Gran Reserva 1975 • $26 • (03/31/92) • **89**
Rioja Gran Reserva 1973 • $30 • (03/31/92) • **83**
Rioja Reserva 1989: Solid, well-made red still has a long life ahead. Deeply colored, it offers ripe plum, coffee and vanilla flavors, adding firm but not drying tannins. Drinkable now, should improve through 1997. • $20 • (03/31/96) • **87**
Rioja Reserva 1986: Balanced and complete, with generous plum flavors and firm, toasty tannins, this wine has freshness and elegance. Good now, but should improve through 1997. 40,000 cases made. • $12 • (04/15/94) • **88**
Rioja Reserva 1985 • $19 • (03/31/92) • **87**
Rioja Reserva 1982 • $25 • (03/31/92) • **83**
Rioja Reserva 1981 • $20 • (03/31/90) • **69**
Rioja Reserva 1975 • $9 • (12/01/85) • **67**
Rioja Rosé 1993: A perennial good value for the red and white, and this rosé stays true to form. From the strawberry, cherry, melon and spice flavors to the dry finish, this is loaded with personality. The vibrant acidity should make this a versatile match with food. 114,000 cases made. • $7 • (08/31/95) BB • **86**
Rioja Satinela 1994: This is lively and quite sweet, a vivid wine with orange and berry flavors that would make a good base for a wine punch. • $8 • (02/29/96) • **78**
Rioja Satinela 1993 • $7 • **72**

CADIZ

Brut Cava Reserva NV • $7 • (05/31/88) • **79**

CAMPAÑAS, LAS

Cabernet Sauvignon Navarra 1989: Full-bodied, full-flavored, with ripe fruit and firm tannins. Robust and rich, but a bit heavy handed. Drinkable now. 3,000 cases made. • $8 • (04/15/94) • **80**
Navarra 1984 • $6 • (03/31/90) BB • **86**
Navarra Crianza 1990: Well-balanced and medium-bodied, with a nice layer of spicy oak over fresh strawberry and cherry flavors. Compact, focused and complete. 15,000 cases made. • $7 BB • **84**

CAMPILLO, BODEGAS

Rioja Crianza 1987 • $12 • (06/15/93) • **80**
Rioja Reserva 1985 • $19 • (08/31/93) • **79**

CAMPO LEONADO

Chardonnay Viño de Levante 1992: Rather dull and unappealing. The stale, earthy flavors aren't appetizing. • $5 • (02/28/95) • **72**

CAMPO VIEJO, BODEGAS

Rioja 1988 • $NA • (03/31/92) • **83**
Rioja 1987 • $6 • (03/31/92) BB • **83**
Rioja 1986 • $6 • (03/31/92) • **81**
Rioja 1985 • $6 • (03/15/90) BB • **83**
Rioja 1984 • $5 • (01/31/88) BB • **82**
Rioja Albor 1993: Soft flavors of pears and vanilla raise some interest, but it lacks depth and fades into slight mustiness on the finish. 15,000 cases made. • $6 • (07/31/95) • **77**
Rioja Albor 1992: Soft and smooth, with vanilla custard flavors, this wine tastes more of the barrel than the grape, with a pleasant hint of apricots on the finish. Low acidity makes it easy to drink. • $5 • (4/15/94) • **78**
Rioja Albor 1991 • $6 • (04/15/94) BB • **85**

Key: SS—Spectator Selection. CS—Cellar Selection. BB—Best Buy. $NA—Price not available. (BT)—Barrel tasting. Ⓐ—Auction Price.
Dates in parentheses represent the issues in which the ratings were published.

Rioja Commemorative Label Crianza 1992: Very light and spicy, with pepper and curry accents, but already on the downward slope. 75,000 cases made. • $7 • (01/31/96) • **73**
Rioja Crianza 1990: Simple, drinkable red. It's straightforward in flavor, a bit rough with tannins and acidity and drying on the finish. 75,000 cases made. • $7 • (01/31/95) • **78**
Rioja Crianza 1989: A simple wine with balance and some fruit flavor, but lacking depth and distinctive character. 100,000 cases made. • $8 • (4/15/94) • **77**
Rioja Gran Reserva 1981 • $NA • (03/31/92) • **83**
Rioja Gran Reserva 1980 • $15 • (09/30/91) • **88**
Rioja Gran Reserva 1978 • $14 • (09/30/90) • **83**
Rioja Marqués de Villamagna Gran Reserva 1982 • $20 • (03/31/92) • **81**
Rioja Marqués de Villamagna Gran Reserva 1978 • $19 • (11/15/91) • **84**
Rioja Marqués de Villamagna Gran Reserva 1975 • $20 • (03/31/92) • **88**
Rioja Marqués de Villamagna Gran Reserva 1973 • $25 • (03/31/92) • **74**
Rioja Marqués de Villamagna Gran Reserva 1970 • $28 • (03/31/92) • **87**
Rioja Reserva 1989: Rustic and mature, with good spice and coffee flavors and aromas. Appealing, though fairly subdued, with a gamy, leathery component. 50,000 cases made. • $10 • (03/31/95) • **79**
Rioja Reserva 1987 • $NA • (04/15/94) • **77**
Rioja Reserva 1985 • $9 • (03/31/92) • **83**
Rioja Reserva 1983 • $9 • (03/31/92) • **81**
Rioja Reserva 1982 • $9 • (03/31/92) • **84**
Rioja Reserva 1981 • $7 • (11/15/88) • **78**
Rioja Viña Alcorta 1985 • $10 • (09/30/90) • **85**
Rioja Viña Alcorta 1981 • $7 • (10/31/88) • **76**
Rioja Viña Alcorta Crianza 1989: Soft and spicy, with brown sugar and cinnamon notes and sweet berry flavor in the center. Should please fans of traditional Rioja. It's silky and quaffable, but lacks depth. Ready to drink now. • $7 • **83**
Rioja Viña Alcorta Reserva 1987: Light and simple, with smoky, meaty and dried cherry flavors. It's fully mature and is drinkable now. • $10 • **78**
Rioja Viña Alcorta Reserva 1982 • $NA • (11/15/87) • **87**
Tempranillo Rioja Viña Alcorta 1981 • $7 • (03/31/90) • **64**

CAN FEIXES

Penedès Blanc Selecció 1993: A basic white, with pleasant peach aromas and flavors that are matched by an herbal note. It also has a hint of spritz. Lacks a finish. 3,000 cases made. • $8 • **80**
Penedès Negre Selecció 1991: Quite rich, with a firm tannic core, this wine offers cherry flavors with an attractive peppery accent. A blend of Cabernet Sauvignon and Ull de Llebre (Tempranillo). Drinkable now. 1,900 cases made. • $12 • (4/15/94) • **82**

CAN RAFOLS DELS CAUS

Penedès Gran Caus 1989 • $14 • (04/15/94) • **80**

CARO, MARQUES DE

Vinedos del Valle de Albaida Reserva Gar Valencia 1982 • $6 • (12/15/88) BB • **83**

CARRERAS, BODEGAS JAIME

Valencia 1985 • $4 • (03/31/90) BB • **80**

CASTANO, BODEGAS

Pozuelo Crianza Cosecha Yecla 1987 • $8 • (03/31/93) • **83**
Pozuelo Reserva Yecla 1990: Smooth and simple, this light-bodied red offers spicy black pepper and dried cherry flavors. Finish is a bit dry. Agreeable, if not distinctive. Drink now. 8,000 cases made. • $10 • **82**

CASTELLBLANCH

Brut Cava Brut Zero 1987 • $7 • (05/15/94) BB • **86**
Brut Cava Extra NV • $6 • (02/29/92) BB • **82**
Brut Cava Zero 1987 • $8 • (03/31/93) • **77**
Brut Cava Zero 1985 • $6 • (12/31/88) • **73**

Brut Cava Zero 1982 • $6 • (05/31/88) • **81**

CASTILLO DE ALMANSA

Viño de Crianza Almansa 1989: Simple, pleasant cherry and vanilla flavors are overshadowed by strong barnyard aromas. An earthy, austere style. 25,000 cases made. • $9 • (03/31/95) • **77**

CAVAS HILL

Brut Blanc de Blancs Cava Nature Reserva Oro 1987 • $12 • (03/31/93) • **81**
Seco Blanc de Blancs Cava Reserva Oro 1990 • $9 • (03/31/93) • **80**
Seco Blanc de Blancs Cava Reserva Oro NV • $8 • (05/31/88) • **83**

CENALSA-MURCHANTE, BODEGAS

Navarra Campo-Nuevo Tinto 1991 • $6 • (03/31/93) • **77**

CHENEAU, PAUL

Brut Cava Blanc de Blancs NV • $7 • (06/15/94) • **82**
Brut Cava Vintage Cuvée Spéciale 1981 • $9 • (05/31/88) • **69**

CHIVITE, BODEGAS JULIAN

Navarra 125 Aniversario 1988: Ripe and generous, full-bodied, offering vibrant plum, toast and spice flavors in a round, mature style. Drinking nicely now. 25,000 cases made. • $19 • (04/15/95) • **85**
Navarra 125 Aniversario 1985: Maturity brings out characteristic earthy mushroom and leather notes in this silky wine. It's soft and still balanced, but not much fruit left. 25,000 cases made. • $25 • **82**
Navarra 125 Aniversario Gran Reserva 1988: Attractive aromas and well-integrated flavors of spice, dried cherry and vanilla. This is a well-made example of a traditional Tempranillo. Drinkable now. • $31 • (8/31/93) • **87**
Navarra 125 Aniversario Gran Reserva 1985 • $31 • (08/31/93) • **82**
Navarra Colleccion 125 1993: Tastes like an oaky, full-blown Chardonnay with its toasty, buttery aromas and ripe pear flavors accented by vanilla and smoke on the finish. A bit extreme in style. 3,000 cases made. • $20 • (03/31/95) • **84**
Navarra Gran Feudo Crianza 1993: Smooth and well balanced. Juicy black cherry and blackberry flavors backed by light, firm tannins. Clean and vibrant, for current drinking. • $8 • **84**
Navarra Gran Feudo Crianza 1991: The bright cherry flavors with berry and spicy accents make you want to refill the glass. A balanced, lively wine that has tannins firm enough to go with food. Drinkable now. 70,000 cases made. • $7 BB • **85**
Navarra Gran Feudo Crianza 1990: A solid red wine with good cherry and plum flavors accented by spicy, gamey aromas. Moderately tannic. Drink now. 20,000 cases made. • $8 • **83**
Navarra Gran Feudo Rosado 1993: A hint of oxidation mars this otherwise floral, spicy offering. Dry and full-bodied, with some alcohol on the finish. 150,000 cases made. • $6 • (08/31/95) • **79**
Navarra Reserva 1991: Balanced, and maturing nicely. Black cherry, spice and coffee flavors with well-integrated tannins. Supple yet firm on the finish. Attractive now, it should improve through 1998. • $10 • **86**
Navarra Reserva 1990: Smoky plum and light leather flavors make for attractive depth and roundness. The tannins are soft, the finish clean, it's balanced and still improving. Drinkable now. 50,000 cases made. • $9 • **85**
Navarra Reserva 1988 • $10 • (12/15/93) • **79**
Navarra Reserva 1987 • $10 • (06/15/93) • **81**
Navarra Viña Marcos 1992: Round and fresh, this wine shows bright grapey flavors that taste as much like candy as wine. Crisp acidity and light tannins make it appealing now. • $NA • **78**
Navarra Viña Marcos 1991 • $6 • (06/15/93) • **77**

CLOS DOFI

Costers del Siurana 1989 • $40 • (01/31/92) • **89**
Priorato Selecció Terrasses 1990 • $35 • (08/31/93) • **85**

CODORNIU

Blanc de Blancs Cava 1984 • $9 • (05/31/88) • **72**
Blanc de Blancs Penedès 1989 • $9 • (06/15/94) • **83**
Brut Anna de Codorniu 1989 • $8 • (05/15/92) • **79**
Brut Blanc de Blancs Cava 1988 • $10 • (03/31/93) • **80**
Brut Blanc de Blancs Cava 1986 • $8 • (07/31/89) • **77**
Brut Cava 1985 • $7 • (05/31/88) • **79**
Brut Cava Anna de Codorniu 1988 • $9 • (03/31/93) • **82**
Brut Cava Anna de Codorniu 1987 • $7 • (08/31/90) • **75**
Brut Cava Anna de Codorniu 1985 • $6 • (07/31/89) • **76**
Brut Cava Anna de Codorniu 1984 • $7 • (05/31/88) • **73**
Brut Cava Chardonnay 1986 • $12 • (07/31/89) • **84**
Brut Cava Clásico 1990 • $6 • (06/15/94) • **78**
Brut Cava Clásico 1986 • $6 • (05/15/89) BB • **82**
Brut Cava Clásico 1983 • $6 • (04/01/86) • **55**
Brut Cava Gran Reserve 1983 • $14 • (05/31/88) • **73**
Brut Chardonnay 1988 • $15 • (05/15/92) • **85**
Brut Clásico 1989 • $9 • (05/15/92) • **75**
Brut Penedès Clásico 1990 • $6 • (06/15/94) • **78**
Extra Dry Cava 1985 • $7 • (05/31/88) • **72**

COLEGIATA

Toro Gran Colegiata Tinto de Crianza 1986 • $7 • (11/30/89) • **77**
Toro Tinto 1986 • $5 • (11/30/89) BB • **82**
Toro Tinto 1985 • $5 • (11/30/89) BB • **88**

CONTINO

Rioja Reserva 1987 • $15 • (04/15/94) • **88**
Rioja Reserva 1985 • $14 • (12/15/90) • **88**
Rioja Reserva 1984 • $12 • (03/31/90) • **84**
Rioja Reserva 1983 • $13 • (03/31/92) • **89**
Rioja Reserva 1982 • $12 • (03/31/92) • **92**
Rioja Reserva 1980 • $11 • (01/31/87) • **83**

CORRAL, BODEGAS

Rioja 1993: Earthy and resin aromas and flavors mar this wine, and there's very little fruit or acidity to give it life. • $6 • (07/31/95) • **74**
Rioja Don Jacobo 1985 • $8 • (03/31/90) • **79**
Rioja Don Jacobo 1982 • $7 • (11/15/87) • **79**
Rioja Don Jacobo Crianza 1989: Round but firm and polished. Plum and chocolate flavors marry nicely. Could use more concentration, but should improve with age. Drinkable now. • $7 • (04/30/95) • **86**
Rioja Don Jacobo Crianza 1988: Seductive plum and spicy vanilla aromas lead to chewy fruit flavors, with lively spice accents and a firm grip. Drinkable now, but there's enough concentration to age well through 1998. • $7 BB • **87**
Rioja Don Jacobo Reserva 1985: A classy, traditional wine loaded with vanilla and fine leather flavors, the fruit and tannins are nicely balanced. It's smooth, firm and drinkable now. • $11 • **85**
Rioja Don Jacobo Reserva 1981 • $11 • (03/31/90) • **86**
Rioja Don Jacobo Rosé 1993: There is a pleasant black currant taste, but the high acidity results in a thin, tart impression. • $6 • (08/31/95) • **78**
Rioja Gran Reserva 1983: In typical traditional Rioja style, it shows some cherry fruit dominated by vanilla, earthy and tea flavors. Smooth, light, but tired. Drinkable now. • $16 • **80**

COSTERS DEL SIURANA

Clos de L'Obac Priorato 1993: Full-bodied, and packed with fruit, oak and tannin. Impressive concentration beneath attractive blackberry and cassis flavors with vanilla and licorice accents. Very firm now, and should improve through 1998. 1,000 cases made. • $45 • **88**
Clos de L'Obac Priorato 1990: Ripe plum and prune flavors, with coffee and chocolate notes that mark maturity. Full-bodied, still tannic. Concentrated, but a bit clumsy, drink with rich food or try in 1997. 1,000 cases made. • $45 • **86**

Miserere Priorato 1993: Lush blackberry flavor and punchy notes of licorice, toast and tar combine in this rich wine. Well-integrated, even subtle, despite its size. 1,000 cases made. • $30 • **85**
Miserere Priorato 1990: You can taste the heat in this rich, ripe monster. There's great concentration on the palate, where chocolate, coffee, plum and prune flavors mingle under the thumb of massive tannins. Yet it doesn't cloy or burn. Drinkable now. 800 cases made. • $30 • (04/30/95) • **91**

COTO, BODEGAS EL

Rioja Coto de Imaz Gran Reserva 1982 • $NA • (11/30/91) • **85**
Rioja Coto de Imaz Reserva 1981 • $9 • (03/31/90) • **81**
Rioja Crianza 1990: A ripe tasting red that's low in tannins and soft in texture with spicy, gamey aromas and pruny flavors. Drinkable now. Tasted twice. • $6 • **80**
Rioja Crianza 1987 • $11 • (09/30/91) • **79**
Rioja Crianza 1985 • $5 • (03/31/90) BB • **81**
Rioja Crianza 1984 • $7 • (03/31/90) BB • **81**
Rioja Gran Reserva 1982: Mature now, this offers tea and cinnamon aromas and smooth, vanilla-accented fruit, thick and soft in texture. Traditional, pleasant and ready to drink. • $10 • **83**

COVISA

Elena Talier "La Pyramida" Somontano 1994: Fresh, firm and fruity. Exuberant blackberry and cassis flavors with a touch of herb for interest, and just enough tannin for food. Unsophisticated, but pleasant drinking. 20,000 cases made. • $6 • **84**

CUEVA DEL GRANERO, BODEGAS

La Mancha Crianza 1988 • $6 • (10/15/92) • **80**

CUNE

Rioja Clarete 1987 • $7 • (11/15/91) • **78**
Rioja Clarete 1986 • $7 • (03/31/92) BB • **84**
Rioja Clarete 1985 • $7 • (03/31/90) • **88**
Rioja Clarete 1984 • $6 • (10/15/88) BB • **80**
Rioja Clarete 1982 • $4 • (06/01/85) • **83**
Rioja Clarete 1978 • $5 • (06/16/85) • **78**
Rioja Clarete Crianza Rioja 1990: Rich, complex aromas, and mature, ripe flavors make this an appealing wine to drink now. Light in tannins. Tasted twice. • $8 • **81**
Rioja Contino Reserva 1989: A well-integrated marriage of black cherry, coffee and earthy flavors with firm tannins and a spicy finish. Maturing now, it's probably near its best. • $16 • **84**
Rioja Contino Reserva 1988: While this estate has been a leader in Rioja, this vintage has been problematic for us. Several bottles were marred by a penetrating musty note, and others showed burnt chicory and slightly rubbery flavors. Nonetheless, all have been concentrated and rip • $16 • **84**
Rioja Imperial Gran Reserva 1987: There's plenty of fruit left in this round, soft, smooth red, delivering flavors of plum, raisin, tobacco and spice. Tannins are an asset. Well-made Rioja from a difficult year. Drinkable now. • $27 • (03/31/96) • **87**
Rioja Imperial Gran Reserva 1986 • $25 • (04/15/94) • **86**
Rioja Imperial Gran Reserva 1985 • $25 • (04/15/94) • **89**
Rioja Imperial Gran Reserva 1982 • $22 • (03/31/92) • **86**
Rioja Imperial Gran Reserva 1981 • $26 • (03/31/92) • **82**
Rioja Imperial Gran Reserva 1978 • $15 • (03/31/90) • **70**
Rioja Imperial Gran Reserva 1975 • $24 • (03/31/92) • **84**
Rioja Imperial Gran Reserva 1973 • $28 • (03/31/90) • **85**
Rioja Imperial Reserva 1986 • $NA • (03/31/92) • **87**
Rioja Reserva 1986 • $10 • (04/15/94) • **76**
Rioja Reserva 1985 • $8 • (03/31/90) • **85**

Key: SS—Spectator Selection. CS—Cellar Selection. BB—Best Buy. $NA—Price not available. (BT)—Barrel tasting. Ⓐ—Auction Price.
Dates in parentheses represent the issues in which the ratings were published.

Rioja Viña Real 1990: Good spice and berry flavors run through this well-made wine. Balanced, though not particularly intense, with cinnamon and clove accents on the finish. • $9 • (03/31/95) • **84**
Rioja Viña Real 1988 • $10 • (03/31/92) • **87**
Rioja Viña Real 1987 • $10 • (03/31/92) • **86**
Rioja Viña Real 1986 • $8 • (03/31/90) • **81**
Rioja Viña Real 1985 • $7 • (03/31/90) • **85**
Rioja Viña Real 1980 • $5 • (06/01/85) • **75**
Rioja Viña Real Crianza 1989: An aromatic cacaphony-gamy, smoky, herbal, fruity-resolves on the palate to give this wine an intensity and complexity rare in crianzas. It's balanced, not too tannic, and will drink well now through 1997. 50,000 cases made. • $9 BB • **87**
Rioja Viña Real Gran Reserva 1986: This wine shows ripeness and firm structure, but earthy and bitter flavors overwhelm the cherry and spice. Lacks harmony and appeal. • $19 • (03/31/95) • **77**
Rioja Viña Real Gran Reserva 1985 • $18 • (04/15/94) • **91**
Rioja Viña Real Gran Reserva 1981 • $17 • (03/31/90) • **88**
Rioja Viña Real Gran Reserva 1973 • $24 • (03/31/92) • **84**
Rioja Viña Real Gran Reserva 1970 • $24 • (03/31/92) • **85**

DELAPIERRE

Brut Cava Carte Noir NV • $8 • (03/31/93) • **78**

DIAZ, J.

Madrid 1985 • $5 • (03/31/90) BB • **85**
Madrid Tinto de Madrid 1985 • $6 • (06/30/88) • **72**

DUBOSC

Brut Cava NV • $10 • (03/31/93) • **81**

EGLI, BODEGAS C. AUGUSTO

Utiel-Requena Casa lo Alto 1983 • $9 • (07/31/89) • **82**

ENVERO

Viño de Mesa Reserva Limousin 1987 • $10 • (08/31/93) • **85**

ERMITA DE PIO

Jumilla 1994: Firm and rich but lacking fruit, showing coffee, herb and licorice flavors. The finish is dry and chewy. 400,000 cases made. • $8 • (04/30/96) • **79**

ESTOLA

La Mancha Crianza Reserva 1987 • $10 • (12/15/92) • **78**
La Mancha Reserva 1985 • $10 • (02/15/92) • **80**
La Mancha Reserva 1982 • $6 • (11/15/89) BB • **87**

FARINA, BODEGAS

Fin del Duero Castilla y Leon 1990: A ripe wine with lush, jammy flavors of plum and black cherry, generous but with enough tannin to keep it firm. Straightforward and enjoyable. A new wine. • $12 • (03/31/95) • **85**
Tinto Crianzano Tierra del Viño 1986 • $7 • (11/30/89) • **79**
Toro 1994: Ripe and fruity, soft and grapey, with light tannins. It's easy-drinking, but doesn't have the stuffing to last. Try it lightly chilled. 5,000 cases made. • $7 • **81**
Toro 1993: Fruity enough, but the texture is slightly spritzy. Has drying tannins and a coarse feel. 2,000 cases made. • $6 • (01/31/95) • **74**
Toro 1992 • $6 • (04/15/94) • **55**
Toro Colegiata 1994: Clean, well-balanced, almost neutral in flavor, but light pear and hazelnut flavors linger on the finish. Simple but well-made. 3,000 cases made. • $7 • (07/31/95) • **80**
Toro Colegiata 1993: A full-bodied white with spritzy texture and simple flavors. 1,000 cases made. • $7 • (02/28/95) • **78**

Toro Colegiata 1991: Barnyardy, gamy and herbal flavors make an unpalatable stew in this clumsy wine. Tasted twice, with consistent notes. 3,000 cases made. • $7 • **63**

Toro Colegiata Tinto 1990: The gamy, meaty aromas are a bit offputting, but the plum, prune and licorice flavors save it. It's jammy and rich, though lacking focus. Drinkable now. • $9 • **77**

Toro Dama de Toro Reserva 1989: A muscular wine with plum and chocolate flavors, this shows good concentration without much complexity. It's mature and drinking well now. 2,000 cases made. • $10 • **83**

Toro Gran Colegiata Crianza 1990: A ripe, supple red with spicy vanilla aromas, plenty of prune, plum and chocolate flavor and a simple finish. Not very tannic, drinkable now. 800 cases made. • $10 • (01/31/95) • **81**

Toro Gran Colegiata Riserva 1988: Sweet oak and wet leather dominate. Has vanilla and cherry notes, with soft tannins. Mature, syrupy fruit and a drying finish. 900 cases made. • $12 • **79**

Toro Gran Colegiata Riserva 1987: This big wine is beginning to fade now. There are still plenty of tannin and alcohol, but the fruit has evolved to tea, dried cherry and leather flavors. 700 cases made. • $12 • (03/31/95) • **80**

Toro Gran Colegiata Riserva 1986: Cola and nutmeg are the dominant flavors, dry tannins the primary texture. This is past its peak. 600 cases made. • $20 • (03/31/95) • **76**

Toro Gran Colegiata Tinto Crianza 1989 • $11 • (04/15/94) • **83**

Toro Reserva 1987 • $12 • (10/15/92) • **80**

Toro Tinto 1990 • $8 • (10/15/92) • **81**

Toro Viño Primero 1995: Candylike flavors of table grapes, bananas and cherries give this a youthful appeal but little depth. Best as a chilled apéritif. 4,000 cases made. • $8 • (04/30/96) • **77**

Zamora 1991 • $5 • (04/15/94) • **79**

Zamora Gran Peromato 1990: This smooth, solid red isn't showy, but it offers ripe, chunky flavors of plums and prunes, adding hints of vanilla and herbs and firm tannins. 5,000 cases made. • $6 • (04/30/96) • **82**

Zamora Gran Peromato Viño de Mesa 1989: Nicely developed aromas of spice and mint lend interest to this oak-influenced, mature and lean-flavored red. 1,000 cases made. • $9 • (02/28/95) • **82**

Zamora Peromato Tinto 1990 • $6 • (04/15/94) • **77**

Zamora Peromato Viño de la Tierra 1991: Smooth and mellow, with subtle plum and cranberry flavors and moderate tannins. 2,000 cases made. • $5 • (02/28/95) • **81**

Zamora Viño de la Tierra 1992: Soft, fruity and simple. It tastes clean and fresh, but is very uncomplicated. 4,000 cases made. • $6 • (02/28/95) • **79**

FAUSTINO MARTINEZ, BODEGAS

Brut Cava Reserva NV • $15 • (03/31/93) • **71**

Rioja 1989 • $10 • (03/31/93) • **83**

Rioja Faustino I Gran Reserva 1987: A smooth, mature wine with ripe cherry, tea and earthy flavors. It's typical and pleasant but not exciting. 31,500 cases made. • $16 • **82**

Rioja Faustino I Gran Reserva 1986 • $21 • (03/31/93) • **86**

Rioja Faustino I Gran Reserva 1982 • $25 • (03/31/92) • **82**

Rioja Faustino I Gran Reserva 1981 • $12 • (10/31/88) • **88**

Rioja Faustino I Gran Reserva 1978 • $NA • (03/31/92) • **76**

Rioja Faustino I Gran Reserva 1973 • $NA • (03/31/92) • **82**

Rioja Faustino I Gran Reserva 1970 • $NA • (03/31/92) • **89**

Rioja Faustino V 1985 • $7 • (10/15/88) • **83**

Rioja Faustino V Reserva 1991: Firm and harmonious, this rich red offers plum, tobacco and light earth notes in a rather somber package that's best accompanied by food. Drinkable now. • $10 • (03/31/96) • **84**

Rioja Faustino V Reserva 1989: Hints of dry leaves and woodsmoke carry through the deep cherry flavor and firm tannins in this muscular wine. It's rich but rough. Drinkable now. 63,000 cases made. • $10 • **83**

Rioja Faustino V Reserva 1988 • $14 • (03/31/93) • **81**

Rioja Faustino V Reserva 1987 • $13 • (01/31/92) • **81**

Rioja Faustino V Reserva 1986 • $16 • (03/31/92) • **86**

Rioja Faustino V Reserva 1985 • $18 • (03/31/92) • **82**

Rioja Faustino VII 1991: Earthy, barnyardy aromas and vanilla and cherry flavors add up to a traditional style of Rioja. It's silky in texture, long on the finish, but it won't appeal to everyone. • $6 • (01/31/95) • **81**

Rioja Faustino VII 1990: Black cherry fruit mingles with an earthy, gamy flavor often found in traditional Riojas. For those who like the style, it's balanced and firm. Drinkable now. 174,000 cases made. • $7 • **81**

Rioja Faustino VII 1988 • $8 • (01/31/92) BB • **85**

FERNANDEZ, BODEGAS ALEJANDRO

Ribera del Duero Pesquera 1990 • $20 • (12/15/93) • **89**

Ribera del Duero Pesquera 1989 • $20 • (04/15/92) CS • **91**

Ribera del Duero Pesquera 1988 • $17 • (09/30/91) • **89**

Ribera del Duero Pesquera 1987 • $17 • (09/30/90) • **84**

Ribera del Duero Pesquera 1986 • $19 • (04/30/89) • **91**

Ribera del Duero Pesquera 1985 • $16 • (04/30/88) • **89**

Ribera del Duero Pesquera 1984 • $14 • (11/15/87) • **89**

Ribera del Duero Pesquera 1983 • $12 • (11/15/87) • **94**

Ribera del Duero Pesquera 1982 • $NA • (11/15/87) • **89**

Ribera del Duero Pesquera 1979 • $NA • (11/15/87) • **90**

Ribera del Duero Pesquera 1978 • $NA • (11/15/87) • **89**

Ribera del Duero Pesquera 1975 • $NA • (11/15/87) • **88**

Ribera del Duero Pesquera Crianza 1991 • $18 • (04/15/94) • **91**

Ribera del Duero Pesquera Gran Reserva 1990: Seductive aromas of blackberry and cocoa give way to rich, ripe, vibrant flavors of fruit and spice. Concentrated and chewy, it has firm tannins and a long, licorice-scented finish. Approachable now, should be better in 1997. 2,500 cases made. • $70 • (04/30/96) • **91**

Ribera del Duero Pesquera Janus Reserva Especial 1982 • $75 • (09/15/88) • **94**

Ribera del Duero Pesquera Reserva 1991: Here's a delicious fruit bomb. From the exuberant blackberry aromas to the sweet, concentrated berry, cherry and plum flavors, this just keeps on coming. There's enough vanilla, oak and firm tannin to frame it and keep the wine in balance. Approachable now. 5,000 cases made. • $26 • (04/30/95) • **91**

Ribera del Duero Pesquera Reserva 1990 • $27 • (04/15/94) • **89**

Ribera del Duero Pesquera Reserva 1986 • $26 • (09/30/90) • **92**

Ribera del Duero Pesquera Reserva 1985 • $NA • (03/31/90) • **89**

Ribera del Duero Reserva 1990: Powerful yet harmonious, this has exuberant ripe plum and black cherry flavors, lots of toasty oak and tannin and enough polish to match the concentration. Tasty now, it will improve with aging. 2,500 cases made. • $27 • **89**

FERRET

Brut Cava NV • $11 • (09/30/87) • **67**

Brut Nature Cava 1984 • $14 • (05/31/88) • **78**

Brut Nature Cava NV • $12 • (09/30/87) • **78**

Brut Nature Cava Rosat 1984 • $15 • (05/31/88) • **85**

FINO ALAIZ

Navarra NV • $4 • (10/31/88) • **78**

FORNELOS, LAGAR DE

Lagar de Cervera Albariño Rias Baixas 1994: A generously flavored, enticingly dry style of white with fig, peach and grapefruit notes and a crisp finish. Has great balance and concentration. • $15 • (03/31/95) • **87**

Lagar de Cervera Albariño Rias Baixas 1993: A good, earthy flavor runs through this racy wine. Concentrated pear and fig flavors, with a hint of butter. Elegant, with a long finish. • $16 • **86**

FREIXENET

Brut Cava Carta Nevada NV • $8 • (05/15/94) • **82**

Brut Cava Cordon Negro NV • $10 • (06/15/94) • **80**

Brut Cordon Negro NV • $9 • (02/29/92) • **80**

Brut Nature 1987 • $10 • (05/15/92) • **80**

Brut Nature Cava 1988 • $10 • (06/15/94) • **86**

Brut Nature Cava 1985 • $10 • (12/31/90) • **81**

Brut Nature Cava 1984 • $8 • (05/31/88) • **75**

Brut Rosé Cava NV • $10 • (06/15/94) • **84**

Extra Dry Cava Cordon Negro NV • $10 • (06/15/94) • **77**

Extra Dry Cava Seco NV • $6 • (05/31/88) • **77**

Extra Dry Cordon Negro NV • $9 • (02/29/92) • **80**
Seco Cava Carta Nevada NV • $7 • (12/31/90) • **71**
Semi-Seco Cava Carta Nevada NV • $8 • (06/15/94) • **76**

GANDIA

Cabernet Sauvignon Utiel-Requena 1993: Good structure, concentration and firm tannins, but the coffee and earth notes detract from the black cherry flavors. 20,000 cases made. • $6 • **78**
Chardonnay Utiel-Requena 1993: Light and crisp, with green apple and lemon flavors that fade quickly, this is a simple, basically neutral wine. 20,000 cases made. • $6 • (04/30/95) • **75**
Merlot Utiel-Requena 1993: A solidly-built wine with firm tannins, ripe cherry flavors and an attractive mineral note. A bit austere. 20,000 cases made. • $6 • (03/31/95) BB • **83**
Utiel-Requena Hoya de Cadenas Reserva 1989: This is about as neutral as red wine gets: light but firm vegetal notes and a hint of red cherries on the short finish. 22,000 cases made. • $7 • (04/30/96) • **74**
Utiel-Requena Marques de Chivé 1989: A pleasant wine with berry fruit and soft tannins. It's simple but balanced and will marry well with hearty food. Drinkable now. 50,000 cases made. • $6 • **81**
Valencia Castillo de Liria White NV • $5 • (04/15/94) BB • **80**

GRAN CAUS

Cabernet Sauvignon Cabernet Franc Merlot Penedès 1986 • $12 • (04/30/89) • **77**
Cabernet Sauvignon Cabernet Franc Merlot Penedès 1985 • $12 • (10/15/88) • **77**
Can Ràfols dels Caus Penedès 1987 • $11 • (10/15/90) • **78**
Penedès 1984 • $12 • (09/15/88) • **68**

GRAN CONDAL

Rioja 1987 • $6 • (03/31/90) • **80**
Rioja Gran Reserva 1982 • $10 • (11/15/87) • **79**
Rioja Gran Reserva 1981 • $8 • (11/30/87) • **80**
Rioja Reserva 1980 • $7 • (11/30/87) BB • **82**

GRAN CORPAS

Tarragona 1988 • $5 • (10/15/92) BB • **84**

GRINON, MARQUES DE

Castilla y Leon Durius 1993: Lively, packed with ripe plum, blackberry and coffee flavors, adding soft tannins and bright acidity. It's clean and lingers on the finish. Drinkable now. 25,000 cases made. • $9 • (04/30/96) • **83**
Castilla y Leon Durius 1991: Vivid and jammy, this wine has lively cherry and blackberry flavors, but there's a candied, spicy note that's not quite clean. Attractive, but with a bit too much make-up. 25,000 cases made. • $9 • (03/31/95) • **78**
Colección Personal Reserva Rioja 1988: Aromas of spice, leather and smoke presage black cherry and plum flavors. It's bold yet utterly harmonious. Drink now or hold. 6,000 cases made. • $15 • (04/30/95) • **88**
Dominio Valdepusa Tinto Malpica 1992: Almost black in color, bursting with chocolate, black pepper and ripe plum and prune flavors, mouth-filling tannins and plenty of alcohol. Should improve. 3,500 cases made. • $19 • (04/30/95) • **87**
Rioja 1994: Pretty vanilla and berry flavors are soft and lush in this drink-me-now red. It's bright and lively, and finishes with nice spicy notes. Delicacy and vivacity are its strong points. 30,000 cases made. • $10 • (06/30/96) BB • **88**
Rioja 1991: Full-bodied, rich, balanced and smooth, with mature flavors of plum, prune and spice, a pleasant gamy component throughout and a dollop of brown sugar on the finish. 200,000 cases made. • $10 • (03/31/95) • **86**

Key: SS—Spectator Selection. CS—Cellar Selection. BB—Best Buy. $NA—Price not available. (BT)—Barrel tasting. Ⓐ—Auction Price.
Dates in parentheses represent the issues in which the ratings were published.

Tinto do Toledo 1985 • $12 • (02/28/90) • **86**

GUELBENZU, BODEGAS

Navarra 1994: Harmonious, firm and ripe, offering black cherry, spice and light herbal flavors in a well-knit, though not showy, package. A good wine with food, drinkable now. 3,000 cases made. • $10 • (04/30/96) • **84**
Navarra 1992: Deeply colored, tasty and intriguing. Has lush cherry and blackberry flavors accented by spice. Moderately tannic, but drink now for its freshness. 1,000 cases made. • $9 • **84**
Navarra 1990 • $9 • (12/15/93) • **82**
Navarra 1989 • $11 • (04/15/92) • **87**
Navarra Evo 1992: Unusually powerful for the region. Deeply colored, toasty oak and plum aromas and flavors, international style. Drinkable now. 2,000 cases made. • $17 • (04/30/95) • **87**
Navarra Evo 1989 • $20 • (04/15/92) • **85**
Navarra Jardin 1995: Spicy and fruity, blackberry jam-like flavors dominate this round, fresh wine. Lacks the structure to age, but chill lightly now and take it on a picnic. 5,000 cases made. • $8 • **84**

GURPEGUI MUGA, BODEGAS LUIS

Navarra Mendiani 1993: An attractive red in a lighter style. The cherry flavor is sweet and fresh, backed by black pepper and vanilla accents. Drinkable now. • $NA • **82**
Navarra Mendiani 1992: Earthy and plummy flavors mingle in this soft, fleshy wine. It has enough concentration to stand up to food, but lacks definition. Drinkable now. 30,000 cases made. • $4 • **78**
Navarra Mendiani White 1992: Reminds us of a dry German Riesling with its piney, peachy flavors and zippy acidity. Lean, crisp and refreshing. • $4 • (03/31/95) • **83**
Rioja Viña Berceo 1993: Bright cherry and berry flavors give this immediate appeal. It's light and fresh, if a bit diluted. Drinkable now. • $NA • **80**
Rioja Viña Berceo 1992: A fresh, clean wine with plenty of cinnamon-scented spice to brighten the berry fruit flavors. Light tanning make it easy to drink now. 150,000 cases made. • $5 • (05/10/95) BB • **84**
Rioja Viña Berceo White 1992: Bludgeoned into insensibility with oak barrels, offering only burnt toast and turpentine flavors. Like an experiment gone wrong. 40,000 cases made. • $6 • (07/31/95) • **72**

HERMANOS LURTON

Rueda 1992 • $4 • (06/15/93) • **77**

HUGUET

Brut Nature Cava Gran Reserva 1989 • $20 • (03/31/93) • **82**

IBERNOBLE

Ribera del Duero 1993 • $8 • **68**
Ribera del Duero 1992 • $8 • **63**
Ribera del Duero Crianza 1992: Oak aging adds vanilla and coffee flavors, which dominate the dried berry and tobacco notes. It's smooth, light and silky. • $15 • (04/30/96) • **78**
Ribera del Duero Crianza 1989: Chocolate aromas and flavors follow through to the long finish. There are also ripe plum and raisin tones, but basically it's a beautiful, one-note wine. Drinkable now. 10,000 cases made. • $15 • (04/30/95) • **87**
Ribera del Duero Reserva 1986: An attractive, polished wine with soft plum fruit and plenty of chocolate flavor. Harmonious, though not complex, it flows over the palate into a long finish, rich and ripe with no hard edges. Drinkable now. 6,000 cases made. • $27 • (04/30/95) • **87**

INVIOSA, BODEGAS

Tierra de Barros Lar de Barros 1992: Ripe yet firm, this rustic red shows coffee, earth and plum flavors over muscular tannins. A good barbecue wine, drinkable now. 15,000 cases made. • $10 • **83**

Tierra de Barros Lar de Barros Tinto Reserva 1991: Vivid but a bit unbalanced. Shows coffee, vanilla and raspberry jam flavors, sharp acidity and gripping tannins. Perhaps it will mellow. 10,000 cases made. • $9 • **79**
Tierra de Barros Lar de Barros Tinto Reserva 1990: Assertive, flavorful, mature. Extreme in style. Flavors of respberry, leather, vanilla and spice. Drink immediately. 10,000 cases made. • $10 • (12/15/94) • **82**
Tierra de Barros Lar de Barros Tinto Reserva 1989 • $8 • (12/15/93) BB • **86**
Tierra de Barros Lar de Barros Tinto Reserva 1988 • $10 • (04/15/92) • **79**
Tierra de Barros Lar de Barros Tinto Reserva 1986 • $8 • (10/15/90) SS • **91**
Tierra de Barros Lar de Barros Tinto Reserva 1983 • $7 • (10/15/87) • **77**
Tierra de Barros Lar de Barros Tinto Reserva 1982 • $5 • (05/15/87) BB • **87**

IRACHE, BODEGAS

Navarra Castillo Irache Reserva 1978 • $12 • (03/31/90) • **81**

JUMILLA, CASTILLO

Jumilla 1985 • $5 • (07/31/89) • **75**
Jumilla Bodegas Bleda 1989 • $8 • (12/15/92) • **79**

JUVE Y CAMPS

Brut Cava Extra Reserva de la Familia 1986 • $16 • (03/31/93) • **76**
Brut Cava Grand Cru NV • $13 • (05/31/88) • **74**
Brut Cava Natural Reserva de la Familia 1983 • $10 • (05/31/88) • **79**
Brut Cava Natural Reserva de la Familia 1981 • $10 • (07/16/86) • **80**

LAN, BODEGAS

Lancorta Crianza Rioja 1989: An intriguing blend of cedar, coffee and cherry flavors combine in this firm-textured, rather tannic wine. Drink now. 150,000 cases made. • $9 • (01/31/95) • **84**

LAR DE LARES

Tierra de Barros Gran Reserva 1989: Rustic but generous, round and mature, mingling raisin, tea, vanilla and light earth flavors in a solid, simple structure. Drinkable now. 2,500 cases made. • $16 • (04/30/96) • **78**
Tierra de Barros Gran Reserva 1982 • $14 • (06/15/91) • **90**

LAVERNOYA, CAVAS

Brut Cava Lacrima Baccus Gran Reserva NV • $10 • (06/15/94) • **77**
Brut Cava Lacrima Baccus Primerisimo NV • $13 • (06/15/94) • **76**
Brut Cava Summum NV • $18 • (08/31/93) • **82**
Cabernet Sauvignon Penedès 1989: Spicy, fruity and mellow, supple in texture but full-bodied and rich in flavor. A very complete and satisfying red wine. • $9 •(04/15/94) BB • **88**
Cabernet Sauvignon Penedès 1988 • $11 • (03/31/93) • **85**

LEMBEY

Brut 1988 • $6 • (05/15/92) BB • **83**
Brut Cava 1985 • $6 • (05/31/88) • **74**
Brut Cava 1984 • $6 • (05/31/88) • **70**
Brut Cava 1982 • $6 • (12/16/85) BB • **72**
Brut Cava Pedro Domecq 1991 • $6 • (06/15/94) • **79**
Brut Cava Pedro Domecq 1986 • $7 • (07/15/90) • **79**
Brut Cava Première Cuvée 1985 • $14 • (03/31/93) • **87**
Brut Cava Première Cuvée 1982 • $12 • **79**

LEON, JEAN

Cabernet Sauvignon Penedès 1988: Rich and quite firm, showing good concentration but less definition. The flavors mingle dried cherry, black olive and tobacco as tannins take over on aftertaste. It could still improve. • $26 • (03/31/96) • **85**
Cabernet Sauvignon Penedès 1984 • $12 • (03/31/91) • **77**
Cabernet Sauvignon Penedès 1983 • $8 • (03/31/90) • **85**
Cabernet Sauvignon Penedès 1980 • $NA • **62**
Cabernet Sauvignon Penedès 1978 • $6 • (04/16/84) • **66**
Cabernet Sauvignon Penedès Reserva 1982: Supple and quite elegant, this features plum, coffee and light herbal flavors in a surprisingly delicate texture, then toughens up somewhat on the finish. Probably at its best now. • $31 • (03/31/96) • **84**
Cabernet Sauvignon Penedès Reserva 1979: Attractive spice and cedar aromas give way to light but firm texture and flavors of dried cherry, herb and chocolate. It turns a bit tough on the finish, though, drink now with food. • $34 • (03/31/96) • **85**
Penedès 1987: Solid and flavorful, a hearty, blackberry flavored red with ample tannins, expressive fruit and full body. A bit rough around the edges, but quite enjoable. • $15 • **84**

LLANOS, BODEGAS LOS

Señorio de Los Llanos Gran Reserva Valdepeñas 1984 • $13 • (01/31/93) • **85**
Señorio de Los Llanos Reserva Valdepeñas 1987 • $9 • (01/31/93) • **81**
Señorio de Los Llanos Reserva Valdepeñas 1984 • $6 • (10/15/92) • **79**

LOPEZ DE HEREDIA VINA TONDONIA, R.

Rioja Bosconia 1982 • $6 • (12/31/87) • **70**
Rioja Bosconia Full Red Rioja 1987: Vanilla, tea and berry flavors predominate in this traditional-style Rioja. Firm tannins may dry out before they soften, however. Drinkable now. • $NA • (03/31/95) • **83**
Rioja Bosconia Gran Reserva 1976 • $14 • (03/31/90) • **72**
Rioja Bosconia Gran Reserva 1973 • $14 • (03/31/90) • **80**
Rioja Bosconia Reserva 1986 • $13 • (03/31/92) • **79**
Rioja Bosconia Reserva 1983 • $13 • (03/31/92) • **78**
Rioja Bosconia Reserva 1982 • $5 • (11/15/87) • **84**
Rioja Cubillo 1987 • $9 • (03/31/92) • **84**
Rioja Cubillo 1984 • $5 • (03/31/90) • **70**
Rioja Tondonia 1981 • $6 • (12/31/87) • **78**
Rioja Tondonia Gran Reserva 1981 • $NA • (03/31/92) • **79**
Rioja Tondonia Gran Reserva 1976 • $37 • (03/31/92) • **85**
Rioja Tondonia Gran Reserva 1973 • $44 • (03/31/92) • **87**
Rioja Tondonia Gran Reserva 1970 • $44 • (03/31/92) • **75**
Rioja Tondonia Reserva 1985 • $13 • (03/31/92) • **86**
Rioja Tondonia Reserva 1983 • $5 • (03/31/90) • **79**
Rioja Viña Tondonia 1987: Getting tired in taste and brown in color. A fully mature wine with cola and tea flavors. Thin on fruit. Tasted twice with consistent notes. 25,000 cases made. • $10 • **77**
Rioja Viña Tondonia Gran Reserva 1976: Fully mature, this is a silhouette of a wine. Light tea and leather flavors accompanied by a silky mouth-feel and a faint finish. For fans of old wine. Drink up. • $NA • (03/31/95) • **82**

LORINON

Rioja Reserva 1989: Plum, spice and caramel flavors give this round, soft wine appeal. It's ripe, with soft tannins, made in a traditional style and ready to drink. 2,500 cases made. • $17 • (04/30/95) •**82**

MAESE JOAN, BODEGAS

Rioja Armorial Crianza 1986 • $8 • (12/15/92) • **82**
Rioja Crianza 1989: Firm and balanced, with spicy cherry and vanilla flavors, this wine also shows an earthy, gamy note that won't appeal to everyone. • $NA • **80**
Rioja El Coro 1990: Ripe cherry fruit is dominated by a chalky, earthy aroma and a dry, dusty finish. An off-balance wine with some attractive elements. 19,000 cases made. • $7 • **72**

MAGANA, BODEGAS

Merlot Navarra Viña Magaña Reserva 1985 • $35 • (04/15/94) • **78**

Navarra 1982 • $14 • (03/31/90) • **73**
Navarra Viña Magaña Gran Reserva 1982 • $30 • (04/15/94) • **74**

MARQUERITE DE BOURGOGNE, CHATEAU

Conde de Valdemar Rioja 1989 • $8 • (12/15/93) • **81**
Conde de Valdemar Reserva Rioja 1987 • $12 • (12/15/93) • **84**
Rioja 1984 • $9 • (03/31/90) • **58**

MARTINEZ BUJANDA, BODEGAS

Rioja Conde de Valdemar 1991 • $7 • (09/30/92) BB • **84**
Rioja Conde de Valdemar Crianza 1993: Lush blackberry and a streak of licorice give this red punch, but the flavors are somewhat muddled. It has enough structure for food, though. 40,000 cases made. • $9 • (03/31/96) • **79**
Rioja Conde de Valdemar Crianza 1990 • $9 • (03/31/94) BB • **87**
Rioja Conde de Valdemar Crianza 1988 • $8 • (03/31/93) • **85**
Rioja Conde de Valdemar Crianza 1987 • $8 • (03/31/92) BB • **90**
Rioja Conde de Valdemar Crianza 1986 • $7 • (03/31/92) • **83**
Rioja Conde de Valdemar Crianza 1985 • $7 • (12/15/88) BB • **89**
Rioja Conde de Valdemar Gran Reserva 1989: Beautifully crafted, well knit, harmonious, featuring classic spice, tea and black cherry and a lingering mineral note that adds depth. Not overly tannic, it's drinkable now but will improve through at least 1997. 10,000 cases made. • $20 • (03/31/96) • **89**
Rioja Conde de Valdemar Gran Reserva 1985 • $21 • (04/15/94) • **90**
Rioja Conde de Valdemar Gran Reserva 1982 • $22 • (11/30/91) • **89**
Rioja Conde de Valdemar Gran Reserva 1981 • $24 • (03/31/92) • **89**
Rioja Conde de Valdemar Gran Reserva 1975 • $NA • (03/31/92) • **87**
Rioja Conde de Valdemar Gran Reserva 1973 • $30 • (03/31/92) • **86**
Rioja Conde de Valdemar Gran Reserva 1970 • $NA • (03/31/92) • **89**
Rioja Conde de Valdemar Reserva 1991: Lush fruit and firm tannins give this red some impact. Flavors of blackberry, coffee and licorice are rich and dark. Sturdy for drinking now. 25,000 cases made. • $12 • (03/31/96) • **84**
Rioja Conde de Valdemar Reserva 1986 • $10 • (03/31/92) • **83**
Rioja Conde de Valdemar Reserva 1985 • $9 • (03/31/92) • **91**
Rioja Conde de Valdemar Reserva 1983 • $14 • (03/31/92) • **88**
Rioja Conde de Valdemar Reserva 1982 • $NA • (03/31/92) • **89**
Rioja Crianza 1990 • $9 • (04/15/94) BB • **87**
Rioja Gran Reserva 1985 • $21 • (04/15/94) • **90**
Rioja Gran Reserva Vendimia Seleccionada 1985 • $25 • (12/15/92) • **83**
Rioja Reserva Especial 1989: Delicious and polished, with nice spice, plum and brown sugar flavors. It is a focused and fairly rich wine with lingering vanilla and cardamon flavors on the finish and a leathery aroma. 2,000 cases made. • $25 • (04/30/95) • **87**
Rioja Reserva Garnacha 1989: Vivid, almost hyperreal aromas of ripe currants, buttery oak and brown sugar carry through on the generous palate, but the wine lacks finesse and structure. A slightly exaggerated style that's drinking well now. 2,000 cases made. • $22 • (04/30/95) • **86**
Rioja Valdemar Vino Tinto 1991 • $7 • (03/31/93) BB • **83**
Rioja Valdemar Vino Tinto 1989 • $7 • (06/30/90) BB • **83**
Rioja Vendimia Seleccionada Garnacha Reserva 1990: Quite expressive, if unconventional, showing exotic flavors of eucalyptus, blueberry and marmalade. It veers between sweet and earthy, soft and tannic. A walk on the wild side of Rioja. 3,000 cases made. • $25 • (03/31/96) • **82**
Rioja Vendimia Seleccionada Reserva 1990: A lush Rioja, boasting toast, coffee and ripe plum flavors. Tannins are firm enough to carry it, and if some focus is lacking on the palate, the lingering finish is elegant. Drinkable now through 1997. 2,000 cases made. • $26 • (03/31/96) • **87**

Key: SS—Spectator Selection. CS—Cellar Selection. BB—Best Buy. $NA—Price not available. (BT)—Barrel tasting. Ⓐ—Auction Price.
Dates in parentheses represent the issues in which the ratings were published.

MARTINSANCHO

Verdejo Rueda 1993: Decadent, tropical-fruit-cocktail flavors dominate. Full with decent acidity, though the finish gets a bit metallic. 1,700 cases made. • $9 • **78**

MAURO, BODEGAS

Ribera del Duero 1991: A solid wine that shows chewy plum, chocolate and earth flavors over firm tannins. It's not very expressive, but will stand up to strong foods. Drinkable now. • $22 • **83**
Ribera del Duero 1990: A muscular wine with firm tannins and lively plum and tar flavors. It's coming into focus now. 7,500 cases made. • $22 • (04/15/94) • **83**
Ribera del Duero 1987 • $17 • (10/15/90) • **82**
Ribera del Duero 1986 • $17 • (03/31/90) • **76**
Ribera del Duero 1985 • $15 • (03/31/90) • **88**
Ribera del Duero 1984 • $16 • (03/31/90) • **78**
Ribera del Duero 1983 • $15 • (10/15/87) • **82**

MENDIANI

Navarra 1990 • $4 • (04/15/92) • **72**

MIRO

Brut Cava NV • $10 • (03/31/93) • **80**
Brut NV • $9 • (02/29/92) • **78**

MOLLINA, BODEGAS DE

Ribera del Duero Urbion 1992: A light, crisp, vegetal tasting red that is tart and lean on the plate. Awkward and green. Tasted twice. 14,000 cases made. • $7 • **70**
Ribera del Duero Urbion 1991: Coffee and earthy flavors mingle with tart cherry fruit, and the tannins are a bit dry, a rustic wine for rustic food. Drinkable now but may soften. 8,000 cases made. • $7 • **80**
Ribera del Duero Urbion 1990: There's plenty of extract and tannin here, but the wine lacks balance and the vegetal flavors are unattractive. It might soften. 12,000 cases made. • $7 • **76**
Ribera del Duero Urbion Crianza 1989: Attractive floral and berry notes carry all the way through this plush wine. It has good balance and lush, ripe fruit. Drinkable now. 3,000 cases made. • $11 • **89**
Tio Vito NV • $4 • (04/15/94) • **79**

MONASTERIO, HACIENDA

Ribera del Duero 1992: Beautiful aromas of toast, tar and cassis are reminiscent of classified-growth Bordeaux. The flavors don't quite match up, but still offer ripe, full plum notes and smoke, licorice and cedar accents. Drinkable now through 1998. 6,000 cases made. • $23 • (04/30/96) • **88**

MONISTROL, MARQUES DE

Brut Blanc de Blancs Cava NV • $7 • (05/31/88) • **79**

MONT-MARCAL

Brut Cava 1991 • $8 • (06/15/94) • **79**
Brut Cava 1990 • $9 • (03/31/93) • **78**
Brut Cava NV • $8 • (07/15/90) • **78**
Brut Cava Gran Reserva NV • $13 • (05/31/88) • **86**
Brut Cava Tradición NV • $7 • (05/31/88) • **81**
Cabernet Sauvignon Penedès 1989 • $9 • (12/15/93) • **82**
Penedès Tinto 1988 • $8 • (03/31/91) • **83**

MONTE DUCAY

Cariñena Gran Reserva 1982 • $8 • (11/30/89) • **85**
Cariñena Vinedos Propios Tinto Gran Reserva 1978 • $8 • (10/31/88) • **82**

MONTE VANNOS

Ribera del Duero 1994: Earth and walnut flavors dominate this broad, thick red, showing accents of herbs, dried fruits and coffee. Powerful, but not all that pleasant. 45,000 cases made. • $11 • (04/30/96) • **77**
Ribera del Duero 1992 • $10 • (12/15/93) • **82**
Ribera del Duero Reserva 1989: Lively in texture, concentrated in oak flavors of smoke and vanilla. Mature, focused, moderately tannic, with a lingering finish. Drinkable now. 3,500 cases made. • $16 • (02/28/95) • **85**
Ribera del Duero Reserva Baños de Valdearados 1985 • $28 • (01/31/93) • **84**
Ribera del Duero Tinto 1992 • $10 • (04/15/94) • **86**
Ribera del Duero Tinto 1991 • $10 • (12/15/92) • **77**

MONTE VELAZ

Rioja 1981 • $4 • (10/15/87) • **73**

MONTECILLO, BODEGAS

Rioja Crianza 1988 • $NA • (03/31/92) • **89**
Rioja Crianza 1987 • $6 • (03/31/92) • **79**
Rioja Especial Gran Reserva 1978 • $30 • (03/31/90) • **85**
Rioja Gran Reserva 1975 • $29 • (12/15/88) • **85**
Rioja Gran Reserva 1973: It's elegant, with light spice and leather flavors and a grip like an old man holding his cane. But it already has one foot in the grave. 3,000 cases made. • $30 • (03/31/95) • **80**
Rioja Gran Reserva 1970: An attractive mix of dried cherry, spice, coffee and herbal notes keeps this lively and harmonious. Silky on the palate, good acidity, but the tannins are beginning to dry out. In good shape for its age, but probably won't improve. • $45 • (01/31/96) • **87**
Rioja Viña Cumbrero 1993: Soft and has some pleasant pear and vanilla notes, but it lacks concentration. A simple quaff. 21,000 cases made. • $7 • (07/31/95) • **79**
Rioja Viña Cumbrero 1991 • $6 • (06/15/93) • **79**
Rioja Viña Cumbrero 1987 • $6 • (08/31/91) BB • **85**
Rioja Viña Cumbrero 1986 • $5 • (03/31/90) • **66**
Rioja Viña Cumbrero 1985 • $5 • (03/31/90) • **59**
Rioja Viña Cumbrero 1984 • $4 • (11/30/87) • **69**
Rioja Viña Cumbrero 1982 • $4 • (11/15/87) • **79**
Rioja Viña Cumbrero 1981 • $4 • (06/01/86) BB • **73**
Rioja Viña Cumbrero Crianza 1991: A big Rioja. Dark color, full, firm tannins and deep notes of currant, coffee and chocolate give this red presence. Drinkable now, but the flavors may come into focus in late 1996. • $7 • (03/31/96) • **84**
Rioja Viña Monty 1978 • $7 • (09/30/86) • **81**
Rioja Viña Monty 1976 • $6 • (05/16/86) • **70**
Rioja Viña Monty Gran Reserva 1986: Barnyardy, vegetal flavors dominate this thick, chewy, astringent wine. It's clumsy and lacks fruit and freshness. Tasted twice, with consistent notes. 17,000 cases made. • $16 • **73**
Rioja Viña Monty Gran Reserva 1985 • $15 • (03/31/94) • **89**
Rioja Viña Monty Gran Reserva 1982 • $14 • (03/31/92) • **87**
Rioja Viña Monty Gran Reserva 1981 • $13 • (03/31/92) • **88**
Rioja Viña Monty Gran Reserva 1980 • $7 • (11/30/87) • **79**
Rioja Viña Monty Gran Reserva 1978 • $28 • (03/31/92) • **82**
Rioja Viña Monty Gran Reserva 1975 • $28 • (03/31/92) • **86**
Rioja Viña Monty Gran Reserva 1973 • $35 • (03/31/92) • **85**
Rioja Viña Monty Gran Reserva 1970 • $40 • (03/31/92) • **87**
Viña Cumbrero Crianza Rioja 1990: Like a cup of good coffee-rich and full-flavored. Fresh and lively, nice cherry and bittersweet chocolate flavors mingling on the finish with spice and vanilla. 80,000 cases made. • $7 • (04/30/95) • **87**
Viña Cumbrero Crianza Rioja 1989: Smooth texture and mature flavors of tomato, vanilla and raspberry mark this soft, easygoing wine. Pleasant drinking now. 75,000 cases made. • $7 BB • **84**

MONTELEIVA, BODEGAS

Rioja Viña Saseta Gran Reserva 1985: Almost creamy in texture, with vanilla, brown sugar, cherry and berry flavors that follow through to the sweet, long finish. Not a blockbuster, but appealing to drink now. 3,000 cases made. • $31 • (03/31/95) • **83**

MONTESIERRA

Somontano 1993: Nouveau aromas and light, fruity flavors make this an easy, fresh-tasting red wine to drink now. 2,750 cases made. • $5 • (01/31/95) • **78**
Somontano 1988 • $6 • (03/31/90) • **81**
Somontano 1987 • $5 • (09/15/88) • **80**
Somontano 1986 • $5 • (11/15/87) • **77**
Somontano Moristel 1995: Light, soft and fruity. Herbal notes perk up the grape flavors. Tastes more like a barrel sample than a finished wine, but served chilled it goes down easily. 4,000 cases made. • $6 • **79**

MORALES, BODEGAS HERMANOS

Gran Creacion Crianza La Mancha 1992: A healthy shot of oak gives this some pleasing chocolate and clove accents, firm tannins and sweet vanilla flavors on the finish. Just enough black cherry to balance it. Try now. 5,000 cases made. • $7 BB • **84**

MORGADIO

Rias Baixas 1994: Very crisp, almost green, with a bright lemon-lime flavor. Quite light and sharp, but would make a clean apéritif. 1,500 cases made. • $18 • (07/31/95) • **80**
Rias Baixas 1993: Lush fruit flavors of peach, apricot and banana give this wine a soft and flavorful profile. Cleanly made and well-balanced, with a good, firm finish. Reminiscent of Riesling. 500 cases made. • $18 • **85**
Rias Baixas 1992 • $18 • (06/15/93) • **80**
Rias Baixas Albariño 1991 • $20 • (05/31/92) • **82**
Torre Fornelos Albariño Rias Baixas 1994: This is crisp, clean and balanced, with light grapefruit, pear and almond flavors. Not complex, but draws you back for more. 1,500 cases made. • $13 • (07/31/95) • **82**

MUERZA, BODEGAS

Rioja Vega 1989 • $7 • (03/31/91) • **77**
Rioja Vega Crianza 1986 • $10 • (03/31/91) • **75**
Rioja Vega Crianza Rioja 1990: A solid core of fruit flavor accented by orange peel and spice. Balanced, dry and refreshing. 20,000 cases made. • $9 • **84**
Rioja Vega Crianza Rioja 1989 • $9 • (04/15/94) • **85**

MUGA, BODEGAS

Rioja 1990: A very gamy wine, with dried tomato and plum flavors. Still tannic, it is fairly rustic and may be best to try now. 35,000 cases made. • $13 • (03/31/95) • **82**
Rioja 1986 • $12 • (05/31/91) • **81**
Rioja 1985 • $12 • (03/31/90) • **83**
Rioja 1984 • $8 • (04/30/89) • **82**
Rioja 1982 • $7 • (11/15/87) • **77**
Rioja Gran Reserva 1976 • $20 • (03/31/90) • **77**
Rioja Prado Enea Gran Reserva 1985: Brown sugar and coffee aromas and vibrant plum flavors. Lively, clean and full-bodied with a long, smoky finish. Drinkable now. 14,000 cases made. • $35 • (04/30/95) • **87**
Rioja Prado Enea Gran Reserva 1982 • $40 • (11/30/91) • **84**
Rioja Prado Enea Gran Reserva 1981 • $35 • (03/31/90) • **79**
Rioja Prado Enea Gran Reserva 1976 • $24 • (03/31/90) • **84**
Rioja Prado Enea Reserva 1981 • $20 • (04/30/89) • **80**
Rioja Reserva 1991: A lush texture and a little spice, but not much fruit. Flavors are slightly dull and cooked, though might perk up with food. It's tannic, too, try in 1997. 6,000 cases made. • $13 • **80**
Rioja Reserva 1989 • $13 • (04/15/94) • **85**
Rioja Reserva 1988 • $13 • (04/15/94) • **87**

MUGA-VILLFRANCA, BODEGAS

Navarra Mendiani 1989 • $4 • (06/15/91) BB • **82**

MURRIETA, MARQUES DE

Rioja 1985 • $17 • (02/28/90) • **87**
Rioja Castillo Ygay Gran Reserva 1968 • $85 • (03/31/90) • **92**
Rioja Castillo Ygay Gran Reserva 1952 • $150 • (03/31/90) • **94**
Rioja Crianza 1991: Smooth, fruity, sculpted, with lots of color and flavor. Medium-bodied and just moderately tannic. Tastes fresh and lively. Drinkable now. • $11 • (12/15/94) • **86**
Rioja Crianza 1990 • $10 • (04/15/94) BB • **88**
Rioja Crianza White 1991: Mature aromas of vanilla and fig lend some interest to this woody, spicy and tart white wine. Not for everybody, because there's little fruit, but it's different. • $10 • (02/28/95) • **80**
Rioja Gran Reserva 1983: A well-made wine with plenty of fresh fruit and firm tannins despite its decade of age. Coffee and spice notes keep it interesting. Drinkable now. Tasted twice. 10,000 cases made. • $20 • **88**
Rioja Gran Reserva 1982: Fruit flavors of raisins and raspberries enlivened by spicy, smoky notes give this wine a delicious complexity as it edges into full maturity. It's rich but not overly tannic and has a long, complex finish. Drink now or hold. Tasted twice. 18,000 cases made. • $60 • **89**
Rioja Gran Reserva 1978 • $30 • (03/31/92) • **87**
Rioja Gran Reserva 1975 • $35 • (03/31/92) • **93**
Rioja Gran Reserva 1973 • $NA • (03/31/92) • **89**
Rioja Gran Reserva 1970 • $NA • (03/31/92) • **83**
Rioja Reserva 1990: The bright cherry flavors are slightly damped by sharp herbaceous aromas. Lean and tart, but vanilla and spice emerge on the finish. Tasted twice, with consistent notes. • $15 • **81**
Rioja Reserva 1988: Round and lively, this wine is shows vivid, fresh plum fruit and toasty oak flavors. It's balanced, firm and young. Attractive now. 57,500 cases made. • $12 • **87**
Rioja Reserva 1986 • $20 • (03/31/92) • **88**
Rioja Reserva 1985 • $20 • (03/31/92) • **90**
Rioja Reserva 1983 • $13 • (03/31/92) • **85**
Rioja Reserva 1982 • $39 • (03/31/92) • **84**
Rioja Reserva 1981 • $39 • (03/31/92) • **88**
Rioja Reserva 1980 • $27 • (03/31/90) • **83**

NAVARRA, VINICOLA

Navarra Castillo de Tiebas Reserva 1976 • $7 • (01/31/88) • **80**
Navarra Las Campanas 1993: Lean, dry and spicy, ending with notes of herbs and watermelon. A firm, dry style that begs for Mediterranean salads or seafood. 5,000 cases made. • $7 • (08/31/95) • **83**
Navarra Las Campanas Crianza 1991: Sweet vanilla and raspberry flavors are enticing in this soft, maturing red, but ultimately seem somewhat simple. Still, a pleasant quaff. 15,000 cases made. • $7 • (04/30/96) • **83**
Navarra Las Campanas Tino Tinto 1982 • $5 • (01/31/88) • **77**

NEKEAS, BODEGA

Merlot Navarra Vega Sindoa 1993: Bright fruit and sweet oak give immediate appeal. Plump with plum and blackberry flavors and a strong vanilla note on the finish. Balanced and firm, should evolve well through 1997. 2,000 cases made. • $10 • **85**
Navarra Vega Sindoa 1993: Firm and well-knit, this lean wine shows spice, tobacco and cherry flavors with dry tannins in a compact structure. A traditional style. 5,000 cases made. • $6 • **81**

NUESTRA SENORA DE LA ANTIGUA

Rioja 1982 • $NA • (11/15/87) • **84**

OCHOA

Cabernet Sauvignon Navarra 1987 • $14 • (09/30/91) • **77**

Key: SS—Spectator Selection. CS—Cellar Selection. BB—Best Buy. $NA—Price not available. (BT)—Barrel tasting. (A)—Auction Price.
Dates in parentheses represent the issues in which the ratings were published.

Navarra 1990: A soft, fruity wine with pleasant vanilla notes and enough tannin to give it the backbone needed for food. Drinkable now. • $NA • **82**
Navarra 1988 • $8 • (09/30/91) BB • **83**
Navarra 1987 • $14 • (09/30/91) • **79**
Navarra 1986 • $5 • (04/15/89) • **73**
Navarra Crianza 1986 • $10 • (11/15/91) • **73**
Navarra Crianza 1984 • $7 • (04/15/89) • **82**
Navarra Reserva 1985: This wine shows spice and tea notes more typical of Rioja, it's soft, with lots of sweet vanilla flavor. A bit clumsy, perhaps, but it has more stuffing than many Navarras, perhaps due to Cabernet Sauvignon in the blend. Drinkable now. • $NA • (04/15/94) • **83**
Navarra Reserva 1982 • $14 • (09/30/91) • **73**
Navarra Reserva 1980 • $11 • (04/15/89) • **85**

OLARRA, BODEGAS

Rioja 1982 • $NA • (11/15/87) • **86**
Rioja Añares 1987 • $6 • (03/31/92) • **79**
Rioja Añares 1985 • $6 • (02/28/89) BB • **82**
Rioja Añares 1983 • $6 • (02/28/90) • **76**
Rioja Añares Gran Reserva 1983 • $19 • (03/31/92) • **75**
Rioja Añares Gran Reserva 1982 • $27 • (11/30/91) • **75**
Rioja Añares Gran Reserva 1981 • $25 • (03/31/92) • **76**
Rioja Añares Reserva 1985 • $25 • (03/31/92) • **83**
Rioja Añares Reserva 1983 • $12 • (02/28/90) • **73**
Rioja Añares Reserva 1981 • $8 • (09/30/86) • **88**
Rioja Cerro Añon 1984 • $4 • (12/01/85) • **70**
Rioja Cerro Añon 1980 • $4 • (04/01/85) • **75**
Rioja Cerro Añon Gran Reserva 1983 • $19 • (03/31/92) • **83**
Rioja Cerro Añon Gran Reserva 1982 • $27 • (11/30/91) • **71**
Rioja Cerro Añon Gran Reserva 1981 • $25 • (03/31/92) • **87**
Rioja Cerro Añon Gran Reserva 1973 • $NA • (03/31/92) • **81**
Rioja Cerro Añon Gran Reserva 1970 • $NA • (03/31/92) • **75**
Rioja Cerro Añon Reserva 1985 • $NA • (03/31/92) • **73**
Rioja Cerro Añon Reserva 1983 • $11 • (03/31/90) • **61**
Rioja Cerro Añon Reserva 1981 • $8 • (09/30/86) • **78**
Rioja Cerro Añon Reserva 1978 • $8 • (03/01/85) • **83**
Rioja Reserva 1978 • $7 • (03/16/85) • **82**
Rioja Tinto 1983 • $5 • (09/30/86) BB • **87**
Rioja Tinto 1980 • $4 • (03/16/85) BB • **87**

ONDARRE, BODEGAS

Rioja Brut Ondarre NV • $11 • (12/31/88) • **81**
Rioja Ondarre 1984 • $5 • (11/15/88) BB • **80**
Rioja Reserva 1981 • $7 • (12/15/88) BB • **84**
Rioja Tidon 1986 • $4 • (12/15/88) • **78**

ONIX

Collita Priorato 1992: Rich and dense, this brawny red shows ripe plum and tomato flavors, muscular tannins and enough acidity to keep it all in balance. A straightforward wine that makes an impact. Try now. 20,000 cases made. • $7 • (04/30/95) • **86**
Priorato 1992 • $7 • (04/15/94) BB • **84**

PADORNINA

El Bierzo 1987 • $8 • (03/31/90) • **81**
El Bierzo 1985 • $7 • (06/30/90) • **74**

PALACIO DE LA VEGA

Navarra Crianza 1991: More complex than many Navarras, this lean wine adds spicy, gamy accents to a polished black cherry core. An unusual blend of 70 percent Cabernet Sauvignon, 30 percent Tempranillo. Drinkable now. • $NA • **83**

PALACIO, BODEGAS

Rioja Cosme Palacio y Hermanos 1989 • $13 • (09/30/92) • **84**

Rioja Cosme Palacio y Hermanos 1988 • $13 • (09/30/92) • **84**
Rioja Cosme Palacio y Hermanos 1987 • $13 • (03/31/90) • **83**
Rioja Cosme Palacio y Hermanos 1986 • $9 • (02/28/89) • **88**
Rioja Glorioso 1986 • $8 • (03/31/90) • **80**
Rioja Glorioso 1985 • $7 • (02/28/89) BB • **85**
Rioja Glorioso Gran Reserva 1982 • $19 • (11/30/91) • **84**
Rioja Glorioso Gran Reserva 1981 • $20 • (03/31/93) • **85**
Rioja Glorioso Gran Reserva 1978 • $15 • (02/28/89) • **88**
Rioja Glorioso Reserva 1982 • $18 • (03/31/90) • **79**
Rioja Glorioso Reserva 1981 • $10 • (02/28/89) • **83**

PALACIOS REMONDO, BODEGAS

Rioja Herencia Remondo 1987 • $6 • (03/31/92) • **84**
Rioja Herencia Remondo 1986 • $6 • (03/31/92) • **76**
Rioja Herencia Remondo 1985 • $NA • (03/31/90) • **81**
Rioja Herencia Remondo 1982 • $NA • (11/15/87) • **90**
Rioja Herencia Remondo Gran Reserva 1982 • $13 • (03/31/92) • **75**
Rioja Herencia Remondo Gran Reserva 1981 • $NA • (03/31/92) • **59**
Rioja Herencia Remondo Gran Reserva 1975 • $NA • (03/31/92) • **79**
Rioja Herencia Remondo Gran Reserva 1973 • $NA • (03/31/92) • **77**
Rioja Herencia Remondo Gran Reserva 1970 • $NA • (03/31/92) • **59**
Rioja Herencia Remondo Reserva 1986 • $9 • (03/31/92) • **79**
Rioja Herencia Remondo Reserva 1985 • $NA • (03/31/92) • **71**

PARXET

Brut Nature Chardonnay NV • $22 • (05/15/92) • **76**

PASCUAS, BODEGA HNOS. PEREZ

Ribera del Duero Viña Pedrosa 1992: Vivid and balanced, rich, featuring an attractive blend of cassis, spice, toast and herbal flavors. It's not a powerhouse, but though drinkable now it should improve through at least 1997. 3,000 cases made. • $23 • (04/30/96) • **87**
Ribera del Duero Viña Pedrosa 1991: A lighter style for Ribera, this is tart and slightly disjointed. Herbal berry and spice flavors, with light, dry tannins. 4,000 cases made. • $20 • **78**
Ribera del Duero Viña Pedrosa 1990: Vanilla-scented oak marries nicely with ripe cassis flavors in this lush, polished wine. Drinkable now, but the balance and concentration promise improvement with time. • $16 • (04/15/94) • **88**
Ribera del Duero Viña Pedrosa 1989 • $18 • (04/15/92) • **86**
Ribera del Duero Viña Pedrosa 1988 • $16 • (05/31/91) • **82**
Ribera del Duero Viña Pedrosa 1987 • $15 • (09/30/90) • **77**
Ribera del Duero Viña Pedrosa 1986 • $14 • (03/31/90) • **88**
Ribera del Duero Viña Pedrosa 1985 • $16 • (09/15/88) • **83**
Ribera del Duero Viña Pedrosa Reserva 1990: For a great vintage, this is straightforward and slightly simple, but raspberry flavors are pleasant until tannins kick in and dry out the finish. 110 cases made. • $100 • (04/30/96) • **77**

PATERNINA, FREDERICO

Rioja Banda Azul 1985 • $5 • (03/15/90) BB • **80**
Rioja Banda Azul Crianza 1993: The silky texture and flavors of light cherry, spice and tea are all characteristic of Rioja, but this is a bit diluted and finishes dry. Drinkable now. 150,000 cases made. • $9 • (03/31/96) • **78**
Rioja Gran Reserva 1987: Tiring now, this traditional red offers tea, earth and leather flavors on a lean, tannic frame. It's drinkable, but doesn't give much pleasure. 15,000 cases made. • $20 • (03/31/96) • **76**
Rioja Viña Vial Reserva 1991: Traditional notes of spice, leather and tea predominate in this lean, somewhat tart red. Expressive but lacks harmony. Better with food. 30,000 cases made. • $14 • (03/31/96) • **79**

PENALBA

Ribera del Duero 1983 • $12 • (02/28/90) • **86**
Ribera del Duero Crianza 1985 • $9 • (02/28/90) • **87**
Ribera del Duero Gran Reserva 1980 • $NA • (03/31/90) • **73**
Ribera del Duero Reserva 1982 • $NA • (03/31/90) • **70**

PERELADA, CASTILLO DE

Ampurdán-Costa Brava Tinto Reserva 1983 • $8 • (10/15/92) • **74**
Cabernet Sauvignon Empordà-Costa Brava 1991: Smooth and light mix of herbal and raisin flavors that finishes a bit dry. Drinkable with food but don't wait. • $10 • (04/30/96) • **80**
Empordà-Costa Brava Reserva 1990: Mature, smooth and sweet, showing raisin, brown sugar and light herbal flavors, then turning dry on the finish. Drinkable now. • $9 • (04/30/96) • **80**
Empordà-Costa Brava Tinto Crianza 1993: This light, smooth red shows herbal, dried cherry and raisin flavors. It's solid but one-dimensional. • $7 • (04/30/96) • **77**

PIQUERAS, BODEGAS

Almansa Castillo de Almansa Viño de Crianza 1987 • $9 • (01/31/93) • **79**
Almansa Castillo de Almansa Viño de Crianza 1986 • $8 • (04/15/92) BB • **83**
Almansa Castillo de Almansa Viño de Crianza 1985 • $8 • (09/30/91) BB • **85**
Almansa Castillo de Almansa Viño de Crianza 1983 • $7 • (03/31/90) • **74**
Almansa Crianza 1988 • $NA • (04/15/94) • **82**

PORTO, BODEGAS

Toro Tinto Colegiata 1985 • $4 • (12/31/87) BB • **84**
Toro Tinto de Crianza Gran Colegiata 1985 • $5 • (12/31/87) • **85**
Toro Tinto de Crianza Gran Colegiata 1982 • $5 • (11/30/87) • **78**

POVEDA, SALVADOR

Alicante Tinto Reserva Monastrell 1989: A quaffable red showing berry, raisin, orange peel and walnut flavors. This is still quite lively but wants drinking now. 100,000 cases made. • $8 • (04/30/96) • **80**
Tinto Gran Reserva 1985 Alicante No. 1 • $9 • (11/15/91) • **79**
Viña Vermeta Tinto Reserva-Monastrell 1988 • $9 • (04/15/94) BB • **83**
Viña Vermeta Tinto Reserva-Monastrell Alicante 1987 • $9 • (03/31/93) • **82**

PRINCIPE DE VIANA, BODEGAS

Cabernet Sauvignon Navarra 1989 • $8 • (03/31/91) BB • **83**
Navarra Crianza 1990 • $NA • (04/15/94) • **82**

PRIVILEGIO DEL RAY SANCHO

Rioja 1978 • $3 • (04/01/84) • **76**

PUERTO, MARQUES DEL

Rioja 1984 • $7 • (02/28/90) • **78**
Rioja 1982 • $6 • (11/15/87) • **78**
Rioja Crianza 1988 • $12 • (03/31/93) • **85**
Rioja Gran Reserva 1985: Traditional Rioja flavors of spice, strawberry and tea mingle in this mature, lean yet still fresh wine. It's silky on the palate, with good balance and a firm finish. Well-made, it's at its best now. 5,000 cases made. • $16 • (04/30/95) • **86**
Rioja Gran Reserva 1978 • $20 • (03/31/90) • **85**
Rioja Reserva 1987: Round plum flavor adds heft to the brown sugar, vanilla and clove nuances, giving this good balance. Still, it's mature, with silky tannins and a slightly drying finish. Drinkable now. 10,000 cases made. • $10 • **83**

PUIG & ROCA, CELLERS

Cabernet Sauvignon Augustus Penedès 1991: There are impressive elements here, from the smoky, toasty oak to the firm acidity and rich tannins, but it's not showing much fruit now. Drinkable now. 1,250 cases made. • $11 • (03/31/95) • **84**

RAIMAT

Cabernet Sauvignon Costers del Segre 1989 • $8 • (01/31/93) • **81**
Cabernet Sauvignon Costers del Segre 1988 • $8 • (12/15/92) • **80**
Cabernet Sauvignon Costers del Segre 1986 • $10 • (03/31/90) • **81**
Costers del Segre Abadia 1989: Nicely balanced berry fruit and bright acidity keep this wine lively and fresh. The tannins are soft and it's at its peak now. A blend of Tempranillo and Cabernet Sauvignon. • $8 • (04/15/94) • **83**
Costers del Segre Abadia 1987 • $9 • (03/31/90) • **84**
Merlot Costers del Segre 1990: The ripe, plump fruit offers appealing cherry and herbal flavors, but the wine lacks depth and dry tannins clamp down on the finish. • $8 • **79**
Tempranillo Costers del Segre 1990: Firm and polished, this wine has good balance and ripe fruit. The plum fruit flavor is accented with herbal, meaty and tar notes. Drinkable now. • $8 BB • **85**

RAVENTOS, JOAN

Brut Cava Rosell Reserva NV • $13 • (03/31/93) • **78**
Brut Nature Cava NV • $14 • (06/15/94) • **78**

REMELLURI

Rioja 1989 • $NA • (03/31/92) • **82**
Rioja 1988 • $NA • (03/31/92) • **75**
Rioja 1986 • $11 • (12/15/90) • **87**
Rioja 1985 • $10 • (03/31/90) • **88**
Rioja 1984 • $9 • (03/31/90) • **77**
Rioja 1983 • $12 • (03/31/90) • **77**
Rioja 1982 • $12 • (03/31/90) • **82**
Rioja Alavesa Labastida 1982 • $8 • (09/30/86) • **84**
Rioja Gran Reserva 1985 • $40 • (03/31/92) • **84**
Rioja Gran Reserva 1982 • $40 • (11/30/91) • **87**
Rioja Reserva 1990: Polished yet rich, deeply colored, aromatic, stuffed with coffee, plum, spice and cedar flavors. This is balanced, even elegant. Approachable now. 23,000 cases made. • $14 • (04/30/95) • **88**
Rioja Reserva 1989: Full-bodied, deeply colored and packed with earthy-gamey-smokey flavors. It's an assertive, bold style of Rioja with firm tannins and just enough fruit. Drinkable now. 25,000 cases made. • $14 • (04/15/94) • **83**
Rioja Reserva 1987 • $14 • (03/31/92) • **76**
Rioja Reserva 1986 • $14 • (03/31/92) • **78**

RIBERALTA, BODEGAS

Ribera del Duero Vega Izan Crianza 1991: There's much oak in this smooth-textured, spicy red. One could ask for more fruit, but it's tasty to drink now. 1,500 cases made. • $11 • (02/28/95) • **83**
Ribera del Duero Vega Izan Tinto Joven 1992: Round and grapey and quaffable, but an earthy note mars the ripe fruit. Made for early drinking. 10,000 cases made. • $7 • **75**
Ribera del Duero Vega Izan Tinto Joven 1991: Dull, earthy aromas and simple, tired flavors make this light red drinkable but not very pleasant. 8,000 cases made. • $7 • (02/28/95) • **72**

RICAVI

Rioja 1994: Soft and fruity, medium body, light tannins and just enough spice to give it interest. Easy drinking now. 5,000 cases made. • $6 • (03/31/96) • **81**
Rioja 1993: Smooth and harmonious, made for early drinking. The smoky cherry and lightly spicy flavors are appealing. Enjoy now while it's fresh. • $6 • **82**

Key: SS—Spectator Selection. CS—Cellar Selection. BB—Best Buy. $NA—Price not available. (BT)—Barrel tasting. Ⓐ—Auction Price.
Dates in parentheses represent the issues in which the ratings were published.

Rioja 1992: A smooth, light-bodied red with plum, herb and coffee flavors and light tannins. A simple, fruity quaffing wine. Drinkable now. 40,000 cases made. • $5 • (04/15/94) • **78**
Rioja Crianza 1991: Silky and charming, if light, this offers typical strawberry, tea and vanilla flavors, fresh and lean, achieving some intensity. Drinkable now. 1,500 cases made. • $8 • (03/31/96) • **83**
Rioja Crianza 1990: A sweet berry flavor is framed nicely in this lean, polished, balanced wine. Not much depth, but the flavors are bright and clean. • $7 • **81**

RIOJA ALTA, LA

Alta Reserva 890 Gran Reserva 1981: The deep mahogany color is unsettling, but distinctive walnut, raisin and brown sugar aromas and flavors give it personality. It's silky on the palate with hints of orange and game. A well-made, traditional Rioja at its peak. • $65 • (06/30/96) • **86**
Rioja Reserva 890 Gran Reserva 1978: A fine example of a mature Rioja. The mahogany color is still vibrant, and the flavors are complex, with coffee, leather and spice notes and enough bright cherry fruit for balance. It's on the plateau, drink now. 1,100 cases made. • $50 • (04/30/95) • **89**
Rioja Reserva 890 Gran Reserva 1973 • $55 • (03/31/92) • **77**
Rioja Reserva 904 Gran Reserva 1982 • $NA • (03/31/92) • **84**
Rioja Reserva 904 Gran Reserva 1981 • $29 • (03/31/92) • **82**
Rioja Reserva 904 Gran Reserva 1976 • $17 • (03/31/90) • **90**
Rioja Reserva 904 Gran Reserva 1975 • $NA • (03/31/92) • **82**
Rioja Reserva 904 Gran Reserva 1973 • $10 • (09/30/86) • **84**
Rioja Reserva 904 Gran Reserva 1970 • $NA • (03/31/92) • **75**
Rioja Viña Alberdi 1991: Mature, with leathery, cedary notes. Tannic but still light-bodied, without enough fruit for balance. • $13 • (06/30/96) • **78**
Rioja Viña Alberdi 1989 • $12 • (04/15/94) • **77**
Rioja Viña Alberdi 1988 • $11 • (04/15/94) • **86**
Rioja Viña Alberdi 1987 • $12 • (03/31/92) • **79**
Rioja Viña Alberdi 1986 • $12 • (03/31/92) • **83**
Rioja Viña Alberdi 1985 • $8 • (03/15/90) BB • **85**
Rioja Viña Alberdi Reserva Lot 2 1989: Good spice and plum flavors, but a murky streak runs through this wine. Hints of vanilla and clove on the finish give it a boost. 22,000 cases made. • $12 • (03/31/95) • **82**
Rioja Viña Arana Reserva 1988: Quite mature, offering some sweet chocolate and licorice flavors to balance the dry tea and leather notes. Sweet finish. A good example of the traditional style, drinkable now. • $17 • (06/30/96) • **83**
Rioja Viña Arana Reserva 1986: Round and soft, with well-defined chocolate and spice flavors. The fruit has mellowed into prune and leather flavors, but it's still balanced and clean. 27,000 cases made. • $16 • (03/31/95) • **82**
Rioja Viña Arana Reserva 1985 • $15 • (04/15/94) • **76**
Rioja Viña Ardanza Reserva 1989: Very mature, showing browning colors, leather and tea aromas, spice and tea flavors and a drying finish. A traditional style that's not going to improve. • $22 • (06/30/96) • **79**
Rioja Viña Ardanza Reserva 1987 • $20 • (04/15/94) • **72**
Rioja Viña Ardanza Reserva 1986 • $20 • (04/15/94) • **85**
Rioja Viña Ardanza Reserva 1985 • $18 • (03/31/92) • **85**
Rioja Viña Ardanza Reserva 1983 • $18 • (03/31/92) • **81**
Rioja Viña Ardanza Reserva 1982 • $17 • (03/31/92) • **84**
Rioja Viña Ardanza Reserva 1978 • $6 • (09/30/86) • **65**

RIOJA SANTIAGO, BODEGAS

Rioja 1991 • $6 • (04/15/94) • **82**
Rioja Gran Reserva 1984: A light, smooth wine with dried berry, tea and leather flavors. It's easy to drink, but the maturing flavors lack much life. Drinkable now. 20,000 cases made. • $16 • (04/15/94) • **82**
Rioja Reserva 1986: Has smoky, earthy aromas and tired, raisiny fruit flavors. Drinkable, but could be fresher. Tasted twice. 14,000 cases made. • $12 •(04/15/94) • **76**

RIOJANAS, BODEGAS

Rioja Canchales 1987 • $4 • (03/15/90) • **75**

Rioja Monte Real Gran Reserva 1985: A dark, attractive wine. Balanced, harmonious and complex, it shows dark fruit, licorice and spice flavors with firm structure and a long finish. Drinkable now. • $22 • (04/15/94) • **88**

Rioja Monte Real Gran Reserva 1982 • $19 • (03/31/92) • **82**

Rioja Monte Real Gran Reserva 1981 • $19 • (03/31/92) • **89**

Rioja Monte Real Gran Reserva 1975 • $NA • (03/31/92) • **78**

Rioja Monte Real Gran Reserva 1973 • $NA • (03/31/92) • **85**

Rioja Monte Real Gran Reserva 1970 • $NA • (03/31/92) • **72**

Rioja Monte Real Reserva 1986: There's pleasant plum fruit here, but a vegetal note, gripping tannins and an earthy finish keep the wine from coming together. Drinkable now. • $14 • (04/15/94) • **77**

Rioja Monte Real Reserva 1985 • $NA • (03/31/92) • **87**

Rioja Monte Real Reserva 1983 • $7 • (03/31/90) BB • **83**

Rioja Monte Real 1991 • $6 • (05/31/92) • **83**

Rioja Puerta Vieja Crianza 1988: Balanced and smooth, showing ripe black cherry fruit on a simple frame, this wine is ready for drinking now. • $9 • (04/15/94) • **80**

Rioja Viña Albina 1983 • $7 • (03/31/90) • **68**

Rioja Viña Albina Gran Reserva 1985: Plum, prune and vanilla flavors are pleasant, but marred by a persistent earthy note, and it's beginning to dry out on the finish. Still has some class, but catch it soon. • $22 • (04/15/94) • **83**

Rioja Viña Albina Gran Reserva 1982 • $19 • (03/31/92) • **87**

Rioja Viña Albina Gran Reserva 1981 • $19 • (03/31/92) • **86**

Rioja Viña Albina Gran Reserva 1975 • $NA • (03/31/92) • **85**

Rioja Viña Albina Gran Reserva 1973 • $NA • (03/31/92) • **81**

Rioja Viña Albina Gran Reserva 1970 • $NA • (03/31/92) • **70**

Rioja Viña Albina Reserva 1986: Roasted coffee and gamy notes give this wine impact, and there are pleasant plum and spicy flavors, though the overall impression is muddy. It's soft and full, ready for drinking now. • $14 • **82**

Rioja Viña Albina Reserva 1985 • $NA • (03/31/92) • **78**

RISCAL, MARQUES DE

Rioja 1984 • $9 • (11/15/88) • **68**

Rioja 1982 • $7 • (11/15/87) • **84**

Rioja Baron de Chirel Reserva 1988: A complex wine that unfolds as you drink it. Subtle spice and chocolate aromas give way to lively plum flavors backed by firm tannins and plenty of oak, then tobacco and brandied cherry notes linger on the long finish. Drink now or hold till 1997. 2,000 cases made. • $36 • (04/30/95) • **90**

Rioja Baron de Chirel Reserva 1986: Rich, ripe and lively in flavor, almost bursting with plum and cherry notes. Big and full-bodied, but not too tannic-it's balanced. Polished and nearing maturity. Drink now through 1997. Tasted twice, with consistent notes. 2,000 cases made. • $36 • (04/15/94) • **90**

Rioja Gran Reserva 1982 • $NA • (11/30/91) • **84**

Rioja Reserva 1991: Appealing, spicy aromas give way to expressive flavors of plum, chocolate and tobacco in this modestly structured yet well-balanced Rioja. Accessible now. • $13 • (03/31/96) • **85**

Rioja Reserva 1990: Soft tea and cinnamon flavors run through this maturing wine. It finishes sweet, but with drying tannins. Drink now. • $13 • (01/31/96) • **82**

Rioja Reserva 1989: Great concentration and style. It's full-bodied, well balanced and ripe with toasty, spicy black cherry flavors. Well-integrated tannins and a long finish keep you coming back for more. Drinkable now, but age-worthy, too. 20,000 cases made. • $11 • (04/30/95) • **90**

Rioja Reserva 1988: This is light but tough, with vanilla, cherry and tea flavors, maturing into traditional Rioja character. If it were softer, the balance would be more pealing. • $12 • (04/15/94) • **83**

Rioja Reserva 1985 • $9 • (03/31/90) • **62**

Rueda 1994: Clean and fresh, this offers a streak of tropical fruit to add interest to its basic white wine character. • $8 • (02/29/96) • **82**

Rueda 1993: Tastes like a full-bodied Sauvignon Blanc, revealing pineapple and ripe grapefruit flavors accented by herbal notes. A buttery, smoky aroma and lingering finish add interest. • $7 • (03/31/95) • **85**

Sauvignon Blanc Rueda 1994: Light nectarine and melon flavors float on a wave of tartness. It's clean and fresh, and finishes soft and short. • $10 • (02/29/96) • **79**

Sauvignon Blanc Rueda 1992: Worth discovering. Distinctive, full in body and smooth-textured, smells smoky and flinty and tastes ripe, with generous apple and pear flavors. Lingering, lively finish. • $9 • (03/31/95) • **87**

ROMERO, BODEGA

Navarra La Cruceta 1994: This understated red is balanced and clean yet not showing much fruit now, delivering light herbal, orange and spice notes. Pleasant but not memorable. 5,000 cases made. • $7 • (04/30/96) • **81**

Navarra La Cruceta 1993: Light, smooth and simple, with basic berry flavors and a hint of vanilla. Soft tannins make it drinkable now. • $6 • (03/31/95) • **79**

Navarra La Cruceta Crianza 1990: Silky and maturing, but still fresh. The vanilla, light tea and spicy notes add to the cherry and berry flavors. Clean and well balanced. Drinkable now. • $8 BB • **84**

Navarra Malón de Echaide 1993: Some herbal, raspberry notes beg for attention underneath its tough, dry structure. 3,500 cases made. • $7 • (08/31/95) • **80**

Navarra Señorio de Yaniz 1993: Earthy, rustic flavors mark this smooth and light red. Drinkable but very simple. 100,000 cases made. • $4 • (03/31/95) • **75**

Navarra Via Corel 1993: Clean and refreshing, silky, offering black cherry, licorice and spice flavors, bright acidity and light tannins. Good for food. 3,000 cases made. • $6 • (04/30/96) • **82**

Navarra Via Corel 1992: Fresh black cherry and light herbal flavors give this soft but vivid wine immediate appeal. It's clean, balanced and drinkable now. 25,000 cases made. • $5 • **83**

ROQUEVALE

Alentejo Terras de Xisto 1990: Drinkable and smooth, but nondescript. Has vague fruit flavors and moderate tannins. 38,000 cases made. • $5 • **77**

Alentejo Tinto da Talha 1992: Soft, generous and fruity, with oodles of blackberry and blueberry flavor. Almost sweet, drink immediately. 3,000 cases made. • $7 • **79**

Redondo Vinho de Redondo 1990: Simple, drinkable red wine with enough fruit flavor to give it life. Not too tannic, drink now. 13,000 cases made. • $6 • **77**

ROSELL, JOAN RAVENTOS

Brut Cava Reserva NV • $13 • (08/31/93) • **78**

ROVELLATS

Brut Cava Imperial NV • $13 • (12/31/90) • **83**

Brut Nature Cava Gran Reserva NV • $17 • (12/31/90) • **78**

ROVIRA, BODEGAS PEDRO

Tarragona Catalonia Reserve 1987 • $6 • (03/31/93) BB • **82**

Tarragona Gran Corpas 1989 • $6 • (08/31/93) • **79**

Tarragona Señorio del Mar 1989: Some strawberry fruit pokes through, but mostly the wine is musty, astringent and sour. • $NA • **70**

Tarragona Viño Tinto Gran Reserva 1982 • $10 • (03/31/93) • **86**

SAN VALERO, BODEGA

Cariñena Don Mendo Tinto Especial 1987 • $5 • (11/30/89) BB • **81**

SANCHO, BODEGAS MANUEL

Mont-Marçal Tinto Reserva Penedès 1989: A well-built wine with concentration and balance. The attractive flavors run from plum and cocoa to licorice and spice. It's still fresh, with enough muscle to stand up to rich food. Drinkable now. 5,000 cases made. • $9 • (04/30/95) • **88**

SANTA DARIA

Rioja 1991: Elegant, light and fragrant. This smooth, supple Rioja does a good imitation of a light Burgundy. Strawberry, spice and cherry flavors make it interesting. 40,000 cases made. • $6 BB • (04/15/94) • **83**
Rioja Crianza 1988 • $10 • (04/15/94) • **74**
Rioja Reserva 1985 • $13 • (04/15/94) • **87**

SARDA

Brut Cava NV • $10 • (03/31/93) • **80**
Brut Cava Borbones NV • $9 • (03/31/93) • **77**
Brut Cava Extra Reserva NV • $16 • (03/31/93) • **80**

SCALA DEI

Priorato 1993: Vivid fruit aromas of blueberries and plums give way to a tannic wine with bright fruit and black pepper flavors. Lighter than many Prioratos. Try now. 2,750 cases made. • $7 • (04/30/95) • **82**
Priorato Cartoixa Gran Reserva 1987: Dense with ripe prune and licorice flavors, it's jammy and lush until the muscular tannins kick in on the finish. This will appeal to fans of Amarone or late-harvest Zinfandel. Drink now or hold and hope for smoother sailing. Improves with decanting. 3,500 cases made. • $18 • (04/15/94) • **83**
Priorato Cartoixa Gran Reserva 1978: Full-bodied and well-structured, this rich wine has enough ripe plum, prune and licorice flavors to balance its firm tannins. Soft enough to drink now, it still has youthful freshness and should improve through 1997. Improves with decanting. Tasted twice 3,500 cases made. • $25 • (04/15/94) • **86**
Priorato El Cipres 1994: Light-bodied yet highly-tannic and acoholic, it lacks balance but still oozes plenty of ripe blackberry, plum and licorice flavors. • $NA • **84**
Priorato Negre Crianza 1991: A round, harmonious wine with expressive flavors of blueberry, cranberry and plum, this shows firm tannins and good balance. Not a blockbuster, but tasty, and approachable now. 1,440 cases made. • $9 • (04/30/95) • **85**
Priorato Negre Crianza 1989: A big, brawny wine with plenty of gusto-full tannins, jammy plum and cassis flavors, black pepper and licorice accents. Drink it now to appreciate its exuberant richness. Improves with decanting. Tasted twice. • $10 • (04/15/94) • **85**

SEGURA VIUDAS

Brut Blanc de Blancs Cava NV • $6 • (05/31/88) • **70**
Brut Cava 1983 • $7 • (05/31/88) • **78**
Brut Cava 1981 • $7 • (11/30/86) BB • **87**
Brut Cava NV • $7 • (06/15/94) • **75**
Brut Cava Aria NV • $10 • (06/15/94) • **78**
Brut Cava Aria Estate NV • $14 • (03/31/93) • **83**
Brut Cava Reserva NV • $7 • (06/15/94) • **80**
Brut Cava Reserva Heredad NV • $20 • (03/31/93) • **82**
Extra Dry Cava Aria NV • $10 • (06/15/94) • **79**
Extra Dry Cava Aria Estate NV • $14 • (03/31/93) • **80**

SENDA GALIANA, BODEGAS

Rioja Conde Alegre 1993: A weedy aroma gives way to a fairly soft wine dominated by smoky cherry and berry flavors. It finishes with a silky texture. 10,000 cases made. • $5 • (04/30/95) • **81**
Rioja Cosecha Reserva 1987: Delicate, even a bit diluted, this is fully mature, with vanilla, berry and nutmeg flavors. The tannins are rather firm for the light fruit. Drink now. 1,000 cases made. • $10 • (03/31/95) • **81**
Rioja Crianza 1990: Maturing now, light, this lacks fresh fruit and shows weedy, earthy flavors and hints of tea and leather. Dry on the finish, drink up. 3,000 cases made. • $7 • (03/31/96) • **72**

Key: SS—Spectator Selection. CS—Cellar Selection. BB—Best Buy. $NA—Price not available. (BT)—Barrel tasting. Ⓐ—Auction Price.
Dates in parentheses represent the issues in which the ratings were published.

Rioja Crianza 1989: The brownish color and tea-like flavors indicate a fully mature wine. Has a smooth texture and lingering finish, but the fruit has faded. 3,500 cases made. • $7 • (01/31/95) • **79**
Rioja Reserva 1989: Elegant in the traditional style. Flavors of berries, tea and vanilla mingle in this firm but light-bodied red. A nice match with light dishes, but drinkable now. 1,000 cases made. • $10 • (03/31/96) • **83**

SEÑORÍO DE NAVA

Ribera del Duero 1986 • $8 • (11/15/89) • **81**

SEÑORÍO DE SARRIA

Navarra 1985 • $5 • (07/31/89) • **77**
Navarra Cosecha 1984 • $5 • (02/28/90) BB • **83**
Navarra Gran Reserva 1981 • $11 • (03/31/90) • **65**

SEÑORÍO DE TORO, EL

Toro Etiqueta Blanca 1989 • $10 • (04/15/92) • **82**

SEÑORÍO DEL MAR

Viño Tinto Seco 1987 • $4 • (10/31/91) BB • **81**

SERRA, JAUME

Brut Cava 1991 • $NA • **75**
Brut Cava Cristalino 1989 • $10 • (03/31/93) • **76**
Brut Cava Cristalino NV: Vanilla and spice aromas and flavors dominate this bubbly. Dry and lean with fairly simple flavors. 50,000 cases made. • $7 • **81**
Merlot Penedès 1991 • $13 • (06/15/93) • **72**
Penedès 1985 • $7 • (04/15/92) BB • **80**
Penedès Crianza 1992: Tobacco and light barnyard aromas give way to a round, soft texture and ripe flavors of plum, herb and vanilla. It's generous, straightforward and drinkable now. 20,000 cases made. • $7 • (03/31/96) • **83**
Penedès Crianza 1991: The wine is thin, with lean, drying tannins and faint echoes of tart cherry. Drink up. 40,000 cases made. • $6 • **71**
Penedès Crianza 1989 • $7 • (03/31/93) BB • **83**
Penedès Macabeo 1993: Tart and lean, displaying dusty aromas and green-apple flavors. Severe. 25,000 cases made. • $5 • (02/28/95) • **73**
Penedès Reserva 1988: Mature and traditional: Light tobacco, tea and dried cherry flavors are mellow, finishing light and a bit dry. It's pleasant now. 25,000 cases made. • $9 • **79**
Penedès Reserva 1986: Mature and simple, with earthy and herbal flavors that aren't much fun. 25,000 cases made. • $9 • (04/15/94) • **74**
Seco Cava Cristalino NV • $10 • (03/31/93) • **81**
Seco Dry Cristalino NV • $8 • (02/29/92) BB • **82**
Seco Rosé Cava Cristalino NV • $8 • (03/31/93) • **72**
Tempranillo Penedès 1993: Fleshy and supple, this bright red offers pleasant raspberry and light herbal flavors, adding just enough grip to balance with food. Drinkable now. 30,000 cases made. • $5 • (03/31/96) • **82**
Tempranillo Penedès 1992: Prematurely aging, this lacks fruit and is already drying on the finish. Silky coffee and mushroom flavors, but drink up. 50,000 cases made. • $5 • **75**
Tempranillo Penedès 1991: A light, silky, mature red that offers earthy mushroom and brown sugar flavors on a lean frame. Fine for drinking now, but sure to fade. 25,000 cases made. • $5 • **76**
Tempranillo Penedès 1990 • $6 • (03/31/93) • **71**
Tempranillo Penedès 1988 • $6 • (04/15/92) BB • **80**

SIERRA CANTABRIA, BODEGAS

Rioja 1992 • $5 • (04/15/94) • **77**
Rioja 1991: Pleasant spice and black cherry flavors are still fresh, but firm tannins close down on the finish. It has life ahead of it, and may soften with food. 12,000 cases made. • $8 • (06/30/96) • **81**

Rioja Codice 1993: There's some berry flavor here, with accents of vanilla and spice, but it's diluted with a drying finish. It might soften with food. 7,000 cases made. • $7 • (06/30/96) • **81**

Rioja Codice 1992: The clove, cinnamon and vanilla notes are a bit too prominent, but some candied berry and strawberry flavors balance it. Exotic and not typical of Rioja. 15,000 cases made. • $6 • (04/15/94) • **79**

Rioja Codice 1990 • $6 • (04/15/94) • **84**

Rioja Codice 1989 • $6 • (04/15/92) • **77**

Rioja Codice 1988 • $6 • (06/15/91) • **78**

Rioja Crianza 1989: Chewy and concentrated, offering delicious chocolate and plum flavors and a nice, tarry aroma. Loads of vanilla and spice in addition. Ready to drink now. 15,000 cases made. • $7 • (03/31/95) • **85**

Rioja Gran Reserva 1982 • $35 • (04/15/94) • **78**

Rioja Reserva 1987: Rich and thick for the vintage. This has plum, prune and chocolate flavors, with muscular tannins and high alcohol. It's concentrated but clumsy. Let it mellow a bit. 2,000 cases made. • $11 • (03/31/95) • **82**

SOLAGUEN

Rioja Reserva 1985: Smooth in texture and complex in aroma, but the modest raisin and cherry flavors are dropping out already. Has a certain faded elegance, but we would have preferred more vitality. • $NA • (04/15/94) • **85**

SOLANA

Cencibel Valdepeñas 1993: Lively and bracing, fruity and fresh. Cranberry and raspberry flavors and moderate tannins give it some punch. Drink now. 28,000 cases made. • $8 • (02/28/95) • **83**

Torrontés & Treixadura Ribeiro 1993: Herbal and severe, with oniony flavors and a dull finish. Delicate, but verging on non-descript. 10,000 cases made. • $8 • **75**

SONSIERRA

Rioja 1993: Tannic, though not out of balance, with good berry and cherry flavors. Turns a bit astringent on the finish. 35,000 cases made. • $5 • (03/31/95) • **80**

Rioja Crianza 1990: A soft and sweetly fruity wine. This is ripe, fleshy and pleasant to drink, though it lacks the Rioja elegance. Drinkable now. 15,000 cases made. • $7 • **79**

Rioja Viña Mindiarte Reserva 1988: Cinnamon and tobacco aromas carry through on the silky palate. Balanced and pleasantly mature, subtle and appealing, with complex coffee, spice and cherry flavors. 8,000 cases made. • $9 • (04/30/95) • **86**

SUMARROCA

Brut Cava NV: A straightforward, generally fruity bubbly with honey and pine flavors. Nearly dry and smooth in texture. Clean and simple in style. • $9 • (07/31/95) • **82**

Brut Nature Cava NV: Refreshing but nearly neutral in flavor. This is a well-balanced, crisp and clean, with simple fruit flavors. • $9 • (07/31/95) • **81**

TAJA

Jumilla 1994: Firm and juicy, spice and earth notes accenting the black cherry flavor. It's straightforward but balanced and bright. • $5 • (04/30/96) • **83**

Jumilla 1988 • $6 • (10/15/92) • **73**

Jumilla 1987 • $6 • (03/31/90) BB • **80**

TINOS, BODEGA LOS

Casa Barco Cafayate-Colchaquíes Valley NV: A soft, fleshy wine with pleasant plum and cherry flavors. Soft tannins make it drinkable now. Good with simple, hearty foods. 75,000 cases made. • $4 BB • **81**

Casa Barco NV: Thick, soft, ripe berry flavor and hints of vanilla. Simple and a bit dull, but drinkable. 25,000 cases made. • $4 • (04/30/96) • **76**

Gran Casa Barco Viño de Mesa NV: This light, silky wine is made in traditional Spanish style, with tea, dried cherry and sweet vanilla flavors. • $5 • (03/31/95) • **78**

TORRECILLA

Navarra 1993: Smooth, clean, light with enough cherry and raspberry character to make it enjoyable. 8,000 cases made. • $6 • **83**

Navarra 1992 • $5 • (08/31/93) BB • **80**

Navarra 1991: A light, pretty, soft red that reminds us of Pinot Noir with its strawberry and cherry flavors. Simple and enjoyable for drinking now. 50,000 cases made. • $5 • (04/15/94) • **81**

Navarra Crianza 1990: Fully mature, spicy, entering its old age, but still a good dinner companion. Smooth in texture, light on tannins. 2,500 cases made. • $7 • **82**

TORRES

Cabernet Sauvignon Penedès Gran Coronas Reserva 1991: A clean, focused wine with food-friendly balance. Cherry, mint and smoky flavors mingle nicely, the wine is smooth and well-defined. Already showing some maturity, drinkable through 1997. • $15 • (04/30/95) • **86**

Chardonnay Penedès Gran Viña Sol 1994: Lively and zesty, flaunting its youthful exuberance and lack of refinement. There's plenty of fruit, though. 33,333 cases made. • $11 • (02/29/96) • **80**

Chardonnay Penedès Milmanda 1993: This shows winemaking skill and refinement, but the oak is too dominant, despite its attractive flavors of toast and honey. Ripe melon flavors need more acidity for liveliness, but this is creamy and smooth. 1,670 cases made. • $40 • (02/29/96) • **84**

Merlot Penedès Viña Las Torres 1990 • $12 • (11/15/91) • **86**

Merlot Penedès Viña Las Torres 1989 • $13 • (10/15/90) • **82**

Merlot Penedès Viña Las Torres 1988 • $10 • (03/31/90) • **83**

Penedès Coronas 1989 • $8 • (04/15/92) • **81**

Penedès Coronas 1988 • $7 • (06/15/91) BB • **81**

Penedès Coronas 1987 • $6 • (10/15/90) BB • **80**

Penedès Coronas 1986 • $6 • (11/30/89) • **78**

Penedès Coronas 1985 • $5 • (11/30/88) BB • **86**

Penedès Coronas 1983 • $4 • (06/30/87) BB • **84**

Penedès Coronas 1982 • $4 • (02/16/86) • **76**

Penedès Fransola 1993: Well rounded, firm and clean. This shows some complexity in its herb and melon flavors, with a touch of vanilla on the finish. 6,300 cases made. • $18 • (02/29/96) • **85**

Penedès Fransola Green Label 1992: Lively, clean and citruslike in flavor with medium body and a crisp texture. Made mostly from Sauvignon Blanc. Simple and direct, for drinking now while it's fresh. • $16 • (04/15/94) • **80**

Penedès Fransola Green Label 1991 • $17 • (08/31/93) • **81**

Penedès Fransola Green Label Vineyard Selection 1991 • $16 • (12/31/92) • **86**

Penedès Gran Coronas 1985 • $11 • (11/30/88) • **89**

Penedès Gran Coronas 1979 • $9 • (02/16/86) • **75**

Penedès Gran Coronas Gran Reserva 1988: 100% Cabernet Sauvignon • $NA • **79**

Penedès Gran Coronas Más La Plana Black Label Gran Reserva 1987 • $33 • (12/15/92) • **85**

Penedès Gran Coronas Más La Plana Black Label Gran Reserva 1985 • $32 • (10/15/90) • **85**

Penedès Gran Coronas Más La Plana Black Label Gran Reserva 1983 • $26 • (03/31/90) • **85**

Penedès Gran Coronas Más La Plana Black Label Gran Reserva 1982 • $29 • (06/15/88) • **85**

Penedès Gran Coronas Más La Plana Black Label Gran Reserva 1981 • $23 • (10/15/87) • **83**

Penedès Gran Coronas Más La Plana Black Label Gran Reserva 1978 • $65 • (02/16/86) • **85**

Penedès Gran Coronas Más La Plana Estate Gran Reserva 1990: A well-made wine entering its prime. Mature and complex flavors of ripe cherry, plum, tar and mushrooms. Well integrated, with smooth tannins and a lingering finish. 13,583 cases made. • $34 • **88**

Penedès Gran Coronas Reserva 1988: Mature, light on fruit flavor, with tarry, earthy aromas and an easy texture. Drink now if you like them mature. • $15 • (04/15/94) • **79**

Penedès Gran Coronas Reserva 1987 • $15 • (04/15/92) • **84**

Penedès Gran Coronas Reserva 1986 • $12 • (11/30/89) • **86**

Penedès Gran Coronas Reserva 1985 • $12 • (03/31/90) • **77**

Penedès Gran Sangre de Toro 1989 • $13 • (12/15/93) • **84**

Penedès Gran Sangre de Toro 1984 • $9 • (09/15/88) • **78**

Penedès Gran Sangre de Toro 1979 • $9 • (02/16/86) • **79**

Penedès Gran Sangre de Toro Reserva 1991: Meaty, and chock full of ripe berry, smoke and licorice flavors, what it lacks in refinement, it makes up in exuberance. Drinkable now, but can hold into 1997. 87,614 cases made. • $11 • **83**

Penedès Gran Sangre de Toro Reserva 1988 • $11 • (12/15/92) • **82**

Penedès Gran Sangre de Toro Reserva 1987 • $10 • (11/15/91) • **83**

Penedès Gran Sangre de Toro Reserva 1986 • $10 • (10/15/90) • **83**

Penedès Gran Sangre de Toro Reserva 1985 • $9 • (11/30/89) • **87**

Penedès Gran Sangre de Toro Reserva 1983 • $9 • (06/15/88) SS • **91**

Penedès Gran Sangre de Toro Reserva 1981 • $5 • (06/15/87) • **80**

Penedès Gran Viña Sol 1993: Floral, appley aromas and a tangy fruitiness make this lively and appealing. Brings you back for another sip. 36,600 cases made. • $11 • (02/28/95) • **83**

Penedès Gran Viña Sol 1992: Vanilla and spice aromas and buttery flavors make a nice profile, but it lacks fruit and liveliness. A bit tannic and chalky on the finish. • $11 • **78**

Penedès Gran Viña Sol 1991 • $11 • (12/31/92) • **76**

Penedès Más Borrás 1991: Awkward, disjointed, with tomato and beet aromas, sweet-sour flavors of cherry and butterscotch and a thick finish. 1,620 cases made. • $20 • **76**

Penedès Más Borrás 1990: A full-bodied, sweet-seeming Pinot Noir with honey and brown sugar aromas, strawberry and rhubarb flavors and a soft finish. Decent quality but lacks personality. 19,500 cases made. • $20 • (04/15/94) • **78**

Penedès Más Borrás 1989 • $20 • (11/15/91) • **79**

Penedès Más Borrás 1988 • $18 • (10/15/90) • **79**

Penedès Milmanda 1992: A full-bodied white wine that's reasonably ripe, nicely accented with spicy oak flavors and long on the finish. Balanced and harmonious, but less rich and flavorful than previous vintages. • $43 • **86**

Penedès Milmanda 1991 • $40 • (12/31/92) • **90**

Penedès Sangre de Toro 1990: A rich, jammy wine with firm tannins and good acidity to frame its plum and licorice flavors. Good concentration, drinkable now but should age well through 1997. • $8 BB • (04/15/94) • **85**

Penedès Sangre de Toro 1989 • $7 • (04/15/92) BB • **82**

Penedès Sangre de Toro 1988 • $6 • (03/31/91) BB • **82**

Penedès Sangre de Toro 1987 • $5 • (11/30/89) BB • **82**

Penedès Sangre de Toro 1986 • $4 • (12/15/88) BB • **80**

Penedès Sangre de Toro 1985 • $5 • (06/15/88) BB • **81**

Penedès Sangre de Toro 1983 • $4 • (06/15/87) • **79**

Penedès Sangre de Toro 1982 • $NA • (02/16/86) • **83**

Penedès Viña Esmeralda 1991 • $10 • (05/31/92) • **80**

Penedès Viña Esmeralda 1993: The perfumey floral and herbal notes remind us of cologne. This is tart on the palate, with a floral finish. Distinctive, but doesn't come together. 81,000 cases made. • $11 • (02/29/96) • **77**

Penedés Viña Esmeralda Gewürztraminer 1994: Perfumed with floral and spice notes—reminiscent of many household products. It's clean and crisp in structure. An odd duck, but drinkable. 79,000 cases made. • $11 • (02/29/96) • **76**

Penedès Viña Las Torres 1993: Pleasant plum and spice flavors mingle in this round, approachable red. Not much structure for aging, but it's easy to drink now. 7,400 cases made. • $12 • **81**

Key: SS—Spectator Selection. CS—Cellar Selection. BB—Best Buy. $NA—Price not available. (BT)—Barrel tasting. (A)—Auction Price.
Dates in parentheses represent the issues in which the ratings were published.

Penedès Viña Las Torres 1992: A fresh, ripe, juicy Merlot with plum and herb flavors, moderate tannins and a hint of sweetness. Drinkable now. • $12 • **82**

Penedès Viña Magdala 1986 • $14 • (11/15/91) • **82**

Penedès Viña Magdala 1984 • $11 • (07/31/89) • **76**

Penedès Viña Magdala 1983 • $9 • (06/15/88) • **74**

Penedès Viña Magdala 1979 • $NA • (02/16/86) • **72**

Penedès Viña Sol 1991 • $7 • (12/31/92) • **78**

TORRES FILOSO, BODEGAS

La Mancha Arboles de Castillejo 1986 • $7 • (04/15/92) • **79**

ULECIA, FAUSTINO RIVERO

Rioja Reserva 1985 • $9 • (03/31/93) • **79**

URBION

Ribera del Duero Crianza Cosecha Excelente 1989 • $11 • (12/15/92) • **87**

Ribera del Duero Tinto 1991 • $7 • (06/15/93) BB • **82**

Ribera del Duero Tinto Cosecha Excelente 1990 • $7 • (12/15/92) • **81**

VALDAMOR

Albariño Rias Baixas 1993: An overblown style with a deep gold color, buttery aromas, but dull fruit flavors. It comes off as awkward. • $14 • (03/31/95) • **79**

VALDEOBISPO

Bierzo Tinto 1990 • $7 • (04/15/92) • **80**

Bierzo Unfiltered 1989 • $10 • (04/15/92) • **87**

VALDUMIA

Rias Baixas Albariño 1991 • $18 • (12/31/92) • **83**

VALLFORMOSA

Brut Cava NV • $11 • (03/31/93) • **79**

Brut Nature Cava NV • $14 • (03/31/93) • (04/15/94) • **78**

Brut Penedès NV • $7 • (04/30/88) • **82**

Penedès Gran Baron Crianza 1988: Mature and smooth, with brown sugar and tea flavors taking over from the fruit component. Soft and easy to drink, but simple. 3,000 cases made. • $6 • **78**

Penedès Gran Baron Reserva 1987: Brown sugar is the dominant flavor in this flabby, tired wine. It's a few years past its prime. Tasted twice. 2,000 cases made. • $8 • (04/15/94) • **74**

Penedès Vall Fort 1986 • $7 • (05/31/91) • **76**

Penedès Vall Fort 1984 • $7 • (03/31/91) BB • **84**

Penedès Vall Fort Crianza 1990: A soft, agreeably fruity red with a spicy, mature accent to the plum and brown sugar flavors. Drink now. 5,000 cases made. • $7 BB • (04/15/94) • **81**

Penedès Vall Reserva 1987: Smooth but tired, its fruit has faded to tea and brown sugar flavors. Won't offend, though. 10,500 cases made. • $9 • (04/15/94) • **77**

Sparkling Penedès Gran Baron NV • $10 • (06/15/94) • **83**

VEGA DE LA REINA, BODEGAS

Castilla y Leon 1985: Light and mature, with fading flavors of strawberry and spice. Well-balanced in a delicate style. Drink now. • $15 • **82**

VEGA DE MORIZ

Cencibel Valdepeñas 1989 • $5 • (06/15/91) BB • **81**

VEGA SICILIA, BODEGAS

Ribera del Duero Unico 1980 • $132 • (12/15/92) • **86**

Ribera del Duero Unico 1979 • $80 • (03/31/90) • **95**

Ribera del Duero Unico 1976 • $82 • (04/30/89) • **91**

Ribera del Duero Unico 1974: Very youthful for its age, with lively plum fruit and sweet vanilla flavors, smooth and rich. A musky note gives it added lift but won't appeal to everyone. At its peak now, but should hold. • $160 • **87**

Ribera del Duero Unico 1973 • $82 • (03/31/90) • **90**

Ribera del Duero Unico 1962 • $113 • (03/31/90) • **89**

Ribera del Duero Unico Reserva 1983: Matured to a pleasant drinkability. Spice, leather and cedar aromas, ripe fruit, tobacco and leather flavors. Good concentration and harmony. Enjoy now with refined dishes. • $120 • (04/30/95) • **89**

Ribera del Duero Unico Reserva 1970: A silky, seamless package of pleasure. Surprisingly dark color, then mature aromas of spice and cherry, with an elegant, soft palate impression that holds coffee, raisin and cherry flavors. It's balanced and long, with a slightly volatile character. • $180 • (04/30/95) • **92**

Ribera del Duero Unico Reserva Especial NV: A harmonious, well-made wine that sticks firmly to the middle of the road. There's pleasant cherry, spice and tobacco flavors, adequate tannins and a reasonable finish. It makes for good drinking, especially with food. • $225 • (04/30/95) • **88**

Ribera del Duero Valbuena 1990: Beginning to show maturity, this offers coffee, roasted plum and spice flavors in a soft, velvety style. Well balanced and approachable now, but should hold through 1997. • $75 • (04/30/95) • **86**

Ribera del Duero Valbuena 3 Años 1986 • $47 • (12/15/90) • **90**

Ribera del Duero Valbuena 3 Años 1985 • $55 • (03/31/90) CS • **92**

Ribera del Duero Valbuena 3 Años 1984 • $28 • (04/30/89) • **79**

Ribera del Duero Valbuena 3 Años 1983 • $22 • (10/15/88) • **88**

Ribera del Duero Valbuena 3 Años 1982 • $25 • (10/15/88) • **90**

Ribera del Duero Valbuena 5 Años 1988: A well-made, very attractive wine. The blackberry, toasty oak and spicy flavors harmonize beautifully, the tannins are firm yet don't get in the way. Still fresh, it's drinkable now but will age well through at least 1997. • $75 • **90**

Ribera del Duero Valbuena 5 Años 1984 • $49 • (03/31/90) • **90**

Ribera del Duero Valbuena 5 Años 1982 • $37 • (03/31/90) • **91**

VEGA VIEJA

Rioja Crianza 1987 • $7 • (09/30/92) • **77**

Rioja Gran Reserva 1981 • $16 • (12/15/92) • **67**

Rioja Reserva 1985 • $12 • (12/15/92) • **79**

VEGAVAL PLATA

Valdepeñas Reserva 1987: It's alive! Smooth and one-dimensional, showing a cherry note from the aroma through the finish. 30,000 cases made. • $10 • (04/30/96) • **79**

VIÑA BERCEO

Rioja Carta de Plata 1991 • $5 • (09/30/91) • **70**

Rioja Crianza 1988 • $5 • (11/15/89) • **77**

Rioja Crianza 1987 • $5 • (04/15/89) BB • **86**

Rioja Crianza 1986 • $7 • (09/30/90) BB • **87**

Rioja Crianza 1984 • $5 • (10/15/88) • **76**

Rioja Reserva 1985 • $10 • (03/31/90) • **76**

Rioja Reserva 1983 • $10 • (11/15/89) • **69**

Rioja Reserva 1982 • $8 • (10/15/88) • **76**

Rioja Reserva 1980 • $8 • (10/15/88) • **77**

Rioja Gran Reserva 1982 • $25 • (11/30/91) • **87**

VIÑA, CASA DE LA

Cencibel Valdepeñas 1985 • $6 • (03/31/90) • **82**

VIÑA IJALBA

Rioja Crianza Múrice 1992: A light-bodied wine whose oak dominates the cherry, chocolate and vanilla flavors. 20,000 cases made. • $13 • (06/30/96) • **79**

Rioja Livor 1994: A strong earthy note and dry tannins make this tough to like, though it has concentration and some chocolate and plum flavors underneath. 4,000 cases made. • $10 • (06/30/96) • **77**

Rioja Ljalba Reserva 1990: The ripe plum and pleasant spicy accents add personality, and firm, round tannins give it grip. Tastefully oaked and enjoyable now, this wine still has life ahead of it. 3,550 cases made. • $16 • (06/30/96) • **88**

VIÑA MAGANA

Navarra 1982 • $16 • (11/15/87) • **77**

Navarra Eventum Crianza Finca Paso de la Reina 1990: A gutsy, "chewy" Spanish red with nicely smoky aromas, lavish fruit flavor, pleasant oak accents and a lingering finish. Packed with fine tannins. It's drinkable now through 1997. 10,000 cases made. • $9 • (04/30/95) • **88**

Navarra Viña Magaña Reserva 1989: A big wine, but somewhat clumsy. Aggressive herbaceous notes detract from the cherry and plum flavors, and the tannins are dull. Drinkable now. 9,000 cases made. • $14 • **77**

VIÑA PEDROSA

Tinto Cosecha Ribera del Duero 1990 • $18 • (12/15/93) • **86**

VIÑA SALCEDA

Rioja 1990: Shows maturity, with plum and brown sugar flavors and a woody component that hangs through to the finish. Tasty and satisfying, with a nice, spicy character. 15,000 cases made. • $11 • (03/31/95) • **83**

Rioja Crianza 1991: Though not big, this packs a lot of flavor, ranging from berry to spice, from light earthiness to vanilla. It's balanced and lingers on the finish. 80,000 cases made. • $11 • (03/31/96) • **85**

Rioja Crianza 1989: A round, fleshy wine with pleasant jammy blackberry fruit and a long, spicy finish. There's not much muscle, though, drink now. 65,000 cases made. • $10 • (04/15/94) • **83**

Rioja Cuvée Especial 25 Aniversario Reserva 1987: Silky and lean, offering a clean core of spice and cherry flavors. It's well integrated and balanced, though a bit light and already quite mature. Drinkable now. 2,000 cases made. • $16 • (03/31/95) • **84**

Rioja Gran Reserva 1985: Plenty of power here, yet the wine is beautifully balanced, with rich, ripe plum, licorice and toasty flavors, firm tannins and a long, complex finish. A great wine for food. Drinkable now, but should hold through 1998. • $20 • (04/15/94) • **89**

VIÑA VALORIA

Rioja 1993: Raspberry and kirsch aromas are assertive and promising, but a heavy texture dulls the flavors. The concentration shows on the finish. 3,000 cases made. • $10 • (08/31/95) • **82**

Rioja 1991: Already browning in color, showing traditional brown sugar and tea aromas, but the chocolate and dried cherry flavors are thin and dry, sapped by premature age. 12,500 cases made. • $8 • **78**

Rioja 1989: Already maturing into earthy flavors, it lacks depth and structure. The berry fruit has a bitter, vegetal edge. Drink now. 1,133 cases made. • $8 • (04/15/94) • **75**

Rioja Crianza 1987: There's not much life left here. It shows a browning color, brown sugar aromas, drying tannins and a hint of strawberry flavor. Drink up. 9,166 cases made. • $12 • (04/15/94) • **76**

Rioja Reserva 1985: Full and soft, the chocolate and prune flavors are full-blown and mature, it's ripe, balanced and attractive. Drink now. 1,125 cases made. • $15 • (04/15/94) • **85**

VIÑA VERMETA

Tinto 1987 • $6 • (11/15/91) • **76**

VIÑADRIAN

Tinto Rioja 1986 • $3 • (10/15/88) • **77**

VIÑAS DE GAIN

Rioja 1988 • $10 • (12/15/92) • **82**

VIÑAS DEL VERO

Chardonnay Barrel Fermented Somontano Saint Marc Reserve 1993: A full-bodied white that's not heavy or dull, showing clean flavors of honey, melon and almond. It can stand up to rich foods. 5,000 cases made. • $11 • (02/29/96) • **83**

Chardonnay Somontano Saint Marc Estate 1993: A smooth and subtle, full-bodied white with spicy, pearlike flavors and good balance. Nutmeg and vanilla accents develop on the finish. 5,000 cases made. • $7 • (03/31/95) • **85**

Chardonnay Somontano Saint Marc Estate Barrel Select 1994: Buttery and soft, offering ripe melon flavors that give a sweet impression, quaffable but simple. 14,000 cases made. • $9 • (02/29/96) • **79**

Chardonnay Somontano Saint Marc Estate Reserve 1994: An overenthusiastic dose of oak gives this aromas of white chocolate and black coffee, while a thick texture and flavors of vanilla and butter show on the palate. Enough melon flavor peeps through to keep it pleasant, but it's for barrel lovers. 8,000 cases made. • $9 • (02/29/96) • **80**

Gewürztraminer Somontano 1994: Thick and quite sweet, showing pineapple and apricot flavors and a clean finish. It's character is blunt but persuasive. • $10 • (02/29/96) • **79**

Merlot Somontano Saint Marc 1993: Fruit, fruit and more fruit. Loads of blueberry and blackberry flavors with a good structure and enough tannins to let it age. Nicely concentrated with a lingering, chocolately finish. Better in 1997. 4,000 cases made. • $8 • (12/31/95) • **86**

Pinot Noir Somontano Saint Marc Estate 1991: A pretty core of raspberry in this young, vibrant wine, but a smoky note turns bitter on the finish. 6,000 cases made. • $10 • (03/31/95) • **78**

Somontano 1992: A light, simple Chardonnay with apple, earth and mineral flavors. Drinkable but not interesting. 6,000 cases made. • $8 • **75**

Somontano Saint Marc 1992: An overlay of oak flavor-vanilla, honey-needs more fruit to back it up. Has the roundness and interest of a good Chardonnay, but seems incomplete. Very dry. 5,000 cases made. • $9 • (04/15/94) • **76**

Somontano Saint Marc 1990: Tannic and very flavorful, with ripe cherry and currant notes and good balance. Rough to drink now, but should develop more complexity and a smoother texture with time. 10,000 cases made. • $9 BB • (04/15/94) • **86**

Somontano Saint Marc Duque de Azara Crianza 1991: Solid, fresh, ripe fruit, mingling black cherry, herbal and chocolate flavors with good backbone and a clean finish. Somewhat rustic, but good food accompaniment. 15,000 cases made. • $9 • (04/30/96) • **83**

Somontano Saint Marc Estate Duque de Azara 1994: Round and soft, with light herbal and apple flavors, this is dry and clean. Fine with food. 20,000 cases made. • $8 • (02/29/96) • **81**

Somontano Saint Marc Estate Reserva Especial 1991: A solid, rustic red offering ripe flavors of plums and blackberries. It's almost jammy, but firm tannins give it grip. 8,000 cases made. • $9 • (04/30/96) • **81**

Somontano Saint Marc Reserva Especial 1990: A solid, four-square wine with gobs of blackberry flavor, a hint of oak, and ample tannins to back it all up. Rich and satisfying. 1,500 cases made. • $9 BB • (04/15/94) • **86**

Tempranillo Somontano Tinto Joven 1994: Flat and dull, as if the heart had been stripped out of it. Simple cherry flavors and light tannins. 3,000 cases made. • $9 • **77**

VIÑOS DE LEON

Tinto Palacio de Leon 1985 • $4 • (11/15/89) BB • **85**

XENIUS

Brut Cava NV • $7 • (07/15/90) BB • **82**
Brut Cava Reserva NV • $9 • (12/15/92) • **83**
Brut Penedès Cava Reserva NV • $9 • (06/15/94) • **83**
Sparkling Penedès Cava Brut Reserva NV • $9 • (06/15/94) • **83**

XIPELLA

Blanc de Blancs Conca de Barberá 1988 • $6 • (03/31/90) • **74**

SPAIN

Key: SS—Spectator Selection. CS—Cellar Selection. BB—Best Buy. $NA—Price not available. (BT)—Barrel tasting. Ⓐ—Auction Price.
Dates in parentheses represent the issues in which the ratings were published.

Other International

• Argentina •

BIANCHI, VALENTIN

Cabernet Sauvignon Mendoza Elsa's Vineyard 1990 • $5 • (06/15/94) • **78**
Cabernet Sauvignon Mendoza Elsa's Vineyard 1987 • $7 • (07/15/91) • **77**
Chenin Blanc Mendoza Elsa's Vineyard 1994: This pleasantly fruity wine is soft yet refreshing. Clean floral and peach aromas give way to smooth flavors of peach and pear with a slight honey note. A lovely apéritif. 20,000 cases made. • $5 • (05/15/95) • **84**
Chenin Blanc Mendoza Elsa's Vineyard 1993: A refreshing and different style, it smells sweet and tastes dry. It has exuberant apple, floral and peach aromas, followed by crisp and almost austere flavors of apple and spice. A good change of pace in white wine from Argentina. 20,000 cases made. • $6 • (07/31/94) BB • **84**
Chenin Blanc Mendoza Elsa's Vineyard 1992 • $5 • (05/31/94) BB • **81**
Malbec Mendoza Elsa's Vineyard 1992: Lively black pepper notes perk up the black cherry flavor. Tannins are somewhat strong for the fruit, but it can handle simple meat dishes. Drinkable now. 30,000 cases made. • $5 • (07/31/95) • **81**
Malbec Mendoza Elsa's Vineyard 1991 • $6 • (06/15/94) BB • **84**
Malbec Mendoza Elsa's Vineyard 1985 • $6 • (07/15/91) • **76**
Sauvignon Blanc Mendoza 1993: It's light and appley in aroma, but turns heavy and dull in flavor, with lots of body but not much fruit. 5,000 cases made. • $6 • (07/31/94) • **74**

BOUVET

Brut Rosé Cafayate-Colchaquíes Valley Excellence NV: A simple, frothy rosé that smells like canned fruit and tastes sweet and candied. • $13 • (10/31/95) • **76**

CADEAUX

Brut Cafayate-Colchaquíes Valley Royal Crown NV: An easy-to-drink bubbly with mature flavors, soft texture and a bit of sweetness. Simple but good. 60,000 cases made. • $9 • (02/28/95) • **80**

CATENA

Cabernet Sauvignon Mendoza Reserve 1990 • $15 • (03/31/93) • **84**
Chardonnay Mendoza Reserve 1991 • $14 • (03/31/93) • **87**

ESMERALDA, BODEGAS

Cabernet Sauvignon Mendoza Catena Agrelo Vineyard 1992: This classy wine takes Argentine Cab to another level. From the deep color to the complex aromas of black cherry, cassis, tobacco and tar through the rich, full-bodied flavors and long finish, this shows concentration, focus and depth. Drinkable now. 2,700 cases made. • $16 • (04/30/95) • **91**
Cabernet Sauvignon Mendoza Catena Reserve 1990 • $14 • (05/31/94) • **85**
Cabernet Sauvignon Mendoza Trumpeter 1992: A core of sweet cherry fruit is appealing but dry tannins and an earthy note detract a bit from the pleasure. It's maturing already and should be drunk now. 8,000 cases made. • $7 • (04/30/95) • **80**
Cabernet Sauvignon Mendoza Trumpeter 1991 • $10 • (06/15/94) • **77**
Chardonnay Mendoza Catena Agrelo Vineyard 1993: This rich wine shows concentration and balance in a restrained, elegant style. There's deft use of oak in the vanilla and toast flavors, and ripe pear and melon fruit with vibrant acidity. Brings you back for another sip. 2,700 cases made. • $15 • (04/30/95) • **89**
Chardonnay Mendoza Catena Reserve 1992 • $13 • (05/31/94) • **84**
Chardonnay Mendoza Trumpeter 1993: Harmonious and balanced, soft-textured, demonstrating light oak and ripe fruit flavors. It's supple and complete, in a lower key, and shows finesse and length. 10,000 cases made. • $7 • (04/30/95) • **84**
Chardonnay Mendoza Trumpeter 1992 • $10 • **79**

ETCHART

Malbec Mendoza 1993: There's plenty of blackberry and black cherry fruit here, and lean tannins add backbone. It's straightforward and clean. • $6 • (09/30/95) • **84**
Merlot Mendoza 1993: It's a decent, drinkable red wine, but the weedy, herbaceous aromas and flavors and a sharp texture make this a bit harsh for a Merlot. • $6 • (09/30/95) • **78**

FAURY, PHILIPPE

Cafayate-Colchaquíes Valley 1985: Perhaps not as powerful as expected but the pure flavors in this wine are impressive. Wonderful berry, raspberry, cherry character, full bodied and silky tannins. Drinkable now. • $70 • **90**
Cafayate-Colchaquíes Valley 1983: Well-focused, succulent and delicate wine with dried cherries and tobacco aromas and flavors. Medium bodied with a delicate finish. Drinkable now. • $NA • **86**
Cafayate-Colchaquíes Valley 1981: A harmonious, caressing wine definitely at or slightly past its peak. Medium ruby/garnet color with chocolate cedar aromas, medium body with a soft texture, light integrated tannins and a delicate chocolate, earthy finish. Drink as soon as possible. • $NA • **83**

FAZIO, NICOLAS E.

Cabernet Sauvignon Mendoza 1986: There's not much left in this soft, browning wine. The flavors are tired and earthy, the tannins grab hold of the finish. Drink up. 3,000 cases made. • $12 • (04/30/95) • **71**
Cabernet Sauvignon Mendoza 1980 • $11 • (09/15/92) • **70**
Chardonnay Mendoza 1993: A flat, dull wine without much flavor. After simple apple and citrus notes a hint of mustiness mars the finish. 2,080 cases made. • $12 • (04/30/95) • **74**
Chardonnay Mendoza Fazio & Joyaux 1994: Banana aromas are a pleasant surprise, but there's very little happening on the palate, with a soft texture and only hints of pear and honey flavors. 1,588 cases made. • $12 • (04/30/95) • **77**
Malbec Mendoza 1978 • $12 • (09/15/92) • **79**
Malbec Mendoza Malbeck 1982: Cherry, raisin, tea and spice flavors in a polished, if somewhat diluted, structure. This has reached maturity safely, drink now. 3,000 cases made. • $12 • (07/31/95) • **83**
Merlot Rio Negro Fabre Montmayou 1988: Chewy, jammy fruit, earth and herb flavors. Tannins are still firm. It's thick and lacks definition, but will stand up to a steak. Drinkable now. 1,767 cases made. • $11 • (11/15/95) • **82**

FLICHMAN, FINCA

Argenta Mendoza 1992 • $5 • (04/30/94) • **75**
Argenta Mendoza 1990: This tastes more like jelly than wine, sweet, soft and grapey. It's round and fruity, without noticeable structure or depth. 30,000 cases made. • $6 • (09/30/94) • **75**
Argenta Mendoza 1988 • $4 • (03/15/91) BB • **84**
Cabernet Sauvignon Mendoza 1991: An odd mix of wet-paint aromas and hard candy flavors, distinctive character-but it's not Cabernet. Tough and short. 10,000 cases made. • $6 • (04/30/95) • **74**
Cabernet Sauvignon Mendoza 1989 • $8 • (06/15/94) • **80**

ARGENTINA

Cabernet Sauvignon Mendoza Caballero de la Cepa 1990: Ripe and jammy, featuring soft raspberry and currant flavors, sharp herbal notes and dry tannins. Drinkable now. 20,000 cases made. • $10 • (04/30/95) • **79**

Cabernet Sauvignon Mendoza Caballero de la Cepa 1989: Full-bodied, fully ripe red that tastes like Port. Reminds us of raisins and prunes. Heavy. 30,000 cases made. • $11 • (01/31/95) • **80**

Cabernet Sauvignon Mendoza Caballero de la Cepa 1987 • $11 • (06/15/94) • **74**

Cabernet Sauvignon Mendoza Caballero de la Cepa 1985 • $8 • (03/15/91) • **68**

Cabernet Sauvignon Mendoza Proprietors Private Reserve 1990: Oozing with ripe, soft fruit flavors, very fresh and light in tannins. Drink now for its charm and exuberance. 30,000 cases made. • $8 • (01/31/95) • **84**

Cabernet Sauvignon Mendoza Proprietors Private Reserve 1989 • $7 • (06/15/93) • **81**

Cabernet Sauvignon Mendoza Proprietors Private Reserve 1988 • $7 • (09/15/92) BB • **82**

Cabernet Sauvignon Mendoza Proprietors Private Reserve 1987 • $6 • (03/15/91) BB • **81**

Chardonnay Mendoza Caballero de la Cepa 1992 • $9 • (06/15/93) • **83**

Chardonnay Mendoza Proprietors Private Reserve 1991 • $7 • (06/15/93) • **79**

Chardonnay Mendoza Proprietors Reserve 1993 • $6 • (04/30/94) BB • **84**

Mendoza 1989 • $5 • (09/15/92) BB • **83**

Merlot Mendoza Proprietors Private Reserve 1988 • $6 • (03/15/91) • **66**

Sangiovese Mendoza 1992: Light cherry and herb notes are pleasant but evanescent, not offering much distinction. Drinkable now. 10,000 cases made. • $6 • (11/15/95) • **78**

Selection Mendoza 1988 • $4 • (03/15/91) BB • **79**

Syrah Mendoza 1990 • $9 • (04/30/94) • **84**

FOND DE CAVE

Cabernet Sauvignon Mendoza 1982 • $7 • (02/15/89) • **76**

MALVIRA

Cafayate-Colchaquíes Valley Red 1990: Firm and focused, a chewy wine with wild berry and perfumy character, plus a whiff of the forest. Needs until 1998 to sort out the tannins. • $15 • **81**

NAVARRO CORREAS

Cabernet Sauvignon Mendoza 1981 • $8 • (02/15/89) • **79**

Cabernet Sauvignon Mendoza Coleccion Privada 1990: This fully mature, soft, light red shows brown sugar, tea and smoke flavors. Fading fast, drink up. 17,500 cases made. • $11 • (04/30/95) • **75**

Cabernet Sauvignon Mendoza Coleccion Privada 1988 • $12 • (05/31/94) • **82**

Cabernet Sauvignon Mendoza Coleccion Privada 1985 • $10 • (03/31/93) • **79**

Chardonnay Mendoza Maipu 1994: Very heavy oak influence results in strong smoky, toast and meaty flavors that overwhelm the light melon and pear notes. An ambitious effort, but out of balance. 3,000 cases made. • $12 • (04/30/95) • **79**

Chardonnay Mendoza Maipu 1993 • $12 • **76**

Malbec Mendoza 1988 • $10 • (03/31/93) • **80**

Malbec Mendoza Maipu Russell Vineyard 1988 • $10 • (05/31/94) • **86**

Malbec Mendoza Russell Vineyard 1991: A tough red that lacks focus and depth, revealing stewed fruit, vanilla and leather flavors. Drinkable now. 20,000 cases made. • $10 • (07/31/95) • **78**

Key: SS—Spectator Selection. CS—Cellar Selection. BB—Best Buy. $NA—Price not available. (BT)—Barrel tasting. Ⓐ—Auction Price.
Dates in parentheses represent the issues in which the ratings were published.

Pinot Noir Mendoza 1989: Light and silky, with sweet strawberry, spice and toasty flavors, this manages a passable resemblance to mature Pinot Noir but begins to cloy on the second sip. 2,000 cases made. • $11 • (07/31/94) • **72**

Syrah Mendoza 1991: This straightforward red has some cherry fruit and firm tannins, but it lacks varietal character. It's clean and ready to drink. 6,000 cases made. • $12 • **79**

PROVIAR

Clos du Moulin Mendoza 1985: Soft, fruity and offering easy drinking now. Strawberry and smoky flavors, very supple tannins and a clean, short finish. Drinkable now. Tasted twice. 20,000 cases made. • $10 • (09/30/94) • **76**

ST. ANTONY

Riesling Cafayate-Colchaquíes Valley Niersteiner Hipping 1993: Great dessert wine here. Wonderful dried apricot, super ripe fruit aromas and flavors. Close to Beerenauslese quality. Full bodied, spicy, fruity and very sweet yet the terrific acidity keeps it very fresh. Drink now or hold. • $NA • **90**

Riesling Cafayate-Colchaquíes Valley Niersteiner Olberg 1993: Excellent for food. Dry and massive like a top-notch Alsace Riesling, with loads of spicy, dried apricot aromas and flavors. Excellent acidity and exceptionally intense character. Drink now or hold. • $NA • **91**

Riesling Cafayate-Colchaquíes Valley Niersteiner Orbel 1993: Big and full bodied with masses of spicy, mineral character. Medium sweet and spicy on the finish with a slightly bitter aftertaste. Drink now. • $NA • **86**

SAN TELMO, BODEGAS

Cabernet Sauvignon Mendoza 1985 • $10 • (03/31/93) • **81**

Cabernet Sauvignon Mendoza Cuesta Del Madero 1987 • $4 • (03/31/93) BB • **83**

Malbec Mendoza Malbeck 1986 • $8 • (03/31/93) • **79**

SANTA ANA

Cabernet Sauvignon Mendoza Reserve 1990: Looks, smells and tastes old for its age. Brownish in color, woody in aroma and resinous in flavor. Not our style of red wine. • $5 • (08/31/95) • **74**

Chardonnay Mendoza Reserve 1992: Weak, watery and simple. What flavor is there is green, thin and vegetal. No fun to drink. Not recommended. • $5 • (08/31/95) • **60**

SANTA JULIA

Cabernet Sauvignon Mendoza Oak Reserve 1993: A sturdy but dull Cabernet with mature aromas, vague fruit flavors and a tough texture. 3,350 cases made. • $9 • **77**

SELECCIÓN MENDOZA

60% San Giovese 40% Malbeck Mendoza NV • $4 • (03/31/93) • **72**

SUTER

Merlot Mendoza 1989: Diluted and thin. The weak cherry flavor is marred by a burnt, earthy character and drying tannins. Tasted twice, with consistent notes. 3,000 cases made. • $7 • (09/30/94) • **64**

TOSO, PASCUAL

Cabernet Sauvignon Mendoza 1992: Showing some age now, this layers tea and smoke flavors on top of the cherry core. It's silky, but still has tannin, best with light foods. 5,000 cases made. • $8 • (09/30/95) • **82**

Cabernet Sauvignon Mendoza 1991 • $8 • (06/15/94) • **78**

Cabernet Sauvignon Mendoza 1990: The brown color isn't kidding. This tastes of brown sugar, tobacco and mud. Drink up. 5,000 cases made. • $7 • (04/30/95) • **72**

Cabernet Sauvignon Mendoza 1988 • $7 • (03/15/91) • **79**

Chardonnay Mendoza 1994: Basic white wine, with little fruit and less varietal character, it has enough acidity to make a refreshing spritzer. 5,000 cases made. • $8 • (09/30/95) • **76**

Malbec Mendoza 1994: Ripe and jammy, this shows blackberry and plum flavors with hints of game and smoke. Lush and drinkable, but without much tannin, it goes down easy. 10,000 cases made. • $6 • (09/30/95) • **83**

Malbec Mendoza 1990 • $6 • (05/31/94) • **74**

Mendoza Red Mendoza 1994: Soft and jammy, this has cherry and spicy flavors and it goes down easy. Not sophisticated, but fine for a picnic. 20,000 cases made. • $6 • (09/30/95) • **79**

Mendoza Red Mendoza 1991 • $6 • (05/31/94) • **76**

White Mendoza 1994: Light and simple, this nearly neutral white offers some peach and apple flavors, then finishes short. A quaffer at best. 20,000 cases made. • $6 • (09/30/95) • **76**

TRAPICHE

Cabernet Sauvignon Mendoza 1982 • $4 • (02/15/89) BB • **81**

Cabernet Sauvignon Mendoza Fond de Cave 1991: This accessible, well-made wine offers black cherry and tobacco notes in a supple, medium-bodied style, nicely balanced between youth and maturity. Pleasant drinking now. • $12 • **83**

Cabernet Sauvignon Mendoza Fond de Cave 1990 • $13 • (06/15/94) • **79**

Cabernet Sauvignon Mendoza Maipu County 1990 • $8 • (05/31/94) • **83**

Cabernet Sauvignon Mendoza Oak Cask Maipu County 1991: An odd mix of tart cranberry, musty, earthy notes and oaky vanilla flavors keeps this off-balanced. It's rich, though, ripe and concentrated. Drinkable now. • $8 • (04/30/95) • **80**

Cabernet Sauvignon Mendoza Oak Cask Reserve Vintner's Selection 1986 • $9 • (10/15/91) • **82**

Cabernet Sauvignon Mendoza Reserve 1992: Here's a thick, chewy wine with ripe plum and tomato flavors, but the tannins are heavy and an offputting animal note mars the aroma. It's rich but clumsy. Tasted three times with consistent results. • $6 • **77**

Cabernet Sauvignon Mendoza Reserve 1988 • $7 • (09/15/92) • **79**

Cabernet Sauvignon Mendoza Reserve 1986 • $5 • (09/15/90) • **77**

Cabernet Sauvignon Mendoza Vintner's Selection Oak Cask Reserve 1986 • $8 • (07/15/91) • **69**

Chardonnay Mendoza Fond de Cave 1993: A clean, straightforward wine, this offers light apple and pear flavors without embellishment. The balance is good, the finish short. • $12 • (09/30/94) • **82**

Chardonnay Mendoza Medalla 1994: The apple and floral aromas are enticing, but the flavors are subdued, with simple apple character. It's fresh and clean. • $20 • (04/30/95) • **80**

Chardonnay Mendoza Oak Cask Vintner's Selection Tupungato V 1992: A plump, generous wine with plenty of oak, this offers ripe tropical fruit and lots of creamy vanilla flavor. A bit exaggerated, but tasty. • $8 • (04/30/95) • **83**

Chardonnay Mendoza Reserve 1993: Flabby without much structure or fruit, offering some apple and fennel flavors. It lacks acidity and length. • $6 • (04/30/95) • **75**

Chardonnay Mendoza Reserve 1991 • $7 • (09/15/92) • **76**

Chardonnay Mendoza Tupungato Valley 1992 • $8 • (05/31/94) • **80**

Cuvée de Trapiche Merlot/Malbec Mendoza 1994: Sweet raspberry and vanilla aromas turn a bit sour on the palate of this light, lean wine. It's simple and quaffable, but that's all. • $4 • **76**

Malbec Mendoza Lujan de Cuyo County 1990 • $8 • (05/31/94) BB • **86**

Malbec Mendoza Oak Cask Reserve 1988 • $8 • (03/31/93) • **81**

Malbec Mendoza Oak Cask Reserve Vintner's Selection 1988 • $6 • (10/15/91) • **81**

Malbec Mendoza Oak Cask Vintner's Selection Lujan de Cuyo County 1991: Oodles of ripe black currant flavors are marked by sweet American oak, lending immense appeal. This Argentine version of the French variety is straightforward, with good balance and structure. A good value and drinkable now. 15,000 cases made. • $8 • (08/31/95) BB • **87**

Malbec Mendoza Oak Cask Vintner's Selection Lujan de Cuyo County 1990: This round, vivid wine shows good depth and polish, with deep black cherry fruit and appealing notes of smoke, toast and spice. It's a sturdy, basic red that stays with you. Drink now. 15,000 cases made. • $8 • (07/31/95) BB • **86**

Malbec Mendoza Reserve 1991: Thin and rather hard, showing cherry, black pepper and some rubbery flavors in a lean, tannic package. Drink now. • $6 • (07/31/95) • **78**

Malbec Mendoza Reserve 1987 • $5 • (09/15/90) BB • **83**

Malbec Mendoza Vintner's Selection Oak Cask Reserve 1988 • $8 • (07/15/91) • **74**

Medalla Mendoza 1993: Delicate peach and floral aromas carry through on the palate in this light, easy-drinking wine. It's clean and well balanced, subtle yet appealing. Delightful for a summer afternoon. • $18 • (09/30/94) • **84**

Medalla Mendoza 1991: A still-youthful red that offers dark color, jammy, black fruit aromas and firm tannins wrapped around ripe blackberry and plum flavors, with vanilla and toast on the finish. Drinkable now. 2,225 cases made. • $18 • (09/30/94) • **87**

Pinot Noir Mendoza Reserve 1988 • $7 • (09/15/92) • **80**

Sauvignon Blanc Mendoza Cuvée de Trapiche 1994: Straightforward and a bit dull, this offers ripe apple fruit with a hint of earth. It's rich but lacks personality. • $4 • **79**

TROCADERO

Brut Blanc de Blancs Cafayate-Colchaquíes Valley NV: Light and well rounded, with appealing peach and apple flavors. It also has some nice toasty notes, extremely effervescent. 25,000 cases made. • $7 • **79**

WEINERT, BODEGA Y CAVAS DE

Cabernet Sauvignon Mendoza Weinert 1985: Fully mature, aged, soft and thick, offering raisin, dried cherry and cedar flavors. Still in balance, it wants drinking now. 10,000 cases made. • $16 • **80**

Cabernet Sauvignon Mendoza Weinert 1983 • $16 • (05/31/94) • **81**

Carrascal Mendoza 1989: Mature earthy and raisin aromas give way to murky earth and vegetal flavors in this thick, dull wine. Drink up. 30,000 cases made. • $10 • **76**

Carrascal Mendoza 1988 • $10 • (05/31/94) • **82**

Carrascal Mendoza 1985 • $10 • (03/31/93) • **75**

Cavas de Weinert Mendoza 1989: This mature wine remains balanced and fruity. Alluring cedar, plum and tobacco aromas give way to a lush palate, rich with ripe plum, raisin and tobacco flavors. A bit rustic, but it shows good concentration. Drinkable now. 7,000 cases made. • $17 • **86**

Cavas de Weinert Mendoza 1985 • $17 • (05/31/94) • **83**

Cavas de Weinert Mendoza 1983 • $16 • (03/31/93) • **77**

Merlot Mendoza Weinert 1990: Prune and tobacco notes dominate this thick, maturing wine. Though it shows some concentration, it's overripe and aging quickly. Drink now. Tasted twice. 15,000 cases made. • $12 • (09/30/94) • **72**

Merlot Mendoza Weinert 1988 • $13 • (03/31/93) • **76**

• Austria •

SCHLUMBERGER

Brut Vienna 1987: A serious, nicely mature sparkling wine with generous toasty-nutty aromas, a smooth, full texture and a lingering finish. A distinctive, dry style. • $17 • (02/28/95) • **87**

SERVUS

Burgenland Cuvée Burgenland 1992: This crisp, clean white shows citrus and light herbal flavors enlivened by a keen edge of acidity. It's light-bodied, a refreshing apéritif. 10,000 cases made. • $5 • (09/30/94) BB • **83**

Burgenland White 1994: A spicy wine that delivers flavors of white pepper and cream. Medium-bodied, dry and easy to like. Drinkable now. From Lenz Moser. • $NA • **82**

• Brazil •

JAMES, MARCUS

White Zinfandel Aurora Valley 1987 • $4 • (06/15/89) • **78**

• Bulgaria •

BALKAN CREST

Cabernet Sauvignon Stara Zagora Oriahovitza Vineyards Reserve 1985 • $6 • (07/15/91) • **58**

BULGARE

Chardonnay Varna 1993: Powerfully aromatic, floral, honey and apricot notes turn hollow on the palate and finish with a nutty, oxidized character. From Bulgaria. 16,000 cases made. • $4 • (06/30/95) • **73**

Merlot & Pinot Noir Sliven 1993: An unbelievably great value from Bulgaria. Generous in flavor, easygoing in texture, with light tannins and good fruit flavors. This has fresh cherry and raspberry accents and an enticing balance. 16,000 cases made. • $4 • (06/30/95) • **84**

DALINA, CHATEAU

Cabernet Sauvignon Russe 1994: Fruity and fresh, with raspberry and sweet cherry flavors and a hint of tobacco. Light and drinkable now. • $5 • (12/31/95) • **82**

Cabernet Sauvignon Russe 1993: Jam aromas give way to fairly lean and astringent flavors, with only modest plum and currant flavors. Good varietal character and a decent finish. • $4 • **80**

Cabernet Sauvignon Russe 1992: Light bodied, simple and fruity with raspberry and plum flavors. A nice touch of herbalness gives this wine some substance as well. Clean flavors and a well-balanced structure. Enjoy with your summer barbecue. A great buy from Bulgaria. • $4 BB • **84**

Chardonnay Russe 1994: Awkward and somewhat coarse, showing honey and butter flavors and a sharp, cheesy note on the finish. • $5 • (05/15/96) • **75**

Chardonnay Russe 1993: Thick and soft, with top-heavy pear and vanilla flavors, this is an entry-level wine without any hard edges or scary depths. • $4 • (03/31/95) BB • **80**

Merlot Russe 1994: Satisfying but not complex. There's a good focus to the nice cherry, plum and berry flavors. Also a good touch of spice, with a tart, zingy finish. • $5 • (12/31/95) • **83**

Merlot Russe 1993: Crisp and flavorful, with good berry and currant flavors and a hint of spice. Typical Merlot, with a nice combination of herbal and fruit flavors, though it has a short finish. • $4 • **84**

HASKOVO ESTATES

Merlot Haskovo 1993: A resinous quality runs through this Bulgarian wine that has decent plum and black currant flavors. Good and fruity-offering a lot in this price range-with a mouth-filling texture and a spicy finish. 4,800 cases made. • $5 • (12/31/95) BB • **84**

NAZDRAVE

Cabernet Sauvignon Korten 1989: Smells and tastes of cassis, with a hint of plum and spice. It is also jammy, with a wallop of tannins and a hot, alcoholic finish. 30,000 cases made. • $5 • **81**

Cabernet Sauvignon Sliven Reserve 1988: Tastes tired, with menthol aromas and flavors. The plum flavors are interesting, but fail to carry this past the menthol. 26,000 cases made. • $6 • **77**

Key: SS—Spectator Selection. CS—Cellar Selection. BB—Best Buy. $NA—Price not available. (BT)—Barrel tasting. Ⓐ—Auction Price.
Dates in parentheses represent the issues in which the ratings were published.

Chardonnay Russe 1993: Apple juice and buttery flavors add to an off-putting finish that's reminiscent of green cider. 42,000 cases made. • $5 • (05/15/96) • **70**

Chardonnay Russe 1992: 42,666 cases made. • $5 • **50**

Country Red Russe NV: A pleasant, well-rounded, easy-drinking red with jammy, plummy flavors. Low in tannin, soft in texture and ready to drink now. 250,000 cases made. • $4 • (06/30/95) • **82**

Merlot Sliven Reserve 1988: A good, firm style, with herbal and currant flavors and a hint of pickle. Crisp for its age and still quite tannic, with a nice, spicy finish. 11,000 cases made. • $6 • **80**

PULDEN

Cabernet Sauvignon Plovdiv 1989: The ripe plum and currant flavors are nicely interwoven with a hint of chocolate. The lengthy finish is full of smoky and spicy notes. • $5 • **84**

Merlot Plovdiv 1990: Lean and extremely earthy, with a bizarre mix of flavors. Ends up cloying on the finish. • $NA • **71**

SVISHTOV, VINPROM

Cabernet Sauvignon Svischtov Amphora Series 1988: A light, simple wine with raisin and weedy flavors. It's inoffensive but doesn't offer much pleasure. The label claims an AOC, but it's only a misleading marketing ploy. 8,333 cases made. • $9 • (03/31/95) • **73**

VINEX PRESLAV

Chardonnay Novi Pazar 1991: This simple wine shows tart citric flavors and light apple fruit. It's lean and diluted. 17,000 cases made. • $5 • (03/31/95) • **73**

VINPROM

Chardonnay Varna Bulgare 1993: Powerfully aromatic, with floral, honey and apricot notes, this wine turns hollow on the palate and finishes with a nutty, oxidized character that lacks finesse and freshness. 16,000 cases made. • $4 • (06/30/95) • **73**

Merlot Haskovo 1989: Tastes tired and mature, with some plum and herbal flavors that are fading. It also has an astringent finish. 125,000 cases made. • $5 • **74**

Merlot Haskovo Reserve 1987: Spicy and plummy, with a nice liveliness for its age. It has nice Merlot character with herbal notes and a hint of wood on the finish. Drinkable now. 25,000 cases made. • $6 • **82**

Merlot & Pinot Noir Bulgare Sliven 1993: A great value. Generous in flavor, easy-going in texture, with light tannins and good fruit flavors. This has fresh cherry and raspberry accents and an enticing balance. 16,000 cases made. • $4 • (06/30/95) BB • **84**

• Canada •

INNISKILLIN NIAGARA

Chardonnay Niagara Peninsula 1992: Straightforward, clean and fresh, with simple apple flavors and good acidity. • $8 • (09/30/94) • **78**

Chardonnay Niagara Peninsula Beamsville Bench 1991: A lot of butter and smoke flavor shows through the thin core of fruit in this medium-bodied Chardonnay. It lacks definitive fruit flavor, and turns thin and candied on the finish. 1,000 cases made. • $14 • (09/30/94) • **77**

Chardonnay Niagara Peninsula Klose Vineyard 1992: A vivid, powerful, high-tension white. Considerable oak shows through in the buttery flavors, but it's solid with acidity and clean in taste. Intriguing, because each sip reveals nuances of pear, vanilla and nutmeg flavors that linger on the finish. 1,100 cases made. • $14 • (09/30/94) • **86**

Chardonnay Niagara Peninsula Reserve 1992: A firmly textured, international style of Chardonnay, with an evident oak-aged character, and good acidity. The nutmeg, cinnamon and vanilla notes give it interest, and the finish is spicy and lingering. Seems slightly sweet, but not overdone. • $12 • (09/30/94) • **85**

Chardonnay Niagara Peninsula Reserve 1991: A simple and fruity white that is of decent quality, but has little Chardonnay character. Soft and clean, but just bland. • $12 • (09/30/94) • **78**

Chardonnay Niagara Peninsula Seeger Vineyard 1992: An extremely oaky style of Chardonnay, from the butterscotch aromas, to the thick, chewy texture, to the seemingly sweet, vanilla flavors on the finish. Some will find it intriguing, but we think it lacks fruit character and finesse. • $14 • (09/30/94) • **79**

Chardonnay Niagara Peninsula Seeger Vineyard 1991: This is a heavy-handed wine with butterscotch aromas and flavors that crowd out the meager fruit flavors underneath. Drinkable, but lacks balance and freshness. 1,200 cases made. • $14 • (09/30/94) • **78**

Pinot Noir Niagara Peninsula Reserve 1992: Soft spice and brown sugar aromas give way to light cherry and leather flavors. It's light and simple. Drink up. 856 cases made. • $15 • (05/15/95) • **77**

Pinot Noir Niagara Peninsula Reserve 1991: Round and generous, this offers ripe fruit, with black cherry, light raisin and spice flavors, on a soft, ample frame that shows some concentration. A friendly, drinkable wine. 475 cases made. • $15 • (05/15/95) • **82**

PELLER ESTATES

Niagara Peninsula Vidal Ice Wine 1991: Flavors of raisins, walnuts and licorice give this wine a Sherry-like quality, it's sweet but lacks the acidity of most ice-wines. Clean and pleasant but atypical. Drink now. • $38 • **80**

Okanagan Valley Ehrenfelser Ice Wine 1993: Smoke and spice notes add interest to this fresh, tart wine. It's bright and clean, with modest apricot and apple flavors and moderate sweetness in a lean frame. Drinkable now. 40 cases made. • $25 • **83**

QUAILS' GATE

Riesling British Columbia Ice Wine 1993: Vivid and fresh, this shows well-defined Riesling peach and floral flavors. It's rich but not heavy, subtle and even delicate, with a nice balance of moderate sweetness and acidity. 104 cases made. • $33 • **86**

REIF ESTATE

Ontario Vidal Ice Wine 1991: More delicate than many Vidals, this shows peach and apple flavors in a sweet but balanced wine. It's fresh and clean. • $32 • **83**

STONECHURCH

Ontario Ice Wine 1991: Sweet raisin and honey notes mark this velvety, very sweet wine. It's thick but short and finishes a bit rough. 2,000 cases made. • $50 • **79**

STONEY RIDGE

Ontario Riesling/Traminer Ice Wine 1992: Expressive aromas of apricot, honey and toast draw you into this rich, very sweet wine. It's luscious on the palate, with nut and caramel flavors, moderate acidity and a lingering finish. Drink now. 25 cases made. • $33 • **85**

SUMMERHILL

Brut British Columbia Cipes NV: A range of flavors, but not all pleasant: cooked apple, maple syrup, canned pear. Aggressively foamy and a bit cloying on the finish. 6,000 cases made. • $19 • (12/15/95) • **79**

Chardonnay British Columbia Reserve 1992: Intriguing. Smells and tastes like a Champagne without the bubbles. It has doughy, mineral-like aromas and subtle buttery, figgy flavors. There's not much fruit, but it has good balance and a nice austerity. • $NA • (06/30/95) • **83**

Pinot Noir British Columbia 1993: Lots of ripe fruit in this medium-bodied, lightly tannic Pinot, but there's not much complexity. It smells like prunes and smoke, tastes smooth. Drink now while it's fresh. • $NA • (06/30/95) • **81**

Riesling British Columbia Ice Wine 1992: Honey, dried apricot and pineapple flavors are intense and focused in this very rich, ripe wine. It's full-bodied and very sweet, with enough acidity on the finish to keep it lively. Drink now. 100 cases made. • $33 • **86**

VINELAND ESTATES

Niagara Peninsula Vidal Ice Wine 1992: Very brown in color, with a spicy apple cider aroma, this achieves a balance of sweet and tart but lacks depth. Simple but vivid, try with a tart dessert. 552 cases made. • $32 • **81**

Niagara Peninsula Vidal Ice Wine 1989: Vegetal notes overwhelm modest apple cider and toffee flavors in this sweet, simple wine. 240 cases made. • $85 • **70**

• Greece •

BOUTARI

Red Goumenissa 1993: Nicely balanced and sufficiently crisp to accompany a wide variety of foods, offering enough raspberry flavor to make it attractive. Very dry, somewhat tannic. • $11 • (05/15/96) • **83**

Red Naoussa 1993: Crisp, solidly made, somewhat tannic, showing enough depth in the berry and anise flavors to keep it interesting. Nicely balanced to drink now. • $8 • (05/15/96) • **84**

Red Naoussa Grande Reserve 1990: Fully mature, featuring spicy, almost sweet fruit flavors and leathery, tealike aromas. • $13 • (05/15/96) • **82**

Red Nemea 1993: A ripe-tasting red that's fairly lush and fruity, offering spicy accents and medium body. Soft and not too tannic, drink now while it's fresh. 40,000 cases made. • $8 • (05/15/96) • **82**

Red Paros 1993: Rustic and tannic, fruity flavors carrying a resinous note. Starts out rich and full and finishes lean. • $13 • (05/15/96) • **78**

CAVA TSANTALIS

Red Greece 1990: Sturdy, showing a lean, moderately tannic texture and modest fruit character. • $7 • (05/15/96) • **81**

HATZIMICHALIS, DOMAINE

20th Anniversary Central Greece 1993: A rustic, smoky-tasting red, presenting tomatolike flavors, soft tannins and short finish. • $NA • (06/30/95) • **77**

Cabernet Sauvignon Central Greece 1992: Plum and meaty flavors show good raw materials, but offputting earthy, plastic notes and aggressive tannins detract from the pleasure. A bit harsh to drink now, but may not improve. Tasted twice with consistant notes. • $12 • (04/30/95) • **69**

Chardonnay Central Greece 1993: Dull, flabby and bland, providing smooth texture but lacking varietal character or personality. It's simple, soft and forgettable. • $12 • (06/30/95) • **75**

ODYSSEY

Cava Premium Dry 1981 • $3 • (12/15/87) • **78**

RAPSANI

Red Greece 1991: A nice note of spicy maturity in the aroma and flavor of this lean but fruity red makes it intriguing. Tannins request hearty food. • $11 • (05/15/96) • **83**

• Hungary •

BODROGVARHEGY LTD.

Tokay Aszú 3 Puttonyos 1988: Slightly sweet, very flavorful and thick in texture. Aromas of nuts, peaches and apricots, with crisp, zingy fruit flavors. A bit short on the finish. • $16 • (09/15/95) • **83**

Tokay Aszú 5 Puttonyos Messzelátö Dülö 1988: Traditional, old-fashioned Tokay. The intense, concentrated raisin, nut and lemon flavors turn a bit hollow. Somewhat bitter finish. • $20 • (09/15/95) • **81**

BORFOK

Cabernet Sauvignon Villányi 1992 • $7 • **55**

DISZNOKO

Furmint Tokay 1994: Clean, fresh lemon, banana and vanilla character, light body and tart finish. • $NA • (09/15/95) • **77**

Furmint Tokay 1993: A well-made, crisp, balanced, straightforward white that offers almond, citrus and green apple flavors, but not much complexity. Tasted twice, with consistent notes. • $7 • (09/15/95) • **78**

Tokay Aszú 4 Puttonyos 1989: Somewhat rustic and tough, with dried apricot and spice character. Smoky and bitter on the finish. • $NA • (09/15/95) • **80**

Tokay Aszú Eszencia 1988: Disappointing for an Eszencia. Starts out nicely, with spice, orange peel and honey aromas, but turns somewhat hollow in the palate and short on the finish. • $NA • (09/15/95) • **83**

Tokay Aszú 5 Puttonyos 1988: Old style-full body, sweet and oxidized-offering marzipan, toffee, spice and coffee flavors. Lacks finesse, as would be expected from a wine pasteurized several times. • $18 • (09/15/95) • **86**

Tokay Aszú 6 Puttonyos 1989: Smooth, silky and viscous, delivering orange peel, lime, almond and spice aromas and flavors. Nicely preserved, but packs less punch than expected from a 6 Puttonyos. • $NA • (09/15/95) • **84**

Tokay Edes Szamorodni 1993: Delicious apéritif and an example of the new style of basic sweet wines made by Westerners. Fresh and medium sweet, offering lovely pineapple, dried apricot and fig flavors. • $NA • (09/15/95) • **86**

Tokay Száraz Szamorodni 1990: Pleasant roasted almond and orange marmalade flavors and medium body. Close to an amontillado style of Sherry. Tasted twice, with consistent notes. • $NA • (09/15/95) • **82**

HETSZOLO

Furmint Tokay 1994: A clean and refreshing dry table wine that reveals melon, pear and green apple flavors, which turn tart and simple on the finish. • $NA • (09/15/95) • **79**

Hárslevelü Tokay 1994: Clean, fresh and slightly off-dry, revealing almond, wet earth and banana flavors. Light in body. Pleasant finish for an apéritif. • $NA • (09/15/95) • **79**

Muscat Tokay 1994: Lovely floral, beeswax and lemon flavors and a touch of honey. Medium-bodied and off-dry, showing a refreshing, delicious, fruity finish. • $NA • (09/15/95) • **83**

Tokay Aszú 5 Puttonyos Dessewffy 1988: A mature, old-style, full-bodied Tokay that has a silky texture and shows almond, fig and raisin notes. Bitter finish. • $NA • (09/15/95) • **80**

Tokay Fordítás Dessewffy 1990: Fresh and flavorful, medium sweet like a light Sauternes. Medium-bodied, slightly oxidized, featuring nut, pineapple and dried apricot. • $NA • (09/15/95) • **81**

HICKORY RIDGE

Chardonnay Hincesti 1994: A basic white showing some butter flavors and slightly sweet notes. Disjointed and overdone. • $5 • (05/15/96) • **78**

MEGYER, CHATEAU

Chardonnay Tokay 1994: Hard to believe this is Chardonnay. Tired, light-bodied and some odd, cooked apple flavors mingle with pear and almond notes. • $NA • (09/15/95) • **75**

Chardonnay Zempléni Tokay 1993: Doesn't taste like Chardonnay. Crisp, tart lemon and apricot flavors on the mid-palate, light in body. • $NA • (09/15/95) • **75**

Furmint Tokay 1994: Decent and dry, offering almond, melon and pear flavors and a touch of cream. Medium in body, pleasant finish. • $NA • (09/15/95) • **78**

Furmint Tokay 1993: Dry and tart, offering fruit cocktail flavors and a chalky character. Medium-bodied and turns a bit sharp and acidic on the finish. • $NA • (09/15/95) • **76**

Tokay Aszú 4 Puttonyos 1988: A bit disjointed: raisin, spice and nut character, medium body, mature and oxidized. Turns bitter and astringent on the finish. • $NA • (09/15/95) • **78**

OREMUS

Tokay Aszú 5 Puttonyos 1988: Shows character and intensity, but could use more balance. Mature nut, lemon and apricot flavors and full body, but simple, short and astringent on the finish. • $NA • (09/15/95) • **82**

Tokay Aszú 6 Puttonyos 1972: An old-style Aszú, but delicious and creamy. Dark amber color and mature character. Attractively ripe and rich with very sweet raisin and dried apricot flavors and a velvety finish. • $NA • (09/15/95) • **89**

Tokay Fordítás 1983: Bitter and heavily oxidized, revealing some dried apricot and raisin character. Sweet, medium body and short finish. • $NA • (09/15/95) • **74**

Tokay Furmint Mandulás 1993: Dry, light and somewhat flat, offering a hint of almond, lemon and apple character. • $NA • (09/15/95) • **73**

Tokay Száraz Szamorodni 1986: Good intensity in this dry, medium-bodied, Sherry-like wine that has peanut, almond and smoke flavors. Try as an apéritif with tapas. • $NA • (09/15/95) • **83**

PAJZOS, CHATEAU

Tokay 1992: Apple, celery and melon flavors mingle in this rich but slightly dull white. The round mouthfeel is pleasant, but it's soft and a bit cloying in the finish. 2,000 cases made. • $7 • **78**

Tokay Aszú 4 Puttonyos 1988: Rich and syrupy. Starts well, with a nice orange peel, spice and raisin character, but turns odd on the mature, drying and bitter finish. • $NA • (09/15/95) • **79**

Tokay Aszú 5 Puttonyos 1988: An older wine that has held up well. Raisin, almond and dried apricot flavors are delicious. Smooth texture and a balanced finish. • $21 • (09/15/95) • **82**

Tokay Furmint 1994: Light and tart aromas and flavors of lime, freshly cut grass and avocado. Very sharp, tongue-twisting finish. • $NA • (09/15/95) • **72**

Tokay Furmint 1993: It's fresh but has some burnt match aromas. Lime, grapefruit and almond flavors and light body. Not much there, really. • $8 • (09/15/95) • **76**

ROYAL TOKAJI WINE CO., THE

Tokay Aszú 5 Puttonyos 1990: Rich and vivid tangerine, honey and citrus aromas and flavors. Medium in body, rather thick and sweet, with a nutty character on the mature finish. • $NA • (09/15/95) • **86**

Tokay Aszú 5 Puttonyos Betsek 1990: Amazingly rich and sweet, but not cloying. Shows delicious floral, marzipan, dried apricot and honey character. Traditional style, but lots going on here. • $50 • (09/15/95) • **91**

Tokay Aszú 5 Puttonyos Birsalma's 1990: Bold and rich, offering plenty of coconut, cream, pear and bread dough flavors. Delicious, but hints at bitter almond on the finish. • $50 • (09/15/95) • **87**

Tokay Aszú 5 Puttonyos Bojta 1990: Balanced and complex, very traditional, with great botrytis character. Flavors of dried apricots and nuts, a round, velvety texture and long finish. • $28 • (09/15/95) • **88**

Tokay Aszú 5 Puttonyos Nyulászó 1990: Seductive and very sweet, the acidity keeping it on track, showing vanilla bean and almond character. Medium to full body and long finish. • $65 • (09/15/95) • **89**

Tokay Betsek 1991: Smooth and honeyed, this shows the nutty, caramel and spice flavors of the traditional, oxidized style of Tokay. It's medium-sweet, with enough acidity for balance. • $48 • **88**

Tokay Birsalma's 1991: A nice marriage of spice and dried fruit flavors give depth. Shows good concentration, and tastes of raisins, dried apricots and honey. Quite sweet, but without much spark. • $48 • **87**

Key: SS—Spectator Selection. CS—Cellar Selection. BB—Best Buy. $NA—Price not available. (BT)—Barrel tasting. (A)—Auction Price.
Dates in parentheses represent the issues in which the ratings were published.

Tokay Blue Label 1991: Fresh, complex and lingering. Good balance of sweet and sour with its spicy vanilla, peach and passion fruit flavors. Lively and attractive—would be great with fruit desserts. • $32 • **89**

Tokay Bojta 1991: Thick, but a bit coarse. Offers sweetness but lacks fresh fruit, showing quite a bit of the traditional oxidation. A pleasant accompaniment to dessert, not as intriguing on its own. • $28 • **84**

Tokay Nyula'szó 1991: Rich, fresh and juicy, with raisin, orange-peel, nut and spice flavors. Quite sweet, but has plenty of acidity to balance. Intriguing and tempting—take another sip. • $65 • **91**

Tokay Szt. Tamás 1991: Concentrated and quite sweet, this rich white offers apricot, dried pineapple and honey flavors, with enough acidity to maintain freshness. A serious meditation wine. • $65 • **90**

ST. DONATUS

Chardonnay Balatonlellei 1993: Fat and rather candied, this wine shows sweet canned pear and nutty flavors, with a dull, earthy finish. It's generous, but lacks refinement. • $6 • (03/31/95) • **78**

STRUCTURE

Tokay Aszú 3 Puttonyos 1990: Medium sweet and oxidized, with mature orange, spice and almond flavors. Bitter and dry on the finish. • $NA • (09/15/95) • **77**

VINUM BONUM

Chardonnay Etyeki 1993: This big, showy wine falls cleanly within the new international style, with its tropical fruit flavors, crisp acidity and sweet vanilla accents. • $10 • (03/31/95) • **80**

Sauvignon Blanc Etyeki 1993: This richly-textured wine fills the mouth nicely, but the flavors lean towards artichokes and chalk, and the finish is slightly bitter. • $10 • (03/31/95) • **77**

• Israel •

CARMEL

Cabernet Sauvignon Israel Galil 1989 • $6 • (03/31/91) • **72**

Cabernet Sauvignon Israel Galil 1981 • $7 • (06/30/87) • **69**

Cabernet Sauvignon Samson 1986 • $7 • (03/31/91) • **78**

Sauvignon Blanc Galil Baron Edmond de Rothschild 1993: Badly oxidized, deep gold, this is flat and dull, with swampy flavors and no life. 6,000 cases made. • $10 • **65**

GAMLA

Cabernet Sauvignon Galil 1990: A sweet, ripe fruity character makes this straightforward and flavorful wine. Soft and full-bodied with raspberry and herbal flavors. 5,700 cases made. • $12 • **83**

Cabernet Sauvignon Galil 1989 • $12 • • **78**

Cabernet Sauvignon Galil 1988 • $10 • (07/15/93) • **77**

Cabernet Sauvignon Galil 1987 • $9 • (03/31/91) • **75**

Cabernet Sauvignon Galil Special Reserve 1986 • $12 • (03/31/91) • **83**

Chardonnay Galil 1991 • $12 • **76**

Sauvignon Blanc Late Harvest Galil 1988 • $14 • (03/31/91) • **75**

GOLAN

Cabernet Sauvignon Galil 1989: Herbal and soft, with surprisingly nice bell pepper and plum flavors. Simple, with inviting flavors, though a bit astringent. 2,000 cases made. • $12 • **81**

Cabernet Sauvignon Galil 1987 • $12 • (04/15/92) • **83**

Cabernet Sauvignon Galil 1986 • $11 • (03/31/91) • **85**

Chardonnay Galil 1991 • $12 • **83**

Sauvignon Blanc Galil 1992 • $10 • **75**

Sauvignon Blanc Galil 1991 • $9 • (07/15/93) • **79**

YARDEN

Brut Galil NV: Grassy aromas and nutty flavors that linger on the finish make this an unusual and disjointed sparkling wine. Drinkable, but not much fun, especially at this price. 3,200 cases made. • $24 • **74**

Cabernet Sauvignon Galil 1990: An herbal style, with good raspberry and cassis flavors. There is some richness and flesh on this wine, with a nice spicey finish. • $18 • **82**

Cabernet Sauvignon Galil 1989: Starts out fruity, but it turns tart and astringet. Herbs, cassis and sweet plum flavors mesh fairly well, but it still tastes medicinal in the end. Drinkable now. 4,200 cases made. • $18 • **79**

Cabernet Sauvignon Galil 1986 • $14 • (06/30/90) • **79**

Cabernet Sauvignon Galil 1985 • $14 • (06/30/90) • **82**

Merlot Galil Special Reserve 1988 • $14 • (03/31/91) • **77**

Merlot Galil Special Reserve 1986 • $12 • (06/30/90) • **79**

Mt. Hermon Red Galil 1989 • $7 • (03/31/91) • **70**

Sauvignon Blanc Galil 1992 • $12 • • **77**

• Lebanon •

MUSAR, CHATEAU

Lebanon White 1992: Aggressive grassy and almond aromas and flavors give this wine a distinctive character, reminiscent in taste and texture of a fino sherry. But it lacks fruit and delicacy. 3,000 cases made. • $16 • (09/30/94) • **77**

Lebanon Red 1987: This wine shows the expressive, mature tea and vanilla aromas of an aged Rioja. On the palate, it's smooth and supple, with ripe fruit and earthy notes. Elegant and easy to drink. 15,000 cases made. • $18 • (09/30/94) • **85**

Lebanon Red 1983 • $17 • (07/15/91) • **86**

Lebanon Red 1982 • $17 • (07/15/91) • **87**

Lebanon Red 1981 • $18 • (07/15/91) • **84**

Lebanon Red 1980 • $17 • (07/31/88) • **91**

• New Zealand •

ARARIMU

Cabernet Sauvignon Hawke's Bay 1991: Fresh, with good plum and berry flavors and a pleasing velvety texture. From Matua Valley. Drink now. • $NA • (05/15/94) • **80**

Chardonnay Gisborne 1991: Flattened by the oak, dark gold-colored, very thick and waxy, lacking vivacity. From Matua Valley. • $NA • (05/15/94) • **79**

ATA RANGI

Pinot Noir 1991: A pleasant Pinot with spicy, berry, smoky aromas and flavors, light body, soft tannins and a fruity finish. Drink now. • $NA • (05/15/94) • **81**

BABICH

Cabernet Blend Hawke's Bay Irongate 1990: Pleasant but light, with cherry and plum character, light tannins and finish. • $NA • (05/15/94) • **79**

Cabernet Sauvignon Hawke's Bay 1989 • $10 • (07/15/91) • **74**

Chardonnay Hawke's Bay 1992: Good, clean, well-made Chardonnay, with apple and pineapple flavors and a nice balance of acidity. • $11 • (05/15/94) • **86**

Chardonnay Hawke's Bay 1991 • $10 • (05/31/93) • **88**

Chardonnay Hawke's Bay Irongate 1992: Hay, apple and honey flavors mingle in this balanced, harmonious mixture of opulence and structure. • $20 • (05/15/94) • **87**

Pinot Noir Henderson Valley 1992: Pleasant raspberry and strawberry flavors are marred by barnyard-like notes, flat on the finish. • $NA • (05/15/94) • **77**

NEW ZEALAND

Sauvignon Blanc Hawke's Bay 1993: Pleasant, offers light celery and fruit character, light body and a crisp finish. • $10 • (05/15/94) • **80**
Sauvignon Blanc Hawke's Bay 1992 • $9 • (12/15/93) • **85**
Sauvignon Blanc Marlborough 1993: Offers broader flavors than many, showing apple and floral character, medium body and a fresh finish. • $11 • (05/15/94) • **82**
Sémillon-Chardonnay Gisborne 1992: Cloying and odd, with canned asparagus, slightly rotten aromas and flavors. • $NA • (05/15/94) • **65**

CASTLE HILL

Sauvignon Blanc Hawke's Bay 1993: Another reserved Sauvignon with pear, green apple and some celery character, clean, fresh and simple. • $NA • (05/15/94) • **82**

CHURCH ROAD

Cabernet Sauvignon Hawke's Bay 1991: Shows good velvety texture with some plum, prune and tobacco character, medium-bodied with a light finish. • $NA • (05/15/94) • **78**
Chardonnay Hawke's Bay Chruch Road 1992: A smooth, solid wine, with apple, vanilla and honey character, medium body and good acidity. • $NA • (05/15/94) • **85**

CLOUDY BAY

Cabernet Merlot 1991: Rather neutral and simple with a light finish. • $NA • (05/15/94) • **75**
Chardonnay Marlborough 1992: An ambitious wine with masses of fruit and wood but an excellent undercarriage of acidity and alcohol. Try after 1994. • $19 • (05/15/94) • **91**
Chardonnay Marlborough 1991: A bit on the green and vegetal side, with lean minty and green pineapple and pear flavors that turn crisp and spicy. • $19 • (05/15/94) • **83**
Sauvignon Blanc Marlborough 1993: Wild and exotic, with grassy, flinty, fruity aromas and flavors. Medium body, fresh acidity and a long, intensely flavored finish. Refreshing. Tasted twice. • $15 • (05/15/94) • **88**
Sauvignon Blanc Marlborough 1991 • $13 • (09/15/93) • **83**

COLLARDS

Chardonnay Auckland Rothsay Vineyard 1991: A tight and muscular style with pineapple and vanilla character, beautiful acidity. In great shape. • $NA • (05/15/94) • **90**
Riesling Marlborough Corners Vineyards 1992: A big, rich style offers spice, apple and grapefruit aromas and flavors, crisp acidity and a long fruity finish. • $NA • (05/15/94) • **86**
Sauvignon Blanc Marlborough 1993: Exciting with intense grapefruit aromas and flavors, crisp and clean, the fresh finish has a hint of vanilla. • $NA • (05/15/94) • **88**
Sémillon Auckland Henderson Estate Vineyard Barrique Fermented 1992: Like biting into a bar of soap. Extremely unpleasant and an unusual misstep for this fine producer. Tasted twice. • $NA • (05/15/94) • **62**

COOPERS CREEK

Cabernet Blend Huapai 1991: Fairly green with some plum and smoky character, but light-bodied and short. • $NA • (05/15/94) • **77**
Cabernet Sauvignon Huapai 1990 • $12 • (08/31/93) • **83**
Cabernet Sauvignon Huapai 1989 • $10 • (04/15/92) • **79**
Chardonnay Gisborne 1993: A rich combination of vanilla, honey and melon lends immediate appeal, ripe, but balanced with fresh acidity. • $11 • (05/15/94) • **85**
Chardonnay Gisborne 1992 • $11 • (08/31/93) • **88**
Chardonnay Hawke's Bay 1991 • $12 • (08/31/93) • **88**

Key: SS—Spectator Selection. CS—Cellar Selection. BB—Best Buy. $NA—Price not available. (BT)—Barrel tasting. Ⓐ—Auction Price.
Dates in parentheses represent the issues in which the ratings were published.

Merlot Hawke's Bay 1992: Thin, sour and lacking in fruit. Very light. • $NA • (05/15/94) • **70**
Sauvignon Blanc Gisborne 1992: Quite thick, with a buttered asparagus and tropical fruit character and tart acidity on the finish. 20 percent Sémillon, oak-aged. • $NA • (05/15/94) • **80**
Sauvignon Blanc Marlborough 1993: Brisk and crisp with celery and grapefruit on the nose and palate, and a refreshing finish. • $NA • (05/15/94) • **84**
Sauvignon Blanc Marlborough 1992 • $10 • (09/15/93) • **86**
Sauvignon Blanc Marlborough 1991 • $10 • (10/31/92) • **82**

CORBANS

Chardonnay Gisborne Private Bin 1992: Understated and firm, with toasted oak, apple and mango flavors, medium body, medium acidity and a tasty finish. • $14 • (05/15/94) • **86**
Merlot Marlborough Private Bin 1991: Crisp and flavorful, beautifully focused and oozing with currant, black cherry, toast and herb flavors. Smooth enough to drink now, but best from 1995. 600 cases made. • $15 • (05/15/94) • **88**
Sauvignon Blanc Marlborough Private Bin 1993: A bit dull and diluted, with a celery, vegetal character and a light finish. • $13 • (05/15/94) • **76**

DASHWOOD

Sauvignon Blanc Marlborough 1993: A little off-kilter, showing green asparagus character and a finish like slightly rancid butter. Thick and unbalanced. • $NA • (05/15/94) • **75**

DE REDCLIFFE

Cabernet Merlot Hawke's Bay 1990: Tired and leafy, with a diluted, astringent character. Tasted twice with consistent notes. • $NA • (05/15/94) • **68**
Pinot Noir Hawke's Bay 1991: Very light and fruity but diluted, with stalky, strawberry flavors, very light tannins and a light finish. Drink now. • $NA • (05/15/94) • **78**
Sauvignon Blanc Marlborough 1993: Attractive flinty, celery character but slightly diluted on the finish. • $NA • (05/15/94) • **79**

DELEGATS

Cabernet Blend Hawke's Bay 1992: White wine masquerading as red, diluted with a hint of raspberry flavor. • $NA • (05/15/94) • **71**
Cabernet Sauvignon Hawke's Bay 1991: A moderate red with licorice, cigar box and vanilla aromas and flavors, clean and fresh with a balance of light tannins and good acidity. Drink now. • $NA • (05/15/94) • **83**
Chardonnay Hawke's Bay 1992: Diluted and watery, tries to make up with overly sweet oak what it lacks in fruit. • $NA • (05/15/94) • **75**
Chardonnay Hawke's Bay Proprietor's Reserve 1991: An exotic style of Chardonnay, with very ripe papaya, lemon and lime character, full body and a long fresh finish. • $NA • (05/15/94) • **89**
Merlot Hawke's Bay Proprietor's Reserve 1990: Acidic and light with green, earthy flavors and a dry finish. • $NA • (05/15/94) • **70**
Sauvignon Blanc Hawke's Bay 1993: More elegant and reserved than most, with hay, apple and grassy character, medium body and a fine balance of acidity. • $NA • (05/15/94) • **84**

ELSTON

Chardonnay Hawke's Bay 1992: Masses of new oak taste like toothpicks, almost sweet. From Te Mata Estate. • $NA • (05/15/94) • **78**

ESK VALLEY

Cabernet Blend Hawke's Bay 1992: A light structured red with bright fruit and tar, cherry character and a hint of bellpepper. Slightly spritzy finish and lacks tannin backbone. Drink now. • $NA • (05/15/94) • **78**
Cabernet Blend Hawke's Bay Reserve 1991: A more assertive style of red, with bright blueberry, blackberry and vanilla character, medium body, medium tannins and a long finish. Drink or hold. • $NA • (05/15/94) • **86**

Chardonnay Hawke's Bay 1991: Smooth, viscous and thick with oak, showing bright lemon flavors, not crisp enough to balance the sweet vanilla taste. • $NA • (05/15/94) • **81**

Chardonnay Hawke's Bay Reserve 1991: The apple and vanilla aromas are tempting, but sweet oak dominates the melon and pineapple flavors. For fans of vanilla ice cream. • $NA • (05/15/94) • **83**

Hawke's Bay Private Bin Wood Aged 1991: Fruity but over-oaked, showing vanilla coconut flavors and not much else. • $NA • (05/15/94) • **78**

Sauvignon Blanc Hawke's Bay 1993: Fresh and straightforward, offering apple and melon flavors and a crisp finish. • $NA • (05/15/94) • **83**

FORREST ESTATE

Chardonnay Marlborough 1993: A clean Chardonnay, with milky, lemon aromas and flavors. Light-bodied with fresh acidity. • $NA • (05/15/94) • **81**

FRENCH FARM

Sauvignon Blanc Marlborough Oak Aged 1992: Some decent celery and fruit aromas, but green and tart on the palate. • $NA • (05/15/94) • **78**

Sauvignon Blanc Waipara 1993: Rather light and neutral with some celery character, but it's marred by high acidity and a short finish. • $NA • (05/15/94) • **78**

GIESEN

Sauvignon Blanc Marlborough Rapura Road 1992: Round and easy to drink, with melon and pie crust aromas and flavors, medium body and pleasant acidity. • $NA • (05/15/94) • **83**

GOLDWATER

Cabernet Blend Waiheke Island 1990: Fresh and harmonious, well-made red with plum, vanilla and blackberry character, medium body, firm tannins and a long finish. 1,500 cases made. • $30 • (05/15/94) • **84**

Cabernet Blend Waiheke Island 1985 • $27 • (07/15/88) • **73**

Chardonnay Marlborough 1992: A little tired from the new oak, with butterscotch and apple aromas and flavors, medium body and thick finish. Better in previous tasting. 5,500 cases made. • $12 • (05/15/94) • **77**

GROVE MILL

Chardonnay Marlborough 1993: Medium-bodied, with an abundance of grapefruit, pineapple and vanilla character, crisp and lively. • $NA • (05/15/94) • **83**

Sauvignon Blanc Marlborough 1993: Another clean, no-nonsense Sauvignon with celery and grapefruit flavors and lively acidity. • $NA • (05/15/94) • **83**

HUNTER'S

Cabernet Sauvignon Marlborough 1990: A strong dose of new wood provides some vanilla, tar and fruit character, but it's just light and simple. • $NA • (05/15/94) • **77**

Chardonnay Marlborough 1991: An attractive Chardonnay, with medium-intensity vanilla, cream and lemon character and balanced acidity. • $NA • (05/15/94) • **84**

Pinot Noir Marlborough 1992: More like fruit juice than wine. It lacks tannins, grip and varietal character. • $NA • (05/15/94) • **76**

Riesling Marlborough 1991: Aromas of dry ice and apricots mingle in this medium-bodied yet intense wine. It's clean and fresh. • $NA • (05/15/94) • **82**

Sauvignon Blanc Marlborough 1993: Thick and funky, with slightly candied aromas and flavors and a sweaty character. • $NA • (05/15/94) • **76**

Sauvignon Blanc Marlborough Oak Aged 1992: Seductive with rich, ripe flavors. It has more complexity than its peers, with mango, pineapple and licorice aromas and flavors, full-bodied and firm with a long finish. Eight months in wood. • $NA • (05/15/94) • **90**

JACKSON ESTATE

Chardonnay Marlborough 1992: Rich and thick, with ripe tropical fruit and toasty vanilla flavors. This wine is saved from its alcoholic strength by firm underlying acidity. • $NA • (05/15/94) • **82**

Sauvignon Blanc Marlborough 1993: Finishes well, with dried herbs and fruit and a hint of mintiness, medium-bodied with good acidity. • $NA • (05/15/94) • **84**

KUMEU RIVER

Chardonnay Kumeu 1992: Big and rich, putting it all together: opulent, smoky oak, firm, fresh acidity, and intense apple and melon flavors. Luscious. Also rated outstanding in a previous tasting. 3,000 cases made. • $28 • (05/15/94) • **92**

Chardonnay Kumeu 1991 • $28 • (10/31/92) • **92**

Merlot Cabernet Kumeu 1987 • $18 • (12/31/90) • **87**

Sauvignon Blanc Kumeu 1992: Distinctive, tasting almost like a dry Sauternes, with flavors of vanilla, almonds, smoke, honey and melon. A winemaker's wine, 14 percent Sémillon, barrel-fermented. • $21 • (05/15/94) • **85**

LONGRIDGE

Cabernet Blend Hawke's Bay 1992: A bit more structure here than other reds in our tasting, a berry finish. • $9 • (05/15/94) • **78**

Cabernet Sauvignon Hawke's Bay 1987 • $10 • (09/15/91) • **68**

Chardonnay Hawke's Bay 1993: Very fresh style with waxy, vanilla, lemon character, medium body and a fresh finish. • $9 • (05/15/94) • **84**

Chardonnay Hawke's Bay 1992 • $10 • (12/15/93) • **84**

Chardonnay Hawke's Bay 1991 • $10 • (08/31/93) • **74**

Merlot Hawke's Bay 1991 • $10 • (08/31/93) • **80**

MARTINBOROUGH

Chardonnay 1992: Truly sophisticated, with alluring, toasty oak and well-defined tropical fruit flavors. This is focused and classy. • $NA • (05/15/94) • **92**

Chardonnay 1991: Shows a wonderful combination of ripe fruit and toasted oak, medium-bodied, fine acidity, very long and silky on the palate. • $NA • (05/15/94) • **90**

Pinot Noir 1992: A delicate red with smoky, black cherry and leather aromas and flavors, it's light-bodied with light tannins. Drink now. • $NA • (05/15/94) • **80**

Riesling 1993: Unbalanced, with sweet, almost cloying fruit clashing with high, almost green acidity. • $NA • (05/15/94) • **76**

Sauvignon Blanc 1993: Offers an attractive combination of melon, grass and celery, with an almost sweet finish. • $NA • (05/15/94) • **80**

MATUA VALLEY

Cabernet Sauvignon Hawke's Bay Smith-Darmoor Estate 1990: Out of balance. Unacceptably high in acidity. • $NA • (05/15/94) • **66**

Cabernet Sauvignon New Zealand 1986 • $20 • **75**

Chardonnay Gisborne 1992: Medium intensity with attractive honey and butterscotch aromas, slightly less impressive on the palate. • $NA • (05/15/94) • **79**

Chardonnay Gisborne Judd Estate 1992: Dull and over-oaked, dark gold, with intense butterscotch and milky aromas and flavors, fat and thick. • $NA • (05/15/94) • **76**

Muscat Lake Harvest Hawke's Bay 1991: Pretty but not complex, with sweet lemon, lime and custard character, medium body and a fruity finish. Not overly sweet but fresh. • $NA • (05/15/94) • **86**

Sauvignon Blanc Hawke's Bay 1992: A bit diluted but it shows some pleasant creamy, grapefruit and apricot flavors and a light crisp finish. • $NA • (05/15/94) • **79**

Sauvignon Blanc Marlborough 1992: This tastes like an excellent glass of Sancerre, with celery, green apple and lime character, medium body and fresh acidity. • $NA • (05/15/94) • **87**

NEW ZEALAND

MILLS REEF

Chardonnay Hawke's Bay 1991: The generous use of oak marries well with ripe lemon and mango flavors. Good acidity. • $NA • (05/15/94) • **86**

Riesling Hawke's Bay Dry 1992: Though this shows some pleasant spicy and melon flavors, it's tired and well past its prime. • $NA • (05/15/94) • **72**

Sauvignon Blanc Hawke's Bay Clifton Road 1993: Pleasant grassy and lemon-lime aromas and flavors and a touch of sweetness on the finish. • $NA • (05/15/94) • **83**

MONTANA

Cabernet Sauvignon Marlborough 1991: Light and diluted with bellpepper, muted fruit character and light tannins. Drink now. • $NA • (05/15/94) • **75**

Chardonnay Marlborough 1992: An attractive, floral, butter, lemon character, but slightly diluted on the finish. • $NA • (05/15/94) • **79**

Riesling Marlborough Rhine Riesling 1991: Sophisticated, with lime and peach character, excellent acidity and a crisp finish. • $NA • (05/15/94) • **87**

Sauvignon Blanc Marlborough 1993: It presents some pretty vanilla, pie crust and fruit aromas, but turns rather dull on the palate. Simple and straightforward. • $NA • (05/15/94) • **80**

MORTON

Brut New Zealand NV: This soft, delicate sparkler is very creamy, with apple and toast flavors and a hint of tropical fruit. It lacks a bit of intensity, though. • $NA • (05/15/94) • **83**

Cabernet Blend Hawke's Bay Black Label 1991: Diluted and soft with simple cherry, green flavors and a tart finish. Drink now. • $NA • (05/15/94) • **76**

Cabernet Blend Hawke's Bay White Label 1992: A low-tannin red with simple plum and cherry character and high acidity. Drink now. • $NA • (05/15/94) • **74**

Chardonnay Hawke's Bay Black Label 1991: Very good richness and structure, loads of smoky, toasted oak and a medium body of ripe fruit. 3,000 cases made. • $25 • (05/15/94) • **87**

Chardonnay Hawke's Bay White Label 1991: Dominated by oak, but some pleasant lemon and pear flavors come through. 7,000 cases made. • $15 • (05/15/94) • **78**

Sauvignon Blanc Hawke's Bay White Label 1992: Rotten cabbage, sweaty socks, flawed and undrinkable. • $11 • (05/15/94) • **58**

NAUTILUS

Chardonnay Marlborough 1992 • $9 • (08/31/93) BB • **87**

Chardonnay Marlborough 1991 • $9 • (02/15/93) BB • **87**

Sauvignon Blanc Hawke's Bay 1992 • $9 • (09/15/93) • **83**

Sauvignon Blanc Hawke's Bay 1991 • $9 • (05/31/93) • **82**

NEUDORF

Chardonnay Moutere 1992: A dead ringer for Puligny-Montrachet. Sophisticated and powerful, yet elegant and refined. Beautiful pineapple, lemon and toasted oak character with fine acidity. • $NA • (05/15/94) • **91**

Pinot Noir 1992: Some Pinot character here, delicate, with leather, spice, smoke character and light tannins. Drink now. • $NA • (05/15/94) • **79**

Sauvignon Blanc 1993: Like crushed grapes, fresh and zingy, but lacking varietal character. Good spritzer base. • $NA • (05/15/94) • **78**

Sémillon Moutere 1992: This is cloying and vegetal, and tastes like sweetened canned asparagus. • $NA • (05/15/94) • **68**

Key: SS—Spectator Selection. CS—Cellar Selection. BB—Best Buy. $NA—Price not available. (BT)—Barrel tasting. Ⓐ—Auction Price.
Dates in parentheses represent the issues in which the ratings were published.

NGATARAWA

Cabernet Blend Hawke's Bay Glazebrook 1991: Pleasant and lively, with simple berry and chocolate aromas and flavors and a light finish. Drink now. • $NA • (05/15/94) • **79**

Chardonnay Hawke's Bay 1991: A subtle Chardonnay, with lovely proportions and flavors of apple and lemon, fine acidity and toasty oak. Well integrated. • $NA • (05/15/94) • **87**

Sauvignon Blanc Hawke's Bay 1992: This is a thick Sauvignon with creamy mango flavor and full body, but it's a little dull on the finish. • $NA • (05/15/94) • **81**

NOBILO, HOUSE OF

Cabernet Sauvignon Hawke's Bay Reserve 1990: Sour and decaying, like rotten cabbage. Tasted twice with consistent notes. • $NA • (05/15/94) • **62**

Chardonnay Gisborne 1992 • $13 • (08/31/93) • **81**

Chardonnay Gisborne Dixon Vineyard Reserve 1991: Not much left here, drying out by excess oak. Rather an odd combination of lemon, honey and acidity. • $NA • (05/15/94) • **74**

Chardonnay Gisborne Poverty Bay 1992: Simple and clean, with melon, lemon and waxy aromas and flavors, medium body and a fresh acidity. • $NA • (05/15/94) • **83**

Chardonnay Marlborough Reserve 1991: Rich and ripe, with pear, apple and vanilla aromas and flavors, medium body and fresh acidity. • $16 • (05/15/94) • **86**

Pinotage Huapai 1991: Attractive gamy, earthy and fruity aromas and flavors, medium-bodied with light tannins. Drink now. • $NA • (05/15/94) • **83**

Pinotage Huapai 1988 • $15 • (07/15/91) • **82**

Sauvignon Blanc Marlborough 1993: Subtlety with good intensity of melon and pineapple flavors, it's round yet has crisp acidity. • $NA • (05/15/94) • **86**

White Cloud New Zealand 1993: Fresh, crisp and clean, offering a creamy lime, mango character and a hint of grass. A blend of Müller-Thurgau and Sauvignon Blanc. • $NA • (05/15/94) • **83**

OYSTER BAY

Chardonnay Marlborough 1993: Crisp, clean and fresh, with lemon and grapefruit flavors and pleasant acidity. A no-nonsense, no-wood white. • $NA • (05/15/94) • **84**

Sauvignon Blanc Marlborough 1993: Elegant, with lemon, grapefruit and green apple aromas and flavors and crisp acidity. • $NA • (05/15/94) • **85**

PALLISER ESTATE

Pinot Noir Martinborough 1992: Light, clean and fruity, with simple strawberry and cherry character and a hint of smoke. Drink now. • $NA • (05/15/94) • **78**

Sauvignon Blanc Martinborough 1993: Pungent, with sage, grapefruit and herbal aromas which turn slightly sweaty and diluted on the palate. • $NA • (05/15/94) • **77**

PASK, C.J.

Cabernet Blend Hawke's Bay Gimblett Road 1992: Very simple and soft with stewed tomato, herbal and asparagus flavors. Drink now. • $NA • (05/15/94) • **73**

Chardonnay Hawke's Bay Gimblett Road 1992: Straightforward Chardonnay, with plenty of pineapple and vanilla character, medium body and a crisp finish. • $NA • (05/15/94) • **86**

Sauvignon Blanc Hawke's Bay Gimblett Road 1993: A vibrant, intense lemon and melon character, medium-bodied and crisp with a long finish. • $NA • (05/15/94) • **86**

REDWOOD VALLEY

Chardonnay Nelson 1992: A big-boned Chardonnay with lots of elements, from toasty wood to ripe tropical fruit, full-bodied and very long, with excellent acidity. • $NA • (05/15/94) • **88**

Rhine Riesling Late Harvest Nelson 1991: Like an excellent ice wine with honey, cream, dried apricot and pie crust flavors, super sweet and rich with a wonderful acidity. • $NA • (05/15/94) • **91**

Sauvignon Blanc Nelson 1993: Very good intensity here, with pineapple, celery and apple character, good acidity and a flavorful finish. Bursting with Loire-like gooseberry and celery flavors, balancing ripe fruit and crisp acidity. • $NA • (05/15/94) • **86**

RONGOPAI

Chardonnay Late Harvest Te Kauwhata Botrytised Reserve 1991: A lovely balance of toasted oak, coconut, pineapple and ripe apple flavors, medium-bodied with a long finish. • $NA • (05/15/94) • **86**

Chardonnay Te Kauwhata 1991: Very thick and voluptuous, with loads of vanilla, melon, canteloupe and pear character. Very sweet, but also plenty of good acidity. Drink now. • $NA • (05/15/94) • **88**

Riesling Late Harvest Te Kauwhata 1993: Superb balance here, with wonderful aromas of honey, spice, toast and fruit. Full-bodied, with amazingly sweet honey, orange and apricot flavors and fabulous acidity. Drinkable now, but has excellent aging potential. • $NA • (05/15/94) • **92**

Sauvignon Blanc Te Kauwhata 1993: An intriguing style, with vanilla, honey and tropical fruit character, but it's thick and tiring to drink. • $NA • (05/15/94) • **79**

ST. HELENA

Pinot Blanc 1991: Big with lots of melon, apple and honey flavors and a hint of herbs on the finish. Good acidity. • $NA • (05/15/94) • **83**

ST. NESBIT

Cabernet Blend Auckland 1988: Cheesy, light and way past its prime. Green and decaying. Tasted twice with consistent notes. • $NA • (05/15/94) • **68**

SCOTT, ALLAN

Chardonnay Marlborough 1993: The pineapple and banana flavors are appealing but simple in this ripe, straightforward white. • $NA • (05/15/94) • **82**

Chardonnay Marlborough 1992: Soft and accessible, offering pineapple and vanilla flavors, slightly diluted, on a simple frame. • $NA • (05/15/94) • **81**

Riesling Marlborough 1993: A lovely apéritif. It's super fresh with melon and pineapple character, crisp acidity and a long flavorful finish. • $NA • (05/15/94) • **83**

Sauvignon Blanc Marlborough 1993: A more reserved, softer style, with melon and grapefruit character, medium body and medium acidity. • $NA • (05/15/94) • **83**

SELAKS

Chardonnay Marlborough 1992: An interesting, exaggerated style, like drinking melted butter, dark gold with intense butterscotch and oily character, full-bodied with good acidity. • $NA • (05/15/94) • **81**

Sauvignon Blanc Marlborough 1993: Brisk lemon-lime and light celery flavors, light body and a fresh finish. • $13 • (05/15/94) • **85**

Sauvignon Blanc Marlborough 1991 • $14 • (05/31/93) • **80**

STONELEIGH

Cabernet Sauvignon Marlborough 1991: Thin, rhubarb and strawberry flavors and aromas. Very watery. • $NA • (05/15/94) • **75**

Chardonnay Marlborough 1992 • $11 • (08/31/93) • **80**

Sauvignon Blanc Marlborough 1993: A reserved style with green apple and grapefruit aromas and flavors and a full finish. Good acidity. • $9 • (05/15/94) • **83**

Sauvignon Blanc Marlborough 1992 • $9 • (09/15/93) • **85**

Sauvignon Blanc Marlborough 1991 • $8 • (05/31/93) BB • **84**

TE MATA

Cabernet Merlot Hawke's Bay Coleraine 1991: Long considered New Zealand's best red. It shows plum and jammy aromas and flavors, medium body and a velvety texture. Good tannin backbone. Drink or hold. • $NA • (05/15/94) • **87**

TIMARA

Cabernet Sauvignon Marlborough 1990: Diluted and mature with earthy, berry character and a very light finish. From Montana. • $NA • (05/15/94) • **71**

VAVASOUR

Cabernet Sauvignon Marlborough Reserve 1991: Fairly well-structured red with plum and tar character, medium body and firm tannins. Drink now. • $NA • (05/15/94) • **84**

Chardonnay Marlborough Reserve 1993: Simple, with nice wood, intense tropical fruit and vanilla aromas and flavors and a hint of wax. • $NA • (05/15/94) • **83**

Pinot Noir New Zealand Reserve 1992: A decent red but it doesn't taste like Pinot. More like a hybrid, with tar and stewed fruit character. • $NA • (05/15/94) • **74**

VIDAL

Cabernet Blend Hawke's Bay Private Bin 1992: A wine with a little fruit, a little oak and a lot of acidity. • $NA • (05/15/94) • **75**

Sauvignon Blanc Hawke's Bay Private Bin 1993: A bit odd with melon, cardboard character and a flat finish. Corked? • $NA • (05/15/94) • **74**

VILLA MARIA

Cabernet Blend Hawke's Bay Reserve 1991: Pretty use of new wood, with licorce, tobacco and berry character, medium body and a velvety finish. Drink now. • $NA • (05/15/94) • **84**

Cabernet Sauvignon Auckland Reserve 1986 • $30 • (07/15/88) • **74**

Cabernet Sauvignon Hawke's Bay Private Bin 1992: High-acid red with some pleasant, plump, smoky oak character, but rather unbalanced. • $NA • (05/15/94) • **74**

Cabernet Sauvignon Hawke's Bay Reserve 1990: Quite thick, showing some velvety tannins and earthy, berry character. Drink now. • $NA • (05/15/94) • **78**

Gewürztraminer Private Bin 1993: Crisp and clean with lovely pinenut and apricot character, medium-bodied with a long dry finish. • $NA • (05/15/94) • **84**

Riesling Marlborough Private Bin 1993: Great as an apéritif or on summer afternoons. It offers flavors of mangos, coconuts and intense dried apricots, held together with excellent acidity. • $NA • (05/15/94) • **88**

Sauvignon Blanc Marlborough Private Bin 1993: Pretty and aromatic, with pineapple, cream and tropical fruit character, medium body and a fruity finish. • $NA • (05/15/94) • **85**

WAIMARAMA

Cabernet Blend Hawke's Bay 1992: Plenty of chocolate, oak and berry character, with a hint of barnyard, medium body and light tannins. Drink now. • $NA • (05/15/94) • **81**

WAIPARA SPRINGS

Chardonnay Canterbury Premiere Reserve 1992: Distinctive, creamy, rose petal and orange character, full body and a silky texture. No great aging potential, but delicious. • $NA • (05/15/94) • **83**

Sauvignon Blanc Marlborough Premiere Reserve 1992: A fresh, clean Sauvignon with celery and grapefruit aromas and flavors and crisp acidity. • $NA • (05/15/94) • **83**

WAIRAU RIVER

Chardonnay Marlborough 1992: Thick, simple and slightly overdone with loads of oak, some fruit and a lot of alcohol. • $NA • (05/15/94) • **79**
Sauvignon Blanc Marlborough 1993: Plenty of melon and canteloupe flavors here, with a hint of grassiness, it has clean acidity and a lemony finish. • $NA • (05/15/94) • **85**

• Romania •

LEGACY

Cabernet Sauvignon Murfatlar 1991: Tart and simple, with only modest currant and cranberry flavors. • $7 • **74**
Chardonnay Murfatlar 1992: Floral and peach flavors have some appeal, but there's little Chardonnay character and less depth. Quaffable, but simple. • $7 • (06/30/95) • **76**
Dessert Murfatlar Special Reserve Muscat Ottonel 1992: Very aromatic, nicely fruity and moderately sweet, with appealing peach and apricot flavors and a soft, smooth texture. • $10 • (06/30/95) • **80**

PREMIAT

Brut Transylvania Méthode Champenoise NV • $6 • (06/01/86) • **55**

VAMPIRE

Cabernet Sauvignon Dealul Mare 1991: Overripe aromas give way to modest plum and green olive flavors and a candied finish. Has a mature character, but too astringent. • $6 • (12/31/95) • **79**
Merlot Dealul Mare 1991: A little tired. The mature, leathery aromas give way to dull dried cherry flavors. Overripe and cloying on the finish. • $6 • (12/31/95) • **76**

• Slovenia •

LJUTOMER WINERY

Chardonnay Slovenia 1994: Very earthy with canned fruit flavors and an off-putting finish. 9,000 cases made. • $8 • (05/15/96) • **70**

MOVIA ESTATES

Chardonnay Slovenia 1993: Simple, slightly spritzy apple and lemon flavors. A bit earthy and chessy on the finish. 850 cases made. • $17 • (05/15/96) • **77**

• South Africa •

AFRICA COLLECTION, THE

Cabernet Sauvignon Stellenbosch 1991: Smoky, herbal, may be past its prime already. Good cherry flavors, but earthiness and browning color are suspicious. 10,000 cases made. • $7 • (09/30/95) • **79**
Chardonnay Stellenbosch 1992: Made in a crisp, lean style, this has modest appley, buttery flavors and comparatively light texture. Charming and well balanced. 12,000 cases made. • $6 • (09/30/95) • **82**
Merlot Stellenbosch 1992: Already past its prime, but some people might still enjoy the mature aromas and dried fruit flavors. Crisp and medium-bodied. 12,000 cases made. • $7 • (09/30/95) • **77**

Key: SS—Spectator Selection. CS—Cellar Selection. BB—Best Buy. $NA—Price not available. (BT)—Barrel tasting. Ⓐ—Auction Price.
Dates in parentheses represent the issues in which the ratings were published.

ALLESVERLOREN

Cabernet Sauvignon Swartland Region 1989: Complex Cabernet showing intriguingly mature aromas and flavors of mint, tobacco and cherry. Firm-textured, adding moderate tannins and a lingering aftertaste. Drinkable now through 1998. 2,000 cases made. • $15 • (09/30/95) • **89**

BACKSBERG

Cabernet Sauvignon Merlot Paarl Klein Babylonstoren 1992: Ripe and spicy, with mature flavors and aromas, the rich plum and cherry matched by subtle chocolate and cinnamon notes. Still firm, but ready to drink. 1,400 cases made. • $13 • (12/31/95) • **84**
Cabernet Sauvignon Paarl 1992: This solid red shows good balance, firm structure and ripe fruit. It's clean and well. Drinkable now. 4,500 cases made. • $10 • (03/31/95) • **85**
Cabernet Sauvignon Paarl 1990: This a sold, Bordeaux-style wine. Still lively, with plum and cherry flavors, it also has nice spicey and herbal components that linger on the finish. Good structure and ripe with earthy aromas, you could drink it now. 4,500 cases made. • $11 • (06/30/94) • **88**
Chardonnay Paarl 1993: Everything nice and spice in this one. Medium bodied, viscous texture and plenty apple, spice and honey flavors. Fresh acidity. • $10 • (06/15/95) • **87**
Chardonnay Paarl 1991 • $12 • (06/15/94) • **78**
Klein Babylonstoren Paarl 1991: Intense barnyard and stewed tomato aromas and flavors, light finish. A blend of Merlot and Cabernet Sauvignon. 1,500 cases made. • $13 • (09/30/95) • **78**
Merlot Paarl 1993: Very concentrated Merlot with tobacco, cherry, berry, and black olive aromas and flavors. Full bodied with velvety tannins and a long rich finish. Drink or hold. 750 cases made. • $10 • (06/15/95) • **87**
Pinotage Paarl 1992: Meaty, berry, smoky aromas and flavors, medium body, firm tannins and soft finish. Drinkable now. 3,000 cases made. • $8 • (06/15/95) • **86**
Pinotage Paarl Estate Wine 1990 • $10 • (02/15/93) • **86**
Sauvignon Blanc Paarl 1992 • $7 • (07/15/93) • **82**
Shiraz Paarl 1992: A solid, flavorful, gamy-tasting and exotic red offering firm tannins and raspberry and pepper notes. Turns rather lean and dry on the finish. 800 cases made. • $10 • (04/30/96) • **85**
Shiraz Paarl 1991: Completely ready to drink. Meaty, berry and earthy aromas and flavors, medium body, soft tannins and tasty finish. 1,500 cases made. • $10 • (09/30/95) • **84**
Syrah Paarl 1990 • $10 • (06/30/94) • **57**

BECK, GRAHAM

Chardonnay Robertson Madeba Valley 1991 • $15 • (10/15/92) • **78**

BELLINGHAM

Pinotage Paarl 1990 • $10 • (02/15/93) • **80**

BERGSIG

Pinotage South Africa Breede River Valley 1990 • $9 • (10/15/92) • **84**
Sauvignon Blanc South Africa Breede River Valley 1992 • $9 • (10/15/92) • **79**

BERTRAMS

Pinotage South Africa 1988 • $10 • (02/15/93) • **76**

BLAAUWKLIPPEN

Cabernet Sauvignon Stellenbosch 1989: Delicious, soft red offering tobacco, cigar-box and berry aromas and flavors, medium body, delicate tannins and sweet fruit finish. Drink now. 2,425 cases made. • $20 • (09/30/95) • **84**
Cabernet Sauvignon Stellenbosch Reserve Guild Auction Label 1989: Complex earth, berry, tobacco and mineral aromas and flavors, full

body, exuberant fruit, tannins and acidity. Drinkable now, but would benefit from age. 391 cases made. • $24 • **88**

Zinfandel Reserve Stellenbosch 1990: Aged aromas mingle with accents of vanilla and maple syrup in this smooth but green-tasting red. Reminiscent of a Rioja. 142 cases made. • $20 • (06/30/95) • **79**

Zinfandel Stellenbosch 1990: This has odd aromas and flavors of honey and vinegar that make it taste overly mature. Drinkable, but not our cup of tea. 1,557 cases made. • $16 • (06/30/95) • **75**

BOPLAAS

South Africa Port 1989: More baked in character than some, offering nut, berry and raisin aromas and flavors. Medium-bodied, very sweet, good fruit and a nutty, salty finish. Drinkable now. • $NA • **82**

BOSCHENDAL

Chardonnay Paarl 1994: Straight forward, well crafted Chardonnay with vanilla, apple and mineral aroms and flavors. Medium bodied with fine acidity and an appley finish. 1,800 cases made. • $13 • (06/15/95) • **85**

Chardonnay Paarl 1991 • $13 • (06/15/94) • **86**

Chardonnay Paarl Jean Le Long Bin 102 Auction Reserve 1991: This is a delicious, mature Chardonnay sporting toasted almond, honey, pineapple and other tropical fruits. Full-bodied and ultrarich, long, delicious finish. Drink now. • $NA • **90**

Le Petit Pavillon Paarl 1994: Suspiciously earthy aromas mar this simple, slightly sweet and soft white. Dull. 12,000 cases made. • $8 • (06/30/95) • **74**

Le Petit Pavillon Paarl 1993 • $7 • **82**

Sauvignon Blanc Paarl 1994: Subtle and intriguing wine with mineral, pine needle and peaches on the nose and palate. Medium bodied and almost off-dry with a fresh and fruity finish. A blend of 40 percent Sauvignon and 60 percent Chenin Blanc. Drink or hold. 3,500 cases made. • $9 • (06/15/95) • **87**

Sauvignon Blanc Paarl 1992: A refreshing but straightforward white wine with crisp acidity, lean texture and good flavors of green apple, lemon and herbs. 4,500 cases made. • $8 • **82**

Sauvignon Blanc Paarl 1991 • $8 • (09/15/93) • **74**

Sauvignon Blanc Paarl Grand Cuvée 1993: Rich and full-bodied, but featuring enough acidity to keep it fresh, ripe melon and apple flavors and a touch of vanilla from aging in oak. 4,000 cases made. • $10 • (03/31/95) • **85**

BOUCHARD FINLAYSON

Blanc de Mer Overberg 1994: Fresh and crisp lemony, steely, haylike character, medium body and acidity and a dry finish. • $11 • **84**

Chardonnay Overberg 1994: A bit dumb now with some good vanilla and melon character, but slightly coarse in texture. Drinkable now. • $NA • **82**

Chardonnay Overberg 1993: Somewhat oily and heavy-handed, but some interesting butter, apple skin and toasted oak character. Full in body, medium acidity. • $17 • **82**

Pinot Noir Walker Bay 1994: A fresh red offering smoky, cherry, berry aromas and flavors, medium body, very firm acidity and medium tannins. Drinkable. 1,600 cases made. • $NA • (06/15/95) • **84**

Pinot Noir Walker Bay 1993: Muscular and firmly structured red with lovely bright black berry, plummy and smoky aromas and flavors. Full bodied with firm tannins and a long finish. Drinkable now. • $NA • (06/15/95) • **85**

Sauvignon Blanc Overberg 1994: Crisp and clean pear, apple and slightly tropical character. Medium-bodied, fresh acidity and light finish. • $13 • (06/15/95) • **84**

BOVLEI WINERY

Cabernet Sauvignon Wellington 1992: Well rounded, marked by vegetal aromas, but there's a lot of oak flavor and just enough cranberry, cherry and herb to keep it lively. 2,000 cases made. • $NA • (06/30/95) • **81**

Grand Rouge Wellington 1992: A generous, fruity red wine with oak accents that sits lightly on the palate. Has ample cherry flavors and spicy nuances to make it interesting, and the flavors linger on the finish. Moderately tannic, but ready to drink now. • $NA • (06/30/95) • **85**

Pinotage Wellington 1994: A tightly wound, medium-bodied red showing firm texture, berrylike flavors and good, crisp acidity. Fairly tannic, but drink now while it's fresh. 2,000 cases made. • $NA • (06/30/95) • **81**

Sauvignon Blanc Wellington 1994: Easy-going Sauvignon Blanc with herb and grapefruit flavors that are dry, clean but simple. • $NA • (06/30/95) • **77**

Shiraz Wellington 1991: This wants to be a light, fresh red, judging by the aromas, but it has heavy smoky notes and an astringent finish that hold it back. • $NA • (06/30/95) • **75**

BREDELL'S

Stellenbosch Vintage Reserve Port Limited Release 1991: Great inky color. Close to the best of Portugal. Full-bodied and sweet, ripe plum, licorice and earth aromas and flavors, fine tannins and long finish. Better in 1997. • $NA • **87**

BUITENVERWACHTING

Buiten Blanc Coastal Region 1994: An austere white showing flavors of grapefruit, herb and burnt toast, this needs food to soften its tart acidity but would be refreshing on a hot day. • $NA • (09/30/95) • **80**

Chardonnay Constantia 1993: Still not giving all it should. Lovely toasted oak, honey and fruit aromas and flavors. Medium-bodied, full acidity and slightly coarse finish. Needs time. 1,700 cases made. • $18 • **83**

Christine Constantia 1989: Like a lovely glass of claret, offering tobacco, cherry and cedar aromas and flavors, velvety tannins, medium body and succulent finish. Drink now. Contains 15 percent Cabernet Sauvignon. 500 cases made. • $20 • **88**

Grand Vin Constantia 1990: Rather hard and astringent. Berry and mint character is compromised by a rubbery component. 950 cases made. • $22 • **77**

Sauvignon Blanc Constantia 1994: Pleasant, clean spice and melon character, medium body and acidity and fresh finish. Tasted twice, with consistent notes. 3,150 cases made. • $16 • **82**

Sauvignon Blanc Constantia 1991 • $13 • (10/15/92) • **85**

CABRIERE, CLOS

Brut Franschhoek Valley Pierre Jourdan NV: Herbal, citrus aromas add a bit of life to this very dry, austere bubbly. The flavors are lean and green. • $14 • (02/28/95) • **78**

Brut Franschhoek Valley Pierre Jourdan Sauvage NV: A Champagne-style sparkling wine that has an attractive, doughy aroma, rich, mouth-filling texture and good fruit. • $20 • (02/28/95) • **85**

CAPE COUNTRY

Cabernet Sauvignon South Africa 1991: A thick, muddled wine, with tomatoey and pruny flavors that makes for a tired taste. An overripe ripe style that finishes with the tannins still clamping down. 5,000 cases made. • $6 • (06/30/94) • **75**

Chardonnay Coastal Region Breede River Valley 1992 • $6 • (06/15/94) • **74**

Pinotage Coastal Region 1990: A decent quality red with smoky aromas, herb and cherry flavors and a crisp finish. Moderate tannins and good acidity give it some bite. 15,000 cases made. • $6 • (06/30/94) • **78**

Pinotage Coastal Region 1989 • $5 • (02/15/93) • **77**

CAPE INDABA

Pinotage Coastal Region 1995: Extremely bright, fruity and clean. A young red for enjoying now, featuring ample strawberry flavor, soft texture and clear finish. 6,000 cases made. • $9 • (04/30/96) • **84**

CAPE SELECTION

Chardonnay Robertson 1991 • $7 • (10/15/92) BB • **82**

Pinotage Stellenbosch 1991 • $8 • (02/15/93) • **83**

SOUTH AFRICA

CATHEDRAL CELLAR

Cabernet Sauvignon Coastal Region 1992: Already at its peak, showing lovely chocolate, tobacco and blackberry flavors. Medium-bodied, silky tannins and cedary finish. Drink now. 3,000 cases made. • $10 • (06/15/95) • **85**

Cabernet Sauvignon Coastal Region 1990: Pleasant and fruity with good raspberry and plum flavors. A rounded structure and herbal notes adds substance to this refreshing wine. A good shot of spice and chocolate flavors on the finish. 2,500 cases made. • $11 • (06/30/94) • **85**

Chardonnay Coastal Region 1993: Some nice oak here and plenty of coconut and vanilla character, but it falls down slightly on the palate and its diluted finish. 3,000 cases made. • $10 • **80**

Chardonnay Coastal Region 1991 • $11 • (06/15/94) • **84**

Pinotage Coastal Region 1992: Old-style Pinotage, with a jammy tobacco and earthy character, medium body, strawberry and cherry flavors and a cedary, resiny finish. 3,000 cases made. • $10 • **80**

Triptych Coastal Region 1992: A red to smell and enjoy lovely tobacco and cedar notes, however, the palate appears rather dry and astringent. Drink now. 2,000 cases made. • $10 • **82**

Triptych Coastal Region 1990: Dressed-up and ready to drink. Finely-textured with soft, lush flavors. There are some sweet oak overtones to the nice cherry and herbal notes. Moderately tannic and fairly ripe. Forty-five percent Cabernet Franc. 2,500 cases made. • $11 • (06/30/94) • **84**

CENTAURUS

Cabernet Sauvignon Durbanville 1991: Full-flavored and tannic, but turning nicely mature. It has complex earthy-spicy aromas, solid fruit flavors and a finish that lingers. 6,300 cases made. • $12 • (04/30/96) • **84**

Pinotage Durbanville 1991: Tannic, crisp cherry and raspberry flavors, but not opening up much for a 5-year-old wine, and we don't know if it will. Currently it tastes tight and hard. 5,000 cases made. • $12 • (04/30/96) • **83**

CLOS MALVERNE

Auret Stellenbosch 1989 • $20 • (10/15/92) • **77**

Cabernet Sauvignon Stellenbosch 1989 • $16 • (10/15/92) • **77**

Pinotage Stellenbosch 1990 • $10 • (02/15/93) • **87**

COOP WINEGROWERS' ASSC. OF SOUTH AFRICA

Pinotage Paarl Limited Specially Selected 1971 • $NA • (02/15/93) • **78**

DE WETSHOF

Chardonnay Robertson Bateleur 1993 • $13 • **65**

Chardonnay Robertson D'Honneur 1994: Some pretty earth, vanilla and hay aromas, but rather candied and slightly oxidized on the finish. Not fresh. 2,500 cases made. • $12 • **76**

Chardonnay Robertson D'Honneur 1993: Ripe, fruity and easy to like, with pear, pineapple and spice flavors, a very smooth, easy texture and a hint of sweetness. Enjoy it now for its richness and fruit. 800 cases made. • $12 • (07/31/94) • **84**

Chardonnay Robertson Lesca 1994: A ringer for a very good Chablis. This Chardonnay shows loads of apple, mineral and honey aromas and flavors. Medium bodied with super fresh, green apple acidity on the finish. 12,000 cases made. • $8 • (06/15/95) BB • **86**

Chardonnay Robertson Lesca 1993: A soft and pleasant style of white wine from South Africa, with delicate apple, peach and floral flavors that linger nicely on the finish. Has good acidity and freshness. Draws you back for another sip. 5,000 cases made. • $8 • (07/31/94) BB • **85**

Key: SS—Spectator Selection. CS—Cellar Selection. BB—Best Buy. $NA—Price not available. (BT)—Barrel tasting. (A)—Auction Price.
Dates in parentheses represent the issues in which the ratings were published.

DELHEIM

Chardonnay Stellenbosch 1993: Over the top and oxidized, showing intense, buttered popcorn character. • $12 • **72**

Gewürztraminer Stellenbosch 1994: Lightly sweet spice, mineral and citrus aromas and flavors, medium-bodied, sweet finish. Good as an apéritif. • $10 • **83**

Grand Reserve Stellenbosch 1991: Absolutely delicious with minty, mineral, black berry and currant aromas and flavors. Medium bodied with fine tannins and a long supple finish. Drink now. • $18 • (06/15/95) • **87**

Grand Reserve Stellenbosch 1989 • $17 • (10/15/92) • **57**

Heerensijn Dry White Stellenbosch 1994: Crisp, clean and fresh-tasting. This is refreshing but very simple in flavor. • $7 • (06/30/95) • **78**

Pinotage Stellenbosch 1989 • $10 • (02/15/93) • **81**

Roodenwijn Dry Red Stellenbosch 1994: A stewed and dry tobacco, cherry and earthy character, medium body, hard tannins and light finish. • $7 • **78**

Shiraz Stellenbosch 1991: Tired, thin and weedy, showing tea and cedar character and a light finish. Drink as quickly as possible. • $10 • **77**

DESTINARE

Chardonnay Franschhoek Valley 1995: An awkward white that's candied and slightly bitter at the same time. Finishes on a cloying note. • $7 • (05/15/96) • **76**

DROSTDY-HOF

Merlot Coastal Region 1992: Plums, spices, touches of herbs-this shows good varietal character in a fresh, balanced red. It's polished and has enough tannin to stand up to food. Drinkable now. 3,000 cases made. • $10 • (09/30/95) • **86**

Pinotage Coastal Region SFW 1989 • $8 • (02/15/93) • **87**

ELLIS, NEIL

Cabernet Sauvignon Stellenbosch 1993: Extremely minty, herbal and tart, with modest cherry and berry flavors. A bit thin in the middle, though some nice spicy notes linger on the finish. 2,000 cases made. • $14 • (12/31/95) • **84**

Cabernet Sauvignon Stellenbosch 1992: Ripe and polished. This wine offers toast, chocolate, mint and plum flavors, soft on the palate and a bit short in the finish. It's drinkable now. 800 cases made. • $14 • (03/31/95) • **82**

Cabernet Sauvignon Stellenbosch 1990: Crisp and lean, with strong minty-eucalyptus flavors. This is still fruity, however, with raspberry and cherry notes that slice through the mint. Well-balanced and tannic, this may be best to drink from now to 1998. 2,200 cases made. • $13 • (06/30/94) • **86**

Chardonnay Stellenbosch 1993: Thick and simple, offering sweet, canned-peach flavors and hints of almonds and herbs. Rich with ample acidity but lacking finesse. 800 cases made. • $13 • (06/30/95) • **79**

Chardonnay Stellenbosch 1992 • $13 • (06/15/94) • **82**

Sauvignon Blanc Elgin Whitehall 1992 • $9 • • **77**

FAIRVIEW ESTATE

Shiraz Paarl 1992: Good to drink now. A jammy, medium-bodied red showing smoky aromas and raspberry tones. Richly flavored, but light in tannins and short on the finish. • $8 • (09/30/95) • **83**

Shiraz-Merlot Paarl 1991: Bright aromas of black cherry and mint give way to round, soft plum, cherry and chocolate flavors. It's still lively and very accessible. Drink now, while the fruit is fresh. • $8 • (09/30/95) • **85**

FLEUR DU CAP

Chardonnay Coastal Region 1994: Not really giving much at the moment but presenting some pretty lemon, vanilla, spice character. Medium in body and acidity, oaky finish. Drinkable now. • $8 • (06/15/95) • **85**

Chardonnay Coastal Region 1992: Crisp and refreshing, although a bit lean and simple in flavor. Has modest apple and herb flavors and a rather coarse texture. • $8 • (02/28/95) • **79**

Dessert Coastal Region Noble Late Harvest 1990: Time to clean out the cellar, use strong detergent. • $8 • **64**

Merlot Coastal Region 1992: Pretty herbal, tobacco styled Cabernet with medium body, medium tannins and a succulent, silky finish. Drink now. • $8 • (06/15/95) • **84**

Merlot Coastal Region 1991: A smoky characater runs through this wine, with herbal aromas and flavors. Lean a bit diluted, with a murky finish. • $8 • **78**

Pinotage Coastal Region 1990: Simple plum, milk chocolate and tobacco character, medium in body and hard texture. A bit tired. • $9 • **78**

Pinotage Coastal Region 1989: A wine with big ambitions but slightly falls short. Full bodied with lovely cherry, raspberry aromas and flavors, full tannins and a medium finish. Drink now but better after 1996. Tasted twice. • $8 • (06/15/95) • **84**

Pinotage Coastal Region 1988 • $10 • (02/15/93) • **88**

GLEN CARLOU

Cabernet Sauvignon Paarl 1993: Lovely balanced wine with plenty of tobacco, lead pencil, cassis character and fine, racy tannins. Give it time. Better after 1997. 400 cases made. • $20 • (06/15/95) • **88**

Chardonnay Paarl 1994: Incredibly complex. Like a premier cru white Burgundy. Wonderful toasted oak, mineral, earthy and fruit components combined with full body and great acidity make this wine a superb package. Drink or hold. 2,000 cases made. • $18 • (06/15/95) • **90**

Chardonnay Paarl 1993: Tart and a bit green-tasting, with strong acidity and a likeable streak of mineral that adds some complexity to the otherwise simple fruit flavors. • $20 • (02/28/95) • **83**

Chardonnay Paarl Reserve 1994: Why buy white Burgundy? Lots of style, rich and viscous, featuring nutmeg, vanilla, clove and apple aromas and flavors. Full in body and round, long, tasty finish. 250 cases made. • $35 • **90**

Chardonnay Paarl Reserve Guild Auction Label 1993: Surprisingly mature nutty, almond, tropical fruit aromas. Full-bodied and oily, rich fruit and delicious finish. 50 cases made. • $NA • **85**

Grande Classique Reserve Paarl 1992: Monster wine. Incredibly expressive tobacco, coconut, cassis and blackberry flavors. Full in body and full, velvety tannins. Perhaps a little overdone? Try in 1998. 650 cases made. • $22 • **88**

Les Trois Paarl 1993: Wonderful red exhibiting cassis, mint and tar aromas and flavors. Full in body, fine tannins and long coffee, berry finish. Drinkable now, but better after 1997. 650 cases made. • $17 • **89**

Merlot Paarl 1993: Big, giant Merlot. Masses of boysenberry, cherry, minty aromas and flavors. Full bodied with fine tannins and a long fruity finish. Drinkable now. 600 cases made. • $18 • (06/15/95) • **89**

Pinot Noir Paarl 1994: This luscious Pinot shows lovely cherry, berry and leaf aromas and flavors, medium body, firm tannins and silky finish. Drinkable now. Tasted twice, with consistent notes. 300 cases made. • $18 • (06/15/95) • **87**

GOOD HOPE WINES

Chairman's Selection Durbanville 1992: A solid, attractive red that's nearly mature but definitely tannic. Ample cherry and plum flavors last on the finish. Needs hearty food, drinkable through 1998. 5,000 cases made. • $11 • (04/30/96) • **84**

Pinotage Paarl 1994: A solid, serious red showing touches of pepper accenting the cherry-strawberry flavors. Moderately tannic, very dry, nicely smooth. 8,000 cases made. • $9 • (04/30/96) • **85**

GRANGEHURST

Cabernet Sauvignon Stellenbosch 1992: Super intense with floral, berry, minty and eucaplytus aromas and flavors. Medium to full bodied with fine tannins and plenty of flavor. Rich yet balanced with a long finish. Try after 1998. • $16 • (06/15/95) • **90**

Pinotage Stellenbosch 1992: A superdark and rich red, boasting loads of ripe fruit character ranging from cassis to plum. Full-bodied, firm tannins and concentrated finish. Drink now, but better in 1998. • $15 • (06/15/95) • **89**

GREEN, DOUGLAS

Cabernet Sauvignon Coastal Region Superior 1981 • $21 • (10/15/92) • **83**

Pinotage Coastal Region Superior 1981 • $NA • (02/15/93) • **83**

Pinotage Coastal Region Superior 1980 • $21 • (10/15/92) • **81**

St. Augustine Coastal Region 1980 • $21 • (10/15/92) • **82**

GROOT CONSTANTIA

Cabernet Sauvignon Constantia 1990: Cassis, mint and raspberry flavors don't hold together in this lean, austere wine. Awkward and ungenerous, with a tough, herbal component. 4,000 cases made. • $12 • (06/30/94) • **78**

Chardonnay Constantia 1992 • $13 • (06/15/94) • **84**

Constantia Blanc Constantia 1994: Simple and straightforward white providing apple and herb flavors and good balance. Dry and nicely crisp. 4,800 cases made. • $7 • (06/30/95) • **80**

Constantia Rood Constantia 1990 • $7 • (06/30/94) • **80**

Pinotage Constantia 1992: Rustic and slightly tired, showing volatile berry and earthy character. 3,000 cases made. • $9 • **78**

Pinotage Constantia 1990: Starts out with weedy aromas and rhubarb flavors, then turns very hard and tannic on the finish. Awkward but drinkable. 3,000 cases made. • $8 • (06/30/94) • **75**

Pinotage Constantia 1989 • $7 • (02/15/93) • **81**

Riesling Constantia Weisser Riesling 1994: This tastes bright, slightly sweet and very fruity, presenting peach flavors and a fairly smooth, rich texture. Hints of ripe fruit linger on the finish. 600 cases made. • $9 • (06/30/95) • **84**

Sauvignon Blanc Constantia 1994: Pretty and easy with floral, tropical fruit character. Medium bodied with a oily texture and fruity finish. A bit simple. 500 cases made. • $10 • (06/15/95) • **84**

Syrah Constantia 1989: Well-balanced, broad and rich with roasted flavors and plum and cherry notes. Finishes tart and tannic. Drinkable now. 2,500 cases made. • $9 • (06/30/94) • **84**

HAMILTON RUSSELL VINEYARDS

Chardonnay Walker Bay 1994: Makes a great first impression, offering toasty oak, crisp lemony acidity and enough tropical fruit to carry through the rich, almost sweet palate. Not one to hold, drink and enjoy. • $12 • (06/30/95) • **87**

Pinot Noir Walker Bay 1992: Like a premature red Burgundy, showing lots of body and delicate and aged flavors. It has an exotic, toasty-spicy aroma, subtle cherry notes and lingering finish. • $16 • (06/30/95) • **82**

JACOBSDAL

Pinotage Stellenbosch 1988 • $10 • (02/15/93) • **86**

KANONKOP

Cabernet Sauvignon Stellenbosch 1991: Rich but rustic tobacco, dried cherry and chestnut character. Full-bodied and thick with velvety tannins, yet slightly dry on the finish. Drink now. • $20 • **81**

Cabernet Sauvignon Stellenbosch 1990: Solid red showing tobacco, cherry, berry and earth character, medium body, lots of tannins and dry, simple finish. Drink now. • $20 • **82**

Paul Sauer Stellenbosch 1991: Unctuous red boasting currant and almost blueberry character, full body, velvety tannins and long, delicious finish. Drinkable now. • $25 • (06/15/95) • **90**

Pinotage South Africa 1990 • $18 • (10/15/92) • **83**

Pinotage Stellenbosch 1993: Big and beautiful. Wonderful pure cherries and toasted oak open to a lush and velvety palate. The tannins are firm but well integrated in the fruit. Drink now or hold. • $14 • (06/15/95) • **88**

Pinotage Stellenbosch Estate Bottled 1990 • $10 • (02/15/93) • **84**

Pinotage Stellenbosch Reserve 1993: Fabulous wine exhibiting great concentration of fruit and toasted oak, yet extremely well balanced and refined. Full in body with firm tannins and a long, rich finish. Drinkable now, but better in 1999. • $18 • **91**

Pinotage Stellenbosch Reserve 1992: Soft, round and velvety blackberry and chocolate aromas and flavors, full body and long aftertaste. Drink now but will improve. • $NA • **87**

KLEINDAL

Pinotage Stellenbosch 1990 • $10 • (02/15/93) • **78**

Cabernet Sauvignon Stellenbosch 1990: A nice mouthful, offering lots of ripe fruit amply supported by sweet oak accents. It's moderately tannic and supple in texture. 1,500 cases made. • $15 • (09/30/95) • **86**

Cabernet Sauvignon Stellenbosch Landgoedwyn 1987 • $16 • (10/15/92) • **75**

Merlot Stellenbosch Landgoedwyn 1988 • $13 • (10/15/92) • **77**

KRONENDAL

Dessert Robertson Port 1991: A good ruby Port, featuring spice, berry and plum aromas and flavors, medium body, soft tannins and sweet finish. Drink now. • $NA • **84**

Sauvignon Blanc Breede River 1994: This is not much fun to drink. It smells and tastes watery and sour. • $7 • (06/30/95) • **72**

KWV

Chenin Blanc Coastal Region 1992: Lemony crispness makes this wine fresh and appealing, but there's not much fruit or depth to it. It makes a nice apéritif. • $6 • (07/31/94) • **78**

Breede River Valley Jerepigo Hanepoot 1975: Thick-textured and mature, amber-colored, nutty in aroma, tasting like coffee and herbs. It's strong, not elegant, but has gained some nuances with age. 1,000 cases made. • $10 • (06/30/95) • **85**

Breede River Valley Red Muscatel 1975: A coffee-colored, molasses-scented sweet wine showing fig and maple-syrup notes, lots of body and lingering finish. Flavorful and mature. 1,000 cases made. • $17 • (06/30/95) • **84**

Coastal Region Noble Late Harvest 1988: Sweet, late-harvest style, mature, intriguing nutty aromas and peachy flavors. It's smooth, still fresh and lively, drink soon. 300 cases made. • $10 • (06/30/95) • **84**

Roodeberg Coastal Region 1992: Baked tomatoes and a burnt rubber character. 70,000 cases made. • $7 • **70**

Roodeberg Coastal Region 1991: Tastes like a cross between Côtes du Rhône and Beaujolais, sporting peppery aromas and sweet-seeming, simple fruit flavors. 60,000 cases made. • $6 • (06/30/95) • **77**

Roodeberg Coastal Region 1989: Some pleasant cherry and chocolate flavors provide a lively component to this, but watch out for the leather and smoke. A full-bodied red that's ready to drink now. 75,000 cases made. • $7 • (06/30/94) • **78**

South Africa Full Cream Sherry NV: A nicely balanced sweet wine yielding mature flavors and lingering finish. It smells like molasses, tastes like black-walnut pie, yet remains subtle and enjoyable. 40,000 cases made. • $7 • (06/30/95) • **86**

South Africa Full Ruby Port NV: Nutty and sweet, featuring a baked apple, toffee, caramel character and slightly burnt finish. 10,000 cases made. • $7 • **81**

South Africa Full Tawny Port NV: Very good Madeira, unfortunately, it's labled Port. Cooked, ripe fruit aromas and flavors, medium body and sweetness, fresh finish. Drink now. 10,000 cases made. • $7 • **84**

South Africa Renasans Pale Medium Dry Sherry NV: Tastes like a well-aged sherry, with briny, nutty aromas, and seemingly dry, bracing flavors and a long-lasting finish. 25,000 cases made. • $7 • (06/30/95) BB • **84**

Stellenbosch Vintage Port 1982: Sweet, baked and sickly, full-bodied and cloying, adding a nutty, raisiny, dried cherry finish. Tough to like. 1,000 cases made. • $17 • **74**

Key: SS—Spectator Selection. CS—Cellar Selection. BB—Best Buy. $NA—Price not available. (BT)—Barrel tasting. Ⓐ—Auction Price.
Dates in parentheses represent the issues in which the ratings were published.

L'ORMARINS

Chardonnay Franschhoek Valley 1993: Gingerbread aromas and pineapple flavors lend distinction, well integrated in an exaggerated style. Unusual but interesting. • $NA • (09/30/95) • **82**

Chardonnay Franschhoek Valley 1992: Fruity, crisp and direct, sporting firm acidity and lemon-grapefruit flavors. • $10 • (02/28/95) • **79**

Sauvignon Blanc Franschhoek Valley Blanc Fumé 1992: A strong licorice note adds interest to this soft, round white, but there's not much fruit. Ripe and easy to drink. • $9 • (03/31/95) • **79**

LANDSKROON

Cabernet Sauvignon Paarl Estate Wine 1990: A moderately tannic Cabernet offering rather lean flavors of berry, herb and olive, smooth-textured. Drinkable now. • $11 • (01/31/95) • **82**

Pinotage Paarl 1994: A generous, ripe red chock-full of black cherry, gamy and bitter chocolate flavors, bright acidity and moderate tannins. Not complex, but exuberant and easy to drink. • $NA • (09/30/95) • **84**

Pinotage Paarl Estate Wine 1990 • $10 • (02/15/93) • **83**

Steen Dry Chenin Blanc Paarl 1995: Light and crisp, this dry chenin blanc shows simple apple flavors and firm acidity. A pleasant, if rather neutral, apéritif. • $NA • (09/30/95) • **80**

LANZERAC

Chardonnay Stellenbosch 1994: Light and crisp in style, this offers simple apple and nutmeg flavors. It's clean and easy to drink. 3,000 cases made. • $8 • (08/31/95) • **81**

LEUWEN JAGT, DE

Cabernet Franc Paarl 1993: Very well-made, smooth red that's true to type, featuring herbaceous and olivelike flavors, supple texture, mild tannins and lingering finish. 250 cases made. • $11 • (09/30/95) • **84**

LIBERTAS, CHATEAU

Coastal Region 1988: Fully mature with brown sugar and tea flavors. Simple and soft, featuring a load of leather and earth. • $10 • (06/30/94) • **75**

LIEVLAND

DVB Stellenbosch 1992: A wild bronco of a wine, with rustic flavors and assertive tannins. Herb, black currant, and a hint of tobacco round out the flavors. A bit tough on the finish. 600 cases made. • $19 • (12/31/95) • **84**

Shiraz Stellenbosch 1991: A perfumed aroma is the best aspect of this solid, straightforward red. It turns leaner and drier in flavor. Moderately tannic, drinkable now. 1,000 cases made. • $18 • (04/30/96) • **81**

LOUISVALE

Chardonnay Stellenbosch 1993: Stylish, almost sweet, appealing and elegant. Ripe-tasting but not obvious, featuring subtle peach, vanilla, cream and butter flavors that mingle nicely and linger on the finish. • $15 • (07/31/95) • **86**

Chardonnay Stellenbosch Devon Valley 1991 • $16 • (10/15/92) • **88**

MEERENDAL

Pinotage Durbanville Estate Wine 1988 • $10 • (02/15/93) • **75**

MEERLUST

Cabernet Sauvignon Stellenbosch 1991: Extremely well crafted, loads of fruit and tannins yet a supple finish. Full in body, featuring wonderful concentration of plum, tobacco and black cherry flavors. Drinkable now. • $16 • (06/15/95) • **89**

Cabernet Sauvignon Stellenbosch 1986: An average red wine with smoke and plum flavors that finishes dry. Mature, but not much interest. • $16 • (11/30/94) • **78**

Chardonnay Stellenbosch 1992: The greatest white wine ever made in South Africa. This competes with grand cru Burgundy. Fabulously rich, boasting tons of toasted oak, pear, apple, pineapple, mineral, grilled nuts ... you name it. It's stupendous, full body, lovely acidity and long finish. • $NA • **93**

Merlot Stellenbosch 1989: Rich and dense with raisin, tar and dried purne character with hint of earth. Full bodied and soft with a slightly dry finish. Drink now. • $16 • (06/15/95) • **84**

Rubicon Stellenbosch 1989: Concentrated and distinctive, offering loads of fruit flavor nicely accented by roasted, peppery nuances. Intensity and harmony, lingering finish. Drink now through 1997. • $16 • (06/30/95) • **88**

MIDDELVLEI

Pinotage Stellenbosch 1990: Soft and fruity, offering meat, berry and cherry flavors. Slightly dry on the finish and unbalanced, however. • $10 • **76**

Pinotage Stellenbosch 1989 • $10 • (02/15/93) • **78**

Shiraz Stellenbosch 1990: Turning old without turning mature. Has very ripe, even overripe fruit flavors, harsh tannins and a slightly bitter finish. • $11 • (04/30/96) • **78**

MOTTE, LA

Cabernet Sauvignon Franschhoek Valley 1992: Straightforward, solid herb and berry flavors and a touch of green olives. Medium body, fine tannins. Drinkable now. • $NA • **83**

Cabernet Sauvignon Franschhoek Valley 1989: A young and wild wine with violet, berry, olives, mineral aromas and flavors. Full bodied with fine, silky tannins. Needs time. Try after 1998. • $15 • (06/15/95) • **86**

Cabernet Sauvignon Franschhoek Valley 1987: Extremely tannic, with smoky and black currant flavors and eucalyptus aromas. Very astringent and lean. An overdone style. • $15 • **74**

Estate Franschhoek Valley 1990: Pretty, aromatic red sporting licorice and toasted oak aromas and flavors. Full-bodied and fresh, loads of tannin and a fresh finish. Drink now. • $11 • (06/15/95) • **86**

Millenium Franschhoek Valley 1992: Decent red, featuring green olive and berry aromas and flavors, medium body, light tannins and slightly hot finish. • $NA • **81**

Shiraz Franschhoek Valley 1992: Plenty of spice, berry and rich fruit, medium to full body, firm tannins and a vanilla, tobacco finish. Drinkable now. • $NA • **87**

MORGENHOF

Chardonnay Stellenbosch 1994: Sweet vanilla and coconut notes show the influence of oak here, hints of tangerine and pineapple. It's smooth and pleasant, but a bit dull. • $12 • (06/30/95) • **83**

Merlot Stellenbosch 1993: Dark-colored, opulently flavored Merlot that reminds us of Pomerol in its richness of fruit, lush texture and lingering finish. Oak accents add to intense currant and cherry flavors. Drinkable now through 1997. • $14 • (06/30/95) • **87**

Sauvignon Blanc Stellenbosch 1994: Light and lean, this has good acidity and nice citrusy, herbal notes, but lacks fruit and finishes a bit tart. Serviceable, but not much more. • $12 • (09/30/95) • **80**

MULDERBOSCH

Faithful Hound Merlot-Cabernet Sauvignon Stellenbosch 1993: Rich and thick, showing black cherry, herb and coffee flavors, but it's somewhat heavy-handed, tannic and muddy on the palate, seeming to lack fresh fruit. • $NA • (09/30/95) • **82**

Sauvignon Blanc Stellenbosch 1995: Fresh and clean, this shows good varietal typicity of herbal, grassy and citric flavors. It's lively and refreshing. • $NA • (09/30/95) • **85**

Sauvignon Blanc Stellenbosch 1994: Very crisp, tart with lemon and lime flavors, this also shows marked herbal and grassy notes that won't appeal to everyone but fall well within the varietal character. A Sancerre-style wine. 3,000 cases made. • $15 • (03/31/95) • **84**

NEDERBURG

Baronne Coastal Region 1989: This shows maturity in its earthy flavors, but we wonder if it wasn't better a few years ago. Thin on fruit, rather tart, reasonably tannic. • $10 • (06/30/95) • **77**

Cabernet Sauvignon Paarl 1991: Weedy and earthy, offering berry, cherry, mineral, salty character and an almost spritzy finish. Drink now. • $10 • **76**

Cabernet Sauvignon Paarl 1989: Ripe and full-bodied with currant, plum and chocolate flavors that make for a well-rounded Cabernet. Solid with plenty of flavor, though not particularly complex, adds a nice finish. Drink now. • $10 • (06/30/94) • **84**

Cabernet Sauvignon Paarl Superior 1981: Thick, rustic and stinky, showing earth and sweet fruit character. • $25 • **76**

Chardonnay Paarl 1994: Solid Chardonnay sporting lively acidity, medium body and vanilla, apple and butter character, fresh finish. Drinkable now. • $10 • **84**

Chardonnay Paarl 1991 • $10 • (06/15/94) • **83**

Edelrood Paarl 1989: Looks and tastes mature. Turning lean, losing its fruit flavor and developing earthy, tealike accents. • $10 • (06/30/95) • **77**

Pinotage Paarl 1990: Tired and light, showing some tobacco and cherry character. Almost finished. • $10 • **73**

Pinotage Paarl 1988: Burnt-rubber aromas and tart, lean flavors make this difficult to like. Tough and astringent, too. • $10 • (06/30/94) • **73**

Prelude Paarl 1991 • $10 • **81**

Prelude Sauvignon Blanc/Chardonnay Paarl 1993: A full-bodied, modestly flavored white that tastes crisp and grapefruitlike. It's clean, fresh and bracing, subtle in character. • $10 • (06/30/95) • **81**

Riesling Paarl 1992: A pleasant and agreeable Riesling with sound fruit flavors and good balance. Its light peach and lemon notes are packaged in a round, soft texture. • $10 • (07/31/94) • **80**

NEETHLINGSHOF

Cabernet Sauvignon Stellenbosch 1990: Sturdy, solid style of Cabernet that packs in plenty of ripe currant and cherry flavor, little oak influence. Tight and firm in texture and a tannic grip on the finish. • $10 • (09/30/95) • **84**

Merlot Stellenbosch 1993: This tastes old and tired for a new release, and there's a green, woody streak running through it. • $10 • (09/30/95) • **72**

Riesling Stellenbosch Weisser Riesling 1993: Crisp and clean, this combines racy acidity and tropical fruitiness accented by spicy vanilla notes. It's vivid and refreshing. • $10 • (08/31/95) • **84**

Riesling Stellenbosch Weisser Riesling Off-Dry 1993: Big-boned and sturdy, showing melon and herbal flavors, fine intensity and acidity. Not much sweetness. Good for food, though lacking clear Riesling character. • $10 • (08/31/95) • **84**

Shiraz Stellenbosch 1992: Heavy, brooding, full-bodied, smoky, almost bitter, coffee and meaty notes are more prominent than the blackberry flavors. Drinkable now. • $10 • (09/30/95) • **81**

REDHILL

Pinotage Coastal Region 1993: Lacks a bit of definition. Loads of smoky, jammy character, medium body, velvety texture and slightly bitter finish. 15,000 cases made. • $6 • **82**

ROOIBERG

Cabernet Sauvignon Robertson 1992: Rather weird and funky, showing candied berry aromas and flavors. Tasted twice, with consistent notes. 2,000 cases made. • $8 • **69**

Chardonnay Robertson 1994: Delicate lemon and floral aromas give way to clean, simple flavors of apple and pear in this smooth, chewy, easy-to-drink Chardonnay. 1,200 cases made. • $8 • (06/30/95) • **80**

Pinotage Eilandia 1991: • $9 • (06/30/94) • **60**

Pinotage Robertson 1992: Delicious red with tobacco and plum aromas and flavors. Medium bodied and firm yet velvety texture and a slightly dry finish. Drink now. 2,000 cases made. • $8 • (06/15/95) • **84**
Sauvignon Blanc Robertson 1994: A wine with interesting lemon custard, chalky, mineral character. Medium bodied with fresh acidity and good flavors. 1,800 cases made. • $8 • (06/15/95) • **85**
Sauvignon Blanc Robertson 1991 • $8 • (04/15/92) • **84**
Syrah Goree 1989 • $11 • (04/15/92) • **82**
Syrah Vinkrivier 1991: Straightforward and fruity with pleasant strawberry and orange peel flavors, and some nice black cherry notes as well. Ripe and broad with moderate tannins and spice. • $9 • (06/30/94) • **84**

ROOSENVELDT

Cabernet Sauvignon Franschhoek Valley 1993: A broad, reasonably rich and appealing Cabernet offering plenty of fruit flavor, spicy oak accents and lingering finish. Firmly tannic, drinkable now through 1997. 3,000 cases made. • $14 • (04/30/96) • **83**
Chardonnay Franschhoek Valley 1995: Extremely buttery, delivering surprisingly mature flavors for its age. Falls a bit short in the middle, but still tasty. Caramel notes come out on the finish. • $12 • (05/15/96) • **82**
Merlot Franschhoek Valley 1994: A big, stiff young Merlot delivering lots of fruit flavor but needing time for the tannins to mellow. Packed with black cherry and strawberry notes, full-bodied, lingering finish. Hold until 1998. 3,000 cases made. • $14 • (04/30/96) • **87**

ROZENDAL

Stellenbosch 1990: Mature red providing barnyard and leather aromas, tart fruit flavors and earthy finish. A good one for fans of funk. • $18 • (06/30/95) • **78**
Stellenbosch 1989: Delicious and decadent leaf, earth, berry and tobacco character. Medium in body, soft tannins and slightly dry finish. Ready now. • $18 • (06/15/95) • **86**

RUST EN VREDE

Cabernet Sauvignon Stellenbosch 1989: Textbook Cabernet flavors and aromas. Rich and round on the palate, with black currant, olive and eucyalyptus notes. Well balanced and ready to drink. Finishes with a nice note of chocolate. 1,800 cases made. • $20 • (11/30/94) • **87**
Estate Wine Stellenbosch 1991: Delicious to drink today. Alluring minty, cherry, berry, and spice aromas and flavors. Full bodied with a silky texture and a chocolate finish. Perfect now. • $25 • (06/15/95) • **89**
Estate Wine Stellenbosch 1990: Beautiful fruit combines with tons of new oak in this vivid wine. Raspberry and tart cherry flavors are almost overwhelmed by vanilla, spice, toast and smoke notes. Right now the oak isn't in harmony. Drinkable now. • $NA • (11/30/94) • **88**
Merlot Stellenbosch 1993: Earthy and mature, with modest plum and cherry flavors. It has a gamy note as well, which makes this a fairly muddled wine. 1,500 cases made. • $12 • (12/31/95) • **80**
Merlot Stellenbosch 1992: Rustic and burnt aromas, with an odd rubbery, ripe fruit character. • $11 • **73**
Merlot Stellenbosch 1991: A good middle-of-the-road Merlot, with spicy, plummy flavors. Not a lot of complexity, but well made with a hint of oak, some tannins and a pleasant finish. 1,200 cases made. • $12 • (11/30/94) • **84**
Shiraz Stellenbosch 1990: Mature and enjoyable for its complex bottle bouquet, concentrated fruit flavor, moderate tannins and spicy accents. Yet it's getting tired, so drink it soon. 2,000 cases made. • $15 • (04/30/96) • **83**
Shiraz Stellenbosch 1989: Nicely integrated, mature and spicy, with smoky flavors and aromas. Lean and lively for its age and ready to drink. Attractive plum flavors linger on the finish. 1,500 cases made. • $16 • (11/30/94) • **85**

Key: SS—Spectator Selection. CS—Cellar Selection. BB—Best Buy. $NA—Price not available. (BT)—Barrel tasting. Ⓐ—Auction Price.
Dates in parentheses represent the issues in which the ratings were published.

RUSTENBERG

Cabernet Sauvignon 1988 • $14 • (10/15/92) • **74**
Cabernet Sauvignon Stellenbosch 1990: Medium-bodied Cabernet featuring tar, tobacco and cherry aromas and flavors and a soft finish. Ready now. • $12 • **84**
Dry Red Stellenbosch 1991: A little tired, but offering some pretty tobacco, cedar and milk chocolate aromas and flavors. Medium-bodied and soft. Drink now. Blend includes Cinsault. • $11 • **82**
Gold Label Stellenbosch 1990: Middle-of-the-road Cabernet blend featuring tobacco, cherry and berry character and a hint of barnyard, medium-bodied and soft. Drink now. • $17 • **84**
Merlot Cabernet Sauvignon Stellenbosch 1991: Tired and stewed, with herbal and berry aromas and flavors. Fermented carrot juice. • $12 • **76**
Rustenberg Gold Stellenbosch 1989 • $19 • (10/15/92) • **82**

SABLE VIEW

Cabernet Sauvignon Coastal Region 1990: A mature and medium-bodied Cabernet with tea and cassis flavors. Tastes old for its age, with an odd menthol finish. Drink now before it loses what little vigor it has. • $8 • (06/30/94) • **78**
Chardonnay Coastal Region 1992 • $8 • (06/15/94) • **74**
Pinotage Coastal Region 1989: The peppery, smoky, meaty flavors are interesting, but it's too lean and tannic, especially on the finish. Acceptable, though • $8 • (06/30/94) • **76**
Sauvignon Blanc Coastal Region 1992 • $8 • **74**

SAXENBURG

Shiraz Stellenbosch Private Collection 1993: Gorgeous, deeply flavored red sporting the exuberance of an Aussie Shiraz but the elegance of a Northern Rhône. Has enticing raspberry and violet aromas, rich, peppery tones and lingering finish. Drinkable now through 1999. 800 cases made. • $16 • (04/30/96) • **90**

SIMONSIG

Cabernet Sauvignon Stellenbosch 1989 • $14 • (10/15/92) • **84**
Chardonnay Stellenbosch 1991 • $14 • (10/15/92) • **84**
Pinotage Stellenbosch 1989 • $11 • (10/15/92) • **82**
Pinotage Stellenbosch Private Reserve Estate Wine 1989 • $NA • (02/15/93) • **87**

SORGVLIET

Grand Vin Rouge Stellenbosch 1992: An intriguing earthy, spicy aroma marks this full-bodied, moderately tannic red. Reminiscent of Cabernet Sauvignon, adding some nice oaky accents to the ripe cherry and plum flavors. 1,500 cases made. • $7 • (09/30/95) • **87**

SPRINGBOK

Cabernet Sauvignon Coastal Region 1992: Earth, tomato and herb aromas and flavors. Very thin and tired. 22,000 cases made. • $7 • **73**
Cabernet Sauvignon Coastal Region 1991: A good combination of spice and tart cherry fruit flavors makes this a fairly lean wine. Clamps down with tannins on the finish. 25,000 cases made. • $6 • **79**
Cabernet Sauvignon Coastal Region 1990: Full-bodied, smooth and fully mature. The flavors are dominated by brown sugar and spice with a touch of plum, finishing with a hint of chocolate. 5,000 cases made. • $7 • (06/30/94) • **82**
Chardonnay Coastal Region 1995: An obvious style, sporting oak and caramel flavors and a touch of lemon and citrus. Simple, but tasty with good acidity. 30,000 cases made. • $7 • (05/15/96) • **82**
Chardonnay Coastal Region 1994: Rich with flavor and lively with acidity, a spicy, buttery, generous wine that offers a lot of satisfaction. Has fine balance and a lingering finish. 35,000 cases made. • $6 • (02/28/95) BB • **86**
Chardonnay Coastal Region 1992 • $7 • (06/15/94) • **77**
Pinotage Coastal Region 1993: Serious, tannic, engaging Pinotage boasting depth and complexity in the cherry and strawberry flavors

and a dry, firm texture. Lingering finish, too. Drinkable now through 1998. 12,000 cases made. • $6 • (04/30/96) • **87**

Pinotage Coastal Region 1991: Not very impressive. Sweet, weedy and tired. 40,000 cases made. • $6 • **74**

Pinotage Coastal Region 1990: A crisp and zingy red whose tart fruit flavors linger on the finish. The good acidity should make it versatile at the table. 25,000 cases made. • $7 • (06/30/94) • **80**

Pinotage Coastal Region 1989 • $6 • (02/15/93) • **82**

Sauvignon Blanc Coastal Region 1994: Fresh and clean but rather neutral, featuring light body, light fruit and light finish. 30,000 cases made. • $6 • **79**

Sauvignon Blanc Coastal Region 1993: Melon and pear flavors mingle in this full-bodied yet very crisp wine. It has good structure, but lacks depth and finishes a bit short. 50,000 cases made. • $6 • (03/31/95) • **80**

Sauvignon Blanc Coastal Region 1992 • $6 • (07/15/93) BB • **85**

Syrah Coastal Region 1989: Not much to get excited about. Tastes mature and tired, with simple brown sugar and plum flavors. 3,500 cases made. • $7 • (06/30/94) • **74**

SPRINGHILL

Shiraz Stellenbosch 1989: A nicely integrated wine that's mature and spicey with smoky aromas and flavors. Lean and lively for its age, smooth and ready to drink. Attractive plummy flavors linger on the finish. 1,500 cases made. • $16 • **85**

STELLENRYCK

Cabernet Sauvignon Coastal Region 1989: Like a fine graves with firm, sleek tannin structure and rich stony, berry, chocolate flavors. Medium bodied with a medium finish. Give it time. Try after 1997. • $13 • (06/15/95) • **87**

Cabernet Sauvignon Coastal Region 1988: Inviting, jammy aromas give way to very soft black currant and cassis flavors. A vegetal note runs through it as well. • $13 • (11/30/94) • **82**

Chardonnay Coastal Region 1994: Buttery, simple, pleasant caramel and baked apple flavors. • $9 • (05/15/96) • **78**

Chardonnay Coastal Region 1992: Deft winemaking completmented by incredible youth. Full bodied, firm acidity and masses of pear, apple, hay and earth character. Needs more time. Try in 1996. • $9 • (06/15/95) • **87**

Chardonnay Coastal Region 1991: Tart, tight and lemony, but it rounds out on the finish with butter and candy notes. A bit stiff to drink now, but it should improve if cellared until 1996. • $9 • (02/28/95) • **83**

STELLENZICHT

Chardonnay Stellenbosch 1993: Attractive toast and butter aromas give way to maturing flavors of pear and toast and an earthy, leesy finish. This ambitious effort still has appeal. 1,000 cases made. • $7 • (08/31/95) • **82**

SWARTLAND WINERY

Cabernet Sauvignon Swartland Region 1993: Solid, fruity-tasting, enjoyable cherry and black currant last from first whiff through the finish. Has supple texture, mild tannins and accents of vanilla from oak aging. Drink now. • $9 • (09/30/95) • **85**

Dry Red Swartland Region NV: A robust red, offering plenty of fruit flavors and smoky accents yet soft on the tannins, so it's smooth enough to drink now. Jammy tasting and enjoyable. • $NA • (09/30/95) • **81**

Merlot Swartland Region 1995: Lushly textured and opulent, featuring deep, dark color and rich fruit flavors generously accented with oak. Tempting to drink now for its exuberant fruitiness, but may improve through 1999. 8,000 cases made. • $10 • (04/30/96) • **87**

Pinotage Swartland Region 1995: A nouveau-style red, quite like Beaujolais, offering lots of jammy and ripe fruit flavors, soft tannins and lingering finish. 6,000 cases made. • $9 • (04/30/96) • **83**

Pinotage Swartland Region 1994: A good quaffing wine that reminds us of Beaujolais. Smells and tastes like strawberry jam, light in tannins and ready to drink. • $6 • (09/30/95) • **83**

Sauvignon Blanc Swartland Region 1994: A clean, drinkable white offering little character. It's slightly herbal or floral on the finish. • $6 • (09/30/95) • **77**

Shiraz Swartland Region 1992: A hint of greenness combines with nice mint and vanilla character. Medium in body, enough fruit flavor, plus light tannins so you can drink it now. • $9 • (09/30/95) • **80**

THELEMA

Cabernet Sauvignon Merlot Stellenbosch 1992: Classy and refined mint, coffee, cedar and dried plum character. Full-bodied and elegant, adding fine tannins and a silky finish. Superbly made. Drinkable now. 1,200 cases made. • $20 • (06/15/95) • **90**

Cabernet Sauvignon Stellenbosch 1991: Luscious mint, chocolate and bright cherry flavors. Full-bodied, offering fine tannins and a wonderful vanilla, toasted oak finish. Drinkable now, but better in 1997. 3,800 cases made. • $19 • (06/15/95) • **89**

Cabernet Sauvignon Stellenbosch 1990: Nicely balanced and intriguingly earthy. Cedar, coffee and cassis flavors blend seamlessly together, firm tannins and lively acidity. Best from now through 1998. • $18 • (01/31/95) • **87**

Cabernet Sauvignon Stellenbosch Reserve 1991: This red caresses your palate with masses of silky tannins and plenty of earthy, berry, minty aromas and flavors. Really polished. Drinkable but better in 1998. 300 cases made. • $22 • **91**

Chardonnay Stellenbosch 1994: Delicious tropical style of Chardonnay with plenty of apple, butter and pineapple character. Full bodied and oily with a long flavorful finish. 3,700 cases made. • $18 • (06/15/95) • **88**

Chardonnay Stellenbosch Reserve 1993: Well-crafted Chardonnay with plenty of pear, spice and vanilla character. Full bodied with fine acidity and a toasted oak, apple flavors. 600 cases made. • $22 • (06/15/95) • **87**

Sauvignon Blanc Stellenbosch 1994: Excellent intensity which builds on your palate. Subtle mineral and grapefruit aromas. Medium bodied with super acidity and loads of spicy, rich fruit flavors. Drink now or hold. 5,500 cases made. • $14 • (06/15/95) • **87**

UITERWYK

Pinotage Stellenbosch 1992: A serious red, quite supple, rich and enjoyable, featuring lots of color, fruit flavor and significant tannins. Full-bodied and layered with accents of roasted meats, violets and blackberries. 1,500 cases made. • $12 • (09/30/95) • **88**

VAN LOVEREN

Blush Robertson Blanc de Noir Red Muscadel 1991 • $9 • (10/15/92) • **82**

Chardonnay Robertson 1991 • $14 • (10/15/92) • **84**

Pinot Gris Robertson 1991 • $10 • (10/15/92) • **86**

VEENWOUDEN

Merlot Coastal Region 1993: Luscious black cherry and spicy oak flavors are focused and bright in this balanced, accessible Merlot. It has grip and character, enjoyable now, it should improve through 1997. • $NA • (09/30/95) • **87**

VERGELEGEN

Chardonnay Coastal Region 1993 • $NA • (06/15/94) • **80**

VILLIERA ESTATE

Blue Ridge Blanc Paarl 1994: Some delicious fruit but lacks a bit of definition. Medium-bodied, simple apple and peach flavors.
A blend of Chenin Blanc and Sauvignon Blanc. • $8 • **82**

Brut South Africa Tradition Carte Rouge NV: Good quality, if not exactly elegant. Fresh and fruity in aroma and flavor, then it turns heavy and less appealing on the finish. • $14 • (07/31/95) • **81**

Cabernet Sauvignon Paarl 1993: Thick and unbalanced, jammy, herbal, grassy character. Try now. Tasted twice, with consistent notes. • $NA • **77**

Cru Monro Blanc Fumé Oak Matured Paarl 1994: Another zippy Sauvignon with plenty of toasted almond, melon and coconut aromas

and flavors. Medium bodied with fresh, ripe and round character. • $NA • (06/15/95) • **88**
Cru Monro Limited Release Oak Matured Paarl 1993: Big, rich blackberry, plum and salty character, full body, firm tannins, an impressive concentration of fruit and long, long finish. Try in 1997. • $16 • **88**
Cru Monro Limited Release Paarl 1992: Beautiful, refined red featuring mint, blackberry and cherry aromas and flavors. Full-bodied, silky tannins and a long, delicious finish. Drinkable now. • $16 • **89**
Gewürztraminer Paarl 1993: Simple, straightforward, pleasant apricot, honey and spice aromas and flavors. Medium in body and lightly sweet, oily finish. • $NA • **82**
Merlot Paarl 1993: Extremely well-crafted cedar, tobacco, berry, stony aromas and flavors. Medium in body, medium to firm tannins and lengthy, fruity finish. Delicious now. • $15 • (06/15/95) • **89**
Merlot Paarl 1992: More mature style with elegant minty, berry, and cassis character. Medium bodied with medium tannins and a silky finish. Drink now. • $15 • (06/15/95) • **86**
Sauvignon Blanc Paarl 1994: Plenty of Sauvignon character in this one. Rich and refreshing with grapefruit, mineral aromas and flavors and hint of grass. Medium bodied and oily yet very fresh on the finish. • $10 • (06/15/95) • **86**

VRIESENHOF

Cabernet Sauvignon Stellenbosch 1990: A lean wine, with sparse raspberry and cherry flavors. An herbal, astringent finish doesn't help. 2,200 cases made. • $12 • (06/30/94) • **75**
Chardonnay Stellenbosch 1992 • $13 • (06/15/94) • **82**
Kallista Stellenbosch 1991: Beautiful to drink now with minty, violet and berry aromas and flavors. Medium odied with firm tannins and a silky finish. Drinkable now or hold. 750 cases made. • $14 • (06/15/95) • **87**
Kallista Stellenbosch 1989: An awkward Cabernet with a leathery, earthy edge. Dry and astringent, murky, ends up overly tannic, despite some ripe plum flavors. 2,000 cases made. • $13 • (06/30/94) • **75**

WARWICK

Cabernet Franc Stellenbosch 1993: Generous oak accents give this bright, fruity red some extra style. Cherry and herb flavors, nutmeg and clove are nicely integrated from the oak barrels in which it was aged. Lingering finish, too. • $15 • (06/30/95) • **85**
Cabernet Sauvignon Stellenbosch 1991: Deep, dark color and generous fruit flavors, impressive, silky-smooth texture. Moderate tannins, with cherry and currant notes lingering on the finish. Drink now through 1997. • $15 • (06/30/95) • **85**
Merlot Stellenbosch 1992: Tart fruit flavors of cherry and cranberry are muddied by earthy aromas and tough tannins. It's awkward and severe. • $15 • (06/30/95) • **78**
Trilogy Stellenbosch 1992: Quite flavorful, balanced toward tartness, showing ample cherry and berry aromas, crisp texture and clean finish. A solid, sturdy red to drink now. • $17 • (06/30/95) • **83**

WELMOED WINERY

Sauvignon Blanc Stellenbosch 1994: Crisp and clean. Characteristic grassy aromas and dry, juicy flavors remind us of a good French Sancerre. Should be versatile at the table. 1,200 cases made. • $8 • (09/30/95) • **85**

WELTEVREDE

Chardonnay Robertson 1993 • $12 • (06/15/94) • **77**
Privé du Bois Robertson 1993: Dry and crisp, but watery in flavor. Simple refreshment, palatable but not interesting. A blend of Sauvignon Blanc and Chardonnay. 2,200 cases made. • $9 • (06/30/95) • **76**
Privé du Bois Robertson 1992 • $8 • **83**

ZANDVLIET

Shiraz Robertson 1989: Old and tired. Barely drinkable. Tea, tobacco and coffee grinds. Drink if you must. • $11 • (09/30/95) • **70**

ZONNEBLOEM

Cabernet Sauvignon Stellenbosch 1989: Simple and flavorful, with good plum, currant and spice flavors. Smooth and uncomplicated, with a touch of chocolate on the finish. Try with pasta. • $11 • (06/30/94) • **82**
Chardonnay Stellenbosch 1992 • $12 • (06/15/94) • **78**
Dessert Stellenbosch Noble Late Harvest 1990 • $10 • **64**
Grand Soleil Stellenbosch 1991 • $11 • **86**
Grand Soleil Vintner's Selection Stellenbosch 1991: An earthy-smelling white that's very dry, almost austere in flavor, and then turns metallic on the finish. • $10 • (06/30/95) • **74**
Merlot Stellenbosch 1991: Raisiny and slightly overripe, rubbery character. Drink if you must. • $10 • (09/30/95) • **76**
Pinotage Stellenbosch 1990: Lean and green tasting, with hefty tannins and a dry finish. There is a bit of charm in the spicy, cherrylike aroma, but it fades quickly. • $10 • (06/30/94) • **75**
Pinotage Stellenbosch Vintner's Selection 1988 • $10 • (02/15/93) • **82**
Sauvignon Blanc Stellenbosch 1992 • $10 • (07/15/93) • **82**
Syrah Stellenbosch 1989: This is past its prime. Tired and rustic, with cola and tea flavors. Earthy and leathery, a cloying finish. • $10 • (06/30/94) • **71**

• Yugoslavia •

AVIA

Cabernet Sauvignon Primorska Region 1985 • $3 • (03/31/89) • **77**
Merlot Primorska Hrvatska-Istra 1985 • $3 • (03/31/89) • **75**

CANTERBURY

Cabernet Sauvignon Istria 1985 • $5 • (09/30/89) BB • **81**

SABLE, LE

Cabernet Sauvignon Primorski 1986 • $4 • (03/31/91) • **64**
Pinot Noir Oplenac 1987 • $4 • (03/31/91) • **70**

Key: SS—Spectator Selection. CS—Cellar Selection. BB—Best Buy. $NA—Price not available. (BT)—Barrel tasting. Ⓐ—Auction Price.
Dates in parentheses represent the issues in which the ratings were published.

USA

CALIFORNIA

California's first vines were planted by Spanish missionaries only about 200 years ago—not a long time by world wine trade standards. Yet today California produces almost 90 percent of the wine made in the U.S.A. The Mission grape planted by the Spaniards is still cultivated in a few areas, but California's greatest success has been in the cultivation of classic European varietals, such as Cabernet Sauvignon, Chardonnay, Pinot Noir, Merlot and Sauvignon Blanc. These classic vinifera varietals, which are used almost exclusively for making wine (as opposed to being used as table grapes), now total about one-third of the 365,000 acres of grapes planted in the state. Along with France and Italy, California is now regarded as one of the truly great wine-producing regions of the world.

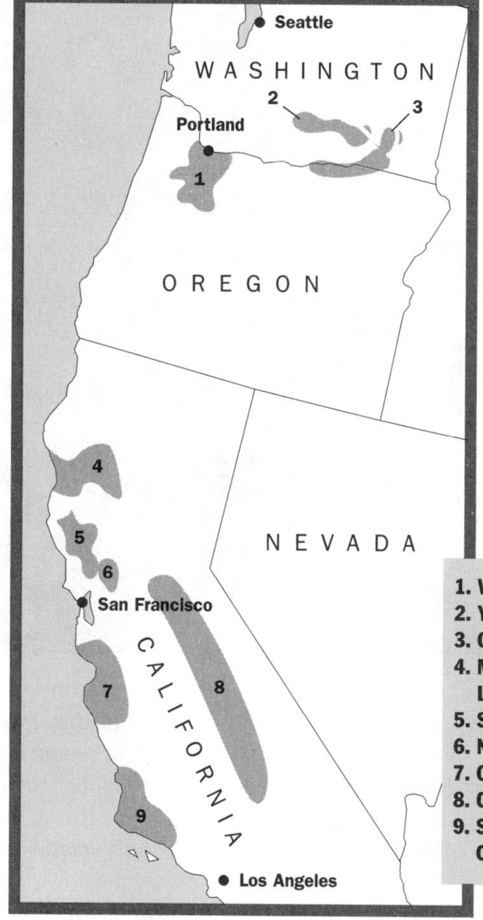

Varietal Labeling

California wines are marketed primarily by varietal categories—by the grape variety (Chardonnay, for instance) that makes up all or most of the wine in the bottle. This method differs from the classic European approach, which is based primarily on such geographic locations and/or appellations as Bordeaux and the Rhône. The implications of California's system have been enormous. Instead of being limited to a few grape types allowed under an appellation law, California's winemakers have been free to experiment and plant whatever grape variety they wish. This has given them great flexibility in choosing what wines to make and how to make them.

Major California Grape Varieties

Although regional soil differences and variations in microclimate have a significant impact on wine flavors, maintaining and enhancing varietal character remains a key objective of California winemaking. Thus, a knowledge of the leading grape varietals grown in California is central to understanding the state's wines.

Chardonnay. With over 55,000 acres now in production, Chardonnay recently displaced French Colombard as the state's most widely planted grape. California Chardonnay displays flavors of fresh-cut yellow fruit, especially apples, melon, pineapple and other tropical fruits. Winemakers build more complexity into these flavors through the use of such techniques as barrel fermentation, *sur lie* aging and malolactic fermentation. California Chardonnay tends to be more full-bodied and plump than French Chardonnay-based wines such as white Burgundy.

With over 11,000 acres planted in the Alexander Valley, Russian River Valley, and Carneros, Sonoma County leads the state in Chardonnay acreage. It is followed by Monterey County, Napa Valley, Santa Barbara, Mendocino and other areas. In recent years, the tendency has been to plant Chardonnay in cooler areas of these regions, leading to wines with less alcohol but with a better balance of fruit and acidity. While many California Chardonnays are quite ordinary, the better ones are undoubtedly among the world's best.

Cabernet Sauvignon. Generally regarded as the king of California red wine. California Cabernet displays the classic varietal characteristics of fresh herbs, cedar, cassis, mint, black currant and violets. In the cooler areas, it can take on a distinct vegetal/bell pepper characteristic, which is increasingly viewed as undesirable.

For many years, it was thought that California Cabernet was sufficiently soft and complex—that it did not benefit from blending with other varietals. While some of the best California Cabernets are still made from 100 percent Cabernet Sauvignon, the trend in recent years has been to add Merlot and other Bordeaux varietals, such as Petit Verdot and Cabernet Franc. Most of the better Cabernet Sauvignons today are aged in small barrels, of both French and American oak, to add appealing vanilla and spice notes. Although many areas of the state now produce top-notch Cabernet, Napa Valley still produces a disproportionate share of the best examples.

St. Clement, Napa.

Zinfandel. The most widely planted red grape in California. Zinfandel lends itself to an enormous variety of styles, ranging from the rosé style called "white" Zinfandel at one extreme, to inky black late-harvest Zinfandels at the other. Leaving the highly commercial white Zinfandels aside, the true red Zinfandel has a zesty, spicy varietal character, and is loaded with notes of raspberry, plum and red-berry fruit. Winemakers often choose to emphasize one or more of these characteristics. Thus, some Zinfandels are made in a medium-weight, claret style that emphasizes the grape's subtler elements and innate fruitiness. Amador County and a few other regions specialize in blockbusters, characterized by high levels of tannin, extract, and alcohol. Another popular style emphasizes Zinfandel's grapey, Beaujolais character.

Sauvignon Blanc. California Sauvignon Blanc is an often under-appreciated and usually bargain-priced white. Many California Sauvignon Blancs are made in a Loire style, and offer strong grassy, herbal, mineral and citrus (particularly grapefruit) tastes with minimal or no oak flavors. A more recent trend, most in evidence in the Napa Valley, has been to emphasize barrel fermentation, lees stirring, and blending with Sémillon, all of which yields a rich style closer to that of a white Bordeaux.

Merlot. Though once thought of as a blending grape, California Merlot has now emerged as a hot new variety on its own. Merlot has been called the "kinder and gentler" alternative to Cabernet Sauvignon: it is softer than the latter, and offers more cherry, plum and red fruit flavors. In California, as elsewhere, Merlot is often blended with Cabernet Sauvignon and other Bordeaux grapes to add complexity to the finished wine. Merlot seems to thrive mainly in the regions where Cabernet Sauvignon does best; the finest California examples tend to be from Napa and Sonoma.

Pinot Noir. This grape variety has had a checkered history in California. Many early examples were a bit clumsy and lacked the elegance expected of a good Pinot Noir. But that has very much changed. Today, good California Pinot Noir has layers of pure strawberry, raspberry and other red and black fruits that expand across the palate on the finish. Pinot Noir seems to have found a natural home in the cooler regions of California, including the Carneros region, the Russian River Valley and Santa Barbara.

Rhône Varieties. The term "Rhône Rangers" has become a catch-all description for a number of California winemakers who are working with grape varieties that originated in France's Rhône Valley; many have already achieved great success with several grape types. Among the red wines, Syrah seems to be achieving the most acclaim at the moment, displaying dense red berry fruit with hints of bacon fat, tar and spice. (Note: Petite Sirah appears to be an unrelated variety; it was long thought to be the Durif of southeastern France, but recent DNA testing has cast doubt on this hypothesis.) Mourvèdre displays characteristics similar to Syrah, but with a bit more earthiness and dustier tannins on the finish. Among whites, Viognier is showing exceptional promise. Its primary characteristics are peach and honeysuckle notes, with an alcoholic fullness and gentle roundness on the finish.

Major California Wine Regions

Napa Valley. Undoubtedly the best known wine region of California, the Napa Valley produces a vast array of fine wines. More than 35,000 acres of the Napa Valley are planted with vines today. Chardonnay and Cabernet Sauvignon account for about 10,000 acres each. Sauvignon Blanc, Riesling, Pinot Noir, Merlot and Zinfandel account for most of the rest.

The Napa Valley includes a wide range of microclimates and soil types. The northern portion of the Valley, near Calistoga, tends to be the warmest, while the southern end, near Carneros and extending up through Yountville, is cooler due to the moderating influence of the San Francisco Bay.

Many of Napa's best known wineries are situated in the central part of the Valley, around Oakville, Rutherford and St. Helena. They include some of the area's oldest wineries—Beaulieu, Robert Mondavi, Beringer and Louis Martini, for instance. Many of the best vineyards are situated on the so-called Rutherford Bench, a narrow strip of soft loam that is renowned for producing classic, long-lived Cabernet Sauvignon.

A number of sub-regions of Napa have developed individual winemaking identities, and several have been granted appellation status. The Stags Leap District, east of Yountville, is known for its supple, Bordeaux-like Cabernets. It is home to Stag's Leap Wine Cellars, Stags' Leap Winery, Safer Vineyards, Pine Ridge, Chimney Rock, S. Anderson and others.

Los Carneros, which straddles the southern ends of Napa and Sonoma, has developed a reputation for Burgundy-style wines made from Pinot Noir and from Chardonnay. Well-known Carneros wineries include Acacia, Bouchaine, Saintsbury and Carneros Creek.

In recent years, several regions in the hilly mountainsides of the Valley have achieved special recognition. Howell Mountain, located to the northeast of St. Helena, has volcanic soil that produces especially rich wines. Howell Mountain wineries such as Dunn and La Jota have established well deserved reputations for producing powerful Cabernets and Zinfandels.

To the west of Yountville is Mount Veeder, a part of the Mayacamas Mountains, which has become known for Cabernet Sauvignon, Chardonnay and Sauvignon Blanc. Leading Mount Veeder wineries include Mayacamas Vineyards, Mount Veeder Winery, Hess Collection and Château Potelle. The best known wineries further north in the Mayacamas Mountains include Diamond Creek, Stony Hill and Philip Togni, most of which specialize in Cabernet, Merlot and Chardonnay.

Sonoma County. Sonoma County presents a more varied picture than the Napa Valley. Geographically diverse, with numerous microclimates, it supports many grape varieties and wine styles.

The historic heart of Sonoma County is the Sonoma Valley, where many of its oldest wineries are located. Cabernet Sauvignon has fared well here, as has Zinfandel. Chardonnay and Pinot Noir seem especially well suited to the southern part of the Sonoma Valley. Leading wineries of Sonoma Valley include Kenwood, B.R. Cohn, Kunde, Laurel Glen, Glen Ellen and Sebastiani, although the latter two also get grapes from elsewhere throughout the state.

Alexander Valley is planted mostly to Cabernet Sauvignon and Chardonnay. The Cabernets produced here have proven to be well balanced and elegant, with many showing a hint of eucalyptus. This region's Chardonnays tend to be full and rich, without the tropical buttery notes found in many other California Chardonnays. Jordan Winery is located here and produces a luxury sparkling wine cuvée called J at new facilities. The region's other well-known wineries include Alexander Valley Vineyards, Murphy-Goode, Simi and Stonestreet.

Dry Creek Valley parallels Alexander Valley, but has a different, often warmer, microclimate. Zinfandel seems to thrive in its benchland soil, but lately Cabernet is making significant inroads. Among whites, Sauvignon Blanc does particularly well here. Leading wineries include Dry Creek Vineyard, Mazzocco, Quivira and Preston.

Because of its proximity to the ocean, Russian River Valley's climate is cool and damp, which for some years discouraged extensive planting. However, recently Pinot Noir and Chardonnay have been shown to thrive under these conditions, which can be likened to those of Burgundy. Russian River Valley also encompasses two smaller sub-regions that are attracting increasing attention, Chalk Hill and Green Valley. Both excel in Chardonnay, and Green Valley has been developed by Iron Horse Vineyards as a source of high quality sparkling wines.

The 19th-century house on the estate of Grace Family Vineyards, in Napa.

The areas of Santa Clara, Monterey and Saint Luis Obispo contain a vast number of fine properties. Important viticultural regions in these areas include the Santa Cruz Mountains, Livermore Valley, Carmel, Arroyo Seco, Paso Robles and Edna Valley. These regions produce a full range of varietal types and make wines that often reach the highest levels of quality.

Other Important Regions. Santa Barbara County includes two distinct viticultural areas with excellent potential. In northern Santa Barbara County, the Santa Maria Valley is becoming best known for Pinot Noir and Chardonnay; both varieties take on a special intensity and richness of fruit here. Au Bon Climat, Byron, Wild Horse and Cambria are among the leading producers. In southern Santa Barbara, the Santa Ynez Valley has also shown an affinity for cool-climate varieties, including Pinot Noir and Chardonnay. The Sanford & Benedict Vineyard in the eastern part of the Valley supplies grapes for some of Sanford Winery's best wines, and supplies other wineries as well. Also in Santa Barbara, experiments with Syrah have produced excellent results; Zaca Mesa's is one of the best.

Just north of Napa lies Lake County, which has become an important producer of Chardonnay, Cabernet, Sauvignon Blanc, Merlot and Pinot Noir. Lake County is the home of Kendall-Jackson Winery and Guenoc Winery, among others.

Located just to the west of Lake County, Mendocino is home to a wide array of varietal wines, many of which sell at very modest prices. For many years, Parducci was the only well-known producer in Mendocino. Today, however, Fetzer and several other successful enterprises have joined its ranks.

OREGON

More than 6,000 acres of vines are planted in Oregon today, and three-quarters of its total wine production comes from the Willamette Valley. The state has shown a particular affinity for the Pinot Noir grape, which constitutes 40 percent of plantings here. The top Oregon Pinot Noirs are competitive with the best of Burgundy and California. Chardonnay, Riesling and other varieties are also widely and successfully cultivated.

Better-known Oregon producers include Eyrie Vineyards, Ponzi, Adelsheim, Knudsen Erath, Sokol Blosser, Elk Cove, Bethel Heights and Henry Estate. Oregon is also the home of Domaine Drouhin, which is owned and operated by the important Burgundian firm of Joseph Drouhin.

WASHINGTON

While Oregon wine has a Burgundian tilt, Washington State's leans toward Bordeaux. Cabernet Sauvignon and Merlot do extremely well here, and now represent nearly a third of Washington's total vine acreage. (Washington Merlot may even have an edge over California's.) Most Washington wineries are located in the Columbia River Valley, which includes the smaller Yakima Valley and Walla Walla districts within its borders. The best known Washington winery is Chateau Ste. Michelle; other major producers include Columbia Winery, Leonetti Cellars, Arbor Crest, and Covey Run.

1 ACRE | CALIFORNIA

Rhône Blend California Cuvée du Soleil 1993: Marked by an earthy, leathery edge before the smoky plum flavors emerge, the lasting impression is one of chewy leather. 270 cases made. • $13 • (02/29/96) • **80**

ABADIA DEL ROBLE | WASHINGTON

Cana's Feast Columbia Valley 1992: Big and brooding, not terribly tannic but submerging its plum, black cherry and currant flavors in the soft, soupy texture. Try in 1997. 206 cases made. • $25 • **85**

Chardonnay California Barrel Fermented 1994: Ripe with honey, peach, pear and spice notes, but also a good dose of oak, which gives it a dry, woody edge on the finish. 4,000 cases made. • $10 BB • **87**

Chardonnay Napa Valley Clos Fontaine du Mont Reserve 1993: Well oaked, with smoky, toasty flavors, but the ripe pear, fig and apple flavors match up well, adding extra flavor dimensions. 1,874 cases made. • $20 • **88**

ABBY D'OR | CALIFORNIA

Zinfandel Late Harvest Paso Robles 1991: Austere, with drying tannins and woody flavors that override the ripe jammy fruit flavors. 352 cases made. • $9 • (10/15/94) • **78**

ABREU | CALIFORNIA

Cabernet Sauvignon Napa Valley Madrona Ranch 1991: A touch earthy and closed, but it's impressive for its rich, dark color and solid core of currant, spice, cedar, anise and tar, altogether complex, dense and tannic, a wine that will be benefit from another three to five years cellaring. Try in 1998. 380 cases made. • $31 • **89**

Cabernet Sauvignon Napa Valley Madrona Ranch 1987 • $25 • (07/31/91) • **89**

ACACIA | CALIFORNIA

Brut Carneros 1988: Rich and full-bodied, with ripe, intense pear, spice, vanilla and hazelnut flavors. Finishes with a tight core of fruit that lingers. Ready now. • $25 • (12/31/94) • **88**

Brut Carneros 1987 • $25 • (12/31/93) • **81**

Brut Carneros 1986 • $25 • (12/31/92) • **87**

Cabernet Sauvignon Napa Valley 1984 • $15 • (12/15/86) • **75**

Chardonnay Carneros 1994: This California Chardonnay serves up a juicy array of tropical fruit flavors, featuring hints of mango, pear, spice and light, toasty oak shadings which add to its finesse and elegance. A nice, complex aftertaste rounds this out. 21,000 cases made. • $18 • (04/30/96) SS • **90**

Chardonnay Carneros 1993: Lightly fruity with an earthy edge to the pear and citrus notes. Good but nothing more. 18,200 cases made. • $17 • (07/31/95) • **84**

Chardonnay Carneros 1992: Crisp and flinty, with an austere core of citrus and pineapple flavors that pick up toasty oak and spicy notes. Still a bit coarse, but short-term cellaring should soften it. 19,000 cases made. • $16 • (06/30/94) • **87**

Chardonnay Carneros Reserve 1993: Firm and intense, boasting rich, full-bodied honey, pear, toast and grapefruit flavors that are well focused and lively through the finish. Given its intensity and vibrancy, some aging should make it even smoother. 3,650 cases made. • $25 • (04/30/96) • **90**

Chardonnay Carneros Reserve 1992: Crisp and flinty, displaying tart citrus, pear, apple and pineapple flavors that are tightly reined in. Acacia's first Reserve. 5,171 cases made. • $22 • (05/15/95) • **89**

Chardonnay Napa Valley 1991 • $11 • (03/15/93) • **85**

Chardonnay Napa Valley Carneros 1991 • $17 • (03/15/93) • **83**

Chardonnay Napa Valley Carneros Marina Vineyard 1991 • $20 • (08/31/93) • **89**

Merlot Napa Valley 1984 • $15 • (02/28/87) • **83**

Pinot Noir Carneros 1994: Supple, harmonious young red sporting ripe cherry, cedar, spice and plum flavors and smooth, polished texture. Elegant and refined. 13,400 cases made. • $18 • (04/30/96) • **89**

Pinot Noir Carneros 1993: A touch earthy, with lightly oaked, modest berry and cherry flavors that pick up a green, tannic feel on the finish. 12,200 cases made. • $15 • (06/30/95) • **83**

Pinot Noir Carneros Reserve 1993: Firm and well focused, featuring pretty cherry, spice, cedar and tea flavors and a tight finish of slightly green tannins, so cellaring into 1997 should help. 2,630 cases made. • $25 • (04/30/96) • **86**

Pinot Noir Napa Valley 1991 • $7 • (02/28/93) • **75**

Pinot Noir Napa Valley Carneros 1991 • $15 • (02/28/94) • **83**

Pinot Noir Napa Valley Carneros 1990 • $15 • (02/28/93) • **80**

Pinot Noir Napa Valley Carneros 1989 • $14 • (11/15/91) • **71**

Pinot Noir Napa Valley Carneros 1988 • $19 • (02/28/91) • **89**

Pinot Noir Napa Valley Carneros 1987 • $18 • (02/15/90) • **87**

Pinot Noir Napa Valley Carneros 1986 • $18 • (06/15/88) • **88**

Pinot Noir Napa Valley Carneros 1985 • $19 • (12/15/87) • **84**

Pinot Noir Napa Valley Carneros 1984 • $20 • (12/15/86) SS • **95**

Pinot Noir Napa Valley Carneros Iund Vineyard 1991 • $21 • (02/28/94) • **82**

Pinot Noir Napa Valley Carneros Iund Vineyard 1984 • $15 • (03/15/87) • **81**

Pinot Noir Napa Valley Carneros Iund Vineyard 1983 • $16 • (08/31/86) • **77**

Pinot Noir Napa Valley Carneros Iund Vineyard 1982 • $31 • (07/16/84) CS • **91**

Pinot Noir Napa Valley Carneros Lee Vineyard 1983 • $20 • (08/31/86) • **89**

Pinot Noir Napa Valley Carneros Lee Vineyard 1982 • $15 • (07/16/84) • **90**

Pinot Noir Napa Valley Carneros Madonna Vineyard 1986 • $25 • (06/15/88) • **88**

Pinot Noir Napa Valley Carneros Madonna Vineyard 1985 • $22 • (12/15/87) • **88**

Pinot Noir Napa Valley Carneros Madonna Vineyard 1984 • $22 • (03/15/87) • **88**

Pinot Noir Napa Valley Carneros Madonna Vineyard 1983 • $22 • (08/31/86) • **93**

Pinot Noir Napa Valley Carneros St. Clair Vineyard 1991 • $25 • (02/28/94) • **83**

Pinot Noir Napa Valley Carneros St. Clair Vineyard 1990 • $21 • (02/28/93) • **84**

Pinot Noir Napa Valley Carneros St. Clair Vineyard 1989 • $21 • (10/31/91) • **86**

Pinot Noir Napa Valley Carneros St. Clair Vineyard 1988 • $20 • (02/28/91) • **91**

Pinot Noir Napa Valley Carneros St. Clair Vineyard 1987 • $22 • (02/15/90) • **89**

Pinot Noir Napa Valley Carneros St. Clair Vineyard 1986 • $25 • (06/15/88) • **91**

Pinot Noir Napa Valley Carneros St. Clair Vineyard 1985 • $23 • (12/15/87) • **91**

Pinot Noir Napa Valley Carneros St. Clair Vineyard 1984 • $28 • (11/30/86) • **93**

Pinot Noir Napa Valley Carneros St. Clair Vineyard 1983 • $30 • (10/01/85) CS • **95**

Pinot Noir Napa Valley Carneros St. Clair Vineyard 1982 • $25 • (07/16/84) • **89**

Pinot Noir Napa Valley Carneros St. Clair Vineyard Reserve 1992: Firm and a touch tannic, but the core of ripe cherry, berry and toasty oak fold together nicely on the finish. Try now. 1,800 cases made. • $25 • (06/30/95) • **87**

Pinot Noir Napa Valley Carneros Winery Lake Vineyard 1983 • $15 • (11/16/85) • **78**

Pinot Noir Napa Valley Carneros Winery Lake Vineyard 1982 • $15 • (07/16/84) • **90**

Zinfandel Napa Valley Caviste 1992: Captures the essence of Zin with its bright wild berry and cherry notes, fine balance and long, fruity aftertaste. Drinks well now, tasted twice. 1,985 cases made. • $11 • (10/15/94) • **85**

Zinfandel Napa Valley Caviste 1991 • $12 • (09/30/93) • **87**

Zinfandel Napa Valley Caviste 1990 • $12 • (10/15/92) • **86**

Zinfandel Napa Valley Old Vines 1993: Appealingly ripe, supple and complex with its berry, cherry, spice and light oak shadings. Well mannered and the tannins are soft. 2,000 cases made. • $10 • (10/15/95) • **85**

ADELAIDA | CALIFORNIA

Cabernet Sauvignon Paso Robles 1988 • $15 • (11/15/92) • **87**

Cabernet Sauvignon Paso Robles 1987 • $14 • (02/28/91) • **89**

Cabernet Sauvignon Paso Robles 1983 • $12 • (12/15/89) • **75**

Cabernet Sauvignon Paso Robles 1981 • $7 • (03/01/84) • **88**

Cabernet Sauvignon San Luis Obispo County 1990: A solid red wine with a vegetal edge to the modest Cabernet fruit, firm and tannic enough to want until 1998. 1,682 cases made. • $22 • (11/15/93) • **81**

Chardonnay San Luis Obispo County 1991 • $18 • (07/15/93) • **88**

Chardonnay San Luis Obispo Reserve 1991: Serves up rich and complex honey, pear and butterscotch flavors, with hints of nutmeg, vanilla and spice. A big, full-blown style that packs in lots of flavor, could use a little more finesse. 1,300 cases made. • $28 • (06/30/94) • **87**

Sangiovese San Luis Obispo County 1993: Smooth and creamy, toasty buttery oak flavors leading to a tight core of cranberry and blackberry. Fine-tuned Sangiovese. 284 cases made. • $23 • (04/30/96) • **87**

Zinfandel Late Harvest Paso Robles 1992: Dark, ripe, intense and hot, a big mouthful of late-harvest Zinfandel for those who yearn for the days of yesteryear. Despite its size, it manages to maintain balance. 615 cases made. • $18 • (04/30/96) • **84**

Zinfandel Paso Robles 1989 • $12 • (10/15/92) • **83**

Zinfandel Paso Robles 1988 • $12 • (04/30/91) • **88**

Zinfandel San Luis Obispo County 1992: Big, intense and hot, but food will take the edge off the jammy berry and cherry flavors. Fans of late-harvest Zin will find the ripeness of the grapes appealing, in the 16 percent alcohol range. 1,079 cases made. • $16 • (04/30/96) • **87**

Zinfandel San Luis Obispo County 1991: An oaky style, with lots of toast and butter flavors and a firm tannic edge, but the ripe cherry, tar and plum peek through on the finish. Drinkable now. 1,088 cases made. • $14 • (10/15/94) • **87**

Zinfandel San Luis Obispo County 1990 • $13 • (09/30/93) • **82**

ADLER FELS | CALIFORNIA

Cabernet Sauvignon Napa Valley 1980 • $10 • (10/01/84) • **74**

Chardonnay Sonoma County 1993: Bold, ripe and complex flavors of pear, apple and honey with buttery tones. The fruit holds on through a long, concentrated finish. One of the best Chardonnays ever from this winery. 2,110 cases made. • $12 • (03/31/96) • **91**

Chardonnay Sonoma County 1992: Marked by a strong muscat and spice edge, but it holds together with ripe pear and light oak shadings. 1,700 cases made. • $12 • (07/31/95) • **84**

Chardonnay Sonoma County Coleman Reserve 1993: Shows mature flavors, a slightly metallic note mingling with the oaky pear and spice flavors. Not as complex and openly fruity as the regular bottling. 969 cases made. • $14 • (03/31/96) • **84**

Chardonnay Sonoma County Coleman Reserve 1992: Earthy with a slight bitter oak edge which detracts from the ripe fruit flavors. 2,000 cases made. • $14 • (07/31/95) • **81**

Chardonnay Sonoma County Coleman Reserve 1991 • $12 • (03/31/94) • **86**

Fumé Blanc Sonoma County 1992: So floral it could even pass as a Riesling, an appealing wine with nice fruit, too. Drinkable now. 3,225 cases made. • $9 • (08/31/94) • **83**

Fumé Blanc Sonoma County 1991 • $8 • (09/15/93) • **82**

Gewürztraminer Sonoma County 1993: Lightly sweet, resiny and floral with smooth orange and pear notes. 3,000 cases made. • $9 • (01/31/95) • **80**

Gewürztraminer Sonoma County 1992 • $8 • (01/31/94) • **84**

Gewürztraminer Sonoma County 1991 • $9 • (11/15/92) • **81**

Sparkling Sonoma County Melange à Deux 1985 • $15 • (10/15/87) • **74**

Key: SS—Spectator Selection. CS—Cellar Selection. BB—Best Buy. $NA—Price not available. (BT)—Barrel tasting. (A)—Auction Price.
Dates in parentheses represent the issues in which the ratings were published.

AETNA SPRINGS | CALIFORNIA

Cabernet Sauvignon Napa Valley 1991: Crisp and earthy, offering a few hints of forest floor to go along with the austere toast and berry flavors. Best to drink now. 250 cases made. • $18 • (05/15/94) • **81**

AHERN | CALIFORNIA

Zinfandel Amador County 1980 • $6 • (02/15/84) • **78**

AHLGREN | CALIFORNIA

Cabernet Sauvignon Napa Valley 1978 • $20 • (11/15/92) • **80**

Cabernet Sauvignon Santa Cruz Mountains Bates' Ranch 1988 • $20 • (11/15/92) • **76**

Chardonnay Santa Cruz Mountains Buerge Vineyard 1991: Crisp and earthy, lean with modest peach and mineral flavors. 186 cases made. • $15 • (06/30/94) • **79**

Chardonnay Santa Cruz Mountains Mayers Vineyard 1991: Earthy, mineral aromas and sweet pineapple flavors are a little jarring. 322 cases made. • $15 • (06/30/94) • **73**

ALATERA | CALIFORNIA

Cabernet Sauvignon Napa Valley 1978 • $NA • (11/15/92) • **82**

ALBAN | CALIFORNIA

Grenache Edna Valley 1993: A rare bird, Grenache from Edna Valley, but showing tasty floral, plum, wild berry, mint and spice features. Drinks well now but has enough depth and full-bodied fruit to hold into 1997. 115 cases made. • $28 • (04/30/96) • **86**

Roussanne San Luis Obispo County 1994: Strives for complexity with its bold, ripe, oaky tones, but it's a touch oxidized, offering honey, pear, nut and nectarine notes. Doesn't shortchange you on flavor, yet it comes across as somewhat heavy. 100 cases made. • $32 • (02/29/96) • **85**

Syrah Edna Valley Reva 1993: Leans toward the earthy side of Syrah, with peppery, plummy character, and a dry, tannic finish. A few months aging will help soften it. 950 cases made. • $18 • (06/15/96) • **87**

Viognier Central Coast 1994: Appealing for its zesty flavors, featuring spicy pear and Muscatlike notes which dominate. Comes across as one-dimensional. 750 cases made. • $20 • (02/29/96) • **84**

Viognier Edna Valley Alban Estate Vineyard 1994: Elegant, spicy, oaky edge to ripe pear and apricot flavors, showing pretty floral overtones on the finish. 950 cases made. • $28 • (02/29/96) • **87**

Viognier San Luis Obispo County 1992 • $28 • (09/30/93) • **84**

Viognier San Luis Obispo County 1991 • $28 • (11/30/92) • **86**

ALDERBROOK | CALIFORNIA

Chardonnay Dry Creek Valley 1993: Marked by an herbal edge, with just a hint of pear and spice coming through. • $12 • (07/31/95) • **83**

Chardonnay Dry Creek Valley 1992: Appealing for nectarine and tangerine edge flavors and spicy nuances. • $15 • (07/31/95) • **85**

Duet Dry Creek Valley 1992: Smooth and flavorful, silky at the core and jumping with green berry, citrus and anise flavors. Finishes lively. 1,100 cases made. • $11 • (08/31/95) • **87**

Pinot Noir Russian River Valley 1994: Well oaked and medium-bodied, with tart, ripe plum, cherry and berry flavors and finishing with mild tannins. Appealing now through 1997. 608 cases made. • $15 • (01/31/96) • **87**

Sauvignon Blanc Dry Creek Valley 1994: Plays its lively pear and green apple against a nice thread of spicy oak, weaving touches of herb through it all. 6,658 cases made. • $8 • (08/31/95) • **85**

Sauvignon Blanc Dry Creek Valley 1993: Soft, generous spicy orange and pear flavors. 4,272 cases made. • $8 • (08/31/95) • **82**

Sauvignon Blanc Late Harvest 1989 • $24 • (06/15/92) • **88**

Sémillon Dry Creek Valley 1993: Bright and fruity, a friendly wine with melon and tobacco flavors. 851 cases made. • $8 • (08/31/95) • **83**

Zinfandel Dry Creek Valley 1993: Tight and intense, with sharp, earthy raspberry and currant flavors. A big, rambunctious style that can use some age to soften it. 3,000 cases made. • $14 • (10/15/95) • **85**

ALEXANDER VALLEY FRUIT & TRADING CO. CALIFORNIA

Zinfandel Dry Creek Valley 1992: Lean and tannic, with a narrow band of spicy strawberry flavors, but it's diluted on the finish. 1,000 cases made. • $9 • (10/15/94) • **81**

Zinfandel Late Harvest Alexander Valley 1991: Lightly sweet and brightly fruity, sort of a junior version of a junior port, offering substantial berry and vanilla flavors. Ready now. 1,000 cases made. • $12 • (10/31/95) • **85**

Zinfandel Late Harvest Alexander Valley 1990: Ripe and sweet, with hints of ripe cherry and plum jam flavors. Supple and medium-bodied. 1,000 cases made. • $12 • (10/15/94) • **82**

ALEXANDER VALLEY VINEYARDS CALIFORNIA

Cabernet Sauvignon Alexander Valley 1989 • $13 • (08/31/92) • **87**

Cabernet Sauvignon Alexander Valley 1988 • $17 • (09/30/91) • **88**

Cabernet Sauvignon Alexander Valley 1987 • $17 • (05/31/90) • **87**

Cabernet Sauvignon Alexander Valley 1986 • $18 • (03/01/89) • **88**

Cabernet Sauvignon Alexander Valley 1985 • $18 • (03/01/89) • **88**

Cabernet Sauvignon Alexander Valley 1984 • $21 • (03/01/89) • **92**

Cabernet Sauvignon Alexander Valley 1983 • $22 • (03/01/89) • **90**

Cabernet Sauvignon Alexander Valley 1982 • $23 • (03/01/89) • **90**

Cabernet Sauvignon Alexander Valley 1981 • $22 • (03/01/89) • **87**

Cabernet Sauvignon Alexander Valley 1980 • $20 • (03/01/89) • **83**

Cabernet Sauvignon Alexander Valley 1979 • $20 • (03/01/89) • **86**

Cabernet Sauvignon Alexander Valley 1978 • $28 • (11/15/92) • **78**

Cabernet Sauvignon Alexander Valley 1976 • $18 • (03/01/89) • **60**

Cabernet Sauvignon Alexander Valley 1975 • $22 • (03/01/89) • **75**

Cabernet Sauvignon Alexander Valley Library Reserve 1986 • $18 • (06/15/93) • **80**

Cabernet Sauvignon Alexander Valley Wetzel Family Estate 1994: Serves up lots of flavor and is well oaked at this stage, but the cherry and currant flavors are bright, lively and long on the finish. 14,600 cases made. • $15 • (05/31/95) • **85-89** (BT)

Cabernet Sauvignon Alexander Valley Wetzel Family Estate 1992: Lean and earthy, with a cedar and tobacco edge to the plum and berry notes. Needs short-term cellaring until 1997. 12,700 cases made. • $14 • (05/31/95) • **86**

Cabernet Sauvignon Alexander Valley Wetzel Family Estate 1991: Ripe and fruity with spice, mint, cherry and currant flavors that are appealing to drink now. 9,000 cases made. • $13 • (11/15/93) • **84**

Cabernet Sauvignon Alexander Valley Wetzel Family Estate 1990: Smooth and supple, with a tinge of bell pepper and herb to add depth to the currant and plum aromas and flavors, supple and round on the finish. Should be best now to 1998. Tasted twice. • $14 • (06/15/93) • **88**

Chardonnay Alexander Valley Wetzel Family Estate 1992: Pleasanty fruity, sporting tart green apple and subtle grassy notes. 4,800 cases made. • $11 • (05/15/95) • **84**

Chardonnay Alexander Valley Wetzel Family Estate 1991 • $10 • (06/30/93) • **88**

Gewürztraminer Alexander Valley 1992 • $8 • (01/31/93) • **80**

Gewürztraminer Alexander Valley 1991 • $8 • (11/30/92) • **75**

Johannisberg Riesling 1991 • $8 • (05/31/92) • **86**

Merlot Alexander Valley 1990 • $13 • (03/31/93) • **87**

Merlot Alexander Valley 1989 • $13 • (11/15/91) • **84**

Merlot Alexander Valley 1985 • $11 • (10/31/87) • **88**

Merlot Alexander Valley Wetzel Family Estate 1993: Simple but clean and correct, with a crisp band of plum and cherry that have some depth. 8,500 cases made. • $15 • (05/15/96) • **83**

Merlot Alexander Valley Wetzel Family Estate 1992: Dark, tight and compact, with a firm core of currant, cedar and tobacco. Needs time to soften a bit and let the tannins subside. 9,500 cases made. • $15 • (07/31/95) • **86**

Merlot Alexander Valley Wetzel Family Estate 1991: Earthy, mulchy flavors take some of the charm out of this sturdy, chunky Merlot. Drinkable now. 8,000 cases made. • $14 • (09/15/94) • **77**

Pinot Noir Alexander Valley 1989 • $10 • (10/31/91) • **65**

Pinot Noir Alexander Valley 1987 • $9 • (05/31/90) • **74**

Pinot Noir Alexander Valley 1985 • $8 • (04/15/88) • **81**

Pinot Noir Alexander Valley 1984 • $7 • (02/15/88) • **87**

Pinot Noir Alexander Valley 1982 • $6 • (11/01/84) • **75**

Pinot Noir Alexander Valley Wetzel Family Estate 1990 • $11 • (02/28/94) • **83**

Zinfandel Alexander Valley 1987 • $9 • (03/31/90) • **82**

Zinfandel Alexander Valley Sin Zin 1993: An odd wine: earthy and tarry, with some ripe plum and raisin flavors. It lacks focus and comes across as clumsy. 1,441 cases made. • $13 • (10/15/95) • **78**

Zinfandel Alexander Valley Sin Zin 1989 • $11 • (10/15/92) • **76**

ALISON, ROBERT | CALIFORNIA

Cabernet Sauvignon California 1993: A strong tobacco flavor runs through the light currant flavors in this soft-textured red. • $6 • (12/15/95) • **81**

Cabernet Sauvignon California 1989 • $5 • (11/15/92) • **78**

Chardonnay California 1994: Soft, almost sweet, with a pleasant note of peach flavor ringing through. Ready now. • $6 • (12/31/95) • **82**

ALMADEN | CALIFORNIA

Cabernet Sauvignon Monterey County 1981 • $5 • (07/01/84) • **80**

Cabernet Sauvignon Monterey County Vintage Classic Selection 1983 • $5 • (10/15/87) • **74**

Pinot Noir San Benito County 1982 • $5 • (06/30/87) • **69**

Premium California 1982 • $7 • (12/31/86) • **79**

ALPEN | CALIFORNIA

Chardonnay Trinity County 1994: Soft in texture, with vanilla aromas and a modest level of pear, spice and toast flavors. Appealing now. 735 cases made. • $7 • (06/15/96) • **82**

ALTAMURA | CALIFORNIA

Cabernet Sauvignon Napa Valley 1992: Dark and complex, with spicy currant, plum and chocolate-cherry flavors that run deep and full into the finish, where it picks up a mineral edge. 1,000 cases made. • $28 • **92**

Cabernet Sauvignon Napa Valley 1991: Full-bodied, with a modest core of ripe cherry and plum flavors, but it loses it focus and intensity on the finish. 1,000 cases made. • $25 • (05/31/96) • **88**

Cabernet Sauvignon Napa Valley 1990: Showy, elegant, ripe, smooth, supple black cherry, currant and vanilla-tinged oak shadings, finishing with mild, polished tannins. Appealing already. 800 cases made. • $25 • (09/15/95) • **88**

Cabernet Sauvignon Napa Valley 1988 • $18 • (11/15/92) • **85**

Sangiovese Napa Valley 1993: Complex, broad array of stewed plum, tar, coffee, mineral and blackberry flavors. Shows a smooth, supple texture and finishes with firm tannins, but the fruit shines through. Impressive. Drinkable now or can age short-term. 800 cases made. • $18 • (04/30/96) • **90**

AMADOR FOOTHILL | CALIFORNIA

Fumé Blanc Shenandoah Valley Amador Fumé 1992: Crisp and refreshing, a solid wine with an earthy edge to the decent pear fruit. 2,300 cases made. • $8 • (08/31/94) • **82**

Sangiovese Shenandoah Valley Festa Dell'Uva 1993: Very light and simple, smooth-textured, offering modest berry and leather flavors. 945 cases made. • $12 • (11/30/95) • **80**

Sangiovese Shenandoah Valley Festa Dell'Uva 1992: Light and softly spicy, a simple with modest currant fruit. Drinkable now. • $12 • (09/15/94) • **79**

Sémillon Shenandoah Valley 1993: Soft, floral, edging toward sour on the finish. 265 cases made. • $9 • (05/31/96) • **76**

Zinfandel Fiddletown Eschen Vineyard 1991: Solid if rustic, with earthy wild berry and spice notes, but lacking polish. Ready now. 674 cases made. • $10 • (10/15/94) • **78**
Zinfandel Fiddletown Eschen Vineyard 1990 • $10 • (09/30/93) • **82**
Zinfandel Fiddletown Eschen Vineyard 1988 • $10 • (10/15/92) • **73**
Zinfandel Fiddletown Eschen Vineyard 1986 • $9 • (06/15/89) • **82**
Zinfandel Fiddletown Eschen Vineyard 1984 • $9 • (10/15/88) • **86**
Zinfandel Fiddletown Eschen Vineyard Special Selection 1982 • $9 • (04/15/87) • **74**
Zinfandel Shenandoah Valley Ferrero Vineyard 1991: Crisp but earthy, the cherry, raspberry are lightly shaded by oak, though it's showing more mature flavors at this stage than expected. 1,003 cases made. • $10 • (10/15/95) • **83**
Zinfandel Shenandoah Valley Ferrero Vineyard 1990 • $10 • (09/30/93) • **82**
Zinfandel Shenandoah Valley Ferrero Vineyard Special Selection 1989 • $10 • (03/31/92) • **81**
Zinfandel Shenandoah Valley Grand-Père Vineyard 1990 • $10 • (09/30/93) • **83**
Zinfandel Shenandoah Valley Grand-Père Vineyard 1989 • $10 • (10/15/92) • **79**
Zinfandel Shenandoah Valley Grand-Père Vineyard Special Selection 1988 • $10 • (08/31/91) • **75**

AMIZETTA | CALIFORNIA

Cabernet Sauvignon Napa Valley 1985 • $16 • (05/31/88) • **70**

ANCIEN | CALIFORNIA

Pinot Noir Carneros 1993: Complex and quite earthy, sporting a dry, tannic edge and some intriguing touches of ripe plum, cherry and forest floor. Dry, leathery tannins on aftertaste, can stand short-term cellaring into 1997. 192 cases made. • $18 • (04/30/96) • **87**

ANDERSON, S. | CALIFORNIA

Blanc de Noirs Napa Valley 1991: Attractive, ripe, complex pear, spice, hazelnut and nutmeg notes turn smooth and polished on the finish, where flavors linger on. 2,200 cases made. • $23 • (12/31/95) • **88**
Blanc de Noirs Napa Valley 1990: Smooth, creamy and complex with vanilla, pear and nutmeg flavors that are rich, deep and focused. Finishes with a long, full aftertaste that echoes vanilla and pear flavors. 1,800 cases made. • $20 • (11/30/94) SS • **90**
Blanc de Noirs Napa Valley 1989 • $20 • (12/31/93) • **86**
Blanc de Noirs Napa Valley 1988 • $20 • (12/31/92) • **87**
Blanc de Noirs Napa Valley 1987 • $19 • (06/15/91) • **86**
Blanc de Noirs Napa Valley 1986 • $20 • (12/31/90) • **83**
Blanc de Noirs Napa Valley 1985 • $16 • (05/31/89) • **87**
Blanc de Noirs Napa Valley 1984 • $16 • (10/15/88) • **79**
Blanc de Noirs Napa Valley 1983 • $28 • (05/31/89) • **85**
Blanc de Noirs Napa Valley Tivoli Brut Noir NV • $12 • (06/15/91) • **73**
Brut Napa Valley 1990: Marked by ripe pear, ginger and spice notes, the emphasis being on fruitiness, and in that regard it succeeds. Finishes with a good dose of pear and spice. 2,200 cases made. • $23 • (11/30/95) • **88**
Brut Napa Valley 1989: Fresh and aromatic, with pretty pear, spice and vanilla flavors that turn smooth and creamy, finishing with a yeasty edge that adds complexity. 2,200 cases made. • $18 • (11/30/94) • **89**
Brut Napa Valley 1987 • $18 • (12/31/93) • **86**
Brut Napa Valley 1986 • $18 • (12/15/91) • **86**
Brut Napa Valley 1985 • $18 • (06/15/91) • **87**
Brut Napa Valley 1984 • $18 • (10/15/88) • **82**
Brut Napa Valley 1983 • $16 • (05/31/87) • **72**
Cabernet Sauvignon Stags Leap District Richard Chambers Vineyard 1992: Strikes a nice balance with rich, earthy currant and cherry flavors, framed by a nice toasty oak edge. A touch of leather sneaks through on the finish. Has the tannins to age into 1999. 900 cases made. • $46 • (12/15/95) • **89**
Cabernet Sauvignon Stags Leap District Richard Chambers Vineyard 1991: Young and tight, with a ripe, supple band of spicy black cherry, herb and currant flavors. Firms up on the finish, where the tannins are more evident. Another impressive Cabernet from this California vineyard. Best starting in 1997. 600 cases made. • $46 • (12/31/94) • **91**
Cabernet Sauvignon Stags Leap District Richard Chambers Vineyard 1990: Smooth, ripe and polished, laced with sweet, buttery oak, bursting with ripe currant and plum aromas and flavors, finishing spicy and silky. Beautifully made, elegant and flavorful. Drinkable now for its suppleness, but could improve through 1997. 600 cases made. • $42 • (11/15/93) • **90**
Cabernet Sauvignon Stags Leap District Richard Chambers Vineyard 1989 • $36 • (11/15/92) • **90**
Chardonnay Napa Valley Carneros 1994: Marked by strong citrus and spice character, just enough pear and apple notes coming through to make it interesting. Lacks the extra dimensions hoped for. 1,250 cases made. • $18 • (05/15/96) • **86**
Chardonnay Napa Valley Carneros 1993: Young and vibrant, sporting a citrus-grapefruit edge to the pear and spice flavors. 1,200 cases made. • $18 • (04/30/95) • **86**
Chardonnay Stags Leap District 1994: Trim and well balanced, as pleasant spice, vanilla and pear flavors fan out on the finish, delivering a measure of harmony and finesse. This has a reputation for gaining in the bottle. 1,350 cases made. • $20 • (04/30/96) • **90**
Chardonnay Stags Leap District 1992: Lean and firm, with a coarse, earthy edge to the ripe pear and pineapple flavors. Can stand short-term cellaring, which should allow it to show more complexity and finesse. 1,750 cases made. • $20 • (06/30/94) • **85**
Chardonnay Stags Leap District 1991 • $18 • (07/15/93) • **85**
Chardonnay Stags Leap District Proprietor's Reserve 1991 • $25 • (07/15/93) • **89**
Rosé Napa Valley 1991: Ripe and fruity, the appealing dried cherry, earth, spice and vanilla flavors folding together well on aftertaste. 340 cases made. • $25 • (12/31/95) • **86**

ANDERSON VALLEY | NEW MEXICO

Cabernet Sauvignon New Mexico 1986 • $11 • (07/31/89) • **80**
Cabernet Sauvignon New Mexico Reserve 1987 • $14 • (02/29/92) • **84**

ANDERSON'S CONN VALLEY | CALIFORNIA

Cabernet Sauvignon Napa Valley Estate Reserve 1992: A beautifully crafted red with rich, complex cherry, plum, wild berry, anise, toast and vanilla notes that turn harmonious and supple on the finish, where the tannins are smooth. Better from 1999 on. 4,243 cases made. • $30 • (11/15/95) • **93**
Cabernet Sauvignon Napa Valley Estate Reserve 1991: This has an earthy, leathery edge to the currant and cherry flavor, but it turns supple and elegant on the finish. Best to cellar until 1999. Tasted twice. 4,088 cases made. • $30 • (11/15/94) • **88**
Cabernet Sauvignon Napa Valley Estate Reserve 1990: Firm and intense with rich, chewy, concentrated currant, chocolate and buttery oak flavors. Packs in lots of flavor and reveals a complex aftertaste of ripe Cabernet fruit and mineral notes. Needs until 1997 to soften. 4,020 cases made. • $25 • (11/15/93) • **90**
Cabernet Sauvignon Napa Valley Estate Reserve 1989 • $25 • (11/15/92) • **88**
Cabernet Sauvignon Napa Valley Estate Reserve 1988 • $24 • (11/15/91) • **92**
Pinot Noir Napa Valley 1992: Smoky and meaty, with spicy, peppery, herbal accents to ripe plum and cherry flavors. Mild tannins, ready now. Tasted twice, with consistent notes. 328 cases made. • $25 • (03/31/95) • **85**
Pinot Noir Napa Valley Valhalla Vineyards 1993: Somewhat earthy in aroma, but enough concentration and depth to hold your interest. Meaty, beefy, dried cherry finish and dry tannins. Cellar into 1997 for best results. 110 cases made. • $40 • (04/30/96) • **86**
Pinot Noir Napa Valley Valhalla Vineyards 1989 • $25 • (02/28/93) • **84**

Key: SS—Spectator Selection. CS—Cellar Selection. BB—Best Buy. $NA—Price not available. (BT)—Barrel tasting. Ⓐ—Auction Price.
Dates in parentheses represent the issues in which the ratings were published.

ANDREW WILL | WASHINGTON

Cabernet Sauvignon Washington 1992: Tart and tannic up front, with the appealing cherry and currant notes built on a tight framework. 400 cases made. • $21 • (05/31/95) • **88**

Cabernet Sauvignon Washington 1991: Austere and tight, but there's enough currant and cherry flavor coming through to hold your attention. Finishes with a gritty tannic edge. Hold until 1997 or 1998. 140 cases made. • $20 • (09/30/94) • **85**

Cabernet Sauvignon Washington Reserve 1991: Firm and ripe, tucking in a lot of flavor between the tannins, echoing ripe blackberry and black cherry notes on the finish. Has enough intensity to need until 1997 to 1999 to settle down. 100 cases made. • $22 • (09/30/94) • **88**

Chenin Blanc Washington Cuvée Lu Lu 1993: Lean and somewhat bitter, trying to resemble Coulée de Serrant, but a sour edge detracts from any charm. 125 cases made. • $10 • (09/30/95) • **73**

Merlot Washington 1993: Ripe, generous currant and black cherry flavors, echoing vanilla and currant on the wide-open finish. Beautifully built and artfully made. Tasted twice, with consistent notes. 600 cases made. • $21 • (06/15/95) • **89**

Merlot Washington 1992: Rich and ripe, packed with focused blackberry, currant and spice aromas and flavors, a little chewy, but give it until 1997 to absorb the tannins. Solidly built, but you could drink it now with hearty food. 520 cases made. • $19 • (09/30/94) • **90**

Merlot Washington Ciel du Cheval 1993: Strives for complexity with its core of cherry, wild berry and spicy oak flavors. Turns smooth at mid-palate, then more substantial tannins emerge. 100 cases made. • $25 • (08/31/95) • **89**

Merlot Washington Pepperbridge 1993: Medium body, has a disjointed core of cedary oak, but nice wild berry and spice flavors. Finishes with chewy tannins. Try in 1997. 100 cases made. • $25 • (08/31/95) • **86**

Merlot Washington Reserve 1993: Lean and earthy, showing stalky green bean and blackberry flavors and a tough, tannic finish. Best in 1997. 200 cases made. • $28 • (09/30/95) • **84**

Merlot Washington Sunshine 1991: Bright and supple, a polished and lively Merlot that pours out its currant, black cherry and minty-cedary flavors in a smooth stream. Finishes elegant and flavorful, drinkable now, best through 1997. 350 cases made. • $19 • (09/30/94) • **89**

Merlot Washington Sunshine Reserve 1992: Sharp and smoky, lean and zingy, starts off with a mouthful of berry and black cherry flavor but fades a little on the finish. Drinkable now. 180 cases made. • $21 • (09/30/94) • **82**

Merlot Washington Sunshine Reserve 1991: Bright and spicy, youthful and exuberant, balances its ripe berry and red cherry flavors against a chorus of spicy oak and delicate herbal overtones. Easy to appreciate now for its freshness. Drinkable now. 150 cases made. • $21 • (09/30/94) • **88**

ANGELINE | CALIFORNIA

Zinfandel California Old Vine Cuvée 1992: Notes of earth, tar and berry accompany chewy tannins, finishing leathery. Has lots of flavor but rustic. 6,000 cases made. • $8 • (10/15/95) • **83**

ANGELS CREEK | CALIFORNIA

Merlot California 1989 • $9 • (05/31/92) • **71**

ANNAPOLIS | CALIFORNIA

Sauvignon Blanc Sonoma Coast Reserve Scalabrini Vineyards 1992: Extremely dark in color and exceedingly floral in flavor. 230 cases made. • $9 • (08/31/94) • **77**

ANTELOPE VALLEY | CALIFORNIA

Merlot California Bien Nacido Vineyards 1990: Earthy, gamy flavors predominate in this supple wine. 500 cases made. • $9 • (09/15/94) • **79**

APEX | WASHINGTON

Cabernet Sauvignon Columbia Valley 1990: Elegant and refined, displaying focused cherry, currant, cedar and buttery oak notes that are intense and concentrated, finishes with a pretty array of complex flavors and fine tannins. Impeccably well balanced, drink now through 2000. 490 cases made. • $18 • (10/15/93) • **88**

Chardonnay Yakima Valley 1993: Buttery, pleasant-tasting Chardonnay offering modest flavors and a spicy finish. 582 cases made. • $16 • (09/30/95) • **82**

Chardonnay Yakima Valley 1991: Earthy, lively and spicy, a distinctive Chardonnay that comes up a little short on fruit but otherwise has appealing character. 860 cases made. • $15 • (09/30/94) • **82**

Gewürztraminer Yakima Valley Barrel Fermented 1993: Nicely balanced between floral, rose petal and toasty apple flavors. Distinctive and full of character, if ever so slightly bitter. Ready now. 176 cases made. • $13 • (09/30/95) • **85**

Gewürztraminer Yakima Valley Barrel Fermented 1992: A bizarre example of a white whose floral character clashes with the toasty oak. Doesn't work for us. 258 cases made. • $16 • (09/30/94) • **74**

Gewürztraminer Yakima Valley Ice Wine 1991: Spice and piney aromas are appealing and carry through on the palate, but there's not much else to back them up. It's modestly sweet, light-bodied and simple. 2,500 cases made. • $14 • (04/15/95) • **77**

Gewüztraminer Late Harvest Yakima Valley Ice Wine 1991: The floral, rose petal-like flavors come through in spades in this sweet but well-balanced dessert wine. Drinkable now, but worth waiting until 1997 to see what develops. 150 cases made. • $16 • (09/30/94) • **86**

Merlot Columbia Valley 1990 • $15 • (09/30/93) • **84**

Merlot Yakima Valley 1992: Appealing for its pure fruit flavors, supple texture and elegant berry and chocolate notes. Approachable now, best in 1996. 834 cases made. • $18 • (09/30/95) • **87**

Merlot Yakima Valley 1989 • $17 • (03/15/93) • **83**

ARAUJO | CALIFORNIA

Cabernet Sauvignon Napa Valley Eisele Vineyard 1992: A classic California Cabernet that is well oaked, with distinct vanilla bean and toasty oak accents, but it also shows compelling cherry and berry flavors that develop complex nuances. The fruit shows a remarkable measure of finesse and harmony on the finish. 810 cases made. • $40 • (11/15/95) CS • **96**

Cabernet Sauvignon Napa Valley Eisele Vineyard 1991: Remarkably dark and intense, with a solid core of rich currant, plum and black cherry flavors that are framed by toasty, buttery oak. Holds together extremely well. The fruit flavors are powerful and compact, flowing right through the long finish. Tannins are firm and dry, best to cellar through 1997 or 1998. 860 cases made. • $40 • (10/15/94) CS • **90**

ARBOR CREST | WASHINGTON

Brut Washington 1990: A spicy, exotic style, with a Muscat-like edge, but if you don't like that one flavor it will wear you out. Turns flat on the finish. 238 cases made. • $13 • (12/31/94) • **80**

Cabernet Franc Columbia Valley 1993: A bright and fruity, airy texture allows the berry flavors to float through. Could stand a little more concentration. Ready now. • $12 • (04/30/95) • **82**

Cabernet Merlot Columbia Valley 1993: Ripe, broad and spicy. A mouthful of plum, cherry and toasty oak keeps singing in harmony through the finish. Needs time to soften the tannins, try in 1998. • $12 • (07/31/95) • **88**

Cabernet Merlot Columbia Valley 1992: Supple and plush, rolls smoothly across the palate, leaving a trail of berry, chocolate, black cherry, mint and cedar. Immensely appealing already. 1,100 cases made. • $11 • (08/31/94) • **89**

Cabernet Sauvignon Columbia Valley 1988 • $11 • (09/30/91) • **87**

Cabernet Sauvignon Columbia Valley Bacchus Vineyard 1985 • $11 • (10/15/89) • **80**

Cabernet Sauvignon Columbia Valley Bacchus Vineyard 1983 • $13 • (12/15/87) • **77**

Cabernet Sauvignon Columbia Valley Dionysus Vineyard Block Sixteen 1991: Elegant and spicy, with pretty vanilla and berry flavors that hang with you. Drinks well now through 1998. 887 cases made. • $11 • (03/15/94) • **83**

Chardonnay Columbia Valley Cameo Reserve 1993: Brightly fruity and distinctly spicy, fresh and lively, but rounded off by a nice tang of smoky oak. 660 cases made. • $9 • (04/30/95) • **86**

Johannisberg Riesling Columbia Valley Dionysus Vineyard 1992: Light, fruity and a little bit sweet, showing mostly fresh grapefruit and pear aromas and flavors. 2,900 cases made. • $5 • (09/30/94) • **80**

Johannisberg Riesling Late Harvest Columbia Valley Select 1994: Sweet, simple and marked by a whiff of pine needle through the peach-centered finish. 396 cases made. • $9 • (09/15/95) • **82**

Merlot Columbia Valley 1991 • $10 • (06/15/93) • **85**

Merlot Columbia Valley 1990 • $12 • (04/15/92) • **88**

Merlot Columbia Valley 1988 • $9 • (08/31/91) • **81**

Merlot Columbia Valley 1987 • $8 • (10/15/89) • **83**

Merlot Columbia Valley Bacchus Vineyard 1985 • $8 • (07/31/87) • **75**

Merlot Columbia Valley Bacchus Vineyard 1982 • $8 • (11/01/84) • **82**

Merlot Columbia Valley Bacchus Vineyard Cameo Reserve 1985 • $10 • (12/15/87) • **83**

Merlot Columbia Valley Cameo Reserve 1992: Firm in texture, fruity in flavor, weaving some spicy oak through the generous berry and plum flavors. Approachable now, better in 1996. 600 cases made. • $13 • (08/31/95) • **88**

Merlot Columbia Valley Cameo Reserve 1991: Crisp in texture but generous in flavor, brimming with black cherry and currant notes plus a nice hint of cedar and a touch of tannin on the finish. Drinkable now. 300 cases made. • $13 • (09/30/94) • **86**

Merlot Columbia Valley Cameo Reserve 1989 • $12 • (03/31/92) • **77**

Merlot Columbia Valley Cameo Reserve 1988 • $12 • (08/31/91) • **83**

Merlot Columbia Valley Cameo Reserve 1987 • $11 • (06/15/90) • **85**

Merlot Columbia Valley Rosebud Vineyard Cameo Reserve 1990 • $14 • (01/31/93) • **86**

Muscat Canelli Columbia Valley 1994: A frankly sweet dessert wine with rich pear, litchi and gentle spice flavors. Drink while it's still fresh. 1,513 cases made. • $6 • (08/31/95) • **85**

Riesling Columbia Valley Dry Dionysus Vineyard 1993: Light and piney, on the dry side, with just enough green apple flavor to keep it in balance. 1,300 cases made. • $5 • (09/30/94) • **83**

Sauvignon Blanc Columbia Valley Bacchus Vineyard 1994: Light, simple and slightly floral. 4,373 cases made. • $7 • (09/30/95) • **79**

Sauvignon Blanc Columbia Valley Bacchus Vineyard 1993: Bright and fruity, a simple wine with appealing pear and grapefruit flavors that echo on the finish. 6,000 cases made. • $7 • (07/31/94) • **85**

Sauvignon Blanc Columbia Valley Bacchus Vineyard 1992 • $7 • (07/31/93) BB • **85**

Sauvignon Blanc Columbia Valley Cameo Reserve 1994: Spicy pear and floral flavors are bright, fruity and refreshing, lingering finish. 431 cases made. • $9 • (09/15/95) • **86**

Sémillon Columbia Valley Dionysus Vineyard 1994: Light, crisp and a little floral, turning toward apple and spice onthe finish. • $6 • (07/31/95) • **84**

Sémillon Columbia Valley Dionysus Vineyard 1993: Lean and austere at first, a bit earthy, but bright enough to balance with some pear and honey notes. Finishes a little sweet. 550 cases made. • $6 • (09/30/94) • **85**

Sémillon Columbia Valley Dionysus Vineyard 1992 • $6 • (09/30/93) BB • **83**

Sémillon Columbia Valley Dionysus Vineyard 1991 • $7 • (11/30/92) • **79**

ARCIERO | CALIFORNIA

Cabernet Sauvignon Paso Robles 1992: Light and silky behind the chewy tannins, showing appealing raspberry and toasty flavors on a modest scale. Best after 1998-1999. 1,090 cases made. • $9 • (12/15/95) • **82**

Cabernet Sauvignon Paso Robles 1991: A bizarre wine, earthy and funky, with a tanky, barnyardy edge to the flavors. Misses the mark with pungent celery, vegetal flavors. 1,410 cases made. • $9 • (12/15/95) • **72**

Cabernet Sauvignon Paso Robles 1990: Lightly fruity but with surprisingly big, dry tannins that dominate. Has a hollowness in the middle. 3,150 cases made. • $7 • (11/15/94) • **78**

Cabernet Sauvignon Paso Robles 1989 • $NA • (11/15/93) • **79**

Cabernet Sauvignon Paso Robles 1987 • $8 • (11/15/92) • **81**

Cabernet Sauvignon Paso Robles 1986 • $8 • (11/15/90) • **80**

Cabernet Sauvignon Paso Robles 1985 • $6 • (12/31/87) • **77**

Cabernet Sauvignon Paso Robles Reserve 1990: Has a sour edge to the basic generic berry flavors, finishing crisp. 175 cases made. • $14 • (12/15/95) • **78**

Chardonnay Paso Robles 1994: Ripe and generous with its spicy, citrusy pear and apple flavors that are focused and precise. The soft, round structure and reasonable price tag on this California white add to the appeal. 5,500 cases made. • $9 • (06/15/96) BB • **86**

Chardonnay Paso Robles 1993: Has spicy, racy aromas but surprisingly tart and unyielding in flavor. Drinkable now. 8,200 cases made. • $9 • (12/31/95) • **81**

Chardonnay Paso Robles 1992: Crisp and flinty, with simple citrus and pineapple flavors. Ready now. 5,000 cases made. • $8 • (06/30/94) • **79**

Chardonnay Paso Robles 1991 • $8 • (05/31/93) • **86**

Merlot Paso Robles 1993: Marked by a distinctive note of dill and green olive, though it manages to pull out enough currant and berry flavors to keep itself in balance. 2,440 cases made. • $12 • (03/31/96) • **82**

Muscat Canelli Paso Robles 1994: Light, soft and decidely floral, sporting a peppery edge to the modest pear flavor. 2,400 cases made. • $6 • (11/30/95) • **81**

Nebbiolo Paso Robles 1991: Soft, simple and fruity. An easy-going red that bears little resemblance to an Italian Nebbiolo. 3,500 cases made. • $11 • (09/30/94) • **79**

Petite Sirah Paso Robles 1989 • $8 • (06/15/93) • **81**

Sauvignon Blanc Paso Robles 1994: Soft and generous with its passion fruit, peach and pear flavors, smooth and appealing to drink now. 1,500 cases made. • $6 • (05/31/96) • **87**

Sauvignon Blanc Paso Robles 1993: Soft, vegetal flavors running through the modest fruit. 1,660 cases made. • $7 • (08/31/95) • **77**

White Riesling Late Harvest Santa Barbara County December Harvest 1985 • $11 • (12/15/89) • **84**

Zinfandel Paso Robles 1992: Has intense, jammy aromas, but not too rich on the palate, where pleasant, earthy wild berry flavors dominate. 810 cases made. • $7 • (10/15/95) • **83**

Zinfandel Paso Robles 1988 • $7 • (10/15/92) • **77**

Zinfandel Paso Robles 1985 • $7 • (12/15/89) • **78**

ARIES | CALIFORNIA

Pinot Noir Los Carneros 1994: Marked by spicy, toasty oak and a supple core of cherry and wild berry flavor. Very appealing, ready-to-drink-now style, appealing price, too. 6,800 cases made. • $10 • (01/31/96) BB • **86**

Pinot Noir Los Carneros 1992 • $10 • (02/28/94) BB • **85**

Pinot Noir Los Carneros Cuvée Vivace 1989 • $8 • (04/30/91) • **70**

ARMAGAN | CALIFORNIA

Brut California NV • $13 • (12/31/93) • **85**

ARMIDA | CALIFORNIA

Chardonnay Russian River Valley 1992: Relies a little too heavily on coarse oak flavor for its personality, overshadowing the pear and nectarine flavors. Can stand short-term cellaring. 3,000 cases made. • $10 • (06/30/94) • **82**

Merlot Russian River Valley 1993: Medium-weight and a tad spicy. Plum and cherry flavors. 975 cases made. • $14 • **81**

Merlot Russian River Valley 1990 • $14 • (05/31/92) • **78**

Pinot Noir Russian River Valley 1992: Earthy, hollow and gamy, it lacks richness and substance, turning dry and tannic on the finish. 1,100 cases made. • $13 • (03/31/95) • **72**

Pinot Noir Russian River Valley 1991 • $12 • (02/28/93) • **84**

Key: SS—Spectator Selection. CS—Cellar Selection. BB—Best Buy. $NA—Price not available. (BT)—Barrel tasting. Ⓐ—Auction Price.
Dates in parentheses represent the issues in which the ratings were published.

ARMSTRONG RIDGE | CALIFORNIA

Brut California NV • $8 • (12/31/93) • **82**

ARROWOOD | CALIFORNIA

Cabernet Sauvignon Sonoma County 1992: A big, ripe and well-oaked style, packs in lots of ripe plum and black cherry-laced fruit that runs deep and complex, finishing with smooth tannins and fine length. Finishes with a touch of herb and tobacco. Best after 1997. 10,658 cases made. • $25 • (11/15/95) • **92**

Cabernet Sauvignon Sonoma County 1991: Supple and elegant, with a wide range of spicy Cabernet flavors. The herb, currant, wild berry, coffee and cedary oak overtones blend in together, yielding complex and satisfying flavors. Offers delicacy and finesse. Can be enjoyed now or cellared. Best around 9,650 cases made. • $25 • (09/30/94) SS • **91**

Cabernet Sauvignon Sonoma County 1990: Smooth, ripe and elegant, a generous wine on a lean frame, beautifully balanced, showing plenty of currant and blackberry fruit, spicy-herbal overtones and a lively zing of berry on the finish. Drinkable now, but shows the stuff to improve through 1999. 9,200 cases made. • $24 • (10/31/93) SS • **91**

Cabernet Sauvignon Sonoma County 1989 • $24 • (11/15/92) • **88**

Cabernet Sauvignon Sonoma County 1988 • $26 • (11/15/91) • **88**

Cabernet Sauvignon Sonoma County 1987 • $26 • (11/15/90) • **87**

Cabernet Sauvignon Sonoma County 1986 • $30 • (10/15/89) • **92**

Cabernet Sauvignon Sonoma County 1985 • $35 • (12/15/88) • **94**

Cabernet Sauvignon Sonoma County Domaine du Grand Archer 1992: Firm and intense, with a good dose of smoky, toasty oak up front, the currant and cherry flavor hangs in to the finish. Has the tannins to age, but is drinkable now. 1,500 cases made. • $9 • (11/15/94) • **87**

Cabernet Sauvignon Sonoma County Réserve Spéciale 1992: Dark, rich and intense, with a seam of elegance to the bright, lively black cherry, plum and wild berry flavors. The finish brings up anise and spice notes. Try in 1998. 500 cases made. • $35 • (12/15/95) • **92**

Cabernet Sauvignon Sonoma County Réserve Spéciale 1989 • $70 • (11/15/93) • **88**

Chardonnay Sonoma County 1994: Ripe, smooth and supple, with a pretty core of spicy pear, apple and melon notes, finishing with a fruity honey aftertaste. Fans of pure Chardonnay fruit will find this especially pleasing. 7,374 cases made. • $21 • (05/31/96) • **88**

Chardonnay Sonoma County 1993: Well focused, with a nice balance between ripe pear, spice and toasty oak flavors that picks up a ginger edge. 6,088 cases made. • $20 • (06/15/95) • **87**

Chardonnay Sonoma County 1992: Starts out slowly but the flavors build, with pretty pear, peach and nectarine, picking up smoky, toasty oak on the finish. Approachable now but probably better this summer. Tasted twice with consistent results. 5,304 cases made. • $20 • (04/30/94) • **89**

Chardonnay Sonoma County 1991 • $19 • (07/15/93) • **88**

Chardonnay Sonoma County Cuvée Michel Berthoud 1992: Lean and crisp, with a tight spicy band of tobacco, pear and light oak shadings. Time in the bottle will give a little more dimension. A fully barrel-fermented malolactic style of Chardonnay. 993 cases made. • $24 • (06/30/94) • **85**

Chardonnay Sonoma County Cuvée Michel Berthoud Réserve Spéciale 1994: Strikes a nice balance between the crisp, well-focused honey, pear, spice and mineral flavors and the lightly toasty oak. It comes together in a nice refrain on the lingering finish. 1,200 cases made. • $27 • (05/31/96) • **92**

Chardonnay Sonoma County Cuvée Michel Berthoud Réserve Spéciale 1993: A well-oaked white, showing toasty, buttery notes, but then the fruit pours through, with focused pear and apple flavors that turn elegant and spicy. Drinkable now. 1,050 cases made. • $24 • (06/15/95) • **91**

Chardonnay Sonoma County Réserve Spéciale 1991 • $50 • (11/30/93) • **89**

Domaine du Grand Archer Sonoma County 1991: A gentle young Cabernet with a sense of elegance and finesse. The ripe plum, currant and spicy flavors are well integrated and balanced, finishing with just the right touch of tannins. Drinkable now. 1,015 cases made. • $8 • (04/30/94) SS • **89**

Merlot Sonoma County 1992: Ripe and supple, striking a nice balance between black cherry, plum and toasty oak flavors. Can stand short-term cellaring to soften the tannins somewhat, but it's elegant and well balanced. • $28 • (12/15/95) • **89**

Merlot Sonoma County 1991: Complex and flavorful, with a rich, supple core of intense currant, cherry and spicy Merlot fruit. Picks up enough tannin on the finish to merit cellaring, but our experience with Merlot suggests that it would be better earlier than later. Try now through 1997. 3,029 cases made. • $28 • (07/31/94) • **90**

Merlot Sonoma County 1990 • $25 • (05/31/93) • **89**

Merlot Sonoma County 1988 • $25 • (05/31/92) • **88**

Merlot Sonoma County Domaine du Grand Archer 1991: Lean and firm with a tight band of currant and cherry fruit, but it turns hard and tannic on the finish. Drinkable now. 1,514 cases made. • $9 • (09/15/94) • **82**

Pinot Blanc Russian River Valley Saralee's Vineyard 1994: Fruity and truly exotic, packing in lots of litchi nut, fig, melon and butterscotch flavors that start out elegant and understated and build to a rich and satisfying finish. 450 cases made. • $28 • (04/30/96) • **91**

Viognier Late Harvest Russian River Valley Saralee's Vineyard Select 1994: Strong, spicy aroma and rich, complex flavors—honey, apricot, vanilla and nectarine—that linger on the finish. 480 cases made. • $28 • **88**

Viognier Russian River Valley Saralee's Vineyard 1993: Bright and spicy, ripe, sweet pear flavor and a resiny background note persist on the snappy finish. 1,680 cases made. • $25 • (01/31/95) • **88**

Viognier Russian River Valley Saralee's Vineyard 1992 • $25 • (09/30/93) • **83**

White Riesling Late Harvest Russian River Valley Oak Meadow Vineyard Select 1991 • $20 • (06/30/93) • **87**

White Riesling Late Harvest Russian River Valley Oak Meadow Vineyard Special Select 1993: Gloriously sweet, rich, supple and complex. A dessert wine from California that unfolds a many-layered swirl of honey, caramel, apricot, pear and exotic tropical fruit and spices, all balanced gorgeously on a fine thread of acidity. Wonderful now, but should be fine through 1998, or even 2000. 300 cases made. • $28 • (04/30/95) • **96**

ARROYO, VINCENT | CALIFORNIA

Cabernet Sauvignon Napa Valley 1990: Strikes a nice balance between oak and supple fruit concentration, with ripe, focused black cherry, raspberry and currant flavors, finishing with spicy anise notes. Drink now. 750 cases made. • $15 • (11/15/92) • **88**

Cabernet Sauvignon Napa Valley 1989 • $15 • (11/15/92) • **81**

Cabernet Sauvignon Napa Valley 1988 • $18 • (11/15/92) • **85**

Cabernet Sauvignon Napa Valley 1987 • $12 • (11/15/90) • **91**

ASHBY, HUNTER | CALIFORNIA

Merlot Napa Valley 1985 • $9 • (07/31/89) • **84**

Merlot Napa Valley 1982 • $6 • (12/15/87) • **65**

ASHLAND PARK | CALIFORNIA

Cabernet Sauvignon Napa Valley 1989 • $5 • (11/15/92) • **75**

ATLAS PEAK | CALIFORNIA

Cabernet Sauvignon Atlas Peak 1992: Well crafted, showing pretty, toasty accents and plenty of currant, cherry, plum and raspberry flavors. Remarkably supple and elegant with lots of harmony. Best yet from Atlas Peak. 1,600 cases made. • $18 • (12/15/95) • **89**

Cabernet Sauvignon Atlas Peak 1991: Dark, deep, detailed and well oaked, adding cedar to black cherry and currant flavors. Features firm tannins and a peppery edge on the finish. Hold into 1997. 900 cases made. • $18 • (09/15/95) • **86**

Chardonnay Atlas Peak 1993: A touch earthy and oaky, but enough ripe pear and apple flavors come through to hold your interest. 1,600 cases made. • $16 • (07/31/95) • **85**

Consenso Atlas Peak 1990: Smooth and supple, with coffee, currant, herb and spice flavors that weave together neatly, finishing with a pretty aftertaste. Complex and well balanced. 2,600 cases made. • $22 • (12/15/95) • **87**

Consenso Atlas Peak 1989: Mature and drying, showing an earth, cedar and coffee edge to the currant and berry notes, turning leathery. • $22 • (03/31/95) • **83**

Consenso Napa Valley 1990: Solid, chunky and modestly flavorful, a rough-textured wine with stalky berry flavors, remaining tannic on the finish. Needs until 1998 to 2000. • $22 • (11/15/93) • **83**

Consenso Napa Valley 1989 • $22 • (03/31/93) • **82**

Sangiovese Atlas Peak 1993: Supple and easy to drink, a gentle backbone of tannin supporting the light earthy, berry and floral flavors. Drinkable now. 12,000 cases made. • $16 • (11/30/95) • **84**

Sangiovese Atlas Peak 1992: Earthy, spicy aromas lead to medium-bodied strawberry and cherry flavors and a smoky finish. 7,200 cases made. • $16 • (02/28/95) • **84**

Sangiovese Atlas Peak 1991 • $16 • (05/31/94) • **83**

Sangiovese Atlas Peak Reserve 1992: Firm in texture, tannic, with strong blackberry and black cherry flavors and a sweet, vanilla finish. Approachable now with hearty food. 1,000 cases made. • $24 • (02/28/95) • **88**

Sangiovese Napa Valley 1990 • $24 • (02/15/93) • **85**

Sangiovese Napa Valley 1989 • $24 • (11/15/91) • **86**

AU BON CLIMAT | CALIFORNIA

Chardonnay Arroyo Grande Valley Talley Reserve 1992: Serves up a pretty array of tropical fruit, with guava, pineapple, honey and pear flavors that remain spicy and long on the finish. 800 cases made. • $25 • (05/31/94) • **91**

Chardonnay Arroyo Grande Valley Talley Vineyard Talley Reserve 1993: Medium bodied but well focused and flavorful, with toasty oak, ripe pear, honey and spicy citrus notes, turning complex and elegant on the finish. 800 cases made. • $25 • (07/31/95) • **90**

Chardonnay Santa Barbara County 1994: Ripe, juicy pear, peach and spice flavors showcase the Chardonnay grape without letting the oak get in the way. • $15 • (01/31/96) • **88**

Chardonnay Santa Barbara County 1993: Well focused with appealing fruit flavors, combining ripe pineapple, citrus and spicy oak flavors, folding together on the finish. • $16 • (07/31/95) • **87**

Chardonnay Santa Barbara County Le Bouge D'àcôté 1992: Rich and earthy, with complex, concentrated pear, pineapple, oak and spice notes that turn elegant, gaining finesse and grace on a long finish, where the honey and pear flavors shine through. Ready now. 1,113 cases made. • $25 • (05/31/94) • **92**

Chardonnay Santa Maria Valley Gold Coast Vineyard 1993: Bold and oaky, with a rich leesy edge to the ripe pear and pineapple flavors, gaining intensity and depth on the finish, where it turns complex. • $20 • (07/31/95) • **89**

Chardonnay Santa Ynez Valley Sanford & Benedict Reserve 1993: A deceptively subtle style that builds richness and intensity. Tiers of spice, pear and pineapple flavors are joined up with nicely toasty oak flavors on the finish. Beautiful aftertaste. • $34 • (01/31/96) • **93**

Chardonnay Santa Ynez Valley Sanford & Benedict Reserve 1992: Young and tight, with crisp pear, citrus and oak flavors that fold together nicely, finishing with good length. • $35 • (07/31/95) • **87**

Pinot Blanc Santa Barbara County Bien Nacido Vineyard 1994: Simple and pleasant enough, with a hint of pear, nectarine and spice, but it doesn't have the extra richness and complexity often found in ABC's best. 1,000 cases made. • $12 • (01/31/96) • **86**

Pinot Noir Arroyo Grande Valley Rosemary's Talley Vineyard 1993: Ripe and smoky, with a toasty oak character and a pretty array of black cherry, plum and anise flavors, showing uncommon richness and depth. Finishes with plush, firm tannins, but the flavors keep pouring through. Drinkable now. 200 cases made. • $40 • (12/31/95) • **91**

Pinot Noir Arroyo Grande Valley Talley and Paragon Vineyards 1993: Medium-bodied, firmly tannic, spicy cherry and leathery notes are tightly wound. Can age, but lacks the extra richness found in great vintages. • $20 • (09/15/95) • **87**

Pinot Noir Santa Barbara County 1989 • $16 • (09/30/92) • **87**

Pinot Noir Santa Barbara County 1988 • $16 • (04/30/91) • **80**

Pinot Noir Santa Barbara County 1987 • $16 • (12/15/89) • **84**

Pinot Noir Santa Barbara County 1985 • $12 • (06/15/88) • **73**

Pinot Noir Santa Barbara County La Bauge Au-dessus 1990 • $30 • (02/28/93) • **87**

Pinot Noir Santa Barbara County La Bauge Au-dessus Bien Nacido Vineyard 1993: Very ripe dried cherry and berry notes pick up pleasant tea leaf and anise tones, retaining flavor while finishing with firm tannins. • $25 • (09/15/95) • **85**

Pinot Noir Santa Barbara County La Bauge Au-dessus Bien Nacido Vineyard 1991 • $25 • (02/28/94) • **91**

Pinot Noir Santa Maria Valley 1994: Combines ripe, bright and lively cherry, berry and cola notes, with good richess and intensity. Deftly balanced. 2,000 cases made. • $18 • (02/29/96) • **88**

Pinot Noir Santa Maria Valley 1993: Well oaked, showing herb, cola and black cherry flavors that turn supple despite firm tannins. Try now. 2,500 cases made. • $14 • (01/31/95) • **86**

Pinot Noir Santa Maria Valley 1990 • $11 • (02/28/93) • **86**

Pinot Noir Santa Maria Valley Rancho Vinedo Vineyard 1992 • $15 • (02/28/94) • **86**

Pinot Noir Santa Ynez Valley 1989 • $30 • (09/30/92) • **81**

Pinot Noir Santa Ynez Valley Benedict Vineyard 1987 • $30 • (12/15/89) • **88**

Pinot Noir Santa Ynez Valley Rancho Vinedo Vineyard 1988 • $13 • (12/15/89) • **83**

Pinot Noir Santa Ynez Valley Sanford & Benedict Vineyard 1993: Well oaked, but with enough wild berry and cherry fruit to keep it in balance, as the flavors are well tapered on the finish, fanning out and turning complex. 250 cases made. • $35 • (12/31/95) • **89**

Pinot Noir Santa Ynez Valley Sanford & Benedict Vineyard 1991 • $35 • (02/28/94) • **91**

AUDUBON | CALIFORNIA

Audubon Rouge California NV • $4 • (10/15/88) • **79**

Cabernet Sauvignon Napa Valley 1985 • $11 • (06/15/88) • **77**

Chardonnay Sonoma County Carneros Sangiacomo Barrel Fermented 1992: Sappy with sweet-tasting pear and honey flavors, picking up charred and smoky oak on the finish. 1,000 cases made. • $12 • (06/30/94) • **79**

Chardonnay Sonoma Valley Carneros Sangiacomo Barrel Fermented 1993: Earthy with a spicy grapefruit and pear edge, turning perfumed. 1,200 cases made. • $12 • (07/31/95) • **83**

Sauvignon Blanc Napa Valley Dry Juliana Vineyards Audubon Collection 1992: Flavorful but a bit raucous and coarse in texture, finishing with a nice array of pear and herb character. Drinkable now. 1,000 cases made. • $9 • (08/31/94) • **80**

Sauvignon Blanc Napa Valley Juliana Vineyards 1994: Lean and focused, tobacco and cedar notes accenting the pear flavor. 1,200 cases made. • $9 • (08/31/95) • **84**

Zinfandel San Luis Obispo County 1983 • $7 • (07/15/88) • **84**

Zinfandel Sonoma County 1990 • $9 • (10/15/92) • **81**

AUSTIN | CALIFORNIA

A Genoux Santa Barbara County 1986 • $15 • (12/15/89) • **74**

Cabernet Franc Santa Barbara County 1988 • $12 • (11/15/90) • **76**

Cabernet Sauvignon Santa Barbara County Mille Delices 1991: Ripe, supple and fleshy with toasty buttery oak and smooth cherry and plum-tinged fruit. Drinkable now. 89 cases made. • $20 • (11/15/93) • **84**

Cabernet Sauvignon Santa Barbara County Perry's Reserve 1991: Austere with spicy herbal notes, but not quite the rich fruit concentration to stand up to the tannins. Finishes with a spicy, cola edge. Drink now. 550 cases made. • $15 • (11/15/93) • **80**

Johannisberg Riesling Late Harvest Santa Barbara County Botrytis 1986 • $8 • (12/15/89) • **81**

Pinot Noir Santa Barbara County 1993: A touch earthy and closed, but it's impressive for its rich, dark color and solid core of currant, spice, cedar, anise and tar, altogether complex, dense and tannic, a wine that

Key: SS—Spectator Selection. CS—Cellar Selection. BB—Best Buy. $NA—Price not available. (BT)—Barrel tasting. Ⓐ—Auction Price.
Dates in parentheses represent the issues in which the ratings were published.

UNITED STATES

will benefit from another three to five years cellaring. Try in 1998. 450 cases made. • $13 • (02/29/96) • **74**

Pinot Noir Santa Barbara County 1987 • $15 • (12/15/89) • **77**

Pinot Noir Santa Barbara County 1983 • $25 • (12/15/89) • **78**

Pinot Noir Santa Barbara County Artist Series 1988 • $10 • (12/15/89) • **75**

Pinot Noir Santa Barbara County Bien Nacido Vineyard 1982 • $10 • (03/16/85) • **88**

Pinot Noir Santa Barbara County Reserve 1991 • $16 • (02/28/94) • **79**

Pinot Noir Santa Barbara County Sierra Madre Vineyards 1982 • $12 • (05/01/84) • **87**

Sauvignon Blanc Late Harvest Santa Barbara County Botrytis Sierra Madre Vineyards 1985 • $10 • (12/15/89) • **72**

Sauvignon Blanc Santa Barbara County Lucas Vineyard 1991 • $10 • (09/15/93) • **70**

Sauvignon Blanc Santa Barbara County Reserve 1991 • $12 • (09/15/93) • **72**

AZALEA SPRINGS | CALIFORNIA

Merlot Napa Valley 1992: Currant, coffee, cherry and anise notes are ripe, supple and well proportioned, turning crisp and tannic on aftertaste. Enough body and flavor hold your interest. Best in 1998. 1,100 cases made. • $22 • (12/15/95) • **88**

Merlot Napa Valley 1991: Smooth, plush and elegant, with a ripe, rich, spicy core of currant, black cherry and plum flavors. Stays focused and lively on a long, full finish. Beautifully crafted, tempting now but a solid bet to gain through 1998. 1,200 cases made. • $22 • (09/15/94) • **88**

BABCOCK | CALIFORNIA

Chardonnay San Luis Obispo Talley Vineyard 1993: Firm and crisp, with a narrow band of citrus and pear and some coarseness on the finish. Drinkable now. 550 cases made. • $25 • (01/31/95) • **85**

Chardonnay Santa Barbara County 1993: Ripe and spicy, featuring fresh pear and apple notes. Fruity and solid but lacking extra dimension. 1,826 cases made. • $16 • (01/31/95) • **85**

Chardonnay Santa Ynez Valley 1991 • $18 • (07/15/93) • **78**

Chardonnay Santa Ynez Valley Grand Cuvée 1992: Distinctive, bright and lively, sporting crisp, intense, spicy lemon, pear and grapefruit notes. Turns elegant and refined on aftertaste, where the flavors linger. • $25 • (09/30/95) • **88**

Chardonnay Santa Ynez Valley Mt. Carmel Vineyard 1994: A touch earthy, but it holds together. This has ripe pear and peach flavors with light oak shadings. An elegant and polished style. • $27 • (01/31/96) • **88**

Chardonnay Santa Ynez Valley Mt. Carmel Vineyard 1993: A slight bitter edge detracts from the modest pear and spice notes, but it lingers on the finish. The $25 price is out of line. 438 cases made. • $25 • (07/31/95) • **83**

Johannisberg Riesling Late Harvest Santa Ynez Valley Cluster Selected 1987 • $14 • (12/15/89) • **89**

Pinot Noir Santa Barbara County Bien Nacido Vineyard 1994: A touch earthy, with a trim band of cherry flavors. Picks up a peppery note on the finish. Drinkable now. 350 cases made. • $18 • (01/31/96) • **84**

Pinot Noir Santa Ynez Valley 1991 • $22 • (02/28/93) • **79**

Pinot Noir Santa Ynez Valley Benedict Vineyard 1991 • $25 • (02/28/94) • **87**

Pinot Noir Santa Ynez Valley Estate Grown 1993: Despite its firm, dry tannins, there's a pretty glimpse of ripe black cherry, herb and cola notes. Still the tannins win on the finish; needs short-term cellaring. 290 cases made. • $30 • **84**

Pinot Noir Santa Ynez Valley Estate Grown 1992: Dark, intense, spicy herb, black cherry and earth notes, finishing on the austere and tannic side. Needs time to soften, try in 1997. 223 cases made. • $30 • (03/31/95) • **85**

Pinot Noir Santa Ynez Valley Sanford & Benedict Vineyard 1993: A touch earthy, with a chunky, oaky core of fruit in a tough rustic style. 150 cases made. • $25 • (12/31/95) • **83**

Pinot Noir Santa Ynez Valley Sanford & Benedict Vineyard 1992: Young and a bit green, with fruit that's barely ripe. Hints of cherry and currant come through with the herb and spice notes. Tannic enough to cellar until 1997. 228 cases made. • $25 • (11/30/94) • **85**

Pinot Noir Santa Ynez Valley Selected Barrels Reserve 1989 • $35 • (02/28/93) • **70**

Sangiovese Santa Ynez Valley Eleven Oaks 1993: Soft and ripe, a prune flavor running through the velvety berry and floral notes. Modest tannins make it ready now. 71 cases made. • $22 • (11/30/95) • **85**

Sauvignon Blanc Santa Ynez Valley Eleven Oaks 1994: Crisp and lively, with sharply focused onion-skin-scented pear, apple and citrus flavors. Long finish has herbal notes. 1,670 cases made. • $20 • **89**

Sauvignon Blanc Santa Ynez Valley Eleven Oaks 1992 • $20 • (05/15/94) • **89**

Sauvignon Blanc Santa Ynez Valley Eleven Oaks Ranch 1991 • $21 • (07/15/93) • **83**

BACCALA, ESTATE WILLIAM | CALIFORNIA

Chardonnay Sonoma County 1993: Smooth and silky, showing some simple citrus liveliness to balance the spicy pear flavors. Ready now. 2,560 cases made. • $13 • (02/29/96) • **85**

Chardonnay Sonoma County 1992: Ripe and spicy with lively pear and peach notes that turn simple and fruity on the finish. Ready now. 2,500 cases made. • $11 • (06/30/94) • **82**

Chardonnay Sonoma County 1991 • $9 • (02/28/94) BB • **86**

Merlot Alexander Valley 1984 • $10 • (02/28/87) • **72**

Merlot Napa Valley 1992: Austere, dry and tannic, with rustic, mature cherry and berry flavors that have a stale edge. Dries out, with a metallic taste on the finish. 2,450 cases made. • $15 • (06/15/96) • **74**

Merlot Napa Valley 1991: Bright and lively, with vivid currant and cherry notes, picking up a spicy edge on the finish. Drinkable now. 3,000 cases made. • $14 • (07/31/94) • **86**

Merlot Napa Valley 1990 • $10 • (08/31/93) • **90**

BADGER MOUNTAIN | WASHINGTON

Cabernet Franc Columbia Valley 1992: Soft and fragrant, a supple red with lightly spicy accents. Drinkable now. 650 cases made. • $13 • (09/30/94) • **84**

Cabernet Franc Columbia Valley Certified Organic Vineyard 1993: Firm, chewy and focused, backing up its tannins with a shot of concentrated berry flavors. Best in 1997. 1,000 cases made. • $13 • (09/30/95) • **85**

Cabernet Franc Columbia Valley Certified Organic Vineyard 1992: Light, elegant and fragrant berry and meaty notes add depth and interest to the proceedings. Tasty now. 1,000 cases made. • $13 • (09/30/95) • **85**

Chardonnay Columbia Valley Certified Organic Vineyard 1994: Light, bright, lively green apple, pear and spice flavors maintain vibrancy through the finish. 1,512 cases made. • $9 • (09/30/95) • **86**

Chardonnay Columbia Valley Certified Organic Vineyard 1993: Smooth, refreshing, lively citrus and pear flavors plus a touch of oak on the finish. 1,000 cases made. • $9 • (09/30/95) • **84**

Gewürztraminer Columbia Valley Mountain Blush Certified Organic Vineyard 1994: Light salmon color is pretty and simple pear flavor finishes a bit quickly. 1,105 cases made. • $6 • (09/30/95) • **76**

Johannisberg Riesling Columbia Valley Certified Organic Vineyard 1994: Light and simple, showing fresh peach and apple flavors that remain crisp on the finish. 819 cases made. • $6 • (09/30/95) • **79**

Seyval Blanc Columbia Valley Sevé Certified Organic Vineyard 1994: Bright and flavorful, floral and lively, echoing pear and a bit of vanilla on the long finish. 2,492 cases made. • $6 • (09/30/95) • **85**

BAILEYANA | CALIFORNIA

Chardonnay Edna Valley 1994: Tastes ripe and mature, marked by honey, pear and light hazelnut notes that may be a bit heavy-handed for some. 1,500 cases made. • $15 • (06/15/96) • **82**

Chardonnay Edna Valley 1991 • $14 • (07/15/93) • **76**

Chardonnay Edna Valley Paragon Vineyard 1993: Serves up a ripe, well focused beam of pear and pineapple, with complex oak shadings that fold together neatly on the finish. Long aftertaste. 1,500 cases made. • $15 • (07/31/95) • **88**

Chardonnay Edna Valley Paragon Vineyard 1992: A Chardonnay name that's new to me. It exhibits ripe, juicy pear, pineapple, honey and butterscotch flavors that are rich and harmonious. Turns smooth and silky on the finish. Ready now. 1,300 cases made. • $14 • (05/31/94) • **88**

BAILLY, ALEXIS | MINNESOTA

Country Red Minnesota NV • $7 • (02/29/92) • **78**
Léon Millot Minnesota 1990 • $9 • (02/29/92) • **74**
Maréchal Foch Minnesota 1990 • $9 • (02/29/92) • **77**

BAINBRIDGE ISLAND | WASHINGTON

Siegerrebe Botrytis Affected Washington 1987 • $15 • (10/15/89) • **71**

BALCOM & MOE | WASHINGTON

Cabernet Sauvignon Washington 1992: Very ripe, almost jammy flavors of blackberry and raspberry and spicy toast overtones. Nicely focused, smoothly integrated tannins. Best now through 1997. 370 cases made. • $14 • (09/30/95) • **87**
Cabernet Sauvignon Washington 1991: Distinctly minty in flavor, a chewy Cabernet that packs in enough black cherry and herb flavors to balance the tannins. Best from 1998 to 1999. 350 cases made. • $14 • (09/30/95) • **84**
Merlot Washington 1992: Strives for elegance, with an airy texture, lovely plum and blackberry flavors and a velvety finish. It needs until 1997 to resolve the modest tannins. 1,540 cases made. • $14 • (08/31/95) • **87**
Sauvignon Blanc Washington 1994: Crisp and juicy, featuring ripe pear, spice and a touch of green. • $9 • (09/15/95) • **84**

BALD MOUNTAIN | CALIFORNIA

Zinfandel Napa Valley 1992: Intense, with pronounced pepper and spice flavors, but they subdue the fruit flavors. A bit lean and trim. • $11 • (10/15/95) • **78**

BALDINELLI | CALIFORNIA

Cabernet Sauvignon Amador County 1989 • $10 • (08/31/92) • **70**
Cabernet Sauvignon Shenandoah Valley 1983 • $7 • (11/30/88) • **86**
Zinfandel Shenandoah Valley 1988 • $7 • (12/31/90) • **82**
Zinfandel Shenandoah Valley 1987 • $8 • (05/15/90) • **85**
Zinfandel Shenandoah Valley Reserve 1986 • $6 • (12/15/88) BB • **83**

BALDWIN | NEW YORK

Landot Noir New York 1982 • $6 • (03/16/86) • **95**

BALLATORE | CALIFORNIA

California Gran Spumante NV • $7 • (05/15/93) • **84**
California NV • $4 • (05/01/86) BB • **87**

BALLENTINE | CALIFORNIA

Cabernet Franc Napa Valley 1992: Medium weight with herb and dill notes that pick up a trace of berry and currant on the finish. Ready. 500 cases made. • $15 • (07/31/95) • **82**
Merlot Napa Valley 1992: Medium weight with cedary herb and dill flavors that dominate. 900 cases made. • $18 • (07/31/95) • **80**
Zinfandel Napa Valley 1992: Firm and compact, with ripe plum and cherry notes that are well focused. Drinks well now. 300 cases made. • $14 • (10/15/95) • **85**

BALVERNE | CALIFORNIA

Cabernet Sauvignon Chalk Hill Laurel Vineyard 1983 • $13 • (02/15/89) • **86**
Cabernet Sauvignon Sonoma County 1982 • $12 • (08/31/88) • **88**

Key: SS—Spectator Selection. CS—Cellar Selection. BB—Best Buy. $NA—Price not available. (BT)—Barrel tasting. (A)—Auction Price.
Dates in parentheses represent the issues in which the ratings were published.

BANCROFT | CALIFORNIA

Chardonnay Howell Mountain 1992: Intense and flinty, with a focused core of earthy citrus, pear and light oak shadings. 1,516 cases made. • $16 • (07/31/95) • **86**

BANDIERA | CALIFORNIA

Cabernet Sauvignon Napa Valley 1993: Pleasant for its ripe plum, spice and berry flavors and mild tannins. A light dash of oak adds interest in this value red. 26,328 cases made. • $8 • (11/30/95) BB • **85**
Cabernet Sauvignon Napa Valley 1992: Pleasant fruity in an easy to drink style that features its cherry and berry flavors. 20,000 cases made. • $8 • (09/30/95) • **83**
Cabernet Sauvignon Napa Valley 1991: Marked by herb and light oak shadings, this is another excellent Bandiera Cabernet. It delivers plenty of currant and cherry flavors at a price that's hard to beat. Best now through 1998. 12,000 cases made. • $6 • (09/30/94) BB • **85**
Cabernet Sauvignon Napa Valley 1990: Broad, supple and flavorful, a fine-textured wine with generous berry, currant and plum fruit echoing on the long finish. Drinkable now. 14,000 cases made. • $6 • (04/15/94) BB • **87**
Cabernet Sauvignon Napa Valley 1989 • $6 • (10/31/92) BB • **86**
Cabernet Sauvignon Napa Valley 1988 • $6 • (04/15/92) BB • **80**
Cabernet Sauvignon Napa Valley 1987 • $7 • (11/15/91) BB • **89**
Cabernet Sauvignon Napa Valley 1986 • $6 • (10/31/89) BB • **85**
Cabernet Sauvignon Napa Valley Reserve 1993: Spicy, peppery edge to vanilla and toasty oak flavors. Ripe plum, cherry and berry notes underneath emerge on aftertaste to yield a nice sense of balance and proportion. 2,500 cases made. • $12 • (11/30/95) • **87**
Chardonnay Napa Valley 1994: Bright and flavorful, with lively apple and citrus flavors tempered by a touch of sweet vanilla. Good subtlety makes this a value. 22,832 cases made. • $8 • (09/30/95) BB • **86**
Chardonnay Napa Valley 1993: A little broader than most 1993s, with toasty pear and vanilla flavors that work in a touch of honey on the finish. 20,000 cases made. • $8 • (07/31/95) • **84**
Chardonnay Napa Valley 1992: Fruity and generous, offering a bright beam of nectarine and apricot flavors that linger on the finish. 12,000 cases made. • $6 • (05/15/94) BB • **85**
Chardonnay Napa Valley 1991 • $6 • (01/31/94) BB • **85**
Merlot Napa Valley Reserve 1993: Dry and tannic. A green, unripe edge pervades the earthy, wild berry flavors. 700 cases made. • $12 • **77**
Sauvignon Blanc Napa Valley 1994: Crisp and generally fruity, hinting at nectarine and a touch of herb on the finish. 6,100 cases made. • $5 • (08/31/95) • **83**
Sauvignon Blanc Napa Valley 1993 • $5 • (06/15/94) BB • **86**
White Zinfandel California 1994: Somewhat earthy, with good strawberry and currant flavors. Finishes a little bitter. 43,000 cases made. • $5 • (09/15/95) • **78**
White Zinfandel California 1988 • $5 • (06/15/89) • **74**
White Zinfandel North Coast 1986 • $4 • (03/31/87) • **70**

BANNISTER | CALIFORNIA

Chardonnay Russian River Valley 1991 • $NA • (07/15/93) • **84**
Chardonnay Russian River Valley Allen Vineyard 1994: Opens with a band of citrus and orange blossom, picking up ripe pear and tart apple notes, a subtle, understated style that finishes with a hint of smoky, toasty oak. 622 cases made. • $20 • (05/31/96) • **88**
Chardonnay Russian River Valley Allen Vineyard 1993: Medium-weight apple, spice and hazelnut flavors turn elegant and delicate on the finish. Well crafted. 792 cases made. • $18 • (06/15/95) • **89**
Chardonnay Russian River Valley Allen Vineyard 1992: Serves up a lot of ripe flavor, with pear, apple and spice shadings, and finishes with light vanilla notes. Elegant and balanced, drink it now. 775 cases made. • $17 • (04/30/94) • **86**
Pinot Noir Russian River Valley 1994: A touch woody, this medium-weight wine is well balanced but not especially rich or concentrated. Features ripe plum and cherry flavors of modest proportion. 162 cases made. • $18 • (05/31/96) • **85**

Zinfandel Dry Creek Valley 1992: Spicy and cedary, turning tight and austere on the palate, the finish echoes tar and caramel. Drinkable now. 385 cases made. • $12 • (01/31/95) • **84**
Zinfandel Dry Creek Valley 1991 • $12 • (09/30/93) • **83**
Zinfandel Dry Creek Valley Bradford Mountain Vineyard 1993: Well balanced and appealing, the core of spicy, peppery raspberry and cherry achieving modest depth and richness. Elegant and refined. 352 cases made. • $15 • (10/15/95) • **86**

BARBOURSVILLE | VIRGINIA

Cabernet Franc Monticello 1993: Herbal and black currant flavors dominate this soft and well-rounded wine. Cedar and smoke notes linger on the finish. Drinkable now. 800 cases made. • $12 • (12/31/95) • **81**
Cabernet Sauvignon Monticello Reserve 1991: A medium-bodied wine with flavors tending to the herbal side. Some nice cherry and spice flavors also add to its appeal. Soft and simple. 600 cases made. • $19 • (12/31/95) • **80**
Cabernet Sauvignon Reserve 1983 • $15 • (02/29/92) • **73**
Chardonnay Monticello Reserve 1994: Vanilla and bread-dough aromas from oak dominate, which makes for a pleasantly smooth texture and sweet flavors, but not much fruit underneath. It's quaffable. 900 cases made. • $15 • (06/30/95) • **80**
Pinot Noir Monticello 1993: After an ugly creosote aroma blows off, a hint of burnt cherry fruit emerges, but the tannins are dry and the finish is short and bitter. 1,200 cases made. • $12 • (05/31/95) • **73**
Riesling Monticello 1994: Lean, even austere, this shows flinty, earthy and some vegetal flavors over crisp acidity. A bit diluted and short. 1,200 cases made. • $9 • (08/31/95) • **76**
Sauvignon Blanc Monticello 1993: Clean and fresh, this lean wine shows some peach and grassy flavors but stays basically neutral. A hint of spritz keeps it lively. 1,000 cases made. • $10 • (05/31/95) • **79**
Sparkling Virginia Brut NV: A smooth, fresh and light sparkler that tastes a bit like apples and pears. Clean, even delicate, and straightforward. 3,000 cases made. • $13 • (06/30/95) • **82**

BARGETTO, LAWRENCE J. | CALIFORNIA

Blanc de Noir Santa Maria Valley 60th Anniversary 1991 • $11 • (12/31/93) • **79**
Cabernet Sauvignon Central Coast Cyrpress 1991: Light and fruity, with an herbal edge to the Cabernet flavors. Ready now. 1,500 cases made. • $9 • (11/15/94) • **82**
Cabernet Sauvignon Napa Valley Komes Ranch 1988 • $15 • (11/15/93) • **84**
Cabernet Sauvignon Santa Cruz Mountains 1986 • $18 • (08/31/92) • **84**
Cabernet Sauvignon Santa Cruz Mountains Bates Ranch 1990: Firm and nicely balanced between chewy tannins and ripe plum and blackberry flavors, the finish is fresh. Best from 1997. 500 cases made. • $16 • (12/15/95) • **85**
Cabernet Sauvignon Santa Cruz Mountains Bates Ranch 1989: Lean and earthy with diluted cherry and cedary flavors. 900 cases made. • $18 • (05/31/95) • **77**
Cabernet Sauvignon Santa Cruz Mountains Bates Ranch 1988: Earthy and herbal, light in color, but typical of the 1988 vintage in its hollowness. Ready now. 601 cases made. • $15 • (11/15/94) • **78**
Cabernet Sauvignon Santa Cruz Mountains Bates Ranch 1987 • $15 • (11/15/93) • **83**
Cabernet Sauvignon Sonoma County Cypress 1985 • $8 • (11/15/89) • **79**
Chardonnay Central Coast Cypress 1994: Floral and perfumed, with a pleasant core of pear and citrus flavors. Medium-bodied, soft and ready. 4,400 cases made. • $9 • (05/15/96) • **84**
Chardonnay Central Coast Cypress 1993: Simple and easy to drink, with a crisp edge of green apple to the basic flavors. 4,800 cases made. • $9 • (07/31/95) • **80**
Chardonnay Central Coast Cypress 1992: Ripe and fruity with spicy pear and apple notes. 5,000 cases made. • $9 • (01/31/95) • **82**
Chardonnay Central Coast Cypress 1991 • $9 • (10/15/93) BB • **85**
Chardonnay Santa Cruz Mountains 1993: Straightforward, fruity and spicy, apple and oak flavors nicely wrapped together to balance. Ready now. 880 cases made. • $16 • (07/31/95) • **84**
Chardonnay Santa Cruz Mountains 1992: Lean and leesy, with an earthy citrus edge to the pear and spice notes. Drinks well now. 600 cases made. • $16 • (01/31/95) • **83**
Gewürztraminer Monterey County 1993: A little sweet and gentle, offering a spicy edge to the simple melony flavor. 1,200 cases made. • $9 • (01/31/95) • **80**
Gewürztraminer Monterey County 1992 • $8 • (09/30/93) • **83**
Gewürztraminer Monterey County 1991 • $8 • (07/31/92) • **80**
Gewürztraminer Santa Cruz Mountains Barrel Fermented Dry 1994: Has pretty fruit and spice up front that fades quickly but offers a nice zip before it disappears. Ready now. 580 cases made. • $10 • (11/15/95) • **80**
Gewürztraminer Santa Cruz Mountains Dry 1995: Dry and distinctly floral, with rose petal and apple flavors shining nicely through the finish. 275 cases made. • $12 • (06/30/96) • **86**
Gewürztraminer Santa Cruz Mountains Dry 1993: Lean and a little earthy, with more mineral notes than fruit. 800 cases made. • $9 • (01/31/95) • **77**
Merlot California 1994: Bland and uninteresting, crisp, narrow flavors defy description. 1,700 cases made. • $17 • **72**
Merlot California 1993: Lean and trim, medium bodied with leafy herb, tea and light cherry notes. Finishes with a sour cherry edge. • $14 • **78**
Merlot Central Coast 1989 • $13 • (12/31/93) • **80**
Merlot San Ysidro 1992: Marked by toasty, buttery oak, so much so it has a bitter edge that overrides the fruit. 675 cases made. • $14 • (06/15/95) • **78**
Pinot Noir Carneros Madonna Vineyard 1985 • $13 • (09/15/88) • **83**
Pinot Noir Central Coast Cypress 1989 • $9 • (09/30/92) • **77**
Pinot Noir Santa Cruz Mountains 1992: Smells fruity but turns more austere, tannic and earthy on the palate. Finishes with pepper and berry notes. Drinkable now. • $23 • (12/31/95) • **83**
Pinot Noir Santa Cruz Mountains 1989 • $15 • (02/28/94) • **78**
Pinot Noir Santa Cruz Mountains Sessantesimo 1991 • $18 • (02/28/94) • **87**
Pinot Noir Santa Maria Valley 1987 • $16 • (02/28/91) • **81**

BARNETT | CALIFORNIA

Cabernet Sauvignon Napa Valley 1990: A deep colored, peppery tasting red that's more like a Côtes du Rhône than a Cabernet. Herbal, vegetal notes affect the core of ripe plum and prune flavors. Moderately tannic and full bodied. 230 cases made. • $25 • (11/15/93) • **83**
Cabernet Sauvignon Napa Valley 1989 • $18 • (11/15/93) • **86**
Cabernet Sauvignon Spring Mountain 1994: Effusively fruity—in fact the fruitiest in this tasting—with tiers of black cherry, currant, plum and spice. Still showing its youthful edges as you might expect, but the raw material is impressive. • $NA • (05/31/95) • **90-94** (BT)
Cabernet Sauvignon Spring Mountain 1993: Tannic, with an earthy, leathery edge to the ripe cherry, anise and currant flavors. Flavors hang on through the finish. Cellar into 1998. 467 cases made. • $32 • **85**
Cabernet Sauvignon Spring Mountain 1992: Chunky, spicy, toasty oak and a chewy core of cherry and currant flavors, strong tannic finish. Best to cellar into 1997. 556 cases made. • $32 • (05/31/95) • **87**
Pinot Noir Carneros 1994: A strong minty flavor dominates. Turns a bit funky and peppery on the finish, missing the mark for 1994. 280 cases made. • $23 • **80**

BARON | CALIFORNIA

Cabernet Sauvignon Paso Robles 1987 • $9 • (11/15/92) • **72**

BARON HERZOG | CALIFORNIA

Cabernet Sauvignon California 1992: Smooth, ripe and generous, with vanilla aromas and cranberry-currant flavors. Has a supple finish and it's drinkable now. 7,000 cases made. • $9 • (12/31/94) BB • **86**
Cabernet Sauvignon California Selection 1990: Simple, earthy and slightly muddy, with a watery finish that manages to get around to berry flavors. Drinkable, but unexceptional. • $11 • (06/15/93) • **75**
Cabernet Sauvignon Sonoma County 1989 • $11 • (03/31/91) • **73**
Cabernet Sauvignon Sonoma County Special Reserve 1986 • $16 • (03/31/91) • **74**

BARROW GREEN

Chardonnay California 1992: Reasonably fruity and herbal in flavor, inviting at first, but it turns soft and semi-sweet on the finish. Acceptable but simple. 16,000 cases made. • $11 • **78**
Chenin Blanc California 1993: Simple and grassy in aroma, simple and off-dry in flavor. A soft, semi-sweet bland-tasting white wine that comes off as dull. Drinkable, but uninteresting. 10,000 cases made. • $6 • **74**
Johannisberg Riesling Late Harvest California 1989 • $8 • (03/31/91) • **86**
Sauvignon Blanc California 1991 • $9 • (09/15/93) • **74**
Zinfandel Sonoma County Special Cuvée 1990 • $10 • (03/31/93) • **86**

BARROW GREEN | CALIFORNIA

Pinot Noir California 1987 • $15 • (10/31/91) • **79**
Pinot Noir California 1986 • $16 • (10/15/89) • **76**

BAY CELLARS | CALIFORNIA

Pinot Noir Los Carneros 1985 • $15 • (06/15/88) • **77**

BAYVIEW CELLARS | CALIFORNIA

Cabernet Sauvignon Napa Valley 1991: An earthy style with a leathery edge to the currant, spice and cedary oak flavors. Needs time to soften, but may always be on the tannic side. Best after 1997. 612 cases made. • $12 • (05/31/95) • **83**
Charbono Napa Valley 1992: Firm and chunky, with a nice thread of currant and blackberry flavors running through it. Polished finish makes it approachable now, best from 1997. 630 cases made. • $14 • (11/15/95) • **86**
Chardonnay Napa Valley Carneros 1993: A simple wine, with nice pear, spice and nutmeg notes. A little more pizzaz would have helped. 414 cases made. • $12 • (06/30/96) • **83**
Chardonnay Napa Valley Carneros 1992: Ripe, smooth and creamy, with pretty pear, honey, toast and apricot flavors that are rich and complex. A new winery part-owned by Ingelnook's John Richburg. 320 cases made. • $12 • (12/15/94) • **88**
Gewürztraminer Napa Valley 1993: Fruity and a bit sweet, with little spice or floral character to identify it as Gewürz. 300 cases made. • $7 • (02/28/95) • **77**
Merlot Napa Valley 1992: A rustic style with a mineral edge to the cherry flavor. The cedary, toasty oak that gives it a troubling dryness, which makes us wonder whether it will ever come into balance. Best after 1997. 167 cases made. • $14 • (06/15/96) • **82**

BEARBOAT | CALIFORNIA

Pinot Noir Russian River Valley 1992: Light and thin, with a shallow band of spicy cherry fruit. Marginal quality, but the label's cute. 204 cases made. • $16 • (03/31/95) • **77**

BEAUCANON | CALIFORNIA

Cabernet Sauvignon Napa Valley 1991: Light in texture, ultimately austere, with modest berry and earth flavors that don't quite mesh yet. Try in 1997. 3,000 cases made. • $12 • (12/15/95) • **79**
Cabernet Sauvignon Napa Valley 1990: Smooth and flavorful, with appealing, smoky oak, currant and spice nuances. One of Beaucanon's better efforts. 3,000 cases made. • $11 • (02/28/95) • **86**
Cabernet Sauvignon Napa Valley 1988 • $12 • (12/15/92) • **70**
Cabernet Sauvignon Napa Valley 1986 • $15 • (12/31/88) • **85**
Chardonnay Late Harvest Envie 1991: Sweet and cloying, with more bubble gum flavors than fruit. Not much excitement in this unbalanced effort. • $11 • (04/15/93) • **76**
Chardonnay Napa Valley 1994: Very soft, almost flat, with modest fruit character. 3,000 cases made. • $12 • (06/15/96) • **78**

Key: SS—Spectator Selection. CS—Cellar Selection. BB—Best Buy. $NA—Price not available. (BT)—Barrel tasting. Ⓐ—Auction Price.
Dates in parentheses represent the issues in which the ratings were published.

Chardonnay Napa Valley 1993: Ripe and fragrant, with spice and floral aromas, leading to ripe pear, peach and spicy flavors, picking up an earthy edge on the finish. 2,500 cases made. • $12 • **87**
Chardonnay Napa Valley 1992: Serves up distinct oaky, toasty, buttery flavors up front, but pulls in enough pear and spice to keep it interesting. Balanced with a sweet smoky aftertaste. Drink now. 7,000 cases made. • $11 • (02/28/94) • **85**
Chardonnay Napa Valley 1991 • $10 • (12/15/92) • **83**
Merlot Napa Valley 1994: Tough, dry and tannic, with just a hint of mint and currant to the earthy, tarry flavors. 1,000 cases made. • $14 • **79**
Merlot Napa Valley 1993: Coffee, currant and berry flavors that quickly fade. Finish is tannic and dry. 2,000 cases made. • $14 • **81**
Merlot Napa Valley 1991: Marked by a weedy, dill edge that turns earthy and funky. 5,000 cases made. • $12 • (02/28/95) • **77**
Merlot Napa Valley 1990 • $12 • (07/15/93) • **81**
Merlot Napa Valley 1989 • $10 • (05/31/92) • **73**
Merlot Napa Valley 1988 • $13 • (03/31/91) • **84**
Merlot Napa Valley 1986 • $13 • (12/31/88) • **78**

BEAULIEU | CALIFORNIA

Brut Napa Valley 1982 • $12 • (05/31/89) • **81**
Brut Napa Valley Champagne de Chardonnay 1982 • $16 • (05/31/89) • **87**
Burgundy Napa Valley 1987 • $5 • (01/31/91) BB • **80**
Burgundy Napa Valley 1984 • $5 • (08/31/89) • **78**
Burgundy Napa Valley 1982 • $5 • (10/15/88) • **79**
Cabernet Sauvignon Napa Valley Beautour 1991: Crisp and austere, with an herb-and-bell-pepper edge to the ripe Cabernet flavors. Mature now. • $9 • (09/30/94) • **82**
Cabernet Sauvignon Napa Valley Beautour 1990: Light with herb, currant and tarry notes that turn simple on the finish. A reliable everyday kind of Cabernet. • $8 • (11/15/93) • **80**
Cabernet Sauvignon Napa Valley Beautour 1988 • $7 • (09/30/90) • **79**
Cabernet Sauvignon Napa Valley Beautour 1987 • $8 • (05/31/89) BB • **81**
Cabernet Sauvignon Napa Valley Beautour 1986 • $7 • (10/31/88) • **83**
Cabernet Sauvignon Napa Valley Beautour 1985 • $7 • (06/15/88) • **83**
Cabernet Sauvignon Napa Valley Beautour 1982 • $7 • (10/15/86) • **64**
Cabernet Sauvignon Napa Valley Claret Special Release 1990: Weedy and herbal. This is labeled "Special Release" Claret, but it tastes more like the old Beautour Cabernet. A fair price in a ripe, balanced Cabernet. Drinkable now. • $7 • (11/15/92) • **79**
Cabernet Sauvignon Napa Valley Georges de Latour Private Reserve 1992: Young and austere yet well crafted, with a firm edge to the plum and cherry flavors, turning smooth and supple on the finish, where the tannins are well integrated. • $40 • (12/15/95) • **89**
Cabernet Sauvignon Napa Valley Georges de Latour Private Reserve 1991: Smooth and elegant, with a cedar and spicy edge to the cherry and currant flavors, finishing with a firm tannic edge. Best to cellar into 1999 to soften. Fits in well with the BV style. Should only get better. • $40 • (12/15/95) • **90**
Cabernet Sauvignon Napa Valley Georges de Latour Private Reserve 1990: Ripe and spicy, showing rich plum and cherry flavor and finishing with fleshy tannins and good length. Impressive for its subtlety and finesse. Approachable now, probably better in 1997. First BV Private Reserve aged in French oak barrels. • $40 • (11/15/94) • **89**
Cabernet Sauvignon Napa Valley Georges de Latour Private Reserve 1989 • $40 • (06/15/94) • **85**
Cabernet Sauvignon Napa Valley Georges de Latour Private Reserve 1988 • $37 • (11/15/92) • **77**
Cabernet Sauvignon Napa Valley Georges de Latour Private Reserve 1987 • $38 Ⓐ • (11/15/91) • **92**
Cabernet Sauvignon Napa Valley Georges de Latour Private Reserve 1986 • $38 Ⓐ • (03/31/91) • **93**
Cabernet Sauvignon Napa Valley Georges de Latour Private Reserve 1985 • $55 Ⓐ • (03/31/91) • **95**
Cabernet Sauvignon Napa Valley Georges de Latour Private Reserve 1984 • $42 Ⓐ • (03/31/91) • **92**
Cabernet Sauvignon Napa Valley Georges de Latour Private Reserve 1983 • $24 Ⓐ • (03/31/91) • **82**
Cabernet Sauvignon Napa Valley Georges de Latour Private Reserve 1982 • $35 Ⓐ • (03/31/91) • **90**

Cabernet Sauvignon Napa Valley Georges de Latour Private Reserve 1981 • $36 • (03/31/91) • **86**

Cabernet Sauvignon Napa Valley Georges de Latour Private Reserve 1980 • $39 Ⓐ • (03/31/91) • **93**

Cabernet Sauvignon Napa Valley Georges de Latour Private Reserve 1979 • $33 Ⓐ • (03/31/91) • **87**

Cabernet Sauvignon Napa Valley Georges de Latour Private Reserve 1978 • $45 Ⓐ • (03/31/91) • **90**

Cabernet Sauvignon Napa Valley Georges de Latour Private Reserve 1977 • $59 • (03/31/91) • **79**

Cabernet Sauvignon Napa Valley Georges de Latour Private Reserve 1976 • $76 • (03/31/91) • **88**

Cabernet Sauvignon Napa Valley Georges de Latour Private Reserve 1975 • $55 • (03/31/91) • **83**

Cabernet Sauvignon Napa Valley Georges de Latour Private Reserve 1974 • $56 Ⓐ • (11/15/94) • **86**

Cabernet Sauvignon Napa Valley Georges de Latour Private Reserve 1973 • $41 Ⓐ • (03/31/91) • **75**

Cabernet Sauvignon Napa Valley Georges de Latour Private Reserve 1972 • $53 • (03/31/91) • **71**

Cabernet Sauvignon Napa Valley Georges de Latour Private Reserve 1971 • $36 Ⓐ • (03/31/91) • **79**

Cabernet Sauvignon Napa Valley Georges de Latour Private Reserve 1970 • $110 Ⓐ • (03/31/91) • **93**

Cabernet Sauvignon Napa Valley Georges de Latour Private Reserve 1969 • $95 • (03/31/91) • **92**

Cabernet Sauvignon Napa Valley Georges de Latour Private Reserve 1968 • $130 Ⓐ • (03/31/91) • **92**

Cabernet Sauvignon Napa Valley Georges de Latour Private Reserve 1967 • $95 • (03/31/91) • **82**

Cabernet Sauvignon Napa Valley Georges de Latour Private Reserve 1966 • $130 • (03/31/91) • **87**

Cabernet Sauvignon Napa Valley Georges de Latour Private Reserve 1965 • $72 Ⓐ • (03/31/91) • **77**

Cabernet Sauvignon Napa Valley Georges de Latour Private Reserve 1964 • $125 • (03/31/91) • **72**

Cabernet Sauvignon Napa Valley Georges de Latour Private Reserve 1963 • $100 • (03/31/91) • **74**

Cabernet Sauvignon Napa Valley Georges de Latour Private Reserve 1962 • $100 • (03/31/91) • **75**

Cabernet Sauvignon Napa Valley Georges de Latour Private Reserve 1961 • $140 • (03/31/91) • **77**

Cabernet Sauvignon Napa Valley Georges de Latour Private Reserve 1960 • $160 • (03/31/91) • **85**

Cabernet Sauvignon Napa Valley Georges de Latour Private Reserve 1959 • $340 • (03/31/91) • **89**

Cabernet Sauvignon Napa Valley Georges de Latour Private Reserve 1958 • $400 Ⓐ • (03/31/91) • **97**

Cabernet Sauvignon Napa Valley Georges de Latour Private Reserve 1957 • $300 • (03/31/91) • **69**

Cabernet Sauvignon Napa Valley Georges de Latour Private Reserve 1956 • $600 • (03/31/91) • **88**

Cabernet Sauvignon Napa Valley Georges de Latour Private Reserve 1955 • $530 • (03/31/91) • **85**

Cabernet Sauvignon Napa Valley Georges de Latour Private Reserve 1954 • $280 • (03/31/91) • **86**

Cabernet Sauvignon Napa Valley Georges de Latour Private Reserve 1953 • $680 • (03/31/91) • **91**

Cabernet Sauvignon Napa Valley Georges de Latour Private Reserve 1952 • $600 • (03/31/91) • **91**

Cabernet Sauvignon Napa Valley Georges de Latour Private Reserve 1951 • $950 • (03/31/91) • **92**

Cabernet Sauvignon Napa Valley Georges de Latour Private Reserve 1950 • $750 • (03/31/91) • **88**

Cabernet Sauvignon Napa Valley Georges de Latour Private Reserve 1949 • $748 Ⓐ • (03/31/91) • **88**

Cabernet Sauvignon Napa Valley Georges de Latour Private Reserve 1948 • $1500 • (03/31/91) • **79**

Cabernet Sauvignon Napa Valley Georges de Latour Private Reserve 1947 • $1450 • (03/31/91) • **89**

Cabernet Sauvignon Napa Valley Georges de Latour Private Reserve 1946 • $1500 • (03/01/89) • **88**

Cabernet Sauvignon Napa Valley Georges de Latour Private Reserve 1945 • $700 • (03/31/91) • **70**

Cabernet Sauvignon Napa Valley Georges de Latour Private Reserve 1944 • $680 • (03/31/91) • **75**

Cabernet Sauvignon Napa Valley Georges de Latour Private Reserve 1943 • $1250 • (03/31/91) • **87**

Cabernet Sauvignon Napa Valley Georges de Latour Private Reserve 1942 • $460 Ⓐ • (03/31/91) • **85**

Cabernet Sauvignon Napa Valley Georges de Latour Private Reserve 1941 • $958 Ⓐ • (03/31/91) • **89**

Cabernet Sauvignon Napa Valley Georges de Latour Private Reserve 1940 • $1250 • (03/31/91) • **89**

Cabernet Sauvignon Napa Valley Georges de Latour Private Reserve 1939 • $1550 • (03/31/91) • **91**

Cabernet Sauvignon Napa Valley Georges de Latour Private Reserve 1936 • $1550 • (03/31/91) • **86**

Cabernet Sauvignon Napa Valley Rutherford 1992: Well crafted, striking a nice balance between ripe plummy flavor and spicy oak. Doesn't dazzle, but hits most of the right notes. • $12 • (11/30/95) • **86**

Cabernet Sauvignon Napa Valley Rutherford 1991: Firm and compact, with a pretty core of currant and cherry that picks up spicy, cedary oak notes on the finish. Elegant and well crafted, may still need cellaring to soften. • $13 • (10/15/94) • **87**

Cabernet Sauvignon Napa Valley Rutherford 1990: Firm in texture, with wide-open, spicy currant and black cherry aromas and flavors, not at all heavy. Tannins clamp down on the finish—enough to warrant cellaring until 1997-98. • $11 • (10/31/93) • **85**

Cabernet Sauvignon Napa Valley Rutherford 1989 • $11 • (03/31/92) • **81**

Cabernet Sauvignon Napa Valley Rutherford 1988 • $15 • (07/15/91) • **86**

Cabernet Sauvignon Napa Valley Rutherford 1987 • $11 Ⓐ • (12/15/90) • **85**

Cabernet Sauvignon Napa Valley Rutherford 1986 • $29 Ⓐ • (09/15/89) • **85**

Cabernet Sauvignon Napa Valley Rutherford 1985 • $17 Ⓐ • (06/15/88) • **85**

Cabernet Sauvignon Napa Valley Rutherford 1984 • $15 • (08/31/87) • **78**

Cabernet Sauvignon Napa Valley Rutherford 1983 • $12 • (06/15/87) • **80**

Cabernet Sauvignon Napa Valley Rutherford 1982 • $20 • (04/16/86) • **81**

Cabernet Sauvignon Napa Valley Rutherford 1981 • $17 • (05/16/85) • **81**

Cabernet Sauvignon Napa Valley Rutherford 1980 • $30 • (06/01/85) • **88**

Cabernet Sauvignon Napa Valley Rutherford 1979 • $12 Ⓐ • (06/01/85) • **89**

Cabernet Sauvignon Napa Valley Rutherford 1970 • $NA • (06/01/85) • **90**

Chardonnay Carneros 1992: Strikes a nice balance between ripe pear and apple flavors with spicy, toasty oak, finishing with good length and pretty, complex flavors. A solid value. • $10 • (06/30/94) BB • **86**

Chardonnay Napa Valley Beaufort 1991 • $8 • (07/15/93) • **82**

Chardonnay Napa Valley Beautour 1994: Simple and a little green around the edges, with a straightforward apple flavor. • $9 • (06/15/96) • **80**

Chardonnay Napa Valley Beautour 1993: Strikes a nice balance between the apple and pear flavors and the subtle, creamy oak. It's elegant and refined on the finish, and a bargain for California Chardonnay. 40,000 cases made. • $10 • (04/30/95) BB • **86**

Chardonnay Napa Valley Beautour 1992: Crisp and focused, with ripe apple and pear shadings that are concentrated and a touch coarse, turning spicy on the finish. Good value, drink now. • $8 • (06/30/94) • **83**

Chardonnay Napa Valley Beautour 1991 • $9 • (07/15/93) • **82**

Chardonnay Napa Valley Carneros 1994: Smooth and elegant, with a pretty band of pear, spice, apple and honey flavors that are well focused and long on the finish. • $13 • (02/29/96) • **88**

Chardonnay Napa Valley Carneros 1993: A crisp Chardonnay, adding an earthy edge to the ripe pear and spice notes. Appealing for its direct fruitiness. • $13 • (09/30/95) • **85**

Chardonnay Napa Valley Carneros Barrel Fermented Reserve 1991: Ripe, smooth and buttery, with spicy pear, honey and butterscotch flavors that are rich and intense. A solid BV Carneros Reserve that can stand short-term cellaring. Tasted twice. • $16 • (06/30/94) • **88**

Chardonnay Napa Valley Carneros Reserve 1994: Ripe, rich, smooth and harmonious, offering tiers of pear, honey, vanilla and spice as flavors fan out on the finish, gaining a sense of elegance and finesse. 4,674 cases made. • $18 • (04/30/96) • **91**

Chardonnay Napa Valley Carneros Reserve 1993: Serves up fig, pear, apple and spice flavors in a round and forward style where toasty oak meshes in neatly on the finish. 2,100 cases made. • $18 • (12/31/95) • **88**

Chardonnay Napa Valley Carneros Reserve 1992: Ripe and spicy, supporting some appealing pear, peach and pineapple flavors that turn elegant and refined, with an earthy edge. 5,200 cases made. • $16 • (04/30/95) • **88**

Chardonnay Napa Valley Carneros Reserve 1991: This wine has a hollow middle, with hints of pear and oak around the edges. Never quite comes together. Ready now. • $16 • (06/30/94) • **81**

Gamay Beaujolais Napa Valley 1988 • $6 • (08/31/89) • **73**

Gamay Beaujolais Napa Valley 1987 • $6 • (09/30/88) • **76**

Meritage Napa Valley 1990: An elegant style with supple herb, plum and cherry notes, finishing with light tannins. Drinks well now but has the depth and flavor to hold and gain through 1998. BV's debut Meritage. • $20 • (11/15/94) • **85**

Merlot Napa Valley 1993: Appealing for its spicy currant and berry-laced fruit. Turns hard and tannic on the finish, with less fruit than it starts with. • $16 • **84**

Merlot Napa Valley 1993: Appealing for its spicy currant and berry flavors. Turns hard and tannic on the finish, with less fruit than it starts with. • $16 • (06/15/96) • **82**

Merlot Napa Valley Beautour 1993: Light and berryish, with a pleasant smoky edge. • $12 • (06/30/96) • **82**

Merlot Napa Valley Beautour 1991: Tough and chewy, firm tannins overriding the berry, herb and cherry flavors. Best after 1997. • $10 • (01/31/95) • **82**

Pinot Noir California Beautour 1994: Light and fruity, with an appealing core of cherry and berry fruit of modest proportion. • $10 • (12/31/95) • **82**

Pinot Noir Napa Valley 1991 • $8 • (02/28/94) • **81**

Pinot Noir Napa Valley 1990 • $8 • (02/28/93) • **73**

Pinot Noir Napa Valley Beaumont 1986 • $7 • (06/15/88) • **74**

Pinot Noir Napa Valley Beaumont 1985 • $6 • (06/15/88) • **78**

Pinot Noir Napa Valley Beautour 1993: Light and easy to drink, with a spicy edge to the modest raspberry flavors. • $10 • (12/31/95) • **81**

Pinot Noir Napa Valley Beautour 1992: Lightly fruity, offering simple cherry and plum notes. Ready now. • $9 • (03/31/95) • **79**

Pinot Noir Napa Valley Carneros 1994: Simple but pleasant, with a modest core of plum and cherry character. Picks up a trace of herb on the finish. • $12 • (03/31/96) • **84**

Pinot Noir Napa Valley Carneros 1993: Somewhat earthy, offering a light band of cherry and spice but turning complex on the finish. Appealing fruity, delicate style. • $13 • (10/15/95) • **86**

Pinot Noir Napa Valley Carneros 1992: Simple with a spicy menthol edge to light cherry fruit. Disappointing given BV's efforts of late to upgrade quality. • $13 • (03/31/95) • **78**

Pinot Noir Napa Valley Carneros Reserve 1994: An elegant and exotic style that captures a wide range of flavors—black cherry, herb, spice and toasty, buttery oak. It all folds together rather nicely on the finish, where the tannins are smooth and polished. Impressive for its depth and finesse. • $19 • (03/31/96) • **90**

Pinot Noir Napa Valley Carneros Reserve 1993: Marked by strong, overriding minty flavors, so much so it dominates the flavors, making it taste one dimensional. Perhaps with time in the bottle more fruit will emerge and the mintiness will subside. • $18 • (12/31/95) • **83**

Pinot Noir Napa Valley Carneros Reserve 1992: Marked by minty plum and cherry notes, it's ripe and supple with good balance. Drinkable now. 2,470 cases made. • $18 • (05/15/95) • **86**

Pinot Noir Napa Valley Carneros Reserve 1991 • $15 • (02/28/94) • **85**

Pinot Noir Napa Valley Carneros Reserve 1990 • $17 • (02/28/93) • **84**

Pinot Noir Napa Valley Carneros Reserve 1989 • $13 • (04/30/91) • **85**

Pinot Noir Napa Valley Carneros Reserve 1988 • $9 • (04/15/90) • **87**

Pinot Noir Napa Valley Carneros Reserve 1987 • $9 • (12/31/88) • **90**

Pinot Noir Napa Valley Los Carneros 1980 • $10 • (08/31/86) • **88**

Pinot Noir Napa Valley Los Carneros Reserve 1986 • $9 • (09/15/88) • **88**

Pinot Noir Napa Valley Los Carneros Reserve 1985 • $9 • (01/31/88) • **74**

Sauvignon Blanc California Beautour 1994: Lean and harmonious, offering lots of nice pear and herb flavors that zip through the finish. • $7 • (06/30/95) • **83**

Key: SS—Spectator Selection. CS—Cellar Selection. BB—Best Buy. $NA—Price not available. (BT)—Barrel tasting. Ⓐ—Auction Price.
Dates in parentheses represent the issues in which the ratings were published.

Sauvignon Blanc Napa Valley 1994: Strongly floral, with rose petal and anise scents. Pear flavors finish with lively intensity. • $8 • **88**

Sauvignon Blanc Napa Valley 1993: Bright and fruity, showing simple pear and mint flavors that finish a little short. • $10 • (09/15/95) • **80**

Sauvignon Blanc Napa Valley 1992: Light and frangrant, a perfumey wine with citrusy tang. • $9 • (12/31/94) • **83**

Tapestry Red Napa Valley Reserve 1992: Young and tight, featuring pretty mineral, currant, cherry and toasty oak flavors, all folding together in a neat, supple package. Crisp acidity and firm tannins. A marked improvement over the '91. Drinkable in 1998. 2,000 cases made. • $20 • (04/30/96) • **88**

Tapestry Signet Collection Napa Valley 1991: Young and intense, an austere style with spice, currant, cherry and cedary oak flavors, all tightly wound and finishing with tannic, herbal edge. • $20 • (12/15/95) • **87**

Tapestry Signet Collection Napa Valley 1990: 2,000 cases made. • $20 • **84**

Zinfandel Napa Valley Signet Collection 1994: Smooth and complex medley of spicy berry, cherry and plum flavors. Impressively fruity and direct finish. BV's first Zinfandel. 800 cases made. • $16 • **88**

BEAUX HAUTS, CHATEAU | CALIFORNIA

Brut Russian River Valley Blanc de Meunier Hopkins Ranch NV • $18 • (12/31/93) • **87**

Brut Russian River Valley Cuvée de Meunier Hopkins Ranch NV • $15 • (12/31/93) • **88**

BEDELL | NEW YORK

Cabernet Sauvignon North Fork of Long Island 1988 • $15 • (06/30/91) • **86**

Eis North Fork of Long Island 1992: The aromas of honey, spice and minerals are pleasant, but don't prepare you for the searing acidity in the finish. A big, sweet, apricot-flavored wine, if it softens, it will be very pleasant. Drinkable now. 100 cases made. • $24 • (04/15/95) • **84**

Merlot North Fork of Long Island 1987 • $18 • (03/31/90) • **90**

Merlot North Fork of Long Island 1986 • $11 • (12/15/88) • **88**

Merlot North Fork of Long Island Reserve 1988 • $14 • (06/30/91) • **90**

BEL ARBORS | CALIFORNIA

Cabernet Sauvignon American Cask 88 NV • $6 • (11/15/91) • **78**

Cabernet Sauvignon American Founder's Selection NV • $5 • (10/15/89) BB • **82**

Cabernet Sauvignon California 1993: Soft and generous, centered around appealing vanilla-scented raspberry and red currant flavors that linger gently on the finish. A fair price for a Cabernet of good quality. Approachable now. 30,000 cases made. • $7 • (12/15/95) • **84**

Cabernet Sauvignon California 1992: Simple, with spicy cherry and cranberry notes. 50,000 cases made. • $7 • (01/31/95) • **78**

Cabernet Sauvignon California 1990: Straightforward and nicely flavorful, with cherry and plum accents. An easy, light texture and soft balance make it drinkable now. 30,000 cases made. • $6 • (03/15/93) BB • **82**

Cabernet Sauvignon California Founder's Selection 1990: Light and fruity with simple cherry and plum notes and soft tannins. Ready now. 30,000 cases made. • $6 • (11/15/93) • **80**

Chardonnay California 1991 • $7 • (11/30/92) • **78**

Chardonnay California Founder's Selection 1992: Soft, simple and appealing, with generous vanilla and spice notes adding to the core of pear flavor. Drinkable now. 215,000 cases made. • $6 • (07/15/93) • **80**

Chardonnay California Vintner's Selection 1994: Fresh and appealing for its scent of lime and the pineapple and pear flavors, which echo nicely on the finish. Offers some excitement, and a steal at this price. 150,000 cases made. • $5 • (05/31/96) BB • **85**

Merlot American Cask 89 NV • $6 • (11/15/91) BB • **81**

Merlot American Founder's Selection American Grown NV • $5 • (06/15/90) • **72**

Merlot California 1990 • $7 • (10/31/92) BB • **84**

Merlot California Vintner's Selection 1994: Light, smooth and refreshing, with rasberry and spice flavors that linger gently on the finish. 35,000 cases made. • $6 • (06/30/96) BB • **84**

White Zinfandel California 1994: Modest strawberry and cherry flavors taste stale. Simple and innocuous. • $5 • (09/15/95) • **75**

Zinfandel California Founder's Selection 1990 • $6 • (09/30/92) BB • **85**

BELL | CALIFORNIA

Cabernet Sauvignon Baritelle Vineyards 1991: Crisp in texture with currant and blackberry flavors that push out into a wide band of flavors that finish with a tingle of acidity. Give it until 1997. New wine from Anthony Bell, former manager of Beaulieu Vineyard. 460 cases made. • $40 • (12/15/95) • **83**

BELL MOUNTAIN | TEXAS

Cabernet Sauvignon Bell Mountain 1989 • $13 • (02/29/92) • **85**

Pinot Noir Bell Mountain 1989 • $12 • (02/29/92) • **76**

Pinot Noir Bell Mountain Oberhellmann Vineyards 1990 • $12 • (02/28/93) • **64**

BELLEROSE | CALIFORNIA

Cabernet Sauvignon Dry Creek Valley Reserve Cuvée 1987 • $18 • (11/15/91) • **83**

Cuvée Bellerose Sonoma County 1986 • $11 Ⓐ • (01/31/90) • **83**

Cuvée Bellerose Sonoma County 1985 • $19 Ⓐ • (12/15/88) • **82**

Cuvée Bellerose Sonoma County 1984 • $14 • (11/15/87) • **77**

Cuvée Bellerose Sonoma County 1983 • $8 Ⓐ • (01/31/87) • **74**

Cuvée Bellerose Sonoma County 1980 • $11 • (11/01/84) • **79**

Merlot Dry Creek Valley Reserve 1988 • $16 • (05/31/92) • **84**

Merlot Sonoma County 1986 • $16 • (04/15/90) • **69**

Merlot Sonoma County 1985 • $16 • (02/28/89) • **73**

Merlot Sonoma County 1984 • $12 • (12/31/87) • **77**

BELVEDERE | CALIFORNIA

Cabernet Sauvignon Alexander Valley Robert Young Vineyard Gifts of the Land 1985 • $16 • (01/31/91) • **81**

Cabernet Sauvignon Alexander Valley Robert Young Vineyards 1984 • $13 • (07/15/88) • **88**

Cabernet Sauvignon Alexander Valley Robert Young Vineyards 1983 • $12 • (05/15/87) • **88**

Cabernet Sauvignon Alexander Valley Robert Young Vineyards 1982 • $18 • (12/01/85) SS • **95**

Cabernet Sauvignon Lake County Discovery Series 1982 • $4 • (04/01/85) BB • **80**

Cabernet Sauvignon Napa Valley Discovery Series 1982 • $4 • (02/16/86) • **71**

Cabernet Sauvignon Napa Valley York Creek Vineyard 1983 • $12 • (12/31/87) • **79**

Cabernet Sauvignon Napa Valley York Creek Vineyard 1982 • $12 • (09/15/86) • **72**

Cabernet Sauvignon Sonoma County 1992: Trim but well balanced, with a pleasant band of currant, cherry, cedar and spice. 3,545 cases made. • $12 • (03/31/96) • **82**

Cabernet Sauvignon Sonoma County 1991: Lean and a bit green, with cedar, tart plum and black cherry notes that pick up a tobacco and light oak flavor on the finish. Ready now through 1998. 1,880 cases made. • $10 • (11/15/94) • **82**

Cabernet Sauvignon Sonoma County Discovery Series 1987 • $6 • (06/15/90) • **75**

Cabernet Sauvignon Sonoma County Preferred Stock 1988 • $18 • (11/15/93) • **84**

Chardonnay Alexander Valley 1994: Effusively fruity style sporting a canned fruit cocktail flavor. Shows off ripe fig, pear and apple notes and touches of spice. 6,250 cases made. • $12 • (04/30/96) • **86**

Chardonnay Alexander Valley 1992: Serves up attractive pear, apple and spice notes that pick up a honey edge on the finish. Light oak adds dimension. Ready now. 11,216 cases made. • $9 • (11/15/94) BB • **87**

Chardonnay Alexander Valley 1991 • $8 • (06/30/93) BB • **86**

Chardonnay Russian River Valley 1994: Ripe and full-bodied, appealing melon, fig and spice notes picking up a touch of honey and fig on the finish. 5,600 cases made. • $13 • (02/29/96) • **88**

Chardonnay Russian River Valley 1993: Elegant and refined, with earthy pear and apple flavors that offer an appealing core of flavors. 3,700 cases made. • $12 • (10/15/95) • **87**

Chardonnay Russian River Valley 1991 • $12 • (04/15/94) • **87**

Chardonnay Sonoma County 1994: Ripe, bright, vivid pear, peach and nectarine notes pick up a trace of oak and hazelnut on the lingering finish. A well-crafted white that delivers a load of flavors. 25,000 cases made. • $9 • (02/29/96) BB • **88**

Chardonnay Sonoma County 1993: Medium in weight, adding a spicy, nutty touch to the ripe pear flavors. 18,000 cases made. • $9 • (05/31/95) • **84**

Chardonnay Sonoma County Preferred Stock 1992: Strikes a nice balance between its ripe, supple pear, vanilla and spice flavors and the light, toasty oak shadings. Turns smooth and creamy on a complex finish, where the flavors echo on. Ready now. 1,250 cases made. • $18 • (11/30/94) • **90**

Chardonnay Sonoma County Preferred Stock 1991 • $18 • (04/15/94) • **90**

Discovery Series Red Table Wine Sonoma County 1983 • $3 • (07/31/88) • **78**

Merlot Alexander Valley Robert Young Vineyards 1986 • $13 • (06/30/89) • **87**

Merlot Alexander Valley Robert Young Vineyards 1984 • $13 • (08/31/88) • **90**

Merlot Alexander Valley Robert Young Vineyards 1983 • $12 • (12/31/87) • **70**

Merlot Alexander Valley Robert Young Vineyards 1982 • $12 • (03/16/86) • **94**

Merlot Sonoma County 1993: Dry and earthy, not showing much in the way of fruit. Dry and bitter on the finish. 1,680 cases made. • $14 • **77**

Merlot Sonoma County 1991: Crisp and lean with simple cherry and plum-scented fruit. A good wine that lacks depth and richness. Drink now. 3,000 cases made. • $12 • (09/15/94) • **82**

Muscat Canelli Late Harvest 1990 • $10 • (06/15/92) • **80**

Pinot Noir Los Carneros Winery Lake 1983 • $12 • (12/15/87) • **73**

Pinot Noir Los Carneros Winery Lake 1982 • $12 • (08/31/86) • **58**

Pinot Noir Sonoma County Bacigalupi 1985 • $12 • (06/15/88) • **73**

Pinot Noir Sonoma County Bacigalupi 1982 • $12 • (11/16/85) • **65**

Zinfandel 1989 • $9 • (05/15/92) BB • **85**

Zinfandel Dry Creek Valley 1993: Marked by pretty plum and cherry flavors, drying up a bit on the finish and turning tannic. It also picks up a slight metallic taste. 1,015 cases made. • $11 • (03/31/96) • **84**

Zinfandel Dry Creek Valley 1991 • $10 • (03/31/94) • **84**

Zinfandel Dry Creek Valley 1990 • $10 • (06/15/93) • **74**

BENHAM | CALIFORNIA

Sangiovese California 1992: Lean and simple, its flavors muddled by a lot of wood, finishing slightly bitter. Not light enough to let out the fruit. 3,500 cases made. • $9 • (11/30/95) • **77**

BENZIGER | CALIFORNIA

A Tribute Sonoma Mountain 1992: Crisp in texture, nicely harmonious in the way in weaves its spicy, toasty-onion nuances through the fig and lemon fruit. Ready now. 200 cases made. • $16 • (08/31/95) • **86**

A Tribute Sonoma Mountain 1990: Pleasant enough, with spice, herb and currant notes, but it lacks the richness and depth found in the best from this vintage. Ready now. 1,170 cases made. • $27 • (11/15/94) • **84**

A Tribute Sonoma Mountain 1989 • $26 • (11/15/92) • **88**

A Tribute Sonoma Mountain 1988 • $26 • (01/31/92) • **88**

A Tribute Sonoma Mountain 1987 • $20 • (12/31/90) • **85**

Aleatico California Blanc de Noirs Lagomarsino Vineyard Imagery Series 1991 • $12 • (11/30/93) • **83**

Blanc de Blancs Carneros Late Disgorged 1989: Serves up nice pear, floral, honey and toast flavors of modest depth and concentration, but they hang in there. Ready now. • $14 • (11/30/94) • **86**

Brut Blanc de Blancs Carneros 1988 • $14 • (12/31/92) • **84**

Brut Carneros Imagery Series 1990: Spicy ripe pear and subtle hazelnut flavors turn complex, lingering on the finish. Appealing style. 360 cases made. • $16 • (05/31/95) • **87**

Cabernet Blend Sonoma Mountain Estate Tribute 1991: Dominated by spicy, minty flavors, but with a pleasant core of currant and cherry flavors sitting underneath. Finishes with crisp tannins. Tasted twice, with consistent results. 1,904 cases made. • $20 • (03/31/96) • **84**

Cabernet Franc Alexander Valley Blue Rock Vineyard Imagery Series 1989 • $16 • (10/15/93) • **85**

Cabernet Franc Alexander Valley Imagery Series 1992: Well oaked, with just enough weedy black currant fruit to stand up to it. 840 cases made. • $16 • (02/28/95) • **83**

Cabernet Sauvignon Sonoma County 1992: Medium-bodied, showing spicy, toasty oak and supple cherry and currant flavors underneath. Well balanced and pleasant enough to drink now. 30,994 cases made. • $13 • (09/15/95) • **87**

Cabernet Sauvignon Sonoma County 1991: Complex and pleasing with a nice core of currant and cherry and pretty toasty, buttery oak flavors. Has a long, lingering finish. Perfectly enjoyable now through 1998. 40,000 cases made. • $12 • (03/15/94) • **88**

Cabernet Sauvignon Sonoma County 1990: A solid wine, offering concentrated plum, berry and currant fruit in good measure with a thwack of spicy on the finish. Needs until 1997 or 1998 for the pieces to fall into place. 15,000 cases made. • $13 • (09/30/93) • **86**

Cabernet Sauvignon Sonoma County 1989 • $12 • (07/15/92) • **84**

Cabernet Sauvignon Sonoma County 1988 • $12 • (11/15/91) • **84**

Cabernet Sauvignon Sonoma County 1987 • $10 • (09/30/90) SS • **93**

Cabernet Sauvignon Sonoma County 1986 • $10 • (07/31/89) • **82**

Cabernet Sauvignon Sonoma Mountain 1989: Crisp and firm, with a narrow band of mint, currant and black cherry flavor. Well balanced for a 1989, but the tannins turn dry on the finish, best to drink soon. 2,000 cases made. • $22 • (11/15/94) • **84**

Cabernet Sauvignon Sonoma Mountain 1988 • $25 • (11/15/91) • **85**

Cabernet Sauvignon Sonoma Valley 1986 • $17 • (04/30/90) • **78**

Cabernet Sauvignon Sonoma Valley 1985 • $16 • (12/15/88) • **83**

Cabernet Sauvignon Sonoma Valley Estate Bottled 1987 • $12 • (11/15/90) • **85**

Chardonnay Carneros 1994: Appealing for its elegance and ripe peach and pear flavors. Smooth and polished in a medium-bodied style. 30,500 cases made. • $13 • (05/15/96) • **84**

Chardonnay Carneros 1993: Smoky, toasty oak leads to a core of ripe pear and spice flavors that have length. Medium body. 16,929 cases made. • $13 • (06/30/95) • **85**

Chardonnay Carneros Premiere Vineyard 1992: Smooth and polished, a nicely balanced wine that offers plenty of pear and pineapple flavors. Finishes with a flourish of fresh fruit and spice. 2,000 cases made. • $16 • (06/15/94) • **88**

Chardonnay Carneros Premiere Vineyard 1991 • $16 • (07/15/93) • **88**

Chardonnay Carneros Reserve 1994: A supple and complex core of creamy pear, spice, honey and smoky, toasty oak flavors lingers well into the aftertaste. An elegant and stylish white that's appealing now. 30,522 cases made. • $13 • (03/31/96) • **89**

Chardonnay Sonoma County 1992: Bright, spicy and generous, pumps a lot of apple and nutmeg flavors through a lean framework. Drinkable now. 25,000 cases made. • $13 • (05/31/94) • **85**

Chardonnay Sonoma County 1991 • $12 • (07/15/93) • **88**

Estate Tribute Sonoma Mountain 1994: Crisp and lightly spicy, a refreshing wine that finishes with smoothly blended herb, citrus and nutmeg flavors. Drinkable now. 764 cases made. • $16 • (06/15/96) • **87**

Estate Tribute Sonoma Mountain 1991: Marked by earthy currant, cedary oak and herbal notes, none of which dominates or is in focus. Finishes with a murky edge. 1,907 cases made. • $20 • (12/15/95) • **84**

Fumé Blanc Sonoma County 1994: Nicely focused and lean, centering around spice, pear and herb flavors. Drink now. 37,000 cases made. • $10 • (06/30/95) • **84**

Key: SS—Spectator Selection. CS—Cellar Selection. BB—Best Buy. $NA—Price not available. (BT)—Barrel tasting. Ⓐ—Auction Price.
Dates in parentheses represent the issues in which the ratings were published.

Fumé Blanc Sonoma County 1993: Simple and refreshing, a citrusy white offering pear and herb notes that finish a bit short. 10,600 cases made. • $9 • (02/28/95) • **80**

Fumé Blanc Sonoma County 1992 • $9 • (03/31/94) BB • **87**

Fumé Blanc Sonoma County 1991 • $9 • (11/30/92) • **88**

International Imagery Series (From France, Australia, Chile, California NV) • $28 • (11/15/93) • **82**

Merlot Sonoma County 1993: Firm, with a modest band of chunky cherry and currant on the palate that finish up with firm, dry tannins. 21,041 cases made. • $14 • (03/31/96) • **82**

Merlot Sonoma County 1992: Firm and tannic, but enough cherry, herb and oak flavors come through on the finish to hold your interest. 28,000 cases made. • $14 • (02/28/95) • **87**

Merlot Sonoma County 1991: This has an unripe, green, tea-like edge up front, but shows more fruit and flavor on the finish, where the cherry and plum notes emerge. Can stand cellaring. 12,000 cases made. • $14 • (09/15/94) • **83**

Merlot Sonoma County 1990 • $14 • (10/15/93) • **85**

Merlot Sonoma County 1989 • $14 • (05/31/92) • **81**

Merlot Sonoma County 1988 • $12 • (11/15/91) • **87**

Merlot Sonoma Valley 1987 • $12 • (03/31/91) • **86**

Merlot Sonoma Valley 1986 • $16 • (07/31/89) • **84**

Moss Oak Vineyard Imagery Series Sonoma County 1993: Soft and round, a gentle giant of a wine, big in structure but brimming with simple fruit. 250 cases made. • $16 • (01/31/95) • **83**

Petite Sirah Paso Robles Shell Creek Vineyard Imagery Series 1989 • $16 • (10/15/93) • **80**

Pinot Blanc Sonoma County 1992: Smooth and spicy, a toasty wine with a nice core of pear and vanilla flavor that keeps echoing on the finish. Ready now. 1,200 cases made. • $13 • (04/15/95) • **85**

Pinot Blanc Sonoma County 1991 • $10 • (12/31/93) • **82**

Pinot Blanc Sonoma Mountain Skinner Vineyard Imagery Series 1993: Elegant and fruity, with soft pear and apple notes that linger and pick up a hint of citrus. 699 cases made. • $16 • (08/31/95) • **84**

Pinot Noir California 1993: A pretty wine that strikes a nice balance between ripe cherries, berries and toasty oak. A little age should help soften it. 1,722 cases made. • $14 • (06/15/96) • **88**

Pinot Noir California 1992: Cherry and herb flavors are hidden beneath the buttery wood, but it's coming together. 2,400 cases made. • $14 • (01/31/95) • **86**

Pinot Noir Sonoma County 1991: Ripe cherry and spice notes. Finishes with an oaky, firmly tannic edge, approachable now. 700 cases made. • $14 • (08/31/94) • **87**

Pinot Noir Sonoma County 1990 • $14 • (02/28/94) • **87**

Pinot Noir Sonoma County 1989 • $13 • (02/28/93) • **85**

Riesling Late Harvest Santa Maria Valley Imagery Series Bien Nacido Vineyard 1994: Very sweet and honeyed, round and generous with its apricot, honey and pear flavors as they swirl through the sugary finish. Delicious, although a bit more acidity would balance it better. 140 cases made. • $16 • (06/15/96) • **89**

Sangiovese Dry Creek Valley Larga Vista Vineyard Imagery Series 1993: Ripe and fruity, well oaked too, with pretty cherry, currant and berry flavors that expand and develop complexity on the finish. Has the tannic strength to cellar into 1998. 250 cases made. • $16 • (06/15/96) • **88**

Sauvignon Blanc Sonoma Mountain 1991 • $14 • (03/31/94) • **84**

Sémillon Sonoma Mountain 1991 • $14 • (03/31/94) • **87**

Syrah Santa Maria Valley Bien Nacido Vineyard Imagery Series 1990 • $16 • (10/31/93) • **70**

White Burgundy Napa Valley Yountmill Vineyard Imagery Series 1994: Smooth, ripe and generous with its dark pear and slightly raisiny flavors, finishing with a touch of spice. 1,000 cases made. • $20 • (06/15/96) • **87**

Zinfandel Port Dry Creek Valley Mayo Family & Carreras Vineyard Imagery 1990: Refreshing, complex and well balanced, with jammy plum, black cherry and juniper berry flavors. Complete and harmonious, approachable now but capable of cellaring. 600 cases made. • $22 • (10/15/94) • **87**

Zinfandel Sonoma County 1993: Strikes a nice balance between spicy, toasty oak and the wild berry, cherry and raspberry flavors. Finishes fruity. 3,177 cases made. • $14 • (10/15/95) • **85**

Zinfandel Sonoma County 1992: Lean and spicy, a peppery red with enough blackberry flavor to keep it balanced. 3,465 cases made. • $13 • (02/28/95) • **86**

Zinfandel Sonoma County 1991: Supple and charming, with smooth, ripe wild berry and black cherry flavors that turn elegant and spicy on the finish. Drinks well now. 1,200 cases made. • $13 • (10/15/94) • **87**

Zinfandel Sonoma County 1990 • $11 • (09/30/93) • **85**

Zinfandel Sonoma County 1989 • $10 • (10/15/92) • **83**

BERGFELD | CALIFORNIA

Cabernet Sauvignon Napa Valley 1988 • $14 • (11/15/91) • **83**

Merlot 1989 • $15 • (05/31/92) • **87**

BERINGER | CALIFORNIA

Cabernet Sauvignon Knights Valley 1992: A solid, chunky core of currant and berry flavors, finishing with firm tannins and a good dose of oak. Can age short-term. 38,000 cases made. • $15 • (08/31/95) • **87**

Cabernet Sauvignon Knights Valley 1991: Offers a pretty array of rich fruit, with layers of currant, wild berry and spicy flavors that turn elegant. Picks up tannins on the finish, but it's well balanced and you can drink it now. • $13 • (05/31/94) • **87**

Cabernet Sauvignon Knights Valley 1990: Firm and ripe, a medium-weight wine with a fleshy texture and spicy, cedary currant and mineral aromas and flavors, all of it smoothly shaped into a wine that should continue to improve through 1999. 35,000 cases made. • $13 • (11/15/93) SS • **90**

Cabernet Sauvignon Knights Valley 1989 • $16 • (11/15/92) • **85**

Cabernet Sauvignon Knights Valley 1988 • $16 • (11/15/91) • **86**

Cabernet Sauvignon Knights Valley 1987 • $16 • (11/15/90) • **90**

Cabernet Sauvignon Knights Valley 1985 • $12 • (05/31/88) • **87**

Cabernet Sauvignon Knights Valley 1983 • $9 • (04/15/87) • **83**

Cabernet Sauvignon Knights Valley 1982 • $9 • (04/15/87) • **90**

Cabernet Sauvignon Knights Valley 1981 • $9 • (10/01/85) • **86**

Cabernet Sauvignon Knights Valley 1980 • $8 • (02/15/84) • **88**

Cabernet Sauvignon Napa Valley Chabot Vineyard 1988 • $35 • (11/15/93) • **83**

Cabernet Sauvignon Napa Valley Chabot Vineyard 1986 • $NA • (03/01/89) • **93**

Cabernet Sauvignon Napa Valley Chabot Vineyard 1985 • $30 • (11/15/91) • **90**

Cabernet Sauvignon Napa Valley Chabot Vineyard 1984 • $30 • (09/15/90) • **85**

Cabernet Sauvignon Napa Valley Chabot Vineyard 1983 • $27 • (03/01/89) • **85**

Cabernet Sauvignon Napa Valley Chabot Vineyard 1982 • $25 • (03/01/89) • **89**

Cabernet Sauvignon Napa Valley Chabot Vineyard 1981 • $23 • (03/01/89) • **87**

Cabernet Sauvignon Napa Valley Private Reserve 1992: Packs a load of ripe, juicy, complex fruit. The tiers of plum, black cherry, currant and spice flavors are all framed nicely by toasty, buttery oak. Combines power with grace. Best in 1999 or later. 5,000 cases made. • $45 • (11/15/95) CS • **95**

Cabernet Sauvignon Napa Valley Private Reserve 1991: Remarkably complex and concentrated, with tiers of currant, anise, cedar and black cherry, finishing with a long, lingering aftertaste. Rich and bright. 14,000 cases made. • $40 • (03/31/95) CS • **94**

Cabernet Sauvignon Napa Valley Private Reserve 1990: Ripe and focused, with a pretty array of rich currant, smoke, toasty oak and spicy mineral flavors that fold together nicely. Impressive for its richness and proportions. Tasted four times with noticeable bottle variation, but two were clearly outstanding. 9,000 cases made. • $40 • (11/15/94) CS • **92**

Cabernet Sauvignon Napa Valley Private Reserve 1989 • $40 • (07/15/93) CS • **90**

Cabernet Sauvignon Napa Valley Private Reserve 1988 • $40 • (06/15/93) • **88**

Cabernet Sauvignon Napa Valley Private Reserve 1987 • $63 Ⓐ • (10/31/91) • **94**

Cabernet Sauvignon Napa Valley Private Reserve 1986 • $69 Ⓐ • (09/15/90) CS • **95**

Cabernet Sauvignon Napa Valley Private Reserve 1985 • $30 • (12/15/89) SS • **95**

Cabernet Sauvignon Napa Valley Private Reserve 1984 • $43 Ⓐ • (03/01/89) • **94**

Cabernet Sauvignon Napa Valley Private Reserve 1983 • $19 • (03/01/89) • **89**

Cabernet Sauvignon Napa Valley Private Reserve 1982 • $19 • (03/01/89) • **92**

Cabernet Sauvignon Napa Valley Private Reserve 1981 • $18 • (03/01/89) • **91**

Cabernet Sauvignon Napa Valley Private Reserve 1978 • $NA • (11/15/92) • **95**

Cabernet Sauvignon Napa Valley Private Reserve Lemmon-Chabot Vineyard 1981 • $25 • (04/15/87) • **93**

Cabernet Sauvignon Napa Valley Private Reserve Lemmon-Chabot Vineyard 1980 • $20 • (03/01/89) • **89**

Cabernet Sauvignon Napa Valley Private Reserve Lemmon Ranch Vineyard 1978 • $15 • (03/01/89) • **92**

Cabernet Sauvignon Napa Valley Private Reserve Lemmon Ranch Vineyard 1977 • $12 • (03/01/89) • **88**

Cabernet Sauvignon Napa Valley Private Reserve State Lane Vineyard 1980 • $15 • (03/01/89) • **85**

Cabernet Sauvignon Napa Valley Private Reserve State Lane Vineyard 1979 • $15 • (03/01/89) • **89**

Chardonnay Napa Valley 1994: Appealing for its purity of fruit, focusing on ripe pear, nectarine, peach and honey. A complex and well-balanced white with a nicely fruity aftertaste. What a find at this price. 50,000 cases made. • $11 • (03/31/96) SS • **90**

Chardonnay Napa Valley 1993: Lean and trim, displaying a narrow, earthy band of pear and citrus flavor. • $11 • (04/30/95) • **84**

Chardonnay Napa Valley 1992: Crisp, firm and focused, with a tight band of spicy pear, hazelnut and herb-tinged flavors. Well-balanced with light oak shading on the finish, but the fruit that comes through is fresh and lively. • $10 • (05/31/94) • **87**

Chardonnay Napa Valley 1991 • $11 • (03/31/93) • **84**

Chardonnay Napa Valley Private Reserve 1994: Ripe, rich, intense and deeply concentrated, packing in tiers of ripe pear, honey, hazelnut and butterscotch. An altogether complex and wonderfully crafted Chardonnay that's long and flavorful on the finish. 19,000 cases made. • $20 • (04/30/96) SS • **95**

Chardonnay Napa Valley Private Reserve 1993: An outstanding Chardonnay that is marked by a leesy edge which stretches the strong core of rich fig, pear and honey flavors. It picks up a nice, flinty accent on the finish. 13,500 cases made. • $20 • (03/31/95) SS • **92**

Chardonnay Napa Valley Private Reserve 1992: Bold, ripe and deftly balanced, with rich fig, pear, citrus and melon notes that finish with a pretty toasty oak edge. Complex and concentrated and should hold through 1997. Tasted twice. • $17 • (06/30/94) • **91**

Chardonnay Napa Valley Private Reserve 1991 • $19 • (07/15/93) • **89**

Chardonnay Napa Valley Sbragia Limited Release 1994: A big, toasty style that supports its fruit with lots of oak flavors. The tiers of pear, fig, honey, melon and spice are rich and concentrated, leading to a tremendous aftertaste. 900 cases made. • $25 • (05/15/96) • **94**

Chardonnay Napa Valley Sbragia Limited Release 1992: A stunning Chardonnay, tight and focused, with pretty nectarine, peach, pear and toasty nuances, picking up an earthiness on the finish. A well-balanced, elegant and spicy aftertaste. Delicious now. 300 cases made. • $25 • (05/31/94) • **93**

Chardonnay Napa Valley Sbragia Limited Release 1991 • $19 • (07/15/93) • **92**

Fumé Blanc Napa Valley 1992: A sturdy white wine with floral flavors and chunky fruit character. • $8 • (08/31/94) • **83**

Fumé Blanc Napa Valley 1991 • $8 • (09/15/93) • **84**

Gamay Beaujolais California 1994: This wine is soft, has a slightly acetone aroma, but is otherwise pleasant and fruity. • $7 • **79**

Gamay Beaujolais California Nouveau 1995: Very light, striving for delicacy in color and flavor and showing a modicum of pleasant berry notes. • $7 • (02/29/96) • **81**

Meritage Knights Valley 1992: Dark, ripe and well oaked, with strong toasty oak and roasted wood flavors that dominate the currant and black cherry underneath. Lots of flavor, but could use a little bottle age. 9,000 cases made. • $13 • (11/15/95) • **87**

Meritage Knights Valley 1991: Beringer's first red Meritage, this is ripe and firmly tannic with spicy currant and plum flavor. Tight and compact, it will benefit from short-term cellaring. A blend of Cabernet Sauvignon, Merlot and Cabernet Franc. Drinkable now. 5,000 cases made. • $13 • (09/15/94) • **88**

Meritage White Knights Valley 1992: Earthy, weedy flavors hardley leave room for the modest citrusy fruit. • $9 • **75**

Merlot Bancroft Ranch 1989 • $29 • (05/31/92) • **91**

Merlot Bancroft Ranch 1988 • $28 • (05/31/92) • **90**

Merlot Howell Mountain Bancroft Ranch 1992: Smooth and harmonious, with a supple core of black cherry, currant, earth and toasty oak that folds together nicely on the finish, the flavors becoming more complex and elegant as it progresses. This vintage adds one more to this California vineyard's fine track record for world-class Merlot. 9,000 cases made. • $29 • (12/15/95) SS • **92**

Merlot Howell Mountain Bancroft Ranch 1991 • $29 • (05/31/94) CS • **90**

Merlot Howell Mountain Bancroft Ranch 1990 • $29 • (08/31/93) • **90**

Merlot Howell Mountain Bancroft Ranch 1987 • $29 • (12/31/90) • **91**

Sauvignon Blanc Napa Valley 1993: Buttery, spicy and round, a generous wine that's less Sauvignon than Chardonnay-and a pretty good one, if somewhat woody. 25,000 cases made. • $8 • (08/31/95) • **84**

Sauvignon Blanc-Sémillon Meritage Knights Valley 1993: A smooth and round Bordeaux-style white blend from this California winery. This is buttery, with just a touch of herb in the background under the honey and pear. Drinkable now. 12,000 cases made. • $9 • (08/31/95) BB • **87**

Sauvignon Blanc-Sémillon Meritage Knights Valley 1991 • $9 • (07/15/93) • **82**

White Zinfandel California 1994: Flavorful, sweet and fruity, featuring decent cherry and berry notes. There's enough acidity here to make it balanced. • $5 • (09/15/95) • **81**

White Zinfandel North Coast 1988 • $7 • (06/15/89) • **72**

Zinfandel 1988 • $8 • (02/29/92) BB • **85**

Zinfandel Napa County 1989 • $8 • (10/15/92) • **85**

Zinfandel Napa Valley 1992: Strikes a nice balance between the ripe and supple cherry and raspberry flavors and the spicy anise notes. Manages to pull off a smooth and supple style, even with its tannins showing. Good value for this kind of complexity. 28,000 cases made. • $9 • (09/15/95) BB • **87**

Zinfandel Napa Valley 1991: Solid and well balanced, with a tight core of cherry, wild berry and spice flavors. Finishes with firm tannins and good length. Drinkable now. 18,000 cases made. • $7 • (08/31/94) BB • **86**

Zinfandel Napa Valley 1990 • $8 • (09/30/93) • **86**

Zinfandel North Coast 1992: Well-balanced, bright berry and cherry flavors, hints of spice, fine tannins and clean finish. Drinkable now. 28,000 cases made. • $10 • (12/31/95) • **85**

Zinfandel North Coast 1987 • $8 • (09/15/90) • **86**

Zinfandel North Coast 1985 • $6 • (04/30/88) BB • **87**

BERNARDUS | CALIFORNIA

Chardonnay California 1991 • $12 • (07/15/93) • **89**

Chardonnay Monterey County 1994: A bold, ripe and full-bodied white from California that offers lots of rich pear, spice, honey flavors, all presented with a light shading of hazelnut. This has a sense of elegance and grace that goes on through the finish. 22,000 cases made. • $15 • (05/15/96) SS • **90**

Chardonnay Monterey County 1993: Solid, featuring an appealing range of apple, pear, spice and light oak flavors that develop complexity on the finish. 22,000 cases made. • $15 • (06/30/95) • **87**

Chardonnay Monterey County 1992: Bold, rich and spicy, with layers of complex pear, toast, honey and vanilla flavors that are intense and concentrated, with a long, full finish. Delicious now. 12,000 cases made. • $13 • (11/15/94) SS • **91**

Key: SS—Spectator Selection. CS—Cellar Selection. BB—Best Buy. $NA—Price not available. (BT)—Barrel tasting. Ⓐ—Auction Price.
Dates in parentheses represent the issues in which the ratings were published.

Pinot Noir Santa Barbara County Bien Nacido Vineyard 1993: An elegant style that's spicy and peppery, with cherry and berry notes. Medium-bodied and pleasant for drinking now. 1,200 cases made. • $25 • (01/31/96) • **86**

Pinot Noir Santa Barbara County Bien Nacido Vineyard 1992: Richly flavored layers of herb, tea, cola and berry. The finish demonstrates tannins, smoky, meaty notes and spicy nuances. Probably best to drink soon. 262 cases made. • $18 • (02/28/95) • **86**

Sauvignon Blanc Monterey County 1994: Bright and pure, pouring out its generous pear, pineapple and citrus flavors. An incredible value in a California white that's fresh and lively through the long finish. Delicious now. 2,700 cases made. • $10 • (12/31/95) BB • **90**

Sauvignon Blanc Monterey County 1993: A broad, ripe, spicy style from this California coastal region. It weaves oaky nuances through pear and apple flavors. Toasty and honey-scented. Drink now. 7,000 cases made. • $9 • (02/28/95) BB • **87**

Sauvignon Blanc Monterey County 1992 • $8 • (01/31/94) BB • **85**

BETTINELLI | CALIFORNIA

Cabernet Sauvignon Napa Valley 1991: Tight and cedary, presenting hints of black cherry and currant that turn thin and austere. 635 cases made. • $14 • (05/31/95) • **82**

Chardonnay Napa Valley 1993: Soft and spicy, featuring toasty oak flavors and a hint of pineapple on the finish. 950 cases made. • $12 • (05/15/96) • **82**

Chardonnay Napa Valley 1992: Marked by ripe pear and apple notes with spicy nuances, it picks up a cedary oak edge before coming up short on the finish. 1,008 cases made. • $11 • (07/31/95) • **83**

Merlot Napa Valley 1993: Ripe and flavorful, with an appealing range of plum, red cherry and spicy flavors. Finishes with a touch of oak and firm tannins. Ready. Tasted twice with consistent notes. 550 cases made. • $25 • (03/31/96) • **88**

BIALE, ROBERT | CALIFORNIA

Zinfandel Napa Valley Aldo's Vineyard Proprietor's Series 1994: A Zinfandel in a rich yet elegant style, showing nuances of ripe cherry, raspberry, mint and spice. The toasty oak flavors fold in nicely on the finish. The best yet from this winery. 780 cases made. • $19 • (05/15/96) • **93**

Zinfandel Napa Valley Aldo's Vineyard Proprietor's Series 1993: Well focused, ripe and complex, with a seam of elegant cherry, plum and wild berry flavors that pick up a nice, toasty nuance on the finish. Has a measure of finesse and grace uncommon for Zinfandel. 615 cases made. • $18 • (10/15/95) • **91**

Zinfandel Napa Valley Aldo's Vineyard Proprietor's Series 1992: Supple and fruity, with spicy strawberry and cherry notes that turn smooth and elegant on the finish. Ready now. 533 cases made. • $14 • (10/15/94) • **84**

Zinfandel Napa Valley Aldo's Vineyard Proprietor's Series 1991 • $15 • (09/30/93) • **86**

BIDWELL | NEW YORK

Cabernet Sauvignon North Fork of Long Island 1988 • $12 • (06/30/91) • **82**

Cabernet Sauvignon North Fork of Long Island 1987 • $12 • (06/30/91) • **81**

Merlot North Fork of Long Island 1988 • $11 • (06/30/91) • **85**

Merlot North Fork of Long Island Reserve 1987 • $16 • (03/31/90) • **83**

BILTMORE, CHATEAU | NORTH CAROLINA

Blanc de Blanc North Carolina NV • $21 • (02/29/92) • **68**

Cabernet Sauvignon North Carolina 1987 • $16 • (02/29/92) • **76**

BILTMORE ESTATE | NORTH CAROLINA

Brut Blanc de Blancs North Carolina NV: Crisp and quite austere, this very foamy sparkler offers crisp green apple flavors, bright but without much depth. Try as an apéritif of a mixer. 2,000 cases made. • $17 • (12/15/95) • **79**

Cabernet Sauvignon American 1987 • $16 • (02/29/92) • **84**

Cabernet Sauvignon North Carolina 1993: A straightforward wine with black cherry, currant and pepper flavors. Good, but lacks intensity. Finishes with a touch of spice. 2,100 cases made. • $13 • (12/31/95) • **81**

Cabernet Sauvignon North Carolina Chateau Biltmore 1993: Austere and tannic, with vegetal flavors and aromas. Very tightly wound, with only modest cherry and plum flavors to back it up. 1,000 cases made. • $20 • (12/31/95) • **79**

Cabernet Sauvignon North Carolina George Washington Vanderbilt Centennial Release 1992: For those who like a Cabernet on the herbal side. Green olive and currant flavors dominate this fairly rich wine. Well rounded and ready to drink now. 330 cases made. • $25 • (12/31/95) • **83**

Chardonnay North Carolina Cheateau Biltmore 1994: Aggressively oaked, this rich white lacks balance but features toast, coffee and earth aromas and flavors and appley pear accents. 2,000 cases made. • $13 • **79**

Chardonnay North Carolina Sur Lies 1993: Straightforward and well balanced, rather austere, offering pear, melon and toast flavors, good acidity and a clean finish. It would be fine with food. 7,000 cases made. • $9 • **81**

George Washington Vanderbilt Centennial Release Vanderbilt Claret North Carolina 1993: Pleasant and flavorful, with good cherry, chocolate and spice components. It is well balanced and has a decent finish. Drinkable now. 584 cases made. • $30 • (12/31/95) • **83**

Johannisberg Riesling North Carolina Cheateau Biltmore 1993: An awkward combination of smoky, candied fruit and citrus flavors mar this otherwise balanced, simple white. 830 cases made. • $10 • (01/31/96) • **73**

Sparkling North Carolina George Washington Vanderbilt Centennial Release 1990: Clean and well-knit, this sparkler offers ripe apple and light honey flavors, though showing mature aromas, it's still crisp and dry on the palate. 214 cases made. • $35 • (12/15/95) • **81**

White Zinfandel North Carolina American Zinfandel Blanc de Noir 1994: Dried cherry and watermelon flavors dominate this well-made wine. It has some body with good acidity. Overall, a refreshing and tasty quaff. 10,000 cases made. • $6 • (09/15/95) • **83**

BLACK MOUNTAIN | CALIFORNIA

Cabernet Sauvignon Alexander Valley Fat Cat 1990: Tight and tannic, an astringent wine, with a lean beam of earth and berry aromas and flavors. Finishes tough. Needs until 2000 to sort itself out. 1,082 cases made. • $18 • (06/15/93) • **80**

Cabernet Sauvignon Alexander Valley Fat Cat 1988 • $18 • (11/15/92) • **85**

Cabernet Sauvignon Alexander Valley Fat Cat 1986 • $20 • (11/15/91) • **86**

Cabernet Sauvignon Alexander Valley Fat Cat 1985 • $18 • (04/30/90) • **87**

Chardonnay Alexander Valley Douglass Hill 1991 • $11 • (05/15/93) • **87**

Petite Sirah Alexander Valley Bosun Crest 1990 • $10 • (06/15/93) • **77**

Petite Sirah Alexander Valley Bosun Crest 1987 • $8 • (10/31/91) BB • **87**

Petite Sirah Alexander Valley Bosun Crest 1986 • $8 • (10/31/91) • **67**

Petite Sirah Alexander Valley Bosun Crest 1985 • $9 • (02/15/89) • **81**

Zinfandel Alexander Valley Cramer Ridge 1990 • $10 • (05/31/93) • **78**

Zinfandel Alexander Valley Cramer Ridge 1987 • $10 • (09/30/91) • **77**

Zinfandel Alexander Valley Cramer Ridge 1986 • $9 • (03/31/90) • **82**

BLACKSTONE | CALIFORNIA

Chardonnay Monterey County Grand Reserve 1994: Soft and generous with its citrus and melon flavors that lose just a bit of focus on the finish. Drinkable now. 15,000 cases made. • $10 • (06/15/96) • **82**

Chardonnay Monterey County Reserve 1993: Earthy with a bitter oak edge to the ripe pear and spice flavors. 7,000 cases made. • $8 • (07/31/95) • **79**

Merlot California Barrel Reserve 1994: Simple, with diluted earthy and berry flavors. Lacks depth and concentration. 18,000 cases made. • $10 • **77**

Merlot Napa County Grand Reserve 1994: Hardly living up to its grand reserve billing, this wine offers a nice range of Merlot flavors but is unbalanced by a charred, slightly bitter and vegetal edge. Tasted twice with consistent notes. 12,000 cases made. • $14 • **77**

Merlot Napa County Reserve 1993: Serves up ripe, polished cherry, currant and light, smoky oak shadings. A red of finesse and grace, aging into 1997 or '98 should only help. Hard to beat at this price. 9,500 cases made. • $10 • (04/30/96) BB • **89**

Pinot Noir Santa Barbara County 1990 • $8 • (02/28/93) • **81**

BLOCKHEADIA RINGNOSII | CALIFORNIA

Zinfandel Rutherford 1993: Light but appealing, showing earthy raspberry, peppermint and spice nuances. Finishes with mild tannins. 200 cases made. • $15 • (10/15/95) • **85**

Zinfandel Rutherford 1992: Ripe, smooth and polished, exhibiting pretty peppery, cherry Zinfandel flavors and mild tannins. Made from grapes grown at Niebaum-Coppola Estate. 231 cases made. • $15 • (02/28/95) • **88**

BOCAGE | CALIFORNIA

Cabernet Sauvignon Monterey Proprietor's Cuvée 1990: Pungently weedy and vegetal. 1,270 cases made. • $10 • (11/15/94) • **70**

Merlot Monterey Proprietor's Cuvée 1990: Leans toward the weedy, herbaceous spectrum of Merlot flavors, but it's balanced and appealing on those counts. Ready now. 1,680 cases made. • $10 • (09/15/94) • **84**

Merlot Monterey Proprietor's Cuvée 1989 • $10 • (10/31/92) • **74**

BOEGER | CALIFORNIA

Barbera El Dorado 1993: Firm in texture with focused blackberry and black cherry fruit that picks up a touch of citrus on the crisp finish. 1,950 cases made. • $12 • (11/15/95) • **86**

Barbera El Dorado 1992: Smooth and spicy, its low-key black cherry fruit rounded out with spicy oak. Ready now. 1,200 cases made. • $12 • (07/31/95) • **84**

Barbera El Dorado 1991 • $11 • (10/31/93) • **84**

Barbera El Dorado 1990 • $11 • (11/30/92) • **81**

Barbera El Dorado 1989 • $10 • (10/31/91) • **85**

Cabernet Sauvignon El Dorado 1991: Smells good up front, but ends up tasting cooked. Not for everyone. 1,800 cases made. • $12 • (12/15/95) • **78**

Cabernet Sauvignon El Dorado 1990: Mature color, with cedar and herb flavors. A good red that's drinkable now. 1,200 cases made. • $12 • (11/15/94) • **83**

Cabernet Sauvignon El Dorado 1989 • $12 • (11/15/92) • **83**

Cabernet Sauvignon El Dorado 1987 • $11 • (03/15/91) • **85**

Cabernet Sauvignon El Dorado 1985 • $11 • (02/15/89) • **77**

Cabernet Sauvignon El Dorado 1984 • $11 • (05/31/88) • **81**

Cabernet Sauvignon El Dorado 1983 • $10 • (08/31/87) • **82**

Cabernet Sauvignon El Dorado 1980 • $8 • (04/16/84) • **76**

Cabernet Sauvignon Napa Valley Joseph A. Nichelini Vineyards 1989 • $12 • (11/15/93) • **77**

Chardonnay El Dorado 1991 • $12 • (09/15/93) • **87**

Hangtown Red California 1988 • $5 • (08/31/90) • **78**

Hangtown Red California 1987 • $5 • (02/28/90) BB • **82**

Hangtown Red California 1985 • $5 • (12/31/88) • **73**

Hangtown Red California 1984 • $4 • (01/31/88) • **77**

Hangtown Red California 1983 • $4 • (06/30/87) • **71**

Hangtown Red Lot No. 16 California NV • $5 • (10/31/91) BB • **80**

Johannisberg Riesling El Dorado 1992: Light and fragrant, slightly sweet and bright, with apple and floral aromas and flavors. 1,100 cases made. • $7 • (02/28/95) • **84**

Meritage El Dorado 1992: Marked by earthy, leathery flavors and hard currant and berry character. An unusually austere style for this winery. 1,000 cases made. • $15 • (03/31/96) • **77**

Meritage El Dorado 1991: Smooth and silky, flavors running strongly toward mint and herbs with a black cherryish streak of fruit extending into the finish. Needs until 1997-1998. 700 cases made. • $15 • (12/15/95) • **86**

Meritage El Dorado 1989 • $14 • (10/15/92) • **83**

Merlot El Dorado 1993: Solid, though somewhat lacking in finesse and polish on the finish where the currant, tar and cedary oak flavors turn dry, vegatal and a bit rustic. 1,250 cases made. • $13 • **82**

BOGLE

Merlot El Dorado 1991 • $13 • (10/15/93) • **86**
Merlot El Dorado 1990 • $13 • (01/31/93) • **78**
Merlot El Dorado 1988 • $13 • (03/31/91) • **78**
Merlot El Dorado 1987 • $13 • (07/15/90) • **81**
Merlot El Dorado 1986 • $13 • (01/31/89) • **73**
Merlot El Dorado 1985 • $13 • (02/15/88) • **82**
Merlot El Dorado 1982 • $10 • (10/01/84) • **74**
Merlot El Dorado Estate Bottled 1992: Marked by smoky, toasty oak and a supple texture, it delivers enough cherry and raspberry flavor to complement the wood. 1,400 cases made. • $14 • (03/31/95) • **86**
Miglióre Reserve El Dorado 1993: A nice blend of spicy fruit and tangy acidity in a ready-to-drink red, finishing lean and zingy enough to call for a special plate of pasta. 680 cases made. • $14 • (11/30/95) • **85**
Sauvignon Blanc El Dorado 1993: Light, floral and lively, with a core of green apple and pear flavor that carries through the finish. 1,800 cases made. • $8 • (01/31/95) • **83**
Sauvignon Blanc El Dorado 1992: Light and spicy, zingy with peach and pear flavors, finishing with a floral flourish. 800 cases made. • $8 • (08/31/94) • **84**
Zinfandel El Dorado 1993: Tastes earthy, with spicy, peppery juniper berry notes and finishing dry and tannic. Remains earthy throughout. 850 cases made. • $10 • (03/31/96) • **76**
Zinfandel El Dorado 1992: The buttery oak and the spicy, tarry raspberry flavors make this complex and intriguing, despite some rough edges. Ready now. 1,300 cases made. • $10 • (10/15/94) • **84**
Zinfandel El Dorado Walker Vineyard 1993: Typical black pepper aromas, along with intense, very ripe wild berry and cherry flavors that turn a touch coarse on the finish. Firmly tannic. 1,260 cases made. • $12 • (10/15/95) • **85**
Zinfandel El Dorado Walker Vineyard 1992: An oaky style that's toasty and buttery, but there's plenty of cherry and raspberry for complexity and finesse. Drinks well now. The best Zinfandel from this winery. 875 cases made. • $12 • (10/15/94) • **87**
Zinfandel El Dorado Walker Vineyard 1991 • $10 • (09/30/93) • **87**
Zinfandel El Dorado Walker Vineyard 1990 • $10 • (10/15/92) • **90**
Zinfandel El Dorado Walker Vineyard 1989 • $9 • (09/30/91) • **84**
Zinfandel El Dorado Walker Vineyard 1988 • $8 • (02/15/91) • **85**
Zinfandel El Dorado Walker Vineyard 1987 • $8 • (03/31/90) • **86**
Zinfandel El Dorado Walker Vineyard 1986 • $7 • (07/31/88) • **73**
Zinfandel El Dorado Walker Vineyard 1981 • $6 • (07/16/85) • **76**
Zinfandel Napa Valley Joseph A. Nichelini Vineyards 1990 • $10 • (04/30/93) • **81**
Zinfandel Napa Valley Joseph A. Nichelini Vineyards 1989 • $12 • (10/15/92) • **80**
Zinfandel Napa Valley Joseph A. Nichelini Vineyards 1988 • $12 • (08/31/91) • **85**

BOGLE | CALIFORNIA

Cabernet Sauvignon California 1993: Good flavor for the price. Simple and nicely focused currant and blackberry flavors echo nicely on the finish. Drinkable now. 7,000 cases made. • $6 • (11/30/95) BB • **85**
Cabernet Sauvignon California 1992: Smooth, appealing and youthful, with modest red cherry and spice flavors. Drinkable now. • $6 • (05/15/94) • **81**
Cabernet Sauvignon California 1990: Soft and fruity, with ripe black cherry aromas and flavors, turning a bit watery on the palate, but finishing with a solid chord of spicy oak. Drinkable now. 5,000 cases made. • $6 • (11/15/92) BB • **83**
Cabernet Sauvignon California 1989 • $7 • (11/15/92) • **77**
Chardonnay California 1993: Crisp and fruity, lively, simple and appealing for its nectarine flavor. Drinkable now. 14,000 cases made. • $6 • (01/31/95) BB • **82**
Chardonnay California 1992: Simple, with tart pear and spicy notes that finish with a slight citrus bite. Ready now. Much better than a bottle tasted earlier. 12,000 cases made. • $6 • (06/15/94) • **81**

Key: SS—Spectator Selection. CS—Cellar Selection. BB—Best Buy. $NA—Price not available. (BT)—Barrel tasting. Ⓐ—Auction Price.
Dates in parentheses represent the issues in which the ratings were published.

Chardonnay California Barrel Fermented Cuvée 1994: A touch earthy, with hints of pineapple and citrus. Also marked by a lightly tinny character. • $6 • (03/31/96) • **81**
Chardonnay California Barrel Fermented Reserve 1992: Ripe and full bodied, with intense pear, apple and spicy notes, that finishing with a light oak edge. Well crafted. 300 cases made. • $10 • (07/31/95) • **86**
Chardonnay California Reserve 1993: Floral and mildly aromatic, showing a core of citrus, pear and spice. Clean and well balanced. • $12 • (05/15/96) • **84**
Chenin Blanc Clarksburg 1993: Light, soft and appealing, delicately sweet, as apple and a touch of floral flavor linger on the finish. 200 cases made. • $6 • (10/15/95) • **84**
Fumé Blanc California 1994: Focused and fruity, this Sauvignon Blanc has bright pear, nectarine and modestly herbal flavors swirling through its smooth, sturdy texture. A fair price for this kind of character, which makes it all the easier to enjoy now. 5,000 cases made. • $5 • (05/15/96) BB • **86**
Fumé Blanc Lake County 1992 • $5 • (07/31/93) BB • **85**
Fumé Blanc Lake County Dry 1993: Crisp and citrusy, a light herbal edge adding a touch of complexity. 5,000 cases made. • $5 • (04/30/95) • **83**
Merlot California 1994: Earthy, sweaty and gamy, with strong minty-herbal flavors that miss the mark. Tasted twice with consistent notes. 24,000 cases made. • $9 • **72**
Merlot California 1992: Supple and fruity, nicely balanced and contained, a red that shows some reserve and polish. Drinkable now. 15,000 cases made. • $8 • (09/15/94) BB • **83**
Merlot California 1991 • $8 • (07/15/93) BB • **85**
Merlot California 1990 • $8 • (05/31/92) • **82**
Petite Sirah California 1993: Smooth and remarkably polished, a solid red with appealing berry, spice and vanilla flavors that roll languidly across the palate. Approachable now with food, best from 1997. 5,000 cases made. • $7 • (11/15/95) BB • **86**
Petite Sirah California 1992: Spicy, earthy notes add a little extra to the soft plum and berry flavors that linger through the finish. Tannins are soft. 3,000 cases made. • $7 • (02/28/95) BB • **85**
Petite Sirah California 1991 • $6 • (07/31/93) BB • **88**
Petite Sirah Clarksburg 1988 • $7 • (10/31/89) • **70**
White Zinfandel California 1994: Funky, oniony aromas give way to cherry and strawberry flavors. 4,000 cases made. • $5 • (09/15/95) • **76**
Zinfandel California 1993: Well-oaked, so the toasty wood flavors stand out, but the wild berry, cherry and blueberry flavors keep it interesting. 2,000 cases made. • $6 • (10/15/95) • **83**
Zinfandel California 1992: Dense and chewy, but the ripe plum and berry jam notes rise to the forefront, lending balance and depth. Better than bottles previously tasted. 2,000 cases made. • $6 • (05/15/95) • **84**

BOISSET | CALIFORNIA

Cabernet Sauvignon Napa Valley 1984 • $7 • (12/31/87) • **72**
Cabernet Sauvignon Napa Valley 1981 • $9 • (05/01/85) • **80**
Cabernet Sauvignon Sonoma County 1990: Earthy and gritty, a charmless wine that hits the bottom. • $15 • (11/15/94) • **70**
Chardonnay Sonoma County 1992: Smooth, rich and creamy with ripe pear, citrus, nutmeg and honeyed notes that are focused and lingering on the finish. 1,750 cases made. • $15 • (06/30/94) • **85**
Merlot Sonoma County 1991: Tough and chewy, with a solid oak frame that dominates the Merlot fruit underneath. Cellaring a year may make it more appealing and generous. • $15 • (09/15/94) • **82**

BON MARCHE | CALIFORNIA

Cabernet Sauvignon Alexander Valley 1989 • $8 • (02/28/91) BB • **87**
Cabernet Sauvignon Napa Valley 1992: Light and fruity with a leathery oak edge to the flavors. Ready now. 4,500 cases made. • $8 • (03/31/94) • **82**
Cabernet Sauvignon Sonoma County 1991: Bright and flavorful, with fresh currant, plum and blackberry aromas and flavors vying for attention. A vibrant wine that's drinkable now. 3,995 cases made. • $7 • (03/31/93) BB • **84**

Chardonnay Sonoma County 1992: Fresh and fruity, soft and simple, with appealing apple and vanilla flavors. A hint of bitterness detracts from the finish. 14,000 cases made. • $8 • (01/31/94) • **79**
Chardonnay Sonoma County 1991 • $8 • (03/15/93) BB • **84**
Pinot Noir Napa Valley 1990 • $7 • (11/15/91) • **79**
Pinot Noir Sonoma County 1991 • $8 • (12/31/92) BB • **86**

BONNY DOON | CALIFORNIA

Cabernet Franc California Pacific Rim 1994: Young and still showing fermentation aromas, but the fruit is ripe and pure, with currant and cherry notes, lacking extra dimensions but pleasant enough. 700 cases made. • $10 • (11/30/95) • **83**
Charbono California La Farfalla 1994: Smells floral and fruity, but is tight and compact on the palate with hints of cherry and berry flavors. 1,500 cases made. • $10 • **82**
Chenin Blanc California Pacific Rim 1994: Bright and fresh, bubbling with youthful grapey and citric flavors, finishing soft but dry. 2,600 cases made. • $8 • (10/15/95) • **84**
Chenin Blanc California Pacific Rim 1993: Simple, earthy, off-dry white with only modest apple fruit. • $8 • (05/31/95) • **78**
Framboise Santa Cruz Mountains NV: Talk about a mouthful of raspberries! Delicious ripe fruit and plenty of it in this lightly sweet, rich fruit wine. Sensational stuff. 3,200 cases made. • $9 • (07/31/95) • **90**
Grahm Crew Vin Rouge California 1989 • $7 • (10/31/90) BB • **82**
Grahm Crew Vin Rouge California 1988 • $7 • (02/15/90) • **83**
Grahm Crew Vin Rouge California 1987 • $8 • (11/30/88) • **85**
Grahm Crew Vin Rouge California 1985 • $6 • (09/30/87) BB • **80**
Grenache American Clos de Gilroy Cuvée St. Marcel NV: Snappy, crushed pepper, cherry and wild berry flavors in a fresh and lively, nouveau style. 3,764 cases made. • $8 • **84**
Grenache California Clos de Gilroy 1994: Medium weight, with pretty, supple plum and cherry notes that linger on the finish, turning a bit grapey. 4,500 cases made. • $8 • (11/15/95) BB • **87**
Grenache California Clos de Gilroy 1993 • $8 • (04/15/94) BB • **87**
Grenache California Clos de Gilroy 1992 • $8 • (02/15/93) • **84**
Grenache California Clos de Gilroy 1991 • $8 • (07/31/92) • **84**
Grenache California Clos de Gilroy 1990 • $8 • (02/15/91) BB • **87**
Grenache California Clos de Gilroy 1989 • $7 • (02/15/90) BB • **88**
Grenache California Clos de Gilroy 1988 • $6 • (02/15/89) BB • **85**
Grenache California Clos de Gilroy 1987 • $6 • (02/29/88) BB • **87**
Grenache California Clos de Gilroy 1986 • $6 • (04/30/87) • **84**
Grenache Late Harvest Vin de Glacière 1987 • $15 • (12/31/88) • **90**
Le Cigare Volant California 1993: Smooth-textured and lively wild berry and red cherry flavors tighten up on the finish. 3,400 cases made. • $20 • (10/15/95) • **85**
Le Cigare Volant California 1991 • $18 • (03/31/94) • **88**
Le Cigare Volant California 1990 • $18 • (11/30/92) • **87**
Le Cigare Volant California 1989 • $20 • (03/15/92) • **80**
Le Cigare Volant California 1988 • $19 • (12/31/90) • **86**
Le Cigare Volant California 1987 • $15 • (12/15/89) • **85**
Le Cigare Volant California 1986 • $22 Ⓐ • (11/15/88) • **92**
Le Cigare Volant California 1985 • $13 • (01/31/88) • **90**
Le Cigare Volant California 1984 • $11 • (08/31/86) • **87**
Le Gaucher California 1992 • $12 • (03/31/94) • **82**
Le Meunier California Blanc de Meunier 1994: Smooth, spicy and inviting, with generous lemon, nutmeg and vanilla flavors. Drinkable now. 461 cases made. • $15 • (03/31/96) • **88**
Le Sophiste Santa Cruz Mountains 1993: Ripe, open-textured, generous and floral, pear and citrus flavors linger on the finish. Drinkable now. Made from Roussanne, with 8 percent Marsanne. 900 cases made. • $25 • (05/15/95) • **87**
Le Sophiste Santa Cruz Mountains 1992 • $25 • (03/31/94) • **89**
Le Sophiste Santa Cruz Mountains 1991 • $25 • (02/15/93) • **88**
Malvasia Bianca Monterey Vin de Glacière 1991 • $15 • (12/15/92) • **85**
Mourvèdre California Old Telegram 1993: Firm and spicy, a little chewy, but showing plenty of focused blackberry and tar flavors. Best in 1997. 450 cases made. • $20 • (12/15/95) • **83**
Mourvèdre California Old Telegram 1991 • $20 • (03/31/94) • **81**
Mourvèdre California Old Telegram 1990 • $20 • (02/15/93) • **84**
Mourvèdre California Old Telegram 1988 • $20 • (12/31/90) • **85**
Mourvèdre California Old Telegram 1986 • $14 • (11/15/88) • **90**
Muscat Canelli Late Harvest California Vin de Glacière 1994: Sweet, rich and profound, a Muscat of astounding depth and complexity. The rich apricot, golden raisin and honey flavors persist on the long finish. A wonderful dessert wine. 5,000 cases made. • $15 • (09/30/95) • **94**
Muscat Canelli Late Harvest California Vin de Glacière 1992: Brilliantly spicy, fruity and generous, showing its flavors with digital clarity—nutmeg, cinnamon, pear, apple, and honey—finishing sweet, rich , and amazingly balanced. Drinkable now. • $15 • (11/15/93) • **92**
Muscat Canelli Late Harvest California Vin de Glacière 1990 • $15 • (03/31/92) • **91**
Muscat Canelli Late Harvest California Vin de Glacière 1987 • $15 • (12/31/88) • **91**
Muscat Canelli Late Harvest Monterey Vin de Glacière 1993: There's good fruit here, orange and peach and melon, and moderate sweetness. It's light-bodied, even delicate, for an icewine, but has balance and freshness. Drink now. 4,200 cases made. • $15 • **82**
Orange Muscat Late Harvest Monterey Vin de Glacière 1993: This fresh, shy wine has good structure—it's quite thick, sweet, with good acidity—but only moderate fruit character, with soft grapefruit and peach notes. It's clean and balanced. 600 cases made. • $15 • **83**
Pear Eau-de-vie Washington NV • $18 • (03/31/92) • **90**
Pinot Meunier California 1991 • $15 • (12/31/93) • **87**
Pinot Noir California 1994: Ripe and spicy, with dried cherry, plum and wild berry flavors. Turns simpler on the finish, but the flavors linger. 910 cases made. • $20 • **87**
Pinot Noir Sonoma County 1981 • $9 • (03/01/84) • **65**
Riesling California Pacific Rim 1994: A stylishly delicate, dry and fragrant white that offers varietal character in a value package. Throws out peach, floral and citrus flavors that linger appealingly on the finish. 7,000 cases made. • $8 • (09/15/95) BB • **88**
Riesling California Pacific Rim 1993: Light and crisp, lively, floral, slightly resiny, keeps singing prettily on the finish. 8,000 cases made. • $8 • (02/28/95) • **85**
Riesling California Pacific Rim 1992 • $8 • (09/30/93) BB • **87**
Riesling California Pacific Rim 1991 • $8 • (12/31/92) BB • **88**
Sparkling Pinot Meunier California Le Canard Froid 1993: Soft, fruity and little sweet and floral, but the berry flavors make this Pinot Meunier sparkler an enjoyable between-meal sipper. • $9 • (12/31/94) • **83**
Syrah Santa Cruz Mountains 1988 • $25 • (02/15/91) • **88**
Vin Gris de Cigare California 1994: Rosé-style, but adding a little spritz. Very dry and almost austere, offering dried currant and herbal flavors. Well balanced. • $7 • (09/15/95) • **82**
Vin Gris De Cigare California 1993: Broader and richer than most rosés, but it keeps the lively strawberry, leather and watermelon flavors in delicate balance. Drink soon. 8,300 cases made. 8,300 cases made. • $8 • (12/31/94) BB • **86**
Vin Gris de Cigare California 1992 • $8 • (08/31/93) • **82**
Vin Gris de Cigare California 1990 • $7 • (07/15/91) BB • **84**
Viognier Late Harvest California Vin de Glacière 1987 • $NA • • **94**

BONTERRA | CALIFORNIA

Cabernet Sauvignon Mendocino County 1993: A modest wine that strikes a nice balance between its ripe currant and cherry flavors and correct tannins. Drinkable now. 13,000 cases made. • $12 • (03/31/96) • **81**
Chardonnay Mendocino 1994: Floral and spicy flavors dominate an otherwise straightforward style that finishes with a bit of bitterness from the oak. 40,000 cases made. • $12 • (03/31/96) • **83**
Sangiovese Mendocino County 1993: Smooth, polished, smoky, earthy plum and currant flavors offer modest varietal character. 120 cases made. • $22 • (04/30/96) • **85**
Syrah Mendocino County 1993: Starts with a strong, cedary edge, giving way to ripe, spicy plum and berry notes. Becomes more interesting on the finish, where the flavors fold together. 675 cases made. • $22 • (04/30/96) • **86**

BONVERRE | CALIFORNIA

Cabernet Sauvignon California Lot Number 9 1991: A good, afforable Cabernet, with bright, fresh, currant, herb and oak shadings. Balanced and pleasing to drink. Ready now. 2,800 cases made. • $7 • (05/15/94) • **83**

Chardonnay California Lot Number 14 1992: Bright and fruity, simple. Lively citrus and peach flavor echoes on the finish. Drinkable now. • $7 • (02/28/95) • **80**

Merlot California Famille Lot Number 8 NV • $8 • (05/31/93) BB • **84**

Merlot California Lot Number 11 1992: Light and fruity, with simple wild berry flavors. 5,071 cases made. • $8 • (09/15/94) • **76**

Sauvignon Blanc Napa Valley Lot Number 10 1992 • $6 • (01/31/94) • **77**

BOOKWALTER | WASHINGTON

Cabernet Sauvignon Washington 1992: Beautifully articulated Cabernet fruit jumps out of the glass. Right to the final echo of the finish, this is smoothly balanced and lightly touched by spicy oak. Best now through 1997. 183 cases made. • $16 • (08/31/95) • **89**

Cabernet Sauvignon Washington 1990: Fruity from the start, smooth enough to show off the generous berry and plum flavors and firm enough to keep them sailing on the finish. Drinkable now. 189 cases made. • $16 • (09/30/94) • **88**

Cabernet Sauvignon Washington Reserve 1989: Ripe and exotic, a chewy red that delivers a mouthful of spicy, tarry currant and plum flavor plus a few hints of tropical fruit on the finish. Best from 1997. 100 cases made. • $20 • (09/30/94) • **88**

Chardonnay Washington 1994: Ripe and round, spicy around the edges, offering pear and toasty vanilla flavors at the core and a firm texture. Drink now. 1,365 cases made. • $9 • (09/30/95) • **87**

Chardonnay Washington 1992: Bright and fruity, not flashy, but brimming with crisply defined pear and apricot flavors that echo on the finish. Tasty. 1,900 cases made. • $8 • (09/30/94) BB • **86**

Chardonnay Washington Barrel Fermented Reserve 1993: Spicy, toasty and gently fruity, a subtle white that spreads out its flavors on the finish. Gets better with each sip. 224 cases made. • $14 • (09/30/95) • **86**

Chenin Blanc Washington 1993: Frankly sweet, a simple white with melon and peach flavor. 2,030 cases made. • $6 • (09/30/94) • **80**

Merlot Washington 1993: Oak shows prominently on the nose, but ripe black cherry and berry weave through the flavors and bring it into balance. Wait until 1997. 316 cases made. • $14 • (09/30/95) • **87**

Merlot Washington 1992: Smells like blackberries and herbs, and the flavors balance a little more toward sweet fruit, finishes smooth and polished. Drinkable now, but it should continue to improve through 1997. 370 cases made. • $12 • (09/30/94) • **88**

Muscat Washington 1993: Very light and soft, with floral overtones to the modest melon and cream flavors. 1,111 cases made. • $8 • (09/30/94) • **80**

Red Table Wine Washington NV: Smooth, generous, drinkable blend of Cabernet and Merlot that has some richness and a velvety finish. 365 cases made. • $9 • (09/30/95) • **83**

White Riesling Late Harvest Washington 1994: Sweet, silky and delicate peach, honey and spice notes. Feels about half as sweet as it is, but needs time to show its depth. Better in 1997. 396 cases made. • $7 • (09/15/95) • **85**

White Riesling Late Harvest Washington 1987 • $5 • (10/15/89) • **78**

BOORDY | MARYLAND

Cabernet Sauvignon Maryland 1989 • $11 • (02/29/92) • **73**

Chardonnay Maryland 1992: A trip to the lumberyard. Heavy oak flavors overwhelm diluted fruit, finishes sweet and dull. 568 cases made. • $10 • **72**

Seyval Blanc Maryland Sur Lie Reserve 1993: Smooth and thick, this offers apple cider and light piney notes, with some vanilla oak accents. It's balanced but a bit dull. 630 cases made. • $8 • **80**

Vidal Blanc Maryland Semi Dry 1994: Tastes like apple-rhubarb pie, sweet and thick. Light citrusy acidity perks it up, but there's not much depth. 700 cases made. • $6 • **77**

Key: SS—Spectator Selection. CS—Cellar Selection. BB—Best Buy. $NA—Price not available. (BT)—Barrel tasting. (A)—Auction Price.
Dates in parentheses represent the issues in which the ratings were published.

BORDONI | CALIFORNIA

Chardonnay Solano County 1994: Marked by lime and citrus flavors, but bordering on unripe, making it seem tart and acidic. 56 cases made. • $16 • (03/31/96) • **78**

BOUCHAINE | CALIFORNIA

Cabernet Franc Sonoma Valley Limited Release 1991: Lean and stalky with a green tealike edge to the currant flavor. 350 cases made. • $14 • (02/28/95) • **79**

Cabernet Franc Sonoma Valley Limited Release 1990 • $14 • (03/31/93) • **83**

Chardonnay California Q.C. Fly 1994: Simple and appealing for its fresh, floral apple flavors. 5,000 cases made. • $9 • (06/15/96) • **82**

Chardonnay California Q.C. Fly 1993: Lingering floral and pear flavors characterize this crisp, spicy and smoothly appealing Chardonnay. Ready now. 1,615 cases made. • $8 • (10/15/95) • **84**

Chardonnay California Q.C. Fly 1992: A spicy style, appealing pear, apple and light oak shadings. 2,500 cases made. • $8 • (04/15/95) • **84**

Chardonnay California Q.C. Fly 1991 • $8 • (09/30/92) BB • **85**

Chardonnay Carneros 1993: Austere, showing a trim band of citrus, pear and spice, where the flavors become more interesting. 4,000 cases made. • $15 • (02/29/96) • **85**

Chardonnay Carneros 1992: Fresh and lively, with a zingy acidity that freshens up the pear, apple and spice notes. 4,000 cases made. • $15 • (02/28/95) • **86**

Chardonnay Carneros 1991: Crisp, firm and a touch earthy, but the spicy pear and butterscotch flavors come through and the texture is smooth and supple, with a pretty finish. Ready now. 5,300 cases made. • $15 • (06/30/94) • **87**

Chardonnay Carneros Napa Valley Reserve 1991: Ripe, smooth and creamy, showing mature, spicy pear and toasty oak flavors that linger on the finish. 600 cases made. • $20 • (02/28/95) • **88**

Chardonnay Carneros Unfiltered Limited Release 1991: Elegant and refined, with spicy apple, pear and light oak shadings, this is a new bottling from Bouchaine. It can stand short-term cellaring. Perhaps more bottle time will reveal that this is the superior one. 136 cases made. • $20 • (06/30/94) • **86**

Chardonnay Napa Valley Carneros Estate Reserve 1993: Floral, with hints of earth and wood, and enough ripe pear and citrus notes to hold your interest. 400 cases made. • $22 • (06/30/96) • **85**

Gewürztraminer Russian River Valley Dry 1994: Soft in texture but dry and floral, a light wine with more rose petal than fruit flavor. 1,400 cases made. • $8 • (05/31/96) • **81**

Gewürztraminer Russian River Valley Dry 1993: Bright and floral, generous, exhibiting a spicy edge to the pear and cream flavors. 1,200 cases made. • $8 • (02/28/95) • **85**

Gewürztraminer Russian River Valley Dry 1992 • $8 • (04/15/94) • **82**

Gewürztraminer Russian River Valley Dry 1991 • $8 • (06/15/93) • **84**

Pinot Noir California Q.C. Fly 1993: Light and smooth, nice toast and cherry flavors running through it. 2,500 cases made. • $8 • (12/31/95) • **82**

Pinot Noir California Q.C. Fly 1992: Lean and simple, showing a narrow band of spice and plum notes. Turns tannic on the finish. • $8 • (03/31/95) • **81**

Pinot Noir California Q.C. Fly 1991 • $8 • (02/28/94) • **82**

Pinot Noir California Q.C. Fly 1990 • $8 • (09/30/92) BB • **81**

Pinot Noir Carneros 1992: Smooth and polished, with attractive cherry, herb, toast and berry flavors that are elegant on the finish. 3,000 cases made. • $15 • (06/30/95) • **86**

Pinot Noir Carneros Napa Valley 1991: Earth, herb, cola and wild berry flavors thin out on the finish, where the tannins become more evident. 5,000 cases made. • $15 • (03/31/95) • **82**

Pinot Noir Carneros Napa Valley Reserve 1991: Smooth and supple in texture; earth, berry and cherry flavors pick up a pleasant mushroomy edge. Drinkable now. 400 cases made. • $20 • (01/31/95) • **88**

Pinot Noir Los Carneros 1985 • $7 • (06/30/87) • **76**

Pinot Noir Napa Valley 1982 • $20 • (06/30/87) • **81**

Pinot Noir Napa Valley Carneros 1990 • $15 • (02/28/93) • **86**

Pinot Noir Napa Valley Carneros 1989 • $15 • (09/30/92) • **84**

Pinot Noir Napa Valley Carneros 1988 • $15 • (07/31/91) • **78**

Pinot Noir Napa Valley Carneros 1987 • $13 • (10/31/90) • **82**

Pinot Noir Napa Valley Carneros 1986 • $12 • (05/31/89) • **86**
Pinot Noir Napa Valley Carneros 1985 • $12 • (12/31/88) • **82**
Pinot Noir Napa Valley Carneros Estate Bottled 1989 • $20 • (02/28/93) • **75**
Pinot Noir Napa Valley Carneros Reserve 1990 • $20 • (04/30/94) • **82**
Pinot Noir Napa Valley Carneros Reserve 1988 • $25 • (03/31/92) • **83**
Pinot Noir Napa Valley Carneros Reserve 1987 • $20 • (10/31/90) • **85**
Pinot Noir Napa Valley Los Carneros 1982 • $13 • (07/16/85) • **87**
Pinot Noir Napa Valley Los Carneros Winery Lake Vineyard 1982 • $18 • (03/01/86) CS • **91**
Pinot Noir Russian River Valley Limited Release 1991: Crisp, with herbal, earthy aromas that lead into barnyardy flavors. A hint of black cherry sneaks through, then it takes on leathery notes on the finish. 197 cases made. • $17 • (06/30/95) • **82**

BRANDBORG | CALIFORNIA

Charbono Napa Valley 1989 • $12 • (10/31/91) • **85**
Pinot Noir Anderson Valley 1989 • $11 • (11/15/91) • **86**
Pinot Noir Mendocino 1992: Medium-weight red, showing lean, tannic cherry flavor. 600 cases made. • $13 • (03/31/95) • **82**
Pinot Noir Mendocino County 1991 • $12 • (02/28/94) • **84**
Pinot Noir Mendocino County 1990 • $11 • (02/28/93) • **73**
Pinot Noir Santa Barbara County 1989 • $13 • (11/15/91) • **87**
Pinot Noir Santa Maria Valley Bien Nacido Vineyard 1992: Herb and tart black cherry flavors, young and compact, tightly wound. Short-term cellaring should help. 700 cases made. • $15 • (03/31/95) • **86**
Pinot Noir Santa Maria Valley Bien Nacido Vineyard 1991 • $14 • (02/28/94) • **84**
Pinot Noir Santa Maria Valley Bien Nacido Vineyard 1990 • $13 • (02/28/93) • **78**
Zinfandel Napa Valley 1989 • $10 • (10/15/92) • **84**

BRANDER | CALIFORNIA

Bouchet Tête de Cuvée Santa Ynez Valley 1993: Lean and chewy, but the berry flavors burst through the firm tannins, extending into hints of earth, toast and spice. Try in 2000. 380 cases made. • $22 • (12/15/95) • **86**
Bouchet Tête de Cuvée Santa Ynez Valley 1990: Intense in vegetal and herb-scented Cabernet flavors and finishing with dry, slightly coarse tannins. Strives for complexity with its blend (14 percent Merlot, 16 percent Cabernet Franc), but in the end the vegetal profile wins out. Drinkable now. 1,200 cases made. • $18 • (11/15/93) • **79**
Bouchet Tête de Cuvée Santa Ynez Valley 1989 • $20 • (03/31/92) • **84**
Bouchet Tête de Cuvée Santa Ynez Valley 1988 • $20 • (07/15/92) • **83**
Cabernet Franc Santa Ynez Valley High Density Vineyard 1993: Smooth and polished up front, although it turns a little leathery at mid-palate where the herb and currant notes emerge. Tannins gain momentum on the finish. Wait until 1997. 25 cases made. • $35 • (04/30/96) • **84**
Chardonnay Santa Ynez Valley Tête de Cuvée 1993: Distinctive for its citrus and nectarine flavors, it picks up a pleasant earthy edge on the finish. 700 cases made. • $15 • (07/31/95) • **84**
Chardonnay Santa Ynez Valley Tête de Cuvée 1992: Intense with tinny grapefruit and pineapple flavors that stretch a bit too far. 600 cases made. • $15 • (06/30/94) • **78**
Chardonnay Santa Ynez Valley Tête de Cuvée 1991 • $16 • (07/15/93) • **78**
Cuvée Natalie Santa Ynez Valley 1994: Light and floral, offering a nice mouthful of peach, pear and rose petal flavors that stay lively on the soft, extended finish. Made from Sauvignon Blanc, Gewürztraminer and Riesling. 250 cases made. • $13 • (08/31/95) • **89**
Cuvée Natalie Santa Ynez Valley 1993: Lean and crisp, with a narrow band of bright pear, citrus and grapefruit flavors, turning a touch coarse. Drinks well now. Tasted three times. 146 cases made. • $13 • (12/15/94) • **86**
Merlot Santa Ynez Valley 1994: Earthy and pungent, with tarry tobacco flavors. Not much in the way of fruit. 1,200 cases made. • $15 • **78**
Merlot Santa Ynez Valley Reserve 1993: Marked by spicy herb, currant and tobacco flavors. This wine delivers more than the 1994 Merlot, as expected from a reserve bottling. 150 cases made. • $18 • **83**
Merlot Santa Ynez Valley Three Flags 1989 • $12 • (05/31/92) • **82**
Merlot Santa Ynez Valley Three Flags 1988 • $12 • (05/31/92) • **81**
Novissimo Santa Ynez Valley 1991 • $9 • (03/15/92) • **82**
Sauvignon Blanc Santa Ynez Valley 1994: Lean and even somewhat austere, herbal flavors edging past the modest apple tones. A green, leafy note on the finish. 2,000 cases made. • $10 • (06/30/95) • **84**
Sauvignon Blanc Santa Ynez Valley 1993: Distinctly herbal, showing an almost oniony edge to the fig and honey flavors. A substantial Sauvignon Blanc with strong flavors. Ready now. 730 cases made. • $10 • (04/30/95) • **86**
Sauvignon Blanc Santa Ynez Valley 1992: Ripe and generous, a distinctive wine that layers its pear, spice and floral-rose petal aromas and flavors artfully, echoing sweet fruit on the finish. • $9 • (05/15/94) • **87**
Sauvignon Blanc Santa Ynez Valley Cuvée Nicolas 1994: Exotic, capturing lots of flavors which range from ripe fig to sautéed onion, from garlic to citrus and pepper. All-in-all a complex if controversial style that will wow some yet trouble others. 270 cases made. • $21 • (04/30/96) • **90**
Sauvignon Blanc Santa Ynez Valley Cuvée Nicolas 1993: Lithe and vibrant, with passion fruit and citrus competing for attention. Exciting tropical flavors—bright and appealing from start to finish. 420 cases made. • $21 • (06/30/95) • **89**
Sauvignon Blanc Santa Ynez Valley Cuvée Nicolas 1992: Soft, ripe and round, so generous and spicy that it resembles a Chardonnay more than a Sauvignon. A little herb-citrus character comes through on the finish. • $21 • (06/15/94) • **87**
Sauvignon Blend Santa Ynez Valley Cuvée Natalie 1995: Rich, ripe, polished and flavorful. The grapefruit, spice, apricot and apple flavors are balanced harmoniously. Appealing now, but should improve through 1998. 275 cases made. • $14 • **89**
Sémillon Santa Ynez Valley 1994: Crisp, fruity and lively apple, lemon and herb flavors swirl with some complexity on the finish. 300 cases made. • $12 • (10/15/95) • **87**

BRAREN PAULI | CALIFORNIA

Cabernet Sauvignon Dry Creek Valley 1990: Smooth and elegant, with lots of juicy raspberry, anise, cherry and spice aromas and flavors, finishing with a light bite of tannin that should keep it going through 1998 or so. Appealing for its beautifully realized fruit flavors and silky texture. 1,250 cases made. • $13 • (10/31/93) • **89**
Cabernet Sauvignon Dry Creek Valley Mauritson Vineyard 1989 • $12 • (11/15/93) • **78**
Cabernet Sauvignon Mendocino 1987 • $8 • (03/31/91) BB • **84**
Merlot Alexander Valley 1992: Clean and correct, with a modest core of spicy cherry and plum flavors that run into a dry and firmly tannic finish. 2,750 cases made. • $12 • (03/31/96) • **84**
Merlot Alexander Valley 1991: Seamless, elegant and polished, with a pretty beam of currant and cherry flavor. Modest tannins on the finish make it approachable now, but it's capable of aging through 1997. 1,300 cases made. • $13 • (09/15/94) • **85**
Merlot Alexander Valley Mauritson Vineyard 1989 • $12 • (05/31/92) • **77**
Merlot Alexander Valley Mauritson Vineyard 1987 • $11 • (03/31/91) • **84**

BRETON, DOMAINE | CALIFORNIA

Zinfandel Lake County 1989 • $8 • (02/29/92) • **79**
Zinfandel Lake County 1988 • $8 • (02/15/91) • **82**

BRIDGEHAMPTON | NEW YORK

Cabernet Sauvignon Long Island 1988 • $14 • (06/30/91) • **84**
Cabernet Sauvignon Long Island 1987 • $14 • (06/30/91) • **87**
Cabernet Sauvignon Long Island 1986 • $12 • (12/15/88) • **79**
Merlot Long Island 1988 • $16 • (06/30/91) • **89**
Merlot Long Island 1986 • $11 • (12/15/88) • **78**
Merlot Long Island 1985 • $11 • (12/15/88) • **79**
Pinot Noir Long Island 1984 • $8 • (03/16/86) • **75**
Reserve Red Grand Vineyard North Fork of Long Island 1987 • $17 • (06/30/91) • **80**

BRIDGMAN, W.B. | WASHINGTON

Cabernet Sauvignon Yakima Valley 1991: Lean, firm and juicy, packing its berry and herbal flavors into a narrow beam that gets a little tannic on the finish. 762 cases made. • $11 • (07/31/95) • **86**

Chardonnay Yakima Valley 1993: Smooth and rich, sporting a distinct black pepper and dusky spice undertone to the buttery pear flavors. Drink now. 576 cases made. • $9 • (09/30/95) • **88**

Chardonnay Yakima Valley 1992: Ripe, round and a little grassy at the edge, an earthy white that unfolds some nice nectarine and apple flavor on a smooth frame. Drinkable now. 1,500 cases made. • $9 • (09/30/94) • **86**

Merlot Yakima Valley 1992: Broad and velvety, focusing its blackberry and toasty chocolate flavors. Needs to lose some tannin. Best from 1996 to 1997. 800 cases made. • $11 • (09/30/95) • **86**

Sauvignon Blanc Yakima Valley 1992: Light and spicy, a creamy-textured Sauvignon Blanc with low-level pear and vanilla flavors at the finish. 1,200 cases made. • $8 • (09/30/94) • **82**

BRINDIAMO | CALIFORNIA

Cabernet Sauvignon California Limited Bottling 1991: Weedy with an herbal, earthy edge. 1,200 cases made. • $8 • (11/15/94) • **76**

Chardonnay California 1992: Fresh and lively, with buttery oak and pear flavors that turn elegant and spicy, with a clove edge. Ready now. 4,275 cases made. • $8 • (06/15/94) • **81**

Chardonnay California Limited Bottling 1993: Simple with ripe pear and cedary oak flavors of modest proportion. 2,600 cases made. • $10 • (07/31/95) • **79**

Gioveto Limited Bottling 1993: Very well oaked, showing its toasty vanilla flavors, and some appealing black cherry, strawberry and raspberry flavors that fold together nicely. 350 cases made. • $14 • (08/31/95) • **86**

Il Bacio Temecula 1990 • $13 • (11/30/92) • **71**

Muscat Alexandria San Diego County Moscato Aromatico Limited Bottling 1994: Despite perfumey, almost soapy aromas, it's a simple, lightly sweet, drinkable dessert wine. 950 cases made. • $6 • **80**

Nebbiolo Limited Bottling 1993: Firm in texture, moving toward elegance, as focused blackberry flavors hint at anise on the finish. Approachable now, best in 1997. 600 cases made. • $14 • (12/15/95) • **85**

Pinot Noir Edna Valley Limited Bottling 1993: Firm and tannic, medium in weight, showing pleasant cherry, berry and cola notes. 1,200 cases made. • $10 • (10/15/95) • **84**

Pinot Noir Santa Barbara County Santa Maria Hills Vineyard Limited Bottling 1990 • $9 • (09/30/92) • **77**

Rosso Vecchio Limited Bottling 1993: Combines intensity and finesse with a solid core of currant, anise and cedar flavors that blend nicely. A new brand from Thornton in Temecula. 875 cases made. • $10 • (06/30/95) • **86**

Rosso Vecchio Limited Bottling 1992: Crisp and spicy, mature, revealing berry and orange-peel notes on the finish. A blend of Mourvèdre, Grenache and Petite Sirah. 560 cases made. • $10 • (05/15/95) • **80**

BRITTHILL | CALIFORNIA

Pinot Noir Napa County 1989 • $13 • (02/28/93) • **81**

BROTHER & SISTER WINERY | CALIFORNIA

Chardonnay Central Coast Epoch 1992: Earthy with a slight cloying edge to the pear and apple notes. Drinks easy and is fair priced. • $5 • (07/31/95) • **83**

Key: SS—Spectator Selection. CS—Cellar Selection. BB—Best Buy. $NA—Price not available. (BT)—Barrel tasting. Ⓐ—Auction Price.
Dates in parentheses represent the issues in which the ratings were published.

BROTHERHOOD | NEW YORK

Johannisberg Riesling New York Late Harvest Eiswein 1991: Simple and candied, it's a dead ringer for cough syrup, but not so tasty. Tasted twice, with consistent notes. 200 cases made. • $15 • **60**

Johannisberg Riesling New York Late Harvest Eiswein 1988: Tired and flabby. There's little fruit and the sweetness tastes more like candy than wine. 250 cases made. • $NA • **62**

BRUCE, DAVID | CALIFORNIA

Cabernet Sauvignon California Vintner's Select 1983 • $13 • (09/30/86) • **79**

Cabernet Sauvignon Santa Cruz Mountains 1978 • $20 • (11/15/92) • **72**

Chardonnay San Ysidro 1991 • $15 • (09/15/93) • **74**

Chardonnay Santa Cruz Mountains Meyley Vineyard 1991 • $18 • (09/15/93) • **70**

Chardonnay Santa Cruz Mountains Split Rail Vineyard 1991 • $18 • (09/15/93) • **73**

Cote de Shandon Vin Rouge San Luis Obispo County 1987 • $7 • (12/31/88) • **81**

Mr. Baggins California 1990 • $10 • (11/30/92) • **80**

Mrs. Baggins California 1990 • $10 • (06/30/92) • **84**

Petite Sirah California Vintner's Select 1991 • $12 • (10/15/93) • **78**

Petite Sirah Central Coast Vintner's Select 1994: Smooth and harmonious. Ripe, spicy plum and wild berry flavors, and a nice tannin level. Spicy, leathery notes to the finish. 1,568 cases made. • $12 • **86**

Pinot Noir Mendocino Vintner's Select 1990 • $12 • (02/28/94) • **84**

Pinot Noir Russian River Valley Reserve 1993: Lacks focus, with nutty, earthy cherry and berry flavors that seem out of sync. Finishes with firm, drying tannins, time in the bottle may round out the rough edges. 882 cases made. • $25 • **83**

Pinot Noir Santa Cruz Mountains 1989 • $18 • (09/30/92) • **75**

Pinot Noir Santa Cruz Mountains 1986 • $18 • (03/31/90) • **59**

Pinot Noir Santa Cruz Mountains 1984 • $15 • (06/30/87) • **81**

Pinot Noir Santa Cruz Mountains 1983 • $15 • (08/31/86) • **78**

Pinot Noir Santa Cruz Mountains Estate Reserve 1993: A touch earthy and leathery, with a drying edge, but just enough cherry and berry fruit to hold your attention. 342 cases made. • $35 • **82**

Pinot Noir Santa Cruz Mountains Estate Reserve 1992: Peppery and leathery, but it turns smooth and plush, with hints of cherry, anise and evident tannins on the finish. Drinkable now. 1,000 cases made. • $30 • (03/31/95) • **88**

Pinot Noir Santa Cruz Mountains Estate Reserve 1990 • $30 • (02/28/94) • **91**

Pinot Noir Santa Cruz Mountains Thirtieth Anniversary 1992: Dense and chewy, with spicy, peppery accents and tightly wound, typical Pinot Noir flavors of black cherry, herb, mineral and anise. Earthy and tannic on the finish. Needs until 1998 to soften, but it clearly delivers a lot of depth and flavor. 66 cases made. • $100 • (03/31/95) • **91**

Pinot Noir Sonoma County Vintner's Select 1993: Medium weight, with modest cherry and tarry aromas and flavors, but it lacks richness and concentration and is ultimately simple. 4,800 cases made. • $12 • **82**

Pinot Noir Sonoma County Vintner's Select 1992: A bit funky, with a leathery, barnyardy edge. But it blends well with the bright, ripe cherry and spice notes. Finishes with earthy tannins. 4,200 cases made. • $12 • (03/31/95) • **83**

Zinfandel San Luis Obispo County 1990 • $12 • (05/15/92) • **90**

BRUCHER | CALIFORNIA

Pinot Noir Santa Barbara County 1992: Lean, crisp and tannic, herbal and vegetal, drinkable now. A new wine from Peter Brucher, a founder of Vichon. 600 cases made. • $16 • (03/31/95) • **78**

BRUTOCAO | CALIFORNIA

Cabernet Sauvignon Mendocino 1988 • $13 • (03/31/92) • **83**

Cabernet Sauvignon Mendocino 1986 • $13 • (03/31/92) • **82**

Cabernet Sauvignon Mendocino 1982 • $9 • (11/30/88) • **83**

Cabernet Sauvignon Mendocino Albert Vineyard 1993: Pleasant enough, with wild cherry and berry notes, a touch of tannin and a green edge. Can age into 1997. 709 cases made. • $13 • (12/15/95) • **82**

Cabernet Sauvignon Mendocino Albert Vineyard 1992: A bit funky, with tart berry and spicy notes that taste disjointed. 800 cases made. • $13 • (07/31/95) • **82**

Cabernet Sauvignon Mendocino Proprietor's Special Reserve 1991: Ripe and smooth black cherry, anise and wild berry flavors that, while distinctive, don't remind us much of Cabernet. 800 cases made. • $35 • (07/31/95) • **83**

Cabernet Sauvignon Mendocino Unfiltered Unfined 1990: Lean and crisp for a 1990, with medium-bodied herb, tea and tart black cherry flavors, finishing with fine tannins. Approachable now through 1998. 800 cases made. • $13 • (05/15/94) • **82**

Chardonnay Mendocino 1991 • $10 • (07/15/93) • **88**

Chardonnay Mendocino Bliss Vineyard 1993: Spicy with a perfumed aroma, it's elegant and subtle with pear and apple notes. 1,100 cases made. • $10 • (07/31/95) • **83**

Chardonnay Mendocino Bliss Vineyard 1992: Intense and lively, with ripe, spicy pear and buttery oak flavors that turn smooth and elegant on the finish. Ready now. • $10 • (06/30/94) • **84**

Merlot Mendocino 1994: Tastes like stewed vegetable soup, heavy on the tomato and vegetal flavors. 1,200 cases made. • $15 • **73**

Merlot Mendocino 1991 • $15 • (08/31/93) • **87**

Merlot Mendocino 1988 • $13 • (05/31/92) • **84**

Merlot Mendocino Unfiltered Unfined 1993: Earthy with tart wild berry flavors that miss the mark for Merlot. 1,200 cases made. • $15 • (07/31/95) • **78**

Merlot Mendocino Unfiltered Unfined 1992: A big, ripe and oaky style, but it doesn't have the fruit to stand up to the wood, rendering it tough and gnarly with firm, drying tannins. Try it after 1996. • $15 • (09/15/94) • **78**

Pinot Noir Anderson Valley Special Reserve 1993: Bizarre and rustic cherry and wild berry flavors. Better described as a generic red. 500 cases made. • $20 • (03/31/95) • **78**

Sauvignon Blanc Mendocino 1994: Soft at first, citrusy-tart on the finish. A stewed onion edge doesn't compliment the pear flavors. 2,500 cases made. • $9 • **80**

Sauvignon Blanc Mendocino 1993: Simple, fruity wine that echoes a floral note to mix with the basic pear flavors. • $8 • (08/31/95) • **80**

Sauvignon Blanc Mendocino 1992 • $8 • (09/15/93) • **83**

Sauvignon Blanc Mendocino 1991 • $8 • (07/31/93) • **90**

Zinfandel Mendocino 1992 • $17 • (06/15/94) • **84**

Zinfandel Mendocino Hopland Ranch 1993: Ripe and juicy, with pretty wild berry and black cherry flavors that turn elegant. 800 cases made. • $12 • (06/15/95) • **84**

Zinfandel Mendocino Proprietor's Reserve 1991 • $17 • (09/30/93) • **85**

BRYANT FAMILY | CALIFORNIA

Cabernet Sauvignon Napa Valley 1992: Marked by a ripe, spicy quality, tightly wound and firmly tannic, but with a nice core of currant and berry flavors peeking through. 1,000 cases made. • $32 • (05/31/96) • **89**

BUEHLER | CALIFORNIA

Cabernet Sauvignon California 1993: Earthy, simple, a little chewy but flavorful enough to make it appealing now. 4,310 cases made. • $8 • (12/15/95) • **79**

Cabernet Sauvignon Napa Valley 1992: Tight and austere, with firm tannins and a decent core of black cherry and currant flavors, but on the finish the tannins clamp down. 2,495 cases made. • $14 • (12/15/95) • **84**

Cabernet Sauvignon Napa Valley 1991: Young and compact, tightly wound, oaky and loaded with ripe berry and plum notes. Finishes with a firm tannic edge, but the fruit keeps pumping through. Best to cellar through 1997. 2,942 cases made. • $13 • (09/15/94) • **86**

Cabernet Sauvignon Napa Valley 1990: Firm and fleshy, with a modest level of tightly wound currant and leather aromas and flavors. Could improve through 1997 or 1998. 3,423 cases made. • $12 • (11/15/93) • **83**

Cabernet Sauvignon Napa Valley 1989 • $16 • (11/15/92) • **79**

Cabernet Sauvignon Napa Valley 1987 • $21 • (07/31/90) • **85**

Cabernet Sauvignon Napa Valley 1986 • $20 • (04/30/89) • **85**

Cabernet Sauvignon Napa Valley 1985 • $19 Ⓐ • (03/01/89) • **93**

Cabernet Sauvignon Napa Valley 1984 • $22 • (03/01/89) • **87**

Cabernet Sauvignon Napa Valley 1983 • $25 • (03/01/89) • **91**

Cabernet Sauvignon Napa Valley 1982 • $26 • (03/01/89) • **88**

Cabernet Sauvignon Napa Valley 1981 • $21 • (03/01/89) • **85**

Cabernet Sauvignon Napa Valley 1980 • $25 • (03/01/89) • **82**

Cabernet Sauvignon Napa Valley 1978 • $35 • (03/01/89) • **87**

Cabernet Sauvignon Napa Valley Reserve 1991: The best Buehler in years. Bold, ripe and complex, boasting attractive plum, currant and black cherry flavor that's rich and lively, with hints of mineral and earth. Best in 1997. 264 cases made. • $25 • (09/30/95) • **91**

Chardonnay Russian River Valley 1994: Appealing for its up-front pear, peach and spicy Chardonnay flavors and light oak shadings on the finish. 5,352 cases made. • $13 • (05/15/96) • **85**

Chardonnay Russian River Valley 1993: Young and vibrant, with crisp, tart pear, peach and citrus notes. Drinkable now. 4,020 cases made. • $13 • (01/31/95) • **85**

Pinot Noir Central Coast 1993: A bit smoky and oaky, with a bitter edge, but it has enough fruit showing. 4,400 cases made. • $9 • (03/31/95) • **79**

White Zinfandel Napa Valley 1994: Green apple and cherry flavors provide a tart edge. Simple, with an oxidized component to it. • $6 • (09/15/95) • **79**

Zinfandel Napa Valley 1994: Starts out somewhat earthy and gamy but works its way into a fruitier profile, including hints of cherry and spice. Drinkable now. 5,321 cases made. • $12 • (04/30/96) • **87**

Zinfandel Napa Valley 1993: Ripe and earthy, the intense cherry, leather, oak and anise flavors folding together nicely. Better than a previous bottle tasted. 3,275 cases made. • $10 • (10/15/95) • **84**

Zinfandel Napa Valley 1992 • $8 • (04/30/94) BB • **88**

Zinfandel Napa Valley 1990 • $9 • (10/15/92) • **77**

Zinfandel Napa Valley 1989 • $9 • (03/31/92) • **83**

Zinfandel Napa Valley 1987 • $9 • (05/15/90) • **89**

Zinfandel Napa Valley 1986 • $8 • (12/15/88) • **83**

Zinfandel Napa Valley 1985 • $8 • (12/31/87) • **89**

Zinfandel Napa Valley 1983 • $6 • (03/15/87) • **71**

Zinfandel Napa Valley 1982 • $6 • (03/01/85) • **91**

Zinfandel Napa Valley 1981 • $6 • (09/16/84) • **80**

BUENA VISTA | CALIFORNIA

Cabernet Sauvignon Carneros 1992: Leans toward the earthy, barnyardy side of Cabernet, but typical of what Buena Vista's been producing the past few vintages. Lacks the fruitiness to keep it in balance. 30,250 cases made. • $12 • (12/15/95) • **80**

Cabernet Sauvignon Carneros 1991: Lean and tannic, tightly wound and still young. Offers a narrow band of herb, currant and spicy oak flavors, but the tannins dominate on the finish. Best to cellar until 1998. 24,000 cases made. • $12 • (10/15/94) • **87**

Cabernet Sauvignon Carneros 1990: Despite a barnyardy edge, this is a pleasant young wine. Intense and modestly flavored with berry, cherry notes and firm tannins, it could use a little more finesse. Drinkable now. • $11 • (09/15/93) • **82**

Cabernet Sauvignon Carneros 1989 • $9 • (11/15/92) • **74**

Cabernet Sauvignon Carneros 1988 • $8 • (11/15/91) • **79**

Cabernet Sauvignon Carneros 1987 • $11 • (10/15/90) • **83**

Cabernet Sauvignon Carneros 1986 • $11 • (10/15/89) • **91**

Cabernet Sauvignon Carneros 1985 • $10 • (11/15/88) • **84**

Cabernet Sauvignon Carneros 1984 • $10 • (08/31/87) • **94**

Cabernet Sauvignon Carneros 1983 • $9 • (06/15/87) • **77**

Cabernet Sauvignon Carneros 1982 • $11 • (09/16/85) • **85**

Cabernet Sauvignon Carneros 1981 • $11 • (02/16/85) • **89**

Cabernet Sauvignon Carneros Grand Reserve 1990: Earthy and vegetal, marked more by herb and bell pepper than typical Cabernet flavors. Could age through 1998. 800 cases made. • $24 • (10/15/94) • **83**

Cabernet Sauvignon Carneros Grand Reserve 1988 • $23 • (03/31/93) • **86**

Cabernet Sauvignon Carneros Private Reserve 1986 • $23 Ⓐ • (03/15/91) • **89**

Cabernet Sauvignon Carneros Private Reserve 1985 • $18 • (10/15/89) SS • **94**

Cabernet Sauvignon Carneros Private Reserve 1984 • $25 • (03/01/89) • **90**

Cabernet Sauvignon Carneros Private Reserve 1983 • $25 • (03/01/89) • **87**

BULLY HILL

Cabernet Sauvignon Carneros Private Reserve 1982 • $30 • (03/01/89) • **85**
Cabernet Sauvignon Carneros Private Reserve 1981 • $18 • (03/01/89) SS • **86**
Cabernet Sauvignon Carneros Special Selection 1980 • $25 • (03/01/89) • **84**
Cabernet Sauvignon Carneros Special Selection 1979 • $35 • (03/01/89) • **92**
Cabernet Sauvignon Carneros Special Selection 1978 • $60 • (03/01/89) • **90**
Cabernet Sauvignon Sonoma County 1986 • $11 • (11/15/89) • **90**
Cabernet Sauvignon Sonoma Valley 1978 • $30 • (06/01/86) • **94**
Cabernet Sauvignon Sonoma Valley 1976 • $40 • (03/01/89) • **66**
Cabernet Sauvignon Sonoma Valley 1975 • $30 • (03/01/89) • **64**
Cabernet Sauvignon Sonoma Valley Cask 25 1974 • $29 • (03/01/89) • **68**
Cabernet Sauvignon Sonoma Valley Cask 34 1977 • $40 • (03/01/89) • **72**
Cabernet Sauvignon Sonoma Valley Special Selection 1978 • $60 • (11/15/92) • **89**
Chardonnay Carneros 1992: Lightly fruity, with simple pear, apple and pineapple notes that finish with a soft aftertaste. • $10 • (12/31/94) • **83**
Chardonnay Carneros 1991: Lean and austere, with tart, earthy pineapple and citrus flavors. Needs a little more flesh and body. 85,000 cases made. • $11 • (06/30/94) • **78**
Chardonnay Carneros Grand Reserve 1994: A big, ripe but somewhat understated style that frames its citrus and pear in a trace of oak. Maintains a sense of elegance and grace. 903 cases made. • $22 • (06/15/96) • **88**
Chardonnay Carneros Grand Reserve 1991: Tastes mature with earthy, toasty flavors framing the ripe, spicy pear and pineapple notes. Solid, ready now. 622 cases made. • $20 • (12/31/94) • **86**
Gamay Beaujolais Carneros 1988 • $7 • (07/15/89) • **84**
Gamay Beaujolais Sonoma Valley Carneros 1987 • $7 • (02/29/88) • **82**
Gamay Beaujolais Sonoma Valley Carneros 1986 • $7 • (05/31/87) • **83**
Gewürztraminer Carneros 1993: Soft and fruity, simple in flavor, a little sweet, tastes of apricots on the finish. 1,790 cases made. • $7 • (02/28/95) • **80**
Gewürztraminer Carneros 1992: Lean and crisp but not very flavorful, generally vinous rather than demonstrably varietal. • $7 • (11/15/94) • **78**
L'Année Carneros 1986 • $35 • (02/28/91) • **87**
L'Année Carneros 1984 • $32 • (02/15/88) • **88**
Late Harvest Carneros Ingrid's Vineyard White 1989 • $18 • (04/30/91) • **87**
Merlot Carneros 1993: Smooth and simple, with a strong herbal streak running through the light cherry flavor. Drinkable now. 8,474 cases made. • $13 • (06/30/96) • **83**
Merlot Carneros 1992: Marked by thin herb and vegetal notes, which overshadow the berry flavor. 4,250 cases made. • $13 • (05/15/95) • **82**
Merlot Carneros 1991 • $12 • (12/31/93) • **82**
Merlot Carneros 1990 • $11 • (10/31/92) • **86**
Merlot Carneros 1989 • $11 • (05/31/92) • **71**
Merlot Carneros 1985 • $11 • (06/30/88) • **80**
Merlot Carneros Grand Reserve 1989 • $20 • (05/31/93) • **82**
Merlot Carneros Private Reserve 1988 • $17 • (05/31/92) • **82**
Merlot Carneros Private Reserve 1987 • $18 • (03/31/91) • **84**
Merlot Carneros Private Reserve 1986 • $17 • (10/31/89) • **86**
Merlot Carneros Private Reserve 1984 • $15 • (02/15/88) • **87**
Merlot Sonoma County 1987 • $11 • (07/31/90) • **86**
Pinot Noir Carneros 1993: Light and appealing for its lively vanilla-scented berry flavors that linger on the finish. Another winner from this value-oriented California winery. 8,514 cases made. • $10 • (10/15/95) BB • **86**
Pinot Noir Carneros 1992: Lean and thin, ordinary, barely ripe, earthy tea and herb flavors. Drinkable now. 5,800 cases made. • $10 • (03/31/95) • **77**
Pinot Noir Carneros 1991 • $10 • (02/28/94) • **80**
Pinot Noir Carneros 1990 • $9 • (09/30/92) • **81**

Key: SS—Spectator Selection. CS—Cellar Selection. BB—Best Buy. $NA—Price not available. (BT)—Barrel tasting. Ⓐ—Auction Price.
Dates in parentheses represent the issues in which the ratings were published.

Pinot Noir Carneros 1989 • $7 • (07/31/91) • **81**
Pinot Noir Carneros 1988 • $11 • (12/15/90) • **82**
Pinot Noir Carneros 1983 • $14 • (08/31/86) • **75**
Pinot Noir Carneros 1980 • $7 • (04/16/84) • **71**
Pinot Noir Carneros Grand Reserve 1994: Complex, earthy edge to the cherry and berry flavors, turning tannic on the finish. 941 cases made. • $20 • (02/29/96) • **84**
Pinot Noir Carneros Grand Reserve 1991: Lean and a bit earthy, it strives for complexity with its buttery oak flavors, but the plum and berry flavors thin out on the finish. Well made, ready now. • $20 • (10/31/94) • **86**
Pinot Noir Carneros Grand Reserve 1990 • $16 • (02/28/93) HR • **89**
Pinot Noir Carneros Private Reserve 1987 • $14 • (06/30/91) • **80**
Pinot Noir Carneros Private Reserve 1986 • $14 • (03/31/90) • **85**
Pinot Noir Carneros Private Reserve 1984 • $15 • (02/15/88) • **81**
Pinot Noir Carneros Private Reserve 1981 • $14 • (08/31/86) • **88**
Sauvignon Blanc Lake County 1995: Light-bodied, with a welcome crispness that complements the melon and citrus flavors. 50,000 cases made. • $8 • **87**
Sauvignon Blanc Lake County 1994: A light, lively and youthful California Sauvignon that's a bargain for this level of quality. It's bright with apple, pear and herbal flavors that linger on the finish. 48,000 cases made. • $7 • (09/15/95) BB • **87**
Sauvignon Blanc Lake County 1993: Bright and almost sweet, a fruity wine with a candied edge to the pear flavors. Lacks subtlety and grace. 26,000 cases made. • $7 • (12/31/94) • **79**
Sauvignon Blanc Lake County 1992 • $7 • (01/31/94) BB • **85**
Sauvignon Blanc Lake County 1991 • $7 • (09/30/92) BB • **86**
Zinfandel North Coast 1984 • $7 • (04/30/88) • **77**
Zinfandel Sonoma County 1982 • $6 • (04/01/85) • **80**

BULLY HILL | NEW YORK

Brut Seyval Blanc Finger Lakes 1988 • $15 • (12/31/90) • **74**

BURGESS | CALIFORNIA

Cabernet Sauvignon Napa Valley Vintage Selection 1991: Austere and tannic, with a narrow band of spicy currant and berry. Lacks the extra dimensions often found in this wine. 8,160 cases made. • $20 • (12/15/95) • **83**
Cabernet Sauvignon Napa Valley Vintage Selection 1990: Strikes a nice balance between ripe, spicy, supple Cabernet fruit and light oak shadings. The result is elegant and complex. It should benefit from short-term cellaring, try after 1998. 7,000 cases made. • $18 • (10/15/94) • **88**
Cabernet Sauvignon Napa Valley Vintage Selection 1989 • $18 • (11/15/93) • **86**
Cabernet Sauvignon Napa Valley Vintage Selection 1988 • $17 • (07/31/92) • **85**
Cabernet Sauvignon Napa Valley Vintage Selection 1987 • $20 • (10/15/91) • **85**
Cabernet Sauvignon Napa Valley Vintage Selection 1986 • $20 • (07/15/90) • **88**
Cabernet Sauvignon Napa Valley Vintage Selection 1985 • $24 • (07/15/89) • **92**
Cabernet Sauvignon Napa Valley Vintage Selection 1984 • $31 • (03/01/89) • **93**
Cabernet Sauvignon Napa Valley Vintage Selection 1983 • $24 • (03/01/89) • **87**
Cabernet Sauvignon Napa Valley Vintage Selection 1982 • $28 • (03/01/89) • **88**
Cabernet Sauvignon Napa Valley Vintage Selection 1981 • $28 • (03/01/89) • **88**
Cabernet Sauvignon Napa Valley Vintage Selection 1980 • $31 • (03/01/89) • **88**
Cabernet Sauvignon Napa Valley Vintage Selection 1979 • $32 • (03/01/89) • **87**
Cabernet Sauvignon Napa Valley Vintage Selection 1978 • $52 • (11/15/92) • **93**
Cabernet Sauvignon Napa Valley Vintage Selection 1977 • $45 • (03/01/89) • **92**

Cabernet Sauvignon Napa Valley Vintage Selection 1976 • $68 • (03/01/89) • **87**
Cabernet Sauvignon Napa Valley Vintage Selection 1975 • $40 • (03/01/89) • **88**
Cabernet Sauvignon Napa Valley Vintage Selection 1974 • $55 • (11/15/94) • **74**
Chardonnay Napa Valley Barrel Fermented Debourbage 1993: Supple and fruity, with appealing apple and pear notes of modest proportion. Picks up a light note on an elegant finish. 11,712 cases made. • $15 • (07/31/95) • **86**
Chardonnay Napa Valley Triere Vineyard 1992: Lean and smooth, peachy and spicy, with a caramel edge. Drinkable now. 16,870 cases made. • $16 • (06/30/94) • **83**
Chardonnay Napa Valley Triere Vineyard 1991 • $16 • (08/31/93) • **86**
Merlot Napa Valley 1993: Lean and a bit tannic, with a modest band of plum, herb and tobacco notes. A little more interesting on the finish, but it lacks depth and complexity. 3,348 cases made. • $20 • (05/31/96) • **84**
Zinfandel Napa Valley 1992: Tart, earthy and the wild berry flavors don't taste fully ripe. Lacks charm. 4,752 cases made. • $11 • (10/15/95) • **79**
Zinfandel Napa Valley 1991: Earthy and gamy, showing just enough peppery flavor to hold your interest. Can stand short-term cellaring. 5,560 cases made. • $12 • (10/15/94) • **81**
Zinfandel Napa Valley 1990 • $12 • (09/30/93) • **84**
Zinfandel Napa Valley 1989 • $10 • (10/15/92) • **80**
Zinfandel Napa Valley 1988 • $12 • (07/31/91) • **80**
Zinfandel Napa Valley 1987 • $10 • (05/31/90) • **82**
Zinfandel Napa Valley 1986 • $9 • (07/31/89) • **82**
Zinfandel Napa Valley 1985 • $9 • (06/30/88) • **87**
Zinfandel Napa Valley 1984 • $8 • (11/15/87) • **89**
Zinfandel Napa Valley 1983 • $7 • (10/31/86) • **81**
Zinfandel Napa Valley 1982 • $6 • (07/16/85) • **85**
Zinfandel Napa Valley 1981 • $6 • (04/16/84) • **81**

BUTTERFLY CREEK | CALIFORNIA

Chardonnay California 1991 • $18 • (07/15/93) • **81**
Merlot California 1989 • $15 • (05/31/92) • **77**
Merlot Sierra Foothills Mariposa County 1991: A rough and chunky style with ripe, chewy cherry and currant notes and gritty tannins. Drinkable now. 51 cases made. • $10 • (09/15/94) • **82**

BUTTONWOOD FARM | CALIFORNIA

Sauvignon Blanc Santa Ynez Valley 1993: Crisply focused and lean, sporting citrusy apple and slightly leafy flavors. Has some zing on the finish. 1,686 cases made. • $12 • (08/31/95) • **85**
Sauvignon Blanc Santa Ynez Valley 1991 • $10 • (09/15/93) • **78**

BYINGTON | CALIFORNIA

Cabernet Sauvignon Alexander Valley Smith Reichel Vineyard 1992: Ripe with bright, tart black cherry and wild berry flavors. Keeps its balance and intensity on the finish, where the fruit flavors stay lively. Best after 1997. 500 cases made. • $15 • (12/15/95) • **87**
Cabernet Sauvignon Napa Valley 1987 • $16 • (11/15/91) • **86**
Cabernet Sauvignon Santa Cruz Mountains Bates Ranch 1992: Tight and compact, with a slight green tannic edge to the flavors, which dominates the berry and cherry fruit. Finishes with gritty tannic edge. 460 cases made. • $22 • (12/15/95) • **83**
Chardonnay Mount Veeder 1993: A touch earthy with a bitter seam, but enough pear, hazelnut and spice to make it palatable. 1,100 cases made. • $14 • (07/31/95) • **83**
Chardonnay Santa Cruz Mountains 1993: Better balanced than most 1993s, with supple pear, citrus and light oak shadings, finishing with a pleasant aftertaste. 900 cases made. • $18 • (07/31/95) • **84**
Chardonnay Santa Cruz Mountains Redwood Hill Vineyard 1993: Medium bodied with modest pear and oak shadings, picking up subtle nuances on the finish. 350 cases made. • $23 • (07/31/95) • **84**
Chardonnay Santa Cruz Mountains Redwood Hill Vineyard 1991 • $18 • (03/31/93) • **89**
Chardonnay Santa Cruz Mountains Special Reserve Vineyards 1994: Smooth and spicy, with appealing ripe pear, honey and apple notes. Impressive for its purity of fruit and elegance. 800 cases made. • $18 • (06/30/96) • **87**
Chardonnay Santa Cruz Mountains Special Reserve Vineyards Spring Ridge Vineyard 1994: Smooth, rich and creamy, with an alluring, substantial core of pear, spice, honey and vanilla. Altogether impressive for its complexity and finesse. 400 cases made. • $23 • (06/30/96) • **90**
Fumé Blanc San Luis Obispo French Camp Vineyard Dry 1992: A pleasant wine, soft and a little sweet, with an herbal edge to the pear fruit. 1,333 cases made. • $8 • (08/31/94) • **80**
Merlot Sonoma County Bradford Mountain 1991: Tart but flavorful, raucous and juicy, echoes plum and berry on the finish. Rough enough to want until 1997 to 1998 to gain some polish. 262 cases made. • $15 • (09/15/94) • **83**
Pinot Noir California 1988 • $15 • (04/30/91) • **83**
Pinot Noir Napa Valley 1987 • $15 • (04/30/91) • **74**
Pinot Noir Santa Barbara County Bien Nacido Vineyard 1991: Pungent and earthy, offering a dry leathery streak to the herb and berry flavors. 900 cases made. • $15 • (03/31/95) • **78**
Pinot Noir Santa Cruz Mountains St. Charles Vineyard Special Reserve Vineyards 1993: Firmly tannic, adding a smoky, meaty, peppery edge to the earthy cherry and berry flavors. Best to cellar into 1997 in hopes the tannins subside. 100 cases made. • $30 • (02/29/96) • **85**
Pinot Noir Santa Cruz Mountains Special Reserve Vineyards 1994: Intense and well-focused spice, cherry, wild berry and subtle earth nuances. Firm tannins on aftertaste, but the fruit stands up better than in the 1993 bottling. Drinkable now. 300 cases made. • $25 • (02/29/96) • **88**
Sauvignon Blanc San Luis Obispo County French Camp Vineyard 1993: A spicy feeling runs through the honeysuckle and pear flavors. Crisp and peppery. 1,100 cases made. • $8 • (08/31/95) • **84**
Zinfandel Howell Mountain 1992: Ripe and appealing for its wild berry and plum-laced flavors, picking up a hint of prune on the finish. Tannins are in the right proportion. 540 cases made. • $10 • (03/31/96) • **86**
Zinfandel Paso Robles Sunny Slope Vineyard 1990 • $12 • (09/30/93) • **85**
Zinfandel Santa Clara County Calle Cielo Vineyard 1992: Holds together well, but an awkward Zin, with a green, unripe edge to the berry flavors. Drinkable now. 204 cases made. • $15 • (10/15/94) • **82**

BYNUM, DAVIS | CALIFORNIA

Cabernet Sauvignon Napa Valley Reserve Bottling 1984 • $7 • (12/15/87) • **71**
Cabernet Sauvignon Sonoma County 1989 • $11 • (11/15/92) • **81**
Cabernet Sauvignon Sonoma County 1987 • $11 • (11/15/90) • **79**
Cabernet Sauvignon Sonoma County 1986 • $10 • (11/15/89) • **84**
Chardonnay Russian River Valley Allen-Griffen Vineyards 1992: Clean, ripe and fruity, with creamy apple, pear and spice flavors that stay with you. Ready now. 1,279 cases made. • $17 • (04/30/94) • **84**
Chardonnay Russian River Valley Allen-Griffin Vineyards Limited Release 1991 • $17 • (07/15/93) • **81**
Chardonnay Sonoma County 1991 • $10 • (07/15/93) • **69**
Fumé Blanc Russian River Valley Shone Farm 1992 • $8 • (02/28/94) • **85**
Fumé Blanc Russian River Valley Shone Farm Dry 1994: Appealing for its simple pear and gooseberry flavors. 5,000 cases made. • $8 • (08/31/95) • **82**
Gewürztraminer Russian River Valley 1992 • $8 • (01/31/94) • **74**
Merlot Russian River Valley Laureles Vineyard 1991: Lean and crisp, with a modest level of berry and herb flavors, finishing earthy. 486 cases made. • $20 • (09/15/94) • **81**
Pinot Noir Russian River Valley 1993: Light in color, body and flavor, with herb, tea and spice notes and just a trace of cherry flavor. 1,522 cases made. • $12 • **82**
Pinot Noir Russian River Valley 1991 • $17 • (02/28/94) • **84**
Pinot Noir Russian River Valley 1990 • $18 • (02/28/94) • **72**
Pinot Noir Russian River Valley Artist Series 1985 • $15 • (06/15/88) • **82**
Pinot Noir Russian River Valley Limited Edition 1992: Crisp with a trim band of cherry and plum fruit. Pleasant enough but lacks extra dimensions. 486 cases made. • $21 • (09/15/95) • **84**

Pinot Noir Russian River Valley Limited Release 1991: An elegant, refined, harmonious style, with pretty black cherry, spice and raspberry notes. Finishes with a delicate touch. Drinks well now but should hold through 1997. 1,312 cases made. • $18 • (10/31/94) • **88**
Pinot Noir Russian River Valley Limited Release 1990 • $18 • (09/30/92) • **84**
Pinot Noir Russian River Valley Limited Release 1988 • $16 • (04/30/91) • **86**
Pinot Noir Russian River Valley Limited Release 1986 • $14 • (03/31/90) • **83**
Pinot Noir Russian River Valley Limited Release 1984 • $14 • (05/31/88) • **89**
Pinot Noir Russian River Valley Westside Road 1983 • $10 • (07/16/86) • **71**
Pinot Noir Sonoma County Reserve Bottling 1986 • $9 • (09/15/88) • **82**
Pinot Noir Sonoma County Reserve Bottling 1985 • $7 • (01/31/88) • **67**
Zinfandel Russian River Valley 1992: Ripe and full-bodied, with rich, spicy black cherry, plum and wild berry flavors that stay in there from start to finish. Well balanced and appealing now. 1,580 cases made. • $12 • (10/15/95) • **88**
Zinfandel Russian River Valley 1991: Ripe and jammy, with a pretty core of black cherry, plum and raspberry flavors that turn smooth and plush. Drinks well now. 2,864 cases made. • $12 • (10/15/94) • **87**
Zinfandel Russian River Valley 1990 • $12 • (10/15/92) • **84**

BYRON | CALIFORNIA

Cabernet Sauvignon Central Coast 1985 • $14 • (12/15/89) • **76**
Cabernet Sauvignon Santa Barbara County 1990: Youthful and tight, with lean, rough-hewn cherry, plum and currant notes. It's also quite tannic and a touch earthy on the finish. Try now. • $16 • (08/31/92) • **85**
Cabernet Sauvignon Santa Barbara County 1989 • $16 • (11/15/93) • **82**
Chardonnay Santa Barbara County 1994: Pleasant enough, with ripe pear, honey, apple and spice notes and then a hint of lemon and tangerine on the finish. Well balanced. 20,000 cases made. • $16 • (05/31/96) • **88**
Chardonnay Santa Barbara County 1993: Well oaked, with toasty vanilla and buttery notes, but lots of pretty ripe pear, apple, spice and honey notes. Turns complex and fruity. 14,000 cases made. • $15 • (07/31/95) SS • **90**
Chardonnay Santa Barbara County 1992: A pleasing style, complex and concentrated, with hints of pear, spice, butterscotch and honey on the finish. Can stand short-term cellaring to soften and evolve. 10,817 cases made. • $15 • (04/30/94) • **88**
Chardonnay Santa Barbara County 1991 • $14 • (05/31/93) SS • **92**
Chardonnay Santa Barbara County Reserve 1994: An elegant, understated style with flavors that grow on you. It has ripe pear with hints of pineapple and citrus framed in spicy, vanilla-scented oak. Picks up a nice hazelnut taste on the finish. 4,252 cases made. • $23 • (05/31/96) • **90**
Chardonnay Santa Barbara County Reserve 1993: Good richness, depth and intensity, a well-focused and complex wine with tiers of honey, pear and smoky oak. Remarkably complex and concentrated. 3,636 cases made. • $23 • (07/31/95) • **91**
Chardonnay Santa Barbara County Reserve 1992: An outstanding reserve-style wine that comes at you with green apple and spice flavors that soften and swirl into honey and cream notes on the long finish. Drink now. 2,816 cases made. • $23 • (11/30/94) SS • **92**
Chardonnay Santa Barbara County Reserve 1991 • $20 • (07/15/93) • **88**
Chardonnay Santa Maria Valley Estate 1993: A bold, complex style that packs in lots of ripe pear, fig, honey and butterscotch flavors and frames them with toasty, smoky oak. It all adds up to a rich, full-bodied mouthful of Chardonnay from this premier California winery. 2,772 cases made. • $28 • (04/30/96) • **93**
Chardonnay Santa Maria Valley Estate 1992: Well focused, with intense pear, spice, nutmeg and toasty oak, all folding together in a rich and complex package. Holds its flavors on the finish. 2,100 cases made. • $25 • (07/31/95) • **91**
Chardonnay Santa Maria Valley Estate 1991 • $23 • (04/30/94) • **91**
Pinot Blanc Santa Maria Valley 1994: Strives for a subtle, understated style, but the flavors build in a pure core of rich fig, honey, pear and butterscotch persisting on a long, full finish. 779 cases made. • $14 • (04/30/96) • **90**
Pinot Noir Santa Barbara County 1994: Intense and lively, offering ample tannins too, as supple cherry and berry flavors pick up an herb and anise edge. Drinkable now. 4,181 cases made. • $16 • (02/29/96) • **87**
Pinot Noir Santa Barbara County 1992 • $15 • (02/28/94) • **83**
Pinot Noir Santa Barbara County 1986 • $12 • (06/15/88) • **88**
Pinot Noir Santa Barbara County 1985 • $12 • (06/15/88) • **81**
Pinot Noir Santa Barbara County Reserve 1992: Firm and crisp, with an earthy, leathery herb and cola edge to the spicy black cherry flavor. Drinkable now. 5,392 cases made. • $23 • (03/31/95) • **86**
Pinot Noir Santa Barbara County Reserve 1991 • $23 • (02/28/94) • **88**
Pinot Noir Santa Barbara County Reserve 1990 • $20 • (02/28/93) • **87**
Pinot Noir Santa Barbara County Reserve 1987 • $16 • (12/15/89) • **85**
Pinot Noir Santa Barbara County Reserve 1986 • $12 • (06/15/88) • **84**
Pinot Noir Santa Barbara County Sierra Madre Vineyards 1984 • $13 • (08/31/86) • **85**
Sauvignon Blanc Santa Barbara County 1993: Firm and nicely focused, modest fruit and a pleasant touch of herbs sneak in on the finish. 2,897 cases made. • $11 • (08/31/95) • **82**
Sauvignon Blanc Santa Barbara County 1992 • $9 • (07/15/93) • **90**
Sauvignon Blanc Santa Barbara County 1991 • $9 • (02/15/93) • **85**

CA' DEL SOLO | CALIFORNIA

Big House Red California 1992 • $8 • (10/15/93) BB • **84**
Big House Red California 1991 • $7 • (11/30/92) BB • **84**
Big House Red California 1990 • $7 • (06/30/92) BB • **85**
Big House White California 1994: Light and fragrant like a Muscat, but with extra citrus and somewhat underripe peach notes to make it more interesting. Finishes dry. A good price for a pleasant white. 1,600 cases made. • $7 • (10/15/95) BB • **86**
Big House White California 1993: Smooth and ripe, a simple, appealing wine with a citrusy edge to the gentle fruit. Drink soon. 1,600 cases made. • $7 • (04/15/95) • **83**
Il Pescatore American 1991 • $12 • (03/15/93) • **80**
Il Pescatore California 1993: Soft and fragrant, a supple wine with generous, spicy pear and almond flavors and a silky texture. Very nice to drink now. Uses Pinot Noir, Pinot Meunier, Chardonnay and Riesling. 4,500 cases made. • $12 • (04/15/95) • **85**
Malvasia Bianca Monterey 1994: Soft and broad, a mouthful of fresh pear and spicy grape flavors. Drink soon, though. • $8 • (09/30/95) • **85**
Malvasia Bianca Monterey 1993: Soft and floral, an earthy wine with a nice core of pear and almond flavor that lingers nicely on the finish. Drink soon. 3,700 cases made. • $8 • (04/15/95) • **85**
Malvasia Bianca Monterey 1992 • $8 • (09/30/93) • **85**
Moscato Monterey Moscato del Solo 1993: A disarmingly fresh and appealing dessert wine, not very aromatic, but the spicy, peppery flavors float lightly and keep lingering on the sweet, honeyed finish. 2,700 cases made. • $9 • (12/31/94) • **85**
Muscat Monterey Moscato del Solo 1992 • $9 • (10/15/93) • **85**
Muscat Monterey Moscato del Solo 1991 • $9 • (02/15/93) • **83**
Prunus California Dessert NV • $15 • (03/31/92) • **92**

CAFARO | CALIFORNIA

Cabernet Sauvignon Napa Valley 1992: Intense, broad shouldered, with chunky fruit flavors that echo currant, chocolate and wild berry. Finishes with a rustic core of fruit and firm tannins, so cellaring into 1998 or 1999 is recommended. 930 cases made. • $26 • (12/15/95) • **88**
Cabernet Sauvignon Napa Valley 1991: Smooth and supple, showing attractive, understated spicy currant and plum flavors followed by cedary oak and tannins. Best to cellar into 1997. Tasted out of magnum. • $28 • (09/15/95) • **88**
Cabernet Sauvignon Napa Valley 1990: A spicy, peppery edge to the cherry and currant notes. Lean and elegant, it's modestly concentrated

Key: SS—Spectator Selection. CS—Cellar Selection. BB—Best Buy. $NA—Price not available. (BT)—Barrel tasting. Ⓐ—Auction Price.
Dates in parentheses represent the issues in which the ratings were published.

UNITED STATES

and mildly tannic. Drink now through 1997. Tasted twice. • $24 • (11/15/93) • **84**
Cabernet Sauvignon Napa Valley 1989 • $16 Ⓐ • (11/15/92) • **85**
Cabernet Sauvignon Napa Valley 1988 • $25 • (11/15/91) • **81**
Cabernet Sauvignon Napa Valley 1987 • $20 • (11/15/90) • **84**
Cabernet Sauvignon Napa Valley 1986 • $18 • (11/15/89) • **93**
Merlot Napa Valley 1988 • $20 • (11/15/91) • **89**
Merlot Napa Valley 1987 • $18 • (12/31/90) • **86**
Merlot Napa Valley 1986 • $18 • (12/31/89) • **84**

CAIN | CALIFORNIA

Cabernet Sauvignon Napa Valley 1986 • $16 • (08/31/90) • **85**
Cabernet Sauvignon Napa Valley 1985 • $16 • (04/15/89) • **81**
Cabernet Sauvignon Napa Valley 1984 • $14 • (05/31/88) • **79**
Cabernet Sauvignon Napa Valley 1983 • $14 • (08/31/87) • **75**
Cabernet Sauvignon Napa Valley 1982 • $11 • (09/30/86) • **78**
Cabernet Sauvignon Napa Valley Estate 1987 • $25 • (10/15/90) • **92**
Cuvée Napa Valley 1992: A touch earthy with a leathery edge, giving it a dry taste, with just a trace of spicy currant emerging. Trim and lean, with dry tannins. 8,300 cases made. • $16 • (12/15/95) • **83**
Cuvée Napa Valley 1991: A bit on the green side, with herb, cedar and simple currant flavors. Finishes with firm tannins. 5,000 cases made. • $15 • (12/31/94) • **83**
Cuvée Napa Valley 1989 • $12 • (11/15/93) • **84**
Cuvée Napa Valley 1988 • $12 • (03/31/93) • **87**
Five Napa Valley 1994: Complex and well constructed, with a complex array of currant, earth, spice and cedary notes, especially impressive on the finish for its length and focus. • $NA • (05/31/95) • **90-94** (BT)
Five Napa Valley 1991: A touch earthy, but complex and distinctive, with intense currant, herb, spice and cedary oak, finishing with firm tannins. Still a touch green, but less so than six months ago. Best for cellaring into 1997. 4,000 cases made. • $40 • (12/15/95) • **89**
Five Napa Valley 1990: Another tremendous Cain Five. Plush and complex, with rich, supple currant, spice and black cherry notes that fold together nicely on the palate. The flavors run deep and are concentrated, finishing with a long, lingering, chocolaty aftertaste. Drink now through 1998. 2,000 cases made. • $34 • (09/15/94) CS • **93**
Five Napa Valley 1987 • $30 • (04/30/91) • **91**
Five Napa Valley 1986 • $30 • (02/15/90) • **91**
Five Napa Valley 1985 • $43 Ⓐ • (06/15/89) • **87**
Merlot Napa Valley 1986 • $14 • (02/28/89) • **83**
Merlot Napa Valley 1984 • $12 • (09/30/88) • **89**
Merlot Napa Valley 1982 • $11 • (02/01/85) • **78**
Sauvignon Blanc Monterey Musqué 1994: Light and crisp. Distinct herbal and olive notes complement the citrusy apple flavors. Classic varietal flavors highlight a finish that just doesn't quit. 1,850 cases made. • $15 • **89**
Sauvignon Blanc Monterey Musqué 1993: Unabashedly herbal, with spicy oak flavors to take the edge off the flavors. 1,200 cases made. • $14 • (08/31/95) • **80**
Sauvignon Blanc Monterey Musqué 1992 • $12 • (06/15/94) • **87**
Sauvignon Blanc Monterey Musqué 1991 • $12 • (09/15/93) • **78**

CAKEBREAD | CALIFORNIA

Cabernet Sauvignon Napa Valley 1991: Serves up a pretty core of ripe black cherry and plum flavor before the tannins kick in and turn it crisp with a bite. Wait until around 1998 when it should be softer. 13,000 cases made. • $22 • (11/15/94) • **88**
Cabernet Sauvignon Napa Valley 1990: Spicy and herbal, with an elegant core of currant and cherry flavors. A solid, straightforward Cabernet that's ready to drink now. 9,000 cases made. • $21 • (09/15/93) • **83**
Cabernet Sauvignon Napa Valley 1989 • $22 • (07/15/92) • **87**
Cabernet Sauvignon Napa Valley 1988 • $24 • (11/15/91) • **86**
Cabernet Sauvignon Napa Valley 1987 • $25 • (10/15/90) • **90**
Cabernet Sauvignon Napa Valley 1986 • $20 • (08/31/89) • **90**
Cabernet Sauvignon Napa Valley 1985 • $17 • (03/01/89) • **84**
Cabernet Sauvignon Napa Valley 1984 • $25 • (03/01/89) • **89**
Cabernet Sauvignon Napa Valley 1983 • $31 Ⓐ • (03/01/89) • **77**
Cabernet Sauvignon Napa Valley 1982 • $25 • (03/01/89) • **86**
Cabernet Sauvignon Napa Valley 1981 • $23 • (03/01/89) • **88**
Cabernet Sauvignon Napa Valley 1980 • $27 • (03/01/89) • **84**
Cabernet Sauvignon Napa Valley 1979 • $27 • (03/01/89) • **82**
Cabernet Sauvignon Napa Valley 1978 • $26 • (03/01/89) • **85**
Cabernet Sauvignon Napa Valley Lot 2 1978 • $33 • (03/01/89) • **86**
Cabernet Sauvignon Napa Valley Lot 2 1974 • $100 • (11/15/94) • **91**
Cabernet Sauvignon Napa Valley Rutherford Reserve 1990: Dense and compact, with a chewy, weedy, earthy edge to the currant and berry notes, finishing with firm tannins. Will need short-term cellaring into 1997 or 1998, but it may always be on the tannic side. 900 cases made. • $42 • (12/15/95) • **87**
Cabernet Sauvignon Napa Valley Rutherford Reserve 1987 • $23 • (09/15/93) • **91**
Cabernet Sauvignon Napa Valley Rutherford Reserve 1986 • $43 • (11/15/91) • **89**
Cabernet Sauvignon Napa Valley Rutherford Reserve 1985 • $40 • (03/01/89) • **85**
Cabernet Sauvignon Napa Valley Rutherford Reserve 1984 • $35 • (02/15/90) • **85**
Cabernet Sauvignon Napa Valley Rutherford Reserve 1983 • $35 • (03/01/89) • **88**
Chardonnay Napa Valley 1994: A pleasantly fruity style with earthy peach and pear notes. Should age a little to soften it and let the flavors develop. Finishes crisp. 36,000 cases made. • $23 • (01/31/96) • **87**
Chardonnay Napa Valley 1993: A bit on the green side, with tart, zesty green apple flavors that are one dimension but focused. • $22 • (07/31/95) • **84**
Chardonnay Napa Valley 1992: Austere with firm acidity and crisp lemon, pineapple, pear and piney flavors that linger. Can stand short-term cellaring, try through 1997. 19,000 cases made. • $20 • (06/30/94) • **87**
Chardonnay Napa Valley 1991 • $23 • (03/31/93) • **81**
Chardonnay Napa Valley Reserve 1992: Clean and correct, with ripe pear, spice and cedary oak of moderate porportions, finishing with a pleasant fruity edge. 1,000 cases made. • $30 • (07/31/95) • **87**
Rutherford Reserve Napa Valley 1988 • $39 • (11/15/93) • **81**
Sauvignon Blanc Napa Valley 1994: Nicely-balanced, ripe flavors are centered around grapefruit and a touch of anise and linger nicely. 9,000 cases made. • $13 • (08/31/95) • **87**
Sauvignon Blanc Napa Valley 1992 • $13 • (11/15/93) • **87**
Sauvignon Blanc Napa Valley 1991 • $14 • (09/15/93) • **80**
Zinfandel Howell Mountain 1992: Intense and spicy, with loads of peppery Zinfandel fruit that's ripe and rich on the palate. Lush, full-bodied raspberry and wild berry flavors. Finishes with firm tannins and a long, smoky aftertaste. 1,000 cases made. • $17 • (09/15/94) • **90**

CALE | CALIFORNIA

Chardonnay Carneros Sangiacomo Vineyard 1994: Strikes a nice balance between smoky, toasty oak and ripe pear and vanilla notes. An elegant and refined style that's pleasant to drink. 2,300 cases made. • $20 • (05/15/96) • **87**
Chardonnay Carneros Sangiacomo Vineyard 1993: Intense and spicy, sporting a sweetish, litchi-nut edge to the ripe pear and buttery oak flavors. 2,000 cases made. • $18 • (06/15/95) • **88**
Chardonnay Carneros Sangiacomo Vineyard 1992: Creamy and complex, with pretty honey, pear, toast and butter flavors that pick up a smoky, toasty edge from oak barrels. Drinkable now. 1,500 cases made. • $18 • (03/31/94) • **90**
Chardonnay Carneros Sangiacomo Vineyard 1991 • $18 • (10/31/93) • **88**

CALERA | CALIFORNIA

Chardonnay Central Coast 1994: A smooth and polished California white with toasty oak, pear, spice and honey notes. It turns elegant and refined on the finish, where the flavors linger. 11,325 cases made. • $15 • (12/31/95) SS • **90**
Chardonnay Central Coast 1993: Earthy, with a juniper berry edge but also a pretty core of smooth, creamy pear and vanilla flavors. Finishes better than it starts. 10,385 cases made. • $15 • (02/28/95) • **88**

Chardonnay Central Coast 1992: Smooth, ripe and creamy with vanilla, pear and spicy Chardonnay flavors that turn silky and elegant on the finish. Drink now. 10,000 cases made. • $15 • (02/28/94) SS • **89**
Chardonnay Central Coast 1991 • $14 • (04/15/93) • **89**
Chardonnay Mount Harlan 1992: Compact and concentrated, with ripe pear, pineapple, butterscotch and toasty oak flavors, distinctive, graceful and harmonious. Needs short-term cellaring to evolve, but the finish is pretty and lively. 1,466 cases made. • $33 • (05/31/94) • **89**
Chardonnay Mount Harlan 1991 • $33 • (07/15/93) • **80**
Pinot Noir Blanc California 1990 • $7 • (10/31/91) BB • **84**
Pinot Noir Central Coast 1994: Marked by herb, tea and black cherry notes and a pretty core of currant and spice. Lengthy finish. Drink now. 6,853 cases made. • $16 • (02/29/96) • **85**
Pinot Noir Central Coast 1993: Marked by smoky, meaty flavors, it serves up enough cherry and berry notes to keep in balance. 10,513 cases made. • $15 • **83**
Pinot Noir Central Coast 1992 • $15 • (02/28/94) • **73**
Pinot Noir Central Coast 1991 • $14 • (02/28/93) • **84**
Pinot Noir Central Coast 1990 • $14 • (03/31/92) • **87**
Pinot Noir Central Coast 1989 • $14 • (11/15/91) • **85**
Pinot Noir Central Coast 1987 • $14 • (02/15/90) • **82**
Pinot Noir Mount Harlan 1993: Simple but pleasant with cherry, berry and spice notes of modest proportion. Shows more depth and complexity than many 1993s, but shares the vintage's medium weight. 1,336 cases made. • $35 • **85**
Pinot Noir Mount Harlan Jensen 1991: Aromatic, ripe, exotic wild berry and raspberry flavors turn elegant and silky. Impressive for its ripeness and delicacy. 1,200 cases made. • $34 • (03/31/95) • **88**
Pinot Noir Mount Harlan Jensen 1990 • $38 • (02/28/94) • **87**
Pinot Noir Mount Harlan Jensen 1989 • $35 • (02/28/94) • **87**
Pinot Noir Mount Harlan Jensen 1988 • $35 • (11/15/91) • **92**
Pinot Noir Mount Harlan Jensen 1987 • $30 • (04/30/91) • **93**
Pinot Noir Mount Harlan Jensen 1986 • $45 • (05/31/89) • **88**
Pinot Noir Mount Harlan Jensen 1985 • $25 • (06/15/88) • **88**
Pinot Noir Mount Harlan Jensen 1983 • $22 • (08/31/86) • **80**
Pinot Noir Mount Harlan Jensen 1982 • $23 • (01/01/85) • **88**
Pinot Noir Mount Harlan Mills 1989 • $32 • (11/15/92) • **91**
Pinot Noir Mount Harlan Mills 1988 • $30 • (11/15/91) • **89**
Pinot Noir Mount Harlan Reed 1992: Comes across as simple at this stage, offering spice and plum flavors that turn a bit coarse on the finish. May be better in about a year. 605 cases made. • $35 • (03/31/95) • **84**
Pinot Noir Mount Harlan Reed 1988 • $36 • (11/15/91) • **85**
Pinot Noir Mount Harlan Reed 1987 • $35 • (04/30/91) • **80**
Pinot Noir Mount Harlan Reed 1982 • $23 • (08/31/86) • **75**
Pinot Noir Mount Harlan Selleck 1987 • $30 • (11/15/91) • **92**
Pinot Noir Mount Harlan Selleck 1986 • $30 • (03/31/90) • **85**
Pinot Noir Santa Barbara County Bien Nacido Vineyard 1985 • $13 • (06/15/88) • **82**
Pinot Noir Santa Barbara County Los Alamos Vineyard 1982 • $10 • (11/16/85) • **62**
Rouge de Rouge California NV • $4 • (01/31/87) BB • **80**
Viognier Mount Harlan 1994: Elegant and refined, with attractive pear, spice and nectarine flavors, showing more complexity and finesse than most Viogniers. 816 cases made. • $30 • (01/31/96) • **89**
Zinfandel California NV • $5 • (07/31/88) • **71**
Zinfandel Cienega Valley 1981 • $7 • (04/16/84) • **81**
Zinfandel Cienega Valley Reserve 1981 • $8 • (01/01/85) • **82**

CALISTOGA VINEYARDS | CALIFORNIA

Chardonnay Napa Valley 1992: A fruity style with ripe apple, pear and melon notes that finishes with a cedary edge. 4,500 cases made. • $11 • (07/31/95) • **82**

Key: SS—Spectator Selection. CS—Cellar Selection. BB—Best Buy. $NA—Price not available. (BT)—Barrel tasting. Ⓐ—Auction Price.
Dates in parentheses represent the issues in which the ratings were published.

CALLAWAY | CALIFORNIA

Cabernet Sauvignon California 1990: A full-bodied, tannic young Cabernet, with modest fruit and herb flavors. Has the outline of a good Cabernet, but could use more stuffing. • $8 • (11/15/93) • **79**
Cabernet Sauvignon California 1989 • $9 • (03/31/93) • **80**
Cabernet Sauvignon California America's Cup 1989 • $10 • (11/15/91) • **82**
Cabernet Sauvignon California Hawk Watch 1991: Simple with grapey Cabernet flavors, a serviceable red that's ready. • $10 • (11/15/94) • **79**
Chardonnay Temecula Calla-Lees 1991 • $8 • (07/15/93) • **78**
Chardonnay Temecula Calla-Lees Hawk Watch Classic Sur Lie Style 1991: Earthy with tinny, canned pear and pineapple flavors. 121,900 cases made. • $10 • (06/30/94) • **75**
Chardonnay Temecula Hawk Watch Calla-Lees 1993: Crisp and simple, a lively wine with gentle pear and vanilla flavors that linger on the finish. 68,200 cases made. • $9 • (07/31/95) • **84**
Chardonnay Temecula Hawk Watch Classic Sur Lie Style Calla-Lees 1992: Ripe and fruity, showing complex apple, pear and spice flavors that turn elegant and supple. 70,750 cases made. • $8 • (04/15/95) • **83**
Chenin Blanc Temecula Sweet Nancy Late Harvest NV: Sweet and deeply honeyed, but it stops short of syrupy and remains nicely balanced between apricot and honey. A lovely dessert wine. 2,400 cases made. • $22 • (02/29/96) • **88**
Fumé Blanc Temecula Hawk Watch 1993: Floral and distinctly peppery, perhaps a little sweet on the finish, making it feel unbalanced. Not for the faint of heart. 11,000 cases made. • $8 • (08/31/95) • **74**
Pinot Gris Hawk Watch Temecula 1993: Light and fruity, with snappy pear and citrus flavors, and finishing sturdily. 478 cases made. • $14 • (12/15/95) • **84**
Sauvignon Blanc Temecula Hawk Watch 1994: Lean, somewhat sweet, herb and apple flavors. 14,280 cases made. • $7 • (08/31/95) • **78**
Sauvignon Blanc Temecula Hawk Watch 1993: Soft, a little sweet, showing apple and spice flavors that linger. • $7 • (04/30/95) • **80**
Sauvignon Blanc Temecula Hawk Watch 1992: Floral flavors persist through the finish on this medium-weight, lean-textured wine. 15,141 cases made. • $8 • (08/31/94) • **79**
Temecula Sweet Nancy 1991: Sweet and vaguely floral, a little touch of honey and a wisp of vinegar on the finish. 505 cases made. • $25 • (09/30/95) • **79**
Viognier Temecula 1993: Soft and fruity, with mild but exotic tropical fruit overtones. • $16 • (09/15/94) • **81**
White Riesling Temecula 1991 • $7 • (06/15/93) • **77**

CAMARADERIE | WASHINGTON

Cabernet Sauvignon Washington 1992: Drifts over to the woody side, showing more spice, oak and smoke than any fruit character. Try in 1997. 200 cases made. • $17 • (09/30/95) • **82**

CAMBIASO | CALIFORNIA

Cabernet Sauvignon Dry Creek Valley 1981 • $4 • (06/16/84) • **60**

CAMBRIA | CALIFORNIA

Chardonnay Santa Barbara County 1994: Complex, intriguing array of ripe pear, peach, spice and toasty oak flavors, adding a lingering aftertaste. • $15 • (02/29/96) • **88**
Chardonnay Santa Maria Valley Katherine's Vineyard 1994: Appealing core of ripe peach and pear. Adds a trace of honey and oak on the finish. • $18 • (02/29/96) • **86**
Chardonnay Santa Maria Valley Katherine's Vineyard 1993: Bright and lively, medium-bodied, showing vivid pear, spice, honey and hazelnut notes that turn elegant. 50,000 cases made. • $16 • (02/28/95) • **87**
Chardonnay Santa Maria Valley Katherine's Vineyard 1991 • $16 • (07/15/93) • **85**
Chardonnay Santa Maria Valley Reserve 1994: Well balanced, with a nice range of spicy, toasty pear and pineapple flavors, all blending well on the finish. Complex and elegant. • $30 • (06/15/96) • **88**
Chardonnay Santa Maria Valley Reserve 1993: Bold, ripe and harmonious, with rich, spicy pear, honey and butterscotch nuances. Picks up

a smoky, somewhat leesy note and leaves a wonderful aftertaste. Drinkable through 1997. 4,000 cases made. • $25 • (05/31/95) SS • **91**

Chardonnay Santa Maria Valley Reserve 1992: Ripe and complex, with pretty pear, peach and nectarine flavors that are focused and concentrated, framed by toasty, buttery oak. Intense and lively, yet elegant and refined, it's delicious to drink through 1997. • $25 • (06/30/94) • **91**

Chardonnay Santa Maria Valley Reserve 1991: Dense and compact, with spicy pear, citrus and nutmeg flavors that are tightly wound. Not as rich and generous as the 1992 Reserve. Drink now. 815 cases made. • $25 • (06/30/94) • **85**

Pinot Noir Santa Maria Valley Julia's Vineyard 1994: Serves up a ripe core of plum, cherry and wild berry notes in an openly fruity, appealing, well-crafted red. Rich finish, smooth texture. • $22 • (02/29/96) • **89**

Pinot Noir Santa Maria Valley Julia's Vineyard 1993: Intensely spicy, and the exotic cherry, herb, and black cherry flavors fold together nicely with the mild tannins. • $18 • (02/28/95) • **86**

Pinot Noir Santa Maria Valley Julia's Vineyard 1992 • $16 • (02/28/94) • **87**

Pinot Noir Santa Maria Valley Julia's Vineyard 1991 • $16 • (02/28/93) • **83**

Pinot Noir Santa Maria Valley Julia's Vineyard 1989 • $15 • (09/30/92) • **80**

Pinot Noir Santa Maria Valley Julia's Vineyard 1988 • $16 • (12/15/90) • **88**

Pinot Noir Santa Maria Valley Reserve 1993: A lighter style with pretty herb, cola and black cherry fruit of modest proportion. Turns elegant on the finish, but lacks the extra dimensions you might expect at this price. 475 cases made. • $35 • **85**

Pinot Noir Santa Maria Valley Reserve 1992: Pleasantly fruity, offering herb and black cherry flavors. Firm tannins and a cola edge on the finish. Best after 1997. 225 cases made. • $30 • (03/31/95) • **86**

Sangiovese Santa Maria Valley Tepusquet Vineyard 1993: Light in texture and flavor, showing a nice thread of persistent raspberry and spice accents that linger on the finish. 950 cases made. • $18 • (08/31/95) • **86**

Syrah Santa Maria Valley Tepusquet Vineyard 1992: Supple, rich and fruity with wild berry character, enhanced by cedar, spice, leather and tobacco notes. Turns smooth and complex on the finish. 120 cases made. • $30 • (05/15/95) • **88**

CAMELOT | CALIFORNIA

Cabernet Sauvignon Central Coast 1992: A lighter style, it still delivers enough spicy oak and currant and cherry flavor to keep your interest. Ready now. • $11 • (11/15/94) • **83**

Cabernet Sauvignon North Coast 1993: Marked by herb, dill and ripe Cabernet flavors, picking up a toasty oak edge on the finish, where the flavors linger. • $12 • (12/15/95) • **87**

Chardonnay Central Coast 1994: Strives for elegance and finesse and succeeds at it. The tiers of honey, pear, nectarine and peach work well together. Impressive for its balance. • $11 • (06/15/96) • **89**

Chardonnay Central Coast 1993: Appealing for its medium bodied pear, spice, light oak and cedary notes. The flavors fan out a gain more depth on the finish. • $12 • (07/31/95) • **88**

Chardonnay Monterey Reserve 1994: A bit musty, with ripe, spicy pear and pineapple flavors. A good solid white. 978 cases made. • $22 • (06/15/96) • **85**

Chardonnay Santa Barbara County 1994: Smooth and polished, with a delicate balance between the ripe pear, apple and honey notes. Picks up a trace of citrus and spice on the finish. • $18 • (06/15/96) • **87**

Chardonnay Santa Barbara County 1993: Crisp and focused, zingy with green apple and spice. The flavors extend into a lively finish. It's stylish and quite charming. Drinkable now. • $12 • (01/31/95) • **90**

Pinot Noir Central Coast 1994: Supple and focused, with a smooth core of cherry, herb and vanilla flavors that are elegant. Long and lingering on the finish. • $12 • (02/29/96) • **84**

Pinot Noir Central Coast 1993: Supple and focused, with a smooth core of cherry, herb and vanilla flavors that are elegant, with a long, lingering finish. • $12 • (03/31/95) • **86**

CANARD | CALIFORNIA

Zinfandel Napa Valley 1990: Mature red featuring a pleasant band of cherry, plum, cedar, pepper and spice. Mild tannins and good length on the finish. 500 cases made. • $12 • (04/30/96) • **85**

CANEPA | CALIFORNIA

Chardonnay Alexander Valley 1991 • $19 • (07/15/93) • **88**

Chardonnay Alexander Valley Canepa Vineyard 1993: Marked by strong smoky, earthy and slightly bitter tones, it nonetheless delivers a rich mouthful of pear and spice. More appealing on the finish than during initial impressions. • $20 • (12/15/95) • **88**

Chardonnay Alexander Valley Gauer Vineyard Adobe 111 1994: There's much to like here in the ripe pear and fig notes, but woody tones on the finish come across as heavy-handed and dominating. Lacks grace, despite its attempt to pack in all the flavor. 605 cases made. • $24 • (04/30/96) • **85**

CANOE RIDGE | WASHINGTON

Chardonnay Columbia Valley 1994: Bright and fruity, effusive peach, apple and vanilla-spice overtones. Ready now. 1,782 cases made. • $12 • (09/30/95) • **86**

Merlot Columbia Valley 1993: Brilliantly focused, its bright blackberry, currant and toasty oak flavors weaving harmoniously through to the spicy finish. Ready now. 2,517 cases made. • $14 • (09/30/95) • **88**

Red Table Wine Columbia Valley 1992: Spicy and elegant, featuring supple currant, black cherry and cedary oak notes. Finishes with soft tannins, which makes it appealing to drink now. • $12 • (03/31/95) • **86**

CANTERBURY | CALIFORNIA

Cabernet Sauvignon California 1990: Ripe and flavorful, a simple, ready-to-drink Cabernet. Ripe plum and currant notes finish with a firm tannic aftertaste. Drinkable now. Tasted twice. 2,350 cases made. • $7 • (11/15/92) • **81**

Cabernet Sauvignon California 1989 • $6 • (11/15/91) BB • **80**

Merlot California 1991 • $8 • (08/31/93) • **74**

Merlot California 1990 • $7 • (05/31/92) • **79**

Zinfandel California 1990 • $5 • (07/15/92) BB • **84**

CANYON ROAD | CALIFORNIA

Cabernet Sauvignon California 1993: Light and fragrant, with a candle wax edge to the raspberry and currant fruit. Ready now. 30,000 cases made. • $6 • (11/15/95) BB • **85**

Cabernet Sauvignon California 1992: Pleasantly balanced with ripe cherry, plum and raspberry flavors. Not too tannic, so you can enjoy it now. 6,000 cases made. • $7 • (11/15/94) • **83**

Cabernet Sauvignon California 1991: Shows decent Cabernet flavors, hints of berries and spices and enough tannin to firm it up on the finish. Drinkable now. 6,000 cases made. • $7 • (06/15/93) • **81**

Chardonnay California 1994: Light, lean and a little grassy behind the narrow beam of spicy apple flavor. Drinkable now. 50,000 cases made. • $7 • (05/15/96) • **81**

Chardonnay California 1993: Light and fruity, a little lean, simple on the finish. Drinkable now. 50,000 cases made. • $7 • (01/31/95) • **78**

Chardonnay California 1992: Guilelessly refreshing, offering plenty of spicy apple and grapefruit aromas and flavors that extend into a lively finish. Not especially complex, but has plenty of appeal. Drinkable now. 20,000 cases made. • $7 • (06/15/93) BB • **84**

Merlot California 1994: Light in texture, with plummy, spicy notes that never quite come into focus. Maybe best in 1997. 10,000 cases made. • $7 • (06/15/96) • **80**

Merlot California 1993: Lacks focus, but the currant, herb and tea notes are complex enough, and certainly a bargain at this level. Better than many Merlots at twice its price. 10,000 cases made. • $8 • (12/15/95) • **84**

Sauvignon Blanc California 1995: Fresh and bright apple and pineapple flavors that narrow a bit on the finish. 15,000 cases made. • $7 • **80**

Sauvignon Blanc California 1994: Bright, fruity and crisp, soft around the edges, showing off apple and grass flavors that mingle nicely. 10,000 cases made. • $6 • (08/31/95) • **83**

Sauvignon Blanc California 1993: Lively and citrusy, showing exuberant fruit and bright acidity. Mouth-filling and delicious. Ready now. 10,000 cases made. • $6 • (09/30/94) BB • **85**

Sauvignon Blanc California 1992 • $6 • (09/15/93) BB • **82**

CAPARONE | CALIFORNIA

Cabernet Sauvignon Santa Maria Valley Tepusquet Vineyard 1981 • $10 • (03/16/84) • **80**
Merlot Santa Maria Valley Tepusquet Vineyard 1981 • $10 • (03/16/84) • **88**

CAREY | CALIFORNIA

Cabernet Sauvignon Santa Ynez Valley 1985 • $10 • (11/15/89) • **83**
Cabernet Sauvignon Santa Ynez Valley 1984 • $9 • (03/31/88) • **72**
Cabernet Sauvignon Santa Ynez Valley Alamo Pintado Vineyard 1981 • $9 • (06/16/84) • **76**
Cabernet Sauvignon Santa Ynez Valley La Cuesta Vineyard 1983 • $9 • (12/15/89) • **83**
Cabernet Sauvignon Santa Ynez Valley La Cuesta Vineyard Reserve 1989 • $16 • (11/15/92) • **77**
Cabernet Sauvignon Santa Ynez Valley La Cuesta Vineyard Reserve 1987 • $16 • (05/31/91) • **81**
Merlot Santa Ynez Valley La Cuesta Vineyard 1988 • $16 • (05/31/92) • **68**
Merlot Santa Ynez Valley La Cuesta Vineyard 1986 • $12 • (12/15/89) • **82**

CARMENET | CALIFORNIA

Cabernet Franc Sonoma Valley Moon Mountain Vineyard 1992: Lean and simple, showing modest fruit flavors and dry, tannic, stalky character. 819 cases made. • $20 • (04/30/96) • **82**
Cabernet Sauvignon Sonoma County Moon Mountain Dynamite Cabernet 1992: Smooth and polished cherry, currant and spice flavors pick up light toasted oak on the finish. Has a nice sense of balance and proportion. 11,270 cases made. • $15 • (09/15/95) • **87**
Cabernet Sauvignon Sonoma Valley Dynamite Cabernet 1991: Ripe and spicy with pretty earth and black cherry flavors that are shaded by toasty notes, finishing with a pleasing fruit aftertaste. Tempting now and probably best in the near future while the fruit's bright and lively. Drink now to 1998. 6,662 cases made. • $15 • (11/15/93) • **85**
Chardonnay Carneros Sonoma Valley Sangiacomo Vineyard 1992: Tight and taut, with flinty grapefruit, citrus and spicy pear flavors that pick up an earthy edge. Tasted twice with consistent notes. 8,011 cases made. • $17 • (06/30/94) • **82**
Chardonnay Carneros Sonoma Valley Sangiacomo Vineyard Private Selection 1991 • $17 • (06/30/93) SS • **90**
Chardonnay Sonoma Valley Carneros Sangiacomo Vineyard 1994: Appealing for its fresh, clean, ripe and fruity flavors, with a nice array of pear, apple, honey, spice and vanilla flavors that fold together nicely. 2,185 cases made. • $16 • **89**
Chardonnay Sonoma Valley Carneros Sangiacomo Vineyard 1993: A touch earthy, but has enough ripe pear, citrus, honey and light oak shadings to balance it out. Turns complex on the finish, where the flavors expand and intensify. Serves up a lot of intriguing flavors. 7,106 cases made. • $16 • (06/30/96) SS • **91**
Meritage Edna Valley 1991 • $12 • (07/15/93) • **82**
Meritage Sonoma Valley Moon Mountain Estate Vineyard 1990: Firm and chunky, with a solid core of black currant and tar aromas and flavors, showing some gritty tannins on the finish. Best to drink in 1998. 11,058 cases made. • $25 • (11/15/93) • **85**
Meritage Sonoma Valley Moon Mountain Estate Vineyard 1989 • $18 • (11/15/92) • **86**
Meritage Vin de Garde Sonoma Valley Moon Mountain Estate Vineyard Reserve 1989 • $35 • (11/15/93) • **83**
Meritage White Paragon Vineyard Edna Valley 1993: Lean, crisp, spicy white sporting a toasted onion edge and some melon flavor that livens the finish. 5,898 cases made. • $12 • (08/31/95) • **83**
Merlot Washington Carmen B 1990 • $10 • (11/30/92) • **86**
Paragon Vineyard Edna Valley 1992: Goes beyond herbal into vegetal flavors but the fig and tobacco character wins out in the end, making for a balanced and appealing, full flavored wine. 4,082 cases made. • $12 • (08/31/94) • **85**
Red Sonoma Valley 1988 • $21 • (11/15/91) • **87**
Red Sonoma Valley 1987 • $20 • (11/15/90) • **89**
Red Sonoma Valley 1986 • $20 • (07/31/89) • **91**
Red Sonoma Valley 1985 • $35 • (03/01/89) • **91**
Red Sonoma Valley 1984 • $27 • (03/01/89) • **92**
Red Sonoma Valley 1983 • $24 • (03/01/89) • **85**
Red Sonoma Valley 1982 • $29 • (03/01/89) • **87**

CARNEROS, DOMAINE | CALIFORNIA

Blanc de Blancs Carneros 1989: Ripe and intense, with a core of earthy pineapple and black cherry flavors that linger on the finish. Packs in lots of concentrated flavors. Ready now through 1999. 1,200 cases made. • $25 • (12/15/94) • **88**
Brut Blanc de Blancs Carneros 1988 • $24 • (12/31/93) • **88**
Brut Carneros 1991: Showing some mature earth, toast, pear and spice notes, it turns complex and smooth on the finish, where the flavors fold together nicely. • $20 • (12/31/95) • **89**
Brut Carneros NV • $17 • (12/31/93) • **80**
Brut Carneros Blanc de Blancs 1989: Complex, creamy texture and pretty, tart apple and spice notes fan out on the palate and add a pleasantly earthy finish. • $25 • (05/15/96) • **90**
Brut Carneros Taittinger NV: A touch coarse and earthy, but enough rich pear, honey and toasty notes pour through to keep it interesting. Ready now. 35,000 cases made. • $18 • (12/31/94) • **87**
Pinot Noir Carneros 1994: Young and tight, sporting an appealing band of plum and cherry flavors and a hint of spice. Fans out and turns complex on the finish. 2,300 cases made. • $20 • (02/29/96) • **87**
Pinot Noir Carneros 1993: Smooth and elegant, with a supple, polished texture, letting the elegant black cherry, vanilla and plum flavors flow through, finishing with a silky edge and creamy aftertaste. Impressive debut for this sparking wine producer. 760 cases made. • $20 • **90**
Pinot Noir Carneros The Famous Gate 1993: Medium bodied, with an earthy, spicy edge to the ripe plum and black cherry fruit. Turns austere and tannic with a slight edge on the finish. Not quite the finesse of the regular Carneros bottling. 400 cases made. • $30 • (12/31/95) • **87**

CARNEROS CREEK | CALIFORNIA

Cabernet Sauvignon Los Carneros 1985 • $15 • (10/31/89) • **90**
Cabernet Sauvignon Napa Valley 1983 • $11 • (08/31/87) • **62**
Cabernet Sauvignon Napa Valley 1982 • $11 • (02/16/86) • **71**
Cabernet Sauvignon Napa Valley 1981 • $12 • (12/16/84) • **77**
Cabernet Sauvignon Napa Valley Fay Vineyard 1982 • $14 • (05/15/87) • **70**
Cabernet Sauvignon Napa Valley Reserve 1983 • $14 • (10/15/88) • **83**
Chardonnay California Fleur de Carneros 1993: Clean and fruity, with ripe pear, honey and apple notes that develop depth and complexity on the finish. It offers much for this price. 5,000 cases made. • $9 • (09/30/95) BB • **87**
Chardonnay Los Carneros 1992: Lean and austere, seems to be holding back its fruit, so all it shows now is smoke and spice. Try now. 6,000 cases made. • $14 • (06/30/94) • **84**
Chardonnay Los Carneros 1991 • $13 • (02/15/93) • **84**
Merlot Napa Valley 1985 • $13 • (02/15/88) • **84**
Merlot Napa Valley 1984 • $11 • (08/31/87) • **87**
Merlot Napa Valley 1982 • $9 • (02/16/86) • **80**
Merlot Napa Valley Truchard Vineyard 1983 • $10 • (10/01/85) • **84**
Pinot Noir Carneros 1994: Medium-bodied, with a meaty, herbal edge to the cherry and berry falvors. Gains complexity and finesse on the finish and has the tannic strength to cellar into 1997. 6,000 cases made. • $16 • (02/29/96) • **87**
Pinot Noir Carneros Fleur de Carneros 1994: Tight and tannic, yet styled for early drinking. The wild berry and cherry flavors come through, and it's a bargain for California Pinot. 16,000 cases made. • $10 • (11/30/95) BB • **85**
Pinot Noir Carneros Fleur de Carneros 1993: The light and simple cherry, herb and strawberry flavors are a bit cloying. Drinkable now. 11,000 cases made. • $9 • (01/31/95) • **82**
Pinot Noir Carneros Fleur de Carneros 1992 • $9 • (02/28/94) • **79**
Pinot Noir Carneros Fleur de Carneros 1991 • $9 • (02/28/94) • **83**

Key: SS—Spectator Selection. CS—Cellar Selection. BB—Best Buy. $NA—Price not available. (BT)—Barrel tasting. Ⓐ—Auction Price.
Dates in parentheses represent the issues in which the ratings were published.

Pinot Noir Carneros Fleur de Carneros 1990 • $9 • (02/28/93) • **80**
Pinot Noir Carneros Fleur de Carneros 1989 • $9 • (04/30/91) • **82**
Pinot Noir Carneros Fleur de Carneros 1988 • $10 • (02/15/90) • **85**
Pinot Noir Carneros Fleur de Carneros 1987 • $9 • (02/28/89) SS • **92**
Pinot Noir Carneros Las Lomas 1994: Ripe and intense, with a crisp band of cherry and spice-laced Pinot Noir fruit. Well crafted but in need of short-term cellaring, as it is still tannic and rough hewn. Best in 1997. 300 cases made. • $18 • (02/29/96) • **86**
Pinot Noir Carneros Signature Reserve 1993: Firmly tannic and a bit dry, but the cherry and plum flavors are ripe and showing more depth and richness than most from this vintage. 600 cases made. • $28 • (11/15/95) • **88**
Pinot Noir Carneros Signature Reserve 1991 • $28 • (02/28/93) • **81**
Pinot Noir Carneros Signature Reserve 1989 • $28 • (09/30/92) • **80**
Pinot Noir Carneros Signature Reserve 1988 • $28 • (10/31/90) • **89**
Pinot Noir Carneros Signature Reserve First Release 1987 • $28 • (10/31/90) • **87**
Pinot Noir Los Carneros 1993: Appealing for its cherry and cola notes and smooth texture. Finishes with fruity aftertaste and shows a measure of delicacy and finesse. 4,000 cases made. • $13 • (09/15/95) • **88**
Pinot Noir Los Carneros 1992: Intense and spicy, with a distinct peppery feel to the black cherry flavor. Finishes with firm tannins. 6,000 cases made. • $15 • (03/31/95) • **86**
Pinot Noir Los Carneros 1991 • $15 • (01/31/94) • **88**
Pinot Noir Los Carneros 1990 • $15 • (02/28/93) • **86**
Pinot Noir Los Carneros 1989 • $15 • (03/31/92) • **85**
Pinot Noir Los Carneros 1988 • $16 • (10/31/90) • **83**
Pinot Noir Los Carneros 1987 • $15 • (02/15/90) • **85**
Pinot Noir Los Carneros 1986 • $15 • (12/31/88) • **92**
Pinot Noir Los Carneros 1985 • $13 • (04/15/88) • **88**
Pinot Noir Los Carneros 1984 • $15 • (03/15/87) • **92**
Pinot Noir Los Carneros 1983 • $13 • (08/31/86) • **92**

CARNEROS QUALITY ALLIANCE | CALIFORNIA

Pinot Noir Carneros 1986 • $23 • (07/31/89) • **81**
Pinot Noir Carneros 1985 • $25 • (12/31/87) • **90**

CARPE DIEM | CALIFORNIA

Chardonnay San Luis Obispo County 1994: Offers an attractive core of pear, peach and spice notes, picking up a trace of honey and light oak on the finish. Well focused. New from Deutz. 1,000 cases made. • $19 • (02/29/96) • **87**
Pinot Blanc San Luis Obispo 1994: Tight, but revealing a band of pear, peach and citrus flavors that expand on the finish as the oak folds in neatly. 100 cases made. • $19 • (01/31/96) • **88**

CARRIE, MAURICE | CALIFORNIA

Chardonnay Temecula 1991 • $7 • (06/30/94) • **77**
Chardonnay Temecula Private Reserve 1991 • $10 • (06/30/94) • **77**
Pinot Noir Santa Barbara County 1990 • $8 • (02/28/93) • **67**

CARTLIDGE & BROWNE | CALIFORNIA

Chardonnay California 1993: Light and simple, offering a modest core of spicy fruit flavors. • $6 • (04/30/95) • **78**

CASA LARGA | NEW YORK

Blanc de Blancs Finger Lakes NV • $13 • (12/31/90) • **78**
Brut Blanc de Blancs Finger Lakes NV • $11 • (12/31/90) • **77**

CASA SENA, LA | CALIFORNIA

Chardonnay Monterey 1992: Light and simple with toasty pear notes and a hint of spice on the finish. Ready now. 388 cases made. • $20 • (12/31/93) • **81**
Chardonnay Monterey La Reina Vineyard 1991 • $19 • (03/31/93) • **83**
Chardonnay Santa Clara Valley 1994: Mature and a bit herbal in flavor, hitting some pineapple and pine notes as it reaches the finish. Best in 1997. 1,194 cases made. • $12 • (04/30/96) • **81**

CASK ONE | CALIFORNIA

Sauvignon Blanc Mendocino County 1994: Crisp and lively. Sharply focused pear, green apple and herbal flavors are balanced and refreshing. 3,000 cases made. • $6 • **88**

CASTALIA | CALIFORNIA

Pinot Noir Russian River Valley Rochioli Vineyard 1993: A touch earthy, but the plum and cherry flavors work their way through and lead into spicy notes. Lacks the finesse of better wines from this vineyard. 150 cases made. • $18 • (03/31/96) • **83**

CASTLE | CALIFORNIA

Merlot Sonoma Valley 1993: Strong mint aromas and flavors charge through the spicy berry flavors in this medium-weight, well-oaked wine. 60 cases made. • $17 • (06/30/96) • **82**
Pinot Noir Carneros 1994: Simple, with a modest core of spicy cherry and wild berry. It's just missing the extra richness and fruitiness that distinguish the best. 325 cases made. • $16 • (01/31/96) • **84**
Zinfandel Sonoma Valley 1993: Has pleasant but modest cherry and wild berry flavors. 90 cases made. • $15 • (10/15/95) • **83**

CASTLE ROCK | CALIFORNIA

Chardonnay Napa Valley Barrel Fermented 1993: Subtle with polished pear and apple flavors, finsihing with a spicy nutmeg edge. 578 cases made. • $10 • (07/31/95) • **84**
Merlot Napa Valley 1993: Flavorful, though a touch funky, earthy currant flavors turn mulchy on the finish. 1,150 cases made. • $13 • **82**

CASTLEVIEW | CALIFORNIA

Cabernet Sauvignon Napa Valley Private Reserve 1993: Marked by herb and oaky flavors and modest plum and cherry notes, but the cedary oak flavors stand out. 4,600 cases made. • $9 • (12/15/95) • **84**
Chardonnay Carneros Private Reserve 1993: Lean, simple and hinting at tasty flavors on the fruity finish. Ready now. 6,000 cases made. • $10 • (10/15/95) • **82**
Chardonnay Russian River Valley Private Reserve 1993: Woody, slightly bitter flavors in this unsubtle white. 6,800 cases made. • $10 • (12/15/95) • **76**
Chardonnay Sonoma County Private Reserve 1993: Light, floral and appealing, charming for its simple melon and spice flavors. 4,700 cases made. • $9 • (10/15/95) • **83**
Merlot Napa Valley Private Reserve 1993: Cherry and currant notes highlight the predominatly earthy, musty flavors. 4,100 cases made. • $12 • **74**

CASTORO | CALIFORNIA

Cabernet Sauvignon Paso Robles 1989 • $9 • (07/31/92) • **84**
Cabernet Sauvignon Paso Robles Hope Farms 1986 • $8 • (12/15/89) • **80**
Cabernet Sauvignon Paso Robles Reserve 1991: Lean and compact, with hints of spice, currant and berry peeking through. Firm tannins on the finish, best after 1996. 213 cases made. • $12 • (11/15/94) • **82**
Cabernet Sauvignon Paso Robles Reserve 1990: Firm, intense and tannic, but on the finish a core of currant and berry flavor comes through before the tannins clamp down. Drinkable now. 481 cases made. • $12 • (11/15/93) • **82**
Cabernet Sauvignon Paso Robles The Wine 1991: Trim and compact, with a narrow band of earthy plum and cherry flavors. Ready now. 1,500 cases made. • $10 • (11/15/94) • **83**
Chardonnay Paso Robles Reserve 1993: Lacks focus, with earthy pear and spice notes of modest proportions. 202 cases made. • $12 • (07/31/95) • **78**

Chardonnay San Luis Obispo County 1993: Light and simple, with a citrus edge to the pear and spice notes. 1,650 cases made. • $10 • (07/31/95) • **82**

Chardonnay San Luis Obispo County 1992: Light, refreshing and charming, with appealing vanilla-scented pear and floral aromas and flavors. Remains lively and fresh on the finish. Drinkable now. 2,600 cases made. • $10 • (07/15/93) • **84**

Chardonnay San Luis Obispo County 1991 • $9 • (06/30/93) • **84**

Chardonnay San Luis Obispo County The Wine 1992: A thin, tart, sour edge to the pear and citrus notes. 2,600 cases made. • $10 • (02/28/95) • **78**

Dieci Anni Paso Robles 1991: A solid but high-priced Cabernet blend that features 14 percent Zinfandel and 44 percent Cabernet Franc. Spicy with moderate fruit intensity, it's drinkable now. 229 cases made. • $16 • (11/15/93) • **79**

Pinot Noir Central Coast 1987 • $4 • (12/15/89) BB • **82**

Pinot Noir Santa Barbara County 1991 • $11 • (02/28/94) • **77**

Pinot Noir Santa Barbara County 1990 • $11 • (02/28/93) • **73**

Zinfandel Paso Robles 1992: Mature, earthy and cedary, but it holds together, turning fruitier on the finish where the cherry and berry notes fill it out. 1,388 cases made. • $10 • (10/15/95) • **84**

Zinfandel Paso Robles 1990 • $8 • (10/15/92) • **82**

Zinfandel Paso Robles 1987 • $7 • (12/15/89) • **90**

Zinfandel Paso Robles The Wine 1991: Crisp and intense, with earthy spice, tar and wild berry flavors, finishing with firm tannins. Drinks well now. 1,688 cases made. • $9 • (10/15/94) • **84**

CATERINA | WASHINGTON

Cabernet Sauvignon Columbia Valley 1993: Gently perfumy at first, exploding on the palate in spicy raspberry and blackberry flavors. Tempting now, but give until 1997 to tone its exuberance. 647 cases made. • $13 • (09/30/95) • **89**

Cabernet Sauvignon Columbia Valley 1992: Crisp, almost citrusy, with a bright beam of black currant and berry fruit shining through the chewy tannins. Best after 1997. 250 cases made. • $13 • (04/15/95) • **85**

Chardonnay Columbia Valley 1994: Smooth and gentle in texture, featuring lively, juicy citrus and pear flavors that linger on the finish. 1,411 cases made. • $10 • (09/30/95) • **87**

Chardonnay Columbia Valley 1993: A fruity and vibrant Washington white. Delicious from the first sip to the last echo of peach, apple and grapefruit flavors. 1,445 cases made. • $10 • (02/28/95) SS • **89**

Chardonnay Columbia Valley 1992: A spicy and fruity young wine that's appealing if a bit simple and one-dimensional. Has a Muscat edge that stays with it from start to finish. Ready now. 900 cases made. • $11 • (04/15/94) • **81**

Chardonnay Columbia Valley Reserve 1993: Straightforward and flavorful, showing fresh pineapple and spice notes and expanding on the toasty vanilla finish. Drink now. 200 cases made. • $14 • (04/15/95) • **85**

Johannisberg Riesling Late Harvest Columbia Valley 1994: Sweet and concentrated, adding an off-note to ripe peach and apricot flavors, lacks any honey richness. Ready now. 114 cases made. • $10 • (09/30/95) • **76**

Merlot Columbia Valley 1993: Spicy and lean, tasting strongly of oak, finishing on the sour side. Seems out of balance. May be better in 1998. 970 cases made. • $13 • (09/30/95) • **78**

Merlot Columbia Valley 1992: Smooth and supple, the ripe blackberry and dried cherry flavors gliding nicely through the finish. Drinkable now. 630 cases made. • $13 • (02/28/95) • **86**

Merlot Columbia Valley 1991: Lean and woody, with tannic currant and plum flavors coming through on the finish, where the oak turns dry and buttery. 400 cases made. • $13 • (09/30/94) • **81**

Sauvignon Blanc Columbia Valley 1994: Bright and spicy, a lively wine with nice sparks of citrus, green apple and peach, plus an herbal zing on the finish. 713 cases made. • $7 • (05/31/96) • **87**

Sauvignon Blanc Columbia Valley 1993: Soft and toasty, a little tired and watery at the edges. Drinkable. 670 cases made. • $8 • (02/28/95) • **77**

CATOCTIN | MARYLAND

Cabernet Sauvignon Maryland 1985 • $8 • (02/29/92) BB • **82**

CAVATAPPI | WASHINGTON

Nebbiolo Washington Maddalena Red Willow Vineyards 1988 • $19 • (06/15/91) • **83**

CAYMUS | CALIFORNIA

Cabernet Sauvignon Napa Valley 1992: Supple and harmonious black cherry, currant, plum and herb flavors pick up an olive and spice edge on aftertaste, where the tannins are polished. Appealing now through 1999. 25,000 cases made. • $25 • (09/30/95) • **89**

Cabernet Sauvignon Napa Valley 1991: Deep, rich and plush, with a ripe core of seductive currant and black cherry flavors framed by toasty, buttery oak. It all adds up to one delicious mouthful of Cabernet. Finishes with a long, complex aftertaste. Tempting to drink now, but will improve at least through 1998. 22,000 cases made. • $20 • (11/15/94) SS • **93**

Cabernet Sauvignon Napa Valley 1990: Firm and focused, with spicy tobacco and chocolate overtones on the ripe prune and currant aromas and flavors. Tannins may need until 1997, but it is drinkable now with hearty food. • $115 Ⓐ • (12/15/93) SS • **90**

Cabernet Sauvignon Napa Valley 1989 • $20 • (11/15/92) • **88**

Cabernet Sauvignon Napa Valley 1988 • $20 • (01/31/92) • **87**

Cabernet Sauvignon Napa Valley 1987 • $96 Ⓐ • (09/15/90) • **93**

Cabernet Sauvignon Napa Valley 1986 • $106 Ⓐ • (03/15/90) SS • **94**

Cabernet Sauvignon Napa Valley 1985 • $24 Ⓐ • (03/01/89) • **92**

Cabernet Sauvignon Napa Valley 1984 • $187 Ⓐ • (03/01/89) • **91**

Cabernet Sauvignon Napa Valley 1983 • $72 Ⓐ • (03/01/89) • **87**

Cabernet Sauvignon Napa Valley 1982 • $112 Ⓐ • (03/01/89) • **90**

Cabernet Sauvignon Napa Valley 1981 • $50 • (03/01/89) • **88**

Cabernet Sauvignon Napa Valley 1980 • $54 • (03/01/89) • **90**

Cabernet Sauvignon Napa Valley 1979 • $68 • (03/01/89) • **92**

Cabernet Sauvignon Napa Valley 1978 • $64 Ⓐ • (03/01/89) • **87**

Cabernet Sauvignon Napa Valley 1977 • $49 • (03/01/89) • **77**

Cabernet Sauvignon Napa Valley 1976 • $10 • (03/01/89) • **85**

Cabernet Sauvignon Napa Valley 1975 • $80 • (03/01/89) • **89**

Cabernet Sauvignon Napa Valley 1974 • $82 Ⓐ • (02/15/90) • **91**

Cabernet Sauvignon Napa Valley 1973 • $125 • (03/01/89) • **93**

Cabernet Sauvignon Napa Valley 1972 • $110 • (03/01/89) • **86**

Cabernet Sauvignon Napa Valley Cuvée 1986 • $15 • (08/31/89) • **90**

Cabernet Sauvignon Napa Valley Cuvée 1985 • $12 • (07/15/88) • **92**

Cabernet Sauvignon Napa Valley Cuvée 1984 • $12 • (08/31/87) • **88**

Cabernet Sauvignon Napa Valley Special Selection 1992: Serves up elegant ripe cherry, currant, cola and spice flavors and frames them in toasty oak to round it all out nicely. Finishes smooth, but its still somewhat chunky overall. Hold off until 1997, but it should last a decade beyond that. 2,000 cases made. • $100 • (05/15/96) CS • **92**

Cabernet Sauvignon Napa Valley Special Selection 1991: Another great wine from arguably California's best Cabernet maker. Bold, rich and massive, with tiers of plum, blackberry, vanilla bean, spice and tobacco flavors that unfold to reveal a wine of uncommon depth, complexity, finesse and, yes, even grace. Drinkable between 1998 and 2008. 2,000 cases made. • $100 • (04/15/95) CS • **99**

Cabernet Sauvignon Napa Valley Special Selection 1990: Beautifully proportioned, smooth, plush, rich and concentrated, featuring tiers of complex cherry, plum, currant and spice flavors, with sweet tannins and pretty, toasty, buttery oak and vanilla notes that linger on a long, full finish. Best between 1996 and 2004. 1,000 cases made. • $192 Ⓐ • (03/31/94) CS • **98**

Cabernet Sauvignon Napa Valley Special Selection 1989 • $60 • (06/30/93) CS • **93**

Cabernet Sauvignon Napa Valley Special Selection 1988 • $60 • (09/30/92) CS • **94**

Cabernet Sauvignon Napa Valley Special Selection 1987 • $115 • (10/31/91) CS • **98**

Key: SS—Spectator Selection. CS—Cellar Selection. BB—Best Buy. $NA—Price not available. (BT)—Barrel tasting. Ⓐ—Auction Price.
Dates in parentheses represent the issues in which the ratings were published.

Cabernet Sauvignon Napa Valley Special Selection 1986 • $182 Ⓐ • (01/31/91) CS • **98**
Cabernet Sauvignon Napa Valley Special Selection 1985 • $240 • (04/30/90) • **99**
Cabernet Sauvignon Napa Valley Special Selection 1984 • $211 Ⓐ • (07/15/89) CS • **98**
Cabernet Sauvignon Napa Valley Special Selection 1983 • $110 • (03/01/89) • **91**
Cabernet Sauvignon Napa Valley Special Selection 1982 • $160 • (03/01/89) • **92**
Cabernet Sauvignon Napa Valley Special Selection 1981 • $120 • (03/01/89) • **93**
Cabernet Sauvignon Napa Valley Special Selection 1980 • $96 Ⓐ • (03/01/89) • **92**
Cabernet Sauvignon Napa Valley Special Selection 1979 • $210 • (03/01/89) • **97**
Cabernet Sauvignon Napa Valley Special Selection 1978 • $40 • (03/01/89) • **97**
Cabernet Sauvignon Napa Valley Special Selection 1976 • $345 Ⓐ • (03/01/89) • **90**
Cabernet Sauvignon Napa Valley Special Selection 1975 • $420 • (03/01/89) • **92**
Conundrum California 1994: Distinctive for its ripe, complex array of flavors, focusing on pear, spice, fig and vanilla. Picks up undertones of citrus on the elegant finish. This has always been, and remains, a one-of-a-kind white wine from this innovative winery. 8,000 cases made. • $17 • (10/15/95) SS • **91**
Conundrum California 1992 • $16 • (04/15/94) • **88**
Conundrum California 1991 • $18 • (04/15/93) SS • **92**
Pinot Noir Napa Valley 1981 • $7 • (05/01/84) BB • **85**
Pinot Noir Napa Valley 1980 • $6 • (03/16/84) • **81**
Pinot Noir Napa Valley Special Selection 1990 • $18 • (02/28/94) • **84**
Pinot Noir Napa Valley Special Selection 1989 • $18 • (09/30/92) • **78**
Pinot Noir Napa Valley Special Selection 1988 • $18 • (11/15/91) • **82**
Pinot Noir Napa Valley Special Selection 1987 • $14 • (12/15/90) • **86**
Pinot Noir Napa Valley Special Selection 1986 • $15 • (12/31/89) • **82**
Pinot Noir Napa Valley Special Selection 1985 • $15 • (12/31/88) • **90**
Pinot Noir Napa Valley Special Selection 1984 • $13 • (02/15/88) • **79**
Pinot Noir Napa Valley Special Selection 1982 • $13 • (08/31/86) • **85**
Sauvignon Blanc Napa Valley Barrel Fermented 1993: Marked by herb and vegetal notes, it's smooth and supple, adding a spicy aftertaste. 13,000 cases made. • $13 • (04/30/95) • **85**
Sauvignon Blanc Napa Valley Barrel Fermented 1992 • $10 • (04/15/94) SS • **91**
Sauvignon Blanc Napa Valley Barrel Fermented 1991 • $10 • (07/15/93) • **85**
Zinfandel California 1976 • $33 • (06/16/85) • **79**
Zinfandel California 1974 • $29 • (06/16/85) • **83**
Zinfandel California Lot 31-J 1975 • $40 • (06/16/85) • **77**
Zinfandel Napa Valley 1992: The best Caymus Zin of recent vintages. Combines ripe, spicy, intense berry and cherry flavors with firm tannins and an overlay of vanilla. Drinks well now, but concentrated enough to cellar through 1997. 4,000 cases made. • $13 • (09/30/94) SS • **89**
Zinfandel Napa Valley 1991 • $11 • (09/30/93) • **85**
Zinfandel Napa Valley 1990 • $10 • (10/15/92) • **82**
Zinfandel Napa Valley 1989 • $10 • (11/15/91) • **83**
Zinfandel Napa Valley 1988 • $9 • (10/15/90) • **80**
Zinfandel Napa Valley 1987 • $13 • (10/31/89) • **85**
Zinfandel Napa Valley 1986 • $15 • (12/15/88) • **89**
Zinfandel Napa Valley 1985 • $15 • (12/31/87) • **85**
Zinfandel Napa Valley 1984 • $15 • (05/15/87) • **90**
Zinfandel Napa Valley 1983 • $15 • (12/31/86) • **79**
Zinfandel Napa Valley 1982 • $15 • (05/16/86) • **92**
Zinfandel Napa Valley 1981 • $15 • (12/01/84) • **84**

CECCHETTI SEBASTIANI | CALIFORNIA

Cabernet Sauvignon Alexander Valley 1989 • $9 • (11/15/92) • **74**
Cabernet Sauvignon Alexander Valley 1988 • $11 • (08/31/92) • **83**
Cabernet Sauvignon Alexander Valley 1986 • $8 • (04/15/89) • **83**
Cabernet Sauvignon Sonoma County 1983 • $13 • (09/30/86) • **76**
Chardonnay Napa Valley 1991 • $10 • (07/15/93) • **83**
Merlot Sonoma County 1990 • $10 • (06/15/93) • **78**
Merlot Sonoma County 1989 • $10 • (05/31/92) • **83**

CEDAR BROOK | CALIFORNIA

Cabernet Sauvignon Napa Valley 1993: Smooth and inviting, a lighter style that unfolds some appealing currant and anise flavors. Drinkable now. 8,500 cases made. • $7 • (12/15/95) • **84**
Cabernet Sauvignon Napa Valley 1992: Firmly oaked and tannic, compact, youthful and tightly wound, offering hints of cherry and currant before the tannins clamp down. Best after 1997. 10,000 cases made. • $8 • (11/15/94) • **84**
Pinot Noir California 1993: Light in texture, but it has a Port-like, smoky, ripe edge to the flavors, making it intriguing through the spicy finish. Drinkable now. 5,000 cases made. • $7 • (11/15/95) BB • **85**

CEDAR CREEK | WISCONSIN

American 1990 • $6 • (02/29/92) • **78**

CEDAR MOUNTAIN | CALIFORNIA

Cabernet Sauvignon Livermore Valley Blanches Vineyard 1990: Very ripe and spicy, it smells richer than it tastes, finishing a bit raisiny and simple. Drink now. 20 cases made. • $20 • (11/15/93) • **83**
Chardonnay Livermore Valley Blanches Vineyard 1993: Spicy and mature already, showing more raisin and toasty overtones than fresh fruit flavors. Ready now. 520 cases made. • $15 • (11/15/95) • **80**
Chardonnay Livermore Valley Blanches Vineyard 1991 • $15 • (07/15/93) • **79**

CHADDSFORD | PENNSYLVANIA

Chambourcin Pennsylvania Proprietor's Reserve 1989 • $10 • (02/29/92) • **80**
Chambourcin Pennsylvania Seven Valleys Vineyard 1989 • $13 • (02/29/92) • **81**
Chardonnay Pennsylvania Philip Roth Vineyard 1991: Big, bold and dramatic in aroma, it smells intensely rich and toasty, has a thick texture and assertive fruit flavors. It finishes a bit rough, but it's distinctive. 126 cases made. • $26 • (02/28/95) • **87**
Chardonnay Pennsylvania Stargazers Vineyard 1991: Dramatic and beautifully mature in aroma, lighter in flavor, but satisfying and complex. It has toast, vanilla, pear and hazelnut accents. 639 cases made. • $24 • (02/28/95) • **88**
Pinot Noir Lake Erie 1988 • $28 • (02/28/93) • **78**
Pinot Noir Pennsylvania Lake Erie Region 1988 • $28 • (02/29/92) • **82**
Proprietor's Reserve Pennsylvania 1990 • $9 • (02/29/92) • **78**
Spring Wine Pennsylvania 1994: A rich, off-dry white with apple and honey flavors and good acidity. Clean and refreshing. 2,170 cases made. • $8 • (10/31/95) • **82**

CHALK HILL | CALIFORNIA

Cabernet Sauvignon Chalk Hill 1991: Leans on earthy, leathery flavors but also delivers a complex core of currant, herb and cedar notes. Will always be on the tannic side and can stand a few years' cellaring. Best after 1998. • $21 • (11/15/94) • **85**
Cabernet Sauvignon Chalk Hill 1990: Cedary, gamy aromas and flavors turn tough on the finish, but the core of coffee- and spice-scented black cherry and berry flavors bodes well. Tasted three times. 8,000 cases made. • $17 • (12/15/93) • **86**
Cabernet Sauvignon Chalk Hill 1989 • $13 • (07/15/92) • **75**
Cabernet Sauvignon Chalk Hill 1988 • $12 • (06/15/91) • **87**
Cabernet Sauvignon Chalk Hill 1983 • $10 • (11/15/86) • **78**
Cabernet Sauvignon Chalk Hill 1982 • $9 • (11/01/85) • **66**
Cabernet Sauvignon Chalk Hill 1981 • $8 • (04/01/84) • **83**
Chardonnay Chalk Hill 1994: Rich, intense and full-bodied, the ripe pear, spice, fig and honey flavors framed nicely by toasty oak. An altogether complex and concentrated California white that's brimming

with flavor and the finish goes on and on. Drinkable now, but still young. 44,500 cases made. • $20 • (06/15/96) SS • **93**

Chardonnay Chalk Hill 1993: A bold, ripe and spicy California Chardonnay, with an intriguing earthy edge to the rich, creamy fig and apple flavors. There are notes of vanilla and toast, followed by a complex aftertaste. Drinkable now, but should develop through 1997. 15,938 cases made. • $19 • (05/15/95) SS • **91**

Chardonnay Chalk Hill 1992: A blunt and coarse young Chardonnay that's intense and concentrated, with ripe pear and oak flavors that are not yet in sync. Drinkable now. 34,777 cases made. • $18 • (05/15/94) • **84**

Chardonnay Chalk Hill 1991 • $10 • (03/15/93) • **83**

Sauvignon Blanc Chalk Hill 1994: Has a welcome subtlety and depth that's missing from many Sauvignon Blancs. Offers plush pear, tobacco and spice flavors and delicate touches of citrus and parsley on the finish. 12,950 cases made. • $14 • **90**

Sauvignon Blanc Chalk Hill 1993: Ripe, round and generous. Beautifully proportioned to show off the spicy, lemony pear and honey flavors that linger enticingly on the finish. 16,411 cases made. • $16 • (08/31/95) • **88**

Sauvignon Blanc Chalk Hill 1992 • $16 • (11/30/93) • **87**

Sauvignon Blanc Chalk Hill 1991 • $10 • (07/31/93) • **83**

Sémillon Late Harvest Chalk Hill 1986 • $10 • (06/15/92) • **91**

CHALONE | CALIFORNIA

Chardonnay Chalone 1994: Strikes a nice balance between its ripe fig, honey, pear, mineral and melon flavors, then expands to show its complexity on the finish. Intense flavors and good length in this. Drinkable now, but will improve through 1999. 13,000 cases made. • $27 • (06/15/96) CS • **91**

Chardonnay Chalone 1993: Smooth and polished, with spicy pear, fig and light toasty oak shadings, more complete than most 1993s. 10,149 cases made. • $27 • (07/31/95) • **87**

Chardonnay Chalone 1992: Tight, firm and focused, with a pretty beam of pear, spice, honey and buttery notes that pick up an oaky edge on a long full finish. Complex and concentrated, it is an excellent Chalone that should've aged very well over the past five years. Better than in previous tasting. 10,791 cases made. • $26 • (06/15/94) • **91**

Chardonnay Chalone 1991 • $25 • (12/31/92) SS • **91**

Chardonnay Chalone Gavilan 1994: Bold, rich and complex, with honeyed pear and spicy melon flavors. This is concentrated, yet manages to maintain its elegance and finesse. 6,500 cases made. • $16 • (06/15/96) • **88**

Chardonnay Chalone Gavilan 1993: Serves up a modest core of ripe pear, apple and vanilla notes that are well balanced for what's there. 4,405 cases made. • $14 • (07/31/95) • **84**

Chardonnay Chalone Gavilan 1992: Crisp and fruity, with pear and spice notes. Finishes clean and simple, but missing some dimensions. Drinkable now. 11,300 cases made. • $13 • (02/28/94) • **86**

Chardonnay Chalone Gavilan 1991 • $13 • (03/31/93) • **84**

Chardonnay Chalone Reserve 1994: Combines ripe, intense fruit with a sense of elegance and finesse. The ripe pear, honey and butterscotch flavors play into the aftertaste that expands on the theme. 1,400 cases made. • $45 • (05/31/96) • **90**

Chardonnay Chalone Reserve 1992: Ripe, smooth and creamy, with a pretty array of earthy pear, spice, honey and butterscotch flavors, picking up vanilla and toasty notes on a long, full finish. Uncommon finesse and complexity for California Chardonnay. Ready now through 1998. Tasted twice with consistent results. Sold only to stockholders. 1,405 cases made. • $35 • (06/30/94) • **93**

Chardonnay Chalone Reserve 1991: Bright and lively pear, spice, citrus and pineapple flavors are ripe, rich and focused, with light buttery oak shadings finishing with a silky texture. Ready now through 1997. Sold only to Chalone stockholders. 784 cases made. • $35 • (06/30/94) • **91**

Chenin Blanc Chalone 1992: Round and spicy, definitely touched by oak, a polished, smooth-textured wine that wears its toasty oak flavors lightly over a core of apple and melon. Very Chardonnay-like. Drinkable now through 1997. 1,099 cases made. • $15 • (07/31/94) • **86**

Key: SS—Spectator Selection. CS—Cellar Selection. BB—Best Buy. $NA—Price not available. (BT)—Barrel tasting. (A)—Auction Price.
Dates in parentheses represent the issues in which the ratings were published.

Pinot Blanc Chalone 1993: Ripe, round and generous, with a spicy tang to the pear and apple flavors that last on the finish. 4,963 cases made. • $18 • (05/31/96) • **88**

Pinot Blanc Chalone 1992 • $20 • (03/31/94) • **86**

Pinot Blanc Chalone 1991 • $18 • (01/31/93) CS • **92**

Pinot Blanc Chalone Gavilan 1992: Broad and spicy, a round wine with unfocused fruit and earthy flavors. Ready now. 3,165 cases made. • $13 • (04/15/95) • **81**

Pinot Noir Chalone 1991: Smooth, supple and well focused, with a pleasant core of spicy, earthy cherry flavor that develops nuances and depth on the finish. 3,000 cases made. • $22 • (06/30/95) • **88**

Pinot Noir Chalone 1990 • $30 • (02/28/94) • **90**

Pinot Noir Chalone 1989 • $30 • (02/28/93) • **77**

Pinot Noir Chalone 1986 • $25 • (12/15/90) • **89**

Pinot Noir Chalone 1985 • $18 • (02/15/90) • **85**

Pinot Noir Chalone 1984 • $19 • (12/15/87) • **88**

Pinot Noir Chalone 1983 • $19 • (08/31/86) • **89**

Pinot Noir Chalone 1982 • $20 • (08/31/86) • **66**

Pinot Noir Chalone 1981 • $19 • (12/16/84) • **83**

Pinot Noir Chalone Gavilan 1992: Light but pleasant, with ripe, spicy cherry, oak and earth notes that persist. But it's not a grand wine and should be consumed soon. 6,830 cases made. • $14 • (10/31/94) • **84**

Pinot Noir Chalone Gavilan 1991 • $13 • (02/28/94) • **78**

Pinot Noir Chalone Gavilan 1990 • $13 • (02/28/93) • **85**

Pinot Noir Chalone Red Table Wine 1983 • $9 • (08/31/86) • **71**

Pinot Noir Chalone Reserve 1990: Lean and firm, displaying tightly wound herb, black cherry, anise and tar flavors and finishing with chewy tannins. Drinkable now. 854 cases made. • $48 • (03/31/95) • **88**

Pinot Noir Chalone Reserve 1989: Firm, showing herb and tobacco flavors. Hints of cherries and spice peek through, but it turns dry and tannic. Drinkable now. 919 cases made. • $32 • (03/31/95) • **84**

Pinot Noir Chalone Reserve 1988: Mature, with an earthy, smoky, leathery edge to the cherry and berry notes, but it's rough going most of the way, drying on the finish. Drinkable now. 521 cases made. • $25 • (03/31/95) • **84**

Pinot Noir Chalone Reserve 1987 • $20 • (02/28/93) • **86**

Pinot Noir Chalone Reserve 1981 • $28 • (08/31/86) • **92**

CHAMISAL | CALIFORNIA

Chardonnay Edna Valley 1991 • $14 • (03/31/93) • **86**

CHANDON, DOMAINE | CALIFORNIA

Blanc de Noirs California Cuvée 390 NV: Smooth and creamy, adding a fleeting snatch of berry notes to enrich the toasty, peppery flavors. Different and appealing. 146,000 cases made. • $14 • (09/15/95) • **86**

Blanc de Noirs Carneros NV: Pale in color, flavorful, delicate, boasting a sense of elegance and finesse, marked by subtle cherry, earth and hazelnut notes and a complex aftertaste. 146,000 cases made. • $14 • (12/15/95) • **89**

Blanc de Noirs Napa Sonoma Counties NV • $12 • (08/31/92) • **82**

Blanc de Noirs Napa Valley NV • $14 • (05/31/89) • **84**

Brut Blanc de Noirs Carneros NV: Smooth and supple, with a pretty core of black cherry, vanilla and spice notes. Turns delicate and fleshy on the finish, where the flavors linger. Ready now. 200,000 cases made. • $12 • (12/31/94) • **87**

Brut Napa County Cuvée NV: Ripe and intense, with a floral, spicy edge to the pear and pineapple flavors. Drinks well now. 200,000 cases made. • $12 • (12/31/94) • **85**

Brut Napa County Cuvée 190 NV: Focused and spicy, a bright beam of cherry-tinged toasty flavors shining through the lively finish. 223,000 cases made. • $14 • (09/15/95) • **87**

Brut Napa County Étoile NV • $23 • (12/31/91) • **85**

Brut Napa Sonoma Counties NV • $15 • (12/31/89) • **80**

Brut Napa Sonoma Counties Chandon Réserve NV • $16 • (12/31/93) • **85**

Brut Napa Sonoma Counties Cuvée NV • $12 • (08/31/92) • **82**

Brut Napa Sonoma Counties Étoile NV • $22 • (12/31/93) • **85**

Brut Napa Sonoma Counties Reserve NV: A mature-tasting bubbly, with earthy, yeasty flavors that pick up pear, black cherry and spice notes on a smooth, full finish. Ready now. 8,000 cases made. • $16 • (12/31/94) • **87**

Brut Napa Valley Club Cuvée NV • $17 • (06/15/91) • **77**

Brut Napa Valley NV • $28 • (05/31/89) • **85**

Brut Napa Valley Étoile NV: Intense and concentrated, adding an earthy, nutty edge to the ripe pear and spice notes. Has a long, full aftertaste and lots of flavor. 5,600 cases made. • $24 • **88**

Brut Napa Valley Réserve NV • $18 • (12/31/92) • **86**

Rosé Napa County Cuvée 291 Club Selection NV: Pale salmon in color, featuring yeast and black cherry aromas and flavors to match. A finishing touch of anise and earthiness adds dimension. 2,900 cases made. • $19 • **87**

Sparkling Napa County Reserve Cuvée 490 NV: A touch earthy with a slight nutty edge, but the ripe pear and spicy flavors work through that and show more richness, depth and concentration on the finish. 6,600 cases made. • $18 • **89**

CHAPPELL FAMILY | CALIFORNIA

Omega Cuvée Sonoma Valley 1990 • $11 • (12/31/93) • **80**

Pinot Noir Carneros Sangiacomo Vineyards 1990 • $14 • (02/28/94) • **80**

Pinot Noir Carneros Sangiacomo Vineyards 1989 • $14 • (02/28/93) • **82**

Zinfandel Sonoma Valley 75-Year-Old Vines Unfiltered 1990 • $12 • (06/15/93) • **84**

CHAPPELLET | CALIFORNIA

Cabernet Sauvignon Napa Valley 1992: Intense, spicy, leathery currant and anise flavors. Finishes with gritty tannins. Aging into 1998 should help, as Chappellet Cabernets often struggle to shake their tannic character. 2,800 cases made. • $20 • (03/31/96) • **83**

Cabernet Sauvignon Napa Valley 1991: Firm and compact, with a tight, earthy band of currant and herb flavor that fans out on the finish. Picks up hints of oak and spice along the way, hold until around 1999. 4,100 cases made. • $20 • (11/15/94) • **89**

Cabernet Sauvignon Napa Valley 1990: A bizarre wine with earthy minty overtones that dominate the cedary currant fruit underneath. Finishes with a good dose of wood and cedar. Drinkable now. 2,100 cases made. • $25 • (11/15/93) • **81**

Cabernet Sauvignon Napa Valley 1983 • $22 • (02/15/93) • **90**

Cabernet Sauvignon Napa Valley 1982 • $21 • (02/15/93) • **74**

Cabernet Sauvignon Napa Valley 1981 • $23 • (02/15/93) • **85**

Cabernet Sauvignon Napa Valley 1980 • $35 • (02/15/93) • **88**

Cabernet Sauvignon Napa Valley 1979 • $30 • (02/15/93) • **89**

Cabernet Sauvignon Napa Valley 1978 • $41 • (02/15/93) • **75**

Cabernet Sauvignon Napa Valley 1977 • $24 • (02/15/93) • **86**

Cabernet Sauvignon Napa Valley 1976 • $31 • (02/15/93) • **91**

Cabernet Sauvignon Napa Valley 1975 • $16 Ⓐ • (02/15/93) • **81**

Cabernet Sauvignon Napa Valley 1974: Dry and bitter, with green earthy flavors. 3,500 cases made. • $50 • (11/15/94) • **68**

Cabernet Sauvignon Napa Valley 1973 • $64 • (02/15/93) • **77**

Cabernet Sauvignon Napa Valley 1972 • $41 • (02/15/93) • **73**

Cabernet Sauvignon Napa Valley 1971 • $40 • (02/15/93) • **78**

Cabernet Sauvignon Napa Valley 1970 • $95 • (02/15/93) • **93**

Cabernet Sauvignon Napa Valley 1969 • $105 • (02/15/93) • **90**

Cabernet Sauvignon Napa Valley 1968 • $90 • (03/01/89) • **88**

Cabernet Sauvignon Napa Valley Pritchard Hill Estates 1992: Firm and substantially tannic, showing a cedary rim to the tightly wound currant, tobacco and earth notes. Will need time to soften. 3,100 cases made. • $15 • (09/15/95) • **86**

Cabernet Sauvignon Napa Valley Reserve 1988 • $14 • (02/15/93) • **85**

Cabernet Sauvignon Napa Valley Reserve 1987 • $27 • (02/15/93) • **92**

Cabernet Sauvignon Napa Valley Reserve 1986 • $20 • (02/15/93) • **89**

Cabernet Sauvignon Napa Valley Reserve 1985 • $25 • (02/15/93) • **93**

Cabernet Sauvignon Napa Valley Reserve 1984 • $24 • (02/15/93) • **90**

Cabernet Sauvignon Napa Valley Signature 1989 • $27 • (03/31/93) • **82**

Chardonnay Napa Valley 1994: Lean and flinty, with a trim band of spicy pear and fig, but it lacks finesse and harmony. Finishes a tad on the bitter side. 4,291 cases made. • $15 • (06/15/96) • **80**

Chardonnay Napa Valley 1993: Medium-bodied, appealing apple, toast and spice flavors hang with you. 4,650 cases made. • $15 • (10/31/95) • **86**

Chardonnay Napa Valley 1992: Ripe and smoky, with spicy pear and light oak shadings. Modest richness and intensity, an understated style. 4,700 cases made. • $14 • (12/31/94) • **85**

Chardonnay Napa Valley Signature 1994: Marked spicy, citrusy accents on its pear and lightly toasty flavors. Its finish is more sublty defined as the flavors trail off. 66 cases made. • $24 • (06/15/96) • **87**

Chenin Blanc Napa Valley Dry 1994: Crisp and flavorful, a dry wine with pretty apple and spice flavors that linger on the finish. 1,900 cases made. • $9 • (06/15/96) • **86**

Chenin Blanc Napa Valley Dry 1993: Dry, light and modestly fruity, with honey and floral accents to the sweet apple flavors. Makes an amiable drink at a friendly price. 2,340 cases made. • $7 • (10/15/95) BB • **86**

Chenin Blanc Napa Valley Dry 1992: Bright and fruity, but dry on the palate. Spicy enough to weave some nice nuances around the delicate apple flavor-an agreeable and friendly wine at this price. It's drinkable now. 5,200 cases made. • $7 • (05/31/95) BB • **85**

Chenin Blanc Napa Valley Dry 1991 • $7 • (11/30/93) BB • **85**

Chenin Blanc Napa Valley Old Vine Cuvée Special Select 1994: Dry and appealing with its soft pear and almond flavors. 3,200 cases made. • $11 • (06/15/96) • **85**

Chenin Blanc Napa Valley Old Vine Cuvée Special Select 1993: Distinctive, ripe and spicy, fashioned like a Chardonnay with prominent nutmeg-oak flavors and soft, honey pear notes. Ready now. 1,940 cases made. • $11 • (10/15/95) • **88**

Dessert Napa Valley Moelleux 1993: Sweet, dried apricot and earthy tobacco flavors. A bit coarse and short on the finish. Drinks well now. 14 cases made. • $40 • **85**

Merlot Napa Valley 1993: Elegant, earthy currant and berry flavors, with a slight mineral edge. Turns leathery and a bit peculiar on the finish. 410 cases made. • $18 • **85**

Merlot Napa Valley 1992: Supple and elegant, with spicy plum and cedary oak flavors that make it appealing to drink now. 575 cases made. • $17 • (06/15/95) • **84**

Merlot Napa Valley 1989 • $16 • (05/31/92) • **68**

Merlot Napa Valley 1988 • $15 • (04/15/92) • **85**

Merlot Napa Valley 1987 • $15 • (12/31/90) • **89**

Merlot Napa Valley 1986 • $15 • (01/31/90) • **80**

Merlot Napa Valley 1985 • $12 • (12/31/88) • **78**

CHARTRONS | CALIFORNIA

Claret California 1986 • $15 • (11/15/91) • **78**

CHASE-LIMOGERE | CALIFORNIA

Brut California NV • $5 • (05/15/92) • **79**

Brut Rosé California NV • $7 • (12/31/89) • **68**

CHATOM | CALIFORNIA

Cabernet Sauvignon Calaveras County 1992: Well oaked, with an odd toasted grain edge, but the fruit is ripe and supple, albeit a bit dry and tannic. 350 cases made. • $12 • (06/15/95) • **84**

Cabernet Sauvignon Calaveras County 1991: Supple and generous showing pretty, toasty vanilla oak flavors and a crisp band of spicy cherry notes. Firm tannins on the finish, drinkable now. 276 cases made. • $12 • (11/15/94) • **83**

Cabernet Sauvignon Calaveras County 1989 • $14 • (11/15/92) • **84**

Chardonnay Calaveras County 1993: Intense and spicy, with a grassy edge to the pear and apple flavors. 250 cases made. • $10 • (07/31/95) • **82**

Chardonnay Calaveras County 1991: Earthy and funky with green oak flavors. Misses the mark. 326 cases made. • $12 • (06/30/94) • **71**

Fumé Blanc Calaveras County 1991: Lean, simple and refreshing, a lighter style of Sauvignon with some floral overtones and a hint of honey on the finish. 721 cases made. • $6 • (08/31/94) • **80**

Merlot Calaveras County 1992: Light with modest varietal character and a strong woody component that turns earthy and rubbery. 600 cases made. • $14 • (07/31/95) • **74**

Merlot Calaveras County 1991: An oaky style with toasty, buttery wood flavors. Fruit purists will find this a bit overdone, but it's smooth and flavorful, with currant and herb notes. Ready now through 1998. 244 cases made. • $14 • (09/15/94) • **85**

Sangiovese Calaveras County 1992: Lean and awfully woody, with a fresh-sawdust character that obliterates the modest fruit. 100 cases made. • $14 • (09/30/94) • **70**

Sauvignon Blanc Calaveras County 1993: Smooth and generous, showing nicely defined pear and floral flavors that just keep coming and coming on the finish. A terrific Sauvignon Blanc that tones down the varietal character but keeps enough to render it outstanding. 850 cases made. • $8 • (05/15/95) • **90**

Sauvignon Blanc Calaveras County Reserve 1994: Light and straightforward, not a big wine, but has modest pear flavors with nice butter and tobacco notes. 564 cases made. • $11 • (05/31/96) • **83**

Sauvignon Blanc Calaveras County Select 1991 • $12 • (05/15/94) • **86**

Sémillon Calaveras County 1993: Bright, focused and layered with appealing fruit aromas and flavors, centering around peach, pear and pineapple. Lasts on the finish, too. 300 cases made. • $8 • (06/30/95) • **87**

Zinfandel Calaveras County 1993: Looks like a rosé and has similar weight, showing modest cherry and spice flavors. 325 cases made. • $9 • (04/30/96) • **77**

Zinfandel Calaveras County 1992: Shows the smoky, buttery flavors of oak, an elegant core of wild berry and cherry fruit adding nice dimensions. 450 cases made. • $8 • (07/31/95) • **84**

Zinfandel Calaveras County 1991: Well mannered, with toasty, buttery, intense wild berry flavors, but it's also quite gritty and tannic on the finish, drinkable now. 225 cases made. • $8 • (10/15/94) • **81**

Zinfandel Calaveras County 1989 • $8 • (09/30/93) • **84**

CHAUFFE-EAU | CALIFORNIA

Cabernet Sauvignon Alexander Valley 1987 • $16 • (08/31/92) • **85**

Chardonnay Carneros Sangiacomo Sans Filtrage 1993: Moderately rich, with light honey, pear and butterscotch flavors that build on the finish. Flavors linger on the finish. 305 cases made. • $17 • (07/31/95) • **87**

Chardonnay Carneros Sangiacomo Sans Filtrage 1992: Smooth and polished, brightly spicy, with honey and apple echoing on the finish. Has elegance and lovely balance. 424 cases made. • $17 • (04/30/94) • **89**

Chardonnay Russian River Valley Sans Filtrage Dutton 1993: Ripe and floral, with pear, spice and apple notes that are medium weight, with smoky toasty oak notes, turning a bit coarse on the finish. 269 cases made. • $18 • (07/31/95) • **86**

Merlot Sonoma Valley Kunde Vineyards 1992: Offers austere, hard tannins and a green tea character to the flavors. Tightly wound and highly tannic style. 191 cases made. • $17 • (09/30/95) • **82**

Pinot Noir Carneros 1993: Earthy with a musty edge to the ripe plum and berry fruit, picking up that musty edge again on the finish. 113 cases made. • $19 • (03/31/96) • **71**

CHERRY HILL | WASHINGTON

Chardonnay Columbia Valley 1994: Focused, lively, resiny pear and vanilla flavors remain zingy through the finish, folding in a touch of oak. 2,571 cases made. • $6 • (09/30/95) • **87**

Key: SS—Spectator Selection. CS—Cellar Selection. BB—Best Buy. $NA—Price not available. (BT)—Barrel tasting. (A)—Auction Price.
Dates in parentheses represent the issues in which the ratings were published.

CHESTNUT HILL | CALIFORNIA

Cabernet Sauvignon California 1988 • $7 • (10/15/91) BB • **81**

Cabernet Sauvignon California Coastal Cuvée 1991: Smells tired and a bit stale, and the fruit bears the mark of Coastal Cabernet with its herb and vegetal notes. Still, its texture is smooth and it picks up focused currant and berry-scented flavors. Ready now. 1,300 cases made. • $9 • (05/15/94) • **82**

Cabernet Sauvignon California Coastal Cuvée 1990: An appealing herbal style that's ripe and robust. The dominant olive and cherry flavors have just enough smoke and spice nuances to give it a nice roasted character. Gutsy and flavorful. Tasted twice. • $8 • (05/15/93) • **84**

Cabernet Sauvignon Napa Valley 1983 • $7 • (10/31/86) BB • **91**

Cabernet Sauvignon Sonoma County 1987 • $9 • (03/31/90) • **80**

Cabernet Sauvignon Sonoma County 1985 • $7 • (10/15/88) • **77**

Chardonnay California 1991 • $8 • (03/31/93) • **74**

Merlot Napa Valley 1989 • $10 • (11/15/91) • **81**

Merlot North Coast 1985 • $8 • (12/15/87) • **84**

Merlot North Coast Coastal Cuvée 1992: Chunky, with a narrow band of earthy currant and oaky flavors. May be more forthcoming in time. 1,300 cases made. • $10 • (09/15/94) • **78**

Merlot North Coast Coastal Cuvée 1991 • $9 • (03/31/93) • **78**

Zinfandel California Old Vines Cuvée 1990 • $6 • (09/30/93) • **75**

Zinfandel San Luis Obispo 1989 • $6 • (07/31/92) • **83**

Zinfandel San Luis Obispo 1988 • $6 • (08/31/91) BB • **86**

Zinfandel San Luis Obispo County Lot 2 1989 • $6 • (04/30/93) • **77**

CHESTNUT MOUNTAIN | GEORGIA

Cabernet Sauvignon Georgia Mossy Creek Vineyard 1989 • $16 • (02/29/92) • **83**

Merlot Georgia 1990 • $14 • (02/29/92) • **83**

CHEURLIN, DOMAINE | NEW MEXICO

Brut New Mexico NV • $12 • (02/29/92) • **82**

Extra Dry New Mexico NV • $12 • (02/29/92) • **77**

CHEVALIER, CHATEAU | CALIFORNIA

Cabernet Sauvignon Napa Valley 1980 • $12 • (01/01/84) • **82**

CHEVRE, CHATEAU | CALIFORNIA

Cabernet Franc Napa Valley 1985 • $16 • (07/31/88) • **85**

Chardonnay Napa Valley 1992: Offers light and elegant pear, apple and toasty oak notes that pick up a spicy edge on the finish. 328 cases made. • $11 • (06/30/94) • **83**

Chev Reserve Napa Valley 1986 • $25 • (07/31/89) • **88**

Merlot Napa Valley 1985 • $16 • (08/31/88) • **87**

Merlot Napa Valley 1984 • $13 • (10/31/87) • **91**

Merlot Napa Valley 1983 • $13 • (10/15/87) • **85**

Merlot Napa Valley 1982 • $12 • (10/01/85) • **84**

Merlot Napa Valley Reserve 1986 • $25 • (07/31/89) • **80**

Merlot Napa Valley Reserve 1984 • $15 • (12/15/87) • **78**

CHIMÉRE | CALIFORNIA

Chardonnay Santa Barbara County 1993: Very ripe, with fig, honey and a slight botrytis edge, turning cloying onthe finish. 750 cases made. • $13 • (07/31/95) • **82**

Merlot Santa Barbara County 1992: Smooth and supple, silky-textured and fine-grained, nicely focused berry and spice flavors lingering on the finish. Best from 1996. 225 cases made. • $16 • (07/31/95) • **83**

Nebbiolo Santa Barbara County 1992: Lean, citrusy and tart, modestly endowed with flavor. 318 cases made. • $15 • (12/15/95) • **77**

Pinot Blanc Santa Barbara County 1993: Earthy and has somewhat of a tin-can character in the pineapple and honey notes. Awkward. 200 cases made. • $10 • (08/31/95) • **76**

CHIMNEY ROCK | CALIFORNIA

Cabernet Sauvignon Stags Leap District 1992: Spicy currant, earth and anise mark this medium-weight red, which lacks richness and depth. Ready now. • $22 • (05/15/96) • **83**

Cabernet Sauvignon Stags Leap District 1990: An earthy, herbal style, with rugged tannins and a tight, closed band of currant and oak. Best to cellar until 1997 in hopes it's more forthcoming. 9,300 cases made. • $20 • (04/30/94) • **85**

Cabernet Sauvignon Stags Leap District 1989 • $18 • (03/31/93) • **76**

Cabernet Sauvignon Stags Leap District 1988 • $18 • (08/31/92) • **87**

Cabernet Sauvignon Stags Leap District 1987 • $29 • (07/31/91) SS • **90**

Cabernet Sauvignon Stags Leap District 1986 • $19 • (09/30/89) • **87**

Cabernet Sauvignon Stags Leap District 1985 • $15 • (03/01/89) • **87**

Cabernet Sauvignon Stags Leap District 1984 • $19 • (03/01/89) • **82**

Cabernet Sauvignon Stags Leap District Reserve 1994: Ripe with bright cherry and cedary flavors of medium weight and intensity. • $24 • (05/31/95) • **85-89** (BT)

Chardonnay Carneros 1994: Strikes a good balance between the citrus and pear flavors and the mild oak shadings. 4,300 cases made. • $16 • (06/30/96) • **84**

Chardonnay Carneros 1993: Blunt and a touch earthy, with a muted grapefruit edge to the Chardonnay flavors. • $16 • (07/31/95) • **82**

Chardonnay Stags Leap District 1992: Leans a little too heavily on wood flavors, which give it a dry oaky mouthfeel. On the finish the spicy pear flavors are appealing, but it lacks harmony. 6,000 cases made. • $15 • (06/30/94) • **82**

Chardonnay Stags Leap District 1991 • $15 • (03/31/94) • **79**

Elevage Stags Leap District 1994: Strives for elegance, with supple cherry and currant fruit that stays focused. • $35 • (05/31/95) • **85-89** (BT)

Elevage Stags Leap District 1992: Appealing for its bright, ripe and supple plum, berry and cherry flavors. Well balanced, it has harmony and finesse. Finishes with mild tannins. Can stand cellaring into 1998. • $30 • (12/15/95) • **88**

Elevage Stags Leap District 1991: Strives for complexity with its smoky oak aroma and rich core of black cherry, currant and buttery flavors, showing more depth, substance and persistence than previous Chimney Rock reds. Firm tannins on the finish, but lots of flavor too. Best after 1997 400 cases made. • $30 • (11/15/94) • **90**

Elevage Stags Leap District 1990: Ripe and flavorful, with a generous beam of currant and blueberry aromas and flavors, finishing spicy and fresh. Has lots of appeal, balanced enough to want until 1997. 40 percent Cabernet Franc, 40 percent Merlot and 20 percent Cabernet Sauvignon. • $30 • (11/15/93) • **88**

Fumé Blanc Napa Valley 1994: Smooth, gentle, modest fruit and spice flavors fade a bit on the finish. • $11 • (08/31/95) • **80**

Fumé Blanc Napa Valley 1993: Lean and herbal, the citrusy flavors keeping it lively. 2,000 cases made. • $11 • (08/31/94) • **82**

Fumé Blanc Napa Valley 1992 • $10 • (12/15/93) • **77**

Reserve Stags Leap District 1992: Smooth and harmonious, with a pretty core of currant, coffee, cedar and spice, turning rich and complex on the finish. The tannins are rich and plush, but the fruit keeps pouring through. Best after 1998. • $30 • (12/15/95) • **92**

CHINA BEND | WASHINGTON

Gewürztraminer Washington Organic Table Wine 1993: Flavors run toward floral and citrusy in this dry, crisp white. 20 cases made. • $12 • (09/30/95) • **82**

Nouveau Organic Red Wine Washington 1994: Soft, grapey and slightly fizzy, a decent quaffing wine showing somewhat more intensity than most. 20 cases made. • $16 • (09/30/95) • **81**

White Riesling Washington Organic Table Wine 1993: Dark color, earthy notes finish with a bite and oxidized flavors that do not make for a charmer. 20 cases made. • $12 • (09/30/95) • **72**

CHINOOK | WASHINGTON

Merlot Washington 1986 • $13 • (10/15/89) • **83**

CHOUINARD | CALIFORNIA

Chardonnay Monterey Ventana Vineyard 1993: Sappy with cloying ripe pear and apple flavors. 250 cases made. • $12 • (07/31/95) • **80**

CHRISTIAN BROTHERS | CALIFORNIA

Cabernet Sauvignon Napa Valley 1988 • $6 • (11/15/91) • **76**

Cabernet Sauvignon Napa Valley 1987 • $7 • (10/15/91) • **79**

Cabernet Sauvignon Napa Valley 1986 • $9 • (11/15/90) • **88**

Cabernet Sauvignon Napa Valley 1985 • $8 • (06/15/88) • **90**

Cabernet Sauvignon Napa Valley 1984 • $7 • (10/15/87) BB • **87**

Cabernet Sauvignon Napa Valley 1980 • $6 • (10/01/85) • **58**

Merlot Napa Valley 1985 • $8 • (08/31/88) • **80**

Montage Premier Cuvée Bordeaux & Napa Valley NV • $15 • (10/15/88) • **84**

Zinfandel Napa Valley 1986 • $5 • (06/30/88) • **79**

CHRISTOPHE | CALIFORNIA

Cabernet Sauvignon California 1989 • $6 • (08/31/92) • **77**

Cabernet Sauvignon California 1988 • $9 • (03/31/91) • **83**

Cabernet Sauvignon California 1982 • $4 • (12/16/85) BB • **85**

Cabernet Sauvignon Napa County 1992: Light, bright and simple, fragrant with berry and vanilla flavors. Approachable now. 2,281 cases made. • $9 • (12/15/95) • **84**

Cabernet Sauvignon Napa County 1991: A bit funky, with earthy, gamy edges that turn musty on the finish. • $8 • (12/15/95) • **75**

Cabernet Sauvignon Napa Valley 1990: Firm in texture, with cherry and currant aromas, lean fruit flavors and a finish that thins out. Tannic for the modest level of fruit, but acceptable for drinking now . Tasted twice, with consistent notes. 7,400 cases made. • $9 • (07/15/93) • **78**

Cabernet Sauvignon Napa Valley Reserve 1987 • $8 • (08/31/92) • **80**

Cabernet Sauvignon Napa Valley Reserve 1986 • $12 • (11/15/90) • **78**

Cabernet Sauvignon Napa Valley Reserve 1985 • $13 • (11/15/89) • **74**

Cabernet Sauvignon Napa Valley Reserve 1983 • $9 • (03/31/88) • **82**

Chardonnay Napa County 1994: Light and a tad earthy, but the bright apple flavor wins in the end. 12,000 cases made. • $9 • (06/15/96) • **82**

Chardonnay Napa County 1993: Crisp and flinty, with a coarse, grapefruity edge to the pear flavor. Ready now. • $8 • (09/30/94) • **79**

Chardonnay Napa Valley Reserve 1991 • $11 • (01/31/93) • **86**

Chardonnay North Coast 1993: Serves up ripe pear and apple notes with a touch of toast and spice. Medium bodied. 15,000 cases made. • $8 • (07/31/95) • **84**

Joliesse California 1987 • $5 • (02/28/90) • **79**

Pinot Noir Napa Valley Carneros Reserve 1989 • $9 • (09/30/92) • **84**

Pinot Noir Napa Valley Los Carneros 1992: A pleasant drink, with peppery plum and currant flavors that are supple. 2,000 cases made. • $8 • (03/31/95) • **83**

Pinot Noir Sonoma County Reserve 1990 • $10 • (02/28/93) • **75**

Sauvignon Blanc Napa Valley 1993: Bright and fresh, a soft, fruity wine with pleasant apple and herb flavors. • $6 • (08/31/94) • **83**

CHRISTOPHER CREEK | CALIFORNIA

Chardonnay Russian River Valley 1993: Elegant with floral aromas and citrus-laced pear and fig notes of modest proportions. 209 cases made. • $14 • (07/31/95) • **84**

Petite Sirah Russian River Valley 1988 • $11 • (10/15/93) • **79**

Syrah Russian River Valley 1992: Elegant, spicy currant, cherry and spice aromas and flavors, but it could use a shade more richness. 1,284 cases made. • $14 • (05/15/95) • **84**

Syrah Russian River Valley 1990 • $14 • (10/31/93) • **86**

CILURZO | CALIFORNIA

Chardonnay Temecula Barrel Fermented 1992: Bizarre smoky, acrylic flavors miss the mark by a long shot. 1,400 cases made. • $8 • (06/30/94) • **65**

Chardonnay Temecula Barrel Fermented Reserve 1991: Earthy and funky with bizarre acrylic, musty notes. Tasted twice with consistent notes. 1,500 cases made. • $12 • (06/30/94) • **60**

Merlot Temecula Unfiltered Proprietor's Reserve 1991: Lean, austere and earthy, a meager red with little generosity. 1,800 cases made. • $12 • (09/15/94) • **70**
Merlot Temecula Unfiltered Proprietor's Reserve 1990 • $12 • (05/31/92) • **79**
Sauvignon Blanc Temecula Reserve Barrel Fermented Luiseno Vineyard 1992: Sweet, floral, with a stalky edge that is not appealing. Tasted twice with consistent results. 1,200 cases made. • $9 • (08/31/94) • **72**

CINNABAR | CALIFORNIA

Cabernet Sauvignon Santa Cruz Mountains 1994: Dark and plush, with a rich earthy currant and tobacco edge and bold but polished tannins. • $NA • (05/31/95) • **90-94** (BT)
Cabernet Sauvignon Santa Cruz Mountains 1990: Austere and peppery, a rough-and-tumble red with coarse texture and gritty tannins. This needs cellaring to soften a bit, but it may always be on the tannic side. 2,250 cases made. • $20 • (11/15/94) • **84**
Cabernet Sauvignon Santa Cruz Mountains 1989 • $20 • (03/31/93) • **82**
Cabernet Sauvignon Santa Cruz Mountains 1987 • $18 • (03/31/91) • **84**
Cabernet Sauvignon Santa Cruz Mountains 1986 • $15 • (11/15/89) • **93**
Cabernet Sauvignon Santa Cruz Mountains Saratoga Vineyard 1992: Ripe, intense and flavorful, with a distinct tobacco leaf edge to the ripe plum and berry flavors. Finishes with earthy tannins, which should soften by 1999. 1,360 cases made. • $20 • (12/15/95) • **88**
Cabernet Sauvignon Saratoga Vineyard 1988 • $20 • (03/15/92) • **82**
Chardonnay Santa Cruz Mountains 1992: Young and tight, with a leafy green edge to the pear, fig and spice notes. Should improve in the short term. 1,971 cases made. • $20 • (03/31/95) • **86**
Chardonnay Santa Cruz Mountains 1991 • $20 • (02/28/94) SS • **90**
Chardonnay Santa Cruz Mountains Saratoga Vineyard 1994: Rich and enticing, with complex notes of ripe pear, toasty oak, honey and spice. The wood stands out somewhat and the finish is a bit hot, but it should mellow with a little age. 1,500 cases made. • $23 • (06/15/96) • **88**

CIRRI | CALIFORNIA

Cabernet Sauvignon Alexander Valley 1992: Firm in texture, with anise and smoke overtones to the jammy blackberry flavors, the finish is tannic but should soften. 400 cases made. • $10 • (12/15/95) • **86**
Cabernet Sauvignon Alexander Valley 1991: Hard-edged, woody and tannic, whatever fruit lies beneath is buried. Drinkable now. 701 cases made. • $10 • (11/15/94) • **79**
Chardonnay Carneros 1992: A new brand using Carneros-grown grapes exhibits ripe pear, honey and buttery notes that linger on the finish. A solid effort at a very reasonable price, the only catch is that there are only 211 cases, and distribution is probably limited to California. 211 cases made. • $11 • (06/30/94) • **85**
Chardonnay Sonoma County 1993: Good intensity for the vintage, with spicy citrus and pear notes that are crisp and clean. 700 cases made. • $9 • (07/31/95) • **83**
Merlot Sonoma Valley 1992: A ripe and chunky style, with hard oak and firm tannins that dominate the plum and berry fruit. Awkward now, best to cellar into 1997 in hopes it will soften. 300 cases made. • $10 • (03/31/96) • **79**
Merlot Sonoma Valley 1991: Tightly wound and firmly tannic, this young Merlot will need cellaring until 1997 or so to soften, but the berry and wild cherry flavors are appealing, it finishes with cedar and earthy notes. 660 cases made. • $11 • (09/15/94) • **85**

CLAIBORNE & CHURCHILL | CALIFORNIA

Chardonnay Edna Valley MacGregor Vineyard 1994: Clean and correct, with a spicy edge to the ripe pear and pineapple notes. The flavors stay with you on the finish, as the fruit keeps pumping out. 125 cases made. • $18 • (05/31/96) • **88**

Key: SS—Spectator Selection. CS—Cellar Selection. BB—Best Buy. $NA—Price not available. (BT)—Barrel tasting. Ⓐ—Auction Price.
Dates in parentheses represent the issues in which the ratings were published.

Chardonnay Edna Valley MacGregor Vineyard 1993: Medium bodied, but with enough pear, spice and lemony flavors to keep your interest, as the flavors fan out on the finish. 225 cases made. • $17 • (07/31/95) • **87**
Chardonnay Edna Valley MacGregor Vineyard 1991 • $16 • (07/15/93) • **80**
Gewürztraminer Central Coast Dry Alsatian Style 1994: Soft and effusively fruity, but dry, unfolding its black pepper, spice and orange cream flavors elegantly. Ready now. 1,283 cases made. • $10 • (11/15/95) • **87**
Gewürztraminer Central Coast Dry Alsatian Style 1993: Crisp and a little austere. This California Gewürz is dry and begins with a little reserve, then offers a haunting whiff of spice on the long finish. Drinkable now. 1,810 cases made. • $10 • (05/15/95) BB • **88**
Gewürztraminer Central Coast Dry Alsatian Style 1991 • $9 • (11/15/92) • **82**
Pinot Noir Edna Valley MacGregor Vineyard 1992: Strives for complexity with its smoky, toasty oak, but there's enough tart berry and cherry underneath to hold your interest. Finishes with a long, lingering aftertaste. 125 cases made. • $15 • (12/31/94) • **88**
Pinot Noir Edna Valley MacGregor Vineyard 1991 • $15 • (02/28/94) • **82**
Pinot Noir Edna Valley MacGregor Vineyard 1990 • $12 • (02/28/93) • **78**
Pinot Noir Edna Valley Runestone 1993: Marked by a strong vegetal edge to the funky black cherry flavors. Rings true for the appellation, but skirts the outer edge of Pinot Noir. 144 cases made. • $16 • **78**
Riesling Central Coast Dry Alsatian Style 1994: Tart and citrusy, light enough to be a refreshing apéritif. 810 cases made. • $10 • (09/30/95) • **84**
Riesling Central Coast Dry Alsatian Style 1993: Sharply focused pear and peach fruit on a light, simple frame. Could use a smoother texture. 831 cases made. • $10 • (06/15/95) • **82**
Riesling Central Coast Dry Alsatian Style 1991 • $9 • (05/31/92) • **85**
Riesling Late Harvest Central Coast 1987 • $15 • (12/15/89) • **81**

CLAIRVAUX | CALIFORNIA

Grenache California 1989 • $7 • (03/31/92) BB • **83**
Merlot Napa Valley 1989 • $12 • (05/31/92) • **85**

CLARCK, DOMAINE DE | CALIFORNIA

Chardonnay Carneros Première Réserve 1991 • $20 • (03/15/93) • **90**
Chardonnay Monterey County 1991 • $14 • (03/15/93) • **87**
Pinot Noir Monterey County Unfiltered 1991 • $20 • (02/28/94) • **81**
Pinot Noir Monterey County Villages 1992 • $10 • (02/28/94) BB • **85**
Pinot Noir Monterey County Villages 1991 • $11 • (02/28/93) • **77**
Pinot Noir Monterey County Villages 1990 • $10 • (03/31/92) • **82**
Pinot Noir Monterey Première 1989 • $15 • (04/30/91) • **77**
Pinot Noir Sonoma County Villages 1989 • $10 • (03/31/92) • **72**

CLAUDIA SPRINGS | CALIFORNIA

Chardonnay Anderson Valley 1993: Well balanced, with vanilla-tinged oak flavors and ripe pear and spice notes. 350 cases made. • $10 • (07/31/95) • **83**
Pinot Noir Anderson Valley 1991 • $13 • (02/28/93) • **86**
Zinfandel Mendocino 1992: Firm and tannic, with a lean band of earthy, tarry fruit flavors that turns dry on the finish. 330 cases made. • $10 • (10/15/94) • **81**
Zinfandel Mendocino Pacini Vineyard 1993: Smooth and elegant, with simple cherry and wild berry flavors that hang with you. Well made, mild tannins and drinks easy. 450 cases made. • $14 • (10/15/95) • **85**

CLINE | CALIFORNIA

Carignane Contra Costa County 1990 • $9 • (12/15/92) • **86**
Côtes d'Oakley Contra Costa County 1991 • $7 • (12/31/93) BB • **82**
Côtes d'Oakley Contra Costa County 1990 • $7 • (11/15/92) BB • **85**
Côtes d'Oakley Contra Costa County 1989 • $7 • (05/31/91) • **80**
Côtes d'Oakley Contra Costa County 1988 • $9 • (04/30/90) • **83**
Merlot California 1989 • $17 • (05/31/92) • **75**
Mourvèdre Contra Costa County 1990: Lean, chewy prune and tobacco flavors tighten up somewhat on the finish. Best in 1997. 2,569 cases made. • $20 • (12/15/95) • **81**

Mourvèdre Contra Costa County 1989 • $18 • (11/30/91) • **86**
Mourvèdre Contra Costa County 1988 • $18 • (04/30/90) • **91**
Mourvèdre Contra Costa County Reserve 1989 • $26 • (03/15/92) • **78**
Oakley Cuvée Contra Costa County 1990: Firm and chewy, its leathery, smoky notes adding some depth to the modest black cherry flavors that persist on the finish. Better in 1997. 3,597 cases made. • $12 • (08/31/95) • **85**
Oakley Cuvée Contra Costa County 1989 • $12 • (05/31/91) • **88**
Oakley Cuvée Contra Costa County 1988 • $12 • (02/28/90) • **90**
Syrah Contra Costa County 1991 • $15 • (10/31/93) • **84**
Zinfandel Contra Costa County 1994: Intense and concentrated, offering tight currant, plum and cherry and a peppermint quality that gives it an unusual flavor profile. Needs short-term cellaring into 1997. 6,019 cases made. • $12 • (04/30/96) • **87**
Zinfandel Contra Costa County 1993: Well proportioned, sporting crisp berry and earth notes that become muddled on the finish. Solid, but lacks finesse. 6,019 cases made. • $12 • (09/15/95) • **85**
Zinfandel Contra Costa County 1992: Zesty, spicy, chunky oregano flavors, but not much in the way of fruit. Finishes with gritty tannins and complex flavors. Try in 1995. 4,889 cases made. • $10 • (10/15/94) • **84**
Zinfandel Contra Costa County 1991 • $10 • (09/30/93) • **84**
Zinfandel Contra Costa County 1990 • $10 • (10/15/92) • **83**
Zinfandel Contra Costa County 1989 • $9 • (05/15/91) • **86**
Zinfandel Contra Costa County 1987 • $9 • (05/15/90) • **89**
Zinfandel Contra Costa County Big Break 1993: Distinct for its ripe, chunky plum, berry and tar flavors and chewy tannins. Best to cellar it short-term for softening. Try now or in 1997. 647 cases made. • $18 • (09/15/95) • **87**
Zinfandel Contra Costa County Bridgehead 1993: Appealing bright, ripe cherry and raspberry flavors that turn vibrant and complex, finishing with firm tannins. 647 cases made. • $18 • (09/15/95) • **87**
Zinfandel Contra Costa County Reserve 1993: Dense and chewy, showing intense tar, plum, spice and nutmeg flavors that turn complex and tannic on the finish. Needs until 1997. 1,469 cases made. • $16 • (09/15/95) • **88**
Zinfandel Contra Costa County Reserve 1992: A bright, vibrant, firm and compact young Zin that's weighted toward tar berry and jam notes. Rich and concentrated, could use short-term cellaring to soften and evolve. Impressive length on the finish. 851 cases made. • $12 • (09/15/94) • **89**
Zinfandel Contra Costa County Reserve 1991 • $14 • (09/30/93) • **86**
Zinfandel Contra Costa County Reserve 1990 • $14 • (10/15/92) • **82**
Zinfandel Contra Costa County Reserve 1989 • $12 • (12/31/91) • **84**
Zinfandel Contra Costa County Reserve 1987 • $12 • (05/15/90) • **87**

CLONINGER | CALIFORNIA

Cabernet Sauvignon Monterey 1990: Smooth, supple and generous, with a solid core of ripe berry and currant flavors. Finishes with a touch of sage and other dusky herbs. Drink soon, while the fruit is still prominent. 906 cases made. • $15 • (07/15/93) • **82**
Chardonnay Monterey 1992: Spicy, earthy, honeyed and candied fruit flavors make an odd mix. They stay with you, but they're out there in style. 11,000 cases made. • $11 • (04/30/96) • **80**
Chardonnay Monterey 1991 • $15 • (07/15/93) • **79**

CLOS DANIELLE | CALIFORNIA

Chardonnay Carneros Private Reserve 1993: A ripe, honeyed and rich-textured California Chardonnay, with beautifully delineated flavors that last and last on the finish. 11,000 cases made. • $9 • (01/31/95) BB • **87**
Merlot Napa Valley 1993: Forward and fruity, throwing a wild berry spin on the fruit flavors. Appealing now. 3,900 cases made. • $10 • (05/15/95) • **82**

CLOS DU BOIS | CALIFORNIA

Cabernet Sauvignon Alexander Valley 1991: Supple and elegant, easy to drink with pretty currant, toast and berry flavors. Mild tannins on the finish make it it alluring now and there is a pretty, toasty oak aftertaste. • $12 • (02/28/94) • **86**
Cabernet Sauvignon Alexander Valley 1990: Surprisingly rich, concentrated and complex, but shows the potential of the 1990 vintage. A pleasing wine that offers ripe currant, berry and spice flavors and a nice dose of toasty, buttery oak. Firmly tannic, but drinkable now through 1998. • $13 • (03/31/93) • **87**
Cabernet Sauvignon Alexander Valley 1989 • $11 • (11/15/92) • **80**
Cabernet Sauvignon Alexander Valley 1988 • $14 • (07/15/91) • **77**
Cabernet Sauvignon Alexander Valley 1987 • $11 • (02/15/90) • **86**
Cabernet Sauvignon Alexander Valley 1986 • $12 • (05/31/89) • **86**
Cabernet Sauvignon Alexander Valley 1985 • $19 Ⓐ • (04/15/88) • **87**
Cabernet Sauvignon Alexander Valley 1984 • $10 • (06/15/87) • **87**
Cabernet Sauvignon Alexander Valley 1981 • $9 • (03/01/86) • **91**
Cabernet Sauvignon Alexander Valley Briarcrest Vineyard 1992: Attractive for its plum, floral and wild berry flavors that are intense and complex, turning supple and elegant on the finish. 5,300 cases made. • $20 • (11/30/95) • **89**
Cabernet Sauvignon Alexander Valley Briarcrest Vineyard 1991: A pleasant, well-balanced red with pretty plum and currant flavors that stay with you. Medium in body, an elegant style appealing to drink now. • $18 • (11/15/94) • **87**
Cabernet Sauvignon Alexander Valley Briarcrest Vineyard 1990: Firm and intense, with well focused, concentrated currant, cherry and wild berry flavors that are framed by toasty, smoky notes on the finish. Impressive for its focus and length, the finish is complex and alluring. Drink now or hold. 4,019 cases made. • $19 • (04/15/94) • **89**
Cabernet Sauvignon Alexander Valley Briarcrest Vineyard 1989 • $19 • (08/31/93) • **80**
Cabernet Sauvignon Alexander Valley Briarcrest Vineyard 1987 • $18 • (11/15/91) • **88**
Cabernet Sauvignon Alexander Valley Briarcrest Vineyard 1986 • $17 • (08/31/90) • **87**
Cabernet Sauvignon Alexander Valley Briarcrest Vineyard 1985 • $16 • (06/15/89) • **86**
Cabernet Sauvignon Alexander Valley Briarcrest Vineyard 1984 • $16 • (03/01/89) • **87**
Cabernet Sauvignon Alexander Valley Briarcrest Vineyard 1983 • $12 • (03/01/89) • **74**
Cabernet Sauvignon Alexander Valley Briarcrest Vineyard 1982 • $12 • (03/01/89) • **66**
Cabernet Sauvignon Alexander Valley Briarcrest Vineyard 1981 • $12 • (03/01/89) • **88**
Cabernet Sauvignon Alexander Valley Briarcrest Vineyard 1980 • $12 • (03/01/89) • **80**
Cabernet Sauvignon Alexander Valley Winemaker's Reserve 1991: Intense and concentrated, with layers of complex currant, black cherry and herb-laced Cabernet fruit. It keeps pumping out the flavors on the long, full finish. A beautiful combination of ripe fruit and spicy oak. Best after 1998. 600 cases made. • $30 • (10/15/94) CS • **92**
Cabernet Sauvignon Dry Creek Valley Proprietor's Reserve 1982 • $19 • (09/15/87) • **88**
Cabernet Sauvignon Sonoma County 1993: Simple but pleasant enough, with supple plum and cherry notes. 79,000 cases made. • $13 • (12/15/95) • **82**
Cabernet Sauvignon Sonoma County Dry Creek 1974 • $NA • (02/15/90) • **74**
Chardonnay Alexander Valley Barrel Fermented 1994: Tight and compact, showing a narrow band of pear and apple flavor. Decent but nothing more. 240,000 cases made. • $13 • (04/30/96) • **82**
Chardonnay Alexander Valley Barrel Fermented 1993: Crisp and fruity with a leafy edge to the appealing, slightly sappy apple and pear flavors. Drinkable now. 125,000 cases made. • $13 • (01/31/95) • **84**
Chardonnay Alexander Valley Barrel Fermented 1992: A successful wine in a light, elegant style. Pear, vanilla, spice and toasty notes are focused and bright. Ready to drink now. (3/15/94) 133,000 cases made. • $12 • (03/15/94) • **85**
Chardonnay Alexander Valley Barrel Fermented 1991 • $13 • (03/31/93) • **83**
Chardonnay Alexander Valley Calcaire Vineyard 1994: Bright and lively, featuring a pretty core of ripe pear, grapefruit, honey and light toasty oak notes that fold together nicely on a tapered finish. Flavors linger on and on, revealing an attractive mineral character. A wonderful

white from this California leader. 11,500 cases made. • $18 • (04/30/96) SS • **91**

Chardonnay Alexander Valley Calcaire Vineyard 1993: Rich and creamy, well crafted, featuring a pretty band of pear, vanilla and nutmeg. Picks up a trace of honey on the finish. 7,000 cases made. • $18 • (05/15/95) • **89**

Chardonnay Alexander Valley Calcaire Vineyard 1992: Strikes a nice balance between ripe Chardonnay fruit and toasty oak flavors, it's complex and concentrated, with pear, spice and citrus notes. Drinks well now but can age short-term. • $18 • (05/15/94) • **89**

Chardonnay Alexander Valley Calcaire Vineyard 1991 • $18 • (07/15/93) • **86**

Chardonnay Dry Creek Valley Flintwood Vineyard 1994: Distinctive for melon and pear flavors in a straightforward style, delivering ripe, full-bodied fruit and light oak shadings. The finish picks up traces of grapefruit. Could profit from a little time in the bottle. 5,650 cases made. • $17 • (04/30/96) • **89**

Chardonnay Dry Creek Valley Flintwood Vineyard 1993: Marked by nut and honey notes, well oaked by a slight toasty bitter edge that may dissipate with time. 4,500 cases made. • $17 • (07/31/95) • **86**

Chardonnay Dry Creek Valley Flintwood Vineyard 1991: Ripe and spicy with a pretty core of citrus, pear and spice flavors that linger on the finish. Well balanced and ready to drink now, but cellaring it a year or two won't hurt. • $17 • (06/30/94) • **87**

Gewürztraminer Early Harvest Alexander Valley 1993: Soft and simple, nice pear flavor echoing on the finish. 3,300 cases made. • $8 • (02/28/95) • **79**

Gewürztraminer Early Harvest Alexander Valley 1991 • $8 • (06/15/93) • **78**

Gewürztraminer Late Harvest Alexander Valley Individual Bunch Selected 1986 • $18 • (08/31/87) • **80**

Johannisberg Riesling Late Harvest Alexander Valley Individual Bunch Selected 1986 • $15 • (08/31/87) • **89**

Malbec Alexander Valley L'Etranger Winemaker's Reserve 1991 • $19 • (03/31/94) • **82**

Malbec Alexander Valley L'Etranger Winemaker's Reserve 1987 • $20 • (01/31/91) • **87**

Marlstone Vineyard Alexander Valley 1992: Well oaked, sporting toasty, buttery flavors and just enough ripe cherry and plum notes to hold its balance. A touch of herb and coffee on aftertaste. 12,000 cases made. • $21 • (11/30/95) • **89**

Marlstone Vineyard Alexander Valley 1991: Ripe and focused, with plum, cranberry, cherry and cedary oak flavors and a smooth, tannic finish. 12,000 cases made. • $18 • (01/31/95) • **88**

Marlstone Vineyard Alexander Valley 1990: Forward and fleshy, with lots of appealing berry and plum aromas and flavors that stay with you on the finish, dressed up with spicy oak. Texture is open and not especially focused, but should be fine through at least 1999 or 2000 . • $20 • (11/15/93) • **88**

Marlstone Vineyard Alexander Valley 1989 • $20 • (03/31/93) • **85**

Marlstone Vineyard Alexander Valley 1987 • $27 • (07/31/91) • **90**

Marlstone Vineyard Alexander Valley 1986 • $24 • (08/31/90) • **85**

Marlstone Vineyard Alexander Valley 1985 • $34 • (06/15/89) • **81**

Marlstone Vineyard Alexander Valley 1984 • $26 • (03/01/89) • **89**

Marlstone Vineyard Alexander Valley 1983 • $25 • (03/01/89) • **70**

Marlstone Vineyard Alexander Valley 1982 • $32 • (03/01/89) • **79**

Marlstone Vineyard Alexander Valley 1981 • $15 Ⓐ • (03/01/89) • **85**

Marlstone Vineyard Alexander Valley 1980 • $38 • (03/01/89) • **77**

Marlstone Vineyard Alexander Valley 1979 • $47 • (03/01/89) • **75**

Marlstone Vineyard Alexander Valley 1978 • $26 • (03/01/89) • **72**

Merlot Sonoma County 1993: Ripe and fruity, with complex cherry, berry and spice flavors. No extra dimensions, but solid Merlot, with a chunky core of fruit. • $16 • (06/15/96) • **84**

Merlot Sonoma County 1992: Ripe and intense with focused wild berry and cherry flavor. Light oak shadings add dimension on the finish. Ready now through 1998. 96,000 cases made. • $15 • (01/31/95) • **88**

Merlot Sonoma County 1991 • $15 • (04/15/94) • **86**

Merlot Sonoma County 1990 • $15 • (06/15/93) • **82**

Key: SS—Spectator Selection. CS—Cellar Selection. BB—Best Buy. $NA—Price not available. (BT)—Barrel tasting. Ⓐ—Auction Price.
Dates in parentheses represent the issues in which the ratings were published.

Merlot Sonoma County 1989 • $15 • (05/31/92) • **82**

Merlot Sonoma County 1988 • $15 • (05/31/91) • **81**

Merlot Sonoma County 1987 • $12 • (04/15/90) • **89**

Merlot Sonoma County 1986 • $11 • (10/15/88) • **86**

Merlot Sonoma County 1985 • $10 • (10/31/87) SS • **92**

Merlot Sonoma County 1984 • $9 • (05/16/86) • **87**

Merlot Sonoma County 1983 • $9 • (10/01/85) • **86**

Muscat of Alexandria Late Harvest Alexander Valley Fleur d'Alexandra 1986 • $10 • (05/31/88) • **90**

Pinot Noir Dry Creek Valley Proprietor's Reserve 1980 • $11 • (07/16/84) • **86**

Pinot Noir Sonoma County 1990 • $12 • (02/28/93) • **82**

Pinot Noir Sonoma County 1989 • $13 • (10/31/91) • **78**

Pinot Noir Sonoma County 1988 • $12 • (04/30/91) • **80**

Pinot Noir Sonoma County 1987 • $12 • (05/31/90) • **73**

Pinot Noir Sonoma County 1986 • $11 • (10/15/89) • **87**

Pinot Noir Sonoma County 1985 • $11 • (06/15/88) • **70**

Pinot Noir Sonoma County 1984 • $8 • (08/31/86) • **86**

Pinot Noir Sonoma County 1983 • $8 • (08/31/86) • **70**

Pinot Noir Sonoma County 1982 • $8 • (07/16/85) • **60**

Sauvignon Blanc Alexander Valley Barrel Fermented 1993: Simple and subdued, a pleasant wine with pear and modest spice flavors. • $8 • (08/31/94) • **80**

Sauvignon Blanc Alexander Valley Barrel Fermented 1992 • $7 • (07/15/93) BB • **87**

Sauvignon Blanc Alexander Valley Barrel Fermented 1991 • $8 • (11/30/92) • **76**

Sauvignon Blanc Sonoma County 1994: Very fresh, lively and bright, showing apple and floral flavors. 65,000 cases made. • $8 • (08/31/95) • **84**

Zinfandel Sonoma County 1993: A simple and modest band of berry and cherry notes turn to tar and earth on the finish. 12,000 cases made. • $13 • (10/15/95) • **83**

Zinfandel Sonoma County 1992: Firm, intense and lively, with spicy cherry, raspberry and cedary flavors. Finishes with firm but fine tannins and good length. Drinkable now through 1998. 7,000 cases made. • $13 • (10/15/94) • **87**

Zinfandel Sonoma County 1991 • $13 • (09/30/93) • **87**

CLOS DU VAL | CALIFORNIA

Cabernet Sauvignon Napa Valley 1990: Austere and very tannic, this is a difficult wine to judge because of the tannic grip. Also atypical of Clos Du Val in its tannin level. You get hints of Cabernet fruit and cedar notes, but that's all now. Perhaps with time it will be more appealing. Cellar until 1997. • $12 • (06/30/94) • **84**

Cabernet Sauvignon Napa Valley 1989 • $15 • (11/15/92) • **83**

Cabernet Sauvignon Napa Valley 1976 • $22 Ⓐ • (03/01/89) • **82**

Cabernet Sauvignon Napa Valley 1974: Fully mature and holding, but beginning to fade, with spicy, cedary Cabernet flavors. Tasted out of magnum. Best to drink up soon. 7,600 cases made. • $83 • (11/15/94) • **82**

Cabernet Sauvignon Napa Valley Gran Val 1985 • $8 • (05/31/88) • **88**

Cabernet Sauvignon Napa Valley Gran Val 1984 • $8 • (02/15/87) BB • **85**

Cabernet Sauvignon Napa Valley Gran Val 1982 • $7 • (04/16/84) • **88**

Cabernet Sauvignon Napa Valley Joli Val 1988 • $13 • (07/31/91) • **82**

Cabernet Sauvignon Napa Valley Joli Val 1986 • $13 • (12/15/89) • **87**

Cabernet Sauvignon Napa Valley Reserve 1990: Strikes a nice balance between subtle earth, tobacco and currant notes, exhibiting supple texture and soft tannins and finishing with a black cherry accent. 706 cases made. • $45 • (04/30/95) • **89**

Cabernet Sauvignon Stags Leap District 1991: Tight and compact, a narrow band of cherry, earth and berry flavors finishing with dry cedary overtones and firm tannins. 18,835 cases made. • $20 • (09/30/95) • **87**

Cabernet Sauvignon Stags Leap District 1990: An elegant red with simple currant, oak and berry flavors that are pleasant enough but not as rich and plush as most of the best 1990s. 15,232 cases made. • $18 • (11/15/94) • **83**

Cabernet Sauvignon Stags Leap District 1988 • $18 • (03/31/92) • **86**

Cabernet Sauvignon Stags Leap District 1987 • $17 • (06/30/91) • **92**

Cabernet Sauvignon Stags Leap District 1986 • $18 • (05/31/90) • **91**

Cabernet Sauvignon Stags Leap District 1985 • $32 • (06/15/89) • **90**
Cabernet Sauvignon Stags Leap District 1984 • $15 • (03/01/89) • **92**
Cabernet Sauvignon Stags Leap District 1983 • $22 • (03/01/89) • **86**
Cabernet Sauvignon Stags Leap District 1982 • $31 • (03/01/89) • **88**
Cabernet Sauvignon Stags Leap District 1981 • $28 • (03/01/89) • **82**
Cabernet Sauvignon Stags Leap District 1980 • $40 • (03/01/89) • **88**
Cabernet Sauvignon Stags Leap District 1979 • $29 • (03/01/89) • **90**
Cabernet Sauvignon Stags Leap District 1978 • $45 • (11/15/92) • **91**
Cabernet Sauvignon Stags Leap District 1977 • $29 • (03/01/89) • **89**
Cabernet Sauvignon Stags Leap District 1975 • $38 • (03/01/89) • **89**
Cabernet Sauvignon Stags Leap District 1974 • $83 • (03/01/89) • **91**
Cabernet Sauvignon Stags Leap District 1973 • $64 • (03/01/89) • **86**
Cabernet Sauvignon Stags Leap District 1972 • $70 • (03/01/89) • **90**
Cabernet Sauvignon Stags Leap District Reserve 1979 • $25 • (03/01/89) • **92**
Cabernet Sauvignon Stags Leap District Reserve 1978 • $NA • (11/15/92) • **94**
Cabernet Sauvignon Stags Leap District Reserve 1977 • $20 • (03/01/89) • **87**
Cabernet Sauvignon Stags Leap District Reserve 1973 • $10 • (03/01/89) • **90**
Chardonnay Carneros 1992: Lean and firm, showing a narrow band of pear and spice flavor. Turns coarse on the finish. Drinkable now. 15,289 cases made. • $15 • (01/31/95) • **84**
Chardonnay Carneros 1991 • $15 • (07/15/93) • **87**
Chardonnay Carneros Napa Valley 1993: Fresh in flavor, a little reticent to show its tropical fruit, pear and spice character. Drink now. 15,870 cases made. • $15 • (12/15/95) • **85**
Chardonnay Carneros Special Select 1993: Marked by earthy, funky notes that override the ripe pear and buttery oak flavors. Tastes better on the aftertaste. 125 cases made. • $20 • (04/30/95) • **86**
Le Clos Napa Valley NV • $5 • (08/31/90) BB • **85**
Merlot Stags Leap District 1992: Tart and austere, with a lean band wild berry and cherry, but the flavors build. Ready. Tasted twice with consistent results. 4,050 cases made. • $30 • (07/31/95) • **84**
Merlot Stags Leap District 1991 • $21 • (05/31/94) • **89**
Merlot Stags Leap District 1990 • $22 • (06/15/93) • **86**
Merlot Stags Leap District 1989 • $21 • (05/31/92) • **86**
Merlot Stags Leap District 1988 • $20 • (03/31/91) • **89**
Merlot Stags Leap District 1987 • $17 • (03/31/90) • **85**
Merlot Stags Leap District 1986 • $16 • (08/31/89) • **86**
Merlot Stags Leap District 1985 • $16 • (04/30/88) • **87**
Merlot Stags Leap District 1984 • $15 • (07/31/87) • **88**
Merlot Stags Leap District 1983 • $14 • (06/16/86) • **92**
Merlot Stags Leap District 1982 • $13 • (10/01/85) • **80**
Merlot Stags Leap District 1981 • $14 • (02/15/84) • **88**
Pinot Noir Carneros Napa Valley 1994: Appealing for its spicy red berry and cherry-laced fruit, but ultimately it's simple with hints of floral and berry. 2,000 cases made. • $15 • (02/29/96) • **83**
Pinot Noir Carneros Napa Valley 1990: Light and thin, with a narrow band of tea- and herb-laced Pinot Noir flavor. 2,500 cases made. • $13 • (03/31/95) • **78**
Pinot Noir Carneros Napa Valley 1989 • $13 • (02/28/94) • **81**
Pinot Noir Carneros Napa Valley 1988 • $14 • (09/30/92) • **80**
Pinot Noir Napa Valley 1987 • $14 • (04/30/91) • **84**
Pinot Noir Napa Valley 1986 • $16 • (02/15/90) • **80**
Pinot Noir Napa Valley 1985 • $13 • (06/15/88) • **80**
Pinot Noir Napa Valley 1984 • $12 • (09/30/87) • **78**
Pinot Noir Napa Valley 1983 • $12 • (08/31/86) • **66**
Pinot Noir Napa Valley 1982 • $11 • (09/01/84) • **75**
Pinot Noir Napa Valley Carneros 1994: Appealing for its spicy red berry and cherry flavors, but ultimately it's simple with hints of floral and berry. 2,000 cases made. • $15 • (02/29/96) • **83**
Reserve Napa Valley 1988 • $48 • (11/15/93) • **88**
Reserve Stags Leap District 1987 • $45 • (07/15/92) CS • **92**
Reserve Stags Leap District 1985 • $45 • (11/15/90) • **94**
Reserve Stags Leap District 1982 • $28 • (03/01/89) • **90**
Sémillon Stags Leap District 1991: Goes beyond floral: aromas of rotting flowers make this decadent and unpleasant. Tasted twice, with consistent notes. 1,518 cases made. • $12 • (06/30/95) • **73**
Zinfandel Stags Leap District 1991: An earthy style, offering modest berry and spice flavors that are elegant. 3,931 cases made. • $15 • (07/31/95) • **84**
Zinfandel Stags Leap District 1990: Light and vegetal, with more herb than fruit flavors. Taste three times. 3,450 cases made. • $14 • (10/15/94) • **74**
Zinfandel Stags Leap District 1989 • $14 • (09/30/93) • **86**
Zinfandel Stags Leap District 1988 • $15 • (10/15/92) • **85**
Zinfandel Stags Leap District 1987 • $16 • (05/31/90) • **83**
Zinfandel Stags Leap District 1986 • $12 • (05/31/89) • **87**
Zinfandel Stags Leap District 1985 • $12 • (04/30/88) • **90**
Zinfandel Stags Leap District 1984 • $19 • (05/31/87) • **81**
Zinfandel Stags Leap District 1981 • $18 • (05/16/84) CS • **90**
Zinfandel Stags Leap District 1974 • $55 • (06/16/85) • **77**
Zinfandel Stags Leap District 1973 • $50 • (06/16/85) • **86**
Zinfandel Stags Leap District 1972 • $60 • (06/16/85) • **90**

CLOS LACHANCE | CALIFORNIA

Cabernet Sauvignon Santa Cruz Mountains 1993: Smooth, supple cherry and berry flavor, turning earthy and slightly meaty on the finish. Medium- bodied, well proportioned. Drinkable now and into 1998. 700 cases made. • $23 • (04/30/96) • **86**
Cabernet Sauvignon Santa Cruz Mountains 1992: Good intensity and depth, featuring ripe cherry, currant and wild berry flavors that are focused and complex. Firmly tannic finish, best to cellar into 1998. 325 cases made. • $20 • (07/31/95) • **88**
Chardonnay Santa Cruz Mountains 1994: Bold, ripe and generous, with buttery pear, fig and melon notes and finishing with a smoky, toasty oak edge. Shows off its ripe fruit on the finish. 1,125 cases made. • $18 • (05/31/96) • **89**
Chardonnay Santa Cruz Mountains 1993: Ripe, smooth and creamy, with pear, hazelnut, and toasty buttery oak, turning rich and complex on the finish, where the flavors fan out. 1,325 cases made. • $18 • (07/31/95) • **89**
Chardonnay Santa Cruz Mountains 1992: Strikes a nice balance between spicy, toasty oak and ripe pear and apple notes. Gains complexity on the finish where the flavors are most interesting, fanning out on the toast and pear notes. Drink through 1997. 1,000 cases made. • $18 • (06/30/94) • **87**
Pinot Noir Santa Cruz Mountains 1993: Tough and tannic, with hard earthy edge to the cherry and spice fruit. Straightens out on the finish. 285 cases made. • $19 • (12/31/95) • **85**

CLOS PEGASE | CALIFORNIA

Cabernet Franc California 1988 • $15 • (10/15/91) • **69**
Cabernet Sauvignon Napa Valley 1993: Smooth and harmonious, with an earthy edge to the plum and currant flavors. Finishes with firm, plush tannins, but its well-balanced and the flavors come through. Best in 1998. 7,400 cases made. • $20 • (03/31/96) • **87**
Cabernet Sauvignon Napa Valley 1992: Tightly wound, rich, firm core of cherry, currant and anise flavors, picking up an earthy, toasted oak edge. Best in 1997. 3,100 cases made. • $19 • (10/15/95) • **88**
Cabernet Sauvignon Napa Valley 1991: This is firmly tannic, but it's also quite flavorful, with layers of currant, cedar, spice and tobacco. The tannins clamp down on the finish, cellaring may have improved it. Try now. 7,300 cases made. • $17 • (06/30/94) • **88**
Cabernet Sauvignon Napa Valley 1990: Firm and intense with a solid core of cherry, currant, plum and spice flavors that gently unfold into a spicy, concentrated, impeccably balanced wine that finishes with pretty cedary oak notes and fine tannins. Tempting now for its plush texture, but sure to pick up complexity. Drink now to 2002. Tasted twice, with consistent notes. 2,400 cases made. • $17 • (11/15/93) SS • **91**
Cabernet Sauvignon Napa Valley 1987 • $17 • (08/31/92) • **82**
Cabernet Sauvignon Napa Valley 1986 • $17 • (09/30/90) • **88**
Cabernet Sauvignon Napa Valley 1985 • $17 • (05/31/88) • **86**
Chardonnay Carneros Napa Valley 1993: Marked by smoky, toasty notes and tight beam of spicy pear and apple, finishing in a short, somewhat coarse manner. 16,800 cases made. • $15 • (09/30/95) • **86**

Chardonnay Napa Valley 1992: Strikes a nice balance between spicy vanilla-tinged oak and ripe pear flavor, but fails to go beyond those basic up-front notes. Elegant and ready to drink now. 16,700 cases made. • $9 • (06/30/94) BB • **84**

Chardonnay Napa Valley 1991 • $13 • (07/15/93) • **87**

Chardonnay Napa Valley Carneros Mitsuko's Vineyard 1994: Young and tart, adding a distinct lemony flair to the ripe pear and spice flavors. Picks up some toasty oak on the finish, where it turns elegant. 11,300 cases made. • $17 • (05/15/96) • **88**

Chardonnay Napa Valley Carneros Pegase Circle Reserve 1994: An elegant, medium-weight, subtle style, featuring supple texture and bright, lively citrus, pear and nutmeg flavors that finish in a complex and lingering aftertaste. Just misses rating outstanding. 983 cases made. • $23 • (05/15/96) • **89**

Chardonnay Napa Valley Carneros Pegase Circle Reserve 1993: Marked by ripe fruit and spicy nuances, with spicy apple and pear notes that pick up a nectarine edge on the finish. 500 cases made. • $20 • (07/31/95) • **87**

Grenache California 1989 • $9 • (08/31/91) • **84**

Hommage California 1989 • $20 • (11/15/93) • **83**

Hommage California 1988 • $25 • (10/15/92) • **84**

Hommage California 1987 • $20 • (08/31/91) • **90**

Hommage Napa Valley 1991: A good red with ripe currant and plum flavors, but it comes across as awkward and hollow in the middle, finishing with crisp tannins. 1,500 cases made. • $25 • (11/15/94) • **86**

Hommage Napa Valley 1990: Crisp and harmonious, gaining some flesh and silkiness as it unfolds its cherry, prune and spice flavors. Approachable now, best from 1997. 2,000 cases made. • $20 • (04/15/94) • **87**

Merlot Napa Valley 1993: Appealing for its direct fruitiness, with ripe plum, currant and berry notes, finishing with firm, crisp tannins. Can stand short term cellaring into 1997. 5,400 cases made. • $19 • (02/29/96) • **87**

Merlot Napa Valley 1992: Supple and harmonious, with pleasant cherry, wild berry and plum flavors that turn smooth and polished. The complexity really shows on the finish. 6,181 cases made. • $17 • (09/30/95) • **90**

Merlot Napa Valley 1991: Tough and tannic, a chunky Merlot with a smoky, stalky edge to the modest cherry and tea flavors. Best from 1997 7,100 cases made. • $16 • (09/15/94) • **79**

Merlot Napa Valley 1990 • $16 • (06/15/93) • **83**

Merlot Napa Valley 1989 • $15 • (10/31/92) • **81**

Merlot Napa Valley 1988 • $15 • (11/15/91) • **82**

Merlot Napa Valley 1986 • $16 • (07/15/90) • **84**

Pegaso Napa Valley 1988 • $12 • (08/31/92) • **82**

Petite Syrah Napa Valley 1988 • $15 • (10/31/91) • **83**

Sauvignon Blanc Napa Valley 1992 • $9 • (01/31/94) • **79**

CLOS ROBERT | CALIFORNIA

Cabernet Sauvignon Napa Valley Proprietor's Reserve 1984 • $7 • (12/31/87) • **71**

CLOS ST. THOMAS | CALIFORNIA

Chardonnay California 1993: A simple, fruity style with spice, pear and apple notes of modest proportion. 8,000 cases made. • $7 • (03/31/95) • **80**

Pinot Noir California 1993: Floral and fruity, with supple berry flavors, tastes like a Gamay. 1,500 cases made. • $8 • (03/31/95) • **78**

Sauvignon Blanc California 1993: Fruity, straightforward, a little on the light side, but a pleasant drink with herbal overtones. 2,500 cases made. • $6 • (03/31/95) • **79**

Key: SS—Spectator Selection. CS—Cellar Selection. BB—Best Buy. $NA—Price not available. (BT)—Barrel tasting. Ⓐ—Auction Price.
Dates in parentheses represent the issues in which the ratings were published.

CLOVERDALE RANCH | CALIFORNIA

Cabernet Sauvignon Alexander Valley Estate Cuvée 1991: A red of medium body with cedary currant and spice notes. Drinkable now. 1,300 cases made. • $12 • (11/15/94) • **83**

Cabernet Sauvignon Alexander Valley Estate Cuvée 1989 • $11 • (03/31/92) • **84**

COASTAL CELLARS | CALIFORNIA

Chardonnay California 1992: Medium-bodied and well proportioned, with spicy oak, ripe pear and fig notes and a smooth, elegant finish. 1,200 cases made. • $5 • (07/31/95) • **84**

Chardonnay Yakima Valley 1993: Remarkably fresh and spicy, the core of nectarine and apple flavors shines through, and the finish is crisp and focused. 2,500 cases made. • $6 • (06/30/96) • **87**

Pinot Noir California 1989 • $5 • (02/28/94) • **68**

CODORNIU NAPA | CALIFORNIA

Brut Napa Valley NV: Serves up a ripe beam of spice, pear and apple, then a touch of subtle black cherry emerges. It all adds up to an elegant and refined style. A tremendous value for such a sparkling wine. 15,000 cases made. • $13 • (12/15/95) SS • **90**

COHN, B.R. | CALIFORNIA

Cabernet Sauvignon Napa County Silver Label 1989 • $12 • (08/31/92) • **82**

Cabernet Sauvignon Napa Valley Silver Label 1988 • $12 • (09/30/91) • **87**

Cabernet Sauvignon Sonoma Valley 1991: Tannic and coarse, a rustic style with hearty Cabernet flavors but lacking polish and finesse. Probably best to drink soon before whatever fruit exists drops out. 3,000 cases made. • $12 • (11/15/94) • **83**

Cabernet Sauvignon Sonoma Valley Olive Hill Vineyard 1993: Dark, dense and tannic, with a rich, well-focused core of currant and cherry flavors. Turns substantially tannic on the finish, where the plush texture collides with the firmness. Ripe, fruity finish. 2,000 cases made. • $32 • (04/30/96) • **90**

Cabernet Sauvignon Sonoma Valley Olive Hill Vineyard 1991: Very ripe and fruity, with lovely plum, cherry and currant flavors and smooth tannins. It finishes with delicate grace. 2,800 cases made. • $28 • (04/15/95) • **91**

Cabernet Sauvignon Sonoma Valley Olive Hill Vineyard 1990: Ripe, smooth, rich and complex with pretty toasty, buttery oak and layers of cherry, currant, anise and plum-tinged fruit, with flavors that stay with you from start to finish. A very pretty young wine that's approachable now but sure to gain through 1997. 4,000 cases made. • $25 • (11/15/93) • **90**

Cabernet Sauvignon Sonoma Valley Olive Hill Vineyard 1989 • $25 • (08/31/92) • **86**

Cabernet Sauvignon Sonoma Valley Olive Hill Vineyard 1988 • $25 • (05/15/91) • **89**

Cabernet Sauvignon Sonoma Valley Olive Hill Vineyard 1987 • $31 Ⓐ • (06/30/90) • **92**

Cabernet Sauvignon Sonoma Valley Olive Hill Vineyard 1986 • $34 Ⓐ • (05/31/89) • **94**

Cabernet Sauvignon Sonoma Valley Olive Hill Vineyard 1985 • $16 • (03/01/89) • **94**

Cabernet Sauvignon Sonoma Valley Olive Hill Vineyard 1984 • $48 Ⓐ • (03/01/89) • **93**

Chardonnay Carneros 1993: Offers a range of citrus and apricot flavors, but turns a little earthy on the finish. 3,000 cases made. • $28 • (07/31/95) • **84**

Chardonnay Carneros Joseph Herman Vineyard Reserve 1993: Tight with a narrow band of pear and green nectarine flavors. 200 cases made. • $20 • (07/31/95) • **82**

Chardonnay Napa Valley Silver Label 1991 • $12 • (03/31/93) • **88**

Chardonnay Sonoma Valley Carneros 1992: Rough and raw in texture and flavor, packed with peach-scented apple and pear flavors, extending into a solid finish, echoing a touch of oak. Tasted twice. 3,500 cases made. • $12 • (11/30/93) • **87**

Merlot Napa-Sonoma Counties 1992: Smooth, generous and supple with gamy overtones to the basic berry flavors, turning a little tough and tannic on the finish. Best from 1997. 1,200 cases made. • $14 • (11/15/94) • **80**

Merlot Napa-Sonoma Counties 1990 • $14 • (10/31/92) • **84**

Merlot Napa Valley Silver Label 1989 • $14 • (11/15/91) • **82**

Merlot Sonoma Valley Olive Hill Vineyard 1994: Marked by a strong oaky character, the dill and berry flavors are pleasant but it turns astringent on the finish. 906 cases made. • $20 • (06/30/96) • **83**

COLBY | CALIFORNIA

Chardonnay Napa Valley 1993: Clean and well balanced, a modest style of appealing pear, apple and spice flavors. Citrus character on the finish. 846 cases made. • $12 • (05/15/96) • **83**

Chardonnay Napa Valley 1992: Lean and crisp, revealing a slight bitter undertone to the tart Chardonnay flavors. 1,191 cases made. • $12 • (05/15/95) • **83**

Chardonnay Napa Valley 1991: Tart and spicy, with green apple and citrus notes of modest weight. 2,100 cases made. • $14 • (03/31/95) • **83**

COLGIN | CALIFORNIA

Cabernet Sauvignon Napa Valley Herb Lamb Vineyard 1992: Dark, intense and compact, the focused black cherry and currant flavors giving a rich feel on the palate. A spicy anise finish brings out the supple tannins. Best after 1998. An impressive debut, but this wine will only be available directly from the winery, or in restaurants. 250 cases made. • $29 • (10/15/95) • **92**

COLONY | CALIFORNIA

Cabernet Sauvignon Sonoma County 1982 • $7 • (03/16/86) BB • **89**

COLORADO CELLARS | COLORADO

Alpenglo Riesling Turley Vineyards Colorado 1990 • $8 • (02/29/92) • **77**

Cherry Wine Colorado 1990 • $5 • (02/29/92) • **73**

Grand Gamé Rocky Mountain 1988 • $8 • (02/29/92) • **79**

COLUMBIA | WASHINGTON

Cabernet Franc Yakima Valley Red Willow Vineyard Signature Series 1993: Ripe, soft and appealing, laying out its berry flavor under a touch of spice, weaving in firm tannins that could use until 1997 or 1998. 450 cases made. • $16 • (09/30/95) • **87**

Cabernet Franc Yakima Valley Red Willow Vineyard Signature Series 1992: Bright and fruity, soft-textured, sharply focused, with marvelous berry and cranberry flavors and none of the stalkiness that afflicts other Cabernet Francs. Drinkable now. 400 cases made. • $16 • (09/30/94) • **87**

Cabernet Franc Yakima Valley Red Willow Vineyard Signature Series 1991 • $15 • (02/28/93) • **86**

Cabernet Sauvignon Columbia Valley 1992: Odd, foxy flavors keep this one a little off balance, but its intensity and richness suggest that aging until 1998 can bring it around. 14,500 cases made. • $13 • (03/31/96) • **86**

Cabernet Sauvignon Columbia Valley 1991: Smooth and silky, a lightly tannic red that should show off its well-turned blueberry, plum and spice flavors to best advantage by 1997. 300 cases made. • $13 • (09/30/94) • **86**

Cabernet Sauvignon Columbia Valley 1990: Herbal, minty overtones gallop through this lean, spicy wine, the mint and sage character outflanking the fruit right through the finish. Maybe best after 1996. 5,000 cases made. • $13 • (11/30/93) • **81**

Cabernet Sauvignon Columbia Valley 1989 • $12 • (10/15/92) SS • **90**

Cabernet Sauvignon Columbia Valley 1988 • $10 • (03/31/91) • **86**

Cabernet Sauvignon Columbia Valley 1987 • $9 • (06/15/90) • **87**

Cabernet Sauvignon Columbia Valley 1986 • $10 • (10/15/89) • **85**

Cabernet Sauvignon Columbia Valley 1985 • $9 • (07/15/88) • **79**

Cabernet Sauvignon Columbia Valley Otis Vineyard Signature Series 1988 • $20 • (04/15/92) • **89**

Cabernet Sauvignon Columbia Valley Red Willow Vineyard Signature Series 1988 • $20 • (04/15/92) • **86**

Cabernet Sauvignon Columbia Valley Sagemoor Vineyard 1985 • $15 • (10/15/89) • **85**

Cabernet Sauvignon Columbia Valley Sagemoor Vineyard Signature Series 1989 • $18 • (03/31/93) • **83**

Cabernet Sauvignon Columbia Valley Sagemoor Vineyard Signature Series 1988 • $20 • (04/30/92) • **81**

Cabernet Sauvignon Columbia Valley Sagemoor Vineyard Signature Series 1986 • $16 • (05/15/91) • **85**

Cabernet Sauvignon Columbia Valley Sagemoor Vineyards Signature Series 25th 1987: Firm and focused, with a rich core of currant, chocolate and spice flavors. The texture is supple and polished, with a long, full and tannic aftertaste. Drinks well now but should hold up well into 2000. 927 cases made. • $20 • (06/30/94) • **89**

Cabernet Sauvignon Washington Bacchus Vineyard 1981 • $12 • (08/01/84) • **86**

Cabernet Sauvignon Yakima Valley 1981 • $8 • (08/01/84) • **76**

Cabernet Sauvignon Yakima Valley Otis Vineyard 1985 • $15 • (10/15/89) • **91**

Cabernet Sauvignon Yakima Valley Otis Vineyard 1981 • $13 • (08/01/84) • **83**

Cabernet Sauvignon Yakima Valley Otis Vineyard Signature Series 1990: Tight and firm, with an austere band of herb, bell pepper and currant-laced Cabernet fruit. This will require cellaring to soften and evolve, but it may always be on the lean side. The tannin level suggests cellaring until 1997. 350 cases made. • $19 • (06/30/94) • **85**

Cabernet Sauvignon Yakima Valley Otis Vineyard Signature Series 1989 • $18 • (06/15/93) • **85**

Cabernet Sauvignon Yakima Valley Red Willow Vineyard 1985 • $15 • (10/15/89) • **82**

Cabernet Sauvignon Yakima Valley Red Willow Vineyard 1981 • $35 • (10/15/89) • **84**

Cabernet Sauvignon Yakima Valley Red Willow Vineyard David Lake Signature Series 1992: Firm and flavorful, sporting nice blackberry, currant and vanilla notes that remain juicy through the finish. Ready now. 950 cases made. • $21 • (05/15/96) • **87**

Cabernet Sauvignon Yakima Valley Red Willow Vineyard Signature Series 1991: Firm and focused, its tannins weaving through the slightly gamy black cherry and gently herbal flavors. Strives for elegance and should get there by 1998 or 1999. 850 cases made. • $20 • (08/31/95) • **88**

Cabernet Sauvignon Yakima Valley Red Willow Vineyard Signature Series 1989 • $18 • (05/31/93) • **89**

Cabernet Sauvignon Yakima Valley Red Willow Vineyard Signature Series 25th Anniversary 1987: Showing mature Cabernet flavors, with spicy currant, herb and cedary oak notes. Picks up substantial tannins on the finish, but it's also developing a plush texture. Ready now through 1999. 997 cases made. • $20 • (06/30/94) • **87**

Chardonnay Columbia Valley Woodburne Cuvée 1994: Refreshingly citrusy and delicately fruity, a mild mannered wine that's clean and immediately drinkable. 14,000 cases made. • $11 • (03/31/96) • **84**

Chardonnay Columbia Valley Woodburne Cuvée 1993: Fresh and lively, a beautifully balanced Chardonnay that shows off its pear, apple and spice notes with style. Flavors expand on the finish. 16,000 cases made. • $12 • (09/30/94) • **88**

Chardonnay Columbia Valley Woodburne Cuvée 1992: Crisp in texture and bright in flavor, with an orange-citrusy character at the core and some nice pineapple and toasty overtones. Drinkable now. 10,053 cases made. • $12 • (12/15/93) • **86**

Chardonnay Columbia Valley Woodburne Cuvée 1991 • $12 • (01/31/93) • **91**

Chardonnay Yakima Valley Wyckoff Vineyard David Lake Signature Series 1994: Fresh and floral, a silky-textured white that sneaks a delicious, honey edge onto the pear and spice flavors of the finish. Drinkable now. 2,250 cases made. • $15 • (04/30/96) • **88**

Chardonnay Yakima Valley Wyckoff Vineyard Signature Series 1993: Crisp, lively and brilliantly focused, presenting apple, pear and citrus flavors engagingly balanced to echo on the finish. 1,400 cases made. • $17 • (04/15/95) • **88**

COLUMBIA CREST

Chardonnay Yakima Valley Wyckoff Vineyard Signature Series 1991 • $15 • (02/28/94) • **82**

Chenin Blanc Yakima Valley 1994: Soft and effusively fruity, a gentle white offering lots of appealing pear flavor and a slightly floral finish. 2,700 cases made. • $6 • (09/30/95) • **84**

Gewürztraminer Yakima Valley 1995: Frankly sweet, with a delicate rose petal note persisting from first whiff to the finish, echoing pear and honey. 6,500 cases made. • $6 • (06/15/96) • **85**

Gewürztraminer Yakima Valley 1994: On the sweet side, flabby in texture, echoing grapey peach and honey notes. 4,500 cases made. • $6 • (09/30/95) • **78**

Gewürztraminer Yakima Valley 1993: Floral and succulent, pouring out distinctive rose petal and pineapple flavors. 6,500 cases made. • $6 • (09/30/94) • **85**

Gewürztraminer Yakima Valley 1992 • $6 • (05/31/94) • **79**

Johannisberg Riesling Columbia Valley 1994: Lightly sweet and generous apricot, peach and apple flavors and a refreshing touch of orange peel on the finish. 6,900 cases made. • $6 • (09/30/95) • **83**

Johannisberg Riesling Columbia Valley 1993: Soft and a little sweet, showing lots of pleasant apple and floral flavors. Drink soon. • $6 • (09/30/94) • **82**

Johannisberg Riesling Columbia Valley 1992 • $6 • (07/31/93) • **79**

Johannisberg Riesling Columbia Valley Cellarmaster's Reserve 1994: A little sugary, offering nice pear and honey notes. 13,000 cases made. • $6 • (09/30/95) • **82**

Johannisberg Riesling Columbia Valley Cellarmaster's Reserve 1993: Frankly sweet, with a spicy, honeyed edge to the apricot and pear flavors. Drinkable now. 8,000 cases made. • $7 • (09/30/94) • **85**

Johannisberg Riesling Columbia Valley Cellarmaster's Reserve 1992 • $7 • (07/31/93) • **79**

Johannisberg Riesling Late Harvest Columbia Valley Cellarmaster's Reserve 1988 • $7 • (10/15/89) BB • **85**

Merlot Red Willow Vineyard Milestone Signature 1989 • $18 • (06/15/92) • **88**

Merlot Columbia Valley 1993: Light-textured and simple in flavor, offering pleasant berry and spice flavors that linger. Best in 1997. 24,000 cases made. • $13 • (05/15/96) • **85**

Merlot Columbia Valley 1992: Bright and appealing, playing out its berry and currant flavors with style and grace, echoing nicely on the lively finish. 10,100 cases made. • $13 • (05/31/95) • **87**

Merlot Columbia Valley 1991: On the austere side, but well packed with berry, chocolate, currant and spice flavors that persist on the solid finish. Drinkable now. • $13 • (09/30/94) • **87**

Merlot Columbia Valley 1990 • $13 • (06/15/93) • **80**

Merlot Columbia Valley 1989 • $12 • (03/31/92) • **80**

Merlot Columbia Valley 1988 • $10 • (03/31/91) • **81**

Merlot Columbia Valley 1986 • $10 • (10/15/89) • **84**

Merlot Columbia Valley 1985 • $9 • (05/31/88) • **86**

Merlot Washington 1984 • $9 • (05/15/87) • **75**

Merlot Washington 1981 • $8 • (08/01/84) • **78**

Merlot Yakima Valley Milestone Merlot Signature Series 1992: Very firm and chewy, a tannic red that unfolds its spicy berry and black cherry flavors gradually. Needs until 1998 to show what it has. 1,800 cases made. • $20 • (09/30/94) • **85**

Merlot Yakima Valley Red Willow Vineyard Milestone 1987 • $15 • (10/15/89) • **80**

Merlot Yakima Valley Red Willow Vineyard Milestone David Lake Signature Series 1993: Ripe mouthful of spicy red berry and plum flavors, adding overtones of cedar and a touch of spice on the firm finish. Best in 1998. 2,350 cases made. • $20 • (05/15/96) • **87**

Merlot Yakima Valley Red Willow Vineyard Milestone David Lake Signature Series 1991 • $20 • (06/15/93) • **84**

Merlot Yakima Valley Red Willow Vineyard Milestone David Lake Signature Series 1988 • $16 • (03/31/91) • **82**

Merlot Yakima Valley Red Willow Vineyard 1989 • $20 • (11/15/91) • **89**

Pinot Noir Washington The Woodburne Collection 1987 • $10 • (03/31/91) • **88**

Key: SS—Spectator Selection. CS—Cellar Selection. BB—Best Buy. $NA—Price not available. (BT)—Barrel tasting. Ⓐ—Auction Price.
Dates in parentheses represent the issues in which the ratings were published.

Pinot Noir Washington Woodburne Cuvée 1993: Light in texture, sporting nicely focused currant and spice flavors that linger through the airy finish. Best in 1996. 2,400 cases made. • $11 • (09/30/95) • **85**

Pinot Noir Washington Woodburne Cuvée 1992: Light and spicy, with an earthy note that plays against the modest plum flavor. Drinkable now. • $12 • (09/30/94) • **82**

Pinot Noir Washington Woodburne Cuvée 1991 • $12 • (02/28/93) • **72**

Pinot Noir Washington Woodburne Cuvée 1990 • $12 • (03/31/92) • **77**

Pinot Noir Washington Woodburne Cuvée 1989 • $12 • (06/15/92) • **84**

Pinot Noir Washington Yakima County 1981 • $7 • (09/01/84) • **71**

Sauvignon Blanc Columbia Valley 1994: SImple, austere, haylike notes. 3,000 cases made. • $8 • (09/30/95) • **82**

Sauvignon Blanc Columbia Valley 1993: Crisp and tart, showing a strong grapefruit component that persists, clean and refreshing, from start to lively finish. 1,800 cases made. • $8 • (07/31/94) BB • **88**

Sémillon Columbia Valley 1994: This is a lean and refreshing white, offering lively peach and floral flavors. A great value from Washington. Drinkable now. 9,000 cases made. • $6 • (08/31/95) BB • **85**

Sémillon Columbia Valley 1993: Crisp and fruity. Fragrant, with tobacco and haylike notes to the bright lemon and pear flavors. Appealing, and best to drink now while it's fresh. 8,000 cases made. • $8 • (08/31/94) BB • **86**

Sémillon Columbia Valley 1992 • $6 • (09/30/93) BB • **85**

Sémillon Columbia Valley Chevrier Sur Lie 1994: Very pretty floral, citrusy flavors dance lightly on a delicate frame, then linger nicely on the finish. 1,950 cases made. • $9 • (05/15/96) • **88**

Sémillon Columbia Valley Chevrier Sur Lie 1993: Smooth, spicy and rich, with a floral edge to the pear and tobacco flavors. Drinkable now. 1,100 cases made. • $8 • (08/31/95) • **86**

Sémillon Columbia Valley Chevrier Sur Lie 1992: Somewhat flat and stale-tasting, but it picks up some nice honey and caramel notes on the long finish. 8,000 cases made. • $10 • (02/28/95) • **80**

Sémillon Columbia Valley Chevrier Sur Lie 1991 • $11 • (06/15/93) • **88**

Sémillon-Chardonnay Columbia Valley 1993: Firm and fruity, nectarine flavors taking the forefront, finishing with a flair of fresh fruit. Drinkable now. 2,500 cases made. • $8 • (09/15/94) BB • **87**

Sémillon-Chardonnay Washington 1994: Toasty, spicy flavors dominate this smooth and engaging white. Ready now. 3,500 cases made. • $8 • (09/30/95) • **84**

Seyval Blanc Washington 1994: Toasty, spicy flavors dominate this smooth, engaging wine, ready now. 3,500 cases made. • $8 • (09/30/95) • **84**

Syrah Yakima Valley Red Willow Vineyard 1993: Has smoky, slightly burnt additions to the pretty berry and spice flavors. Needs until 1998 or '99 for softening, but should be a beauty. 925 cases made. • $21 • (05/15/96) • **88**

Syrah Yakima Valley Red Willow Vineyard 1992: Rich and focused, firm-textured, spilling over with blackberry, black cherry and spice flavors that keep echoing on the finish. Tempting now, best from 1997 to 1998. 875 cases made. • $20 • (09/30/95) • **88**

Syrah Yakima Valley Red Willow Vineyard 1991: Firm in texture, a little gamy in flavor, with a chewy finish that echoes just enough blackberry flavor to suggest it might improve by 1997. 800 cases made. • $18 • (09/30/94) • **83**

Syrah Yakima Valley Red Willow Vineyard 1990 • $20 • (12/31/93) • **88**

Syrah Yakima Valley Red Willow Vineyard 1989 • $25 • (11/30/92) • **87**

Syrah Yakima Valley Red Willow Vineyard 1988 • $25 • (05/15/91) • **90**

COLUMBIA CREST | WASHINGTON

Cabernet Sauvignon Columbia Valley 1993: Dense and chewy without being rough, packed with ripe cherry and spice flavors that turn toward elegance on the finish. Delicious now, better in 1997. 130,000 cases made. • $9 • (06/15/96) • **87**

Cabernet Sauvignon Columbia Valley 1992: A firm and flavorful Washington red, showing true currant and berry flavors and a touch of leafy herbal character on the chewy finish. Try in 1998. 120,000 cases made. • $9 • (07/31/95) BB • **85**

Cabernet Sauvignon Columbia Valley 1991: Crisp and a little spicy, with enough plum and currant flavor to keep it interesting. Drinkable now, may be best in 1997. 41,000 cases made. • $9 • (09/30/94) • **84**

Cabernet Sauvignon Columbia Valley 1990: Supple and polished, with fine-textured, chewy tannins surrounding a modest core of berry and spice flavors. Tries hard to be supple and subtle, but ends up a bit too tannic for the rest of it. Try in 1997. • $10 • (11/30/93) • **82**
Cabernet Sauvignon Columbia Valley 1989 • $8 • (10/15/93) • **82**
Cabernet Sauvignon Columbia Valley 1988 • $9 • (07/31/92) SS • **89**
Cabernet Sauvignon Columbia Valley 1987 • $10 • (08/31/91) • **85**
Cabernet Sauvignon Columbia Valley 1986 • $8 • (01/31/91) BB • **88**
Cabernet Sauvignon Columbia Valley 1985 • $8 • (10/15/89) • **81**
Cabernet Sauvignon Columbia Valley 1984 • $7 • (07/15/88) • **79**
Cabernet Sauvignon Columbia Valley Barrel Select 1991: Lean, spicy oak flavors, the woody character overshadowing ripe cherry and tar notes pushing through tannins on the finish. Hard-edged, but may be best in 1998. • $15 • (05/31/96) • **85**
Cabernet Sauvignon Columbia Valley Barrel Select 1990: Earthy, meaty undertones add a little depth to this smooth-textured, spicy Cabernet. The black cherry and currant flavors sneak in on the finish. Drinkable now. 2,500 cases made. • $15 • (09/30/94) • **87**
Cabernet Sauvignon Columbia Valley Barrel Select 1989: 3,031 cases made. • $15 • (06/30/94) • **80**
Chardonnay Columbia Valley 1994: Light, juicy peach and apple flavors, smooth texture. Drinkable now. 330,000 cases made. • $8 • (04/30/96) • **84**
Chardonnay Columbia Valley 1993: A bright and fresh Washington white that's distinctive for its spicy nectarine and pear flavors that remain lively through the ripe finish. Drinkable now. 300,000 cases made. • $8 • (01/31/95) BB • **88**
Chardonnay Columbia Valley 1992: Juicy and polished. Its spicy vanilla overtones and silky texture show off the well-rounded pear and apple flavors. Elegant for the price. 300,000 cases made. • $8 • (01/31/94) SS • **88**
Chardonnay Columbia Valley 1991 • $8 • (03/31/93) BB • **84**
Chardonnay Columbia Valley Barrel Select 1993: Smooth and lively, butterscotch flavors yielding ultimately to zingy citrus and ripe pear on the harmonious finish. Delicious now. 1,083 cases made. • $10 • (09/30/95) • **88**
Chardonnay Columbia Valley Barrel Select 1992: Spicy, toasty notes fold together nicely with pear and grapefruit at the core, making this an appealing white to drink now for its range of flavors. 1,000 cases made. • $10 • (09/30/94) • **88**
Chardonnay Columbia Valley Barrel Select 1991 • $14 • (12/15/93) • **86**
Chardonnay Columbia Valley Reserve 1993: Its barrel-fermented and tastes like it, but terrific fruit pokes through on the finish and balances the oak with refreshing melon and citrus character. Smooth and potentially harmonious, this should be best from 1997. 180 cases made. • $14 • (03/31/96) • **89**
Gamay Beaujolais Columbia Valley 1993: Light and fruity, delicately spicy too, very pleasant and long on the finish. Best served slightly chilled. 13,000 cases made. • $7 • (09/30/94) • **85**
Gewürztraminer Columbia Valley 1995: Sweet, citrusy flavors show little Gewurztraminer character, but this makes a pleasant sipper. 23,000 cases made. • $6 • (06/15/96) • **80**
Gewürztraminer Columbia Valley 1994: Soft, simple and slightly sweet, showing modest nectarine and spice flavors. 13,000 cases made. • $6 • (09/30/95) • **80**
Gewürztraminer Columbia Valley 1993: A soft and refreshingly fruity Washington wine. The litchi, pear and grapefruit flavors pick up a touch of rose petal on the finish. Lovely to drink now. 8,000 cases made. • $6 • (02/28/95) BB • **85**
Gewürztraminer Columbia Valley 1992 • $6 • (05/31/94) • **82**
Johannisberg Riesling Columbia Valley 1995: Brightly aromatic, with a rush of apple and floral aromas that become soft and less lively on the palate. A pleasant sipper from Washington that's easy on the wallet. 25,000 cases made. • $6 • (06/15/96) BB • **84**
Johannisberg Riesling Columbia Valley 1994: Fresh and delicately sweet, a mouthful of nectarine and floral flavors that echo nicely on the finish. It makes a nice package at an attractive price. 26,000 cases made. • $6 • (09/30/95) • **86**
Johannisberg Riesling Columbia Valley 1993: Bright and fruity, light on its feet, deftly balancing a real moutfhul of spicy nectarine and peach fruit on an easy-drinking frame. 10,000 cases made. • $6 • (09/30/94) BB • **87**
Johannisberg Riesling Columbia Valley 1992 • $6 • (07/31/93) • **77**
Johannisberg Riesling Columbia Valley 1991 • $6 • (11/30/92) • **74**
Merlot Columbia Valley 1993: Ripe, smooth and distinctly gamy, making this a Washington red that gives you some character for the money. There's a hint of the barnyard in the delicious blackberry and currant flavors. Fine tannins should be about right in 1997 or '98. 230,000 cases made. • $10 • (05/31/96) BB • **88**
Merlot Columbia Valley 1992: Light and zingy, a lively red that puts some zip behind its raspberry and currant flavors, finishing with a pleasant touch of vanilla and spice. Tasty to drink now. 163,000 cases made. • $10 • (09/30/94) • **87**
Merlot Columbia Valley 1991 • $10 • (04/15/94) BB • **88**
Merlot Columbia Valley 1990 • $10 • (05/31/93) • **85**
Merlot Columbia Valley 1989 • $10 • (02/29/92) SS • **88**
Merlot Columbia Valley 1987 • $8 • (09/30/90) BB • **86**
Merlot Columbia Valley 1985 • $8 • (10/15/89) • **85**
Merlot Columbia Valley 1984 • $7 • (05/31/88) • **78**
Merlot Columbia Valley Barrel Select 1992: Light in texture, nicely focused, as basic blackberry flavors and black pepper overtones emerge on the finish. Drinkable now. 5,600 cases made. • $15 • (05/15/96) • **88**
Merlot Columbia Valley Barrel Select 1991: Beguiling stuff, brash and oaky up front, then a firm touch of tannin and toasty anise flavors and finally more berry and currant. Approachable now, best in 1997. 5,200 cases made. • $15 • (09/30/95) • **87**
Merlot Columbia Valley Barrel Select 1990: Smooth, ripe and spicy, not a huge wine, but it delivers a nice mouthful of chocolate-scented plum, blackberry and cedar flavors. Drinkable now. 6,000 cases made. • $15 • (09/30/94) • **86**
Merlot Columbia Valley Barrel Select 1989 • $15 • (05/31/93) • **88**
Merlot Columbia Valley Barrel Select 1988 • $15 • (07/31/92) • **87**
Merlot Columbia Valley Barrel Select 1987 • $15 • (05/31/91) • **84**
Red Reserve Columbia Valley 1992: Lithe and elegant, deftly balanced to show off its smoothly integrated berry, red plum and spice flavors, hinting at smoke on the finish. Try in 1997 or 1998. 227 cases made. • $18 • (07/31/95) • **90**
Riesling Columbia Valley Dry 1991 • $6 • (11/30/92) BB • **82**
Sauvignon Blanc Columbia Valley 1993: Light, lean and fruity, nicely balanced if not especially distinctive. 27,000 cases made. • $7 • (07/31/94) • **82**
Sauvignon Blanc Columbia Valley 1992 • $7 • (01/31/94) BB • **86**
Sauvignon Blanc Columbia Valley 1991 • $7 • (08/31/93) • **80**
Sémillon-Chardonnay Columbia Valley 1994: Lean, floral and fragrant, balanced by just enough citrusy fruit. 40,000 cases made. • $7 • (05/15/96) • **84**
Sémillon-Chardonnay Columbia Valley 1993: Smooth and a little sweet, with a fruit cocktail-pear character that hangs on through the bright finish. Drinkable now. 23,000 cases made. • $7 • (09/30/94) • **84**
Sémillon-Chardonnay Columbia Valley 1992 • $7 • (05/15/94) BB • **83**
Sémillon-Chardonnay Columbia Valley 1991 • $7 • (02/15/93) BB • **85**
Sémillon Columbia Valley 1994: Bright and citrusy, shaded by a touch of smoke and tobacco, finishing buttery and smooth. A bargain from Washington made to enjoy now. 14,000 cases made. • $6 • (05/15/96) BB • **85**
Sémillon Columbia Valley 1993: Light and fruity, simple, appealing for its citrusy pear flavors. Drinkable now. Tasted twice. 13,000 cases made. • $6 • (09/30/94) • **84**
Sémillon Columbia Valley 1992 • $6 • (05/15/94) BB • **82**
Sémillon Columbia Valley 1991 • $6 • (02/15/93) BB • **87**
Sémillon Late Harvest Columbia Valley 1992: Beautifully rich, focused and exquisitely balanced, this has it all. Its honey-scented pear, pineapple and apricot flavors linger and echo on the finish, supported by just the right amount of zingy acidity. Drinkable now, but should improve through 2001, maybe 2005. 420 cases made. • $8 • (04/30/95) • **93**
Sémillon-Sauvignon Columbia Valley 1992: Bright and fruity, with a spice-pineapple streak running through the pear flavors, fresh and appealing to drink now. Tasted twice. 2,700 cases made. • $7 • (08/31/94) • **83**
Vineyard Reserve Columbia Valley 1986 • $5 • (10/15/89) • **64**

CONCANNON | CALIFORNIA

Assemblage Livermore Valley 1993: Soft and appealing, with a touch of spice and honey sneaking in on the light finish. 983 cases made. • $15 • (08/31/95) • **80**

Assemblage Livermore Valley 1991: Earthy and herbal, a bit on the murky side, with muddled, chalky Cabernet fruit. Hard to predict whether this one will improve. 635 cases made. • $15 • (11/15/94) • **80**

Assemblage Reserve Central Coast 1992: Smooth and flavorful, sneaking in a cola edge to the black cherry flavors that keep sailing through the finish. Best from 1997. 990 cases made. • $15 • (12/15/95) • **86**

Cabernet Sauvignon Central Coast Selected Vineyard 1992: Supple and spicy, with an herb and cedar edge to the Cabernet flavors. Still, plenty of fruit comes through on the finish. Ready now. 9,200 cases made. • $10 • (11/15/94) • **84**

Cabernet Sauvignon Livermore Valley 1983 • $12 • (06/15/87) • **77**

Cabernet Sauvignon Livermore Valley 1981 • $12 • (12/16/84) • **82**

Cabernet Sauvignon Livermore Valley Concannon Estate Vineyard 1991: A wine with a smoky, herbal and bell pepper edge, but not much else. Those flavors turn to tobacco and spice on the finish. Drink now. 8,101 cases made. • $9 • (11/15/93) • **79**

Cabernet Sauvignon Livermore Valley Concannon Estate Vineyard 1989 • $10 • (11/15/93) • **78**

Cabernet Sauvignon Livermore Valley Reserve 1987 • $16 • (07/15/91) • **83**

Cabernet Sauvignon Livermore Valley Reserve 1985 • $14 • (02/15/89) • **87**

Chardonnay Central Coast Selected Vineyards 1993: Well crafted, striking a nice balance between ripe the ripe pear and apple notes and light oak flavors, finishing with a grassy edge. 21,000 cases made. • $10 • (07/31/95) • **84**

Chardonnay Central Coast Selected Vineyards 1992: Strikes a nice balance between ripe, bright peach- and apple-laced Chardonnay and light oak shadings, finishes with a pretty fruity aftertaste. Ready now. 21,600 cases made. • $11 • (05/15/94) • **86**

Chardonnay Central Coast Selected Vineyards 1991 • $10 • (07/15/93) • **82**

Chardonnay Livermore Valley Limited Bottling Reserve 1991: Bright and fruity, but it has a metallic streak that robs it of much of its charm. 1,032 cases made. • $15 • (06/30/94) • **77**

Chardonnay Livermore Valley Reserve 1993: Offers attractive ripe pear, apple and spice notes with light toasty oak shadings, turning complex on the finish. Well crafted. 298 cases made. • $15 • (07/31/95) • **87**

Petite Sirah Central Coast Selected Vineyard 1991: An earthy character colors the black cherry flavor. It finishes soft and a little short. Drinkable now. 32,000 cases made. • $10 • (02/28/95) • **81**

Petite Sirah Livermore Valley 1987 • $11 • (08/31/91) • **77**

Petite Sirah Livermore Valley Reserve 1985 • $15 • (08/31/91) • **83**

Sangiovese Central Coast Rosé of Sangiovese 1993: Raspberry jam comes to mind when smelling this fruit bomb, which reminds us more of juice than wine. • $8 • (09/15/95) • **76**

Sauvignon Blanc Livermore Valley 1992 • $8 • (05/15/94) • **81**

Sauvignon Blanc Livermore Valley James Concannon Vineyard 1993: Simple and soft, a little floral but only vaguely fruity. 3,606 cases made. • $8 • (08/31/95) • **78**

CONGRESS SPRINGS | CALIFORNIA

Brut Santa Clara County Brut de Pinot 1986 • $8 • (03/31/88) • **77**

Cabernet Franc Santa Cruz Mountains 1986 • $18 • (07/31/89) • **88**

Merlot Santa Clara County 1988 • $14 • (03/31/91) • **74**

Pinot Noir Santa Clara County 1989 • $10 • (04/30/91) • **84**

Pinot Noir Santa Clara County San Ysidro Vineyard 1988 • $9 • (03/31/90) • **87**

Zinfandel Santa Cruz Mountains 1987 • $12 • (03/15/90) • **83**

Key: SS—Spectator Selection. CS—Cellar Selection. BB—Best Buy. $NA—Price not available. (BT)—Barrel tasting. (A)—Auction Price.
Dates in parentheses represent the issues in which the ratings were published.

CONN CREEK | CALIFORNIA

Anthology Napa Valley 1992: Firm and tannic, but the ripe fruit flavors are pretty, with plum, wild berry and cherry notes filling out the sage and spice notes. Has the tannins to age into 1999, but it may still be tannic. 1,175 cases made. • $30 • (12/15/95) • **90**

Anthology Napa Valley 1991: Complex and elegant, with supple, polished currant, black cherry, plum and vanilla flavors that fold together nicely, finishing with a long, full aftertaste and pretty fruit flavors that linger. A wine of harmony and grace. Best after 1998 or 1999. 1,062 cases made. • $30 • (09/30/94) CS • **93**

Cabernet Sauvignon Napa Valley 1992: Firm and tight with a pretty band of floral- and currant-scented fruit. Young and unevolved, but balanced, showing toasty oak. 5,000 cases made. • $NA • (05/31/93) BT • **886**

Cabernet Sauvignon Napa Valley 1981 • $18 • (03/01/89) • **85**

Cabernet Sauvignon Napa Valley 1980 • $35 • (03/01/89) • **88**

Cabernet Sauvignon Napa Valley 1979 • $17 (A) • (03/01/89) • **77**

Cabernet Sauvignon Napa Valley 1977 • $27 • (03/01/89) • **90**

Cabernet Sauvignon Napa Valley 1976 • $40 • (03/01/89) • **86**

Cabernet Sauvignon Napa Valley 1974: Deeply colored and richly concentrated, with spice, currant, cedar and leather notes. This high-extract, complex Cabernet has begun to dry out, leaving considerable tannin on the long minerally finish. Made from Eisele Vineyard grapes. 900 cases made. • $250 • (11/15/94) • **88**

Cabernet Sauvignon Napa Valley Barrel Select 1991: Firm and tight, showing a narrow, compact band of cherry and currant flavor. Finishes with earthy tannins and a dash of oak. Needs cellaring until 1998. 1,000 cases made. • $18 • (11/15/94) • **85**

Cabernet Sauvignon Napa Valley Barrel Select 1988 • $15 • (10/31/92) • **84**

Cabernet Sauvignon Napa Valley Barrel Select 1987 • $17 • (07/15/91) • **87**

Cabernet Sauvignon Napa Valley Barrel Select 1986 • $18 • (02/28/91) • **55**

Cabernet Sauvignon Napa Valley Barrel Select 1985 • $29 • (09/15/90) • **90**

Cabernet Sauvignon Napa Valley Barrel Select 1983 • $30 • (03/01/89) • **82**

Cabernet Sauvignon Napa Valley Barrel Select 1982 • $22 • (03/01/89) • **85**

Cabernet Sauvignon Napa Valley Barrel Select Lot 79 1984 • $22 • (03/01/89) • **86**

Cabernet Sauvignon Napa Valley Barrel Select Private Reserve 1986 • $40 • (12/15/90) • **91**

Cabernet Sauvignon Napa Valley Barrel Select Private Reserve 1985 • $45 • (09/15/90) • **91**

Cabernet Sauvignon Napa Valley Collins Vineyard Private Reserve 1984 • $28 • (03/31/89) • **94**

Cabernet Sauvignon Napa Valley Collins Vineyard Proprietor's Special Selection 1983 • $70 • (03/01/89) • **87**

Cabernet Sauvignon Napa Valley Collins Vineyard Proprietor's Special Selection 1982 • $70 • (03/01/89) • **85**

Cabernet Sauvignon Napa Valley Collins Vineyard Proprietor's Special Selection 1981 • $70 • (03/01/89) • **86**

Cabernet Sauvignon Napa Valley Collins Vineyard Proprietor's Special Selection 1980 • $55 • (03/01/89) • **93**

Cabernet Sauvignon Napa Valley Limited Release 1992: Ripe and fruity, with spicy plum, cherry and currant flavors. An elegant, well-crafted wine that's tempting to drink now, but has intensity and depth. 1,500 cases made. • $18 • (12/15/95) • **88**

Cabernet Sauvignon Napa Valley Limited Release 1991: Well focused, with supple currant and black cherry flavors that turn smooth and polished, finishing with a spicy anise edge. Medium-bodied, with good length. Approachable now. • $18 • (11/15/94) • **88**

Cabernet Sauvignon Napa Valley Lot 2 1978 • $43 • (11/15/92) • **86**

Cabernet Sauvignon Napa Valley Reserve 1987 • $23 • (08/31/92) • **87**

Cabernet Sauvignon Stags Leap District 1973 • $53 • (03/01/89) • **92**

Merlot Napa Valley Barrel Select 1990: Crisp and firm, with intriguing flavors that range from ripe plum to tobacco, spice and herb notes. Firm tannins on the finish suggest short-term cellaring. 530 cases made. • $14 • (09/15/94) • **84**

Merlot Napa Valley Barrel Select 1989 • $16 • (10/31/92) • **80**
Merlot Napa Valley Barrel Select 1988 • $22 • (11/15/91) • **86**
Merlot Napa Valley Collins Vineyard 1985 • $14 • (03/31/88) • **84**
Merlot Napa Valley Collins Vineyard Barrel Select Limited 1987 • $22 • (12/31/90) • **87**
Merlot Napa Valley Limited Release 1991: Despite its bottle age and late release, there's not much to this wine. It comes across as simple, with light cherry and berry flavors. 500 cases made. • $15 • (06/30/96) • **83**
Triomphe Napa Valley 1987 • $26 • (07/15/92) • **89**
Zinfandel Napa Valley 1979 • $7 • (03/16/84) • **60**
Zinfandel Napa Valley Barrel Select 1988 • $10 • (10/15/92) • **82**
Zinfandel Napa Valley Barrel Select 1987 • $10 • (11/15/91) • **80**
Zinfandel Napa Valley Barrel Select 1986 • $9 • (10/15/90) • **86**
Zinfandel Napa Valley Collins Vineyard 1983 • $10 • (12/15/88) • **84**

COOK, R & J | CALIFORNIA

Delta Clarksburg Red Table Wine NV • $3 • (11/15/87) • **75**
Merlot Clarksburg 1989 • $9 • (05/31/92) • **82**
Petite Sirah Clarksburg 1984 • $6 • (12/31/87) • **73**
Petite Sirah Clarksburg 1981 • $5 • (12/16/84) • **86**

COOK'S | CALIFORNIA

Brut American Champagne NV • $4 • (03/31/92) • **74**
Brut American Imperial Grand Reserve Extremely Dry NV • $6 • (12/31/87) • **75**
Cabernet Sauvignon California Captain's Reserve 1988 • $5 • (07/15/92) BB • **80**
Extra Dry American NV • $4 • (03/31/92) • **76**
Extremely Dry Grand Reserve American NV • $4 • (03/31/92) • **70**
Merlot California Captain's Reserve 1992: Light and fruity, with appealing currant and berry flavors. Drinkable now. 150,000 cases made. • $5 • (09/15/94) BB • **81**
Merlot California Captain's Reserve 1989 • $5 • (05/31/92) • **77**
Rosé American Blush NV • $4 • (10/15/88) • **72**

COOPER-GARROD | CALIFORNIA

Cabernet Franc Santa Cruz Mountains 1994: Light and uncomplicated, showing a very modest band of cherry and herb. Lacks depth and concentration. 850 cases made. • $18 • (04/30/96) • **77**
Cabernet Franc Santa Cruz Mountains Premier Release 1992: Marked by a wild berry and spritzy edge, it delivers decent flavor but lacks focus and harmony. 140 cases made. • $16 • (02/28/95) • **80**
Cabernet Sauvignon Santa Cruz Mountains 1992: A touch earthy, but with enough plum and cherry showing to hold your interest. Finishes with supple tannins. 240 cases made. • $20 • (03/31/96) • **82**
Chardonnay Santa Cruz Mountains 1994: Strives for complexity with its layers of flavor. Serves up a rich core of pear, apple and oak flavors. Finishes with a long aftertaste. 770 cases made. • $18 • (02/29/96) • **89**
Chardonnay Santa Cruz Mountains Premier Release 1992: Firm and fruity, exhibiting pretty pear, peach, nectarine and spicy oak flavors that fold together nicely, finishing with an elegant, complex aftertaste. Impressive and ready now. 520 cases made. • $16 • (12/15/94) • **90**

COOPERS' LEGACY | CALIFORNIA

Chardonnay Sonoma County 1993: Perfumed with ripe pear and honeyed notes of medium weight. 1,002 cases made. • $9 • (07/31/95) • **82**
Merlot Sonoma County 1993: Dry and chunky, with hints of currant and berry flavors. Finish is tannic and slightly green. 909 cases made. • $12 • **79**

CORBETT CANYON | CALIFORNIA

Cabernet Sauvignon Alexander Valley Reserve 1989 • $8 • (11/15/92) BB • **85**
Cabernet Sauvignon California Coastal Classic 1991: A generous beam of blackberry and currant flavors streaks through this light, simple, fruity wine that finishes lively and refreshing. Drink soon. Tasted twice, with consistent notes. • $6 • (06/15/93) • **80**
Cabernet Sauvignon California Coastal Classic 1989 • $7 • (11/15/91) • **76**
Cabernet Sauvignon Central Coast 1983 • $7 • (05/16/86) BB • **80**
Cabernet Sauvignon Central Coast Coastal Classic 1986 • $6 • (12/15/89) • **80**
Cabernet Sauvignon Central Coast Reserve 1987 • $9 • (11/15/91) • **82**
Cabernet Sauvignon Central Coast Select 1984 • $8 • (02/15/87) • **82**
Cabernet Sauvignon Napa Valley Reserve 1991: A grapey style of Cabernet with a coarse, tannic edge. Packs intense flavors, but is short on finesse. Ready now through 1997. • $9 • (09/30/94) • **82**
Cabernet Sauvignon Napa Valley Reserve 1990: Deftly balanced and easy to drink, this full-flavored Cabernet is soft on tannins and long on fruit flavors. Throws in hints of spice and sweet vanilla to complement the solid cherry and currant flavors. • $9 • (09/15/93) BB • **84**
Cabernet Sauvignon Santa Barbara-San Luis Obispo Counties Select 1985 • $10 • (05/31/88) • **79**
Cabernet Sauvignon Sonoma-Napa Counties Reserve 1989 • $8 • (11/15/92) • **74**
Chardonnay California Coastal Classic 1995: Light and refreshing for its youthful grapefruit and pineapple flavors. 40,000 cases made. • $6 • (06/15/96) • **82**
Chardonnay Central Coast Coastal Classic 1993: Light and fruity, displaying a slight metallic edge to the peach and pear flavors. Drinkable now. 105,000 cases made. • $5 • (01/31/95) • **80**
Chardonnay Central Coast Coastal Classic 1992: Has an ashy, spoiled fruit edge to the otherwise appealing apple and pear flavors, finishing crisp and slightly sweet. Drinkable now. 30,000 cases made. • $5 • (03/31/94) • **79**
Chardonnay Central Coast Coastal Classic 1991 • $6 • (11/30/92) • **77**
Chardonnay Santa Barbara County Reserve 1993: Simple, rather like canned pears in flavor, finishing fresh. Drinkable now. 3,700 cases made. • $9 • (01/31/95) • **81**
Chardonnay Santa Barbara County Reserve 1992: Moderate intensity and depth, with spice, pear and light oak shadings, it drinks well now. 2,100 cases made. • $9 • (06/30/94) • **82**
Chardonnay Santa Barbara County Reserve 1991 • $9 • (07/15/93) • **75**
Merlot California Coastal Classic 1992: Simple and fruity. More like a light style of Zinfandel than Merlot, but pleasant and quaffable. 12,000 cases made. • $7 • (09/15/94) BB • **82**
Merlot California Coastal Classic 1991 • $6 • (11/30/92) • **79**
Merlot California Coastal Classic 1989 • $7 • (11/15/91) BB • **81**
Pinot Noir Central Coast Reserve 1989 • $9 • (11/15/91) • **81**
Pinot Noir Central Coast Reserve 1986 • $8 • (12/15/89) • **83**
Pinot Noir Santa Barbara County Coastal Classic 1990 • $7 • (02/28/93) • **71**
Pinot Noir Santa Barbara County Reserve 1992: Simple but pleasant, with light cherry, earth and spice notes. Drinkable now. 1,300 cases made. • $9 • (03/31/95) • **82**
Pinot Noir Santa Barbara County Reserve 1991 • $9 • (02/28/93) • **72**
Pinot Noir Santa Barbara County Reserve 1990 • $8 • (02/28/93) • **73**
Pinot Noir Santa Maria Valley Sierra Madre Vineyard Reserve 1985 • $12 • (02/15/88) • **81**
Sauvignon Blanc California Coastal Classic 1995: Earthy, cardboardy flavors are unpleasant. • $NA • **74**
Sauvignon Blanc Central Coast Coastal Classic 1992 • $4 • (06/30/93) BB • **82**
Sauvignon Blanc Central Coast Costal Classic 1994: A strong vegetal flavor pervades this smooth, oaky white, making it seem off-balanced. 10,000 cases made. • $5 • (08/31/95) • **77**
Zinfandel San Luis Obispo County Select 1984 • $7 • (05/15/88) • **87**

CORISON | CALIFORNIA

Cabernet Sauvignon Napa Valley 1992: Bold, ripe, rich and concentrated, with layers of plum and currant flavors, accented by anise, toasty oak and tobacco character. Finishes firmly tannic, long and full. Try in 1998 or later. 2,500 cases made. • $28 • (11/30/95) CS • **92**
Cabernet Sauvignon Napa Valley 1991: Strives for complexity with its leathery coffee and currant flavors. It turns dry and tannic on the finish, although the fruit still sneaks through. Needs time, try after 1999. 2,500 cases made. • $26 • (10/15/94) • **89**
Cabernet Sauvignon Napa Valley 1990: Smooth and generous, with ripe currant, cherry and chocolate aromas and flavors, all of it holding

together in elegance and harmony. Has all the pieces to continue developing though 2000. 2,500 cases made. • $24 • (10/15/93) • **91**
Cabernet Sauvignon Napa Valley 1989 • $26 • (11/15/92) • **88**
Cabernet Sauvignon Napa Valley 1988 • $25 • (11/15/91) • **89**
Cabernet Sauvignon Napa Valley 1987 • $20 • (11/15/90) • **92**

CORNERSTONE | CALIFORNIA

Cabernet Sauvignon Howell Mountain Beatty Ranch 1992: Elegant and well mannered, with a well-focused band of currant, spice and black cherry, finishing with complex flavors and fine but firm tannins. Best after 2000. 975 cases made. • $33 • (12/15/95) • **90**
Cabernet Sauvignon Howell Mountain Beatty Ranch 1991: Ripe and generous, with a tight, focused band of currant, plum and black cherry flavors that are plush and concentrated, finishing with a long, complex aftertaste. Has the tannins to age, best around 2000. 500 cases made. • $33 • (11/15/94) • **93**

COSENTINO | CALIFORNIA

Cabernet Franc Napa County 1987 • $13 • (09/30/89) • **75**
Cabernet Franc North Coast 1990 • $16 • (11/15/92) • **83**
Cabernet Franc North Coast 1989 • $16 • (11/15/92) • **78**
Cabernet Franc North Coast 1988 • $16 • (11/15/91) • **80**
Cabernet Franc North Coast 1986 • $14 • (07/31/88) • **92**
Cabernet Sauvignon Napa County 1990: Ripe and jammy, with straightforward Cabernet flavors that show hints of plum and cherry and spicy oak notes around the edges. Drinkable now. 2,000 cases made. • $15 • (11/15/93) • **81**
Cabernet Sauvignon Napa County 1989 • $15 • (03/31/92) • **86**
Cabernet Sauvignon Napa Valley 1991: Young and tight, with a compact band of spice, herb, mineral and currant flavors that are well focused and lingering on the finish. It's quite tannic and concentrated, it should be softer by 1997. 1,400 cases made. • $16 • (10/31/94) • **86**
Cabernet Sauvignon Napa Valley 1990: Young and tight, a bit austere with chewy currant and cedary notes. Tough to judge at this stage, but perhaps with time it will have become more forthcoming. 2,000 cases made. • $15 • (11/15/93) • **86**
Cabernet Sauvignon Napa Valley Punched Cap Fermented Unfined 1992: Offers a pretty array of ripe plum and cherry flavors before tannins step in, adding cedar and tobacco to the finish. Try in 1997. 2,500 cases made. • $16 • (09/15/95) • **88**
Cabernet Sauvignon Napa Valley Reserve 1994: A touch earthy, but the toasty oak and currant flavors are medium-weight, but not especially concentrated. 600 cases made. • $24 • (05/31/95) • **85-89** (BT)
Cabernet Sauvignon Napa Valley Reserve 1991: Lithe, juicy and refreshing, flavors focusing on plum, berry and vanilla, matching grace with strength on the distinctive finish. Tannins are fine, best from 1998. 300 cases made. • $30 • (12/15/95) • **90**
Cabernet Sauvignon Napa Valley Reserve 1990: Very ripe with a cherry jam and raspberry edge, elegant and supple on the finish, where the flavors linger. Mild tannins make it approachable now, will gain through 1999. 250 cases made. • $25 • (11/15/94) • **87**
Cabernet Sauvignon Napa Valley The Winemaster 1989 • $20 • (11/15/92) • **80**
Cabernet Sauvignon North Coast 1988 • $15 • (05/31/91) • **88**
Cabernet Sauvignon North Coast 1987 • $16 • (06/30/90) • **80**
Cabernet Sauvignon North Coast 1985 • $11 • (09/15/88) • **84**
Cabernet Sauvignon North Coast Reserve 1988 • $25 • (08/31/92) • **81**
Cabernet Sauvignon North Coast Reserve 1987 • $28 • (02/28/91) • **86**
Cabernet Sauvignon North Coast Reserve 1986 • $18 • (05/15/90) • **90**
Cabernet Sauvignon North Coast Reserve 1985 • $18 • (04/30/89) • **81**
Cabernet Sauvignon North Coast Reserve 1984 • $14 • (03/31/88) • **78**
Chardonnay Napa County 1992: Ripe and creamy with an elegant framework and spicy pear, vanilla, fig and melon notes that build intensity on the finish. Well balanced with a flavorful aftertaste. Ready now. 2,000 cases made. • $15 • (03/31/94) • **86**

Key: SS—Spectator Selection. CS—Cellar Selection. BB—Best Buy. $NA—Price not available. (BT)—Barrel tasting. Ⓐ—Auction Price.
Dates in parentheses represent the issues in which the ratings were published.

Chardonnay Napa Valley 1994: Strikes a nice balance between the ripe pear, citrus and honey notes and the light oak flavors. 2,600 cases made. • $14 • (06/30/96) • **85**
Chardonnay Napa Valley 1993: Tart with a lemony edge to the pear and spice notes. Medium weight and well balanced. 2,500 cases made. • $15 • (07/31/95) • **83**
Chardonnay Napa Valley 1991 • $14 • (01/31/93) • **87**
Chardonnay Napa Valley The Sculptor 1992: Crisp and fruity, a simple wine with appealing apple and nectarine flavors. A little too much sculpted off it? 600 cases made. • $20 • (06/30/94) • **81**
Chardonnay Napa Valley The Sculptor 1991 • $20 • (07/15/93) • **85**
Chardonnay Napa Valley The Sculptor Reserve 1994: Delivers nice oak and ripe fruit flavors that aim for complexity, but come up just a bit short. 1,050 cases made. • $25 • (06/30/96) • **85**
Chardonnay Napa Valley The Sculptor Reserve 1993: Lean and trim, with an earthy edge to the ripe pear and apple flavors. 900 cases made. • $24 • (02/28/95) • **86**
M. Coz Napa Valley Meritage 1992: Well oaked, with a stylish vanilla bean and wood edge, packing in lots of plush currant, black cherry, anise and spice flavors. Big, bold and complex, with a wonderful sense of harmony and finesse. 400 cases made. • $45 • (12/15/95) • **92**
M. Coz Napa Valley Meritage 1991: Strikes a nice balance between ripe, spicy Cabernet fruit and buttery oak, but it needs a good three years' cellaring to soften and round out the rough edges. Best after 1999. • $45 • (11/15/94) • **89**
M. Coz Napa Valley Meritage 1990: An elegant and richly fruity wine with wonderful texture and detail, as the currant, black cherry, vanilla and cedar flavors gently unfold, finishing with excellent length, fine tannins and a burst of fruit. Refined enough to drink tonight, but it should age well through the decade. 330 cases made. • $45 • (11/15/93) • **92**
M. Coz Napa Valley Meritage 1989 • $45 • (11/15/92) • **90**
M. Coz Napa Valley Meritage 1988 • $45 • (11/15/91) • **89**
Merlot Napa County 1988 • $18 • (04/15/91) • **82**
Merlot Napa County 1986 • $14 • (09/30/88) • **85**
Merlot Napa County Reserve 1987 • $18 • (07/31/90) • **80**
Merlot Napa Valley 1992: Supple and elegant, with ripe, fleshy currant, black cherry, herb and buttery oak shadings. This is a fine effort by Cosentino, one that combines finesse with polished fruit flavors. 1,000 cases made. • $19 • (09/15/94) • **88**
Merlot Napa Valley 1991: Tight and firm, with a very narrow band of cedary cherry flavors that are wrapped in drying tannins. May come around with time in the bottle. 1,124 cases made. • $18 • (09/15/94) • **77**
Merlot Napa Valley 1990 • $18 • (06/15/93) • **84**
Merlot Napa Valley 1989 • $18 • (05/31/92) • **85**
Merlot Napa Valley Oakville 1994: Smooth and polished, with a rich core of currant, chocolate and berry notes that finish with soft tannins. 465 cases made. • $38 • (06/30/96) • **87**
Merlot Napa Valley Oakville 1993: Ripe, nicely balanced, appealing plum, black cherry, herb, cedar and toasty oak notes. The finish features a complex interplay of flavors and mild tannins. Best in 1997. 200 cases made. • $30 • (12/15/95) • **89**
Merlot Napa Valley Oakville 1992: Not as rich and chewy as the other, non-vineyard-designated bottling, but makes up for it with its suppleness, elegance and complexity. This Oakville-grown Merlot serves up a pretty range of silky currant, coffee, vanilla and spice notes that glide across the palate. Drinks well now. 52 cases made. • $28 • (09/15/94) • **89**
Pinot Noir Carneros 1994: Light in color and body, offering earthy cherry, berry and toasty oak flavors that build intensity on the finish. Picks up a tea and tannic edge. 800 cases made. • $25 • (02/29/96) • **84**
Pinot Noir Carneros 1991 • $18 • (02/28/94) • **82**
Pinot Noir Carneros Unfined & Unfiltered 1993: Modest herb and cola flavors are framed by toasty, buttery oak. Drinkable now. 700 cases made. • $25 • (03/31/95) • **84**
Pinot Noir Carneros Unfined & Unfiltered 1992 • $20 • (02/28/94) • **89**
Pinot Noir Napa Valley 1990 • $14 • (09/30/92) • **83**
Pinot Noir Napa Valley LZ 1994: Well oaked, featuring toasty, buttery wood notes and a decent core of cherry and berry flavors. Has more depth and substance than the Carneros bottling. 500 cases made. • $20 • (02/29/96) • **87**

Pinot Noir Napa Valley Punched Cap Fermented Unfiltered and Unfined 1993: Herb, oak and cola flavors predominate, but enough black cherry and plum flavor comes through to hold your interest. 700 cases made. • $25 • (05/15/95) • **86**

Pinot Noir Napa Valley Unfined & Unfiltered 1993: Leans toward an herb and cola character. Picks up oak flavors on the finish, but a little simple. 800 cases made. • $18 • (03/31/95) • **83**

Pinot Noir Russian River Valley 1994: Smooth-textured range of smoky cherry, herb, cola and mushroom flavors. Finish is complex, with fine tannins. Ready now and into 1998. 500 cases made. • $38 • **88**

Pinot Noir Sonoma County 1990 • $18 • (09/30/92) • **83**

Pinot Noir Sonoma County 1989 • $13 • (06/30/91) • **82**

The Novelist Napa Valley Meritage 1995: Classy, rich and distinctive. Nice balance of earthy, citrusy pear and herbal flavors, and a nice note of greengage plum on the finish. 1,300 cases made. • $14 • **87**

The Novelist Napa Valley Meritage 1994: Strike a subtle balance between lively pear and apple flavors and delicate spice, toast and herb nuances. Supple and elegant, echoing spicy notes on a long finish. 525 cases made. • $15 • (12/31/95) • **88**

The Novelist Napa Valley Meritage 1992 • $18 • (04/15/94) • **85**

The Poet California Meritage 1990: Tightly wound, showing chunky cedar, currant and oak flavors. Needs time, best after 1998. 1,200 cases made. • $23 • (05/15/95) • **86**

The Poet California Meritage 1989 • $25 • (11/15/93) • **79**

The Poet California Meritage 1988 • $27 • (05/31/91) • **85**

The Poet California Meritage 1987 • $25 • (09/15/90) • **85**

The Poet California Meritage 1986 • $22 • (07/31/89) • **86**

The Poet California Meritage 1985 • $18 • (08/31/88) • **79**

The Poet Napa Valley Meritage 1992: Clean and correct, with a ripe plum and currant edge, turning firm and chunky on the finish, with pure fruit flavors. Well balanced, with firm tannins. Best after 1997. 1,100 cases made. • $24 • (12/15/95) • **87**

Zinfandel Napa County Sonoma County The Zin 1994: Smooth and complex, offering a pretty array of cherry, wild berry, spice and toasty, buttery oak. The texture is supple, providing harmony and adding more complexity on the finish. 600 cases made. • $21 • (04/30/96) • **90**

Zinfandel Russian River Valley The Zin 1991 • $15 • (12/31/92) • **89**

Zinfandel Sonoma County The Zin 1992: Pretty and harmonious, with toasty oak notes adding dimension and richness to the core of spicy cherry and raspberry. Firmly tannic, but it drinks well now. 250 cases made. • $16 • (07/31/94) • **88**

Zinfandel Sonoma County The Zin 1990 • $15 • (10/15/92) • **88**

Zinfandel Sonoma County The Zin Unfined and Unfiltered 1993: Earthy and tannic, chewy, peppery berry and plum flavors pack a wallop. 1,160 cases made. • $18 • (09/15/95) • **87**

COTES DE SONOMA | CALIFORNIA

Cabernet Sauvignon Sonoma County 1993: Earthy, with a mature color and flavors, dried fruit and a decadent edge. Spicy currant and cherry flavors hold it together. • $8 • (12/15/95) • **83**

Cabernet Sauvignon Sonoma County 1990: A toasty, oaky characteristic gives a nice spicy accent to the smooth cherry and plum flavors in this medium-bodied, moderately tannic wine. It's a pleasure to drink now. 4,000 cases made. • $6 • (10/31/92) BB • **83**

Cabernet Sauvignon Sonoma County 1989 • $7 • (11/15/91) BB • **83**

Chardonnay Sonoma County 1995: Emphasizes fruit, with green apple and green plum flavors and a lively, almost Muscat-like personality. 9,000 cases made. • $9 • (06/15/96) • **84**

Chardonnay Sonoma County 1994: Lean and crisp, showing plenty of floral, citrus and apple flavors that remain vibrant on the finish. A Chardonnay that still delivers some charm without charging a premium. 10,000 cases made. • $8 • (10/15/95) BB • **86**

Chardonnay Sonoma County 1993: Fresh and flavorful, simple but brimming with pear and nectarine character that lingers on the finish. Drinkable now. 10,000 cases made. • $8 • (04/15/95) • **84**

Chardonnay Sonoma County 1992: Fresh and spicy, with a bright beam of pear and nutmeg aromas and flavors and a smooth, elegant finish. Has a soft feel overall. Drinkable now, while it's fresh. 4,000 cases made. • $7 • (07/15/93) BB • **86**

Deux Cépages Sonoma County 1990 • $6 • (11/15/91) • **73**

Sauvignon Blanc Sonoma County 1995: Bright and flavorful, an appealing wine brimming with melon, vanilla and green berry flavors. 2,000 cases made. • $9 • (06/15/96) • **86**

Sauvignon Blanc Sonoma County 1994: A crisp and lively touch of floral character spikes up the green apple and green berry flavors. • $7 • (08/31/95) • **83**

Sauvignon Blanc Sonoma County 1993: A gentle wine, showing plenty of pear and a touch of herb flavor, echoing a bit of anise on the finish. Drinkable now. 2,000 cases made. • $7 • (11/30/94) BB • **85**

Sauvignon Blanc Sonoma County 1992 • $6 • (08/31/93) BB • **81**

COTTONWOOD CANYON | CALIFORNIA

Chardonnay Santa Barbara County 1991: Extremely dark color and sherrylike aromas; flavors just turn woody on the finish. 1,200 cases made. • $20 • (07/31/95) • **70**

Pinot Noir Santa Barbara County 1991: A touch earthy, but enough black cherry, plum and berry notes come through to give it a pleasant balance. Ready even if a shade tannic. 364 cases made. • $29 • **85**

Pinot Noir Santa Barbara County 1990 • $20 • (02/28/94) • **79**

Pinot Noir Santa Barbara County 1989 • $25 • (02/28/93) • **88**

Pinot Noir Santa Barbara County Barrel Select 1991: Mature with earthy cherry and berry fruit flavors and a whif of vegetal aromas, but it hangs together finishing with good intensity, length, and spicy nuances. 179 cases made. • $38 • **87**

Pinot Noir Santa Barbara County Barrel Select 1989 • $25 • (02/28/93) • **82**

COTURRI | CALIFORNIA

Zinfandel Sonoma Valley Chauvet Vineyards 1990 • $17 • (10/15/92) • **83**

COVEY RUN | WASHINGTON

Cabernet Sauvignon Yakima Valley 1993: Light and fruity, but dark in flavor, with more black cherry and blackberry than anything lighter. Drinkable now. 2,100 cases made. • $7 • (09/30/94) • **80**

Cabernet Sauvignon Yakima Valley 1992: Lean, a little chewy, offering a chocolate and tobacco edge to the solid Cabernet fruit. Drinkable now. 3,500 cases made. • $11 • (03/31/95) • **84**

Cabernet Sauvignon Yakima Valley 1990: Lean and spicy, with flavors that veer toward cedar and toast. 1,700 cases made. • $9 • (03/15/94) • **78**

Cabernet Sauvignon Yakima Valley 1989 • $12 • (03/15/93) • **78**

Cabernet Sauvignon Yakima Valley 1988 • $11 • (04/30/92) • **85**

Cabernet Sauvignon Yakima Valley 1986 • $10 • (10/15/89) • **80**

Cabernet Sauvignon Yakima Valley Whiskey Canyon 1992: Woody, pickle-barrel aromas and harsh tannins make this unyielding, although the finish shows ripe berry flavor. 500 cases made. • $20 • (09/30/95) • **79**

Cabernet Sauvignon Yakima Valley Whiskey Canyon 1991: Very firm and chewy, its tannins clamp down on the modest plum and berry flavor. Try in 1998 or 1999. 200 cases made. • $20 • (09/30/95) • **85**

Cabernet Sauvignon Yakima Valley Whiskey Canyon Vineyard Reserve 1991: Smoky, acrid, ashy flavors takes this one down a few notches. 225 cases made. • $20 • (09/30/94) • **69**

Chardonnay Washington 1992: A bit heavy-handed with the oak, which gives it a slightly bitter edge, but spicy pear and apple notes come through. Ready now. 20,000 cases made. • $11 • (02/28/94) • **80**

Chardonnay Washington 1991 • $10 • (06/15/93) • **79**

Chardonnay Washington Celilo Vineyard 1992: Lean and firm, sharply focused, slides some earthy, mineral undertones into the peach and apple flavors. Drinkable now. 225 cases made. • $20 • (09/30/94) • **85**

Chardonnay Yakima Valley 1993: Earthy, sour flavors detract from the modest apple and spice notes, taking this one down a few notches. 25,000 cases made. • $10 • (04/15/95) • **74**

Chardonnay Yakima Valley Reserve 1992: Bright, spicy and lively; a lithe Chardonnay with fresh citrus, pear and honey flavors echoing on the finish. Drinkable now. 2,000 cases made. • $15 • (09/30/94) • **87**

Chardonnay Yakima Valley Reserve 1991 • $15 • (02/28/94) • **87**

Fumé Blanc Washington 1993: A bright, fruity and spicy Washington white with polished, citrusy edges that allow the pear and apple flavors to shine. There's a hint of herb on the finish. 7,000 cases made. • $8 • (03/31/95) BB • **88**

Fumé Blanc Washington Dry 1992: Bright and fruity; a refreshing white with pleasant melon and grapefruit aromas and flavors. 4,500 cases made. • $8 • (07/31/94) • **83**

Gewürztraminer Washington 1994: Smells distinctly varietal, but the sweet rose petal flavors get a little too mushy on the finish. 2,000 cases made. • $7 • (09/30/95) • **78**

Gewürztraminer Washington Celilo Vineyard Reserve 1992: Weedy, herbal flavors take the charm from this one. 200 cases made. • $10 • (09/30/94) • **72**

Gewürztraminer Yakima Valley 1993: On the dry side, modestly flavorful, with enough spicy notes to let you know it's Gewürztraminer. 4,000 cases made. • $7 • (09/30/94) • **82**

Johannisberg Riesling Yakima Valley 1994: Fruity and lightly sweet, accenting peach and vanilla. 11,000 cases made. • $7 • (09/30/95) • **83**

Merlot Yakima Valley 1993: Chewy, grapey and somewhat tannic, but generous enough to show a nice minty note to accompany the ripe fruit. Drinkable now. 10,000 cases made. • $11 • (05/31/95) • **83**

Merlot Yakima Valley 1992 • $11 • (05/15/94) • **74**

Merlot Yakima Valley 1990 • $12 • (01/31/93) • **82**

Merlot Yakima Valley 1989 • $11 • (06/15/92) • **79**

Merlot Yakima Valley 1988 • $10 • (03/31/91) • **87**

Merlot Yakima Valley 1986 • $9 • (10/15/89) • **82**

Merlot Yakima Valley 1985 • $9 • (04/15/89) • **85**

Merlot Yakima Valley 1984 • $8 • (11/15/87) • **82**

Merlot Yakima Valley Reserve 1993: Extremely oaky and minty, unbalanced away from fruit, finishing with a strong taste of wood. Fruit sneaks in on the finish. May be best in 1998. 750 cases made. • $15 • (09/30/95) • **80**

Merlot Yakima Valley Reserve 1989 • $17 • (03/31/92) • **83**

Muscat Yakima Valley Morio Muskat 1994: Not too sweet, a dessert wine showing delicate spice and floral overtones to the modest fruit. 2,000 cases made. • $7 • (09/30/95) • **81**

Muscat Yakima Valley Morio Muskat 1993: Sour and unpleasant, like rotting flowers. 3,000 cases made. • $7 • (09/30/94) • **70**

Riesling Columbia Valley Dry 1994: Soft and fruity, adding a resiny edge to the pear and peach flavors. 1,500 cases made. • $7 • (09/30/95) • **83**

Riesling Yakima Valley Dry 1993: Fresh and lively, showing some nice green apple and floral flavors, but it could be finer in texture. Drinkable now. 1,900 cases made. • $7 • (09/30/94) • **81**

Riesling Yakima Valley Ice Wine 1990: This modest wine isn't as sweet as some, but it's well-balanced, with pleasant apple and melon flavors and an exotic note of cocoa. Drinkable now. • $20 • **83**

Sémillon Yakima Valley 1993: Smells nice and fruity, but the flavors have a smoky, slightly acrid note that just won't quit. Needs food. Tasted twice. 2,000 cases made. • $8 • (09/30/94) • **79**

White Riesling Late Harvest Yakima Valley 1994: This is sweet and brilliantly focused, wrapping its intense apricot, pear and honey flavors in a sheen of sweet spices. Such distinctiveness makes this an almost inconceivable deal. Delicious now. 2,000 cases made. • $7 • (09/15/95) BB • **91**

White Riesling Late Harvest Yakima Valley 1993: Sweet and rich, a little on the sugary side, but showing enough bright pear and vanilla flavors to make a delicious dessert wine on its own terms. Finishes long and sweet. 1,700 cases made. • $7 • (09/30/94) BB • **88**

White Riesling Late Harvest Yakima Valley Ice Wine 1990: Ripe and generous, layered with honey, spice and floral flavors between the concentrated pineapple, pear and tropical fruit notes that keep echoing in the long finish. Delicious now. 500 cases made. • $20 • (09/30/94) • **90**

White Riesling Late Harvest Yakima Valley Ice Wine 1987 • $24 • (10/15/89) • **87**

White Riesling Late Harvest Yakima Valley Mahre Vyds Botrytis 1986 • $7 • (10/15/89) • **83**

COYNE, THOMAS | CALIFORNIA

Merlot El Dorado Quartz Hill Vineyard 1990 • $12 • (06/30/93) • **84**

Merlot Sonoma County 1990 • $12 • (06/30/93) • **84**

Key: SS—Spectator Selection. CS—Cellar Selection. BB—Best Buy. $NA—Price not available. (BT)—Barrel tasting. (A)—Auction Price.

Dates in parentheses represent the issues in which the ratings were published.

CRAIG, ROBERT | CALIFORNIA

Cabernet Sauvignon Howell Mountain 1993: Smooth and harmonious given its youth; the dark cherry, plum, currant and cedary oak flavors turn smoky on the mineral finish. Could age into 1998. 300 cases made. • $25 • (10/15/95) • **89**

Cabernet Sauvignon Mount Veeder 1993: Plush and harmonious, complex and well crafted, featuring currant, earth, anise and cedary oak flavors. Bold and intense, with a long, full finish; needs cellaring into 1998. 370 cases made. • $25 • (10/15/95) • **90**

Cabernet Sauvignon Napa Valley 1992: Intense and concentrated, crisp, austere and tannic, showing currant, plum and anise flavors. Could use more flesh and a little less tannin, so short-term cellaring should help. 250 cases made. • $20 • (10/15/95) • **87**

Cabernet Sauvignon Napa Valley Affinity 1993: Smells complex with currant and cherry flavor but turns austere, adding crisp acidity and firm tannins. Softens somewhat on aftertaste, needs cellaring into 1997. 870 cases made. • $25 • (10/15/95) • **87**

CRANE CANYON | CALIFORNIA

Knights Valley Rosé 1994: Dry, rich and flavorful, mouth-filling, spreads its orange-scented watermelon and strawberry notes thick. Very tasty. 90 cases made. • $13 • (09/15/95) • **86**

Mourvèdre Sonoma Valley 1993: Ripe and spicy, with bright cherry and berry flavors that turn smooth and supple. Drinks easy. 70 cases made. • $18 • (08/31/95) • **86**

Zinfandel Sonoma Valley 1993: Supple and medium-bodied, with attractive cherry and raspberry flavors of modest proportions. Finishes with a touch of toasty oak. 35 cases made. • $18 • (10/15/95) • **83**

CREMA, LA | CALIFORNIA

Chardonnay California 1992: A bit oaky at this youthful stage, but the ripe, rich, concentrated pear and butterscotch flavors stand up to it, adding dimension and complexity. Finishes with a combination of ripe fruit and vanilla-laced oak flavors. Drinkable now. • $12 • (06/30/94) • **87**

Chardonnay California Grand Cuvée 1993: Elegant and ripe pear, nutmeg, spice and light toasty oak shadings. Appealing now. • $20 • (05/31/95) • **85**

Chardonnay California Reserve 1993: Hits the right notes—clean and correct. The pear, light oak and spice flavors finish with a crisp edge. • $12 • (05/31/95) • **85**

Chardonnay California Reserve 1992: Firm, ripe and intense, with complex, concentrated pear, pineapple, and spice notes framed by toasty, buttery oak flavors that are well integrated and lively through the finish. Ready now through 1997. • $20 • (06/30/94) • **88**

Chardonnay Sonoma County 1994: Marked by spicy oak and spicy fruit, with hints of pear and nutmeg coming through. It's solid and finishes with a creamy mouth-feel. • $15 • (03/31/96) • **88**

Pinot Noir Blanc California Vin Gris 1986 • $8 • (10/31/87) • **70**

Pinot Noir California 1992 • $12 • (02/28/94) • **78**

Pinot Noir California 1991 • $12 • (02/28/94) • **78**

Pinot Noir California 1986 • $12 • (12/31/88) • **89**

Pinot Noir California 1985 • $11 • (09/30/87) • **90**

Pinot Noir California 1984 • $11 • (03/15/87) • **89**

Pinot Noir California Grand Cuvée 1993: Elegant and delicate, with creamy vanilla, spice and black cherry flavors leading into a long, lingering finish. Drink now. 2,000 cases made. • $19 • (03/31/95) • **86**

Pinot Noir California Reserve 1993: Has a lean profile, with a narrow, earthy beam of berry flavors that turn tannic and spicy. 11,000 cases made. • $11 • (03/31/95) • **84**

Pinot Noir California Reserve 1992 • $20 • (02/28/94) • **83**

Pinot Noir California Reserve 1991 • $20 • (02/28/94) • **79**

Pinot Noir California Reserve 1990 • $17 • (02/28/93) • **85**

Pinot Noir California Reserve 1986 • $22 • (05/31/89) • **85**

Pinot Noir California Reserve 1985 • $18 • (12/31/87) • **82**

Pinot Noir Sonoma County 1994: Hits a lot of the right notes, with its ripe plum and cherry flavors, picking up a trace of oak and spice on the finish. Best to let it soften a bit. • $17 • (03/31/96) • **88**

Pinot Noir Sonoma County Reserve 1994: Medium-bodied, showing a simple core of plum and cherry flavor and a slight toasty oak finish. Should benefit from short-term cellaring. • $14 • (02/29/96) • **87**

CRESTON | CALIFORNIA

Cabernet Sauvignon Central Coast Winemaker's Selection 1985 • $17 • (12/15/89) • **75**

Cabernet Sauvignon Central Coast Winemaker's Selection 1984 • $16 • (12/15/87) • **71**

Cabernet Sauvignon Paso Robles 1992: Distinct for its wild berry and cherry fruit, but comes across as one dimensional, finishing with firm, dry oak and tannins. 2,176 cases made. • $10 • (12/15/95) • **83**

Cabernet Sauvignon Paso Robles 1989 • $10 • (11/15/93) • **85**

Cabernet Sauvignon Paso Robles 1988 • $10 • (11/15/92) • **81**

Cabernet Sauvignon Paso Robles 1987 • $10 • (11/15/91) • **79**

Cabernet Sauvignon Paso Robles Winemaker's Selection 1989: Elegant and oaky, with supple herb and currant notes. Fits the Creston style, but not as rich and complex as earlier bottlings. Ready now. 632 cases made. • $17 • (11/15/94) • **83**

Cabernet Sauvignon Paso Robles Winemaker's Selection 1988 • $16 • (11/15/92) • **80**

Cabernet Sauvignon Paso Robles Winemaker's Selection 1987 • $16 • (11/15/91) • **82**

Cabernet Sauvignon San Luis Obispo 1990: Firm and intense, with a narrow band of cranberry flavor that bows to the tannins. • $10 • (11/15/94) • **81**

Cabernet Sauvignon San Luis Obispo County 1985 • $12 • (12/15/89) • **68**

Chardonnay Paso Robles 1993: Ordinary, with simple grapey pear and citrus notes, finishing with a light oak edge. 4,187 cases made. • $10 • (07/31/95) • **80**

Chardonnay Paso Robles 1992: Relies a little too heavily on oak for its flavor and structure, which gives it a woody, astringent edge. Ready. 3,088 cases made. • $10 • (06/30/94) • **77**

Chardonnay Paso Robles 1991 • $10 • (07/15/93) • **83**

Chevrier Blanc Paso Robles 1994: Smooth and lavishly perfumed, a brightly appealing white that shows a nice touch of pear on the finish. This one calls itself by an alternate moniker for Sémillon, but has 20 percent Sauvignon in the mix. 750 cases made. • $9 • (08/31/95) • **86**

Merlot Paso Robles 1991 • $13 • (12/31/93) • **85**

Pinot Noir Paso Robles 1994: Light, with modest wild berry and cherry flavors. A wine to drink now. 2,157 cases made. • $10 • (01/31/96) • **82**

Pinot Noir Paso Robles 1993: Simple, with modest varietal character and more cedary oak than ripe berry fruit. 1,674 cases made. • $10 • **80**

Pinot Noir Paso Robles 1992 • $9 • (01/31/94) • **83**

Pinot Noir Paso Robles 1991 • $9 • (02/28/93) • **74**

Pinot Noir Paso Robles 1990 • $8 • (11/15/91) • **70**

Pinot Noir San Luis Obispo County Petit d'Noir 1987 • $8 • (08/31/88) • **80**

Pinot Noir San Luis Obispo County Petit d'Noir Maceration Carbonique 1988 • $8 • (12/15/89) • **74**

Sauvignon Blanc Paso Robles 1995: Ripe and a bit thick in texture, but pleasant for its peach and apple flavors. 664 cases made. • $10 • **83**

Sauvignon Blanc Paso Robles 1994: Anise and apple flavors compete for attention. Lean and distinctly herbal, also a little bitter. 750 cases made. • $9 • (08/31/95) • **79**

Zinfandel Paso Robles 1991 • $10 • (09/30/93) • **78**

Zinfandel Paso Robles 1990 • $9 • (10/15/92) • **87**

CRICHTON HALL | CALIFORNIA

Merlot Napa Valley 1993: Earthy with a leathery edge, picking up a spicy currant and cherry edge, thinning out on the finish where the earthiness comes through. 1,200 cases made. • $21 • (06/15/96) • **84**

Pinot Noir Napa Valley 1993: Dry and earthy, with a slightly musty edge to the modest cherry and berry notes. Marginal. 700 cases made. • $22 • (01/31/96) • **74**

Pinot Noir Napa Valley 1993: Supple and elegant, appealing for its complex earth, cherry and mineral flavors. Finishes with crisp acidity and firm tannins, enjoyable now and into 1998. 700 cases made. • $22 • (04/30/96) • **86**

CRISTOM | WASHINGTON

Chardonnay Columbia Valley 1993: Washington grapes give this a bright, livelier aspect than most Oregon Chardonnays, echoing melon, citrus and apple fruit on the finish. Ready now. 275 cases made. • $16 • (01/31/96) • **87**

CRONIN | CALIFORNIA

Cabernet Sauvignon Santa Cruz Mountains 1991: Somewhat rustic, firm tannins and slight metallic edge, opening up to reveal a tight core of mineral and currant, and a dry tannic finish. Needs cellaring to soften and develop. Best in 1998. 154 cases made. • $17 • (04/30/96) • **89**

Cabernet Sauvignon Santa Cruz Mountains 1990: Lean and earthy, with currant and cherry notes struggling to break loose. Potent oak on the finish. Best after 1996. 112 cases made. • $17 • (02/28/95) • **85**

Cabernet Sauvignon Santa Cruz Mountains 1989 • $17 • (03/15/94) • **88**

Cabernet Sauvignon-Merlot San Mateo County Shaw & Cronin 1986 • $15 • (02/28/91) • **88**

Cabernet Sauvignon-Merlot Santa Cruz Mountains 1988 • $17 • (03/31/93) • **83**

Cabernet Sauvignon-Merlot Santa Cruz Mountains 1987 • $17 • (03/31/92) • **84**

Cabernet Sauvignon-Merlot Stags Leap District Robinson Vineyard 1989 • $17 • (03/31/93) • **90**

Cabernet Sauvignon-Merlot Stags Leap District Robinson Vineyard 1988 • $17 • (03/31/92) • **88**

Cabernet Sauvignon-Merlot Stags Leap District Robinson Vineyard 1987 • $17 • (02/28/91) • **89**

Cabernet Sauvignon-Merlot Stags Leap District Robinson Vineyard 1986 • $16 • (02/15/90) • **88**

Chardonnay Alexander Valley Stuhlmuller Vineyard 1993: Spicy with a cedary oak edge to the modest pear and citrus notes. Well balanced for the fruit it has. 334 cases made. • $18 • (07/31/95) • **85**

Chardonnay Alexander Valley Stuhlmuller Vineyard 1992: Pleasantly balanced between ripe, spicy pear and light oak shadings. Finishes with a good dose of toasty, buttery oak, so cellaring for the short term won't hurt. 285 cases made. • $18 • (11/15/94) • **88**

Chardonnay California Nancy's Cuvée 1991: Crisp and intense with spicy pear and apple flavors; simple but pleasant. Drinkable now. 96 cases made. • $27 • (06/30/94) • **82**

Chardonnay Monterey County Ventana Vineyard 1992: Fresh and lively, with a zingy acidity that freshens up the pear, apple and spice notes. 192 cases made. • $18 • (04/15/95) • **86**

Chardonnay Monterey County Ventana Vineyard 1991 • $18 • (08/31/93) • **83**

Chardonnay Napa Valley 1993: Ripe and spicy, with apple, pear, honey and toasty oak flavors of modest proportions. 280 cases made. • $18 • (07/31/95) • **85**

Chardonnay Napa Valley 1992: Intense and earthy, with a firm, narrow band of pear, nutmeg and spice notes. Drinkable now. 333 cases made. • $18 • (11/15/94) • **88**

Chardonnay Napa Valley 1991 • $18 • (08/31/93) • **87**

Chardonnay Santa Cruz Mountains 1993: Pleasant enough, but lacking richness and depth, with spicy pear, toasty oak and light honey notes. Medium bodied. 876 cases made. • $20 • (07/31/95) • **84**

Chardonnay Santa Cruz Mountains 1992: Ripe and intense, with spice, pear, pineapple and light oak shadings. Picks up an earthy edge on the finish, but overall it's complex and well proportioned. 624 cases made. • $22 • (11/15/94) • **88**

Chardonnay Santa Cruz Mountains 1991 • $20 • (08/31/93) • **91**

Concerto Stags Leap District Robinson Vineyard 1992: Young, vibrant, ripe, rich cherry, currant and plum flavors, picking up a pretty dash of spice and cedary oak on the finish. The texture is pure Stags Leap in its suppleness. Tempting though it may be, it's best to cellar into 1998. 219 cases made. • $17 • (04/30/96) • **93**

Concerto Stags Leap District Robinson Vineyard 1991: Solid and intense, displaying ripe cherry and currant flavors flanked by anise and cedary oak. Firmly tannic, best after 1996. 192 cases made. • $17 • (02/28/95) • **87**

Concerto Stags Leap District Robinson Vineyard 1990: Lean and a bit green with a tight oak overlay. The currant, berry and cherry flavors are appealing, but it's tannins that carry the finish. Drinkable now. 216 cases made. • $17 • (03/15/94) • **82**

Joe's Cuvée California 1990: Heavy handed with cedary oak, currant, green olive, herb and tobacco flavors. A blend of Cabernet, Cabernet Franc and Merlot in equal parts. Try now. 72 cases made. • $27 • (03/15/94) • **86**

Pinot Noir Santa Clara County 1989 • $17 • (02/28/94) • **81**

Pinot Noir Santa Cruz Mountains Peter Martin Ray Vineyard 1992: Mature and somewhat earthy, offering a complex array of dried cherry, sage, mushroom and tobacco notes, dry finish and firm tannins. The texture is smooth and silky. 77 cases made. • $22 • (04/30/96) • **89**

Pinot Noir Santa Cruz Mountains Peter Martin Ray Vineyard 1991: Lean, thin and tannic, exhibiting a narrow beam of cherry, earth and juniper berry flavors. 93 cases made. • $20 • (03/31/95) • **82**

Pinot Noir Santa Cruz Mountains Peter Martin Ray Vineyard 1990 • $20 • (04/30/94) • **83**

Pinot Noir Santa Cruz Mountains Peter Martin Ray Vineyard 1988 • $27 • (03/31/92) • **81**

Sauvignon Blanc-Chardonnay Napa Valley 1992: Very ripe and buttery, spicy and mouth-filling, with rich oak notes, pear flavor and a little bit of an herbal edge. Drinkable now. 120 cases made. • $10 • (10/15/94) • **88**

Sauvignon Blanc-Chardonnay Napa Valley 1991 • $10 • (09/15/93) • **84**

Zinfandel Santa Clara County 1992: On the austere side, with a tart, green character to the wild berry and spice notes. Not as ripe or complex as the Sonoma Valley bottling, but true to this appellation. 24 cases made. • $12 • (10/15/95) • **85**

Zinfandel Sonoma Valley 1992: Ripe and jammy, the pretty plum, raspberry and cherry notes turning smooth and supple on the palate. A well-proportioned, even elegant, rendering that's delicious now. 48 cases made. • $15 • (10/15/95) • **91**

CROSSE, LA | CALIFORNIA

Cabernet Sauvignon Napa Valley 1991: Offers modest currant and berry notes. 5,000 cases made. • $7 • (02/28/95) • **77**

Cabernet Sauvignon Napa Valley 1989 • $6 • (12/15/92) • **77**

Chardonnay Napa Valley 1993: Well oaked, presenting subdued pear and apple flavors that turn soft on the finish. Drinkable now. 10,000 cases made. • $7 • (04/30/95) • **83**

Chardonnay Napa Valley 1992: Nice tension between oak and fruit in this medium-weight, smooth-textured white that echoes peach and spice on the finish. 9,000 cases made. • $6 • (05/31/94) BB • **84**

Chardonnay Napa Valley 1991 • $6 • (12/31/92) BB • **85**

Merlot Napa Valley 1993: Supple and fruity, offering a pleasant band of herb, black cherry and spice notes that turn smooth on the mildly tannic finish. 2,500 cases made. • $8 • (05/15/95) • **85**

CROSSWOODS | NEW YORK

Merlot North Fork of Long Island Ressler Vineyards 1987 • $10 • (02/29/92) • **84**

CRUVINET | CALIFORNIA

Cabernet Sauvignon Alexander Valley 1985 • $7 • (09/15/88) BB • **85**

CRYSTAL VALLEY | CALIFORNIA

Cabernet Sauvignon Napa Valley Unfined 1989 • $12 • (09/15/93) • **80**

Cabernet Sauvignon North Coast 1983 • $8 • (08/31/86) BB • **89**

Cabernet Sauvignon North Coast Reserve Edition 1984 • $14 • (10/15/87) • **75**

Pinot Blanc Napa Valley 1991 • $12 • (06/15/93) • **77**

Pinot Noir North Coast Reserve Edition 1986 • $11 • (06/15/88) • **74**

Sauvignon Blanc Napa Valley 1992 • $8 • (11/15/93) • **82**

Key: SS—Spectator Selection. CS—Cellar Selection. BB—Best Buy. $NA—Price not available. (BT)—Barrel tasting. Ⓐ—Auction Price.
Dates in parentheses represent the issues in which the ratings were published.

CULBERTSON | CALIFORNIA

Blanc de Noir California 1983 • $14 • (05/16/86) • **68**

Blanc de Noir California NV • $14 • (12/31/90) • **77**

Blanc de Noir California NV • $12 • (12/31/92) • **78**

Brut California 1987 • $16 • (12/31/93) • **82**

Brut California 1985 • $14 • (05/31/89) • **83**

Brut California 1983 • $14 • (05/16/86) • **66**

Brut California NV: Complex and distinctive with rich yeast, toast and spicy pear flavors that are concentrated and long on the finish. Impressive for its style and length, particularly at this price. Ready now. 5,000 cases made. • $12 • (11/15/94) • **89**

Brut California American-European Train Deluxe NV • $20 • • **70**

Brut California Pinot Noir Cuvée Rouge NV • $12 • (12/31/92) • **82**

Brut California Reserve 1988 • $18 • (12/31/93) • **87**

Brut Rosé California 1987 • $16 • (12/31/93) • **85**

Brut Rosé California 1986 • $18 • (05/31/89) • **80**

Demi-Sec Cuvée de Frontignan California NV • $12 • (05/15/92) • **81**

Natural California 1987 • $16 • (12/31/93) • **74**

Natural California 1986 • $19 • (12/31/90) • **74**

Natural California 1985 • $18 • (05/31/89) • **81**

Natural California 1983 • $17 • (05/16/86) • **72**

Cuvée de Frontignan California Artist Series 1994 NV: Sweet with just enough ripe pear and apple flavors to ward off the slight bitterness that creeps in on the finish. 1,200 cases made. • $10 • (05/31/95) • **78**

Cuvée Rouge Artist Series California 1994 NV: The dark-ruby color may throw you, but this is a sparkling wine for red wine drinkers, offering grapey cherry, strawberry and plum notes. 1,200 cases made. • $12 • (05/31/95) • **84**

CUNEO CELLARS | WASHINGTON

Cana's Feast Columbia Valley 1992: Big and brooding, not terribly tannic but submerging its plum, black cherry and currant flavors in the soft, soupy texture. Try in 1997. 206 cases made. • $25 • (05/15/96) • **85**

CUNEO, RICHARD | CALIFORNIA

Sparkling Sonoma County Cuvée de Chardonnay 1991: Intense and lively, with a pretty band of honey, butter and pear flavors that fold together nicely, gaining depth and length on the finish. Ready now. • $15 • (12/15/94) • **88**

Cuvée de Chardonnay Sonoma County 1988 • $15 • (12/15/93) • **88**

Cuvée de Chardonnay Sonoma County 1987 • $14 • (11/15/91) • **84**

CUTLER | CALIFORNIA

Cabernet Sauvignon Sonoma Valley 1990: Ripe and fruity, with an herb and bell pepper edge to the currant and cherry flavor. Finishes with elegance and finesse, along with firm tannins. Best after 1998. 900 cases made. • $19 • (11/15/94) • **88**

Cabernet Sauvignon Sonoma Valley Batto Ranch 1987 • $17 • (03/31/92) • **90**

Cabernet Sauvignon Sonoma Valley Batto Ranch 1986 • $17 • (11/15/90) • **86**

Cabernet Sauvignon Sonoma Valley Batto Ranch 1985 • $20 • (07/31/89) • **91**

Satyre Sonoma Valley 1989: Smooth and nicely focused, showing its maturity in the form of a harmonious balance between the black cherry and cedar flavors and the firm backbone. Approachable now. 600 cases made. • $20 • (12/15/95) • **87**

Satyre Sonoma Valley 1987 • $20 • (07/15/92) • **89**

Satyre Sonoma Valley 1986 • $20 • (02/28/91) • **85**

CUVAISON | CALIFORNIA

Cabernet Sauvignon Napa Valley 1992: An austere style, with a trim band of currant, earth, cedar and spice, finishing with firm tannins that clamp down. Best after 1999. 3,900 cases made. • $26 • (12/15/95) • **88**

Cabernet Sauvignon Napa Valley 1991: Firm and intense, with a ripe, rich core of currant, cherry and spicy oak flavors. Well balanced and tannic now, it needs cellaring to soften the rough edges, best after 1998. 5,714 cases made. • $22 • (11/15/94) • **88**

Cabernet Sauvignon Napa Valley 1990: Tight and a little on the tough side; a beam of berry flavor pushing through on the finish. Drink now. 3,500 cases made. • $18 • (03/31/94) • **85**

Cabernet Sauvignon Napa Valley 1989 • $22 • (02/15/93) • **82**

Cabernet Sauvignon Napa Valley 1988 • $19 • (11/15/91) • **82**

Cabernet Sauvignon Napa Valley 1987 • $25 • (10/31/90) • **92**

Cabernet Sauvignon Napa Valley 1986 • $30 • (07/15/89) • **94**

Cabernet Sauvignon Napa Valley 1985 • $40 • (03/31/89) • **91**

Cabernet Sauvignon Napa Valley 1984 • $24 • (03/01/89) • **89**

Cabernet Sauvignon Napa Valley 1983 • $18 • (03/01/89) • **75**

Cabernet Sauvignon Napa Valley 1982 • $22 • (03/01/89) • **82**

Cabernet Sauvignon Napa Valley 1981 • $21 • (03/01/89) • **74**

Cabernet Sauvignon Napa Valley 1980 • $22 • (03/01/89) • **77**

Cabernet Sauvignon Napa Valley 1979 • $22 • (03/01/89) • **75**

Cabernet Sauvignon Napa Valley 1978 • $30 • (03/01/89) • **72**

Cabernet Sauvignon Napa Valley 1977 • $30 • (03/01/89) • **79**

Cabernet Sauvignon Napa Valley 1976 • $30 • (03/01/89) • **79**

Cabernet Sauvignon Napa Valley 1975 • $33 • (03/01/89) • **79**

Cabernet Sauvignon Napa Valley Philip Togni Signature 1975 • $40 • (03/01/89) • **88**

Chardonnay Carneros Napa Valley 1993: Pleasantly fruity with ripe, medium weight apple, pear, spice and citrus notes that stay focused. 35,000 cases made. • $15 • (07/31/95) • **86**

Chardonnay Napa Valley Carneros 1992: Plenty of bright pear and spicy pineapple flavors that are moderatly rich and intense, but the wood notes stand out on the finish. Drink now. 42,000 cases made. • $15 • (09/15/94) • **89**

Chardonnay Napa Valley Carneros 1991 • $14 • (07/15/93) • **87**

Chardonnay Napa Valley Carneros Reserve 1994: Well focused ripe pear, honey, apple and citrus flavors. Holds its fruitiness through the finish. Smoky oak and creamy vanilla flavors aren't overblown. • $30 • **92**

Chardonna Napa Valley Carneros Reserve 1993: Well mannered, ripe and fruity with pear, citrus and light oak shadings that fold together nicely on the finish. 1,215 cases made. • $28 • (07/31/95) • **88**

Chardonnay Napa Valley Carneros Reserve 1992: 1,250 cases made. • $25 • (05/15/95) • **88**

Chardonnay Napa Valley Carneros Twenty-fifth Anniversary Harvest 1994: Pleasing for its ripe pineapple and apple flavors, it picks up flinty mineral and citrus notes on the finish. 36,959 cases made. • $16 • (06/30/96) • **85**

Meritage Reserve Napa Valley 1991: Elegant and well balanced if on the crisp side. Enough cherry and berry fruit to sustain your interest, finishing with a crisp edge. Appealing now through 1999. 227 cases made. • $50 • (12/15/95) • **86**

Merlot Napa Valley 1991: A touch on the green side, with cedary wood and herb flavors and just enough currant-laced Merlot fruit to stand up to it. 5,172 cases made. • $24 • (09/15/94) • **83**

Merlot Napa Valley 1990 • $23 • (06/15/93) • **82**

Merlot Napa Valley 1990 • $23 • (08/31/93) • **87**

Merlot Napa Valley 1989 • $23 • (05/31/92) • **89**

Merlot Napa Valley 1988 • $24 • (04/15/91) • **86**

Merlot Napa Valley 1985 • $19 • (06/30/88) • **89**

Merlot Napa Valley Anniversary Release 1984 • $14 • (08/31/87) • **90**

Pinot Noir Napa Valley Carneros 1993: Funky, with a dry, earthy streak in the dried cherry and berry flavors, finishing leathery. Tasted three times, with consistent notes. 1,335 cases made. • $24 • (01/31/96) • **76**

Pinot Noir Napa Valley Carneros 1992: Spicy, showing a green leafy edge to the cherry plum notes. Turns thin and tannic on the finish, where the flavors taper off. 1,500 cases made. • $22 • (03/31/95) • **84**

Pinot Noir Napa Valley Carneros 1991 • $19 • (02/28/94) • **85**

Zinfandel Napa Valley 1986 • $10 • (03/15/89) • **85**

Zinfandel Napa Valley 1983 • $8 • (09/15/87) • **75**

D-CUBED | CALIFORNIA

Zinfandel Howell Mountain 1994: Brimming with ripe, juicy, spicy wild berry, raspberry and cherry notes. Turns slightly hot and tarry at mid-palate and holds that heat through the finish, yet delivers a lot of flavor and long aftertaste. 450 cases made. • $15 • (04/30/96) • **90**

DALLA VALLE | CALIFORNIA

Cabernet Sauvignon Napa Valley 1992: Ripe, dark, complex and concentrated, with a solid core of ripe black cherry and currant flavors. Picks up toasty, spicy oak accents and finishes with a firm wall of tannins. Best from 1998 on. 2,700 cases made. • $30 • (12/15/95) CS • **92**

Cabernet Sauvignon Napa Valley 1991: An exotic style with ripe, spicy black cherry and wild berry flavors that make up an intriguing flavor profile. Well balanced, with richness, depth and concentration, finishes with firm tannins. Drink soon. 2,100 cases made. • $25 • (11/15/94) SS • **92**

Cabernet Sauvignon Napa Valley 1990: Deep, dense and delicious, bursting with plum, currant, chocolate and spice aromas and flavors, generous and concentrated, an elegant wine with power. Echoes anise and fruit on the long finish. Has enough tannin to want until 1998-2000. 2,000 cases made. • $25 • (09/30/93) • **93**

Cabernet Sauvignon Napa Valley 1989 • $25 • (11/15/92) • **85**

Cabernet Sauvignon Napa Valley 1988 • $25 • (11/15/91) • **85**

Cabernet Sauvignon Napa Valley 1986 • $20 • (06/30/90) • **85**

Maya Napa Valley 1992: Dark, intense and enormously complex, with a wonderfully rich core of currant, black cherry, mineral and spice. Finishes long and full, with firm, concentrated tannins. Maintains a sense of elegance and finesse. A single-vineyard blend of roughly equal parts Cabernet Sauvignon and Cabernet Franc. Better in 1998. 500 cases made. • $75 • (12/15/95) • **94**

Maya Napa Valley 1991: Bold and ripe, with delicious currant, black cherry and plum flavors before the firm tannins kick in. This tightly-wound red finishes on the short side, but cellaring until 1998 should make it more appealing. 500 cases made. • $50 • (11/15/94) • **90**

Maya Napa Valley 1990: Dark and inky in color with ripe, rich, complex currant, plum, cherry and spice flavors that turn smoky and buttery on the finish. Deep in flavor with mineral and herbal notes on the firmly tannic finish. Try 1997 to 2003. 250 cases made. • $50 • (09/30/93) • **89**

Maya Napa Valley 1989 • $50 • (10/15/92) • **91**

Maya Napa Valley 1988 • $45 • (11/15/91) • **86**

Pietre Rosse Napa Valley NV: A touch cedary, with ripe plum and cherry-berry flavors, but ultimately it lacks focus and doesn't really succeed as either Californian or Italian. 325 cases made. • $35 • (06/15/96) • **82**

Zinfandel Napa Valley 1986 • $25 • (02/15/91) • **84**

DANIEL | CALIFORNIA

Cabernet Sauvignon Napa Valley 1984 • $21 • (07/15/88) • **89**

Cabernet Sauvignon Napa Valley 1983 • $20 • (04/30/89) • **79**

DE BAUN, CHATEAU | CALIFORNIA

Russian River Valley Finale 1993: Aromatic and smooth, a little simple at first, but the floral, honey and pear flavors swirl around nicely as they grow on the finish. 950 cases made. • $10 • (07/31/95) • **88**

Brut Rosé Sonoma County NV: An off-beat style that's pungently spicy, turning cloying on the finish. Lacks focus and appeal. Drinkable, but marginal. 1,500 cases made. • $10 • (12/31/94) • **73**

Brut Rosé Sonoma County Symphony Rhapsody 1988 • $11 • (07/15/91) • **83**

Brut Rosé Sonoma County Symphony Rhapsody 1987 • $12 • (05/31/90) • **78**

Brut Rosé Sonoma County Symphony Rhapsody 1986 • $12 • (09/15/88) • **88**

Brut Sonoma County NV • $10 • (12/31/93) • **77**

Brut Sonoma County Symphony Romance 1988 • $11 • (07/15/91) • **84**

Brut Sonoma County Symphony Romance 1987 • $12 • (04/30/90) • **80**

Brut Sonoma County Symphony Romance 1986 • $12 • (07/31/88) • **74**

Chardonnay Russian River Valley 1994: Simple, ordinary pear and spice flavors. Good but nothing more. 12,015 cases made. • $10 • (05/15/96) • **81**

Chardonnay Russian River Valley 1993: Appealing for its tangerine and nectarine flavors, it turns smooth and creamy, picking up a buttery edge on the finish. 9,600 cases made. • $10 • (04/30/95) • **87**

Chardonnay Russian River Valley 1992: Serves up ripe, spicy pear- and apple-tinged flavor with a nice buttery oak edge coming through on the finish. Smooth and silky, it drinks well now. 8,200 cases made. • $10 • (04/15/94) BB • **85**

Chardonnay Russian River Valley 1991 • $10 • (06/30/93) • **86**

Chardonnay Russian River Valley Creekside Vineyard Reserve 1993: Smooth, ripe, rich and creamy, with tiers of honey, pear, spice and hazelnut notes, a remarkably elegant and refined style with flavor to burn. Best Chardonnay ever from the winery. 400 cases made. • $18 • (02/29/96) • **92**

Pinot Noir California Barrel Select Rouge 1991: Earthy and tarry, revealing a dirty edge to the mature plum flavors. 7,087 cases made. • $5 • (03/31/95) • **73**

Pinot Noir California Chateau Rouge Barrel Select 1990 • $5 • (02/28/93) • **75**

Pinot Noir Russian River Valley 1993: Light and uncomplicated, marked by toasty oak with a narrow band of dried cherry flavor underneath. 500 cases made. • $10 • (12/31/95) • **82**

Pinot Noir Russian River Valley 1992: Very light, with raspberry flavors and earthy, animal notes that linger gently on the finish. Best from 1996. 2,905 cases made. • $10 • (12/31/95) • **83**

Pinot Noir Sonoma County 1991 • $10 • (02/28/94) • **82**

Symphony Late Harvest Sonoma County Finale 1989 • $6 • (11/15/93) • **87**

Symphony Late Harvest Sonoma County Finale 1988 • $12 • (04/30/91) • **87**

Symphony Late Harvest Sonoma County Finale 1987 • $14 • (04/30/89) • **85**

Symphony Late Harvest Sonoma County Finale 1986 • $14 • (09/15/87) • **81**

Symphony Russian River Valley Stellé 1994: Light, fragrant and slightly fizzy, delicately sweet with litchi and pear notes. 1,000 cases made. • $12 • (09/30/95) • **84**

DE LEU, CHATEAU | CALIFORNIA

Brunolino North Coast 1991 • $6 • (10/15/93) BB • **85**

Brulino North Coast 1990 • $6 • (07/31/92) • **83**

Chardonnay Solano County Green Valley 1992: Earthy with tart grapefruit flavors that turn lemony on the finish. 682 cases made. • $10 • (06/30/94) • **78**

Pinot Noir Napa Valley 1991 • $9 • (02/28/94) • **83**

Pinot Noir Napa Valley 1990 • $11 • (02/28/93) • **75**

Pinot Noir Solano County Green Valley 1985 • $7 • (02/28/89) • **77**

DE LOACH | CALIFORNIA

Cabernet Sauvignon Dry Creek Valley 1984 • $11 • (12/15/87) • **89**

Cabernet Sauvignon Dry Creek Valley 1983 • $11 • (09/30/86) • **85**

Cabernet Sauvignon Dry Creek Valley 1981 • $11 • (04/01/85) • **80**

Cabernet Sauvignon Russian River Valley 1992: Marked by earthy flavors, it pulls together enough cherry and berry fruit to keep it interesting; the tannins are substantial for this medium-bodied wine. Best after 1997. 5,800 cases made. • $15 • (12/15/95) • **86**

Cabernet Sauvignon Russian River Valley 1991: Lean and a bit green, with an herbal, green bean edge to the Cabernet flavors. Tannins have bite on the finish. Not quite ripe. • $15 • (11/15/94) • **78**

Cabernet Sauvignon Russian River Valley 1990: Tight and firm, with a range of flavors that stretches from herbs and spices to ripe currants and raspberries. Vegetal hints peek through at points, but it's a solid effort, if a bit on the green side. Firmly tannic and in need of cellaring, try in 1997. 4,100 cases made. • $16 • (03/31/93) • **85**

Cabernet Sauvignon Russian River Valley 1989 • $16 • (11/15/91) • **86**

Cabernet Sauvignon Russian River Valley O.F.S. 1991: Young and somewhat compact but the flavors are well focused, offering pleasant earth, berry and cherry notes and a long finish. 900 cases made. • $25 • (09/30/95) • **89**

Cabernet Sauvignon Russian River Valley O.F.S. 1987 • $22 • (10/15/90) • **85**

Chardonnay Russian River Valley 1994: Clean and correct, with modest pear and spice notes, and a light, citrusy finish. Solid and well-balanced, but lacking in richness and concentration. 25,000 cases made. • $15 • (06/30/96) • **85**

Key: SS—Spectator Selection. CS—Cellar Selection. BB—Best Buy. $NA—Price not available. (BT)—Barrel tasting. Ⓐ—Auction Price.
Dates in parentheses represent the issues in which the ratings were published.

Chardonnay Russian River Valley 1993: Ripe and vibrant, with an appealing core of spice, apple, pear and honey notes. Finishes with an elegant aftertaste. 25,000 cases made. • $15 • (02/29/96) • **85**

Chardonnay Russian River Valley 1991 • $15 • (03/31/93) • **88**

Chardonnay Russian River Valley O.F.S. 1994: Pleasant fruit, featuring an attractive array of pear, citrus, honey and butterscotch which hangs together nicely, adding a fruity aftertaste. 5,000 cases made. • $25 • (05/15/96) • **89**

Chardonnay Russian River Valley O.F.S. 1993: An intense and compelling style from California that pours out lots of ripe pear, apple, spice and toasty oak. The bright and lively flavors develop complexity on the long finish, where the oak blends in with the rich fruit. 4,000 cases made. • $25 • (09/30/95) • **90**

Chardonnay Russian River Valley O.F.S. 1991 • $25 • (07/15/93) • **91**

Chardonnay Sonoma County Sonoma Cuvée 1993: Clean and fruity, with spicy pear, apple and nutmeg notes. Offers a nice value. 25,000 cases made. • $10 • (05/15/96) • **84**

Fumé Blanc Russian River Valley 1992 • $10 • (11/15/93) • **84**

Fumé Blanc Russian River Valley 1991 • $10 • (12/31/92) • **88**

Fumé Blanc Russian River Valley Dry Sauvignon Blanc 1993: Strongly varietal, with herbal, vegetal flavors that keep playing on the finish. 5,500 cases made. • $10 • (12/31/94) • **84**

Gewürztraminer Early Harvest Russian River Valley 1993: Bright citrusy, and smooth-textured, with a nectarine note to the lemon and grapefruit flavors. 2,400 cases made. • $8 • (01/31/95) • **84**

Gewürztraminer Early Harvest Russian River Valley 1992 • $8 • (01/31/94) SS • **88**

Gewürztraminer Early Harvest Russian River Valley 1991 • $8 • (11/15/92) • **80**

Gewürztraminer Late Harvest Russian River Valley 1991 • $14 • (10/15/92) • **86**

Gewürztraminer Late Harvest Russian River Valley 1989 • $10 • (04/30/91) • **88**

Gewürztraminer Late Harvest Russian River Valley 1987 • $10 • (12/31/88) • **93**

Gewürztraminer Late Harvest Russian River Valley 1984 • $10 • (10/01/85) BB • **92**

Merlot Russian River Valley 1994: Medium weight, with a nice range of cherry, currant, anise and light oak flavors. Comes up short on the finish. 6,500 cases made. • $15 • **84**

Merlot Russian River Valley 1993: Dark, ripe, rich and chewy, showing earthy currant, berry and cherry flavor which picks up a cedary oak edge on the complex finish. 4,000 cases made. • $14 • (09/30/95) • **87**

Merlot Russian River Valley 1992: Soft, fruity and appealing, the tannins nicely integrated but prominent enough to need until 1997 to show off the currant and berry flavors to their best advantage. 5,472 cases made. • $14 • (07/31/94) • **86**

Pinot Noir Russian River Valley 1994: Tastes mature for such a young wine and it's marked by a green, stemmy edge. Decent but lacks pizzazz. 435 cases made. • $25 • (02/29/96) • **79**

Pinot Noir Russian River Valley 1992: A rustic, tight style offering tart, earthy Pinot Noir flavors. Turns gamy on the finish. 2,820 cases made. • $13 • (03/31/95) • **82**

Pinot Noir Russian River Valley 1991 • $13 • (02/28/94) • **74**

Pinot Noir Russian River Valley 1990 • $13 • (09/30/92) • **80**

Pinot Noir Russian River Valley 1986 • $12 • (05/31/90) • **87**

Pinot Noir Russian River Valley 1985 • $12 • (06/15/88) • **72**

Pinot Noir Russian River Valley 1983 • $10 • (03/01/86) • **75**

Pinot Noir Russian River Valley 1982 • $10 • (08/31/86) • **76**

Pinot Noir Russian River Valley O.F.S. 1994: Complex and inviting, featuring cherry, currant, herb and spice notes and pretty oak flavors too. Shows off a measure of finesse and polish, building on the finish. Cellar into late 1996 or 1997. 435 cases made. • $25 • (02/29/96) • **89**

Pinot Noir Russian River Valley O.F.S. 1992: Moves past its initial earthiness to reveal a supple core of plum and cherry-laced Pinot Noir fruit. Finishes with smooth tannins. 300 cases made. • $25 • **88**

Pinot Noir Russian River Valley O.F.S. 1990 • $26 • (02/28/93) • **82**

Pinot Noir Russian River Valley O.F.S. 1987 • $25 • (10/31/90) • **82**

Sauvignon Blanc Russian River Valley 1993: Lean in texture, a floral wine with a sweet edge to the modest pear flavor. 1,600 cases made. • $10 • (12/31/94) • **81**

Sauvignon Blanc Russian River Valley 1991 • $10 • (11/30/92) • **85**

White Zinfandel Russian River Valley 1994: Reminds us of bubble gum, showing sweet, candied flavors of fruit cocktail and pineapple. • $7 • (09/15/95) • **74**
White Zinfandel Russian River Valley 1990 • $7 • (03/31/91) • **77**
Zinfandel Russian River Valley 1994: A bit uneven in flavor but has appeal, offering notes that run from ripe cherry and berry to green tea and herb. Drinkable now. 4,500 cases made. • $14 • (04/30/96) • **86**
Zinfandel Russian River Valley 1993: Medium-bodied, with a pleasant core of cherry and plum flavors that linger on the finish. 5,800 cases made. • $13 • (10/15/95) • **85**
Zinfandel Russian River Valley 1991 • $11 • (05/31/93) • **83**
Zinfandel Russian River Valley 1990 • $12 • (05/15/92) • **89**
Zinfandel Russian River Valley 1989 • $11 • (09/30/91) • **82**
Zinfandel Russian River Valley 1988 • $11 • (09/15/90) • **78**
Zinfandel Russian River Valley 1987 • $10 • (09/15/89) • **90**
Zinfandel Russian River Valley 1986 • $9 • (10/15/88) • **88**
Zinfandel Russian River Valley 1984 • $8 • (07/31/87) • **84**
Zinfandel Russian River Valley 1983 • $8 • (10/15/86) • **69**
Zinfandel Russian River Valley 1982 • $8 • (11/01/85) • **77**
Zinfandel Russian River Valley 1981 • $7 • (06/01/85) • **89**
Zinfandel Russian River Valley Barbieri Ranch 1994: Tightly wound, as tart plum, cherry and berry flavors build on the finish. Can stand short-term cellaring to soften and open up. 500 cases made. • $15 • (04/30/96) • **85**
Zinfandel Russian River Valley Barbieri Ranch 1993: Elegant, well focused and pouring out its bright, lively cherry, raspberry and peppery notes. Finishes with firm tannins, so with a little age, it should be ideal. 500 cases made. • $14 • (10/15/95) • **88**
Zinfandel Russian River Valley Barbieri Ranch 1991 • $14 • (01/31/93) • **82**
Zinfandel Russian River Valley Barbieri Ranch 1990 • $14 • (05/15/92) • **82**
Zinfandel Russian River Valley Gambogi Ranch 1994: This tightly wound, young red is marked by tart cherry and berry notes, but wait until the finish, when the flavors fan out. Drinkable now and into 1997. 500 cases made. • $15 • (04/30/96) • **87**
Zinfandel Russian River Valley Gambogi Ranch 1993: A touch earthy and austere, but it opens up to show off a range of cherry and berry flavors. Tight and compact. 500 cases made. • $14 • (10/15/95) • **86**
Zinfandel Russian River Valley O.F.S. 1994: Complex, broad, ripe range of cherry, herb and wild berry flavors. Shows a nice measure of finesse and balance, featuring light oak shadings, smooth tannins and long finish. First O.F.S. Zin. 500 cases made. • $25 • (04/30/96) • **88**
Zinfandel Russian River Valley Papera Ranch 1994: Slightly earthy and tannic, but enough wild berry and cherry flavor emerges to achieve a nice balance, finishing in a tart, berry edge. Drinkable now. 500 cases made. • $15 • (04/30/96) • **87**
Zinfandel Russian River Valley Papera Ranch 1993: Medium body and color, but the zesty, earthy berry and cherry flavors are elegant and well focused. Finishes with supple tannins. 500 cases made. • $14 • (10/15/95) • **86**
Zinfandel Russian River Valley Papera Ranch 1991 • $14 • (01/31/93) • **85**
Zinfandel Russian River Valley Papera Ranch 1990 • $14 • (05/15/92) • **81**
Zinfandel Russian River Valley Pelletti Ranch 1994: Impressive for its pretty cherry, berry and cranberry flavors, finishing with a beam of fruit and earthy tannins. 500 cases made. • $15 • (04/30/96) • **86**
Zinfandel Russian River Valley Pelletti Ranch 1993: Full and rich, ripe with cherry jam and raspberry flavors, turning smooth and polished on the lingering finish. 750 cases made. • $14 • (10/15/95) • **88**
Zinfandel Russian River Valley Pelletti Ranch 1991 • $14 • (01/31/93) • **86**
Zinfandel Russian River Valley Pelletti Ranch 1990 • $14 • (05/15/92) • **87**
Zinfandel Russian River Valley Sonoma County 1992 • $12 • (06/15/94) • **88**

DE LORIMIER | CALIFORNIA

Chardonnay Alexander Valley 1993: Good intensity and focus, adding a spicy, citrus edge to the pear and tart apple notes. 800 cases made. • $14 • (02/29/96) • **85**
Chardonnay Alexander Valley 1992: Spicy, with floral notes and ripe pear and apple flavors. 800 cases made. • $15 • (02/28/95) • **85**
Chardonnay Alexander Valley Clonal Select 1994: A medium-weight style of wine, with appealing peach, smoky oak and honey notes, and distinct for its spicy qualities. 208 cases made. • $20 • (06/30/96) • **88**
Chardonnay Alexander Valley Clonal Select 1992: Intense and oaky, but ripe pear, apple and fig notes emerge, finishing with a complex range of toasty oak flavors. 120 cases made. • $20 • (02/28/95) • **87**
Chardonnay Alexander Valley Prism 1991 • $15 • (03/31/94) • **84**
Mosaic Alexander Valley Meritage 1992: Offers a tightly wound core of currant, black cherry, spice and cedary oak. This trim and compact wine can stand to soften a bit, but drinkable now. 780 cases made. • $18 • (03/31/96) • **85**
Mosaic Alexander Valley Meritage 1991: Well balanced, with a supple core of plum and cherry offsetting the cedary notes and mild tannins. Young and vibrant. Try now. 860 cases made. • $18 • (08/31/95) • **85**
Mosaic Alexander Valley Meritage 1990: Lean and simple, with plum and vegetal notes that turn thin and bland. Disappointing. 1,532 cases made. • $18 • (06/15/94) • **77**
Mosaic Alexander Valley Meritage 1988 • $18 • (06/15/93) • **81**
Mosaic Alexander Valley Meritage 1987 • $18 • (03/31/92) • **81**
Mosaic Alexander Valley Meritage 1986 • $16 • (10/31/89) • **84**
Sauvignon Blanc Late Harvest Alexander Valley Lace 1986 • $11 • (02/29/88) • **82**
Spectrum Alexander Valley Meritage 1994: Definitely herbal, with a peppery edge to the modest fig and floral flavors. 1,200 cases made. • $10 • (06/30/96) • **84**
Spectrum Alexander Valley Meritage 1993: Distinctly herbal, with vanilla and citrus overtones to the creamy, perfumy flavors. Ready now. 935 cases made. • $10 • **83**
Spectrum Alexander Valley Meritage 1992: A delicate Bordeaux-style blend from California, with plenty of nuances for a good price. Has understated fig, melon, cigar box and butterscotch flavors that fold together nicely. 900 cases made. • $10 • (05/15/95) BB • **89**
Spectrum Alexander Valley Meritage 1991: Lean and herbal, with a greenish edge to the citrusy apple flavors. 2,800 cases made. • $10 • (08/31/94) • **82**

DEBONNE | OHIO

Chambourcin Ohio Lake Erie 1989 • $6 • (02/29/92) • **79**

DECOY | CALIFORNIA

Migration Red Napa Valley 1993: Ripe, well-focused, spicy black cherry, herb and cedar flavors are bright and lively. Well proportioned and moderately tannic, it's approachable now but better in 1997 after softening. Deliciously complex and terrific at this price. 4,900 cases made. • $12 • (02/29/96) SS • **90**
Migration White Napa Valley 1994: Austere, adding a lean edge to the onion and spice notes. Citric finish. 1,200 cases made. • $7 • (02/29/96) • **82**

DEER PARK | CALIFORNIA

Cabernet Sauvignon Howell Mountain Beatty Ranch Reserve 1990: Distinct for its spicy, peppery flavors and austere tannins. Full-bodied but turns lean and crisp on the finish. Best to cellar this until 1997 or 1998, even then it will be on the tannic side. 300 cases made. • $24 • (10/31/94) • **88**
Cabernet Sauvignon Howell Mountain Beatty Ranch Reserve 1988 • $24 • (11/15/92) • **87**
Petite Sirah Howell Mountain Parks/Muscatine Vineyards 1987 • $14 • (10/31/91) • **82**
Zinfandel Howell Mountain Beatty Ranch 1991: Light in color, showing earthy, dried fruit flavors and picking up a pleasant spiciness on the finish. 420 cases made. • $14 • (10/15/95) • **83**
Zinfandel Howell Mountain Beatty Ranch 1990: Tight, with earthy pepper and tar notes and prune flavor on the finish. Best after 1995. 700 cases made. • $14 • (10/15/94) • **81**
Zinfandel Howell Mountain Beatty Ranch 1988 • $13 • (10/15/92) • **83**
Zinfandel Howell Mountain Beatty Ranch 1987 • $14 • (08/31/91) • **79**
Zinfandel Howell Mountain Beatty Ranch Reserve 1987 • $18 • (08/31/91) • **85**
Zinfandel Napa Valley 1991: Showing cedary flavors and just a touch of spicy dried fruit. It's mature-tasting, but at the expense of riper fruit flavors. 122 cases made. • $16 • (10/15/95) • **83**

DEER VALLEY | CALIFORNIA

Cabernet Sauvignon Monterey 1985 • $5 • (12/31/87) • **72**
Chardonnay Monterey County 1993: Distinctively spicy in a Muscat sort of way, broad-textured, showing some bitter almond and grapefruit on the finish. Drinkable now. • $7 • (10/31/95) • **81**
Merlot 1990 • $6 • (05/31/92) • **77**
Merlot California 1992: Lean and simple, with cedary oak flavors overriding the fruit. • $6 • (09/15/94) • **79**

DEHLINGER | CALIFORNIA

Cabernet Franc Russian River Valley 1989 • $12 • (03/31/92) • **75**
Cabernet Franc Russian River Valley 1988 • $13 • (04/30/91) • **84**
Cabernet Sauvignon Russian River Valley 1992: Ripe and spicy layers of plum, cherry and currant flavors. Finish hold the fruit and has firm but balanced tannins. 975 cases made. • $18 • **86**
Cabernet Sauvignon Russian River Valley 1991: Ripe, supple and elegant, presenting a rich core of currant, herb, mineral and toasty oak, all well proportioned. The finish provides rich tannins and fine length. 1,100 cases made. • $15 • (05/15/95) • **88**
Cabernet Sauvignon Russian River Valley 1990: Firm and tannic, austere, exhibiting crisp, lean, herb-laced Cabernet fruit that finishes with a dry, tannic edge. Not quite ripe when last tasted. Try now. 900 cases made. • $15 • (11/15/94) • **80**
Cabernet Sauvignon Russian River Valley 1989 • $15 • (08/31/93) • **79**
Cabernet Sauvignon Russian River Valley 1988 • $15 • (03/31/92) • **83**
Cabernet Sauvignon Russian River Valley 1987 • $13 • (02/28/91) • **88**
Cabernet Sauvignon Russian River Valley 1986 • $13 • (03/15/90) • **90**
Cabernet Sauvignon Russian River Valley 1985 • $13 • (05/31/89) • **74**
Cabernet Sauvignon Russian River Valley 1984 • $12 • (02/15/88) • **76**
Cabernet Sauvignon Russian River Valley 1983 • $11 • (06/15/87) • **85**
Cabernet Sauvignon Russian River Valley 1982 • $11 • (08/31/86) • **73**
Cabernet Sauvignon Sonoma County 1981 • $9 • (05/16/85) • **87**
Chardonnay Russian River Valley 1994: Smooth and subtle, with a polished texture and ripe pear, spice and hazelnut notes. Shows off a tart edge on the finish, where the flavors linger. Some age should help. 2,850 cases made. • $16 • (05/31/96) • **88**
Chardonnay Russian River Valley 1993: Lively and intense, showing a focused band of pear, citrus, spice and light oak shadings. 2,800 cases made. • $15 • (05/31/95) • **88**
Chardonnay Russian River Valley 1992: Relies heavily on wood and toasty oak flavors, but has a rich core of spicy pear fruit underneath. Can stand cellaring, which may bring more fruit to the forefront. 2,700 cases made. • $15 • (06/30/94) • **84**
Chardonnay Russian River Valley 1991 • $13 • (05/15/93) • **89**
Chardonnay Russian River Valley The Montrachet Cuvée 1992: Serves up lots of ripe fruit, with elegant pear, spice and honey flavors; vanilla notes add dimension to the rich and smoky finish. Drinkable now. 300 cases made. • $20 • (11/15/94) • **90**
Merlot Sonoma County 1986 • $13 • (07/31/89) • **83**
Merlot Sonoma County 1985 • $11 • (04/30/88) • **89**
Merlot Sonoma County 1984 • $12 • (06/15/87) SS • **94**
Pinot Noir Russian River Valley 1993: Medium-bodied, featuring a modest core of black cherry jam. Smells more intriguing than it tastes; picks up on the finish. Right on track for the vintage. 2,000 cases made. • $20 • (11/30/95) • **88**
Pinot Noir Russian River Valley 1992: A bit coarse and closed, but the black cherry and cedary oak flavors that do emerge are pleasing. It finishes with firm, chewy tannins, so short-term cellaring is advised. 1,300 cases made. • $18 • (12/31/94) • **88**
Pinot Noir Russian River Valley 1991 • $17 • (02/28/94) • **87**
Pinot Noir Russian River Valley 1990 • $18 • (02/28/93) • **85**
Pinot Noir Russian River Valley 1989 • $17 • (03/31/92) • **80**
Pinot Noir Russian River Valley 1987 • $14 • (02/15/90) • **91**
Pinot Noir Russian River Valley 1986 • $13 • (05/31/89) • **88**
Pinot Noir Russian River Valley 1985 • $12 • (02/15/88) • **85**
Pinot Noir Russian River Valley 1984 • $11 • (06/30/87) • **89**
Pinot Noir Russian River Valley 1983 • $10 • (08/31/86) • **89**
Pinot Noir Russian River Valley 1982 • $10 • (10/01/85) • **86**
Pinot Noir Russian River Valley Reserve 1992: An intense and tightly wound California Pinot, with lots of depth and flavor. Mineral, black cherry and cedar aromas lead to matching flavors, but it finishes with a firm, tannic grip. Drinkable now. 300 cases made. • $25 • (12/31/94) • **91**
Pinot Noir Russian River Valley Reserve 1991 • $23 • (02/28/94) • **91**
Pinot Noir Sonoma County Selection 1990 • $10 • (02/28/93) • **81**
Syrah Russian River Valley 1993: A dark and chewy Rhône-style red from California that packs in plenty of plum, black cherry, mineral and spice notes, finishing with a hint of leather and tobacco. Approachable now, but also age-worthy. 990 cases made. • $18 • (05/31/96) • **90**
Syrah Russian River Valley 1992: Uncommonly dark with deep purple hues and a rich, plush core of plum, cherry, currant and mineral flavors. Serves up a big, bold mouthful of California Syrah. Ready now, but worthy of short-term cellaring. 200 cases made. • $16 • (05/15/95) • **93**
Young Vines Russian River Valley 1985 • $9 • (04/15/89) • **68**
Zinfandel Sonoma County 1983 • $8 • (07/31/87) • **73**

DELICATO | CALIFORNIA

Cabernet Sauvignon California 1985 • $6 • (06/30/88) • **66**
Cabernet Sauvignon Carneros Napa Valley 1983 • $10 • (06/15/87) • **72**
White Zinfandel California 1988 • $5 • (06/15/89) • **73**

DELILLE | WASHINGTON

Chaleur Estate Yakima Valley 1993: Ripe, rich, supple and glowing with plum, black cherry, blueberry and gently spicy flavors that last and last on the generous finish. 950 cases made. • $28 • **91**
Chaleur Estate Yakima Valley 1992: Ripe, velvety and distinctly herbal, as bay leaf and menthol notes weave through the solid blackberry and anise flavors. 1,000 cases made. • $28 • (09/30/95) • **85**
Red Yakima Valley D2 1993: Ripe and distinguished for its currant, prune and plum flavors, chocolate, coffee and spice overtones—all of which swirl smoothly through the long finish. Has fine tannins that don't get in the way now, but try to keep it through 2000-2002. 475 cases made. • $18 • **92**

DEMOOR | CALIFORNIA

Cabernet Sauvignon Napa Valley 1989 • $14 • (05/15/94) • **86**
Cabernet Sauvignon Napa Valley 1987 • $16 • (11/15/91) • **76**
Cabernet Sauvignon Napa Valley 1985 • $14 • (03/01/89) • **79**
Cabernet Sauvignon Napa Valley 1984 • $14 • (03/01/89) • **88**
Cabernet Sauvignon Napa Valley 1983 • $12 • (03/01/89) • **86**
Cabernet Sauvignon Napa Valley 1982 • $12 • (03/01/89) • **86**
Cabernet Sauvignon Napa Valley Napa Cellars 1981 • $12 • (03/01/89) • **86**
Cabernet Sauvignon Napa Valley Napa Cellars 1980 • $12 • (03/01/89) • **80**
Cabernet Sauvignon Napa Valley Napa Cellars 1979 • $10 • (03/01/89) • **85**
Cabernet Sauvignon Napa Valley Napa Cellars 1978 • $10 • (03/01/89) • **89**
Cabernet Sauvignon Napa Valley Owners Select 1986 • $16 • (02/28/91) • **78**
Cabernet Sauvignon Napa Valley Owners Select 1982 • $12 • (03/01/89) • **88**
Chardonnay Napa Valley 1993: Marked by a grassy edge, with a lean band of pear and citrus notes. 1,800 cases made. • $12 • (07/31/95) • **80**
Chardonnay Napa Valley 1992: Ripe and fruity with spicy pear and pineapple flavors that turn simple on the finish. Ready now. 1,500 cases made. • $12 • (06/30/94) • **83**
Chardonnay Napa Valley 1991 • $13 • (07/15/93) • **80**
Sauvignon Blanc Late Harvest Fie Doux 1989 • $12 • (03/15/92) • **84**
Sauvignon Blanc Napa Valley 1992: Hay-like aromas, plus a whiff of barnyard, make this a distinctive wine that not everyone can warm up to. 1,100 cases made. • $9 • (08/31/94) • **76**
Zinfandel Napa Valley 1991 • $10 • (09/30/93) • **87**
Zinfandel Napa Valley 1988 • $10 • (04/30/91) • **72**

Key: SS—Spectator Selection. CS—Cellar Selection. BB—Best Buy. $NA—Price not available. (BT)—Barrel tasting. Ⓐ—Auction Price.
Dates in parentheses represent the issues in which the ratings were published.

DE NATALE | CALIFORNIA

Pinot Noir Russian River Valley 1991 • $9 • (02/28/93) • **59**
Pinot Noir Russian River Valley 1990 • $8 • (02/28/93) • **82**

DEUX AMIS | CALIFORNIA

Cabernet Sauvignon Dry Creek Valley 1987 • $14 • (11/15/91) • **83**
Zinfandel Sonoma County 1993: Medium-bodied and elegant, the cherry and raspberry flavors showing well-proportioned contours. 1,600 cases made. • $12 • (10/15/95) • **86**

DEVLIN | CALIFORNIA

Cabernet Sauvignon Santa Cruz Mountains Beauregard Ranch 1991: Laced with herb and funky oak flavors, it has an earthy, tanky character. • $9 • (02/28/95) • **73**
Cabernet Sauvignon Sonoma County 1981 • $6 • (08/01/85) • **83**
Merlot Central Coast 1982 • $8 • (07/16/85) • **80**

DI STEFANO | WASHINGTON

Cabernet Sauvignon Columbia Valley 1991: Bright and fruity, open-textured, with plum and berry flavors up front, a vanilla-spicy edge and a very soft finish. Drinkable now. 100 cases made. • $16 • (09/30/94) • **84**
Fumé Blanc Columbia Valley 1992: Light and fruity, a little watery, but the melon and vanilla flavors are pleasant. 225 cases made. • $8 • (09/30/94) • **78**

DIABLO VISTA | CALIFORNIA

Merlot Dry Creek Valley 1981 • $7 • (05/01/84) • **79**

DIAMOND CREEK | CALIFORNIA

Cabernet Sauvignon Napa Valley Gravelly Meadow 1994: Medium weight with an elegant core of currant, cherry and earthy notes, finishing with a nice focus. Borders on outstanding. 650 cases made. • $50 • (05/31/95) • **85-89** (BT)
Cabernet Sauvignon Napa Valley Gravelly Meadow 1993: Marked by mint and herbal flavors, it manages to counter with enough coffee and currant notes to keep it in balance. Complex aftertaste. Best to age into 1998. 650 cases made. • $50 • (12/15/95) • **86**
Cabernet Sauvignon Napa Valley Gravelly Meadow 1992: Firm and compact, with a tight band of currant, cedar and cherry flavors. Still needs cellaring to soften and evolve. Best after 1999. 650 cases made. • $50 • (11/15/94) CS • **92**
Cabernet Sauvignon Napa Valley Gravelly Meadow 1992: Elegant with supple, spicy black cherry fruit that turns earthy on the finish. Crisp and tannic. 3,600 cases made. • $NA • (05/31/93) BT • **888**
Cabernet Sauvignon Napa Valley Gravelly Meadow 1991: Chewy in texture, but brightly focused currant and plum flavors shine through the layer of fine tannins, making this an elegant wine, echoing fruit on the finish. Tightly wrapped now, but should be at its best after 1997. 600 cases made. • $50 • (10/31/93) CS • **92**
Cabernet Sauvignon Napa Valley Gravelly Meadow 1990: Extremely youthful and full of extract, with concentrated currant, cedar and herb aromas and flavors. Hints of cola and tea on the long, smooth finish. A complete wine, drink now or hold through 1998. 447 cases made. • $50 • (11/15/92) • **89**
Cabernet Sauvignon Napa Valley Gravelly Meadow 1989 • $50 • (01/31/92) • **83**
Cabernet Sauvignon Napa Valley Gravelly Meadow 1988 • $60 • (11/15/90) • **87**
Cabernet Sauvignon Napa Valley Gravelly Meadow 1987 • $50 • (12/15/89) • **90**
Cabernet Sauvignon Napa Valley Gravelly Meadow 1986 • $53 • (03/01/89) • **94**
Cabernet Sauvignon Napa Valley Gravelly Meadow 1985 • $29 Ⓐ • (03/01/89) • **92**
Cabernet Sauvignon Napa Valley Gravelly Meadow 1984 • $55 • (03/01/89) • **94**
Cabernet Sauvignon Napa Valley Gravelly Meadow 1983 • $54 • (03/01/89) • **89**
Cabernet Sauvignon Napa Valley Gravelly Meadow 1982 • $55 • (03/01/89) • **89**
Cabernet Sauvignon Napa Valley Gravelly Meadow 1981 • $60 • (03/01/89) • **89**
Cabernet Sauvignon Napa Valley Gravelly Meadow 1980 • $54 • (03/01/89) • **92**
Cabernet Sauvignon Napa Valley Gravelly Meadow 1979 • $85 • (03/01/89) • **91**
Cabernet Sauvignon Napa Valley Gravelly Meadow 1978 • $13 • (03/01/89) • **93**
Cabernet Sauvignon Napa Valley Gravelly Meadow 1978 • $67 Ⓐ • (11/15/92) • **95**
Cabernet Sauvignon Napa Valley Gravelly Meadow 1977 • $75 • (03/01/89) • **89**
Cabernet Sauvignon Napa Valley Gravelly Meadow 1976 • $77 • (03/01/89) • **85**
Cabernet Sauvignon Napa Valley Gravelly Meadow 1975 • $95 • (03/01/89) • **85**
Cabernet Sauvignon Napa Valley Gravelly Meadow 1974: This wine showed the best of the three Diamond Creek bottlings. Rich and earthy, but deeply colored and very concentrated, it has uncommon depth and intensity for a Cabernet this age. While exhibiting exceptionally well now, it appears to have the kind of richness and intensity to improve for another decade. Still, it's best to drink soon rather than risk its drying out. 105 cases made. • $160 • (11/15/94) • **94**
Cabernet Sauvignon Napa Valley Gravelly Meadow Lake Blend 1991: Bright and chewy, with a solid core of currant and berry flavors, almost floral at the edges; a youthful wine with a light feel behind the layer of tannins. Nicely balanced, it should be at its best after 1996 or 1997. 50 cases made. • $50 • (11/15/93) • **90**
Cabernet Sauvignon Napa Valley Gravelly Meadow Special Selection 1982 • $20 • (03/01/89) • **84**
Cabernet Sauvignon Napa Valley Lake 1990: Bright and lively, packed with broad currant, herb, mineral, tobacco and hints of prune flavors that gain complexity and depth with oak shadings. A serious wine that commands your attention. Try now. 117 cases made. • $176 Ⓐ • (02/15/93) • **90**
Cabernet Sauvignon Napa Valley Lake 1987 • $220 Ⓐ • (11/15/90) • **91**
Cabernet Sauvignon Napa Valley Lake 1984 • $153 Ⓐ • (03/01/89) • **92**
Cabernet Sauvignon Napa Valley Lake 1978 • $528 Ⓐ • (11/15/92) • **98**
Cabernet Sauvignon Napa Valley Red Rock Terrace 1994: Firm and compact, with a pleasantly focused band of toasty oak and currant notes, picking up a complex earthy edge on the finish. • $NA • (05/31/95) • **90-94** (BT)
Cabernet Sauvignon Napa Valley Red Rock Terrace 1993: Medium-bodied, intense and tannic, with a modest core of currant, cedar and berry notes. Comes across as lacking richness and concentration. 750 cases made. • $50 • (12/15/95) • **85**
Cabernet Sauvignon Napa Valley Red Rock Terrace 1992: Ripe and spicy, displaying a rich core of black cherry, currant, anise and cedary oak flavors. Well focused with intensity and depth, needs cellaring until 1998 to soften. 750 cases made. • $50 • (11/15/94) • **90**
Cabernet Sauvignon Napa Valley Red Rock Terrace 1991: Earthy, herbal and chewy, with a solid core of cherry fruit to carry it to a long finish and a cedar-tobacco character that makes it distinctive; a chunky wine that needs until 1997-1999 to soften its edges. 700 cases made. • $50 • (11/15/93) • **90**
Cabernet Sauvignon Napa Valley Red Rock Terrace 1990: Chunky, chewy and tannic, with a solid core of black cherry and currant flavors. Still rustic and rough in texture, but solid enough to be expected to gain through 1997 to '99. 634 cases made. • $50 • (11/15/92) • **91**
Cabernet Sauvignon Napa Valley Red Rock Terrace 1989 • $50 • (01/31/92) • **89**
Cabernet Sauvignon Napa Valley Red Rock Terrace 1988 • $47 • (11/15/90) • **89**
Cabernet Sauvignon Napa Valley Red Rock Terrace 1987 • $52 • (12/15/89) • **94**
Cabernet Sauvignon Napa Valley Red Rock Terrace 1986 • $51 • (03/01/89) • **96**

Cabernet Sauvignon Napa Valley Red Rock Terrace 1985 • $29 Ⓐ • (03/01/89) • **93**
Cabernet Sauvignon Napa Valley Red Rock Terrace 1984 • $60 • (03/01/89) • **96**
Cabernet Sauvignon Napa Valley Red Rock Terrace 1983 • $49 • (03/01/89) • **88**
Cabernet Sauvignon Napa Valley Red Rock Terrace 1982 • $51 • (03/01/89) • **87**
Cabernet Sauvignon Napa Valley Red Rock Terrace 1981 • $63 • (03/01/89) • **91**
Cabernet Sauvignon Napa Valley Red Rock Terrace 1980 • $53 • (03/01/89) • **86**
Cabernet Sauvignon Napa Valley Red Rock Terrace 1979 • $85 • (03/01/89) • **92**
Cabernet Sauvignon Napa Valley Red Rock Terrace 1978 • $63 Ⓐ • (11/15/92) • **95**
Cabernet Sauvignon Napa Valley Red Rock Terrace 1976 • $77 • (03/01/89) • **85**
Cabernet Sauvignon Napa Valley Red Rock Terrace 1975 • $77 • (03/01/89) • **88**
Cabernet Sauvignon Napa Valley Red Rock Terrace 1974: Deeply colored, with wonderful complex and youthful aromas. The spicy, grapey currant flavors pick up an anise note on a long, full finish. A second bottle showed more mature flavors and faded with a metallic edge. Best now. • $140 • (11/15/94) • **92**
Cabernet Sauvignon Napa Valley Red Rock Terrace 1972 • $200 • (03/01/89) • **74**
Cabernet Sauvignon Napa Valley Red Rock Terrace First Pick 1977 • $75 • (03/01/89) • **88**
Cabernet Sauvignon Napa Valley Red Rock Terrace Micro-Climate 3 1991: Spicy, peppery, bursting with currant and jammy blackberry fruit, marvelously dense and deep, flashing all sorts of nuances to make it interesting, all of it centered around the concentrated fruit. Muscular enough to want until 2000-2005 to settle down. 50 cases made. • $50 • (11/15/93) CS • **94**
Cabernet Sauvignon Napa Valley Red Rock Terrace Second Pick 1977 • $10 • (03/01/89) • **75**
Cabernet Sauvignon Napa Valley Red Rock Terrace Special Selection 1982 • $20 • (03/01/89) • **80**
Cabernet Sauvignon Napa Valley Three Vineyard Blend 1992: A rare blend of the three Diamond Creek vineyards, it is also the least distinctive. Tight, firm and tannic with an earthy currant edge. • $NA • (05/31/93) BT • **88**
Cabernet Sauvignon Napa Valley Three Vineyard Blend 1990: Austere, but packed with herb, currant, tobacco and plum flavors framed by spicy, toasty oak notes. Rich, intense, concentrated, well focused and in need of cellaring. The finish is thick with tannins and fruit. Try after 1997. • $75 • (02/15/93) • **88**
Cabernet Sauvignon Napa Valley Three Vineyard Blend 1985 • $100 • (03/01/89) • **89**
Cabernet Sauvignon Napa Valley Three Vineyard Blend 1984 • $100 • (03/01/89) • **89**
Cabernet Sauvignon Napa Valley Three Vineyard Blend 1981 • $100 • (03/01/89) • **90**
Cabernet Sauvignon Napa Valley Volcanic Hill 1994: Firm, dark, ripe and richly flavored, with tiers of currant, toasty oak and cherry flavors that fold together nicely through a long, full finish. Impressive for its balance of flavors. • $NA • (05/31/95) • **90-94** (BT)
Cabernet Sauvignon Napa Valley Volcanic Hill 1993: Ripe and intense, with a tightly wound core of earthy currant, herb, tobacco and spice. Finishes with good balance and finesse and just-so tannins. Should soften by 1998. 1,400 cases made. • $50 • (12/15/95) • **88**
Cabernet Sauvignon Napa Valley Volcanic Hill 1992: Supple and elegant, with polished currant, black cherry and plum flavors. Finishes with good length and firm tannins. Best after 1998. 1,400 cases made. • $50 • (11/15/94) • **91**

Key: SS—Spectator Selection. CS—Cellar Selection. BB—Best Buy. $NA—Price not available. (BT)—Barrel tasting. Ⓐ—Auction Price.
Dates in parentheses represent the issues in which the ratings were published.

Cabernet Sauvignon Napa Valley Volcanic Hill 1991: Lean and trim, a harmonious wine offering a burst of currant, cherry and berry aromas and flavors, a bit raw and youthful now, but it has the balance and grace to improve through 1998 at least. 800 cases made. • $50 • (11/15/93) CS • **91**
Cabernet Sauvignon Napa Valley Volcanic Hill 1990: Solid and flavorful, with raspberry and currant flavors bursting through the fine veil of tannins, echoing fruit and spice on the long finish. A great choice for laying down in your cellar. Drink from 1997 to 2010. 981 cases made. • $50 • (11/15/92) CS • **92**
Cabernet Sauvignon Napa Valley Volcanic Hill 1989 • $50 • (01/31/92) • **86**
Cabernet Sauvignon Napa Valley Volcanic Hill 1988 • $26 Ⓐ • (11/15/90) • **88**
Cabernet Sauvignon Napa Valley Volcanic Hill 1987 • $58 • (12/15/89) • **95**
Cabernet Sauvignon Napa Valley Volcanic Hill 1986 • $43 Ⓐ • (03/01/89) • **96**
Cabernet Sauvignon Napa Valley Volcanic Hill 1985 • $32 Ⓐ • (03/01/89) • **93**
Cabernet Sauvignon Napa Valley Volcanic Hill 1984 • $46 Ⓐ • (03/01/89) • **94**
Cabernet Sauvignon Napa Valley Volcanic Hill 1983 • $50 • (03/01/89) • **89**
Cabernet Sauvignon Napa Valley Volcanic Hill 1982 • $38 Ⓐ • (03/01/89) • **89**
Cabernet Sauvignon Napa Valley Volcanic Hill 1981 • $62 • (03/01/89) • **92**
Cabernet Sauvignon Napa Valley Volcanic Hill 1980 • $57 • (03/01/89) • **90**
Cabernet Sauvignon Napa Valley Volcanic Hill 1978 • $85 Ⓐ • (11/15/92) • **94**
Cabernet Sauvignon Napa Valley Volcanic Hill 1977 • $75 • (03/01/89) • **84**
Cabernet Sauvignon Napa Valley Volcanic Hill 1976 • $77 • (03/01/89) • **87**
Cabernet Sauvignon Napa Valley Volcanic Hill 1975 • $100 • (03/01/89) • **93**
Cabernet Sauvignon Napa Valley Volcanic Hill 1974: This showed consistently in two tastings, with an austere, tannic edge to the Cabernet fruit. At this stage it is still tightly wound, with just a trace of racy currant flavor coming through on the finish. Ready now. 485 cases made. • $130 • (11/15/94) • **88**
Cabernet Sauvignon Napa Valley Volcanic Hill 1973 • $200 • (03/01/89) • **80**
Cabernet Sauvignon Napa Valley Volcanic Hill 1972 • $200 • (03/01/89) • **85**
Cabernet Sauvignon Napa Valley Volcanic Hill First Pick 1979 • $90 • (03/01/89) • **95**
Cabernet Sauvignon Napa Valley Volcanic Hill Micro-Climate 4 1991: Firm and brilliantly focused, a dense wine with concentrated plum, currant and raspberry fruit shaded by more than a hint of cedar. A real mouthful of Cabernet, lithe and muscular, but balanced enough to hit its stride around 1998-2000. 50 cases made. • $50 • (11/15/93) CS • **93**
Cabernet Sauvignon Napa Valley Volcanic Hill Second Pick 1979 • $15 • (03/01/89) • **82**
Cabernet Sauvignon Napa Valley Volcanic Hill Special Selection 1982 • $20 • (03/01/89) • **79**

DIANA, CHATEAU | CALIFORNIA

Blanc de Noirs Monterey Special Reserve 1986 • $7 • (06/15/91) • **71**
Cabernet Sauvignon California Limited Edition 1989 • $5 • (11/15/91) • **69**
Cabernet Sauvignon California Limited Edition 1988 • $5 • (10/15/91) • **72**
Cabernet Sauvignon California Limited Edition 1986 • $5 • (10/15/91) BB • **82**
Cabernet Sauvignon Central Coast Limited Edition 1984 • $6 • (11/30/88) BB • **82**

DICKERSON | CALIFORNIA

Cabernet Sauvignon Napa Valley Ruby Cabernet Limited Reserve 1991: Pretty and deeply colored, with exotic wild berry and cherry flavor. This rich, high-extract red combines classic Cabernet notes with a hint of Zinfandel-like fruit. 256 cases made. • $11 • (11/15/94) • **87**
Merlot Napa Valley Limited Reserve 1993: Young and intense, with a vibrant core of plum, black cherry, herb and toasty oak. Has a big,

firm tannic structure, so cellaring into 1998 is advised—but even then it may be tannic. 229 cases made. • $16 • **87**

Merlot Napa Valley Limited Reserve 1992: Intense and lively, with a solid core of currant, cherry and light oak shadings that give it richness, depth and complexity. Delicious now, but should drink well through 1998. 200 cases made. • $17 • (02/28/95) • **90**

Ruby Cabernet Limited Reserve Napa Valley 1993: Aromatic, with complex wild berry, mint and cherry flavors. Doesn't fit the Cabernet mold because the grape is a cross of Cabernet and Carignane. 225 cases made. • $9 • (12/15/95) • **88**

Ruby Cabernet Napa Valley 1992: Ripe and chunky, spicy black cherry, currant and plum flavors finish in a firm, tannic grip. Try now. 228 cases made. • $10 • (05/15/95) • **85**

Ruby Cabernet Napa Valley 1988 • $9 • (02/28/91) • **79**

Zinfandel Napa Valley Limited Reserve 1993: Very ripe and fruity, bordering on jammy, as black cherry, raspberry and wild berry flavors turn up the volume. A hot, high alcohol aftertaste. 180 cases made. • $17 • (12/31/95) • **88**

Zinfandel Napa Valley Limited Reserve 1991: Intensely ripe, with a spicy, minty edge. Loaded with complex black cherry and raspberry flavors. Tannic on the finish, but the fruit comes through. Tempting now, but worth waiting until 1999. 200 cases made. • $19 • (10/15/94) • **92**

DOLAN | CALIFORNIA

Cabernet Sauvignon Mendocino 1984 • $12 • (05/31/88) • **88**

Cabernet Sauvignon Mendocino 1983 • $12 • (02/29/88) • **86**

DOLAN, R.W. | CALIFORNIA

Merlot California 1986 • $8 • (01/31/89) • **88**

DOLCE | CALIFORNIA

Dessert California 1990 • $50 • (11/15/93) • **92**

Dessert California Late Harvest 1989 • $50 • (06/15/92) • **91**

Dessert Napa Valley Late Harvest 1992: Sweet, rich, complex honey, pear, fig, nectarine and peach flavors lead to a concentrated aftertaste that echoes ultra ripe fruit. Ready now through 1998. 1,050 cases made. • $50 • (12/31/95) • **90**

DOMAINE, LE | CALIFORNIA

Brut California NV • $5 • (02/28/89) • **67**

DOMINUS | CALIFORNIA

Napanook Vineyard Napa Valley 1991: Marked by an earthy, cedary edge, it manages to showcase a supple, harmonious core of currant, tobacco, mineral and anise flavors. Finishes with thick but polished tannins. Best to cellar into 1997. 6,500 cases made. • $55 • (11/15/95) CS • **93**

DOMINUS ESTATE | CALIFORNIA

Napa Valley 1989 • $45 • (11/15/93) • **89**

Napa Valley 1988 • $45 • (12/15/92) • **87**

Napa Valley 1987 • $43 Ⓐ • (11/15/91) • **89**

Napa Valley 1986 • $45 Ⓐ • (02/28/91) • **91**

Napa Valley 1985 • $69 Ⓐ • (02/15/90) • **84**

Napa Valley 1984 • $40 • (03/01/89) • **90**

Napa Valley 1983 • $48 Ⓐ • (04/15/89) • **86**

Cabernet Sauvignon Napa Valley 1990: Deeply flavored, rich and complex, with tiers of currant, coffee, spice and chocolate. While it's young, intense and tannic, it's developing a supple texture, which allows the flavors to glide through on the finish. Best to cellar short-term, try in 1997. Tasted twice. 4,600 cases made. • $64 Ⓐ • (06/30/94) SS • **91**

DONNA MARIA | CALIFORNIA

Pinot Noir Chalk Hill 1981 • $6 • (09/16/84) • **79**

DORCICH | CALIFORNIA

Cabernet Sauvignon Santa Clara County 1991: Hard edged and firmly tannic, with a grapey currant and red cherry flavor, but in the end it turns dry and chewy. Best after 1998. 1,250 cases made. • $18 • (07/31/95) • **86**

Cabernet Sauvignon Santa Clara County 1990: Grapey with ripe black cherry and plummy fruit that's rustic and tannic, but it hangs in there despite the rough edges. Best after 1997. 1,100 cases made. • $20 • (07/31/95) • **85**

DORCICH CELLARS | CALIFORNIA

Cabernet Sauvignon Santa Clara County 1991: Hard-edged and firmly tannic, presenting grapey currant and red cherry flavors, but in the end it turns dry and chewy. Best after 1998. 1,250 cases made. • $18 • (07/31/95) • **86**

Cabernet Sauvignon Santa Clara County 1990: Grapey, ripe black cherry and plum flavors in a rustic, tannic style, but it hangs in there despite the rough edges. Try in 1997. 1,100 cases made. • $20 • (07/31/95) • **85**

DORE | CALIFORNIA

Cabernet Sauvignon California 1984 • $5 • (12/31/87) • **64**

Cabernet Sauvignon California Limited Release Lot 102 1987 • $8 • (11/15/91) • **80**

DOUGLASS HILL | CALIFORNIA

Cabernet Sauvignon Napa Valley 1992: Smooth and polished, with a gamy, earthy edge to the cherry and berry flavors. Simple and pleasant. 800 cases made. • $15 • (12/15/95) • **84**

Chardonnay Napa Valley 1993: Goes for a strong, spicy overlay to the ripe pineapple and pear, finishing somewhat off-balanced and leaning toward caramel on the finish. Drinkable now. 1,000 cases made. • $15 • (12/31/95) • **84**

DREYER SONOMA | CALIFORNIA

Cabernet Sauvignon Sonoma County 1989 • $15 • (08/31/92) • **79**

Chardonnay Sonoma County 1994: Fresh and floral, a Chardonnay of modest scale but charming for its spicy pear flavors. Ready now. 3,000 cases made. • $9 • (04/30/96) • **87**

DRY CREEK | CALIFORNIA

Cabernet Franc Dry Creek Valley 1990 • $18 • (10/15/93) • **83**

Cabernet Sauvignon Dry Creek Valley 1993: Very ripe and somewhat cedary from oak. Plum and cherry notes are bright and jammy, finishing with dry tannins as flavors linger through. Best in 1998. 9,300 cases made. • $16 • (11/30/95) • **88**

Cabernet Sauvignon Dry Creek Valley 1992: Elegant, smooth and polished, sporting refined cherry, currant, berry and spice notes. Shows more depth and flavor than most Dry Creek Cabernets. 10,100 cases made. • $16 • (10/15/95) • **89**

Cabernet Sauvignon Dry Creek Valley 1974: Hanging on but its best years are well behind. Ripe with mature Cabernet flavors that echo herb, earth and currant notes. 817 cases made. • $55 • (11/15/94) • **83**

Cabernet Sauvignon Dry Creek Valley Reserve 1993: Offers a decent core of wild berry, black berry and cherry flavors of some depth and concentration. Finishes with crisp tannins and a touch of dill from the oak. 2,000 cases made. • $22 • (03/31/96) • **83**

Cabernet Sauvignon Dry Creek Valley Reserve 1991: Firm, tight and tannic, but with enough rich currant and plum flavors to hold your interest. Finishes with pretty oak shadings and crisp acidity that keeps the flavors going. Needs time to soften and evolve, best after 1997. 1,720 cases made. • $20 • (10/31/94) • **89**

DUCKHORN

Cabernet Sauvignon Sonoma County 1991: Ripe, rich, intense and spicy with high extract, jammy currant, raspberry and plum flavors that pack a wallop. Drink now to 2000. Tasted three times. 15,000 cases made. • $15 • (11/15/93) • **87**
Cabernet Sauvignon Sonoma County 1989 • $14 • (03/31/92) • **86**
Cabernet Sauvignon Sonoma County 1988 • $14 • (05/31/91) • **81**
Cabernet Sauvignon Sonoma County 1987 • $13 • (04/15/90) • **84**
Cabernet Sauvignon Sonoma County 1986 • $11 • (03/31/89) • **88**
Cabernet Sauvignon Sonoma County 1985 • $11 • (05/31/88) SS • **91**
Cabernet Sauvignon Sonoma County 1984 • $10 • (05/15/87) • **85**
Cabernet Sauvignon Sonoma County 1982 • $9 • (02/01/85) • **81**
Cabernet Sauvignon Sonoma County 1980 • $9 • (04/16/84) • **78**
Cabernet Sauvignon Sonoma County Special Reserve 1980 • $13 • (05/01/86) • **78**
Chardonnay Dry Creek Valley Reserve 1994: A smooth, rich and complex young white, boasting well-integrated pear, fig, melon and toasty oak notes. Turns elegant and flavorful on the finish. 6,000 cases made. • $17 • (05/15/96) • **90**
Chardonnay Dry Creek Valley Wolcott Vineyard Barrel Fermented Reserve 1994: Bold, ripe and full-bodied, offering rich fig, citrus and honey notes. It picks up a good dose of smoky, toasty oak. Packs in lots of flavor. 310 cases made. • $22 • (02/29/96) • **88**
Chardonnay Sonoma County 20th Vintage Anniversary Reserve 1991: Tastes smooth and mature, with honey, pear and toast notes of moderate richness and complexity. Ready now. 5,000 cases made. • $15 • (11/15/94) • **87**
Chardonnay Sonoma County Barrel Fermented 1994: Serves up a pleasing core of ripe, juicy pear, honey and butterscotch notes, turning elegant and complex on the finish. Altogether complex and well balanced. Ready. 25,000 cases made. • $14 • (03/31/96) • **89**
Chardonnay Sonoma County Barrel Fermented 1993: Marked by spicy pear and apple notes of modest proportion. Pleasant if on the light side. 30,700 cases made. • $14 • (07/31/95) • **84**
Chardonnay Sonoma County Barrel Fermented 1992: Herbal and leafy, with a lean edge to the pear and apple notes. May be more appealing with time in the bottle. 24,000 cases made. • $14 • (06/30/94) • **80**
Chardonnay Sonoma County Barrel Fermented 1991 • $13 • (03/15/93) • **85**
Chardonnay Sonoma County Barrel Fermented Reserve 1992: A touch racy with pear, nectarine and honey notes of modest proportion, although the flavors fan out on the finish. 5,000 cases made. • $16 • (07/31/95) • **86**
Chenin Blanc California Dry 1993: Smooth, off-dry, a generous wine with nicely compact pear and melon fruit. Ready now. 11,200 cases made. • $7 • (05/31/95) • **82**
Chenin Blanc Clarksburg Dry 1994: Soft, spicy apple and almond flavors are pleasant to drink soon. 7,310 cases made. • $7 • (06/15/96) • **83**
David S. Stare Vintner's Reserve Sonoma County 1984 • $18 • (05/31/88) • **88**
David S. Stare Vintner's Selection Dry Creek Valley 1983 • $15 • (12/31/86) • **74**
Fumé Blanc Dry Creek Valley Barrel Fermented Reserve 1994: Complex, well oaked, but flavorful too, offering tiers of fig, melon and spice. Holds its notes on the finish. 2,200 cases made. • $15 • (02/29/96) • **88**
Fumé Blanc Dry Creek Valley Barrel Fermented Reserve 1991: Round and generous, featuring honey accents on the fig and herb flavors. 1,000 cases made. • $14 • (03/31/95) • **85**
Fumé Blanc Dry Creek Valley Reserve 1991 • $14 • (03/15/94) • **84**
Fumé Blanc Sonoma County 1991 • $9 • (04/15/93) • **84**
Fumé Blanc Sonoma County Dry 1993: Simple, sturdy and nicely focused, showing pear and green, leafy notes. 22,500 cases made. • $9 • (08/31/95) • **84**
Fumé Blanc Sonoma County Dry 1992 • $9 • (04/30/94) • **82**
Meritage Dry Creek Valley 1993: Effusive cherry, berry and currant flavors. Holds its fruitiness through the finish, avoiding excessive oak or tannins. Tempting now, but can age into 1997. 2,000 cases made. • $20 • (11/30/95) • **89**

> **Key:** SS—Spectator Selection. CS—Cellar Selection. BB—Best Buy. $NA—Price not available. (BT)—Barrel tasting. Ⓐ—Auction Price.
> **Dates in parentheses represent the issues in which the ratings were published.**

Meritage Dry Creek Valley 1990: An herbal, oaky style with ripe, chunky currant, plum and wild berry flavors. This offers good richness and depth, but it's best to cellar until 1997. 1,450 cases made. • $18 • (11/15/94) • **89**
Meritage Dry Creek Valley 1988 • $24 • (10/15/93) • **86**
Meritage Dry Creek Valley 1987 • $24 • (01/31/92) • **87**
Meritage Dry Creek Valley 1986 • $22 • (09/15/90) • **80**
Meritage Dry Creek Valley 1985 • $22 • (11/15/89) • **89**
Merlot Dry Creek Valley 1992: Marked by a cedary oak edge to the herb and cherry-laced fruit, finishing with a crisp tannic edge. 10,200 cases made. • $15 • (06/15/95) • **84**
Merlot Dry Creek Valley 1991 • $15 • (03/15/94) • **84**
Merlot Dry Creek Valley 1990 • $14 • (03/31/93) • **85**
Merlot Dry Creek Valley 1989 • $14 • (04/15/92) • **86**
Merlot Dry Creek Valley 1988 • $15 • (03/31/91) • **83**
Merlot Dry Creek Valley 1985 • $7 • (02/15/88) • **80**
Merlot Dry Creek Valley Bullock House Vineyard 1991: Crisp and focused, spicy, with enough berry flavor to keep it lively. Drinkable now. 1,362 cases made. • $20 • (09/15/94) • **85**
Merlot Dry Creek Valley Reserve 1993: Ripe and full-bodied, with firm tannins. Delivers lots of ripe cherry and plum flavors with jammy anise and cedary oak shadings. Now through 1998. 2,000 cases made. • $22 • **87**
Merlot Sonoma County 1986 • $15 • (03/31/89) • **78**
Sauvignon Blanc Late Harvest Dry Creek Valley Soleil Vintner's Reserve David S. Stare 1986 • $15 • (06/15/89) • **90**
Sauvignon Blanc Late Harvest Sonoma County Soliel NV: Generally sweet and smooth, sporting a sort of herbal honey flavor that lingers on the finish. Tasty now. 875 cases made. • $18 • (04/30/95) • **85**
Zinfandel Dry Creek Valley 1986 • $9 • (04/15/89) • **85**
Zinfandel Dry Creek Valley Old Vines 1991 • $12 • (08/31/93) • **88**
Zinfandel Dry Creek Valley Old Vines 1990 • $11 • (10/15/92) • **85**
Zinfandel Dry Creek Valley Old Vines 1989 • $11 • (05/15/92) • **85**
Zinfandel Dry Creek Valley Old Vines 1988 • $11 • (02/15/91) • **86**
Zinfandel Sonoma County Old Vines 1993: Well balanced, serving up nice, ripe wild berry and cherry flavors and a sense of elegance and finesse. Drinkable now. 7,300 cases made. • $15 • (09/15/95) • **88**
Zinfandel Sonoma County Old Vines 1992: Lean, with tannic wild berry and raspberry flavors, but without the depth or richness you might expect from an "old vines" wine. 8,200 cases made. • $14 • (02/28/95) • **83**
Zinfandel Sonoma County Reserve 1993: Medium in weight, smooth and spicy, adding a touch of strawberry jam. Loses its focus on aftertaste, where the flavors turn simple. 1,000 cases made. • $20 • (05/15/96) • **83**
Zinfandel Sonoma County Reserve 1991: Despite an odd woody component, the fruit is pure and supple, with cherry and plum flavors. Drinks well now. 500 cases made. • $20 • (10/15/94) • **84**

DUCKHORN | CALIFORNIA

Cabernet Sauvignon Napa Valley 1992: Smooth and harmonious, even at this youthful age, with pretty plum, black cherry and currant notes. The finish shows off its complexity and finesse. The firm tannins have a slight gritty edge now, so it's best to age into 1998. 5,000 cases made. • $24 • (10/31/95) SS • **90**
Cabernet Sauvignon Napa Valley 1990: Young, firm and intense, with a rich, complex, concentrated core of currant, cherry, anise and toasty, buttery oak flavors. A wine of great harmony, finesse, elegance and grace. Well-articulated fruit flavors stay focused on the long, rich finish. Delicious 3,646 cases made. • $20 • (07/31/93) CS • **93**
Cabernet Sauvignon Napa Valley 1989 • $36 Ⓐ • (12/15/92) • **83**
Cabernet Sauvignon Napa Valley 1988 • $20 • (07/31/91) • **85**
Cabernet Sauvignon Napa Valley 1987 • $20 • (06/30/90) CS • **95**
Cabernet Sauvignon Napa Valley 1986 • $39 Ⓐ • (07/31/89) SS • **94**
Cabernet Sauvignon Napa Valley 1985 • $40 Ⓐ • (03/01/89) • **92**
Cabernet Sauvignon Napa Valley 1984 • $50 • (03/01/89) • **92**
Cabernet Sauvignon Napa Valley 1983 • $26 Ⓐ • (03/01/89) • **88**
Cabernet Sauvignon Napa Valley 1982 • $47 • (03/01/89) • **90**
Cabernet Sauvignon Napa Valley 1981 • $53 • (03/01/89) • **87**
Cabernet Sauvignon Napa Valley 1980 • $35 Ⓐ • (03/01/89) • **91**
Cabernet Sauvignon Napa Valley 1978 • $64 Ⓐ • (11/15/92) • **92**

Howell Mountain 1991: Serves up lots of ripe, spicy black cherry, currant and anise flavors before the chewy tannins kick in. Needs cellaring until about 1998. 1,400 cases made. • $25 • (11/15/94) • **88**

Howell Mountain 1990: Tight and firm, a young and intense wine with spicy, cedary currant and berry flavors that are focused in a narrow band. Finishes with intensity and fine tannins and an earthy tobacco edge. Tasted twice. Drinkable now. 2,700 cases made. • $25 • (11/15/93) • **86**

Howell Mountain 1989 • $25 • (11/15/92) • **89**

Merlot Napa Valley 1993: An intense and well-focused Merlot that has a rich, supple core of earthy currant, herb and cherry flavors that fold together nicely. Finishes with firm tannins that show just enough polish to encourage you to wait and see how this develops, try in 1998. 10,000 cases made. • $24 • (01/31/96) • **90**

Merlot Napa Valley 1992: Tart and grapey, showing a tight beam of herb and spice-laced currant and cherry flavor that finishes with a cedary oak edge and firm tannins. 9,500 cases made. • $23 • (03/31/95) • **88**

Merlot Napa Valley 1990 • $21 • (12/15/92) SS • **89**

Merlot Napa Valley 1989 • $25 • (04/15/92) • **82**

Merlot Napa Valley 1988 • $50 • (12/31/90) • **86**

Merlot Napa Valley 1987 • $33 • (12/31/89) • **91**

Merlot Napa Valley 1986 • $49 • (01/31/89) • **86**

Merlot Napa Valley 1985 • $35 • (12/31/87) CS • **93**

Merlot Napa Valley 1984 • $38 • (12/31/86) SS • **94**

Merlot Napa Valley 1983 • $45 • (11/01/85) CS • **94**

Merlot Napa Valley 1982 • $49 • (10/01/85) • **81**

Merlot Napa Valley Three Palms Vineyard 1991: An elegant and spicy young Merlot that seems a bit out of balance, with a range of flavors that runs from ripe cherry to greener notes. The tart acidity holds it together, but is also dominant. 1,600 cases made. • $25 • (09/15/94) • **84**

Merlot Napa Valley Three Palms Vineyard 1990 • $25 • (08/31/93) • **83**

Merlot Napa Valley Three Palms Vineyard 1989 • $45 • (05/31/92) • **89**

Merlot Napa Valley Three Palms Vineyard 1988 • $45 • (11/15/91) • **84**

Merlot Napa Valley Three Palms Vineyard 1987 • $60 • (07/31/90) • **92**

Merlot Napa Valley Three Palms Vineyard 1986 • $63 • (07/31/89) • **88**

Merlot Napa Valley Three Palms Vineyard 1985 • $63 • (06/30/88) • **91**

Merlot Napa Valley Three Palms Vineyard 1984 • $75 • (07/31/87) • **89**

Merlot Napa Valley Vine Hill Ranch 1987 • $18 • (07/31/90) • **87**

Merlot Napa Valley Vine Hill Ranch 1986 • $18 • (07/31/89) • **80**

Merlot Napa Valley Vine Hill Ranch 1985 • $16 • (06/30/88) • **91**

Sauvignon Blanc Napa County 1992 • $11 • (03/15/94) • **89**

Sauvignon Blanc Napa Valley 1994: Crisp-textured but smooth and spicy in flavor, weaving a touch of celery and apple flavors through the polished finish. Ready now. 15,000 cases made. • $12 • (12/31/95) • **89**

Sauvignon Blanc Napa Valley 1993: Bright and straightforward, distinctly herbal on the smooth, generous finish. 11,800 cases made. • $12 • (04/30/95) • **85**

Sauvignon Blanc Napa Valley 1991 • $11 • (12/31/92) • **87**

DUNCAN PEAK | CALIFORNIA

Cabernet Sauvignon Mendocino County 1993: Lean and trim, offering pleasant cherry, currant and berry flavors of modest depth and proportion. Well balanced, but the finish comes up short, has the tannic strength to cellar into 1997. 600 cases made. • $18 • (04/30/96) • **86**

Cabernet Sauvignon Mendocino County 1992: The ripe cherry and currant flavors are bright and lively yet somewhat one-dimensional. Drinkable now. 346 cases made. • $16 • (11/15/94) • **85**

Cabernet Sauvignon Mendocino County 1991: Packs in lots of fruit, with ripe, rich plum, cherry and herb-tinged Cabernet fruit that turns lighter and simpler on the finish. Well balanced. Drinkable now. 385 cases made. • $12 • (10/31/93) • **88**

Cabernet Sauvignon Mendocino County 1989 • $10 • (11/15/92) BB • **88**

DUNN | CALIFORNIA

Cabernet Sauvignon Howell Mountain 1991: Dark, dense, tannic and earthy, but it works its way into a rich and concentrated core of currant, mineral, cedar and anise flavors. An outstanding California Cabernet that finishes with thick, dry tannins, so it's best to age this into 2001. 2,300 cases made. • $39 • (12/15/95) CS • **91**

Cabernet Sauvignon Howell Mountain 1990: Dark in color, with very ripe, opulent, fleshy Cabernet fruit and a woody oak edge. It's tightly wound and compact now, in need of cellaring through 1999. Chewy tannins on the finish and a hint of cherry and spice. • $39 • (05/15/94) • **89**

Cabernet Sauvignon Howell Mountain 1989 • $39 • (07/31/93) • **88**

Cabernet Sauvignon Howell Mountain 1988 • $66 • (02/29/92) • **86**

Cabernet Sauvignon Howell Mountain 1987 • $NA • (11/30/91) • **95**

Cabernet Sauvignon Howell Mountain 1986 • $NA • (11/30/91) • **96**

Cabernet Sauvignon Howell Mountain 1985 • $110 • (11/30/91) • **88**

Cabernet Sauvignon Howell Mountain 1984 • $140 • (11/30/91) • **96**

Cabernet Sauvignon Howell Mountain 1983 • $115 • (11/30/91) • **91**

Cabernet Sauvignon Howell Mountain 1982 • $140 • (11/30/91) • **94**

Cabernet Sauvignon Howell Mountain 1981 • $160 • (11/30/91) • **93**

Cabernet Sauvignon Howell Mountain 1980 • $180 • (11/30/91) • **95**

Cabernet Sauvignon Howell Mountain 1979 • $200 • (11/30/91) • **94**

Cabernet Sauvignon Napa Valley 1992: Young and grapey, a high-extract style with rich currant, mineral, leather and herb flavors. Finishes with a tannic wallop. Best to cellar into 1999. Tasted twice, with consistent notes. 2,100 cases made. • $33 • (12/15/95) • **88**

Cabernet Sauvignon Napa Valley 1991: Despite its deep color, firm tannins and fruit concentration, this is still rough-and-tumble, with earthy, oaky flavors that override the backward berry and currant notes. Tasted twice. 2,100 cases made. • $28 Ⓐ • (11/15/94) • **88**

Cabernet Sauvignon Napa Valley 1990: Dense, ripe and concentrated, with a tough edge of tannin but plenty of berry, currant and plum fruit showing through. A massive wine that holds together nicely on the finish, should be at its best after 1998-2000. Tasted twice. 1,900 cases made. • $41 Ⓐ • (11/15/93) CS • **92**

Cabernet Sauvignon Napa Valley 1989 • $33 Ⓐ • (04/30/93) • **90**

Cabernet Sauvignon Napa Valley 1988 • $31 Ⓐ • (11/30/91) • **90**

Cabernet Sauvignon Napa Valley 1987 • $49 Ⓐ • (11/30/91) • **94**

Cabernet Sauvignon Napa Valley 1986 • $53 Ⓐ • (11/30/91) • **93**

Cabernet Sauvignon Napa Valley 1985 • $64 Ⓐ • (11/30/91) • **93**

Cabernet Sauvignon Napa Valley 1984 • $53 Ⓐ • (11/30/91) • **97**

Cabernet Sauvignon Napa Valley 1983 • $38 Ⓐ • (11/30/91) • **91**

Cabernet Sauvignon Napa Valley 1982 • $72 Ⓐ • (11/30/91) • **91**

DUNNEWOOD | CALIFORNIA

Cabernet Sauvignon Alexander Valley Seven Arches Vineyard Gold Label Select 1992: Marked by green olive and herb flavors with a touch of dill and bell pepper flavors that override the cherry and plum notes. Finishes with firm tannins. 3,000 cases made. • $10 • (02/29/96) • **82**

Cabernet Sauvignon California 1986 • $7 • (06/15/90) • **73**

Cabernet Sauvignon Napa Valley Napa Reserve 1986 • $11 • (06/15/90) • **82**

Cabernet Sauvignon Napa Valley Reserve 1984 • $11 • (12/31/88) • **85**

Cabernet Sauvignon North Coast Barrel Select 1991: Firm, austere and tannic with rough edges, but there's enough plum and currant-laced Merlot fruit here to admire. Drink now. • $7 • (11/15/94) • **84**

Chardonnay Carneros Gold Label Select 1993: Medium weight, with a modest smoky pear edge. 1,301 cases made. • $10 • (07/31/95) • **83**

Chardonnay Carneros Gold Label Select 1992: Serves up lots of flavor, with tiers of honey, pear, butter and vanilla that are rich and complex. Retains its elegance and finesse with a long, full finish that keep echoing the flavors. Drink now. 970 cases made. • $9 • (06/30/94) BB • **88**

Chardonnay North Coast Barrel Select 1993: Simple and fruity, showing hints of pear, apple and spice, turns grassy on the finish. 70,000 cases made. • $8 • (02/28/95) • **80**

Chardonnay North Coast Barrel Select 1992: Fresh and lively with spicy nectarine, peach and pear-tinged flavors that are elegant and floral on the finish. Ready now. 60,000 cases made. • $7 • (06/30/94) BB • **83**

Chardonnay North Coast Barrel Select 1991 • $6 • (11/30/92) BB • **84**

Merlot California Barrel Select 1990 • $6 • (04/15/93) BB • **83**

Merlot North Coast Barrel Select 1992: Very ripe, almost pruny, with gobs of currant and blackberry flavors. The finish is soft but persistent. Drinkable now for its individuality. 5,000 cases made. • $7 • (09/15/94) BB • **82**

Reserve Red California NV • $3 • (02/28/89) • **76**

Sauvignon Blanc North Coast Barrel Select 1993: Light and simple, creamy enough to show off some nice pear and spice flavors. 5,000 cases made. • $7 • (08/31/95) • **80**

Sauvignon Blanc North Coast Barrel Select 1992: Herbal, weedy flavors never quite let go so the fruit can emerge. Tasted twice with consistent results. 5,000 cases made. • $6 • (08/31/94) • **78**

Zinfandel Sonoma Valley Barrel Select 1992: Austere, with an earthy, cedary edge to the muted berry flavors. 4,871 cases made. • $10 • (02/28/95) • **80**

DURNEY | CALIFORNIA

Cabernet Sauvignon Carmel Valley 1990: Ripe and spicy, with intense currant and black cherry flavors that turn complex on the finish. Despite firm tannins, it's not as tannic as most Durney Cabernets. 1,180 cases made. • $17 • (11/15/94) • **89**

Cabernet Sauvignon Carmel Valley 1981 • $13 • (09/01/84) • **82**

Cabernet Sauvignon Carmel Valley 1978 • $NA • (11/15/92) • **69**

Cabernet Sauvignon Carmel Valley Dances On Your Palate Private Reserve 1992: Very ripe and spicy, with an elegant core of herb, currant, cedar and tobacco, finishing smooth before the tannins kick in. 1,480 cases made. • $31 • (05/31/96) • **86**

Cabernet Sauvignon Carmel Valley Private Reserve 1989: Simple, with spicy herb and currant notes and gritty, drying tannins. True to the Durney style with its tannins, but lacking the substance you would expect from a reserve-designated wine. 95 cases made. • $26 • (11/15/94) • **83**

Cabernet Sauvignon Carmel Valley Private Reserve 1988: Ripe and jammy, with intense, compact and tannic fruit. Austere almost to a fault, may always be tannic. 95 cases made. • $31 • (11/15/94) • **82**

Cabernet Sauvignon Carmel Valley Private Reserve 1985 • $20 • (11/15/92) • **86**

Cabernet Sauvignon Carmel Valley Private Reserve 1983 • $20 • (04/30/91) • **86**

Cabernet Sauvignon Carmel Valley Reserve 1978 • $NA • (11/15/92) • **69**

Chardonnay Carmel Valley Cachagua Dances On Your Palate 1993: Earthy, adding a slight bitter edge to the pear and spice notes. • $11 • (05/15/96) • **76**

Chardonnay Carmel Valley Dances On Your Palate 1992: Serves up plenty of bold ripe Chardonnay flavors, with hints of pear, apple and spice flavors. • $18 • (02/29/96) • **87**

Chenin Blanc Carmel Valley 1993: Light, simple and fruity, off-dry but nicely balanced to show off the melon and apple fruit. Ready now. 2,840 cases made. • $9 • (05/31/95) • **85**

Pinot Noir Carmel Valley 1990: Showing mature Pinot Noir flavors, with an herb, tea and mint edge to the black cherry notes. Picks up an earthy tone on the finish. 188 cases made. • $18 • (03/31/95) • **80**

Pinot Noir Carmel Valley 1989 • $18 • (02/28/94) • **80**

Pinot Noir Carmel Valley 1988 • $16 • (04/30/91) • **80**

Pinot Noir Carmel Valley Dances On Your Palate 1992: Heavily oaked and marked by earthy tannins lacking obvious charm. Still it has to grow out of some chewy tannins. 350 cases made. • $24 • **81**

Red Carmel Valley NV • $7 • (11/15/92) • **73**

DUXOUP | CALIFORNIA

Charbono Napa Valley 1987 • $9 • (06/15/89) • **88**

Napa Gamay Dry Creek Valley 1988 • $7 • (02/28/90) • **76**

Napa Gamay Dry Creek Valley 1987 • $7 • (02/28/89) BB • **86**

Napa Gamay Dry Creek Valley 1990-1991 NV • $9 • (03/31/93) • **85**

Syrah Dry Creek Valley 1987 • $12 • (04/15/89) • **87**

Syrah Dry Creek Valley 1986 • $9 • (04/15/89) • **85**

Syrah Sonoma County 1982 • $9 • (03/16/84) • **78**

Key: SS—Spectator Selection. CS—Cellar Selection. BB—Best Buy. $NA—Price not available. (BT)—Barrel tasting. Ⓐ—Auction Price.
Dates in parentheses represent the issues in which the ratings were published.

E.B. FOOTE | WASHINGTON

Cabernet Sauvignon Columbia Valley 1993: Has a strong streak of pickle-barrel flavor that cuts through the modest fruit. Try it in 1999. 390 cases made. • $10 • **79**

Cabernet Sauvignon Columbia Valley 1992: Firm and a little chewy, but flavorful, with a floral edge to the ripe blackberry and plum notes. Drinkable now. 166 cases made. • $13 • (09/30/94) • **85**

Chardonnay Columbia Valley 1993: Smooth and inviting, generous with its spicy green apple and leesy flavors which linger on the finish. Tiny quantity, thus hard to find. Ready now. 77 cases made. • $9 • (09/30/95) • **88**

Merlot Columbia Valley 1994: Brilliant blackberry, currant and delicate toast flavors swirl appetizingly. Notes of fruit and spice on the long finish. 183 cases made. • $10 • **88**

Merlot Columbia Valley 1993: Smooth and nicely focused, sporting black cherry and currant flavor and a buzz of tannin on the finish. Best from 1997 to 1998. 100 cases made. • $8 • (09/30/95) • **85**

Pinot Noir Washington NV: Very light in color, with earthy-beet aromas and flavors that turn tart and raw on the finish. 99 cases made. • $7 • (09/30/94) • **73**

Pinot Noir Washington Jacobson's Eagle Crest Vineyard 1991: Light in color, smoky and a little sour. Over the hill at this young age. 70 cases made. • $7 • (09/30/94) • **69**

Pinot Noir Washington La Center Vineyard 1993: Smoky aromas and flavors dominate the modest currant and berry notes, which could come through by 1997. 55 cases made. • $7 • (09/30/95) • **80**

EAGLE RIDGE | CALIFORNIA

Zinfandel Amador County Grand Pere Vineyard 1989 • $12 • (10/15/92) • **76**

EASTON | CALIFORNIA

Riesling El Dorado County 1994: Soft and appealing for its peach-almond flavors. 200 cases made. • $12 • (06/15/96) • **80**

Zinfandel Fiddletown 1993: Tastes overly mature for its age, with earthy berry and pepper flavors that dry out on the tannic finish. 475 cases made. • $15 • (03/31/96) • **77**

EBERLE | CALIFORNIA

Barbera Paso Robles Norman Vineyard 1992: Ripe berry flavors have an earthy, animal edge, turning citrusy and tart on the finish. Give it until 1997 to settle down. 288 cases made. • $18 • (11/15/95) • **83**

Cabernet Sauvignon Paso Robles 1991: Supple texture marked by weedy herb, black olive and currant flavors, picking up a touch of cedar and toasty oak. Best Eberle in several vintages. 4,131 cases made. • $16 • (04/15/95) • **88**

Cabernet Sauvignon Paso Robles 1990: This has an earthy, leathery edge to the spicy cherry and currant notes, but it holds together. Has the tannins to age through the decade; drinkable now. 5,100 cases made. • $15 • (09/15/94) • **84**

Cabernet Sauvignon Paso Robles 1989 • $15 • (11/15/93) • **83**

Cabernet Sauvignon Paso Robles 1988 • $15 • (11/15/92) • **86**

Cabernet Sauvignon Paso Robles 1987 • $22 • (11/15/91) • **76**

Cabernet Sauvignon Paso Robles 1986 • $15 • (11/15/89) • **85**

Cabernet Sauvignon Paso Robles 1985 • $17 • (03/01/89) • **89**

Cabernet Sauvignon Paso Robles 1984 • $17 • (03/01/89) • **86**

Cabernet Sauvignon Paso Robles 1983 • $18 • (03/01/89) • **84**

Cabernet Sauvignon Paso Robles 1982 • $22 • (03/01/89) • **72**

Cabernet Sauvignon Paso Robles 1981 • $24 • (03/01/89) • **85**

Cabernet Sauvignon Paso Robles 1980 • $24 • (03/01/89) • **78**

Cabernet Sauvignon Paso Robles Reserve 1987: Herbal with bell pepper and black olive notes, turning tannic and gritty on the finish. Released way too late. 560 cases made. • $28 • (11/15/94) • **78**

Cabernet Sauvignon Paso Robles Reserve 1982 • $30 • (03/01/89) • **71**

Cabernet Sauvignon Paso Robles Reserve 1981 • $35 • (03/01/89) • **80**

Cabernet Sauvignon San Luis Obispo 1979 • $25 • (03/01/89) • **82**

Chardonnay Paso Robles 1993: Funky and earthy, with a bitter edge to the buttery pear and oak notes. 3,520 cases made. • $12 • (07/31/95) • **78**

Chardonnay Paso Robles 1992: Serves up a solid core of spicy pear- and nectarine-laced Chardonnay fruit. What it's lacking now are the extra dimensions of flavor and complexity, perhaps with time those will develop. Drink now. 3,710 cases made. • $12 • (06/30/94) • **83**

Chardonnay Paso Robles 1991 • $12 • (07/15/93) • **82**

Muscat Canelli Paso Robles 1994: Light, sweet and simple, a solid wine of delicate litchi flavors that needs light dessert fare to balance it. 1,000 cases made. • $9 • (09/30/95) • **82**

Syrah Paso Robles 1991 • $16 • (10/31/93) • **85**

Syrah Paso Robles Fralich Vineyard 1993: Dark, ripe and intense, with a rich, earthy edge to the supple black cherry and currant flavors. Turns complex on the finish, where the toasty oak folds in. 340 cases made. • $16 • (08/31/95) • **89**

Syrah Paso Robles Fralich Vineyard 1992: Firm and spicy, a supple wine with generous plum and berry fruit that gets spicy on the finish. Drinkable now. 94 cases made. • $16 • (07/31/94) • **86**

Viognier Paso Robles Fralich Vineyard 1993: Dark in color, soft in texture, not very fresh in flavors, spicy with simple notes. Drink soon. 74 cases made. • $16 • (09/15/94) • **78**

Zinfandel Paso Robles 1989 • $12 • (10/15/92) • **86**

Zinfandel Paso Robles Sauret Vineyard 1994: Slightly dusty and earthy but the flavors develop nicely, as a band of anise, cherry and berry turns supple and polished on the finish, even adding a trace of heat. 1,200 cases made. • $16 • (04/30/96) • **87**

Zinfandel Paso Robles Sauret Vineyard 1993: Rough and tumble now, presenting sharp, edgy tannins, but the appealing wild berry and cherry flavors persist. 1,200 cases made. • $13 • (06/15/95) • **86**

Zinfandel Paso Robles Sauret Vineyard 1992: Coarse and tannic, with a thin band of earthy raspberry flavor. The tannins turn gritty on the finish. Give it a year to soften up. 1,058 cases made. • $13 • (10/15/94) • **82**

Zinfandel Paso Robles Sauret Vineyard 1991 • $12 • (08/31/93) • **89**

Zinfandel Paso Robles Sauret Vineyard 1990 • $12 • (12/31/92) • **88**

L'ECOLE NO. 41 | WASHINGTON

Cabernet Sauvignon Columbia Valley 1992: Luxurious berry and black cherry flavors, shaded with spicy oak and a touch of bay leaf on the moderately tannic finish. Approachable now, better in 1997. 670 cases made. • $22 • (07/31/95) • **88**

Cabernet Sauvignon Washington 1991: Ripe, chewy and supple, under the veneer of fine tannins, shining a nice beam of black cherry and currant flavor through the gritty texture. Echoes fruit and spice on the finish. Best from 1997. 280 cases made. • $19 • (09/30/94) • **87**

Cabernet Sauvignon Washington 1989 • $18 • (05/31/93) • **88**

Chardonnay Washington 1993: Ripe, spicy and supple, smooth in texture, showing off its clove-scented pear and pineapple on the long finish. 658 cases made. • $16 • (09/30/95) • **88**

Chardonnay Washington 1992: Ripe, round and spicy, generously complex, with buttery pear, honey and spice flavors that keep singing in harmony on the finish. Drinkable now. 700 cases made. • $15 • (08/31/94) • **89**

Chardonnay Washington 1991 • $16 • (06/15/93) • **78**

Merlot Columbia Valley 1993: A smooth and inviting Merlot that focuses its generous beam of plum, currant and spice flavors into the sweet tannins. Has a gentle structure that folds together nicely. Best to wait until 1997. 2,464 cases made. • $19 • (08/31/95) SS • **90**

Merlot Columbia Valley 1992: Ripe and polished, a spicy red with butter and tobacco overtones, finishing with an exotic, spicy twist. Drinkable now. 2,000 cases made. • $17 • (09/30/94) • **87**

Merlot Walla Walla Valley Seven Hills Vineyard 1993: Smooth and elegant, pouring out its plum and currant flavor, wrapped in a light cloak of sweet oak and fine tannin. Rich and tempting now, best in 1997. 170 cases made. • $22 • (09/30/95) • **91**

Merlot Washington 1990 • $17 • (04/15/94) • **83**

Merlot Washington 1989 • $16 • (05/31/93) • **82**

Merlot Washington 1987 • $13 • (11/30/91) • **90**

Sémillon Washington Barrel Fermented 1993: Ripe, smooth and generous, with a caramel edge to the honey and grapefruit flavors. 1,033 cases made. • $12 • (08/31/95) • **88**

Sémillon Washington Barrel Fermented 1992: Toasty, tobacco aromas and flavors characterize this orange-scented, lemony white, round in texture from barrel fermentation. Has a lot of personality. 1,100 cases made. • $12 • (08/31/94) • **86**

Sémillon Washington Barrel Fermented 1991 • $12 • (06/15/93) • **72**

EDDY, TOM | CALIFORNIA

Cabernet Sauvignon Napa Valley 1992: Attractive plum, herb, cherry and cedary oak flavors, losing its focus a bit on the finish, but then again it's young and tannic. Try in 1997 or '98. 300 cases made. • $36 • (05/15/96) • **88**

Cabernet Sauvignon Napa Valley 1991: Firm and intense, boasting a tight core of currant, cherry and cedary oak flavors, turning to coffee and anise. 240 cases made. • $32 • (04/30/95) • **90**

EDEN ROC | CALIFORNIA

Brut California NV • $4 • (05/15/92) • **76**

Extra Dry California Naturally Fermented NV • $3 • (07/31/93) • **76**

Extra Dry California NV • $4 • (05/15/92) • **78**

EDMEADES | CALIFORNIA

Chardonnay Anderson Valley 1994: Smooth and elegant fig, pear, spice and honey notes. Turns somewhat simple on the finish, where it takes on a candied edge. • $18 • (05/15/96) • **88**

Chardonnay Anderson Valley Anderson Crest Vineyard 1994: Serves up a fruity core of mango, ripe pear and apple flavors complimented by lightly toasty, spicy notes. • $20 • (06/15/96) • **87**

Chardonnay Anderson Valley Dennison Vineyard 1993: Hits the right notes, with ripe pear, toast, spice and nutmeg notes, turning elegant with a grapefruit edge. • $20 • (07/31/95) • **85**

Chardonnay Mendocino 1993: A touch spritzy. The earthy pear and apple notes show modest depth. 2,000 cases made. • $12 • (04/15/95) • **82**

Gewürztraminer Anderson Valley 1994: Light and gently spicy over a nice thread of pear and coffee flavors. Goes for delicacy over intensity. Ready now. • $13 • (11/15/95) • **84**

Pinot Noir Anderson Valley 1994: Well focused, with attractive plum and black cherry laced Pinot Noir fruit. Finishes with a mild tannic edge. • $16 • **87**

Pinot Noir Anderson Valley 1982 • $10 • (02/16/85) • **89**

Pinot Noir Anderson Valley Anderson Crest Vineyard 1994: Dark and intense, with a solid core of tannin, but the plum and wild berry flavors that peek through are appealing. Best to age a little to let this soften a bit. • $23 • (03/31/96) • **85**

Pinot Noir Anderson Valley Dennison Vineyard 1993: Firm and somewhat oaky now, but ripe plum and cherry flavors pick up a spice and anise edge on the finish. 143 cases made. • $20 • (09/15/95) • **86**

Zinfandel Mendocino 1994: Smooth, elegant, supple texture and attractive cherry, berry, spice and vanilla flavors. Finishes with firm but mild tannins. Drinkable now. • $16 • (04/30/96) • **88**

Zinfandel Mendocino Ciapusci Vineyard 1994: A claret style that's somewhat austere, as cedar, sage and tar flavors are more evident than ripe fruit, which peeks through on the finish accompanied by hints of berry. Drinkable now. • $29 • (04/30/96) • **85**

Zinfandel Mendocino Ciapusci Vineyard 1993: Tough and tannic, with the wild berry flavors barely squeezing through the tannins on the finish. Drinkable now. 50 cases made. • $20 • (10/15/95) • **86**

Zinfandel Mendocino Ciapusci Vineyard 1990 • $20 • (10/15/92) • **86**

Zinfandel Mendocino Ciapusci Vineyard 1981 • $9 • (03/01/85) • **87**

Zinfandel Mendocino Zeni Vineyard 1994: Somewhat earthy, adding sage and juniper and wild berry underneath. The finish has a slight green edge. Drinkable now. • $29 • (04/30/96) • **84**

Zinfandel Mendocino Zeni Vineyard 1993: Tight and firm, with a hard, tannic character. The chewy core of earthy raspberry and spice takes a while to work through, then it picks up oak and peppery notes on the finish. 250 cases made. • $20 • (08/31/95) • **88**

Zinfandel North Coast 1992: A solid, chunky Zinfandel showing pepper, wild berry and spice notes that are fresh and vibrant. Ready now through 1998. 900 cases made. • $12 • (01/31/95) • **86**

EDMUNDS ST. JOHN | CALIFORNIA

El Niño California Red 1992: Lean, firm and tannic, with a narrow band of leathery berry and tar flavors that are appealing. • $11 • (06/30/95) • **84**
Les Côtes Sauvages California Red 1992: Intense and spicy, with a distinct, peppery character in the grape and currant flavors. Turns tannic and leathery on the finish. • $16 • (06/30/95) • **88**
Les Côtes Sauvages California Red 1989 • $19 • (07/15/91) • **79**
Les Côtes Sauvages California Red 1986 • $14 • (04/15/89) • **88**
Les Côtes Sauvages Cuvée Wahluke 90 American NV • $14 • (01/31/94) • **86**
Les Fleurs du Chaparral Napa Valley 1987 • $15 • (08/31/90) • **91**
Mourvèdre California L'Enfant Terrible 1994: A touch earthy, with a slightly bitter edge. Meager fruit just barely catches your attention. • $12 • **76**
Mourvèdre Napa Valley 1986 • $15 • (04/15/89) • **87**
Port O'Call New World Red California Red 1989 • $9 • (08/31/91) • **84**
Syrah California 1994: Distinct, spicy fruit flavors, and on the tannic side. Finishes with a leathery accent, but plenty of plum and cherry come through. 550 cases made. • $12 • **86**
Syrah California 1987 • $18 • (12/15/89) • **81**
Syrah Sonoma County 1986 • $12 • (04/15/89) • **91**
Syrah Sonoma Valley 1988 • $19 • (08/31/91) • **85**
Syrah Sonoma Valley Durrell Vineyard 1991 • $20 • (12/31/93) • **89**
Viognier Knights Valley 1992 • $18 • (02/28/94) • **88**
Zinfandel Amador County 1993: Ripe and rustic, with cherry and raspberry jam flavors that stretch the limits of ripeness, yet it manages to hang together. 250 cases made. • $16 • (10/15/95) • **86**
Zinfandel Mendocino County Pallini Rosso 1993: Medium-bodied, with zesty raspberry and earthy anise notes. A good effort, but doesn't quite reach the heights it tries for. 250 cases made. • $11 • (10/15/95) • **83**
Zinfandel Napa Valley Amaronese 1988 • $12 • (10/15/92) • **80**

EDNA VALLEY | CALIFORNIA

Brut Edna Valley 1987: A rich, winey style of full-bodied sparkler that unfolds its honey and spice-scented pear and toast flavors gracefully. Finishes long and throws in some mature flourishes. Delicious now. 220 cases made. • $25 • (12/31/94) • **90**
Chardonnay Edna Valley 1993: Ripe, smooth and polished, with pleasant honey, pear and citrus flavors that combine nicely on the finish. Has more depth and richness than most 1993s. 47,335 cases made. • $15 • (06/30/95) • **88**
Chardonnay Edna Valley 1992: Dense, rich and earthy, with a lean streak of citrus- and pear-laced fruit. In several tastings this wine has shown bottle variation, but at its best it reflects the Edna Valley appellation quite well with a Burgundian earthiness. Drinkable now. 56,000 cases made. • $15 • (06/30/94) • **84**
Chardonnay Edna Valley 1991 • $15 • (12/31/92) • **88**
Chardonnay Edna Valley Paragon Vineyard Reserve Bottling 1991: Stretches to the extremes with funky, earthy flavors, picking up peach and apple on the aftertaste with a touch of vanilla and spice. Best on the finish, where the flavors fold into butterscotch. 1,448 cases made. • $20 • (06/30/94) • **85**
Pinot Noir Edna Valley 1993: Earthy, mixing musty mushroom flavors with ripe black cherry. Troubling. Tasted twice, with consistent results. 3,672 cases made. • $15 • (03/31/95) • **73**
Pinot Noir Edna Valley 1992: Ripe and supple, displaying herb, cherry, spice and cedar notes. Ready now despite the tannins. 2,424 cases made. • $15 • (03/31/95) • **83**
Pinot Noir Edna Valley 1990 • $15 • (02/28/93) • **84**
Pinot Noir Edna Valley 1986 • $15 • (12/15/89) • **76**
Pinot Noir Edna Valley 1985 • $15 • (06/15/88) • **78**
Pinot Noir Edna Valley 1984 • $10 • (12/15/87) • **85**
Pinot Noir Edna Valley 1983 • $10 • (04/15/87) • **57**

Key: SS—Spectator Selection. CS—Cellar Selection. BB—Best Buy. $NA—Price not available. (BT)—Barrel tasting. Ⓐ—Auction Price.
Dates in parentheses represent the issues in which the ratings were published.

Pinot Noir Edna Valley 1982 • $12 • (08/31/86) • **80**
Pinot Noir Edna Valley Paragon Vineyard Reserve 1992: Firm and compact, offering herb, black cherry and plum notes that pick up a sweetish edge. Drinkable now. 206 cases made. • $18 • (03/31/95) • **86**
Pinot Noir Edna Valley Reserve 1988 • $18 • (02/28/93) • **82**

EHLERS GROVE | CALIFORNIA

Cabernet Sauvignon Napa Valley 1993: Firm and chewy, a lean wine with just about enough berry flavor to sneak through on the finish. Best from 1997. 2,000 cases made. • $11 • (12/15/95) • **83**
Cabernet Sauvignon Napa Valley 1992: Tight and firm, with marked herb, cedar and black cherry flavors. The well-focused, complex aftertaste lingers. Well proportioned, and shows promise for drinking in 1997 or 1998. 200 cases made. • $15 • (12/15/95) • **88**
Chardonnay California 1993: Medium bodied, with appealing pear, citrus and light cedary wood flavors. • $10 • (07/31/95) • **80**
Sauvignon Blanc Napa Valley 1994: Veers strongly toward the herbal side, offering a touch of green apple to balance the celery and herb flavors. Ready now. 700 cases made. • $9 • (12/15/95) • **81**

EHLERS LANE | CALIFORNIA

Cabernet Sauvignon Napa Valley 1983 • $12 • (06/15/87) • **79**

EL MOLINO | CALIFORNIA

Chardonnay Napa County 1992: Bold, ripe and racy, with a leafy, earthy edge to the pear and apple-laced Chardonnay fruit. Picks up oaky, somewhat earthy flavors on the finish, but holds together. Best now. 425 cases made. • $30 • (06/30/94) • **86**
Chardonnay Napa County 1991 • $30 • (07/15/93) • **89**
Chardonnay Napa Valley 1994: Grows on you, offering ripe pear, spice and honey notes, with light oak shadings folding in on the finish. An elegant, understated wine of great finesse. Will benefit from aging, so look to some future enjoyment from this. 530 cases made. • $35 • (05/31/96) • **91**
Chardonnay Napa Valley 1993: Complex with an appealing core of ripe pear and apple notes with just the right amount of oak shading. 425 cases made. • $30 • (07/31/95) • **88**
Pinot Noir Napa County 1990 • $30 • (02/28/94) • **84**
Pinot Noir Napa County 1989 • $30 • (09/30/92) • **82**
Pinot Noir Napa County 1988 • $30 • (11/15/91) • **82**
Pinot Noir Napa County 1987 • $29 • (10/31/91) • **85**
Pinot Noir Napa Valley 1993: Solid with a pleasant core of ripe plum and cherry, but not much in the way of finesse or grace. Firmly tannic now, a little age should help soften it. 650 cases made. • $35 • (05/31/96) • **87**
Pinot Noir Napa Valley 1992: Bold, ripe, rich and complex. It's still tightly wound, but the layers of cherry, plum and spice flavors open up nicely and linger on the finish. Drinkable now. 625 cases made. • $30 • (02/28/95) • **91**
Pinot Noir Napa Valley 1991: Firmly tannic, an austere, compact wine with a tight band of smoky cherry, leather and spice flavors. Drinkable now. 620 cases made. • $30 • (02/28/95) • **89**

ELAN, CHATEAU | GEORGIA

Blush Georgia Essence de Cabernet Founder's Reserve 1988 • $11 • (02/29/92) • **76**
Cabernet Sauvignon Napa Valley 1978 • $NA • (11/15/92) • **77**

ELIZABETH | CALIFORNIA

Zinfandel Mendocino 1992: Smooth, ripe and complex, with layers of supple black cherry, plum and wild berry flavors. Thick but polished tannins let the fruit glide through. Ready now through 1997. 239 cases made. • $10 • (10/15/94) • **86**
Zinfandel Mendocino 1990 • $10 • (10/15/92) • **85**

ELKHORN PEAK | CALIFORNIA

Chardonnay Napa Valley Fagan Creek Vineyards 1993: Complex with toasty, smoky oak and ripe pear, spice and hazelnut notes that gain intensity and nuance on the finish. 543 cases made. • $15 • (07/31/95) • **85**

Chardonnay Napa Valley Fagan Creek Vineyards 1992: For fans of ultra-ripe, woody, smoky Chardonnay. Has excesses, but enough ripe pear and apple flavors to keep it barely in balance. From a new winery that's using grapes harvested in Jamison Canyon. 350 cases made. • $15 • (12/15/94) • **87**

Pinot Noir Napa Valley Fagan Creek Vineyards 1993: Medium weight, with a modest core of wild berry and cherry fruit that finsihes with a simple aftertaste. What's there is appealing for everyday drinking. 469 cases made. • $21 • **83**

Pinot Noir Napa Valley Fagan Creek Vineyards 1992: Light and simple, hints of unripe strawberries. 160 cases made. • $21 • (03/31/95) • **79**

ELLISTON | CALIFORNIA

Cabernet Sauvignon Central Coast Sunol Valley Vineyard 1985 • $16 • (11/15/91) • **74**

Captain's Claret California NV: Leans toward the weedy, herbal side of Cabernet and is well oaked as well, giving it a dill and pickle barrel edge to the fruit. Drinkable now. 271 cases made. • $14 • (11/15/94) • **82**

Captain's Claret Napa Valley 1992: Shows off its pretty wild berry, cherry and currant flavors in a medium-bodied style. Firm but mild tannins and good length. 530 cases made. • $14 • (08/31/95) • **84**

Chardonnay Central Coast Sunol Valley Vineyard 1991 • $12 • (11/30/92) • **85**

Cuvée des Trois Sunol Valley Vineyard Central Coast 1993: Sturdy, spicy, straightforward white, round and slightly honeyed, more distinctive for its structure and texture than for its flavors. Ready now. 1,150 cases made. • $10 • (12/15/95) • **83**

Pinot Blanc Central Coast Sunol Valley Vineyard 1991 • $10 • (01/31/93) • **82**

Pinot Noir Santa Cruz Mountains Unfiltered Unfined 1993: Simple but pleasantly balanced, with the cherry, berry and vanilla flavors well focused for its weight. 48 cases made. • $22 • **83**

ELYSE | CALIFORNIA

Cabernet Sauvignon Napa Valley Morisoli Vineyard 1994: Dark, intense with a black cherry jam flavor that holds its focus, finishing with a rich fruity aftertaste. Borders on outstanding. • $NA • (05/31/95) • **90-94** (BT)

Cabernet Sauvignon Napa Valley Morisoli Vineyard 1992: Marked by a strong anise and black cherry quality, young, intense and firmly tannic, featuring compact, tightly wound flavors. Strong and potent tannins just barely let the fruit pass through. Definitely needs time, try in 2002. 312 cases made. • $30 • (04/30/96) • **89**

Nero Misto Napa Valley 1992: Mostly Petite Sirah and Zinfandel, this hearty red shows chewy tannins and ample raspberry and spice notes. Drink now. 620 cases made. • $14 • (01/31/95) • **84**

Nero Misto Napa Valley 1991 • $14 • (06/15/93) • **86**

Nero Misto Napa Valley 1990 • $15 • (06/30/92) • **86**

Zinfandel Howell Mountain 1994: Ripe and perfumed, sporting pretty aromatics, firm tannins and bright, elegant cherry and berry flavors. Can stand short-term cellaring to soften a bit, but is true to the appellation. 1,221 cases made. • $16 • (04/30/96) • **87**

Zinfandel Howell Mountain 1993: Tight and firm, with an austere band of earthy, spicy wild berry flavors. Hard tannins on the finish. 1,104 cases made. • $16 • (10/15/95) • **85**

Zinfandel Howell Mountain 1992: Pure Zinfandel from start to finish, with spicy, peppery wild berry and raspberry notes that pick up a pleasant earthy nuance on the finish. Crisp, dry tannins. Best now through 1997. 770 cases made. • $14 • (10/15/94) • **87**

Zinfandel Howell Mountain 1991 • $14 • (09/30/93) • **85**

Zinfandel Napa Valley Coeur du Val 1994: Tight and firm, adding an austere edge to the spicy cherry and wild berry flavors and a pretty, fruity aftertaste. 952 cases made. • $14 • (04/30/96) • **87**

Zinfandel Napa Valley Coeur du Val 1993: Hard and tight, with a narrow band of wild berry and cherry flavors that have a green, tannic bite. May be more appealing with age. 863 cases made. • $14 • (10/15/95) • **83**

Zinfandel Napa Valley Coeur du Val 1992: Firm and tight, crisp and flavorful, serving up spicy cherry and raspberry flavors until the tannins clamp down. Drink soon, over the next year. 402 cases made. • $14 • (10/15/94) • **85**

Zinfandel Napa Valley Morisoli Vineyard 1993: Floral and aromatic, followed by tight raspberry and cherry flavors of modest depth and richness. 812 cases made. • $16 • (10/15/95) • **84**

Zinfandel Napa Valley Morisoli Vineyard 1992: Bright and lively black cherry and raspberry flavors, well focused and spicy. Turns firm and tannic on the finish. Enjoyable now for its vivid flavors, but probably best from 1997. 650 cases made. • $14 • (10/15/94) • **88**

Zinfandel Napa Valley Morisoli Vineyard 1991 • $14 • (09/30/93) • **87**

Zinfandel Napa Valley Morisoli Vineyard 1990 • $13 • (10/15/92) • **88**

Zinfandel Napa Valley Morisoli Vineyard 1989 • $13 • (08/31/91) • **85**

Zinfandel Napa Valley Rutherford Bench Morisoli Vineyard 1994: Well balanced and pleasant to drink, in a claret style that avoids excess. Flavorful, with bright ripe cherry, strawberry and spice. 1,080 cases made. • $16 • **88**

ENCANTOS, LOS | CALIFORNIA

Cabernet Sauvignon Napa Valley Covenant Reserve 1992: Ripe but elegant, with spicy cherry and plum-laced fruit and a firm core of tannins on the finish. Well mannered, finishing with a touch of toasty oak, best after 1997. 5,000 cases made. • $14 • (02/29/96) • **85**

Chardonnay Santa Maria Covenant Reserve 1994: Firm and tight, with a pretty focus to the spice, pear and apple notes, turning complex on the finish. Young and vibrant, it's well crafted. 5,000 cases made. • $14 • (02/29/96) • **88**

Pinot Noir Edna Valley Covenant Reserve 1994: Simple, with modest cherry and berry flavors, but it has some appeal. 1,200 cases made. • $14 • (01/31/96) • **84**

EPOCH | CALIFORNIA

Chardonnay Central Coast 1993: Thin, stale and earthy, finishing with modest, tart grapefruit notes. 6,000 cases made. • $7 • (10/31/95) • **77**

ESTANCIA | CALIFORNIA

Cabernet Sauvignon Alexander Valley 1994: Elegant and medium weight, but the currant and cherry flavors gain, adding dimension on the finish. 54,000 cases made. • $10 • (05/31/95) • **85-89** (BT)

Cabernet Sauvignon Alexander Valley 1992: Earthy, dry and tannic, with just enough fruit coming through to hold your interest. 55,000 cases made. • $10 • (11/15/94) • **82**

Cabernet Sauvignon Alexander Valley 1991: Serves up ripe plum and cherry fruit, but it turns leathery on the finish. Despite that it's a well balanced and attractive wine that's elegant and spicy. Drinkable now. 40,000 cases made. • $9 • (10/31/93) BB • **86**

Cabernet Sauvignon Alexander Valley 1990: Lean and hard-edged, with an ashy component that tends to overpower the ripe blackberry and currant aromas and flavors. It echoes fruit on the finish, which bodes well. Try it in 1997. 30,000 cases made. • $9 • (06/15/93) BB • **86**

Cabernet Sauvignon Alexander Valley 1989 • $10 • (11/15/92) • **85**

Cabernet Sauvignon Alexander Valley 1988 • $9 • (05/31/91) • **81**

Cabernet Sauvignon Alexander Valley 1987 • $7 • (07/15/90) BB • **80**

Cabernet Sauvignon Alexander Valley 1986 • $8 • (04/15/89) BB • **85**

Cabernet Sauvignon Alexander Valley 1985 • $6 • (06/15/88) BB • **87**

Cabernet Sauvignon Alexander Valley 1984 • $6 • (12/31/87) • **79**

Cabernet Sauvignon Alexander Valley 1982 • $6 • (04/15/87) BB • **87**

Cabernet Sauvignon Sonoma Napa Counties 1993: Tight with an earthy, cedary edge to the wild berry and spice notes. Well balanced. • $10 • (12/15/95) • **84**

Chardonnay Monterey 1991 • $8 • (05/31/93) BB • **86**

Chardonnay Monterey County 1993: Pleasantly fruity at a great price, with elegant pear, toast and spice flavors that expand and turn complex on the finish. 130,000 cases made. • $9 • (04/15/95) BB • **87**

Chardonnay Monterey County 1992: Complex and well balanced, with ripe, creamy pear, vanilla, spice and toast flavors that turn silky and elegant on the finish. Ready now. 100,000 cases made. • $8 • (02/28/94) SS • **88**

Chardonnay Monterey County Reserve 1993: Clean and well balanced, with light pear, apple, honey and toast notes that turn elegant. 2,900 cases made. • $20 • (07/31/95) • **87**

Chardonnay Monterey Reserve 1994: Smooth and creamy, with nice, ripe core of pear, apple, melon and spice flavors. It finishes with toasty oak shadings that make an elegant statement. 4,000 cases made. • $20 • (05/31/96) • **90**

Meritage Alexander Valley 1992: A nice balance between ripe plum, cherry, herb and cedary oak, harmonious and supple. Turns complex and elegant on the finish, where flavors fold together cleanly. • $15 • (09/30/95) • **89**

Meritage Alexander Valley 1991: An oaky style with an herbal and gamy edge to the Cabernet fruit. Finishes with hints of currant and mint and firm, chewy tannins. Best to cellar this one until 1997. 10,000 cases made. • $14 • (09/15/94) • **85**

Meritage Alexander Valley 1989 • $14 • (11/15/92) • **85**

Meritage Alexander Valley 1988 • $14 • (11/15/91) • **83**

Meritage Alexander Valley 1987 • $12 • (01/31/91) • **88**

Meritage Red Alexander Valley 1990: Ripe and distinctive, with a toffee, spice-scented tone to the supple currant and blackberry flavors, finishing rich and elegant. Has the style and concentration to mature through 1998. 70 percent Cabernet Sauvignon, 25 percent Cabernet Franc and 5 percent Merlot. 8,000 cases made. • $14 • (10/15/93) SS • **90**

Meritage White Monterey 1993: Rich, spicy and round, starting off like a barrel fermented Chardonnay and hinting at herb and butter on the generous finish. Achieves substantial depth. 3,000 cases made. • $14 • (05/15/95) • **87**

Meritage White Monterey 1992: Soft, round and aromatic, a spicy wine with a nice core of fig and tobacco flavors, finishing with a touch of honey and oak. • $13 • (08/31/94) • **87**

Meritage White Monterey 1991 • $12 • (12/31/92) • **82**

Merlot Alexander Valley 1992: Supple and complex, with pretty herb, currant and cedary flavors that are well focused and long on the finish. Drinks well now, but has the richness and depth to cellar. 5,000 cases made. • $10 • (11/15/94) BB • **88**

Pinot Noir Monterey 1994: Pleasantly fruity in an uncomplicated way. Supple, offering plum and cherry notes of modest proportion. • $10 • (10/15/95) • **84**

Pinot Noir Monterey County 1993: Lighter style featuring strawberry jam and spicy flavors made in a fruity, delicate manner. 6,000 cases made. • $10 • (05/15/95) • **84**

Sangiovese Alexander Valley 1993: Medium-bodied, adding a cedary oak edge to the cherry and berry flavors. Pleasantly balanced for ready enjoyment. • $20 • (11/30/95) • **85**

Sangiovese Alexander Valley 1991 • $12 • (12/15/93) • **83**

Sauvignon Blanc Monterey 1994: Broad and spicy, adding an undertone of vegetal flavors that sneak through the modest pear and toast on the finish. 9,300 cases made. • $8 • (08/31/95) • **82**

Sauvignon Blanc Monterey 1991 • $7 • (02/15/93) • **74**

Sauvignon Blanc Monterey County 1993: Soft and fruity, a nicely balanced wine for drinking while it's still fresh. 6,000 cases made. • $7 • (08/31/94) • **82**

ESTRELLA RIVER | CALIFORNIA

Blanc de Blancs Paso Robles Star Cuvée 1983 • $13 • (02/29/88) • **81**

Cabernet Sauvignon Paso Robles 1985 • $9 • (11/15/89) • **67**

Cabernet Sauvignon Paso Robles 1983 • $8 • (04/15/88) • **80**

Cabernet Sauvignon Paso Robles 1982 • $10 • (06/15/87) • **85**

Cabernet Sauvignon Paso Robles 1981 • $9 • (05/01/85) • **88**

Cabernet Sauvignon Paso Robles Founders Epic Collection 1983 • $12 • (12/15/89) • **65**

Cabernet Sauvignon San Luis Obispo County 1980 • $10 • (03/16/85) • **77**

Cabernet Sauvignon San Luis Obispo County 1979 • $6 • (03/01/84) BB • **84**

Cabernet Sauvignon San Luis Obispo County 1978 • $20 • (11/15/92) • **74**

Chardonnay California Proprietor's Reserve 1992: Tastes sweet beyond ripeness, but delivers pretty peach and pineapple flavors that linger, turning slightly cloying. Ready now. 25,000 cases made. • $6 • (06/30/94) BB • **82**

Sauvignon Blanc California Proprietor's Reserve 1993: Soft and fragrant, spicy enough make the slightly buttery pear flavors interesting. Drinkable now. • $5 • (09/30/94) • **80**

Sauvignon Blanc California Proprietor's Reserve 1992: Soft and fruity with a strong undercurrent of herb and onion overtones. 5,000 cases made. • $5 • (08/31/94) • **77**

Sauvignon Blanc California Proprietor's Reserve 1991 • $6 • (08/31/93) BB • **84**

Syrah Paso Robles 1986 • $8 • (09/30/89) • **82**

Syrah Paso Robles 1985 • $6 • (03/31/88) • **79**

Syrah Paso Robles 1983 • $6 • (01/31/88) BB • **80**

Zinfandel Paso Robles 1987 • $8 • (12/15/89) • **72**

Zinfandel San Luis Obispo County 1980 • $6 • (12/01/84) • **77**

ETUDE | CALIFORNIA

Cabernet Sauvignon California 1985 • $16 • (12/15/88) • **92**

Cabernet Sauvignon Napa Valley 1992: Dark, rich and harmonious, with complex plum, currant, cherry, vanilla and toasty oak flavors, all neatly wound together. Finishes with a wall of tannins and a trace of coffee and cedar. Best to hold off until 1999. 1,500 cases made. • $30 • (11/30/95) • **93**

Cabernet Sauvignon Napa Valley 1989 • $24 Ⓐ • (03/31/93) • **89**

Cabernet Sauvignon Napa Valley 1987 • $24 • (11/10/90) • **85**

Cabernet Sauvignon Napa Valley 1986 • $24 Ⓐ • (09/30/89) • **92**

Pinot Noir Carneros 1993: Light in body and flavor, with an earthy, slightly bitter edge to the cherry and berry. Turns crisp and austere on the finish. 3,800 cases made. • $27 • **84**

Pinot Noir Carneros 1992: Smooth and elegant, with ripe black cherry, currant and light oak shadings. Has delicate accents on the finish. Drinkable now through 1998. 3,500 cases made. • $24 • (01/31/95) • **89**

Pinot Noir Carneros 1990 • $25 • (02/28/93) • **88**

Pinot Noir Carneros 1989 • $20 • (11/15/91) • **85**

Pinot Noir Napa Valley 1988 • $20 • (12/15/90) • **86**

Pinot Noir Napa Valley 1985 • $16 • (06/15/88) • **83**

EVEREST | CALIFORNIA

Cabernet Sauvignon Dry Creek Valley 1989 • $16 • (11/15/93) • **77**

Cabernet Sauvignon Dry Creek Valley 1987 • $16 • (08/31/92) • **84**

EXPRESSIONS | CALIFORNIA

Cabernet Sauvignon Napa Valley 1993: Ripe and harmonious, offering supple plum and cherry flavors and a dry, tannic finish. Tempting now at this price, but best to wait until 2000. 11,300 cases made. • $10 • (04/30/96) BB • **87**

Chardonnay Sonoma County 1994: Harmonious and focused, letting its peach, pear and vanilla flavors emerge gently on the round finish. A great value that's drinkable now. From Glen Ellen. 35,700 cases made. • $10 • (04/30/96) BB • **88**

Merlot Sonoma County 1994: Light in texture but it wraps its delicious berry and delicate plum flavors in a sweet layer of spicy oak. Maybe a bit too much oak, but the texture and flavors are appealing and the flavors linger. 9,400 cases made. • $12 • (06/15/96) • **87**

Sangiovese California 1994: Medium-weight, featuring modest flavors of spicy cherry and berry. While not overwhelming in richness or concentration, it offers a measure of finesse. Don't be thrown by the blue bottle—red wine is inside. By Glen Ellen. 500 cases made. • $12 • (04/30/96) • **86**

Zinfandel Sonoma County 1993: Ripe and very intense, offering a tight core of cherry and wild berry that's well focused, but it turns hot and doesn't gain much complexity on the finish. By Glen Ellen. 400 cases made. • $12 • (04/30/96) • **85**

Key: SS—Spectator Selection. CS—Cellar Selection. BB—Best Buy. $NA—Price not available. (BT)—Barrel tasting. Ⓐ—Auction Price.
Dates in parentheses represent the issues in which the ratings were published.

EYE OF THE SWAN | CALIFORNIA

Cabernet Sauvignon California Limited Edition NV • $7 • (03/31/92) • **77**
Pinot Noir California 1989 • $6 • (04/30/92) • **77**

FACELLI | WASHINGTON

Cabernet Sauvignon Columbia Valley 1992: Supple and smooth, modest tannins wrapping around the straightforward berry and herb flavors. Best in 1997. 218 cases made. • $20 • (09/30/95) • **82**
Cabernet Sauvignon Columbia Valley 1991: Lean in texture and a little on the gamy side, tough, and barely squeezes out a little berry and currant flavor on the finish. May be best by 1997 or 1999. 163 cases made. • $25 • (07/31/94) • **83**
Chardonnay Columbia Valley 1991: Bright and flavorful, beautifully balanced, plays its citrus and pear notes against a delicate tinge of spicy oak. Everything echoes nicely on the finish. Drinkable now. 459 cases made. • $14 • (08/31/94) • **89**
Fumé Blanc Columbia Valley 1993: Smooth and lightly floral, simple and graced by a touch of vanilla. 615 cases made. • $9 • (09/30/95) • **82**
Fumé Blanc Columbia Valley Dry 1992: Soft and fruity, with an onion-skin character running through the basic pear flavor. 476 cases made. • $9 • (09/30/94) • **78**
Johannisberg Riesling Columbia Valley Dry 1993: Lean, citrusy and a little sour, not very charming. 259 cases made. • $8 • (09/30/95) • **74**
Lemberger Yakima Valley Limited Bottling 1993: Bright, crisp, fruity and nicely focused, like a mouthful of fresh plum. Ready now. 191 cases made. • $12 • (09/30/95) • **85**
Merlot Columbia Valley 1992: Distinctly minty and herbal, showing more spice than fruit in the formidable flavors. Best from 1997 to 1998. 351 cases made. • $15 • (09/30/95) • **81**
Merlot Columbia Valley 1991: Has a bitter edge to the toasty berry flavors, but it's balanced and spicy. Drinkable now. 423 cases made. • $15 • (09/30/94) • **83**
Pinot Noir Washington 1992: Light and fruity, appealing for its plum, berry and spice notes on a delicate frame. Fresh and drinkable now, and the flavors do persist on the finish. 153 cases made. • $20 • (09/30/94) • **85**
Sémillon Columbia Valley 1993: Intensely floral, a touch bitter, an odd wine with little charm. 251 cases made. • $9 • (09/30/95) • **73**
Sémillon Columbia Valley 1992: A little heavy and strongly floral, with a tart pineapple edge. 222 cases made. • $9 • (09/30/94) • **79**

FALCONER | CALIFORNIA

Brut Blanc de Blancs Russian River Valley 1984 • $15 • (03/15/91) • **89**

FALL CREEK | TEXAS

Cabernet Sauvignon 1989 • $13 • (02/29/92) • **75**
Cabernet Sauvignon 1988 • $13 • (07/15/91) • **78**
Carnelian Llano County 1988 • $13 • (07/15/91) • **73**

FALLENLEAF | CALIFORNIA

Chardonnay Carneros Sonoma Valley 1991: Light and crisp, with a tinny edge to the modest pear and apple flavors. 2,000 cases made. • $12 • (06/30/94) • **77**
Sauvignon Blanc Sonoma Valley 1991: Frankly vegetal, with more celery and pepper than fruit, but it finishes crisp and refreshing. Drink soon. 2,500 cases made. • $9 • (08/31/94) • **80**

FANUCCHI VINEYARDS | CALIFORNIA

Zinfandel Russian River Valley Old Vine 1994: Ripe and spicy, medium-bodied and showing pleasant earthy raspberry flavors. Drinks well now, even at this young stage. 187 cases made. • $22 • (10/15/95) • **84**

FAR NIENTE | CALIFORNIA

Cabernet Sauvignon Napa Valley 1993: Big, ripe and intense. Lots of plum and currant flavors that continue to emerge through the finish, where they gain a leathery, slightly bitter edge. 10,700 cases made. • $45 • **86**
Cabernet Sauvignon Napa Valley 1992: Big, ripe and complex, with tiers of rich plum, currant and black cherry. Yet for all its size, it manages to show off its finesse and harmony. Finishes with smooth, polished tannins. A remarkably well-balanced wine. Try in 1998. 12,000 cases made. • $45 • (11/15/95) • **93**
Cabernet Sauvignon Napa Valley 1991: Supple and elegant, with a finely crafted band of spicy currant, black cherry, cedar, anise and light oak shadings. Impressive for its balance and delicacy. Finishes with firm but fine tannins. Appealing now, but has the depth and concentration to last into the next decade. Best after 1997. 11,000 cases made. • $40 • (09/15/94) • **89**
Cabernet Sauvignon Napa Valley 1990: Young, firm, tannic and leathery, showing toasty new oak notes, but also a nice core of currant and spice flavors that stays with you on the finish. Needs time to soften and develop, but has all the right ingredients. Drink after 1997. 9,500 cases made. • $36 • (09/15/93) • **88**
Cabernet Sauvignon Napa Valley 1989 • $36 • (11/15/92) • **86**
Cabernet Sauvignon Napa Valley 1988 • $36 • (11/15/91) • **85**
Cabernet Sauvignon Napa Valley 1987 • $33 • (11/15/90) • **88**
Cabernet Sauvignon Napa Valley 1986 • $30 • (09/30/89) • **91**
Cabernet Sauvignon Napa Valley 1985 • $41 Ⓐ • (03/01/89) • **92**
Cabernet Sauvignon Napa Valley 1984 • $32 Ⓐ • (03/01/89) • **92**
Cabernet Sauvignon Napa Valley 1983 • $25 • (03/01/89) • **87**
Cabernet Sauvignon Napa Valley 1982 • $20 Ⓐ • (03/01/89) • **82**
Chardonnay Napa Valley 1994: A subtle style that shows off its citrus and pear notes, starting out crisp and refreshing and adding more flavor development on the finish. Typical of Far Niente, it can stand short-term cellaring. 20,000 cases made. • $32 • (02/29/96) • **86**
Chardonnay Napa Valley 1993: A wine of medium intensity, with spicy citrus and pear flavors that are clean and simple. 21,000 cases made. • $32 • (07/31/95) • **85**
Chardonnay Napa Valley 1992: Broad and ripe, with spicy toast and pear flavors that are young and a bit on the green side. Needs short-term cellaring, as the spicy pear notes on the finish are the most pleasing. Typically young and backward at this stage. 24,000 cases made. • $30 • (06/30/94) • **86**
Chardonnay Napa Valley 1991 • $30 • (07/15/93) • **87**

FARELLA-PARK | CALIFORNIA

Cabernet Sauvignon Napa Valley 1991: Supple and smooth, herb, currant, cedar and anise flavors fold together nicely. Soft tannins predominate. Approachable now through 1999. 50 cases made. • $25 • (02/28/95) • **85**
Chardonnay Napa Valley 1991 • $15 • (10/15/93) • **84**
Chardonnay Napa Valley Barrel Fermented 1992: Earthy, with a funky edge to the mature pear and spice flavors, although it straightens out. 500 cases made. • $14 • (02/28/95) • **83**
Merlot Napa Valley 1990: Laced with currant flavors, this is still a tightly knit and tannic young red. Needs time to soften a bit. 60 cases made. • $20 • (02/28/95) • **84**
Merlot Napa Valley 1988 • $18 • (08/31/93) • **84**
Sauvignon Blanc Napa Valley 1993: Earthy and funky, a lean wine with little charm. 190 cases made. • $9 • (08/31/95) • **74**
Sauvignon Blanc Napa Valley 1991 • $9 • (09/15/93) • **75**

FARRELL, GARY | CALIFORNIA

Cabernet Sauvignon Sonoma County 1987 • $16 • (10/31/90) • **87**
Cabernet Sauvignon Sonoma County Ladi's Vineyard 1992: Full-bodied, unfolding ripe cherry and currant flavors slowly to reveal depth and richness on the finish. Just showing its potential, should be excellent around 1997. 500 cases made. • $20 • (07/31/95) • **89**
Cabernet Sauvignon Sonoma County Ladi's Vineyard 1991: Deeply colored, firm and intense, with spicy black cherry, currant and plum notes that pick up cedary oak flavors on the finish. A crisp tannic edge suggests cellaring until 1998. 560 cases made. • $18 • (08/31/94) • **87**
Cabernet Sauvignon Sonoma County Ladi's Vineyard 1990: Rich, smooth and supple, with intense, sharply focused currant, chocolate,

cedar and spice—the full range of oak-aged Cabernet flavors—that turn broad and polished on the aftertaste. A charming, youthful wine that's sure to hold through the decade. Drinkable now. 900 cases made. • $18 • (11/15/92) • **90**

Cabernet Sauvignon Sonoma County Ladi's Vineyard 1989 • $18 • (11/15/92) • **81**

Cabernet Sauvignon Sonoma County Ladi's Vineyard 1988 • $18 • (08/31/91) • **86**

Chardonnay Russian River Valley 1994: Openly ripe, sweet-tasting and exotic, distinctive for its range of tangerine, orange and nectarine notes and pouring on more flavors of pear and fig. Delicious now and for the next few years. 325 cases made. • $17 • (05/15/96) • **92**

Chardonnay Russian River Valley 1991 • $16 • (04/15/93) • **86**

Chardonnay Russian River Valley Allen Vineyard 1994: Bold and intense, boasting rich pear, honey, toast and spice, an altogether mouth-filling white with lots of ripe, bright flavors but also a measure of finesse. 600 cases made. • $20 • (04/30/96) • **92**

Chardonnay Russian River Valley Allen Vineyard 1993: A tight, compact California Chardonnay with nice, toasty oak blending with pear, apple and spice. Expands on the complex finish, where butterscotch flavors lend more richness. 610 cases made. • $18 • (04/15/95) • **92**

Chardonnay Russian River Valley Allen Vineyard 1992: Firm and tight, with a compact band of pear, honey, spice and cedary oak. This wine needs time in the bottle to soften and evolve, but it is complex and concentrated, with a long aftertaste. 750 cases made. • $18 • (06/15/94) • **88**

Chardonnay Russian River Valley Allen Vineyard 1991 • $18 • (07/15/93) • **86**

Chardonnay Russian River Valley Westside Farms 1993: Medium weight, with ripe pear, peach and apple notes picking up a spicy, toasty oak edge on the finish, where the flavors fan out and turn complex. 300 cases made. • $18 • (07/31/95) • **89**

Merlot Sonoma County Ladi's Vineyard 1993: Attractive for its cherry and currant flavors, and it's well balanced, but this Merlot lacks the richness and depth to merit a higher rating. Can benefit from aging into 1997. 950 cases made. • $20 • (04/30/96) • **87**

Merlot Sonoma County Ladi's Vineyard 1992: A touch earthy, with leather, currant and cedary notes that turn dry and tannic. Tasted twice with consistent results. 813 cases made. • $20 • (07/31/95) • **83**

Merlot Sonoma County Ladi's Vineyard 1991 • $16 • (06/15/94) • **88**

Merlot Sonoma County Ladi's Vineyard 1990 • $16 • (04/15/93) • **88**

Pinot Noir Russian River Valley 1991 • $18 • (02/28/93) • **88**

Pinot Noir Russian River Valley 1989 • $16 • (07/31/91) • **88**

Pinot Noir Russian River Valley 1988 • $16 • (10/31/90) • **88**

Pinot Noir Russian River Valley 1986 • $15 • (06/15/88) • **90**

Pinot Noir Russian River Valley 1985 • $14 • (06/15/88) • **62**

Pinot Noir Russian River Valley 1984 • $12 • (04/15/87) • **79**

Pinot Noir Russian River Valley 1983 • $12 • (08/31/86) • **88**

Pinot Noir Russian River Valley Allen Vineyard 1992: Serves up ripe plum and raspberry flavors of moderate richness and intensity, but it turns tight, tannic and compact on the finish, indicating it needs more time to develop. 500 cases made. • $32 • (11/30/94) • **88**

Pinot Noir Russian River Valley Allen Vineyard 1991 • $32 • (02/28/94) • **87**

Pinot Noir Russian River Valley Allen Vineyard 1990 • $28 • (12/31/92) • **94**

Pinot Noir Russian River Valley Allen Vineyard 1988 • $25 • (10/31/90) • **87**

Pinot Noir Russian River Valley Olivet Lane Vineyard 1994: Young and tight, with a crisp edge to the plum and berry flavors. Picks up a trace of herb and toasty oak on the finish. 325 cases made. • $30 • (06/30/96) • **88**

Pinot Noir Russian River Valley Sonoma County 1990 • $16 • (12/31/92) • **87**

Pinot Noir Santa Barbara County Bien Nacido Vineyard 1992: Intense and spicy, with peppery notes and a firm, tannic backbone. The herb, tea and berry flavors bearly sneak past the tannins, hands off until 1997. 300 cases made. • $28 • (11/30/94) • **85**

Pinot Noir Santa Barbara County Bien Nacido Vineyard 1990 • $24 • (09/30/92) • **88**

Pinot Noir Sonoma County Howard Allen Vineyard 1987 • $20 • (02/15/90) • **84**

Pinot Noir Sonoma County Howard Allen Vineyard 1986 • $15 • • **78**

Sauvignon Blanc Russian River Valley Rochioli Vineyard 1992 • $10 • (06/15/93) • **86**

Zinfandel Russian River Valley 1992: Beautifully crafted, with amazingly complex fruit. The cherry, raspberry and boysenberry are bright, intense and lively until the tannins clamp down. Tar and cedary oak flavors add complexity and dimension on the finish. 650 cases made. • $15 • (08/31/94) • **92**

Zinfandel Russian River Valley 1991 • $15 • (04/30/93) • **88**

Zinfandel Russian River Valley Collins Vineyard 1994: Solid, complex black cherry, cedar, spice and tar notes characterize this young and somewhat unevolved red that will clearly benefit from short-term cellaring. Drinkable now, best in 1997. 850 cases made. • $16 • (04/30/96) • **88**

Zinfandel Russian River Valley Collins Vineyard 1993: Dark, tight and intensely wound, needs short-term cellaring. Chunky currant and raspberry flavors, though, are appealing, rich and well focused. 800 cases made. • $15 • (07/31/95) • **89**

Zinfandel Russian River Valley Collins Vineyard 1990 • $14 • (10/15/92) • **88**

Zinfandel Sonoma County 1985 • $10 • (04/30/88) • **91**

FARVIEW FARM | CALIFORNIA

Merlot California Templeton 1980 • $6 • (03/16/84) • **78**

Zinfandel San Luis Obispo Reserve 1980 • $7 • (03/16/84) • **62**

FATHOM | CALIFORNIA

Cabernet Franc Santa Ynez Valley 1992: Marked by earthy, horsy flavors that turn dry and leathery. 240 cases made. • $17 • (02/28/95) • **70**

Cabernet Sauvignon Santa Ynez Valley 1992: Tight and compact, with a trim layer of currant, anise and cedar flavors and firm tannins. Needs cellaring to soften into a more supple and approachable red. Try after 1998. 300 cases made. • $24 • (11/15/94) • **86**

Merlot Santa Ynez Valley 1992: Crisp and firm, displaying a tight band of spice, currant and earth notes, turning austere on the finish. 107 cases made. • $18 • (02/28/95) • **84**

FELTA SPRINGS | CALIFORNIA

Cabernet Sauvignon Sonoma County 1983 • $5 • (03/31/87) • **78**

FELTON EMPIRE | CALIFORNIA

Pinot Noir California Tonneaux Français 1984 • $12 • (05/15/87) • **77**

FENESTRA | CALIFORNIA

Cabernet Sauvignon Livermore Valley 1991: Leans toward the herb and vegetal side of Cabernet, with just enough berry fruit to keep in interesting. Firmly tannic. 438 cases made. • $11 • (06/15/95) • **79**

Cabernet Sauvignon Livermore Valley 1990: An improvement from the 1989, but it's still tough and tannic, with just a hint of currant and berry fruit showing through. Drinkable now. 304 cases made. • $12 • (11/15/93) • **82**

Cabernet Sauvignon Livermore Valley 1989 • $13 • (11/15/92) • **79**

Cabernet Sauvignon Livermore Valley 1988 • $12 • (11/15/91) • **85**

Cabernet Sauvignon Monterey Smith & Hook Vineyard 1989 • $14 • (11/15/93) • **79**

Cabernet Sauvignon Monterey Smith & Hook Vineyard 1988 • $15 • (11/15/92) • **86**

Cabernet Sauvignon Monterey Smith & Hook Vineyard 1987 • $14 • (11/15/91) • **75**

Cabernet Sauvignon Monterey Smith & Hook Vineyard 1986 • $14 • (11/15/93) • **83**

Key: SS—Spectator Selection. CS—Cellar Selection. BB—Best Buy. $NA—Price not available. (BT)—Barrel tasting. Ⓐ—Auction Price.
Dates in parentheses represent the issues in which the ratings were published.

Chardonnay Livermore Valley Toy Vineyard 1993: Lean and earthy, with a leesy edge to the pear and pineapple flavors. 373 cases made. • $12 • (07/31/95) • **82**

Chardonnay Livermore Valley Toy Vineyard 1992: Tastes awkward and disjointed, with earthy Chardonnay and oak flavors. 437 cases made. • $12 • (06/30/94) • **75**

Chardonnay Livermore Valley Toy Vineyard 1991 • $12 • (07/15/93) • **81**

Merlot Livermore Valley 1991: Light, bright and crisp, offering pleasant berry and currant flavor that lingers. 460 cases made. • $11 • (09/15/94) • **83**

Merlot Livermore Valley 1990: Modest, with a chewy texture and low-intensity flavors that fade quickly. 410 cases made. • $13 • (09/15/94) • **78**

Merlot Livermore Valley 1989 • $13 • (05/31/92) • **87**

Merlot Livermore Valley Special Reserve 1989 • $40 • (05/31/92) • **89**

Merlot Sonoma County 1986 • $11 • (10/15/89) • **83**

Semonnay Livermore Valley 1992: Broad, spicy and generously scented with oak, this has a nice core of citrusy flavor. Appealing now. 104 cases made. • $13 • (05/15/95) • **85**

Sémillon Livermore Valley 1992: Round and generous, very pretty for its honey-scented pear and apricot. Tasty now. 278 cases made. • $9 • (06/30/95) • **86**

White Zinfandel Livermore Valley 1987 • $5 • (06/15/89) • **80**

Zinfandel Livermore Valley 1990 • $8 • (09/30/93) • **80**

Zinfandel Livermore Valley 1989 • $8 • (10/15/92) • **87**

Zinfandel Livermore Valley Special Reserve 1991: Dry and earthy, with chewy tannins and a waxy berry flavor. 210 cases made. • $11 • (10/15/95) • **78**

FENN VALLEY | MICHIGAN

Chancellor Lake Michigan Shore 1989 • $9 • (02/29/92) • **81**

FENSALIR | CALIFORNIA

Cabernet Sauvignon Napa Valley 1989 • $10 • (11/15/92) • **83**

Cabernet Sauvignon Napa Valley 1988 • $14 • (11/15/91) • **85**

FERMENTATIONS AND MORE | CALIFORNIA

Chardonnay Edna Valley MacGregor Vineyard 1994: Crisp and refreshing for its lively pineapple and spice flavors, although there is a candied edge that lowers the charm quotient somewhat. • $13 • (04/30/96) • **86**

Zinfandel Paso Robles Benito Dusi Vineyard 1993: Ripe and jammy, sporting lots of cherry, berry and plummy flavors. A touch of heat and mix of pepper and spice on the finish. Drinkable now. 25 cases made. • $14 • (04/30/96) • **88**

FERRARI-CARANO | CALIFORNIA

Cabernet Sauvignon Alexander Valley 1988 • $14 • (08/31/92) • **84**

Cabernet Sauvignon Alexander Valley 1987 • $18 • (07/15/91) • **84**

Cabernet Sauvignon Alexander Valley 1986 • $18 • (09/15/90) • **80**

Cabernet Sauvignon Alexander Valley Reserve 1988 • $40 • (11/15/93) • **86**

Cabernet Sauvignon Alexander Valley Special Selection 1987 • $24 • (03/31/93) • **83**

Cabernet Sauvignon Sonoma County 1991: Well oaked, as the currant, herb and berry flavors are just able to balance out, subtle tobacco finish. 13,000 cases made. • $16 • (09/15/95) • **86**

Cabernet Sauvignon Sonoma County 1990: Bright and vibrant, with a lively array of ripe currant and black cherry flavors. It picks up an intriguing cedar and toasty oak edge, which adds another dimension. Best after 1997. 9,900 cases made. • $15 • (09/30/94) • **89**

Chardonnay Alexander Valley 1994: Serves up a pretty array of fig, pear, spice and smoky, toasty oak flavors. This California Chardonnay turns on the elegance and complexity on the finish, where the flavors take on a sense of delicacy. 30,000 cases made. • $22 • (05/15/96) SS • **90**

Chardonnay Alexander Valley 1993: Deliciously fruity California Chardonnay with a solid core of spice, pear and apple. The flavors are framed by smoky, toasty oak, followed up with a long, lingering finish. Drinkable now. 30,000 cases made. • $20 • (04/30/95) SS • **91**

Chardonnay Alexander Valley 1992: Serves up a lot of ripe, generous fruit flavors. Layers of pear, pineapple, honey, vanilla and almond flavors are deftly balanced, finishing with an amazingly long and complex aftertaste. Delicious now through 1997. 30,000 cases made. • $20 • (04/30/94) SS • **93**

Chardonnay Alexander Valley 1991 • $20 • (06/30/93) • **91**

Chardonnay Alexander Valley Tre Terre 1994: Openly fruity, remarkably complex and subtle, sporting ripe pear, peach, nectarine and pretty toasty, smoky oak shadings and a long, elegant aftertaste. 467 cases made. • $24 • (05/15/96) • **91**

Chardonnay Alexander Valley Tre Terre 1993: Brimming with bright, rich and complex fruit flavors. Tiers of honey, pear, spice and nectarine pick up a hint of hazelnut and buttery oak. Elegant and refined, finishing long and rich. • $22 • (02/29/96) • **93**

Chardonnay Napa-Sonoma Counties Reserve 1993: Smooth and polished, an elegant style boasting ripe pear, fig, apple and pineapple notes, finishing with crisp acidity and some citrus and nutmeg. The flavors linger in a long, complex aftertaste. 2,900 cases made. • $30 • (05/15/96) • **91**

Chardonnay Napa-Sonoma Counties Reserve 1992: A complex Chardonnay with ripe pear and apple flavors and a rich, creamy texture. It picks up an exotic hint of tangerine that lingers. Drink now. 3,000 cases made. • $27 • (05/31/95) • **91**

Chardonnay Sonoma-Napa Counties Reserve 1991 • $28 • (04/30/94) • **90**

Fumé Blanc Sonoma County 1994: Fresh and lively, more complex than most, offering peach, citrus and anise flavors that linger nicely on the finish. 30,000 cases made. • $11 • (12/15/95) • **88**

Fumé Blanc Sonoma County 1993: Fruity, citrusy, showing some nice orange and cream flavors and a touch of oak, a smooth wine that keeps its flavors nicely balanced and elegant. • $11 • (08/31/94) • **88**

Fumé Blanc Sonoma County 1992 • $10 • (08/31/93) • **89**

Fumé Blanc Sonoma County 1991 • $11 • (11/30/92) • **87**

Fumé Blanc Sonoma County Reserve 1994: Ripe, rich, round and spicy featuring new oak flavors backed by a mouthful of nectarine, pear and orange notes that expand on the finish. Superbly crafted in its supple, oak-centered style. 4,500 cases made. • $15 • (12/15/95) • **90**

Fumé Blanc Sonoma County Reserve 1993: Bright and fruity, tart enough to lend some zing to the concentrated apricot and apple flavors. Drinkable now. 1,000 cases made. • $14 • (11/30/94) • **87**

Merlot Alexander Valley 1987 • $17 • (07/31/90) • **84**

Merlot Alexander Valley 1986 • $15 • (06/30/89) • **87**

Merlot Sonoma County 1993: Crisp, with a trim band of ripe plum and cherry flavors. Good, albeit without the extra dimensions and richness of the best. 14,500 cases made. • $23 • (06/30/96) • **83**

Merlot Sonoma County 1992: Showcases its ripe, crisp black cherry, plum and currant flavors and integrated tannins. Picks up pretty anise and spice notes along the way to a supple finish. 15,000 cases made. • $20 • (09/30/95) • **89**

Merlot Sonoma County 1991 • $17 • (05/31/94) • **89**

Merlot Sonoma County 1990 • $15 • (07/15/93) • **81**

Merlot Sonoma County 1989 • $15 • (05/31/92) • **86**

Merlot Sonoma County 1988 • $18 • (08/31/91) • **85**

Pinot Noir Napa-Sonoma Counties Rhonda's Reserve 1990 • $30 • (02/28/93) • **82**

Reserve Sonoma County 1990: Dark, ripe, bold and opulent, boasting plush black cherry, plum, anise and mineral flavors and a dash of herb and tobacco on the finish. Intense, complex and concentrated, yet with smooth, polished tannins. Best in 1998. 1,076 cases made. • $47 • (11/30/95) • **91**

Reserve Sonoma County 1989: Austere with firm, gritty tannins yet it's more complete than most '89s, offering an intense core of very ripe Cabernet fruit and hints of plum and prune. Cellar until 1997. 7,006 cases made. • $40 • (11/15/94) • **85**

Sauvignon Blanc Late Harvest Alexander Valley Eldorado Gold 1989 • $17 • (09/15/91) • **88**

Sauvignon Blanc Late Harvest Sonoma County Eldorado Gold 1991 • $17 • (04/15/93) • **83**

Sauvignon Blend Dry Creek Valley Eldorado Gold Late Harvest 1994: Silky, elegant, round and sweet, layering its floral pear, pineapple, apricot and vanilla flavors in great style, finishing smooth and long.

Drinkable now through 1998. Tasted twice with consistent notes. 388 cases made. • $18 • (12/31/95) • **91**

Siena Sonoma County 1993: A smooth and harmonious Sangiovese-Cabernet blend with a supple core of black cherry, wild berry, coffee and spice flavors that weave into a nice tapestry of fruit and spice on the finish. 2,800 cases made. • $24 • (11/30/95) • **90**

Siena Sonoma County 1992: Stretches the flavors, sporting an elegant range of blackberry, currant, tar and anise and a cedary oak finish. Needs short-term cellaring. 2,800 cases made. • $20 • (09/30/95) • **89**

Siena Sonoma County 1991: The best Sangiovese blend we've seen, a solid wine with beautifully articulated currant, spice and vanilla aromas and flavors, smooth and generous on the long finish. Has style and grace to age through at least 1998 . 375 cases made. • $20 • (11/15/93) • **90**

Zinfandel Dry Creek Valley 1992: Fresh, lively and vibrant, with a pretty core of spicy black cherry, wild berry and light oak shadings. Rich, complex and turns elegant on the finish. Delicious now through 1997. 2,300 cases made. • $15 • (09/30/94) • **89**

Zinfandel Dry Creek Valley 1991 • $14 • (09/30/93) • **85**

Zinfandel Dry Creek Valley 1990 • $15 • (01/31/93) • **90**

Zinfandel Sonoma County 1993: Toasty raspberry aromas lead to flavors that match, giving this an appealing core of fruit and oak, followed by a complex aftertaste and firm tannins. 4,000 cases made. • $14 • (08/31/95) • **88**

FERRER, GLORIA | CALIFORNIA

Blanc de Noirs Sonoma County NV: A ripe and fruity style that showcases its black cherry and strawberry notes. Impressive for its suppleness and overt fruit flavors. Ready now. 9,800 cases made. • $14 • (12/31/94) • **87**

Brut Carneros Cuvée 1985 • $20 • (04/30/90) • **81**

Brut Carneros Cuvée NV • $14 • (05/15/92) • **84**

Brut Carneros Late Disgorged Cuvée 1987: Serves up a ripe, rich core of spice and pineapple flavors up front, but the flavors lose some of their intensity on the finish. Ready now. 1,000 cases made. • $25 • (12/31/94) • **87**

Brut Carneros Royal Cuvée 1988: Appealing for its aromatic cherry and vanilla notes. Ripe, complex and concentrated, with a smooth texture and the extra dimensions one can imagine will only improve with additional bottle age. 15,000 cases made. • $18 • (12/15/95) SS • **91**

Brut Carneros Royal Cuvée 1987: Shows mature pear, black cherry and spice notes that turn a bit earthy on the finish. Ready now. 13,000 cases made. • $17 • (12/31/94) • **85**

Brut Carneros Royal Cuvée 1986 • $17 • (12/31/91) • **84**

Brut Rosé Sonoma County NV: Fresh and lively, with a modest dose of black cherry, rose petal and spicy flavors that finish with delicate edge. Ready now. 2,000 cases made. • $20 • (11/15/94) • **87**

Brut Sonoma County NV: Good intensity but the flavors are a bit muted and subtle, as earthy cherry and spice tones fail to develop into something more complex and interesting. 35,000 cases made. • $15 • **86**

Brut Sonoma County Royal Cuvée 1986 • $16 • (04/30/91) • **84**

Brut Sonoma County Royal Cuvée 1985 • $16 • (03/15/91) • **83**

Brut Sonoma County Royal Cuvée 1984 • $15 • (04/15/88) • **89**

Chardonnay Carneros 1993: This combines delicacy with finesse: The creamy pear, honey, spice and nutmeg flavors lead into a complex aftertaste. 8,000 cases made. • $15 • (03/31/95) SS • **91**

Chardonnay Carneros 1991 • $15 • (07/15/93) • **90**

Chardonnay Carneros Freixenet Vineyards 1992: Rich, fruity and generous wine that keeps pumping out the apple, pear and pineapple flavors, while remaining balanced and smooth. Try now. 2,800 cases made. • $15 • (04/30/94) • **91**

Natural Sonoma County Cuvée Emerald NV • $11 • (05/16/86) • **89**

Pinot Noir Carneros 1994: Light in color, texture and flavor, a shade darker than a rosé, delivering modest cherry and herb notes. 3,000 cases made. • $16 • (02/29/96) • **79**

Key: SS—Spectator Selection. CS—Cellar Selection. BB—Best Buy. $NA—Price not available. (BT)—Barrel tasting. Ⓐ—Auction Price.
Dates in parentheses represent the issues in which the ratings were published.

Pinot Noir Carneros 1993: A touch earthy, with oak and sage notes, it offers just enough ripe fruit to hold your interest. The 1992 is superior. 3,000 cases made. • $16 • **81**

Pinot Noir Carneros 1992: Marked by creamy, toasty oak, there's enough cherry and berry fruit to keep in balance. Ready now. 2,400 cases made. • $16 • **86**

Pinot Noir Carneros 1991 • $15 • (02/28/94) • **85**

FERRONNIERE, LA | CALIFORNIA

Cabernet Sauvignon Napa Valley 1985 • $14 • (01/31/90) • **80**

FETZER | CALIFORNIA

Bonterra Organically Grown Grapes Mendocino County 1993: Bright and appealing, its pear and apple flavors shaded nicely with touches of herb and celery. The fruit wins on the finish. • $7 • (07/31/95) BB • **87**

Bonterra Organically Grown Grapes Mendocino County 1991 • $9 • (03/31/94) • **83**

Cabernet Sauvignon California 1988 • $8 • (01/31/91) BB • **81**

Cabernet Sauvignon California Barrel Select 1990: Spicy and complex with a pretty, ripe and supple core of currant and cherry-scented Cabernet fruit that's framed by light cedary oak and finishing with firm tannins that let just enough fruit through to keep you coming back for another sip. Drinkable now 27,000 cases made. • $12 • (11/15/93) • **87**

Cabernet Sauvignon California Barrel Select 1989 • $11 • (03/15/93) • **87**

Cabernet Sauvignon California Barrel Select 1988 • $11 • (08/31/92) • **86**

Cabernet Sauvignon California Barrel Select 1983 • $8 • (06/15/87) • **70**

Cabernet Sauvignon California Bel Arbors 1993: Soft and generous, centered around appealing vaniulla-scented raspberry and red currant flavors that linger gently on the finish. Approachable now. • $7 • (12/15/95) BB • **84**

Cabernet Sauvignon California Reserve 1985 • $17 • (11/15/89) • **87**

Cabernet Sauvignon California Valley Oaks 1993: Light, straightforward, showing nice plum and berry flavors that fade a bit on the finish. Ready now. • $8 • (12/15/95) • **82**

Cabernet Sauvignon California Valley Oaks 1990: Smooth and correct, a good, easy-to-drink wine, with modest fruit and herb flavors and moderate tannins. Fine for everyday drinking. 200,000 cases made. • $8 • (03/15/93) • **83**

Cabernet Sauvignon California Valley Oaks 1989 • $8 • (08/31/92) BB • **85**

Cabernet Sauvignon California Valley Oaks 1988 • $8 • (11/15/91) • **82**

Cabernet Sauvignon Lake County 1985 • $6 • (08/31/87) BB • **82**

Cabernet Sauvignon Lake County 1984 • $8 • (05/15/87) • **74**

Cabernet Sauvignon Lake County 1983 • $5 • (05/01/86) • **83**

Cabernet Sauvignon Lake County 1982 • $5 • (05/16/84) • **78**

Cabernet Sauvignon Mendocino Barrel Select 1985 • $10 • (12/15/88) • **85**

Cabernet Sauvignon Mendocino Barrel Select 1984 • $9 • (11/30/87) • **82**

Cabernet Sauvignon Mendocino Barrel Select 1982 • $7 • (02/01/85) • **73**

Cabernet Sauvignon Mendocino County 1981 • $7 • (12/16/84) • **86**

Cabernet Sauvignon Mendocino Special Reserve 1984 • $14 • (12/31/88) • **85**

Cabernet Sauvignon North Coast Barrel Select 1992: A beefy wine, with a meaty, smoky oak edge to the ripe plum and currant laced-fruit. Turns tannic and chunky on the finish. • $12 • (12/15/95) • **85**

Cabernet Sauvignon North Coast Barrel Select 1991: Sturdy with a tight core of currant and oak flavor that turns dry and tannic on the finish. Best to cellar short-term, allowing it to soften. Try in 1997. 33,000 cases made. • $12 • (11/15/94) • **83**

Cabernet Sauvignon Sonoma County Reserve 1989: Lean and compact, with a trim band of cedar and currant, turning earthy and drying out on the finish. Decent but fairly typical of the 1989s, best now into 1997. • $24 • (12/15/95) • **85**

Cabernet Sauvignon Sonoma County Reserve 1988: Crisp and austere, featuring a lean band of herb, currant and cedary oak and finishing with dry tannins. Ready now through 1999. 2,692 cases made. • $24 • (11/15/94) • **83**

Cabernet Sauvignon Sonoma County Reserve 1987 • $22 • (09/30/93) • **88**

Cabernet Sauvignon Sonoma County Reserve 1986 • $24 • (09/30/91) • **88**

Cabernet Sauvignon Sonoma County Reserve 1985 • $24 • (08/31/90) • **86**

Chardonnay California Sundial 1993: Smooth and fruity, a generous wine with simple flavors that taper on the finish. 626,000 cases made. • $8 • (07/31/95) • **81**

Chardonnay California Sundial 1992: A simple, fruity, soft-textured wine, with appealing tropical fruit and lemon aromas and flavors and a fresh, soft finish. Drinkable now. 700,000 cases made. • $8 • (07/15/93) • **80**

Chardonnay California Sundial 1992: Light and fruity with ripe pear and spice notes. Ready now. 700,000 cases made. • $8 • (06/30/94) BB • **83**

Chardonnay California Sundial 1991 • $8 • (08/31/92) • **76**

Chardonnay Mendocino County Barrel Select 1992: An oaky style but it has the fruit intensity to match, with spice, pear, toast and honey notes coming through on the finish. It should be enjoyed now. 77,000 cases made. • $11 • (04/15/94) • **85**

Chardonnay Mendocino County Barrel Select 1991 • $11 • (07/15/93) • **84**

Chardonnay Mendocino County Bonterra Organically Grown Grapes 1993: Smooth and spicy, generous with its pear and nutmeg flavors, glides gently into the finish. Drinkable now. 39,000 cases made. • $9 • (06/30/95) • **84**

Chardonnay Mendocino County Bonterra Organically Grown Grapes 1992: Ripe, smooth and supple with pretty pear, honey and butterscotch notes. Picks up a hint of oak and hazelnut on the finish, but the flavors hang with you. Ready now. 20,087 cases made. • $9 • (04/15/94) BB • **85**

Chardonnay Mendocino County Organically Grown Grapes 1991 • $9 • (04/30/93) BB • **88**

Chardonnay Mendocino Reserve 1993: Complex with attractive flavors, ranging from ripe pear, spice, honey and toasty oak, all folding together on the finish, where the flavors linger. 1,200 cases made. • $24 • (07/31/95) • **88**

Chardonnay Mendocino Reserve 1991 • $18 • (07/15/93) • **83**

Chardonnay North Coast Barrel Select 1994: Smooth in texture, with spicy apple and pear flavors in balance and echoing nicely on the finish. • $10 • (06/15/96) • **86**

Chardonnay North Coast Barrel Select 1993: Appealing for its ripe apple, pear and light, spicy oak shadings that hang on through the finish. Well made. 87,000 cases made. • $11 • (06/30/95) • **87**

Chardonnay North Coast Sundial 1995: Ripe, bright and attractive for its citrusy melon and pear flavors that remain fresh through the finish. • $7 • (06/15/96) • **84**

Fumé Blanc California Dry 1992 • $7 • (05/15/94) BB • **85**

Fumé Blanc Mendocino County 1995: A mouthful of vivid, fruit flavors—crisp apple, citrus and peach—that have just a hint of herb. 50,000 cases made. • $6 • **86**

Gamay Beaujolais Mendocino 1987 • $6 • (07/15/88) • **83**

Gamay Beaujolais Mendocino County 1988 • $5 • (07/15/89) • **74**

Gamay Beaujolais Mendocino County 1986 • $4 • (01/31/88) • **80**

Gewürztraminer California 1992 • $7 • (09/30/93) • **81**

Gewürztraminer California 1991 • $6 • (07/31/92) BB • **84**

Johannisberg Riesling California 1992 • $6 • (11/15/93) BB • **86**

Johannisberg Riesling California 1991 • $6 • (07/31/92) BB • **86**

Johannisberg Riesling Late Harvest Sonoma County Reserve 1988 • $10 • (03/31/91) • **91**

Merlot California Eagle Peak 1994: The flavors edge strongly toward black cherry and a hint of chocolate on a light, open-textured frame. A bit tannic, should be fine with hearty food. At this price, it's a good off-the-shelf red. 300,000 cases made. • $8 • (06/15/96) BB • **85**

Merlot California Eagle Peak 1992: Lean, crisp and chewy, with modest berry and plum flavors. Tannic enough to need until 1997 to soften. 70,000 cases made. • $8 • (09/15/94) • **81**

Merlot North Coast Barrel Select 1994: Supple and ripe, with bright berry and vanilla flavors that echo nicely on the velvety finish. • $12 • (06/30/96) • **85**

Petite Sirah California Petite Syrah Reserve 1986 • $14 • (08/31/90) • **74**

Petite Sirah Mendocino Petite Syrah 1982 • $5 • (04/16/85) • **78**

Pinot Noir California Barrel Select 1991 • $13 • (02/28/94) • **88**

Pinot Noir California Reserve 1990 • $13 • (02/28/93) • **85**

Pinot Noir California Special Reserve 1980 • $13 • (08/31/86) • **65**

Pinot Noir Mendocino 1981 • $5 • (04/01/84) • **80**

Pinot Noir Mendocino County Reserve 1986 • $18 • (10/31/90) • **87**

Pinot Noir Mendocino County Special Reserve 1985 • $13 • (06/15/88) • **78**

Pinot Noir North Coast Barrel Select 1994: Complex with an appealing array of ripe fig, toast, spice and pear-laced flavors. Strikes a nice balance between its ripe fruit and toasty oak. Ready now. • $13 • (02/29/96) • **81**

Pinot Noir North Coast Barrel Select 1992: Lean, tart and leathery, with firm tannins that override the modest cherry and herb flavors. 13,000 cases made. • $13 • (01/31/95) • **82**

Pinot Noir Santa Barbara County Bien Nacido Vineyards 1994: Simple, modest plum and cherry flavors pick up a trace of spice and oak. • $17 • (02/29/96) • **82**

Pinot Noir Santa Barbara County Bien Nacido Vineyards 1992: A sound red displaying buttery oak shadings which dominate the earthy cola, herb and cherry notes. 600 cases made. • $24 • (01/31/95) • **86**

Pinot Noir Sonoma County Olivet Lane Vineyard 1992: Strikes a nice balance between buttery oak and firm, spicy Pinot Noir fruit. 450 cases made. • $24 • (01/31/95) • **87**

Port Mendocino County Eagle Point 1993: Has Zinfandel fruit and spice flavors running through it, a sweeter, lighter style that goes for early drinkability. Best in 1998. • $19 • (05/15/96) • **85**

Premium Red California 1985 • $4 • (03/15/88) • **78**

Red Mendocino County Organically Grown Grapes 1990 • $9 • (05/31/93) • **83**

Sauvignon Blanc California Barrel Select 1991 • $9 • (02/28/93) • **85**

Sauvignon Blanc Mendocino County Barrel Select 1993: Soft and simple, a little citrusy and a little spicy, not much intensity. • $10 • (08/31/95) • **79**

Sauvignon Blanc Mendocino County Barrel Select 1992 • $10 • (11/30/93) • **85**

Sauvignon Blanc North Coast Barrel Select 1994: Light-bodied and crisp. Has citrusy apple flavors with a distinctly herbal tang. 18,000 cases made. • $10 • **85**

White Zinfandel California 1994: Sweeter style yielding strawberry flavors and a hint of butter on the finish. It has enough acidity to balance the sugar. • $7 • (09/15/95) • **80**

White Zinfandel California 1988 • $7 • (06/15/89) • **85**

Zinfandel California 1989 • $6 • (11/30/90) • **76**

Zinfandel California 1986 • $6 • (09/15/88) • **78**

Zinfandel California Barrel Select 1989 • $9 • (07/31/92) • **84**

Zinfandel Lake County 1986 • $6 • (02/15/88) BB • **83**

Zinfandel Lake County 1984 • $5 • (04/15/87) • **81**

Zinfandel Lake County 1983 • $4 • (07/16/86) BB • **83**

Zinfandel Mendocino 1982 • $5 • (04/01/85) • **81**

Zinfandel Mendocino 1980 • $5 • (04/01/84) • **78**

Zinfandel Mendocino County Barrel Select 1992: Firm and compact, with spicy cherry, earth and raspberry flavors that pick up a buttery oak flavor on the finish. 35,000 cases made. • $9 • (09/30/94) BB • **86**

Zinfandel Mendocino County Barrel Select 1991 • $9 • (12/31/93) BB • **86**

Zinfandel Mendocino County Reserve 1991 • $13 • (03/31/94) • **87**

Zinfandel Mendocino County Reserve 1986 • $14 • (07/31/90) • **83**

Zinfandel Mendocino Home Vineyard 1982 • $8 • (11/01/84) • **77**

Zinfandel Mendocino Lolonis Vineyards 1982 • $8 • (11/01/84) • **79**

Zinfandel Mendocino Ricetti Vineyard 1985 • $14 • (10/15/88) • **79**

Zinfandel Mendocino Ricetti Vineyard 1983 • $8 • (02/16/86) • **82**

Zinfandel Mendocino Ricetti Vineyard 1982 • $8 • (10/16/84) • **79**

Zinfandel Mendocino Ricetti Vineyard Reserve 1986 • $14 • (07/31/90) • **74**

Zinfandel Mendocino Scharffenberger Vineyard 1982 • $8 • (10/16/84) • **85**

Zinfandel Mendocino Special Reserve 1985 • $14 • (12/15/88) • **81**

Zinfandel Mendocino Special Reserve 1983 • $8 • (05/01/86) • **63**

FICKLIN | CALIFORNIA

Port California Special Bottling No. 5 1980 • $19 • (04/30/91) • **84**

Port California Special Bottling No. 6 1983 • $25 • (11/30/91) • **87**

Port California Tinta NV • $10 • (04/30/91) • **78**

Tawny Port Madera County Aged 10 Years NV: Smooth, sweet and spicy, as chocolate, caramel and toast flavors blend together nicely on the rich finish. 600 cases made. • $20 • (05/15/96) • **87**

FIDDLEHEAD | CALIFORNIA

Pinot Noir Santa Maria Valley 1993: Strikes a nice blalance between spicy cherry, light herb and berry notes, with good structure and fine balance. Flavors linger on the finish. 940 cases made. • $25 • (05/31/96) • **88**

Pinot Noir Santa Maria Valley 1992: Attractive for its delicate texture and alluring black cherry, cola, herb and spice flavors. Unfolds gently, turning supple and complex. 850 cases made. • $25 • (02/28/95) • **88**

Pinot Noir Santa Maria Valley 1990 • $25 • (02/28/94) • **82**

Sauvignon Blanc Santa Ynez Valley 1994: Has some nice citrus and pear flavors, but in striving for a lighter style much of the character got trimmed away. 850 cases made. • $17 • (05/31/96) • **84**

FIELD STONE | CALIFORNIA

Cabernet Sauvignon Alexander Valley 1991: Medium-bodied and a bit light for this vintage. The currant and plum flavors pick up a cedary oak edge on the finish before the tannins take over. Best after 1997. 3,400 cases made. • $14 • (11/15/94) • **84**

Cabernet Sauvignon Alexander Valley 1989 • $14 • (11/15/92) • **85**

Cabernet Sauvignon Alexander Valley 1987 • $14 • (02/28/91) • **85**

Cabernet Sauvignon Alexander Valley 1983 • $11 • (10/15/88) • **74**

Cabernet Sauvignon Alexander Valley Home Ranch Vineyard 1985 • $14 • (04/15/89) • **70**

Cabernet Sauvignon Alexander Valley Hoot Owl Barrel Select 1990: Dominated by drying tannins, leaving the simple cherry and plum flavors overwhelmed. Cellaring may make it more appealing, best after 1997. 763 cases made. • $16 • (05/15/94) • **80**

Cabernet Sauvignon Alexander Valley Hoot Owl Creek Vineyards 1985 • $20 • (03/31/89) • **87**

Cabernet Sauvignon Alexander Valley Hoot Owl Creek Vineyards 1984 • $14 • (10/15/88) • **82**

Cabernet Sauvignon Alexander Valley Hoot Owl Reserve 1986 • $20 • (12/15/90) • **85**

Cabernet Sauvignon Alexander Valley Staten Family Reserve 1990: Firm and intense, with a crisp, lean core of currant, coffee and herb flavors. Turns austere and dry on the finish, worth cellaring until 1998. 600 cases made. • $20 • (11/15/94) • **84**

Cabernet Sauvignon Alexander Valley Staten Family Reserve 1989 • $20 • (11/15/92) • **82**

Cabernet Sauvignon Alexander Valley Staten Family Reserve 1987 • $25 • (11/15/91) • **72**

Cabernet Sauvignon Alexander Valley Turkey Hill Vineyard 1985 • $18 • (02/28/91) • **84**

Cabernet Sauvignon Alexander Valley Turkey Hill Vineyard 1984 • $16 • (12/31/88) • **88**

Cabernet Sauvignon Alexander Valley Turkey Hill Vineyard 1982 • $12 • (03/16/86) • **78**

Cabernet Sauvignon Alexander Valley Vineyard Blend 1990: Ripe, intense and spicy with a good dose of cedary oak, but the cherry and currant-scented Cabernet fruit measures up to it, finishing with mild tannins that make it drinkable through 1997. 1,500 cases made. • $14 • (11/15/93) • **84**

Chardonnay Sonoma County 1993: Ripe and perfumed, with a dash of honey and pear notes, turning earthy on the finish. 1,300 cases made. • $14 • (07/31/95) • **82**

Chardonnay Sonoma County 1992: A decent Chardonnay, but it comes across as flat and one-dimensional with spicy pear and oak flavors that taste separated rather than united. Ready now. 1,200 cases made. • $14 • (06/30/94) • **80**

Chardonnay Sonoma County 1991 • $14 • (07/15/93) • **89**

Gewürztraminer Sonoma County 1992 • $9 • (09/30/93) • **81**

Petite Sirah Alexander Valley 1988 • $15 • (12/31/90) • **85**

Petite Sirah Alexander Valley 1987 • $15 • (12/31/90) • **84**

Petite Sirah Alexander Valley 1986 • $15 • (09/30/89) • **79**

Key: SS—Spectator Selection. CS—Cellar Selection. BB—Best Buy. $NA—Price not available. (BT)—Barrel tasting. (A)—Auction Price.
Dates in parentheses represent the issues in which the ratings were published.

Petite Sirah Alexander Valley 1985 • $11 • (02/15/89) • **83**

Petite Sirah Alexander Valley 1984 • $11 • (10/15/88) • **88**

Petite Sirah Alexander Valley 1982 • $8 • (07/01/86) • **69**

Petite Sirah Alexander Valley Old Vines 1990 • $16 • (06/15/93) • **83**

Sauvignon Blanc Sonoma County 1994: Smooth and fruity, nicely balanced to show its pear and peppery spice flavors. 1,500 cases made. • $9 • (08/31/95) • **83**

Sauvignon Blanc Sonoma County Proprietor's Blend 1991 • $9 • (09/15/93) • **82**

FIELDBROOK | CALIFORNIA

Chardonnay Mendocino County Redwood Valley Vineyard 1992: Marked by a tart, grassy edge and hints of pear and herb notes. 197 cases made. • $12 • (02/28/95) • **81**

Merlot Napa Valley Frediani Vineyard 1991: Supple and elegant, with ripe, spicy cherry, wild berry and plum flavors. Drinkable now. 164 cases made. • $15 • (09/15/94) • **84**

Pinot Noir Napa Valley Beard Vineyard 1992: Delicate and spicy, with pretty herb, tea, plum and cherry flavors that are ripe and focused. Finishes with firm tannins, but the fruit keeps pumping through. Drinks well now. 172 cases made. • $18 • (10/31/94) • **87**

Pinot Noir Napa Valley Beard Vineyard 1988 • $12 • (02/28/93) • **77**

Sauvignon Blanc California Trinity County Meredith Vineyard 1992: Soft, fruity and appealing, echoing pear and spice flavors, not very varietal but fun to drink. 120 cases made. • $9 • (08/31/94) • **85**

Sauvignon Blanc Mendocino County Quillen Vineyard 1992 • $9 • (07/31/93) • **89**

Sauvignon Blanc Mendocino County Webb Vineyard 1994: Light, juicy, crisp-textured, sappy citrus and pear flavors. 182 cases made. • $10 • (08/31/95) • **83**

Sauvignon Blanc Mendocino County Webb Vineyard 1993: Bright and fruity, flavors centered around grapefruit and sweet vanilla, echoing nicely on the crisp, smoothly balanced finish. Drinkable now for its fresh, lively character. 490 cases made. • $9 • (09/30/94) • **87**

Zinfandel Mendocino County Pacini Vineyard 1993: Deep in color and serving up plenty of pure, ripe Zinfandel fruit-cherry jam, wild berry and spicy raspberry flavors. Finishes with firm tannins and a pretty aftertaste. Drinks well now, but can age. 344 cases made. • $12 • (10/15/94) • **87**

Zinfandel Mendocino County Pacini Vineyard 1991 • $11 • (03/15/93) • **84**

Zinfandel Mendocino County Pacini Vineyard Reserve 1992: A touch earthy and gamy, the tart berry and cherry notes finishing with tar and spice. 246 cases made. • $10 • (04/30/96) • **82**

FIELDS OF FAIR | KANSAS

Concord Kansas 1991 • $5 • (02/29/92) • **70**

Flint Hills Red Proprietor's Reserve Kansas 1990 • $6 • (02/29/92) • **70**

Vintage One Proprietor's Reserve Kansas 1991 • $7 • (02/29/92) • **70**

FIFE | CALIFORNIA

Petite Sirah Napa Valley Les Vieilles Vignes 1991 • $16 • (06/15/93) • **87**

Zinfandel Napa Valley Les Vieilles Vignes 1992: Ripe, intense black cherry and plum flavors, adding hints of anise, cedar, blueberry and spice. Some heat and firm tannins on the finish. Drinking well now through 1998. 700 cases made. • $16 • (09/15/95) • **89**

Zinfandel Napa Valley Les Vieilles Vignes 1991 • $16 • (06/15/93) • **85**

FILIPPI, JOSEPH | CALIFORNIA

Angelica Elena Cucamonga Valley Limited Release Winemaker's Reserve NV: Toasty, walnut-caramel flavors are surprisingly gentle, making this a soft dessert wine for easy sipping. 112 cases made. • $10 • (06/15/96) • **82**

Chardonnay Monterey Limited Release Winemaker's Reserve 1992: Light and simple with a brackish edge to the apple and pear flavors. 507 cases made. • $7 • (06/30/94) • **73**

Ruby Port California Limited Release Winemaker's Reserve NV: The color is more like a tawny, but the sweet flavors center around strawberry and vanilla, with hints of caramel and coffee. 325 cases made. • $8 • (06/15/96) • **81**

Sauvignon Blanc Biane Guasti Vineyard Limited Release Winemaker's Reserve 1994: Soft and floral, supple, a little vegetal in flavor. Drinkable now. 480 cases made. • $8 • (08/31/95) • **80**

Sauvignon Blanc Monterey Winemaker's Reserve Limited Release 1992: Aggressively vegetal and earthy, not for the faint of heart, but soft and fruity enough overall to stay in bounds. 504 cases made. • $6 • (08/31/94) • **80**

Zinfandel Cucamonga Valley Limited Release Winemaker's Reserve 1994: Modest in varietal character, showing an odd hay, wild berry and beet flavor. Decent. 200 cases made. • $9 • (04/30/96) • **76**

FIRELANDS | OHIO

Brut American Champagne NV • $12 • (02/29/92) • **73**

Cabernet Sauvignon Ohio Lake Erie 1988 • $10 • (02/29/92) • **82**

FIRESTONE | CALIFORNIA

Blanc de Noirs Santa Ynez Valley 1985 • $15 • (12/31/88) • **79**

Cabernet Sauvignon Santa Barbara County 1978 • $20 • (11/15/92) • **65**

Cabernet Sauvignon Santa Ynez Valley 1992: Broad and spicy, spreading its berry and cinnamon flavors along a layer of chewy tannins. Best from 1999. 8,500 cases made. • $12 • (12/15/95) • **83**

Cabernet Sauvignon Santa Ynez Valley 1991: Firm and compact, with toasty wood flavors and medium-weight currant and cherry notes that pick up an earthy edge on the finish. Best after 1996. 8,500 cases made. • $12 • (11/15/94) • **84**

Cabernet Sauvignon Santa Ynez Valley 1990: An herbal style with hints of vegetables along with currant and cedar, but the texture is smooth and the tannins are soft, so if you like this flavor profile this should be a pleasing wine. Drink now. 9,800 cases made. • $12 • (11/15/93) • **81**

Cabernet Sauvignon Santa Ynez Valley 1989 • $12 • (11/15/92) • **78**

Cabernet Sauvignon Santa Ynez Valley 1988 • $12 • (11/15/91) • **75**

Cabernet Sauvignon Santa Ynez Valley 1987 • $11 • (05/31/90) • **82**

Cabernet Sauvignon Santa Ynez Valley 1986 • $10 • (12/15/89) • **81**

Cabernet Sauvignon Santa Ynez Valley 1985 • $9 • (08/31/88) • **72**

Cabernet Sauvignon Santa Ynez Valley 1984 • $9 • (03/31/88) • **72**

Cabernet Sauvignon Santa Ynez Valley 1983 • $9 • (06/15/87) • **77**

Cabernet Sauvignon Santa Ynez Valley 1981 • $8 • (03/01/85) • **89**

Cabernet Sauvignon Santa Ynez Valley Reserve 1990: Earthy, with a tobacco, herb and bell pepper edge but enough Cabernet flavors to hold your interest. Try after 1996. 1,700 cases made. • $20 • (11/15/94) • **85**

Cabernet Sauvignon Santa Ynez Valley Reserve 1988 • $18 • (02/28/91) • **84**

Cabernet Sauvignon Santa Ynez Valley Special Release 1977 • $9 • (04/16/85) • **77**

Cabernet Sauvignon Santa Ynez Valley Vintage Reserve 1990: Firm and spicy, with a pleasant smack of vanilla and spice-scented oak to round out the modest blackberry and currant flavors. Finishes smooth and spicy. Drink now. 1,700 cases made. • $20 • (02/15/93) • **84**

Cabernet Sauvignon Santa Ynez Valley Vintage Reserve 1985 • $25 • (12/15/89) • **67**

Cabernet Sauvignon Santa Ynez Valley Vintage Reserve 1979 • $12 • (03/16/86) • **73**

Chardonnay Santa Ynez Valley Barrel Fermented 1994: Clean, ripe, appealing apple, pear and spice flavors. The finish is somewhat coarse, but time may soften it a bit. • $13 • (05/15/96) • **84**

Chardonnay Santa Ynez Valley Barrel Fermented 1993: A fruity style with pretty pear, spice and honey notes framed by light oak shadings. Elegant and refined. Ready now. 30,738 cases made. • $12 • (11/30/94) • **87**

Chardonnay Santa Ynez Valley Barrel Fermented 1992: Ripe and elegant, with beautifully defined pineapple, pear and slightly herbal, spicy aromas and flavors, stylish and forward enough to drink now. 15,000 cases made. • $12 • (11/30/93) • **86**

Chardonnay Santa Ynez Valley Barrel Fermented 1991 • $13 • (02/15/93) • **90**

Gewürztraminer California 1992 • $9 • (01/31/94) • **84**

Gewürztraminer Santa Barbara County 1994: Soft in texture and innocuous in flavor, not much there. 3,200 cases made. • $9 • (05/31/96) • **77**

Gewürztraminer Santa Ynez Valley 1991 • $8 • (11/15/92) • **88**

Johannisberg Riesling Late Harvest Santa Barbara County Selected Harvest 1991 • $12 • (12/15/92) • **84**

Johannisberg Riesling Late Harvest Santa Barbara County Selected Harvest 1989 • $12 • (04/30/91) • **84**

Johannisberg Riesling Late Harvest Santa Ynez Valley Ambassador's Vyd Sel Harvest 1988 • $9 • (12/15/89) • **79**

Johannisberg Riesling Late Harvest Santa Ynez Valley Ambassador's Vyd Selected 1986 • $9 • (02/28/89) • **89**

Johannisberg Riesling Santa Ynez Valley Selected Harvest 1993: Sweet, unctuous, chewy with orange-scented honey and caramel flavors. Finishes a bit soft. 800 cases made. • $15 • (06/15/96) • **85**

Merlot Santa Ynez Valley 1993: Marked by spicy, peppery flavors, firmly tannic, but with herbal cherry and berry flavors that make it pleasant enough. 25,000 cases made. • $13 • (03/31/96) • **84**

Merlot Santa Ynez Valley 1992: A spicy, herbal style exhibiting green pepper and racy vegetable tones. Supple enough to drink now, fans of this flavor profile will find it appealing. 18,082 cases made. • $12 • (11/15/94) • **81**

Merlot Santa Ynez Valley 1991 • $12 • (12/31/93) • **83**

Merlot Santa Ynez Valley 1990 • $13 • (11/30/92) • **79**

Merlot Santa Ynez Valley 1989 • $12 • (08/31/91) • **86**

Merlot Santa Ynez Valley 1988 • $11 • (03/31/91) • **82**

Merlot Santa Ynez Valley 1987 • $9 • (12/15/89) • **83**

Merlot Santa Ynez Valley 1986 • $9 • (09/30/88) • **83**

Merlot Santa Ynez Valley 1985 • $9 • (04/30/88) • **78**

Merlot Santa Ynez Valley 1981 • $6 • (05/16/86) • **50**

Pinot Noir Santa Ynez Valley 1986 • $10 • (12/15/89) • **77**

Pinot Noir Santa Ynez Valley 1983 • $9 • (11/15/87) • **71**

Pinot Noir Santa Ynez Valley 1981 • $8 • (05/16/86) • **73**

Prosperity Red Santa Ynez Valley NV • $5 • (03/31/93) • **75**

Red Table Wine Santa Ynez Valley 1990 • $6 • (04/30/92) • **74**

Rosé of Cabernet Sauvignon Santa Ynez Valley 1984 • $4 • (02/01/86) • **74**

Sauvignon Blanc Santa Ynez Valley 1994: Soft and fragrant, showing nice almond and herb notes to complement the pear flavor. Ready now. 5,000 cases made. • $NA • (02/29/96) • **87**

Sauvignon Blanc Santa Ynez Valley 1993: Strongly floral and distinctly herbal and peppery, showing enough bright fruit to balance things on the finish. 7,166 cases made. • $7 • (08/31/95) • **81**

Sauvignon Blanc Santa Ynez Valley 1992: Soft and fruity, with a strong earthy-weedy streak. Not for everyone. 5,000 cases made. • $7 • (08/31/94) • **81**

Sauvignon Blanc Santa Ynez Valley 1991 • $7 • (11/30/92) • **79**

Vintage Reserve Santa Ynez Valley 1991: Rich, ripe and generous, supple in texture but focusing its currant, berry and herbal flavors beautifully. Delicious now, but fine tannins can use until 1998-1999 to soften further. 500 cases made. • $22 • (12/15/95) • **89**

FISHER | CALIFORNIA

Cabernet Sauvignon Napa-Sonoma Counties Coach Insignia 1992: Supple and fruity with spicy, plummy Cabernet fruit that's round and fleshy, finishing with firm tannins. Fine balance and length, could be outstanding. • $NA • (05/31/93) BT • **788**

Cabernet Sauvignon Napa-Sonoma Counties Coach Insignia 1990: Firm and flavorful, with generous currant and vanilla aromas and flavors. Finishes with style and harmony. Can grow through 1997. 1,706 cases made. • $20 • (06/15/93) • **86**

Cabernet Sauvignon Napa-Sonoma Counties Coach Insignia 1989 • $18 • (03/31/92) • **82**

Cabernet Sauvignon Napa-Sonoma Counties Coach Insignia 1987 • $20 • (11/15/91) • **84**

Cabernet Sauvignon Napa Valley Coach Insignia 1994: Young and tight, but the cherry and currant fruit that emerges is bright and lively. Flirts with outstanding. 2,200 cases made. • $24 • (05/31/95) • **85-89** (BT)

Cabernet Sauvignon Napa Valley Coach Insignia 1991: Framed by toasty, cedary oak, tightly wound and tannic, with a rich, intense core of plum and currant flavors. Best after 1999. 1,105 cases made. • $20 • (11/15/94) • **84**

Cabernet Sauvignon Napa Valley Lamb Vineyard 1994: Medium weight, with ripe, but light cherry and berry notes. 500 cases made. • $30 • (05/31/95) • **85-89** (BT)
Cabernet Sauvignon Sonoma County 1983 • $13 • (06/15/87) • **73**
Cabernet Sauvignon Sonoma County 1982 • $13 • (11/01/85) • **88**
Cabernet Sauvignon Sonoma County 1981 • $12 • (12/01/84) • **85**
Cabernet Sauvignon Sonoma County Coach Insignia 1986 • $20 • (01/31/90) • **87**
Cabernet Sauvignon Sonoma County Coach Insignia 1985 • $18 • (03/01/89) • **90**
Cabernet Sauvignon Sonoma County Coach Insignia 1984 • $18 • (03/01/89) • **89**
Cabernet Sauvignon Sonoma County Wedding Vineyard 1994: Tight and dense, but the beam of currant and cherry is well focused and firm at this youthful stage. Fine structure. • $NA • (05/31/95) • **85-89** (BT)
Cabernet Sauvignon Sonoma County Wedding Vineyard 1991: A gamy style with dry, plush tannins and an earthy streak, but also interesting currant and chocolate flavors. Cleans up with aeration, best after 1999. 426 cases made. • $28 • (11/15/94) • **88**
Chardonnay Sonoma County Coach Insignia 1994: The spicy, earthy pear, toast, honey and apple flavors weave together intricately on the finish. 3,300 cases made. • $18 • (06/15/96) • **86**
Chardonnay Sonoma County Coach Insignia 1992: Light and spicy, nicely crafted, with a vanilla-clove streak running through the fresh apple. 2,004 cases made. • $16 • (06/30/94) • **86**
Chardonnay Sonoma County Coach Insignia 1991 • $16 • (07/15/93) • **87**
Chardonnay Sonoma County Whitney's Vineyard 1994: Ripe and flavorful, but a touch on the mature side, which gives a leesy quality to the pear, pineapple and butterscotch flavors. 430 cases made. • $26 • (06/15/96) • **87**
Chardonnay Sonoma County Whitney's Vineyard 1993: Medium weight with herb, pear, spice and citrus notes, but not the richness and concentration this wine achieves in top years. Finishes with smoky oak. 443 cases made. • $26 • (07/31/95) • **85**
Chardonnay Sonoma County Whitney's Vineyard 1992: Marked by toasty, spicy oak flavors, but enough ripe pear and apple fruit emerges to give it depth focus. 400 cases made. • $26 • (07/31/95) • **87**
Merlot Napa Valley RCF Vineyard 1993: Clean and correct, with ripe cherry and plum flavors that become elegant on the finish. 1,600 cases made. • $26 • (06/30/96) • **84**
Merlot Napa Valley RCF Vineyard 1991 • $22 • (10/31/93) • **84**

FITCH MOUNTAIN | CALIFORNIA

Cabernet Sauvignon Napa Valley 1985 • $9 • (04/15/89) • **74**
Merlot Napa Valley 1986 • $9 • (09/30/88) • **84**
Merlot Napa Valley 1985 • $9 • (12/15/87) • **89**
Zinfandel Dry Creek Valley 1989 • $10 • (03/31/92) • **86**

FIVE PALMS | CALIFORNIA

Cabernet Sauvignon Napa Valley 1984 • $6 • (03/31/87) BB • **87**

FLEUR DE CARNEROS CELLARS
CALIFORNIA

Chardonnay California 1992: Simple and correct with ripe, earthy pear-laced Chardonnay fruit framed by toasty oak flavors that stay with you. A good value in everyday Chardonnay. 3,500 cases made. • $9 • (06/30/94) • **82**

FLORA SPRINGS | CALIFORNIA

Cabernet Sauvignon Napa Valley 1986 • $15 • (03/15/90) • **85**
Cabernet Sauvignon Napa Valley 1985 • $15 • (07/31/89) • **90**
Cabernet Sauvignon Napa Valley 1984 • $25 • (07/31/88) • **71**
Cabernet Sauvignon Napa Valley 1983 • $20 • (12/15/86) • **79**

Key: SS—Spectator Selection. CS—Cellar Selection. BB—Best Buy. $NA—Price not available. (BT)—Barrel tasting. (A)—Auction Price.
Dates in parentheses represent the issues in which the ratings were published.

Cabernet Sauvignon Napa Valley 1982 • $9 • (10/15/86) • **78**
Cabernet Sauvignon Napa Valley 1981 • $25 • (12/16/84) • **82**
Cabernet Sauvignon Napa Valley 1980 • $28 • (03/01/89) • **85**
Cabernet Sauvignon Napa Valley Cellar Select 1988 • $24 • (02/29/92) • **85**
Cabernet Sauvignon Napa Valley Cellar Select 1987 • $25 • (11/15/90) • **91**
Cabernet Sauvignon Napa Valley Reserve 1991: Easily the best Flora Springs red, period. This is stylish, packing in lots of ripe, rich flavors with a polish of toasty, buttery oak. The currant, plum and cherry flavors are bright and lively, picking up spicy herb and tobacco notes on a long, full finish. The tannins are firm but fine. 350 cases made. • $33 • (09/30/94) CS • **97**
Cabernet Sauvignon Napa Valley Reserve 1990: Correct and balanced, with a leathery edge to the currant, herb and berry flavors. May have softened with cellaring by now. • $33 • (02/28/94) • **85**
Cabernet Sauvignon Napa Valley Reserve 1989 • $25 • (11/15/92) • **88**
Cabernet Sauvignon Napa Valley Rutherford Reserve 1992: Serves up a broad range of complex flavors-tiers of currant, plum, black cherry and spice-then finishes with prune and anise nuances that add some exciting dimensions. Finishes long and rich, with smooth, polished tannins. Better in 1998 or 1999. 500 cases made. • $40 • (11/15/95) • **96**
Chardonnay Carneros 1994: Strikes a nice balance between the ripe pear, apple and nectarine flavors and the toasty oak. An elegant, well-crafted Chardonnay that's new from Flora Springs. 200 cases made. • $20 • (06/30/96) • **89**
Chardonnay Napa Valley Barrel Fermented 1993: Marked by earthy, woody flavors that dominate the spicy pear and grapefruit notes. Comes across as a bit coarse and disjointed, atypical of this wine in the past. Tasted three times with consistent notes. 6,800 cases made. • $20 • (07/31/95) • **84**
Chardonnay Napa Valley Barrel Fermented 1992: Bold, rich and flavorful, plush and supple, with layers of pear, spice and hazelnut framed by toasty buttery oak flavors that linger. Ready now. Tasted twice. 5,000 cases made. • $23 • (06/30/94) • **88**
Chardonnay Napa Valley Barrel Fermented 1991 • $23 • (06/15/93) SS • **91**
Chardonnay Napa Valley Floréal 1992: Tastes ripe beyond sweetness with a slightly candied edge, but it straightens out on the finish, picking up toasty notes. Ready now. 8,000 cases made. • $11 • (06/30/94) • **83**
Chardonnay Napa Valley Floréal 1991 • $12 • (07/15/93) • **81**
Merlot Napa Valley 1994: Pleasant, with a supple band of cherry and currant flavors. The finish is cedary, best to drink in 1997. 6,300 cases made. • $14 • (06/30/96) • **87**
Merlot Napa Valley 1993: Supple and harmonious black cherry, plum and currant flavors and smooth tannins. Medium in body, it's appealing now. 4,400 cases made. • $12 • (09/30/95) • **87**
Merlot Napa Valley 1988 • $15 • (08/31/91) • **83**
Merlot Napa Valley 1987 • $17 • (07/31/90) • **87**
Merlot Napa Valley 1985 • $15 • (06/30/88) • **82**
Merlot Napa Valley Floréal 1991 • $12 • (10/31/93) • **86**
Merlot Napa Valley Floréal 1990 • $14 • (11/30/92) • **79**
Pinot Noir Napa Valley Floréal 1989 • $12 • (09/30/92) • **78**
Sangiovese Napa Valley 1993: Marked by tart, crisp wild berry, herb and spicy oak flavors, this young and tannic Sangiovese needs short-term cellaring to open, but it's impressive. • $15 • (02/28/95) • **86**
Sauvignon Blanc Napa Valley 1993: Straightforward, soft and fruity, pleasant pear flavors and a flash of spice on the finish. 1,300 cases made. • $8 • (08/31/95) • **85**
Sauvignon Blanc Napa Valley Floréal 1992 • $8 • (04/30/94) BB • **88**
Sauvignon Blanc Napa Valley Floréal 1991 • $9 • (11/30/92) • **77**
Sauvignon Blanc Napa Valley Soliloquy 1994: Pleasant and distinctive mineral, floral and grassy qualities give a gratifying sense of weightiness. 2,000 cases made. • $15 • **87**
Sauvignon Blanc Napa Valley Soliloquy 1993: Earthy, tired flavors detract from this simple, straightforward white. 1,000 cases made. • $15 • (08/31/95) • **77**
Soliloquy Napa Valley 1991 • $20 • (09/15/93) • **82**
Trilogy Napa Valley 1992: Well oaked, dark and intense, with a rich core of black cherry, currant, olive and toasty oak character. A big, bold interpretation of a Bordeaux-style red that packs in lots of intense flavor. Given its weight, it strikes a nice balance between fruit and oak. Hold off until 1998. 1,500 cases made. • $27 • (11/30/95) CS • **92**

Trilogy Napa Valley 1991: A gamy style showing earthy currant, black cherry and spicy oak. Youthful and tightly wound with chewy tannins, it will need some cellaring, best after 1998. 2,500 cases made. • $25 • (11/15/94) • **86**

Trilogy Napa Valley 1990: Lean and austere, with a tight band of currant, berry and cedary oak flavors. It's pleasing, but has more tannin and acid than suppleness. Try it after 1997. • $33 • (02/28/94) • **85**

Trilogy Napa Valley 1989 • $33 • (11/15/92) • **87**

Trilogy Napa Valley 1988 • $33 • (02/29/92) • **86**

Trilogy Napa Valley 1987 • $33 • (05/15/91) • **90**

Trilogy Napa Valley 1986 • $37 Ⓐ • (02/15/90) • **94**

Trilogy Napa Valley 1985 • $30 • (03/01/89) • **88**

Trilogy Napa Valley 1984 • $30 • (03/01/89) • **84**

FOGARTY, THOMAS | CALIFORNIA

Blanc de Blancs Santa Cruz Mountains 1989 • $22 • (12/31/93) • **80**

Brut Blanc de Blancs Santa Cruz Mountains 1989 • $22 • (12/31/92) • **74**

Brut Santa Cruz Mountains 1990: Somewhat disjointed, adding a toasty oak and cedary edge to ripe pear and citrus flavors and turning slightly coarse on the finish. Still, it holds together. 811 cases made. • $22 • **87**

Cabernet Sauvignon Napa Valley 1985 • $15 • (07/15/91) • **70**

Cabernet Sauvignon Napa Valley Vallerga Vineyards 1992: Well-oaked style of pronounced herb, wood and butter flavors, enough supple plum and cherry notes and a complex coffee and cedary edge on the finish. Has the tannic strength to cellar, best to lay it down until 1999. 125 cases made. • $25 • (04/30/96) • **90**

Chardonnay Santa Cruz Mountains 1994: Ripe and intense, with an elegant core of earthy pear, honey and hazelnut flavors that are well focused and lively right through to the long, lingering finish. Has a lot of finesse and grace. 1,394 cases made. • $17 • (02/29/96) • **90**

Chardonnay Santa Cruz Mountains 1992: Smooth and silky, showing pleasant spice and pear flavors that finish gently. 1,643 cases made. • $16 • (07/31/95) • **82**

Chardonnay Santa Cruz Mountains Estate Reserve 1994: Complex, with a pretty array of smoky, toasty oak and ripe pear, citrus and melon notes. The flavors expand and linger on the long, elegant finish. 550 cases made. • $23 • (06/30/96) • **91**

Chardonnay Santa Cruz Mountains Estate Reserve 1992: Smooth and elegant, boasting ripe, rich pear, honey, toast and hazelnut notes and a soft, creamy texture. Finishes with good length and complex flavors. 550 cases made. • $18 • (02/29/96) • **90**

Chardonnay Santa Cruz Mountains Estate Reserve 1992: Smooth and elegant, with ripe, rich pear, honey, toast and hazelnut flavors and a soft creamy texture. Finishes with good length and complex flavors. 550 cases made. • $18 • (02/29/96) • **90**

Gewürztraminer Monterey Ventana Vineyards 1994: Dry to the taste and lipsmacking with its spicy, honeyed apricot, melon and rose petal flavors. Finishes with a touch of pepper. Ready now. • $12 • (11/15/95) • **88**

Gewürztraminer Monterey Ventana Vineyards 1991 • $10 • (01/31/93) • **82**

Pinot Noir Carneros Napa Valley 1985 • $15 • (06/15/88) • **73**

Pinot Noir Napa Valley 1988 • $15 • (02/28/91) • **86**

Pinot Noir Santa Cruz Mountains 1992: A touch earthy and tannic, with a crisp bite to the black cherry fruit. Finishes with an earthy edge. 1,028 cases made. • $21 • **84**

Pinot Noir Santa Cruz Mountains Estate 1989 • $16 • (02/28/93) • **74**

Pinot Noir Santa Cruz Mountains Estate 1988 • $15 • (02/28/91) • **83**

Pinot Noir Santa Cruz Mountains Estate 1986 • $20 • (06/15/88) • **64**

Pinot Noir Santa Cruz Mountains Estate 1985 • $20 • (06/15/88) • **58**

FOLIE À DEUX | CALIFORNIA

Brut Napa Valley Fantasie 1989 • $18 • (06/15/91) • **81**

Cabernet Sauvignon Napa Valley 1993: Marked by a spicy anise edge, this is a ripe and fruity style. The plum and currant flavors pick up leathery notes on the finish. 1,200 cases made. • $14 • (12/15/95) • **85**

Cabernet Sauvignon Napa Valley 1988 • $18 • (08/31/92) • **83**

Cabernet Sauvignon Napa Valley 1987 • $18 • (11/15/90) • **92**

Cabernet Sauvignon Napa Valley 1986 • $17 • (04/15/90) • **85**

Cabernet Sauvignon Napa Valley 1984 • $15 • (05/31/88) • **88**

Merlot Napa Valley 1988 • $18 • (03/31/91) • **82**

Merlot Napa Valley Reserve 1993: Marked by minty, cedary flavors that override the ripe plum and berry falvors. It comes across and disjointed and out of balance, certainly lacking in harmony and finesse. 1,000 cases made. • $25 • **81**

FOPPIANO | CALIFORNIA

Cabernet Sauvignon Russian River Valley 1990: Looks and tastes mature for a wine this young. Finishes with stewed plum and spice notes and soft tannins. Ready now. 2,000 cases made. • $9 • (11/15/94) • **80**

Cabernet Sauvignon Russian River Valley 1985 • $9 • (06/30/89) • **71**

Cabernet Sauvignon Russian River Valley 1984 • $8 • (04/30/88) • **77**

Cabernet Sauvignon Russian River Valley 1981 • $7 • (04/16/85) • **81**

Cabernet Sauvignon Sonoma County 1989 • $9 • (03/15/92) • **82**

Cabernet Sauvignon Sonoma County 1986 • $9 • (11/15/90) • **79**

Merlot Russian River Valley 1994: Tough and tannic, with a dry, austere edge. Plum and currant flavors make it interesting—but just barely. 4,600 cases made. • $12 • **82**

Merlot Russian River Valley 1992: Firm and compact, with a tight, narrow band of cherry and currant flavors that pick up an herb and spice edge on the finish. Needs short-term cellaring to soften. 2,450 cases made. • $10 • (09/15/94) • **83**

Petite Sirah Napa Valley La Grande Petite Reserve 1991: Inky dark in color, a little earthy around the edges, but solid berry flavors carry through the finish. Best after 1996. 1,200 cases made. • $20 • (04/30/95) • **80**

Petite Sirah Russian River Valley 1988 • $8 • (08/31/90) • **86**

Petite Sirah Russian River Valley 1986 • $8 • (06/15/89) • **83**

Petite Sirah Russian River Valley 1984 • $7 • (05/31/88) • **84**

Petite Sirah Russian River Valley Reserve Le Grande Petite 1987 • $20 • (08/31/90) • **79**

Petite Sirah Sonoma County 1992: Chewy and tannic at first, but the solid plum and berry flavors come through as the tannins become more polished on the finish. Best from 1997. 12,000 cases made. • $9 • (11/15/95) • **82**

Petite Sirah Sonoma County 1991: Firm in texture, with bright black cherry and toast flavors that echo on the tannic finish. Give it until 1997. 9,000 cases made. • $11 • (02/28/95) • **82**

Petite Sirah Sonoma County 1990 • $10 • (06/30/92) • **87**

Sauvignon Blanc Dry Creek Valley 1993: Focuses its ripe, generous pear and citrusy orange flavors into a lively finish. Somewhat hot at the end, but ready now. 724 cases made. • $8 • (08/31/95) • **85**

Sauvignon Blanc Dry Creek Valley 1992: Crisp and straightforward, a simple wine with bright fruit. 1,600 cases made. • $8 • (08/31/94) • **81**

Zinfandel Dry Creek Valley 1993: Spritzy, offering earthy berry and spice notes that are light and elegant. 4,000 cases made. • $11 • (06/15/95) • **81**

Zinfandel Dry Creek Valley 1991 • $10 • (09/30/93) • **87**

Zinfandel Dry Creek Valley Proprietor's Reserve 1987 • $12 • (12/31/90) • **86**

FOREST GLEN | CALIFORNIA

Cabernet Sauvignon Sonoma County 1991: This young wine offers bright, lively cherry and plum-tinged flavors that are crisp and pleasing, finishing with a burst of fruit on the finish. Tannins are in proportion. Ready now through 1997. 25,000 cases made. • $10 • (04/30/94) • **85**

Cabernet Sauvignon Sonoma County 1990: Firm and austere, offering a narrow band of spicy currant, cedar and herb flavors that pick up a trace of tobacco on the finish. Perhaps with time, this wine will be more generous and interesting, but for now it's very tight and closed. Drink after 1996. • $12 • (09/15/93) • **83**

Cabernet Sauvignon Sonoma County Barrel Select 1992: Earthy, with a narrow range of spicy currant and Cabernet flavors, turns tannic on the finish. Cellar until 1998. 5,000 cases made. • $10 • (11/15/94) • **83**

Chardonnay California Barrel Fermented 1994: Distinctive for its core of butterscotch flavors, it also has a nice band of pear and spice, at a very attractive price. 30,000 cases made. • $10 • (05/15/96) • **85**

Chardonnay California Barrel Fermented 1991 • $12 • (07/15/93) • **80**

Chardonnay Sonoma County 1992: A bold, ripe and richly flavored young California Chardonnay that offers ripe pear, spice, honey and toasty oak flavors that linger on a long finish. More flavor and depth than you get from most California Chardonnays-even at much higher prices. Ready now. 12,000 cases made. • $10 • (06/30/94) SS • **90**

Chardonnay Sonoma County Barrel Fermented 1993: Clean and lightly fruity, with pear, spice and vanilla notes. 25,000 cases made. • $10 • (12/31/94) • **83**

Merlot California 1992: Simple and direct, with grapey currant and cherry notes that turn tannic on the finish. Good value, ready now. 2,500 cases made. • $10 • (09/15/94) • **82**

Merlot Sonoma County Barrel Select 1994: An odd mixture of ripe fruit and pickle flavors lead to an offbeat wine. 25,000 cases made. • $10 • (05/31/96) • **77**

FOREST HILL | CALIFORNIA

Chardonnay Napa Valley Private Reserve 1994: Simple, with a modest band of citrus and pear, and crisp acidity, which a little age should soften. 750 cases made. • $32 • (06/30/96) • **83**

Chardonnay Napa Valley Private Reserve 1993: Crisp and narrow, with ripe pear and spicy oak flavors that fan out a bit, but it could use a little more richness and depth. 1,000 cases made. • $28 • (07/31/95) • **85**

Chardonnay Napa Valley Private Reserve 1992: Tight and flinty, with a narrow range of citrus, pear and spicy, toasty oak flavors that fan out on the long, full finish, giving it greater depth and complexity. Drink now. 1,000 cases made. • $26 • (06/30/94) • **90**

Chardonnay Napa Valley Private Reserve 1991 • $26 • (07/15/93) • **90**

FOREST LAKE | CALIFORNIA

Cabernet Sauvignon California 1991: Soft and fruity, bright, generous and supple, finishes clean and simple. Drinkable now. • $6 • (05/31/94) BB • **83**

Cabernet Sauvignon California 1989 • $6 • (11/15/92) BB • **82**

Cabernet Sauvignon California 1988 • $6 • (11/15/91) • **81**

Chardonnay California 1992: Lightly fruity with simple spicy pear flavors. Ready now. • $6 • (06/30/94) • **76**

FORESTVILLE | CALIFORNIA

Cabernet Sauvignon California 1992: Simple with grapey flavors that taste off-dry. 25,000 cases made. • $6 • (11/15/94) • **78**

Chardonnay California 1994: Light, simple and appealing for its almond-scented apple flavors that persist on the smooth finish. 12,000 cases made. • $6 • (06/30/96) BB • **84**

Chardonnay California 1993: Crisp, simple and slightly metallic, but fruity enough to be drinkable. • $6 • (01/31/95) • **77**

Merlot California 1992: Simple and fruity, with berry, cherry and spice notes. Ready now. 4,000 cases made. • $6 • (09/15/94) • **79**

Sauvignon Blanc California 1994: Simple, fruity and refreshing, echoing apple and spice. 3,000 cases made. • $5 • (10/31/95) • **81**

Zinfandel California 1993: Simple, earthy cherry and wild berry notes pick up a jammy edge on the finish. 5,000 cases made. • $5 • (10/15/95) • **83**

FORIS | WASHINGTON

Cabernet Sauvignon Washington Klipsun Vineyard 1992: Firm and a little chewy, packing some solid blackberry and leafy flavors into its lean frame. Maybe better from 1997. 342 cases made. • $15 • **82**

FORMAN | CALIFORNIA

Cabernet Sauvignon Napa Valley 1993: Crisp cedar, cherry and currant flavor and firmly tannic finish. This is a well-crafted young Cabernet which lacks the richness of the 1991 or '92 vintages but is impressive nonetheless. 1,800 cases made. • $32 • (04/30/96) • **88**

Cabernet Sauvignon Napa Valley 1992: An intense wine that weaves together a pretty array of ripe cherry, currant and spicy oak flavors, and adds a trim of earthy character. Very well focused, young and vibrant, but needs at least until 1999. Tasted twice, with consistent notes. 2,000 cases made. • $30 • (06/15/95) CS • **93**

Cabernet Sauvignon Napa Valley 1991: Dark and inky, young and raw like a barrel sample, but with lots of concentrated currant, spice and cherry flavors and a peppery finish. The tannins are raw too, so wait until 1997 or 1998. 2,000 cases made. • $30 • (03/15/94) CS • **89**

Cabernet Sauvignon Napa Valley 1990: This massive young wine is packed with currant, berry and cherry flavors and substantial tannins. A big, blockbuster style that will require a decade or so to settle down. Best to cellar until 1998. Tasted twice. 2,100 cases made. • $30 • (07/15/93) • **89**

Cabernet Sauvignon Napa Valley 1989 • $22 Ⓐ • (07/15/92) • **87**

Cabernet Sauvignon Napa Valley 1988 • $32 • (08/31/91) • **88**

Cabernet Sauvignon Napa Valley 1987 • $30 Ⓐ • (09/30/90) CS • **93**

Cabernet Sauvignon Napa Valley 1986 • $37 Ⓐ • (06/15/89) • **93**

Cabernet Sauvignon Napa Valley 1985 • $45 Ⓐ • (03/01/89) • **93**

Cabernet Sauvignon Napa Valley 1984 • $60 • (03/01/89) • **92**

Cabernet Sauvignon Napa Valley 1983 • $57 • (03/01/89) • **90**

Chardonnay Napa Valley 1994: A delicious young wine that balances intensity with elegance in a ripe, fruity, moderately rich style. Features ripe pear, spice, melon and fig notes, finishing with toasty oak and smoky nuances. 1,800 cases made. • $23 • **91**

Chardonnay Napa Valley 1992: Crisp and lean with lots of spice, but also apple, pear and nectarine flavors. Can stand cellaring. 1,500 cases made. • $22 • (03/31/94) • **86**

Chardonnay Napa Valley 1991 • $24 • (04/15/93) • **86**

FOSS CREEK | CALIFORNIA

Cabernet Sauvignon Sonoma County 1991: Simple but pleasing, with cedar, coffee, herb and currant flavors that finish with a tannic edge. Priced fairly at $7, drink now. 150 cases made. • $7 • (11/15/94) • **82**

Chardonnay Central Coast Barrel Fermented 1992: Smooth and fruity, sliding its apple, earth and honey flavors nicely through the lingering finish. Drinkable now. 500 cases made. • $7 • (01/31/95) • **86**

Chardonnay Sonoma County 85% Barrel Fermented 1992: Lean and lively, citrusy apple and pear flavors. Drinkable now. 100 cases made. • $6 • (01/31/95) • **81**

FOUR CHIMNEYS | NEW YORK

Cabernet Sauvignon New York 1984 • $17 • (03/16/86) • **51**

FOXEN | CALIFORNIA

Cabernet Franc Santa Maria Valley Tinaquaic Vineyard 1993: Elegant and complex, boasting pretty cherry, plum, spice, smoke and mineral flavors, fine concentration and balance and a sense of harmony and finesse. 400 cases made. • $24 • (04/30/96) • **90**

Cabernet Sauvignon Santa Barbara County 1993: Smooth and generous, with some vegetal aromas, but the flavors center around currant and raspberry. Delicious now. 1,000 cases made. • $22 • (12/15/95) • **86**

Cabernet Sauvignon Santa Barbara County 1992: Firm and intense, with a spicy core of currant, herb and cedary oak flavors. Finishes with a supple texture and good length. Ready now through 2000. 900 cases made. • $20 • (10/31/94) • **87**

Cabernet Sauvignon Santa Barbara County 1991: Smooth and generous, offering a mouthwatering range of black cherry, plum, anise and other spice flavors, all lingering nicely on the finish. Best now. 850 cases made. • $20 • (02/28/94) • **90**

Cabernet Sauvignon Santa Barbara County 1990: Smells fruity and forward, but turns simple on the palate, with plum and black cherry flavors that pick up a trace of oak on the finish. Drink now. 950 cases made. • $20 • (11/15/92) • **84**

Cabernet Sauvignon Santa Barbara County 1989 • $20 • (11/15/91) • **91**

Cabernet Sauvignon Santa Barbara County 1988 • $18 • (11/15/91) • **89**

Key: SS—Spectator Selection. CS—Cellar Selection. BB—Best Buy. $NA—Price not available. (BT)—Barrel tasting. Ⓐ—Auction Price.
Dates in parentheses represent the issues in which the ratings were published.

Chardonnay Santa Maria Valley 1993: A concentrated Chardonnay offering many tiers of honey, pear, apple, spice and toasty oak shadings. Finishes with good complexity. 900 cases made. • $20 • (04/15/95) • **90**

Chardonnay Santa Maria Valley 1992: Strives for complexity with its earthy, toasty and creamy texture, but it comes up short on depth and the finish turns simple. Drink now. 950 cases made. • $20 • (04/15/94) • **85**

Chardonnay Santa Maria Valley Tinaquaic Vineyard 1993: Earthy with a strong leesy edge to the pear and pineapple flavors, but offers more depth and intensity than many 1993's. 400 cases made. • $28 • (07/31/95) • **85**

Chardonnay Santa Maria Valley Tinaquaic Vineyard 1992: Spicy and toasty, with a crisp, rich core of nectarine, peach, pear and nutmeg flavors that are complex and concentrated. Finishes with a burst of fruit that stays rich and focused. Tasted twice with consistent notes. 250 cases made. • $28 • (05/15/94) • **92**

Chenin Blanc Santa Barbara County 1993: Smells and tastes like a barrel-fermented Chardonnay at first, kicking in its bright apple and melon flavors. Sacrifices charm for flavor and seems a little sweet on the finish. Tasty to drink now. 350 cases made. • $12 • (05/31/95) • **83**

Chenin Blanc Santa Barbara County 1992: Has all the earmarks of a barrel-fermented Chardonnay—spicy, toasty overtones, polished texture, buttery fruit—but it carries them all lightly and with a sense of elegance. Drinkable now. 3,000 cases made. • $12 • (07/31/94) • **87**

Merlot Santa Barbara County 1992: Marked by a green, stalky edge and lean olive and herbal flavors, as just hints of cherry and tart plum come through on the finish. 300 cases made. • $22 • (12/15/95) • **84**

Merlot Santa Barbara County 1991 • $22 • (03/15/94) • **88**

Merlot Santa Maria Valley Tinaquaic Vineyard 1993: Supple and complex, boasting ripe, rich black cherry, currant and anise flavors and finishing with fine depth and firm tannins. Graceful and harmonious. Best now and through 1999. • $24 • (04/30/96) • **90**

Pinot Noir Santa Maria Valley 1994: Medium-bodied and well balanced, with good intensity and attractive notes of cherry, wild berry, herbs and tea. Should improve into 1997. 800 cases made. • $20 • (01/31/96) • **87**

Pinot Noir Santa Maria Valley 1993: Pleasantly fruity, with supple cherry and plum notes of modest depth and proportion. Gains depth and complexity on the finish, where the flavors fan out. 800 cases made. • $20 • (11/15/95) • **88**

Pinot Noir Santa Maria Valley 1992: Intense and focused, with a narrow beam of herb, cola and black cherry flavors. Finishes with firm tannins, but the fruit pours through. Has the depth and tannic structure to age through 1999. 250 cases made. • $30 • (11/30/94) • **87**

Pinot Noir Santa Maria Valley 1991 • $20 • (01/31/94) • **89**

Pinot Noir Santa Maria Valley 1990 • $20 • (09/30/92) • **89**

Pinot Noir Santa Maria Valley 1987 • $16 • (12/15/89) • **78**

Pinot Noir Santa Maria Valley Bien Nacido Vineyard 1993: Offers a pleasant core of ripe cherry, plum and currant fruit that's well focused, turning supple and complex on the finish. 200 cases made. • $26 • (11/15/95) • **90**

Pinot Noir Santa Ynez Valley Sanford & Benedict Vineyard 1993: Serves up pretty array of ripe, intense fruit, with hints of cherry, plum, wild berry and spice, all folding together neatly on the finish. Drinkable now. 250 cases made. • $30 • (11/15/95) • **90**

Pinot Noir Santa Ynez Valley Sanford & Benedict Vineyard 1992: Intense and tightly wound, with herb, tea, cola and black cherry flavors. Cellaring should round out the tannins. 250 cases made. • $30 • (01/31/95) • **87**

Pinot Noir Santa Ynez Valley Sanford & Benedict Vineyard 1991 • $30 • (02/28/94) • **89**

FOXHOLLOW | CALIFORNIA

Cabernet Sauvignon Paso Robles 1991: A good wine with ripe currant and cherry flavors that finishes with firm tannins and an oaky edge. Can stand short-term cellaring to soften. • $10 • (06/30/94) • **82**

Merlot California 1992: Herbal, floral overtones give this crisp, slightly tannic red a little extra interest. • $10 • (09/15/94) • **81**

FOX MOUNTAIN | CALIFORNIA

Cabernet Sauvignon Russian River Valley Reserve 1986 • $20 • (11/15/92) • **87**

Cabernet Sauvignon Russian River Valley Reserve 1985 • $19 • (09/15/89) • **75**

Cabernet Sauvignon Russian River Valley Reserve 1982 • $18 • (12/31/87) • **77**

Cabernet Sauvignon Russian River Valley Reserve 1981 • $16 • (12/15/86) • **79**

Cabernet Sauvignon Sonoma County Reserve 1987: Simple, with earthy, tarry, mature Cabernet flavors, dries out on the finish. Drink up. 1,600 cases made. • $15 • (11/15/94) • **79**

FOX RUN | NEW YORK

Brut Finger Lakes 1993: A drinkable but simple sparkling wine with plenty of buttery aroma, but little fruit flavor. It turns heavy on the palate and then goes flat on the finish. • $NA • (06/30/95) • **78**

Brut Finger Lakes 1991: A drinkable but simple bubbly with plenty of buttery aroma, but little fruit flavor. Heavy on the palate and flat on the finish. • $NA • (06/30/95) • **78**

Riesling Finger Lakes 1994: Generous, featuring ripe peach and pineapple flavors and crisp acidity underlying the fruity sweetness. It's ripe and clean. 450 cases made. • $9 • (01/31/96) • **85**

FRANCAL | CALIFORNIA

Mourvèdre California 1988 • $7 • (02/15/93) • **78**

FRANCISCAN | CALIFORNIA

Cabernet Sauvignon Alexander Valley 1980 • $7 • (10/16/84) • **86**

Cabernet Sauvignon Napa Valley 1979 • $18 • (03/01/89) • **79**

Cabernet Sauvignon Napa Valley Library Selection 1985 • $18 • (03/01/89) • **88**

Cabernet Sauvignon Napa Valley Oakville Estate 1994: Pleasantly fruity, with ripe plum, cherry, spice and floral notes. Medium bodied, turning elegant. 23,300 cases made. • $14 • (05/31/95) • **85-89** (BT)

Cabernet Sauvignon Napa Valley Oakville Estate 1992: Medium bodied, with ripe, spicy cherry and plummy fruit. A well crafted, elegant style of wine with mild tannins. Ready now. • $15 • (12/15/95) • **87**

Cabernet Sauvignon Napa Valley Oakville Estate 1991: Ripe and fleshy, showing herb, cherry and toasty oak flavors. Finishes with a good dose of oak and tannins, best after 1997. 15,000 cases made. • $13 • (11/15/94) • **82**

Cabernet Sauvignon Napa Valley Oakville Estate 1990: Dense and chewy, with tough-textured tannins up front that make it hard to pick out all the flavors, but the currant, berry and plum fruit is bright and compact. Should be best with cellaring until 1998-2000. 9,000 cases made. • $13 • (10/31/93) • **88**

Cabernet Sauvignon Napa Valley Oakville Estate 1989 • $13 • (05/15/93) • **87**

Cabernet Sauvignon Napa Valley Oakville Estate 1988 • $12 • (08/31/92) • **81**

Cabernet Sauvignon Napa Valley Oakville Estate 1987 • $12 • (02/15/91) • **89**

Cabernet Sauvignon Napa Valley Oakville Estate 1986 • $11 • (07/15/90) • **84**

Cabernet Sauvignon Napa Valley Oakville Estate 1985 • $11 • (05/15/89) • **86**

Cabernet Sauvignon Napa Valley Oakville Estate 1984 • $9 • (09/15/88) • **84**

Cabernet Sauvignon Napa Valley Oakville Estate 1983 • $9 • (04/30/87) • **75**

Cabernet Sauvignon Napa Valley Oakville Estate Reserve 1988 • $18 • (03/15/93) • **81**

Cabernet Sauvignon Napa Valley Oakville Estate Reserve 1985 • $15 • (05/31/90) • **88**

Cabernet Sauvignon Napa Valley Private Reserve 1984 • $9 • (03/01/89) • **87**

Cabernet Sauvignon Napa Valley Private Reserve 1983 • $8 • (03/01/89) • **85**
Cabernet Sauvignon Napa Valley Reserve 1978 • $15 • (03/01/89) • **78**
Cabernet Sauvignon Napa Valley Reserve 1975 • $12 • (03/01/89) • **82**
Chardonnay Napa Valley Oakville Estate 1992: Crisp in texture, with generous nectarine and apple flavors that pick up a tinge of vanilla on the finish. Drinkable now. 18,000 cases made. • $11 • (06/30/94) • **87**
Chardonnay Napa Valley Oakville Estate 1991 • $12 • (07/15/93) • **89**
Chardonnay Napa Valley Oakville Estate Barrel Fermented 1994: Complex and well focused, boasting a solid core of ripe, spicy pear and apple flavors and pretty dashes of toasty oak. Finishes with intensity and concentration and a long aftertaste. Terrific value. • $13 • (04/30/96) • **90**
Chardonnay Napa Valley Oakville Estate Barrel Fermented 1993: A great-value Chardonnay that's marked by smoky, toasty oak and a ripe core of pear, apple and spice flavors that become complex and concentrated on the finish. 18,000 cases made. • $12 • (04/15/95) SS • **90**
Chardonnay Napa Valley Oakville Estate Cuvée Sauvage 1993: Ripe, elegant pear, hazelnut, toasty oak and spice flavors that turn complex on the lingering finish. 2,705 cases made. • $30 • (05/31/95) • **89**
Chardonnay Napa Valley Oakville Estate Cuvée Sauvage 1992: Dsplays toasty oak and ripe pear flavors that are compact and concentrated, especially pleasing on the finish where it shows more depth and richness. 3,000 cases made. • $24 • (06/30/94) • **90**
Chardonnay Napa Valley Oakville Estate Cuvée Sauvage 1991 • $25 • (07/15/93) SS • **91**
Johannisberg Riesling Late Harvest Napa Valley Select 1983 • $10 • (01/31/88) • **88**
Meritage Magnificat Napa Valley 1990: Lean and crisp, displaying a tight, narrow band of spice, currant and herb flavors. Drinkable now. 5,000 cases made. • $20 • (11/15/94) • **85**
Meritage Magnificat Napa Valley 1989 • $18 • (11/15/93) • **86**
Meritage Magnificat Oakville Estate Napa Valley 1991: Well oaked, with a buttery edge and a medium-bodied core of plum, cherry, anise and spice. Merits attention for its suppleness and finesse. Picks up a pruny edge on the aftertaste. • $20 • (12/15/95) • **89**
Meritage Napa Valley 1988 • $18 • (07/15/92) • **89**
Meritage Napa Valley 1987 • $17 • (04/30/91) • **87**
Meritage Napa Valley 1986 • $15 • (07/31/90) • **79**
Meritage Napa Valley 1985 • $16 • (03/31/90) • **90**
Merlot Napa Valley 1981 • $8 • (10/01/85) • **91**
Merlot Napa Valley Oakville Estate 1993: Smooth and polished, a harmonious if somewhat oaky style as toasty oak and smoke nuances add dimension to black cherry and plum flavors. An attractive herbal edge appears on the finish. • $16 • (12/15/95) • **89**
Merlot Napa Valley Oakville Estate 1990 • $12 • (07/15/93) • **87**
Merlot Napa Valley Oakville Estate 1989 • $12 • (05/31/92) • **79**
Merlot Napa Valley Oakville Estate 1987 • $13 • (06/15/90) • **88**
Merlot Napa Valley Oakville Estate 1986 • $12 • (07/31/89) • **80**
Merlot Napa Valley Oakville Estate 1985 • $9 • (05/31/88) • **89**
Merlot Napa Valley Oakville Estate 1984 • $8 • (06/30/87) SS • **90**
Merlot Napa Valley Oakville Estate 1983 • $8 • (02/28/87) • **88**
Merlot Napa Valley Oakville Estate Reserve 1991: Well oaked, with toasty vanilla, herb, currant and cherry flavors that turn decadent on the tannic finish. Tempting now. 200 cases made. • $25 • (01/31/95) • **89**
Zinfandel Napa Valley 1980 • $6 • (03/16/85) • **55**
Zinfandel Napa Valley Oakville Estate 1993: Strikes a nice balance between toasty, buttery oak and peppery, berry-laced Zinfandel fruit. 7,000 cases made. • $11 • (06/15/95) • **86**
Zinfandel Napa Valley Oakville Estate 1992: A range of flavors, but it's hard to look past the earthiness. Ready now. Tasted twice. 7,500 cases made. • $12 • (10/15/94) • **80**
Zinfandel Napa Valley Oakville Estate 1991 • $10 • (09/30/93) • **85**
Zinfandel Napa Valley Oakville Estate 1990 • $10 • (07/31/92) • **87**
Zinfandel Napa Valley Oakville Estate 1989 • $10 • (07/31/91) • **88**
Zinfandel Napa Valley Oakville Estate 1988 • $9 • (05/31/90) • **87**

Key: SS—Spectator Selection. CS—Cellar Selection. BB—Best Buy. $NA—Price not available. (BT)—Barrel tasting. (A)—Auction Price.
Dates in parentheses represent the issues in which the ratings were published.

FRANK, CHATEAU | NEW YORK

Brut Finger Lakes 1985 • $18 • (12/31/90) • **80**
Sparkling Finger Lakes Brut 1987: Still fresh for an eight-year old wine, this has vanilla, citrus and apple tart flavors. Though it hasn't developed much complexity, it's still firm and clean. 1,800 cases made. • $15 • (12/15/95) • **82**
Sparkling Finger Lakes Crémant Célèbre NV: Quite mature, this combines a gentle mousse, low acidity and flavors of toast, vanilla and pineapple, marred by a light rubbery note. 1,400 cases made. • $10 • (12/15/95) • **78**

FRANK, DR. KONSTANTIN | NEW YORK

Cabernet Sauvignon Finger Lakes 1993: The deep color and spicy aromas are promising, but it turns lean, tart and green on the palate. Has some cranberry and tart cherry flavor, along with sweet oak, but we would like more ripe fruit. 150 cases made. • $22 • (06/30/95) • **79**
Cabernet Sauvignon Finger Lakes 1991: A lean but enjoyable Cabernet with great balance and a sense of harmony between its cherry and herb flavors, oak accents and moderate tannins. 200 cases made. • $22 • (06/30/95) • **84**
Chardonnay Finger Lakes 1992: Simple and extremely nutty, with a buttery, almost stale quality to the flavors. There's little finesse in this wine, with lots of acidity, but it does have a clean finish. • $12 • **78**
Chardonnay Finger Lakes Reserve 1993: This crisp, simple white offers clean flavors of apples and peaches, then fades quickly. A good apéritif. 815 cases made. • $15 • **79**
Gewürztraminer New York 1994: Smoky, spicy flavors typical of Gewürz, but they are blurred by vegetal notes that leave this rather flat and dull. 350 cases made. • $12 • (01/31/96) • **76**
Johannisberg Riesling Finger Lakes Dry 1994: A vivid lime flavor enlivens this tight, tart wine. It has a round, almost unctuous mouthfeel. Almost candylike right now, but it may gain some breadth. 1,470 cases made. • $9 • (08/31/95) • **79**
Johannisberg Riesling Finger Lakes Dry 1993: Generous in texture, ripe in flavor, firm in acidity, showing crisp apple and peach notes accented by grassy aromas. Overall it's clean, fruity and easy to drink.\ 500 cases made. • $8 • (09/15/94) • **85**
Johannisberg Riesling Finger Lakes Select Late Harvest 1991: An impressive, extremely flavorful late-harvest Riesling with a full array of honey, nut and apricot flavors, a rich texture and full body. The hot, alcoholic finish holds it back a bit. 60 cases made. • $24 • (09/15/94) • **86**
Johannisberg Riesling Finger Lakes Semi-Dry 1994: An easy-drinking wine with apple, peach and pine flavors, plus enough sweetness to round out any hard edges. Clean and straightforward. 1,120 cases made. • $9 • (08/31/95) • **84**
Johannisberg Riesling New York Semi-Dry 1993: Very complete and harmonious wine, with bright, ripe fruit flavors, great balance and acidity, a smooth, rich texture and not enough sweetness to make it cloying. 430 cases made. • $8 • (09/15/94) BB • **86**
Pinot Noir Finger Lakes 1992: Round but soft, this wine shows some berry and spice flavors reminiscent of Pinot Noir, but a distracting smoky, rubbery note emerges on the finish. It's got some life, though. 400 cases made. • $18 • (05/15/95) • **79**
Pinot Noir Finger Lakes 1990: A rustic wine that does show Pinot Noir character, this mingles cherry, spice and earthy flavors in a medium-bodied wine with some grip. The finish lingers with pleasant tobacco and spice notes. 300 cases made. • $18 • (05/15/95) • **83**
Pinot Noir Finger Lakes 1985 • $15 • (06/15/88) • **75**
Rkatsiteli Finger Lakes 1993: A mouthfilling, smooth-textured white wine with nondescript fruit flavors and a dusty, musky aroma. 210 cases made. • $12 • (06/30/95) • **77**
Sereksia Finger Lakes Late Harvest 1991: A very sweet but well-balanced dessert wine, with herbal, earthy aromas, nice but vague flavors and a sweet, lingering finish. 126 cases made. • $15 • (06/30/95) • **80**

FRANUS | CALIFORNIA

Zinfandel Mount Veeder Brandlin Ranch 1993: 550 cases made. • $15 • **85**

Zinfandel Mount Veeder Brandlin Ranch 1991 • $13 • (09/30/93) • **86**

Zinfandel Mount Veeder Brandlin Vineyard 1992: Typical Zin flavors of spice, pepper and wild berry that stay focused. Has intensity and firm tannins. Drinkable now. 900 cases made. • $16 • (01/31/95) • **88**

Zinfandel Napa Valley Hendry Vineyard 1993: Compact, with somewhat of a green tea character and leathery notes. It offers just enough Zinfandel fruitiness to balance it out. 850 cases made. • $14 • (10/15/95) • **85**

Zinfandel Napa Valley Hendry Vineyard 1992: Ripe and spicy, with bright, rich, lively raspberry, anise and black cherry flavors that are firmly tannic and framed by light oak. Captures the essence of Zinfandel. Ready now. 900 cases made. • $13 • (07/31/94) • **88**

Zinfandel Napa Valley Hendry Vineyard 1991 • $13 • (09/30/93) • **88**

Zinfandel Napa Valley Hendry Vineyard 1989 • $13 • (10/15/92) • **83**

FREEMARK ABBEY | CALIFORNIA

Cabernet Sauvignon Napa Valley 1991: Correct and well balanced with a firm band of earthy currant and light oak shadings. Short-term cellaring until around 1997 should help a bit. 11,000 cases made. • $17 • (11/15/94) • **85**

Cabernet Sauvignon Napa Valley 1990: Tight, lean and compact, with a thin band of currant and spice flavor that picks up an oaky edge on the finish. Should be a little better in 1995 or '96 when its tannins soften. • $16 • (11/15/94) • **83**

Cabernet Sauvignon Napa Valley 1989 • $16 • (11/15/93) • **81**

Cabernet Sauvignon Napa Valley 1988 • $16 • (08/31/92) • **81**

Cabernet Sauvignon Napa Valley 1987 • $22 Ⓐ • (07/31/91) • **86**

Cabernet Sauvignon Napa Valley 1986 • $15 • (11/15/90) • **83**

Cabernet Sauvignon Napa Valley 1985 • $21 Ⓐ • (10/31/89) • **79**

Cabernet Sauvignon Napa Valley 1984 • $14 • (02/15/89) • **84**

Cabernet Sauvignon Napa Valley 1983 • $12 • (02/15/88) • **68**

Cabernet Sauvignon Napa Valley 1982 • $12 • (02/15/87) • **84**

Cabernet Sauvignon Napa Valley 1981 • $20 Ⓐ • (10/01/85) • **79**

Cabernet Sauvignon Napa Valley 1980 • $15 • (05/16/84) • **84**

Cabernet Sauvignon Napa Valley 1979 • $29 Ⓐ • (01/01/84) • **89**

Cabernet Sauvignon Napa Valley 1974: Drying out, with earthy, metallic flavors, this one's headed over the hill but still enjoyable. 7,800 cases made. • $50 • (11/15/94) • **83**

Cabernet Sauvignon Napa Valley 1969 • $40 • (04/01/86) • **68**

Cabernet Sauvignon Napa Valley Bosché 1989: Compact but focused, a smoky wood edge to the ripe currant and cherry flavors. Finishes with firm tannins. Ready now. • $25 • (11/15/94) • **85**

Cabernet Sauvignon Napa Valley Bosché 1987 • $25 • (11/15/91) • **87**

Cabernet Sauvignon Napa Valley Bosché 1986 • $24 • (07/31/90) • **76**

Cabernet Sauvignon Napa Valley Bosché 1985 • $39 • (07/31/89) • **90**

Cabernet Sauvignon Napa Valley Bosché 1984 • $31 • (03/01/89) • **88**

Cabernet Sauvignon Napa Valley Bosché 1983 • $33 • (03/01/89) • **86**

Cabernet Sauvignon Napa Valley Bosché 1982 • $40 • (03/01/89) • **88**

Cabernet Sauvignon Napa Valley Bosché 1981 • $35 • (03/01/89) • **86**

Cabernet Sauvignon Napa Valley Bosché 1980 • $47 • (03/01/89) • **88**

Cabernet Sauvignon Napa Valley Bosché 1979 • $35 • (03/01/89) • **93**

Cabernet Sauvignon Napa Valley Bosché 1978 • $56 • (11/15/92) • **86**

Cabernet Sauvignon Napa Valley Bosché 1977 • $25 • (03/01/89) • **88**

Cabernet Sauvignon Napa Valley Bosché 1976 • $39 • (03/01/89) • **85**

Cabernet Sauvignon Napa Valley Bosché 1975 • $50 • (03/01/89) • **90**

Cabernet Sauvignon Napa Valley Bosché 1974: Showing its age but retaining an elegant personality, the Bosché is drying out and losing fruit, but there's just enough complexity and finesse to hold your interest. Drink up, if you still have a bottle. 4,127 cases made. • $75 • (11/15/94) • **85**

Cabernet Sauvignon Napa Valley Bosché 1973 • $79 • (03/01/89) • **88**

Cabernet Sauvignon Napa Valley Bosché 1972 • $30 • (03/01/89) • **80**

Cabernet Sauvignon Napa Valley Bosché 1971 • $38 • (03/01/89) • **86**

Cabernet Sauvignon Napa Valley Bosché 1970 • $100 • (03/01/89) • **91**

Cabernet Sauvignon Napa Valley Sycamore Vineyards 1990: Ripe, round and generous, packing a mouthful of black cherry and spicy toast flavors into a balanced frame. Tannins hang around in the background, making this ready now, but could improve through 2000. 1,460 cases made. • $23 • (12/15/95) • **88**

Cabernet Sauvignon Napa Valley Sycamore Vineyards 1989: Tries to be soft and supple, but the structure gets rough and is starting to crumble. 3,050 cases made. • $20 • (12/15/95) • **80**

Cabernet Sauvignon Napa Valley Sycamore Vineyards 1988: A good 1988, with lean, tannic and earthy Cabernet flavors that pick up a spicy vanilla edge on the finish. Well balanced and ready to drink now. • $25 • (11/15/94) • **84**

Cabernet Sauvignon Napa Valley Sycamore Vineyards 1987 • $25 • (11/15/93) • **90**

Cabernet Sauvignon Napa Valley Sycamore Vineyards 1986 • $25 • (11/15/91) • **91**

Cabernet Sauvignon Napa Valley Sycamore Vineyards 1985 • $25 • (10/31/89) • **88**

Cabernet Sauvignon Napa Valley Sycamore Vineyards 1984 • $20 • (12/15/88) • **91**

Chardonnay Napa Valley 1993: Well balanced and appealing for its ripe, spicy pear, light oak and honey notes. 7,400 cases made. • $16 • (06/30/96) • **84**

Chardonnay Napa Valley 1992: Has just enough ripe pear, spice and light oak shadings to hold together. Simple but pleasant. 17,000 cases made. • $16 • (07/31/95) • **83**

Chardonnay Napa Valley 1991: Bright and fruity, simple with nice pineapple and spice aromas and flavors. 17,302 cases made. • $16 • (06/30/94) • **81**

Chardonnay Napa Valley Carpy Ranch 1991: Firm and compact, with a slight leesy edge to the ripe pear and apple. Picks up pretty toasty oak on the finish, and the flavors linger. Ready now to 1997. 1,447 cases made. • $22 • (06/30/94) • **88**

Johannisberg Riesling Late Harvest Napa Valley Edelwein Gold 1991 • $25 • (10/15/92) CS • **92**

Johannisberg Riesling Late Harvest Napa Valley Edelwein Gold 1989 • $22 • (07/15/90) • **92**

Johannisberg Riesling Late Harvest Napa Valley Edelwein Gold 1988 • $18 • (06/15/89) • **87**

Johannisberg Riesling Late Harvest Napa Valley Edelwein Gold 1986 • $19 • (06/15/87) • **87**

Johannisberg Riesling Late Harvest Napa Valley Edelwein Gold 1973 • $NA • (02/28/87) • **91**

Merlot Napa Valley 1993: Smooth and harmonious, with a pretty core of plum and cherry fruit framed by light toasty oak. Finishes with a pretty fruity aftertaste and firm tannins, so cellaring into 1997 should help. 4,800 cases made. • $16 • **87**

Merlot Napa Valley 1992: A medium-weight red showing a narrow band of herb and currant flavors, finishing with a light tobacco edge. 4,300 cases made. • $15 • (03/31/95) • **83**

Merlot Napa Valley 1991 • $15 • (04/15/94) • **86**

Merlot Napa Valley 1989 • $15 • (07/15/93) • **80**

Merlot Napa Valley 1985 • $10 • (12/31/88) • **90**

Petite Sirah Napa Valley 1980 • $NA • (02/01/88) • **78**

Petite Sirah Napa Valley 1979 • $NA • (02/01/88) • **87**

Petite Sirah Napa Valley 1978 • $NA • (02/01/88) • **80**

Petite Sirah Napa Valley 1977 • $NA • (02/01/88) • **82**

Petite Sirah Napa Valley 1976 • $NA • (02/01/88) • **77**

Petite Sirah Napa Valley 1975 • $NA • (02/01/88) • **73**

Petite Sirah Napa Valley 1974 • $NA • (02/01/88) • **80**

Petite Sirah Napa Valley 1973 • $NA • (02/01/88) • **86**

Petite Sirah Napa Valley 1972 • $NA • (02/01/88) • **76**

Petite Sirah Napa Valley 1971 • $NA • (02/01/88) • **90**

Petite Sirah Napa Valley 1969 • $NA • (02/01/88) • **81**

FREMONT CREEK | CALIFORNIA

Cabernet Sauvignon Mendocino County 1988 • $10 • (11/15/92) • **77**

Cabernet Sauvignon Mendocino-Napa Counties 1986 • $8 • (04/30/91) BB • **85**

Cabernet Sauvignon Mendocino-Napa Counties 1985 • $9 • (03/31/88) • **78**

Cabernet Sauvignon Napa-Mendocino Counties Beckstoffer Vineyards 1990: Simple, with herb and cedar notes. Ready. 486 cases made. • $9 • (11/15/94) • **77**

Cabernet Sauvignon Napa-Mendocino Counties Beckstoffer Vineyards 1989 • $9 • (11/15/93) • **71**

Chardonnay Napa-Mendocino Counties Beckstoffer Vineyards 1992: Crisp and light with pear, nutmeg and oak flavors that fade on the finish. 969 cases made. • $9 • (06/30/94) • **80**
Chardonnay Napa-Mendocino Counties Beckstoffer Vineyards 1991 • $9 • (07/15/93) • **75**

FRENCH CREEK | WASHINGTON

Cabernet Sauvignon Washington 1988 • $9 • (04/15/92) • **73**
Cabernet Sauvignon Washington 1985 • $8 • (10/15/88) • **82**
Merlot Washington 1985 • $12 • (12/31/88) • **83**

FREY | CALIFORNIA

Pinot Noir Mendocino 1991 • $11 • (02/28/93) • **62**
Sauvignon Blanc Late Harvest Mendocino NV: Earthy, gamy flavors run through this sweet, soft wine. Lacks backbone and fruit. 1,600 cases made. • $8 • **72**
Sauvignon Blanc Mendocino Grapes Grown Organically No Sulfites Added 1993: Sweet and floral, unbalanced and slightly candied on the finish. 4,416 cases made. • $7 • (08/31/95) • **73**
Syrah Mendocino Bulow Vineyard 1986 • $10 • (04/15/89) • **82**
Zinfandel Mendocino 1993: Stays in bounds while stretching the limits, with medium-weight black cherry, spice and light tannins. 4,000 cases made. • $8 • (10/15/95) • **83**
Zinfandel Mendocino 1992: Very ripe and fruity, with layers of cherry, raspberry and plum. Drinkable now through 1998. 5,846 cases made. • $8 • (10/15/94) BB • **84**
Zinfandel Mendocino 1990 • $8 • (10/15/92) • **84**

FRICK | CALIFORNIA

Grenache Napa County 1985 • $7 • (04/15/89) • **86**
Petite Sirah Monterey County 1985 • $8 • (02/15/89) • **87**
Pinot Noir California 1981 • $12 • (08/31/86) • **89**
Pinot Noir Santa Maria Valley 1984 • $12 • (02/28/89) • **75**
Zinfandel Dry Creek Valley 1991: Intense and aromatic, but sharp and tart on the palate, coming up short on depth and ripeness. 405 cases made. • $13 • (10/15/94) • **79**
Zinfandel Russian River Valley 1990 • $13 • (09/30/93) • **70**

FRITZ, J. | CALIFORNIA

Cabernet Sauvignon Alexander Valley 1985 • $10 • (12/31/88) • **57**
Cabernet Sauvignon Dry Creek Valley 1989 • $12 • (08/31/92) • **86**
Chardonnay Russian River Valley Barrel Select 1992: Appealing for its complex blend spicy, toasty oak and ripe pear and fig flavors. 230 cases made. • $18 • (07/31/95) • **85**
Chardonnay Sonoma County 1993: Marked by a grassy edge, it offers a narrow beam of spicy pear flavors of modest proportions. 9,900 cases made. • $10 • (07/31/95) • **82**
Chardonnay Sonoma County 1992: Despite an earthy, grassy edge, it hangs together, with spicy pear and apple notes that are simple but pleasant enough. Fair price. Drink now. 7,800 cases made. • $10 • (06/15/94) • **83**
Melon Russian River Valley 1994: Straightforward and solidly fruity, a little raucous but appealing for its zip. 725 cases made. • $12 • (05/31/96) • **83**
Sauvignon Blanc Dry Creek Valley 1994: Solid and flavorful, featuring generous pear, spice and slightly herbal notes. 4,000 cases made. • $9 • (08/31/95) • **83**
Sauvignon Blanc Dry Creek Valley 1993: Light and fragrant, balancing spicy pear flavor with a nice touch of sweet peas. Drinkable now. 2,900 cases made. • $8 • (06/30/94) BB • **86**
Sauvignon Blanc Dry Creek Valley 1992 • $9 • (09/15/93) • **84**
Zinfandel Dry Creek Valley 1986 • $9 • (03/15/89) • **86**
Zinfandel Dry Creek Valley 1984 • $7 • (02/15/88) • **84**

Key: SS—Spectator Selection. CS—Cellar Selection. BB—Best Buy. $NA—Price not available. (BT)—Barrel tasting. (A)—Auction Price.
Dates in parentheses represent the issues in which the ratings were published.

Zinfandel Dry Creek Valley Eighty-Year-Old Vines 1993: Austere, with a dry, tannic aspect to the wild berry and cherry flavors. A little aging may soften the edges a bit. 1,500 cases made. • $12 • (10/15/95) • **84**
Zinfandel Dry Creek Valley Eighty-Year-Old Vines 1992: Firm and intense, with wild cherry, raspberry and spice notes. Drinks well now. 1,500 cases made. • $10 • (10/15/94) • **83**
Zinfandel Dry Creek Valley Eighty-Year-Old Vines 1991 • $10 • (09/30/93) • **82**
Zinfandel Dry Creek Valley Eighty-Year-Old Vines 1990 • $10 • (10/15/92) • **82**
Zinfandel Dry Creek Valley Eighty-Year-Old Vines 1989 • $10 • (03/31/92) • **84**
Zinfandel Dry Creek Valley Eighty-Year-Old Vines 1988 • $10 • (07/31/91) • **79**

FROG'S LEAP | CALIFORNIA

Cabernet Sauvignon Napa Valley 1990: Firm in texture, a tightly wound wine with generous ripe plum, black berry and spice aromas and flavors, opening up and show more on the finish that at the start. Worth cellaring until 1997. 7,000 cases made. • $17 • (09/30/93) • **88**
Cabernet Sauvignon Napa Valley 1989 • $17 • (07/15/92) • **79**
Cabernet Sauvignon Napa Valley 1988 • $17 • (12/15/90) • **88**
Cabernet Sauvignon Napa Valley 1987 • $39 • (12/31/89) SS • **94**
Cabernet Sauvignon Napa Valley 1986 • $42 • (12/31/88) • **94**
Cabernet Sauvignon Napa Valley 1985 • $24 • (03/01/89) • **85**
Cabernet Sauvignon Napa Valley 1984 • $32 • (03/01/89) • **92**
Cabernet Sauvignon Napa Valley 1983 • $22 • (03/01/89) • **80**
Cabernet Sauvignon Napa Valley 1982 • $25 • (03/01/89) • **87**
Chardonnay Carneros 1992: Relies a little too much on oak for flavor, but has enough spicy pear and citrus notes to keep it interesting. A good but unexceptional Frog's Leap. Tasted twice. 7,000 cases made. • $16 • (06/30/94) • **83**
Chardonnay Carneros 1991 • $16 • (07/15/93) • **89**
Merlot Napa Valley 1993: Ripe, fruity, its supple core of cherry and wild berry framed by medium-toast oak. Young and vibrant, it can stand short-term cellaring into 1997. • $NA • (04/30/96) • **87**
Merlot Napa Valley 1991 • $17 • (05/31/94) • **88**
Merlot Napa Valley 1990 • $17 • (01/31/93) • **84**
Sauvignon Blanc Late Harvest Napa Valley Late Leap 1989 • $14 • (10/31/91) • **84**
Sauvignon Blanc Late Harvest Napa Valley Late Leap 1986 • $9 • (09/30/88) • **85**
Sauvignon Blanc Napa Valley 1994: Tart and slightly bitter, leaning toward the herbal end of the spectrum, but not as fresh and lively as it could be. 22,000 cases made. • $11 • (09/15/95) • **80**
Sauvignon Blanc Napa Valley 1992 • $10 • (09/15/93) • **82**
Zinfandel Napa Valley 1992: Earthy and a bit funky, with an odd, woody streak to the flavors. Tasted twice. 7,448 cases made. • $13 • (10/15/94) • **68**
Zinfandel Napa Valley 1991 • $12 • (09/30/93) • **85**
Zinfandel Napa Valley 1990 • $12 • (10/15/92) • **80**
Zinfandel Napa Valley 1989 • $12 • (11/15/91) • **83**
Zinfandel Napa Valley 1988 • $12 • (12/15/90) • **88**
Zinfandel Napa Valley 1987 • $11 • (03/15/90) • **86**
Zinfandel Napa Valley 1986 • $10 • (12/15/88) • **85**
Zinfandel Napa Valley 1985 • $9 • (11/15/87) • **79**

FURST, J. | CALIFORNIA

Fumé Blanc California 1991 • $9 • • **82**
Fumé Blanc California 1991: An herbal-smelling, green-tasting Sauvignon with flavors of green bean, tarragon and lemon. It's fresh and bracing, with decent fruit flavors and touch of toasty flavor presumably from oak aging. 2,500 cases made. • $9 • **82**

GABRIELLI | CALIFORNIA

Ascenza Mendocino 1991 • $12 • (09/30/93) • **84**
Chardonnay Mendocino 1992: Lean and simple with a narrow band of pear and oak flavors. 1,700 cases made. • $14 • (06/30/94) • **80**
Chardonnay Mendocino 1991 • $14 • (07/15/93) • **87**

Chardonnay Mendocino Reserve 1992: Simple and fruity with spicy pear, herb and grassy notes that are elegant and understated. Drinks well now, but not quite up to Reserve status. 400 cases made. • $20 • (06/30/94) • **83**

Chardonnay Mendocino Reserve 1991 • $20 • (07/15/93) • **78**

Zinfandel Mendocino 1993: Ripe but not overdone, with hints of plum and cherry jam turning spicy and tannic. Appealing now. 2,250 cases made. • $12 • (07/31/95) • **86**

Zinfandel Mendocino 1992: Lean and compact, with a tight band of spicy cherry, raspberry and tar notes. Turns crisp and tannic on the finish, cellar until 1996. 1,225 cases made. • $12 • (10/15/94) • **85**

Zinfandel Mendocino 1991 • $10 • (12/31/93) • **85**

Zinfandel Mendocino 1990 • $10 • (10/15/92) • **85**

Zinfandel Mendocino Reserve 1992: Firm and tannic, with a core of spicy cherry, raspberry and gamy, oaky flavors. Intense and chunky, needing until 1996 to soften. 400 cases made. • $18 • (10/15/94) • **84**

Zinfandel Mendocino Reserve 1991 • $16 • (03/31/94) • **84**

Zinfandel Mendocino Reserve 1990 • $16 • (10/15/92) • **82**

GAINEY | CALIFORNIA

Cabernet Franc Santa Ynez Valley Limited Selection 1990 • $16 • (10/15/93) • **88**

Cabernet Sauvignon 1988 • $13 • (03/15/92) • **77**

Cabernet Sauvignon Santa Barbara County 1987 • $13 • (11/15/90) • **82**

Cabernet Sauvignon Santa Barbara County Limited Selection 1989 • $20 • (11/15/92) • **83**

Cabernet Sauvignon Santa Barbara County Limited Selection 1986 • $15 • (12/15/89) • **89**

Cabernet Sauvignon Santa Ynez Valley 1989 • $13 • (11/15/92) • **77**

Cabernet Sauvignon Santa Ynez Valley Limited Selection 1988 • $20 • (03/10/92) • **75**

Chardonnay Santa Barbara County 1993: Has enough of a core of pear, spice and honey to hold your interest. Medium weight and well focused. 1,813 cases made. • $14 • (07/31/95) • **86**

Chardonnay Santa Barbara County 1991 • $13 • (07/15/93) • **84**

Chardonnay Santa Ynez Valley Limited Selection 1994: Pleasantly balanced, ripe and elegant, with layers of rich pear, honey, vanilla and spice. The flavors become delicate and elegant on the finish. 701 cases made. • $25 • (06/30/96) • **88**

Chardonnay Santa Ynez Valley Limited Selection 1993: Tight and intense, with a sharply focused core of pear, nectarine, honey and smoky, toasty oak, all folding together neatly on the finish, where the flavors linger. 431 cases made. • $25 • (07/31/95) • **91**

Chardonnay Santa Ynez Valley Limited Selection 1992: A racy style, with lots of spice, oak, ripe pear and pineapple flavors that are rich, intense, complex and concentrated, finishing with a honeyed edge. Tasted three times with consistent notes. Drink now. 310 cases made. • $25 • (06/15/94) • **91**

Johannisberg Riesling Santa Barbara County 1995: Soft, sweet and generous with its citrusy peach and lightly floral aromas and flavors. 1,925 cases made. • $9 • (06/15/96) • **83**

Johannisberg Riesling Santa Ynez Valley 1994: Lightly sweet, delicate in texture, but rich with apricot-scented pear flavors. Drinkable now. 2,500 cases made. • $8 • (09/15/95) • **87**

Johannisberg Riesling Santa Ynez Valley 1992 • $8 • (05/15/93) • **85**

Johannisberg Riesling Santa Ynez Valley 1991 • $8 • (07/31/92) • **83**

Merlot Limited Selection 1988 • $20 • (02/29/92) • **89**

Merlot Santa Barbara County 1989 • $14 • (05/31/92) • **70**

Merlot Santa Barbara County 1988 • $13 • (04/15/91) • **82**

Merlot Santa Ynez Valley 1990 • $14 • (07/15/93) • **83**

Merlot Santa Ynez Valley Limited Selection 1990 • $20 • (10/15/93) • **76**

Pinot Noir Santa Barbara County 1990 • $15 • (02/28/94) • **87**

Pinot Noir Santa Barbara County 1986 • $15 • (12/15/89) • **88**

Pinot Noir Santa Maria Valley 1989 • $18 • (09/30/92) • **74**

Pinot Noir Santa Ynez Valley Limited Reserve 1991 • $30 • (02/28/94) • **88**

Pinot Noir Santa Ynez Valley Limited Selection 1990 • $25 • (02/28/94) • **85**

Pinot Noir Santa Ynez Valley Limited Selection 1989 • $25 • (02/28/93) • **83**

Pinot Noir Santa Ynez Valley Limited Selection 1988 • $25 • (11/15/91) • **86**

Pinot Noir Santa Ynez Valley Sanford and Benedict Vineyard 1993: Smooth and polished up front, showing earthy cherry and berry notes and finishing with drying and chunky tannins. Can stand cellaring into 1997. 575 cases made. • $30 • (04/30/96) • **84**

Sauvignon Blanc Santa Ynez Valley 1992: Crisp and lively, with a generous layer of pear and spice aromas and flavors, hinting at herbs on the finish. 1,278 cases made. • $9 • (08/31/94) • **82**

Sauvignon Blanc Santa Ynez Valley 1991 • $9 • (08/31/93) • **86**

Sauvignon Blanc Santa Ynez Valley Limited Selection 1993: Definitely on the oaky side. Spicy, toasty and woody through the finish, but not harshly so. 891 cases made. • $16 • (08/31/95) • **83**

Sauvignon Blanc Santa Ynez Valley Limited Selection 1991 • $16 • (08/31/93) • **88**

GALLO, E. & J. | CALIFORNIA

Cabernet Sauvignon California NV • $5 • (08/31/92) BB • **80**

Cabernet Sauvignon California Limited Release Reserve 1980 • $8 • (11/15/86) • **78**

Cabernet Sauvignon California Reserve NV • $6 • (11/15/91) • **84**

Cabernet Sauvignon Dry Creek Valley Frei Ranch Vineyard Gallo Sonoma 1992: Ripe, rich and intense, with a tightly wound core of currant, anise, plum and cherry flavors. Finishes with thick but plush tannins. Well crafted and built to age, begin trying in 1997. This is the first bottling of Frei Ranch with the Dry Creek appellation. 2,000 cases made. • $16 • (11/15/95) • **89**

Cabernet Sauvignon Northern Sonoma 1991: Young and vibrant, with ripe, rich, supple Cabernet fruit that runs deep and full. Concentrated spicy cherry and berry flavors last through a long and full finish. Best starting in 1997. 4,000 cases made. • $50 • (11/15/94) • **91**

Cabernet Sauvignon Northern Sonoma 1990: Ripe and spicy, supple and complex with rich, concentrated currant, spice, cedar and black cherry fruit that's beautifully focused, rich and elegant. Combines a wealth of flavor with elegance and finesse. Delicious on the finish, where the soft tannins keep the flavors alive and vanilla toast notes add dimension. 2,016 cases made. • $60 • (10/31/93) CS • **93**

Cabernet Sauvignon Northern Sonoma 1985 • $8 • (08/31/92) • **80**

Cabernet Sauvignon Northern Sonoma Limited Release 1981 • $5 • (12/31/88) • **75**

Cabernet Sauvignon Northern Sonoma Reserve 1984 • $7 • (10/15/91) • **80**

Cabernet Sauvignon Northern Sonoma Reserve 1982 • $6 • (05/31/91) BB • **82**

Cabernet Sauvignon Sonoma County Gallo Sonoma 1992: Intense and well focused, with a slight leathery edge to the currant and berry flavors. Finishes with dry tannins, but hangs together nicely. 50,000 cases made. • $12 • (11/15/95) • **87**

Sauvignon Sonoma County Gallo Sonoma 1991: Lavishly oaked, with heavy toast flavors, but the fruit is elegant and polished, focusing in on wild berry and black cherry on the finish. 41,000 cases made. • $12 • (03/31/95) SS • **90**

Cabernet Sauvignon Sonoma County Gallo Sonoma 1990: An herbal style, with spicy red pepper flavor adding dimension to the currant and berry notes. Finishes with a supple edge. Ready now. 41,600 cases made. • $10 • (11/15/94) BB • **86**

Chardonnay Dry Creek Valley Stefani Vineyard 1994: Clean, vibrant, appealing pear and spice notes finish in light, toasty oak shadings. Solid, if unspectacular. 4,108 cases made. • $16 • (05/15/96) • **87**

Chardonnay Northern Sonoma Estate 1991 • $30 • (06/30/93) • **92**

Chardonnay Northern Sonoma Estate Bottled 1993: Serves up attractive ripe pear, peach, honey and spice, all in a lighter, delicate style. Tasted twice with consistent results. 1,800 cases made. • $30 • (07/31/95) • **88**

Chardonnay Northern Sonoma Estate Bottled 1992: Gallo's second vintage of this high-class Chardonnay is complex and enticing, with a rich core of toasty, buttery oak and ripe, spicy pear flavors that are focused and long on the finish. Has a sense of style and finesse. 1,500 cases made. • $30 • (09/15/94) • **91**

Chardonnay Russian River Valley Laguna Ranch Vineyard Gallo Sonoma 1994: The seductive, complex smoky oak and exotic fruit flavors turn more elegant and refined on the palate as the tiers of earthy pear, grapefruit and spice show through. Finishes with a delciate touch.

The first Gallo Chardonnay from Laguna Ranch Vineyard. 6,195 cases made. • $16 • (04/30/96) • **92**

Chardonnay Sonoma County Gallo Sonoma 1993: Serves up lots of flavor, with ripe apple, pear, citrus and honey wrapped in an elegant package. Finishes clean and fruity. 50,000 cases made. • $12 • (06/30/95) • **87**

Chardonnay Sonoma County Gallo Sonoma 1991: Smooth and polished, with ripe, rich, spicy melon, pear and apple notes that develop complexity and nuance on the long, full finish. New from Gallo Sonoma. • $9 • (06/30/94) • **89**

Hearty Burgundy Limited Release California NV • $2 • (03/15/88) BB • **80**

Merlot Dry Creek Valley Frei Ranch Vineyard Gallo Sonoma 1992: Crisp and lean, offering tart, trim cherry and plum flavors. 2,038 cases made. • $15 • (05/15/95) • **82**

Merlot Dry Creek Valley Frei Ranch Vineyard Gallo Sonoma 1991: Firm and compact, with a tight, narrow band of cherry and currant, finishing with an herbal edge and crisp tannins. Gallo's first Merlot, needs cellaring until 1997 to soften. 1,950 cases made. • $15 • (09/15/94) • **84**

Merlot Northern Sonoma Vineyard Designation Gallo Sonoma 1993: Somewhat chunky, adding a tannic edge to the ripe plum and wild berry flavors and showing good oak too. Tannins are firm and edgy, if not the dominant force at this point. Cellar into 1997. 5,000 cases made. • $15 • (04/30/96) • **87**

White Grenache California 1987 • $3 • (04/15/89) • **72**

White Zinfandel California 1994: Rich and sweet, with bright watermelon and plum flavors. • $3 • (09/15/95) • **79**

White Zinfandel California 1988 • $5 • (06/15/89) • **79**

Zinfandel Dry Creek Valley Frei Ranch Vineyard Gallo Sonoma 1993: Supple, ripe cherry and berry flavor, finishing with fine tannins and a soft edge. 2,059 cases made. • $14 • (04/30/96) • **87**

Zinfandel Dry Creek Valley Frei Ranch Vineyard Gallo Sonoma 1992: Has an earthy character, but with enough berry and cherry flavors to hang together. Tasted twice, with consistent results. 2,400 cases made. • $15 • (09/15/95) • **85**

Zinfandel Dry Creek Valley Frei Ranch Vineyard Gallo Sonoma 1991: Rich, smooth and supple, with complex raspberry, anise, earth and tar flavors and aromas that unfold gently, revealing even greater depth. 2,800 cases made. • $14 • (02/28/95) SS • **90**

Zinfandel Dry Creek Valley Frei Ranch Vineyard Gallo Sonoma 1990: Bright and lively, with spicy black cherry, raspberry and peppery notes that are deep and complex, finishing with a long, lingering aftertaste. Debut Frei Ranch Zin from Gallo. 3,600 cases made. • $14 • (07/31/94) SS • **90**

Zinfandel North Coast 1992: A touch leathery, but enough wild berry and cherry flavors hang in there to keep it in balance. 50,000 cases made. • $6 • (08/31/95) • **82**

Zinfandel Northern Sonoma 1990: Lots of ripe, juicy black cherry, blueberry and raspberry flavors that pick up a spicy, buttery oak note on the finish. Crisp, with lean tannins. Drinks well now, but should hold through 1997. 40,000 cases made. • $5 • (08/31/94) BB • **88**

Zinfandel Northern Sonoma 1987 • $5 • (09/30/93) BB • **84**

GAN EDEN | CALIFORNIA

Black Muscat 1993: Soft, sweet plum and spice flavors linger lightly on the finish. • $7 • (05/15/95) • **80**

Cabernet Sauvignon Alexander Valley 1989: Well oaked with a gamy edge, but enough rustic, earthy currant flavors pull through to keep it intersting. Firmly tannic, best in 1997. 4,200 cases made. • $14 • (07/31/95) • **83**

Cabernet Sauvignon Alexander Valley 1988 • $18 • (03/31/93) • **77**

Cabernet Sauvignon Alexander Valley 1987 • $18 • (03/31/91) • **90**

Cabernet Sauvignon Alexander Valley 1986 • $15 • (02/15/89) • **86**

Key: SS—Spectator Selection. CS—Cellar Selection. BB—Best Buy. $NA—Price not available. (BT)—Barrel tasting. (A)—Auction Price.
Dates in parentheses represent the issues in which the ratings were published.

Chardonnay Sonoma County 1993: Tart with a green, leesy edge to the apple, pear and melon flavors, but it holds together nicely though the finish. 2,800 cases made. • $12 • (07/31/95) • **88**

Chardonnay Sonoma County Reserve 1993: Stretches the range of flavors, taking the earthy canned grapefruit and pineapple flavors to the edge. Not especially varietal. 1,000 cases made. • $14 • (07/31/95) • **78**

Gewürztraminer Late Harvest Monterey County 1993: Frankly sweet, offering peach and apricot flavors that fade a little on the finish. 1,300 cases made. • $8 • (09/30/95) • **81**

Sauvignon Blanc Sonoma County 1993: Crisp and lively, a fruity wine with green apple at the core and distinctive nuances of celery and sweet peas. 2,500 cases made. • $8 • (08/31/94) • **83**

Sémillon Sonoma County 1993: Light and lively, a brightly fruity example of an early-drinking Sémillon. 800 cases made. • $14 • (06/30/95) • **83**

GARLAND RANCH | CALIFORNIA

Cabernet Sauvignon Central Coast 1986 • $6 • (10/31/89) • **70**

Cabernet Sauvignon Monterey County 1984 • $6 • (08/31/88) BB • **84**

Chardonnay California 1991 • $6 • (07/15/92) • **72**

Merlot California 1986 • $6 • (05/31/92) • **76**

White Zinfandel Monterey 1987 • $6 • (06/15/89) • **75**

GAUER ESTATE | CALIFORNIA

Cabernet Sauvignon Alexander Valley 1988 • $18 • (08/31/92) • **84**

Chardonnay Alexander Valley 1991 • $16 • (06/15/93) • **84**

Merlot Alexander Valley 1990 • $16 • (06/15/93) • **84**

GEHRS, DANIEL | CALIFORNIA

Chardonnay Monterey County 1991 • $11 • (07/15/93) • **84**

Chenin Blanc Monterey County Le Chenay 1993: Gehrs adds 20 percent Chardonnay to this cuvée which gives it a little more body, but it's still a trim, compact wine with tart apricot and pear flavors. 539 cases made. • $8 • (12/31/94) • **84**

Chenin Blanc Monterey County Le Cheniere Carmel Vineyard 1994: Dry and flavorful, with a profile like apple cider and a light finish. 1,250 cases made. • $8 • (06/15/96) • **82**

Chenin Blanc Santa Barbara County Le Cheniere 1993: Has complexity with its toasty oak outline which makes for an interesting wine. Serves up spicy pear and apple notes that ring true for Chenin Blanc. 1,012 cases made. • $8 • (12/31/94) • **83**

Muscadet Monterey County 1993: Part of Gehrs Loire-style wines, this is a crisp, flinty wine with a narrow band of spice, tart pear and mineral tones. Drinks well now. 318 cases made. • $8 • (12/15/94) • **84**

Muscadet Monterey County Carmel Vineyard 1994: Simple, fruity and round, centering around pear and almond flavors. 495 cases made. • $8 • (05/31/96) • **82**

Pinot Blanc Monterey County 1993: Simple with fruity pear and herb notes, the least interesting of the new Gehrs wines. 548 cases made. • $10 • (12/15/94) • **81**

Pinot Blanc Monterey County Carmel Vineyard 1994: Simple, earthy edge to the vanilla and pear flavors. Succeeds in its delicacy and finesse. 698 cases made. • $10 • (04/30/96) • **84**

Sauvignon Blanc Monterey County Fumé En Vogue 1993: A Loire-style Sauvignon Blanc with grapey, racy flavors that pick up honey and pear notes on the finish. 330 cases made. • $9 • (12/15/94) • **83**

GEMELLO | CALIFORNIA

Zinfandel Mendocino 1993: Medium-bodied, earthy and tannic, with berry flavors. 294 cases made. • $16 • (10/15/95) • **80**

Zinfandel Mendocino 60th Anniversary 1934-1994 1992: Has ripe, mature berry flavors that trail off on the finish. Could be a touch heavy-handed, but drinkable now. 492 cases made. • $16 • (10/15/95) • **82**

Zinfandel Mendocino County 1990 • $16 • (09/30/93) • **84**

GEORIS | CALIFORNIA

Merlot Carmel Valley 1992: Smooth, polished and tannic, offering cherry and wild berry notes and hints of sage and spice. Firm tannins on the finish, good depth of flavor. 800 cases made. • $28 • **89**
Merlot Carmel Valley 1989 • $25 • (05/15/93) • **87**
Merlot Carmel Valley 1987 • $27 • (03/31/91) • **89**
Merlot Carmel Valley 1986 • $25 • (12/31/90) • **77**
Merlot Carmel Valley 1985 • $20 • (04/15/89) • **83**

GEYSER PEAK | CALIFORNIA

Cabernet Sauvignon Alexander Valley 1993: Clean and well balanced, with spicy berry and cherry flavors. Drink now. 38,000 cases made. • $10 • (12/15/95) • **83**
Cabernet Sauvignon Alexander Valley 1989 • $9 • (11/15/92) • **82**
Cabernet Sauvignon Alexander Valley 1984 • $7 • (03/15/88) • **77**
Cabernet Sauvignon Alexander Valley 1983 • $7 • (03/15/87) BB • **87**
Cabernet Sauvignon Alexander Valley 1982 • $7 • (09/15/86) • **68**
Cabernet Sauvignon Alexander Valley 1980 • $6 • (01/01/85) • **57**
Cabernet Sauvignon Alexander Valley Estate Reserve 1989 • $14 • (11/15/92) • **87**
Cabernet Sauvignon Alexander Valley Estate Reserve 1987 • $14 • (06/15/91) • **89**
Cabernet Sauvignon Alexander Valley Estate Reserve 1986 • $15 • (09/30/90) • **85**
Cabernet Sauvignon Alexander Valley Estate Reserve 1985 • $15 • (05/15/89) • **77**
Cabernet Sauvignon Alexander Valley Reserve 1993: Smooth and polished, with a marked herbal edge to the ripe berry and cherry flavors. Appealing now and into 1997. 2,733 cases made. • $20 • (12/15/95) • **88**
Cabernet Sauvignon Alexander Valley Reserve 1991: Ripe and generous, a smooth-texture wine that focuses a broad beam of currant, black cherry and berry fruit right down the middle, shading it with spicy oak and a touch of herb. Tannic enough to want until 1998 or 2002. 1,825 cases made. • $20 • (03/15/94) SS • **90**
Cabernet Sauvignon Alexander Valley Reserve 1990: Strives for complexity and elegance, offering bright, ripe currant and raspberry flavors that are intense, yet is crisp and spicy, with pretty oak seasoning. Balanced and supple enough to enjoy now, but has the depth and complexity to age. Best now to 1998. 2,500 cases made. • $15 • (06/15/93) • **90**
Cabernet Sauvignon Sonoma County 1991: Appealing for its balance and flavor. Serves up pretty, focused berry and cherry notes with a spicy oak and herb edge to the tannic finish. Drinks well now. 20,000 cases made. • $10 • (03/15/94) • **84**
Cabernet Sauvignon Sonoma County 1990: Ripe, round and spicy, with generous red cherry, raspberry and clove aromas and flavors and hints of herb and vanilla on the finish. Drink soon. 13,500 cases made. • $10 • (06/15/93) • **81**
Cabernet Sauvignon Sonoma County 1987 • $8 • (11/30/90) BB • **88**
Cabernet Sauvignon Sonoma County 1981 • $7 • (06/16/85) • **83**
Chardonnay Alexander Valley Reserve 1994: Strikes a nice balance between ripe pear, fig and honey notes and traces of citrus and spice. Turns elegant on the finish, but loses some of its intensity. 3,500 cases made. • $20 • (05/15/96) • **89**
Chardonnay Alexander Valley Reserve 1993: Strikes a nice balance between ripe pear and apple flavors that are framed nicely by toasty, buttery oak. Outstanding. 2,900 cases made. • $20 • (04/15/95) • **90**
Chardonnay Alexander Valley Reserve 1991 • $17 • (07/15/93) • **81**
Chardonnay Sonoma County 1993: Ripe and juicy, with spicy pear, apple and nutmeg flavors that smooth out on the finish. Ready now. 40,000 cases made. • $10 • (12/15/94) BB • **85**
Chardonnay Sonoma County 1992: Light and simple with watery grapefruit and pear flavors. Drink now. 70,000 cases made. • $10 • (03/15/94) • **80**
Chardonnay Sonoma County 1991 • $10 • (07/15/93) • **80**
Gewürztraminer California 1995: Soft and generous with its pineapple, citrus, honeysuckle and spice flavors, and it finishes characteristically for this variety, off-dry and round. A definite good value. 12,000 cases made. • $7 • (06/15/96) BB • **86**
Gewürztraminer North Coast 1993: Soft, smooth and bubbling with fresh fruit flavors, centering around pear, floral and sweet orange. 10,000 cases made. • $6 • (01/31/95) • **84**
Gewürztraminer Sonoma County 1992 • $6 • (09/30/93) • **80**
Johannisberg Riesling California Soft 1995: Fresh and openly sweet, this is nicely balanced to show off the peach, spice and floral flavors on a polished frame. Good, typical flavors for this grape at a bargain. 40,000 cases made. • $7 • (06/15/96) BB • **84**
Johannisberg Riesling Late Harvest Mendocino County Selected Dried Berry 1990 • $13 • (08/31/91) • **93**
Johannisberg Riesling Late Harvest Russian River Valley Selected Dried Berry 1991 • $16 • (10/15/92) • **90**
Johannisberg Riesling North Coast Soft 1994: A fresh, youthful style, lightly sweet and showing exuberant peach and floral flavors. Finishes with a touch of a resiny quality. Great price, too. 40,000 cases made. • $6 • (09/30/95) BB • **85**
Malbec Alexander Valley 1991 • $10 • (03/31/94) • **85**
Malbec Alexander Valley Trione Vineyards Winemaker's Selection 1993: A touch herbal, with a hint of green tobacco, also a bit stalky, with modest plum and currant notes. 200 cases made. • $18 • (03/31/96) • **83**
Merlot Alexander Valley 1992: Smoky, toasty oak complements ripe cherry and berry flavors. Finishes with a peppery edge, thanks to 9 percent Syrah. Best after 1997. 1,500 cases made. • $12 • (01/31/95) • **85**
Merlot Alexander Valley 1991 • $13 • (06/15/93) • **87**
Merlot Alexander Valley 1989 • $9 • (05/31/92) • **79**
Merlot Alexander Valley 1987 • $8 • (07/15/90) • **82**
Merlot Alexander Valley 1985 • $7 • (10/15/88) • **77**
Merlot Alexander Valley 1984 • $7 • (02/29/88) • **69**
Merlot Alexander Valley 1983 • $7 • (12/31/86) • **80**
Opulence California NV • $7 • (01/31/87) • **80**
Petite Sirah Alexander Valley 1989 • $15 • (06/30/92) • **79**
Pinot Noir Sonoma County Carneros 1985 • $6 • (06/15/88) • **82**
Pinot Noir Sonoma County Carneros 1981 • $5 • (08/31/86) • **82**
Port Sonoma County Shiraz Trione Vineyards Henry's Reserve 1993: Ripe, broad and peppery, round enough to keep the earthy fruit flavors feeling round and polished, but it finishes flabby. Where's the grip? 400 cases made. • $15 • **73**
Red Trione Vineyards California 1987 • $3 • (02/28/90) • **77**
Réserve Alexandre Alexander Valley 1991: Ripe, intense and elegantly crafted. This serves up a pretty array of plum, currant, herb and cherry notes, finishing with an earthy edge and crisp tannins. Approachable now but also worthy of cellaring. Best after 1996. 2,397 cases made. • $30 • (07/31/94) CS • **91**
Réserve Alexandre Alexander Valley 1990: Firm, ripe, intense and complex with layers of spice, cedar, plum and currant flavors that are bright and lively, staying with you on a long, full, supple finish. Wonderful balance and sense of finesse. Drinkable now but sure to hold and gain through the decade. 2,500 cases made. • $30 • (11/15/93) • **90**
Réserve Alexandre Alexander Valley 1987 • $21 • (05/15/93) • **87**
Réserve Alexandre Alexander Valley 1986 • $20 • (09/30/90) • **89**
Réserve Alexandre Alexander Valley 1985 • $19 • (09/30/89) • **88**
Réserve Alexandre Alexander Valley 1984 • $19 • (08/31/88) • **89**
Réserve Alexandre Alexander Valley 1983 • $15 • (04/30/87) • **80**
Reisling Late Harvest Sonoma County Trione Vineyards Reserve 1993: Very sweet and rich, smooth and syrupy, with spicy, floral overtones to the modest honey and apricot flavors. Best from 1997. 400 cases made. • $16/375ml • (07/31/95) • **87**
Sauvignon Blanc Sonoma County 1995: The zingy, citrusy flavors show delicious shadings of passion fruit, lemongrass and spice, making for a lively, distinctive white to drink soon. Can't argue with the price either. 10,000 cases made. • $8 • (05/15/96) BB • **89**
Sauvignon Blanc Sonoma County 1994: A lean and lively white that's distinctive for adding anise and herbal overtones to the basic apple and kiwi flavors. 18,000 cases made. • $7 • (08/31/95) • **85**
Sauvignon Blanc Sonoma County 1992 • $7 • (07/15/93) BB • **82**
Sauvignon Blanc Sonoma County 1991 • $6 • (12/31/92) BB • **86**
Semchard California 1993: Herbal, almost vegetal flavors sneak in around the edges of the mostly apple and leafy flavors, finishing crisp. 3,500 cases made. • $7 • (12/15/94) • **81**
Semchard California 1992 • $7 • (07/31/93) BB • **83**
Semchard California 1991 • $9 • (12/15/92) BB • **88**

Syrah Alexander Valley Reserve 1991 • $18 • (12/31/93) • **91**
Syrah Alexander Valley Shiraz 1993: Well crafted, deftly balanced, with pretty black cherry, currant and anise flavors, finishing with a spicy edge and plush tannins. Very appealing now, softer in 1997. 3,500 cases made. • $12 • (06/15/96) • **89**
Zinfandel Alexander Valley 1984 • $7 • (07/31/88) • **79**

GICOMA CELLARS | CALIFORNIA

Cabernet Sauvignon Napa Valley Pointer Run Vineyards 1992: Tart with a slight green unripe edge to the currant and plum flavors. 360 cases made. • $14 • (03/31/96) • **78**

GIRARD | CALIFORNIA

Cabernet Sauvignon Napa Valley 1994: Well focused, with a pretty beam of cherry, currant and cedary oak, with flavors that build on the finish. Flirts with outstanding. 2,800 cases made. • $22 • (05/31/95) • **85-89** (BT)
Cabernet Sauvignon Napa Valley 1991: Serves up pretty floral, plum and cherry notes before the tannins clamp down on the finish. Elegant, compact and tightly wound, best to cellar until 1997. 2,638 cases made. • $18 • (05/31/94) • **86**
Cabernet Sauvignon Napa Valley 1989 • $20 Ⓐ • (11/15/92) • **82**
Cabernet Sauvignon Napa Valley 1988 • $16 • (11/15/91) • **85**
Cabernet Sauvignon Napa Valley 1987 • $16 • (11/15/90) • **86**
Cabernet Sauvignon Napa Valley 1986 • $16 • (11/15/89) • **89**
Cabernet Sauvignon Napa Valley 1985 • $22 Ⓐ • (09/15/88) • **88**
Cabernet Sauvignon Napa Valley 1984 • $35 Ⓐ • (11/30/87) • **88**
Cabernet Sauvignon Napa Valley 1983 • $15 • (12/15/86) • **71**
Cabernet Sauvignon Napa Valley 1982 • $29 • (03/01/89) • **87**
Cabernet Sauvignon Napa Valley 1981 • $26 • (03/01/89) • **86**
Cabernet Sauvignon Napa Valley 1980 • $27 • (03/01/89) • **92**
Cabernet Sauvignon Napa Valley Estate Grown 1990: Intense and flavorful with ripe, spicy cherry and currant flavors that turn crisp and tannic on the finish. Well balanced and richly flavored, it may still need until 1997 to soften and mellow. 2,782 cases made. • $16 • (11/15/93) • **87**
Cabernet Sauvignon Napa Valley Reserve 1994: Firm and well focused, with ripe, rich, complex currant, cherry, spice and cedary oak flavors. Uncommon depth and dimension in this tasting. • $NA • (05/31/95) • **90-94** (BT)
Cabernet Sauvignon Napa Valley Reserve 1992: Trim and austere, with a light band of currant, earth and cherry flavors, picking up subtle herbal tones on the finish. Tightly wound, young and needs to age until 1998. 750 cases made. • $40 • (12/15/95) • **88**
Cabernet Sauvignon Napa Valley Reserve 1991: Young and austere with dry, gripping tannins but also plenty of ripe cherry and currant notes. A bit chunky and awkward now, it can stand cellaring until 1998. 935 cases made. • $35 • (11/15/94) • **87**
Cabernet Sauvignon Napa Valley Reserve 1990: Firm, chunky and herbal, with a range of aromas that includes forest underbrush along with currant and spice. Try it now. • $25 • (04/15/94) • **86**
Cabernet Sauvignon Napa Valley Reserve 1989 • $25 • (11/15/93) • **84**
Cabernet Sauvignon Napa Valley Reserve 1988 • $25 • (11/15/92) • **84**
Cabernet Sauvignon Napa Valley Reserve 1987 • $25 • (11/15/91) • **88**
Cabernet Sauvignon Napa Valley Reserve 1986 • $34 • (11/15/90) • **87**
Cabernet Sauvignon Napa Valley Reserve 1985 • $35 • (02/15/90) • **86**
Cabernet Sauvignon Napa Valley Reserve 1984 • $35 • (03/01/89) • **92**
Cabernet Sauvignon Napa Valley Reserve 1983 • $18 • (03/01/89) • **87**
Chardonnay Napa Valley 1994: Combines ripe, rich fruit with a sound measure of finesse and harmony. Lots of juicy pear, honey and butterscotch flavors dovetail on the finish and linger. 7,700 cases made. • $18 • (06/15/96) SS • **91**
Chardonnay Napa Valley Estate 1992: Smooth and creamy, with ripe spicy pear, vanilla and toasty notes that are rich and focused, finishing with good length and flavor. 7,349 cases made. • $18 • (06/30/94) • **88**
Chardonnay Napa Valley Estate 1991 • $18 • (07/15/93) • **90**
Chardonnay Napa Valley Old Vines 1993: Bold, ripe and creamy, boasting pretty pear, spice, custard and toasty oak. Packs in lots of flavor and oak, and pulls it off. 6,700 cases made. • $19 • (12/15/95) • **88**
Chardonnay Napa Valley Reserve 1994: A bold, ripe, rich and dramatic style that's loaded with concentrated pear, spice, honey, toast and pineapple flavors. It shows the extra depth and dimensions of a great wine in the making. 800 cases made. • $32 • (05/31/96) • **93**
Chardonnay Napa Valley Reserve 1992: A spicy style, with creamy pear, vanilla and nutmeg flavors that hang together nicely, finishing with a complex aftertaste. Drinks well now but can age short-term. 446 cases made. • $28 • (06/30/94) • **89**
Chardonnay Napa Valley Viridian Vineyard 1993: Very ripe, floral and perfumed aromas and flavors. Big and bold, marked by strong oaky notes, but fruit rises to the occasion, adding a complex aftertaste. 241 cases made. • $38 • (12/15/95) • **87**
Chenin Blanc Napa Valley Dry 1992: Dry, lean and spicy, almost austere, doling out its melon and apple flavors in a fine spray of flavor on the finish. 800 cases made. • $9 • (07/31/94) • **82**

GLASS MOUNTAIN QUARRY | CALIFORNIA

Cabernet Sauvignon California 1992: Light, refreshing and straightforward, offering berry and spice flavors that stay with you on the supple finish. Ready now. 27,300 cases made. • $10 • (12/15/95) • **84**
Cabernet Sauvignon California 1990: Ripe, supple and beautifully balanced, offering generous currant, red plum and herb aromas and flavors that come together harmoniously on the finish. A terrific wine to drink now. From Markham. 12,000 cases made. • $9 • (06/15/93) • **84**
Cabernet Sauvignon Napa Valley 1988 • $8 • (10/15/91) BB • **85**
Chardonnay California 1993: Well oaked, with toasty, buttery aromas and just the right mix of ripe pear and spice notes to achieve balance. 20,000 cases made. • $9 • (06/30/95) • **84**
Chardonnay California 1991 • $9 • (06/15/93) • **82**
Petite Sirah Napa Valley 1988 • $8 • (10/31/91) BB • **81**
Rubis du Val Napa Valley 1988 • $8 • (10/31/91) BB • **82**

GLEN ELLEN | CALIFORNIA

Aleatico California Blanc de Noirs Barrel Fermented Imagery 1990 • $12 • (03/31/92) • **87**
Cabernet Franc Alexander Valley Imagery Series 1988 • $16 • (03/31/92) • **86**
Cabernet Sauvignon California Proprietor's Reserve 1993: Light, focused around raspberry and a touch of mint, smooth and drinkable now. • $6 • (12/15/95) • **82**
Cabernet Sauvignon California Proprietor's Reserve 1991: Light and fruity with simple berry flavors. Drinkable now. 50,000 cases made. • $6 • (11/15/93) • **78**
Cabernet Sauvignon California Proprietor's Reserve 1989 • $6 • (11/15/92) BB • **84**
Cabernet Sauvignon California Proprietor's Reserve 1988 • $6 • (11/15/91) BB • **79**
Cabernet Sauvignon California Proprietor's Reserve 1987 • $6 • (01/31/91) • **79**
Cabernet Sauvignon California Proprietor's Reserve 1986 • $4 • (07/15/88) BB • **82**
Cabernet Sauvignon Sonoma Valley Benziger Family Selection 1984 • $14 • (10/15/87) • **82**
Cabernet Sauvignon Sonoma Valley Benziger Family Selection 1983 • $9 • (05/15/87) • **91**
Cabernet Sauvignon Sonoma Valley Glen Ellen Estate 1982 • $9 • (02/01/85) • **85**
Cabernet Sauvignon Sonoma Valley Imagery Series 1985 • $13 • (02/15/89) • **86**
Chardonnay California Proprietor's Reserve 1993: Features ripe, lively pineapple and grapefruit flavors that hang with you. Well made. 227,000 cases made. • $5 • (07/31/95) BB • **85**
Chardonnay California Proprietor's Reserve 1992: Light and fruity, with gentle melon, peach and vanilla aromas and flavors and a

Key: SS—Spectator Selection. CS—Cellar Selection. BB—Best Buy. $NA—Price not available. (BT)—Barrel tasting. Ⓐ—Auction Price.
Dates in parentheses represent the issues in which the ratings were published.

touch of spice on the finish. Ultimately tastes simpler than it sounds, but appealing. Drinkable now. 999,999 cases made. • $6 • (07/15/93) BB • **81**

Chardonnay California Proprietor's Reserve 1991 • $6 • (01/31/93) BB • **84**

Fumé Blanc California Proprietor's Reserve 1994: Light, spicy, with a vanilla edge to the modest citrus flavors. • $6 • (05/31/96) • **82**

Merlot California Proprietor's Reserve 1992: Pleasing for its light and fruity cherry and vanilla flavors. Ready now. • $5 • (09/15/94) • **82**

Merlot California Proprietor's Reserve 1991 • $6 • (04/15/93) BB • **82**

Merlot California Proprietor's Reserve 1990 • $6 • (05/31/92) • **79**

Merlot California Proprietor's Reserve 1986 • $6 • (01/31/89) BB • **84**

Petit Verdot Alexander Valley Imagery Series 1988 • $16 • (03/31/92) • **88**

Riesling Late Harvest Santa Maria Valley Imagery Series 1989 • $10 • (03/31/92) • **79**

Sauvignon Blanc California Proprietor's Reserve 1993: Lean, fruity and spicy, but fairly modest flavors. Drinkable now. 135,000 cases made. • $5 • (06/30/95) • **80**

White Zinfandel California Proprietor's Reserve 1994: A middle-of-the-road blush wine, offering slightly sweet flavors dominated by peach and strawberry. • $5 • (09/15/95) • **79**

White Zinfandel California Proprietor's Reserve 1989 • $5 • (12/31/90) • **80**

White Zinfandel California Proprietor's Reserve 1988 • $5 • (06/15/89) • **84**

White Zinfandel California Proprietor's Reserve 1985 • $4 • (02/16/86) • **73**

GLENORA | NEW YORK

Blanc de Blancs Finger Lakes 1987 • $12 • (12/31/90) • **85**

Blancs de Blancs New York 1991: Fresh-tasting and lightly fruity, with good balance and a smooth texture. It tastes appley and slightly herbal. Refreshing and well made. 3,029 cases made. • $15 • (02/28/95) • **84**

Brut New York 1989: The ripe fruit, toast and bread-dough flavors give it Champagne character. Enjoyable, but rough-cut. Tasted twice, with consistent notes. 4,200 cases made. • $13 • **84**

Brut New York 1987 • $12 • (12/31/90) • **81**

Brut Rose New York 1991: This crisp, clean rosé has cherry aromas and sweet-tart flavors of apple and cranberry that grow on you. Nicely balanced and refreshing. 407 cases made. • $20 • (02/28/95) • **84**

Chardonnay Finger Lakes 1992: A spicy, vanilla aroma and flavor isn't backed up by much fruit flavor or acidity in this medium-bodied white wine. It turns rather simple on the finish. Average quality. 6,200 cases made. • $9 • **79**

Chardonnay Finger Lakes 1991: A pleasant, harmonious Chardonnay with a soft texture, nicely ripe flavors and good balance. Attractive, if fairly straightforward. 4,100 cases made. • $9 • (09/15/94) • **81**

Chardonnay Finger Lakes Barrel Fermented 1991 • $15 • • **79**

Extra Dry New York NV: Nice in texture, off-dry, but with earthy, tealike flavors that are simple, rustic and lack depth. 1,060 cases made. • $13 • **75**

Johannisberg Riesling Finger Lakes 1994: Rather heavy and full-bodied, showing ripe, cooked apple flavors with simple sweetness and not quite enough acidity for balance. • $8 • (01/31/96) • **78**

Johannisberg Riesling Finger Lakes 1993: Sweet, appley wine that is soft in texture, cleanly made, with touches of cinnamon and honey. 962 cases made. • $8 • **79**

Riesling Finger Lakes Dry 1994: Delicate floral and citrus aromas and flavors give this a light, Mosel-like character, offering peach notes that linger on the finish. • $8 • (01/31/96) • **85**

Riesling Finger Lakes Dry 1992: Drinkable but an extreme mix. The buttery, floral aromas and lemon and green apple notes clash with the milky, candied flavors. 1,500 cases made. • $8 • **75**

GODSPEED | CALIFORNIA

Cabernet Sauvignon Mount Veeder 1991: Firm, intense and tannic, with an earthy band of currant and herb flavors, but what sticks with you is the dry chewy tannins. May never outgrow that quality. 320 cases made. • $15 • (12/15/95) • **82**

Chardonnay Mount Veeder 1993: Tart and intense, with a tight beam of lemon, citrus and pear flavors. 375 cases made. • $15 • (07/31/95) • **85**

GODWIN | CALIFORNIA

Chardonnay Alexander Valley 1994: Toasty, smoky notes add class to the aromas, and it does seem rich, although losing some charm as wood covers the fruit on the medium-weight palate. 600 cases made. • $20 • (04/30/96) • **82**

GOLD HILL | CALIFORNIA

Merlot El Dorado 1991: Soft and chewy, chunky, with only a modest level of dark fruit flavors. May be best from 1996. 290 cases made. • $11 • (09/15/94) • **79**

GOLD SEAL | NEW YORK

Blanc de Blancs American Charles Fournier Special Selection NV • $10 • (06/30/90) • **77**

Brut Bottle Fermented New York NV • $7 • (12/31/90) • **69**

GOLDEN CREEK | CALIFORNIA

Caberlot Reserve Sonoma County 1991: Ripe and spicy, exhibiting solid plum and currant flavor and finishing with herb and light oak shadings. A 50-50 blend of Cabernet and Merlot. Ready now. 200 cases made. • $15 • (11/15/94) • **83**

Cabernet Sauvignon Sonoma County 1990: Simple with light plum and cherry notes. Ready now. 330 cases made. • $12 • (11/15/94) • **80**

Merlot Reserve 1989 • $16 • (05/31/92) • **87**

Merlot Sonoma County 1989 • $13 • (05/31/92) • **81**

Merlot Sonoma County Reserve 1991: Ripe and grapey, with spicy cherry, currant and wild berry flavors that turn crisp with leathery tannins on the finish. Best after 1997. • $15 • (09/15/94) • **84**

Merlot Sonoma County Reserve 1990: Lean and earthy, with a leathery edge to the Merlot fruit. Finishes with chewy tannins. Drinkable now. 330 cases made. • $15 • (09/15/94) • **82**

GORDON BROTHERS | WASHINGTON

Cabernet Sauvignon Washington 1991: Chewy-textured but bright and open in flavor, sending its solid Cabernet fruit through the veil of soft tannins on the finish. Best in 1997 or 1998. 1,115 cases made. • $15 • (09/30/95) • **85**

Cabernet Sauvignon Washington 1990: Hard and tannic, but packed with cedar and coffee flavors. May be better after 1997. 1,100 cases made. • $14 • (03/15/94) • **77**

Cabernet Sauvignon Washington 1989 • $16 • (07/31/92) • **83**

Cabernet Sauvignon Washington 1988 • $19 • (11/15/91) • **89**

Chardonnay Washington 1992: Smooth and generous, a little spicy and toasty around the edges, shining a bright beam of apple and pear right through the finish. 1,664 cases made. • $9 • (12/31/94) • **85**

Chardonnay Washington Reserve 1992: Soft and somewhat tired already, offering a rose petal edge to the vanilla and pear flavors. Drink soon. 420 cases made. • $15 • (09/30/95) • **80**

Merlot Washington 1992: Smooth, supple and glowing berry flavors wrap softly around the finish. Nicely done. Drinkable now. 976 cases made. • $15 • (09/30/95) • **87**

Merlot Washington 1990 • $14 • (06/15/93) • **78**

Tradition Cabernet Blend Washington 1991: Solidly built, framing a ripe mouthful of currant and blackberry with fine tannins and a touch of spicy oak. Nicely balanced and appealing through and through. Drinkable now. 100 cases made. • $20 • (01/31/95) • **88**

GRACE FAMILY | CALIFORNIA

Cabernet Sauvignon Napa Valley 1993: A lean, trim, leathery style, offering more oak and cedary flavors than obvious fruit, which is usually the most evident feature of this wine. Tasted twice, with consistent notes. 187 cases made. • $75 • (05/15/96) • **85**

Cabernet Sauvignon Napa Valley 1991: This is a lean, earthy bottling of Grace, which usually shows more ripe, opulent fruit. It's tightly wound and compact, with spicy currant, cedar and spice notes. Tasted three times. • $225 Ⓐ • (11/15/94) • **88**

Cabernet Sauvignon Napa Valley 1990: Offers wonderfully complex aromas and flavors, showing a toasty, smoky, buttery oak overlay to the ripe currant and cherry flavors underneath. The tannins are chewy and firm, but soft for a wine this young. Will need time to develop, but has elegance and 154 cases made. • $225 Ⓐ • (08/31/93) • **90**

Cabernet Sauvignon Napa Valley 1988 • $144 Ⓐ • (06/30/91) • **92**

Cabernet Sauvignon Napa Valley 1987 • $260 Ⓐ • (06/30/90) • **97**

Cabernet Sauvignon Napa Valley 1986 • $40 • (03/01/89) • **93**

Cabernet Sauvignon Napa Valley 1985 • $260 Ⓐ • (03/01/89) • **95**

Cabernet Sauvignon Napa Valley 1984 • $280 • (03/01/89) • **92**

Cabernet Sauvignon Napa Valley 1983 • $188 Ⓐ • (03/01/89) • **91**

Cabernet Sauvignon Napa Valley 1982 • $200 Ⓐ • (03/01/89) • **89**

Cabernet Sauvignon Napa Valley 1981 • $230 • (03/01/89) • **88**

Cabernet Sauvignon Napa Valley 1980 • $320 • (03/01/89) • **92**

Cabernet Sauvignon Napa Valley 1979 • $380 • (03/01/89) • **92**

Cabernet Sauvignon Napa Valley 1978 • $500 • (03/01/89) • **86**

GRAESER | CALIFORNIA

Cabernet Sauvignon Napa Valley 1991: Austere, tannic and earthy, with chewy tannins and a leathery streak to the Cabernet flavors. Finishes with a dry stalky, green bean edge. 1,300 cases made. • $14 • (12/15/95) • **79**

Chardonnay Napa Valley Silverado Summers Vineyard 1992: Lean and thin with lemony citrus flavors but not much ripe fruit. 450 cases made. • $13 • (07/31/95) • **78**

GRAFF, RICHARD | CALIFORNIA

Mourvèdre Chalone 1992: Complex and intriguing for its mineral, smoke, dried cherry and berry flavors and mild tannins. Young and taut, it's drinkable now. 125 cases made. • $16 • (01/31/96) • **86**

GRAHAM, G. | CALIFORNIA

Pinot Noir Carneros 1992: Spicy and elegant, marked by herb and black cherry flavors of modest proportions, finishing with a toasty edge. • $18 • (03/31/95) • **86**

GRAND CRU | CALIFORNIA

Cabernet Sauvignon Premium Selection 1988 • $12 • (03/15/92) • **84**

Cabernet Sauvignon Alexander Valley Collector's Reserve 1986 • $22 • (05/15/90) • **85**

Cabernet Sauvignon Alexander Valley Collector's Reserve 1985 • $18 • (07/15/89) • **81**

Cabernet Sauvignon Alexander Valley Collector's Reserve 1982 • $15 • (09/30/87) • **70**

Cabernet Sauvignon Alexander Valley Collector's Reserve 1980 • $15 • (11/01/84) • **85**

Cabernet Sauvignon Sonoma County 1984 • $8 • (12/31/87) • **75**

Cabernet Sauvignon Sonoma County 1983 • $8 • (11/16/85) • **68**

Cabernet Sauvignon Sonoma County Premium Selection 1987 • $12 • (11/15/91) • **85**

Cabernet Sauvignon Sonoma County Premium Selection 1986 • $12 • (04/30/90) • **79**

Cabernet Sauvignon Sonoma County Premium Selection 1985 • $9 • (06/15/89) • **79**

Chardonnay California Premium Selection 1994: Simple and refreshing, with nectarine and citrus flavors lingering briefly on the finish. 7,000 cases made. • $8 • (06/30/96) • **83**

Key: SS—Spectator Selection. CS—Cellar Selection. BB—Best Buy. $NA—Price not available. (BT)—Barrel tasting. Ⓐ—Auction Price.
Dates in parentheses represent the issues in which the ratings were published.

Gewürztraminer California Premium Selection 1993: Brassy color, modest flavors, soft and sweet, hinting at peach on the finish. • $7 • (02/28/95) • **80**

Gewürztraminer Late Harvest Sonoma County Select 1987 • $10 • (03/31/90) • **72**

Johannisberg Riesling California Premium Selection 1993: Odd sappy, citrus peel flavors won't be to everyone's taste, but this off-dry wine has character and style, finishing with a touch of apricot. 7,000 cases made. • $7 • (06/15/95) • **83**

Merlot California Premium Selection 1992: Light and fruity, with grapey, cherry and currant notes. Drinks easy now. 2,500 cases made. • $8 • (09/15/94) • **81**

Sauvignon Blanc California 1994: Soft and floral, with a nice hint of peach on the finish. 2,500 cases made. • $7 • (05/31/96) • **83**

Sauvignon Blanc California Premium Selection 1991 • $6 • (09/15/93) • **75**

White Zinfandel California 1988 • $5 • (06/15/89) • **73**

Zinfandel California Premium Selection 1992: This is simple, with ripe cherry and wild berry flavors. • $7 • (10/15/95) • **78**

GRAND TRAVERSE, CHATEAU | MICHIGAN

Johannisberg Riesling Late Harvest Michigan 1990 • $10 • (02/29/92) • **78**

GRANDE ROCHE, CHATEAU LA | CALIFORNIA

Napa Valley Red 1988 • $13 • (10/15/90) • **86**

Pinot Noir Napa Valley 1991 • $16 • (02/28/94) • **85**

GRANITE SPRINGS | CALIFORNIA

Zinfandel El Dorado 1990 • $8 • (09/30/93) • **82**

Zinfandel El Dorado 1989 • $8 • (10/15/92) • **75**

GREAT WESTERN | NEW YORK

Blanc de Blancs New York NV • $14 • (06/30/90) • **76**

Blanc de Noirs American NV • $14 • (03/31/90) • **70**

Brut Very Dry New York NV • $9 • (12/31/90) • **69**

Extra Dry New York NV • $9 • (12/31/90) • **68**

Natural New York NV • $14 • (06/30/90) • **74**

Rosé New York NV • $9 • (12/31/90) • **71**

GREEN & RED | CALIFORNIA

Chardonnay Napa Valley Catacula Vineyard 1994: A medium-bodied white serving up a nice core of ripe, spicy pear and citrus flavors, and finishing with a light dash of oak. 690 cases made. • $18 • (06/30/96) • **84**

Chardonnay Napa Valley Catacula Vineyard 1993: Pleasant enough, with a core of ripe pear, vanilla and earthy notes on the finish. Lacks focus. 750 cases made. • $16 • (07/31/95) • **84**

Chardonnay Napa Valley Catacula Vineyard 1992: An odd wine with a gluey edge to the pear-laced Chardonnay fruit. Good, but only average considering how many fine 1992s there are out there. 1,340 cases made. • $15 • (06/30/94) • **80**

Chardonnay Napa Valley Catacula Vineyard 1991 • $16 • (07/15/93) • **88**

Zinfandel Napa Valley 1989 • $11 • (10/15/92) • **81**

Zinfandel Napa Valley 1987 • $9 • (02/15/91) • **77**

Zinfandel Napa Valley 1986 • $9 • (03/15/90) • **76**

Zinfandel Napa Valley 1985 • $8 • (06/15/89) • **73**

Zinfandel Napa Valley 1984 • $7 • (11/15/87) • **82**

Zinfandel Napa Valley 1983 • $7 • (07/31/87) • **64**

Zinfandel Napa Valley 1982 • $7 • (12/16/85) • **82**

Zinfandel Napa Valley Chiles Mill Vineyard 1994: Elegant, refined, tart cherry and berry flavor gains a spicy, anise edge on aftertaste, where the texture is smooth and tannins fine. 1,000 cases made. • $16 • (04/30/96) • **88**

Zinfandel Napa Valley Chiles Mill Vineyard 1992: A big brawny style, intense and chewy, with firm dry tannins and a wallop of oak and a lot of fruit, too. Drinkable now. 1,000 cases made. • $14 • (07/31/94) • **88**

Zinfandel Napa Valley Chiles Mill Vineyard 1991 • $12 • (09/30/93) • **85**
Zinfandel Napa Valley Chiles Mill Vineyard 1990 • $12 • (03/15/93) • **90**
Zinfandel Napa Valley Chiles Mill Vineyard Unfiltered 1993: Intense yet elegant, focused on the spicy cherry, wild berry and light jammy notes. Has firm tannins to frame the flavors. Drinkable now through 1998. 1,350 cases made. • $15 • (09/30/95) • **90**

GREENSTONE | CALIFORNIA

Zinfandel Amador County 1990 • $9 • (09/30/93) • **84**
Zinfandel Amador County Special Release 1987 • $10 • (09/30/93) • **84**

GREENWOOD RIDGE | CALIFORNIA

Cabernet Sauvignon Anderson Valley 1992: Dark, thick and plush, sporting rich, chunky, earthy currant, toasty oak and black cherry notes that are intense and concentrated. Packs in lots of flavor. 300 cases made. • $18 • (09/15/95) • **89**
Cabernet Sauvignon Anderson Valley 1991: Lean, earthy and oaky, so that the woody flavors dominate the currant and berry notes. Try now. 1,000 cases made. • $14 • (11/15/94) • **82**
Cabernet Sauvignon Anderson Valley 1989 • $12 • (08/31/92) • **74**
Cabernet Sauvignon Anderson Valley Estate Reserve 1990: Fresh green bean and green pepper aromas and flavor cut a swath through this wine, robbing it of its fruit. Not for most Cabernet fans. 400 cases made. • $16 • (06/15/93) • **75**
Cabernet Sauvignon Anderson Valley Estate Reserve 1989 • $16 • (11/15/92) • **87**
Cabernet Sauvignon Mendocino 1988 • $15 • (02/29/92) • **83**
Chardonnay Anderson Valley Du Pratt Vineyard 1994: Ripe and refreshing, featuring complex pear, tangerine, honey and spice flavors and a delicate finish. Impressive for its finesse and grace. 500 cases made. • $19 • (04/30/96) • **90**
Chardonnay Anderson Valley Du Pratt Vineyard 1992: Smooth and generous, a mouthful of pear, peach and spice flavors that balance elegantly on a crisp structure. Finishes with style. Drinkable now. 650 cases made. • $19 • (05/31/94) • **90**
Chardonnay Late Harvest Anderson Valley 1993 • $18 • (06/15/94) • **85**
Chardonnay Mendocino 1991 • $16 • (03/31/93) • **83**
Merlot Anderson Valley 1993: Rich and well focused, with chewy currant, black cherry, plum and berry notes. Picks up a spicy anise edge with light toasty oak. Finishes with firm tannins. Best after 1996. 950 cases made. • $20 • **89**
Merlot Anderson Valley 1992: Firm and compact, with a lean, chunky core of currant and wild berry flavors. 927 cases made. • $20 • (04/15/95) • **86**
Merlot Anderson Valley 1991 • $16 • (03/15/94) • **78**
Merlot Anderson Valley 1989 • $16 • (11/15/91) • **85**
Pinot Noir Anderson Valley 1994: Dark in color, with ripe, rich and intense flavors. The cherry and berry notes show nicely through the supple tannins. Impressive for its purity of flavor. Young and intense, but aging into 1997 should bring out its best. 915 cases made. • $16 • (01/31/96) • **90**
Pinot Noir Anderson Valley 1990 • $15 • (09/30/92) • **87**
Pinot Noir Anderson Valley 1989 • $14 • (06/30/91) • **87**
Pinot Noir Anderson Valley Roederer Estate Vineyards 1993: Ripe, smooth and polished, with elegant black cherry, currant and wild berry flavors, finishing with fine tannins and a grapey character. 997 cases made. • $15 • (03/31/95) • **89**
Pinot Noir Anderson Valley Roederer Estate Vineyards 1992: Deep color, with ripe, rich, well-focused black cherry, wild berry and raspberry flavors that are complex and concentrated. Distinctive and makes a strong statement about the quality and potential of Pinot Noir from this California appellation. 750 cases made. • $15 • (10/31/94) SS • **90**
Pinot Noir Mendocino County 1991 • $15 • (02/28/93) • **87**
Sauvignon Blanc Anderson Valley 1994: Bright and citrusy, a nice mouthful of grapefruit, peach and herb. Easy-drinking and appealing. 576 cases made. • $9 • (02/29/96) • **87**
Sauvignon Blanc Anderson Valley 1993: Earthy, minty flavors dominate this toasty wine, a little sharp with oak flavor on the finish. 1,000 cases made. • $9 • (08/31/95) • **80**
Sauvignon Blanc Anderson Valley 1992 • $9 • (01/31/94) • **84**
Sauvignon Blanc Anderson Valley 1991 • $9 • (09/15/93) • **70**
White Riesling Anderson Valley 1994: Soft and creamy in texture, lightly sweet, with a delicate vanilla note floating over the gentle pear flavors. 638 cases made. • $8 • (06/15/96) • **84**
White Riesling Anderson Valley 1993: Bright, fruity and appealing, a light white that's a little spritzy on the palate, balancing the sweet peach and nectarine flavor. 1,380 cases made. • $8 • (02/28/95) • **85**
White Riesling Anderson Valley 1992 • $8 • (05/15/93) • **83**
White Riesling Anderson Valley 1991 • $8 • (05/31/92) • **82**
White Riesling Late Harvest Mendocino 1989 • $18 • (08/31/91) • **89**
Zinfandel Sonoma County 1991 • $12 • (05/31/93) • **85**
Zinfandel Sonoma County 1990 • $13 • (07/31/92) • **86**
Zinfandel Sonoma County 1989 • $12 • (10/15/92) • **81**
Zinfandel Sonoma County 1988 • $11 • (05/15/91) • **86**
Zinfandel Sonoma County Scherrer Vineyards 1994: Complex and graceful, featuring lots of cherry and raspberry notes and gaining a sense of elegance and finesse on the finish, where the flavors fold together nicely. 917 cases made. • $15 • (04/30/96) • **90**
Zinfandel Sonoma County Scherrer Vineyards 1993: Bright, youthful, dark cherry yields to vanilla, toast and bitter almond on the finish. Tannic, wait until 1997. 953 cases made. • $14 • (01/31/95) • **87**
Zinfandel Sonoma County Scherrer Vineyards 1992: Tight and compact, with chewy tannins. The wild berry and plummy flavors are wrapped in tannins now, but a wonderful core of fruit emerges on the finish. Drinkable now. 760 cases made. • $14 • (09/15/94) • **88**
Zinfandel Sonoma County Scherrer Vineyards 1991 • $12 • (08/31/93) • **91**

GRGICH HILLS | CALIFORNIA

Cabernet Sauvignon Napa-Sonoma Counties 1980 • $27 Ⓐ • (03/01/89) • **90**
Cabernet Sauvignon Napa Valley 1992: Lean, tart and tannic, with just a glimpse of cherry and cedar flavors peeking through. Lacks the charm and harmony usual to Grgich. Cellaring into1998 advised. 9,000 cases made. • $26 • **79**
Cabernet Sauvignon Napa Valley 1991: Trim with a green tea and herbal edge to the flavors, it lacks the richness, depth and concentration of the best 1991s. 12,000 cases made. • $24 • (12/15/95) • **83**
Cabernet Sauvignon Napa Valley 1990: Sturdy rather than elegant, exhibiting bold, ripe plum and black cherry flavors and spicy, cedary oak. Needs short-term cellaring into 1997. 8,000 cases made. • $22 • (04/30/95) • **87**
Cabernet Sauvignon Napa Valley 1989: Austere and oaky, showing more wood and tannins than fruit. A surprisingly awkward effort given Grgich's usually deft hand at balancing. Tasted three times with consistent notes. 11,500 cases made. • $22 • (11/15/94) • **81**
Cabernet Sauvignon Napa Valley 1988 • $22 • (11/15/93) • **84**
Cabernet Sauvignon Napa Valley 1987 • $22 • (11/15/92) • **87**
Cabernet Sauvignon Napa Valley 1986 • $20 • (11/15/91) • **88**
Cabernet Sauvignon Napa Valley 1985 • $35 Ⓐ • (10/31/90) • **90**
Cabernet Sauvignon Napa Valley 1984 • $35 Ⓐ • (04/30/89) • **87**
Cabernet Sauvignon Napa Valley 1983 • $17 • (03/01/89) • **88**
Cabernet Sauvignon Napa Valley 1982 • $17 • (03/01/89) • **87**
Cabernet Sauvignon Napa Valley 1981 • $17 • (03/01/89) • **86**
Cabernet Sauvignon Napa Valley Yountville Selection 1991: Straightforward, sturdy style of Cabernet, showing currant fruit at first and hinting at plum and vanilla as the finish revs up. Drink now. 1,255 cases made. • $35 • (12/15/95) • **89**
Chardonnay Napa Valley 1994: Crisp and flinty, with a well-focused core of pear, citrus, lemon and spice, graced by a pretty overlay of smoky, toasty oak. Impressive for its balance and length. Will age well. 35,000 cases made. • $26 • (05/31/96) • **90**
Chardonnay Napa Valley 1993: Smooth and generous, a little light overall but tasty for its pear, resin and spice flavors. Ready now. 30,000 cases made. • $24 • (12/15/95) • **86**
Chardonnay Napa Valley 1992: Supple, with elegant pear, honey and apple flavors that pick up a citrus edge on the finish. Drinks well now but it's worth tucking a few bottles. • $24 • (12/15/94) • **88**

Chardonnay Napa Valley 1991 • $24 • (03/15/94) • **87**

Chardonnay Napa Valley Carneros Selection 1992: Starts out tight and firm but expands on the palate, where citrus, toast, pear and spice flavors fan out. 3,000 cases made. • $35 • (04/30/95) • **89**

Fumé Blanc Napa Valley 1994: Crisp and citrusy, with a slight oniony edge to the floral and apple flavors. 12,000 cases made. • $14 • (06/30/96) • **83**

Fumé Blanc Napa Valley 1991 • $13 • (02/15/93) • **84**

Fumé Blanc Napa Valley Dry 1993: Crisp, adding a flinty grapefruit and citrus edge and lingering flavors. 9,700 cases made. • $13 • (03/31/95) • **85**

Fumé Blanc Napa Valley Dry 1992 • $13 • (03/31/94) • **84**

Johannisberg Riesling Late Harvest Napa Valley 1993: Sweet, deep honey flavors, folding in a floral character that keeps echoing on the smooth and elegant finish. Shows some restraint. Delicious now. 2,000 cases made. • $50 • (04/30/95) • **88**

Sauvignon Blanc Napa Valley Fumé Blanc Dry 1994: Lean and herbal, a celery note harmonizing with the toasted onion and citrus flavors. • $14 • (02/29/96) • **82**

Zinfandel Alexander Valley 1986 • $19 • (05/15/90) • **85**

Zinfandel Alexander Valley 1985 • $19 • (07/31/89) • **84**

Zinfandel Alexander Valley 1984 • $19 • (03/15/87) • **90**

Zinfandel Alexander Valley 1983 • $19 • (05/01/86) • **85**

Zinfandel Alexander Valley 1982 • $18 • (05/16/85) SS • **91**

Zinfandel Sonoma County 1992: Oaky, earthy, adding mature, cedary tones to cherry and berry notes. Flavors turn to pepper and berry, which lacks focus. Tasted twice with consistent results. 10,000 cases made. • $14 • (07/31/95) • **84**

Zinfandel Sonoma County 1991: Ripe and chunky, with rich, tannic raspberry and tart cherry flavors and cedary oak notes on the finish. Needs time to soften. Best from now to 1998. 4,700 cases made. • $13 • (10/15/94) • **84**

Zinfandel Sonoma County 1990 • $13 • (04/30/94) • **85**

Zinfandel Sonoma County 1989 • $13 • (04/30/93) • **85**

Zinfandel Sonoma County 1988 • $12 • (03/31/92) • **85**

Zinfandel Sonoma County 1987 • $22 • (10/15/90) • **84**

Zinfandel Sonoma County 1984 • $11 • (10/31/88) • **86**

Zinfandel Sonoma County 1981 • $10 • (04/01/84) • **80**

GRIFFIN, BARNARD | WASHINGTON

Cabernet Merlot Columbia Valley 1992: A little chewy, but the berry and currant flavors come through nicely. Give it until 1997 to polish the tannins. 1,100 cases made. • $10 • (08/31/94) • **86**

Cabernet Merlot Columbia Valley 1990: Ripe and generous, a polished wine with distinctive currant, berry and spice aromas and flavors, shaded by oak on the finish. A delicious wine. Drinkable now. 1,600 cases made. • $10 • (03/15/94) BB • **88**

Cabernet Sauvignon Columbia Valley 1993: Rich, supple and generous, loaded with spicy plum, black cherry and lightly smoky flavors that linger and swirl on the finish. Modest tannins can use until 1997 or 1998 to settle. 490 cases made. • $15 • (03/31/96) • **88**

Cabernet Sauvignon Columbia Valley 1991: Supple and generous, its tannins showing a somewhat hard edge but finishing in nice coffee, dried blackberry and toast flavors. Best in 1998. 450 cases made. • $15 • (09/30/95) • **86**

Cabernet Sauvignon Columbia Valley 1990: Dense and chewy, earthy, with coarse tannins and a moderate level of beet and berry flavors. May be better after 1997 to 1998. 400 cases made. • $15 • (09/30/94) • **78**

Chardonnay Columbia Valley 1994: Nicely focused pear and vanilla flavors remain clear and bright in this easy-to-drink Chardonnay. • $13 • (04/30/96) • **86**

Chardonnay Columbia Valley Barrel Fermented 1993: Ripe, spicy and just a little earthy, nicely balanced and generous enough to show off its pear and resiny flavors through the delicate finish. Ready now. 4,500 cases made. • $13 • (09/30/95) • **84**

Key: SS—Spectator Selection. CS—Cellar Selection. BB—Best Buy. $NA—Price not available. (BT)—Barrel tasting. (A)—Auction Price.
Dates in parentheses represent the issues in which the ratings were published.

Chardonnay Columbia Valley Barrel Fermented 1992: Bright, straightforward style of Chardonnay, solidly fruity and refreshing, apple and nectarine flavors predominating. Drinkable now. 4,800 cases made. • $13 • (04/15/95) SS • **84**

Chardonnay Columbia Valley Barrel Fermented 1991 • $13 • (06/15/93) • **84**

Fumé Blanc Columbia Valley 1994: Crisp and lively, sprightly with juicy pear, citrus and delicate herb flavors that last on the finish. Good fun and value. 4,400 cases made. • $9 • (09/30/95) • **87**

Fumé Blanc Columbia Valley Dry 1993: Soft and fruity, light enough to sip by itself, generous enough with its citrusy pear flavors to match up with dinner. Drinkable now. 4,900 cases made. • $9 • (09/15/94) • **83**

Merlot Washington 1993: Firm in texture, featuring chewy blackberry and currant flavors that hint at tar and smoke on the modestly tannic finish. Best in 1997. 1,610 cases made. • $15 • (09/30/95) • **85**

Merlot Washington 1992: Firm and a little tannic around the edges but showing a nice core of supple fruit, leaning toward bright currant and cherry. Drinkable now. 1,250 cases made. • $15 • (12/31/94) • **82**

Merlot Washington 1991: Herbal, bell pepper flavors dominate the fruit in this lean, somewhat austere Merlot. May be best from 1997. 1,000 cases made. • $15 • (09/30/94) • **78**

GRISTINA | NEW YORK

Cabernet Sauvignon North Fork of Long Island 1988 • $14 • (06/30/91) • **90**

Chardonnay North Fork of Long Island Andy's Field 1993: Floral and buttery aromas lead to fresh, light appley and sweet vanilla flavors on the palate, balanced and delicate. 250 cases made. • $19 • **83**

GROTH | CALIFORNIA

Cabernet Sauvignon Napa Valley 1992: Starts out a bit rough but turns more complex as the flavors unfold, revealing layers of currant, cedar, coffee and spice. Turns to herbal and cedary accents on the finish. Has the tannic strength to age, but best from 1997 to 1998. 13,500 cases made. • $20 • (09/30/95) CS • **91**

Cabernet Sauvignon Napa Valley 1991: Laced with cedary oak and herbal notes, but the currant and coffee flavors underneath are rich and intense. Finishes with a weedy black currant and chocolate edge. Firmly tannic, it needs cellaring until 1999. 12,000 cases made. • $18 • (10/15/94) SS • **90**

Cabernet Sauvignon Napa Valley 1990: Dense and concentrated, a dark, chunky wine that has plenty of flavor, running from plum and currant to herb and tobacco, echoing coffee and spice on the finish. Best to drink after 1997. 12,000 cases made. • $17 • (09/30/93) SS • **90**

Cabernet Sauvignon Napa Valley 1989 • $17 • (11/15/92) • **81**

Cabernet Sauvignon Napa Valley 1988 • $20 • (11/15/91) • **75**

Cabernet Sauvignon Napa Valley 1987 • $20 • (10/31/90) • **81**

Cabernet Sauvignon Napa Valley 1986 • $18 • (11/15/89) • **92**

Cabernet Sauvignon Napa Valley 1985 • $16 • (03/01/89) • **91**

Cabernet Sauvignon Napa Valley 1984 • $14 • (03/01/89) • **92**

Cabernet Sauvignon Napa Valley 1983 • $13 • (03/01/89) • **88**

Cabernet Sauvignon Napa Valley 1982 • $13 • (03/01/89) • **88**

Cabernet Sauvignon Napa Valley Reserve 1992: Dark, thick, smooth and polished, this plush young Cabernet is brimming with ripe cherry, currant and berry flavors. It's well shaded by smoky, toasty oak that gives it coffee and cedary accents on the finish. Truly exotic, about as complex and concentrated as it gets, suggesting a long life ahead. 1,400 cases made. • $70 • (04/30/96) CS • **98**

Cabernet Sauvignon Napa Valley Reserve 1991: From an estate with a great track record. This is distinctive for its richness and depth, marked by herb, bell pepper and racy currant flavors that offer uncommon complexity in a unique style. Drinkable between 1998 and 2008. 1,250 cases made. • $50 • (04/15/95) CS • **95**

Cabernet Sauvignon Napa Valley Reserve 1990: Distinctive and has a lot of personality. Packs in ripe currant, black cherry, herb and coffee flavors that are deep and complex. Framed by toasty, buttery oak, it finishes with a broad range of flavors and firm but supple tannins. The winery's best since the '85 Reserve. Approachable now but better after 1996. 725 cases made. • $45 • (11/15/94) CS • **94**

Cabernet Sauvignon Napa Valley Reserve 1989 • $40 • (11/15/93) • **88**

Cabernet Sauvignon Napa Valley Reserve 1988 • $40 • (06/15/93) • **85**
Cabernet Sauvignon Napa Valley Reserve 1987 • $58 Ⓐ • (03/31/92) • **88**
Cabernet Sauvignon Napa Valley Reserve 1986 • $31 Ⓐ • (04/30/91) • **91**
Cabernet Sauvignon Napa Valley Reserve 1985 • $135 Ⓐ • (04/15/90) • **95**
Cabernet Sauvignon Napa Valley Reserve 1984 • $25 • (04/15/89) • **84**
Cabernet Sauvignon Napa Valley Reserve 1983 • $25 • (03/01/89) • **92**
Chardonnay Napa Valley 1994: Ripe pear, nut, light oak and spice flavors add up to an enjoyable wine. Finishes with a fruity aftertaste. 9,000 cases made. • $15 • (06/30/96) • **84**
Chardonnay Napa Valley 1993: Tart and earthy, showing a pungent, grassy edge to the spicy pear flavors. 12,000 cases made. • $14 • (04/15/95) • **84**
Chardonnay Napa Valley 1992: Coarse and simple with earthy fig, pear and spice flavors that turn chunky on the finish. Lacks the finesse and grace you find in the best 1992s. Tasted three times with consistent notes. 11,960 cases made. • $14 • (03/31/94) • **83**
Chardonnay Napa Valley 1991 • $14 • (04/30/93) • **86**
Merlot Napa Valley 1992: Intense and lively, yet despite its weight this Merlot offers a seam of elegance and early finesse and ripe cherry, plum and currant flavor. 1,770 cases made. • $20 • (09/30/95) • **89**
Merlot Napa Valley 1991: Tart and earthy, with cedary oak dominating the cherry- and herb-laced Merlot fruit underneath. Finishes with a good dose of tannin. Drinkable now. 18,000 cases made. • $17 • (09/15/94) • **82**
Merlot Napa Valley 1990 • $15 • (08/31/93) • **83**
Sauvignon Blanc Napa Valley 1994: Lean and definitely herbal, showing an onion-skin edge to the peppery pear flavors. 11,500 cases made. • $9 • (08/31/95) • **83**
Sauvignon Blanc Napa Valley 1992 • $8 • (05/15/94) • **83**

GROVE STREET | CALIFORNIA

Cabernet Sauvignon California Vineyard Select 1992: Lean and tannic, has just enough fruit to sneak past. 12,000 cases made. • $7 • (11/15/94) • **75**
Chardonnay Sonoma County 1992: Tastes sweet and simple with light fruit notes. 19,000 cases made. • $6 • (06/30/94) • **75**
Chardonnay Sonoma County Healdsburg Vineyard Select 1993: Simple and flavorful, with an unfortunate rubbery edge to the pear fruit. 25,000 cases made. • $7 • (07/31/95) • **77**
Chardonnay Sonoma County Vintage Select 1992: Intense and somewhat earthy, putting grassy tones on the pear and pineapple flavors. Drinks well now. A second label from the owner of Belvedere Winery. 28,000 cases made. • $7 • (05/15/95) • **84**

GRUET | NEW MEXICO

Brut Blanc de Noirs New Mexico NV • $15 • (12/15/92) • **82**
Brut New Mexico NV • $15 • (12/15/92) • **79**

GUENOC | CALIFORNIA

Cabernet Franc Lake County 1985 • $12 • (02/15/89) • **70**
Cabernet Franc Napa Valley 1990 • $14 • (11/15/93) • **83**
Cabernet Sauvignon Guenoc Valley Premier Cuvée 1985 • $17 • (10/15/90) • **84**
Cabernet Sauvignon Guenoc Valley Tephra Ridge Reserve 1993: Appealing for its ripe, bright fruit flavors of cherry, plum and wild berry, turning tart and simple on the finish. 310 cases made. • $30 • (12/15/95) • **86**
Cabernet Sauvignon Lake County 1992: Medium weight, with a supple core of dill, cherry and spice. Well crafted in a smooth, easy drinking style. 10,930 cases made. • $15 • (12/15/95) • **85**
Cabernet Sauvignon Lake County 1991: Firm and compact, with an earthy edge to the currant and plum Cabernet flavors. Drinkable now. 4,201 cases made. • $15 • (11/15/94) • **85**
Cabernet Sauvignon Lake County 1990: Lean and firmly tannic, but with a pleasasnt core of currant and cedary oak flavors. Loses intensity on the finish, where the tannins gain the upper hand, but at • $11 it's a good value in quality Cabernet. Drink now. 10,000 cases made. • $11 • (04/15/94) • **84**
Cabernet Sauvignon Lake County 1989 • $12 • (11/15/92) • **77**
Cabernet Sauvignon Lake County 1987 • $12 • (07/15/91) • **89**
Cabernet Sauvignon Lake County 1986 • $13 • (04/30/91) • **78**
Cabernet Sauvignon Lake County 1985 • $33 • • **68**
Cabernet Sauvignon Lake County 1983 • $9 • (09/30/86) • **89**
Cabernet Sauvignon Lake County 1981 • $8 • (12/16/84) • **78**
Cabernet Sauvignon Napa Valley Beckstoffer IV Vineyard Reserve 1992: Tight and intense, with a trim band of spice, currant, black cherry and tobacco, turning tannic on the finish. A young and complex wine that needs cellaring to soften and evolve. Best after 1999. 2,833 cases made. • $40 • (12/15/95) • **90**
Cabernet Sauvignon Napa Valley Beckstoffer Vineyard Reserve 1991: Young and a bit austere at first, it is well focused, concentrated and serves up complex herb, currant and black cherry flavors that turn supple and elegant on the finish. Shows a measure of finesse and restraint. Ready in 1998. 1,311 cases made. • $35 • (09/30/94) CS • **94**
Cabernet Sauvignon Napa Valley Beckstoffer Vineyard Reserve 1990: Ripe and aromatic, rich and flavorful with a tight, solid core of black cherry, cedar, currant and spice flavors that fan out on your palate. Supple and generous, yet with a firm backbone. Needs cellaring until 1998 for the tannins to soften. 1,362 cases made. • $35 • (11/15/93) • **92**
Cabernet Sauvignon Napa Valley Beckstoffer Vineyard Reserve 1989 • $30 • (03/31/93) • **85**
Cabernet Sauvignon Napa Valley Beckstoffer Vineyard Reserve 1987 • $24 • (06/30/91) • **92**
Cabernet Sauvignon Napa Valley Bella Vista Vineyard Reserve 1992: Tight and compact, with a firm band of anise, currant, black cherry and cedary oak. Turns austere on the finish, where the tannins dominate. Best in 1999. 821 cases made. • $25 • (12/15/95) • **90**
Cabernet Sauvignon North Coast 1991: Simple, with earthy, tannic dill and herbal flavors. Best now, given the tannic edge on the finish and modest richness of the fruit. 16,914 cases made. • $12 • (11/15/94) • **82**
Cabernet Sauvignon North Coast 1988 • $12 • (08/31/92) • **79**
Chardonnay Guenoc Valley 1994: Sleek and elegant, a trim and focused style showing nectarine, pear and citrus flavors that turn flinty on the finish. 11,913 cases made. • $15 • (04/30/96) • **87**
Chardonnay Guenoc Valley 1993: Marked by gamy, woody flavors, leading to ripe pear and pineapple notes on the finish that turn smooth and supple. • $15 • (02/28/95) • **86**
Chardonnay Guenoc Valley 1992: Crisp and pleasing with pretty pear and apple notes that turn slightly tinny on the finish. Drinkable now. 11,700 cases made. • $15 • (02/28/94) • **84**
Chardonnay Guenoc Valley 1991 • $14 • (04/30/93) • **85**
Chardonnay Guenoc Valley Genevieve Magoon Unfiltered Reserve 1994: Intense, elegant, attractive pear, spice, fig and melon notes. This is a solid Chardonnay that holds together well. 396 cases made. • $30 • (05/15/96) • **88**
Chardonnay Guenoc Valley Genevieve Magoon Vineyard 1992: Aims for complexity with its rich core of spicy pear, honey, hazelnut and buttery oak. Complex and concentrated, a young, elegant and graceful wine. Ready now. 3,043 cases made. • $25 • (05/15/94) • **89**
Chardonnay Guenoc Valley Genevieve Magoon Vineyard Estate Reserve 1994: Marked by grassy nuances to the pear and tangerine flavors, but it holds together nicely on the palate, finishing in a slight citrus edge. 3,200 cases made. • $23 • (04/30/96) • **88**
Chardonnay Guenoc Valley Genevieve Magoon Vineyard Reserve 1993: It's marked by smoky, toasty aromas, but with juicy pear and apple flavors to accompany them. The whole symphony turns elegant and lively on the finish, where a note of quince appears. Try now. 3,207 cases made. • $25 • (05/31/95) • **90**
Chardonnay Guenoc Valley Genevieve Magoon Vineyard Reserve 1991 • $25 • (10/15/93) • **88**
Chardonnay North Coast 1991 • $12 • (09/15/92) • **77**
Langtry Guenoc Valley 1992: A white Meritage blend that is classy, firm, intense and lively, with lots of spice, pear, fig and herb flavors. Lavishly oaked, with smoky butter notes, it gains richness and complexity on a long, full finish. Drink now through 1998. 2,860 cases made. • $17 • (12/15/94) SS • **90**
Langtry Guenoc Valley Meritage White 1993: Classy, aromatic white. Spice, herb and honey notes surround a core of pear and melon. Has a lingering, subtle finish. Drinkable now. 1,100 cases made. • $17 • (04/30/95) • **88**

Langtry Lake County Meritage 1990: Lively, ripe and spicy, a graceful wine with concentrated plum, currant and black cherry flavors and vanilla and spice overtones, supple enough to be tempting to drink now. 2,731 cases made. • $35 • (11/15/93) • **91**

Langtry Meritage White Guenoc Valley 1991 • $17 • (02/15/93) • **84**

Meritage Lake County 1992: A touch on the green side, but elegant and appealing, with a pretty core of plum, wild berry and spice. Finishes with smooth, plush tannins that clamp down on the finish. 4,946 cases made. • $15 • (12/15/95) • **88**

Meritage Lake County 1991: A firm, crisp and chunky Bordeaux-style red, with a solid core of ripe black cherry, currant and plum flavors. It picks up a spice and buttery oak flavor on the finish, but its intense flavors and tannins still need to soften. Hold off until 1997. 3,938 cases made. • $15 • (10/31/94) SS • **89**

Meritage Lake County 1990: Comes alive with rich, complex Cabernet fruit that echoes currant, spice and cherry, with a pretty toasty, buttery character from new oak. Balanced and concentrated, adding a long, full finish that keeps pumping out the flavor. 66 percent Cabernet Sauvignon, 18 percent Cabernet Franc, 15 percent Merlot. 4,672 cases made. • $18 Ⓐ • (11/15/93) SS • **91**

Meritage Lake County 1989 • $17 • (11/15/92) • **83**

Meritage Langtry California 1992: Elegant and harmonious, a big, ripe style with plum and black cherry flavors and a good dose of tannin. Backward and tightly wound, it definitely needs cellaring into 1998 to soften and mature. 2,233 cases made. • $35 • (12/15/95) • **89**

Meritage Langtry California 1991: A stylish young wine with lots of flavor. Layers of plum, red cherry, raspberry and herb stay focused and linger on a long finish. Picks up cedary oak notes in the aftertaste and the tannins are firm but polished. Best after 1997 or 1998. 16,914 cases made. 1,265 cases made. • $35 • (09/30/94) • **91**

Meritage Langtry Lake County 1989 • $35 • (11/15/92) • **88**

Meritage Langtry Lake-Napa Counties 1988 • $35 • (11/15/91) • **86**

Meritage Langtry Lake-Napa Counties 1987 • $35 • (04/15/91) • **88**

Merlot Guenoc Valley 1985 • $15 • (03/31/89) • **85**

Merlot Lake-Napa Counties 1987 • $14 • (11/15/91) • **86**

Merlot Lake-Napa Counties 1986 • $12 • (06/15/90) • **80**

Petite Sirah Guenoc Valley 1988 • $10 • (08/31/91) • **86**

Petite Sirah Guenoc Valley 1985 • $7 • (02/15/89) • **83**

Petite Sirah Guenoc Valley 1984 • $7 • (11/15/87) • **77**

Petite Sirah North Coast 1992: Supple and aromatic, with pretty floral and fruity aromas. Lots of pure cherry and berry flavors with mineraly nuances. Manages to tame the tannins throughout. 6,180 cases made. • $14 • **89**

Petite Sirah North Coast 1990: Ripe and plummy, a generous red with a chewy texture and a spicy finish. Drinkable now, although the fine-textured tannins can use until 1997. • $13 • (09/30/94) • **84**

Petite Sirah North Coast 1989 • $14 • (06/30/92) • **82**

Port California 1992: Sweet and decidedly plummy, showing a distinctive range of spice and fruit flavors that echo plum on the solid finish. Tempting now, better from 1998. 912 cases made. • $15 • (05/31/95) • **89**

Sauvignon Blanc Guenoc Valley 1994: Snappy and fruity, a wine with a lot of zip and character, echoing peach, vanilla and herb on the lively finish. 2,277 cases made. • $11 • (07/31/95) • **87**

Sauvignon Blanc Guenoc Valley 1993: A smooth-textured, light and earthy white that's a dead-ringer for Chardonnay. 5,200 cases made. • $11 • (01/31/95) • **82**

Sauvignon Blanc Guenoc Valley 1992 • $11 • (03/15/94) • **87**

Sauvignon Blanc Guenoc Valley 1991 • $9 • (07/15/93) • **86**

Zinfandel California 1991 • $9 • (09/30/93) • **86**

Zinfandel California 1990 • $10 • (09/30/92) • **84**

Zinfandel California 1989 • $9 • (05/15/92) • **85**

Zinfandel California 1988 • $7 • (09/15/90) • **76**

Zinfandel Guenoc Valley 1987 • $8 • (05/15/90) • **84**

Zinfandel Guenoc Valley 1984 • $5 • (09/15/87) • **67**

Zinfandel Lake County 1985 • $5 • (03/31/89) • **79**

Zinfandel Lake County 1981 • $5 • (05/16/84) • **78**

Key: SS—Spectator Selection. CS—Cellar Selection. BB—Best Buy. $NA—Price not available. (BT)—Barrel tasting. Ⓐ—Auction Price.
Dates in parentheses represent the issues in which the ratings were published.

GUGLIELMO | CALIFORNIA

Cabernet Sauvignon Monterey County 1989: Mature, with earthy, vegetal flavors and more oak than it needs. 1,000 cases made. • $8 • (11/15/94) • **74**

Cabernet Sauvignon Santa Clara County Private Reserve 1986 • $12 • (11/15/93) • **75**

Chardonnay Monterey County 1992: Light and spicy, appealing for its apple and peach flavors, finishing bright. Drinkable now. 1,000 cases made. • $8 • (03/31/94) • **82**

Merlot Napa Valley 1990: Lean and a little astringent, but the toasty tobacco and grapey flavors come through. 1,000 cases made. • $8 • (09/15/94) • **78**

Pinot Noir Santa Clara Valley Private Reserve 1990 • $10 • (02/28/93) • **75**

Zinfandel Santa Clara Valley Private Reserve 1991: Tart and spicy, with notes of berry, pepper and mint. Turns earthy and metallic on the finish. 1,688 cases made. • $9 • (10/15/95) • **78**

Zinfandel Santa Clara Valley Private Reserve 1989: Earthy and gamy, with a ripe, raisiny edge to the flavors. Finishes with crisp, dry tannins and cedary oak. • $NA • (10/15/94) • **79**

Zinfandel Santa Clara Valley Private Reserve 1988 • $8 • (09/30/93) • **84**

GUILLIAMS | CALIFORNIA

Cabernet Sauvignon Napa Valley Spring Mountain District 1990: Supple and elegant, with herb, spice, light oak and ripe currant flavors. Well crafted, understated, pleasant enough to drink now, but should hold well through 1998. 420 cases made. • $15 • (11/15/94) • **86**

Cabernet Sauvignon Spring Mountain 1991: Appealing for its ripe plum and berry fruit flavors and supple, polished texture. Finishes with mild tannins, light oak and a dash of spice. Attractive now but smoother in 1998. 1,100 cases made. • $17 • (12/15/95) • **88**

GUNDLACH BUNDSCHU | CALIFORNIA

Bearitage Sonoma Valley 1990: Fruity, but sharp and aggressive, dominated by a mix of raspberry and strong herbal flavors. An intense wine that tastes more like Zinfandel than Cabernet. Crisp and exuberant, with a nice touch of cherry on the finish. 60 percent Cabernet Sauvignon, 30 percent Merlot and 10 percent Zinfandel. 2,200 cases made. • $10 • (05/15/93) • **81**

Cabernet Franc Rhinefarm Vineyards 1989 • $12 • (02/29/92) • **87**

Cabernet Franc Sonoma Valley Rhinefarm Vineyards 1987 • $12 • (09/15/90) • **89**

Cabernet Sauvignon Sonoma Valley 1986 • $9 • (11/15/89) • **87**

Cabernet Sauvignon Sonoma Valley 1981 • $7 • (03/01/89) • **84**

Cabernet Sauvignon Sonoma Valley Batto Ranch 1984 • $14 • (03/01/89) • **79**

Cabernet Sauvignon Sonoma Valley Batto Ranch 1983 • $10 • (03/01/89) • **77**

Cabernet Sauvignon Sonoma Valley Batto Ranch 1982 • $10 • (03/01/89) • **70**

Cabernet Sauvignon Sonoma Valley Batto Ranch 1981 • $10 • (03/01/89) • **88**

Cabernet Sauvignon Sonoma Valley Batto Ranch 1980 • $8 • (03/01/89) • **80**

Cabernet Sauvignon Sonoma Valley Batto Ranch 1979 • $8 • (03/01/89) • **80**

Cabernet Sauvignon Sonoma Valley Batto Ranch 1977 • $8 • (03/01/89) • **89**

Cabernet Sauvignon Sonoma Valley Rhinefarm Vineyards 1994: Herbaceous with a wild berry edge, turning to bell pepper on the finish. 7,000 cases made. • $15 • (05/31/95) • **80-84** (BT)

Cabernet Sauvignon Sonoma Valley Rhinefarm Vineyards 1992: Ripe, juicy cherry and plum flavors turn supple and polished. The pretty aftertaste echoes fruit. Has enough tannic structure to cellar into 1997. 5,114 cases made. • $15 • (10/31/95) • **87**

Cabernet Sauvignon Sonoma Valley Rhinefarm Vineyards 1991: Laced with herb, green olive and spicy bell pepper notes, this is supple and polished. Picks up complexity on the finish where the currant flavors come together. Can stand short-term cellaring. 5,400 cases made. • $15 • (10/31/94) • **88**

Cabernet Sauvignon Sonoma Valley Rhinefarm Vineyards 1990: Firm and chunky, an austere style that never quite shows enough flavor to beat the tannins, flavors edging toward green olive and tobacco rather than fruit. Best after 1998. Tasted twice with consistent results. 3,200 cases made. • $14 • (11/15/93) • **83**

Cabernet Sauvignon Sonoma Valley Rhinefarm Vineyards 1989 • $15 • (11/15/92) • **80**

Cabernet Sauvignon Sonoma Valley Rhinefarm Vineyards 1987 • $15 • (05/15/91) • **85**

Cabernet Sauvignon Sonoma Valley Rhinefarm Vineyards 1986 • $12 • (03/01/89) • **89**

Cabernet Sauvignon Sonoma Valley Rhinefarm Vineyards 1985 • $12 • (03/31/89) • **78**

Cabernet Sauvignon Sonoma Valley Rhinefarm Vineyards 1984 • $9 • (03/01/89) • **85**

Cabernet Sauvignon Sonoma Valley Rhinefarm Vineyards 1983 • $9 • (03/01/89) • **73**

Cabernet Sauvignon Sonoma Valley Rhinefarm Vineyards 1982 • $9 • (03/01/89) • **65**

Cabernet Sauvignon Sonoma Valley Rhinefarm Vineyards 1974: Turns thin and metallic with a mature, weedy Cabernet edge. Finishes with earthy, gitty tannins. • $40 • (11/15/94) • **74**

Cabernet Sauvignon Sonoma Valley Rhinefarm Vineyards Reserve 1989 • $24 • (11/15/93) • **84**

Cabernet Sauvignon Sonoma Valley Rhinefarm Vineyards Reserve 1986 • $25 • (08/31/91) • **83**

Cabernet Sauvignon Sonoma Valley Rhinefarm Vineyards Reserve 1982 • $20 • (09/15/87) • **71**

Cabernet Sauvignon Sonoma Valley Rhinefarm Vineyards Reserve 1981 • $20 • (03/01/89) • **90**

Cabernet Sauvignon Sonoma Valley Rhinefarm Vineyards Vintage Reserve 1994: Bold and ripe, with a cherry jam edge to the currant and berry notes. Finishes with good depth and extract. • $NA • (05/31/95) • **85-89** (BT)

Cabernet Sauvignon Sonoma Valley Rhinefarm Vineyards Vintage Reserve 1987 • $22 • (07/31/92) • **89**

Chardonnay Sonoma Valley 1991 • $12 • (10/31/93) • **83**

Chardonnay Sonoma Valley Sangiacomo Ranch Special Selection 1993: Soft, almost plush with apple, pear and spice flavors that glide smoothly through the fresh, lively finish. Ready now. 1,300 cases made. • $15 • (11/15/95) • **89**

Chardonnay Sonoma Valley Sangiacomo Ranch Special Selection 1991 • $16 • (07/15/93) • **85**

Gewürztraminer Sonoma Valley 1994: Dry but distinctly fruity, centering its flavors around peach and melon. Not much to say Gewurz, but a nice sipping wine. 4,000 cases made. • $9 • (11/15/95) • **84**

Gewürztraminer Sonoma Valley Rhinefarm Vineyards 1992 • $8 • (01/31/94) • **77**

Gewürztraminer Sonoma Valley Rhinefarm Vineyards 1991 • $7 • (11/15/92) • **78**

Merlot Sonoma Valley Rhinefarm Vineyards 1993: Tart and earthy, with dry wild berry and cherry flavors. Finishes with a tannic edge. 9,900 cases made. • $15 • **81**

Merlot Sonoma Valley Rhinefarm Vineyards 1992: A wild berry and black cherry edge leads to a slightly oaky finish. 9,000 cases made. • $16 • (01/31/95) • **88**

Merlot Sonoma Valley Rhinefarm Vineyards 1990 • $16 • (10/15/93) • **85**

Merlot Sonoma Valley Rhinefarm Vineyards 1989 • $16 • (05/31/92) • **80**

Merlot Sonoma Valley Rhinefarm Vineyards 1988 • $20 • (05/31/91) • **81**

Merlot Sonoma Valley Rhinefarm Vineyards 1987 • $18 • (10/31/89) SS • **93**

Merlot Sonoma Valley Rhinefarm Vineyards 1986 • $19 • (12/31/88) • **91**

Merlot Sonoma Valley Rhinefarm Vineyards 1985 • $20 • (02/29/88) SS • **92**

Merlot Sonoma Valley Rhinefarm Vineyards 1984 • $20 • (02/28/87) • **88**

Merlot Sonoma Valley Rhinefarm Vineyards 1983 • $15 Ⓐ • (05/01/86) • **92**

Merlot Sonoma Valley Rhinefarm Vineyards 1982 • $19 • (10/01/85) • **88**

Pinot Noir Sonoma Valley Rhinefarm Vineyards 1993: Offers a medium bodied core of cedar, plum and currant, finishing with a spicy oak edge. Drink now. 2,000 cases made. • $14 • **85**

Pinot Noir Sonoma Valley Rhinefarm Vineyards 1992: Lean and trim, medium-bodied, exhibiting a crisp, narrow band of spice and cherry. Drinkable now. 2,800 cases made. • $14 • (03/31/95) • **82**

Pinot Noir Sonoma Valley Rhinefarm Vineyards 1991 • $14 • (02/28/94) • **78**

Pinot Noir Sonoma Valley Rhinefarm Vineyards 1989 • $14 • (10/31/91) • **83**

Pinot Noir Sonoma Valley Rhinefarm Vineyards 1988 • $12 • (02/28/91) • **88**

Pinot Noir Sonoma Valley Rhinefarm Vineyards 1986 • $10 • (06/15/88) • **89**

Pinot Noir Sonoma Valley Rhinefarm Vineyards 1985 • $10 • (02/29/88) • **81**

Pinot Noir Sonoma Valley Rhinefarm Vineyards 1984 • $10 • (06/30/87) • **53**

Pinot Noir Sonoma Valley Rhinefarm Vineyards 1982 • $9 • (05/01/84) • **75**

Riesling Sonoma Valley Dresel's Sonoma Riesling 1993: Light and fruity, showing nice pear and nectarine flavors that linger softly on the finish. 1,200 cases made. • $9 • (06/15/95) • **83**

Riesling Sonoma Valley Dresel's Sonoma Riesling 1992 • $9 • (08/31/93) • **82**

Sonoma Red #2 Sonoma Valley NV • $5 • (11/15/89) • **77**

Zinfandel Sonoma Valley 1992: A claret style that's fresh and vibrant, with black cherry, plum and buttery toast flavors. Folded neatly together in complex and enticing style. Drinks well now. 1,325 cases made. • $10 • (09/15/94) SS • **92**

Zinfandel Sonoma Valley 1991 • $10 • (09/30/93) • **85**

Zinfandel Sonoma Valley 1989 • $7 • (07/31/91) • **84**

Zinfandel Sonoma Valley 1988 • $7 • (05/31/90) BB • **88**

Zinfandel Sonoma Valley 1987 • $7 • (03/31/89) • **87**

Zinfandel Sonoma Valley Rhinefarm Vineyards 1993: A touch earthy, but the bright, lively berry flavors balance it out. Picks up some sour cherry nuances on the elegant finish. Well crafted. 1,200 cases made. • $14 • (10/15/95) • **88**

Zinfandel Sonoma Valley Rhinefarm Vineyards 1990 • $9 • (09/30/92) • **87**

Zinfandel Sonoma Valley Rhinefarm Vineyards 1989 • $12 • (07/31/91) • **87**

Zinfandel Sonoma Valley Rhinefarm Vineyards 1988 • $10 • (12/15/90) • **88**

Zinfandel Sonoma Valley Rhinefarm Vineyards 1987 • $8 • (09/15/89) • **71**

Zinfandel Sonoma Valley Rhinefarm Vineyards 1986 • $8 • (09/15/88) • **90**

Zinfandel Sonoma Valley Rhinefarm Vineyards 1985 • $8 • (02/29/88) • **84**

Zinfandel Sonoma Valley Rhinefarm Vineyards 1984 • $7 • (04/30/87) BB • **87**

Zinfandel Sonoma Valley Rhinefarm Vineyards 1982 • $7 • (02/16/86) • **87**

HACIENDA | CALIFORNIA

Antares Sonoma County 1987 • $28 • (11/15/90) • **91**

Antares Sonoma County 1986 • $28 • (07/31/89) • **91**

Cabernet Sauvignon California Clair de Lune 1992: Earthy, with a shallow band of sweet-tasting Cabernet. An oddity. 5,000 cases made. • $7 • (11/15/94) • **72**

Cabernet Sauvignon Sonoma County 1987 • $15 • (11/15/92) • **81**

Cabernet Sauvignon Sonoma County 1986 • $15 • (11/15/91) • **87**

Cabernet Sauvignon Sonoma County 1985 • $15 • (09/30/90) • **83**

Cabernet Sauvignon Sonoma Valley 1983 • $11 • (05/31/88) • **86**

Cabernet Sauvignon Sonoma Valley 1982 • $11 • (09/01/85) • **63**

Cabernet Sauvignon Sonoma Valley Estate Reserve 1985 • $18 • (11/15/92) • **78**

Cabernet Sauvignon Sonoma Valley Estate Reserve 1984 • $18 • (05/31/91) • **87**

HAGAFEN

Cabernet Sauvignon Sonoma Valley Selected Reserve 1982 • $18 • (03/31/87) • **86**
Chardonnay California Clair de Lune 1994: Soft, fragrant floral and honey notes, but a little funky, too, its modest fruit hanging on the finish. Ready now. 6,000 cases made. • $7 • (05/15/96) • **81**
Chardonnay California Clair de Lune 1993: Soft and ripe, gentle enough to show off the pear and floral flavors with delicacy. Drinkable now. 16,000 cases made. • $6 • (02/28/95) • **83**
Chardonnay California Clair de Lune 1992: Shows some interesting peach and nectarine flavors that are elegant and racy, picking up crisp grapefruit notes on the finish. Ready now. 4,000 cases made. • $7 • (06/30/94) • **84**
Merlot California Clair de Lune 1992: Light and fruity, with currant and strawberry notes and mild tannins. 4,000 cases made. • $8 • (09/15/94) • **81**
Pinot Noir Sonoma Valley 1982 • $12 • (12/16/84) • **85**
Pinot Noir Sonoma Valley Estate Reserve 1989 • $17 • (11/30/92) • **81**
Pinot Noir Sonoma Valley Estate Reserve 1987 • $15 • (10/31/90) • **78**
Pinot Noir Sonoma Valley Estate Reserve 1986 • $15 • (06/15/88) • **80**
Pinot Noir Sonoma Valley Estate Reserve 1985 • $15 • (06/15/88) • **86**

HAGAFEN | CALIFORNIA

Cabernet Sauvignon Napa Valley 1994: Intense, deeply colored and marked by a potent menthol-herbal edge which tends to dominate. 1,000 cases made. • $24 • (05/31/95) • **85-89** (BT)
Cabernet Sauvignon Napa Valley 1993: Smooth and graceful, a veil of tough tannins covering the bright currant and blackberry flavors. Try in 1998. 900 cases made. • $20 • (12/15/95) • **83**
Cabernet Sauvignon Napa Valley 1990: Heavy-handed with dusty, woody oak flavors, the lingering impression is a one-dimensional wine. 1,200 cases made. • $20 • (05/15/94) • **77**
Cabernet Sauvignon Napa Valley 1989 • $20 • (12/15/92) • **68**
Cabernet Sauvignon Napa Valley 1988 • $20 • (03/31/91) • **88**
Cabernet Sauvignon Napa Valley 1987 • $20 • (04/30/90) • **88**
Cabernet Sauvignon Napa Valley Reserve 1989: Smoky and well oaked with a strong cedar and dill edge, the currant and cherry fruit struggles to work its way through. Comes across as clumsy and disjointed, cellaring into 1998 may help. 600 cases made. • $28 • (12/15/95) • **84**
Cabernet Sauvignon Napa Valley Reserve 1988 • $28 • (03/31/93) • **85**
Chardonnay Napa Valley 1992: Crisp, spicy and fruity, a simple wine with a nice range of peach, pear, honey and vanilla aromas and flavors, all in a lean package. Drinkable now. 1,300 cases made. • $14 • (06/30/94) • **85**
Chardonnay Napa Valley 1991 • $13 • (07/15/93) • **86**
Chardonnay Napa Valley Reserve 1991: Soft and generous, ripe with appealing pear and spice flavors. 1,991 cases made. • $17 • (06/30/94) • **82**
Harmonia Napa Valley 1994: Tough and leathery, showing hard tannins and just a trace of fruit. • $8 • (11/30/95) • **77**
Johannisberg Riesling 1991 • $9 • (05/31/92) • **84**
Johannisberg Riesling Napa Valley 1994: Fresh, fruity and appealing, lightly sweet and loaded with peach, nectarine and floral flavors. Drink it young. • $8 • (06/15/95) • **86**
Pinot Noir Blanc California 1989 • $6 • (03/31/91) • **74**
Pinot Noir Napa Valley 1991 • $11 • (02/28/94) • **77**
Red Table Wine Napa Valley NV • $7 • (06/30/92) • **75**

HAHN | CALIFORNIA

Cabernet Sauvignon Monterey 1989 • $10 • (06/15/93) • **73**
Cabernet Sauvignon Monterey 1988 • $10 • (11/15/92) • **80**
Cabernet Sauvignon Santa Lucia Highlands 1992: Austere, with firm tannins and a rustic, cedary edge to the Cabernet fruit, focusing on cherry and plum. 7,984 cases made. • $10 • (08/31/95) • **83**
Cabernet Sauvignon Santa Lucia Highlands 1991: An herbaceous style with modest fruit and gritty tannins. 4,159 cases made. • $10 • (11/15/94) • **80**
Cabernet Sauvignon Santa Lucia Highlands 1990: Simple and correct, with herb, wood and currant notes that turn tannic and spicy on the finish. A good value at • $10. Ready now. 10,080 cases made. • $10 • (05/15/94) • **80**
Chardonnay Monterey 1994: Crisp, simple and appealing, a little short on fruit but adding citrus notes on the finish. 12,391 cases made. • $10 • (10/31/95) • **81**
Chardonnay Monterey 1993: Young and fruity, offering ripe pear and apple notes that pick up a spice edge on the finish. Drinkable now. 2,868 cases made. • $10 • (03/31/95) • **85**
Chardonnay Monterey 1992: Ripe, spicy and generous, nicely polished, smooth-textured, with oodles of pineapple, pear and honey flavor cascading across the palate. Delicious now through 1997. 8,090 cases made. • $10 • (05/31/94) SS • **89**
Chardonnay Monterey 1991 • $10 • (06/15/93) • **83**
Merlot 1990 • $10 • (05/31/92) • **83**
Merlot 1989 • $10 • (05/31/92) • **86**
Merlot Monterey 1992: Chewy and tannic, hard to get a handle on it. The modest currant flavors struggle to break free of the tannin. Try after 1997, but no promises. 15,000 cases made. • $10 • (09/15/94) • **81**
Merlot Monterey 1991 • $10 • (06/15/93) • **84**
Merlot Santa Lucia Highlands 1994: Cedary oak flavors, punctuated by strong herb, particularly dill, and green bean accents. 18,000 cases made. • $11 • **78**
Merlot Santa Lucia Highlands 1993: A vegetal streak adds flashes of bell pepper, but it gathers enough plum and cherry flavor to create interest. 25,000 cases made. • $10 • (12/15/95) • **82**

HALLCREST | CALIFORNIA

Barbera El Dorado Ritchie Vineyard 1990 • $12 • (11/30/92) • **80**
Cabernet Sauvignon El Dorado County Covington Vineyard 1990: Ripe and vibrant, with rich, spicy black cherry, currant and earth notes. This is a well-crafted Cabernet that can stand cellaring for the short term, try in 1997. 540 cases made. • $19 • (11/15/94) • **86**
Cabernet Sauvignon El Dorado County De Cascabel Vineyard Proprietors Reserve 1990: Distinctive for its ripe wild berry and cherry flavors, firm and compact, with ample tannins. Best after 1998. 54 cases made. • $13 • (11/15/94) • **85**
Cabernet Sauvignon El Dorado Covington Vineyard 1989 • $12 • (11/15/92) • **76**
Cabernet Sauvignon El Dorado De Cascabel Vineyard 1989 • $14 • (06/15/93) • **70**
Cabernet Sauvignon El Dorado De Cascabel Vineyard 1988 • $15 • (11/15/92) • **81**
Cabernet Sauvignon El Dorado De Cascabel Vineyard 1987 • $13 • (11/15/91) • **83**
Cabernet Sauvignon Santa Cruz Mountains Beauregard Ranch Proprietors Reserve 1990: A rustic style showing an earthy streak to the wild cherry and raspberry flavors. Finishes with firm, crisp tannins that suggest cellaring until about 1999. 33 cases made. • $23 • (11/15/94) • **84**
Chardonnay California Fortuyn Cuvée 1991: Earthy, bordering on sour, misses the mark. Finishes with strong, oaky flavors. Marginal. 586 cases made. • $9 • (03/31/95) • **72**
Chardonnay Santa Cruz Mountains Meyley Vineyard 1991: Firm, compact and exotic-if not funky-caramel, pineapple and pear flavors and an earthy finish. 616 cases made. • $17 • (03/31/95) • **77**
Clos de Jeannine California 1990 • $7 • (05/31/93) • **84**
Clos de Jeannine California 1989 • $8 • (10/31/91) • **82**
Merlot El Dorado County De Cascabel Vineyard 1989 • $15 • (05/31/92) • **74**
Merlot El Dorado County De Cascabel Vineyard 1988 • $15 • (05/31/92) • **78**
Merlot El Dorado County De Cascabel Vineyards Proprietors Reserve 1991: Firm and compact, but with a pretty beam of plum and currant that peeks through and stays on a long, full finish. Has the tannins to age, best after 1997. Another impressive wine from Hallcrest. 60 cases made. • $19 • (11/15/94) • **87**

Key: SS—Spectator Selection. CS—Cellar Selection. BB—Best Buy. $NA—Price not available. (BT)—Barrel tasting. Ⓐ—Auction Price.
Dates in parentheses represent the issues in which the ratings were published.

Merlot El Dorado De Cascabel Vineyard 1991 • $14 • (07/15/93) • **83**
Syrah California Doe Mill Cuvée 1989 • $7 • (04/30/91) • **86**
Veilig (Sanctuary) Cabernet Blend California NV: Leans heavily on spicy bell pepper and pickle barrel flavors. Ready now. 1,022 cases made. • $11 • (11/15/94) • **79**
White Riesling Santa Cruz Mountains Estate Vineyard 1991 • $19 • (06/15/93) • **73**
Zinfandel California Doe Mill Vineyard 1990 • $8 • (10/15/92) • **83**
Zinfandel Santa Cruz Mountains Beauregard Ranch Proprietors Reserve 1988 • $13 • (10/15/92) • **76**

HAMBRECHT | CALIFORNIA

Cabernet Sauvignon Dry Creek Valley Bradford Mountain 1991: Austere and tannic, with a narrow range of currant and cherry flavor. Best after 1998. 500 cases made. • $14 • (11/15/94) • **83**
Cabernet Sauvignon Dry Creek Valley Bradford Mountain Vineyard 1990: Firm and chunky, with a nice core of currant and plum fruit, shaded by hints of spice and smoke. A solid wine that seems a bit raw now, but should be at its best from 1997. 250 cases made. • $13 • (11/15/93) • **86**
Zinfandel Dry Creek Valley 1992: Supple and generous, with an earthy edge to the cherry and wild berry flavors. Drinks well now, but can age through 1997. 250 cases made. • $14 • (10/15/94) • **86**

HAMPTON | NEW YORK

Sunset Blush North Fork of Long Island 1987 • $6 • (12/15/88) • **83**

HANDLEY | CALIFORNIA

Blanc de Blancs Anderson Valley 1990: Ripe and elegant, featuring fresh apple, toast, pear and melon notes, an altogether complex and refreshing style that puts the fruit up front. 970 cases made. • $18 • (12/15/95) • **88**
Blanc de Blancs Anderson Valley 1989: Crisp and refreshing, with a tight band of pear, vanilla and spice notes that turn earthy on the finish. Ready now. 1,000 cases made. • $18 • (12/31/94) • **84**
Blanc de Blancs Anderson Valley 1988 • $18 • (12/31/93) • **84**
Brut Anderson Valley 1990: Clean and correct, offering ripe, spicy pear, apple, toast and vanilla flavors that play straight ahead, showing less focus on the finish. 812 cases made. • $15 • (12/31/95) • **87**
Brut Anderson Valley 1989: Crisp and focused, with spicy black cherry, pear and vanilla notes that finish slightly astringent. Shows off the Pinot Noir (70 percent of the blend) more than the Chardonnay. 1,374 cases made. • $15 • (12/31/94) • **86**
Brut Anderson Valley 1988 • $15 • (05/31/93) • **86**
Brut Anderson Valley 1984 • $15 • (10/15/88) • **81**
Brut Rosé Anderson Valley 1990: Pretty color, with fresh black cherry and strawberry flavors that pick up a slightly tannic edge on the finish. Ready now. 200 cases made. • $17 • (12/31/94) • **85**
Brut Rosé Anderson Valley 1989 • $17 • (12/31/93) • **83**
Brut Rosé Anderson Valley 1988 • $17 • (05/31/93) • **86**
Brut Rosé Anderson Valley 1984 • $17 • (12/31/88) • **75**
Chardonnay Anderson Valley 1993: A strong leesy character adds a slightly sour note to this otherwise solid white. 1,266 cases made. • $11 • (06/15/96) • **81**
Chardonnay Anderson Valley 1992: Crisp and elegant, with ripe apple and citrus notes, finishing with a grapefruit edge. 2,000 cases made. • $12 • (07/31/95) • **83**
Chardonnay Anderson Valley 1991: Lightly fruity with simple spice and pear flavors. Drinks easy now. 3,100 cases made. • $12 • (06/30/94) • **80**
Chardonnay Dry Creek Valley 1993: Marked by a refreshing lemon-citrus edge, it's an elegant, subtle style that's best paired with delicate fare. 2,500 cases made. • $15 • (06/30/96) • **87**
Chardonnay Dry Creek Valley 1992: Tart with crisp grapefruit, citrus and spicy pear notes on the finish. 2,600 cases made. • $16 • (07/31/95) • **84**
Chardonnay Dry Creek Valley 1991: Simple, light and fruity with spice, pear and toasty oak notes. Solid but unexceptional. Ready now. 4,200 cases made. • $16 • (06/30/94) • **80**
Gewürztraminer Anderson Valley 1994: Light in flavor and in texture, a modest wine on all counts but pleasant to sip. 850 cases made. • $9 • (11/15/95) • **79**
Gewürztraminer Anderson Valley 1993: On the dry side, but the nectarine and melon flavors are appealing. Should make a wonderful apéritif. 1,550 cases made. • $8 • (02/28/95) • **85**
Pinot Noir Anderson Valley 1994: Serves up lots of ripe plum and cherry flavor but it comes across as one-dimensional, adding a tannic edge to the texture. 487 cases made. • $15 • (02/29/96) • **84**
Pinot Noir Anderson Valley 1993: Medium weight, with crisp plum and cherry fruit of modest depth. Appealing now. 1,050 cases made. • $15 • (12/31/95) • **84**
Pinot Noir Anderson Valley 1992: Laced with herb, cola and cherry flavors. Medium-bodied, young, and has an alluring, supple texture. 1,140 cases made. • $14 • (10/31/94) • **84**
Pinot Noir Anderson Valley 1991 • $13 • (06/15/93) • **84**
Sauvignon Blanc Dry Creek Valley 1993: Ripe, nicely focused pear, spice and a touch of herb, beautifully balanced style that centers around fruit. 2,400 cases made. • $9 • (08/31/95) • **87**
Sauvignon Blanc Dry Creek Valley 1992: Soft, fruity and pleasant, its slightly citrusy overtones adding a nice extra touch. 3,000 cases made. • $9 • (08/31/94) • **85**
Sauvignon Blanc Dry Creek Valley 1991 • $8 • (07/31/93) • **81**

HANNA | CALIFORNIA

Cabernet Sauvignon Alexander Valley 1992: Marked by a gamy edge, it offers enough cherry and berry fruit to hold your interst. Finishes with mild tannins. 1,400 cases made. • $16 • (12/15/95) • **84**
Cabernet Sauvignon Alexander Valley 1991: Ripe and firmly tannic, showing a tight core of black cherry and cedary oak flavors. Drinkable now. 3,095 cases made. • $14 • (02/28/95) • **85**
Cabernet Sauvignon Alexander Valley 1990: Soft, supple, with an underlying intensity of currant and blackberry aromas and flavors that persist into a solid finish that echoes fruit nicely. Drinkable now. 1,300 cases made. • $18 • (11/15/93) • **87**
Cabernet Sauvignon Sonoma County 1988 • $16 • (11/15/91) • **86**
Cabernet Sauvignon Sonoma County 1987 • $16 • (08/31/90) • **80**
Cabernet Sauvignon Sonoma County 1986 • $16 • (07/31/89) • **87**
Cabernet Sauvignon Sonoma Valley 1985 • $14 • (06/30/88) • **86**
Chardonnay Russian River Valley Reserve 1993: Pleasant, with a spicy edge to the ripe pear and apple flavors. Finishes with nice toasty oak and vanilla notes. 555 cases made. • $18 • (06/30/96) • **85**
Chardonnay Russian River Valley Reserve 1992: Supple and fruity, displaying a spicy, toasty edge to the ripe pear and creamy vanilla flavors. 487 cases made. • $16 • (02/28/95) • **85**
Chardonnay Sonoma County 1994: Smooth, adding a peppermint note to the modest apple and spice flavors. Ready now. 1,820 cases made. • $14 • (04/30/96) • **84**
Chardonnay Sonoma County 1992: An earthy, leafy edge leads to complex, toasty pear and spice flavors. Tasted twice, with consistent notes. 2,960 cases made. • $14 • (04/30/95) • **84**
Chardonnay Sonoma County 1991 • $14 • (04/15/94) • **86**
Merlot Alexander Valley 1993: Ripe and spicy, with intense wild berry, plum and cherry flavors, turning chunky and tannic on the finish. Could use a little more polish, which age may provide. Try now. 1,075 cases made. • $16 • (06/15/96) • **87**
Merlot Alexander Valley 1991 • $14 • (12/31/93) • **82**
Merlot Alexander Valley 1990 • $14 • (12/15/92) • **87**
Pinot Noir Russian River Valley 1992 • $14 • (01/31/94) • **86**
Sauvignon Blanc Sonoma County 1994: Bright and fruity. Snappy, vibrant anise-scented pear and vanilla flavors. 11,000 cases made. • $10 • (08/31/95) • **87**
Sauvignon Blanc Sonoma County 1993: Crisp and lemony, a spicy wine with polished texture, finishing light but persistent. 6,000 cases made. • $10 • (08/31/94) • **85**
Sauvignon Blanc Sonoma County 1992 • $8 • (08/31/93) BB • **86**

HANZELL | CALIFORNIA

Cabernet Sauvignon Sonoma Valley 1990: A racy style typical of Hanzell, with weedy bell pepper, olive and earth flavors. Best to cellar until 1997. 360 cases made. • $20 • (11/15/94) • **83**

Cabernet Sauvignon Sonoma Valley 1989 • $19 • (11/15/93) • **82**

Cabernet Sauvignon Sonoma Valley 1988 • $22 • (11/15/92) • **82**

Cabernet Sauvignon Sonoma Valley 1987 • $22 • (11/15/91) • **84**

Cabernet Sauvignon Sonoma Valley 1986 • $22 • (10/31/90) • **90**

Cabernet Sauvignon Sonoma Valley 1982 • $20 • (03/31/87) • **76**

Chardonnay Sonoma Valley 1992: Clean, compact, featuring a ripe core of pear, apple and light oak shadings. Not the extra dimensions usually found in this wine, but it should improve in the cellar. Try in 1998. 1,700 cases made. • $25 • (10/31/95) • **87**

Chardonnay Sonoma Valley 1991: Big, ripe and assertive, with nectarine, pear and spice notes that stay focused on the finish. Can stand short-term cellaring for the wood flavors to soften and fold into the others. 1,550 cases made. • $25 • (06/30/94) • **87**

Pinot Noir Sonoma County 1989 • $19 • (02/28/94) • **87**

Pinot Noir Sonoma Valley 1991: Earthy and firm, with intense tannins. Has spicy stewed plum and anise flavors. Best to age until 1997 and let soften a bit. 750 cases made. • $19 • (06/30/95) • **86**

Pinot Noir Sonoma Valley 1990: Rustic, with chunky, earthy plum and black cherry flavor that's in an awkward phase, but the core of fruit is complex. 800 cases made. • $21 • (03/31/95) • **85**

Pinot Noir Sonoma Valley 1988 • $19 • (02/28/93) • **88**

Pinot Noir Sonoma Valley 1987 • $19 • (02/15/92) • **84**

Pinot Noir Sonoma Valley 1986 • $19 • (10/31/90) • **84**

Pinot Noir Sonoma Valley 1985 • $19 • (03/31/90) • **82**

Pinot Noir Sonoma Valley 1984 • $17 • (05/31/89) • **78**

Pinot Noir Sonoma Valley 1983 • $17 • (04/15/88) • **70**

Pinot Noir Sonoma Valley 1981 • $17 • (08/31/86) • **93**

HARBOR WINERY | CALIFORNIA

Merlot Napa Valley Narsai David Vineyard 1991: Lean and earthy, a crisp red with modest flavors. 337 cases made. • $9 • (09/15/94) • **78**

HARGRAVE | NEW YORK

Cabernet Franc North Fork of Long Island 1988 • $14 • (06/30/91) • **81**

Cabernet Sauvignon North Fork of Long Island 1986 • $22 • (12/15/88) • **87**

Cabernet Sauvignon North Fork of Long Island 1985 • $22 • (12/15/88) • **82**

Cabernet Sauvignon North Fork of Long Island 1983 • $22 • (12/15/88) • **86**

Cabernet Sauvignon North Fork of Long Island Reserve 1982 • $22 • (12/15/88) • **70**

Cabernet Sauvignon North Fork of Long Island Vintner's Signature 1981 • $29 • (12/15/88) • **78**

Cabernet Sauvignon North Fork of Long Island Vintner's Signature 1980 • $NA • (12/15/88) • **79**

Merlot North Fork of Long Island 1988 • $18 • (06/30/91) • **81**

Merlot North Fork of Long Island 1985 • $19 • (12/15/88) • **85**

Merlot North Fork of Long Island 1980 • $NA • (12/15/88) • **78**

HARLAN | CALIFORNIA

Napa Valley 1991: Tough and chewy, but very flavorful. Tiers of currant, leather, anise and cherry all fold together in a tight aftertaste. Tannins pack a wallop, best in 1999 or 2000. Tasted twice, with consistent notes. 935 cases made. • $65 • (11/30/95) • **90**

Key: SS—Spectator Selection. CS—Cellar Selection. BB—Best Buy. $NA—Price not available. (BT)—Barrel tasting. (A)—Auction Price.
Dates in parentheses represent the issues in which the ratings were published.

HARMONY CELLARS | CALIFORNIA

Cabernet Sauvignon Paso Robles 1990: Mature with earthy, cedary, tarry flavors that miss the mark for a young wine. Turns to tea and tobacco on the finish. 450 cases made. • $12 • (11/15/93) • **77**

Cabernet Sauvignon Paso Robles 1989 • $12 • (11/15/92) • **85**

Chardonnay Paso Robles 1992: An oaky style with toast, butter and vanilla flavors, but also nice pear and peach notes. Ready now. 425 cases made. • $11 • (06/30/94) • **82**

Pinot Noir Paso Robles 1990 • $11 • (02/28/93) • **88**

HARRISON | CALIFORNIA

Cabernet Sauvignon Napa Valley 1994: Austere with trim cherry and currant flavors that hold their own, but don't at this point show extra dimensions. 950 cases made. • $35 • (05/31/95) • **85-89** (BT)

Cabernet Sauvignon Napa Valley 1992: Packs in lots of flavor, layered with currant, plum, cherry and mint, showing excellent depth and richness through the long, full aftertaste. Best from 1997 on. 916 cases made. • $33 • (11/15/95) • **90**

Cabernet Sauvignon Napa Valley 1991: Lean and a bit green around the edges with a narrow, crisp band of cherry and currant flavor. Needs cellaring to soften and evolve, best after 1998. 830 cases made. • $30 • (11/15/94) • **82**

Cabernet Sauvignon Napa Valley 1990: Young, ripe and intense, with a tight, firm core of currant, cherry and spicy oak flavors. Raw and unevolved now, but shows intensity and depth, may reveal more harmony and finesse with time in the bottle. Drink after 1996. • $30 • (07/15/93) • **87**

Cabernet Sauvignon Napa Valley 1989 • $30 • (04/15/92) • **91**

Cabernet Sauvignon Napa Valley Reserve 1990: Ripe, rich, smooth and supple, with polished currant, oak and spice flavors. Full-bodied, compact and tightly wound, finishing with chewy tannins. Best to cellar into 1998. 45 cases made. • $40 • (10/15/94) • **91**

Chardonnay Napa Valley 1994: Smooth, ripe and creamy, the pretty honey, pear, spice and vanilla flavors picking up a trace of tangerine and nutmeg on the finish. Wonderful sense of harmony and finesse. 870 cases made. • $26 • (04/30/96) • **90**

Chardonnay Napa Valley 1993: Pleasantly fruity in a medium-weight style, with pear, apple and spicy flavors that fold together nicely. 920 cases made. • $26 • (07/31/95) • **86**

Chardonnay Napa Valley 1992: Young and firm, with a strong woody flavor, but it has the ripe pear and spicy Chardonnay fruit to stand up to the oak. The alcohol stands out on the finish, but this is ready now through 1997. 950 cases made. • $24 • (06/30/94) • **87**

Chardonnay Napa Valley 1991 • $24 • (07/15/93) • **88**

HART | CALIFORNIA

Cabernet Sauvignon Temecula Hansen Vineyard 1989 • $15 • (11/15/92) • **82**

Merlot Temecula 1989 • $15 • (05/31/92) • **80**

HARTFORD COURT | CALIFORNIA

Pinot Noir Russian River Valley Arrendell Vineyard 1994: Smooth, ripe, rich and polished, delivering a complex array of plum, cherry, wild berry and toasty oak. The finish shows off a range of lingering flavors. 400 cases made. • $42 • (02/29/96) • **89**

Pinot Noir Russian River Valley Dutton Ranch-Sanchietti Vineyard 1994: Appealing for its ripe, sweet plum and black cherry flavor, it shows a shade more tannin on the finish, so short-term cellaring is advised. Finishes with a meaty edge. 400 cases made. • $35 • (02/29/96) • **86**

Zinfandel Russian River Valley Hartford Vineyard 1994: An oaky style, boasting prominent buttery, toasty notes which lead to a rich core of currant and cherry and finish in complex flavors and aromas. Can stand short-term cellaring into 1997. 500 cases made. • $30 • (04/30/96) • **92**

HART'S DESIRE | CALIFORNIA

Chardonnay Edna Valley MacGregor Vineyard 1992: Crisp, with a trim band of citrus and pear flavors. Drinkable now. 190 cases made. • $14 • (03/31/95) • **84**

Zinfandel Russian River Valley Ponzo Vineyard 1994: Ripe, flavorful plum and berry in a rustic style that lacks the special qualities of the best. 150 cases made. • $14 • (05/15/96) • **85**

HARTWELL | CALIFORNIA

Cabernet Sauvignon Stags Leap District 1992: Supple and harmonious, with a pretty core of polished cherry and berry flavors, finishing with a nice dash of toasty oak, spice and mild tannins. Try in 1998. 200 cases made. • $50 • (11/15/95) • **90**

Cabernet Sauvignon Stags Leap District 1991: Ripe, round, smooth and supple, this wine delivers a pretty core of currant, cedar and spice, finishing with smooth tannins and toasty oak nuances. Needs short-term cellaring to soften, best after 1996. • $55 • (11/15/94) • **92**

HAVENS | CALIFORNIA

Merlot Carneros Napa Valley Truchard Vineyard 1988 • $20 • (08/31/91) • **76**

Merlot Carneros Napa Valley Truchard Vineyard Reserve 1989 • $20 • (05/31/92) • **82**

Merlot Carneros Truchard Vineyard Reserve 1990 • $20 • (06/15/93) • **88**

Merlot Napa Valley 1991 • $15 • (07/15/93) • **90**

Merlot Napa Valley 1990 • $15 • (06/15/93) • **87**

Merlot Napa Valley 1989 • $14 • (05/31/92) • **84**

Merlot Napa Valley 1988 • $14 • (03/31/91) • **82**

Merlot Napa Valley 1987 • $14 • (07/15/90) • **89**

Merlot Napa Valley 1986 • $14 • (03/31/90) • **72**

Merlot Napa Valley 1985 • $13 • (05/31/88) • **84**

Sauvignon Blanc Napa Valley Clock Vineyard 1994: Smooth and fruity, featuring nectarine, spice and slightly grassy and vanilla overtones. 800 cases made. • $10 • (08/31/95) • **84**

HAVILAND | WASHINGTON

Merlot Washington 1982 • $8 • (10/01/84) • **76**

HAWK CREST | CALIFORNIA

Cabernet Sauvignon California 1991: Lightly fruity, with meaty herb, dill and oak flavors that make for a good table wine, but not much more. Ready now. • $9 • (03/31/94) • **78**

Cabernet Sauvignon California 1990: Fruity and supple. An interesting roasted quality runs through this wine that's smooth and slightly on the sweet side, showing nice cherry and plum flavors and a touch of vanilla on the finish. • $9 • (04/30/93) • **82**

Cabernet Sauvignon California 1989 • $9 • (03/15/92) • **77**

Cabernet Sauvignon Mendocino 1981 • $5 • (03/16/85) BB • **84**

Cabernet Sauvignon North Coast 1987 • $8 • (03/31/90) • **79**

Cabernet Sauvignon North Coast 1986 • $7 • (10/15/88) BB • **82**

Cabernet Sauvignon North Coast 1985 • $6 • (07/31/88) • **75**

Cabernet Sauvignon North Coast 1984 • $7 • (10/15/87) • **76**

Cabernet Sauvignon North Coast 1981 • $5 • (02/01/86) • **65**

Chardonnay California 1994: Nice enough, with simple pear, spice and apple notes. Good but nothing exceptional. • $9 • (05/15/96) • **82**

Chardonnay California 1992: This earthy, simple wine has little to offer until the finish, where it picks up nice apple and peach flavors. Drinkable now. • $9 • (07/15/93) • **76**

Sauvignon Blanc California 1994: Bright and fruity, appealing for its clear apple and citrus flavors. Ready now. • $8 • (02/29/96) • **85**

Sauvignon Blanc California 1993: Light, simple and slightly earthy around a light core of pear flavor. 3,200 cases made. • $6 • (08/31/95) • **79**

Sauvignon Blanc California 1992 • $6 • (03/31/94) • **81**

HAYWOOD | CALIFORNIA

Cabernet Sauvignon California 1991: Firm and intense, compact and young, with spice, currant and light oak shadings. Finishes with a tannic edge. Best now to 1998. • $8 • (11/15/94) • **83**

Cabernet Sauvignon California Vintner's Select 1993: Smells funky, but the flavors pick up lovely raspberry accents, polished by spicy, toasty notes. Drinkable now. 25,000 cases made. • $8 • (12/15/95) • **84**

Cabernet Sauvignon California Vintner's Select 1990: Light and smooth, with a nice interplay of plum, currant and buttery spice aromas and flavors. Drinkable now. • $8 • (03/15/93) • **82**

Cabernet Sauvignon California Vintner's Select 1989 • $8 • (03/15/92) • **80**

Cabernet Sauvignon Sonoma Valley 1988 • $16 • (02/28/91) • **82**

Cabernet Sauvignon Sonoma Valley 1986 • $19 • (11/15/89) • **92**

Cabernet Sauvignon Sonoma Valley 1985 • $20 • (03/01/89) • **89**

Cabernet Sauvignon Sonoma Valley 1984 • $20 • (03/01/89) • **88**

Cabernet Sauvignon Sonoma Valley 1983 • $20 • (03/01/89) • **77**

Cabernet Sauvignon Sonoma Valley 1982 • $20 • (03/01/89) • **79**

Cabernet Sauvignon Sonoma Valley 1981 • $20 • (03/01/89) • **85**

Cabernet Sauvignon Sonoma Valley 1980 • $20 • (03/01/89) • **86**

Cabernet Sauvignon Sonoma Valley Los Chamizal Vineyards 1989: Crisp and narrow, showing more earth and leathery flavors than fruit although a splash of currant sneaks through on the finish. Perhaps short-term cellaring will help, best after 1996. 2,800 cases made. • $12 • (11/15/94) • **84**

Cabernet Sauvignon Sonoma Valley Los Chamizal Vineyards 1988 • $16 • (11/15/91) • **85**

Chardonnay California Vintner's Select 1994: Soft and broad in texture, centered around citrusy pear and toasty earthy flavors that spread on the finish. Ready now. 60,000 cases made. • $8 • (11/15/95) BB • **85**

Chardonnay California Vintner's Select 1993: Tastes off-dry, with a spicy, Riesling-like edge to the subtle pear and apple notes. 27,000 cases made. • $8 • (02/28/95) • **82**

Chardonnay California Vintner's Select 1992: Serves up a pleasant core of spicy pear and cedary oak flavors that stay with you. Ready now. Tasted twice. 8,963 cases made. • $8 • (06/30/94) BB • **84**

Chardonnay California Vintner's Select 1991 • $8 • (03/31/93) • **81**

Spaghetti Red California NV • $6 • (02/15/90) • **74**

Spaghetti Red Sonoma County NV • $4 • (04/30/87) • **74**

Zinfandel Sonoma Valley 1986 • $11 • (09/15/88) • **89**

Zinfandel Sonoma Valley 1985 • $9 • (11/15/87) • **85**

Zinfandel Sonoma Valley 1984 • $9 • (05/31/87) • **92**

Zinfandel Sonoma Valley 1983 • $8 • (01/01/86) • **85**

Zinfandel Sonoma Valley 1982 • $8 • (11/01/84) • **89**

Zinfandel Sonoma Valley Los Chamizal Vineyard 1992: Smooth, medium body, with pleasant cherry and spice notes. Straightforward. 4,590 cases made. • $14 • (10/15/95) • **84**

Zinfandel Sonoma Valley Los Chamizal Vineyards 1991: Dry and tannic, with a tarry, smoky edge to the fruit flavors, which seem trapped in the tannins. Drinkable now. 7,330 cases made. • $14 • (10/15/94) • **84**

Zinfandel Sonoma Valley Los Chamizal Vineyards 1990 • $14 • (10/15/92) • **83**

Zinfandel Sonoma Valley Los Chamizal Vineyards 1989 • $14 • (11/15/91) • **85**

Zinfandel Sonoma Valley Los Chamizal Vineyards 1988 • $13 • (11/30/90) • **89**

Zinfandel Sonoma Valley Rocky Terrace 1992: An oaky style that's woody and tannic, but the Zinfandel character comes through with spicy cherry, cedar and anise notes. Well balanced and polished compared with the other Haywood Zins. 478 cases made. • $18 • (10/15/94) • **88**

HECKER PASS | CALIFORNIA

Zinfandel Santa Clara Valley 1988 • $7 • (10/15/92) • **75**

HEDGES | WASHINGTON

Cabernet Merlot Columbia Valley 1994: Light and velvety, as modest red berry and cedary flavors linger tentatively on the finish. Ready now. 39,500 cases made. • $9 • (05/15/96) • **83**

Cabernet Merlot Columbia Valley 1990: Firm and focused, with currant and plum aromas and flavors shaded by oak and cedar on the finish. A nicely balanced wine. Drinkable now. 29,500 cases made. • $9 • (06/15/92) BB • **88**

Cabernet Merlot Columbia Valley 1989 • $7 • (09/30/91) BB • **89**

Caberne Merlot Washington 1993: Ripe and generous, showing nicely articulated berry and black cherry flavors that extend into a delicious finish, shading with herb flavors at the end. 55,000 cases made. • $9 • (08/31/94) BB • **87**

Cabernet Merlot Washington 1992: Ripe and smooth, a velvety wine with generous black cherry and currant aromas and flavors. Drinkable now. 31,200 cases made. • $9 • (12/31/93) BB • **86**

Cabernet Merlot Washington 1991: Elegant and spicy, with lush, fleshy black currant, cherry and anise notes that glide across the palate. Goes down easy and the fruit flavors keep repeating on the long, lingering finish. Drinkable now. 28,500 cases made. • $9 • (03/31/93) BB • **88**

Fumé Chardonnay Columbia Valley 1994: Fruity and bright, light on its feet but zesty in its grapefruit and apple flavors. 5,000 cases made. • $6 • (05/15/96) • **85**

Fumé Chardonnay Washington 1993: Sweet and fruity, crisp enough to balance the sweetness and pleasant to drink by itself. The melon and apple flavor is appealing. 16,400 cases made. • $8 • (09/30/94) • **80**

Fumé Chardonnay Washington 1992: Light and fresh, with a floral-spicy edge to the fruity flavors. 5,700 cases made. • $9 • (09/30/94) • **83**

Proprietors' Selection Red Mountain Reserve Columbia Valley 1992 • $15 • (05/15/94) • **83**

Red Mountain Reserve Columbia Valley 1991: Tough and tannic up front, but there's enough ripe plum and a touch of prune flavor to keep it rich and lively through the finish. Best in 1998. 990 cases made. • $23 • (09/30/95) • **85**

Red Mountain Reserve Columbia Valley 1990: A big, dense, chewy wine that aims for complexity and concentration, but the finish turns dry and tannic and the wood picks up an ashlike flavor. Will need time to settle down. Drinkable now. 408 cases made. • $25 • (03/15/94) • **84**

Red Mountain Reserve Columbia Valley 1989 • $25 • (03/31/93) • **87**

HEITZ | CALIFORNIA

Blush Napa Valley Grignolino Rosé 1994: A serious wine that tastes like a rosé. Its wild side is dominated by earthy, spicy berry flavors. Extremely pungent and dry as well as full-bodied. • $5 • (09/15/95) • **82**

Cabernet Sauvignon Napa Valley 1991: Marked by a dank, earthy, rustic aroma, it's more satisfying on the palate as the spicy Cabernet flavors unfold slowly, turning supple in texture. Somewhat backward, short-term cellaring into 1997 is advised. 15,000 cases made. • $19 • (04/30/96) • **85**

Cabernet Sauvignon Napa Valley 1990: Strikes a lively balance between spicy, cedary oak and ripe cherry and currant flavors, turning smooth and supple on the finish. Has plenty of intensity and depth. Tasted twice, with consistent results. 13,900 cases made. • $18 • (04/30/95) • **90**

Cabernet Sauvignon Napa Valley 1989: Intense and lively, rich and supple, featuring tiers of spicy currant and black cherry flavors and a toasty vanilla note. Finishes with firm, dry tannins, best after 1997. 12,000 cases made. • $15 • (07/31/94) • **88**

Cabernet Sauvignon Napa Valley 1988 • $18 • (03/31/93) • **88**

Cabernet Sauvignon Napa Valley 1987 • $20 • (04/15/92) SS • **90**

Cabernet Sauvignon Napa Valley 1986 • $18 • (04/15/91) • **88**

Cabernet Sauvignon Napa Valley 1985 • $34 • (05/15/90) • **80**

Cabernet Sauvignon Napa Valley 1984 • $30 • (01/31/90) • **89**

Cabernet Sauvignon Napa Valley 1983 • $20 • (01/31/90) • **85**

Cabernet Sauvignon Napa Valley 1982 • $30 • (01/31/90) • **80**

Cabernet Sauvignon Napa Valley 1981 • $30 • (01/31/90) • **86**

Cabernet Sauvignon Napa Valley 1980 • $28 • (01/31/90) • **88**

Cabernet Sauvignon Napa Valley 1979 • $18 Ⓐ • (01/31/90) • **86**

Cabernet Sauvignon Napa Valley 1978 • $30 • (01/31/90) • **90**

Cabernet Sauvignon Napa Valley 1977 • $48 • (01/31/90) • **83**

Cabernet Sauvignon Napa Valley 1973 • $49 • (01/31/90) • **78**

Key: SS—Spectator Selection. CS—Cellar Selection. BB—Best Buy. $NA—Price not available. (BT)—Barrel tasting. Ⓐ—Auction Price.
Dates in parentheses represent the issues in which the ratings were published.

Cabernet Sauvignon Napa Valley 1970 • $100 • (01/31/90) • **74**

Cabernet Sauvignon Napa Valley NV • $NA • (01/31/90) • **68**

Cabernet Sauvignon Napa Valley Bella Oaks Vineyard 1990: Solid but unexciting, presenting a chewy core of currant, mint and spice, turning austere and tannic on the finish. Tasted twice, with consistent results. 2,481 cases made. • $27 • (04/30/95) • **85**

Cabernet Sauvignon Napa Valley Bella Oaks Vineyard 1989: The lightest of the Heitz Cabernets and the least interesting, it displays elegant cedar, currant and cherry flavor but loses intensity on the finish. Approachable now, can cellar to 2000. 100 cases made. • $23 • (07/31/94) • **85**

Cabernet Sauvignon Napa Valley Bella Oaks Vineyard 1988 • $32 • (03/31/93) • **81**

Cabernet Sauvignon Napa Valley Bella Oaks Vineyard 1987 • $33 • (06/30/92) • **85**

Cabernet Sauvignon Napa Valley Bella Oaks Vineyard 1986 • $26 Ⓐ • (04/15/91) • **89**

Cabernet Sauvignon Napa Valley Bella Oaks Vineyard 1985 • $36 Ⓐ • (05/15/90) CS • **92**

Cabernet Sauvignon Napa Valley Bella Oaks Vineyard 1984 • $43 • (05/15/89) • **86**

Cabernet Sauvignon Napa Valley Bella Oaks Vineyard 1983 • $39 • (03/01/89) • **86**

Cabernet Sauvignon Napa Valley Bella Oaks Vineyard 1982 • $48 • (03/01/89) • **85**

Cabernet Sauvignon Napa Valley Bella Oaks Vineyard 1981 • $60 • (03/01/89) • **90**

Cabernet Sauvignon Napa Valley Bella Oaks Vineyard 1980 • $31 Ⓐ • (03/01/89) • **93**

Cabernet Sauvignon Napa Valley Bella Oaks Vineyard 1978 • $79 • (03/01/89) • **89**

Cabernet Sauvignon Napa Valley Bella Oaks Vineyard 1977 • $63 • (03/01/89) • **91**

Cabernet Sauvignon Napa Valley Bella Oaks Vineyard 1976 • $53 • (03/01/89) • **85**

Cabernet Sauvignon Napa Valley Fay Vineyard 1978 • $52 • (02/16/84) • **80**

Cabernet Sauvignon Napa Valley Fay Vineyard 1977 • $35 • (02/16/84) • **78**

Cabernet Sauvignon Napa Valley Martha's Vineyard 1991: Typical Martha's Vineyard character, sporting its minty currant overtones. On the palate, sage and cherry notes add dimension, but it is still unevolved. As with many other '91s, this is tightly wound. With aeration, the supple texture shows its polish and the flavors turn elegant. Should be drinking well in 1997, but should last another decade or more. 7,624 cases made. • $65 • (04/30/96) CS • **91**

Cabernet Sauvignon Napa Valley Martha's Vineyard 1990: One of California's benchmark Cabernets, this has lovely depth and intensity. Marked by mint and currant flavors with a cedary accent, all turning smooth and supple. Firm tannins on the finish. Drink from 1997 to 2007. 2,462 cases made. • $65 • (04/30/95) CS • **90**

Cabernet Sauvignon Napa Valley Martha's Vineyard 1989: Dark, rich and intensely flavored, this is a young and tightly wound wine that's opening up with spicy mint, cherry and currant flavors that turn supple and generous on the finish. Has the tannins and richness to cellar through this decade and probably well into the next. Try in 1997. 5,200 cases made. • $64 Ⓐ • (06/30/94) CS • **90**

Cabernet Sauvignon Napa Valley Martha's Vineyard 1988 • $71 • (03/31/93) • **87**

Cabernet Sauvignon Napa Valley Martha's Vineyard 1987 • $86 Ⓐ • (03/31/92) CS • **95**

Cabernet Sauvignon Napa Valley Martha's Vineyard 1986 • $76 • (04/15/91) CS • **95**

Cabernet Sauvignon Napa Valley Martha's Vineyard 1985 • $163 Ⓐ • (04/30/90) • **98**

Cabernet Sauvignon Napa Valley Martha's Vineyard 1984 • $92 Ⓐ • (03/15/89) SS • **97**

Cabernet Sauvignon Napa Valley Martha's Vineyard 1983 • $90 • (03/01/89) • **89**

Cabernet Sauvignon Napa Valley Martha's Vineyard 1982 • $55 Ⓐ • (03/01/89) • **88**

Cabernet Sauvignon Napa Valley Martha's Vineyard 1981 • $78 • (03/01/89) • **89**

Cabernet Sauvignon Napa Valley Martha's Vineyard 1980 • $48 Ⓐ • (03/01/89) • **89**

Cabernet Sauvignon Napa Valley Martha's Vineyard 1979 • $68 Ⓐ • (03/01/89) • **93**

Cabernet Sauvignon Napa Valley Martha's Vineyard 1978 • $105 • (11/15/92) • **92**

Cabernet Sauvignon Napa Valley Martha's Vineyard 1977 • $88 • (01/31/90) • **90**

Cabernet Sauvignon Napa Valley Martha's Vineyard 1976 • $80 • (03/01/89) • **85**

Cabernet Sauvignon Napa Valley Martha's Vineyard 1975 • $80 Ⓐ • (03/01/89) • **92**

Cabernet Sauvignon Napa Valley Martha's Vineyard 1974: In four separate tastings, this showed mature, well-developed Cabernet flavors in its lesser moments and extraordinary richness, depth and complexity at its best. Here is a classic exercise in bottle variation. Two bottles had deep currant, mint, spice and cassis flavors, but there was less intensity and depth in two others. 4,543 cases made. • $298 Ⓐ • (11/15/94) • **97**

Cabernet Sauvignon Napa Valley Martha's Vineyard 1973 • $102 Ⓐ • (03/01/89) • **92**

Cabernet Sauvignon Napa Valley Martha's Vineyard 1972 • $105 • (03/01/89) • **79**

Cabernet Sauvignon Napa Valley Martha's Vineyard 1970 • $312 Ⓐ • (03/01/89) • **98**

Cabernet Sauvignon Napa Valley Martha's Vineyard 1969 • $257 Ⓐ • (03/01/89) • **93**

Cabernet Sauvignon Napa Valley Martha's Vineyard 1968 • $477 Ⓐ • (03/01/89) • **99**

Cabernet Sauvignon Napa Valley Martha's Vineyard 1967 • $165 Ⓐ • (03/01/89) • **86**

Cabernet Sauvignon Napa Valley Martha's Vineyard 1966 • $290 Ⓐ • (03/01/89) • **92**

Cabernet Sauvignon Napa Valley MZ-1 NV • $NA • (01/31/90) • **75**

Cabernet Sauvignon Napa Valley Trailside Vineyard 1990: Offers some mature cedar and coffee notes, accompanied by complex anise, cherry, plum and currant flavors that are well focused and harmonious. Finishes with firm tannins and a sense of finesse. The second vintage from this vineyard, which is in a good site for Cabernet. Drink now through 2000. 1,022 cases made. • $45 • (10/15/95) CS • **91**

Cabernet Sauvignon Napa Valley Trailside Vineyard 1989: Intense and lively, rich and supple, with tiers of spicy currant and black cherry flavors with a toasty vanilla note. A wonderful sense of harmony and finesse for this vintage. Finishes with firm, dry tannins, but the fruit pours through. Best after 1997. 1,304 cases made. 1,304 cases made. • $35 • (09/30/94) • **89**

Cabernet Sauvignon Napa Valley Z-91 NV • $NA • (01/31/90) • **90**

Chardonnay Napa Valley Estate Selection 1993: Lacks focus, with an modest range of earthy pear and oak notes. 854 cases made. • $18 • (07/31/95) • **78**

Port Napa Valley Grignolino Port 1992: Light-textured for a port but sweet and plummy in flavor, adding spicy vanilla and caramel on the soft finish. 265 cases made. • $13 • (09/30/95) • **85**

Ryan's Red Napa Valley NV • $6 • (02/28/89) • **74**

Zinfandel Napa Valley Heitz Vineyard 1989 • $8 • (09/30/93) • **67**

Zinfandel Napa Valley Heitz Vineyard 1988 • $7 • (10/15/92) • **78**

HENDRY | CALIFORNIA

Zinfandel Mount Veeder Brandlin Vineyard 1992: Has the typical briar and black pepper flavors, but the finish clamps down. Dry and tightly wound, may not grow out of its tannins. 200 cases made. • $15 • (10/15/95) • **86**

Zinfandel Napa Valley Hendry Block 7 1992: Young and intense, a tightly wound core of wild berry, cherry, anise and spice flowing through it. The complex aftertaste echoes the fruit and tannins. 250 cases made. • $14 • (10/15/95) • **88**

HERMANOS, LOS | CALIFORNIA

White Zinfandel California 1988 • $8 • (06/15/89) • **61**

HERON HILL | NEW YORK

Johannisberg Riesling Late Harvest Finger Lakes Ingles Vineyard 1983 • $6 • (03/16/86) • **64**

HERON LAKE | CALIFORNIA

Chardonnay Wild Horse Valley 1992: Crisp and nicely focused, a mouthful of bright pear, apple and nectarine fruit that lingers on the finish. 370 cases made. • $12 • (07/31/95) • **87**

Pinot Noir Wild Horse Valley 1994: Brimming with fresh, ripe pear, apricot, peach and spicy fruit flavors, a rich and forward style with a pretty creamy, fruity aftertaste. Hard to beat at this price—or even twice this price. 500 cases made. • $24 • (02/29/96) • **87**

Pinot Noir Wild Horse Valley 1990: Earthy with a mature black cherry and vegetal edge, picking up a trace of spice on the finish. Gains points for its smooth texture. Ready. 276 cases made. • $12 • **82**

HESS COLLECTION, THE | CALIFORNIA

Cabernet Sauvignon Napa Valley 1992: Very rich and intense, deeply complex and concentrated, offering tiers of plum, blackberry, currant and spice, and picking up nice, spicy oak notes on the finish. Packs a wallop. Best to wait until 1999 or 2000 at least. 18,000 cases made. • $18 • (11/15/95) SS • **94**

Cabernet Sauvignon Napa Valley 1991: Has a wonderful sense of harmony and finesse. Ripe, spicy, concentrated currant, plum and black cherry flavors, with spicy oak notes for added dimension. Finishes with a long, rich and fruity aftertaste. Try after 1997. 10,000 cases made. • $18 • (11/15/94) SS • **92**

Cabernet Sauvignon Napa Valley 1990: Firm and compact, with a tight band of currant, plum, spice and oak flavors that need short-term cellaring to soften and evolve. While the fruit is chunky, the style is elegant and it's our guess that time will be kind to this wine. Try in 1998. 10,000 cases made. • $18 • (04/15/94) CS • **90**

Cabernet Sauvignon Napa Valley 1989 • $17 • (02/15/93) • **82**

Cabernet Sauvignon Napa Valley 1988 • $18 • (01/31/92) CS • **90**

Cabernet Sauvignon Napa Valley 1987 • $17 • (04/15/91) SS • **94**

Cabernet Sauvignon Napa Valley 1986 • $15 • (11/15/89) • **90**

Cabernet Sauvignon Napa Valley 1985 • $13 • (03/01/89) • **96**

Cabernet Sauvignon Napa Valley 1983 • $13 • (03/01/89) • **84**

Cabernet Sauvignon Napa Valley Reserve 1991: Very intense and minty, a rich, concentrated, vibrant and tightly wound young red that slowly opens to reveal a complex core of plum and currant. Needs cellaring into 1997 or '98 to soften slightly, as the tannins are major-league. 380 cases made. • $39 • (04/30/96) • **91**

Cabernet Sauvignon Napa Valley Reserve 1990: Bold, rich and intensely concentrated, with compact, tannic Cabernet fruit. The spicy black cherry, currant and mineral notes are focused and complex on the finish. Simply needs cellaring until 1998 to 2000 to show its best. 300 cases made. • $38 • (11/15/94) • **90**

Cabernet Sauvignon Napa Valley Reserve 1989 • $35 • (11/15/93) • **84**

Cabernet Sauvignon Napa Valley Reserve 1986 • $33 • (09/15/90) • **93**

Cabernet Sauvignon Napa Valley Reserve 1984 • $22 • (03/01/89) • **93**

Cabernet Sauvignon Napa Valley Reserve 1983 • $22 • (03/01/89) • **88**

Chardonnay Mount Veeder 1991: A spicy style with Muscat-like flavors that dominate the apple and pear notes underneath. Comes across as simple and one-dimensional, picking up a light toast note on the finish. 350 cases made. • $22 • (06/30/94) • **84**

Chardonnay Napa Valley 1993: Medium bodied, with ripe pear and peach notes that pick up a light toasty oak shading. 15,000 cases made. • $15 • (07/31/95) • **84**

Chardonnay Napa Valley 1992: Starts out lean and a bit coarse, with ripe pear, toast and spicy notes. Gains richness and depth on the finish, where smoky oak notes come into play. Best to cellar short-term to let it soften and smooth out. 14,000 cases made. • $15 • (12/15/94) • **89**

Chardonnay Napa Valley 1991 • $14 • (07/15/93) • **87**

Merlot Napa Valley 1992: Marked by nice herb, spice and dill notes, and showing a good core of cherry and plum flavors, it suffers somewhat from a thin finish. 600 cases made. • $18 • (06/30/96) • **88**

Merlot Napa Valley 1991: Decidedly minty, as that flavor dominates. Picks up a hint of cherry and berry, but overall it's weighted toward mintiness. Sold only at the winery. 350 cases made. • $18 • **83**

Merlot Napa Valley 1989 • $25 • (05/31/92) • **86**

Zinfandel Napa Valley 1992: Tight and firm, with a compact band of cherry, spice, herb and pepper notes. A young and vibrant wine that finishes with firm tannins. Best after 1996. This Zinfandel is only available at the winery. 250 cases made. • $15 • (10/15/95) • **87**

HESS SELECT | CALIFORNIA

Cabernet Sauvignon California 1993: Ripe and compact, with attractive cherry and berry flavors that are well focused. This delivers a good bang for the buck, finishing with spicy, earthy notes. 50,000 cases made. • $9 • (11/30/95) BB • **85**

Cabernet Sauvignon California 1992: Ripe and fruity, with a pretty array of black cherry, plum, cedar and spice flavors. Finishes with mild tannins, good length and a hint of mint. Ready now. 40,000 cases made. • $9 • (11/15/94) BB • **87**

Cabernet Sauvignon California 1991: Lean and crisp, with modest berry and tobacco aromas and flavors. Finishes green and tight, drinkable now. 30,000 cases made. • $9 • (02/28/94) • **82**

Cabernet Sauvignon California 1990: Soft and fragrant, with generous red cherry and plum aromas and flavors. Simple, sturdy and drinkable now. Tasted twice. 15,000 cases made. • $9 • (11/15/92) • **80**

Cabernet Sauvignon California 1988 • $9 • (03/31/91) • **86**

Chardonnay California 1994: Fresh and flavorful, with apricot and pear flavors swirling refreshingly through it. Drinkable now. 80,000 cases made. • $9 • (06/30/96) BB • **87**

Chardonnay California 1993: Firm and lively, with intense grapefruit, citrus and pear-laced fruit. Turns complex and supple on the finish, where the flavors linger on. 50,000 cases made. • $9 • (12/15/94) BB • **86**

Chardonnay California 1992: Simple and spicy, with a pretty core of pear, citrus and oak flavors, picking up a grapefruit edge on the finish. Drinkable now. 62,000 cases made. • $9 • (03/31/94) • **84**

Chardonnay California 1991 • $10 • (12/15/92) • **82**

Pinot Noir Santa Barbara County Bien Nacido Vineyards 1994: Lean and somewhat leathery, showing a trim band of tart cherry and berry flavors. Good but nothing more. 3,900 cases made. • $11 • (02/29/96) • **83**

Pinot Noir Santa Barbara County Bien Nacido Vineyards Unfiltered 1993: Solid if lacking in extra dimensions, with attractive earthy cherry, herb and cola notes of modest depth. Ready now. 350 cases made. • $14 • **84**

HIDDEN CELLARS | CALIFORNIA

Alchemy Mendocino County 1992: Ripe and spicy and generous, presenting a woody edge to the honeyed fig and citrus flavors. Drink now. 1,440 cases made. • $20 • (02/28/95) • **87**

Alchemy Mendocino County 1991 • $18 • (04/15/93) • **82**

Cabernet Sauvignon Mendocino County Mountanos Vineyard 1984 • $12 • (08/31/88) • **88**

Chanson d'Or Mendocino County Bailey J. Lovin Vineyard 1989 • $15 • (09/15/91) • **84**

Chardonnay Mendocino County 1993: Pleasantly fruity with ripe pear, apple and nectarine notes. 3,100 cases made. • $10 • (07/31/95) • **83**

Chardonnay Mendocino County 1992: Focused and elegant with a tight beam of pear, lemon, toast and butter flavors that gain intensity and length on the finish. Wonderful balance, with a sense of harmony and finesse. Drink now. 3,300 cases made. • $12 • (02/28/94) • **88**

Chardonnay Mendocino County 1991 • $14 • (07/15/93) • **78**

> **Key:** SS—Spectator Selection. CS—Cellar Selection. BB—Best Buy. $NA—Price not available. (BT)—Barrel tasting. Ⓐ—Auction Price.
> **Dates in parentheses represent the issues in which the ratings were published.**

Chardonnay Mendocino County Organically Grown Grapes 1992: Intense and lively, with tiers of citrus, pineapple and pear flavors that pick up a slightly tart edge on the finish. Ready now. 1,450 cases made. • $14 • (03/31/94) • **84**

Chardonnay Mendocino County Organically Grown Grapes 1991 • $14 • (12/15/92) • **83**

Chardonnay Mendocino County Reserve 1992: Impressive for its ripe, rich and complex flavors, with layers of concentrated pear, honey, spice and vanilla that linger on a long, full finish. Drinks well now. 800 cases made. • $17 • (11/30/94) • **89**

Chardonnay Mendocino County Reserve 1991 • $16 • (07/15/93) • **78**

Chardonnay Mendocino Organically Grown Grapes 1993: Smooth, round, spicy, focusing its pear, nutmeg and caramel flavors through a tight finish. Drinkable now. 1,400 cases made. • $10 • (09/30/95) • **86**

Chauché Gris Mendocino Organically Grown Grapes 1994: Soft, vaguely spicy in flavor, a simple white with enough roundness to carry the modest fruit and cream notes. 900 cases made. • $8 • (09/30/95) • **81**

Johannisberg Riesling Mendocino County 1993: Fragrant and distinctly floral, a nice bead of apricot flavor carrying through the off-dry finish. Tasty now. 1,900 cases made. • $8 • (02/28/95) • **86**

Johannisberg Riesling Mendocino County 1992 • $8 • (08/31/93) • **83**

Riesling Late Harvest Mendocino Bailey Lovin Vineyard 1984 • $10 • (10/16/85) • **94**

Sauvignon Blanc California 1991 • $9 • (02/15/93) • **78**

Sauvignon Blanc Mendocino 1994: Soft and pleasantly fruity, adding a tobacco edge to the lingering citrus and peach flavors. Ready now. 5,000 cases made. • $9 • (12/15/95) • **85**

Sauvignon Blanc Mendocino 1993: Smooth, round and more complex than most Sauvignons, featuring an earthy, mineral edge to the honeyed pear flavors. Drink now. 5,000 cases made. • $8 • (04/30/95) • **85**

Sauvignon Blanc Mendocino County 1992 • $9 • (01/31/94) • **85**

Sauvignon Blanc Mendocino County Organically Grown Grapes 1993: 1,950 cases made. • $8 • **76**

Sauvignon Blanc Mendocino County Organically Grown Grapes 1992 • $9 • (03/31/94) • **85**

Sémillon Sauvignon Blanc Mendocino Alchemy 1993: Ripe, smooth and spicy, a rich, buttery wine with a melon note at the center and just a hint of pepper on the finish. 1,400 cases made. • $18 • (06/30/96) • **87**

Zinfandel Mendocino County 1992: Solid and rustic, with bright, ripe cherry, spice and earthy raspberry flavors, finishing with firm tannins. Best from 1995 to 1996. 1,800 cases made. • $10 • (10/15/94) • **85**

Zinfandel Mendocino County 1991 • $11 • (09/15/93) • **88**

Zinfandel Mendocino County 1990 • $10 • (10/15/92) • **85**

Zinfandel Mendocino County Pacini Vineyard 1989 • $10 • (02/29/92) • **81**

Zinfandel Mendocino County Pacini Vineyard 1988 • $10 • (12/31/90) • **85**

Zinfandel Mendocino County Pacini Vineyard 1986 • $7 • (10/31/88) • **86**

Zinfandel Mendocino County Pacini Vineyard 1984 • $7 • (04/15/87) • **88**

Zinfandel Mendocino McAdams Vineyard 1993: Modest but balanced, with appealing berry and cherry notes. Tasted twice, with consistent notes. 683 cases made. • $10 • (10/15/95) • **83**

HILL, WILLIAM | CALIFORNIA

Cabernet Sauvignon Napa Valley 1992: Medium weight, with cedar, herb and tobacco notes folding in with the currant and cherry fruit. Finishes with firm tannins. 16,500 cases made. • $14 • (12/15/95) • **84**

Cabernet Sauvignon Napa Valley Gold Label 1983 • $18 Ⓐ • (03/01/89) • **85**

Cabernet Sauvignon Napa Valley Gold Label 1982 • $40 • (03/01/89) • **90**

Cabernet Sauvignon Napa Valley Gold Label 1981 • $42 • (03/01/89) • **85**

Cabernet Sauvignon Napa Valley Gold Label 1980 • $38 • (03/01/89) • **87**

Cabernet Sauvignon Napa Valley Gold Label 1979 • $42 • (03/01/89) • **93**

Cabernet Sauvignon Napa Valley Gold Label 1978 • $46 Ⓐ • (11/15/92) • **94**

Cabernet Sauvignon Napa Valley Reserve 1992: Earthy with a leathery edge and drying tannins, the currant and berried flavors struggle to emerge from the veil of tannins. Tastes disjointed, needs cellaring into 1999 to 2000. Tasted twice with consistent results. 5,400 cases made. • $24 • (12/15/95) • **85**

Cabernet Sauvignon Napa Valley Reserve 1991: Lean and austere, with a narrow band of spicy cedar and currant flavors. Perhaps it will reveal more complexity with time. Best after 1995. Tasted three times. • $14 • (10/15/94) • **84**

Cabernet Sauvignon Napa Valley Reserve 1990: Green olive and herbal notes tend to obscure the modest currant and berry fruit in this smooth-textured, appealing wine. Has the stuff to improve through 1997. • $24 • (11/15/93) • **88**

Cabernet Sauvignon Napa Valley Reserve 1989 • $29 • (03/31/93) • **87**

Cabernet Sauvignon Napa Valley Reserve 1988 • $26 • (11/15/91) • **84**

Cabernet Sauvignon Napa Valley Reserve 1987 • $39 • (11/15/90) SS • **95**

Cabernet Sauvignon Napa Valley Reserve 1986 • $29 • (11/15/89) • **91**

Cabernet Sauvignon Napa Valley Reserve 1985 • $46 • (03/01/89) • **94**

Cabernet Sauvignon Napa Valley Reserve 1984 • $41 • (03/01/89) • **91**

Cabernet Sauvignon Napa Valley Silver Label 1989 • $14 • (03/31/93) • **82**

Cabernet Sauvignon Napa Valley Silver Label 1987 • $14 • (11/15/90) • **85**

Cabernet Sauvignon Napa Valley Silver Label 1985 • $12 • (04/30/88) • **90**

Cabernet Sauvignon Sonoma County Silver Label 1988 • $14 • (11/15/91) • **82**

Chardonnay Napa Valley 1992: Tight, firm and focused, still a bit green, with intense, tart pear and apple flavors, light oak shadings on the finish add dimension. • $13 • (01/31/95) • **88**

Chardonnay Napa Valley Reserve 1992: Straightforward, ripe, spicy pear and honey notes that linger. Drinks well now. 10,000 cases made. • $18 • (01/31/95) • **85**

Chardonnay Napa Valley Silver Label 1991: Stale and simple, with light apple and spice notes, but below average. • $12 • (06/30/94) • **78**

Merlot Napa Valley 1994: A touch of green, cedary herb to the cherry and currant flavors. Finishes with crisp tannins. 9,000 cases made. • $16 • **82**

Merlot Napa Valley 1992: Earthy, with a chunky herbal and weedy edge and chewy tannins. Needs short-term cellaring, but may always be tannic, best after 1997. • $18 • (01/31/95) • **82**

Merlot Napa Valley Premier Release 1991: An elegant young red with a spicy minty edge to the earthy Merlot flavors. This is good now. • $15 • (09/15/94) • **84**

Sauvignon Blanc Napa Valley Napa 1993: Smooth-textured, citrusy pear and floral flavors that linger. 8,000 cases made. • $9 • (08/31/95) • **81**

Sauvignon Blanc Napa Valley Premiere Release 1992 • $10 • (06/15/94) • **85**

HILL & MAYES, DOMAIN HILL | CALIFORNIA

Cabernet Sauvignon Napa Valley Clos Fontaine du Mont Reserve 1992: Big, ripe, dense and tannic, a hard-edged, young wine whose tannins overshadow its cherry and currant flavors. Finishes with a smoky, toasty oak edge. Best to cellar until 2000. 850 cases made. • $32 • (12/15/95) • **87**

Chardonnay Napa Valley Clos Fontaine du Mont Reserve 1993: Ripe and mature, with a plump core of pear, spice, honey and light oak shadings, finishing with a hot aftertaste along with plenty of flavor. 1,840 cases made. • $20 • (05/31/96) • **88**

HILL & MAYES, DOMAINE | CALIFORNIA

Cabernet Sauvignon Napa Valley Clos Fontaine du Mont Reserve 1991: Lean and tart, with a narrow band of earthy herb and oak laced currant and wild berry flavors. Best after 1997, but may always be on the austere side. • $32 • (12/31/94) • **85**

Chardonnay Napa Valley Clos Fontaine du Mont 1992: William Hill's first wine under his new label. It is ripe and supple with moderately rich pear, honey and spice notes, picking up a light oak shading on the finish. Ready now. • $20 • (12/31/94) • **87**

HINZERLING | WASHINGTON

Gewüztraminer Late Harvest Yakima Valley Selected Cluster Die Sonne 1985 • $12 • (10/15/89) • **82**

HITCHING POST | CALIFORNIA

Pinot Noir Santa Barbara County 1994: Forward and appealing now, with a delicate mix of earthy cherry, cola herbs and spice. Turns light and simple on the finish. 400 cases made. • $14 • (12/31/95) • **84**

Pinot Noir Santa Barbara County Sierra Madre and Gold Coast Vineyards 1993: Smooth and polished, with a subtle band of cola, cherry, spice and light oak shadings. A well balanced, well proptioned wine, that's appealing now. 400 cases made. • $14 • (12/31/95) • **86**

Pinot Noir Santa Maria Valley 1993: Trim and compact. Currant, spice and cedar flavors become more complex and interesting on aftertaste-a good sign. Not quite the depth of the Bien Nacido bottling. 420 cases made. • $16 • (10/15/95) • **87**

Pinot Noir Santa Maria Valley Bien Nacido Vineyard 1993: Supple and refined plum, cherry, cola and spice flavors remain focused. Gains complexity and finesse on the finish. Drink now. 200 cases made. • $25 • (10/15/95) • **88**

Pinot Noir Santa Ynez Valley Sanford & Benedict Vineyard 1993: Intense and lively cherry and currant flavors, somewhat astringent with a green tea edge. 175 cases made. • $25 • (10/15/95) • **88**

HMR | CALIFORNIA

Pinot Noir Paso Robles 1979 • $6 • (02/01/85) • **72**

HOBBS, PAUL | CALIFORNIA

Cabernet Sauvignon Carneros Napa Valley Hyde Vineyard 1992: Intense and concentrated, a big, complex wine marked by earthy currant, mineral, berry and spice flavors. Despite its size, the tannins are smooth and polished, although cellaring into 1997-98 should do the trick. 694 cases made. • $30 • (12/15/95) • **93**

Cabernet Sauvignon Carneros Napa Valley Hyde Vineyard 1991: Firm, ripe and intense, with a rich, focused core of currant, black cherry, mineral and herb notes. Supple and complex on the finish, when the tannins kick in, and the buttery oak flavors add dimension to the aftertaste. 784 cases made. • $30 • (10/31/94) • **91**

Cabernet Sauvignon Howell Mountain Liparita Vineyard 1992: Earthy and beefy herb and currant notes, turning thin and tannic on the finish. Lacks richness, depth and concentration. 568 cases made. • $35 • (05/15/96) • **84**

Chardonnay Sonoma Mountain Richard Dinner Vineyard 1994: An openly oaky style, with mature, medium-bodied honey, citrus and earthy pear notes, and an elegant finish. Well balanced and drinkable now. Tasted twice with consistent notes. 1,800 cases made. • $28 • (06/30/96) • **89**

Chardonnay Sonoma Mountain Richard Dinner Vineyard 1993: Understated with a ripe core of pear, honey and toasty oak flavors that are pleasant but missing the extra dimensions you might hope for. 1,067 cases made. • $28 • (07/31/95) • **86**

Chardonnay Sonoma Mountain Richard Dinner Vineyard 1991 • $27 • (12/31/93) • **92**

Pinot Noir Carneros Hyde Vineyard 1992: Earthy to the point of being funky, strays into more barnyardy flavors, although it picks up a hint of black cherry on the finish. 962 cases made. • $24 • (03/31/95) • **81**

Pinot Noir Carneros Hyde Vineyard 1991 • $25 • (02/28/94) • **86**

Pinot Noir Napa Valley Carneros Hyde Vineyard 1993: Medium-garnet in color, adding tarry character to the cherry and berry flavors. Pleasant enough in an elegant, earthy style. 878 cases made. • $23 • (05/15/96) • **84**

HOGUE | WASHINGTON

Blush Washington 1988 • $6 • (10/15/89) • **82**

Brut Yakima Valley NV • $12 • (10/15/89) • **82**

Cabernet Sauvignon Columbia Valley 1991: Medium-weight, with attractive cherry and berry notes of modest proportions and soft tannins. Drinks easy. 6,400 cases made. • $14 • (06/15/95) • **85**

Cabernet Sauvignon Washington 1990: Smooth tannins, generous black cherry and currant flavors and a solid finish add up to a pleasant red. Drinkable now. 6,400 cases made. • $14 • (09/30/94) • **85**

Cabernet Sauvignon Washington 1989 • $12 • (11/15/91) • **84**

Cabernet Sauvignon Washington 1988 • $12 • (03/31/92) • **88**

Cabernet Sauvignon Washington Reserve 1990: Ripe, supple and generous, nicely balanced to display its toasty berry and currant flavors that keep swirling gently on the finish. Drink now. 970 cases made. • $18 • (09/30/95) • **90**

HOMEWOOD

Cabernet Sauvignon Washington Reserve 1989: Dense and chewy, tannic at first, but enough of the black cherry and currant flavors sneak through on the smoky finish to suggest that cellaring until 1997 or 1998 will bring it around. 770 cases made. • $18 • (09/30/94) • **86**

Cabernet Sauvignon Washington Reserve 1988 • $18 • (11/15/91) • **89**

Cabernet Sauvignon Washington Reserve 1987 • $19 • (03/31/91) • **88**

Cabernet Sauvignon Washington Reserve 1985 • $18 • (10/15/89) • **81**

Chardonnay Columbia Valley 1994: A smooth and spicy white from Washington that's nicely balanced to show off its pineapple, pear and nutmeg flavors. The finish lingers pleasantly, and this looks good for its value, too. Drinkable now. 59,200 cases made. • $9 • (08/31/95) BB • **88**

Chardonnay Columbia Valley 1993: Beautifully articulated pear and apple flavors pick up citrusy, spicy notes on the finish. A lively and utterly beguiling Chardonnay from Washington-to drink while it's fresh. 49,640 cases made. • $10 • (04/15/95) SS • **89**

Chardonnay Columbia Valley 1992: Bright and flavorful, with beautifully articulated peach, nectarine and pear aromas and flavors, finishing with a kiss of spice. Drinkable now. 40,000 cases made. • $10 • (04/15/94) SS • **91**

Chardonnay Washington Reserve 1993: Smooth and enticing, focusing its spicy pear, honey and caramel flavors into a gentle stream that keeps flowing though the finish. Delicious now. 3,201 cases made. • $13 • (08/31/95) • **89**

Chardonnay Washington Reserve 1992: Just delicious with its apple, pear and spice aromas and flavors, slipping in a ring of spicy oak on the finish. Drinkable now. 3,500 cases made. • $12 • (04/15/94) • **89**

Chenin Blanc Columbia Valley 1994: Fresh, fruity and appealing, off-dry and richened by peach and melon flavors. 8,300 cases made. • $6 • (09/30/95) • **84**

Chenin Blanc Columbia Valley 1993: Light and flavorful, centered around pear and apple and finishing with a silky texture and lingering fruit. 17,400 cases made. • $6 • (09/30/94) • **84**

Chenin Blanc Columbia Valley Dry 1994: Melon and pear flavors linger on the off-dry finish in this light and somewhat resiny Chenin. 2,420 cases made. • $6 • (09/30/95) • **84**

Chenin Blanc Columbia Valley Dry 1993: Fruity and simple, with fine melon and apple flavors and a strong floral note. 4,800 cases made. • $6 • (09/30/94) • **82**

Fumé Blanc Columbia Valley 1994: Distinctly spicy and varietal, a touch of vanilla echoing on the finish. This dry wine from Washington offers a lot of character for its price. 45,350 cases made. • $7 • (09/15/95) BB • **86**

Fumé Blanc Columbia Valley 1992 • $8 • (08/31/93) BB • **87**

Fumé Blanc Columbia Valley Dry 1993: A brilliantly fruity Sauvignon from a Washington winery. It is brimming with peach, apricot, pear and citrus flavors that keep vibrating on the lively finish. 32,000 cases made. • $7 • (12/31/94) BB • **88**

Fumé Blanc Columbia Valley Dry 1992: Bright and fresh, a lively wine centered around appealing apple and lemon fruit and a grace notes of fig and grass. Drinkable now. 38,200 cases made. • $7 • (09/15/94) BB • **88**

Gewürztraminer Columbia Valley 1994: Soft and floral, frankly sweet and full of appealing pear and spice flavors. 3,200 cases made. • $6 • (09/30/95) • **83**

Gewürztraminer Columbia Valley 1993: Bright and fruity with a welcome edge of rose petal and spice that reflects the varietal character in spades. A little soft on the finish, but otherwise nicely done. 5,690 cases made. • $6 • (09/30/94) • **84**

Johannisberg Riesling Columbia Valley Dry 1994: Fresh and faintly sweet, like biting into a green apple, adding some apricot on the finish. Ready now. 17,850 cases made. • $6 • (09/30/95) • **85**

Johannisberg Riesling Yakima Valley 1993: Soft and fruity, generous with its peach and apple fruit, hinting at honey on the finish. 22,800 cases made. • $6 • (09/30/94) • **83**

Key: SS—Spectator Selection. CS—Cellar Selection. BB—Best Buy. $NA—Price not available. (BT)—Barrel tasting. (A)—Auction Price.
Dates in parentheses represent the issues in which the ratings were published.

Johannisberg Riesling Yakima Valley Dry 1993: Dry, but not particularly crisp or lively, a simple white with modest pear flavor. 9,660 cases made. • $6 • (09/30/94) • **81**

Lemberger Columbia Valley 1992: Light-textured, fairly bold in flavor, featuring black cherry and slightly herbal notes. 970 cases made. • $9 • (09/30/95) • **82**

Lemberger Yakima Valley 1993: Fruity, sturdy and simple, showing a nice touch of blackberry flavor. Ready now. 1,000 cases made. • $9 • (09/30/95) • **82**

Lemberger Yakima Valley 1991 • $10 • (12/31/93) • **85**

Merlot Columbia Valley 1992: Medium in weight, with a decent core of black cherry and cedary flavors, moderate depth and concentration. 23,200 cases made. • $14 • (06/15/95) • **86**

Merlot Columbia Valley 1991: Crisp and herbal, a little chewy, with a moderate level of tarry cherry flavors. Drinkable now, probably best from 1997. 33,700 cases made. • $14 • (09/30/94) • **84**

Merlot Washington 1990 • $12 • (01/31/93) • **86**

Merlot Washington 1989 • $12 • (10/15/91) SS • **92**

Merlot Washington 1986 • $12 • (04/15/89) • **85**

Merlot Washington 1985 • $12 • (11/15/87) • **80**

Merlot Washington Reserve 1991: Crisp and beautifully focused, playing out its black cherry, currant and spicy oak flavors harmoniously. Good now. 1,000 cases made. • $18 • (09/30/95) • **89**

Merlot Washington Reserve 1990: Crisp in texture, with sharply focused berry and currant flavors that echo nicely on the finish. Drinkable now, but give it unti 1997 to add some nuances. 2,500 cases made. • $18 • (09/30/94) • **87**

Merlot Washington Reserve 1989 • $18 • (06/15/93) • **88**

Merlot Washington Reserve 1988 • $18 • (11/15/91) • **90**

Merlot Washington Reserve 1987 • $19 • (03/31/91) • **89**

Sémillon Chardonnay Columbia Valley 1993: Crisp and refreshing, a lively blend featuring spicy pear and vanilla flavors that linger nicely on the citrusy finish. 4,750 cases made. • $7 • (04/30/95) • **85**

Sémillon Chardonnay Columbia Valley 1992: Crisp and fruity, offering a beguiling tang of grapefruit and peach that lingers on the generous finish. Definitely fruit-centered, and drinkable now. 4,960 cases made. • $7 • (08/31/94) BB • **89**

Sémillon Columbia Valley 1994: Round-textured, generous in flavor, spicy and toasty, adding a citrusy edge on the finish. Ready now. 3,550 cases made. • $7 • (09/30/95) • **85**

Sémillon Columbia Valley 1993: Light and fragrant, with tobacco accents to the nicely defined citrus and pineapple flavors. A Washington white with a fresh finish. 4,840 cases made. • $8 • (03/31/95) BB • **85**

Sémillon Columbia Valley 1992 • $8 • (06/15/93) BB • **86**

Seyval Blanc Columbia Valley 1994: Ripe and tasty, striking a balance between apple and pear flavors and nice hints of herb and spice. Ready now. 7,800 cases made. • $7 • (09/30/95) • **86**

White Riesling Late Harvest Columbia Valley 1994: This Riesling is frankly sweet, but crisply balanced. It keeps the ripe apricot, honey and citrus flavors humming. Offers style and complexity for an agreeable price. Drinkable now. 10,300 cases made. • $6 • (08/31/95) BB • **88**

White Riesling Late Harvest Columbia Valley 1993: Sweet and ripe without being unctuous, melon and nectarine flavors echoing right through the finish. Nicely balanced. 9,660 cases made. • $6 • (09/30/94) • **85**

White Riesling Late Harvest Yakima Valley Markin Vineyard 1987 • $7 • (10/15/89) • **79**

HOMEWOOD | CALIFORNIA

Cabernet Sauvignon Alexander Valley 1989 • $14 • (11/15/92) • **80**

Cabernet Sauvignon Alexander Valley 1988 • $13 • (11/15/92) • **83**

Zinfandel Dry Creek Valley Quinn Vineyard 1993: Austere and crisp, as tannins dominate the cherry and berry flavor. Turns hollow at mid-palate and finishes in a hard, dry edge. Some aging might help somewhat. 600 cases made. • $12 • (04/30/96) • **80**

Zinfandel Dry Creek Valley Quinn Vineyard 1992 • $9 • (03/31/94) • **79**

Zinfandel Sonoma Valley 110-Year-Old Vines 1992 • $12 • (03/31/94) • **83**

HONIG | CALIFORNIA

Cabernet Sauvignon Napa Valley 1988 • $14 • (08/31/92) • **83**

Sauvignon Blanc Napa Valley 1991 • $9 • (02/28/93) • **80**
Sauvignon Blanc Napa Valley Barrel Fermented 1993: Herbal, vegetal notes tip this into the "odd" but good category. 10,076 cases made. • $10 • (08/31/95) • **80**

HOODSPORT | WASHINGTON

Chenin Blanc Washington 1992: Fresh and fruity, on the dry side, but showing plenty of grassy melon and pear flavors. Drink soon, while it's fresh. 1,015 cases made. • $8 • (09/30/94) • **83**
Gewürztraminer Washington 1994: Bright and fruity and off-dry, a mouthful of fresh pear and delicate floral overtones. 2,062 cases made. • $8 • (09/30/95) • **83**
Gewürztraminer Washington 1993: Light and delicately spicy, soft and simple, with little oomph to the flavors. 1,706 cases made. • $8 • (09/30/94) • **78**
Johannisberg Riesling Washington 1994: Smells and tastes like crushed wildflowers, adding a touch of nectarine on the finish. 2,514 cases made. • $8 • (09/15/95) • **85**
Johannisberg Riesling Washington 1993: Soft and refreshing, a simple white with a piney edge to the melon flavors. 2,200 cases made. • $8 • (09/30/94) • **80**
Lemberger-Cab Washington 1993: Lean and a little metallic, nicely fruity but also somewhat bitter. 1,664 cases made. • $10 • (09/30/95) • **77**
Lemberger Washington 1992: Soft and spicy with an unfortunate acrid, burnt edge to the flavor. 726 cases made. • $8 • (09/30/94) • **73**
Merlot Washington 1992: Veers off strongly toward the minty-vegetal end of the flavor spectrum, highly distinctive, but otherwise smooth-textured and drinkable now. 409 cases made. • $11 • (09/30/94) • **80**
Sémillon Washington 1993: Simple, somewhat stale, adding a floral edge, slightly bitter. 515 cases made. • $8 • (09/30/95) • **76**
Sémillon Washington 1992: Crisp and nicely herbal, a lively white with very pretty pear and floral flavors that extend into a fresh finish. 450 cases made. • $8 • (08/31/94) BB • **86**
Sémillon Washington Limited Aritist Edition 1994: Floral, perfumy flavors dominate the fruit and finish a bit flat. 430 cases made. • $8 • (05/15/96) • **79**

HOP KILN | CALIFORNIA

Cabernet Sauvignon Alexander Valley 1984 • $10 • (03/31/88) • **77**
Cabernet Sauvignon Dry Creek Valley 1986 • $12 • (06/15/89) • **69**
Cabernet Sauvignon Dry Creek Valley 1985 • $10 • (10/15/88) • **75**
Cabernet Sauvignon Russian River Valley 1991: Firm and intense, with racy black cherry and cider flavors. This young and vibrant Cabernet needs short-term cellaring to soften the rough edges. Best after 1997. 454 cases made. • $14 • (11/15/94) • **83**
Cabernet Sauvignon Russian River Valley 1990: Ripe and straightforward, this is a young, intense and firmly tannic wine, with a narrow band of spice, raspberry and cherry notes. Finishes with a touch of buttery oak. Best now to 2000. 565 cases made. • $14 • (09/15/93) • **84**
Cabernet Sauvignon Sonoma County 1989 • $14 • (11/15/92) • **73**
Chardonnay Russian River Valley 1992: Crisp in texture, packs a lot of fruit and spice into its elegant frame, offering pear and apple notes with a touch of nutmeg. Drink now. 900 cases made. • $15 • (06/30/94) • **87**
Chardonnay Russian River Valley M. Griffin Vineyards 1993: Intense and spicy, featuring complex pear, vanilla, toast and butter notes that fan out, giving added depth and richness. 570 cases made. • $15 • (02/28/95) • **89**
Chardonnay Russian River Valley M. Griffin Vineyards 1991 • $15 • (07/15/93) • **85**
Gewürztraminer Russian River Valley M. Griffin Vineyards 1993: Dry, modest in scope, with rose petal and apple flavors that emerge gently on the finish. 420 cases made. • $7 • (11/15/94) • **82**
Gewürztraminer Russian River Valley M. Griffin Vineyards 1992 • $7 • (09/30/93) • **85**
Johannisberg Riesling Russian River Valley M. Griffin Vineyards 1993: Sweet but balanced, and it keeps the peach, honey and floral flavors in check. Tasty now. 600 cases made. • $8 • (02/28/95) • **83**
Johannisberg Riesling Russian River Valley M. Griffin Vineyards 1992 • $8 • (11/15/93) • **82**
Marty Griffin's Big Red Russian River Valley 1988 • $7 • (11/30/90) BB • **85**
Marty Griffin's Big Red Russian River Valley 1987 • $7 • (12/15/89) BB • **89**
Marty Griffin's Big Red Russian River Valley 1986 • $6 • (06/15/89) BB • **85**
Marty Griffin's Big Red Russian River Valley 1984 • $5 • (12/31/87) • **68**
Marty Griffin's Big Red Sonoma County 1991 • $8 • (09/15/93) BB • **88**
Petite Sirah Russian River Valley M. Griffin Vineyards 1987 • $11 • (02/28/90) • **82**
Petite Sirah Russian River Valley M. Griffin Vineyards 1985 • $11 • (03/31/88) • **77**
Petite Sirah Russian River Valley M. Griffin Vineyards 1984 • $10 • (02/15/87) • **90**
Petite Sirah Sonoma County 1991 • $15 • (10/15/93) • **84**
Valdiguié M. Griffin Vineyards Russian River Valley 1991 • $15 • (10/15/93) • **82**
Valdiguié M. Griffin Vineyards Russian River Valley 1990 • $15 • (06/30/92) • **77**
Zinfandel Russian River Valley 1992: Rich, spicy and complex, offering peppery cherry and wild berry flavors that pick up a tar and oak edge. Appealing now. 1,472 cases made. • $14 • (06/15/95) • **86**
Zinfandel Russian River Valley 1988 • $12 • (12/15/90) • **88**
Zinfandel Russian River Valley 1987 • $10 • **74**
Zinfandel Russian River Valley 1986 • $10 • (06/15/89) • **85**
Zinfandel Russian River Valley 1982 • $8 • (11/01/85) • **85**
Zinfandel Russian River Valley Marty Griffin's Big Red 1990 • $8 • (04/30/93) • **81**
Zinfandel Russian River Valley Primitivo 1992: Ripe and racy, displaying a gamy edge to the wild raspberry and cherry flavors. Tasty now but can age through 1997. 454 cases made. • $18 • (02/28/95) • **85**
Zinfandel Russian River Valley Primitivo Reserve 1985 • $12 • (06/15/89) • **90**
Zinfandel Sonoma County 1991: Bright and lively, with ripe, lush, spicy cherry and raspberry flavors that pick up an anise edge on the finish. Ready now through 1998. 1,057 cases made. • $12 • (10/15/94) • **84**
Zinfandel Sonoma County 1990 • $12 • (10/15/92) • **85**
Zinfandel Sonoma County Marty Griffin's Big Red 1992: Austere, with a thin, earthy band of dried cherry flavor and a metallic edge on the finish. 2,438 cases made. • $8 • (02/28/95) • **81**
Zinfandel Sonoma County Marty Griffin's Big Red Reserve NV: Tightly wound and compact, with rich, sharply focused cherry and raspberry flavors. Finishes with a burst of ripe fruit. Drinkable now. 2,700 cases made. • $8 • (09/15/94) BB • **87**
Zinfandel Sonoma County Primitivo 1993: Firm and tight, its compact band of earthy cherry and raspberry flavors picking up notes of tar. Should soften a bit. 450 cases made. • $18 • (10/15/95) • **86**
Zinfandel Sonoma County Primitivo 1991 • $15 • (09/15/93) • **87**
Zinfandel Sonoma County Primitivo 1990 • $15 • (10/15/92) • **85**
Zinfandel Sonoma County Primitivo 1988 • $14 • (12/31/90) • **89**

HOPE FARMS | CALIFORNIA

Cabernet Sauvignon Paso Robles 1990: An oaky Cabernet marked by toasty, buttery notes, but enough anise and cherry flavor emerges on the finish to merit attention. Ready now. 88 cases made. • $9 • (11/15/94) • **84**
Cabernet Sauvignon Paso Robles 1989 • $16 • (11/15/93) • **84**
Claret Paso Robles 1991: Light with spicy herb and cedar notes. Finishes with a hint of cherry and currant and mild tannins. Ready now. 401 cases made. • $10 • (11/15/94) • **81**
Sauvignon Blanc Paso Robles 1994: Bright and simple, showing some nice pear fruit. 167 cases made. • $NA • (05/31/96) • **81**
Zinfandel Paso Robles NV • $7 • (09/30/93) BB • **84**

HORIZON'S EDGE | WASHINGTON

Muscat Canelli Yakima Valley Nouveaux Riche 1993: Clever name, but fruit comes up short on intensity and spice and fails to balance the sweetness. 191 cases made. • $10 • (09/30/95) • **81**

HORTON | Virginia

Chardonnay Monticello Montdomaine Reserve 1993: Understated yet muscular, this full-bodied Chardonnay shows melon and light herb flavors and firm acidity. A good accompaniment to food. • $13 • **82**

Chardonnay Virginia 1994: Pleasant, sweet vanilla-oaky aromas and flavors dominate this light-bodied white, adding some melon and fig notes underneath. It's clean and rather simple, best for fans of oak. • $15 • **83**

Marsanne Virginia Orange County 1992 • $15 • (09/30/93) • **84**

Viognier Virginia 1993: Peachy aromas and flavors add up to an attractive wine. Aromatic, with nice butterscotch notes on the finish. Luscious and tasty, with a nice richness. 1,021 cases made. • $23 • **86**

Viognier Virginia Orange County 1992 • $20 • (09/30/93) • **82**

HOUTZ | California

Cabernet Sauvignon Santa Ynez Valley 1985 • $8 • (12/15/89) • **63**

Chardonnay Santa Ynez Valley 1991 • $12 • (07/15/93) • **73**

HOWELL MOUNTAIN VINEYARD | California

Zinfandel Howell Mountain 1988 • $11 • (10/15/92) • **74**

HULTGREN & SAMPERTON | California

Pinot Noir Sonoma County 1980 • $5 • (09/01/84) • **55**

HUNT COUNTRY VINEYARDS | New York

Chardonnay Finger Lakes 1991: A modestly fruity but indistinct wine with light body, smooth texture and a tart finish. Simple and lacking Chardonnay character. • $10 • **76**

Johannisberg Riesling Finger Lakes 1992: Sweet, easy-going and simply fruity, with apple and peach flavors. A decent dessert drink, but nothing special. • $8 • **77**

Ravat Blanc Finger Lakes Late Harvest #51 1988: • $6 • **73**

Seyval Blanc Finger Lakes 1992: Unusual flavors of banana and butter turn to a sweet-sour impression on the finish. Not pleasant. • $6 • (06/30/95) • **72**

Vidal Finger Lakes Ice Wine 1992: Exaggerated vegetal and hard cider flavors make this wine difficult to swallow. Funky and acrid. Tasted twice with consistent results. • $15 • **55**

White Finger Lakes 1992: A sweet, flavorful white that smells herbal and tastes like sweetened rhubarb or peaches. Try as an apéritif or with a fruit dessert. • $7 • (06/30/95) • **80**

HUNTER, ROBERT | California

Blanc de Noirs Sonoma Valley Brut de Noirs 1991: Pleasant enough, a modest core of creamy cherry and spice flavor turns simple on aftertaste. Drinks well now. Better than a previous tasting of this vintage. 1,000 cases made. • $25 • (09/15/95) • **85**

Blanc de Noirs Sonoma Valley Brut de Noirs 1984 • $15 • (10/15/88) • **84**

Blanc de Noirs Sonoma Valley Brut de Noirs 1983 • $15 • (01/31/88) • **84**

Blanc de Noirs Sonoma Valley Brut de Noirs 1982 • $14 • (12/31/86) • **90**

Blanc de Noirs Sonoma Valley Brut de Noirs 1981 • $14 • (12/16/84) • **87**

Blanc de Noirs Sonoma Valley Brut de Noirs Later Disgorged 1981 • $14 • (02/01/86) • **69**

HUNTINGTON | California

Cabernet Sauvignon Alexander Valley 1989 • $8 • (08/31/92) • **68**

Key: SS—Spectator Selection. CS—Cellar Selection. BB—Best Buy. $NA—Price not available. (BT)—Barrel tasting. Ⓐ—Auction Price.
Dates in parentheses represent the issues in which the ratings were published.

HUSCH | California

Cabernet Sauvignon Mendocino 1986 • $12 • (02/15/90) • **84**

Cabernet Sauvignon Mendocino La Ribera Cabernet 1989 • $8 • (11/15/93) • **79**

Cabernet Sauvignon Mendocino La Ribera Cabernet 1985 • $5 • (11/30/87) BB • **84**

Cabernet Sauvignon Mendocino La Ribera Red 1992: Tight and firm, with a narrow band of spicy currant Cabernet fruit. Best to drink now through 1997. • $8 • (11/15/94) • **83**

Cabernet Sauvignon Mendocino La Ribera Vineyard 1991: Lean and simple, with modest cherry and currant notes, but it's better balanced than the woody North Field Select. Drinkable now. 1,289 cases made. • $14 • (03/31/95) • **84**

Cabernet Sauvignon Mendocino La Ribera Vineyards 1990: An elegant, complex, young wine that has finesse and grace. Layers of spice, cherry, toast and currant flavors fold together on the finish, where the crisp acidity keeps the flavors alive. Supple enough to enjoy now. • $14 • (08/31/93) • **88**

Cabernet Sauvignon Mendocino La Ribera Vineyards 1989 • $14 • (11/15/92) • **81**

Cabernet Sauvignon Mendocino La Ribera Vineyards 1988 • $12 • (06/30/91) • **86**

Cabernet Sauvignon Mendocino La Ribera Vineyards 1987 • $12 • (11/15/90) • **90**

Cabernet Sauvignon Mendocino La Ribera Vineyards 1984 • $10 • (12/31/87) • **73**

Cabernet Sauvignon Mendocino North Field Select 1991: Relies too heavily on strong, dill-laced oak flavors, which overshadow the narrow band of currant. 797 cases made. • $18 • (03/31/95) • **81**

Cabernet Sauvignon Mendocino North Field Select 1990: Firm and intense with ripe cherry, currant, anise and spice flavors that turn chunky and tannic on the finish. Drinkable now. 600 cases made. • $18 • (11/15/93) • **87**

Cabernet Sauvignon Mendocino North Field Select 1989 • $18 • (08/31/93) • **87**

Cabernet Sauvignon Mendocino North Field Select 1988 • $18 • (08/31/92) • **84**

Cabernet Sauvignon Mendocino North Field Select 1987 • $16 • (11/15/90) • **87**

Chardonnay Anderson Valley Special Reserve 1992: Distinct for its ripe pear and spicy notes, but it loses its intensity and focus on the finish. 473 cases made. • $18 • (07/31/95) • **85**

Chardonnay Mendocino 1993: Intense and lively, with a grassy edge to the pear and apple notes. Drink now. • $12 • (11/30/94) • **85**

Chardonnay Mendocino 1992: Crisp and flinty with tart pear, apricot and spicy flavors that string out on the finish. Balanced and ready to drink now. • $11 • (03/15/94) • **84**

Chardonnay Mendocino 1991 • $11 • (04/15/93) • **89**

Chenin Blanc Mendocino La Ribera Vineyard 1994: Light, charming and generous with its green apple and sweet pear fruit. Not too sweet. Ready now. • $8 • (06/15/95) • **85**

Chenin Blanc Mendocino La Ribera Vineyards 1993: Lightly sweet and lightly fruity, with a leafy-herbal streak running through the green apple flavor. Drinkable now. 1,923 cases made. • $7 • (07/31/94) • **82**

Gewürztraminer Anderson Valley 1993: Light and soft, an airy-textured white featuring simple citrus and peach flavors. • $9 • (01/31/95) • **81**

Gewürztraminer Anderson Valley 1992 • $8 • (01/31/94) • **82**

Gewürztraminer Anderson Valley 1991 • $8 • (01/31/93) • **85**

Gewürztraminer Late Harvest Anderson Valley 1993: Soft and sweet, with recognizable Gewürztraminer spice and a touch of bitterness to enliven the syrupy finish. Very tasty and the flavors persist nicely. • $14 • (07/31/95) • **87**

Pinot Noir Anderson Valley 1993: Light—almost watery—with the thinnest thin band of earthy berry flavors. 3,297 cases made. • $15 • **72**

Pinot Noir Anderson Valley 1992: Ripe and intense, with a pretty core of black cherry, plum and spicy flavors, with an aftertaste that keeps pumping out the fruit. Drinks well now. • $14 • (11/30/94) • **88**

Pinot Noir Anderson Valley 1991 • $14 • (04/30/94) • **84**

Pinot Noir Anderson Valley 1990 • $14 • (02/28/93) • **81**

Pinot Noir Anderson Valley 1989 • $14 • (11/15/91) • **87**

Pinot Noir Anderson Valley 1988 • $13 • (12/15/90) • **84**

Pinot Noir Anderson Valley 1987 • $13 • (02/15/90) • **80**
Pinot Noir Anderson Valley 1986 • $13 • (10/15/89) • **81**
Pinot Noir Anderson Valley 1985 • $10 • (06/15/88) • **84**
Pinot Noir Anderson Valley 1983 • $9 • (05/31/88) • **74**
Pinot Noir Anderson Valley 1982 • $9 • (08/31/86) • **88**
Sauvignon Blanc Mendocino 1994: Light and juicy, a nice mouthful of passion fruit, grapefruit and pineapple flavor that persists on the lively finish. 10,950 cases made. • $9 • (08/31/95) • **87**
Sauvignon Blanc Mendocino La Ribera Vineyards 1992 • $8 • (05/15/94) BB • **86**

HYATT | WASHINGTON

Black Muscat Yakima Valley 1994: More spicy flavor than aroma in this lightly sweet pink wine that gives up more generous cinnamon and strawberry flavors on the long finish. 11,670 cases made. • $7 • (03/31/96) • **85**
Black Muscat Yakima Valley Royale 1993: Off-dry, soft and lively, with a peppery-spicy streak running through the modest apple flavor. Drinkable now. 1,740 cases made. • $7 • (09/30/94) • **82**
Cabernet Merlot Yakima Valley 1992: Lighter than most, chewy, picks up enough berryish flavor to remain in balance. Drinkable now. 1,000 cases made. • $9 • (08/31/94) • **84**
Cabernet Sauvignon Yakima Valley 1991: A tough and tannic red that has some berry and gamy flavors struggling to peek through the tannins. Needs until 2000 at least. 1,008 cases made. • $13 • (03/31/96) • **83**
Cabernet Sauvignon Yakima Valley Reserve 1992: Gamy, leathery flavors tend to overpower the moderately plummy accents in this firm Cabernet that is otherwise nicely focused. Has enough personality to suggest aging until 1999. 209 cases made. • $25 • (03/31/96) • **84**
Cabernet Sauvignon Yakima Valley River's Bend Vineyard 1990: Distinctive for its wild raspberry flavors, this fresh, crisp, medium-bodied young Cabernet seems almost like a Zinfandel. Fine tannins on the finish make it enjoyable now. 1,000 cases made. • $13 • (10/15/93) • **82**
Chardonnay Yakima Valley 1993: Crisp, spicy and sharply focused, leaning a little toward oak for flavor but there's a nice, citrusy bite to the finish. Drinkable now. • $8 • (04/30/96) • **84**
Chardonnay Yakima Valley 1992: Crisp and fresh, not especially rich or complex, but it has a little spiciness to accent the citrusy flavors. Drinkable now. 2,300 cases made. • $10 • (09/30/94) • **83**
Chardonnay Yakima Valley 1991 • $9 • (12/15/93) • **80**
Fumé Blanc Yakima Valley 1992: Crisp and refreshing, simple, with appealing peach and slightly herbal aromas and flavors. 1,080 cases made. • $7 • (09/30/94) • **81**
Johannisberg Riesling Yakima Valley 1992: Sweet and fruity, a simple Riesling with a hint of apricot added to the melon flavor. Finishes a little sweet. 1,200 cases made. • $5 • (09/30/94) • **81**
Merlot Columbia Valley 1991 • $11 • (05/15/94) • **75**
Merlot Columbia Valley 1989 • $11 • (11/30/92) • **87**
Merlot Yakima Valley 1993: Soft, fruity, gentle with its tannins, and echoing its tasty plum and black cherry flavors on the airy finish. Drinkable now. 6,450 cases made. • $11 • (03/31/96) • **85**
Merlot Yakima Valley 1992: Ripe and juicy, lacing spicy oak into the bold black cherry and blackberry flavors. Finishes smooth and almost plush. 5,800 cases made. • $11 • (08/31/95) • **88**
Merlot Yakima Valley 1990 • $13 • (06/15/93) • **85**
Merlot Yakima Valley Reserve 1993: Firm, chewy and offers a nice mouthful of berry and spice flavors. Still needs to lose some of its gritty tannins. Best from late 1997. 313 cases made. • $25 • (03/31/96) • **84**
Riesling Late Harvest Yakima Valley 1994: Sweet, elegant and light, with pretty honey, melon and floral flavors that linger on the balanced finish. Drinkable now. 227 cases made. • $9 • (03/31/96) • **87**
Riesling Late Harvest Yakima Valley 1987 • $8 • (10/15/89) • **87**

INDIAN SPRINGS | CALIFORNIA

Cabernet Sauvignon Nevada County 1991: Strikes a nice balance between cedary oak and ripe currant flavors. Picks up a hint of coffee on the finish before the tannins kick in. 1,000 cases made. • $9 • (11/15/94) • **82**
Cabernet Sauvignon Nevada County 1990: A rustic young Cabernet with earthy, tannic currant flavors that turn spicy on the finish, but in the end the tannins hang tough. Drinkable now. 500 cases made. • $8 • (11/15/93) • **80**
Chardonnay Nevada County Sierra Foothills Reserve 1991 • $17 • (03/31/93) • **75**
Merlot Nevada County 1992: Smooth and supple, with a nice range of currant, herb and spicy Merlot flavors. Drinks well now but has the intensity and tannins for short-term cellaring. 1,500 cases made. • $12 • (09/15/94) • **84**
Merlot Nevada County 1991 • $12 • (08/31/93) • **84**
Merlot Nevada County Sierra Foothills 1990 • $12 • (06/15/93) • **84**
Merlot Sierra Foothills 1989 • $10 • (11/30/92) • **85**
Sémillon Nevada County 1993: Strongly herbal, earthy flavors are too much for the lemony notes. 250 cases made. • $8 • (10/15/95) • **74**

INGLENOOK | CALIFORNIA

Cabernet Sauvignon California Claret-Medoc Type 1897 • $NA • (03/01/89) • **87**
Cabernet Sauvignon Napa Valley 1989 • $10 • (11/15/92) • **80**
Cabernet Sauvignon Napa Valley 1988 • $10 • (11/15/92) • **80**
Cabernet Sauvignon Napa Valley 1987 • $10 • (11/15/91) • **86**
Cabernet Sauvignon Napa Valley 1986 • $10 • (02/28/91) BB • **85**
Cabernet Sauvignon Napa Valley 1985 • $10 • (03/31/89) • **83**
Cabernet Sauvignon Napa Valley 1983 • $10 • (03/15/88) • **80**
Cabernet Sauvignon Napa Valley 1980 • $14 Ⓐ • (02/15/84) • **87**
Cabernet Sauvignon Napa Valley 1960 • $125 • (06/01/85) • **89**
Cabernet Sauvignon Napa Valley 1958 • $125 • (06/01/85) • **88**
Cabernet Sauvignon Napa Valley 1946 • $600 • (03/01/89) • **87**
Cabernet Sauvignon Napa Valley 1943 • $1,500 • (03/01/89) • **91**
Cabernet Sauvignon Napa Valley 1941 • $1,450 • (03/01/89) • **100**
Cabernet Sauvignon Napa Valley 1933 • $1,650 • (03/01/89) • **95**
Cabernet Sauvignon Napa Valley Cask 1980 • $22 • (03/01/89) • **88**
Cabernet Sauvignon Napa Valley Cask 1979 • $23 • (03/01/89) • **77**
Cabernet Sauvignon Napa Valley Cask 1978 • $35 • (03/01/89) • **86**
Cabernet Sauvignon Napa Valley Cask 1977 • $25 • (03/01/89) • **84**
Cabernet Sauvignon Napa Valley Cask 1976 • $19 • (03/01/89) • **72**
Cabernet Sauvignon Napa Valley Cask 1974 • $59 • (03/01/89) • **86**
Cabernet Sauvignon Napa Valley Cask 1973 • $60 • (03/01/89) • **67**
Cabernet Sauvignon Napa Valley Cask 1972 • $28 • (03/01/89) • **67**
Cabernet Sauvignon Napa Valley Cask 1971 • $50 • (03/01/89) • **73**
Cabernet Sauvignon Napa Valley Cask 1970 • $90 • (03/01/89) • **85**
Cabernet Sauvignon Napa Valley Cask 1969 • $62 • (03/01/89) • **80**
Cabernet Sauvignon Napa Valley Cask 1968 • $83 • (03/01/89) • **85**
Cabernet Sauvignon Napa Valley Cask 1967 • $110 • (03/01/89) • **73**
Cabernet Sauvignon Napa Valley Cask 1966 • $89 • (03/01/89) • **73**
Cabernet Sauvignon Napa Valley Cask 1960 • $140 • (03/01/89) • **80**
Cabernet Sauvignon Napa Valley Cask 1958 • $400 • (03/01/89) • **94**
Cabernet Sauvignon Napa Valley Cask 1955 • $400 • (03/01/89) • **93**
Cabernet Sauvignon Napa Valley Cask 1949 • $700 • (03/01/89) • **92**
Cabernet Sauvignon Napa Valley Cask A-4 Limited Cask 1974: Never a great Inglenook. The fruit has completely disappeared, leaving a thin tobacco and tea-like edge. 11,864 cases made. • $59 • (11/15/94) • **67**
Cabernet Sauvignon Napa Valley Cask A-8 1974 • $59 • (02/15/90) • **79**
Cabernet Sauvignon Napa Valley Cask F-11 1958 • $NA • (02/28/87) • **79**
Cabernet Sauvignon Napa Valley Reserve Cask 1988 • $19 • (03/15/94) • **84**
Cabernet Sauvignon Napa Valley Reserve Cask 1987 • $21 • (11/15/92) • **89**
Cabernet Sauvignon Napa Valley Reserve Cask 1986 • $25 • (10/31/91) • **91**
Cabernet Sauvignon Napa Valley Reserve Cask 1985 • $19 • (02/15/91) CS • **90**
Cabernet Sauvignon Napa Valley Reserve Cask 1984 • $22 • (07/31/90) • **90**
Cabernet Sauvignon Napa Valley Reserve Cask 1983 • $22 • (03/01/89) • **89**
Cabernet Sauvignon Napa Valley Reserve Cask 1982 • $32 • (03/01/89) • **91**
Cabernet Sauvignon Napa Valley Reserve Cask 1981 • $25 • (03/01/89) • **93**
Charbono Napa Valley 1984 • $8 • (04/15/88) • **82**
Charbono Napa Valley 1980 • $8 • (03/01/85) • **79**
Chardonnay Napa Valley 1991: Crisp and firm, with moderately intense pear and pineapple flavors, picking up a citrus note on the finish. 12,800 cases made. • $9 • (06/30/94) • **83**
Gewürztraminer Late Harvest Napa Valley 1986 • $9 • (05/15/88) • **78**
Merlot Reserve 1988 • $12 • (05/31/92) • **83**

Merlot Napa Valley 1981 • $12 • (10/01/85) • **77**
Merlot Napa Valley Limited Bottling 1982 • $8 • (05/16/86) • **67**
Merlot Napa Valley Reserve 1986 • $12 • (10/31/89) • **81**
Merlot Napa Valley Reserve 1985 • $14 • (10/15/88) SS • **91**
Merlot Napa Valley Reserve 1983 • $9 • (10/15/87) • **85**
Merlot Napa Valley Reserve 1981 • $12 • (02/16/85) • **80**
Niebaum Claret Napa Valley 1986 • $13 • (06/30/91) • **74**
Niebaum Claret Napa Valley 1985 • $12 • (03/15/89) • **82**
Niebaum Claret Napa Valley 1983 • $12 • (11/30/87) • **88**
Petite Sirah Napa Valley 1982 • $5 • (12/31/86) BB • **87**
Petite Sirah Napa Valley 1981 • $6 • (02/01/85) BB • **86**
Pinot Noir Napa Valley 1985 • $9 • (06/15/88) • **82**
Pinot Noir Napa Valley 1982 • $7 • (12/31/86) • **64**
Pinot Noir Napa Valley 1981 • $7 • (02/01/85) • **62**
Pinot Noir Napa Valley 1980 • $6 • (03/01/84) • **71**
Reunion Napa Valley 1986 • $NA • (03/01/89) • **92**
Reunion Napa Valley 1985 • $35 • (07/15/89) • **91**
Reunion Napa Valley 1984 • $35 • (03/01/89) • **92**
Reunion Napa Valley 1983 • $38 • (03/01/89) • **93**
Zinfandel Napa Valley 1986 • $8 • (04/30/91) • **73**
Zinfandel Napa Valley 1983 • $7 • (03/15/88) • **81**
Zinfandel Napa Valley 1981 • $7 • (02/01/85) • **79**

INGLENOOK-NAVALLE | CALIFORNIA

White Zinfandel California NV • $7/1.5L • (06/15/89) • **69**

INNISFREE | CALIFORNIA

Cabernet Sauvignon Napa Valley 1990: Intense, focused, rich and spicy, with incredibly fruity flavors. The cherry, currant and oak flavors blend together well and good chocolate notes emerge on the finish. Drinkable now. • $11 • (04/30/93) • **88**
Cabernet Sauvignon Napa Valley 1988 • $11 • (04/30/91) • **84**
Cabernet Sauvignon Napa Valley 1986 • $11 • (06/30/90) • **73**
Cabernet Sauvignon Napa Valley 1985 • $9 • (03/15/89) • **86**
Cabernet Sauvignon Napa Valley 1984 • $9 • (12/15/87) • **68**
Cabernet Sauvignon Napa Valley 1983 • $9 • (11/15/86) • **82**
Cabernet Sauvignon Napa Valley 1982 • $9 • (12/16/85) • **80**
Pinot Noir California 1990 • $11 • (09/30/92) • **84**
Pinot Noir California 1989 • $11 • (04/30/91) • **84**

INTAGLIA | CALIFORNIA

Pinot Noir Russian River Valley Saralee's Vineyard 1992: Earthy, dirty, a funky menthol edge. Tasted twice, with consistent notes. 130 cases made. • $14 • (03/31/95) • **70**

IRON HORSE | CALIFORNIA

Blanc de Blancs Sonoma County Green Valley 1989: Lean, firm and focused, with a narrow band of spicy pear and vanilla flavors, turning more complex on the finish. Shows a measure of delicacy and finesse. Ready now. 3,111 cases made. • $24 • (12/31/94) • **88**
Blanc de Blancs Sonoma County Green Valley 1988 • $24 • (07/31/93) • **90**
Blanc de Blancs Sonoma County Green Valley 1987 • $25 • (12/31/91) • **89**
Blanc de Blancs Sonoma County Green Valley 1986 • $22 • (12/31/90) • **87**
Blanc de Blancs Sonoma County Green Valley 1985 • $21 • (12/31/89) • **85**
Blanc de Blancs Sonoma County Green Valley 1984 • $19 • (12/31/88) • **79**
Blanc de Blancs Sonoma County Green Valley 1982 • $17 • (05/16/86) • **78**
Blanc de Blancs Sonoma County Green Valley 1981 • $18 • (11/01/84) • **86**
Blanc de Blancs Sonoma County Green Valley Late Disgorged 1982 • $24 • (12/31/87) • **85**
Blanc de Noirs Sonoma County Green Valley Wedding Cuvée 1992: Shows off the Pinot Noir's dried cherry and floral notes in a solid if unspectacular offering. 1,536 cases made. • $24 • **84**
Blanc de Noirs Sonoma County Green Valley 1989 • $23 • (08/31/92) • **82**
Blanc de Noirs Sonoma County Green Valley Wedding Cuvée 1990 • $25 • (07/31/93) • **86**
Blanc de Noirs Sonoma County Green Valley Wedding Cuvée 1988 • $24 • (10/31/91) • **84**
Blanc de Noirs Sonoma County Green Valley Wedding Cuvée 1986 • $19 • (05/31/89) • **90**
Blanc de Noirs Sonoma County Green Valley Wedding Cuvée 1985 • $17 • (12/31/88) • **86**
Blanc de Noirs Sonoma County Green Valley Wedding Cuvée 1984 • $17 • (12/31/87) • **85**
Blanc de Noirs Sonoma County Green Valley Wedding Cuvée 1983 • $17 • (12/31/86) • **82**
Brut Rosé Sonoma County Green Valley 1990: Mature spice and dried cherry flavors turn coarse and heavy on the finish. Drinking with food should soften some of the rough edges. 850 cases made. • $28 • (12/31/94) • **84**
Brut Rosé Sonoma County Green Valley 1989 • $28 • (12/31/93) • **81**
Brut Rosé Sonoma County Green Valley 1988 • $28 • (12/15/91) • **87**
Brut Rosé Sonoma County Green Valley 1987 • $28 • (12/31/90) • **84**
Brut Rosé Sonoma County Green Valley 1986 • $23 • (12/31/89) • **80**
Brut Rosé Sonoma County Green Valley 1985 • $20 • (12/31/88) • **88**
Brut Sonoma County Green Valley 1991: Smooth and well focused, marked by spice, ginger, pear and vanilla notes and picking up a toasty edge on the finish. 14,882 cases made. • $24 • **88**
Brut Sonoma County Green Valley 1990: A rich and earthy style with complex layers of toast, pear and spice notes that return to the earthy character on the finish. Ready now. 8,062 cases made. • $24 • (12/31/94) • **87**
Brut Sonoma County Green Valley 1989 • $20 • (12/31/93) • **85**
Brut Sonoma County Green Valley 1988 • $23 • (08/31/92) • **84**
Brut Sonoma County Green Valley 1987 • $21 • (11/15/90) • **89**
Brut Sonoma County Green Valley 1986 • $20 • (12/31/89) • **82**
Brut Sonoma County Green Valley 1985 • $18 • (12/31/88) • **83**
Brut Sonoma County Green Valley 1984 • $17 • (12/31/87) • **79**
Brut Sonoma County Green Valley 1983 • $17 • (12/31/86) • **87**
Brut Sonoma County Green Valley 1982 • $17 • (05/16/86) • **80**
Brut Sonoma County Green Valley Late Disgorged 1989: Creamy, smooth and complex, featuring a pippin apple and spicy fruit edge that lingers on the finish. Well focused and stylistic. 1,017 cases made. • $45 • (12/31/95) • **88**
Brut Sonoma County Green Valley Late Disgorged 1988 • $25 • (12/31/93) • **82**
Brut Sonoma County Green Valley Late Disgorged 1987 • $25 • (12/31/92) • **87**
Brut Sonoma County Green Valley Late Disgorged 1984 • $23 • (12/31/89) • **80**
Brut Sonoma County Green Valley Late Disgorged Vrais Amis 1986 • $25 • (12/15/91) • **90**
Brut Sonoma County Green Valley Vrais Amis 1989 • $25 • (12/31/93) • **87**
Cabernet Sauvignon Alexander Valley 1984 • $20 • (03/01/89) • **86**
Cabernet Sauvignon Alexander Valley 1983 • $18 • (03/01/89) • **82**
Cabernet Sauvignon Alexander Valley 1982 • $22 • (03/01/89) • **83**
Cabernet Sauvignon Alexander Valley 1981 • $24 • (03/01/89) • **79**
Cabernet Sauvignon Alexander Valley 1980 • $25 • (03/01/89) • **86**
Cabernet Sauvignon Alexander Valley 1979 • $23 • (03/01/89) • **91**
Cabernet Sauvignon Alexander Valley 1978 • $30 • (03/01/89) • **80**
Cabernet Sauvignon Alexander Valley T-T Reserve 1992: Tough and chewy, showing hard tannins. Enough cherry and berry flavor emerges to maintain your interest, but it's difficult to warm up to. Lacks finesse and harmony. Keep until 1998 for softening. 600 cases made. • $20 • (04/30/96) • **82**
Cabernets Alexander Valley 1990: A raw, awkward wine that trips over its tannins before finding its balance. The currant and berry fruit is ripe and chunky and the tannins are substantial, if a bit raw. On the finish it turns complex with hints of sour cherry and spice. Best to cellar until 1997 to allow it to soften. 1,001 cases made. • $19 • (11/15/93) • **88**
Cabernets Alexander Valley 1988 • $22 • (03/31/92) • **85**
Cabernets Alexander Valley 1987 • $20 • (03/15/91) • **86**
Cabernets Alexander Valley 1986 • $22 • (04/15/90) • **90**
Cabernets Alexander Valley 1985 • $21 • (03/01/89) • **87**

Key: SS—Spectator Selection. CS—Cellar Selection. BB—Best Buy. $NA—Price not available. (BT)—Barrel tasting. Ⓐ—Auction Price.
Dates in parentheses represent the issues in which the ratings were published.

Cabernets Alexander Valley T-T 1991: Smooth and elegant, with bright cherry and wild berry flavors, turning supple and polished on the finish where the tannins are mild. 4,260 cases made. • $19 • (12/15/95) • **87**

Cabernets Alexander Valley T-T Vineyards 1990: Firm and taut, with a narrow band of currant, black cherry and oak flavors that hold their focus through the finish, where the tannins become more evident. 1,001 cases made. • $15 • (10/31/94) • **86**

Cabernets Alexander Valley T-T Vineyards 1989 • $15 • (05/15/94) • **86**

Chardonnay Sonoma County Cuvée Joy 1993: An intense, crisp, juicy core of grapefruit and citrus flavor picks up a nice, oaky accent on the finish. Tight and complex. 500 cases made. • $19 • (05/15/95) • **90**

Chardonnay Sonoma County Green Valley 1994: Lean and tart, a trim band of pippin apple flavors giving it tangy character. 11,702 cases made. • $18 • (05/15/96) • **87**

Chardonnay Sonoma County Green Valley 1993: Marked by tight, compact green apple and pear notes. Crisp and refreshing, with fruity aftertaste. 12,400 cases made. • $18 • (05/15/95) • **87**

Chardonnay Sonoma County Green Valley 1991 • $18 • (04/30/93) • **91**

Chardonnay Sonoma County Green Valley Lot #2 1992: Crisp and lean, with spicy apple and pear flavors that turn elegant on the finish. Well-proportioned and ready to enjoy now. 8,690 cases made. • $17 • (06/30/94) • **86**

Demi-Sec Sonoma County Green Valley 1989 • $20 • (12/31/93) • **82**

Fumé Blanc Alexander Valley T-T Vineyards 1995: Bright, vibrant and citrusy, with a resiny streak that echoes floral and pear notes on the zingy finish. 2,100 cases made. • $13 • (06/30/96) • **88**

Fumé Blanc Alexander Valley T-T Vineyards 1994: Ripe, round floral and tropical fruit flavors finish soft and focused. 25 percent Viognier creates an unusual blend, filling the palate without much wood. 2,680 cases made. • $12 • (08/31/95) • **87**

Fumé Blanc Alexander Valley T-T Vineyards 1993: Ripe and fruity, soft-textured and spilling out nectarine and herbal vanilla flavors. Drinkable now. 1,073 cases made. • $12 • (11/30/94) • **87**

Fumé Blanc Alexander Valley T-T Vineyards 1992 • $11 • (03/31/94) • **85**

Fumé Blanc Alexander Valley T-T Vineyards 1991 • $13 • (11/30/92) • **86**

Pinot Noir 1986 • $18 • (06/15/88) • **92**

Pinot Noir 1985 • $18 • (06/15/88) • **77**

Pinot Noir Sonoma County Green Valley 1994: Just ripe, with cola, tea and herb flavors and a trace of black cherry. Finishes with a slightly green accent. 1,900 cases made. • $18 • **82**

Pinot Noir Sonoma County Green Valley 1993: An austere style with a trim band of cherry and black berry flavors that fails to take off. 3,489 cases made. • $18 • **84**

Pinot Noir Sonoma County Green Valley 1992: Intense and tannic, dense and oaky, packing in lots of flavor, with chunky ripe plum notes that turn diffuse and coarse on the finish. 940 cases made. • $19 • (10/31/94) • **87**

Pinot Noir Sonoma County Green Valley 1987 • $19 • (10/31/90) • **72**

Pinot Noir Sonoma County Green Valley 1982 • $10 • (10/01/85) • **76**

Sangiovese Alexander Valley T-T Vineyards 1993: Ripe and lively, delivering attractive black cherry, spice and raspberry flavors and an elegant aftertaste. Has the tannic strength to age into 1997. Contains 14 percent Cabernet Sauvignon. 144 cases made. • $18 • (04/30/96) • **87**

Sonoma County Green Valley Vrais Amis 1987 • $25 • (12/31/92) • **85**

Sonoma County Green Valley Wedding Cuvée 1993: Fresh and vibrant, featuring pretty cherry, strawberry and watermelon flavors that are ripe and pure. Lovely delicacy and finesse. 4,000 cases made. • $19 • (04/30/96) • **87**

Sonoma County Green Valley Wedding Cuvée 1991: Bright and fruity, with grapefruit notes paired with delicate raspberry flavors. Drinkable now. 2,982 cases made. • $20 • (11/15/94) • **87**

Sonoma County Green Valley Wedding Cuvée 1990 • $20 • (12/31/93) • **86**

Sparkling Sonoma County Green Valley Vrais Amis 1990: Tight, intense, crisp, flinty band of pear, earth and citrus, lively aftertaste and a burst of spice. 606 cases made. • $25 • **88**

Zinfandel Alexander Valley 1982 • $7 • (10/16/84) • **81**

IRURTIA, VINOS DANTE | NEW YORK

Ca' del Sacramento Carmelo 1985: There's not much left here. Light strawberry and herbal notes, the loosening grip of tannin, watery flavors and a short finish. Still quaffable, drink up. • $6 • (11/30/94) • **76**

JACKSON VALLEY | CALIFORNIA

Chardonnay Amador County 1994: Spicy, toasty flavors characterize this wine that finishes a bit short on fruit. 200 cases made. • $7 • (06/15/96) • **80**

Zinfandel Amador County 1990 • $9 • (10/15/92) • **83**

JADE MOUNTAIN | CALIFORNIA

Cabernet Sauvignon Alexander Valley Icaria Creek Vineyard deCarteret 1984 • $8 • (06/30/88) • **75**

Cotes Du Soleil California Red 1994: Has dusty, meaty flavors and ripe cherry too, but it's coarse and tannic on the finish. • $8 • **81**

Grenache American NV • $8 • (03/31/92) • **82**

La Provençale California Red 1994: Rustic and tannic. Wild berry and cherry flavors have a strong, meaty, peppery edge. Finishes with firm tannins and a touch of heat. • $15 • **84**

La Provençale California Red 1992: Firm and tight, with an earthy band of cherry, wild berry, anise and mineral flavors. Finishes with crisp tannins and good length. Can take a little aging. • $14 • (06/30/95) • **88**

La Provençale California Red 1990 • $12 • (03/15/92) • **80**

Les Jumeaux California Red 1994: Distinct, smoky, meaty and peppery flavors. Nice touches of berry and cherry come through on the finish, giving balance to the hard, green tannins. • $18 • **85**

Merlot Napa Valley 1993: Firm and chunky, with an intense core of plum, cherry and spice flavors that linger. Can age into 1997 to soften a bit. • $25 • (03/31/96) • **87**

Mourvèdre California 1991: Earthy, gamy, ashlike flavors run through this tough-textured red. 185 cases made. • $15 • (12/15/95) • **74**

Mourvèdre California 1990 • $15 • (03/15/92) • **81**

Mourvèdre Unfiltered 1990 • $15 • (03/15/92) • **83**

Syrah Napa Valley 1993: Firm and intense, with ripe currant, cherry and anise flavors. The fruit is pure and focused, but it struggles to stand up to the tannins, which are dry and coarse. Anyone's guess as to whether the tannins will soften. • $18 • **85**

Syrah Napa Valley 1992: Well crafted, elegant in style and body, with an attractive core of currant and cherry flavors, although it loses its intensity on the finish. Mildly tannic. • $18 • (06/30/95) • **87**

Zinfandel California 1991: A touch earthy, but the wild berry and raspberry flavors come through to give it balance. Finishes with a spicy anise edge. 190 cases made. • $13 • (10/15/95) • **85**

JAEGER | CALIFORNIA

Merlot Inglewood Vineyard 1986 • $15 • (05/31/92) • **88**

Merlot Napa Valley Inglewood Vineyard 1989: Crisp, lean and tannic. A hollow wine with shallow flavors. Disappointing, but typical of the vintage. • $19 • (09/15/94) • **77**

Merlot Napa Valley Inglewood Vineyard 1988 • $17 • (08/31/93) • **81**

Merlot Napa Valley Inglewood Vineyard 1987 • $15 • (05/31/92) • **81**

Merlot Napa Valley Inglewood Vineyard 1986 • $15 • (03/31/91) • **83**

Merlot Napa Valley Inglewood Vineyard 1985 • $16 • (02/15/90) • **89**

Merlot Napa Valley Inglewood Vineyard 1983 • $14 • (02/29/88) • **87**

JAFFURS | CALIFORNIA

Chardonnay Santa Barbara County Bien Nacido Vineyard 1994: Smooth and elegant, with a pleasant band of typical Chardonnay flavors that center on pear and citrus. Finishes simple, with a tart edge. 150 cases made. • $15 • (03/31/96) • **84**

Syrah Santa Barbara County Thompson Vineyard 1994: Dark, ripe, rich and intense, packing a wallop with its ripe, vivid wild berry and black cherry flavors. Well defined and focused, right tannin level on the finish, making it appealing now or worthy of cellaring into 1997. 250 cases made. • $14 • (02/29/96) • **91**

JAMESPORT | New York

Cabernet Sauvignon North Fork of Long Island North House 1987 • $10 • (06/30/91) • **78**

Merlot North Fork of Long Island 1986 • $9 • (06/30/91) • **72**

JANKRIS | California

Chardonnay Paso Robles 1992: Seriously flawed, with gluey, toasty, bitter flavors. Avoid. 236 cases made. • $10 • (06/30/94) • **62**

Merlot Paso Robles 1992: Bright and fruity, oozing with blackberry flavors that echo on the crisp, polished finish. Drinkable now through 1997. 303 cases made. • $12 • (09/15/94) • **85**

Merlot Paso Robles 1991 • $11 • (08/31/93) • **84**

Zinfandel Paso Robles 1993: Features bright, ripe, juicy Zinfandel flavors, with notes of black cherry and strawberry jam. Fine tannins and drinkable now. 470 cases made. • $9 • (10/15/95) • **87**

Zinfandel Paso Robles 1992: Has buttery oak shadings, but it doesn't have the fruity richness to match. Ready now. 159 cases made. • $10 • (10/15/94) • **78**

Zinfandel Paso Robles 1991 • $8 • (09/30/93) • **81**

JARVIS | California

Cabernet Franc Napa Valley 1992: Marked by some stalky tobacco and green herb accents, but enough of the currant and cedary oak flavors come into play to keep up the balancing act. • $40 • (08/31/95) • **86**

Cabernet Sauvignon Napa Valley 1993: A 100-percent Cabernet, smooth, elegant and polished, showing slightly more tannin than its companion blend Lake William, but similar currant, cedar, cherry and spice flavors. Appealing now, will age well through 2001. 400 cases made. • $48 • (05/15/96) • **88**

Cabernet Sauvignon Napa Valley 1992: Supple and polished, a wine of finesse and grace, with ripe black cherry, currant, cedar and tobacco notes, finishing with mild, integrated tannins, light oak shadings and good length. • $48 • (08/31/95) • **90**

Chardonnay Napa Valley 1992: Elegant and well balanced, with a smooth core of creamy pear, honey and butterscotch notes. The lingering finish is laced with light, toasty oak. • $34 • (08/31/95) • **90**

Lake William Red Napa Valley 1993: Well-crafted blend of Cabernet Sauvignon (64 percent) and Cabernet Franc (34 percent), exhibiting an elegant, spicy cherry, cedar and currant range of flavors and finishing with mild tannins and good length. 500 cases made. • $45 • (05/15/96) • **88**

JEKEL | California

Cabernet Franc Monterey 1990: Marked by cedary oak flavors, a narrow band of cherry and currant emerges, but it turns stalky on the finish. 2,072 cases made. • $13 • (07/31/95) • **82**

Cabernet Sauvignon Arroyo Seco 1990: Firm, intense and tannic, but with enough currant and berry notes to sustain your interest, there is a light oak finish. 10,160 cases made. • $13 • (11/15/94) • **84**

Cabernet Sauvignon Arroyo Seco 1989 • $13 • (04/30/93) • **81**

Cabernet Sauvignon Arroyo Seco 1988 • $12 • (03/15/93) • **80**

Cabernet Sauvignon Arroyo Seco 1986 • $13 • (11/15/90) • **83**

Cabernet Sauvignon Arroyo Seco Home Vineyard 1980 • $25 • (02/01/86) • **63**

Cabernet Sauvignon Arroyo Seco The Sanctuary Estate 1992: Smooth and generous, a mouthful of supple berry, black cherry and tobacco flavors that finishes round and almost drinkable. Best from 1997-1998. 8,000 cases made. • $13 • (12/15/95) • **87**

Cabernet Sauvignon Monterey 1984 • $12 • (07/31/89) • **63**

Cabernet Sauvignon Monterey 1983 • $8 • (02/15/89) • **67**

Cabernet Sauvignon Monterey 1982 • $11 • (01/31/87) • **71**

Key: SS—Spectator Selection. CS—Cellar Selection. BB—Best Buy. $NA—Price not available. (BT)—Barrel tasting. (A)—Auction Price.
Dates in parentheses represent the issues in which the ratings were published.

Cabernet Sauvignon Monterey Home Vineyard Private Reserve 1982 • $20 • (02/01/86) • **69**

Cabernet Sauvignon Monterey Home Vineyard Private Reserve 1981 • $20 • (02/01/86) • **76**

Cabernet Sauvignon Monterey Home Vineyard Private Reserve 1979 • $18 • (02/01/86) • **77**

Cabernet Sauvignon Monterey Home Vineyard Private Reserve 1978 • $16 • (02/01/86) • **70**

Cabernet Sauvignon Monterey Private Reserve 1978 • $22 • (11/15/92) • **68**

Chardonnay Arroyo Seco Gravelstone Vineyard 1993: Lean and spicy, simple and pleasant with its apple and toast flavors. 18,500 cases made. • $10 • (07/31/95) • **82**

Chardonnay Arroyo Seco Gravelstone Vineyard 1992: Coarse and flinty, with crisp apple and pear flavors that finish with a rough texture. Drink now. 11,500 cases made. • $10 • (06/30/94) • **80**

Chardonnay Arroyo Seco Gravelstone Vineyard 1991 • $10 • (05/31/94) BB • **86**

Johannisberg Riesling Arroyo Seco 1991 • $7 • (08/31/93) • **85**

Meritage Arroyo Seco The Sanctuary Estate 1992: Marked by an herbal-vegetal edge, it offers just enough cherry and berry fruit to achieve balance. 3,000 cases made. • $13 • (12/15/95) • **83**

Meritage Symmetry Arroyo Seco 1989 • $20 • (11/15/93) • **85**

Meritage Symmetry Arroyo Seco The Sanctuary Estate 1987 • $25 • (03/31/93) • **77**

Merlot Arroyo Seco The Sanctuary Estate 1993: Clean and correct, with cedar, herb and some very nice dried cherry notes. 10,000 cases made. • $13 • **82**

Merlot Arroyo Seco The Sanctuary Estate 1992: Intense and tannic, with firm herb, spice, mineral and currant flavors, but it turns dry and tannic on the finish. Best after 1996. • $15 • (09/15/94) • **83**

Pinot Noir Arroyo Seco 1992 • $14 • (02/28/94) • **84**

Pinot Noir Arroyo Seco Gravelstone Vineyard 1993: Medium-bodied, with a tannic edge to the modest cherry and berry flavors. Good but nothing more. 2,600 cases made. • $15 • (01/31/96) • **82**

Pinot Noir Arroyo Seco Home Vineyard 1982 • $20 • (06/30/87) • **57**

Riesling Late Harvest Arroyo Seco Gravelstone Vineyard 1987 • $14/375ml • (02/28/89) • **77**

JENNER VINEYARDS | California

Cabernet Sauvignon Dry Creek Valley 1992: A rustic style with many curious flavors, but not much in the way of focus or finesse. Doubtful whether it can improve. • $6 • (03/31/96) • **75**

JEPSON | California

Blanc de Blancs Mendocino 1989: Smooth and elegant, with spicy pear, vanilla and crisp apple notes. Finishes with a soft aftertaste. Ready now. 2,500 cases made. • $16 • (12/31/94) • **85**

Blanc de Blancs Mendocino 1988 • $16 • (12/15/93) • **88**

Blanc de Blancs Mendocino 1986 • $16 • (04/30/91) • **86**

Brut Mendocino 1985 • $16 • (12/31/88) • **82**

Chardonnay Mendocino 1992: Ripe and juicy, with a flinty edge to the pear and apple notes and spicy oak notes. 2,700 cases made. • $14 • (02/28/95) • **87**

Chardonnay Mendocino 1991: Decadent flavors go over the top, robbing this of freshness and making it seem spoiled. 2,950 cases made. • $14 • (06/30/94) • **68**

Chardonnay Mendocino County Estate Select 1994: Lean and spicy, with prominent oak flavors that stand out more than fruit. • $14 • (06/15/96) • **82**

Sauvignon Blanc Mendocino 1993: Smooth and refreshing, lively and fruity enough to show off the mildly herbal pear flavors, soft finish. 3,000 cases made. • $8 • (08/31/95) • **82**

Sauvignon Blanc Mendocino 1992: Soft and fruity, almost sweet on the palate, with a candied edge to the finish. 3,000 cases made. • $8 • (08/31/94) • **77**

Sauvignon Blanc Mendocino County Estate Select 1994: Smooth and juicy, with some nice peppery notes wrapped in a ripe nectarine package. Drinkable now. 2,300 cases made. • $8 • (05/31/96) • **87**

JESSANDRA VITTORIA | CALIFORNIA

Santa Vittoria Sonoma Valley 1994: A blend of Cabernet (70 percent) and Sangiovese. A touch leathery, but enough cherry and currant flavors emerge to give it polish and a measure of finesse. 396 cases made. • $25 • **83**

JOHNSON TURNBULL | CALIFORNIA

Cabernet Sauvignon Napa Valley 1991: Shows the classic mint and bay leaf aromas of this vineyard, but it also delivers enough juicy currant and cherry-laced Cabernet fruit to keep it interesting. Has the tannic strength for cellaring, best after 1998. 3,400 cases made. • $18 • (10/31/94) • **89**

Cabernet Sauvignon Napa Valley 1990: Decidedly minty, a lean wine with an austere feel to it, showing just a touch of fruit to balance out the finish. Try in 1997. 3,000 cases made. • $16 • (03/31/94) • **81**

Cabernet Sauvignon Napa Valley 1989 • $16 • (08/31/93) • **85**

Cabernet Sauvignon Napa Valley 1988 • $16 • (11/15/91) • **84**

Cabernet Sauvignon Napa Valley 1987 • $16 • (11/15/90) • **80**

Cabernet Sauvignon Napa Valley 1985 • $18 • (03/01/89) • **83**

Cabernet Sauvignon Napa Valley 1984 • $20 • (03/01/89) • **90**

Cabernet Sauvignon Napa Valley 1983 • $19 • (03/01/89) • **88**

Cabernet Sauvignon Napa Valley 1982 • $25 • (03/01/89) • **82**

Cabernet Sauvignon Napa Valley 1981 • $31 • (03/01/89) • **87**

Cabernet Sauvignon Napa Valley 1980 • $29 • (03/01/89) • **87**

Cabernet Sauvignon Napa Valley 1979 • $31 • (03/01/89) • **85**

Cabernet Sauvignon Napa Valley Vineyard Selection 67 1990: Potently minty, but with a nice currant and plum edge underneath. The texture is supple and the tannins on the finish firm up. Best to cellar until 1997 for more nuance and complexity. 300 cases made. • $34 • (04/30/94) • **87**

Cabernet Sauvignon Napa Valley Vineyard Selection 67 1989 • $16 • (11/15/93) • **87**

Cabernet Sauvignon Napa Valley Vineyard Selection 67 1988 • $22 • (08/31/93) • **86**

Cabernet Sauvignon Napa Valley Vineyard Selection 67 1987 • $22 • (06/30/91) • **89**

Cabernet Sauvignon Napa Valley Vineyard Selection 67 1986 • $25 • (04/15/90) • **86**

Cabernet Sauvignon Napa Valley Vineyard Selection 82 1986 • $15 • (08/31/89) • **95**

JOLIESSE | CALIFORNIA

Chardonnay California Reserve 1994: Zingy, fruity and a bargain too. This offers a real mouthful of complex peach, pear and spice flavors. 15,000 cases made. • $7 • (05/31/96) BB • **86**

Sauvignon Blanc California Reserve 1994: Generous herb and sweet pear flavors make this a pleasant, easy-to-drink wine. 15,000 cases made. • $7 • (05/31/96) • **82**

JORDAN | CALIFORNIA

Cabernet Sauvignon Alexander Valley 1994: Light in this tasting, with grapey cherry and berry notes of modest proportion. Does not appear to have seen any oak. • $30 • (05/31/95) • **80-84** (BT)

Cabernet Sauvignon Alexander Valley 1991: A touch green, with a lean, cedary edge to the herb and cherry notes. Finishes with firm tannins, but not much length or complexity. • $25 • (06/15/95) • **84**

Cabernet Sauvignon Alexander Valley 1990: Tight, young and chunky, especially for Jordan, but the flavors are familiar, with herb, currant and spicy wood flavors. The tannin level on the finish suggests this wine be cellared another three to five years, but it has richness, depth and good extract. • $25 • (06/30/94) • **87**

Cabernet Sauvignon Alexander Valley 1989 • $24 • (11/15/93) • **80**

Cabernet Sauvignon Alexander Valley 1988 • $27 • (11/15/92) • **85**

Cabernet Sauvignon Alexander Valley 1987 • $36 Ⓐ • (11/15/91) • **90**

Cabernet Sauvignon Alexander Valley 1986 • $22 • (11/15/90) • **88**

Cabernet Sauvignon Alexander Valley 1985 • $46 Ⓐ • (09/15/89) • **88**

Cabernet Sauvignon Alexander Valley 1984 • $43 Ⓐ • (10/10/90) • **80**

Cabernet Sauvignon Alexander Valley 1983 • $51 • (03/01/89) • **78**

Cabernet Sauvignon Alexander Valley 1982 • $38 • (03/01/89) • **73**

Cabernet Sauvignon Alexander Valley 1981 • $46 • (03/01/89) • **84**

Cabernet Sauvignon Alexander Valley 1980 • $24 Ⓐ • (03/01/89) • **80**

Cabernet Sauvignon Alexander Valley 1979 • $29 Ⓐ • (03/01/89) • **79**

Cabernet Sauvignon Alexander Valley 1978 • $NA • (11/15/92) • **80**

Cabernet Sauvignon Alexander Valley 1977 • $36 Ⓐ • (03/01/89) • **77**

Cabernet Sauvignon Alexander Valley 1976 • $38 Ⓐ • (03/01/89) • **79**

Chardonnay Alexander Valley 1992: Medium-weight, with crisp pear and apple shadings, finishing with a crisp snappy edge. Reflects a different style for Jordan, as it's less opulent and oaky. • $21 • (07/31/95) • **86**

Chardonnay Alexander Valley 1991: Soft and floral with a ripe apple edge that picks up a slight candied note on the finish. Nice oak shading shows Jordan's progress with Chardonnay, but it's still not among the Alexander Valley elite. Ready now. • $19 • (06/30/94) • **84**

Chardonnay Sonoma County 1993: Pleasant enough, with modest pear, apple and spice notes, turns simple on the finish. • $20 • (06/30/96) • **84**

Sonoma County J 1990: Offers more complexity and finesse than most other California sparkling wines. This is intense and concentrated, with bright, lively, well-defined pear, spice and black cherry flavors. The complex and creamy aftertaste is long and lingering. 25,000 cases made. • $23 • (11/30/95) SS • **91**

Sonoma County J 1989 • $24 • (07/31/93) • **89**

Sonoma County J 1987 • $22 • (05/15/91) • **88**

JORY | CALIFORNIA

Black Hand Mano Nera California 1993: Dark-colored, ripe, intense, spicy band of raspberry flavor. A blend of Zinfandel, Mourvèdre and Syrah. 573 cases made. • $13 • (04/30/95) • **85**

Chardonnay California White Zeppelin Blimp de Blanc 1992: A fat, round wine (seems appropriate, doesn't it?), but the flavors veer off into a sweet, candied earthiness before returning to the flight pattern with a core of pear and peach. Drinkable now. 423 cases made. • $10 • (06/30/94) • **83**

Chardonnay Monterey Reserve 1991 • $23 • (03/31/93) • **84**

Chardonnay Santa Clara County Selected Clone 1992: Earthy with a strong caramel streak to add an extra dimension to the apple and grapefruit flavors. Try now. 499 cases made. • $17 • (06/30/94) • **86**

Claret Old Barrister California 1990 • $13 • (10/15/92) • **84**

Pinot Noir California Santa Clara County San Ysidro 1989 • $20 • (02/28/93) • **81**

Pinot Noir Santa Clara County 1986 • $19 • (06/15/88) • **76**

Pinot Noir Santa Clara Valley San Ysidro Bon Jory 1989 • $9 • (02/28/93) • **76**

Red Zeppelin Bon Jory Red California 1991: Light and definitely gamy. A hollow wine that shows more earthy flavor than fruit. Drinkable now. 673 cases made. • $10 • (09/30/94) • **80**

Red Zeppelin Bon Jory Red California 1989 • $10 • (11/30/92) • **88**

Red Zeppelin II The Emperor's Reserve Red California 1990 • $15 • (10/15/93) • **86**

Zinfandel California Old Barrister Cuvée 91 1991: Earthy and tannic, with a medicinal edge to the raspberry and wild berry flavors. Very dry and tannic on the finish. 492 cases made. • $13 • (10/15/94) • **81**

JOULLIAN | CALIFORNIA

Cabernet Sauvignon Carmel Valley 1990: Warm and ripe, with a cooked edge to the berry and plum fruit, edging toward earth and smoke on the finish. Best from 1999. 1,520 cases made. • $14 • (12/15/95) • **83**

Cabernet Sauvignon Carmel Valley 1989: Firm and tannic, with a narrow band of earthy Cabernet fruit. Doubtful this one's going anywhere. 1,298 cases made. • $14 • (11/15/94) • **81**

Cabernet Sauvignon Carmel Valley 1987 • $14 • (07/31/91) • **81**

Chardonnay Carmel Valley Family Reserve 1991: Strives for complexity with its smoky, toasty oak overlay, but that can't quite shield the charred, earthy notes that come through. Solid but perhaps a bit overproduced. Ready now. 168 cases made. • $18 • (06/30/94) • **84**

Chardonnay Monterey 1994: Smooth and spicy, showing some nice pear and subtle, raisinlike flavors that linger. 4,410 cases made. • $12 • (06/15/96) • **87**

Chardonnay Monterey 1993: Medium-bodied with enough ripe pear and citrus notes to hold your interest, even if the flavors are modest. 3,543 cases made. • $11 • (07/31/95) • **82**

Chardonnay Monterey 1992: Woody flavors stand out and dominate in this young Chardonnay. You get hints of pear and peach before the oak takes over. Ready now. 2,900 cases made. • $11 • (06/30/94) • **81**

Chardonnay Monterey 1991 • $10 • (06/15/93) • **84**

Chardonnay Monterey Family Reserve 1993: A crisp, eye-opening acidity to balance the ripe pineapple and spice flavors. Finishes in a pleasing harmony. 200 cases made. • $20 • (06/15/96) • **86**

Chardonnay Monterey Family Reserve 1992: Bold, ripe and complex, with a rich and complex core of honey, pear, toast and spice, all folding together for a wonderful aftertaste echoing fruit and oak. 200 cases made. • $18 • (07/31/95) • **89**

Sauvignon Blanc Carmel Valley 1994: Lots of mineral aromas and flavors come to the fore in this lean, spicy wine. A hint of oak on the finish. 2,057 cases made. • $9 • **81**

Sauvignon Blanc Carmel Valley 1993: Lean and modest in scope, adding a waxy edge to the tinge of pear and citrus flavors sneaking in on the finish. 2,432 cases made. • $8 • (08/31/95) • **81**

Sauvignon Blanc Carmel Valley 1992: Sturdy, spicy and round, maybe a little sweet, but balanced and drinkable. 1,805 cases made. • $7 • (08/31/94) BB • **84**

Sauvignon Blanc Carmel Valley Family Reserve 1994: Crisp and lively in the mouth. Spicy, citrus flavors include an attractive essence of orange peel. 200 cases made. • $14 • **85**

Sauvignon Blanc Carmel Valley Family Reserve 1993: Shows a little more oak than most, modest levels of spicy grapefruit character never get going very fast. 200 cases made. • $13 • (08/31/95) • **83**

Sauvignon Blanc Carmel Valley Family Reserve 1992: Spicy, toasty flavors dominate this soft-textured, buttery wine. Pleasant to drink now. 168 cases made. • $12 • (08/31/94) • **85**

JOYA | CALIFORNIA

Pinot Blanc Napa Valley 1991: Smooth and buttery, with a floral edge to the modest flavors, finishing soft and a little spicy. Ready now. 350 cases made. • $8 • (04/15/95) • **83**

Zinfandel Napa Valley 1992: A big, ripe, jammy style with tannins to match. A wild, juniper berry flavor gives it an earthy edge. Finishes with crisp tannins. Drinkable now. 200 cases made. • $9 • (08/31/94) • **86**

JUDD'S HILL | CALIFORNIA

Cabernet Sauvignon Napa Valley 1994: Firm but with an appealing core of wild berry jam flavors and toasty oak that are complex. • $NA • (05/31/95) • **90-94** (BT)

Cabernet Sauvignon Napa Valley 1992: Rich and plush, with an exotic core of rich currant, black cherry and wild berry flavors. Turns tight and tannic on the finish, but the fruit pushes through. Best after 1999. 1,500 cases made. • $26 • (12/15/95) • **91**

Cabernet Sauvignon Napa Valley 1991: Packs in lots of ripe, juicy plum and currant flavors that pick up subtle herb, tea, spice and tobacco notes. Has an elegant, supple, polished texture, with oaky vanilla notes lingering in the background. Impressive for its subtlety and finesse. Best after 1998. 1,500 cases made. • $24 • (09/30/94) SS • **93**

Cabernet Sauvignon Napa Valley 1989 • $20 • (04/15/92) • **89**

JULIEN, CHATEAU | CALIFORNIA

Cabernet Sauvignon Monterey County Private Reserve 1989 • $20 • (08/31/92) • **79**

Chardonnay Monterey County Barrel Fermented 1991 • $8 • (07/15/93) • **79**

Key: SS—Spectator Selection. CS—Cellar Selection. BB—Best Buy. $NA—Price not available. (BT)—Barrel tasting. (A)—Auction Price.
Dates in parentheses represent the issues in which the ratings were published.

Chardonnay Monterey County Grand Reserve 1993: Marked by an earthy, sour, grapefruit edge and vegetal notes. Offers enough flavors, even if they miss the mainstream for this varietal. • $7 • (05/15/96) • **79**

Chardonnay Monterey County Private Reserve 1991: Mature with ripe apricot flavors that take on a rich but earthy edge, picking up a honeyed edge on the finish. Tastes overly mature. 690 cases made. • $15 • (07/31/95) • **80**

Chardonnay Monterey County Sur Lie Private Reserve 1993: Light and simple, bordering on sweet, as just a tinge of nectarine makes it interesting. Ready now. 600 cases made. • $17 • (12/15/95) • **75**

Chardonnay Monterey County Sur Lie Private Reserve 1991: Ripe and broad but the flavors are strange, more meaty than fruity, an earthy Chardonnay that has plenty of personality but a strange one. 1,200 cases made. • $11 • (06/30/94) • **83**

Merlot Monterey County 1989 • $9 • (05/31/92) • **86**

Merlot Monterey County 1991 • $10 • (05/31/93) • **84**

Merlot Monterey County 1988 • $9 • (05/31/92) • **72**

Merlot Monterey County 1986 • $10 • (04/15/89) • **60**

Merlot Monterey County Grand Reserve 1994: Light and appealing, with ripe currant and blueberry flavors and a smooth finish. Drinkable now. 2,400 cases made. • $9 • (06/30/96) • **85**

Merlot Monterey County Private Reserve 1991: Supple and elegant, with a ripe core of cherry, currant and cedary oak flavors that linger on the finish. This winery continues to make a fine-value Merlot. Ready now through 1997. 1,200 cases made. • $9 • (09/15/94) BB • **85**

Merlot Santa Barbara County Bien Nacido Vineyard 1984 • $12 • (02/29/88) • **76**

JUSTIN | CALIFORNIA

Blanc de Noir Paso Robles 1985 • $23 • (12/31/91) • **84**

Cabernet Blend Reserve Paso Robles 1988 • $23 • (11/15/91) • **75**

Cabernet Blend Reserve Paso Robles 1987 • $20 • (02/15/91) • **90**

Cabernet Franc Paso Robles 1989 • $20 • (11/15/92) • **86**

Cabernet Franc San Luis Obispo 1991: Deep color and rich, chewy tannins to match. This has an intriguing array of plum and black cherry flavors peeking through on the finish that makes for a complex aftertaste. Cellar until 1997, when the tannins should be more manageable. 500 cases made. • $20 • (12/31/94) • **87**

Cabernet Sauvignon Paso Robles 1989 • $19 • (11/15/92) • **81**

Cabernet Sauvignon Paso Robles 1988 • $19 • (11/15/91) • **72**

Cabernet Sauvignon San Luis Obispo County 1992: Complex and inviting, with pretty, toasty oak, wild berry and cherry flavors, finishing with mild tannins and good length. Well proportioned and supple. 1,500 cases made. • $18 • (12/15/95) • **88**

Cabernet Sauvignon San Luis Obispo County 1990: Strives for complexity with its earthy currant and cherry flavors, but it turns tannic and leathery at mid-palate. On the finish it straightens out, but the finish is muddled and out of focus. Try now. 875 cases made. • $19 • (11/15/93) • **80**

Cabernet Sauvignon San Luis Obispo County Obtuse 1992: Smooth and fruity, centering around currant, raspberry and spice flavors that finish in a tight grip of alcohol and minimal tannin. Best from 1997 to 1999. 230 cases made. • $23 • (09/30/95) • **84**

Cabernet Sauvignon San Luis Obispo Society Reserve 1991: Ripe and juicy, with plump plum and cherry flavors and light oak shadings. An appealing and forward style of Cabernet. Tempting to drink now, probably best after 1997. 1,237 cases made. • $19 • (11/15/94) • **88**

Isosceles Reserve Cabernet Blend San Luis Obispo County 1992: Smooth and polished for such a rich wine. This California red packs in lots of complex flavors, weaving together currant, coffee, cedar and cherry into a complex and compelling style. Delicious now, but better in 1997. 1,100 cases made. • $25 • (12/15/95) • **92**

Isosceles Reserve Cabernet Blend San Luis Obispo 1991: Big and ripe with bright black cherry and plum flavor. Picks up earthy tannins along with a gamy metallic edge on the long finish. Best after 1998. 1,056 cases made. • $23 • (11/15/94) • **84**

Isosceles Reserve Cabernet Blend San Luis Obispo County 1990: Ripe, smooth and complex with strong, focused, earthy currant flavors that run through it. Picks up toasty, buttery oak and an earthy note on the finish. Drinkable now. 430 cases made. • $23 • (11/15/93) • **88**

Isosceles Reserve Cabernet Blend Paso Robles 1989 • $23 • (11/15/92) • **86**
Justification Cabernet Blend San Luis Obispo County 1992: Leans toward the vegetal side, but it puts a racy kick into the cherry and plum flavors. Smooth texture, ample tannins and doesn't shortchange you on flavor. 975 cases made. • $20 • (05/15/95) • **87**
Merlot San Luis Obispo County 1992: A ripe and complex California red with a rich core of juicy plum and cherry flavors. Has a nice sense of depth and proportion, picking up herb, coffee, cedar and chocolate notes, finishing with firm tannins. Tempting now for its vibrant fruit, but worth aging into 1997. 1,500 cases made. • $20 • (12/31/95) • **91**

KALIN | CALIFORNIA

Cabernet Sauvignon Sonoma County Reserve 1988 • $26 • (08/31/92) • **81**
Cabernet Sauvignon Sonoma County Reserve 1985 • $23 • (04/15/91) • **83**
Pinot Noir Sonoma County Cuvée DD 1986 • $20 • (04/30/91) • **80**

KALINDA | CALIFORNIA

Zinfandel Paso Robles 1991: Appealing for its supple raspberry and cherry notes, this also adds a nice spicy twist on the finish. • $9 • (10/15/95) • **84**

KARLY | CALIFORNIA

Cabernet Sauvignon El Dorado Stromberg Carpenter Vineyard 1991: An earthy, herbal style with muddled currant and plum flavors. Drinkable now. • $15 • (11/15/94) • **82**
Chardonnay Edna Valley MacGregor Vineyard 1992: Sturdy flavorful white with a spice-honey edge to the apple flavor. 892 cases made. • $14 • (06/30/94) • **81**
Chardonnay Edna Valley MacGregor Vineyard 1991 • $14 • (07/15/93) • **84**
Petite Sirah Amador County 1989 • $12 • (03/15/92) • **65**
Petite Sirah Amador County Not So Petite Sirah 1991: Smooth and flavorful, with a wild edge to the berry character, finishing slightly gamy. Drinkable now. 504 cases made. • $12 • (09/30/94) • **83**
Petite Sirah Amador County Not So Petite Sirah 1988 • $14 • (12/31/90) • **81**
Sauvignon Blanc Amador County 1993: Smooth and fruity, generous and definitive, leafy, herbal overtones add to the pear and melon flavors. 2,243 cases made. • $8 • (01/31/95) • **83**
Sauvignon Blanc Amador County 1992 • $8 • (01/31/94) • **82**
Sauvignon Blanc Amador County 1991 • $8 • (04/15/93) • **79**
Syrah Amador County 1992: A ripe, chewy, solid red that beams its plum and berry flavors brightly through the chunky tannins. 745 cases made. • $13 • (01/31/95) • **85**
White Zinfandel Amador County 1988 • $7 • (06/15/89) • **76**
Zinfandel Amador County 1994: Ruggedly earthy, powerful style adds a leathery rim to the plum and wild berry flavors. Big and ripe, lots of tannin, comes across as clumsy. 2,734 cases made. • $12 • (04/30/96) • **79**
Zinfandel Amador County 1993: An earthy, gamy style that is slightly funky, but it holds together. Enough wild berry flavors keep your interest. 2,453 cases made. • $10 • (10/15/95) • **82**
Zinfandel Amador County 1992: Intense and a bit raw, but with enough spicy cherry and raspberry flavors to hold your interest. Drink now. 970 cases made. • $9 • (10/15/94) • **82**
Zinfandel Amador County 1990 • $9 • (09/15/93) • **86**
Zinfandel Amador County 1989 • $9 • (10/15/92) • **74**
Zinfandel Amador County 1988 • $9 • (12/31/90) • **83**
Zinfandel Amador County 1987 • $9 • (03/31/90) • **83**
Zinfandel Amador County 1986 • $9 • (03/31/89) • **79**
Zinfandel Amador County 1985 • $8 • (12/31/87) • **72**
Zinfandel Amador County Pokerville 1993: A touch earthy, but the cherry and wild berry flavors are very ripe and floral in this bargain of a California red. Hints of jam seep in around the palate and the fruity finish shows dry tannins. 2,000 cases made. • $8 • (10/15/95) • **87**
Zinfandel Amador County Pokerville 1990 • $6 • (09/15/93) BB • **88**
Zinfandel Amador County Sadie Upton Vineyard 1992: A ripe, jammy style that gushes with fresh black cherry, raspberry and plum flavors plus earthy notes on the tannic finish. Enjoy now. • $14 • (01/31/95) • **88**
Zinfandel Amador County Sadie Upton Vineyard 1991: Earthy and gamy, with coarse, leathery flavors. 500 cases made. • $15 • (10/15/94) • **77**
Zinfandel Amador County Sadie Upton Vineyard 1989 • $15 • (03/31/92) • **81**

KAUTZ (IRONSTONE) | CALIFORNIA

Chardonnay California Gold Canyon 1991 • $10 • (04/15/93) • **81**
Merlot California Highlands 1990 • $10 • (03/31/93) • **76**

KEDEM | NEW YORK

Charmat Kosher New York NV • $6 • (12/31/90) • **72**

KEEBLE, ROBERT | CALIFORNIA

Cabernet Franc Sonoma County 1988 • $12 • (11/15/91) • **79**
Cabernet Sauvignon Napa Valley 1989 • $14 • (11/15/92) • **80**
Cabernet Sauvignon Napa Valley 1987 • $14 • (10/15/91) • **89**

KEENAN | CALIFORNIA

Cabernet Sauvignon Napa Valley 1992: Hard-edged and leathery with a young, green streak to the currant and cedar flavors. Aggressive tannins are unpleasant. 2,349 cases made. • $20 • **74**
Cabernet Sauvignon Napa Valley 1991: With a strong mint and menthol streak, this has more character than most, tending toward earthy flavors over fruit. Best from 1997. 1,850 cases made. • $21 • (12/15/95) • **85**
Cabernet Sauvignon Napa Valley 1989 • $18 • (11/15/93) • **83**
Cabernet Sauvignon Napa Valley 1988 • $18 • (03/31/92) • **85**
Cabernet Sauvignon Napa Valley 1987 • $19 • (05/31/90) • **86**
Cabernet Sauvignon Napa Valley 1986 • $20 • (08/31/89) • **93**
Cabernet Sauvignon Napa Valley 1985 • $15 • (03/31/89) • **79**
Cabernet Sauvignon Napa Valley 1984 • $25 • (03/01/89) • **92**
Cabernet Sauvignon Napa Valley 1983 • $17 • (03/01/89) • **87**
Cabernet Sauvignon Napa Valley 1982 • $35 • (03/01/89) • **88**
Cabernet Sauvignon Napa Valley 1981 • $22 • (03/01/89) • **84**
Cabernet Sauvignon Napa Valley 1980 • $25 • (03/01/89) • **80**
Cabernet Sauvignon Napa Valley 1979 • $28 • (03/01/89) • **74**
Cabernet Sauvignon Napa Valley 1978 • $28 • (11/15/92) • **78**
Cabernet Sauvignon Napa Valley 1977 • $25 • (03/01/89) • **69**
Chardonnay Napa Valley 1993: Tart and crisp lemon, grapefruit and hints of pear, an elegant and refined style that finishes in a fruity aftertaste. 2,025 cases made. • $15 • (10/15/95) • **88**
Chardonnay Napa Valley 1992: Rich and smoky, with toasty oak flavors that add dimension and depth to the ripe pear and apple notes. • $15 • (12/31/94) • **87**
Chardonnay Napa Valley 1991 • $15 • (04/15/93) • **83**
Chardonnay Napa Valley Hillside 1994: A juicy wine with spicy citrus, grapefruit and tart pear notes that finish crisply. 1,750 cases made. • $15 • (06/15/96) • **83**
Merlot 1988 • $18 • (05/31/92) • **84**
Merlot Napa Valley 1993: Smooth and harmonious, with a supple band of ripe cherry, currant and vanilla flavors. Nice sense of balance and proportion, although the tannins are quite assertive on the finish. 2,700 cases made. • $25 • (06/30/96) • **86**
Merlot Napa Valley 1992: Firm and a bit austere, showing trim bands of currant, tea and herb flavors, but what stands out is the crispness and acidity. 2,500 cases made. • $17 • (09/30/95) • **83**
Merlot Napa Valley 1990 • $18 • (07/15/93) • **83**
Merlot Napa Valley 1989 • $18 • (05/31/92) • **82**
Merlot Napa Valley 1987 • $20 • (03/31/90) • **88**
Merlot Napa Valley 1986 • $18 • (06/30/89) • **90**
Merlot Napa Valley 1985 • $19 • (05/31/88) • **83**
Merlot Napa Valley 1984 • $30 • (07/31/87) CS • **94**
Merlot Napa Valley Vintners Selection 1990 • $25 • (07/15/93) • **88**

KELTIE BROOK | CALIFORNIA

Pinot Noir Carneros Unfiltered 1991 • $10 • (02/28/93) • **84**

KENDALL-JACKSON | CALIFORNIA

Cabernet Franc California Vintner's Reserve 1992: A green herbal and cedary oak edge adds to the spicy currant and berry notes. Firmly tannic finish, but drinkable now through 1997. • $15 • (01/31/95) • **82**

Cabernet Sauvignon California Cardinale 1986 • $65 • (11/15/90) • **91**

Cabernet Sauvignon California Cardinale 1985 • $45 • (11/15/89) • **97**

Cabernet Sauvignon California Grand Reserve 1994: Trim and firm, with a tight band of currant, toasty oak and black cherry fruit that unfolds nicely on the finish. Firmly tannic, borders on outstanding. • $30 • (05/31/95) • **85-89** (BT)

Cabernet Sauvignon California Grand Reserve 1992: Dense and chewy, but has all the ingredients for greatness, with tiers of black cherry, currant, anise and plum, finishing with chunky tannins that let the fruit glide through. Finishes spicy. • $35 • (11/30/95) • **91**

Cabernet Sauvignon California Grand Reserve 1991: This features bright, ripe and rich currant, black cherry and spice flavors that are focused and concentrated. Finishes with a burst of sweet fruit, best after 1998. • $30 • (11/15/94) • **89**

Cabernet Sauvignon California Grand Reserve 1990: Ripe and generous, with a strong current of Cabernet fruit, firm tannins and enough generosity to warrant cellaring this wine until 1998-2000. Flavors are distinctive, with an herbal edge that keeps echoing on the finish. • $30 • (11/15/93) • **90**

Cabernet Sauvignon California Proprietor's Grand Reserve 1988 • $23 • (03/15/93) • **83**

Cabernet Sauvignon California Proprietor's Grand Reserve 1987 • $16 • (03/31/92) • **87**

Cabernet Sauvignon California Proprietor's Reserve 1985 • $20 • (12/15/88) • **95**

Cabernet Sauvignon California The Proprietor's 1986 • $24 • (03/15/90) • **85**

Cabernet Sauvignon California Vintner's Reserve 1993: Supple and harmonious, with a range of cherry, herb and olive flavors that linger. Drinks well now. • $15 • (03/31/96) • **85**

Cabernet Sauvignon California Vintner's Reserve 1992: A firm, tight core of currant, cedar and tobacco notes that pick up a minty tone and chewy tannins. • $14 • (04/30/95) • **82**

Cabernet Sauvignon California Vintner's Reserve 1991: Pleasantly fruity with grape, herb, cherry and currant notes framed by light oak, but finishing with firm tannins. Ready now. • $15 • (07/31/94) • **83**

Cabernet Sauvignon California Vintner's Reserve 1990: Light and fruity, with straight-on Cabernet flavor that offers hints of plum and cherry, but the finish turns dry and oaky and ends rather abruptly. Drinkable now. • $13 • (11/15/92) • **83**

Cabernet Sauvignon California Vintner's Reserve 1989 • $13 • (07/31/92) • **84**

Cabernet Sauvignon California Vintner's Reserve 1987 • $14 • (11/15/91) • **82**

Cabernet Sauvignon California Vintner's Reserve 1986 • $11 • (12/31/88) • **85**

Cabernet Sauvignon Lake County 1986 • $7 • (07/31/88) • **74**

Cabernet Sauvignon Lake County 1984 • $7 • (11/15/87) BB • **81**

Cabernet Sauvignon Lake County 1983 • $7 • (05/01/86) • **69**

Cardinale California 1990: Bold, ripe, smooth and polished. The layers of plum, currant, cherry and blueberry flavors are focused and lively right through the finish. Has the tannin and concentration for cellaring through the decade. 3,190 cases made. • $50 • (10/15/94) • **91**

Cardinale California 1988 • $50 • (11/15/93) • **85**

Cardinale California 1984 • $45 • (07/31/87) • **84**

Cardinale California 1983 • $50 • (10/16/85) • **82**

Cardinale California Meritage 1988 • $51 • (11/15/92) • **88**

Cardinale California Meritage 1987 • $44 Ⓐ • (03/31/92) • **95**

Chardonnay California Grand Reserve 1994: Intense yet with a sense of elegance and finesse, with ripe pear, melon, nutmeg and apple flavors. Finishes with a light touch of oak and a fruity aftertaste. • $26 • (03/31/96) • **90**

Key: SS—Spectator Selection. CS—Cellar Selection. BB—Best Buy. $NA—Price not available. (BT)—Barrel tasting. Ⓐ—Auction Price.
Dates in parentheses represent the issues in which the ratings were published.

Chardonnay California Grand Reserve 1993: Effusively fruity, with pretty pear, spice, pineapple and creamy vanilla flavors that fold together nicely in a seamless, elegant package. Approachable now. Tasted twice, with consistent notes. • $24 • (06/30/95) • **90**

Chardonnay California Grand Reserve 1992: Strikes a nice balance between ripe, polished pear and hazelnut flavors with light oak shadings. Elegant and refined, it turns smooth and spicy on the finish. Ready now. • $22 • (06/30/94) • **87**

Chardonnay California Proprietor's Grand Reserve 1991 • $23 • (03/31/93) • **85**

Chardonnay California Vintner's Reserve 1994: Openly fruity, with ripe pear, melon, apple and spice notes, a straightforward and appealing wine that's ready to drink now. • $14 • (12/15/95) • **86**

Chardonnay California Vintner's Reserve 1993: Ripe and fruity with a pretty band of pear and spice, finishing with honey and vanilla notes. Ready now. • $14 • (09/15/94) • **85**

Chardonnay California Vintner's Reserve 1992: Fresh and lively, with appealing, lemony apple aromas and flavors. Finishes simple and refreshing. Drinkable now. • $13 • (07/15/93) • **80**

Chardonnay California Vintner's Reserve 1991 • $13 • (07/15/92) • **84**

Chardonnay Late Harvest California Select 1993: Ripe and honeyed, centered around some pretty pear fruit that persists into a gentle finish. Ready now. • $15 • (07/31/95) • **85**

Chardonnay Santa Maria Valley Camelot Vineyard 1994: Smooth, ripe and creamy, striking a nice balance between its rich pear, fig, melon and spice character and the toasty, buttery oak. Finishes with a creamy flavor and texture. Keeps up the track record for this leading California winery. 10,000 cases made. • $18 • (03/31/96) SS • **90**

Chardonnay Santa Maria Valley Camelot Vineyard 1993: Offers attractive ripe pear, apple, honey and citrus notes and holds its focus on the finish, where it turns elegant. • $16 • (07/31/95) • **88**

Chardonnay Santa Maria Valley Camelot Vineyard 1992: Wonderfully delicious Santa Maria Chardonnay. Broad, ripe, smooth, rich and creamy with pretty pear, spice and hazelnut flavors that are elegant and lively, showing toasty oak notes on the finish. Bracing acidity keeps the fruit fresh and lively. Ready now through 1997. • $15 • (06/30/94) • **90**

Chardonnay Santa Maria Valley Camelot Vineyard 1991 • $16 • (01/31/93) • **89**

Chardonnay Sonoma Valley Durell Vineyard 1991 • $16 • (11/30/92) • **80**

Chenin Blanc California Vintner's Reserve 1992: Light and direct, off-dry, showing fresh apple and leafy flavors, polished on the finish. Ready now. • $10 • (05/31/95) • **84**

Gewürztraminer California Vintner's Reserve 1993: Bright and refreshing, simple, revealing pleasant pear and spice flavors. Ready now. • $10 • (02/28/95) • **82**

Gewürztraminer Vintner's Reserve 1991 • $9 • (07/31/92) • **80**

Johannisberg Riesling California Vintner's Reserve 1993: Soft, a little sweet, with modest apple and citrus flavors. • $9 • (06/15/95) • **80**

Johannisberg Riesling California Vintner's Reserve 1992 • $9 • (11/15/93) • **84**

Johannisberg Riesling California Vintner's Reserve 1991 • $9 • (10/31/92) • **81**

Meritage Cardinale California 1991: Shows off its ripe black cherry, currant and wild berry flavors that stretch to a jammy edge, adding pretty spice and anise and firm tannins. Well crafted, best in 1999. • $60 • (12/15/95) • **91**

Meritage Cardinale California 1989 • $50 • (05/15/94) • **88**

Meritage Royale California 1994: Bright and intriguing, with passion fruit, citrus and pear flavors that just don't quit. If there is oak, it is well submerged. Delicious to drink now. • $15 • (07/31/95) • **89**

Merlot Alexander Valley 1986 • $16 • (12/31/88) • **93**

Merlot California Grand Reserve 1993: Serves up an attractive core of ripe plum, cherry and berry flavors with light toasty oak shadings, but loses its focus on the finish, when the flavors become more diffuse. 2,200 cases made. • $42 • (06/30/96) • **86**

Merlot California Grand Reserve 1992: Rich and fruity, boasting lots of plum, black cherry, currant and spicy mint notes, cedary oak and plush tannins. Packs a wallop with its flavor. • $30 • (09/30/95) • **90**

Merlot California Grand Reserve 1991: Serves up a pretty array of ripe, supple cherry, plum and strawberry fruit with appealing spice notes.

Finishes with firm tannins and it turns diffuse. Ready now through 1998. 1,400 cases made. • $30 • (09/15/94) • **86**

Merlot California Vintner's Reserve 1993: Pleasant enough, with its uncomplicated ripe cherry and light oak flavors. • $NA • **84**

Merlot California Vintner's Reserve 1992: Crisp and austere, with a narrow band of spicy currant and herb notes, picking up a cedary edge on the finish. Ready now through 1997. • $15 • (09/15/94) • **82**

Merlot California Vintner's Reserve 1991 • $14 • (10/15/93) • **87**

Merlot California Vintner's Reserve 1990 • $14 • (01/31/93) • **83**

Merlot California Vintner's Reserve 1988 • $14 • (11/15/91) • **84**

Merlot Sonoma County The Proprietor's 1987 • $20 • (12/31/90) • **87**

Merlot Vintner's Reserve 1989 • $14 • (05/31/92) • **75**

Pinot Noir California Proprietor's Grand Reserve 1992: A smooth, supple, elegant Pinot, with herb, cola and spicy cherry flavors that turn silky, picking up buttery oak on the finish. Well balanced and ready to drink now through 1997. • $30 • (10/31/94) • **86**

Pinot Noir California Proprietor's Grand Reserve 1991 • $30 • (02/28/94) • **82**

Pinot Noir California Unfiltered Grand Reserve 1993: Supple and elegant, marked by toasty oak, and the ripe cherry and spicy plum flavors glide past the soft tannins. • $30 • (03/31/95) • **88**

Pinot Noir California Vintner's Reserve 1994: Smooth and polished, with complex black cherry, anise, spice and tasty oak. All well-balanced, finishing with an alluring, even delicate aftertaste. Ready now. • $14 • (11/15/95) • **88**

Pinot Noir California Vintner's Reserve 1993: Firm and spicy, with a narrow band of herb and black cherry flavors. Drinkable now. • $14 • (03/31/95) • **83**

Pinot Noir California Vintner's Reserve 1992 • $13 • (02/28/94) • **82**

Pinot Noir California Vintner's Reserve 1991 • $13 • (09/15/93) • **80**

Pinot Noir California Vintner's Reserve 1990 • $13 • (02/28/93) • **82**

Pinot Noir Santa Maria Valley Julia's Vineyard 1988 • $14 • (11/15/91) • **82**

Riesling Late Harvest California Select 1993: Ripe and very sweet, soft enough that it seems syrupy, more unctuous than rich. Echoes honey and floral notes on the finish. • $15 • (07/31/95) • **86**

Royale Meritage California 1992: Soft and fragrant, offering pear, spice and herb character in a gentle package. Ready now. • $15 • (04/30/95) • **85**

Sauvignon Blanc California Grand Reserve 1994: Fresh and spicy, a simple, fruity wine with bright, citrusy flavors that last and last on the lively finish. • $20 • (06/30/96) • **87**

Sauvignon Blanc California Grand Reserve 1993: A sweet layer of smoky oak character runs through the pear and honey flavors in this ripe, broad, harmonious white. • $14 • (12/31/94) • **86**

Sauvignon Blanc California Grand Reserve 1992: Crisp and bright, offering some nice herbal grace notes to the lemony melody. A stylish wine that remains lively through the long finish. Refreshing to drink now. • $14 • (08/31/94) • **87**

Sauvignon Blanc California Vintner's Reserve 1995: Fresh and citrusy. A lively wine with refreshing grapefruit and floral flavors. • $10 • **84**

Sauvignon Blanc California Vintner's Reserve 1994: Light, lean and somewhat sweet, finishing with a floral flourish and delicate vanilla notes. • $9 • (08/31/95) • **82**

Sauvignon Blanc California Vintner's Reserve 1993: Sturdy, simple and lightly herbal, softly fruity at the core. • $9 • (01/31/95) • **82**

Sauvignon Blanc California Vintner's Reserve 1991 • $9 • (02/15/93) • **81**

Sémillon California Vintner's Reserve 1994: Delicious floral, pear and citrus flavors finish with focus and elegance. Nicely balanced, drinkable now. • $12 • (06/30/96) • **87**

Syrah California Grand Reserve 1991: A rich and mouth-filling, beautifully balanced red, with blackberry, black cherry and black pepper flavors competing for attention. Drinkable now as an effusively fruity wine, may be best from 1996. • $20 • (09/30/94) • **88**

Syrah California Proprietor's Grand Reserve 1990 • $16 • (02/15/93) • **88**

Syrah California Vintner's Reserve 1990 • $14 • (10/31/93) • **83**

Syrah Sonoma Valley Durell Vineyard 1990: Smooth and supple, polished herb, currant and spice flavors. Mild tannins make it approachable now. • $16 • (05/15/95) • **85**

Syrah Sonoma Valley Durell Vineyard 1988 • $24 • (08/31/91) • **89**

Syrah Sonoma Valley Durell Vineyard 1987 • $17 • (12/15/89) • **90**

Syrah Sonoma Valley Durell Vineyard 1986 • $14 • (11/30/88) • **92**

Zinfandel Anderson Valley DePatie-DuPratt Vineyard 1986 • $16 • (12/15/89) • **85**

Zinfandel Anderson Valley DuPratt Vineyard 1990 • $20 • (09/30/93) • **88**

Zinfandel Anderson Valley DuPratt Vineyard 1987 • $20 • (07/31/91) • **90**

Zinfandel Anderson Valley DuPratt-DePatie Vineyard 1983 • $10 • (11/01/85) • **76**

Zinfandel California Grand Reserve 1993: Lean and spicy, with more herb and dried cherry than ripe fruit flavors. Unexpectedly modest, given the price and reserve status. • $25 • **82**

Zinfandel California Grand Reserve 1992: Lightly fruity, exhibiting simple berry notes and firm tannins. A good Zin but it lacks the extra dimensions one expects in a reserve-style wine. • $20 • (01/31/95) • **84**

Zinfandel California Grand Reserve 1991: Crisp, firm and very tannic, with a lean core of spicy berry flavor that hangs with you. Cellaring could soften it a bit. Drinkable now. • $20 • (10/15/94) • **86**

Zinfandel California Proprietor's Grand Reserve 1990 • $16 • (01/31/93) • **89**

Zinfandel California Vintner's Reserve 1994: A medium-weight style delivering pleasant cherry and berry flavors. Drinks well now. • $14 • (04/30/96) • **83**

Zinfandel California Vintner's Reserve 1993: A subdued style that shows trim wild berry, cherry, earth and tar notes. Shows good intensity and depth, finishing with mild tannins. • $14 • (10/15/95) • **83**

Zinfandel California Vintner's Reserve 1992: Firm and tannic, with a gritty texture. Hints of wild berry and spicy raspberry come through on the finish, where the flavors get more interesting. • $12 • (10/15/94) • **83**

Zinfandel California Vintner's Reserve 1991 • $10 • (09/30/93) • **84**

Zinfandel California Vintner's Reserve 1990 • $9 • (12/15/92) • **78**

Zinfandel California Vintner's Reserve 1989 • $11 • (09/30/91) • **84**

Zinfandel Clear Lake Vina Las Lomas Vineyard 1983 • $7 • (06/01/85) • **80**

Zinfandel Mendocino 1987 • $9 • (03/15/90) • **88**

Zinfandel Mendocino 1986 • $9 • (09/15/88) • **86**

Zinfandel Mendocino Ciapusci Vineyard 1989 • $20 • (10/15/92) • **82**

Zinfandel Mendocino Ciapusci Vineyard 1988 • $20 • (10/15/92) • **77**

Zinfandel Mendocino Ciapusci Vineyard 1984 • $16 • (12/15/89) • **86**

Zinfandel Mendocino County DuPratt Vineyard Proprietor's Grand Reserve 1990 • $23 • (10/15/92) • **84**

Zinfandel Mendocino Zeni Vineyard 1990 • $20 • (10/15/92) • **83**

KENNEDY, KATHRYN | CALIFORNIA

Cabernet Sauvignon Santa Cruz Mountains 1991: This walks a tightrope between earthy juniper berry and peppery cherry notes. Tight and tannic, it will need until at least 1997, for now it's best to lay away in the cellar. 600 cases made. • $54 • (11/15/94) • **87**

Cabernet Sauvignon Santa Cruz Mountains 1990: Earthy and oaky, with a potent tannin level, it is nonetheless a rich and powerful young wine that will need another three to five years minimum to show its full potential. Best after 1997. 180 cases made. • $54 • (06/15/94) • **89**

Cabernet Sauvignon Santa Cruz Mountains 1989 • $54 • (03/31/93) • **87**

Cabernet Sauvignon Santa Cruz Mountains 1988 • $60 • (11/15/91) • **88**

Cabernet Sauvignon Santa Cruz Mountains 1987 • $46 • (01/31/91) • **89**

Cabernet Sauvignon Santa Cruz Mountains 1986 • $37 • (03/15/90) • **81**

Cabernet Sauvignon Santa Cruz Mountains 1985 • $33 • (12/15/88) • **93**

Lateral California 1993: Openly fruity, with jammy cherry and berry notes of medium depth and richness. Mild tannins and pleasant aftertaste. Best after 1997. 700 cases made. • $25 • (12/15/95) • **86**

Lateral California 1991: Ripe and pleasant in flavor, with an austere bite of tannin on the finish, echoing currant, plum and tar on the full-bodied finish. A nice mouthful to try now. 50 percent Cabernet Franc, 40 percent Merlot and 10 percent Cabernet Sauvignon. 650 cases made. • $18 • (11/15/93) • **86**

Lateral California 1990: Firm, focused and spicy, with generous cherry, cinnamon and raspberry flavors melding nicely on the balanced, harmonious finish. Drinkable now. 600 cases made. • $17 • (10/15/92) • **88**

Lateral California 1989 • $17 • (11/15/91) • **86**

Lateral California 1988 • $15 • (10/15/90) • **87**

KENWOOD | CALIFORNIA

Cabernet Sauvignon Artist Series 1988 • $35 • (03/15/92) • **83**

Cabernet Sauvignon Sonoma County Artist Series 1976 • $10 • (03/01/89) • **77**

Cabernet Sauvignon Sonoma County Artist Series 1975 • $6 • (03/01/89) • **73**
Cabernet Sauvignon Sonoma Valley 1994: Tight and tannic, with a hard edge and not much fruit showing at this stage. 3,000 cases made. • $20 • (05/31/95) • **80**
Cabernet Sauvignon Sonoma Valley 1991: Austere and tannic, with chunky herb and currant notes framed by oak. A tough red to warm up to. Best after 1998. 21,000 cases made. • $16 • (11/15/94) • **82**
Cabernet Sauvignon Sonoma Valley 1990: Distinctively minty, a moderately tannic wine of moderate intensity that weaves plenty of mint aroma and flavor through the cherry and currant fruit. Seems a little green, but it should be fine by 1998. 11,000 cases made. • $17 • (11/15/93) • **84**
Cabernet Sauvignon Sonoma Valley 1989 • $15 • (11/15/92) SS • **91**
Cabernet Sauvignon Sonoma Valley 1987 • $15 • (07/15/91) • **90**
Cabernet Sauvignon Sonoma Valley 1986 • $15 • (09/30/89) • **86**
Cabernet Sauvignon Sonoma Valley 1985 • $15 • (02/15/89) • **91**
Cabernet Sauvignon Sonoma Valley 1984 • $12 • (05/31/88) • **83**
Cabernet Sauvignon Sonoma Valley 1983 • $10 • (02/15/88) • **85**
Cabernet Sauvignon Sonoma Valley 25th Anniversary Vintage 1992: Tight, compact core of earthy berry and currant flavor. Oak and tannins dominate, giving it quite a bite, so it's best to cellar into 1998. 20,000 cases made. • $16 • (10/31/95) • **86**
Cabernet Sauvignon Sonoma Valley Artist Series 1991: Firm and compact, with a tight, narrow band of spicy currant, cedary oak and mineral notes. Picks up an earthy edge on the finish but hangs together. Best after 1998. • $40 • (11/15/94) • **89**
Cabernet Sauvignon Sonoma Valley Artist Series 1990: Minty, herbal aromas and flavors course through this focused, tough-textured wine that turns gnarly on the finish. Has a core of berry flavor trying to break through the cedar and bark character. Drink after 1997. Tasted three times with consistent results. • $30 • (12/15/93) • **86**
Cabernet Sauvignon Sonoma Valley Artist Series 1989 • $36 • (10/31/92) CS • **93**
Cabernet Sauvignon Sonoma Valley Artist Series 1987 • $35 • (11/15/90) • **88**
Cabernet Sauvignon Sonoma Valley Artist Series 1986 • $25 Ⓐ • (11/30/89) CS • **95**
Cabernet Sauvignon Sonoma Valley Artist Series 1985 • $39 • (03/01/89) • **91**
Cabernet Sauvignon Sonoma Valley Artist Series 1984 • $32 Ⓐ • (03/01/89) • **93**
Cabernet Sauvignon Sonoma Valley Artist Series 1983 • $44 • (03/01/89) • **87**
Cabernet Sauvignon Sonoma Valley Artist Series 1982 • $37 • (03/01/89) • **87**
Cabernet Sauvignon Sonoma Valley Artist Series 1981 • $13 Ⓐ • (03/01/89) • **89**
Cabernet Sauvignon Sonoma Valley Artist Series 1980 • $70 • (03/01/89) • **80**
Cabernet Sauvignon Sonoma Valley Artist Series 1979 • $20 • (03/01/89) • **91**
Cabernet Sauvignon Sonoma Valley Artist Series 1978 • $NA • (11/15/92) • **90**
Cabernet Sauvignon Sonoma Valley Artist Series 1977 • $160 • (03/01/89) • **82**
Cabernet Sauvignon Sonoma Valley Jack London Vineyard 1994: Green and tough, with a tanky edge to the herb and bell pepper notes. Finishes better than it starts, as it takes on a tarry, earthy edge. Clearly a wine that will need some time. 12,000 cases made. • $15 • (05/31/95) • **80**
Cabernet Sauvignon Sonoma Valley Jack London Vineyard 1992: Ripe and plush, showing herb- and currant-laced Cabernet fruit, toasty oak and supple tannins on the finish. 15,000 cases made. • $20 • (10/31/95) • **87**
Cabernet Sauvignon Sonoma Valley Jack London Vineyard 1991: Light in color due to 15 percent Sangiovese in the blend, this serves up ripe plum and cherry before gathering a trace of bitterness from the wood. Best after 1996. 12,000 cases made. • $20 • (11/15/94) • **83**
Cabernet Sauvignon Sonoma Valley Jack London Vineyard 1989 • $20 • (11/15/92) • **89**
Cabernet Sauvignon Sonoma Valley Jack London Vineyard 1987 • $19 • (01/31/91) • **92**
Cabernet Sauvignon Sonoma Valley Jack London Vineyard 1986 • $18 • (09/15/89) • **90**
Cabernet Sauvignon Sonoma Valley Jack London Vineyard 1985 • $21 • (10/15/88) • **89**
Cabernet Sauvignon Sonoma Valley Jack London Vineyard 1984 • $21 • (11/30/87) • **91**
Cabernet Sauvignon Sonoma Valley Jack London Vineyard 1983 • $21 • (02/15/87) • **86**
Cabernet Sauvignon Sonoma Valley Jack London Vineyard 1980 • $25 • (05/16/84) • **80**
Chardonnay Sonoma County 25th Anniversary Vintage 1994: Light, lean, fresh and fruity, zingy apple and melon flavors lingering spicily on the finish. Ready now. 17,700 cases made. • $14 • (12/15/95) • **87**
Chardonnay Sonoma Valley 1993: Ripe and pleasantly fruity, with pear, citrus and spicy notes that hang together. 11,000 cases made. • $14 • (07/31/95) • **84**
Chardonnay Sonoma Valley 1992: Clean and simple with spicy pear, apple and peach flavors that are tight and compact, picking up a spicy oak note on the finish. Ready now. • $14 • (06/30/94) • **83**
Chardonnay Sonoma Valley Beltane Ranch 1993: Medium weight with spicy pear, apricot and spicy oak notes of modest proportion. 500 cases made. • $18 • (07/31/95) • **84**
Chardonnay Sonoma Valley Reserve 1993: Simple and correct, with modest pear and spice notes, but as good as the 1992, as it's light and uncomplicated. 3,500 cases made. • $18 • (07/31/95) • **84**
Chardonnay Sonoma Valley Reserve 1992: Ripe and spicy, soft and earthy, with modest pineapple flavor lurking in the background. Picks up some nice intensity on the finish. Drink now. 3,000 cases made. • $18 • (06/30/94) • **87**
Chardonnay Sonoma Valley Reserve 1991 • $18 • (06/15/93) • **91**
Chardonnay Sonoma Valley Yulupa 1993: Marked by a minty edge that turns to a piney oak flavor that overrides pear and apple fruit. Disjointed at this stage. 20,000 cases made. • $14 • (07/31/95) • **83**
Chardonnay Sonoma Valley Yulupa Vineyard 1992: An elegant young white that serves up pretty ripe pear, spice and vanilla flavors, picking up a hint of nutmeg on the finish. Ready now. 10,000 cases made. • $14 • (06/30/94) • **85**
Chardonnay Sonoma Valley Yulupa Vineyard 1991 • $14 • (06/15/93) • **87**
Johannisberg Riesling Late Harvest Sonoma Valley 1985 • $10 • (02/28/87) BB • **89**
Johannisberg Riesling Late Harvest Sonoma Valley 1984 • $8 • (09/16/85) • **79**
Merlot Sonoma County 1992: Lean with a cedar and tobacco edge, but it thins out and the plum flavors lack depth. 12,000 cases made. • $16 • (07/31/95) • **83**
Merlot Sonoma County 1991: Firm and spicy, toasty, with a generous beam of berry flavor, finishing with a burnt edge. Drinkable now. 5,500 cases made. • $16 • (09/15/94) • **80**
Merlot Sonoma County 1990 • $16 • (06/15/93) • **86**
Merlot Sonoma County 1989 • $15 • (01/31/93) • **83**
Merlot Sonoma County Jack London Vineyard 1992: Intense and focused, featuring ripe plum, currant, herb and spice notes which pick up a cedary oak edge on the lingering finish. • $18 • (09/30/95) • **88**
Merlot Sonoma Mountain Jack London Vineyard 1991: A little rough around the edges, but there's a lot going for this wine. Dark in color, aromatic, with spicy cedar, plum and currant notes. It comes up a bit tight and tannic on the finish. Best to cellar until 1997 to allow it to soften and evolve. 2,800 cases made. • $18 • (06/30/94) • **87**
Merlot Sonoma Mountain Jack London Vineyard 1990 • $18 • (06/15/93) • **82**
Merlot Sonoma Valley Massara Vineyards 1992: Tight and cedary, cherry- and currant-flavored. Needs short-term cellaring to soften as the tannins are substantial. 1,000 cases made. • $18 • (02/28/95) • **84**
Pinot Noir Russian River Valley 1993: First Russian River bottling for Kenwood, it succeeds in its medium-bodied herb, cherry and plum

Key: SS—Spectator Selection. CS—Cellar Selection. BB—Best Buy. $NA—Price not available. (BT)—Barrel tasting. Ⓐ—Auction Price.
Dates in parentheses represent the issues in which the ratings were published.

notes, elegant aftertaste and smooth tannins. 1,056 cases made. • $14 • (10/15/95) • **84**

Pinot Noir Russian River Valley Olivet Lane 1993: Tight and a bit lean and tannic, but just enough Pinot Noir fruit comes through to make it palatable. Can stand short-term cellaring. 900 cases made. • $22 • (10/15/95) • **87**

Pinot Noir Sonoma Valley Jack London Vineyard 1992: Earthy and somewhat funky, with one-dimensional candied cherry flavors. Drinkable now, but may benefit from short-term cellaring. 1,200 cases made. • $18 • (03/31/95) • **80**

Pinot Noir Sonoma Valley Jack London Vineyard 1990 • $18 • (09/30/92) • **85**

Pinot Noir Sonoma Valley Jack London Vineyard 1989 • $15 • (10/31/91) • **80**

Pinot Noir Sonoma Valley Jack London Vineyard 1984 • $15 • (05/31/89) • **77**

Sauvignon Blanc Sonoma County 1995: Simple and direct, with appealing citrus and spicy nectarine flavors. 50,000 cases made. • $9 • **83**

Sauvignon Blanc Sonoma County 1994: A fresh and lively value of a Sauvignon Blanc. This offers a mouthful of grapefruit, pear and subtle herb flavors. Delicious now. 41,000 cases made. • $9 • (12/15/95) BB • **87**

Sauvignon Blanc Sonoma County 1993: Crisp, floral and lively, featuring smoothly integrated apple character. 30,000 cases made. • $9 • (05/31/95) • **84**

Sauvignon Blanc Sonoma County 1992 • $9 • (03/31/94) • **86**

Sauvignon Blanc Sonoma County 1991 • $9 • (11/30/92) • **84**

Sauvignon Blanc Sonoma Valley Reserve 1994: Crisp, lively, straightforward, focused pear flavors last on the finish. Drinkable now. 1,000 cases made. • $15 • (12/15/95) • **85**

Vintage Red California 1988 • $5 • (12/31/90) • **77**

Vintage Red California 1986 • $5 • (11/30/88) • **74**

Vintage Red Sonoma County 1983 • $4 • (05/31/88) • **77**

White Zinfandel Sonoma Valley 1988 • $6 • (06/15/89) • **86**

White Zinfandel Sonoma Valley 1986 • $5 • (03/31/87) • **80**

Zinfandel Sonoma County Geyserville Mazzoni 1993: Smoky, buttery notes are well oaked, gaining a ripe core of cherry and berry flavor that turns complex and elegant on the aftertaste. 700 cases made. • $15 • (09/30/95) • **89**

Zinfandel Sonoma Mountain Jack London Vineyard 1991 • $14 • (09/30/93) • **86**

Zinfandel Sonoma Valley 1992: Supple and spicy, with an elegant band of peppery berry flavors. Finishes with firm tannins, ready now. 8,000 cases made. • $12 • (07/31/95) • **84**

Zinfandel Sonoma Valley 1991: Firm and compact, with a narrow band of spicy cherry flavor that picks up gritty tannins on the finish. Drinkable now. 8,000 cases made. • $12 • (10/15/94) • **82**

Zinfandel Sonoma Valley 1990 • $12 • (09/30/93) • **86**

Zinfandel Sonoma Valley 1988 • $14 • (12/31/90) • **82**

Zinfandel Sonoma Valley 1987 • $15 • (10/31/89) • **90**

Zinfandel Sonoma Valley 1985 • $15 • (05/15/88) • **89**

Zinfandel Sonoma Valley 1984 • $16 • (09/15/87) • **90**

Zinfandel Sonoma Valley 1983 • $16 • (11/15/86) • **88**

Zinfandel Sonoma Valley 1982 • $16 • (07/16/86) • **90**

Zinfandel Sonoma Valley Barricia Estate 1993: Intense and a bit rustic, with chunky berry and cherry fruit flavors, finishing with firm tannins, a kiss of toasty oak and a slight coarse edge. Needs short-term cellaring. 1,100 cases made. • $16 • **85**

Zinfandel Sonoma Valley Barricia Estate Vineyard 1991: A big, oaky, tannic style that still needs to soften and evolve. Packed with rich, briary, wild berry and cherry flavors, but the tannins are dry. Drinkable now. 2,000 cases made. • $16 • (10/15/94) • **84**

Zinfandel Sonoma Valley Barricia Estate Vineyard 1990 • $12 • (10/15/92) • **89**

Zinfandel Sonoma Valley Jack London Vineyard 1993: Smooth, medium-bodied, offering modest proportions of tar, plum and spicy-peppery notes. 3,359 cases made. • $14 • (10/15/95) • **84**

Zinfandel Sonoma Valley Jack London Vineyard 1992: Light and fruity, with simple, earthy berry flavors. Elegant, if somewhat simple. Ready now. Tasted twice. 6,000 cases made. • $14 • (10/15/94) • **82**

Zinfandel Sonoma Valley Jack London Vineyard 1990 • $14 • (10/15/92) • **84**

Zinfandel Sonoma Valley Jack London Vineyard 1989 • $14 • (09/30/91) • **83**

Zinfandel Sonoma Valley Jack London Vineyard 1987 • $12 • (12/15/89) • **88**

Zinfandel Sonoma Valley Nuns Canyon 1993: Well oaked, with toasty vanilla flavors, the ripe cherry and wild berry flavors come through in fine fashion, giving this wine a smooth, silky texture and finishing with classic Zinfandel peppery notes. 1,300 cases made. • $16 • (04/30/96) • **90**

KERR, J. | CALIFORNIA

Chardonnay Santa Barbara County 1991: Fresh and simple, slightly syrupy in texture but fruity and generous with its nectarine and spice flavors. 400 cases made. • $30 • (06/30/94) • **81**

Pinot Noir Santa Barbara County 1991: Wild cherry, berry, earth and spice notes unfold in an elegant, subtle style. Drinks well now but has depth and richness to merit short-term cellaring. 350 cases made. • $19 • (08/31/94) • **85**

Pinot Noir Santa Barbara County 1990: A funky style showing pungent, earthy beet root and cola flavors that have a bitter oaky edge on the finish. Good but nothing more. Drinkable now. 300 cases made. • $19 • (03/31/95) • **80**

KINDERWOOD | CALIFORNIA

Chardonnay Monterey County 1992: Earthy with a slightly sour edge, but the ripe pear flavors come through. Still, a fair value at $6. 15,000 cases made. • $6 • (06/30/94) • **79**

Merlot California 1992: Intense, with grapey, floral and currant-laced flavor. An excellent value in everyday Merlot. 1,600 cases made. • $6 • (09/15/94) BB • **83**

KIONA | WASHINGTON

Cabernet Sauvignon Washington 1991: On the tannic side, a rough-textured Cabernet that shows a decent level of currant and plum flavor. Should be best from 1997. 1,100 cases made. • $12 • (09/30/94) • **86**

Cabernet Sauvignon Washington 1990: Lean and lithe, a nicely polished red with a modest level of berry flavor and herbal notes. Drinkable now. • $12 • (07/31/94) • **84**

Cabernet Sauvignon Yakima Valley 1991: Very firm and focused, a chewy red that shows a nice core of black cherry and dark plum flavor and finishes with enough tannin to want until 1997. 750 cases made. • $18 • (09/30/95) • **86**

Cabernet Sauvignon Yakima Valley 1990: Smooth and supple, velvety in texture and ripe with coffee- and vanilla-scented black cherry and blackberry flavors that extend into a rich finish. Best in 1997. 400 cases made. • $18 • (08/31/95) • **89**

Cabernet Sauvignon Yakima Valley 1989: With a firm structure and supple texture, this shows off its spicy-chocolate, currant and berry flavors with more than the usual style. Drinkable now. • $15 • (07/31/94) • **87**

Cabernet Sauvignon Yakima Valley Estate Bottled 1986 • $14 • (10/15/89) • **89**

Cabernet Sauvignon Yakima Valley Tapteil Vineyard 1989 • $12 • (03/15/93) • **89**

Cabernet Sauvignon Yakima Valley Tapteil Vineyard 1988 • $12 • (03/31/92) • **85**

Chardonnay Yakima Valley Barrel Fermented 1992: Ripe, spicy, somewhat bitter around the edges. Has a creamy finish, which makes it appealing. 900 cases made. • $12 • (09/30/95) • **83**

Chardonnay Yakima Valley Barrel Fermented 1991: Bright, spicy and generous, almost apricotty it's so ripe, but it remains balanced and lively through the fruit-centered finish. 3,000 cases made. • $11 • (09/15/94) • **88**

Chenin Blanc Late Harvest Yakima Valley Ice Wine 1993: Sweet and fruity, lean, with focused pear and spice flavors but not a lot of other extra dimensions. 300 cases made. • $19 • (09/30/94) • **80**

Chenin Blanc Yakima Valley 1994: Bright and fruity, off-dry and focused, featuring pear and almond flavors that swirl nicely on the finish. 1,200 cases made. • $6 • (09/30/95) • **85**

Chenin Blanc Yakima Valley 1993: Fruity, spicy and lively, a mouthful of citrusy peach and melon flavor that keeps spilling over on the finish. A wonderful sipper. 1,000 cases made. • $6 • (09/30/94) • **87**

Chenin Blanc Yakima Valley 1992: Soft and fruity, the melon and apple flavors settling smoothly on the finish. Drink it soon. 1,000 cases made. • $6 • (09/30/94) • **83**

Chenin Blanc Yakima Valley Ice Wine 1993: Light-bodied and not very sweet for an ice wine, this shows apple, light peach and herbal flavors with firm acidity. It lacks concentration and length. 339 cases made. • $19 • **78**

Chenin Blanc Yakima Valley Ice Wine 1989: If you can get past the swampy, rhubarb aromas, you'll find raspberry jam and milk chocolate flavors, along with even more rhubarb. 259 cases made. • $20 • **68**

Gewürztraminer Late Harvest Yakima Valley 1994: Complex spice flavors weave through this sweet dessert wine, balanced by a refreshing touch of bitter almond on the finish. 400 cases made. • $7 • (09/30/95) • **87**

Gewürztraminer Late Harvest Yakima Valley 1993: Sweet and unctuous, a spicy, floral white that picks up some melon, apricot and vanilla notes on the long, supple finish. Drinkable now. 650 cases made. • $6 • (09/30/94) • **89**

Lemberger 1989 • $9 • (05/15/92) • **76**

Lemberger Yakima Valley 1993: Light and vibrant blackberry and spice flavors, appealing to drink right now and firm enough to be there through 1996. 1,200 cases made. • $10 • (09/30/95) • **85**

Lemberger Yakima Valley 1992: Smoky, almost burnt on the nose, but the flavors are polished and generously fruity, echoing raspberry and spice. Drinkable now. 1,000 cases made. • $10 • (09/30/94) • **84**

Lemberger Yakima Valley 1990: Soft in texture, a little tannic, a little tired and oaky, but still flavorful enough to be modestly appealing. 1,000 cases made. • $10 • (09/30/94) • **79**

Merlot Columbia Valley 1992: Rich, plush and elegant, a high-fidelity voice that sings out its plum, black cherry, vanilla and spice flavors. A Washington Merlot that echoes ripe fruit and oak on the long finish. Drinkable now. 1,800 cases made. • $12 • (09/30/95) • **91**

Merlot Columbia Valley 1991: Firm in texture, with a nice range of berry and currant flavors that seem to suspend themselves in midair, echoing on the finish. If it kick-starts when the tannin softens, it should be best around 1997. 600 cases made. • $12 • (09/30/94) • **87**

Merlot Columbia Valley 1990 • $12 • (06/15/93) • **81**

Merlot Columbia Valley 1989 • $12 • (03/31/92) • **86**

Merlot Columbia Valley 1988 • $12 • (05/31/91) • **84**

Muscat Late Harvest Yakima Valley 1994: Sweet and spicy, a nutmeg note dominating the fruit in this fresh-tasting dessert wine. 400 cases made. • $7/375ml • (09/30/95) • **82**

Muscat Late Harvest Yakima Valley 1993: Flavorful and direct, a refreshing, clean-tasting example of pure varietal fruit. Sweet but not unctuous, beautifully balanced. 500 cases made. • $7/375ml • (09/30/94) • **89**

Vintage Rosé Washington 1993: Fruity, generous and popping in cherry and vaguely cinnamonlike flavors, finishing on the dry side. Don't drink this too cold. 600 cases made. • $6 • (09/30/95) • **85**

White Riesling Columbia Valley 1994: Vibrant and refreshing, with exciting floral, peach and apple flavors, a classic off-dry Riesling for summer sipping. 1,400 cases made. • $6 • (06/30/96) • **86**

White Riesling Late Harvest Yakima Valley 1994: Sweet and fresh-tasting, showing peach and hints of apricot. On the light side for such a sweet wine. 800 cases made. • $6 • (09/15/95) • **85**

White Riesling Late Harvest Yakima Valley 1991: Sweet but balanced with enough acidity to taste almost delicate, showing appealing honey-scented floral, peach and almond flavors. 1,700 cases made. • $6 • (09/30/94) • **86**

White Riesling Yakima Valley 1993: Soft, lightly sweet and fruity, offering a ripe apricot note to the fresh pear and apple flavors, generous and delicious to drink now. 1,200 cases made. • $6 • (09/30/94) • **87**

Key: SS—Spectator Selection. CS—Cellar Selection. BB—Best Buy. $NA—Price not available. (BT)—Barrel tasting. Ⓐ—Auction Price.
Dates in parentheses represent the issues in which the ratings were published.

White Riesling Yakima Valley Dry 1994: Light and appealing, a delicate white showing modest peach and resin flavors. 1,200 cases made. • $6 • (09/30/95) • **81**

White Riesling Yakima Valley Dry 1993: Lightly sweet and pleasantly fruity, with appealing melon and apple flavors that pick up a citrusy tinge on the finish. 1,200 cases made. • $6 • (09/30/94) • **86**

White Riesling Yakima Valley Dry 1992: Light, bright and fruity, shining its nectarine and apricot flavors through a narrow beam. Clean and drinkable, off-dry on the finish. • $6 • (09/30/94) • **84**

KISTLER | CALIFORNIA

Cabernet Sauvignon California Kistler Estate Vineyard 1990: Rich and velvety, with a coffee-tobacco streak running through the modest berry and beet flavors. Has the potential to improve through 1998. 563 cases made. • $30 • (02/28/94) • **86**

Cabernet Sauvignon Napa Valley Veeder Hills Vineyard 1983 • $25 • (03/01/89) • **78**

Cabernet Sauvignon Napa Valley Veeder Hills Vineyard 1982 • $26 • (03/01/89) • **86**

Cabernet Sauvignon Napa Valley Veeder Hills-Veeder Peak 1981 • $30 • (03/01/89) • **87**

Cabernet Sauvignon Napa Valley Veeder Hills-Veeder Peak 1980 • $36 • (03/01/89) • **85**

Cabernet Sauvignon Sonoma Valley Glen Ellen Vineyard 1980 • $36 • (03/01/89) • **84**

Cabernet Sauvignon Sonoma Valley Kistler Estate Vineyard 1988 • $25 • (08/31/92) • **86**

Cabernet Sauvignon Sonoma Valley Kistler Estate Vineyard 1987 • $33 • (02/28/91) • **83**

Cabernet Sauvignon Sonoma Valley Kistler Estate Vineyard 1986 • $26Ⓐ • (09/30/89) • **84**

Cabernet Sauvignon Sonoma Valley Kistler Estate Vineyard 1985 • $36Ⓐ • (03/01/89) • **93**

Cabernet Sauvignon Sonoma Valley Kistler Vineyard 1991: Marked by herb, coffee and black olive notes, it's smooth and supple with polished currant and plum flavors, finishing with a complex aftertaste and fine tannins. Ready now through 2000. Shows more restraint with tannins than past vintages. 1,136 cases made. • $30 • (06/15/95) • **90**

Chardonnay Russian River Valley Dutton Ranch 1993: Smooth-textured, elegant and understated, with a nice core of citrus, pear and cream. The flavors linger on the finish, picking up hints of hazelnut and honey. 1,872 cases made. • $35 • (06/30/96) • **89**

Chardonnay Russian River Valley Dutton Ranch 1992: Intense and lively, with layers of tightly wound pear, spice, vanilla and nutmeg, held together by crisp acidity and finishing with a long, full lingering aftertaste. Drink now. 2,800 cases made. • $30 • (05/15/94) • **92**

Chardonnay Russian River Valley Dutton Ranch 1991 • $33 • (02/15/93) • **90**

Chardonnay Russian River Valley Vine Hill Vineyard 1993: Aromatically complex, with flavors to match, offering tiers of rich honey, pear and hazelnut flavors that expand and linger. The texture is smooth and polished, leading to an altogether complex and fascinating aftertaste. 1,857 cases made. • $35 • (06/30/96) • **92**

Chardonnay Russian River Valley Vine Hill Vineyard 1992: Ripe, rich and exotic, with layers of pear, toast, hazelnut and smoky oak, all folding together into a complex and concentrated Chardonnay. 2,764 cases made. • $32 • (03/31/95) • **91**

Chardonnay Russian River Valley Vine Hill Vineyard 1991 • $32 • (05/31/93) • **92**

Chardonnay Sonoma Coast 1993: Has smoky, toasty oak flavors, but a pretty core of elegant pear and spice picks up hazelnut notes, ending with a complex aftertaste. 6,423 cases made. • $26 • (06/15/95) • **89**

Chardonnay Sonoma County 1992: Packs in lots of ripe, fresh, lively pear, nectarine, spice and honey notes that turn smooth and elegant with a fleshy texture and a long, full, complex finish. Drinkable now. At this stage, this is the showiest of the Kistler wines. Tasted twice. 7,320 cases made. • $26 • (05/15/94) SS • **93**

Chardonnay Sonoma County Cuvée Cathleen 1993: An ultra-rich and flavorful style of wine, with layers of ripe pear, honey, butterscotch and spice that unfold into a long, complex aftertaste. 531 cases made. • $50 • (06/30/96) • **90**

Chardonnay Sonoma County Cuvée Cathleen 1992: Remarkably complex, with ripe, rich pear, fig and smoky oak flavors. Lingers on the finish. This should develop even more complexity over the next year. First Cuvée Cathleen bottling. 522 cases made. • $50 • (06/30/95) • **92**

Chardonnay Sonoma Mountain McCrea Vineyard 1993: Rich and concentrated, with subtle flavors of honey, pear, vanilla and hazelnut. The long, full aftertaste develops traces of pineapple and spice as it lingers on the palate. 2,760 cases made. • $35 • (06/30/96) • **91**

Chardonnay Sonoma Mountain McCrea Vineyard 1992: Young and tight, with smoky, toasty pear and spice flavors slowly unfolding, revealing more depth and complexity on the finish. Try now. 3,686 cases made. • $35 • (04/30/95) • **90**

Chardonnay Sonoma Mountain McCrea Vineyard 1991 • $32 • (05/31/93) • **90**

Chardonnay Sonoma Valley Durell Vineyard 1993: A smooth, ripe and harmonious Chardonnay that has rich and complex flavors of pear, hazelnut, honey and spice, following through to a smoky aftertaste. Try now. 2,758 cases made. • $34 • (06/15/95) • **91**

Chardonnay Sonoma Valley Durell Vineyard Sand Hill 1992: Ripe and assertive, brimming with rich pear and apple notes, framed by toasty oak flavor. The finish is pretty with spicy pear and honey notes. Drinkable now. 2,857 cases made. • $28 • (05/15/94) • **91**

Chardonnay Sonoma Valley Durell Vineyard Sand Hill 1991 • $32 • (05/31/93) • **88**

Chardonnay Sonoma Valley Kistler Vineyard 1993: Smooth and creamy, with rich, subtle flavors that develop and expand to reveal a complex core of ripe pear, butter, hazelnut and smoky oak. In all, very harmonious wine. The finish lingers on and on, revealing nuance after nuance. 929 cases made. • $40 • (06/30/96) CS • **94**

Chardonnay Sonoma Valley Kistler Vineyard 1992: A rich, enormously complex blend of ripe pear, apple and spice flavors, with toasty, smoky, buttery nuances. Has a long, full aftertaste. 1,874 cases made. • $40 • (03/31/95) SS • **94**

Chardonnay Sonoma Valley Kistler Vineyard 1991 • $32 • (02/28/94) • **90**

Pinot Noir Russian River Valley Cuvée Catherine Kistler Estate Vineyard 1992: Shows complex toasty, buttery oak and pretty plum and black cherry fruit to match. Adds up to a wine of extra diminsion and finesse, with a particularly appealing aftertaste where the flavors flow together. 274 cases made. • $40 • **90**

Pinot Noir Russian River Valley Dutton Ranch 1987 • $15 • (03/31/90) • **85**

Pinot Noir Russian River Valley Dutton Ranch 1986 • $14 • (06/15/88) • **89**

Pinot Noir Sonoma Mountain McCrea Vineyard 1992: Serves up a ripe, supple core of black cherry, anise and currant flavors that turn smooth and polished despite a firm tannic backbone. 650 cases made. • $22 • (03/31/95) • **88**

KLEIN | CALIFORNIA

Cabernet Sauvignon Santa Cruz Mountains 1990: Deep and dark in color, it turns earthy and mulchy on the palate with unripe Cabernet flavors and a dose of bad oak. Misses the mark. • $25 • (11/15/93) • **81**

Cabernet Sauvignon Santa Cruz Mountains 1989 • $25 • (08/31/92) • **85**

Cabernet Sauvignon Santa Cruz Mountains 1988 • $25 • (01/31/92) • **83**

Cabernet Sauvignon Santa Cruz Mountains 1987 • $19 • (10/15/90) • **87**

Cabernet Sauvignon Santa Cruz Mountains 1986 • $22 • (09/30/89) • **89**

KNAPP | NEW YORK

Brut Finger Lakes NV: An extremely doughy aroma and flavor makes this difficult to appreciate at first. But it turns more appealing as you sip. Crisp, appley. 350 cases made. • $18 • **78**

Cabernet Sauvignon New York 1982 • $16 • (03/16/86) • **52**

Chardonnay Finger Lakes Barrel Fermented 1992: The spicy, nutmeg and cinnamon flavors don't mesh well with the green apple and pineapple notes in this light-bodied, tart wine. Has pleasing elements, but lacks harmony. 560 cases made. • $14 • **78**

Pinot Noir Finger Lakes 1992: This is a tart wine with cranberry flavors and a little spice. A strong vegetal note dominates its aroma. A tight, tannic wine that verges on being lean. 400 cases made. • $13 • (11/15/94) • **78**

Prism Finger Lakes 1993: A very deep-colored, aromatic, tannic and tart red wine that smells like Port and tastes like cider. It doesn't have the stuffing of flavor to measure up to the color and aroma, though. • $NA • (06/30/95) • **76**

Riesling Finger Lakes Cayuga Lake 1992: Very sweet and sugary in flavor, without much fruit except for some lemon and green apple that doesn't blend in well. This is awkward-tart and cloying at the same time. 400 cases made. • $8 • **76**

Vignoles Finger Lakes Late Harvest 1991: Luscious late-harvest wine with an earthy, mushroomy aroma that segues to nut, honey and subtle apricot flavors on the palate. The nuances linger on the finish, too. 150 cases made. • $17 • (06/30/95) • **86**

KNIPPRATH | WASHINGTON

Chardonnay Columbia Valley Reserve 1991: Earthy tobacco and toast aromas and flavors dominate this oaky white, although a beam of sweet pineapple and lemonade notes comes through. 104 cases made. • $10 • (09/30/94) • **79**

Lemberger Yakima Valley Pleasant Vineyards 1992: Dark, dense and spicy, with a modest level of blackberry flavor sneaking in to balance the toasty spice notes. Drinkable now. 116 cases made. • $8 • (09/30/94) • **81**

KONOCTI | CALIFORNIA

Cabernet Franc Lake County 1988 • $9 • (02/28/91) • **83**

Cabernet Sauvignon Lake County 1990: Light and simple, with a bit of an herb and beet edge to the currant flavors, finishing with a touch of tar. Drink now. 6,249 cases made. • $10 • (11/15/93) • **82**

Cabernet Sauvignon Lake County 1989 • $9 • (11/15/92) • **81**

Cabernet Sauvignon Lake County 1986 • $9 • (04/30/90) • **80**

Cabernet Sauvignon Lake County 1985 • $7 • (11/15/89) BB • **89**

Cabernet Sauvignon Lake County 1984 • $7 • (02/15/89) • **76**

Cabernet Sauvignon Lake County 1983 • $6 • (06/15/87) BB • **84**

Cabernet Sauvignon Lake County 1982 • $7 • (11/15/86) • **78**

Chardonnay California Mount Konocti Kelsey 1992: Simple and fruity, with an anise edge to the basic apple flavors. Drinkable now. 6,000 cases made. • $10 • (07/15/93) • **76**

Chardonnay California Mount Konocti Reserve 1992: Complex and intense with concentrated pear, spice, vanilla and butterscotch flavors. Finishes with flavors that fan out and stay with you. Drink now. 333 cases made. • $15 • (02/28/94) • **87**

Fumé Blanc Clear Lake Grand Fumé Reserve 1992 • $10 • (12/15/93) • **86**

Fumé Blanc Lake County 1991 • $7 • (12/31/92) • **84**

Fumé Blanc Lake County Kelsey 1992 • $7 • (09/15/93) BB • **84**

Meritage Clear Lake 1987 • $17 • (11/15/92) • **84**

Meritage Red Clear Lake 1987 • $17 • (04/15/91) • **85**

Merlot 1989 • $10 • (02/29/92) • **85**

Merlot Lake County 1988 • $9 • (03/31/91) BB • **83**

Merlot Lake County 1987 • $9 • (12/31/90) • **73**

Merlot Lake County 1985 • $8 • (12/31/88) • **83**

Merlot Lake County Mount Konocti Kelsey 1992: Rich and fruity, with a pretty band of currant, herb and oak flavors that fold together nicely. Finishes with firm tannins and spicy oak notes. Best from 1996 to 1997. 5,800 cases made. • $10 • (06/30/94) BB • **86**

Mount K Select Reserve Clear Lake 1991 • $11 • (09/15/93) • **79**

Red Table Wine Lake County NV • $5 • (11/15/92) BB • **80**

Sauvignon Blanc Lake County Grand Fumé Barrel Fermented 1991 • $10 • (11/30/92) • **83**

KONRAD | CALIFORNIA

Barbera Amador County 1992: Light and airy in texture, with nicely focused plum and blackberry fruit that keeps coming on the finish. 400 cases made. • $12 • (07/31/95) • **85**

Charbono Mendocino 1992: Earthy, barnyardy flavors weave their way through this chewy, supple wine. A touch of cherry fruit echoes on the finish. Maybe best from 1997-1998. 500 cases made. • $11 • (11/15/95) • **81**

Chardonnay Mendocino 1993: A sturdy white with spicy, slightly resiny apple flavors, starting to show some maturity. 880 cases made. • $11 • (06/15/96) • **83**

Chardonnay Mendocino 1992: Simple with modest toast and apple flavors. 1,100 cases made. • $11 • (02/28/95) • **77**

Chardonnay Mendocino County 1991 • $11 • (04/15/94) • **88**

Mélange à Trois Mendocino 1992: Pleasant enough with wild berry and cherry-laced fruit, finishing with firm tannins, a touch of heat and a leathery edge. Can stand cellaring into 1997 to soften. 900 cases made. • $13 • (12/15/95) • **85**

Mélange à Trois Mendocino 1991: Crisp in texture, jammy and intense in flavor, showing currant and berry and nice hints of vanilla and toast on the finish. • $12 • (03/15/94) • **86**

Mélange à Trois Mendocino County 1989 • $16 • (07/15/92) • **87**

Petite Sirah Mendocino 1991 • $11 • (05/31/94) • **84**

Petite Sirah Mendocino County 1991: Bright in flavor, chunky in texture, slipping some nice blackberry and spice flavor through the tannins. Best from 1997-1998. • $11 • (09/30/94) • **84**

Port Mendocino Petite Sirah Port Admiral's Quinta 1990 • $18 • (11/15/93) • **74**

Zinfandel Mendocino 1992: Lacks focus, the earthy, tarry Zinfandel flavors ending on a leathery note. 888 cases made. • $10 • (10/15/95) • **79**

Zinfandel Mendocino 1991: Crisp and austere, with more drying tannins than fruit showing through. 900 cases made. • $9 • (10/15/94) • **80**

Zinfandel Mendocino County 1990 • $9 • (09/30/93) BB • **88**

Zinfandel Mendocino County 1989 • $10 • (03/31/92) • **84**

KORBEL | CALIFORNIA

Blanc de Blancs NV • $14 • (05/15/92) • **72**

Blanc de Blancs California Private Reserve 1981 • $34 • (02/29/88) • **69**

Blanc de Noirs NV • $14 • (05/15/92) • **80**

Blanc de Noirs California Cuvée Master's Reserve NV • $15 • (12/31/93) • **80**

Blanc de Noirs California Cuvée Master's Reserve 1990: Tastes sweet with crisp, tinny pear, cherry and citrus notes. 5,000 cases made. • $15 • (05/31/95) • **78**

Brut California NV • $11 • (12/31/93) • **83**

Brut Rosé California NV • $11 • (12/31/93) • **83**

Cabernet Sauvignon Alexander Valley 1991: Earthy, leathery, dry and tannic. Just a hint of fruit sneaks through. Marginal. 1,000 cases made. • $13 • (11/15/94) • **73**

California Rouge NV • $13 • (12/31/93) • **81**

Chardonnay Russian River Valley 1993: Smooth, creamy and medium-bodied, showing ripe pear, fig and apricot flavors and a spicy finish. Well crafted. 900 cases made. • $15 • (06/30/95) • **85**

Chardonnay Sonoma County 1992: Strikes a nice balance between light pear and apple notes with spicy oak flavors. 1,275 cases made. • $10 • (06/30/94) • **82**

Chardonnay Sonoma County 1991: Has an odd earthy streak that runs through the ripe pear and spice flavors. Marginal. 2,500 cases made. • $10 • (06/30/94) • **70**

Extra Dry California NV • $11 • (12/31/93) • **79**

Natural California NV: Tastes off-dry with a cherry and candied fruit flavor profile, but it's crisp and clean. 30,000 cases made. • $13 • (05/31/95) • **80**

Sec California NV • $10 • (08/31/89) • **73**

KORNELL, HANNS | CALIFORNIA

Blanc de Blancs California 1982 • $15 • (11/30/86) • **77**

Blanc de Noirs California 1987 • $15 • (06/15/91) • **87**

Blanc de Noirs California 1986 • $15 • (05/31/89) • **69**

Key: SS—Spectator Selection. CS—Cellar Selection. BB—Best Buy. $NA—Price not available. (BT)—Barrel tasting. Ⓐ—Auction Price.
Dates in parentheses represent the issues in which the ratings were published.

Brut California NV • $12 • (06/15/91) • **79**

Extra Dry California NV • $11 • (05/31/89) • **73**

Sparkling California Sehr Trocken 1984 • $15 • (06/15/91) • **74**

KRISTONE | CALIFORNIA

Blanc de Blancs California 1991: Mature-appearing with its deep gold color and flavors to match, which seem a bit tired for a wine this young. The toasty, earthy pear notes pick up a trace of honey and butterscotch on the finish. • $60 • (11/30/95) • **87**

Blanc de Noirs California 1991: Smooth and polished, with complex, mature black cherry, honey, toast and hazelnut notes, all folding together into a harmonious and distinctive wine. Flavors linger on the finish. • $60 • (11/30/95) • **91**

Brut Rosé California 1991: A classy rosé, pretty in color, with ripe, complex cherry and berry flavors, picking up hints of floral, spicy notes. Keeps its fruity edge through the finish. • $60 • (11/30/95) • **90**

KRUG, CHARLES | CALIFORNIA

Cabernet Sauvignon 1988 • $12 • (03/15/92) • **73**

Cabernet Sauvignon Napa Valley 1992: Marked by supple herb and leathery flavors, the fruit struggles to emerge from the cloak of tannins, as it finishes with a slight bitter edge. • $12 • (12/15/95) • **84**

Cabernet Sauvignon Napa Valley 1991: Firm and compact, with an herbaceous, earthy edge to the flavors. 38,000 cases made. • $12 • (11/15/94) • **81**

Cabernet Sauvignon Napa Valley 1990: Firm and tight, but with a nice core of black cherry, currant and plum flavor underneath. It's young and tannic, but the fruit that peeks through is complex and concentrated. Needs time to evolve, best after 1997. • $12 • (10/31/93) • **88**

Cabernet Sauvignon Napa Valley 1989 • $12 • (11/15/92) • **77**

Cabernet Sauvignon Napa Valley 1987 • $11 • (11/15/91) • **79**

Cabernet Sauvignon Napa Valley 1986 • $11 • (02/28/91) • **87**

Cabernet Sauvignon Napa Valley 1985 • $23 Ⓐ • (01/31/90) • **77**

Cabernet Sauvignon Napa Valley 1982 • $7 • (10/31/87) • **79**

Cabernet Sauvignon Napa Valley 1965 • $35 • (07/16/85) • **74**

Cabernet Sauvignon Napa Valley 1962 • $65 • (07/16/85) • **84**

Cabernet Sauvignon Napa Valley 1961 • $125 • (07/16/85) • **84**

Cabernet Sauvignon Napa Valley 1952 • $250 • (07/16/85) • **86**

Cabernet Sauvignon Napa Valley 1951 • $250 • (07/16/85) • **80**

Cabernet Sauvignon Napa Valley 1947 • $300 • (07/16/85) • **89**

Cabernet Sauvignon Napa Valley 1944 • $420 • (03/01/89) • **88**

Cabernet Sauvignon Napa Valley Vintage Select 1986 • $NA • (03/01/89) • **87**

Cabernet Sauvignon Napa Valley Vintage Select 1985 • $29 • (03/15/92) • **89**

Cabernet Sauvignon Napa Valley Vintage Select 1984 • $26 • (06/30/90) • **87**

Cabernet Sauvignon Napa Valley Vintage Select 1983 • $24 • (06/30/90) • **81**

Cabernet Sauvignon Napa Valley Vintage Select 1981 • $25 • (09/30/90) • **90**

Cabernet Sauvignon Napa Valley Vintage Select 1980 • $23 • (03/01/89) • **79**

Cabernet Sauvignon Napa Valley Vintage Select 1979 • $32 • (03/01/89) • **82**

Cabernet Sauvignon Napa Valley Vintage Select 1978 • $NA • (11/15/92) • **78**

Cabernet Sauvignon Napa Valley Vintage Select 1977 • $30 • (03/01/89) • **74**

Cabernet Sauvignon Napa Valley Vintage Select 1974 • $44 • (02/15/90) • **87**

Cabernet Sauvignon Napa Valley Vintage Select 1973 • $35 • (03/01/89) • **73**

Cabernet Sauvignon Napa Valley Vintage Select 1972 • $57 • (03/01/89) • **77**

Cabernet Sauvignon Napa Valley Vintage Select 1971 • $31 • (03/01/89) • **79**
Cabernet Sauvignon Napa Valley Vintage Select 1970 • $65 • (03/01/89) • **75**
Cabernet Sauvignon Napa Valley Vintage Select 1969 • $65 • (03/01/89) • **81**
Cabernet Sauvignon Napa Valley Vintage Select 1968 • $77 • (03/01/89) • **80**
Cabernet Sauvignon Napa Valley Vintage Select 1966 • $53 • (06/01/85) • **87**
Cabernet Sauvignon Napa Valley Vintage Select 1965 • $70 • (03/01/89) • **87**
Cabernet Sauvignon Napa Valley Vintage Select 1964 • $70 • (03/01/89) • **86**
Cabernet Sauvignon Napa Valley Vintage Select 1963 • $42 • (03/01/89) • **74**
Cabernet Sauvignon Napa Valley Vintage Select 1962 • $55 • (03/01/89) • **78**
Cabernet Sauvignon Napa Valley Vintage Select 1961 • $70 • (03/01/89) • **89**
Cabernet Sauvignon Napa Valley Vintage Select 1960 • $50 • (03/01/89) • **79**
Cabernet Sauvignon Napa Valley Vintage Select 1959 • $60 • (03/01/89) • **85**
Cabernet Sauvignon Napa Valley Vintage Select 1958 • $200 • (03/01/89) • **88**
Cabernet Sauvignon Napa Valley Vintage Select 1957 • $135 • (07/16/85) • **81**
Cabernet Sauvignon Napa Valley Vintage Select 1956 • $185 • (03/01/89) • **90**
Cabernet Sauvignon Napa Valley Vintage Select 1952 • $530 • (03/01/89) • **92**
Cabernet Sauvignon Napa Valley Vintage Select 1951 • $350 • (03/01/89) • **85**
Cabernet Sauvignon Napa Valley Vintage Select 1950 • $500 • (03/01/89) • **79**
Cabernet Sauvignon Napa Valley Vintage Select 1946 • $750 • (03/01/89) • **88**
Cabernet Sauvignon Napa Valley Vintage Select Lot F-1 1974 • $44 • (03/01/89) • **88**
Cabernet Sauvignon Napa Valley Vintage Selection 1991: Firm in texture, with solid currant flavors, a touch of earth and a buzz of tannin on the finish. Best from 1999. 1,500 cases made. • $28 • (12/15/95) • **89**
Cabernet Sauvignon Napa Valley Vintage Selection 1988 • $28 • (07/31/93) • **87**
Cabernet Sauvignon Napa Valley Vintage Selection 1986 • $28 • (10/31/92) • **92**
Cabernet Sauvignon Napa Valley Vintage Selection 1974: Noticeable bottle variation in two tastings. One sample was very tired and metallic, the second showed better, but with an earthy edge to the supple currant and plum flavors. Dry and simple on the finish. Best to drink up soon. 8,246 cases made. • $44 • (11/15/94) • **81**
Chardonnay Napa Valley 1993: Light and simple, presenting delicate pear and spice flavors. 28,000 cases made. • $11 • (05/15/95) • **81**
Chardonnay Napa Valley 1992: Young and a bit coarse, but with ripe pear, citrus and oak flavors that come together better on the finish, where it picks up a toasty, buttery edge. Best now. 29,000 cases made. • $12 • (03/31/94) • **84**
Chardonnay Napa Valley 1991 • $12 • (12/31/92) • **85**
Chardonnay Napa Valley Carneros Reserve 1992: Unlike the 1991 Reserve, which has a strong leesy edge, this one hits the mark. It combines supple ripe pear and honey flavors with spicy oak and a hint of nutmeg and spice on the finish. Moderately rich and concentrated. Drink now. Tasted twice. 2,000 cases made. • $17 • (06/15/94) • **89**
Chardonnay Napa Valley Carneros Reserve 1991 • $16 • (06/15/94) • **87**
Gamay Beaujolais Napa Valley 1983 • $4 • (05/31/87) • **62**
Merlot 1989 • $13 • (05/31/92) • **84**
Merlot Napa Valley 1993: A touch earthy and leathery, with just enough plum and berry flavors to create a balance. Let it breathe.... 6,800 cases made. • $14 • **79**
Merlot Napa Valley 1992: Lean and trim, offering some currant and spice flavors. Appealing, but lacks extra dimensions. 4,600 cases made. • $14 • (03/31/95) • **83**
Merlot Napa Valley 1991: This has a green tobacco edge to the plummy Merlot fruit. Finishes with firm tannins. Drinkable now. 3,200 cases made. • $13 • (09/15/94) • **81**
Merlot Napa Valley 1990 • $14 • (06/15/93) • **85**
Pinot Noir 1989 • $10 • (02/15/92) • **82**
Pinot Noir Carneros 1987 • $8 • (02/28/91) BB • **87**
Pinot Noir Carneros Napa Valley 1993: Light and simple, with cherry-berry flavors of modest depth and proportion. 5,150 cases made. • $9 • **81**
Pinot Noir Carneros Napa Valley 1992: Tart and earthy, a spicy, wild raspberry edge turns funky on the finish. Drinkable now. 5,800 cases made. • $9 • (01/31/95) • **82**
Pinot Noir Carneros Napa Valley 1991 • $9 • (02/28/94) • **78**
Pinot Noir Carneros Napa Valley 1990 • $9 • (02/28/93) • **78**
Pinot Noir Carneros Napa Valley 1985 • $8 • (02/15/90) • **81**
Sauvignon Blanc Napa Valley 1993: Crisp, floral, lightly fruity. Finishes smooth. Ready now. 1,200 cases made. • $9 • (10/31/95) • **81**
White Zinfandel North Coast 1988 • $6 • (06/15/89) • **72**
Zinfandel Napa Valley 1992: Simple, with earthy notes of modest proportion and distinction. Ready now. 3,078 cases made. • $7 • (10/15/94) • **81**
Zinfandel Napa Valley 1990 • $6 • (09/30/93) • **74**
Zinfandel Napa Valley 1989 • $6 • (12/15/90) BB • **83**

KUNDE | CALIFORNIA

Cabernet Sauvignon Sonoma Valley 1990: Ripe and complex, with generous berry, currant and toast aromas and flavors, finishing firm but flavorful. Has a broad range of flavor that remains focused on the finish. Best to drink after 1996. 81 percent Cabernet Sauvignon, 12 percent Merlot and 7 percent Cabernet Franc. 6,000 cases made. • $15 • (03/15/93) • **88**
Cabernet Sauvignon Sonoma Valley Estate Reserve 1990: Rough texture, stalky flavors and modest intensity combine to make this less than exciting, although the green olive and currant flavors that come through on the finish help to lift it into the "could be" category. Try in 1997. 2,100 cases made. • $23 • (11/15/93) • **82**
Cabernet Sauvignon Sonoma Valley Reserve 1991: Tight, tannic and chewy, with a leathery quality in the currant and cherry flavors, turns dry and austere on the finish, and may never tame its tannic nature. 2,000 cases made. • $23 • (05/31/96) • **85**
Chardonnay Sonoma Valley 1994: A pleasant wine that offers spicy pear and apple notes, with a smooth and creamy mouth-feel. 23,000 cases made. • $14 • (01/31/96) • **86**
Chardonnay Sonoma Valley 1992: Ripe and spicy, with a pretty core of buttery pear- and fig-laced Chardonnay fruit that picks up light hazelnut shadings on the finish. Tasted three times. 13,900 cases made. • $14 • (06/30/94) • **88**
Chardonnay Sonoma Valley 1991 • $14 • (04/15/93) • **89**
Chardonnay Sonoma Valley Estate Reserve 1992: Spicy and concentrated, with pretty pear, fig and anise notes that are firm and focused, finishing with a tight beam of Chardonnay fruit that lingers. Drinks well now but can age through 1997. 2,900 cases made. • $20 • (06/30/94) • **89**
Chardonnay Sonoma Valley Kinneybrook 1994: An elegant and detailed young wine with bright, vivid pear, spice and citrus flavors that keeps its focus on a long, complex finish. 500 cases made. • $20 • (05/31/96) • **89**
Chardonnay Sonoma Valley Kinneybrook Unfiltered 1993: Serves up lots of flavor, with lively pear, spice, citrus, hazelnut and honey notes. It's complex and rich on the finish. 450 cases made. • $17 • (01/31/96) • **90**
Chardonnay Sonoma Valley Kinneybrook Vineyard 1992: Intense and focused, with chunky pear and butterscotch flavors that turn heavy-handed with oak on the finish. A rough-and-tumble Kunde that lacks the polish and finesse so evident in earlier vintages. 350 cases made. • $17 • (06/30/94) • **82**
Chardonnay Sonoma Valley Reserve 1994: A subtle, elegant style that opens up an attractive core of ripe pear, apple and honey notes, then adds a trace of hazelnut on the finish. 3,000 cases made. • $22 • (06/15/96) • **87**

Chardonnay Sonoma Valley Reserve 1993: Smooth, ripe and buttery, sporting tiers of honey, pear, fig and toast notes that fold together nicely on the finish. Impressive for its flavor and balance. 3,000 cases made. • $20 • **89**
Chardonnay Sonoma Valley Wildwood 1994: Smooth, rich and creamy, with tiers of honey, pear, vanilla and spice. A complex and well-crafted wine that finishes with a pleasant aftertaste. 500 cases made. • $20 • (05/31/96) • **89**
Chardonnay Sonoma Valley Wildwood Unfiltered 1993: Good intensity and flavor, with spicy pear, apple and honey notes. The texture is a bit coarse, but a little age should help it. 440 cases made. • $17 • (01/31/96) • **89**
Chardonnay Sonoma Valley Wildwood Vineyard 1992: Firm and tight, compact, with ripe spicy pear and oak flavors that turn coarse on the finish. Perhaps with time it will soften and settle out. 350 cases made. • $17 • (06/30/94) • **82**
Claret Sonoma Valley Louis Kunde Founder's Reserve 1990: Firm and focused, a spicy, toasty, chocolate-scented wine with a modest core of currant and plum flavor that persists into an elegant finish. Balanced for harmony in the long run. Best 1998 to 2000. 1,000 cases made. • $17 • (11/15/93) • **88**
Louis Kunde Founder's Reserve Sonoma Valley 1989 • $15 • (11/15/92) • **90**
Merlot Sonoma Valley 1993: Smooth and harmonious, adding supple currant, black cherry, herb and smoky oak shadings. Impressive, elegant, graceful. Complex aftertaste. 5,800 cases made. • $17 • (12/31/95) • **88**
Merlot Sonoma Valley 1991: Surprisingly earthy and tarry, void of fruit and well off the pace that Kunde set with its other wines earlier on. Tasted three times with consistent notes. 3,900 cases made. • $15 • (09/15/94) • **77**
Sauvignon Blanc Sonoma Valley Magnolia Lane 1994: Toasted onion notes waft through the green pear flavors in this smooth and distinctly herbal white. Ready now. 9,700 cases made. • $10 • (10/31/95) • **82**
Sauvignon Blanc Sonoma Valley Magnolia Lane 1993: Smooth and distinctly herbal, a light white with a resiny edge. 4,000 cases made. • $10 • (02/28/95) • **80**
Sauvignon Blanc Sonoma Valley Magnolia Lane 1992: Intense and spicy, with focused pear and grapefruit flavors that are rich and lively. Good depth and concentration, ready now. 3,900 cases made. • $10 • (06/30/94) BB • **87**
Sauvignon Blanc Sonoma Valley Magnolia Lane 1991 • $9 • (04/15/93) • **82**
Sonoma Valley Red 1994: Very fruity and fresh, its spicy flavors hinting at almond and pine nut on the finish. Drink now. 1,400 cases made. • $17 • (09/30/95) • **85**
Viognier Sonoma Valley 1993: Deliciously fresh, floral and spicy, bright and fruity, with exotic overtones, focused and supple on the finish. 300 cases made. • $15 • (09/15/94) • **88**
Zinfandel Sonoma Valley Shaw Vineyard 1990 • $14 • (12/31/92) • **84**
Zinfandel Sonoma Valley The Shaw Vineyard Century Vines 1993: Intense, firm tannins and a modest core of spice, wild berry, pepper and oak. Could stand to soften a bit in the cellar. 5,800 cases made. • $14 • (03/31/96) • **85**
Zinfandel Sonoma Valley The Shaw Vineyard Century Vines 1992: Earthy and a bit funky, with drying fruit flavors. Off the mark. Tasted three times. 2,900 cases made. • $14 • (10/15/94) • **74**
Zinfandel Sonoma Valley The Shaw Vineyard Century Vines 1991 • $14 • (06/15/94) • **82**

JOTA, LA | CALIFORNIA

Barrel Fermented Howell Mountain Red 1993: A bright, floral, full-bodied white that leans more toward piney, resiny flavors than fruit. Drink now. 300 cases made. • $24 • (01/31/95) • **80**
Cabernet Franc Howell Mountain 1993: Starts out sporting spicy cherry, berry and pepper flavors, but turns tight and chunky at mid-palate. Adds some anise and a good dose of tannin. 350 cases made. • $28 • (04/30/96) • **88**

Key: SS—Spectator Selection. CS—Cellar Selection. BB—Best Buy. $NA—Price not available. (BT)—Barrel tasting. Ⓐ—Auction Price.
Dates in parentheses represent the issues in which the ratings were published.

Cabernet Franc Howell Mountain 1992: Well oaked but not overdone, with buttery, spicy overtones and a pretty core of currant and cherry flavors that fan out. 350 cases made. • $28 • (07/31/95) • **89**
Cabernet Franc Howell Mountain 1991: Firm, compact and well oaked, with a dense core of chocolate and berry flavors that are tightly wound. Best to cellar this one another year or two, try after 1996. 325 cases made. • $28 • (12/31/94) • **84**
Cabernet Franc Howell Mountain 1990 • $28 • (11/15/93) • **80**
Cabernet Franc Howell Mountain 1988 • $28 • (08/31/91) • **89**
Cabernet Franc Howell Mountain 1986 • $25 • (10/15/89) • **81**
Cabernet Sauvignon Howell Mountain 1990: Firm and supple with intense currant, anise and herbal notes that turn smooth and fleshy on the finish. Drink now. 2,500 cases made. • $28 • (11/15/93) • **85**
Cabernet Sauvignon Howell Mountain 1989 • $28 • (11/15/92) • **78**
Cabernet Sauvignon Howell Mountain 1988 • $17 Ⓐ • (08/31/91) • **85**
Cabernet Sauvignon Howell Mountain 1987 • $31 Ⓐ • (07/31/90) SS • **95**
Cabernet Sauvignon Howell Mountain 1986 • $38 Ⓐ • (10/15/89) • **85**
Cabernet Sauvignon Howell Mountain 1985 • $26 Ⓐ • (03/01/89) • **88**
Cabernet Sauvignon Howell Mountain 1984 • $34 • (03/01/89) • **88**
Cabernet Sauvignon Howell Mountain 1983 • $41 • (03/01/89) • **84**
Cabernet Sauvignon Howell Mountain 1982 • $43 • (03/01/89) • **84**
Cabernet Sauvignon Howell Mountain 10th Anniversary Release 1991: Very pretty and charming, with elegant, spicy cherry, chocolate and vanilla flavors that are rich and focused, finishing with good length and firm tannins. Drinkable now. 1,400 cases made. • $38 • (06/15/94) CS • **90**
Cabernet Sauvignon Howell Mountain 11th Anniversary Release 1992: 950 cases made. • $38 • **92**
Cabernet Sauvignon Howell Mountain 12th Anniversary Release 1993: A well oaked style, featuring lots of vanilla and toasty, smoky oak. Underneath, the currant, cherry and mineral flavors are full-blown, finishing in strong wood and plush tannins. Can stand aging into 1999—maybe longer. 1,450 cases made. • $42 • (04/30/96) • **91**
Cabernet Sauvignon Howell Mountain 13th Anniversary 1994: Austere with a green, unripe edge to the currant and berry flavors. Borders on a stale edge. • $NA • (05/31/95) • **80-84** (BT)
Cabernet Sauvignon Howell Mountain Selection 1993: Tight and a touch earthy, sporting cedar, currant, cherry and pepper notes. Chewy, chalky tannins on the finish, best to cellar into 1998 or '99. 1,240 cases made. • $24 • (04/30/96) • **87**
Cabernet Sauvignon Howell Mountain Selection 1992: Solid, chunky core of earthy currant and tobacco, turning supple in texture but adding ample tannins. 950 cases made. • $18 • (06/15/95) • **88**
Cabernet Sauvignon Howell Mountain Selection 1991: Heavy handed, with oaky flavors and drying tannins, seemingly void of fruit at this stage. Hard to warm up to. • $18 • (06/15/94) • **79**
Cabernet Sauvignon Napa Valley Little J NV • $9 • (10/15/92) • **81**
Cold Fermented Howell Mountain Red 1993: Firm, full-bodied and fruity, packed with rambunctious melon, pear and spice flavors. 300 cases made. • $24 • (01/31/95) • **87**
Petite Sirah Howell Mountain 1992: Ripe and chewy, showing typical Petite Sirah tannins that are refined enough for the spicy, oaky blackberry flavor to shine through. 325 cases made. • $18 • (02/28/95) • **87**
Viognier Howell Mountain 1991 • $24 • (11/30/92) • **89**
Viognier Howell Mountain Sweet 1993: Very ripe, honeyed and unctuous, with haylike overtones to the sweet pear and cereal flavors. Tasty now, if highly unusual. 95 cases made. • $36 • (04/30/95) • **85**
Zinfandel Howell Mountain 1987 • $12 • (10/31/89) • **83**
Zinfandel Howell Mountain 1986 • $10 • (10/31/88) • **89**
Zinfandel Howell Mountain 1985 • $10 • (04/30/88) • **85**
Zinfandel Howell Mountain 1984 • $10 • (11/15/87) • **88**

LAFAYETTE | FLORIDA

Blush Florida Sunblush NV • $7 • (02/29/92) • **75**

LAKE SONOMA | CALIFORNIA

Cinsault Vintner's Reserve Dry Creek Valley 1991 • $16 • (02/15/93) • **73**
Merlot Yoakim Bridge Ranch 1990 • $14 • (05/31/92) • **86**
Merlot Dry Creek Valley Yoakim Bridge Ranch 1991 • $14 • (03/31/93) • **83**

Zinfandel Dry Creek Valley 1990 • $10 • (09/30/93) • **72**
Zinfandel Dry Creek Valley 1989 • $9 • (10/15/92) • **84**

LAKERIDGE | FLORIDA

Sparkling Florida Crescendo NV • $12 • (02/29/92) • **79**

LAKESPRING | CALIFORNIA

Cabernet Sauvignon Napa Valley 1993: Medium-bodied, with a modest band of currant, cedar and spicy flavors. • $12 • (03/31/96) • **80**
Cabernet Sauvignon Napa Valley 1990: Firm and chewy, showing a solid beam of currant and berry flavor shining through the thick veil of tannin. Best from 1997 or 1998. • $10 • (05/15/94) • **87**
Cabernet Sauvignon Napa Valley 1987 • $17 • (10/15/91) • **84**
Cabernet Sauvignon Napa Valley 1986 • $17 • (03/01/89) • **88**
Cabernet Sauvignon Napa Valley 1985 • $19 • (03/01/89) • **88**
Cabernet Sauvignon Napa Valley 1983 • $11 • (03/01/89) • **85**
Cabernet Sauvignon Napa Valley 1981 • $22 • (03/01/89) • **86**
Cabernet Sauvignon Napa Valley 1980 • $21 • (03/01/89) • **88**
Cabernet Sauvignon Napa Valley Reserve Selection 1988 • $18 • (11/15/92) • **74**
Cabernet Sauvignon Napa Valley Reserve Selection 1984 • $20 • (03/01/89) • **92**
Cabernet Sauvignon Napa Valley Vintage Selection 1982 • $28 • (03/01/89) • **88**
Chardonnay Napa Valley 1994: Complex, appealing array of fig, toast, spice and pear flavors. Strikes a nice balance between its ripe fruit and toasty oak. Ready now. • $12 • (02/29/96) • **88**
Chardonnay Napa Valley 1992: Crisp and flavorful, turning a bit astringent on the finish, but it has enough fruit to carry it through. Drink now. 3,450 cases made. • $10 • (06/30/94) • **81**
Dessert Napa Valley Elixia Late Harvest 1989 • $12 • (03/01/92) • **75**
Merlot Napa Valley 1994: Medium body and showing only modest levels of grapey Merlot flavors. Finishes dry and oaky, a bit heavy-handed. 3,500 cases made. • $14 • (03/31/96) • **78**
Merlot Napa Valley 1987 • $14 • (06/15/90) • **85**
Merlot Napa Valley 1986 • $14 • (03/31/89) • **79**
Merlot Napa Valley 1985 • $15 • (03/31/88) SS • **91**
Merlot Napa Valley 1984 • $12 • (05/15/87) • **88**
Merlot Napa Valley 1983 • $11 • (05/16/86) • **87**
Merlot Napa Valley 1982 • $10 • (10/01/85) • **78**
Merlot Napa Valley Yount Mill Vineyard 1990 • $14 • (07/15/93) • **88**
Merlot Yount Mill Vineyard 1988 • $15 • (02/29/92) • **85**
Sauvignon Blanc Napa Valley Yount Mill Vineyard 1993: Fresh and herbal, with a nice core of peach and melon fruit to keep it lively. 6,300 cases made. • $8 • (08/31/94) • **83**
Sauvignon Blanc Napa Valley Yount Mill Vineyard 1992 • $8 • (01/31/94) • **84**
Sauvignon Blanc Napa Valley Yount Mill Vineyard 1991 • $8 • (08/31/93) • **84**

LAKEWOOD | CALIFORNIA

Chevriot Clear Lake 1993: Crisp and focused, bright, toasty green apple and spice flavors. Livelier than most oak-apparent Sauvignons. • $12 • (08/31/95) • **86**
Chevriot Clear Lake 1992: A 50-50 blend of Sémillon and Sauvignon Blanc, it strikes a fine balance between the two, with rich, smoky fig, sweet pea and pear-laced flavors. More complexity and depth than most of this breed. Ready. • $12 • (12/15/94) • **88**
Sauvignon Blanc Clear Lake 1994: Bright, crisp and disarming for its lively green apple, fennel and spice flavors that linger on the finish. Ready now. • $10 • (12/31/95) • **87**
Sauvignon Blanc Clear Lake 1993: Lean and crisp, with hints of herb, melon and grass. • $9 • (12/15/94) • **84**
Sauvignon Blanc Clear Lake 1992: Lean and tart, a simple wine with citrusy, spicy flavors. • $NA • (08/31/94) • **81**
Sémillon Clear Lake 1993: A little rough around the edges, but the ripe fig, herb and pear flavors ring true. Short-term cellaring should soften it a bit. Ready. • $12 • (12/15/94) • **85**
Sémillon Clear Lake 1991 • $12 • (03/31/94) • **80**
White Table Wine Clear Lake 1991: Floral, herbal flavors come off as stale in this medium-weight, tired white. • $NA • (08/31/94) • **73**

LAKEWOOD (NY) | NEW YORK

Dessert Finger Lakes Glaciovinum Delaware Ice Wine 1993: The grapey, foxy notes of Labrusca are evident here, but not displeasing, wrapped in unctuous sweetness and lemony acidity. It packs a punch, but the overall impression is of grape jelly. 168 cases made. • $9 • **81**

LAMBERT BRIDGE | CALIFORNIA

Cabernet Sauvignon Dry Creek Valley Crane Creek 1989 • $28 • (11/15/92) • **80**
Cabernet Sauvignon Sonoma County 1993: Clean and correct, with ripe plum, spice and berry notes, finishing with mild oak and tannins. Well proportioned. 420 cases made. • $15 • (12/15/95) • **86**
Cabernet Sauvignon Sonoma County 1992: Dry and well oaked, with a smoky wood edge that overrides the ripe plum and currant flavors. Finishes with a good dose of wood and fruit, with cellaring into 1998 recommended. 1,549 cases made. • $15 • (12/15/95) • **87**
Cabernet Sauvignon Sonoma County 1991: Dark, firm and tannic. A tightly wound Cabernet with spicy currant notes, but not showing much at this stage. Best to cellar until 1997 or 1998. 1,947 cases made. • $14 • (10/15/94) • **84**
Cabernet Sauvignon Sonoma County 1984 • $10 • (04/15/87) • **80**
Cabernet Sauvignon Sonoma County 1981 • $12 • (01/01/85) • **75**
Chardonnay Sonoma County 1992: Soft and fruity, simple, with a brash, sappy streak running through it. Drinkable now. 2,103 cases made. • $13 • (06/30/94) • **80**
Chardonnay Sonoma County Barrel Fermented 1993: Nicely focused and flavorful, pointing its apple and pear notes deliciously through the lively finish. Drink now. 3,683 cases made. • $13 • (04/15/95) • **86**
Fumé Blanc Sonoma County Fumé 1992: Simple, herbal aromas and flavors characterize this sturdy, slightly sweet wine. 530 cases made. • $7 • (08/31/94) • **78**
Merlot Sonoma County 1993: Marked by cedary oak, an austere band of cherry and plum flavors and chewy tannins. Can use cellaring into 1997, but may always be on the tannic side. 2,150 cases made. • $15 • (12/15/95) • **86**
Merlot Sonoma County 1992: Smooth and polished, with a supple currant, berry and cherry flavor that's well focused, finishing with a smoky, toasty oak edge. Tannins are round and fleshy, firming up on the finish. Best after 1997. 1,783 cases made. • $14 • (09/15/94) • **87**
Merlot Sonoma County 1991: Austere with firm tannins and a narrow band of herb and wild berry flavors. Short-term cellaring should make it softer and perhaps more appealing. 493 cases made. • $14 • (09/15/94) • **79**
Merlot Sonoma County 1985 • $10 • (12/15/87) • **69**
Merlot Sonoma County 1982 • $12 • (12/16/84) • **79**
Merlot Sonoma County Library Reserve 1989 • $24 • (11/30/92) • **85**
Sauvignon Blanc Sonoma County Fumé 1993: Light, fruity and appealing, with pear and smoky herbal flavors lingering on the delicate finish. 560 cases made. • $8 • (02/28/95) • **81**
Zinfandel Dry Creek Valley 1992: Earthy and tannic, with a hard-edged core of tarry fruit flavors. Needs a year or two in the cellar to soften. 475 cases made. • $11 • (10/15/94) • **84**

LAMBORN FAMILY | CALIFORNIA

Zinfandel Howell Mountain 1990 • $12 • (10/15/92) • **80**
Zinfandel Howell Mountain 1988 • $11 • (02/15/91) • **89**
Zinfandel Howell Mountain 1987 • $10 • (03/15/90) • **84**
Zinfandel Howell Mountain The Phoenix Vintage 1991 • $12 • (09/30/93) • **82**

LAMOREAUX LANDING | NEW YORK

Blanc de Noirs Finger Lakes 1990: An exotic, spicy mix of nutmeg, vanilla, orange and lemon flavors make this an interesting, full-blown bubbly. 325 cases made. • $15 • **83**

Brut Finger Lakes 1990: Modest apple and spice aromas and subtle apple flavors add up to a subdued but enjoyable wine. 400 cases made. • $15 • **80**

Chardonnay Finger Lakes 1993: This lively Chardonnay shows good freshness and sweet fruit character, offering melon, peach and a strong dose of oak. It's balanced and brings you back for another sip. 419 cases made. • $12 • **85**

Chardonnay Finger Lakes 1992: A lively, fresh Chardonnay with bright lemon and piney aromas, citrus flavors and a definite overlay of oak. Drinkable now. 550 cases made. • $12 • (09/15/94) • **84**

Chardonnay Finger Lakes 1991: Butterscotch aromas give way to ripe apple flavors that turn almost sweet. The fruit is nearly overwhelmed by the butter. 400 cases made. • $12 • (09/15/94) • **82**

Chardonnay Finger Lakes Reserve 1991: Nicely flavorful and complete, with toasty, smoky aromas, ripe pear and vanilla flavors and a lingering finish that echoes fruit and spice. It's balanced and harmonious. 328 cases made. • $16 • (09/15/94) • **85**

Finger Lakes 1992: There is lots of sweet oak in this lush-textured, lavish tasting white wine. Doesn't have much fruit flavor, but it's enjoyable for its opulence and style. Nicely priced, too. 306 cases made. • $7 • (06/30/95) • **83**

Pinot Noir Finger Lakes 1993: Attractive cherry and spicy aromas give way to a light, fresh wine with cherry flavors and lean, slightly green tannins. Drinkable now, it's got clean varietal character in a delicate style. 195 cases made. • $12 • (09/30/95) • **82**

Pinot Noir Finger Lakes 1991: A nice combination of cherry, cedar and spice flavors makes this a refreshing quaff. This wine is well balanced, medium-bodied and has moderate tannins. 200 cases made. • $12 • (11/15/94) • **82**

Riesling Finger Lakes Dry 1994: Generous aromas of mango and lime give way to a more austere palate and steely acidity. It's clean and refreshing. 543 cases made. • $8 • (01/31/96) • **83**

Riesling Finger Lakes Dry 1993: A dry, clean-tasting Riesling with nice floral and piney aromas, crisp acidity and light body. Brisk, fruity and nicely balanced, clean on the finish.\ 209 cases made. • $8 • (09/15/94) • **83**

Riesling Finger Lakes Semi-Dry 1994: This pleasant quaff offers ripe peach and vanilla flavors and a good balance of bright acidity and moderate sweetness. A good apéritif. 543 cases made. • $8 • (01/31/96) • **83**

Riesling Finger Lakes Semi-Dry 1993: Definitely sweet, but it's supported by lively acidity and plenty of fresh orange and pineapple flavors, to make a rich and vivid wine. 134 cases made. • $8 • **82**

Riesling Ice Wine Finger Lakes 1991: A straightforward, simple wine with modest apple and nut flavors and moderate sweetness. There's little complexity or varietal flavor, but it's pleasant. Drink now. 56 cases made. • $25 • **78**

LANDMARK | CALIFORNIA

Chardonnay Alexander Valley Damaris Reserve 1993: Ripe, smooth and creamy, with lush pear, vanilla and light toast shadings that turn smooth and silky on the finish. 900 cases made. • $19 • (12/31/94) • **90**

Chardonnay Alexander Valley Damaris Reserve 1992: Fresh and lively, with apple- and pear-laced Chardonnay fruit that comes across as simple and one-dimensional. Ready now. 1,600 cases made. • $16 • (06/30/94) • **82**

Chardonnay Alexander Valley Damaris Reserve 1991 • $17 • (06/15/93) • **91**

Chardonnay Sonoma County Damaris Reserve 1994: Rich and creamy, with a good dose of toasty, buttery oak and just the right amount of spicy pear and honey-laced Chardonnay. Finishes with a complex encore of fruit and smoky oak. 1,400 cases made. • $23 • (03/31/96) • **89**

Chardonnay Sonoma County Overlook 1994: A fabulous California Chardonnay. Well oaked, rich and creamy, with a pretty core of melon, fig, honey and pear flavors that hold on through the finish. This builds on the palate, offering more complexity as it goes. 17,000 cases made. • $16 • (03/31/96) SS • **91**

Key: SS—Spectator Selection. CS—Cellar Selection. BB—Best Buy. $NA—Price not available. (BT)—Barrel tasting. Ⓐ—Auction Price.
Dates in parentheses represent the issues in which the ratings were published.

Chardonnay Sonoma County Overlook 1993: Firm and compact, spicy pear, fig and citrus notes that pick up a light toasty accent on the finish. 9,000 cases made. • $14 • (02/28/95) • **88**

Chardonnay Sonoma County Overlook 1992: Serves up pretty pear, nectarine and apple flavors that zing across the palate, picking up toasty oak notes on the finish. Drinkable now. 2,500 cases made. • $12 • (03/31/94) • **87**

Chardonnay Sonoma County Overlook 1991 • $12 • (04/15/93) • **88**

Chardonnay Sonoma Valley Two Williams Vineyards 1992: Packed with flavor, a polished, flinty wine that throws off sparks of apple, vanilla and spice along the way. Has style and personality to spare. Drinkable now. 750 cases made. • $14 • (06/30/94) • **90**

LANG | CALIFORNIA

Zinfandel El Dorado Twin Rivers Vineyards 1992: Adds a ripe, fruity, spicy, peppery edge to the plum and cherry flavors. Holds together nicely. 380 cases made. • $6 • (09/15/95) • **87**

LATAH CREEK | WASHINGTON

Cabernet Sauvignon Washington 1993: Firm in texture, with soft plum and currant flavors that linger on the finish. Drinkable now. 800 cases made. • $12 • (09/30/95) • **85**

Cabernet Sauvignon Washington 1986 • $13 • (10/15/88) • **80**

Cabernet Sauvignon Washington Limited Bottling 1992: Earthy, gamy notes dominate this. The fruit is present, but it veers off into too many vegetal flavors. 850 cases made. • $12 • (09/30/94) • **77**

Cabernet Sauvignon Washington Limited Bottling 1990: Firm and focused, with a solid core of currant and spice aromas and flavors, a straightforward wine with enough intensity to repay cellaring through 1997. • $12 • (06/15/93) • **85**

Cabernet Sauvignon Washington Limited Bottling 1988 • $13 • (10/15/91) • **91**

Cabernet Sauvignon Washington Limited Bottling 1987 • $13 • (10/15/89) • **83**

Cabernet Sauvignon Washington Reserve 1991: Tight texture, but supple underneath the tannins. Shows some elegance and reserve. Black cherry and spice flavors echo on the finish. Best after 1996. 605 cases made. • $20 • (12/31/93) • **85**

Chardonnay Washington 1993: Smooth, supple and generous, folding some nice spicy notes in with the well articulated pear and peach flavors. Immensely appealing for its taste and price. 1,250 cases made. • $10 • (04/30/95) BB • **88**

Chardonnay Washington 1992: Bright and polished, a smooth-textured wine with orange, pear and fig aromas and flavors. Finishes with a touch of sweet oak. Drinkable now. 1,460 cases made. • $10 • (12/31/93) • **84**

Chardonnay Washington 1991 • $10 • (06/15/93) • **82**

Chardonnay Washington Feather 1993: Simple and fruity, lively enough to show off the Mâcon-like apple and mineral flavors. Drinkable now. 3,500 cases made. • $7 • (09/30/94) • **82**

Chenin Blanc Late Harvest Washington 1990: Dark in color and nasty in aroma, like rotten celery, syrupy on the finish, not at all pleasant. 420 cases made. • $8 • (09/30/94) • **62**

Chenin Blanc Washington 1994: Sweet but balanced with lemony acidity, centered around pear and apple flavors. Ready now. 700 cases made. • $6 • (09/30/95) • **83**

Gewürztraminer Washington 1993: Lean and crisp and not much else. Tasted twice with consistent notes. 500 cases made. • $6 • (09/30/94) • **73**

Johannisberg Riesling Washington 1994: Simple, fruity and refreshing, lightly sweet, featuring pear and floral flavors. 800 cases made. • $6 • (09/30/95) • **80**

Johannisberg Riesling Washington Dry 1992: Floral in flavor and a little thick in texture, simple, drink soon. 900 cases made. • $6 • (09/30/94) • **78**

Lemberger Washington 1992 • $8 • (12/31/93) • **80**

Lemberger Washington 1991 • $8 • (04/30/93) • **82**

Lemberger Washington 1990 • $8 • (01/31/92) • **85**

Merlot Washington 1993: Lean, chewy and somewhat tannic for its lingering light plum and cherry flavors, finishes with a touch of anise. Best in 1997. 2,500 cases made. • $12 • (09/30/95) • **85**
Merlot Washington 1986 • $10 • (05/31/88) • **89**
Merlot Washington Limited Bottling 1992 • $12 • (12/31/93) • **82**
Merlot Washington Limited Bottling 1991 • $12 • (05/31/93) • **87**
Merlot Washington Limited Bottling 1989 • $11 • (09/30/91) • **91**
Merlot Washington Limited Bottling 1987 • $10 • (10/15/89) • **90**
Muscat Canelli Washington 1994: Sweet and simple, soft-textured, offering subtle grapey, spicy flavors. 700 cases made. • $6 • (09/30/95) • **80**
Muscat Canelli Washington 1993: Off-dry, zingy and spicy, with a piney edge to the lean, green apple flavor. 650 cases made. • $6 • (09/30/94) • **79**
Sauvignon Blanc Washington 1994: Smooth, lively and intriguing in the way it weaves together its pear, apple, herb and vanilla flavors. 700 cases made. • $8 • (09/15/95) • **87**
Sauvignon Blanc Washington 1991 • $8 • (12/31/93) • **79**

LAURA'S | CALIFORNIA

Cabernet Sauvignon Paso Robles 1985 • $12 • (12/15/89) • **71**
Cabernet Sauvignon Paso Robles 1983 • $8 • (12/31/87) • **80**

LAUREL ESTATE | CALIFORNIA

Cabernet Sauvignon North Coast 1989 • $8 • (11/15/92) • **77**
Chardonnay North Coast 1991 • $8 • (11/30/92) • **83**

LAUREL GLEN | CALIFORNIA

Cabernet Sauvignon Napa Valley Terra Rosa 1990: Starts off lean and austere, but expands on the palate to show some appealing currant, spice and toasty oak aromas and flavors, finishing firm and lively. Best to drink after 1996. 15 percent Merlot and 10 percent Cabernet Franc. 15,000 cases made. • $9 • (09/30/93) BB • **89**
Cabernet Sauvignon North Coast Terra Rosa 1992: A ripe California red that has smooth and supple cherry, berry and spice flavors with an attractive buttery oak backbone. Offers depth and intensity, with firm tannins. 30,000 cases made. • $10 • (04/30/95) SS • **88**
Cabernet Sauvignon Sonoma County Counterpoint 1988 • $13 • (07/15/91) • **83**
Cabernet Sauvignon Sonoma County Terra Rosa 1989 • $9 • (07/15/92) • **86**
Cabernet Sauvignon Sonoma Mountain 1992: Dense and firmly tannic, giving it a dry, austere edge, but the plum, cherry and currant notes are pretty. Whether it will ever outgrow its tannins is the major question. 16 cases made. • $33 • (12/15/95) • **85**
Cabernet Sauvignon Sonoma Mountain 1991: Dense and concentrated with an earthy edge opening up to spicy currant and black cherry flavors that turn elegant on the finish. Try now, or cellar until '97 or '98. 1,500 cases made. • $30 • (11/15/94) • **89**
Cabernet Sauvignon Sonoma Mountain 1990: Firm and flavorful, its spicy plum and berry aromas and flavors fanning across the palate, hinting at bell pepper and herb on the finish. Almost drinkable now, but the tannins should be softer in 1997. 1,000 cases made. • $30 • (11/15/93) • **89**
Cabernet Sauvignon Sonoma Mountain 1989 • $34 • (08/31/92) • **88**
Cabernet Sauvignon Sonoma Mountain 1988 • $35 • (05/15/91) CS • **90**
Cabernet Sauvignon Sonoma Mountain 1987 • $34 • (09/15/90) • **90**
Cabernet Sauvignon Sonoma Mountain 1986 • $29 ⓐ • (05/15/89) • **87**
Cabernet Sauvignon Sonoma Mountain 1985 • $85 ⓐ • (03/01/89) • **93**
Cabernet Sauvignon Sonoma Mountain 1984 • $55 • (03/01/89) • **89**
Cabernet Sauvignon Sonoma Mountain 1983 • $40 • (03/01/89) • **59**
Cabernet Sauvignon Sonoma Mountain 1982 • $33 • (03/01/89) • **85**
Cabernet Sauvignon Sonoma Mountain 1981 • $73 • (03/01/89) • **92**
Cabernet Sauvignon Sonoma Mountain 1978 • $NA • (11/15/92) • **92**
Cabernet Sauvignon Sonoma Mountain Counterpoint 1992: Intense and concentrated, with a well focused core of plum, currant, black cherry and spice, picking up a slight mineral edge on the finish. Can age into 1998. 900 cases made. • $16 • (12/15/95) • **88**
Cabernet Sauvignon Sonoma Mountain Counterpoint 1991: A rough and tumble young wine with great potential. It shows remarkable depth of black cherry, blackberry and currant flavors and lots of fascinating shades of bay leaf, smoke and tar. Tannins need until 1998 or 2000 to subside. 2,750 cases made. • $15 • (11/30/93) SS • **90**
Cabernet Sauvignon Sonoma Mountain Counterpoint 1990: Firmly tannic, lean and youthful, with tightly wound herb, currant and leather notes and dry, biting tannins. Concentrated and structured, and the finish fans out with tobacco and plum notes. Best to drink now or cellar until '97. • $15 • (03/15/93) • **87**
Cabernet Sauvignon Sonoma Mountain Counterpoint 1989 • $15 • (01/31/92) • **85**
Cabernet Sauvignon Sonoma Mountain Counterpoint 1987 • $13 • (10/31/89) • **94**
Cabernet Sauvignon Sonoma Mountain Counterpoint Cuvée 85-86 NV • $11 • (05/31/88) • **89**
Cabernet Sauvignon Sonoma Mountain Reserve 1990: Firm in texture, with restrained berry, plum, cedar and tobacco flavors that keep trying to peek through on the long finish. Drinkable now or wait until 1998. 300 cases made. • $75 • (11/15/93) • **88**
Reds Rouge Rosso Tinto California 1993: A firm and tight value wine that has some herbal tones in its wild berry and plum aromas and flavors. Finishes firmly tannic, so aging into 1997 is advised. 7,000 cases made. • $7 • (11/30/95) BB • **87**
Terra Rosa Napa Valley 1988 • $12 • (11/15/90) • **85**
Terra Rosa Napa Valley 1987 • $14 • (07/31/90) • **86**

LAURENT CELLARS | CALIFORNIA

Chardonnay Napa Valley 1991 • $25 • (07/15/93) • **88**
Napa Valley 1988 • $30 • (06/30/93) • **87**

LAURIER | CALIFORNIA

Cabernet Sauvignon Sonoma County Green Valley 1982 • $12 • (02/16/85) • **82**
Chardonnay Sonoma County 1993: Medium-weight, with ripe pear, apple, spice and buttery oak that picks up a vanilla and butterscotch edge on the finish. Complex and well balanced. Ready. 3,100 cases made. • $15 • (03/31/96) • **88**
Chardonnay Sonoma County 1992: Tart and lean, but elegant and refined, with a crisp edge to the apple and pear flavors. Picks up intensity on the finish, where toasty oak comes into play, giving it a pretty aftertaste. Ready now. 7,250 cases made. • $15 • (06/30/94) • **88**
Pinot Noir Sonoma County 1994: Smooth and elegant, with a pretty core of ripe black cherry, spice, plum and berry, all framed by a nice dose of toasty, buttery oak. Finishes with soft tannins, making it appealing to drink now. 5,900 cases made. • $15 • (03/31/96) • **88**
Pinot Noir Sonoma County Green Valley 1986 • $10 • (06/15/88) • **90**
Pinot Noir Sonoma County Green Valley 1982 • $10 • (11/15/87) • **63**
Pinot Noir Sonoma County Green Valley 1981 • $10 • (02/16/85) • **78**

LAVA CAP | CALIFORNIA

Cabernet Sauvignon El Dorado 1989 • $10 • (11/15/93) • **85**
Fumé Blanc El Dorado 1991 • $7 • (09/15/93) • **73**
Merlot El Dorado 1990 • $13 • (07/15/93) • **84**
Zinfandel El Dorado 1991: Tired, with earthy, gamy oak flavors and not much fruit. 500 cases made. • $10 • (10/15/94) • **73**
Zinfandel El Dorado 1990 • $8 • (09/30/93) • **77**
Zinfandel El Dorado 1989 • $8 • (10/15/92) • **77**

LAZY CREEK | CALIFORNIA

Chardonnay Anderson Valley 1993: A little earthy, with simple orange-scented apple flavors. 1,000 cases made. • $10 • (07/31/95) • **75**
Chardonnay Anderson Valley 1992: Smells and tastes more like Gewürztraminer than Chardonnay, with its spice and litchi fruit character, but it's tasty and appealing. Drinkable now. 1,900 cases made. • $9 • (04/15/94) • **87**
Chardonnay Anderson Valley 1991 • $10 • (07/15/93) • **86**
Pinot Noir Anderson Valley 1991 • $12 • (02/28/93) • **83**

LEEWARD | CALIFORNIA

Cabernet Sauvignon Alexander Valley 1991: Tough and chewy, a tannic red with only modest currant and berry flavors struggling to poke through on the stubby finish. Could develop with cellaring until 1998. • $15 • (11/30/93) • **81**
Cabernet Sauvignon Alexander Valley 1988 • $13 • (11/15/92) • **78**
Cabernet Sauvignon Alexander Valley 1987 • $13 • (11/15/90) • **84**
Cabernet Sauvignon Alexander Valley 1986 • $12 • (10/15/89) • **79**
Cabernet Sauvignon Alexander Valley 1985 • $12 • (10/31/87) • **83**
Chardonnay Central Coast 1993: Plays out its round, generous pear and earth flavors in a straightforward way. Drink now. 5,130 cases made. • $11 • (10/15/95) • **83**
Chardonnay Central Coast 1992: Stretches the range of flavors a bit too far, with strong leesy, ripe and almost sour pineapple notes. It straightens out on the finish where it's more pleasing, but the flavors are powerful. Ready now. 10,270 cases made. • $11 • (06/30/94) • **82**
Chardonnay Central Coast 1991 • $11 • (11/30/92) • **85**
Chardonnay Edna Valley Paragon Vineyard Reserve 1991 • $15 • (07/15/93) • **74**
Chardonnay Edna Valley Reserve 1993: A fruity style with tart apple, pineapple and spice notes, solid and well made. 1,544 cases made. • $15 • (05/31/95) • **86**
Chardonnay Edna Valley Reserve 1992: Shows off ripe and exotic guava, pineapple and tropical fruit flavors, but it loses its focus on the finish where the woodiness stands out and dominates. Still, it's a solid effort from the sometimes erratic Edna Valley winery. Best now. 1,427 cases made. • $15 • (06/30/94) • **85**
Chardonnay Monterey County 1991: Tart and spicy, citrusy, and seems to jangle a little on the finish. 395 cases made. • $14 • (06/30/94) • **84**
Chardonnay Ventura County 1992: Earthy with a sour pineapple edge to the spicy pear flavors, offers lots of taste notes but they're difficult to warm up to. Consistent with the Leeward style of stretching the flavors, but many will feel they've gone too far. Drink now. 522 cases made. • $12 • (06/30/94) • **81**
Merlot Napa Valley 1993: Firm and compact with a trim band of cedar, currant, anise and oak flavors. Finishes with a hard tannic edge. Best after 1998. 621 cases made. • $15 • (02/29/96) • **84**
Merlot Napa Valley 1992: Lean and hollow, with a slim, bland streak of simple Merlot fruit. Tasted twice with consistent notes. 320 cases made. • $15 • (09/15/94) • **74**
Merlot Napa Valley 1991: An oaky style, with chunky currant and cherry notes that come through on the finish. A good wine, but the flavors appear as flat and one-dimensional. • $15 • (09/15/94) • **81**
Merlot Napa Valley 1989 • $14 • (11/15/91) • **83**
Merlot Napa Valley 1985 • $10 • (05/15/87) • **88**
Pinot Noir 1989 • $16 • (02/15/92) • **59**
Pinot Noir Santa Barbara County 1993: Ripe, full-bodied, plum, cherry and earthy berry flavors are a bit muddled on the finish, where oak kicks in. 327 cases made. • $14 • (09/15/95) • **86**
Pinot Noir Santa Barbara County 1990 • $14 • (02/28/93) • **76**
Pinot Noir Santa Barbara County 1989 • $16 • (02/28/93) • **82**

LEFRANC, CHARLES | CALIFORNIA

Cabernet Sauvignon Monterey County 1981 • $8 • (09/16/85) • **76**
Cabernet Sauvignon Napa County 1984 • $12 • (10/15/87) • **80**
Gewürztraminer Late Harvest San Benito County Selected 1984 • $11 • (03/16/86) • **75**
Merlot Monterey County San Lucas Ranch 1984 • $8 • (12/15/87) • **70**
White Zinfandel California 1985 • $5 • (05/01/86) • **61**

LENZ | NEW YORK

Merlot North Fork of Long Island 1987 • $12 • (06/30/91) • **80**
Merlot North Fork of Long Island 1986 • $12 • (12/15/88) • **83**
Merlot North Fork of Long Island 1985 • $11 • (12/15/88) • **84**
Merlot North Fork of Long Island 1984 • $12 • (12/15/88) • **74**
Sparkling North Fork of Long Island 1986 • $18 • (12/31/90) • **68**

LEONETTI | WASHINGTON

Cabernet Sauvignon Columbia Valley 1992: Not quite the concentration as in earlier vintages, but another winner from this Washington leader. This has toasty, buttery flavors and a core of cherry and currant that matches the wood quite well. Mild tannins make it attractive to drink now or age short-term. 1,500 cases made. • $33 • (06/15/95) • **91**
Cabernet Sauvignon Columbia Valley 1986 • $20 • (10/15/89) • **81**
Cabernet Sauvignon Walla Walla Valley Seven Hills Vineyard 1988 • $25 • (08/31/91) • **91**
Cabernet Sauvignon Walla Walla Valley Seven Hills Vineyard 1985 • $22 • (10/15/89) • **85**
Cabernet Sauvignon Walla Walla Valley Seven Hills Vineyard Reserve 1990: Well oaked, with a strong vanilla bean edge. Picks up gamy cherry and currant flavors that blend together well and are long on the finish. Tempting now, but age-worthy. 450 cases made. • $50 • (08/31/95) • **90**
Cabernet Sauvignon Washington 1991: Another tremendous effort by Leonetti. This is a richly flavored Cabernet, with amazingly supple, complex currant, herb, spice and toasty buttery oak. But as in most of Gary Figgins' wines, the flavors are beautifully integrated, finishing with a long, lingering aftertaste. Drinks well now through 2002. 2,000 cases made. • $29 • (06/30/94) CS • **95**
Cabernet Sauvignon Washington 1990: Smooth, rich and opulent, exotically spicy, deep and concentrated. Lays out plum, prune, nutmeg, cedar and black cherry flavors with almost digital definition, echoing licorice on the finish. Fabulous, supple and delicious now. Best from 1995 to 2002. 915 cases made. • $26 • (06/15/93) CS • **96**
Cabernet Sauvignon Washington 1989 • $25 • (07/31/92) • **96**
Cabernet Sauvignon Washington 1988 • $22 • (08/31/91) • **87**
Cabernet Sauvignon Washington 1987 • $22 • (06/15/90) • **91**
Cabernet Sauvignon Washington Reserve 1985 • $40 • (06/15/91) • **84**
Merlot Columbia Valley 1987 • $16 • (10/15/89) • **88**
Merlot Washington 1993: Dark in color and lavishly oaked, but with plenty of fruit to match the buttery, toasty notes. Black cherry, currant and wild berry flavors lead into a rich and lingering finish. Drinkable now through 1997. 1,600 cases made. • $29 • (06/15/95) SS • **91**
Merlot Washington 1992 • $25 • (05/15/94) CS • **96**
Merlot Washington 1991 • $22 • (05/31/93) • **92**
Merlot Washington 1990 • $22 • (06/15/92) • **92**
Merlot Washington 1989 • $18 • (05/31/91) • **93**
Merlot Washington 1988 • $17 • (04/15/90) • **90**
Select Walla Walla Valley 1990: Big and brawny, this youthful, two-fisted wine has herb- and cedar-scented currant and blackberry aromas and flavors, a solid layer of fine tannin and flavor to burn on the finish. Needs cellaring until 1998 to 2001 to sort itself out but should be spectacular when it gets there. 50 percent Cabernet Sauvignon, 30 percent Merlot and 20 percent Cabernet Franc. 487 cases made. • $28 • (06/15/93) • **90**

LEWIS CELLARS | CALIFORNIA

Cabernet Sauvignon Napa Valley Oakville Ranch 1993: Young, tight, vibrant cedar, currant and spice pick up bright cherry flavors on the finish, where the tannins fold in. Best to cellar into 1999 to 2001 to let it soften a bit. 1,200 cases made. • $32 • (04/30/96) • **88**
Cabernet Sauvignon Napa Valley Oakville Ranch 1992: Has a wonderful sense of harmony and finesse, with tiers of currant, plum, cherry and tobacco flavors enhanced by hints of toast and vanilla from oak. Finishes with firm, fine tannins. Better still in 1998. 700 cases made. • $30 • (11/30/95) • **94**
Chardonnay Napa Valley Oakville Ranch Reserve 1994: Big, ripe, complex pear, apple, fig and melon notes accompany lots of pretty, smoky, toasty oak. Shortens up somewhat on the finish, but give this a few more months for the flavors to round out. 1,400 cases made. • $28 • (05/15/96) • **90**
Chardonnay Napa Valley Oakville Ranch Reserve 1993: Ripe and spicy, with a pretty core of fig, pear, nectarine and toasty oak, all folding

Key: SS—Spectator Selection. CS—Cellar Selection. BB—Best Buy. $NA—Price not available. (BT)—Barrel tasting. Ⓐ—Auction Price.
Dates in parentheses represent the issues in which the ratings were published.

together, finishing with complex aftertaste that picks up fruit and oak. 600 cases made. • $26 • (07/31/95) • **90**

LIBERTY SCHOOL | CALIFORNIA

Cabernet Sauvignon Alexander Valley Lot 13 NV • $6 • (01/01/86) • **64**
Cabernet Sauvignon California Lot 17 NV • $6 • (02/29/88) • **73**
Cabernet Sauvignon California Lot 18 NV • $7 • (04/30/89) BB • **81**
Cabernet Sauvignon California Lot 19 NV • $7 • (11/15/89) • **77**
Cabernet Sauvignon California Vintner Select Series Three 1990: A fresh, lively Cabernet that's light and straightforward, with cola and cherry flavors that verge on jamminess and a small hint of vanilla and spice on the finish. Soft tannins and vibrant fruit make this drinkable now. • $7 • (06/15/93) • **83**
Cabernet Sauvignon California Vintner Select Series Two NV • $7 • (11/15/91) BB • **82**
Three Valley Select California White 1991 • $7 • (02/15/93) BB • **85**

LIMERICK LANE | CALIFORNIA

Sauvignon Blanc Russian River Valley Collins Vineyard 1992 • $7 • (09/15/93) • **71**
Zinfandel Russian River Valley 1991 • $12 • (06/15/93) • **88**
Zinfandel Russian River Valley 1990 • $13 • (10/15/92) • **88**
Zinfandel Russian River Valley Collins Vineyard 1993: An austere style, with just enough black cherry and raspberry flavors to hold your interest. Finishes with a flash of fruit and firm tannins. 2,460 cases made. • $14 • (10/15/95) • **85**

LIMUR | CALIFORNIA

Chardonnay Napa Valley 1992: Tart and a bit green, with a narrow band of spicy apple and peach flavors. Can stand short-term aging. 345 cases made. • $16 • (06/30/94) • **83**
Chardonnay Napa Valley 1991 • $16 • (07/15/93) • **83**

LINDEN | VIRGINIA

Cabernet 1988 • $15 • (02/29/92) • **84**
Cabernet Sauvignon Virginia 1990: Firm and tight, with fruity, floral aromas and ripe, intense Cabernet fruit on the palate. This is a solid wine, with highly extracted plum and currant flavors. Tannins are firm and chewy. Drinkable now. • $16 • (09/30/93) • **86**
Cabernet Virginia 1991: A big, bold wine with plenty of stuffing. Ripe, rich and tannic with loads of chocolate and spice flavors as well as plum and cherry notes. Rich but not jammy with a hint of herbalness on the finish. A pleasant surprise. 420 cases made. • $16 • (12/31/95) • **88**
Chardonnay Virginia 1991 • $14 • (12/15/93) • **83**

LIPARITA | CALIFORNIA

Cabernet Sauvignon Howell Mountain 1994: Well focused, with bright, ripe currant, plum and jam notes of medium depth. Well made, shy of outstanding. 2,100 cases made. • $28 • (05/31/95) • **85-89** (BT)
Cabernet Sauvignon Howell Mountain 1992: A touch earthy and spritzy, with a wild berry and cherry edge and firm tannins. Not the blockbuster you might expect from Howell Mountain. 1,250 cases made. • $28 • (12/15/95) • **84**
Cabernet Sauvignon Howell Mountain 1991: Intense, rustic and compact with an earthy, leathery edge to the tannic currant and mineral flavors. Tightly wound, needs cellaring until 1997 to 1998 to soften. 600 cases made. • $28 • (11/15/94) • **86**
Cabernet Sauvignon Howell Mountain 1990: Smooth and flavorful, a dense, chewy young wine that's packed with currant, anise and black cherry fruit and finishing with a long echo of the pretty fruit. Drinkable now through 1998. 450 cases made. • $28 • (11/15/93) • **89**
Chardonnay Howell Mountain 1994: Tight and firm, a crisp, well-focused style that gently unfolds, revealing complex mineral, pear, spice, honey and vanilla notes. Deceptively subtle and understated, but the flavors are wonderful and they grow on you. 800 cases made. • $18 • (04/30/96) • **92**
Chardonnay Howell Mountain 1993: Serves up an intriguing array of flavors, with smoky, buttery oak and a core of pear and apple. Well crafted and deftly balanced, the best yet from this California winery. 1,350 cases made. • $16 • (10/31/95) • **90**
Chardonnay Howell Mountain 1992: Bright and fruity, a lively wine that keeps lobbing zingers of apricot, apple and grapefruit flavor across the palate. Fresh and appealing, drink now. 1,100 cases made. • $16 • (06/15/94) • **88**
Chardonnay Howell Mountain 1991 • $16 • (03/15/94) • **82**
Merlot Howell Mountain 1993: Serves up a pretty core of ripe cherry, berry and spice, all in an elegant style, offering very pleasant aftertaste and supple texture. Can stand short-term cellaring. 800 cases made. • $26 • (04/30/96) • **88**
Merlot Howell Mountain 1991: An earthy, leathery, oaky edge dominates the Merlot fruit in this young and compact red. Cellaring may give it a chance to grow out of this initial taut stage. 700 cases made. • $24 • (09/15/94) • **83**
Sauvignon Blanc Howell Mountain 1994: Soft, perfumy, appealing for its peach and herb flavors that linger on the finish. 300 cases made. • $14 • (10/31/95) • **85**

LITTORAI | CALIFORNIA

Chardonnay Russian River Valley Mays Canyon 1993: Bold, ripe and buttery, boasting an array of rich pear, honey, toast and smoke flavors that fold together nicely. Complex, concentrated aftertaste. Debut from Littorai's Ted Lemon. 166 cases made. • $25 • (12/31/95) • **91**

LIVINGSTON | CALIFORNIA

Cabernet Sauvignon Napa Valley Moffett Vineyard 1992: Marked by strong toasty oak flavors and hard tannins, this is a tight and compact wine with a core of spicy currant flavors. Needs to soften, try around 2000. 1,500 cases made. • $30 • (12/15/95) • **89**
Cabernet Sauvignon Napa Valley Moffett Vineyard 1991: Very ripe and decadent with earthy black cherry and currant flavor. Finishes with gritty tannins and a mineral edge. Needs cellaring until about 2000 to soften. 1,200 cases made. • $30 • (11/15/94) • **89**
Cabernet Sauvignon Napa Valley Moffett Vineyard 1990: Firm, tight and concentrated with a spicy, herbal edge to the rich currant and cherry flavors that are sharply focused, finishing with firm, chewy tannins and a cedary oak edge. A young and vibrant wine that needs time to soften. Best after 1997. 1,200 cases made. • $30 • (11/15/93) • **91**
Cabernet Sauvignon Napa Valley Moffett Vineyard 1989 • $30 • (11/15/92) • **81**
Cabernet Sauvignon Napa Valley Moffett Vineyard 1988 • $30 • (11/15/91) • **85**
Cabernet Sauvignon Napa Valley Moffett Vineyard 1987 • $30 • (11/15/90) • **94**
Cabernet Sauvignon Napa Valley Moffett Vineyard 1986 • $19 Ⓐ • (11/30/89) • **88**
Cabernet Sauvignon Napa Valley Moffett Vineyard 1985 • $33 Ⓐ • (03/01/89) • **86**
Cabernet Sauvignon Napa Valley Moffett Vineyard 1984 • $42 • (03/01/89) • **87**
Cabernet Sauvignon Napa Valley Stanley's Selection 1992: Firm, tight and tannic, with a core of earthy currant and cedary oak, menthol peeking through underneath. 1,500 cases made. • $18 • (08/31/95) • **87**
Cabernet Sauvignon Napa Valley Stanley's Selection 1991: Herbal and smoky, with an austere band of currant and spice notes. Lacks richness and depth. Ready now through 1998. 1,600 cases made. • $20 • (11/15/94) • **83**
Cabernet Sauvignon Napa Valley Stanley's Selection 1990: Tight, firm and tannic, but not out of line for a 1990 Cabernet. Concentrated, intense and loaded with ripe currant, black cherry and spice flavors and just the right touch of oak seasoning. The finish is pleasing, with focused, lively flavors. Drink from 1997 to 2004. 1,200 cases made. • $20 • (03/15/93) • **88**
Cabernet Sauvignon Napa Valley Stanley's Selection 1989 • $20 • (07/15/92) • **85**

LIVINGSTONE, STEVEN THOMAS
WASHINGTON

Merlot Columbia Valley 1990 • $13 • (11/30/92) • **89**
Merlot Columbia Valley 1989 • $11 • (08/31/91) • **84**

LLANO ESTACADO | TEXAS

Cabernet Sauvignon 1988 • $12 • (02/29/92) • **81**
Cabernet Sauvignon Texas High Plains 1992: Lean and lively, showing nice concentration of berry and currant flavors and a touch of cedar and herb on the edge. Ready now. • $12 • (01/31/95) • **85**
Chardonnay Texas 1991 • $12 • (12/15/93) • **83**
Merlot Texas 1991 • $12 • (06/30/93) • **81**
Sauvignon Blanc Texas 1992: Crisp and lightly spicy, lively with modest flavors. 2,550 cases made. • $8 • (09/15/94) BB • **84**
Signature Edition White Texas 1992: Slightly sweet, fruity and pleasant to drink soon. 5,600 cases made. • $8 • (09/15/94) • **79**
Signature Red Signature Edition Texas 1992: Light and somewhat spicy, fresh tasting, with berry flavors and a hint of mint. Drinkable now. 8,000 cases made. • $8 • (01/31/95) BB • **83**

LLORDS & ELWOOD | CALIFORNIA

Cabernet Sauvignon Napa Valley 1982 • $8 • (12/15/87) • **79**

LOCKWOOD | CALIFORNIA

Cabernet Sauvignon Monterey 1992: A well oaked style with vanilla and toasty flavors, but enough supple cherry and herb notes to balance and give it some dimension. • $14 • (09/30/95) • **86**
Cabernet Sauvignon Monterey 1991: Complex and inviting with a broad, ripe array of toasty buttery oak and a smooth core of currant, herb and spicy flavors that stay with you on a long, full finish. Drinks well now but has the intensity and depth to age through 1998. 8,150 cases made. • $11 • (10/31/93) • **88**
Cabernet Sauvignon Monterey Partners Reserve 1991: Firm and compact, with currant, plum and cherry notes framed by cedary oak. This is a well balanced red that should age well, try now. • $16 • (11/15/94) • **84**
Cabernet Sauvignon Monterey Partners Reserve 1990: Firm, intense, lean and lively with ripe, spicy boysenberry, cherry and currant flavors that stay with you from start to finish. The flavors are pretty, drinkable now. 840 cases made. • $18 • (10/31/93) • **88**
Chardonnay Monterey 1994: Spicy and generous with its oak-wrapped pineapple and honey flavors, smooth and rich through the finish. 8,004 cases made. • $15 • (04/30/96) • **87**
Chardonnay Monterey 1993: Smooth and generous, playing out its honey-scented apple and nutmeg flavors. Nicely balanced for current drinking. 1,478 cases made. • $15 • (12/15/95) • **86**
Chardonnay Monterey 1992: Strikes a nice balance between ripe pear, peach and spicy flavors and light toasty oak shadings that turn smoky on the finish. Balanced and ready to drink. 10,200 cases made. • $10 • (05/31/94) • **84**
Chardonnay Monterey 1991 • $9 • (07/15/93) • **84**
Chardonnay Monterey Partners Reserve 1993: Serves up ripe pear, pineapple and spice notes in a rich, full-bodied style. The flavors linger on the aftertaste. 1,037 cases made. • $17 • (06/30/96) • **86**
Chardonnay Monterey Partners Reserve 1992: Earthy with a citrus and grapefruit edge to the ripe pear and honeyed flavors. • $18 • (07/31/95) • **83**
Chardonnay Monterey Partners Reserve 1991 • $14 • (07/15/93) • **89**
Merlot Monterey 1993: Well balanced currant and cherry flavors play off notes of light cedary oak. Appealing, but pricey. 8,050 cases made. • $16 • **85**

Key: SS—Spectator Selection. CS—Cellar Selection. BB—Best Buy. $NA—Price not available. (BT)—Barrel tasting. Ⓐ—Auction Price.
Dates in parentheses represent the issues in which the ratings were published.

Merlot Monterey 1992: Smooth, polished and appealingly spicy, sweet cedary overtones marking the soft raspberry flavors. A little on the oaky side, but tempting to drink now. 3,850 cases made. • $15 • (09/15/94) • **86**
Merlot Monterey 1991 • $12 • (05/31/94) • **89**
Pinot Blanc Monterey 1994: Lean and focused, showing a narrow band of spice, raisin and pear flavors that linger on the finish. 465 cases made. • $11 • (05/31/96) • **86**
Pinot Blanc Monterey 1993: Ripe, round and spicy, sturdy rather than supple, finishing with concentrated flavor. • $9 • (11/15/95) • **82**
Sauvignon Blanc Monterey 1995: Mouth-filling butterscotch, citrus and herb flavors seem a little raucous at this point, but the crisp finish brings it together nicely. 6,450 cases made. • $10 • **87**
Sauvignon Blanc Monterey 1994: Extremely floral, soft and earthy, with a pleasing fig motif singing on the finsh. Richer in texture than most, making it distinctive and a bargain in California Sauvignon. 5,335 cases made. • $9 • (05/31/96) BB • **88**
Sauvignon Blanc Monterey 1993: Lean, fruity and charming. Nice herbal notes weave through the bright green apple and spice flavors. 3,757 cases made. • $9 • (08/31/95) • **86**
Sauvignon Blanc Monterey 1992 • $7 • (05/15/94) BB • **89**

LOGAN | CALIFORNIA

Chardonnay Monterey 1994: A touch earthy with a slight tinny edge to the pear and pineapple notes, but it folds together nicely, keeping the fruit up front. 7,500 cases made. • $14 • (05/15/96) • **87**
Chardonnay Monterey 1993: Earthy with a pungent, grassy edge to the pear and apple notes, but it has appealing flavors and is elegant. • $14 • (07/31/95) • **84**
Chardonnay Monterey 1992: An elegant and simple Chardonnay with pleasant, soft pear, peach and spice notes. Enjoy it now. 6,500 cases made. • $14 • (06/30/94) • **84**
Chardonnay Monterey 1991 • $14 • (07/15/93) • **84**

LOHR, J. | CALIFORNIA

Cabernet Sauvignon California 1987 • $7 • (02/15/90) BB • **84**
Cabernet Sauvignon California 1986 • $6 • (04/15/89) BB • **84**
Cabernet Sauvignon California 1984 • $5 • (11/30/86) BB • **82**
Cabernet Sauvignon California Cypress 1993: Bright, fruity and simple, generous with its berry flavors, finishing soft. 45,000 cases made. • $8 • (12/15/95) • **82**
Cabernet Sauvignon California Cypress 1992: Ripe, smooth and polished enough to show off its plum, currant and spice flavors that mingle harmoniously and linger on the finish. Tannins are well integrated. A fair-priced red that's approachable now. 46,000 cases made. • $9 • (11/30/95) BB • **86**
Cabernet Sauvignon California Cypress 1991: Shows off its toasty, buttery oak and has enough Cabernet fruit to match. A good value. 25,000 cases made. • $8 • (11/15/94) • **82**
Cabernet Sauvignon California Cypress 1990: Despite a toasty, smoky wood overlay, there's a nice spice core of Cabernet fruit underneath and on the finish the fruit and wood hang together nicely. Lots of flavor and character, especially at this price. Drinkable now. 25,000 cases made. • $7 • (11/15/93) BB • **86**
Cabernet Sauvignon California Cypress 1989 • $7 • (05/15/93) BB • **83**
Cabernet Sauvignon California Cypress 1988 • $7 • (11/15/91) • **80**
Cabernet Sauvignon Napa Valley Carol's Vineyard Reserve 1985 • $15 • (12/15/88) • **89**
Cabernet Sauvignon Napa Valley Carol's Vineyard Reserve Lot 2 1985 • $18 • (09/30/90) • **88**
Cabernet Sauvignon Paso Robles Seven Oaks 1993: Marked by strong toasty, buttery oak flavor, it matches this with ripe, complex plum, currant and cherry notes. 65,000 cases made. • $12 • (11/30/95) • **87**
Cabernet Sauvignon Paso Robles Seven Oaks 1991: Relies on toasty, buttery oak for much of its flavor—as the label implies—and that's pleasing, but it also has enough ripe Cabernet fruit to maintain interest. Best now through 1998. 34,000 cases made. • $11 • (07/31/94) • **84**
Cabernet Sauvignon Paso Robles Seven Oaks 1990: A ripe and showy style with its buttery oak flavors, but underneath the spicy wood flavors is a pretty core of cherry and currant-scented fruit. The texture is

smooth and polished, finishing with firm tannins and crisp acidity. A tasty young Cabernet that's fun to drink through 1997. 30,000 cases made. • $11 • (11/15/93) • **88**

Cabernet Sauvignon Paso Robles Seven Oaks 1989 • $12 • (11/15/92) • **89**

Cabernet Sauvignon Paso Robles Seven Oaks 1987 • $12 • (04/30/91) • **86**

Cabernet Sauvignon Paso Robles VS. 1991: Well oaked, offering toasty vanilla and spice nuances which add dimension and texture to plum and cherry notes and complex aftertaste. 1,500 cases made. • $22 • (11/30/95) • **87**

Cabernet Sauvignon Paso Robles VS.1 1990: Supple and spicy, displaying attractive cherry, currant and berry notes and finishing with mild tannins. 1,300 cases made. • $22 • (03/31/95) • **88**

Cabernet Sauvignon Seven Oaks 1988 • $13 • (03/15/92) • **83**

Chardonnay Arroyo Seco VS. 1994: A complex white with an enticing array of ripe pear, fig and celery flavors, picking up some nicely smoky, toasty oak character to help carry it all through the long finish. 1,200 cases made. • $23 • (06/15/96) • **89**

Chardonnay California Cypress 1993: Light and fragrant, smooth-textured, showing plenty of spicy, leesy pear and apple flavor and a lingering finish. Drink now. 66,000 cases made. • $9 • (12/15/95) • **85**

Chardonnay California Cypress 1992: A simple but pleasant young Chardonnay with spicy apple and pear notes, with light oak. This winery has been producing some excellent Chardonnay and Cabernet values of late. 47,000 cases made. • $8 • (06/30/94) BB • **83**

Chardonnay California Cypress 1991 • $7 • (07/15/93) • **76**

Chardonnay Monterey Riverstone 1994: A complex array of elegant pear, spice, honey and hazelnut notes, leading up to a nice, smoky, toasted oak finish. Combines richness with depth, concentration and finesse. Has the flavor and complexity of wines two to three times its price. 86,000 cases made. • $12 • (02/29/96) SS • **90**

Chardonnay Monterey Riverstone 1993: Crisp and lively, featuring bright pear and vanilla flavors and a touch of caramel on the aftertaste. Ready now. 78,000 cases made. • $12 • (12/15/95) • **87**

Chardonnay Monterey Riverstone 1992: Combines ripe peach and pear flavors with creamy, toasty, buttery oak. Balanced and appealing. 50,000 cases made. • $12 • (05/15/94) • **85**

Chardonnay Monterey Riverstone 1991 • $12 • (07/15/93) • **89**

Fumé Blanc California Cypress 1993: Ripe, round and generous, with pleasant honey and fig notes on the finish. A little sweet, but smooth-textured and balanced. 4,100 cases made. • $7 • (03/31/95) BB • **86**

Fumé Blanc California Cypress 1992: Ripe and spicy, an oaky wine with modest fruit flavors, not especially varietal but drinkable now. 2,500 cases made. • $6 • (08/31/94) BB • **81**

Gamay Monterey County Monterey Gamay 1987 • $5 • (07/15/88) • **78**

Gamay Monterey Wildflower 1993: There's some jammy raspberry fruit here, but the overall effect is marred by an underlying rubbery note. 1,400 cases made. • $8 • (09/15/95) • **78**

Johannisberg Riesling Late Harvest Monterey Bay Mist 1993: Has the depth and richness of wines many times its price. A sweet, rich and spicy California dessert wine with honey, pepper and floral aromas that add complexity to the ripe apricot and dried pear flavors. Delicious now, but should improve through 2000. One of the best values we have seen in botrytized wines. 400 cases made. • $10 • (10/31/95) • **93**

Johannisberg Riesling Monterey Bay Mist 1992 • $7 • (05/15/94) BB • **83**

Merlot California Cypress 1993: Strives for complexity with its toasty, smoky oak, but comes across as a bit disjointed. Short-term cellaring should help. 17,300 cases made. • $10 • (12/31/95) • **86**

Merlot California Cypress 1992 • $9 • (06/15/94) BB • **86**

Merlot California Cypress 1991 • $9 • (05/31/93) • **82**

Merlot Cypress 1989 • $8 • (02/29/92) BB • **85**

Pinot Blanc Monterey October Night 1994: Elegant and complex, with smoky pear, honey and light toasty notes that unfold and increase in nuance and finesse on the finish. 2,500 cases made. • $14 • (06/30/96) • **88**

Syrah Paso Robles South Ridge 1993: Dark color and hard, chewy tannins are promising, but insufficient flavor and a hollowness in the middle detract. 2,500 cases made. • $14 • **80**

LOLONIS | CALIFORNIA

Cabernet Sauvignon Mendocino County Lolonis Vineyard Private Reserve 1989 • $15 • (11/15/91) • **86**

Cabernet Sauvignon Mendocino County Private Reserve 1989 • $16 • (08/31/92) • **84**

Cabernet Sauvignon Mendocino County Private Reserve 1986 • $15 • (05/15/90) • **83**

Chardonnay Mendocino County Estate Reserve 1991 • $12 • (07/15/93) • **83**

Chardonnay Mendocino County Private Reserve 1991 • $19 • (07/15/93) • **82**

Fumé Blanc Mendocino County Estate Reserve 1991 • $9 • (09/15/93) • **79**

Merlot Mendocino County Private Reserve 1993: Ultra fruity, ripe and jammy, with a racy edge to the wild berry, raspberry and spicy flavors. Not your typical Merlot, but a distinctive wine nonetheless. Best after 1996. 900 cases made. • $18 • **88**

Zinfandel Mendocino County 1992: A touch meaty, but the wild berry and cherry flavors come through in this lean and crisp wine. It's not the Private Reserve, but a good value. 1,000 cases made. • $10 • (10/15/95) • **84**

Zinfandel Mendocino County 1991: Ripe, with a berry jam character, finishing with crisp tannins. Ready now. 1,800 cases made. • $10 • (10/15/94) • **83**

Zinfandel Mendocino County 1990 • $10 • (09/30/93) • **85**

Zinfandel Mendocino County Lolonis Vineyards Private Reserve 1989 • $12 • (08/31/91) • **83**

Zinfandel Mendocino County Lolonis Vineyards Private Reserve Lot 2 1989 • $8 • (10/15/92) • **76**

Zinfandel Mendocino County Private Reserve 1992: Appealing for its ripe, bright cherry and berry flavors, hints of anise and spice enhancing the fruit. Finishes with firm tannins. Well crafted and ready to drink. 700 cases made. • $16 • (10/15/95) • **88**

Zinfandel Mendocino County Private Reserve 1991: Lean and firm, with spicy raspberry, leather and anise notes that are complex and build on the finish. Turns diffuse on the finish, but the fruit comes through. Ready now. 500 cases made. • $16 • (10/15/94) • **85**

Zinfandel Mendocino County Private Reserve 1990 • $13 • (10/15/92) • **89**

LONE OAK | CALIFORNIA

Cabernet Sauvignon Monterey 1992: An herbal style with spice and bell pepper notes. Ready. 411 cases made. • $6 • (11/15/94) • **79**

LONG | CALIFORNIA

Cabernet Sauvignon Napa Valley 1994: Dark, ripe, rich and intense, with a solid core of currant and wild berry fruit that holds together, finishing with a spicy edge. Borders on outstanding. 150 cases made. • $150 • (05/31/95) • **85-89** (BT)

Cabernet Sauvignon Napa Valley 1993: Young and tannic, with strong wood flavors. Offers hints of ripe raisin and plum, but a hot, tannic aftertaste presides on the finish. 200 cases made. • $32 • **84**

Cabernet Sauvignon Napa Valley 1990: Thick, dense and tannic, with a rich core of currant, chocolate, mint and berry flavors that spread out on the palate. A big, ripe, opulent, complex style that will need nearly a decade to soften and mellow. Picks up mineral and spice notes on the finish • $30 • (08/31/93) • **89**

Cabernet Sauvignon Napa Valley 1986 • $45 • (03/01/89) • **86**

Cabernet Sauvignon Napa Valley 1985 • $40 • (03/01/89) • **92**

Cabernet Sauvignon Napa Valley 1984 • $50 • (03/01/89) • **88**

Cabernet Sauvignon Napa Valley 1983 • $36 • (03/01/89) • **78**

Cabernet Sauvignon Napa Valley 1980 • $45 • (03/01/89) • **91**

Cabernet Sauvignon Napa Valley 1979 • $45 • (03/01/89) • **90**

Chardonnay Napa Valley 1993: Attractive for its purity of ripe pear and apple flavors. It's a crisp and refreshing style that showcases the fruit, with just a trace of oak way in the background. • $30 • (01/31/96) • **90**

Chardonnay Napa Valley 1992: Firm and intense, offering a tight core of spice, pear, apple and toasty oak shadings which give it depth and a sense of elegance. 1,500 cases made. • $29 • (04/15/95) • **89**

Chardonnay Napa Valley 1991 • $29 • (07/15/93) • **91**

Johannisberg Riesling Late Harvest Napa Valley Botrytis 1990 • $18 • (09/15/91) • **86**
Sauvignon Blanc Napa Valley 1994: Bright and flavorful, showing a slight oniony edge to the pineapple and pear notes. Tasty now. 650 cases made. • $14 • (05/15/96) • **87**

LONGORIA | CALIFORNIA

Cabernet Franc Santa Ynez Valley Blues Cuvée 1993: An austere style, offering a trim band of spice, currant, mineral and berry notes, but bottle time may soften the edges and round it out. 270 cases made. • $20 • (11/30/95) • **84**
Cabernet Sauvignon Santa Ynez Valley 1990: Lean and racy, showing more spicy oak aromas and flavors than fruit, although berry notes come through on the finish. An herbal streak runs through it, as well, making for a distinctive if unusual wine. 105 cases made. • $15 • (06/15/93) • **83**
Chardonnay Santa Barbara County 1992: Marked by a strong leesy and toasty oak edge, the ripe pear and pineapple flavors gain intensity on the finish. 336 cases made. • $18 • (07/31/95) • **87**
Chardonnay Santa Ynez Valley Huber Vineyard 1994: Smooth and elegant, with a ripe, spicy core of pear, cream and vanilla notes, finishes with a trace of earthiness. 555 cases made. • $21 • (06/30/96) • **88**
Chardonnay Santa Ynez Valley Huber Vineyard 1993: A cedary oak edge dominates at this stage, with ripe pear, spice and apple notes underneath. Well balanced, with flavors that stay focused. 585 cases made. • $16 • (07/31/95) • **86**
Merlot Santa Ynez Valley 1990 • $16 • (07/15/93) • **85**
Pinot Noir Santa Maria Valley Bien Nacido Vineyard 1994: Smooth and harmonious, smoky, toasty oak flavors leading to a trim band of currant and berry notes and delicate aftertaste. Drinkable now and into 1997. 225 cases made. • $23 • (04/30/96) • **86**
Pinot Noir Santa Maria Valley Bien Nacido Vineyard 1993: Intense and well focused, adding earth and herbs to the cherry and cola notes. Try now. 135 cases made. • $20 • (09/15/95) • **86**
Pinot Noir Santa Ynez Valley Benedict Vineyard 1989 • $28 • (02/28/93) • **86**

LYETH | CALIFORNIA

A Red Blend Alexander Valley 1992: Supple and polished cedar, coffee, cherry and berry flavors. This is elegant, finishing with firm tannins and good length. Drinkable now. • $18 • (08/31/95) • **87**
A Red Blend Alexander Valley 1991: Firm and austere, with a tannic edge, but the ripe cherry, plum and wild berry flavors are appealing. Some cellar time should soften the rough edges. Best in 1997. Made from Cabernet Sauvignon, Merlot and Cabernet Franc. 15,000 cases made. • $14 • (10/15/94) SS • **89**
A Red Blend Alexander Valley 1990: Crisp and focused, with spicy herb, currant and cherry flavors that turn elegant and supple on the finish, picking up toasty oak, chocolate and spice notes. Drinkable now. • $13 • (06/30/93) • **87**
A White Blend Sonoma County 1991 • $8 • (09/15/93) • **79**
Chardonnay Sonoma County 1994: Elegant with a pretty band of pear, apple and spice, finishing with a trace of oak and a lingering finish. 8,000 cases made. • $11 • (02/29/96) • **87**
Chardonnay Sonoma County 1993: Young and unfocused, with coarse, spicy Chardonnay flavors that may have benefitted from short-term cellaring, try now. • $12 • (12/15/94) • **82**
Chardonnay Sonoma County 1992: Smooth and creamy, with ripe apple, pineapple and spicy citrus flavors that are elegant and lively, finishing with a nutmeg edge. Drinks well now. 6,000 cases made. • $11 • (06/30/94) • **88**
Chardonnay Sonoma County 1991 • $12 • (07/15/93) • **83**
Meritage California 1993: Soft around the edges, but the bright berry and herb flavors shine through brightly. Approachable now, but better in 1997. 25,000 cases made. • $13 • (11/15/95) • **86**

Key: SS—Spectator Selection. CS—Cellar Selection. BB—Best Buy. $NA—Price not available. (BT)—Barrel tasting. Ⓐ—Auction Price.
Dates in parentheses represent the issues in which the ratings were published.

Meritage White Sonoma County 1994: Crisp and fruity, with a floral thread running through the green apple flavors. Ready now. 10,000 cases made. • $7 • (06/15/96) • **86**
Red Alexander Valley 1988 • $12 • (11/15/92) • **84**
Red Alexander Valley 1987 • $15 • (10/15/92) • **83**
Red Alexander Valley 1986 • $23 • (11/15/90) • **88**
Red Alexander Valley 1985 • $19 Ⓐ • (05/31/89) • **86**
Red Alexander Valley 1984 • $24 • (03/01/89) • **90**
Red Alexander Valley 1983 • $17 • (03/01/89) • **78**
Red Alexander Valley 1982 • $18 • (03/01/89) • **85**
Red Alexander Valley 1981 • $20 • (03/01/89) • **77**

LYNMAR | CALIFORNIA

Pinot Noir Russian River Valley 1993: Trim and spicy, with just enough cherry and berry flavors to hold your interest. Drinkable now. • $17 • (03/31/96) • **83**
Pinot Noir Russian River Valley 1992: Smooth, supple and elegant cherry, cola, oak and spice notes have a delicate feel. 600 cases made. • $16 • (05/15/95) • **88**
Pinot Noir Russian River Valley Quail Hill Vineyard 1992: Complex and enticing, elegant, ripe, smooth, polished cherry, plum and spicy oak flavors all dovetail together on the finish. 400 cases made. • $24 • (05/15/95) • **90**

LYTTON SPRINGS | CALIFORNIA

Cabernet Sauvignon Mendocino County Private Reserve 1988 • $18 • (11/15/91) • **80**
Cabernet Sauvignon Mendocino County Private Reserve 1987 • $18 • (09/15/90) • **88**
Palette Sonoma-Mendocino Counties NV • $10 • (11/15/91) • **83**
Zinfandel Sonoma County 1994: Delivers a bold, ripe core of cherry and wild berry flavor, an elegant aftertaste and some pretty hints of floral and berry notes. 6,672 cases made. • $18 • (04/30/96) • **88**
Zinfandel Sonoma County 1992: Deep color, thick and rich, but still tight and compact, packing black cherry, blueberry and wild raspberry flavors. Finishes with a burst of flavor and crisp tannins. For all its power, it's sleek and polished. Drinkable now. 7,900 cases made. • $16 • (08/31/94) • **89**
Zinfandel Sonoma County 1989 • $15 • (08/31/91) • **84**
Zinfandel Sonoma County 1988 • $12 • (07/31/90) • **90**
Zinfandel Sonoma County 1987 • $12 • (05/31/89) • **88**
Zinfandel Sonoma County 1986 • $10 • (10/15/88) • **87**
Zinfandel Sonoma County 1985 • $8 • (08/31/87) • **90**
Zinfandel Sonoma County 1984 • $36 Ⓐ • (10/31/86) • **70**
Zinfandel Sonoma County Valley Vista Vineyard Private Reserve 1981 • $12 • (01/01/85) • **85**

MAACAMA CREEK | CALIFORNIA

Cabernet Sauvignon Alexander Valley Melim Vineyard Reserve 1991: An oaky style where the wood overshadows the simple Cabernet fruit. An easy drinking style without much character. Drinkable now. 6,000 cases made. • $9 • (11/15/93) • **75**
Cabernet Sauvignon Alexander Valley Reserve 1992: Lean, dry and tannic, which doesn't give the fruit much chance. 4,462 cases made. • $12 • (11/15/94) • **77**
Cabernet Sauvignon Alexander Valley Reserve 1990: A light, fruity Cabernet, with plum, cherry and cedar notes that are well balanced in an easy-to-drink style. 700 cases made. • $14 • (11/15/92) • **81**
Cabernet Sauvignon Sonoma County Melim Vineyard 1989 • $8 • (11/15/91) BB • **86**
Chardonnay Alexander Valley Melim Vineyard Reserve 1992: Crisp and lively, simple and citrusy, with a tart finish. 200 cases made. • $10 • (06/30/94) • **80**

MACKINAW | CALIFORNIA

Chardonnay California 1993: Ripe and generous, built around a core of pear and citrus flavor and playing a touch of spice and honey as counterpoint. • $10 • (03/31/95) • **85**

Chardonnay California 1992: Crisp, spicy and light with a little kick of toast and nutmeg. Probably would taste good with the trout on the label. 1,400 cases made. • $9 • (01/31/94) • **80**

MACROSTIE | CALIFORNIA

Chardonnay Carneros 1994: Bold, ripe and delicious, brimming with ripe pear, honey, hazelnut and light oak shadings. Gets extra marks for its silky texture and long aftertaste. Has a wonderful sense of harmony and finesse. 6,500 cases made. • $17 • (04/30/96) • **91**

Chardonnay Carneros 1993: Straightforward and bright against a supple background, laying out its fresh, youthful pear and floral flavors. Appealingly fresh. 6,000 cases made. • $16 • (02/28/95) • **85**

Chardonnay Carneros 1992: Crisp and spicy, a toasty wine with relatively modest fruit intensity. Drinkable now. 6,500 cases made. • $16 • (06/30/94) • **86**

Chardonnay Carneros 1991 • $16 • (12/15/92) • **88**

Chardonnay Carneros Reserve 1993: The complexity builds on the palate, starting out with a spicy, grassy character, then picking up attractive pear, spice and toasty oak nuances. Impressive for its refinement and length. 200 cases made. • $23 • (01/31/96) • **92**

Chardonnay Carneros Reserve 1992: This subtle white folds in some lovely spice and honey notes on the long, elegant finish, all wrapped around a nice core of apple and quince. 200 cases made. • $20 • (02/28/95) • **91**

Merlot Carneros 1993: Austere, delivering a crisp tannic edge to the herb, cherry and leather flavors. Can stand short-term cellaring into 1997 in hopes it will soften somewhat. 900 cases made. • $19 • (02/29/96) • **86**

Merlot Carneros 1992: Lean and trim, with a cedary vanilla-bean edge to a tight core of berry and currant flavor. 1,000 cases made. • $18 • (02/28/95) • **87**

Merlot Carneros 1991: Lean, firm and earthy, with a barnyardy edge to the currant and cherry notes, picking up a cedary edge on the finish. 1,000 cases made. • $18 • (09/15/94) • **82**

Pinot Noir Carneros 1994: Subtle, with understated spicy cola, cherry and earthy mushroom flavors. Finishes with enough tannin to merit cellaring into 1997. 700 cases made. • $17 • **85**

Pinot Noir Carneros 1993: Dry and earthy, with mature Pinot Noir flavors that echo dried plum and cherry. Finishes with a touch of buttery oak, which adds some flavor and texture. 900 cases made. • $17 • (01/31/96) • **87**

Pinot Noir Carneros 1992 • $16 • (02/28/94) • **84**

MADDALENA | CALIFORNIA

Cabernet Sauvignon Alexander Valley Reserve 1986 • $10 • (03/31/90) • **77**

Cabernet Sauvignon Alexander Valley Reserve 1985 • $11 • (06/30/89) • **78**

Cabernet Sauvignon Sonoma County 1990: Earthy and funky, with drying tannins and not much fruit. 10,000 cases made. • $8 • (11/15/94) • **76**

Cabernet Sauvignon Sonoma County 1988 • $7 • (03/31/92) • **79**

Cabernet Sauvignon Sonoma County 1985 • $6 • (05/31/88) • **74**

Cabernet Sauvignon Sonoma County Vintner's Reserve 1984 • $9 • (03/31/87) • **82**

Chardonnay Central Coast 1992: Lean and earthy, but with some pear and apple flavors peeking through. Best now. 25,000 cases made. • $7 • (06/30/94) • **80**

Chardonnay Central Coast San Simeon Collection 1991: Ripe and fruity with exotic tropical fruit flavors that echo guava, nectarine and peach, finishing with a soft fleshy edge. Ready now. 3,000 cases made. • $10 • (06/30/94) • **82**

Johannisberg Riesling Central Coast 1993: Soft and gentle, off-dry, slightly honey-toned in color and flavor, finishing with a floral, grassy edge. 6,000 cases made. • $6 • (02/28/95) • **78**

Merlot Central Coast San Simeon Collection 1990: Dank and earthy, with pungent vegetal flavors. Missing the fruit. 3,000 cases made. • $9 • (09/15/94) • **77**

Merlot Central Coast San Simeon Collection 1989 • $12 • (05/31/92) • **73**

Muscat Canelli Central Coast 1993: Spicy and exotic, with a peppery allspice-clove character that is unusual and appealing, but not too sweet. 2,000 cases made. • $6 • (12/31/94) • **82**

MADIGAN | CALIFORNIA

Cabernet Sauvignon Napa Valley 1991: Simple and fruity with spice, ash and currant notes that turn tannic on the finish. Drinkable now. 700 cases made. • $10 • (11/15/93) • **79**

Cabernet Sauvignon Napa Valley 1989 • $10 • (11/15/93) • **78**

MADRON LAKE HILLS | MICHIGAN

White Riesling Late Harvest Lake Erie Semi-Dry Heartland Vineyards 1990 • $10 • (02/29/92) • **74**

MADRONA | CALIFORNIA

Cabernet Franc El Dorado 1986 • $11 • (03/31/92) • **73**

Cabernet Sauvignon El Dorado 1991: Elegant with a floral and grapey currant edge that's pleasing to drink now. 1,700 cases made. • $11 • (05/31/95) • **81**

Cabernet Sauvignon El Dorado 1985 • $12 • (04/15/92) • **82**

Chardonnay El Dorado 1993: Clean and appealing for its ripe pear and custard flavors that turn elegant and refined on the finish. 440 cases made. • $12 • (07/31/95) • **85**

Chardonnay El Dorado 1992: Ripe and spicy with pretty pear, apple and cedary oak flavors. Ready now. 873 cases made. • $10 • (06/30/94) • **84**

Chardonnay El Dorado 1991: Elegant and understated with pretty pear, spice and buttery oak flavors. A good white on a small scale. 2,406 cases made. • $10 • (06/30/94) • **82**

White Zinfandel El Dorado 1988 • $5 • (06/15/89) • **76**

Zinfandel El Dorado 1993: Clean and pleasant enough but nothing special, adding hints of spice, pepper and wild berry. Firmly tannic. 620 cases made. • $9 • (04/30/96) • **83**

Zinfandel El Dorado 1992: Medium-bodied and smooth, with cherry and berry flavors that are simple but pleasing. 850 cases made. • $8 • (10/15/95) • **84**

Zinfandel El Dorado 1989 • $8 • (10/15/92) • **64**

MAGNOLIA | CALIFORNIA

Chardonnay Napa Valley 1991 • $16 • (07/15/93) • **74**

MAISON DEUTZ | CALIFORNIA

Blanc de Noirs San Luis Obispo County NV • $15 • (12/31/93) • **82**

Blanc de Noirs San Luis Obispo & Santa Barbara Counties NV: Round, spicy and charming, with modest cherry flavors that finish soft and creamy. Has a sense of elegance. 8,000 cases made. • $16 • (12/31/94) • **85**

Brut Cuvée NV • $15 • (01/31/88) • **85**

Brut Rosé NV • $24 • (05/15/92) • **85**

Brut Rosé San Luis Obispo NV: A little funky, but the floral and spicy flavors pick up the charm on the finish. 1,000 cases made. • $20 • (12/31/94) • **81**

Brut Rosé San Luis Obispo County NV: Offers distinctive cherry and wild berry notes, serving up appealing, ripe fruit flavors with a sense of elegance and finesse. 400 cases made. • $20 • **86**

Brut San Luis Obispo & Santa Barbara Counties Cuvée NV: The very intense, ripe and rich flavors stay with you and echo pear, earth, spice and toast at the end. Still a bit awkward, so some time in the cellar wouldn't hurt. 20,000 cases made. • $15 • (12/31/94) • **87**

Brut San Luis Obispo County Reserve 1990: Tart and spicy, with a narrow band of citrus, herb and pear flavors. Intense and concentrated, with unusual flavors on the long, full finish. Ready now. 1,000 cases made. • $23 • (12/31/94) • **85**

Brut San Luis Obispo County Reserve 1987 • $22 • (10/31/91) • **88**

Brut San Luis Obispo County Reserve 1986 • $22 • (04/30/91) • **77**

Brut Santa Barbara County Cuvée NV • $15 • (10/31/86) • **89**
Brut Santa Barbara County Cuvée 3 NV • $17 • (05/31/89) • **89**

MAKOR | CALIFORNIA

Pinot Blanc Santa Barbara County Bien Nacido Vineyards 1995: Good, with appealing pear and subtle peach flavors. 329 cases made. • $11 • **83**

MANISCHEWITZ | CALIFORNIA

Pinot Noir Russian River Valley 1989 • $9 • (03/31/91) • **74**
White Zinfandel Sonoma County 1989 • $6 • (03/31/91) • **77**

MANZANITA RIDGE | CALIFORNIA

Zinfandel Alexander Valley 1988 • $8 • (07/15/92) BB • **89**

MARBLE CREST | WASHINGTON

Cabernet Sauvignon Columbia Valley 1993: Soft and generous, centered around gentle plum and berry flavors. Ready now. 4,200 cases made. • $8 • (09/30/95) • **82**
Chardonnay Columbia Valley 1993: Tasty and bright, adding a spicy edge to the pear flavor that keeps flowing generously on the finish. 5,100 cases made. • $8 • (09/30/95) • **84**
Merlot Columbia Valley 1993: A lean and spicy, pickle-barrel character overtakes the fruit. Drinkable now. 3,400 cases made. • $10 • (09/30/95) • **80**

MARCASSIN | CALIFORNIA

Chardonnay Alexander Valley Gauer Vineyard Upper Barn 1994: Bold, ripe, ultrarich and creamy, loaded with tiers of pear, fig and melon flavors, adding some complexity on the finish with its echoes of anise and spice. A real mouthful of Chardonnay from this leading California winery that will do well in the cellar. 275 cases made. • $39 • (05/15/96) CS • **94**
Chardonnay Alexander Valley Gauer Vineyard Upper Barn 1993: An ultrarich and toasty California white with intense and complex pear, pineapple, spice, honey and hazelnut flavors. Develops delicate nuances on the finish. Uncommon complexity and depth for this vintage. 275 cases made. • $36 • (06/30/95) • **92**
Chardonnay Alexander Valley Gauer Vineyard Upper Barn 1992: Bold, ultra rich and flavorful, with loads of exotic spice, honey, pear and vanilla. Turns smooth and supple on the finish, where the flavors linger with a long, smoky aftertaste. Delicious now. 50 cases made. • $50 • (09/30/94) • **92**
Chardonnay Carneros Hudson Vineyard 1994: Serves up a mouthful of ripe pear, grapefruit and lemon flavors framed by toasty, smoky oak. The texture is smooth and polished, leading to its long, rich, complex aftertaste. 200 cases made. • $39 • (05/15/96) • **93**
Chardonnay Carneros Hudson Vineyard 1993: Smoky and perfumey, with polished honey, pear and butterscotch nuances that develop complexity and depth on the finish. Has a sense of harmony and finesse. 225 cases made. • $36 • (06/30/95) • **90**
Chardonnay Sonoma Coast Lorenzo Vineyard 1993: Well oaked, with bold, rich, concentrated honey, pear, toasty oak flavors that are ripe and well focused. The finish is long and complex. 200 cases made. • $36 • (06/30/95) • **91**

MARGARITE, CHATEAU | CALIFORNIA

Cabernet Sauvignon Napa Valley 1992: Medium weight, with simple but pleasant cherry and berry notes. Appealing now with its modest tannins. 272 cases made. • $15 • (12/15/95) • **85**
Cabernet Sauvignon Napa Valley 1991: Smooth and fruity, with exuberant berry, cherry and spice aromas and flavors, finishing bright and tasty. Tempting to drink now through 1997. 315 cases made. • $15 • (11/15/93) • **87**
Cabernet Sauvignon Napa Valley 1990: Ripe and chunky, with generous blackberry, black cherry and Brazil nut aromas and flavors, soften a bit more than we would like on the finish, but worth continuing to cellar until 1997 to see what develops. 189 cases made. • $12 • (11/15/93) • **86**
Cabernet Sauvignon Napa Valley 1989 • $15 • (11/15/93) • **74**

MARIETTA | CALIFORNIA

Cabernet Sauvignon Sonoma County 1987 • $10 • (02/28/91) • **87**
Cabernet Sauvignon Sonoma County 1985 • $10 • (06/30/90) • **83**
Cabernet Sauvignon Sonoma County 1984 • $10 • (12/31/87) • **78**
Cabernet Sauvignon Sonoma County 1981 • $9 • (06/16/84) • **78**
Old Vine Red Lot No. Eight Sonoma County NV • $5 • (05/31/90) BB • **81**
Old Vine Red Lot No. Eleven Sonoma County NV • $6 • (03/31/93) • **79**
Old Vine Red Lot No. Five Sonoma County NV • $5 • (12/31/87) • **77**
Old Vine Red Lot No. Seven Sonoma County NV • $6 • (11/15/89) BB • **82**
Old Vine Red Lot No. Ten Sonoma County NV • $6 • (04/30/92) • **79**
Old Vine Red Lot No. Three Sonoma County NV • $4 • (04/16/86) BB • **85**
Old Vine Red Lot No. Fourteen Sonoma County NV: Ripe, sweet cherry and berry flavors that turn soft and supple. Appealing now. 12,000 cases made. • $8 • (04/30/95) • **83**
Petite Sirah 1988 • $10 • (03/15/92) • **84**
Port Alexander Valley 1989: Smells and tastes like a really good late harvest Zinfandel, smooth and berryish, not too sweet, with a solid mouthful of fruit and spice on the finish. Best from 1998-2000. 530 cases made. • $16 • (05/31/95) • **86**
Zinfandel Sonoma County 1992: A ripe, jammy, effusively fruity style, showing wild berry, black cherry and raspberry flavors. Has lots of tannin too, but it's appealing now. 3,300 cases made. • $11 • (09/15/95) • **85**
Zinfandel Sonoma County 1988 • $8 • (12/31/91) BB • **87**
Zinfandel Sonoma County 1987 • $8 • (11/30/90) • **79**
Zinfandel Sonoma County 1985 • $7 • (12/31/87) • **87**
Zinfandel Sonoma County 1984 • $7 • (01/31/87) • **90**
Zinfandel Sonoma County 1982 • $6 • (06/16/84) • **73**
Zinfandel Sonoma County Reserve 1985 • $10 • (12/31/87) • **88**

MARILYN MERLOT | CALIFORNIA

Merlot 1989 • $14 • (05/31/92) • **87**
Merlot Napa Valley 1990 • $14 • (06/15/93) • **85**
Merlot Napa Valley 1988 • $13 • (05/31/91) • **85**
Merlot Napa Valley 1986 • $13 • (12/31/88) • **85**

MARION | CALIFORNIA

Cabernet Sauvignon California 1989 • $9 • (11/15/91) • **83**
Cabernet Sauvignon California 1985 • $5 • (12/31/87) • **62**
Chardonnay Sonoma County 1992: Simple and correct, with spicy pear and apple flavors. Fairly priced and drinkable now. 8,500 cases made. • $8 • (09/15/93) • **82**
Chardonnay Sonoma County 1991 • $8 • (07/15/93) • **80**
Merlot Napa Valley 1991 • $9 • (04/15/93) • **84**
Pinot Noir Sonoma County 1991 • $8 • (02/28/94) • **75**
Sauvignon Blanc Sonoma County 1992 • $6 • (09/15/93) BB • **83**

MARK WEST | CALIFORNIA

Blanc de Noirs Russian River Valley 1984 • $17 • (12/31/88) • **71**
Chardonnay Russian River Valley 1993: A ripe and juicy California white that delivers a pleasant mouthful of pear, tropical fruit and spice flavors right through the nice, lingering finish. Drinkable now. 6,388 cases made. • $13 • (05/31/96) SS • **89**
Chardonnay Russian River Valley 1991 • $12 • (02/15/93) • **86**
Chardonnay Russian River Valley Barrel Fermented 1991 • $11 • (07/15/93) • **82**
Chardonnay Russian River Valley Estate Reserve 1991 • $14 • (07/15/93) • **81**

Key: SS—Spectator Selection. CS—Cellar Selection. BB—Best Buy. $NA—Price not available. (BT)—Barrel tasting. Ⓐ—Auction Price.
Dates in parentheses represent the issues in which the ratings were published.

Gewürztraminer Russian River Valley 1994: A wine with generous peach, litchi and grapefruit flavors. The finish is dry and refreshingly open in texture. Drinkable now. 286 cases made. • $9 • (06/30/96) • **86**

Gewürztraminer Russian River Valley 1991 • $8 • (01/31/93) • **85**

Johannisberg Riesling Late Harvest Russian River Valley 1983 • $10 • (03/16/86) • **79**

Pinot Noir Russian River Valley 1991 • $10 • (02/28/94) • **84**

Pinot Noir Russian River Valley 1990 • $14 • (02/28/93) • **82**

Pinot Noir Russian River Valley 1983 • $10 • (05/16/86) • **67**

Pinot Noir Russian River Valley Ellis Vineyard 1986 • $14 • (03/31/90) • **81**

Pinot Noir Russian River Valley Ellis Vineyard 1984 • $10 • (03/15/87) • **84**

Pinot Noir Sonoma County 1986 • $8 • (02/28/89) • **80**

Sauvignon Blanc Russian River Valley 1994: Distinctive peppery-floral notes charaterize this medium-weight wine. 426 cases made. • $9 • (05/31/96) • **83**

Zinfandel Robert Rue Vineyard 1987 • $17 • (05/15/92) • **86**

Zinfandel Sonoma County Robert Rue Vineyard 1986 • $14 • (03/15/90) • **83**

Zinfandel Sonoma County Robert Rue Vineyard 1985 • $14 • (07/31/88) • **85**

MARKHAM | CALIFORNIA

Cabernet Sauvignon Napa Valley 1992: Ripe, fruity, supple black cherry, spice and berry notes. A complex aftertaste picks up hints of light oak and spice. Drinks well now but should age well into 1998. 10,700 cases made. • $17 • (11/30/95) • **88**

Cabernet Sauvignon Napa Valley 1991: This is a spicy red with pretty currant, plum and cherry notes that add dimension and depth. It also packs in lots of tannins, so it's best to cellar until 1999. 10,500 cases made. • $17 • (11/15/94) • **88**

Cabernet Sauvignon Napa Valley 1990: Ripe in flavor but firmly tannic, an opulent wine trapped under a swarm of tannins, with spicy, chocolaty plum, berry and currant flavors pushing through the tannins on the finish. Has power and style. Best to cellar until 1998-2000. 13,500 cases made. • $17 • (11/15/93) SS • **90**

Cabernet Sauvignon Napa Valley 1989 • $17 • (11/15/92) • **88**

Cabernet Sauvignon Napa Valley 1988 • $16 • (11/15/92) • **80**

Cabernet Sauvignon Napa Valley 1987 • $17 • (08/31/91) • **87**

Cabernet Sauvignon Napa Valley 1986 • $16 • (04/30/91) • **87**

Cabernet Sauvignon Napa Valley 1985 • $17 • (04/15/90) • **91**

Cabernet Sauvignon Napa Valley 1984 • $20 • (03/01/89) • **91**

Cabernet Sauvignon Napa Valley 1983 • $26 • (07/31/89) • **90**

Cabernet Sauvignon Napa Valley 1982 • $26 • (03/01/89) • **90**

Cabernet Sauvignon Napa Valley 1981 • $29 • (03/01/89) • **86**

Cabernet Sauvignon Napa Valley 1980 • $25 • (03/01/89) • **89**

Cabernet Sauvignon Napa Valley 1979 • $31 • (03/01/89) • **88**

Cabernet Sauvignon Napa Valley 1978 • $30 • (11/15/92) • **86**

Chardonnay Napa Valley 1994: Bold, ripe, complex and showing a broad spectrum of pear, honey, spice and mineral notes. It picks up a toasty oak character, then keeps echoing fruit in its long, complex aftertaste. 26,700 cases made. • $15 • (06/15/96) SS • **90**

Chardonnay Napa Valley 1992: Ripe, smooth and complex, with layers of creamy vanilla, pear, spice and honey that stay with you on a long, full finish. Picks up pretty hazelnut notes on the aftertaste. Delicious now. 20,000 cases made. • $15 • (03/15/94) SS • **90**

Chardonnay Napa Valley 1991 • $15 • (04/30/93) • **88**

Chardonnay Napa Valley Barrel Fermented 1993: A distinctive wine with personality and finesse. Deliciously ripe and full-bodied, showing attractive pear, ginger, quince and spice aromas and flavors. Has a style that carries through to the finish. 17,000 cases made. • $17 • (06/15/95) SS • **91**

Laurent Reserve Cabernet Blend Napa Valley 1990: Supple and elegant, with spicy, cedary oak, black cherry and currant flavors that turn smooth and silky. Doesn't quite deliver the richness and depth one might expect from a 1990, but it is elegant and polished. Ready now through 1998. • $25 • (12/31/94) • **85**

Merlot Napa Valley 1993: Supple, harmonious and smooth, showing pretty black cherry, plum and currant notes. Very well balanced, finishing with fleshy tannins. 33,000 cases made. • $16 • (12/15/95) • **89**

Merlot Napa Valley 1992: Ripe and chewy, with chunky black cherry, currant and mineral flavors, finishing with firm tannins and fine length. Drink now. 32,000 cases made. • $17 • (04/15/95) • **88**

Merlot Napa Valley 1991 • $16 • (05/31/94) • **87**

Merlot Napa Valley 1990 • $15 • (05/31/93) • **91**

Merlot Napa Valley 1989 • $15 • (05/31/92) • **85**

Merlot Napa Valley 1988 • $14 • (04/15/91) • **90**

Merlot Napa Valley 1987 • $14 • (10/15/89) • **91**

Merlot Napa Valley 1985 • $11 • (04/30/88) • **88**

Merlot Napa Valley 1981 • $8 • (08/01/84) • **86**

Sauvignon Blanc Napa Valley 1994: Bright and focused, showing lots of sweet tropical fruit, floral and herb flavors that swirl through the finish. A good value for immediate enjoyment. 25,000 cases made. • $8 • (08/31/95) BB • **87**

Sauvignon Blanc Napa Valley 1993: This is floral and spicy—juicier than most California '93s. A passion fruit character runs through it and lingers on the finish. Easy-drinking, terrific value. 15,000 cases made. • $8 • (06/30/95) SS • **89**

Sauvignon Blanc Napa Valley 1992 • $9 • (02/28/94) BB • **88**

Sauvignon Blanc Napa Valley 1991 • $9 • (04/15/93) • **90**

MARKKO | OHIO

Cabernet Sauvignon Conneaut 1988 • $10 • (02/29/92) • **76**

Pinot Noir Conneaut 1989 • $15 • (02/29/92) • **76**

MARTIN BROTHERS | CALIFORNIA

Aleatico California 1990 • $10 • (03/15/92) • **78**

Cabernet Etrusco Paso Robles 1993: Bright and lively, with a pretty, toasty oak overlay to the ripe plum and cherry flavors, finishing with a smoky edge to the fruit. 1,500 cases made. • $16 • (12/15/95) • **90**

Cabernet Sauvignon Paso Robles 1989 • $12 • (11/15/91) • **77**

Chardonnay Paso Robles in Botti 1994: Light and silky, showing the effects of barrel fermentation with spicy, leesy flavors and smooth texture, some length on aftertaste. Drink now. 2,328 cases made. • $12 • (09/30/95) • **84**

Chardonnay Paso Robles in Botti 1993: Marked by juicy pear, earth and pineapple flavors, turning earthier on the finish. 2,643 cases made. • $12 • (07/31/95) • **81**

Etrusco Paso Robles 1992: Herb and tar flavors with medium body and depth, but it doesn't hold your interest. 1,682 cases made. • $18 • (02/28/95) • **79**

Etrusco Paso Robles 1991: The best wine we've tasted from Martin Brothers. This Cabernet blends in Sangiovese, and the result is an elegant, spicy, complex young red that serves up pretty currant, black cherry, anise and berry flavors. The long, fruity finish makes it delicious and drinkable now. • $18 • (06/30/93) • **89**

Etrusco Paso Robles 1990: A light, fruity style of Cabernet that's appealing to drink now. The lovely plum and currant flavors are spicy and have a hint of strawberry and raspberry on the finish. Not too tannic. 15 percent Sangiovese. • $18 • (11/15/92) • **85**

Gemelli Paso Robles NV: Firm in texture, a chunky red that has dense blackberry, spice and black pepper flavors buried under firm tannins. Give it until 1997 or 1998 to open. 887 cases made. • $25 • (10/15/95) • **86**

Muscat Paso Robles Allegro Moscato 1994: Lightly sparkling, sweet and fruity, featuring a definite peppery-floral flavor that lingers on the finish. Drink soon. 3,481 cases made. • $10 • (11/30/95) • **85**

Nebbiolo California 1989 • $9 • (11/15/91) • **76**

Nebbiolo California 1987 • $12 • (12/15/89) • **75**

Nebbiolo California 1986 • $12 • (12/15/89) • **75**

Nebbiolo California 1982 • $7 • (04/01/84) • **78**

Nebbiolo California Vecchio 1992: Light and smooth, nice fruit up front, featuring spicy, new oak flavors and finishing with sweet vanilla and plum notes. 395 cases made. • $20 • (12/15/95) • **84**

Nebbiolo California Vecchio 1990 • $18 • (05/31/93) • **83**

Nebbiolo Central Coast 1993: Fruity, light, showing nice raspberry and vanilla flavors that echo on the supple finish. Ready now. 1,434 cases made. • $10 • (12/15/95) • **84**

Nebbiolo Paso Robles 1987 • $12 • (12/15/89) • **85**

MARTINELLI

Pinot Grigio Central Coast 1994: Light and appealing for its supple pear and apricot flavors. Drink now. 890 cases made. • $12 • (11/30/95) • **84**
Pinot Grigio Central Coast 1993: Soft, fruity and a little spicy on the finish, centering around citrus and apple flavors. 100 cases made. • $12 • **85**
Sangiovese Paso Robles Il Palio 1994: A touch earthy, but the cherry and strawberry flavors are ripe and attractive, if medium-bodied. 1,117 cases made. • $12 • (06/15/96) • **84**
Sangiovese Paso Robles Il Palio 1992 • $12 • (05/31/94) • **82**
Sparkling California Moscato Allegro 1992 • $10 • (05/15/93) • **77**
Sparkling California Moscato Frizzante 1991 • $9 • (03/31/92) • **88**
Vin Santo Sweet Malvasia Bianca 1990 • $15 • (03/15/92) • **81**
Zinfandel Paso Robles 1986 • $8 • (12/15/89) • **78**
Zinfandel Paso Robles 1985 • $6 • (02/15/88) • **83**
Zinfandel Paso Robles La Primitiva 1993: Tight and compact, with a narrow band of spicy berry and cherry flavors and firm tannins. 577 cases made. • $10 • (10/15/95) • **84**
Zinfandel Paso Robles La Primitiva 1992: Simple and fruity, with a light color and modest berry flavors. 817 cases made. • $10 • (06/15/95) • **83**
Zinfandel Paso Robles La Primitiva 1991: Firm and intense, with an earthy, gamy edge to the wild berry flavors. Holds together well through finish. Drinkable now. 936 cases made. • $10 • (10/15/94) • **84**
Zinfandel Paso Robles Primitivo 1990 • $9 • (03/31/93) • **82**
Zinfandel Port Primitivo Appassito 1990 • $12 • (03/15/92) • **83**

MARTINELLI | CALIFORNIA

Sauvignon Blanc Russian River Valley 1993: Sweet and peppery, an off-putting wine. 800 cases made. • $9 • (08/31/94) • **71**
Zinfandel Russian River Valley 1989 • $13 • (10/15/92) • **71**
Zinfandel Russian River Valley 1988 • $11 • (04/30/91) • **85**
Zinfandel Russian River Valley Jackass Vineyard 1992: Intense and lively, with earthy, tarry raspberry and cherry flavors that are ripe and focused. Finishes with a burst of fruit and firm tannins. Drinks well now. 600 cases made. • $14 • (10/15/94) • **88**
Zinfandel Russian River Valley Jackass Vineyard 1991 • $12 • (05/31/93) • **81**
Zinfandel Russian River Valley Jackass Vineyard 1990 • $13 • (12/15/92) • **91**
Zinfandel Russian River Valley Martinelli Vineyard 1989 • $13 • (12/15/92) • **81**

MARTINI & PRATI | CALIFORNIA

Zinfandel Sonoma County 1991: Tart and bordering on sour, with marginally ripe flavors. 420 cases made. • $7 • (10/15/94) • **72**

MARTINI, LOUIS M. | CALIFORNIA

Barbera California 1991: Distinctly Barbera, featuring wild berry, cherry, earth and tar notes, good intensity and depth and a mildly tannic finish. 1,969 cases made. • $12 • (10/15/95) • **85**
Barbera California 1987 • $6 • (12/31/90) BB • **83**
Barbera California 1984 • $7 • (11/15/89) • **80**
Barbera Napa Valley 1981 • $6 • (12/31/87) BB • **80**
Blush California Fresco Rosso 1991 • $6 • (11/30/92) • **75**
Cabernet Sauvignon California Private Reserve 1962 • $70 • (03/01/89) • **73**
Cabernet Sauvignon California Private Reserve 1956 • $52 • (03/01/89) • **77**
Cabernet Sauvignon California Private Reserve 1952 • $NA • (02/28/87) • **93**
Cabernet Sauvignon California Private Reserve Villa del Rey 1943 • $400 • (03/01/89) • **70**
Cabernet Sauvignon California Special Reserve 1939 • $850 • (03/01/89) • **90**

Key: SS—Spectator Selection. CS—Cellar Selection. BB—Best Buy. $NA—Price not available. (BT)—Barrel tasting. Ⓐ—Auction Price.
Dates in parentheses represent the issues in which the ratings were published.

Cabernet Sauvignon California Special Selection 1978 • $23 • (03/01/89) • **86**
Cabernet Sauvignon California Special Selection 1977 • $20 • (03/01/89) • **70**
Cabernet Sauvignon California Special Selection 1976 • $25 • (03/01/89) • **86**
Cabernet Sauvignon California Special Selection 1974: Dried out, earthy and weedy, with pickle flavors and a metallic edge on the finish. 5,411 cases made. • $45 • (11/15/94) • **68**
Cabernet Sauvignon California Special Selection 1972 • $50 • (03/01/89) • **63**
Cabernet Sauvignon California Special Selection 1970 • $65 • (03/01/89) • **88**
Cabernet Sauvignon California Special Selection 1968 • $40 • (03/01/89) • **90**
Cabernet Sauvignon California Special Selection 1966 • $65 • (03/01/89) • **87**
Cabernet Sauvignon California Special Selection 1964 • $100 • (03/01/89) • **85**
Cabernet Sauvignon California Special Selection 1961 • $100 • (03/01/89) • **80**
Cabernet Sauvignon California Special Selection 1959 • $140 • (03/01/89) • **87**
Cabernet Sauvignon California Special Selection 1958 • $125 • (03/01/89) • **88**
Cabernet Sauvignon California Special Selection 1957 • $85 • (03/01/89) • **91**
Cabernet Sauvignon California Special Selection 1955 • $120 • (03/01/89) • **87**
Cabernet Sauvignon California Special Selection 1952 • $140 • (03/01/89) • **93**
Cabernet Sauvignon California Special Selection 1951 • $300 • (03/01/89) • **87**
Cabernet Sauvignon California Special Selection 1947 • $450 • (03/01/89) • **90**
Cabernet Sauvignon California Special Selection 1945 • $400 • (03/01/89) • **75**
Cabernet Sauvignon Napa Valley Reserve 1989: Lean and a bit earthy, displaying currant flavor and finishing with crisp, firm and dry tannins. Best after 1996. Tasted twice with consistent notes. 5,810 cases made. • $14 • (11/15/94) • **81**
Cabernet Sauvignon Napa Valley Reserve 1988 • $14 • (11/15/92) • **78**
Cabernet Sauvignon Napa Valley Reserve 1987 • $14 • (10/15/90) • **87**
Cabernet Sauvignon North Coast 1992: Light and modestly fragrant, a simple wine with berry and spice notes. Drink now. 29,597 cases made. • $9 • (12/15/95) • **82**
Cabernet Sauvignon North Coast 1990: Green, tannic and herbal, surprisingly hard-edged, was in need of short-term cellaring, try now. 28,000 cases made. • $8 • (11/15/94) • **79**
Cabernet Sauvignon North Coast 1986 • $9 • (09/15/89) • **80**
Cabernet Sauvignon North Coast 1985 • $8 • (10/31/88) • **76**
Cabernet Sauvignon North Coast 1983 • $7 • (03/31/87) • **69**
Cabernet Sauvignon North Coast 1981 • $6 • (03/01/85) • **83**
Cabernet Sauvignon North Coast Special Selection 1984 • $NA • (03/01/89) • **85**
Cabernet Sauvignon North Coast Special Selection 1980 • $12 • (03/01/89) • **84**
Cabernet Sauvignon Sonoma County 1988 • $9 • (04/30/91) BB • **81**
Cabernet Sauvignon Sonoma Valley Monte Rosso 1990: Firm, intense and lean, with a tight, tannic core of currant, herb and mint notes, finishing with slightly green tannins. Can stand short-term cellaring, best after 1997. 991 cases made. • $23 • (09/30/94) • **85**
Cabernet Sauvignon Sonoma Valley Monte Rosso 1988 • $25 • (11/15/91) • **81**
Cabernet Sauvignon Sonoma Valley Monte Rosso 1987 • $20 • (11/15/90) • **93**
Cabernet Sauvignon Sonoma Valley Monte Rosso 1986 • $20 • (03/01/89) • **86**
Cabernet Sauvignon Sonoma Valley Monte Rosso 1985 • $22 • (03/01/89) • **80**
Cabernet Sauvignon Sonoma Valley Monte Rosso 1984 • $22 • (03/01/89) • **89**

Cabernet Sauvignon Sonoma Valley Monte Rosso 1983 • $22 • (03/01/89) • **86**
Cabernet Sauvignon Sonoma Valley Monte Rosso 1982 • $22 • (03/01/89) • **85**
Cabernet Sauvignon Sonoma Valley Monte Rosso 1981 • $15 • (12/15/86) • **90**
Cabernet Sauvignon Sonoma Valley Monte Rosso Los Niños 1983 • $25 • (03/01/89) • **83**
Cabernet Sauvignon Sonoma Valley Monte Rosso Los Niños 1982 • $25 • (03/01/89) • **82**
Cabernet Sauvignon Sonoma Valley Monte Rosso Los Niños 1981 • $25 • (03/01/89) • **85**
Cabernet Sauvignon Sonoma Valley Monte Rosso Lot 2 1979 • $10 • (03/01/89) • **84**
Cabernet Sauvignon Sonoma Valley Monte Rosso Vineyard 1991: Tannic and oaky, with a leathery edge to the modest Cabernet flavors. Tasted twice with consistent notes. 1,129 cases made. • $22 • (12/15/95) • **78**
Cabernet Sauvignon Sonoma Valley Monte Rosso Vineyard 1989: Green, stemmy, earthy and tough, not a likable wine at all. 1,100 cases made. • $23 • (12/15/95) • **71**
Chardonnay Napa Valley 1994: Has more going for it than most Chardonnays at this price. Spice and tobacco nuances support the pear and apple flavors and it finishes with pizzazz. Drinkable now. 21,385 cases made. • $11 • (06/15/96) • **87**
Chardonnay Napa Valley 1992: Very fruity and forward, ripe, creamy pear, apple and spice flavors are rich and focused. Finishes with a long, fruity aftertaste that gains complexity. 24,800 cases made. • $8 • (11/15/94) BB • **86**
Chardonnay Napa Valley 1991 • $8 • (06/30/93) • **82**
Chardonnay Napa Valley Reserve 1991 • $14 • (02/28/94) • **89**
Gewürztraminer Russian River Valley 1992 • $7 • (01/31/94) • **85**
Merlot North Coast 1994: Light, bright and lively, with modest strawberry flavors and a hint of mint on the finish. 29,538 cases made. • $9 • (06/30/96) • **83**
Merlot North Coast 1993: Light, simple and fragrant with berry and modest toast flavors. 29,538 cases made. • $9 • (06/15/96) • **81**
Merlot North Coast 1992: Light and crisp, simple berry flavors on a lively structure. Drinkable now. 37,103 cases made. • $9 • (07/31/95) • **81**
Merlot North Coast 1991: Simple and fruity, with a cranberry and cherry streak that becomes tart and a bit earthy on the finish. Drinkable now. 27,720 cases made. • $8 • (09/15/94) • **82**
Merlot North Coast 1990 • $10 • (08/31/93) • **79**
Merlot North Coast 1989 • $9 • (05/31/92) • **74**
Merlot North Coast 1988 • $10 • (08/31/91) • **85**
Merlot North Coast 1986 • $12 • (10/31/89) • **79**
Merlot North Coast 1984 • $6 • (02/15/88) • **79**
Merlot North Coast 1982 • $5 • (02/16/86) • **71**
Merlot Russian River Valley Los Vinedos del Rio 1990: Ripe and supple, with a crisp, focused band of currant, bell pepper and herbal notes that fold together neatly on the finish. The tannins are smooth, making this one easy to enjoy now through 1997. 1,000 cases made. • $20 • (09/15/94) • **87**
Merlot Russian River Valley Los Vinedos del Rio 1988 • $22 • (05/31/92) • **74**
Merlot Russian River Valley Los Vinedos del Rio 1986 • $20 • (03/31/90) • **79**
Merlot Russian River Valley Los Vinedos del Rio 1984 • $12 • (02/15/88) • **82**
Merlot Russian River Valley Los Vinedos del Rio 1981 • $10 • (10/01/85) • **81**
Merlot Russian River Valley Los Vinedos del Rio Vineyard Selection 1991: Simple, with earthy and light berry flavors that turn dry and almost sour on the finish. Disappointing, given this vineyard's track record. 400 cases made. • $20 • **78**
Merlot Russian River Valley Reserve 1992: Nice array of smoky herb, plum and cherry flavors. Texture is a bit coarse and the finish turns rustic. 928 cases made. • $15 • **84**
Petite Sirah Napa Valley 1985 • $7 • (10/31/89) BB • **85**
Petite Sirah Napa Valley 1983 • $6 • (12/31/87) • **76**
Petite Sirah Napa Valley 1982 • $5 • (09/15/86) BB • **80**
Petite Sirah Napa Valley Reserve 1987 • $11 • (11/30/91) • **85**
Petite Sirah Napa Valley Reserve 1986 • $12 • (10/31/90) • **81**
Pinot Noir Carneros Napa Valley 1992: Smooth and ripe, offering attractive plum, cherry and anise notes and a delicate aftertase with mild tannins. A bargain in Pinot Noir. Drinkable now. 3,814 cases made. • $7 • (05/15/95) BB • **86**
Pinot Noir Carneros Napa Valley 1990 • $8 • (02/28/93) • **67**
Pinot Noir Carneros Napa Valley 1987 • $7 • (02/28/91) BB • **82**
Pinot Noir Carneros Napa Valley La Loma Vineyard 1988 • $18 • (03/31/92) • **75**
Pinot Noir Carneros Napa Valley Las Amigas Vineyard Selection 1982 • $12 • (03/31/90) • **85**
Pinot Noir Carneros Napa Valley Las Amigas Vineyard Selection 1980 • $10 • (03/15/87) • **68**
Pinot Noir Los Carneros 1993: A touch earthy, with dried cherry and plum flavors, finishing with a pleasant mushroom edge. Very appealing, and a wonderful buy at this price. Has 14 percent Petite Sirah, which pushes the tannins a bit. 3,943 cases made. • $8 • (01/31/96) BB • **85**
Pinot Noir Los Carneros 1988 • $8 • (07/15/91) BB • **85**
Pinot Noir Los Carneros La Loma Vineyard 1990 • $16 • (02/28/94) • **82**
Pinot Noir Los Carneros Napa Valley 1990 • $8 • (02/28/94) • **79**
Pinot Noir Napa Valley 1986 • $8 • (12/31/89) BB • **85**
Sauvignon Blanc Napa Valley 1994: Light and lean, adding a peachy edge to the modest floral flavors. 911 cases made. • $8 • (02/29/96) • **81**
White Zinfandel Napa Valley 1988 • $5 • (06/15/89) • **81**
Zinfandel California 1974 • $NA • (06/16/85) • **78**
Zinfandel California 1973 • $NA • (06/16/85) • **87**
Zinfandel North Coast 1985 • $6 • (03/31/89) • **80**
Zinfandel North Coast 1984 • $6 • (02/15/88) BB • **84**
Zinfandel North Coast 1983 • $7 • (10/15/86) • **87**
Zinfandel Paso Robles 1989 • $8 • (08/31/91) • **83**
Zinfandel Sonoma County 1986 • $7 • (10/31/89) • **79**
Zinfandel Sonoma Valley 1992: Well oaked and a bit murky, with the focus on cedar and spice, but hints of cherry and berry come through on the finish to give it more appeal. 5,767 cases made. • $8 • (08/31/95) • **84**
Zinfandel Sonoma-Napa Counties 1989 • $7 • (06/15/93) • **73**
Zinfandel Sonoma-Napa Counties 1988 • $7 • (10/15/92) • **79**

MASO | CALIFORNIA

Cabernet Blend Napa Valley 1991: Hard and tannic, showing herb- and oak-laced fruit. The finish is smoky, dry and leathery, tough to like. A curious blend of Sangiovese, Cabernet Sauvignon, Cabernet Franc and Pinot Noir. 10,000 cases made. • $8 • (03/31/95) • **80**
Rosé California Rosatta 1993: Herbal and sweet, offering rhubarblike flavors and a stale finish. • $5 • (09/15/95) • **73**
White Table Wine Napa Valley 1992: Oak, oak and more oak, a spicy, toasty, round-textured wine that finally gets around to some honey and pear notes on the finish. Primarily Chardonnay. Drinkable now. 5,000 cases made. • $8 • (04/15/95) • **81**

MASON | CALIFORNIA

Merlot Napa Valley 1993: Ripe and complex, sporting cherry and berry notes, spicy, toasty oak shadings and smooth, supple aftertaste. Drinkable now and into 1997. An impressive new offering from Randy Mason, the former winemaker for Lakespring. 650 cases made. • $20 • (04/30/96) • **89**

MASSON, PAUL | CALIFORNIA

Blanc de Noirs Monterey Centennial Cuvée 1984 • $9 • (12/31/87) • **83**
Cabernet Sauvignon California Vintners Selection 1986 • $6 • (06/30/89) • **84**
Cabernet Sauvignon Monterey County Vintage Selection 1986 • $9 • (11/15/89) • **79**
Cabernet Sauvignon Monterey County Vintage Selection 1985 • $8 • (09/15/88) • **78**
Chardonnay Monterey County 1993: Soft and spicy, smooth in texture and modest with its vanilla-scented pear flavors. Ready now. • $10 • **78**
Merlot Monterey County 1988 • $8 • (05/31/92) • **79**

Merlot Monterey County Vintage Selection 1987 • $8 • (07/15/90) • **83**
Merlot Vintners Selection 1989 • $4 • (04/15/92) BB • **80**
White Zinfandel California 1988 • $7 • (06/15/89) • **74**

MASTANTUONO | CALIFORNIA

Carminello California 1988 • $7 • (07/15/91) • **79**
Zinfandel San Luis Obispo County Dante Dusi Vineyards 1986 • $9 • (08/31/91) • **84**
Zinfandel San Luis Obispo County Dante Dusi Vineyards 1984 • $18 • (07/31/91) • **73**
Zinfandel San Luis Obispo County Templeton Dante Dusi Vineyards 1989 • $9 • (09/30/93) • **77**

MATANZAS CREEK | CALIFORNIA

Cabernet Sauvignon Sonoma Valley 1983 • $14 • (07/16/86) • **75**
Cabernet Sauvignon Sonoma Valley 1982 • $14 • (08/01/85) • **88**
Cabernet Sauvignon Sonoma Valley 1981 • $16 • (04/16/84) • **84**
Chardonnay Sonoma Valley 1994: An openly fruity style with appealing floral aromas to match the hints of apple, pear and spice, and flavors to match. Finishes rich and fruity, with just a kiss of smoky oak tones. 16,195 cases made. • $28 • (05/31/96) • **90**
Chardonnay Sonoma Valley 1993: Rich, round and distinctively spicy, this is an elegant mouthful of pear, apple and nutmeg. Buttery, creamy notes chime in on the finish. Stylish and graceful. Delicious now and at its best through 1998. 15,000 cases made. • $23 • (09/30/95) SS • **91**
Chardonnay Sonoma Valley 1992: Austere and flinty, offering bright green apple and spicy pear notes that taste young and vibrant. Can stand short-term cellaring to develop more nuances. • $22 • (11/15/94) • **88**
Chardonnay Sonoma Valley 1991 • $20 • (11/30/93) • **90**
Chardonnay Sonoma Valley Journey 1992: Well-oaked, rich, complex, bold and ripe, the toasty, buttery notes popping out, but it has creamy layers of pear, honey and spice to match the wood. Packs in lots of flavors yet manages a measure of finesse and smoky aftertaste. 271 cases made. • $70 • (12/31/95) • **91**
Merlot Sonoma County 1992 • $NA • (05/31/93) • **886**
Merlot Sonoma County 1987 • $25 • (06/15/90) SS • **92**
Merlot Sonoma County 1986 • $20 • (06/30/89) • **92**
Merlot Sonoma Valley 1993: Smooth and polished, with appealing ripe plum, cherry, cedar and spice flavors, picking up a trace of earthiness on the finish. A little age should improve it, try in 1997 or 1998. 6,400 cases made. • $38 • (06/30/96) • **88**
Merlot Sonoma Valley 1992: Perennially one of California's tip-top Merlots. Dark in color, with lots of rich currant, herb, tobacco and buttery oak, but it retains a sense of elegance, even for such substantial weight and flavor. 6,700 cases made. • $30 • (04/15/95) SS • **91**
Merlot Sonoma Valley 1991: A rich, tight and compact young Merlot that has lots of ripe currant, cherry, herb and vanilla notes from oak aging. Picks up a pretty coffee and cola edge on the finish. Drinkable now. • $29 • (09/15/94) • **89**
Merlot Sonoma Valley 1990 • $28 • (05/15/93) • **89**
Merlot Sonoma Valley 1989 • $28 • (04/15/92) • **90**
Merlot Sonoma Valley 1988 • $28 • (08/31/91) • **88**
Merlot Sonoma Valley 1985 • $29 Ⓐ • (05/31/88) • **88**
Merlot Sonoma Valley 1984 • $23 Ⓐ • (06/30/87) • **91**
Merlot Sonoma Valley 1982 • $14 • (10/01/85) • **88**
Merlot Sonoma Valley 1981 • $13 • (04/16/84) • **80**
Pinot Noir Sonoma County Quail Hill Ranch 1980 • $9 • (07/01/84) • **82**
Sauvignon Blanc Sonoma County 1994: A racier style, featuring intense grass, herb and citrus flavors that ring true for Sauvignon Blanc. Not quite up to its usual, but solid. 12,000 cases made. • $15 • (02/29/96) • **87**
Sauvignon Blanc Sonoma County 1993: Crisp and bright, with appealing pear and vanilla flavors shaded by a light touch of grapefruit and herb. • $14 • (12/31/94) • **87**

> **Key:** SS—Spectator Selection. CS—Cellar Selection. BB—Best Buy. $NA—Price not available. (BT)—Barrel tasting. Ⓐ—Auction Price.
> **Dates in parentheses represent the issues in which the ratings were published.**

Sauvignon Blanc Sonoma County 1992 • $13 • (02/28/94) • **87**
Sauvignon Blanc Sonoma County 1991 • $13 • (02/15/93) • **88**

MATTHEWS | WASHINGTON

Cabernet Blend Washington 1994: Supple and generous at first, takes a dip after the first sip, then redeems itself with a chewy licorice-tobacco streak and plum flavors. Best from 1999. 191 cases made. • $21 • **85**
Cabernet Sauvignon Washington Reserve 1994: Has a burnt, ashy edge and astringent texture that detract from a narrow core of berry flavors. 98 cases made. • $30 • **78**
Merlot Washington Reserve 1993: Very smoky, almost like ash. Lean berry flavors turn tart on the finish. Not much charm. • $NA • **77**

MATTITUCK HILLS | NEW YORK

Cabernet Sauvignon North Fork of Long Island 1987 • $9 • (06/30/91) • **82**

MAYACAMAS | CALIFORNIA

Cabernet Sauvignon California 1969 • $95 • (03/01/89) • **89**
Cabernet Sauvignon California 1968 • $155 • (03/01/89) • **88**
Cabernet Sauvignon California 1967 • $125 • (03/01/89) • **65**
Cabernet Sauvignon California 1966 • $150 • (03/01/89) • **75**
Cabernet Sauvignon California 1965 • $150 • (03/01/89) • **65**
Cabernet Sauvignon California 1963 • $130 • (03/01/89) • **69**
Cabernet Sauvignon California 1962 • $150 • (03/01/89) • **68**
Cabernet Sauvignon Napa Valley 1990: Leans toward the herbal spectrum of Cabernet with a stalky, green edge to the currant and berry notes. Picks up a coffee and cedar edge and turns tannic on the finish. Tasted twice with consistent notes. 1,300 cases made. • $25 • (12/15/95) • **85**
Cabernet Sauvignon Napa Valley 1989: Light with earthy cedar, herb, cherry and spice notes, turning dry and earthy on the finish. Decent, but lacks pizzazz. 1,390 cases made. • $20 • (12/15/95) • **82**
Cabernet Sauvignon Napa Valley 1987 • $41 • (11/15/92) • **81**
Cabernet Sauvignon Napa Valley 1986 • $45 • (11/15/91) • **82**
Cabernet Sauvignon Napa Valley 1985 • $49 • (01/31/90) • **92**
Cabernet Sauvignon Napa Valley 1984 • $45 • (04/15/89) • **80**
Cabernet Sauvignon Napa Valley 1983 • $25 • (03/01/89) • **90**
Cabernet Sauvignon Napa Valley 1982 • $30 • (03/01/89) • **77**
Cabernet Sauvignon Napa Valley 1981 • $44 • (03/01/89) • **91**
Cabernet Sauvignon Napa Valley 1980 • $65 • (03/01/89) • **92**
Cabernet Sauvignon Napa Valley 1979 • $74 • (03/01/89) • **95**
Cabernet Sauvignon Napa Valley 1978 • $82 • (11/15/92) • **88**
Cabernet Sauvignon Napa Valley 1977 • $75 • (03/01/89) • **92**
Cabernet Sauvignon Napa Valley 1976 • $68 • (03/01/89) • **84**
Cabernet Sauvignon Napa Valley 1975 • $70 • (03/01/89) • **89**
Cabernet Sauvignon Napa Valley 1974: Holding its deep color, aromas of earthy currant, berry and spice turn drier on the palate with a short finish. The tannins have softened and it's still tight and concentrated. Tasted three times with noticeable bottle variaton. 2,300 cases made. • $125 • (11/15/94) • **88**
Cabernet Sauvignon Napa Valley 1973 • $65 • (03/01/89) • **87**
Cabernet Sauvignon Napa Valley 1972 • $80 • (03/01/89) • **82**
Cabernet Sauvignon Napa Valley 1971 • $75 • (03/01/89) • **86**
Cabernet Sauvignon Napa Valley 1970 • $110 • (03/01/89) • **96**
Chardonnay Napa Valley 1993: Marked by citrus and grapefruit character, this emphasizes the flinty, grassy side of Chardonnay, turning crisp and lemony on the finish. 1,500 cases made. • $18 • (05/15/96) • **88**
Chardonnay Napa Valley 1992: Young and closed, but that's typical of Mayacamas at this stage. Crisp and flinty, with pleasant, earthy pear and spice notes. Not much oak to please fans of that style. Drinkable now, but should age well, too. 1,477 cases made. • $16 • (08/31/95) • **88**
Pinot Noir Napa Valley 1988 • $14 • (02/28/93) • **68**
Pinot Noir Napa Valley 1987 • $14 • (04/30/91) • **80**
Pinot Noir Napa Valley 1986 • $14 • (03/31/90) • **67**
Pinot Noir Napa Valley 1985 • $12 • (06/15/88) • **72**
Pinot Noir Napa Valley 1984 • $12 • (12/31/88) • **71**
Sauvignon Blanc Napa Valley 1994: Bright and citrusy, zingy for its grapefruit, vanilla and gentle herbal flavors. Drinkable now. 580 cases made. • $12 • (05/15/96) BB • **86**

Sauvignon Blanc Napa Valley 1993: Clean and crisp, boasting pretty pear, spice, citrus and floral notes. Altogether elegant and refreshing, ideal for summertime. 600 cases made. • $10 • (08/31/95) • **88**

Zinfandel Late Harvest Napa Valley 1984 • $18 • (11/15/89) • **84**

MAZZOCCO | CALIFORNIA

Cabernet Sauvignon Alexander Valley Claret Style 1988 • $18 • (03/15/92) • **85**

Cabernet Sauvignon Alexander Valley Claret Style 1987 • $20 • (08/31/90) • **93**

Cabernet Sauvignon Alexander Valley Claret Style 1986 • $20 • (07/31/89) • **78**

Cabernet Sauvignon Sonoma County 1992: Supple and elegant, marked by herb, chocolate and currant flavors which turn complex and harmonious on the finish. Tempting to enjoy now. 3,000 cases made. • $18 • (04/30/96) • **88**

Cabernet Sauvignon Sonoma County 1991: Supple and spicy with ripe, smooth black cherry, earth and currant flavors. Finishes with polished tannins, approachable now but worthy of short-term cellaring. 2,875 cases made. • $18 • (11/15/94) • **88**

Cabernet Sauvignon Sonoma County 1989 • $15 • (06/15/93) • **81**

Chardonnay Sonoma County River Lane 1994: An elegant style that's fresh and vibrant. Has an attractive core of ripe pear, citrus and melon flavors and finishes with traces of light oak. 7,000 cases made. • $14 • (06/30/96) • **87**

Chardonnay Sonoma County River Lane 1993: A touch earthy, with grapefruit, citrus and pear shadings, but turning tart and lean on the finish. 5,000 cases made. • $15 • (07/31/95) • **83**

Chardonnay Sonoma County River Lane 1992: Lean and simple, offering some pleasant apple and spice flavors that linger on the finish. Shows some promise. Drink now. 6,750 cases made. • $15 • (06/30/94) • **85**

Chardonnay Sonoma County River Lane 1991 • $15 • (03/31/93) • **86**

Chardonnay Sonoma County Winemaker's Select 1993: An oaky style with lots of smoky, woody flavors. The pear and spice notes struggle to match the woodiness. 200 cases made. • $18 • (06/30/96) • **84**

Chardonnay Sonoma County Winemaker's Select 1992: Pleasantly fruity, featuring ripe, clean pear, apple and spice flavors that turn refined and elegant on the finish. Ready now. 200 cases made. • $18 • (10/15/95) • **88**

Matrix Dry Creek Valley 1992: Firm and tight, with focused currant, cherry and cedary oak flavors and a hint of anise. Finishes with a nice burst of fruit, and the tannins are soft and round. 350 cases made. • $28 • **87**

Matrix Dry Creek Valley 1991: Light but focused, drawing a bead of currant and black cherry that jumps to life on the lively finish. Stylish, with personality. Give it until 1997-1998. 300 cases made. • $28 • (12/15/95) • **87**

Matrix Sonoma County 1990: Lean and compact, with a narrow band of spice, currant and bell pepper flavor that hangs together, but it could use a little more depth, richness and texture. Drinkable now. 550 cases made. • $28 • (11/15/94) • **82**

Matrix Sonoma County 1989 • $28 • (11/15/93) • **86**

Matrix Sonoma County 1987 • $28 • (01/31/92) • **91**

Merlot Dry Creek Valley 1992: Serves up an attractive range of cherry, berry, herb and spice notes, but is a shade on the crisp side as the acidity and tannin stand out. Try in 1997. 850 cases made. • $15 • (05/31/96) • **84**

Merlot Dry Creek Valley 1991: Lean, a bit green and tannic, void of fruit. Hard-edged and unyielding, try after 1998. 900 cases made. • $15 • (11/15/94) • **78**

Merlot Dry Creek Valley 1989 • $14 • (06/15/93) • **78**

Merlot Estate Unfiltered 1989 • $14 • (05/31/92) • **89**

Zinfandel Dry Creek Valley Cuneo & Saini 1993: Clean and correct, with crisp and earthy raspberry flavors of modest proportions. 200 cases made. • $20 • (10/15/95) • **83**

Zinfandel Sonoma County 1993: Intense and well focused, with pretty floral, wild berry and raspberry notes. Finishes a bit tannic. 3,200 cases made. • $14 • (08/31/95) • **86**

Zinfandel Sonoma County 1992: Elegant and fruity, with ripe strawberry and raspberry flavors that pick up firm tannins on the finish. Ready now. 2,600 cases made. • $14 • (10/15/94) • **86**

Zinfandel Sonoma County 1991 • $14 • (09/30/93) • **88**

Zinfandel Sonoma County Traditional Style 1988 • $13 • (10/15/90) • **89**

Zinfandel Sonoma County Traditional Style 1986 • $10 • (12/15/88) • **90**

Zinfandel Sonoma Valley 1990 • $13 • (10/15/92) • **87**

MCCOY, PETER | CALIFORNIA

Chardonnay Knights Valley Clos des Pierres 1993: Lean and flinty, with a hint of tart apple and a mature finish. 1,800 cases made. • $20 • (06/15/96) • **85**

Chardonnay Knights Valley Clos des Pierres 1992: Medium weight, with earthy citrus and pear notes that linger on the finish. 1,800 cases made. • $19 • (07/31/95) • **85**

MCCREA | WASHINGTON

La Mer Columbia Valley 1991 • $10 • (06/15/93) • **78**

MCDOWELL | CALIFORNIA

Bistro Red LVC Mendocino NV • $7 • (06/30/92) • **79**

Cabernet Sauvignon California 1988 • $10 • (11/15/91) • **78**

Cabernet Sauvignon California 1987 • $9 • (11/15/90) • **78**

Cabernet Sauvignon McDowell Valley 1986 • $8 • (04/30/90) • **70**

Cabernet Sauvignon McDowell Valley 1983 • $11 • (04/15/88) • **76**

Cabernet Sauvignon McDowell Valley 1982 • $11 • (12/15/86) • **89**

Cabernet Sauvignon McDowell Valley 1981 • $11 • (12/16/84) • **78**

Cabernet Sauvignon Mendocino 1992: Firm and chunky, with a decent core of currant, plum and cedary oak flavors that fold together nicely. Best after 1997. 12,000 cases made. • $10 • (12/15/95) • **85**

Cabernet Sauvignon Mendocino 1990: This firm, flavorful wine has a decadent edge to the basic black cherry flavors and finishes with a wisp of almond. Drinkable now. • $9 • (07/15/93) • **82**

Cabernet Sauvignon Mendocino 1989 • $9 • (11/15/92) • **75**

Chardonnay Mendocino 1994: Simple and pleasant enough, delivering a modest range of pear, spice, apple and melon flavors. • $10 • (05/15/96) • **84**

Chardonnay Mendocino 1992: Well-turned, shading its solid pear flavor with hints of spice, toast and vanilla. Drink now. • $9 • (01/31/94) • **86**

Chardonnay Mendocino 1991 • $9 • (06/30/93) • **83**

Grenache Rosé McDowell Valley Les Vieux Cépages 1990 • $7 • (06/15/91) BB • **82**

Grenache Rosé McDowell Valley Les Vieux Cépages 1989 • $6 • (10/31/90) BB • **82**

Grenache Rosé McDowell Valley Les Vieux Cépages 1988 • $6 • (11/15/89) BB • **80**

Grenache Rosé Mendocino 1993: There's plenty of dried fruit and spice in the aromas and flavors, underscored by lively acidity. Vibrant and refreshing, a substantial finish. • $7 • (09/15/95) • **83**

Les Vieux Cépages Les Trésor McDowell Valley Red 1988 • $12 • (06/30/92) • **75**

Les Vieux Cépages Les Trésor McDowell Valley Red 1987 • $14 • (08/31/90) • **82**

Les Vieux Cépages Les Trésor McDowell Valley Red 1986 • $13 • (09/30/89) • **86**

Les Vieux Cépages McDowell Valley Red 1990 • $13 • (10/15/93) • **86**

Syrah McDowell Valley 1985 • $12 • (09/30/89) • **90**

Syrah McDowell Valley 1984 • $9 • (02/15/89) • **86**

Syrah McDowell Valley 1983 • $10 • (05/31/88) • **69**

Syrah McDowell Valley 1982 • $10 • (01/31/87) • **75**

Syrah McDowell Valley 1981 • $10 • (12/16/84) • **90**

Syrah McDowell Valley Bistro Syrah LVC 1991 • $9 • (03/31/93) • **79**

Syrah McDowell Valley Bistro Syrah LVC 1990 • $9 • (06/30/92) • **76**

Syrah McDowell Valley Les Vieux Cépages 1987 • $16 • (03/31/91) • **74**

Syrah McDowell Valley Les Vieux Cépages 1986 • $14 • (08/31/90) • **80**

Syrah Mendocino 1993: Ripe and generous, focusing its plum and berry flavors nicely against the velvety background. Good value for a California Syrah with this much character. Drink now. 3,000 cases made. • $10 • (10/15/95) BB • **87**

Syrah Mendocino 1990: Ripe and chunky, a chewy wine with plum and pepper flavors sneaking in, not as generous as it could be. Drinkable now. 1,500 cases made. • $17 • (07/31/94) • **82**

MCGREGOR

Syrah Mendocino Bistro 1992: Bright and fruity, a light style that shows lots of appealing strawberry and raspberry flavors. Drinkable now. 3,000 cases made. • $10 • (07/31/94) • **85**

Syrah Mendocino McDowell Valley Estate 1992: A very ripe style with a cooked tinge, giving a meaty quality to the ripe plum and wild berry flavors. Finishes with crisp acidity and firm tannins. 2,500 cases made. • $15 • (05/31/96) • **84**

Viognier McDowell Valley Les Vieux Cépages 1991 • $25 • (11/30/92) • **88**

Viognier Mendocino 1992 • $25 • (02/28/94) • **84**

Zinfandel McDowell Valley 1990 • $9 • (04/30/93) • **79**

Zinfandel McDowell Valley 1989 • $9 • (10/15/92) • **80**

Zinfandel McDowell Valley 1988 • $9 • (12/31/90) • **80**

Zinfandel McDowell Valley 1987 • $8 • (12/15/89) BB • **87**

MCGREGOR | NEW YORK

Blanc de Blancs Finger Lakes 1985 • $15 • (12/31/90) • **64**

Pinot Noir Finger Lakes 1986 • $13 • (06/15/88) • **70**

Pinot Noir Finger Lakes Reserve 1983 • $14 • (03/16/86) • **67**

MCHENRY | CALIFORNIA

Pinot Noir Santa Cruz Mountains 1985 • $13 • (06/15/88) • **75**

MEADOW GLEN | CALIFORNIA

Merlot Napa Valley 1989 • $8 • (05/31/92) • **81**

MEEKER | CALIFORNIA

Cabernet Sauvignon Dry Creek Valley 1988 • $14 • (08/31/92) • **85**

Cabernet Sauvignon Dry Creek Valley 1987 • $14 • (10/15/91) • **87**

Cabernet Sauvignon Dry Creek Valley 1986 • $19 • (02/15/90) • **72**

Cabernet Sauvignon Dry Creek Valley 1985 • $18 • (04/30/89) • **76**

Cabernet Sauvignon Dry Creek Valley 1984 • $18 • (06/15/88) • **78**

Cabernet Sauvignon Dry Creek Valley Gold Leaf Cuvée 1991: Lean and firm, with a very narrow band of currant and cherry flavor that doesn't quite come to life. 1,500 cases made. • $14 • (11/15/94) • **78**

Cabernet Sauvignon Dry Creek Valley Gold Leaf Cuvée 1990: Tight and lean, with a narrow band of cedar and currant flavors. It comes up short on richness, flavor and depth. Drinkable now. 850 cases made. • $14 • (09/15/93) • **82**

Cabernet Sauvignon Dry Creek Valley Scharf Family Vineyard 1990: Ripe and intense, displaying spicy, peppery aromas and a solid, compact core of black cherry and currant flavor. Finishes with firm, crisp tannins, best after 1997. 560 cases made. • $14 • (11/15/94) • **84**

Cabernet Sauvignon Second Rack Dry Creek Valley NV: A serviceable red table wine with chunky, chewy Cabernet flavors. Ready now. 860 cases made. • $8 • (11/15/94) • **79**

Chardonnay Dry Creek Valley White Table Wine Second Rack 1992: Earthy, adding a funky edge, like the bark of a tree. 728 cases made. • $8 • (02/28/95) • **76**

Fumé Blanc Dry Creek Valley Gold Label Cuveé 1993: Light and distinctly herbal, a little pear flavor at the core and a hint of sweet peas around the edges. Drinkable now. 300 cases made. • $9 • (10/15/94) • **85**

Merlot Sonoma County Winemakers' Handprint Collection 1992: A big, ripe style with lots of oak seasoning, with bold black berry and cherry flavors and firm dry tannins. This tense and tannic wine definitely needs cellaring, but may always be on the tannic side. 200 cases made. • $18 • **87**

Sauvignon Blanc Late Harvest Dry Creek Valley Gold Leaf Cuveé 1992: Sweet, supple, subtle, elegant, sporting delicious orange overtones to pear and honey flavors. Ready now. 160 cases made. • $16 • (09/30/95) • **88**

Zinfandel Dry Creek Valley 1991 • $8 • (09/30/93) • **82**

Zinfandel Dry Creek Valley 1989 • $10 • (10/15/92) • **80**

Zinfandel Dry Creek Valley 1988 • $10 • (08/31/91) • **82**

Key: SS—Spectator Selection. CS—Cellar Selection. BB—Best Buy. $NA—Price not available. (BT)—Barrel tasting. (A)—Auction Price.
Dates in parentheses represent the issues in which the ratings were published.

Zinfandel Dry Creek Valley 1987 • $10 • (03/31/90) • **85**

Zinfandel Dry Creek Valley 1986 • $9 • (03/15/89) • **83**

Zinfandel Dry Creek Valley 1985 • $8 • (05/15/88) • **90**

Zinfandel Dry Creek Valley Gold Leaf Cuvée 1992: Lean and simple, with barely ripe fruit flavors. Turns dry and tannic on the finish. 1,800 cases made. • $12 • (10/15/94) • **80**

Zinfandel Dry Creek Valley Gold Leaf Cuvée 1991 • $11 • (09/30/93) • **84**

Zinfandel Dry Creek Valley Gold Leaf Cuvée 1990 • $10 • (01/31/93) SS • **90**

Zinfandel Dry Creek Valley Gold Leaf Reserve 1989 • $14 • (10/15/92) • **81**

Zinfandel Dry Creek Valley Red Table Wine First Rack 1991 • $8 • (09/30/93) BB • **86**

Zinfandel Sonoma County Sonoma Cuvée 1992: Smooth and polished, with elegant wild berry and cherry flavors. A solid Zin that will be best from now to 1998. Tasted twice. 1,000 cases made. • $10 • (10/15/94) • **84**

MEITZ | CALIFORNIA

Merlot Sonoma County 1991 • $15 • (04/15/94) • **85**

MENDOCINO ESTATE | CALIFORNIA

Cabernet Sauvignon Mendocino 1985 • $5 • (02/15/88) • **61**

Cabernet Sauvignon Mendocino 1984 • $4 • (06/15/87) • **78**

Cabernet Sauvignon Mendocino 1982 • $4 • (10/15/86) BB • **87**

Zinfandel Mendocino 1985 • $4 • (02/15/88) • **79**

Zinfandel Mendocino 1984 • $4 • (05/31/87) • **68**

MENDOCINO HILL | CALIFORNIA

Cabernet Sauvignon Mendocino County 1989 • $15 • (03/31/93) • **88**

MENDOCINO VINEYARDS | CALIFORNIA

Cabernet Sauvignon Mendocino County NV • $6 • (04/15/89) • **73**

MER & SOLEIL | CALIFORNIA

Chardonnay Central Coast 1994: A bold, ripe, rich and full-bodied style of California Chardonnay that laces the honey, pear and pineapple flavors with nice spicy, toasty shadings. A concentrated white with a long, lingering aftertaste. Delicious. 2,400 cases made. • $32 • (05/31/96) • **93**

Chardonnay Central Coast 1992: A new California Chardonnay from Chuck Wagner of Caymus-on his own. This is well oaked, showing toasty, buttery nuances, but it's also richly fruity, with exotic pear, tropical fruit, honey and spice flavors. Packs lots of complexity into a bold style. Sold only outside of California. Drinkable now. 1,100 cases made. • $25 • (08/31/95) SS • **91**

MERCER RANCH | WASHINGTON

Cabernet Sauvignon Columbia Valley Mercer Ranch Vineyard Block 1 1985 • $13 • (10/15/89) • **81**

MEREDYTH | VIRGINIA

Cabernet Sauvignon Virginia 1989 • $11 • (02/29/92) • **79**

Merlot 1989 • $25 • (02/29/92) • **81**

MERIDIAN | CALIFORNIA

Cabernet Sauvignon Paso Robles 1990: Intense and fruity with tart cherry and berry flavors that are clean and correct, but rather one dimensional now. Picks up toasty oak flavors on the finish. Best now. • $14 • (09/30/93) • **87**

Cabernet Sauvignon Paso Robles 1989 • $14 • (07/31/92) • **85**

Cabernet Sauvignon Paso Robles 1988 • $12 • (09/30/91) SS • **92**

Chardonnay Edna Valley 1993: Simple, offering a modest band of earth, spice and light pear flavors. • $14 • (04/30/95) • **85**

Chardonnay Edna Valley 1992: Firm and compact with an earthy edge to the ripe pear and spicy butterscotch flavors. Picks up an oaky edge on the finish. Young and unevolved, it can stand short-term cellaring. Drinkable now. Tasted twice.-JL • $14 • (06/30/94) • **86**

Chardonnay Edna Valley 1991 • $14 • (03/31/93) • **88**

Chardonnay Edna Valley Reserve 1994: Serves up a modest band of citrus and pineapple notes, becomes simple on the finish while maintaining the fruit. • $14 • (06/30/96) • **85**

Chardonnay Santa Barbara County 1994: Brimming with fresh, ripe pear, apricot, peach and spicy fruit flavors, a rich and forward style that leads into a pretty, creamy, fruity aftertaste. Hard to beat at this price-or even twice this price. 100,000 cases made. • $10 • (02/29/96) BB • **89**

Chardonnay Santa Barbara County 1993: Offers medium-weight pear, apple and spice notes that are ripe and pleasing. • $10 • (06/15/95) • **85**

Chardonnay Santa Barbara County 1992: Has an earthy edge but also a nice concentrated core of pear and pineapple flavor that picks up wood and citrus notes on the finish. Drink now.-JL • $10 • (03/15/94) • **85**

Chardonnay Santa Barbara County 1991 • $10 • (07/15/93) • **85**

Chardonnay Santa Barbara County Limited Release 1994: Soft and pillowy, a gentle wine with a nice core of apple and peach flavors. Drinkable now. • $17 • (06/30/96) • **86**

Merlot California 1993: Lovely currant and chocolate flavors. Finish is a bit coarse, as the tannins kick in. • $16 • **82**

Pinot Blanc Santa Barbara County 1993: Subtle with ripe pear, spice and a hint of orange blossom in the background. • $14 • (04/15/95) • **86**

Pinot Noir Edna Valley Reserve 1991 • $16 • (04/30/94) • **86**

Pinot Noir Santa Barbara County 1994: Elegant and well crafted, with refined notes of cherry, toasty oak, spice and subtle herbal qualities. An appealing young wine that drinks well now. • $14 • (03/31/96) • **86**

Pinot Noir Santa Barbara County 1992: Lean and fruity, with spice, cherry, herb and tea notes. Simple but well balanced. • $14 • (11/30/94) • **83**

Pinot Noir Santa Barbara County 1991 • $14 • (02/28/94) • **80**

Pinot Noir Santa Barbara County 1990 • $14 • (02/28/93) • **80**

Pinot Noir Santa Barbara County Riverbench Vineyard 1988 • $14 • (02/28/91) • **86**

Pinot Noir Santa Barbara County San Luis Obispo County 1993: Light with simple cherry, herb and berry notes, picking up an earthy edge on the finish. Ready now. • $14 • (09/15/95) • **82**

Pinot Noir Santa Barbara County San Luis Obispo County Reserve 1993: Refined and elegant, adding a spicy, peppery edge to the plum and black cherry flavors. Finishes with smooth tannins. Drinkable now. • $16 • (11/30/95) • **87**

Sauvignon Blanc California 1994: Lightly spicy, simple and pleasant enough, without any special qualities. • $8 • (06/15/96) • **79**

Sauvignon Blanc California 1993: Bright, fragrant, lively apple and pear flavors, shaded by a touch of herb, smooth finish. • $8 • (05/15/95) • **86**

Sauvignon Blanc California 1992 • $8 • (11/30/93) • **83**

Syrah Paso Robles 1991: Soft, broad and spicy, with jammy berry and pepper notes reverberating on the palate. Finishes tough, needing until 1997 to soften. • $14 • (07/31/94) • **83**

Syrah Paso Robles 1990 • $15 • (03/31/93) • **85**

Syrah Paso Robles 1988 • $14 • (03/31/91) • **91**

Zinfandel Paso Robles 1990 • $14 • (09/30/93) • **86**

Zinfandel Paso Robles 1989 • $9 • (10/15/92) • **85**

MERLION | CALIFORNIA

Cabernet Sauvignon Napa Valley 1986 • $17 • (11/15/90) • **84**

Cabernet Sauvignon Napa Valley 1985 • $14 • (08/31/88) • **85**

Pinot Noir Los Carneros Hyde Vineyards 1986 • $14 • (02/28/89) • **66**

MERRYVALE | CALIFORNIA

Cabernet Sauvignon Napa Valley 1992: Marked by an earthy, leathery edge, it regains its balance to reveal a dense core of currant and black cherry flavors, finishing with firm, chewy tannins. Needs until 1999 to soften and evolve. 2,400 cases made. • $24 • (12/15/95) • **88**

Cabernet Sauvignon Napa Valley 1991: Dense, chewy and tannic with a rich core of minty currant and mineral flavor. Tightly wound and compact, best after 1997. Tasted twice. 2,500 cases made. • $23 • (11/15/94) • **87**

Cabernet Sauvignon Napa Valley 1990: Ripe and round, with a generous streak of currant, plum and vanilla flavors running through the lively, youthful structure. Has the concentration to keep developing through 1997. • $20 • (06/30/93) • **88**

Cabernet Sauvignon Napa Valley 1989 • $16 • (10/31/92) SS • **92**

Cabernet Sauvignon Napa Valley 1988 • $18 • (07/15/91) • **86**

Cabernet Sauvignon Napa Valley Profile 1992: Dark, dense and chewy with a rich, solid and complex core of Cabernet fruit that's wrapped in tight, firm tannins. Intense and balanced, it should be a long-lived wine. • $NA • (05/31/93) BT • **90-94**

Cabernet Sauvignon Napa Valley Profile 1991: Smooth and polished up front, with supple currant, coffee, mineral and spice flavors before the substantial tannins kick in. Finishes with a hint of mint and drying tannins. Best to cellar into 1998. 1,430 cases made. • $36 • (12/15/95) • **90**

Cabernet Sauvignon Napa Valley Profile 1987 • $25 • (11/15/91) • **83**

Chardonnay Napa Valley Reserve 1993: Medium-bodied, with smoky, toasty oak and ripe pear flavors, elegant and refined for the vintage. Finishes with an appealing aftertaste. 2,500 cases made. • $25 • (07/31/95) • **88**

Chardonnay Napa Valley Reserve 1992: An awkward young wine with tart green pear and pineapple flavors. May fill out with time, as the finish shows more complexity and depth. Not up to par with the past Merryvale vintage. Tasted three times with consistent notes. 2,900 cases made. • $25 • (06/30/94) • **84**

Chardonnay Napa Valley Reserve 1991 • $25 • (05/31/93) • **91**

Chardonnay Napa Valley Silhouette 1993: Ripe, smooth and harmonious, with a complex core of honey, pear, toasty and vanilla notes, showing off a pretty array of flavors and smoky toasty oak. 900 cases made. • $36 • (05/31/96) • **89**

Chardonnay Napa Valley Starmont 1994: Starts out with subtle notes that gradually build into a more interesting wine, with ripe pear, apple, citrus and honey notes. Doesn't rely on heavy oak for its flavors. 10,000 cases made. • $16 • (05/31/96) • **88**

Chardonnay Napa Valley Starmont 1993: Appealing for its forward fruitiness, with ripe pear, peach and apple notes of modest depth, but not up to Merryvale's standards. 10,000 cases made. • $16 • (07/31/95) • **84**

Chardonnay Napa Valley Starmont 1992: A solid Chardonnay that balances ripe, spicy pear with toasty nutmeg and hazelnut flavors. Complex and concentrated, it drinks well now but can age short-term.-JL 10,000 cases made. • $16 • (06/30/94) • **88**

Chardonnay Napa Valley Starmont 1991 • $16 • (05/31/93) • **90**

Late Harvest Alexander Valley Solstice 1989 • $24 • (06/30/93) • **85**

Meritage Napa Valley 1993: A disappointment, showing way too much wood. Round and spicy, strongly marked by oak, with just a hint of herb behind the woody pear flavors. Ready now. 3,500 cases made. • $14 • (08/31/95) • **78**

Meritage Napa Valley 1992 • $13 • (09/15/93) • **87**

Meritage Napa Valley 1991 • $12 • (11/30/92) • **87**

Merlot Napa Valley 1992: Strikes a pleasant balance between ripe cherry and plum flavors, but the tannins are somewhat rugged and chewy. Should soften by 1997. 3,000 cases made. • $24 • (09/30/95) • **85**

Merlot Napa Valley 1991: Tight and firm, striking a nice balance between oak, currant and bay leaf flavors that turn austere and tannic on the finish. Best to cellar a year or two in hopes it softens and develops. 1,200 cases made. • $28 • (09/15/94) • **84**

Merlot Napa Valley 1990 • $18 • (12/15/92) • **85**

Merlot Napa Valley 1989 • $16 • (05/31/92) • **84**

Muscat de Frontignan Napa Valley Antigua NV • $12 • (11/30/91) • **86**

Profile Napa Valley 1990: Rustic with a strong oaky edge and earthy leathery flavors, turning bitter. 1,300 cases made. • $36 • (12/15/95) • **78**

Profile Napa Valley 1989 • $30 • (06/30/93) • **86**

Profile Napa Valley 1988 • $25 • (11/15/92) • **85**

Red Table Wine Napa Valley 1986 • $24 • (10/15/90) • **86**

Red Table Wine Napa Valley 1985 • $24 • (03/01/89) • **91**

Red Table Wine Napa Valley 1984 • $24 • (03/01/89) • **86**

Red Table Wine Napa Valley 1983 • $18 • (03/01/89) • **88**

Sauvignon Blanc Napa Valley 1993: Simple and fruity, sturdy enough to carry through the spicy pineapple flavors on the finish. 4,300 cases made. • $10 • (06/30/95) • **83**

Sauvignon Blanc Napa Valley 1992 • $9 • (09/15/93) • **83**

MESSINA HOF | TEXAS

Cabernet Sauvignon Texas Barrel Reserve 1989 • $10 • (03/15/93) • **84**

Cabernet Sauvignon Texas Private Reserve 1990: Lean and herbal, a lithe red with appealing spice and mint flavors. 800 cases made. • $15 • (01/31/95) • **81**

Pinot Noir Texas Reflections 1991 • $10 • (02/28/93) • **80**

Reflections 1988 • $15 • (02/29/92) • **77**

MICHAEL, PETER | CALIFORNIA

Cabernet Sauvignon Knights Valley Les Pavots 1992: Defines elegance with its supple texture, fine balance and pretty currant and cherry flavors. Finishes with a nice dose of creamy oak and fine tannins. Has a complex aftertaste. • $29 • (12/15/95) • **90**

Cabernet Sauvignon Knights Valley Les Pavots 1991: Turns earthy and leathery and somewhat gamy, but there's enough currant and cherry flavor to maintain a delicate balance. 1,400 cases made. • $26 • (05/15/95) • **87**

Cabernet Sauvignon Knights Valley Les Pavots 1989 • $24 • (12/15/92) • **79**

Cabernet Sauvignon Knights Valley Les Pavots 1988 • $25 • (11/15/91) • **90**

Chardonnay Napa County Clos du Ciel 1994: Pleasant, spicy notes accent the ripe pear and honey flavors that glide into an elegant finish. 2,800 cases made. • $32 • (06/15/96) • **87**

Chardonnay Napa County Clos du Ciel 1992: Smooth, elegant and polished, with pretty pear, honey, hazelnut and floral notes that are rich and focused, finishing with a long, lingering aftertaste. Picks up a hint of vanilla and spice on the finish. • $26 • (06/30/94) • **91**

Chardonnay Napa County Clos du Ciel 1991 • $25 • (07/15/93) • **88**

Chardonnay Sonoma County Cuvée Indigène 1993: A Chardonnay of elegance and finesse, with subtle hints of ripe pear, hazelnut, spice and citrus. This is especially attractive for its aftertaste that echoes fruit and oak. A classy wine from start to finish. • $40 • (01/31/96) • **93**

Chardonnay Sonoma County Mon Plaisir 1993: Beautifully crafted, with ripe, rich, complex pear, peach, honey and hazelnut flavors, gaining complexity and nuance with subtle buttery oak flavors. A rich and complex wine that's delicious now, but will improve over the next year. • $35 • (01/31/96) • **93**

MICHAEL'S | CALIFORNIA

Cabernet Sauvignon Napa Valley Summit Vineyard Reserve 1984 • $15 • (03/31/88) • **75**

MICHAELS, RICHARD | CALIFORNIA

Cabernet Sauvignon California 1985 • $10 • (09/30/88) • **78**

MICHEL, DOMAINE | CALIFORNIA

Cabernet Sauvignon Dry Creek Valley Michel Vineyard Reserve 1988 • $25 • (11/15/93) • **81**

Cabernet Sauvignon Sonoma County 1992: Rich, intense and potent with layers of spicy black cherry and currant-scented fruit. A chewy, tannic finish gives you a mouthful of Cabernet. • $NA • (05/31/93) BT • **888**

Cabernet Sauvignon Sonoma County 1990: Tough and oaky, with hints of currant and berry on the finish, could use more generosity. Tasted twice. 6,200 cases made. • $12 • (11/15/94) • **79**

Cabernet Sauvignon Sonoma County 1989 • $15 • (11/15/93) • **81**

Cabernet Sauvignon Sonoma County 1988 • $19 • (03/31/93) • **82**

Cabernet Sauvignon Sonoma County 1987 • $20 • (08/31/92) • **81**

Key: SS—Spectator Selection. CS—Cellar Selection. BB—Best Buy. $NA—Price not available. (BT)—Barrel tasting. Ⓐ—Auction Price.
Dates in parentheses represent the issues in which the ratings were published.

Cabernet Sauvignon Sonoma County 1986 • $19 • (06/30/90) • **75**

Cabernet Sauvignon Sonoma County 1984 • $19 • (09/15/87) • **86**

Chardonnay Dry Creek Valley 1991 • $13 • (02/28/94) • **79**

Merlot Dry Creek Valley 1991: Lean and hard, with a tannic, narrow band of fruit that dries out on the finish. Needs a little more stuffing, but it's typical of the Domaine Michel wines. 400 cases made. • $15 • (09/15/94) • **80**

MICHEL-SCHLUMBERGER | CALIFORNIA

Cabernet Sauvignon Dry Creek Valley 1991: Ripe and spicy showing a grapey Cabernet edge, but it doesn't take off from there. Finishes with dry tannins and oaky notes. 2,600 cases made. • $18 • (11/15/94) • **81**

Cabernet Sauvignon Dry Creek Valley Reserve 1990: Austere and tannic with an oaky edge, but just enough currant and cherry flavor emerges to hold your attention. Best after 1997. 440 cases made. • $35 • (11/15/94) • **82**

Cabernet Sauvignon Sonoma County 1994: Somewhat unfocused, but the fruit is ripe and it's well balanced, coming across as simple at this point. • $35 • (05/31/95) • **85-89** (BT)

Chardonnay Dry Creek Valley 1992: Lean and smoky, offering a tight, thin band of spice and pear flavor that fades on the finish. 1,800 cases made. • $18 • (03/31/95) • **83**

MIETZ | CALIFORNIA

Merlot Sonoma County 1994: Simple, with uncomplicated cherry, cedar and oak flavors. 2,250 cases made. • $18 • (06/30/96) • **82**

Merlot Sonoma County 1993: Tannic with a green herbal edge to the modest core of plum and berry fruit, but overall the impression is of barely ripe fruit. 1,855 cases made. • $17 • **81**

Merlot Sonoma County 1990 • $14 • (11/30/92) • **81**

Merlot Sonoma County 1989 • $14 • (04/15/92) • **91**

MILANO | CALIFORNIA

Cabernet Sauvignon Mendocino County Sanel Valley Vineyard 1985 • $18 • (09/30/89) • **80**

Cabernet Sauvignon Mendocino County Sanel Valley Vineyard 1982 • $13 • (12/15/87) • **83**

Zinfandel Mendocino County 1981 • $6 • (10/01/84) • **80**

Zinfandel Mendocino County Sanel Valley Vineyard 1993: Intense and well-focused cherry, wild berry and raspberry notes are ripe, elegant and supple. 400 cases made. • $10 • (10/15/95) • **85**

Zinfandel Mendocino County Sanel Valley Vineyard 1990: Ripe, supple, fruity flavors with notes of maturity. Turns soft and fleshy on the finish. Ready now through 1997. 500 cases made. • $8 • (09/15/94) • **85**

Zinfandel Mendocino County Sanel Valley Vineyard 1988 • $8 • (04/30/91) • **85**

MILAT | CALIFORNIA

Cabernet Sauvignon Napa Valley 1990: Ripe and intense, showing a spicy, minty edge to the cherry and plum notes. Finishes with crisp tannins, so cellaring should soften it a bit. Best after 1997. 433 cases made. • $14 • (11/15/94) • **83**

MILL CREEK | CALIFORNIA

Cabernet Sauvignon Dry Creek Valley 1992: Ripe and ready, generous with its plum and currant fruit, wrapped in a cloak of minty, leafy, herbal notes. Modest tannins need until 1997. 550 cases made. • $12 • (12/15/95) • **85**

Cabernet Sauvignon Dry Creek Valley 1991: Firm and tight, with a narrow band of herb, currant and berry notes. Cellar until 1997. 570 cases made. • $12 • (11/15/94) • **83**

Cabernet Sauvignon Dry Creek Valley 1990: There's a slight beam of spicy berry fruit peeking through this otherwise earthy, oaky young Cabernet. Needs food to soften the round edges. Tasted twice. 464 cases made. • $12 • (11/15/93) • **74**

Cabernet Sauvignon Dry Creek Valley 1988 • $12 • (11/15/91) • **78**

Cabernet Sauvignon Dry Creek Valley 1982 • $9 • (06/15/88) • **68**

Chardonnay Dry Creek Valley 1994: Light and bright, with nectarine and spice flavors that linger nicely on the finish. Tasty now, best from 1997. 1,559 cases made. • $12 • (06/30/96) • **86**
Chardonnay Dry Creek Valley 1993: Up-front fruitness is appealing as apple, pear and spice flavors turn a touch coarse on the finish. 1,000 cases made. • $12 • (05/15/95) • **87**
Chardonnay Dry Creek Valley 1992: A bit heavy-handed with toasty, buttery oak, but there's enough pear, apple and vanilla flavor to match, making it more interesting on the finish, where the flavors spread out. Drink now.-JL 1,070 cases made. • $12 • (02/28/94) • **87**
Gewürztraminer Dry Creek Valley 1993: Soft and lively, brightly fruity, offering pear and spicy-floral aromas and flavors. 725 cases made. • $7 • (02/28/95) • **84**
Gewürztraminer Dry Creek Valley 1992 • $7 • (09/30/93) • **82**
Gewürztraminer North Coast 1994: Soft, off-dry and appealing for its rose petal fragrance and light pear notes. 742 cases made. • $8 • (06/15/96) • **83**
Merlot Dry Creek Valley 1994: Achieves a nice balance between its ripe cherry and currant flavors and light oak shadings. Impressive finish. 5,896 cases made. • $14 • **86**
Merlot Dry Creek Valley 1993: Smoky, toasty oak notes add dimension to the ripe cherry and plum flavors. 2,848 cases made. • $14 • **84**
Merlot Dry Creek Valley 1991: Oaky and leathery, with ripe currant and cherry flavor underneath. Needs short-term cellaring for the tannins to soften. Best after 1996. 3,000 cases made. • $12 • (09/15/94) • **83**
Merlot Dry Creek Valley 1990 • $14 • (10/15/93) • **84**
Merlot Dry Creek Valley 1989 • $12 • (03/31/93) • **82**
Merlot Dry Creek Valley 1988 • $12 • (05/31/92) • **77**
Merlot Dry Creek Valley 1987 • $12 • (11/15/91) • **84**
Merlot Dry Creek Valley 1984 • $8 • (02/15/88) • **68**
Merlot Dry Creek Valley 1983 • $9 • (10/01/85) • **80**
Merlot Dry Creek Valley 1982 • $8 • (04/01/85) • **85**
Pinot Noir Dry Creek Valley 1982 • $6 • (08/31/86) • **71**
Sauvignon Blanc Dry Creek Valley 1994: Smooth and spicy, balancing crisp grapefruit against spicy oak in a light- to medium-weight wine. 2,150 cases made. • $8 • (10/31/95) • **86**
Sauvignon Blanc Dry Creek Valley 1993: Smooth and spicy, balancing crisp grapefruit against spicy oak in a light- to medium-weight wine. Drinkable now. 1,184 cases made. • $8 • (10/15/94) BB • **86**

MILLBROOK | NEW YORK

Cabernet Franc Hudson River Region 1993: 800 cases made. • $14 • **55**
Cabernet Sauvignon Hudson River Region Proprietor's Special Reserve 1993: Fairly rich with a nice mix of herbal and plum flavors. Tannic with a lingering finish that has some nice spice nuances. A ripe and well-rounded wine. 260 cases made. • $17 • (12/31/95) • **85**
Chardonnay Central Coast Mistral Vineyard 1993: A serious Chardonnay from the toasty aromas to the ripe and layered fruit to the lasting finish. Fine balance, a touch of oak flavor and velvety texture add to its appeal. 1,750 cases made. • $8 • (02/28/95) • **89**
Chardonnay Hudson River Region 1992: There's an earthy edge to the buttery aromas and flavors. Good, but somewhat short and a bit coarse on the finish. 6,100 cases made. • $11 • (02/28/95) • **80**
Chardonnay Hudson River Region Proprietor's Special Reserve 1993: An exotic style of Chardonnay with effusive honey and apricot flavors and a rich texture. Mellow, nutty nuances develop on the long finish, indicating a wine with depth and some aging potential. Drinkable now. 1,200 cases made. • $16 • (02/28/95) • **88**
Pinot Noir Central Coast Mistral Vineyard 1993: A ripe and fruity Pinot with black cherry and tea flavors and a touch of leather. Full-bodied and balanced, but a little murky. • $9 • (11/15/94) • **80**

MILLSTREAM | CALIFORNIA

Cabernet Sauvignon California 1993: Smooth and exuberantly fruity, wheeling its raspberry, tobacco and spice flavors through the polished finish. Ready now. 3,000 cases made. • $5 • (12/15/95) • **84**

MIRABELLE | CALIFORNIA

Brut North Coast NV • $12 • (05/15/92) • **84**

MIRASSOU | CALIFORNIA

Blanc de Noirs Cuvée 1989 • $13 • (05/15/92) • **82**
Blanc de Noirs Monterey 1983 • $11 • (12/31/88) • **69**
Blanc de Noirs Monterey 1982 • $10 • (08/31/87) • **66**
Blanc de Noirs Monterey Cuvée 1987 • $12 • (11/15/91) • **77**
Brut Blanc de Noirs Monterey Fifth Generation Cuvée 1991 • $14 • (12/31/93) • **80**
Brut Monterey 1983 • $10 • (07/31/88) • **66**
Brut Monterey 1982 • $12 • (09/16/85) • **78**
Brut Monterey Au Naturel Fifth Generation Cuvée Reserve 1989 • $14 • (12/31/93) • **82**
Brut Monterey County 1987 • $13 • (12/31/91) • **76**
Brut Monterey County Fifth Generation Cuvée 1991: Ripe and intense, showing a slight green edge to the flavors and some coarseness in texture. Good, but lacking the extra dimensions. 10,000 cases made. • $12 • **84**
Brut Monterey Cuvée 1989 • $13 • (12/31/92) • **87**
Brut Monterey Cuvée 1988 • $13 • (05/15/92) • **78**
Brut Monterey Cuvée 1984 • $12 • (06/15/91) • **84**
Brut Monterey Cuvée Reserve 1985 • $15 • (12/31/92) • **82**
Brut Monterey Cuvée Reserve 1984 • $15 • (12/31/91) • **85**
Brut Monterey Fifth Generation Cuvée 1990 • $12 • (07/31/93) • **83**
Brut Monterey Fifth Generation Cuvée Reserve 1988 • $14 • (12/31/93) • **73**
Brut Monterey Reserve 1983 • $15 • (12/31/89) • **76**
Cabernet Sauvignon California Family Selection 1986 • $9 • (05/31/91) • **83**
Cabernet Sauvignon Monterey County Fifth Generation Family Selection 1991: Marked by earthy, gamy, vegetal flavors, with green tannins. 12,800 cases made. • $9 • (12/15/95) • **74**
Cabernet Sauvignon Monterey County Fifth Generation Family Selection 1990: Solid and medium-bodied, showing ample fruit flavors and not-too-heavy tannins. A deep color, eucalyptus aromas and black cherry flavors give it good substance and balance. Drink now. • $9 • (09/15/93) • **81**
Cabernet Sauvignon Monterey County Fifth Generation Harvest Reserve 1991: Minty and fresh, with ripe berry flavors running through the velvety structure, making it drinkable now. Finish is long enough to want until 1997-1998. 2,137 cases made. • $12 • (12/15/95) • **87**
Cabernet Sauvignon Monterey County Fifth Generation Harvest Reserve Limited 1990: Austere for a 1990 with crisp herb and currant flavors that thin out on the finish. A ready-to-drink now style. 3,397 cases made. • $12 • (11/15/93) • **79**
Cabernet Sauvignon Monterey County Harvest Reserve 1988 • $13 • (11/15/92) • **76**
Cabernet Sauvignon Monterey County Harvest Reserve 1987 • $13 • (11/15/91) • **86**
Cabernet Sauvignon Monterey County Harvest Reserve 1986 • $13 • (07/31/91) • **60**
Cabernet Sauvignon Napa Valley Harvest Reserve 1985 • $12 • (11/15/89) • **81**
Cabernet Sauvignon Napa Valley Harvest Reserve 1983 • $12 • (12/15/86) • **67**
Cabernet Sauvignon Napa Valley Harvest Reserve 1982 • $12 • (04/16/86) • **82**
Cabernet Sauvignon North Coast 1982 • $7 • (10/16/85) BB • **82**
Chardonnay Monterey County Family Selection 1991: Crisp and fruity with light oak shadings and a hint of pear and spice.-JL 19,000 cases made. • $9 • (06/30/94) • **79**
Chardonnay Monterey County Fifth Generation Family Selection 1994: Light, fragrant and supple, showing off lovely pear, spice and toast flavors that swirl deliciously and elegantly through the finish. 16,500 cases made. • $11 • (06/15/96) • **88**
Chardonnay Monterey County Fifth Generation Harvest Reserve 1993: Well focused, with good intensity to the ripe pear, apple and honeyed notes and pretty oak shadings. Impressive for its fruit and balance. 5,593 cases made. • $12 • (07/31/95) • **87**
Chardonnay Monterey County Fifth Generation Harvest Reserve 1992: Strikes a pleasant balance between ripe pear, fig and smoky oak flavors, with a long, lingering aftertaste. Another impressive Mirassou Chardonnay. 5,300 cases made. • $12 • (07/31/95) • **87**

■ ■ ■ ■

MISSION CANYON

Chardonnay Monterey County Harvest Reserve 1992: Combines intensity with richness and flavor, ripe, spicy pear, toast, butter and honeyed notes linger. Turns elegant on the finish.-JL 5,300 cases made. • $12 • (05/31/94) • **85**

Chardonnay Monterey County Harvest Reserve 1991 • $12 • (05/31/94) • **83**

Chardonnay Santa Clara County 140th Anniversary Selection Anniversary Bottling 1992: Tight and well focused, with a pretty toasty oak frame around the spicy fig and pear flavors. Well crafted. 1,212 cases made. • $14 • (07/31/95) • **87**

Chenin Blanc Monterey County Fifth Generation Family Selection Dry 1993: Lively, citrusy and generous. A dry wine with appealing orange and pear flavors that linger. Drinkable now. 3,300 cases made. • $6 • (06/30/95) • **85**

Johannisberg Riesling Late Harvest Monterey Fifth Generation Harvest Reserve Select 1992 • $13 • (04/15/94) • **85**

Johannisberg Riesling Late Harvest Monterey Select Harvest Reserve 1987 • $13 • (08/31/91) • **87**

Merlot Central Coast Family Selection 1991 • $9 • (06/15/93) • **80**

Merlot Central Coast Fifth Generation Family Selection 1992: Bright and floral, the currant flavors sneaking in on the slightly tannic finish. Best from 1997. 9,453 cases made. • $9 • (04/15/95) • **84**

Merlot Central Coast Fifth Generation Family Selection 1991: Soft and fruity, simple, with pleasant currant flavor that lingers. 10,200 cases made. • $9 • (09/15/94) • **84**

Merlot Monterey County Family Selection 1990 • $9 • (03/31/93) • **80**

Natural Cuvée Au Naturel 1988 • $15 • (05/15/92) • **85**

Natural Monterey Cuvée Au Naturel 1989 • $15 • (12/31/92) • **72**

Natural Monterey Cuvée Au Naturel 1987 • $15 • (11/15/91) • **85**

Natural Monterey Cuvée Au Naturel 1984 • $15 • (06/15/91) • **83**

Petite Sirah Monterey County Family Selection 1989 • $7 • (03/15/92) • **79**

Petite Sirah Monterey County Family Selection Commemorative Bottling 1990 • $9 • (03/31/93) • **75**

Petite Sirah Monterey County Fifth Generation Family Selection 1991: A little coarse in texture, but the flavors of berry and pepper are true. Drinkable now. 4,984 cases made. • $9 • (02/28/95) • **81**

Pinot Blanc Monterey County Family Selection 1991 • $7 • (01/31/93) BB • **86**

Pinot Blanc Monterey County Fifth Generation Family Selection White 1993: Light but sturdy, with a tarry, spicy edge to the basic pear fruit. Ready now. 32,325 cases made. • $7 • (04/15/95) • **81**

Pinot Blanc Monterey County Fifth Generation Harvest Reserve 1993: Medium in body and a touch earthy, with a touch of juniper berry to the ripe pear notes. 3,200 cases made. • $12 • (08/31/95) • **82**

Pinot Blanc Monterey County Harvest Reserve 1991 • $12 • (06/15/93) • **86**

Pinot Noir Monterey County 1990 • $7 • (09/30/92) • **72**

Pinot Noir Monterey County Family Selection 1990 • $7 • (02/28/93) • **75**

Pinot Noir Monterey County Family Selection 1988 • $7 • (04/30/91) BB • **81**

Pinot Noir Monterey County Fifth Generation Family Selection 1992: Light, straightforward, modest in flavor, offering some nice plum and toast flavors. 5,600 cases made. • $7 • **80**

Pinot Noir Monterey County Fifth Generation Harvest Reserve 1992: Ripe but gentle, adding a coffee-cola edge to the black cherry flavor as texture becomes velvety on the finish. 2,244 cases made. • $12 • (10/15/95) • **86**

Pinot Noir Monterey County Fifth Generation Harvest Reserve Limited 1991: Lean and trim, with meaty, smoky overtones to the berry flavors, turning tannic on the finish. Drinkable now. 1,884 cases made. • $12 • (03/31/95) • **83**

Pinot Noir Monterey County Harvest Reserve 1989 • $13 • (09/30/92) • **80**

Pinot Noir Monterey County Harvest Reserve 1988 • $13 • (04/30/92) • **84**

Pinot Noir Monterey County Harvest Reserve 1986 • $12 • (04/30/91) • **78**

Sauvignon Blanc California 1993: Soft and simple, showing nice grapefruit and floral flavors that linger on the finish. 18,000 cases made. • $6 • (08/31/95) • **85**

Sauvignon Blanc California 1992: Simple and soft, an appealing white wine with a slight herbal edge. 20,000 cases made. • $5 • (06/30/94) BB • **80**

White Zinfandel California 1994: Very fruity, offering some body and zippy acidity. Only a hint of sweetness, nice strawberry and cherry flavors. 12,458 cases made. • $10 • (09/15/95) • **82**

White Zinfandel California 1988 • $6 • (06/15/89) • **75**

Zinfandel California 1989 • $5 • (04/30/93) • **72**

Zinfandel California Dry Red Lot No. 3 NV • $5 • (07/31/91) • **73**

Zinfandel California Lot No. 4 NV • $5 • (07/31/91) BB • **81**

Zinfandel California Lot No. 6 NV • $5 • (09/15/92) • **73**

Zinfandel Central Coast Fifth Generation Family Selection 1992: On the lighter side, both in color and body, but has appealing cherry and berry notes of modest proportions. 2,500 cases made. • $7 • (08/31/95) • **83**

Zinfandel Santa Clara Valley Fifth Generation Harvest Reserve 1992: A claret style, medium-bodied, toasty nuances and with cherry and berry notes. 783 cases made. • $12 • (10/15/95) • **83**

Zinfandel Santa Clara Valley Fifth Generation Harvest Reserve Limited 1991: Earthy and gamy, with a strong woody edge to the flavors. Ready now. 1,400 cases made. • $12 • (10/15/94) • **79**

Zinfandel Santa Clara Valley Harvest Reserve 1990 • $13 • (03/15/93) • **82**

Zinfandel Santa Clara Valley Harvest Reserve 1988 • $13 • (10/15/92) • **85**

MISSION CANYON | CALIFORNIA

Chardonnay Santa Barbara County 1994: Round and herbal, with pine-like nuances adding to the apple and spice flavors. 400 cases made. • $9 • (06/15/96) • **84**

Chardonnay Santa Barbara County 1993: Lean and simple with a narrow band of spicy fruit. 1,850 cases made. • $8 • (07/31/95) • **79**

MISSION MOUNTAIN | WASHINGTON

Cabernet Sauvignon Columbia Valley 1990: Chewy and lean, a strong mint and herbal streak runs past the austere, modest berry flavors. Try in 1997. 420 cases made. • $15 • (03/31/95) • **79**

MISSION VIEW | CALIFORNIA

Cabernet Sauvignon Paso Robles 1990: Straightforward style with ripe currant and cherry notes. Drinks well now. 691 cases made. • $12 • (11/15/94) • **82**

Cabernet Sauvignon Paso Robles 1989 • $12 • (11/15/92) • **85**

Cabernet Sauvignon Paso Robles 1988 • $12 • (11/15/92) • **86**

Cabernet Sauvignon Paso Robles 1986 • $12 • (12/15/89) • **72**

Chardonnay Paso Robles 1995: A strong resiny streak cuts through the spicy fruit flavors in this oaky white. 1,074 cases made. • $10 • (06/15/96) • **79**

Chardonnay Paso Robles 1994: Soft and fragrant, a chunky white which adds a spicy, perfumy edge to the pear and orange flavors. Ready now. 294 cases made. • $10 • (10/31/95) • **85**

Chardonnay San Luis Obispo 1993: Dull and a bit earthy, but it's palatable. 196 cases made. • $10 • (07/31/95) • **77**

Fumé Blanc Paso Robles Barrel Fermented & Aged 1994: Smooth and fruity, appealing for its sweet apple and lightly herbal flavors. 305 cases made. • $9 • (09/15/95) • **84**

Merlot Paso Robles Limited Release 1992: Light with an herbal edge to the modest cherry and berry fruit. 217 cases made. • $14 • (06/15/95) • **76**

Pinot Noir Monterey County Limited Release 1990 • $14 • (02/28/93) • **77**

Sauvignon Blanc Paso Robles 1995: Soft, smooth and decidedly vegetal, offering more green pepper and celery than fruit. 1,072 cases made. • $9 • (06/15/96) • **79**

Sauvignon Blanc San Luis Obispo 1993: Oddly vegetal, with a celery-like edge to the modest apple fruit. 209 cases made. • $9 • (08/31/95) • **78**

Zinfandel Paso Robles 1993: Ripe with a supple core of jammy cherry and plum-laced fruit, a distinctive style that pushes the ripeness. 230 cases made. • $12 • **85**

Zinfandel Paso Robles 1990 • $11 • (09/30/93) • **81**

Key: SS—Spectator Selection. CS—Cellar Selection. BB—Best Buy. $NA—Price not available. (BT)—Barrel tasting. (A)—Auction Price.
Dates in parentheses represent the issues in which the ratings were published.

MISTY MOUNTAIN | VIRGINIA

Cabernet Sauvignon Virginia 1988 • $18 • (02/29/92) • **82**
Merlot Virginia 1988 • $18 • (02/29/92) • **77**

MITCHELL, CHARLES B. | CALIFORNIA

Cabernet Sauvignon El Dorado Reserve 1993: Light and straightforward, with an earthy edge to the modest strawberry flavors. 157 cases made. • $14 • (12/15/95) • **80**
Chenin Blanc El Dorado Dry 1994: Soft and a little sweet, with an off-flavor component that kills the fruit. 250 cases made. • $6 • (06/15/96) • **77**
Fumé Blanc El Dorado 1994: Pear and spice flavors are soft, fruity and pleasant. 350 cases made. • $7 • (08/31/95) • **82**
Port California NV: Big and rangy, a chewy wine with black cherry, anise and coffee flavors, not terribly sweet, finishing with a touch of cola. A bit soft. 1,000 cases made. • $15 • (06/15/96) • **83**
Sauvignon Blanc El Dorado 1993: Soft, generous vanilla-scented pear and slightly leafy green berry flavors. 800 cases made. • $6 • (08/31/95) • **83**

MONDAVI, CK | CALIFORNIA

Cabernet Sauvignon California 1993: Light and gently fruity, hinting at plum and currant on the modest finish. • $6 • (12/15/95) • **80**
Cabernet Sauvignon Napa Valley 1983 • $4 • (10/15/87) • **65**
Chardonnay California 1994: Soft, fruity and appealing for its snappy tropical fruit and floral flavors. Ready now. 36,000 cases made. • $6 • (05/15/96) • **80**
Chardonnay California 1992: Tastes more like an off-dry Chenin Blanc, but it delivers ripe pear and apple flavors that are pleasant enough. Ready now.-JL 86,500 cases made. • $6 • (06/30/94) • **79**
Sauvignon Blanc California 1992: Simple, slightly sweet and fruity, floral notes on the finish. 9,900 cases made. • $5 • (08/31/94) • **78**
White Zinfandel California 1988 • $5 • (06/15/89) • **85**
Zinfandel California 1992: A solid Zin, with an earthy, barnyardy edge that adds an interesting dimension. Ready now. 4,900 cases made. • $5 • (10/15/94) • **81**
Zinfandel California 1991: Earthy, with a barnyardy streak in the ripe cherry and plum flavors. Finishes with fine tannins. Ready now. • $5 • (10/15/94) • **79**

MONDAVI, ROBERT | CALIFORNIA

Barbera California La Famiglia di Robert Mondavi 1993: Supple and lively, medium-bodied, with plum, black cherry and cedar flavors. Drinkable now. 212 cases made. • $15 • (08/31/95) • **85**
Brut Napa Valley Chardonnay Reserve 1987 • $28 • (12/31/93) • **86**
Brut Napa Valley Chardonnay Reserve 1985 • $35 • (12/31/91) • **85**
Brut Napa Valley Reserve 1987 • $28 • (12/31/93) • **90**
Brut Napa Valley Reserve 1985 • $35 • (12/31/91) • **90**
Cabernet Sauvignon 1992: Supple and harmonious, with rich, earthy currant, cherry and sage notes. Shows fine depth and concentration with a long, full finish and plush tannins. Can age until 1998 or '99 to soften. • $28 • (09/30/95) • **91**
Cabernet Sauvignon California Cabernet 1986 • $5 • (12/15/88) BB • **80**
Cabernet Sauvignon California Cabernet 1985 • $4 • (10/31/87) BB • **78**
Cabernet Sauvignon California Woodbridge 1992: An herbal style, with spicy currant and berry notes. Simple but appealing. 500,000 cases made. • $6 • (11/15/94) BB • **82**
Cabernet Sauvignon California Woodbridge 1991: Herbal and oaky with weedy currant flavors that turn earthy and bitter on the finish. Drinkable now. 450,000 cases made. • $7 • (11/15/93) • **80**
Cabernet Sauvignon California Woodbridge 1990: Soft and simple, with herb, cherry and berry flavors that seem sweet on the finish. Drinkable, but not interesting. • $8 • (10/31/92) • **81**
Cabernet Sauvignon California Woodbridge 1988 • $6 • (02/28/91) BB • **81**
Cabernet Sauvignon California Woodbridge 1987 • $6 • (09/15/89) • **74**
Cabernet Sauvignon Napa Valley 1990: Dark, dense and tannic, but remarkably supple for such a big wine, offering lots of currant, cherry and bitter almond flavors, finishing with a bite that will need until 1998-2003 to soften. 103,000 cases made. • $15 • (10/31/93) SS • **90**
Cabernet Sauvignon Napa Valley 1989 • $18 • (03/31/93) • **84**
Cabernet Sauvignon Napa Valley 1988 • $18 • (11/15/92) • **84**
Cabernet Sauvignon Napa Valley 1987 • $46 Ⓐ • (05/31/90) • **87**
Cabernet Sauvignon Napa Valley 1986 • $35 • (07/31/89) • **93**
Cabernet Sauvignon Napa Valley 1985 • $27 Ⓐ • (12/15/88) SS • **94**
Cabernet Sauvignon Napa Valley 1984 • $31 • (12/31/87) • **80**
Cabernet Sauvignon Napa Valley 1983 • $26 • (04/15/87) • **94**
Cabernet Sauvignon Napa Valley 1982 • $26 • (07/01/85) • **90**
Cabernet Sauvignon Napa Valley 1981 • $27 • (12/16/84) • **90**
Cabernet Sauvignon Napa Valley 1979 • $29 • (07/16/85) • **85**
Cabernet Sauvignon Napa Valley 1978 • $26 Ⓐ • (11/15/92) • **86**
Cabernet Sauvignon Napa Valley 1977 • $17 Ⓐ • (07/16/85) • **89**
Cabernet Sauvignon Napa Valley 1976 • $40 • (07/16/85) • **84**
Cabernet Sauvignon Napa Valley 1975 • $35 • (11/30/91) • **85**
Cabernet Sauvignon Napa Valley 1974 • $30 Ⓐ • (02/15/90) • **79**
Cabernet Sauvignon Napa Valley 1973 • $24 Ⓐ • (07/16/85) • **86**
Cabernet Sauvignon Napa Valley 1972 • $30 • (03/01/89) • **75**
Cabernet Sauvignon Napa Valley 1971 • $43 • (07/16/85) • **87**
Cabernet Sauvignon Napa Valley 1970 • $90 • (11/30/91) • **92**
Cabernet Sauvignon Napa Valley 1969 • $60 • (11/30/91) • **91**
Cabernet Sauvignon Napa Valley 1968 • $81 • (11/30/91) • **88**
Cabernet Sauvignon Napa Valley 1967 • $70 • (11/30/91) • **79**
Cabernet Sauvignon Napa Valley 1966 • $110 • (11/30/91) • **88**
Cabernet Sauvignon Napa Valley Reserve 1994: Dark with a rich, elegant core of currant and cherry, turning supple with polished tannnins. • $NA • (05/31/95) • **90-94** (BT)
Cabernet Sauvignon Napa Valley Reserve 1992: Dense and compact, with a tightly wound, rich core of earthy currant, cedar, spice and cherry flavors, finishing with chewy tannins. Great length, but will need to age at least until 1998. 18,000 cases made. • $55 • (07/31/95) CS • **91**
Cabernet Sauvignon Napa Valley Reserve 1991: Dense, compact and tightly wound, showing a rich, focused beam of minty currant and chocolate flavors. Complex, concentrated and firmly tannic, it needs cellaring to soften, best after 1996. Tasted twice with one bottle superior to the other. 16,811 cases made. • $56 • (11/15/94) • **90**
Cabernet Sauvignon Napa Valley Reserve 1990: Deeply colored and richly flavored, this one offers an intriguing array of spicy black cherry, currant, mineral and cedary oak flavors that keep on repeating themselves on a long, full, tannic finish. Tempting now for its fruit velocity, it should age well through the decade. Start drinking in 1998. 17,000 cases made. • $55 • (10/31/93) • **91**
Cabernet Sauvignon Napa Valley Reserve 1989 • $19 Ⓐ • (11/15/92) • **85**
Cabernet Sauvignon Napa Valley Reserve 1988 • $26 Ⓐ • (11/30/91) • **91**
Cabernet Sauvignon Napa Valley Reserve 1987 • $74 Ⓐ • (11/30/91) • **94**
Cabernet Sauvignon Napa Valley Reserve 1986 • $44 Ⓐ • (11/30/91) • **95**
Cabernet Sauvignon Napa Valley Reserve 1985 • $55 Ⓐ • (11/30/91) • **94**
Cabernet Sauvignon Napa Valley Reserve 1984 • $40 Ⓐ • (11/30/91) • **90**
Cabernet Sauvignon Napa Valley Reserve 1983 • $22 Ⓐ • (11/30/91) • **82**
Cabernet Sauvignon Napa Valley Reserve 1982 • $21 Ⓐ • (11/30/91) • **82**
Cabernet Sauvignon Napa Valley Reserve 1981 • $26 Ⓐ • (11/30/91) • **85**
Cabernet Sauvignon Napa Valley Reserve 1980 • $18 Ⓐ • (11/30/91) • **86**
Cabernet Sauvignon Napa Valley Reserve 1979 • $30 Ⓐ • (11/30/91) • **91**
Cabernet Sauvignon Napa Valley Reserve 1978 • $57 Ⓐ • (11/15/92) • **91**
Cabernet Sauvignon Napa Valley Reserve 1977 • $28 Ⓐ • (11/30/91) • **89**
Cabernet Sauvignon Napa Valley Reserve 1976 • $27 Ⓐ • (11/30/91) • **84**
Cabernet Sauvignon Napa Valley Reserve 1975 • $34 Ⓐ • (03/01/89) • **86**
Cabernet Sauvignon Napa Valley Reserve 1974: Mature with ripe currant, coffee and cedar flavors and a smooth, plush texture, showing its age, but it was elegant in this grouping. Best to drink up soon. 9,000 cases made. • $100 • (11/15/94) • **87**
Cabernet Sauvignon Napa Valley Reserve 1973 • $31 Ⓐ • (11/30/91) • **92**
Cabernet Sauvignon Napa Valley Reserve 1972 • $NA • (11/30/91) • **78**
Cabernet Sauvignon Napa Valley Reserve 1971 • $NA • (11/30/91) • **91**
Cabernet Sauvignon Napa Valley Unfiltered 1991: A racy style with lots of ripe, juicy Cabernet fruit. Echoes currant, plum and black cherry notes before picking up some toasty oak on the finish. Needs cellaring until 1997 or so. 73,460 cases made. • $18 • (11/15/94) SS • **90**
Cabernet Sauvignon Napa Valley Unfined 1970 • $90 • (03/01/89) • **89**
Cabernet Sauvignon Napa Valley Unfined 1969 • $37 Ⓐ • (03/01/89) • **86**

MONDAVI, ROBERT

Cabernet Sauvignon Napa Valley Unfined 1968 • $48 Ⓐ • (03/01/89) • **83**
Cabernet Sauvignon North Coast Coastal 1993: Ripe, smooth and harmonious, laced with plum, herb and currant flavors, picking up a trace of mineral and spice on the finish, where the tannins become more prominent. New from Mondavi. • $11 • (02/29/96) • **85**
Cabernet Sauvignon North Coast Coastal 1991: Intense and spicy, with a solid core of wild black cherry and currant flavors, turns dry and tannic on the finish, suggesting it needs another two years in the cellar. • $11 • (09/30/94) • **83**
Cabernet Sauvignon Oakville 1992: Somewhat earthy and spritzy, adding a wild berry and cherry edge and firm tannins. Not the blockbuster you might expect from Howell Mountain. • $28 • (09/30/95) • **84**
Chardonnay California Woodbridge 1992: Crisp and simple, a light wine with bright citrusy flavor. • $8 • (01/31/94) • **80**
Chardonnay California Woodbridge 1991 • $8 • (12/31/92) • **80**
Chardonnay Carneros 1993: Smooth, ripe, creamy, adding a touch of fig, pear and spice and delicate aftertaste. Drinks well now. 6,000 cases made. • $23 • (05/15/96) • **88**
Chardonnay Carneros 1992: Ripe and spicy, with intense but elegant pineapple, pear and citrus notes that turn smooth and creamy on the finish, where the flavors fan out and turn extra spicy. Try now. Tasted twice with consistent results. 5,000 cases made. • $22 • (06/30/94) • **92**
Chardonnay Carneros 1991 • $20 • (05/15/93) • **90**
Chardonnay Central Coast Coastal 1994: Ripe and spicy, showing a juicy, almost-sweet core of citrus and grapefruit flavors. 200,000 cases made. • $10 • (05/15/96) • **82**
Chardonnay Central Coast Coastal 1993: A fruity style with pretty pear, citrus and spice notes. Elegant and ready to drink now. 50,000 cases made. • $11 • (12/15/94) • **84**
Chardonnay Central Coast Coastal 1992: A spicy style with ripe, sweet-tasting pear and apple flavors, finishing with a creamy oak texture and honey notes. Ready now. • $11 • (09/15/94) • **87**
Chardonnay Napa Valley 1994: Young and vibrant, with a focused core of spicy pear, citrus and lemon flavors, picking up a trace of toasty oak on the finish. Impressive for its length. 100,000 cases made. • $17 • (05/31/96) • **89**
Chardonnay Napa Valley 1992: Intense and compact, with a tight band of spicy pear, honey and hazelnut flavors that are sharply focused. Finishes with good flavors that linger on the palate. Try now • $15 • (06/15/94) • **88**
Chardonnay Napa Valley 1991 • $15 • (04/30/93) SS • **90**
Chardonnay Napa Valley Reserve 1993: Elegant and refined, with a tantalizing array of flavors-ripe pear, smoky, toasty oak and hints of vanilla and nutmeg. A seamless wine that's rich and complex, showing great finesse and style. 11,000 cases made. • $29 • (07/31/95) • **91**
Chardonnay Napa Valley Reserve 1992: Remarkably elegant and complex, with tiers of ripe, polished pear, peach, nectarine and honey flavors framed by toast and vanilla-laced oak. Finishes with a long, full, elegant aftertaste. Drink now or hold. Tasted twice with consistent results. • $28 • (06/15/94) • **92**
Chardonnay Napa Valley Reserve 1991 • $28 • (04/30/93) • **90**
Chardonnay Napa Valley Unfiltered 1993: Lean and tart, with narrow band of apple, pear and light oak, that folds together on the finish. • $15 • (07/31/95) • **85**
Chenin Blanc Napa Valley 1991 • $8 • (11/30/93) • **75**
Fumé Blanc Napa Valley 1994: Simple, fruity, citrusy, adding a hint of floral character to make it interesting. Some spicy oak on the finish. Ready now. 64,000 cases made. • $11 • (05/15/96) • **85**
Fumé Blanc Napa Valley 1993: Crisply flavorful and exceptionally complex for this price. Harmonizes its pear, citrus, toast and herb tones well and hints at anise on the lively finish. 71,000 cases made. • $10 • (05/31/95) BB • **88**
Fumé Blanc Napa Valley 1992: Ripe and distinctly herbal, with grapefruit and pear at the core, a clear expression of full-fledged Sauvignon Blanc flavor that keeps reverberating without going over the edge. For those who want the full impact without excessive herbaceousness. Drinkable now. 71,100 cases made. • $10 • (12/15/94) SS • **89**

Key: SS—Spectator Selection. CS—Cellar Selection. BB—Best Buy. $NA—Price not available. (BT)—Barrel tasting. Ⓐ—Auction Price.
Dates in parentheses represent the issues in which the ratings were published.

Fumé Blanc Napa Valley 1991 • $11 • (11/30/93) • **81**
Fumé Blanc Napa Valley To-Kalon Vineyard Reserve 1994: Rich and round, though spicy oak character somewhat overwhelms the nice, pear flavors. 3,900 cases made. • $20 • **83**
Fumé Blanc Napa Valley To-Kalon Vineyard Reserve 1993: Lots of green, herbal notes weave through the brisk pear and apple flavors in this lively white. Drinkable now. • $19 • (05/31/95) • **86**
Fumé Blanc Napa Valley To-Kalon Vineyard Reserve 1992 • $11 • (04/30/94) • **87**
Fumé Blanc Napa Valley To-Kalon Vineyard Reserve 1991 • $19 • (04/15/93) • **82**
Fumé Blanc Stags Leap District 1994: Tangy and refreshing aromas and flavors—herb, sweet pea and melon—that linger nicely on the finish. 5,000 cases made. • $18 • **88**
Johannisberg Riesling Napa Valley 1991 • $8 • (11/15/93) • **76**
Merlot Napa Valley 1993: Appealing for its chocolate and cherry notes up front, but the tannins turn a touch bitter and leathery on the finish. 100,000 cases made. • $19 • (05/31/96) • **84**
Merlot Napa Valley 1992: Dense and cedary, with a tightly wound core of earthy currant, tobacco, mineral and spice. Finishes with firm but supple tannins, so cellaring into 1997-98 is advised. 9,500 cases made. • $19 • **87**
Merlot Napa Valley 1991 • $21 • (06/15/94) • **89**
Merlot Napa Valley 1990 • $21 • (03/31/93) • **86**
Merlot Napa Valley 1989 • $21 • (05/31/92) • **87**
Muscat Napa Valley Moscato d'Oro 1991 • $12 • (10/15/92) • **70**
Pinot Noir Carneros 1991 • $20 • (02/28/94) • **83**
Pinot Noir Carneros Napa Valley Unfiltered 1993: Distinctive for rich, smoky, toasty oak aromas, but also for its silky smooth black cherry, herb, spice and plum notes. Finesse, sophistication. 4,600 cases made. • $26 • (11/30/95) • **89**
Pinot Noir Carneros Unfiltered 1992: Crisp and firm, displaying a delicate band of cherry, cola and spice flavors, framed by light oak. Drinks well now. Tasted twice, with consistent notes. 4,000 cases made. • $24 • (03/31/95) • **86**
Pinot Noir Central Coast Coastal 1994: A touch earthy with a tart edge to the cherry and wild berry flavors. Medium weight, it's pleasant if unexciting. 10,000 cases made. • $11 • (05/31/96) • **82**
Pinot Noir Napa Valley 1991 • $14 • (02/28/94) • **85**
Pinot Noir Napa Valley 1990 • $18 • (03/31/92) • **86**
Pinot Noir Napa Valley 1989 • $15 • (04/30/91) • **86**
Pinot Noir Napa Valley 1988 • $13 • (02/15/90) • **89**
Pinot Noir Napa Valley 1987 • $12 • (07/31/89) • **88**
Pinot Noir Napa Valley 1985 • $11 • (06/15/88) • **79**
Pinot Noir Napa Valley 1984 • $8 • (11/15/87) • **75**
Pinot Noir Napa Valley 1982 • $9 • (08/31/86) • **79**
Pinot Noir Napa Valley 1981 • $7 • (11/01/84) • **80**
Pinot Noir Napa Valley Reserve 1993: A touch earthy, but enough plum and cherry fruit emerges to keep it in balance. An elegant and supple style that's appealing to drink now. 6,000 cases made. • $30 • (05/31/96) • **89**
Pinot Noir Napa Valley Reserve 1991 • $28 • (02/28/94) • **89**
Pinot Noir Napa Valley Reserve 1990 • $30 • (03/31/92) • **92**
Pinot Noir Napa Valley Reserve 1988 • $26 • (10/31/90) • **82**
Pinot Noir Napa Valley Reserve 1986 • $22 • (10/15/89) • **91**
Pinot Noir Napa Valley Reserve 1985 • $31 • (04/15/89) SS • **92**
Pinot Noir Napa Valley Reserve 1983 • $25 • (11/15/87) • **80**
Pinot Noir Napa Valley Reserve 1982 • $25 • (08/31/86) • **78**
Pinot Noir Napa Valley Reserve 1981 • $17 • (08/31/86) • **86**
Pinot Noir Napa Valley Reserve 1980 • $13 • (08/01/84) • **81**
Pinot Noir Napa Valley Unfiltered 1993: Modest range of herb, cherry, tea and spice finishes with smooth tannins and a slight tobacco edge. Elegant and supple, drinkable now through 1997. • $16 • (09/15/95) • **86**
Pinot Noir Napa Valley Unfiltered 1992: Lean with an herb and cola flavor that doesn't offer much richness or depth. Finishes with a leathery, tannic edge. • $14 • (11/30/94) • **84**
Pinot Noir Napa Valley Unfiltered Reserve 1992: Firm and compact, showing flavors of spice, smoke, black cherry and cola. Mild tannins, best now. Tasted twice, with consistent notes. 6,000 cases made. • $29 • (03/31/95) • **87**
Red California 1984 • $5 • (01/31/87) • **75**
Rosé California 1986 • $5 • (03/31/87) • **80**

Sangiovese California La Famiglia di Robert Mondavi 1993: Lean and earthy, with briar, berry and cherry notes that pick up a hint of cedar and mint. Tasted twice, with consistent notes. 104 cases made. • $22 • (08/31/95) • **83**
Sauvignon Blanc California Woodbridge 1992 • $5 • (05/15/94) BB • **85**
Sauvignon Blanc California Woodbridge 1991 • $6 • (12/31/92) BB • **84**
Sauvignon Blanc North Coast Coastal 1994: Floral, oddly foxy flavors characterize this soft, lightly citrusy white. Ready now. 40,000 cases made. • $9 • (02/29/96) • **83**
Sauvignon Blanc Stags Leap District 1993: Intensely varietal, this new bottling of Sauvignon Blanc captures the essence of the grape, offering its grassy, herbal and lemony flavors. Finishes with a tart grapefruit edge. • $18 • (09/15/95) • **88**
White Zinfandel California 1988 • $5 • (06/15/89) • **80**
White Zinfandel California 1985 • $5 • (06/16/86) • **69**
White Zinfandel California Woodbridge 1994: • $NA • **65**
Zinfandel California Woodbridge 1992: Light and diluted, with simple cherry and strawberry notes. Ready now. 25,000 cases made. • $6 • (10/15/94) • **77**
Zinfandel California Woodbridge 1991 • $5 • (06/15/93) • **79**
Zinfandel California Woodbridge 1990 • $7 • (07/15/92) BB • **84**
Zinfandel Napa Valley 1994: A well-mannered Zin that captures the wild berry, plum and cherry notes, adding nice touches of cedar and spice without going overboard. Rich and full-bodied, the flavors are plush and concentrated. Drinkable now. 5,800 cases made. • $16 • (04/30/96) • **91**
Zinfandel Napa Valley 1993: Tough and tannic, an intense core of wild cherry and raspberry notes; finishes with a chewy aftertaste. Drinkable now. 4,000 cases made. • $16 • (07/31/95) • **86**
Zinfandel Napa Valley 1992: Ripe, rich and supple, with plush cherry, raspberry and plum-laced Zinfandel fruit. Carries its flavors exceptionally well, finishing with a long burst of fruit and smooth, polished tannins. Drinks well now, but short-term cellaring should soften it. Made with grapes from Howell Mountain, West Napa and Mount Veeder. 1,188 cases made. • $14 • (10/15/94) SS • **92**
Zinfandel Rosé California 1986 • $4 • (10/31/87) • **78**
Zinfandel Rosé California 1985 • $3 • (09/30/86) • **74**

MONT ST. JOHN | CALIFORNIA

Cabernet Sauvignon Napa Valley 1987 • $14 • (11/15/92) • **70**
Cabernet Sauvignon Napa Valley 1986 • $14 • (04/30/91) • **87**
Cabernet Sauvignon Napa Valley 1983 • $15 • (07/31/89) • **78**
Cabernet Sauvignon Napa Valley 1982 • $15 • (03/15/89) • **82**
Cabernet Sauvignon Napa Valley Private Reserve 1980 • $12 • (05/16/84) • **75**
Chardonnay Carneros 1994: Soft and spicy, with a moderate level of citrus to balance the toasty flavors. 2,800 cases made. • $13 • (06/15/96) • **80**
Chardonnay Carneros Napa Valley Madonna Vineyards 1993: Simple with a crisp band of earthy citrus and pear notes. Medium weight. 113 cases made. • $18 • (07/31/95) • **82**
Chardonnay Carneros Napa Valley Madonna Vineyards 1992: Lean in texture but sharply focused, with a nice tension between fruit and oak, the apple and pear flavors winning out in the end. Drink now.-HS 147 cases made. • $18 • (06/30/94) • **87**
Chardonnay Carneros Organically Grown Grapes 1993: Intense and earthy, but it holds together, with a solid core of grapefruit and citrus notes and a hint of pear. • $13 • (07/31/95) • **85**
Chardonnay Carneros Organically Grown Grapes 1992: Smooth and polished, a lighter style of Chardonnay with pretty pear and floral flavors.-HS • $13 • (06/30/94) • **85**
Pinot Noir Carneros 1993: Lean and crisp, with a trim band of tea, herb and cherry fruit. Lacks body and richness. 1,500 cases made. • $15 • (12/31/95) • **81**
Pinot Noir Carneros Napa Valley 1989 • $11 • (09/30/92) • **85**
Pinot Noir Carneros Napa Valley 1988 • $14 • (04/30/91) • **81**
Pinot Noir Carneros Napa Valley 1987 • $15 • (03/31/90) • **76**
Pinot Noir Carneros Napa Valley 1985 • $15 • (10/15/89) • **82**
Pinot Noir Carneros Napa Valley 1981 • $9 • (05/16/84) • **73**
Pinot Noir Carneros Napa Valley Madonna Vineyard 1985 • $11 • (06/15/88) • **78**

MONTDOMAINE | VIRGINIA

Heritage Monticello 1988 • $14 • (02/29/92) • **82**
Merlot Monticello Reserve 1987 • $15 • (02/29/92) • **86**

MONTE CARASSO | CALIFORNIA

Sangiovese Napa Valley 1994: Ripe and fruity range of anise, cedar, plum and coffee. Softly tannic finish. • $17 • (02/29/96) • **84**

MONTE VERDE | CALIFORNIA

Cabernet Sauvignon California Proprietor's Reserve 1988 • $5 • (12/15/92) • **79**
Cabernet Sauvignon California Proprietor's Reserve 1987 • $6 • (12/15/89) • **80**

MONTE VOLPE | CALIFORNIA

Barbera California 1992: Simple, earthy and a little tart, with modest beet and berry flavors sneaking in on the finish. Maybe best from 1997. 815 cases made. • $9 • (11/15/95) • **82**
Barbera Mendocino 1991 • $8 • (03/31/93) BB • **87**
Moscato Mendocino 1991 • $8 • (10/15/92) • **80**
Peppolino Mendocino 1992: Smooth, supple and charming, offering pretty berry, vanilla and spice flavors that glide through the finish. A mishmash of Italian varieties (Nebbiolo, Barbera, Sangiovese, Malvasia Nera) that works. 200 cases made. • $14 • (10/15/95) • **85**
Pinot Bianco Mendocino 1993: Bright and fruity, a zingy wine with lively pear and resin flavors that linger on the finish. Ready now. 1,109 cases made. • $9 • (04/15/95) • **84**
Sangiovese Mendocino 1992: Supple and fruity, gently unfolding its soft currant and berry flavors. A very nicely balanced, graceful wine with a smooth texture. Drinkable now. 230 cases made. • $14 • (09/30/94) • **86**

MONTELENA, CHATEAU | CALIFORNIA

Cabernet Calistoga Cuvée Napa Valley 1993: Well balanced, with pleasant cherry, plum and spice notes, with firm tannins on the finish. Best after 1997. 10,000 cases made. • $18 • (12/15/95) • **86**
Cabernet Sauvignon Alexander Valley Sonoma 1979 • $45 • (03/01/89) • **88**
Cabernet Sauvignon Alexander Valley Sonoma 1978 • $68 • (11/15/92) • **86**
Cabernet Sauvignon Alexander Valley Sonoma 1977 • $55 • (03/01/89) • **91**
Cabernet Sauvignon Alexander Valley Sonoma 1974: Mature, complex and full-bodied, with spicy cedar, herb, currant and anise notes, beginning to dry out and the high tannin level makes for a chewy, gritty finish. It is still deeply concentrated. 6,000 cases made. • $57 Ⓐ • (11/15/94) • **88**
Cabernet Sauvignon Alexander Valley Sonoma 1973 • $95 • (03/01/89) • **87**
Cabernet Sauvignon Napa Valley 1989 • $30 • (11/15/93) • **85**
Cabernet Sauvignon Napa Valley 1988 • $30 • (11/15/92) • **87**
Cabernet Sauvignon Napa Valley 1987 • $91 Ⓐ • (10/31/91) SS • **95**
Cabernet Sauvignon Napa Valley 1986 • $53 Ⓐ • (10/15/90) • **93**
Cabernet Sauvignon Napa Valley 1985 • $59 Ⓐ • (11/15/89) CS • **92**
Cabernet Sauvignon Napa Valley 1984 • $50 Ⓐ • (03/01/89) • **94**
Cabernet Sauvignon Napa Valley 1983 • $32 Ⓐ • (03/01/89) • **92**
Cabernet Sauvignon Napa Valley 1982 • $55 • (03/01/89) • **92**
Cabernet Sauvignon Napa Valley 1981 • $40 • (03/01/89) • **80**
Cabernet Sauvignon Napa Valley 1980 • $60 • (03/01/89) • **86**
Cabernet Sauvignon Napa Valley 1979 • $51 • (03/01/89) • **87**
Cabernet Sauvignon Napa Valley 1978 • $119 Ⓐ • (11/15/92) • **96**
Cabernet Sauvignon Napa Valley 1977 • $53 Ⓐ • (03/01/89) • **94**
Cabernet Sauvignon Napa Valley 1974: After years of drinking exceptionally well this is showing transition, with more dried-out and earthy flavors than pure fruit. There are hints of ripe plum and raisin on the finish but also a metallic streak. Probably best soon. 1,100 cases made. • $140 • (11/15/94) • **83**

Cabernet Sauvignon Napa Valley Calistoga Cuvée 1992: Bold, ripe and supple, with a rich, focused core of currant, black cherry, plum and exotic spice flavors. Builds richness, intensity and depth on a long, complex finish. Beautifully crafted. Best now. 12,000 cases made. • $15 • (11/15/94) SS • **90**

Cabernet Sauvignon Napa Valley The Montelena Estate 1991: Uncommonly dark and intense, even for this vintage, with a rich core of leathery currant, spice, cedar and anise flavors that are young and rambunctious. This is a massive wine that needs to age through 1999. 12,000 cases made. • $40 • (05/31/95) SS • **92**

Cabernet Sauvignon Napa Valley The Montelena Estate 1990: A new designation for this wine, which indicates a style change-less tannic and more elegant. While the currant and black cherry flavors are focused and still ring true, this is more forward and supple than those in the past. Best after 1997. 9,500 cases made. • $46 Ⓐ • (11/15/94) CS • **90**

Cabernet Sauvignon North Coast 1976 • $89 • (03/01/89) • **90**

Cabernet Sauvignon North Coast 1975 • $75 • (03/01/89) • **86**

Chardonnay Napa Valley 1993: Marked by a tart, crisp, green edge but it holds together, with tart apple and citrus notes. 10,000 cases made. • $23 • (07/31/95) • **84**

Chardonnay Napa Valley 1991: A spicy style with a tart Muscat edge and light pear and apple notes, but the flavors taper off on the finish. Ready now, but this has a history of gaining in the bottle. 14,000 cases made. • $23 • (06/30/94) • **83**

Chardonnay Napa Valley 1972-1992 Anniversary 1992: Ripe, rich pear, apple, melon and spice notes turn smooth and polished on the finish, where the oak folds in. 12,000 cases made. • $23 • (06/15/95) • **88**

Zinfandel Napa-Alexander Valleys 1974 • $40 • (06/16/85) • **92**

Zinfandel Napa Valley 1991: Has an earthy, tarry edge to it, but hints of stewed plum and pepper come through on the finish, along with a gamy edge and a coarse texture. Drink now. • $12 • (10/15/94) • **84**

Zinfandel Napa Valley 1989 • $12 • (10/15/92) • **80**

Zinfandel Napa Valley 1987 • $10 • (07/31/90) • **69**

Zinfandel Napa Valley 1986 • $15 • (09/15/89) • **80**

Zinfandel Napa Valley 1985 • $15 • (04/30/88) • **90**

Zinfandel Napa Valley 1983 • $11 • (05/01/86) • **84**

Zinfandel Napa Valley 1982 • $18 • (05/01/84) • **91**

Zinfandel Napa Valley 1981 • $20 • (04/16/84) • **80**

Zinfandel Napa Valley 1973 • $29 • (06/16/85) • **90**

Zinfandel Napa Valley John Rolleri Vineyard 1984 • $18 • (05/15/87) • **91**

Zinfandel Napa Valley The Montelena Estate 1992: Starts out oaky and a touch gamy, but the wild berry and raspberry flavors work through and rise to the forefront, giving it greater balance and definition. 1,900 cases made. • $12 • (07/31/95) • **87**

Zinfandel North Coast 1976 • $25 • (06/16/85) • **78**

MONTEREY PENINSULA | CALIFORNIA

Barbera California Vineyard View Pleasant Hill 1989 • $12 • (10/31/93) • **78**

Black Burgundy California NV • $6 • (10/15/93) • **75**

Cabernet Sauvignon Monterey County 1991: Crisp and tannic, a tough little wine that manages to poke some Cabernet fruit through the chewy tannins. Try in 1998. 1,000 cases made. • $12 • (12/15/95) • **80**

Cabernet Sauvignon Monterey County 1986: A good value in mature Cabernet, with supple herb and currant notes that pick up a chocolate edge on the finish. Best now through 1998. 1,100 cases made. • $10 • (11/15/94) • **84**

Cabernet Sauvignon Monterey County 1985 • $12 • (11/15/92) • **82**

Cabernet Sauvignon Monterey County 1982 • $11 • (03/31/87) • **74**

Cabernet Sauvignon Monterey County Doctors' Reserve 1986: Mature herb and spice flavors with a solid core of currant and plum notes. Approachable now but has the depth and intensity for further cellaring. 1,000 cases made. • $18 • (11/15/94) • **86**

Cabernet Sauvignon Monterey County Doctors' Reserve 1985 • $25 • (11/15/92) • **76**

Key: SS—Spectator Selection. CS—Cellar Selection. BB—Best Buy. $NA—Price not available. (BT)—Barrel tasting. Ⓐ—Auction Price.
Dates in parentheses represent the issues in which the ratings were published.

Cabernet Sauvignon Monterey County Doctors' Reserve 1984 • $18 • (11/15/92) • **78**

Cabernet Sauvignon Monterey County Monterey Cellars 1986 • $8 • (11/15/92) • **77**

Cabernet Sauvignon Monterey Doctors' Reserve 1984 • $16 • (02/28/91) • **81**

Cabernet Sauvignon Monterey Doctors' Reserve Lot II 1982 • $14 • (06/15/87) • **83**

Chardonnay California 1992: Earthy and gamy flavors turn leathery on the finish, overriding the fruit. Marginal. 500 cases made. • $10 • (07/31/95) • **72**

Merlot Doctors' Reserve 1986 • $16 • (05/31/92) • **83**

Merlot Monterey County Doctors' Reserve Unfiltered Unfined 1987 • $18 • (07/15/93) • **81**

Merlot Monterey Doctors' Reserve 1986 • $16 • (03/31/91) • **84**

Merlot Monterey Doctors' Reserve 1985 • $14 • (01/31/89) • **83**

Merlot Monterey Doctors' Reserve 1984 • $12 • (12/15/87) • **74**

Pinot Noir Monterey County Sleepy Hollow 1989 • $12 • (02/28/93) • **76**

Pinot Noir Monterey County Sleepy Hollow Vineyard 1992: Supple and elegant, offering attractive cherry, vanilla and spice flavors that stay through the finish. Drinkable now. 150 cases made. • $12 • (01/31/95) • **85**

Pinot Noir Monterey Sleepy Hollow 1987 • $18 • (02/28/91) • **86**

White Riesling Late Harvest Monterey County Sleepy Hollow 1989 • $15 • (06/30/93) • **89**

Zinfandel Amador County Ferrero Ranch 1990 • $10 • (09/30/93) • **80**

Zinfandel Amador County Ferrero Ranch Doctors' Reserve 1987 • $15 • (05/15/91) • **83**

Zinfandel Amador County Ferrero Ranch Doctors' Reserve 1982 • $10 • (02/29/88) • **83**

Zinfandel Amador County Ferrero Vineyard 1991: Intense and tannic, with earthy, tarry raspberry flavor. Can stand short-term cellaring to soften. 500 cases made. • $9 • (10/15/94) • **80**

MONTEREY VINEYARD | CALIFORNIA

Cabernet Sauvignon Classic 1989 • $6 • (03/15/92) BB • **83**

Cabernet Sauvignon Monterey County Classic 1990: A straightforward, sturdy Cabernet, with plum, herb and earth flavors, a full body and moderate tannins. Drink now. 16,309 cases made. • $6 • (03/31/93) BB • **80**

Cabernet Sauvignon Monterey County Classic 1987 • $6 • (01/31/91) BB • **83**

Cabernet Sauvignon Monterey County Classic 1986 • $5 • (10/31/89) • **76**

Cabernet Sauvignon Monterey County Limited Release 1990: Marked by spicy, toasty oak, delivering enough cedary Cabernet fruit to make it interesting. Well balanced and easy to drink. 500 cases made. • $11 • (11/15/94) • **84**

Cabernet Sauvignon Monterey County Limited Release 1986 • $8 • (08/31/92) • **79**

Cabernet Sauvignon Monterey County Limited Release 1985 • $10 • (08/31/88) • **75**

Cabernet Sauvignon Monterey-Sonoma-San Luis Obispo Counties Classic 1985 • $5 • (02/15/89) • **73**

Chardonnay Monterey County Classic 1993: An earthy style that has a strong citrus and grapefruit edge to the Chardonnay flavors. 250,000 cases made. • $6 • (02/28/95) • **79**

Chardonnay Monterey County Classic 1992: Delivers pure spicy pear- and apple-tinged flavors and modest oak nuances. Ready.-JL • $6 • (06/30/94) BB • **82**

Chardonnay Monterey County Limited Release 1993: Smooth and polished, unfolding its generous pear, citrus and spicy oak flavors over a gentle structure, its flavors lingering nicely. Ready now. 550 cases made. • $13 • (07/31/95) • **85**

Classic Red California 1982 • $4 • (06/16/86) • **74**

Classic Red Monterey 1984 • $4 • (11/15/87) • **74**

Classic Red Monterey County 1990 • $5 • (03/31/93) • **76**

Merlot Monterey Classic 1989 • $6 • (02/29/92) BB • **84**

Merlot Monterey County 1992: Hard-edged but on the light side, with modest plum and berry flavors. A bit tannic on the finish. • $6 • (09/15/94) • **80**

Merlot Monterey County Classic 1988 • $6 • (12/31/90) • **76**

Pinot Noir Monterey County 1987 • $8 • (03/31/90) • **84**
Pinot Noir Monterey County 1986 • $7 • (06/15/88) • **83**
Pinot Noir Monterey County Classic 1992: Lean and earthy, with a smoky, meaty edge to the flavors. 7,400 cases made. • $6 • (03/31/95) • **77**
Pinot Noir Monterey County Classic 1991 • $6 • (02/28/94) • **79**
Pinot Noir Monterey County Limited Release 1990 • $8 • (02/28/93) • **78**
Pinot Noir Monterey County Limited Release 1989 • $8 • (09/30/92) • **71**
Pinot Noir Monterey County Limited Release 1988 • $9 • (02/28/91) • **80**
Sauvignon Blanc Central Coast Classic 1994: Crisp and floral, some wood flavor shows through the modest fruit. 12,000 cases made. • $5 • (08/31/95) • **82**
Sauvignon Blanc Monterey County Classic 1992: Light and simple, slightly spicy, a pleasant white wine with a floral edge. • $5 • (08/31/94) • **79**
White Zinfandel Central Coast Classic White Zinfandel 1994: Sweet and simple, with light strawberry and cherry flavors, tasting as much like fruit juice as wine, but it will appeal to summertime sippers. • $5 • **78**

MONTERRA | CALIFORNIA

Cabernet Sauvignon Monterey 1991: Earthy and spicy, displaying bell pepper and herb flavors. Finishes on the short side, with drying tannins. Drinkable now. 2,000 cases made. • $7 • (11/15/94) • **81**
Chardonnay California 1992: Simple with light pear and oak flavors, good for the price.-JL 4,500 cases made. • $7 • (06/30/94) • **80**
Merlot Monterey 1991 • $7 • (05/31/94) BB • **86**
Merlot Monterey Sand Hill 1992: Elegant and fruity, adding just a trace of herb. Bright cherry and berry flavors are well defined. Medium-bodied, mild tannins. Drinks well now. • $10 • (02/29/96) • **86**

MONTEVINA | CALIFORNIA

Aleatico Amador County 1993: Very light red, very light aromas and flavors, moderately sweet and simple. 800 cases made. • $7 • **78**
Barbera Amador County 1993: An elegant, medium-weight style, showing bright, tart cherry and berry flavors. 1,712 cases made. • $9 • (05/15/96) • **84**
Barbera Amador County Reserve 1990 • $15 • (12/15/92) • **82**
Barbera Amador County Reserve Selection 1987 • $14 • (05/31/91) • **89**
Barbera Amador County Terra d'Oro 1993: Medium in weight, featuring a pleasant band of cherry, berry and earthy notes and finishing with fine tannins. Ready now or into 1997. 575 cases made. • $16 • (05/15/96) • **86**
Barbera Shenandoah Valley 1984 • $6 • (10/15/88) • **78**
Cabernet Sauvignon California 1992: Firm and chewy, a tight little wine that manages to sneak in some lovely berry flavor on the finish. Try in 1998. 13,000 cases made. • $9 • (12/15/95) • **83**
Cabernet Sauvignon California 1990: An herbal style that's fairly simple, showing decent plum and cherry flavors. Smooth and drinkable now. • $9 • (05/15/93) • **80**
Cabernet Sauvignon California 1989 • $9 • (08/31/92) • **78**
Cabernet Sauvignon California 1988 • $8 • (02/15/90) • **77**
Cabernet Sauvignon Shenandoah Valley Limited Release 1984 • $7 • (08/31/88) BB • **86**
Chardonnay California 1993: Strong earthy canned pineapple flavors dominate this one-dimensional wine. 10,000 cases made. • $8 • (07/31/95) • **78**
Fumé Blanc California 1993: Herbal, toasty-oniony flavors, finishing soft. 15,000 cases made. • $7 • (08/31/95) • **78**
Matrimonio Amador County 1992: Crisp in texture, with a nice thread of smooth black currant and berry flavors that bring some suppleness to the finish. Better in 1997. 571 cases made. • $8 • (08/31/95) • **84**
Montanaro Amador County 1992: Light in texture and a little chewy with tannins, but the plum and black cherry flavors hold their own on the finish. Drink now with hearty food, or age until 1998. 717 cases made. • $7 • (08/31/95) • **85**
Montanaro Amador County 1989 • $10 • (11/30/92) • **80**
Sangiovese Amador County 1992: A dead ringer for a Zinfandel-full body, spicy and rippling with plum and blackberry flavors that turn to stewed plums on the finish. Drinkable now. 900 cases made. • $12 • (08/31/95) • **86**
Sangiovese Amador County Terra d'Oro 1993: Offers modest varietal character at best, but there's enough plum and wild berry flavor to keep your interest. Drinkable now. 929 cases made. • $15 • (04/30/96) • **80**
White Zinfandel Shenandoah Valley 1985 • $5 • (02/16/86) • **63**
Zinfandel Amador County 1993: Rustic and shows a meaty side to the tannic wild berry flavors. Starts to grow on you, though, by the second or third sip. 10,500 cases made. • $7 • (10/15/95) • **83**
Zinfandel Amador County 1992: Smooth and supple, with appealing accents of cherry, wild berry and tar that hang with you. 3,500 cases made. • $7 • (10/15/95) • **84**
Zinfandel Amador County 1990 • $6 • (06/15/94) BB • **83**
Zinfandel Amador County 1989 • $8 • (10/15/92) • **72**
Zinfandel Amador County 1987 • $7 • (03/31/90) • **75**
Zinfandel Amador County Brioso 1994: A lighter style marked by fresh berry and strawberry flavors. Might work well served slightly chilled. Drinkable now. 6,000 cases made. • $6 • (04/30/96) • **83**
Zinfandel Amador County Brioso 1993: A lighter style marked by ripe strawberry and cherry jam flavors and aromas. Supple and appealing. 4,000 cases made. • $7 • (10/15/95) • **83**
Zinfandel Amador County Brioso 1992 • $7 • (09/30/93) • **83**
Zinfandel Amador County Brioso 1991 • $7 • (06/15/93) • **77**
Zinfandel Amador County Brioso 1990 • $7 • (07/15/92) BB • **86**
Zinfandel Amador County Reserve 1991: Ripe with wild berry and cherry jam flavors, but it comes across as one-dimensional. Ready now through 1997. 1,590 cases made. • $12 • (10/15/94) • **82**
Zinfandel Amador County Reserve 1989 • $12 • (10/15/92) • **87**
Zinfandel Amador County Terra d'Oro 1993: Elegant, complex, pleasant array of ripe plum, berry, spice and smoky oak flavors, finishing with a smooth, berried aftertaste and polished tannins. Impressive new wine from this property. 1,800 cases made. • $15 • (04/30/96) • **89**
Zinfandel Shenandoah Valley Montino 1985 • $5 • (10/15/88) • **75**
Zinfandel Shenandoah Valley Winemaker's Choice 1984 • $9 • (08/31/87) • **75**
Zinfandel Shenandoah Valley Winemaker's Choice 1980 • $9 • (04/16/84) • **78**

MONTHAVEN | CALIFORNIA

Cabernet Sauvignon Napa Valley 1993: Pleasant enough, with ripe cherry, currant and berry flavors of modest proportion. 3,000 cases made. • $8 • (03/31/96) • **81**
Chardonnay Napa Valley 1994: Clean and spicy, with a modest core of citrus, pear and spice flavors. A decent wine for the price. 3,000 cases made. • $8 • (03/31/96) • **82**
Malbec Napa Valley 1993: Austere and stalky, the unripe character of the modest plum and currant flavors barely holding your interest. 300 cases made. • $8 • (03/31/96) • **81**
Sauvignon Blanc Napa Valley 1994: A crisp white marked by a core of grassy citrus, lemon and herb flavors. Elegant and refined, easy-drinking. 2,000 cases made. • $6 • (03/31/96) • **83**

MONTICELLO | CALIFORNIA

Cabernet Sauvignon Napa Valley 1981 • $14 • (07/16/84) • **74**
Cabernet Sauvignon Napa Valley Corley Reserve 1990: Uncommonly dark in color, with ultra-ripe porty aromas. On the palate it's chunky and ripe, but the flavors don't go overboard, with ripe plum and currant notes that stay with you on a long, full finish. Lots of tannin to shed, but it's tasty. Try around 1997. 1,200 cases made. • $25 • (11/15/93) • **88**
Cabernet Sauvignon Napa Valley Corley Reserve 1989 • $25 • (11/15/92) • **85**
Cabernet Sauvignon Napa Valley Corley Reserve 1987 • $25 • (11/15/90) • **90**
Cabernet Sauvignon Napa Valley Corley Reserve 1986 • $30 • (03/15/90) • **92**
Cabernet Sauvignon Napa Valley Corley Reserve 1985 • $35 • (07/31/89) • **92**
Cabernet Sauvignon Napa Valley Corley Reserve 1984 • $30 • (03/01/89) • **91**

Cabernet Sauvignon Napa Valley Corley Reserve 1983 • $24 • (03/01/89) • **88**
Cabernet Sauvignon Napa Valley Corley Reserve 1982 • $33 • (03/01/89) • **90**
Cabernet Sauvignon Napa Valley Corley Select Reserve 1992: Marked by an odd, off-putting charred oak edge, turning earthy and drying on the finish. Turns unusually tannic on the finish. Tasted twice with consistent results. 864 cases made. • $28 • (12/15/95) • **83**
Cabernet Sauvignon Napa Valley Corley Select Reserve 1991: Firm and austere, with good intensity and ripe chewy cherry and earthy currant flavors that are big and rambunctuous. Will need time in the bottle to soften. Try after 2001. 1,200 cases made. • $25 • (12/15/95) • **85**
Cabernet Sauvignon Napa Valley Jefferson Cuvée 1992: Serves up an appealing core of ripe, plush fruit, with delicate cherry, currant and plum notes, finishing with spice, light oak and mild tannins. Complex aftertaste. 2,607 cases made. • $18 • (12/15/95) • **89**
Cabernet Sauvignon Napa Valley Jefferson Cuvée 1989 • $15 • (11/15/93) • **86**
Cabernet Sauvignon Napa Valley Jefferson Cuvée 1988 • $16 • (11/15/91) • **85**
Cabernet Sauvignon Napa Valley Jefferson Cuvée 1987 • $14 • (09/30/90) • **90**
Cabernet Sauvignon Napa Valley Jefferson Cuvée 1986 • $14 • (04/15/89) • **89**
Cabernet Sauvignon Napa Valley Jefferson Cuvée 1985 • $12 • (02/29/88) • **87**
Cabernet Sauvignon Napa Valley Jefferson Cuvée 1984 • $11 • (11/30/87) • **90**
Cabernet Sauvignon Napa Valley Jefferson Cuvée 1983 • $10 • (11/30/86) • **77**
Cabernet Sauvignon Napa Valley Jefferson Cuvée 1982 • $10 • (02/01/86) • **91**
Chardonnay Napa Valley 1991 • $9 • (01/31/94) • **83**
Chardonnay Napa Valley Corley Estate Reserve 1993: Marked by a slight bitter note from oak, the citrus and pear flavors struggling to work their way through. Nowhere near the quality of the 1992. Tasted twice, with consistent notes. 725 cases made. • $26 • (05/15/96) • **82**
Chardonnay Napa Valley Corley Estate Reserve 1992: Bold, rich and concentrated, with attractive pear, honey, spice and apple flavors that turn smooth and creamy as the toasty oak nuances chime in. 492 cases made. • $26 • (04/15/95) • **94**
Chardonnay Napa Valley Corley Family Vineyards 1992: Well crafted, striking a fine balance between ripe pear, apple and spice notes and light oak shadings. Turns rich and complex on the finish. • $15 • (09/30/95) • **89**
Chardonnay Napa Valley Corley Reserve 1992: Straightforward, with ripe pear, apple and toasty oak flavors that are moderately rich and complex. It gets most interesting on the finish, where the flavors come together for a buttery aftertaste. Tasted twice. 500 cases made. • $18 • (06/30/94) • **87**
Chardonnay Napa Valley Corley Reserve 1991 • $17 • (07/15/93) • **86**
Chardonnay Napa Valley Corley Wild Yeast Estate Reserve 1994: Has a cedary edge to the the pear and citrus notes, and a tart, leesy quality emerges on the finish. A touch too oaky now, but should pull together by 1997. 230 cases made. • $33 • (06/15/96) • **85**
Merlot Napa Valley 1990 • $17 • (07/15/93) • **86**
Merlot Napa Valley Corley Family Vineyard 1992: Appealing for its ripe fruit flavors, but the tannins weigh in heavily as well. Dense and chewy, needs cellaring. Cedary oak edge on aftertaste. • $18 • (09/30/95) • **88**
Pinot Noir Napa Valley 1991 • $18 • (02/28/94) • **81**
Pinot Noir Napa Valley 1990 • $18 • (09/30/92) • **86**
Pinot Noir Napa Valley 1987 • $15 • (10/15/89) • **85**
Pinot Noir Napa Valley 1986 • $12 • (06/15/88) • **89**
Pinot Noir Napa Valley 1985 • $12 • (12/15/87) • **89**
Pinot Noir Napa Valley Corley Family Vineyards 1992: Elegant and well focused, featuring deft balance between ripe cherry, spice, wild berry and pretty vanilla notes. Classy, well-defined fruit and long aftertaste. 2,000 cases made. • $18 • (09/15/95) • **88**
Pinot Noir Napa Valley Monticello Vineyards Estate Reserve 1993: Complex plum, black cherry, cedary oak and spice notes turn smooth and polished on the finish. Has a long, rich aftertaste. 230 cases made. • $30 • (11/30/95) • **89**

MONTPELLIER | CALIFORNIA

Cabernet Sauvignon California 1990: An earthy style that pulls through with supple currant and berry flavor and finishes with a coffee and floral edge. 10,000 cases made. • $8 • (11/15/94) • **83**
Cabernet Sauvignon California 1988 • $7 • (07/31/91) BB • **83**
Chardonnay California 1994: A light, simple wine, with pleasant floral and apple flavors. Drinkable now. 12,000 cases made. • $8 • (06/30/96) • **83**
Chardonnay California 1992: Earthy, gamy and bitter, a disappointingly sour and awkward wine. Misses the mark. Tasted twice with consistent notes.-JL 8,400 cases made. • $8 • (06/30/94) • **70**
Merlot California 1993: Openly fruity, with ripe, juicy cherry, plum and berry notes that are medium bodied. Simple but pleasant. 7,000 cases made. • $8 • (11/15/95) • **83**
Merlot California 1992: Offers spicy strawberry and raspberry flavors in a light and simple style. Ready now. 8,000 cases made. • $8 • (09/15/94) • **80**
Pinot Noir California 1993: Modestly varietal, with a hint of cherry, berry flavors and light oak. 1,500 cases made. • $8 • **78**
Sauvignon Blanc California 1992: Herbal and peppery, but it's smooth and graceful enough to remain in balance. 1,250 cases made. • $7 • (08/31/94) • **82**
Sauvignon Blanc California 1991 • $6 • (09/15/93) • **73**
Zinfandel California 1993: Strikes a pleasant balance between the ripe cherry, plum and wild berry flavors and the modest tannins. 1,250 cases made. • $7 • (10/15/95) • **83**

MONTREAUX | CALIFORNIA

Brut Napa Valley 1987: An intense and exotic style that focuses on ripe pear, honey and vanilla flavors before picking up an earthy edge. Drinks well now. 2,000 cases made. • $26 • (12/31/94) • **86**
Brut Napa Valley 1986 • $26 • (12/31/93) • **76**
Brut Napa Valley 1985 • $32 • (12/31/90) • **79**

MOONDANCE | CALIFORNIA

Cabernet Sauvignon Napa Valley 1992: Marked by cedary tobacco and earthy nuances, just enough herb and currant flavors coming through to maintain balance. Best in 1997, but it may always be tannic. 1,125 cases made. • $10 • (07/31/95) • **82**
Merlot Napa Valley 1993: Ripe and openly fruity, with wild berry, cherry and currant notes. Finishes with firm tannins and a slightly coarse texture. Short-term cellaring advised. 1,000 cases made. • $15 • **83**
Merlot Napa Valley 1992: Smooth, open and generous, a little chewy but flavorful and focused, with black currant, blackberry and toast notes that carry through to the finish. Drinkable now. 1,000 cases made. • $12 • (11/15/94) • **87**
Merlot Napa Valley 1990 • $10 • (03/31/93) • **86**
Petite Sirah Napa Valley 1992: Very smooth and generous, velvety, cascading its plum, berry and lightly spicy flavors. Drink now. 200 cases made. • $16 • (09/30/95) • **88**
Sangiovese Alexander Valley 1993: Light in color and flavor, featuring simple, wispy berry and violet notes. A little tough in tannin for the modest accents. 430 cases made. • $13 • (11/30/95) • **80**
Zinfandel Sonoma Valley 1992: Smooth, ripe and polished, offering ripe cherry, currant and wild berry notes that turn complex on the finish with buttery oak flavors. Drinks well now, but has enough depth to age through 1998. 130 cases made. • $12 • (10/15/94) • **88**

MOORE, Z | CALIFORNIA

Danato Zinfandel Blend Sonoma-Mendocino Counties 1990 • $22 • (09/30/93) • **87**

Key: SS—Spectator Selection. CS—Cellar Selection. BB—Best Buy. $NA—Price not available. (BT)—Barrel tasting. (A)—Auction Price.
Dates in parentheses represent the issues in which the ratings were published.

Gewürztraminer Russian River Valley Barrel Fermented 1991 • $9 • (09/30/93) • **89**
Gewürztraminer Russian River Valley Martinelli Vineyard Barrel Fermented New Barrel Select 1991 • $18 • (09/30/93) • **86**
Gewürztraminer Russian River Valley McIlroy/Martinelli Barrel Fermented Puncheon Select 1991 • $12 • (09/30/93) • **82**

MORAGA | CALIFORNIA

Cabernet Sauvignon Bel Air 1990: Smoky and earthy, showing a burnt tar edge to the flavors and not much fruit. It improves upon aeration but finishes with dry, bitter tannins. Very disappointing. Tasted three times. 226 cases made. • $50 • (11/15/94) • **80**
Cabernet Sauvignon Bel Air 1989 • $50 • (06/30/93) • **87**

MORGAN | CALIFORNIA

Cabernet Sauvignon Carmel Valley 1991: Lavishly oaked and firmly tannic, this chewy young red is complex and concentrated, with intense currant and cherry flavor. Best to cellar until 1998. 1,600 cases made. • $15 • (11/15/94) • **88**
Cabernet Sauvignon Carmel Valley 1990: Harsh, burnt-tobacco flavors rob this one of its charm. Just seems way too tight, tart and harsh. Tasted twice with consistent results. 2,800 cases made. • $14 • (11/15/93) • **77**
Cabernet Sauvignon Carmel Valley 1989 • $15 • (08/31/92) • **83**
Cabernet Sauvignon Carmel Valley 1988 • $19 • (11/15/91) • **81**
Cabernet Sauvignon Carmel Valley 1987 • $16 • (09/30/90) • **92**
Cabernet Sauvignon Carmel Valley 1986 • $16 • (09/15/89) • **90**
Chardonnay Monterey 1992: Gamy with a slightly sour edge, still there are pleasant flavors, with spice, pear and vanilla notes, finishing with a toasty edge. Drinkable now. • $15 • (12/31/93) • **85**
Chardonnay Monterey 1991 • $16 • (07/15/93) • **77**
Chardonnay Monterey Reserve 1993: Solid, though somewhat understated at first, delivering a pleasant core of apple, pear and lightly toasty oak. It expands and develops more complexity on the finish. 1,100 cases made. • $23 • (06/15/96) • **88**
Chardonnay Monterey Reserve 1992: Intense and sharply focused, featuring a rich band of honey, pear, spice and nutmeg flavors that fold together nicely, turning complex. 2,500 cases made. • $25 • (04/30/95) • **88**
Chardonnay Monterey Reserve 1991 • $23 • (12/31/93) • **86**
Pinot Noir California 1994: Decent earthy, cherry and tarry notes and light oak shadings. Shows more depth and substance than most Pinot Noirs carrying the California appellation. 5,000 cases made. • $18 • (02/29/96) • **85**
Pinot Noir California 1993: Medium-bodied, with modest herb and cherry flavors and aromas. 4,900 cases made. • $15 • (06/30/95) • **83**
Pinot Noir California 1992: Well oaked and intense, with hints of herb and spicy black cherry. A blend of Carneros and Monterey grapes. 3,800 cases made. • $15 • (03/31/95) • **85**
Pinot Noir California 1991 • $15 • (02/28/93) • **81**
Pinot Noir California 1990 • $15 • (09/30/92) • **89**
Pinot Noir California 1989 • $14 • (03/31/92) • **85**
Pinot Noir California 1988 • $14 • (04/30/91) • **75**
Pinot Noir California 1987 • $15 • (07/31/89) • **81**
Pinot Noir California 1986 • $14 • (06/15/88) • **84**
Pinot Noir Carneros Reserve 1992: Firm and intense, somewhat tannic, but the black cherry, spice and herb notes are focused and concentrated. 500 cases made. • $27 • (03/31/95) • **87**
Pinot Noir Carneros Reserve 1991 • $23 • (02/28/94) • **84**
Pinot Noir Carneros Reserve 1990 • $23 • (09/30/92) • **89**
Pinot Noir Monterey 1991 • $25 • (02/28/94) • **81**
Pinot Noir Monterey Reserve 1993: Light in color and medium weight in flavor, with a range of cherry, herb and tea notes, maintaining a nice balance. Has a sense of harmony and finesse missing in many 1993s. Ready. 600 cases made. • $25 • **86**
Pinot Noir Monterey Reserve 1992: A pretty, supple and elegant array of herb, tea and black cherry flavors are ripe and focused, finishing with soft tannins and good length. Ready now through 1998. 500 cases made. • $27 • (03/31/95) • **87**
Pinot Noir Monterey Reserve 1990 • $24 • (09/30/92) • **90**
Sauvignon Blanc Sonoma County 1992 • $9 • (04/30/94) • **89**
Sauvignon Blanc Sonoma County Unfiltered Barrel Fermented 1994: Crisp and juicy, fairly glowing with vanilla-scented pear and tropical fruit flavors. Just a touch of herb on the finish. 8,500 cases made. • $11 • (06/30/95) • **86**
VNA Sonoma County Red 1994: Surprisingly lean and crisp, an attempt to rein in the exuberance of Viognier. 175 cases made. • $18 • (11/30/95) • **82**
Zinfandel Sonoma County 1993: Tough and tannic, with dry, leathery pepper and berry notes. 2,200 cases made. • $14 • (10/15/95) • **82**

MORO VINO | CALIFORNIA

Sauvignon Blanc Santa Barbara County 1995: Tart, crisp and tangy, with citrusy herbal flavors that hold on through a zingy finish. 350 cases made. • $10 • **85**

MORRIS, J.W. | CALIFORNIA

Cabernet Sauvignon Alexander Valley 1985 • $8 • (02/15/89) • **74**
Cabernet Sauvignon California Private Reserve 1989 • $6 • (11/15/92) • **79**
Cabernet Sauvignon California Private Reserve 1988 • $7 • (11/15/91) • **74**
Cabernet Sauvignon California Private Reserve 1987 • $8 • (03/31/90) • **83**
Chardonnay California Private Reserve 1991 • $7 • (07/15/93) BB • **81**
Private Reserve California Red 1987 • $3 • (06/30/90) • **70**
Private Reserve California Red 1986 • $3 • (12/31/88) • **78**
Private Reserve California Red 1984 • $3 • (11/15/87) BB • **79**
White Zinfandel California 1988 • $5 • (06/15/89) • **73**

MORRISETTE, CHATEAU | VIRGINIA

Chardonnay Virginia 1993: Lemony aromas give way to sweet lemon pie flavors in this ripe, soft wine. A bit vegetal and cloying on the finish. 1,000 cases made. • $10 • (06/30/95) • **77**
Chardonnay Virginia Rocky Knob 1991 • $12 • (06/30/93) • **78**

MORRO BAY | CALIFORNIA

Chardonnay Central Coast Special Edition 1994: Has a distinctly earthy edge that hints of celery on top of the sweet apple flavor. It definitely has personality. Drink soon. 35,000 cases made. • $10 • (12/31/95) • **83**
Chardonnay Central Coast Special Edition 1993: Soft and pleasantly fruity, providing pear, apple and light spice shadings. 15,000 cases made. • $10 • (05/15/95) • **84**

MOSBY | CALIFORNIA

Gewürztraminer Dry Santa Barbara County Barrel Fermented Select 1992: Mature, focused and concentrated, weaving rose petal and spice flavors through the honey-scented fruit. Delicious to drink now, but it's still improving. 375 cases made. • $16 • (11/15/95) • **89**
Nebbiolo Santa Barbara County Rosso di Nebbiolo 1991: Soft and slightly chewy, but this has a distinctive profile, offering currant, raspberry and anise flavors that linger on the slightly tannic finish. Drinkable now with hearty food. 518 cases made. • $12 • (09/30/94) • **83**
Pinot Grigio Santa Barbara County 1994: Silky, smooth and supple, showing lovely almond and floral nuances to the appealing peach flavor. Captures an Italian character. 700 cases made. • $11 • (12/15/95) • **86**
Sangiovese Santa Barbara County Vigna Della Casa Vecchia 1993: Chewy, simple, modest in flavor, but tannic enough to need until 1997 or '98 to settle. 500 cases made. • $16 • (08/31/95) • **79**

MOSHIN | CALIFORNIA

Blush Russian River Valley Blanc de Noir Dry Barrel Fermented 1993: Broad and lightly fruity, touches of berry on the palate and some color giving it a fleshy look. Finishes dry. 100 cases made. • $9 • (09/15/95) • **86**
Pinot Noir Russian River Valley 1992: A shade more depth and flavor than the 1991, but still on the modest side, herb, cherry and spice notes. 630 cases made. • $13 • (03/31/95) • **83**
Pinot Noir Russian River Valley 1989 • $9 • (02/28/93) • **75**

Pinot Noir Russian River Valley Reserve 1991: Light, with subtle herb, tea and cranberry flavors of modest proportion. 113 cases made. • $25 • (03/31/95) • **81**

MOUNT BAKER | WASHINGTON

Cabernet Sauvignon Washington 1989: Very spicy and fruity, with an acetic edge that takes some of the fun out of it. Needs food to show well. Drinkable now. • $19 • (09/30/94) • **83**
Cabernet Sauvignon Washington 1988 • $16 • (03/31/92) • **84**
Gewürztraminer Washington 1992: The fruit tastes stale in this coarse-textured white. • $8 • (09/30/94) • **72**

MOUNT EDEN | CALIFORNIA

Cabernet Sauvignon Santa Cruz Mountains 1993: Marked by strong oak and chewy tannins, dense and backward, tasting more like a raw barrel sample than a finished wine. Will require patience and may always be tannic. Best to wait until 2002. 1,261 cases made. • $18 • (04/30/96) • **84**
Cabernet Sauvignon Santa Cruz Mountains 1992: Lean, tannic and leathery, with the currant and berry fruit buried underneath. Turns dry and austere on the finish. 1,036 cases made. • $16 • (05/31/95) • **83**
Cabernet Sauvignon Santa Cruz Mountains 1989 • $25 • (11/15/92) • **86**
Cabernet Sauvignon Santa Cruz Mountains 1988 • $26 • (11/15/92) • **86**
Cabernet Sauvignon Santa Cruz Mountains 1987 • $28 • (04/30/91) • **65**
Cabernet Sauvignon Santa Cruz Mountains 1986 • $29 • (08/31/90) • **83**
Cabernet Sauvignon Santa Cruz Mountains 1985 • $40 • (11/15/89) • **81**
Cabernet Sauvignon Santa Cruz Mountains 1984 • $34 • (03/01/89) • **84**
Cabernet Sauvignon Santa Cruz Mountains 1983 • $35 • (03/01/89) • **79**
Cabernet Sauvignon Santa Cruz Mountains 1982 • $35 • (03/01/89) • **70**
Cabernet Sauvignon Santa Cruz Mountains 1981 • $32 • (03/01/89) • **86**
Cabernet Sauvignon Santa Cruz Mountains 1980 • $40 • (03/01/89) • **85**
Cabernet Sauvignon Santa Cruz Mountains 1979 • $32 • (03/01/89) • **69**
Cabernet Sauvignon Santa Cruz Mountains 1978 • $24 Ⓐ • (11/15/92) • **84**
Cabernet Sauvignon Santa Cruz Mountains 1977 • $41 • (03/01/89) • **91**
Cabernet Sauvignon Santa Cruz Mountains 1976 • $81 • (03/01/89) • **83**
Cabernet Sauvignon Santa Cruz Mountains 1975 • $19 Ⓐ • (03/01/89) • **90**
Cabernet Sauvignon Santa Cruz Mountains 1974: Mature, ripe, rich and concentrated, showing a deep, dark color and flavors to match, packed with complex currant, cherry, tar and spice notes that turn earthy and tannic on the finish. A monumental red that can age for years. 437 cases made. • $75 • (11/15/94) • **88**
Cabernet Sauvignon Santa Cruz Mountains 1973 • $75 • (03/01/89) • **91**
Cabernet Sauvignon Santa Cruz Mountains 1972 • $50 • (03/01/89) • **84**
Cabernet Sauvignon Santa Cruz Mountains Kennedy Vineyard 1978 • $NA • (11/15/92) • **85**
Cabernet Sauvignon Santa Cruz Mountains Lathweisen Ridge 1990: Ripe, generous and muscular, with thick-textured, herb- and earth-scented currant and black cherry aromas and flavors. The tannins are present, but fine in texture and well integrated. Should be at its best after 1998. 1,054 cases made. • $15 • (06/15/93) • **88**
Cabernet Sauvignon Santa Cruz Mountains Lathweisen Ridge 1989 • $14 • (08/31/92) • **85**
Cabernet Sauvignon Santa Cruz Mountains Lathweisen Ridge 1988 • $12 • (04/30/91) • **87**
Cabernet Sauvignon Santa Cruz Mountains Old Vine Reserve 1992: Dark, ripe, and intense, marked by plum, prune, cherry, currant and mineral notes. Finishes with firm tannins and a sense of finesse. Best after 1999. 496 cases made. • $35 • (06/15/96) • **90**
Cabernet Sauvignon Santa Cruz Mountains Old Vine Reserve 1991: Lean and firm, with a tight core of herb, black cherry and cedary flavors that turn supple on the finish, although the tannins are tight on the finish. Best after 1997. 344 cases made. • $35 • (04/15/95) • **88**
Cabernet Sauvignon Santa Cruz Mountains Old Vine Reserve 1990: Dark and dense, a sturdy wine with solid currant, black cherry, smoke and caramel aromas and flavors, finishing with a silky texture that shows off the spicy, toasty notes. Should be ready now. Tasted twice. 448 cases made. • $30 • (11/15/93) • **85**
Cabernet Sauvignon Santa Cruz Mountains Young Vine Cuvée 1987 • $12 • (04/15/90) • **85**
Chardonnay Edna Valley MacGregor Vineyard 1994: Moderate pear and citrus notes float through this. Doesn't have the richness of some earlier vintages, but good nonetheless. 5,000 cases made. • $16 • (06/15/96) • **84**
Chardonnay Edna Valley MacGregor Vineyard 1993: A decadent style that's earthy and funky, but the rich, complex pear, honey, toast and spice flavors build to a full, complex aftertaste. 4,597 cases made. • $15 • (03/31/95) SS • **90**
Chardonnay Edna Valley MacGregor Vineyard 1992: Firm and focused, with delicate layers of honey, pear and hazelnut flavors that turn elegant and spicy on the finish. Well balanced and ready to drink now through 1997.-JL 4,994 cases made. • $15 • (06/15/94) • **89**
Chardonnay Edna Valley MacGregor Vineyard 1991 • $15 • (07/15/93) • **85**
Pinot Noir Edna Valley 1991 • $15 • (02/28/94) • **83**
Pinot Noir Santa Cruz Mountains 1990 • $30 • (02/28/94) • **86**
Pinot Noir Santa Cruz Mountains 1989 • $30 • (02/28/94) • **85**
Pinot Noir Santa Cruz Mountains 1987 • $25 • (04/15/90) • **79**
Pinot Noir Santa Cruz Mountains 1985 • $35 • (06/15/88) • **90**
Pinot Noir Santa Cruz Mountains 1984 • $35 • (04/15/88) • **86**
Pinot Noir Santa Cruz Mountains 1983 • $35 • (08/31/86) • **77**

MOUNT KONOCTI | CALIFORNIA

Cabernet Franc Lake County Kelsey 1992: Light, with an herb and cedary oak edge to the berry flavors. Drinkable now. 1,487 cases made. • $7 • (02/28/95) • **84**
Cabernet Sauvignon Lake County 1993: A bit rustic, with chewy tannins and earthy wild berry flavors. 4,500 cases made. • $10 • (12/15/95) • **82**
Cabernet Sauvignon Lake County Kelsey 1992: Young and still a bit grapey, not to mention firmly tannic. Drinkable now or hold until 1997. 4,800 cases made. • $10 • (11/15/94) • **84**
Fumé Blanc Lake County 1994: Bright and tasty, generous with its pear, papaya and spice flavors and hinting at honey on the finish. 10,000 cases made. • $8 • (08/31/95) • **85**
Fumé Blanc Lake County 1993: A lean and citrusy California wine, with distinct grapefruit character running through the finish. 12,000 cases made. • $7 • (12/31/94) BB • **85**
Fumé Blanc Lake County Grand Fumé Barrel Fermented Reserve 1993: Light and delicate, round enough to display some spicy honey and pear flavors. Not much that says Sauvignon Blanc, however. 500 cases made. • $12 • (08/31/95) • **84**
Sémillon-Chardonnay Lake County 1993: Simple and a little herbal, with a sappy edge to the basic apple fruit. Ready now. 4,974 cases made. • $7 • (04/15/95) • **82**

MOUNT MADONNA | CALIFORNIA

Merlot San Luis Obispo County 1987 • $8 • (05/31/92) • **69**

MOUNT MADRONA | CALIFORNIA

Chardonnay Napa Valley Certified Kosher 1992: Tart and earthy, with a modest band of smoky oak, grapefruit and ripe pear flavors. 10,000 cases made. • $14 • (07/31/95) • **83**

MOUNT PALOMAR | CALIFORNIA

Cabernet Sauvignon Temecula 1991: Earthy and funky, with weedy bell pepper flavors that turn leathery on the finish. 1,281 cases made. • $10 • (11/15/94) • **74**
Cabernet Sauvignon Temecula 1990: Firm and focused, with herbal notes accenting the raspberry and blackberry flavors. Has a touch of fine tannin and plenty of flavor on the finish. Drink now. 1,175 cases made. • $12 • (07/15/93) • **83**
Castelletto Cortese Temecula 1993: Cortese is the grape that makes Gavi in the Piedmont region of Italy, fresh and enticing, a lively wine

Key: SS—Spectator Selection. CS—Cellar Selection. BB—Best Buy. $NA—Price not available. (BT)—Barrel tasting. Ⓐ—Auction Price.
Dates in parentheses represent the issues in which the ratings were published.

with pear and floral flavors that linger nicely on the finish. 495 cases made. • $16 • (12/31/94) • **87**

Chardonnay Temecula 1993: Austere, with a tart band of flinty herb and spice accents. 2,000 cases made. • $10 • (02/28/95) • **79**

Chardonnay Temecula 1992: Doesn't quite make it with the gluey canned pineapple flavors. Marginal quality. Ready now.-JL 2,198 cases made. • $10 • (06/30/94) • **72**

Chardonnay Temecula 1991 • $10 • (08/31/92) • **83**

Chardonnay Temecula Reserve 1993: Clean and correct, with a spicy, grassy edge to the pear-laced flavors. 325 cases made. • $16 • (07/31/95) • **83**

Chardonnay Temecula Reserve 1992: An elegant, reserved style, with light pear, oak and spice flavors, finishing with a citrus and grapefruit edge. Ready now.-JL 291 cases made. • $16 • (06/30/94) • **84**

Chardonnay Temecula Reserve 1991 • $16 • (08/31/92) • **79**

Johannisberg Riesling Temecula 1993: Tart and sweet, like a sugared vinegar. Not for every taste. 4,500 cases made. • $6 • (09/15/95) • **73**

Sangiovese Temecula Castelletto 1992: Light and earthy, with some unwelcome barnyard notes. 588 cases made. • $18 • (08/31/95) • **73**

Sangiovese Temecula Castelletto 1991: A modestly ripe and smoky Sangiovese with floral, herb, olive and spicy cherry notes. Medium-bodied, it is light in tannins and drinks well now. Better than bottle previously tasted. 360 cases made. • $20 • (09/30/94) • **82**

Sauvignon Blanc Temecula 1993: Light and refreshing, a delicately herbal wine that finishes slightly sweet. 958 cases made. • $7 • (08/31/94) • **79**

Sauvignon Blanc Temecula 1992 • $7 • (09/15/93) • **78**

Sauvignon Blanc Temecula Reserve 1993: Earthy flavors, modest intensity, soft structure add up to a drinkable but unexceptional wine. 226 cases made. • $10 • (08/31/94) • **74**

MOUNT PLEASANT | MISSOURI

Augusta Port 1988 • $19 • (02/29/92) • **80**

Vidal Late Harvest Augusta Ice Wine 1989 • $20 • (02/29/92) • **78**

MOUNT VEEDER | CALIFORNIA

Cabernet Sauvignon Mount Veeder 1992: Supple and forward but with an earthy edge to the Cabernet fruit. Round around the edges, but not atypical for this wine at this stage. • $NA • (05/31/93) BT • **85**

Cabernet Sauvignon Napa Valley 1992: Intense and tannic, with a tightly wound core of currant, cherry, anise and berry flavors, but in the end its the tannins that stand out in this wine, giving it a hard, biting edge. Hands off until 1999, but even then it may be tannic. • $25 • (12/15/95) • **87**

Cabernet Sauvignon Napa Valley 1991: Very good, but not in the same class as the spectacular 1990. Ripe currant and black cherry flavors pick up cedar and spice on the tough, tannic finish. Tasted three times, with consistent notes. Best after 1996. 2,600 cases made. • $18 • (01/31/95) • **85**

Cabernet Sauvignon Napa Valley 1990: Opulent and chewy with lots of ripe fruit flavors and spicy, buttery oak shadings. Serves up a rich core of black cherry, currant and plum-tinged fruit and finishes with a delicious encore of fruit and oak. Wonderful depth, richness, balance and finesse. 2,400 cases made. • $15 • (10/31/93) SS • **94**

Cabernet Sauvignon Napa Valley 1989 • $15 • (06/15/93) • **82**

Cabernet Sauvignon Napa Valley 1987 • $22 • (04/30/91) • **85**

Cabernet Sauvignon Napa Valley 1986 • $20 • (11/15/90) • **83**

Cabernet Sauvignon Napa Valley 1985 • $20 • (03/01/89) • **87**

Cabernet Sauvignon Napa Valley 1984 • $24 • (03/01/89) • **88**

Cabernet Sauvignon Napa Valley 1983 • $24 • (03/01/89) • **84**

Cabernet Sauvignon Napa Valley 1982 • $18 • (03/01/89) • **68**

Cabernet Sauvignon Napa Valley 1981 • $24 • (03/01/89) • **77**

Cabernet Sauvignon Napa Valley 1974: Still sturdy with ample dry oak flavors and ripe, lean, earthy currant and cedar notes. The tannins have mellowed but this Cabernet remains dry and austere, picking up a gamy edge on the finish. Drinkable now. Tasted twice, with one superior bottle. 650 cases made. • $53 • (11/15/94) • **85**

Cabernet Sauvignon Napa Valley 1973 • $70 • (03/01/89) • **90**

Cabernet Sauvignon Napa Valley Bernstein Vineyards 1980 • $30 • (03/01/89) • **87**

Cabernet Sauvignon Napa Valley Bernstein Vineyards 1979 • $39 • (03/01/89) • **92**

Cabernet Sauvignon Napa Valley Bernstein Vineyards 1978 • $31 • (11/15/92) • **78**

Cabernet Sauvignon Napa Valley Bernstein Vineyards 1977 • $32 • (03/01/89) • **85**

Cabernet Sauvignon Napa Valley Bernstein Vineyards 1976 • $23 • (03/01/89) • **77**

Cabernet Sauvignon Napa Valley Bernstein Vineyards 1975 • $29 • (03/01/89) • **83**

Cabernet Sauvignon Napa Valley Niebaum-Coppola 1977 • $60 • (03/01/89) • **88**

Cabernet Sauvignon Napa Valley Sidehill Ranch 1978 • $40 • (03/01/89) • **86**

Chardonnay Napa Valley 1992: Pleasantly balanced, with ripe spicy pear and toasty oak flavors that fan out and gain complexity on the finish, picking up peach and smoky notes.-JL 4,000 cases made. • $14 • (06/30/94) • **88**

Chardonnay Napa Valley 1991 • $16 • (07/15/93) • **76**

Meritage Cabernet Blend Napa Valley 1989 • $24 • (06/15/93) • **88**

Meritage Cabernet Blend Napa Valley 1988 • $24 • (07/15/92) • **83**

Meritage Cabernet Blend Napa Valley 1986 • $25 • (03/01/89) • **93**

Reserve Cabernet Blend Napa Valley 1992: Tightly-wound currant, cherry and berry flavors and lively tannins on the finish. Vibrant and young, needs cellaring into 1998-99. 3,000 cases made. • $40 • **88**

Reserve Cabernet Blend Napa Valley 1991: Elegant, attractive earth, anise and currant, turning crisp and lean on the palate of beet and cedar flavors. 3,000 cases made. • $40 • (09/15/95) • **84**

Reserve Cabernet Blend Napa Valley 1990: Elegant and supple, with a rich, spicy blend of currant, berry and buttery oak flavors. Has a wonderful sense of harmony and finesse, finishing with firm, plush tannins. Best to cellar this one through 1997. 2,400 cases made. • $25 • (09/15/94) CS • **92**

Zinfandel Napa County 1982 • $8 • (03/16/85) • **86**

Zinfandel Napa Valley 1993: Clean and correct, with a modest core of plum, earth and berry that's appealing though chunky and somewhat unevolved. A little age may soften it up a bit. 438 cases made. • $20 • (03/31/96) • **83**

MOUNTAIN DOME | WASHINGTON

Brut Rosé Washington NV: Coppery color, smooth texture, delicate toasty flavors and a hint of melon add up to an enjoyable pre-dinner sipper. 450 cases made. • $20 • (09/15/95) • **85**

Brut Washington 1991: Has a slightly sour edge to the spicy, slightly gamy flavors. Not for everyone. 550 cases made. • $17 • (09/30/95) • **78**

Brut Washington 1990: Smooth and spicy, a soft-textured bubbly with ginger and vanilla overtones to the toasty pear flavors. 2,000 cases made. • $16 • (09/30/94) • **85**

MOUNTAIN VALLEY | TENNESSEE

Dessert Tennessee Blackberry Table Wine 1991 • $8 • (02/29/92) • **75**

MOUNTAIN VIEW | CALIFORNIA

Cabernet Sauvignon Mendocino County 1986 • $6 • (03/31/90) • **79**

Cabernet Sauvignon Mendocino County 1985 • $6 • (02/15/89) • **77**

Cabernet Sauvignon North Coast 1992: Correct but simple, with cedary oak and light, grapey Cabernet flavors. 8,500 cases made. • $6 • (11/15/94) • **79**

Cabernet Sauvignon North Coast 1990: Crisp, tart and earthy, with a beet edge to the caramel-tinged, modest cherry flavors. Finishes a bit gamy. An odd duck, but drinkable. 8,000 cases made. • $6 • (06/15/93) • **76**

Cabernet Sauvignon North Coast 1989 • $6 • (11/15/92) • **71**

Cabernet Sauvignon North Coast 1988 • $6 • (04/30/91) BB • **80**

Cabernet Sauvignon North Coast 1980 • $5 • (04/16/84) • **62**

Chardonnay Monterey 1993: Light and citrusy, with a strong oaky streak running through the narrow flavors. Ready now. 50,000 cases made. • $6 • **80**

Chardonnay Monterey 1992: Lean with a tinny canned pineapple and grapefruit edge.-JL 72,000 cases made. • $6 • (06/30/94) • **75**

Chardonnay Monterey County 1991 • $6 • (03/31/93) • **78**
Merlot Napa County 1989 • $6 • (05/31/91) • **72**
Pinot Noir Carneros 1986 • $6 • (02/28/89) BB • **80**
Pinot Noir Monterey-Napa Counties 1992 • $6 • (02/28/94) • **81**
Pinot Noir Monterey-Napa Counties 1991 • $6 • (02/28/93) • **74**
Pinot Noir Monterey-Napa Counties 1990 • $6 • (04/30/92) BB • **82**
Pinot Noir Monterey-Napa Counties 1989 • $6 • (02/28/91) BB • **82**
Pinot Noir Monterey-Napa Counties 1988 • $6 • (03/31/90) • **72**
Zinfandel Amador County Lot #91 NV: Intense, chewy and tannic. A hearty style with rustic flavors. 3,000 cases made. • $5 • (10/15/94) • **79**
Zinfandel Amador County Lot #93 NV: Medium-bodied and pleasant enough to be a good value that offers pure berry and spice notes. 3,300 cases made. • $6 • (10/15/95) • **82**

MOYER | TEXAS

Brut Texas NV • $13 • (02/29/92) • **80**
Brut Texas Especial NV • $9 • (02/29/92) • **78**
Brut Texas Natural NV • $11 • (07/31/89) • **79**
Extra Dry Texas NV • $9 • (02/29/92) • **81**

MUELLER | CALIFORNIA

Chardonnay Alexander Valley Gauer Ranch 1994: Begins with spicy, toasty oak and turns toward lean citrus and pear flavors. 508 cases made. • $15 • (05/15/96) • **89**
Chardonnay Russian River Valley 1994: Clean and lively, as an attractive band of citrus, apple, pear and spice finishes in a subtle nutmeg and honey aftertaste. Complex and refined style that offers lots of finesse and grace. 592 cases made. • $13 • (05/15/96) • **90**
Chardonnay Russian River Valley Barrel Fermented 1991 • $13 • (10/15/93) • **91**
Chardonnay Russian River Valley LB Barrel Fermented 1992: Smooth and ripe, with rich pear, smoke and toasty oak shadings. Big and generous, rich aftertaste. 481 cases made. • $13 • (12/15/94) • **88**
Chardonnay Russian River Valley LB Reserve 1992: Intense and spicy, with rich apricot, pear, honey and oak flavors that fold together nicely, with a rich smoky aftertaste. 32 cases made. • $30 • (07/31/95) • **90**
Chardonnay Sonoma County Gauer Ranch 1993: A complex and sophisticated style that combines ripe, bold Chardonnay fruitiness with subtle oak shadings. Hints of pear, honey and nutmeg blend together on the finish. 306 cases made. • $15 • (03/31/96) • **88**
Pinot Noir Russian River Valley Emily's Cuvée 1994: Serves up a complex array of ripe, juicy Pinot Noir fruit, sporting tiers of cherry, spice, herb and pretty, buttery oak. An elegant and understated style: smooth, silky texture and long, lingering aftertaste. 266 cases made. • $20 • (04/30/96) • **91**

MUMM CUVÉE NAPA | CALIFORNIA

Brut Blanc de Blancs Napa Valley NV: Somewhat earthy, but there's enough ripe cherry and wild berry flavor to maintain balance. Finishes with a spicy, toasty edge and delicate touch. 2,500 cases made. • $18 • (12/15/95) • **89**
Brut Blanc de Noirs Napa Valley NV: Attractive for its ripe, earthy black cherry and spice flavors. Holds together nicely, finishing with richness and depth. Ready now. • $14 • (12/31/94) • **87**
Brut Carneros Winery Lake 1990: Intense and complex, sporting well-focused pear, spice and citrus notes and an appealing, fruity aftertaste. Drinks well now. 4,500 cases made. • $18 • (11/30/95) • **89**
Brut Carneros Winery Lake 1989: Smooth and elegant, with ripe pear, vanilla, toast and spice notes that linger. Drinks well now. • $20 • (12/31/94) • **86**
Brut Carneros Napa Valley Winery Lake Cuvée Napa 1988 • $22 • (11/15/91) • **89**
Brut Carneros Winery Lake Cuvée Napa 1987 • $22 • (11/15/90) • **91**

Key: SS—Spectator Selection. CS—Cellar Selection. BB—Best Buy. $NA—Price not available. (BT)—Barrel tasting. Ⓐ—Auction Price.
Dates in parentheses represent the issues in which the ratings were published.

Brut Carneros Winery Lake Cuvée Napa 1986 • $23 • (12/10/90) • **87**
Brut Napa Valley Prestige NV: This grows on you with its subtle cherry, vanilla and spice flavors that start out simple but gain some nuances on the finish. Ready now. • $14 • (12/15/94) • **88**
Brut Napa Valley Reserve Cuvée Napa 1989 • $18 • (10/15/93) • **89**
Brut Napa Valley Reserve Cuvée Napa 1987 • $22 • (12/31/90) • **87**
Brut Napa Valley Reserve Cuvée Napa 1985 • $21 • (05/31/89) • **86**
Sparkling Napa Valley DVX 1991: Ripe, bright pear, apple, vanilla and spice notes. Intensity, depth and concentration on aftertaste, but fruit rises to the occasion, giving it a complex finish. 3,000 cases made. • $30 • **89**
Sparkling Napa Valley DVX 1990: Crisp and clean, with a band of toast, ginger, pear and spice. Gains depth and complexity on the finish, where the flavors fan out. Mumm's new prestige cuvée. 3,000 cases made. • $25 • (12/15/94) SS • **91**
Sparkling Napa Valley Vintage Reserve 1989: A solid bubbly, with modest spice, pear and hazelnut flavors that build on the finish, where they turn spicy. An elegant wine that's ready now. • $18 • (12/31/94) • **87**

MURPHY-GOODE | CALIFORNIA

Alexander Valley 1994: Light and smooth, its vibrant nectarine and spice flavors humming nicely on the finish. Not much that says Sauvignon, but tasty and long. 20,000 cases made. • $10 • (07/31/95) • **87**
Cabernet Sauvignon Alexander Valley 1987 • $17 • (05/31/90) • **89**
Cabernet Sauvignon Alexander Valley Estate Vineyard 1988 • $16 • (11/15/91) • **87**
Cabernet Sauvignon Alexander Valley Goode-Ready The Second Cabernet 1989 • $10 • (06/15/91) • **80**
Cabernet Sauvignon Alexander Valley Murphy Ranch 1993: Dense and compact, with chewy tannins and rich plum and cherry-laced Cabernet flavors. Still a bit rustic, but a little aging into 1998 should do the trick. 2,900 cases made. • $16 • (11/15/95) • **88**
Cabernet Sauvignon Alexander Valley Murphy Ranch 1992: Firm and crisp, offering a narrow band of dried cherry, chocolate and plum flavors that finish with a good dose of tannin and toasty oak. 3,300 cases made. • $15 • (05/15/95) • **87**
Cabernet Sauvignon Alexander Valley Murphy Ranch 1991: Marked by strong smoky oak flavors. Perhaps with time the spicy currant notes will be able to overcome the oakiness, but for now the fruit takes a backseat. Tasted twice. • $15 • (11/15/94) • **83**
Cabernet Sauvignon Alexander Valley Murphy Ranch 1990: A ripe and pleasing young wine that serves up moderately rich plum, chocolate and currant flavors that turn supple and spicy on the finish. It's well proportioned and tasty through the finish. Drinkable now. 3,300 cases made. • $15 • (10/15/93) • **87**
Cabernet Sauvignon Alexander Valley Murphy Ranch 1989 • $16 • (11/15/92) • **84**
Cabernet Sauvignon Alexander Valley Premier Vineyard 1986 • $16 • (11/15/89) • **90**
Chardonnay Alexander Valley Barrel Fermented 1994: Soft and fruity, offering tasty, bright melon and green grape flavors and a nice addition of resiny oak. Ready now. • $14 • (12/31/95) • **86**
Chardonnay Alexander Valley Barrel Fermented 1993: Tastes a little disjointed, with the acidity standing apart, but the ripe pear and apple-laced flavors hold together. 17,000 cases made. • $13 • (07/31/95) • **86**
Chardonnay Alexander Valley Barrel Fermented 1992: Clean, elegant and lively with crisp pear, citrus and hazelnut flavors that fan out on the finish. Balanced and ready to drink now.-JL 16,100 cases made. • $13 • (03/15/94) • **86**
Chardonnay Alexander Valley Estate Vineyard 1991 • $13 • (12/15/92) • **80**
Chardonnay Alexander Valley Island Block Reserve 1994: Serves the ripe pear and pineapple flavors up front, with a spicy oak dimension that's complex and compelling. An openly fruity white that finishes with a rich, smoky aftertaste. 1,400 cases made. • $24 • (01/31/96) • **89**
Chardonnay Alexander Valley Reserve 1992: A rich, creamy and utterly delicious new wine from Murphy-Goode. It serves up layers of ripe apple, pear and honeyed notes and then adds a pretty overlay of spicy, toasty oak. The finish is long and complex, with a smoky aftertaste. 1,000 cases made. • $22 • (06/30/94) • **92**

Chardonnay Russian River Valley J & K Murphy Vineyard Reserve 1994: Marked by an openly spicy edge, it's an elegant and refined style with flavors that build on the finish, picking up a smoky, toasty edge. Very appealing now. 1,350 cases made. • $24 • (05/31/96) • **89**

Chardonnay Russian River Valley J & K Murphy Vineyard Reserve 1993: A lot of oaky flavors, but it wears it well, with floral and spicy aromas with a tangerine edge to the pear and oak flavors, but it folds together nicely on the finish where it turns smoky. 1,000 cases made. • $24 • (07/31/95) • **90**

Fumé Blanc Alexander Valley Barrel Fermented Reserve 1992 • $15 • (03/15/94) • **88**

Fumé Blanc Alexander Valley Barrel Fermented Reserve 1991 • $14 • (02/15/93) • **83**

Fumé Blanc Alexander Valley Dry 1993: Light and slightly herbal. A crisp wine with bright grapefruit and sage flavors that's drinkable now. • $10 • (09/30/94) • **86**

Fumé Blanc Alexander Valley Estate Vineyard 1991 • $9 • (11/30/92) • **82**

Fumé Blanc Alexander Valley Reserve 1993: Smooth and elegant, featuring a buttery, creamy texture and flavors of pear and citrus on the balanced finish. 9,400 cases made. • $15 • (02/28/95) • **89**

Merlot Alexander Valley 1992: Deeply colored, well oaked and firmly tannic, offering currant and cherry flavors. This young Merlot needs cellaring, best after 1996. • $15 • (01/31/95) • **83**

Merlot Alexander Valley Murphy Ranch 1990 • $15 • (03/31/93) • **83**

Merlot Alexander Valley Murphy Ranch 1989 • $15 • (05/31/92) • **82**

Merlot Alexander Valley Murphy Ranches 1993: Firm, compact, balanced, featuring a trim band of plum and cherry flavor, solid tannins and good length. Drinkable now through 1998. 1,650 cases made. • $16 • (12/15/95) • **85**

Merlot Alexander Valley Murphy Ranches 1991 • $15 • (03/15/94) • **83**

Merlot Alexander Valley Premier Vineyard 1986 • $14 • (01/31/89) • **90**

Pinot Blanc Alexander Valley 1992 • $13 • (12/31/93) • **83**

Pinot Blanc Alexander Valley Barrel-Fermented 1994: Bright, fruity and straightforward, showing apple and spice flavors. Nicely balanced with just a hint of oak. 2,900 cases made. • $13 • (11/15/95) • **83**

Pinot Blanc Alexander Valley G.M.S. Redux Barrel Fermented Melon de Bourgogne 1991 • $13 • (12/31/92) • **83**

Pinot Blanc Alexander Valley Melon de Bourgogne Barrel Fermented 1993: Soft and fruity, a delicate wine with a spicy edge to the pretty pear and citrus flavors, finishing smooth and with a light touch of oak. Ready now. 3,000 cases made. • $13 • (04/15/95) • **88**

Sauvignon Blanc Alexander Valley Reserve Fumé 1994: Smooth and generous, offering a nice touch of herb, pear and citrus and ripe aftertaste. 11,000 cases made. • $16 • (02/29/96) • **85**

MURRIETA'S WELL | CALIFORNIA

Vendimia Livermore Valley 1992: Smooth and polished, round in texture, an elegant wine that shows citrus-tinged pear and spicy vanilla flavors. Ready now. 2,400 cases made. • $23 • (07/31/95) • **88**

Vendimia Livermore Valley 1991: Earthy with a tarry, smoky edge to the currant and berry flavors. 2,240 cases made. • $28 • (05/31/95) • **84**

Vendimia Livermore Valley 1990: Lean and green, with a stalky, vegetal edge to the modest currant fruit, balanced and lively in texture, with a nice spiciness on the finish, hinting at tobacco at the end. Drink after 1997. 1,492 cases made. • $28 • (11/15/93) • **86**

Vendimia Red Livermore Valley 1990: Strikes a nice balance between spicy, buttery oak and pretty currant and plum notes. Flavors linger on the finish, where the tannins are smooth and plush. 1,492 cases made. • $28 • (11/15/94) • **89**

Zinfandel Livermore Valley 1991: Brimming with fresh, ripe, juicy fruit. Exotic and serves up lots of rich wild berry, cherry and raspberry jam flavors. Smooth tannins make it appealing now, but it's rich and concentrated enough to cellar. 880 cases made. • $16 • (10/15/94) • **89**

Zinfandel Livermore Valley 1989: Ripe, with characteristic raspberry and pepper aromas. Has a tar note that turns funky and earthy on the long finish. Best to drink it soon. 311 cases made. • $16 • (10/15/94) • **83**

NALLE | CALIFORNIA

Cabernet Sauvignon Dry Creek Valley 1990: Firm and focused, with bright blackberry and currant aromas and flavors, chunky tannins and an austere finish. It has enough intensity to warrant cellaring until 1997 or 1998. 200 cases made. • $18 • (11/15/93) • **85**

Cabernet Sauvignon Dry Creek Valley 1987 • $18 • (01/31/91) • **89**

Zinfandel Dry Creek Valley 1993: Well balanced, with supple cherry and raspberry flavors and light oak shadings that turn elegant. The flavors linger, but it's a shade lighter than in past vintages. 2,500 cases made. • $16 • (08/31/95) • **87**

Zinfandel Dry Creek Valley 1992: Pleasing, ripe, supple fruit and hints of floral and wild berry notes. The tannins are firm and intense, but drinkable now. 2,500 cases made. • $15 • (10/15/94) • **85**

Zinfandel Dry Creek Valley 1991 • $14 • (09/30/93) • **86**

Zinfandel Dry Creek Valley 1990 • $14 • (10/15/92) • **89**

Zinfandel Dry Creek Valley 1989 • $14 • (07/31/91) • **85**

Zinfandel Dry Creek Valley 1988 • $25 • (07/31/90) • **89**

Zinfandel Dry Creek Valley 1987 • $22 • (05/31/89) SS • **92**

Zinfandel Dry Creek Valley 1986 • $9 • (06/30/88) • **90**

Zinfandel Dry Creek Valley 1985 • $8 • (09/15/87) • **91**

Zinfandel Dry Creek Valley 1984 • $7 • (10/15/86) • **91**

NAPA, DOMAINE | CALIFORNIA

Cabernet Sauvignon Napa Valley 1987 • $13 • (12/15/92) • **75**

Cabernet Sauvignon Napa Valley 1985 • $12 • (12/15/88) • **81**

Chardonnay Napa Valley 1991 • $13 • (07/15/93) • **82**

Merlot Napa Valley 1990 • $15 • (05/31/92) • **84**

Sauvignon Blanc Napa Valley Michel A. Perret 1992: Lean and a bit austere, with an earthy edge to the modest vanilla and pear fruit. 2,000 cases made. • $9 • (08/31/94) • **81**

NAPA CELLARS | CALIFORNIA

Cabernet Sauvignon California 1990: Green and herbal with pungent bell pepper and earth flavors. Turns dry and tannic on the finish. Drinkable now. 1,100 cases made. • $8 • (11/15/94) • **78**

Chardonnay Napa Valley 1993: Earthy and sweaty, with pungent canned grapefruit flavors that are unappetizing. 3,500 cases made. • $7 • (07/31/95) • **72**

Chardonnay Napa Valley 1991 • $7 • (07/15/93) • **82**

Merlot California 1990 • $7 • (05/31/92) • **79**

Merlot California 1989 • $7 • (05/31/91) • **70**

NAPA CREEK | CALIFORNIA

Cabernet Sauvignon Napa Valley 1991: Earthy and leathery, with chewy tannins that dominate the fruit. Will need cellaring to soften and hopefully show more flavor. 2,500 cases made. • $12 • (11/15/94) • **82**

Merlot Napa Valley 1988 • $13 • (03/31/91) • **75**

Merlot Napa Valley 1987 • $14 • (06/15/90) • **83**

NAPA RIDGE | CALIFORNIA

Cabernet Sauvignon Central Coast 1992: Ripe and fruity, with a core of jammy black cherry and wild berry flavors that have a tannic edge. Needs only a little aging to enhance its value even more. 45,000 cases made. • $8 • (10/15/95) BB • **87**

Cabernet Sauvignon Central Coast Oak Barrel 1991: Supple and generous, with pretty wild berry and cherry flavors. Mildly tannic, you can drink now or cellar for a year or so to allow it to soften. • $8 • (11/15/94) • **84**

Cabernet Sauvignon Napa Valley Coastal Reserve 1989 • $12 • (07/15/93) • **85**

Cabernet Sauvignon North Coast 1982 • $5 • (03/31/87) • **72**

Cabernet Sauvignon North Coast Coastal 1989 • $6 • (11/15/91) • **79**

Cabernet Sauvignon North Coast Coastal Oak Barrel 1993: Has appealing spicy berry and toasty oak flavors that are pleasantly well proportioned. Another terrific value from this California winery. 38,000 cases made. • $7 • (11/30/95) BB • **87**

Cabernet Sauvignon North Coast Coastal Oak Barrel 1992: Austere with crisp currant and cherry notes of modest depth and proportion. Ready now. • $8 • (11/15/94) • **79**

Cabernet Sauvignon North Coast Coastal Oak Barrel 1991: Light and fruity, a simple young Cabernet with berry and cherry overtones and soft tannins. Drinkable now. • $8 • (11/15/93) • **77**

Cabernet Sauvignon North Coast Coastal Reserve 1991: An intense, tight core of cherry, plum, anise and cedar flavors. It's also quite tannic, so cellaring into 1997 is advised. • $13 • (10/15/95) • **87**

Cabernet Sauvignon North Coast Coastal Reserve 1990: A good but ultimately simple Cabernet, with ripe, coarse fruit notes and firm tannins but not much in the way of finesse or focus. Ready now. • $13 • (11/15/94) • **82**

Cabernet Sauvignon North Coast Coastal Reserve 1989 • $13 • (11/15/93) • **87**

Chardonnay Central Coast 1993: Wonderful flavor and complexity, especially at this price. Rich, with creamy pear, honey and vanilla notes that are firm and compact. Excellent value. Santa Barbara-grown grapes. • $7 • (06/15/94) BB • **87**

Chardonnay Central Coast 1991 • $7 • (07/15/93) • **80**

Chardonnay Central Coast Coastal Vines 1994: Soft, creamy and disarmingly tasty, showing spicy orange and pear flavors that glide smoothly through the supple finish. • $7 • (10/15/95) • **85**

Chardonnay Central Coast Coastal Vines 1993: Lightly fruity with spicy pear and grapefruit notes that are harmonious. Easy to drink and a great value. • $8 • (11/30/94) BB • **85**

Chardonnay Napa Valley Coastal Frisinger Vineyard 1994: Toasty, spicy, earthy notes add some extra dimension to the pear flavors. Best after 1996. 224 cases made. • $11 • (06/30/96) • **85**

Chardonnay Napa Valley Coastal Frisinger Vineyard 1993: An elegant, deft balance between bright pear and lemon flavors and light, spicy oak shadings. Gains richness on the finish. 200 cases made. • $11 • (04/15/95) • **88**

Chardonnay Napa Valley Coastal Reserve 1994: Broad and ripe, with floral, earthy notes that add complexity, and just a hint of honey on the aftertaste. Ready now. 850 cases made. • $12 • (06/30/96) • **86**

Chardonnay Napa Valley Coastal Reserve 1993: Appealing for its compex fruit flavors, with tiers of citrus, pear and spice that stay focused, gaining complexity and length. • $13 • (07/31/95) • **86**

Chardonnay North Coast Coastal Reserve 1992: A spicy style with pretty pear, oak and honeyed notes that are elegant and lively. Fine balance of fruit and wood shadings.-JL • $13 • (05/31/94) • **86**

Chardonnay North Coast Coastal Reserve 1991 • $12 • (07/15/93) • **80**

Chardonnay North Coast Coastal Vines 1992: Bright and fruity, with a sappy streak that takes down some of the charm.-HS • $8 • (06/30/94) • **80**

Merlot North Coast Coastal 1993: Smooth and flavorful, with tasty black cherry, spice and herbal flavors that linger delicately on the finish. • $10 • (06/30/96) BB • **85**

Merlot North Coast Coastal 1992: A chewy California red with a pretty core of herb, currant and vanilla flavors that fold together nicely. It finishes with an attractive cherry and spice edge. 30,000 cases made. • $9 • (03/31/95) BB • **87**

Merlot North Coast Coastal 1991: A lighter style, but well balanced, with spicy Merlot fruit that echoes currant and cherry. Finishes with smooth tannins. Ready now. • $9 • (09/15/94) • **84**

Merlot North Coast Coastal 1990 • $7 • (06/15/93) • **81**

Pinot Noir North Coast 1991 • $6 • (02/28/94) BB • **83**

Pinot Noir North Coast Coastal 1994: Smooth and polished, with a pretty core of cherry and plum and a toasty oak overlay. Attractive for its value. 49,000 cases made. • $7 • (01/31/96) BB • **86**

Pinot Noir North Coast Coastal 1993: Leans toward the herb- and tealike aspects of Pinot Noir, finishing with a nice touch of toasty oak and black cherry. 30,000 cases made. • $8 • (12/15/94) BB • **84**

Pinot Noir North Coast Coastal 1989 • $7 • (07/31/91) BB • **82**

Sauvignon Blanc North Coast Coastal 1994: A bright and crisp California white that folds in some lively herbal aromas and flavors to go along with the citrus and melon notes. Drinkable now, and what an attractive price. 22,000 cases made. • $5 • (12/15/95) BB • **86**

Key: SS—Spectator Selection. CS—Cellar Selection. BB—Best Buy. $NA—Price not available. (BT)—Barrel tasting. Ⓐ—Auction Price.
Dates in parentheses represent the issues in which the ratings were published.

Sauvignon Blanc North Coast Coastal 1993: Simple and appealing, offering peach and pear flavors with an earthy, herbal edge. • $4 • (03/31/95) • **81**

Sauvignon Blanc North Coast Coastal 1992: Crisp and simple, a nice white wine with little to identify it as Sauvignon Blanc. • $6 • (08/31/94) • **79**

White Zinfandel Lodi 1988 • $6 • (06/15/89) • **75**

Zinfandel Central Coast Coastal 1990 • $7 • (09/30/93) • **76**

NAPA SUN | CALIFORNIA

Cabernet Sauvignon Napa Valley 1980 • $5 • (03/16/84) • **75**

NAVARRO | CALIFORNIA

Brut Anderson Valley Gewürztraminer 1989 • $8 • (05/15/92) • **82**

Brut Anderson Valley NV: Tastes off-dry, showing ripe, spicy pear, hazelnut and vanilla notes. Simple but appealing. 610 cases made. • $17 • (05/31/95) • **83**

Brut Mendocino 1988 • $16 • (12/31/93) • **81**

Cabernet Sauvignon Mendocino 1990: A complete and complex young red, supple and harmonious, showing rich herb, chocolate, cherry and vanilla notes and plush tannins. Best in 1997. 520 cases made. • $17 • (10/15/95) • **88**

Cabernet Sauvignon Mendocino 1989: An herbal, earthy style that manages to deliver sufficient currant and spice flavors to maintain interest. The finish is tannic enough to warrant cellaring through 1996. 793 cases made. • $16 • (11/15/94) • **82**

Cabernet Sauvignon Mendocino 1988 • $16 • (10/15/93) • **86**

Cabernet Sauvignon Mendocino 1987 • $16 • (11/15/92) • **88**

Cabernet Sauvignon Mendocino 1986 • $16 • (10/15/91) • **87**

Cabernet Sauvignon Mendocino 1985 • $14 • (11/15/90) • **87**

Chardonnay Anderson Valley 1993: Solid with ripe, appealing pear, apple and spicy notes, finishing with a light oak shading. 1,920 cases made. • $8 • (07/31/95) • **83**

Chardonnay Anderson Valley Première Reserve 1994: Bright and lively, with a tight core of pear, peach, honey and nectarine flavors, yet maintains its delicacy and finesse. Young and vibrant, it can age too. 3,272 cases made. • $15 • (06/15/96) • **89**

Chardonnay Anderson Valley Première Reserve 1993: Clean, ripe and fruity, sporting pretty pear, apple, peach and nectarine notes and spicy aftertaste. Young and vibrant, it drinks well now but can stand short-term aging. • $NA • (02/29/96) • **88**

Chardonnay Anderson Valley Première Reserve 1992: Supple and fruity, with ripe pear, apple and light oak shadings. Harmonious and can stand short-term cellaring. • $15 • (11/30/94) • **87**

Chardonnay Anderson Valley Première Reserve 1991 • $15 • (10/31/93) SS • **91**

Chardonnay Anderson Valley Table Wine 1992: Smooth and creamy, with a spicy wood and nutmeg edge to the ripe pear and apple flavors. Try now.-JL 1,189 cases made. • $7 • (04/15/94) BB • **86**

Chardonnay Mendocino 1994: Ripe and spicy, with a juicy core of citrus, pear and spice. Drinks well now. 1,258 cases made. • $8 • (02/29/96) • **85**

Edelzwicker Mendocino 1993: A little sweet, but the snappy acidity balances nicely, showing off the appealing apple, citrus and spice flavors. Ready. • $6 • (12/31/94) • **86**

Gewürztraminer Anderson Valley Cuvée Traditional Dry 1991 • $8 • (06/15/93) • **86**

Gewürztraminer Anderson Valley Dry 1994: Bright, focused and on-the-mark with its rose petal, grapefruit and nectarine flavors that finish dry and round. Delicious now. 4,053 cases made. • $11 • (05/31/96) • **88**

Gewürztraminer Anderson Valley Dry 1993: Light and floral, a touch of grapefruit and pear sneaks in behind the floral, spicy notes, finishing a little flat. Drink soon. 4,194 cases made. • $9 • (02/28/95) • **84**

Gewürztraminer Anderson Valley Dry 1992 • $9 • (04/15/94) BB • **88**

Gewürztraminer Late Harvest Anderson Valley Sweet 1989 • $12 • (04/30/91) • **86**

Gewürztraminer Late Harvest Anderson Valley Sweet Cluster Selected 1989 • $15 • (03/15/92) • **86**

Gewürztraminer Late Harvest Anderson Valley Vineyard Selection 1986 • $19 • (02/28/89) • **93**

Gewürztraminer Late Harvest North Coast Sweet 1991 • $14 • (12/31/93) • **90**

Petits Villages Mendocino 1993: Very light and fruity, a Beaujolais-style wine with appealing berry and watermelon character. Ready now. A blend of several varieties, including Grenache, Pinot Noir and Gamay. 760 cases made. • $8 • (04/30/95) • **83**

Pinot Gris Anderson Valley 1994: Light in weight but broad-flavored, showing pear, nectarine and spice notes on a simple frame. Ready now. 566 cases made. • $12 • (11/30/95) • **85**

Pinot Gris Anderson Valley 1993: Smooth, polished and creamy, lovely for its peach and orange cream flavors that linger delicately on the finish. 477 cases made. • $8 • **87**

Pinot Noir Anderson Valley 1984 • $12 • (01/31/88) • **91**

Pinot Noir Anderson Valley 1982 • $9 • (04/15/87) • **82**

Pinot Noir Anderson Valley Clone 54 1992: Beaujolais-like with its fresh, snappy, grapey edge, but rich and complex, with black cherry and wild berry flavors that stay focused on the finish. Not too tannic, so you can drink it now or age it short-term. • $12 • (11/30/94) • **87**

Pinot Noir Anderson Valley Cuvée 90/91 • $9 • (02/28/94) BB • **83**

Pinot Noir Anderson Valley Deep End Blend 1989 • $18 • (02/28/93) • **88**

Pinot Noir Anderson Valley Méthode à l'Ancienne 1992: Pleasant enough with its ripe plum and cherry notes and hints of spice and oak on the finish. Smooth tannins make it appealing now. 3,216 cases made. • $15 • (03/31/96) • **85**

Pinot Noir Anderson Valley Méthode à l'Ancienne 1991: Elegant with delicate cherry and blackberry that are bright and vivid, and a finish that echoes those flavors. 3,308 cases made. • $15 • (12/31/94) • **86**

Pinot Noir Anderson Valley Méthode à l'Ancienne 1990 • $15 • (02/28/94) • **86**

Pinot Noir Anderson Valley Méthode à l'Ancienne 1989 • $15 • (02/28/93) • **87**

Pinot Noir Anderson Valley Méthode à l'Ancienne 1988 • $14 • (03/31/92) • **89**

Pinot Noir Anderson Valley Méthode à l'Ancienne 1987 • $14 • (04/30/91) • **85**

Pinot Noir Anderson Valley Méthode à l'Ancienne 1986 • $14 • (03/31/90) • **87**

Pinot Noir Anderson Valley Méthode à l'Ancienne 1985 • $14 • (02/28/89) • **85**

Pinot Noir Anderson Valley Table Wine 1993: Simple but pleasant with cherry and berry flavors of modest proportion. Ready now, might even work well slightly chilled. 1,630 cases made. • $10 • **81**

Pinot Noir Anderson Valley Whole Berry Fermentation 1987 • $9 • (02/28/89) • **81**

Sauvignon Blanc Mendocino Cuvée 128 1994: Zesty, ripe, lively core of ripe pear, citrus, fig and melon, turning richer and more complex on the finish, where the flavors linger on. 1,429 cases made. • $11 • (02/29/96) • **90**

Sauvignon Blanc Mendocino Cuvée 128 1993: Light and smooth texture, with vibrant flavors. Melon, pear and floral notes compete for attention on the citrusy finish. 1,039 cases made. • $10 • (04/30/95) • **88**

Sauvignon Blanc Mendocino Cuvée 128 1992 • $9 • (04/30/94) BB • **88**

Sauvignon Blanc Mendocino Cuvée 128 1991 • $10 • (07/15/93) • **87**

White Riesling Anderson Valley 1992: Light and slightly sweet, with apricot and floral flavors that extend into a solid finish. Could be a little more delicate. 705 cases made. • $8 • (06/15/95) • **83**

White Riesling Anderson Valley 1991 • $8 • (11/30/92) • **85**

White Riesling Late Harvest Anderson Valley Cluster Selected 1985 • $10 • (05/15/87) • **81**

White Riesling Late Harvest Anderson Valley Sweet Cluster Selected 1989 • $15 • (03/31/92) • **83**

White Riesling Late Harvest Anderson Valley Sweet Cluster Selected 1986 • $25 • (03/31/90) • **85**

Zinfandel Mendocino 1993: Clean and correct, but not especially exciting, with a decent core of plum and wild berry. 883 cases made. • $15 • (03/31/96) • **83**

Zinfandel Mendocino 1992: Ripe, with a wild, gamy, jammy edge to the cherry and plum flavors. Drinkable now. 672 cases made. • $15 • (02/28/95) • **85**

Zinfandel Mendocino 1991 • $14 • (03/31/94) • **86**

NAYLOR | PENNSYLVANIA

Chambourcin York County 1986 • $10 • (02/29/92) • **70**

Dessert York County Ekem 1990 • $9 • (02/29/92) • **77**

NEGOCIANTS, THE | CALIFORNIA

Cabernet Sauvignon Napa Valley 1990: Firm and focused. This is a tightly wound young wine, with cedar, currant and mineral flavors that manage to muscle their way through chewy tannins on the finish. It may be wise to drink up now, this isn't known for aging. 1,000 cases made. • $10 • (03/31/94) • **85**

Chardonnay Central Coast 1993: Lean and earthy, adding a weedy herbal edge to the flavors. 2,000 cases made. • $7 • (02/28/95) • **74**

Chardonnay Central Coast 1992: Lean and trim, but the smoky pear and spice flavors fan out on the finish, where they get more interesting, finishing with toasty aftertaste. Tremendous value. 2,666 cases made. • $6 • (11/30/94) BB • **87**

Chardonnay Central Coast Barrel Fermented 1992: Lean and simple, with pear, spice and cedary oak flavors. • $7 • (12/15/94) • **80**

Chardonnay Napa Valley Barrel Select 1992: Light and simple, with a strong earthy edge to the basic apple flavors. 1,366 cases made. • $6 • (01/31/94) • **77**

Merlot Napa Valley Reserve 1992: Focused herb, cherry and currant notes shorten up with firm tannins. Best after 1996. 680 cases made. • $8 • (03/31/95) • **84**

NELSON ESTATE | CALIFORNIA

Cabernet Franc Sonoma County 1990: Tastes underripe, with a cedary edge to the tart flavors. 2,900 cases made. • $15 • (02/28/95) • **78**

Cabernet Franc Sonoma County 1987 • $16 • (04/30/91) • **82**

NEUHARTH | WASHINGTON

Merlot Washington 1991: A tart, green, young wine with a pickley edge. Marginal quality. 200 cases made. • $14 • (09/30/94) • **71**

NEVADA CITY | CALIFORNIA

Cabernet Sauvignon Sierra Foothills Nevada County 1989 • $11 • (11/15/92) • **81**

Chardonnay Nevada County Barrel Fermented 1993: Refreshingly fruity with appealing pear, apple and light citrus notes, holding its flavor through the finish. 545 cases made. • $11 • (07/31/95) • **86**

Chardonnay Nevada County Barrel Fermented 1992: Light and fruity with an earthy mineral edge on the finish. Balanced and pleasing.-JL 620 cases made. • $10 • (06/30/94) • **83**

Claret Sierra Foothills The Directors' Reserve 1990: Clean and correct with ripe berry and plum-scented Cabernet fruit. An easy-drinking style that doesn't quite fit its $14 price tag. 120 cases made. • $14 • (11/15/93) • **79**

Claret The Director's Reserve 1989 • $15 • (05/31/92) • **83**

Merlot Nevada County 1989 • $14 • (05/31/92) • **80**

Merlot Sierra Foothills 1991: Bitter, ashy aromas and flavors bring this down to the average level. 220 cases made. • $14 • (09/15/94) • **74**

Zinfandel Sierra Foothills 1991 • $9 • (09/30/93) • **85**

Zinfandel Sierra Foothills 1990 • $8 • (10/15/92) • **84**

NEVADA COUNTY WINE GUILD | CALIFORNIA

Pinot Noir Nevada County 1991 • $11 • (02/28/93) • **70**

NEW LAND | NEW YORK

Pinot Noir Finger Lakes Reserve 1993: Aromatic and intriguing, the fresh fruit complemented by generous oak shadings-cinnamon, vanilla and nutmeg. Light in texture and body, but has intensity of flavor. 400 cases made. • $15 • (06/30/95) • **82**

NEWLAN | CALIFORNIA

Cabernet Sauvignon Napa Valley 1991: Lots of oak up front, but fruit makes this a rich, fleshy red as plum, raspberry and vanilla flavors wind effortlessly through the finish. Delicious now, best in 1997. 761 cases made. • $16 • (11/30/95) • **89**

Cabernet Sauvignon Napa Valley 1990: Broad and ripe black cherry, currant and wild berry flavors are tightly wound, finishing with dry, gritty tannins. Best after 1996. 355 cases made. • $26 • (02/28/95) • **86**

Cabernet Sauvignon Napa Valley 1988: Tight and peppery, with a lean core of currant and earthy berry flavors. 1,192 cases made. • $16 • (02/28/95) • **84**

Cabernet Sauvignon Napa Valley 1987 • $15 • (11/15/92) • **88**

Cabernet Sauvignon Napa Valley 1986 • $15 • (04/30/91) • **89**

Cabernet Sauvignon Napa Valley 1985 • $15 • (03/31/90) • **87**

Century Selection Napa Valley 1989 • $11 • (11/30/92) • **78**

Chardonnay Napa Valley 1991: A little disjointed now, with fruit and oak not quite married. The pear, apple and spice flavors are pure and appealing, picking up vanilla and toast on the finish. Best by summer or fall.-JL 296 cases made. • $19 • (06/30/94) • **86**

Chardonnay Napa Valley Napa-Villages 1992: Smooth and spicy, a streak of honey running through the silky pear and spice flavors which linger on the finish. Ready now. 735 cases made. • $10 • (09/30/95) • **86**

Chardonnay Napa Valley Reserve 1991 • $20 • (07/15/93) • **83**

Johannisberg Riesling Late Harvest Napa Valley 1993: Very sweet, unctuous and rich, balanced artfully with hints of citrusy acidity, rolling its apricot, raisin, honey and spice flavors across the palate and through the long finish. Delicious now, best from 1997. Tasted twice with consistent results. 140 cases made. • $22 • **94**

Johannisberg Riesling Late Harvest Napa Valley 1992: Sweet and syrupy, a mouthful of spice, honey, apricot and floral flavors that become unctuous and round on the silky finish. 168 cases made. • $22 • (04/30/95) • **88**

Johannisberg Riesling Late Harvest Napa Valley 1991 • $20 • (12/31/93) • **89**

Pinot Noir Napa County School House Vieilles Vignes 1991: Tart, with a green-tealike edge to the barely ripe cherry flavor. Last of the Newlan School House Pinot Noirs. 25 cases made. • $25 • (03/31/95) • **79**

Pinot Noir Napa Valley 1993: Young, tight, firm, slightly green tannins and a pleasant core of earthy cherry and berry flavors. It can stand some aging into 1997. 519 cases made. • $18 • (05/15/96) • **87**

Pinot Noir Napa Valley 1992: Lean and crisp but it lacks richness and depth, coming across as one-dimensional, exhibiting a firm, tannic, minty edge. 654 cases made. • $18 • (03/31/95) • **83**

Pinot Noir Napa Valley 1991 • $18 • (02/28/94) • **80**

Pinot Noir Napa Valley 1989 • $18 • (02/28/93) • **87**

Pinot Noir Napa Valley 1988 • $18 • (11/15/91) • **81**

Pinot Noir Napa Valley 1987 • $16 • (03/31/90) • **81**

Pinot Noir Napa Valley 1985 • $12 • (06/15/88) • **88**

Pinot Noir Napa Valley Napa-Villages 1991: Light but pleasant strawberry and cranberry notes, picking up an earthy, smoky edge on the finish. Drinkable now. 898 cases made. • $10 • (03/31/95) • **81**

Pinot Noir Napa Valley Reserve 1993: Tough and chewy, adding an earthy, leathery touch to the cherry and berry flavor. Shows a stemmy quality on the finish. 510 cases made. • $28 • (05/15/96) • **82**

Pinot Noir Napa Valley Reserve 1991 • $28 • (02/28/94) • **84**

Pinot Noir Napa Valley Vieilles Vignes 1986 • $19 • (03/31/90) • **76**

Pinot Noir Napa Valley Vieilles Vignes 1985 • $16 • (06/15/88) • **80**

Zinfandel Napa Valley 1992: Spicy and peppery, but a lean and compact style that has firm, drying tannins overshadowing the fruit at this stage. Finishes with a tarry edge. Try now. 1,976 cases made. • $14 • (10/15/94) • **86**

Zinfandel Napa Valley 1991 • $15 • (03/31/94) • **86**

Zinfandel Napa Valley 1990 • $12 • (09/30/93) • **88**

Key: SS—Spectator Selection. CS—Cellar Selection. BB—Best Buy. $NA—Price not available. (BT)—Barrel tasting. Ⓐ—Auction Price.
Dates in parentheses represent the issues in which the ratings were published.

NEWTON | CALIFORNIA

Cabernet Sauvignon Napa Valley 1989 • $19 • (11/15/93) • **84**

Cabernet Sauvignon Napa Valley 1988 • $17 • (11/15/92) • **87**

Cabernet Sauvignon Napa Valley 1987 • $17 • (11/15/91) • **87**

Cabernet Sauvignon Napa Valley 1986 • $16 • (05/31/90) • **91**

Cabernet Sauvignon Napa Valley 1985 • $16 • (03/01/89) • **89**

Cabernet Sauvignon Napa Valley 1984 • $14 • (03/01/89) • **87**

Cabernet Sauvignon Napa Valley 1983 • $13 • (03/01/89) • **92**

Cabernet Sauvignon Napa Valley 1982 • $13 • (03/01/89) • **66**

Cabernet Sauvignon Napa Valley 1981 • $13 • (03/01/89) • **83**

Cabernet Sauvignon Napa Valley 1980 • $12 • (03/01/89) • **55**

Cabernet Sauvignon Napa Valley 1979 • $12 • (03/01/89) • **85**

Chardonnay Napa Valley 1994: Combines ripe fig and pear flavors with light smoky notes from oak. Develops more nuances on the creamy finish. Elegant and well crafted. • $19 • (03/31/96) • **90**

Chardonnay Napa Valley 1992: Ripe fruit gives a sweet impression, with the spicy pear, apricot and nectarine flavors that are focused and lively. Drinks well now. • $16 • (03/15/94) • **87**

Chardonnay Napa Valley 1991 • $15 • (07/15/93) • **89**

Claret Napa Valley 1992: Spicy, with ripe plum and cherry flavors that are moderately rich and well focused. This young, compact red needs cellaring to begin showing its full potential. • $13 • (11/15/94) • **88**

Claret Napa Valley 1991: Rich and supple, hitting the right flavor notes with cherry and currant and a hint of toast and spice, finishing smooth and subtle on the finish. Drinkable now. • $12 • (06/15/93) • **87**

Claret Napa Valley 1990: Appealing for its youthful fruit, with light currant, chocolate and plum-tinged flavors that stay with you. Not too tannic, soft and approachable now. • $12 • (08/31/92) • **83**

Claret Napa Valley 1988 • $11 • (03/15/91) • **89**

Merlot Napa Valley 1989 • $20 • (05/31/92) • **88**

Merlot Napa Valley 1987 • $17 • (07/31/90) • **81**

Merlot Napa Valley 1986 • $15 • (12/31/88) • **83**

Merlot Napa Valley 1985 • $14 • (03/31/88) • **93**

Merlot Napa Valley 1983 • $12 • (02/28/87) • **90**

Merlot Napa Valley 1982 • $13 • (02/16/86) • **83**

Merlot Napa Valley 1981 • $13 • (12/16/84) • **91**

NEYERS | CALIFORNIA

Cabernet Franc Napa Valley 1987 • $16 • (11/15/90) • **79**

Cabernet Sauvignon Napa Valley 1988 • $15 • (11/15/91) • **82**

Cabernet Sauvignon Napa Valley 1985 • $14 • (07/15/89) • **83**

Cabernet Sauvignon Napa Valley 1984 • $13 • (04/30/88) • **75**

Cabernet Sauvignon Napa Valley 1983 • $12 • (08/31/87) • **79**

Chardonnay Carneros 1994: Bold, ripe and complex, with lots of ripe pear, honey, toast and hazelnut flavors. Finishes with a concentrated aftertaste and lots of finesse. Impressive. 1,053 cases made. • $18 • (06/30/96) • **91**

Chardonnay Carneros 1993: Serves up ripe pear, apple and pineapple flavors and adds light oak shadings. 700 cases made. • $16 • (02/28/95) • **86**

Merlot Napa Valley 1992: Tightly joined core of cedar, currant and black cherry flavor that finishes with firm tannins. 300 cases made. • $18 • (05/15/95) • **84**

NICHELINI | CALIFORNIA

Cabernet Sauvignon Napa Valley 1988 • $15 • (11/15/93) • **81**

Cabernet Sauvignon Napa Valley Joseph A. Nichelini Vineyards 1989: Earthy, demonstrating a lean, cedary edge that's drying and tannic. 1,100 cases made. • $12 • (06/15/95) • **77**

Merlot Napa Valley 1992: Earthy, dry and leathery, a gamy style where those flavors dominate the plum and cherry fruit underneath. Perhaps the earthiness will subside with bottle age, but that's only a guess. 100 cases made. • $20 • (03/31/96) • **81**

Sauvignon Blanc Napa Valley Joseph A. Nichelini Vineyards 1993: Ripe and floral, creamy and supple, providing a modest level of pear and vanilla flavors. 458 cases made. • $9 • (05/15/95) • **82**

Sauvignon Vert Joseph A. Nichelini Vineyard Napa Valley 1994: A fruit-centered wine that plays out its orange-scented pear and vanilla flavors smoothly, right through the finish. 458 cases made. • $9 • (05/31/96) • **83**

Zinfandel Napa Valley 1991: Serves up an attractive array of ripe, spicy Zinfandel flavors, with hints of anise, stewed plum and wild berry. Tannins are tame on the finish, letting the purity of the fruit come through. 900 cases made. • $12 • (03/31/96) • **87**

Zinfandel Napa Valley Centennial Vintage 1990: An earthy style that has just enough wild berry and spice to hold its balance. 900 cases made. • $10 • (06/15/95) • **79**

NICHOLS | CALIFORNIA

Chardonnay Arroyo Grande Valley Talley Vineyards 1994: Bold, ripe and juicy notes of rich pear, honey, peach and nectarine pick up toasty, smoky oak on the finish, where the flavors linger on and on. 1,100 cases made. • $23 • (04/30/96) • **92**

Chardonnay Arroyo Grande Valley Talley Vineyards 1993: Trim and compact, featuring a pretty array of pear, citrus and spice flavors. Good focus and balance. 700 cases made. • $20 • (12/31/95) • **87**

Pinot Noir Santa Barbara County Sierra Madre Vineyard 1994: Complex and well focused, offering tart cherry, berry and spicy, earthy nuances that add dimension and depth. Fine, tannic finish and a touch of herbaceous quality. 770 cases made. • $24 • (04/30/96) • **89**

Pinot Noir Santa Barbara County Sierra Madre Vineyard 1993: Smooth and polished, with supple black cherry, wild berry, spice and pretty toasty oak shadings. A remarkably elegant and refined wine that showcases the finesse of this grape. 440 cases made. • $24 • (12/31/95) • **91**

NIEBAUM-COPPOLA | CALIFORNIA

Cabernet Franc Napa Valley Family Wines 1991: Earthy, leathery flavors dominate along with a slight bitter edge. Hints of currant and sage make it drinkable. Best after 1996. 190 cases made. • $14 • (01/31/95) • **81**

Cabernet Franc Napa Valley Francis Coppola Family Wines 1990 • $12 • (03/31/93) • **84**

Merlot Napa Valley 1993: Complex and supple, with smoky oak, herb, black cherry and currant flavors. Turns elegant and polished on the finish, where the flavors linger on. Well crafted. Drinkable now through 1997. • $18 • (05/15/96) • **89**

Merlot Napa Valley Francis Coppola Family Wines 1991 • $16 • (10/15/93) • **86**

Rubicon Napa Valley 1990: Ripe, smooth and polished, with pretty plum, black cherry, herb, mineral and cedar flavors. Well focused and showing a more supple texture than previous vintages. Finishes with fine but firm tannins and good length. Ready in 1997. 1,980 cases made. • $35 • (12/15/95) • **90**

Rubicon Napa Valley 1989: Tough and chewy, with hard-core tannins that override the smoky herb and currant flavors. Has just enough texture to fend off the dry tannins. Cellaring recommended, try after 1997. 2,000 cases made. • $30 • (11/15/94) • **83**

Rubicon Napa Valley 1988: Herb and mint aromas give way to taut, chewy currant and cherry flavors, but this wine is still austere and tannic, needing some cellar time. 2,100 cases made. • $30 • (11/15/94) • **83**

Rubicon Napa Valley 1987 • $30 • (11/15/93) • **88**

Rubicon Napa Valley 1986 • $29 • (11/15/92) • **88**

Rubicon Napa Valley 1985 • $29 Ⓐ • (11/15/90) • **87**

Rubicon Napa Valley 1984 • $37 • (03/01/89) • **85**

Rubicon Napa Valley 1982 • $40 • (10/15/89) • **88**

Rubicon Napa Valley 1981 • $41 • (03/01/89) • **87**

Rubicon Napa Valley 1980 • $36 • (03/01/89) • **87**

Rubicon Napa Valley 1979 • $46 • (03/01/89) • **75**

Rubicon Napa Valley 1978 • $53 • (11/15/92) • **88**

Rubicon Napa Valley 1977 • $NA • (02/28/87) • **93**

Zinfandel Napa Valley Edizione Pennino 1993: Intense and a bit austere, the lean but spicy cherry and raspberry flavors expanding into more depth on the finish, where firm tannins kick in. 500 cases made. • $16 • (10/15/95) • **87**

Zinfandel Napa Valley Edizione Pennino 1992: Ripe and lush, with pretty tar, earth and berry flavors framed by toasty oak. Drinkable now. 340 cases made. • $15 • (10/15/94) • **88**

Zinfandel Napa Valley Edizione Pennino 1991: Ripe, intense and spicy, with a band of rich, chunky pepper and plum flavors. Finishes with a good dose of tannin, but the fruit keeps up. Ready now through 1998. 220 cases made. • $14 • (10/15/94) • **88**

Zinfandel Napa Valley Edizione Pennino 1990 • $14 • (09/30/93) • **88**

Zinfandel Napa Valley Edizione Pennino 1989 • $14 • (09/30/93) • **87**

NIEBAUM, GUSTAVE | CALIFORNIA

Cabernet Sauvignon Napa Valley Mast Vineyard 1987 • $14 • (08/31/92) • **89**

Cabernet Sauvignon Napa Valley Reference 1989 • $11 • (07/31/92) • **85**

Cabernet Sauvignon Napa Valley Reference 1985 • $14 • (10/31/89) • **89**

Cabernet Sauvignon Napa Valley Tench Vineyard 1988 • $15 • (07/31/92) • **80**

Cabernet Sauvignon Napa Valley Tench Vineyard 1986 • $16 • (10/15/89) • **93**

Chardonnay Napa Valley Reference 1991 • $11 • (03/31/93) • **81**

Merlot Napa Valley Reference 1989 • $11 • (10/31/92) • **72**

NOCETO | CALIFORNIA

Sangiovese Shenandoah Valley 1994: Ripe and attractive layers of currant and black cherry flavors, with spice and anise notes. Well balanced, nicely focused and flavorful on the finish. 1,338 cases made. • $10 • **87**

Sangiovese Shenandoah Valley 1993: Chewy in texture, with a modest level of ripe blackberry and spice flavors sneaking through. 1,600 cases made. • $10 • (08/31/95) • **82**

Sangiovese Shenandoah Valley 1992: A lean, chewy, modest wine with more tannin than fruit. Drinkable now. 1,100 cases made. • $8 • (09/30/94) • **77**

Sangiovese Shenandoah Valley 1991 • $8 • (07/31/93) • **81**

NOMINEE | CALIFORNIA

Cabernet Sauvignon Napa Valley 1992: Austere, dry and leathery, needs fruit. 10,000 cases made. • $7 • (11/15/94) • **75**

Cabernet Sauvignon Napa Valley 1991: Tight, dense and firm, with chewy, tannic currant and berry flavors that were closed and hard. Needed time to soften, but may be more generous and forthcoming now. Drink now. 7,000 cases made. • $7 • (07/15/93) • **83**

Cabernet Sauvignon Paso Robles 1993: Firm and tight, with a well balanced band of currant, cedar and spice. 10,000 cases made. • $7 • (12/15/95) • **83**

Chardonnay Paso Robles 1994: Harmoniously plays its light, smooth spice and fruit flavors off a touch of toasty oak. Ready now. 32,000 cases made. • $7 • (12/15/95) • **83**

Chardonnay Paso Robles 1993: Simple and fruity with apple and pear notes. Ready now. 35,000 cases made. • $6 • (06/30/94) • **79**

Chardonnay Paso Robles Central Coast 1992: Spicy, fruity and appealing, a light-style of white wine, with appealing apple, nectarine and nutmeg aromas and flavors. Drinkable now. • $6 • (03/31/93) BB • **84**

Merlot Napa Valley 1992: Crisp and flavorful, chunky, with a nice plum-and-currant streak, finishing generous and unfocused. Drinkable now. • $8 • (09/15/94) • **83**

NORMAN | CALIFORNIA

Cabernet Sauvignon Paso Robles 1992: Supple and elegant, showing a pretty band of herb, cherry and currant flavor. Finishes with mild tannins, making it approachable now. 550 cases made. • $13 • (11/15/94) • **87**

Cabernet Sauvignon Paso Robles No Nonsense Red 1992: Herb, cedar, currant and berry flavors are tight and compact, finishing with firm tannins. Best after 1996. 275 cases made. • $9 • (11/15/94) • **82**

Chardonnay San Luis Obispo County 1994: Vibrant and fruity, sporting pretty pear, nectarine and tangerine flavors that turn elegant and refined on the finish. Especially attractive price. 600 cases made. • $12 • (05/15/96) • **88**

Zinfandel Late Harvest Paso Robles 1994: Lightly sweet and fruity, but not bold enough to make a statement. Some berryish flavors on its soft frame. 85 cases made. • $15 • (10/31/95) • **79**

Zinfandel Paso Robles 1993: Ripe and plush, with rich, supple black cherry, raspberry and wild berry flavors that are bright and lively. A firm, tannic edge on the finish is smooth, not biting. 250 cases made. • $13 • (10/15/95) • **90**

Zinfandel Paso Robles 1992: Ripe and spicy, with a pretty band of herb and cherry-laced Zinfandel fruit that turns rich and supple on the finish. Captures the essense of the grape. Ready now through 1998. 120 cases made. • $11 • (07/31/94) • **88**

Zinfandel Paso Robles The Classic 1994: Intense and lively, featuring a core of cherry and wild berry flavor framed by cedary oak. Strikes a nice balance between fruit, oak and tannin. Can age into 1997. 350 cases made. • $13 • (04/30/96) • **88**

NORTH COAST CELLARS | CALIFORNIA

White Zinfandel North Coast 1987 • $6 • (06/15/89) • **68**

OAK FALLS | CALIFORNIA

Chardonnay Napa Valley Private Reserve 1991 • $7 • (02/15/93) • **80**

Merlot Napa Valley 1992: Light in texture and not very concentrated, but it should be nice when the currently coarse tannins subside. Try in 1997-1998. 4,200 cases made. • $9 • (06/15/95) • **80**

Merlot Napa Valley Private Reserve 1990 • $8 • (03/31/93) • **82**

Sauvignon Blanc California 1993: Extremely herbal, almost like licorice, on the sharp finish. Interesting, but not for everyone. 6,700 cases made. • $4 • (02/28/95) • **76**

Zinfandel Amador County 1991: Medium-bodied, with a range of flavors from tart berry to anise and ripe wild berry flavors. Tar shows up on the finish. 5,000 cases made. • $6 • (10/15/95) • **82**

OAK RIDGE VINEYARDS | CALIFORNIA

Chardonnay California Bighorn 1993: Curious, lacks focus, very ripe fruit flavors take on a sour-candied edge. 1,500 cases made. • $7 • (06/30/94) • **74**

Fumé Blanc California Swan Lake 1993: Soft and watery, a disappointing wine that seems sweet and insipid. Tasted twice with consistent results. 1,000 cases made. • $4 • (08/31/94) • **73**

OAKFORD | CALIFORNIA

Cabernet Sauvignon Napa Valley 1991: Intense and spicy, with a lively core of currant, plum and berry notes, picking up a nice trace of spicy oak on the finish. Shows more depth than previous vintages. Best after 1999. 800 cases made. • $30 • (12/15/95) • **88**

Cabernet Sauvignon Napa Valley 1990: Young and compact, with tightly-wound currant, herb and earth notes. Concentrated and rich, it needs cellaring until 1998 to show its best. 1,000 cases made. • $25 • (11/15/94) • **88**

Cabernet Sauvignon Napa Valley 1989: Offers spice, mint and currant flavors and finishes with firm tannins. Ready now but it should drink well over the next few years. 1,000 cases made. • $25 • (11/15/94) • **88**

Cabernet Sauvignon Napa Valley 1988: Crisp and compact, with a pleasant band of cherry and currant flavor framed by light oak shadings. Drinks well now but can hold through 1997. 1,000 cases made. • $25 • (11/15/94) • **87**

Cabernet Sauvignon Napa Valley 1987 • $25 • (11/15/90) • **91**

OAKVILLE BENCH | CALIFORNIA

Cabernet Sauvignon Napa County 1990: Crisp and simple, with some nice plum flavors and a greenish edge that keeps it from becoming fleshy. Drinkable now. 1,000 cases made. • $12 • (05/15/94) • **82**

Key: SS—Spectator Selection. CS—Cellar Selection. BB—Best Buy. $NA—Price not available. (BT)—Barrel tasting. (A)—Auction Price.
Dates in parentheses represent the issues in which the ratings were published.

Cabernet Sauvignon Napa Valley 1989 • $12 • (03/15/92) • **87**

OAKVILLE RANCH | CALIFORNIA

Cabernet Sauvignon Napa Valley 1992: Austere and tightly wound, a firm band of currant and black cherry, with a long, full finish where the fruit emerges from the significant tannins. Best into 1998. 900 cases made. • $24 • (12/15/95) • **90**

Cabernet Sauvignon Napa Valley 1991: Serves up a rich, supple core of ripe and flavorful Cabernet fruit. Layers of currant, cherry, plum and chocolate flavors finish up with a good dose of oak. Needs until 1998 to soften and mature. 1,500 cases made. • $24 • (09/30/94) • **89**

Cabernet Sauvignon Napa Valley 1990: Smooth and stylish, with a strong spicy streak of cedary currant and plum aromas and flavors, finishing silky and elegant with flavor to spare. Has the concentration and balance to become a beauty by 1997 or so. 650 cases made. • $23 • (10/15/93) • **93**

Cabernet Sauvignon Napa Valley 1989 • $20 • (11/15/92) • **90**

Cabernet Sauvignon Napa Valley Lewis Select 1991: Ripe and plush, with rich currant, cherry and chocolate notes framed by toasty, buttery oak. Has depth, concentration and complexity, finishing with a long, full finish. Best to cellar until 1998. 450 cases made. • $28 • (09/30/94) • **91**

Cabernet Sauvignon Napa Valley Reserve 1991: Packs in lots of black cherry, currant, mineral and spice flavors, turning smooth and supple on the palate, finishing with a long, rich, concentrated aftertaste. Mild tannins make it approachable, but it's best to cellar short-term into 1997. 400 cases made. • $32 • (05/15/95) • **92**

Chardonnay Napa Valley 1991 • $18 • (07/15/93) • **89**

Chardonnay Napa Valley ORV 1994: Young and tight, showing citrus, pear and toasty vanilla flavors and long, complex aftertaste. Picks up a trace of herb on the finish and it's slightly tannic, some aging should help. 400 cases made. • $28 • (05/15/96) • **89**

Chardonnay Napa Valley ORV 1992: Ripe, smooth and creamy, with a pretty core of pear and toasty oak that turns smoky on the finish. A big, round, flavorful wine. Drink now. 750 cases made. • $24 • (09/30/94) • **88**

Chardonnay Napa Valley Vista Vineyard 1994: Not quite together when tasted, it certainly has enough ripe and complex pear, pineapple and spice flavors that are a bit tannic and woody on the finish. Some aging should help. 1,400 cases made. • $20 • (05/15/96) • **88**

Chardonnay Napa Valley Vista Vineyards 1993: Elegant and understated, but ripe with pear and melon flavors that turn smooth and polished on the finish. This is drinkable now. 1,500 cases made. • $18 • **90**

Chardonnay Napa Valley Vista Vineyards 1992: A big, ripe, buttery style with spicy pear, nectarine and vanilla flavors, picking up smoky notes on the finish, but the fruit hangs in there, giving it richness and depth. Drink now. 1,000 cases made. • $18 • (06/30/94) • **87**

Chardonnay Napa Valley Vista Vineyards 1991 • $18 • (07/15/93) • **88**

Merlot Napa Valley 1992: Smells earthy and leathery, with hard tannins and just a hint of tart cherry and currant flavors. It may always be on the tannic side, but it should soften by 1997. 200 cases made. • $24 • (05/15/96) • **83**

Old Vine Field Blend Napa Valley 1993: Ripe and fruity, featuring a grapey edge to spicy berry flavor. Doesn't quite come together on the finish, as it picks up an herbal tinge. 200 cases made. • $18 • (11/30/95) • **87**

OAKWOOD | WASHINGTON

Cabernet Sauvignon Yakima Valley 1989: Mature enough to be smooth in texture, but feels like it needs until 1997 to let the berry, tar and smoke flavors settle down. 800 cases made. • $14 • (09/30/95) • **87**

Cabernet Sauvignon Yakima Valley Reserve 1987 • $20 • (11/30/93) • **92**

Lemberger Yakima Valley 1991: Soft and simple, playing its volatile acidity against the simple berry flavor. 700 cases made. • $10 • (09/30/95) • **78**

Muscat Canelli Yakima Valley 1993: Lightly sweet, glowing with freshness, offering nectarine, spice and litchi flavors that echo on the long finish. 450 cases made. • $6 • (09/30/95) • **85**

OASIS | VIRGINIA

Brut Virginia Cuvée D'Or 1990: Fruity, lively, tart sparkling wine that has modest apple and pear flavors, a mouthfilling texture, but a trace of earthiness. 500 cases made. • $25 • **81**

Brut Virginia NV: A bit sweet, this sparkling wine is light and fizzy in texture. Acceptable, but simple. 2,000 cases made. • $16 • (12/15/95) • **78**

Cabernet Franc Virginia 1993: 530 cases made. • $15 • **58**

Cabernet Sauvignon Virginia Bleu Rock Vineyard 1990: 100 cases made. • $15 • **60**

Chardonnay Virginia 1994: Clumsy, mingling celery and canned peach aromas. Sweet and syrupy on the palate. Flavorful, but doesn't hold together. 2,400 cases made. • $10 • (06/30/95) • **77**

Chardonnay Virginia 1993: A good, serviceable and fruity wine whose flavors are on the lean side. Rather tart, too. 3,500 cases made. • $10 • (02/28/95) • **82**

Chardonnay Virginia Barrel Select 1992: Rich honey and maple sugar aromas give way to a smooth, polished mouthfeel and sweet butter and hazelnut flavors. It's attractive, but lacks the acidity to marry well with food. Drink now. 2,000 cases made. • $15 • (06/30/95) • **82**

Chardonnay Virginia Bleu Rock Vineyard 1992: This lively, tightly-wound wine shows bright lemony fruit, sweet vanilla oak and crisp acidity. It's still young and fresh. A clean, well-made wine. 350 cases made. • $10 • (06/30/95) • **85**

Chardonnay Virginia White Eagle Vineyards 1992: A rich, oaky Chardonnay that's packed with honey and sweet vanilla flavors, but underneath there's tropical fruit and lemony acidity. Drink now to enjoy the bright, fresh fruit. 180 cases made. • $15 • (06/30/95) • **85**

Extra Dry Virginia NV: Simple flavors of apple and pineapple and a coarse, tart texture make this pretty ordinary stuff. 2,000 cases made. • $16 • **75**

Great Falls Vineyard Vidal Blanc Virginia 1994: Green apple, herbal and light rubbery flavors mingle in this thick, somewhat cloying wine. 154 cases made. • $15 • (10/31/95) • **77**

Meritage Virginia 1993: On the lean and green side of the flavor spectrum, with herbal aromas and flavors, and a strong streak of wood throughout. Drinkable, but awkward. 101 cases made. • $15 • (06/30/95) • **77**

Merlot Virginia 1992: Overwhelming cinammon flavors and aromas make this a bit unbalanced. Soft cherry flavors lean towards the candied side. 800 cases made. • $12 • (12/31/95) • **74**

Riesling Virginia 1992: There are pleasant elements here — apple and piney flavors, an easy balance of light sweetness and lemony acidity — but some earthy and candied notes detract slightly. 1,500 cases made. • $8 • (08/31/95) • **80**

OBESTER | CALIFORNIA

Chardonnay Mendocino County 1991: Austere and flinty, but well focused with its band of pear and apple flavors. Lively acidity on the finish keeps the flavors alive.-JL • $15 • (06/30/94) • **85**

Gewürztraminer Anderson Valley 1992 • $8 • (04/15/94) • **84**

Pinot Noir Anderson Valley 1992 • $15 • (04/30/94) • **78**

Sangiovese Mendocino County 1993: Soft in texture and bright, showing modest strawberry flavor and a mildly grapey character. Drinkable now. 1,400 cases made. • $10 • (08/31/95) • **83**

Sangiovese Mendocino County 1992 • $14 • (03/31/94) • **79**

Sauvignon Blanc Mendocino County 1993: Slightly raisiny, earthy edge to the modest fruit keeps this a little off balance. Drinkable now. 1,000 cases made. • $8 • (08/31/95) • **80**

Sauvignon Blanc Mendocino County 1992 • $9 • (04/15/94) BB • **85**

Sauvignon Blanc Mendocino County 1991 • $9 • (06/30/93) • **85**

Zinfandel Mendocino County 1991 • $11 • (06/15/94) • **84**

OCTOPUS MOUNTAIN | CALIFORNIA

Cabernet Sauvignon Anderson Valley Dennison Vineyard 1991: Ripe and intense, with a grapey currant and cherry edge to the flavors. Firm tannins on the finish, drinkable now. 190 cases made. • $13 • (11/15/94) • **82**

Cabernet Sauvignon Anderson Valley Dennison Vineyards 1989 • $13 • (07/31/91) • **83**

Pinot Noir Anderson Valley 1989 • $13 • (10/31/91) • **86**

Pinot Noir Anderson Valley Dennison Vineyard 1991 • $14 • (12/15/93) • **85**

Sauvignon Blanc Anderson Valley 1991: Crisp and fruity, lively with sweet pear and spice flavors. 400 cases made. • $8 • (08/31/94) • **83**

OJAI | CALIFORNIA

Cabernet Sauvignon Syrah Red California 1986 • $7 • (04/15/89) • **74**

Chardonnay Arroyo Grande Valley 1993: A medium bodied style with a modest range of spice, pear and light oak shadings. Holds together through the finish. 700 cases made. • $18 • (07/31/95) • **86**

Chardonnay Arroyo Grande Valley Reserve 1992: An oaky style with rich, honeyed Chardonnay fruit to match the hints of apricot, pear and smoky oak. Drinkable now. 384 cases made. • $21 • (01/31/95) • **88**

Chardonnay Arroyo Grande Valley Reserve 1991 • $21 • (12/31/93) • **89**

Chardonnay Santa Barbara County 1992: Clean and correct, with spicy pear, honey and pine-oak shadings. Finishes with a touch of pineapple and spice. Delicate and smooth drinking now. 300 cases made. • $15 • (12/31/93) • **88**

Chardonnay Santa Barbara County Reserve 1993: Ripe and appealing, with spicy pear, pineapple and melon notes that are moderately complex, folding together on the finish. 250 cases made. • $21 • (07/31/95) • **87**

Chardonnay Santa Barbara County Reserve 1992: Compact and flavorful, with a band of pear, toast and spice notes that hang with you. 200 cases made. • $21 • (01/31/95) • **86**

Pinot Noir Santa Barbara County 1993: Well balanced, with ripe plum, black cherry and vanilla shadings. Focused and flavorful. Finishes with tight tannins. 400 cases made. • $25 • (06/30/95) • **86**

Syrah California 1992: Distinctive for its spice and pepper, it serves up complex black cherry, plum and cedar flavors. Short-term cellaring would help. 800 cases made. • $15 • (01/31/95) • **84**

Syrah California 1991 • $15 • (12/31/93) • **87**

Syrah California 1986 • $7 • (04/15/89) • **77**

OL BLUE JAY | CALIFORNIA

Zinfandel California Blue Blood NV • $11 • (12/31/92) • **81**

OLIVER | INDIANA

Merlot Indiana 1988 • $15 • (02/29/92) • **82**

OLIVET LANE | CALIFORNIA

Chardonnay Russian River Valley 1992: A light and simple young Chardonnay that doesn't show much aroma or flavor up front, but picks up a little intensity on the finish where the spicy pear and wood flavors come forth. Drink now. 2,200 cases made. • $12 • (03/15/94) • **84**

Chardonnay Russian River Valley Pellegrini Family Vineyards 1994: Strives for complexity in its honey and butterscotch notes. An elegant, subtle style where flavors build on the palate, fanning out on aftertaste. 2,595 cases made. • $12 • (02/29/96) • **87**

Pinot Noir Russian River Valley 1993: Medium bodied, with an earthy edge to the cherry and wild berry flavors, finishing with firm tannins and a cola edge. Ready now through 1998. 2,581 cases made. • $13 • **84**

Pinot Noir Russian River Valley 1992 • $12 • (02/28/94) • **84**

Pinot Noir Russian River Valley 1991 • $10 • (02/28/93) • **84**

Pinot Noir Russian River Valley 1988 • $9 • (06/30/91) BB • **85**

Pinot Noir Russian River Valley Pellegrini Family Vineyards 1994: Appealing for its ripe, earthy cherry and berry flavors and light oak shadings. 3,400 cases made. • $15 • (01/31/96) • **86**

OLIVOS VINTNERS, LOS | CALIFORNIA

Chardonnay Santa Barbara County 1993: Well oaked with vanilla and smoky, toasty notes, but also offering an appealing core of ripe, exotic pear, guava, honey and butterscotch flavors that linger. 900 cases made. • $18 • (09/30/95) • **90**

Pinot Noir Santa Barbara County 1993: An odd style, showing an earthy, beefy edge and not much in the way of varietal character. Vegetal finish. 325 cases made. • $20 • (02/29/96) • **75**

OLSON | CALIFORNIA

Merlot California 1989 • $11 • (05/31/92) • **76**

ONE | CALIFORNIA

Cabernet Sauvignon Napa Valley 1989 • $18 • (03/31/93) • **72**
Cabernet Sauvignon Napa Valley 1988 • $15 • (11/15/92) • **77**
Sauvignon Blanc Napa Valley 1992: Floral, herbal and vaguely fruity, finishing chalky, a flat wine that could use a little more zip and backbone. 601 cases made. • $9 • (08/31/94) • **79**

ONE WORLD WINERY | CALIFORNIA

Cabernet Sauvignon Russian River Valley 1991: Crisp and tasty, a lighter style, austere but nicely balanced. Drinkable now. 250 cases made. • $15 • (05/15/94) • **82**
Sauvignon Blanc Russian River Valley 1993: Herbal and earthy, showing little charm. 125 cases made. • $9 • (08/31/94) • **70**
Zinfandel Russian River Valley 1993: Tastes old and tired, with mature cedar and earth flavors. 350 cases made. • $14 • (04/30/96) • **70**
Zinfandel Russian River Valley 1992 • $11 • (04/30/94) • **85**

OPTIMA | CALIFORNIA

Cabernet Sauvignon Alexander Valley 1992: Ripe and supple, with an herbal edge to the ripe plum and cherry flavors. Smooth tannins clamp down on the finish. Should be drinkable in 1997. • $25 • (12/15/95) • **89**
Cabernet Sauvignon Alexander Valley 1991: Young and tight, but it opens to reveal ripe black cherry and currant flavors that stay focused. Drinkable now through 2000. 2,204 cases made. • $25 • (02/28/95) • **88**
Cabernet Sauvignon Alexander Valley 1990: A tough, hard-edged, tannic and oaky Optima, with spicy currant, chocolate and berry flavors, lacks focus and harmony and finishes with a heavy dose of woody oak. Best after 1997. Tasted three times. • $27 • (06/15/94) • **82**
Cabernet Sauvignon Sonoma County 1989 • $25 • (11/15/92) • **88**
Cabernet Sauvignon Sonoma County 1987 • $22 • (12/15/90) • **92**
Cabernet Sauvignon Sonoma County 1986 • $22 • (02/15/90) • **91**
Cabernet Sauvignon Sonoma County 1985 • $19 • (12/15/88) • **93**
Cabernet Sauvignon Sonoma County 1984 • $17 • (02/29/88) • **90**
Chardonnay Carneros 1994: An elegant style, with a medium-bodied core of pear, spice, hazelnut and anise, turning complex on the finish. 300 cases made. • $28 • (02/29/96) • **87**
Chardonnay Carneros Unfiltered 1993: Complex pear, honey, toast and hazelnut notes turn elegant and refined on the finish where the flavors linger on. 300 cases made. • $25 • (10/15/95) • **89**
Chardonnay Sonoma County 1992: An oaky style that holds in there, with toasty, cedary oak dominating. Underneath you pick up hints of pear and nectarine. 300 cases made. • $25 • (04/30/94) • **85**
Chardonnay Sonoma County 1991 • $25 • (07/15/93) • **84**
Pinot Noir Russian River Valley 1994: Slightly funky, cheesy edge, straightening out on the palate where the flavors are more integrated, revealing pleasant plum and cherry. Time in the bottle will help round out some of the rough spots. 110 cases made. • $40 • (04/30/96) • **87**

OPUS ONE | CALIFORNIA

Napa Valley 1992: Young and vibrant, with ripe, rich black cherry, currant and cedar flavors that are just now coming together. Has a supple, forward appeal and seemingly fits in well with the vintage. It's impressive now and may become even more compelling. 26,000 cases made. • $75 • (12/15/95) CS • **91**
Napa Valley 1991: Highly concentrated and richly flavored, packing lots of dense currant, anise and black cherry flavors before picking up a chalky chocolate edge on the finish. Big and tannic, but manages a glimpse of elegance on the finish. While most Opus Ones show a supple texture, this is still a bit chunky. Cellaring until 1998 should be about perfect. 22,000 cases made. • $65 • (11/15/94) CS • **93**
Napa Valley 1990: A chunky, chewy, sturdy wine that shows some perfumey currant and berry flavors, all wrapped in several layers of fine tannins. Rich, complex and needs until 1997 to 1999 to soften. 21,000 cases made. • $65 • (11/30/93) CS • **92**
Napa Valley 1989 • $63 • (12/15/92) • **89**
Napa Valley 1988 • $91 Ⓐ • (10/31/91) • **92**
Napa Valley 1987 • $96 Ⓐ • (11/15/90) CS • **97**
Napa Valley 1986 • $79 Ⓐ • (11/30/89) • **95**
Napa Valley 1985 • $95 Ⓐ • (06/15/89) • **95**
Napa Valley 1984 • $73 Ⓐ • (03/01/89) • **94**
Napa Valley 1983 • $66 Ⓐ • (03/01/89) • **89**
Napa Valley 1982 • $92 Ⓐ • (03/01/89) • **90**
Napa Valley 1981 • $79 Ⓐ • (03/01/89) • **88**
Napa Valley 1980 • $79 Ⓐ • (03/01/89) • **93**
Napa Valley 1979 • $195 • (03/01/89) • **90**

ORFILA VINEYARDS | CALIFORNIA

California Tawny Port NV: A lighter style of Port, not quite as spicy or nutty as one expects from a tawny, finishing a little bitter. 300 cases made. • $13 • (05/31/95) • **78**
Chardonnay California Barrel Fermented 1992: Lean and spicy, with citrus and pear flavors and a honeyed finish. 2,600 cases made. • $10 • (05/31/95) • **84**
Merlot California 1992: Light and chewy, reveals a floral nuance in the basic berry flavors. Try now. 672 cases made. • $15 • (05/15/95) • **79**
Merlot California 1991: Berry and spice flavors lose intensity in this trim and lean red. 900 cases made. • $16 • (03/31/95) • **79**
Merlot San Diego County 1991: Rather thin, with dill, cedar and barnyardy flavors that turn austere and crisp on the finish. 392 cases made. • $25 • (03/31/95) • **78**
Merlot San Diego County Ambassador's Reserve 1992: Lavishly oaked, but the fruit struggles to compete, with cherry and berry flavors outflanked by woodiness. 268 cases made. • $25 • (03/31/95) • **85**

ORGANIC WINE WORKS | CALIFORNIA

à Notre Terre California 1992 • $8 • (07/31/93) • **79**
à Notre Terre California 1991 • $7 • (05/31/93) • **83**
Barbera El Dorado 1991 • $9 • (06/15/93) • **76**
Chardonnay Mendocino County Redwood Valley Vineyards 1992: Fresh apple and pear aromas and buttery apple cider flavors make this unusual but palatable. A candied streak runs through it, too. It's a controversial style that's good on its own merits, but not what we look for in a Chardonnay. Organically grown and processed. • $12 • (04/15/93) • **77**
Chardonnay Sonoma County Freiberg Vinyard 1991 • $9 • (07/15/92) • **72**
Fumé Blanc Napa Valley 1992 • $7 • (09/15/93) • **71**
Merlot Thompson Ranch 1991 • $13 • (05/31/92) • **84**
Merlot Butte County 1992 • $12 • (08/31/93) • **80**
Pinot Noir Mendocino County 1992 • $12 • (06/15/93) • **73**
Sémillon Napa Valley 1992 • $8 • (07/31/93) • **67**
Zinfandel California 1991 • $8 • (10/15/92) • **86**
Zinfandel Napa County 1992 • $10 • (05/31/93) • **80**

PACHECO RANCH | CALIFORNIA

Cabernet Sauvignon Marin County 1985 • $10 • (11/15/91) • **76**

PAGE MILL | CALIFORNIA

Cabernet Sauvignon Napa Valley V. & L. Eisele Vineyard 1990: Simple with cedar and berry notes of modest proportion. Lacks the flair of the best 1990s. 225 cases made. • $18 • (03/31/96) • **80**
Cabernet Sauvignon Napa Valley V. & L. Eisele Vineyard 1989 • $22 • (11/15/93) • **74**
Cabernet Sauvignon Napa Valley V. & L. Eisele Vineyard 1988 • $18 • (11/15/93) • **84**
Chardonnay California Cuvée Select 1992: Light and spicy, with a generous, focused beam of slightly sweet, nutty pear flavors. Finishes soft,

Key: SS—Spectator Selection. CS—Cellar Selection. BB—Best Buy. $NA—Price not available. (BT)—Barrel tasting. Ⓐ—Auction Price.
Dates in parentheses represent the issues in which the ratings were published.

with a touch of honey. Drinkable now. 50 cases made. • $24 • (07/15/93) • **79**

Chardonnay Santa Clara County Elizabeth Garbett Vineyard 1992: Simple, fruity and spicy, showing focused pear, peach and honey aromas and flavors that glide smoothly to a satisfying finish, echoing fruit and honey. 265 cases made. • $17 • (07/15/93) • **86**

Merlot Santa Maria Valley Bien Nacido Vineyard 1993: Marked by earthy herb and olive flavors, it offers a modest band of berry laced Merlot fruit. 150 cases made. • $12 • (03/31/96) • **80**

Pinot Noir Santa Barbara County Bien Nacido Vineyard 1990 • $18 • (02/28/93) • **68**

Pinot Noir Santa Barbara County Bien Nacido Vineyard 1985 • $13 • (06/15/88) • **87**

Pinot Noir Santa Maria Valley Bien Nacido Vineyard 1991 • $18 • (02/28/94) • **86**

PAGOR | CALIFORNIA

Cabernet Sauvignon California 1992: Oaked to a fault, with a heavy dose of smoky, toasty, buttery wood that dominates the slight cherry flavor. • $12 • (03/31/96) • **73**

Merlot Santa Maria Valley 1984 • $11 • (04/30/88) • **70**

Pinot Noir Santa Barbara County 1990 • $14 • (02/28/93) • **65**

Pinot Noir Santa Barbara County 1987 • $11 • (12/15/89) • **85**

PAHLMEYER | CALIFORNIA

Caldwell Vineyard Napa Valley 1990: Ripe and intense with a pretty array of flavors ranging from herb, mint, spice and currant. The texture is rich and smooth and the flavors keep repeating themselves on a long, full finish, where you pick up tobacco and cherry notes. Drinkable now. 1,800 cases made. • $32 • (10/15/93) • **90**

Caldwell Vineyard Napa Valley 1989 • $24 • (10/15/92) • **83**

Caldwell Vineyard Napa Valley 1988 • $24 • (11/15/91) • **89**

Caldwell Vineyard Napa Valley 1987 • $41 • (11/15/90) • **91**

Caldwell Vineyard Napa Valley 1986 • $39 • (11/15/89) • **89**

Caldwell Vineyard Napa Valley Minty Cuvée 1990: Potently minty, a flavor that overrides all else, with just a hint of currant and cedar emerging on the finish. For fans of mint-dominated Cabernet. Best after 1996. 130 cases made. • $NA • **82**

Chardonnay Napa Valley 1994: Starts out with a smoky, toasty oak aroma and follows up with elegant, spicy pear, honey and butterscotch flavors that blend together. Finishes with complex and concentrated flavors. 2,100 cases made. • $34 • (05/31/96) • **92**

Chardonnay Napa Valley 1993: Strikes a nice balance between spicy oak and ripe pear, peach and pineapple flavors, the finish has good depth and richness. 1,600 cases made. • $30 • (04/30/95) • **89**

Chardonnay Napa Valley 1991 • $24 • (06/30/93) • **94**

Chardonnay Napa Valley Not Filtered 1992: Mature in color and flavor, with slightly oxidized pear, honey and toast notes that turn rich and smoky, losing fruit on the finish. Not nearly as interesting as the stunning 1991, not likely to gain. 600 cases made. • $26 • (11/15/94) • **86**

Jayson Napa Valley 1992: Dense and chewy, but it turns supple, fanning out with currant, herb, tobacco and leathery notes. Ample tannins on the finish suggest short-term cellaring, but you can drink it now if you like big, rich wines. • $20 • (12/31/94) • **88**

Merlot Napa Valley 1991: Tight and firm, with an earthy mint and cedary edge to the herb and currant-laced Merlot flavors. Smells more complex than what it delivers, picking up cherry and currant before finishing with cedary herbal notes and firm but supple tannins. Pahlmeyer's second Merlot. Best to cellar short-term and see what happens. 400 cases made. • $24 • (09/15/94) • **85**

Merlot Napa Valley Caldwell Vineyard 1990 • $24 • (10/15/93) • **85**

Napa Valley Cabernet Blend 1993: A ripe, rich, full-bodied Bordeaux-style red that shows its plush and complex side already, though still young. The tiers of cherry, currant, anise and spice finish with thick but polished tannins and a rich aftertaste. Impressive for its depth and concentration. 3,000 cases made. • $36 • (05/31/96) CS • **91**

Napa Valley Cabernet Blend 1992: Supple and fleshy, displaying ripe, spicy currant and berry flavors, with tobacco and leather accents. Finishes with smooth tannins. Best after 1998. 1,800 cases made. • $34 • (12/15/95) • **89**

Napa Valley Cabernet Blend 1991: Mintiness to the extreme, where that one-flavor component dominates the currant and plum notes. Finishes with gritty tannins. Hands off for now, best after 1998. 2,000 cases made. • $32 • (11/15/94) • **82**

PALMER | NEW YORK

Cabernet Franc North Fork of Long Island Proprietor's Reserve 1991: Subtle mushroom flavors give this wine a nice mature edge. A bit herbal, with some dried cherry and currant notes as well. A workmanlike wine. 340 cases made. • $15 • (12/31/95) • **79**

Cabernet Franc North Fork of Long Island Proprietor's Reserve 1989 • $13 • (11/15/91) • **76**

Cabernet Sauvignon North Fork of Long Island 1988 • $14 • (06/30/91) • **83**

Cabernet Sauvignon North Fork of Long Island 1986 • $10 • (12/15/88) • **82**

Chardonnay North Fork of Long Island 1991 • $13 • (11/15/93) • **80**

Chardonnay North Fork of Long Island Barrel Fermented 1992: A rough and ready Chardonnay with a vivid color, effusive toasty aromas and bold, tart flavors of grapefruit and pineapple. Chock full of flavor, only lacks finesse. 1,344 cases made. • $15 • (02/28/95) • **85**

Merlot North Fork of Long Island 1989 • $13 • (07/31/92) • **82**

Merlot North Fork of Long Island 1988 • $13 • (06/30/91) • **86**

Merlot North Fork of Long Island 1986 • $10 • (12/15/88) • **80**

Pinot Noir Blanc Blush North Fork of Long Island NV • $6 • (12/15/88) • **75**

Riesling North Fork of Long Island 1993: Round, soft and offers apricot, butter-cookie and marzipan flavors, with more sweetness than crispness. It's simple but pleasant. 238 cases made. • $8 • (08/31/95) • **80**

Riesling North Fork of Long Island 1992: Unusual wine, with spicy, doughy, mature aromas and tart, apple cider flavors. Disjointed and hard to warm up to. 265 cases made. • $8 • **74**

Sauvignon Blanc North Fork of Long Island 1993: A healthy dollop of toasty oak adds interest to this bright wine. The fruit is clean and ripe, with mango and citrus flavors, and crisp acidity keeps it lively. 306 cases made. • $9 • **86**

PARADIGM | CALIFORNIA

Cabernet Sauvignon Napa Valley 1992: Dark and intense, with a hard tannic and oaky edge, so much so the currant and berry fruit struggles to work its way through the green tannins. Time in the bottle should soften the rough edges, but it may always be on the tannic side. 1,800 cases made. • $28 • (12/15/95) • **87**

Cabernet Sauvignon Napa Valley 1991: Firm, supple and complex, with pretty anise, currant and cherry flavors framed by toasty, smoky oak. Impressive for its richness, depth and finish. Needs short-term cellaring to soften, best after 1997. 1,610 cases made. • $26 • (11/15/94) • **90**

PARAISO SPRINGS | CALIFORNIA

Chardonnay Monterey County Barrel Fermented 1991: Earthy and buttery notes override the spicy pear and fig, but the flavors grow on you after a couple of sips. Especially appealing for those who like their Chardonnays with buttery oak. 1,200 cases made. • $10 • (06/30/94) • **84**

Chardonnay Santa Lucia Highlands 1994: Soft and pillowy, with honey, spice and earthy notes that linger on the finish. Unusually mature at this stage, so drink soon. 1,200 cases made. • $12 • (06/30/96) • **83**

Chardonnay Santa Lucia Highlands Barrel Fermented 1993: Well oaked, with a grapey perfumed aroma, turning more complex and focused on the finish where the citrus, pear and toasty oak flavors turn elegant. 860 cases made. • $12 • (07/31/95) • **86**

Gewürztraminer Monterey County Santa Lucia Highlands 1993: With its rose petal and pear aromas and flavors, this dryish white performs lightly and appealingly through the fine finish. 650 cases made. • $7 • (02/28/95) • **84**

Pinot Blanc Monterey County 1991: Crisp and spicy around a light core of pear and apple fruit. Ready now. 1,400 cases made. • $8 • (04/15/95) • **82**

Pinot Blanc Santa Lucia Highlands 1994: Very spicy style, with more oak apparent than fruit, finishing smooth. 650 cases made. • $9 • (05/31/96) • **80**

Pinot Blanc Santa Lucia Highlands 1993: Ripe, smooth and supple, beautifully balanced to show off the spicy pear fruit and the satiny texture, with just a hint of kiwi fruit on the finish. Ready now. 780 cases made. • $9 • (11/15/95) • **87**

Pinot Blanc Santa Lucia Highlands Reserve 1995: Lean and trim. Delicate peach and nectarine flavors have a spicy accent and pick up a note of citrus on the finish. 220 cases made. • $15 • **85**

Pinot Noir Carneros 1991 • $8 • (02/28/94) • **77**

Santa Lucia Highlands Hand Selected 1993: Light, sweet and very smooth, a little sugary but the floral apricot flavors sneak in on the finish. Best from 1997. 900 cases made. • $20 • (07/31/95) • **85**

PARDUCCI | CALIFORNIA

Bono-Sirah Mendocino 1990 • $7 • (11/15/92) BB • **82**

Cabernet Franc Mendocino County 1989 • $10 • (11/15/91) • **85**

Cabernet Merlot Cellarmaster Selection Mendocino County 1986 • $15 • (11/15/92) • **80**

Cabernet Merlot Cellarmaster Selection Mendocino County 1978 • $12 • (02/01/86) • **75**

Cabernet Sauvignon Mendocino County 1992: Not much on the nose from this California value wine, but it's ripe and chewy on the palate, concentrating its plum and black currant flavors in a thick, rich finish that lasts. Not too tannic, but should be better in 1998. 2,400 cases made. • $8 • (11/15/95) BB • **88**

Cabernet Sauvignon Mendocino County 1991: Smooth and polished, with more depth and character than in other recent vintages. This shows off ripe plum and smoky oak flavors. 10,000 cases made. • $8 • (02/28/95) BB • **84**

Cabernet Sauvignon Mendocino County 1989 • $7 • (04/15/94) • **84**

Cabernet Sauvignon Mendocino County 1984 • $8 • (07/31/88) • **74**

Cabernet Sauvignon Mendocino County 1981 • $6 • (02/01/86) • **73**

Cabernet Sauvignon Mendocino County 1980 • $6 • (02/01/86) • **79**

Cabernet Sauvignon Mendocino County 1979 • $8 • (02/01/86) • **69**

Cabernet Sauvignon Mendocino County 1978 • $5 • (02/01/86) • **75**

Cabernet Sauvignon North Coast 1990: Herbal with a green bell pepper edge, although hints of cherry sneak through on the finish. 15,000 cases made. • $7 • (11/15/94) • **79**

Cabernet Sauvignon North Coast 1988 • $8 • (11/15/92) • **80**

Cabernet Sauvignon North Coast 1987 • $9 • (04/30/91) • **80**

Cabernet Merlot Cellarmaster Selection Mendocino County 1993: Smooth and generous, round-textured, with focused berry, vanilla and spice flavors that linger on the finish. • $15 • (11/15/95) • **88**

Chardonnay Mendocino County 1994: Smooth, fruity and distinctly spicy, weaving a nutmeg-cinnamon character through its pear and smoke flavors. It's a good value to boot. 25,000 cases made. • $8 • (09/30/95) BB • **87**

Chardonnay Mendocino County 1993: Tart and green, but offering crisp pear and apple notes. For fans of non-oaked Chardonnay. • $8 • (02/28/95) • **81**

Chardonnay Mendocino County 1991 • $8 • (07/15/93) • **81**

Merlot California 1994: Smooth and polished, with pretty coffee, toasty oak and wild berry flavors that pick up nice, spicy notes on the finish. Hard to find a better value in Merlot anywhere. 34,166 cases made. • $8 • (12/31/95) BB • **88**

Merlot Mendocino County 1983 • $8 • (12/15/87) • **75**

Merlot North Coast 1992 • $9 • (06/15/94) • **85**

Merlot North Coast 1990 • $8 • (10/31/92) BB • **82**

Merlot North Coast 1989 • $10 • (11/15/91) • **85**

Merlot North Coast 1988 • $9 • (04/30/91) • **78**

Petite Sirah Mendocino County 1992: Smooth and concentrated, with plum and bright strawberry flavors that weave neatly through the vanilla-scented finish. Offers elegance and value. 5,000 cases made. • $6 • (09/30/95) BB • **86**

Key: SS—Spectator Selection. CS—Cellar Selection. BB—Best Buy. $NA—Price not available. (BT)—Barrel tasting. Ⓐ—Auction Price.
Dates in parentheses represent the issues in which the ratings were published.

Petite Sirah Mendocino County 1991: This California red is tannic, with vanilla-scented strawberry and plum flavors that linger sweetly on the finish. Drinkable now. 11,000 cases made. • $7 • (02/28/95) BB • **84**

Petite Sirah Mendocino County 1989 • $7 • (11/30/92) • **80**

Pinot Noir Mendocino County 1994: Complex and well oaked for this price category, with a strong toasty oak and vanilla edge to the ripe cherry and wild berry flavors. 10,000 cases made. • $8 • (01/31/96) BB • **87**

Pinot Noir Mendocino County 1993: Tries a little too hard, with tannic extract. Leaving an overly tannic young wine with modest berry and cherry fruit. 17,000 cases made. • $7 • **79**

Pinot Noir Mendocino County 1992 • $7 • (01/31/94) BB • **83**

Pinot Noir Mendocino County 1990 • $7 • (09/30/92) BB • **85**

Pinot Noir Mendocino County 1988 • $7 • (04/15/90) BB • **85**

Pinot Noir Mendocino County 1986 • $7 • (06/15/88) • **70**

Pinot Noir Mendocino County 1985 • $5 • (11/15/87) • **76**

Pinot Noir Mendocino County 1983 • $6 • (08/31/86) • **65**

Pinot Noir Mendocino County 1980 • $5 • (08/01/84) • **56**

Pinot Noir Mendocino County Cellarmaster Selection 1987 • $15 • (04/30/91) • **84**

Sauvignon Blanc Mendocino County 1992 • $6 • (09/15/93) • **77**

Sauvignon Blanc North Coast 1993: Simple, floral flavors on a lean frame. Ready to drink now. • $6 • (02/28/95) • **79**

Zinfandel Mendocino County 1993: Earthy and tannic, with diluted, murky wild berry notes. Lacks focus and charm. 17,000 cases made. • $7 • (10/15/95) • **77**

Zinfandel Mendocino County 1992: Crisp and a bit woody, with the oak overshadowing the light berry flavor. Still, it comes together on the finish. Ready now. 12,000 cases made. • $6 • (10/15/94) BB • **82**

Zinfandel Mendocino County 1991 • $6 • (09/15/93) BB • **82**

Zinfandel Mendocino County 1990 • $6 • (09/30/93) • **78**

Zinfandel Mendocino County 1986 • $5 • (07/15/88) • **80**

Zinfandel Mendocino County Cellarmaster Selection 1990: Lean and crisp, with a narrow band of cherry and spice notes that turn tannic. Ready now. 4,200 cases made. • $12 • (10/15/94) • **83**

Zinfandel North Coast 1988 • $6 • (10/15/92) • **74**

PARKER, FESS | CALIFORNIA

Chardonnay Santa Barbara County 1994: Shows off its ripe pear, peach and nectarine flavors in a clean, correct, well-balanced style. The flavors linger on the finish. 7,683 cases made. • $16 • (06/30/96) • **87**

Chardonnay Santa Barbara County 1993: Forward, ripe and generous with broad and complex pear, peach and spice flavors. 4,800 cases made. • $13 • (01/31/95) • **87**

Chardonnay Santa Barbara County 1992: Ripe and succulent, with layers of plum, berry and spice flavors that turn almost silky on the finish. Try now. 4,300 cases made. • $15 • (02/28/94) • **85**

Chardonnay Santa Barbara County American Tradition Reserve 1993: Smooth and polished, displaying ripe pear, honey and spice notes, framed by light, toasty oak shadings. 1,600 cases made. • $18 • (06/15/95) • **88**

Chardonnay Santa Barbara County Reserve 1992: Ripe and round, generous, with smooth texture and plenty of pear and spice flavors at the core. Drinkable now. 800 cases made. • $16 • (04/30/94) • **88**

Johannisberg Riesling Santa Barbara County 1993: Light and refreshing, a little sweet, exhibiting prominent peach and apple flavors. 1,600 cases made. • $9 • (02/28/95) • **84**

Pinot Noir Santa Barbara County 1994: Somewhat earthy, featuring a leathery edge and modest core of cherry and anise Pinot Noir character. Finishes with soft, fleshy tannins. 2,692 cases made. • $16 • (02/29/96) • **86**

Pinot Noir Santa Barbara County 1993: Supple and fruity, with exotic wild berry, cherry and plum flavors. Finishes with a fruity aftertaste that lingers. 1,600 cases made. • $15 • (12/31/94) • **86**

Pinot Noir Santa Barbara County American Tradition Reserve 1994: Smooth, supple, polished texture and appealing cherry, plum and berry notes. An elegant and refined style that's long and lingering on the finish. Very well made. 800 cases made. • $25 • (02/29/96) • **88**

Pinot Noir Santa Barbara County American Tradition Reserve 1993: Ripe, clean and fruity, with appealing cherry and berry-laced flavors, finishing with a dash of spice, anise, tar and light oak shadings. • $22 • (02/29/96) • **86**

Syrah Santa Barbara County 1992: Ripe and succulent, a sturdy wine with layers of plum, berry and spice flavors that turn almost silky on the finish. Drinkable now. 1,725 cases made. • $15 • (09/30/94) • **85**

Syrah Santa Barbara County American Tradition Reserve 1993: Smooth and polished, with an appealing core of anise, plum, celery and spice. Finishes with a buttery oak edge and good but not exceptional length. 773 cases made. • $34 • (05/31/96) • **87**

PARSONS CREEK | CALIFORNIA

Brut Mendocino County Reserve NV • $15 • (05/31/89) • **79**
Cabernet Sauvignon Sonoma County 1986 • $13 • (11/15/89) • **75**
Cabernet Sauvignon Sonoma County 1985 • $13 • (06/30/89) • **76**

PATZ & HALL | CALIFORNIA

Chardonnay Mount Veeder Carr Vineyard 1994: Bold, ultrarich and complex, with tiers of concentrated pear, spice, honey and hazelnut flavors that fan out on the finish. Shows uncommon richness and depth of flavor, with a long, full aftertaste. A new vineyard designated wine from Patz & Hall. 350 cases made. • $38 • (02/29/96) • **94**

Chardonnay Napa Valley 1994: Another winner from this exceptional California winery. A rich yet elegant white, that's brimming with complex flavors of pear, spice, vanilla and hazelnut, with lovely length. 2,000 cases made. • $28 • (02/29/96) • **91**

Chardonnay Napa Valley 1993: Delivers a mouthful of ripe pear, peach, honey and hazelnut flavors that persist on the finish, where it turns rich and elegant. Beautifully crafted. 1,200 cases made. • $25 • (06/15/95) • **91**

Chardonnay Napa Valley 1992: A lively wine that's spicy, with generous fruit-distinctive nectarine, vanilla and spice aromas and flavors. Drinkable now. 1,300 cases made. • $25 • (04/15/94) • **91**

Chardonnay Napa Valley 1991 • $24 • (12/15/92) • **91**

PAUL, PATRICK M. | WASHINGTON

Cabernet Franc Walla Walla Valley 1988 • $12 • (02/29/92) • **84**

Cabernet Franc Walla Walla Valley Reserve 1992: Looks, smells and tastes awfully mature for a '92, spicy and earthy rather than fruity. Drinkable now. 90 cases made. • $14 • (09/30/94) • **78**

Cabernet Franc Washington 1993: Ripe and generous, full-bodied, bordering on plush, a mouthful of berry and black cherry flavor wrapped in sweet, cedary oak. Tempting to drink now, best now through 1997. 95 cases made. • $9 • (09/30/95) • **89**

PAULSEN, PAT | CALIFORNIA

American Gothic California 1984 • $6 • (12/31/86) BB • **80**
Cabernet Sauvignon Alexander Valley 1984 • $11 • (04/30/87) • **70**
Cabernet Sauvignon Alexander Valley 1983 • $11 • (07/01/86) • **84**
Cabernet Sauvignon Alexander Valley 1982 • $10 • (03/01/85) BB • **85**
Cabernet Sauvignon Sonoma County 1985 • $11 • (12/31/87) • **78**
Cabernet Sauvignon Sonoma County 1981 • $8 • (01/01/84) • **78**

PAUMANOK | NEW YORK

Assemblage North Fork of Long Island 1993: A plush and flavorful wine that is ripe and well-structured. Rich and full-bodied with lovely chocolate, mint and plum flavors. Spice notes linger on the finish. May be best in 1997. 400 cases made. • $22 • (12/31/95) • **88**

Cabernet Sauvignon North Fork of Long Island 1991: A tight and lean wine with modest cherry and currant flavors. Tough and astringent on the finish. • $12 • (12/31/95) • **75**

Cabernet Sauvignon North Fork of Long Island 1991: A tight and lean wine with modest cherry and currant flavors. Tough and astringent on the finish. • $12 • (12/31/95) • **75**

Cabernet Sauvignon North Fork of Long Island Grand Vintage 1993: This is a young wine with plenty of plush toasty oak. Minty aromas and flavors predominate, with loads of berry and plum flavors as well. It finishes with a nice shot of chocolate and spice. Try in 1996. 335 cases made. • $22 • (12/31/95) • **88**

Chardonnay North Fork of Long Island Barrel Fermented 1993: Ripe and sweet, a bit top-heavy, with syrupy honey and canned peach flavors. Plenty of vanilla, piecrust and spice notes. Appealing at first, it fades quickly on the finish. • $15 • (06/30/95) • **82**

Merlot North Fork of Long Island 1992: A solid wine with herbal flavors and a touch of oak. A bit austere, with some modest cherry and spice flavors. Drink now. • $13 • (12/31/95) • **81**

Merlot North Fork of Long Island 1991: Slightly rich and appealing for its spice, cherry and chocolate flavors. Very tannic and a bit resinous. • $13 • (12/31/95) • **82**

Merlot North Fork of Long Island Grand Vintage 1993: Plenty of oaky aromas and flavors with enough fruit to make it worthwhile. Blackberry, currant, cherry and plum flavors are well-integrated into a blanket of spice and chocolate. Finishes tannic, but not harsh, with some nice coffee and butterscotch notes. Wait until at least 1997 to try. 560 cases made. • $19 • (12/31/95) • **87**

PAVONA | CALIFORNIA

Pinot Blanc Monterey County Paraiso Springs Vineyard 1994: Smooth and spicy, a silky wine with toast and nutlike overtones to the apple flavors. Echoes spice on the finish. 600 cases made. • $12 • (05/31/96) • **87**

Pinot Noir Monterey County Paraiso Springs Vineyard 1994: Ripe and full-bodied, offering an appealing band of plum, cherry and sage. Keeps its focus through mid-palate, finishing in dried cherries and firm tannins. Best to cellar into 1997. 500 cases made. • $15 • (04/30/96) • **86**

PEACHY CANYON | CALIFORNIA

Cabernet Blend Central Coast Para Siempré 1993: Starts out with dusty oak and currant notes with flavors to match, it picks up a trace of black cherry and anise on the finish, where the tannins are smooth and integrated. 140 cases made. • $28 • (03/31/96) • **87**

Cabernet Sauvignon Central Coast 1993: Smooth and supple, with pretty black cherry, plum and currant notes of modest depth and richness. Pleasant, relying more on finesse and balance than sheer power. 400 cases made. • $20 • (12/15/95) • **88**

Cabernet Sauvignon Central Coast 1992: A very ripe style, displaying intense black cherry and berry flavors. Finishes with firm tannins and good length, but it's best to wait until 1998. 500 cases made. • $18 • (11/15/94) • **87**

Cabernet Sauvignon Paso Robles 1991: Bold, ripe, intense and fleshy with gorgeous cherry, currant and plum-tinged fruit, picking up an earthy herbal edge on the finish, but for most of the ride you get a load of delicious, ripe fruit and not much tannin. Tasty now through 1997. Tasted twice. 500 cases made. • $18 • (11/15/93) • **90**

Cabernet Sauvignon Paso Robles 1990: Tough, tannic and chewy, this youthful, backward wine offers ripe plum and raspberry flavors and lots of oak seasoning before finishing with drying tannins. It's hard to tell how this will evolve, although it's balanced and flavorful. Drink now to 2002. 500 cases made. • $15 • (03/31/93) • **85**

Merlot Paso Robles 1993: Serves up an appealing core of supple currant and black cherry fruit. Well focused, with nice detail to the mineral, toasty oak and spice flavors. Drinks well now. 400 cases made. • $22 • (03/31/96) • **88**

Merlot Paso Robles 1992: Well oaked, but the ripe plum and cherry-laced fruit stands up to it, turning complex and elegant on the finish, where the flavors marry well. 200 cases made. • $22 • (07/31/95) • **91**

Zinfandel Paso Robles 1989 • $10 • (12/31/91) • **82**

Zinfandel Paso Robles Dusi Ranch 1993: Firm, ripe and intense, offering well-focused black cherry, plum and raspberry flavors that are fresh and lively. Finishes with crisp but mild tannins. 600 cases made. • $20 • (10/15/95) • **88**

Zinfandel Paso Robles Dusi Ranch 1992: Lean-textured, with earthy, spicy flavors that build on the finish. Tasted twice. Drinkable now. 400 cases made. • $18 • (10/15/94) • **85**

Zinfandel Paso Robles Eastside 1993: Marked by earthy, leathery tones, but the fruit manages to pull through. There's enough wild berry and cherry flavors to keep it in balance. 600 cases made. • $12 • (10/15/95) • **87**

Zinfandel Paso Robles Especial 1991 • $18 • (06/15/94) • **85**
Zinfandel Paso Robles Especial 1990 • $13 • (08/31/93) • **90**
Zinfandel Paso Robles Especial Reserve 1989 • $12 • (12/31/91) • **89**
Zinfandel Paso Robles Incredible Red Bin 102 NV: Light and fruity, with simple but pleasant cherry and berry flavors. Drinkable now. 1,860 cases made. • $9 • (03/31/96) • **83**
Zinfandel Paso Robles Westside 1993: Impressive for its focus on the bright, lively black cherry and wild berry flavors that even show some modest depth. 1,600 cases made. • $15 • (10/15/95) • **86**
Zinfandel Paso Robles Westside 1992: Supple and generous, with ripe cherry and blackberry flavors that last through the finish. Complex and concentrated. Drinks well now, but has the depth and richness to cellar through 1997. Tasted twice. 1,900 cases made. • $12 • (10/15/94) • **88**
Zinfandel Paso Robles Westside 1991 • $12 • (08/31/93) • **84**
Zinfandel Paso Robles Westside 1990 • $12 • (10/15/92) • **91**

PEBBLEWOOD | CALIFORNIA

Merlot Alexander Valley Limited Release 1987 • $9 • (05/31/92) • **76**

PECONIC BAY | NEW YORK

Cabernet Sauvignon North Fork of Long Island 1988 • $13 • (06/30/91) • **81**
Cabernet Sauvignon North Fork of Long Island 1987 • $13 • (06/30/91) • **78**
Cabernet Sauvignon North Fork of Long Island 1986 • $11 • (12/15/88) • **84**
Cabernet Sauvignon North Fork of Long Island 1985 • $11 • (12/15/88) • **78**
Merlot North Fork of Long Island 1989 • $13 • (06/30/91) • **78**

PECOTA, ROBERT | CALIFORNIA

Cabernet Sauvignon Napa Valley 1982 • $12 • (03/01/89) • **85**
Cabernet Sauvignon Napa Valley Kara's Vineyard 1993: Offers a decent core of ripe plum and currant flavors with a spicy edge, finishing with mild tannins and medium weight. Well balanced. Ready now through 1997. 1,300 cases made. • $20 • (12/15/95) • **86**
Cabernet Sauvignon Napa Valley Kara's Vineyard 1991: A classy, elegant young wine that blends toasty, buttery oak with a supple core of bright, lively cherry and currant flavors. Finishes with a broad, complex aftertaste and fine tannins. Tempting now but sure to improve through 1997 and age into the next century. 1,200 cases made. • $20 • (09/15/94) • **91**
Cabernet Sauvignon Napa Valley Kara's Vineyard 1990: Firm and fleshy, offering a generous beam of spicy currant and cherry flavors shaded by hints of toast and mineral. A nicely proportioned wine that should be at its best already. 1,200 cases made. • $16 • (09/15/93) • **86**
Cabernet Sauvignon Napa Valley Kara's Vineyard 1989 • $17 • (11/15/92) • **78**
Cabernet Sauvignon Napa Valley Kara's Vineyard 1988 • $16 • (11/15/91) • **89**
Cabernet Sauvignon Napa Valley Kara's Vineyard 1987 • $16 • (10/15/90) • **90**
Cabernet Sauvignon Napa Valley Kara's Vineyard 1986 • $16 • (09/15/89) • **86**
Cabernet Sauvignon Napa Valley Kara's Vineyard 1985 • $16 • (03/01/89) • **86**
Cabernet Sauvignon Napa Valley Kara's Vineyard 1984 • $14 • (03/01/89) • **85**
Merlot Napa Valley Steven André Vineyard 1992: Ripe and oaky but well proportioned, displaying pretty cherry and currant notes that blend in well with the wood on the finish. Given the tannins, it's best to cellar until 1997. • $18 • (11/15/94) • **87**
Merlot Napa Valley Steven André Vineyard 1991 • $18 • (10/31/93) • **89**
Merlot Napa Valley Steven André Vineyard 1990 • $17 • (06/15/93) • **86**
Merlot Napa Valley Steven André Vineyard 1989 • $17 • (11/15/91) • **86**

Key: SS—Spectator Selection. CS—Cellar Selection. BB—Best Buy. $NA—Price not available. (BT)—Barrel tasting. (A)—Auction Price.
Dates in parentheses represent the issues in which the ratings were published.

Merlot Napa Valley Steven André Vineyard Unfiltered 1993: Serves up a decent core of ripe cherry and wild berry flavors, turning crisp and simple on the finish. Appealing now. 2,600 cases made. • $20 • (12/15/95) • **85**
Muscat Napa Valley Moscato d'Andrea 1994: Sweet and spicy, stopping just short of syrupy, showing off the pure Muscat flavors with moderate intensity. • $11 • (09/30/95) • **84**
Muscato di Andrea Late Harvest Napa Valley Sweet Andrea Select 1990 • $16 • (12/15/92) • **81**
Muscato di Andrea Napa Valley 1992 • $10 • (05/15/93) • **84**
Muscato di Andrea Napa Valley 1991 • $9 • (12/15/92) • **83**
Sauvignon Blanc Napa Valley 1995: Round and flavorful. Pear flavors have a strong herbal-weedy edge that persists through the finish. 4,200 cases made. • $7 • **84**
Sauvignon Blanc Napa Valley 1994: Light and flavorful, showing herb and peach notes that linger nicely on the bright finish. 7,000 cases made. • $7 • (08/31/95) • **85**
Sauvignon Blanc Napa Valley 1993: Sturdy, fruity and spicy, drinkable now for its freshness. 4,000 cases made. • $7 • (08/31/94) BB • **83**
Sauvignon Blanc Napa Valley 1992 • $7 • (11/15/93) BB • **87**
Sauvignon Blanc Napa Valley 1991 • $6 • (08/31/93) BB • **82**

PEDRONCELLI, J. | CALIFORNIA

Brut Rosé Sonoma County 1986 • $10 • (07/31/89) • **84**
Cabernet Sauvignon Alexander Valley Fay Vineyard 1992: Simple, straightforward berry and earthy flavors stay with you on the tight finish. Best from 1997. 1,800 cases made. • $13 • (12/15/95) • **84**
Cabernet Sauvignon Alexander Valley Morris Fay Vineyards Single Vineyard Selection 1992: Strikes a nice balance between anise and currant laced fruit and spicy, cedary oak. This wine shows more depth and richness than Pedroncelli Cabernets of late, it is also the first vineyard designated Cabernet. 1,800 cases made. • $13 • (03/31/96) • **84**
Cabernet Sauvignon Dry Creek Valley 1991: Lean and earthy, with a bitter, oaky edge. Dries out. • $9 • (11/15/94) • **75**
Cabernet Sauvignon Dry Creek Valley 1990: Very light and herbal for a 1990, and lacking the character you usually find in Pedroncelli reds. Drink now. Tasted twice. 8,000 cases made. • $9 • (11/15/93) • **73**
Cabernet Sauvignon Dry Creek Valley 1989 • $9 • (08/31/92) • **75**
Cabernet Sauvignon Dry Creek Valley 1987 • $8 • (11/15/90) BB • **85**
Cabernet Sauvignon Dry Creek Valley 1986 • $7 • (09/15/89) BB • **83**
Cabernet Sauvignon Dry Creek Valley 1985 • $7 • (10/15/88) • **79**
Cabernet Sauvignon Dry Creek Valley 1983 • $6 • (08/31/87) • **75**
Cabernet Sauvignon Dry Creek Valley 1981 • $6 • (12/01/84) BB • **80**
Cabernet Sauvignon Dry Creek Valley Reserve 1988 • $14 • (11/15/92) • **78**
Cabernet Sauvignon Dry Creek Valley Reserve 1986 • $14 • (11/15/92) • **78**
Cabernet Sauvignon Dry Creek Valley Reserve 1985 • $14 • (03/31/90) • **85**
Cabernet Sauvignon Dry Creek Valley Reserve 1982 • $13 • (10/15/89) • **73**
Cabernet Sauvignon Sonoma County 1988 • $9 • (10/15/91) • **83**
Cabernet Sauvignon Sonoma County 1974: Mature brown color, with aromas to match, a hint of cedar and chocolate before drying out and turning earthy. Past its prime, but drinkable. 3,000 cases made. • $40 • (11/15/94) • **78**
Chardonnay Dry Creek Valley 1993: Simple, straightforward and spicy, with a touch of a tannic bite on the finish. 6,700 cases made. • $9 • (07/31/95) • **80**
Chardonnay Dry Creek Valley 1992: Lean and a bit earthy with simple pear and grapefruit notes. 9,500 cases made. • $10 • (06/30/94) • **79**
Chardonnay Dry Creek Valley 1991 • $9 • (03/31/94) • **80**
Fumé Blanc Dry Creek Valley 1994: Fruity and floral, with citrus and pear flavors. Some zingy herb and chocolate overtones. 4,800 cases made. • $8 • **86**
Fumé Blanc Dry Creek Valley 1992 • $7 • (01/31/94) • **77**
Gamay Beaujolais Sonoma County 1987 • $4 • (01/31/88) • **77**
Gamay Beaujolais Sonoma County 1984 • $4 • (08/31/87) BB • **87**
Merlot Dry Creek Valley 1991: Dense and earthy, with a pungent, funky, leathery edge. Finishes with chewy tannins. Best after 1996. 7,000 cases made. • $10 • (09/15/94) • **82**
Merlot Dry Creek Valley 1990 • $10 • (08/31/93) • **83**
Merlot Dry Creek Valley Benchlands 1994: Oaky for Pedroncelli, but plenty of light cherry and berry flavors pull it into balance. 6,300 cases made. • $12 • **83**

Merlot Sonoma County 1989 • $13 • (02/29/92) • **76**
Pinot Noir Dry Creek Valley 1993: Simple, with and earthy, cedary edge to the modest plum and berry. 3,900 cases made. • $9 • **78**
Pinot Noir Dry Creek Valley 1992: Earthy, with a tarry edge to the cranberry flavors, turns tannic on the finish. 3,800 cases made. • $9 • (03/31/95) • **79**
Pinot Noir Dry Creek Valley 1991 • $8 • (01/31/94) • **82**
Pinot Noir Dry Creek Valley 1990 • $8 • (02/28/93) • **79**
Pinot Noir Dry Creek Valley 1989 • $8 • (03/31/92) • **75**
Pinot Noir Dry Creek Valley 1988 • $8 • (02/28/91) BB • **84**
Pinot Noir Dry Creek Valley 1986 • $7 • (05/31/90) • **70**
Pinot Noir Dry Creek Valley 1985 • $7 • (06/15/88) • **76**
Pinot Noir Sonoma County 1983 • $6 • (04/15/88) • **67**
Pinot Noir Sonoma County 1982 • $5 • (06/30/87) • **68**
Primitivo Misto Sonoma County 1991: Earthy and gamy, it comes up short on fruit. 4,500 cases made. • $6 • (01/31/95) • **75**
White Zinfandel Sonoma County 1988 • $6 • (06/15/89) • **87**
White Zinfandel Sonoma County 1986 • $4 • (03/31/87) • **82**
White Zinfandel Sonoma County 1985 • $4 • (02/16/86) BB • **83**
Zinfandel Dry Creek Valley 1991: Medium-bodied, with earthy raspberry and cherry flavors. Finishes with crisp tannins and a touch of spice. Ready now. Tasted twice. 4,500 cases made. • $7 • (10/15/94) • **83**
Zinfandel Dry Creek Valley 1990 • $7 • (04/30/93) • **80**
Zinfandel Dry Creek Valley 1989 • $7 • (10/15/92) • **77**
Zinfandel Dry Creek Valley 1988 • $7 • (11/30/90) BB • **84**
Zinfandel Dry Creek Valley 1987 • $7 • (07/31/90) • **65**
Zinfandel Dry Creek Valley 1986 • $6 • (03/31/89) BB • **86**
Zinfandel Dry Creek Valley 1984 • $5 • (07/15/88) BB • **88**
Zinfandel Dry Creek Valley Mother Clone Special Vineyard Selection 1993: Pleasantly balanced, with spicy, tarry facets to the plum and cherry flavors. Finishes with mild tannins. 1,900 cases made. • $11 • (10/15/95) • **85**
Zinfandel Dry Creek Valley Pedroni-Bushnell Vineyard Single Vineyard 1993: A solid core of black cherry and raspberry flavors are tightly wound. 1,800 cases made. • $12 • (10/15/95) • **84**
Zinfandel Rosé Sonoma County 1994: Simple and sweet, showing cherry, raspberry and candied flavors. • $5 • (09/15/95) • **76**
Zinfandel Sonoma County 1983 • $4 • (09/15/87) • **77**
Zinfandel Sonoma County 1982 • $4 • (10/31/86) BB • **79**
Zinfandel Sonoma County 1981 • $4 • (01/01/85) • **78**
Zinfandel Sonoma County Reserve 1981 • $8 • (11/15/87) • **82**

PEIRANO ESTATE | CALIFORNIA

Zinfandel Lodi 1993: Dense and plush, with a firm, tannic aspect to the cherry and plum flavors. Well crafted. Drinks well now. 1,478 cases made. • $10 • (08/31/95) • **87**
Zinfandel Lodi 1992: Ripe and juicy, with intense, jammy wild berry, cherry and plum flavors that hang with you. 543 cases made. • $10 • (06/15/95) • **86**

PEJU | CALIFORNIA

Cabernet Sauvignon Napa Valley 1992: Chunky with modest plum and currant fruit that has an earthy edge to it. Finishes on the short side. 800 cases made. • $18 • (12/15/95) • **84**
Cabernet Sauvignon Napa Valley 1991: A touch rustic, earthy and vinegary, but cherry and plum flavors come through on the finish, even if they lack focus and turn chewy and tannic. 900 cases made. • $18 • (09/15/95) • **85**
Cabernet Sauvignon Napa Valley 1989 • $15 • (08/31/92) • **85**
Cabernet Sauvignon Napa Valley HB Vineyard 1992: Very ripe—almost jammy—with rich, complex plum and currant flavors, picking up a complex floral and spicy quality that adds dimension and complexity. The texture turns smooth and polished. Best after 1999. 600 cases made. • $35 • (12/15/95) • **91**
Cabernet Sauvignon Napa Valley HB Vineyard 1991: Dark and well focused, sporting spicy plum, cherry and currant flavors that are tight and a bit austere now. Better in 1997. 800 cases made. • $35 • (09/15/95) • **86**
Cabernet Sauvignon Napa Valley HB Vineyard 1990: Smooth and plush, with a rich core of smoky currant, spice and mineral flavors, needs cellaring to soften but has a lot of flavor and depth. Best after 1998. 2,500 cases made. • $35 • (11/15/94) • **88**
Cabernet Sauvignon Napa Valley HB Vineyard 1989 • $30 • (08/31/92) • **84**
Cabernet Sauvignon Napa Valley HB Vineyard 1988 • $30 • (08/31/91) • **82**
Cabernet Sauvignon Napa Valley HB Vineyard 1987 • $20 • (11/15/90) • **87**
Cabernet Sauvignon Napa Valley HB Vineyard 1986 • $20 • (11/15/89) • **92**
Cabernet Sauvignon Napa Valley HB Vineyard Special Selection 1988 • $24 • (08/31/92) • **87**
Chardonnay Late Harvest Napa Valley Select 1989 • 13 (03/15/92) • 88
Chardonnay Napa Valley 1994: An attractive core of ripe pear, spice, honey and nectarine flavors. Picks up a butterscotch note on the finish. 1,050 cases made. • $15 • (06/30/96) • **86**
Chardonnay Napa Valley 1993: A touch earthy, with smoky toasty oak edge, but just enough ripe pear and apple-laced fruit to keep it in balance. 1,500 cases made. • $16 • (07/31/95) • **86**
Chardonnay Napa Valley 1992: Serves up a range of spicy citrus notes, with grapefruit, pear and apple flavors that are fresh and lively. Ready now. 600 cases made. • $14 • (06/30/94) • **85**
Chardonnay Napa Valley 1991 • $15 • (07/15/93) • **75**
Chardonnay Napa Valley Barrel Fermented HB Vineyard 1993: Complex, with ripe, rich pear and smoky, toasty oak flavors. Try now. 550 cases made. • $22 • (12/31/94) • **88**
Chardonnay Napa Valley HB Vineyard 1994: An unusual wine, with ripe, sweet-tasting tangerine and floral flavors, not quite a classic Chardonnay, but enjoyable nonetheless. 950 cases made. • $22 • (06/30/96) • **83**
Chardonnay Napa Valley HB Vineyard 1992: Relies a little too much on toasty oak, which dominates the flavor. You get a hint of pear and apple on the coarse finish, but surely the fruit should be more prominent. 450 cases made. • $18 • (06/30/94) • **83**
Chardonnay Napa Valley HB Vineyard 1991 • $18 • (07/15/93) • **83**
Karma Blush North Coast 1991 • $8 • (11/30/92) • **79**
Meritage Napa Valley 1992: Very ripe and juicy, with bright black cherry and plum flavors. Firm tannins stand out on the finish, so cellar it until 1998. 850 cases made. • $24 • (11/15/94) • **87**
Sauvignon Blanc Late Harvest Napa Valley Special Select 1992 • $14 • (06/15/94) • **87**
Sauvignon Blanc Late Harvest Napa Valley Special Select 1991 • $15 • (01/31/93) • **81**

PELLEGRINI FAMILY | CALIFORNIA

Barbera Sonoma Valley Old Vines 1993: Lighter with watery berry, earth and spice notes. 750 cases made. • $10 • (07/31/95) • **81**
Cabernet Sauvignon Alexander Valley Cloverdale Ranch Estate Cuvée 1988 • $12 • (06/15/91) • **82**
Côtes de Sonoma Deux Cépages Sonoma County Red 1991 • $6 • (03/31/93) BB • **83**
Zinfandel Sonoma County Old Vines 1993: Crisp and compact, displaying a narrow band of simple berry flavor. 963 cases made. • $9 • (02/28/95) • **81**

PELLEGRINI VINEYARDS | NEW YORK

Cabernet Sauvignon North Fork of Long Island 1991: A ripe style with intense fruit aromas and flavors. Concentrated currant and black cherry flavors nicely restrained by firm tannins and acidity. Drinkable now. • $15 • (11/15/94) • **86**
Chardonnay North Fork of Long Island Vintner's Pride 1992: Nicely mature in aroma, with toasty, buttery, figgy accents, more lean and simple on the palate and finish. A good drink. • $13 • (02/28/95) • **83**
Encore North Fork of Long Island Vintner's Pride Cabernet Blend 1992: A modest and tannic wine with a loads of spice flavors, but light on fruit. Fairly lean and simple. 146 cases made. • $20 • (12/31/95) • **81**
Finale North Fork of Long Island 1993: Candy apple and cinnamon flavors mark this heavy, sweet wine. It's rich, but soft and clumsy, and finishes a bit burnt and bitter. 215 cases made. • $25 • **78**
Finale North Fork of Long Island 1992: A blowsy, honeyed wine with modest peach flavors and plenty of sweetness. It's viscous, but simple and a bit hollow. 30 cases made. • $25 • **79**
Merlot North Fork of Long Island 1992: Appealing cranberry and cherry flavors are bound up by some fairly tough tannins. Flavorful, but ends

up rather lean and closed on the finish. Difficult to say whether it will improve with time. • $16 • (11/15/94) • **84**

PENARD | CALIFORNIA

Chardonnay Carneros 1992: Ripe and juicy, with delicious peach- and pear-laced Chardonnay fruit that turn smooth and silky on a long, lingering finish. 361 cases made. • $16 • (12/15/94) • **89**
Chardonnay Carneros 1991 • $19 • (03/31/93) • **83**

PEPI, ROBERT | CALIFORNIA

Cabernet Sauvignon Napa Valley Vine Hill Ranch 1991: Serves up ripe, chunky currant, black cherry and anise notes before the earthy tannins kick in. Closed and tight, will need cellaring into 1999 to soften. • $18 • (12/15/95) • **86**
Cabernet Sauvignon Napa Valley Vine Hill Ranch 1989: Serves up a moderately rich core of currant and cherry flavor. Finishes with firm tannins and enough fruit to keep it interesting. Best after 1996. 3,000 cases made. • $18 • (11/15/94) • **85**
Cabernet Sauvignon Napa Valley Vine Hill Ranch 1988 • $18 • (11/15/92) • **89**
Cabernet Sauvignon Napa Valley Vine Hill Ranch 1987 • $24 • (04/30/91) • **90**
Cabernet Sauvignon Napa Valley Vine Hill Ranch 1986 • $18 • (10/31/90) • **88**
Cabernet Sauvignon Napa Valley Vine Hill Ranch 1985 • $16 • (07/31/90) • **85**
Cabernet Sauvignon Napa Valley Vine Hill Ranch 1984 • $21 • (08/31/89) • **80**
Cabernet Sauvignon Napa Valley Vine Hill Ranch 1983 • $22 • (03/01/89) • **80**
Cabernet Sauvignon Napa Valley Vine Hill Ranch 1982 • $24 • (03/01/89) • **88**
Cabernet Sauvignon Napa Valley Vine Hill Ranch 1981 • $25 • (03/01/89) • **86**
Chardonnay Napa Valley Puncheon Fermented 1992: Medium weight, with ripe pear and apricot notes of modest proportions, but lacks the extra dimensions. Finishes with an earthy, oaky edge. 5,000 cases made. • $15 • (07/31/95) • **85**
Chardonnay Napa Valley Puncheon Fermented 1991 • $16 • (12/31/93) • **88**
Sangiovese Grosso Napa Valley Colline di Sassi 1990 • $25 • (02/15/93) • **75**
Sangiovese Grosso Napa Valley Colline di Sassi 1989 • $25 • (10/31/91) • **83**
Sangiovese Grosso Napa Valley Colline di Sassi 1988 • $25 • (11/10/90) • **87**
Sangiovese Napa Valley Colline Di Sassi 1991: Lean but nicely focused, with ripe berry and tobacco flavors shining through on the finish. Drinkable now. 1,500 cases made. • $20 • (11/30/95) • **87**
Sauvignon Blanc Napa Valley Reserve Selection 1994: An oaky style that succeeds. Ripe and intense with a pretty array of pear, grass, herb, melon and cedary oak, finishing with a smoky, toasty edge and plenty of flavor. • $20 • (03/31/96) • **89**
Sauvignon Blanc Napa Valley Reserve Selection 1993: Round and generous, filling the mouth with citrusy pear, peach and vanilla flavors that remain lively through the richly balanced finish. • $20 • (06/30/95) • **88**
Sauvignon Blanc Napa Valley Reserve Selection 1991 • $18 • (02/15/93) • **88**
Sauvignon Blanc Napa Valley Selection Reserve 1992: Crisp and delicately fruity, but the flavors never quite come into focus, finishing a bit simple. Drinkable now. 500 cases made. • $18 • (11/30/94) • **84**
Sauvignon Blanc Napa Valley Two-Heart Canopy 1995: Very direct peach and spicy apple flavors are appealing, though atypical of Sauvignon Blanc. • $12 • **84**
Sauvignon Blanc Napa Valley Two-Heart Canopy 1994: Distinctly herbal and toasty, a lean wine with modest fruit to balance. • $11 • (08/31/95) • **84**

Key: SS—Spectator Selection. CS—Cellar Selection. BB—Best Buy. $NA—Price not available. (BT)—Barrel tasting. Ⓐ—Auction Price.
Dates in parentheses represent the issues in which the ratings were published.

Sauvignon Blanc Napa Valley Two-Heart Canopy 1993: Bright and fruity, offering generous pear and vanilla flavors and a slight oniony, varietal edge. 12,000 cases made. • $9 • (01/31/95) BB • **86**
Sauvignon Blanc Napa Valley Two-Heart Canopy 1992 • $9 • (03/31/94) BB • **87**
Sauvignon Blanc Napa Valley Two-Heart Canopy 1991 • $9 • (09/15/93) • **85**

PEPPERWOOD GROVE | CALIFORNIA

Cabernet Sauvignon California 1993: Strongly herbal, almost medicinal and not as charming as some others. 8,400 cases made. • $6 • (12/15/95) • **78**
Cabernet Sauvignon California 1991: Light, simple and fruity, with hints of plum and spice. At $6, it's easy on the pocketbook. Drink up. 12,000 cases made. • $6 • (06/15/93) • **77**
Cabernet Sauvignon California 1990: A simple, rustic red, with beet and green bean flavors that are pretty basic. Drinkable, but not much fun. 2,500 cases made. • $5 • (11/15/92) • **74**
Chardonnay California 1992: This light, simple wine offers basic apple flavors and a watery texture. Drinkable now. 8,000 cases made. • $6 • (07/15/93) • **76**
Pinot Noir California 1993: Straightforward, with fleshy herb and cedar accents, finishing with spicy cherry flavors. 10,500 cases made. • $6 • (02/28/95) BB • **83**
Pinot Noir California Cask Lot 1 1993: Light and plummy, keeping its fruit singing on the light finish. Has style. 16,300 cases made. • $6 BB • **83**
Pinot Noir California Cask Lot 1 1992 • $5 • (02/28/94) • **78**
Pinot Noir California Cask Lot 2 1992 • $5 • (01/31/94) BB • **86**
Pinot Noir California Cask Lot 3 1992: Lightly fruity, with herb, tar an spice notes that add dimension to the plum and berry flavors. Another terrific value from this producer. 3,300 cases made. • $5 | • (11/30/94) BB • **84**
Zinfandel California 1993: Correct and well proportioned. Has wild berry, cherry and strawberry notes. Good price, too. 1,400 cases made. • $6 • (10/15/95) • **83**

PEPPERWOOD SPRINGS | CALIFORNIA

Pinot Noir Anderson Valley Estate Bottled 1991 • $15 • (02/28/93) • **79**
Pinot Noir Mendocino County Vidmar Vineyard 1991 • $10 • (02/28/93) • **74**

PERELLI-MINETTI, MARIO | CALIFORNIA

Cabernet Sauvignon Napa Valley 1991: Smooth, ripe and plush, with a complex core of currant, herb, cherry and cedar flavors. Turns tannic and dry on the finish, try after 1997. Significantly better than in an earlier tasting. 2,700 cases made. • $13 • (05/31/96) • **86**
Cabernet Sauvignon Napa Valley 1990: Firm and compact, with a tight band of plum, currant, spice and cedary oak. Flavors are rich and the texture supple. Needs time, best after 1998. 1,970 cases made. • $15 • (11/15/94) • **88**
Cabernet Sauvignon Napa Valley 1988 • $13 • (11/15/92) • **86**
Cabernet Sauvignon Napa Valley 1987 • $12 • (04/30/91) • **83**
Chardonnay Napa Valley 1991: Ripe and generous in flavor, firmly structured, keeps its earthy, slightly herbal pear and honey flavors in check. 3,350 cases made. • $13 • (09/30/95) • **87**

PESENTI | CALIFORNIA

Cabernet Sauvignon Paso Robles Family Reserve 1990: Herbal, oaky, ripe and well balanced, showing plum and currant-tinged Cabernet flavors, but lacking extra dimensions. Perhaps with time it will develop more nuance. Drink now. 517 cases made. • $12 • (11/15/92) • **82**
Cabernet Sauvignon Paso Robles Family Reserve 1989 • $13 • (11/15/92) • **82**
Cabernet Sauvignon San Luis Obispo County Family Reserve 1987 • $8 • (12/15/89) • **84**
Cabernet Sauvignon San Luis Obispo County Family Reserve 1985 • $13 • (12/15/89) • **77**
Zinfandel Paso Robles 1993: Elegant and well focused, featuring a complex array of black cherry, raspberry and anise notes framed by pretty

oak shadings. Appealing now through 1998. 682 cases made. • $12 • (09/30/95) • **88**

Zinfandel Paso Robles 1992: Light in color, with strawberry and cherry flavors that dry out. Lacks concentration. 395 cases made. • $12 • (10/15/94) • **78**

Zinfandel Paso Robles Dry Late Harvest Family Reserve 1990: Ripe and jammy, but tannic and hollow on the palate, drying out. 2,340 cases made. • $7 • (10/15/94) • **72**

Zinfandel San Luis Obispo County Family Reserve 1984 • $6 • (12/15/89) • **79**

PETERSON | CALIFORNIA

Cabernet Sauvignon Dry Creek Valley 1992: Medium-bodied, offering a leathery edge to the cedar and berry flavors and finishing somewhat dry and tannic. Should soften in time. 200 cases made. • $16 • (09/15/95) • **83**

Chardonnay Anderson Valley 1993: Firm and compact, with a medium-weight beam of pear and citrus flavors that fold together on the finish. 185 cases made. • $13 • (07/31/95) • **84**

Zinfandel Dry Creek Valley 1993: Tart, tight and tannic, showing a crisp and earthy facet to the cherry and wild berry flavors. Needs some aging. 725 cases made. • $15 • (10/15/95) • **84**

PETITE VIGNE, LA | CALIFORNIA

Chenin Blanc Napa Valley 1993: A serious attempt at oak-aged Chenin Blanc that exhibits light toasty oak aromas that match up well with the rich and spicy apple, pear, honey and melon notes. It drinks well now and should hold up for a few years. 500 cases made. • $14 • (07/31/94) • **88**

PHEASANT RIDGE | TEXAS

Cabernet Franc Lubbock County Cox Family Vineyards 1988 • $12 • (02/29/92) • **79**

Cabernet Sauvignon Lubbock County 1988 • $13 • (02/29/92) • **83**

Pinot Noir Texas 1989 • $14 • (02/28/93) • **67**

PHELPS, JOSEPH | CALIFORNIA

Cabernet Sauvignon Napa Valley 1993: Dry and a bit rustic, cedary, currant flavors have an earthy accent. Struggles a bit to open up. Best cellared into 1998. 12,167 cases made. • $22 • **86**

Cabernet Sauvignon Napa Valley 1992: Dark and intense, featuring black cherry, currant and anise flavors which turn earthy and leathery on the finish. 16,000 cases made. • $20 • (09/30/95) • **87**

Cabernet Sauvignon Napa Valley 1991: Young and a bit raw, but the black cherry and currant flavors are pure and ripe. Finishes with a light oak and spice edge. Impressive for its focus and elegance, has the tannins to age through 1998. 12,740 cases made. • $18 • (10/15/94) • **89**

Cabernet Sauvignon Napa Valley 1990: Firm and flavorful, a solid red wine, with basic currant and cherry aromas and flavors that gain a little speed on the finish. Tannins are well-integrated, but it needs until 1997 or 1998 to settle down. 10,000 cases made. • $24 • (06/15/93) • **85**

Cabernet Sauvignon Napa Valley 1989 • $20 • (04/15/92) • **78**

Cabernet Sauvignon Napa Valley 1988 • $23 • (11/15/91) • **86**

Cabernet Sauvignon Napa Valley 1987 • $50 • (07/15/91) • **75**

Cabernet Sauvignon Napa Valley 1985 • $61 • (05/15/89) • **84**

Cabernet Sauvignon Napa Valley 1984 • $24 • (10/31/88) • **91**

Cabernet Sauvignon Napa Valley 1983 • $36 • (08/31/87) • **84**

Cabernet Sauvignon Napa Valley 1982 • $24 • (12/15/86) • **82**

Cabernet Sauvignon Napa Valley 1981 • $34 • (09/01/85) • **86**

Cabernet Sauvignon Napa Valley 1980 • $41 • (07/01/84) • **89**

Cabernet Sauvignon Napa Valley Backus Vineyard 1992: Ripe, smooth and harmonious, with complex plum, cherry and wild berry flavors. Shortens up a bit on the finish, where the tannins dominate. Give it until 1999. 1,200 cases made. • $45 • (12/15/95) • **89**

Cabernet Sauvignon Napa Valley Backus Vineyard 1991: A bare-knuckled, hard-edged, dark and inky wine. Packed with chewy, tannic plum and cherry flavors. This is big and powerful, probably needing a decade to mature and soften. And even then it will be on the brutish side. Try it after 1999. 1,565 cases made. • $35 • (10/15/94) BB • **90**

Cabernet Sauvignon Napa Valley Backus Vineyard 1990: Shows its toasty, buttery oak right from the start, but there's also a nice core of cherry, currant and plum-tinged fruit to stand up to it. Intense and concentrated, it finishes with a woody, cedary edge. Needs time to round out. Drink 1997 to 2005. 1,000 cases made. • $30 • (11/15/93) • **88**

Cabernet Sauvignon Napa Valley Backus Vineyard 1989 • $30 • (11/15/92) • **88**

Cabernet Sauvignon Napa Valley Backus Vineyard 1987 • $35 • (07/15/91) • **88**

Cabernet Sauvignon Napa Valley Backus Vineyard 1986 • $38 • (01/31/90) • **83**

Cabernet Sauvignon Napa Valley Backus Vineyard 1985 • $49 • (03/01/89) • **90**

Cabernet Sauvignon Napa Valley Backus Vineyard 1984 • $45 • (03/01/89) • **86**

Cabernet Sauvignon Napa Valley Backus Vineyard 1983 • $42 • (03/01/89) • **85**

Cabernet Sauvignon Napa Valley Backus Vineyard 1981 • $37 • (03/01/89) • **91**

Cabernet Sauvignon Napa Valley Backus Vineyard 1978 • $50 • (03/01/89) • **89**

Cabernet Sauvignon Napa Valley Backus Vineyard 1977 • $59 • (03/01/89) • **86**

Cabernet Sauvignon Napa Valley Eisele Vineyard 1991: Lifts off with spicy black cherry and currant flavors, then the chewy tannins creep in. Intense and compact, needing a few more years to soften and develop. Try in 1999. 1,158 cases made. • $45 • (10/15/94) • **89**

Cabernet Sauvignon Napa Valley Eisele Vineyard 1989 • $40 • (06/15/93) • **83**

Cabernet Sauvignon Napa Valley Eisele Vineyard 1986 • $40 • (08/10/90) • **77**

Cabernet Sauvignon Napa Valley Eisele Vineyard 1985 • $56 • (05/31/89) • **81**

Cabernet Sauvignon Napa Valley Eisele Vineyard 1984 • $45 • (03/01/89) • **87**

Cabernet Sauvignon Napa Valley Eisele Vineyard 1983 • $41 • (03/01/89) • **86**

Cabernet Sauvignon Napa Valley Eisele Vineyard 1982 • $46 • (03/01/89) • **85**

Cabernet Sauvignon Napa Valley Eisele Vineyard 1981 • $52 • (03/01/89) • **89**

Cabernet Sauvignon Napa Valley Eisele Vineyard 1979 • $64 • (03/01/89) • **92**

Cabernet Sauvignon Napa Valley Eisele Vineyard 1978 • $89 • (11/15/92) • **97**

Cabernet Sauvignon Napa Valley Eisele Vineyard 1977 • $70 • (03/01/89) • **82**

Cabernet Sauvignon Napa Valley Eisele Vineyard 1975 • $155 • (03/01/89) • **97**

Chardonnay Los Carneros 1993: A bold, ripe and intense Chardonnay from a California appellation that's proving itself worthy. A rich core of pear, spice, honey and toasty oak flavors finish up with good concentration and depth. Well crafted. 17,000 cases made. • $17 • (08/31/95) • **89**

Chardonnay Los Carneros 1992: Firm and intense, with toasty, buttery oak flavors that add dimension to the ripe pear and apple notes. Balanced and elegant, it drinks well now but can age short-term. 13,000 cases made. • $17 • (05/15/94) • **88**

Chardonnay Napa Valley 1991 • $16 • (07/15/93) • **86**

Gewürztraminer California 1994: Smooth and ever-so-slightly sweet, with a peppery, modestly bitter edge to the focused pear fruit. Ready now. 1,200 cases made. • $14 • (11/15/95) • **82**

Gewürztraminer California 1992 • $12 • (09/30/93) • **82**

Gewürztraminer California 1991 • $11 • (11/15/92) • **90**

Grenache Rosé California Vin du Mistral 1994: Overtly fruity, with aromas and concentrated flavors of raspberry and strawberry. A bit soft and simple though the finish lingers. • $NA • **80**

Grenache Rosé California Vin du Mistral 1993: A pretty rosé, bright with strawberry and raspberry flavors that extend into a lively finish. Drink it fresh. 2,500 cases made. • $10 • (06/30/95) • **87**

Grenache Rosé California Vin du Mistral 1992 • $9 • (07/31/93) • **87**

Grenache Rosé California Vin du Mistral 1990 • $9 • (07/31/92) • **85**
Grenache Rosé California Vin du Mistral 1989 • $9 • (11/30/90) • **84**
Insignia Napa Valley 1992: Well oaked but well balanced, too, with pretty currant and cherry flavors that work their way through the initial oakiness. This Cabernet blend combines ripe, rich, intense fruit with a supple texture and a sense of harmony and finesse. Better still in 1998. 4,733 cases made. • $50 • (09/30/95) CS • **90**
Insignia Napa Valley 1991: Dark and intense, with attractive black currant aromas and tight, dense currant, mineral and tar flavors. The cedary accents from oak are a touch astringent, though, and this needs cellaring until 1998 to soften. 6,000 cases made. • $50 • (05/31/95) CS • **90**
Insignia Napa Valley 1990: Firm and compact with a narrow band of herb and currant flavor, turning lean and tannic on the finish. Lacks generosity now but cellaring should help by 1998 or 1999. Tasted three times. 5,725 cases made. • $40 • (11/15/94) • **86**
Insignia Napa Valley 1989 • $35 • (11/15/93) • **87**
Insignia Napa Valley 1988 • $35 • (11/15/91) • **86**
Insignia Napa Valley 1986 • $40 • (08/31/90) CS • **93**
Insignia Napa Valley 1985 • $52 • (07/31/89) CS • **93**
Insignia Napa Valley 1984 • $44 • (03/01/89) • **89**
Insignia Napa Valley 1983 • $46 • (03/01/89) • **89**
Insignia Napa Valley 1982 • $50 • (03/01/89) • **85**
Insignia Napa Valley 1981 • $25 • (03/01/89) • **92**
Insignia Napa Valley 1980 • $60 • (03/01/89) • **90**
Insignia Napa Valley 1979 • $51 • (03/01/89) • **90**
Insignia Napa Valley 1978 • $85 • (11/15/92) • **92**
Insignia Napa Valley 1977 • $63 • (03/01/89) • **91**
Insignia Napa Valley 1976 • $105 • (03/01/89) • **93**
Insignia Napa Valley 1975 • $80 • (03/01/89) • **85**
Insignia Napa Valley 1974: Aging well, with a tight, compact core of spice, mineral and racy Cabernet fruit. Tasted out of magnum, the fruit was mature but vibrant, finishing with rich, chewy tannins and a coffee and cedar aftertaste. Ready now. 670 cases made. • $155 • (11/15/94) • **88**
Johannisberg Riesling Late Harvest Napa Valley 1985 • $12 • (12/15/86) • **93**
Johannisberg Riesling Late Harvest Napa Valley Special Select 1983 • $25 • (03/16/86) H • **75**
Johannisberg Riesling Late Harvest Napa Valley Special Select 1982 • $23 • (04/16/84) • **92**
Le Mistral California Red 1993: Bright, youthful, exuberant, a mouthful of rich berry, plum and spice flavors, finishing with some peppery smoke. Appealing now. 4,500 cases made. • $15 • (12/15/95) • **88**
Merlot Napa Valley 1993: Starts out tannic and intense, with a leathery quality to the currant and cherry flavors, finishing with a slight bitter edge and hard oak flavors. 4,364 cases made. • $22 • (06/15/96) • **83**
Merlot Napa Valley 1991: Crisp and austere, a tough-textured red that has a modest beam of currant flavor to keep it in bounds. Drink from now to 1997. 4,000 cases made. • $18 • (09/15/94) • **83**
Merlot Napa Valley 1990 • $16 • (06/15/93) • **83**
Merlot Napa Valley 1989 • $15 • (05/31/92) • **88**
Merlot Napa Valley 1987 • $18 • (07/31/90) • **80**
Merlot Napa Valley 1986 • $15 • (06/30/88) • **84**
Sauvignon Blanc Napa Valley 1993: Herbal, bordering on bitter, with a toasty edge to the modest fruit. 6,000 cases made. • $12 • (08/31/95) • **77**
Sauvignon Blanc Napa Valley 1992: Crisp and focused, with pear and apple at the core and some nice lemon and herb overtones. Delicious to drink now. 7,000 cases made. • $10 • (06/30/94) BB • **87**
Sauvignon Blanc Napa Valley 1991 • $9 • (09/15/93) • **87**
Scheurebe Late Harvest 1990 • $13 • (06/15/92) • **81**
Scheurebe Late Harvest Napa Valley 1985 • $15 • (08/31/86) SS • **94**
Scheurebe Late Harvest Napa Valley 1983 • $15 • (09/16/84) • **87**
Scheurebe Late Harvest Napa Valley 1982 • $15 • (04/16/84) CS • **90**
Scheurebe Late Harvest Napa Valley Special Select 1989 • $18 • (04/30/91) • **88**
Scheurebe Late Harvest Napa Valley Special Select 1982 • $25 • (05/16/85) • **88**

Key: SS—Spectator Selection. CS—Cellar Selection. BB—Best Buy. $NA—Price not available. (BT)—Barrel tasting. (A)—Auction Price.
Dates in parentheses represent the issues in which the ratings were published.

Sémillon Late Harvest Napa Valley Délice du Sémillon 1989 • $13 • (04/30/91) • **89**
Sémillon Late Harvest Napa Valley Délice du Sémillon 1985 • $8 • (08/31/87) • **91**
Sémillon Late Harvest Napa Valley Délice du Sémillon 1983 • $15 • (01/31/87) • **61**
Syrah Napa Valley 1984 • $8 • (11/15/88) • **89**
Syrah Napa Valley 1983 • $8 • (11/15/87) • **71**
Syrah Napa Valley 1979 • $7 • (09/16/84) • **78**
Syrah Napa Valley Vin du Mistral 1992: Intense and tightly wound, with a ripe, complex core of pepper and currant flavors. It picks up an earthy, oaky tone on the finish before the tannins clamp down. Given its weight, it has a remarkably smooth texture at mid-palate. 500 cases made. • $22 • (12/15/95) • **92**
Syrah Napa Valley Vin du Mistral 1991: Firm and chewy, bright blackberry and black pepper flavors poke through the tannic finish. Best from 1997 or 1998. 500 cases made. • $22 • (01/31/95) • **88**
Syrah Napa Valley Vin du Mistral 1990 • $18 • (10/31/93) • **81**
Syrah Napa Valley Vin du Mistral 1989 • $18 • (12/31/92) • **81**
Syrah Napa Valley Vin du Mistral 1988 • $16 • (06/30/92) • **87**
Syrah Napa Valley Vin du Mistral 1987 • $14 • (08/31/91) • **81**
Syrah Napa Valley Vin du Mistral 1986 • $14 • (10/31/90) • **88**
Vin du Mistral California Red 1989 • $14 • (07/15/91) • **85**
Vin du Mistral Le Mistral California 1991 • $14 • (07/31/93) • **84**
Vin du Mistral Le Mistral California 1990 • $14 • (11/30/92) • **85**
Vin du Mistral Napa Valley Red 1993: Smooth, ripe, round and generous, featuring pear and melon flavor that adds floral vanilla notes on the long finish. 1,350 cases made. • $27 • (01/31/95) • **89**
Viognier Napa Valley Vin du Mistral 1994: A rich and fruity style, boasting appealing spice, peach and nectarine flavors that fan out and broaden on the palate. Shows more finesse and depth than do most Viogniers. 1,081 cases made. • $27 • (02/29/96) • **89**
Viognier Napa Valley Vin du Mistral 1992 • $25 • (08/31/93) • **90**
Viognier Napa Valley Vin du Mistral 1991 • $25 • (11/30/92) • **89**
Zinfandel Alexander Valley 1990 • $12 • (10/15/92) • **88**
Zinfandel Alexander Valley 1989 • $12 • (10/15/92) • **82**
Zinfandel Alexander Valley 1985 • $10 • (07/31/87) • **74**
Zinfandel Alexander Valley 1981 • $6 • (04/16/85) • **80**
Zinfandel Alexander Valley 1980 • $6 • (07/16/84) • **85**
Zinfandel Napa Valley 1985 • $6 • (12/31/86) • **82**
Zinfandel Napa Valley 1980 • $6 • (01/01/86) • **60**
Zinfandel Napa Valley 1979 • $6 • (04/16/84) • **60**

PHILIPPE, DOMAINE | CALIFORNIA

Cabernet Sauvignon Napa Valley Select Cuvée 1984 • $6 • (05/15/88) BB • **87**

PHILIPPE-LORRAINE | CALIFORNIA

Cabernet Sauvignon Napa Valley 1990: Overripe, showing some pruny notes along with currant and toast flavors. Full-bodied, almost thick in texture. An odd wine that could use more elegance, but has plenty of raw material. Try in 1997. 990 cases made. • $10 • (09/15/93) • **82**
Cabernet Sauvignon Napa Valley 1989 • $10 • (07/15/92) • **84**
Chardonnay Napa Valley 1991 • $9 • (03/31/93) • **75**
Merlot Napa Valley 1989 • $15 • (05/31/92) • **89**

PHILLIPS, R.H. | CALIFORNIA

Alliance California 1992: Rustic, rough-and-tumble style that relies too much on high-extract tannins. Cherry, berry and waxy flavors are submerged underneath and really don't shine through. Slightly bitter finish. Mourvèdre and Syrah. 2,500 cases made. • $9 • (04/30/96) • **80**
Alliance California 1990 • $10 • (05/31/93) • **80**
Alliance California 1989 • $10 • (11/30/91) • **88**
Cabernet Sauvignon California 1992: Medium-bodied with a cedary accent on the ripe plum and cherry flavors. Offers modest depth. 32,000 cases made. • $7 • (05/15/96) • **82**
Cabernet Sauvignon California 1991: Crisp and straightforward, light and simple, with an herbal edge. Drinkable now. 8,800 cases made. • $8 • (05/15/94) • **82**

Cabernet Sauvignon California 1990: Firm and fruity, with a nice band of berry flavors stretching across a layer of slightly scratchy tannins. Drinkable now. 8,800 cases made. • $8 • (11/15/92) • **80**

Cabernet Sauvignon California 1989 • $8 • (07/31/91) BB • **82**

Cabernet Sauvignon California 1985 • $6 • (11/30/88) • **80**

Cabernet Sauvignon California Night Harvest NV • $4 • (11/30/88) BB • **83**

Chardonnay California Barrel Cuvée 1993: Attractive, well-balanced pear, spice and light oak shadings, all focused together, with a lingering aftertaste. Drinkable now. 89,000 cases made. • $7 • (06/30/95) BB • **85**

Chardonnay California Barrel Cuvée 1992: Crisp and simple, with a spicy edge to the modest pear and apple flavors, finishing solid. 82,500 cases made. • $8 • (06/15/94) BB • **83**

Chardonnay California Barrel Cuvée 1991 • $8 • (08/31/92) BB • **81**

Chardonnay Dunnigan Hills Barrel Cuvée 1994: Light, elegant and surprisingly deep in flavor, which makes this low-priced California white quite notable. This adds extra facets of spice and hazelnut to the pear and apricot flavors. 160,000 cases made. • $8 • (05/31/96) BB • **87**

Mistura Night Harvest Dunnigan Hills 1994: Simple, modest fruit flavors that develop a dry, clay-like edge when mixed with the tannins. 32,500 cases made. • $6 • **80**

Mourvèdre California EXP 1990 • $15 • (10/15/93) • **83**

Mourvèdre California EXP 1988 • $13 • (04/30/91) • **74**

Night Harvest Cuvée California NV • $5 • (05/15/89) BB • **86**

Night Harvest Cuvée Rouge California NV • $3 • (11/15/92) BB • **80**

Sauvignon Blanc Night Harvest 1994: Light and simple, offering a nice core of apple and spice flavors. 73,000 cases made. • $5 • (12/15/95) • **83**

Sauvignon Blanc Night Harvest 1991 • $3 • (06/15/92) BB • **86**

Sauvignon Blanc California Night Harvest 1992 • $4 • (06/15/93) BB • **84**

Sauvignon Blanc Dunnigan Hills Night Harvest 1995: Open-textured and bright. Pear and vanilla flavors gain a hint of herb on the finish. 70,600 cases made. • $5 • **84**

Syrah California EXP 1993: Smooth and polished, with a core of supple cherry and berry flavors. Firms up on the finish where the tannins become more evident. Try now or cellaring until may 1997 do the trick. 2,500 cases made. • $10 • (12/31/95) BB • **88**

Syrah California EXP 1989 • $15 • (12/31/92) • **86**

Syrah California EXP 1988 • $15 • (11/15/91) • **91**

Syrah California Reserve 1987 • $13 • (12/31/90) • **80**

Viognier EXP 1993: Ripe, round and bubbling over with fruit, mixing its nectarine, pear and almond flavors artfully, finishing supple and smooth. 2,469 cases made. • $10 • (07/31/95) • **86**

Viognier California EXP 1992 • $15 • (02/28/94) • **79**

Viognier California EXP 1991 • $15 • (11/30/92) • **84**

Viognier Dunnigan Hills EXP 1994: Somewhat earthy, adding a slight vegetal edge to the sweetish-tasting pear and apricot flavors. Good, but lacks focus. • $NA • (02/29/96) • **82**

PHOENIX | CALIFORNIA

Hillside Rogue Napa Valley 1992: A blend of Cabernet Sauvignon and Syrah where neither grape benefits. Intense, tannic and hard-edged, overdone, heavy-handed, lacking charm and polish. Ready in 1998, perhaps. • $16 • (04/30/96) • **77**

PIEDMONT | VIRGINIA

Chardonnay Virginia Special Reserve 1993: Opulent, luscious and yummy to drink now. Shows plenty of new oak character-vanilla, nutmeg and butter-along with ripe fruit and a creamy-smooth texture. The generous flavors linger beautifully on the finish. 774 cases made. • $15 • (02/28/95) • **91**

PIETRA SANTA | CALIFORNIA

Sangiovese California Sassolino 1993: A touch earthy, as the drying tannins don't leave much room for fruit. Hints of dried cherry and olive persist on the finish. • $13 • (04/30/96) • **83**

Sangiovese San Benito County 1993: A difficult wine to like. Crisp with a stalky, tannic edge and a very narrow band of cherry fruit, turns crisp and a touch volatile on the aftertaste. 380 cases made. • $19 • (02/29/96) • **74**

Sangiovese San Benito County 1992: Earthy, gamy tones add character to the black cherry notes in this solid, flavorful red. Not to everyone's taste, for sure, but worth a try. • $12 • (02/28/95) • **84**

PINDAR | NEW YORK

Brut North Fork Premier Cuvée North Fork of Long Island 1986 • $13 • (12/31/90) • **80**

Cabernet Sauvignon North Fork of Long Island 1986 • $13 • (12/15/88) • **86**

Cabernet Sauvignon North Fork of Long Island 1984 • $9 • (03/16/86) • **71**

Cabernet Sauvignon North Fork of Long Island Reserve 1988 • $14 • (06/30/91) • **85**

Champagne North Fork of Long Island NV • $13 • (12/15/88) • **86**

Merlot North Fork of Long Island 1987 • $13 • (12/15/90) • **80**

Merlot North Fork of Long Island 1986 • $13 • (12/15/88) • **84**

Merlot North Fork of Long Island Reserve 1988 • $14 • (06/30/91) • **83**

Mythology North Fork of Long Island 1988 • $20 • (06/30/91) • **83**

Mythology North Fork of Long Island 1987 • $20 • (06/30/91) • **81**

Pinot Noir North Fork of Long Island 1985 • $15 • (06/15/88) • **56**

PINE RIDGE | CALIFORNIA

Andrus Reserve Howell Mountain 1988 • $15 • (11/15/91) • **82**

Andrus Reserve Stags Leap District 1988 • $15 • (11/15/91) • **82**

Cabernet Sauvignon 1994: Well focused, with currant and black cherry flavors that are elegant and well defined, finishing with toasty oak. Better than the Stags Leap bottling. • $NA • (05/31/95) • **85-89** (BT)

Cabernet Sauvignon Howell Mountain 1994: Intense and well focused, but also firmly tannic, with earthy currant and cherry fruit emerging on the finish. 1,500 cases made. • $28 • (05/31/95) • **85-89** (BT)

Cabernet Sauvignon Howell Mountain 1993: Well oaked, with a smoky edge to the currant and berry edge. Tight and a bit lean, though it fans out on the finish. Age into 1997. 1,526 cases made. • $31 • (12/15/95) • **88**

Cabernet Sauvignon Napa Valley Andrus Reserve 1991: Crisp and straightforward for such a luxuriously packaged wine, with a tobacco edge to the Cabernet fruit. Drinkable now. 600 cases made. • $60 • (11/15/93) • **85**

Cabernet Sauvignon Napa Valley Andrus Reserve 1986 • $45 • (05/15/90) • **80**

Cabernet Sauvignon Napa Valley Andrus Reserve 1984 • $37 • (03/01/89) • **93**

Cabernet Sauvignon Napa Valley Andrus Reserve 1983 • $29 • Ⓐ (03/01/89) • **88**

Cabernet Sauvignon Napa Valley Andrus Reserve 1980 • $55 • (03/01/89) • **96**

Cabernet Sauvignon Napa Valley Andrus Reserve Cuvée Duet 1985 • $40 • (03/01/89) • **92**

Cabernet Sauvignon Napa Valley Diamond Mountain 1987 • $35 • (11/15/90) • **84**

Cabernet Sauvignon Napa Valley Diamond Mountain 1986 • $30 • (11/30/89) • **92**

Cabernet Sauvignon Napa Valley Rutherford Cuvée 1992: Smooth and elegant, with a supple core of currant, coffee, toasty oak and spice flavors. Hangs together well and has a complex aftertaste that lingers on. Tempting now, but better in 1997 or 1998. 8,900 cases made. • $16 • (11/15/95) SS • **91**

Cabernet Sauvignon Napa Valley Rutherford Cuvée 1991: Supple and generous, with forward cherry and berry flavors that firm up on the finish. Well balanced and may still need short-term cellaring. 10,000 cases made. • $17 • (11/15/94) • **84**

Cabernet Sauvignon Napa Valley Rutherford Cuvée 1990: Strives for complexity with its marriage of rich fruit and oak, and while the currant and cherry flavors are supple and pleasing the wood has a smoky green edge to it. Best after 1996. 6,000 cases made. • $16 • (11/15/93) • **84**

Cabernet Sauvignon Napa Valley Rutherford Cuvée 1987 • $16 • (03/15/92) • **77**

Cabernet Sauvignon Napa Valley Rutherford Cuvée 1986 • $19 • (05/31/90) • **90**

Cabernet Sauvignon Napa Valley Rutherford Cuvée 1985 • $20 • (03/01/89) • **93**

Cabernet Sauvignon Napa Valley Rutherford Cuvée 1984 • $29 • (03/01/89) • **90**
Cabernet Sauvignon Napa Valley Rutherford Cuvée 1983 • $30 • (03/01/89) • **84**
Cabernet Sauvignon Napa Valley Rutherford Cuvée 1982 • $22 • (03/01/89) • **90**
Cabernet Sauvignon Napa Valley Rutherford Cuvée 1981 • $24 • (03/01/89) • **88**
Cabernet Sauvignon Napa Valley Rutherford District 1980 • $12 • (03/01/89) • **91**
Cabernet Sauvignon Napa Valley Rutherford District 1979 • $9 • (03/01/89) • **85**
Cabernet Sauvignon Napa Valley Rutherford District 1978 • $7 • (03/01/89) • **89**
Cabernet Sauvignon Stags Leap District 1994: Medium weight, austere with a leafy, herbal edge to the flavors. Good but not impressive. • $NA • (05/31/95) • **85-89** (BT)
Cabernet Sauvignon Stags Leap District 1992: Ripe and complex, with rich, complex flavors, with tiers of currant, coffee, cedar and black cherry. Has a wonderful sense of harmony and finesse, with distinctive features. Best after 1998. 2,346 cases made. • $31 • (12/15/95) • **90**
Cabernet Sauvignon Stags Leap District 1991: Nice balance between ripe, supple black cherry, currant and spice notes and light cedary oak flavors. Tannins are firm but polished, best in 1997. 1,655 cases made. • $30 • (11/15/94) • **88**
Cabernet Sauvignon Stags Leap District 1990: A drying, charred green oak edge takes away from what would otherwise be a successful wine. The black cherry and currant flavors are elegant and crisp, but it's hard looking past the greenness and overt woody flavors. Drink after 1997. 1,800 cases made. • $30 • (11/15/93) • **83**
Cabernet Sauvignon Stags Leap District 1987 • $28 • (01/31/92) • **85**
Cabernet Sauvignon Stags Leap District Cuvée 1981 • $20 • (02/01/85) • **88**
Cabernet Sauvignon Stags Leap District Pine Ridge Stags Leap Vineyard 1986 • $29 • (03/01/89) • **91**
Cabernet Sauvignon Stags Leap District Pine Ridge Stags Leap Vineyard 1985 • $30 • (04/10/89) • **80**
Cabernet Sauvignon Stags Leap District Pine Ridge Stags Leap Vineyard 1984 • $33 • (03/01/89) • **93**
Cabernet Sauvignon Stags Leap District Pine Ridge Stags Leap Vineyard 1983 • $46 • (03/01/89) • **85**
Cabernet Sauvignon Stags Leap District Pine Ridge Stags Leap Vineyard 1982 • $32 • (03/01/89) • **90**
Cabernet Sauvignon Stags Leap District Pine Ridge Stags Leap Vineyard 1981 • $50 • (03/01/89) • **92**
Chardonnay Napa Valley Knollside Cuvée 1994: Strikes a nice balance between ripe, juicy pear, apple and honey notes and smoky, toasty oak shadings. Flavors linger on the finish. 3,300 cases made. • $16 • (05/31/96) • **88**
Chardonnay Napa Valley Knollside Cuvée 1992: Good intensity and range of flavors, with spice, pear and dried apricot nuances that flow throughout. 7,611 cases made. • $14 • (06/30/95) • **86**
Chardonnay Stags Leap District 1994: A well-oaked style from California that matches its toasty, creamy, buttery flavors against a rich core of fig, honey and pear. Remarkably elegant and refined on the finish, and the flavors keep coming through. 1,250 cases made. • $25 • (05/31/96) • **93**
Chardonnay Stags Leap District 1993: Shows more depth and flavor than most Chardonnays from this vintage. The ripe pear, apple and honey notes pick up nice hints of toasty oak on the finish. 1,166 cases made. • $25 • (06/30/95) • **89**
Chardonnay Stags Leap District Vieille Vigne 1992: Intense and smoky, with a rich, complex core of focused and lively spice, pear, honey and vanilla flavors. Ripe, concentrated, picks up an earthy edge on the finish. 280 cases made. • $35 • (11/15/94) • **89**
Diamond Mountain Andrus Reserve Napa Valley 1988 • $32 • (11/15/91) • **82**

Key: SS—Spectator Selection. CS—Cellar Selection. BB—Best Buy. $NA—Price not available. (BT)—Barrel tasting. Ⓐ—Auction Price.
Dates in parentheses represent the issues in which the ratings were published.

Merlot Carneros 1993: A shade more depth than the Napa bottling, with a core of earthy black cherry and anise flavors, thinning and turning simple on the finish. 633 cases made. • $28 • **85**
Merlot Napa Valley Carneros 1994: Smells attractive, but tastes simple and thin, with cedar and charred oak notes to the currant and cherry flavors. Finishes with firm tannins, so cellaring into 1997 is advised. 800 cases made. • $29 • (06/30/96) • **87**
Merlot Napa Valley Selected Cuvée 1993: Has a spectrum of cherry, tar, earth and light oak shadings. Good but lacks the extra dimensions one might hope for. 7,800 cases made. • $18 • (05/15/96) • **84**
Merlot Napa Valley Selected Cuvée 1991: A little strong on the earthy-herbal overtones at first, but the fruit comes through in the smooth finish. Drinkable now through 1997. • $17 • (09/15/94) • **85**
Merlot Napa Valley Selected Cuvée 1989 • $17 • (05/31/92) • **73**
Merlot Napa Valley Selected Cuvée 1988 • $17 • (08/31/91) • **80**
Merlot Napa Valley Selected Cuvée 1987 • $15 • (04/15/90) • **88**
Merlot Napa Valley Selected Cuvée 1986 • $15 • (06/30/89) • **80**
Merlot Napa Valley Selected Cuvée 1985 • $13 • (02/15/88) SS • **91**
Merlot Napa Valley Selected Cuvée 1984 • $18 • (05/15/87) • **80**
Merlot Napa Valley Selected Cuvée 1983 • $13 • (12/16/85) • **83**
Merlot Napa Valley Selected Cuvée 1982 • $13 • (10/01/85) • **90**
Merlot Napa Valley Selected Cuvée 1981 • $13 • (03/16/84) • **82**
Rutherford Cuvée Andrus Reserve Napa Valley 1988 • $19 • (11/15/91) • **65**

PINNACLES | CALIFORNIA

Chardonnay Monterey 1992: Serves up lots of ripe, rich, generous flavors, with ripe pear, mineral, spice and butterscotch flavors that are complex and concentrated. Finishes with a long, full aftertaste, with the kind of depth and character that should bode well for short-term cellaring. 4,000 cases made. • $15 • (06/15/94) • **89**
Chardonnay Monterey 1991 • $16 • (07/15/93) • **84**
Pinot Noir Monterey Pinnacles Vineyard 1991 • $16 • (02/28/93) • **84**
Pinot Noir Monterey Pinnacles Vineyard 1990 • $16 • (02/28/93) • **79**
Pinot Noir Monterey Pinnacles Vineyard 1988 • $16 • (10/31/91) • **74**

PINTLER | IDAHO

Cabernet Sauvignon Idaho 1988 • $16 • (02/29/92) • **81**

PIPER SONOMA | CALIFORNIA

Blanc de Noirs Sonoma County NV • $NA • (12/31/93) • **87**
Blanc de Noirs Sonoma County Select Cuvée NV: Delicate style, with crisp, fresh cherry, spice and light pear shadings of modest depth and proportion. Turns simple on the finish. Ready now. • $14 • (12/31/94) • **84**
Blanc de Noirs Sonoma County 1988 • $14 • (12/31/92) • **86**
Blanc de Noirs Sonoma County 1987 • $16 • (06/15/91) • **83**
Blanc de Noirs Sonoma County 1986 • $15 • (05/31/89) • **87**
Blanc de Noirs Sonoma County 1983 • $15 • (12/31/86) • **88**
Blanc de Noirs Sonoma County 1982 • $15 • (04/01/86) • **86**
Brut Rosé Sonoma County 1990: Pale salmon in color, with light, floral and Pinot Noir aromas that come across as somewhat coarse and simple. 750 cases made. • $19 • **84**
Brut Rosé Sonoma County 1989: No mistaking the fruit here: ripe, spicy black cherry and subtle plum notes. This also keeps its flavors on the finish. Ready now. 200 cases made. • $19 • (11/15/94) • **88**
Brut Sonoma County 1988 • $14 • (01/31/92) • **88**
Brut Sonoma County 1987 • $16 • (06/15/91) • **87**
Brut Sonoma County 1986 • $14 • (05/31/89) • **82**
Brut Sonoma County 1985 • $14 • (07/15/88) • **79**
Brut Sonoma County 1983 • $22 • (01/31/88) • **74**
Brut Sonoma County 1982 • $13 • (05/01/86) • **62**
Brut Sonoma County Reserve 1982 • $20 • (12/31/89) • **93**
Brut Sonoma County Select Cuvée NV: This has an earthy streak running through the pear, black cherry and spice notes, but it comes together on the finish, where the fruit prevails. Ready now. 48,000 cases made. • $14 • (12/31/94) • **87**
Brut Sonoma County Tête de Cuvée 1981 • $29 • (05/31/89) • **88**
Sparkling Sonoma County Tête De Cuvée 1985: Lean and trim, with tightly wound, earthy citrus flavors that gain modest depth on the fin-

ish. Not the complexity you expect from a tête de cuvée, but a solid effort. 1,000 cases made. • $28 • (12/31/94) • **86**

PLAM | CALIFORNIA

Cabernet Sauvignon California 1992: Smooth and polished, with earthy herb, cherry and a spicy pickley edge, finishing with fine tannins. Ready. 18,000 cases made. • $6 • (12/15/95) • **82**

Cabernet Sauvignon Napa Valley 1988 • $28 • (09/30/91) • **79**

Cabernet Sauvignon Napa Valley 1986 • $24 • (09/15/89) • **92**

Cabernet Sauvignon Napa Valley 1985 • $24 • (06/30/88) • **91**

Merlot Napa Valley 1993: A touch earthy, with a bitter, meaty, leathery overtone to the plum and currant flavors. Lacks charm. 391 cases made. • $25 • (03/31/96) • **78**

PLANE'S CAYUGA | NEW YORK

Chancellor Finger Lakes 1983 • $5 • (03/16/86) • **76**

PODERE DELL' OLIVOS IL | CALIFORNIA

Barbera California Ragazzo Legnoso Riserva 1993: Barbera doesn't get much better in California. Brilliantly fruity, velvety in texture and exuberant with blackberry, currant and a floral touch on the finish. Appealing now, fine through 1998. 325 cases made. • $18 • (10/15/95) • **90**

Riserva Ragazzo Legnoso California 1994: A blend of Barbera and Nebbiolo that doesn't optimize the qualities of either. Shows tart plum and berry flavors with modest depth and richness. 300 cases made. • $18 • **81**

PONTIN DEL ROZA | WASHINGTON

Cabernet Sauvignon Columbia Valley 1993: Has a distinct pickle-barrel note that runs through the modest blackberry flavors. Approachable now, best from 1997. 375 cases made. • $22 • **84**

Chenin Blanc Columbia Valley 1995: Soft and pleasant. Slightly sweet pear and almond flavors. Drink it soon. 500 cases made. • $6 • **82**

Merlot Columbia Valley 1993: Fresh, lively and focused, playing out its berry, spice and vanilla flavors with style and flair. Tasty now, maybe best in 1997-1998. 540 cases made. • $11 • **87**

Roza Sunset Blush Columbia Valley NV: Sweaty, leathery flavors are not appealing. 650 cases made. • $6 • **70**

Roza Sunset Yakima Valley 1988 • $6 • (10/15/89) • **80**

POPE VALLEY CELLARS | CALIFORNIA

Cabernet Sauvignon Napa Valley 1990: Very ripe and tannic, with a pruny edge to the currant and cherry flavors. Dense and compact, the finish has a strong, chewy character. Best after 1997. 300 cases made. • $14 • (11/15/94) • **84**

Cabernet Sauvignon Napa Valley La Dolce DeVita Vineyard 1992: Tightly wound with a firm core of black cherry, currant and cedary oak, this compact young wine will need cellaring into 1998 or beyond to soften and mature. May always be on the tannic side. 300 cases made. • $15 • (12/15/95) • **87**

Port Napa Valley 1994: Exuberant, polished currant, raspberry and blackberry flavors shine through the fine tannins. A solid port that bursts with fruit. Best from 2000 to 2002. 360 cases made. • $18 • (10/31/95) • **88**

Port Napa Valley 1993: Soft and jammy, not terribly sweet but loaded with raspberry jam flavor that extends into a slightly tannic finish. Maybe best from 1997. 85 cases made. • $18 • (05/31/95) • **83**

POPLAR RIDGE | NEW YORK

Foch New York 1981 • $7 • (03/16/86) • **54**

POPPY HILL | CALIFORNIA

Cabernet Sauvignon California 1987 • $7 • (05/31/91) • **78**

Merlot Napa Valley Founder's Selection 1991: Ripe and inviting, with a pretty core of supple currant, cherry and herb flavors. Drinkable now. • $10 • (09/15/94) • **84**

PORTER CREEK | CALIFORNIA

Chardonnay Russian River Valley 1993: Austere with a flinty edge to the lean pear and apple notes. 750 cases made. • $14 • (07/31/95) • **82**

Chardonnay Russian River Valley Unfiltered Reserve 1993: Lacks focus, with an earthy edge to the modest pear and oak flavors. 200 cases made. • $23 • (07/31/95) • **83**

PORTTEUS | WASHINGTON

Cabernet Sauvignon Yakima Valley 1991: Soft in texture,with juicy currant and berry notes, plus some tobacco, spice and prune tones on the finish. Interesting range of flavors, but the structure seems a little soft. Drinkable now. 600 cases made. • $19 • (09/30/94) • **71**

Cabernet Sauvignon Yakima Valley 1990: Smoky aromas and vegetal flavors end up tasting sour and unpleasant. Not our style. 1,000 cases made. • $19 • (09/30/95) • **72**

Cabernet Sauvignon Yakima Valley 1988 • $19 • (02/28/93) • **85**

Cabernet Sauvignon Yakima Valley 1987 • $18 • (03/31/92) • **86**

Cabernet Sauvignon Yakima Valley Estate Bottled 1991: Soft in texture, with juicy currant and berry notes, plus some tobacco, spice and prune tones on the finish. Interesting range of flavors, but the structure seems a little soft. Drinkable now. 250 cases made. • $23 • (09/30/94) • **85**

Chardonnay Yakima Valley Estate Bottled 1991: Floral and flavorful in a light frame, hinting at citrus and apple on the finish. Drinkable now. 800 cases made. • $11 • (09/30/94) • **82**

Lemberger Yakima Valley 1992: Sturdy and fruity with generous blackberry, anise and cola aromas and flavors that keep echoing on the finish. Appealing. 250 cases made. • $12 • (09/30/94) • **85**

POTELLE, CHATEAU | CALIFORNIA

Cabernet Sauvignon Alexander Valley 1988 • $18 • (11/15/92) • **87**

Cabernet Sauvignon Alexander Valley 1987 • $16 • (08/31/91) • **83**

Cabernet Sauvignon Alexander Valley 1986 • $15 • (10/31/90) • **84**

Cabernet Sauvignon Alexander Valley 1984 • $13 • (12/31/88) • **83**

Cabernet Sauvignon Napa Valley Cuvée 95 1990: Austere and tannic, with intense currant, plum and spice notes. Will need cellaring until about 1999 for the tannins to soften. 2,000 cases made. • $16 • (10/15/94) • **86**

Chardonnay Mount Veeder V.G.S. 1992: Rich and concentrated, offering an earthy, mature edge to the tiers of smoky pear, honey and toast. It finishes in a burst of buttery oak and the hazelnut flavors linger on and on. 1,500 cases made. • $34 • (04/30/96) • **91**

Chardonnay Mount Veeder V.G.S. 1991: A ripe and vibrant array of creamy pear, spice, honey and peach notes that give way to a long, rich aftertaste. 700 cases made. • $32 • (06/15/95) • **91**

Chardonnay Napa Valley 1991 • $9 • (03/15/94) BB • **88**

Chardonnay Napa Valley-Central Coast 1994: Intense and earthy with pronounced grassy overtones, straying into Sauvignon Blanc territory where it takes a citrus and grapefruit edge. 13,000 cases made. • $9 • (10/15/95) • **85**

Sauvignon Blanc Napa Valley 1994: Light, crisp, refreshing tropical fruit and citrusy flavors that linger. 7,000 cases made. • $9 • (08/31/95) • **87**

Sauvignon Blanc Napa Valley 1993: Fruity and bright, lively and exuberant, echoes citrus and pear flavors. • $9 • (01/31/95) • **85**

Sauvignon Blanc Napa Valley 1992 • $9 • (11/30/93) SS • **88**

Zinfandel Mount Veeder V.G.S. 1992: Beautifully crafted and delicious. Layers of ripe, rich, supple raspberry, cherry and plum flavors. Smooth and polished on the finish, where the toasty, buttery oak adds depth and dimension. Ready now through 2001. 1,000 cases made. • $28 • (10/15/94) • **92**

Zinfandel Mount Veeder V.G.S. 1990 • $27 • (04/30/93) • **90**

Zinfandel Napa Valley V.G.S. 1993: Intense and firmly tannic, but rings true for Zinfandel with its spice, pepper and wild berry flavors. Should age to soften the rough edges. 1,700 cases made. • $28 • (12/31/95) • **88**

POWERS | WASHINGTON

Cabernet Sauvignon Columbia Valley 1993: Silky smooth and beautifully polished, a mouthful of sweet plum, blackberry and vanilla flavor that glides smoothly through the finish. Approachable now but could improve through 1998. 300 cases made. • $12 • (09/30/95) • **91**

Cabernet-Merlot Columbia Valley 1994: Bright, plummy flavors make this a lively blend, balancing its zesty fruit against a firm frame of fine tannin and some spiciness. Best in 1998. 1,000 cases made. • $10 • (05/15/96) • **87**

Cabernet-Merlot Columbia Valley 1993: Packs a rich vein of spicy plum, currant and berry flavor on an airy, elegant frame. Disarming in its purity of sweet fruit combined with polished texture and nice touches of minty oak. Approachable now, best in 1998. 550 cases made. • $10 • (05/15/96) • **91**

Cabernet-Merlot Columbia Valley 1992: A chunky red with rough edges, more aromatic than flavorful, showing some nice currant and toasty oak aromas that turn simple on the palate. Drinkable now. 500 cases made. • $8 • (10/15/93) • **79**

Chardonnay Columbia Valley 1994: Light and spicy, sneaking some toasty oak into the mix on the finish. 1,500 cases made. • $8 • (09/30/95) • **82**

Chardonnay Columbia Valley 1993: Bright and brimming with apple, vanilla and citrus flavors. Ready now. 500 cases made. • $8 • (09/30/95) • **87**

Chardonnay Columbia Valley 1991 • $7 • (12/15/93) • **81**

Fumé Blanc Columbia Valley Dry 1994: Toasty, herbal notes run through this lively and citrusy white, finishing lean and jazzy. 400 cases made. • $8 • (09/30/95) • **83**

Merlot Columbia Valley 1993: Lighter style, with spicy dill notes in the modest tobacco-scented berry flavors. Finishes firm, needs until 1998. 1,000 cases made. • $13 • (05/31/96) • **85**

Merlot Columbia Valley 1992: Light but buttery and spicy with flavors from oak aging, a smooth-textured Merlot that balances away from the modest plum and berry notes lurking in the background. Drinkable now. 1,100 cases made. • $12 • (09/30/94) • **80**

PRADEL, BERNARD | CALIFORNIA

Cabernet Sauvignon Howell Mountain Ranch 1991: Offers hints of cherry and berry jam before dense, earthy tannins clamp down. Packs a wallop, but needs considerable cellar time to soften. Try in 1998. 600 cases made. • $21 • (09/15/95) • **87**

Cabernet Sauvignon Napa Valley 1987 • $20 • (10/15/90) • **86**

Cabernet Sauvignon Napa Valley 1986 • $12 • (01/31/90) • **82**

Cabernet Sauvignon Napa Valley 1985 • $12 • (04/30/89) • **91**

Cabernet Sauvignon Napa Valley 1984 • $11 • (02/29/88) • **88**

Cabernet Sauvignon Napa Valley Limited Barrel Selection 1990: Smooth and supple, adding a mineral and cedar edge to cherry and plum notes, smooth, mature tannins on the finish. 2,000 cases made. • $14 • (09/15/95) • **85**

Cabernet Sauvignon Napa Valley Limited Barrel Selection 1989 • $18 • (08/31/92) • **81**

Cabernet Sauvignon Napa Valley Limited Barrel Selection 1988 • $20 • (11/15/91) • **80**

Sauvignon Blanc Late Harvest Napa Valley Allais Vineyard Botrytis 1985 • $9 • (05/31/88) • **75**

PRESTON | CALIFORNIA

Barbera Dry Creek Valley 1992: Supple and generous up front, packed with blackberry and spicy, peppery overtones, finishing with focused fruit flavors that linger and pick up a touch of lime-tinged acidity. Ready now. 999 cases made. • $13 • (11/15/95) • **89**

Barbera Dry Creek Valley 1990 • $13 • (11/30/92) • **82**

Barbera Dry Creek Valley 1989 • $13 • (03/15/92) • **86**

Key: SS—Spectator Selection. CS—Cellar Selection. BB—Best Buy. $NA—Price not available. (BT)—Barrel tasting. Ⓐ—Auction Price.
Dates in parentheses represent the issues in which the ratings were published.

Barbera Dry Creek Valley 1985 • $8 • (01/31/88) • **85**

Cabernet Sauvignon Dry Creek Valley 1990: Compact and tightly wound, exhibiting currant, black cherry and spice flavors that linger on. Firmly tannic, so best to cellar until 1998. 2,000 cases made. • $12 • (11/15/94) • **88**

Cabernet Sauvignon Dry Creek Valley 1989 • $12 • (11/15/93) • **81**

Cabernet Sauvignon Dry Creek Valley 1988 • $14 • (03/15/92) • **80**

Cabernet Sauvignon Dry Creek Valley 1987 • $14 • (10/31/90) • **88**

Cabernet Sauvignon Dry Creek Valley 1986 • $12 • (03/15/90) • **87**

Cabernet Sauvignon Dry Creek Valley 1985 • $11 • (03/01/89) • **89**

Cabernet Sauvignon Dry Creek Valley 1984 • $11 • (03/01/89) • **87**

Cabernet Sauvignon Dry Creek Valley 1983 • $11 • (03/01/89) • **86**

Cabernet Sauvignon Dry Creek Valley 1982 • $11 • (03/01/89) • **87**

Chenin Blanc Dry Creek Valley Barrel Aged 1992: Soft and fruity, but dry, with a lemony edge to liven up the spicy melon and almond flavors, finishing with welcome generosity. Drink while it's fresh. 2,334 cases made. • $7 • (07/31/94) • **86**

Dry Creek Valley Red 1993: Bright, spicy and lively, full-bodied but not too weighty, showing some pretty floral and hazelnut notes on the lingering finish. 670 cases made. • $18 • (01/31/95) • **87**

Estate Red Dry Creek Valley 1989 • $5 • (06/30/90) • **77**

Estate Red Dry Creek Valley 1988 • $5 • (08/31/89) BB • **82**

Faux Dry Creek Valley 1993: Smooth and generous, medium-weight, spicy, black cherry and berry flavors linger on the solid finish. Ready now. Blend includes Syrah, Grenache and Mourvèdre. 2,550 cases made. • $9 • (04/30/95) • **85**

Faux Dry Creek Valley 1992 • $9 • (12/31/93) BB • **83**

Faux-Castel Dry Creek Valley 1991 • $9 • (11/30/92) • **85**

Faux-Castel Dry Creek Valley 1990 • $9 • (06/30/92) • **82**

Gamay Beaujolais Dry Creek Valley 1995: Youthful, ripe and disarmingly delicious, sporting bright berry and dusky spice flavors. Drink it soon. 1,650 cases made. • $9 • (02/29/96) • **86**

Gamay Beaujolais Dry Creek Valley 1994: Dark in color, effusively fruity, sporting bright berry flavors and smooth texture. To drink while it's fresh and zingy. 1,400 cases made. • $8 • (04/30/95) • **87**

Gamay Beaujolais Dry Creek Valley 1988 • $7 • (02/15/89) • **85**

Gamay Beaujolais Dry Creek Valley 1987 • $6 • (01/31/88) • **78**

Gamay Beaujolais Dry Creek Valley 1986 • $6 • (02/15/87) • **88**

Gamay Beaujolais Dry Creek Valley 1985 • $5 • (02/01/86) • **88**

Marsanne Dry Creek Valley 1992 • $18 • (07/31/93) • **88**

Marsanne Dry Creek Valley 1991 • $17 • (11/30/92) • **88**

Marsanne Dry Creek Valley Organically Grown Grapes 1994: Soft, ripe and silky, with a vanilla note running through the fruit bowl flavors. Finishes bright and appealing. 750 cases made. • $18 • (07/31/95) • **87**

Muscat Canelli Late Harvest Dry Creek Muscat Brûlée 1989 • $12 • (03/15/92) • **82**

Muscat Canelli Late Harvest Dry Creek Valley Muscat Brûlée 1987 • $12 • (08/31/89) • **91**

Sauvignon Blanc Dry Creek Valley 1994: Bright and appealing for its simple pear and slightly herbal flavors. 522 cases made. • $12 • (02/29/96) • **82**

Sauvignon Blanc Dry Creek Valley Cuvée de Fumé 1994: Soft and weedy, with a sweet vanilla overtone to the floral flavors. Lacks fruit, not the norm for Preston. 1,594 cases made. • $9 • **78**

Sauvignon Blanc Dry Creek Valley Cuvée de Fumé 1993: A lean, crisp and racy white that has slight green accents to the tobacco-scented pear flavor. Drink now. 4,000 cases made. • $9 • (05/31/95) BB • **86**

Sauvignon Blanc Dry Creek Valley Cuvée de Fumé 1992 • $9 • (03/15/94) • **84**

Sauvignon Blanc Dry Creek Valley Cuvée de Fumé 1991 • $9 • (07/31/92) • **85**

Sauvignon Blanc Dry Creek Valley Organically Grown Grapes 1993: Round in texture but citrusy at the core, dressed up with a touch of ripe pear and toast. 238 cases made. • $12 • (08/31/95) • **83**

Sémillon Dry Creek Valley Barrel Fermented 1994: Soft, round and modestly fuity, a pleasant wine with pretty peach and citrus flavors. 537 cases made. • $13 • (05/31/96) • **83**

Syrah Dry Creek Valley 1993: Ripe and lively, sporting a well-focused if tannic core of wild berry and cherry flavor. The complex aftertaste picks up an anise edge. 750 cases made. • $18 • (02/29/96) • **88**

Syrah Dry Creek Valley 1990 • $18 • (12/31/92) • **85**

Syrah Dry Creek Valley Unfiltered 1992: Dark in color, offering an alluring core of earthy currant, cedar and spice flavors that are tightly wound, richly tannic finish. 1,011 cases made. • $18 • (05/15/95) • **88**

Syrah-Sirah Dry Creek Valley 1989 • $18 • (03/15/92) • **78**

Syrah-Sirah Dry Creek Valley 1986 • $11 • (02/15/89) • **90**

Syrah-Sirah Dry Creek Valley 1985 • $9 • (01/31/88) • **91**

Viognier Dry Creek Valley 1992 • $18 • (07/31/93) • **85**

Viognier Dry Creek Valley 1991 • $18 • (11/30/92) • **86**

Viognier Dry Creek Valley Barrel Fermented 1994: Spicy, soft and fresh, a peppery edge to the simple pear flavors that last on the finish. 830 cases made. • $17 • (07/31/95) • **85**

White Zinfandel Dry Creek Valley Le Petit Faux 1994: Fruity and almost candied watermelon and cherry flavors. Simple and finishes somewhat astringent. 370 cases made. • $10 • (09/15/95) • **78**

Zinfandel Dry Creek Valley 1992: Ripe and chunky, with rich, complex raspberry, cherry and blackberry flavors. A bit rustic, but has depth. The tannins should soften through 1998, may be Preston's best to date. 3,400 cases made. • $12 • (09/15/94) SS • **89**

Zinfandel Dry Creek Valley 1991 • $11 • (09/30/93) • **88**

Zinfandel Dry Creek Valley 1990 • $12 • (12/15/92) • **87**

Zinfandel Dry Creek Valley 1989 • $11 • (10/15/92) • **86**

Zinfandel Dry Creek Valley 1988 • $10 • (10/15/90) • **86**

Zinfandel Dry Creek Valley 1987 • $10 • (03/15/90) • **83**

Zinfandel Dry Creek Valley 1986 • $8 • (12/15/88) • **84**

Zinfandel Dry Creek Valley 1985 • $8 • (11/15/87) • **91**

Zinfandel Dry Creek Valley 1984 • $8 • (12/31/86) • **80**

Zinfandel Dry Creek Valley Old Vines Old Clones 1993: Rich, solid core of cedary oak and berry flavors. A complete package that turns spicy, complex and tannic. 2,325 cases made. • $13 • (06/15/95) • **88**

PRESTON WINE CELLARS | WASHINGTON

Cabernet Sauvignon Washington 1992: Simple, with tart wild berry and cherry notes and firm tannins. Best to drink it now while the flavors are fresh and lively. 2,100 cases made. • $12 • (03/15/94) • **82**

Cabernet Sauvignon Washington 1982 • $8 • (05/31/88) • **84**

Cabernet Sauvignon Washington Oak Aged 1993: Smooth, ripe and generous, opening up to a cascade of berry, plum, spice and vanilla flavors that swirl around elegantly on the finish. Approachable now, better in 1997. 1,600 cases made. • $10 • (09/30/95) • **89**

Cabernet Sauvignon Washington Oak Aged 1989 • $10 • (05/15/91) • **85**

Cabernet Sauvignon Washington Preston Vineyard Oak Aged 1990: Decidedly herbal, vegetal and oaky, with hints of barely ripe plum and currant. Stylistic, but some may like the greenish, herbal character. Drinkable now. • $12 • (04/30/92) • **76**

Cabernet Sauvignon Washington Preston Vineyard Reserve 1990: Complex and harmonious, with lovely currant, anise, cherry and spice flavors framed by toasty, buttery oak nuances. Balanced and long on the finish. A delicious wine that should age well throughout the decade. 125 cases made. • $21 • (03/31/92) • **91**

Cabernet Sauvignon Washington Preston Vineyard Selected Reserve 1987 • $14 • (10/15/89) • **62**

Cabernet Sauvignon Washington Reserve 1992: Smooth and round, a real mouthful of blackberry, tar, vanilla and spice flavor that keeps bubbling up as the soft tannins kick in on the finish. Impressive now, best from 1997 to 1998. 300 cases made. • $27 • (09/30/95) • **90**

Cabernet Sauvignon Washington Reserve 1991: Crisp in texture, with a tart streak running through the ripe currant, cedar and coffee flavors. Finishes more mature than you might expect. Drinkable now. • $28 • (10/15/93) • **84**

Cabernet Sauvignon Washington Reserve 1989 • $24 • (08/31/91) • **90**

Cabernet Sauvignon Washington Western White Oak Aged 1992: Grapey, floral flavors are odd, but this red has an odd charm. Needs a little more richness on the finish. 75 cases made. • $24 • (04/30/96) • **81**

Cabernet Sauvignon Washington Western White Oak Aged 1991: A light style, displaying crisp berry, earth, oak and cherry notes that turn simple and watery, with a touch of herb on the finish. Drink now. • $18 • (10/15/93) • **81**

Chardonnay Washington 1993: Lean and spicy, with a nasty, bitter edge to the modest pear flavors. • $9 • (12/31/94) • **73**

Chardonnay Washington 1992: Crisp, austere and lean, with more floral and mineral flavors than fruit. Finishes hard and acidic. Drinkable now. • $12 • (06/15/93) • **76**

Chardonnay Washington All Around Cowboy Limited Edition 1993: Excessively earthy at first, but the bright, spicy apple and lemon flavors linger nicely. Ready now. • $14 • (04/30/95) • **84**

Chardonnay Washington Barrel Fermented 1992: Tastes tired and a little oxidized, spicy rather than showing much fruit. Drinkable. 600 cases made. • $12 • (12/31/94) • **75**

Fumé Blanc Washington Bareback Riding Limited Edition 1993: Light and herbal, more floral than other flavors. • $9 • (09/30/95) • **77**

Gamay Beaujolais Rosé Blush Washington 1994: Light and effusively fruity, sporting lively raspberry and watermelon flavors and finishing slightly sweet. 1,900 cases made. • $5 • (09/30/95) • **82**

Gewürztraminer Washington 1993: Fresh, floral and brightly fruity, an off-dry, lightly textured white offering beguiling litchi and vanilla flavors. 400 cases made. • $5 • (09/30/95) • **85**

Merlot Washington Bareback Riding Limited Edition 1992: Very ripe, almost raisiny, offering dried cherry and Port-like berry flavors that slide smoothly into the finish. Ready now. • $18 • (06/15/95) • **84**

Merlot Washington Oak Aged 1993: Rich and full-bodied, a strong herbal, earthy streak cutting through the chunky black cherry flavors. May be best in 1998. 1,500 cases made. • $10 • (09/30/95) • **83**

Merlot Washington Oak Aged 1988 • $7 • (08/31/91) • **77**

Merlot Washington Reserve 1990 • $26 • (09/30/93) • **80**

Riesling Washington Ice Wine 1986: Almost worn out. Soft, a bit threadbare, with hints of apple cider and spice on the palate, it fades out gently on the finish. Drink up. 66 cases made. • $32 • **79**

Riesling Washington Ice Wine 1978: Lean, earthy and bitter. It's barely sweet, and lacks fruit. Doesn't show its age, but hasn't improved either. • $42 • **72**

White Riesling Late Harvest Washington Ice Wine 1986 • $38 • (10/15/89) • **80**

PRIDE | CALIFORNIA

Cabernet Franc Napa Valley 1992: Dense, chewy and firmly tannic, with an intriguing tobacco accent to the currant and leathery flavors. Best after 1997. 94 cases made. • $18 • (12/31/94) • **83**

Cabernet Franc Sonoma County 1993: Despite firm tannins, there's a nice core of rich cherry, currant, anise and mineral and the finish adds extra dimension. Some touches of smoky oak, cellar into 1997 or '98 450 cases made. • $20 • (04/30/96) • **88**

Cabernet Sauvignon Napa Valley 1992: A touch earthy, with mineral, leather, currant and mineral flavors. Not quite the richness and depth of the 1991, but it's pleasant enough and well balanced. 1,000 cases made. • $18 • (12/15/95) • **87**

Cabernet Sauvignon Napa Valley 1991: Ripe, smooth and polished, with plush cherry, currant and toasty oak flavors, but picks up richness, depth and concentration on the finish, not to mention firm but supple tannins and a long, complex aftertaste. Tempting now, but it should begin to peak around 1998 or 2000. 475 cases made. • $18 • (05/15/94) • **92**

Chardonnay Napa Valley 1994: Strikes a nice balance between its ripe pear and spicy oak flavors. Finesse and grace characterize this Chardonnay. 700 cases made. • $18 • (05/15/96) • **87**

Chardonnay Napa Valley 1993: Ripe with spicy, creamy pear and apple-laced fruit, turning elegant and delicate on the finish. 1,100 cases made. • $18 • (07/31/95) • **87**

Chardonnay Napa Valley 1992: Tight and firm, a sleek young wine with a narrow beam of apricot, pear and vanilla flavors that turn to hazelnut and honey on the finish. Tasty now. 780 cases made. • $18 • (02/28/94) • **88**

Chardonnay Napa Valley 1991 • $18 • (04/30/94) • **85**

Merlot Napa Valley 1993: Smooth, supple, ripe, polished cherry, currant and anise flavors turn elegant and complex on the finish, where tannins are fine and well integrated. Drinkable now or cellar into 1997. 3,300 cases made. • $20 • (12/15/95) • **89**

Merlot Napa Valley 1992: A bit green and herbal now, showing black cherry and cedar on the pleasing finish. Best to cellar a short time, drink after 1997. 2,400 cases made. • $18 • (01/31/95) • **85**

Merlot Napa Valley 1991 • $18 • (03/15/94) • **89**

Viognier Napa Valley 1994: Impressive for its ripe, spicy, exotic fruit flavors, tiers of honeysuckle, pear and citrus notes, and for its richness and complexity. 35 cases made. • $24 • (05/31/96) • **89**

PRINCE MICHEL | VIRGINIA

Cabernet Sauvignon American De Rapidan Cask 92 NV: Smooth and a little earthy, supple, featuring modest flavors, nicely balanced to drink soon. 2,000 cases made. • $12 • (01/31/95) • **83**
Cabernet-Merlot Virginia Reserve 1990: Deeply colored and supple, in the Bordeaux style. Black cherry and berry flavors are accented by stylish, oaky tones of nutmeg, chocolate and cedar. Has lots of soft tannins and a lingering finish. Drinkable now. • $15 • (01/31/93) • **87**
Chardonnay Virginia 1991 • $10 • (03/15/93) • **85**
Chardonnay Virginia Barrel Select 1991 • $15 • (03/15/93) • **88**
Chardonnay Virginia De Virginia 1992: Shows a definite earthy edge to the simple grapey flavors, but it cleans up on the finish. 6,500 cases made. • $11 • (09/15/94) • **82**
De Virginia Reserve Cabernet Blend Virginia 1991: Herbal, gamy flavors pervade this highly unusual, otherwise smooth-textured wine, not for most tastes. 900 cases made. • $16 • (01/31/95) • **76**
Le Ducq Lot 87 Cabernet Blend NV • $50 • (02/29/92) • **79**
Le Ducq Lot 88 Cabernet Blend American NV: Smooth, supple and decidedly gamy, a nicely balanced red that outlines a range of earthy flavors. Approachable now. 450 cases made. • $65 • (01/31/95) • **84**

PURPLE MOUNTAIN | CALIFORNIA

Chardonnay Monterey Barrel Fermented 1991 • $10 • (03/31/93) • **80**

QUADY | CALIFORNIA

Black Muscat California Elysium 1993: Smooth and lightly sweet, displaying plum and litchi notes that dance delicately. Appealing for its unique fruit flavors. 3,130 cases made. • $13 • (05/15/95) • **87**
Black Muscat California Elysium 1992 • $12 • (11/15/93) • **82**
Black Muscat California Elysium 1990 • $12 • (11/30/91) • **86**
Black Muscat California Elysium 1989 • $12 • (10/15/90) • **85**
Black Muscat California Elysium 1988 • $11 • (08/31/89) • **90**
Black Muscat California Elysium 1987 • $11 • (09/30/88) • **82**
Black Muscat California Elysium 1985 • $11 • (09/15/86) • **85**
Black Muscat California Elysium 1984 • $11 • (08/01/85) • **87**
Orange Muscat California Electra 1993: Light and sweet, exhibiting orange and peach flavors that glide smoothly across the palate. Drink soon while it's fresh. 1,156 cases made. • $9 • (04/30/95) • **83**
Orange Muscat California Electra 1992 • $9 • (06/30/93) BB • **86**
Orange Muscat California Electra 1991 • $9 • (06/15/92) • **84**
Orange Muscat California Essensia 1993: Appealingly sweet, adding a definite citrusy edge to the honey and pear flavors. Drinkable now. 9,407 cases made. • $13 • (05/15/95) • **84**
Orange Muscat California Essensia 1990 • $12 • (11/30/91) • **83**
Orange Muscat California Essensia 1989 • $12 • (10/15/90) • **89**
Orange Muscat California Essensia 1987 • $11 • (08/31/89) • **78**
Orange Muscat California Essensia 1985 • $11 • (09/30/86) • **79**
Orange Muscat California Essensia 1984 • $11 • (07/01/85) • **88**
Port Amador County 1984 • $9 • (10/01/85) • **82**
Port Amador County Frank's Vineyard 1986 • $12 • (10/15/90) • **75**
Port Amador County Frank's Vineyard 1985 • $16 • (08/31/89) • **65**
Port Amador County Starboard Frank's Vineyard 1989 • $20 • (12/15/92) • **87**
Port California 1985 • $9 • (08/31/89) • **73**
Port California LBV 1991: Light in color, lightly plummy and spicy in flavor, a smooth wine that is ready to drink already. 851 cases made. • $9 • (05/31/95) • **81**
Starboard Amador County 1987 • $25 • (03/31/91) • **81**
Starboard Batch 88 California NV • $16 • (04/15/93) • **85**

Key: SS—Spectator Selection. CS—Cellar Selection. BB—Best Buy. $NA—Price not available. (BT)—Barrel tasting. (A)—Auction Price.
Dates in parentheses represent the issues in which the ratings were published.

Starboard Batch 88 Rich Ruby Amador County 1988 • $15 • (11/30/91) • **87**

QUAFF | CALIFORNIA

White Riesling Monterey County 1993: Light and lively, just off-dry, sporting orange, apple and vanilla flavors. Ready now. 2,000 cases made. • $7 • (10/15/95) • **85**

QUAIL RIDGE | CALIFORNIA

Cabernet Sauvignon Napa Valley 1990: Medium-bodied and modestly fruity with hints of anise and currant. Can stand short-term cellaring to soften, but it lacks the depth and richness for greatness. Best after 1996. • $13 • (11/15/94) • **85**
Cabernet Sauvignon Napa Valley 1989 • $16 • (06/15/93) • **82**
Cabernet Sauvignon Napa Valley 1988 • $16 • (08/31/92) • **80**
Cabernet Sauvignon Napa Valley 1987 • $16 • (09/30/91) • **93**
Cabernet Sauvignon Napa Valley 1986 • $15 • (11/15/90) • **89**
Cabernet Sauvignon Napa Valley 1985 • $15 • (07/31/89) • **82**
Cabernet Sauvignon Napa Valley 1984 • $15 • (03/31/89) • **88**
Cabernet Sauvignon Napa Valley 1982 • $13 • (09/16/85) • **86**
Cabernet Sauvignon Napa Valley Reserve 1987 • $25 • (11/15/92) • **87**
Cabernet Sauvignon Napa Valley V. & L. Eisele Vineyard Reserve 1989: A touch earthy and leathery, with a narrow band of mature currant and anise flavors. Lacks depth and richness. 500 cases made. • $30 • (12/15/95) • **82**
Merlot Napa Valley 1991: Crisp and intense, offering cherry and berry flavor, firmly tannic finish and an earthy edge. Can stand short-term cellaring into 1997 to soften. 7,200 cases made. • $14 • (12/15/95) • **82**
Merlot Napa Valley 1990: Menthol and tobacco overtones make this distinctive, but it finishes with an austere bite. Drinkable now. • $15 • (09/15/94) • **82**
Merlot Napa Valley 1989 • $15 • (07/15/93) • **79**
Merlot Napa Valley 1988 • $15 • (05/31/92) • **84**
Merlot Napa Valley 1987 • $15 • (06/15/90) • **86**
Merlot Napa Valley 1985 • $14 • (03/31/89) • **90**
Sauvignon Blanc Napa Valley 1993: Perfumy, floral flavors never resolve into anything attractive or smooth, making this a funky white without much charm. 3,009 cases made. • $11 • (05/15/96) BB • **75**
Sauvignon Blanc Napa Valley 1992: Soft, floral and fruity, a generous wine with a profile that includes pear, honey and oak. • $10 • (08/31/94) • **85**
Sauvignon Blanc Napa Valley 1991 • $8 • (04/15/93) • **88**

QUARRY LAKE | WASHINGTON

Cabernet Sauvignon Washington 1986 • $10 • (10/15/89) • **78**
Merlot Washington 1986 • $10 • (10/15/89) • **81**

QUILCEDA CREEK | WASHINGTON

Cabernet Sauvignon Washington 1990: Tight and firm, with a cedary aroma and ripe currant, toast and berry flavors on the palate. Elegant and well balanced, drinking well now but with depth and intensity to carry it through the decade. Best from now to 2000. 925 cases made. • $24 • (05/15/94) • **89**
Cabernet Sauvignon Washington 1989 • $24 • (10/15/93) • **87**
Cabernet Sauvignon Washington 1988 • $22 • (02/28/93) • **89**
Cabernet Sauvignon Washington 1985 • $17 • (10/15/89) • **74**
Cabernet Sauvignon Washington Reserve 1992: A titanic wine, packed with flavor and built to age gracefully. Firm and chewy at first, it bristles with blackberry, black cherry and coffee flavors that build up momentum through the solid finish. Tannins are firm but integrated. Best to age until 2000 or 2003. 150 cases made. • $49 • (09/30/95) • **95**

QUIVIRA | CALIFORNIA

Cabernet Cuvée Dry Creek Valley 1991: Lean and earthy, a narrow band of cherry and cedar, but needing some more flesh and flavor. • $15 • (07/31/95) • **82**

Cabernet Cuvée Dry Creek Valley 1990: Supple and spicy, with an herb and bell pepper streak that runs through the currant and berry flavors. Modest tannins make this approachable now, but it can age through 1999. 4,000 cases made. • $15 • (11/15/94) • **85**

Cabernet Cuvée Dry Creek Valley 1989 • $15 • (11/15/92) • **84**

Cabernet Sauvignon Dry Creek Valley 1988 • $18 • (11/15/91) • **84**

Cabernet Sauvignon Dry Creek Valley 1987 • $15 • (11/15/90) • **87**

Dry Creek Cuvée Dry Creek Valley Red 1994: Simple and drinkable, with nicely spicy plum and berry notes. 1,000 cases made. • $13 • **82**

Dry Creek Cuvée Dry Creek Valley Red 1993: A ripe and fruity style, with ripe grape and cherry flavors. Can be served chilled. A blend of Grenache, Mourvèdre, Syrah and Zinfandel. • $12 • (06/30/95) • **84**

Dry Creek Cuvée Dry Creek Valley Red 1992: Firm in texture, with a nice fruit profile that includes plum and berry flavors along with toast and earth notes that add interest. Finishes a little short. • $12 • (09/30/94) • **83**

Sauvignon Blanc Dry Creek Valley 1994: Bright, crisp and lively with pear, spice and a hint of celery. Ready now. 5,500 cases made. • $10 • (06/15/96) • **86**

Sauvignon Blanc Dry Creek Valley 1993: Light and fragrant, more floral than herbal, offering citrusy flavors on the finish. 5,000 cases made. • $10 • (08/31/95) • **85**

Sauvignon Blanc Dry Creek Valley 1992 • $9 • (04/30/94) • **89**

Sauvignon Blanc Dry Creek Valley 1991 • $9 • (02/15/93) • **76**

Sauvignon Blanc Dry Creek Valley Reserve 1993: A bit of resiny flavor adds some interest to the light and snappy, bright pear notes. 1,500 cases made. • $14 • (08/31/95) • **84**

Sauvignon Blanc Dry Creek Valley Reserve 1992: Bright and buttery, medium-weight, smooth in texture, with a touch of fig to balance the basic butterscotch flavors. Drinkable now. • $14 • (09/30/94) • **84**

Zinfandel Dry Creek Valley 1994: Pleasing for its ripe, pure cherry, currant and berry flavors. A medium-weight style that finishes in light oak and hints of herb and cedar. 4,906 cases made. • $15 • (04/30/96) • **88**

Zinfandel Dry Creek Valley 1993: Supple and well balanced, adding a pleasant, earthy edge to the cherry and wild berry flavors. Finishes with mild tannins and a tarry aftertaste. Drinkable now. 4,000 cases made. • $14 • (04/30/96) • **87**

Zinfandel Dry Creek Valley 1992: Smooth, rich and complex, with a ripe, concentrated core of wild berry, raspberry and spice notes that are well focused. Finishes long and full with toasty oak. Impressive and drinks well now, but should improve through 1998. 4,200 cases made. • $14 • (09/30/94) • **89**

Zinfandel Dry Creek Valley 1991 • $13 • (09/30/93) • **88**

Zinfandel Dry Creek Valley 1990 • $13 • (10/15/92) • **90**

Zinfandel Dry Creek Valley 1989 • $13 • (07/31/91) • **84**

Zinfandel Dry Creek Valley 1988 • $12 • (05/31/90) • **88**

Zinfandel Dry Creek Valley 1987 • $11 • (07/31/89) • **88**

Zinfandel Dry Creek Valley 1986 • $9 • (12/15/88) • **88**

Zinfandel Dry Creek Valley 1984 • $7 • (04/15/87) • **88**

Zinfandel Dry Creek Valley 1983 • $7 • (01/01/86) • **75**

QUPE | CALIFORNIA

Bien Nacido Cuvée White Santa Barbara County 1994: Attractive for its pure flavors of juicy pear, peach and honey, ending in a spicy aftertaste that shows off the Viognier half of this blend, with Chardonnay making up the rest. 768 cases made. • $15 • (01/31/96) • **88**

Chardonnay Santa Barbara County Sierra Madre Reserve 1994: Shows off a hint of honeyed botrytis on the nose and palate, but the apple and pear notes fold in nicely on the finish and it's well balanced. 680 cases made. • $25 • (05/31/96) • **88**

Chardonnay Santa Barbara County Sierra Madre Reserve 1993: Marked by a slight botrytis edge, with honey and fig notes that straightens out on the finish, where the flavors linger. • $25 • (07/31/95) • **88**

Chardonnay Santa Barbara County Sierra Madre Vineyards 1993: Bold, ripe and creamy, with a pretty array of complex pear, honey, toast and spicy flavors that are concentrated and long on the finish. Beautifully crafted. 2,300 cases made. • $11 • (04/30/95) SS • **90**

Los Olivos Cuvée Santa Barbara County 1993: Firm and trim, with an intense, compact band of plum and cherry flavors that pick up earthy, leathery tones. Finishes with firm tannins. 442 cases made. • $15 • (08/31/95) • **88**

Los Olivos Cuvée Santa Barbara County 1989 • $15 • (08/31/91) • **85**

Marsanne Santa Barbara County Los Olivos Vineyard 1994: Broad, soft and gentle, not distinctive, a solid but uneventful white. 1,500 cases made. • $12 • (11/30/95) • **81**

Syrah Central Coast 1993: Distinct for its pepper and green olive notes, but balanced by ripe cherry and plum. Turns complex and spicy on the finish. 4,000 cases made. • $11 • (08/31/95) • **88**

Syrah Central Coast 1988 • $11 • (12/15/89) • **90**

Syrah Central Coast 1987 • $9 • (04/15/89) • **88**

Syrah Central Coast 1986 • $9 • (04/15/89) • **79**

Syrah Central Coast 1985 • $5 • (04/15/88) • **78**

Syrah Santa Barbara County Bien Nacido Reserve 1993: A well-focused California version of the Rhône variety that's ripe and plummy, with spicy, peppery notes. Shows fine depth and concentration, while maintaining a sense of elegance and finesse. The finish goes on and on. Delicious now through 2001. 850 cases made. • $17 • (08/31/95) SS • **91**

Syrah Santa Barbara County Bien Nacido Vineyard 1989 • $20 • (08/31/91) • **89**

Syrah Santa Barbara County Bien Nacido Vineyard 1987 • $20 • (02/28/90) • **81**

Syrah Santa Barbara County Los Olivos Reserve 1993: Complex, toasty oak and ripe currant notes pick up a spicy aniselike edge on the finish. Has a sense of elegance and finesse, and carries through a lingering aftertaste. 95 cases made. • $20 • (08/31/95) • **88**

Viognier Santa Barbara County Los Olivos Vineyard 1994: Smooth, round and generous, a mouthful of floral fruit basket flavor that persists into an exuberant, tasty finish. Ready now. 200 cases made. • $22 • (09/30/95) • **89**

RABBIT RIDGE | CALIFORNIA

Allure California Red 1991: A touch herbaceous, but it serves up enough pleasant fruit flavors to keep it in balance. 3,000 cases made. • $7 • (06/30/95) • **82**

Allure California Red 1990 • $8 • (10/15/93) • **83**

Allure California Red 1989 • $7 • (05/31/93) • **81**

Cabernet Sauvignon Sonoma County 1989: Heavy-handed, oaky and tannic with little to offer. Marginal. 800 cases made. • $12 • (11/15/94) • **77**

Cabernet Sauvignon Sonoma County 1988 • $12 • (08/31/91) • **89**

Cabernet Sauvignon Sonoma County Rabbit Ridge Ranch Estate Reserve 1990: Firm, compact and tannic, opening up with currant, anise and spicy wood flavors before turning dry and finishing chewy. Drinkable now. 504 cases made. • $20 • (11/15/94) • **86**

Chardonnay Russian River Valley Rabbit Ridge Ranch 1991 • $16 • (04/30/93) • **89**

Chardonnay Russian River Valley Rabbit Ridge Ranch Estate Reserve 1994: Pleasant enough, as its ripe, spicy pear and melon notes persist to the finish, where toasty oak folds in nicely. 1,400 cases made. • $16 • (05/15/96) • **87**

Chardonnay Russian River Valley Rabbit Ridge Ranch Estate Reserve 1993: Intensely spicy with lichee nut, pear and honeyed notes, a bold and full bodied Chardonnay with good depth. 850 cases made. • $16 • (07/31/95) • **88**

Chardonnay Sonoma County 1992: Tastes sweet beyond ripeness, with a slightly sour pineapple edge. The alcohol stands out too, overriding the apple and pear notes. 1,500 cases made. • $12 • (06/30/94) • **82**

Chardonnay Sonoma County 1991 • $12 • (10/15/93) • **84**

Merlot Carneros Sangiacomo Vineyard 1992: Smooth and polished, spice-scented berry and black cherry flavors folding neatly between the delicate sparks of toasty oak. Nicely balanced all the way around. Drink now. 840 cases made. • $15 • (06/15/95) • **86**

Mystique North Coast 1993: Light and bright, simple and straightforward, showing off its fresh, buttery pear flavor. Drinkable now. 2,500 cases made. • $7 • (06/30/95) • **85**

Mystique Sonoma County 1992: Smooth and creamy, a mouthfilling wine that spills its vanilla- and spice-scented citrusy pear flavors gently through the long and appealing finish. Sauvignon Blanc, Sémillon, and Gewürztraminer. Ready. 3,000 cases made. • $7 • (12/15/94) BB • **88**

Mystique Sonoma County 1991 • $7 • (04/15/93) BB • **83**

Oddux Reserve Red California 1990 • $15 • (03/31/93) • **78**

Petite Sirah Sonoma County 1990 • $10 • (03/31/93) • **80**

Sangiovese Dry Creek Valley Coniglio Selezione 1992: Supple and polished, with cedary tones and ripe cherry and berry flavors. 750 cases made. • $12 • (08/31/95) • **84**

Sangiovese Sonoma County Coniglio Selezione 1993: Smooth, velvety, focusing ripe black cherry and plum flavors in a generous mouthful that echoes fruit and spice on the finish. Appealing now. 600 cases made. • $13 • (11/30/95) • **85**

Zinfandel Dry Creek Valley 1993: Mild-mannered, presenting spicy berry and cherry flavors of modest proportions. 2,500 cases made. • $11 • (06/15/95) • **85**

Zinfandel Dry Creek Valley 1992: An oaky style, with gritty tannins and coarse core of tarry fruit flavors. Lacks finesse. 2,600 cases made. • $11 • (10/15/94) • **80**

Zinfandel Dry Creek Valley 1991 • $10 • (05/31/93) • **87**

Zinfandel Dry Creek Valley 1990 • $9 • (10/15/92) • **73**

Zinfandel Dry Creek Valley Olsen Vineyard 1994: Remarkably complex, featuring pretty spice, oak and berry aromas and flavors to match and adding tiers of wild berry, cherry, currant and spice. Finishes with a long, full aftertaste. Given all its richness and flavor, it's still an elegant and refined style. 420 cases made. • $16 • (04/30/96) • **92**

Zinfandel Russian River Valley Rabbit Ridge Ranch 1988 • $8 • (04/30/91) • **86**

Zinfandel Sonoma County 1994: Ripe and spicy, with pretty plum, cherry and berry jam notes of modest proportion. Drinks well now. 3,000 cases made. • $10 • (03/31/96) • **84**

Zinfandel Sonoma County 1989 • $9 • (08/31/91) • **86**

Zinfandel Sonoma County San Lorenzo Vineyard Reserve 1993: Dark, rich and complex, with splendidly ripe plum, black cherry and raspberry flavors that expand to reveal greater depth and concentration. Has a satisfying, full aftertaste. 622 cases made. • $18 • (09/15/95) • **93**

Zinfandel Sonoma County San Lorenzo Vineyard Reserve 1991 • $14 • (09/30/93) • **90**

RADANOVICH | CALIFORNIA

Cabernet Sauvignon Sierra Foothills Mariposa County 1989 • $18 • (12/15/92) • **77**

Merlot Sierra Foothills Mariposa County 1991: Simple, fruity and a little earthy, a medium-weight red with modest but appealing flavors and moderate tannins. 125 cases made. • $15 • (09/15/94) • **82**

Sauvignon Blanc Sierra Foothills 1994: Simple, tart and minty, with a citrusy finish. 550 cases made. • $8 • (05/31/96) • **80**

Zinfandel Sierra Foothills 1993: Pleasant enough, offering a tarry plum edge and mild tannins. Drinkable now. 1,800 cases made. • $9 • (04/30/96) • **80**

Zinfandel Sierra Foothills Mariposa County 1989 • $11 • (12/15/92) • **72**

RAFANELLI, A. | CALIFORNIA

Cabernet Sauvignon Dry Creek Valley 1988 • $13 • (08/31/91) • **90**

Cabernet Sauvignon Dry Creek Valley 1987 • $12 • (08/31/90) • **91**

Cabernet Sauvignon Dry Creek Valley 1986 • $9 • (09/30/89) • **91**

Cabernet Sauvignon Dry Creek Valley 1985 • $8 • (09/15/88) • **78**

Cabernet Sauvignon Dry Creek Valley Unfiltered 1992: Beautifully focused, ripe, rich and complex, with layers of currant, black cherry and cedar flavors, all well proportioned. A long, complex aftertaste plays a lingering melody. Firmly tannic, and a good bet to age into 1998. 2,700 cases made. • $17 • (09/30/95) SS • **92**

Cabernet Sauvignon Dry Creek Valley Unfiltered 1991: Firm and intense, with ripe, juicy Cabernet fruit that echoes currant, black cherry and spicy oak flavors. It comes across as a bit rustic and chunky, but this doesn't shortchange you on rich, deep flavors. Drink now. 2,300 cases made. • $15 • (09/15/94) SS • **90**

Cabernet Sauvignon Dry Creek Valley Unfiltered 1990: Intense, spicy and elegant, a lavish wine that stays reined in, showing plenty of appealing berry, currant and nutmeg aromas and flavors, and hinting at vanilla bean and coffee on the finish. Drinkable now. 2,300 cases made. • $15 • (09/15/93) • **90**

Cabernet Sauvignon Dry Creek Valley Unfiltered 1989 • $14 • (09/30/92) • **84**

Zinfandel Dry Creek Valley 1993: Smooth, elegant, supple core of cherry and wild berry flavor is followed by a clean, fruity aftertaste. Ready now. 5,300 cases made. • $14 • (12/31/95) • **88**

Zinfandel Dry Creek Valley 1989 • $11 • (09/30/91) • **85**

Zinfandel Dry Creek Valley 1988 • $9 • (09/15/90) • **90**

Zinfandel Dry Creek Valley 1987 • $9 • (12/15/89) • **84**

Zinfandel Dry Creek Valley 1986 • $7 • (09/15/88) • **91**

Zinfandel Dry Creek Valley 1985 • $6 • (12/31/87) • **77**

Zinfandel Dry Creek Valley 1983 • $6 • (03/01/86) BB • **91**

Zinfandel Dry Creek Valley Unfiltered 1992: Starts out with rich fruit and pretty, toasty oak, then shows complex, concentrated blackberry and cherry flavors that linger on the finish. This is intense and tannic, needing some time in the cellar. Try this after 1995. 5,700 cases made. 5,700 cases made. • $13 • (10/15/94) SS • **88**

Zinfandel Dry Creek Valley Unfiltered 1991 • $13 • (12/15/93) SS • **89**

Zinfandel Dry Creek Valley Unfiltered 1990 • $12 • (09/30/92) • **88**

RAMSAY | CALIFORNIA

Merlot Napa Valley 1992: Has high points, with bright plum, wild berry and cherry notes, but turns lean and austere on the finish, suggesting that cellaring should give it softer edges. 1,100 cases made. • $14 • (09/15/94) • **87**

Merlot Napa Valley 1991 • $13 • (06/15/93) • **88**

Merlot Napa Valley 1989 • $12 • (04/15/92) • **86**

Pinot Noir Carneros 1993: Pleasantly ripe and fruity, with black cherry, plum and jam notes in a well focused, elegant style. Appealing now. 1,500 cases made. • $12 • **86**

Pinot Noir Carneros 1992: Firm and tightly tannic, the fruit is compact, accompanied by hints of dried cherry and tobacco, but it could be more generous. 700 cases made. • $12 • (03/31/95) • **82**

Pinot Noir Carneros 1991 • $12 • (02/28/94) • **81**

Sangiovese California 1993: Light, austere and tannic, not showing much fruit. Decent but lacks varietal character, and its disappointingly shallow. 1,793 cases made. • $14 • (02/29/96) • **74**

Sangiovese California 1992: Lean and a little leathery, earthy, berry flavors shoot through the finish. Drink now. • $14 • (02/28/95) • **82**

Trebbiano California 1993: Oxidized, and it smells and tastes like vinegar, with honey on the finish. 582 cases made. • $8 • (12/15/95) • **76**

RAMSPECK | CALIFORNIA

Pinot Noir Napa Valley 1994: Young and intense, with a ripe, rich, complex core of cherry, wild berry and toasty oak flavors. Has a long, fruity aftertaste and supple tannins. 770 cases made. • $16 • (01/31/96) • **88**

RANCHO SISQUOC | CALIFORNIA

Cabernet Sauvignon Santa Maria Valley 1992: A touch earthy with a vegetal streak, there's just enough cherry and berry fruit to keep it in balance. 450 cases made. • $15 • (12/15/95) • **82**

Cabernet Sauvignon Santa Maria Valley 1991: An herbaceous style that's moderately rich and spicy, picking up cherry and plum flavors on the finish where a little bell pepper sneaks through. 800 cases made. • $15 • (11/15/94) • **84**

Cabernet Sauvignon Santa Maria Valley 1990: Light and simple, with a sour edge to the modest plum and currant flavors, and a green edge on the finish that does not bode well. May be better after 1996. 800 cases made. • $14 • (11/15/93) • **76**

Cabernet Sauvignon Santa Maria Valley 1989 • $14 • (11/15/92) • **85**

Cabernet Sauvignon Santa Maria Valley 1986 • $10 • (12/15/89) • **73**

Cabernet Sauvignon Santa Maria Valley 1974: Pungently vegetal and concentrated, void of classic Cabernet flavors, yet with its own personality. Stylistic, past its peak but holding. • $NA • (11/15/94) • **74**

Cellar Select Red Santa Maria Valley 1990: Ripe and fleshy with bright, complex, concentrated cherry, currant and spice flavors that show a delicate balance. Flavors stay with you on a long, lively finish. Ready now

Key: SS—Spectator Selection. CS—Cellar Selection. BB—Best Buy. $NA—Price not available. (BT)—Barrel tasting. Ⓐ—Auction Price.
Dates in parentheses represent the issues in which the ratings were published.

through 1997. 50 percent Cabernet Franc, 25 percent Cabernet Sauvignon and 25 percent Merlot. 150 cases made. • $25 • (11/15/93) • **88**

Cellar Select Red Wine Santa Maria Valley 1989 • $25 • (11/15/92) • **87**

Chardonnay Santa Maria Valley 1993: Medium bodied, with crisp, earthy pear and citrus flavors of modest proportions. 1,200 cases made. • $15 • (07/31/95) • **82**

Chardonnay Santa Maria Valley 1991 • $14 • (07/15/93) • **88**

Johannisberg Riesling Late Harvest Santa Maria Valley Special Select 1986 • $18 • (12/15/89) • **68**

Merlot Santa Maria Valley 1991: Lean and slightly astringent, but it has modest flavors of chocolate and berry that echo lightly on the finish. 900 cases made. • $13 • (09/15/94) • **80**

Merlot Santa Maria Valley 1989 • $12 • (05/31/92) • **81**

Merlot Santa Maria Valley 1986 • $9 • (12/15/89) • **77**

Sauvignon Blanc Santa Maria Valley 1994: Some nice orange, cream and earthy flavors that fade a bit on the finish. 1,800 cases made. • $12 • **79**

Sauvignon Blanc Santa Maria Valley 1993: Definitely wrapped in a layer of sweet oak. Ripe and spicy, balanced and fruity enough to stay lively through the finish. 1,200 cases made. • $10 • (08/31/95) • **87**

Sauvignon Blanc Santa Maria Valley 1992: Ripe and broad, with flavors that lean more toward pineapple and grapefruit than herbs, finishing a little chunky. 600 cases made. • $9 • (08/31/94) • **81**

RANDOM RIDGE | CALIFORNIA

Sangiovese Mount Veeder 1993: Lean and herbal, showing a trim band of black cherry and berry flavor that has slight green, earthy notes. Offers only moderate richness and depth. • $27 • (02/29/96) • **83**

Zinfandel Sonoma Valley Old Wave 1993: Starts out with a flash of cherry and berry, but loses some of that intensity to gain elegance. Spicy finish, with firm tannins. • $14 • (10/15/95) • **85**

RAPIDAN RIVER | VIRGINIA

Chardonnay Virginia 1991 • $9 • (03/15/93) • **73**

Merlot Virginia 1991 • $9 • (01/31/93) • **86**

Riesling Virginia Dry 1992: A light white with pretty floral, peach and apple flavors singing brightly over the crisp structure. 2,200 cases made. • $9 • (09/15/94) • **85**

White Riesling Virginia Semi-dry 1992: Off-dry and flavorful, a light Riesling, peppery and floral, with a distinctive range of fruit notes. 3,200 cases made. • $9 • (09/15/94) • **83**

RASMUSSEN, KENT | CALIFORNIA

Cabernet Sauvignon Napa Valley 1988 • $20 • (11/15/91) • **83**

Chardonnay Napa Valley 1994: Serves up a nice core of ripe pear and apple, but the flavors lack the extra dimensions and finesse you might hope for at this price. 1,100 cases made. • $21 • (02/29/96) • **86**

Chardonnay Napa Valley 1992: Firm and supple, with spicy pear, toasty oak and light, earthy flavors, finishing with a burst of fruit. Drinks well now. 692 cases made. • $19 • (12/31/94) • **88**

Chardonnay Napa Valley 1991 • $18 • (07/15/93) • **90**

Dolcetto Napa Valley 1990 • $20 • (03/15/92) • **85**

Pinot Noir Carneros 1993: Serves up a pretty array of ripe plum and strawberry jam flavors, with a smooth, polished texture and fine length. Offers a measure of elegance and grace. Drinks well now. 1,200 cases made. • $20 • **87**

Pinot Noir Carneros 1992: Tight and firm, softening a bit in texture, with herb, cherry and cedar notes. Drink now. 880 cases made. • $19 • (01/31/95) • **87**

Pinot Noir Carneros 1991 • $18 • (02/28/94) • **88**

Pinot Noir Carneros 1990 • $19 • (02/28/93) • **86**

Pinot Noir Carneros 1988 • $22 • (10/31/90) • **84**

RATTLESNAKE RIDGE | WASHINGTON

Lemberger Yakima Valley 1992: Simple, with a slightly bitter edge to the modest plum and smoke flavors. 1,000 cases made. • $6 • (09/30/94) • **74**

RAVENSWOOD | CALIFORNIA

Cabernet Sauvignon California 1979 • $8 • (03/01/89) • **59**

Cabernet Sauvignon California 1978 • $20 • (03/01/89) • **81**

Cabernet Sauvignon El Dorado County Madrona Vineyards 1977 • $8 • (03/01/89) • **82**

Cabernet Sauvignon Sonoma County 1993: Dry and austere with a touch of wild berry and spice. Hangs together with chunky fruit flavors, but the tannins tend to dominate. Needs to age into 1998, but the tannins may still prevail. 3,600 cases made. • $15 • (12/15/95) • **87**

Cabernet Sauvignon Sonoma County 1992: Heavy-handed up front with smoky, toasty oak that gives this high-extract Cabernet a slightly bitter edge. Still, there's enough currant and plum to hold your interest. Best after 1997. 3,136 cases made. • $15 • (11/15/94) • **86**

Cabernet Sauvignon Sonoma County 1991: Tight and chewy, with a narrow, compact band of currant and tarry Cabernet flavor. Will require several years of cellaring and even then it may be on the tannic side. Try in 1998. • $14 • (11/15/94) • **84**

Cabernet Sauvignon Sonoma County 1989 • $14 • (11/15/92) • **84**

Cabernet Sauvignon Sonoma County 1986 • $12 • (03/01/89) • **86**

Cabernet Sauvignon Sonoma County 1985 • $20 • (03/01/89) • **85**

Cabernet Sauvignon Sonoma County 1984 • $25 • (03/01/89) • **80**

Cabernet Sauvignon Sonoma County 1983 • $19 • (03/01/89) • **76**

Cabernet Sauvignon Sonoma County 1982 • $25 • (03/01/89) • **84**

Cabernet Sauvignon Sonoma County 1980 • $20 • (03/01/89) • **79**

Cabernet Sauvignon Sonoma Valley 1988 • $14 • (03/15/91) • **89**

Cabernet Sauvignon Sonoma Valley 1987 • $11 • (05/31/90) • **84**

Cabernet Sauvignon Sonoma Valley Gregory 1993: Marked by minty notes and hints of sage and herb, but enough currant and cherry come through. Supple and harmonious on the finish, even with substantial tannins. Try in 1998. 960 cases made. • $20 • (12/15/95) • **89**

Cabernet Sauvignon Sonoma Valley Gregory Vineyard 1990: Definitely herbal, with strong mint, sage and tarragon aromas and flavors. Finishes soft and minty more than fruity. Does show a core of fruit, however, and should be fine now. 500 cases made. • $18 • (04/30/93) • **84**

Cabernet Sauvignon Sonoma Valley Gregory Vineyard 1989 • $18 • (11/15/92) • **85**

Cabernet Sauvignon Sonoma Valley Gregory Vineyard 1988 • $18 • (11/15/91) • **80**

Cabernet Sauvignon Sonoma Valley Olive Hill 1978 • $31 • (11/15/92) • **80**

Chardonnay North Coast Vintners Blend 1993: Tart and flinty, with a greed edge to the pear and apple flavors. 2,737 cases made. • $9 • (07/31/95) • **84**

Chardonnay Sonoma Valley Estate 1991 • $11 • (04/30/93) • **71**

Merlot Carneros Sangiacomo 1990 • $20 • (12/15/92) • **88**

Merlot Carneros Sangiacomo 1989 • $20 • (11/15/91) • **90**

Merlot North Coast Vintners Blend 1992: Well proportioned, with supple, earthy berry and cherry flavors that pick up a spicy edge. Can stand short-term cellaring. • $10 • (09/15/94) • **84**

Merlot North Coast Vintners Blend 1991 • $10 • (05/31/93) • **83**

Merlot North Coast Vintners Blend 1990 • $9 • (05/31/92) BB • **84**

Merlot Sonoma County 1992: Tight and tough, offering a band of minty currant that peeks through, best to cellar through 1996 to soften, but it may always be on the tannic side. 5,400 cases made. • $15 • (02/28/95) • **85**

Merlot Sonoma County 1990 • $15 • (06/15/93) • **85**

Merlot Sonoma County 1989 • $15 • (05/31/92) • **86**

Merlot Sonoma County 1987 • $18 • (01/31/90) • **87**

Merlot Sonoma County 1986 • $18 • (12/31/88) • **80**

Merlot Sonoma County 1984 • $11 • (02/28/87) • **85**

Merlot Sonoma County 1983 • $11 • (05/16/86) • **61**

Merlot Sonoma County Vintners Blend 1989 • $18 • (03/31/91) BB • **84**

Merlot Sonoma Valley Sangiacomo 1992: Dense, chewy and tannic, but there's enough currant, herb and cedary oak flavors to hold your interest, picking up a nice tobacco edge on the finish. Drinkable now. 1,500 cases made. • $20 • (06/15/95) • **86**

Mountain Claret Sonoma County 1992: Marked by herb and cedar notes, the narrow band of currant and cherry emerges on aftertaste, giving it more depth and shape. Drink now. 1,116 cases made. • $12 • (09/15/95) • **84**

Pickberry Vineyards Sonoma Mountain Cabernet Blend 1994: Complex and earthy currant aromas lead to similar flavors in this solid young wine. Maintains its elegant style with medium-rich flavors and good but not great depth. • $NA • (05/31/95) • **85-89** (BT)
Pickberry Vineyards Sonoma Mountain Cabernet Blend 1990: Ripe, smooth and polished, a supple wine with prune, chocolate and cola aromas and flavors, echoing a hint of cherry on the finish. Best to drink in 1997. 1,000 cases made. • $26 • (11/15/93) • **86**
Pickberry Vineyards Sonoma Mountain Cabernet Blend 1989 • $37 • (11/15/92) • **89**
Pickberry Vineyards Sonoma Mountain Cabernet Blend 1988 • $27 • (04/30/91) • **82**
Pickberry Vineyards Sonoma Mountain Cabernet Blend 1986 • $38 • (03/01/89) • **89**
Zinfandel Napa Valley Canard 1988 • $12 • (08/31/91) • **75**
Zinfandel Napa Valley Canard 1986 • $11 • (03/15/90) • **81**
Zinfandel Napa Valley Canard 1985 • $10 • (03/15/89) • **85**
Zinfandel Napa Valley Dickerson 1993: Effusively fruity, complex and ripe, offering pretty black cherry, plum and raspberry jam notes, mild tannins and long, fruity aftertaste. 690 cases made. • $20 • (09/15/95) • **89**
Zinfandel Napa Valley Dickerson 1992: Firm, tight, crisp and tannic, but the spicy raspberry, wild berry and black cherry flavors are ripe, intense and sharply focused. Has a minty edge on the finish. Drinkable now. 1,297 cases made. • $18 • (09/15/94) SS • **91**
Zinfandel Napa Valley Dickerson 1990 • $16 • (09/30/92) SS • **92**
Zinfandel Napa Valley Dickerson 1989 • $13 • (11/15/91) • **87**
Zinfandel Napa Valley Dickerson 1988 • $13 • (08/31/91) • **84**
Zinfandel Napa Valley Dickerson 1987 • $13 • (03/15/90) • **86**
Zinfandel Napa Valley Dickerson 1986 • $12 • (12/15/88) • **88**
Zinfandel Napa Valley Dickerson 1985 • $11 • (12/31/87) • **80**
Zinfandel Napa Valley Vintners Blend 1985 • $6 • (05/31/87) • **80**
Zinfandel North Coast Vintners Blend 1992: Simple and fruity, with plum and cherry flavors that turn spicy and earthy on the finish. Mild tannins make it drinkable now. • $8 • (10/15/94) • **83**
Zinfandel North Coast Vintners Blend 1991 • $7 • (05/31/93) • **84**
Zinfandel North Coast Vintners Blend 1990 • $7 • (10/15/92) • **81**
Zinfandel North Coast Vintners Blend 1989 • $7 • (07/31/91) BB • **83**
Zinfandel North Coast Vintners Blend 1988 • $7 • (10/15/90) BB • **81**
Zinfandel Russian River Valley Wood Road Belloni 1993: Rambunctious, intense young Zin marked by chewy tannins, offering just enough plum and wild berry flavors to maintain balance. Drinkable now. 3,490 cases made. • $20 • (09/15/95) • **87**
Zinfandel Sonoma County 1993: Smooth and polished, sporting ripe raspberry, cherry, anise and cedar notes. Finishes with a complex tarry edge and fine tannins. Appealing now through 2000. 7,056 cases made. • $15 • (09/15/95) • **89**
Zinfandel Sonoma County 1992: Bright and lively, with lots of spicy cherry, raspberry, plum and currant notes. Elegant, supple texture and light, toasty oak shadings. Focused, complex and tasty now, but should drink well through 1998. 6,200 cases made. • $12 • (08/31/94) SS • **91**
Zinfandel Sonoma County 1987 • $11 • (03/15/90) • **88**
Zinfandel Sonoma County 1986 • $9 • (12/15/88) • **90**
Zinfandel Sonoma County 1985 • $8 • (12/31/87) • **80**
Zinfandel Sonoma County 1983 • $8 • (05/01/86) • **57**
Zinfandel Sonoma County Belloni 1992: Big, rich, intense and tannic, with loads of Zinfandel fruit. Tiers of black cherry, wild berry, spice and floral notes. Beautifully crafted but still young and should be cellared until 1995. 996 cases made. • $18 • (09/15/94) • **89**
Zinfandel Sonoma County Dry Creek Benchland 1981 • $6 • (04/01/84) • **81**
Zinfandel Sonoma County Old Vine 1990 • $11 • (10/15/92) • **89**
Zinfandel Sonoma County Old Vine 1989 • $11 • (12/31/91) • **82**
Zinfandel Sonoma County Old Vine 1988 • $11 • (11/30/90) • **87**
Zinfandel Sonoma County Vintners Blend 1987 • $6 • (06/15/89) BB • **88**
Zinfandel Sonoma County Vogensen Vineyard 1981 • $8 • (04/16/84) • **68**
Zinfandel Sonoma Valley Belloni 1991 • $18 • (09/30/93) • **89**
Zinfandel Sonoma Valley Cooke 1993: Austere but very compact and concentrated, featuring crisp cherry and wild berry notes, firm, dry tannins and tealike aftertaste. Drinkable now. 410 cases made. • $20 • (09/15/95) • **89**
Zinfandel Sonoma Valley Cooke 1992: Tight and compact, with a firm tannic edge, it opens up to reveal bright, ripe cherry, raspberry and spicy flavors that are rich and focused. Finishes with a long, full aftertaste. Given the tannin level, I'd cellar this short-term, perhaps up to a year, 394 cases made. • $18 • (10/15/94) • **91**
Zinfandel Sonoma Valley Cooke 1991 • $18 • (09/30/93) • **88**
Zinfandel Sonoma Valley Cooke 1990 • $16 • (10/15/92) • **90**
Zinfandel Sonoma Valley Cooke 1987 • $13 • (03/15/90) • **84**
Zinfandel Sonoma Valley Dickerson 1991 • $18 • (09/30/93) • **87**
Zinfandel Sonoma Valley Monte Rosso 1993: A compact, supple core of cherry and raspberry flavor turns to spice and anise, adding firm tannins and an elegant finish. 1,440 cases made. • $20 • (09/15/95) • **88**
Zinfandel Sonoma Valley Old Hill Vineyard 1993: Ripe and well proportioned, with a ripe core of black cherry, wild berry, tar and spice. It all folds together into a complex wine that is drinkable now. 685 cases made. • $22 • (09/15/95) • **90**
Zinfandel Sonoma Valley Old Hill Vineyard 1992: Perfumey and floral, with bright, ripe, intense cherry and raspberry flavors that border on the exotic. Holds its focus, finishing with crisp tannins and lots of spicy fruit flavors. Drinkable now. 842 cases made. • $20 • (10/15/94) • **92**
Zinfandel Sonoma Valley Old Hill Vineyard 1991 • $20 • (09/30/93) • **87**
Zinfandel Sonoma Valley Old Hill Vineyard 1990 • $18 • (10/15/92) • **89**
Zinfandel Sonoma Valley Old Hill Vineyard 1987 • $15 • (03/15/90) • **87**
Zinfandel Sonoma Valley Old Hill Vineyard 1986 • $13 • (12/15/88) • **92**
Zinfandel Sonoma Valley Old Hill Vineyard 1985 • $12 • (12/31/87) • **87**
Zinfandel Sonoma-Napa Counties Vintners Blend 1986 • $5 • (06/30/88) BB • **85**

RAY, MARTIN | CALIFORNIA

Cabernet Sauvignon California Saratoga Cuvée 1993: Ripe cherry and currant flavors are generous—avoiding the hollow middle found in so many 1993 Cabernets. Finishes with a fruity aftertaste and crisp tannins. Ready now and into 1997. 650 cases made. • $32 • **86**
Cabernet Sauvignon California Saratoga Cuvée 1992: Trim, compact, a backward, restrained style, boasting wild berry, cherry and currant notes of modest depth and proportion. Firmly tannic finish. Hold until 1999. 400 cases made. • $28 • (10/31/95) • **89**
Cabernet Sauvignon Napa Valley 1993: Well balanced, given the vintage, and there's plenty of cherry, coffee and currant flavors to offset the crisp tannins. Try in 1998. 875 cases made. • $32 • **86**
Cabernet Sauvignon Napa Valley 1992: Austere, dry and firmly tannic, crisp and lean, offering hints of plum, cherry, smoke and tobacco, but in the end the tannins dominate. 450 cases made. • $28 • (10/31/95) • **86**
Cabernet Sauvignon Napa Valley 1991: Rich, ripe, supple and intense, packing lots of currant, black cherry, plum and spice notes, gaining depth and nuance from toasty, buttery oak. Keeps pumping out the fruit on the long, full finish. Defines concentration and complexity. Try after 1997. 400 cases made. • $28 • (11/15/94) • **94**
Chardonnay California Mariage 1994: Ripe, complex and elegant, with tiers of bright, spicy pear, apple, honey and light citrus shadings. Impressive for its purity of flavor and long, lingering finish. A wonderful Chardonnay from this upstart winery. 700 cases made. • $25 • (05/31/96) • **93**
Chardonnay California Mariage 1993: A smooth, elegant style, with lemon, citrus and pear flavors that are tightly wound but persistent and lingering. The aftertaste keeps echoing the fruit nuances. 600 cases made. • $24 • (08/31/95) • **89**
Chardonnay California Mariage 1992: Intense and lively, a ripe, supple and complex Chardonnay offering layers of spicy pear, honey, toasty and smoky oak flavors. Finishes with a long, rich aftertaste. Try now. 600 cases made. • $24 • (11/30/94) • **91**

RAYMOND | CALIFORNIA

Cabernet Sauvignon California Amberhill California Selection 1991: Pleasantly balanced, with spicy, toasty oak and supple currant and cherry flavor. Ready now. 10,000 cases made. • $8 • (11/15/94) • **84**
Cabernet Sauvignon California Amberhill California Selection 1990: Chunky, with grapey cherry flavor that's good for a red table wine. 7,258 cases made. • $8 • (11/15/94) • **78**

Key: SS—Spectator Selection. CS—Cellar Selection. BB—Best Buy. $NA—Price not available. (BT)—Barrel tasting. Ⓐ—Auction Price.
Dates in parentheses represent the issues in which the ratings were published.

Cabernet Sauvignon Napa Valley 1991: Medium-weight, pleasantly balanced red with spice, currant, smoke and herb flavors. Turns smooth and supple on the finish without hard-core tannins. Best after 1997. 15,000 cases made. • $17 • (11/15/94) • **88**
Cabernet Sauvignon Napa Valley 1990: Firm, chunky and pleasantly fruity, a solid wine that reins itself in to remain lithe and spicy, offering some buttery oak and cedar overtones to the core of currant and plum fruit. Best to drink now. 20,000 cases made. • $17 • (11/15/93) • **88**
Cabernet Sauvignon Napa Valley 1989 • $17 • (02/15/93) • **88**
Cabernet Sauvignon Napa Valley 1988 • $18 • (08/31/92) • **85**
Cabernet Sauvignon Napa Valley 1987 • $17 • (02/28/91) • **83**
Cabernet Sauvignon Napa Valley 1986 • $16 • (05/31/90) • **90**
Cabernet Sauvignon Napa Valley 1985 • $16 • (12/15/89) • **84**
Cabernet Sauvignon Napa Valley 1984 • $28 • (02/15/89) • **90**
Cabernet Sauvignon Napa Valley 1983 • $30 • (02/15/88) • **89**
Cabernet Sauvignon Napa Valley 1982 • $22 • (11/15/86) • **91**
Cabernet Sauvignon Napa Valley 1981 • $22 • (03/01/89) • **85**
Cabernet Sauvignon Napa Valley 1980 • $25 • (03/01/89) • **82**
Cabernet Sauvignon Napa Valley 1979 • $24 • (03/01/89) • **85**
Cabernet Sauvignon Napa Valley 1978 • $31 • (11/15/92) • **86**
Cabernet Sauvignon Napa Valley 1977 • $25 • (03/01/89) • **84**
Cabernet Sauvignon Napa Valley 1976 • $35 • (03/01/89) • **78**
Cabernet Sauvignon Napa Valley 1974: Smooth for a wine in this tasting, laced with herb and cedar notes that turn earthy on the finish. Drinkable. 800 cases made. • $40 • (11/15/94) • **78**
Cabernet Sauvignon Napa Valley Estates 1993: Supple and harmonious, with a pleasant core of plum and cherry flavors. Appealing now. 9,000 cases made. • $12 • (03/31/96) • **84**
Cabernet Sauvignon Napa Valley Private Reserve 1991: Clean and correct, with a modest band of currant and cherry fruit, but not the extra dimensions usually found in this wine. 3,000 cases made. • $25 • (12/15/95) • **84**
Cabernet Sauvignon Napa Valley Private Reserve 1990: Pleasing integration of spicy, buttery oak and ripe Cabernet fruit, finishing with smooth fleshy tannins. Serves up lots of complex flavors on the finish. Best after 1997. 5,000 cases made. • $25 • (10/31/94) • **88**
Cabernet Sauvignon Napa Valley Private Reserve 1988 • $26 • (07/31/93) • **88**
Cabernet Sauvignon Napa Valley Private Reserve 1987 • $28 • (08/31/92) • **82**
Cabernet Sauvignon Napa Valley Private Reserve 1986 • $28 • (11/15/91) • **88**
Cabernet Sauvignon Napa Valley Private Reserve 1985 • $30 • (07/15/90) CS • **91**
Cabernet Sauvignon Napa Valley Private Reserve 1984 • $25 • (07/15/89) • **87**
Cabernet Sauvignon Napa Valley Private Reserve 1983 • $35 • (03/01/89) • **84**
Cabernet Sauvignon Napa Valley Private Reserve 1982 • $36 • (03/01/89) • **85**
Cabernet Sauvignon Napa Valley Private Reserve 1981 • $28 • (03/01/89) • **87**
Cabernet Sauvignon Napa Valley Private Reserve 1980 • $34 • (03/01/89) • **85**
Cabernet Sauvignon Napa Valley Reserve 1993: Smooth and harmonious, featuring a supple core of cherry, currant and berry notes. Turns complex and fleshy on aftertaste where the flavors unfold, revealing anise and spice. 20,500 cases made. • $17 • (04/30/96) • **90**
Chardonnay California Amberhill 1994: Oddly spicy and medicinal around the edge of the tangy apple flavor. 100,000 cases made. • $10 • (06/15/96) • **76**
Chardonnay California Amberhill California Selection 1993: Pleasantly fruity, with ripe pear, apple and citrus notes. 80,000 cases made. • $11 • (02/28/95) • **83**
Chardonnay California Amberhill California Selection 1992: Bold, ripe and creamy, this new line of Amberhill wines under the Raymond label extends the range of values from this Napa-based winery. Plenty of ripe apple, pear and spice flavors. Ready now. 80,000 cases made. 80,000 cases made. • $11 • (05/15/94) • **84**
Chardonnay California Selection 1991 • $8 • (07/15/93) BB • **83**
Chardonnay Monterey Estates 1994: A racy style, with a distinctive grassy edge to the grapefruit and citrus flavors, graced by pear and spice notes. Comes together on the finish, where the flavors evolve. 30,000 cases made. • $12 • (03/31/96) • **87**
Chardonnay Napa Valley 1993: Bright, fruity and straightforward, a nice mouthful of apple, pineapple and resiny flavors. Drink now. 26,000 cases made. • $14 • (12/15/95) • **87**
Chardonnay Napa Valley 1992: Lean and crisp, showing a narrow band of tart apple and pear flavors that are well focused. 30,000 cases made. • $14 • (04/30/95) • **85**
Chardonnay Napa Valley 1991 • $15 • (02/28/94) • **85**
Chardonnay Napa Valley Private Reserve 1994: An oaky style, with lots of buttery, smoky wood flavors, but enough ripe pear, apple and honey notes arrive to keep it in balance. 3,500 cases made. • $18 • (05/31/96) • **89**
Chardonnay Napa Valley Private Reserve 1992: Ripe, smooth, polished, offering an elegant core of spicy pear, apple and light vanilla oak shadings but not the usual gusto found in Raymond reserve Chardonnay. 6,500 cases made. • $18 • (04/30/95) • **87**
Chardonnay Napa Valley Private Reserve 1991 • $18 • (07/15/93) • **89**
Chardonnay Napa Valley Reserve 1994: Grows into a complex and attractive wine, marked by cedar, toast and spicy wood shadings that add dimensions and richness to the ripe pear, grapefruit and melon notes. 35,000 cases made. • $14 • (05/31/96) • **89**
Johannisberg Riesling Late Harvest Napa Valley 1985 • $8 • (09/15/86) • **91**
Meritage Napa Valley 1989 • $35 • (11/15/93) • **89**
Meritage Private Reserve Napa Valley 1991: Ripe and jammy, with wild berry, cherry and raspberry fruit, picking up a touch of spicy oak on the finish. Clean and well balanced, with an sense of elegance and finesse. 1,000 cases made. • $40 • (12/15/95) • **87**
Meritage Private Reserve Napa Valley 1990: This offers bright, lively black cherry, currant and plum flavors that are rich, focused and elegant. Finishes with a long, fruity aftertaste and smooth, polished tannins. Delicious now with its complex array of flavors, but age-worthy, too. 1,000 cases made. • $40 • (10/31/94) • **90**
Merlot Napa Valley 1992: Supple and harmonious, with an elegant band of cherry, currant and spice, finishing with a nice dash of oak and spice. Finishes with a strong fruity aftertaste and hints of coffee and herbs. 8,000 cases made. • $17 • (11/15/95) • **89**
Merlot Napa Valley Reserve 1993: An oaky style, with firm tannins and a trim band of cherry and chocolate flavors, becomes more complex on the finish. 4,000 cases made. • $17 • (06/30/96) • **83**
Pinot Noir Napa Valley 1992: Tight with an earthy, stemmy edge, but enough fruit to comes through make it appealing, with hints of dried cherry. 1,750 cases made. • $17 • (09/15/95) • **83**
Sauvignon Blanc Napa Valley 1994: Earthy, musty flavors intrude on the modest fruit in this lean, hard-edged white. Difficult to warm up to. 6,200 cases made. • $9 • (12/31/95) • **77**
Sauvignon Blanc Napa Valley 1993: Spicy, floral flavors run through this straightforward, slightly vegetal wine. 6,500 cases made. • $9 • (08/31/95) • **81**
Sauvignon Blanc Napa Valley 1992 • $8 • (09/15/93) • **77**
Sauvignon Blanc Napa Valley 1991 • $9 • (02/28/93) • **76**
Sauvignon Blanc Napa Valley Reserve 1995: Bright and fruity pear and floral flavors with a smoky accent. 9,800 cases made. • $10 • **85**
Vintage Select Red California 1984 • $4 • (02/15/88) • **75**
Vintage Select Red California 1983 • $4 • (08/31/87) • **69**
Vintage Select Red North Coast 1982 • $4 • (04/01/86) BB • **82**

RED HILL | CALIFORNIA

Chardonnay California 1993: Tastes sweet, with a cloying, candied edge to the apple-laced fruit. • $4 • (07/31/95) • **79**
Sauvignon Blanc California 1993: Light and crisp, distinctly fruity, but ultimately fairly simple. 1,000 cases made. • $3 • (05/15/95) • **81**

REDWOOD CANYON | CALIFORNIA

Cabernet Sauvignon Napa Valley 1993: Ripe and fruity, with a spicy edge to the plum and berry flavors. Simple but pleasant. 7,000 cases made. • $13 • (12/15/95) • **84**

REDWOOD VALLEY | CALIFORNIA

White Zinfandel California 1987 • $6 • (06/15/89) • **66**

REMICK RIDGE | CALIFORNIA

Cabernet Sauvignon Sonoma Valley 1992: Strikes a nice balance between its ripe currant and plum flavors and thick tannins. Should soften a bit by 1997 or '98. 296 cases made. • $19 • (05/31/96) • **88**

Chardonnay Sonoma Valley 1994: Distinctive for its fresh, ripe peach, pear and melon notes, and it finishes with complex toasty oak accents. The texture turns a bit coarse, but only a bit. A little age should bring it in line. 300 cases made. • $16 • (06/15/96) • **88**

Merlot Sonoma Valley Marcy's Vineyard 1992: Complex and inviting, with a pretty range of flavors. The ripe plum, cherry, anise and cedar notes are well focused and well proportioned. Picks up nice tobacco and buttery oak notes on the finish. 199 cases made. • $30 • (05/31/96) • **88**

RENAISSANCE | CALIFORNIA

Cabernet Sauvignon North Yuba 1991: Lean and chewy, a tannic wine with modestly proportioned flavors. Finishes a little bitter. 10,000 cases made. • $12 • (12/15/95) • **78**

Cabernet Sauvignon North Yuba 1990: Ripe with a slight raisiny edge, but it turns coarse and finishes with gritty tannins. Try in1997. 6,000 cases made. • $14 • (11/15/94) • **81**

Cabernet Sauvignon North Yuba 1988 • $12 • (11/15/93) • **76**

Cabernet Sauvignon North Yuba 1987 • $15 • (08/31/92) • **76**

Cabernet Sauvignon North Yuba 1986: Crisp and firm, with a narrow band of earthy currant, dries out on the finish. Drink up soon. 5,000 cases made. • $21 • (11/15/94) • **78**

Cabernet Sauvignon North Yuba Reserve 1987: Smooth and generous, a mature wine with a lovely truffle character that runs through the berry and anise flavors. Ready now, but could improve through 1999. 987 cases made. • $35 • (12/15/95) • **88**

Cabernet Sauvignon North Yuba Reserve 1985 • $45 • (11/15/92) • **82**

Chardonnay North Yuba Barrel Select 1993: Earthy with a bitter grapefruit and canned fruit edge, although it straightens out on the finish. Needs food. Marginal. 1,700 cases made. • $20 • (07/31/95) • **76**

Merlot North Yuba 1993: Pungently earthy and leathery with a bitter edge to it all, overriding the currant and berry fruit underneath. Finishes with full-scale, drying tannins, hard to imagine this one ever outgrowing its tannins. On the other hand, if you like leathery tannins galore. . . . 270 cases made. • $16 • (03/31/96) • **74**

Riesling Late Harvest North Yuba Special Select 1986: Almost amber-colored yet light in structure and flavor, definitely sweet but balanced short of syrupy. Notes of honey, apricot and pear. Best from 1997 or 1998. 3,475 cases made. • $15 • (09/30/95) • **89**

Riesling North Yuba Dry 1992: Light and refreshing, flavors centered around grapefruit, finishing a tad sweet. • $9 • (06/15/95) • **85**

Riesling North Yuba Dry 1991 • $8 • (08/31/93) • **65**

Sauvignon Blanc Late Harvest North Yuba 1990 • $12 • (12/31/93) • **78**

Sauvignon Blanc Late Harvest North Yuba Select 1991: Sweet and fresh, nice pear and apricot flavors linger on the solid finish. Tasty now, may be best from 1997. 300 cases made. • $13 • (05/15/95) • **85**

Sauvignon Blanc Late Harvest North Yuba Select 1985: Deliciously sweet and mature, a little sugary but accented by caramel, honey, floral and some raisiny flavor. Drink now. 2,875 cases made. • $13 • (09/30/95) • **89**

Sauvignon Blanc North Yuba 1994: Pear and grassy flavors that are typical of this varietal. Earthy, spicy and floral notes add flair and complexity. 2,033 cases made. • $9 • **87**

Sauvignon Blanc North Yuba 1993: Floral, slightly bitter flavors make this one seem charmless. 10,000 cases made. • $9 • (08/31/95) • **77**

Sauvignon Blanc North Yuba 1992: Aggressively floral aromas and flavors mark this as an unusual style, but there are some nice pear and apple notes behind it. Drinkable now. • $10 • (12/31/94) • **83**

Sauvignon Blanc North Yuba 1991 • $8 • (09/15/93) • **80**

Key: SS—Spectator Selection. CS—Cellar Selection. BB—Best Buy. $NA—Price not available. (BT)—Barrel tasting. Ⓐ—Auction Price.
Dates in parentheses represent the issues in which the ratings were published.

Sauvignon Blanc North Yuba Barrel Select 1994: Rich and mouth-filling, with butterscotch accents to the bright pear and caramel flavors. Finish is soft and plush. 190 cases made. • $12 • **89**

RENWOOD | CALIFORNIA

Barbera Amador County 1992: Firm and fruity, but strays toward an undertone of horsy flavor. Finishes with firm black cherry flavors. Ready now. 1,905 cases made. • $16 • (07/31/95) • **82**

Port Shenandoah Valley Late Bottled Vintage 1989: A lighter style of Port, with nicely focused black cherry and blackberry flavors, slightly smoky and with a delicate grip on the finish. Solid to drink now, best from 1997-1998. 902 cases made. • $18 • (05/31/95) • **85**

Zinfandel Amador County 1991 • $12 • (03/31/94) • **83**

Zinfandel Amador County Old Vine 1993: Ripe, flavorful, well endowed with tannins. A thick, heady dose of berry jam, pepper and raspberry pushes limits for extract and intensity. For fans of this style. 2,870 cases made. • $15 • (09/15/95) • **89**

Zinfandel Fiddletown Old Vine 1993: Firm and intense, compact and concentrated, but the flavors are a bit murky and unevolved, adding hints of cedar, spice and earthy berry. The finish is more interesting, but it's still dense and tannic getting there. Try in 1997. 634 cases made. • $22 • (04/30/96) • **87**

Zinfandel Shenandoah Valley Grandpère 1993: An austere character, the ripe raisin notes paired with biting tannins, but it holds together and finishes with a flash of berry, spice and more tannin. Drink now. 1,904 cases made. • $21 • (10/15/95) • **87**

Zinfandel Shenandoah Valley Grandpère 1992: Dark in color, with very ripe raisin, plum and black cherry flavors. Finishes with firm tannins, but the fruit, despite a rustic edge, are intense and concentrated. Drinkable now. 800 cases made. • $18 • (08/31/94) • **88**

Zinfandel Shenandoah Valley Grandpère 1991 • $16 • (03/31/94) • **86**

RETZLAFF | CALIFORNIA

Cabernet Sauvignon Livermore Valley 1991: Intensely oaky with a bitter, charred edge that spoils the Cabernet fruit. Marginal quality. 317 cases made. • $16 • (11/15/93) • **68**

Meritage Livermore Valley 1990: Firm, intense, oaky and tannic. Underneath you get a chewy, rustic beam of currant flavor that turns tarry and cedary, finishing with a woody edge. Drinkable now. 390 cases made. • $18 • (11/15/93) • **81**

Merlot Livermore Valley 1991: This is austere with a strong cedar and oak edge that dominates the flavors and overrides the fruit. Short-term cellaring may make the flavors taste more integrated. 329 cases made. • $14 • (09/15/94) • **79**

REVE, LA | NEW YORK

Cabernet Sauvignon North Fork of Long Island American Series 1986 • $12 • (12/15/88) • **78**

Merlot North Fork of Long Island American Series 1986 • $13 • (12/15/88) • **86**

REVERE | CALIFORNIA

Chardonnay Napa Valley Berlenbach Vineyards 1992: Crisp, austere, almost astringent, with a nice shot of citrusy apple flavor sneaking in on the finish. 152 cases made. • $20 • (06/30/94) • **80**

Chardonnay Napa Valley Berlenbach Vineyards 1991: Crisp and fruity, simple with nectarine flavor predominating, finishing soft and generous. 218 cases made. • $20 • (06/30/94) • **83**

Chardonnay Napa Valley Reserve 1992: Crisp but more earthy than fruity, lean, never gets much flavor going. 149 cases made. • $22 • (06/30/94) • **80**

Chardonnay Napa Valley Reserve 1991: Fresh, generous and sturdy, full-bodied, with pear and pineapple flavors, finishing with a chunky texture. 427 cases made. • $22 • (06/30/94) • **84**

REY SOL | CALIFORNIA

Syrah Temecula 1994: Earthy, musty notes divert the focus of the modest pepper and berry flavors. More characteristic of a a red table wine than a Syrah. 300 cases made. • $10 • **81**

RICH PASSAGE | WASHINGTON

Fumé Blanc Washington 1993: Smooth-textured, floral in flavor, offering a definte oaky note on the finish. 250 cases made. • $9 • (09/30/95) • **83**
Fumé Blanc Washington Dry 1992: Dark in color, with smoky, mineral overtones to the buttery apple flavors. Takes a stab at extra depth, but comes off a little woody. 220 cases made. • $9 • (07/31/94) • **85**
Pinot Noir Washington Morgan Vineyard 1990 • $12 • (02/28/93) • **68**

RICHARDSON | CALIFORNIA

Cabernet Franc Sonoma Valley Giles Vineyard 1993: Medium in weight, delivering tart cherry and berry flavors of modest proportions. 200 cases made. • $15 • (05/15/96) • **83**
Cabernet Sauvignon Sonoma Valley 1985 • $12 • (11/30/88) • **78**
Cabernet Sauvignon Sonoma Valley Horne 1992: An earthy, minty style that turns rustic and tannic, missing the usual charm found in Richardson's wines. Best after 1997. 500 cases made. • $12 • (11/15/94) • **81**
Cabernet Sauvignon Sonoma Valley Horne 1991: Ripe, intense and jammy with lush, complex black berry and currant flavors that turn spicy and chewy on the finish where the tannins kick in. Balanced and richly textured, this is a big, potent young Cabernet that should develop nicely through the decade. 650 cases made. • $14 • (11/15/93) • **89**
Cabernet Sauvignon Sonoma Valley Horne 1990: Firm, focused and decidedly earthy, showing a barnyardy streak that seems to take over on the finish. Not for all tastes. 850 cases made. • $12 • (11/15/93) • **73**
Cabernet Sauvignon Sonoma Valley Horne 1989 • $14 • (11/15/91) • **78**
Merlot Carneros Sangiacomo 1993: Tart and trim, with a narrow band of cedar, tart black cherry, plum and wild berry. Tastes better on the finish, where the oak flavors fold in together nicely with the fruit. Cellar into 1997. 750 cases made. • $18 • **87**
Merlot Sonoma Valley Carneros Gregory 1990 • $15 • (05/31/92) • **89**
Merlot Sonoma Valley Carneros Gregory 1989 • $14 • (03/31/91) • **83**
Merlot Sonoma Valley Carneros Sangiacomo 1990 • $15 • (05/31/92) • **87**
Merlot Sonoma Valley Los Carneros 1992: Builds complexity and finesse with every sip, with tiers of ripe cherry, plum and spice flavors that stay with you on the finish. Ready now but sure to hold through 1997. 952 cases made. • $15 • (09/15/94) • **87**
Merlot Sonoma Valley Los Carneros Gregory 1991 • $18 • (06/15/93) • **86**
Merlot Sonoma Valley Los Carneros Sangiacomo & Gregory Vineyards 1991 • $15 • (06/15/93) • **85**
Pinot Noir Carneros Sangiacomo 1993: Tight and firm, with a minty, tannic edge to the wild berry flavors. Drinkable now. 750 cases made. • $15 • (03/31/95) • **84**
Pinot Noir Carneros Sonoma Valley Sangiacomo 1991 • $15 • (02/28/93) • **80**
Pinot Noir Carneros Sonoma Valley Sangiacomo 1990 • $14 • (09/30/92) • **81**
Pinot Noir Sonoma Valley Carneros Sangiacomo 1989 • $14 • (04/30/91) • **86**
Pinot Noir Sonoma Valley Carneros Sangiacomo 1987 • $12 • (10/15/89) • **88**
Pinot Noir Sonoma Valley Carneros Sangiacomo 1986 • $12 • (06/15/88) • **87**
Pinot Noir Sonoma Valley Los Carneros Sangiacomo 1992: 752 cases made. • $14 • **74**
Synergy California 1989 • $15 • (11/15/91) • **83**
Synergy Los Carneros 1989 • $15 • (05/31/92) • **84**
Synergy Sonoma Valley 1994: A touch earthy and leathery, though it still serves up well-proportioned currant and cherry flavors. Hold off until 1999 for smoother tannins. 1,000 cases made. • $15 • (12/15/95) • **86**
Zinfandel Sonoma Valley NV • $9 • (07/31/89) • **76**
Zinfandel Sonoma Valley Nora's Vineyard 1993: Austere, but the firm tannins and trim band of spicy cherry flavors pull through. 450 cases made. • $15 • (10/15/95) • **84**
Zinfandel Sonoma Valley Nora's Vineyard 1992: Bold, ripe and intense, with layers of spicy raspberry, tar and cedar notes. Rich and focused, with fine balance and a long, full finish. Drinks well now or can age through 1998. 572 cases made. • $12 • (08/31/94) • **89**

RIDGE | CALIFORNIA

Cabernet Santa Cruz Mountains 1993: Pleasant, with a touch of herb and currant, this medium weight wine reflects the character of the 1993 vintage with its trim band of flavors. 7,193 cases made. • $20 • (12/15/95) • **83**
Cabernet Sauvignon Howell Mountain 1983 • $12 • (03/16/86) • **83**
Cabernet Sauvignon Howell Mountain 1982 • $12 • (06/01/85) • **88**
Cabernet Sauvignon Napa County 1981 • $12 • (02/15/84) • **63**
Cabernet Sauvignon Napa County York Creek 1991: Intense and compact, with a firm core of currant, lead pencil and cedary oak. Rich and concentrated but backward and in need of cellaring. Best after 1999, but even then it may still be tannic. 7,444 cases made. • $16 • (11/15/94) • **85**
Cabernet Sauvignon Napa County York Creek 1990: Solid, chunky in texture with a green, herbal edge to the prune and berry flavors at the core, finishing with enough follow-through to make it worth cellaring until 1998. 2,227 cases made. • $16 • (11/15/93) • **88**
Cabernet Sauvignon Napa County York Creek 1987 • $21 • (11/15/92) • **85**
Cabernet Sauvignon Napa County York Creek 1986 • $20 • (03/01/89) • **88**
Cabernet Sauvignon Napa County York Creek 1985 • $21 • (06/10/89) • **78**
Cabernet Sauvignon Napa County York Creek 1984 • $23 • (03/01/89) • **88**
Cabernet Sauvignon Napa County York Creek 1983 • $21 • (03/01/89) • **73**
Cabernet Sauvignon Napa County York Creek 1982 • $25 • (03/01/89) • **73**
Cabernet Sauvignon Napa County York Creek 1981 • $28 • (03/01/89) • **76**
Cabernet Sauvignon Napa County York Creek 1980 • $35 • (03/01/89) • **88**
Cabernet Sauvignon Napa County York Creek 1979 • $38 • (03/01/89) • **88**
Cabernet Sauvignon Napa County York Creek 1978 • $33 • (11/15/92) • **87**
Cabernet Sauvignon Napa County York Creek 1977 • $35 • (03/01/89) • **88**
Cabernet Sauvignon Napa County York Creek 1976 • $29 • (03/01/89) • **68**
Cabernet Sauvignon Napa County York Creek 1975 • $60 • (03/01/89) • **87**
Cabernet Sauvignon Napa County York Creek 1974 • $87 • (03/01/89) • **87**
Cabernet Sauvignon Santa Barbara County Tepusquet Vineyard 1981 • $9 • (04/16/84) • **83**
Cabernet Sauvignon Santa Cruz Mountains 1992: Intense and focused, with supple, elegant currant, earth and black cherry flavor framed by toasty, cedary oak. Finishes with a nice burst of fruit, but it needs cellaring, try after 1999. 5,551 cases made. • $16 • (11/15/94) • **89**
Cabernet Sauvignon Santa Cruz Mountains 1991: A tough, chewy, earthy style that packs in lots of flavor, with layers of currant, chocolate and tar. Thick without being too tough and tannic without being overbearing. Hints of spice and mineral keep the flavors pumping. Drink after 1996. 7,443 cases made. • $16 • (10/15/93) • **89**
Cabernet Sauvignon Santa Cruz Mountains 1989 • $12 • (03/31/92) • **82**
Cabernet Sauvignon Santa Cruz Mountains 1986 • $15 • (10/31/89) • **68**
Cabernet Sauvignon Santa Cruz Mountains 1985 • $12 • (06/15/89) • **64**
Cabernet Sauvignon Santa Cruz Mountains 1984 • $12 • (06/15/87) • **64**
Cabernet Sauvignon Santa Cruz Mountains 1983 • $20 • (03/01/89) • **84**
Cabernet Sauvignon Santa Cruz Mountains Jimsomare 1985 • $16 • (02/15/89) • **87**
Cabernet Sauvignon Santa Cruz Mountains Jimsomare 1984 • $16 • (10/31/87) • **69**
Cabernet Sauvignon Santa Cruz Mountains Jimsomare 1983 • $10 • (11/30/86) • **78**
Cabernet Sauvignon Santa Cruz Mountains Jimsomare/Monte Bello 1981 • $12 • (01/01/85) • **87**
Cabernet Sauvignon Santa Cruz Mountains Monte Bello 1988 • $26 Ⓐ • (01/31/92) • **84**
Cabernet Sauvignon Santa Cruz Mountains Monte Bello 1987 • $58 • (11/15/90) • **88**
Cabernet Sauvignon Santa Cruz Mountains Monte Bello 1986 • $48 Ⓐ • (09/15/89) • **82**
Cabernet Sauvignon Santa Cruz Mountains Monte Bello 1985 • $115 Ⓐ • (03/01/89) • **95**
Cabernet Sauvignon Santa Cruz Mountains Monte Bello 1984 • $90 Ⓐ • (03/01/89) • **97**

Cabernet Sauvignon Santa Cruz Mountains Monte Bello 1982 • $32 • (03/01/89) • **75**
Cabernet Sauvignon Santa Cruz Mountains Monte Bello 1981 • $62 Ⓐ • (03/01/89) • **92**
Cabernet Sauvignon Santa Cruz Mountains Monte Bello 1980 • $68 Ⓐ • (03/01/89) • **80**
Cabernet Sauvignon Santa Cruz Mountains Monte Bello 1978 • $95 Ⓐ • (11/15/92) • **92**
Cabernet Sauvignon Santa Cruz Mountains Monte Bello 1977 • $77 Ⓐ • (03/01/89) • **94**
Cabernet Sauvignon Santa Cruz Mountains Monte Bello 1976 • $80 • (03/01/89) • **83**
Cabernet Sauvignon Santa Cruz Mountains Monte Bello 1975 • $100 • (03/01/89) • **88**
Cabernet Sauvignon Santa Cruz Mountains Monte Bello 1974: The first bottle showed poorly, but the second was quite impressive. With its deep ruby color and ripe, spicy currant and anise flavors that are fresh, rich and focused, it turns smooth and elegant on the finish. There's a wonderful sense of harmony and proportion with mild tannins. Drinking exceptionally well, but with proper cellaring it can hold a few more years. 1,260 cases made. • $175 • (11/15/94) • **94**
Cabernet Sauvignon Santa Cruz Mountains Monte Bello 1973 • $100 • (03/01/89) • **87**
Cabernet Sauvignon Santa Cruz Mountains Monte Bello 1972 • $110 • (03/01/89) • **84**
Cabernet Sauvignon Santa Cruz Mountains Monte Bello 1971 • $180 Ⓐ • (03/01/89) • **85**
Cabernet Sauvignon Santa Cruz Mountains Monte Bello 1970 • $200 • (03/01/89) • **96**
Cabernet Sauvignon Santa Cruz Mountains Monte Bello 1969 • $200 • (03/01/89) • **92**
Cabernet Sauvignon Santa Cruz Mountains Monte Bello 1968 • $330 • (03/01/89) • **87**
Cabernet Sauvignon Santa Cruz Mountains Monte Bello 1965 • $200 • (03/01/89) • **86**
Cabernet Sauvignon Santa Cruz Mountains Monte Bello 1964 • $210 • (03/01/89) • **90**
Cabernet Sauvignon Santa Cruz Mountains Monte Bello 1963 • $400 • (03/01/89) • **70**
Chardonnay Santa Cruz Mountains 1994: The ripe pear and smoky oak flavors finish a bit astringent at this point, but it should smooth out, needs time for the fruit and oak to blend. 761 cases made. • $16 • (06/15/96) • **82**
Chardonnay Santa Cruz Mountains 1992: Ripe and complex aromas and flavors of spice, pear and honey that persist and build through the finish. A toasty, buttery character accents it nicely. Another beauty from Ridge. 3,300 cases made. • $20 • (03/31/95) SS • **92**
Chardonnay Santa Cruz Mountains 1991 • $20 • (07/15/93) • **85**
Chardonnay Santa Cruz Mountains Monte Bello Ridge Vineyards 1994: Smells complex, featuring creamy pear, fig and vanilla notes, and it's elegant and refined, as young, vibrant, concentrated flavors finish with a trace of tannin and hint of mineral. 809 cases made. • $20 • (05/15/96) • **90**
Geyserville Sonoma County 1993: This is well oaked, with an interesting band of flavors. A hint of dill accompanies the ripe plum and cherry notes and it's smooth and supple on the finish. This Zinfandel-based blend gains complexity and depth on the palate as the flavors expand. Drinkable now. 6,300 cases made. • $20 • (09/15/95) SS • **91**
Geyserville Sonoma County 1992: Lush, ripe fruit and earthy, leathery character. The finish has a horsy, barnyardy edge that's troubling. Still, it has a lot going for it. Drinkable now. 8,900 cases made. • $18 • (08/31/94) • **86**
Geyserville Sonoma County 1991 • $18 • (09/15/93) • **90**
Geyserville Sonoma County 1990 • $16 • (10/15/92) • **87**
Geyserville Sonoma County 1989 • $14 • (11/15/91) • **84**
Lytton Springs Dry Creek Valley 1993: A wonderfully complex and concentrated Zinfandel-based blend from California. Deliciously ripe, rich and supple, offering intense, jammy cherry, plum, tar and spice. A long, plush aftertaste keeps pumping out the flavors. Drinkable now, but should improve. 11,086 cases made. • $19 • (07/31/95) SS • **91**
Merlot Napa County York Creek 1991: Light and spicy, showing an austere, woody edge to the modest blackberry flavors. Drinkable now. 2,271 cases made. • $18 • (11/15/94) • **80**
Merlot Santa Cruz 1992: Leans toward the earthy, decadent side of Merlot with its dried fruit, leather, anise and toasty oak flavors, but it doesn't shortchange you on flavor. Has more of a Pomerol character than you might expect from a Santa Cruz Merlot. Try in 1997. 918 cases made. • $16 • (01/31/96) • **91**
Merlot Santa Cruz Mountains Monte Bello 1974: Maintaining a deep ruby color with plenty of herb, coffee and cedary oak flavors, this is a rare wine from Ridge's Monte Bello vineyard. It picks up a hint of plum on the finish, turning dry and chewy. 250 cases made. • $175 • (11/15/94) • **84**
Merlot Santa Cruz Mountains Monte Bello Ridge 1993: Rich and full bodied, with dark, dense currant, mineral, anise and cedary oak. Packs in lots of flavor. Hold into 1997 or 1998. 1,253 cases made. • $24 • (06/15/96) • **88**
Merlot Sonoma County Bradford Mouintain 1990 • $18 • (03/15/94) • **89**
Merlot Sonoma County Bradford Mountain 1989 • $18 • (10/31/92) • **82**
Merlot Sonoma County Bradford Mountain 1987 • $17 • (07/15/90) • **75**
Merlot Sonoma County Bradford Mountain 1986 • $16 • (07/31/89) • **64**
Monte Bello Santa Cruz Mountains 1994: Dark, intense with black cherry and wild berry notes and supple tannins. • $480/case as futures. 3,000 cases made. • $480 • (05/31/95) • **85**
Monte Bello Santa Cruz Mountains 1992: Ripe, intense and focused with layers of currant, cherry, toast and spice. A big, flavorful but elegant style that's long on the finish. Worth watching. • $NA • (05/31/93) BT • **88**
Monte Bello Santa Cruz Mountains 1991: Complex and inviting red from California with a pleasant range of currant, vanilla and herb flavors that fold together nicely, finishing with depth, richness and concentration. Best to age into 1997, but it should last another decade beyond. 3,000 cases made. • $75 • (11/15/95) CS • **91**
Monte Bello Santa Cruz Mountains 1990: Earthy, cedary flavors dominate this chunky, solidly built wine, dark and a bit tannic on the palate, finishing with an echo of black cherry and spice. Has a solid future. Drinkable in 1998. 2,368 cases made. • $60 • (11/15/93) • **89**
Monte Bello Santa Cruz Mountains 1989 • $40 • (11/15/92) • **91**
Mourvèdre Evangelo Vineyards Mataro 1990 • $14 • (03/15/92) • **73**
Mourvèdre Contra Costa County Bridgehead Mataro 1993: Smooth and fruity, a mouthful of berry and smoke flavor that lingers on the finish. 2,212 cases made. • $16 • (12/15/95) • **84**
Petite Sirah California York Creek 1991: Firm-textured but soft enough to let blackberry and black pepper flavors ooze through on the finish. 2,200 cases made. • $18 • (09/30/95) • **85**
Petite Sirah Napa County York Creek 1990: Firm and a little spicy, showing just enough plummy flavor to balance the chewy tannins. Best now. 2,099 cases made. • $18 • (09/30/94) • **83**
Petite Sirah Napa County York Creek 1990 • $18 • (05/31/94) • **83**
Petite Sirah Napa County York Creek 1987 • $12 • (08/31/91) • **76**
Petite Sirah Napa County York Creek 1985 • $9 • (10/31/89) • **87**
Petite Sirah Napa County York Creek 1984 • $10 • (01/31/88) • **70**
Petite Sirah Napa County York Creek 1983 • $9 • (03/15/87) • **86**
Petite Sirah Napa County York Creek 1981 • $8 • (10/01/84) • **90**
Petite Sirah Napa Valley 1988 • $16 • (03/15/92) • **80**
Zinfandel Dry Creek Valley Lytton Springs 1992: Lean and elegant, with a spicy edge. The wild berry, jam and pepper notes hang together extremely well. Focused and delivers lots of flavor. Ready now but it should age well through 1998. 12,100 cases made. • $18 • (08/31/94) SS • **90**
Zinfandel Dry Creek Valley Lytton Springs 1991 • $18 • (08/31/93) CS • **91**
Zinfandel Howell Mountain 1990 • $12 • (10/15/92) • **80**
Zinfandel Howell Mountain 1989 • $12 • (03/31/92) • **87**
Zinfandel Howell Mountain 1988 • $12 • (07/31/91) • **82**
Zinfandel Howell Mountain 1987 • $10 • (05/31/90) • **83**
Zinfandel Howell Mountain 1985 • $9 • (05/15/88) • **73**
Zinfandel Howell Mountain 1984 • $9 • (06/30/87) • **81**
Zinfandel Howell Mountain 1983 • $9 • (05/01/86) • **89**
Zinfandel Howell Mountain 1982 • $9 • (06/01/85) • **85**
Zinfandel Napa County York Creek 1985 • $11 • (12/31/87) • **82**

Key: SS—Spectator Selection. CS—Cellar Selection. BB—Best Buy. $NA—Price not available. (BT)—Barrel tasting. Ⓐ—Auction Price.
Dates in parentheses represent the issues in which the ratings were published.

Zinfandel Napa County York Creek 1984 • $11 • (03/15/87) • **86**
Zinfandel Napa County York Creek 1982 • $22 • (07/16/85) SS • **91**
Zinfandel Napa County York Creek 1981 • $9 • (01/01/84) • **89**
Zinfandel Paso Robles 1991 • $12 • (09/15/93) • **90**
Zinfandel Paso Robles 1990 • $10 • (10/15/92) • **84**
Zinfandel Paso Robles 1989 • $10 • (11/15/91) • **84**
Zinfandel Paso Robles 1987 • $10 • (03/15/90) • **85**
Zinfandel Paso Robles 1986 • $7 • (10/31/88) • **81**
Zinfandel Paso Robles 1982 • $8 • (01/01/85) • **90**
Zinfandel Paso Robles Dusi Ranch 1993: Smooth and elegant, showing a pleasant band of cherry and spice and picking up an anise and raspberry edge on the finish. 1,876 cases made. • $14 • (09/30/95) • **86**
Zinfandel Paso Robles Dusi Ranch 1992: Bold, ripe and jammy in an older style of Zin. Ripe, incredibly lush black cherry and plum flavors. Enticing now, but it should hold through 1998. 4,100 cases made. • $14 • (08/31/94) • **90**
Zinfandel Sonoma County 1993: Beautifully balanced, supple and harmonious, wild berry, black cherry, plum and anise turn smooth and polished on the finish. Blended with Carignane, Petite Sirah, Grenache and Alicante Bouschet. 3,400 cases made. • $12 • (09/15/95) • **88**
Zinfandel Sonoma County 1991 • $10 • (08/31/93) SS • **90**
Zinfandel Sonoma County 1990 • $8 • (12/31/92) BB • **86**
Zinfandel Sonoma County 1989 • $8 • (03/31/92) • **80**
Zinfandel Sonoma County 1988 • $8 • (02/15/91) BB • **88**
Zinfandel Sonoma County Geyserville 1988 • $19 • (11/30/90) SS • **90**
Zinfandel Sonoma County Geyserville 1987 • $15 • (10/31/89) • **90**
Zinfandel Sonoma County Geyserville 1986 • $30 • (10/31/88) • **79**
Zinfandel Sonoma County Geyserville 1985 • $25 • (09/15/87) • **83**
Zinfandel Sonoma County Geyserville 1984 • $18 • (12/31/86) • **79**
Zinfandel Sonoma County Geyserville 1982 • $32 • (09/16/84) • **90**
Zinfandel Sonoma County Geyserville 1975 • $35 • (06/16/85) • **67**
Zinfandel Sonoma County Geyserville 1974 • $44 • (06/16/85) • **79**
Zinfandel Sonoma County Geyserville 1973 • $55 • (06/16/85) • **80**
Zinfandel Sonoma County Lytton Springs 1990 • $15 • (10/15/92) • **89**
Zinfandel Sonoma County Lytton Springs 1989 • $13 • (11/15/91) • **82**
Zinfandel Sonoma County Lytton Springs 1988 • $12 • (11/30/90) • **82**
Zinfandel Sonoma County Lytton Springs 1987 • $18 • (10/31/89) • **91**
Zinfandel Sonoma County Lytton Springs 1986 • $25 • (10/15/88) • **88**
Zinfandel Sonoma County Lytton Springs 1985 • $22 • (09/15/87) • **81**
Zinfandel Sonoma County Lytton Springs 1984 • $17 • (11/15/86) • **79**
Zinfandel Sonoma Valley Pagani Ranch 1993: A pleasantly balanced Zinfandel that has well-focused ripe plum, raspberry and cherry flavors. It turns smooth and elegant on the finish, even with its mild tannic grip. It's tasty now, but also a good bet to age. 5,076 cases made. • $20 • (09/15/95) CS • **90**
Zinfandel Sonoma Valley Pagani Ranch 1991 • $14 • (09/30/93) • **86**
Zinfandel Sonoma Valley Pagani Ranch Late Picked 1992: This packs in lots of ripe, jammy flavors, yet maintains its elegance and finesse. Plenty of intense and concentrated black cherry, wild berry and currant, finishing with a long, full, rich finish. Delicious now through 1998. 2,689 cases made. • $16 • (10/15/94) SS • **93**

RITCHIE CREEK | CALIFORNIA

Cabernet Sauvignon Napa Valley 1991: Ripe and raisiny, with a dry, gamy, smoked meat edge to the plum and berry notes. Altogether a funky, earthy wine that doesn't fit the Napa Cabernet profile. • $18 • (04/15/95) • **85**
Cabernet Sauvignon Napa Valley 1978 • $22 • (11/15/92) • **78**

RIVER OAKS | CALIFORNIA

Cabernet Sauvignon North Coast 1984 • $6 • (10/15/87) • **75**
Cabernet Sauvignon Sonoma County 1983 • $6 • (12/15/86) • **75**
Cabernet Sauvignon Sonoma County 1982 • $6 • (04/01/85) BB • **82**
Cabernet Sauvignon Sonoma County 1981 • $6 • (07/01/84) • **76**

RIVER ROAD | CALIFORNIA

Cabernet Sauvignon Napa County 1993: Light, smooth and appealing, its berry and currant flavors nicely integrated. 2,400 cases made. • $9 • (12/15/95) • **83**

RIVERSIDE FARM | CALIFORNIA

Cabernet Sauvignon California 1990: Light and fruity, with jammy plum and raspberry flavors of modest depth and richness. Best to drink now, while it's fresh and fruity. Tasted twice. 12,000 cases made. • $7 • (11/15/92) • **79**
Cabernet Sauvignon California 1985 • $4 • (05/31/88) • **72**
Cabernet Sauvignon North Coast 1983 • $3 • (09/15/86) • **77**
Chardonnay California 1992: A sweet-tasting Chardonnay, but if you like it that way this one delivers pleasing fruit. Ready now. • $6 • (06/30/94) • **79**
Chardonnay California 1991 • $7 • (07/15/92) BB • **82**
White Zinfandel California 1988 • $5 • (06/15/89) • **80**
Zinfandel California 1992 • $6 • (09/30/93) • **82**
Zinfandel California 1990 • $5 • (04/30/93) • **79**

RIVERSIDE VINEYARDS | CALIFORNIA

Cabernet Sauvignon California 1991: Lean and earthy, with just enough cherry and plum flavor to keep it together. • $7 • (11/15/94) • **78**
Chardonnay California 1992: Lightly fruity with cedary oak flavors that turn smoky. Decent. • $7 • (06/30/94) • **79**
Fumé Blanc Sonoma County 1992: Smooth but dominated by earthy-floral flavors around a lean core of apple and spice flavor. • $6 • (08/31/94) • **83**
White Zinfandel California NV: Pleasant and fruity, offering nice strawberry and watermelon flavors, slightly sweet and a little candied. 20,000 cases made. • $6 • (09/15/95) • **78**
Zinfandel California 1992: Earthy and gamy. A simple wine of little distinction. • $7 • (10/15/94) • **74**

ROCHE | CALIFORNIA

Chardonnay Carneros 1991 • $15 • (07/15/93) • **85**
Chardonnay Carneros Barrel Select Reserve 1992: Strikes a nice balance between spicy, toasty oak and ripe pear and apple flavors, giving it depth and complexity along with an elegant finish. 500 cases made. • $20 • (06/30/94) • **85**
Pinot Noir Carneros 1990 • $15 • (09/30/92) • **83**
Pinot Noir Carneros 1989 • $15 • (04/30/91) • **81**
Pinot Noir Carneros 1988 • $14 • (12/31/89) • **89**
Pinot Noir Carneros Reserve 1990 • $19 • (02/28/93) • **83**
Pinot Noir Carneros Unfiltered 1991 • $16 • (12/31/93) • **84**
Pinot Noir Carneros Unfiltered 1989 • $19 • (04/30/91) • **78**

ROCHIOLI | CALIFORNIA

Cabernet Sauvignon Russian River Valley J. Rochioli Neoma's Vineyard Reserve 1990: Smooth and ripe, with generous currant and blackberry aromas and flavors and hints of vanilla and spice on the long finish. A gentle wine that shows a lot of potential. Should be best now. 125 cases made. • $24 • (06/15/93) • **86**
Cabernet Sauvignon Russian River Valley Neoma's Vineyard Reserve 1993: Attractive for its bright, tart cherry, currant and raspberry flavor. It's intense and balanced well and shows good depth and concentration. Best to cellar into 1997 or '98. 146 cases made. • $28 • (04/30/96) • **86**
Cabernet Sauvignon Russian River Valley Neoma's Vineyard Reserve 1991: Firm and chunky, with ripe plum and cherry fruit and a dry oak and tannic aftertaste, picking up a trace of herb and chocolate on the finish. Best after 1998. 140 cases made. • $26 • (12/15/95) • **87**
Chardonnay Russian River Valley 1994: A delicate style that laces its spicy ripe pear flavors with hints of honey, then floats them nicely through the finish. 1,800 cases made. • $17 • (06/15/96) • **89**
Chardonnay Russian River Valley 1993: Combines ripe pear and apricot flavor with deft oak shadings, in a clean and well balanced wine. 1,700 cases made. • $16 • (07/31/95) • **85**
Chardonnay Russian River Valley 1992: Creamy and spicy, with supple pear, honey and apple notes that are ripe, rich and focused. Finishes with a long, lingering, spicy aftertaste. Hangs together nicely. Drink now.1,600 cases made. • $15 • (05/31/94) SS • **90**
Chardonnay Russian River Valley 1991 • $15 • (07/15/93) • **90**

Chardonnay Russian River Valley J. Rochioli Reserve 1991 • $24 • (07/15/93) • **91**

Chardonnay Russian River Valley Reserve 1994: Amazingly ripe, rich and complex, tiers of concentrated pear, hazelnut, honey and toasty oak flavors all folding together into a remarkably sophisticated Chardonnay. A tremendous effort that matches intensity of fruit, elegance and grace. 210 cases made. • $28 • (04/30/96) • **95**

Chardonnay Russian River Valley Reserve 1993: Serves up plenty of elegant flavors, with apple, pear, carmel and honey notes that are of medium weight but persistent. 182 cases made. • $28 • (06/15/95) • **90**

Chardonnay Russian River Valley Reserve 1992: Ripe, rich and elegant, complex and concentrated, with layers of honey, pear, spice, hazelnut and apple flavors that are pure and focused. It finishes with a long, lingering aftertaste that keeps pumping out the flavors. 150 cases made. • $26 • (05/31/94) • **93**

Pinot Noir Russian River Valley 1992: Firm, tight and compact, with a young tannic edge to the ripe cherry and plum-laced fruit. Flavors expand on the finish, revealing more depth and complexity. Best now to 1999. 1,662 cases made. • $18 • (12/15/94) • **88**

Pinot Noir Russian River Valley 1991 • $19 • (02/28/94) SS • **90**

Pinot Noir Russian River Valley 1989 • $16 • (11/15/91) • **84**

Pinot Noir Russian River Valley 1988 • $15 • (10/31/90) • **85**

Pinot Noir Russian River Valley 1987 • $15 • (05/31/90) • **89**

Pinot Noir Russian River Valley 1986 • $15 • (10/15/89) • **87**

Pinot Noir Russian River Valley 1985 • $13 • (06/15/88) • **92**

Pinot Noir Russian River Valley 1984 • $12 • (11/15/87) • **84**

Pinot Noir Russian River Valley 1982 • $13 • (08/31/86) • **89**

Pinot Noir Russian River Valley J. Rochioli Reserve 1990 • $30 • (11/15/92) • **92**

Pinot Noir Russian River Valley Reserve 1991 • $35 • (02/28/94) SS • **92**

Pinot Noir Russian River Valley West Block Reserve 1993: Pretty aromatics and well-defined cherry, plum, mineral and spice flavors fold together nicely. Complex, mildly tannic, medium in weight. Ready now through 1997. 204 cases made. • $38 • (10/15/95) • **89**

Pinot Noir Russian River Valley West Block Reserve 1992: Deep, saturated color, with a rich, ripe core of black currant, anise and spicy oak shadings that run deep and long on the finish. 228 cases made. • $36 • (12/15/94) • **92**

Pinot Noir Sonoma County 1990 • $16 • (02/28/93) • **80**

Sauvignon Blanc Russian River Valley 1994: Lean and lively, showing herbal and floral overtones to the basic green apple flavors. Finishes a bit simple. 2,800 cases made. • $11 • (08/31/95) • **84**

Sauvignon Blanc Russian River Valley 1993: Spicy and flavorful, a flowery wine with crisp apple character and lingering finish. 2,600 cases made. • $10 • (06/30/94) BB • **87**

Sauvignon Blanc Russian River Valley 1991 • $9 • (11/30/92) • **81**

Sauvignon Blanc Russian River Valley J. Rochioli Reserve 1991 • $17 • (11/30/92) • **88**

Sauvignon Blanc Russian River Valley Old Vines Reserve 1994: Elegant, lively and balanced, weaving its spice, herb and rich pear flavors around a smooth, focused beam of cream. Flavors last and last on the finish. 102 cases made. • $19 • **91**

Sauvignon Blanc Russian River Valley Reserve 1993: Ripe, broad and aromatic, leaning toward oaky flavors, but adding a strong flourish of fruit on the finish. Drink now. 116 cases made. • $19 • (02/28/95) • **88**

Sauvignon Blanc Russian River Valley Reserve 1992 • $20 • (11/30/93) • **83**

Zinfandel Russian River Valley Sodini Vineyard 1993: Well oaked, with toasty vanilla and cedar accents, but the wild berry and cherry flavors give it balance and depth. On the finish it shows its finesse and complexity. Drinkable now. 202 cases made. • $15 • (08/31/95) • **88**

Zinfandel Russian River Valley Sodini Vineyard 1992: Smooth, ripe and polished, with bright, lively cherry, raspberry and currant notes that become elegant and refined on the finish. Intriguing floral aromas give it complexity and finesse. Drinks well now, but should hold through 1998. 202 cases made. • $14 • (09/30/94) • **91**

Key: SS—Spectator Selection. CS—Cellar Selection. BB—Best Buy. $NA—Price not available. (BT)—Barrel tasting. (A)—Auction Price.

Dates in parentheses represent the issues in which the ratings were published.

ROCKING HORSE | CALIFORNIA

Cabernet Sauvignon Napa Valley Garvey Family Vineyard 1993: Somewhat earthy and leathery but the Cabernet fruit rises, giving it a sense of balance and finesse. Should drink well early, as the tannins are modest. 1,000 cases made. • $20 • (04/30/96) • **87**

Cabernet Sauvignon Napa Valley Hillside Cuvée 1991: Chewy, chunky, tannic and sturdy, without showing much grace or style at this stage, sneaking in some currant, blackberry and tar on the finish. Best from 1998. 230 cases made. • $18 • (03/15/94) • **84**

Cabernet Sauvignon Napa Valley Hillside Cuvée 1989 • $17 • (03/31/92) • **85**

Cabernet Sauvignon Stags Leap District Robinson Vineyard 1993: Appealing, fruity flavors that turn spicy and simple at mid-palate. Drinks well now with its soft tannins. 200 cases made. • $28 • **83**

Cabernet Sauvignon Stags Leap District Robinson Vineyard 1992: Firm and tight, with a supple core of currant and cherry fruit that's framed by light oak shadings. Drinkable now. 400 cases made. • $24 • (04/15/95) • **86**

Cabernet Sauvignon Stags Leap District Robinson Vineyard 1991: Smooth and stylish, a wine that can show many facets, offering generous plum and berry, chocolate-scented vanilla and spice aromas and flavors, finishing silky and seductive. Best to drink soon. 230 cases made. • $24 • (03/31/94) • **90**

Cabernet Sauvignon Stags Leap District Robinson Vineyard 1990: Firm, tight, youthful and flavorful, with focused plum and currant flavors that are fleshy and balanced, finishing with fine tannins and fruit that lingers. Drinkable now. 300 cases made. • $22 • (02/15/93) • **91**

Zinfandel Howell Mountain Lamborn Family Vineyard 1993: Intense, earthy as Howell Mountain goes, rich and peppery, sporting spicy wild berry flavors, firm tannins and a supple texture. Best in 1997. 1,000 cases made. • $15 • (04/30/96) • **89**

Zinfandel Howell Mountain Lamborn Vineyard 1991 • $14 • (03/31/94) • **88**

Zinfandel Howell Mountain Lamborn Vineyard 1989 • $13 • (10/15/92) • **81**

ROCKLAND | CALIFORNIA

Cabernet Sauvignon Napa Valley 1993: Smooth, ripe and polished, marked by spicy plum, currant and cherry notes and finishing with soft, fleshy tannins and a touch of cedar. Well balanced and enjoyable now, should age well into 2000. 80 cases made. • $30 • (05/15/96) • **89**

Petite Sirah Napa Valley 1993: Dark, spicy, peppery, floral aromas and the requisite firm tannins, but there's more flesh to the texture than you find in most Petite Sirahs. Similar flavors on aftertaste. 185 cases made. • $17 • (05/15/96) • **89**

ROEDERER ESTATE | CALIFORNIA

Brut Anderson Valley NV: Elegant and delicate in style, with complex pear, hazelnut, spice and toast nuances. Its real finesse and polish shows through best on the finish, where the flavors linger on and on. 45,000 cases made. • $16 • (11/30/95) SS • **90**

Brut Anderson Valley L'Ermitage 1990: Smooth, ripe and marked by crisp, tart apple and pear notes, turning complex and creamy on the finish. Well-crafted, rich, complex flavors. 2,600 cases made. • $35 • (12/31/95) • **90**

Brut Anderson Valley L'Ermitage 1989 • $35 • (11/30/93) SS • **92**

Brut Rosé Anderson Valley NV: Aromatically attractive floral, rose petal and wild berry flavors, turning smooth and supple on the finish. 1,500 cases made. • $21 • (11/30/95) • **88**

ROLLING HILLS | CALIFORNIA

Cabernet Sauvignon California 1987 • $7 • (12/15/89) BB • **86**

Pinot Noir Santa Maria Valley 1985 • $6 • (06/15/88) • **77**

ROMBAUER | CALIFORNIA

Cabernet Franc Napa Valley 1990 • $16 • (07/15/93) • **87**

Cabernet Sauvignon Napa Valley 1991: A touch earthy and leathery, with drying tannins, the ripe cherry and currant flavors struggle for center stage. Finishes with a green, tannic edge. 2,000 cases made. • $20 • (12/15/95) • **84**

Cabernet Sauvignon Napa Valley 1990: A moderately rich and ripe Cabernet showing spicy cherry and currant flavors. Finishes with firm tannins and a touch of oak. Best to cellar short-term, drink after 1996. 2,240 cases made. • $18 • (11/15/94) • **86**

Cabernet Sauvignon Napa Valley 1989 • $15 • (11/15/93) • **78**

Cabernet Sauvignon Napa Valley 1987 • $17 • (11/15/91) • **87**

Cabernet Sauvignon Napa Valley 1986 • $18 • (04/15/90) • **88**

Cabernet Sauvignon Napa Valley 1985 • $20 • (04/30/89) • **85**

Cabernet Sauvignon Napa Valley 1984 • $20 • (03/01/89) • **84**

Cabernet Sauvignon Napa Valley 1983 • $19 • (03/01/89) • **73**

Cabernet Sauvignon Napa Valley 1982 • $32 • (03/01/89) • **83**

Cabernet Sauvignon Napa Valley 1981 • $21• (03/01/89) • **82**

Cabernet Sauvignon Napa Valley 1980 • $25 Ⓐ • (03/01/89) • **86**

Chardonnay Carneros 1994: An oaky California style, with ripe fig, pear, spice and hazelnut flavors that are smooth and opulent, finishing with a long, rich aftertaste that keeps pumping out the flavor. The smoky oak finish adds a nice dimension. 9,000 cases made. • $21 • (12/31/95) SS • **93**

Chardonnay Carneros 1993: Serves up lots of ripe and juicy pear, fig and pineapple flavors that are framed by toasty, buttery oak. It all folds together into one delicious California white. 5,000 cases made. • $18 • (03/31/95) SS • **92**

Chardonnay Carneros 1992: Packs in lots of flavor, with ripe pear, honey, smoke and vanilla notes that turn rich and complex on the finish. Drinks well now. • $16 • (11/15/94) • **88**

Chardonnay Carneros 1991 • $15 • (09/15/93) SS • **91**

Le Meilleur Du Chai Napa Valley 1989: Mature with a medium weight range of currant and plum flavors, pleasant enough for a 1989. Drinks well now. 570 cases made. • $35 • (12/15/95) • **84**

Le Meilleur du Chai Napa Valley 1987 • $35 • (11/15/93) • **83**

Le Meilleur du Chai Napa Valley 1986 • $45 • (05/15/91) • **84**

Le Meilleur du Chai Napa Valley 1985 • $48 • (10/31/89) • **90**

Le Meilleur du Chai Napa Valley 1984 • $33 • (03/31/89) • **94**

Le Meilleur du Chai Napa Valley 1983 • $33 • (03/01/89) • **90**

Merlot Napa Valley 1991 • $20 • (03/15/94) • **82**

Merlot Napa Valley 1990 • $16 • (07/15/93) • **84**

Merlot Napa Valley 1989 • $16 • (11/15/91) • **84**

Merlot Napa Valley 1987 • $14 • (02/15/90) • **87**

Merlot Napa Valley 1986 • $14 • (07/31/89) • **78**

Zinfandel Napa Valley 1993: Combines toasty buttery oak with zesty Zinfandel flavors, picking up lots of spice, earth and raspberry notes. Strikes a nice balance of fruit and oak. 550 cases made. • $18 • (07/31/95) • **88**

ROSENBLUM | CALIFORNIA

Cabernet Sauvignon Napa Valley 1989 • $17 • (08/31/92) • **80**

Cabernet Sauvignon Napa Valley George Hendry Vineyard 1990: Distinctive for its minty herbal notes, the currant flavor takes on a dill and oak flavor on the way to a dense, chewy, tannic finish. Young and in need of cellaring, it's best to lay away until 1998. 800 cases made. • $14 • (11/15/93) • **84**

Cabernet Sauvignon Napa Valley George Hendry Vineyard Reserve 1991: Ripe and intense, with a firm band of racy raspberry, cherry and currant flavors. This is crisp and tannic, but has enough fruit to merit cellaring until 1998. 500 cases made. • $30 • (11/15/94) • **88**

Cabernet Sauvignon Napa Valley Holbrook Mitchell Vineyard 1991: Well proportioned, complex and inviting. Has typical ripe, smooth, polished Cabernet flavors of plum, cherry and currant that pick up spicy oak flavors on the long finish. Drink now. 311 cases made. • $14 • (10/31/94) • **90**

Holbrook Mitchell Trio Napa Valley 1993: Simple with light spice and berry notes of modest proportion. Picks up a trace of herb on the finish. Ready now. 600 cases made. • $23 • (12/15/95) • **80**

Holbrook Mitchell Trio Napa Valley 1992: An odd wine with sweet-tasting stewed plum and black cherry flavor that turns soft and fleshy on the finish. Best to cellar this one short-term in hopes it will come together. 675 cases made. • $23 • (11/15/94) • **85**

Holbrook Mitchell Trio Napa Valley 1991: Strongly herbal, with powerful mint, oregano and vanilla aromas and flavors running through the solid currant and earth notes. Hints at ash on the finish. Drinkable now. 47 percent Cabernet Franc, 35 percent Merlot and 18 percent Cabernet Sauvignon. 420 cases made. • $22 • (11/15/93) • **86**

Holbrook Mitchell Trio Napa Valley 1990: A complex arrangement of currant, cherry and mint flavors that are focused, intense and balanced. Still a bit rough and tannic, picking up a nice touch of rosemary on the aftertaste. Cellar through 1997. A blend of 37 percent Cabernet Sauvignon, 35 percent Cabernet Franc and 28 percent merlot. 400 cases made. • $22 • (11/15/92) • **87**

Merlot Napa Valley Holbrook Mitchell Vineyard 1989 • $20 • (05/31/92) • **80**

Merlot Russian River Valley 1989 • $14 • (05/31/92) • **85**

Merlot Russian River Valley Lone Oak Vineyard 1990 • $15 • (07/15/93) • **81**

Petite Sirah Napa Valley 1992: Almost velvety in texture, offering supple wild berry and plum flavor and a touch of smoke and leather on aftertaste. Best in 1998. 1,000 cases made. • $13 • (09/30/95) • **86**

Pinot Noir Napa Valley George Hendry Vineyard 1990 • $12 • (02/28/93) • **73**

Pinot Noir Russian River Valley Ellis Ranch 1991 • $9 • (02/28/94) • **80**

Zinfandel Alexander Valley Harris-Kratka Vineyard 1993: Rustic, earthy, woody and tannic, with wild berry flavors. Lacks the focus and finesse of most Rosenblum Zinfandels, but pleasant. 520 cases made. • $15 • (10/15/95) • **83**

Zinfandel California Vintners Cuvée X NV: Earthy but shows hints of wild berry and spice. A solid Zin for everyday drinking. 5,000 cases made. • $8 • (10/15/95) • **83**

Zinfandel California Vintners Cuvée IX NV: Supple and elegant, with light strawberry and cherry notes. Drinks well now. 4,000 cases made. • $8 • (10/15/94) • **81**

Zinfandel California Vintners Cuvée VI NV • $7 • (09/30/93) BB • **85**

Zinfandel California Vintners Cuvée V NV • $7 • (10/15/92) BB • **82**

Zinfandel California Vintners Cuvée IV NV • $7 • (10/15/92) • **84**

Zinfandel Contra Costa County 1994: Appealing for its ripe, forward fruitiness and layers of ripe cherry, plum and berry. Finishes in a flash of mild tannins, but it's the purity of fruit that's striking. 4,240 cases made. • $11 • (04/30/96) • **89**

Zinfandel Contra Costa County 1993: Firm, compact and earthy cherry and wild berry flavors. Finishes with unyielding tannins and doesn't bend much now. 2,600 cases made. • $11 • (09/30/95) • **86**

Zinfandel Contra Costa County 1992: Lean, earthy and gamy, with some fruit coming through on the finish. Needs until 1995 to soften, but it may never lose its gamy edge. 2,000 cases made. • $10 • (10/15/94) • **83**

Zinfandel Contra Costa County 1991 • $9 • (09/30/93) • **90**

Zinfandel Contra Costa County 1990 • $9 • (10/15/92) • **87**

Zinfandel Mount Veeder Brandlin Ranch 1993: Starts out firm and tight, showing off earthy wild berry and raspberry flavors, but it slowly reveals more fruit and depth. Drinkable now. 770 cases made. • $19 • (10/15/95) • **87**

Zinfandel Mount Veeder Brandlin Ranch 1992: Tight and firm, with a chewy core of plum and wild berry flavors. Turns austere and tannic on the finish, so it's best to cellar a year or two. 1,250 cases made. • $19 • (10/15/94) • **86**

Zinfandel Mount Veeder Brandlin Ranch 1991 • $15 • (09/30/93) • **88**

Zinfandel Napa Valley 1993: Firm and tight, an elegant style offering crushed black pepper and cherry-berry flavors that are fresh and vibrant. 3,400 cases made. • $14 • (04/30/96) • **87**

Zinfandel Napa Valley 1987 • $9 • (10/31/89) • **77**

Zinfandel Napa Valley George Hendry Vineyard 1989 • $13 • (10/15/92) • **84**

Zinfandel Napa Valley George Hendry Vineyard Reserve 1993: Smooth, plush, ripe plum and black cherry flavors are well focused and complex, picking up a spicy anise edge on the finish. Impressive for its vibrancy and texture. Has firm tannins, but they're well integrated. 1,450 cases made. • $22 • (04/30/96) • **90**

Zinfandel Napa Valley George Hendry Vineyard Reserve 1992: Ripe and fruity up front, with spicy cherry, raspberry and buttery oak flavors, turning elegant and supple. Drinkable now to 1997. 950 cases made. • $20 • (10/15/94) • **86**

Zinfandel Napa Valley Hendry Vineyard Reserve 1988 • $14 • (04/30/91) • **84**

Zinfandel Napa Valley Michael Marston Vineyard 1990 • $14 • (10/15/92) • **84**

Zinfandel Paso Robles 1990 • $10 • (10/15/92) • **87**

Zinfandel Paso Robles Richard Sauret Vineyard 1994: Tightly wound, showing intense cherry, plum and berry flavors and a finish of crisp acidity and firm tannins. 1,600 cases made. • $12 • (04/30/96) • **87**
Zinfandel Paso Robles Richard Sauret Vineyard 1993: Marked by well-defined cherry and plum notes that pick up a jammy edge on the finish, where tannins are smooth and round. Supple and polished. 1,320 cases made. • $12 • (09/30/95) • **88**
Zinfandel Paso Robles Richard Sauret Vineyard 1992: Lots of ripe, supple, focused black cherry and raspberry flavors that are fresh and lively. Finishes with firm tannins and a smooth aftertaste. 1,100 cases made. • $11 • (10/15/94) • **87**
Zinfandel Paso Robles Richard Sauret Vineyard 1991 • $10 • (09/30/93) • **88**
Zinfandel Sonoma County 1991 • $11 • (09/30/93) • **86**
Zinfandel Sonoma County 1990 • $12 • (09/30/92) • **90**
Zinfandel Sonoma County Old Vines 1993: Ripe and juicy, pretty plum, cherry and berry notes turning smooth and supple on the finish, where flavors linger. 3,330 cases made. • $13 • (09/30/95) • **88**
Zinfandel Sonoma County Old Vines 1992: Firm and compact, with a narrow band of currant and earthy flavors that turn tannic. Drinkable now. 2,700 cases made. • $12 • (10/15/94) • **85**
Zinfandel Sonoma Valley Samsel Vineyard Maggie's Reserve 1993: Tart and intense, sporting bright cherry, raspberry and anise notes that are ripe and elegant. Adds a burst of blackberry on the finish. 780 cases made. • $22 • (09/30/95) • **89**
Zinfandel Sonoma Valley Samsel Vineyard Maggie's Reserve 1992: Quintessential Zin, with lots of ripe cherry, berry, raspberry and plum notes that turn spicy on the finish. Elegant, medium-bodied and approachable now through 1997. 650 cases made. • $22 • (10/15/94) • **87**
Zinfandel Sonoma Valley Samsel Vineyard Maggie's Reserve 1991 • $16 • (09/30/93) • **91**
Zinfandel Sonoma Valley Samsel Vineyard Maggie's Reserve 1990 • $15 • (10/15/92) • **90**

ROSENTHAL | CALIFORNIA

Cabernet Sauvignon California 1992: Starts out promising ripe currant and cherry flavors, turns earthy and leathery, then regains its balance to finish with attractive currant and anise notes. Hangs together as it opens up. Best after 1999. 750 cases made. • $22 • (12/15/95) • **89**
Cabernet Sauvignon California 1991: First wine from this Beverly Hills-based estate. Elegant and concentrated, successfully combining tart, ripe, spicy Cabernet fruit with toasty, buttery oak. The finish has lots of flavor and finesse and a good dose of tannins. 200 cases made. • $20 • (11/15/94) • **91**

ROSEWOOD | CALIFORNIA

Chardonnay Monterey 1994: Ripe, spicy and sturdy, with slightly bitter but solid pineapple and caramel flavors. Second wine of Talbott. 1,000 cases made. • $10 • (06/15/96) • **80**

ROSS VALLEY | CALIFORNIA

Merlot Sonoma Valley 1992: Tart and a bit sour, concentrated cherry and berry flavors have a distinctly grapey accent. Finish is dry, and has a tannic edge it may or may not outgrow. • $13 • **82**
Zinfandel Russian River Valley Tom and Kelly Parsons' Vineyard 1993: Ruggedly tannic, showing a dense, earthy rim to the pepper and wild berry notes, but in the end tannins dominate. Hold another year in hopes it softens. 350 cases made. • $12 • (05/15/96) • **83**
Zinfandel Sonoma County Tom and Kelley Parsons' Vineyard 1988 • $11 • (08/31/91) • **83**

ROUDON-SMITH | CALIFORNIA

Cabernet Sauvignon California 1991: A safe and correct Cabernet that's fairly priced, but has no real distinctive features. Light Cabernet and oak flavors are pleasant. Drink now. 260 cases made. • $10 • (11/15/93) • **77**
Cabernet Sauvignon Santa Cruz Mountains 1986 • $12 • (03/15/91) • **81**
Cabernet Sauvignon Santa Cruz Mountains 1984 • $12 • (06/30/88) • **78**
Cabernet Sauvignon Santa Cruz Mountains 1978 • $20 • (11/15/92) • **65**
Chardonnay Central Coast 1991: Simple with woody pear and citrus notes. Ready. 1,043 cases made. • $10 • (06/30/94) • **78**
Claret Cuvée Five California NV • $4 • (03/31/89) • **78**
Petite Sirah San Luis Obispo County 1984 • $8 • (09/30/88) • **84**
Pinot Noir Santa Cruz Mountains 1989 • $15 • (02/28/93) • **70**
Pinot Noir Santa Cruz Mountains 1985 • $15 • (06/15/88) • **86**
Pinot Noir Santa Cruz Mountains Cox Vineyard 1989 • $15 • (06/15/93) • **82**
Pinot Noir Santa Cruz Mountains Cox Vineyard 1987 • $15 • (02/28/91) • **84**
Zinfandel San Luis Obispo County 1989 • $8 • (10/15/92) • **80**
Zinfandel San Luis Obispo County Beckwith Vineyard 1990 • $10 • (05/31/93) • **81**
Zinfandel Sonoma County 1988 • $12 • (02/15/91) • **87**
Zinfandel Sonoma Valley Chauvet Vineyard 1985 • $8 • (03/31/89) • **80**

ROUGETTE, LA | CALIFORNIA

Pinot Noir Carneros Truchard Vineyard 1992: Smooth and supple, with creamy, delicate cherry, vanilla and smoky oak flavors that build into a complex finish. 196 cases made. • $11 • (03/31/95) • **86**

ROUND HILL | CALIFORNIA

Cabernet Sauvignon California 1992: Soft and generous, a simple wine with strawberry and light plum fruit that hangs in there on the finish. Ready now. 22,000 cases made. • $7 • (12/15/95) • **83**
Cabernet Sauvignon California 1991: Simple but correct with mature Cabernet and oak flavors. Firmly tannic, but best consumed soon. 6,500 cases made. • $7 • (11/15/94) • **80**
Cabernet Sauvignon California 1990: Crisp and flavorful, a bit on the austere side, but tasty and zingy enough to echo leafy, spicy currant flavors on the finish. 2,716 cases made. • $7 • (05/31/94) BB • **84**
Cabernet Sauvignon California 1989 • $6 • (12/15/92) BB • **82**
Cabernet Sauvignon California House Lot 89 NV • $6 • (11/15/92) BB • **80**
Cabernet Sauvignon California House Lot 8 NV • $6 • (07/31/91) • **79**
Cabernet Sauvignon California House Lot 7 NV • $6 • (10/31/90) • **79**
Cabernet Sauvignon California House Lot 6 NV • $5 • (10/15/87) • **72**
Cabernet Sauvignon California House Lot 5 NV • $5 • (09/30/86) BB • **76**
Cabernet Sauvignon Napa Valley 1992: Chewy tannins wrap around a nice beam of currant and plum flavor that persists into a finish that's trying to be soft. Give it until 1999-2000. 4,492 cases made. • $12 • (12/15/95) • **85**
Cabernet Sauvignon Napa Valley 1988 • $9 • (11/15/91) • **81**
Cabernet Sauvignon Napa Valley 1986 • $8 • (10/15/88) • **82**
Cabernet Sauvignon Napa Valley 1984 • $8 • (05/31/88) • **84**
Cabernet Sauvignon Napa Valley 1982 • $9 • (05/16/86) • **88**
Cabernet Sauvignon Napa Valley 1981 • $9 • (03/16/85) • **86**
Cabernet Sauvignon Napa Valley 1980 • $7 • (04/16/84) • **81**
Cabernet Sauvignon Napa Valley Reserve 1990: Firm and chunky, with a narrow band of earthy currant and mineral flavor. Fans out a bit on the finish before the tannins clamp down. Best after 1997. 2,883 cases made. • $11 • (11/15/94) • **84**
Cabernet Sauvignon Napa Valley Reserve 1989: Austere, with crisp, firm, chunky currant and black cherry flavor, cellaring should soften this and make it more palatable. Better than bottle previously tasted. Drink 1995 to 2002. 3,000 cases made. • $11 • (11/15/94) • **83**
Cabernet Sauvignon Napa Valley Reserve 1988 • $10 • (02/15/93) • **75**
Cabernet Sauvignon Napa Valley Reserve 1987 • $11 • (11/15/91) • **77**
Cabernet Sauvignon Napa Valley Reserve 1986 • $9 • (06/30/90) • **80**
Cabernet Sauvignon Napa Valley Reserve 1985 • $11 • (05/31/88) • **86**
Cabernet Sauvignon Napa Valley Reserve 1984 • $10 • (10/31/87) • **88**
Cabernet Sauvignon Napa Valley Reserve 1983 • $9 • (12/15/86) • **92**
Chardonnay California 1993: Young and crisp, with a green character to the pear and apple flavors, but it fans out on the finish, where the fruit intensifies and gains complexity. A good wine at a good price. 100,000 cases made. • $7 • (04/30/95) BB • **86**

Key: SS—Spectator Selection. CS—Cellar Selection. BB—Best Buy. $NA—Price not available. (BT)—Barrel tasting. Ⓐ—Auction Price.
Dates in parentheses represent the issues in which the ratings were published.

Chardonnay California 1992: Light and simple, showing some nice peach and vanilla aromas and flavors. • $7 • (01/31/94) • **81**
Chardonnay California 1991 • $6 • (02/15/93) BB • **83**
Chardonnay Napa Valley Reserve 1993: Hard and woody, with a toasty oak flavors dominating the pear and grapefruit flavors, finishing with a touch of bitterness from wood. 3,200 cases made. • $11 • (07/31/95) • **82**
Chardonnay Napa Valley Reserve 1991 • $11 • (07/15/93) • **81**
Chardonnay Napa Valley Van Asperen Reserve 1991 • $11 • (07/15/93) • **84**
Chardonnay Napa Valley Van Asperen Selection Reserve 1993: Bright and fruity, with a cidery apple flavor at the core and spicy oak on the finish. Ready now. 250 cases made. • $12 • (07/31/95) • **83**
Chardonnay Napa Valley Van Asperen Selection Reserve 1992: Crisp and lean with simple earthy, grassy pear flavors. 450 cases made. • $12 • (06/30/94) • **81**
Fumé Blanc Napa Valley 1993: Immediately appealing peach and vanilla flavors linger in this bright, fruity, exuberant white. 1,244 cases made. • $7 • (08/31/95) • **85**
Fumé Blanc Napa Valley 1991 • $7 • (02/28/93) BB • **84**
Merlot California 1993: Simple and rustic, with cedary, cherry flavors that are dry at the start and become even dryer on the finish. 24,000 cases made. • $8 • **80**
Merlot California 1992: Earthy, oaky flavors override the simple Merlot notes. Ready now. • $7 • (09/15/94) • **77**
Merlot California 1990 • $7 • (01/31/93) BB • **84**
Merlot Napa Valley 1993: Pleasant, if unassuming, with plum and currant flavors. Turns thin and tannic on the finish, where the flavors taper off. 5,700 cases made. • $14 • **80**
Merlot Napa Valley 1984 • $9 • (05/15/87) • **87**
Merlot Napa Valley 1983 • $7 • (01/31/87) SS • **92**
Merlot Napa Valley 1982 • $7 • (02/16/86) • **65**
Merlot Napa Valley Reserve 1991: The strong leathery oak flavors dominate the fruit, so much so that this detracts from the quality. 1,120 cases made. • $11 • (09/15/94) • **78**
Merlot Napa Valley Reserve 1990 • $11 • (06/15/93) • **78**
Merlot Napa Valley Reserve 1989 • $11 • (05/31/92) • **78**
Merlot Napa Valley Reserve 1988 • $11 • (11/15/91) • **80**
Merlot Napa Valley Reserve 1986 • $11 • (12/31/88) • **82**
Merlot Napa Valley Reserve 1985 • $10 • (05/31/88) • **84**
Zinfandel Napa Valley 1993: Firm and tannic, with strong tar and anise flavors. There is just enough spicy cherry and berry to keep your attention. Good, but off-pace for this winery, which usually does better. 844 cases made. • $10 • (03/31/96) • **83**
Zinfandel Napa Valley 1992: Intense and lively, with spicy, minty aromatics and attractive wild berry and cherry flavors. Well crafted. 3,403 cases made. • $8 • (10/15/95) • **85**
Zinfandel Napa Valley 1990 • $6 • (10/15/92) BB • **85**
Zinfandel Napa Valley 1989 • $6 • (03/31/92) BB • **81**
Zinfandel Napa Valley 1988 • $6 • (02/15/91) BB • **89**
Zinfandel Napa Valley 1985 • $5 • (05/15/88) BB • **82**
Zinfandel Napa Valley 1981 • $5 • (04/16/84) • **84**
Zinfandel Napa Valley Select 1987 • $6 • (03/31/90) BB • **84**

ROYCE | CALIFORNIA

Cabernet Sauvignon Napa Valley 1989 • $10 • (12/15/92) • **77**
Cabernet Sauvignon Sonoma County 1987 • $12 • (11/15/92) • **80**
Chardonnay California 1991 • $10 • (02/15/93) • **78**
Merlot Napa Valley Reserve 1990 • $16 • (01/31/93) • **81**
Merlot Sonoma County 1991 • $12 • (06/30/93) • **85**

RUBISSOW-SARGENT | CALIFORNIA

Cabernet Sauvignon Mount Veeder 1991: Ripe and soft, showing rich currant and plum flavors, edging toward earthy tannins on the finish. Best from 1998. 1,344 cases made. • $16 • (12/15/95) • **84**
Cabernet Sauvignon Mount Veeder 1990: Lean and a bit green, with austere cedar, currant and spice notes, it could use a little more richness and depth. Best after 1997. 1,008 cases made. • $16 • (11/15/94) • **84**
Cabernet Sauvignon Mount Veeder 1988 • $16 • (04/15/92) • **87**
Les Trompettes Mount Veeder 1990: Firm and compact, with a narrow band of earthy Cabernet flavor that finishes with crisp tannins. Needs short-term cellaring to soften, best after 1997. 455 cases made. • $18 • (11/15/94) • **85**
Les Trompettes Mount Veeder 1989: Lean, tannic and earthy, typical of the 1989 vintage with its hollow murky flavors. 288 cases made. • $18 • (11/15/94) • **79**
Merlot Mount Veeder 1992: Pleasant enough, with pretty plum, currant, herb and spice notes of moderate proportion. Finishes with a smoky oak and anise edge, has the tannic strength to age into 1997. 790 cases made. • $16 • (05/15/96) • **85**
Merlot Mount Veeder 1990: Rich and lavishly oaked, but with enough complex fruit to stand up to it. Shows spicy currant, cherry and plum notes, finishing with fleshy tannins. 794 cases made. • $15 • (09/15/94) • **86**
Merlot Mount Veeder 1989 • $15 • (08/31/93) • **76**
Merlot Mount Veeder 1988 • $15 • (05/31/92) • **84**

RUSTRIDGE | CALIFORNIA

Cabernet Sauvignon Napa Valley 1991: Medium bodied, with a trim band of currant and cedar. Less tannic than the 1990 Reserve, but still in need of cellaring in hopes the tannins subside. 550 cases made. • $20 • (12/15/95) • **87**
Cabernet Sauvignon Napa Valley 1990: Firmly tannic, almost to a fault, as it's dry and austere, with a narrow band of cedar and coffee laced Cabernet fruit, but doesn't measure up to its • $30 price tag. 220 cases made. • $30 • (12/15/95) • **82**
Cabernet Zinfandel Napa Valley 1991 • $18 • (09/30/93) • **82**

RUTHERFORD ESTATE | CALIFORNIA

Cabernet Sauvignon Napa Valley 1991: Austere and tannic, with drying flavors of modest depth and proportion. Tough and chewy, hard to warm up to, perhaps cellaring will soften it. • $7 • (11/15/94) • **81**
Cabernet Sauvignon Napa Valley 1987 • $6 • (08/31/92) BB • **84**
Cabernet Sauvignon Napa Valley 1986 • $7 • (11/15/91) • **80**
Cabernet Sauvignon Napa Valley 1984 • $5 • (11/15/87) • **72**
Chardonnay California Barrel Select 1994: Bright and citrusy, a lively mouthful of peach and citrus flavor, softening on the finish. Drinkable now. • $7 • (05/15/96) • **84**
Chardonnay Napa Valley 1992: Has a distinct peppery edge, which is unusual for Chardonnay, but there's also a nice core of pear and cedary oak flavors to latch onto. Ready now. • $7 • (06/30/94) • **80**
Merlot Napa Valley 1991: Bright and fruity, soft in texture and fragrant, with berry and currant flavors. Drinkable now. 14,000 cases made. • $7 • (06/30/94) BB • **84**
Pinot Noir Napa Valley 1992: Supple and fruity, with simple plum and cherry notes. Drinkable now. 9,000 cases made. • $7 • (01/31/95) • **81**
Sauvignon Blanc Napa Valley 1992: Light and smooth, offering a mild vanilla edge to the herbal pear notes. 7,500 cases made. • $6 • (08/31/95) • **82**
White Zinfandel California 1994: Off-dry, showing nice cherry and berry notes. Has some body and balance and loads of good fruit aromas and flavors. Clean, well made, good dose of apricot on the finish. • $7 • (09/15/95) • **83**

RUTHERFORD HILL | CALIFORNIA

Cabernet Sauvignon Napa Valley 1991: Austere and tannic, with drying flavors of modest depth and proportion. Tough and chewy, hard to warm up to, perhaps cellaring will soften it. 13,000 cases made. • $14 • (11/15/94) • **81**
Cabernet Sauvignon Napa Valley 1987 • $16 • (11/15/92) • **85**
Cabernet Sauvignon Napa Valley 1986 • $14 • (02/28/91) • **68**
Cabernet Sauvignon Napa Valley 1985 • $17 • (04/30/90) • **82**
Cabernet Sauvignon Napa Valley 1984 • $22 • (03/01/89) • **88**
Cabernet Sauvignon Napa Valley 1983 • $21 • (03/01/89) • **83**
Cabernet Sauvignon Napa Valley 1982 • $18 • (03/01/89) • **83**
Cabernet Sauvignon Napa Valley 1981 • $18 • (03/01/89) • **85**
Cabernet Sauvignon Napa Valley 1980 • $21 • (03/01/89) • **82**
Cabernet Sauvignon Napa Valley 1979 • $20 • (03/01/89) • **87**
Cabernet Sauvignon Napa Valley 1978 • $25 • (11/15/92) • **78**
Cabernet Sauvignon Napa Valley 1977 • $22 • (03/01/89) • **72**

Cabernet Sauvignon Napa Valley 1976 • $32 • (03/01/89) • **73**
Cabernet Sauvignon Napa Valley 1975 • $18 • (03/01/89) • **69**
Cabernet Sauvignon Napa Valley Cask Lot 2 Limited Edition 1980 • $21 • (03/01/89) • **88**
Cabernet Sauvignon Napa Valley XVS 1987 • $26 • (11/15/92) • **86**
Cabernet Sauvignon Napa Valley XVS 1986 • $22 • (03/01/89) • **88**
Cabernet Sauvignon Napa Valley XVS 1985 • $29 • (04/30/89) • **88**
Chardonnay Napa Valley Exceptional Vineyard Selection Reserve 1992: Marked by ripe, spicy pear and light oak shadings, but ultimately simple. • $20 • (07/31/95) • **83**
Chardonnay Napa Valley Exceptional Vineyard Selection Reserve 1991: Crisp, spicy and toasty with grapefruit and pineapple flavors sneaking in on the finish. 1,203 cases made. • $19 • (06/30/94) • **83**
Merlot Napa Valley 1991: Lean and trim, with simple berry and cherry flavors that turn simple and light on the finish. 45,000 cases made. • $16 • (09/15/94) • **82**
Merlot Napa Valley 1989 • $14 • (05/31/92) • **70**
Merlot Napa Valley 1988 • $15 • (05/31/92) • **82**
Merlot Napa Valley 1987 • $14 • (03/31/91) • **74**
Merlot Napa Valley 1986 • $13 • (06/15/90) • **68**
Merlot Napa Valley 1985 • $12 • (01/31/89) • **92**
Merlot Napa Valley 1984 • $11 • (04/30/88) • **84**
Merlot Napa Valley 1983 • $10 • (08/31/87) • **87**
Merlot Napa Valley 1982 • $11 • (05/16/86) • **79**
Merlot Napa Valley 1981 • $10 • (10/01/85) • **78**
Merlot Napa Valley Exceptional Vineyard Selections Reserve 1993: Thin and earthy, with narrow stripe of leathery flavors. Lacks focus and depth, and turns almost sour on the finish. 50,000 cases made. • $15 • **77**
Merlot Napa Valley Twentieth Anniversary 1994: A good balance of ripe cherry and currant flavors, light oak accents and firm tannins. On the finish, the fruit comes through. 58,000 cases made. • $15 • **85**
Merlot Napa Valley XVS Reserve 1992: Tight and intense, with a woody, cedary edge to the rich currant and black cherry flavors. Finishes with a firm tannic edge. 1,335 cases made. • $21 • (06/15/95) • **85**
Port Napa Valley Vintage 1983 • $18 • (11/15/87) • **66**

RUTHERFORD RANCH | CALIFORNIA

Cabernet Sauvignon Napa Valley 1991: Tart and intense, with spicy black cherry and currant notes that pick up an anise and cedar edge on the finish. Holds together nicely. Best after 1997. 3,480 cases made. • $10 • (11/15/94) • **86**
Cabernet Sauvignon Napa Valley 1987 • $13 • (04/30/91) • **83**
Cabernet Sauvignon Napa Valley 1985 • $11 • (05/15/90) SS • **92**
Cabernet Sauvignon Napa Valley 1984 • $13 • (05/31/89) • **85**
Cabernet Sauvignon Napa Valley 1983 • $11 • (12/31/87) • **83**
Cabernet Sauvignon Napa Valley 1982 • $11 • (06/15/87) • **84**
Chardonnay Napa Valley 1993: Sturdy and nicely focused, generous with its spicy pear flavors. Ready now. 5,432 cases made. • $9 • (07/31/95) • **82**
Chardonnay Napa Valley 1992: Fresh, lively, focused, bright apple and pear flavors keep bouncing through the finish. Drinkable now. 4,857 cases made. • $9 • (05/31/95) BB • **86**
Meritage Quintessence Napa Valley 1991: Lean and juicy, on the tart side, almost Barbera-like with bright berry and currant fruit and modest tannins. Well made and drinkable now. 500 cases made. • $20 • (12/15/95) • **86**
Meritage Quintessence Napa Valley 1989: Crisp and lean showing a narrow acidic band of spice, oak and black cherry flavor and finishing with firm tannins. A good 1989 but typical of the vintage and its austerity. Drink from now to 2000. • $16 • (11/15/94) • **83**
Merlot Napa Valley 1992: Lean and a little chewy, showing a bead of blackberry and tar flavor that extends into the finish. Best from 1997. 6,564 cases made. • $10 • (04/15/95) • **82**
Merlot Napa Valley 1990 • $9 • (03/31/93) • **82**
Merlot Napa Valley 1988 • $12 • (08/31/91) • **80**
Merlot Napa Valley 1986 • $12 • (12/31/88) • **87**

Key: SS—Spectator Selection. CS—Cellar Selection. BB—Best Buy. $NA—Price not available. (BT)—Barrel tasting. (A)—Auction Price.
Dates in parentheses represent the issues in which the ratings were published.

Merlot Napa Valley 1985 • $11 • (04/30/88) • **92**
Merlot Napa Valley 1984 • $9 • (10/15/87) • **83**
Sauvignon Blanc Napa Valley 1993 • $7 • (05/15/94) • **85**
Zinfandel Napa Valley 1992: Ripe and jammy, showing hints of raisin and tar, which give this some unique flavors. Turns spicy and elegant on the finish, and reveals a touch of heat. 1,287 cases made. • $8 • (08/31/95) • **85**
Zinfandel Napa Valley 1986 • $7 • (10/31/88) • **62**
Zinfandel Napa Valley 1985 • $7 • (03/15/88) • **89**
Zinfandel Napa Valley 1982 • $6 • (09/16/85) • **80**

RUTHERFORD VINEYARDS | CALIFORNIA

Cabernet Sauvignon Napa Valley Rutherford Bench 1992: Smooth, supple and generous with its plum, berry, spice and vanilla flavors that keep weaving through . Tannins can use until 1998, but it's appealing now. 5,000 cases made. • $8 • (12/15/95) • **87**
Chardonnay Napa Valley 1993: Light and easy to drink, inserting a hint of passion fruit among the pear and toast flavors. Drinkable now. 3,000 cases made. • $8 • (06/15/95) BB • **86**
Fumé Blanc Napa Valley 1993: Bright, citrusy, lively, generous peach, apple and grapefruit flavors remain fresh through the finish. 2,500 cases made. • $8 • (08/31/95) • **87**

RUTZ CELLARS | CALIFORNIA

Chardonnay Russian River Valley 1993: Ripe and fruity, with a smoky edge to the pear, honey, melon and spice notes. Picks up a slight bitter edge from oak on the finish. • $18 • **83**
Pinot Noir Russian River Valley Dutton Ranch 1993: Mature-looking in color, with earthy tea, dried cherry, tar and spice notes. The texture is smooth and plush, with drying tannins on the finish. • $24 • (01/31/96) • **85**
Pinot Noir Russian River Valley Quail Hill Vineyard 1993: Showing some maturity, but the dried cherry, cedar and spice flavors are a shade fresher than in the Dutton Ranch bottling. • $24 • (01/31/96) • **87**

SADDLE MOUNTAIN | WASHINGTON

Blush White Riesling Columbia Valley 1988 • $5 • (10/15/89) • **59**

SADDLEBACK | CALIFORNIA

Cabernet Sauvignon Napa Valley 1993: Dark, ripe, plush and concentrated, with layers of currant, plum, black cherry and mineral. Finishes with a hint of anise and cedar, all adding to its complexity. Ready in 1997, but should age well into 2000 and beyond. • $19 • (05/31/96) • **92**
Cabernet Sauvignon Napa Valley 1992: Marked by pronounced olive and vegetal flavors with a burnt bell pepper flavors, but it counters with just enough currant and cherry fruit to keep it in balance. Turns complex on the finish where the flavors fold together. 986 cases made. • $17 • (12/15/95) • **87**
Cabernet Sauvignon Napa Valley 1991: A rich and oaky style, with currant, black cherry and buttery oak flavors that fold together nicely, leading into a complex and flavorful finish. Plush and supple enough to drink now or you can cellar it through 1997. 960 cases made. • $17 • (10/31/94) • **90**
Cabernet Sauvignon Napa Valley 1990: Ripe, smooth and spicy with a pretty, supple core of Cabernet fruit. Mild tannins on the finish make this drinkable now. 900 cases made. • $15 • (11/15/93) • **84**
Cabernet Sauvignon Napa Valley 1988 • $14 • (08/31/92) • **73**
Cabernet Sauvignon Napa Valley Family Reserve 1989: A weedy, herbal style but true to the vintage. Finishes with just enough ripe Cabernet fruit to hold your interest, but it's doubtful if it will get much better. 100 cases made. • $25 • (11/15/94) • **85**
Cabernet Sauvignon Napa Valley Family Reserve 1988 • $24 • (11/15/93) • **81**
Chardonnay Napa Valley 1993: Modest pear and apple flavors are ripe and floral, but there's a coarseness to the texture. 650 cases made. • $13 • (07/31/95) • **81**

Chardonnay Napa Valley Nils Venge 1992: Simple and coarse, grassy in flavor like biting into an unripe apple. 889 cases made. • $13 • (06/30/94) • **73**

Chardonnay Napa Valley Nils Venge 1991: Tart and simple, with green apple and unripe pine-apple aromas and flavors that become almost minty on the finish. 869 cases made. • $12 • (06/30/94) • **78**

SADDLEGROVE | CALIFORNIA

Chardonnay California 1991 • $7 • (07/15/93) • **73**

ST. AMANT | CALIFORNIA

Port Amador County Late Bottled 1991: Soft, plush, ripe-and-ready style that balances its fresh plum and spice flavors without a hard bite of alcohol. Ready now. 350 cases made. • $12 • (05/15/96) • **86**

Port Amador County Reserve 1992: Hard-edged and spicy around black cherry and anise flavors, finishing under a gentle grip of tannin and alcohol. Best in 2000. 450 cases made. • $18 • (05/15/96) • **88**

ST. ANDREW'S VINEYARD | CALIFORNIA

Chardonnay Napa Valley 1993: Simple with floral and pear notes that finish with a cloying edge. • $12 • (07/31/95) • **82**

Chardonnay Napa Valley 1992: Simple and appealing, has some reserve, seems to be holding back its spicy pear and apple flavors. Drink now. • $10 • (06/30/94) • **83**

Chardonnay Napa Valley Limited Reserve 1991: Serves up elegant pear, spice and light oak flavors, but it lacks the richness and concentration of the best wines of the vintage. Ready now. • $18 • (06/30/94) • **84**

ST. ANDREW'S WINERY | CALIFORNIA

Cabernet Sauvignon Napa Valley 1986 • $15 • (04/30/90) • **87**
Cabernet Sauvignon Napa Valley 1985 • $11 • (05/15/88) • **89**
Chardonnay Napa Valley 1991 • $10 • (07/15/93) • **86**
Sauvignon Blanc Napa Valley 1991 • $6 • (09/15/93) • **77**

ST. CLEMENT | CALIFORNIA

Cabernet Sauvignon Howell Mountain 1994: Young with a grapey edge to the plush currant and cherry fruit. Turns supple and elegant. 250 cases made. • $30 • (05/31/95) • **85-89** (BT)

Cabernet Sauvignon Napa Valley 1994: Still a touch grapey, but the floral and berry notes are attractive in a medium-bodied style. 3,500 cases made. • $25 • (05/31/95) • **85-89** (BT)

Cabernet Sauvignon Napa Valley 1992: Beautiful core of ripe, rich currant, berry and plum-scented fruit. Floral, supple yet firmly tannic, with pretty toasty oak shadings. Very tasty even at this stage. • $NA • (05/31/93) BT • **790**

Cabernet Sauvignon Napa Valley 1992: Pleasantly balanced between ripe plum and cherry flavors and light oak shadings. Finishes with good focus and a fruity aftertaste. Age into 1998 to 1999. 3,200 cases made. • $24 • (10/31/95) • **90**

Cabernet Sauvignon Napa Valley 1991: Tight and compact, but well focused, with intense, spicy currant, black cherry and anise notes that turn elegant and supple on the finish. Has the richness, depth and concentration to improve into the next century, best to cellar until 1997 or 1998. 4,600 cases made. • $23 • (09/30/94) SS • **90**

Cabernet Sauvignon Napa Valley 1990: Firm and chunky, with a full complement of currant, berry and spice aromas and flavors, picking up hints of herb and toast on the long finish. Has style and power, with enough tannin to want until 1998-2000. 2,600 cases made. • $22 • (10/31/93) • **90**

Cabernet Sauvignon Napa Valley 1989 • $23 • (11/15/92) • **84**
Cabernet Sauvignon Napa Valley 1988 • $22 • (03/31/92) • **86**
Cabernet Sauvignon Napa Valley 1987 • $23 • (09/30/91) CS • **90**
Cabernet Sauvignon Napa Valley 1986 • $18 • (03/01/89) • **87**
Cabernet Sauvignon Napa Valley 1985 • $17 • (03/01/89) • **93**
Cabernet Sauvignon Napa Valley 1984 • $28 • (03/01/89) • **89**
Cabernet Sauvignon Napa Valley 1983 • $25 • (03/01/89) • **91**
Cabernet Sauvignon Napa Valley 1982 • $29 • (03/01/89) • **91**
Cabernet Sauvignon Napa Valley 1981 • $33 • (03/01/89) • **85**
Cabernet Sauvignon Napa Valley 1980 • $25 • (03/01/89) • **82**
Cabernet Sauvignon Napa Valley 1979 • $38 • (03/01/89) • **90**
Cabernet Sauvignon Napa Valley 1978 • $33 • (03/01/89) • **88**
Cabernet Sauvignon Napa Valley 1977 • $31 • (03/01/89) • **90**
Cabernet Sauvignon Napa Valley 1975-76 • $50 • (03/01/89) • **87**
Chardonnay Carneros Abbotts Vineyard 1991 • $18 • (07/15/93) • **88**

Chardonnay Carneros Napa Valley Abbotts Vineyard 1993: Simple and uncomplicated, with spicy pear and honey notes. 3,500 cases made. • $18 • (07/31/95) • **84**

Chardonnay Napa Valley 1991 • $16 • (04/15/93) • **86**

Chardonnay Napa Valley Carneros 1992: Complex and enticing, with firm, sharply focused pear, spice, toast and honeyed notes that are rich and concentrated, fanning out on the finish. Another finely crafted St. Clement Chardonnay. Ready now. 4,090 cases made. • $16 • (03/31/94) SS • **90**

Chardonnay Napa Valley Carneros Abbotts Vineyard 1994: Light and simple, with a modest band of pear, spice and vanilla flavors that fan out on the finish. A pleasant, easy-drinking wine. 3,000 cases made. • $21 • (06/30/96) • **84**

Chardonnay Napa Valley Carneros Abbotts Vineyard 1991 • $18 • (12/31/93) • **90**

Merlot Napa Valley 1993: Openly fruity, not relying on smoky, toasty oak for its flavor yet offering pleasant plum, cherry, currant and spice. Loses its focus on the finish where the notes become diffuse. Best in 1997. 5,000 cases made. • $18 • (04/30/96) • **87**

Merlot Napa Valley 1992: Ripe and chunky, exhibiting cherry, earth, currant and light oak shadings that turn spicy and fruity on the finish. Just misses, but might get there soon. 2,900 cases made. • $21 • (03/31/95) • **88**

Merlot Napa Valley 1991: An austere Merlot that's tough and tannic around the edges. Once you dig into the currant and black cherry fruit it's inviting, but getting there is tough and tannic. Drinkable now. Tasted twice with consistent notes. 2,000 cases made. • $20 • (09/15/94) • **83**

Merlot Napa Valley 1990 • $20 • (05/31/93) • **88**
Merlot Napa Valley 1989 • $18 • (05/31/92) • **87**
Merlot Napa Valley 1987 • $16 • (12/31/90) • **85**
Merlot Napa Valley 1986 • $15 • (10/31/89) • **74**
Merlot Napa Valley 1985 • $15 • (03/31/89) • **91**
Merlot Napa Valley 1983 • $15 • (05/31/88) • **81**

Oroppas Napa Valley 1993: Strikes a fine balance between toasty, buttery oak and ripe, juicy plum and currant flavors-a wine of elegance and finesse. Doesn't have quite the depth and richness of the past two vintages, but still impressive. 650 cases made. • $30 • (10/31/95) • **92**

Oroppas Napa Valley 1992: A solid wine with a rich core of ripe plum, black cherry, currant and new-oak flavors, all of which are bright and well focused. Finishes with a long, full, rich aftertaste. Has the depth and concentration to age well into the next decade. Delicious and merits special attention. 650 cases made. • $25 • (09/30/94) CS • **95**

Oroppas Napa Valley 1991: Bold, ripe, rich and generous with tiers of supple black cherry, currant, spice and anise, all sharply focused and picking up pretty toasted oak and coffee notes on a long, lingering finish. Beautifully crafted and impeccably balanced, it's tasty now but should reach its peak around 1998. 150 cases made. • $22 • (10/31/93) • **94**

Sauvignon Blanc Napa Valley 1994: Lean and focused, offering definite cigar box, cedary overtones to the pear and fig flavors. Drink now. 2,800 cases made. • $12 • (08/31/95) • **87**

Sauvignon Blanc Napa Valley 1993: Floral pear flavors and a soft texture linger nicely on the delicate finish. 2,300 cases made. • $11 • (02/28/95) • **84**

Sauvignon Blanc Napa Valley 1992 • $11 • (09/15/93) • **84**
Sauvignon Blanc Napa Valley 1991 • $11 • (11/30/92) • **84**

ST. FRANCIS | CALIFORNIA

Brut Sonoma Valley 1984 • $9 • (12/16/85) • **82**
Cabernet Franc Sonoma Valley 1989 • $14 • (11/15/93) • **83**
Cabernet Sauvignon California 1985 • $9 • (11/30/87) • **88**

Cabernet Sauvignon Sonoma County 1993: Ripe and intense, with earthy plum, cherry, anise and leather, finishing with firm tannins and crisp acidity. Hangs together but not as much complexity as previous vintages. 25,000 cases made. • $12 • (11/30/95) • **85**

Cabernet Sauvignon Sonoma County 1992: Serves up a nice array of bright, ripe Cabernet fruit, but it's still a little rough around the edges where the tannins kick in. Ready now through 1998. • $10 • (11/15/94) • **85**

Cabernet Sauvignon Sonoma County 1991: Intense and earthy, with bell pepper notes, and chocolate, herb and currant flavors. Drinkable now. • $10 • (09/15/93) • **84**

Cabernet Sauvignon Sonoma County 1990: Smooth and ripe, with a generous beam of plum and currant fruit, with a nice touch of toasty oak on the finish. Drinkable now. 1,300 cases made. • $10 • (09/30/93) • **89**

Cabernet Sauvignon Sonoma County 1989 • $10 • (09/30/93) • **84**

Cabernet Sauvignon Sonoma County 1988 • $14 • (08/31/91) • **90**

Cabernet Sauvignon Sonoma County 1986 • $12 • (01/31/90) • **89**

Cabernet Sauvignon Sonoma County Reserve 1994: Ripe and complex, with a pretty array of black cherry, currant and cedary oak, especially impressive for its finish, where the flavors fold together nicely. 4,000 cases made. • $25 • (05/31/95) • **90-94** (BT)

Cabernet Sauvignon Sonoma County Reserve 1992: This is deep, dark and intense, with a complex core of currant, chocolate, black cherry and toasty oak. A distinct and well-crafted wine that oozes with complex flavors. Best to age until 1998. 2,000 cases made. • $24 • (11/30/95) • **92**

Cabernet Sauvignon Sonoma County Reserve 1991: Complex and enticing, with exotic cedar, coffee and vanilla aromas and supple currant, cherry and chocolate flavors. Tight and tannic now, give it until 1997. 2,500 cases made. • $24 • (11/15/94) • **88**

Cabernet Sauvignon Sonoma County Reserve 1990: Firm, focused and flavorful, a narrow beam of berry, currant, coffee and cedar flavors dancing brightly, hinting at chocolate on the fine-textured finish. Drinkable now, probably best 1997-2000. 2,500 cases made. • $24 • (09/30/93) • **91**

Cabernet Sauvignon Sonoma Valley Reserve 1989 • $24 • (11/15/92) • **89**

Cabernet Sauvignon Sonoma Valley Reserve 1988 • $24 • (08/31/91) • **87**

Cabernet Sauvignon Sonoma Valley Reserve (Black Label) 1986 • $20 • (11/30/89) • **94**

Chardonnay Sonoma County 1994: A sweet and fruity white that's light and straightforward, a good value at this price. 50,000 cases made. • $10 • (05/15/96) • **84**

Chardonnay Sonoma County 1993: A little heavy-handed with buttery oak flavors now, overriding the pear and spice notes. May be more appealing with time in the bottle. • $12 • (11/30/94) • **82**

Chardonnay Sonoma County 1992: Young and compact with tight pear, hazelnut, spice and oak flavors that finish with a blunt edge. Needs time in the bottle. • $10 • (05/31/94) • **84**

Chardonnay Sonoma County 1991 • $9 • (08/31/92) • **84**

Chardonnay Sonoma Valley Reserve 1993: A distinctive style that blends its smoky, toasty oak flavors nicely with the ripe, spicy pear and fig flavors. 2,000 cases made. • $19 • (04/15/95) • **90**

Chardonnay Sonoma Valley Reserve Estate 1994: Strives for complexity in toast and butterscotch flavors. Ripe pear and smoky oak notes fold in nicely on the finish, as its depth becomes more evident. 4,500 cases made. • $20 • (05/15/96) • **90**

Chardonnay Sonoma Valley Reserve Estate 1992: Complex and concentrated, beautifully crafted, exhibiting pretty, smoky, toasty oak that leads to ripe, spicy pear, apple and pineapple flavors. Turns smooth and creamy on a long, full finish. Delicious now through 1997. 2,500 cases made. • $15 • (04/30/94) SS • **91**

Chardonnay Sonoma Valley Reserve Estate 1991 • $15 • (07/15/93) • **85**

Gewürztraminer Sonoma County 1992: Soft, almost watery, with bitter almond and sweet grapey flavors trying to achieve a varietal intensity. It falls short. • $11 • (11/15/94) • **73**

Gewürztraminer Sonoma County 1991 • $10 • (01/31/93) • **82**

Merlot Sonoma Valley 1992: 1,300 cases made. • $20 • **87**

Merlot Sonoma Valley 1991: Atypical in varietal character, it keeps you guessing with its wild meaty and spicy flavors. But on the palate it hangs together, with herb, oak and currant flavors and a supple texture. Ready now through 1998. 13,000 cases made. • $18 • (07/31/94) • **86**

Merlot Sonoma Valley 1990 • $18 • (05/31/93) • **88**

Merlot Sonoma Valley 1989 • $14 • (05/31/92) • **79**

Merlot Sonoma Valley 1988 • $16 • (11/15/91) • **82**

Merlot Sonoma Valley 1987 • $14 • (06/15/90) • **80**

Merlot Sonoma Valley 1986 • $14 • (06/30/89) • **85**

Merlot Sonoma Valley 1985 • $12 • (10/15/88) • **66**

Merlot Sonoma Valley 1984 • $12 • (10/31/87) • **88**

Merlot Sonoma Valley 1983 • $11 • (07/31/87) • **80**

Merlot Sonoma Valley 1982 • $11 • (10/01/85) • **78**

Merlot Sonoma Valley Estate Reserve 1993: Smooth and supple, with ripe cherry, currant and berry notes. Holds its fruity flavors through the finish, when the sweet toasty oak folds in. Drinkable now. 5,000 cases made. • $26 • (08/31/96) • **88**

Merlot Sonoma Valley Estate Reserve 1990 • $24 • (05/31/93) • **91**

Merlot Sonoma Valley Reserve 1991: An herbal style with lots of spicy flavors, but it turns richly fruity on the palate, where the currant and cherry are evident. Lavishly oaked, and the texture is smooth and supple. Ready now. 2,500 cases made. • $24 • (09/15/94) • **89**

Merlot Sonoma Valley Reserve 1989 • $24 • (05/31/92) • **90**

Merlot Sonoma Valley Reserve 1988 • $24 • (11/15/91) • **82**

Merlot Sonoma Valley Reserve 1986 • $20 • (01/31/90) • **94**

Merlot Sonoma Valley Reserve 1985 • $15 • (12/31/88) • **81**

Merlot Sonoma Valley Reserve 1984 • $16 • (02/15/88) • **74**

Pinot Noir Sonoma Valley 1986 • $14 • (06/15/88) • **74**

Zinfandel Sonoma Valley Old Vines 1993: Complex and appealing, the minty, spicy notes are followed by pretty cherry and raspberry flavors. Turns smooth and supple, with mild tannins. A big, bold style that manages to hang in balance. 1,680 cases made. • $18 • (10/15/95) • **91**

Zinfandel Sonoma Valley Old Vines 1992: Spicy and aromatic, with bay and dill notes, but the ripe Zinfandel fruit comes through, revealing a dark berry and gamy edge. Packs in lots of flavor. Drinkable now. 1,750 cases made. • $14 • (10/15/94) • **87**

Zinfandel Sonoma Valley Old Vines 1990 • $12 • (10/15/92) • **88**

Zinfandel Sonoma Valley Old Vines 1989 • $12 • (03/31/92) • **76**

ST. GEORGE, DOMAINE | CALIFORNIA

Cabernet Sauvignon California Vintage Reserve 1992: Supple and generous, with ripe, bright, fleshy cherry and plum flavors. Very appealing and easy to drink now. 15,000 cases made. • $6 • (11/15/94) BB • **85**

Cabernet Sauvignon Russian River Valley Premier Cuvée Reserve 1989: Spicy, with a cedary oak frame and chewy tannins, it delivers just enough ripe Cabernet fruit to keep in balance. Ready now. 800 cases made. • $10 • (11/15/94) • **83**

Cabernet Sauvignon Russian River Valley Select Reserve 1986 • $9 • (05/31/90) • **79**

Cabernet Sauvignon Sonoma County 1988 • $6 • (11/15/90) BB • **83**

Cabernet Sauvignon Sonoma County Premier Cuvée Reserve 1989: A solid, chunky red displaying earth, herb and currant flavor and finishing with firm tannins. Ready now. 3,000 cases made. • $9 • (11/15/94) • **84**

Cabernet Sauvignon Sonoma County Premier Cuvée Reserve 1988 • $8 • (11/15/93) • **77**

Cabernet Sauvignon Sonoma County Vintage Reserve 1989 • $5 • (11/15/92) • **74**

Chardonnay California Vintage Reserve 1993: Tastes sweet beyond ripeness, with cloying pear and apple flavors. Drinkable now. 50,000 cases made. • $6 • (01/31/95) • **80**

Merlot Chalk Hill Premier Cuvée Reserve 1989 • $11 • (12/31/93) • **69**

Zinfandel California 1989 • $5 • (02/15/91) • **77**

SAINT GREGORY | CALIFORNIA

Chardonnay Mendocino 1992: Medium-weight pear, spice and apple notes and a slight caramel finish. Drink now. 946 cases made. • $12 • (04/15/95) • **85**

Chardonnay Mendocino 1991 • $14 • (04/15/94) • **86**

Pinot Noir Mendocino 1993: Medium weight, middle of the road style, with modest varietal character, and hints of oak and berry. 450 cases made. • $14 • **81**

Key: SS—Spectator Selection. CS—Cellar Selection. BB—Best Buy. $NA—Price not available. (BT)—Barrel tasting. (A)—Auction Price.
Dates in parentheses represent the issues in which the ratings were published.

Pinot Noir Mendocino 1992: Lean and crisp, revealing a range of wild berry and cherry flavors. 389 cases made. • $14 • (03/31/95) • **81**
Pinot Noir Mendocino 1991 • $14 • (02/28/94) • **84**
Pinot Noir Mendocino 1990 • $14 • (09/30/92) • **86**

ST. JEAN, CHATEAU | CALIFORNIA

Brut Blanc de Blancs Sonoma County 1987 • $12 • (12/31/89) • **81**
Brut Blanc de Blancs Sonoma County 1984 • $11 • (05/31/89) • **88**
Brut Blanc de Blancs Sonoma County 1983 • $11 • (07/31/87) • **76**
Brut Blanc de Blancs Sonoma County 1982 • $13 • (05/16/86) • **79**
Brut Blanc de Blancs Sonoma County 1981 • $14 • (11/01/84) • **82**
Brut Blanc de Blancs Sonoma County NV: Intense and focused, with a pretty core of spice, pear and vanilla. Turns smooth and elegant on the finish, where the flavors linger. Ready now. • $11 • (11/30/94) SS • **88**
Brut Sonoma County 1987 • $12 • (04/30/90) • **82**
Brut Sonoma County 1986 • $12 • (12/31/89) • **87**
Brut Sonoma County 1985 • $11 • (12/31/88) • **86**
Brut Sonoma County 1984 • $11 • (07/15/88) • **84**
Brut Sonoma County 1983 • $11 • (05/31/87) • **67**
Brut Sonoma County 1982 • $13 • (05/16/86) • **67**
Brut Sonoma County 1981 • $14 • (11/01/84) • **81**
Brut Sonoma County NV • $11 • (12/31/93) • **85**
Brut Sonoma County Grande Cuvée 1985 • $19 • (12/31/93) • **88**
Brut Sonoma County Grande Cuvée 1982 • $19 • (06/15/91) • **80**
Cabernet Franc Sonoma Valley Jeanette Vineyards 1989 • $24 • (07/15/93) • **83**
Cabernet Sauvignon Alexander Valley 1987 • $16 • (06/30/91) SS • **92**
Cabernet Sauvignon Alexander Valley 1986 • $19 • (10/15/89) • **90**
Cabernet Sauvignon Alexander Valley 1985 • $19 • (11/15/88) • **86**
Cabernet Sauvignon Alexander Valley Reserve 1987 • $38 • (07/31/92) CS • **92**
Cabernet Sauvignon Sonoma County 1989 • $18 • (06/30/93) • **80**
Cabernet Sauvignon Sonoma County 1988 • $18 • (07/31/92) • **87**
Cabernet Sauvignon Sonoma County 1981 • $15 • (11/30/86) • **72**
Cabernet Sauvignon Sonoma County Cinq Cépages 1992: Young and tight, as currant, herb, coffee and cedar flavors wrestle with the tannins but emerge on aftertaste. Needs cellaring to soften the rough spots, best in 1999. 8,500 cases made. • $18 • (02/29/96) • **89**
Cabernet Sauvignon Sonoma County Cinq Cépages 1991: Rich and complex, with full bodied currant, anise, cherry and berry fruit, all framed by pretty toasty oak that adds texture and finesse to this beautifully crafted wine. 5,000 cases made. • $18 • (11/15/95) • **91**
Cabernet Sauvignon Sonoma County Cinq Cépages 1990: A big, rich and dense young Cabernet that serves up chunky currant and oak flavors. In a rustic style that will need cellaring to make it softer and more inviting. Best to start drinking in 1997 or '98. 7,500 cases made. • $18 • (09/30/94) • **87**
Cabernet Sauvignon Sonoma County Reserve 1990: A bold, smooth, rich and exotic style of Cabernet that packs in lots of extra flavors. The well-focused currant, cherry, mineral and toasty oak flavors are deftly balanced, expanding on the finish where the herb, chocolate and smoke notes enhance the pure fruit. This should hold well through 1999. 1,000 cases made. • $38 • (04/30/96) CS • **95**
Cabernet Sauvignon Sonoma County Reserve 1989: Pleasant enough for an '89, with a trim, crisp band of cherry and plum-laced fruit, finishing with a dry tannic edge. May always be on the tannic side. 400 cases made. • $38 • (11/15/95) • **87**
Cabernet Sauvignon Sonoma County Reserve 1988 • $38 • (10/15/93) • **91**
Cabernet Sauvignon Sonoma Valley Wildwood Vineyards 1980 • $17 • (09/01/85) • **82**
Cabernet Sauvignon Sonoma Valley Wildwood Vineyards 1979 • $17 • (07/01/84) • **76**
Chardonnay Alexander Valley Belle Terre Vineyards 1994: Rich and full-bodied, showing a complex core of ripe pear, nectarine, honey, spice and toasty oak flavors that are well focused and long on the finish. A terrific California white from a vineyard that is showing consistently good results. 5,000 cases made. • $18 • (04/30/96) • **92**
Chardonnay Alexander Valley Belle Terre Vineyards 1993: Ripe and spicy, with medium-weight pear, apple and light oak shadings. 5,000 cases made. • $18 • (07/31/95) • **86**
Chardonnay Alexander Valley Belle Terre Vineyards 1992: Strikes a lovely balance between ripe pear and peach flavors, surrounded by pretty, toasty, buttery oak. An enticingly complex and flavorful young wine that has a pretty aftertaste. 5,000 cases made. • $18 • (05/15/94) • **90**
Chardonnay Alexander Valley Belle Terre Vineyards 1991 • $17 • (05/15/94) • **85**
Chardonnay Alexander Valley Belle Terre Vineyards Reserve 1991: Disjointed now but remarkably youthful, pine, spice and apple flavors and smoky, toasty oak. Finish is somewhat coarse and woody. Drink now. 100 cases made. • $40 • (04/30/95) • **88**
Chardonnay Alexander Valley Robert Young Vineyards 1992: Serves up a bowlful of ripe fruit, with layers of pear, peach, nectarine and apple, and shades it with very light oak nuances, letting the flavors pour through on the finish. Can stand cellaring. 5,000 cases made. • $22 • (05/15/94) • **88**
Chardonnay Alexander Valley Robert Young Vineyards 1991 • $22 • (05/15/94) • **90**
Chardonnay Alexander Valley Robert Young Vineyards Reserve 1992: Aromatically complex, boasting a pretty array of honey, floral, pear and spice notes and following up with rich, deeply concentrated flavors that are bright, lively and long on the finish. This classy white also adds a deft touch of smoky oak. 1,000 cases made. • $50 • (04/30/96) • **94**
Chardonnay Alexander Valley Robert Young Vineyards Reserve 1991: A dramatic wine from this respected California winery. It is ripe and fruity, with a complex, supple core of pear, peach and toasty oak flavors that integrate nicely. The finish is long and lingering. 500 cases made. • $50 • (04/30/95) • **91**
Chardonnay Sonoma County 1994: Serves up a ripe and refreshing core of pear, honey, spice and nectarine flavors. A beautifully crafted Chardonnay that delivers the fruit and just a hint of oak. 95,000 cases made. • $11 • (04/30/96) SS • **90**
Chardonnay Sonoma County 1993: Features a spicy note that dominates the flavor, with just enough pear and apple underneath. 90,000 cases made. • $11 • (05/15/96) • **85**
Chardonnay Sonoma County 1992: Fruity and spicy, with racy peach and honey notes of modest depth and intensity. 75,000 cases made. • $12 • (11/15/94) • **84**
Chardonnay Sonoma County 1991 • $10 • (07/15/93) • **85**
Fumé Blanc Russian River Valley La Petite Etoile 1994: Complex aromas offer celery, herb, fig and melon, turning smooth and polished on the palate where the flavors show good depth and richness. Finishes with a trace of grapefruit and oak. 5,000 cases made. • $12 • (04/30/96) • **88**
Fumé Blanc Russian River Valley La Petite Etoile 1991 • $11 • (09/15/93) • **80**
Fumé Blanc Russian River Valley La Petite Étoile 1993: Light, simple and vaguely fruity, not much definition but pleasant and mildly herbal. 5,000 cases made. • $12 • (08/31/95) • **84**
Fumé Blanc Sonoma County 1994: Ripe and refreshing, delivering complex herb, citrus and fig flavors. Drinkable now. 22,000 cases made. • $8 • (04/30/96) • **87**
Fumé Blanc Sonoma County 1991 • $8 • (03/15/94) BB • **88**
Fumé Blanc Sonoma County Dry 1993: Straightforward, a sturdy white featuring simple pear flavor and hints of spice on the finish. 30,000 cases made. • $8 • (08/31/95) • **82**
Fumé Blanc Sonoma County Dry 1992: Crisp and citrusy, the herbal overtones adding a nice dimension to the lemony flavors. 19,500 cases made. • $8 • (08/31/94) BB • **85**
Gewürztraminer Late Harvest Alexander Valley Robert Young Vineyards 1982 • $18 • (07/16/84) • **91**
Gewürztraminer Late Harvest Alexander Valley Robert Young Vineyards Select 1983 • $14 • (11/01/84) • **92**
Gewürztraminer Sonoma County 1992 • $8 • (01/31/94) • **82**
Johannisberg Riesling Late Harvest Alexander Valley Robert Young Vineyards 1984 • $15 • (03/16/86) • **86**
Johannisberg Riesling Late Harvest Alexander Valley Robert Young Vineyards 1983 • $25 • (08/01/85) SS • **92**
Johannisberg Riesling Late Harvest Alexander Valley Robert Young Vineyards Special Select 1982 • $22 • (09/01/84) • **92**
Johannisberg Riesling Late Harvest Alexander Valley Select 1988 • $20 • (01/31/93) • **88**

Johannisberg Riesling Late Harvest Alexander Valley Select 1987 • $25 • (01/31/93) • **90**
Johannisberg Riesling Late Harvest Alexander Valley Special Select 1989 • $25 • (11/15/93) CS • **95**
Johannisberg Riesling Late Harvest Alexander Valley Special Select 1986 • $25 • (01/31/93) • **94**
Johannisberg Riesling Late Harvest Alexander Valley Special Select Hoot Owl Creek Vineyards 1989 • $22 • (01/31/93) • **93**
Johannisberg Riesling Late Harvest Russian River Valley Select 1985 • $12 • (08/31/87) • **84**
Merlot Sonoma County 1992: Firm with a supple beam of black cherry, black berry and plum notes, turning tannic on the finish. 11,000 cases made. • $12 • (04/15/95) • **86**
Merlot Sonoma County 1991: Firm and compact, yet developing a supple texture, with ripe plum and currant notes that turn spicy on the finish. Cellaring for a year or two may give it more generosity. 5,000 cases made. • $12 • (09/15/94) • **84**
Merlot Sonoma County 1990 • $12 • (03/15/94) • **85**
Merlot Sonoma County 1989 • $12 • (12/31/93) • **80**
Merlot Sonoma County Reserve 1991: Ripe and intense, boasting a pretty core of rich, spicy Merlot fruitiness with echoes of black cherry, tar, earth and anise, picking up a pleasant, earthy character on the finish. Classy, firmly tannic, and offers lots of flavor while maintaining its finesse. Tempting now, smoother in 1997. 500 cases made. • $32 • (02/29/96) CS • **92**
Mourvèdre Sonoma Valley 1990 • $17 • (06/15/93) • **83**
Pinot Noir Sonoma County 1991 • $16 • (02/28/94) • **86**
Pinot Noir Sonoma County 1990 • $19 • (02/28/93) • **80**
Pinot Noir Sonoma Valley McCrea Vineyards 1983 • $12 • (09/30/87) • **75**
Sauvignon Blanc Late Harvest Sonoma County Sauvignon d'Or 1982 • $15 • (07/01/84) • **85**
Sémillon Late Harvest Sonoma Valley Sémillon D'Or St. Jean Vineyard 1984 • $15 • (11/30/86) • **86**

ST. JULIAN | MICHIGAN

Chambourcin Lake Michigan Shore 1989 • $8 • (02/29/92) • **76**
Solera Light Cream Sherry Michigan NV • $12 • (02/29/92) • **88**

ST. SUPERY | CALIFORNIA

Cabernet Sauvignon Napa Valley Dollarhide Ranch 1990: Exotic for its ripe strawberry and currant jam flavors, but not typical in its range of flavors. On the finish the flavors gain intensity and added dimensions. Ready to drink now through 1999. 14,200 cases made. • $14 • (05/15/94) • **86**
Cabernet Sauvignon Napa Valley Dollarhide Ranch 1989: Hints of chocolate and berry peek through, but it's lean and tannic and could use short-term cellaring. 599 cases made. • $19 • (07/31/94) • **86**
Cabernet Sauvignon Napa Valley Dollarhide Ranch 1988 • $14 • (09/30/91) • **85**
Cabernet Sauvignon Napa Valley Dollarhide Ranch 1987 • $13 • (07/15/90) • **85**
Chardonnay Napa Valley Dollarhide Ranch 1993: Lean and simple, with coarse pear and citrus notes, but it lacks focus and harmony. 17,000 cases made. • $13 • (07/31/95) • **81**
Chardonnay Napa Valley Dollarhide Ranch 1992: Chunky, straightforward and flavorful, offering decent pear and citrus flavors, but it flattens out a little on the finish. 8,000 cases made. • $12 • (06/30/94) • **83**
Chardonnay Napa Valley Dollarhide Ranch 1991 • $13 • (03/31/93) • **86**
Merlot Napa Valley Dollarhide Ranch 1993: Complex and appealing with currant, black cherry, herb and tobacco flavors. A well-crafted wine with substance and depth. 17,215 cases made. • $17 • **86**
Merlot Napa Valley Dollarhide Ranch 1992: The modest concentration of berry and cherry flavors leaves the tannins more exposed. 11,800 cases made. • $15 • (05/15/95) • **80**
Merlot Napa Valley Dollarhide Ranch 1991 • $14 • (12/31/93) • **85**

Key: SS—Spectator Selection. CS—Cellar Selection. BB—Best Buy. $NA—Price not available. (BT)—Barrel tasting. Ⓐ—Auction Price.
Dates in parentheses represent the issues in which the ratings were published.

Merlot Napa Valley Dollarhide Ranch 1990 • $14 • (11/30/92) • **86**
Merlot Napa Valley Dollarhide Ranch 1989 • $14 • (05/31/92) • **89**
Moscato California 1992 • $11 • (05/15/93) • **76**
Moscato California 1989 • $11 • (12/15/92) • **72**
Sauvignon Blanc Napa Valley Dollarhide Ranch 1993: Simple and a little tired, but the grapefruit flavors persist on the finish. 21,000 cases made. • $8 • (08/31/95) • **80**
Sauvignon Blanc Napa Valley Dollarhide Ranch 1992 • $9 • (04/30/94) • **84**
Sauvignon Blanc Napa Valley Dollarhide Ranch 1991 • $9 • (04/15/93) • **82**

STE. CHAPELLE | WASHINGTON

Brut Chardonnay Washington NV • $9 • (03/15/88) • **80**
Cabernet Sauvignon Idaho 73% Arena Valley Vineyard/27% Symms Old 1990: Looks, smells and tastes mature with cedar and currant notes. Decent, but nothing more. 428 cases made. • $12 • (03/31/94) • **74**
Cabernet Sauvignon Idaho Reserve 1988 • $20 • (02/29/92) • **74**
Cabernet Sauvignon Washington 1993: Firm in texture, with brightly focused grapey berry flavors that remain lively on the finish. Drinkable now. 2,773 cases made. • $10 • (11/15/95) BB • **87**
Cabernet Sauvignon Washington 1992: Tough and chewy, a little syrupy with its berry and currant flavors, finishing soft and tannic enough to need until 1998. Idaho winery, Washington grapes. • $10 • (01/31/95) • **83**
Cabernet Sauvignon Washington 1989 • $10 • (03/15/93) • **79**
Cabernet Sauvignon Washington 1988 • $10 • (02/29/92) • **84**
Cabernet Sauvignon Washington 1986 • $10 • (08/31/91) • **83**
Cabernet Sauvignon Washington 1983 • $9 • (04/30/88) • **77**
Cabernet Sauvignon Washington 1981 • $9 • (05/15/87) • **80**
Cabernet Sauvignon Washington Canyon 1992: An Idaho Cab made from Washington grapes that's ripe, chunky and firm-textured. Has black cherry, currant and cedar flavors that echo on the finish. Drinkable now. 2,800 cases made. • $7 • (01/31/95) BB • **86**
Cabernet Sauvignon Washington Collectors Series 1988 • $16 • (10/15/93) • **73**
Cabernet Sauvignon Washington Collectors' Series 1981 • $18 • (10/15/89) • **81**
Cabernet Sauvignon Washington Mercer Ranch Vineyard 1989 • $16 • (01/31/94) • **80**
Chardonnay Idaho 1992: Bright and fruity, a light-textured wine that picks up some nice pear and spice flavors. Ready. 4,800 cases made. • $10 • (05/31/95) • **84**
Chardonnay Idaho Reserve 1994: Spicy, butterscotch flavors come to the fore in this broad-structured wine that finishes with an herbal note. 601 cases made. • $15 • (06/15/96) • **85**
Chenin Blanc Idaho Dry 1992 • $5 • (11/15/93) • **80**
Fumé Blanc Idaho 1993: Simple, bright and fruity, showing green-edged peach and vanilla flavors that linger. Ready now. 1,194 cases made. • $7 • (05/31/95) • **82**
Johannisberg Riesling Idaho 1992 • $6 • (08/31/93) BB • **88**
Johannisberg Riesling Idaho Winery Hill Vineyard Special Harvest 1992 • $9 • (11/15/93) • **87**
Johannisberg Riesling Late Harvest Idaho Botrytis 1986 • $15 • (02/15/88) • **79**
Merlot Idaho 1992: Intense, with bright, lively wild berry and cherry flavor that's ripe and focused. Finishes with firm tannins and smoky oaky notes. Best after 1996. Impressive for its flavor and balance. • $10 • (09/15/94) • **85**
Merlot Washington 1987 • $10 • (09/30/90) • **73**
Merlot Washington Dionysus Vineyard 1986 • $12 • (05/31/88) • **81**
Pinot Noir Idaho 1988 • $8 • (02/29/92) • **74**
Sparkling Johannisberg Riesling Washington Sec NV • $7 • (03/15/88) • **76**
Syrah Idaho Reserve 1994: Soft and pleasant, with plummy, slightly tarry flavors. Drinkable now. 203 cases made. • $20 • (06/30/96) • **84**

STE. CLAIRE | CALIFORNIA

Cabernet Sauvignon California 1992: An oaky style but it holds together, with plum and cherry notes adding dimension. • $11 • (11/15/94) • **82**
Chardonnay California Barrel Select 1992: Clean and well balanced, with attractive apple, pear and fig notes of modest proportion. • $11 • (07/31/95) • **84**

STE. MICHELLE, CHATEAU | WASHINGTON

Blanc de Blanc Columbia Valley 1986 • $15 • (12/31/90) • **85**
Blanc de Blanc Columbia Valley NV: Toasty, spicy flavors characterize this crisp sparkler from Washington. An appealing price, and it's made for drinking now. 45,000 cases made. • $10 • (09/15/95) BB • **87**
Blanc de Blancs Columbia Valley 1986 • $14 • (01/31/92) • **86**
Blanc de Noir Columbia Valley 1987 • $20 • (11/15/93) • **80**
Blanc de Noirs Columbia Valley 1986 • $17 • (01/31/92) • **80**
Blanc de Noirs Columbia Valley 1985 • $20 • (12/31/90) • **86**
Brut Columbia Valley NV • $9 • (03/31/93) • **80**
Blush Riesling Columbia Valley 1988 • $5 • (10/15/89) • **75**
Cabernet Franc Columbia Valley Cold Creek Vineyard 1992: Soft and velvety, showing a band of plum and berry flavors that finish gently. Approachable now, but best in 1997. 480 cases made. • $22 • (09/30/95) • **85**
Cabernet Sauvignon Benton County Cold Creek Vineyards Château Reserve 1980 • $21 • (10/15/89) • **85**
Cabernet Sauvignon Columbia Valley 1993: Richly fruit-flavored and elegant in style, showing impressive depth in black cherry, currant, vanilla and spice notes that echo on the finish. Fine tannins are present but not intrusive. Best in 1997. 66,000 cases made. • $14 • (04/30/96) • **89**
Cabernet Sauvignon Columbia Valley 1992: Lean and chewy, bay leaf and other herbal notes adding interest to the dark fruit flavors. Could use until 1998 to soften. 60,000 cases made. • $14 • (07/31/95) • **86**
Cabernet Sauvignon Columbia Valley 1991: Ripe and generous, supple and elegant, showing off the pretty currant, black cherry and spice flavors echoing appealingly on the finish. • $14 • (09/30/94) • **88**
Cabernet Sauvignon Columbia Valley 1990: Nicely crafted from start to finish, firm in texture, bright and fruity in flavor, centered around blackberry and vanilla as the notes echo on the finish. • $14 • (07/31/94) • **87**
Cabernet Sauvignon Columbia Valley 1989 • $14 • (03/15/93) • **88**
Cabernet Sauvignon Columbia Valley 1988 • $13 • (08/31/91) • **84**
Cabernet Sauvignon Columbia Valley 1986 • $12 • (09/30/90) • **88**
Cabernet Sauvignon Columbia Valley Cold Creek Vineyard 1993: Dense and chewy—a serious wine. Focused berry and chocolate flavors persist on the solid finish. Seems closed at this point, needing more richness on the finish. Allow until 1999-2000 to soften. 2,500 cases made. • $26 • **87**
Cabernet Sauvignon Columbia Valley Cold Creek Vineyard 1992: Ripe and rich, but exceedingly gentle with its fine tannins and nicely tuned acidity-just enough to show off the beautiful plum, berry and vanilla flavors that lace themselves through the long, elegant finish. A fine Washington Cabernet. Best to age until 1997. 2,500 cases made. • $26 • (12/15/95) SS • **92**
Cabernet Sauvignon Columbia Valley Cold Creek Vineyard 1991: Firm, focused and zingy, with ripe blackberry and currant flavors, tannins need until 1997 to resolve. Tasted twice, with consistent notes. 1,200 cases made. • $22 • (01/31/95) • **88**
Cabernet Sauvignon Columbia Valley Cold Creek Vineyard Limited Bottling 1987 • $20 • (08/31/91) • **83**
Cabernet Sauvignon Columbia Valley Horse Heaven Vineyard 1993: Deliciously focused berry and currant flavors over a velvety frame. Echoes of spice and fruit on the lively, complex finish. Best from 1997-1998.Ⓐ • $27 • **87**
Cabernet Sauvignon Columbia Valley River Ridge Vineyard Limited Bottling 1987 • $18 • (08/31/91) • **87**
Cabernet Sauvignon Columbia Valley Twentieth Vintage 1987 • $12 • (09/30/90) • **85**
Cabernet Sauvignon Washington 1985 • $12 • (10/15/89) • **85**
Cabernet Sauvignon Washington 1984 • $11 • (12/31/88) • **89**
Cabernet Sauvignon Washington 1983 • $10 • (11/15/87) • **81**
Cabernet Sauvignon Washington 1980 • $9 • (03/01/85) • **65**
Cabernet Sauvignon Washington Cold Creek Vineyard Limited Bottling 1985 • $19 • (12/15/90) • **83**
Cabernet Sauvignon Washington River Ridge Vineyard Limited Bottling 1985 • $17 • (11/30/90) • **90**
Chardonnay Columbia Valley 1994: Bright on a smaller scale, featuring nicely focused peach, apple and spice flavors. Ready now. 150,000 cases made. • $13 • (05/15/96) • **87**
Chardonnay Columbia Valley 1991 • $12 • (03/31/93) • **88**
Chardonnay Columbia Valley Barrel Fermented 1993: Crisp and spicy, a zinger on the palate, focusing its citrus, apple and spice flavors on a narrow beam. Oak flavors are very subtle. Drink now. 125,000 cases made. • $13 • (08/31/95) • **87**
Chardonnay Columbia Valley Barrel Fermented 1992: Ripe and polished, layering its spice, pear, butter and honey flavors in a round package that's delicious to drink now. 93,000 cases made. • $13 • (09/15/94) • **88**
Chardonnay Columbia Valley Canoe Ridge Estate Vineyard 1993: Ripe, round and distinctly spicy, adding duskiness to the pear and honey. Drink now. First Chardonnay from this vineyard and the vines are young. 1,200 cases made. • $26 • (09/30/95) • **86**
Chardonnay Columbia Valley Chateau Reserve 1993: Combines elegance with finesse and ripe, smooth, creamy pear, honey and hazelnut flavors. This Washington white turns complex and picks up nice smoky tones on the finish, where the flavors linger. 1,300 cases made. • $30 • (12/31/95) • **91**
Chardonnay Columbia Valley Chateau Reserve 1992: Spicy, ripe, generous and silky, with layers of pear, apple, peach and honey aromas and flavors, deftly balanced between ripe fruit and spicy oak. Pretty notes linger on the long finish. Delicious now, so why wait? 1,200 cases made. • $22 • (09/15/94) • **92**
Chardonnay Columbia Valley Cold Creek Vineyard 1993: Subtle, harmonious and beautifully balanced, blending together pear, spice, vanilla, honey and toast flavors right through to the smooth finish. An intriguing Washington white that's drinkable already, but should improve through 1997. 3,600 cases made. • $25 • (08/31/95) SS • **90**
Chardonnay Columbia Valley Cold Creek Vineyard 1991 • $18 • (03/31/93) • **89**
Chardonnay Columbia Valley Cold Creek Vineyard Barrel Fermented 1992: Fresh and lively, with a spicy floral tone to the buttery pear and apple flavors, finishing with an elegant edge and graceful fruit notes. Drinkable now. 2,500 cases made. • $19 • (09/15/94) • **87**
Chardonnay Columbia Valley Indian Wells Vineyard 1993: Smooth, round and elegant, its nectarine, pear and spice flavors unfolding in the silky texture and finishing long and generous. Delicious now and should improve through 1997. 640 cases made. • $20 • (08/31/95) • **91**
Chenin Blanc Columbia Valley 1993: Bright and fruity, slightly off-dry and bursting with melon and pear flavors that keep singing on the finish. Drink soon for the fruit. • $7 • (09/30/94) • **84**
Gewürztraminer Columbia Valley 1993: Light and a little bitter, on the dry side but not exactly brimming with fruit. Drinkable now. • $7 • (09/30/94) • **79**
Gewürztraminer Columbia Valley 1992 • $7 • (05/31/94) BB • **85**
Gewürztraminer Columbia Valley 1991 • $7 • (11/30/92) • **80**
Johannisberg Riesling Columbia Valley 1992 • $7 • (07/31/93) • **84**
Johannisberg Riesling Columbia Valley 1991 • $7 • (11/30/92) • **82**
Meritage Washington 1993: Crisp and fruity at first, offering nicely articulated berry flavors, although the tannins sneak past these notes by the finish. Try in 1998. 1,250 cases made. • $30 • (04/30/96) • **88**
Merlot Columbia Valley 1993: Firm and nicely focused, showing bright berry fruit and spicy overtones, lingering enticingly on the finish. 60,000 cases made. • $15 • (05/31/96) • **87**
Merlot Columbia Valley 1992: Firm in texture, featuring smoky, earthy prune and spice flavors. Needs until 1996 to smooth itself out. 50,000 cases made. • $15 • (09/30/95) • **83**
Merlot Columbia Valley 1990 • $14 • (04/15/94) • **87**
Merlot Columbia Valley 1989 • $14 • (06/15/93) • **85**
Merlot Columbia Valley 1988 • $15 • (03/31/92) • **84**
Merlot Columbia Valley 1987 • $12 • (09/30/90) • **84**
Merlot Columbia Valley 1986 • $12 • (09/30/90) • **84**
Merlot Columbia Valley Canoe Ridge Estate Vineyard 1993: Supple and generous with its plum and berry flavors, a solid wine that lingers on the finish. Approachable now, but needs until 1998 to sort out the fine tannins. 1,200 cases made. • $28 • (06/15/96) • **88**
Merlot Columbia Valley Cold Creek Vineyard 1993: Silky, spicy and generous with its plum, anise and gently peppery flavors, smooth and inviting on the finish. This Washington red is approachable now, but will be better in 1998. 1,500 cases made. • $28 • (06/15/96) • **90**
Merlot Columbia Valley Cold Creek Vineyard 1987 • $19 • (06/15/93) • **79**

STE. VINCENT, DOMAINE

Merlot Columbia Valley Cold Creek Vineyard Limited Bottling 1987 • $19 • (08/31/91) • **81**

Merlot Columbia Valley Horse Heaven Vineyard 1993: A solid mouthful of anise-scented, slightly raisiny blackberry, plum and black pepper flavors that linger distinctively on the finish. Best in 1997 or 1998. 1,000 cases made. • $27 • (06/15/96) • **88**

Merlot Columbia Valley Indian Wells Vineyard 1992: Well oaked, but pretty, spicy cherry, currant and wild berry flavors fold together nicely, adding firm but smooth tannins on the finish. 1,200 cases made. • $30 • (09/30/95) • **90**

Merlot Columbia Valley Indian Wells Vineyard 1991: Smooth and polished, showing a nice overlay of tobacco and spice that adds depth and richness to the ripe berry and plum flavor. Very tasty now. 1,200 cases made. • $20 • (09/30/94) • **88**

Merlot Columbia Valley River Ridge Vineyard 1985 • $18 • (09/30/90) • **89**

Merlot Washington 1983 • $10 • (12/31/88) • **80**

Merlot Washington River Ridge Vineyard 1985 • $14 • (10/15/89) • **87**

Merlot Washington River Ridge Vineyard Château Reserve 1983 • $15 • (12/31/88) • **87**

Pinot Noir Columbia Valley Limited Bottling 1987 • $11 • (08/31/91) • **79**

Riesling Columbia Valley Dry 1993: Light and lively, showing an airy texture but a bright core of floral apple flavors that echo on the finish. Not sweet. • $7 • (09/30/94) • **85**

Riesling Columbia Valley Dry 1992 • $7 • (07/31/93) • **82**

Riesling Columbia Valley Dry River Ridge Vineyard 1991 • $7 • (11/30/92) • **74**

Riesling Washington Ice Wine 1978: Aging nicely, this still has fresh acidity and pleasant floral, apple and light cherry flavors that linger on the palate. It's soft and moderately sweet. A well-made wine. • $NA • **85**

Sauvignon Blanc Columbia Valley 1993: Light, airy and refreshing, adding a citrusy edge to the pear and faintly herbal flavors. 50,000 cases made. • $9 • (09/15/95) • **84**

Sauvignon Blanc Columbia Valley 1992 • $9 • (08/31/93) • **88**

Sémillon Columbia Valley 1993: Soft and harmonious, showing some nice pear and tobacco notes. 4,500 cases made. • $7 • (07/31/95) • **82**

Sémillon Columbia Valley Barrel Fermented 1994: Lively, zingy flavors of spice, herb and pear show plenty of character and length. 5,000 cases made. • $7 • (07/31/95) BB • **86**

Sémillon Late Harvest Columbia Valley Reserve 1992: Rich, honeyed and pure, with buttery pear, vanilla and a touch of fig swirling around and through the long and impressive finish. Tasty now, but worth waiting until 1998 or 2000 to see what develops. 400 cases made. • $20 • (04/30/95) • **90**

White Riesling Columbia Valley Sweet Select 1992 • $7 • (07/31/93) • **78**

White Riesling Late Harvest Columbia Valley Chateau Reserve 1991: A ripe, sweet, generous and elegant dessert wine from Washington. The silky mouth-feel and gorgeous honey, apricot and spice flavors blend beautifully, joined by a touch of almond on the lovely finish. Wonderful now, and it should last through 1999 and beyond. 1,000 cases made. • $9 • (09/15/95) • **93**

White Riesling Late Harvest Columbia Valley River Ridge Vyd Hand-Selected Cluster 1989 • $18 • (09/30/91) • **82**

White Riesling Late Harvest Yakima Valley Château Reserve Hand-Selected Cluster 1985 • $22 • (07/31/89) • **91**

STE. VINCENT, DOMAINE | CALIFORNIA

Cabernet Sauvignon Sonoma County Reserve 1986 • $8 • (11/15/92) • **77**

SAINTSBURY | CALIFORNIA

Chardonnay Carneros 1993: Appealing for its direct pear, spice and creamy vanilla notes. Medium weight, ready now. Tasted twice with consistent results. 12,768 cases made. • $15 • (07/31/95) • **85**

Key: SS—Spectator Selection. CS—Cellar Selection. BB—Best Buy. $NA—Price not available. (BT)—Barrel tasting. (A)—Auction Price.
Dates in parentheses represent the issues in which the ratings were published.

Chardonnay Carneros 1992: Young and spicy, it shows off ripe pear, apple and oaky flavors that finally pull together on the finish. Elegant and stylish, it's drinkable now but worthy of short-term cellaring. • $15 • (06/30/94) • **85**

Chardonnay Carneros 1991 • $15 • (12/15/92) • **87**

Chardonnay Carneros Reserve 1994: Bold, ripe, smooth and creamy, a real mouthful of Chardonnay. Its tiers of ripe pear, fig and honey flavors are framed by smoky, toasty oak. An altogether complex and beautifully crafted young wine, with a rich butterscotch aftertaste that still has all those delicious flavors chiming in. Kudos to this California winery. 1,130 cases made. • $25 • (05/31/96) • **95**

Chardonnay Carneros Reserve 1993: Intense and spicy, with ripe pear, apple and butterscotch flavors that turn complex and smoky on the finish. 1,451 cases made. • $25 • (05/31/95) • **89**

Chardonnay Carneros Reserve 1991 • $22 • (05/31/94) • **92**

Pinot Noir Carneros 1994: Smooth and elegant, striking a nice balance between ripe fruit and oak, with a finish that showcases the fig, melon, toasty oak and pear flavors. Shows more complexity and depth on the finish. 18,227 cases made. • $18 • (02/29/96) • **88**

Pinot Noir Carneros 1992: Delicate, with fresh, crisp cherry, strawberry and spice, picking up a pleasant earthy edge on the finish. Very appealing now. • $16 • (02/28/95) • **85**

Pinot Noir Carneros 1991 • $17 • (02/28/94) • **87**

Pinot Noir Carneros 1989 • $17 • (02/15/92) • **85**

Pinot Noir Carneros 1988 • $15 • (12/15/90) SS • **91**

Pinot Noir Carneros 1987 • $15 • (07/31/89) • **86**

Pinot Noir Carneros 1986 • $14 • (06/15/88) • **92**

Pinot Noir Carneros 1985 • $13 • (11/30/87) • **92**

Pinot Noir Carneros 1984 • $12 • (12/15/86) • **93**

Pinot Noir Carneros 1983 • $12 • (12/01/85) • **93**

Pinot Noir Carneros 1982 • $8 • (11/30/87) • **86**

Pinot Noir Carneros Garnet 1994: Appealing now with its supple berry, cherry, earth and spice notes. Finishes with a clean, fruity aftertaste and mild tannins. 9,726 cases made. • $11 • (11/15/95) • **85**

Pinot Noir Carneros Garnet 1993: Spicy and lively, with cherry and spice flavors and subtle, earthy notes. Perfect for drinking now through the next year. 10,313 cases made. • $11 • (12/15/94) • **86**

Pinot Noir Carneros Garnet 1992 • $10 • (02/28/94) • **84**

Pinot Noir Carneros Garnet 1991 • $10 • (12/31/92) • **88**

Pinot Noir Carneros Garnet 1990 • $10 • (02/15/92) • **86**

Pinot Noir Carneros Garnet 1989 • $9 • (12/15/90) • **88**

Pinot Noir Carneros Garnet 1988 • $9 • (03/31/90) • **84**

Pinot Noir Carneros Garnet 1987 • $9 • (12/31/88) • **91**

Pinot Noir Carneros Garnet 1986 • $8 • (12/15/87) • **87**

Pinot Noir Carneros Garnet 1985 • $9 • (03/15/87) • **86**

Pinot Noir Carneros Garnet 1984 • $8 • (08/31/86) • **76**

Pinot Noir Carneros Garnet 1983 • $8 • (11/30/87) • **73**

Pinot Noir Carneros Rancho 1981 • $NA • (11/30/87) • **80**

Pinot Noir Carneros Reserve 1993: Smells more complex than it tastes with its ripe cherry and oaky nuance. Well balanced for the vintage. Drinkable now. 1,522 cases made. • $30 • **88**

Pinot Noir Carneros Reserve 1992: Much like the 1991, complex and flavorful, blending ripe, spicy black cherry with herb, cedar and earthy nuances. Smooth and supple, finishing with a smoky anise aftertaste and moderate tannins. Cellaring until 1995 to '96 advised. 2,022 cases made. • $30 • (12/15/94) • **89**

Pinot Noir Carneros Reserve 1991 • $30 • (02/28/94) • **88**

Pinot Noir Carneros Reserve 1990 • $30 • (12/31/92) • **91**

SALAMANDRE | CALIFORNIA

Chardonnay Arroyo Seco 1993: Earthy with a sweaty matchstick and canned grapefruit edge. Marginal. 300 cases made. • $16 • (07/31/95) • **77**

Chardonnay Santa Cruz Mountains Matteson Vineyard 1993: Medium weight but well focused, with a narrow beam of lemon, grapefruit and light pear notes, which fan out and pick up an oaky note. 150 cases made. • $16 • (07/31/95) • **86**

SALISHAN | WASHINGTON

Cabernet Sauvignon Washington 1992: Light, simple and unassuming, its fruit flavors seeming a little cooked. Drinkable now. 172 cases made. • $12 • (09/30/95) • **78**

Chardonnay Washington 1991: Simple, straightforward, spicy enough to keep echoing on the finish. 257 cases made. • $8 • (09/30/95) • **83**

Pinot Noir Washington 1991: Very light notes lean toward spice and toast, a slight thread of cherry flavor weaving through the finish. Ready now. 318 cases made. • $9 • (09/30/95) • **83**

Pinot Noir Washington Lot 1 1989 • $9 • (02/28/93) • **77**

SALMON CREEK | CALIFORNIA

Chardonnay Carneros 1993: Relies heavily on oak at this stage, but enough ripe pear and pineapple fruit comes through on the finish to hold your edge. • $12 • (07/31/95) • **85**

SAN MARTIN, DOMAIN | CALIFORNIA

Cabernet Sauvignon Central Coast 1981 • $7 • (10/01/85) • **76**

White Zinfandel Central Coast 1985 • $4 • (03/31/87) • **67**

SAN SABA | CALIFORNIA

Cabernet Sauvignon Monterey 1990: A nice blend of spicy, toasty oak and supple currant and herb flavors, finishing with a caramel edge and fine, polished tannins. Tasty. 740 cases made. • $15 • (11/15/94) • **88**

SANDERLING | CALIFORNIA

Zinfandel Amador County 1984 • $6 • (05/01/86) • **70**

SANFORD | CALIFORNIA

Chardonnay Santa Barbara County 1994: Hits all the right notes with its ripe pear, light oak shadings and hints of vanilla, pineapple and citrus. An elegant and complex Chardonnay from this California Winery. 19,000 cases made. • $17 • (05/31/96) SS • **90**

Chardonnay Santa Barbara County 1993: A bold wine that makes a statement about Santa Barbara Chardonnay. Complex and full-bodied, well oaked and flavorful, with ripe pear, honey and earthy notes that turn rich and complex on the finish. Drinkable now. 22,000 cases made. • $18 • (06/30/95) SS • **90**

Chardonnay Santa Barbara County 1992: Firm and focused, with a tight band of pear, spice and honeyed notes that turn elegant and spicy on the finish. Drinks well now. 11,000 cases made. • $16 • (06/30/94) • **88**

Chardonnay Santa Barbara County 1991 • $17 • (03/15/93) • **91**

Chardonnay Santa Barbara County Barrel Select 1993: Ripe and fruity, offering an elegant core of earthy pear and apple tones. Picks up light oak, hazelnut and spice notes on the finish, where the flavors turn complex and tropical. 1,500 cases made. • $30 • **90**

Chardonnay Santa Barbara County Barrel Select 1992: Well crafted, presenting a nice marriage of honey, pear and citrus with spicy, toasty oak. It all folds together neatly on the finish, where the flavors echo. 2,000 cases made. • $30 • (06/30/95) • **90**

Chardonnay Santa Barbara County Barrel Select 1991 • $30 • (06/30/93) • **91**

Chardonnay Santa Ynez Valley 1993: Lean and crisp, with spicy pear, citrus and pineapple notes, turning complex and well focused. • $24 • (07/31/95) • **86**

Chardonnay Santa Ynez Valley 1992: Ripe, creamy pear, honey and apple flavors gain depth and complexity on the finish. A new wine and style from Sanford that does not undergo malolactic fermentation. • $24 • (05/15/95) • **88**

Merlot Santa Barbara County 1984 • $18 • (12/31/87) • **66**

Pinot Noir Blanc Santa Barbara County Vin Gris 1994: An attempt to make an interesting wine that didn't work, overly oaked and little fruit. Tastes stripped and woody. • $10 • (09/15/95) • **74**

Pinot Noir Central Coast 1984 • $12 • (05/15/87) • **85**

Pinot Noir Santa Barbara County 1994: Shows off some pretty ripe Pinot Noir fruit with hints of cherry, cola, herb and spice, finishing with a nice touch of oak. Well balanced and appealing now. 9,000 cases made. • $18 • **88**

Pinot Noir Santa Barbara County 1992: Spice, herb and ripe black cherry flavors lead to earthy anise notes on the mildly tannic finish. Drink now. 6,000 cases made. • $18 • (01/31/95) • **88**

Pinot Noir Santa Barbara County 1991 • $17 • (09/15/93) • **87**

Pinot Noir Santa Barbara County 1990 • $17 • (11/30/92) SS • **90**

Pinot Noir Santa Barbara County 1989 • $15 • (03/31/92) • **85**

Pinot Noir Santa Barbara County 1988 • $15 • (06/30/91) • **78**

Pinot Noir Santa Barbara County 1987 • $14 • (02/28/91) • **76**

Pinot Noir Santa Barbara County 1986 • $14 • (12/15/89) • **75**

Pinot Noir Santa Barbara County 1985 • $14 • (06/15/88) • **74**

Pinot Noir Santa Barbara County Barrel Select 1986 • $20 • (12/15/89) • **78**

Pinot Noir Santa Barbara County Barrel Select 1985 • $20 • (06/15/88) • **75**

Pinot Noir Santa Barbara County Sanford & Benedict Vineyard Barrel Select 1992: Firm and compact, with herb, spice and dried cherry flavors, mild tannins and good length. Drink now. 1,000 cases made. • $30 • (01/31/95) • **88**

Pinot Noir Santa Barbara County Sanford & Benedict Vineyard Barrel Select 1991 • $30 • (02/28/94) • **88**

Pinot Noir Santa Barbara County Sanford & Benedict Vineyard Barrel Select 1990 • $30 • (02/28/93) • **89**

Pinot Noir Santa Maria Valley 1982 • $11 • (12/01/84) • **63**

Pinot Noir Santa Ynez Valley Barrel Select 1994: Smooth and polished, with rich flavors—cherry, herb, spice and dried berry. Complex, well-crafted and long on the finish, where the supple tannins fold in. 1,300 cases made. • $30 • **91**

Pinot Noir Santa Ynez Valley Barrel Select 1993: Tight and compact, with a trim band of black cherry, herb and anise and spice notes, showing a sense of harmony and finesse, with a lingering aftertaste. Drinkable now. 1,000 cases made. • $30 • **88**

Sauvignon Blanc Santa Barbara County 1993: Smooth, supple, modest fruit flavors pop through on the finish. 6,000 cases made. • $9 • (08/31/95) • **82**

Sauvignon Blanc Santa Barbara County 1991 • $9 • (11/30/92) • **83**

SANTA BARBARA WINERY | CALIFORNIA

Cabernet Sauvignon Santa Ynez Valley 1991: Strong herb, bell pepper and earth flavors are hard to look past in this one. 772 cases made. • $11 • (11/15/94) • **75**

Cabernet Sauvignon Santa Ynez Valley 1990: Intense and herbaceous with spice, onion, cherry and currant notes, but the texture is a bit wooly and the tannins on the finish turn crisp and austere. 660 cases made. • $11 • (11/15/93) • **83**

Cabernet Sauvignon Santa Ynez Valley 1989 • $11 • (11/15/92) • **79**

Cabernet Sauvignon Santa Ynez Valley 1988 • $12 • (11/15/91) • **83**

Cabernet Sauvignon Santa Ynez Valley Reserve 1992: A touch austere, with firm tannins and a dusty oak edge, but the currant and cherry fruit that emerges is rich and full bodied. Best after 1997. 432 cases made. • $16 • (12/15/95) • **86**

Cabernet Sauvignon Santa Ynez Valley Reserve 1990: Smells like a saute of onions and bell pepper, but once you get past that you pick up hints of cherry and spice and it gets better. Tastes better on the palate and on the finish than in the initial aromas. Drink now through 1997. 763 cases made. • $16 • (11/15/93) • **83**

Cabernet Sauvignon Santa Ynez Valley Reserve 1989 • $16 • (11/15/92) • **82**

Cabernet Sauvignon Santa Ynez Valley Reserve 1988 • $18 • (11/15/91) • **83**

Cabernet Sauvignon Santa Ynez Valley Reserve 1987 • $18 • (11/15/90) • **77**

Cabernet Sauvignon Santa Ynez Valley Reserve 1984 • $14 • (10/31/87) • **81**

Cabernet Sauvignon Santa Ynez Valley Reserve 1974 • $16 • (12/15/89) • **81**

Cabernet Sauvignon Santa Ynez Valley Unfiltered Reserve 1991: Intense and spicy, showing a racy bell pepper and herb edge to the currant and cherry flavor. Finishes with crisp tannins. Drinks well now but can age short-term. 310 cases made. • $16 • (11/15/94) • **84**

Chardonnay Santa Ynez Valley 1991 • $12 • (07/15/93) • **86**

Chardonnay Santa Ynez Valley Lafond Vineyard 1993: Distinctive for its smooth, creamy fig, smoke and butterscotch flavors. Bold and full-bodied, turning more elegant on the finish. 206 cases made. • $30 • (05/15/96) • **90**

Chardonnay Santa Ynez Valley Lafond Vineyard 1991 • $30 • (04/30/94) • **88**

Chardonnay Santa Ynez Valley Lafond Vineyard Unfiltered 1992: Strives for complexity with its array of toasty oak and ripe pear and butterscotch, turning supple and elegant. 193 cases made. • $30 • (07/31/95) • **89**
Chardonnay Santa Ynez Valley Reserve 1994: Ripe and spicy, with a pleasant band of pear, melon and apricot flavors that become complex on the finish and linger. 1,859 cases made. • $22 • (06/30/96) • **87**
Chardonnay Santa Ynez Valley Reserve 1993: Rich and buttery, with an attractive butterscotch flavor that adds complexity to the ripe pear and honey notes that linger on the finish. Well made. 1,372 cases made. • $20 • (07/31/95) • **89**
Chardonnay Santa Ynez Valley Reserve 1992: Firm and focused, brimming with fresh, ripe pear and pineapple flavors that are framed by light toasty, smoky oak. Complex and concentrated, it picks up a slight astringent edge on the finish, but that should dissipate with time. Best now to 1998. 510 cases made. • $20 • (04/30/94) • **89**
Chardonnay Santa Ynez Valley Reserve 1991 • $20 • (07/15/93) • **86**
Johannisberg Riesling Late Harvest Santa Ynez Valley Botrytised Grapes 1986 • $15 • (10/15/87) • **88**
Johannisberg Riesling Santa Barbara County 1992 • $8 • (08/31/93) • **82**
Pinot Noir Santa Barbara County 1994: Austere, showing a narrow band of earthy cherry, herb and spice notes of modest depth and proportion. 1,757 cases made. • $15 • (02/29/96) • **84**
Pinot Noir Santa Barbara County 1993: Pleasantly fruity, with spicy herb and black cherry flavors that run into crisp tannins on the finish. Drinkable now. 2,334 cases made. • $12 • (03/31/95) • **83**
Pinot Noir Santa Barbara County 1991 • $11 • (02/28/94) • **82**
Pinot Noir Santa Barbara County 1990 • $11 • (02/28/93) • **87**
Pinot Noir Santa Barbara County 1989 • $11 • (07/31/91) • **84**
Pinot Noir Santa Barbara County 1986 • $11 • (06/15/88) • **80**
Pinot Noir Santa Barbara County Reserve 1994: Tough and tannic, adding an austere, stemmy edge to the modest herb and cherry flavors. May not outgrow its tannins. Best to cellar in hopes it will soften. 468 cases made. • $24 • (02/29/96) • **82**
Pinot Noir Santa Barbara County Reserve 1991 • $20 • (02/28/94) • **79**
Pinot Noir Santa Barbara County Reserve 1990 • $20 • (09/30/92) • **89**
Pinot Noir Santa Barbara County Reserve 1989 • $20 • (11/15/91) • **87**
Pinot Noir Santa Barbara County Unfiltered Reserve 1993: Smooth and elegant, with a pretty array of cola, black cherry, and spice. Comes up a bit short on the finish, where the tannins kick in. 400 cases made. • $20 • (12/31/95) • **84**
Pinot Noir Santa Barbara County Unfiltered Reserve 1992: Tight, firm, lean, complex cherry, oak and anise flavors, but not the extra dimensions you might expect. Needs short-term cellaring. 160 cases made. • $20 • (03/31/95) • **86**
Pinot Noir Santa Ynez Valley Reserve 1987 • $20 • (12/15/89) • **89**
Sauvignon Blanc Late Harvest Santa Ynez Valley 1994: Juicy, ripe peach and nectarine flavors, finishing with an earthy, sweaty accent. 563 cases made. • $18 • **83**
Sauvignon Blanc Late Harvest Santa Ynez Valley 1993: Sweet and elegant, showing off its pure pineapple, honey and vanilla flavors, finishing just a little syrupy and sweet. Finish is very long. Delicious now, but try it in 1998. 970 cases made. • $14 • (05/15/95) • **90**
Sauvignon Blanc Late Harvest Santa Ynez Valley Late Harvest Lafond Vineyard 1990 • $12 • (03/10/92) • **72**
Sauvignon Blanc Santa Ynez Valley 1993: Accented by rose petal and herb flavors, this keeps a solid core of pear and ginger floating through the finish. 625 cases made. • $8 • (08/31/95) • **83**
Sauvignon Blanc Santa Ynez Valley Reserve 1993: Lean and spicy, more oak than fruit, sneaking in a touch of herb on the finish. 200 cases made. • $12 • (08/31/95) • **80**
Sauvignon Blanc Santa Ynez Valley Reserve 1992: Herbal, almost vegetal on the nose, but the pineapple and citrus flavors come up nicely on the palate. Perhaps a little sweet, but an enjoyable drink. 510 cases made. • $12 • (08/31/94) • **85**
Syrah Santa Ynez Valley 1994: Dark and a bit gamy, adding leathery character to the ripe plum and cherry flavor. This is chewy and tannic and, although pleasant enough, doesn't quite have the richness or depth. 95 cases made. • $16 • (05/15/96) • **85**
White Riesling Santa Ynez Valley Paradis 1993: String resiny, piney notes dominate the fruit in this dry, austere wine. 626 cases made. • $8 • (06/15/96) • **78**
Zinfandel Central Coast Beaujour 1991 • $7 • (07/31/92) BB • **84**
Zinfandel Late Harvest Santa Ynez Valley Essence 1993: A sweet Zinfandel. This is more syrupy than grape juice, with some nice plum and black cherry fruit, free of any raisiny, pruny flavors and not very alcoholic. An usual wine that can substitute for dessert. 136 cases made. • $20 • (05/31/95) • **87**
Zinfandel Late Harvest Santa Ynez Valley Essence 1987 • $15 • (12/15/89) • **74**
Zinfandel San Luis Obispo County Saucelito Canyon Vineyard 1990 • $11 • (10/15/92) • **84**
Zinfandel San Luis Obispo County Saucelito Canyon Vineyard 1989 • $11 • (10/15/92) • **82**
Zinfandel Santa Ynez Valley 1987 • $8 • (12/15/89) • **82**
Zinfandel Santa Ynez Valley Beaujour 1994: Ripe and grapey, a Beaujolais-styled red that's best served chilled. 720 cases made. • $9 • (02/28/95) • **82**
Zinfandel Santa Ynez Valley Beaujour 1993: Has deep color, but the flavors don't quite match. It's pleasant enough, with grapey notes. Drinks well now, can be served chilled. 1,086 cases made. • $9 • (10/15/94) • **84**
Zinfandel Santa Ynez Valley Beaujour 1992 • $8 • (03/15/93) • **80**
Zinfandel Santa Ynez Valley Beaujour 1988 • $7 • (12/15/89) • **80**
Zinfandel Santa Ynez Valley Lafond Vineyard 1992: Ripe and spicy, with a rustic core of tarry Zinfandel fruit that turns dry and tannic on the finish. Some cellaring will soften the cherry and wild berry notes. Try in 1996. 1,150 cases made. • $10 • (10/15/94) • **85**
Zinfandel Santa Ynez Valley Lafond Vineyard 1991 • $10 • (09/30/93) • **83**

SANTA CRUZ MOUNTAIN | CALIFORNIA

Cabernet Sauvignon Santa Cruz Mountains Bates Ranch 1990: Marked by an earthy edge to the currant and berry-laced fruit, it shows off intense mineral and leathery tannins and for now the tannins have the upper hand. Truly needs cellaring to soften, but may always be on the tannic side. 746 cases made. • $15 • (12/15/95) • **85**
Cabernet Sauvignon Santa Cruz Mountains Bates Ranch 1989 • $15 • (11/15/93) • **71**
Cabernet Sauvignon Santa Cruz Mountains Bates Ranch 1988 • $14 • (11/15/93) • **87**
Cabernet Sauvignon Santa Cruz Mountains Bates Ranch 1987 • $16 • (11/15/92) • **91**
Cabernet Sauvignon Santa Cruz Mountains Bates Ranch 1986 • $15 • (11/15/91) • **89**
Cabernet Sauvignon Santa Cruz Mountains Bates Ranch 1985 • $18 • (03/01/89) • **92**
Cabernet Sauvignon Santa Cruz Mountains Bates Ranch 1984 • $15 • (03/01/89) • **87**
Cabernet Sauvignon Santa Cruz Mountains Bates Ranch 1983 • $27 • (06/15/89) • **80**
Cabernet Sauvignon Santa Cruz Mountains Bates Ranch 1982 • $23 • (03/01/89) • **72**
Cabernet Sauvignon Santa Cruz Mountains Bates Ranch 1981 • $25 • (03/01/89) • **79**
Cabernet Sauvignon Santa Cruz Mountains Bates Ranch 1980 • $25 • (03/01/89) • **86**
Cabernet Sauvignon Santa Cruz Mountains Bates Ranch 1979 • $23 • (03/01/89) • **79**
Cabernet Sauvignon Santa Cruz Mountains Bates Ranch 1978 • $35 • (11/15/92) • **88**
Merlot California 1993: Ripe and jammy, brimming with black cherry, currant and a Portlike edge. It's a mouthful of Merlot that defies varietal definition but packs in lots of flavor. Best in 1998. 866 cases made. • $15 • (04/30/96) • **86**
Merlot California 1991: A deeply colored and richly fruity wine, with an abundance of ripe and grapey flavors that pick up a pretty undertone of currant. The fruit stays with you a long time on the finish before the weight of the tannin is felt. Best to cellar this one until 1997. 535 cases made. • $14 • (07/31/94) • **89**

Key: SS—Spectator Selection. CS—Cellar Selection. BB—Best Buy. $NA—Price not available. (BT)—Barrel tasting. Ⓐ—Auction Price.
Dates in parentheses represent the issues in which the ratings were published.

Merlot California 1989 • $12 • (11/30/92) • **83**
Merlot California 1983 • $10 • (10/01/85) • **82**
Pinot Noir Santa Cruz Mountains 1990 • $18 • (02/28/94) • **81**
Pinot Noir Santa Cruz Mountains 1989 • $15 • (02/28/93) • **90**
Pinot Noir Santa Cruz Mountains 1985 • $15 • (06/15/88) • **89**
Pinot Noir Santa Cruz Mountains Estate Vineyard 1987 • $18 • (02/28/94) • **84**
Pinot Noir Santa Cruz Mountains Jarvis Vineyard 1981 • $15 • (08/31/86) • **89**
Pinot Noir Santa Cruz Mountains Matteson Vineyard 1992: Smells of beguiling, ripe cherry and berry aromas, leading to complex flavors of truffle, earth and cedar. This distinctive red has reached a nice drinking plateau. 300 cases made. • $16 • (04/30/96) • **89**
Pinot Noir Santa Cruz Mountains Matteson Vineyard 1991: Mature, offering a soft core of earth and mushroom and just hints of cherry and pepper on the finish. Tannins have softened and the texture is smooth. Ready now and into 1997. 449 cases made. • $15 • (04/30/96) • **88**
Pinot Noir Santa Cruz Mountains Matteson Vineyard 1990 • $15 • (02/28/93) • **87**
Pinot Noir Santa Cruz Mountains Matteson Vineyard 1989 • $18 • (02/28/93) • **87**

SANTA YNEZ VALLEY | CALIFORNIA

Cabernet Merlot Santa Barbara County 1987 • $13 • (03/31/90) • **72**
Pinot Noir Santa Maria Valley 1987 • $13 • (03/31/90) • **62**
Zinfandel Paso Robles 1987 • $8 • (03/31/90) • **84**

SANTINO | CALIFORNIA

Alfresco Amador County Red NV • $6 • (08/31/91) BB • **83**
Barbera Amador County Aged Release 1988 • $12 • (10/31/91) • **85**
Johannisberg Riesling Late Harvest Sonoma County Dry Berry Select 1989 • $18 • (11/30/91) • **92**
Satyricon California Red 1988 • $14 • (10/31/91) • **83**
White Zinfandel Amador County 1988 • $5 • (06/15/89) • **87**
Zinfandel Amador County Aged Release 1990 • $9 • (09/30/93) • **84**
Zinfandel Amador County Aged Release 1989 • $7 • (10/15/92) • **81**
Zinfandel Amador County Aged Release 1988 • $7 • (02/29/92) • **75**
Zinfandel Amador County Aged Release 1984 • $7 • (03/31/89) • **67**
Zinfandel Fiddletown Eschen Vineyards 1983 • $7 • (04/15/87) • **84**
Zinfandel Shenandoah Valley Grandpère Vineyards 1989 • $12 • (10/15/92) • **83**
Zinfandel Shenandoah Valley Grandpère Vineyards 1988 • $12 • (08/31/91) • **79**

SARAFORNIA | CALIFORNIA

Zinfandel Napa Valley 1988 • $8 • (02/15/91) • **81**
Zinfandel Napa Valley 1987 • $7 • (03/15/90) • **78**

SARAH'S VINEYARD | CALIFORNIA

Chardonnay Santa Clara County 1993: Combines intense citrus and grapefruit flavors with touches of honey, pear and peach, adding up to a complex and elegant wine with fine length and an earthy note. Ready. 200 cases made. • $42 • (07/31/95) • **89**
Chardonnay Santa Clara County 1992: Ripe and intense, with spicy peach, pear, honey and light toasty oak shadings. Combines richness with finesse and polish. 250 cases made. • $42 • (07/31/95) • **89**
Chardonnay Santa Clara County Lot II 1992: Ripe with apricot, honey and toasty buttery oak, a full-bodied and well oaked wine that holds together. 450 cases made. • $24 • (07/31/95) • **88**
Grenache California Cadenza 1988 • $NA • (04/15/89) • **80**
L'Audace Santa Clara County Cabernet Blend 1988 • $30 • (11/15/92) • **82**
Merlot San Luis Obispo County John Radike Vineyard 1987 • $30 • (05/31/92) • **65**
Pinot Noir Santa Clara County 1993: Rich and flavorful, boasting a full array of plum, cherry and wild berry notes that turn plush and complex on the finish. Tannins are firm but well integrated. Has the extra dimensions one hopes for. 160 cases made. • $50 • (10/15/95) • **92**

SATTUI, V. | CALIFORNIA

Cabernet Sauvignon Napa Valley 1991: Tight and compact, with spicy black cherry and plum flavors that are pure and focused. Could use a little more richness and depth, best after 1997. 2,500 cases made. • $14 • (11/15/94) • **85**
Cabernet Sauvignon Napa Valley Julian Schwinger Reserve Stock 1992: Young and intense, tightly wound, spicy, peppery, filling out the palate but also packing in lots of tannin and oak. Given the dry finish, it may be a bit overdone. Cellaring into 1998 or '99 should help. 800 cases made. • $50 • (04/30/96) • **87**
Cabernet Sauvignon Napa Valley Mario's Stock Reserve 1991: Serves up nice portions of spice, plum and black cherry, turning smooth and supple on the finish, where the flavors build richness and depth. Tasty now but worthy of short-term cellaring through 1997. 585 cases made. • $35 • (11/15/94) • **90**
Cabernet Sauvignon Napa Valley Preston Vineyard 1988 • $20 • (11/15/91) • **86**
Cabernet Sauvignon Napa Valley Preston Vineyard 1986 • $20 • (03/01/89) • **88**
Cabernet Sauvignon Napa Valley Preston Vineyard 1985 • $20 • (03/01/89) • **87**
Cabernet Sauvignon Napa Valley Preston Vineyard 1984 • $20 • (03/01/89) • **86**
Cabernet Sauvignon Napa Valley Preston Vineyard 1983 • $20 • (03/01/89) • **81**
Cabernet Sauvignon Napa Valley Preston Vineyard Reserve 1982 • $75 • (03/01/89) • **78**
Cabernet Sauvignon Napa Valley Preston Vineyard Reserve 1980 • $85 • (03/01/89) • **85**
Cabernet Sauvignon Napa Valley Preston Vineyard Rutherford District 1991: Strikes a nice balance between spicy oak and sweet ripe Cabernet fruit. Not too tannic, so you can drink it now or cellar it through 2000. 600 cases made. • $22 • (11/15/94) • **87**
Cabernet Sauvignon Napa Valley Preston Vineyards Reserve Stock 1988 • $35 • (11/15/92) • **87**
Cabernet Sauvignon Napa Valley Preston Vineyards Reserve Stock 1987 • $35 • (11/15/92) • **88**
Cabernet Sauvignon Napa Valley Suzanne's Vineyard 1991: Firm and compact, with ample tannins to shed, it reveals a crisp core of cherry and currant flavor, will need cellaring until 1999 to soften. 1,900 cases made. • $16 • (11/15/94) • **86**
Cabernet Sauvignon Napa Valley Suzanne's Vineyard 1989 • $15 • (11/15/92) • **82**
Chardonnay Napa Valley 1992: Simple and direct, fruity with a spicy edge. 700 cases made. • $14 • (06/30/94) • **82**
Chardonnay Napa Valley Carsi Vineyard Barrel Fermented 1993: A real zinger, balancing its spicy, almost peppery pear and vanilla flavors against a silky background. Stylish and appealing. Drinkable now. 1,400 cases made. • $18 • (02/28/95) • **89**
Chardonnay Napa Valley Carsi Vineyard Barrel Fermented 1992: Nicely put together, seductive, with generous pineapple, citrus and pear aromas and flavors that persist on the lively spicy finish. Should improve through 1995. 2,000 cases made. • $18 • (06/30/94) • **89**
Chardonnay Napa Valley Carsi Vineyard Barrel Fermented 1991: Crisp and lively, spicy, with a bright beam of apple and peach flavor shining through the zippy finish. 2,000 cases made. • $23 • (06/30/94) • **86**
Merlot Napa Valley 1989: Light and grapey, appealing to drink now. 800 cases made. • $16 • (09/15/94) • **80**
Sauvignon Blanc Napa Valley 1994: Light and smoothly reined-in, balancing slightly toward oak, fresh nectarine and spice on the finish. 2,100 cases made. • $11 • (08/31/95) • **83**
Sauvignon Blanc Napa Valley 1993: Brightly focused and flavorful, earthy, herbal notes echo only a touch of grapefruit to balance it. 2,150 cases made. • $10 • (01/31/95) • **82**
Sauvignon Blanc Napa Valley 1992: Crisp and frankly sweet, a fruity wine with a floral edge. 1,700 cases made. • $10 • (06/30/94) • **79**
Sauvignon Blanc Napa Valley Suzanne's Vineyard Barrel Fermented Reserve Stock 1992: Broad and spicy, a juicy wine with a frank overlay of oak but plenty of peach and citrus flavors to keep it lively. Solid but unexciting. 600 cases made. • $13 • (06/30/94) • **84**

Zinfandel Howell Mountain 1993: Spicy and peppery on the nose, offering rich wild berry and cherry flavors but little in the way of finesse. Hard tannins on aftertaste. Best to cellar into 1997 in hopes it softens. 1,000 cases made. • $18 • (04/30/96) • **84**

Zinfandel Howell Mountain 1991: A rustic style, offering cedar, pepper, raspberry and exotic spices, turning smooth and tarry on the finish. Mild tannins. 650 cases made. • $14 • (02/28/95) • **86**

SAUCELITO CANYON | CALIFORNIA

Zinfandel Arroyo Grande Valley 1993: A ripe and refreshing California Zinfandel that offers pretty floral notes and strawberry jam, cherry and wild berry flavors. Elegant, well focused and finishes with mild tannins. Drinkable now. 1,947 cases made. • $14 • (10/15/95) SS • **91**

Zinfandel Arroyo Grande Valley 1992: Very ripe and jammy, with wild berry, black cherry and plum flavors that are fleshy and focused, with a long, fruity aftertaste. 2,030 cases made. • $12 • (08/31/94) • **87**

Zinfandel Arroyo Grande Valley 1991 • $12 • (09/30/93) • **88**

Zinfandel Arroyo Grande Valley 1990 • $13 • (10/15/92) • **85**

Zinfandel Arroyo Grande Valley 1989 • $13 • (10/15/92) • **89**

Zinfandel San Luis Obispo County 1986 • $9 • (12/15/89) • **87**

SAUSAL | CALIFORNIA

Cabernet Sauvignon Alexander Valley 1992: Young and vibrant, somewhat disjointed, but a core of cherry and currant flavor is rich and ripe and persists to the finish. Best after 1997. 570 cases made. • $14 • (10/31/95) • **88**

Cabernet Sauvignon Alexander Valley 1988 • $14 • (07/15/93) • **80**

Cabernet Sauvignon Alexander Valley 1987 • $14 • (11/15/92) • **79**

Cabernet Sauvignon Alexander Valley 1985 • $12 • (07/31/89) • **74**

White Zinfandel Alexander Valley 1988 • $6 • (06/15/89) • **70**

Zinfandel Alexander Valley 1994: A solid value, featuring earthy berry and spice flavors and adding firm tannins and good intensity on the finish. 6,000 cases made. • $10 • (04/30/96) • **84**

Zinfandel Alexander Valley 1993: A firm and intense red from California, with well-focused, earthy plum, cherry and raspberry flavors and aromas that are rich and concentrated. Packs in lots of intenstiy. Best in 1997. 3,500 cases made. • $9 • (07/31/95) BB • **88**

Zinfandel Alexander Valley 1992: A big wine from California but it's smooth. Ripe in flavor, oozing plum and blackberry flavors through its satiny texture. Drinkable now. 2,500 cases made. • $9 • (01/31/95) SS • **89**

Zinfandel Alexander Valley 1990 • $9 • (12/15/92) • **82**

Zinfandel Alexander Valley 1989 • $8 • (03/31/92) • **79**

Zinfandel Alexander Valley 1988 • $8 • (04/30/91) • **82**

Zinfandel Alexander Valley 1987 • $7 • (09/15/89) • **83**

Zinfandel Alexander Valley 1986 • $6 • (03/31/89) SS • **90**

Zinfandel Alexander Valley 1985 • $6 • (10/15/88) • **72**

Zinfandel Alexander Valley 1984 • $6 • (05/31/88) • **78**

Zinfandel Alexander Valley 1983 • $5 • (09/15/87) BB • **82**

Zinfandel Alexander Valley Century Vines 1993: Solid and chunky cherry and currant, picking up notes of anise and leather. Has the density and richness for the cellar, but the heavy-handed style makes this difficult to warm up to. 500 cases made. • $15 • (03/31/96) • **84**

Zinfandel Alexander Valley Private Reserve 1992: Soft, ripe and generous, round and fully packed, with vanilla, plum and berry flavors that linger. Drinkable now. 1,000 cases made. • $14 • (01/31/95) • **87**

Zinfandel Alexander Valley Private Reserve 1991: Lean, firm and tannic, with a compact band of spice, raspberry and peppery flavors that build and gain depth through on the finish. 500 cases made. • $14 • (10/15/94) • **87**

Zinfandel Alexander Valley Private Reserve 1988 • $14 • (04/30/91) • **88**

Zinfandel Alexander Valley Private Reserve 1984 • $10 • (02/15/88) • **86**

SBARBORO | CALIFORNIA

Cabernet Sauvignon Sonoma County 1983 • $10 • (11/15/87) • **71**

Key: SS—Spectator Selection. CS—Cellar Selection. BB—Best Buy. $NA—Price not available. (BT)—Barrel tasting. Ⓐ—Auction Price.
Dates in parentheses represent the issues in which the ratings were published.

SCHARFFENBERGER | CALIFORNIA

Blanc de Blancs Mendocino County 1988 • $22 • (08/31/92) • **90**

Blanc de Blancs Mendocino County 1987 • $20 • (12/31/91) • **83**

Blanc de Blancs Mendocino County 1986 • $20 • (03/15/91) • **91**

Blanc de Blancs Mendocino County 1985 • $18 • (12/31/88) • **85**

Blanc de Blancs Mendocino County 1984 • $18 • (12/31/87) • **78**

Brut Blanc de Blancs Mendocino County 1989 • $20 • (12/31/93) • **89**

Brut Blanc de Blancs Mendocino County Prestige Cuvée 1991: Complex, well-focused range of earthy pear and pineapple notes, turning smooth and flavorful on the finish. Has a sense of harmony and finesse. 3,500 cases made. • $23 • **90**

Brut Blanc de Blancs Mendocino County Prestige Cuvée 1989: Ripe, smooth and elegant, with spicy pear, vanilla and light toasty flavors that are fresh and vibrant. Finishes with a delicate edge. Ready now. 7,000 cases made. • $20 • (12/15/94) • **89**

Brut Mendocino County 1983 • $13 • (09/30/87) • **84**

Brut Mendocino County 1982 • $13 • (02/01/86) • **85**

Brut Mendocino County NV: Supple and balanced, with ripe, spicy pear, toast and honey notes that linger. Drinks well now. 15,000 cases made. • $17 • (12/31/94) • **86**

Brut Rosé Mendocino County 1989: Smooth and elegant, with spice, black cherry and raspberry flavors that fold together nicely, with a long finish that echoes the fruit. Ready now. 2,500 cases made. • $18 • (12/31/94) • **87**

Brut Rosé Mendocino County NV • $15 • (12/31/93) • **88**

Crémant Mendocino County NV • $18 • (12/31/91) • **83**

Crémant Mendocino Extra Dry NV: Tastes off-dry with a hint of sweetness, but the toast, pear and vanilla flavors are focused and pleasing. Drinks well now. 1,500 cases made. • $17 • (12/31/94) • **87**

SCHERRER, F. | CALIFORNIA

Zinfandel Alexander Valley Old & Mature Vines 1993: Tight and compact, with a dense, earthy character to the black cherry and raspberry. Finishes with chewy tannins, try now. 1,000 cases made. • $15 • (10/15/95) • **87**

Zinfandel Alexander Valley Old Vines 1992: Firm and fleshy, with a ripe, supple core of black cherry, plum and spice flavors that are focused right through the finish. Has the tannin to age, but it's approachable now. 620 cases made. • $14 • (09/15/94) • **90**

Zinfandel Alexander Valley Old Vines Unfiltered 1991 • $14 • (08/31/93) • **87**

SCHOOL HOUSE | CALIFORNIA

Pinot Noir Spring Mountain 1993: Lacks charm, with a hard edge tobacco, sage and stemmy cherry flavors, the tannins dominate on the finish, where it turns dry and austere. Drinkable now. 98 cases made. • $35 • **77**

SCHRAMSBERG | CALIFORNIA

Blanc de Blancs Napa Valley 1989: Tastes mature with a slightly oxidized pear note, but it turns to smooth, spicy vanilla on the finish. Ready now. 15,000 cases made. • $22 • (12/31/94) • **87**

Blanc de Blancs Napa Valley 1988 • $22 • (12/31/93) • **87**

Blanc de Blancs Napa Valley 1987 • $21 • (12/15/91) • **87**

Blanc de Blancs Napa Valley 1986 • $20 • (12/31/90) • **89**

Blanc de Blancs Napa Valley 1985 • $20 • (05/31/89) • **84**

Blanc de Blancs Napa Valley 1983 • $18 • (05/16/86) • **82**

Blanc de Blancs Napa Valley Late Disgorged 12/90 1985 • $27 • (06/15/91) • **87**

Blanc de Noirs Napa Valley 30th Anniversary 1965-1995 1984: Mature with pleasant dried cherry, spice, sage and vanilla flavors. Holding its fruit quite well, a ginger edge on the finish. Ready now. 1,000 cases made. • $32 • **88**

Blanc de Noirs Napa Valley 1987: Smooth and complex, with black cherry, vanilla and strawberry flavors that linger. Well balanced and ready now. 8,000 cases made. • $24 • (12/31/94) • **87**

Blanc de Noirs Napa Valley 1986 • $24 • (12/31/93) • **87**

Blanc de Noirs Napa Valley 1985 • $22 • (12/31/91) • **83**

Blanc de Noirs Napa Valley 1984 • $22 • (12/31/90) • **82**
Blanc de Noirs Napa Valley 1983 • $21 • (05/31/89) • **90**
Blanc de Noirs Napa Valley 1981 • $20 • (05/16/86) • **91**
Blanc de Noirs Napa Valley Late Disgorged 12/90 1983 • $28 • (06/15/91) • **87**
Brut Napa Valley Reserve 1983 • $29 • (12/31/90) • **82**
Brut Napa Valley Reserve 1982 • $28 • (05/31/89) • **85**
Brut Napa Valley Reserve 1981 • $27 • (07/31/87) • **78**
Brut Napa Valley Reserve 1980 • $30 • (05/16/86) • **61**
Brut Rosé Napa Valley Cuvée de Pinot 1990: Offers a firm and lively array of ripe cherry and strawberry flavors, finishing with a clean, fruity aftertaste. Ready now. 2,000 cases made. • $23 • (12/31/94) • **87**
Brut Rosé Napa Valley Cuvée de Pinot 1989 • $22 • (12/31/93) • **84**
Brut Rosé Napa Valley Cuvée de Pinot 1987 • $20 • (12/31/90) • **81**
Brut Rosé Napa Valley Cuvée de Pinot 1986 • $19 • (05/31/89) • **76**
Brut Rosé Napa Valley Cuvée de Pinot 1985 • $17 • (04/30/88) • **80**
Brut Rosé Napa Valley Cuvée de Pinot 1984 • $17 • (05/31/87) • **83**
Demi-Sec Crémant Napa Valley 1989: Off-dry, with a trace of honey, pear and spice that finish with a rich aftertaste. Ready now. 2,000 cases made. • $22 • (12/31/94) • **87**
Demi-Sec Crémant Napa Valley 1987 • $20 • (12/31/91) • **80**
Demi-Sec Crémant Napa Valley 1986 • $20 • (12/31/90) • **77**
Demi-Sec Crémant Napa Valley 1985 • $19 • (05/31/89) • **85**
J. Schram Sparkling Napa Valley 1989: Everything you want in a bottle-aged sparkling wine. Bold, ripe and spicy, with honey, pear, nut and vanilla flavors that turn rich and creamy on the finish. Impressive for its finesse and concentration. 2,000 cases made. • $50 • (06/30/95) • **90**
J. Schram Sparkling Napa Valley 1988 • $50 • (12/31/93) • **90**
J. Schram Sparkling Napa Valley 1987 • $50 • (12/31/92) • **85**
Reserve Sparkling Napa Valley 1987: Fresh and aromatic, with spice, pear and vanilla scents that are firm and focused, only the flavors don't quite show the same complexity. Ready now. 2,000 cases made. • $32 • (12/31/94) • **86**
Reserve Sparkling Napa Valley 1986 • $32 • (12/31/93) • **85**

SCHUETZ OLES | CALIFORNIA

Chardonnay Napa Valley Chappell Vineyard 1993: Medium-weight and crisp, with an earthy, leesy edge to the pear and citrus flavors. 1,004 cases made. • $14 • (07/31/95) • **82**
Zinfandel Napa Valley Korte Ranch 1993: Intense and earthy, with some tar accents to the wild berry flavors. Finishes firmly tannic. Try now. 2,208 cases made. • $14 • (10/15/95) • **88**
Zinfandel Napa Valley Korte Ranch 1992: Firm and compact, well proportioned, striking a nice balance between currant, black cherry and toasty oak flavors. Has a measure of finesse. 2,000 cases made. • $14 • (06/15/95) • **89**

SCHUG | CALIFORNIA

Cabernet Sauvignon Sonoma Valley Heritage Reserve 1992: Youthful and a bit grapey, with the rough edges you'd expect from a barrel sample. Currant, black cherry, mineral and spicy oak flavors show promise, cellar through 1997. 300 cases made. • $25 • (11/15/94) • **86**
Chardonnay Carneros 1994: A medium-bodied white, with a trim, somewhat tart band of light oak, spice and pear. Appealing for its fruit. 1,800 cases made. • $18 • (06/30/96) • **85**
Chardonnay Carneros 1993: Marked by an earthy edge to the ripe pear and apple flavors, finishing with a funky leesy edge. 1,000 cases made. • $16 • (07/31/95) • **78**
Chardonnay Carneros Barrel Fermented 1992: Firm and one-dimensional, with light fruit aromas and flavors that fail to excite. The oak tastes hard and disjointed. Perhaps more interesting with time in the bottle. Tasted twice with consistent notes. 1,750 cases made. • $16 • (06/30/94) • **80**
Chardonnay Carneros Barrel Fermented 1991 • $15 • (07/15/93) • **80**
Chardonnay Carneros Heritage Reserve 1994: Marked by earthy citrus and tart pineapple notes, it becomes elegant and spicy on the finish. Well-crafted. The wines from this winery just keep getting more complex and interesting. 300 cases made. • $25 • (06/30/96) • **88**
Chardonnay Carneros Heritage Reserve 1993: Appealing for its ripe pear, apple and spice notes with a toasty oak edge, with a finish that echos fruit and oak. 200 cases made. • $25 • (07/31/95) • **88**
Chardonnay Sonoma Valley 1994: A pleasant white with a good band of citrus, pear and apple flavors. 1,950 cases made. • $14 • (06/30/96) • **85**
Chardonnay Sonoma Valley 1993: On the simple side now, but it's young, with ripe pear, toast and vanilla notes. Try now. 2,350 cases made. • $12 • (11/30/94) • **85**
Chardonnay Sonoma Valley 1992: Lean with shallow flavors that echo pear and apple notes. A good wine, but a little too austere. 1,200 cases made. • $12 • (06/30/94) • **82**
Pinot Noir Carneros 1994: Well-crafted smoky, toasty oak flavors and a pretty core of cherry and plum underneath. Intense and concentrated, it's young and vibrant and in need of short-term cellaring. 3,000 cases made. • $16 • (02/29/96) • **87**
Pinot Noir Carneros 1993: Tight and firm, with a band of earthy cherry, spice and cedary oak, but it fills out on the finish, where the flavors come to life. Shows Schug is making progress. 1,500 cases made. • $16 • **86**
Pinot Noir Carneros 1992: Tough and leathery, showing drying tannins and just a trace of fruit. Turns bitter, with a tealike edge. 1,250 cases made. • $15 • (03/31/95) • **78**
Pinot Noir Carneros 1991: Earthy, with leathery, gamy Pinot Noir flavors that dry out on the finish, where the tannins are potent. 1,295 cases made. • $15 • (03/31/95) • **78**
Pinot Noir Carneros 1990 • $14 • (02/28/94) • **78**
Pinot Noir Carneros Beckstoffer Vineyard 1990 • $16 • (02/28/94) • **80**
Pinot Noir Carneros Beckstoffer Vineyard 1989 • $14 • (02/28/93) • **74**
Pinot Noir Carneros Beckstoffer Vineyard 1988 • $13 • (09/30/92) • **79**
Pinot Noir Carneros Beckstoffer Vineyard 1987 • $13 • (02/28/91) • **81**
Pinot Noir Carneros Beckstoffer Vineyard 1986 • $13 • (10/31/90) • **87**
Pinot Noir Carneros Heritage Reserve 1991: Intense and spicy, offering pretty, elegant herb, black cherry and earthy raspberry flavors. Balanced and drinking well now. 200 cases made. • $25 • (12/15/94) • **87**
Pinot Noir Carneros Heritage Reserve Barrel Aged 25 Months 1992: Complex with ripe cherry, plum and currant notes, picking up an earthy gamy edge, with tarry notes. Tannins are softening. 200 cases made. • $25 • **86**
Pinot Noir Napa Valley Heinemann Vineyard Reserve 1989 • $18 • (02/28/94) • **80**
Pinot Noir Napa Valley Heinemann Vineyard Reserve 1985 • $15 • (11/15/91) • **83**
Rouge de Noirs Pinot Noir Carneros 1992: Distinctly red color, with Pinot Noir aromas and flavors. Dry and nicely balanced. Unusual, but worth trying with dinner. 250 cases made. • $20 • (12/31/94) • **85**
Rouge de Noirs Pinot Noir Carneros 1987 • $18 • (12/15/91) • **85**
Sauvignon Blanc Sonoma Valley 1993: Strange, vegetal, piney flavors in a coarse-textured white. 900 cases made. • $8 • (01/31/95) • **73**

SCOTLAND CRAIG | CALIFORNIA

Pinot Noir Russian River Valley Rochioli Vineyard 1993: Medium-bodied, with spicy berry, cola and light oak shadings. A good first vintage from this new producer, but it's not yet in the league of Rochioli or Williams Selyem bottlings. 168 cases made. • $35 • (12/31/95) • **85**

SCREAMING EAGLE | CALIFORNIA

Cabernet Sauvignon Napa Valley 1992: Dark, intense and concentrated, with a rich earthy core of mint, currant and leathery flavors. Packs in lots of complex flavors yet maintains a measure of finesse. Has richness and depth with a full long aftertaste. 175 cases made. • $50 • (02/29/96) • **92**

SEA RIDGE | CALIFORNIA

Merlot Sonoma Coast Occidental Vineyards 1989 • $15 • (05/31/92) • **86**
Pinot Noir Sonoma Coast Hirsch Vineyard 1990 • $20 • (03/31/92) • **82**
Pinot Noir Sonoma Coast Hirsch Vineyard 1989 • $18 • (03/31/92) • **81**
Pinot Noir Sonoma County 1982 • $11 • (08/31/86) • **72**

Zinfandel Late Harvest Sonoma Coast Morelli Vineyards 1991: Very ripe, intense and jammy, with spicy cherry and wild berry flavors. Carries off the tannin and alcohol well. 225 cases made. • $12 • (10/15/94) • **83**

Zinfandel Sonoma Coast Occidental Vineyard 1991: Intensely ripe and jammy, with wild blackberry and raspberry flavors, but it's mostly raw power. Approachable now. 300 cases made. • $12 • (10/15/94) • **82**

Zinfandel Sonoma Coast Occidental Vineyard 1990 • $12 • (09/30/93) • **80**

SEAVEY | CALIFORNIA

Cabernet Sauvignon Napa Valley 1991: Tight and compact, firmly tannic and earthy. Intense currant and cedar flavors lead to rich complex cherry and berry notes on the finish. Try in 1997. 840 cases made. • $26 • (07/31/95) • **89**

Cabernet Sauvignon Napa Valley 1990: Dark, rich, chewy and supple, jam-packed with layers of high-extract currant, anise, cherry and cedary oak flavors and plush tannins. Should age up to 20 years, best to cellar until 1997. • $24 • (08/31/94) • **89**

Chardonnay Napa Valley 1994: Fragrant, delicate honey, pear, peach and nectarine notes of moderate concentration and richness. A subtle, understated style. Tasted twice, with consistent notes. 395 cases made. • $16 • (05/15/96) • **88**

Chardonnay Napa Valley 1992: Firm and focused, tightly wound, offering rich, intense pear, spice and smoky, buttery oak flavors that linger on a long, full finish. Drinkable now, can age through 1998. 500 cases made. • $16 • (03/31/95) • **87**

SEBASTIANI | CALIFORNIA

Barbera Sonoma County 1989 • $10 • (03/31/93) • **81**

Barbera Sonoma Valley 1992: Crisp and juicy, lively with blackberry, black cherry and spice flavors that jump lightly through the finish. Ready now. 3,900 cases made. • $14 • (07/31/95) • **86**

Barbera Sonoma Valley 1987 • $11 • (04/30/91) • **86**

Blanc de Noirs Sonoma County Five Star NV • $11 • (04/30/90) • **77**

Brut Sonoma County Five Star NV • $11 • (04/30/90) • **72**

Cabernet Franc California 1988 • $8 • (07/15/91) • **77**

Cabernet Franc Sonoma County 1989 • $10 • (03/31/93) • **88**

Cabernet Sauvignon California Proprietor's Reserve 1974: Dried out and earthy with a pickle barrel aroma and flavor. • $40 • (11/15/94) • **68**

Cabernet Sauvignon North Coast Emilia 1986 • $13 • (03/31/92) • **71**

Cabernet Sauvignon North Coast Proprietor's Reserve 1979 • $11 • (08/01/84) • **58**

Cabernet Sauvignon Sonoma County 1992: Light and jammy, packing in plenty of raspberry and cola flavors that glide smoothly through the finish. Approachable now, best from 1997. 40,500 cases made. • $10 • (11/15/95) BB • **87**

Cabernet Sauvignon Sonoma County 1991: Distinctive for its spicy, minty notes, this elegant red serves up pretty currant and berry flavor, finishing with spice and firm tannins. Best after 1997. 44,000 cases made. • $10 • (11/15/94) • **85**

Cabernet Sauvignon Sonoma County 1990: Lean with a narrow band of oak and currant notes. Drinks well now but lacks the opulence of the vintage's best. 30,000 cases made. • $10 • (11/15/94) • **80**

Cabernet Sauvignon Sonoma County 1989 • $9 • (04/30/93) • **82**

Cabernet Sauvignon Sonoma County 1988 • $8 • (11/15/92) • **77**

Cabernet Sauvignon Sonoma County Family Selection 1985 • $8 • (10/15/88) • **80**

Cabernet Sauvignon Sonoma County Reserve 1988 • $12 • (10/31/92) • **83**

Cabernet Sauvignon Sonoma County Reserve 1986 • $13 • (01/31/91) • **86**

Cabernet Sauvignon Sonoma County Reserve 1985 • $13 • (11/15/90) • **86**

Cabernet Sauvignon Sonoma County Reserve 1978 • $NA • (11/15/92) • **83**

Cabernet Sauvignon Sonoma Valley Cherryblock 1987 • $14 • (07/15/92) • **84**

Cabernet Sauvignon Sonoma Valley Cherryblock 1985 • $17 • (03/31/90) • **89**

Key: SS—Spectator Selection. CS—Cellar Selection. BB—Best Buy. $NA—Price not available. (BT)—Barrel tasting. (A)—Auction Price.
Dates in parentheses represent the issues in which the ratings were published.

Cabernet Sauvignon Sonoma Valley Cherryblock Old Vines 1991: Firm and intense, with moderately rich and concentrated cherry, spice and currant flavors. A long, full, elegant finish, tempting now, but better in 1997. 1,720 cases made. • $24 • (11/15/94) • **88**

Cabernet Sauvignon Sonoma Valley Cherryblock Old Vines 1989 • $15 • (06/15/93) • **82**

Cabernet Sauvignon Sonoma Valley Eagle Vineyards 1982 • $27 • (09/15/86) • **75**

Cabernet Sauvignon Sonoma Valley Eagle Vineyards 1981 • $25 • (08/01/85) • **91**

Cabernet Sauvignon Sonoma Valley Reserve 1982 • $11 • (12/31/87) • **74**

Chardonnay Russian River Valley Dutton Ranch 1994: Delivers a nice core of ripe pear, peach and nectarine flavors with a light dash of oak. Well balanced, with a lingering aftertaste. 2,000 cases made. • $18 • (06/30/96) • **86**

Chardonnay Russian River Valley Dutton Ranch 1993: Perfumed with ripe pear and apple flavors that pick up a toasty, smoky buttery edge on the finish. Best Sebastiani Chardonnay-maybe ever. 1,200 cases made. • $18 • (05/31/95) • **89**

Chardonnay Sonoma County 1993: Smooth and creamy. The shades of appealing apple, pear and vanilla flavors unfold and hang together on the finish, where they pick up a toasty note. Drinkable now. 20,000 cases made. • $10 • (06/15/95) BB • **87**

Chardonnay Sonoma County 1992: Pleasant spicy pear and nutmeg flavors hang together, simple but drinkable with light oak shadings on the finish. 55,000 cases made. • $12 • (06/30/94) • **83**

Chardonnay Sonoma County 1991 • $9 • (05/15/93) • **84**

Chardonnay Sonoma County Reserve 1991 • $13 • (07/15/93) • **86**

Merlot Sonoma County 1994: Light and simple, appealing for its modest plum and spice flavors. Ready now. • $14 • (06/30/96) • **82**

Merlot Sonoma County 1993: Firm and compact, with a trim band of herb, toasty oak and currant flavors, finishing with firm tannins. Best to cellar into 1997 or 1998. 70,000 cases made. • $12 • (11/15/95) • **87**

Merlot Sonoma County 1992: Lean and chewy. A tannic wine that never quite gets its flavors revved up, barely showing its grapey currant character. May be better after 1997. 20,000 cases made. • $12 • (09/15/94) • **79**

Merlot Sonoma County 1991 • $8 • (05/15/93) BB • **84**

Merlot Sonoma County 1990 • $9 • (03/31/93) • **82**

Merlot Sonoma County 1989 • $9 • (05/31/92) • **85**

Merlot Sonoma County Family Selection 1985 • $7 • (09/30/88) • **85**

Mourvèdre California Old Vines 1993: Smooth and supple core of mineral, currant and wild berry flavors that hold together nicely on the finish. • $14 • **85**

Red Hill Vineyard Sonoma Valley 1989 • $14 • (11/15/93) • **79**

Sauvignon Blanc California Propreietor's 1993: Simple, fruity and neutral. 126,000 cases made. • $6 • (08/31/94) • **75**

Syrah Sonoma County 1992: Ripe, rich and smoky, complex and focused, currant and spice flavors lead to a short, tannic finish. Drinkable now. 1,200 cases made. • $14 • (01/31/95) • **86**

White Zinfandel California 1988 • $5 • (06/15/89) • **69**

White Zinfandel California Proprietor's White Zinfandel 1994: Strange mix of peach and cherry flavors gives this a spicy edge. • $7 • (09/15/95) • **75**

Wildwood Sonoma Valley 1987 • $15 • (08/31/91) • **86**

Zinfandel Dry Creek Valley Cuneo-Saini Vineyard 1994: Well-oaked, elegant and refined, with pretty cherry and currant notes that turn supple. Finishes with a touch of buttery oak. 1,550 cases made. • $12 • (10/15/95) • **88**

Zinfandel Sonoma County 1991: Has a shallow band of spicy flavors that picks up hints of cherry and raspberry on the finish. Ready now. 24,000 cases made. • $8 • (10/15/94) • **83**

Zinfandel Sonoma County 1989 • $7 • (03/31/93) BB • **85**

Zinfandel Sonoma County 1988 • $6 • (09/15/92) • **78**

Zinfandel Sonoma County Family Selection 1985 • $5 • (09/15/88) BB • **88**

Zinfandel Sonoma Valley Proprietor's Reserve Black Beauty 1980 • $9 • (12/16/85) • **76**

SEBASTIANI, AUGUST | CALIFORNIA

Merlot California Country NV • $4 • (05/31/92) • **72**

White Zinfandel California 1988 • $7 • (06/15/89) • **65**

SEGHESIO | CALIFORNIA

Cabernet Sauvignon Northern Sonoma 1986 • $8 • (06/30/90) • **76**
Cabernet Sauvignon Northern Sonoma 1985 • $5 • (04/15/89) BB • **84**
Cabernet Sauvignon Northern Sonoma 1983 • $6 • (07/15/88) • **69**
Cabernet Sauvignon Northern Sonoma 1982 • $5 • (04/30/87) • **77**
Cabernet Sauvignon Sonoma County 1992: Firm and intense, showing a pretty core of grapey Cabernet fruit and finishing with hints of currant and cherry. Drinkable now. • $9 • (11/15/94) • **84**
Cabernet Sauvignon Sonoma County 1991: Tart and lean, with crisp cherry and raspberry-tinged flavors. A medium-bodied young Cabernet that is tasty now, but has enough intensity and tannin for short-term cellaring. 10,000 cases made. • $9 • (03/31/94) • **83**
Cabernet Sauvignon Sonoma County 1990: A simple, direct style that features ripe cherry and currant flavors and turns chewy and tannic on the finish. It's nothing special, but it's priced fairly and is easy to drink. 5,000 cases made. • $9 • (06/15/93) • **79**
Cabernet Sauvignon Sonoma County 1989 • $9 • (11/15/92) • **82**
Cabernet Sauvignon Sonoma County 1987 • $9 • (04/30/91) • **85**
Cabernet Sauvignon Sonoma County Home Ranch 1993: Good intensity, with lively mint, cherry and plum-laced flavors before the tannins kick in. A solid value at this price. 13,000 cases made. • $9 • (02/29/96) • **84**
Carignane Alexander Valley Old Vine 1992 • $12 • (12/31/93) • **84**
Chardonnay Russian River Valley Family Home 1994: Somewhat coarse, featuring spicy pear and vanilla notes. Straightfoward style that's a decent value. 10,000 cases made. • $10 • (05/15/96) • **84**
Chardonnay Sonoma County 1993: Crisp and fruity, generous with its spiced apple and vanilla flavors that lose a little focus on the finish. • $9 • (07/31/95) • **82**
Chardonnay Sonoma County 1992: Smooth and generous, a mouthful of fresh peach and apple flavor, finishing bright and lively. Drinkable now. 18,000 cases made. • $9 • (03/31/94) BB • **87**
Chardonnay Sonoma County 1991 • $9 • (06/30/93) • **83**
Pinot Noir Northern Sonoma 1983 • $5 • (04/15/87) • **72**
Pinot Noir Russian River Valley 1991 • $9 • (02/28/94) • **81**
Pinot Noir Russian River Valley 1990 • $9 • (02/28/93) • **78**
Pinot Noir Russian River Valley 1988 • $9 • (10/31/91) • **83**
Pinot Noir Russian River Valley 1987 • $8 • (04/15/90) • **84**
Pinot Noir Russian River Valley Reserve 1987 • $13 • (04/15/90) • **83**
Pinot Noir Sonoma County 1993: Well balanced, with a solid core of earthy black cherry, spice, tea and plum notes-complex on a medium-weight frame. Try now. 4,300 cases made. • $12 • (11/15/95) • **86**
Pinot Noir Sonoma County 1989 • $9 • (04/30/92) • **79**
Pinot Noir Sonoma-Mendocino Counties 1984 • $6 • (05/31/88) • **84**
Sangiovese Alexander Valley Chianti Station Old Vine 1990 • $30 • (12/15/92) • **86**
Sangiovese Alexander Valley Vitigno Toscano 1992 • $14 • (05/31/94) • **87**
Sangiovese Alexander Valley Vitigno Toscano 1991 • $14 • (12/15/92) • **80**
Sauvignon Blanc Dry Creek Valley 1992 • $7 • (11/30/93) • **82**
Sauvignon Blanc Sonoma County 1994: Light, lean and lively, bright pear and floral flavors. 6,500 cases made. • $9 • (08/31/95) • **85**
Sauvignon Blanc Sonoma County 1993: Crisp and lively, grapefruity at the core and distinctly herbal at the edges. Bright, appealing and keeps pumping out the flavors. 4,000 cases made. • $7 • (09/30/94) BB • **88**
Sonoma Red Lot 4 Sonoma County NV • $5 • (06/30/90) • **75**
Sonoma Red Lot 3 Sonoma County NV • $4 • (05/31/88) • **78**
White Zinfandel Northern Sonoma 1988 • $5 • (06/15/89) • **84**
Zinfandel Alexander Valley Old Vine Reserve 1990 • $14 • (12/15/92) • **83**
Zinfandel Alexander Valley Reserve 1988 • $12 • (08/31/91) • **88**
Zinfandel Alexander Valley Reserve 1986 • $9 • (10/31/89) • **80**
Zinfandel Dry Creek Valley 1993: Strikes a pleasant balance between ripe berry and cherry flavors and finishes with firm tannins. It may become more supple with age. 600 cases made. • $12 • (10/15/95) • **85**
Zinfandel Northern Sonoma 1987 • $6 • (07/31/90) BB • **85**
Zinfandel Northern Sonoma 1986 • $6 • (05/15/90) BB • **80**
Zinfandel Northern Sonoma 1985 • $5 • (03/15/89) BB • **80**
Zinfandel Northern Sonoma 1984 • $5 • (06/30/88) • **76**
Zinfandel Sonoma County 1993: Tight, firm and tannic, with a narrow band of earthy berry and cherry. Tannins clamp down on the finish, but enough fruit sneaks past to hold your interest. Can age a little. 18,000 cases made. • $9 • (10/15/95) • **85**
Zinfandel Sonoma County 1992: Clean, flavorful and youthful, with bright, fresh black cherry, wild berry and raspberry flavors that are crisp and focused. Deftly balanced. 19,000 cases made. • $9 • (09/15/94) BB • **88**
Zinfandel Sonoma County 1991 • $7 • (09/30/93) • **84**
Zinfandel Sonoma County 1990 • $7 • (10/15/92) BB • **85**
Zinfandel Sonoma County 1989 • $7 • (07/31/92) BB • **84**
Zinfandel Sonoma County 1988 • $6 • (09/30/91) BB • **86**

SEGURA VIUDAS | CALIFORNIA

Brut Napa Valley NV • $12 • (07/31/93) • **82**

SELBY | CALIFORNIA

Chardonnay Sonoma County 1994: Big, ripe and intense, loaded with bold tropical fruit notes and layers of ripe pear, guava, honeysuckle and spice, an altogether rich and fruity style that doesn't shortchange you on flavor. • $18 • (04/30/96) • **90**
Pinot Noir Russian River Valley 1994: Well oaked, dry and tannic, delivering simple but pleasant cherry and berry flavors. Lacks the richness and depth of the best Pinot Noirs from this appellation. Tasted twice, with consistent notes. 200 cases made. • $16 • (05/15/96) • **85**

SELENE | CALIFORNIA

Merlot Napa Valley 1993: Serves up a modest band of earth, currant and oak flavors with firm tannins, lacks the extra flavor dimensions found in finer vintages. Drinkable now. • $25 • (06/15/96) • **84**
Merlot Napa Valley 1992: Ripe, with layers of herb, currant, cherry and cedar flavors. Complex through the finish, where the flavors fold together. Delicious now, but worthy of short-term cellaring. • $NA • **89**
Merlot Napa Valley 1991: An intriguing style, with lots of pretty fruit flavors, echoing wild berry, cherry, spice and tobacco, picking up an earthy, chocolaty edge on a firmly tannic finish. Drinkable now. • $22 • (07/31/94) • **88**
Sauvignon Blanc Carneros Hyde Vineyards 1994: Packs a lot of citrusy, appley flavor into its lively, slightly raw frame. Has the length to repay holding until 1997, but it's very good now. • $18 • (02/29/96) • **88**
Sauvignon Blanc Carneros Napa Valley Hyde Vineyards 1993: Balanced toward fruity, appealing for its pear and ever-so-slightly herbal flavors that last on the smooth finish. 650 cases made. • $18 • (08/31/95) • **86**

SELTZNER | CALIFORNIA

Merlot Stags Leap District 1991: Generous aromas of plum and currant, but the tannins clamp down on the flavors, leaving the wine struggling to maintain its balance on the finish. 1,354 cases made. • $17 • (09/15/94) • **83**

SEQUOIA GROVE | CALIFORNIA

Cabernet Sauvignon Estate Reserve 1992: Serves up a complex range of flavors, with tiers of currant, coffee, cedar and toasty oak, all well focused, finishing with firm tannins and a leathery edge. Best to short-term cellar into 1997. 3,147 cases made. • $30 • (07/31/95) • **89**
Cabernet Sauvignon Alexander Valley 1981 • $28 Ⓐ • (03/01/89) • **84**
Cabernet Sauvignon Napa County 1986 • $16 • (09/30/89) • **78**
Cabernet Sauvignon Napa County 1985 • $16 • (03/01/89) • **86**
Cabernet Sauvignon Napa Valley 1992: Deep, intense fruit and lively acidity, with a rich core of earthy currant, chocolate, cedar and vanilla, finishing with a long, tannic and complex aftertaste. Impressive for its harmony and finesse. 7,490 cases made. • $18 • (07/31/95) SS • **90**
Cabernet Sauvignon Napa Valley 1991: Firm, ripe and focused, with a beam of currant, black cherry and plum flavors. Tightens up on the finish, where the earthy tannins weigh in, but altogether it's rich and pleasing. Best after 1997. • $18 • (11/15/94) • **88**
Cabernet Sauvignon Napa Valley 1990: Firm and compact, with a rich, chewy core of currant, tobacco, earth and mineral notes that are com-

plex and concentrated. May still need time to soften and develop, but try now. 7,000 cases made. • $16 • (03/31/94) SS • **90**

Cabernet Sauvignon Napa Valley 1989 • $16 • (11/15/92) • **80**
Cabernet Sauvignon Napa Valley 1988 • $20 • (11/15/92) • **87**
Cabernet Sauvignon Napa Valley 1987 • $19 • (11/15/91) • **70**
Cabernet Sauvignon Napa Valley 1984 • $20 • (03/01/89) • **85**
Cabernet Sauvignon Napa Valley 1981 • $28 • (03/01/89) • **80**
Cabernet Sauvignon Napa Valley Cask One 1980 • $30 • (03/01/89) • **85**
Cabernet Sauvignon Napa Valley Cask Two 1980 • $30 • (03/01/89) • **87**
Cabernet Sauvignon Napa Valley Estate 1988 • $25 • (11/15/92) • **87**
Cabernet Sauvignon Napa Valley Estate 1987 • $31 • (11/15/91) • **87**
Cabernet Sauvignon Napa Valley Estate 1986 • $28 • (09/30/89) • **84**
Cabernet Sauvignon Napa Valley Estate 1985 • $30 • (08/31/88) • **92**
Cabernet Sauvignon Napa Valley Estate 1982 • $30 • (03/01/89) • **82**
Cabernet Sauvignon Napa Valley Estate Reserve 1991: Ripe, firm and focused, with an intense core of currant, cherry, plum and spice, and it's developing a supple texture. Develops a rich, smoky aftertaste on the finish, where the flavors are most appealing. Best after 1998. 2,000 cases made. • $26 • (07/31/94) • **91**
Cabernet Sauvignon Napa Valley Estate Reserve 1990: Smooth and supple, a very soft-textured wine with a nice array of spicy, chocolaty currant and prune aromas and flavors that slide across the finish without a ripple. Flavorful in a gentle sort of way. Drinkable now. Tasted twice. 1,995 cases made. • $25 • (12/15/93) • **90**
Cabernet Sauvignon Napa Valley Estate Reserve 1989 • $25 • (10/31/92) • **93**
Cabernet Sauvignon Napa-Alexander Valleys 1983 • $18 • (03/01/89) • **77**
Cabernet Sauvignon Napa-Alexander Valleys 1982 • $25 • (03/01/89) • **78**
Cabernet Sauvignon Rutherford Estate Reserve 1992: Tiers of well-focused currant, coffee, cedar and toasty oak finish with firm tannins and a leathery edge. Best to cellar short-term into 1997. 3,147 cases made. • $30 • (12/31/95) • **89**
Chardonnay Carneros 1991 • $14 • (07/15/93) • **82**
Chardonnay Carneros Napa Valley 1993: Earthy with a marked grapefruit and citrus edge, turning lean and simple on the finish. 6,639 cases made. • $14 • (07/31/95) • **83**
Chardonnay Carneros Napa Valley 1992: Clean and crisp, with juicy peach, citrus and nectarine flavors that are tightly wound but well proportioned. Try now. 6,725 cases made. • $14 • (06/30/94) • **86**
Chardonnay Napa Valley Carneros 1991: Lean and thin with a narrow band of pear and spice flavors. Not nearly as rich and flavorful as it usually is. Best in 1995. Tasted twice with consistent results. 7,074 cases made. • $14 • (06/30/94) • **80**
Chardonnay Napa Valley Estate Reserve 1993: Leans toward the earthy citrus and grapefruit side of Chardonnay, which isn't very pretty absent more fruit. 1,711 cases made. • $18 • (07/31/95) • **82**
Chardonnay Napa Valley Estate Reserve 1992: Lean and intense, displaying ripe pear and apple flavors that turn rich and spicy on the finish, where it picks up a smoky edge. • $19 • (03/31/95) • **88**
Chardonnay Napa Valley Estate Reserve 1991: Tight and compact, with a narrow band of buttery pear flavors, but the finish comes up short. This is unusually simple and bland for Sequoia Grove, which usually excels with the grape. Tasted twice with consistent notes. Ready now. 2,800 cases made. • $21 • (06/30/94) • **82**

SEVEN HILLS | WASHINGTON

Merlot Walla Walla Valley Seven Hills Vineyard 1993: Supple, velvety, bright berry and black cherry flavors, nicely integrated to spicy oak on the lingering finish. Best in 1996. 1,000 cases made. • $22 • (09/30/95) • **88**
White Riesling Columbia Valley 1995: Off-dry, bright and lively, with disarmingly fresh peach and floral flavors. 900 cases made. • $7 • **85**
White Riesling Columbia Valley 1994: Simple and easy to drink, like biting into a juicy peach, adds resiny overtones on the finish. Ready now. 720 cases made. • $7 • (09/30/95) • **85**

Key: SS—Spectator Selection. CS—Cellar Selection. BB—Best Buy. $NA—Price not available. (BT)—Barrel tasting. Ⓐ—Auction Price.
Dates in parentheses represent the issues in which the ratings were published.

SHADOW CREEK | CALIFORNIA

Blanc de Blancs California 1984 • $15 • (01/31/88) • **77**
Blanc de Blancs Sonoma County 1983 • $15 • (05/16/86) • **88**
Blanc de Blancs Sonoma County 1982 • $15 • (10/16/85) • **89**
Blanc de Noirs California 1984 • $13 • (05/31/87) • **86**
Blanc de Noirs California NV • $11 • (06/15/91) • **80**
Blanc de Noirs Sonoma County 1982 • $13 • (05/16/86) • **79**
Brut Blanc de Noirs California NV • $11 • (12/31/92) • **86**
Brut California NV • $11 • (12/31/92) • **86**
Brut California Reserve Cuvée 1983 • $20 • (05/31/89) • **87**

SHADOWBROOK | CALIFORNIA

Cabernet Sauvignon Napa Valley 1985 • $9 • (07/15/91) • **84**
Pinot Noir Napa Valley 1990 • $9 • (09/30/92) • **79**

SHAFER | CALIFORNIA

Cabernet Sauvignon Stags Leap District 1992: Ripe and fruity, with attractive plum and cherry notes that progress to more depth and complexity. The flavors fold neatly into a smooth and harmonious finish. 6,500 cases made. • $22 • (09/30/95) CS • **91**
Cabernet Sauvignon Stags Leap District 1991: Rich and supple, with a focused core of earth, tobacco and currant flavor that picks up a cedary oak edge and mineral notes. Has the tannic structure for cellaring, best after 1997. 5,000 cases made. • $21 • (08/31/94) • **90**
Cabernet Sauvignon Stags Leap District 1990: Ripe and generous, with a broad array of plum, blackberry, prune and chocolate flavors driving across the palate, pumping strong into the finish. Echoes of fruit and spice keep it going. Has outstanding potential, which it should have reached by now or in 1997. 5,500 cases made. • $20 • (11/15/93) • **90**
Cabernet Sauvignon Stags Leap District 1989 • $19 • (08/31/92) • **86**
Cabernet Sauvignon Stags Leap District 1988 • $20 • (08/31/91) • **88**
Cabernet Sauvignon Stags Leap District 1987 • $19 • (07/31/90) • **92**
Cabernet Sauvignon Stags Leap District 1986 • $20 • (09/30/89) SS • **93**
Cabernet Sauvignon Stags Leap District 1985 • $22 • (03/01/89) • **91**
Cabernet Sauvignon Stags Leap District 1984 • $20 • (03/01/89) • **91**
Cabernet Sauvignon Stags Leap District 1983 • $20 • (03/01/89) • **87**
Cabernet Sauvignon Stags Leap District 1982 • $27 • (03/01/89) • **88**
Cabernet Sauvignon Stags Leap District 1980 • $30 • (03/01/89) • **77**
Cabernet Sauvignon Stags Leap District 1979 • $40 • (03/01/89) • **89**
Cabernet Sauvignon Stags Leap District 1978 • $50 • (11/15/92) • **91**
Cabernet Sauvignon Stags Leap District Hillside Select 1991: Sleek and elegant, with appealing black cherry, raspberry, spice and toast shadings. Offers a supple texture, with bright, ripe flavors and good length. Tempting now for its elegance and finesse, but it has the stuffing to age through another decade. 2,000 cases made. • $45 • (11/15/95) CS • **93**
Cabernet Sauvignon Stags Leap District Hillside Select 1989 • $35 • (05/15/94) • **90**
Cabernet Sauvignon Stags Leap District Hillside Select 1988 • $35 • (03/31/93) • **88**
Cabernet Sauvignon Stags Leap District Hillside Select 1987 • $36 • (07/31/92) • **88**
Cabernet Sauvignon Stags Leap District Hillside Select 1986 • $45 • (03/15/91) • **91**
Cabernet Sauvignon Stags Leap District Hillside Select 1985 • $48 Ⓐ • (05/31/90) CS • **91**
Cabernet Sauvignon Stags Leap District Hillside Select 1984 • $35 • (04/30/89) • **89**
Cabernet Sauvignon Stags Leap District Hillside Select 1983 • $32 Ⓐ • (03/01/89) • **89**
Cabernet Sauvignon Stags Leap District Hillside Select 1990: Marked by herb and tobacco notes, but with sufficient plum and cherry fruit to balance. Finishes with good length, fine tannins and a supple, polished texture. Showing hints of maturity, but it's also tighly wound, so cellaring into 1997 is advised. 2,000 cases made. • $38 • (12/15/95) • **90**
Cabernet Sauvignon Stags Leap District Reserve 1982 • $35 • (03/01/89) • **89**
Chardonnay Napa Valley Barrel Select 1993: A tight and narrow band of pear and nutmeg fans out on the finish of this well-crafted white. • $16 • (04/30/95) • **87**

Chardonnay Napa Valley Barrel Select 1992: Strikes a nice balance between clean, fresh pear and vanilla flavors, and they linger on the finish. Appealing to drink now. 6,000 cases made. • $16 • (03/31/94) • **86**
Chardonnay Napa Valley Barrel Select 1991 • $15 • (03/15/93) • **91**
Chardonnay Napa Valley Carneros Red Shoulder Ranch 1994: Big, ripe, intense and juicy, loaded with rich, complex flavors. The echoes of ripe pear, anise, fig and spice are cast nicely in a full-bodied style. Yet for all its size and depth, it maintains a sense of elegance and finesse right through the long finish. 3,500 cases made. • $23 • (06/15/96) • **93**
Firebreak Stags Leap District Red 1993: Medium weight, with ripe plum and cherry flavors before finishing with crisp tannins. 400 cases made. • $24 • (02/29/96) • **84**
Firebreak Stags Leap District Sangiovese 1992: Rich in flavor, sinewy in structure, lacing its ripe black cherry and berry with anise and gamy notes. The flavors keep pumping out on the chewy, somewhat tannic finish. Drinkable now. 500 cases made. • $22 • (11/30/94) • **89**
Firebreak Stags Leap District Cabernet Blend 1991: Firm and flavorful, a soft-textured wine with solid currant and violet aromas and flavors, finishing with an echo of fruit. Drinkable now through 1997. 500 cases made. • $20 • (12/15/93) • **85**
Merlot Napa Valley 1993: Medium-weight, supple and flavorful, featuring currant, cherry, herb and berry notes, very good balance and mild tannins. Missing the extra dimensions of some vintages, but well crafted nonetheless. 6,000 cases made. • $24 • (12/15/95) • **88**
Merlot Napa Valley 1992: A smooth and elegant wine with cedary oak and currant flavors that are well integrated, finishing with a pretty berry aftertaste. • $21 • (06/15/95) • **88**
Merlot Napa Valley 1991: Leans toward the herb and coffee spectrum of flavors, with a hint of dried prune, but it's an awkward young Merlot that lacks charm, surprising for Shafer, which has hit the mark so often with this wine. Drinkable now. 6,000 cases made. • $20 • (09/15/94) • **83**
Merlot Napa Valley 1990 • $18 • (05/31/92) • **91**
Merlot Napa Valley 1989 • $18 • (08/31/91) • **87**
Merlot Napa Valley 1988 • $17 • (12/31/90) • **83**
Merlot Napa Valley 1987 • $15 • (10/15/89) • **92**
Merlot Napa Valley 1986 • $13 • (12/31/88) • **91**
Merlot Napa Valley 1985 • $13 • (12/15/87) • **90**
Merlot Napa Valley 1984 • $13 • (02/28/87) • **87**
Merlot Napa Valley 1983 • $10 • (02/16/86) • **93**
Zinfandel Napa Valley Last Chance 1983 • $7 • (02/16/86) • **73**

SHAW, CHARLES | CALIFORNIA

Gamay Beaujolais Napa Valley 1988 • $6 • (07/15/89) • **78**
Gamay Blanc Napa Valley 1986 • $4 • (03/31/87) • **70**
Gamay Napa Valley 1986 • $6 • (05/31/87) • **77**

SHENANDOAH | CALIFORNIA

Black Muscat Amador County 1992 • $10 • (11/15/93) • **84**
Cab-Shiraz Amador County 1993: Broad and chewy, providing a nice mouthful of berry and spice flavors wrapped in a layer of tannin that requires until 1997 or 1998 to soften. 450 cases made. • $10 • (12/15/95) • **85**
Cabernet Franc Amador County Varietal Adventure Series 1989 • $10 • (08/31/91) • **87**
Cabernet Sauvignon Amador County 1992: This is another solid effort from Shenandoah, with its bright, juicy black cherry, plum and currant flavors. Picks up a nice touch of spice and toasty oak on the finish, but the flavors keep pumping through. Ready now. 1,800 cases made. • $10 • (11/15/94) BB • **88**
Cabernet Sauvignon Amador County 1991: An earthy style that needs food to tame the flavors. Ready now. 450 cases made. • $10 • (11/15/94) • **79**
Cabernet Sauvignon Amador County 1990: Earthy and vegetal, with a strong bell pepper and green bean edge to the currant and tobacco flavors. Will appeal to some more than others, but is drinkable. Tasted twice. 900 cases made. • $10 • (11/15/92) • **74**
Cabernet Sauvignon Amador County Artist Series 1987 • $10 • (02/28/91) • **80**
Cabernet Sauvignon Amador County Artist Series 1986 • $12 • (10/31/88) • **86**
Cabernet Sauvignon Amador County Artist Series 1984 • $9 • (08/31/87) • **89**
Orange Muscat Amador County 1992 • $10 • (11/15/93) • **84**
Orange Muscat Amador County 1990 • $10 • (06/15/92) • **84**
Port Amador County 1989: Sweet and distinctive in flavor, leaning toward prune and caramel, finishing soft, with just the lightest grip. Good now, better in 1998 to 2000. 387 cases made. • $7 • (09/30/95) • **81**
Sangiovese Amador County 1994: Ripe and intense, distinctly minty, muscular core of cherry and currant. Chewy tannins and a touch of heat on the finish. Best into 1997. 156 cases made. • $12 • (04/30/96) • **84**
Sauvignon Blanc Amador County 1995: Bright and nimble, an invigorating mouthful of passion fruit, citrus and fig flavors that keep swirling through the finish. 1,620 cases made. • $8 • (05/31/96) • **89**
Sauvignon Blanc Amador County 1994: Definitely floral and herbal, a soft, round-textured white that adds a noticeable dose of oak on the finish. 646 cases made. • $7 • (08/31/95) • **84**
Sauvignon Blanc Amador County 1993: Smooth and polished, a silky white containing citrusy pear and mineral flavors. 1,600 cases made. • $8 • (02/28/95) • **82**
Sauvignon Blanc Amador County California 1991: Crisp and nicely made, a well proportioned wine that shows appealing apple and sweet pea flavors. 5,600 cases made. • $7 • (06/30/94) • **84**
Serene Varietal Adventure Series Amador County 1989 • $8 • (03/31/91) • **74**
White Zinfandel Amador County 1988 • $6 • (06/15/89) • **81**
White Zinfandel Amador County 1986 • $5 • (03/31/87) • **82**
Zinfandel Special Reserve 1989 • $8 • (02/29/92) • **84**
Zinfandel Amador County 1991 • $6 • (06/15/93) • **76**
Zinfandel Amador County Classico Varietal Adventure Series 1990 • $6 • (09/15/92) BB • **82**
Zinfandel Amador County Classico Varietal Adventure Series 1989 • $6 • (04/30/91) BB • **82**
Zinfandel Amador County Special Reserve 1994: Young and still somewhat raw and tannic but well balanced, featuring a pleasant core of smoky, toasty, berry flavors. Finishes on the short side, aging into 1997 is advised. 1,850 cases made. • $8 • (04/30/96) • **87**
Zinfandel Amador County Special Reserve 1993: Firm, ripe and intense, with a full-bodied core of chewy wild berry and raspberry flavors couched in earthy tannins. Drink now. 1,594 cases made. • $8 • (10/15/95) • **87**
Zinfandel Amador County Special Reserve 1992: Smells floral and fruity but tastes a bit earthier, anise and wild berry notes appear before the tannins close in. 1,700 cases made. • $8 • (02/28/95) • **83**
Zinfandel Amador County Special Reserve 1990 • $8 • (06/15/93) • **78**
Zinfandel Amador County Special Reserve 1987 • $8 • (07/31/89) • **81**
Zinfandel Amador County Special Reserve 1986 • $7 • (07/15/88) • **86**
Zinfandel Amador County Special Reserve 1985 • $7 • (02/15/88) • **85**
Zinfandel Fiddletown Special Reserve 1983 • $7 • (10/15/86) • **74**
Zinfandel/Sirah Late Harvest Sierra Foothills 1991: Bold, ripe and Port-like, with dense, dry, chewy tannins. The ripe plum flavor doesn't quite fight through. Best after 1998, but likely to remain tannic. • $8 • (10/15/94) • **81**
Zingiovese Amador County 1993: Dry and tannic, with just enough fruit to hold your interest, but doesn't do justice to either the Zin or Sangiovese in the blend. 336 cases made. • $9 • (05/15/95) • **77**

SHOOTING STAR | CALIFORNIA

Cabernet Franc Clear Lake 1992: This has a weedy, herbal edge to the light berry and currant notes, but it holds its focus and gains complexity on the finish. Ready now. 1,000 cases made. • $9 • (12/31/94) • **84**
Cabernet Franc Clear Lake 1991 • $9 • (10/15/93) BB • **85**
Chardonnay Mendocino 1993: An odd style, with an earthy edge to the pear and spice flavors. Drinkable now. 900 cases made. • $9 • (11/15/94) • **82**
Chardonnay Mendocino 1992: An excellent value in Chardonnay, with spicy, lively pear and buttery oak flavors. Jed Steele's second label. 600 cases made. • $9 • (06/30/94) BB • **84**

SHOWN AND SONS

Chardonnay Sonoma County 1994: Distinctive for its nectarine and tangerine accents, featuring complex flavors of modest proportions. 800 cases made. • $10 • (05/15/96) • **84**

Grenache Washington Côte de Columbia 1994: Smooth, fruity and generous with its blackberry, plum and spice flavors. From a California winery, but with Washington grapes. 500 cases made. • $8 • (09/30/95) • **85**

Merlot Clear Lake 1992: Light in color, but very flavorful, showing pretty, toasty, buttery oak, spicy cherry and currant and a long, full finish. Best now until 1997. 400 cases made. • $9 • (06/30/94) • **87**

Pinot Noir Mendocino 1993: Well oaked, with vanilla and toast flavors that complement the black cherry and spice. Drinkable now. 600 cases made. • $9 • (02/28/95) BB • **86**

Zinfandel Lake County 1994: Serves up pleasant toasty, buttery oak character and ripe plum and cherry flavor in an elegant, easy-to-drink-and-enjoy style. Drink this while you're waiting for the Steele Zin to soften. 300 cases made. • $8 • (04/30/96) • **89**

Zinfandel Lake County 1993: A supple, polished red with wild berry, raspberry and blueberry flavors that are ripe and appealing. Drinks well now, and will hold up through 1997. 900 cases made. • $8 • (02/28/95) BB • **87**

Zinfandel Mendocino Zin Gris Pacini Vineyard 1994: Dry and a little funky. This has an earthy character, with only modest charms. 400 cases made. • $8 • (10/15/95) • **78**

SHOWN AND SONS | CALIFORNIA

Cabernet Sauvignon Napa Valley Rutherford 1979 • $15 • (04/01/84) • **63**

Zinfandel Napa Valley 1981 • $7 • (04/16/84) • **85**

SIDURI | CALIFORNIA

Pinot Noir Anderson Valley Rose Vineyard 1994: Complex and rich, offering dark cherry, wild berry, plum and spice notes that gain a measure of depth and flavor from the spicy, toasty oak. An impressive new wine. 107 cases made. • $30 • (01/31/96) • **89**

SIERRA VISTA | CALIFORNIA

Cabernet Sauvignon El Dorado 1989 • $11 • (11/15/92) • **76**

Cabernet Sauvignon El Dorado 1988 • $11 • (04/15/92) • **84**

Cabernet Sauvignon El Dorado 1984 • $9 • (03/31/88) • **86**

Cabernet Sauvignon El Dorado Five Star Reserve 1991: Pleasantly earthy with supple spice and currant notes. 250 cases made. • $22 • (11/15/94) • **86**

Syrah El Dorado Sierra Syrah 1985 • $9 • (04/15/89) • **82**

Syrah El Dorado Sierra Syrah 1983 • $9 • (04/15/89) • **89**

Zinfandel El Dorado 1990 • $9 • (10/15/92) • **73**

Zinfandel El Dorado 1989 • $9 • (03/31/92) • **78**

Zinfandel El Dorado Herbert Vineyards 1986 • $8 • (03/31/89) • **84**

Zinfandel El Dorado Reeves Vineyard Special Reserve 1985 • $12 • (04/30/88) • **73**

SIGNORELLO | CALIFORNIA

Cabernet Sauvignon Napa Valley Founder's Reserve 1993: Ripe and fruity, as complex flavors echo black cherry, currant, anise and light oak shadings. Has the tannic strength to cellar into 1998 or '99. 575 cases made. • $32 • (05/15/96) • **88**

Cabernet Sauvignon Napa Valley Founder's Reserve 1992: Smooth and polished for such a young wine, with an appealing array of black cherry, currant, plum and spice flavors. The finish shows up the light oak shadings and firm tannins. Hold onto this until 1997. 825 cases made. • $32 • (09/15/95) CS • **90**

Cabernet Sauvignon Napa Valley Founder's Reserve 1991: Rich and intense, packed with currant, mineral, herb and tobacco flavors that lead to a firm, tannic edge and pretty oak shadings. The texture is chewy and a bit coarse, but still in bounds for a wine this young. Will need cellaring until 1998. 750 cases made. • $30 • (09/30/94) • **90**

Cabernet Sauvignon Napa Valley Founder's Reserve 1990: Ripe, round and chewy, a complex wine with a brilliantly focused beam of currant, chocolate and buttery oak flavor that keeps singing on the long finish. Has style and intensity, worth cellaring until 2000 to 2005, although it is approaching drinkability. 425 cases made. • $30 • (10/15/93) • **92**

Cabernet Sauvignon Napa Valley Founder's Reserve 1989 • $25 • (07/15/92) • **85**

Cabernet Sauvignon Napa Valley Founder's Reserve 1988 • $25 • (05/15/91) • **92**

Chardonnay Napa Valley 1994: An elegant style where the ripe fig, pear and melon flavors are shaded by toasty oak. Turns complex and spicy on the finish, where the smoky flavors are a touch astringent. 1,200 cases made. • $20 • (03/31/96) • **89**

Chardonnay Napa Valley 1993: Lavishly oaked, demonstrating smoky, charred, almost bitter edges, but the creamy pear and vanilla flavors unfold into a long, complex aftertaste. 800 cases made. • $20 • (04/15/95) • **88**

Chardonnay Napa Valley 1991 • $20 • (07/15/93) • **85**

Chardonnay Napa Valley Founder's Reserve 1994: Bold, ripe, rich and complex, offering tiers of ripe fig, pear, apple and honeysuckle notes before picking up pleasant, toasty oak and hazelnut. Still a bit tannic, but very concentrated and deep in flavor. 475 cases made. • $30 • (05/15/96) • **92**

Chardonnay Napa Valley Founder's Reserve 1993: Intense and concentrated, with ripe pear, pineapple and nectarine notes that turn complex, with a long aftertaste, picking up a citrus. 525 cases made. • $30 • (07/31/95) • **90**

Chardonnay Napa Valley Founder's Reserve 1992: Firm and compact, with a tight, narrow, flinty band of citrus, nutmeg and pineapple flavors that are complex and concentrated. Should drink well into 1997. 500 cases made. • $28 • (06/30/94) • **88**

Il Taglio Napa Valley 1991 • $9 • (03/31/94) • **86**

Merlot Napa Valley 1990 • $25 • (03/15/94) • **82**

Petite Sirah Napa Valley Unfined Unfiltered 1990 • $15 • (10/15/93) • **84**

Pinot Noir Napa Valley 1988 • $25 • (02/28/91) • **85**

Pinot Noir Napa Valley Founder's Reserve 1992: Black cherry, watermelon and wild berry flavors turn elegant and refined on the finish. Ripe and spicy, ready through 1998. 500 cases made. • $28 • (03/31/95) • **87**

Pinot Noir Napa Valley Founder's Reserve 1991 • $28 • (02/28/94) • **87**

Pinot Noir Napa Valley Founder's Reserve 1990 • $25 • (02/28/93) • **82**

Pinot Noir Napa Valley Founder's Reserve 1989 • $25 • (11/15/91) • **78**

Pinot Noir North Coast Unfiltered Founder's Reserve 1993: Medium weight with spicy plum and black cherry fruit of modest proportion, it's a delicate style with a measure of finesse. 625 cases made. • $28 • **86**

Sauvignon Blanc Napa Valley 1993: Broad, generous and supple, glowing with honey-scented pear, citrus and spicy vanilla flavors that linger. Ready now. 400 cases made. • $15 • (02/28/95) • **89**

Sauvignon Blanc Napa Valley 1992 • $15 • (03/15/94) • **87**

Sauvignon Blanc Napa Valley Barrel Fermented 1991 • $15 • (06/30/93) • **85**

Sémillon Napa Valley 1994: Has nice buttery character in addition to the citrusy pear flavor that lingers on the spicy finish. Drinkable now. 650 cases made. • $18 • (05/15/96) • **87**

Sémillon Napa Valley 1992: Ripe and spicy, lavishly layered and rich in texture, a generous wine that wraps its pear and pineapple fruit in a plush coat of spice and honey. Ready. 100 cases made. • $18 • (12/15/94) • **88**

Sémillon Napa Valley Barrel Fermented 1993: Ripe and spicy, generous with its oaky pear and lanolin flavors, finishing strong. 250 cases made. • $18 • (08/31/95) • **86**

Sémillon Napa Valley Barrel Fermented 1991 • $18 • (09/30/93) • **86**

Zinfandel Napa Valley Unfined Unfiltered 1993: Lots of toasty, smoky oak-so much that fruit flavors struggle to peek through. Has hints of earthy berry and spice that might show better with age. 100 cases made. • $18 • (09/15/95) • **86**

Zinfandel Napa Valley Unfined Unfiltered 1990 • $15 • (06/15/93) • **75**

Key: SS—Spectator Selection. CS—Cellar Selection. BB—Best Buy. $NA—Price not available. (BT)—Barrel tasting. Ⓐ—Auction Price.
Dates in parentheses represent the issues in which the ratings were published.

SILVER HORSE | CALIFORNIA

Cabernet Sauvignon Paso Robles 1993: Medium-weight, with a simple band of cherry and berry fruit and a vegetal edge. 1,000 cases made. • $13 • (03/31/96) • **79**

Cabernet Sauvignon Paso Robles 1990: Simple but pleasant enough, with light berry and cola notes. Ready now. 150 cases made. • $10 • (11/15/94) • **82**

Chardonnay Paso Robles 1994: Clean and well crafted, with lots of smoky, toasty oak and a nice core of pear and apple fruit. 1,200 cases made. • $11 • (02/29/96) • **87**

Pinot Noir Paso Robles 1994: Marked by a menthol edge that dominates. Clean and pleasant enough, adding spicy nuances to the plum flavor. 700 cases made. • $13 • (02/29/96) • **81**

Zinfandel Paso Robles 1992: An earthy, austere and cedary style of Zin, showing hints of wild blackberry coming through on the finish. 300 cases made. • $12 • (02/28/95) • **84**

SILVER LAKE | WASHINGTON

Cabernet Sauvignon Columbia Valley 1991: Firm in texture, a chewy red with modest plum and herb flavors sneaking through. Best from 1997. 975 cases made. • $13 • (09/30/94) • **80**

Cabernet Sauvignon Columbia Valley Reserve 1989: Soft and generous, showing a lot of honey and floral character, an intriguing red that is very mature. Drinkable now. 450 cases made. • $16 • (09/30/94) • **86**

Chardonnay Columbia Valley 1993: Supple, generous up front and dripping with pear and citrusy flavors, narrowing a bit on the finish. 2,600 cases made. • $8 • (09/30/95) • **83**

Chardonnay Columbia Valley Reserve 1993: Smooth, generous, spicy and floral, focused grapefruit and pear flavors turning a little bitter on the finish. 675 cases made. • $13 • (09/30/95) • **82**

Chardonnay Columbia Valley Reserve 1992: Round and spicy, delicately scented by peach, toast and nutmeg. Leans a little too strongly toward oak, but try now. 450 cases made. • $13 • (09/30/95) • **84**

Chardonnay Columbia Valley Reserve 1991: Rich, round, smooth and elegant, a supple wine with gorgeous pear, earth, spice and honey flavors competing for attention, all wrapped in a silky texture that lets the flavors mingle enticingly on the long finish. Drinkable now, but should be fine through 1998. 450 cases made. • $16 • (12/31/94) • **90**

Chardonnay Columbia Valley Sentinel Peak 1993: Lean and spicy, crisp in texture, as citrusy pear and floral flavors extend into a lively finish. 2,100 cases made. • $7 • (09/30/95) • **84**

Fumé Blanc Columbia Valley Dry 1993: Smoky notes resembling toasted onion skins intrude on the spicy nectarine flavor, but the finish is fresh. 900 cases made. • $6 • (09/30/95) • **80**

Ice Wine Columbia Valley 1989 • $25/375ml • (06/15/91) • **85**

Merlot Columbia Valley 1990: Bright, firm and fruity, the tannins smoothly integrated into a slightly chewy red with scents of berry and plum. Drinkable now. 700 cases made. • $16 • (09/30/94) • **86**

Merlot Columbia Valley Sentinel Peak 1993: Lean and earthy, adding a stemmy-menthol edge to the modest black cherry flavors. Try in 1997. 1,950 cases made. • $8 • (09/30/95) • **78**

Red Wine Reserve Columbia Valley 1990: Soft and smooth, generous with its smoky plum flavors, finishing broad. Drink now. 200 cases made. • $16 • (09/30/95) • **84**

Riesling Columbia Valley Dry 1992: Light and sappy, with piney notes adding an extra touch to the simple melon and peach flavors. 1,500 cases made. • $7 • (09/30/94) • **82**

Riesling Columbia Valley Ice Wine 1989: Maturing Riesling aromas of petrol, mineral and apricot draw you in and follow through on the medium-bodied, somewhat delicate palate. It's not exceptionally sweet, but offers balance and good fruit. 250 cases made. • $25 • **85**

Sauvignon Blanc Columbia Valley 1991 • $8 • (06/15/93) • **81**

Sentinel Peak Cabernet Blend Columbia Valley 1993: Lean and tangy, offering an unusual zing of acidity. The flavors are reminiscent of unripe berry. 1,800 cases made. • $7 • (09/30/95) • **79**

Sentinel Peak Fumé Chardonnay Columbia Valley 1993: Lean and floral, adding a bit of spice on the finish. 1,400 cases made. • $6 • (09/30/95) • **78**

SILVER MOUNTAIN | CALIFORNIA

Chardonnay Monterey 1991: Elegant and stylish with ripe pear, peach, light toasty oak and spicy Chardonnay flavors. Drinkable now. 500 cases made. • $14 • (06/30/94) • **84**

SILVER OAK | CALIFORNIA

Cabernet Sauvignon Alexander Valley 1991: Lavishly oaked, with an herb and dill edge to the currant and berry fruit. It is a rich and harmonious style, with layers of flavor. Firmly tannic, it can stand cellaring into 1998 to 2000 and still be massive. 35,000 cases made. • $32 • (11/15/95) • **91**

Cabernet Sauvignon Alexander Valley 1990: An herbal style showing a dill and pepper edge, it turns smooth and supple, finishing with plum and cherry notes and soft tannins. Drinkable now 28,000 cases made. • $32 • (11/15/94) • **89**

Cabernet Sauvignon Alexander Valley 1989 • $29 • (11/15/93) • **82**
Cabernet Sauvignon Alexander Valley 1988 • $38 • (10/31/92) • **91**
Cabernet Sauvignon Alexander Valley 1987 • $45 • (10/15/91) • **89**
Cabernet Sauvignon Alexander Valley 1986 • $48 • (10/31/90) SS • **93**
Cabernet Sauvignon Alexander Valley 1985 • $60 • (10/31/89) • **86**
Cabernet Sauvignon Alexander Valley 1984 • $57 • (03/01/89) • **89**
Cabernet Sauvignon Alexander Valley 1983 • $40 • (03/01/89) • **86**
Cabernet Sauvignon Alexander Valley 1982 • $57 Ⓐ • (03/01/89) • **90**
Cabernet Sauvignon Alexander Valley 1981 • $65 Ⓐ • (03/01/89) • **86**
Cabernet Sauvignon Alexander Valley 1980 • $69 Ⓐ • (03/01/89) • **88**
Cabernet Sauvignon Alexander Valley 1979 • $71 Ⓐ • (03/01/89) • **85**
Cabernet Sauvignon Alexander Valley 1978 • $90 Ⓐ • (11/15/92) • **91**
Cabernet Sauvignon Alexander Valley 1977 • $85 Ⓐ • (03/01/89) • **88**
Cabernet Sauvignon Alexander Valley 1976 • $75 • (03/01/89) • **86**
Cabernet Sauvignon Alexander Valley 1975 • $60 Ⓐ • (03/01/89) • **88**

Cabernet Sauvignon Napa Valley 1991: A big, ripe, dark and intense style yet it manages to offer enough finesse and grace to keep in balance. Offers ripe cherry, currant and meaty edge on the finish, where the oak kicks in. Best after 1997. 8,800 cases made. • $36 • (11/15/95) • **90**

Cabernet Sauvignon Napa Valley 1990: Lavishly oaked, with a pretty band of complex spice, herb, currant and black cherry flavors that pick up a smoky edge on the finish. The texture is smooth and supple, giving it the appeal to drink now. 6,000 cases made. • $32 • (11/15/94) CS • **91**

Cabernet Sauvignon Napa Valley 1989 • $29 • (11/15/93) • **86**
Cabernet Sauvignon Napa Valley 1988 • $40 • (10/31/92) • **88**
Cabernet Sauvignon Napa Valley 1987 • $44 • (10/15/91) • **89**
Cabernet Sauvignon Napa Valley 1986 • $26 • (10/31/90) CS • **94**
Cabernet Sauvignon Napa Valley 1985 • $85 • (10/31/89) • **88**
Cabernet Sauvignon Napa Valley 1984 • $70 Ⓐ • (03/01/89) • **86**
Cabernet Sauvignon Napa Valley 1983 • $48 • (03/01/89) • **74**
Cabernet Sauvignon Napa Valley 1982 • $74 Ⓐ • (03/01/89) • **88**
Cabernet Sauvignon Napa Valley 1981 • $65 Ⓐ • (03/01/89) • **79**
Cabernet Sauvignon Napa Valley 1980 • $85 Ⓐ • (03/01/89) • **73**
Cabernet Sauvignon Napa Valley 1979 • $60 Ⓐ • (03/01/89) • **82**

Cabernet Sauvignon Napa Valley Bonny's Vineyard 1987 • $87 • (10/31/92) • **89**

Cabernet Sauvignon Napa Valley Bonny's Vineyard 1986 • $95 • (10/15/91) • **88**

Cabernet Sauvignon Napa Valley Bonny's Vineyard 1985 • $95 • (11/15/90) • **83**

Cabernet Sauvignon Napa Valley Bonny's Vineyard 1984 • $85 • (10/15/89) • **84**

Cabernet Sauvignon Napa Valley Bonny's Vineyard 1983 • $50 • (03/01/89) • **82**

Cabernet Sauvignon Napa Valley Bonny's Vineyard 1982 • $61 • (03/01/89) • **78**

Cabernet Sauvignon Napa Valley Bonny's Vineyard 1981 • $75 • (03/01/89) • **77**

Cabernet Sauvignon Napa Valley Bonny's Vineyard 1980 • $60 Ⓐ • (03/01/89) • **70**

Cabernet Sauvignon Napa Valley Bonny's Vineyard 1979 • $100 Ⓐ • (03/01/89) • **72**

Cabernet Sauvignon North Coast 1974: Two bottles each showed their age. The better was light in color with mature, smoky currant and stewed plum flavors that turned smooth and soft on the finish. Past its

peak yet enjoyable, best to drink soon. 4,000 cases made. • $110 Ⓐ • (11/15/94) • **83**
Cabernet Sauvignon North Coast 1973 • $130 • (03/01/89) • **81**
Cabernet Sauvignon North Coast 1972 • $110 • (03/01/89) • **86**

SILVER RIDGE | CALIFORNIA

Cabernet Sauvignon Napa Valley 1989: A good 1989 with ripe currant, spice and oak shadings. Best to drink soon. 2,500 cases made. • $10 • (11/15/94) • **84**
Chardonnay California Barrel Fermented 1994: Ripe and spicy, with generous nutmeg, toast and pear flavors that narrow to a sharp focus on the finish. 5,000 cases made. • $10 • (06/30/96) • **86**
Chardonnay California Barrel Fermented 1991 • $10 • (06/15/93) • **83**
Merlot California 1992: Light and grapey, with currant and cherry notes, but has enough fruit to keep it interesting. 3,000 cases made. • $12 • (09/15/94) • **80**
Merlot California Barrel Select 1992: Medium bodied, with simple cherry and berry fruit flavors and light oak shadings with mild tannins. Good but nothing more. 2,000 cases made. • $10 • **81**

SILVERADO HILL CELLARS | CALIFORNIA

Chardonnay Napa Valley 1994: A light style that's harmonious and delicately spicy, accenting the green apple flavor. 3,500 cases made. • $10 • (06/15/96) • **85**
Chardonnay Napa Valley 1992: Smooth and polished on the surface and crisp-textured underneath, offering plenty of pear and grapefruit flavor that rings on through the finish. 3,870 cases made. • $10 • (06/30/94) BB • **87**
Chardonnay Napa Valley Winemaker's Traditional Methode 1994: Distinctive, with a character reminisicent of apple cider that persists on the supple finish. 4,500 cases made. • $10 • (06/15/96) • **83**
Chardonnay Napa Valley Winemaker's Traditional Methode 1993: Crisp and simple, with a lean band of pear and citrus notes that pick up a light floral edge. 1,500 cases made. • $10 • (07/31/95) • **83**

SILVERADO VINEYARDS | CALIFORNIA

Cabernet Sauvignon Napa Valley 1993: Well crafted, with attractive herb, cherry and currant flavors. Finishes with the requisite tannins, but they're not excessive for a wine this young. 9,500 cases made. • $20 • **87**
Cabernet Sauvignon Napa Valley 1992: Firm and rich, with complex cherry, anise, currant and cedar flavors. Young, intense and tannic, so it needs some time in the cellar. Best after 1998. 15,000 cases made. • $19 • (03/31/95) SS • **90**
Cabernet Sauvignon Napa Valley Limited Reserve 1990: A beautifully crafted Cabernet that combines ripe, rich, complex currant, black cherry, cedar, vanilla bean and spice. Wonderful depth, beautifully articulated flavors that keep pumping out the flavors. Delicious now, but should hold and gain through the decade. Start drinking around 1997. 2,994 cases made. • $40 • (10/31/93) CS • **97**
Cabernet Sauvignon Stags Leap District 1991: A ripe and richly concentrated wine, with focused cherry, berry and currant flavors. On the finish, the tannins really kick in, but it also delivers a lot of fruit. This is a tremendous wine, especially in its price range. Best in 1997 and thereafter. 12,850 cases made. • $17 • (04/30/94) SS • **93**
Cabernet Sauvignon Stags Leap District 1990: Smooth, polished and elegant, offering complex plum, currant, spice and vanilla aromas and flavors smoothly blended into a harmonious whole. Finishes rich and supple. Tannic and smoothly integrated, making this tempting to drink now, but best after 1999. 9,628 cases made. • $16 • (06/30/93) • **90**
Cabernet Sauvignon Stags Leap District 1989 • $19 • (08/31/92) • **81**
Cabernet Sauvignon Stags Leap District 1988 • $18 • (03/31/91) • **86**
Cabernet Sauvignon Stags Leap District 1987 • $25 • (04/15/90) SS • **92**
Cabernet Sauvignon Stags Leap District 1986 • $25 • (08/31/89) SS • **94**

Key: SS—Spectator Selection. CS—Cellar Selection. BB—Best Buy. $NA—Price not available. (BT)—Barrel tasting. Ⓐ—Auction Price.
Dates in parentheses represent the issues in which the ratings were published.

Cabernet Sauvignon Stags Leap District 1985 • $30 • (03/01/89) • **92**
Cabernet Sauvignon Stags Leap District 1984 • $21 • (03/01/89) • **91**
Cabernet Sauvignon Stags Leap District 1983 • $22 • (03/01/89) • **88**
Cabernet Sauvignon Stags Leap District 1982 • $25 • (03/01/89) • **88**
Cabernet Sauvignon Stags Leap District 1981 • $33 • (03/01/89) • **90**
Cabernet Sauvignon Stags Leap District Limited Reserve 1991: Ripe, complex, with tiers of black cherry, plum and currant aromas and flavors. Gains richness on the palate, revealing uncommon depth and concentration, finishing with firm tannins and a long, rich aftertaste. Try after 1998. 2,000 cases made. • $40 • (11/15/94) CS • **93**
Cabernet Sauvignon Stags Leap District Limited Reserve 1987 • $45 • (10/31/91) • **93**
Chardonnay Napa Valley 1993: Crisp, tart apple, peach and citrus flavors. What's there is pretty, could use some development on the finish. Tasted twice, with consistent notes. 28,385 cases made. • $15 • (05/31/95) • **87**
Chardonnay Napa Valley 1992: Well balanced and nicely proportioned, with creamy pear, hazelnut and spicy notes that turn delicate on the finish. Enjoy it now. 44,500 cases made. • $16 • (04/30/94) • **87**
Chardonnay Napa Valley 1991 • $14 • (07/15/93) • **89**
Chardonnay Napa Valley Limited Reserve 1992: An exciting new release that is ripe and racy, with tart pear, citrus, honey and toasty flavors that are rich and concentrated. It finishes with a long, full aftertaste. 2,400 cases made. • $33 • (12/31/94) SS • **92**
Merlot Napa Valley 1992: Firm and focused, with a nice core of cherry and mint flavors poking through the chewy tannins. Drinkable now. • $18 • (01/31/95) • **85**
Merlot Napa Valley 1991: A solid red with plenty of currant and berry flavor, finishing with a bit of a tannic bite. Drinkable now. 3,600 cases made. • $17 • (09/15/94) • **85**
Merlot Napa Valley Limited Reserve 1992: Supple and fruity, with bright, lively, juicy cherry and currant fruit, picking up a trace of herb and chocolate. Finishes with crisp acidity and firm tannins, but they're not overbearing. 1,279 cases made. • $45 • **89**
Merlot Stags Leap District 1990 • $17 • (06/15/93) • **87**
Merlot Stags Leap District 1989 • $16 • (04/15/92) • **87**
Merlot Stags Leap District 1988 • $16 • (05/31/91) • **86**
Merlot Stags Leap District 1987 • $14 • (04/15/90) • **92**
Merlot Stags Leap District 1986 • $12 • (08/31/89) • **91**
Merlot Stags Leap District 1984 • $13 • (12/15/87) • **78**
Sauvignon Blanc-Chardonnay-Sémillion Late Harvest Napa Valley Limited Reserve NV: Very ripe and sweet, a dark-colored, spicy, pineapple-scented wine that echoes honey on the finish. Delicious now. 500 cases made. • $25/375ml • (04/30/95) • **90**
Sauvignon Blanc Napa Valley 1995: Ripe, mouth-filling and flavorful, a core of pear, citrus and smoky flavors and a smooth, round finish. 21,411 cases made. • $10 • **86**
Sauvignon Blanc Napa Valley 1994: Crisp and refreshing, zesty, marked by herb, citrus and light fig shadings. 22,425 cases made. • $9 • (02/29/96) • **86**
Sauvignon Blanc Napa Valley 1993: Crisp and grapefruity up front, a refreshing wine that fades a little as it approaches the finish. 19,700 cases made. • $9 • (08/31/94) • **84**
Sangiovese Napa Valley 1993: Heavily oaked, with chewy tannins and a lean core of currant and spice, turning dry on the finish. Lacks varietal character, as it seems overoaked and overly tannic. 417 cases made. • $18 • (01/31/96) • **78**
Sauvignon Blanc Napa Valley 1992 • $9 • (12/15/93) • **79**
Sauvignon Blanc Napa Valley 1991 • $9 • (11/30/92) • **84**

SILVERWOOD | CALIFORNIA

Claret Napa Valley 1988 • $9 • (10/15/92) • **70**

SIMI | CALIFORNIA

Altaire North Coast Red 1992 • $8 • (07/31/93) • **78**
Cabernet Sauvignon Alexander Valley 1992: Ripe and plush, offering supple texture and lots of rich, earthy currant and cherry flavor. Finishes with firm, chewy tannins, so cellaring into 1998 is advised. 30,000 cases made. • $15 • (10/15/95) • **89**
Cabernet Sauvignon Alexander Valley 1989 • $14 • (06/15/93) • **77**

Cabernet Sauvignon Alexander Valley 1988 • $15 • (07/31/92) • **84**
Cabernet Sauvignon Alexander Valley 1981 • $20 • (11/01/85) • **79**
Cabernet Sauvignon Alexander Valley 1980 • $28 • (07/01/84) • **81**
Cabernet Sauvignon Alexander Valley 1979 • $28 • (04/01/84) SS • **91**
Cabernet Sauvignon Alexander Valley 1975 • $32 • (03/01/89) • **85**
Cabernet Sauvignon Alexander Valley 1973 • $25 • (03/01/89) • **72**
Cabernet Sauvignon Alexander Valley 1972 • $31 • (03/01/89) • **80**
Cabernet Sauvignon Alexander Valley 1971 • $30 • (03/01/89) • **75**
Cabernet Sauvignon Alexander Valley 1970 • $35 • (03/01/89) • **73**
Cabernet Sauvignon Alexander Valley Reserve 1991: Supple and harmonious, with well-focused cherry, currant, mineral and spice notes that lead to firm tannins and an excellent, long finish. This ample California Cab needs to age into 1998 or 1999 to show its best. 3,500 cases made. • $35 • (10/15/95) • **92**
Cabernet Sauvignon Alexander Valley Reserve 1988 • $33 • (03/31/93) • **87**
Cabernet Sauvignon Alexander Valley Reserve 1987 • $37 • (07/15/92) • **88**
Cabernet Sauvignon Alexander Valley Reserve 1986 • $36 • (07/31/91) • **89**
Cabernet Sauvignon Alexander Valley Reserve 1985 • $25 • (08/31/90) SS • **94**
Cabernet Sauvignon Alexander Valley Reserve 1984 • $25 • (03/01/89) • **92**
Cabernet Sauvignon Alexander Valley Reserve 1981 • $30 • (12/15/88) • **86**
Cabernet Sauvignon Alexander Valley Reserve 1980 • $40 • (03/01/89) • **84**
Cabernet Sauvignon Alexander Valley Reserve 1979 • $40 • (03/01/89) • **87**
Cabernet Sauvignon Alexander Valley Reserve 1978 • $50 • (03/01/89) • **72**
Cabernet Sauvignon Alexander Valley Reserve 1974 • $54• (02/15/90) • **85**
Cabernet Sauvignon Alexander Valley Reserve Vintage 1974 • $54 • (03/01/89) • **87**
Cabernet Sauvignon Alexander Valley Special Reserve 1974: Distinctive for its weedy, herbal Cabernet edge, well past its peak,finishing with a spicy, tarry edge. Drink up. 2,000 cases made. • $54 • (11/15/94) • **82**
Cabernet Sauvignon Alexander Valley Special Selection 1977 • $30 • (03/01/89) • **70**
Cabernet Sauvignon Sonoma County 1987 • $17 • (05/15/91) • **89**
Cabernet Sauvignon Sonoma County 1985 • $21 • (09/30/89) • **91**
Cabernet Sauvignon Sonoma County 1984 • $20 • (10/31/88) • **86**
Cabernet Sauvignon Sonoma County 1982 • $15 • (11/15/86) • **90**
Cabernet Sauvignon Sonoma County Centennial Edition 1990: An earthy style, displaying just enough supple plum and cherry flavor to maintain your interest. Finishes with good length, but not the richness and depth you might expect from this vintage. • $14 • (11/15/94) • **84**
Cabernet Sauvignon Sonoma-Napa Counties Reserve 1982 • $50 • (04/15/89) • **90**
Chardonnay Mendocino-Sonoma-Napa Counties 1991 • $12 • (07/15/93) • **85**
Chardonnay Sonoma County Reserve 1993: Clean and lively, with a pretty array of ripe pear and apple flavors set off by lightly toasty oak shadings. It finishes with a sense of elegance and finesse. Impeccibly balanced and attractive. 2,000 cases made. • $28 • (06/15/96) • **92**
Pinot Noir North Coast 1981 • $7 • (09/16/85) • **64**
Rosé of Cabernet Sauvignon Sonoma County 1990 • $7 • (04/30/92) • **77**
Rosé of Cabernet Sauvignon Sonoma County 1988 • $7 • (11/15/89) • **81**
Rosé of Cabernet Sauvignon Sonoma County 1985 • $7 • (07/16/86) • **81**
Sauvignon Blanc Sonoma County 1993: Soft and fruity, offering a floral edge to the slightly honeyed pear flavors. 20,000 cases made. • $9 • (08/31/95) • **84**
Sauvignon Blanc Sonoma County 1991 • $9 • (02/28/93) • **85**
Sendal Sonoma County 1994: Lemon and spice flavors jump smartly to the fore in this polished, oak-accented Sauvignon Blanc-Sémillon blend. 1,100 cases made. • $16 • **85**
Sendal Sonoma County 1992: Broad and toasty, a bit of onion intruding around the edges of the light, herbal, smoky pear flavors. 700 cases made. • $16 • (08/31/95) • **84**
Sendal Sonoma County 1991: Ripe and generous, with a figgy edge to the buttery pineapple flavors that shows some extra dimensions. A smooth wine that's drinkable now. 755 cases made. • $18 • (09/30/94) • **88**
Zinfandel Sonoma County 1982 • $6 • (05/01/86) • **60**

SINEANN | WASHINGTON

Zinfandel Columbia Valley Old Vine 1994: Ripe and generous with its blackberry, wild strawberry and black pepper flavors that show plenty of richness on a supple frame. Ready now, but best in 1998. 128 cases made. • $15 • (04/30/96) • **88**

SINSKEY, ROBERT | CALIFORNIA

Cabernet Sauvignon Napa Valley Aries 1990: Intense and vibrant with chewy plum and currant flavors that are ripe and complex, picking up anise and spice notes on a firm, tannic finish. Was balanced and young, should have developed into a nice wine by about now. Tasted twice. 600 cases made. • $11 • (10/31/93) • **87**
Cabernet Sauvignon Stags Leap District 1989 • $22 • (11/15/92) • **89**
Chardonnay Carneros 1993: Tart with a green apple and pear edge, this is a young wine with a definite lemony streak. Can stand short-term cellaring. 1,000 cases made. • $20 • (07/31/95) • **87**
Chardonnay Los Carneros 1992: Tart, tight and intense with crisp citrus, pear and pineapple flavors that are lean and focused, picking up a pretty toasty oak edge on the finish. Ready now. 400 cases made. • $20 • (06/30/94) • **87**
Chardonnay Los Carneros 1991 • $16 • (07/15/93) • **90**
Claret RSV Carneros 1990: Tight, firm and focused, with cedar aromas and ripe cherry, plum and wild berry flavors that are medium-bodied and supple on the palate. Relies heavily on Merlot (52 percent), which gives it a soft mouth-feel and smooth tannins. Appealing now, but worth aging short-term. 1,660 cases made. • $28 • (05/15/94) • **87**
Claret RSV Carneros 1989 • $28 • (02/15/93) • **85**
Claret RSV Carneros 1988 • $28 • (11/15/91) • **89**
Claret RSV Stags Leap District 1991: Dark, intense and firmly tannic, with enough currant, spice, mineral and cherry notes to merit cellaring through 1997. Should develop into something special. 1,100 cases made. • $28 • (11/15/94) • **88**
Merlot Aries 1989 • $18 • (05/31/92) • **86**
Merlot Carneros 1991 • $18 • **80**
Merlot Carneros Napa Valley 1992: Trim, medium-bodied band of cedar and currant picks up an earthy edge on the finish. Supple tannins. Drinkable now. 3,400 cases made. • $18 • (04/30/96) • **85**
Merlot Carneros Napa Valley 1989 • $18 • (05/31/92) • **83**
Merlot Carneros Napa Valley Aries 1989 • $11 • (11/30/92) • **84**
Merlot Los Carneros Napa Valley 1990 • $18 • (12/31/93) • **86**
Merlot Napa Valley 1987 • $18 • (03/31/91) • **88**
Merlot Napa Valley 1986 • $17 • (10/15/89) • **83**
Pinot Noir Carneros Napa Valley 1992: Strongly oaked, showing a meaty, smoky, gamy cover that dominates the ripe plum and cherry flavor beneath. A heavy-handed style where the fruit gets overwhelmed. 4,100 cases made. • $19 • (03/31/95) • **83**
Pinot Noir Carneros Napa Valley 1990 • $18 • (09/30/92) • **85**
Pinot Noir Carneros Napa Valley 1988 • $18 • (02/28/91) • **81**
Pinot Noir Carneros Napa Valley 1987 • $14 • (03/31/90) • **86**
Pinot Noir Carneros Napa Valley 1986 • $12 • (06/15/88) • **79**
Pinot Noir Carneros Napa Valley Aries 1991 • $9 • (02/28/93) • **84**
Pinot Noir Carneros Napa Valley RSV Reserve 1990 • $32 • (11/30/92) • **80**
Pinot Noir Napa Valley Los Carneros 1991 • $19 • (02/28/94) • **82**

SKY | CALIFORNIA

Zinfandel Mount Veeder 1990 • $16 • (09/30/93) • **88**
Zinfandel Mount Veeder 1989 • $13 • (10/15/92) • **87**
Zinfandel Napa Valley 1988 • $12 • (08/31/91) • **78**
Zinfandel Napa Valley 1987 • $17 • (10/15/90) • **90**
Zinfandel Napa Valley 1985 • $9 • (10/31/88) • **88**

SLAUGHTER LEFTWICH | TEXAS

Cabernet Sauvignon 1989 • $9 • (02/29/92) • **76**

SMITH, W.H. | CALIFORNIA

Pinot Noir Sonoma Coast Hellenthal Vineyard Young Vines 1994: Big, bold, ripe and complex, featuring tiers of ripe cherry, plum and wild berry, shaded by pretty, toasty oak and mineral flavors that come through on the finish. Has a measure of finesse and grace. 180 cases made. • $22 • (04/30/96) • **91**

SMITH & HOOK | CALIFORNIA

Cabernet Sauvignon Monterey 1983 • $14 • (11/15/87) • **78**
Cabernet Sauvignon Monterey County 1981 • $14 • (12/16/84) • **90**
Cabernet Sauvignon Monterey Santa Lucia Highlands 1988 • $15 • (11/15/91) • **80**
Cabernet Sauvignon Napa County 1985 • $12 • (09/30/89) • **88**
Cabernet Sauvignon Napa County 1982 • $17 • (06/15/87) • **79**
Cabernet Sauvignon Santa Lucia Highlands 1992: Tough and chewy, a nice core of currant and plum fruit trying to push through the layers of tannin. Needs until 1999-2001. 4,088 cases made. • $18 • (12/15/95) • **83**
Cabernet Sauvignon Santa Lucia Highlands 1991: A big, ripe, herbal style, with layers of cedar, currant, coffee and spice notes that are deep and concentrated. Finishes with firm tannins, best after 1996. 2,487 cases made. • $18 • (11/15/94) • **86**
Cabernet Sauvignon Santa Lucia Highlands 1990: An oaky style that's complex and concentrated, with herb, currant, tobacco and spicy flavors framed by toasty, buttery wood. Full-bodied and finishing with a smoky, meaty edge and firm tannins. Drinkable now through 1998 and beyond. 10,261 cases made. • $18 • (03/31/94) • **87**
Cabernet Sauvignon Santa Lucia Highlands Masterpiece Edition 1992: Firm and chewy, the currant, plum and spice flavors are generous enough to sail past the fine tannins on the finish. A harmonious wine. Best from 1998. 416 cases made. • $30 • (12/15/95) • **88**
Merlot Napa County 1987 • $15 • (12/31/90) • **83**
Merlot Napa County 1986 • $20 • (08/31/89) • **86**
Merlot Santa Lucia Highlands 1993: Lean and tough, with a band of cedar, herb, light cherry and currant flavors. 2,783 cases made. • $18 • **83**
Merlot Santa Lucia Highlands 1992: Well oaked with herb and currant flavors that pick up a spicy wood flavor on the finish. 2,783 cases made. • $18 • (07/31/95) • **85**
Merlot Santa Lucia Highlands 1991: Earthy, rubbery aromas and flavors dominate this soft, flavorful red. Not for everyone. 2,573 cases made. • $18 • (09/15/94) • **78**
Merlot Santa Lucia Highlands 1990: Lean and tart, with an austere vegetal, bell-pepper edge. But there are some cherry notes framed by toasty, buttery oak. Drink now through 1997. 2,059 cases made. • $18 • (09/15/94) • **81**
Merlot Santa Lucia Highlands 1989 • $15 • (05/31/92) • **70**
Merlot Santa Lucia Highlands 1988 • $15 • (05/31/92) • **80**

SMITH-MADRONE | CALIFORNIA

Cabernet Sauvignon Napa Valley 1985 • $19 • (04/15/90) • **74**
Cabernet Sauvignon Napa Valley 1984 • $25 • (03/01/89) • **91**
Cabernet Sauvignon Napa Valley 1983 • $16 • (03/01/89) • **84**
Cabernet Sauvignon Napa Valley 1982 • $16 • (03/01/89) • **79**
Cabernet Sauvignon Napa Valley 1981 • $18 • (03/01/89) • **78**
Cabernet Sauvignon Napa Valley 1980 • $18 • (03/01/89) • **79**
Cabernet Sauvignon Napa Valley 1979 • $25 • (03/01/89) • **86**
Cabernet Sauvignon Napa Valley 1978 • $25 • (03/01/89) • **84**
Pinot Noir Napa Valley 1984 • $10 • (12/15/87) • **65**

SMOTHERS BROTHERS | CALIFORNIA

Cabernet Sauvignon Sonoma Valley 1988: An earthy style with tobacco, green bean and leathery currant flavors that turn meaty and tannic on the finish. 467 cases made. • $17 • (11/15/94) • **82**
Cabernet Sauvignon Sonoma Valley Remick Ridge Ranch 1990: Offers more substance and depth than the '89. Of medium weight with moderately rich currant, cherry and oak flavors. Approachable now but can be cellared short-term, best after 1998. 780 cases made. • $18 • (11/15/94) • **87**
Cabernet Sauvignon Sonoma Valley Remick Ridge Ranch 1989: Light and simple with herb, currant and spice notes. Ready now. 681 cases made. • $16 • (11/15/94) • **82**

Key: SS—Spectator Selection. CS—Cellar Selection. BB—Best Buy. $NA—Price not available. (BT)—Barrel tasting. Ⓐ—Auction Price.
Dates in parentheses represent the issues in which the ratings were published.

SNOQUALMIE | WASHINGTON

Cabernet Merlot Columbia Valley 1992: This serves up an attractive medium-weight range of wild berry and cherry flavors. Drinkable now. 4,000 cases made. • $8 • (02/28/95) BB • **85**
Cabernet Sauvignon Columbia Valley 1989 • $11 • (03/15/94) • **87**
Cabernet Sauvignon Columbia Valley 1987 • $10 • (09/30/90) • **90**
Gewürztraminer Columbia Valley 1994: A little sweet but nicely balanced to show off the nectarine and delicate rose petal flavors. 5,000 cases made. • $6 • (09/30/95) • **83**
Gewürztraminer Columbia Valley 1993: Soft and fruity, a simple white with a little sweetness. • $7 • (09/30/94) • **78**
Johannisberg Riesling Columbia Valley 1994: Light and somewhat tart, citrusy, showing appealing floral and apple flavor and a touch of sweetness. Ready now. 5,000 cases made. • $6 • (09/30/95) • **84**
Johannisberg Riesling Columbia Valley 1993: A bright and immaculate Washington white that shows off its peach, pear and zippy citrus flavors as they sail smoothly through the finish. Utterly beguiling for its taste and price. 6,000 cases made. • $6 • (09/15/95) BB • **87**
Johannisberg Riesling Columbia Valley Dry 1994: Generous, harmonious and spilling over with fruit, offering nectarine, pear and a hint of floral spice. Enjoy it now. 2,000 cases made. • $6 • (09/30/95) • **86**
Merlot Columbia Valley Reserve 1987 • $12 • (09/30/90) • **91**
Muscat Canelli Columbia Valley 1994: Simple, sweet but not quite syrupy. Generous pear and litchi flavors follow through on the lingering finish. 6,500 cases made. • $8 • (09/30/95) • **82**
Muscat Canelli Columbia Valley 1993: Lightly sweet and oddly vegetal, not as pretty as it could be. • $7 • (09/30/94) • **78**
Sémillon Columbia Valley 1994: Crisp, light and distinctly herbal, finishing delicately and with a touch of pear. 5,000 cases made. • $6 • (07/31/95) • **81**
Sémillon Columbia Valley 1993: Light and perfumy, a refreshing white with delicate herb and floral overtones to the citrusy pear flavors. Drinkable now. • $7 • (09/30/94) • **84**
White Riesling Late Harvest Columbia Valley 1988 • $7 • (10/15/89) • **84**

SOBON ESTATE | CALIFORNIA

Blush Shenandoah Valley Rosé 1994: Dry, fresh and lively, gently unfolding its watermelon and spice flavors. 495 cases made. • $6 • (09/15/95) • **82**
Cabernet Franc Shenandoah Valley 1990 • $12 • (08/31/92) • **81**
Cabernet Sauvignon Shenandoah Valley 1988 • $14 • (08/31/92) • **78**
Cabernet Sauvignon Shenandoah Valley 1987 • $15 • (11/30/90) • **83**
Fumé Blanc Shenandoah Valley 1991 • $8 • (01/31/94) • **78**
Rhône Rouge Shenandoah Valley Red 1992: Intensely spicy, combining earthy, tarry, bell-pepper accents with currant and cherry flavors. 600 cases made. • $8 • (05/15/95) • **86**
Syrah Shenandoah Valley 1993: Earthy, gamy flavors dominate this gutsy, chewy red. Has a little black cherry note on the finish. Best in 1997 or '98. 593 cases made. • $10 • (09/30/95) • **82**
Syrah Shenandoah Valley 1991: Intense and deeply colored, with compact, concentrated flavors turning meaty and spicy on the tannic finish. Drinkable now or cellar into 1997. 1,019 cases made. • $12 • (01/31/95) • **82**
Syrah Shenandoah Valley 1990 • $12 • (12/31/92) • **86**
Viognier Shenandoah Valley 1994: Exuberant aromas of fruit, flowers and spices become soft on the palate, bordering on flabby. A nice drink, but it needs more backbone. 666 cases made. • $17 • (09/30/95) • **80**
Viognier Shenandoah Valley 1993: Ripe and broad, a mouth-filling white with tropical fruit, spice and slightly earthy overtones. Tastes generous. For drinking soon. 511 cases made. • $17 • (09/15/94) • **86**
Viognier Shenandoah Valley 1992 • $16 • (09/30/93) • **78**
Zinfandel Fiddletown Lubenko 1993: Dark, intense, ripe and jammy, with plum, cherry and wild berry flavors that are on the rustic side. 389 cases made. • $13 • (03/31/96) • **83**
Zinfandel Fiddletown Lubenko 1992: Very ripe, though the prunelike edge is dry and tannic. 239 cases made. • $14 • (06/15/95) • **82**
Zinfandel Shenandoah Valley 1992: A rustic style, with cherry and berry jam flavors and a tarry character. Tannic and earthy on the finish. 830 cases made. • $10 • (10/15/95) • **81**

Zinfandel Shenandoah Valley 1988 • $10 • (11/30/90) • **88**

Zinfandel Shenandoah Valley Cougar Hill 1993: Ripe and intense, with a firm, tannic core of earthy wild berry and cherry. 388 cases made. • $13 • (03/31/96) • **83**

Zinfandel Shenandoah Valley Old Vines Sobon Estate 1990 • $16 • (09/30/93) • **78**

Zinfandel Shenandoah Valley Rocky Top 1993: Strikes a nice balance between ripe cherry, plum and berry flavors, light oak shadings and supple tannins. Finishes with good length and chunky fruit character. 395 cases made. • $13 • (03/31/96) • **85**

Zinfandel Shenandoah Valley Rocky Top 1992: Ripe-almost jammy-featuring wild berry and cherry flavors that turn exotic, then finish with chewy tannins. 292 cases made. • $14 • (02/28/95) • **82**

Zinfandel Sierra Foothills 1990 • $10 • (09/30/93) • **81**

Zinfandel Sierra Foothills 1989 • $10 • (07/31/92) • **86**

SODA CANYON | CALIFORNIA

Chardonnay Napa Valley 13th Leaf 1991: Relies heavily on smoky, oaky notes, but this delivers enough spicy fig-and pear-tinged flavor to keep it interesting. Excellent value. Ready now. 2,856 cases made. • $10 • (06/30/94) • **85**

Chardonnay Napa Valley 14th Leaf 1992: Simple with spicy pear and light cedary notes that fan out on the finish. 1,812 cases made. • $10 • (07/31/95) • **83**

SOLARI | CALIFORNIA

Cabernet Sauvignon Napa Valley Larkmead Vineyards 1985 • $10 • (03/15/90) • **80**

Cabernet Sauvignon Napa Valley Larkmead Vineyards 1984 • $12 • (04/15/88) • **80**

SOLETERRA | CALIFORNIA

Pinot Noir Napa Valley Three Palms Vineyard 1982 • $12 • (10/16/84) • **80**

SOLIS | CALIFORNIA

Chardonnay Santa Clara County Barrel Fermented 1991 • $10 • (11/30/92) • **85**

Merlot Monterey County 1988 • $11 • (05/31/92) • **73**

Merlot Santa Clara County 1991 • $11 • (11/30/92) • **81**

Pinot Noir Santa Clara County 1988 • $9 • (04/30/91) • **78**

SOLITUDE | CALIFORNIA

Chardonnay Carneros Sangiacomo Vineyard 1994: Serves up pretty peach and nectarine flavors, a fruit-driven wine that's smooth and refreshing. The finish brings out more pretty fruit couched in light oak shadings. • $19 • (01/31/96) • **91**

Chardonnay Carneros Sangiacomo Vineyard 1993: An overtly fruity California Chardonnay. The ripe pear, apple and attractive spice flavors are elegant and appealing. It even picks up spicy, smoky oak flavors on the finish. Tempting now for the fruit, but should age well. 1,298 cases made. • $18 • (05/31/95) • **90**

Chardonnay Carneros Sangiacomo Vineyard 1991 • $18 • (07/15/93) • **90**

Pinot Noir Carneros Sangiacomo Vineyard 1993: Tough and hard-edged, but has typical Pinot Noir fruit. Cherry and plum flavors peek through the chewy tannins. A little bottle age should soften this a bit. 523 cases made. • $18 • (01/31/96) • **84**

Pinot Noir Carneros Sangiacomo Vineyard 1991 • $18 • (02/28/94) • **75**

Pinot Noir Sonoma County 1992: Ripe and supple, featuring herb, black cherry and spice notes that turn simple on the finish. Drinkable now. 382 cases made. • $17 • (03/31/95) • **84**

SONOITA | ARIZONA

Cabernet Sauvignon Soñoita Private Reserve 1987 • $15 • (02/29/92) • **79**

Cabernet Sauvignon Soñoita Private Reserve 1985 • $22 • (02/29/92) • **71**

Pinot Noir Soñoita 1989 • $30 • (02/29/92) • **75**

SONOMA CREEK | CALIFORNIA

Cabernet Sauvignon Napa Valley Reserve 1991: Ripe with a racy wild berry and herbal edge, firm tannins on the finish, so cellaring short-term is advised. 1,200 cases made. • $15 • (11/15/94) • **84**

Cabernet Sauvignon Sonoma Valley 1991: Intensely tannic, this austere young red is laced with herbal and tarry notes. Finishes with an oaky, tannic edge, best to wait until 1997. 1,200 cases made. • $15 • (11/15/94) • **82**

Cabernet Sauvignon Sonoma Valley 1988 • $12 • (11/15/91) • **74**

Chardonnay Carneros Barrel Fermented 1992: Crisp and thin, with a candied, earthy, oxidized edge. Marginal quality. 6,000 cases made. • $10 • (09/30/94) • **70**

Chardonnay Carneros Organically Grown 1992: Elegant and refined, with pretty pear, spice and hazelnut flavors framed by light, toasty oak notes lingering on the finish. 2,000 cases made. • $15 • (12/15/94) • **87**

Merlot Sonoma Valley Sangiacomo Vineyard 1992: Deep, dark, dense and tannic, with herb, cedar and currant notes. Packs in lots of flavor, but it's tightly wound and in need of cellaring to soften. Best after 1998. 800 cases made. • $25 • (11/15/94) • **85**

Pinot Noir Carneros 1992: Light and simple, showing a hollow strip of spicy cherry and oak flavors. Marginal. 3,000 cases made. • $10 • (03/31/95) • **77**

Pinot Noir Sonoma County 1993: A lighter style with herb, tea and spice notes, finishing with a light black cherry edge. 5,000 cases made. • $10 • **83**

Zinfandel Sonoma County 1992: Earthy and gamy, with a dry, leathery edge to the flavors. Needs decanting. 5,000 cases made. • $10 • (10/15/94) • **78**

Zinfandel Sonoma Valley 1990 • $9 • (10/15/92) • **78**

SONOMA-CUTRER | CALIFORNIA

Chardonnay Russian River Valley 1991 • $13 • (07/15/93) • **84**

Chardonnay Sonoma Coast Cutrer Vineyard 1992: Well focused, with a pretty core of pear, spice, oak and honey, finishing with a spicy oak edge. • $21 • (07/31/95) • **88**

Chardonnay Sonoma Coast Cutrer Vineyard 1991: Creamy and smooth with pretty pear, vanilla and nutmeg and hints of citrus and spice, turns a little oaky on the finish. Ready now. Tasted twice. • $20 • (06/30/94) • **87**

Chardonnay Sonoma Coast Les Pierres 1991: A subtle, flinty style with mature pear, spice, honey and light toast shadings that acquire a citrus edge. Drinkable now. • $19 • (03/31/95) • **88**

Chardonnay Sonoma Coast Russian River Ranches 1993: Young and crisp, showing citrus and grapefruit flavor that has a bitter edge. It may come around. • $14 • (04/30/95) • **84**

Chardonnay Sonoma Coast Russian River Ranches 1992: Tight and flinty, with a narrow band of earthy pear and spice flavors that turn perfumed on the finish. Tasted twice. • $14 • (06/30/94) • **83**

SONOMA MISSION | CALIFORNIA

Chardonnay Sonoma County 1993: A little light in flavor and intensity, but the spicy pear fruit dances lightly over the finish. 841 cases made. • $8 • (07/31/95) • **82**

Chardonnay Sonoma County 1992: Light and simple with apple and pear notes. 1,000 cases made. • $8 • (06/30/94) • **78**

SONOMA VINEYARDS | CALIFORNIA

Cabernet Sauvignon Sonoma County Alexander's Crown 1974: Earthy-bordering on dirty-with tarry, dried-out Cabernet flavors. This one's well beyond its prime. • $50 • (11/15/94) • **74**

SONOMA-LOEB | CALIFORNIA

Cabernet Sauvignon Alexander Valley 1988 • $10 • (02/29/92) • **82**

Chardonnay Sonoma County 1992: Pleasant if undistinctive, with spice, pear, vanilla and honey notes that lighten up on the finish. Drink now. 813 cases made. • $15 • (03/31/94) • **84**

Chardonnay Sonoma County 1991 • $15 • (01/31/93) • **91**

Chardonnay Sonoma County Ambassador John L. Loeb Jr.'s 1994: Smooth and polished, with ripe pear and buttery oak flavors that show a moderate level of richness and complexity, followed by a spicy, smoky aftertaste. 1,257 cases made. • $18 • (03/31/96) • **88**

Chardonnay Sonoma County Ambassador John L. Loeb Jr.'s 1993: Young and spicy, with ripe, lively Chardonnay flavors that echo pear and lots of spice, finishing with a light oaky aftertaste. Ready. 800 cases made. • $16 • (07/31/95) • **86**

Chardonnay Sonoma County Ambassador John L. Loeb Jr.'s Private Reserve 1994: Ripe, complex pear, spice and apple notes pick up a pretty, toasty oak edge on the finish. Try now. 372 cases made. • $25 • (02/29/96) • **88**

Chardonnay Sonoma County Ambassador John L. Loeb Jr.'s Private Reserve 1993: A touch woody at first, but it opens up with ripe pear, peach and vanilla flavors that turn smooth and elegant. Ready. 200 cases made. • $26 • (07/31/95) • **89**

Chardonnay Sonoma County Ambassador John L. Loeb Jr.'s Private Reserve 1992: Smooth and creamy, with a leesy, earthy edge. It turns soft and fleshy, with spicy pear, honey and vanilla flavors. But it also reveals a coarse edge on the finish. Drinkable now. • $26 • (09/30.94) • **89**

Chardonnay Sonoma County Private Reserve 1991 • $28 • (03/15/93) • **89**

SOOS CREEK | WASHINGTON

Cabernet Sauvignon Columbia Valley 1991: Distinctive, lively, spicy range of red currant, leather and gently toasty flavors, finishing with unobtrusive tannins. May need until 1999 to 2001 to settle down. 148 cases made. • $15 • (04/30/96) • **84**

Cabernet Sauvignon Columbia Valley 1989 • $15 • (10/15/93) • **86**

SOQUEL | CALIFORNIA

Cabernet Sauvignon Santa Cruz Mountains 1991: Firm, tannic and intense, with a distinctive meaty, peppery edge to the currant flavors which persist on the finish. Young and tight, it may still need cellaring, try in 1997. 429 cases made. • $20 • (04/15/94) • **86**

Cabernet Sauvignon Santa Cruz Mountains 1990: Supple and fruity, with spicy plum and black currant flavors that turn spicy, firm and tannic on the finish, with a firmness you'd expect from a young Cabernet Sauvignon. A dash of spicy oak comes through on the aftertaste. Best to cellar until 1997 or so. 486 cases made. • $16 • (03/31/93) • **88**

Cabernet Sauvignon Santa Cruz Mountains Special Reserve 1989 • $25 • (08/31/92) • **85**

Cabernet Sauvignon Stags Leap District 1991: Tart and lean, with a green edge to the cherry and plum flavors, but if you like your Cabernet on the tart side, this one will serve you well. Not what we've come to expect from Stags Leap District Cabernet, though. Ready now through 1998. 262 cases made. • $18 • (05/15/94) • **83**

Cabernet Sauvignon Stags Leap District 1990: Crisp and austere, with firm tannins dominating the flavor and texture profile. Hints of mint, menthol and berry come through, but in the end the tannins win. 254 cases made. • $20 • (02/29/96) • **80**

Cabernet Sauvignon Stags Leap District 1989 • $16 • (02/15/93) • **85**

Chardonnay California Coastal Cellars 1993: Smooth and fruity, with a spicy edge to the grapefruit flavors that keep resonating on the finish. • $NA • **86**

Pinot Noir Santa Cruz Mountains 1991 • $16 • (02/28/94) • **80**

Pinot Noir Santa Cruz Mountains 1990 • $18 • (09/30/92) • **86**

Pinot Noir Santa Cruz Mountains Longridge Vineyard 1994: Young and grapey, showing a simple core of cherry and berry flavor and firm tannins. Drinkable now or cellar through 1997. 77 cases made. • $25 • (02/29/96) • **85**

Pinot Noir Santa Cruz Mountains Special Reserve 1994: Relies a little too much on wood for flavor and the fruit doesn't quite stand up to it. Good, but it leaves you expecting more. 76 cases made. • $25 • (03/31/96) • **83**

Key: SS—Spectator Selection. CS—Cellar Selection. BB—Best Buy. $NA—Price not available. (BT)—Barrel tasting. (A)—Auction Price.
Dates in parentheses represent the issues in which the ratings were published.

Pinot Noir Santa Cruz Mountains Special Reserve 1993: Medium bodied, with simple cherry and berry notes, turning leathery, dry and tannic on the finish. 66 cases made. • $25 • **81**

Zinfandel Alexander Valley 1991 • $8 • (06/15/93) • **79**

SOTOYOME | CALIFORNIA

Syrah Russian River Valley 1986 • $7 • (04/15/89) • **85**

Syrah Russian River Valley 1985 • $7 • (04/15/89) • **77**

SOUVERAIN, CHATEAU | CALIFORNIA

Cabernet Sauvignon Alexander Valley 1992: Beneath the dominating oak, the currant, cherry and spice flavors are elegant and polished, finishing with a coffee and toasty oak aftertaste. 45,000 cases made. • $12 • (03/31/95) • **85**

Cabernet Sauvignon Alexander Valley 1991: Dense and chocolaty, with spicy currant, vanilla and toasty oak flavors that are tight and compact, finishing with firm tannins. Drinkable now. 36,000 cases made. • $11 • (06/30/94) • **85**

Cabernet Sauvignon Alexander Valley 1990: Solidly built, well packed with currant, plum, toast and tobacco aromas and flavors, persisting and spreading on the finish. Gets a little tannic, but it should be terrific after 1998. 33,381 cases made. • $11 • (11/15/93) SS • **90**

Cabernet Sauvignon Alexander Valley 1989 • $10 • (11/15/92) • **85**

Cabernet Sauvignon Alexander Valley 1988 • $10 • (11/15/91) • **85**

Cabernet Sauvignon Alexander Valley 1987 • $9 • (11/15/90) • **87**

Cabernet Sauvignon Alexander Valley 1986 • $8 • (11/15/89) BB • **85**

Cabernet Sauvignon Alexander Valley Private Reserve 1987 • $15 • (05/15/91) • **83**

Cabernet Sauvignon Alexander Valley Winemaker's Reserve 1992: Rich and supple, with a pretty core of currant, plum and cherry. Picks up a nice overlay of oak on the finish, where the flavors fold together nicely. 900 cases made. • $16 • (12/15/95) • **89**

Cabernet Sauvignon Alexander Valley Winemaker's Reserve 1991: A big, ripe and chewy red, with layers of black cherry, plum and currant flavors framed by toasty, buttery oak. Deeply concentrated and packs in lots of flavor. Plush enough to drink now but smoother in 1997. 425 cases made. • $14 • (10/31/94) • **91**

Cabernet Sauvignon Alexander Valley Winemaker's Reserve 1990: A solid young Cabernet, rich and focused, with supple currant, spice and cedary oak flavors, picking up a peppery edge on the finish. Has the tannins to age, yet the texture is developing a plush edge. Best after 1997. 2,400 cases made. • $13 • (05/31/94) • **89**

Cabernet Sauvignon Alexander Valley Winemaker's Reserve 1988 • $14 • (11/15/92) • **83**

Cabernet Sauvignon North Coast Vintage Selection 1980 • $13 • (09/16/85) • **83**

Cabernet Sauvignon Sonoma County 1985 • $8 • (11/30/88) • **87**

Cabernet Sauvignon Sonoma County 1984 • $8 • (08/31/87) • **83**

Cabernet Sauvignon Sonoma County 1978 • $50 • (11/15/92) • **82**

Cabernet Sauvignon Sonoma County Vintage Selection 1978 • $28 • (11/15/92) • **83**

Cabernet Sauvignon Sonoma County Vintage Selection 1974 • $50 • (02/15/90) • **84**

Chardonnay Carneros Winemaker's Reserve 1994: Ripe, smooth and elegant, with an alluring spectrum of spicy pear, honey, vanilla and toasty oak flavors that weave into each other nicely. The lingering finish keeps you intrigued. 1,200 cases made. • $16 • (06/15/96) • **91**

Chardonnay Russian River Valley Allen Vineyard Reserve 1992: A nice balance between ripe pear, apple and fig flavors and cedary oak, finishing with a slightly coarse edge from the wood. Short-term cellaring may give it a more harmonious edge. 375 cases made. • $14 • (06/30/94) • **86**

Chardonnay Russian River Valley Allen Vineyard Reserve 1991 • $14 • (07/15/93) • **90**

Chardonnay Russian River Valley Rochioli Vineyard Reserve 1993: Marked by creamy oak, it turns smoky with ripe, fleshy pear and spicy vanilla notes and a complex aftertaste. 450 cases made. • $16 • (04/30/95) • **89**

Chardonnay Sonoma County 1994: Smooth and spicy, ripe with pear and a hint of pineapple, harmonious in the way it folds its sweet oak, vanilla and fruit together. Delicious, amazingly long and drinkable now. An excellent value. 32,000 cases made. • $12 • (04/30/96) SS • **91**

Chardonnay Sonoma County Barrel Fermented 1993: Medium in weight, ripe pear and spice notes pick up a touch of smoky oak and vanilla on the finish. 30,000 cases made. • $12 • (06/15/95) • **85**

Chardonnay Sonoma County Barrel Fermented 1992: Spicy pear and apple flavors are simple and direct, with light oak shadings and a toasty aftertaste. Best soon. 44,000 cases made. • $11 • (06/30/94) • **84**

Chardonnay Sonoma County Barrel Fermented 1991 • $9 • (03/15/93) • **85**

Chardonnay Sonoma Valley Durell Vineyard Reserve 1991 • $13 • (07/15/93) • **88**

Merlot 1990 • $10 • (05/31/92) • **86**

Merlot 1989 • $10 • (05/31/92) • **89**

Merlot Alexander Valley 1993: Somewhat earthy, adding a cedary oak edge, but it pulls together at mid-palate where currant and cherry flavors become more prominent. Well balanced and ready to drink. 20,000 cases made. • $13 • (12/15/95) • **86**

Merlot Alexander Valley 1992: Relies heavily on cedary oak for its flavor and structure, but the tannic plum, currant and cherry notes come through. Give it a year to two tc soften, then it should be more supple and harmonious. 24,000 cases made. • $12 • (06/30/94) • **85**

Merlot Alexander Valley 1991: Smooth and round, bordering on opulent, the currant and berry flavors shaded nicely by spice, caramel and tobacco notes. The tannins could use until 1996 or 1997. 22,000 cases made. • $12 • (06/30/94) • **87**

Merlot Alexander Valley 1990 • $10 • (05/31/93) • **86**

Merlot Alexander Valley 1989 • $10 • (02/29/92) • **77**

Merlot North Coast 1981 • $6 • (10/01/85) • **89**

Merlot Sonoma County 1986 • $10 • (03/31/89) • **74**

Merlot Sonoma County 1984 • $8 • (07/31/87) • **86**

Pinot Noir Carneros Winemaker's Reserve 1993: Supple and refined, with modest herb, cherry, spice and toasty oak shadings. Drinkable now. 600 cases made. • $16 • (03/31/95) • **84**

Pinot Noir Carneros Winemaker's Reserve 1992 • $14 • (04/30/94) • **85**

Pinot Noir Carneros Winemaker's Reserve 1991 • $15 • (02/28/94) • **85**

Sauvignon Blanc Alexander Valley 1992 • $7 • (04/30/94) BB • **86**

Sauvignon Blanc Alexander Valley Barrel Fermented 1994: Lean and lively, flavors centered around nectarine, grapefruit and a touch of grass. 12,000 cases made. • $8 • (08/31/95) • **85**

Sauvignon Blanc Alexander Valley Barrel Fermented 1993: Fresh and lively, with snappy pear, sweet pea, fig and citrus notes. Medium-bodied with good depth and richness. Ready now. 3,125 cases made. • $7 • (12/15/94) BB • **87**

White Zinfandel California 1988 • $5 • (06/15/89) • **77**

Zinfandel 1989 • $7 • (05/15/92) BB • **82**

Zinfandel Dry Creek Valley 1993: Smooth and well integrated, with modest cherry, spice and wild berry flavors that finish off with soft tannins and a touch of oak. Nice subtleties in a California red of this price range. 13,000 cases made. • $9 • (08/31/95) BB • **87**

Zinfandel Dry Creek Valley 1992: Smooth and smoky, with a spicy core of raspberry and black cherry. Intense and lively. Delicious now, but should hold through 1997. 11,000 cases made. • $9 • (08/31/94) BB • **87**

Zinfandel Dry Creek Valley 1991 • $8 • (09/15/93) BB • **87**

Zinfandel Dry Creek Valley 1990 • $7 • (10/15/92) • **84**

Zinfandel Dry Creek Valley 1987 • $9 • (05/15/90) • **82**

Zinfandel Dry Creek Valley 1986 • $5 • (03/31/89) BB • **81**

Zinfandel Dry Creek Valley Bradford Mountain Vineyard 1987 • $15 • (05/15/90) • **85**

SPARROW LANE | CALIFORNIA

Zinfandel North Coast 1993: An elegant, well-balanced style, with a pleasant band of cedar, cherry, berry and anise flavors that turn smooth and elegant on the finish. 700 cases made. • $12 • (10/15/95) • **88**

SPOTTSWOODE | CALIFORNIA

Cabernet Sauvignon Napa Valley 1992: A young and tightly wound Cabernet that's dark and plummy, with rich, well-focused currant and black cherry flavors. Nice peppery and mineral notes on the finish. Substantial but polished tannins suggest aging until 1998 or longer. 5,000 cases made. • $39 • (11/30/95) CS • **90**

Cabernet Sauvignon Napa Valley 1991: Ripe, smooth and polished, loaded with pretty currant, black cherry and anise flavors that are rich and focused, complex and concentrated. Has the tannins to age, but just turning drinkable. Best after 1998. 5,000 cases made. • $40 • (11/15/94) CS • **93**

Cabernet Sauvignon Napa Valley 1990: Ripe, opulent, rich and intense with pretty plum, berry, currant and spice, with cedary, buttery oak flavors that stay with you from start to finish. Fine balance, with firm tannins that bode well for aging. Start drinking around 1997. 4,500 cases made. • $56 • (10/31/93) CS • **91**

Cabernet Sauvignon Napa Valley 1989 • $46 • (11/15/92) • **89**

Cabernet Sauvignon Napa Valley 1988 • $52 •(11/15/91) • **90**

Cabernet Sauvignon Napa Valley 1987 • $85 Ⓐ • (09/15/90) SS • **96**

Cabernet Sauvignon Napa Valley 1986 • $82 Ⓐ • (09/15/89) • **95**

Cabernet Sauvignon Napa Valley 1985 • $105 Ⓐ • (03/01/89) • **95**

Cabernet Sauvignon Napa Valley 1984 • $77 Ⓐ • (03/01/89) • **90**

Cabernet Sauvignon Napa Valley 1983 • $95 • (03/01/89) • **89**

Cabernet Sauvignon Napa Valley 1982 • $105 Ⓐ • (03/01/89) • **90**

Sauvignon Blanc Napa Valley 1995: Smooth, silky and almost sweet, with ripe apricot, pear and lightly minty-herbal overtones. A distinctive wine that finishes with a polished feel. 4,150 cases made. • $15 • **89**

Sauvignon Blanc Napa Valley 1994: Smooth, supple and harmonious, sporting tropical fruit and spice flavors and just a hint of anise on the finish. 4,000 cases made. • $14 • (06/30/95) • **87**

Sauvignon Blanc Napa Valley 1993: Fresh and floral, a little more concentrated than most, with focused grapefruit, pear and earth-mineral flavors. 3,100 cases made. • $12 • (08/31/94) • **85**

SPRING MOUNTAIN | CALIFORNIA

Cabernet Sauvignon Napa Valley 1986 • $NA • (03/01/89) • **90**

Cabernet Sauvignon Napa Valley 1985 • $20 • (10/15/89) • **85**

Cabernet Sauvignon Napa Valley 1984 • $15 • (03/15/89) • **89**

Cabernet Sauvignon Napa Valley 1983 • $19 • (03/01/89) • **79**

Cabernet Sauvignon Napa Valley 1982 • $18 • (03/01/89) • **66**

Cabernet Sauvignon Napa Valley 1981 • $18 • (03/01/89) • **78**

Cabernet Sauvignon Napa Valley 1980 • $19 • (03/01/89) • **86**

Cabernet Sauvignon Napa Valley 1979 • $27 • (03/01/89) • **87**

Cabernet Sauvignon Napa Valley 1978 • $30 Ⓐ • (03/01/89) • **83**

Cabernet Sauvignon Napa Valley 1977 • $39 • (03/01/89) • **85**

STAGLIN FAMILY | CALIFORNIA

Cabernet Sauvignon Napa Valley 1993: Appealing for its spicy, zesty cherry and plum notes, this medium-weight red offers a nice core of flavors, inserting hints of smoky oak on the firmly tannic finish. 3,000 cases made. • $30 • (04/30/96) • **89**

Cabernet Sauvignon Napa Valley 1992: Tightly wound, a touch austere, but it opens up to reveal more richness and depth, with tiers of fleshy plum and black cherry flavors, finishing with firm tannins and a long aftertaste. 1,900 cases made. • $28 • (12/15/95) • **91**

Cabernet Sauvignon Napa Valley 1991: Intense and lively, tightly wound, serves up lovely, supple plum and currant flavors before acquiring a spicy, cedary note on the finish. Best after 1998. 1,392 cases made. • $26 • (11/15/94) • **89**

Cabernet Sauvignon Napa Valley 1990: Tight, firm and oaky, with vanilla and chocolate notes showing through, but a band of black cherry and currant flavors underneath is tightly wound and in need of cellaring. Already showing signs of elegance and grace, should evolve into a very pleasant wine. Drink after 1998. 998 cases made. • $24 • (03/31/93) • **88**

Cabernet Sauvignon Napa Valley 1989 • $22 • (11/15/92) • **87**

Sangiovese Napa Valley Stagliano 1994: Strikes a nice balance between ripe yet tart cherry and berry flavors. Oaky and tannic, so cellaring into 1997 should give it some softness. 150 cases made. • $34 • (04/30/96) • **87**

Sangiovese Napa Valley Stagliano 1993: Framed by supple toasty oak, the cherry, currant and wild berry flavors stay focused. A pleasant, spicy accent is very appealing. 90 cases made. • $34 • (02/28/95) • **88**

STAG'S LEAP WINE CELLARS | CALIFORNIA

Cabernet Sauvignon Napa Valley 1991: Firm, focused and supple, with herb, leather, berry and currant flavors, finishing with a bite of tannin and a hint of vanilla. Drinkable now. 10,000 cases made. • $18 • (03/31/94) • **87**

Cabernet Sauvignon Napa Valley 1990: Sleek and flavorful, this pretty, almost exotic wine has lots of fruit and spice flavors and a long finish. Mint and currant aromas, a smooth texture, supple tannins and great balance add to its appeal. Drinkable now, but so nicely proportioned that it should age though at least 1997. 10,000 cases made. • $18 • (05/15/93) SS • **91**

Cabernet Sauvignon Napa Valley 1989 • $18 • (09/30/92) • **83**

Cabernet Sauvignon Napa Valley 1988 • $18 • (06/15/91) • **90**

Cabernet Sauvignon Napa Valley 1987 • $18 • (08/31/90) • **75**

Cabernet Sauvignon Napa Valley 1986 • $18 • (06/15/89) • **82**

Cabernet Sauvignon Napa Valley 1985 • $16 • (09/15/88) • **90**

Cabernet Sauvignon Napa Valley 1984 • $15 • (07/15/87) • **83**

Cabernet Sauvignon Napa Valley 1981 • $15 • (12/16/84) • **82**

Cabernet Sauvignon Napa Valley Cask 23 1974: One bottle was off, but the second revealed a rich core of supple, vibrant and complex Cabernet fruit that echoed currant, tar and tobacco notes before smoothing out on a long, full finish. Silky and elegant, it remains in excellent condition and has the potential to hold for a few more years with proper storage. Impressive youthful and intense fruit, best bottle in a decade. 100 cases made. • $150 • (11/15/94) • **94**

Cabernet Sauvignon Napa Valley Fay 1992: Supple and polished, with an herbal, leathery edge to the ripe, rich currant and black cherry flavors. Finishes with a complex interplay of fruit and light oak shadings. Tempting now, but worthy of cellaring into 1997 or 1998. 5,000 cases made. • $35 • (12/15/95) CS • **91**

Cabernet Sauvignon Napa Valley Fay 1991: Rich and intense, with an earthy edge to the flavors. There is an underripe quality to the currant and cherry flavors that pick up tobacco and herb accents. • $30 • (12/31/94) • **88**

Cabernet Sauvignon Napa Valley Fay 1990: It's aromatic, but lean and spicy on the palate, turning generous on the finish. Well defined, earthy berry and spice flavors. A bit tannic, but full enough to carry it past 2000. 2,500 cases made. • $30 • (03/31/94) • **88**

Cabernet Sauvignon Napa Valley S.L.V. 1992: Shows some oak, dryness and austerity at this stage, but this is concentrated. The tightly wound herb, currant and anise flavors lead to a firmly tannic finish. Better in 1998. 5,000 cases made. • $35 • (12/15/95) • **88**

Cabernet Sauvignon Napa Valley S.L.V. 1990: Fleshy and earthy, an herb- and chocolate-scented wine with deep cherry and spice flavors lacing through the finish. A flavorful red that should be at its best from 1998. 2,500 cases made. • $30 • (03/31/94) • **89**

Cabernet Sauvignon Napa Valley S.L.V. Fay 1989 • $25 • (11/15/92) • **80**

Cabernet Sauvignon Stags Leap District S.L.V. 1988 • $38 • (11/15/91) • **85**

Cabernet Sauvignon Stags Leap District S.L.V. 1987 • $33 • (11/15/90) • **77**

Cabernet Sauvignon Stags Leap District S.L.V. 1986 • $32 • (11/30/89) • **91**

Cabernet Sauvignon Stags Leap District S.L.V. 1985 • $49 • (03/01/89) • **94**

Cabernet Sauvignon Stags Leap District S.L.V. 1984 • $39 • (03/01/89) • **92**

Cabernet Sauvignon Stags Leap District Stag's Leap Vineyards 1983 • $37 • (03/01/89) • **73**

Cabernet Sauvignon Stags Leap District Stag's Leap Vineyards 1982 • $30 • (03/01/89) • **75**

Cabernet Sauvignon Stags Leap District Stag's Leap Vineyards 1981 • $40 • (03/01/89) • **91**

Cabernet Sauvignon Stags Leap District Stag's Leap Vineyards 1979 • $44 • (03/01/89) • **68**

Cabernet Sauvignon Stags Leap District Stag's Leap Vineyards 1978 • $52 • (03/01/89) • **89**

Cabernet Sauvignon Stags Leap District Stag's Leap Vineyards 1977 • $29 • (03/01/89) • **85**

Key: SS—Spectator Selection. CS—Cellar Selection. BB—Best Buy. $NA—Price not available. (BT)—Barrel tasting. Ⓐ—Auction Price.
Dates in parentheses represent the issues in which the ratings were published.

Cabernet Sauvignon Stags Leap District Stag's Leap Vineyards 1976 • $61 • (03/01/89) • **73**

Cabernet Sauvignon Stags Leap District Stag's Leap Vineyards 1975 • $54 • (03/01/89) • **74**

Cabernet Sauvignon Stags Leap District Stag's Leap Vineyards 1974 • $95 • (02/15/90) • **83**

Cabernet Sauvignon Stags Leap District Stag's Leap Vineyards 1973 • $100 • (03/01/89) • **86**

Cabernet Sauvignon Stags Leap District Stag's Leap Vineyards 1972 • $110 • (03/01/89) • **70**

Cabernet Sauvignon Stags Leap District Stag's Leap Vineyards Cask 23 1984 • $120 • (03/01/89) • **93**

Cabernet Sauvignon Stags Leap District Stag's Leap Vineyards Cask 23 1983 • $80 • (03/01/89) • **88**

Cabernet Sauvignon Stags Leap District Stag's Leap Vineyards Cask 23 1979 • $85 • (03/01/89) • **88**

Cabernet Sauvignon Stags Leap District Stag's Leap Vineyards Cask 23 1978 • $200 • (11/15/92) • **92**

Cabernet Sauvignon Stags Leap District Stag's Leap Vineyards Cask 23 1977 • $79 • (03/01/89) • **91**

Cabernet Sauvignon Stags Leap District Stag's Leap Vineyards Cask 23 1974 • $150 • (02/15/90) • **80**

Cabernet Sauvignon Stags Leap District Stag's Leap Vineyards Lot 2 1978 • $56 • (11/15/92) • **88**

Cabernet Sauvignon Stags Leap District Stag's Leap Vineyards Lot 2 1977 • $56 • (03/01/89) • **90**

Cabernet Sauvignon Stags Leap District Stag's Leap Vineyards Lot 2 1976 • $23 • (03/01/89) • **80**

Chardonnay Napa Valley 1994: Clean and sound, with ripe pear, apple and spice flavors than grow on the finish. A subtle style that draws you in. 15,000 cases made. • $22 • (06/15/96) • **89**

Chardonnay Napa Valley 1993: Ripe and spicy, with pretty pear, light oak, hazelnut and buttery flavors, turning elegant and refined. 15,000 cases made. • $19 • (07/31/95) • **88**

Chardonnay Napa Valley 1992: Broad and ripe, with a spicy nutmeg edge to the pear, apple, toast and vanilla flavors, picking up a grassy edge on the finish. A harmonious style that's delicious now. 12,000 cases made. • $18 • (06/30/94) SS • **90**

Chardonnay Napa Valley 1991 • $18 • (07/15/93) • **82**

Chardonnay Napa Valley Beckstoffer Ranch 1994: Openly fruity, with an elegant core of ripe pear, apple, fig and melon notes framed by toasty, creamy oak. Finishes with echoes of the fruit and smoky oak. Only available at the winery. 400 cases made. • $24 • (05/31/96) • **91**

Chardonnay Napa Valley Reserve 1993: Ripe with buttery pear, tropical fruit and spice notes that are focused and elegant through the finish. 2,500 cases made. • $28 • (05/31/95) • **89**

Chardonnay Napa Valley Reserve 1992: Ripe, smooth and polished, with pear, fig, citrus and spicy oak flavors. Has an elegant and refined Chardonnay character. 1,200 cases made. • $28 • (12/31/94) • **90**

Chardonnay Napa Valley Reserve 1991 • $28 • (03/15/94) • **91**

Merlot Napa Valley 1992: Ripe and well oaked, showing dense and chewy herb, currant, chocolate and vanilla flavors and a tannic finish. Best to cellar into 1997. 3,000 cases made. • $24 • (12/15/95) • **88**

Merlot Napa Valley 1991 • $22 • (05/31/94) • **86**

Merlot Napa Valley 1990 • $22 • (03/31/93) • **87**

Merlot Napa Valley 1985 • $16 • (05/31/88) • **86**

Merlot Napa Valley 1984 • $15 • (05/15/87) • **78**

Merlot Napa Valley 1982 • $14 • (10/01/85) • **78**

Merlot Napa Valley 1981 • $14 • (04/16/84) • **82**

Petite Sirah Napa Valley 1992: Chewy, earthy, spicy and distinctive with leathery, peppery notes. This is a small-scale wine with possibilities. Should be best from 1999-2000. 600 cases made. • $18 • (09/30/95) • **83**

Petite Sirah Napa Valley 1991: Dark-colored and tannic, but light in flavor, with some plum and berry sneaking in on the finish. Drinkable now. 7,184 cases made. • $19 • (02/28/95) • **85**

Petite Sirah Napa Valley 1987 • $12 • (08/31/90) • **87**

Petite Sirah Napa Valley 1985 • $9 • (10/15/88) • **85**

Petite Sirah Napa Valley 1982 • $7 • (12/01/85) • **73**

S.L.V. Cask 23 Napa Valley 1992: Elegant and refined, with well-focused, pure and complex currant, cherry, spice and earth flavors. Picks up anise leather notes on the finish, where the tannins are smooth and polished. Has the depth and intensity to age into 1999 and beyond, but it's approachable now. 2,000 cases made. • $80 • (12/15/95) CS • **94**

S.L.V. Cask 23 Napa Valley 1991: Young and tightly wound, with a firm, tannic spine, but loaded with rich currant, coffee, herb and anise flavors that run deep and long. Complex and concentrated. Best from 1997 to 2004, maybe longer. 2,500 cases made. • $70 • (12/31/94) CS • **92**

S.L.V. Cask 23 Napa Valley 1990: Rich and chocolaty with intense, focused herb, currant, coffee and cedar flavors that pick up earthy tobacco, mineral, silk and grace notes on the long, full, rich and complex finish. Tasty now but should age well through the decade. 1,000 cases made. • $65 • (10/31/93) CS • **92**

S.L.V. Cask 23 Stags Leap District 1987 • $60 • (11/15/91) • **87**

S.L.V. Cask 23 Stags Leap District 1986 • $70 • (11/15/90) • **93**

S.L.V. Cask 23 Stags Leap District 1985 • $180 • (11/30/89) • **96**

Sauvignon Blanc Napa Valley 1992 • $11 • (03/31/94) • **82**

Sauvignon Blanc Napa Valley Rancho Chimiles 1993: Extremely floral and a little candied, not as fresh and appealing as it could be. 5,000 cases made. • $11 • (08/31/95) • **77**

Sauvignon Blanc Napa Valley Rancho Chimiles 1991 • $10 • (07/15/93) • **82**

White Riesling Late Harvest Napa Valley Birkmyer Vyds Selected Bunches 1983 • $14 • (10/01/84) • **85**

White Riesling Napa Valley 1992 • $8 • (05/15/94) BB • **86**

STAGS' LEAP WINERY | CALIFORNIA

Burgundy Napa Valley 1983 • $5 • (09/15/87) • **71**

Cabernet Sauvignon Napa Valley 1991: Austere with a peppery edge to the Cabernet flavors and lots of chewy tannins to shed. Tannic finish, but cellaring until after 1998 should soften some of the rough spots. 9,897 cases made. • $20 • (11/15/94) • **85**

Cabernet Sauvignon Napa Valley 1989 • $19 • (03/15/93) • **86**

Cabernet Sauvignon Stags Leap District 1987 • $18 • (06/30/91) • **89**

Cabernet Sauvignon Stags Leap District 1986 • $NA • (03/01/89) • **86**

Cabernet Sauvignon Stags Leap District 1985 • $18 • (03/01/89) • **85**

Cabernet Sauvignon Stags Leap District 1984 • $26 • (03/01/89) • **87**

Cabernet Sauvignon Stags Leap District 1983 • $20 • (03/01/89) • **80**

Cabernet Sauvignon Stags Leap District 1982 • $20 • (03/01/89) • **71**

Cabernet Sauvignon Stags Leap District 1981 • $20 • (03/01/89) • **85**

Merlot Napa Valley 1990 • $18 • (06/15/93) • **78**

Merlot Napa Valley 1989 • $17 • (05/31/92) • **88**

Merlot Napa Valley 1987 • $17 • (11/15/91) • **85**

Merlot Napa Valley 1986 • $17 • (12/31/90) • **84**

Merlot Napa Valley 1981 • $12 • (02/16/85) • **83**

Petite Sirah Napa Valley 1990: Firm in texture, but not overly tannic, modest in flavor, flashing a bit of prune and chocolate on the finish. 5,335 cases made. • $17 • (09/30/94) • **81**

Petite Sirah Napa Valley 1988 • $15 • (11/30/92) • **88**

Petite Sirah Napa Valley Petite Syrah 1987 • $14 • (10/31/91) • **82**

Petite Sirah Napa Valley Petite Syrah 1980 • $10 • (03/01/85) • **84**

STAIGER, P & M | CALIFORNIA

Chardonnay Santa Cruz Mountains 1994: A flinty style that serves up an attractive range of ripe pear, spice and fig flavors. Finishes somewhat coarse, but should soften by 1997. 230 cases made. • $12 • (06/15/96) • **86**

Chardonnay Santa Cruz Mountains 1992: Displays a strong green apple and oak edge, complete with an astringent mouthfeel on the finish. Lacks the extra dimensions you might hope for in this vintage. Ready now. 250 cases made. • $12 • (06/30/94) • **80**

Pinot Noir Monterey 1987 • $12 • (02/28/93) • **67**

STANFORD | CALIFORNIA

Brut California Governor's Cuvée NV • $5 • (12/31/90) • **76**

Extra Dry California Governor's Cuvée NV • $5 • (12/31/90) • **73**

STAR HILL | CALIFORNIA

Cabernet Sauvignon Napa Valley Bartolucci Vineyard Doc's Reserve 1990: Firm and flavorful, with a tobacco, juniper edge to the basic black currant flavor. A solid wine with room to grow, try now. • $24 • (02/15/93) • **82**

Cabernet Sauvignon Napa Valley Doc's Reserve 1987 • $24 • (11/15/91) • **88**

Pinot Noir Napa Valley Doc's Reserve 1988 • $19 • (02/15/92) • **82**

Pinot Noir Napa Valley Doc's Reserve 1987 • $19 • (05/31/90) • **87**

STATON HILLS | WASHINGTON

Blanc de Noir Washington NV • $16 • (10/15/89) • **77**

Brut Rosé Washington NV • $16 • (04/30/92) • **84**

Cabernet Sauvignon Washington 1992: Firm in texture and forward in flavor, with bright black cherry, anise and spice flavors in profusion and in balance. Try in 1998 or 1999. 4,960 cases made. • $12 • (06/15/96) • **87**

Cabernet Sauvignon Washington 1989: Ripe and generous, with currant, mint and spice flavors gliding smoothly through the finish. Drinkable now. 5,241 cases made. • $14 • (01/31/95) • **87**

Cabernet Sauvignon Washington 1988 • $15 • (03/31/92) • **81**

Cabernet Sauvignon Washington 1987 • $13 • (03/31/91) • **86**

Cabernet Sauvignon Washington 1986 • $12 • (10/15/89) • **80**

Cabernet Sauvignon Washington Estate 1987 • $20 • (02/29/92) • **79**

Cabernet Sauvignon Washington Estate 1986 • $20 • (03/31/91) • **83**

Cabernet Sauvignon Washington Reserve 1987 • $22 • (03/31/92) • **85**

Cabernet Sauvignon Washington Reserve 1986 • $22 • (08/31/91) • **83**

Chardonnay Washington 1991: An extreme wine, very spicy, toasty and oxidized, finishing flat but showing honey and caramel notes. 2,000 cases made. • $9 • (01/31/95) • **79**

Fumé Blanc Washington 1994: Light, crisp and fruity, with pear and gentle spice flavors that persist nicely on the finish. 3,400 cases made. • $9 • (05/31/96) • **84**

Fumé Blanc Washington 1993: Sturdy and flavorful, edging toward earthy, mineral tones, but there are enough apple notes to keep it in balance. 3,000 cases made. • $7 • (07/31/94) • **83**

Merlot Washington 1992: Lean and peppery, but it shows a core of berry flavor that needs until 1998 to soften the tannins. 6,000 cases made. • $13 • (06/15/96) • **85**

Merlot Washington 1988 • $15 • (03/31/92) • **82**

Merlot Washington 1987 • $14 • (08/31/91) • **79**

Merlot Washington Reserve 1987 • $22 • (10/15/92) • **87**

Phoenix Red Yakima Valley 1992: Light and a little bit cooked in flavor, finishing with a nice touch of spice. 1,100 cases made. • $18 • (06/15/96) • **82**

Riesling Late Harvest Washington 1987 • $10 • (03/31/92) • **82**

STAUB'S, RUSTY | CALIFORNIA

Cabernet Sauvignon California 1992: A fruity style with wild berry and raspberry notes, turning smooth and polished on the finish. Simple and pleasing. 2,000 cases made. • $10 • (12/15/95) • **83**

STEELE | CALIFORNIA

Cabernet Sauvignon Anderson Valley 1993: Shows off pretty toast, vanilla and smoky oak before the currant and cherry flavors come through, adding hints of anise and spice. Has a nice sense of balance and proportion, despite firm tannins. 250 cases made. • $22 • (04/30/96) • **90**

Chardonnay California 1994: Bold, ripe and exotic, boasting complex fig, apricot, honey, pear and vanilla notes, an altogether opulent and mouth-filling bottle of Chardonnay. Packs in lots of flavor, yet manages to maintain its finesse. 5,000 cases made. • $18 • (05/15/96) SS • **92**

Chardonnay California 1993: Spicy with modest ripe pear and light oak shadings. Elegant and well balanced, but not especially complex. 500 cases made. • $18 • (07/31/95) • **86**

Chardonnay California 1992: Spicy and a bit earthy, but it serves up lots of pretty pear, spice, vanilla and oaky flavors that turn elegant. Finishes long and clean, with pretty honeyed flavors. 4,000 cases made. • $18 • (06/15/94) • **90**

Chardonnay California 1991 • $18 • (02/15/93) • **87**

Chardonnay Carneros Sangiacomo Vineyard 1994: Well oaked, with ripe, rich, complex fruit to match. The layers of pear, spice, honey, fig and melon all meld together quite nicely on the finish and linger on. 500 cases made. • $22 • (05/31/96) • **93**

Chardonnay Carneros Sangiacomo Vineyard 1992: Spicy, buttery oak flavors and a touch of pear: crisp and lively. Not as rich and opulent as the Durell Vineyard, but still impressive. Drinkable now. 200 cases made. • $22 • (03/31/94) • **90**

Chardonnay Carneros Sangiacomo Vineyard 1991 • $22 • (03/15/93) • **89**

Chardonnay Mendocino Dennison Vineyard 1994: A subtle white that grows on you, with an elegant band of spicy, toasty oak, ripe pear and apple notes. A graceful style with flavors that expand on the finish. 250 cases made. • $22 • (05/31/96) • **90**

Chardonnay Mendocino Dennison Vineyard 1992: Tight and firm, with a compact band of citrus, pear and cedary oak flavors that turn smoky on the finish. Complex and concentrated, it's approachable now, but worthy of cellaring through 1996. 70 cases made. • $20 • (06/15/94) • **89**

Chardonnay Mendocino DuPratt Vineyard 1994: Smooth and complex, with a pretty array of ripe pear, honey and apple flavors set in a creamy texture. Shows fine depth and integration of the fruit and oak flavors that continue to expand on the finish. 400 cases made. • $24 • (05/31/96) • **92**

Chardonnay Mendocino DuPratt Vineyard 1993: Bright and fruity with a focused beam of pear, spice, apple and buttery notes, turning supple and complex. 200 cases made. • $24 • (07/31/95) • **91**

Chardonnay Mendocino DuPratt Vineyard 1992: An elegant style, with ripe, spicy pear, honey and spice notes that hang together nicely, turning simple on the finish. Ready now. 300 cases made. • $22 • (06/30/94) • **86**

Chardonnay Mendocino DuPratt Vineyard 1991 • $24 • (03/15/93) • **92**

Chardonnay Mendocino Lolonis Vineyard 1994: Serves up an attractive array of ripe pear and tangerine flavors in a smooth and elegant style. Lacks the extra dimensions and complexity of the best from this vintage. 600 cases made. • $26 • (05/31/96) • **88**

Chardonnay Mendocino Lolonis Vineyard 1993: Ripe and spicy, with a smooth texture and pretty pear, toasty oak and buttery notes, turning complex on the finish. 280 cases made. • $20 • (07/31/95) • **90**

Chardonnay Mendocino Lolonis Vineyard 1992: Crisp and focused, with pretty peach, spice, apple and fig flavors that fan out on the palate, giving it added richness and dimension on the finish. Delicious now. 300 cases made. • $26 • (06/15/94) • **92**

Chardonnay Mendocino Lolonis Vineyard 1991 • $26 • (03/15/93) • **90**

Chardonnay Santa Barbara County Bien Nacido Vineyard 1994: An elegant, refined style with smooth, polished pear and honey flavors laced with hints of toasty oak. Has a creamy texture, and the flavors sail on and on. A beautifully crafted white. 400 cases made. • $24 • (05/31/96) • **91**

Chardonnay Santa Barbara County Bien Nacido Vineyard 1993: Smooth and polished, with appealing creamy vanilla, pear, honey and spice, turning elegant and refined on the finish. 350 cases made. • $22 • (07/31/95) • **88**

Chardonnay Santa Barbara County Bien Nacido Vineyard 1992: Firm and tightly wound. The spicy pear and hazelnut flavors are just beginning to open up and reveal their depth and richness. 100 cases made. • $22 • (03/31/94) • **90**

Chardonnay Santa Barbara County Goodchild Vineyard 1994: A wonderfully crafted, ripe, rich and complex white that takes you through tiers of honey, spice, fig and melon flavors, then gives you a lovely hazelnut finish. A complex and racy yet elegant and refined style. 350 cases made. • $24 • (05/31/96) • **92**

Chardonnay Sonoma Valley Durell Vineyard 1994: A complex array of ripe tropical fruit, with tiers of honey, pear and butterscotch flavors. Picks up a toasty oak edge on the finish. 400 cases made. • $24 • (05/31/96) • **88**

Chardonnay Sonoma Valley Durell Vineyard 1992: Firm, intense and lively, this is a complex and compelling young Chardonnay with layers of fig, vanilla, honey and hazelnut flavors that are sharply focused, concentrated and long on the finish. Drink now. 70 cases made. • $24 • (03/31/94) • **92**

Key: SS—Spectator Selection. CS—Cellar Selection. BB—Best Buy. $NA—Price not available. (BT)—Barrel tasting. (A)—Auction Price.
Dates in parentheses represent the issues in which the ratings were published.

Pinot Blanc Santa Barbara County Bien Nacido Vineyard 1994: Fruity, spicy, generous and round, still fresh enough to show its citrusy pear flavors in profusion. Drink it soon. 1,200 cases made. • $14 • (11/15/95) • **85**

Pinot Blanc Santa Barbara County Bien Nacido Vineyard 1993: Smooth and spicy, showing a lot of nutmeg and almond personality to liven up the melon and apple, and some real depth. 700 cases made. • $14 • (12/31/94) • **89**

Pinot Blanc Santa Barbara County Bien Nacido Vineyard 1992 • $13 • (12/31/93) • **83**

Pinot Noir Carneros 1993: A smooth and elegant California Pinot, with ripe black cherry flavors and attractive, toasty oak flavors graced by a tinge of vanilla. It all melds together nicely and shows increasing depth on the finish. 3,000 cases made. • $18 • (09/15/95) • **90**

Pinot Noir Carneros 1992 • $16 • (02/28/94) • **87**

Pinot Noir Carneros 1991 • $18 • (02/15/93) • **90**

Pinot Noir Carneros Durell Vineyard 1993: Lush and complex tiers of toasty, buttery oak and black cherry and currant flavors fold together in a ripe, supple manner. • $19 • (09/15/95) • **88**

Pinot Noir Carneros Durell Vineyard 1992 • $20 • (02/28/94) • **87**

Pinot Noir Carneros Sangiacomo Vineyard 1993: Well-oaked, smoky, toasty aromas and enough ripe cherry and wild berry flavors to match, coming together on the finish. 280 cases made. • $22 • (09/15/95) • **88**

Pinot Noir Carneros Sangiacomo Vineyard 1991 • $22 • (02/28/93) • **88**

Pinot Noir Mendocino DuPratt Vineyard 1992 • $26 • (02/28/94) • **86**

Pinot Noir Santa Barbara County Bien Nacido Vineyard 1994: Ripe, spicy, rich and complex young red delivering supple cherry, tar, currant and berry notes. Has a measure of grace and harmony, finishing in fine tannins. Ready now and into 1997. 900 cases made. • $20 • (04/30/96) • **90**

Pinot Noir Santa Barbara County Bien Nacido Vineyard 1993: Marked by a spicy, peppery edge, almost Syrahlike, but the cherry and earth nuances come through. 280 cases made. • $22 • (09/15/95) • **86**

Zinfandel Clear Lake Catfish Vineyard 1994: A classy Zin, boasting complex black cherry and wild berry flavors, pretty, toasty oak and lots of finesse. Dense, dark, compact, packing in lots of extras, but should age into 1997 for best results. 500 cases made. • $16 • (04/30/96) • **90**

Zinfandel Clear Lake Catfish Vineyard 1993: Complex balance between spicy, toasty oak and the ripe cherry and raspberry flavors. Turns supple on a long, fruity finish. Tasted twice, with consistent notes. 800 cases made. • $13 • (09/30/95) • **89**

Zinfandel Clear Lake Catfish Vineyard 1992: Shows off smoky, buttery oak and pretty currant and blackberry flavors in a smooth, polished style faintly reminiscent of a Pinot Noir. A complex, original style of Zinfandel with a peppery finish. 800 cases made. • $13 • (09/15/94) • **90**

Zinfandel Clear Lake Catfish Vineyard 1991 • $13 • (09/30/93) • **90**

Zinfandel Mendocino DuPratt Vineyard 1993: Beautifully crafted, rich and complex, featuring layers of spice, wild berry, cherry and toasty, buttery oak, an altogether supple and harmonious red that packs in flavor while maintaining its elegance. Picks up a peppery note on the finish. Delicious now and into 1997. Tasted twice, with consistent notes. 1,100 cases made. • $18 • (04/30/96) • **91**

Zinfandel Mendocino DuPratt Vineyard 1993: • $NA • (02/29/96) • **91**

Zinfandel Mendocino Pacini Vineyard 1994: Firm, intense and tannic too, but underneath is a solid core of dense cherry and wild berry flavor, finishing with hints of tar and spice. Aging into 1997 is advised. 1,100 cases made. • $15 • (04/30/96) • **88**

Zinfandel Mendocino Pacini Vineyard 1993: Tight, firm, well-oaked, toasty, buttery flavors, but also a good core of wild berry and cherry notes and firmly tannic aftertaste. Tasted twice, with consistent notes. 700 cases made. • $14 • (09/30/95) • **87**

Zinfandel Mendocino Pacini Vineyard 1992: Lean and a bit earthy, striving for elegance and finesse but doesn't quite make it. Still, it's nice and ready now. 800 cases made. • $13 • (10/15/94) • **82**

Zinfandel Mendocino Pacini Vineyard 1991 • $13 • (09/30/93) • **84**

STELTZNER | CALIFORNIA

Cabernet Sauvignon Napa Valley 1994: Austere with hard-edged berry and currant fruit. Tough and tough to judge. • $150/case as futures. 4,200 cases made. • $20 • (05/31/95) • **80-84** (BT)

Cabernet Sauvignon Napa Valley 1991: Chunky, with ripe cherry and currant flavor that turns earthy and tannic. Best after 1996. 4,000 cases made. • $18 • (03/31/95) • **85**
Cabernet Sauvignon Stags Leap District 1988 • $19 • (11/15/92) • **82**
Cabernet Sauvignon Stags Leap District 1987 • $25 • (11/15/91) • **86**
Cabernet Sauvignon Stags Leap District 1986 • $18 • (03/01/89) • **90**
Cabernet Sauvignon Stags Leap District 1985 • $25 • (03/01/89) • **93**
Cabernet Sauvignon Stags Leap District 1984 • $33 • (03/01/89) • **91**
Cabernet Sauvignon Stags Leap District 1983 • $14 • (03/01/89) • **90**
Cabernet Sauvignon Stags Leap District 1982 • $31 • (03/01/89) • **90**
Cabernet Sauvignon Stags Leap District 1981 • $32 • (03/01/89) • **89**
Cabernet Sauvignon Stags Leap District 1980 • $30 • (03/01/89) • **88**
Cabernet Sauvignon Stags Leap District 1979 • $42 • (03/01/89) • **89**
Cabernet Sauvignon Stags Leap District 1978 • $45 • (11/15/92) • **87**
Cabernet Sauvignon Stags Leap District 1977 • $45 • (03/01/89) • **85**
Cabernet Sauvignon Stags Leap District Commemorative 1991: Earthy and tannic, revealing a leathery edge to the currant and cherry flavors. Opens up a bit with aeration, best after 1996. 800 cases made. • $45 • (03/31/95) • **85**
Claret Stags Leap District 1993: Light and simple, coming across a bit watery, lacking focus and depth. 3,200 cases made. • $11 • (12/15/95) • **77**
Claret Stags Leap District 1992: Tight and taut, exhibiting hard currant, cedary oak and earth notes, firm tannins. 3,500 cases made. • $11 • (03/31/95) • **84**
Claret Stags Leap District 1991: Lean and focused, but has some pretty, ripe, juicy cherry and berry flavors. Earthy on the finish, but the flavors stay on. Drinkable now. 3,434 cases made. • $10 • (02/28/94) • **84**
Claret Stags Leap District 1990: Ripe and juicy, with intense plum and black cherry flavors that are lively and supple. Not too tannic or concentrated, finishing with spicy oak notes on aftertaste. Drinkable already, but sure to hold through 1997. A blend of 65 percent Cabernet Franc, 30 percent Cabernet Sauvignon and 5 percent Merlot. 1,100 cases made. • $11 • (11/15/92) • **88**
Merlot Stags Leap District 1993: Marked by ripe fruity flavors, with hints of spice, cherry and plum, but the texture is a bit coarse and the tannins stand out on the finish. Best into 1998. 2,120 cases made. • $19 • **83**
Merlot Stags Leap District 1992: Trim, lean, reveals a narrow band of cedar and berry flavor. Drinkable now. 1,800 cases made. • $19 • (03/31/95) • **82**
Merlot Stags Leap District 1990 • $20 • (08/31/93) • **85**
Merlot Stags Leap District 1989 • $15 • (11/15/91) • **85**
Sauvignon Blanc Napa Valley Oak Knoll Ranch 1991 • $7 • (09/15/93) • **81**

STEMMLER, ROBERT | CALIFORNIA

Cabernet Sauvignon Sonoma County 1982 • $15 • (04/01/85) • **66**
Pinot Noir Sonoma County 1992: Light in color, with smooth mature plum, earth and cedary flavors. Ready. 3,121 cases made. • $20 • **84**
Pinot Noir Sonoma County 1991: Light, modest herb, tea and spicy cherry notes. 6,457 cases made. • $20 • (03/31/95) • **78**
Pinot Noir Sonoma County 1990 • $20 • (02/28/94) • **80**
Pinot Noir Sonoma County 1989 • $20 • (02/28/93) • **71**
Pinot Noir Sonoma County 1988 • $20 • (02/28/93) • **71**
Pinot Noir Sonoma County 1987 • $19 • (10/31/90) • **82**
Pinot Noir Sonoma County 1986 • $18 • (06/15/88) • **84**
Pinot Noir Sonoma County 1985 • $18 • (09/30/87) • **79**
Pinot Noir Sonoma County 1984 • $15 • (08/31/86) • **90**
Pinot Noir Sonoma County 1983 • $15 • (03/16/85) SS • **93**
Sauvignon Blanc Late Harvest Sonoma County 1985 • $10 • (09/30/88) • **68**

STEPHENS | CALIFORNIA

Cabernet Sauvignon Napa Valley 1981 • $8 • (02/15/84) • **74**

STERLING | CALIFORNIA

Cabernet Blanc Napa Valley 1985 • $6 • (04/01/86) • **86**
Cabernet Sauvignon Napa Valley 1992: Austere and tannic, adding a spicy, minty edge to the currant and berry flavor. Could use some more finesse and generosity. 51,065 cases made. • $14 • (11/30/95) • **85**
Cabernet Sauvignon Napa Valley 1991: An earthy, gamy flavor dominates the fruit here, turning dry and leathery on the finish. Short-term cellaring and aeration helps clean up some of the earthy notes. Tasted three times. • $14 • (11/15/94) • **82**
Cabernet Sauvignon Napa Valley 1990: Tightly wound, firm-textured with a compact array of berry, currant and leather aromas and flavors, fading a bit on the finish. Could improve through 1998. 39,000 cases made. • $14 • (11/15/93) • **83**
Cabernet Sauvignon Napa Valley 1989 • $18 • (11/15/92) • **83**
Cabernet Sauvignon Napa Valley 1988 • $15 • (11/15/91) • **80**
Cabernet Sauvignon Napa Valley 1987 • $14 • (05/15/90) • **91**
Cabernet Sauvignon Napa Valley 1986 • $18 • (03/31/89) • **91**
Cabernet Sauvignon Napa Valley 1985 • $17 • (05/15/88) • **89**
Cabernet Sauvignon Napa Valley 1983 • $18 • (02/15/87) • **81**
Cabernet Sauvignon Napa Valley 1982 • $16 • (05/16/86) • **66**
Cabernet Sauvignon Napa Valley 1981 • $20 • (08/01/85) • **88**
Cabernet Sauvignon Napa Valley 1980 • $28 • (02/15/84) • **84**
Cabernet Sauvignon Napa Valley 1978 • $22 • (06/01/86) • **95**
Cabernet Sauvignon Napa Valley 1974 • $41 • (11/15/94) • **82**
Cabernet Sauvignon Napa Valley Diamond Mountain Ranch Vineyard 1992: Ripe, harmonious, supple currant, black cherry, anise and cedary notes finish with crisp acidity and firm tannins. Can stand cellaring into 1997 or 1998. 6,539 cases made. • $17 • (10/31/95) • **88**
Cabernet Sauvignon Napa Valley Diamond Mountain Ranch Vineyard 1991: Earthy, dry and leathery. Hints of herb, currant and mineral come through on the tannic finish. Hands off until 1999 to 2001. • $18 • (11/15/94) • **86**
Cabernet Sauvignon Napa Valley Diamond Mountain Ranch Vineyard 1990: A young and firmly tannic wine where the fruit is tightly wound and in need of time to soften and develop. Hard-edged and a bit green around the edges, but may have taken a turn for the better by now. 4,000 cases made. • $18 • (11/15/93) • **81**
Cabernet Sauvignon Napa Valley Diamond Mountain Ranch Vineyard 1989 • $18 • (11/15/92) • **79**
Cabernet Sauvignon Napa Valley Diamond Mountain Ranch Vineyard 1987 • $16 • (11/15/90) • **91**
Cabernet Sauvignon Napa Valley Diamond Mountain Ranch Vineyard 1986 • $15 • (03/15/90) • **91**
Cabernet Sauvignon Napa Valley Diamond Mountain Ranch Vineyard 1985 • $21 • (05/31/89) • **88**
Cabernet Sauvignon Napa Valley Diamond Mountain Ranch Vineyard 1984 • $18 • (03/01/89) • **85**
Cabernet Sauvignon Napa Valley Diamond Mountain Ranch Vineyard 1983 • $20 • (03/01/89) • **87**
Cabernet Sauvignon Napa Valley Diamond Mountain Ranch Vineyard 1982 • $33 • (03/01/89) • **82**
Cabernet Sauvignon Reserve Napa Valley 1992: Well oaked with firm, dry tannins, but enough cherry and currant fruit emerges to keep in balance. Finishes with a light toasty oak edge and very tough tannins. Will need more time to show what it's made of. 2,115 cases made. • $40 • (12/15/95) • **87**
Cabernet Sauvignon Reserve Napa Valley 1991: Crisp and youthful, exhibiting a grapey, peppery edge to the ripe Cabernet flavors. Finishes with firm, chewy tannins, best to cellar until 1999. • $30 • (11/15/94) • **88**
Cabernet Sauvignon Reserve Napa Valley 1990: Elegant, with spicy oak and vanilla flavors and supple currant and black cherry notes. A well-made red that should be cellared until 1998. Tasted three times. • $30 • (11/15/94) • **87**
Cabernet Sauvignon Napa Valley Reserve 1989 • $35 • (06/30/93) • **88**
Cabernet Sauvignon Napa Valley Reserve 1988 • $40 • (03/31/92) • **85**
Cabernet Sauvignon Napa Valley Reserve 1987 • $43 • (11/15/90) • **93**
Cabernet Sauvignon Napa Valley Reserve 1986 • $43 • (03/15/90) CS • **95**
Cabernet Sauvignon Napa Valley Reserve 1985 • $42 • (07/15/89) SS • **96**
Cabernet Sauvignon Napa Valley Reserve 1984 • $47 • (03/31/89) CS • **92**
Cabernet Sauvignon Napa Valley Reserve 1983 • $31 • (03/01/89) • **82**
Cabernet Sauvignon Napa Valley Reserve 1982 • $30 • (03/01/89) • **75**
Cabernet Sauvignon Napa Valley Reserve 1981 • $24 • (03/01/89) • **85**
Cabernet Sauvignon Napa Valley Reserve 1980 • $37 • (03/01/89) • **91**

Cabernet Sauvignon Napa Valley Reserve 1979 • $36 • (03/01/89) • **85**
Cabernet Sauvignon Napa Valley Reserve 1978 • $41 • (11/15/92) • **90**
Cabernet Sauvignon Napa Valley Reserve 1977 • $56 • (03/01/89) • **93**
Cabernet Sauvignon Napa Valley Reserve 1976 • $48 • (03/01/89) • **76**
Cabernet Sauvignon Napa Valley Reserve 1975 • $51 • (03/01/89) • **78**
Cabernet Sauvignon Napa Valley Reserve 1974 • $77 • (11/15/94) • **83**
Cabernet Sauvignon Napa Valley Reserve 1973 • $100 • (03/01/89) • **89**
Chardonnay Napa Valley 1993: Earthy and a touch bitter, but it straightens out on the finish where the pear and spice flavors are more appealing. • $14 • (04/30/95) • **82**
Chardonnay Napa Valley 1992: Spicy, sappy flavors tend to overshadow the modest fruit in this medium-weight, straightforward Chardonnay. • $14 • (06/30/94) • **81**
Chardonnay Napa Valley 1991 • $14 • (07/15/93) • **78**
Chardonnay Napa Valley Carneros Winery Lake Vineyard 1993: Lean and earthy, with a coarse edge to the grapefruit and citrus notes. 6,000 cases made. • $18 • (07/31/95) • **78**
Chardonnay Napa Valley Carneros Winery Lake Vineyard 1992: Earthy and bitter, void of ripe fruit, with a papery, filter-pad edge. Tasted four times with consistent notes. • $18 • (06/30/94) • **67**
Chardonnay Napa Valley Carneros Winery Lake Vineyard 1991: This one has a strong earthy, leesy edge, but it picks up spicy apple and pear notes and the texture is smooth and supple. • $18 • (09/30/94) • **84**
Chardonnay Napa Valley Diamond Mountain Ranch Vineyard 1992: A tightly reined-in style, adding flintiness to the spicy pear, apple, nutmeg and toasty oak shadings. • $18 • (04/30/95) • **84**
Chardonnay Napa Valley Diamond Mountain Ranch Vineyard 1991: Crisp and restrained, almost too much so, comes off simple and muted. Has some nice apple and honey on the finish. Drinkable now. 3,300 cases made. • $18 • (06/30/94) • **84**
Chardonnay Napa Valley Sterling Collections Z Lot 1993: Ripe, smooth and creamy, with a slight bitter edge from oak, but the fruit rises to the occasion, with enough pear and spice to keep balance. 300 cases made. • $20 • (07/31/95) • **85**
Dolcetto Napa Valley Sterling Collections 25 Years Silver Anniversary 1994: Smells bright and youthful, but the flavors seem raw and a little bitter. Only available at the winery. 1,068 cases made. • $10 • **80**
Merlot Napa Valley 1993: Firm and intense, with an austere band of cedar, currant and anise flavors. Could use a little more suppleness and flavor, as it comes across as lean and trim. 47,000 cases made. • $14 • (03/31/96) • **82**
Merlot Napa Valley 1991: The green, cedary wood dominates this, both in aroma and on the palate. Unfortunately, there's not enough fruit to stand up to it and make it more appealing. • $14 • (09/15/94) • **74**
Merlot Napa Valley 1990 • $14 • (06/15/93) • **82**
Merlot Napa Valley 1989 • $15 • (05/31/92) • **82**
Merlot Napa Valley 1988 • $15 • (04/15/91) • **83**
Merlot Napa Valley 1987 • $13 • (06/15/90) • **83**
Merlot Napa Valley 1986 • $14 • (03/31/89) • **85**
Merlot Napa Valley 1985 • $14 • (03/31/88) • **87**
Merlot Napa Valley 1984 • $12 • (04/30/87) • **93**
Merlot Napa Valley 1983 • $11 • (06/01/86) • **91**
Merlot Napa Valley 1982 • $12 • (10/01/85) • **83**
Merlot Napa Valley 1981 • $11 • (03/01/84) • **83**
Merlot Napa Valley Carneros Winery Lake 1987 • $25 • (12/31/90) • **90**
Merlot Napa Valley Three Palms Vineyard 1992: An austere style with firm, crisp tannins and a lean band of cedary oak and dry tannins. Could use a little more richness and flavor, but this is often what the vineyard yields. 4,000 cases made. • $22 • (03/31/96) • **83**
Merlot Napa Valley Three Palms Vineyard 1990 • $18 • (04/15/94) • **85**
Pinot Grigio Sterling Collections Napa Valley 1994: Simple, sturdy, dusky. Spicy notes lift the low-level apricot flavors. 300 cases made. • $12 • (12/15/95) • **80**
Pinot Noir Napa Valley Carneros Winery Lake Vineyard 1994: Lean, trim band of cherry and spice notes of modest proportion. Lacks richness and depth, but it's better than in the past few vintages. 6,200 cases made. • $18 • (02/29/96) • **82**

Key: SS—Spectator Selection. CS—Cellar Selection. BB—Best Buy. $NA—Price not available. (BT)—Barrel tasting. (A)—Auction Price.
Dates in parentheses represent the issues in which the ratings were published.

Pinot Noir Napa Valley Carneros Winery Lake Vineyard 1993: Simple with tart cherry and berry notes of modest depth and proportion. Still, an improvement from the previous few efforts. 6,400 cases made. • $18 • **82**
Pinot Noir Napa Valley Carneros Winery Lake Vineyard 1992: A bit clumsy, with sharp tannins and a streak of wild berry flavors that turn earthy and bitter. • $15 • (03/31/95) • **73**
Pinot Noir Napa Valley Carneros Winery Lake Vineyard 1991 • $18 • (02/28/93) • **78**
Pinot Noir Napa Valley Carneros Winery Lake Vineyard 1990 • $14 • (11/30/92) • **73**
Pinot Noir Napa Valley Carneros Winery Lake Vineyard 1989 • $14 • (03/31/92) • **87**
Pinot Noir Napa Valley Carneros Winery Lake Vineyard 1988 • $14 • (04/30/91) • **87**
Pinot Noir Napa Valley Carneros Winery Lake Vineyard 1987 • $18 • (12/31/89) • **86**
Pinot Noir Napa Valley Carneros Winery Lake Vineyard 1986 • $18 • (02/28/89) • **89**
Sangiovese Atlas Peak Sterling Collections 1993: Light and fruity, showing subtle black cherry and spicy plum notes on an airy texture. Ready now. 1,500 cases made. • $14 • (11/30/95) • **82**
Sauvignon Blanc Napa Valley 1995: Crisp and appealing for its bright apple, vanilla and grapefruit flavors that linger nicely on the finish. 80,000 cases made. • $8 • **85**
Sauvignon Blanc Napa Valley 1994: Serves up a modest band of herb, melon, spice and a touch of celery, turning elegant and refined on the finish. Captures the essence of the grape in a stylish wine. • $9 • (03/31/96) • **85**
Sauvignon Blanc Napa Valley 1993: Clean and bright, with just a narrow streak of tobacco and herb running through the modest pear and peach flavors. Ready now. • $9 • (05/31/95) • **80**
Sauvignon Blanc Napa Valley 1992 • $8 • (12/15/93) • **72**
Sauvignon Blanc Napa Valley 1991 • $8 • (11/30/92) • **74**
Three Palms Vineyard Napa Valley Cabernet Blend 1988 • $19 • (11/15/92) • **85**
Three Palms Vineyard Napa Valley 1987 • $23 • (11/15/90) • **87**
Three Palms Vineyard Napa Valley 1986 • $22 • (12/31/89) • **86**
Three Palms Vineyard Napa Valley 1985 • $22 • (12/31/88) • **93**

STEVENOT | CALIFORNIA

Cabernet Sauvignon Amador County Grand Reserve 1988 • $10 • (11/15/92) • **83**
Cabernet Sauvignon Calaveras County 1985 • $7 • (06/30/89) • **76**
Cabernet Sauvignon Calaveras County Grand Reserve 1987 • $9 • (03/31/92) • **82**
Cabernet Sauvignon Calaveras County Grand Reserve 1984 • $15 • (12/31/87) • **75**
Cabernet Sauvignon Calaveras County Reserve 1992: Manages to balance its ripe berry and cherry flavors against the earthy, somewhat rubbery notes. 3,000 cases made. • $10 • (07/31/95) • **82**
Cabernet Sauvignon Calaveras County Reserve 1991: Rich, intense and spicy, with floral, plum and cedary oak flavors. A solid red that's firm and compact, at a fair price. • $11 • (11/15/94) • **84**
Cabernet Sauvignon Calaveras County Reserve 1990: A stylish, solidly fruity Cabernet, with plenty of new oak flavor to give it class. Has a deep color, plum flavor, firm but fine tannins and a lingering finish. Drinkable now. • $10 • (07/31/93) • **86**
Cabernet Sauvignon Calaveras County Reserve 1989 • $10 • (03/15/93) • **82**
Cabernet Sauvignon California 1991: A light, fruity Cabernet that's smooth and supple, with a strong layer of oak. Straightforward, with strawberry and cherry flavors and a nice touch of spice. Drinkable now. 2,000 cases made. • $8 • (04/30/93) BB • **83**
Cabernet Sauvignon California 1990: A sweet oak character, with its components of vanilla and nutmeg, dominates this smooth, medium-bodied Cabernet. Has modest fruit flavor and a soft texture. Drinkable now. 2,000 cases made. • $8 • (11/15/92) • **79**
Cabernet Sauvignon California 1989 • $7 • (11/15/92) • **79**
Cabernet Sauvignon Sierra Foothills 1993: Strikes a nice balance between smoky, toasty oak and ripe, spicy berry flavor. 7,000 cases made. • $7 • (12/15/95) • **83**

Chardonnay Calaveras County Barrell Fermented 1992: Earthy with tart grapefruit and citrus notes. A good white table wine, but lacks true varietal expression. 2,200 cases made. • $11 • (06/30/94) • **74**
Chardonnay Calaveras County Reserve 1994: Good intensity, showing pear and peach notes of modest proportions and a strong citrus finish. 1,500 cases made. • $10 • (05/15/96) • **84**
Chardonnay Calaveras County Reserve 1993: Crisp and flinty, showing a grapefruit edge to the flavors. • $11 • (02/28/95) • **82**
Chardonnay Calaveras County Reserve 1991 • $10 • (06/30/93) • **86**
Chardonnay California 1992: Crisp, lean and simple, with tart pear and apple flavors. Drink now. • $8 • (09/15/93) • **79**
Chardonnay California 1991 • $8 • (04/15/93) • **77**
Chardonnay Sierra Foothills 1993: Crisp, with a flinty, earthy edge to the pear and apple notes. • $8 • (02/28/95) • **82**
Merlot North Coast Reserve 1991 • $10 • (03/31/93) • **75**
Merlot North Coast Reserve 1990 • $10 • (11/30/92) • **80**
Merlot Reserve 1989 • $10 • (05/31/92) • **83**
Merlot Sierra Foothills Reserve 1992: A burnt-rubber smell permeates this otherwise nicely balanced and flavorful Merlot. 6,000 cases made. • $11 • (09/15/94) • **77**
Sauvignon Blanc Calaveras County Barrel Fermented 1992: Lean and spicy, with an earthy-mineral undertone to the peachy fruit. 650 cases made. • $7 • (08/31/94) • **80**
Sauvignon Blanc Calaveras County Reserve 1993: Light, simple, easy to drink, modestly fruity, period. 1,000 cases made. • $7 • (08/31/95) • **79**
Zinfandel Amador County Grand Reserve 1985 • $7 • (12/31/87) • **72**
Zinfandel Calaveras County 1986 • $7 • (07/31/89) BB • **84**
Zinfandel Calaveras County 1984 • $6 • (06/30/87) • **73**
Zinfandel Calaveras County Reserve 1991 • $10 • (06/15/94) • **73**
Zinfandel Calaveras County Reserve 1990 • $10 • (06/15/93) • **77**
Zinfandel California 1989 • $6 • (04/30/93) • **79**
Zinfandel Sierra Foothills Reserve 1993: Light but has some simple spice, berry and oaky notes that are pleasant. 2,000 cases made. • $8 • (10/15/95) • **80**

STEWART | WASHINGTON

Cabernet Sauvignon Columbia Valley 1988 • $11 • (08/31/91) • **79**
Chardonnay Columbia Valley 1993: Firm, focused and flavorful but not showing much finesse at this stage, toast and peach notes carrying through to the finish. Drink now. 497 cases made. • $9 • (09/30/95) • **85**
Chardonnay Columbia Valley Barrel Fermented Reserve 1993: Lean, lithe and snappy, offering a resiny edge to the spicy pear flavors. Drink now. 220 cases made. • $14 • (09/30/95) • **85**
Gewüztraminer Late Harvest Yakima Valley 1994: Sweet and beguiling bite-of-fresh-peach immediacy, finishing with a touch of apricot and distinctive spice. Delicious now. 699 cases made. • $8 • (09/30/95) • **88**
Gewürztraminer Yakima Valley 1993: Fruit seems to be fading in this lean, off-dry, slightly floral Gewürz. 1,019 cases made. • $5 • (09/30/95) • **79**
Johannisberg Riesling Columbia Valley 1994: Fresh, off-dry, fruity and bright, featuring Golden Delicious apple and floral flavors. Drink now. 652 cases made. • $5 • (09/30/95) • **84**
White Riesling Late Harvest Columbia Valley 1987 • $8 • (07/31/89) • **83**
White Riesling Late Harvest Columbia Valley Select 1986 • $6 • (10/15/89) • **80**

STILLMAN BROWN | CALIFORNIA

Sauvignon Blanc Paso Robles 1994: Well oaked, perhaps to a fault, as this thoroughly dominates the flavors now, adding a smoky, acrid aftertaste that isn't all that pleasant. 297 cases made. • $14 • (02/29/96) • **74**

STONE CELLARS | WASHINGTON

Cabernet Sauvignon Columbia Valley 1993: Youthful, with plenty of fruit and some tannin that should round out nicely by 1997 or '98. 20,000 cases made. • $5 • (05/31/95) • **83**
Chardonnay Columbia Valley 1993: A subdued, subtle white exhibiting nice nectarine and spice flavors that linger on the delicate finish. Ready now. 20,000 cases made. • $5 • (01/31/95) • **81**
Merlot Columbia Valley 1993: Crisp, flavorful and generous with its meaty black cherry and berry notes. Tannins are a little chewy, may be better in 1997. 20,000 cases made. • $6 • (05/31/95) BB • **83**

STONE CREEK | CALIFORNIA

Cabernet Sauvignon California Special Selection 1989 • $6 • (11/15/93) • **72**
Cabernet Sauvignon Napa Valley Chairman's Reserve 1990: Overbearingly earthy and woody with potent cedary and tarry notes. Tastes void of fruit. Marginal quality. 4,500 cases made. • $10 • (11/15/93) • **68**
Cabernet Sauvignon Napa Valley Limited Bottling 1986 • $10 • (06/15/90) • **85**
Cabernet Sauvignon Napa Valley Special Selection 1986 • $10 • (11/15/91) • **80**
Cabernet Sauvignon Napa Valley Special Selection 1983 • $8 • (05/31/87) BB • **91**
Chardonnay California 1991 • $7 • (09/30/92) • **78**
Chardonnay California Special Selection 1994: Light and a little spicy, centered around simple peach fruit that lingers on the finish. Ready now. 40,000 cases made. • $7 BB • **83**
Chardonnay Napa Valley Chairman's Reserve 1994: Bright, fresh and smooth, lively with nectarine and vanilla flavors on a silky frame. Ready now. 2,500 cases made. • $15 • (11/15/95) • **87**
Merlot California Special Selection 1990 • $7 • (11/30/92) • **80**
Merlot California Special Selection 1989 • $6 • (05/31/92) • **79**
Merlot Columbia Valley 1989 • $7 • (05/31/91) BB • **86**
Merlot Columbia Valley 1988 • $6 • (09/30/90) • **78**
Merlot Washington Special Selection 1993: A distinctly floral character spices up this light-textured, flavorful red that echoes spice and berry. Has enough tannin to warrant waiting until 1997 or '98. A good price for all that. 25,000 cases made. • $8 • (05/15/96) BB • **84**
Zinfandel California 1991: Firm, tannic and dry, with a compact band of black cherry and wild berry flavors that are tart and persistent. Finishes with a tannic edge. Ready now. 7,000 cases made. • $6 • (09/30/94) BB • **85**
Zinfandel California Special Selection 1991: Mature and earthy, with notes of berry and tar. Finishes crisply acidic, with firm tannins. 5,000 cases made. • $7 • (10/15/95) • **83**

STONE HILL | MISSOURI

Port Missouri 1992: Thick, fruity and sweet, this offers dark chocolate, walnut and grapey flavors in a soft, round package. Doesn't have the backbone or depth of true Port, but appealing nonetheless. • $NA • (10/31/95) • **83**

STONEGATE | CALIFORNIA

Cabernet Franc Napa Valley 1990 • $NA • (11/15/93) • **81**
Cabernet Sauvignon Napa Valley 1991: A touch earthy and gamy, but enough Cabernet fruit emerges to sustain short-term interest. 2,200 cases made. • $18 • (12/15/95) • **82**
Cabernet Sauvignon Napa Valley 1990: An earthy style with a gamy streak that runs through the Cabernet flavors. Perhaps time in the bottle will smooth things out. Try after 1997. 1,900 cases made. • $14 • (11/15/94) • **81**
Cabernet Sauvignon Napa Valley 1989 • $15 • (11/15/93) • **80**
Cabernet Sauvignon Napa Valley 1988 • $14 • (11/15/92) • **84**
Cabernet Sauvignon Napa Valley 1987 • $14 • (03/31/92) • **82**
Cabernet Sauvignon Napa Valley 1986 • $17 • (02/28/91) • **86**
Cabernet Sauvignon Napa Valley 1985 • $17 • (08/31/90) • **86**
Cabernet Sauvignon Napa Valley 1984 • $17 • (03/01/89) • **88**
Cabernet Sauvignon Napa Valley 1982 • $22 • (03/01/89) • **80**
Cabernet Sauvignon Napa Valley 1981 • $17 • (03/01/89) • **79**
Cabernet Sauvignon Napa Valley 1980 • $27 • (03/01/89) • **86**
Cabernet Sauvignon Napa Valley 1979 • $25 • (03/01/89) • **84**
Cabernet Sauvignon Napa Valley 1978 • $27 • (11/15/92) • **87**
Cabernet Sauvignon Napa Valley 1977 • $25 • (03/01/89) • **81**
Chardonnay Sonoma County Bella Vista Vineyard 1991 • $14 • (11/30/93) • **83**

Felicity Napa Valley 1991 • $7 • (12/15/92) • **77**
Late Harvest Napa Valley 1990 • $9 • (03/31/92) • **83**
Late Harvest Napa Valley 1989 • $13 • (04/30/91) • **87**
Meritage Reserve Napa Valley 1988 • $17 • (11/15/93) • **85**
Meritage Reserve Napa Valley 1987 • $17 • (11/15/93) • **86**
Merlot Napa Valley 1989 • $17 • (10/31/92) • **86**
Merlot Napa Valley 1988 • $17 • (05/31/92) • **81**
Merlot Napa Valley 1986 • $15 • (04/15/90) • **84**
Merlot Napa Valley Pershing Vineyard 1987 • $17 • (03/31/91) • **83**
Merlot Napa Valley Spaulding Vineyard 1987 • $17 • (03/31/91) • **86**
Merlot Napa Valley Spaulding Vineyard 1984 • $15 • (12/31/88) • **85**
Merlot Napa Valley Spaulding Vineyard 1982 • $14 • (02/28/87) • **84**
Merlot Napa Valley Spaulding Vineyard 1980 • $12 • (10/01/85) • **68**
Reserve Napa Valley 1989: Firm and focused, showing plenty of currant and blackberry fruit against a counterpoint of toast and spice. Stays lively on the finish. Best from 1998. 630 cases made. • $24 • (12/15/95) • **88**
Sauvignon Blanc Napa Valley 1993: Herbal, oniony notes are a little hard to enjoy in this sturdy white. 1,600 cases made. • $9 • (08/31/95) • **76**
Sauvignon Blanc Napa Valley 1991 • $9 • (08/31/94) • **72**

STONEHEDGE | CALIFORNIA

Cabernet Sauvignon Napa Valley Winemaker's Reserve 1993: Earthy and tannic, with just enough currant and berry showing through to make it palatable, but it won't lose its tannins. 1,500 cases made. • $10 • (03/31/96) • **79**
Cabernet Sauvignon Napa Valley Winemaker's Reserve 1992: Smooth and elegant, with a supple band of cherry, currant and raspberry flavors couched in light oak shadings. Finishes with firm, fine tannins. Needs until 1999 to show its best. 3,500 cases made. • $10 • (11/30/95) BB • **89**
Malbec Napa Valley 1993: A touch earthy, with a funky streak in the currant and plum flavors. Lacks focus, and somewhat marginal as an example of this variety. 500 cases made. • $15 • (03/31/96) • **79**

STONESTREET | CALIFORNIA

Cabernet Sauvignon Alexander Valley 1992: Tight and compact, with well-focused cherry, currant and cedar flavors that are complex and concentrated. Smooth and polished on the finish despite firm tannins. 1,660 cases made. • $25 • (10/31/95) • **91**
Cabernet Sauvignon Alexander Valley 1991: Appealingly supple cherry, currant, spice and cedary oak, in a full-bodied, elegant style. Can stand cellaring into 1997 to make it softer. 2,500 cases made. • $22 • (05/15/95) • **88**
Cabernet Sauvignon Alexander Valley 1990: Ripe and spicy with a pretty core of ripe cherry and raspberry flavor. Finishes with firm tannins and good length. Drinkable now. • $20 • (11/15/94) • **87**
Cabernet Sauvignon Alexander Valley 1989 • $24 • (11/15/92) • **84**
Cabernet Sauvignon Alexander Valley 1988 • $24 • (08/31/92) • **82**
Chardonnay Sonoma County 1994: A smooth, rich and complex white that has an attractive array of honey, pear and butterscotch flavors kissed by spicy toasty oak. Deep and concentrated, finishing with a satisfying complexity. 13,018 cases made. • $25 • (05/31/96) SS • **91**
Chardonnay Sonoma County 1993: Another remarkable Chardonnay from Stonestreet. This is a rich, toasty, complex wine with tiers of pear, spice, toast and smoky oak flavors, followed by a long finish. A real mouthful. 7,500 cases made. • $21 • (04/30/95) SS • **92**
Chardonnay Sonoma County 1992: Ripe, rich and oaky, with a pleasant range of toasty, buttery pear and spicy flavors that fan out and turn complex. 3,600 cases made. • $20 • (01/31/95) SS • **90**
Chardonnay Sonoma County 1991: Serves up ripe pear and appley flavors that turn spicy and a bit cloying on the finish. Picks up a trace of toasty oak on the aftertaste. • $24 • (06/30/94) • **84**

Key: SS—Spectator Selection. CS—Cellar Selection. BB—Best Buy. $NA—Price not available. (BT)—Barrel tasting. (A)—Auction Price.
Dates in parentheses represent the issues in which the ratings were published.

Gewürztraminer Anderson Valley 1993: Soft and very spicy, with strong nutmeg, allspice and rose petal notes, light fruit echoes on the finish. Drink soon. • $13 • (02/28/95) • **85**
Gewürztraminer Sonoma County 1991 • $12 • (01/31/93) • **78**
Legacy Alexander Valley 1992: Supple, complex and harmonious, with layers of smoky oak, currant, cherry and spice. Finishes with smooth, thick tannins and excellent length. A beautifully crafted red wine from this California winery. 784 cases made. • $35 • (09/30/95) CS • **92**
Legacy Alexander Valley 1991: Smooth, plush and elegant, with a rich, focused core of plum and currant flavor. Mildly tannic with a long full finish, it drinks well now but is sure to hold through the decade. • $35 • (11/15/94) • **91**
Legacy Alexander Valley 1990: Crisp and spicy, with a chocolate-spice edge to the modest core of berry and currant flavor, finishing lean and elegant. Drinkable now. • $35 • (11/15/93) • **85**
Merlot Alexander Valley 1993: Marked by earthy currant and leathery flavors, picks up herb and mineral notes on the finish, when the tannins kick in. A little age should soften it. 4,941 cases made. • $30 • (06/30/96) • **86**
Merlot Alexander Valley 1992: The best yet from this California winery and one of the rare Merlots that is outstanding in quality. This is appealing now for its rich, earthy, toasty oak and tobacco scents and plush currant and mineral flavors. Turns complex and lingers on the finish. 6,272 cases made. • $22 • (05/15/95) SS • **90**
Merlot Alexander Valley 1991: With its charred edge and tight tannins, it clamps down at the beginning with a firm bit but you get hints of currant, herb and oak on the finish. May always be on the tannic side, drinkable now. • $24 • (09/15/94) • **85**
Merlot Alexander Valley 1990: Shows off herb, cola and currant flavors, but ultimately a simple wine that's dry and tannic, lacking extra dimensions. Drink now. • $20 • (09/15/94) • **82**
Merlot Alexander Valley 1989 • $24 • (05/31/92) • **88**
Pinot Noir Russian River Valley 1994: Complex, earthy edge to the ripe plum and cherry flavors. A toasty oak and tannic finish. Can stand short-term cellaring. • $30 • (02/29/96) • **87**
Pinot Noir Russian River Valley 1990 • $30 • (09/30/92) • **84**
Pinot Noir Sonoma County 1993: A touch earthy with a cedary oak edge, with gamy cherry and plum notes. It holds together on the finish where the flavors come together. Best after 1996. • $25 • **87**
Pinot Noir Sonoma County 1992: The fruit struggles to rise above the herb and tobacco flavors. Turns chunky and a bit tannic on the finish. Drinkable now. • $20 • (03/31/95) • **86**
Pinot Noir Sonoma County 1991 • $30 • (02/28/94) • **89**
Pinot Noir Sonoma County Reserve 1992: Smooth in texture, with a pretty band of cherry, herb, spice and cola notes that are ripe and focused. Finishes with firm tannins. Drinkable now. • $34 • (12/15/94) • **89**

STONY HILL | CALIFORNIA

Chardonnay Napa Valley 1993: Tastes simple and uncomplicated at first, with modest pear and spice notes, but picks up a trace of honey and mineral on the crisp finish. 3,100 cases made. • $21 • (06/15/96) • **85**
Chardonnay Napa Valley 1992: Austere and earthy, with a metallic edge to the pineapple and citrus flavors. Tasted twice with consistent notes. • $30 • (07/31/95) • **83**
Chardonnay Napa Valley 1991: Clean and crisp, with pretty peach, nectarine and spicy nuances, elegant and vibrant, it keeps pumping out fresh fruit flavors on a long, lingering finish. Ready now, but cellaring it a few years won't hurt, up to 2000. • $42 • (06/30/94) • **88**
Chardonnay Napa Valley SHV 1993: Despite floral aromas, it's tight and trim to drink, with a narrow band of pear and spice that fans out on the finish. Best to cellar short-term. • $23 • (07/31/95) • **86**
Chardonnay Napa Valley SHV 1991 • $14 • (03/31/93) • **74**

STONY RIDGE | CALIFORNIA

Cabernet Sauvignon California 1989 • $6 • (08/31/92) • **78**
Cabernet Sauvignon Napa Valley Limited Release 1989 • $9 • (11/15/92) • **78**
Chardonnay California 1991 • $6 • (11/30/92) • **81**
Merlot North Coast Limited Release 1991 • $10 • (06/30/93) • **85**

Merlot North Coast Limited Release 1990 • $9 • (11/30/92) • **82**
Zinfandel Livermore Valley 1980 • $7 • (06/16/84) • **75**

STORRS | CALIFORNIA

Chardonnay Santa Cruz Mountains Christie Vineyard Mountain Vineyard Collection 1993: More complete than most 1993s, with supple pear, honey and light oak notes. • $17 • (07/31/95) • **85**
Chardonnay Santa Cruz Mountains Vanumanutagi Vineyards 1993: Young and fruity. The attractive peach, pear and vanilla notes are clean and well proportioned. 750 cases made. • $19 • (05/31/95) • **86**
Zinfandel Beauregard Ranch 1992: Austere, with a crisp, leathery, earthy character and just a trace of berry flavor. 554 cases made. • $15 • (10/15/95) • **82**
Zinfandel California Ben Lomond Mountain Beauregard Ranch 1990 • $15 • (10/15/92) • **82**
Zinfandel California Ben Lomond Mountain Beauregard Ranch 1989 • $13 • (10/15/92) • **81**

STORY | CALIFORNIA

Zinfandel Amador County 1987 • $8 • (04/30/91) • **84**
Zinfandel Amador County 1986 • $8 • (08/31/91) • **80**
Zinfandel Amador County 1980 • $6 • (04/01/84) • **73**
Zinfandel Amador County Shenandoah Valley Private Reserve 1984 • $14 • (04/30/91) • **79**
Zinfandel Shenandoah Valley 1992: The earthy, tarry character dominates the simple cherry and berry notes, but the flavors grow on you. Will show better with food. 1,100 cases made. • $10 • (10/15/95) • **83**
Zinfandel Shenandoah Valley 1991 • $10 • (09/30/93) • **86**
Zinfandel Shenandoah Valley 1990 • $8 • (09/30/93) • **83**
Zinfandel Shenandoah Valley 1989 • $9 • (09/30/93) • **82**
Zinfandel Shenandoah Valley Picnic Hill Vineyard Old Vines 1993: Tough and tannic, but the solid core of earthy berry, cherry and mineral flavors are pleasant and pick up a touch of anise and spice on the finish. 750 cases made. • $16 • (10/15/95) • **84**
Zinfandel Shenandoah Valley Private Reserve 1992: Mature and earthy, a slight pickle-barrel edge to the wild berry flavors. It straightens out a bit on the finish. 350 cases made. • $16 • (10/15/95) • **82**

STORYBOOK MOUNTAIN | CALIFORNIA

Zinfandel Howell Mountain 1992: Tart and relatively modest, showing crisp black cherry and strawberry notes. Not the blockbuster you expect from this appellation. 700 cases made. • $14 • (10/15/95) • **83**
Zinfandel Howell Mountain 1991: Austere with a tight, firm and focused core of black cherry, raspberry and spice notes. • $15 • (10/15/94) • **87**
Zinfandel Napa Valley 1992: Intense but well balanced, with firm acidity and lively berry and pepper flavors that finish austere and tannic. Should improve by 1997, but will remain tannic. 7,000 cases made. • $14 • (10/15/95) • **86**
Zinfandel Napa Valley 1991 • $14 • (09/30/93) • **87**
Zinfandel Napa Valley 1990 • $14 • (03/15/93) • **83**
Zinfandel Napa Valley 1989 • $15 • (03/31/92) • **80**
Zinfandel Napa Valley 1988 • $13 • (12/31/90) • **75**
Zinfandel Napa Valley 1987 • $12 • (12/15/89) • **88**
Zinfandel Napa Valley 1986 • $11 • (12/15/88) • **88**
Zinfandel Napa Valley 1985 • $10 • (12/31/87) • **90**
Zinfandel Napa Valley 1984 • $9 • (03/15/87) • **80**
Zinfandel Napa Valley 1983 • $8 • (04/16/86) • **90**
Zinfandel Napa Valley 1982 • $8 • (12/01/84) • **86**
Zinfandel Napa Valley Eastern Exposures 1992: A new bottling from this winery. This is warm, ripe, supple and harmonious, the pretty plum and black cherry flavors turning smooth on the finish. Well done. 858 cases made. • $17 • (10/15/95) • **89**
Zinfandel Napa Valley Estate Reserve 1991: Ripe, intense and spicy, but it turns hollow in the middle. Has a pruny edge with gritty tannins that turns earthy and gamy. Best to cellar until 1997. • $25 • (10/15/94) • **82**
Zinfandel Napa Valley Estate Reserve 1989 • $19 • (06/15/93) • **71**
Zinfandel Napa Valley Reserve 1991: Tightly wound, with austere berry, pepper and sage notes. Intense and tannic, so it can stand some aging, but the tannins may remain for years. 955 cases made. • $25 • (10/15/95) • **86**
Zinfandel Napa Valley Reserve 1988 • $20 • (03/31/92) • **84**
Zinfandel Napa Valley Reserve 1987 • $25 • (12/31/90) • **89**
Zinfandel Napa Valley Reserve 1986 • $27 • (05/15/90) • **82**
Zinfandel Napa Valley Reserve 1985 • $29 • (05/31/89) • **88**
Zinfandel Napa Valley Reserve 1984 • $22 • (04/30/88) • **92**
Zinfandel Napa Valley Reserve 1983 • $22 • (07/31/87) • **81**
Zinfandel Napa Valley Reserve 1981 • $9 • (04/16/84) • **86**
Zinfandel Sonoma County 1986 • $8 • (10/15/88) • **87**
Zinfandel Sonoma County 1982 • $7 • (09/16/85) • **81**

STRATFORD | CALIFORNIA

Cabernet Sauvignon California 1990: Light and fruity, with a floral edge to the basic currant flavors, finishing firm with modest tannins. Drink now. 2,233 cases made. • $12 • (11/15/92) • **81**
Cabernet Sauvignon California 1985 • $10 • (11/30/88) • **83**
Cabernet Sauvignon California 1983 • $8 • (02/15/87) • **86**
Cabernet Sauvignon Napa Valley 1993: A lean wine with flavors that run toward pickle barrel and toast, modest on the fruit. Tannic enough to want until 1998 or even 2000. 3,000 cases made. • $10 • (12/15/95) • **81**
Cabernet Sauvignon Napa Valley 1987 • $12 • (04/30/90) • **85**
Cabernet Sauvignon Napa Valley Partners' Reserve 1988 • $16 • (03/15/92) • **68**
Cabernet Sauvignon Napa Valley Partners' Reserve 1987 • $16 • (04/30/91) • **90**
Chardonnay California 1991 • $9 • (07/15/93) • **82**
Dolcetto Napa Valley 1994: Lightly floral, fruity and simple, an easy wine to drink as an apéritif or with light lunch. 713 cases made. • $8 • (11/15/95) • **83**
Merlot California 1991 • $11 • (07/15/93) • **84**
Merlot California 1990 • $9 • (05/31/92) BB • **85**
Merlot California 1987 • $13 • (10/31/89) • **83**
Merlot California 1986 • $10 • (01/31/89) • **78**
Merlot California 1983 • $8 • (09/30/86) • **79**
Sauvignon Blanc California Partners' Reserve 1991 • $9 • (06/15/93) • **85**
Zinfandel California 1991 • $7 • (06/15/93) BB • **83**

STRAUS | CALIFORNIA

Merlot Napa Valley 1991: A smooth, elegant, smoky oak character blend with the currant, black cherry and mineral flavors. 1,450 cases made. • $17 • (05/15/95) • **85**
Merlot Napa Valley 1990 • $16 • (08/31/93) • **85**
Merlot Napa Valley 1989 • $15 • (11/15/91) • **81**
Merlot Napa Valley 1988 • $14 • (12/31/90) • **82**
Merlot Napa Valley 1987 • $12 • (02/15/90) • **90**
Merlot Napa Valley 1986 • $11 • (02/28/89) • **93**
Merlot Napa Valley 1985 • $10 • (02/15/88) • **81**

STREBLOW | CALIFORNIA

Cabernet Sauvignon Napa Valley 1987 • $16 • (10/15/90) • **79**
Cabernet Sauvignon Napa Valley 1986 • $16 • (07/31/89) • **87**
Cabernet Sauvignon Napa Valley 1985 • $15 • (06/15/88) • **89**
Merlot Napa Valley 1989 • $20 • (05/31/92) • **89**

STRONG, RODNEY | CALIFORNIA

Cabernet Sauvignon Alexander Valley Alexander's Crown Vineyard 1987 • $17 • (07/15/91) • **89**
Cabernet Sauvignon Alexander Valley Alexander's Crown Vineyard 1985 • $17 • (05/31/91) • **87**
Cabernet Sauvignon Alexander Valley Alexander's Crown Vineyard 1984 • $12 • (04/30/89) • **80**
Cabernet Sauvignon Alexander Valley Alexander's Crown Vineyard 1982 • $12 • (10/31/88) • **80**
Cabernet Sauvignon Alexander Valley Alexander's Crown Vineyard 1981 • $12 • (11/30/87) • **77**
Cabernet Sauvignon Alexander Valley Alexander's Crown Vineyard 1980 • $11 • (04/16/85) • **86**

STUERMER

Cabernet Sauvignon Alexander Valley Alexander's Crown Vineyard 1979 • $12 • (04/16/84) • **79**

Cabernet Sauvignon Alexander Valley Alexander's Crown Vineyard 1978 • $12 • (01/01/84) • **80**

Cabernet Sauvignon Alexander Valley Reserve 1988 • $30 • (11/15/92) • **84**

Cabernet Sauvignon Alexander Valley Reserve 1987 • $28 • (09/30/91) • **92**

Cabernet Sauvignon Northern Sonoma Alexander's Crown Vineyard 1991: Light and spicy, with a fine thread of bright berry fruit to keep it lively. Approachable now, best from 1997. 11,300 cases made. • $20 • (12/15/95) • **86**

Cabernet Sauvignon Northern Sonoma Alexander's Crown Vineyard 1990: Firm and tasty, a soft-textured wine with a green bean edge to the plum and currant fruit, tannins sneaking in to bite a bit on the finish. Drink after 1997. 5,800 cases made. • $20 • (11/15/93) • **86**

Cabernet Sauvignon Northern Sonoma Alexander's Crown Vineyard 1988 • $18 • (09/30/92) • **91**

Cabernet Sauvignon Northern Sonoma Reserve 1991: Intense if a bit murky in its focus, with spicy, toasty oak and a range of cherry and currant fruit underneath. Hangs together where the finish picks up a spicy edge. • $30 • (12/15/95) • **86**

Cabernet Sauvignon Northern Sonoma Reserve 1990: Displays many pleasing facets, with ripe, tightly-wound cherry, currant and light toasty oak flavors. Capable of aging through this decade and into the next. • $30 • (06/15/94) • **88**

Cabernet Sauvignon Sonoma County 1993: Well balanced, with pretty oak, currant and plum flavors, a well-executed style that turns complex on the finish. Best after 1996. • $11 • (12/15/95) • **86**

Cabernet Sauvignon Sonoma County 1992: A rustic style marked by cedary oak, currant and berry flavors, with firm tannins. Best after 1996. • $10 • (06/15/95) • **83**

Cabernet Sauvignon Sonoma County 1991: Firm, intense and tannic, with a narrow band of spicy Cabernet fruit. Can stand cellaring a year or two to soften and flush out the flavors. • $10 • (11/15/94) • **82**

Cabernet Sauvignon Sonoma County 1990: Lean and a bit on the green side, with herb, bell pepper and green bean notes. Shows a hint of plum and spice, along with oak, on the finish, but it could use a little more flavor and finesse. Drink now. • $11 • (11/15/93) • **81**

Cabernet Sauvignon Sonoma County 1989 • $10 • (09/30/92) • **84**

Cabernet Sauvignon Sonoma County 1988 • $10 • (11/15/91) • **80**

Cabernet Sauvignon Sonoma County 1987 • $10 • (06/30/91) • **85**

Cabernet Sauvignon Sonoma County 1982 • $7 • (12/15/86) • **69**

Cabernet Sauvignon Sonoma Valley 1981 • $7 • (12/16/84) • **86**

Chardonnay Chalk Hill Vineyard 1994: Fruit-centered white packs some concentration on a medium frame, offering apple, spice and vanilla notes and a touch of green flavor on the finish. • $14 • (04/30/96) • **85**

Chardonnay Chalk Hill Vineyard 1993: Well balanced in a medium-bodied style, with ripe pear, apple, honey and spice notes. • $14 • (07/31/95) • **85**

Chardonnay Chalk Hill Vineyard 1992: Subdued aromas of spice, pear and oak turn elegant and spicy on the palate. A good, complete young Chardonnay that drinks well now. • $13 • (06/30/94) • **85**

Chardonnay Chalk Hill Vineyard 1991 • $13 • (07/15/93) • **74**

Chardonnay Sonoma County 1994: A fruity style that adds a touch of hazelnut to its pear, honey and melon flavors. The understated toastiness lets the ripe fruit shine. • $11 • (06/15/96) • **87**

Chardonnay Sonoma County 1993: Simple and straightforward, with ripe pear and apple-laced fruit. 60,000 cases made. • $11 • (04/30/95) • **83**

Chardonnay Sonoma County 1992: A ripe, spicy, floral style, with hints of peach and honey. Drinks easy, at a fair price. Ready now. • $10 • (10/15/93) • **82**

Chardonnay Sonoma County 1991 • $9 • (11/15/92) BB • **84**

Merlot Russian River Valley River West Vineyard 1985 • $12 • (02/28/89) • **79**

Key: SS—Spectator Selection. CS—Cellar Selection. BB—Best Buy. $NA—Price not available. (BT)—Barrel tasting. (A)—Auction Price.
Dates in parentheses represent the issues in which the ratings were published.

Merlot Sonoma County 1993: Supple and well oaked, with a toasty, buttery edge to the plum and cherry-laced fruit. Firm and chunky now, in need of cellaring into 1996-97, but well made, with a complex aftertaste. • $16 • **87**

Merlot Sonoma County 1992: Lean and crisp, with a narrow band of herb, plum and spice notes that turn elegant. • $14 • (02/28/95) • **84**

Pinot Noir Russian River Valley River East Vineyard 1993: Smooth and harmonious, a medium-weight style with pleasant cherry, creamy oak, spice and earthy notes. Well balanced. • $16 • (12/31/95) • **87**

Pinot Noir Russian River Valley River East Vineyard 1992: Earthy and herbal, but delivering enough black cherry notes to keep in balance. Finishes with green tannins and a tea-flavored edge. 5,000 cases made. • $14 • (03/31/95) • **83**

Pinot Noir Russian River Valley River East Vineyard 1991 • $14 • (02/28/94) • **87**

Pinot Noir Russian River Valley River East Vineyard 1990 • $14 • (09/30/92) • **82**

Pinot Noir Russian River Valley River East Vineyard 1985 • $10 • (02/28/91) • **83**

Pinot Noir Russian River Valley River East Vineyard 1984 • $8 • (11/15/87) • **78**

Pinot Noir Russian River Valley River East Vineyard 1981 • $8 • (08/31/86) • **63**

Pinot Noir Russian River Valley River East Vineyard 1980 • $10 • (07/01/84) • **78**

Sauvignon Blanc Northern Sonoma Charlotte's Home Vineyard 1995: Bright and citrusy, nicely polished to show off its nectarine and grapefruit flavors. • $10 • (06/15/96) • **86**

Sauvignon Blanc Northern Sonoma Charlotte's Home Vineyard 1994: Smooth and flavorful in a tropical-fruit sort of way, as waves of leafy, herbal notes wash over the finish. • $9 • (08/31/95) • **84**

Sauvignon Blanc Northern Sonoma Charlotte's Home Vineyard 1993: Soft and fruity, spicy and generous, echoing nectarine and spicy vanilla flavors. 5,000 cases made. • $10 • (08/31/94) • **85**

Sauvignon Blanc Northern Sonoma Charlotte's Home Vineyard 1992 • $9 • (09/15/93) • **87**

Sauvignon Blanc Northern Sonoma Charlotte's Home Vineyard 1991 • $9 • (02/28/93) • **82**

Zinfandel Northern Sonoma Old Vines 1993: Marked by spicy, peppery flavors and a touch of earthy jam. It's a rustic style with firm, drying tannins. 5,400 cases made. • $14 • (03/31/96) • **84**

Zinfandel Russian River Valley River West Vineyard Old Vines 1992: Well oaked but with a bright core of cherry and raspberry fruit to match it. Drinks well now, with a long, fruity aftertaste. Drinkable now. • $14 • (07/31/95) • **86**

Zinfandel Russian River Valley River West Vineyard Old Vines 1991 • $14 • (04/30/94) • **82**

Zinfandel Russian River Valley River West Vineyard Old Vines 1990 • $14 • (12/15/92) • **86**

Zinfandel Russian River Valley River West Vineyard Old Vines 1988 • $15 • (10/15/92) • **89**

Zinfandel Russian River Valley River West Vineyard Old Vines 1987 • $14 • (08/31/91) • **82**

Zinfandel Russian River Valley River West Vineyard Old Vines 1980 • $12 • (11/15/87) • **68**

Zinfandel Russian River Valley River West Vineyard Old Vines 1979 • $10 • (03/15/87) • **71**

Zinfandel Sonoma County 1986 • $5 • (03/31/89) • **79**

Zinfandel Sonoma County 1982 • $5 • (12/31/87) • **70**

STUERMER | CALIFORNIA

Cabernet Sauvignon Lake County 1984 • $15 • (09/30/89) • **66**

SUGARLOAF RIDGE | CALIFORNIA

Cabernet Sauvignon Sonoma Valley 1986 • $13 • (03/31/90) • **82**

SULLBERG, MICHAEL | CALIFORNIA

Cabernet Sauvignon Central Coast 1992: Dry and intense, with a leathery oak edge to the currant- and berry-laced fruit. Finishes with a strong dose of sage and mint. 1,200 cases made. • $6 • (12/15/95) • **84**

Cabernet Sauvignon Napa Valley 1991: Gamy with a pickle and herb edge, decent, offering enough flavor, fair price. Ready now. 1,000 cases made. • $7 • (11/15/94) • **79**

Chardonnay Atlas Peak Lot 55 Barrel Fermented 1991: Mature with an earthy edge to the pear and honey notes, finishing with a slight brackish taste. 1,256 cases made. • $6 • (05/15/96) • **82**

Chardonnay Central Coast Barrel Fermented 1992: Relies a little too heavily on wood for its flavor, but some apple and pear notes pop through on the finish. Ready now. 1,200 cases made. • $6 • (06/30/94) • **79**

Chardonnay Knights Valley Lot 54 Barrel Fermented 1994: Light in texture but bright, featuring pear and vanilla flavors that finish with some restraint. Ready now. 2,200 cases made. • $8 • (02/29/96) • **86**

Chardonnay Sonoma County 1992: Simple, fruity and spicy, nicely balanced, echoes fruit and vanilla on the finish. 2,600 cases made. • $6 • (06/30/94) BB • **84**

Merlot-Cab Cuvée Reserve Mount Veeder NV: Light and airy, aiming for delicacy over power, with more berry flavor up front than on the finish. 2,000 cases made. • $6 • (12/15/95) • **80**

Merlot California Barrel Reserve 1991: Soft and fruity, chunky, with modest flavor intensity. 300 cases made. • $7 • (09/15/94) • **81**

Pinot Noir Anderson Valley 1992: Supple and spicy, a medium-bodied Pinot Noir displaying modest cherry and oak flavors. 1,600 cases made. • $6 • (03/31/95) • **81**

Zinfandel California Old Vine Reserve 1990: Lean and minty, with a simple core of earthy raspberry flavors. Drinkable now. 950 cases made. • $5 • (10/15/94) • **79**

SULLIVAN | CALIFORNIA

Cabernet Sauvignon Napa Valley 1991: Intense and tannic, displaying an earthy streak that runs through the hard-edged Cabernet fruit. Dry finish which suggests the need for short-term cellaring. 1,200 cases made. • $23 • (11/15/94) • **85**

Cabernet Sauvignon Napa Valley 1989 • $23 • (11/15/92) • **85**

Coeur de Vigne Private Reserve Napa Valley 1991: Tight and intense, with chewy, chunky tannins and a rugged core of currant and black cherry flavor. At this stage the wood and tannins win out, best to cellar until 1997 or 1998. 280 cases made. • $30 • (11/15/94) • **82**

Meritage Coeur de Vigne Napa Valley 1989 • $25 • (08/31/92) • **82**

Meritage Coeur de Vigne Napa Valley 1988 • $25 • (07/15/92) • **83**

Merlot Napa Valley 1991: Lean, tart and spicy, with a wild streak to the berry, beet and currant flavors that are bright but shallow, lacking the extra depth. Finishes with firm tannins. Drinkable now. 800 cases made. • $22 • (09/15/94) • **83**

Merlot Napa Valley 1990 • $20 • (06/15/93) • **87**

Merlot Napa Valley 1989 • $20 • (04/15/92) • **92**

SUMMERFIELD | CALIFORNIA

Chardonnay California Vintner's Reserve 1994: Balances its spicy oak and fresh pear flavors nicely on a medium-bodied frame. 15,000 cases made. • $8 • (06/15/96) • **82**

Chardonnay California Vintner's Reserve 1993: Simple and correct, with a citrus and lees edge to the pear and light oak shadings. 850 cases made. • $6 • (07/31/95) • **82**

Sauvignon Blanc California 1993: Pleasant, with simple, muddled flavors on a soft frame that mix vanilla and pear. • $4 • (06/30/95) • **81**

SUMMERS RANCH | CALIFORNIA

Merlot Knights Valley 1992: Crisp but appealing, offering a range of black cherry, tar, anise and cedar. Hangs together well, if somewhat on the lean side. Drinks well now but should be a shade softer in 1997. • $21 • (02/29/96) • **87**

SUMMIT LAKE | CALIFORNIA

Zinfandel Howell Mountain 1992: Tart and spicy, with a marked peppery edge to the rustic cherry and berry flavors. Finishes with earthy notes and firm tannins. 12,000 cases made. • $13 • (03/31/96) • **83**

Zinfandel Howell Mountain 1991: Ripe and intense, but turning mature. The spicy berry flavors have a note of tar on them. At its peak, but likely to hold on for a few more years. 822 cases made. • $12 • (10/15/95) • **87**

Zinfandel Howell Mountain 1989 • $9 • (08/31/93) • **84**

Zinfandel Howell Mountain 1988 • $11 • (10/15/92) • **82**

Zinfandel Howell Mountain 1987 • $11 • (02/15/91) • **87**

Zinfandel Howell Mountain 1986 • $11 • (03/15/90) • **84**

Zinfandel Howell Mountain 1985 • $9 • (12/15/88) • **88**

Zinfandel Howell Mountain 1984 • $8 • (04/30/88) • **90**

SUNCREST | WASHINGTON

Gewürztraminer Washington 1992: Vaguely floral and slightly earthy, but not very distinctive, simple and light with a rose petal edge. 784 cases made. • $7 • (09/30/94) • **78**

Gewürztraminer Washington Organically Grown Grapes 1993: Stale floral aromas are not too pleasant. • $7 • (09/30/95) • **72**

Johannisberg Riesling Washington 1992: Fruity and generous, a mouthful of pretty peach and apple flavor, plus a touch of honey on the finish. 280 cases made. • $7 • (09/30/94) • **85**

Johannisberg Riesling Washington Organically Grown Grapes 1991: A mature Riesling that has lost its youthful fruit without gaining much depth. • $7 • (09/30/95) • **79**

SUNNY ST. HELENA | CALIFORNIA

Cabernet Sauvignon California 1989 • $10 • (11/15/91) • **86**

Cabernet Sauvignon Napa Valley 1985 • $9 • (10/31/87) • **81**

Cabernet Sauvignon North Coast 1988 • $13 • (04/30/91) • **85**

SUNRIDGE | CALIFORNIA

Cabernet Sauvignon Napa Valley 1989 • $6 • (08/31/92) • **78**

SUNRISE | CALIFORNIA

Pinot Noir Santa Clara County San Ysidro Vineyard 1985 • $12 • (06/15/88) • **71**

Pinot Noir Sonoma County Green Valley Dutton Ranch Vineyard 1986 • $10 • (06/15/88) • **60**

SUNSTONE | CALIFORNIA

Chardonnay Santa Barbara County 1993: Simple with bland pear and spicy oak flavors. Serviceable but unexciting. 400 cases made. • $14 • (07/31/95) • **78**

SUTTER HOME | CALIFORNIA

Cabernet Sauvignon California 1991: Dry and tannic, with herb and cedar flavors. A solid everyday Cabernet. 390,000 cases made. • $6 • (11/15/94) • **81**

Cabernet Sauvignon California 1990: Simple, sturdy and flavorful, with a light enough texture to show off the pure currant and blueberry flavors. Drinkable now. Tasted twice. • $6 • (09/15/93) BB • **81**

Cabernet Sauvignon California 1989 • $5 • (10/15/91) BB • **83**

Cabernet Sauvignon California 1988 • $5 • (11/15/90) BB • **81**

Cabernet Sauvignon California 1987 • $5 • (06/30/89) • **77**

Cabernet Sauvignon California 1986 • $5 • (11/30/88) • **79**

Cabernet Sauvignon Napa Valley Centennial Selection Reserve 1990: Crisp and flavorful, with a generous beam of wild berry Zinfandel-ish fruit that persists on the finish. Tannins are rough enough to want until 1997. 2,200 cases made. • $12 • (10/31/93) • **87**

Cabernet Sauvignon Napa Valley Reserve 1991: This has an earthy green pepper and herbaceous edge to the Cabernet flavors and is quite tannic. Best to cellar until 1998 in hopes it will be smoother. 2,000 cases made. • $12 • (11/15/94) • **82**

Chardonnay California 1993: Marred by a tinny, canned grapefruit edge. About average. 800,000 cases made. • $6 • (04/30/95) • **74**

Chardonnay California 1992: Crisp and simple, offering a glint of apple in the background. 285,000 cases made. • $6 • (01/31/94) • **79**

Chardonnay California 1991 • $6 • (03/31/93) • **76**

Chenin Blanc California 1993: An attempt to make a more complex style of Chenin Blanc, but it veers off toward earthiness rather than centering around pretty fruit. 65,000 cases made. • $4 • (06/15/95) • **79**

Gewürztraminer California 1994: Light and vaguely floral, simple and modestly fruity, not especially varietal. 35,000 cases made. • $5 • **79**

Gewürztraminer California 1992 • $6 • (09/30/93) • **75**

Merlot California 1992: Firm in texture but low on intensity. What's there is pleasant, though. Softens on the finish and gets a wee bit sweet. 80,000 cases made. • $6 • (09/15/94) • **79**

Merlot California 1991 • $6 • (08/31/93) • **78**

Muscat Alexandria California 1994: Light and sweet, but a generous wine for this price. Pours out its spicy pear and litchi flavors on the palate. Drink it as, or with, dessert. 35,000 cases made. • $5 • (09/30/95) BB • **84**

Muscat Alexandria California 1991 • $5 • (10/15/92) • **79**

Sauvignon Blanc California 1993: Light, fruity and simple, sturdy enough to display appealing apple and spice flavors. 270,000 cases made. • $5 • (02/28/95) • **82**

Sauvignon Blanc California 1992 • $4 • (01/31/94) • **79**

White Zinfandel California 1994: Very pale in color, this is closer to sugar water than wine. It's sweet and simple, with light berry flavors. Tasted twice, with consistent notes. • $4 • (09/15/95) • **73**

Zinfandel Amador County 1981 • $6 • (05/16/84) • **80**

Zinfandel Amador County 1973 • $NA • (06/16/85) • **86**

Zinfandel Amador County 1972 • $NA • (06/16/85) • **85**

Zinfandel Amador County 1970 • $NA • (06/16/85) • **80**

Zinfandel Amador County Centennial Selection Reserve 1990: Strikes a nice balance between intense, spicy fruit flavors and buttery oak notes. Drinks well now, but could stand some cellaring. 8,100 cases made. • $10 • (10/15/94) • **83**

Zinfandel Amador County Reserve 1989 • $10 • (10/15/92) • **79**

Zinfandel Amador County Reserve 1988 • $10 • (03/31/92) • **84**

Zinfandel Amador County Reserve 1987 • $9 • (05/15/91) • **79**

Zinfandel Amador County Reserve 1984 • $9 • (07/31/89) • **82**

Zinfandel California 1993: Modest, light in color, delivering cedar, earth and light berry notes. 130,000 cases made. • $5 • (04/30/96) • **77**

Zinfandel California 1992: Light and simple, with hints of raspberry and strawberry. 200,000 cases made. • $5 • (10/15/94) • **75**

Zinfandel California 1991 • $5 • (04/30/93) BB • **82**

Zinfandel California 1990 • $5 • (09/15/92) • **77**

Zinfandel California 1989 • $5 • (05/15/91) BB • **85**

Zinfandel California 1988 • $5 • (03/31/91) • **72**

Zinfandel California 1987 • $5 • (07/31/89) • **78**

Zinfandel California 1986 • $7 • (10/15/88) • **76**

Zinfandel California 1984 • $6 • (12/31/86) • **77**

SUTTER RIDGE | CALIFORNIA

Chardonnay Amador County 1994: A round wine with modest pear and spice flavors. 300 cases made. • $8 • (06/15/96) • **81**

SWAN, JOSEPH | CALIFORNIA

Cabernet Sauvignon Sonoma Mountain Steiner Vineyard 1990: Pickle barrel aromas and flavors pervade this wine, but it has plenty of blueberry and plum fruit to counterbalance. Echoes a touch of vinegar on the finish. A stylish wine not everyone will love. Drink now. 360 cases made. • $18 • (11/15/93) • **84**

Côtes du Rosa Russian River Valley Red 1991 • $10 • (11/30/92) • **88**

Key: SS—Spectator Selection. CS—Cellar Selection. BB—Best Buy. $NA—Price not available. (BT)—Barrel tasting. Ⓐ—Auction Price.

Dates in parentheses represent the issues in which the ratings were published.

Pinot Noir Russian River Valley 1993: Austere and fairly tannic for the level of fruit, which is crisp with a band of citrus and tart berry. Lacks body and richness, but is in sync with the vintage. 500 cases made. • $14 • **82**

Pinot Noir Russian River Valley 1992: Mature with supple black cherry, plum and spice notes, finishing with a complex aftertaste and fine tannins. Ready now through 1997. 350 cases made. • $22 • **87**

Pinot Noir Russian River Valley 1991: Tight and chewy, showing an earthy streak to the wild berry flavors. Turns gamy and tannic on the finish. Drinkable now. 476 cases made. • $20 • (03/31/95) • **83**

Pinot Noir Russian River Valley 1990 • $20 • (02/28/93) • **84**

Pinot Noir Russian River Valley Sonoma Coast 1988 • $20 • (06/30/91) • **79**

Pinot Noir Russian River Valley Sonoma Coast 1985 • $18 • (06/15/88) • **89**

Pinot Noir Russian River Valley Sonoma Coast 1982 • $13 Ⓐ • (08/31/86) • **82**

Pinot Noir Sonoma Mountain Steiner Vineyard 1994: Smells of mint and spice, but turns trim and narrow on the palate, where the cherry and oregano flavors peek through. Firm, dry, tannic finish. Best in 1997. 266 cases made. • $17 • (04/30/96) • **86**

Pinot Noir Sonoma Mountain Steiner Vineyard 1993: Round and earthy, with a tart, green cherry and wild berry flavors. Drink now. 135 cases made. • $15 • (03/31/95) • **84**

Pinot Noir Sonoma Mountain Steiner Vineyard 1992: Appealing for its black cherry, wild berry and tar accents. Drinkable now. 281 cases made. • $16 • (02/28/95) • **88**

Pinot Noir Sonoma Mountain Wolfspierre Vineyard 1992: Tart and crisp, exhibiting an earthy edge to the wild berry and raspberry flavors. Drinkable now. 141 cases made. • $14 • (03/31/95) • **86**

Zinfandel California 1973 • $NA • (06/16/85) • **84**

Zinfandel California 1969 • $NA • (06/16/85) • **83**

Zinfandel Russian River Valley Frati Ranch 1993: Dark, ripe and rich, with complex cherry, plum, spice and raspberry flavors. It has a nice tannic edge and finishes with herbs and spice. The fullest and most complex of the 1993 Swan Zins. Drinkable now through 1998. 240 cases made. • $18 • (10/15/95) • **90**

Zinfandel Russian River Valley Frati Ranch 1992: Has jammy aromas, with flavors to match. As ripe and intense as it can get without going overboard. Delivers layers of ripe wild berry, black cherry and plum flavors. Drinkable now, or cellar through 1998. 210 cases made. • $16 • (10/15/94) • **92**

Zinfandel Russian River Valley V.H.S.R. Bohn Vineyard 1993: A touch earthy, but it stays in bounds with its tightly wound core of flavors. Lacks the bright fruit flavors of the best Swan 1993 Zins, but it still has appeal. 235 cases made. • $15 • (10/15/95) • **85**

Zinfandel Russian River Valley V.H.S.R. Vineyard 1992: Dark, rich and chocolaty, with intense, focused wild berry and black cherry flavors. It's ripe and lively-very impressive for this ultraripe style-and the finish goes on and on. 285 cases made. • $15 • (10/15/94) • **92**

Zinfandel Sonoma County 1989 • $13 • (10/15/92) • **80**

Zinfandel Sonoma County 1988 • $16 • (08/31/91) • **82**

Zinfandel Sonoma County 1987 • $16 • (07/31/90) • **86**

Zinfandel Sonoma County 1986 • $16 • (03/15/90) • **89**

Zinfandel Sonoma County 1985 • $17 • (03/15/89) • **82**

Zinfandel Sonoma County Ziegler Vineyard 1993: Medium-bodied, has some earthy berry flavors. Good but almost watery compared with other Swan 1993 Zins and lacks their depth. 445 cases made. • $15 • (10/15/95) • **81**

Zinfandel Sonoma County Ziegler Vineyard 1987 • $16 • (09/15/90) • **86**

Zinfandel Sonoma Valley Stellwagen Vineyard 1993: A classy Zin, with smooth, ripe, peppery flavors, lush with cherry and raspberry. Has a wonderful sense of harmony and finesse. Finishes long, full and fruity. Drinkable now. 450 cases made. • $16 • (10/15/95) • **88**

Zinfandel Sonoma Valley Stellwagen Vineyard 1992: Reeks of dill, oregano and bay leaf, making it difficult to find the fruit. 380 cases made. • $14 • (10/15/94) • **77**

Zinfandel Sonoma Valley Stellwagen Vineyard 1989 • $14 • (10/15/92) • **80**

Zinfandel Sonoma Valley Stellwagen Vineyard 1987 • $13 • (09/15/90) • **86**

SWANSON | CALIFORNIA

Cabernet Sauvignon Napa Valley 1993: Marked by spicy currant, tobacco and cedary oak flavors. Balanced enough for early drinking, despite the tannin level. Finishes on the dry side, cellaring into 1998 advised. 1,093 cases made. • $22 • **83**
Cabernet Sauvignon Napa Valley 1992: Dark, ripe and intense, with well-focused currant, black cherry, spice and mineral flavors framed by toasty, spicy oak. Needs until 1999 to soften, but has all the ingredients for greatness. 1,106 cases made. • $22 • (12/15/95) • **90**
Cabernet Sauvignon Napa Valley 1991: Supple and complex, rich and flavorful, laced with buttery oak and full of ripe cherry, currant and spice flavors. Tightly wound and firmly tannic, cellar through 1997. 1,150 cases made. • $20 • (11/15/94) • **89**
Cabernet Sauvignon Napa Valley 1990: Deep, dense and elegant, its ripe berry, cherry and currant flavors wrapped in a tight blanket of fine tannin, echoing toast and spice on the finish. Should be best after 1998 or 2000. 1,040 cases made. • $23 • (11/15/93) • **89**
Cabernet Sauvignon Napa Valley 1988 • $23 • (11/15/92) • **82**
Cabernet Sauvignon Napa Valley 1987 • $25 • (10/15/91) • **92**
Chardonnay Napa Valley Carneros 1994: Young and tight, offering trim citrus, pear and grapefruit flavors. It fans out a bit on the finish, where toasty oak folds in. 1,489 cases made. • $22 • (05/15/96) • **87**
Chardonnay Napa Valley Carneros 1993: Shows good intensity and breadth of flavor, with ripe pear, peach, spice and honey notes, with a nice touch of oak. 2,310 cases made. • $20 • (07/31/95) • **88**
Chardonnay Napa Valley Carneros 1992: Serves up a bright beam of ripe peach, pear and melon flavors, turning supple and elegant on the finish. Ready. 2,100 cases made. • $18 • (01/31/95) • **89**
Chardonnay Napa Valley Carneros 1991: Firm and intense, with a solid core of ripe pineapple and citrus flavors framed by toasty oak, but the fruit comes through on the finish. Ready now. 1,430 cases made. • $18 • (06/30/94) • **87**
Merlot Napa Valley 1993: Young and intense, with firm tannins and crisp acidity, it's a bit raw and in need of cellaring to soften the tannins and rough edges. Still the earthy currant and berry flavors are appealing if unevolved. 4,272 cases made. • $18 • **85**
Merlot Napa Valley 1992: Marked by cedary oak and a leathery edge, the wild berry and cherry battles the tannins right up to the finish. Needs time. 4,200 cases made. • $16 • (07/31/95) • **86**
Merlot Napa Valley 1991 • $15 • (05/31/94) • **84**
Merlot Napa Valley 1990 • $16 • (05/31/92) • **82**
Sangiovese Napa Valley 1993: Smooth and spicy, with supple cherry and berry flavors, finishing with shadings of anise and leather. Try in 1998. 1,100 cases made. • $18 • (06/15/96) • **88**
Sangiovese Napa Valley 1992: Ripe and generous, round and flavorful. Pours out its pure plum, berry and spicy vanilla character in a supple package that just doesn't quit. Beautifully made. Drinkable now. 1,492 cases made. • $18 • (11/30/94) SS • **90**
Sangiovese Napa Valley 1991 • $16 • (05/31/94) • **84**
Sangiovese Napa Valley Rosato 1994: Dominated by new oak, this has loads of cherry flavor to match. Nuances of vanilla and butter add up to a tasty mouthful and lingering finish. 280 cases made. • $9 • (09/15/95) • **84**
Syrah Napa Valley 1993: Dark-colored, richly flavored and substantial in tannic strength, boasting lots of flavor, earthy currant, mint and herbal overtones and firm aftertaste. Best to cellar into 1997 or 1998; even then it may be tannic. 372 cases made. • $30 • (02/29/96) • **89**
Syrah Napa Valley 1993: 372 cases made. • $30 • (02/29/96) • **89**
Syrah Napa Valley 1992: Dark and inky, with spice, prune, currant and meaty Syrah flavors. Tannins dominate now, but this red holds your interest. Drink now. 335 cases made. • $25 • (01/31/95) • **87**
Sémillon Late Harvest Napa Valley 1992: Rich, sweet and unctuous, a cascade of spicy, cinnamon-nutmeg-scented, toasty almond, pear, honey and apricot flavors weaving through the finish. It lasts and lasts. Seductive now, maybe better in 1998-2000. 123 cases made. • $25 • **97**
Sémillon Late Harvest Napa Valley 1991: Silky and sweet, unfolding delicious fig, tobacco and honey flavors. Gets a bit sugary on the finish, but should be at its best from 1997 to 1998. 240 cases made. • $25 • (05/15/95) • **88**
Sémillon Late Harvest Napa Valley 1988 • $25 • (06/30/93) • **80**
Zinfandel Napa Valley 1988 • $12 • (03/31/93) • **86**

SWEDISH HILL | NEW YORK

Brut Finger Lakes 1990: Aggressive flavors and an overly tart texture make this wine awkward and unappealing. Smells earthy and barnyardy. 420 cases made. • $15 • **71**
Johannisberg Riesling Finger Lakes 1992: An appealing, straightforward, smooth-textured and sweet Riesling with apple and citrus flavors and a touch of vanilla on the finish. 1,600 cases made. • $8 • **81**
Optimus Finger Lakes 1991: Grapey with an odd menthol note. Simple and fruity, but a peculiar mix of flavors. A blend of Merlot and Cabernets. 120 cases made. • $15 • (11/15/94) • **75**
Riesling Finger Lakes Dry 1992: A rich style of dry Riesling, showing peachy, slightly piney aromas, plenty of body, smooth texture and honest, appley flavors. 1,500 cases made. • $8 • (09/15/94) • **83**
Vignoles Finger Lakes Late Harvest 1992: A powerful, flavorful late-harvest with honey, apricot and pineapple flavors that last through the finish. Very sweet, but so crisp that it stays fresh and enjoyable. 120 cases made. • $11 • (06/30/95) • **83**

SYCAMORE CREEK | CALIFORNIA

Cabernet Sauvignon Central Coast 1978 • $NA • (11/15/92) • **70**
Zinfandel California 1982 • $9 • (06/16/84) • **87**
Zinfandel Santa Clara Valley 1988 • $8 • (10/15/92) • **84**

SYLVAN SPRINGS | CALIFORNIA

Cabernet Sauvignon California Vintner's Reserve 1985 • $5 • (09/30/88) BB • **80**

SYLVESTER | CALIFORNIA

Cabernet Sauvignon Paso Robles Kiara Reserve 1988 • $9 • (07/15/93) • **82**
Chardonnay Paso Robles Kiara Reserve 1991 • $9 • (07/15/93) • **60**

T VINE | CALIFORNIA

Zinfandel Napa Valley 1992: Attractive for its ripe wild berry and cherry flavors. Made in a light and simple style. 335 cases made. • $10 • (10/15/95) • **83**

TAFT STREET | CALIFORNIA

Cabernet Sauvignon California 1992: Supple and generous, a mouthful of currant and berry fruit that rolls on through the nicely polished finish. Ready now. 3,100 cases made. • $9 • (12/15/95) • **85**
Cabernet Sauvignon California 1985 • $7 • (10/15/88) • **78**
Cabernet Sauvignon Napa Valley 1983 • $9 • (01/31/87) • **84**
Cabernet Sauvignon Sonoma County 1991: Supple and pleasantly fruity, with herb, currant and light oak shadings. Ready to drink now, fair price. • $11 • (03/15/94) • **81**
Chardonnay Sonoma County 1994: Soft and charming, offering up a nice mouthful of lightly spicy melon and pear flavors. This is a value white for drinking now. 14,400 cases made. • $10 • (06/15/96) BB • **86**
Chardonnay Sonoma County 1993: Smooth and creamy, with ripe pear, apple and spice flavors and aromas that turn elegant and soft on the finish. 18,250 cases made. • $9 • (01/31/95) BB • **86**
Chardonnay Sonoma County 1992: Generous, floral and fruity, a soft wine with appealing wildflower and pear flavors. Drink now. 16,500 cases made. • $8 • (04/30/94) BB • **86**
Chardonnay Sonoma County 1991 • $8 • (05/15/93) BB • **85**
Merlot Sonoma County 1993: Ripe, with spicy cherry, plum and berry flavors and light oak shadings. 4,100 cases made. • $13 • **83**
Merlot Sonoma County 1992: Marked by herb, tea and green tannins, berried Merlot fruit holds your interest. 3,500 cases made. • $11 • (01/31/95) • **81**
Merlot Sonoma County 1991 • $11 • (07/15/93) • **83**
Merlot Sonoma County 1990 • $12 • (05/31/92) • **89**
Merlot Sonoma County 1989 • $12 • (05/31/92) • **85**
Merlot Sonoma County 1985 • $10 • (05/31/88) • **83**
Pinot Noir Monterey County 1982 • $7 • (05/01/84) • **76**

Pinot Noir Santa Maria Valley 1983 • $9 • (04/15/87) • **76**
Sauvignon Blanc Sonoma County 1994: Soft, simple and generous, with interesting citrus accents. 5,300 cases made. • $8 • (05/31/96) • **80**
Sauvignon Blanc Sonoma County 1993: Soft and simple, a gently fruity wine to drink soon. 9,376 cases made. • $6 • (08/31/94) • **77**
Sauvignon Blanc Sonoma County 1991 • $6 • (04/15/93) BB • **86**

TAGARIS | WASHINGTON

Blanc de Noirs Washington 1988 • $12 • (01/31/94) • **79**
Chardonnay Columbia Valley 1993: Nicely fruity, showing apricot, nectarine and pear notes, but the texture comes off as a bit coarse and simple. Drink now. 1,400 cases made. • $6 • (04/15/95) • **81**
Johannisberg Riesling Columbia Valley 1993: Sweet and piney, an odd combination that never lets the fruit come through. 750 cases made. • $6 • (09/30/95) • **77**
Johannisberg Riesling Columbia Valley Reserve 1994: Ripe, generous sweet apricot and pear flavors, delicately balanced to show off the fruit without presenting too much sweetness. Ready now. 780 cases made. • $6 • (09/30/95) • **87**

TALBOTT | CALIFORNIA

Chardonnay Monterey 1992: Ripe and complex, with earthy pear and pineapple flavors and a nice touch of toasty oak on the finish that goes on and on. Delicious, try now. 6,500 cases made. • $25 • (06/30/95) SS • **91**
Chardonnay Monterey 1991: Ripe and opulent with layers of honey, spicy, fig and pear flavors that are rich and concentrated, picking up a nice honeyed aftertaste. Drinks well now but can age through 1997. 6,500 cases made. • $24 • (06/30/94) • **88**
Chardonnay Monterey Diamond T Estate 1993: An elegant and understated style with clean and refreshing pear flavors, spicy nuances and a touch of honey and celery on the finish. A mature-tasting Chardonnay. 980 cases made. • $34 • (05/31/96) • **90**
Chardonnay Monterey Diamond T Estate 1992: A bold, rich and earthy style, loading in scads of complex pear, honey and toasty, buttery oak flavors. 960 cases made. • $34 • **91**
Chardonnay Monterey Diamond T Estate 1991: Fresh and lively, with a pretty array of spice, pear, apple and melon notes that are bright and elegant. Flavors linger on the finish. 850 cases made. • $30 • (09/15/94) • **90**
Chardonnay Monterey Sleepy Hollow Vineyard 1993: Distinctive for its overt fruitiness, with complex earthy fig, pear, honey and apricot flavors. A bold and ripe California Chardonnay with rich, complex flavors. 7,500 cases made. • $26 • (12/31/95) CS • **91**

TALLEY | CALIFORNIA

Chardonnay Arroyo Grande Valley 1993: Pleasantly fruity, with light pear, honey and spice notes that are well focused in a medium-bodied style. Shows more depth and finesse than most 1993's. 3,186 cases made. • $18 • (07/31/95) • **88**
Chardonnay Arroyo Grande Valley 1991 • $16 • (07/15/93) • **81**
Chardonnay Edna Valley Oliver's Vineyard 1994: Attractive for its ripe pear and citrus flavors and light shades of pineapple. Finishes clean and fruity, with just a dash of oak. 680 cases made. • $15 • (06/15/96) • **87**
Pinot Noir Arroyo Grande Valley 1993: Tightly wound and firmly tannic, it offers a spicy core of cherry, anise and wild berry fruit, but needs time to soften and evolve. Best after 1996. 1,258 cases made. • $22 • (12/31/95) • **83**
Pinot Noir Arroyo Grande Valley 1992: Compact, tight, tannic herb and cola flavors. Best after 1996. 1,060 cases made. • $20 • (03/31/95) • **82**
Pinot Noir Arroyo Grande Valley 1990 • $17 • (09/30/92) • **87**
Pinot Noir Arroyo Grande Valley 1989 • $17 • (10/31/91) • **75**
Pinot Noir Arroyo Grande Valley Rincon Vineyard 1993: Well oaked, tight and tannic, with a trim band of spicy cherry and subtle earthy notes. Can stand short-term cellaring into 1996 or 1997 to shed some of its tannins. 62 cases made. • $30 • **85**
Pinot Noir Arroyo Grande Valley Rosemary's Vineyard 1993: Ripe, rich and intense, with a measure of finesse and elegance, showcasing the pretty black cherry, sage, spice and wild berry notes. Finishes with thick, firm tannins. Needs cellaring into 1997. Best of the Talley bottlings. 65 cases made. • $30 • **90**

TALUS | CALIFORNIA

Cabernet Sauvignon California 1993: Ripe and fruity, with supple plum and currant notes of modest proportion. Picks up a spicy edge on the finish. • $8 • (12/15/95) • **84**
Chardonnay California 1994: A solid Chardonnay, with ripe, juicy pear, apple and spice notes. Appealing for its fruitiness. 68,000 cases made. • $8 • (03/31/96) • **83**
Merlot California 1994: Light and peppery, with a blueberry edge to the earthy flavors. Maybe best in 1997. 100,000 cases made. • $8 • (06/30/96) • **82**
Zinfandel California 1993: Solid if rustic, with chunky wild berry and cherry flavors that turn crisp and a touch stemmy on the finish. 25,000 cases made. • $7 • (03/31/96) • **82**

TAMAS, IVAN | CALIFORNIA

Cabernet Sauvignon Livermore Valley 1992: Light in texture, vegetal, bordering on cooked, with berry and beet flavors swinging through. Drinkable now. 10,000 cases made. • $7 • (12/15/95) • **80**
Cabernet Sauvignon Livermore Valley Le Clan des Quatre Vineyards 1991: Smells fruity and floral, but it turns earthy and herbal, drying out on the finish. Decent but nothing more. Drink now. 3,200 cases made. • $8 • (11/15/93) • **77**
Cabernet Sauvignon Mendocino McNab Ranch 1984 • $6 • (02/15/87) BB • **84**
Cabernet Sauvignon North Coast 1985 • $7 • (12/31/87) • **79**
Chardonnay Central Coast 1994: Light and bright, offering a nice core of floral and apple flavors. Drinkable now. 8,000 cases made. • $9 • (06/15/96) • **82**
Chardonnay Livermore Valley Hayes Ranch 1993: Light and pleasantly fruity, generous with its fresh pear and apple fruit that lingers on the finish. Ready now. 6,500 cases made. • $8 • (07/31/95) • **84**
Chardonnay Livermore Valley Hayes Ranch 1992: Lean and a bit earthy, with citrus and pear notes of modest depth. 6,500 cases made. • $8 • (07/31/95) • **82**
Fumé Blanc Livermore Valley Figoni Ranch 1992: Light and crisp, with simple green apple and lemon flavors. Maybe best in 1995. 1,200 cases made. • $7 • (08/31/94) • **82**
Pinot Grigio Monterey 1993: Simple, broad and a little spicy, picking up an almond edge to the modest peach flavors. Drinkable now. 700 cases made. • $9 • (12/15/95) • **82**
Sauvignon Blanc Livermore Valley Figoni Ranch 1994: Varietal herb and citrus flavors lose some of their brightness on the finish. Drink now. 2,813 cases made. • $8 • **83**

TANNER, LANE | CALIFORNIA

Pinot Noir Santa Barbara County 1992: A spicy, peppery style, racy Pinot Noir fruit echoes cherry and vegetal notes. Drinkable now. 800 cases made. • $20 • (03/31/95) • **84**
Pinot Noir Santa Barbara County 1991 • $20 • (02/28/93) • **75**
Pinot Noir Santa Barbara County Benedict Vineyard 1989 • $25 • (11/15/91) • **85**
Pinot Noir Santa Barbara County Sanford & Benedict Vineyards 1992: Thin and tart, offering a lean core of earthy, berry flavor. 191 cases made. • $30 • (03/31/95) • **82**
Pinot Noir Santa Barbara County Sierra Madre Vineyards 1990 • $22 • (09/30/92) • **84**
Pinot Noir Santa Barbara County Sierra Madre Vineyards Hitching Post 1987 • $25 • (02/28/93) • **81**
Pinot Noir Santa Maria Valley Bien Nacido 1994: Trim and tart, sporting ripe, spicy cherry, berry and earthy flavors that are vibrant and lively.

Key: SS—Spectator Selection. CS—Cellar Selection. BB—Best Buy. $NA—Price not available. (BT)—Barrel tasting. Ⓐ—Auction Price.
Dates in parentheses represent the issues in which the ratings were published.

Can stand short-term cellaring into 1997 to soften. 600 cases made. • $20 • (02/29/96) • **86**

Pinot Noir Santa Maria Valley Bien Nacido Vineyards Picked Under A Blue Moon 1993: Serves up a beam of ripe black cherry and wild berry fruit and holds its focus, even if it comes across as one dimensional. 400 cases made. • $22 • **84**

Pinot Noir Santa Maria Valley Sierra Madre Plateau 1994: Good intensity but also earthy and tannic, dominating the cherry and berry flavor at this stage. Cellaring into 1997 should reveal more depth. Impressive for its complexity on the finish. 600 cases made. • $20 • (02/29/96) • **88**

Pinot Noir Santa Ynez Valley Sanford & Benedict Vineyard 1991 • $25 • (02/28/94) • **88**

TANTALUS | CALIFORNIA

Meritage Sonoma County 1991: A fruity style offering plum and cherry notes, but turning ruggedly tannic on the finish. Try in 1997. 750 cases made. • $16 • (07/31/95) • **83**

Meritage Sonoma County 1989 • $15 • (07/15/92) • **86**

TARARA | VIRGINIA

Cabernet Frederick County 1989 • $12 • (02/29/92) • **82**

TAY | CALIFORNIA

Cabernet Sauvignon Napa Valley 1993: Aromatically complex, as pretty currant, black cherry and toasty oak flavors gain nuance and finesse on the finish, where accents of anise and cedar fold in neatly. Rich and concentrated, adding a long, full aftertaste. Tempting now, but best around 1999 or 2000. 150 cases made. • $35 • (04/30/96) • **92**

TAYLOR | NEW YORK

Brut Bottle Fermented New York NV • $6 • (12/31/90) • **61**

TEADERIPPLE | CALIFORNIA

Sauvignon Blanc Napa Valley 1992: Oaky flavors dominate this fulbodied wine, but it never becomes graceful. 200 cases made. • $9 • (08/31/94) • **74**

TEAL LAKE | CALIFORNIA

Pinot Noir Monterey 1991 • $12 • (02/28/93) • **82**

TEDESCHI | CALIFORNIA

Zinfandel Dry Creek Valley 1991: Crisp, lean and refreshing, with herbal aromas, apple flavor and a clean, short finish. 2,000 cases made. • $15 • **85**

TEDESCHI VINEYARDS | HAWAII

Brut Blanc de Noirs Maui 1984 • $19 • (02/29/92) • **79**

Nouveau Maui 1991 • $15 • (02/29/92) • **78**

Rosé Hawaii Ranch Cuvée 1984 • $20 • (02/29/92) • **79**

TEFFT | WASHINGTON

Cabernet Sauvignon Yakima Valley 1992: Ripe, round and supple, spicy with toasty oak and bulging with sweet plum, black cherry and currant flavors that show brilliantly on the long finish. Tannins fold in smothly. Tempting now, but should be best from 1998 to 1999. 210 cases made. • $20 • (09/30/95) • **91**

Cabernet Sauvignon Yakima Valley 1991: Lean and a little watery with ripe Cabernet fruit up front, finishing with a slightly bitter edge. Could be fine by 1997. 200 cases made. • $13 • (09/30/94) • **79**

Merlot Columbia Valley 1991 • $13 • (06/15/93) • **88**

Merlot Yakima Valley 1993: Firm, a little chewy in texture, offering chunky fruit and tar flavors that need until 1997 or 1998 to come together smoothly. 470 cases made. • $14 • (09/30/95) • **83**

Proprietor's Red Columbia Valley NV: Light, smooth and appealingly fruity and spicy, shading the black cherry flavors with hints of anise and nutmeg. Ready now. 265 cases made. • $10 • (09/30/95) • **85**

Red Table Wine Yakima Valley NV: A minty character keeps running through the chunky black cherry flavors in this mouth-filling red. Drinkable now. 200 cases made. • $10 • (09/30/94) • **83**

Sauvignon Blanc Late Harvest Yakima Valley River Mist 1992: Sweet and floral with a bit of a honey edge that picks up some black fig and toast notes on the finish. Nicely made, not too sweet but rich enough. Tasty now. 50 cases made. • $10 • (09/30/94) • **87**

TELDESCHI | CALIFORNIA

Moscato Dry Creek Valley Frontignan NV: Sweet and succulent, not strongly honeyed or spicy, but nicely balanced to accompany a fruit dessert. 390 cases made. • $11 • (12/31/95) • **87**

Zinfandel Sonoma County 1990: Showing its mature flavors, with an earthy, cedary character to the berry and spice notes. Drink now. 2,000 cases made. • $10 • (10/15/95) • **84**

TENNESSEE VALLEY | TENNESSEE

Cabernet Sauvignon Tennessee 1988 • $14 • (02/29/92) • **72**

TENREBAC | WASHINGTON

Port 1989 • $24 • (11/30/91) • **74**

TERRA | CALIFORNIA

Cabernet Franc Napa Valley 1990: A good, hearty, somewhat herbal red wine with pleasant olive and plum flavors and a shot of toasty oak. The aroma has a nice, smoky character. 365 cases made. • $15 • **82**

Cabernet Sauvignon Napa Valley 1990: A ripe and herbal Cabernet that ends up a little harsh. The olive and cherry flavors are overblown and make this an unbalanced wine. 1,403 cases made. • $13 • **79**

Chardonnay Carneros 1992: This wine is dominanted by pleasant buttery and oaky flavors. Tastey and fairly harmonious, though it lacks fruit. 447 cases made. • $16 • **83**

Chardonnay Carneros Sangiacomo Vineyard 1993: Appealing for its ripe tropical fruit flavors, its hints of spice, honey and pear, and the light butterscotch notes on the finish. 400 cases made. • $19 • (06/30/96) • **88**

Merlot Napa Valley 1988 • $14 • (05/31/92) • **84**

TERRA VIN | CALIFORNIA

Napa Valley Red NV: Complex with an appealing array of ripe cherry, plum and berry notes. Hints of herb and spice and finishing with firm tannins, but just enough fruit emerges to hold your interest. 910 cases made. • $11 • (02/29/96) • **88**

TERRACES | CALIFORNIA

Cabernet Sauvignon 1987 • $38 • (02/29/92) • **92**

Cabernet Sauvignon Napa Valley 1991: Tight and austere, offering a trim band of currant, spice, cedar and berry, hints of prune and anise and a firmly tannic finish. Best to cellar into 1998. 250 cases made. • $40 • (10/31/95) • **88**

Cabernet Sauvignon Napa Valley 1990: Extremely leathery and tannic, with hints of cedar, black currant and plum notes, but they're lurking in the background beneath the tannins. Definitely needs time, best after 1999. 230 cases made. • $40 • (11/15/94) • **86**

Cabernet Sauvignon Napa Valley 1989 • $40 • (11/15/93) • **89**

Cabernet Sauvignon Napa Valley 1988 • $40 • (03/31/93) • **88**

Cabernet Sauvignon Napa Valley 1986 • $23 • (01/31/91) • **96**

Zinfandel Napa Valley 1992: Has some mature notes, with an intriguing array of earthy cherry, prune, celery and cedar tones, all of which add up to a complex wine. Smooth at mid-palate, then firm on the finish. Well crafted, drink now through 1998. 400 cases made. • $16 • (10/15/95) • **88**

Zinfandel Napa Valley 1991: A claret style that's rich and full-bodied, with ripe cherry, anise and spice notes that turn smooth and supple on the finish. Has the tannins to age, but it's drinking very well now. 360 cases made. • $13 • (10/15/94) • **87**

Zinfandel Napa Valley 1990 • $15 • (06/15/94) • **84**

Zinfandel Napa Valley 1989 • $13 • (03/31/93) • **87**

Zinfandel Napa Valley 1988 • $13 • (02/29/92) • **86**

Zinfandel Napa Valley 1987 • $13 • (02/15/91) • **89**

Zinfandel Napa Valley Hogue Vineyard 1985 • $13 • (10/31/88) • **87**

TERRE ROUGE, DOMAINE DE LA | CALIFORNIA

Sierra Foothills Red 1986 • $12 • (04/15/89) • **89**

Blush Fiddletown Vin Gris d'Amador 1994: Light, simple and crisp, not sweet but not particularly flavorful either. • $9 • (03/31/96) • **80**

Reserve Red Wine California 1991: Complex and flavorful, with appealing cherry, berry , herb and anise flavors. Moderately rich and firmly tannic, best to cellar into 1997 in hope the tannins subside. 990 cases made. • $15 • (02/29/96) • **86**

Syrah Amador County 1993: Ripe and fruity, with a rich, supple core of anise, spice and wild berries. Finishes with firm tannins and a rich concentration of fruit with a dried berry character. 300 cases made. • $20 • (06/15/96) • **89**

TESSERA | CALIFORNIA

Chardonnay California 1994: Serves up a modest portion of ripe, spicy pear and hints of oak. Straightforward on the finish. 18,800 cases made. • $9 • (06/15/96) • **84**

Merlot California 1994: A crisp, well-focused and mildly tannic wine packed with bright berry and anise flavors. Should be best in 1997 or 1998. 8,500 cases made. • $9 • (06/30/96) BB • **86**

TEWKSBURY | NEW JERSEY

Blush New Jersey Sunset 1990 • $7 • (02/29/92) • **78**

New Jersey Cherry Wine NV • $6 • (02/29/92) • **78**

TEYSHA | TEXAS

Cabernet Sauvignon Late Harvest 1990: An earthy style of red dessert wine, offering plum and prune aromas and flavors. Simple and not terribly tannic. Like a ruby Port without the high alcohol. 5.8 percent residual sugar. Drink soon. • $10 • (02/29/92) • **78**

Rosé of Cabernet Sauvignon Texas Cabernet Royale 1990 • $9 • (02/29/92) • **77**

THACKREY, SEAN H. | CALIFORNIA

Mourvèdre California Taurus 1989 • $24 • (08/31/91) • **86**

Mourvèdre California Taurus 1988 • $24 • (09/30/90) • **86**

Petite Sirah Napa Valley Sirius Marston Vineyard Old Vines 1989 • $24 • (08/31/91) • **87**

Pleiades California Old Vines 1991 • $20 • (10/31/93) • **84**

Pleiades California Old Vines NV: Marked by strong spice and mint flavors, delivering an earthy core of wild berry and plum and a hint of pepper. Best in 1998. 1,460 cases made. • $15 • (12/15/95) • **88**

Syrah California Orion 1992: Dark, ripe and intense, marked by rich pepper, plum, spice and berry flavors. Turns supple and complex on the finish, where anise and earth notes fold together. 620 cases made. • $30 • (12/15/95) • **91**

Syrah Napa Valley Orion 1990 • $NA • (10/31/93) • **83**

Syrah Napa Valley Orion 1989 • $45 • (12/31/91) • **90**

Syrah Napa Valley Orion 1988 • $30 • (09/30/90) • **89**

Syrah Napa Valley Orion 1987 • $30 • (09/30/89) • **92**

Syrah Napa Valley Orion 1986 • $26 • (04/15/89) • **83**

Syrah Napa Valley Rossi Vineyard Orion 1993: Dark, intense and lively, offering a ripe, rich core of spicy, peppery wild berry and currant flavor, fine length and firm tannins. Best beginning in 1997. • $30 • (04/30/96) • **91**

THOMAS-HSI | CALIFORNIA

Chardonnay Napa Valley 1991: Firm and concentrated, with a spicy, earthy citrus and grapefruit edge to the ripe pear and light oak shadings. This tightly wound young Chardonnay is drinkable now, but can stand short-term cellaring. It should be ideal for summer drinking. • $18 • (06/30/94) • **87**

THOMAS, PAUL | WASHINGTON

Cabernet-Merlot Columbia Valley 1993: Delicious blend from Washington that offers ripe, elegant plum, berry and spicy vanilla flavors that remain focused and bright on the finish. Drinkable now. 7,200 cases made. • $9 • (03/31/95) BB • **87**

Cabernet-Merlot Columbia Valley 1992: Fat, bright berry and currant flavors jump right up, edging toward minty-herbal notes as the finish rolls around. Drinkable now. 1,700 cases made. • $10 • (08/31/94) • **87**

Cabernet-Merlot Columbia Valley 1991: Lean and herbal, with a dusty character to the modest black cherry flavor. A bit tannic, try now. 1,164 cases made. • $10 • (12/31/93) • **80**

Cabernet-Merlot Washington 1994: Open-textured and plummy, a bit light on intensity but very pretty. Approachable now. 8,500 cases made. • $9 • (06/15/96) • **84**

Cabernet Sauvignon Columbia Valley 1993: A ripe and nicely focused Washington Cab, showing well-defined plum, currant and spice flavors that linger on the smooth, elegant finish. Drinkable now. 3,600 cases made. • $9 • (03/31/95) BB • **87**

Cabernet Sauvignon Columbia Valley 1992: Light, watery and strongly herbal, with hints of cranberry and tobacco sneaking in on the finish. 1,400 cases made. • $10 • (09/30/94) • **78**

Cabernet Sauvignon Washington 1994: A little light and lean, but showing enough freshness on the finish to make it approachable. Better in 1997. 7,500 cases made. • $9 • (03/31/96) • **84**

Cabernet Sauvignon Washington 1989 • $12 • (03/31/92) • **80**

Cabernet Sauvignon Washington 1986 • $14 • (09/30/90) • **84**

Cabernet Sauvignon Washington 1985 • $20 • (10/15/89) • **88**

Cabernet Sauvignon Washington Reserve 1988 • $15 • (03/15/94) • **80**

Cabernet Sauvignon Washington Reserve 1987 • $16 • (03/31/92) • **86**

Chardonnay Columbia Valley 1993: Fresh, fruity and appealing. A supple Chardonnay with gorgeous fruit flavors that keep getting juicier with every sip, echoing grapefruit, peach and pear notes on the smoothly balanced finish. 6,200 cases made. • $10 • (08/31/94) BB • **90**

Chardonnay Columbia Valley 1992: Crisp and lively, a light-textured wine with appealing pear and spice aromas and flavors, finishing clean and refreshing. 3,950 cases made. • $10 • (12/31/93) • **86**

Chardonnay Columbia Valley 1991 • $10 • (03/31/93) • **84**

Chardonnay Washington 1994: Bright and resiny, a mouthful of green apple and pine flavors that are distinctive and fresh. Drinkable now. 18,500 cases made. • $9 • (05/15/96) • **85**

Chenin Blanc Washington 1993: Charming, crisp and fruity, a delicious mouthful of peach, pear and melon flavors, off-dry but not too sweet. Drink while it's fresh. 1,500 cases made. • $6 • (09/30/94) • **86**

Gewürztraminer Columbia Valley 1994: Soft and simple, appealing for its pretty pear and honey flavors. 1,300 cases made. • $6 • (09/30/95) • **82**

Gewürztraminer Columbia Valley 1993 • $NA • (05/31/94) • **78**

Johannisberg Riesling Columbia Valley 1994: Soft and simple, offering appealing pear and slightly floral flavors. 6,000 cases made. • $6 • (09/30/95) • **80**

Johannisberg Riesling Columbia Valley Dry 1994: Light and charming, rolling out its peach, apricot and apple flavors with finesse. 3,000 cases made. 3,000 cases made. • $6 • (09/15/95) • **84**

Johannisberg Riesling Columbia Valley Select Harvest 1994: Frankly sweet, but still light enough to show off its lightly honeyed pear and pretty floral flavors. 1,200 cases made. • $6 • (09/30/95) • **85**

Johannisberg Riesling Washington 1993: With its bright beam of apricotty-peachy flavor, this is immediately likeable and fresh, finishing just off-dry. Drink soon. 2,500 cases made. • $6 • (09/30/94) • **87**

Key: SS—Spectator Selection. CS—Cellar Selection. BB—Best Buy. $NA—Price not available. (BT)—Barrel tasting. Ⓐ—Auction Price.

Dates in parentheses represent the issues in which the ratings were published.

Lemberger Columbia Valley 1993: Light and fruity, offering simple, charming, spicy berry flavors and a touch of walnut. 1,100 cases made. • $8 • (09/30/95) • **83**
Merlot Columbia Valley 1993: Light and crisp, a simple red of modest, grapey flavors. Drinkable now. 9,000 cases made. • $9 • (06/15/95) • **78**
Merlot Columbia Valley 1992: Earthy, spicy black cherry and blackberry flavors come through strongly in this chewy, cellar-worthy red. Drinkable now, best in 1997. 450 cases made. • $9 • (04/30/95) • **87**
Merlot Washington 1987 • $16 • (09/30/90) • **89**
Merlot Washington Reserve 1990 • $15 • (05/15/94) • **79**
Merlot Washington Reserve 1989 • $15 • (03/31/92) • **79**
Riesling Washington Dry 1993: Bright and fruity, an apricot edge indicating ripeness despite the dry finish. Drink now while it's fresh. 2,500 cases made. • $6 • (09/30/94) • **86**
Sauvignon Blanc Columbia Valley 1994: Very dry, austere, bordering on bitter, but refreshing in its crisp and citrusy intensity. 2,500 cases made. • $8 • (09/30/95) • **82**
Sauvignon Blanc Columbia Valley 1993: Seems a little watery, with herbal flavors that never quite come into focus. Drinkable now. • $9 • (09/30/94) • **77**
Sauvignon Blanc Washington 1992 • $8 • (05/15/94) • **62**
Sémillon Columbia Valley 1993: Simple and modestly fruity, showing some nice fig and herb flavors. Drinkable now. 5,000 cases made. • $6 • (03/31/95) • **80**
Seyval Blanc Columbia Valley 1993: Simple and somewhat earthy, adding a tarry edge to the modest pear flavor. Drink now. 2,000 cases made. • $7 • (09/30/95) • **77**
Seyval Blanc Washington 1994: Firm and flavorful, stuffed with melon and herb notes that take a turn toward austere on the finish. 2,500 cases made. • $8 • (09/30/95) • **83**

THORNHILL | CALIFORNIA

Cabernet Sauvignon Napa Valley 1991: Ripe and pruny, this compact young Cabernet shows currant, black cherry and spice notes before turning austere and tannic on the finish. Lacks finesse and polish, but at this price delivers plenty of flavor. 1,600 cases made. • $10 • (11/15/94) • **83**

THORNTON | CALIFORNIA

Pinot Noir San Luis Obispo County Coastal Reserve 1994: Pungently earthy, dry and tannic, as leathery flavors override whatever fruit exists. 1,100 cases made. • $18 • (02/29/96) • **72**
Zinfandel South Coast Limited Bottling 1994: Strives for complexity with its toasty oak overlay, but the cherry and berry flavors underneath are supple and appetizing. 1,150 cases made. • $12 • (03/31/96) • **85**

TIJSSELING | CALIFORNIA

Blanc de Blancs Mendocino 1986 • $13 • (12/31/91) • **72**
Blanc de Blancs Mendocino Cuvée de Chardonnay 1985 • $13 • (12/31/89) • **80**
Brut Mendocino 1987 • $12 • (12/31/91) • **81**
Brut Mendocino 1986 • $12 • (12/31/89) • **89**
Cabernet Sauvignon Mendocino 1986 • $8 • (01/31/90) BB • **85**
Cabernet Sauvignon Mendocino County 1990: Light and fruity, with modest strawberry and vanilla aromas and flavors. 698 cases made. • $8 • (11/15/92) • **77**

TITUS | CALIFORNIA

Cabernet Sauvignon Napa Valley 1992: A touch earthy, with a leathery streak, but enough plum and berry flavors emerge to keep it balanced, finishing with an earthy aftertaste. Tasted twice, with consistent notes. 680 cases made. • $19 • (12/15/95) • **85**

TOAD HALL | CALIFORNIA

Bodacious Napa Valley Cabernet Blend 1988 • $20 • (11/15/92) • **81**
Bodacious Napa Valley Cabernet Blend 1987 • $20 • (11/15/92) • **83**

TOBIN JAMES | CALIFORNIA

Cabernet Sauvignon Paso Robles Private Stash 1990: Ripe and smooth, with rich currant, plum and black cherry flavors that are a bit awkward now, tannins and acidity stick out on the finish. Drinkable now. 675 cases made. • $12 • (11/15/92) • **84**
Cabernet Sauvignon Paso Robles Private Stash 1989 • $12 • (08/31/92) • **88**
Cabernet Sauvignon San Luis Obispo County Star Light 1993: Ripe and fruity, with a simple core of plum- and cherry-laced fruit that's bright and lively. Finishes with modest tannins. Ready now. 919 cases made. • $14 • (03/31/96) • **84**
Cabernet Sauvignon San Luis Obispo County Twilight 1991: Fresh and fruity, displaying jammy cherry, berry and raspberry flavors that ooze across the palate. Supple, rich, lively and complex. Drinkable now. 950 cases made. • $12 • (11/15/93) • **86**
Chateau Le Cacheflo Central Coast Red NV: Light-textured but snappy in flavor, delivering a nice mouthful of wild berry, raspberry and plum that lingers on the lively finish. Ready now. 969 cases made. • $7 • (11/30/95) • **85**
Chateau le Cacheflo Paso Robles Red NV • $6 • (07/31/93) BB • **82**
Merlot Paso Robles Full Moon 1991 • $14 • (06/15/93) • **86**
Merlot San Luis Obispo Made in the Shade 1992: Bright and fruity, with spicy herb and currant flavor that's quite appealing now. 430 cases made. • $14 • (03/31/95) • **84**
Pinot Noir Santa Barbara County Black Tie 1992: Intense and spicy, revealing a narrow beam of cherry and herb notes. Drinkable now. 490 cases made. • $13 • (03/31/95) • **84**
Pinot Noir Santa Barbara County Sunshine 1990 • $14 • (11/30/92) • **86**
Syrah Paso Robles High Five 1992: Smooth and polished, with a supple texture. An appealing array of stewed plum, spice, black cherry and light cedary oak finish up with fine tannins. 736 cases made. • $13 • (08/31/95) • **87**
Zinfandel Late Harvest Paso Robles Solar Flair 1992: Sweet and ripe, with cherry, berry and spice flavors. A very appealing late harvest Zin that doesn't overpower you with tannins. 350 cases made. • $10 • (10/15/94) • **84**
Zinfandel Late Harvest Paso Robles Solar Flair 1991: An intriguing and elegant style, with bright, lively cherry jam and wild berry flavors. Well balanced and easy to drink. 320 cases made. • $11 • (10/15/94) • **85**
Zinfandel Paso Robles Big Time 1991 • $12 • (06/15/93) • **82**
Zinfandel Paso Robles Blue Moon Reserve 1991 • $14 • (06/15/93) • **84**
Zinfandel Paso Robles Blue Moon Reserve 1990 • $12 • (12/15/92) • **84**
Zinfandel Paso Robles Flag Ship 1993: Bright and jammy, but a crisp, tannic tone overshadows the cherry and wild berry flavors. Hard-edged finish. Best in 1997. 1,100 cases made. • $14 • (04/30/96) • **84**
Zinfandel Paso Robles James Gang Reserve 1993: A late-harvest style that tips the scale at 15.3 alcohol, showing ripe, jammy wild berry and cherry notes, but it comes across as heavy-handed and one-dimensional, adding a hot finish. 330 cases made. • $20 • (04/30/96) • **81**
Zinfandel Paso Robles Sure Fire 1991: An unusual wine, halfway between late harvest and Port, showing very smooth, ripe black cherry and plum flavors and a touch of raisin and a modest Portlike grip on the finish. Not terribly sweet. Ready now. 80 cases made. • $18 • (05/31/95) • **86**

TOGNI, PHILIP | CALIFORNIA

Ca' Togni Napa Valley 1992: Ultra ripe and spicy, with zesty pepper, anise, mint and wild berry flavors. Finishes with an appealing hot-and-sweet tobacco accent. 175 cases made. • $20 • **88**
Cabernet Sauvignon Napa Valley 1993: Starts with an herbal accent-like dill weed-then works its way into a core of currant and cherry before finishing with dry tannins and a hint of olive. 2,000 cases made. • $35 • (05/31/96) • **87**
Cabernet Sauvignon Napa Valley 1992: Distinctive for its racy style: laced with herb, currant, spice and toasty oak flavors, all folding together nicely and finishing with a long, complex aftertaste that echoes herb, currant and black olive. Best after 1999. 1,700 cases made. • $32 • (11/15/94) CS • **91**

Cabernet Sauvignon Napa Valley 1991: Rich, almost opulent, with lovely herb and mineral notes adding complexity to the mouthfilling currant and berry flavors, rich and meaty on the finish. This wine has a great future, best after 1998-2000. 1,800 cases made. • $30 • (11/15/93) • **90**

Cabernet Sauvignon Napa Valley 1990: Plush and flavorful, a wine with concentration and elegance, offering deep plum, currant, blackberry, pepper and anise aromas and flavors that extend into a smooth, supple finish. Tempting now, but should be at its best after 1996 to '98. 650 cases made. • $30 • (11/15/92) • **92**

Cabernet Sauvignon Napa Valley 1989 • $30 • (08/31/92) • **84**

Cabernet Sauvignon Napa Valley 1988 • $26 • (07/15/91) • **92**

Cabernet Sauvignon Napa Valley 1987 • $24 • (08/31/90) • **94**

Cabernet Sauvignon Napa Valley 1986 • $22 • (07/31/89) • **89**

Cabernet Sauvignon Napa Valley 1985 • $20 • (03/01/89) • **89**

Cabernet Sauvignon Napa Valley 1984 • $18 • (03/01/89) • **86**

Cabernet Sauvignon Napa Valley 1983 • $18 • (03/01/89) • **87**

Cabernet Sauvignon Napa Valley Tanbark Hill Vineyard 1988 • $24 • (06/30/91) • **87**

Sauvignon Blanc Napa Valley 1992: Lean and zingy, a distinctly weedy, earthy wine that gets a little sour on the finish. 1,100 cases made. • $14 • (08/31/94) • **77**

Sauvignon Blanc Napa Valley 1991 • $14 • (09/15/93) • **76**

TOPAZ | CALIFORNIA

Rouge de Trois Napa Valley 1991: Marked by mint and bay leaf notes, it's a supple, medium weight wine that's appealing to drink now. 655 cases made. • $17 • (12/15/95) • **84**

Rouge de Trois Napa Valley 1990: A vegetal style, with green bean and herbal notes, but also has hints of currant and berry that add dimension to the flavors. Balanced and not too tannic, drinkable now. 60 percent Cabernet Sauvignon, 25 percent Merlot and 15 percent Cabernet Franc. 600 cases made. • $16 • (06/30/93) • **82**

Rouge de Trois Napa Valley 1988 • $15 • (11/15/91) • **87**

Sauvignon Blanc-Sémillon Late Harvest Napa Valley Special Select 1991 • $19 • (06/15/94) • **87**

Sauvignon Blanc-Sémillon Late Harvest Napa Valley Special Select 1989 • $19 • (08/31/91) • **90**

TOPOLOS | CALIFORNIA

Cabernet Sauvignon Sonoma County 1992: Lean and tannic, with herb, cranberry and raspberry flavors. Cellar until 1998. 624 cases made. • $18 • (11/15/94) • **83**

Chardonnay Sonoma County Dry Farmed Sonoma Mountain Old Vines Bar 1992: Tart and oaky, a mouth-puckering wine that finishes with a touch of lemon. 982 cases made. • $12 • (06/30/94) • **79**

Pinot Noir Sonoma Mountain Dry Farmed 1992 • $12 • (02/28/94) • **79**

Riserva Cabernet Blend Sonoma County 1991: Intense and peppery—almost like a racy Zinfandel or Syrah—but it's a bizarre Cabernet that offers more beet and herb flavors than classic currant or cherry notes. Drinkable now. 188 cases made. • $18 • (11/15/93) • **79**

Sauvignon Blanc Sonoma County 1993: Lean and a little bitter, right through to the finish. 648 cases made. • $8 • (08/31/95) • **76**

Sauvignon Blanc Sonoma County C.C.O.F. Certified 1994: Light and somewhat sappy, resiny flavors detract from the simple fruit. 790 cases made. • $8 • (08/31/95) • **76**

Zinfandel Napa County 1993: Simple wild berry and black cherry flavors and aromas. 50 cases made. • $8 • (10/15/95) • **83**

Zinfandel Sonoma County 1992: Firm, tight, compact and earthy, but enough spicy raspberry flavor sneaks through to hold interest. May be better with another year in the bottle. 2,800 cases made. • $8 • (10/15/94) • **84**

Zinfandel Sonoma County 1991 • $8 • (09/30/93) • **81**

Zinfandel Sonoma County Piner Heights Old Vines Unfined 1994: Clean and correct, with a core of spice, cherry and berry flavors that are modest but appealing nonetheless. 1,781 cases made. • $13 • (10/15/95) • **83**

Zinfandel Sonoma County Piner Heights Old Vines Unfined 1993: Austere, with crisp tannins and pleasant plum and wild berry flavors. Try aging just a little. 400 cases made. • $13 • (10/15/95) • **84**

Zinfandel Sonoma County Rossi Ranch 1992: Austere, with leather and pickle notes and raspberry flavors. A bit too bizarre. 1,600 cases made. • $15 • (10/15/94) • **78**

Zinfandel Sonoma County Rossi Ranch 1990 • $24 Ⓐ • (10/15/92) • **84**

Zinfandel Sonoma County Rossi Ranch 1989 • $10 • (10/15/92) • **84**

Zinfandel Sonoma County Rossi Ranch 80-Year-Old Vines Late Picked 1993: A touch earthy, but the plum and cherry flavors stand up to it. An austere style that finishes earthy and tannic. 1,767 cases made. • $18 • (10/15/95) • **83**

Zinfandel Sonoma County Rossi Ranch Organically Grown 1991 • $14 • (09/30/93) • **85**

Zinfandel Sonoma County Ultimo 1988 • $12 • (05/15/92) • **77**

Zinfandel Sonoma County Ultimo Old Vines 1992: Austere, with a green, unripe edge to the flavors. But on the finish the peppery raspberry and blackberry flavors come through. Needs food. 490 cases made. • $18 • (10/15/94) • **83**

Zinfandel Sonoma County Ultimo Old Vines Unfined 1993: Intense and well focused, with a pretty core of tart black cherry and wild berry flavors that turn supple and elegant until the tannins sneak through. 335 cases made. • $20 • (10/15/95) • **86**

Zinfandel Sonoma County Ultimo Organically Grown 1991 • $18 • (09/30/93) • **84**

TORRES, MARIMAR | CALIFORNIA

Chardonnay Sonoma County Green Valley Don Miguel Vineyard 1993: Lean and bright, a tight wine with focused pear and resiny flavors that linger nicely on the finish. Ready now, could improve through 1997. 5,700 cases made. • $20 • (05/15/96) • **88**

Chardonnay Sonoma County Green Valley Don Miguel Vineyard 1992: A rich, smooth and polished white from this Spanish-owned venture. This has a creamy texture and ripe, broad pear, apple and spice notes that build in intensity. The finish is elegant and refined. 6,745 cases made. • $20 • (04/30/95) SS • **91**

Chardonnay Sonoma County Green Valley Don Miguel Vineyard 1991 • $25 • (07/15/93) • **85**

Pinot Noir Sonoma County Green Valley Don Miguel Vineyard 1993: Medium bodied, pleasant enough, with cola, berry, light oak and spice notes of modest depth. Drinkable now. 1,888 cases made. • $25 • **84**

Pinot Noir Sonoma County Green Valley Don Miguel Vineyard 1992: Ripe and supple plum, herb and cherry flavors. Drinks well now, offering enough tannin. 1,007 cases made. • $25 • (03/31/95) • **86**

Pinot Noir Sonoma County Green Valley Don Miguel Vineyard Vineyard Selection 1992: Hints of tea and cherry at the start, turning soft and elegant with modest fruit richness and concentration. Gets points for its elegance and grace. 250 cases made. • $35 • (04/30/96) • **87**

TOTT'S | CALIFORNIA

Brut NV • $8 • (05/15/92) • **77**

Brut California Reserve Cuvée NV • $8 • (05/31/89) • **80**

Extra Dry NV • $8 • (05/15/92) • **75**

Extra Dry California Reserve Cuvée NV • $8 • (02/28/89) • **75**

TOURNELLE, LA | CALIFORNIA

Chardonnay Monterey 1992: Fresh and lively, with apple- and pear-laced Chardonnay fruit that comes across as simple and one-dimensional. Ready now. 10,000 cases made. • $8 • (01/31/94) • **82**

Chenin Blanc Monterey Ventana Vineyard 1992: Leafy aromas and flavors in this soft, fruity white that finishes with a touch of mint. 1,800 cases made. • $6 • (07/31/94) • **80**

TOYON | CALIFORNIA

Cabernet Sauvignon Alexander Valley 1982 • $10 • (11/15/86) • **83**

Key: SS—Spectator Selection. CS—Cellar Selection. BB—Best Buy. $NA—Price not available. (BT)—Barrel tasting. Ⓐ—Auction Price.
Dates in parentheses represent the issues in which the ratings were published.

TRAULSEN | CALIFORNIA

Zinfandel Napa Valley 1989 • $18 • (09/30/93) • **82**

TREFETHEN | CALIFORNIA

Cabernet Sauvignon Napa Valley 1992: Dark, rich and intense, with a solid core of earthy currant. black cherry and wild berry flavors. Finishes with firm but supple tannins. Drinkable now. 4,670 cases made. • $21 • (02/29/96) • **87**

Cabernet Sauvignon Napa Valley 1991: Marked by a green edge with herb and tea notes. The dark color suggests more ripe dark fruit flavors, but they just don't emerge. Cellaring into 1997 or 1998 may deliver a more complete wine. 6,000 cases made. • $19 • (12/15/95) • **84**

Cabernet Sauvignon Napa Valley 1990: Smooth and polished, with elegant herb, currant, anise and light toasty oak shadings. All well-proportioned with supple tannins. Ready now. 4,900 cases made. • $19 • (11/15/95) • **87**

Cabernet Sauvignon Napa Valley 1989 • $18 • (07/31/94) • **84**
Cabernet Sauvignon Napa Valley 1988 • $16 • (04/30/93) • **82**
Cabernet Sauvignon Napa Valley 1987 • $16 • (11/15/90) • **86**
Cabernet Sauvignon Napa Valley 1986 • $16 • (10/31/89) • **84**
Cabernet Sauvignon Napa Valley 1985 • $15 • (03/01/89) • **80**
Cabernet Sauvignon Napa Valley 1984 • $14 • (03/01/89) • **84**
Cabernet Sauvignon Napa Valley 1983 • $12 • (03/01/89) • **84**
Cabernet Sauvignon Napa Valley 1982 • $11 • (03/01/89) • **58**
Cabernet Sauvignon Napa Valley 1981 • $11 • (03/01/89) • **87**
Cabernet Sauvignon Napa Valley 1980 • $11 • (03/01/89) • **68**
Cabernet Sauvignon Napa Valley 1979 • $11 • (03/01/89) • **86**
Cabernet Sauvignon Napa Valley 1978 • $10 • (03/01/89) • **81**
Cabernet Sauvignon Napa Valley 1977 • $8 • (03/01/89) • **86**
Cabernet Sauvignon Napa Valley 1976 • $7 • (03/01/89) • **76**
Cabernet Sauvignon Napa Valley 1975 • $7 • (03/01/89) • **83**
Cabernet Sauvignon Napa Valley 1974 • $37 • (11/15/94) • **78**
Cabernet Sauvignon Napa Valley Estate Reserve 1989 • $30 • (07/31/94) • **86**
Cabernet Sauvignon Napa Valley Estate Reserve 1986 • $30 • (08/31/92) • **82**
Cabernet Sauvignon Napa Valley Hillside Selection 1986 • $NA • (03/01/89) • **90**
Cabernet Sauvignon Napa Valley Hillside Selection 1985 • $30 • (11/15/90) • **80**
Cabernet Sauvignon Napa Valley Library Selection 1983 • $30 • (10/10/90) • **80**

Chardonnay Napa Valley 1994: A touch earthy, with hints of grapefruit and citrus in the pear and pineapple notes. Finishes with a spicy citrus edge. 25,000 cases made. • $19 • (06/30/96) • **83**

Chardonnay Napa Valley 1993: Distinct for its simple citrus and grapefruit flavors, it fans out a bit on the finish. 18,000 cases made. • $19 • (07/31/95) • **85**

Chardonnay Napa Valley 1992: Crisp and simple, on the austere side, with modest apple and leafy-floral flavors that hang in there on the finish. • $18 • (06/30/94) • **83**

Chardonnay Napa Valley Eshcol 1994: Simple, smooth and generous with its juicy apple and spice flavors. Drinkable now. 15,000 cases made. • $10 • (04/30/96) • **84**

Eshcol Napa Valley Cabernet Blend NV: Light and herbal with simple cherry and currant notes. Ready now. • $8 • (11/15/94) • **80**

Pinot Noir Napa Valley 1986 • $13 • (07/31/89) • **68**
Pinot Noir Napa Valley 1985 • $12 • (06/15/88) • **74**
Pinot Noir Napa Valley 1984 • $9 • (05/31/88) • **80**

Riesling Napa Valley Dry 1994: Smells fruity and open, an off-dry white turning toward lime and floral notes on the tart finish. • $9 • (09/15/95) • **85**

White Riesling Napa Valley 1991 • $9 • (05/15/93) • **74**

TRENTADUE | CALIFORNIA

Cabernet Sauvignon Dry Creek Valley 1989 • $10 • (11/15/93) • **77**

Chardonnay Alexander Valley 1992: Smoky, meaty flavors dominate in this young wine, so much so that the pear and spicy Chardonnay flavors struggle to fight through. Ready now. 500 cases made. • $10 • (06/30/94) • **78**

Zinfandel Sonoma County 1993: Crisp and fruity, with hints of black cherry and spicy wild berry, finishing short and tannic. 3,080 cases made. • $11 • (10/15/95) • **83**

Zinfandel Sonoma County 1992: Firm, ripe and intense, with a solid core of spicy mint and wild cherry fruit that picks up pretty earthy, gamy notes on the finish. Well balanced and easy to drink while maintaining the zesty personality of the grape. 800 cases made. • $10 • (10/15/94) BB • **88**

TRIA | CALIFORNIA

Cabernet Franc Dry Creek Valley 1993: Smells more interesting than it tastes, so there's hope that more of the herb and cherry flavors will fan out. 130 cases made. • $24 • (05/15/96) • **83**

Claret Dry Creek Valley 1993: Drinks well now, highlighting its appealing black cherry flavor with spicy, cedary, earthy tones and finishing with the right amount of tannins. 130 cases made. • $24 • (05/31/96) • **87**

Pinot Noir Late Harvest Carneros 1994: Sweet, with an earthy edge to the cherry and Pinot Noir flavors. An unusual wine, enjoyable, if not to everyone's likes. 90 cases made. • $20 • (06/30/96) • **83**

Syrah Dry Creek Valley 1993: Firm, dark and intense, offering rich, full-bodied, plummy cherry and berry flavor, long, complex aftertaste and a good dose of tannin. Best now and into 1997. 185 cases made. • $20 • (05/15/96) • **89**

Zinfandel Dry Creek Valley 1994: Well balanced, a tad tannic, delivering pleasant cherry and berry flavor and some spice, but lacking the extra dimensions of complexity. 246 cases made. • $16 • (05/15/96) • **83**

Zinfandel Napa Valley 1994: Well proportioned, featuring smoky raspberry and berry flavors and just the right amount of tannin and intensity. Anise and tar on the finish. 456 cases made. • $16 • (05/15/96) • **89**

TRIBAUT | CALIFORNIA

Blanc de Noirs California NV: Lean and trim, sporting a hint of cherry and spice in an otherwise crisp, narrow sparkler. 25,000 cases made. • $9 • (05/31/95) • **81**

Blanc de Noirs Monterey County NV • $10 • (01/31/92) • **82**

Brut California NV: Tastes off-dry, showing a metallic edge to the pear and citrus notes. Simple but serviceable. 25,000 cases made. • $9 • (05/31/95) • **81**

Brut Monterey County 1985 • $13 • (05/31/89) • **91**
Brut Monterey County 1984 • $14 • (12/31/87) • **85**
Brut Monterey County 1983 • $14 • (02/15/87) • **81**
Rosé Monterey County 1984 • $14 • (12/31/87) • **80**
Rosé Monterey County NV • $13 • (01/31/92) • **77**

TRIONE | CALIFORNIA

Cabernet Sauvignon Alexander Valley 1984 • $10 • (12/31/87) • **74**

TROQUATO | CALIFORNIA

Zinfandel Santa Clara County 1991: Ripe and jammy, with bright cherry and blackberry flavors. Tart and intriguing, best with food. Ready now through 1998. 275 cases made. • $8 • (10/15/94) • **85**

TRUCHARD | CALIFORNIA

Cabernet Sauvignon Napa Valley Carneros 1992: Somewhat earthy and tannic, but there's enough currant and cherry flavor to keep in balance. A rustic style that can last into 1998. 1,671 cases made. • $20 • (03/31/96) • **88**

Cabernet Sauvignon Napa Valley Carneros 1991: Young and compact, well balanced and well proportioned, with supple currant and cherry flavors. Still firmly tannic, it needs cellaring until about 1998 to soften. 1,574 cases made. • $18 • (11/15/94) • **87**

Cabernet Sauvignon Napa Valley Carneros 1990: A spicy, peppery style of Cabernet that's richly flavored, deep and complex. Serves up lots of flavor and turns crisp and austere on the finish, with dry tannins. Best to cellar until 1997. Tasted twice with consistent results. 627 cases made. • $18 • (11/15/93) • **87**

Cabernet Sauvignon Napa Valley Carneros 1989 • $18 • (12/15/92) • **87**

Chardonnay Napa Valley Carneros 1994: Bold, ripe, rich and exotic, with layers of pear, honey, toast and smoky oak flavors. An altogether complex and enticing style that is deep and concentrated, with a smooth, supple texture. Finishes with a wonderful display of flavors. 1,120 cases made. • $19 • (03/31/96) • **94**

Chardonnay Napa Valley Carneros 1993: Well crafted, with a nice balance between light spicy oak and ripe pear flavors that turn elegant. 672 cases made. • $17 • (07/31/95) • **87**

Chardonnay Napa Valley Carneros 1992: Intense and lively, with an elegant band of spicy pear, apple, vanilla and nutmeg flavors that fold together nicely on the finish. Drink now. 682 cases made. • $16 • (06/30/94) • **91**

Chardonnay Napa Valley Carneros 1991 • $16 • (07/15/93) • **90**

Merlot Napa Valley Carneros 1993: Marked by spiciness, an elegant, complex, vibrant young red delivering tiers of cherry, currant, toasty oak and mint, picking up a touch of earth and leather. Firmly tannic, drinkable now and into 1997. 1,938 cases made. • $20 • (04/30/96) • **89**

Merlot Napa Valley Carneros 1992: Tight and intense, as a hard cedar and leathery edge and potent tannins override the currant and berry flavors. Can age into 1997. 1,713 cases made. • $18 • (09/30/95) • **87**

Merlot Napa Valley Carneros 1991: Lean and supple, with a generous beam of plum and berry shaded nicely with touches of spice and leather. Drinkable now. 1,310 cases made. • $18 • (06/30/94) • **87**

Merlot Napa Valley Carneros 1990 • $18 • (07/15/93) • **85**

Merlot Napa Valley Carneros 1989 • $18 • (05/31/92) • **81**

Pinot Noir Napa Valley Carneros 1993: Elegant, well focused cherry, plum and berry notes acquire a light oaky edge on aftertaste. Medium in body, smooth-textured and polished, leading to a subtle finish. 1,861 cases made. • $18 • (11/30/95) • **88**

Pinot Noir Napa Valley Carneros 1992 • $18 • (02/28/94) • **84**

Pinot Noir Napa Valley Carneros 1991 • $18 • (02/28/93) • **82**

Pinot Noir Napa Valley Carneros 1990 • $18 • (09/30/92) • **86**

Pinot Noir Napa Valley Carneros 1989 • $18 • (10/31/91) • **90**

Syrah Napa Valley Carneros 1994: Remarkably concentrated and distinctive. Ripe and complex tiers of currant flavor with smoky meaty nuances and just enough oak. Finishes with a long, full aftertaste. Has the tannic strength to age into 1997 or 1998. 888 cases made. • $21 • **91**

Syrah Napa Valley Carneros 1993: Intensely grapey, with exotic, smoky currant and cherry flavors that pick up leather, mineral and tobacco accents on the finish. This California red combines richness with elegance. 640 cases made. • $18 • (05/15/95) • **92**

Syrah Napa Valley Carneros 1992: Very firm and spicy, a rough-and-tumble wine that throws as much at you as flavor. Drinkable now. 294 cases made. • $16 • (07/31/94) • **84**

Zinfandel Napa Valley Carneros 1994: Intense and spicy, with minty, peppery cherry and wild berry flavors. Well focused, with firm but supple tannins, finishing with a nicely fruity aftertaste. 418 cases made. • $15 • (03/31/96) • **88**

TRUMPETVINE | CALIFORNIA

Syrah California Berkeley Red NV • $5 • (04/15/89) • **79**

TUCKER | WASHINGTON

Chardonnay Yakima Valley 1992: Smooth and appealing, modest in scope, showing spicy pear and orange flavors weaving through the soft finish. 500 cases made. • $10 • (09/30/95) • **83**

Gewürztraminer Yakima Valley 1994: Lightly sweet and appealingly flavorful, weaving spicy rose petal overtones through the pear and apricot notes. Drink now. 1,500 cases made. • $6 • (09/30/95) • **86**

Key: SS—Spectator Selection. CS—Cellar Selection. BB—Best Buy. $NA—Price not available. (BT)—Barrel tasting. Ⓐ—Auction Price.
Dates in parentheses represent the issues in which the ratings were published.

Muscat Canelli Yakima Valley 1993: Soft and gently fruity, showing a modest level of distinctive Muscat flavor lingering on the finish. 800 cases made. • $7 • (09/30/95) • **83**

Pinot Noir Yakima Valley 1989 • $8 • (02/28/93) • **72**

TUDAL | CALIFORNIA

Cabernet Sauvignon Napa Valley 1992: Distinct for its vegetal cabbage and dill notes, but it manages to deliver enough currant and cherry fruit to keep it interesting. Flavors are complex and concentrated, if unbalanced. Tasted twice with consistent results. 1,904 cases made. • $18 • (12/15/95) • **83**

Cabernet Sauvignon Napa Valley 1990: Smooth, supple and stylish, a spicy Cabernet with ripe currant and chocolate flavors extending into a generous finish. • $17 • (02/28/94) • **88**

Cabernet Sauvignon Napa Valley 1989 • $17 • (11/15/92) • **74**

Cabernet Sauvignon Napa Valley 1988 • $17 • (11/15/92) • **80**

Cabernet Sauvignon Napa Valley 1986 • $15 • (12/15/89) • **91**

Cabernet Sauvignon Napa Valley 1985 • $15 • (03/01/89) • **89**

Cabernet Sauvignon Napa Valley 1984 • $13 • (03/01/89) • **91**

Cabernet Sauvignon Napa Valley 1983 • $13 • (03/01/89) • **86**

Cabernet Sauvignon Napa Valley 1982 • $12 • (03/01/89) • **72**

Cabernet Sauvignon Napa Valley 1981 • $12 • (03/01/89) • **88**

Cabernet Sauvignon Napa Valley 1980 • $12 • (03/01/89) • **85**

Cabernet Sauvignon Napa Valley 1979 • $11 • (03/01/89) • **90**

TULOCAY | CALIFORNIA

Cabernet Sauvignon Napa Valley 1986 • $12 • (06/30/90) • **70**

Cabernet Sauvignon Napa Valley 1978 • $NA • (11/15/92) • **78**

Cabernet Sauvignon Napa Valley Cliff Vineyard 1991: A touch earthy, displaying a barnyardy streak, it holds enough plum and cherry flavor to maintain your interest. Finishes with firm tannins. Best after 1997. 580 cases made. • $12 • (11/15/94) • **86**

Cabernet Sauvignon Napa Valley Cliff Vineyard 1990: Earthy with a metallic edge to the flavors. Hard to swallow. 150 cases made. • $12 • (11/15/94) • **74**

Cabernet Sauvignon Napa Valley De Celles Vineyard 1991: This is laced with herb and black olive flavor which adds dimension to the spicy cherry and currant notes. Has the tannins for cellaring until 1999. 95 cases made. • $12 • (11/15/94) • **87**

Cabernet Sauvignon Napa Valley Egan Vineyard 1988 • $15 • (11/15/91) • **86**

Cabernet Sauvignon Napa Valley Egan Vineyard 1987 • $17 • (02/15/91) • **74**

Chardonnay Napa Valley De Celles Vineyard 1993: Has a hint of earthiness on the nose, but it's more palatable to drink, with ripe pear and oak shadings of modest depth. • $14 • (07/31/95) • **83**

Chardonnay Napa Valley DeCelles Vineyard 1991 • $13 • (07/15/93) • **87**

Pinot Noir Napa Valley Haynes Vineyard 1992: Appealing for its ripe, bright black cherry- and plum-laced flavors, picking up a spicy, floral edge on the finish. Impressive fruitiness. 492 cases made. • $15 • (11/30/95) • **87**

Pinot Noir Napa Valley Haynes Vineyard 1989 • $16 • (03/31/92) • **76**

Pinot Noir Napa Valley Haynes Vineyard 1988 • $15 • (03/31/92) • **75**

Pinot Noir Napa Valley Haynes Vineyard 1985 • $18 • (02/28/91) • **83**

TURLEY | CALIFORNIA

Petite Sirah Napa Valley Aida Vineyard 1993: Dark and immensely concentrated, packed with rich berry and peppery flavors and the requisite tannins. Big in every way, yet beautiful in its own way. 200 cases made. • $21 • (09/30/95) • **90**

Sauvignon Blanc Napa Valley Turley Vineyard 1994: Smoothly balanced between ripe fig, citrus and pear notes, turning soft and fleshy. 150 cases made. • $16 • (10/31/95) • **87**

Zinfandel Howell Mountain Black-Sears Vineyard 1994: Captures a wonderful array of spicy blackberry and wild berry flavors and manages to deliver substantial finesse, depth and concentration. Gets extra points for elegance, finishing with a roasted meat edge. 275 cases made. • $24 • (04/30/96) • **93**

Zinfandel Napa Valley Aida Vineyard 1994: Doesn't capture the depth, richness or ripeness of the other Turley Zins, but succeeds on its own merits, with pretty plum, sage, cedar and spice notes and firm but not overpowering flavors. 450 cases made. • $20 • (04/30/96) • **90**

Zinfandel Napa Valley Aida Vineyard 1993: Dark, rich and intense, boasting potent wild berry, chocolate, cherry and buttery oak flavors and a chewy, tannic finish. 200 cases made. • $20 • (09/30/95) • **93**

Zinfandel Napa Valley Hayne Vineyard 1994: Even more impressive than the first release from this winery, the 1993 vintage. This is dark, rich and intense, loaded with chocolate, cherry, wild berry and spice flavors, accented by a wonderful dose of smoky, toasty oak. Packs a wallop of flavor, yet manages to hold a measure of finesse and grace. 450 cases made. • $27 • (04/30/96) • **96**

Zinfandel Napa Valley Hayne Vineyard 1993: A truly exciting, beautifully proportioned, rich and vibrant red. Has a delicious core of ripe black cherry, raspberry, anise and plum, finishing with depth and smooth, polished tannins. Drinkable now through 1999. 200 cases made. • $22 • (09/30/95) • **95**

Zinfandel Napa Valley Moore Earthquake Vineyard 1994: Dense, tannic and tightly wound, somewhat more alcoholic than the other Turley Zins, but it delivers a wallop of anise, black cherry, wild berry and spicy nuances. 450 cases made. • $25 • (04/30/96) • **94**

Zinfandel Napa Valley Moore Earthquake Vineyard 1993: Tight and intense, well focused and compact, offering lively wild berry, spice and raspberry flavors and finishing with a blackberry edge. Can stand short-term cellaring. 200 cases made. • $20 • (09/30/95) • **90**

Zinfandel Napa Valley Whitney Vineyard 1994: Packs a bounty of flavor, as tiers of smoky, meaty Zinfandel flavor unfold to reveal dense currant, wild berry, plum and cherry. The finish captures a complex marriage of fruit and oak. 130 cases made. • $22 • (04/30/96) • **91**

TURNBULL | CALIFORNIA

Cabernet Sauvignon Napa Valley 1994: An alluring blend of herbs and fruit. The ripe cherry, currant and plum notes are elegant and linger on the finish, picking up a nice, spicy accent. 4,500 cases made. • $20 • (05/31/95) • **90-94** (BT)

TWIN HILLS | CALIFORNIA

Cabernet Sauvignon Paso Robles 1991: Earthy, with a sour edge. 2,000 cases made. • $7 • (11/15/94) • **72**

Cabernet Sauvignon Paso Robles 1989 • $13 • (11/15/93) • **69**

Cabernet Sauvignon Paso Robles 1988 • $8 • (11/15/92) • **76**

Chardonnay Paso Robles 1993: Light and oaky, with just enough fruit to hold your interest, as the vanilla shadings override the ripe pear notes. 750 cases made. • $9 • (07/31/95) • **79**

Chardonnay Paso Robles A Natural Wine 1992: Coarse in texture, earthy with a syrupy finish. 500 cases made. • $6 • (06/30/94) • **73**

Chardonnay Paso Robles Reserve 1992: Simple and a bit coarse, but the pineapple and spice flavors have appeal. 750 cases made. • $9 • (06/30/94) • **80**

Zinfandel Paso Robles 1991 • $9 • (09/30/93) • **80**

UNIONVILLE VINEYARDS | NEW JERSEY

Hunter's White Reserve New Jersey 1994: A big-boned, aggressively dry wine with some attractive citrus, floral and smoky notes. It's clean and bold. 425 cases made. • $6 • **80**

Seyval Blanc New Jersey Windfall 1994: Aggressive toasty, smoky oak flavors overwhelm the fruit in this thick, chewy wine. Though a bit startling at first sip, it grows on you, finishing with pretty pineapple notes. Unbalanced but appealing. 150 cases made. • $9 • **82**

Seyval Blanc New Jersey Windfall 1993: Apple, vanilla and spice notes are attractive, if somewhat blunt, in this full-bodied white. A touch of oak adds dimension to the flavors. 150 cases made. • $9 • (01/31/96) • **83**

UNISSENT | CALIFORNIA

Cabernet Sauvignon California 1988 • $15 • (11/15/91) • **83**

UVE CELLARS | CALIFORNIA

Vin Santo Napa Valley 1991: A wonderful Vin Santo, vibrating with almond, pear, floral and citrus peel flavors, sweet but not unctuous, rich but not heavy. 150 cases made. • $19 • **89**

VALLEJO, M.G. | CALIFORNIA

Cabernet Sauvignon California 1992: This is smooth and shines with bright fruit flavors, offering raspberry, strawberry, vanilla and a touch of herb on the supple finish. Approachable now, and at an attractive price. 116,500 cases made. • $6 • (11/30/95) BB • **85**

Cabernet Sauvignon California 1990: Simple but correct, with sweetish plum and currant notes and herbal flavors. Balanced and easy to drink. Ready now. 500,000 cases made. • $6 • (11/15/92) BB • **80**

Cabernet Sauvignon California 1986 • $5 • (06/15/90) BB • **82**

Cabernet Sauvignon California 1985 • $4 • (02/15/89) • **78**

Cabernet Sauvignon California 1983 • $4 • (08/31/87) • **67**

Cabernet Sauvignon California Harvest Select 1991: Light and fruity with simple berry notes. Ready now. 69,000 cases made. • $6 • (11/15/94) • **79**

Cabernet Sauvignon California Harvest Select 1990: Smooth, round and pleasant, with appealing, vanilla-tinged berry and herb aromas and flavors. Drink soon. 5,000 cases made. • $7 • (06/15/93) • **78**

Chardonnay California 1994: Smooth and flavorful, showing plenty of vanilla-scented pear and citrus character. Ready now. • $6 • (11/15/95) • **84**

Chardonnay California 1993: Smooth and gently spicy, crisp and appley at the core but smooth around the edges, echoing spice on the finish. 90,000 cases made. • $6 • (07/31/95) • **82**

Chardonnay California 1991 • $5 • (11/30/92) BB • **85**

Chardonnay California Harvest Select 1992: Light and fruity, with a spicy edge that gives it some extra zing. Drinkable now. 67,000 cases made. • $6 • (03/31/95) BB • **84**

Chardonnay California Harvest Select 1991 • $7 • (07/15/93) • **78**

M.G.V. Red California NV • $3 • (05/31/90) • **74**

Merlot California 1991 • $6 • (11/30/92) BB • **84**

Merlot California 1990 • $6 • (05/31/92) BB • **80**

Merlot California 1987 • $5 • (06/15/90) • **77**

Merlot California Harvest Select 1992: Ripe and fruity, with simple cherry, berry and spice notes. Ready now. • $6 • (09/15/94) • **82**

Merlot California Harvest Select 1991 • $7 • (06/15/93) • **79**

Pinot Noir California Harvest Select 1994: Light and simple, with modest fruit flavors that may possibly remind you of Pinot Noir. • $8 • (01/31/96) • **80**

Sauvignon Blanc California 1993: Fresh and simple, nicely balanced between pear and floral fruit and a touch of herbs. 20,000 cases made. • $5 • (08/31/95) • **82**

Sauvignon Blanc California 1992: Still fresh and floral, adding a rose petal edge to the modest pear flavor. 15,200 cases made. • $5 • (08/31/95) • **83**

White Zinfandel California 1994: Well made, tasting of tea and cherry. Quite dry and in balance, but fairly soft. • $6 • (09/15/95) • **80**

VALLEY OF THE MOON | CALIFORNIA

Zinfandel Sonoma Valley 1984 • $9 • (03/15/90) • **76**

Zinfandel Sonoma Valley Reserve 1990: Firm and austere, with spicy fruit, finishing on a tar and herb note. Ready now. 420 cases made. • $10 • (10/15/94) • **80**

VALLEY RIDGE | CALIFORNIA

Cabernet Sauvignon Sonoma County 1989 • $9 • (11/15/91) • **83**

Zinfandel Sonoma County 1988 • $9 • (11/15/91) • **86**

VAN DER HEYDEN | CALIFORNIA

Cabernet Sauvignon Alexander Valley 1987 • $18 • (08/31/92) • **80**

Chardonnay Napa Valley 1991: Funky overall, earthy and gamy, with a perfumed fruit aroma. 1,250 cases made. • $9 • (01/31/95) • **75**

VAN DER KAMP | CALIFORNIA

Brut Rosé Sonoma Valley Midnight Cuvée 1989: Simple, with spicy black cherry flavors that are a bit coarse. Ready now. 3,300 cases made. • $15 • (12/31/94) • **83**
Brut Rosé Sonoma Valley Midnight Cuvée 1988 • $12 • (05/15/92) • **75**
Brut Rosé Sonoma Valley Midnight Cuvée 1987 • $15 • (11/15/90) • **81**
Brut Rosé Sonoma Valley Midnight Cuvée 1986 • $15 • (05/31/89) • **83**
Brut Rosé Sonoma Valley Midnight Cuvée 1985 • $18 • (12/31/87) • **84**
Brut Sonoma Valley 1988 • $15 • (12/15/93) • **86**
Brut Sonoma Valley 1985 • $15 • (12/15/91) • **84**
Brut Sonoma Valley 1984 • $15 • (05/31/89) • **86**
Brut Sonoma Valley 1983 • $18 • (12/31/87) • **86**
Brut Sonoma Valley English Cuvée 1986 • $15 • (12/31/92) • **89**
Brut Sonoma Valley Reserve 1986: A solid bubbly, with spicy pear, earth and vanilla notes that hang together well. Ready now. 1,500 cases made. • $16 • (12/31/94) • **84**

VANINO | CALIFORNIA

Cabernet Sauvignon Sonoma County 1985 • $11 • (09/30/88) • **80**

VEEDERCREST | CALIFORNIA

Cabernet Sauvignon Napa Valley 1978 • $NA • (11/15/92) • **74**

VEGA | CALIFORNIA

Johannisberg Riesling Late Harvest Santa Barbara County Special Selection 1987 • $11 • (12/15/89) • **78**

VENDANGE | CALIFORNIA

Cabernet Sauvignon California 1991: Light and simple with cedary Cabernet flavors. • $6 • (11/15/94) • **76**
Cabernet Sauvignon California 1990: Simple and earthy, with a modest level of sweet currant flavor lurking in the background. Drinkable now. • $6 • (08/31/92) • **73**
Chardonnay California Autumn Harvest 1993: Light and simple, with citrus and pineapple notes. Ready now. 150,000 cases made. • $7 • (06/30/94) • **79**
Merlot California 1990 • $6 • (05/31/92) BB • **80**
Merlot California Autumn Harvest 1992: Lean and earthy, with simple cherry and berry notes. 150,000 cases made. • $7 • (09/15/94) • **78**
Pinot Noir California 1990 • $6 • (02/28/94) • **78**
Pinot Noir California Autumn Harvest 1993: This is light, with weedy, earthy flavors, but serviceable at this price. • $6 • (03/31/95) • **76**
Sauvignon Blanc California Autumn Harvest 1995: Has a flavor like canned fruit juice that has turned. 90,000 cases made. • $5 • **72**
Sauvignon Blanc California Autumn Harvest 1993: Soft and simple, with some orange and leather notes. 45,000 cases made. • $7 • (08/31/94) • **77**
White Zinfandel California Autumn Harvest 1994: A wine showing some character. Smells and tastes like Muscat with an herbal note. Flavors linger on the finish. • $6 • (09/15/95) • **81**
Zinfandel California 1991 • $7 • (12/31/93) • **78**
Zinfandel California 1989 • $6 • (07/31/92) BB • **84**
Zinfandel California 1987 • $5 • (09/15/90) • **78**
Zinfandel California Autumn Harvest 1993: Light and simple, with gamy notes. • $6 • (10/15/94) • **79**

VENEZIA | CALIFORNIA

Bianco Nuovo Mondo Alexander Valley Meritage 1994: Smooth, rich and flavorful, with a pretty core of fig, pear, lemon and grapefruit flavors that expand on the finish, where the oak flavors fold in. 940 cases made. • $18 • (03/31/96) • **89**
Cabernet Sauvignon Alexander Valley 1993: Lots of toasty vanilla notes and tasty black cherry, plum and wild berry flavors, turning tight and firmly tannic on the finish. Can stand aging into 1998. New from Geyser Peak. 400 cases made. • $20 • (04/30/96) • **88**

VENGE | CALIFORNIA

Cabernet Sauvignon Napa Valley Family Reserve 1992: Dark, tight and intense, with a rich core of currant and cherry, finishing with firm tannins and a touch of heat. Best in 1997. • $NA • (06/30/96) • **88**

VENTANA | CALIFORNIA

Chardonnay Monterey Gold Stripe Selection 1992: Appealing for its ripe pear, honey, spice and light oak shadings, all merging well with the butter and vanilla accents. 2,152 cases made. • $12 • (06/30/95) • **88**
Chardonnay Monterey Gold Stripe Selection 1991 • $10 • (02/28/94) BB • **88**
Chenin Blanc Monterey 1993: Soft and fragrant, a leafy, minty character carrying through stronger than the fruit. Drinkable now. 815 cases made. • $6 • (06/30/95) • **81**
Johannisberg Riesling Monterey 1994: Delicately sweet, with modest apricot and apple flavors with pine-like overtones. A nice sipper. 1,200 cases made. • $6 • (06/15/96) • **84**
Johannisberg Riesling Monterey 1992 • $6 • (05/15/94) BB • **82**
Johannisberg Riesling Monterey White Riesling 1993: Smooth and appealing, a soft wine with modest apple and pear flavors that linger on the finish. 500 cases made. • $6 • (06/15/95) • **84**
Magnus Monterey Meritage 1986 • $20 • (10/31/89) • **79**
Riesling Monterey Dry 1994: Light and fragrant, a zesty mouthful of apple, floral and peppery flavors that linger appealingly on the finish. 1,000 cases made. • $6 • (06/15/96) • **85**
Sauvignon Blanc Monterey 1994: Soft and appealing, a nice mouthful of bright pear and apple flavors. Drinkable now. 1,800 cases made. • $9 • (05/31/96) • **85**
Sauvignon Blanc Monterey 1993: Ripe and refreshing while remaining round and harmonious. An example of a fruit-centered Sauvignon that lavishes spice and tobacco nuances on the pear, fig and honey character. 2,100 cases made. • $8 • (04/30/95) BB • **89**
Sauvignon Blanc Monterey 1991 • $8 • (01/31/94) • **77**
White Riesling Late Harvest Monterey Ventana Vyds Hand-Selected Clusters 1987 • $14 • (08/31/89) • **70**

VERITE | CALIFORNIA

Bourguignon Noir Cuvée Ancienne Alexander Valley 1980 • $6 • (01/01/85) • **84**

VIADER | CALIFORNIA

Napa Valley Cabernet Blend 1993: Dark and intense currant, anise, chocolate and berry, adding a nice array of flavors on aftertaste, where the tannins fold in. 2,613 cases made. • $29 • (05/15/96) • **89**
Napa Valley Cabernet Blend 1992: Well oaked, with strong vanilla and chocolate notes and rich currant and cherry flavors to match. Intriguing, and has the tannins to age through 1997. 2,120 cases made. • $28 • (07/31/95) • **88**
Napa Valley Cabernet Blend 1991: Supple and generous, with layers of ripe plum, currant, anise and smoke notes. Turns plush and elegant on the finish, where the fine tannins blend in well with the rich fruit flavors. Best after 1997. 1,843 cases made. • $28 • (11/15/94) • **91**
Napa Valley Cabernet Blend 1990: Ripe, rich and generous, with spicy currant, plum and blackberry flavors framed by toasty, smoky oak notes. The flavors run long and deep and the tannins are smooth and polished, making this tasty to drink now, but it should develop through the decade. Mostly Cabernet Sauvignon, with 32 percent Cabernet Franc. 1,404 cases made. • $25 • (07/15/93) • **91**
Napa Valley Cabernet Blend 1989 • $25 • (11/15/92) • **90**

Key: SS—Spectator Selection. CS—Cellar Selection. BB—Best Buy. $NA—Price not available. (BT)—Barrel tasting. Ⓐ—Auction Price.
Dates in parentheses represent the issues in which the ratings were published.

VIANO | CALIFORNIA

Cabernet Sauvignon California Reserve Selection 1988: Mature, with a cedary aroma and austere currant and spice notes that turn tannic on the finish. Can stand at least another year of cellaring. Best in 1996. • $9 • (11/15/94) • **81**

Zinfandel Contra Costa County Sand Rock Hill Reserve 1991: A very ripe and oaky style that somehow hangs together. The cherry and raspberry flavors border on jammy and it's tannic and hot on the finish. 800 cases made. • $8 • (10/15/94) • **80**

Zinfandel Contra Costa County Sand Rock Hill Reserve Selection 1992: Intense and spicy, packed with well-focused black cherry, currant and plum notes. Turns firmly tannic on the finish, where it picks up a toasty oak flavor. Well balanced. • $9 • (10/15/95) • **89**

Zinfandel Contra Costa County Sand Rock Hill Reserve Selection 1989 • $7 • (06/15/93) • **81**

Zinfandel Late Harvest Contra Costa County Reserve Selection 1989: Sweet Zinfandel without any special characteristics, edging toward medicinal flavors on the finish. • $9 • (12/31/95) • **76**

Zinfandel Late Harvest Contra Costa County Reserve Selection 1988: Dense, dark and chewy, showing off complex tar, smoke and toasty oak flavors with lots of fresh, ripe, bright cherry, raspberry and plum notes. Drinks well now, but has the balance to hold until 1997. • $8 • (10/15/94) • **86**

VIANSA | CALIFORNIA

Cabernet Sauvignon Napa-Sonoma Counties 1988 • $17 • (11/15/92) • **76**

Cabernet Sauvignon Napa-Sonoma Counties 1984 • $13 • (07/31/88) • **85**

Cabernet Sauvignon Napa-Sonoma Counties Reserve 1988 • $23 • (11/15/93) • **78**

Cabernet Sauvignon Sonoma Valley Grand Reserve 1983 • $35 • (10/15/88) • **88**

Cabernet Sauvignon Sonoma Valley Reserve 1983 • $18 • (10/15/88) • **88**

Cabernet Sauvignon Sonoma-Napa Counties 1986 • $15 • (07/31/90) • **77**

Cabernet Sauvignon Sonoma-Napa Counties 1985 • $13 • (09/15/89) • **72**

Cabernet Sauvignon Sonoma-Napa Counties Sam J. Sebastiani 1983 • $15 • (11/30/86) • **88**

Nebbiolo Northern California 1990 • $15 • (11/30/92) • **81**

Obsidian Sonoma-Napa Counties Cabernet Blend 1987 • $65 • (07/15/91) • **85**

Prindelo Sonoma Valley Zinfandel Blend 1993: Brimming with ripe, complex berry and black cherry jam flavors. Remarkably complex and well crafted, with some extra dimensions rarely found in any wine. 725 cases made. • $20 • (10/15/95) • **92**

Prindelo Sonoma Valley Zinfandel Blend 1991 • $16 • (12/31/93) • **82**

Riserva Anatra Rosso Napa-Sonoma Counties 1989 • $18 • (11/15/93) • **80**

Thalia Napa County Red 1990 • $22 • (11/30/92) • **83**

VICHON | CALIFORNIA

Cabernet Sauvignon California Coastal Selection 1992: Complex and elegant, with tiers of black cherry, spice and cedar flavors. Drinkable now. 22,000 cases made. • $9 • (01/31/95) BB • **87**

Cabernet Sauvignon California Coastal Selection 1991: A good but simple wine with grapey Cabernet flavors that pick up herb and oak notes on the finish. Ready now. 8,200 cases made. • $11 • (09/30/94) • **82**

Cabernet Sauvignon California Coastal Selection 1990: Firm, intense and spicy with earthy currant and cedar notes. Balanced and ready to drink now. Flavors stay with you on the finish. Drink now. 10,144 cases made. • $9 • (11/15/93) • **82**

Cabernet Sauvignon California Coastal Selection 1989 • $10 • (11/15/92) • **84**

Cabernet Sauvignon Napa Valley 1992: Firm and intense, with a spicy, minty edge to the currant and black cherry fruit. Flavors fan out on the finish, where they turn more complex. Well crafted. 2,821 cases made. • $16 • (12/15/95) • **87**

Cabernet Sauvignon Napa Valley 1991: In three tastings, it was firm, tight and closed, not revealing much fruit or depth of flavor. Some hints of currant and cherry, but the finish is short. Drink now. 4,700 cases made. • $16 • (04/30/94) • **81**

Cabernet Sauvignon Napa Valley 1990: Young, tight and tannic, but lots of interesting, toasty, currantlike, spicy flavors play off each other and last into the long finish. Has a fine backbone of fruit flavor that should serve it well as it ages into something more mellow. Try after 1997. 3,900 cases made. • $16 • (08/31/93) • **89**

Cabernet Sauvignon Napa Valley 1989 • $16 • (11/15/92) • **89**

Cabernet Sauvignon Napa Valley 1988 • $16 • (05/15/91) • **84**

Cabernet Sauvignon Napa Valley 1985 • $13 • (03/01/89) • **88**

Cabernet Sauvignon Napa Valley 1984 • $12 • (03/01/89) • **88**

Cabernet Sauvignon Napa Valley 1983 • $10 • (03/01/89) • **80**

Cabernet Sauvignon Napa Valley 1982 • $13 • (03/01/89) • **76**

Cabernet Sauvignon Napa Valley 1981 • $13 • (03/01/89) • **80**

Cabernet Sauvignon Napa Valley Volker Eisele Vineyard 1982 • $16 • (03/01/89) • **78**

Cabernet Sauvignon Napa Valley Volker Eisele Vineyard 1980 • $16 • (03/01/89) • **83**

Cabernet Sauvignon Stags Leap District 1992: Tough and chewy, with dense tannins holding the upper hand in this youthful wine. It shows a tight core of earthy currant and cherry, but it will be several years before this wine softens. try in 1997 or 1998. 1,000 cases made. • $31 • (03/31/96) • **84**

Cabernet Sauvignon Stags Leap District Fay Vineyard 1984 • $14 • (03/01/89) • **85**

Cabernet Sauvignon Stags Leap District Fay Vineyard 1982 • $14 • (03/01/89) • **79**

Cabernet Sauvignon Stags Leap District Fay Vineyard 1980 • $16 • (03/01/89) • **85**

Cabernet Sauvignon Stags Leap District SLD 1991: Complete and well crafted, with an elegant beam of currant, coffee, cedar and spice. Lacks the drama and richness of the best of the vintage, but wins points on finesse and grace. 1,100 cases made. • $28 • (12/15/95) • **88**

Cabernet Sauvignon Stags Leap District SLD 1990: Firm, chewy and flavorful, showing a nice glow of plum, currant and anise flavor, finishing with overtones of cedar, tobacco and herb. This is a wine that evolves in the glass, showing more character and smoother texture with each sip. Destined to improve through 1998-2000. 3,100 cases made. • $24 • (11/15/93) • **91**

Cabernet Sauvignon Stags Leap District SLD 1989 • $24 • (11/15/92) • **88**

Cabernet Sauvignon Stags Leap District SLD 1988 • $24 • (11/15/91) • **90**

Cabernet Sauvignon Stags Leap District SLD 1987 • $17 • (07/31/90) • **87**

Cabernet Sauvignon Stags Leap District SLD 1986 • $21 • (10/31/89) • **91**

Cabernet Sauvignon Stags Leap District SLD 1985 • $18 • (03/01/89) • **92**

Cabernet Sauvignon Stags Leap District Tenth Harvest 1989 • $24 • (08/31/93) • **83**

Chardonnay California Coastal Selection 1994: Bright, generous and round, with a spicy character to the pear flavor. 50,000 cases made. • $10 • (06/15/96) • **83**

Chardonnay California Coastal Selection 1993: Clean and fruity, with a citrus note that holds the pear and spice flavors together. • $10 • (01/31/95) • **82**

Chardonnay California Coastal Selection 1992: Lean and simple, with light pear and spice flavors. Ready now. 20,000 cases made. • $10 • (09/30/94) • **80**

Chardonnay California Coastal Selection 1991 • $10 • (01/31/93) • **82**

Chardonnay Napa Valley 1994: Ripe and fruity, moderately rich, as tiers of apple, fig and melon gain depth and complexity on the finish, where the flavors fold together nicely. • $NA • (02/29/96) • **89**

Chardonnay Napa Valley 1993: Light with modest pear and spice notes that hang with you, but ultimately its simple. 5,000 cases made. • $14 • (07/31/95) • **83**

Chardonnay Napa Valley 1992: Smooth, ripe and creamy, with spicy pear, apple, nutmeg and vanilla flavors that are focused and elegant. Pretty aftertaste. 9,000 cases made. • $14 • (06/15/94) • **88**

Chardonnay Napa Valley 1991 • $14 • (06/15/93) • **90**

Chevrignon Napa Valley Sauvignon Blend 1994: Smooth and polished, sporting ripe, rich, complex pear, fig and citrus notes. Appealing to drink now. • $NA • (02/29/96) • **87**

Chevrignon Napa Valley Sauvignon Blend 1993: Smooth, harmonious and delicately herbal atop a layer of pretty apple and pear flavor. 10,600 cases made. • $8 • (05/15/95) • **85**

Chevrignon Napa Valley Sauvignon Blend 1992 • $9 • (04/15/94) BB • **87**

Chevrignon Napa Valley Sauvignon Blend 1991 • $10 • (06/15/93) • **84**

Merlot California Coastal Selection 1992: Crisp and fruity, with simple cherry and currant flavors and mild tannins. • $10 • (01/31/95) • **83**

Merlot Napa Valley 1992: Complex, rich and supple, with distinct herb, current, cherry and chocolate notes, part of the flavor coming from toasty oak. The texture is smooth, which make it quite appealing. • $18 • (01/31/96) • **90**

Merlot Napa Valley 1991: Firm and focused, with an herbal edge to the black cherry flavors, finishing a mite tannic. Drinkable now. 5,400 cases made. • $19 • (09/15/94) • **84**

Merlot Napa Valley 1990 • $18 • (06/30/93) • **89**

Merlot Napa Valley 1989 • $17 • (04/15/92) • **88**

Merlot Napa Valley 1988 • $16 • (12/31/90) • **81**

Merlot Napa Valley 1987 • $16 • (02/15/90) • **91**

Merlot Napa Valley 1986 • $16 • (08/31/89) • **86**

Merlot Napa Valley 1985 • $14 • (12/15/87) • **88**

Sémillon Late Harvest Napa Valley Botrytis 1986 • $15 • (12/31/88) • **86**

Sémillon Late Harvest Napa Valley Botrytis 1985 • $15 • (07/15/88) • **88**

Zyrah California Red 1993: Mature plum and berry notes fold together nicely, while spicy, peppery, gamy notes lend distinction. • $13 • **85**

VIEILLE MONTAGNE, LA | CALIFORNIA

Cabernet Sauvignon Napa Valley 1988 • $15 • (11/15/92) • **81**

Cabernet Sauvignon Napa Valley 1987 • $14 • (06/15/91) • **81**

Cabernet Sauvignon Napa Valley 1986 • $14 • (06/30/90) • **84**

VIGIL | CALIFORNIA

Cabernet Sauvignon Napa Valley NV: Earthy tobacco flavors course through this solid, black cherry-centered wine. It's tannic enough to need until 1997 or 1998 in the cellar. 93 cases made. • $12 • (12/15/95) • **84**

VILLA HELENA | CALIFORNIA

Cabernet Sauvignon Napa Valley Atlas Peak Baron von Kees Vineyard 1990: Dense, weedy and vegetal, this Cabernet is a difficult style to like. Tastes like grapes that didn't quite ripen from young, overcropped vines. Marginal quality. 700 cases made. • $22 • (11/15/93) • **71**

Viognier Napa Valley 1992 • $22 • (08/31/93) • **87**

VILLA MT. EDEN | CALIFORNIA

Cabernet Sauvignon California Cellar Select 1991: A good, simple, correct Cabernet without any extra dimensions. Drinks well now and is fairly priced. • $10 • (05/15/94) • **82**

Cabernet Sauvignon California Cellar Select 1990: Tight, firm and tannic, with a narrow band of plummy currant flavor and a crisp, firm finish. A lean style that could use a little more body and flesh. Drink now. • $10 • (03/31/93) • **83**

Cabernet Sauvignon California Cellar Select 1989 • $10 • (03/31/93) • **85**

Cabernet Sauvignon Mendocino Signature Series 1992: A firm, chunky debut wine that shows a tight, concentrated beam of cherry and currant, finishing with firm tannins and long, toasty aftertaste. 225 cases made. • $45 • (03/31/95) • **92**

Cabernet Sauvignon Napa Valley 1987 • $13 • (02/15/91) • **88**

Cabernet Sauvignon Napa Valley 1986 • $13 • (02/15/91) • **84**

Cabernet Sauvignon Napa Valley 1985 • $13 • (03/01/89) • **82**

Cabernet Sauvignon Napa Valley 1984 • $15 • (03/01/89) • **80**

Cabernet Sauvignon Napa Valley 1983 • $15 • (03/01/89) • **72**

Cabernet Sauvignon Napa Valley 1982 • $15 • (03/01/89) • **70**

Cabernet Sauvignon Napa Valley 1980 • $19 • (03/01/89) • **62**

Cabernet Sauvignon Napa Valley 1979 • $19 • (03/01/89) • **78**

Cabernet Sauvignon Napa Valley 1978 • $45 • (11/15/92) • **85**

Cabernet Sauvignon Napa Valley 1977 • $22 • (03/01/89) • **86**

Cabernet Sauvignon Napa Valley 1976 • $21 • (03/01/89) • **70**

Cabernet Sauvignon Napa Valley 1975 • $95 • (03/01/89) • **89**

Cabernet Sauvignon Napa Valley 1974 • $95 • (11/15/94) • **90**

Key: SS—Spectator Selection. CS—Cellar Selection. BB—Best Buy. $NA—Price not available. (BT)—Barrel tasting. Ⓐ—Auction Price.
Dates in parentheses represent the issues in which the ratings were published.

Cabernet Sauvignon Napa Valley Cellar Select 1988 • $8 • (07/15/92) BB • **85**

Cabernet Sauvignon Napa Valley Grand Reserve 1992: Young and tight, firmly tannic. The minty currant and berry flavors fight through, but on the finish the tannins show their raw side. Needs short-term cellaring to soften. 2,225 cases made. • $16 • (04/30/96) • **88**

Cabernet Sauvignon Napa Valley Grand Reserve 1991: Tight and somewhat green, with firm tannins. Enough ripe currant and berry flavor comes through to hold your interest. Drinkable now. 2,500 cases made. • $14 • (03/31/95) • **83**

Cabernet Sauvignon Napa Valley Grand Reserve 1990: Supple and complex with ripe, intense cherry and currant-scented fruit. Balanced with light oak shadings that peek through on the finish. Drinks well now but should hold through 1997 and beyond. 1,860 cases made. • $16 • (11/15/93) • **86**

Cabernet Sauvignon Napa Valley Grand Reserve 1989 • $14 • (10/31/92) • **84**

Cabernet Sauvignon Napa Valley Grand Reserve 1988 • $12 • (07/15/92) • **87**

Cabernet Sauvignon Napa Valley Reserve 1983 • $13 • (10/10/90) • **90**

Cabernet Sauvignon Napa Valley Reserve 1982 • $17 • (03/01/89) • **84**

Cabernet Sauvignon Napa Valley Reserve 1981 • $17 • (03/01/89) • **85**

Cabernet Sauvignon Napa Valley Reserve 1980 • $20 • (03/01/89) • **70**

Cabernet Sauvignon Napa Valley Reserve 1979 • $39 • (03/01/89) • **75**

Cabernet Sauvignon Napa Valley Reserve 1978 • $59 • (03/01/89) • **88**

Chardonnay California Cellar Select 1994: Crisp and flavorful, with pleasant pear and spice flavors that soften on the finish. 60,000 cases made. • $9 • (06/30/96) • **84**

Chardonnay California Cellar Select 1993: Ripe and fruity, revealing good depth and intensity to pear and apple notes, turns elegant on the finish. 40,000 cases made. • $8 • (04/30/95) • **85**

Chardonnay California Cellar Select 1991 • $10 • (03/15/93) • **84**

Chardonnay Carneros Grand Reserve 1993: Begins flamboyantly with its smoky, toasty, buttery oak and spicy pear and apple flavors, but turns smooth and complex, showing finesse and grace. 2,400 cases made. • $14 • (04/30/95) • **91**

Chardonnay Carneros Grand Reserve 1991 • $15 • (03/31/93) • **87**

Chardonnay Napa Valley Grand Reserve 1994: Rich, smooth and creamy, a complex and exotic style that offers lots of bold pear, spice, vanilla and hazelnut notes, picking up a citrus edge on the finish. Impressive flavor and texture. 3,000 cases made. • $16 • (04/30/96) • **92**

Chardonnay Santa Barbara County Signature Series 1993: Makes quite a statement about where Villa Mt. Eden is headed. Bold, ripe and creamy, with ultra rich tropical fruit, pear, honey, toast and spice flavors that fold together, finishing with excellent length, depth and concentration. Alas only 235 cases. 235 cases made. • $30 • (07/31/95) • **93**

Chardonnay Santa Maria Valley Bien Nacido Vineyard Signature Series 1994: A bold, ripe, rich and seductive style that places its pear, peach, honey and smoke flavors into a smooth, creamy texture. A trace of green plum adds to its complexity. Finishes amazingly plush and elegant. 500 cases made. • $30 • (05/31/96) • **94**

Merlot Napa Valley Grand Reserve 1994: Strives for elegance and grace with its understated cherry and berry flavors. Good, although lacking richness and concentration. 1,800 cases made. • $16 • (06/30/96) • **85**

Merlot Napa Valley Grand Reserve 1993: Elegant and medium bodied, showing pretty currant, cherry, tar and anise notes that finish with crisp tannins and good length. Ready now. • $16 • (12/31/95) • **86**

Merlot Napa Valley Grand Reserve 1991 • $15 • (05/31/94) • **88**

Merlot Napa Valley Grand Reserve 1990 • $15 • (03/31/93) • **88**

Pinot Blanc Santa Maria Valley Bien Nacido Vineyard Grand Reserve 1994: A complex white with an intriguing array of flavors-pretty pear, custard, toast and butterscotch-that play a unique counterpoint on the palate. • $16 • (01/31/96) • **88**

Pinot Blanc Santa Maria Valley Bien Nacido Vineyard Grand Reserve 1993: Bold, ripe and creamy, with a core of spice, pear, apple flavors that fold together nicely. 350 cases made. • $14 • (04/15/95) • **88**

Pinot Noir California Cellar Select 1994: Offers a modest core of plum and cherry flavors, but you won't feel shortchanged at this price. Drinkable now. 5,700 cases made. • $8 • (01/31/96) • **82**

Pinot Noir California Cellar Select 1993: Simple and correct, with a pleasant band of herb, cola, cherry and spice flavors. 3,500 cases made. • $8 • (03/31/95) • **83**

Pinot Noir Carneros Grand Reserve 1991 • $14 • (02/28/94) • **86**
Pinot Noir Napa Valley 1988 • $12 • (02/28/91) • **82**
Pinot Noir Napa Valley Tres Ninos Vineyard 1981 • $5 • (04/16/85) BB • **86**
Pinot Noir Santa Maria Valley Bien Nacido Vineyard Grand Reserve 1994: Good intensity and ripe flavors, with hints of cherry, raspberry and spice. Appealing for its aftertaste and light oak treatment. 1,400 cases made. • $12 • (01/31/96) • **86**
Pinot Noir Santa Maria Valley Bien Nacido Vineyard Grand Reserve 1993: Smooth and polished, with appealing cherry, vanilla and light spice notes. Delicate and pleasing. 374 cases made. • $14 • (03/31/95) • **84**
Sauvignon Blanc Late Harvest Napa Valley 1989 • $13/375ml • (04/30/91) • **83**
Sauvignon Blanc Late Harvest Napa Valley 1986 • $10/375ml • (05/15/88) • **89**
Zinfandel California Cellar Select 1993: Pleasantly balanced, with a nice mix of currant, black cherry and wild berry flavors. Firm tannins and a touch of oak are part of the appeal. Great value, and drinkable now through 1997. 10,000 cases made. • $8 • (09/15/95) BB • **88**
Zinfandel California Cellar Select 1992: Firm and compact, with a tight band of earthy, tarry fruit flavors and a shade of light oak. Drinks well now. 5,976 cases made. • $8 • (10/15/94) BB • **84**
Zinfandel California Cellar Select 1991 • $8 • (08/31/93) BB • **86**
Zinfandel California Cellar Select 1990 • $8 • (09/15/92) • **84**
Zinfandel California Cellar Select 1989 • $8 • (09/15/92) BB • **86**
Zinfandel Napa Valley 1986 • $8 • (12/15/88) • **90**
Zinfandel Sonoma Valley Monte Rosso Vineyard Grand Reserve 1993: Bold, ripe, complex, flavorful, offering rich, concentrated wild berry, plum, cherry and mint notes. Needs a little aging, as the tannins cling. 250 cases made. • $16 • (09/15/95) • **88**

VILLA ZAPU | CALIFORNIA

Cabernet Sauvignon Napa Valley 1988 • $20 • (11/15/91) • **86**
Cabernet Sauvignon Napa Valley 1986 • $16 • (10/31/89) • **79**

VINA VISTA | CALIFORNIA

Merlot 1988 • $12 • (05/31/92) • **86**
Merlot Alexander Valley 1985 • $8 • (10/31/87) • **90**

VINAS, LAS | CALIFORNIA

Cabernet Sauvignon California Private Reserve 1988 • $6 • (10/31/92) • **78**

VINE CLIFF | CALIFORNIA

Cabernet Sauvignon Napa Valley 1992: Lean, austere herb, currant, tobacco and light oak shadings. Could use more fruit generosity and depth and less tannin. 1,950 cases made. • $30 • (05/15/96) • **83**
Cabernet Sauvignon Napa Valley 1991: Well oaked and firmly tannic, but featuring a solid core of earthy currant and mineral flavors. Tannins turn leathery, needs cellaring until 1997 or 1998. 3,100 cases made. • $25 • (04/30/95) • **88**
Cabernet Sauvignon Napa Valley 1990: Tight and firm with hard tannins and a chewy core of cherry and herb. Not showing any finesse or suppleness at this stage and the flavors border on being unripe. Perhaps with time it will be more appealing. Approach after 1998. 3,000 cases made. • $35 • (11/15/93) • **85**
Chardonnay Napa Valley 1994: Remarkably complex and well focused, with a pretty core of ripe pear and citrus flavors couched in light spicy oak shadings. Still a bit rough around the edges, but should improve by 1997. 1,000 cases made. • $23 • (05/31/96) • **90**
Chardonnay Napa Valley Proprietress Reserve 1993: Intensely spicy on the nose and palate, featuring tight apple and pear flavors supported by tart acidity. 675 cases made. • $35 • (05/31/95) • **89**

VINEYARD 29 | CALIFORNIA

Cabernet Sauvignon Napa Valley 1993: Firm and trim, with an attractive band of currant, coffee, anise and cedar. A well-proportioned, moderately rich and complex young red that finishes with mild tannins. New from Tom Paine's and Teresa Norton's vineyard in St. Helena, produced at Grace Family Vineyards. Drinkable now. 200 cases made. • $33 • (03/31/96) • **88**

VITA NOVA | CALIFORNIA

Red Central Coast 1994: Smooth and spicy, with yellow bell pepper and red cherry notes that are elegant and polished on the finish. 200 cases made. • $16 • (06/15/96) • **83**
Reservatum Santa Barbara County Cabernet Blend 1986 • $20 • (12/15/89) • **87**

VON STRASSER | CALIFORNIA

Cabernet Sauvignon Diamond Valley Mountain 1994: Trim and firm, with an earthy edge to the currant and berry notes. Austere tannins on the finish. 1,400 cases made. • $30 • (05/31/95) • **85-89** (BT)
Cabernet Sauvignon Napa Valley Diamond Mountain 1993: Attractive floral and blackberry flavors follow through on the palate, picking up a nice, toasty, smoky oak feel. Firmly tannic but balanced, it should be drinking well around 1998. 1,173 cases made. • $28 • (04/30/96) • **89**
Cabernet Sauvignon Napa Valley Diamond Mountain 1992: Earthy currant and cherry flavors are submerged beneath the tannins, but it's rich and concentrated, needs cellaring until 1997. 987 cases made. • $28 • (02/28/95) • **88**
Cabernet Sauvignon Napa Valley Diamond Mountain 1991: Ripe and chewy, youthful and tannic, so rough in texture thay you might miss the ripe currant, plum and mint fruit rushing in on the finish. Needs until 1998 or 2000 to settle down. 829 cases made. • $25 • (03/31/94) • **88**
Cabernet Sauvignon Napa Valley Diamond Mountain 1990: Firm and chunky in texture, with mint and currant aromas and flavors vying for attention, finishing with a solid core of flavor that shows through the veil of tannins. Best after 1996. 750 cases made. • $25 • (11/15/93) • **87**
Chardonnay Napa Valley 1994: Spicy, mature pear and citrus flavors dominate in this classy Chardonnay. 406 cases made. • $30 • (06/15/96) • **86**

VOSE | CALIFORNIA

Cabernet Sauvignon Napa Valley 1978 • $NA • (11/15/92) • **76**

VOSS | CALIFORNIA

Chardonnay Napa Valley 1993: Smooth and elegant, balanced between ripe fruit and oak, adding a finish that showcases fig, melon, toasty oak and pear flavors. Shows more complexity and depth on aftertaste. • $NA • (02/29/96) • **89**
Chardonnay Napa Valley 1992: Earthy, lively, green and lean, adding a minty edge to the apple flavors. • $13 • (02/28/95) • **85**
Chardonnay Napa Valley 1991 • $16 • (01/31/93) • **85**
Merlot Napa Valley 1993: Austere and astringent with a green, tannic, bitter edge to the plum and currant flavors. 1,300 cases made. • $16 • (05/31/96) • **75**
Merlot Napa Valley 1992: Tight and firm, with a compact band of currant, cedary oak and herb notes. 1,500 cases made. • $15 • (04/15/95) • **83**
Merlot Napa Valley 1991: Lean and green, this is a hard-edged Merlot with more tobacco and cedar flavors than fruit. Drinkable now. Tasted twice with consistent notes. 1,500 cases made. • $18 • (09/15/94) • **75**
Sauvignon Blanc Napa Valley 1994: Ripe and flavorful, the pear and apple fruit laced with distinctly varietal floral and grassy characters. Finishes tasty. 1,900 cases made. • $9 • (07/31/95) • **87**
Sauvignon Blanc Napa Valley 1993: Fresh and lively, with a fruity center and nice anise and herbal overtones, distinctly varietal and nicely balanced. Drink soon while it's fresh. 1,375 cases made. • $10 • (08/31/94) • **88**
Zinfandel Alexander Valley 1992: Soft and raisiny, the tannic, bitter finish seems to bite back. May be better after 1996. • $13 • (01/31/95) • **77**
Zinfandel Alexander Valley 1991 • $13 • (05/31/93) • **88**

WAGNER | New York

Chardonnay Finger Lakes Grace House 1993: Toasty oak notes are pleasant, if dominant, but there's enough green apple flavor to carry this crisp, round white through a clean finish. • $10 • (01/31/96) • **83**

Chardonnay Finger Lakes Grace House 1991: Rather earthy and smoky in flavor, with a creamy flavor that needs more fruit and freshness to support it. Drinkable but dull. 900 cases made. • $12 • **75**

Gewürztraminer Finger Lakes 1993: Bland and has little fruit. The acidity makes this a good palate cleanser, but it lacks Gewürz character. • $8 • (01/31/96) • **78**

Gewürztraminer Finger Lakes 1991: What we like in Gewürztraminer, with fresh fruit and floral aromas and slightly sweet flavors that become more complex as you sip. Has great balance and appeal. • $8 • (06/30/95) • **85**

Johannisberg Riesling Finger Lakes 1994: The Riesling character of peaches is there but a bit diluted, and the full-bodied wine needs more acidity to balance the sweetness. • $8 • (01/31/96) • **80**

Johannisberg Riesling Finger Lakes 1991: Grapey, spicy aromas and nearly dry flavors of apple and herbs make this an interesting, complex white that is evolving well with age. Could use more harmony, but is balanced and drinkable. • $8 • (09/15/94) • **83**

Johannisberg Riesling Finger Lakes Fermented Dry 1994: Round and full in body, this shows a mix of exotic flavors—pineapple, banana and vegetal—that add up to less than the sum of its parts. • $8 • (01/31/96) • **78**

Johannisberg Riesling Finger Lakes Fermented Dry 1991: An austere style of Riesling that's marked by smoky aromas, mineral and earthy flavors, and a narrow band of tart fruit flavors that reminds us of lemon and grapefruit. Clean and bracing in balance, but not very flavorful. 290 cases made. • $8 • **82**

Johannisberg Riesling Finger Lakes Ice Wine 1990: This bold, exotic wine gives you quite a ride, but finally doesn't quite get you home. The flavors are an odd mixture of honey, candied cherry and cabbage, sweet and tart at once. 290 cases made. • $15 • **76**

Johannisberg Riesling Late Harvest Finger Lakes Ice Wine 1989 • $14 • (01/31/92) • **85**

Ravat Blanc Finger Lakes Ice Wine 1990: Attractive aromas of spice, créme brulée and tobacco give way to orange and honey flavors on the palate, which is sweet but also quite tart, even hard. There's character and complexity, but it lacks harmony. Drink now. 600 cases made. • $14 • **79**

WASHINGTON HILLS | Washington

Cabernet-Merlot Columbia Valley 1992: Currant and berry flavors emerge smoothly through a chewy layer of fine tannins, making this approachable now. 4,200 cases made. • $8 • (08/31/94) • **83**

Cabernet-Merlot Columbia Valley Varietal Select 1993: Lean and a little chewy, appealing cherry and tarry flavors showing on the finish. Best in 1997. 3,500 cases made. • $9 • (09/30/95) • **83**

Cabernet Sauvignon Columbia Valley Varietal Select 1993: Lean and chewy, flirting with oak up front, but ripe fruit comes bouncing back on the tannic finish, echoing currant and plum. 3,500 cases made. • $9 • (09/30/95) • **86**

Chardonnay Columbia Valley 1992: Round and generous, a full-bodied white that leans distinctly in the direction of fruit, offering bright nectarine and apple on the lively finish. Drinkable now. 6,000 cases made. • $8 • (09/30/94) • **85**

Chardonnay Columbia Valley Varietal Select 1991 • $9 • (06/15/93) • **76**

Chenin Blanc Columbia Valley Dry 1992: Has a greenish edge to the dry, spicy flavors. • $6 • (09/30/94) • **78**

Gewürztraminer Columbia Valley 1993: Light and soft, with appealing rose petal-scented melon flavors, finishing light and a little sweet. 2,500 cases made. • $6 • (09/30/94) • **81**

Key: SS—Spectator Selection. CS—Cellar Selection. BB—Best Buy. $NA—Price not available. (BT)—Barrel tasting. Ⓐ—Auction Price.
Dates in parentheses represent the issues in which the ratings were published.

Gewürztraminer Columbia Valley Varietal Select 1994: Remarkably fresh and vibrant, off-dry, like biting into a fresh peach with lovely spice and floral overtones. 1,466 cases made. • $7 • (09/30/95) • **85**

Gewürztraminer Columbia Valley Varietal Select 1991 • $6 • (06/15/93) • **80**

Johannisberg Riesling Columbia Valley 1993: Off-dry, smooth and silky, shows very pretty apple and apricot flavors, finishing generously. 4,800 cases made. • $6 • (09/30/94) BB • **86**

Johannisberg Riesling Columbia Valley Varietal Select 1994: Smooth and lightly sweet, generous peach, pear and delicate pine flavors. Drink while it is fresh. 3,118 cases made. • $7 • (09/15/95) • **86**

Merlot Columbia Valley 1992: Firm in texture, spicy and toasty in flavor, a light-weight red with a modest level of plum notes to balance. Drinkable now. • $9 • (09/30/94) • **81**

Merlot Columbia Valley Varietal Select 1993: Broad and supple, concentrating its plum, currant and tar flavors in a slightly chewy package. Best in 1997. 2,700 cases made. • $9 • (09/30/95) • **85**

Riesling Columbia Valley Varietal Select Dry 1993: Lean, light and gently fruity, echoing green apple and peach flavors on the finish. Just off-dry. 1,500 cases made. • $6 • (09/15/95) • **84**

Sauvignon Blanc Columbia Valley Varietal Select 1993: Doesn't quite come together, citrusy and sharp, but some raw nectarine flavor follows through as well. 1,000 cases made. • $7 • (09/30/95) • **80**

Sémillon Chardonnay Columbia Valley 1992: Sturdy, fresh, floral and medium-weight, finishing slightly bitter. • $7 • (09/30/94) • **80**

Sémillon Chardonnay Columbia Valley 1991 • $7 • (04/30/93) • **75**

Sémillon Sauvignon Blanc Columbia Valley 1991 • $7 • (04/30/93) BB • **84**

Seyval Blanc Columbia Valley Varietal Select 1993: Strange medicinal flavors run through this pineapple-scented white, lingering juicily on the finish. Ready now. 1,000 cases made. • $7 • (09/30/95) • **82**

White Riesling Columbia Valley Special Harvest 1993: Lightly sweet and delicately honeyed, not rich, but it offers creamy pineapple and floral flavors. Drinkable now. 1,800 cases made. • $6 • (09/30/94) BB • **86**

White Riesling Columbia Valley Varietal Select Special Harvest 1993: Tries to be crisply balanced, but lacks the intensity to show much fruit up front. Has some nice spicy notes on the finish. 1,786 cases made. • $7 • (09/30/95) • **81**

WATERBROOK | Washington

Cabernet Sauvignon Columbia Valley 1993: Ripe and generous, a mouthful of spicy black cherry and berry flavors, feeling almost thick on the palate. Needs time to open up, at least until 1998 or '99. 1,100 cases made. • $18 • (12/15/95) • **88**

Cabernet Sauvignon Columbia Valley 1992: A ripe, sweet and silky Washington Cab that has spicy black cherry and currant flavors, and is a fine value. It hints at smoke and mocha on the lingering finish. 1,425 cases made. • $16 • (04/15/95) SS • **91**

Cabernet Sauvignon Columbia Valley 1991: Generous, spicy and chewy, with lavish tannins, exotic flavors and a nice core of berry and cherry notes. Marked by oak, it should be fine by 1998 or 1999. 450 cases made. • $15 • (09/30/94) • **88**

Cabernet Sauvignon Columbia Valley 1989 • $13 • (10/15/93) • **86**

Cabernet Sauvignon Columbia Valley 1988 • $14 • (04/15/92) • **85**

Chardonnay Columbia Valley 1994: A bright, ripe and fruity Washington white that offers good flavors for the dollars. A nice thread of spicy oak runs through this to balance it out. Drinkable now. 11,500 cases made. • $10 • (12/15/95) BB • **87**

Chardonnay Columbia Valley 1993: A lean and intensely focused Washington white. Deftly balanced, showing nice hints of nectarine and pear flavors on the lively finish. 14,808 cases made. • $9 • (12/31/94) BB • **88**

Chardonnay Columbia Valley 1992: Strikes a nice balance between fruit, oak and spice, with layers of apple, apricot and nectarine that are framed by toasty oak. Gains intensity on the finish. Drinkable now. 13,000 cases made. • $9 • (12/15/93) SS • **89**

Chardonnay Columbia Valley Barrel Fermented Reserve 1992: Strives for complexity, but it's rough around the edges, with a tart grapefruit and pear edge that finishes with a blunt edge. Drinkable now. 960 cases made. • $12 • (12/15/93) • **81**

Chardonnay Walla Walla Valley Cottonwood Creek Estate 1993: Bright and spicy, a nicely sculpted wine that shows facets of pear, spice, vanilla and citrus. Appealing to drink now. 249 cases made. • $14 • (12/31/94) • **89**

Merlot Columbia Valley 1993: Rich, smooth and spicy, its fine tannins nicely integrated with the dark plum and black cherry flavor, long and fragrant. Approachable now, best in 1997-'98. 2,000 cases made. • $18 • (05/15/96) • **90**

Merlot Columbia Valley 1992: Bright, supple and flavorful, an immediately enjoyable red that displays its vanilla bean-scented berry and black cherry notes on a seductive frame. Ready now. 833 cases made. • $15 • (09/30/95) • **90**

Merlot Columbia Valley 1991 • $14 • (12/31/93) • **86**

Merlot Columbia Valley 1990 • $15 • (06/15/93) • **84**

Merlot Columbia Valley 1989 • $14 • (04/30/92) • **94**

Merlot Columbia Valley Reserve 1992: Smooth, elegant and nicely nuanced as plum, blackberry and spice flavors weave through supple textures. Delicious to drink now, but has the stuffing to improve through 1997. 491 cases made. • $22 • (05/31/95) • **89**

Sauvignon Blanc Columbia Valley 1993: Soft and creamy, with tasty, slightly leafy apple and vanilla flavors that echo a touch of oak. Drinkable now. 1,400 cases made. • $9 • (03/31/95) • **86**

Sauvignon Blanc Columbia Valley 1992 • $9 • (12/31/93) BB • **87**

Sauvignon Blanc Columbia Valley 1991 • $9 • (07/31/93) • **89**

WATSON | CALIFORNIA

Pinot Noir Santa Maria Valley Bien Nacido Vineyard 1986 • $9 • (12/15/89) • **77**

WEIBEL | CALIFORNIA

Brut Mendocino County 1982 • $13 • (09/15/86) • **77**

Cabernet Sauvignon Mendocino County 1988 • $8 • (03/15/92) BB • **81**

Cabernet Sauvignon Mendocino County 1987 • $8 • (02/28/91) BB • **84**

Cabernet Sauvignon Mendocino Limited Reserve 1989 • $10 • (11/15/93) • **77**

Pinot Noir Mendocino County 1988 • $6 • (02/28/91) • **74**

WEINSTOCK | CALIFORNIA

Cabernet Sauvignon Sonoma County 1992: Smoky, herbal flavors finish with a cedary bite, a tough wine that needs until 1997 or so to smooth out the tannic wrinkles. 4,000 cases made. • $9 • (05/31/95) • **85**

Gamay Sonoma County 1989 • $8 • (03/31/91) • **75**

Pinot Noir Sonoma County Winemaker Selection Reserve 1989 • $13 • (11/15/91) • **79**

WELLINGTON | CALIFORNIA

Cabernet Franc Mount Veeder 1990 • $13 • (11/15/92) • **80**

Cabernet Sauvignon Mount Veeder Random Ridge 1992: Firm and tannic, showing a narrow beam of spicy berry flavor. Needs until 1998-2000. 280 cases made. • $16 • (12/15/95) • **83**

Cabernet Sauvignon Mount Veeder Random Ridge 1991: An earthy style with racy flavors but it holds together, delivering just enough currant and plum notes to offset the earthiness. 415 cases made. • $16 • (11/15/94) • **84**

Cabernet Sauvignon Mount Veeder Random Ridge 1990: Ripe and earthy, a mouthful of flavor in a relatively light- textured wine, echoing spices and plums on the silky finish. Needs until 1998 to loosen up the tannins. 234 cases made. • $16 • (10/15/93) • **86**

Cabernet Blend Mount Veeder Random Ridge 1989 • $16 • (11/15/92) • **86**

Cabernet Sauvignon Sonoma County Mohrhardt Ridge Vineyard 1992: Lean, toasty and a little jammy, working in a nice range of raspberry, anise and mineral flavors at a modest level. Needs until 1997-1998. 490 cases made. • $14 • (12/15/95) • **84**

Cabernet Sauvignon Sonoma County Mohrhardt Ridge Vineyard 1991: Spicy, ripe plum, cherry and currant flavors are focused and lively, staying with you on the finish. Well proportioned. 464 cases made. • $14 • (11/15/94) • **85**

Cabernet Sauvignon Sonoma County Mohrhardt Ridge Vineyard 1990: Robust and full-bodied, with plenty of currant and black cherry flavors and plenty of tannins, too. There's not much oak in this solid and fruity—but young and rough—Cabernet. Best to drink now. 390 cases made. • $14 • (09/15/93) • **83**

Cabernet Sauvignon Sonoma County Mohrhardt Ridge Vineyard 1989 • $14 • (08/31/92) • **85**

Cabernet Sauvignon Sonoma Valley Glen Lyon Vineyard 1993: Light and brightly focused, a mouthful of minty, earthy berry flavors that finish solidly, if not with great depth. 215 cases made. • $14 • (12/15/95) • **84**

Chardonnay Sonoma County Barrel Fermented Lot 2 1993: Floral and perfumed, with a narrow band of spicy pear and apricot flavors, finishing with chewy oak notes. 590 cases made. • $8 • (07/31/95) • **81**

Chardonnay Sonoma Valley 1994: Simple, with a modest band of spicy pear, citrus and light oak notes, but nothing more. 520 cases made. • $11 • (06/30/96) • **84**

Chardonnay Sonoma Valley Barrel Fermented 1993: Potently floral and perfumed, with a strong wood and honeysuccle edge that dominates. Gains more fruit on the finish. 450 cases made. • $12 • (07/31/95) • **84**

Chardonnay Sonoma Valley Barrel Fermented 1992: Crisp and perfumed, but not in a grapey way. A strange candied edge doesn't help. 800 cases made. • $11 • (06/30/94) • **70**

Chardonnay Sonoma Valley Barrel Fermented 1991 • $11 • (06/15/93) • **88**

Criolla Sonoma Valley Old Vines Red 1991 • $7 • (06/15/93) • **85**

Criolla Sonoma Valley Old Vines Red 1990 • $7 • (03/31/92) • **85**

Merlot Sonoma County 1992: Tight and firm, with a good dose of tannin too, but enough cherry, herb and plum fruit and cedary oak to give it added dimensions. 784 cases made. • $15 • (11/15/95) • **86**

Merlot Sonoma County 1991: A little chewy, but the minty currant aromas and flavors land solidly around the tannins. Drinkable now. 720 cases made. • $11 • (09/15/94) • **85**

Merlot Sonoma Valley 1993: Crisp and trim, with medium-depth herb, tobacco and cherry flavors. 600 cases made. • $15 • **83**

Syrah Russian River Valley Alegría Vineyards 1993: Ripe and elegant, spreading out its slightly gamy plum, pepper and berry flavors and well-integrated tannins on a round structure. Drink now. 172 cases made. • $12 • (09/30/95) • **89**

Zinfandel Sonoma County Old Vines 1993: Pungently earthy, with a funky barnyard streak that runs through the flavors. Marginal. 540 cases made. • $9 • (10/15/95) • **72**

Zinfandel Sonoma Valley 100-Year-Old Vines 1993: Offers flavors that stretch from tart cherry to ripe wild berry and dark fruit. Finishes earthy and with firm tannins. 203 cases made. • $15 • (10/15/95) • **87**

Zinfandel Sonoma Valley 100-Year-Old Vines 1992: Ripe, bright black cherry, wild berry and plum flavors. Supple and generous, delicious now, but should hold in the cellar. 193 cases made. • $13 • (10/15/94) • **87**

Zinfandel Sonoma Valley Casa Santinamaria 1993: Has potential. Offers attractive wild berry and cherry flavors, but right now, it loses some focus on the finish, which should improve with age. 540 cases made. • $12 • (10/15/95) • **86**

Zinfandel Sonoma Valley Casa Santinamaria 1992: Dark, ripe and intense, with jammy cherry and wild berry flavors that turn supple and earthy on the finish. Drinks well now through 1998. 280 cases made. • $10 • (10/15/94) • **84**

WENTE | CALIFORNIA

Blanc de Blancs Arroyo Seco NV • $14 • (12/31/93) • **82**

Blanc de Noir Arroyo Seco 1983 • $15 • (03/31/89) • **78**

Blanc de Noir Arroyo Seco NV • $14 • (12/31/93) • **85**

Brut Arroyo Seco 1983 • $10 • (08/31/88) • **79**

Brut Arroyo Seco 1982 • $8 • (12/31/86) • **84**

Brut Arroyo Seco 1981 • $8 • (04/01/86) • **78**

Brut Arroyo Seco Grande Brut NV • $12 • (12/31/93) • **82**

Cabernet Sauvignon California 1981 • $7 • (12/16/85) • **65**

Cabernet Sauvignon Central Coast 1985 • $8 • (11/15/89) • **78**

Cabernet Sauvignon Livermore Valley 1991: Leans toward the earthy, leathery spectrum, turning dry on the finish. A good 1991 that's ready to drink. • $10 • (11/15/94) • **82**

Cabernet Sauvignon Livermore Valley Charles Wetmore Vineyard Estate Reserve 1989 • $18 • (11/15/93) • **85**

Cabernet Sauvignon Livermore Valley Charles Wetmore Vineyard Estate Reserve 1987 • $18 • (04/30/91) • **86**

Cabernet Sauvignon Livermore Valley Charles Wetmore Vineyard Reserve 1990: Leans toward the herbal spectrum but has enough currant and spicy Cabernet fruit to maintain interest. The texture is smooth and supple and the flavors linger. Drink after 1996. • $16 • (08/31/94) • **86**
Cabernet Sauvignon Livermore Valley Estate Reserve 1986 • $12 • (10/15/90) • **82**
Cabernet Sauvignon Livermore Valley Wente Family Estate Selection 1993: A sturdy California wine that offers a lot for a fair price. The solid, beet-scented berry and herb flavors pick up interesting notes of spice and pickle barrel on the finish. Drinkable now. 28,000 cases made. • $8 • (11/15/95) BB • **85**
Cabernet Sauvignon Livermore Valley Wente Family Estate Selection 1990: An herbal style with smoky tobacco notes that turn austere and tight. Could use a little more generosity and depth. Fades out on the finish. Drinkable now through 1997. 15,000 cases made. • $8 • (11/15/93) • **81**
Chardonnay Arroyo Seco Riva Ranch 1993: Smooth and satiny, wrapping its light pineapple and pear notes around a core of spicy, toasty flavors. Finishes in a flourish. Ready now. 1,000 cases made. • $8 • (05/15/96) • **85**
Chardonnay Arroyo Seco Riva Ranch 1992: Smooth and silky, with elegant pear, spice and honey notes, medium bodied and well crafted. • $12 • (07/31/95) • **85**
Chardonnay Arroyo Seco Riva Ranch 1991 • $12 • (07/15/93) • **87**
Chardonnay Central Coast 1994: Light and straightforward, with modest apple and vaguely toasty flavors. Drinkable now. 40,000 cases made. • $9 • (06/15/96) • **81**
Chardonnay Central Coast Estate Grown 1992: Fresh and spicy, with pleasant apple, pear and nutmeg aromas and flavors that remain light and fragrant through the finish. Drinkable now. 80,000 cases made. • $9 • (07/15/93) BB • **84**
Chardonnay Central Coast Estate Grown 1991 • $8 • (07/15/92) SS • **91**
Chardonnay Central Coast Wente Family Estate Selection 1993: A crisp, slightly coarse texture, but appealing pear and apple flavors. Drinkable now. 40,000 cases made. • $9 • (04/30/95) • **85**
Chardonnay Livermore Valley Herman Wente Reserve 1994: Elegant and refreshing, with spicy pear, tangerine, citrus and smoky oak flavors that add dimension and complexity to the finish. 2,000 cases made. • $22 • (06/30/96) • **88**
Chardonnay Livermore Valley Herman Wente Vineyard Estate Reserve 1993: Round, spicy and generous, marked by barrel fermentation and aging, finishing smooth and long. Manages substantial richness. 3,000 cases made. • $14 • (09/30/95) • **88**
Chardonnay Livermore Valley Herman Wente Vineyard Reserve 1991 • $15 • (07/15/93) • **88**
Merlot Livermore Valley Crane Ridge 1993: Rings true for the varietal, with herb, currant, cherry and berry flavors that finish with light, toasty oak shadings. 9,000 cases made. • $13 • **84**
Merlot Livermore Valley Crane Ridge 1991: An oaky, earthy style that gets more intersting with every sip, revealing more ripe cherry and plum flavors. Finishes with soft tannins, ready now through 1998. Tasted twice with consistent results. 3,000 cases made. • $12 • (09/15/94) • **84**
Merlot Livermore Valley Crane Ridge 1990 • $12 • (12/31/93) • **84**
Petite Sirah Livermore Valley 1981 • $5 • (12/01/85) • **61**
Riesling Late Harvest Arroyo Seco Auslese 1973 • $NA • (02/28/87) • **95**
Riesling Late Harvest Arroyo Seco November Harvest Reserve Arroyo Seco Vin 1987 • $12 • (07/15/90) • **76**
Sauvignon Blanc Livermore Valley Estate Grown 1991 • $7 • (11/15/93) • **80**
Sauvignon Blanc Livermore Valley Wente Family Estate Selection 1993: Spicy, smooth pineapple and herb flavors extend into a generous finish. Value-priced and drinkable now. 10,000 cases made. • $7 • (06/30/95) BB • **85**
Sauvignon Blanc Livermore Valley Wente Family Estate Selection 1992: Simple and soft, with a hint of apple and a pleasant grassy edge. 5,000 cases made. • $8 • (08/31/94) • **83**
Sémillon Livermore Valley 1991 • $7 • (09/30/93) • **80**
Zinfandel Livermore Valley Special Selection Raboli Vineyards 1985 • $10 • (12/15/89) • **77**

WESTWOOD | CALIFORNIA

Barbera El Dorado Ritchie Vineyard 1991 • $7 • (12/15/92) • **81**
Pinot Noir California 1991 • $10 • (02/28/93) • **73**
Pinot Noir California 1990 • $9 • (09/30/92) • **82**
Pinot Noir California 1989 • $9 • (04/30/91) • **75**
Pinot Noir Napa Valley Haynes Vineyard Reserve 1989 • $18 • (02/28/93) • **82**

WHALER | CALIFORNIA

Zinfandel Mendocino 1992: Firmly tannic, with a supple wild berry and blueberry flavor profile that's pleasing. Drinkable now. 1,251 cases made. • $10 • (10/15/94) • **84**
Zinfandel Mendocino 1991 • $10 • (09/30/93) • **84**
Zinfandel Mendocino 1990 • $10 • (10/15/92) • **81**
Zinfandel Mendocino 1989 • $10 • (10/15/92) • **83**
Zinfandel Mendocino Flagship 1992: The ripe, juicy plum and black cherry flavors are focused and lively. Firm tannins and good length on the finish. 443 cases made. • $14 • (10/15/94) • **87**
Zinfandel Mendocino Flagship 1991 • $14 • (09/30/93) • **87**
Zinfandel Mendocino Flagship 1990 • $14 • (10/15/92) • **85**

WHEELER | CALIFORNIA

Cabernet Sauvignon Dry Creek Valley 1989 • $12 • (06/15/93) • **81**
Cabernet Sauvignon Dry Creek Valley 1988 • $15 • (08/31/92) • **83**
Cabernet Sauvignon Dry Creek Valley 1987 • $14 • (11/15/91) • **84**
Cabernet Sauvignon Dry Creek Valley 1986 • $12 • (08/31/90) • **83**
Cabernet Sauvignon Dry Creek Valley 1985 • $12 • (07/15/89) • **76**
Cabernet Sauvignon Dry Creek Valley 1984 • $11 • (04/15/88) • **75**
Cabernet Sauvignon Dry Creek Valley Norse Vineyard Private Reserve 1985 • $18 • (11/15/90) • **83**
Cabernet Sauvignon Dry Creek Valley Norse Vineyard Private Reserve 1984 • $15 • (07/31/89) • **60**
Cabernet Sauvignon Dry Creek Valley Norse Vineyards Reserve 1991: Firm and compact, with medium-weight spice, vanilla and black cherry flavors that linger on the finish. Drinkable now. 2,200 cases made. • $12 • (11/15/94) • **84**
Chardonnay Sonoma County 1993: Good intensity and depth for the vintage, with a complex core of honey, pear, vanilla and spice, turning elegant on the finsh. 6,000 cases made. • $11 • (07/31/95) • **84**
Chardonnay Sonoma County 1992: Complex and flavorful, with toasty, buttery oak overshadowing the spicy pear flavor underneath, it's rich and focused and the flavors linger. Ready now. 5,500 cases made. • $11 • (04/30/94) • **87**
Chardonnay Sonoma County 1991 • $13 • (04/15/93) • **91**
Fumé Blanc Dry Creek Valley 1991 • $8 • (07/31/93) • **81**
Fumé Blanc Sonoma County 1992: Smooth and distinctly herbal, adding in minty notes that carry through the finish against a citrus-and-pear background. 2,600 cases made. • $7 • (10/15/94) BB • **86**
Merlot Dry Creek Valley 1992: Tries to be ripe and broad, but comes a little off balance, citrusy at the center and chewy at the edges. Best from 1997. 1,500 cases made. • $12 • (04/15/95) • **79**
Quintet California Red 1990 • $7 • (05/31/93) • **76**
RS Reserve California Red 1989 • $11 • (10/31/91) • **77**
RS Reserve California Red 1988 • $10 • (08/31/90) • **83**
Zinfandel Dry Creek Valley 1992: Well oaked and polished, with attractive cherry, wild berry and plum flavors that gain complexity and finesse through the finish. Drinkable now, even with the tannins. 2,500 cases made. • $11 • (08/31/95) • **87**
Zinfandel Dry Creek Valley 1991 • $12 • (09/30/93) • **80**

WHITCRAFT | CALIFORNIA

Chardonnay Santa Maria Valley Bien Nacido Vineyard 1994: Filled with flavors of pear, spice, honey and nectarine. Perhaps in time a little

Key: SS—Spectator Selection. CS—Cellar Selection. BB—Best Buy. $NA—Price not available. (BT)—Barrel tasting. Ⓐ—Auction Price.
Dates in parentheses represent the issues in which the ratings were published.

more polish and finesse will develop as well. 950 cases made. • $17 • (06/15/96) • **88**

Chardonnay Santa Maria Valley Bien Nacido Vineyard 1993: Intense, bright, sharply focused, with tart citrus, pineapple and pear notes that lead to a pretty, nectarine-laced finish. 585 cases made. • $22 • (05/31/95) • **89**

Chardonnay Santa Maria Valley Bien Nacido Vineyard 1992: Broad and buttery, already tasting mature and woody, finishing with a sense of sweetness. Earthy and distinctive, seems a little out of whack. 550 cases made. • $20 • (12/31/93) • **85**

Chardonnay Santa Ynez Valley Sanford & Benedict Vineyard 1994: Clean and correct, showing a trim band of leesy pear and light, toasty oak shadings. Comes across as an elegant, understated white. 120 cases made. • $35 • (05/15/96) • **88**

Pinot Noir Russian River Valley Olivet Lane Vineyard 1992 • $30 • (02/28/94) • **90**

Pinot Noir Russian River Valley Olivet Lane Vineyard 1991 • $25 • (02/28/93) • **81**

Pinot Noir Santa Maria Valley Bien Nacido Vineyard 1994: Dark, rich and intense, with a wonderful array of flavors, tiers of black cherry, mineral and leather accented by a meaty, smoky edge that turns complex and concentrated. Shows a measure of finesse to match its intensity. 200 cases made. • $30 • (12/31/95) • **93**

Pinot Noir Santa Maria Valley Bien Nacido Vineyard 1993: Bright and lively, with fresh, ripe, elegant cherry, strawberry and plum notes, picking up a leathery edge on the finish when the tannins kick in. Drinkable now. 225 cases made. • $30 • (12/31/94) • **88**

Pinot Noir Santa Maria Valley Bien Nacido Vineyard 1992 • $30 • (02/28/94) • **88**

Pinot Noir Santa Maria Valley Bien Nacido Vineyard 1991 • $25 • (02/28/93) • **83**

Pinot Noir Santa Maria Valley Bien Nacido Vineyard 1990 • $25 • (02/28/93) • **88**

Pinot Noir Santa Maria Valley Bien Nacido Vineyard N 1994: Starts out smooth and elegant, as tart black cherry, cola and herb notes pick up earthy mushroom on the finish. Shows its tannic strength on aftertaste, but altogether well proportioned. 160 cases made. • $40 • (05/15/96) • **89**

Pinot Noir Santa Maria Valley Bien Nacido Vineyard N 1993: A touch earthy and gamy with a smoked bacon and leathery, picking up a hint of plum and cherry-laced fruit, which has to work to emerge through the tannins. 200 cases made. • $35 • **87**

Pinot Noir Santa Maria Valley Bien Nacido Vineyard Q 1994: Austere but still quite flavorful, a more tightly reined-in style that shows lots of detail to the flavors. Picks up black cherry, herb and minty notes, finishing with a tannic, slightly coarse edge. 175 cases made. • $35 • **88**

Pinot Noir Santa Maria Valley Bien Nacido Vineyard Q 1993: A shade denser and more compact than the other bottling, it delivers ripe plum and currant flavors on the finish. Modest tannins make it approachable now. Q is a section of Bien Nacido Vineyard that is primarily planted with the Pommard clone. 225 cases made. • $35 • (12/31/94) • **89**

Pinot Noir Santa Maria Valley Bien Nacido Vineyard Q 1992 • $40 • (02/28/94) • **88**

Pinot Noir Sonoma Coast Hirsch Vineyard 1994: Uncommonly dark, rich and exotic, truly distinctive, showing wild berry, black cherry, anise and vanilla flavors. Color and richness of the fruit may throw you, but this is wonderfully complex and compelling. 50 cases made. • $40 • (05/15/96) • **92**

WHITE HERON | WASHINGTON

Chantepierre Washington Cabernet Blend 1992: Lean and a bit tannic, herbal notes mingling with the modest plum and spicy prune flavors. Best in 1996. 500 cases made. • $10 • (09/30/95) • **80**

Chantepierre Washington Cabernet Blend 1990: Chunky, with modest cedar-tinged berry flavors, edging toward tobacco and herbs on the finish. Chewy enough to need until 1997. 500 cases made. • $10 • (09/30/94) • **83**

Chantepierre Washington Cabernet Blend 1989 • $10 • (03/15/93) • **70**

Chantepierre Washington Cabernet Blend 1988 • $11 • (04/15/92) • **80**

Pinot Noir Washington 1990: Light, soft and mature, modest berry and plum flavors echoing against the spicy overtones. Drinkable now. 500 cases made. • $7 • (09/30/94) • **81**

WHITE OAK | CALIFORNIA

Cabernet Franc Alexander Valley 1992: Firm and compact, with chewy tannins and just enough black cherry and berry flavors to hold your interest. Best after 1996. • $17 • (12/31/94) • **85**

Cabernet Franc Alexander Valley 1989 • $12 • (11/15/92) • **84**

Cabernet Sauvignon Alexander Valley 1992: Medium bodied, with appealing plum, cherry and cedary oak. Nothing fancy, but well made. 584 cases made. • $14 • (12/15/95) • **85**

Cabernet Sauvignon Alexander Valley 1991: Despite ample ripe, spicy and exotic wild berry and cherry flavor, it turns simple and loses its focus and intensity on the finish. Drinkable now. 621 cases made. • $14 • (11/15/94) • **84**

Cabernet Sauvignon Alexander Valley 1990: Smooth, soft and pleasant, with grapey flavors that persist on the finish. Not very complex, but it has enough appeal to be worth drinking through 1997 or 1999. 393 cases made. • $14 • (11/15/93) • **87**

Cabernet Sauvignon Alexander Valley 1988 • $14 • (11/15/92) • **85**

Cabernet Sauvignon Alexander Valley Myers Limited Reserve 1985 • $18 • (07/31/89) • **85**

Cabernet Sauvignon Sonoma County 1987 • $14 • (02/29/92) • **85**

Chardonnay Russian River Valley Poplar Ranch Private Reserve 1994: A pleasant, well-oaked wine with intense ripe pear, spice and nutmeg flavors. Could be more complex, ultimately. 250 cases made. • $18 • (06/30/96) • **84**

Chardonnay Russian River Valley Poplar Ranch Private Reserve 1993: A touch earthy and astringent, with just a hint of light pear and oak coming through. 250 cases made. • $18 • (07/31/95) • **82**

Chardonnay Sonoma County 1993: Marked by lean, earthy grapefruit and citrus flavors, but not much in the way of ripe fruit. 3,000 cases made. • $11 • (07/31/95) • **83**

Chardonnay Sonoma County 1991 • $13 • (09/15/92) • **80**

Chardonnay Sonoma County Myers Limited Reserve 1993: Tart, crisp green apple and pear notes add a hint of lemon and citrus. Well crafted, ready now. 426 cases made. • $16 • (10/15/95) • **87**

Chardonnay Sonoma County Myers Limited Reserve 1991: At this youthful stage the toasty oak flavors override the spice and pear-laced Chardonnay fruit, but it holds together on the finish where it gains complexity. 472 cases made. • $20 • (06/30/94) • **88**

Chenin Blanc California 1993: Bright, fruity and utterly charming, unfolding its melon, mint and pear flavors with grace and style. Ready now. 1,200 cases made. • $7 • (06/15/95) • **87**

Sauvignon Blanc Sonoma County 1993: Light, spicy and lean, with pear and herb flavors that soften on the finish. Drinkable now. • $9 • (09/30/94) • **83**

Sauvignon Blanc Sonoma County 1992 • $7 • (09/15/93) • **81**

Sauvignon Blanc Sonoma County 1991 • $9 • (11/30/92) • **80**

Zinfandel Alexander Valley 1993: Ripe and flavorful with its pretty cherry and wild berry accents, finishes with firm tannins and a spicy floral edge. Drinkable now. 200 cases made. • $15 • (10/15/95) • **88**

Zinfandel Alexander Valley 1990 • $10 • (12/15/92) • **75**

Zinfandel Alexander Valley Church Vineyard 1992: Has a wild berry streak in it, with an unripe edge. Overall, a rustic style that hangs together well. Drinkable now. 203 cases made. • $14 • (10/15/94) • **82**

Zinfandel Dry Creek Valley Saunders Vineyard 1992: An earthy, spicy Zin, with tar, pepper and wild berry flavors that lose their focus at mid-palate. Ready now. 228 cases made. • $16 • (10/15/94) • **85**

Zinfandel Dry Creek Valley Saunders Vineyard 1990 • $13 • (10/15/92) • **91**

Zinfandel Dry Creek Valley Saunders Vineyard Unfined Unfiltered 1991 • $16 • (09/15/93) • **89**

Zinfandel Sonoma County 1992: Firm, tight and gamy, with wild berry, cherry and plum flavors. Drinkable now. 3,000 cases made. • $9 • (10/15/94) BB • **85**

Zinfandel Sonoma County 1991 • $10 • (09/15/93) • **87**

Zinfandel Sonoma County 1989 • $10 • (02/29/92) • **87**

Zinfandel Sonoma County Limited Reserve 1993: Marked by a mint-menthol character at first, but it picks up pleasant wild berry and cherry notes and firm tannins. Try after 1996. 625 cases made. • $13 • (10/15/95) • **85**

Zinfandel Sonoma County Limited Reserve 1992: Lean and tarry, with a band of cedar and spice flavors followed by cherry and wild berry.

Dry on the finish, could use short-term cellaring to soften. 406 cases made. • $13 • (10/15/94) • **86**

Zinfandel Sonoma County Limited Reserve 1991 • $13 • (09/15/93) • **88**

Zinfandel Sonoma Valley 1993: A well-built Zin, with a chunky core of cherry and menthol flavors, finishing with a firmly tannic edge. Try now. 2,000 cases made. • $9 • (10/15/95) • **87**

WHITE ROCK | CALIFORNIA

Chardonnay Napa Valley 1992: Crisp and compact, with an elegant core of spicy pear and peach-tinged fruit. This tightly-wound young wine needs short-term cellaring to soften, but the flavors that emerge on the finish are pleasing. 930 cases made. • $17 • (06/30/94) • **87**

Chardonnay Napa Valley 1991 • $16 • (10/15/93) • **88**

Claret Napa Valley 1991: Marked by a stalky, slightly green edge, it walks a tightrope between oak and tannins with a cedary edge to the currant fruit. Best to cellar into 1997, when should be softer and perhaps more alluring. 1,020 cases made. • $22 • (12/15/95) • **85**

Claret Napa Valley 1990: Tight and firm, with a narrow range of spice, cedary oak and plum flavors. On the finish it starts to open up a bit. Will require cellaring, best after 1998. 1,000 cases made. • $19 • (04/15/94) • **88**

Claret Napa Valley 1989 • $18 • (11/15/93) • **83**

Claret Napa Valley 1988 • $18 • (11/15/93) • **84**

Claret Napa Valley 1986 • $18 • (10/31/89) • **80**

WHITEHALL LANE | CALIFORNIA

Cabernet Franc Napa Valley 1990 • $15 • (07/15/93) • **86**

Cabernet Franc Napa Valley 1989 • $18 • (08/31/92) • **79**

Cabernet Franc Napa Valley 1988 • $19 • (11/15/90) • **88**

Cabernet Sauvignon California NV • $7 • (10/15/88) • **70**

Cabernet Sauvignon California Le Petit NV • $8 • (03/31/90) • **81**

Cabernet Sauvignon Napa Valley 1992: Tight and austere and firmly tannic, but currant and black cherry flavor rises to the occasion. Tannins are quite substantial for the amount of fruit. 1,800 cases made. • $15 • (10/15/95) • **87**

Cabernet Sauvignon Napa Valley 1991: Smooth and supple, with a pretty core of ripe currant, cherry, leather and spice. Finishes with firm but polished tannins and lots of flavor. Best after 1997. 1,300 cases made. • $14 • (11/15/94) • **88**

Cabernet Sauvignon Napa Valley 1990: Smooth and polished, offering lots of appealing grapey, currant and violet aromas and flavors, echoing on the finish. Drink now. Tasted twice. 900 cases made. • $13 • (12/15/93) • **88**

Cabernet Sauvignon Napa Valley 1988 • $18 • (11/15/91) • **87**

Cabernet Sauvignon Napa Valley 1987 • $18 • (09/15/90) • **84**

Cabernet Sauvignon Napa Valley 1986 • $16 • (08/31/89) • **89**

Cabernet Sauvignon Napa Valley 1985 • $16 • (11/15/88) • **93**

Cabernet Sauvignon Napa Valley 1984 • $14 • (12/31/87) • **84**

Cabernet Sauvignon Napa Valley 1983 • $14 • (11/30/86) • **77**

Cabernet Sauvignon Napa Valley 1982 • $12 • (02/16/85) • **86**

Cabernet Sauvignon Napa Valley NV • $6 • (12/31/87) • **77**

Cabernet Sauvignon Napa Valley Morisoli Vineyard 1994: A dense, high-extract style, very deep and plush, rich in color and flavor, with tight, complex, plush currant, black cherry and plum-laced fruit. Impressive. • $NA • (05/31/95) • **90-94** (BT)

Cabernet Sauvignon Napa Valley Morisoli Vineyard 1992: Remarkably complex and concentrated, with an appealing core of currant, black cherry, vanilla and spice. Finishes with smooth, polished tannins and a wonderful sense of harmony. 1,000 cases made. • $28 • (10/15/95) • **93**

Cabernet Sauvignon Napa Valley Morisoli Vineyard 1991: Ripe and intense, with a tight core of currant, cherry, spice and cedary oak flavors that fold together nicely. Has the tannic strength to age through the decade, try in 1997. 480 cases made. • $36 • (05/31/95) • **89**

Cabernet Sauvignon Napa Valley Reserve 1992: Firm and tightly wound, beautifully focused, with a dense, complex core of currant, anise, cedar and spice to round out the experience. Needs until 1998 or 1999 to begin softening, but it has all the elements for greatness. 2,000 cases made. • $23 • (10/15/95) • **92**

Cabernet Sauvignon Napa Valley Reserve 1991: Provides a nice core of currant, cherry and berry fruit that's framed by toast and supported by firm tannins. Best to cellar this one into 1997-1998 for it to soften. 2,100 cases made. • $26 • (05/31/95) • **89**

Cabernet Sauvignon Napa Valley Reserve 1990: Firm and compact, featuring cedar, currant, cherry and spice flavors that turn smooth and supple. Best after 1996. 884 cases made. • $23 • (02/28/95) • **88**

Cabernet Sauvignon Napa Valley Reserve 1989 • $19 • (11/15/93) • **89**

Cabernet Sauvignon Napa Valley Reserve 1988 • $27 • (11/15/92) • **86**

Cabernet Sauvignon Napa Valley Reserve 1987 • $28 • (11/15/91) • **90**

Cabernet Sauvignon Napa Valley Reserve 1986 • $30 • (11/15/90) • **77**

Cabernet Sauvignon Napa Valley Reserve 1985 • $30 • (11/30/89) • **88**

Chardonnay Napa Valley 1993: Light, spicy, modest ripe pear and cedary oak notes. 1,800 cases made. • $11 • (05/15/95) • **82**

Chardonnay Napa Valley 1992: Simple and unfocused, with tart green apple, spice and wood flavors that are disjointed until the finish where the smoky, toasty flavors bring it together. Perhaps with time it will be more complete. 1,400 cases made. • $11 • (02/28/94) • **86**

Chardonnay Napa Valley Barrel Fermented 1993: Slightly green from cedary oak, but pear and vanilla flavors are appealing, picking up a smoky, buttery finish. Some age should make it more complete. 300 cases made. • $13 • (05/15/95) • **84**

Johannisberg Riesling Late Harvest Napa Valley 1994: Distinctive, medium-sweet and generous with its apricot and pear flavors, finishing a little spicy. Delicious now. 450 cases made. • $12 • **88**

Late Harvest California Primavera NV • $8 • (10/15/92) • **74**

Meritage Napa Valley 1991: Firm and tannic, with a tightly-wound core of earthy currant and mineral notes. Needs time to soften, but it may always be on the tannic side. Best after 1997. 1,200 cases made. • $15 • (11/15/94) • **85**

Merlot Knights Valley 1992: Cherry and plum flavors turn spicy and tannic on the finish, where toasty oak comes into play. Drinkable now. 3,400 cases made. • $17 • (05/15/95) • **88**

Merlot Knights Valley 1991: Smooth and supple, tasty, with modest berry, spice and tobacco aromas and flavors, finishing with a touch of vanilla. Drinkable now through 1997. 3,400 cases made. • $15 • (09/15/94) • **86**

Merlot Knights Valley 1987 • $16 • (07/15/90) • **77**

Merlot Knights Valley 1984 • $14 • (12/31/87) • **87**

Merlot Knights Valley 1983 • $12 • (10/01/85) • **85**

Merlot Knights Valley 1982 • $10 • (06/01/85) CS • **92**

Merlot Knights Valley Reserve 1986 • $15 • (07/31/89) • **72**

Merlot Knights Valley Summers Ranch 1990 • $16 • (06/15/93) • **86**

Merlot Knights Valley Summers Ranch 1989 • $18 • (04/15/92) • **84**

Merlot Knights Valley Summers Ranch 1988 • $18 • (03/31/91) • **82**

Merlot Napa Valley 1993: Trim and firm, offering an austere edge to the currant and plum notes. Has good balance, yet cellaring into 1997 should soften it somewhat. 2,000 cases made. • $18 • (12/15/95) • **86**

Merlot Napa Valley Leonardini Vineyard Reserve 1993: Dark, intense black cherry, plum and berry notes finish with austere tannins and a dash of oak. Drinkable now. 430 cases made. • $28 • (12/15/95) • **88**

Pinot Noir Alexander Valley 1990 • $12 • (02/28/94) • **82**

Pinot Noir Alexander Valley 1988 • $14 • (10/31/90) • **82**

Pinot Noir Napa Valley 1987 • $12 • (10/15/89) • **88**

Pinot Noir Napa Valley 1985 • $7 • (06/15/88) • **82**

Pinot Noir Napa Valley 1984 • $7 • (03/01/86) • **86**

Sauvignon Blanc Napa Valley Barrel Fermented 1993: Herbal, foxy aromas and flavors are distinctive but could be offputting to some. Ready now. 600 cases made. • $10 • (05/31/95) • **81**

WIEDERKEHR | ARKANSAS

Altus Spumante Arkansas NV • $6 • (02/29/92) • **80**

Cabernet Sauvignon Arkansas Mountain 1978 • $35 • (02/29/92) • **70**

Muscat di Tanta Maria Altus Arkansas 1990 • $9 • (02/29/92) • **71**

Key: SS—Spectator Selection. CS—Cellar Selection. BB—Best Buy. $NA—Price not available. (BT)—Barrel tasting. (A)—Auction Price.

Dates in parentheses represent the issues in which the ratings were published.

WIEMER, HERMANN J. | NEW YORK

Blanc de Noirs Finger Lakes 1989: A stale, coarse quality holds back this dry, smooth-textured but brownish colored bubbly. Tart, almost sour, with apple cider overtones. 458 cases made. • $14 • **74**

Chardonnay Finger Lakes 1992: A simple, full-bodied, drinkable white wine that tastes like fruit cocktail and has little or no Chardonnay character. 1,973 cases made. • $13 • **75**

Chardonnay Finger Lakes Reserve 1994: Fig, banana and brown sugar flavors give this round white personality, if not typical Chardonnay character. It finishes dry and short. 500 cases made. • $16 • (01/31/96) • **80**

Johannisberg Riesling Finger Lakes Dry 1994: This pleasantly fruity white shows typical Riesling flavors of peach, mineral and light herbs. It's full-bodied yet dry and well balanced. 3,500 cases made. • $8 • (01/31/96) • **84**

Johannisberg Riesling Finger Lakes Dry 1992: Soft and simple, an easy-drinking Riesling with peachy aromas and indistinct fruit flavors. 2,320 cases made. • $9 • **77**

Johannisberg Riesling Finger Lakes Semi-Dry 1994: Floral and honey aromas are intriguing, and follow through on the vibrant palate with attractive peach and lime flavors. It's firm, delicate and nicely balanced. A great-value Riesling. 4,000 cases made. • $10 • (01/31/96) BB • **88**

Johannisberg Riesling Finger Lakes Semi-Dry 1992: Earthy, diesel aromas mingle with sweet, simple flavors in this rather awkward wine. It turns sweet and sour on the finish. • $9 • **78**

Johannisberg Riesling Late Harvest Finger Lakes 1994: Delicate yet nervy, this vibrant white offers light floral aromas, then more assertive apricot, honey and spice flavors, sweet yet balanced. A well-made wine. 500 cases made. • $16 • (01/31/96) • **88**

Johannisberg Reisling Late Harvest Finger Lakes 1990: A creamy smooth, elegant and interesting dessert Riesling with complex, delicate flavors of lemon, vanilla, honey and hazelnut in a beautifully textured package. The finish is full and lingering. 839 cases made. • $13 • (09/15/94) • **87**

Johannisberg Riesling Late Harvest Finger Lakes 1984 • $9 • (03/16/86) • **82**

Johannisberg Reisling Late Harvest Finger Lakes Bunch Select 1987: A classy, surprisingly youthful and vital late-harvest wine with ample flavors of honey, apple, apricot, cinnamon and vanilla. Shows good balance of acidity and sweetness, and a lingering finish. 912 cases made. • $16 • (09/15/94) • **87**

Naturel Finger Lakes 1988: A well-balanced sparkling wine with piney, smoky aromas, lemony flavors and rather coarse texture. 1,144 cases made. • $12 • (02/28/95) • **79**

WILD HOG HILL | CALIFORNIA

Pinot Noir Sonoma County 1990 • $14 • (02/28/93) • **82**

WILD HORSE | CALIFORNIA

Cabernet Sauvignon Paso Robles 1987 • $13 • (04/30/91) • **88**

Cabernet Sauvignon Paso Robles Wild Horse Vineyards 1985 • $11 • (06/30/88) • **70**

Chardonnay Central Coast 1994: Smooth and creamy, with a spicy edge to the ripe pear, peach and vanilla notes. Develops elegance and complexity on the finish. 12,943 cases made. • $14 • (06/30/96) SS • **89**

Chardonnay Central Coast 1993: Smooth, supple and nicely balanced earth, caramel and citrusy pear flavors persist on the finish. Drink now. 10,394 cases made. • $13 • (01/31/95) • **88**

Malvasia Bianca Monterey 1993: Bright and open-textured, appealing for its apple, honey and spice flavors that echo smoothly on the finish. Drink soon. 664 cases made. • $13 • (04/15/95) • **84**

Merlot Central Coast 1989 • $15 • (05/31/92) • **76**

Merlot Central Coast 1986 • $11 • (07/31/89) • **77**

Merlot Paso Robles Cheval Sauvage 1990 • $28 • (03/31/93) • **87**

Merlot San Luis Obispo 1991: Firm and compact, displaying a tight band of cherry, herb and currant flavors and finishing with ample tannins, best after 1996. 10,157 cases made. • $14 • (02/28/95) • **85**

Negrette Cienega Valley 1992: Deeply colored, with ripe, supple berry, currant and spice flavors that are complex and hearty. Drinkable now. 182 cases made. • $16 • (01/31/95) • **85**

Pinot Blanc Monterey 1993: Broad, spicy and scented with vanilla, with a fruity pear flavor sneaking in on the finish. Ready now. 2,700 cases made. • $12 • (04/15/95) • **83**

Pinot Blanc Santa Barbara County Bien Nacido Vineyard 1993: Ripe, almost opulent, and supple. Has a rich texture and marvelous pear, spice and honey flavors. This is ready now. 40 cases made. • $13 • (12/31/94) • **90**

Pinot Noir Central Coast 1993: A tight, firm Pinot with a compact profile of cherry, herb and currant flavors and aromas. Drinks well now, but should age well short-term. 2,700 cases made. • $12 • (02/28/95) • **85**

Pinot Noir Central Coast 1992: Lean and tight, with a spicy, peppery edge to the cherry and berry flavors. Drink now. 8,382 cases made. • $14 • (01/31/95) • **84**

Pinot Noir Central Coast 1991 • $16 • (02/28/94) • **87**

Pinot Noir Paso Robles 1987 • $14 • (10/15/89) • **90**

Pinot Noir Paso Robles Cheval Sauvage 1990 • $28 • (02/28/93) • **90**

Pinot Noir Santa Barbara County 1990 • $14 • (02/28/93) • **86**

Pinot Noir Santa Barbara County 1988 • $14 • (04/30/91) • **79**

Pinot Noir Santa Barbara County 1987 • $14 • (03/31/90) • **82**

Pinot Noir Santa Barbara County 1986 • $14 • (06/15/88) • **85**

Pinot Noir Santa Barbara County 1985 • $13 • (06/15/88) • **86**

Pinot Noir Santa Barbara County Cheval Sauvage 1990 • $25 • (02/28/94) • **88**

Pinot Noir Santa Barbara County Cheval Sauvage 1989 • $28 • (02/28/93) • **85**

Zinfandel Paso Robles 1989 • $11 • (09/30/93) • **85**

Zinfandel Paso Robles Unbridled 1990: Ripe and spicy, with a juicy, supple core of blackberry, raspberry and cherry flavors. Finishes with crisp, firm tannins, suggesting it needs short cellaring. 200 cases made. • $16 • (09/15/94) • **88**

WILDCAT | CALIFORNIA

Merlot Sonoma Valley 1989 • $20 • (05/31/92) • **74**

Merlot Sonoma Valley 1988 • $18 • (05/31/92) • **78**

WILDHURST | CALIFORNIA

Cabernet Sauvignon Clear Lake 1991: Simple and oaky with the wood flavors masking the raspberry-scented Cabernet fruit. Soft tannins make it drinkable now. 800 cases made. • $9 • (11/15/93) • **76**

Cabernet Sauvignon Clear Lake 1990: A ripe and smooth medium-weight wine that offers generous currant and plum aromas and flavors. Drinks well now. Tasted twice. 2,700 cases made. • $10 • (07/31/92) • **83**

Chardonnay California 1994: A sturdy, fresh, fragrant white with spicy apple flavors. 1,500 cases made. • $11 • (06/15/96) • **81**

Chardonnay California 1993: Crisp and spicy, with ripe apple, pear, honey and vanilla notes, turing complex and elegant on the finish, where the oak folds in nicely. Very well made. 6,185 cases made. • $10 • (07/31/95) • **85**

Chardonnay Sonoma County 1991 • $8 • (01/31/94) • **80**

Chardonnay Sonoma County Reserve 1993: Smooth, round and spicy, a silky wine that spins out its oak- scented pear and apple fruit through a gentle finish. 5,040 cases made. • $12 • (07/31/95) • **85**

Chardonnay Sonoma County Reserve 1991 • $16 • (03/31/93) • **89**

Fumé Blanc Clear Lake Reserve 1993: Smooth and polished, spicy and fresh like a Chardonnay. 759 cases made. • $11 • (08/31/95) • **84**

Johannisberg Riesling Clear Lake Dry 1991 • $13 • (10/31/92) • **82**

Merlot Clear Lake 1991 • $8 • (03/31/93) BB • **84**

Merlot Lake County Reserve 1992: An oaky style with toasty, buttery flavors dominating, but enough cherry, currant and spice notes to keep it balanced and interesting. Finishes with firm tannins, ready now through 1998. 500 cases made. • $15 • (09/15/94) • **84**

Merlot Lake County Reserve 1991 • $15 • (10/15/93) • **87**

Pinot Noir Mendocino County 1992 • $9 • (02/28/94) • **74**

Sauvignon Blanc Clear Lake 1994: Fruity and straightforward with its anise-scented grapefruit and melon flavors. 1,800 cases made. • $9 • (06/15/96) • **83**

Sauvignon Blanc Clear Lake 1993: Soft and sweet-tasting, with a honeyed, caramel tinge to the citrusy fruit. 1,383 cases made. • $9 • (08/31/95) • **81**
Sauvignon Blanc Clear Lake 1991 • $7 • (12/15/93) BB • **87**
Zinfandel Clear Lake 1992: Intense and tannic, with drying fruit flavors that have an earthy, briary edge. Drink now. 2,023 cases made. • $9 • (10/15/94) • **80**
Zinfandel Clear Lake 1991 • $7 • (09/30/93) BB • **86**
Zinfandel Clear Lake 1990 • $7 • (07/15/92) BB • **85**

WILE & SONS, J. | CALIFORNIA

Cabernet Sauvignon Napa Valley 1991: Simple, light and marginally interesting Cabernet. Drink now. 12,000 cases made. • $7 • (11/15/93) • **74**
Cabernet Sauvignon Napa Valley 1987 • $10 • (05/31/91) • **78**
Cabernet Sauvignon Napa Valley 1986 • $7 • (09/15/88) • **75**
Cabernet Sauvignon Napa Valley 1985 • $7 • (11/15/87) • **78**
Merlot Napa Valley 1989 • $10 • (05/31/92) • **77**

WILLIAMS SELYEM | CALIFORNIA

Chardonnay Russian River Valley Allen Vineyard 1993: Elegant and refined, with a subtle mix of pear, spice, toast and apple flavors that folds together nicely. It all turns smooth and complex on the finish. 206 cases made. • $35 • (06/30/95) • **91**
Chardonnay Russian River Valley Allen Vineyard 1992: Serves up lots of pretty flavors, with ripe, spicy pear, apple and toasty oak flavors. Elegant, subtle and surprisingly balanced for its high alcohol. 190 cases made. • $30 • (04/30/94) • **88**
Pinot Noir Anderson Valley Ferrington Vineyard 1993: Austere, tart edge to the cherry and berry notes. This is a tightly wound young red that can stand short-term cellaring into 1997. • $NA • (02/29/96) • **88**
Pinot Noir Anderson Valley Ferrington Vineyard 1992: Combines ripe black cherry, spice and currant notes with cedary oak flavors. It all folds together nicely with a complex aftertaste and firm tannins. Drink now or cellar short-term. First Ferrington Vineyard bottling by Williams Selyem. Tasted twice, with consistent results. 147 cases made. • $30 • (12/15/94) • **92**
Pinot Noir Russian River Valley 1994: Medium weight, with a light, pleasant band of cherry, plum and spice flavors, which linger on the finish. • $28 • (06/30/96) • **86**
Pinot Noir Russian River Valley 1993: Light and simple, with mild cherry and berry notes of modest proportion. 1,460 cases made. • $23 • (09/15/95) • **83**
Pinot Noir Russian River Valley 1992: Ripe, intense and fruity, with elegant black cherry, plum and currant flavors that turn smooth and silky on the finish. Drinkable now. 1,458 cases made. • $25 • (08/31/94) • **90**
Pinot Noir Russian River Valley 1991 • $23 • (02/28/94) • **93**
Pinot Noir Russian River Valley 1990 • $20 • (11/15/92) • **93**
Pinot Noir Russian River Valley Allen Vineyard 1992: Intense and focused, with a tight, narrow beam of black cherry, plum and appealing, toasty oak. Gradually unfolds, revealing more depth and complexity on the finish. Firmly tannic. Drinkable now. Tasted twice, with consistent results. 780 cases made. • $38 • (12/15/94) • **91**
Pinot Noir Russian River Valley Allen Vineyard 1991 • $35 • (02/28/94) • **89**
Pinot Noir Russian River Valley Allen Vineyard 1990 • $30 • (11/15/92) • **92**
Pinot Noir Russian River Valley Allen Vineyard 1988 • $25 • (05/31/90) • **88**
Pinot Noir Russian River Valley Allen Vineyard 1987 • $20 • (05/31/89) • **92**
Pinot Noir Russian River Valley Cohn Vineyard 1993: Marked by pungent weedy aromas, more flavorful on the palate, but still thin on the finish where the flavors fade. 382 cases made. • $35 • (09/15/95) • **83**
Pinot Noir Russian River Valley Olivet Lane Vineyard 1993: Smooth, supple light cherry, earth and spice notes lead to a finish of firm, green tannins. 1,039 cases made. • $28 • (09/15/95) • **85**
Pinot Noir Russian River Valley Olivet Lane Vineyard 1992: Smells wonderful, with a pretty array of ripe fruit and buttery oak, but it turns austere and tannic. Needs a year of cellaring, but the black cherry and currant notes on the finish are appealing. Tasted three times with consistent results. 1,103 cases made. • $28 • (12/15/94) • **89**
Pinot Noir Russian River Valley Olivet Lane Vineyard 1991 • $28 • (02/28/94) • **92**
Pinot Noir Russian River Valley Olivet Lane Vineyard 1990 • $25 • (09/30/92) • **84**
Pinot Noir Russian River Valley Olivet Lane Vineyard 1989 • $25 • (11/15/91) • **90**
Pinot Noir Russian River Valley Rochioli Vineyard 1993: Smooth and polished, offering supple black cherry, plum and berry notes of medium depth and intensity. Picks up a pretty toasty oak edge on the finish, where the flavors linger on. • $NA • (02/29/96) • **88**
Pinot Noir Russian River Valley Rochioli Vineyard 1992: Beautifully crafted blend of complex, sweet oak and silky black cherry, currant and spice flavors. Rich and focused, with a long, full, lingering aftertaste. Pinot Noir doesn't get much better. Tasted twice, with consistent results. 200 cases made. • $50 • (12/15/94) • **94**
Pinot Noir Russian River Valley Rochioli Vineyard 1991 • $45 • (02/28/94) • **95**
Pinot Noir Russian River Valley Rochioli Vineyard 1988 • $40 • (02/28/91) • **92**
Pinot Noir Sonoma Coast 1994: Ripe and fruity, with pleasing cherry, plum and wild berry flavors. Picks up a trace of tea and oak on the finish. Tannic enough to need until 1997 to soften. • $30 • (06/30/96) • **90**
Pinot Noir Sonoma Coast 1993: Strikes a nice balance between spicy, toasty oak and doses of plum and cherry flavors. Has a smooth and polished texture and mild tannins. 794 cases made. • $26 • (09/15/95) • **85**
Pinot Noir Sonoma Coast 1988 • $18 • (05/31/90) • **92**
Pinot Noir Sonoma Coast Summa & Coastlands Vineyards 1993: Smells more attractive than it tastes, as the plum, cherry and berry notes are austere, adding a touch of tea and herb on the finish. An elegant style that's appealing already. 129 cases made. • $40 • (02/29/96) • **85**
Pinot Noir Sonoma Coast Summa Vineyard 1991 • $100 • (02/28/94) • **95**
Pinot Noir Sonoma Coast Summa Vineyard 1988 • $25 • (05/31/90) • **88**
Pinot Noir Sonoma County 1994: Serves up pleasant tea, herb, olive and spice notes of modest proportion, finishing with a hint of cherry and spice. • $23 • (06/30/96) • **86**
Pinot Noir Sonoma County 1987 • $16 • (05/31/89) • **88**
Pinot Noir Sonoma County 1986 • $16 • (06/15/88) • **91**
Zinfandel Russian River Valley 1992: Ultradark and rich, a big, ripe, intense style that doesn't hide its alcohol but manages to stay balanced, finishing in a burst of dried cherry and wild berry flavor. • $30 • (04/30/96) • **89**
Zinfandel Russian River Valley 1991: Beautifully crafted with layers of bright, ripe, spicy raspberry, cherry and vanilla flavors. Intense and lively through the long, full, lingering aftertaste. Enough tannin to age, but drinkable now while it's youthful and vibrant. 335 cases made. • $20 • (09/30/94) • **92**
Zinfandel Russian River Valley Leno Martinelli Vineyard 1985 • $10 • (07/31/88) • **79**

WILLOW CREEK | CALIFORNIA

Cabernet Sauvignon Napa Valley 1984 • $8 • (03/31/88) • **73**
Cabernet Sauvignon Napa-Alexander Valleys 1986 • $9 • (07/31/89) • **82**

WILRIDGE | WASHINGTON

Cabernet Sauvignon Columbia Valley Crawford Vineyard 1991: Ripe and generous, a mouthful of black cherry, pepper and spice on a smooth texture, immensely appealing but a little soft around the edges. Tempting to drink now, while the fruit is fresh. 150 cases made. • $19 • (09/30/94) • **86**
Cabernet Sauvignon Columbia Valley Klipsun Vineyard 1993: Bright and flavorful, featuring zingy blackberry and herb notes, tannins closing down on the finish. Give it until 1997 or 1998. 200 cases made. • $19 • (09/30/95) • **88**
Cabernet Sauvignon Columbia Valley Klipsun Vineyard 1992: Firm and focused, showing a bright beam of red cherry, raspberry and spice flavor that lingers on the velvety finish. Best now through 1997. 200 cases made. • $19 • (09/30/95) • **87**

Key: SS—Spectator Selection. CS—Cellar Selection. BB—Best Buy. $NA—Price not available. (BT)—Barrel tasting. Ⓐ—Auction Price.
Dates in parentheses represent the issues in which the ratings were published.

Merlot Columbia Valley Klipsun Vineyards 1993: Smooth and generous, playing out its plum and currant flavors over a supple frame. Tasty now, but it doesn't feel like an ager. 200 cases made. • $19 • (09/30/95) • **86**

WILSON DANIELS | CALIFORNIA

Chardonnay Napa Valley 1993: Bright and focused, showing a distinct toasty, spicy streak through the supple pear flavors. Drinkable now. • $10 • (05/15/96) • **87**

Chardonnay Napa Valley 1992: Lean and a bit green, displaying spice, tart pear and apple notes of modest proportions and finishing with light oak shadings. • $10 • (01/31/95) • **85**

WINDEMERE | CALIFORNIA

Cabernet Sauvignon Napa Valley 1991: Tart and a bit earthy, with currant and cherry fruit that has a green edge to it. Comes across as disjointed. 150 cases made. • $16 • (03/31/96) • **82**

Cabernet Sauvignon Napa Valley 1989 • $16 • (08/31/92) • **83**

Cabernet Sauvignon Napa Valley Diamond Mountain 1990: Firm and young, offering lots of fruit complexity and all of its parts in balance. Has plenty of cherry, plum and currant flavors and tight tannins on the finish, ready to drink now. • $14 • (08/31/93) • **88**

Chardonnay Edna Valley MacGregor Vineyard 1992: An intense young wine with tart, ripe pear and pineapple flavors that finish with crisp lemony acidity. Ready now. 800 cases made. • $11 • (03/15/94) • **84**

Chardonnay Edna Valley MacGregor Vineyard 1991 • $12 • (07/15/93) • **77**

Zinfandel Paso Robles Benito Dusi Vineyard 1993: Flavors of ripe plum and cherry jam, really showing off its fruitiness, then finishing nicely spicy and peppery, while staying mild with the tannins. • $15 • (03/31/96) • **86**

WINDSOR | CALIFORNIA

Cabernet Sauvignon Russian River Valley River West Vineyard 1987 • $20 • (11/15/92) • **87**

Cabernet Sauvignon Sonoma County Signature Series 1988 • $26 • (11/15/92) • **83**

Merlot Signature Series 1987 • $25 • (05/31/92) • **84**

Pinot Noir California Signature Series 1993: Well oaked, with toasty, smoky aromas and just enough cherry laced Pinot Noir fruit to hold your interest. • $15 • **82**

Pinot Noir Russian River Valley Winemaster's Private Reserve 1985 • $8 • (06/15/88) • **83**

Pinot Noir Sonoma County Private Reserve 1993: Marked by oak and medium-bodied plum and spice notes, a good if unexciting style that's ready. • $14 • **84**

WINTERBROOK | CALIFORNIA

Cabernet Sauvignon Napa County 1991: Throws out a lot of flavor, with no pretense at finesse or grace. There's a picklelike edge to the cherry and currant notes, but still a decent everyday red table wine. 5,000 cases made. • $8 • (05/15/94) • **81**

Cabernet Sauvignon Napa County 1990: Soft and velvety, with ripe currant and berry aromas and flavors, a touch of vinegar and sweet oak notes on the finish to wrap it up. Drink soon. • $9 • (08/31/92) • **81**

Cabernet Sauvignon Napa Valley Grand Reserve 1991: Tight and earthy, with a leathery edge to the currant and berry flavors, but it should soften a bit. 500 cases made. • $18 • (01/31/95) • **84**

Cabernet Sauvignon Napa Valley Grand Reserve 1990: Tight, firm and a bit lean, with a spicy core of tart black cherry and currant flavors that are framed by toasty, cedary oak. A young, backward wine that will require cellaring until 1997. A new Napa Valley label. 600 cases made. • $19 • (09/15/93) • **85**

Chardonnay Napa Valley Grand Reserve 1992: Tastes very ripe and fruity, with fresh pear, apple and spice notes. Modest oak shadings peek out from the background. 500 cases made. • $15 • (02/28/95) • **87**

Chardonnay Napa Valley Grand Reserve 1991 • $17 • (07/15/93) • **85**

Merlot Sonoma County Reserve 1991: Earthy, funky, cedary flavors that need more fruit. Finishes with a strange, meaty taste that's not very pleasant. 900 cases made. • $12 • **70**

WOLFE, THURSTON | WASHINGTON

Black Muscat Washington 1992: Sweet and fruity, a little plum and black cherry sneaking in amidst the lightly-spicy citrusy flavors. 310 cases made. • $9 • (09/30/94) • **85**

Black Muscat Washington 1987 • $9 • (10/15/89) • **85**

JTW's Columbia Valley Port 1992: Sweet and focused, featuring chewy black cherry, tar and spicy vanilla flavors packed into the finish. Best from 1998 to 2000. 160 cases made. • $17 • (09/30/95) • **85**

JTW's Washington Port 1991: A classically built Port, sweet and juicy with blackcurrant, black cherry and spice flavors that linger on the finish. Could use a little more grip, but should be fine from 1998-2000. 166 cases made. • $10 • (06/15/95) • **87**

Late Bottled Columbia Valley Port 1988: Has the smoothness, richness and spicy, caramelized flavors of a rich tawny port, as threads of blackberry weave through the finish. 97 cases made. • $9 • (09/30/95) • **89**

Lemberger Columbia Valley 1992: A bit harsh and tannic, a chewy red with only a little fruit to give it some charm. Drinkable now. 359 cases made. • $10 • (09/30/94) • **77**

Sweet Rebecca Late Harvest Yakima Valley 1992: Tastes very sweet and honeyed, with a wild, herbal edge to the orange and apricot flavors. Balanced toward sweetness, but doesn't try to be too rich. 325 cases made. • $10 • (09/30/94) • **85**

Sweet Rebecca Sauvignon Blanc Late Harvest Washington 1987 • $9 • (10/15/89) • **83**

Zinfandel Columbia Valley 1992: Distinctly varietal, brightly fruity, with a lively streak of black pepper accenting the berry and vanilla flavors. Nicely done, drinkable now. 210 cases made. • $12 • (09/30/94) • **85**

Zinfandel Port Columbia Valley Burgess Vineyard 1992: Thick, ripe and plummy, a mouthful of fruit and spicy overtones that lingers on the solid finish, tannic enough to show some grip. Best from 1998 to 2000. 28 cases made. • $20 • (09/30/95) • **87**

WOLLERSHEIM | WISCONSIN

Domaine Reserve Wisconsin 1989 • $12 • (02/29/92) • **73**

Domaine du Sac Dry Red Wine Wisconsin 1990 • $8 • (02/29/92) • **81**

Pinot Noir Wisconsin Sugarloaf Hill 1989 • $NA • (02/29/92) • **75**

WOLTNER, CHATEAU | CALIFORNIA

Cabernet Sauvignon North Coast 1979 • $3 • (03/16/84) • **76**

Chardonnay Howell Mountain 1993: Light and fruity, with fresh pear and apple notes that pick up a spicy citrus edge on the finish. Drinkable now. 709 cases made. • $10 • (09/30/94) • **86**

Chardonnay Howell Mountain 1992: Serves up a pleasing array of flavors, with spice, pear, citrus and honey notes that are lively and fruity, and finishes with a tangy zing from acidity. Drink now. 6,280 cases made. • $10 • (09/15/93) • **84**

Chardonnay Howell Mountain 1991 • $12 • (07/15/92) • **84**

Chardonnay Howell Mountain Estate Reserve 1993: Offers modest pear and spice notes with a flinty edge, but little more as the flavors are simple. 1,530 cases made. • $17 • (07/31/95) • **84**

Chardonnay Howell Mountain Estate Reserve 1992: Tight and focused, with a firm band of spicy Chardonnay fruit, and toasty oak- and pear-laced flavors that linger on the finish. Has the richness, depth and concentration for short-term cellaring. Drinkable now. 2,479 cases made. • $17 • (06/30/94) • **90**

Chardonnay Howell Mountain Estate Reserve 1991 • $17 • (09/15/93) • **87**

Chardonnay Howell Mountain Frederique Vineyard 1993: Lean and tart, with a strong citrus edge to the crisp apple and pear notes. Comes across as disjointed. 270 cases made. • $40 • (07/31/95) • **82**

Chardonnay Howell Mountain Frederique Vineyard 1992: Tart and tightly wound, with spicy pear, mineral and light oak shadings, picking up light toasty oak and nutmeg flavors that are crisp and persistent on the finish. Drinkable now. 397 cases made. • $40 • (06/30/94) • **90**

Chardonnay Howell Mountain Frederique Vineyard 1991 • $40 • (09/15/93) • **85**
Chardonnay Howell Mountain St. Thomas Vineyard 1993: Marked by tart, flinty pear and citrus flavors. Simple at best. 810 cases made. • $23 • (07/31/95) • **83**
Chardonnay Howell Mountain St. Thomas Vineyard 1992: Tart and intense, with a tightly wound core of grapefruit, pineapple and light oak shadings, giving you a long, full finish with flavors that linger. Drinkable now. 880 cases made. • $23 • (06/30/94) • **88**
Chardonnay Howell Mountain Titus Vineyard 1993: Tart and flinty, with an earthy citrus edge, but not much more in the way of fruit. 282 cases made. • $40 • (07/31/95) • **82**
Chardonnay Howell Mountain Titus Vineyard 1992: A lean, crisp style with tart citrus- and pear-laced flavors, finishing with a hint of nutmeg and clove. Drinkable now. 457 cases made. • $40 • (06/30/94) • **88**
Chardonnay Howell Mountain Titus Vineyard 1991 • $40 • (09/15/93) • **90**
Merlot Alexander Valley Cask 465 1982 • $4 • (04/16/85) • **60**

WOODS, CHRISTINE | CALIFORNIA

Chardonnay Anderson Valley 1991: Sour, tart and earthy up front, it straightens out a bit on the finish where the toasty, buttery oak flavors add dimension. 500 cases made. • $12 • (06/30/94) • **78**
Chardonnay Anderson Valley Estate Reserve 1992: Spicy with a candied, canned pineapple edge that turns metallic. 300 cases made. • $14 • (07/31/95) • **77**
Pinot Noir Alexander Valley 1989 • $10 • (02/28/93) • **69**
Pinot Noir Anderson Valley 1990 • $12 • (02/28/93) • **72**
Pinot Noir Anderson Valley NV: Old style California Pinot, showing firm tannins and earthy cherry and berry notes, turning crisp and a bit leathery on the finish. 275 cases made. • $10 • **80**
Pinot Noir Anderson Valley Estate Reserve 1992: Lean and trim, showing earthy, grapey aromas that follow through in the flavors, picking up notes reminiscent of a forest floor. 225 cases made. • $16 • (05/15/95) • **79**

WOODBRIDGE | CALIFORNIA

Cabernet Sauvignon California Barrel Aged 1992: Simple but pleasant, with ripe cherry and strawberry jam notes, picking up a spicy edge. 900,000 cases made. • $6 • (12/15/95) • **83**
Chardonnay California Barrel Aged 1993: Ripe with a fruity, earthy edge to the pear and cedary notes. 999,999 cases made. • $6 • (07/31/95) • **81**
Sauvignon Blanc California Barrel Aged 1993: Smooth and appealing, with generous pineapple, passion fruit and citrus flavors that persist on the lively finish. From Robert Mondavi. 800,000 cases made. • $5 • (06/30/95) BB • **85**
Zinfandel California Barrel Aged 1993: A touch earthy, with a greentealike edge, but the wild berry and cherry flavors rise up and make it palatable. 80,000 cases made. • $5 • (08/31/95) • **82**

WOODBURY | CALIFORNIA

Port Alexander Valley Old Vines 1981 • $10 • (01/01/86) • **91**

WOODBURY | NEW YORK

Blanc de Noirs New York 1987 • $12 • (12/31/90) • **70**
Brut Blanc de Blancs New York 1987 • $12 • (12/31/90) • **82**

WOODSIDE | CALIFORNIA

Cabernet Sauvignon Santa Cruz Mountains 1990: Lean, tart and vegetal with odd turnip, burlap and weedy black currant flavors that turn earthy and funky on the finish. Not our style, but drinkable. Perhaps with bottle time it will taste more together. 153 cases made. • $24 • (11/15/93) • **75**
Chardonnay Santa Cruz Mountains 1992: Lean and tart, with green pineapple and floral aromas and flavors. 357 cases made. • $18 • (06/30/94) • **78**
Zinfandel Santa Cruz Mountains Vineyard Hill Vineyards 1991: Very ripe and minty, with jammy, tannic fruit that shows its heat. Not for the faint-of-heart. Drinkable now. 191 cases made. • $14 • (10/15/94) • **77**

WOODWARD CANYON | WASHINGTON

Cabernet Sauvignon Columbia Valley 1991: Deep, dark, rich and intense, this is jam-packed with flavors. Tiers of currant, exotic spices and herb and floral notes, finishing with a rich, buttery oak aftertaste that keeps drawing out the flavors. Tempting now — so try a bottle — but hold a few for down the road. 2,191 cases made. • $29 • (07/31/94) • **93**
Cabernet Sauvignon Columbia Valley 1989 • $27 • (05/15/92) • **92**
Cabernet Sauvignon Columbia Valley 1988 • $24 • (04/15/92) • **93**
Cabernet Sauvignon Columbia Valley 1987 • $35 • (04/15/92) • **95**
Cabernet Sauvignon Columbia Valley 1986 • $35 • (04/15/92) • **87**
Cabernet Sauvignon Columbia Valley 1985 • $30 • (04/15/92) • **86**
Cabernet Sauvignon Columbia Valley 1984 • $27 • (04/15/92) • **81**
Cabernet Sauvignon Columbia Valley 1983 • $30 • (04/15/92) • **88**
Cabernet Sauvignon Columbia Valley 1982 • $28 • (04/15/92) • **83**
Cabernet Sauvignon Columbia Valley 1981 • $30 • (04/15/92) • **85**
Cabernet Sauvignon Columbia Valley Dedication Series #13 1993: On the crisp side, but nicely packed with spicy plum and coffee flavors. Remains lean and balanced toward spicy oak on the finish. Should be best in 1997 or 1998. 2,447 cases made. • $30 • (06/15/96) • **88**
Cabernet Sauvignon Columbia Valley Dedication Series #12 1992: This Washington Cab is firm and chunky in texture, with ripe blackberry, anise and herbal flavors poking through the tannins on the long finish. Richly flavorful. Try in 1998. 2,448 cases made. • $27 • (08/31/95) CS • **90**
Cabernet Sauvignon Columbia Valley Dedication Series #10 1990: Supple, rich and elegant, this is impressive for its toasty, buttery oak notes and pretty core of cherry and currant flavors. Adds up to a complex, engaging young wine that seduces you with flavor, yet has the depth and intensity to keep your interest. 2,000 cases made. • $27 • (07/31/93) • **91**
Cabernet Sauvignon Washington Canoe Ridge Vineyard 1992: Marked by toasty, buttery oak up front and complex currant and berry flavors following up, turning smooth and supple. 304 cases made. • $20 • (05/31/95) • **90**
Cabernet Sauvignon Washington Canoe Ridge Vineyard Artist Series #2 1993: Smooth and inviting for its spicy currant and black cherry flavors that jump right up and show from the first sip, then remain lively through the supple finish. 297 cases made. • $25 • (06/15/96) • **90**
Charbonneau Walla Walla County 1989 • $30 • (05/15/92) • **88**
Charbonneau Walla Walla County 1988 • $NA • (04/15/92) • **95**
Charbonneau Walla Walla County 1987 • $30 • (12/31/90) • **89**
Charbonneau Walla Walla County 1985 • $30 • (04/15/92) • **86**
Chardonnay Columbia Valley 1994: Bright and flavorful, a little astringent around the edges but shining with pear, apple and vanilla flavors. Best from late 1996. 2,000 cases made. • $23 • (03/31/96) • **88**
Chardonnay Columbia Valley 1993: Ripe, generous, harmonious and complex, spreading out its citrus, pineapple, mineral and toast character on a rich, supple frame. 1,820 cases made. • $23 • (01/31/95) SS • **90**
Chardonnay Columbia Valley 1992: Showing more fruit up front than the Reserve bottling, it delivers complex pear, toast, honey and spicy nutmeg flavors and a long, lingering finish. Try now. 1,641 cases made. • $21 • (09/15/94) • **90**
Chardonnay Washington Celilo Vineyard 1994: Bright, flavorful and elegant, weaving some lovely nutmeg and pepper flavors through the silky pear and vanilla core. Echoes the flavors on the long finish, too. 240 cases made. • $30 • (06/15/96) • **91**
Chardonnay Washington Reserve 1994: Ripe, focused and elegant, swirling its pear, spice and honey flavors in a finish that fans out appealingly. Approachable now, but best from 1997. 642 cases made. • $28 • (03/31/96) • **91**
Chardonnay Washington Reserve 1993: Smooth and elegant, fanning out its pear, spice and apple flavors with a nice touch of citrus on the lively finish. Harmonious, graceful and appealing. Ready now. 490 cases made. • $28 • (01/31/95) • **91**

Key: SS—Spectator Selection. CS—Cellar Selection. BB—Best Buy. $NA—Price not available. (BT)—Barrel tasting. Ⓐ—Auction Price.
Dates in parentheses represent the issues in which the ratings were published.

Chardonnay Washington Reserve 1992: Lean and concentrated, with a pretty band of pear, toast and nutmeg flavors that unfold on a long finish. Shows a good winemaker's hand for Chardonnay. Drinkable now. 655 cases made. • $26 • (05/15/94) • **92**

Merlot Columbia Valley 1994: This Washington red offers a solid mouthful of ripe berry, tar and sweet anise flavors that linger on the chewy finish. Artfully balanced to show the lovely fruit character and length. Try in 1997 or 1998. 1,467 cases made. • $27 • (06/15/96) • **91**

Merlot Columbia Valley 1993: Lean, nicely focused, showing currant and berry flavors and a touch of toast, spice and tannin on the finish. Has depth and elegance. At its best now through 1997. 1,211 cases made. • $23 • (09/30/95) • **89**

Merlot Columbia Valley 1992: Leans toward the herb and bell pepper spectrum of Merlot, but hangs in there, picking up currant and cedary notes on the finish. Should drink well now through 1997. Tasted twice with consistent notes. 1,171 cases made. • $21 • (09/30/94) • **86**

Merlot Columbia Valley 1991 • $22 • (11/15/93) • **84**

WORDEN | WASHINGTON

Cabernet-Merlot Washington 1992: Firm and focused, striving for elegance and achieving a nice balance of black cherry and spicy oak. Finishes quietly. Best in 1997. 800 cases made. • $12 • (09/30/95) • **84**

Cabernet-Merlot Washington 1991: Definitely on the spicy-herbal side, a chewy red with a meaty streak running through the basic cherry flavor. 584 cases made. • $12 • (08/31/94) • **83**

Cabernet-Merlot Washington 1990: Muddy, earthy flavors stand in the way of the modest berry notes, and a juniper edge distracts from the finish. Drinkable now. 700 cases made. • $10 • (07/31/92) • **73**

Cabernet-Merlot Washington 1989 • $10 • (02/29/92) • **86**

Cascade Claret Washington 1992: Light and brightly fruity, nicely balanced and immensely appealing, echoing berry and spice on the long finish. Just delicious for drinking now. 400 cases made. • $9 • (09/30/94) • **87**

Chardonnay Washington 1992: Smooth and flavorful, on the earthy side, but balanced with a touch of peach on the finish. Ready now. • $10 • (09/30/95) • **79**

Chardonnay Washington 1991: Crisp and earthy, lean, with a mineral edge to the modest apple flavor. Drinkable now. 1,206 cases made. • $10 • (09/30/94) • **83**

Chenin Blanc Washington 1993: Silky-smooth, oozing with melon and pear flavors, a generously fruity Chenin that finishes light and deftly balanced with a touch of sweetness. 1,206 cases made. • $7 • (09/30/94) • **86**

Claret Washington 1993: Edgy and lean, a metallic component taking some charm from the modest berry flavors. 675 cases made. • $8 • (09/30/95) • **79**

Gewürztraminer Late Harvest Washington 1992: Sweet and pleasantly floral, with a slightly bitter edge to the apricot and pear flavors, finishes sweet and snappy. Drinkable now. 117 cases made. • $7 • (09/30/94) • **83**

Johannisberg Riesling Washington 1993: Lean and a little acrid, sour enough to cut down the modest fruit. 800 cases made. • $6 • (09/30/95) • **73**

Johannisberg Riesling Washington 1992: Light and fruity, with a slightly spicy edge to the apple flavors. Drinkable now. 1,900 cases made. • $7 • (09/30/94) • **81**

Merlot Washington 1993: Light, lean and spicy raspberry and watermelon flavors dance across the finish. Ready now. 1,300 cases made. • $8 • (09/30/95) • **81**

Merlot Washington 1992 • $12 • (05/15/94) • **76**

Oyster White Washington 1992: Light and simple, a little spicy, a little toasty, finishing with an almond and peach character. Drink now. 225 cases made. • $9 • (09/30/95) • **83**

Oyster White Washington 1991: Crisp and lively, showing bright pineapple notes at the core and an herbal edge on the finish. Drinkable now. 204 cases made. • $12 • (09/30/94) • **84**

YAKIMA RIVER | WASHINGTON

Cabernet Sauvignon Columbia Valley 1988 • $15 • (03/31/92) • **74**

Cabernet Sauvignon Yakima Valley 1991: Earthy, gamy flavors dominate this moderately tannic, open-textured red. Better to try again in 1998. 980 cases made. • $13 • (03/31/96) • **79**

Cabernet Sauvignon Yakima Valley 1990: Lean in structure, with focused black currant and pickle-barrel aromas and flavors that point through the softly tannic finish. Best in 1998. 4,350 cases made. • $15 • (04/15/95) • **84**

Cabernet Sauvignon Yakima Valley Winemaker's Reserve 1989: Herbal and tobacco aromas and flavors run through this one, echoing mint and oak on the finish, making this less charming than it could be. 350 cases made. • $25 • (09/30/94) • **83**

Chenin Blanc Yakima Valley 1995: Light, soft, and semisweet. Flavors are simple and nondistinctive. 360 cases made. • $6 • **79**

Fumé Blanc Yakima Valley Dry 1993: Smells like canned fruit cocktail, finishing a tad bitter. 2,350 cases made. • $9 • (09/30/94) • **71**

Johannisberg Riesling Yakima Valley 1995: Fresh apple and peach flavors are soft and appealing. 1,200 cases made. • $6 • **84**

Johns Vintage Port Yakima Valley 1992: Sweet and distinctly spicy, almost bitter, offering cinnamon and nutmeg tones over modest black cherry flavor. May be best from 1999 to 2001. 1,000 cases made. • $16 • (06/15/95) • **82**

Lemberger Rendezvous Yakima Valley 1989 • $7 • (03/31/92) • **81**

Lemberger Sof/Lem Yakima Valley 1995: A simple and dryish rosé. Appealing raspberry and rhubarb flavors linger on the finish. 1,000 cases made. • $8 • **82**

Merlot Columbia Valley 1988 • $15 • (04/15/92) • **83**

Merlot Yakima Valley 1992: Spicy, herbal, sandalwood flavors meld nicely with soft black cherry notes to make this an appealing, distinctly cedary red. Ready now. 2,000 cases made. • $12 • (05/15/96) • **86**

Merlot Yakima Valley 1991: Firm but fleshy, ripe and round, with a chewy undercurrent. Pretty berry and currant flavors weave in a spicy note on the long finish. Best from 1996 to 1997. 4,700 cases made. • $15 • (06/15/95) • **88**

Merlot Yakima Valley 1990: Light, silky and appealing for its delicate plummy berry flavors that glide delicately through the finish, and persist. Drinkable now. 6,700 cases made. • $15 • (09/30/94) • **85**

YORK MOUNTAIN | CALIFORNIA

Cabernet Sauvignon San Luis Obispo 1986 • $15 • (11/15/90) • **84**

Cabernet Sauvignon San Luis Obispo 1985 • $15 • (12/15/89) • **83**

Cabernet Sauvignon San Luis Obispo County 1990: Lean and a little crisp, focusing its berry and red cherry fruit, without ever expanding on the finish. Best from 1997. 700 cases made. • $14 • (12/15/95) • **85**

Cabernet Sauvignon San Luis Obispo County 1989: Tannic with an earthy menthol edge. 550 cases made. • $14 • (11/15/94) • **71**

Cabernet Sauvignon San Luis Obispo County 1988 • $12 • (11/15/92) • **83**

Cabernet Sauvignon San Luis Obispo County 1987 • $12 • (11/15/92) • **84**

Cabernet Sauvignon San Luis Obispo County 1986 • $14 • (11/15/92) • **84**

Cabernet Sauvignon San Luis Obispo County Reserve 1990: Soft, a little watery, with broad berry and beet flavors and supple tannins. Ready now. 200 cases made. • $16 • (12/15/95) • **82**

Chardonnay San Luis Obispo 1993: Strikes a nice balance between ripe, earthy pear and citrus notes and toasty buttery oak, finishing with a lingering aftertaste. 920 cases made. • $12 • (07/31/95) • **84**

Chardonnay San Luis Obispo County 1994: Crisp and brightly fruity, a zippy mouthful of apple and spice flavors. 900 cases made. • $12 • (06/30/96) • **85**

Chardonnay San Luis Obispo County 1992: Surprisingly dark and spicy for a '92, weaving a bit of harsh toast into the otherwise smooth earthy pear flavors. Drinkable now. 410 cases made. • $12 • (06/30/94) • **80**

Chardonnay San Luis Obispo County 1991 • $9 • (07/15/93) • **78**

Merlot 1989 • $13 • (05/31/92) • **84**

Merlot San Luis Obispo 1991: Simple, with a narrow strip of currant, herb and tobacco flavors. Marginal quality, but short-term cellaring should soften it. Tasted twice with consistent results. 1,100 cases made. • $12 • (09/15/94) • **79**

Merlot San Luis Obispo 1990: Earthy, slightly bitter flavors shoulder past the modest fruit. 950 cases made. • $12 • (09/15/94) • **77**

Merlot San Luis Obispo County 1993: Bizarre, with an unattractive prune and vinegary flavor. Hard to warm up to. 350 cases made. • $12 • **70**
Merlot San Luis Obispo County 1986 • $10 • (12/15/89) • **80**
Pinot Noir Central Coast 1986 • $6 • (06/15/88) • **81**
Pinot Noir San Luis Obispo County 1992: Tough, tannic and earthy, those flavors overriding the cherry and berry notes underneath. Rustic in style. 500 cases made. • $10 • (12/31/95) • **78**
Pinot Noir San Luis Obispo County 1991: Earthy, bitter and marked by gamy flavors, it lacks ripe fruit and finesse. Finishes with a stemmy edge. 850 cases made. • $10 • (12/31/95) • **73**
Pinot Noir San Luis Obispo County 1990: Tea, herb and tobacco flavors dominate the fruit. Turns earthy and tannic on the finish, where it picks up a cola and cherry edge. Try now. 360 cases made. • $10 • (03/31/95) • **82**
Pinot Noir San Luis Obispo County 1989 • $9 • (02/28/93) • **76**
Pinot Noir San Luis Obispo County 1985 • $9 • (06/15/88) • **80**
Zinfandel San Luis Obispo County 1991: Ultraripe, jammy and prune-like, but also bearing a subtle pungency. A full-blown style that picks up a tart, earthy, slightly hot aftertaste. 750 cases made. • $9 • (10/15/95) • **83**
Zinfandel San Luis Obispo County 1990 • $9 • (06/15/94) • **82**
Zinfandel San Luis Obispo County 1989 • $7 • (09/30/93) • **78**
Zinfandel San Luis Obispo County 1988 • $9 • (10/15/92) • **74**
Zinfandel San Luis Obispo County 1986 • $8 • (12/15/89) • **85**

YORKVILLE | CALIFORNIA

Sauvignon Blanc Mendocino Randle Hill Vineyard 1994: Leans heavily to the earthy side, with a finish that tastes candied. • $8 • (05/31/96) • **77**
Sauvignon Blanc Mendocino Randle Hill Vineyard Organically Grown Grapes 1993: Crisp and lemony, a little floral as wel, soft enough to settle in with dinner now. 295 cases made. • $8 • (08/31/95) • **80**
Sémillon Mendocino 1993: Round and spicy, scented with oak and ripe with pear and caramel flavors. A hint of mineral on the finish. 100 cases made. • $9 • (08/31/95) • **83**

YORKVILLE CELLARS | CALIFORNIA

Chardonnay Anderson Valley 1993: Simple and marked by medium bodied honey and apricot flavors. 260 cases made. • $10 • (07/31/95) • **81**

Z. MOORE | CALIFORNIA

Gewürztraminer Russian River Valley Barrel Fermented Dry 1992: A dry, fruity style from California that favors citrus, pineapple and melon flavors—until the finish, which echoes spice. 2,000 cases made. • $9 • (01/31/95) BB • **87**
Gewürztraminer Russian River Valley Martinelli Vineyard Puncheon Select 1992: Dry and spicy, showing a golden pineapple edge to the resiny notes. Drink with herb-flavored foods. 415 cases made. • $14 • (01/31/95) • **86**

ZACA MESA | CALIFORNIA

Cabernet Sauvignon Central Coast 1988 • $12 • (11/15/91) • **58**
Cabernet Sauvignon Central Coast Reserve 1987 • $25 • (11/15/91) • **83**
Cabernet Sauvignon Santa Barbara County 1986 • $9 • (12/15/89) • **78**
Cabernet Sauvignon Santa Barbara County 1984 • $8 • (10/31/88) • **79**
Cabernet Sauvignon Santa Barbara County 1981 • $8 • (04/01/84) • **76**
Cabernet Sauvignon Santa Barbara County American Reserve 1983 • $13 • (03/31/87) • **87**
Cabernet Sauvignon Santa Barbara County Reserve 1986 • $15 • (12/15/88) • **80**
Cabernet Sauvignon Santa Barbara County Reserve 1985 • $15 • (10/15/88) • **79**
Chardonnay Santa Barbara County 1991 • $11 • (06/30/93) • **88**

Key: SS—Spectator Selection. CS—Cellar Selection. BB—Best Buy. $NA—Price not available. (BT)—Barrel tasting. Ⓐ—Auction Price.
Dates in parentheses represent the issues in which the ratings were published.

Chardonnay Santa Barbara County Alumni Winemaker Series James A. Clenden 1992: Ripe, creamy and supple with extra dimensions, offering apricot, pear and vanilla flavors that swirl through the finish. Drinkable now. 500 cases made. • $18 • (01/31/95) • **90**
Chardonnay Santa Barbara County Chapel Vineyard 1992: Spicy and intense, with the full Burgundian treatment, a rich, round wine that gets a little soft on the finish, but the fruit comes through on the aftertaste. Drinkable now. 1,300 cases made. • $16 • (06/30/94) • **85**
Chardonnay Santa Barbara County Jim Clendenen Alumni Winemaker Series 1993: A woody style, with spicy pear, butterscotch and honeyed notes that manage to stand up to oak. Loses some of its intensity and richness on the finish. 402 cases made. • $18 • (02/29/96) • **88**
Chardonnay Santa Barbara County Zaca Vineyards 1994: Ripe and spicy, a generous wine that pours out its distinctive herb-tinged pear and caramel flavors on the supple finish. Drinkable now. 20,000 cases made. • $13 • (05/15/96) • **87**
Chardonnay Santa Barbara County Zaca Vineyards 1993: Lean and somewhat leafy in flavor, showing nice apple notes on the lively finish. Drinkable now. 15,000 cases made. • $12 • (01/31/95) • **87**
Cuvée Z Santa Barbara County Red 1993: Lean and flavorful, showing impressive complexity of berry, cherry and tar notes and a hint of barnyard on the finish. Drinkable now. 1,700 cases made. • $14 • (04/30/95) • **85**
Cuvée Z Santa Barbara County Red 1992: A light, smooth, modest wine with gentle berry and earth flavors. Drinkable now. 1,200 cases made. • $14 • (09/30/94) • **78**
Pinot Noir Santa Barbara County American Reserve 1984 • $13 • (02/15/87) • **93**
Pinot Noir Santa Barbara County American Reserve 1983 • $13 • (08/31/86) • **60**
Pinot Noir Santa Barbara County Lane Tanner Alumni Winemaker Series 1993: Lean and trim, with tea, herb and cherry notes that turn elegant and smoky. 500 cases made. • $18 • (03/31/95) • **84**
Pinot Noir Santa Barbara County Reserve 1990 • $16 • (02/28/93) • **74**
Pinot Noir Santa Barbara County Reserve 1989 • $16 • (09/30/92) • **73**
Pinot Noir Santa Barbara County Reserve 1988 • $16 • (10/31/90) • **86**
Pinot Noir Santa Barbara County Reserve 1987 • $15 • (12/15/89) • **82**
Pinot Noir Santa Barbara County Reserve 1986 • $15 • (06/15/88) • **91**
Pinot Noir Santa Barbara County Sierra Madre Vineyard 1990: Solid, but it promises more in aroma than it delivers in flavor. Earthy cola and beet root impressions dominate. Drinkable now. 4,200 cases made. • $16 • (08/31/94) • **82**
Pinot Noir Santa Ynez Valley 1981 • $12 • (04/01/84) • **59**
Syrah Santa Barbara County 1990 • $12 • (12/31/92) • **83**
Syrah Santa Barbara County 1989 • $12 • (08/31/91) • **83**
Syrah Santa Barbara County Alumni Winemaker Series Bob Lindquist 1992: Ripe, round, generous and complex, bursting with blackberry, black cherry, black pepper and anise flavors and a lively finish. Best from 1997. 250 cases made. • $18 • (01/31/95) • **90**
Syrah Santa Barbara County Bob Lindquist Alumni Winemaker Series 1993: Somewhat leathery, herbal and earthy, but enough smoky plum and cherry flavors linger on the finish, where it gains a meaty, peppery, tannic edge. Should drink well into 1997. 413 cases made. • $18 • (02/29/96) • **88**
Syrah Santa Barbara County Chapel Vineyard 1992: Sturdy stuff, showing fresh plum, berry and spice flavor followed by chewy tannins on the leaner finish. Drinkable now. 270 cases made. • $19 • (01/31/95) • **85**
Syrah Santa Barbara County Zaca Vineyards 1993: An outstanding Syrah from this California winery. Rich and fruity, with gobs of ripe cherry, wild berry, currant and raspberry flavors. It picks up anise, cedar and spice notes, then turns smooth and complex on the finish. The tannins are fine and the flavors keep pouring through. Achieves its rich character without the heavy feel. 3,200 cases made. • $13 • (11/30/95) SS • **94**
Z Cuvée Santa Barbara County Red 1994: Strikes a good balance between wild berry and cherry, picking up anise, pepper and spice notes and traces of vegetal flavor. Firmly tannic finish. Grenache, Mourvèdre and Syrah. 2,560 cases made. • $14 • (04/30/96) • **85**

ZAYANTE | CALIFORNIA

Chardonnay Santa Cruz Mountains 1993: Medium bodied with a toasty caramel edge to the ripe pear flavors. 100 cases made. • $14 • (07/31/95) • **83**

ZD WINES | CALIFORNIA

Cabernet Sauvignon California 1982 • $12 • (07/16/86) • **66**
Cabernet Sauvignon Napa Valley 1994: Austere, tannic and marked by earthy, herbal notes, with the fruit lurking beneath. High in extract, but comes across as awkward now. 3,400 cases made. • $30 • (05/31/95) • **85-89** (BT)
Cabernet Sauvignon Napa Valley 1990: Lavishly oaked and well balanced for the vintage, but comes close to having too much wood to match the fruit concentration. Still, you get a pretty core of currant and cherry-scented flavors. Not quite the opulence you'd expect from a '90, but an attract 1,154 cases made. • $20 • (11/15/92) • **86**
Cabernet Sauvignon Napa Valley 1989 • $20 • (11/15/92) • **78**
Cabernet Sauvignon Napa Valley 1988 • $20 • (04/30/91) • **86**
Cabernet Sauvignon Napa Valley 1987 • $16 • (02/15/91) • **78**
Cabernet Sauvignon Napa Valley 1985 • $14 • (05/15/89) • **81**
Cabernet Sauvignon Napa Valley Estate Bottled 1987 • $40 • (01/31/91) • **90**
Cabernet Sauvignon Napa Valley Reserve 1992: Complex and harmonious, as aromas of smoky oak, mushroom and cherry follow through with those flavors on the palate. Finishes with plush tannins and good length. Best to cellar into 1998. 217 cases made. • $34 • (04/30/96) • **88**
Chardonnay California 1993: An exotic style featuring grapefruit, mango and guava flavors. Turns simple and loses its intensity on the finish. • $23 • (02/28/95) • **85**
Chardonnay California 1991 • $21 • (07/15/93) • **82**
Pinot Noir Carneros Napa Valley 1990 • $20 • (09/30/92) • **83**
Pinot Noir Carneros Napa Valley 1989 • $16 • (11/15/91) • **82**
Pinot Noir Carneros Napa Valley 1988 • $17 • (06/30/91) • **82**
Pinot Noir Carneros Napa Valley 1985 • $14 • (07/31/89) • **79**
Pinot Noir Napa Valley 1982 • $13 • (08/31/86) • **75**
Pinot Noir Napa Valley Carneros 1991 • $20 • (02/28/94) • **78**

ZELLERBACH ESTATES | CALIFORNIA

Cabernet Sauvignon Alexander Valley 1988 • $10 • (10/31/90) • **82**
Cabernet Sauvignon Alexander Valley 1984 • $8 • (11/30/88) • **86**
Cabernet Sauvignon Alexander Valley 1982 • $6 • (11/30/86) • **80**
Cabernet Sauvignon Alexander Valley 1980 • $8 • (04/01/85) • **77**
Cabernet Sauvignon California 1991: Oaky and herbaceous, with a drying leathery edge, turns spicy toward the finish. Drink now. 12,000 cases made. • $9 • (03/31/94) • **78**
Cabernet Sauvignon Sonoma County 1978 • $NA • (11/15/92) • **84**
Chardonnay California 1992: Simple with a lean band of spice, oak and pear flavors, but it fails to take off beyond that. Ready now. 40,000 cases made. • $9 • (03/31/94) • **82**
Merlot Alexander Valley 1982 • $8 • (10/01/85) • **84**
Merlot Alexander Valley 1980 • $8 • (05/01/84) • **68**

ZELLERBACH, STEPHEN | CALIFORNIA

Chardonnay California 1994: A fresh and spicy mouthful of nectarine, resin and vanilla flavors that soften on the finish. Drinkable now. • $8 • (10/31/95) • **83**
Chardonnay California 1993: A lightly fruity style, ripe pear, apple and melon flavors finish with a trace of oak. Drinkable now. 20,000 cases made. • $8 • (01/31/95) • **83**
Chardonnay Sonoma County 1994: Bright and fruity, offering a bitter woody streak that takes away some of the charm. Try now. • $12 • (05/15/96) • **80**
Merlot Napa Valley 1993: Earthy with a stalky, herbal edge and a modest core of berries and cherries. 1,346 cases made. • $14 • (06/15/96) • **75**
Sauvignon Blanc California 1992: Veers strongly toward the herbal, vegetal style but softens a little on the finish. • $6 • (01/31/95) • **78**
Sauvignon Blanc Sonoma County 1993: This is frankly herbal and shows distinctively varietal character in its aromas, but it rounds out the flavors with soft, charming pear and apple-a fine balance that enhances its value. 3,200 cases made. • $7 • (08/31/95) BB • **88**

ZIA | CALIFORNIA

Cabernet Sauvignon Napa Valley 1992: Smooth, polished, ripe, complex cherry, currant, coffee and cedar, adding a nice dose of smoky, buttery oak. Shows great finesse and grace for a new red of this proportion. 300 cases made. • $24 • (04/30/96) • **90**

ZILLAH OAKES | WASHINGTON

Aligoté Yakima Valley 1993: Crisp, refreshing, lively apple and citrus flavors, finishing simple and clean as a whistle. Ready now. 500 cases made. • $10 • (09/30/95) • **84**
Cabernet Franc Yakima Valley 1993: Frankly herbal, showing earth, mineral and berry flavors that get a little tough on the finish. 500 cases made. • $10 • (09/30/95) • **79**
Muscat Canelli Yakima Valley 1994: Sweet, fruity and beguiling. This swirls its spicy pear, litchi and citrus flavors in an attractive pattern. A lovely dessert wine. 250 cases made. • $7 • (08/31/95) • **87**
Riesling Late Harvest Yakima Valley 1993: Definitely sweet but light in texture, sporting honey, earth, tobacco and pear flavors that are more like Sémillon than Riesling. 500 cases made. • $9 • (09/15/95) • **84**
Sémillon Yakima Valley 1994: Light, lean and crisp, vibrant, sporting citrusy pear flavor. Drink now. 250 cases made. • $7 • (09/30/95) • **85**

ZODIAC | CALIFORNIA

Chardonnay California Gemini 1991 • $6 • (09/15/93) • **72**
Chardonnay California Pisces 1992: Coarse and chunky, but the toasty oak and pear flavors are solid on the finish. Good value, but only 100 cases made, ready now. 100 cases made. • $6 • (04/15/94) • **82**

Winery Index